READER'S DIGEST

GREAT
ILLUSTRATED
DICTIONARY

READER'S DIGEST

GREAT ILLUSTRATED DICTIONARY

IN TWO VOLUMES

Published by The Reader's Digest Association Limited

LONDON · NEW YORK · SYDNEY · CAPE TOWN · MONTREAL

GREAT ILLUSTRATED DICTIONARY
A Reader's Digest book adapted
and developed from the lexical databases of the
Houghton Mifflin Company of Boston, Massachusetts, with permission.

Lexical Databases, Copyright © 1984
Houghton Mifflin Company of Boston

Reader's Digest GREAT ILLUSTRATED DICTIONARY
First edition, Copyright © 1984
The Reader's Digest Association Limited
25 Berkeley Square, London W1X 6AB

Copyright © 1984
The Reader's Digest Association Far East Limited
Philippines Copyright 1984
The Reader's Digest Association Far East Limited

TYPESETTING: Lehigh ROCAPPI, Pennsauken, New Jersey
Vantage Photosetting Co. Ltd, Eastleigh and London
SEPARATIONS: Aero Offset Reproductions Ltd, Eastleigh
PAPER: Mead Paper, Escanaba, Michigan, USA
PRINTING AND BINDING: Rand McNally & Co., Versailles, Kentucky, USA

® READER'S DIGEST is a registered trademark of
The Reader's Digest Association Inc.
of Pleasantville, New York, USA

Printed in the United States of America

CONTRIBUTORS

CONSULTANT EDITOR
Dr. Robert Ilson
Associate Director of the Survey of English Usage,
University College London

USAGE EDITOR
Professor David Crystal
Professor of Linguistic Science, University of Reading

PRONUNCIATION EDITOR
Dr. John Wells
Department of Phonetics and Linguistics,
University College London

ETYMOLOGY EDITOR
Dr. Thomas Hill Long

CHIEF LEXICOGRAPHER
Faye Carney

LEXICOGRAPHERS
Edwin Carpenter Elizabeth Collingwood
Emily Driver John Kahn
James Harpur Anna Lumley
Sarah Mitchell Sarah Overton
Michael Rundell Michael Scherk

The artists and photographers who
contributed to Great Illustrated Dictionary
are credited on page 1918

VOLUME TWO
L-Z

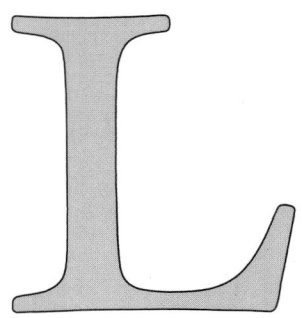

l, L (el) *n., pl.* **l's** or *rare* **ls, L's** or **Ls. 1.** The 12th letter of the modern English alphabet. **2.** Any of the speech sounds represented by this letter. **3.** Anything shaped like the letter **L.**

l, L, I., L. *Note:* As an abbreviation or symbol, *l* may be a small or a capital letter, with or without a full stop. Established forms or those generally preferred precede the definition. When no form is given, all four forms are in general use in that sense. **1. l., L.** lake. **2. L** lambert. **3. L** large. **4. L.** Latin. **5. L** *British.* learner driver. **6. l.** length. **7. L.** Liberal. **8. L.** licentiate (in titles). **9. l.** line. **10. L.** Linnaean. **11. l.** lira. **12. l** litre. **13. L** The Roman numeral for 50. **14. L** *Electricity.* inductor. **15. L** *Physics.* latent heat.

l- *n. comb. form. Chemistry.* Indicates a laevorotatory compound. Usually written in italics: for example, *l*- **glucose.** Compare *d.*

L- *n. comb. form. Chemistry.* Indicating an optically active compound with a molecular structure derived from or related to the structure of laevorotatory glyceraldehyde: for example **L- alanine.** Compare **D-.** An isomer designated L- may itself be laevorotatory (*l*-) but is not necessarily so.

la¹ Variant of **lah.**

la² (law, laa) *interj. Archaic.* Used to express emphasis or to indicate surprise. [Perhaps variant of LO.]

La¹ The symbol for the element lanthanum.

La² (laa). **1.** A respectful title prefixed to the surname of an eminent female artiste: *La Sutherland.* **2.** A title facetiously prefixed to the surname of a woman who is regarded as formidable, temperamental, or troublesome. [Feminine definite article of Romance languages.]

La. Louisiana.

L.A. 1. Legislative Assembly. **2.** Library Association. **3.** local agent. **4.** Los Angeles.

laa·ger, la·ger (laágər) *n. Chiefly South African.* **1.** A defensive encampment encircled by wagons or armoured vehicles. **2.** A narrow and protective social or intellectual environment.

~*v.* **laagered, -gering, -gers.** —*tr.* To form into a laager. —*intr.* To camp in a laager. [Afrikaans *lager,* from Dutch *leger,* camp, LAIR.]

laager mentality *n.* An attitude or policy of isolationism and inflexible opposition to change, especially as thought by its opponents to characterise the ruling Afrikaners of South Africa.

lab (lab) *n. Informal.* A **laboratory** *(see).*

lab. laboratory.

Lab. 1. Labour. **2.** Labrador.

lab·a·rum (lábərəm) *n., pl.* **-ara** (-ərə). **1.** The banner adopted by Constantine the Great after his conversion to Christianity, combining the Roman military standard and Christian symbols. **2.** Any banner, especially an ecclesiastical one. [Late Latin *labarum†.*]

lab·da·num (lábdənəm) *n.* Also **lad·a·num** (ládd'n-əm). A resinous exudation of certain Old World plants of the genus *Cistus,* yielding a fragrant essential oil used in flavourings and perfumes. [Medieval Latin, from Latin *lādanum,* from Greek *ladanon, lēdanon,* from *lēdon,* shrub from which labdanum exudes, from Semitic.]

la·bel (láyb'l) *n.* **1.** Anything functioning as a means of identification; especially: **a.** A piece of paper, card, or the like attached to an article such as a parcel or suitcase to designate its origin, owner, and destination. **b.** A piece of paper or similar material attached to a container such as a bottle or packet, providing printed or written information, about the contents. **2.** A term serving to describe or categorise; an epithet. **3.** The brand or trademark of a particular company, especially of a record company. **4.** A moulding over a door or window; a dripstone. **5.** The heraldic device distinguishing an eldest son, consisting of a horizontal band across the upper part of the shield with a set of usually three downward projections. **6.** *Chemistry.* A radioactive element in a compound, used to trace the pathway of the compound through a system.

~*tr.v.* **labelled** or *U.S.* **labeled, -belling** or *U.S.* **-beling, -bels. 1.** To attach a label to. **2.** To describe, classify, or designate. **3.** To make an atom in (a molecule or compound) radioactive so that the pathway of the molecule or compound can be traced through a system. [Middle English, label, narrow strip, from Old French, ribbon, strip, from Germanic.] —**la·bel·ler** *n.*

la·bel·lum (lə-bélləm) *n., pl.* **-bella** (-béllə). **1.** The often enlarged lip of an orchid. **2.** The lobe at the top of a fly's proboscis. [New Latin, from Latin, "small lip", diminutive of *labrum,* lip.]

la·bi·al (láybi-əl) *adj.* **1.** Of or pertaining to the lips or labia. **2.** Resembling or serving as a lip. **3.** *Music.* Producing tones by the impact of a stream of air upon the edge of a lip, as in a flute or the flue pipes of an organ. **4.** *Phonetics.* Formed mainly by closing or partly closing the lips.

~*n.* A labial sound, such as (b), (m), (v), (w), or a rounded vowel. [Medieval Latin *labiālis,* from Latin *labium,* lip.] —**la·bi·al·ly** *adv.*

la·bi·al·ise, la·bi·al·ize (láybi-ə-līz) *tr.v.* **-ised, -ising, -ises.** *Phonetics.* To round (a vowel); make labial. —**la·bi·al·ism, la·bi·al·isa·tion** (-lī-záysh'n ‖ *U.S.* -li-) *n.*

la·bi·a ma·jo·ra (láybi-ə mə-jáwrə ‖ -jórə) *pl.n.* Two rounded folds of tissue that form the external lateral boundaries of the vulva. [New Latin, "greater lips".]

labia mi·no·ra (mi-náwrə ‖ -nórə) *pl.n.* Two narrow folds of tissue enclosed within the cleft of the labia majora. Also called "nympha". [New Latin, "lesser lips".]

la·bi·ate (láybi-ət, -it, -ayt) *adj.* **1.** Having lips or liplike parts. **2.** *Botany.* **a.** Having or designating flowers with the corolla divided into two liplike parts. **b.** Of or belonging to the family Labiatae, which includes the mints.

~*n.* A labiate plant. [New Latin *labiatus,* from Latin *labium,* lip.]

la·bile (láy-bīl ‖ *U.S. also* -b'l) *adj.* Constantly liable to undergo change or fluctuation; unstable. [Late Latin *lābilis,* from Latin *lābī,* to slide.] —**la·bil·i·ty** (lə-bílləti) *n.*

labio- *comb. form.* Indicates formed with the lips (and another organ); for example, **labiodental.** [Latin *labium,* lip.]

la·bi·o·den·tal (láybi-ō-dént'l) *adj. Phonetics.* Articulated with the lip or lips and teeth.

~*n. Phonetics.* A labiodental sound, such as (f) or (v).

la·bi·o·ve·lar (láybi-ō-véelər) *adj.* Also **la·bi·al·ve·lar** (-əl-). *Phonetics.* Simultaneously labial and velar.

~*n. Phonetics.* A labiovelar sound, such as (w).

la·bi·um (láybi-əm) *n., pl.* **-bia** (-bi-ə). **1.** *Anatomy.* Any of four folds of tissue of the female external genitalia. See **labia majora, labia minora. 2.** *Zoology.* A liplike structure, such as the appendage forming the lower lip in insects. **3.** *Botany.* Any of the liplike divisions of a labiate corolla. [New Latin, from Latin, lip.]

lab·lab (láb-lab) *n.* **1.** A tropical African twining plant, *Dolichos lablab.* **2.** The edible pod or seed of this plant. [Arabic.]

lab·o·ra·to·ry (lə-bórra-təri, -tri ‖ *U.S.* lábbrə-tawri, lábbərə-, -tōri) *n., pl.* **-ries.** *Abbr.* **lab. 1.** A room or building equipped for scientific experimentation, research, or testing. Also used adjectivally: *laboratory conditions; a laboratory assistant.* **2.** A place where drugs and chemicals are manufactured. **3.** Any place equipped for study, practice, or testing, such as a **language laboratory** *(see).* Also informally called "lab". [Medieval Latin *labōrātōrium,* workshop, from Latin *labōrātus,* past participle of *labōrāre,* to LABOUR.]

la·bo·ri·ous (lə-báwri-əss ‖ -bóri-) *adj.* **1.** Requiring long, hard work. **2.** Hard-working; industrious. **3.** Not fluent or spontaneous; laboured: *a laborious explanation.* [Middle English, from Old French *laborieus,* from Latin *labōriōsus,* from *labor,* LABOUR.] —**la·bo·ri·ous·ly** *adv.* —**la·bo·ri·ous·ness** *n.*

la·bour, *U.S.* **la·bor** (láybər) *n.* **1.** Physical or mental exertion of a practical nature, as distinguished from exertion for the sake of pleasure or recreation; work. **2.** A specific task, especially one requiring physical effort. **3.** The contribution made by workers to the production of goods and provision of services in a community; work done for wages as distinguished from work done for profit. **4.** The class of people who make such a contribution; workers collectively, as distinguished from management and employers. **5.** *Capital L.* A political party claiming to represent the interests of this class, such as the Labour Party of Great Britain. **6. a.** The physical effort involved in giving birth; parturition. **b.** An instance or period of such effort: *a long labour; a difficult labour.* —See Synonyms at **work.**

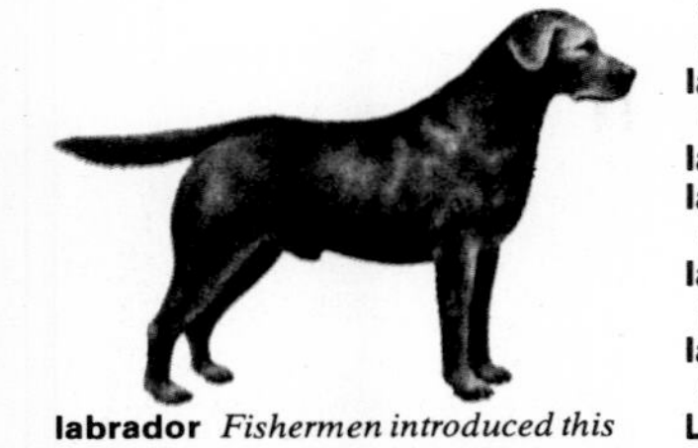

labrador *Fishermen introduced this North American breed into Europe in the early 19th century. Labradors, which usually have black or fawn-coloured fur, were once trained as retrievers and used to pick up shot game. Today they are more often kept as pets or used as guide dogs for the blind.*

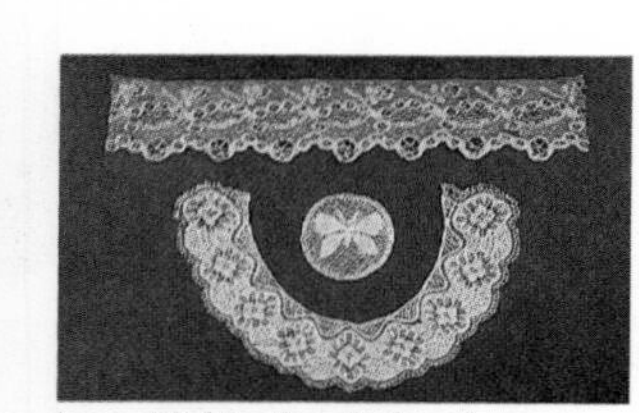

lace *Making lace by hand was an important European industry from the Renaissance to World War I. These examples of handmade English lace are from Honiton in Devon – one of the few centres where the craft still survives despite competition from modern textile machinery.*

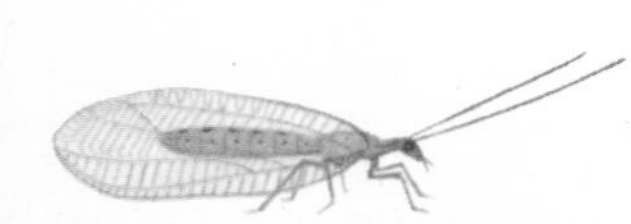

lacewing *A delicate-looking green insect with golden eyes and gauzy wings, from which it gets its name. Both the adults and the larvae are fierce predators, feeding mainly on aphids.*

~*v.* **laboured** or *U.S.* **labored, -bouring** or *U.S.* **-boring, -bours** or *U.S.* **-bors.** —*intr.* **1.** To expend great physical or mental effort; work; toil. **2.** To strive painstakingly or strenuously for a particular end. **3. a.** To proceed slowly; plod. **b.** To pitch and roll. Used of a ship. **4.** To be hampered. Used with *under: labouring under a misconception.* **5.** To undergo the pains of childbirth. —*tr.* **1.** To deal with in exhaustive detail; treat laboriously: *labour a point.* **2.** To cultivate; till. [Middle English, from Old French, from Latin *labor.*]

labour camp *n.* **1.** A penal settlement where the prisoners undertake forced labour. **2.** A camp for migrant workers.

Labour Day *n.* **1.** A public holiday celebrated in many countries in honour of the working class, usually on May 1. **2.** A similar holiday (Labor Day) observed in the United States and Canada on the first Monday in September.

la·boured (láybərd) *adj.* **1.** Done or produced with labour or difficulty: *laboured breathing.* **2.** Showing evidence of labour; lacking natural ease; overworked.

la·bour·er (láy-bərər, -brər) *n.* A person who performs physical work, especially of an unskilled nature.

labour exchange *n. British.* Formerly, an **employment office** *(see).*

la·bour-in·ten·sive (láybər-in-ten-siv, -tén-) *adj.* Requiring a high degree of human as opposed to mechanical work.

la·bour·ite (láybə-rīt) *n. Sometimes capital* **L.** A member or supporter of a Labour Party.

labour of love *n.* A task performed for the enjoyment it brings to oneself or another.

Labour Party *n.* **1.** A British political party, formed in 1900 from the Independent Labour Party and various trade unions, cooperative societies, and other socialist bodies, and claiming to represent the interests of workers. **2.** Any of several similar parties in other countries, especially in the Commonwealth.

la·bour-sav·ing (láybər-sayving) *adj.* Designed to reduce or eliminate the labour required to carry out a task.

labour union *n. U.S.* A trade union.

lab·ra·dor (lábbrə-dawr) *n.* A dog of a breed originating in Newfoundland, having a short, dense, black or yellow-brown coat and a tapering tail. Also called "labrador retriever".

Lab·ra·dor[1] (lábbrə-dawr). Also **Lab·ra·dor-Un·ga·va** (lábbrə-dáwr-ən-gaávə). Peninsula of east Canada, divided between Quebec and Newfoundland provinces. A high plateau, with barren tundra in the north and coniferous forest in the south, it has large mineral, forest, and hydroelectric resources. **—Lab·ra·dor·i·an** (-dáw-ri-ən || -dṓ-) *n. & adj.*

Labrador[2]. The mainland part of Newfoundland province, Canada.

Labrador Current *n.* A cold ocean current flowing southwards from Baffin Bay along the coast of Labrador to unite with the Gulf Stream over the Grand Banks off southeast Newfoundland. Also called "Arctic Current".

lab·ra·dor·ite (lábbrə-dawr-īt, -dáwr-) *n.* A plagioclase feldspar, found in igneous rocks, and characterised by brilliant colours in some specimens. [After LABRADOR.]

la·bret (láy-bret, -brət) *n.* An ornament inserted in a perforation in the lip. [Latin *labrum,* lip + -ET.]

la·brum (láy-brəm) *n., pl.* **-bra** (-brə). A lip or liplike structure, such as the upper lip in insects. [New Latin, from Latin, lip.]

La Bru·yère (laábrōō-yaír; *French* la brü-yaír), **Jean de** (1645–96). French writer. His single work, *Caractères de Théophraste traduits du grec, avec les caractères et les moeurs de ce siècle* (1688–96), satirises society under Louis XIV.

la·bur·num (lə-búrnəm) *n.* Any of several poisonous trees or shrubs of the genus *Laburnum;* especially, *L. anagyroides,* cultivated for its drooping clusters of yellow flowers. Also called "golden chain". [Latin *laburnum,* perhaps from Etruscan.]

lab·y·rinth (lábbə-rinth) *n.* **1. a.** An intricate structure of interconnecting passages; a maze **b.** *Capital* **L.** *Greek Mythology.* The maze in which the Minotaur was confined. **2.** Something highly intricate or tortuous in character, composition, or construction. **3.** *Anatomy.* **a.** A group of communicating anatomical cavities. **b.** The internal ear, comprising the semicircular canals, vestibule, and cochlea. **4.** *Electronics.* A loudspeaker housing containing a number of air chambers, used to reduce the production of standing waves and improve the quality of sound reproduction. [Learned respelling of Middle English *laborintus,* from Latin *labyrinthus,* from Greek *laburinthos,* probably akin to *labrus,* LABYRIS.]

labyrinth fish *n.* Any small freshwater fish of the family Anabantidae, of tropical Africa and Asia, having a lunglike breathing organ.

lab·y·rin·thi·an (lábbə-rínthi-ən) *adj.* Labyrinthine.

lab·y·rin·thine (lábbə-rín-thīn, -theen || -thin) *adj.* **1.** Of, pertaining to, or constituting a labyrinth. **2.** Intricate; complicated.

lab·y·rinth·o·dont (lábbi-rínthə-dont) *n.* Any primitive extinct amphibian of the subclass Labyrinthodontia, having hollow teeth convoluted in cross-section.

~*adj.* Of or pertaining to the Labyrinthodontia. [New Latin *Labyrinthodontia* : LABYRINTH + -ODONT.]

lab·y·ris (lábbi-riss) *n.* Also **lab·rys** (láb-). **1.** In ancient Minoan civilisation, a sacred double-headed axe. **2.** A similarly-shaped modern feminist symbol of strength, especially of lesbian solidarity. [Greek *labrus,* double-headed axe.]

lac[1] (lak) *n.* A resinous secretion of the **lac insect** *(see),* used in making shellac. [Dutch *lak* or French *laque,* from Hindi *lākh,* from Prakrit *lakkha,* from Sanskrit *lākshā.*]

lac[2]. Variant of **lakh.**

L.A.C. leading aircraftman (in Britain).

Laccadive, Minicoy, and Amindivi Islands. See **Lakshadweep.**

lac·co·lith (láckə-lith) *n.* A mushroom-shaped body of igneous rock intruded between layers of sedimentary rock. [Greek *lakkos,* cistern (referring to the shape) + -LITH.]

lace (layss) *n.* **1.** A delicate fabric woven of silk, cotton, nylon, or other thread in an open weblike pattern. **2.** A cord or ribbon threaded through eyelets or around hooks on two opposite edges, as of a shoe or garment, for drawing and tying them together. **3.** Gold or silver braid ornamenting an officer's uniform.

~*v.* **laced, lacing, laces.** —*tr.* **1.** To thread a cord through the eyelets or around the hooks of: *laced her shoes.* **2. a.** To draw together and tie the laces of. Used with *up.* **b.** To pinch in the waist of by tightening corset laces. **3.** To intertwine: *lace shoots of a plant through a trellis.* **4.** To apply lace to. **5.** To add spirits to (a drink). **6.** To streak with colour. **7.** *Informal.* To give a beating to; thrash. —*intr.* To be fastened with a lace. **—lace into.** To attack; assail. [Middle English *lace, laas, las,* braid, cord, from Old French *laz, las,* from Vulgar Latin *lacium* (unattested), from Latin *laqueus,* noose, trap, probably related to *lacere,* to allure.] **—lac·er** *n.*

Lacedaemon. See **Laconia, Sparta.**

lac·er·ate (lássə-rayt) *tr.v.* **-ated, -ating, -ates. 1.** To tear (especially flesh) roughly or jaggedly. **2.** To distress deeply.

~*adj.* (-rayt, -rət, -rit). Also **lac·er·at·ed** (-raytid). **1.** Torn; mangled. **2.** Deeply wounded; distracted. **3.** Having jagged, deeply cut edges: *lacerate leaves.* [Latin *lacerāre,* from *lacer,* torn, rent, mangled.] **—lac·er·a·tion** (-ráysh'n) *n.* **—lac·er·a·tive** (-rətiv) *adj.*

La·cer·ta (lə-súrtə) *n.* A constellation in the Northern Hemisphere near Cygnus and Andromeda. [New Latin, from Latin, LIZARD.]

lace·wing (láyss-wing) *n.* Any of various greenish or brownish insects of the families Chrysopidae and Hemerobiidae, having four gauzy wings, threadlike antennae, and larvae that feed on insect pests such as aphids. [From the texture of the wings.]

lach·es (láychiz, láchiz) *n., pl.* **laches.** *Law.* Culpable negligence; especially, delay in asserting a right or a claim. [Middle English *lachesse,* from Anglo-French, Old French, from *lasche,* lax, from Vulgar Latin *lascus* (unattested), from Latin *laxus,* LAX.]

Lach·e·sis (lácki-siss) *n. Greek Mythology.* One of the three **Fates** *(see).* [Greek *Lakhesis,* "disposer of lots", from *lakhein,* aorist infinitive of *lankhanein*†, to obtain by lot.]

Lach·ry·ma Chris·ti (láckrimə kristi) *n.* A dryish white or occasionally red wine produced from grapes grown on the southern slopes of Vesuvius. [Latin, "tear of Christ".]

lach·ry·mal, lac·ri·mal (láckrim'l) *adj.* **1.** Of or pertaining to tears. **2.** Of or pertaining to the lachrymal glands.

~*n.* **1.** A lachrymatory. **2.** *Plural.* The lachrymal glands. [Medieval Latin *lachrymālis, lacrimālis,* from Latin *lacrima, lacruma,* tear.]

lachrymal duct *n.* The short duct in the inner corner of the eyelid through which tears are drained into the nasal cavity. Also called "tear duct".

lachrymal gland *n.* A gland that lies beneath the upper eyelid in humans and many vertebrates and secretes tears.

lach·ry·ma·tor, lac·ri·ma·tor (láckri-maytər) *n.* Any substance that induces an excessive flow of tears; especially, **tear gas** *(see).* [Latin *lacrima,* tear + -OR.]

lach·ry·ma·to·ry (láckri-mə-təri, -may-, -máy-, -tri) *n., pl.* **-ries.** Formerly, a vase or phial for holding the tears of mourners.

~*adj.* Of, pertaining to, or causing tears. [Medieval Latin *lachrymatōrium,* from Late Latin *lacrimatōrius,* of tears, from Latin *lacrimāre,* to cry, from *lacrima,* tear.]

lach·ry·mose (láckri-mōss, -mōz) *adj.* **1.** Weeping or inclined to weep; tearful. **2.** Causing tears; sorrowful. **3.** Lugubrious; morose. [Latin *lacrimōsus,* from *lacrima,* tear.] **—lach·ry·mose·ly** *adv.*

lac·ing (láy-sing) *n.* **1.** *British.* A course of stone or brick built into a stone or rubble wall so as to bind the facing to the core. **2.** *Informal.* A thrashing.

la·cin·i·ate (lə-sínni-ayt, -ət, -it) *adj.* Also **la·cin·i·a·ted** (-aytid). *Biology.* **1.** Fringed. **2.** Having edges cut into narrow, fringelike segments or lobes: *laciniate petals.* [Latin *lacīnia,* fringe, tuft.] **—la·cin·i·a·tion** (-áysh'n) *n.*

lac insect *n.* Any of various insects of the subfamily Lacciferinae; especially, *Laccifer lacca,* of southern Asia, the female of which secretes the resinous substance lac.

lack (lak) *n.* **1.** A deficiency or want: *a lack of money.* **2.** A need.

~*v.* **lacked, lacking, lacks.** —*tr.* To be entirely without or have too little of (a thing or quality). —*intr.* **1.** To be wanting or deficient. Used with *in* or *for.* **2.** *Archaic.* To be missing. [Middle English *lac, lacke,* perhaps from Middle Dutch, deficiency, fault.]

Usage: Intransitive *lack,* followed by *for,* has attracted criticism: *They lack for nothing; You will not be lacking for support.* In both examples, the transitive use of *lack* provides an alternative: *They lack nothing; You will not lack support.*

lack·a·dai·si·cal (láckə-dáyzik'l) *adj.* Lacking spirit or enthusiasm; languid. [From earlier *lackadaisy,* extended form of LACKADAY.] **—lack·a·dai·si·cal·ly** *adv.* **—lack·a·dai·si·cal·ness** *n.*

lack·a·day (láckə-day, -dáy) *interj. Archaic.* Used to express regret or disapproval. [From the phrase *alack the day.*]

lack·ey (lácki) *n., pl.* **-eys.** Also **lac·quey** *pl.* **-queys. 1.** A liveried male servant; a footman. **2.** A servile follower; a toady.

~*tr.v.* **lackeyed, -eying, -eys.** Also **lac·quey, -queyed, -queying, -queys.** To attend as a lackey. [French *laquais,* from Old French, from Catalan *alacay,* akin to Spanish ALCALDE.]

lack·ing (lácking) *adj. British Informal.* Mentally deficient. **—lacking in.** Deficient in; in need of.

lack·lus·tre, *U.S.* **lack·lus·ter** (láck-lustər) *adj.* Lacking lustre, brightness, or vitality; dull.

La·clos (la-klṓ), **Pierre Choderlos de** (1741–1803). French writer and general. His novel, *les Liaisons dangereuses* (1782), is a study of moral and sexual corruption. He died fighting in Italy.

La·co·ni·a (lə-kṓni-ə). Also **Lac·e·dae·mon** (lássi-déemən). Ancient region of the southern Peloponnese, Greece. Sparta, its capital, stood on the river Evrotás, and dominated the area before the rise of the Achaean League in the third century B.C.

la·con·ic (lə-kónnik) *adj.* Expressed in or using few words; terse; succinct. See Synonyms at **concise.** [Latin *laconicus,* from Greek *Lakōnikos,* of or resembling the Laconians or Spartans (known for their brevity of speech: a famous anecdote concerns Philip of Macedon's warning, "If I enter Laconia, I shall raze Sparta to the ground", to which the Spartans returned the laconic message "If"), from *Lakōn*†, native of Laconia, Spartan.] **—la·con·i·cal·ly** *adv.*

lac·o·nism (láckə-niz'm) *n.* Also **la·con·i·cism** (lə-kónni-siz'm). **1.** Succinctness of expression. **2.** A laconic expression.

La Co·ru·ña (lá kō-ro͞on-yə). *English* **Co·run·na** (kə-rúnnə). City in northwest Spain, capital of the province of La Coruña. It is an Atlantic port and a summer resort. The English commander, Sir John Moore, was killed here in 1809 during the Peninsular campaign against Napoleon.

lac·quer (láckər) *n.* **1.** Any of various clear or coloured synthetic coatings, made by dissolving cellulose derivatives together with plasticisers and pigments in a mixture of volatile solvents, and used to give wood and metal surfaces a high gloss. **2.** Any glossy, often resinous material used as a surface coating, such as the exudation of the lacquer tree. **3.** A baked-on finish on the inside of food and drink tins. **4.** A substance sprayed on hair to keep a style in place. *~tr.v.* **lacquered, -quering, -quers. 1.** To coat with lacquer. **2.** To give a sleek, glossy finish to. [Earlier *lacker,* from obsolete French *lacre,* sealing wax, variant of Portuguese *laca,* LAC (resin).] **—lac·quer·er** *n.*

lacquer tree *n.* A tree, *Rhus verniciflua,* of eastern Asia, having a toxic exudation from which a black lacquer is obtained. Also called "varnish tree".

lacrimal. Variant of **lachrymal.**

lac·ri·ma·tion (láckri-máysh'n) *n.* The secretion of tears, especially in excess.

lacrimator. Variant of **lachrymator.**

la·crosse (lə-króss, la- || -kráwss) *n.* A team game of American Indian origin played with long-handled sticks fitted with nets for catching, carrying, and throwing the ball. [Canadian French, from French *(le jeu de) la crosse,* (the game of) the hooked stick, from Old French *crosse, croce,* staff, crosier, from Germanic.]

lac·tal·bu·min (lak-tál-bew-min, lák-tal-béw-) *n.* The albumin contained in milk. [LACT(O)- + ALBUMIN.]

lac·tam (lák-tam) *n.* Any of various amides containing the group -CONH-. [LACT(ONE) + AM(IDE).]

lac·tase (lák-tayz, -tayss) *n.* An enzyme occurring in certain yeasts and in the intestinal juices of mammals that catalyses the conversion of lactose into glucose and galactose. [LACT(O)- + -ASE.]

lac·tate (lák-tayt, lak-táyt) *intr.v.* **-tated, -tating, -tates.** To secrete or produce milk.
~n. A salt or ester of lactic acid. [Latin *lactāre,* to suckle, from *lac* (stem *lact-*), milk.] **—lac·ta·tion** (-táysh'n) *n.*

lac·te·al (lákti-əl) *adj.* **1.** Of, pertaining to, or like milk; milky. **2.** *Anatomy.* Of or pertaining to the lacteals.
~n. Anatomy. Any of numerous minute lymph-carrying vessels that convey chyle from the intestine to the thoracic duct. [Latin *lacteus,* of milk, from *lac* (stem *lact-*), milk.] **—lac·te·al·ly** *adv.*

lac·tes·cent (lak-téss'nt) *adj.* **1.** Becoming milky. **2.** Milky. **3.** *Biology.* Secreting or yielding a milky juice. Said of certain plants and insects. [Latin *lactescēns* (stem *lactescent-*), present participle of *lactescere,* to become milky, from *lactēre,* to be milky, from *lac* (stem *lact-*), milk.] **—lac·tes·cence** *n.*

lac·tic (láktik) *adj.* Pertaining to or derived from milk. [French *lactique,* from Latin *lac* (stem *lact-*), milk.]

lactic acid *n.* A hygroscopic syrupy liquid, $CH_3CH(OH).CO_2H$, present in sour milk, molasses, various fruits, and wines, and used in foods and beverages as an acidulant, flavouring, and preservative, and in adhesives, plasticisers, and pharmaceuticals.

lac·tif·er·ous (lak-tíffərəss) *adj.* **1.** Producing, secreting, or conveying milk. **2.** *Botany.* Yielding latex or a similar milky juice; laticiferous. [Late Latin *lactifer* : LACT(O)- + -FEROUS.]

lac·ti·fuge (lákti-fewj) *n.* Any drug or other agent used to suppress the secretion of milk in mothers not breast-feeding their babies. [LACTI- + -FUGE.]

lacto–, lact– *comb. form.* Indicates milk; for example, **lactoprotein.** [French, from Late Latin, from Latin *lac* (stem *lact-*), milk.]

lac·to·ba·cil·lus (láktō-bə-sílləss) *n., pl.* **-cilli** (-sílli). Any of various bacilli of the genus *Lactobacillus,* that ferment carbohydrates to produce lactic acid.

lac·to·fla·vin (lák-tō-fláyvin, -tə-) *n. Chemistry.* **Riboflavin** *(see).*

lac·to·gen·ic (láktə-jénnik) *adj.* Inducing lactation: *lactogenic hormone.* [LACTO- + -GENIC.]

lac·tone (lák-tōn) *n.* A cyclic ester of a hydroxyl acid, formed by removing the constituents of water from a molecule of the acid. [LACT(O)- + -ONE.] **—lac·ton·ic** (lak-tónnik) *adj.*

lac·to·pro·tein (láktō-prṓ-teen || -tee-in) *n.* Any protein normally present in milk.

lac·tose (lák-tōss, -tōz) *n.* A white crystalline disaccharide, $C_{12}H_{22}O_{11}$, occurring in milk and used in pharmaceuticals, infant foods, bakery products, and confections. Also called "milk sugar", "sugar of milk". [French : LACT(O)- + -OSE.]

la·cu·na (lə-kéw-nə, la-, -ko͞o-) *n., pl.* **-nae** (-nee) or **-nas. 1.** An empty space or missing part, especially in an ancient manuscript; a gap. **2.** *Biology.* A cavity or depression. [Latin *lacūna,* pool. See **lagoon.**] **—la·cu·nal, la·cu·nar·y** *adj.*

la·cu·nar (lə-kéw-nər, -ko͞o-) *n., pl.* **-nars** or **lacunaria** (láckew-náir-i-ə). *Architecture.* **1.** A ceiling or soffit decorated with a pattern of recessed panels. **2.** A panel in such a pattern.
~adj. Biology. Of, pertaining to, or containing lacunae. [Latin *lacūnar,* from *lacūna,* cavity, cleft, pool. See **lagoon.**]

la·cus·trine (lə-kúss-trīn, la-, -trin) *adj.* **1.** Of or pertaining to a lake. **2.** Living or growing in or along the edges of lakes. [French *lacustre,* of a lake, from Latin *lacus,* LAKE (influenced in form by Latin *palūster,* marshy, from *palus,* swamp).]

L.A.C.W. leading aircraftwoman (in Britain).

lac·y (láy-si) *adj.* **-ier, -iest.** Of, pertaining to, or resembling lace. **—lac·i·ness** *n.*

lad (lad) *n.* **1.** A boy or young man. **2.** *Informal.* A man of any age. Used familiarly. **3.** *British.* A person of any age who looks after horses: *a stable lad.* [Middle English *ladde*†.]

ladanum. Variant of **labdanum.**

lad·der (láddər) *n.* **1.** A device consisting of two long structural members crossed by parallel, equally spaced rungs, used for climbing up or down. **2.** A length of unravelled stitches, as in a stocking. Also called "run". **3. a.** A means of ascent and descent: *ascending the social ladder.* **b.** A series of ranked stages or levels: *high on the executive ladder.* See **fish ladder. 4.** *Sports.* A competition in a game, such as squash or tennis, in which each competitor tries to beat the competitor above him and so take his place.
~v. **laddered, -dering, -ders.** *—intr.* To develop a ladder. Used especially of stockings. *—tr.* To cause (a stocking, for example) to ladder. [Middle English *ladder,* Old English *hlǣd(d)er.*]

lad·der-back (láddər-bak) *n.* **1.** A chair back consisting of two upright posts connected by horizontal slats. **2.** A chair with this type of back. **—lad·der-back** *adj.*

lad·die (láddi) *n.* A young lad.

lade (layd) *v.* **laded, laden** (láyd'n) or **laded, lading, lades.** *—tr.* **1. a.** To load with or as if with cargo. **b.** To ship (cargo). **2.** To take up or remove water with a ladle or the like; bale. *—intr.* To take on cargo. [Lade (infinitive), laden (past participle); Middle English *laden, laden,* Old English *hladan, gehladen.*]

lad·en (láyd'n) *adj.* **1.** Weighed down with a load; heavy. **2.** Oppressed; burdened: *laden with grief.* **3.** Saturated or suffused. Also used in combination: *a guilt-laden atmosphere.*

la-di-da (laá-di-daá) *adj. Informal.* Affectedly genteel; pretentious.
~n. Informal. A person showing such affectation. [Imitative of affected speech.]

la·dies, la·dies' (láydiz) *n. Used with a singular verb. Informal.* A public lavatory for women. Also called "ladies' room".

ladies' fingers *n. Used with a singular or plural verb.* A plant, the **kidney vetch** *(see).* Compare **lady's finger.**

ladies' man *n.* A man who enjoys and attracts the company of women.

la·dies'-tress·es, la·dy's-tress·es (láydiz-tressiz) *n. Used with a singular or plural verb.* Any of various orchids of the genus *Spiranthes,* having a spike of small white flowers usually in a spiral.

La·din (la-déen) *n.* **1.** The Rhaeto-Romanic dialect spoken in southeast Switzerland, contiguous parts of northern Italy, and the Tyrol. It is a distinct Romance language. **2.** An inhabitant of this region who speaks Ladin. [Italian *Ladino,* from Latin *Latīnus,* LATIN.]

La·di·no (lə-déenō) *n.* A Romance language, derived from Spanish with Hebrew elements and modifications, spoken by Sephardic Jews, especially in the Balkans. Also called "Judaeo-Spanish". [Spanish, "Latin", from Latin *Latīnus,* LATIN.]

la·dle (láyd'l) *n.* **1.** A long-handled spoon with a deep bowl for serving liquids. **2.** A large container used to transfer molten metals.
~tr.v. **ladled, -dling, -dles. 1.** To lift out or convey with a ladle. **2.** To distribute (money or food, for example) liberally. Used with *out.* [Middle English *ladel,* Old English *hlædel,* from *hladan,* to draw out, LADE.]

Lad·o·ga (lád-ə-gə, laád-, -ō-). *Russian* **Ladozhskoye Ozero;** *Finnish* **Laatokka.** Largest freshwater lake in Europe, in northwest U.S.S.R. It covers 18 130 square kilometres (7,000 square miles).

la·dy (láydi) *n., pl.* **-dies. 1.** A woman having the refined habits, gentle manners, and other characteristics typically associated with breeding, culture, and high station; the female equivalent of a gentleman. **2. a.** An adult female. Used as a polite term, especially in her presence: *Would you ask the lady to wait?* Also used adjectivally: *a lady doctor.* **b.** *U.S. & South African. Informal.* Madam. Used in direct address: *Can I help you, lady?* **3.** A woman considered especially from the point of view of some specified ability or quality: *She's a very dynamic lady.* **4. a.** A woman to whom a man is romantically attached; a ladylove. **b.** *Informal.* A wife or mistress. **5.** *Capital* **L.** A term prefixed to the title of certain positions of office when such a position is held by a woman: *the Lady Mayor.* **6.** *Capital* **L.** *British.* The general feminine title of nobility and of other rank, used in the following specific ways: **a.** For the wife or widow of a knight or baronet: *Lady Smith* (wife of Sir Harry Smith). **b.** Semiformally for a marchioness, countess, viscountess, or baroness: *Lady Salisbury* (the Marchioness of Salisbury). **c.** As the usual style for the wife or widow of a baron: *Lady Snow* (wife of

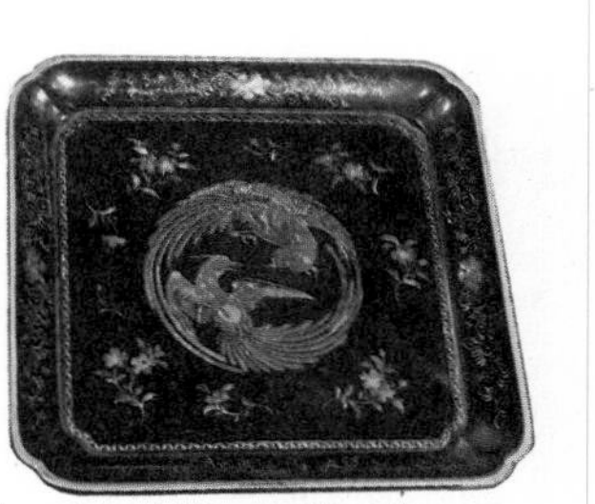

lacquer *A lacquered tray from an 18th-century Chinese picnic set, now in the Victoria and Albert Museum, London.*

PRONUNCIATION KEY

a, trap; aa, father; ai, fair; ar, star; aw, lawn; ay, play; b, bb, stab; rubber; ch, church; ck, ticket; d, dd, dead; ladder; e, dress; ee, bee; er, defer; ew, few; ewr, pure; ə, about; ər, letter; f, ff, fife; differ; g, gg, giggle; h, hat; i, kit; ī, price; īr, fire; j, judge; k, kick; l, ll, let; 'l, needle; m, mm, man; n, nn, no; 'n, sudden; ng, thing; o, lot; ō, no; o͝o, foot; o͞o, shoe; oor, poor; ow, cow; owr, hour; oy, boy; p, pp, pepper; r, rr, red; s, ss, sauce; sh, ship; t, tt, totter; th, thick; th, this; smooth; u, cut; ur, turn; v, vv, valve; w, wet; y, yes; z, zz, zebra; zh, vision; pleasure

IN FOREIGN WORDS:

aN, oN, Saint-Saëns; hl, Llanelli; Hluhluwe; kh, loch; lough; Khaled

STRESS MARK:

ín-sīt, insight; in-sī́t, incite

Lord Snow); **d.** As a courtesy title for the daughter of a duke, marquis, or earl: *Lady Hester Stanhope* (daughter of Earl Stanhope); **e.** As a courtesy title for the wife or widow of a younger son of a duke or marquis: *Lady John Russell* (wife of Lord John Russell, third son of the Duke of Bedford). ***Note:*** In direct address, *my lady* and *your ladyship* are deferential substitutes for any of the above.With all except **a,** the formal usage (as in addressing a letter), is *The Lady Snow, The Lady Ruthven,* and the like. [Middle English *la(ve)di, lafdi,* Old English *hlǣfdige,* "kneader of bread", lady : *hlǣf,* LOAF + *dig-* (unattested), knead.]

Usage: Apart from its special uses with reference to the British aristocracy, *lady* is the normal form to use when referring to a female person in her presence: *Show the lady to her seat; Has one of you ladies dropped a handkerchief? Woman* would be blunt or rude, or imply some kind of nuance, in such contexts. In fixed phrases or special contexts, however, *woman* is a permissible variant for *lady:* one may refer to either the *ladies' finals* or the *women's finals* in a sport, or to a *young lady* or *young woman.* In such cases, *lady* is the form which implies an extra degree of courtesy or formality. On the other hand, in the context of jobs, *woman* is often used adjectivally without any special implication: *a woman teacher, women students.*

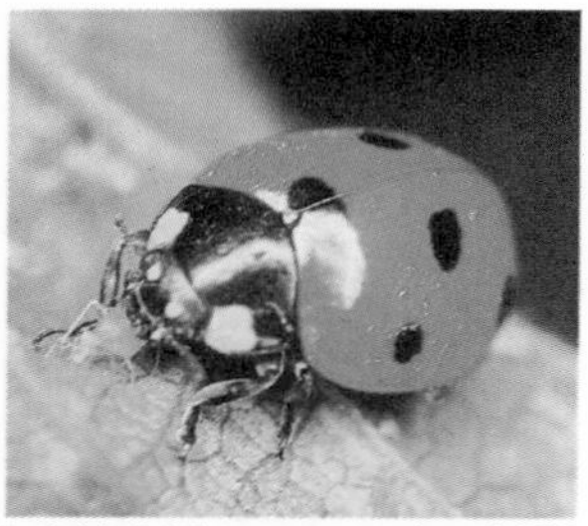

ladybird *There are more than 3,000 species of ladybird, and almost all are among the most beneficial of insects, eating countless numbers of aphids, greenflies, and other pests. In California, they are gathered by the thousands in their breeding grounds and farmers buy them to clean their crops.*

la·dy·bird (láydi-burd) *n.* Any of numerous small beetles of the family Coccinellidae, often reddish with black spots. Also *U.S.* "ladybug". [After OUR LADY.]

Lady Chapel *n. Sometimes small* **l,** *small* **c.** A chapel in a church or cathedral dedicated to the Virgin Mary.

Lady Day *n.* The Feast of the Annunciation, celebrated on March 25, one of the four quarter days in England and Wales.

lady in waiting *n., pl.* **ladies in waiting.** A lady of a court appointed to serve or attend a queen or princess. Also called "lady of the bedchamber".

la·dy·kill·er (láydi-killər) *n. Slang.* A man reputed to be exceptionally successful and often ruthless with women.

la·dy·like (láydi-līk) *adj.* **1.** Characteristic of or befitting a lady; refined; well-bred. **2.** Unduly sensitive to matters of propriety or decorum. **3.** Effeminate. Said of a man.

la·dy·love (láydi-luv) *n.* A beloved woman; a sweetheart.

lady of the house *n.* The female head of a household.

lady's finger *n.* A vegetable, **okra** *(see).* Compare **ladies' fingers.**

la·dy·ship (láydi-ship) *n. Sometimes capital* **L.** Used in addressing or referring to a woman holding the title of Lady, or ironically of any woman. Used with *Your* or *Her.* See Note at **lady.**

lady's mantle *n.* Any of various plants of the genus *Alchemilla,* having clusters of small greenish flowers.

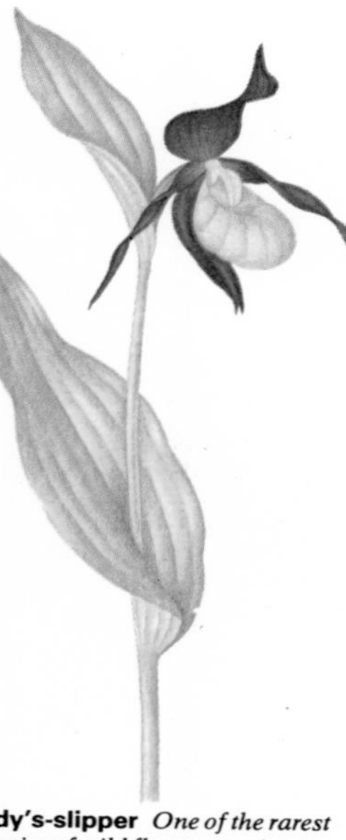

lady's-slipper *One of the rarest species of wild flower growing in Britain. It blooms in shady places in spring.*

La·dy·smith (láydi-smith). Market town in eastern South Africa. During the second Anglo-Boer War, a British garrison there was besieged from November, 1899, until relieved in February, 1900.

la·dy's-slip·per (láydiz-slíppər || -slippər) *n.* Any of various orchids of the genus *Cypripedium,* having variously coloured flowers with an inflated, pouchlike lip.

la·dy's-smock (láydiz-smok) *n.* A plant, the **cuckooflower** *(see).*

lady's-tresses. Variant of **ladies'-tresses.**

La·ën·nec (la-e-nék), **René Théophile Hyacinthe** (1781–1826). French physician who invented the stethoscope.

La·er·tes (lay-ér-teez). *Greek Mythology.* The father of Odysseus.

La·e·trile (láy-ə-tril) *n.* A trademark for a cyanide-containing compound extracted from the seeds of peaches and related plants and used experimentally in the treatment of cancer.

laevo–, *U.S.* **levo–** *comb. form.* Indicates: **1.** Towards the left-hand side; for example, **laevorotatory. 2.** A laevorotatory chemical compound; for example, **laevulose.** [Latin *laevus,* left.]

laevodopa. Variant of **levodopa.**

lae·vo·ro·ta·tion (léevō-rō-táysh'n) *n.* An anticlockwise rotation; a rotation to the left, especially of the plane of polarised light.

lae·vo·ro·ta·to·ry (léevō-rṓtə-tri, -rō-táy-, -təri). *adj.* Also **lae·vo·ro·ta·ry** (-rṓtəri). **1.** In optics, turning or rotating the plane of polarisation of light to the left or anticlockwise. **2.** *Chemistry.* Of or pertaining to a solution that rotates the plane of polarised light in this way. Compare **dextrorotatory.**

laev·u·lin (lévvew-lin, léevew-) *n.* A polysaccharide that occurs in the tubers of certain plants of the genus *Helianthus,* such as the Jerusalem artichoke. [LAEVULOSE + -IN.]

laev·u·lose (lévvew-lōss, léevew-, -lōz) *n.* A sugar, **fructose** *(see).* [LAEVO- + -ULE + -OSE.]

La Fa·yette (laá-fī-ét, lá-, -fay-; *French* la-fa-yét), **Marie Joseph Paul Yves Roch Gilbert du Motier, Marquis de** (1757–1834). French soldier and politician. He served on Washington's staff in the War of American Independence. In France he took part in the 1789 and 1830 revolutions. He designed the modern French flag.

La Fayette, Marie-Madeleine Pioche de la Vergne, Comtesse de (1634–93). French writer. Her novel *la Princesse de Clèves* (1678) examines the conflicts between passion and duty in marriage.

La·fon·taine (lá-fon-táyn, laá-, lə-fón-; *French* la-foN-tén), **Henri-Marie** (1854–1943). Belgian jurist and statesman. He was President of the International Peace Bureau (1907–43), and was awarded the Nobel peace prize in 1913.

La Fon·taine (lá-fon-táyn, laá-, lə-fón; *French* la-foN-tén), **Jean de** (1621–95). French poet, who collected the fables of Aesop and others in his *Fables* (1668–94).

lag[1] (lag) *intr.v.* **lagged, lagging, lags. 1.** To fail to keep up a pace; fall behind; straggle; loiter. Often used with *behind.* **2.** To fail, weaken, or slacken gradually; flag.

~*n.* **1.** The act, process, or condition of lagging. **2.** An extent or duration of lagging; a time lag. [Probably from *lag* (noun), last person; compare dialect *fog, seg, lag,* fanciful distortions of *first, second, last* in children's games.] **—lag·ger** *n.*

lag[2] *n.* Any covering for a cylindrical object, especially the insulating covering of a hot-water cylinder, steam pipes, or the like.

~*tr.v.* **lagged, lagging, lags.** To furnish or cover with lagging. [Perhaps from Scandinavian, akin to Swedish *lagg,* barrel stave.] **—lag·ger** *n.*

lag[3] *tr.v.* **lagged, lagging, lags.** *Slang.* **1.** To arrest. **2.** To send to prison.

~*n. Slang.* **1.** A convict. Used especially in the phrase *an old lag.* **2.** A term of imprisonment. [19th century : origin obscure.]

lag·an (lággən) *n.* Also **li·gan** (lígən), **lag·end** (lággənd). *Law.* Cargo or equipment thrown into the sea from a ship in distress, often attached to a float or buoy to enable it to be recovered. [Old French, perhaps from Old Norse *lögn* (stem *lagn-*), dragnet.]

Lag b'O·mer (lág bṓmər, laág, bə-ṓmər) *n.* A Jewish holiday, originally an agricultural festival, celebrated on the 33rd day after the second day of Passover, on the 18th day of Iyar. [Hebrew, "33rd (day) of the Omer".]

la·ge·na (lə-jéenə) *n.* The structure in the inner ear of fishes and amphibians that is homologous to the cochlea of higher vertebrates. [Latin, from Greek *lagēnos,* flask (referring to the shape).]

la·ger[1] (laágər) *n.* A light, usually effervescent beer of a type originally brewed in Germany, that contains a relatively small amount of hops. [Short for German *Lager(bier),* (beer) for storing, from *lager,* store, lair, from Old High German *legar,* lair.]

lager[2]**.** Variant of **laager.**

La·ger·löf (laágər-löv), **Selma** (1858–1940). Swedish novelist. She wrote *Gösta Berlings Saga* (1891), and in 1909 became the first woman to win the Nobel prize for literature.

lag·gard (lággərd) *adj.* Lagging behind or tending to lag behind; dawdling; straggling. [LAG (fall behind) + -ARD.] **—lag·gard** *n.* **—lag·gard·ly** *adv.* **—lag·gard·ness** *n.*

lag·ging (lágging) *n.* **1.** Insulation used to prevent heat diffusion from steam pipes, boilers, and the like. **2.** A wooden frame built to support the sides of an arch until the keystone is positioned. [From LAG (insulating covering).]

lag·o·morph (lággō-mawrf, lággə-) *n.* Any of various gnawing mammals of the order Lagomorpha, which includes the rabbits and hares. [New Latin *Lagomorpha* : Greek *lagōs,* hare + -MORPH.] **—lag·o·mor·phic** (-mórfik) *adj.*

la·goon (lə-gṑon) *n.* **1.** A body of salt water separated from the sea by sand or shingle bars or coral reefs. **2.** *Australian & N.Z.* A small body of fresh water. [French *lagune* and Italian or Spanish *laguna,* from Latin *lacūna,* pool, cavity, from *lacus,* LAKE.]

La·gos (láy-goss). Largest city of Nigeria, lying on the Gulf of Guinea. It was the country's capital until a new one was inaugurated at Abuja in 1982. Lagos consists of four islands and four mainland sections, joined to one another by bridges and causeways. It is Nigeria's chief port and industrial centre.

lag screw *n.* A heavy screw having a square bolt head. [Originally used in securing barrel staves. See **lag** (insulate).]

Lag·ting, Lag·thing (laág-ting) *n.* The upper house in the Storthing, or parliament, of Norway. Compare **Odelsting.** [Norwegian : *lag,* society, from Old Norse, due place (influenced in meaning by plural *lög,* law) + *ting,* parliament, from Old Norse *thing,* parliament, assembly.]

La Guar·di·a (lə gwárdi-ə), **Fiorello (Henry)** (1882–1947). U.S. politician. He was a congressman (1916–21, 1923–33), and mayor of New York (1934–45). One of the city's airports is named after him.

lah, la (laa) *n. Music.* In tonic sol-fa, a syllable representing the sixth note of a diatonic scale.

La·hore (lə-hór || -hṓr). A city in east central Pakistan, the capital of Punjab province and Pakistan's second largest city. It is notable for its architecture, especially the palace and mausoleum of the emperor Jahangir.

la·ic (láy-ik) *adj.* Also **la·i·cal** (-ik'l). Of or pertaining to the laity; secular.

~*n.* A layman. [Late Latin *lāicus,* LAY.] **—la·i·cal·ly** *adv.*

la·i·cise, la·i·cize (láy-i-sīz) *tr.v.* **-cised, -cising, -cises. 1.** To free from ecclesiastical control; give over to laymen. **2.** To secularise. **—la·i·ci·sa·tion** (-sī-záysh'n || *U.S.* -si-) *n.*

laid. Past tense and past participle of **lay** (verb).

laid-back (láyd-bák) *adj. Informal.* Relaxed; easy-going.

laid paper *n.* **1.** A paper made on wire moulds that give it a characteristic watermark of fine lines. Compare **wove paper. 2.** A machine-made paper imitating this.

laik (layk) *v.* **laiked, laiking, laiks.** *British Regional. —intr.* **1.** To have a day off work; be on holiday. **2.** To be out of work. **3.** To play about. *—tr.* To play (a game). [Middle English *leiken,* to frolic, play, from Old Norse *leika;* akin to LARK.]

lain. Past participle of **lie** (to recline).

Laing (lang, layng), **R(onald) D(avid)** (1927–). British psychiatrist. His controversial theories about the nature of sanity are outlined in *The Politics of Experience* (1967). His other books include *The Divided Self* (1960) and a book of poetry, *Knots* (1970).

lair (lair) *n.* **1.** The den or dwelling of a wild animal. **2.** *British.* An enclosure for cattle to stay in on their way to market. **3.** *Archaic.* A resting place; a couch. **4.** *Informal.* A place of hiding or seclusion.

~*v.* **laired, lairing, lairs.** *—tr.* To put in a lair. *—intr.* To retreat to or lie in a lair. [Middle English *lair, leir,* Old English *leger.*]

laird (laird) *n.* In Scotland, the owner of a landed estate. [Scottish, variant of LORD.]

Laird (laird), **Macgregor** (1808–61). Scottish explorer, who helped to open up the Niger river.

lair·y (laír-i) *adj.* **-ier, -iest.** *Australian Informal.* Flashily dressed; exhibitionistic. [Variant of LEERY.]

lais·sez-al·ler, lais·ser-al·ler (léssay-ál-ay, láy-say-) *n.* Also **lais·ser-aller.** An absence of constraint; uncontrolled freedom. [French, "let go".]

lais·sez-faire, lais·ser-faire (léssay-faír, láy-say-) *n.* **1.** The doctrine that government should not interfere with commerce. **2.** *Informal.* Noninterference in the affairs of others. [French, "allow (them) to do".] **—lais·sez-faire·ism** *n.*

lais·sez-pas·ser, lais·ser-pas·ser (léssay-pássay, láy-say-, -páa-say) *n.* A pass; especially, a permit allowing one to enter a restricted area. [French, "allow (them) to pass".]

la·i·ty (láy-əti) *n., pl.* **-ties. 1.** Laymen collectively, as distinguished from the clergy. **2.** All those persons outside a given profession, art, or other specialised field; nonprofessionals. [From LAY (nonclergy).]

La·ius (lí-əss, láy-əss). *Greek Mythology.* The king of Thebes who was killed by his own unwitting son, Oedipus.

lake[1] (layk) *n. Abbr.* **L., l. 1.** A large inland body of fresh or salt water. **2.** A scenic pond as in a park. **3.** A large pool of any liquid. [Middle English *lac,* from Old French *lac,* from Latin *lacus,* basin for water.]

lake[2] *n.* A pigment consisting of organic colouring matter with an inorganic base or carrier. [Variant of LAC (resin).]

lake[3] *tr.v.* **laked, laking, lakes.** To cause (blood) to become a homogeneous solution by releasing haemoglobin from erythrocytes, as by suspending the erythrocytes in water. [From LAKE (pigment).]

Lake Dis·trict (láyk-distrikt). Scenic district and tourist area of northwest England, lying between Morecambe Bay and the Solway Firth. It includes the Cumbrian mountains and 15 lakes, among them Windermere, Ullswater, and Derwentwater. The Lake District National Park, covering about 32 375 hectares (80,000 acres), was established in 1951.

lake dwelling *n.* A dwelling built on piles in a shallow lake, especially in prehistoric times. **—lake dweller** *n.*

lake herring *n.* **1.** A fish, the **powan** *(see).* **2.** A North American food fish, *Coregonus artedii* (or *Leucichthys artedii*), of the Great Lakes region, related to the whitefishes.

Lake·land terrier (láyk-lənd) *n.* A terrier of a breed developed in the Lake District for flushing foxes from cover.

Lake Plac·id (plássid). Village in northeast New York state, United States. It lies on Mirror Lake in the Adirondack mountains, and was the site of the Winter Olympic Games in 1932 and 1980.

Lake Poets *pl.n.* Coleridge, Wordsworth, and Southey, grouped as a school because they lived for a time in the Lake District.

lakh, lac (laak, lak) *n.* In India: **1.** The number 100,000: *12 lakhs of rupees.* **2.** A very large number. Compare **crore.** [Hindi *lākh,* from Sanskrit *laksha.*]

Lak·shad·weep (lak-shád-weep). Formerly **Laccadive, Minicoy, and Amindivi Islands.** Indian territory off the coast of Kerala, comprising 27 coral islands, 10 of which are inhabited. The total area is only 32 square kilometres (12 square miles). Administered as separate island groups by Britain (1877–1947), it became a single territory, the Laccadive, Minicoy, and Amindivi Islands, in 1956. The name was changed to Lakshadweep in 1973.

lak·y (láyki) *adj.* **-ier, -iest.** Of the colour of lake or of blood.

-lalia *n. comb. form.* Indicates a speech defect; for example, **echolalia.** [New Latin, from Greek *lalia,* chatter, Greek *lalein,* to babble.]

La·lique (la-léek, lə-), **René** (1860–1945). French jeweller and glassmaker, who applied Art Nouveau designs to crystal ware.

Lal·lans (lál-ənz) *n. Used with a singular verb.* The dialect of Scottish English spoken in the Lowlands. **—Lal·lan, Lal·lans** *adj.*

lal·la·tion (la-láysh'n) *n.* The pronunciation of the sound (l) as (r). [Latin *lallāre,* to make lulling sounds.]

lam (lam) *v.* **lammed, lamming, lams.** *Slang.* **—***tr.* To thrash; wallop. **—***intr.* To strike. Used with *into* or *out.* [Of Scandinavian origin, akin to Old Norse *lemja,* to flog, make lame by beating.]

Lam. Lamentations (Old Testament).

la·ma (láamə) *n.* A Buddhist monk of Tibet or Mongolia. [Tibetan *bla-ma,* superior one.]

La·ma·ism (láamə-iz'm) *n.* The religion of Tibet and Mongolia and neighbouring areas, a form of Mahayana Buddhism with an admixture of animism, characterised by elaborate rituals. [From LAMA (priest).] **—La·ma·ist** *n.* & *adj.* **—La·ma·is·tic** (-ístik) *adj.*

La·marck (lə-márk, la-), **Jean Baptiste Pierre Antoine de Monet, Chevalier de** (1744–1829). French naturalist. His idea of human evolution influenced Darwin's theory, but Lamarck believed that acquired characteristics could be inherited, a belief since discredited. **La·marck·i·an** *n.* & *adj.*

La·marck·ism (lə-márk'iz'm) *n.* The theory that adaptive responses to environment cause structural changes capable of being inherited. Compare **Darwinism.** See **acquired characteristic.** [Developed by Chevalier de LAMARCK.]

La·mar·tine (la-maar-téen), **Alphonse Marie Louis de** (1790–1869). French romantic poet who was briefly minister of foreign affairs in 1848.

la·ma·ser·y (láamə-səri ‖ -serri) *n., pl.* **-ies.** A Lamaist monastery.

lamb (lam) *n.* **1.** A young sheep, especially one not yet weaned. **2.** The flesh of a young sheep used as meat. **3.** Lambskin. **4. a.** A sweet, mild-mannered person; a dear. **b.** One who is easily cheated; a dupe. **5.** A member of a Christian flock. **—the Lamb.** Christ. Also called "Lamb of God". **~***intr.v.* **lambed, lambing, lambs.** To give birth to a lamb. **—lamb down.** *Australian Informal.* **1.** To spend one's money wastefully or recklessly. **2.** To persuade (a person) to do this. [Middle English, Old English, from Germanic *lambiz-* (unattested).]

Lamb (lam), **Charles** (1775–1834). English essayist. He and his sister, Mary Lamb (1764–1847), wrote *Tales from Shakespeare* (1807) for children.

lam·baste, lam·bast (lam-báyst, -bást) *tr.v.* **-basted, -basting, -bastes** or **-basts.** *Slang.* **1.** To give a thrashing to; whip; beat. **2.** To attack verbally; berate or criticise. [Perhaps LAM (beat) + BASTE (beat).]

lamb·da (lámdə) *n.* The 11th letter in the Greek alphabet, written Λ, λ. Transliterated in English as *L, l.* [Greek *lambda,* of Semitic origin, akin to Hebrew *lāmedh,* LAMED.]

lambda particle *n. Symbol* Λ *Physics.* An electrically neutral subatomic particle in the baryon family, having a mass 2,183 times that of the electron and a mean lifetime of approximately 2.5×10^{-10} second. [From LAMBDA.]

lambda point *n.* **1.** The temperature at which the transition from helium I to superfluid helium II occurs, approximately 2.19° K. **2.** The temperature of any phase transition in which the specific heat capacity regarded as a function of temperature has a logarithmic singularity.

lamb·doid (lám-doyd) *adj.* Also **lamb·doi·dal** (lam-dóyd'l). Designating the deeply serrated suture in the skull between the two parietal bones and the occipital bone. [French *lambdoïde,* from Greek *lambdoeidēs,* "lambda-shaped" : LAMBDA + -OID.]

lam·bent (lámbənt) *adj.* **1.** Flickering lightly and gently over a surface: *lambent flames.* **2.** Flitting over subjects with effortless brilliance: *a lambent wit.* **3.** Having a gentle glow; luminous. —See Synonyms at **bright.** [Latin *lambens* (stem *lambent-*), present of *lambere,* to lick, tap.] **—lam·ben·cy** *n.* **—lam·bent·ly** *adv.*

lam·bert (lámbərt) *n. Symbol* L A unit of illumination equal to one lumen per square centimetre. [After J.H. *Lambert* (1728–77), German physicist.]

Lam·bert (lámbərt), **Constant** (1905–51). British composer and conductor. Much of his work, notably *The Rio Grande* (1929), a choral piece, experimented with the jazz idiom. His *Music Ho!* (1934) is a noted critical study of the music of the 1920s.

Lam·beth (lámbəth). Borough of central Greater London, lying south of the river Thames. In it are situated the South Bank arts complex, the headquarters of the Greater London Council, and Lambeth Palace, the London residence of the archbishop of Canterbury.

Lambeth Conference *n.* An assembly of all the diocesan bishops of the Anglican Communion throughout the world, held every 10 years at Lambeth Palace to discuss matters of interest.

Lambeth Walk *n. British.* A dance popular in the 1930s and 1940s.

lamb·kin (lám-kin) *n.* **1.** A small lamb. **2.** A small endearing child.

lam·bre·quin (lám-brə-kin, -bər-) *n.* **1. a.** A piece of material worn over a helmet in medieval times. **b.** A heraldic representation of this, **mantling** *(see).* **2.** A scalloped band of colour ornamenting the top of a piece of porcelain. [French, from Dutch *lamperkin* (unattested), diminutive of *lamper,* veil, from Middle Dutch *lampert.*]

lamb·skin (lám-skin) *n.* **1.** The skin of a lamb, especially when dressed without removing the fleece, as for a garment. **2.** Leather made from the dressed hide of a lamb.

lamb's-let·tuce (lámz-lettiss) *n.* A plant, **corn salad** *(see).*

lambs' tails *pl.n. British.* Hazel catkins.

lame[1] (laym) *adj.* **lamer, lamest. 1.** Disabled or crippled in one or more limbs, especially in a leg or foot so that walking is impaired. **2.** Weak and ineffectual; unsatisfactory: *a lame excuse.* **~***tr.v.* **lamed, laming, lames. 1.** To cause to become lame. **2.** To make ineffective; disable. [Middle English *lame,* Old English *lama.*] **—lame·ly** *adv.* **—lame·ness** *n.*

lame[2] *n.* A thin metal plate such as an overlapping plate in medieval armour. [Old French, from Latin *lāmina,* thin plate.]

la·mé (láa-may ‖ U.S. laa-máy) *n.* A fabric in which are woven metallic threads, often of gold or silver. [French, from adjective, "worked with silver and gold thread", from Old French *lame,* thin metal plate, LAME.]

la·med, la·medh (láa-mid, -med) *n.* The 12th letter in the Hebrew alphabet. [Hebrew *lāmedh,* "ox goad" (from the shape of the letter).]

lame duck *n. Informal.* **1.** An ineffectual, helpless, or disabled person. **2.** A company that is chronically unable to achieve profitability. **3.** A speculator on a stock market who is unable to meet all his obligations. **4.** *U.S.* An official or body during the period between an election defeat and the inauguration of a successor.

la·mel·la (lə-méllə) *n., pl.* **-mellae** (-méllee) or **-las. 1.** A thin scale, plate, or layer; especially: **a.** Any of the gills of a mushroom. **b.** Any of the concentric layers of calcified material of which bone is formed. **c.** Any of the layers of membranes in a plant chloroplast. **2.** A thin layer of a fluid. **3.** A wooden, metal, or concrete member forming the frame of a vaulted roof. [New Latin, from Latin *lāmella,* diminutive of *lāmina,* thin plate.] **—la·mel·lar** (-méllər) *adj.* **—la·mel·lar·ly** *adv.*

la·mel·late (lámmi-layt, lət, -lit, lə-mé-) *adj.* Also **lam·el·la·ted** (-laytid). **1.** Having, composed of, or arranged in thin layers or lamellae. **2.** Resembling a lamella. **—lam·el·la·tion** (lámmi-láysh'n) *n.*

lamelli– *comb. form.* Indicates a lamella or lamellae; for example, **lamellibranch**. [From LAMELLA.]

la·mel·li·branch (lə-mélli-brangk) *n.* Any of the molluscs of the class Lamellibranchia (or Bivalvia). See **bivalve**.
~*adj.* Of or pertaining to lamellibranchs. [New Latin *Lamellibranchia*, "plate gilled" : LAMELLI- + BRANCHIA.]

la·mel·li·corn (lə-mélli-kawrn) *n.* A beetle of the superfamily Lamellicornia (or Scarabaeoidea), which includes the scarabs and other beetles having antennae tipped with movable leaflike plates. [New Latin *Lamellicornia*, "plate horned" : LAMELLI- + Latin *cornū*, horn.] —**la·mel·li·corn** *adj.*

la·mel·li·form (lə-mélli-fawrm) *adj.* Having the form of a thin plate or lamella. [LAMELLI- + -FORM.]

la·ment (lə-mént) *v.* -mented, -menting, -ments. —*tr.* 1. To express grief for or about; mourn over: *lament a death.* 2. To regret deeply; deplore. —*intr.* 1. To grieve. 2. To wail; complain.
~*n.* 1. An expression of sorrow or grief; a lamentation. 2. A song or poem expressing grief; an elegy; a dirge. [French *lamenter*, from Old French, from Latin *lāmentārī*, from *lāmentum*, expression of sorrow.] —**la·ment·er** *n.*

lam·en·ta·ble (lámmen-təb'l, lə-mén-) *adj.* 1. To be lamented; deplorable; highly regrettable. 2. *Archaic.* Exhibiting sorrow or grief; mournful. —See Synonyms at **pathetic**. —**lam·en·ta·bly** *adv.*

lam·en·ta·tion (lámmen-táysh'n, lámmən-) *n.* 1. The act of lamenting. 2. An instance of such expression of grief; a lament.

Lam·en·ta·tions (lámmen-táysh'nz, lámmən-) *n. Used with a singular verb. Abbr.* **Lam.** A book of the Old Testament, attributed to Jeremiah.

la·ment·ed (lə-méntid) *adj.* Mourned for. Used chiefly in the phrase *the late lamented.* —**la·ment·ed·ly** *adv.*

la·mi·a (láymi-ə) *n., pl.* -mias or -miae (-ee). 1. *Greek Mythology.* A monster, represented as a serpent with the head and breasts of a woman, reputed to prey upon humans and suck their blood. 2. A sorceress; a vampire. [Middle English, from Latin, from Greek.]

lam·i·na (lámmi-nə) *n., pl.* -nae (-nee) or -nas. 1. A thin plate, sheet, or layer, as of bone or mineral. 2. *Botany.* The expanded area, or blade, of a leaf or thallus. 3. *Zoology.* A scalelike or platelike structure, such as any of the thin layers of sensitive tissue in the hoof of a horse. 4. *Geology.* A narrow bed of rock. [New Latin, from Latin *lāmina*, thin plate.] —**lam·i·nar** (-nər), **lam·i·nal** *adj.*

laminar flow *n.* Nonturbulent flow of a viscous fluid in layers near a boundary, as of lubricating oil in bearings. Compare **streamline flow, turbulent flow.**

lam·i·nar·i·a (lámmi-naíri-ə) *n.* Any seaweed of the genus *Laminaria*, having large, brown, leathery fronds. Also called "oarweed". See **kelp**. [New Latin, from Latin *lamina*, tissue, plate. See **lamina**.]

lam·i·nate (lámmi-nayt) *v.* -nated, -nating, -nates. —*tr.* 1. To beat or compress into a thin plate or sheet. 2. To divide into thin layers. 3. To make by uniting several layers. 4. To cover with thin sheets. —*intr.* To split into thin layers or sheets.
~*adj.* (lámmi-nayt, -nət, -nit). Also **lam·i·nose** (-nōss), **lam·i·nous** (-nəss). Consisting of, arranged in, or covered with a lamina or laminae.
~*n.* A laminated product, such as plywood. [LAMIN(A) + -ATE.] —**lam·i·na·tor** (-naytər) *n.*

lam·i·nat·ed (lámmi-naytid) *adj.* 1. Composed of layers bonded together. 2. Arranged in laminae; laminate.

laminated glass *n.* See **safety glass**.

laminated iron *n.* Thin sheets or iron or a steel-silicon alloy shaped to form the core of a transformer to reduce the eddy current losses that occur with a solid iron core.

lam·i·na·tion (lámmi-náysh'n) *n.* 1. The process or state of being laminated. 2. Something laminated. 3. A lamina.

lam·i·ni·tis (lámmi-nítiss) *n.* Inflammation of the sensitive laminae in the hoof of a horse. Also called "founder". [New Latin : LAMIN(A) + -ITIS.]

Lam·mas (lámməss) *n.* August 1, one of the four Scottish quarter days. [Middle English *Lammasse*, Old English *hlāfmæsse* : *hlāf*, LOAF + *mæsse*, MASS.] —**Lam·mas·tide** *n.*

lam·mer·gei·er, lam·mer·gey·er (lámmər-gī-ər) *n.* A large predatory bird, *Gypaetus barbatus*, of mountainous regions of the Old World, having black bristles around the bill. Also called "bearded vulture" and sometimes "ossifrage". [German *Lämmergeier* : *Lämmer*, genitive plural of *Lamm*, lamb, from Old High German *lamb*, from Germanic *lambiz-* (unattested), LAMB + *Geier*, vulture, from Old High German *gīr*.]

Lam·mer·muir Hills (lámmər-mewr). Range of low-lying mountains in southeast Scotland, southeast of Edinburgh. The highest peak, Meikle Says Law, rises to 535 metres (1,755 feet).

lamp (lamp) *n.* 1. a. Any of various devices that generate light, heat, or therapeutic radiation. b. A vessel containing oil, paraffin, or alcohol burned through a wick for illumination. 2. *Poetic.* A star, planet, meteor, or other celestial body regarded as lighting the heavens. 3. *Literary.* That which illumines the mind or the soul. [Middle English *lampe*, from Old French, from Latin *lampas*, from Greek, torch, from *lampein*, to shine.]

lamp·black (lámp-blak) *n.* A grey or black pigment made from the soot of incompletely burned carbonaceous materials, used as a pigment, and in matches, explosives, lubricants, and fertilisers.

Lam·pe·du·sa (lámpi-dōozə), **Giuseppe (Tomasi) di** (1896-1957). Italian novelist. His best-known work, *The Leopard* (1958), published posthumously, deals with his own experience of the Sicilian aristocracy in decline at the beginning of the century.

lam·per eel (lámpər) *n.* The lamprey. [Variant of LAMPREY.]

lam·pern (lámpərn) *n.* A European lamprey, *Lampetra fluviatilis*, that migrates up rivers from the sea to spawn. [Middle English *laumprun*, from Old French, from *lampreie*, LAMPREY.]

lam·pi·on (lámpi-ən) *n.* An oil-burning lamp, often of coloured glass, for outdoor use. [French, from Italian *lampione*, augmentative of *lampa*, lamp, from Old French *lampe*, LAMP.]

lamp·light (lámp-līt) *n.* The light shed by a lamp.

lamp·light·er (lámp-lītər) *n.* 1. Formerly, a person employed to light and extinguish street lamps. 2. *U.S.* Something, such as a torch or taper, used to light lamps.

lam·poon (lam-pôon) *n.* 1. A bitingly satirical piece of writing that is strongly personal in its flavour and ridicule. 2. A light, good-humoured satire. —See Synonyms at **caricature**.
~*tr.v.* **lampooned, -pooning, -poons.** To assail in a satirical composition; write a lampoon concerning. [French, perhaps from *lampons*, let us drink (used as a refrain in 17th-century poetry), first person plural imperative of *lamper*, to gulp down, guzzle, from Germanic.] —**lam·poon·er, lam·poon·ist** *n.* —**lam·poon·er·y** *n.*

lamp·post (lámp-pōst) *n.* A post supporting a street lamp.

lam·prey (lámpri) *n., pl.* **-preys.** Any of various primitive elongated freshwater or anadromous fishlike vertebrates of the family Petromyzontidae, characteristically having a jawless sucking mouth with a rasping tongue. Also called "lamper eel". [Middle English *lamprei*, from Old French *lampreie*, from Medieval Latin *lamprēda†*. See also **limpet**.]

lam·pro·phyre (lámprə-fīr) *n.* Any of several intermediate igneous rocks comprising feldspar and ferromagnesian minerals that occur as dykes and minor intrusions. [Greek *lampros*, bright + *-phyre*, from PORPHYRY.]

lamp·shade (lámp-shayd) *n.* Any of various protective or ornamental coverings used for screening a light bulb.

lamp shell *n.* A marine invertebrate, a **brachiopod** *(see).* [From the shape of one of the valves in certain species.]

LAN Local area network.

Lan·ark (lánnərk). Town in south central Scotland, lying on the river Clyde. At New Lanark, nearby, Robert Owen built his model industrial village for his mill hands in the early 19th century.

la·nate (láy-nayt) *adj. Biology.* Covered with or consisting of woolly hairs. [Latin *lānātus*, from *lāna*, wool.]

Lancang Jiang. See **Mekong.**

Lan·ca·shire[1] (láng-kə-shər, -sheer). Nonmetropolitan county in northwest England. In the late 18th and early 19th centuries it was the greatest cotton-manufacturing region in the world. Preston is the administrative centre, and Lancaster is the county town. Since 1974 the Liverpool and Manchester areas, Lancashire's old industrial heartland, have been formed into the metropolitan counties of Merseyside and Greater Manchester.

Lancashire[2] *n.* A white, crumbly, English cheese made from cow's milk. [Originally made in Lancashire.]

Lan·cas·ter[1] (láng-kə-stər || -kaa-, -ka-). The family name of the English royal family (1399-1461).

Lancaster[2]. County town of Lancashire, northwest England, lying on the river Lune. It stands on the site of a Roman military station.

Lancaster, Duchy of. Collection of estates scattered throughout England and Wales, with its own administration. Created as an earldom in 1267, it was attached to the Crown when Henry IV became king in 1399, and it still provides revenue for the Crown.

Lan·cas·tri·an (lang-káss-tri-ən) *adj.* 1. Of or pertaining to the English royal house of Lancaster. 2. Of or pertaining to Lancashire or its inhabitants.
~*n.* 1. A member of the Lancastrian faction in the Wars of the Roses (1455-85). 2. An inhabitant of Lancashire.

lance (laanss || lanss) *n.* 1. A thrusting weapon with a long wooden shaft and a sharp metal head, used by horsemen. 2. A similar implement for spearing fish or killing whales. 3. A lancer. 4. A lancet.
~*tr.v.* **lanced, lancing, lances.** 1. To pierce with a lance. 2. *Archaic.* To fling; hurl. 3. To make an incision in with a lancet; cut into: *lance a boil.* [Middle English *la(u)nce*, from Old French *lance*, from Latin *lancea†*.]

lance corporal *n. Abbr.* **L/Cpl.** 1. In the British Army, a noncommissioned officer of the lowest rank. 2. In the U.S. Marine Corps, an enlisted man ranking above a private first class and below a corporal. [Translation from obsolete *lancepesade*, from Old French *lancepessade*, from Old Italian *lancia spezzata*, old soldier, "broken lance" : *lancia*, LANCE + *spezzata*, feminine past participle of *spezzare*, to break in pieces.]

lance-jack (laanss-ják || lánss-) *n. British Slang.* A lance corporal.

lance·let (laanss-lit || lánss-) *n.* Any of various small, flattened marine organisms of the genus *Amphioxus* and subphylum Cephalochordata, allied to the vertebrates but having a notochord rather than a true vertebral column. Also called "amphioxus".

Lan·ce·lot, Laun·ce·lot (laan-slət, -slot, -sə-lət, -lot || lán-). In Arthurian legend, a knight of the Round Table whose love affair with Queen Guinevere resulted in a war with King Arthur

lan·ce·o·late (laan-si-ə-layt, -lət, -lit || lán-) *adj.* Narrow and tapering at each end: *lanceolate leaves.* [Late Latin *lanceolātus*, from Latin *lanceola*, diminutive of *lancea*, LANCE.]

lanc·er (laan-sər || lán-) *n.* 1. Formerly, a cavalryman armed with a lance. 2. A soldier belonging to a regiment that was originally armed with lances. [French *lancier*, from Old French, from LANCE.]

lanc·ers (laan-sərz || lán-) *n.* Also **lan·ciers** (lán-seerz, laan-). *Used*

---

with a singular verb. **1.** A form of quadrille for 8 or 16 couples. **2.** The music for this dance.

lance sergeant *n.* In certain regiments of the British Army, a corporal.

lan·cet (laán-sit || lán-) *n.* **1.** A surgical knife with a short, wide, pointed, double-edged blade. **2.** *Architecture.* **a.** A lancet arch. **b.** A lancet window. [Middle English *lancette,* from Old French, diminutive of *lance,* LANCE.]

lancet arch *n. Architecture.* An arch that is narrow and pointed like the head of a spear. Also called "lancet".

lancet fish *n.* Either of two large marine fishes, *Alepisaurus ferox,* of the Atlantic, or *A. richardsoni,* of the Pacific, having long, sharp teeth and a large dorsal fin.

lancet window *n. Architecture.* A tall narrow window set in a lancet arch. Also called "lancet".

lance·wood (laánss-wood || lánss-) *n.* **1.** Any of several tropical trees, such as *Oxandra lanceolata* of tropical America or *Acacia doratoxylon* of Australia, having hard, durable, uniformly grained wood. **2.** The wood of such a tree.

lan·cin·at·ing (laán-si-nayting || lán-) *adj.* Acute; stabbing. Said of a pain.

land (land) *n.* **1.** The solid ground of the Earth, especially as distinguished from the sea. **2. a.** The soil; the earth: *till the land.* **b.** Any tract of ground considered in terms of its potential or nature: *desert land; prime building land.* **c.** *Plural. South African.* An area of land used for the cultivation of crops. **d.** The rural as opposed to the urban life: *back to the land.* **3. a.** A nation. **b.** A district or region inhabited by a particular people. **c.** *Plural.* Territorial possessions. **d.** A sphere or domain: *no longer in the land of the living.* **4.** Public or private landed property; real estate. **5.** *Law.* **a.** Any tract of land that may be owned, together with everything growing or constructed upon it. **b.** A landed estate. **6. a.** Any of the raised strips in a field that is divided by furrows. **b.** The raised portion of a grooved surface. **—how the land lies.** The nature of the prevailing state of affairs.
~*v.* **landed, landing, lands.** *—tr.* **1. a.** To bring to and unload on land: *land cargo.* **b.** To set or bring down on land or other surface: *land an aircraft.* **2.** To cause to arrive; bring to a specified place or condition: *landed me in trouble.* **3. a.** To catch and pull in (a fish). **b.** *Informal.* To win; secure: *land a big contract.* **4.** To deliver: *land a blow on the head.* *—intr.* **1. a.** To come to shore. **b.** To disembark. **2. a.** To descend towards and settle on the ground or other surface. **b.** To meet or come to rest on a surface in a specified way: *landed on her back.* **—land up.** **1.** To reach a specified place or condition in the end; finish up: *You'll land up in court if you carry on this way.* **2.** To cause to reach a specified place or condition in the end. **—land with.** To present with something that is not wanted or appreciated: *Don't land me with your problems.* [Middle English, Old English.] **—land·less** *adj.*

-land *n. comb. form.* Indicates: **1.** A region of a specified quality or kind; for example, **grassland.** **2.** A realm of a specified nature; for example, **dreamland.**

land agent *n.* **1.** *Chiefly Australian & N.Z.* An estate agent. **2.** A person who manages a landed estate.

lan·dau (lán-daw || -dow) *n.* **1.** A four-wheeled closed carriage with passenger seats facing front and back and a roof made in two sections for lowering or detaching. **2.** An early type of car with a roof similar to this. [First manufactured in *Landau,* Bavaria.]

lan·dau·let, lan·dau·lette (lándaw-lét) *n.* **1.** A small landau. **2.** A early type of U.S. car having a collapsible roof over the back seat and an open driver's seat.

land bank *n.* A bank that issues long-term loans on real estate in return for mortgages.

land breeze *n.* Wind blowing from the land towards the sea or a lake centre in the early part of the day, most commonly in the tropics.

land bridge *n.* **1.** A tract of land once thought to have connected one continent to another, providing a passage for migrating animals and thereby influencing their distribution. **2.** A tract of land, such as the Panama isthmus, joining two continents.

land crab *n.* Any terrestrial crab of the tropical family Gecarcinidae, having a large, square body.

land·drost (lánd-drost || *South African* lúnt-) *n. South African.* Formerly, a government official serving as magistrate or sheriff of a particular district. [Afrikaans, from Dutch : *land,* country + *drost,* sheriff.]

land·ed (lándid) *adj.* **1.** Owning land: *landed gentry.* **2.** Consisting of land or real estate: *a landed estate.*

land·fall (lánd-fawl) *n.* **1.** The sighting or reaching of land on a voyage or flight. **2.** The land sighted or reached.

land·form (lánd-fawrm) *n.* Any physical feature of the earth's surface, such as a mountain or river valley.

land-grab·ber (lánd-grabbər) *n.* One who seizes land illegally or unscrupulously; specifically, one who took over a farm in Ireland following the eviction of its tenant.

land·grave (lánd-grayv) *n.* **1.** In medieval Germany, a count having jurisdiction over a particular territory. **2.** The title of certain German princes. [German *Landgraf,* from Middle High German *lantgrāve* : *lant,* land, + *grāve,* count.]

land·gra·vi·ate (land-gráyvi-ət, -it, -ayt) *n.* The office, jurisdiction, or territory of a landgrave.

land·gra·vine (lánd-grə-veen) *n.* **1.** The wife or widow of a landgrave. **2.** The female ruler of a landgraviate. [German *Landgräfin,* from Middle High German *lantgrævinne,* from *lantgrāve,* LANDGRAVE.]

land·hold·er (lánd-hōldər) *n.* A person who owns or holds land. **—land·hold·ing** *n.*

land·ing (lánding) *n. Abbr.* **ldg. 1. a.** The act or process of coming to land or rest, especially after a sea voyage or flight. **b.** A termination, especially of a sea voyage or flight. **2.** A site for landing. **3. a.** An intermediate platform on a flight of stairs. **b.** The area at the top or bottom of a staircase.

landing beam *n.* A radio beam transmitted from an airfield to enable incoming aircraft to make a landing using instruments only.

landing craft *n. Abbr.* **L.C.** A flat-bottomed naval craft specifically designed to convey troops and equipment from ship to shore.

landing field *n.* A tract of land providing a runway for aircraft.

landing gear *n.* The undercarriage of an aircraft, designed to support the weight of the craft and its load on the ground.

landing strip *n.* An aircraft runway without airport facilities.

land·la·dy (lánd-laydi) *n., pl.* **-dies. 1.** A woman who owns and rents leases land, commercial property, or residential units. **2.** A woman who runs a boarding house or inn. **3.** A female publican or the wife of a publican.

länd·ler (léntlər) *n.* **1.** An Austrian country dance for couples in triple time. **2.** The music for this dance. [German, from dialectal *Landl,* Upper Austria, where the dance originated.]

land line *n.* **1.** A telephone or telegraph link consisting of a cable laid over land rather than under the sea. **2.** A radio link.

land·locked (lánd-lokt) *adj.* **1.** Surrounded or nearly surrounded by land. **2.** Confined to inland waters, as certain salmon are.

land·lop·er (lánd-lōpər) *n. Chiefly Scottish.* A tramp or vagabond. [Dutch : LAND + *loper,* from *loopen,* to walk, LEAP.]

land·lord (lánd-lawrd) *n.* **1.** A person who owns and leases land or buildings. **2.** A man who runs a boarding house or inn. **3.** A man who runs a public house; a publican.

land·lord·ism (lánd-lawr-diz'm) *n.* **1.** A system of land management in which ownership of land is vested in a private individual or group that leases it at a fixed rate to tenants. **2.** The advocacy of such a system.

land·lub·ber (lánd-lubbər) *n.* A person with little or no experience of the sea or seamanship.

land·mark (lánd-maark) *n.* **1.** A fixed marker, such as a concrete block, indicating a boundary line. **2.** A prominent and identifying natural or man-made feature of a landscape. **3.** An event marking an important stage of development or a turning point in history.

land·mass (lánd-mass) *n.* Any large area of land, such as a continent.

land mine *n.* An explosive mine laid usually just below the surface of the ground.

land of milk and honey *n.* A region or country offering the promise of a high standard of living and material comforts. [Referring to the Promised Land and God's promise to Moses to lead the Israelites "unto a land flowing with milk and honey" (Exodus 3:8).]

Land of Nod *n. Informal.* Sleep. [Punning phrase from NOD (to fall asleep) and the biblical Land of Nod: "And Cain . . . dwelt in the land of Nod, on the East of Eden" (Genesis 4:16).]

Land of the Long White Cloud *n.* New Zealand.

Land of the Midnight Sun *n.* **1.** Land lying north of the Arctic circle. It has at least one day in summer when the sun does not set. **2.** Any region or country whose borders lie within this area, especially Lappland.

Land of the Rising Sun *n.* Japan.

Lan·dor (lán-dawr), **Walter Savage** (1775–1864). British writer. A romantic republican, he is best known for his *Imaginary Conversations of Literary Men and Statesmen* (1824–29), written in Florence.

land·own·er (lánd-ōnər) *n.* One who owns land. **—land·own·er·ship** *n.* **—land·own·ing** *n. & adj.*

land-poor (lánd-poor) *adj.* Owning much unprofitable land but lacking the capital to improve or maintain it.

land·race (lánd-rayss) *n.* **1.** A pig of a white, lop-eared breed, yielding good-quality bacon and pork. **2.** Any primitive variety of a cultivated crop. [Danish: *land,* LAND + *race,* breed, RACE.]

land rail *n.* A bird, the **corncrake** *(see).*

Land Registry *n. Law.* In Britain, an office where the title, registrable leases, mortgages, restrictive covenants, or the like, of or affecting a piece of land are registered, and where a purchaser may go to inspect these before buying a piece of land.

Land-Ro·ver (lánd-rōvər) *n.* A trademark for a powerful four-wheel drive motor car that is especially suited for rough terrain.

land·scape (lánd-skayp, *old-fashioned* -skip) *n.* **1.** A wide view or vista of natural scenery: *a desert landscape.* **2.** A painting, photograph, or other pictorial representation depicting such scenery. **3.** The branch of art dealing with the representation of natural scenery. **4. a.** A locality as seen with regard to its natural and man-made features: *an industrial landscape.* **b.** The scenery or appearance, natural or as modified by man, characteristic of a particular locality: *the Highland landscape.* **5.** An extensive mental view; a prospect; a vista: *whole landscapes of thought.*
~*v.* **landscaped, -scaping, -scapes.** *—tr.* To adorn or improve (grounds) by contouring the land and planting flowers, shrubs, or trees. *—intr.* To arrange grounds artistically as a profession. [Dutch *landschap,* from Middle Dutch *landschap, lantscap,* landscape, region : *land,* land + *-schap, -scap,* suffix indicating condition.]

landscape architecture *n.* The decorative and functional alter-

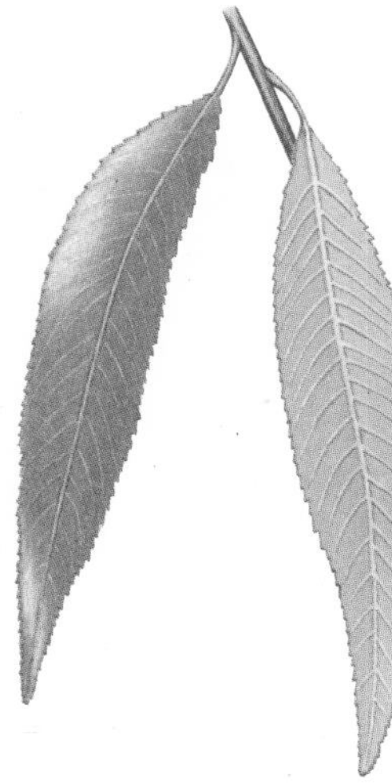

lanceolate *A botanical term describing the narrow leaves of shrubs and trees that taper gently to a point like the head of a lance. These leaves are from a willow tree.*

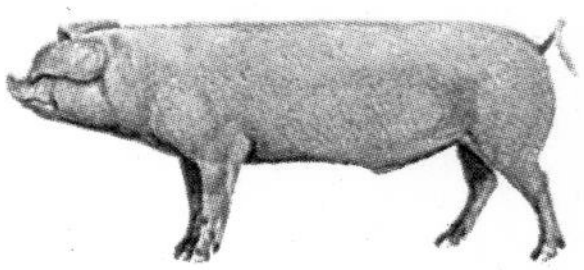

Landrace *A Scandinavian breed of pig, introduced to Britain in the 1950s and reared for its bacon. It is widely used for crossing as well as pure breeding.*

ation, planning, and planting of a piece of land, especially with reference to the siting of buildings. —**landscape architect.** *n.*

landscape gardening *n.* The planning and planting of gardens or grounds in order to obtain a picturesque or harmonious result. —**landscape gardener** *n.*

land·scap·ist (lánd-skaypist) *n.* A painter of landscapes.

Land·seer (lán-seer), **Sir Edwin Henry** (1802–73). British painter. His paintings, often depicting animals, were popular with both Queen Victoria and the public, combining sentimentality with photographic realism; *The Monarch of the Glen* (1851) is probably one of the best known of all animal paintings. He also designed the lions in Trafalgar Square.

Land's End. Rugged, westernmost peninsula of Cornwall and of England. It is the furthest point on the mainland of Great Britain from John O' Groats, which is traditionally considered to be its northernmost point.

land·side (lánd-sīd) *n.* The flat side of a plough opposite the furrow.

lands·knecht (lántsk-nekht, lántsk-) *n.* A European mercenary soldier in the 16th or 17th century; especially, a German foot soldier armed with a pike or lance. [German *Landsknecht : land + knecht,* soldier, KNIGHT.]

land·slide (lánd-slīd) *n.* **1. a.** The dislodging and fall of a mass of earth or rock or both. **b.** The dislodged mass. Also *chiefly British* "landslip". **2. a.** An overwhelming majority of votes for a political party or candidate. **b.** An election that sweeps a party or person into office. **c.** Any great victory.

land·slip (lánd-slip) *n. Chiefly British.* A landslide.

Lands·mål (láantss-mawl) *n.* **Nynorsk** *(see).* [Norwegian *Landsmål,* "country speech".]

lands·man¹ (lándz-mən) *n., pl.* **-men** (-mən). One who lives and works on land as distinguished from a seaman.

lands·man² (lándz-mən, láants-) *n., pl.* **landsleit** (-līt). A fellow Jew coming from one's own district or town in Eastern Europe. [Yiddish, compatriot, from Middle High German *lantsman :* Old High German *lant,* land + *man,* man.]

Land·stei·ner (lánd-stī-nər, láant-, -shtī-), **Karl** (1868–1943). Austrian physician. Noted for his discovery of blood groups (1900), and for devising the ABO classification which enabled blood transfusions to be made, he also discovered the Rh factor, and was the first to isolate the poliomyelitis virus. He was awarded the Nobel prize in 1930.

Land·tag (láant-taak) *n.* **1.** A legislative assembly of a West German state. **2.** In some German states in the 19th century, a diet or assembly. [German, "land-day".]

land tax *n.* Formerly in Britain, a tax paid by the owner of land.

land·ward (lándwərd) *adj.* Being towards the land.

land·wards (lándwərdz) *adv.* Towards the land or the shore.

Land·wehr (láant-vair) *n.* In German-speaking countries, a trained military reserve. [German, "land defence".]

land yacht *n.* A wind-powered vehicle having wheels and sails and used on flat ground, such as beaches. —**land yachting** *n.*

lane¹ (layn) *n.* **1. a.** A narrow way or passage between walls, hedges, or fences. **b.** A narrow road, as in the country. **2.** Any narrow passage, course, or track, such as: **a.** A prescribed course for ships or aircraft. **b.** Any of two or more strips delineated on a road or motorway to accommodate a single line of traffic. **c.** Any of a set of parallel courses marking the bounds for contestants in a race, especially a swimming or running race. **d.** A bowling alley. [Middle English, Old English, akin to Old Frisian *lana,* Middle Dutch *lāne†.*]

lane² *adj. Scottish.* Lone.

Lane (layn), **Sir Allen** (1902–70). British publisher. In 1936 he founded Penguin books, the first paperback publishing house in the United Kingdom.

Lan·franc (lán-frangk) (*c.*1010–89). Italian churchman. He was appointed Archbishop of Canterbury (1070) by William I, in which post he reorganised the English church as a mainstay of the Norman administration.

lang (lang) *adj. Scottish.* Long.

lang. language.

Lang (lang), **Fritz** (1890–1976). German film director. After pioneering the German film industry with such films as *Metropolis* (1926) and *M* (1931), he moved to Hollywood where he made many Westerns and thrillers about their sombreness of tone.

Langerhans, islets of *pl.n.* **Islets of Langerhans** *(see).*

Lang·land (láng-lənd), **William** (*c.*1332–*c.*1400). English poet. Probably a minor cleric, he is attributed with the authorship of *The Vision of William concerning Piers the Plowman* (earliest complete known edition: 1392), one of the greatest literary works of medieval England. Its religious allegory is combined with social comment on inequality and clerical abuse.

lang·lauf (laáang-lowf) *n.* A cross-country ski run. [German *Langlauf,* "long race" : *lang,* long, from Old High German + *Lauf,* a running, from Old High German *hlouf,* a leap, from *hlouffan,* to leap.] —**lang·lauf** *intr.v.* —**läng·lauf·er** (-loyfər) *n.*

lang·ley (lángli) *n.* A unit of illumination used to measure temperature, as of a star, equal to one gram calorie per square centimetre of irradiated surface. [After S.P. *Langley* (1834–1906). U.S. astronomer.]

Lan·go·bard (láng-gə-baard, -gō-) *n., pl.* **-bardi** (-bárdi). A **Lombard** *(see).* —**Lan·go·bar·dic** (-bárdik) *adj.*

lan·gouste (lóng-gōost, long-gōost) *n.* The **spiny lobster** *(see).*

[French, from Old French, from Old Provençal *langosta,* from Vulgar Latin *lacusta* (unattested), perhaps variant of Latin *lŏcusta,* lobster, LOCUST.]

lan·gous·tine (lón-gōoss-téen) *n.* A **Dublin Bay prawn** *(see).* [French, diminutive of LANGOUSTE.]

lan·grage (láng-grij) *n.* Also **lan·grel** (-grəl), **lan·gridge** (-grij). A type of shot consisting of scrap iron loaded into a case, formerly used in naval warfare to damage sails and rigging.

lang·syne, lang syne (láng-sín, -zín) *adv. Scottish.* Long ago. ~*n. Scottish.* Time long past; times past. [Middle English *lang sine : lang,* LONG + *sine,* contraction of *sithen,* SINCE.]

Lang·try (láng-tri), **Lillie,** born Emilie Charlotte le Breton (1853–1929). British actress. Known as the "Jersey Lily", she was already a society figure before making her stage debut (1881). She was for a time the mistress of Edward, Prince of Wales.

lan·guage (láng-gwij) *n. Abbr.* **lang. 1. a.** The aspect of human behaviour that involves the use of vocal sounds in meaningful patterns and, when they exist, corresponding written symbols to form, express, and communicate thoughts and feelings. **b.** The faculty in human beings which enables them to communicate in this way. **2.** A pattern of such behaviour, historically established among a social or cultural group, involving a grammar and vocabulary that offers substantial communication only among its users: *the English language.* **3.** Any method of communicating ideas, as by a system of signs, symbols, gestures, or the like: *the language of algebra; body language.* **4.** The transmission of meaning, feeling, or intent by significance of act or manner: *"There's language in her eye"* (Shakespeare). **5.** The special vocabulary and usages of a scientific, professional, or other group. **6.** A characteristic style of speech or writing: *Miltonic language.* **7. a.** Speech or writing which uses vulgar or abusive terms: *Less of the language!* **b.** A particular manner of utterance or choice of words: *gentle language.* **8.** The manner or means of communication between living creatures other than man: *the language of dolphins.* **9. a.** *Often plural.* A language, especially a foreign language, as a subject of study: *He did languages at university.* **b.** Linguistics. **10.** *Law.* The wording of a document or statute as distinct from its spirit. **11.** A computer programing code enabling human language to be translated into a form intelligible to computers. —**speak the same language.** To have the same background, experience, or understanding as another person. [Middle English *langage,* from Old French, from Gallo-Roman *linguāticum* (unattested), from Latin *lingua,* tongue, language.]

language laboratory *n.* A room designed for learning foreign languages, using audiovisual equipment such as tape recorders and a monitoring device that enables the teacher to listen and speak to students individually or all together.

langue (laangg, loNg) *n. Linguistics.* Language considered as an abstract pattern or system shared by a speech community, as opposed to **parole** *(see),* the actual instances of its use in speech or writing. Compare **competence.** [French (specialised sense introduced by Saussure), tongue, language.]

langue de chat (də shaa) *n.* A thin, flat, finger-shaped, sweet biscuit or piece of chocolate. [French, "cat's tongue".]

langue d'oc (dok) *n.* The Romance language spoken in and around Provence and the Roussillon surviving in Provençal and Occitan. [French, from Old French, "language of *oc*". *Oc* is the word for "yes" in Provençal.]

Langue·doc (lóng-dók). Wine-producing region of southern France, formerly a province, lying on the Mediterranean Sea to the west of the Rhône. Its largest city is Toulouse.

langue d'o·ïl (do-éel) *n.* The Romance language of Gaul north of the Loire on which modern French is based. [French, "language of *oïl*". *Oïl* is the word for "yes" in northern medieval French.]

lan·guet (láng-gwet, -gwit) *n. Rare.* A tonguelike thing or part. [Middle English, from Old French *languette,* diminutive of *langue,* tongue, language, from Latin *lingua.*]

lan·guid (láng-gwid) *adj.* **1.** Lacking energy or vitality; faint; weak. **2.** Showing little or no spirit or animation; listless. **3.** Slow of movement; sluggish. [Old French *languide,* from Latin *languidus,* from *languēre,* to LANGUISH.] —**lan·guid·ly** *adv.* —**lan·guid·ness** *n.*

lan·guish (láng-gwish) *intr.v.* **-guished, -guishing, -guishes. 1. a.** To become weak or feeble; sag with loss of strength or vigour; flag. **b.** To continue in a state of apathy, debility, or suffering; exist under miserable or disheartening conditions. **c.** To be left ignored or neglected. **2.** To fall off; fade. **3.** To become listless as with longing; pine. Often used with *for.* **4.** To affect a mawkish air of nostalgia, tenderness, or wistfulness. [Middle English *languishen,* from Old French *languir* (stem *languiss-*), from Vulgar Latin *languīre* (unattested), from Latin *languēre,* to be faint or weak.] —**lan·guish·er** *n.* —**lan·guish·ment** *n.*

lan·guish·ing (láng-gwishing) *adj.* **1.** Becoming weak; fading. **2.** Slow; lingering. **3.** Expressing languor; full of sentimentality. —**lan·guish·ing·ly** *adv.*

lan·guor (láng-gər ‖ láng-ər) *n.* **1.** Physical or mental lassitude; sluggishness. **2.** Oppressive quiet or stillness. **3.** An atmosphere or feeling of soft or wistful tenderness. **4.** *Archaic.* Debility; sickness. —See Synonyms at **lethargy.** [Middle English, from Old French, from Latin, from *languēre,* to LANGUISH.] —**lan·guor·ous** *adj.* —**lan·guor·ous·ly** *adv.* —**lan·guor·ous·ness** *n.*

lan·gur (lung-góor, laang-) *n.* Any of various slender, long-tailed, leaf-eating, Asian monkeys of the genus *Presbytis* and related genera. Also called "leaf monkey". [Hindi *langūr,* perhaps from Sanskrit *lāṅgūla†,* "tailed".]

language

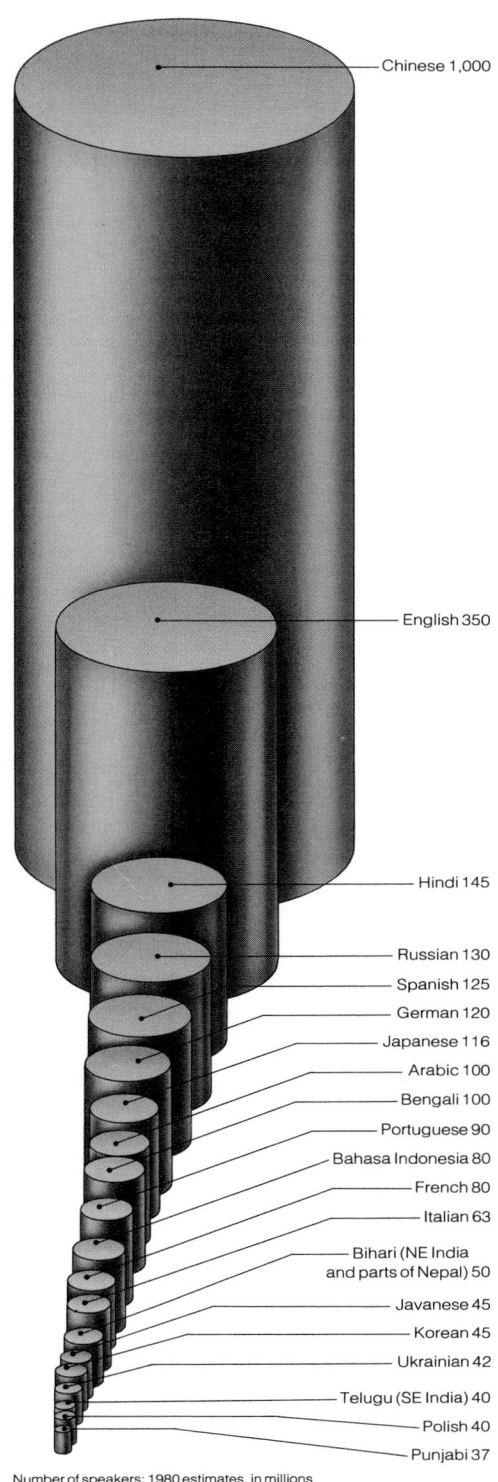

THE TONGUES OF MEN

The 20 most widely spoken languages in the world

Chinese is spoken by the largest number of people, but many dialects, such as Mandarin and Cantonese, are mutually unintelligible when spoken, and could almost be regarded as separate languages. On this basis, English is the most widely spoken language. Like Spanish and Portuguese, it has spread far beyond its land of origin.

Chinese 1,000
English 350
Hindi 145
Russian 130
Spanish 125
German 120
Japanese 116
Arabic 100
Bengali 100
Portuguese 90
Bahasa Indonesia 80
French 80
Italian 63
Bihari (NE India and parts of Nepal) 50
Javanese 45
Korean 45
Ukrainian 42
Telugu (SE India) 40
Polish 40
Punjabi 37

Number of speakers; 1980 estimates, in millions

---

laniard. Variant of **lanyard.**

la·ni·ar·y (lánni-əri ‖ -erri) *adj.* Adapted for tearing. Said of teeth, especially canines.

~*n., pl.* **laniaries.** A laniary tooth; a canine. [Latin *laniāre,* to tear.]

la·nif·er·ous (lə-nífferəss) *adj. Biology.* Having wool or wool-like hair. [Latin *lānifer,* "wool-bearing" : *lāna,* wool + -FEROUS.]

lank (langk) *adj.* **1.** Long and lean; gaunt. **2.** Long, straight, and limp: *lank hair.* —See Synonyms at **lean.** [Old English *hlanc,* loose, hollow, from Germanic.] —**lank·ly** *adv.* —**lank·ness** *n.*

lank·y (lángki) *adj.* **-ier, -iest.** Tall, thin, and ungainly. See Synonyms at **lean.** —**lank·i·ly** *adv.* —**lank·i·ness** *n.*

lan·ner (lánnər) *n.* **1.** A falcon, *Falco biarmicus,* of Africa and the Mediterranean region. **2.** *Archaic.* The female of this species, used in falconry. [Middle English *laner,* from Old French *lanier (faucon),* cowardly (falcon), scornful application of *lanier,* weaver, from Latin *lānārius,* wool worker, from *lāna,* wool.]

lan·ner·et (lánnə-ret) *n. Archaic.* A male lanner, smaller than the female, used in falconry. [Middle English *lanerette,* from Old French *laneret,* diminutive of *lanier,* LANNER.]

lan·o·lin, lan·o·line (lánnə-lin, -leen) *n.* A yellowish-white fatty substance obtained from wool and used in soaps, cosmetics, and ointments. Also called "wool fat". [German *Lanolin* : Latin *lāna,* wool + -OL (hydrocarbon) + -IN.]

la·nose (láy-nōss, -nōz) *adj.* Having woolly hair. [Latin *lānōsus,* from *lāna,* wool.] —**la·nos·i·ty** (lay-nóssəti) *n.*

Lans·bu·ry (lánz-bəri, -bri), **George** (1859–1940). British politician. As an M.P. (1910–12, 1922–40), he espoused women's suffrage and pacifism. He was leader of the Labour Party (1931–35).

lans·que·net (lán-skə-net) *n.* **1.** A card game involving betting. **2.** A landsknecht. [French.]

lan·ta·na (lan-táynə, -táʿanə) *n.* Any of various aromatic, chiefly tropical shrubs of the genus *Lantana,* having dense clusters of small, variously coloured flowers. [New Latin *Lantana†.*]

lan·tern (lántərn) *n.* Also *obsolete* **lant·horn** (lánt-hawrn, lántərn). **1.** A case that has transparent or translucent sides for holding and protecting a light, and is either fixed or portable. **2.** The room at the top of a lighthouse where the light is located. **3.** *Architecture.* A structure built on top of a roof with open or windowed walls to let in light and air. **4.** A **magic lantern** *(see).* [Middle English *lanterne,* from Old French, from Latin *lanterna,* from Greek *lamptēr,* lantern, torch, from *lampein,* to shine.]

lantern fish *n.* Any of numerous small deep-sea fishes of the family Myctophidae, having phosphorescent light organs on the body.

lantern fly *n.* Any of various chiefly tropical insects of the subfamily Fulgorinae, having an enlarged, elongated head. [They were once erroneously thought to be luminous.]

lantern jaw *n.* **1.** A protruding, usually square-shaped, lower jaw. **2.** *Plural.* Long thin jaws with sunken cheeks. —**lan·tern-jawed** *adj.*

lantern slide *n.* A photographic slide for projection, used in a magic lantern.

lantern wheel *n.* A small pinion consisting of circular discs connected by cylindrical bars that serve as teeth, used now chiefly in inexpensive clocks. Also called "lantern pinion".

lan·tha·nide (lánthə-nīd) *n.* Also **lan·tha·non** (-non). A **rare-earth element** *(see).* [LANTHAN(UM) + -IDE.]

lanthanide series *n.* The set of chemically related elements with atomic numbers from 57 to 71; the rare-earth elements.

lan·tha·num (lánthənəm) *n. Symbol* **La** A soft, silvery-white, malleable, ductile, metallic, rare-earth element, obtained chiefly from monazite and bastnaesite, used in glass manufacture and with other rare earths in carbon lights for film and television studio lighting. Atomic number 57, atomic weight 138.91, melting point 920°C, boiling point 3,469°C, relative density 5.98 to 6.186, valency 3. [New Latin, from Greek *lanthanein,* to hide (from the finding of lanthanum concealed in cerium oxide).]

la·nu·gi·nous (lə-néw-ji-nəss ‖ -nōō-) *adj.* Also **la·nu·gi·nose** (-nōss, -nōz). Covered with soft, short hair; downy. [Latin *lānūginōsus,* from *lānūgō,* down, LANUGO.] —**la·nu·gi·nous·ness** *n.*

la·nu·go (lə-néw-gō ‖ -nōō-) *n., pl.* **-gos.** Fine, soft hair, such as that covering a foetus. [Latin *lānūgō,* down, from *lāna,* wool.]

lan·yard, lan·iard (lán-yərd, -yaard) *n.* **1.** *Nautical.* A short rope or gasket for seizing a ladder, for example, or to secure rigging. **2.** A cord worn around the neck for carrying a knife, keys, or a whistle. **3.** A cord with a hook at one end used to fire a cannon. [Middle English *lanyer,* from Old French *laniere, lasniere,* from *lasne,* thong, strap : perhaps *laz,* LACE + *nasle,* string, from Germanic.]

Lao (low) *n., pl.* **Laos** or collectively **Lao.** Also **La·o·tian** (lów-shi-ən, -shən, lay-ṓ-shən). **1.** A member of a Buddhist people of Thai stock living in the area of the Mekong River in Laos and Thailand. **2.** The Thai language of this people, the official language of Laos. ~*adj.* Of the Lao or their language.

La·oc·o·on (lay-óckō-on, -ən). *Greek Mythology.* A Trojan priest of Apollo who was killed with his two sons by two sea serpents for having warned his people against the Trojan horse.

La·od·i·ce·a (láy-ōdi-sée-ə). Name given to several cities built in Asia and Asia Minor by the Greek Seleucid dynasty in the third century B.C. The chief one, Laodicea ad Lycum, near present-day Denizli in western Turkey, was a prosperous market town on the Roman trading route from the Orient and an early centre of Christianity. —**La·od·i·ce·an** *n. & adj.*

la·od·i·ce·an (láy-ōdi-sée-ən) *adj.* Indifferent or lukewarm. [After *Laodicea ad Lycum,* whose early church is reproved in Revelation

lapwing *Vanellus vanellus, the lapwing or peewit of Europe and Asia, nests on the ground and feeds mainly on insects in farmland, moors, and coastal marshes.*

larch *These deciduous conifers, originally mountain trees from central Europe, grow in mild lowland climates. Because they do not cast heavy shadows, they are often used to shelter hardwood saplings in planted forests. This is the European larch, Larix decidua.*

3:14–16 as being "lukewarm, and neither hot nor cold".] **—la·od·i·ce·an** *n.*

Laois. See **Leix.**

Laos (la'a-oss, lowss, lowz). Officially **The Lao People's Democratic Republic.** Country in southeast Asia. It is largely mountainous and forested, most of the population living in the Mekong valley. Rice dominates the economy; teak and tin are exports. Laos was part of French Indochina, becoming fully independent in 1953. Pathet Lao Communists fought two civil wars (1953-54; 1960–73), and finally swept away the 600-year monarchy in 1975. The country aided the Vietnamese invasion of Kampuchea (1979), and by 1980 there was a massive Vietnamese presence in Laos, still racked by guerrilla activity. Area, 236 800 square kilometres (91,428 square miles). Population, 3,700,000. Capital, Viangchan (formerly Vientiane). **—Lao·ti·an** (lówshən) *n. & adj.*

Lao Zi (lów dzȯ), also known as **Lao Tzu** or **Lao Tze** (*c.* 6th century B.C.). Chinese philosopher. In legend he is a hermit from the Imperial Court who became deified as the founder of Taoism and author of Tao-te-Ching (Way of Life). [Chinese, "old master".]

lap¹ (lap) *n.* **1.** The front region or area of a seated person extending from the lower trunk to the knees. **2. a.** The portion of a garment that covers this area. **b.** The front part of a skirt or dress used to hold or carry something. **c.** A hanging or flapping part of a garment. **3.** A hollow or depressed area as in the land. **4.** A secure place or environment: *in the lap of luxury.* **—in (someone's) lap.** Under someone's responsibility. **—in the lap of the gods.** To be decided by fate or some impersonal power. [Middle English *lappe,* Old English *læppa,* flap of a garment, from Germanic.]

lap² *v.* **lapped, lapping, laps.** *—tr.* **1.** To fold, wrap, or wind over or around something: *lap pie crust over a filling.* **2.** To envelop in something; enwrap; swathe: *lapped in sables.* **3. a.** To place (a thing) so as to overlap another. **b.** To lie partly over (something underneath); project onto or over the edge of. **4.** In cabinetmaking, to join as by scarfing. **5.** To get ahead of (an opponent) in a race by one or more complete circuits of the course. **6.** To polish until smooth, especially to hone (two mating parts against each other) with or without an abrasive. **7.** To convert (cotton or other fibres) into a sheet or layer. *—intr.* **1.** To fold or wind around something. **2.** To extend beyond an edge; overlap.

~n. **1.** A part that overlaps. **2. a.** One complete turn or circuit, especially of a racecourse or racetrack. **b.** A segment or stage of a race, journey, or comparable undertaking. **3.** A length, as of rope, required to encircle a drum or wheel, for example. **4.** A continuous band, layer, or sheet of cotton, flax, or other fibres ready for further processing. **5.** A wheel, disc, or slab of leather or metal, either stationary or rotating, used for polishing stone, glass, or the like. [Middle English *lappen,* probably from *lappe,* LAP (as of a garment).]

lap³ *v.* **lapped, lapping, laps.** *—tr.* **1.** To take in (a liquid or food) with the tongue. Often used with *up.* Usually used of animals, especially dogs and cats. **2.** To wash against with a gentle intermittent slapping sound. Used of waves or a body of water. *—intr.* **1.** To drink by lifting a liquid with the tongue. **2.** To dash or slap softly against a shore or other surface. **—lap up.** *Informal.* To receive eagerly and uncritically: *lap up praise.*

~n. **1.** The act or process of lapping. **2.** A watery food for animals. **3.** An amount ingested by a lap. **4.** The sound of lapping water. [Middle English *lappen,* Old English *lapian.*] **—lap·per** *n.*

lap·a·ro·scope (láppərə-skōp) *n.* A surgical instrument that is inserted through the abdominal wall to inspect the abdominal organs.

[Greek *lapara,* flank, from *laparos,* soft + -SCOPE.] **—lap·a·ros·co·py** (láppə-róskəpi) *n.*

lap·a·rot·o·my (láppə-róttəmi) *n., pl.* **-mies.** Surgical incision into the abdominal wall, either as a prelude to further surgery or to aid diagnosis. [Greek *lapara,* flank, from *laparos,* soft + -TOMY.]

La Paz (laa páz, la, *Spanish* páss). Also **La Paz de Ayacucho** (ĭ-ə-kōōchō). Capital of Bolivia, founded in 1548. Independence from Spain was declared there in 1809 and it became the capital in 1898. It is the world's highest capital at 3 577 metres (11,735 feet).

lap·board (láp-bawrd ‖ -bōrd) *n.* A flat board to hold on the lap as a substitute for a table or desk.

lap dissolve *n.* A cinematic technique of overlapping a fade-out and a fade-in so that one scene dissolves into the next.

lap dog *n.* **1.** A small, easily held dog kept as a pet. **2.** *Informal.* A person prepared to do another's bidding out of uncritical love or admiration. Used derogatorily.

la·pel (lə-pél) *n.* Either of two parts of a garment, such as a jacket, that are an extension of the collar and fold back against the breast. [From LAP (flap of a garment).]

lap·ful (láp-fŏol) *n.* As much as the lap can support or hold.

lap·i·dar·i·an (láppi-daír-i-ən) *adj.* Cut in or inscribed on stone. [Latin *lapidārius,* of stone, from *lapis* (stem *lapid*-), stone, perhaps akin to Greek *lepas,* of Mediterranean origin.]

lap·i·dar·y (láppi-dəri ‖ *U.S.* -derri) *n., pl.* **-ies. 1.** A person who works at cutting, polishing, or engraving gemstones. **2.** A dealer in precious or semiprecious stones.

~adj. **1.** Of or pertaining to precious stones or the art of working with them. **2.** Engraved in stone. **3.** Elegant and concise: *lapidary prose.* [Latin *lapidārius,* stoneworker, from *lapis* (stem *lapid*-), stone. See **lapidarian.**]

lap·i·date (láppi-dayt) *tr.v.* **-dated, -dating, -dates.** *Literary.* To pelt with stones or stone to death. [Latin *lapidāre,* to stone, from *lapis* (stem *lapid*-), stone.] **—lap·i·da·tion** (-dáysh'n) *n.*

la·pid·i·fy (lə-píddi-fī) *v.* **-fied, -fying, -fies.** *—tr.* To turn into stone. *—intr.* To become stone. [French *lapidifier,* from Medieval Latin *lapidificāre* : *lapis* (stem *lapid*-), stone + -*ficāre,* -FY.]

la·pil·lus (lə-pílloss) *n., pl.* **-pilli** (-pílli). *Usually plural.* A small solidified fragment of lava. [Latin *lapillus,* small stone, diminutive of *lapis,* stone. See **lapidarian.**]

lap·is laz·u·li (láppiss lázzew-lī, -lee) *n.* **1.** An opaque, azure-blue to deep-blue gemstone of lazurite. **2.** A mineral, **lazurite** (*see*). [Middle English, from Medieval Latin : Latin *lapis,* stone (see **lapidarian**) + Medieval Latin *lazuli,* genitive of *lazulum,* lapis lazuli, from Arabic *lāzaward,* from Persian *lāzhuward*†.]

lap joint *n.* A joint in which the ends or edges are overlapped and fastened together. **—lap-joint·ed** *adj.*

La·place (laa-pláss, la-, lə-), **Pierre Simon, Marquis de** (1749–1827). French mathematician and astronomer. His speculation, in *Mécanique céleste* (1798–1825), that the solar system evolved from a rotating nebula, is thought to be broadly correct.

Laplace operator *n. Mathematics. Symbol* ∇^2 The differential operator $\partial^2/\partial x^2 + \partial^2/\partial y^2 + \partial^2/\partial z^2$. Also called "Laplacian". [After P.S. de LAPLACE.]

La Pla·ta (laa pláatə, la, pláttə). City in eastern Argentina, the capital of Buenos Aires province, lying 8 kilometres (5 miles) inland from Ensenada, its port on the Río de la Plata. It is Argentina's leading oil-refining centre.

lap of honour *n.* A celebratory circuit made of a racetrack, or other sports ground by the winner or winners of a sports event.

Lapp (lap) *n.* Also **Lap·pish** (láppish) (for sense 2). **1.** A member of a people of nomadic tradition who inhabit Lappland. Also called "Lapplander". **2.** The Finno-Ugric language of this people.

~adj. Also **Lappish.** Of the Lapps or their language.

lap·pet (láppit) *n.* **1.** A decorative flap, streamer, or loose fold on a garment or headdress. **2.** A flaplike structure, such as the wattle of a bird. [From LAP (fold or flap).]

lap·pie (lúppi) *n., pl.* **-pies** (-pis, -piz). *South African Informal.* A cloth or rag, as for cleaning. [Afrikaans, diminutive of *lap,* rag, cloth.]

Lapp·land (lápp-land). *Norwegian* **Lapland;** *Finnish* **Lappi.** Vast Arctic region of Europe, extending over the north of Norway, Sweden, Finland, and the Kola peninsula of the U.S.S.R. It consists of tundra, swamps, forests, and mountains, and is inhabited by the reindeer-herding Lapps or Lapplanders, about two-thirds of whom live in Norway. There are large forest and mineral resources. **—Lapp·land·er** *n.*

lapse (laps) *intr.v.* **lapsed, lapsing, lapses. 1. a.** To fall away by degrees; decline; vanish: *My enthusiasm soon lapsed.* **b.** To subside gradually; drift: *lapse into dreaminess.* **c.** To drop in standard or quality, usually temporarily. **d.** To cease practising or adhering to a belief, custom, or the like: *a lapsed Catholic.* **2.** To elapse: *Years had lapsed since we last met.* **3. a.** *Law.* To pass to another through neglect or omission. Said of a right or privilege, a benefice, or an estate. **b.** To become void or ineffective.

~n. **1.** The act of lapsing; a gradual or imperceptible falling or sliding away. **2. a.** A minor slip or failure: *a lapse of the memory.* **b.** A fall from rectitude; moral error. **3.** A slipping into a lower state or degree; a decline: *his lapse into premature senility.* **4. a.** The passage of time. **b.** An interval. **5.** *Law.* The termination of a right, interest, or privilege through disuse, a death, or other failure. **6.** An abandonment of a practice, especially of religious faith. **7.** A failure to renew membership of an organisation. [Latin *lapsus,* error, a sliding, from *lābī* (past participle *lapsus*), to slide.] **—laps·er** *n.*

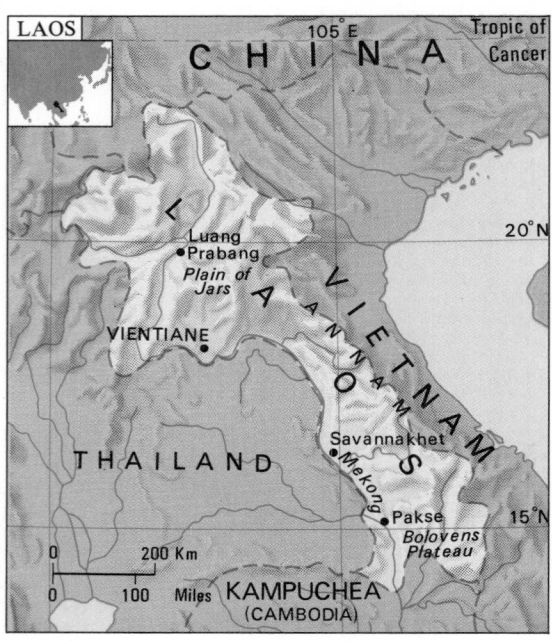

LAOS · CHINA · 105 E · Tropic of Cancer · VIETNAM · ANNAM · 20°N · Luang Prabang · Plain of Jars · VIENTIANE · THAILAND · Savannakhet · Mekong · Pakse · 15°N · Bolovens Plateau · 0 200 Km · 0 100 Miles · KAMPUCHEA (CAMBODIA)

lapse rate *n.* The rate of change of a meteorological parameter with increasing height, such as the rate of change of atmospheric temperature for every 100 metres increase in altitude.

lap·strake (láp-strayk) *adj.* Also **lap·streak** (-streek). *Nautical.* Built with each strake overlapping the one below; clinker-built.
~*n.* Also **lap·streak.** A clinker-built boat. [LAP (to overlap) + STRAKE.]

lap·sus (láp-səss) *n., pl.* **-sus.** *Formal.* A lapse; a slip.

lapsus lin·guae (líng-gwī) *n., pl.* **lapsus linguae.** A slip of the tongue; an inappropriate word or group of words uttered unintentionally. [Latin.]

La·pu·tan (lə-péwt'n) *adj.* Impractical and visionary; absurd. [After *Laputa,* a country in Swift's *Gulliver's Travels* (1726) devoted to absurdly visionary schemes.]

lap·wing (láp-wing) *n.* Any of several Eurasian birds of the genus *Vanellus,* related to the plovers; especially, *V. vanellus,* having a narrow crest. Also called "peewit", "pewit", "green plover". [Middle English *lapwinge,* variant (influenced by *winge,* wing, and *lappen,* to overlap) of *lappewinke,* Old English *hlēapewince* : *hlēapan,* to LEAP + *-wince* (unattested), WINK (referring to its way of flying).]

lar (lar) *n., pl.* **lares** (laír-eez, laár-, -ayz) or **lars.** *Sometimes capital* **L.** A tutelary deity or spirit of an ancient Roman household. [Latin *Lār*†.]

lar·board (lárbərd) *n. Nautical.* The port side.
~*adj. Nautical.* On the port side. [Middle English *lathebord, lad(d)borde,* probably "the loading side" (but influenced by STARBOARD) : *laden,* to load, LADE + *bord,* ship's side, BOARD.]

lar·ce·ny (lár-səni) *n., pl.* **-nies.** *Law.* The felonious taking and removing of another's personal property; theft. In Britain the offence was abolished in 1968 and is now covered by the laws on theft. See **grand larceny, petit larceny.** [Middle English, from Old French *larcin,* from Latin *latrōcinium,* military service for pay, freebooting, from *latrō,* mercenary soldier, from Greek *latron,* pay.] **—lar·ce·nist, lar·ce·ner** *n.* **—lar·ce·nous** *adj.* **—lar·ce·nous·ly** *adv.*

larch (larch) *n.* **1.** Any of several coniferous trees of the genus *Larix,* such as *L. decidua,* the European larch, having deciduous needles and heavy, durable wood. **2.** The wood of a larch. [German *Lärche,* from Middle High German *larche, lerche,* from Old High German *larihha* (unattested), from Latin *larix*† (stem *laric-*).]

lard (lard) *n.* The white solid or semisolid rendered fat of a pig.
~*tr.v.* **larded, larding, lards. 1.** To cover or coat with fat. **2.** To insert strips of bacon or the like in (lean meat or poultry) before cooking. **3.** To enrich (speech or writing) with witticisms, quotations, or similar additions. Often used derogatorily. [Middle English, from Old French, from Latin *lārdum, lāridum*†.] **—lard·y** *adj.*

lar·der (lárdər) *n.* A small room, cupboard, or the like where meat and other foods are kept. [Middle English, from Old French *lardier,* from *lard,* LARD.]

larder beetle *n.* A small black beetle, *Dermestes lardarius,* found in houses, where it feeds on bacon and other fatty foods.

lar·don (lárd'n) *n.* Also **lar·doon** (laar-dóon). A strip of fat for larding meat. [French, from Old French, from *lard,* LARD.]

lardy cake *n.* A breadlike cake containing currants. [From LARD.]

lar·es and pe·na·tes *pl.n.* Esteemed household possessions. [From two kinds of Roman household gods. See **lar, penates.**]

large (larj) *adj.* **larger, largest.** *Abbr.* **L, lg., lge. 1.** Of considerable size, extent, quantity, capacity, or amount; big; not small: *a large house.* **2.** Important; on a considerable scale: *a large steel producer.* **3. a.** Of wide scope or capacity: *a large mind.* **b.** Having breadth or sweep; comprehensive. **4. a.** Liberal; generous: *a large heart.* **b.** Prodigal. **5.** *Rare.* **a.** Pretentious; big. Said of speech or manners. **b.** Unrestrained; loose; gross. Said of speech or language. **6.** *Nautical.* Designating a favourable wind. **—at large. 1.** At liberty; free. **2.** At length; copiously: *He spoke at large on the housing problem.* **3.** As an entity or whole; in general. **—in the large.** On a broad scale. [Middle English, from Old French, from Latin *largus*†, generous, bountiful.] **—large·ness** *n.*

large calorie *n.* A unit of heat, a **calorie** *(see).*

large-heart·ed (lárj-hártid) *adj.* Having a generous disposition; sympathetic. **—large-heart·ed·ness** *n.*

large intestine *n.* The portion of the intestine that extends from the ileum to the anus, forming an arch around the convolutions of the small intestine, and including the caecum, colon, and rectum.

large·ly (lárjli) *adv.* **1.** In a large manner; on a large scale. **2.** To a large extent; mainly.

large-mind·ed (lárj-mīndid) *adj.* Having a breadth of ideas; of liberal views; open-minded. **—large-mind·ed·ness** *n.*

larg·er-than-life, larger than life (lárjər-thən-līf) *adj.* Seeming to belong to the world of fiction rather than to real life; possessing extraordinary qualities.

large-scale (lárj-skáyl, -skayl) *adj.* **1.** Of large scope; conducted as or operating a major undertaking. **2.** Drawn or made large to show detail. Said of maps and models.

lar·gesse, lar·gess (laar-jéss, lár-jess, -zhéss) *n.* **1. a.** Generosity, especially as displayed by an important person on a great occasion. **b.** The money, favours, or gifts bestowed. **2.** Generosity of attitude. [Middle English, from Old French, from *large,* generous, LARGE.]

lar·ghet·to (laar-géttō) *adv. Music.* Moderately slow in tempo. Used as a direction.
~*n., pl.* **larghettos.** *Music.* A larghetto movement or passage.
~*adj. Music.* Moderately slow. [Italian, diminutive of LARGO.]

larg·ish (lárjish) *adj.* Fairly large.

lar·go (lárgō) *adv. Music.* In a slow, solemn manner. Used as a direction.
~*adj. Music.* Slow and solemn.
~*n., pl.* **largos.** *Music.* A largo movement or passage. [Italian, slow, "broad", from Latin *largus,* LARGE.]

lar·i·at (lárri-ət) *n. U.S.* **1.** A long rope with a running noose for catching wild livestock; a lasso. **2.** A rope for picketing grazing horses or mules. [Spanish *la reata,* lasso, rope for tying mules : *la,* the + *reatar,* to tie again : *re-,* again, from Latin + *atar,* to tie, from Latin *aptāre,* to fit, from *aptus,* APT.]

Lá·ri·sa or **La·ris·sa** (lə-ríssə; *Greek* lárree-sa). Capital of ancient Thessaly in Greece. It now produces silk and tobacco.

lark[1] (lark) *n.* **1.** Any of various chiefly Old World birds of the family Alaudidae, having a sustained, melodious song. See **skylark. 2.** Any of several similar birds, such as the meadowlark. **—up with the lark.** Out of bed early. [Middle English *larke,* Old English *lāwerce, lǣwerce,* from West Germanic *larw(a)rikōn* (unattested).]

lark[2] *n. Informal.* **1.** A carefree adventure. **2.** A harmless prank. **3.** An amusing situation or event: *What a lark!*
~*intr.v.* **larked, larking, larks.** *Informal.* **1.** To play or have fun. Often used with *about* or *around.* **2.** To play tricks. [Probably variant of dialectal *lake,* to play, from Middle English *leiken,* from Old Norse *leika.*]

Lar·kin (lár-kin), **Philip** (1922–). British poet, novelist, and editor of *The Oxford Book of Twentieth Century English Verse* (1973). His books of poetry include *The Whitsun Weddings* (1964) and *High Windows* (1974). His novels include *A Girl in Winter* (1947).

lark·spur (lárk-spur) *n.* Any of various plants of the genus *Delphinium,* having spurred, variously coloured flowers.

Lar·mor precession (lár-mər, -mawr) *n.* The precession of the orbit of an electron in an atom subjected to a magnetic field. The frequency of the precession (the *Larmor frequency*) is $eH/4\pi mv$, where H is the field strength and $m,e,$ and v are the mass, charge, and velocity of the electron respectively. [After Sir Joseph *Larmor* (1857–1942), British physicist.]

larn (larn) *v.* **larned, larning, larns.** *Nonstandard.* —*intr.* To learn. Often used humorously. —*tr.* To teach; especially, to teach (a person) a lesson: *That'll larn you!*

Larne (larn). Seaport and resort in Northern Ireland. It is the ferry terminal to Stranraer (Scotland), the shortest sea route between Ireland and Britain.

La Roche·fou·cauld (laa rósh-fōō-kō ‖ rṓsh-; *French* la-rosh-fōō-kṓ), **François, Duc de** (1613–80). French moralist. He wrote *Maximes* (1664), a collection of cynical epigrams suggesting that people are ruled by self-interest.

La Ro·chelle (laa ro-shél; *French* la-ro-shél). City in western France, lying on the Bay of Biscay. It is the chief French Atlantic fishing port. During the 16th-century Wars of Religion it was the most important stronghold of the Protestant Huguenots.

La·rousse (lə-rōōss, la-), **Pierre** (1817–75). French lexicographer, who compiled the *Grand Dictionnaire universel du XIXe Siècle* (1866–76). His company still publishes reference books.

lar·ri·gan (lárrigən) *n. Sometimes capital* **L.** A moccasin with knee-high leggings made of oiled leather. [17th century : origin obscure.]

lar·ri·kin (lárri-kin) *n. Australian & N. Z. Informal.* A rowdy youth; a hooligan. [From English dialect, probably from *Larry* (pet form of *Lawrence*) + -KIN.]

lar·rup (lárrəp) *tr.v.* **-ruped, -ruping, -rups.** *Regional.* To beat; flog.
~*n. Regional.* A blow. [19th century : origin obscure.]

Lars Por·se·na (lárz pór-sinə) (*c.* 6th century B.C.). Etruscan king who, in Roman legend, attacked Rome after the proclamation of the Republic (509 B.C.) but failed to restore the Roman monarchy.

lar·um (lárrəm) *n. Archaic.* An alarm. [Short for ALARUM.]

lar·va (lár-və) *n., pl.* **-vae** (-vee). **1.** The wingless, often wormlike form of a newly hatched insect before metamorphosis. **2.** The newly hatched stage of any of various animals that undergo metamorphosis, differing markedly in appearance from the adult. [Latin *lārva*†, disembodied spirit, mask.] **—lar·val** *adj.*

lar·vi·cide (lárvi-sīd) *n.* An insecticide designed to kill larval pests. [LARV(A) + -CIDE.] **—lar·vi·ci·dal** (-sīd'l) *adj.*

la·ryn·ge·al (lárrin-jée-əl, -jéel, lə-rínji-əl, -rínjəl) *adj.* Also **la·ryn·gal** (lə-ríng-g'l). **1.** Of, pertaining to, affecting, or near the larynx. **2.** *Phonetics.* Produced in or with the larynx; glottal.
~*n.* **1.** A part of the larynx. **2.** *Phonetics.* A laryngeal sound. **3.** Any of a set of sounds reconstructed for Proto-Indo-European, of uncertain character (but originally thought to be laryngeal in nature), manifested in various environments, typically involving loss of the original sound in most languages of the family. [New Latin *laryngeus,* from *larynx* (stem *laryng-*), LARYNX.]

lar·yn·gec·to·my (lárrin-jéktəmi) *n., pl.* **-mies.** Surgical removal of part or all of the larynx, as for the treatment of laryngeal cancer. [LARYNG(O)- + -ECTOMY.]

lar·yn·gi·tis (lárrin-jītiss) *n.* Inflammation of the larynx, causing hoarseness and sometimes temporary loss of speech. [New Latin : LARYNG(O)- + -ITIS.] **—lar·yn·git·ic** (-jíttik) *adj.*

laryngo-, laryng- *comb. form.* Indicates the larynx or pertaining to the larynx; for example, **laryngoscope, laryngitis.** [New Latin, from Greek *larungo-,* from *larunx* (stem *larung-*), LARYNX.]

la·ryn·go·graph (lə-ríng-gə-graaf, -graf) *n.* An instrument used to observe the functioning of the vocal cords by means of electrodes placed on the surface of the neck. [LARYNGO- + -GRAPH.] **—la·ryn·go·graph·ic** (-gráffik) *adj.* **—la·ryn·gog·ra·phy** (lárring-góggrəfi) *n.*

lar·yn·gol·o·gy (lárring-gólləji) *n.* The medical study or treatment

larkspur *The tall spikes of these originally Mediterranean flowers bear showers of blooms in shades of pink, white, or blue.*

larva *The second stage in the four-stage life cycle of most advanced insects. The four stages are egg, larva, pupa, and adult. This is the larva of a dung beetle.*

PRONUNCIATION KEY

a, trap; aa, father; ai, fair; ar, star; aw, lawn; ay, play; b, bb, stab; rubber; ch, church; ck, ticket; d, dd, dead; ladder; e, dress; ee, bee; er, defer; ew, few; ewr, pure; ə, about; ər, letter; f, ff, fife; differ; g, gg, giggle; h, hat; i, kit; ī, price; īr, fire; j, judge; k, kick; l, ll, let; 'l, needle; m, mm, man; n, nn, no; 'n, sudden; ng, thing; o, lot; ō, no; ŏŏ, foot; ōō, shoe; oor, poor; ow, cow; owr, hour; oy, boy; p, pp, pepper; r, rr, red; s, ss, sauce; sh, ship; t, tt, totter; th, thick; th, this; smooth; u, cut; ur, turn; v, vv, valve; w, wet; y, yes; z, zz, zebra; zh, vision; pleasure

IN FOREIGN WORDS:

aN, oN, Saint-Saëns; hl, Llanelli; Hluhluwe; kh, loch; lough; Khaled

STRESS MARK:

ín-sīt, insight; in-sīt, incite

of the larynx and its diseases. [LARYNGO- + -LOGY.] —**lar·yn·go·log·i·cal** (lə-ríng-gə-lójik'l) *adj.* —**lar·yn·gol·o·gist** *n.*

la·ryn·go·scope (lə-ríng-gə-skōp) *n.* A tubular instrument used to observe the interior of the larynx. [LARYNGO- + -SCOPE.] —**la·ryn·go·scop·ic** (-skóppik), **la·ryn·go·scop·i·cal** *adj.* —**la·ryn·go·scop·i·cal·ly** *adv.* —**lar·yn·gos·co·py** (lárring-góskəpi) *n.*

lar·yn·got·o·my (lárring-góttəmi) *n., pl.* **-mies.** Surgical incision into the larynx. [LARYNGO- + -TOMY.]

lar·ynx (lárringks) *n., pl.* **larynges** (lə-rín-jeez) or **-ynxes.** The upper part of the respiratory tract between the pharynx and the trachea, having cartilaginous walls and containing the vocal cords. [New Latin, from Greek *larunx†.*]

la·sa·gne, la·sa·gna (lə-zán-yə, -sán-, -zaán-, -saán-) *n.* **1.** Flat wide noodles. **2.** A dish made by baking such noodles in layers with minced meat, tomatoes, and cheese. [Italian, from Latin *lasanum,* cooking pot, originally "chamber pot", from Greek *lasanon†.*]

La Salle (lə sál, laa, la), **Robert Cavelier, Sieur de** (1643–87). French explorer. He led expeditions to North America and claimed Louisiana for France (1682). He was murdered by mutineers on his final expedition.

las·car (láskər) *n.* A sailor from the East Indies. [Hindi *lashkarī,* soldier, from *lashkar,* army, from Persian, from Arabic *al-'askar,* the army.]

Las Ca·sas (lass kaá-səss), **Bartolomé de** (1474–1566). Spanish planter in the West Indies, who joined the Dominican order and campaigned for the abolition of Indian slavery.

Las·caux (láss-kō; *French* la-skó). Cave near Montignac in southwest France, lying above the Vézère valley in the Dordogne. Discovered in 1940, it is one of the most important sites of prehistoric cave art in Europe. The paintings, mostly of animals, are from the late Aurignacian period.

las·civ·i·ous (lə-sívvi-əss) *adj.* **1.** Of or characterised by lust; lewd; lecherous. **2.** Exciting sexual desires. [Late Latin *lascīviōsus,* from Latin *lascīvia,* licentiousness, wantonness, from *lascīvus,* wanton, lustful.] —**las·civ·i·ous·ly** *adv.* —**las·civ·i·ous·ness** *n.*

Las·dun (láz-dən), **Sir Denys (Louis)** (1914–). British architect, who designed the University of East Anglia, Norwich (1961) and the National Theatre, London (1968–76).

---

larynx

THE MEDIUM OF SPEECH

How sounds are formed in the larynx

The larynx is often known as the voice box because spoken sounds are formed there. As air is expelled from the lungs, it passes through the larynx where it provides the energy for speech. If the vocal cords are tensed, the passage of air makes them vibrate and produce a buzzing, or voiced, sound which is then shaped into spoken words by the tongue, teeth, and lips. In adolescent boys, the larynx enlarges in response to the male sex hormone, and the treble voice of childhood "breaks", or deepens.

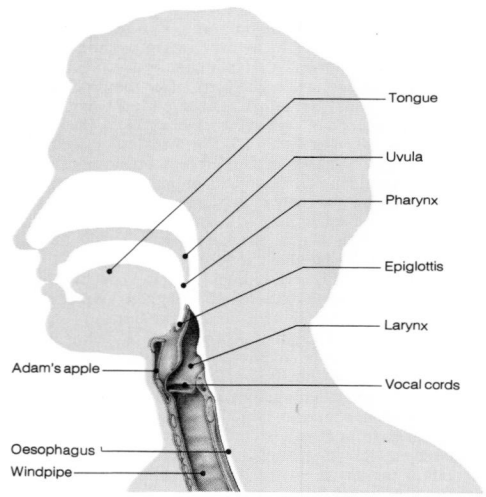

Tongue

Uvula

Pharynx

Epiglottis

Larynx

Vocal cords

Adam's apple

Oesophagus

Windpipe

ANATOMY OF THE LARYNX *The larynx is a structure of cartilage, muscles, and ligaments in the windpipe. It sticks out slightly in the front of the neck to form the Adam's apple, and contains the vocal cords. Muscles control the length and tension of the cords, which can be vibrated by air passing through them to make sounds. To ensure that foods and fluids pass down the oesophagus rather than the windpipe, the epiglottis – a valve-like flap of cartilage behind the tongue – closes during the act of swallowing.*

---

lase (layz) *intr.v.* **lased, lasing, lases.** To function as a laser; emit coherent radiation by the action of a laser. [Back-formation from LASER.]

la·ser (láyzər) *n.* **1.** Any of several devices that convert incident electromagnetic radiation of mixed frequencies to one or more discrete frequencies of highly amplified and coherent visible radiation. Also called "optical maser". **2.** Any such device, including the **ma·ser** *(see),* the output of which is in an invisible region of the electromagnetic spectrum. [*L*ight *a*mplification by *s*timulated *e*mission of *r*adiation.]

lash¹ (lash) *n.* **1.** A stroke or blow with or as if with a whip, rope, or the like. **2.** The thin stinging part or parts of a whip; the thongs. **3.** A remark that insults, reprimands, or ridicules. **4.** A powerful or violent impact: *the lash of rain on the windows.* **5.** An eyelash. —**have a lash.** *Australian Informal.* To attempt; have a go. ~*v.* **lashed, lashing, lashes.** —*tr.* **1.** To strike with or as if with a whip. **2.** To strike against with force or violence: *waves lashing the sides of the ship.* **3.** To move or wave rapidly to and fro: *a lion lashing his tail.* **4.** To make a vehement verbal or written attack on. **5.** To incite or urge as with lashes. —*intr.* **1.** To move a limb, tail, or the like rapidly or suddenly. **2.** To make a sudden or violent attack. Used with *at* or *against.* —**lash out. 1.** To make a sudden or violent attack. **2.** To express vehement criticism. **3.** To kick out violently. Used of a horse. **4.** *Informal.* To spend money in an apparently extravagant way. [Middle English *lashe†.*] —**lash·er** *n.*

lash² *tr.v.* **lashed, lashing, lashes.** To secure or bind, as with a rope, cord, or chain. [Middle English *lasshen,* from Old French *lac(h)ier,* from Latin *laqueāre,* to ensnare, from *laqueus,* snare.] —**lash·er** *n.*

lash·ing (láshing) *n.* **1.** Something used for securing or binding, such as a rope or cord. **2.** A beating or flogging.

lash·ings (láshingz) *pl.n. Chiefly British.* Lavish quantities. [From LASH (whip) in an obsolete sense "lavish".]

Las·ker (láskər), **Emanuel** (1868–1941). German chess player, world champion (1894–1921) until losing to Capablanca.

Las·ki (láski), **Harold (Joseph)** (1893–1950). British socialist and political theorist. He was a professor at the London School of Economics.

Las Pal·mas (lass pál-məss, paál-). Also **Las Palmas de Gran Canaria.** Capital of Spain's Las Palmas province in the Canary Islands, lying on the Isla de Gran Canaria. It was founded in 1478 and named after the palm trees growing there. It was an important station for Spanish trade ships on the African-South American route. Today it is a major tourist resort.

La Spe·zia (laa spét-siə, la, spétss-yə). Seaport in northwest Italy, lying on the Gulf of La Spezia. It has been an important fortified town since the Middle Ages and is today the largest naval station and arsenal in Italy.

lass (lass) *n.* **1.** A girl or young woman. **2.** A sweetheart. [Middle English *lasce, lasse†.*]

Lassa. See **Lhasa.**

Las·sa fever (laá-sə, lássə) *n.* A severe viral disease of Central West Africa, typically causing fever, headache, and muscular pain and often leading to death from heart or kidney failure.

las·si (lassi, lussi) *n.* A sweet or salty cold drink, originating in India, made from yoghurt or buttermilk and spices. [Hindi.]

las·sie (lássi) *n.* A lass. [Diminutive of LASS.]

las·si·tude (lássi-tewd ‖ -tŏŏd) *n.* A state of exhaustion or torpor. See Synonyms at **lethargy.** [Latin *lassitūdō,* from *lassus,* tired, weary.]

las·so (la-sóo, lə-, *rarely* lássō) *n., pl.* **-sos** or **-soes.** A long rope or leather thong with a running noose at one end used especially to catch horses and cattle. ~*tr.v.* **lassoed, -soing, -sos** or **-soes.** To catch with or as if with a lasso; rope. [Spanish *lazo,* from Latin *laqueus,* snare.]

last¹ (laast ‖ last). Alternative superlative of **late.** ~*adj.* **1.** Being or coming after all others: *last on the list.* **2.** Being the only remaining part of a collection or sequence: *my last stamp.* **3.** Most recent; latest: *last year.* **4.** Highest; greatest; utmost: *the last degree.* **5.** Most valid, authoritative, or conclusive:- *The boss always has the last say.* **6.** Least appropriate; most unexpected: *the last man we suspected.* **7.** The lowest in rank, size, or importance: *the last prize.* **8.** Final or ultimate, as just before death: *famous last words.* —See Usage note at **first.** —**every last.** *Informal.* All; omitting none: *He took every last cigarette.* —**last but not least.** Important or significant although coming at the end. ~*adv.* **1.** After all others, as in chronology or sequence: *They left last.* **2.** Most recently: *last heard of in May.* Often used in combination: *the last-mentioned item.* ~*n.* **1.** One that is last: *the last of the Plantagenets.* **2.** The end: *He held out until the last.* **3.** The final mention or appearance of something: *I fear we haven't seen the last of her.* **4.** The person or thing most recently mentioned: *You need glue, string, and paper, the last being the most important.* **5.** The last instance or occasion of something: *This day will be your last.* —**at (long) last.** After a considerable length of time; finally. —**breathe one's last.** To die. [Middle English *last,* Old English *latost,* superlative of *laet, late,* LATE.]

Synonyms: last, final, terminal, eventual, ultimate.

last² *v.* **lasted, lasting, lasts.** —*intr.* **1.** To continue in existence; go on: *The war lasted for four years.* **2.** To remain in good condition; endure: *Clay lasts longer than paper.* **3.** To endure or get through. Often used with *out: His strength won't last out.* **4.** To remain in adequate supply. Often used with *out: Will our water last out?* —*tr.* **1.** To be adequate or sufficient for: *Five pounds will last me till* laser

THE ELEMENTAL POWER OF THE LASER

A beam of intensely pure light that can slice through metal or perform eye surgery

In the laser, man has at his service a device which unlocks an elemental power of nature – the power of light. The laser's beam of intensely pure light can cut through metal or pierce diamond, the hardest natural substance on Earth.

The first laser – *L*ight *A*mplification by means of *S*timulated *E*mission of *R*adiation – was built by the American physicist T. H. Maiman in 1960. But the principles on which the laser depends had been established when the century was young, by physicists unravelling the secrets of the atom. In 1913, Niels Bohr, a Dane, pointed out that atoms exist only in certain states, each with its own energy level. If an

atom changes from a high-energy level to a low-energy level, it gives out surplus energy in the form of radiation. Some atoms give off this excess energy spontaneously. Others, as was observed in 1917 by the German-born physicist Albert Einstein, can be triggered into changing their energy state if they are bombarded with radiation from an outside source. This is known as the stimulated emission of radiation.

For the laser he built in 1960, Maiman used a rod of artificial ruby. Atoms in the rod were excited by high-intensity light from outside, and were stimulated to give off pure red light in brief, penetrating pulses. The pulsed ruby laser is still the most powerful type of

laser, producing light with 10 million times the intensity of sunlight. It was followed by the gas laser, which is less powerful but emits a continuous beam of light, rather than very short pulses.

Laser light differs from ordinary light in several ways. Whereas ordinary white light is made up of light of different wavelengths (that is, colours), laser light is of a single wavelength. Instead of spreading out in all directions from its source, like light from the Sun or from an electric-light bulb, pure laser light stays concentrated, with a beam that is almost perfectly parallel. It is this concentration of energy that makes the laser so powerful.

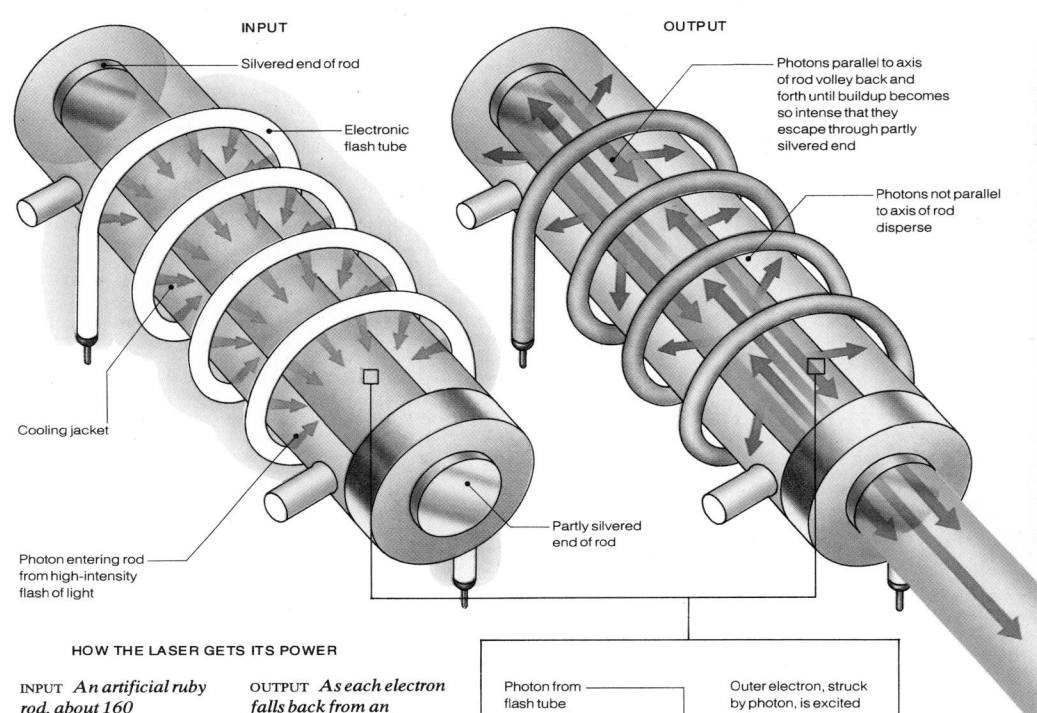

INPUT

- Silvered end of rod
- Electronic flash tube
- Cooling jacket
- Photon entering rod from high-intensity flash of light

OUTPUT

- Photons parallel to axis of rod volley back and forth until buildup becomes so intense that they escape through partly silvered end
- Photons not parallel to axis of rod disperse
- Partly silvered end of rod

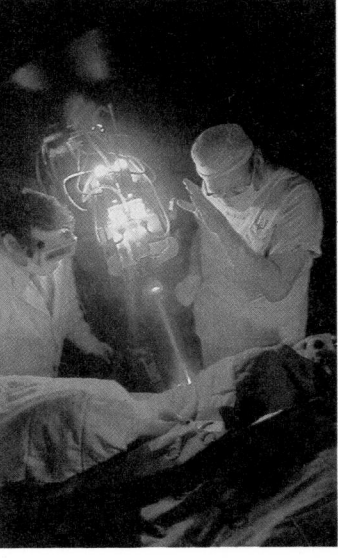

LASERS IN ACTION

Producing bursts of light energy that last for only a few millionths of a second, but are 10 million times more powerful than sunlight, the ruby laser is used in eye surgery and also (above) in the treatment of skin cancer.

The accurately focused laser beam burns away cancerous cells, but without causing damage to surrounding tissue. Laser scalpels can make fine incisions, and at the same time heat-seal the blood vessels, to reduce bleeding.

In industry, lasers are used for cutting and welding, and to guide tunnel-boring machinery on a perfectly straight line. In telecommunications, they are used in fibre optics; and they help to create three-dimensional photographs in holography. Sending out a laser pulse and measuring the time that elapses before its reflection returns, provides a very accurate way of measuring distances. The distance from Earth to Moon, for instance, can be calculated to the nearest metre.

HOW THE LASER GETS ITS POWER

INPUT *An artificial ruby rod, about 160 millimetres (6 inches) long and 12 millimetres (½ inch) across, is silvered at one end and partly silvered at the other. Encompassing the rod is a high-intensity electronic flash tube. When the tube flashes on, chromium atoms in the ruby become excited. This causes the outer electrons to jump from their ground state of energy to a high-energy level; then they fall back – first to an intermediate state, then back to the ground state from which they originally jumped.*

OUTPUT *As each electron falls back from an intermediate to a ground state, it emits a photon of light energy. Some photons collide with electrons still in the intermediate state. The electrons release photons that travel in exactly the same direction as the "striker" photon. Other electrons are struck and release more photons. A chain reaction develops. The silvered ends reflect back and forth those photons travelling parallel to the rod's axis until a hot, red beam builds up and flashes out from the partly silvered end.*

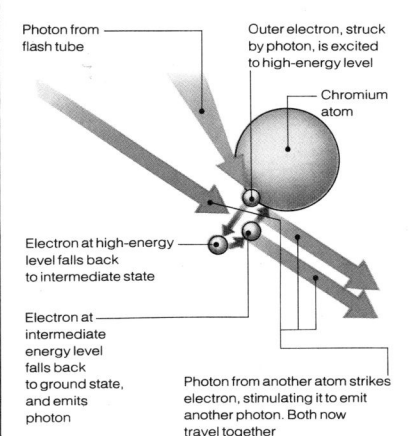

- Photon from flash tube
- Outer electron, struck by photon, is excited to high-energy level
- Chromium atom
- Electron at high-energy level falls back to intermediate state
- Electron at intermediate energy level falls back to ground state, and emits photon
- Photon from another atom strikes electron, stimulating it to emit another photon. Both now travel together

---

tomorrow. **2.** To endure throughout: *He didn't last the course.* **3.** To take or go on for (a specified time): *It lasts half an hour.* [Middle English *lasten,* Old English *lǣstan.*] —**last·er** *n.*

last³ *n.* A block or form shaped like a human foot, used by shoemakers in making or repairing shoes.

~*tr.v.* **lasted, lasting, lasts.** To mould or shape on a last. —**stick to (one's) last.** To do the work to which one is accustomed. [Middle English *laste,* Old English *lǣste,* from *lǣst,* sole, footprint.]

last⁴ *n. Chiefly British.* A unit of weight or volume varying for different commodities and in different districts, and approximating to

80 bushels, 640 gallons, or 2 tons. [Middle English *last,* "load", "burden", Old English *hlæst.*]

last-ditch (laást-dích ‖ lást-) *adj.* Of or designating a final desperate effort: *a last-ditch attempt to save the company.*

last honours *pl.n.* Observances or signs of respect at a funeral. Also called "funeral honours".

last·ing¹ (laást-ing ‖ lást-) *adj.* Continuing for a long time; durable. —**last·ing·ly** *adv.* —**last·ing·ness** *n.*

lasting² *n.* A durable twilled fabric.

Last Judgment *n.* According to the Bible, the final judgment by God of all mankind. Preceded by *the.*

last·ly (laást-li ‖ lást-) *adv.* In the end; in conclusion; finally.

last minute *n.* The moment or time immediately before an event or deadline: *She always does everything at the last minute.* Also called "last moment". —**last-minute** (laást-mínnit) *adj.*

last name *n.* A surname.

last post *n. Sometimes capital* L, *capital* P. *Military.* 1. A bugle call blown as a signal for the hour for retiring to bed. 2. A bugle call blown at funerals.

last resort *n.* A final measure or course of action open to one.

last straw *n.* An additional difficulty, irritation, or trouble that stretches one's tolerance or endurance beyond the limit. Preceded by *the.* [Based on the proverbial phrase, *It's the last straw that breaks the camel's back.*]

Last Supper *n.* Christ's supper with his disciples on the night before his Crucifixion, at which he instituted the Eucharist. Preceded by *the.* Also called the "Lord's Supper".

last thing *adv. Informal.* As the last or final action: *She'll do that last thing before she leaves.*

last word *n.* 1. The final statement in a verbal argument. 2. **a.** A conclusive or authoritative statement or treatment: *the last word in car safety.* **b.** The power or authority of ultimate decision. 3. *Informal.* The newest in fashion; the latest thing. Preceded by *the.*

Las Ve·gas (lass váygəss ‖ *U.S.* laass). City in southern Nevada, in the southwest United States. Set in a remote ranching and mining region, it is nevertheless the leading gambling city in the country and the site of many famous nightclubs.

lat. latitude.

Lat. Latin.

lat·a·ki·a (láttə-kée-ə) *n.* A grade of Turkish tobacco. [After *Latakia,* Syrian port in a tobacco-growing region.]

latch (lach) *n.* 1. A fastening or lock, typically a bar that falls into a groove or cavity and is lifted by a lever. 2. A small spring-lock for an outside door that can be opened from the outside by a key. —*v.* **latched, latching, latches.** —*tr.* To close or lock with a latch. —*intr.* To have a latch for closing or locking. —**latch on.** *Informal.* 1. To attach oneself; cling. Used with *to.* 2. To understand; perceive: *The fool still hasn't latched on.* Often used with *to.* 3. To single out (an idea, for example). Used with *to: latched on to idealism as the key to his work.* [Middle English *lache,* from *lachen,* to latch, seize, Old English *læccan,* to grasp.]

latch·et (láchit) *n. Archaic.* A thong used to fasten a shoe or sandal. [Middle English, from Old French *lachet, lacet,* shoestring, from *las,* noose, snare.]

latch·key (lách-kee) *n.* 1. A key for opening a latch, especially one on an outside door or gate. 2. A symbol of freedom from parental authority.

latchkey child *n.* A child who has a key to his home because both parents are out working when he returns from school.

latch·string (lách-string) *n.* A cord attached to a latch and often passed through a hole in the door to allow lifting of the latch from the outside.

late (layt) *adj.* **later** or *rare* **latter** (láttər), **latest** or **last** (laast ‖ last). 1. Coming or occurring after the correct, usual, or expected time; delayed. 2. **a.** Beginning at, occurring at, or lasting until a relatively advanced hour or time: *a late breakfast.* **b.** Occurring, being, or continuing towards the end: *the late 19th century.* **c.** Coming from near the end of a period or life: *a late Rembrandt.* **d.** At an advanced hour at night: *It was very late by then.* 3. Taking longer than usual to reach a given stage: *a late developer.* 4. Having recently begun or occurred; just previous to the present: *the latest developments.* 5. Being the immediate past occupant of a position or place; former. 6. Dead, especially recently deceased: *the late Mr. Foster.* —See Synonyms at **tardy.** —*adv.* **later, latest.** 1. After the correct, usual, or expected time; tardily. 2. **a.** At a relatively advanced time: *undertaken late in his life.* **b.** At an advanced hour of the night: *called very late.* **c.** Far into a period of time. 3. In the recent past: *As late as last week, he was still alive.* —**of late.** In the near past; lately. [Middle English, Old English *læt.*] —**late·ness** *n.*

lat·ed (láytid) *adj. Poetic.* Belated. [From LATE.]

la·teen (lə-téen) *adj. Nautical.* 1. Designating a triangular sail hung on a long yard attached to a short mast. 2. Rigged with such a sail. —*n.* A lateen-rigged boat. [French *(voile) Latine,* "Latin (sail)" (from its use in the Mediterranean), from Old French, feminine of *Latin,* LATIN.]

Late Greek *n.* Greek during the early Byzantine Empire, from about the fourth to about the seventh century A.D.

Late Latin *n.* Latin from the third to the seventh century A.D.

late·ly (láytli) *adv.* Not long ago; recently.

La Tène (laa tén, la) *adj.* Pertaining to or designating an Iron Age European civilisation dating from the fifth to the first century B.C. [After *La Tène,* on Lake Neuchâtel, Switzerland, where the remains were first discovered.]

la·tent (láyt'nt) *adj.* Present or potential, but not manifest: *latent talent.* [Latin *latēns* (stem *latent-*), present participle of *latēre,* to lie hidden, be concealed.] —**la·ten·cy** *n.* —**la·tent·ly** *adv.*

Synonyms: latent, dormant, potential, quiescent.

latent heat *n. Symbol* L. The quantity of heat absorbed or released by a substance undergoing a change of state, as by ice changing to water or water to steam.

latent image *n.* In photography, an invisible image produced in an emulsion after exposure but before development.

latent period *n.* 1. The incubation period of an infectious disease. 2. The interval between stimulus and response.

lat·er (láytər). Comparative of **late.** ~*adj.* Subsequent.

lat·er·al (láttərəl, láttrəl) *adj.* 1. Of, pertaining to, or situated at or on the side or sides. 2. *Phonetics.* Designating a sound produced by breath passing along one or both sides of the tongue. ~*n.* 1. A lateral part, projection, passage, or appendage. 2. *Phonetics.* A lateral sound, such as (l). [Latin *laterālis,* from *latus*† (stem *later-*), side.] —**lat·er·al·ly** *adv.*

lateral inversion *n.* Inversion between right and left, such as that which occurs in the formation of an image in a plane mirror.

lateral line *n.* A linear series of sensory pores and tubes for sensing sound and vibration, as along the side of a fish.

lateral thinking *n.* A method of solving problems by using an associational, sometimes apparently illogical, approach, especially one that uses the imagination as opposed to step-by-step reasoning. [Coined by Edward de Bono (1933–), British psychologist and author of *The Use of Lateral Thinking* (1967).]

Lat·er·an (láttərən) *n.* 1. The church of Saint John Lateran, the cathedral church of the pope as bishop of Rome. 2. The palace, now a museum, adjoining this church. Preceded by *the.* [Latin *Laterana,* district of ancient Rome, residence of the family Plautii Laterani.]

la·te·ra rec·ta. Plural of **latus rectum.**

lat·er·ite (láttə-rīt) *n.* A reddish-brown earthy substance, the residue produced by leaching of the soil in tropical regions, consisting of a preponderance of hydrated iron oxide with some hydrated aluminium oxide. Compare **bauxite.** [Latin *later*†, brick, tile + -ITE.]

lat·est (láytist). Alternative superlative of **late.** ~*adj.* Most recent, modern, or up-to-date. ~*n. Informal.* The most recent or up-to-date news, fashion, or the like. Preceded by *the.*

la·tex (láy-teks) *n., pl.* **latices** (láyti-seez) or **-texes.** 1. The usually milky, viscous sap of certain trees and plants, such as the rubber tree, that coagulates on exposure to air. 2. An emulsion of rubber or plastic globules in water, used in paints, adhesives, and other products. [New Latin, from Latin *latex,* fluid.] —**la·tex** *adj.*

latex paint *n.* A paint having a binder that is a latex. Also called "rubber-base paint".

lath (laath ‖ lath) *n., pl.* **laths** (laaths, laathz ‖ laths, lathz). 1. A narrow, thin strip of wood or metal, used especially in making a supporting structure for plaster, shingles, slates, or tiles. 2. Any other building material, such as a sheet of metal mesh, used for similar purposes. 3. A slat. 4. Lathing. ~*tr.v.* **lathed, lathing, laths.** To build, cover, or line with laths. [Middle English *lat, lathe,* Old English *lætt.*]

lathe (layth) *n.* 1. A machine on which a piece of wood or metal, for example, is spun on a horizontal axis and shaped by a fixed cutting or abrading tool. 2. A potter's wheel. ~*tr.v.* **lathed, lathing, lathes.** To cut or shape on a lathe. [Perhaps Middle English *lath,* Old Danish *lad,* supporting stand, perhaps a special use of *lad,* pile, from Old Norse *hladh.*]

lath·er (laáth-ər, láth-) *n.* 1. A light foam formed by soap or detergent agitated in water. 2. Froth formed by profuse sweating, as on a horse. —**in a lather.** *Informal.* Highly excited or upset; agitated. ~*v.* **lathered, -ering, -ers.** —*tr.* 1. To put lather on; coat with lather. 2. *Informal.* To give a beating to; whip. —*intr.* 1. To produce lather; foam. 2. To become coated with lather. Used especially of horses. [Revival of Old English *lēathor,* washing soda.] —**lath·er·er** *n.* —**lath·er·y** *adj.*

lath·ing (laáth-ing ‖ laáth-, láth-) *n.* 1. The act or process of building with laths. 2. A structure made of laths. Also called "lath".

lath·y (laáthi ‖ láthi) *adj.* **-ier, -iest.** Tall and thin like a lath.

la·ti·ci·fer (la-tíssifər, lay-) *n.* A cell or vessel containing latex, found in such plants as rubber, poppy, and euphorbia. [New Latin, from *latex* (stem *latic-*) + -FER.]

lat·i·cif·er·ous (látti-síffərəss, láyti-) *adj.* Secreting or exuding latex. [New Latin *latex* (stem *latic-*), LATEX + -FEROUS.]

lat·i·fun·di·um (látti-fúndi-əm) *n., pl.* **-dia** (-ə). A landed estate, especially one in the ancient Roman world or in Latin America. [Latin *lātifundium : lātus,* broad + *fundus,* estate, bottom.]

Lat·i·mer (láttimər), **Hugh** (c. 1485–1555). English churchman during the Reformation, who became Bishop of Worcester (1535). He was martyred at Oxford by Queen Mary I.

Lat·in (láttin ‖ látt'n) *adj.* 1. *Abbr.* L., **Lat.** Of or pertaining to Latium, its people, or its culture. 2. Of or pertaining to ancient Rome, its people, or its culture. 3. Of, pertaining to, or composed in the language of ancient Rome and Latium. 4. Of or pertaining to those countries or peoples using Romance languages, especially the countries of Latin America. 5. Of or pertaining to the Roman Catholic Church, as distinguished from the Eastern Orthodox Church. ~*n. Abbr.* **L., Lat.** 1. The ancient Italic dialect of Latium or the language into which it evolved, which through the political and cultural expansion of Rome became the dominant language of the Western Roman Empire, and survived into the Middle Ages as a language of learning and state documents, and until modern times as the official language of the Roman Catholic Church. See **Late Latin, Medieval Latin, New Latin, Old Latin, Vulgar Latin.** 2. A native or resident of ancient Latium. 3. A member of a Latin people, especially of Latin America. 4. A Roman Catholic.

Latin alphabet *n.* The **Roman alphabet** *(see).*

Latin America. A division of the Americas, consisting broadly of

lateen *In a lateen rig, the luff, or leading edge of the sail, is attached to a very long spar, not the mast. Lateen-rigged boats, like this one on the Nile, are still common in many parts of the world.*

LATIN AMERICA

U N I T E D   S T A T E S   O F   A M E R I C A

Sierra Madre Occidental
Sierra Madre Oriental
Rio Grande
Gulf of California
Baja California
C. San Lucas
MEXICO
Citlaltepetl 5699m
Ixtaccihuatl
Popocatepetl 5452m
Isthmus of Tehuantepec
Yucatán
GUATEMALA
BELIZE
HONDURAS
EL SALVADOR
NICARAGUA
L. Nicaragua
COSTA RICA
Canal Zone (US)
PANAMA

GULF OF MEXICO
Straits of Florida
BAHAMAS
Turks & Caicos Is (UK)
CUBA
Greater Antilles
JAMAICA
Hispaniola
DOMINICAN REP.
HAITI
Puerto Rico (US)
Virgin Is (US) (UK)
Anguilla (UK)
Montserrat (UK)
ANTIGUA
Guadeloupe (FR.)
DOMINICA
Martinique (FR.)
ST LUCIA
BARBADOS
ST VINCENT
GRENADA
TRINIDAD & TOBAGO
St Kitts & Nevis
Lesser Antilles
CARIBBEAN SEA
Curaçao (NETH.)
Leeward Is
Windward Is

A T L A N T I C   O C E A N
Bermuda (UK)
30°N
Tropic of Cancer

VENEZUELA
Llanos
Orinoco
Magdalena
COLOMBIA
Dam
GUYANA
SURINAM
FRENCH GUIANA
Guiana Highlands
Angel Fall
Cuquenan Falls
Caroni

Galapagos Is (ECUADOR)
ECUADOR
Cotopaxi 5896m
Putumayo
Negro
Ucayali
Huascaran 6768m
La Montaña
L. Titicaca
Ancohuma 7014m
Ullimani 6402m
BOLIVIA
Altiplano
Atacama Desert
Llullaillaco 6723m
Ojos del Salado 7084m
Pissis 6858m
Bonete 6872m
Salinas Grandes
Tupungato 6800m
Aconcagua 6960m
Juan Fernandez Is (CHILE)
Bio-Bio

P A C I F I C   O C E A N
Easter I. (CHILE)
Equator

Putumayo
Napo
Marañon
Amazon
Madeira
Purus
Juruá
Tapajos
Xingu
Tocantins
Serra Geral de Goiás
B R A Z I L
Mato Grosso
Brazilian Highlands
Serra do Espinhaço
S. Francisco
Campos
Paraguay
Urubupungá Dam
Paraná
PARAGUAY
Gran Chaco
Entre Rios
Serra do Mar
L. Patos
L. Mirim
URUGUAY
Plate
Pampas
Colorado
Negro
A R G E N T I N A
Patagonia

Tropic of Capricorn
30°S

A T L A N T I C   O C E A N
Falkland Is (UK)

Strait of Magellan
Tierra del Fuego
Cape Horn
Drake Passage
S. Georgia (UK)
60°S

0   1000   2000 Km
0   500   1000 Miles
Equatorial scale

90°W   60°W   30°N   60°W

PRONUNCIATION KEY

a, trap; aa, father; ai, fair;
ar, star; aw, lawn; ay, play;
b, bb, stab; rubber;
ch, church; ck, ticket;
d, dd, dead; ladder; e, dress;
ee, bee; er, defer; ew, few;
ewr, pure; ə, about;
ər, letter; f, ff, fife; differ;
g, gg, giggle; h, hat; i, kit;
ī, price; īr, fire; j, judge;
k, kick; l, ll, let; 'l, needle;
m, mm, man; n, nn, no;
'n, sudden; ng, thing; o, lot;
ō, no; ŏŏ, foot; ōō, shoe;
oor, poor; ow, cow;
owr, hour; oy, boy;
p, pp, pepper; r, rr, red;
s, ss, sauce; sh, ship;
t, tt, totter; th, thick; th, this;
smooth; u, cut; ur, turn;
v, vv, valve; w, wet; y, yes;
z, zz, zebra; zh, vision;
pleasure

IN FOREIGN WORDS:

aN, oN, Saint-Saëns;
hl, Llanelli; Hluhluwe;
kh, loch; lough; Khaled

STRESS MARK:

ín-sīt, insight; in-sít, incite

the countries of Central and South America (specifically those speaking Romance languages), together with Mexico. The region constitutes the fourth largest of the world's major divisions, with 14 per cent of its land, and 8 per cent of its people.

Latin America's backbone of young fold mountains, the Sierra Madre of Mexico and the Andes, is earthquake-prone, and forms part of the Pacific's "Ring of Fire", with active volcanoes. To the east lie highland blocks, and vast lowlands drained by great rivers such as the Amazon and Paraná.

The region has some of the driest places on earth—some 20 per cent is thorn forest, savannah, steppe, or desert—but it also has more tropical rain forest (selvas) than any other region. It covers 30

per cent of the area, and supplies more than 15 per cent of the world's hardwoods.

Less than 25 per cent of Latin America is cultivated; 34 per cent of its workers are in agriculture. It produces much of the world's coffee, sugar cane, and bananas, and also beef and wool.

The area has vast reserves of silver, copper, high-grade iron ore, bauxite, chrome, and nickel. It has little coal but considerable oil and gas, soon to supply most of the energy for its increasing industrialisation, especially in Mexico and Brazil.

The region's basic problems persist, however: a shortage of cultivable land, overpopulation and the drift of people to the cities, social disparities, and political instability.

Lat·in·ate (látti-nayt) *adj.* Imitative of the style of Latin or using many Latinisms: *Latinate English prose.*

Latin Church *n.* The Roman Catholic Church.

Latin cross *n.* A cross with the lower limb longest.

Lat·in·ise, Lat·in·ize (látti-nīz) *v.* **-ised, -ising, -ises.** —*tr.* **1.** To translate into Latin. **2.** To transliterate into the characters of the Latin alphabet; Romanise. **3.** To cause to adopt or acquire Latin characteristics or customs. **4.** To cause to follow or resemble the Roman Catholic Church in dogma or practices. —*intr.* To use Latinisms. —**Lat·in·i·sa·tion** (-nī-záysh'n ‖ *U.S.* -ni-) *n.* —**Lat·in·i·ser** *n.*

Lat·in·ism (láttiniz'm) *n.* An idiom, structure, or word derived from or in imitation of Latin.

Lat·in·ist (láttinist) *n.* A Latin scholar.

La·tin·i·ty (lə-tínnəti, la-) *n.* **1.** The use of Latin. **2.** The manner in which Latin is used in speaking or writing; Latin style.

Latin lover *n.* A vain, ostentatiously seductive man, apparently of Italian or Spanish parentage. Used humorously.

Latin Quarter *n.* A section of Paris on the left bank of the Seine, a centre for university students for many centuries.

Latin square *n. Mathematics.* A set of *n* numbers or symbols arranged in a square array of *n* rows and *n* columns such that each number of symbol occurs only once in each row and column. Such squares are used for the statistical analysis of variability.

lat·ish (láytish) *adj. Informal.* Fairly late. —**lat·ish** *adv.*

lat·i·tude (látti-tewd ‖ -tōod) *n. Abbr.* **l., L., lat. 1.** Extent; breadth; range. **2.** Freedom from normal restraints, limitations, or regulations. **3.** *Geography.* The angular distance north or south of the equator, measured in degrees along a meridian, as on a map, globe, or the celestial sphere. **4.** A region of the Earth considered in relation to its distance from the equator: *temperate latitudes.* **5.** The range of values or conditions over which something operates or is effective; for example, the range of exposures over which a photographic film yields usable images. [Middle English, from Latin *lātitūdō,* from *lātus,* wide, broad.] —**lat·i·tu·din·al** (-téwdin'l) *adj.*

lat·i·tu·di·nar·i·an (látti-téwdi-náiri-ən ‖ -tōodi-) *adj.* Favouring freedom of thought and behaviour, especially in religion. ~*n.* A latitudinarian person. [Latin *lātitūdō* (stem *lātitūdin-*), LATITUDE + -ARIAN.] —**lat·i·tu·di·nar·i·an·ism** *n.*

La·ti·um (láy-shi-əm, -sh'm). **1.** An ancient country in west-central Italy. **2.** See Lazio.

La Tour (la tóor), **Georges de** (1593–1652). French painter. He specialised in genre painting and religious subjects, and is famous for the dramatic lighting of his night scenes, as in *La Madeleine à la veilleuse.*

la·tri·a (lə-trī-ə) *n.* In the Roman Catholic and Eastern Orthodox churches, the special reverence due to God alone. Compare **dulia, hyperdulia.** [Latin, from Greek *latreia,* worship.]

la·trine (lə-tréen) *n.* A lavatory, as in a barracks or camp. [French, from Latin *latrīna,* contraction of *lavātrīna,* bath.]

–latry *n. comb. form.* Indicates the worship of; for example, **idolatry.** [Greek *latreia,* service, worship.]

THE GRID LINES ON THE GLOBE

A method of locating precisely any place on Earth

For purposes of navigation and geography, Earth's surface is divided into degrees, minutes, and seconds of latitude and longitude.

An imaginary line from the equator to the centre of the Earth, and another from the North Pole (or from the South Pole) to the centre of the Earth would meet at an angle of 90°. This angle is divided into degrees, from 0° at the equator to 90°N at the North Pole (or 90°S at the South Pole). The same degree reading is given to every point on the globe's surface that is at the same angle to these imaginary lines. Each degree is subdivided into 60 minutes, and each minute into 60 seconds. A circle joining the points with the same degree reading, forms a line parallel to the equator; it is called a parallel or a line of latitude. Every place on that line has the same latitude.

A line of longitude joins places at which the Sun is at its highest point in the sky at the same time. It is a noon or midday line, hence the term meridian, from the Latin *merides,* "midday". Each meridian runs from Pole to Pole, and is half a Great Circle. In the same way that latitude is measured as angles north and south of the equator (latitude 0°), longitude is measured as angles east and west of the Prime Meridian (longitude 0°), which passes through Greenwich.

Longitude therefore represents difference in time on Earth. Noon occurs an hour earlier for each 15° of longitude to the east of the Prime Meridian, and an hour later for each 15° to the west. Travelling eastwards, an hour must be added to Greenwich time for each 15° of longitude to obtain local time. Travelling westwards, an hour must be subtracted for each 15° of longitude. The 180° meridian is the International Date Line for most of its length. Travellers going eastwards across this line set the calendar back a day; travellers going westwards set it forward a day.

FIXING LATITUDE AND LONGITUDE *An imaginary line inclined at 15° above a line from Earth's centre to the equator would meet the globe surface at what we call the latitude 15°N. Similarly, an imaginary line at a horizontal angle of 15° to a line between Earth's centre and the Prime Meridian would meet the globe surface at what we call the longitude 15° (W or E).*

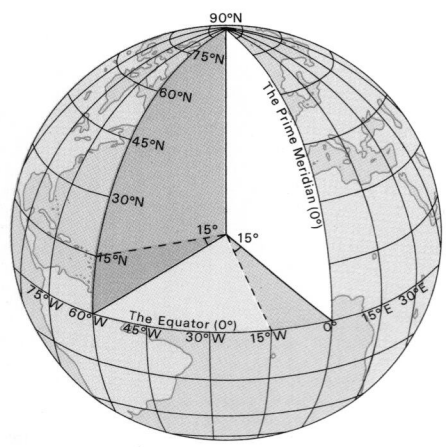

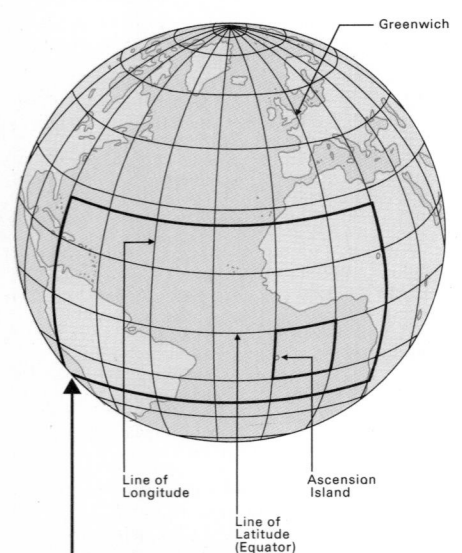

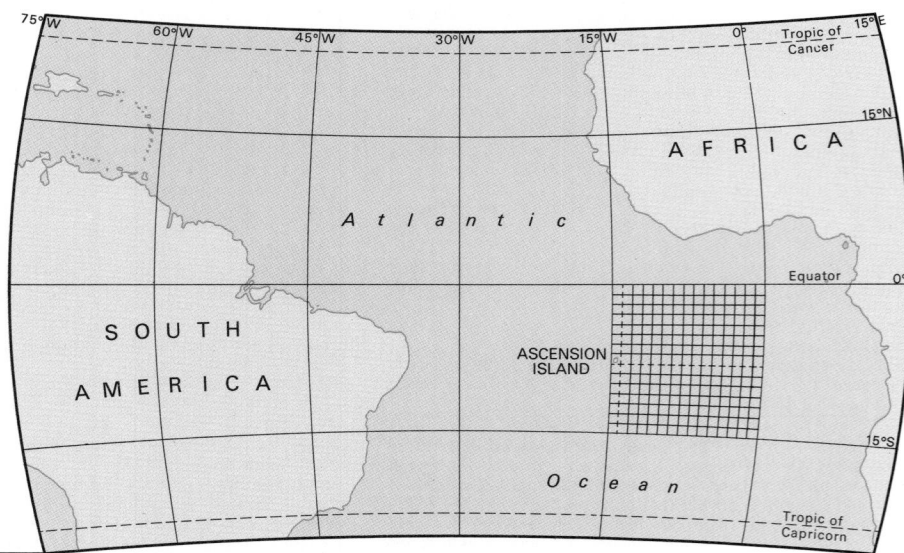

LOCATING ASCENSION ISLAND *The island is about 88 square kilometres (34 square miles) in area. It is located at 14°22′W and 7°57′S; that is 14 degrees 22 minutes west of the Prime Meridian and 7 degrees 57 minutes south of the equator. A degree of longitude at the equator is about 111 kilometres (69 miles); a degree of latitude anywhere is about 111 kilometres. By giving position not just in degrees but accurate to the minute and second, it is possible to locate precisely an airport on the island.*

lat·ten (látt'n) *n.* **1.** An alloy formerly made of or made to resemble brass, hammered thin, and used in the manufacture of church vessels. **2.** Any thin sheet of metal, especially of tin. [Middle English *laton,* from Old French *leiton, laton,* from Arabic *lāṭūn,* copper, from Turkish dialectal *altan,* gold.]

lat·ter (láttər). *Rare.* Alternative comparative of **late**.
~*adj.* **1.** Designating the second of two persons or things mentioned. **2.** Further advanced in time or sequence; later. **3.** Closer to the end: *the latter part of the book.*
~*n.* The second of two persons or things mentioned. [Middle English, Old English *lætra,* comparative of *læt,* LATE.]
Usage: *Latter* is appropriate only in referring to the second of two previously mentioned entities: *We could travel by car or train—the latter would be quicker. Latter* is sometimes loosely used to refer to the last-mentioned item in a sequence of three or more (*We could travel by car, train or boat. . .*), but formal usage prefers an alternative form, such as *the last-named, the last of these,* or simply *the last.* Similarly, *latter* is not acceptable when only one item is referred to: *We could travel by car—the latter is very convenient.*

lat·ter-day (láttər-dáy) *adj.* Belonging to present or recent time; modern.

Latter-day Saint *n.* A **Mormon** *(see).*

lat·ter·ly (láttər-li) *adv.* Recently; lately.

lat·ter·most (láttər-mōst) *adj.* Last.

lat·tice (láttiss) *n.* **1.** An open framework made of strips of metal, wood, or other material interwoven to form regular, patterned spaces. **2.** A screen, window, gate, or the like made of such a framework. **3.** Something, such as a heraldic bearing, that resembles such a framework. **4.** *Chemistry.* A regular, periodic configuration of points, particles, or objects throughout an area or space; especially, the arrangement of ions or molecules in a crystalline solid.
~*tr.v.* **latticed, -ticing, -tices.** To construct or furnish with a lattice or latticework. [Middle English *latis,* from Old French *lattis,* from *latte,* lath, from Germanic, akin to Old English *lætt,* LATH.] **—lat·ticed** *adj.*

lat·tice·work (láttiss-wurk) *n.* **1.** A lattice or something resembling a lattice; trelliswork. **2.** A structure made of lattices.

la·tus rec·tum (láttəss réktəm, laàtəss) *n., pl.* **latera recta** (láttərə réktə). In geometry, a chord through the focus of a parabola, hyperbola, or ellipse parallel to a transverse axis. [New Latin, "straight side".]

Lat·vi·a (látvi-ə). Officially **Latvian Soviet Socialist Republic.** Constituent republic of the U.S.S.R., lying on the Baltic Sea. It consists largely of a fertile lowland, although there are numerous lakes and hills to the east. Latvia came under Russian control in the 18th century. From 1918 to 1940 it was an independent republic, but during World War II it was annexed by the U.S.S.R. Capital, Riga.

Lat·vi·an (látvi-ən) *adj.* Of or pertaining to Latvia, its people, or its language.
~*n.* **1.** A native or inhabitant of Latvia. **2.** The Baltic language of these people. In this sense, also called "Lettish".

lau·an (low-aàn, lōō-) *n.* Timber obtained from any of various trees native to the Philippines, such as *Shorea,* having light yellow to brown, close-grained wood. [Tagalog *lawaan.*]

laud (lawd) *tr.v.* **lauded, lauding, lauds.** To give praise or express devotion to; glorify. See Synonyms at **praise.**
~*n.* **1.** Praise; glorification. **2.** A hymn or song of praise. **3.** *Plural. Usually capital* **L.** *Ecclesiastical.* **a.** An early-morning church service at which psalms of praise are sung. **b.** The service of prayers following the matins and constituting with them the first of the seven canonical hours. [Latin *laudāre,* to praise, from *laus* (stem *laud-*), praise.] **—laud·er** *n.*

Laud (lawd), **William** (1573–1645). Archbishop of Canterbury (1633–45). His attempts to introduce the Book of Common Prayer into Scotland led to the Bishops' Wars, and his eventual imprisonment and execution by Parliament.

Lau·da (lówdə), **Niki** (1949–). Austrian motor-racing driver. He was Formula 1 world champion (1975, 1977). He recovered from severe facial burns sustained in a crash (1976) to continue racing.

laud·a·ble (láwdə-b'l) *adj.* Deserving approbation; commendable; praiseworthy. **—laud·a·bil·i·ty** (-bílləti), **laud·a·ble·ness** *n.* **—laud·a·bly** *adv.*

lau·da·num (lód-nəm, láwd'n-əm) *n.* A tincture of opium. [New Latin *laudanum* (coined by Paracelsus), possibly from Latin *lādanum, labdanum,* resin, LABDANUM.]

laud·a·tion (law-dáysh'n) *n.* The act of lauding; praise.

laud·a·tive (láwdətiv) *adj.* Laudatory.

laud·a·to·ry (láwdə-təri, -tri) *adj.* Including, expressing, or bestowing praise; eulogistic. [Late Latin *laudātōrius,* from Latin *laudāre* (past participle *laudātus*), to praise, LAUD.]

Lau·der (láwdər), **Sir Harry,** born Hugh MacLennan (1870–1950). Scottish music-hall star who created the comic figure of a wry but sentimental Highlander.

laugh (laaf || laf) *v.* **laughed, laughing, laughs.** *—intr.* **1.** To express emotion, typically mirth, by a series of inarticulate sounds, characteristically with the mouth open in a wide smile. **2.** To produce sounds or cries resembling laughter. **3.** To manifest or appear to manifest joy in any way. *—tr.* **1.** To drive, induce, or effect with or by laughter: *They laughed him off the stage.* **2.** To utter or express by or as if by laughing: *laughing their appreciation.* **—be laughing.** *Informal.* To be in a position of good fortune, satisfaction, or easy success. **—laugh at. 1.** To exhibit amusement at. **2.** To poke fun at; ridicule; deride. **3.** To refuse to consider seriously. **—laugh down.** To silence with laughter. **—laugh off** or **away.** To dismiss lightly (especially, something unpleasant or painful), by or as if by laughing.
~*n.* **1.** A burst or sound of laughter. **2.** *Informal.* Something amusing, improbable, or ridiculous; a joke or absurdity: *That's a laugh.* **—have the last laugh.** To enjoy vindication. [Middle English *laughen,* Old English *hliehhan, hlæhhan.*] **—laugh·er** *n.* **—laugh·ing·ly** *adv.*

laugh·a·ble (laàf-əb'l || láff-) *adj.* Causing or deserving of laughter or derision. **—laugh·a·ble·ness** *n.* **—laugh·a·bly** *adv.*

laugh·ing gas (laàfing || láffing) *n.* An anaesthetic, **nitrous oxide** *(see).*

laughing hyena *n.* The **spotted hyena** *(see).*

laughing jackass *n.* A bird, the **kookaburra** *(see).*

laughing stock *n.* An object of jokes or ridicule; a butt; a fool.

laugh·ter (laàf-tər || láf-) *n.* **1.** The act of laughing. **2.** The sound produced by laughing. **3.** The experience or appearance of joy, merriment, amusement, or the like. **4.** *Archaic.* A cause or subject for laughter. [Middle English, Old English *hleahtor.*]

laughter line *n.* A line that forms as a wrinkle on the face as a result of laughing or smiling.

Laugh·ton (láwt'n), **Charles** (1899–1962). British actor. Among many starring Hollywood roles was his screen triumph as Captain Bligh in *Mutiny on the Bounty* (1935).

launce (laanss || lawnss) *n.* A fish, the **sand eel** *(see).* [Perhaps variant of LANCE.]

Launcelot. Variant of **Lancelot.**

Laun·ces·ton (láwn-sə-stən, lón-). City in Tasmania, southeast Australia. It is Tasmania's second largest city and the main port for trade between the island and the Australian mainland.

launch[1] (lawnch, *rarely* laanch) *v.* **launched, launching, launches.** *—tr.* **1.** To move or set in motion with force; propel: *launch a missile; launched a volley of snowballs.* **2.** To slide or lower (a boat) into the water, especially for the first time. **3.** To put into action; inaugurate; initiate. **4.** To set or start (a person or group) on a particular course of action. **5.** To engage (oneself) vigorously and enthusiastically in a new activity. **6.** To introduce (a new book, film, product, or the like) to the public through a publicity campaign. *—intr.* **1.** To begin a new project or venture; especially, to widen or extend one's current activities or enterprises. Usually used with *out: The company is launching out into plastics this year.* **2.** To make a rousing or enthusiastic beginning. Used with *into* or *forth into: The whole crowd launched into song.* **3.** To start talking or writing, especially eagerly and at length. Used with *on* or *forth* or *into: launched forth into a tirade.*
~*n.* An act of launching. Also used adjectivally: *a launch complex.* [Middle English *launchen,* to hurl, pierce, from Old North French *lancher,* variant of Old French *lancier,* from *lance,* LANCE.]

launch[2] *n.* **1.** A large ship's boat formerly sloop-rigged but now powered. **2.** Any large, open motorboat. [Portuguese *lancha,* from Malay, akin to Malay *lancharan,* boat.]

launch·er (láwn-chər, laàn-) *n.* One that launches, such as: **1.** A device for firing grenades. **2.** A device for firing rockets.

launching pad (láwnching) *n.* Also **launch pad.** The base or platform from which a rocket or space vehicle is launched.

launch vehicle *n. Aerospace.* A **booster** *(see).*

laun·der (láwn-dər, *rarely* laàn-) *v.* **-dered, -dering, -ders.** *—tr.* **1.** To wash, or wash and iron (clothes, linen, or the like). **2.** To pass (money from a dubious source) through a bank or other intermediary, in order to obscure its origin. *—intr.* **1.** To withstand washing in a specified way: *This material launders well.* **2.** To wash, or wash and iron, clothes or linens.
~*n.* In mining, a wooden trough for water, used for washing ore. [From obsolete *launder,* launderer, from Middle English *launder,* variant of *lavender,* from Old French *lavandier,* from Vulgar Latin *lavandārius* (unattested), from Latin *lavanda,* things that need washing, from the gerundive of *lavāre,* to wash, LAVE.] **—laun·der·er** *n.*

laun·derette (láwn-də-rét, -drét) *n.* Also **laun·drette** (-drét). A commercial establishment equipped with washing machines and dryers, usually coin-operated and self-service. [LAUNDR(Y) + -OMAT.]

laun·dress (láwn-driss, *rarely* laàn-, -dress) *n.* A woman who launders clothes, linen, or the like, as an occupation.

laun·dry (láwn-dri, *rarely* laàn-) *n., pl.* **-dries. 1.** Soiled or laundered clothes and linens; washing. **2.** A place where laundering is done. [From obsolete *launder,* launderer. See **launder.**]

laun·dry·man (láwn-dri-mən, laàn-) *n., pl.* **-men** (-mən). **1.** A man who makes collections and deliveries for a commercial laundry. **2.** A man who works in a laundry.

laun·dry·wom·an (láwn-dri-wŏŏmən, laàn-) *n., pl.* **-women** (wimmin). A female laundryman.

Laur·as·i·a (law-ráy-shə, -zhə). Ancient supercontinent which formed the northern land mass of the world when the single continent of Pangaea split into two sections at the end of the Palaeozoic era. It comprised North America, Greenland, Europe, and Asia (excluding the Indian subcontinent), and itself split during the Mezozoic era, into North America and Eurasia.

lau·re·ate (láwri-ət, lórri-) *adj.* **1.** Worthy of laurels for one's achievements; pre-eminent. **2.** Crowned or decked with laurel as a mark of honour. **3.** Honoured for achievement in a field. **4.** *Archaic.* Made of laurel sprigs, as a wreath or crown.
~*n.* **1.** A poet laureate. **2.** One honoured with a crown of laurel. **3.** One who has received an honour or award: *a Nobel laureate.* [Latin *laureātus,* crowned with laurel, from *laurea,* laurel tree or

lattice *A latticed window in the Tower of London.*

launcher *A rocket being fired from a hand-held launcher. Since the bazooka of World War II was developed as an antitank weapon, light rocket launchers have been increasingly important in every modern army.*

PRONUNCIATION KEY

a, trap; aa, father; ai, fair; ar, star; aw, lawn; ay, play; b, bb, stab; rubber; ch, church; ck, ticket; d, dd, dead; ladder; e, dress; ee, bee; er, defer; ew, few; ewr, pure; ə, about; ər, letter; f, ff, fife; differ; g, gg, giggle; h, hat; i, kit; ī, price; īr, fire; j, judge; k, kick; l, ll, let; 'l, needle; m, mm, man; n, nn, no; 'n, sudden; ng, thing; o, lot; ō, no; ŏŏ, foot; ōō, shoe; oor, poor; ow, cow; owr, hour; oy, boy; p, pp, pepper; r, rr, red; s, ss, sauce; sh, ship; t, tt, totter; th, thick; th, this; smooth; u, cut; ur, turn; v, vv, valve; w, wet; y, yes; z, zz, zebra; zh, vision; pleasure

IN FOREIGN WORDS:

aN, oN, Saint-Saëns; hl, Llanelli; Hluhluwe; kh, loch; lough; Khaled

STRESS MARK:

ín-sīt, insight; in-sít, incite

laurel *A common garden shrub, particularly in towns. It can stand shade and damp and even neglect and still produce its shiny black fruit.*

crown, from *laureus,* of laurel, from *laurus,* LAUREL.] **—lau·re·ate·ship** *n.*

lau·rel (lórrəl || láwrəl) *n.* **1.** A shrub or tree, the **bay** *(see).* **2.** Any of several similar or related shrubs or trees, such as **California laurel, cherry laurel, mountain laurel, spotted laurel,** and **spurge laurel** *(all of which see).* **3.** *Usually plural.* Leaves or twigs of a laurel, especially *L. nobilis,* formed into a wreath and conferred as a mark of honour in ancient times upon poets, heroes, and victors in athletic contests. **4.** *Plural.* Honour and glory won for achievement. **—look to (one's) laurels.** To protect one's position of eminence against rivals. **—rest on (one's) laurels.** To be content with past achievements and to cease striving.
~*tr.v.* **laurelled** or *U.S.* **-reled, -relling** or *U.S.* **-reling, -rels.** To crown with laurel. [Middle English *lorel, laurer,* laurel tree, from Old French *lorier,* from *lor,* laurel, from Latin *laurus,* perhaps of Mediterranean origin.]

Lau·rel and Har·dy (lórrəl ənd hárdi). Film comedy team, the first great innovative comedians of talking films. Stan Laurel, born Arthur Stanley Jefferson (1890–1965), was British, Oliver Hardy (1892–1957), American. They made many short films between 1926 and 1945. *The Music Box* (1932) won an Academy Award.

lau·ric acid (láwr-ik, lórr-) *n.* A fatty acid, $C_{12}H_{24}O_2$, obtained chiefly from coconut oil, and used in making soaps, cosmetics, insecticides, and alkyd resins. Also called "dodecanoic acid". [Latin *laurus,* LAUREL (from its occurrence in some laurel).]

Lau·ri·er (lórri-ər), **Sir Wilfrid** (1841–1919). The first French-Canadian prime minister of Canada (1896–1911). His Liberal administration fought to improve Canada's status within the Commonwealth.

lau·rus·ti·nus (lórrə-stīnəss || láwrə-) *n.* A Mediterranean shrub, *Viburnum tinus,* often grown for ornament, having glossy, dark green foliage and flattish clusters of small pink or white flowers. [New Latin : Latin *laurus,* laurel + *tinus,* name of a plant (probably laurustinus), probably from Germanic.]

lau·ryl alcohol (láwr-il, lórr-) *n.* A white crystalline solid, $C_{12}H_{25}OH$, used in the manufacture of detergents. [LAURIC ACID + -YL.]

Lau·sanne (lō-zán). A city in western Switzerland, lying on Lake Geneva. It is the trading and marketing centre of a fertile agricultural region and also a popular resort and conference centre.

lav (lav) *n. Chiefly British Informal.* A lavatory.

lav. lavatory.

la·va (laávə || lávvə) *n.* **1.** Molten rock that issues from a volcano or a fissure in the earth's surface. **2.** The same rock when cooled and solidified. [Italian, lava stream from Vesuvius, stream caused by rain, from *lavare,* to wash, from Latin *lavāre,* to wash, LAVE.]

la·va·bo (lə-váy-bō, -vaá-, lávvə-) *n., pl.* **-boes. 1.** *Often capital* **L. a.** In the Roman Catholic and Anglican churches, the ceremonial washing of the celebrant's hands after the offertory of the Mass. **b.** The psalm passage formerly recited at this point. **2.** The basin or small towel used in this ritual. **3.** A washbowl and water tank with a spout used for ablutions in medieval monasteries. [Latin *lavābo,* "I shall wash" (first word in Psalm 26:6), from *lavāre,* to wash, LAVE.]

lav·age (lávvij, la-vaázh) *n. Medicine.* A washing, especially of a hollow organ, such as the stomach or lower bowel, with repeated injections of water. [French, a washing, from Old French, from *laver,* to wash, from Latin *lavāre,* to wash, LAVE.]

La·val (la-vál), **Pierre** (1883–1945). French politician. He twice served as prime minister (1931–32, 1935–36). Following the surrender of France he became premier of the Vichy government (1942). He was executed for treason for collaborating with the Germans.

la·va-la·va (laávə-laávə) *n.* A rectangular strip of printed cotton cloth tied around the waist and worn as a skirt by Polynesians, especially Samoans. [Samoan *lavalava.*]

lav·a·liere (lávvə-léer) *n.* Also **la·val·lière** (lávval-yaír). *U.S.* **1.** A pendant worn on a chain around the neck. **2.** A **neck microphone** *(see).* [French *lavallière,* after Louise de *La Vallière,* a mistress of Louis XIV.]

la·va·tion (la-váysh'n, lay-) *n. Formal.* The process of washing; a cleansing. [Latin *lavātiō* (stem *lavātiōn-*), from *lavāre,* LAVE.]

lav·a·to·ry (lávvə-təri, -tri) *n., pl.* **-ries.** *Abbr.* **lav. 1.** A disposal apparatus consisting of a bowl fitted with a flushing device, used for urination and defecation. **2.** A room equipped with one or more lavatories and usually with washing facilities. [Middle English *lavatorie,* from Late Latin *lavātorium,* washing place, washing vessel, from Latin *lavāre,* to wash, LAVE.] **—la·va·to·ri·al** (-táwri-əl || -tōri-) *adj.*

lavatory paper *n. Chiefly British.* Toilet paper.

lave (layv) *v.* **laved, laving, laves.** *—tr. Archaic & Literary.* **1.** To wash; bathe. **2.** To lap or wash against: *The stream laved the rocks.* *—intr. Archaic & Literary.* To bathe oneself. [Middle English *laven,* from Old French *laver,* from Latin *lavāre.*]

lavender *This fragrant shrub has been associated for centuries with traditional flower gardens.*

lav·en·der (lávv'ndər) *n.* **1.** Any of various aromatic Old World plants of the genus *Lavandula;* especially, *L. officinalis* (or *L. spica* or *L. vera*), having clusters of small purplish flowers and yielding an oil used in perfumery. **2.** The fragrant dried leaves, stems, and flowers of such a plant. **3.** Any of various similar or related plants, such as **sea lavender** and **spike lavender** *(both of which see).* **4.** Pale to light bluish purple, to very light or pale violet. [Middle English *lavendre,* from Anglo-French, from Medieval Latin *lavendula, livendula*†.] **—lav·en·der** *adj.*

la·ver¹ (láyvər) *n.* **1.** A large basin used in ancient Judaism by the priest for ablutions before making a sacrificial offering. **2.** *Archaic.* A stone basin or trough used for washing. **3.** *Archaic.* The baptismal font or the water in it. [Middle English *laver, lavor,* from Old French *laveoir,* perhaps from Late Latin *lavātorium,* LAVATORY.]

la·ver² (laávər) *n.* Any of several edible seaweeds of the genus *Porphyra.* [New Latin, from Latin *laver*†.]

La·ver (láyvər), **Rod(ney George)** (1938–). Australian tennis player. He was Wimbledon champion in 1961, 1962, 1968, and 1969. He won the world's four major singles titles in 1962 as an amateur, and in 1969 as a professional.

La·ve·ran (lávvə-róN), **(Charles Louis) Alphonse** (1845–1922). French physician. He isolated the parasitic protozoa responsible for malaria (1880), for which he was awarded the Nobel prize in physiology and medicine (1907).

laver bread (laávər) *n.* The fronds of laver seaweed dipped in oatmeal, fried and eaten, especially in Wales.

lav·er·ock (lávvərək) *n. Scottish & Archaic.* A skylark. [Middle English *laverok,* Old English *lǣwerce,* LARK.]

lav·ish (lávvish) *adj.* **1.** Extravagant; prodigal. **2.** Characterised by or produced with extravagance and profusion. **3.** Showing unrestrained generosity: *a lavish present.* —See Synonyms at **ornate.**
~*tr.v.* **lavished, -ishing, -ishes.** To give or pour forth unstintingly: *the loving care they lavished on the work.* [Middle English *lavas,* from noun, "an outpouring", profusion, from Old French *lavasse,* torrent of rain, from *laver,* to wash, LAVE.] **—lav·ish·er** *n.* **—lav·ish·ly** *adv.* **—lav·ish·ness** *n.*

La·voi·sier (laa-vwaázi-ay, *French* -vwaz-yáy), **Antoine Laurent de** (1743–94). French chemist, and father of modern chemistry. He isolated the major constituents of air, disproved the phlogiston theory by explaining the role of oxygen in combustion, and organised the classification of compounds. He was guillotined during the Revolution for having held various government posts.

law (law) *n. Abbr.* **l., L. 1.** A rule established by authority, society, or custom. **2. a.** The body of rules governing the affairs of people within a community or among states; a legal system: *the law of nations.* **b.** The condition of social order or justice resulting from the existence of a legal system in a society. **c.** A declaration or position which is not to be questioned or disputed: *His word is law.* **3.** A set of rules or customs dealing with a specified area of a legal system: *the law of contracts; criminal law.* **4.** In Britain: **a.** The body of rules and principles originally followed by the common law courts, as opposed to those which were administered by the courts of equity. **b.** That part of the law which arises out of legislation; statute law as opposed to common law. **5. a.** The system of courts, judicial processes, and legal officers giving effect to the laws of a society: *resort to the law in defence of one's interests.* **b.** An impromptu system of justice, usually illegal, substituted for established juridical procedure: *gang law.* **6.** The science and study of law; jurisprudence. **7.** Knowledge of law: *His law is good.* **8.** The profession of a lawyer. **9.** *Capital* **L. a.** *Often plural.* A code of behaviour of divine origin: *Mosaic Law.* **b.** In the Old Testament, the Pentateuch and the precepts laid down in it. **10. a.** *Often plural.* Principles of conduct conceived to be of natural origin: *the laws of decency.* **b.** A way of life: *law of the jungle.* **11.** *Often plural.* A code of principles and regulations observed by a profession or association or by sportsmen: *the law of the turf.* **12. a.** *Often plural.* A formulation of the observed recurrence, order, relationship, or interaction of natural phenomena: *laws of motion.* **b.** A generalisation based on the observation of repeated events: *Parkinson's law.* **13.** *Mathematics.* A general principle or rule that is obeyed in all cases to which it is applicable. **14.** *Often plural.* The rules of an art; principles or elements: *the laws of harmony; the laws of grammar.* **15.** *Slang.* The police or a policeman. Preceded by *the.* **—be a law unto (oneself).** To disregard established laws and conventions; make one's own rules. **—go to law.** To take a complaint to court for settlement. **—lay down the law.** To speak in a firm, authoritarian way. **—take the law into (one's) own hands.** To redress a wrong or proceed by one's own methods rather than proper authority. [Middle English *law(e),* binding custom or practice, Old English *lagu,* code of rules.]

Law (law), **Andrew Bonar** (1858–1923). Canadian-born leader of the British Conservative Party. He succeeded Lloyd George as prime minister (1922).

law-a·bid·ing (láw-ə-bīding) *adj.* Abiding by the law.

law agent *n.* Formerly in Scotland, a solicitor.

law and order *n. Used with a singular or plural verb.* **1.** A state of peace in a law-abiding society. **2.** The use or advocacy of stringent measures to reduce crime and eliminate violence in a society.

law·break·er (láw-braykər) *n.* A person who breaks the law. **—law·break·ing** *n. & adj.*

law centre *n.* In Britain, an office, often financed by a local authority, that provides free legal advice and information to the public.

law·ful (láwf'l) *adj.* **1.** Within the law; allowed by law: *lawful methods.* **2.** Established or recognised by the law; legally acknowledged: *the lawful heir.* **3.** Legally sanctioned; legitimate: *a lawful marriage.* **—law·ful·ly** *adv.* **—law·ful·ness** *n.*

law·giv·er (láw-givvər) *n.* **1.** One who gives a code of laws to a people. **2.** A lawmaker; a legislator. **—law·giv·ing** *n. & adj.*

lawks (lawks) *interj. British.* Used to express astonishment, dismay, or the like. [Variant of *Lord!* (perhaps influenced by ALACK).]

law·less (láw-ləss, -liss) *adj.* **1. a.** Unrestrained by law; disobedient: *a lawless person.* **b.** Unbridled: *lawless passion.* **2.** Heedless of or contrary to the law: *a lawless act.* **3.** Not governed by law: *the lawless border.* **—law·less·ly** *adv.* **—law·less·ness** *n.*

Law Lord *n.* In Britain, a member of the House of Lords who sits in the highest court of appeal; a Lord of Appeal in Ordinary.

law·mak·er (láw-maykər) *n.* One who draughts or helps to enact laws; a legislator. **—law·mak·ing** *n. & adj.*

law merchant *n.* The rules and regulations applied to trade and commerce, drawn from the customs of merchants in the past; commercial law.

lawn[1] (lawn) *n.* A usually closely mown plot or area planted with grass or similar plants. [Variant of obsolete *laund,* from Middle English *launde, lawnde,* from Old French *launde,* heath, from Germanic.] **—lawn·y** *adj.*

lawn[2] *n.* A very fine fabric of cotton or linen. [Middle English, probably from *Laon,* France, linen-manufacturing town.] **—lawn·y** *adj.*

lawn mower *n.* A machine with a revolving blade or blades for cutting grass.

lawn tennis *n.* **1.** Tennis played on a grass court. **2.** *Formal.* Tennis.

law of averages *n.* The assertion that what happens at one extreme will be counteracted by what happens at the other, thus maintaining an average.

law officer *n.* In Britain, any of various officials who advise the Crown and Parliament on legal matters, and who are sometimes concerned with prosecutions on behalf of the Crown. For England, Wales, and Northern Ireland, they are the Attorney-General and the Solicitor-General, and in Scotland, the Lord Advocate and the Solicitor-General.

law of large numbers *n. Mathematics.* **Bernoulli's law** *(see).*

Law of Moses *n.* **Mosaic Law** *(see).*

law of nations *n.* **International law** *(see).*

Law·rence (lórrənss), **D(avid) H(erbert)** (1885–1930). British novelist, short-story writer, essayist, and poet. Among his novels are *Sons and Lovers* (1913), *The Rainbow* (1915), and *Women in Love* (1920). The sex scenes in his work aroused controversy: publication of *Lady Chatterley's Lover* (1928) was not allowed in Britain until 1961. **—Law·ren·ti·an** (law-rénsh'n) *adj.*

Lawrence, Ernest Orlando (1901–58). U.S. physicist. He designed the cyclotron, a particle accelerator, and was awarded the Nobel prize in physics (1939).

Lawrence, Gertrude (1898–1952). British actress. She formed a memorable partnership with her childhood friend, Noël Coward, notably in his play *Private Lives* (1931). She later appeared in films such as *The King and I* (1951).

Lawrence, Sir Thomas (1769–1830). British portrait painter, artist to George III (1792), and President of the Royal Academy (1820).

Lawrence, T(homas) E(dward), also known as T.E. Shaw, J.H. Ross, Lawrence of Arabia (1888–1935). British soldier and writer. He was sent in 1916 to organise Arab insurgency in the Turkish empire, and led a legendary guerrilla action. He wrote a philosophical record of the desert campaign, *The Seven Pillars of Wisdom* (1926). He was killed in a motor-cycling accident.

law·ren·ci·um (lo-rén-si-əm, law-) *n. Symbol* **Lr** A synthetic transuranic element. The most stable isotope has a mass number 257 and a half-life of 35 seconds. Also called "unniltrium". [After Ernest O. LAWRENCE.]

Law Society *n.* An organisation representing, conducting examinations for, and regulating the admission of solicitors in various countries, such as England, Scotland, and Australia.

law stationer *n.* **1.** A person who sells stationery required by lawyers. **2.** A person who engrosses legal documents.

law·suit (láw-sōōt, -sewt) *n.* A case brought before a court, usually a civil case.

law term *n.* **1.** A word or expression used in legal contexts. **2.** A period of time appointed for the sitting of a lawcourt or lawcourts.

law·yer (láw-yər, lóy-ər) *n.* **1.** One whose profession is to give legal advice and assistance to clients and represent them in court. **2.** *British.* Loosely, a solicitor. **3.** A student or teacher of law. **4.** *Regional.* A burbot. [Middle English *lawyere,* from *lawe,* LAW.]

Usage: *lawyer, solicitor, barrister, advocate, counsel, attorney, counsellor.* These nouns denote members of the legal profession. *Lawyer* is the general and most comprehensive term for one authorised to manage the legal affairs of a client, give legal advice, and represent clients in court. *Solicitor,* especially in Britain and some other Commonwealth countries, refers to a lawyer who gives legal advice, acts as a legal agent, represents clients in lower courts, and prepares cases for trial in higher courts. *Barrister,* in England and some other Commonwealth countries, refers to a lawyer who represents and argues cases for clients in higher courts. *Advocate* refers generally to a person who pleads a case on behalf of another. In Scotland and South Africa, it is the usual term for a *barrister. Counsel* refers to a barrister or group of barristers engaged in pleading a case in court: *counsel for the prosecution. Attorney* refers generally to a person, usually a lawyer, who is appointed or empowered to act for another. In the United States, *attorney* is the usual term for a *lawyer* and in South Africa, for a *solicitor. Counsellor,* in the United States, is used as another term for an *attorney,* especially one who represents clients in court.

lax (laks) *adj.* **1. a.** Showing little concern; remiss; negligent: *lax about paying bills.* **b.** Not strict; unenforced. **2.** Not taut, firm, or compact; slack. **3.** Loose and not easily retained or controlled. Said of bowel movements. **4.** *Phonetics.* Pronounced with the muscles of the tongue and jaw partially relaxed; wide. Said of certain vowel sounds, such as *e* in *let* or *i* in *hid.* Compare **tense.** —See Synonyms at **careless.** [Middle English, from Latin *laxus,* slack, loose.] **—lax·a·tion** (-sáysh'n) *n.* **—lax·ly** *adv.* **—lax·i·ty, lax·ness** *n.*

lax·a·tive (láksətiv) *n. Medicine.* A drug that stimulates evacuation of the bowels. Also called "cathartic", "purgative".
~*adj.* **1.** Stimulating evacuation of the bowels. **2.** Unrestrained. [Middle English *laxatif,* from adjective, "producing looseness", from Old French, from Latin *laxātīvus,* from *laxāre,* to relax, from *laxus,* loose, LAX.]

Lax·ness (laáks-ness), **Halldór (Kiljan)** (1902–). Icelandic novelist, writing in the epic tradition of his country. He was awarded the Nobel prize (1955).

lay[1] (lay) *v.* **laid** (layd), **laying, lays.** *—tr.* **1.** To cause to lie; put in a recumbent position: *lay a child in its cot.* **2.** To place or rest in a particular state or position: *lay the books on the table.* **3.** To put or set down, especially for a particular purpose or as a basis: *lay a trail; lay foundations.* **4.** To produce and deposit: *lay eggs.* **5. a.** To cause to settle or subside: *The fog laid the wind.* **b.** To scotch (a rumour, for example). **c.** To exorcise (a ghost). **6.** To put or apply: *lay an ear to the door.* **7.** To assign or attribute: *laid the blame on him.* **8.** To put in a setting; locate: *laid the story in Italy.* **9.** To bury; sink in the ground: *lay a cable.* **10.** To place in the proper position or spot: *lay a carpet; lay bricks.* **11. a.** To arrange in a required order for use; make ready: *lay a trap; lay a fire.* **b.** To arrange knives, forks, mats, and the like on (a table) ready for eating. **12.** To devise; make: *lay plans.* **13.** To apply in a thick layer or coat: *lay paint on a canvas.* **14.** To place or give (importance): *lay stress on clarity.* **15.** To impose as a burden or punishment. Usually used with *upon: lay a penalty upon him.* **16.** To put forth for examination; present; submit. Often used with *before: lay a case before a committee.* **17.** To place (a bet); stake; wager: *lay ten pounds on a horse.* **18.** To bring or deliver forcefully: *laid a blow on his jaw.* **19.** *Archaic.* To take possession of; annex. **20.** *Military.* To aim (a gun or cannon). **21. a.** To place together (strands) to be twisted into rope. **b.** To make in this manner. Used with *up: lay up cable.* **22.** To inlay: *The floor was laid in semiprecious stones.* **23.** To bring (a ship) to a specified position: *lay the vessel alongside the wharf.* **24.** In hunting, to put (hounds) on a scent. **25.** *Vulgar Slang.* To have sexual intercourse with. Used especially of men. *—intr.* **1.** To produce and deposit eggs. **2. a.** *Nonstandard.* To lie; recline. **b.** *Nautical.* To lie in a specified position: *The ship laid aft.* **—lay about (one).** To hit out in all directions; fight vigorously. **—lay aloft.** *Nautical.* To go up into the rigging of a ship. **—lay aside. 1.** To put off to one side; abandon: *lay aside all hope.* **2.** To put aside for the future; save. **3.** To disregard for the moment. **—lay away. 1.** To reserve for the future; save. **2.** To hold (merchandise) for future delivery. **—lay bare.** To expose to view; reveal. **—lay down. 1.** To store (wine or provisions), especially in a cellar. **2.** To place (a bet); wager. **3.** To relinquish or sacrifice (one's hopes or life, for example). **4.** To begin the construction of (a ship, railway, or the like). **5.** To make or formulate (a rule, principle, or the like). **6.** To convert (land) into pasture: *lay down a field with grass.* **7.** To put down (a chart, diagram, or the like) on paper. **—lay hold of.** To seize; grasp. **—lay in.** To obtain and store (provisions or supplies). **—lay into.** *Informal.* To attack, either physically or verbally. **—lay it on.** *Informal.* **1.** To be effusive with praise, flattery, excuses, or the like. **2.** To inflict blows on; strike. **—lay on. 1.** To provide (refreshments or entertainment, for example). **2.** To install the necessary pipes and fittings for supplying (gas, electricity, or water). **—lay (oneself) open.** To make oneself vulnerable; expose oneself, as to criticism, blame, or the like. **—lay open. 1.** To cut open. **2.** To expose; reveal. **—lay to. 1.** To apply oneself vigorously. **2.** *Nautical.* **a.** To bring (a sailing ship) to a stop in open water, steadying her with a jib or other small sail. **b.** To remain stationary, facing into the wind. **—lay to rest.** To bury. **—lay up. 1.** To store for future needs. **2.** *Informal.* To confine to bed through illness. Used in the passive. **—lay waste.** To ravage (land, for example).
~*n.* **1.** A share of the profits of a whaling or fishing expedition allotted in place of wages. **2. a.** The direction the strands of a rope or cable are twisted in: *a left lay.* **b.** The amount of such twist. **3.** The position, way, or direction in which something, such as land, lies. **4.** *Chiefly British Slang.* A line of activity, especially one of a questionable nature. **5.** *Vulgar Slang.* **a.** An act of sexual intercourse. **b.** A partner in sexual intercourse. **—in lay.** In a period of ovulation. Said of laying hens. [Lay, laid, laid; Middle English *leggen, leide, leid,* Old English *lecgan, lēde, gelēd.*]

Usage: The overlap in the forms of the verbs *lay* and *lie* often leads to uncertain usage. *Lay* has the senses "put, place, prepare", a past tense *laid,* and a past participle *laid. Lie* has the senses "recline, be situated", a past tense *lay,* and a past participle *lain.* The crucial difference in grammar is that *lay* takes a direct object, whereas *lie* does not. Thus one says: *I laid the table* (not *lay*); *The hen has laid an egg* (not *lain*); *I lay down to sleep* (not *laid*). The forms in brackets are sometimes heard in informal speech, and are common in some regional dialects, but only occasionally does the confusion surface in the written language (usually in idiomatic constructions, such as *to lie/lay low; the lie/lay of the land*).

lay[2] *adj.* **1.** Pertaining to, coming from, or serving the laity; secular: *a lay preacher.* **2.** Nonprofessional; not formally qualified or trained. **3.** Of or typical of the average or common man: *a lay opinion.* [Middle English *laie,* from Old French *lai,* from Late Latin *lāicus,* from Greek *laikos,* from *laos*†, the people.]

PRONUNCIATION KEY

a, trap; aa, father; ai, **fair**;
ar, **star**; aw, **lawn**; ay, **play**;
b, bb, **stab**; **rubber**;
ch, **church**; ck, **ticket**;
d, dd, **dead**; **ladder**; e, **dress**;
ee, **bee**; er, **defer**; ew, **few**;
ewr, **pure**; ə, **about**;
ər, **letter**; f, ff, **fife**; **differ**;
g, gg, **giggle**; h, **hat**; i, **kit**;
ī, **price**; īr, **fire**; j, **judge**;
k, **kick**; l, ll, **let**; 'l, **needle**;
m, mm, **man**; n, nn, **no**;
'n, **sudden**; ng, **thing**; o, **lot**;
ō, **no**; ŏŏ, **foot**; ōō, **shoe**;
oor, **poor**; ow, **cow**;
owr, **hour**; oy, **boy**;
p, pp, **pepper**; r, rr, **red**;
s, ss, **sauce**; sh, **ship**;
t, tt, **totter**; th, **thick**; th, **this**;
smooth; u, **cut**; ur, **turn**;
v, vv, **valve**; w, **wet**; y, **yes**;
z, zz, **zebra**; zh, **vision**;
pleasure

IN FOREIGN WORDS:

aN, oN, **Saint-Saëns**;
hl, **Llanelli**; **Hluhluwe**;
kh, **loch**; **lough**; **Khaled**

STRESS MARK:

ín-sīt, insight; in-sī́t, incite

lay³ n. A ballad. [Middle English, from Old French *lai*, akin to Provençal *lais*†.]

lay⁴. Past tense of **lie** (recline).

lay·a·bout (láy-ə-bowt) n. *British Informal.* One who avoids work; an idler.

lay brother n. A man who has taken religious vows but who is not ordained and is usually employed in manual duties.

lay by tr.v. **1.** To keep on hand for future needs; save. **2.** To lay (a sailing vessel) to. —*intr.v.* To lay to. Used of a sailing vessel.

lay-by (láy-bī) n., pl. **-bys. 1.** *Chiefly British.* An area beside a main road where vehicles can stop without obstructing other traffic. **2.** A similar area on a canal or beside a railway for boats or railway coaches. **3.** *Australian & N.Z.* A method of reserving an article in a shop by paying a deposit: *put a dress on lay-by.*

lay clerk n. A lay male member of a cathedral or church choir.

lay-day (láy-day) n. *Finance.* A day in port allowed to the lessee of a ship without charge; a free day. [From LAY (verb).]

lay·er (láy-ər) n. **1. a.** A single thickness, coating, or stratum spread out or covering a surface. **b.** A superimposed level: *layers of meaning.* **2.** One that lays; specifically, a hen. **3.** In horticulture, a stem covered with soil for rooting while still part of a living plant. —v. **layered, -ering, -ers.** —*tr.* **1.** To cut (hair) into layers. **2.** In horticulture, to propagate (a plant) by layering. —*intr.* **1.** To separate or split into layers. **2.** In horticulture, to take root as a result of layering. [Middle English *leyer*, from *leyen, leggen*, to LAY.]

layer cake n. A usually iced cake of two or more layers separated by a filling, such as jam or cream.

lay·ered (láy-ərd) adj. **1.** Having or arranged in layers. **2.** Consisting of one garment or layer of fabric worn over another: *the layered look; a layered skirt.*

lay·er·ing (láy-ər-ing) n. Also **lay·er·age** (-ij). The process of rooting branches, twigs, or stems that are still attached to a parent plant, as by placing a specially treated part in moist soil.

lay·ette (lay-ét) n. Clothing and other accessories for a newborn baby. [French, from Old French, diminutive of *laie*, box, from Middle Dutch *laege*†.]

lay figure n. **1.** A jointed model of the human body used by artists, especially to demonstrate the arrangement of drapery. Also called "mannequin". **2.** A subservient person.

lay·man (láy-mən) n., pl. **-men** (-mən). **1.** A member of a congregation as distinguished from the clergy. **2.** One who does not have special or advanced training or skill.

lay off tr.v. **1.** To suspend (workers) from employment, especially during a slack period. **2.** To mark off; chart the boundaries of. **3.** *Informal.* **a.** To desist from (an activity): *lay off shouting.* **b.** To leave (a person or thing) alone. —*intr.v. Informal.* To desist.

lay-off (láy-off, -awf) n. **1.** The suspension or dismissal of employees. **2.** The interval for which employment has been suspended.

lay out tr.v. **1.** To put or spread out in readiness, as for wear, packing, display, or inspection. **2. a.** To arrange according to plan: *laid out the grounds of the castle.* **b.** To set out (an argument, for example). **3.** *Informal.* To spend or invest (money), especially on a large scale. **4.** To clothe and prepare (a corpse) for burial. **5.** *Informal.* To knock down; especially, to knock unconscious. **6.** *Informal.* to put (oneself) to a lot of trouble.

lay·out (láy-out) n. **1.** The laying out of something. **2.** The arrangement, plan, or structuring of something laid out; the overall picture or form: *the layout of a factory.* **3. a.** The arrangement and juxtaposition of printed matter, photographs, or the like, as for a newspaper or magazine page. **b.** A dummy, sketch, or paste-up for matter to be printed. **4.** A diagram showing how something, such as a machine, is constructed.

lay reader n. A layman in the Anglican and Episcopal churches authorised by a bishop to preach and conduct certain services. Also called "reader".

lay-shaft (láy-shaaft ‖ -shaft) n. A secondary shaft to which motion is transmitted from the main shaft in a gear box.

lay sister n. A female lay brother.

lay·wo·man (láy-wŏŏmən) n., pl. **-women** (-wimmin). A female layman.

la·zar (lázzər ‖ láyzər) n. *Archaic.* A beggar afflicted with some loathsome disease, especially leprosy; a leper. [Middle English, from Medieval Latin *Lazarus*, LAZARUS.]

laz·a·ret·to (lázzə-réttō) n., pl. **-tos.** Also **laz·a·ret, laz·a·rette** (-rét). **1.** Formerly, a hospital treating contagious diseases. Also called "lazar house", "pest house". **2.** A building or ship used as a quarantine station. **3.** A storage space between the decks of a ship. [Italian *lazaretto*, from *lazzaro*, leper, beggar, from Medieval Latin *Lazarus*, LAZARUS.]

Laz·a·rus (lázzərəss). **1.** The brother of Mary and Martha whom Jesus raised from the dead. John 11:1–44. **2.** The diseased beggar in the parable of the rich man and the beggar. Luke 16:19–31.

laze (layz) v. **lazed, lazing, lazes.** —*intr.* To be lazy; loaf. —*tr.* To spend (time) in loafing. Often used with *away.* —n. Time spent in idleness. [Back-formation from LAZY.]

La·zio (látsi-ō, láats-yō). Region of west central Italy, bordering on the Tyrrhenian Sea, embracing ranges of the central Apennines in the east and the lowlands of the Campagna di Roma and Pontine marshes in the west. In ancient times the region was called Latium. The largest city and capital is Rome.

lazuli n. Lapis lazuli (see).

laz·u·lite (lázzew-līt) n. A relatively rare, deep sky-blue or azure mineral, essentially $Mg,Al_2(PO_4)_2(OH)_2$, in which iron usually replaces some of the magnesium. [Medieval Latin *lazulum*, LAPIS LAZULI + -ITE.]

laz·u·rite (lázzewr-īt) n. A relatively rare, azure, violet-blue, or Prussian blue mineral, $3(NaAlSiO_4)\cdot Na_2S$. Also called "lapis lazuli". [German *Lasurit*, from Medieval Latin *lazur*, from Arabic *lāzaward*, LAPIS LAZULI.]

la·zy (láyzi) adj. **-zier, -ziest. 1.** Resistant to work or exertion; given to idleness; slothful. **2.** Slow-moving; sluggish: *a lazy river.* **3.** Conducive to languor or indolence: *a lazy day.* [Perhaps from Low German and akin to *lasich*, idle.] —**la·zi·ly** adv. —**la·zi·ness** n.

la·zy·bones (láyzi-bōnz) n., pl. **-bones.** *Informal.* A lazy person.

lazy tongs pl.n. Tongs having a jointed extensible framework operated by scissor-like handles for grasping an object at a distance.

lb pound [Latin *libra*].

l.b. leg bye (in cricket).

l.b.w. leg before wicket (in cricket).

l.c. 1. letter of credit. **2.** In the place cited [Latin *loco citato*]. **3.** *Printing.* lower-case.

L.C.C. London County Council (formerly in Britain).

L/C letter of credit.

LCD n. A *liquid-crystal display:* a digital display, as in electronic calculators, containing liquid crystal between sheets of glass, the display becoming readable when a voltage is applied.

l.c.d., L.C.D. lowest common denominator.

L.C.J. Lord Chief Justice (in England and Wales).

l.c.m., L.C.M. lowest common multiple.

L/Cpl. lance-corporal.

ld. 1. *Printing.* lead. **2.** load.

Ld. Lord (title).

LD lethal dose. LD_{50} is an index of toxicity indicating the amount of poison that causes the death of 50 per cent of a batch of experimental organisms.

L-D converter n. *Metallurgy.* A converter for producing steel by blowing oxygen through a water-cooled pipe into molten pig iron, thus burning off some of the carbon. [From *Linz-Donawitz*, after two towns in Austria where the method was first used.]

L-do·pa (él-dōpə) n. An amino acid, $C_9H_{11}NO_4$, that occurs naturally in the body and is used to treat Parkinson's disease. Also called "levodopa". [From *L-dihydroxyphenylalanine*.]

L-driver (él-drīvər) n. *British.* A **learner-driver** (see).

lea¹ (lee ‖ U.S. *also* lay) n. Also **ley** (lay ‖ lee). *Poetic.* **1.** Grassland; meadow. **2.** Land sown temporarily with grass. [Middle English *ley(e)*, Old English *lēah, lēa.*]

lea² (lee) n. A measure of yarn that is 300, 200, 120, or 80 yards (275, 183, 110, or 73 metres) depending on the type. [Middle English *lee*, perhaps from French *lier*, from Latin *ligāre*, to bind.]

lea. 1. league (unit of distance). **2.** leather.

L.E.A. local education authority (in Britain).

leach (leech) v. **leached, leaching, leaches.** —*tr.* **1.** To remove soluble constituents from (a substance) by the action of a percolating liquid. **2.** To remove (soluble constituents) from a substance in this way. —*intr.* **1.** To be dissolved and washed out by a percolating liquid. **2.** To lose or yield soluble matter to a percolating liquid. —n. **1.** The process of leaching. **2.** A porous, perforated, or sieve-like vessel that holds material to be leached. **3.** The substance through which a liquid is leached. **4.** The solution thus leached. [Variant of obsolete *letch*, to wet, probably ultimately from Old English *leccan*, to moisten.] —**leach·er** n.

Leach (leech), **Bernard (Howell)** (1887–1979). British potter. He set up a pottery at St. Ives, Cornwall (1920), and described his innovative ideas in *A Potter's Book* (1940).

leach·ing (léeching) n. *Geology.* Separation and removal of soluble components from soil by percolating water. Also called "chemical weathering".

Lea·cock (léekok), **Stephen (Butler)** (1869–1944). British-born Canadian humorist. He was a professor of economics at McGill University, Montreal, while writing humorous essays and books.

lead¹ (léed) v. **led** (led), **leading, leads.** —*tr.* **1. a.** To show the way to by going in advance; conduct, escort, or direct. **b.** To show (the way) by going in advance or by setting an example. **2.** To guide physically, as by taking by the hand or by holding by a rope: *lead a horse.* **3.** To serve as a route for; conduct on a particular course: *The path led him to a cemetery.* **4. a.** To cause to follow some course of action or line of thought; induce: *led him to believe otherwise.* **b.** To influence the answer of (a witness) by phrasing a question in a certain way. **5. a.** To direct the performance or activities of: *lead a battalion.* **b.** To inspire the conduct of: *led the nation.* **6.** To assume leadership in; steer; guide: *lead a discussion.* **7.** To be at the head of: *His name led the list.* **8.** To have an advance over: *led the field in aerodynamics.* **9.** To pursue; live: *leading a hectic life.* **10.** In card games, to begin a round of play by putting down (a card): *lead an ace.* **11.** To aim in front of (a moving target). **12.** *Chiefly British.* To be the principal first violinist in (an orchestra). **13.** To guide (a partner) when dancing. **14.** To be a channel for (water, electricity, or the like). —*intr.* **1.** To be first; be ahead: *leading by a length.* **2.** To go first as a guide. **3.** To act as commander, director, or conductor. **4.** To guide a partner in dance steps. **5.** To be guided: *The horse leads easily.* **6.** To afford a passage, course, or route: *a door leading into the kitchen.* **7.** To tend towards a certain goal or result. Used with *to: led to complications.* **8.** To make the initial play, as in a card game. **9.** *British.* To be the principal first violinist in an orchestra. **10.** In boxing, to deliver attacking punches with a specified fist: *leading with his left.* **11.** To begin a presentation in a given way: *led with the election news.* **12.** In dancing, to start off on a specified foot: *leading with your right foot.* **13.** *Music.* To have a lead in a piece of music. **—lead astray.** To lead into error or wrongdoing. **—lead on.** To draw along; lure; entice, especially by deception. **—lead up to. 1.** To result in by a series of steps. **2.** To proceed towards (one's true purpose or subject) with preliminary remarks.

~*n.* **1.** The first place; the foremost position. **2.** The margin by which one is ahead: *he was losing his lead.* **3. a.** A piece of information of possible use in a search: *several good leads for a job.* **b.** A clue; a hint. **4.** Command; leadership: *take the lead.* **5.** An example; a precedent. **6. a.** The principal role in a dramatic production. **b.** The person playing such a part. **7.** In journalism: **a.** The opening line or paragraph of a news story. **b.** A prominently displayed news story. **8.** In card games: **a.** The first play. **b.** The prerogative of making or turn to make the first play. **c.** The card played. **9.** In boxing: **a.** The arm with which a boxer usually leads. **b.** A punch using this arm. **10.** A leash, rope, or strap for leading an animal. **11.** *Nautical.* The direction in which a rope runs. **12.** *Mining.* **a.** A deposit of gold ore in an old riverbed. **b.** A lode. **13.** A wire or cable for making an electrical connection. **14.** The act of aiming ahead of and firing at a moving target. **15.** *Music.* A major part at the beginning of a piece of music for an instrument or voice. **16.** A stream or other channel leading up to a mill. [Middle English *leden,* Old English *lǣdan, lǣdde, lǣded.*]

lead[2] (led) *n.* **1.** *Symbol* **Pb** A soft, malleable, ductile, bluish-white, dense metallic element, extracted chiefly from galena and used in containers and pipes for corrosives, in solder and type metal, bullets, radiation shielding, paints, and antiknock compounds. Atomic number 82, atomic weight 207.19, melting point 327.5°C, boiling point 1,744°C, relative density 11.35, valencies 2, 4. **2.** A lump of lead suspended by a line, used to make soundings to determine the depth of water. **3.** *Plural. British.* **a.** A flat or slightly pitched roof covered with sheets of lead. **b.** The sheets of lead used for such a roof. **4.** Bullets from or for firearms; shot. **5.** *Plural.* Strips of lead used in fitting windows with small panes or stained glass pieces. **6.** *Printing. Abbr.* **ld.** A thin strip of type metal used to separate lines of type. **7. a.** Any of various, often graphitic, compositions used as the writing substance in pencils. **b.** A thin stick of such material. **—swing the lead.** To shirk one's duties, especially by malingering.

~*adj.* Containing or made of lead.

~*v.* **leaded, leading, leads.** *—tr.* **1.** To cover, line, weight, fill, or treat with lead. **2.** *Printing.* To provide space between (lines of type) with leads. **3.** To secure (window glass) with leads. *—intr.* To become filled, covered, or clogged with lead. [Middle English *lead, lœd,* Old English *lēad,* from West Germanic *lauda* (unattested), akin to Gaelic *luaidh*†.]

lead acetate (led) *n.* A poisonous white crystalline compound, $Pb(C_2H_3O_2)_2{\cdot}3H_2O$, used in dyes, waterproofing compounds, and varnishes. Also called "sugar of lead".

lead arsenate (led) *n.* A poisonous white crystalline compound, $Pb_3(AsO_4)_2$, used in insecticides and herbicides.

Lead·bel·ly (lĕd-belli), born Huddie Ledbetter (1888–1949). Black U.S. songwriter and blues singer. Among his compositions is *Goodnight Irene.*

lead carbonate (led) *n.* A poisonous white amorphous powder, $PbCO_3$, used as a paint pigment.

lead chromate (led) *n.* A poisonous yellow crystalline compound, $PbCrO_4$, used as a paint pigment.

lead·en (lĕdd'n) *adj.* **1.** Made of or containing lead. **2.** Heavy and inert like lead. **3.** Dull and listless; sluggish. **4.** Burdened; weighted down; depressed: *a leaden heart.* **5.** Dull, dark grey: *a leaden sky.* **—lead·en·ly** *adv.* **—lead·en·ness** *n.*

lead·er (lēedər) *n.* **1.** A person who leads others along a way; a guide. **2.** One in charge or in command of others. **3.** The head of a political party or organisation. **4.** *British. Capital* **L. a.** A member of the House of Commons who is responsible for organising the programme of parliamentary business. Also called "Leader of the House of Commons". **b.** A peer who has a similar function in the House of Lords. Also called "Leader of the House of Lords". In both senses, also called "Leader of the House". **5. a.** The principal performer in an orchestra, quartet, choir, or the like; especially, a principal first violinist who represents the orchestra to the conductor and often plays solos. **b.** *U.S.* The conductor of an orchestra, band, or choral group. **6.** The foremost horse, dog, or other animal in a harnessed team. **7.** *British.* The senior counsel, usually a Queen's Counsel, who conducts a case in court. **8.** *Chiefly British.* The main editorial article in a newspaper or periodical. Also called "leading article". **9.** *Plural. Printing.* Dots or dashes in a row leading the eye across a page, as in an index entry. **10.** A pipe for conveying rainwater from the roof to the ground. **11.** A short length of gut, wire, or the like by which the hook is attached to a fishing line. **12.** *Botany.* The growing apex or main shoot of a shrub or tree. **13.** A tab on the end of a film or tape, used to thread it.

lead·er·ship (lēedərship) *n.* **1.** The position, office, or term of a leader. **2.** A group of leaders. **3.** The capacity to be a leader; ability to lead.

lead glance (led) *n.* A mineral, **galena** *(see).*

lead glass (led) *n.* **Flint glass** *(see).*

lead-in (lēed-in) *n.* **1.** An introduction, as to a subject or programme. **2.** The part of an antenna or aerial that leads to an electronic transmitter or receiver.

lead·ing[1] (lēeding) *adj.* **1.** Major; principal: *a leading factor.* **2.** At the head; in the lead; foremost: *the leading candidate.* **3.** Playing a lead or principal role in a theatrical production: *a leading lady.* **4.** Phrased to elicit a desired response: *a leading question.* —See Synonyms at **chief.** **—lead·ing·ly** *adv.*

lead·ing[2] (lĕdding) *n.* **1.** A border or rim of lead, as around a windowpane. **2.** *Printing.* The spacing between lines.

leading aircraftman (lēeding) *n., pl.* **-men.** *Abbr.* **L.A.C..** A serviceman in the Royal Air Force ranking between a senior aircraftman and an aircraftman.

leading aircraftwoman (lēeding) *n., pl.* **-women.** *Abbr.* **L.A.C.W.** A member of the British Women's Royal Air Force holding a rank equivalent to that of a leading aircraftman.

leading edge (lēeding) *n.* **1.** The edge of a sail that faces the wind. **2.** The front edge of an aircraft propeller blade or wing.

leading light (lēeding) *n. Informal.* A person of great importance or value, especially to a group or undertaking.

leading note (lēeding) *n. Music.* The seventh note, or degree, of a scale, a half tone below the tonic; a subtonic.

leading-rein (lēeding-rayn) *n.* A rope or rein attached to a horse's bridle or halter by which to lead it.

leading reins (lēeding) *pl.n.* A harness with straps attached used to support a baby learning to walk. Also called "leading strings".

leading seaman (lēeding) *n., pl.* **-men.** A serviceman in the Royal Navy ranking between a petty officer and an able seaman.

leading strings (lēeding) *pl.n.* **1.** Excessive control or guidance. Used especially in the phrase *keep someone in leading strings.* **2.** Leading reins.

lead lights (led) *pl.n.* Also **lead·ed lights** (lĕddid). Windows made up of small pieces of glass held together by lead strips.

lead line (led) *n. Nautical.* A sounding line with a lump of lead on it used to determine the depth of water.

lead monoxide (led) *n. Chemistry.* **Litharge** *(see).*

lead off (leed) *intr.v.* To make the initial play or move; start.

lead-off (lēed-off, -awf) *n.* **1.** An opening play or move; a start; a beginning. **2.** A person or thing that starts something.

lead pencil (led) *n.* A pencil that contains a thin stick of graphite as its marking substance.

lead poisoning (led) *n.* Acute or chronic poisoning by lead or any of its salts, the acute form causing severe gastroenteritis, and the chronic form anaemia, abdominal pain, constipation, partial paralysis, and convulsions. Also called "plumbism", "saturnism".

lead screw (leed) *n.* A threaded screw along the bed of a lathe, used to drive the tool carriage along at a controlled rate, as in cutting threads.

leads·man (lĕdz-mən) *n., pl.* **-men** (-mən). *Nautical.* The man who uses the lead line in taking soundings.

lead tetraethyl (led) *n.* **Tetraethyl lead** *(see).*

lead time (lēed) *n.* The time needed or available between the decision to start a project and the completion of the work.

lead·wort (lĕd-wurt) *n.* **1.** Any of various plants of the genera *Plumbago* or *Ceratostigma,* having clusters of variously coloured flowers. **2.** Any of several similar plants. Also called "plumbago". [Some species were thought to cure lead poisoning.]

leaf (leef) *n., pl.* **leaves** (leevz). *Abbr.* **l., L. 1.** A usually green, flattened structure of vascular plants, characteristically consisting of a bladelike expansion attached to a stem, and functioning as a principal organ of photosynthesis and transpiration. **2.** A leaflike organ or structure. **3.** Leaves collectively; foliage. **4.** The leaves of a plant used or processed for a specific purpose: *tobacco leaf.* **5.** Any of the sheets of paper bound in a book, each side of which constitutes a page. **6.** Metal in the form of a very thin sheet: *gold leaf.* **7.** A hinged or removable section for a table top. **8.** A hinged or otherwise movable section of a folding door, shutter, or gate. **9.** Any of the metal strips forming a leaf spring. **—in leaf.** Having sprouted or produced leaves; green with foliage. **—turn over a new leaf.** To make a significant change in one's life by mending one's ways.

~*intr.v.* **leafed, leafing, leafs. 1.** To produce leaves; put forth foliage. **2.** To turn pages rapidly; glance: *leafed through the catalogue.* [Middle English *le(e)f,* Old English *lēaf.*]

leaf·age (lēefij) *n.* Leaves; foliage.

leaf beet *n.* A vegetable, **chard** *(see).*

leaf-cutter ant (lēef-kuttər) *n.* Any of various ants of the genus *Atta,* native to South America, that cut away leaf pieces to use them as fertiliser for their fungus gardens.

leaf-cutter bee *n.* Any of various carpenter bees of the genus *Megachile* that use pieces of leaf to construct the walls of their egg cells. *M. centuncularis* is a pest of garden roses.

leaf fat *n.* A dense fat that collects around the kidneys of certain animals, notably pigs.

leaf·hop·per (lēef-hoppər) *n.* Any of numerous insects of the family Cicadellidae, that suck juices from plants.

leaf insect *n.* Any of various chiefly Asiatic insects of the genus *Phyllium* and related genera, that resemble leaves.

leaf-lard (lēef-laard) *n.* High-grade lard made from the leaf fat of a pig.

leaf·less (lēef-ləss, -liss) *adj.* Having or putting forth no leaves.

leaf·let (lēef-lət, -lit) *n.* **1.** Any of the segments of a compound leaf. **2.** A small leaf or leaflike part. **3.** A printed, usually folded sheet of paper for distribution, such as an advertising circular.

~*v.* **leafleted** or **leafletted, -leting** or **-letting, -lets.** *—intr.* To distribute leaflets. *—tr.* **1.** To distribute leaflets in (an area). **2.** To distribute leaflets to (people).

leadwort Plumbago capensis, *one of 12 species in the leadwort genus.*

leaf insect *Related to stick insects, leaf insects live in the forests of tropical Asia and New Guinea, camouflaged from predators by their resemblance to leaves. The insect's eggs are protected by camouflage, too; they resemble plant seeds.*

leaf shape

DIFFERENT SHAPES BUT IDENTICAL FUNCTION
How leaves have adapted to their native habitats

Although leaves differ widely in appearance, the main function they perform is the same – to provide food for the plant. A leaf does this by photosynthesis, the process in which it uses light and its own green colouring, chlorophyll, to make food from the carbon dioxide and water the plant has absorbed.

The shape of its leaves is the result of a plant's evolution in its native habitat – its individual adaptation to carry out photosynthesis with maximum efficiency. A plant may have many small leaves or fewer large ones and they are arranged in a mosaic that secures the greatest possible exposure of leaf surface to light and air. Plants that grow in shade usually have a large leaf area to obtain whatever light is available.

A leaf's second function is to control the plant's loss of water through stomata, or pores, on its underside. In many plants leaves alter their shape by curling at the edges when the weather is dry to reduce the exposed area of the underside and so cut down water loss. Some plants have made the alteration of shape permanent – heathers, thyme, coniferous trees, and other plants have adapted to the exposed conditions of their native habitats by evolving small, narrow leaves to reduce water loss. Succulent plants such as houseleeks have evolved thick leaves to store water, and cacti have reduced their leaves to stems.

SIMPLE LEAVES

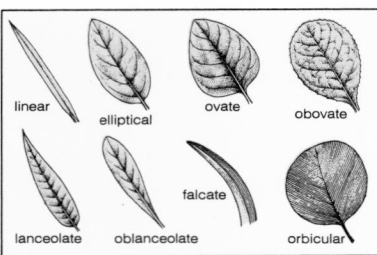

linear, elliptical, ovate, obovate, falcate, lanceolate, oblanceolate, orbicular

LEAF BASE

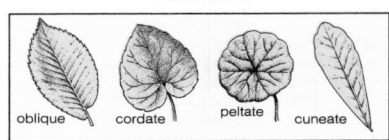

oblique, cordate, peltate, cuneate

LEAF APEX

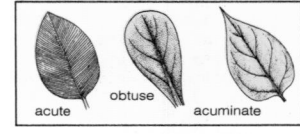

acute, obtuse, acuminate

COMPOUND LEAVES

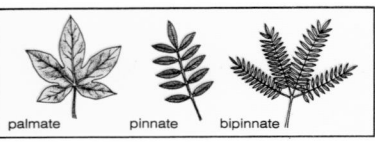

palmate, pinnate, bipinnate

LEAF MARGIN

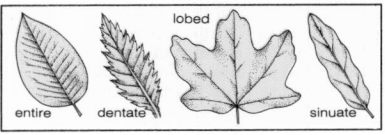

lobed, entire, dentate, sinuate

VENATION

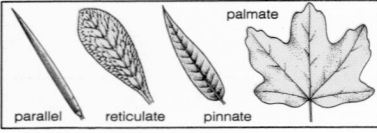

palmate, parallel, reticulate, pinnate

IDENTIFICATION *Leaves are either simple (with a single blade) or compound (with separate leaflets), but their actual shape, design of veins (venation), and position on the stem vary greatly. Terms devised by botanists describe these variations and help to identify the plant.*

leaf miner *n.* Any of numerous small flies and moths that in the larval state dig into and feed on leaf tissue.

leaf monkey *n.* The **langur** (*see*).

leaf mould *n.* Humus or compost consisting of decomposed leaves and other organic material.

leaf spot *n.* Any of various plant diseases resulting in well-defined darkened areas on the leaves.

leaf spring *n.* A composite spring, used especially in vehicle suspensions, consisting of several layers of flexible metallic strips joined to act as a single unit.

leaf·stalk (leef-stawk) *n.* The stalk by which a leaf is attached to a stem; a petiole.

leaf·worm (leef-wurm) *n.* See **cotton leafworm**.

leaf·y (leefi) *adj.* **-ier, -iest. 1.** Having or covered with leaves. **2.** Consisting of leaves. **3.** Leaflike. —**leaf·i·ness** *n.*

league¹ (leeg) *n. Abbr.* **l., L. 1.** An association of states, organisations, or individuals formed to promote common interests; an alliance. **2.** An association of sports teams or clubs that play one another. **3.** *Informal.* A class of competition; a level: *out of his league.* —**in league.** Allied; in close cooperation. —*v.* **leagued, leaguing, leagues.** —*intr.* To come together for a common purpose; unite. —*tr.* To bring together under a common agreement; join. [Middle English *ligg,* from Old French *ligue,* from Italian *liga, lega,* from *legare,* to bind, from Latin *ligāre.*]

league² *n. Abbr.* **lea. 1.** Formerly, a unit of distance, usually equal to three statute miles. **2.** A square league. [Middle English *leg(h)e,* from Late Latin *leuca, leuga,* perhaps from Gaulish.]

League of Nations *n.* An international organisation of nations established in 1920 to promote world peace and dissolved in 1946.

lea·guer¹ (leegər) *n. Archaic.* **1.** A siege; beleaguerment. **2.** A besieging army or its camp.

—*tr.v.* **leaguered, -guering, -guers.** To besiege; beleaguer. [Dutch *leger,* camp, siege, from Middle Dutch, camp, lair.]

leaguer² *n.* A person who belongs to a league.

Le·ah (leer, lée-ə). The elder daughter of Laban and first wife of Jacob. Genesis 29:16–23. [Hebrew, "wild cow".]

leak (leek) *n.* **1.** An escape from normal or proper confinement; especially, an accidental escape from a container or conduit. **2.** Something escaping normal or proper confines, such as: **a.** A liquid or gas abnormally flowing out of a pipe or reservoir. **b.** An electric current diverted through faulty insulation. **c.** Light or other radiation passing through an accidental opening. **3.** A flaw, crack, hole, or passage through which an escape occurs. **4.** The path followed by the escaping material. **5. a.** A disclosure of confidential information, either intentional or deliberate. **b.** The information disclosed. **c.** The source of such information. **6.** *Vulgar Slang.* An act of urinating. —**spring a leak.** To contract or develop an opening or other flaw that allows the escape or entrance of a substance. —*v.* **leaked, leaking, leaks.** —*intr.* **1.** To permit the escape or passage of something through a hole, crack, or similar opening. **2.** To escape or pass through such an opening. **3.** To become publicly known through a breach of secrecy. Often used with *out: The news leaked out.* **4.** *Vulgar Slang.* To urinate. —*tr.* **1.** To permit (a substance) to escape or pass through a hole, crack, or similar opening. **2.** To disclose (information) without authorisation or official sanction. [Middle English *leke,* perhaps from Old Norse *leki.*]

leak·age (leekij) *n.* **1.** The process or an instance of leaking. **2.** That which escapes by leaking. **3.** An allowance made for loss of stock by leaking, as in commerce.

Lea·key (leeki), **Louis (Seymour Bazett)** (1903–72). British palaeontologist. He influenced evolutionary thinking with his account and analysis of the discovery, with his wife Mary Leakey (1913–), of the 1.75 million-year-old *Zinjanthropus* skull at Olduvai Gorge, in Tanzania. Mary Leakey and his son, Richard Leakey (1944–) have continued his research.

leak·y (leeki) *adj.* **-ier, -iest.** Having leaks or tending to leak.

Leam·ing·ton (lémmingtən). Town in Warwickshire, central England, on the river Leam. Its full name is Royal Leamington Spa, and its saline waters made it a popular spa and health resort in the late 18th and 19th centuries.

lean¹ (leen) *v.* **leaned** (lent, leend) or **leant** (lent), **leaning, leans.** —*intr.* **1.** To bend or slant away from the vertical. **2.** To incline the weight of the body so as to be supported: *leaning against the railing.* **3.** To rely for assistance or support: *Lean on me for help.* **4.** To have a tendency or preference. Used with *to* or *towards: She leans towards the group approach.* **5.** *Informal.* To exert pressure. Used with *on: Their boss is leaning on them.* —*tr.* **1.** To set or place so as to be resting or supported. **2.** To cause to incline: *Lean your head back.* —**lean over backwards.** To put oneself to great inconvenience to achieve something.

—*n.* A tilt or inclination away from the vertical. [Middle English *lenen,* Old English *hleonian, hlinian.*]

Usage: Leant is the usual past tense and participle form in British English, *leaned* in American English; the latter is more widespread in the English-speaking world, especially in written English. Many users of British English write *leaned,* but say (lent).

lean² *adj.* **leaner, leanest. 1.** Not fleshy or fat; thin. **2.** Containing little or no fat. Said of meat. **3.** Not productive or abundant: *lean years.* **4. a.** Lacking mineral value: *lean ore.* **b.** Lacking a high proportion of combustible material; containing much air: *lean fuel.* —*n.* Meat with little or no fat. [Middle English *lene,* Old English *hlæne,* from Germanic *hlainjaz* (unattested).] —**lean·ly** *adv.* —**lean·ness** *n.*

Synonyms: *lean, spare, skinny, scrawny, lank, lanky, gaunt.*

Lean (leen), **David** (1908–). British film director. His work includes *The Bridge Over the River Kwai* (1957) and *Lawrence of Arabia* (1962), both of which won Academy Awards.

Le·an·der (li-ándər). *Greek Mythology.* Youth who loved Hero and drowned while swimming the Hellespont one night to be with her.

lean·ing (leening) *n.* A tendency; a proclivity; an inclination.

lean-to (leen-too, -too) *n., pl.* **-tos. 1.** A shed with a single-pitch roof attached to the side of a building. **2.** A shelter made from planks or branches raised in the front on poles.

leap (leep) *v.* **leapt** (lept) or **leaped** (leept), **leaping, leaps.** —*intr.* **1.** To jump off the ground with a spring of the legs. **2.** To jump forwards; vault; bound. **3.** To move quickly, abruptly, or impulsively: *leaps from one loyalty to another.* —*tr.* **1.** To jump over; hurdle: *leap the brook.* **2.** To cause to jump: *leap a horse.* —*n.* **1.** The act of springing up or forwards; a vault; a bound. **2.** The distance cleared in a forward spring. **3.** An abrupt or precipitous passage, shift or transition. **4.** Something, such as a fence, that is or is to be leapt. —**a leap in the dark.** A course of action or a risk taken without knowing what the consequences will be. —**by leaps and bounds.** Very quickly and by large degrees. [Middle English *le(a)pen,* Old English *hlēapan.*] —**leap·er** *n.*

Usage: Leapt is the usual past tense and participle form in British English, *leaped* in American English; the latter is more widespread in the English-speaking world, especially in written English. Many users of British English write *leaped,* but say (lept).

leap·frog (leep-frog ‖ -frawg) *n.* A game in which one player kneels or bends over while the next in line jumps over him straddle-legged. —*v.* **leapfrogged, -frogging, -frogs.** —*tr.* **1.** To jump over in or as if in leapfrog. **2.** *Military.* To advance (two military units) by engaging one with the enemy while moving the other to a forward position. —*intr.* To move forwards or progress by or as if by alternating leaps.

leap year *n.* **1.** A year in the Gregorian calendar having 366 days, with the extra day, February 29, intercalated to compensate for the quarter-day difference between an ordinary year and the astronomical year. Every year whose number is divisible by 4 is a leap year, except centennial numbers, which are leap years only when divisible by 400. **2.** An intercalary year in any calendar.

Lear (leer), **Edward** (1812–88). British artist and writer. He was a skilled painter of birds, but is famous for the whimsical humour of his limericks and works such as his first *Book of Nonsense* (1846).

learn (lern) *v.* **learned** (lernt, lernd) or *chiefly British* **learnt** (lernt), **learning, learns.** —*tr.* **1.** To gain knowledge, comprehension, or mastery of through experience or study. **2.** To fix in the mind or memory; memorise: *learnt the poem by heart.* **3.** To acquire through experience: *learnt humility in the hands of his captors.* **4.** To become informed of; find out. **5.** *Obsolete.* To give information of. **6.** *Nonstandard.* To teach. —*intr.* **1.** To gain knowledge, comprehension, or skill. **2.** To become informed. Used with *of* or *about.* [Middle English *lernen,* Old English *leornian.*] **—learn·er** *n.*

Usage: *Learnt* is the usual past tense and participle form in British English, *learned* in American English; the latter is more widespread in the English-speaking world, especially in written English. *Learned* pronounced as one syllable (lernt *or* lernd) should not be confused with the adjective *learned* (as in *a learned historian),* which is pronounced as two syllables (lérnid). *Learn* in the sense of "teach, impart knowledge" has no status in standard English.

learn·ed (lérnid) *adj.* **1.** Having or demonstrating profound knowledge or scholarship; erudite; scholarly. **2.** Scholarly or directed towards scholars: *a learned journal.* **3.** Designating a member of the legal profession, especially a barrister: *my learned friend.*

learner-driver (lérnər-drīvər) *n.* A driver with a provisional licence who is learning to drive and in Britain has L-plates on his or her car. Also *British* "L-driver".

learn·ing (lérning) *n.* **1.** Instruction; education. **2.** Acquired wisdom, knowledge, or skill. **3.** *Psychology.* The process of development through experience which leads to relatively permanent changes in behaviour. —See Synonyms at **knowledge.**

learning curve *n.* A graph representing progress in learning, usually showing a fairly steady increase, especially at the beginning, and then levelling off towards the end.

lease (leess) *n.* **1. a.** A contract granting use or possession of property for a specified period in exchange for rent. **b.** The legal document granting such use or possession. **2.** The term or duration of use or possession granted by such a contract. **3.** Property used or possessed by contract in exchange for rent. **—a new lease of life.** Renewed strength, enthusiasm, or usefulness.
∼*tr.v.* **leased, leasing, leases. 1.** To grant use or possession of by lease. **2.** To use or possess by lease. [Middle English *les,* from Anglo-French, from *lesser,* to lease, from Old French *laissier,* to let go, leave, from Latin *laxāre,* to let go, loosen, from *laxus,* LAX.] **—leas·a·ble** *adj.*

lease-back (leéss-bak) *n.* The leasing of property by a new owner back to the previous owner: *sale and lease-back.*

lease·hold (leéss-hōld) *n.* **1.** Use or possession by lease. **2.** Property held under a lease for a term of years. Compare **freehold.**
∼*adj.* Designating property held under a lease for a term of years.

lease·hold·er (leéss-hōldər) *n.* A person who uses or possesses property through a lease.

leash (leesh) *n.* **1.** A chain, rope, or strap attached to the collar or harness of an animal and used to hold it in check or lead it. **2.** A control or check kept on something, as if by a leash. **3.** In hunting, a group of three animals, such as hounds, foxes, or hares. **—straining at the leash.** Eager and impatient to start.
∼*tr.v.* **leashed, leashing, leashes.** To restrain with or as if with a leash. [Middle English *lees, leshe,* from Old French *laisse,* from *laissier,* to loosen, let (a dog run slack). See **lease.**]

leas·ing (leé-sing) *n. Archaic.* A lie, or the act of lying; falsehood. [Middle English *le(e)sing,* Old English *lēasung,* from *lēasian,* to lie, from *lēas,* untrue, false.]

least (leest). Alternative superlative of **little.**
∼*adj.* **1.** Lowest in importance or rank. **2.** Smallest in magnitude, amount, or degree. **3.** Slightest; remotest: *He hasn't the least notion.*
∼*adv.* To or in the smallest degree or amount. **—at least. 1.** According to the lowest possible assessment; no less than. **2.** In any event; anyway: *You might at least answer.*
∼*n.* The smallest or slightest degree, amount, or the like. **—at the (very) least.** At the lowest calculation; as a minimum. **—in the least.** At all: *I don't mind in the least.* [Middle English *leest, least,* Old English *lǣst,* from Germanic *loisiz* (unattested), little. See **less.**]

least common denominator *n. Mathematics.* The **lowest common denominator** *(see).*

least common multiple *n. Mathematics.* The **lowest common multiple** *(see).*

least squares *n. Used with a singular verb.* A method of determining the line or curve that best fits an experimental set of data, using the criterion that the sums of the squares of deviations of experimental points from curve ordinates be a minimum.

least·ways (leést-wayz) *adv.* Also *chiefly U.S.* **least·wise** (-wīz). *Informal.* Anyway; at least.

leat (leet) *n.* An open ditch or trench that conducts water to a mill, mining works, or the like. [Old English *-gelǣt* (as in *wætergelǣt,* water-channel), from the root of LET.]

leath·er (lé*th*ər) *n. Abbr.* **lea. 1.** The dressed or tanned hide of an animal, usually with the hair removed. **2.** Any of various articles made of leather, such as a strap or boot. **3.** The flap of a dog's ear.
∼*adj.* Of or made of leather.
∼*tr.v.* **leathered, -ering, -ers. 1. a.** To cover with leather. **b.** To add leather parts to. **2.** *Informal.* To beat with or as if with a leather strap. [Middle English *lether, leder,* Old English *lether.*]

leath·er·back (lé*th*ər-bak) *n.* A large, chiefly tropical marine turtle, *Dermochelys coriacea,* having a leathery, ridged carapace.

Leath·er·ette (lé*th*ə-rét) *n.* A trademark for a paper or cloth imitation leather.

leath·er·head (lé*th*ər-hed) *n.* The **friarbird** *(see).*

leath·er·jack·et (lé*th*ər-jackit) *n.* **1.** The tough-skinned larva of certain crane flies, which feeds on the roots of grasses. **2.** Any of various fish of the genera *Scomberoides* and *Oligoplites,* having a leathery skin. **3.** Any of various triggerfish of the genus *Monacanthus* and related genera.

leath·ern (lé*th*ərn) *adj. Archaic.* **1.** Made of or covered with leather. **2.** Resembling leather.

leath·er·neck (lé*th*ər-nek) *n. U.S. Slang.* A marine. [Referring to the U.S. marine uniform which formerly had a leather neckband.]

leath·er·y (le*th*əri) *adj.* Having the texture or appearance of leather; tough or weathered: *leathery hands.*

leave[1] (leev) *v.* **left** (left), **leaving, leaves.** —*tr.* **1.** To go out of or away from. **2.** To go without taking or removing. Often used with *behind: left his book behind on the train.* **3. a.** To cause to remain as a consequence or aftereffect: *left a trail of smoke.* **b.** To bring to a specified state or condition: *left her in a rage.* **4. a.** To forgo moving, changing, proceeding with, or interfering with; let remain: *Leave the dishes in the sink.* **b.** To allow (a person or thing) or do something without intervening: *left the house to burn down.* **c.** To postpone: *leave packing till the morning.* **5.** To have remaining alive after one's death: *He leaves a son.* **6.** To give as or as if as a bequest. **7.** To submit to another to be done, acted upon, or accomplished: *Leave the hard work for Jones to do.* **8.** To abandon; forsake: *She's leaving home.* **9.** To give (information) to be acted upon at a later stage: *I left my number with his wife.* **10.** To have as remainder: *6 from 12 leaves 6.* —*intr.* To depart; set out; go. **—leave alone.** To refrain from disturbing, upsetting, or dealing with. **—leave be.** To refrain from interfering with, changing, or disturbing. **—leave go or hold of.** *Informal.* To let go of; stop holding. **—leave it at that.** To stop at the point indicated and do or say no more. **—leave much to be desired.** To fall far short of the appropriate standard or quality. **—leave off. 1.** To stop; cease. **2.** To stop doing or using: *leave off alcohol.* **—leave out. 1.** To omit. **2.** To disregard or ignore, especially in social matters. [Leave, left, left; Middle English *leven, left, lefte,* Old English *lǣfan, lǣfde, lǣfed.*]

Usage: In the sense of "refrain from interfering", *leave* and *let* are often interchangeable *(leave him alone/let him alone)* but some users try to maintain a distinction between the verbs: *leave alone* is felt to imply "leave someone in solitude", *let alone* simply "stop interfering with". In the sense of "allow", *let* is the usual form *(let him be, let it go),* though *leave* is often heard in less formal speech.

leave[2] *n.* **1.** Permission: *With your leave, I must go.* **2.** Official permission, as for military personnel, to be absent from work or duty for a considerable length of time: *leave of absence.* **3.** The duration of absence granted by such permission. **4.** Formal or verbal farewell: *took leave of her with a heavy heart.* **—on leave.** Absent with official permission. [Middle English *leve,* Old English *lēaf.*]

leave[3] *intr.v.* **leaved, leaving, leaves.** To put forth foliage; leaf. [Middle English *leven,* from *le(e)f,* LEAF.]

leaved (leevd) *adj.* **1.** Having or bearing a leaf or leaves. **2.** Having a specified number or kind of leaves. Usually used in combination: *three-leaved; wide-leaved.*

leav·en (lévv'n) *n.* **1. a.** A substance, such as yeast, added to batters and doughs to produce fermentation. **b.** A portion of fermented dough used to produce fermentation in a new batch of dough. **2.** Any element or influence which works to lighten or enliven the whole.
∼*tr.v.* **leavened, -ening, -ens. 1.** To add yeast or some other fermenting agent to. **2.** To produce fermentation in. **3.** To pervade with a lightening or enlivening influence: *leavened with a gentle humour.* [Middle English *levain,* from Old French, probably from Latin *levāmen,* alleviation, hence (in Vulgar Latin) "that which raises", from *levāre,* to raise.]

leaves. Plural of **leaf.**

leave-tak·ing (leév-tayking) *n.* **1.** A departure or farewell. **2.** An act of saying farewell.

leav·ings (leévingz) *pl.n.* Scraps or remains; leftovers; residue. See Synonyms at **remainder.**

Lea·vis (leéviss), **F(rank) R(aymond)** (1895–1978). British literary critic. He was editor of *Scrutiny* (1932–53), and his books include *The Great Tradition* (1948) and studies of D.H. Lawrence (1955) and Dickens (1971), this last work in collaboration with his wife, the critic Q.D. Leavis (1900–81). **—Lea·vis·ite** *n. & adj.*

Leb·a·non, Republic of (lébbənən). Small country in the Middle East. It has few resources, but developed as the regional centre of international finance, trade, and tourism. Unlike other Arab countries, it has a large Christian population, mainly Maronite (about 40 per cent of the total). It also has more than 200,000 Palestinian refugees. Lebanon was created as a French League of Nations mandate in 1920, and proclaimed its independence in 1941. It played a minor role in the 1948 and 1956 Arab-Israeli wars, but did not

PRONUNCIATION KEY

a, **trap**; aa, **father**; ai, **fair**; ar, **star**; aw, **lawn**; ay, **play**; b, bb, **stab**; **rubber**; ch, **church**; ck, **ticket**; d, dd, **dead**; **ladder**; e, **dress**; ee, **bee**; er, **defer**; ew, **few**; ewr, **pure**; ə, **about**; ər, **letter**; f, ff, **fife**; **differ**; g, gg, **giggle**; h, **hat**; i, **kit**; ī, **price**; īr, **fire**; j, **judge**; k, **kick**; l, ll, **let**; 'l, **needle**; m, mm, **man**; n, nn, **no**; 'n, **sudden**; ng, **thing**; o, **lot**; ō, **no**; ŏŏ, **foot**; ōō, **shoe**; oor, **poor**; ow, **cow**; owr, **hour**; oy, **boy**; p, pp, **pepper**; r, rr, **red**; s, ss, **sauce**; sh, **ship**; t, tt, **totter**; th, **thick**; *th*, **this**; **smooth**; u, **cut**; ur, **turn**; v, vv, **valve**; w, **wet**; y, **yes**; z, zz, **zebra**; *zh*, **vision**; **pleasure**

IN FOREIGN WORDS:

aN, oN, **Saint-Saëns**; *hl*, **Llanelli**; **Hluhluwe**; *kh*, **loch**; **lough**; **Khaled**

STRESS MARK:

ín-sīt, insight; in-sít, incite

participate in those of 1967 and 1973. Civil war between rival groups occurred in 1958, 1969, 1973, 1975-76; when a Syrian peace-keeping force entered the country, and again in 1977. To counter Palestine Liberation Organisation (PLO) attacks on northern Israel, the Israelis occupied south Lebanon in 1978, after which a U.N. peace-keeping force took over, and again in 1982, when more than 10,000 PLO guerrillas were evacuated, mainly from Beirut, under U.S., French, and Italian supervision. Area, 10 400 square kilometres (4,014 square miles). Population, 2,700,000. Capital, Beirut. See map at Jordan. **—Leb·a·nese** (lébbə-néez ‖ -néess) *n. & adj.*

Le·bens·raum (láybənz-rowm) *n.* **1.** Additional territory deemed, especially by the Nazis, to be necessary to a nation for its economic well-being. **2.** Broadly, any extra space needed to facilitate working or living. [German, "living space".]

Le·blanc process (lə-blón) *n.* A former industrial process for manufacturing sodium carbonate from sodium chloride and sulphuric acid. [After Nicolas *Leblanc* (1742-1806), French chemist.]

Le Corbusier

CONCRETE "MACHINES" FOR LIVING IN
Building high with 20th-century materials

Le Corbusier was the name adopted by Charles Edouard Jeanneret, born at La Chaux-de-Fonds, Switzerland, in 1887. He trained as a designer-engraver at the local art school and went on to become one of the most influential figures in 20th-century architecture.

The most powerful advocate of the modernist architectural school, he believed that in the machine age housing must be functional or utilitarian. "A house is a machine for living in," he said. He produced undecorated buildings modelled on factory architecture, despite his professed fascination with the "ceaseless inexhaustible miracle of proportion".

Le Corbusier studied in Paris in 1908–9, with Auguste Perret, pioneer of building in reinforced concrete. There Le Corbusier learned the techniques of reinforced concrete which he was to employ so frequently. Throughout the 1920s and 1930s he worked with his cousin Pierre Jeanneret, designing such buildings as the five-storey Swiss pavilion at the University of Paris, made of concrete and raised on stilts. His design

for the Ville Contemporaine, a town for three million people, was never built but it inspired other architects with its pedestrian walkways, roof gardens, courtyards, elevated highways, and recreation areas. His pre-World War II work is self-contained and abstract, showing classical influence, but his later work shows more interest in the environment.

His Unité d'Habitation in Marseille (1946–52) is a 17-storey residential block built on stilts and designed to blend with the mountain background. Other projects include the town of Chandigarh, Punjab, India, built to replace Lahore – lost through partition in 1947. Chandigarh is only a partial success because it is not sufficiently adapted to Indian customs.

Le Corbusier built to heights previously unknown in Europe for domestic architecture and was a powerful influence on the building of high-rise flats in postwar Europe. Although he was a pioneer in the use of modern materials, his buildings have been criticised, chiefly for the isolation they impose on their inhabitants.

A SACRED TASK *Le Corbusier's pilgrimage chapel at Ronchamp, Vosges, France, completed in 1952, is his most unconventional work. Its thick roof hangs over the white walls, producing remarkable acoustic effects. The towers act as funnels for light and the irregularly placed windows contain stained glass. A strip of stained glass also runs along the very top of the walls, causing lines of light to climb and descend the interior walls as the sun moves across the sky.*

Le Brun (lə brŏN), **Charles** (1619–90). Artist to Louis XIV. He decorated Versailles, directed the Gobelins works (1663), responsible for royal furnishings, and was a founder of the Académie de France (1666), set up to enable French artists to study abroad.

Le Car·ré (lə kárray), **John**, pen name of David John Moore Cornwell (1931–). British writer of espionage novels. These include *The Spy Who Came in from the Cold* (1963), *Tinker, Tailor, Soldier, Spy* (1974), and *Smiley's People* (1980).

lech, letch (lech) *n. Informal.* **1.** A strong desire or craving, especially of a sexual nature. **2.** A lecherous act.
~intr.v. leched or **letched, leching** or **letching, leches** or **letches.** *Informal.* To behave in a lecherous manner. Often used with *after.* [Back-formation from LECHER.]

Le Cha·te·lier's principle (lə sha-télli-ayz) *n. Chemistry.* The principle that if a chemical reaction is at equilibrium and the conditions (such as pressure, temperature, or concentration) are changed, then there will be a compensating change in the position of equilibrium tending to restore the original conditions. [After H.L. *Le Chatelier* (1850–1936), French chemist.]

lech·er (léchər) *n.* A man given to excessive sexual cravings or indulgence. [Middle English *lech(o)ur,* from Old French *lecheor, lecheur,* from *lechier,* to live in debauchery, lick, from Frankish *likkōn* (unattested).] **—lech·er·ous** *adj.* **—lech·er·ous·ly** *adv.* **—lech·er·ous·ness** *n.*

lech·er·y (léchəri) *n.* **1.** Excessive indulgence in sexual activity. **2.** Prurience; lasciviousness.

lec·i·thin (léssithin) *n.* Any of a group of phospholipids found in all plant and animal tissues, produced commercially from egg yolks, soyabeans, and maize, and used in the processing of foods, pharmaceuticals, cosmetics, paints and inks, and rubber and plastics. [Greek *lekithos†,* egg yolk + -IN.]

le·cith·i·nase (lə-síthi-nayz, léssithi-, -nayss) *n.* Any of several enzymes that break down lecithin.

Le·clan·ché cell (lə-klónshay) *n.* A voltaic cell of a type having a carbon anode, a zinc cathode, and ammonium chloride electrolyte. Manganese dioxide is used as a depolariser. The dry form is widely used in small batteries.

Le Cor·bu·sier (lə kawr-béwzi-ay, *French* -büz-yáy), pseudonym of Charles-Edouard Jeanneret (1887–1965). Swiss-born French architect. His design and use of modular housing units has greatly influenced modern town planning.

lec·tern (léktərn) *n.* **1.** A reading desk with a slanted top holding the books from which Scriptural passages are read during a church service. **2.** Broadly, any stand that serves as a support for notes or books, especially those of a speaker. [Middle English *lectorn, lettron,* from Old French *lettrun,* from Medieval Latin *lectrīnum,* from *lectrum,* from Latin *lectus,* past participle of *legere,* to read.]

lec·tion (léksh'n) *n.* **1.** A variant reading or transcription of a text as given in a particular edition or copy. **2.** A reading from Scripture that forms a part of a church service. [Latin *lectiō* (stem *lectiōn-*), "a reading", from *legere,* to read. See **lectern.**]

lec·tion·ar·y (léksh'n-əri ‖ *U.S.* -erri) *n., pl.* **-ies.** A book containing lessons or a list of lessons from Scripture to be read at services. [Late Latin *lectiōnārium,* from Latin *lectiō,* LECTION.]

lec·tor (lék-tawr ‖ -tər) *n.* **1. a.** A cleric of the second lowest of the four minor orders in the early Christian church and formerly in the Roman Catholic Church, having the office of reading the sacred books in church. **b.** In the Roman Catholic Church, an ordinand who has been admitted to one of the first stages of the priestly ministry. **2.** A person who reads aloud certain of the Scriptural passages used in a church service; a reader. **3.** A lecturer or reader in certain universities. [Late Latin, from Latin, "reader", from *legere,* to read. See **lecture.**] **—lec·tor·ship** *n.*

lec·ture (lékchər) *n.* **1.** An exposition of a given subject delivered before an audience or class for the purpose of instruction; a discourse. **2.** A method of teaching by discourse, as is used in universities. **3.** A sober admonition or correction; a solemn scolding.
~v. lectured, -turing, -tures. **—***intr.* To deliver a lecture. **—***tr.* **1.** To give a lecture to (a class or audience). **2.** To scold soberly and at length. [Middle English, "a reading", from Old French, from Medieval Latin *lectūra,* from *lectus,* past participle of *legere,* to read.]

lec·tur·er (lékchərər) *n.* **1.** A person who gives a lecture. **2. a.** A teacher in a college or university ranking below a reader or professor. **b.** The rank or position of such a teacher.

lec·ture·ship (lékchər-ship) *n.* **1.** The status or position of a lecturer. **2.** An endowment or foundation supporting a series or course of lectures.

led. Past tense and past participle of **lead.**

LED *n. Electronics.* A light-emitting diode: a semiconductor device that emits light when a voltage is applied, used extensively in visual displays on calculators, digital measuring instruments, and the like.

Le·da (léedə). *Greek Mythology.* A queen of Sparta and the mother, by Zeus, who had taken the form of a swan, of Helen and Pollux, and by her husband Tyndareus of Castor and Clytemnestra.

le·der·ho·sen (láydər-hōz'n) *pl.n.* Men's leather shorts worn as part of traditional Tyrolean or Bavarian costume. [German, "leather trousers".]

ledge (lej) *n.* **1.** A horizontal projection forming a narrow shelf on a wall. **2.** A cut or projection forming a shelf on a cliff or rock wall. **3.** A ridge or rock shelf under water. **4.** A level of rock bearing ore; a vein. [Middle English *legge,* a raised strip or bar, perhaps from *leggen,* to lay, Old English *lecgan.*] **—ledged, ledg·y** *adj.*

ledg·er (léjər) *n.* **1. a.** A book in which the monetary transactions of a business are recorded as debits and credits. **b.** A book to which the record of accounts is transferred as final entry from original listings. **2.** A slab of stone laid flat over a grave. **3.** A horizontal timber in scaffolding, attached to the uprights and supporting the putlogs. **4.** In fishing, ledger bait, line, or tackle. [Middle English *legger,* book fixed in one place, probably from Middle Dutch *legger, ligger,* respectively from *leggen,* to lay, and *liggen,* to lie.]

ledger bait *n.* Fishing bait that is designed to rest on the bottom.

ledger board *n.* The top railing of a fence or balustrade.

ledger line, leg·er line (léjər) *n.* **1.** *Music.* A short line placed above or below a staff to accommodate notes higher or lower than the staff's range. **2.** A fishing line used with ledger bait.

ledger tackle *n.* Fishing tackle used with ledger bait.

Le Duc Tho (láy dŏŏk tō) (1911–). Vietnamese politican, who negotiated the North Vietnamese-U.S. ceasefire (1973) with Henry Kissinger. Both were awarded the Nobel peace prize (1973), but Le Duc Tho refused it.

lee (lee) *n.* **1. a.** *Nautical.* The side or quarter away from the direction from which the wind blows; the side sheltered from the wind. **b.** Any place sheltered from the wind. **2.** Cover; shelter: *under the lee of a large tree.*

~adj. Located on or moving in the direction of the side towards which the wind blows: *the lee side of a ship.* Compare **weather.** [Middle English *le(e),* from Old English *hlēo,* covering, shelter.]

Lee (lee), **Robert E(dward)** (1807–70). Commander of the Confederate armies in the U.S. Civil War. He led the U.S. marines when they captured John Brown at Harper's Ferry in 1859. Loyalty to his native Virginia led him to resign from the Federal army in April, 1861, and become a Confederate general. He won victories at Bull Run (1862), Fredericksburg (1862), and Chancellorsville (1863). Lee was appointed Confederate general-in-chief in February 1865, two months before surrending to Grant at Appomatox.

lee·board (lée-bawrd || -bōrd) *n.* Either of a pair of movable boards or plates attached to the sides of certain flat-bottomed sailing vessels, that is lowered into the water on the lee side when the vessel is sailing to windward to prevent its drifting leeward.

leech¹ (leech) *n.* **1.** Any of various chiefly aquatic bloodsucking or carnivorous annelid worms of the class Hirudinea, having suckers at each end of the body. One species, *Hirudo medicinalis,* was formerly used by physicians to bleed patients. **2.** One who preys on or clings to another; a parasite. **3.** *Archaic.* A physician.

~tr.v. **leeched, leeching, leeches.** *Medicine.* **1.** To bleed (someone) with leeches. **2.** To drain in a parasitic way: *leeched them penniless.* **3.** *Archaic.* To heal. [Middle English *leche,* from Old English *lǣce,* leech; akin to Middle Dutch *leke*† and *lǣce,* physician.]

leech² *n. Nautical.* **1.** Either vertical edge of a square sail. **2.** The after edge of a fore-and-aft sail. [Middle English *leche,* earlier *liche,* probably from Middle Low German *līk,* leech line.]

Leech (leech), **John** (1817–64). English illustrator. From 1841 he contributed over 3,000 illustrations to *Punch.* He illustrated the novels of Surtees, and Dickens' *A Christmas Carol.*

Leeds (leedz). City in West Yorkshire, north England, lying on the river Aire. Since the 14th century it has been a centre of the wool industry. It neoclassical town hall (1858) is an example of grandiose Victorian civic architecture.

leek (leek) *n.* **1.** A plant, *Allium porrum,* related to the onion and having a cylindrical bulb that is the base of the flat, overlapping leaves. It is a national emblem of Wales. **2.** The blanched leaves of this plant, used as food. **3.** Any of various similar wild plants of the genus *Allium.* [Middle English *le(e)k,* Old English *lēac.*]

Lee Kuan Yew (lée kwán yōō) (1923–). Singapore politician. In 1954 he helped to found the Socialist People's Action Party, which campaigned for a self-governing constitution. He became Singapore's first prime minister in 1959, and has held the office since.

leer (leer) *intr.v.* **leered, leering, leers.** To look or glance slyly, lasciviously, or with hostile intent: *leered at her with a dirty grin.*

~n. A sly or lascivious look. [Probably from obsolete *leer,* cheek, Middle English *ler(e),* Old English *hlēor.*]

leer·y (léer-i) *adj.* **-ier, -iest.** *Informal.* Suspicious or distrustful; wary. [From LEER, sly look.]

lees (leez) *pl.n.* The sediment or dregs of an alcoholic drink, such as wine. [Plural of obsolete *lee,* sediment, from Middle English *lie,* from Old French, from Medieval Latin *lia,* from Celtic.]

lee shore *n.* A shore towards which the wind is blowing and towards which a ship is likely to be driven.

leet (leet) *n.* **1.** A former manorial court in England. Also called "court-leet". **2.** The jurisdiction of this court. [Middle English *lete,* from Anglo-French *lete* and Medieval Latin *leta*†.]

Leeu·wen·hoek (láy-v'n-hŏŏk, -wən-), **Anton van** (1632–1723). Dutch naturalist. He was a pioneer in microscopy.

lee·ward (lée-wərd; *Nautical* loord) *adj.* Located on or moving in the direction of the side towards which the wind is blowing.

~n. **1.** The lee direction. **2.** The lee side or quarter.

~adv. Towards the lee side. Compare **windward.**

Lee·ward Islands¹ (léewərd). Northern group of the Lesser Antilles in the West Indies, extending from Puerto Rico to the Windward Islands. The chief islands or groups are the Virgin Islands, Guadeloupe, Anguilla, Antigua, Saint Kitts-Nevis, and Montserrat.

Leeward Islands² *French* **Îles sous le Vent** (éel sōō lə vón). The western group of the Society Islands, part of French Polynesia.

Leeward Islands³. Chain of islets to the northwest of Hawaii, United States. Only Midway Island is inhabited.

lee·way (lée-way) *n.* **1.** The drift of a ship or aircraft to leeward of true course. **2.** A margin of freedom or variation, as of activity, time, or expenditure; latitude.

Le Fa·nu (léffə-new, lə-fáanōō), **Joseph Sheridan** (1814–73). Irish writer. His novels of suspense include *The House by the Churchyard* (1863) and *Uncle Silas* (1864).

left¹ (left) *adj.* **1. a.** Designating, belonging to, or located on the side of the body in which most of the heart is located and which has the hand that is weaker in most people: *left arm.* **b.** Designating or located on the corresponding side of anything that can be said to have a front: *the bird's left wing.* **c.** Designating or located on that side of anything which an observer facing it perceives to be on or towards his left side. **2.** *Often capital* **L.** Of, belonging to, or towards the political or intellectual Left.

~n. **1. a.** The left side or direction: *My house is on the left.* **b.** That which is on or towards the left-hand side. **2.** A turn in the direction of the left hand or side: *took a left at the traffic lights.* **3.** *Often capital* **L. a.** The individuals and groups pursuing generally egalitarian political goals by reformist or revolutionary means, as opposed to broadly conservative, established, or reactionary interests. **b.** A stance of favouring such goals, considered as part of a roughly measurable political continuum: *moving further to the left.* **4.** In boxing, the left hand or a blow struck by the left hand.

~adv. On or towards the left side or direction. [Middle English *luft, lift, left,* Old English *left, lyft* (attested only in *lyftādl,* paralysis, "left-disease"), akin to Middle Dutch *luft, lucht*†, weak, useless.]

left². Past tense and past participle of **leave.**

Left Bank *n.* In Paris, a district situated on the left or southern bank of the River Seine, noted for its artistic and bohemian atmosphere. [Translation of French *rive gauche.*]

left-hand (léft-hánd) *adj.* **1.** Of, pertaining to, or located on the left: *a left-hand drive car.* **2.** Moving or turning to the left: *a left-hand turn.* **3.** Intended for the left hand or a left-handed person.

left-hand·ed (léft-hándid) *adj.* **1.** Having more power or skill in the left hand, or using the left hand more easily than the right: *a left-handed batsman.* **2.** Executed with the left hand. **3.** Designed for wear on or use by the left hand. **4.** Awkward; clumsy; maladroit. **5.** Obliquely derisive; dubious; insincere: *a left-handed compliment.* **6.** Of, pertaining to, or born of a morganatic marriage. **7.** Turning or spiralling from right to left; anticlockwise.

~adv. With the left hand. **—left-hand·ed·ly** *adv.* **—left-hand·ed·ness** *n.*

left-hand·er (léft-hándər) *n.* **1.** One who is left-handed or uses the left hand. **2.** A blow with the left hand.

left·ism (léft-iz'm) *n. Often capital* **L.** The ideology of the Left. **—left·ist** *n. & adj.*

left-lug·gage office (léft-lúggij) *n.* A room at a railway station, airport, or the like, where luggage can be stored temporarily for a fee. Also *U.S.* "checkroom".

left·o·ver (léft-ōvər) *adj.* Of or designating something that has been left as an unused remnant or portion.

left·o·vers (léft-ōvərz) *pl.n.* An unused portion or remnant of something, especially of food.

left wing *n.* **1.** The troops on the left-hand side of an army. **2.** In ball games such as soccer or hockey: **a.** An attacking player on the far left-hand side of his team. **b.** The position of such a player. **3.** *Often capital* **L,** *capital* **W.** The radical or leftist faction of a group or party. **—left-wing** (léft-wíng) *adj.* **—left-wing·er** (-wíng-ər) *n.*

left·y (léfti) *n., pl.* **-ies.** *Informal.* **1.** A person on the political Left. **2.** *Chiefly U.S.* A left-handed person.

leg (leg) *n.* **1.** A limb or appendage of an animal, used for locomotion or support. **2.** The lower or hind limb in man and primates. **3.** The edible back part of the hindquarter of an animal such as a chicken or sheep. **4.** Any supporting part resembling a leg in shape or function: *a table leg.* **5.** Either or any of the branches of a forked or jointed object, such as a pair of compasses. **6.** Any part of a garment, especially of a pair of trousers, that covers all or part of the leg. **7.** In geometry, either side of a right-angled triangle that is not the hypotenuse. **8. a.** A stage of a journey, course, or race: *ran the first leg quickly.* **b.** A stage of a sporting contest that counts towards the final result: *won the first leg but lost the second.* **9.** *Nautical.* The distance travelled by a sailing vessel on a single tack. **10.** In cricket, the side of the field that is on the left of or behind the left shoulder of a right-handed batsman who is facing the bowling, or on the right of or behind the right shoulder of a left-handed batsman. Also used adjectivally: *the leg stump.* **—give a leg up.** To assist by boosting or providing support. **—not have a leg to stand on.** To have no justifiable or logical basis for a defence or proposition. **—on (one's) last legs.** On the verge of failure, exhaustion, collapse, or death. **—pull (someone's) leg.** *Informal.* To tease, make fun of, or fool someone. **—shake a leg.** *Slang.* To hasten; hurry. Often used in the imperative. **—show a leg.** *Informal.* To rise from bed in the morning. **—stretch (one's) legs.** To stand or walk, especially after sitting for a long time.

~intr.v. **legged, legging, legs.** *Informal.* To walk or run, especially so as to escape. Usually used with *it: We legged it to the station.* [Middle English *leg, legge,* from Old Norse *leggr*†.]

leg. **1.** legal. **2.** legate. **3.** *Music.* legato. **4.** legislation; legislative; legislature.

leg·a·cy (léggə-si) *n., pl.* **-cies.** **1.** Money or property bequeathed to someone by will. **2.** Something handed down from an ancestor or predecessor, or from the past: *a legacy of madness.* [Middle English

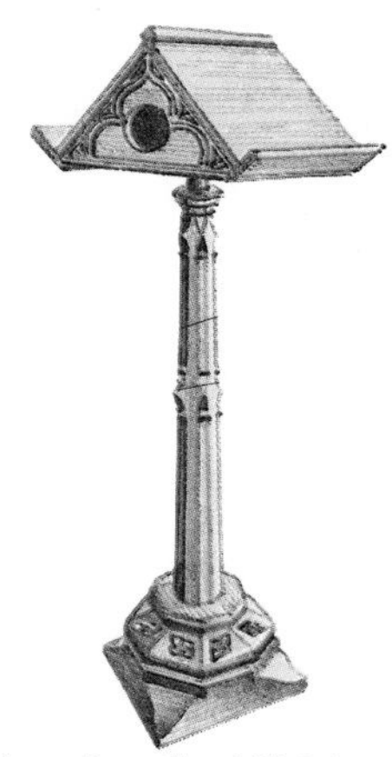

lectern *In medieval Christian churches, pairs of lecterns, or ambos, were often built into the sanctuary – one for the Epistle reading and another for the Gospel. Others, like this double-sided lectern dating from 1500 at Hawstead, in Suffolk, England, were freestanding.*

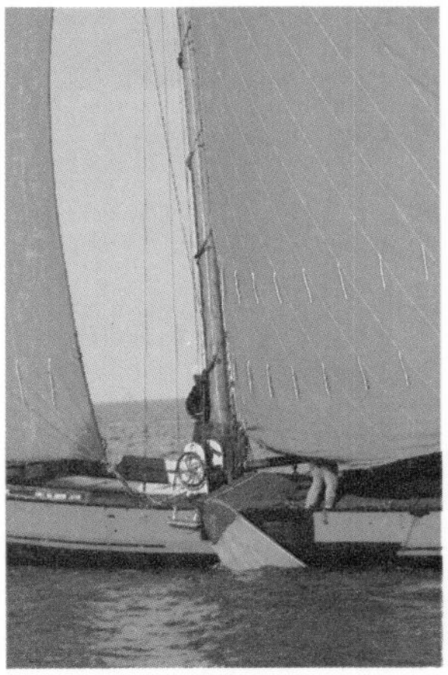

leeboard *On a flat-bottomed vessel the leeboard helps to compensate for the absence of a keel when sailing close to the wind.*

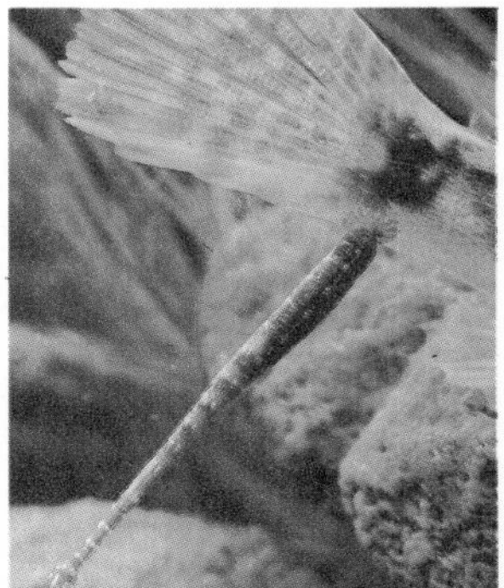

leech *These parasitic worms have suckers at one or both ends of their bodies by which they fasten on to other animals and feed on their blood. Here a leech has attached itself to the tail of a bullhead fish. Leeches were once widely used by doctors to draw off blood from human patients in the belief that this would speed the patients' recovery from a variety of illnesses.*

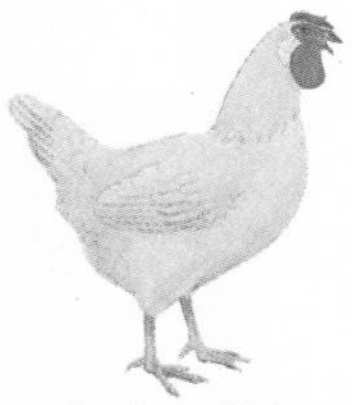

leghorn *Leghorn chickens, which are descended from Mediterranean birds, were first bred in the United States in the mid-19th century. They are excellent layers, but are too light to make good table birds.*

PRONUNCIATION KEY

a, trap; aa, father; ai, fair; ar, star; aw, lawn; ay, play; b, bb, stab; rubber; ch, church; ck, ticket; d, dd, dead; ladder; e, dress; ee, bee; er, defer; ew, few; ewr, pure; ə, about; ər, letter; f, ff, fife; differ; g, gg, giggle; h, hat; i, kit; ī, price; īr, fire; j, judge; k, kick; l, ll, let; 'l, needle; m, mm, man; n, nn, no; 'n, sudden; ng, thing; o, lot; ō, no; ŏŏ, foot; ōō, shoe; oor, poor; ow, cow; owr, hour; oy, boy; p, pp, pepper; r, rr, red; s, ss, sauce; sh, ship; t, tt, totter; th, thick; th, this; smooth; u, cut; ur, turn; v, vv, valve; w, wet; y, yes; z, zz, zebra; zh, vision; pleasure

IN FOREIGN WORDS:

aN, oN, Saint-Saëns; hl, Llanelli; Hluhluwe; kh, loch; lough; Khaled

STRESS MARK:

ín-sīt, insight; in-sít, incite

legacie, from Old French, from Medieval Latin *lēgantia,* from Latin *lēgāre,* to depute, commission, bequeath.]

le·gal (léeg'l) *adj. Abbr.* **leg. 1.** Of, pertaining to, or concerned with law: *legal papers.* **2. a.** Authorised by or based on law: *a legal act.* **b.** Established by law; statutory. **3.** In conformity with or permitted by law. **4.** Recognised or enforced by law rather than by equity. **5.** In terms of or created by the law: *a legal offence.* **6.** Applicable to or characteristic of lawyers or their profession: *legal advice.* **7.** *Theology.* **a.** Of or pertaining to Mosaic law. **b.** Of or pertaining to salvation through works rather than through faith. [Old French, from Latin *lēgālis,* from *lēx* (stem *lēg-*), law.] **—le·gal·ly** *adv.*

legal age *n.* The age of legal responsibility. See **age.**

legal aid *n.* In Britain, financial assistance towards court costs and legal fees given to people whose disposable income and capital assets fall below a certain limit.

legal holiday *n. U.S.* A **bank holiday** *(see).*

le·gal·ise, le·gal·ize (léeg'l-īz) *tr.v.* **-ised, -ising, -ises.** To make legal or lawful. **—le·gal·i·sa·tion** (-ī-záysh'n || *U.S.* -i-) *n.*

le·gal·ism (léeg'l-iz'm) *n.* **1.** Strict, literal adherence to law. **2.** *Theology.* Adherence to the doctrine of salvation by works rather than by faith. **—le·gal·ist** *n.* **—le·gal·is·tic** (-ístik) *adj.* **—le·gal·is·ti·cal·ly** *adv.*

le·gal·i·ty (lee-gál-əti) *n., pl.* **-ties. 1.** The state or quality of being legal; lawfulness. **2.** Adherence to or observance of the law. **3.** A requirement of law: *Legalities prevented the merger.*

legal memory *n. Law.* The period of time required for certain customs to attain legal significance, approximately 20 years in British common law.

legal separation *n.* **Judicial separation** *(see).* Not in technical usage.

legal tender *n.* Currency that may legally be offered in payment of a debt and that a creditor must accept.

leg·ate (lég-ət, -it) *n. Abbr.* **leg. 1.** An official emissary; especially, an official representative of the pope. **2.** In Roman history: **a.** The deputy of a general. **b.** The deputy of a provincial governor. **c.** During the empire, a provincial governor. [Middle English, from Old French, from Latin *lēgātus,* from the past participle of *lēgāre,* to depute, commission, send on an embassy.] **—leg·ate·ship** *n.* **—leg·a·tine** (léggə-tīn || -teen, -tin) *adj.*

leg·a·tee (léggə-tée) *n.* The inheritor of a legacy.

le·ga·tion (li-gáysh'n) *n.* **1.** The sending of a legate. **2.** The mission on which a legate is sent. **3. a.** A diplomatic mission in a foreign country, ranking below an embassy. **b.** The legate and staff of such a mission. **4.** The position or office of a legate. **5.** The premises occupied by a legation. [Middle English *legacioun,* from Old French *legation,* from Latin *lēgātiō* (stem *lēgātiōn-*), from *lēgātus,* LEGATE.]

le·ga·to (li-gaátō) *adv. Abbr.* **leg.** *Music.* In an even, smooth style. Used as a direction.

~n., pl. **legatos.** A smooth, even style, performance, or passage. [Italian, connected, continuous, bound, from *legare,* to bind, from Latin *ligāre.*] **—le·ga·to** *adj.*

leg·a·tor (léggə-tór || *U.S.* lə-gáytər) *n.* A person who makes a will; a testator. [Latin *lēgātōr,* from *lēgāre,* to bequeath. See **legacy.**] **—leg·a·tor·i·al** (léggə-táwri-əl || -tōri-) *adj.*

leg before wicket *n. Abbr.* **l.b.w.** In cricket, a dismissal occurring when a correctly bowled ball, which would otherwise have hit the wicket, strikes the batsman's leg.

leg break *n.* In cricket, a ball bowled with a spin that makes it move from leg to off upon landing.

leg bye *n. Abbr.* **l.b.** In cricket, a run scored when a bowled ball is deflected off the batsman's legs or any other part of his body except his hands.

leg·end (léjənd) *n.* **1. a.** An unverified popular story handed down from earlier times. **b.** A story of the life of a saint. **2.** A body or collection of such stories. **3.** A romanticised or popularised myth of modern times. **4.** A person who achieves legendary fame: *He was a legend in his own lifetime.* **5.** An inscription or title on an object, such as a coat of arms or coin. **6.** An explanatory caption accompanying a map, chart, or illustration. [Middle English *legende,* originally, story of a saint's life, from Old French, from Medieval Latin *legenda,* "things for reading", from Latin *legendus,* gerundive of *legere,* to collect, gather, read.]

leg·en·dar·y (léjən-dəri, -dri || -derri) *adj.* **1.** Of, constituting, based on, or of the nature of a legend. **2.** Famous or described in legend. **3.** Celebrated or notorious to such an extent as to form the basis of a legend.

Lé·ger (lay-zháy), **Fernand** (1881–1955). French painter. One of the early Cubists, he exhibited with the Orphist group (1910–14). His obsession with machinery led to his being called "the primitive of the machine age".

leg·er·de·main (léjərdə-máyn) *n.* **1. Sleight of hand** *(see).* **2.** Any deception or trickery; hocus-pocus. [Middle English *legerdemayn,* from Old French *leger de main,* "light of hand" : *leger,* light, from Vulgar Latin *leviārius* (unattested), from Latin *levis* + *main,* hand, from Latin *manus.*]

leger line. Variant of **ledger line.**

le·ges. Plural of **lex.**

leg·ged (léggid, legd) *adj.* **1.** Having a leg or legs. **2.** Having a specified number or kind of legs. Used in combination: *bowlegged; six-legged.*

leg·gings (léggingz) *pl.n.* Coverings for the legs, as of canvas or leather, usually extending from the knee to the foot.

leg·gy (léggi) *adj.* **-gier, -giest. 1.** Having disproportionately long legs: *a leggy colt.* **2.** *Informal.* Having attractively long and slender legs. **3.** Having long, spindly, often leafless stems.

leg·horn (le-górn, li-; *for senses 1,2,3 also* lég-hawrn || ərn) *n.* **1.** The dried and bleached straw of an Italian variety of wheat. **2.** A plaited fabric made from this straw. **3.** A hat made from this fabric. **4.** *Often capital* **L.** A domestic fowl of a breed of Mediterranean origin, noted for prolific production of eggs. [After LEGHORN.]

Leghorn. See **Livorno.**

leg·i·ble (léji-b'l) *adj.* Capable of being read or deciphered. [Middle English *legibille,* from Late Latin *legibilis,* from Latin *legere,* to read.] **—leg·i·bil·i·ty** (-bílləti), **leg·i·ble·ness** *n.* **—leg·i·bly** *adv.*

le·gion (léejən) *n.* **1.** The major unit of the ancient Roman army consisting of 3,000 to 6,000 infantry troops and 100 to 200 cavalrymen. **2.** *Sometimes plural.* Any large number; a multitude: *He surveyed the massed, singing legions.* **3.** *Usually capital* **L.** Any of several honorary or military organisations: *the Foreign Legion; the British Legion.* —See Synonyms at **multitude.**

~adj. Very numerous; abundant: *Examples are legion.* [Middle English *legioun,* from Old French *legion,* from Latin *legiō,* from *legere,* "to gather", levy troops.]

le·gion·ar·y (léejən-əri, -ri || *U.S.* -erri) *adj.* Of, pertaining to, or constituting a legion.

~n., pl. **legionaries.** A soldier of a legion.

legionary ant *n.* An **army ant** *(see).*

le·gion·naire (léejə-naír) *n.* A member of a legion. [French *légionnaire,* from Old French *legion,* LEGION.]

le·gion·naires' disease (léejə-naírz) *n.* A serious, often fatal, bacterial infection of the lungs, characterised by fever, chest pain, dry cough, and breathlessness. [First identified when it struck members attending an American Legion convention in Philadelphia (1976).]

Legion of Honour *n.* A high French civilian and military decoration, instituted in 1802.

legis. legislation; legislative; legislature.

leg·is·late (léji-slayt) *v.* **-lated, -lating, -lates.** *—intr.* **1.** To pass a law or laws. **2.** *Informal.* To make provision by taking prior measures. Used with *for*: *You can't legislate for a rainy day.* *—tr.* To create or bring about by legislation; enact into law. [Back-formation from LEGISLATOR.]

leg·is·la·tion (leji-sláysh'n) *n. Abbr.* **leg., legis. 1.** The act or procedure of legislating; lawmaking. **2.** A law or laws made by such a procedure.

leg·is·la·tive (léji-slətiv, -slaytiv) *adj. Abbr.* **leg., legis. 1.** Of or pertaining to legislation. **2.** Resulting from or decided by legislation. **3.** Having the power to create laws; designed to legislate: *a legislative body.* **4.** Of or pertaining to a legislature. Compare **executive, judicial.**

~n. The legislative body of a government. **—leg·is·la·tive·ly** *adv.*

legislative assembly *n. Sometimes capital* **L,** *capital* **A. 1.** A bicameral legislature, as in some U.S. states. **2.** A unicameral legislature, as in a Canadian Province. **3.** The lower house of a bicameral legislature, as in Australia.

legislative council *n. Sometimes capital* **L,** *capital* **C. 1.** The upper house of a bicameral legislature, as in Australia. **2.** A unicameral legislature, as in certain dependent states or territories.

leg·is·la·tor (léji-slaytər) *n.* **1.** A person who creates or enacts laws. **2.** A member of a legislative body. [Latin *lēgis lātor,* "proposer of law" : *lēgis,* genitive of *lēx,* law + *lātor,* bearer, proposer, from *lātus,* "carried", past participle of *ferre,* to bear, carry.] **—leg·is·la·to·ri·al** (-slay-táwri-əl || -tōri-) *adj.*

leg·is·la·ture (léji-slaychər) *n. Abbr.* **leg., legis.** An official body of persons having the responsibility and power to legislate for a political unit, such as a nation or state. Compare **executive, judiciary.**

le·gist (léejist) *n.* A specialist in law. [Medieval Latin *lēgista,* from Latin *lēx,* law.]

le·git (lə-jít) *n. Slang.* Legitimate drama; stage plays collectively as opposed to films and musicals.

~adj. Slang. Legitimate.

le·git·i·mate (li-jítti-mət, -mit) *adj.* **1.** In compliance with the law; lawful. **2.** In accordance with traditional or established patterns and standards. **3.** Based on logical reasoning; reasonable: *a legitimate solution.* **4.** *Archaic.* Authentic; genuine. **5.** Born in wedlock. **6.** Of, pertaining to, or ruling by hereditary right. **7.** Of, pertaining to, or designating stage plays as opposed to films, musicals, music-hall, and the like.

~tr.v. (-mayt) **legitimated, -mating, -mates. 1.** To justify as legitimate; authorise. **2.** To make, establish, or declare legitimate. [Middle English, born in wedlock, from Medieval Latin *lēgitimātus,* past participle of *lēgitimāre,* to make lawful, from Latin *lēgitimus,* lawful, legal, from *lēx* (stem *lēg-*), law.] **—le·git·i·ma·cy** (-mə-si) *n.* **—le·git·i·mate·ly** *adv.*

le·git·i·mise, le·git·i·mize (li-jítti-mīz) *tr.v.* Also **le·git·i·ma·tise** (-mə-tīz). To make or claim to be legitimate or acceptable.

le·git·i·mist (li-jíttimist) *n.* A person who believes in or supports legitimate authority; especially, a supporter of rule by hereditary right. **—le·git·i·mism** *n.* **—le·git·i·mist, le·git·i·mis·tic** *adj.*

leg·less (lég-ləss, -liss) *adj.* **1.** Without legs. **2.** *Slang.* So drunk as to be unable to walk.

leg·man (lég-man) *n., pl.* **-men** (-men). *Chiefly U.S.* **1.** A news reporter who gathers news in person away from the office, interviewing people and visiting the scenes of incidents. **2.** A person employed to deliver messages, run errands, and perform other tasks requiring legwork.

Leg·o (léggō) *n.* **1.** A trademark for any of various construction sets consisting of small, plastic interlocking toy bricks. **2.** Such bricks collectively.
~*adj. Often small* **l.** Resembling Lego in being made up of uniform blocks: *a lego housing scheme.*

leg-of-mut·ton (lég-əv-mútt'n) *adj.* Resembling a leg of mutton in shape; tapering sharply from one large end to a point or smaller end, as in a sleeve or sail.

leg-pull (lég-pōōl) *n. Informal.* A humorous deception or hoax; a practical joke.

leg·room (lég-rōōm, -rōōm) *n.* Space that enables one to stretch one's legs, as in a car or cinema.

leg·ume (léggewm, li-géwm) *n.* **1.** A pod, such as that of a pea or bean, that splits into two halves with the seeds attached to the lower edge of one of the halves. **2.** Such a pod or seed, used as food. **3.** Any plant of the family Leguminosae, characteristically bearing such pods. [French *légume,* from Latin *legūmen*†, pulse, bean.]

le·gu·mi·nous (li-géwminəss) *adj.* **1.** Of, belonging to, or characteristic of the family Leguminosae, which includes peas, beans, clover, alfalfa, and other plants. **2.** Resembling or of the nature of a legume. [New Latin *leguminosus,* from Latin *lugūmen,* bean, LEGUME.]

leg·work (lég-wurk) *n. Informal.* Work, such as collecting information, that involves walking or travelling about.

Le·hár (láy-haar, li-hár), **Franz** (1870–1948). Hungarian composer of light operas. His first success was *Viennese Ladies* (1902). His most popular work remains *The Merry Widow* (1905).

Le Ha·vre (lə áavrə). Commercial port on the north coast of France, lying on the Seine estuary. One of France's leading ports, it handles much transatlantic trade, and is the main port for transatlantic passage liners. The city is built around one of the largest central squares in Europe, the Place de l'Hôtel de Ville.

Leh·mann (láymən), **Lotte** (1888–1976). German soprano. She sang chiefly with the Vienna State Opera (1914–38), then settled in the United States, singing at the Metropolitan Opera, New York. She created the role of Ariadne in Richard Strauss's *Ariadne auf Naxos,* and Strauss wrote *Arabella* especially for her.

lehr (leer) *n.* A long oven for annealing glass. [17th century : origin obscure.]

lei[1] (lay, láy-ee) *n., pl.* **leis.** A garland of flowers. [Hawaiian.]

lei[2]. Plural of **leu.**

Leib·niz or **Leib·nitz** (líbnits), **Baron Gottfried Wilhelm von** (1646–1716). German philosopher and mathematician. He devised the infinitesimal calculus independently of Newton. His philosophy includes the theories that the universe is made of indivisible units called **monads** *(see),* and—since God disposes these in the best possible combination—that we live in the best possible world. **—Leib·niz·i·an** *adj.*

Leices·ter[1] (léstər). City in central England, the county town of Leicestershire. It has been an industrial centre, chiefly associated with hosiery and shoe manufacturing, since the 14th century.

Leicester[2] *n.* **1.** A sheep of a breed developed in Leicestershire, having long, fine wool. **2.** A hard, flaky, orange-coloured cheese. In this sense, also called "red Leicester".

Leicester, Robert Dudley, 1st Earl of (*c.* 1532–88). English courtier and favourite of Elizabeth I. In 1553 he helped to place his sister-in-law, Lady Jane Grey, on the throne. He was condemned to death, but pardoned. He was a confidante of Elizabeth, who shortly after her accession made him a privy councillor (1559) and later captain general of her armies (1587).

Leices·ter·shire (léstər-shər, -sheer). Nonmetropolitan county in central England. Although Leicester and other towns in the western part of the county are industrial centres, Leicestershire remains primarily an agricultural county, the home of Stilton cheese.

Lei·den or **Ley·den** (líd'n). City in south Holland, Netherlands. The **Leyden jar** was invented at its famous university, founded (1575) by William of Orange.

Leif Er·ic·sson (léef érrik-sən) (*fl.* 1000). Norse discoverer of America. He was the son of Eric the Red, and probably born in Iceland. According to Norse sagas, on his return from Greenland in 1000 he was blown off course to an unknown land, called Vinland after the vines supposedly growing there. It is thought to lie somewhere between Newfoundland and Virginia.

Leigh (lee), **Vivien,** born Vivien Hartley (1913–67). English actress. She won an Academy Award as best actress for her roles in *Gone with the Wind* (1939) as Scarlett O'Hara and in *A Streetcar Named Desire* (1951) as Blanche Dubois. She was the second wife of Laurence Olivier.

Leigh·ton (láyt'n), **Frederic, 1st Baron** (1830–96). English painter. With Alma-Tadema and Poynter, he revived a fashion for scenes of ancient Greek and Roman life. His first exhibited painting, *Cimabue's Madonna Carried in Procession,* was bought by Queen Victoria in 1855. He was president of the Royal Academy (1878–96), and became a peer in 1896.

Lein·ster (lén-stər). Province in the east of the Republic of Ireland, consisting of the counties of Carlow, Dublin, Kildare, Kilkenny, Leix, Longford, Louth, Meath, Offaly, Westmeath, Wexford, and Wicklow. The major city is Dublin.

Leip·zig (líp-sig || *German* líp-tsikh). City in south central East Germany, one of the great historic industrial and cultural centres of Europe, and now the second largest city in East Germany. Originally a Slav settlement called Lipsk, it developed by the early Middle Ages into a major trading and commercial town, famous from the 15th to the mid-20th centuries for its book and music publishing. Its university was founded in 1409. At the battle of Leipzig (the Battle of the Nations) in 1813, the armies of Russia, Prussia, and Austria inflicted a decisive defeat on the army of Napoleon.

leish·man·i·a·sis (léeshmə-ní-ə-siss) *n.* **1.** Infection with flagellate protozoans of the genus *Leishmania.* **2.** A disease, such as kala-azar or various ulcerative skin diseases, caused by such infection. [New Latin, from *Leishmania,* genus of protozoans, identified by Sir William B. *Leishman* (1865–1926), British medical officer.]

leis·ter (léestər) *n.* A three-pronged spear used for catching fish, such as salmon.
~*tr.v.* **leistered, -tering, -ters.** To spear (a fish) with a leister. [Old Norse *ljōstr,* from *ljōsta*†, to strike.]

lei·sure (lézhər || *U.S. also* léezhər) *n.* Freedom from time-consuming duties, responsibilities, or activities. See Synonyms at **rest. —at leisure. 1.** Having free time. **2.** Not employed, occupied, or engaged. **3.** Unhurried. **—at (one's) leisure.** When one has free time; at one's convenience.
~*adj.* **1.** Not spent in work or compulsory activity; free. **2.** Having much leisure; leisured. [Middle English *leisour, leiser,* freedom, opportunity, from Anglo-French *leisour,* variant of Old French *leisir,* to be permitted, from Latin *licēre*†, to be lawful, be permitted.]

lei·sured (lézhərd || *U.S. also* léezhərd) *adj.* **1.** Having much leisure: *the leisured classes.* **2.** Unhurried; leisurely.

lei·sure·ly (lézhərli || *U.S. also* léezhərli) *adj.* Without haste; unhurried: *a leisurely meal.*
~*adv.* In a steady, relaxed manner; slowly. **—lei·sure·li·ness** *n.*

Leith (leeth). The second largest port in Scotland, absorbed by Edinburgh in 1920.

leit·mo·tif, leit·mo·tiv (lít-mōteef) *n.* **1.** *Music.* A thematic passage, as in Wagnerian opera, associated with a specific character, thing, or element. **2.** A dominant theme or recurring image or use of words, as in a novel. [German *Leitmotiv,* "leading motif".]

Lei·trim (léetrim). County in the north of the Republic of Ireland, having a short border with Northern Ireland. The county town is Carrick on Shannon. The county is divided by Lough Allen into a lowland southern half and a mountainous northern half.

Leix or **Laois** or **Laoighis** (leesh). County in the central part of the Republic of Ireland, occupying the valleys of the upper Nore and upper Barrow rivers. From 1556 to 1922 it was known as the Queen's County. The county town is Port Laoise (Maryborough).

lek[1] (lek) *n.* **1.** The basic monetary unit of Albania, equal to 100 quintars. **2.** A coin worth one lek. [Albanian.]

lek[2] *n.* An area used for courtship display and mock fighting by certain male birds, especially the black grouse. [Probably from Scandinavian; akin to Swedish *lek,* sport, play, Old Norse *leikr,* play; compare LAIK.]

lek·ker (léckər) *adj. South African Informal.* **1.** Very good-tasting; delicious. **2.** Very pleasing, attractive, or enjoyable. **3.** Slightly drunk; tipsy. [Afrikaans, from Dutch.]

Le·ly (léeli), **Sir Peter** (1618–80). Dutch painter. He worked in England from about 1643 and in 1660 was appointed principal painter to Charles II recording in portraits the Restoration court.

LEM (lem) *n. Aerospace.* A *l*unar *e*xcursion *m*odule.

lem·an (lémmən, léemən) *n. Archaic.* **1.** A lover. **2.** A mistress. [Middle English *leofman, lemman* : *lef, leof,* dear, from Old English *lēof* + MAN.]

Léman, Lac. See **Geneva, Lake.**

Le Mans (lə móɴ). City in northwest France, capital of the Sarthe département, lying on the river Sarthe. It was settled from pre-Roman times and was for a time the Merovingian capital. Its Romanesque cathedral is renowned for its flamboyant flying buttresses. Since 1906 Le Mans has been the site of the annual 24-hour motor race.

Lemberg. See **Lvov.**

lem·ma[1] (lémmə) *n., pl.* **-mas** or **lemmata** (lémmətə). **1.** *Logic.* A subsidiary proposition assumed to be valid and used to demonstrate a principal proposition. **2.** A theme, argument, or subject indicated in a title. **3.** A glossed word in a glossary or other listing. [Latin, from Greek *lēmma,* anything received, argument, proof, from *lambanein* (past perfect *eilēmmai*), to grasp, take.]

lem·ma[2] *n., pl.* **-mas** or **lemmata.** *Botany.* The outer, lower bract enclosing the flower in a grass spikelet. [Greek *lemma,* rind, husk, from *lepein,* to peel.]

lem·ma·tise, lem·ma·tize (lémmə-tīz) *tr.v.* **-ised, -ising, -ises.** To arrange (words in a text) in such a way that all words which are inflected or variant forms of the same word are grouped together. [Latin *lemma* (stem *lemmat-*), proposition (see LEMMA) + -ISE.]

lem·ming (lémming) *n.* **1.** Any of various volelike rodents of the genus *Lemmus* and related genera, of northern regions, such as the European species *L. lemmus,* noted for its mass migrations as a result of periodic population increases. **2.** A person who wilfully follows a disastrous course of action; a self-destructive person. [Norwegian *lemming, lemende,* akin to Swedish *lemmel*†.]

lem·nis·cate (lem-nís-kət, -kit) *n.* In geometry: **1.** A plane curve that is the locus of the foot of a perpendicular from the origin to a tangent moving on a rectangular hyperbola. The curve, which has two symmetrical lobes, has the equation $(x^2 + y^2) = a^2 (x^2 - y^2)$, where a is the greatest distance from the node to the curve. Also called "lemniscate of Bernoulli". **2.** A plane curve that is the locus of the vertex of a triangle with the side opposite the vertex of fixed length and the other two sides having a constant product (k) equal to one quarter of the square of the fixed side. Its equation is $[(x + a)^2 + y^2][(x - a)^2 + y^2] = k^4$, where a is one half of the length of

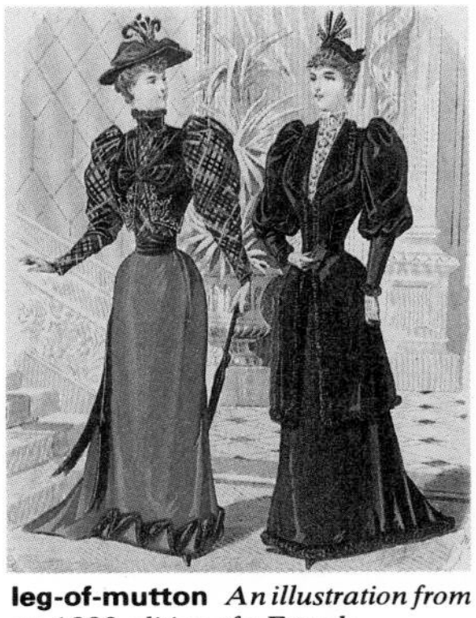

leg-of-mutton *An illustration from an 1892 edition of a French magazine called* Salon de la Mode, *showing leg-of-mutton sleeves on the dresses.*

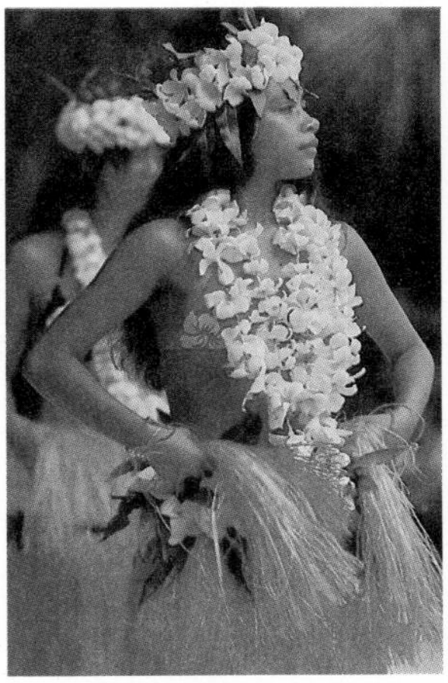

lei *Garlands of beads, shells, or flowers have been used by Hawaiians since ancient times as symbols of welcome and farewell.*

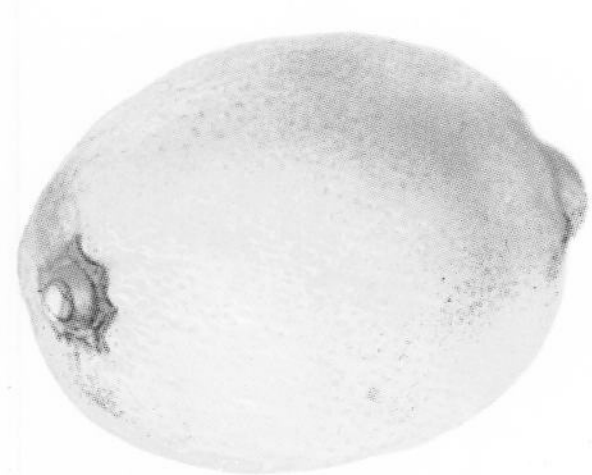

lemon Citrus limon, *the lemon tree, was introduced to Europe after it was discovered in Palestine by the Crusaders. The tree can grow up to 6 metres (20 feet) high.*

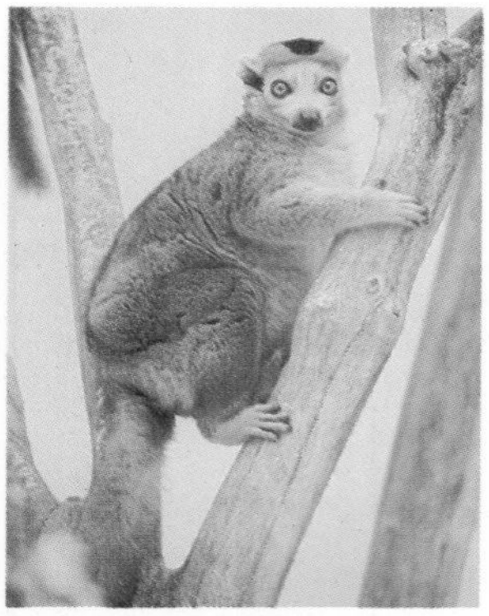

lemur *Found chiefly in Madagascar, the lemur is a primitive primate which lives mainly in trees feeding on fruit, vegetation, and insects. It gets its name from the Latin word for ghosts – lemures – because of its pallid face.*

PRONUNCIATION KEY

a, trap; aa, father; ai, fair; ar, star; aw, lawn; ay, play; b, bb, stab; rubber; ch, church; ck, ticket; d, dd, dead; ladder; e, dress; ee, bee; er, defer; ew, few; ewr, pure; ə, about; ər, letter; f, ff, fife; differ; g, gg, giggle; h, hat; i, kit; ī, price; īr, fire; j, judge; k, kick; l, ll, let; 'l, needle; m, mm, man; n, nn, no; 'n, sudden; ng, thing; o, lot; ō, no; ŏŏ, foot; ōō, shoe; oor, poor; ow, cow; owr, hour; oy, boy; p, pp, pepper; r, rr, red; s, ss, sauce; sh, ship; t, tt, totter; th, thick; th, this; smooth; u, cut; ur, turn; v, vv, valve; w, wet; y, yes; z, zz, zebra; zh, vision; pleasure

IN FOREIGN WORDS:

aN, oN, Saint-Saëns; hl, Llanelli; Hluhluwe; kh, loch; lough; Khaled

STRESS MARK:

ín-sīt, insight; in-sí̄t, incite

the fixed side. Also called "lemniscate of Cassini". [Greek *lēmniskos,* fillet, ribbon.]

lem·nis·cus (lem-nískəss) *n., pl.* **-nisci** (-níssī, -nískī). A bundle of sensory nerve fibres located in the brain. [New Latin, from Latin *lēmniscus,* ribbon, from Greek *lēmniskos*†.]

lem·on (lémmən) *n.* **1.** A spiny evergreen tree, *Citrus limon,* native to Asia, widely cultivated for its yellow, egg-shaped fruit. **2.** The fruit of this tree, having an aromatic rind and acid, juicy pulp. **3. Lemon yellow** *(see).* **4.** *Informal.* Something or someone that is or proves to be defective, inadequate, or unsuitable. [Middle English *lymon,* from Old French *limon,* from Arabic *laymūn,* variant of *līmūn,* from Persian *līmūn*†.] **—lem·on** *adj.*

lem·on·ade (lémmə-náyd) *n.* A cold, often carbonated, drink made of lemon juice or flavouring, water, and sugar. [French *limonade* : obsolete *limon,* LEMON + -ADE.]

lemon balm *n.* A plant, **balm** *(see).*

lemon curd *n.* A sweet, viscous, yellow paste used in tarts or on sandwiches, prepared from lemons, sugar, butter, and eggs. Also called "lemon cheese".

lemon drop *n.* A small, hard, lemon-flavoured sweet.

lemon geranium *n.* A widely cultivated plant, *Pelargonium limoneum* (or *P. mellisimum*), having lemon-scented leaves and small, pale purple flowers.

lem·on·grass (lémmən-graass || -grass) *n.* Any of several tropical grasses of the genus *Cymbopogon;* especially, *C. citratus,* yielding an aromatic oil used in perfumery and as flavouring.

lemon sole *n.* An edible marine flatfish, *Microstomus kitt* (or *Limanda limanda*), having a variegated brown body. Also called "lemon dab". [French *limande,* from Old French, irregularly from *lime,* file, lemon sole (from its shape), from Latin *lima,* file.]

lemon verbena *n.* An aromatic plant, *Lippia citriodora,* native to South America, cultivated for its fragrant foliage and flowers.

lem·on·y (lémməni) *adj.* **1.** Having the characteristic odour or flavour of lemons. **2.** *Australian Slang.* Irritable; peevish.

lemon yellow *n.* Brilliant, vivid yellow to greenish yellow. **—lem·on-yel·low** *adj.*

lem·pi·ra (lem-péer-ə) *n.* **1.** The basic monetary unit of Honduras, equal to 100 centavos. **2.** A coin or note worth one lempira. [After *Lempira,* indigenous Indian leader who resisted the Spanish.]

le·mur (léemər) *n.* Any of several arboreal primates chiefly of the family Lemuridae, of Madagascar and adjacent islands, having large eyes, soft fur, and a long tail. [New Latin, coined by Linnaeus after Latin *lemurēs,* LEMURES, from the ghostly appearance of its face and its nocturnal habits.] **—le·mur·ine** (-īn, lémmewr-, -in), **le·mur·oid** *adj.*

lem·u·res (lémmewr-eez) *pl.n.* In ancient Rome, the spirits of the dead considered as frightening spectres. Compare **manes.** [Latin *lemurēs.*]

Le·na (léenə || *Russian* lyáynə). Easternmost of the great rivers of Siberia, rising near Lake Baikal and flowing northeast for 4 300 kilometres (2,670 miles) into the Arctic Ocean. It broadens into a vast delta about 400 kilometres (250 miles) wide.

Le Nain (lə náN), **Antoine** (*c.*1588-1648) and **Mathieu** (*c.*1607–77). French painters. The brothers worked in Paris after about 1630, painting mostly peasant scenes. They signed their paintings without initials, so it is difficult to separate their work. Mathieu was made painter to the city of Paris in 1633.

lend (lend) *v.* **lent** (lent), **lending, lends.** *—tr.* **1.** To give out or allow the use of (something) temporarily on the condition that it or its equivalent in kind will be returned. **2.** To provide (money) temporarily on the condition that the amount borrowed will be returned, often with an interest fee. **3.** To contribute or impart, especially a desirable attribute or quality; add: *She lent elegance to the proceedings.* **4.** To put at another's service or needs; give. **5.** To accommodate or offer (itself) to something; be suited to. Used reflexively: *This medium lends itself to many styles.* *—intr.* To make a loan or loans. —See Usage note at **loan.** [Middle English *len(d)en,* Old English *lǣnan,* to lend, give.] **—lend·er** *n.*

lending library *n.* A library from which books may be borrowed or rented for a fee. Also *U.S.* "circulating library".

lend-lease (lénd-léess) *n.* The U.S. aid programme during World War II providing food, munitions, and other goods to strategic countries threatened by Germany and Italy.

~tr.v. **lend-leased, -leasing, -leases.** To provide (aid) to a country, as under the provisions of the U.S. Lend-Lease Act (1941).

Leng·len (loN-glóN), **Suzanne** (1899–1938). French tennis player. She won the Wimbledon women's singles championship six times from 1919 to 1925, and also won the French championship six times.

length (length, lengkth || lenth) *n. Abbr.* **l. 1.** The state, quality, or fact of being long. **2. a.** The measurement of the extent of something along its greatest dimension. **b.** The measurement of the extent of something from back to front as distinguished from its width or height. **3.** A piece of something, often of a standard size, normally measured along the greatest dimension: *a length of cloth.* **4.** A unit of measurement based on the approximate extent from front to back of an animal or vehicle in a race: *The boat won by two lengths.* **5.** The extent of a thing from start to finish as measured by space, pages, or words: *the length of a story.* **6.** The amount of time between particular moments; a duration; a period. **7.** The distance between particular points or locations: *the length of their journey.* **8.** The state or quality of extending greatly in time or space. **9.** *Phonetics.* **a.** The quantity or duration of a vowel. **b.** Loosely, the quality of a vowel. **10.** In verse, the quantity or duration of a syllable. **11.** In cricket, the distance in front of the batsman at which the ball strikes the pitch: *bowled a good length.* **12.** The longer side or dimension of a swimming pool, or the distance from end to end: *swam ten lengths.* **—at length. 1.** After some time; eventually. **2.** For a considerable time; fully. **—go to any** or **great length** or **lengths.** To take great trouble. **—keep at arm's length.** To refuse to become closely associated with. **—measure (one's) length.** To fall flat.

~adj. **1.** Extending up to or down to a specified part or point. Used in combination: *shoulder-length hair.* **2. a.** Having a specified length. Used in combination: *a full-length opera.* **b.** Being as long as something specified. Used in combination: *a book-length manuscript.* [Middle English *lengthe,* Old English *lengthu.*]

length·en (léng-th'n, léngk- || lén-) *v.* **-ened, -ening, -ens.** *—tr.* To make longer. *—intr.* To become longer. **—length·en·er** *n.*

length·man (léngth-mən, léngkth- || lénth-) *n., pl.* **-men** (-mən). *British.* A person employed to maintain a stretch of railway line or road.

length·ways (léngth-wayz, léngkth- || lénth-) *adv.* Also *chiefly U.S.* **length·wise** (-wīz). In or along the direction of a length: *He cut the cloth lengthways.* **—length·ways** *adj.*

length·y (léng-thi, léngk- || lén-) *adj.* **-ier, -iest.** Of considerable length, especially in time; drawn-out. **—length·i·ly** *adv.* **—length·i·ness** *n.*

le·ni·en·cy (léeni-ən-si, léen-yən-) *n., pl.* **-cies.** Also **le·ni·ence** (léeni-ənss). **1.** The condition or quality of being lenient. **2.** A lenient action. —See Synonyms at **mercy.**

le·ni·ent (léeni-ənt, léen-yənt) *adj.* **1.** Merciful, restrained, or forgiving; gentle or understanding. **2.** Not austere or strict; liberal; generous: *lenient rules.* **3.** *Archaic.* Soothing or relaxing. [Latin *lēniēns* (stem *lēnient-*), present participle of *lēnīre,* to soothe, make soft, from *lēnis,* soft.] **—le·ni·ent·ly** *adv.*

Le·nin (lénnin; *Russian* lyáy-neen), **Vladimir Ilich,** born Vladimir Ilich Ulyanov; also known as Nikolai Lenin (1870–1924). Russian revolutionary leader. He was exiled to Siberia for subversive activities in 1895. In 1900 he went abroad to study Marx's theories, returning briefly to Russia during the abortive 1905 revolution. Lenin was in Switzerland in 1917 when the revolution broke out in Russia, and the German government secretly helped him to travel to Petrograd. On November 7 (October 25 by the Russian calendar) he led the Bolshevik overthrow of Kerensky's government and was head of the Soviet government until his death following a stroke.

Len·in·grad (lénnin-grad; *Russian* linnin-gráat). City in the west of the U.S.S.R., situated on the banks and delta islands of the river Neva, at the head of the Gulf of Finland. It is the U.S.S.R.'s second largest city, and a leading seaport and commercial and industrial centre. It was founded in 1703 by Peter the Great, was called St. Petersburg, and was the capital of Russia from 1712 until 1918. From 1914 until 1924 it was called Petrograd. The city was laid out on classical lines by French and Italian architects: its central thoroughfare is the celebrated Nevsky Prospect. The city is also the site of the famous Hermitage museum.

Len·in·ism (lénni-niz'm) *n.* The theory and practice of proletarian revolution as developed by Lenin. See **Marxism-Leninism. —Len·in·ist** *n. & adj.*

Lenin Peak. Highest peak in the Trans-Alai range of mountains, in southwest Asian U.S.S.R. It rises to 7 134 metres (23,405 feet) and is the third highest mountain in the U.S.S.R.

le·nis (lée-niss, láy-) *adj. Phonetics.* Articulated with little or no aspiration; weak; soft. The consonants *b* and *d* are lenis compared with *p* and *t.* Compare **fortis.**

~n., pl. **lenes** (lée-neez, láy-). *Phonetics.* A speech sound pronounced with little or no aspiration; a lenis consonant. [Latin *lēnis,* soft, mild, smooth.]

len·i·tive (lénnitiv) *adj.* Capable of easing pain or discomfort.

~n. A lenitive medicine. [Old French *lenitif,* from Medieval Latin *lēnītīvus,* from Latin *lēnīre,* to soothe, soften, from *lēnis,* soft.]

len·i·ty (lén-əti, léen-) *n., pl.* **-ties. 1.** The state, condition, or quality of being lenient; leniency. **2.** A lenient action. [Latin *lēnitas* (stem *lēnitāt-*), gentleness, mildness, from *lēnis,* soft, mild.]

Len·non (lénnən), **John** (1940–80). English pop musician, one of the Beatles. He and Paul McCartney wrote most of the group's songs of the 1960s. Lennon married the singer Yoko Ono in 1969. He was shot dead in New York by Mark Chapman.

le·no (léenō) *n., pl.* **-nos. 1.** A weaving of a type in which the warp yarns are paired and twisted. **2.** A fabric having such a weave. [Probably from French *linon,* fine linen, from *lin,* flax, linen, from Latin *līnum.*]

lens (lenz) *n.* **1.** A carefully ground or moulded piece of glass, plastic, or other transparent material, in which either or both opposite surfaces are curved such that light rays are refracted to converge or diverge and form an image. **2.** A combination of two or more such lenses, sometimes with other optical devices such as prisms, used to form an image for viewing or photographing. Also called "compound lens". **3.** Any device that causes radiation other than light to converge or diverge by an action analogous to that of an optical lens. **4.** A transparent, biconvex body of the eye between the iris and the vitreous humour, that focuses light rays entering through the pupil to form an image on the retina. In this sense, also called "crystalline lens". **5.** A combination of electrodes or magnets used to converge or diverge a beam of electrons or other charged parti-

THE DEVICE THAT FOCUSES REFLECTED RAYS OF LIGHT

Manipulating the lens to capture sharper images

A lens has one or more curved surfaces that refract, or bend, light rays passing through it to form an image on a surface beyond the lens – the retina of the eye or a cinema screen, for example. The distance from the lens to the focal plane is known as the focal length.

In cameras, telescopes, and similar devices, the lens is turned on a screw-thread mounting to adjust the focal length and so focus the images of objects at various distances. In a human eye, focal length is adjusted by muscles that alter the lens curvature.

Light rays of different colours are bent by different amounts as they pass through a curved surface; this causes a distortion of the image, known as "chromatic aberration". In cameras, sharper images are obtained by arranging two or more lenses so that the aberration of one cancels out the aberration of the other. Such an arrangement is collectively called an achromatic lens. A zoom lens may contain 20 separate lenses.

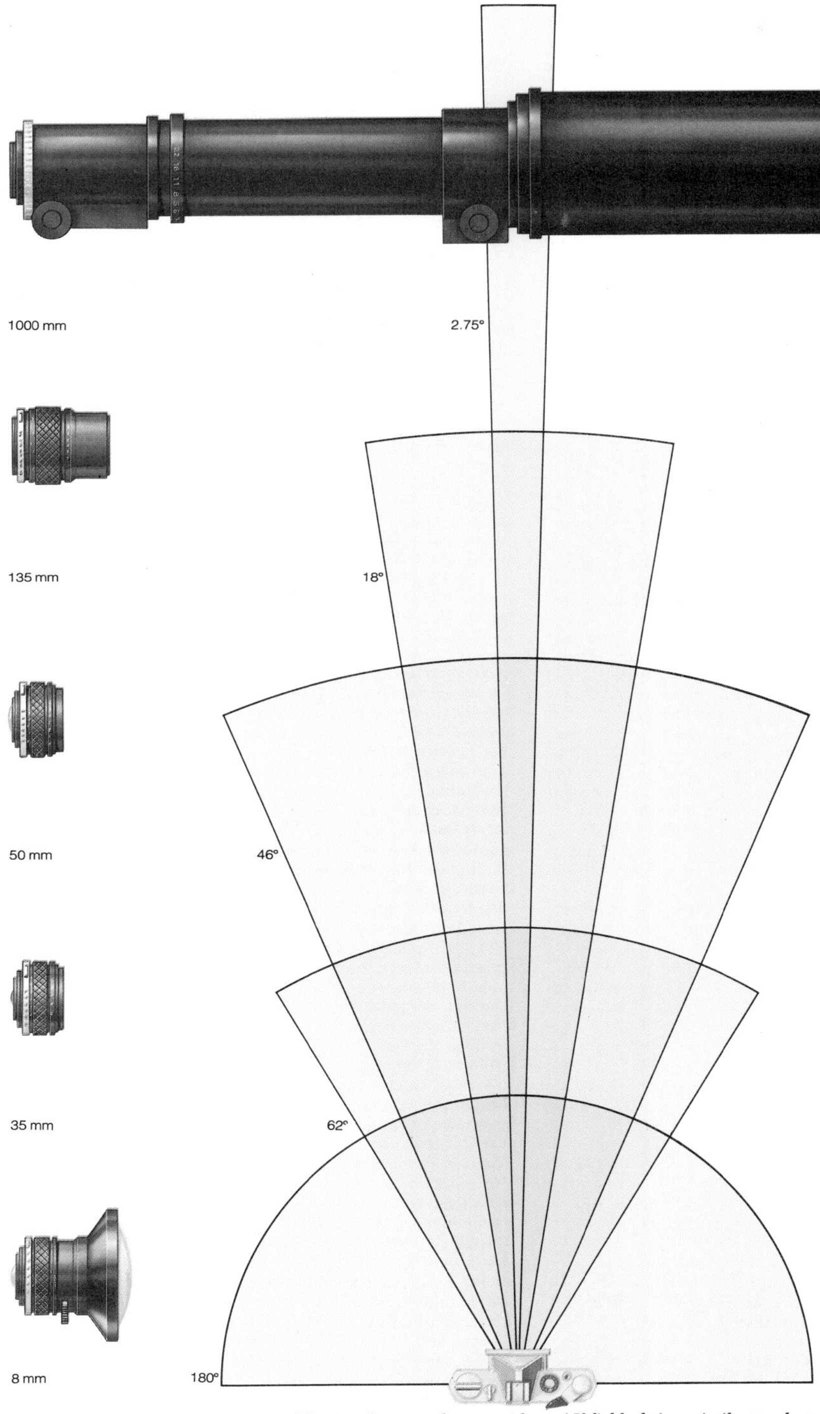

1000 mm   2.75°

135 mm   18°

50 mm   46°

35 mm   62°

8 mm   180°

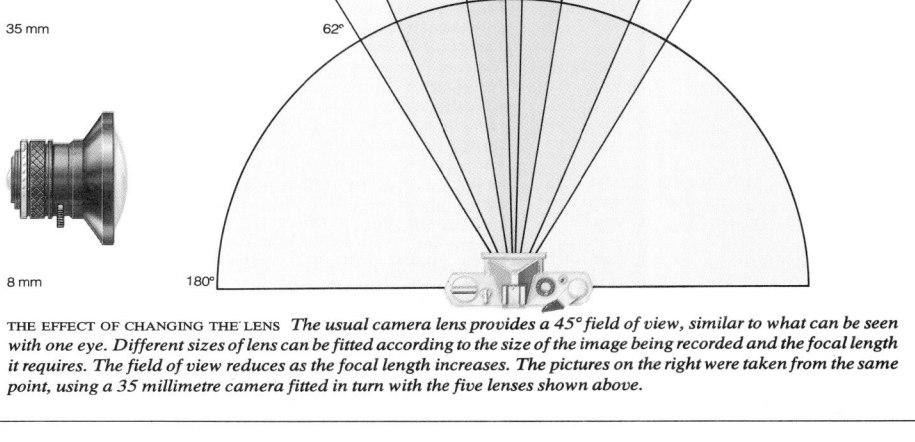

THE EFFECT OF CHANGING THE LENS *The usual camera lens provides a 45° field of view, similar to what can be seen with one eye. Different sizes of lens can be fitted according to the size of the image being recorded and the focal length it requires. The field of view reduces as the focal length increases. The pictures on the right were taken from the same point, using a 35 millimetre camera fitted in turn with the five lenses shown above.*

cles. Also called "electron lens". [New Latin, from Latin *lēns,* LENTIL (from the resemblance of an optical lens to a lentil seed).]
lent. Past tense and past participle of **lend.**
Lent (lent) *n.* **1.** The 40 weekdays before Easter (beginning on Ash Wednesday), observed as a season of penitence. **2.** *Plural.* At Cambridge University, boat races occurring during the Lent term. [Middle English *lente, lenten,* originally "spring", Old English *lencten,* probably from Germanic *lang-* (unattested), LONG (referring to the lengthening days of spring).]
Lent·en (léntən) *adj.* **1.** Of or pertaining to Lent. **2.** *Sometimes small* **l.** *Archaic.* Characteristic of or appropriate to Lent; meagre; sombre: *Lenten fare; a Lenten face.*
len·tic (léntik) *adj.* Of, pertaining to, or designating ecological communities living in still water. Compare **lotic.** [Latin *lentus,* slow, still.]
len·ti·cel (lénti-sel) *n. Botany.* Any of the small pores on the surface of the stems of woody plants, allowing the passage of gases to and from the interior tissue. [New Latin *lenticella,* diminutive of Latin *lēns* (genitive *lentis*), LENTIL.] **—len·ti·cel·late** (-séll-it, -ət) *adj.*
len·tic·u·lar (len-tíckewlər) *adj.* **1. a.** Shaped like a biconvex lens. **b.** Shaped like a lentil seed. **2.** Of or pertaining to a lens, especially that of the eye. [Latin *lenticulāris,* like a lentil, from *lenticula,* LENTIL (compare **lens**).]
len·ti·go (len-tīgō) *n., pl.* **-tigines** (-tíji-neez) **1.** A freckle. **2.** A naevus. [Latin *lentīgo,* freckles, from *lēns,* LENTIL.] **—len·tig·i·nous** (-tíji-nəss), **len·tig·i·nose** (-nōss, -nōz) *adj.*
len·til (léntil, lént'l) *n.* **1.** A leguminous plant, *Lens esculenta* (or *L. culinaris*), native to the Old World, having pods containing edible seeds. **2.** The round, brown or orange, flattened seed of this plant. [Middle English, from Old French *lentille,* from Vulgar Latin *lentīcula* (unattested), variant of Latin *lenticula,* diminutive of *lēns*†, lentil.]
len·tisk (lén-tisk) *n.* The **mastic tree** *(see).* [Middle English, from Latin *lentīscus*†.]
len·to (léntō) *adv. Music.* Slowly. Used as a direction.
~*adj. Music.* Slow.
~*n. Music.* A lento passage. [Italian, from Latin *lentus,* slow.]
len·toid (lén-toyd) *adj.* Lenticular.
Lent term *n.* In some universities, the term during which most of the period of Lent falls.
Len·ya (lén-yə), **Lotte,** born Karoline Wilhelmine Blamauer (1900–81). Austrian singer and actress. In 1926 she married Kurt Weill, who composed *The Seven Deadly Sins* for her.
Lenz's law (léntsiz) *n. Physics.* The principle that if the magnetic flux linked with a circuit changes, the current induced in the circuit flows in such a way as to produce a field opposing the change. [After H.F.E. *Lenz* (1804–65), German physicist.]
Le·o[1] (lée-ō) *n.* **1.** A constellation in the Northern Hemisphere near Cancer and Virgo, containing the bright stars Regulus and Denebola. **2. a.** The fifth sign of the **zodiac** *(see).* Also called the "Lion". **b.** One born under this sign. [New Latin, from Latin *leō,* LION.]
Leo[2]. A name for a lion, as used by children and in folk tales. [Latin, lion.]
Leo I, Saint, known as Leo the Great (*c.* 400–461). Italian pope from 440–61. His negotiations with Attila in 452 and Gaiseric the Vandal in 455 saved Rome from barbarian invasions. *The Leonian Sacramentary,* the oldest existing form of the Roman missal, is named after him though probably not his work. His feast day is April 11.
Leo Minor *n.* A constellation in the Northern Hemisphere near Leo and Ursa Major.
Le·ón (lay-ón). Capital of León province in northwest Spain. It was the capital of the medieval kingdom of León, and is today a major tourist centre.
Le·o·nar·do da Vin·ci (lée-ə-nárdō də vínchi, láy-, -ō-, daa), also known as Leonardo (1452–1519). Italian artistic and scientific genius of the Renaissance. He trained in Florence under Verrocchio, and became engineer and adviser to Duke Ludovico Sforza in Milan, Cesare Borgia in Florence, and finally Francis I in Amboise in France. Few of his paintings survive, but among these are *The Virgin of the Rocks* (1485) and *Mona Lisa* (or *La Gioconda*) (1503).
Le·on·ca·val·lo (láy-ongka-vál-ō), **Ruggiero** (1858–1919). Italian composer. He wrote several operas, including *I Pagliacci* (1892), in the style of Italian *verismo,* or realism.
le·one (lee-ṓni) *n.* **1.** The basic monetary unit of Sierra Leone, equal to 100 cents. **2.** A note worth one leone. [From SIERRA LEONE.]
Le·o·nid (lée-ənid) *n., pl.* **-nids** or **Leonides** (li-ónni-deez). Any of the meteors constituting the shower that recurs annually in mid-November. [New Latin *Leōnidēs,* from Latin *Leō,* lion (the meteors seem to radiate from the constellation Leo).]
Le·on·i·das I (li-ónni-dass) (died 480 B.C.). King of Sparta. He led a handful of Spartans and Thespians in the heroic defence of the pass at Thermopylae in 480 B.C. during the Persian Wars. He was killed in the battle.
le·o·nine (lée-ə-nīn) *adj.* Of, pertaining to, or characteristic of a lion: *a leonine sigh.* [Middle English, from Old French *leonin(e),* from Latin *leōnīnus,* from *leō* (stem *leōn-*), LION.]
Le·o·nine (lée-ə-nīn) *adj.* Of or pertaining to any of the popes called Leo. [Latin *leōnīnus,* of Leo.]
Leonine verse *n.* **1.** A Latin verse of a type written in the Middle Ages, usually consisting of alternating hexameters and pentameters, each line having internal rhyme. **2.** A similar verse in English poetry. [After *Leo* or *Leonius,* medieval poet who used this verse.]
leop·ard (léppərd) *n.* **1.** A large feline mammal, *Panthera pardus,* of Africa and Asia, having a tawny coat with dark rosette-like markings. There is also a black colour variant. See **panther. 2.** Any of several similar felines, such as the cheetah or the snow leopard. **3.** The pelt or fur of a leopard. **4.** *Heraldry.* A lion in side view, having one forepaw raised and the head facing the observer. [Middle English *leopard, leupard,* from Old French, from Late Latin *leopardus,* from Late Greek *leopardos, leontopardos,* "lion pard" (it was thought to be a hybrid) : *leōn* (genitive *leontos*), LION + *pardos,* PARD.]
leop·ard·ess (léppərd-iss, -ess) *n.* A female leopard.
Le·o·par·di (láy-ō-pardee), **Giacomo, Count** (1798–1837). Italian poet. His *Canti* ("Songs") (1816–36) combine patriotic appeals against Austrian rule with lyrical nature poetry.
leopard lily *n.* A tall plant, *Lilium pardalinum,* of the western United States, having orange-red, dark-spotted flowers and long stamens.
leopard moth *n.* A moth, *Zeuzera pyrina,* having black-spotted white wings and larvae that damage trees by boring into the wood.
leop·ard's-bane (léppərdz-bayn) *n.* **1.** Any of several plants of the genus *Doronicum,* especially *D. plantagineum,* having rayed yellow flowers. **2.** Any of several similar or related plants.
Le·o·pold II (1835–1909). King of the Belgians (1865–1909). In 1885 he was given personal rule of the Congo Free State, established in that year at an international congress at Berlin. He imposed slavery on the natives in rubber plantations, and was forced by public opinion to hand over control to the Belgian government in 1908.
Léopoldville. See **Kinshasa.**
le·o·tard (lée-ətaard) *n.* A sleeveless, skin-tight garment worn by dancers, gymnasts, or the like. [After Jules *Léotard,* 19th-century French acrobat who popularised it.]
Le·pan·to, Battle of (li-pántō). A naval battle (1571) in a strait between the Gulf of Corinth and the Ionian Sea, in which Ottoman sea power was temporarily destroyed by a Christian armada.
Lep·cha (lépchə) *n., pl.* **-chas** or collectively **Lepcha. 1.** A member of a Mongoloid people living in Sikkim, India. **2.** The Tibeto-Burman language of this people.
lep·er (léppər) *n.* **1.** A person afflicted with leprosy. **2.** One who is spurned on moral or social grounds. [Middle English, from *leper,* leprosy, from Old French *lepre,* from Late Latin *lepra,* from Greek *lepra,* from *lepros,* scaly, from *lepos, lepis,* a scale.]
lepido-, lepid- *comb. form.* Indicates a scale or flake; for example, **lepidopteran.** [Greek *lepis* (stem *lepid-*), scale.]
le·pid·o·lite (li-píddə-līt, léppidə-) *n.* A lilac or pink to grey mica, $K_2Li_3Al_4Si_7O_2(OH,F)_3$, used as a lithium ore and in glass and ceramic production. [German *Lepidolith* : LEPIDO- + -LITH.]
lep·i·dop·ter·an (léppi-dóptərən) *n., pl.* **-terans** or **-tera** (-tərə). Also **lep·i·dop·ter·on** (-tərən, -təron) *pl.* **-tera** (-tərə). A lepidopterous insect. [New Latin *Lepidoptera,* "scale-winged ones" : LEPIDO- + -PTER.] **—lep·i·dop·ter·an** *adj.*
lep·i·dop·ter·ist (léppi-dóptərist) *n.* An entomologist specialising in the study of butterflies and moths.
lep·i·dop·ter·ous (léppi-dóptərəss) *adj.* Of or belonging to the order Lepidoptera, which includes the butterflies and moths, having four wings covered with small scales, and with caterpillars forming the larval stage.
lep·i·dote (léppi-dōt) *adj.* Covered with small scales. [Greek *lepidōtos,* from *lepis,* scale.]
lep·o·rine (léppə-rīn || -rin, -rən) *adj.* Of or characteristic of hares. [Latin *leporīnus,* from *lepus* (stem *lepor-*), hare.]
lep·re·chaun (léppra-kawn) *n.* In Irish folklore, any of a race of elves who are cobblers and have hidden treasure. [Earlier *lubrican,* from Irish *lupracán, leipracán,* from Middle Irish *luchrupán,* from Old Irish *luchorpán* : *lū,* small + *corp,* body, from Latin *corpus.*]
lep·ro·sar·i·um (léppra-sáir-i-əm) *n., pl.* **-ums** or **-saria** (-i-ə). A hospital for the treatment of lepers. [Medieval Latin, from Late Latin *leprōsus,* LEPROUS.]
lep·rose (lép-rōss, -rōz) *adj.* Scurfy or scaly; leprous. [Late Latin *leprōsus,* LEPROUS.]
lep·ro·sy (léppra-si) *n.* A chronic, infectious, granulomatous disease occurring chiefly in tropical and subtropical regions, caused by a bacillus, *Mycobacterium leprae,* and ranging in severity from noncontagious and spontaneously remitting forms to contagious, malignant forms with progressive anaesthesia, paralysis, ulceration, nutritive disturbances, gangrene, and mutilation. Also called "Hansen's disease". [From LEPROUS.] **—lep·rot·ic** (le-próttik) *adj.*
lep·rous (lépprəss) *adj.* **1.** Having leprosy. **2.** Of, pertaining to, or resembling leprosy. **3.** *Biology.* Having or consisting of loose, scurfy scales. [Middle English *lepro(u)s,* from Late Latin *leprōsus,* from *lepra,* leprosy. See **leper.**] **—lep·rous·ly** *adv.* **—lep·rous·ness** *n.*
-lepsy *n. comb. form.* Indicates a fit or seizure; for example, **narcolepsy.** [Greek *-lēpsia,* from *lēpsis,* taking, seizure, from *lambanein* (future stem *lēps-*), to take, seize.] **—-leptic** *adj. comb. form.*
lepto-, lept- *comb. form.* Indicates slender, thin, fine; for example, **leptocephalus, lepton.** [Greek *leptos,* peeled, fine, small, thin, from *lepein,* to peel.]
lep·to·ceph·a·lus (léptō-séff'l-əss) *n., pl.* **-li** (-lī). Any of the slender, transparent larvae of eels and certain other fishes. [New Latin, "slender-headed" : LEPTO- + -CEPHALOUS.]
lep·ton[1] (lép-ton) *n., pl.* **-ta** (-tə). **1.** A monetary unit equal to $^1/_{100}$ of the drachma of Greece. **2.** An ancient Greek coin. [Modern Greek, from Greek, small coin, from *leptos,* fine, small, from *lepein,* to peel.]

leopard *A large cat found throughout Africa and most of Asia, the leopard hunts at night, feeding on monkeys, rodents, birds, and dogs. It is normally solitary and generally waits in a tree to ambush its prey.*

lep·ton² *n., pl.* **-tons.** Any of a family of elementary particles including the electron, the muon, the tau particle, and their associated neutrinos, all having spin equal to ½ and masses less than those of the mesons. [LEPT(O)- + -ON.]

lepton number *n. Symbol* **L** *Physics.* A quantum number equal to the number of leptons in an interaction minus the number of antileptons. Each type of lepton has its own quantum number that is separately conserved.

lep·to·some (léptə-sōm) *n. Physiology.* A person with a slender, thin, or frail body. [German *Leptosom* : LEPTO- + -SOME (body).] —**lep·to·so·mat·ic** (-sōmáttik) *adj.*

lep·to·spi·ro·sis (léptō-spīr-ō-siss) *n.* An infectious disease caused by bacteria of the genus *Leptospira,* that may be transmitted to humans by contact with rodents, dogs, and other mammals, and is characterised by fever and either jaundice or meningitis. [New Latin *Leptospira* (LEPTO- + Greek *speira,* coil) + -OSIS.]

lep·to·spo·ran·gi·ate (léptō-spə-ránji-ət, -spaw-, -it, -ayt) *adj.* Of or pertaining to ferns in which the sporangium develops from a single cell. Compare **eusporangiate.**

lep·to·tene (lép-tə-teen, -tō-) *n. Biology.* The first stage of prophase in mitosis and meiosis when the nuclear material becomes visible as slender single-stranded threads. [LEPTO- + -tene, from Greek *taina,* band, thread.]

Lep·us (léppəss, léepəss) *n.* A constellation in the Southern Hemisphere near Orion and Columba. [New Latin, from Latin, hare.]

Le Puy (lə pwée). *French* **Le Puy en Ve·lay** (ON və-láy). The administrative centre of the Haute-Loire *département,* south central France, built around towering rock pinnacles. It is a liqueur and lace-making centre.

Lé·ri·da (láyreeda). Capital of Lérida province, Catalonia, northeast Spain. An ancient fortified city on the river Segre, it was taken by Julius Caesar (49 B.C.). The city commanded the approaches to Barcelona during the Spanish Civil War, and fell to the Nationalists in 1938 after a nine-month battle.

Ler·mon·tov (laír-montof || *Russian* -məntəf), **Mikhail Yuryevich** (1814–41). Russian writer. He wrote the novel *A Hero of Our Time* (1840), and many poems. He was killed in a duel.

Ler·ner (lérnər), **Alan Jay** (1918–). U.S. lyricist. He wrote musicals with the composer, Frederick Loewe, including *Brigadoon* (1947) and *My Fair Lady* (1956).

Ler·wick (lér-wik). Most northerly town in the British Isles, in Shetland, Scotland. It has a sheltered harbour with a fishing industry, and serves the North Sea oil industry.

Le Sage (lə saázh), **Alain René** (1668–1747). French writer. His novel *Gil Blas de Santillane* (1715-35) was one of the earliest examples of modern realistic fiction.

Leonardo da Vinci

THE MAN WHO WANTED TO KNOW EVERYTHING
How curiosity drove the artist who became the world's greatest designer

Leonardo da Vinci was one of the outstanding figures of the Renaissance – not only an artist of rare power, but a pioneering scientist as well. His devouring curiosity drove him to explore fields as diverse as anatomy, botany, geology, meteorology, physics, mathematics, geometry, and music. His architectural drawings explored design problems in buildings, harbours, irrigation systems and canals, but no building by him survives. He foretold the future with sketches of submarines, diving suits, tanks, parachutes, flying machines, machine guns, and cluster bombs. All these ideas and observations were recorded in voluminous notebooks; 7,000 pages survive, many annotated by the left-handed designer in mirror writing. Born in Vinci, a village near Florence, in 1452, Leonardo was the illegitimate son of a lawyer and a peasant girl. He died in France in 1519.

TANK PROTOTYPE *Leonardo's hand-cranked tank was never made, but its design foreshadowed the first tanks that were built some 400 years later.*

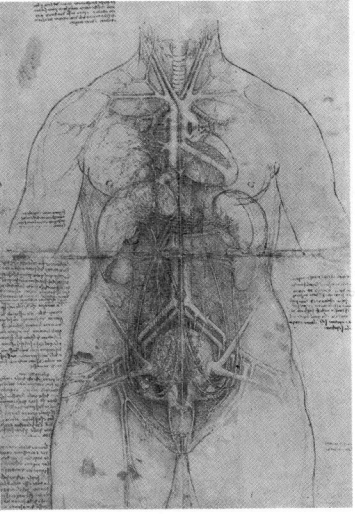

MASTER DRAUGHTSMAN *Few of Leonardo's major artistic works have survived complete and undamaged. Some, like* The Adoration of the Magi *(begun in 1481), were never finished. Others, like* The Last Supper *(1497), a mural in a Milan monastery, have deteriorated because Leonardo used unorthodox techniques. This drawing – of the* Virgin and Child with St. Anne and John the Baptist *– is a rare exception.*

ANATOMY OF ART *To sketch the internal layout of the human body, Leonardo dissected more than 30 corpses. Detailed notes on his painstaking observations are jotted down in his characteristic right-to-left mirror writing.*

PRONUNCIATION KEY

a, trap; aa, father; ai, fair;
ar, star; aw, lawn; ay, play;
b, bb, stab; rubber;
ch, church; ck, ticket;
d, dd, dead; ladder; e, dress;
ee, bee; er, defer; ew, few;
ewr, pure; ə, about;
ər, letter; f, ff, fife; differ;
g, gg, giggle; h, hat; i, kit;
ī, price; īr, fire; j, judge;
k, kick; l, ll, let; 'l, needle;
m, mm, man; n, nn, no;
'n, sudden; ng, thing; o, lot;
ō, no; ŏŏ, foot; ōō, shoe;
oor, poor; ow, cow;
owr, hour; oy, boy;
p, pp, pepper; r, rr, red;
s, ss, sauce; sh, ship;
t, tt, totter; th, thick; <u>th</u>, <u>th</u>is;
smooth; u, cut; ur, turn;
v, vv, valve; w, wet; y, yes;
z, zz, zebra; <u>zh</u>, vision;
pleasure

IN FOREIGN WORDS:

aN, oN, Saint-Saëns;
<u>hl</u>, <u>Ll</u>anelli; <u>Hl</u>uhluwe;
<u>kh</u>, loch; lough; <u>Kh</u>aled

STRESS MARK:

ín-sīt, insight; in-sīt, incite

les·bi·an (lézbi-ən) *n. Sometimes capital* **L.** A female homosexual.
~*adj. Sometimes capital* **L.** Of or pertaining to female homosexuals. [After LESBOS, alluding to the supposed homosexuality of Sappho who lived there.] **—les·bi·an·ism** *n.*

Les·bi·an (lézbi-ən) *n.* **1.** A native or resident of Lesbos. **2.** The Ancient Greek dialect of Lesbos, belonging to Aeolic, used in the lyric poetry of Sappho and Alcaeus.
~*adj.* **1.** Of or pertaining to Lesbos or its people. **2.** Of or pertaining to the Ancient Greek dialect of Lesbos. **3.** Of, pertaining to, or characteristic of Sappho, or her poetry.

Les·bos (lézboss). *Greek* **Lés·vos** (lézvoss). Mountainous Greek island off western Turkey, the home of Sappho and Aristotle.

lese majesty (leez) *n.* Also *French* **lèse ma·jes·té** (láyz mázhess-tay, léz, -táy). **1.** An offence or crime committed against the ruler or supreme power of a state; treason. **2.** The act or an instance of affronting another's dignity or overstepping authority. [Old French *lese-majeste,* from Latin *laesa mājestās,* "violated majesty" : *laesa,* past participle of *laedere,* to injure, damage, offend + MAJESTY.]

le·sion (léezh'n) *n.* **1.** A wound or injury. **2.** A circumscribed pathological alteration of tissue or an organ. **3.** A point or patch of a skin disease. [Middle English *lesioun,* from Old French *lesion,* from Latin *laesiō* (stem *laesiōn-*), from *laedere*†, to injure, damage.]

Le·so·tho, Kingdom of (li-sóotoo, lə-, -sōtō). Independent Commonwealth country, formerly Basutoland, surrounded by the Republic of South Africa. It became a British protectorate in 1868 and an independent kingdom in 1966. It is mountainous, but produces wheat and maize. Area, 30 355 square kilometres (11,720 square miles). Population, 1,400,000. Capital, Maseru. See map at **South Africa.**

less (less). Alternative comparative of **little.**
~*adj.* **1.** Not as great in extent, quantity, magnitude, or degree: *takes less sugar; needs less attention.* **2.** Lower in importance, esteem, or rank: *No less a person than a marquis is considered.* **—no less. 1.** Used, sometimes ironically, as a comment on a preceding statement, when surprised or impressed: *She's going to Oxford, no less.* **2.** None other: *The surprise guest turned out to be no less than the chairman himself.* —See Usage note at **fewer.**
~*adv.* To a smaller extent, degree, or frequency.
~*n.* A smaller amount. **—less of.** To stop or desist from. Used in the imperative: *Less of your cheek!*
~*prep.* Minus; subtracting: *Five less one is four.* [Middle English *less(e),* Old English *lǣssa* (adjective) and *lǣs* (adverb and noun), from Germanic *loisiz* (unattested), little.]

-less *adj. comb. form.* Indicates: **1.** Lack of, free of, not having, or without; for example, **toothless, sleepless, blameless. 2.** Not acting or able to be acted upon in a specified way; for example, **tireless, ceaseless, countless.** [Middle English *-les(se),* Old English *-lēas,* from *lēas,* lacking, free from.]

les·see (le-sée) *n.* One holding a lease. [Middle English, from Anglo-French *lessee,* variant of Old French *lesse,* past participle of *lesser,* to LEASE.] **—les·see·ship** *n.*

less·en (léss'n) *v.* **-ened, -ening, -ens.** *—tr.* **1.** To cause to decrease; make less. **2.** To make little of; minimise; belittle. *—intr.* To become less; decrease. —See Synonyms at **decrease.** [Middle English *lessenen,* from *lesse,* LESS.]

Les·seps (léssəps ‖ *French* le-séps), **Ferdinand Marie, Vicomte de** (1805–94). French engineer and diplomat. He planned and supervised construction of the Suez Canal, opened in 1869. His company began building the Panama Canal in 1881, but went bankrupt in 1888. The canal was completed by the U.S. government.

less·er (léssər) *adj.* Smaller or less in size, amount, value, or importance, especially in a comparison of two elements. [Middle English double comparative, from LESS.]

Lesser Antilles. A chain of islands in the West Indies, forming a barrier between the Atlantic Ocean and the Caribbean Sea. They are made up of the Leeward and Windward Islands. See map at **Latin America.**

lesser brethren *pl.n.* Those members of a group regarded as less important than the other members.

lesser celandine *n.* A plant, *Ranunculus ficaria,* having heart-shaped leaves and yellow flowers. Also called "pilewort".

lesser doxology *n.* The **Gloria Patri** *(see).*

lesser panda *n.* See **panda.**

Les·sing (léssing), **Doris (May)** (1919–). English novelist, born in Iran. She published her first novel, *The Grass is Singing,* in 1950, and her works include the semiautobiographical *Children of Violence* (1952–69), a five-volume series, and several science-fiction works such as *The Sirian Experiments* (1981).

Lessing, Gotthold Ephraim (1729–81). German dramatist and critic. He wrote the plays *Minna von Barnhelm* (1763), and *Nathan der Weise* (1779) which advocated tolerance.

les·son (léss'n) *n.* **1.** Something to be learned. **2. a.** A period of instruction; a class: *a tennis lesson.* **b.** The material taught in one such period. **3. a.** An experience or observation that imparts beneficial new knowledge or wisdom. **b.** The knowledge or wisdom learned in such a manner. **4.** A reprimand or punishment. **5.** A reading from the Bible or other sacred writing as part of a religious service.
~*tr.v.* **lessoned, -soning, -sons.** *Rare.* **1.** To teach a lesson or lessons to; instruct. **2.** To reprimand or punish. [Middle English *lesso(u)n,* a reading, lesson, from Old French *lecon,* from Latin *lectiō,* LECTION.]

les·sor (léssawr, le-sáwr) *n.* One who lets property under a lease; a landlord. [Middle English *lessour,* from Anglo-French, from *lesser,* to LEASE.]

lest (lest) *conj. Literary.* **1.** So as to prevent the possibility that; for fear that: *Tiptoe lest the guard should hear you.* **2.** That. Used after phrases denoting fear, worry, or the like: *anxious lest he should become ill.* [Middle English *leste,* short for *les the,* whereby less, Old English *thȳ lǣs the,* from *lǣs,* LESS.]

let[1] (let) *tr.v.* **let, letting, lets. 1.** Used as an auxiliary followed by an infinitive omitting *to:* **a.** To grant permission to; allow: *She let him continue.* **b.** To cause to. Used with *know* or *hear: He let me know the results.* **2.** Used as an auxiliary in the imperative: **a.** In order to convey a command, request, or proposal: *Let's finish the job!* **b.** In order to convey a warning or threat: *Just let her try!* **c.** In order to convey an assumption or hypothesis: *Let x equal y.* **d.** In order to convey acceptance of or resignation to the inevitable: *Let death come!* **3.** To permit to move or change in a specified manner: *let the dog through.* **4.** To rent or lease: *let a room to a bachelor.* **5.** To assign (a contract for work, for example): *let the construction job to a new firm.* **—let alone.** Not to speak of; much less: *Don't whisper, let alone speak.* **—let in.** To permit to enter: *They let in three goals.* **—let in for.** To involve in: *let them in for a lot of trouble.* **—let in on. 1.** To take into one's confidence; inform: *Were they let in on the secret?* **2.** To allow to participate: *Let him in on the robbery.* **—let into. 1.** To permit to enter or be inserted into. **2.** To take into one's confidence; inform. **—let on. 1.** To allow it to be known: *Don't let on that you helped me.* **2.** To pretend. [Middle English *leten,* Old English *lǣtan,* to leave behind, leave undone.]
Usage: In negative constructions, the form *let's not* has widespread currency in both British and American English speech. *Don't let's* is largely British; *let's don't* is to be found in American English, but is considered nonstandard. *Let* is followed by pronouns in their objective form: *Let Jane and me/him/us decide.* See also **leave.**

let[2] *n.* **1.** An obstacle. Used chiefly in the phrase *without let or hindrance.* **2.** *Sports.* **a.** In certain games such as tennis or squash, a small irregularity in the play that causes the point to be replayed. **b.** A point replayed for this reason.
~*tr.v.* **letted** or **let, letting, lets.** *Archaic.* To obstruct or hinder. [Middle English *let(te),* a hindrance, from *letten,* to hinder, prevent, Old English *lettan.*]

-let *n. suffix.* Indicates: **1.** Diminutive size or minor status; for example, **brooklet, starlet. 2.** An article worn on some part of the body; for example, **bracelet, anklet.** [Middle English *-lette,* from Old French *-elet* : noun ending *-el* + *-et(te),* -ETTE.]

letch. Variant of **lech.**

Letch·worth (léch-wərth, -wurth). Britain's first garden city. It lies in Hertfordshire and was planned in 1903 as an industrial and residential town surrounded by a rural belt.

let down *tr.v..* **1.** To take down; lower: *let down the sails.* **2.** To fail to satisfy; disappoint: *The mayor let down the electorate.* **3.** To undo so as to add length: *let down a dress; let down her hair.* **4.** To release air from: *let down tyres.*

let·down (lét-down) *n.* **1.** A slowing down, relaxing, or decrease, as of effort or energy. **2.** *Informal.* A disappointment. **3.** The descent made by an aircraft in order to land.

le·thal (léeth'l) *adj.* **1.** Sufficient to cause or capable of causing death. **2.** Of, pertaining to, or causing death. —See Synonyms at **fatal.** [Latin *lethālis,* from *lēthum,* death, variant of *lētum.*] **—le·thal·i·ty** (lee-thál-əti) *n.* **—le·thal·ly** *adv.*

lethal dose *n.* See **LD.**

lethal gene *n.* A gene that, under certain conditions, brings about the death of the organism carrying it, usually when its effect is not masked by a normal dominant gene.

lethargic encephalitis *n. Pathology.* **Encephalitis lethargica** *(see).*

leth·ar·gy (léthərji) *n.* **1.** Sluggish indifference or slowness; a feeling of laziness or lack of arousal. **2.** A state of unconsciousness resembling deep sleep, from which an individual can be roused but into which he at once relapses. [Middle English *litargie, letargie,* from Old French *litargie,* from Latin *lēthargia,* drowsiness, from Greek, from *lēthargos,* forgetful, from *lēthē,* forgetfulness.] **—leth·ar·gic** (le-thárjik, li-, lə-) *adj.* **—leth·ar·gic·al·ly** *adv.*
Synonyms: *lethargy, lassitude, sluggishness, torpor, languor.*

Le·the (léethi) *n. Greek Mythology* **1.** The river of forgetfulness in Hades. **2.** Oblivion; loss of memory. [Greek *lēthē,* forgetfulness (later personified).] **—Le·the·an** (li-thée-ən, léethi-) *adj.*

Le·to (léetō). *Greek Mythology.* A consort of Zeus and the mother of Apollo and Artemis.

let off *tr.v.* **1.** To emit or release: *let off steam.* **2.** To excuse or dismiss: *let the workmen off early.* **3.** To give little or no punishment to for an offence: *He was let off with a year on probation.* **4.** To detonate or fire: *let off a bomb.*

let-off (lét-off, -awff) *n.* An escape or reprieve: *a lucky let-off.*

let out *tr.v.* **1.** To release from confinement. **2.** To give forth, emit: *The dog let out a yelp.* **3.** To make known, (a secret, for example); reveal: *Who let that story out?* **4.** To increase the size of (a garment, for example). **5.** To rent or lease (buildings, land, or the like).

let-out (lét-owt) *n.* A way of escape; a loophole.

let's (lets). Contraction of *let us.*

Lett (let) *n.* A Latvian.

let·ter (lettər) *n.* **1.** A written symbol or character representing a speech sound; a component of an alphabet. **2.** A written or printed communication directed to an individual or organisation. **3.** *Often plural.* A formal or legal document giving information or granting rights to its bearer or recipient. **4.** The literal meaning of some-

PRONUNCIATION KEY

a, trap; aa, father; ai, fair; ar, star; aw, lawn; ay, play; b, bb, stab; rubber; ch, church; ck, ticket; d, dd, dead; ladder; e, dress; ee, bee; er, defer; ew, few; ewr, pure; ə, about; ər, letter; f, ff, fife; differ; g, gg, giggle; h, hat; i, kit; ī, price; īr, fire; j, judge; k, kick; l, ll, let; 'l, needle; m, mm, man; n, nn, no; 'n, sudden; ng, thing; o, lot; ō, no; o͝o, foot; o͞o, shoe; oor, poor; ow, cow; owr, hour; oy, boy; p, pp, pepper; r, rr, red; s, ss, sauce; sh, ship; t, tt, totter; th, thick; th, this; smooth; u, cut; ur, turn; v, vv, valve; w, wet; y, yes; z, zz, zebra; zh, vision; pleasure

IN FOREIGN WORDS:

aN, ON, Saint-Saëns; hl, Llanelli; Hluhluwe; kh, loch; lough; Khaled

STRESS MARK:

in-sīt, insight; in-sīt, incite

thing: *the letter of the law.* **5.** *Printing.* **a.** A piece of type that prints a single character. **b.** A specific style of type. **c.** The characters in one style of type. **6.** *Plural.* Honour, distinction, or the like, displayed in a written, abbreviated form: *letters after his name.* —**to the letter.** Precisely as directed, as when following orders. —*tr.v.* **lettered, -tering, -ters. 1.** To write letters on. **2.** To write in letters. [Middle English *letter, lettre,* from Old French *lettre,* from Latin *littera,* letter (of the alphabet), letter, document (in plural only).] —**let·ter·er** *n.*

letter bomb *n.* An explosive device that is thin enough to fit into a large envelope and is designed to explode when the envelope is opened.

let·ter·box, letter box (léttər-boks) *n.* **1.** A postbox (*see*). **2.** A slot in a front door, usually covered with a flap, through which post is delivered. **3.** A private box for receiving incoming letters. Also chiefly *U.S.* "mailbox".

letter card *n.* A card, often with a printed stamp, that has gummed edges and can be folded and sent as a letter.

let·tered (léttərd) *adj.* **1. a.** Educated to read and write; literate. **b.** Erudite; learned. **2.** Of or pertaining to literacy or learning. **3.** Inscribed or marked with letters.

let·ter·head (léttər-hed) *n.* **1.** The printed heading at the top of a sheet of writing paper, usually a person's address or the name and address of an organisation. **2.** Paper with such a printed heading.

let·ter·ing (léttəring) *n.* **1.** The act, process, or art of forming or inscribing with letters. **2.** The letters themselves.

letter of advice *n.* A letter containing specific information about a commercial transaction, as from a consignor to a consignee.

letter of credit *n. Abbr.* **l.c., L/C** A letter issued by a bank authorising the bearer or person named to draw a stated amount of money from it or its branches, or from associated banks or agencies.

let·ter·per·fect (léttər-pér-fikt, -fekt) *adj. Chiefly U.S.* Correct in every detail; word-perfect.

let·ter·press (léttər-press) *n.* **1. a.** The process of printing from a raised inked surface. **b.** Anything printed in this fashion. **2.** The text itself as distinct from illustrations or other ornamentation.

let·ters (léttərz) *n. Used with a singular verb.* Literary culture or learning; literature as a discipline or profession: *a man of letters.*

letters of administration *pl.n.* A legal document entrusting an individual with the administration of a deceased person's estate.

letters of credence *pl.n.* Also **letter of credence.** An official document conveying the credentials of a diplomatic envoy to a foreign government. Also called "letters credential".

letters of marque *pl.n.* Also **letter of marque. 1.** A document issued by a nation allowing a private citizen to seize citizens or goods of another nation. **2.** A document issued by a nation allowing a private citizen to equip a ship with arms in order to attack enemy ships. Also called "letters of marque and reprisal". [Middle English, from Old French *marque,* reprisal, from Old Provençal *marca,* from *marcar,* to seize as a pledge, from Germanic.]

letters patent *pl.n. Law.* A document issued by a government granting a patent to an inventor.

Let·tish (léttish) *adj.* Of or pertaining to the Latvians or their language.
—*n.* A language, **Latvian** (*see*).

let·tre de cac·het (léttrə də ka-sháy) *n., pl.* **lettres de cachet** (*pronounced as singular*). *French.* Formerly, a document issued or sanctioned by the French sovereign, granting powers of arrest or banishment without trial.

let·tuce (léttiss) *n.* **1.** Any of various plants of the genus *Lactuca;* especially, *L. sativa,* cultivated for its edible leaves. **2.** The leaves of *L. sativa,* eaten as salad. **3.** Any of various plants resembling lettuce, such as the sea lettuce. [Middle English *letus(e),* from Old French *laituës,* plural of *laituë,* from Latin *lactūca,* from *lac* (stem *lact-*), milk (from its milky juice).]

let up *intr.v.* **1.** To diminish; slacken; lessen. **2.** To stop.

let·up (lét-up) *n.* **1.** A slackening of pace, force, intensity, or effort; a slowdown. **2.** A temporary stop; a pause.

le·u (láy-ōō) *n., pl.* **lei** (lay). **1.** The basic monetary unit of Romania, equal to 100 bani. **2.** A coin worth one leu. [Romanian, "lion", from Latin *leō* (stem *leōn-*), LION.]

leu·cine (lōō-seen, léw-) *n.* An essential amino acid, $C_6H_{13}NO_2$, derived from the hydrolysis of protein by pancreatic enzymes. [LEUC(O)- + -INE.]

leu·cite (lōō-sīt, léw-) *n.* A white or grey mineral, consisting essentially of $KAl(SiO_3)_2$. [German *Leucit*: LEUC(O)- + -ITE.]

leuco-, leuc-, leuko- *comb. form.* Indicates: **1.** White or colourless; for example, **leucoderma, leucoplast. 2.** Leucocyte; for example, **leucopenia, leukaemia.** [New Latin, from Greek *leukos,* clear, white.]

leu·co base (lōōkō, léwkō) *n. Chemistry.* A colourless dyestuff produced by reducing a dye. It can be oxidised back to the original dye in the fabric. [Greek *leukos,* lacking colour, white.]

leu·co·cyte (lōōkə-sīt, léwkə-) *n.* Any of the white or colourless nucleated cells occurring in blood. Also called "white blood cell", "white corpuscle". [LEUCO- + -CYTE.] —**leu·co·cyt·ic** (-sittik) *adj.*

leu·co·cy·to·poi·e·sis (lōōkō-sītō-pay-ée-siss, léwks-) *n.* Leucopoiesis. [LEUCOCYT(E) + -POIESIS.] —**leu·co·cy·to·poi·et·ic** (-ettik) *adj.*

leu·co·cy·to·sis (lōōkō-sī-tō-siss, léwkō-) *n., pl.* **-ses** (-seez). A large increase in the number of leucocytes in the blood, generally in response to infection. [New Latin : LEUCOCYT(E) + -OSIS.] —**leu·co·cy·tot·ic** (-tóttik) *adj.*

leu·co·der·ma (lōōkō-dérmə, léwkō-) *n.* Partial or total lack of skin

pigmentation. Also called "vitiligo". [New Latin : LEUCO- + -DERMA.] —**leu·co·der·mal, leu·co·der·mic** *adj.*

leu·co·ma (lōō-kṓmə, lew-) *n.* A dense, white opacity of the cornea of the eye. [New Latin, from Greek *leukōma*: LEUC(O)- + -OMA.]

leu·co·pe·ni·a (lōōkō-péeni-ə, léwkō-) *n.* An abnormally low number of leucocytes in the blood. [New Latin : LEUCO- + -PENIA.]

leu·co·plast (lōōkō-plast, léwkō-) *n.* Also **leu·co·plas·tid** (-plásstid). A colourless plastid in the cytoplasm of plant cells, around which starch collects. [LEUCO- + PLAST(ID).]

leu·co·poi·e·sis (lōōkō-poy-ée-siss, léwkō-) *n.* The formation and development of leucocytes. Also called "leucocytopoiesis". [New Latin : LEUCO- + -POIESIS.] —**leu·co·poi·et·ic** (-éttik) *adj.*

leu·cor·rhoe·a (lōōkə-réeə, léwkə-, -rée-ə) *n.* A whitish or yellowish vaginal discharge containing mucus, which in excessive amounts may indicate infection of the lower reproductive tract. [New Latin : LEUCO- + -RRHOEA.]

leu·cot·o·my (lōō-kóttəmi, lew-) *n., pl.* **-omies.** The surgical interruption of certain of the nerve fibres in the brain to relieve severe emotional tension and other mental disorders, especially when all other treatment has failed. The original form of this operation was called "prefrontal lobotomy". [LEUCO- (referring to the white tissue of the frontal lobe) + -TOMY.]

leu·kae·mi·a (lōō-kéemi-ə, léwkō-) *n.* Any of a group of usually fatal diseases of the reticuloendothelial system, involving uncontrolled proliferation of leucocytes, which suppress the production of normal blood cells. [New Latin : LEUC(O)- + -AEMIA.]

leuko-. Variant of leuco-.

Leuven. See **Louvain.**

lev (lef) *n., pl.* **leva** (lévvə). *Abbr.* **L. 1.** The basic monetary unit of Bulgaria, equal to 100 stotinki. **2.** A coin worth one lev. [Bulgarian, "lion", from Old Bulgarian *livu,* probably from Old High German *lewo,* from Latin *leō,* LION.]

Lev. Leviticus (Old Testament).

Lev·al·loi·si·an (lévvə-lóyzi-ən) *adj.* Of or pertaining to a western European stage in lower Palaeolithic culture distinguished by the method of striking off flake tools from pieces of flint. [After *Levallois*-Perret, district near Paris.]

lev·al·lor·phan (li-vál-ər-fan) *n.* A drug used to counteract the slowing in breathing caused by narcotic pain relievers without reducing their analgesic effects. [*Levorotatory* + *all*yl + *morph*ine + *-an* (unsaturated carbon compound).]

le·vant¹ (li-vánt) *n.* A type of heavy, coarse-grained morocco leather often used in bookbinding. Also called "Levant morocco". [Originally imported from the LEVANT.]

le·vant² *intr.v.* **-vanted, -vanting, -vants.** To run away or abscond, usually leaving unpaid debts behind. [Slang use of LEVANT.]

Le·vant (li-vánt). A term for the countries bordering on the eastern Mediterranean. Preceded by *the.* [Middle English *levaunt,* "the Orient", from Old French *levant,* "rising" (said of the sun), present participle of *lever,* to rise, raise.]

le·vant·er (li-vántər) *n.* **1.** One who levants; an absconder. **2.** A strong easterly wind in the extreme west Mediterranean area. In this sense, also called "levante". **3.** *Capital L.* A Levantine.

le·van·tine (lévv'n-tīn, -teen || lə-vánt-) *n.* A strong, closely woven silk fabric. [Originally made in the LEVANT.]

Le·van·tine (lévv'n-tīn || -teen, lə-vánt-) *adj.* Of or pertaining to the Levant.
—*n.* **1.** A native or resident of the Levant. **2.** A ship from the Levant.

le·va·tor (li-váytər) *n., pl.* **levatores** (lévvə-táwr-eez || -tōr-). **1.** *Anatomy.* Any muscle that raises a part of the body. **2.** In surgery, an instrument for lifting the depressed part of a fractured skull. [New Latin, from Latin *levāre,* to raise.]

lev·ee¹ (lévvi, lə-vée) *n.* **1.** A natural embankment built up by a river. **2.** An embankment raised to prevent a river from overflowing. **3.** A small ridge or raised area bordering an irrigated field. **4.** *U.S.* A landing place on a river; a pier. [French *levée,* from Old French *levee,* "raising", from the past participle of *lever,* to raise.]

lev·ee² (lévvi, lévvay) *n.* **1.** A reception held by a monarch or other high-ranking person on rising from bed. **2.** A formal reception, as at a royal court. [French *levé,* variant of *lever,* rising, from *lever,* to rise.]

lev·el (lévv'l) *n.* **1. a.** Relative position or rank on a scale, as in a hierarchy, society, or other grouping. Also used in combination and adjectivally: *high-level talks between diplomats.* **b.** Loosely, any grade or step in a series or position on a range: *a deeper level of meaning; at the spiritual level.* **c.** A natural or proper position, place, or stage: *finally found her own level.* **2.** An amount, degree, standard, or value achieved: *a level of output; sound levels.* **3.** Position along a vertical axis; elevation; height: *the level of the windows.* **4. a.** A horizontal line or plane at right angles to the plumb or vertical. **b.** The position or height of such a line or plane: *eye level.* **5. a.** A flat, horizontal surface. **b.** A layer, as of land or rock. **6.** A tract of land of uniform elevation. **7. a.** A **spirit level** (*see*). **b.** A spirit level combined with a telescope, used in surveying. **c.** A computation of the difference in elevation between two points, using a spirit level. —**on a level with.** Equal to. —**on the level.** *Informal.* Without deception.
—*adj.* **1.** Having a flat, smooth surface. **2.** On a horizontal plane. **3.** Being at the same height as another; even. **4.** Poured or measured into a container so as to be even with its rim: *a level teaspoonful.* **5.** Being of the same degree or rank as another; equal.

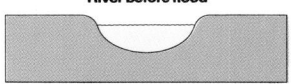

River before flood

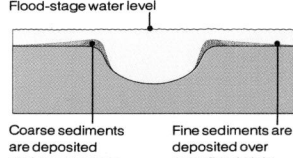

River during flood

Flood-stage water level

Coarse sediments are deposited at channel edges

Fine sediments are deposited over outer flood plain

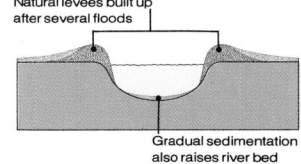

River after many floods

Natural levees built up after several floods

Gradual sedimentation also raises river bed

levee *Rivers which flood regularly can create natural levees. Each time the river bursts its banks, fine sediment is spread over the flood plain, but coarse sediment builds up along the banks. In places, natural levees along the Mississippi in the United States have built up to a height of 12 metres (40 feet) above the river's lowest level.*

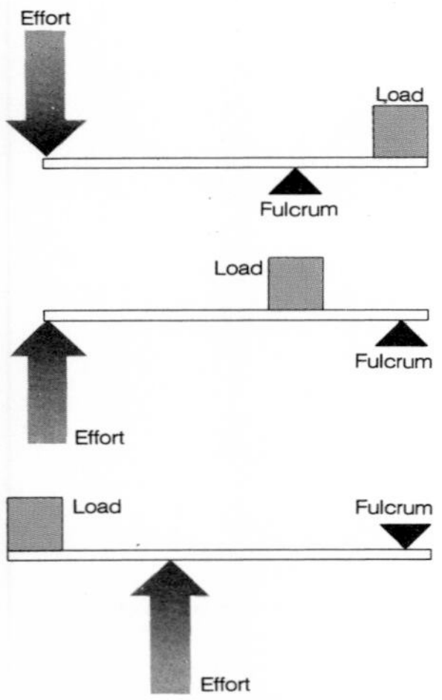

lever *There are three basic types of lever, which differ according to the relative positions of the pivot (or fulcrum), the effort and the load. In the first type (top), effort and load are on opposite sides of the fulcrum – as in a crowbar or see-saw. In the second (centre), the load is between effort and fulcrum – as in a wheelbarrow. In the third (bottom), the effort is between load and fulcrum. The forearm is an example; the elbow joint is the fulcrum and the effort is exerted by the biceps muscle, which pulls on the bones of the forearm to raise a load in the hand.*

6. Without abrupt variations; uniform; consistent. **—(one's) level best.** The best one is capable of doing.
~v. **levelled** or *U.S.* **-leveled, -elling** or *U.S.* **-eling, -els.** *—tr.* **1.** To make horizontal, flat, or even. Often used with *off.* **2.** To tear down; raze. **3.** To knock down with or as if with a blow. **4.** To put (two persons or things) in the same rank, degree, or plane. **5.** To aim along a horizontal plane: *levelled a gun at my head.* **6.** To direct (a gaze or remark, for example) emphatically or forcefully towards someone. **7.** To measure the different elevations of (a tract of land) with a level. *—intr.* **1.** To render persons or things equal, as in rank, importance, or size. **2.** To achieve or come to a level. **3.** To aim a weapon horizontally. **4.** *Chiefly U.S. Informal.* To be frank. Used with *with: Level with me on what happened.* **—level off** or **out. 1.** To move towards stability or consistency. **2.** To manoeuvre an aircraft into horizontal flight after gaining or losing altitude.
~adv. Along a flat or even line or plane. [Middle English *level, livel,* from Old French *livel,* from Vulgar Latin *libellum* (unattested), variant of Latin *lībella,* level, water level, plummet line, diminutive of *lībra,* "a pound", balance, level.] **—lev•el•ly** *adv.* **—lev•el•ness** *n.*
Synonyms: *level, flat, plane, even, smooth, flush.*

level crossing *n.* A place where a railway line crosses a road on the same level, usually having a protective barrier that closes the road when a train is coming. Also *U.S.* "grade crossing".

lev•el•head•ed (lévv'l-héddid) *adj.* Characteristically self-composed; sensible; calm. **—lev•el•head•ed•ly** *adv.* **—lev•el•head•ed•ness** *n.*

lev•el•ler, *U.S.* **lev•el•er** (lévv'l-ər) *n.* **1.** One that levels. **2.** One who advocates the abolition of social inequalities.

Lev•el•ler (lévv'l-ər) *n.* A member of an English radical political movement active in the 1640s that advocated universal male suffrage, parliamentary democracy, and religious tolerance.

lev•el•ling rod (lévv'l-ing) *n.* A graduated pole or stick with a movable marker, used with a surveyor's level to measure differences in elevation. Also called "levelling pole", "levelling staff".

level-pegging (lévv'l-pégging) *n.* A state of equality, especially between contestants.
~adj. Running equal in output, performance, or the like.

Le•ven, Loch (léev'n). Lake in southeast Tayside Region, Scotland. Mary, Queen of Scots was imprisoned on one of its seven islands, Castle Island, in the 16th century.

le•ver (léevər || *U.S. also* lévvər) *n.* **1.** A simple **machine** *(see)* consisting of a rigid body, typically a metal bar, pivoted on a fixed fulcrum. **2.** A projecting handle used to adjust or operate a mechanism. **3.** A means of advancement or accomplishment.
~v. **levered, -vering, -vers.** *—tr.* To move or lift with a lever. *—intr.* To use a lever. [Middle English *lever, levour,* from Old French *levier, leveor,* from *lever,* to raise, from Latin *levāre,* from *levis,* light.]

le•ver•age (léevərij || *U.S. also* lévvərij) *n.* **1.** The action of a lever. **2.** The mechanical advantage of a lever. **3.** Positional advantage; power to act effectively; influence.

lev•er•et (lévvərit) *n.* A young hare, especially one less than a year old. [Middle English, from Anglo-French, diminutive of *levre,* variant of Old French *lievre,* hare, from Latin *lepus* (stem *lepor-*).]

Le•ver•hulme (léevər-hewm), **William Hesketh Lever, 1st Viscount** (1851–1925). English soap magnate. He founded Lever Brothers (1884), developing "Sunlight", a soap made from vegetable oils rather than tallow. Lever became an M.P. in 1906, and was made a baron in 1917 and viscount in 1922.

Le•ver•rier (lə-vérri-ay), **Urbain Jean Joseph** (1811–77). French astronomer. He discovered the planet Neptune in 1846, independently of its discovery by the English astronomer, J.C. Adams.

Le•vesque (lə-véck), **René** (1922–). Canadian politician. In 1967 he co-founded the Parti Québecois, a French-Canadian separatist party. He became premier of Quebec in 1976.

Le•vi¹ (léevī). A son of Jacob and Leah. Genesis 29:34.

Levi² *n.* A tribe of Israel descended from Levi.

lev•i•a•ble (lévvi-əb'l) *adj.* **1.** Liable to be levied, as a tax is. **2.** Liable to be taxed or to have a levy imposed, as imports might be.

le•vi•a•than (li-vī́-əthən) *n.* **1.** A monstrous sea creature mentioned in the Old Testament. Job 41:1. **2.** Any very large animal. **3.** Anything unusually large for its kind. [Middle English, from Late Latin, from Hebrew *libhyāthān.*]

lev•i•gate (lévvi-gayt) *tr.v.* **-gated, -gating, -gates. 1.** To make into a smooth, fine powder, as by grinding when moist. **2.** To suspend in a liquid. **3.** To make smooth; polish.
~adj. Botany. Smooth; glabrous. [Latin *lēvigāre* : *lēvis,* smooth + *agere,* to do, make.] **—lev•i•ga•tion** (-gáysh'n) *n.*

lev•in (lévvin) *n. Archaic.* Lightning. [Middle English *leven(e),* probably from Scandinavian; akin to Old Swedish *liughn(elder),* lightning (flash).]

lev•i•rate (lévvi-rət, -rit) *n.* The practice of marrying the widow of one's brother, as required by ancient Hebrew law. Compare **sororate.** [Latin *lēvir,* husband's brother.] **—lev•i•rat•ic** (-ráttik), **lev•i•rat•i•cal** *adj.*

Le•vis (léevīz) *pl.n.* A trademark for snugly fitting trousers of heavy denim with rivets reinforcing points of strain.

Lé•vi-Strauss (lévvi-strówss; *French* -stráwss), **Claude** (1908–). French social anthropologist, born in Belgium. He is a leading exponent of the theory of structuralism, and believes that there are similar underlying patterns of social life in all cultures, resulting from the unconscious structure of the human mind.

lev•i•tate (lévvi-tayt) *v.* **-tated, -tating, -tates.** *—intr.* To rise into the air and float, in apparent defiance of gravity. *—tr.* **1.** To cause to rise into the air and float. **2.** To support (a patient with severe burns) on an **air bed** *(see).* [From LEVITY.] **—lev•i•ta•tion** (-táysh'n) *n.* **—lev•i•ta•tor** (-taytər) *n.*

Le•vite (léevīt) *n.* A member of the tribe of Levi, the men of which were assistants to the Temple priests.

Le•vit•i•cal (li-víttik'l) *adj.* Also **Le•vit•ic** (-víttik). **1.** Of or pertaining to the Levites. **2.** Of or pertaining to Leviticus.

Le•vit•i•cus (li-víttikəss) *n. Abbr.* **Lev.** The third book of the Old Testament, containing the Hebrew ceremonial laws.

lev•i•ty (lévvəti) *n., pl.* **-ties. 1.** Lightness of speech or manner, especially when inappropriate; frivolity. **2.** Changeableness; inconstancy. **3.** *Archaic.* Lack of weight; lightness; buoyancy. [Latin *levitās* (stem *levitat-*), from *levis,* light.]

levo-. *U.S.* Variant of **laevo-.**

le•vo•do•pa (léevə-dṓpə) *n.* Also *rare* **lae•vo•do•pa. L-dopa** *(see).*

lev•y (lévvi) *v.* **-ied, -ying, -ies.** *—tr.* **1.** To impose or collect (a tax, for example). **2.** To conscript into military service. **3.** To declare, begin, or wage (a war). *—intr.* To confiscate property, especially in accordance with a legal judgment.
~n., pl. **levies. 1.** The act or process of levying. **2. a.** The money, property, or number of soldiers levied. **b.** *Usually plural.* The men or troops levied. [Middle English *leve(e), levie,* from Old French *levee,* a raising, from *lever,* to raise.] **—lev•i•er** *n.*

lewd (lōōd, lewd) *adj.* **lewder, lewdest. 1.** Licentious; lustful. **2.** Obscene; indecent. **3.** *Obsolete.* Wicked. [Middle English *lew(e)d,* originally, ignorant, vulgar, Old English *lǣwede†,* lay (nonclergy).] **—lewd•ly** *adv.* **—lewd•ness** *n.*

Lew•es (lōō-iss, léw-). County town of East Sussex, England. The old market town grew around a Norman castle, still standing.

Lewes, George Henry (1817–78). English writer. His works include *Life of Goethe* (1855) and a five-volume philosophical work, *Problems of Life and Mind* (1874–79). He met George Eliot (Mary Ann Evans) in 1851 and lived with her from 1854.

lew•is (lōō-iss, léw-) *n.* A dovetailed iron tenon made of several parts and designed to fit into a dovetail mortise in a large stone so that it can be lifted by a hoisting apparatus. Also called "lewisson".

Lewis, Cecil Day. See **Day Lewis, Cecil.**

Lew•is (lōō-iss), **C(live) S(taples)** (1898–1963). British author and critic. His works include the medieval study, *The Allegory of Love* (1936), and the autobiographical *Surprised by Joy* (1954). He also wrote poems, theological works, space fantasies, and the famous children's fantasy series of Narnia tales.

Lewis, Sinclair (1855–1951). U.S. novelist. He satirised middle-class America in his 22 novels, including *Main Street* (1920), *Babbit* (1922), and *Elmer Gantry* (1927).In 1930 he became the first American to win a Nobel prize for literature.

Lewis, (Percy) Wyndham (1884–1957). English painter and author, born in the United States. In 1914–15 he edited with Ezra Pound the organ of the Vorticist movement, *Blast.* His writings include *The Apes of God* (1930) and *Self-Condemned* (1954).

Lewis acid *n. Chemistry.* A compound capable of accepting a pair of electrons from a donor to form a coordinate bond. [After G.N. *Lewis* (1875–1946), U.S. chemist.]

Lewis base *n. Chemistry.* A compound capable of donating a pair of electrons to an acceptor to form a coordinate bond. [After G.N. *Lewis* (see **Lewis acid**).]

Lew•i•sham (lōō-ishəm). Borough in Greater London, England.

Lewis with Harris. Largest and most northerly island in the Outer Hebrides off northwest Scotland, now part of Western Isles Region. Lewis is low-lying, Harris mountainous. The largest town is Stornoway. Harris tweed is spun and woven by the island crofters.

lex (leks) *n., pl.* **leges** (léejeez). A law or system of laws. [Latin *lēx.*]

lex. lexicon.

lex•eme (lék-seem) *n.* An abstract linguistic unit, posited as the smallest vocabulary unit in the semantic system of a language, consisting typically of: **1.** A word root abstracted from its inflections, such as *run-* in the group *runs, running, runner.* **2.** A set consisting of a word together with all its inflections and derivations. **3.** An idiomatic phrase that makes no sense when broken down into its components, such as *to kick the bucket* ("to die").

lex•i•cal (lék-sik'l) *adj.* **1.** Of or pertaining to the vocabulary, words, or morphemes of a language. **2.** Of, pertaining to, or appropriate to lexicography or a lexicon. [From LEXICON.]

lex•i•cog•ra•pher (léksi-kóggrəfər) *n.* One who writes, compiles, or edits a dictionary.

lex•i•cog•ra•phy (léksi-kóggrəfi) *n.* The writing or compilation of a dictionary or dictionaries. [LEXICO(N) + -GRAPHY.] **—lex•i•co•graph•ic** (-kə-gráffik), **lex•i•co•graph•i•cal** *adj.* **—lex•i•co•graph•i•cal•ly** *adv.*

lex•i•col•o•gy (léksi-kólləji) *n.* The study of the lexical component of language. [LEXICO(N) + -LOGY.] **—lex•i•co•log•i•cal** (-kə-lójik'l) *adj.* **—lex•i•co•log•i•cal•ly** *adv.* **—lex•i•col•o•gist** *n.*

lex•i•con (lék-si-kən || -kon) *n. Abbr.* **lex. 1.** A dictionary, especially of an ancient language such as Latin or Hebrew. **2.** A vocabulary of terms used in or of a particular profession, subject, or style; a specialised list of terms: *the lexicon of the sports page.* **3.** *Linguistics.* The morphemes of a language. [New Latin, from Greek *lexikon (biblion),* (book) pertaining to words, from *lexis,* speech, word, phrase, from *legein,* to speak.]

lex•i•gra•phy (lek-síggrəfi) *n.* A system of writing, such as that of Chinese, in which each word is represented by a single character or symbol. [Greek *lexis,* word (see **lexis**) + -GRAPHY.] **—lex·i·graph·ic** (-gráffik) *adj.* **—lex·i·graph·ic·al·ly** *adv.*

lex·is (léksiss) *n.* Vocabulary; the total set of words in a language. [Greek, word, from *legein,* to speak.]

lex ta·li·o·nis (tál-i-ṓ-niss) *n.* The principle of retribution according to which the punishment matches the offence in nature and severity, as encapsulated in such phrases as "an eye for an eye". [New Latin, "law of retaliation".]

ley. Variant of **lea** (meadow).

Leyden. See **Leiden.**

Ley·den jar (lī́d'n) *n.* An early form of capacitor, consisting of a glass jar lined inside and out with tinfoil and having a conducting rod connected to the inner foil lining and passing out of the jar through an insulated stopper. [After LEYDEN (Leiden), where it was invented (1745).]

ley farming *n.* The rotation, or alternate growing, of crops and grass on arable land.

Ley·land cypress (láy-lənd, -land) *n.* A fast-growing hybrid conifer tree, *Cupressocyparis leylandii.* [After C. J. *Leyland* (1849–1926), British botanist.]

ley lines (lay || lee) *pl.n.* Straight lines linking hilltops, tumuli, church sites, and other traditional places of sanctity in the British isles. They sometimes appear to correspond with prehistoric tracks. [From LEY, variant of LEA (grassland) : the lines are supposed to have demarcated ancient meadows.]

lf, l.f. **1.** *Printing.* lightface. **2.** low frequency.

LG, L.G. Low German.

lg., lge. large.

LH luteinising hormone.

Lha·sa or **Las·sa** (laá-sə, lá-). Capital of the Tibet Autonomous Region, southwest China. Formerly the national capital of Tibet and centre of Tibetan Buddhism, it had numerous monasteries, temples, and convents, many of which were closed or razed following the Tibetan revolt against the Chinese in 1959. Until 1904 Lhasa was closed to foreign visitors, and known as the "Forbidden City".

Lhasa ap·so (ápsō) *n.* A small dog of a Tibetan breed, having a long, straight coat. [LHASA + Tibetan *apso,* Lhasa apso.]

li (lee) *n., pl.* **li.** A traditional Chinese measure of distance, today standardised at 500 metres (547 yards). [Chinese *lǐ.*]

Li The symbol for the element lithium.

li·a·bil·i·ty (lī́-ə-bílləti) *n., pl.* **-ties. 1.** Something for which one is liable; an obligation or debt. **2.** *Plural.* The financial obligations entered in the balance sheet of a business enterprise. Compare **assets. 3.** A hindrance; a handicap. **4.** Likelihood.

li·a·ble (lī́-əb'l) *adj.* **1.** Legally obliged; responsible. Used with *for: liable for military service.* **2.** Susceptible; subject. Used with *to: liable to fainting fits.* **3.** Likely; apt. Used with an infinitive: *You're liable to get hurt if you fall for her.* —See Synonyms at **responsible.** [Middle English, perhaps from Anglo-French *liable* (unattested), from Old French *lier,* to bind, from Latin *ligāre.*]

li·aise (li-áyz) *intr.v.* **-aised, -aising, -aises.** To contact and communicate, often on a regular or official basis; effect a liaison. Often used with *with* or *between.* [Back-formation from LIAISON.]

li·ai·son (li-áy-z'n, -zon, -ZON) *n., pl.* **-sons. 1.** An instance or means of communication between bodies, groups, or units. **2. a.** A close relationship. **b.** A sexual relationship. **3.** The pronunciation of the usually silent final consonant of a word when followed by a word beginning with a vowel. **4.** In cookery, a thickening agent, such as egg yolks or cream, for sauces, soups, or the like. [French *liaison,* "binding", from Old French, from *lier,* to bind.]

li·an·a (li-aánə || -ánnə) *n.* Also **li·ane** (-aán || -án). Any of various high-climbing, usually woody vines common in the tropics. [French *liane,* perhaps from *lier,* to bind.]

li·as (lī́-əss) *n.* **1.** A pale grey, clayey limestone, usually found with clays and shales, particularly in southwest England. Also used adjectivally: *lias limestone.* **2.** *Capital* **L.** The earliest series of rocks formed in the Jurassic period, consisting of beds of sandstone, clay, lias limestone, and shale, and often containing ammonite fossils. [Middle English, from Old French *liais,* a kind of limestone, probably from Germanic.] **—li·as, li·as·sic** (lī-ássik) *adj.*

lib (lib) *n. Informal.* Liberation. Often used as an abbreviation in titles such as *animal lib* or *gay lib,* and sometimes considered to be offensive, as in *women's lib.*

lib. 1. liberal. **2.** librarian; library.

Lib. Liberal.

li·ba·tion (lī-báysh'n) *n.* **1. a.** The pouring of a liquid offering as a religious ritual. **b.** The liquid poured. **2.** *Informal.* An intoxicating drink. [Middle English *libacioun,* from Latin *lībātiō* (stem *lībātiōn-*), from *lībāre,* to taste, pour out as an offering.]

lib·ber (líbbər) *n. Informal.* **1.** A feminist. Used derogatorily. **2.** A member of or a believer in any of various liberation movements. Usually used in combination: *a gay libber.* [From LIB.]

Lib·by (líbbi), **Willard Frank** (1908–80). U.S. chemist. He developed the method of radiocarbon dating. He won the Albert Einstein award (1959) and the Nobel prize in chemistry (1960).

li·bec·ci·o (li-béchi-ō) *n.* A southwest wind in Italy. [Italian, from Latin *Libs,* the southwest wind, from Greek *Lips*† (stem *lib-*).]

li·bel (lī́b'l) *n.* **1.** *Law.* **a.** Any written, printed, or pictorial statement that damages a person by defaming his character or reputation. **b.** The act of presenting such a statement to the public. Compare **slander. 2.** Any slighting statement. **3.** The written claims presented by a plaintiff to an ecclesiastical court.

~tr.v. **libelled** or *U.S.* **-libeled, -belling** or *U.S.* **-beling, -bels. 1.** To make or publish a defamatory statement about. **2.** To speak slightingly of. **3.** To make a claim or bring an action against in an ecclesiastical court. —See Synonyms at **malign.** [Middle English, formal written claim of a plaintiff, from Old French *libel,* from Latin *libellus,* a little book, diminutive of *liber,* book.] **—li·bel·ist, li·bel·ler** *n.*

li·bel·lant, *U.S.* **li·bel·ant** (lī́b'l-ənt) *n.* The plaintiff in a case of ecclesiastical libel.

li·bel·lous, *U.S.* **li·bel·ous** (lī́b'l-əss) *adj.* Containing or constituting a libel; defamatory. **—li·bel·lous·ly** *adv.*

lib·er·al (líbbrəl, líbbərəl) *adj. Abbr.* **lib. 1.** Having, expressing, or following social or political views or policies that favour nonrevolutionary progress and reform. **2. a.** Having, expressing, or following views or policies that favour the freedom of individuals to act or express themselves in a manner of their own choosing. **b.** Having, expressing, or following a belief in laissez-faire economic policies. **3.** *Capital* **L.** *Abbr.* **Lib.** Of, designating, or belonging to a Liberal political party. **4.** Of, pertaining to, or designating a wide cultural education, as opposed to a technical or specialised one. **5.** Tolerant of the ideas or behaviour of others. **6. a.** Tending to give freely; generous: *a liberal benefactor.* **b.** Generously given; bountiful: *a liberal helping.* **7.** Not strict or literal: *a liberal translation.*

~n. **1.** A person with liberal ideas or opinions. **2.** *Capital* **L.** *Abbr.* **Lib.** A member of a Liberal political party. [Middle English, from Old French, from Latin *līberālis,* of freedom, from *līber,* free.] **—lib·er·al·ly** *adv.* **—lib·er·al·ness** *n.*

liberal arts *pl.n.* Academic disciplines, such as languages, history, philosophy, and pure science, that provide information of general cultural concern, as distinguished from narrow practical training.

lib·er·al·ise, lib·er·al·ize (líbbrə-līz, líbbərə-) *v.* **-ised, -ising, -ises.** *—tr.* To make liberal or more liberal. *—intr.* To become liberal or more liberal. **—lib·er·al·i·sa·tion** (-ī-záysh'n || *U.S.* -i-) *n.*

lib·er·al·ism (líbbrə-líz'm, líbbərə-) *n.* Liberal views and policies, especially with regard to social or political questions.

lib·er·al·i·ty (líbbə-rál-əti) *n., pl.* **-ties. 1.** The quality or state of being liberal. **2.** A generous gift.

Liberal Party *n.* A political party advocating liberalism; especially, a party formed in Great Britain in the 19th century.

liberal studies *n. Usually used with a singular verb.* An arts course consisting of literature, social studies, and the like, taken by students undergoing further education whose main courses are usually technical, professional, or scientific.

lib·er·ate (líbbə-rayt) *tr.v.* **-ated, -ating, -ates. 1.** To free, as from oppression, repression, bondage, or foreign control. **2.** *Chemistry.* To release from combination. Used especially of gases. **3.** *Slang.* To obtain by looting; steal. In this sense, used ironically. [Latin *līberāre,* from *līber,* free.] **—lib·er·a·tion** (-ráysh'n) *n.* **—lib·er·a·tion·ist** *n.* **—lib·er·a·tor** (-raytər) *n.*

liberation theology *n.* A school of theology, especially prevalent in the Catholic Church in Latin America, seeing in the Gospel a call to liberate people from political and material oppression.

Li·be·ri·a, Republic of (lī-beér-i-ə). Africa's oldest independent republic, founded as a home for freed U.S. slaves early in the 19th century. It has a large flag-of-convenience merchant navy. Most Liberians are subsistence farmers, although the country exports iron ore, rubber, rice, coffee, and sugar. Area 111 369 square kilometres (43,000 square miles). Population 2,000,000. Capital, Monrovia. **—Li·be·ri·an** *n. & adj.*

lib·er·tar·i·an (líbbər-taír-i-ən) *n.* **1.** One who believes in freedom, especially individual freedom, of action and thought. **2.** One who believes in free will as opposed to determinism. [From LIBERTY.] **—lib·er·tar·i·an** *adj.* **—lib·er·tar·i·an·ism** *n.*

lib·er·tine (líbbər-teen, -tin, -tīn) *n.* **1.** One who acts without moral or sexual restraint; a dissolute person. **2.** One standing in defiance of established moral precepts.

~adj. Morally or sexually unrestrained. [Middle English *libertyn* (only in the sense "freed slave"), from Latin *lībertīnus,* from *lībertus,* set free, from *līber,* free.]

lib·er·tin·ism (líbbərti-niz'm) *n.* Also **lib·er·tin·age** (-nij). **1.** Sexual promiscuity. **2.** *Rare.* Freedom of thought.

lib·er·ty (líbbərti) *n., pl.* **-ties. 1. a.** The condition of being not subject to restriction or control. **b.** The right to act in a manner of one's own choosing. **2.** The state of not being in confinement or servitude. **3.** Permission or right to do a specific thing; a privilege. **4.** *Often plural.* **a.** A social action regarded as more familiar than polite convention permits: *Is it a liberty to address you by your first name?* **b.** A statement, attitude, or action not warranted by conditions or actualities: *a historical novel that takes liberties with chronology.* **5.** Authorised leave from naval duty. **—at liberty. 1.** Not in confinement or under constraint; free. **2.** Not occupied or in use. [Middle English *liberte,* from Old French, from Latin *lībertās* (stem *lībertāt-*), from *līber,* free.]

liberty bodice *n. Sometimes capital* **L.** A trademark for an item of underwear for women and children, similar to a sleeveless vest, and usually made of thick cotton with buttons down the front.

liberty cap *n.* **1.** A brimless cap that fits snugly around the head and has a soft conical crown. Compare **Phrygian cap. 2.** A **magic mushroom** *(see).* [Adopted as a symbol of liberty during the French Revolution. In ancient Rome such caps were presented to slaves when they were freed.]

liberty hall *n. Informal.* **1.** A place in which one can behave as one likes. **2.** A state of absolute freedom.

PRONUNCIATION KEY

a, trap; aa, father; ai, **fair**; ar, **star**; aw, **lawn**; ay, **play**; b, bb, **stab**; **rubber**; ch, **church**; ck, **ticket**; d, dd, **dead**; **ladder**; e, **dress**; ee, **bee**; er, **defer**; ew, **few**; ewr, **pure**; ə, **about**; ər, **letter**; f, ff, **fife**; **differ**; g, gg, **giggle**; h, **hat**; i, **kit**; ī, **price**; īr, **fire**; j, **judge**; k, **kick**; l, ll, **let**; 'l, **needle**; m, mm, **man**; n, nn, **no**; 'n, **sudden**; ng, **thing**; o, **lot**; ō, **no**; ŏŏ, **foot**; ōō, **shoe**; oor, **poor**; ow, **cow**; owr, **hour**; oy, **boy**; p, pp, **pepper**; r, rr, **red**; s, ss, **sauce**; sh, **ship**; t, tt, **totter**; th, **thick**; th, **this**; **smooth**; u, **cut**; ur, **turn**; v, vv, **valve**; w, **wet**; y, **yes**; z, zz, **zebra**; zh, **vision**; **pleasure**

IN FOREIGN WORDS:

aN, oN, **Saint-Saëns**; hl, **Llanelli**; **Hluhluwe**; kh, **loch**; **lough**; **Khaled**

STRESS MARK:

ín-sīt, insight; in-sī́t, incite

liberty ship *n.* A large U.S. cargo ship of a type produced in large numbers during World War II.

li·bid·i·nous (li-bíddinəss) *adj.* Characterised by or having lustful desires; licentious; lascivious. [Middle English *lybydynous*, from Latin *libīdinōsus*, from *libīdō*, desire, LIBIDO.]

li·bi·do (li-bée-dō, -bī-, libbi-dō) *n., pl.* **-dos. 1.** The psychic and emotional energy associated with instinctual biological drives. **2. a.** Sexual desire. **b.** Manifestation of the sexual drive. [Latin *libīdō*, desire, lust.] —**li·bid·i·nal** (li-biddin'l) *adj.*

li·bra (lí-brə *for sense 1;* lée-brə *for sense 2) n., pl.* **-brae** (-bree) (for sense 1) or **-bras** (-brəz) (for sense 2). **1.** A unit of weight in ancient Rome corresponding to a pound and equivalent to approximately 12 ounces. **2.** A former gold coin of Peru. [Latin *libra*, "pound", balance.]

Li·bra (lée-brə, lí-, libbrə) *n.* **1.** A constellation in the Southern Hemisphere near Scorpius and Virgo. **2. a.** The seventh sign of the **zodiac** *(see).* Also called the "Balance", the "Scales". **b.** One born under this sign. [New Latin, from Latin *libra*, balance. See **libra**.] —**Lib·ran** *n. & adj.*

li·brar·i·an (lī-bráir-i-ən) *n. Abbr.* **lib. 1.** A person in charge of a library. **2.** One trained or employed in library administration.

li·brar·i·an·ship (lī-bráir-i-ən-ship ‖ *U.S.* -brérri-) *n. Chiefly British.* The principles or practice of library administration.

li·brar·y (lí-brəri, -bri ‖ *U.S.* -brerri) *n., pl.* **-ies.** *Abbr.* **lib. 1.** A repository for literary and artistic materials, such as books, periodicals, newspapers, pamphlets, and prints, kept for reading or reference. **2.** A collection of such material, especially when systematically arranged for reference or borrowing. **3. a.** An institution or foundation maintaining such a collection. **b.** A room in a private home set aside to house such a collection. **4.** A series or set of books issued by a publisher. **5.** A collection of standard computer programs. [Middle English *librarie*, from Old French *librairie*, from Vulgar Latin *librāriā* (unattested), alteration of Latin *librāria (taberna)*, book (shop), from *liber†*, book.]

library edition *n.* A special edition of a book, usually large, strongly bound, and of superior quality.

Library of Congress classification *n.* A system of classification of books and other publications using a notation of letters of the alphabet and numbers. Compare **Dewey Decimal System.** [After the *Library of Congress,* the national library of the United States in Washington, D.C. founded in 1800.]

library science *n.* Librarianship.

li·brate (lī-bráyt ‖ lí-brayt) *intr.v.* **-brated, -brating, -brates. 1.** To oscillate; undergo libration. **2.** To balance; hover. [Latin *librāre* (past participle *librātus*), from *libra*, balance.] —**li·bra·to·ry** (-əri, líbrə-tri) *adj.*

li·bra·tion (lī-bráysh'n) *n.* A real or apparent very slow oscillation of a satellite as viewed from its parent celestial body.

li·bret·tist (li-bréttist) *n.* The author of a libretto.

li·bret·to (li-bréttō) *n., pl.* **-tos** or **-bretti** (-bréttee). The text of an opera or other dramatic musical work. [Italian, diminutive of *libro*, book, from Latin *liber †.*]

Li·bre·ville (lée·brə-vil). Capital and chief port of Gabon, lying on the Gabon river estuary. It was founded as a French trading post, and renamed Libreville (1848) after freed slaves were settled there.

Lib·y·a (líbbi-ə, líb-yə). Also **Socialist People's Libyan Arab Jamahiriya.** Republic in North Africa, the first independent state created by the United Nations (1951). Oil discoveries brought great prosperity in the 1970s, and the nationalised oil industry remains the basis of the economy. In 1969 King Idris was deposed by Colonel Gaddafi, and the country has since been run as an Islamic state. Area, 1 759 540 square kilometres (679,362 square miles). Population 3,200,000. Capital, Tripoli.

Lib·y·an (líbbi-ən, Líb-yən) *adj.* Of or pertaining to Libya, its people, or their language.
~*n.* **1.** A native or resident of Libya. **2.** The extinct Hamitic language used in ancient Libya.

lice. Plural of **louse.**

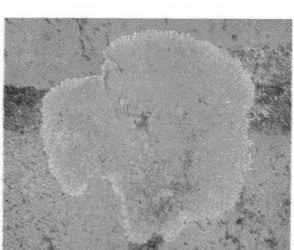

lichen *The lichens – symbiotic plants formed by a partnership between fungi and algae – can survive and thrive in almost any climate. Some flourish even under snow, providing an important food source for animals such as reindeer.*

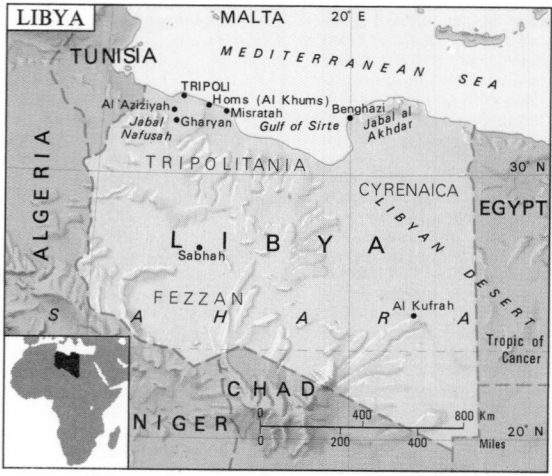

li·cence, *U.S.* **li·cense** (lí-s'nss) *n.* **1.** Official or legal permission to do or own a specified thing. **2.** Proof of permission granted, usually in the form of a document, card, or plate: *a television licence.* Compare **certificate. 3.** Deviation from normal rules, practices, or methods in order to achieve a certain end or effect: *artistic licence.* **4.** An instance of such deviation. **5.** Freedom from strict rules, especially concerning behaviour or speech. **6.** Excessive or undisciplined freedom constituting an abuse of a privilege. **7.** Lust; licentiousness. [See **license.**]

Usage: The spelling of *licence* and *license* is often confused in British English (not so in American English, where *license* is the normal form in all uses). *Licence* is the noun; *license* is the correct form for the verb and derivative uses (as in *licensed premises).*

li·cense (lí-s'nss) *tr.v.* **-censed, -censing, -censes. 1.** To give or yield permission to or for. **2.** To grant a licence to or for; authorise. **3.** To obtain a licence for: *Have you licensed the car yet?* [Middle English *licence*, from Old French *licence*, from Latin *licentia*, freedom, from *licēre*, to be lawful, be permitted. See **leisure.**] —**li·cens·a·ble** *adj.* —**li·cen·ser, li·cen·sor** *n.*

licensed premises *pl.n.* A place, such as a public house or hotel, licensed to sell alcohol to be consumed there. Compare **off-licence.**

li·cen·see (lí-s'n-sée) *n.* One to whom a licence is granted; especially, one licensed to sell beer and spirits.

li·cen·ti·ate (lī-sénshi-ət, -it ‖ li-) *n.* **1. a.** A person who is granted a licence by an authorised body to practise a specific profession. **b.** A person licensed to preach, especially in the Presbyterian Church. **2.** *Abbr.* **L. a.** A degree from certain European universities ranking below that of a doctorate. **b.** One holding such a degree. [Medieval Latin *licentiātus*, from *licentiāre*, to allow, from Latin *licentia*, freedom, LICENCE.]

li·cen·tious (lī-sénshəss) *adj.* **1.** Lacking moral discipline or sexual restraint. **2.** Having no regard for accepted rules or standards. [Latin *licentiōsus*, from *licentia*, freedom, dissoluteness, LICENCE.] —**li·cen·tious·ly** *adv.* —**li·cen·tious·ness** *n.*

lichee. Variant of **lychee.**

li·chen (líkən, líchən) *n.* **1.** Any of numerous plants consisting of a fungus, usually of the class Ascomycetes, in close combination with certain algae, characteristically forming a crustlike, scaly, or branching growth on rocks or tree trunks. **2.** *Pathology.* Any of various skin eruptions occurring primarily in lichen-like patches. ~*tr.v.* **lichened, -chening, -chens.** To cover with lichen or lichens. [Latin *līchēn*, from Greek *leikhēn*, "licker", from *leikhein*, to lick.] —**li·chen·ose** (-ōss, -ōz), **li·chen·ous** *adj.*

li·chen·ol·o·gy (līkə-nólləji) *n.* The botanical study of lichens. —**li·chen·ol·o·gist** *n.*

lich gate, lych gate (lich) *n.* A roofed gateway to a churchyard used originally to rest biers before burial. [Middle English *lycheyaţe* : *lich*, body, corpse, Old English *līc* + *gate, yate,* GATE.]

Lich·ten·stein (líktən-stīn, -steen), **Roy** (1923–). U.S. painter and sculptor. He is a leading exponent of Pop art.

lic·it (líssit) *adj.* Within the law; legal. [Middle English, from Latin *licitus*, from the past participle of *licēre*, to be permitted. See **leisure.**] —**lic·it·ly** *adv.* —**lic·it·ness** *n.*

lick (lik) *v.* **licked, licking, licks.** —*tr.* **1.** To pass the tongue over or along. **2.** To lap up. **3.** To move or flicker over like a tongue: *The waves licked the rocks lining the shore.* **4.** *Informal.* To thrash; whip. **5.** *Informal.* To get the better of; defeat. —*intr.* **1.** To pass over something with or as if with the tongue: *The flames licked at our feet.* **2.** To move rapidly. ~*n.* **1.** The act or process of licking. **2.** A small quantity; a bit: *a lick of paint.* **3.** A place frequented by animals that lick the exposed natural salt deposits. **4.** *Informal.* A blow. **5.** *Informal.* Speed; pace: *at a good lick.* —**lick and a promise.** A quick and not very thorough wash. [Middle English *licken*, Old English *liccian.*] —**lick·er** *n.*

lick·er·ish, li·quor·ish (líckərish) *adj. Archaic.* **1.** Lascivious; lecherous. **2.** Relishing pleasurable sensations. **3.** Greedy. **4.** Arousing hunger; appetising. [Alteration of Middle English *lickerous*, from Anglo-French *likerous* (unattested), variant of Old French *lechereus*, from *lecheor*, LECHER.]

lick·e·ty-split (lícketi-split) *adv. Chiefly U.S. Informal.* With great speed. [From LICK and SPLIT.]

lick·ing (lícking) *n. Informal.* **1.** A beating or spanking. **2.** A resounding defeat.

lick·spit·tle (lik-spitt'l) *n.* A fawning underling; a toady. —**lick·spit·tle** *adj.*

licorice. *U.S.* Variant of **liquorice.**

lic·tor (lík-tər, -tawr) *n.* A Roman functionary who carried fasces in attendance on a magistrate. [Middle English *littour*, from Latin *lictor.*]

lid (lid) *n.* **1.** A removable or sometimes hinged cover for any hollow receptacle. **2.** An eyelid. **3.** *Biology.* A flaplike covering, such as an operculum. **4.** A curb or restraint. **5.** *Slang.* A hat. —**flip (one's) lid.** *Informal.* **1.** To have a sudden and violent feeling, as of rage or infatuation. **2.** To lose one's sanity; go mad. —**put the (tin) lid on.** *British Slang.* **1.** To be the climax of a series of misfortunes. **2.** To put an end to. —**take the lid off.** To expose the scandalous truth about. [Middle English, Old English *hlid*, covering, gate, opening.] —**lid·ded** *adj.*

li·dar (lí-daar) *n.* A type of radar using a directional laser or maser beam. [*Light* + ra*dar.*]

Li·di·ce (líddit-se). Mining village west of Prague, Czechoslovakia, destroyed in 1942 by the German army in retaliation for the assassination of the Nazi chief Reinhard Heydrich. The men were killed and the women and children deported. After the war, a new village was built, the old site being maintained as a memorial.

lid·less (lĭd-ləss, -liss) adj. **1.** Having no lid. **2.** Having no eyelids. Said of animals. **3.** Archaic. Sleepless; watchful.

li·do (léedō ‖ lĭdŏ) n., pl. **-dos. 1.** An open-air swimming pool for public use, often providing other recreational facilities. **2.** A bathing beach. [Italian, beach of sand or silt separated from the mainland by a lagoon, such as the Lido, name of fashionable bathing beach near Venice, from Latin litus, shore.]

li·do·caine (lĭdə-kayn) n. U.S. An anaesthetic, **lignocaine** (see). [From acetanilide + (CO)CAINE.]

lie¹ (lī) intr.v. **lay** (lay), **lain** (layn), **lying, lies. 1.** To be in or place oneself in a prostrate or recumbent position; rest; recline. Often used with down. **2. a.** To be placed on or supported by a surface that is usually horizontal. **b.** To float at anchor. Used of a ship. **3.** To be or remain in a specified condition: The conflict lies dormant. **4.** To exist; be inherent: Her good nature lies within her. **5.** To be located: The spring lies several miles beyond this village. **6.** To be buried or entombed. **7.** To extend: Our land lies between these trees and the river. **8.** Archaic. To stay for a night or short while: The regiment is lying not far from here. **9.** To remain on the ground. Used of game birds. **10.** Law. To be admissible or maintainable. —See Usage note at lay. —lie down. To remain impassive in the face of provocation: She won't take those insults lying down. —lie low. To keep oneself or one's plans hidden. —lie off. Nautical. To anchor away from the shore or from another ship. —lie over. To remain and wait until a future time. —lie to. Nautical. To remain stationary while facing the wind. —lie up. **1.** To remain in one's room, usually when ill. **2.** To be out of use or in need of repair. —lie with. **1.** To be decided by, dependent upon, or up to: The choice lies with you. **2.** Archaic. To have sexual intercourse with.
~n. **1.** The manner or position in which something is situated. **2.** A lair or hiding place of an animal. **3.** In golf, the position of a ball that has come to a stop. —the lie of the land. **1.** The physical characteristics of a piece of land. **2.** A social or political state of affairs, usually in the process of changing. [Lie, lay, lain; Middle English lien or lig(g)en, lay, ley(e)n, Old English licgan, læg, legen.]

lie² n. **1.** A false statement or piece of information deliberately presented as being true; a falsehood. **2.** Anything meant to deceive or give a wrong impression. —give the lie to. **1.** To prove to be untrue; belie. **2.** To accuse of lying; contradict.
~v. **lied, lying, lies.** —intr. **1.** To present false information with the intention of deceiving. **2.** To convey a false image or impression: Appearances often lie. —tr. To put in a specific condition through deceit: lied herself into trouble. [Middle English ligen, lien, Old English lēogan.]

Lie (lee), **Trygve (Halvdan)** (1896–1968). Norwegian politician and first Secretary-General of the United Nations (1946–53).

Lieb·frau·milch (léeb-frow-milk ‖ German léep-, -milkh) n. A white wine from the Rhine region. [German : Liebfrau, the Virgin Mary (to whom the convent where the wine was first produced was dedicated) + Milch, milk.]

Lie·big (lée-big, German -bikh), **Justus, Baron von** (1803–73). German chemist. He discovered chloral, and later revealed the importance in plant growth of atmospheric nitrogen and carbon dioxide and of soil minerals.

Liebig condenser n. Chemistry. A simple laboratory condenser, usually of glass, having a straight central tube surrounded by a jacket through which cold water is passed. [After Justus von LIEBIG.]

Lieb·knecht (German léep-knekht), **Karl** (1871–1919). German politician, son of Wilhelm. Expelled from the Social Democratic Party in 1916, he engaged in illegal antiwar activity with Rosa Luxemburg in the Spartacusbund, which was to become the German Communist Party. In 1919 he led an unsuccessful uprising and was arrested and murdered by army officers.

Liebknecht, Wilhelm (1826–1900). German pacifist politician. With August Bebel, he founded the German Social Democratic Labour party in 1869.

Liech·ten·stein (lĭktən-stīn). German **Für·sten·tum Liech·ten·stein** (fŭrstəntóom léekht'n-shtīn). Small, landlocked Alpine principality in central Europe. It has a currency and customs union with neighbouring Switzerland, which looks after its defence and foreign affairs. Area, 157 square kilometres (61 square miles). Population 25,000. Capital, Vaduz.

lied (leed; German leet) n., pl. **lieder** (léedər). A German song in the style of a ballad for solo voice and piano. [German Lied, song, from Old High German liod.]

lie detector n. A **polygraph** (see) used to detect lying in a person undergoing interrogation.

lief (leef) adv. Archaic. Readily; willingly: as lief go now as later.
~adj. Archaic. **1.** Beloved; dear. **2.** Ready or willing. [Middle English le(e)f, lif, from le(e)f, "beloved", Old English lēof.]

liege (leej, also leezh) n. **1.** A lord or sovereign in feudal law. **2.** A vassal or subject owing allegiance and services to a lord or sovereign under feudal law.
~adj. **1.** Of, pertaining to, or designating the relationship between a vassal or subject and his lord. **2.** Entitled to the loyalty and services of his vassals or subjects. Said of a feudal lord. **3.** Bound to give such allegiance and services to a lord or monarch. Said of a feudal vassal or subject. **4.** Loyal. [Middle English li(e)ge, lege,

from Old French li(e)ge, from Medieval Latin lēticus, laeticus, from lētus, lītus, serf, from Germanic.]

Li·ège (li-áyzh, French -ézh). Flemish **Luik** (loyk); German **Lüt·tich** (lŭttikh). City on the river Meuse, Belgium. It is a centre of the country's steel, engineering, and arms industries.

liege·man (léej-man, -mən) n., pl. **-men** (-men, -mən). **1.** A feudal vassal or subject. **2.** A loyal supporter or follower.

Liegnitz. See **Legnica.**

lie in intr.v. **1.** Archaic. To be in confinement for childbirth. **2.** To stay in bed late into the morning.

lie-in (lī-ín) n. A long sleep or stay in bed late into the morning.

lien (léern, lée-ən ‖ leen) n. Law. The right to take and hold or sell the property of a debtor as security or payment for a debt. [Old French l(o)ien, bond, tie, from Latin ligāmen, from ligāre, to bind.]

li·e·nal (lī-ən'l, lī-éen'l) adj. Of or pertaining to the spleen. [Latin liēn, spleen.]

li·en·ter·y (lī-ən-tri, -təri ‖ -terri) n. Diarrhoea in which the faeces contains undigested food. [French, lientérie, from Greek leienteria : leios, smooth + entera, intestine.]

li·erne (li-érn) n. Architecture. A reinforcing rib used in Gothic vaulting to connect the intersections and bosses of the primary ribs. [French, from Old French, from lier, to bind, from Latin ligāre.]

lieu (lew, lōō) n. Place; stead. Used chiefly in the phrase in lieu of. [Middle English liue, from Old French lieu, from Latin locus, place, LOCUS.]

lieu·ten·ant (lef-ténnənt, ləf-; but for sense 2 lə-ténnənt, le-, lōō-, and for sense 3 lōō-ténnənt) n. Abbr. **Lieut., Lt.** Military. **1.** Either of two officers in the British and other armies and various other military, police, and civilian organisations: **a.** A commissioned officer of the lowest rank, a **second lieutenant** (see). **b.** An officer ranking between a captain and a second lieutenant. In this sense, also U.S. "first lieutenant". **2.** An officer of the British and other navies, ranking between a lieutenant-commander and a sublieutenant, equivalent in rank to a captain in the army. **3.** Either of two officers in the U.S. navy: **a.** A lieutenant junior grade, ranking between a lieutenant senior grade and an ensign. **b.** A lieutenant senior grade, ranking between a lieutenant-commander and a lieutenant junior grade. **4.** One who is second in command to and sometimes acts in place of a superior; a deputy. [Originally, "officer who acts for a superior", from Middle English lieutenaunt, vice regent, from Old French lieutenant : lieu, LIEU + tenant, present participle of tenir, to hold, from Vulgar Latin tenīre (unattested), from Latin tenēre.] —**lieu·ten·an·cy** n.

lieu·ten·ant-colo·nel, U.S. **lieutenant colonel** (lef-ténnənt-kérn'l, ləf- ‖ U.S. lōō-) n. Abbr. **Lt. Col.** Military. An officer of the British army and various other armies, air forces, and marine corps, ranking between a colonel and a major.

lieu·ten·ant-com·mand·er, U.S. **lieutenant commander** (lə-ténnənt-kə-ma'andər, le-, lōō- ‖ -mándər) n. Abbr. **Lt. Comdr.** An officer of the British and other navies ranking between a commander and a lieutenant.

lieu·ten·ant-gen·e·ral, U.S. **lieutenant general** (lef-ténnənt-jénrəl, ləf-, -ərəl ‖ U.S. lōō-) n. Abbr. **Lt. Gen.** An officer of the British army and various other armies, air forces, and marine corps, ranking between a general and a major general.

lieutenant governor n. Abbr. **Lt. Gov. 1.** Also **lieu·ten·ant-gov·er·nor** (lef-ténnənt-gúv-nər, ləf-, -ərnər ‖ U.S. lōō-). A deputy governor. **2.** An elected state official ranking just below the governor of a U.S. state. **3.** The appointed head of government of a Canadian province.

life (līf) n., pl. **lives** (līvz). **1.** The property or quality manifested in functions such as metabolism, growth, response to stimulation, and reproduction, by which living organisms are distinguished from dead organisms or from inanimate matter. **2.** The characteristic state or condition of a living organism. **3.** Living organisms collectively: plant life. **4.** A living being, especially a person, contrasted with one no longer alive: lives lost in battle. **5.** The interval between the birth or inception of an organism and its death. **6. a.** The remainder of one's life: paralysed for life. Also used adjectively: a life sentence. **b.** Slang. A sentence of life imprisonment: For such a vicious murder, he should have got life. **7.** The period of one's life that has already passed: She has suffered from rheumatism all her life. **8.** The interval or amount of time during which anything exists or functions: the operating life of a machine. **9. a.** A spiritual state regarded as a transcending of death. **b.** Salvation. **10.** An account of a person's life; a biography: lives of the saints. **11. a.** Human activities, relationships, and interests collectively: everyday life. **b.** A career; prospects: made a new life for herself in Australia. **c.** A mode of activity or existence: country life. **12.** A pleasant, easy, or luxurious manner of existence: That's the life. **13.** An animating force; a source of vitality. **14.** Animation, spirit, or liveliness: full of life. **15.** Strength or freshness of flavour. **16.** In fine arts: **a.** A living person or model regarded as an artistic subject: painted from life. Also used adjectively: life drawing. **b.** Actual environment or reality; nature. **17. a.** A chance to live again; specifically, an immunity to fatal accident or an exemption from death at the last moment: That cat has nine lives. **b.** In games, any of an allotted number of chances to take part prior to exclusion. —**as big** or **large as life. 1.** Life-size. **2.** Informal. Physically real; living; vital. —**bring to life. 1.** To cause to regain consciousness. **2.** To put spirit into; animate. **3.** To make lifelike. —**come to life. 1.** To regain consciousness. **2.** To become or seem to become animated; grow lively or lifelike. —**for dear life.** Desperately or urgently. —**for**

life. 1. Until the end of one's life. 2. So as to save one's life. **—for the life of (one).** *Informal.* Though trying hard. Used with negative expressions: *For the life of me I couldn't remember her name.* **—lay down (one's) life.** To sacrifice one's life. **—not on your life.** *Informal.* Not for any reason; definitely not. **—take (someone's) life.** To kill. **—the good life.** An affluent, luxurious life-style. **—the life and soul of the party.** An animated or amusing person who is the centre of attention at a social gathering. **—the life of Riley.** *Informal.* An easy or good lifestyle. **—to save (one's) life.** No matter how hard one tries: *I can't dance to save my life.* **—to the life.** Exactly or closely resembling a model or original. **—true to life.** Not deviating from reality; faithfully representing real life. [Middle English *lif(e),* Old English *līf.*]

Life. See **Liffey.**

life assurance *n.* Assurance that guarantees a specific sum of money to a beneficiary when the insured dies or to the insured if he lives beyond a certain age. Also called "life insurance".

life belt *n.* A large ring of buoyant material designed to keep a person afloat.

life•blood (līf-blud, -blúd) *n.* 1. Blood regarded as essential for life. 2. The indispensable vital part of a thing.

life•boat (līf-bōt) *n.* 1. A boat carried on a ship to sustain persons abandoning the ship. 2. A boat used for rescuing people at sea.

life buoy *n.* Any of various devices for keeping people afloat.

life cycle *n.* 1. The course of developmental changes through which an organism passes from its inception as a fertilised zygote to the mature state in which another zygote may be produced. 2. A progression through a series of differing stages of development, as in insect metamorphosis.

life estate *n.* Property which a person can hold during his lifetime, but may not sell or bequeath to anyone else.

life expectancy *n.* The statistically determined number of years that an individual is expected to live.

life•guard (līf-gaard) *n.* An expert swimmer trained and employed to safeguard swimmers or bathers. Also called "lifesaver".

Life Guards *pl.n.* A British regiment, formerly of cavalry and now of armour, making up with the Blues and Royals the mounted section of the Household Division. **—Life Guardsman** *n.*

Life Guards *One of the two mounted regiments in the Household Division – the section of the British army which forms the Queen's personal bodyguard. The Life Guards are seen here parading near Buckingham Palace in London.*

life history *n.* 1. The history of changes undergone by an organism from inception or conception to death. 2. The developmental history of an individual or group in society.

life instinct *n. Psychology.* An instinct that includes the impulses for self-preservation and reproduction.

life insurance *n.* **Life assurance** *(see).*

life interest *n.* Interest payable to a person during his lifetime, which lapses when he dies.

life jacket *n.* An inflatable sleeveless jacket designed to keep the wearer afloat in water.

life•less (līf-ləss, -liss) *adj.* 1. Having no life; inanimate. 2. Having lost life; dead. 3. Incapable of sustaining life; not inhabited by living beings. 4. Lacking vitality or animation; dull; listless. —See Synonyms at **dead. —life•less•ly** *adv.* **—life•less•ness** *n.*

life•like (līf-līk) *adj.* 1. Resembling a living thing. 2. Accurately representing real life. **—life•like•ness** *n.*

life•line (līf-līn) *n.* 1. An anchored line thrown as a support to someone falling or drowning. 2. A line shot to a ship in distress either to connect it with the shore or for hauling aboard other lifesaving devices such as heavier lines or breeches buoys. 3. A line used to raise and lower deep-sea divers. 4. a. Any means or route by which necessary supplies are transported. b. Any person or thing that provides continuous or sustained support in times of difficulty or distress. 5. A diagonal line crossing the palm of the hand and alleged to indicate the length and major events of one's life.

life•long (līf-long, -lóng || -lawng) *adj.* Continuing for a lifetime.

life peer *n. British.* A peer whose title is bestowed for a lifetime only and lapses at death. **—life peerage** *n.*

life preserver *n.* 1. *British.* A weapon, such as a club or bludgeon. 2. *U.S.* A buoyant device, usually in the shape of a ring, belt, or jacket, designed to keep a person afloat in the water.

lif•er (līfər) *n. Slang.* A prisoner serving a life sentence.

life raft *n.* A raft usually made of wood or inflatable material and used in an emergency at sea.

life•sav•er (līf-sayvər) *n.* 1. One that saves a life. 2. A **lifeguard** *(see).* 3. One that provides help in a minor crisis or emergency.

life•sav•ing, life-sav•ing (līf-sayving) *n.* A set of skills or techniques for rescuing and resuscitating the victims of accidents, especially victims of drowning.
~*adj.* 1. Of or pertaining to the techniques studied in lifesaving: *a lifesaving medal.* 2. a. Saving life. b. Providing help in a minor crisis or emergency.

life science *n.* Any of the fields of science dealing with the structure and function of organisms, such as botany, zoology, biochemistry, genetics, or immunology. Compare **physical science.**

life-size (līf-sīz) *adj.* Also **life-sized** (-sīzd). Being of the same size as the person, animal, or thing represented.

life span *n.* The period of time during which an organism or machine remains alive or functional under normal conditions.

life•style, life-style (līf-stīl) *n.* An internally consistent way of life or style of living that reflects the attitudes and values of an individual or a culture.

life-sup•port system (līf-sə-pawrt || -pōrt) *n.* 1. The equipment that provides a viable environment where this would not normally be possible, as in a spacecraft or below the sea. 2. Hospital equipment that artificially sustains life.

life•time (līf-tīm) *n.* 1. The period of time during which an individual is alive. 2. The interval or amount of time during which an object, property, process, or phenomenon exists or functions. 3. *Physics.* The average time of existence of an unstable particle or nucleus. Also called "mean life".
~*adj.* Continuing or lasting for such a period of time: *a lifetime guarantee.*

life•work (līf-wúrk) *n.* Also **life's work.** The chief work or creation of one's lifetime.

Lif•fey (liffi). *Irish* **Li•fe.** River in the Republic of Ireland, flowing from the Wicklow Mountains into the Irish Sea at Dublin.

lift (lift) *v.* **lifted, lifting, lifts.** *—tr.* 1. To direct or carry from a lower to a higher position; raise; elevate: *lift the suitcase; lift one's eyes.* 2. To pick up for the purpose of moving or removing: *lift the child from the sandpit; lift a suitcase down.* 3. a. To take back or remove; revoke; rescind: *lift a ban.* b. To bring an end to (a blockade or siege) by removing forces. c. To cease (artillery fire) on an area. 4. To raise in condition, rank, esteem, or value; exalt: *Her courage lifted her in their eyes.* 5. To remove (plants) from the ground for transplanting. 6. To project or sound in loud, clear tones: *lifted their voices in song.* 7. *Informal.* To steal; pilfer. 8. *Informal.* To plagiarise. 9. *U.S.* To pay off or clear (a debt or mortgage, for example). 10. To perform cosmetic surgery on (the face or breasts), especially to remove wrinkles or sag. 11. a. In golf and cricket, to hit (the ball) very high into the air. b. In golf, to pick up (the ball) in the hand to put in a better position. 12. To carry (a passenger or goods) in a vehicle. *—intr.* 1. To rise; ascend. 2. To disappear or disperse by or as if by rising: *The clouds had lifted.* 3. To use force or energy in or as if in lifting something. 4. To yield to upward force: *The window won't lift.* 5. To stop temporarily.
~*n.* 1. The act or process of raising or rising to a higher position. 2. Power or force available for raising: *the lift of a pump.* 3. An amount or weight raised or capable of being raised at one time; a load. 4. The extent or height to which something is raised; the amount of elevation. 5. The distance or space through which something is raised. 6. A rising of the level of the ground. 7. A rising of spirits; a mood of exhilaration or happiness. 8. A raised, high, or erect position: *the lift of her chin.* 9. A machine or device designed to pick up, raise, or carry something. 10. Any of the layers of leather, rubber, or other material making up the heel of a shoe. 11. a. *Chiefly British.* A platform or enclosure raised and lowered in a vertical shaft to transport goods or people. Also *chiefly U.S.* "elevator". b. An apparatus for transporting people up and down a mountain; a **chair lift** *(see).* 12. A ride given in a vehicle to help someone reach a destination. 13. Any kind of assistance or help. 14. A set of pumps used in a mine. 15. *Aeronautics.* a. The component of the total aerodynamic force acting on an aerofoil, or on an entire aircraft or winged missile, perpendicular to the relative wind and normally exerted in an upward direction, opposing the pull of gravity. b. The upward force on a balloon, airship, or the like. [Middle English *liften,* from Old Norse *lypta.*] **—lift•er** *n.*

Synonyms: *lift, raise, elevate, hoist, heave, boost.*

lifting body *n.* An aircraft or spacecraft that has no wings and gains lift by the action of aerodynamic forces on its body.

lift off *intr.v.* To commence flight. Used of a rocket or other craft.

lift•off (lift-off, -awff) *n.* 1. The initial movement by which a rocket or other craft commences flight. 2. The instant at which this occurs.

lift pump *n.* A simple pump for lifting a liquid to a higher level, typically having a piston with a valve in the base moving vertically in a cylinder.

lig•a•ment (líggə-mənt) *n.* 1. *Anatomy.* A sheet or band of tough, fibrous tissue connecting two or more bones or cartilages, or supporting an organ, fascia, or muscle. 2. Any unifying or connecting tie or bond. [Middle English, from Latin *ligāmentum,* bond, bandage, from *ligāre,* to bind.] **—lig•a•men•tal** (-mént'l), **lig•a•men•ta•ry** (-méntəri), **lig•a•men•tous** (-méntəss) *adj.*

ligan. Variant of **lagan.**

lig•and (líggənd, līgənd) *n. Chemistry.* An atom, ion, group, or molecule that is linked to a central atom in an inorganic coordination compound. [Latin *ligandum,* gerund of *ligāre,* to bind.]

li•gase (lī-gayz, -gayss) *n.* An enzyme that catalyses the linkage of molecules, using ATP as an energy source. [Latin *ligāre,* to bind + -ASE.]

li•gate (lī-gáyt || lī-gayt) *tr.v.* **-gated, -gating, -gates.** To tie up, bind, or constrict with a ligature. [Latin *ligāre,* to bind.]

li•ga•tion (lī-gáysh'n) *n.* 1. The act of binding or applying a ligature. 2. The state of being bound. 3. Something that binds; a ligature.

lig•a•ture (líggə-chər, -tewr) *n.* 1. The act of tying together, binding, or constricting. 2. A cord, wire, or bandage used for tying, binding, or constricting. 3. Something that unites; a bond. 4. In surgery, a thread, wire, cord, or the like, applied in a tight loop, as to close vessels, tie off ducts, or constrict a growth. 5. A character or type combining two or more letters, such as *fi.* 6. *Music.* a. A group of notes intended to be played or sung as one phrase. b. A curved line indicating such a phrase; a slur.
~*tr.v.* **ligatured, -turing, -tures.** To ligate. [Middle English, from Latin *ligātūra,* from *ligāre,* to bind.]

li•ger (līgər) *n.* A hybrid produced by the mating of a female tiger and a male lion. [Blend of *lion* + *tiger.*]

Li•ge•ti (líggeti), **György** (1923–). Hungarian avant-garde composer.

PRONUNCIATION KEY

a, trap; aa, father; ai, fair; ar, star; aw, lawn; ay, play; b, bb, stab; rubber; ch, church; ck, ticket; d, dd, dead; ladder; e, dress; ee, bee; er, defer; ew, few; ewr, pure; ə, about; ər, letter; f, ff, fife; differ; g, gg, giggle; h, hat; i, kit; ī, price; īr, fire; j, judge; k, kick; l, ll, let; 'l, needle; m, mm, man; n, nn, no; 'n, sudden; ng, thing; o, lot; ō, no; ŏŏ, foot; ōō, shoe; oor, poor; ow, cow; owr, hour; oy, boy; p, pp, pepper; r, rr, red; s, ss, sauce; sh, ship; t, tt, totter; th, thick; th, this; smooth; u, cut; ur, turn; v, vv, valve; w, wet; y, yes; z, zz, zebra; zh, vision; pleasure

IN FOREIGN WORDS:

aɴ, ᴏɴ, Saint-Saëns; hl, Llanelli; Hluhluwe; kh, loch; lough; Khaled

STRESS MARK:

in-sīt, insight; in-sīt, incite

light

LIGHT: THE VISIBLE PART OF A VERY WIDE SPECTRUM
Light is a part of the same phenomenon as radio waves and X-rays

Light is that part of the electromagnetic spectrum to which the eye is sensitive. Electromagnetic energy travels in waves at about 300 000 kilometres (about 186,000 miles) per second in a vacuum, which is thought to be the ultimate speed limit in the universe. The spectrum extends from radio waves of very low frequency to gamma rays from radioactive substances, of very high frequency and dangerous to living things.

Within its narrow part of the spectrum, light varies in colour – depending on the frequency, or wavelength, of its waves – from comparatively low-frequency red through orange, yellow, green, and blue to high-frequency violet. Isaac Newton showed in 1666 that white light can be separated into its different colours by passing it through a glass prism. This is because each colour (wavelength) is refracted at a different angle.

A rainbow is a spectrum of light produced by the natural prism of raindrops in the atmosphere. Colour results from the absence or the absorption of other wavelengths. A red object appears red because other colours are absorbed and only red is reflected.

When a light source – for example, a distant galaxy – is receding at a very great speed, the light waves from it are effectively lengthened and appear redder than they should. This "red shift" indicates that the universe is still expanding.

Each chemical element has its own characteristic pattern of lines in the spectrum – a kind of identifying "fingerprint" of colours emitted or absorbed by its atoms. Because of this the composition of heavenly bodies can be discovered by analysing the light that comes from them.

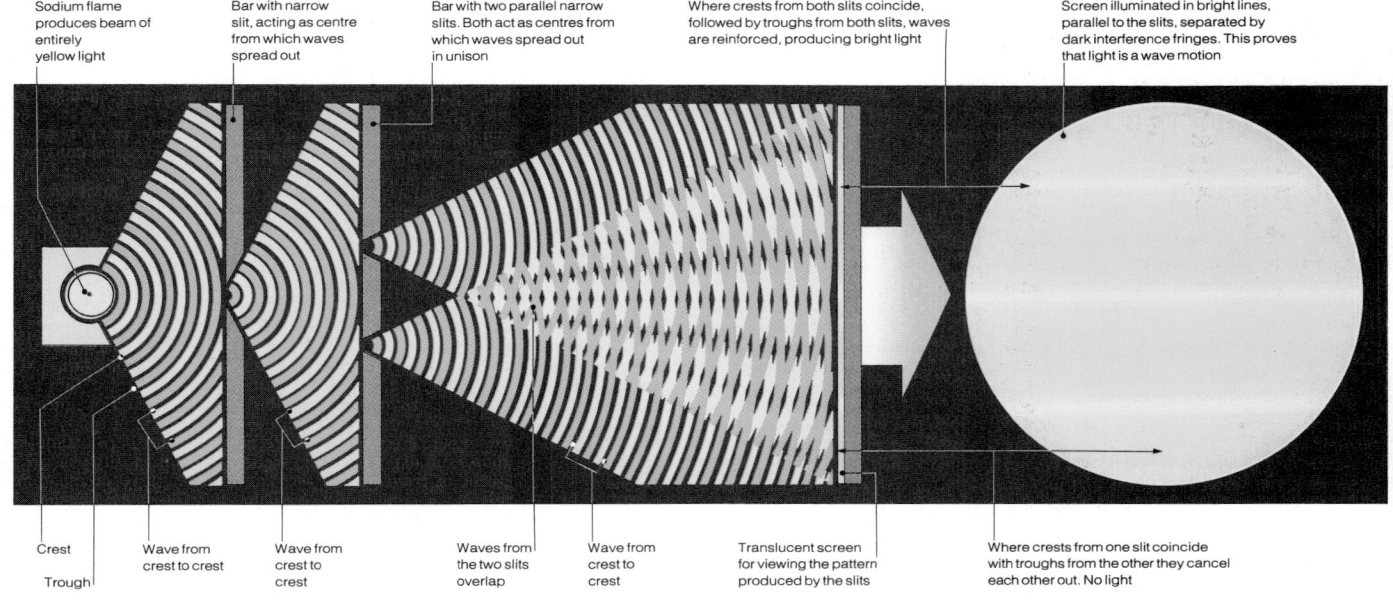

Sodium flame produces beam of entirely yellow light

Bar with narrow slit, acting as centre from which waves spread out

Bar with two parallel narrow slits. Both act as centres from which waves spread out in unison

Where crests from both slits coincide, followed by troughs from both slits, waves are reinforced, producing bright light

Screen illuminated in bright lines, parallel to the slits, separated by dark interference fringes. This proves that light is a wave motion

Crest

Trough

Wave from crest to crest

Wave from crest to crest

Waves from the two slits overlap

Wave from crest to crest

Translucent screen for viewing the pattern produced by the slits

Where crests from one slit coincide with troughs from the other they cancel each other out. No light

PROOF THAT LIGHT TRAVELS IN WAVES *Newton thought that light was a steady stream of particles; his contemporary Christiaan Huygens thought it had a wave motion. They were both right. Light consists of moving quanta (packets) of photons (particles of pure energy). And Thomas Young, an English physicist, proved in 1802 that it does have a wave motion. In his experiment (above), the parallel beams of light should have produced a brighter area where they overlapped, if light were a steady stream. Instead, they produced bright bands separated by dark bands, the result of two sets of waves coinciding or cancelling each other out.*

light¹ (līt) *n.* **1.** *Physics.* **a.** Electromagnetic radiation that has a wavelength in about the range 380–780 nanometres and that may be perceived by the normal, unaided human eye. **b.** Loosely, other electromagnetic radiation that is close to light in wavelength, but not visible: *ultraviolet light.* **2.** The sensation of the perception of such radiation; brightness. **3.** A source of illumination, such as the sun or an electric lamp. **4. a.** The illumination derived from such a source: *by the light of the moon.* **b.** The particular quality or amount of such illumination: *Play was abandoned because of bad light.* **c.** The path by which light reaches a person: *You're standing in my light.* **5.** Daylight. **6.** Dawn; daybreak. **7. a.** Something that admits light, such as a window. **b.** *Often plural.* Daylight falling on a window. See **ancient lights**. **8.** A means or agent, such as a match or cigarette lighter, for igniting something. **9. a.** Something that provides clarification or elucidation: *shed some light on the problem.* **b.** A state of understanding or awareness, especially as derived from a particular source: *saw the light; in the light of experience.* **10.** The state of being visible, publicly available, or generally known; public attention or awareness: *bring new facts to light.* **11.** A way of regarding something; an angle; an aspect: *saw the situation in a new light.* **12.** *Archaic & Poetic.* Eyesight. **13.** *Plural.* One's individual opinions, choices, or life philosophy: *acted according to their own lights.* **14.** A person who inspires or is adored by another: *Her son is the light of her life.* **15.** A prominent or distinguished person, especially one serving as an example for others; a notable or luminary: *the brighter lights of Irish art.* **16.** An expression of the eyes, usually indicative of animation or liveliness. **17. a.** Spiritual illumination. **b.** *Capital* L. In Quaker doctrine, the guiding spirit or divine presence in each person. **18. a.** The representation of light in art. **b.** An area of pronounced illumination in a painting or photograph. **19. a.** A traffic light. **b.** A lighthouse beacon.
~v. lighted or **lit** (līt), **lighting, lights.** —*tr.* **1.** To set on fire; ignite; kindle. **2.** To cause to give out light; make luminous. **3.** To provide, cover, or fill with light; illuminate. **4.** To guide or direct with or as if with lights. **5.** To enliven or animate: *a smile lighting her* face. —*intr.* To start to burn; be ignited or kindled: *Green wood will not light easily.* —See Usage note at **light².** —**light up. 1.** To become or cause to become light, radiant, or bright. **2.** To become or cause to become animated or cheerful. **3.** *Informal.* To start smoking a cigarette, cigar, or pipe.
~adj. lighter, lightest. *Abbr.* **lt. 1.** Having a greater rather than lesser degree of **lightness** (*see*). Said of a colour. **2.** Characterised by or filled with light; radiant; bright. **3.** Pale, as if mixed with white; fair: *a light complexion.* [Middle English *liht, light,* Old English *lēoht, līht.*]

light² *adj.* **lighter, lightest. 1.** Of relatively low weight; not heavy. **2.** Of low weight in proportion to bulk; of relatively low density. **3.** Of less than the correct, standard, or lawful weight; underweight: *a light pound.* **4.** Exerting little pressure; having relatively little force or impact: *a light kick.* **5. a.** Having relatively little volume, quantity, or intensity: *a light rain; light traffic.* **b.** Moderate; abstemious: *a light eater; a light smoker.* **6. a.** Having little importance or value; insignificant: *light chatter.* **b.** Characterised by frivolity; silly; trivial. **7.** Intended as entertainment; not serious or profound: *a light comedy.* **8.** Free from worries or troubles; blithe. **9.** Having little moral discipline; wanton. **10.** Suffering from mild delirium or faintness; dizzy. **11.** Moving quickly and easily; graceful; nimble. **12. a.** Designed for ease and quickness of movement; having a slim structure and little weight: *light aircraft.* **b.** Designed to carry relatively small loads: *a light lorry.* **13.** Concerned with the production of relatively small consumer goods: *light industry.* **14.** Performed or endured without significant difficulty or effort: *Many hands make light work.* **15.** Easily disturbed or woken: *a light sleeper.* **16.** *Military.* Carrying little equipment or arms: *a light brigade.* **17.** Characterised by lightness and elegance in design or construction; not ponderous or massive. **18.** Easily digested. **19.** Having a spongy or flaky texture; well-leavened: *light pastries.* **20.** Having a loose, porous consistency; not packed together or solid: *light earth.* **21.** Containing a relatively small amount of alcohol: *a light wine.* **22.** Faint; not bold. Said of type. **23.** In phonetics and prosody, designating a vowel or syllable pronounced with little or no stress. **24.** *Informal.* Lacking an adequate supply of something. Used with *on.* —**make light of.** To regard or treat as insignificant or petty.

~*adv.* **1.** Lightly. **2.** Without additional weight or burdens; in an unencumbered manner: *travelling light.*

~*intr.v.* **lighted** or **lit** (lit), **lighting, lights. 1.** To get down, as from a mount or vehicle; dismount; alight. **2.** To descend to the ground after flight; perch; land. **3.** To come upon one suddenly; strike suddenly, as a blow or stroke of luck may. Often used with *on* or *upon: Misfortune lighted upon her.* **4.** To come upon an object or idea by chance or accident. Used with *on* or *upon.* —**light into.** *Informal.* To attack verbally or physically; assail. —**light out.** *Informal.* To leave hastily; run off. [Middle English *liht, light,* Old English *lēoht, līht.*]

Usage: The past tense and participle of **light[1]** and **light[2]** is generally *lit. Lighted* is used only in a few special senses; for example, when **light[1]** means "provide with light" (*I was lighted along the corridor by candles*). When **light[2]** is used in the phrases *light on* or *light upon,* meaning "discover", *lighted* and *lit* are both possible: *We lighted/lit upon an old map.* In adjectival use, *lighted* is the usual form, although *lit* is sometimes found, especially if there is a preceding adverb: *a lighted cigarette,* but *a well-lit arcade.*

light air *n.* A wind whose speed is 0.3 to 1.5 metres per second, force 1 on the Beaufort scale.

light breeze *n.* A wind whose speed in 1.6 to 3.3 metres per second, force 2 on the Beaufort scale.

light bulb, light·bulb (līt-bulb) *n.* An electric lamp in which a filament is heated to incandescence by an electric current.

light-emitting diode *n.* See LED.

light·en[1] (līt'n) *v.* **-ened, -ening, -ens.** —*tr.* **1. a.** To make light or lighter; illuminate; brighten. **b.** To make (a colour) lighter. **2.** *Archaic.* To enlighten mentally or spiritually, as by imparting knowledge or wisdom to. —*intr.* **1.** To become light or lighter; brighten. **2.** To be luminous; glow; shine. **3.** To produce or give off flashes of lightning. —See Usage note at **lightning.**

lighten[2] *v.* **-ened, -ening, -ens.** —*tr.* **1.** To make less heavy, as by a reduction in weight or load. **2.** To lessen the oppressiveness, trouble, or severity of. **3.** To relieve of cares or worries; gladden. —*intr.* **1.** To become lighter. **2.** To become less oppressive, severe, or troublesome. **3.** To become cheerful. —See Synonyms at **relieve.**

light·er[1] (līter) *n.* **1.** One that lights or ignites something. **2.** A mechanical device for lighting a cigarette, cigar, or pipe.

lighter[2] *n. Nautical.* A large barge used to transport goods over short distances or to deliver to or unload from a larger cargo ship unable to navigate in shallow water.

~*v.* **lightered, -ering, -ers.** —*tr.* To convey (cargo) in a lighter. —*intr.* To use a lighter to transport cargo. [Middle English, from Middle Dutch *lichter* (unattested), from *lichten,* to lighten, unload.]

light·er·age (līterij) *n.* **1.** The transport of goods on a lighter. **2.** The fee charged for such service.

light-er-than-air (līter-thən-áir) *adj.* Having a weight less than that of the air displaced. Said of certain aircraft.

light·face (līt-fayss) *n. Printing. Abbr.* **lf** A typeface or font of characters having relatively thin, light lines. Compare **boldface.** —**light· face, light·faced** *adj.*

light-fin·gered (līt-fing-gərd) *adj.* **1.** Having quick and nimble fingers. **2.** Skilled at or given to petty thievery. —**light-fin·gered·ness** *n.*

light flyweight *n.* A wrestler or amateur boxer weighing not more than 48 kilograms (106 pounds).

light-foot·ed (līt-foõtid) *adj.* Also *poetic* **light-foot** (-foõt). Treading with light and nimble ease. —**light-foot·ed·ly** *adv.* —**light-foot·ed· ness** *n.*

light-head·ed (līt-héddid) *adj.* **1.** Delirious, giddy, or faint: *light-headed with wine.* **2.** Frivolous; silly. —**light-head·ed·ly** *adv.* —**light-head·ed·ness** *n.*

light-heart·ed (līt-hártid) *adj.* **1.** Blithe; carefree; gay. **2.** Not serious: *a light-hearted look at the week's news.* —See Synonyms at **glad.** —**light-heart·ed·ly** *adv.* —**light-heart·ed·ness** *n.*

light heavyweight *n.* **1. a.** An amateur boxer weighing between 75 and 81 kilograms (165 and 178.5 pounds). **b.** A professional boxer weighing between 160 and 175 pounds (72.5 and 79.5 kilograms). **2.** A wrestler weighing between 82 and 90 kilograms (181 and 198.5 pounds).

light·house (līt-howss) *n.* A tall structure topped by a powerful light used as a beacon or signal to aid marine navigation.

light·ing (līting) *n.* **1.** The state of being lighted; illumination. **2. a.** The method or equipment used to provide artificial illumination. **b.** The illumination so provided.

lighting-up time (līting-úp) *n.* The time by which vehicles must have their lights on along public highways.

light·ly (lītli) *adv.* **1.** With little weight or force; gently. **2.** To a slight extent or amount; sparingly; little: *use lightly.* **3.** With buoyancy or ease; quickly and gracefully. **4.** In a carefree manner; cheerfully; blithely: *take the bad news lightly.* **5.** Without enough care or serious consideration; thoughtlessly; indifferently. **6.** Depreciatingly; slightingly.

light meter *n.* In photography, an **exposure meter** (see).

light middleweight *n.* An amateur boxer weighing between 67 and 71 kilograms (148 and 157 pounds).

light-mind·ed (līt-mīndid) *adj.* Frivolous, silly, or inane; giddy. —**light-mind·ed·ly** *adv.* —**light-mind·ed·ness** *n.*

light·ness[1] (līt-nəss, -niss) *n.* **1.** The dimension of the colour of an

lighthouse *Beacons have been used at least since Roman times to warn shipping away from dangerous waters. This modern lighthouse marks the rocks below Beachy Head on England's Sussex coast.*

---

lightning

SHOWER POWER

How rain generates the awesome voltage of lightning

When drops of water falling through a thundercloud strike other drops, some of the energy in each is transformed into an electric charge. The charges are minute at first, but powerful updraughts in the cloud keep lifting the drops, so that they collide again and again. The charges build up, turning the cloud into a gigantic battery. Within about 15 minutes, the total charge becomes so great – many millions of volts – that it overcomes the insulating effect of the air.

The electricity is discharged as an enormous spark that earths itself to the nearest part of the ground. Lightning travels in a forked path, but sometimes it is seen as a sheet – which is a reflection of forked lightning occurring elsewhere. The spark heats the surrounding air to more than 16,000°C (about 28,800°F) – three times hotter than the Sun's surface – causing it to expand explosively and generate the shock wave we hear as thunder.

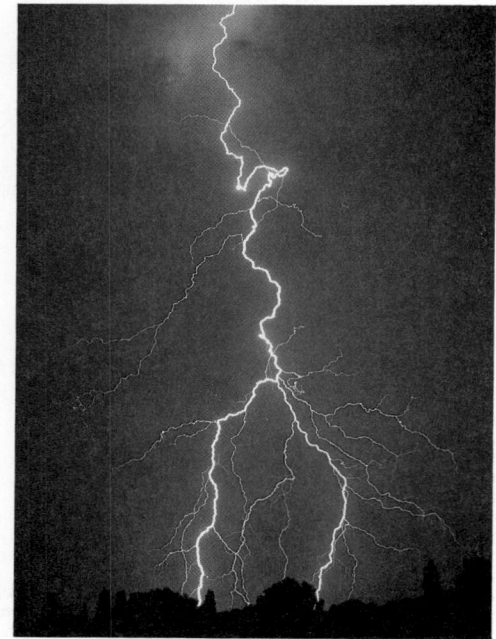

FORKED LIGHTNING *A bolt of lightning can arc across a gap of up to 8 kilometres (5 miles). The spark forks as it flashes through the sky, hunting for the easiest path to Earth. Then, once one or more of the branches makes contact, the bolt discharges itself and the side branches fade in mid-air.*

---

object by which the object appears to reflect or transmit more or less of the incident light, varying from black to white for surface colours, and from black to colourless for transparent volume colours. **2.** The relative paleness of an object or the brightness of a place.

lightness[2] *n.* **1.** The state or quality of having little weight or force. **2.** Ease or quickness of style or movement; agility; nimbleness. **3.** Freedom from worry or trouble; blitheness; gaiety. **4.** Lack of appropriate seriousness; levity.

light·ning (līt-ning) *n.* A large-scale natural electric discharge in the atmosphere in the form of a visible flash of light.

~*intr.v.* **lightninged** (-ningd), **-ning, -nings.** To discharge a flash or flashes of lightning. Sometimes used impersonally.

~*adj.* Moving with extreme alacrity; very fast or sudden, the way a flash of lightning is. [Middle English *light(e)ning,* from *lightenen,* to illuminate, from LIGHT (illumination).]

Usage: Lightning and *lightening* are sometimes confused in spelling, on account of their similar pronunciations. *Lightning* is the noun (as in *thunder and lightning*); *lightening* is a participle form of the verbs *lighten[1]* and *lighten[2].* Note that it is possible, though rare, to use *lighten[1]* to refer to the process that produces lightning: *It was thundering and lightening by the time I returned.*

lightning bug *n. U.S.* A firefly.

lightning conductor *n.* An earthed metal rod placed high on a structure to prevent damage by conducting lightning to the ground. Also *chiefly U.S.* "lightning rod".

lightning strike *n.* **1.** A strike of a work force called at very short notice. **2.** A sudden and intensive military attack.
light opera *n.* An **operetta** *(see).*
light pen *n. Computing.* A photoelectric device shaped like a pen, used to sense and amend data or lines on a visual-display unit.
light ratio *n. Astronomy.* The ratio of the brightness of a star to that of any other star one magnitude fainter, approximately 2.512.
lights (līts) *pl.n.* The lungs, especially of sheep, pigs, or bullocks, used chiefly as pet food. [Middle English *lihte,* from *liht,* LIGHT (not heavy).]
light·ship (līt-ship) *n.* A ship with a powerful light or warning signals anchored in dangerous waters to alert other vessels.
light show *n.* A display of moving coloured lights or slides projected onto a screen or wall, especially in a discotheque.
light·some[1] (līt-səm) *adj.* **1.** Providing light; illuminating; luminous. **2.** Covered with or full of light; bright. **—light·some·ly** *adv.* **—light·some·ness** *n.*
lightsome[2] *adj.* **1.** Light, nimble, or graceful in movement; buoyant. **2.** Carefree; blithe; cheerful. **3.** Frivolous; silly. **—light·some·ly** *adv.* **—light·some·ness** *n.*
lights out *n. Used with a singular verb.* The time when all lights must be extinguished for the night, as in a military camp, boarding school, or the like.
light water *n.* Ordinary water as distinguished from heavy water.
light·weight (līt-wayt) *n.* **1.** A person, animal, or thing that weighs relatively little. **2.** A person of little ability, intelligence, influence, or importance. **3. a.** An amateur boxer weighing between 57 and 60 kilograms (126 and 132 pounds). **b.** A professional boxer weighing between 130 and 135 pounds (59 and 61 kilograms). **4.** A wrestler weighing between 62 and 68 kilograms (137 and 150 pounds).
~adj. Weighing relatively little; not heavy: *lightweight wool.*
light welterweight *n.* An amateur boxer weighing between 60 and 63.5 kilograms (132 and 140 pounds).
light-year, light year (līt-yeer, -yer) *n.* The distance that light covers travelling in a vacuum for a period of one year, approximately 9.4607 × 10^{12} kilometres (5.878 × 10^{12} miles).
lig·ne·ous (líg-ni-əss) *adj.* Consisting of or having the texture or appearance of wood; woody. Said of a plant. [Latin *ligneus,* from *lignum,* wood.]
ligni-, ligno-, lign- *comb. form.* Indicates wood; for example, **lignocellulose, lignin.** [Latin *lignum,* wood.]
lig·ni·fy (líg-ni-fī) *v.* **-fied, -fying, -fies.** *—intr.* To form or turn into wood through the formation and deposit of lignin in cell walls. *—tr.* To make woody or woodlike by the deposit of lignin. [French *lignifier* : LIGNI- + -FY.] **—lig·ni·fi·ca·tion** (-fi-káysh'n) *n.*
lig·nin (líg-nin) *n.* The chief noncarbohydrate constituent of wood, a polymer that functions as a natural binder and support for the cellulose fibres of woody plants. [LIGN(I)- + -IN.]
lig·nite (líg-nīt) *n.* A low-grade, brownish-black coal. Also called "brown coal". [French : LIGN(I)- + -ITE.] **—lig·nit·ic** (-níttik) *adj.*
lig·no·caine (líg-nə-kayn, -nō-) *n.* A local anaesthetic administered by injection or direct application for dental and minor surgical operations. Also *U.S.* "lidocaine". [LIGNO- + (CO)CAINE.]
lig·no·cel·lu·lose (líg-nō-séllew-lōss, -lōz) *n.* Any combination of lignin and cellulose that strengthens plant cells.
lig·num vi·tae (líg-nəm vítī, veé-tī) *n., pl.* **lignum vitaes. 1.** Either of two tropical American trees, *Guaiacum officinale* or *G. sanctum,* having evergreen leaves and heavy, durable, resinous wood. **2.** The wood of either of these trees, used for machine bearings. **3.** Any of several similar or related trees. [New Latin, from Late Latin, "tree or wood of life" : *lignum,* wood + *vītae,* genitive of *vīta,* life.]
lig·ro·in (líggrō-in) *n.* A volatile, flammable fraction of petroleum boiling in the range 70–130°C and used chiefly as a solvent. [20th century : origin obscure.]
lig·u·la (líggew-lə) *n., pl.* **-lae** (-lee) or **-las.** A strap-shaped structure, especially a mouthpart in certain insects. [New Latin, LIGULE.]
lig·u·late (líggew-lət, -lit, -layt) *adj.* **1.** Strap-shaped. **2.** Having a ligule or ligula. [New Latin *ligula,* LIGULE + -ATE.]
lig·ule (líggewl) *n.* A straplike structure, such as a ray flower of a daisy or a sheathlike organ at the base of a grass leaf. [New Latin *ligula,* from Latin, tongue of a shoe, shoe-strap, variant of *lingula,* from *lingua,* tongue.]
lig·ure (líggewr) *n.* A precious stone of ancient Israel. Exodus 28:19. [Middle English *lugre, ligurie,* from Late Latin *ligūrius,* from Greek *ligurion*†, a precious stone.]
Li·gu·ria (li-géwr-i-ə). Autonomous region of northwest Italy. The industrial port of Genoa is the capital.
lik·a·ble, like·a·ble (līk-əb'l) *adj.* Pleasing; attractive. **—lik·a·bil·i·ty** (-ə-bílliti), **lik·a·ble·ness** *n.*
like[1] (līk) *v.* **liked, liking, likes.** *—tr.* **1.** To find pleasant; enjoy. **2.** To feel an attraction, tenderness, or affection for; be fond of. **3.** To want, wish, or prefer. **4.** To feel towards or respond to; view; regard: *How do you like that!* **5.** *Archaic & Poetic.* To agree with; suit or please: *This likes me not.* *—intr.* To have an inclination or preference; desire; choose; wish: *If you like, we can go fishing.*
~n. Plural. Preferences or predilections. Used in the phrase *likes and dislikes.* [Middle English *lik(i)en,* Old English *līcian,* to please, be sufficient.] **—lik·er** *n.*
Synonyms: *like, love, enjoy, relish, fancy, dote.*
Usage: *Like* is often followed by an infinitive form of the verb, which may be preceded by a noun or pronoun: *I would like you to travel by bus.* The insertion of *for* (*I would like for you to travel by bus*) is often heard in informal American English, and occasionally in some other English dialects, but it is not considered standard. The forms *would have/should have liked* are usually followed by a simple infinitive form (*They would have liked to go*), rather than by a perfect infinitive as in *They would have liked to have gone*: the double use of *have* is considered unnecessary.
like[2] *prep.* **1.** Possessing the characteristics of; resembling closely; similar to. **2. a.** In the same way as: *to live like pigs.* **b.** In the typical manner of: *It's not like you to take offence.* **3.** Desirous of; disposed to: *He felt like swimming.* **4.** As if the probability exists for; indicative of: *It looks like a bad season for the English team.* **5.** Such as; for example: *The better wines, like claret, cost more.*
~adj. **1.** Possessing the same or almost the same characteristics; similar: *on this and like occasions.* **2.** Having equivalent value or quality. Usually used in negative phrases: *There's nothing like an open fire.* **3.** Alike: *They are as like as two brothers.* **4.** *Archaic & Regional.* Likely: *He's like to cause trouble.*
~adv. **1.** *Informal.* Probably; likely: *Like as not she'll change her mind.* **2.** *Nonstandard.* As it were. Used to provide an emphasis or pause: *I thought I would just teach him a lesson, like.*
~n. **1.** Similar or related persons or things. Used with *the: He was subject to fevers, coughs, asthma, and the like.* **2.** *Often plural. Informal.* An equivalent or similar person or thing; an equal or match: *I've never seen the likes of this before.*
~conj. Nonstandard. **1.** In the same way that; as: *She talks just like you do.* **2.** As if: *He acts like he owns the place.* [Middle English *lic, lik,* Old English *līc* (unattested), short for *gelīc.*]
Usage: The use of *like* as a conjunction is hardly ever acceptable in formal English, where *as* (or *as if, as though*) is preferred. Such sentences as *He acts like he owns the place* and *It looks like we'll win* would have the *like* replaced by *as if* in formal English. *Sort out the books like I told you* would become *as I told you.* There is, however, one case where *like* is a more acceptable variant of *as,* namely, when it introduces a clause in which the verb is not expressed: *The dress looks like new* (compare *The dress looks as if it is new*). Of course, *like* is quite acceptable in its other uses, and there is no need to use *as* in preference. For example, the prepositional use of *like* expresses comparison—*works like a charm, sings like an angel*—whereas the use of *as* here would instead imply a contrast (of manner or role): compare *He asked a question as a beginner* (i.e. he is a beginner) and *He asked a question like a beginner* (i.e. he is behaving as if he were a beginner).
-like *adj. comb. form.* Indicates: **1.** A resemblance or similarity to something specified; for example, **lifelike. 2.** A characteristic of or appropriateness to something specified; for example, **childlike, ladylike.** [From LIKE (preposition).]
like·li·hood (līkli-hood) *n.* The state of being likely; probability.
like·ly (līkli) *adj.* **-lier, -liest. 1.** Having, expressing, or exhibiting an inclination or probability; apt. Used with an infinitive: *They are likely to become angry with him.* **2.** That can with reasonable confidence be expected to occur; probable: *the likely outcome; More rain is likely.* **3.** Within the realm of credibility; seeming to be true; plausible: *a likely excuse.* **4.** Apparently appropriate or suitable for a purpose: *phoned round all the likely shops.* **5.** Apparently capable of doing well or becoming successful; promising: *a likely lad.* **6.** *Chiefly U.S.* Attractive; pleasant; enjoyable.
~adv. Probably. **—not likely.** Definitely not. [Middle English *likely,* from Old Norse *līkligr,* from *līkr,* like.]
Usage: As an adverb, *likely* normally requires a qualifying word, such as *quite, very,* or *most*: *I will very likely arrive by six.* If you do not wish to use a qualifying word, it is preferable to use an alternative word, such as *probably.*
like-mind·ed (līk-mīndid) *adj.* Of the same turn of mind.
lik·en (līkən) *tr.v.* **-ened, -ening, -ens.** To see, mention, or show as being like or similar; compare. [Middle English *lik(n)en,* from *lik,* LIKE (adjective).]
like·ness (līk-nəss, -niss) *n.* **1.** The state or quality of resembling or being like something. **2.** An imitative appearance; a semblance or guise. **3.** A pictorial, graphic, or sculptured representation of someone or something; an image.
Synonyms: *likeness, similarity, similitude, resemblance, analogy, affinity.*
like·wise (līk-wīz) *adv.* **1.** In the same way; similarly. **2.** As well; also; too. —See Synonyms at **also.**
Usage: *Likewise* is considered to be an adverb (*She did likewise*) in standard English, and its occasional informal use as a conjunction attracts criticism: *Her speech, likewise her manner, upset me.*
lik·ing (līking) *n.* **1.** The state or act of someone who likes. **2.** A feeling of attraction, tenderness, or love; fondness; affection. **3.** Preference; inclination; taste: *Was the meal to your liking?*
li·ku·ta (li-kootaa) *n., pl.* **makuta** (maa-). A coin equal to 1/100 of the zaire of Zaire. [Native word in Zaire.]
li·lac (lī-lək ‖ -lak, -lok) *n.* **1.** Any of various shrubs of the genus *Syringa;* especially, *S. vulgaris,* widely cultivated for its clusters of fragrant purplish or white flowers. **2.** Pale purple; mauve. [Obsolete French, from Spanish, from Arabic *līlak,* from Persian, variant of *nīlak,* from *nīl,* indigo, blue.] **—li·lac** *adj.*
li·la·ngeni (leé-lang-gáyni) *n., pl.* **emalangeni** (émma-). The standard monetary unit of Swaziland equal to 100 cents. [SiSwati : *li-,* singular prefix + *-langeni,* money.]
lil·i·a·ceous (lílli-áyshəss) *adj.* Of, pertaining to, or belonging to the Liliaceae, a family of flowering plants including lilies, tulips, and onions. [Late Latin *līliāceus,* from *līlium,* lily.]
Lil·ith (líllith). **1.** In ancient Semitic legend, an evil female spirit or

lilac *There are 30 species of the lilac genus,* Syringa, *as well as many cultivated varieties. This is* Syringa vulgaris, *or common lilac, thought to come originally from the Romanian province of Transylvania.*

PRONUNCIATION KEY

a, trap; aa, father; ai, fair; ar, star; aw, lawn; ay, play; b, bb, stab; rubber; ch, church; ck, ticket; d, dd, dead; ladder; e, dress; ee, bee; er, defer; ew, few; ewr, pure; ə, about; ər, letter; f, ff, fife; differ; g, gg, giggle; h, hat; i, kit; ī, price; īr, fire; j, judge; k, kick; l, ll, let; 'l, needle; m, mm, man; n, nn, no; 'n, sudden; ng, thing; o, lot; ō, no; ŏŏ, foot; ōō, shoe; oor, poor; ow, cow; owr, hour; oy, boy; p, pp, pepper; r, rr, red; s, ss, sauce; sh, ship; t, tt, totter; th, thick; th, this; smooth; u, cut; ur, turn; v, vv, valve; w, wet; y, yes; z, zz, zebra; zh, vision; pleasure

IN FOREIGN WORDS:

aN, oN, Saint-Saëns; hl, Llanelli; Hluhluwe; kh, loch; lough; Khaled

STRESS MARK:

ín-sīt, insight; in-sít, incite

demon alleged to haunt lonely, deserted places and attack children. **2.** In Hebrew folklore, the first wife of Adam, believed to have been in existence before the creation of Eve. **3.** A witch in medieval legend. [Hebrew *līlīth.*]

Lille (leel). Administrative centre of the Nord département, north France. It was the birthplace of Charles de Gaulle.

Lil·lie (lílli), **Beatrice** (1898–). British actress and singer, born in Canada. She made her London stage debut in 1914 and her first film, *Exit Smiling,* in 1926.

Lil·li·pu·tian (lílli-péwsh'n) *n.* **1.** A very small person or being. **2.** A person of little intelligence, worth, or significance.
~*adj.* **1.** Very small; diminutive. **2.** Trivial; petty. [After *Lilliput,* the land of tiny people, in Swift's *Gulliver's Travels* (1726).]

Li·lō, li·lo (lī́lō) *n., pl.* **-lōs.** A trademark for a type of air bed, popular as a floating mattress in swimming pools.

Li·lon·gwe (li-lóng-gway). Capital of Malawi, lying in its western highlands. It replaced Zomba as the capital in 1975.

lilt (lilt) *n.* **1.** A light, happy tune or song. **2.** A cheerful or lively manner of speaking marked by a pleasantly varied cadence. **3.** A light, springing manner of moving or walking.
~*v.* **lilted, lilting, lilts.** —*tr.* To say, sing, or play in a cheerful, rhythmic manner. —*intr.* To speak, sing, or play with liveliness or rhythm. [Middle English *lulten*†, to sound, sing.]

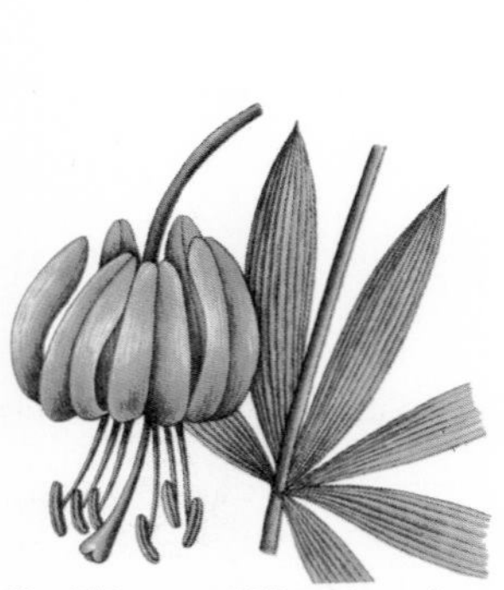

lily *This genus of 80 species and numerous garden hybrids is represented throughout the temperate zone of the Northern Hemisphere. The species shown here, with its large turban-like flowers –* Lilium martagon, *or the Turk's-cap lily – is native to the mountains of central Europe and Russia.*

lil·y (lílli) *n., pl.* **-ies.** **1.** Any of various plants of the genus *Lilium,* having showy, variously coloured, often trumpet-shaped flowers. **2.** Any of various similar or related plants, such as the tiger lily or the water lily. **3.** The flower of such a plant. **—gild the lily.** To try to improve what is already excellent or beautiful. [Middle English *lilie,* Old English, from Latin *līlium,* akin to Greek *leirion,* probably of Mediterranean origin.]

lily iron *n.* A harpoon with a barbed head that may be detached. [From its shape.]

lil·y-liv·ered (lílli-lívvərd) *adj.* Cowardly; timid.

lily of the valley *n., pl.* **lilies of the valley.** A plant, *Convallaria majalis,* having a spike of fragrant, bell-shaped white flowers.

lily pad *n.* Any of the broad, floating leaves of a water lily.

lil·y-trot·ter (lílli-trottər) *n.* A bird, the **jacana** *(see).*

lil·y-white (lílli-wīt, -hwīt) *adj.* **1.** White as a lily. **2.** Beyond reproach; blameless; pure.

Li·ma (léema). Capital of Peru, founded in 1535 by Francisco Pizarro. It is now an industrial centre, joined to its port of Callao.

li·ma bean (lī́mə) *n.* **1.** Any of several varieties of a tropical American plant, *Phaseolus lunatus* (or *P. limensis*), having flat pods containing large, light-green, edible seeds. **2.** The seed of such a plant. See **butter bean.** [After *Lima,* Peru.]

lim·a·cine (límmə-sīn, lī́mə-, -sin) *adj.* Of, pertaining to, or resembling a slug. [New Latin *limacinus* : Latin *līmax* (stem *līmac-*), slug, snail, from *līmus,* slime + -INE.]

li·ma·çon (límmə-son) *n.* In geometry, a type of curve: the locus of a point on a straight line such that the point is always a fixed distance from the intersection of the line with a fixed circle as the line rotates about a point on the circle. [French, snail (named by Pascal with reference to the shape).]

Li·mas·sol (límmə-sol). Seaport on the south coast of Cyprus, centre of the island's wine industry.

lime *The common lime tree, with its heart-shaped leaves (above), is not, despite its name, a relative of the citrus fruit. The name of the tree, which is native to Europe, comes from "lind" or "linden", which is still the U.S. name for the tree.*

limb[1] (lim) *n.* **1.** Any of the jointed appendages of a person or an animal, used for locomotion or grasping, such as an arm, leg, wing, or flipper. **2.** Any of the larger branches of a tree. **3.** Any extension or projecting part, as of a building or a mountain range. **4.** One that is considered to be an extension, member, or representative of a larger body, group, or the like. **5.** *Geology.* Either of the sides of a fold in rock strata, away from the central axis. **6.** *Rare.* An impish or naughty child. **—out on a limb.** *Informal.* **1.** In a difficult, awkward, or vulnerable position. **2.** *British.* Isolated, especially in holding unpopular or controversial opinions. **—tear limb from limb.** To dismember.
~*tr.v.* **limbed, limbing, limbs.** *Rare.* To dismember. [Middle English *lim, lymm,* Old English *lim;* akin to Old Norse *limr*†.] **—limb·less** *adj.*

limb[2] *n.* **1.** *Astronomy.* The circumferential edge of the apparent disc of a celestial body. **2.** The edge of a graduated arc or circle used in an instrument to measure angles. **3.** *Botany.* The expanded tip of a petal or the expanded upper part of a united corolla. [French *limbe,* from Latin *limbus*†, border, hem, seam.]

lim·bate (límbayt) *adj. Botany.* Having an edge of a different colour. [Late Latin *limbātus,* bordered, from *limbus*†, border.]

limbed (limd) *adj.* **1.** Having a limb or limbs. **2.** Having a specified number or kind of limbs: *strong-limbed athletes.*

lim·ber[1] (límbər) *adj.* **1.** Bending or flexing readily; pliable. **2.** Capable of moving, bending, or contorting easily; agile; supple.
~*v.* **limbered, -bering, -bers.** —*tr.* To make limber. Often used with *up.* —*intr.* To make oneself limber. Used with *up: The football players limbered up before the game.* [16th century : perhaps from LIMBER (vehicle).] **—lim·ber·ly** *adv.* **—lim·ber·ness** *n.*

limber[2] *n.* A two-wheeled horse-drawn vehicle that carries ammunition and behind which a field gun may be towed.
~*v.* **limbered, -bering, -bers.** —*tr.* To fasten a limber to (a gun). Often used with *up.* —*intr.* To fasten a limber and a gun together. Often used with *up.* [Middle English *lymo(u)r,* shaft of a carriage, perhaps from Medieval Latin *limōnārius,* of a shaft, from *limō,* shaft, perhaps from Celtic.]

limber[3] *n. Nautical.* A channel on either side of the keelson into which water drains and can then be pumped away. [French *lumière,* hole, limber (literally, light).]

lim·bic system (límbik) *n.* The part of the brain governing basic activities, such as self-preservation, reproduction, and the expression of fear and rage. [French *limbique,* from *limbe,* LIMBUS.]

lim·bo (límbō) *n., pl.* **-bos.** **1.** *Often capital* **L.** *Theology.* The abode of just souls kept from Heaven through circumstance, such as lack of baptism. **2.** A region or condition of oblivion or neglect. **3.** A state or place of confinement. **4.** An intermediate state, usually of an unpleasant or unsatisfactory nature. [Middle English, from Medieval Latin *in limbō,* "(region) on the border (of hell)" : *in,* on + *limbus*†, border.]

limbo[2] *n., pl.* **-bos.** A West Indian dance in which the performer has to pass under a low bar, bending his knees and leaning backwards. [20th century : origin obscure.]

Lim·burg·er, Lim·bourg·er (lím-burgər) *n.* A soft, often pungent, white cheese made with herbs, originally produced in Limburg province, Belgium.

lim·bus (lím-bəss) *n., pl.* **-bi** (-bī). *Biology.* A distinctive border or edge. [Latin *limbus*†, border, hem, seam.]

lime[1] (līm) *n.* **1.** A spiny, evergreen tree, *Citrus aurantifolia,* native to Asia, having fragrant white flowers, and egg-shaped fruit with a green rind and acid juice used as flavouring. **2.** The fruit of this tree. [French, from Provençal *limo,* from Arabic *līmah.*]

lime[2] *n.* Any of several Old World trees of the genus *Tilia,* having sweet-scented flowers; especially the common lime, *T.* × *europaea,* which is a hybrid of the small-leaved lime, *T. cordata,* and the large-leaved lime, *T. platyphyllos.* Also called "linden". [Variant of *line,* dialectal variant of obsolete *lind,* LINDEN.]

lime[3] *n.* **1. a. Calcium oxide** *(see).* **b. Calcium hydroxide** *(see).* **2.** A sticky substance smeared on twigs to catch birds; birdlime.
~*tr.v.* **limed, liming, limes.** **1.** To treat with lime. **2.** To smear with birdlime. **3.** To catch or snare with or as with birdlime. [Middle English *lim,* Old English *līm.*]

lime green *n.* A bright yellowish green. **—lime-green** *adj.*

lime·kiln (līm-kiln, -kil) *n.* A furnace used to reduce naturally occurring forms of calcium carbonate to lime.

lime·light (līm-līt) *n.* **1.** An early type of stage light in which lime was heated to incandescence producing brilliant illumination. **2.** The brilliant light so produced. Also called "calcium light". **3.** The state of being at the centre of public attention. Used especially in the phrase *in the limelight.*

li·men (lī́-men) *n., pl.* **-mens** or **limina** (límminə) The threshold of a physiological or psychological response. [Latin *līmen,* threshold, akin to *līmes,* boundary, LIMIT.] **—lim·i·nal** (límmin'l) *adj.*

lime pit *n.* A pit containing lime and water in which hides are soaked to remove the hair before they are tanned.

lim·er (lī́mər) *n. West Indian Informal.* A person who hangs about the streets; a loafer. **—lim·ing** *n.*

lim·er·ick (límmərik, límrik) *n.* A light humorous or nonsensical verse of five anapaestic lines usually with the rhyme scheme *aabba.* [From the line "Will you come up to Limerick?" (the refrain of a convivial verse in a similar form).]

Lim·e·rick[1] (límmərik). County in Munster province, Republic of Ireland. Its fertile pastures support dairy and beef cattle.

Limerick[2]. Port on the river Shannon, the county town of County Limerick, Republic of Ireland. It was founded by the Vikings on an island on the river. It has long been noted for its lace.

lime·stone (līm-stōn) *n.* A sedimentary rock, chiefly $CaCO_3$. The chief mineral is calcite, but dolomite may also be present. It is used as building stone, and in the manufacture of lime, carbon dioxide, and cement.

lime-twig (līm-twig) *n.* **1.** A twig covered with birdlime to catch birds. **2.** A snare.

lime·wa·ter (līm-wawtər ‖ *U.S. also* -wottər) *n.* A clear, colourless, alkaline, aqueous solution of calcium hydroxide, used in calamine lotion and other skin preparations and as an antacid. It is used in a laboratory test for carbon dioxide, which causes it to go milky.

lim·ey (līmi) *n., pl.* **-eys.** *U.S. Slang.* **1.** A British person. **2.** A British sailor. [From earlier *lime-juicer,* American term for a British sailor or ship (the drinking of lime-juice as an antiscorbutic was compulsory in the Royal Navy).] **—lim·ey** *adj.*

li·mic·o·line (lī-míckə-līn, -lin) *adj.* Of, pertaining to, or designating shore birds, such as sandpipers, of the suborder Charadrii. [New Latin *Limicolae* (former order name), "mud dwellers" : Latin *līmus,* slime, mud + *-colae,* from *-colus,* -COLOUS.]

lim·it (límmit) *n.* **1.** The point, edge, or line beyond which something is no longer possible or allowable; the final or furthest confines or extent of something. **2.** *Usually plural.* The boundary surrounding a specific area; bounds: *within the city limits.* **3.** The maximum or minimum amount or number allowed: *an overdraft limit of £250; no minimum age limit.* **4.** *Informal.* Someone or something that goes beyond the limits of forbearance or acceptability. Preceded by *the.* **5.** *Archaic.* A region or section enclosed within or as if within boundaries. **6.** *Mathematics.* **a.** A number that is approached by a function as the variable approaches zero, infinity, or some other number. **b.** A value that a sequence or series approaches as the number of terms approaches infinity. **7.** Either of the two values between which a definite integral is defined. —See Synonyms at **boundary.** **—off limits.** *Chiefly U.S.* Out of bounds.
~*tr.v.* **limited, -iting, -its.** **1.** To confine or restrict within a limit or limits. **2.** To specify; fix definitely. [Middle English *limite,* from Latin *līmes*† (stem *līmit-*), border between fields, boundary.] **—lim·**

it·a·ble adj. —**lim·i·ta·tive** (límmi-tətiv, -taytiv) adj. —**lim·it·er** n.
Synonyms: limit, restrict, confine, circumscribe, bound.
lim·i·tar·y (límmi-təri, -tri || U.S. -terri) adj. **1. a.** Of or pertaining to a limit or boundary. **b.** Limiting; restrictive. **2.** Limited.
lim·i·ta·tion (límmi-táysh'n) n. **1.** The act of limiting or the state of being limited. **2.** A restriction. **3.** A shortcoming. **4.** Law. A limited period during which, by statute, an action may be brought.
lim·it·ed (límmitid) adj. Abbr. **Ltd., ltd. 1. a.** Having a limit or limits. **b.** Confined or restricted. **2. a.** Not attaining the highest goals or achievement: a limited success. **b.** Having only moderate talent or range of ability: a rather limited writer. **3.** Having governmental or ruling powers restricted by enforceable limitations, as a constitution or legislative body might. **4.** U.S. Designating transport facilities, such as trains or buses, that make few stops and carry relatively few passengers. —**lim·i·ted·ly** adv. —**lim·i·ted·ness** n.
limited edition n. An edition, as of a book or print, limited to a stated number of copies.
limited liability company n. British. Abbr. **Limited, Ltd.** A public or private company in which the liability of a shareholder for the company's debts is limited to his actual investment, such that his other assets are not affected if the company fails.
lim·i·ter (límmitər) n. Electronics. A circuit that cuts off an alternating signal and restricts it to a predetermined maximum or minimum value. Also called "clipper".
lim·it·less (límmit-ləss, -liss) adj. **1.** Having no limit or limits. **2.** Unconfined or unrestricted. —See Synonyms at **infinite.**
limit point n. Mathematics. A limit.
lim·i·trophe (límmi-trōf) adj. Near or on a frontier. Said of a country or region. [French, from Late Latin limitrophus, from Latin līmes (stem limit-), boundary + Greek -trophos, supporting, feeding (referring to frontier land devoted to supporting troops guarding the border).]
limn (lim) tr.v. **limned, limning** (límming, lím-ning), **limns.** Archaic. **1.** To describe. **2.** To depict by painting or drawing. [Middle English limnen, to illuminate (manuscripts), shortened from luminen, from Old French luminer, from Latin lūmināre, from lūmen, light.] —**lim·ner** (lím-nər) n.
lim·net·ic (lim-néttik) adj. Of or occurring in the water of lakes or ponds to the level of light penetration. [Greek limnē†, pool, lake.]
lim·nol·o·gy (lim-nólləji) n. The scientific study of the life and phenomena of lakes, ponds, and streams. [Greek limnē, pool, lake + -LOGY.] —**lim·no·log·i·cal** (-nə-lójik'l) adj. —**lim·no·log·i·cal·ly** adv. —**lim·nol·o·gist** (-nólləjist) n.
lim·o (límmō) n., pl. **-mos.** Informal. A limousine.
Li·moges¹ (li-mōzh). Capital of the Haute-Vienne département, central France.
Limoges² n. A variety of fine porcelain made at Limoges. Also called "Limoges ware".
lim·o·nene (límmə-neen) n. A liquid, $C_{10}H_{16}$, with a characteristic lemon-like fragrance, used as a solvent, wetting agent, and dispersing agent, and in the manufacture of resins. [French limon, lime, from Old French, LEMON + -ENE.]
li·mo·nite (límə-nīt) n. A widely occurring yellowish-brown to black natural iron oxide, essentially $FeO(OH)·nH_2O$, used as an ore of iron. [German Limonit, "meadow ore", bog iron ore : Greek leimōn†, meadow + -ITE.] —**li·mo·nit·ic** (-níttik) adj.
lim·ou·sine (límmə-zeen, -zéen) n. **1.** Formerly, a large car with an enclosed passenger compartment and an open but roofed driver's seat. **2.** Any large and luxurious car. [Originally a cloak popular in Limousin, former province of France, which the projecting roof was thought to resemble.]
limp (limp) intr.v. **limped, limping, limps. 1.** To walk lamely, especially with irregularity, when or as if one leg is weaker or shorter than the other. **2.** To move or proceed haltingly or unsteadily.
~n. An irregular, jerky, or awkward way of walking.
~adj. **limper, limpest. 1.** Lacking or having lost rigidity; flaccid; flabby. **2.** Lacking vitality, vigour, or strength of character; weak. **3.** Not stiffened; paperbacked. Said of a bookbinding. [Probably shortened from obsolete limphalt, lame, ultimately from Old English lemphealt, læmpihalt.] —**limp·ly** adv. —**limp·ness** n.
lim·pet (límpit) n. **1.** Any of numerous, generally marine gastropod molluscs, of the families Acmaeidae and Patellidae, characteristically having a tent-shaped shell and adhering to rocks of tidal areas. **2.** One who clings persistently. **3.** A type of explosive designed to cling to the hull of a ship and detonate on contact or signal. [Middle English lempet, Old English lempedu, from Medieval Latin lamprēda, LAMPREY.]
lim·pid (límpid) adj. **1.** Characterised by transparent clearness; pellucid. **2.** Easily intelligible; clear. Said especially of literary style. **3.** Calm and untroubled; serene. [French limpide, from Latin limpidus†.] —**lim·pid·i·ty** (lim-píddəti), **lim·pid·ness** n. —**lim·pid·ly** adv.
limp·kin (límpkin) n. A brownish wading bird, Aramus guarauna, of warm, swampy regions of the New World, having a distinctive, wailing call. Also called "courlan". [LIMP (referring to its movements) + -KIN.]
Lim·po·po (lim-pópō). River in southern Africa. It flows 1 600 kilometres (1,000 miles) from near Pretoria, Transvaal, South Africa, to the Indian Ocean north of Maputo, Mozambique.
lim·u·lus (límmew-ləss) n., pl. **-li** (-lī). A horseshoe crab; especially, Limulus polyphemus. [New Latin, from Latin, diminutive of limus, sidelong.]
lim·y (lími) adj. **-ier, -iest.** Of, resembling, or containing lime.
lin. **1.** lineal. **2.** linear.

lin·ac (línnak) n. Physics. A **linear accelerator** (see). [From linear accelerator.]
lin·age, line·age (línij) n. **1.** The number of lines of printed or written material. **2.** Payment for written work according to the number of such lines.
lin·al·o·ol (li-nál-ō-ol || -ōl) n. Also **lin·al·ol** (línnə-lol || -lōl). A colourless, fragrant liquid, $C_{10}H_{18}O$, distilled from the oils of rosewood, bergamot, and other plants and trees, and used in perfume manufacture. [Earlier linaloe, fragrant wood of a Mexican tree, from Mexican Spanish linaloe, from Spanish, from Late Latin lignum aloēs, "wood of the aloe" : Latin lignum, wood + aloē, ALOE.]
Lin Biao or **Lin Piao** (lín byów) (1907-71). Chinese Communist politician. He fought with Mao Ze-dong in the communist campaign to gain power in China. He was defence minister after 1959 and heir-apparent to Mao after 1969.
linch·pin, lynch·pin (línch-pin) n. **1.** A locking pin inserted in the end of a shaft, as in an axle to prevent a wheel from slipping off. **2.** A central or cohesive element: the linchpin of the family. [Middle English lynspin : lins, linchpin, Old English lynis, akin to Old Saxon lunisa† + PIN.]
Lin·coln (língkən). County town and market centre of Lincolnshire, England. In the tower of its (11th-15th century) cathedral is the famous bell, Great Tom of Lincoln.
Lincoln, Abraham (1809-65). 16th President of the United States (1861-65). From 1836 he practised law in Illinois, until becoming a Whig congressman (1847-49). Lincoln opposed slavery, and in 1856 joined the new Republican party, winning the 1860 presidential election. He vigorously led the North in the Civil War, and in 1863 issued the Emancipation Proclamation, freeing the slaves in the areas still under Confederate control. He was re-elected president in 1864, and during its session of 1864-65 Congress approved the 13th Amendment to the Constitution, abolishing slavery in the United States. Lincoln was assassinated in April, days after the end of the war, at Ford's Theatre in Washington, by John Wilkes Booth, a southern actor.
Lincoln green n. **1.** A yellowish- or brownish-green colour. **2.** Cloth of this colour, which Robin Hood and his men are supposed to have worn. [After LINCOLN, where the cloth was originally made.] —**Lincoln green** adj.
Lincoln Red n. Any of a breed of short-horned, red-coated beef cattle developed in eastern England.
Lin·coln·shire (língkən-shər, -sheer). Largely flat county in eastern England, intersected by canals and dykes. Much of its fenland has been drained for agricultural use.
Lincoln's Inn n. One of the four legal societies forming the **Inns of Court** (see) in England.
linc·tus (língktəss) n. A liquid, syrupy medicine taken to relieve coughs. [Latin, from the past participle of lingere, to lick.]
Lind (lind), **Jenny,** also known as The Swedish Nightingale (1820-87). Swedish soprano. After 1852, she lived mainly in London, and taught at the Royal College of Music (1883-86).
lin·dane (líndayn) n. A white poisonous powder used as a weed killer and insecticide. It is an isomer of hexachlorocyclohexane. [After T. van den Linden, 20th-century Dutch chemist.]
Lind·bergh (líndberg), **Charles (Augustus)** (1902-74). U.S. pilot. In May, 1927, he made the first solo nonstop transatlantic flight, from New York to Paris. His baby son was kidnapped and murdered in 1932, a notorious case.
lin·den (líndən) n. U.S. A lime tree. Not in current British usage.
Lindisfarne. See **Holy Island.**
Lind·sey (líndzi), **Parts of.** See **Lincolnshire.**
Lind·wall (línd-wawl), **Ray(mond Russell)** (1921-). Australian cricketer. By the time of his retirement in 1959, he had taken 228 Test wickets, then a record for a fast bowler.
line¹ (līn) n. Abbr. **l., L. 1.** In geometry: **a.** The locus of a point having one degree of freedom; a curve. **b.** A set of points (x, y) that satisfy the linear equation $ax + by + c = 0$, where a and b are not both zero. **2.** A thin, continuous mark, such as that made by a pen, pencil, or brush applied to a surface. **3.** A similar mark cut or scratched into a surface. **4.** An indentation or crease in the skin, especially on the face or palm; a wrinkle. **5.** Sports. **a.** A mark on a playing court or field indicating a boundary of play. **b.** A mark or imaginary point at which a race starts or ends. **6.** Chiefly U.S. A border or boundary: the county line. **7.** Any demarcation: a picket line. **8.** A contour or outline. **9.** In art: **a.** A mark used to define a shape or represent a contour. **b.** Any of the marks that make up the formal design of a picture. **10.** A cable, rope, string, cord, or wire, such as: **a.** One used on a ship. **b.** One used for catching fish. **c.** A clothes line. **d.** A string or cord used, as by builders or surveyors, for taking measurements, levelling, or straightening. **e.** A cable transmitting electric power of telecommunications signals: telephone lines. **11.** An open or functioning telephone connection. **12. a.** A system of public transport, as by ship, aircraft, or bus, usually over a definite route. **b.** A company owning or managing such a system. Sometimes used in combination: an airline. **13. a.** A railway track. **b.** A particular section of a railway network: the London to Glasgow line. **14.** A course of progress or movement: the line of flight. **15. a.** A general method, manner, or course of procedure: different lines of thought. **b.** A manner or course of procedure determined by a specified factor: development along communist lines; a society divided along tribal lines. **16.** An official or prescribed policy: the party line. **17.** A state of alignment, conformity, or agreement: brought the front wheels into line; a wages agreement

in line with recent settlements. **18. a.** One's trade or occupation. **b.** The range of one's competence or preferred activity: *not really in my line.* **19.** Merchandise of a similar or related nature: *This store carries a line of small tools.* **20.** A group of persons or things arranged in a row or series, especially abreast. **21.** A series of persons, especially belonging to the same family, who succeed each other chronologically: *comes of a long line of bankers.* **22. a.** A row of words printed or written across a page or a column. **b.** A unit of verse made up of such a row, or formed of a certain number of metrical feet characteristic of the verse. **c.** *Plural. British.* A usually specified number of lines of prose or verse to be written out by a pupil as a punishment. **23.** A brief letter; a note. **24.** *Often plural.* The dialogue of a play or other theatrical presentation: *learning his lines.* **25.** A calculated or glib way of speaking, usually to obtain some undeclared end. **26.** A hint or snippet of information: *tried to get a line on their secret plans.* **27.** A horizontal demarcation in bridge dividing categories of points scored: *Points above the line do not count towards game.* **28.** *Music.* Any of the five parallel marks composing a staff. **29.** *Military.* **a.** A formation in which elements, such as troops, tanks, or ships, are arranged abreast of each other. **b.** The battle area closest to the enemy. **c.** The troops in this area. **d.** A bulwark or trench. **e.** An extended system of such fortifications or defences. **f.** *Capital* **L.** In the British army, the regular numbered regiments, as distinguished from the Guards and auxiliary units. Preceded by *the.* **30.** The equator. Preceded by *the*: *crossed the line.* **31.** Any of the horizontal bands that make up a television picture. **32.** The course followed when hunting a fox. **33.** In cricket, the degree of a bowler's control over the direction of the ball: *good line and length.* **34.** A unit of magnetic flux, one **maxwell** *(see).* **35.** The proportion of an insurance risk assumed by a particular underwriter or company. **—all along the line. 1.** In every place. **2.** At every stage or moment. **—draw the line (at).** To refuse to go as far as or beyond; consider as unacceptable. **—hold the line. 1.** To keep open a telephone connection. **2.** To maintain a firm position. **—in line for.** Likely or due to receive: *in line for promotion.* **—in the line of duty.** As a part of one's responsibilities in a given job. **—keep in line.** To keep in order; restrain. **—lay** or **put on the line.** *Informal.* **1.** To make payment. **2.** To jeopardise; put at risk: *put his reputation on the line.* **3.** To be candid or explicit: *He sure laid it on the line.* **—read between the lines.** To deduce the implicit rather than explicit meaning of a statement. **—shoot a line.** To try to deceive by lying or exaggerating. **—toe the line.** To obey the rules; conform.

~*v.* **lined, lining, lines.** —*tr.* **1.** To mark or incise with a line or lines. **2.** To represent or depict with a line or lines. **3.** To place in a series or row. Often used with *up.* **4.** To form a bordering line along: *Small stalls lined the alleys.* —*intr.* To form a line. Usually used with *up.* See **line up.** [Middle English *ligne, line,* cord, stroke, mark, line, partly from Old French *ligne,* from Vulgar Latin *linja* (unattested), from Latin *līnea,* thread, line, from *līnum,* flax, and partly from Old English *līne,* cord, rope, series, representing a Common Germanic borrowing of Latin *līnea.*]

line² *tr.v.* **lined, lining, lines. 1.** To sew or fit a covering to the inside surface of: *a coat lined with fur.* **2.** To cover the inner surface of: *Moisture lined the cave's walls.* **3.** To fill plentifully, as with money or food. [Middle English *linen,* from *line,* flax, Old English *līn,* from Germanic *līnam* (unattested), from Latin *līnum,* flax.]

lin·e·age¹ (línni-ij) *n.* **1.** Direct descent from a particular ancestor; ancestry. **2.** Derivation. **3.** The descendants of a certain ancestor considered as the founder of the line. [Middle English *linage,* from Old French *li(g)nage,* from *ligne,* LINE.]

line·age². Variant of **linage.**

lin·e·al (línni-əl) *adj. Abbr.* **lin. 1.** Belonging to or being in the direct line of descent from an ancestor. Compare **collateral. 2.** Derived from or pertaining to a particular line of descent: *the lineal rights of royalty.* **3.** Linear. [Middle English, from Old French, from Late Latin *līneālis,* from Latin *līnea,* LINE.] **—lin·e·al·ly** *adv.*

lin·e·a·ment (línni-əmənt) *n.* **1.** A distinctive shape, contour, or line, especially of the face. **2.** A definitive or characteristic mark or feature. [Middle English *liniament,* from Latin *līneāmentum,* from *līneāre,* to make straight, from *līnea,* LINE.]

lin·e·ar (línni-ər) *adj. Abbr.* **lin. 1.** Of, pertaining to, or resembling a line or lines; straight. **2.** In geometry: **a.** In, of, describing, described by, or related to a straight line. **b.** Having only one dimension. **3.** In art, characterised chiefly by forms and shapes that are precisely defined by line. Compare **painterly. 4.** Narrow and elongated: *a linear leaf.* **5.** Designating a form of script made up of lines rather than pictorial symbols. See **Linear A, Linear B.** [Latin *līneāris,* from *līnea,* LINE.] **—lin·e·ar·ly** *adv.*

Linear A *n.* A partly linear, partly pictographic script used in Crete from about 1900 to 1500 B.C., and as yet undeciphered.

linear accelerator *n.* An electron, proton, or heavy-ion **accelerator** *(see)* in which the paths of the particles accelerated are essentially straight lines rather than circles or spirals. Also called "linac".

linear algebra *n.* **1.** A branch of mathematics dealing with the theory of systems of linear equations, matrices, vector spaces, determinants, and linear transformations. **2.** A mathematical ring and vector space with scalars from an associated field, the multiplication of which is of the form $(aA)(bB) = (ab)(AB)$ where a and b are scalars and A and B are vectors.

Linear B *n.* A syllabic script, probably a modification of Linear A, used in Mycenaean Greek documents from the 14th to the 12th century B.C. and deciphered by Michael Ventris in 1952.

linear equation *n.* An algebraic equation, such as $x + y + 5 = 0$, in which the highest degree term in the variable or variables is of the first degree.

linear measure *n.* **1.** Measurement of length. **2.** A unit or system of units for measuring length. Also called "long measure".

linear momentum *n. Physics.* **Momentum** *(see).*

linear motor *n.* A type of electric motor in which the moving and stationary parts are linear and parallel so that a current causes motion along a line. Commonly, the moving part, which may be a vehicle, such as a locomotive, contains horizontal coils which induce a voltage in a long metal rail.

linear perspective *n.* See **perspective.**

linear programming *n. Mathematics.* A technique using successive approximations to find the optimum value of a function that is subject to linear constraints, used extensively in planning industrial processes, economic models, and the like.

lin·e·a·tion (línni-áysh'n) *n.* **1.** A marking or outlining with lines. **2.** An outline. **3.** An arrangement of lines.

line breeding *n.* Selective inbreeding to perpetuate certain qualities or characteristics in a strain of stock.

line cut *n.* A letterpress printing plate made from a line drawing by a photoengraving process. Also called "line engraving".

line drawing *n.* A drawing made with lines only, especially one used as copy for a line engraving.

line engraving *n. Printing.* **1.** A metal plate, used in intaglio printing, on the surface of which design lines have been hand engraved. **2.** The process of making such an engraving. **3.** A print made from such an engraving. **4.** A line cut.

Line Islands (līn). Group of small islands in the central Pacific Ocean. Eight of them are part of Kiribati. The other three are uninhabited, and are dependencies of the United States.

lin·en (línnin) *n.* **1.** Thread made from fibres of the flax plant. **2.** Cloth woven from this thread. **3.** Garments or other articles, such as sheets and tablecloths, made from this or similar cloth. ~*adj.* **1.** Made of flax or linen. **2.** Resembling linen. [Middle English, Old English *līnen, linnen,* "made of flax" (not used of linen cloth), from Germanic *līnin* (unattested), from *līnam* (unattested), flax, from Latin *līnum.*]

line of credit *n.* A **credit line** *(see).*

line of fire *n.* The flight path of a bullet or other missile discharged from a firearm.

line of force *n. Physics.* An imaginary line in a field of force, any tangent to which gives the direction of the field at the point of tangency.

line of scrimmage *n.* In American football, an imaginary line across the field on which the ball rests and at which the teams line up for a new play.

line of sight *n.* An imaginary line from the eye to the object being looked at. Also called "line of vision".

lin·e·o·late (línni-ə-layt) *adj. Biology.* Marked with fine lines. [New Latin *lineolatus,* from Latin *līneola,* diminutive of *līnea,* LINE.]

line-out (lī́n-owt) *n.* In Rugby football, the grouping of the opposing forwards into two parallel lines between which the ball is thrown from the touchline after it has gone out of play.

line printer *n.* A fast printer that prints characters a whole line at a time, used especially for printing the output from computers.

lin·er¹ (lī́nər) *n.* **1.** One that draws or makes a line or lines. **2.** A commercial ship or aircraft, especially one carrying passengers on a regular route. **3. Eyeliner** *(see).*

liner² *n.* **1.** One who makes or puts in linings. **2.** Something used as a lining: *a dustbin liner.*

lines·man (lī́nz-mən) *n., pl.* **-men** (-mən, -men). *Sports.* An official assisting the referee or umpire, as in soccer or tennis, whose main duty is to indicate when the ball has gone out of play.

line spectrum *n.* A spectrum consisting of a set of discrete, fairly narrow lines.

line squall *n.* A band of extremely stormy weather with gusting winds, hail, and thunderstorms, associated with a cold front.

line up *intr.v.* To form or take a place in a line. —*tr.v.* **1.** To put into line or into alignment. **2.** To assemble, organise, or prepare: *lined up a lot of evidence against him.*

line-up, line-up (lī́n-up) *n.* **1.** A line of persons formed for inspection or identification. **2.** A group or arrangement of people or things brought together for a particular purpose: *an interesting line-up of acts for the show; in the Leeds line-up for tonight's game.*

ling¹ (ling) *n., pl.* **lings** or collectively **ling.** Any of various marine food fishes related to or resembling the cod, such as *Molva molva,* of northwest European waters. [Middle English *leng(e),* probably of Low German origin; akin to Dutch *lenghe, linghe.*]

ling² *n.* A plant, **heather** *(see).* [Middle English *lyng,* from Old Norse.]

-ling¹ *n. suffix.* Indicates: **1.** The young of a specified animal; for example, **duckling, gosling. 2.** A smaller, lesser, or inferior version; for example, **princeling, underling. 3.** One produced by or under the care or control of; for example, **earthling, nursling, hireling.** Often used derogatorily. [Middle English, Old English, from Common Germanic *-linga-* (unattested) : noun ending *-ilaz* (unattested) + patronymic ending *-inga-.*]

-ling² *adj. & adv. suffix.* Indicates: **1.** Direction or position; for example, **sideling, flatling. 2.** Condition; for example, **darkling.** [Middle English, from Old English, from West Germanic *-ling-, -lang-* (unattested).]

ling. linguistics.

PRONUNCIATION KEY

a, trap; aa, father; ai, fair; ar, star; aw, lawn; ay, play; b, bb, stab; rubber; ch, church; ck, ticket; d, dd, dead; ladder; e, dress; ee, bee; er, defer; ew, few; ewr, pure; ə, about; ər, letter; f, ff, fife; differ; g, gg, giggle; h, hat; i, kit; ī, price; īr, fire; j, judge; k, kick; l, ll, let; 'l, needle; m, mm, man; n, nn, no; 'n, sudden; ng, thing; o, lot; ō, no; o͝o, foot; o͞o, shoe; oor, poor; ow, cow; owr, hour; oy, boy; p, pp, pepper; r, rr, red; s, ss, sauce; sh, ship; t, tt, totter; th, thick; th, this; smooth; u, cut; ur, turn; v, vv, valve; w, wet; y, yes; z, zz, zebra; zh, vision; pleasure

IN FOREIGN WORDS:

aN, oN, Saint-Saëns; hl, Llanelli; Hluhluwe; kh, loch; lough; Khaled

STRESS MARK:

ín-sīt, insight; in-sī́t, incite

lin·gam (líng-gəm) *n.* Also **lin·ga** (-gə). A stylised phallus worshipped as a symbol of the Hindu god Shiva. [Sanskrit *lingat*†, "distinctive mark", penis.]

ling·cod (líng-kod) *n., pl.* **-cods** or collectively **lingcod.** A food fish, *Ophiodon elongatus,* of northern Pacific waters.

lin·ger (líng-gər) *v.* **-gered, -gering, -gers.** —*intr.* **1.** To delay departure; be slow and reluctant to leave; tarry. **2.** To hover between life and death for some time before dying. **3.** To remain, in dilute form; be slow in disappearing: *The smell of frying lingered on; The memory still lingers.* **4.** To delay; procrastinate. **5.** To proceed slowly; saunter. —*tr. Archaic.* To prolong; protract. Used with *on* or *out.* —See Synonyms at **stay.** [Middle English (northern dialect) *lengeren,* frequentative of *lengen,* to tarry, from Old Norse *lengja.*] —**lin·ger·er** *n.* —**lin·ger·ing·ly** *adv.*

lin·ge·rie (láNzhə-ri, lónzhə-, -ray) *n.* **1.** Women's underwear and night wear. **2.** *Archaic.* Linen articles, especially garments. [French, "linen garments", from *linge,* linen, from Latin *līneus,* made of linen, from *līnum,* flax.]

lin·go (líng-gō) *n., pl.* **-goes.** *Informal.* Language that is distinctive, unintelligible, or unfamiliar through being foreign or a jargon. [Portuguese *lingoa,* "tongue", language, from Latin *lingua.*]

lin·gua (líng-gwə) *n., pl.* **-guae** (-gwee). A tongue or tonguelike organ. [Latin.]

lingua fran·ca (fráng-kə) *n., pl.* **linguae francae** (-kee) or **lingua francas. 1.** Any hybrid language used as a medium of communication between peoples of different languages. **2.** Any mutually intelligible medium of communication. **3.** *Capital* **L.** A mixture of Italian with French, Spanish, Arabic, Greek, and Turkish, formerly spoken in eastern Mediterranean ports. [Italian, "the Frankish tongue".]

lin·gual (líng-gwəl || -gew-əl) *adj.* **1.** Of, pertaining to, or resembling the tongue or a tonguelike organ. **2.** *Phonetics.* Formed with the tongue in conjunction with other organs of speech. **3.** *Rare.* Linguistic.
~*n. Phonetics.* A sound that is pronounced with the tongue in conjunction with other organs of speech, such as the sounds (t), (l), or (n). —**lin·gual·ly** *adv.*

lin·gui·form (líng-gwi-fawrm) *adj.* Having the form of a tongue.

lin·gui·ni (ling-gwéeni) *n.* **1.** *Used with a singular or plural verb.* Pasta in the form of long, thin, flat strands. **2.** A dish consisting of or containing such pasta. [Italian, plural of *linguino,* "small tongue", from *lingua,* tongue, from Latin.]

lin·guist (líng-gwist) *n.* **1.** A person who speaks several languages fluently. **2.** A student of a language or languages. **3.** A specialist in linguistics. **4.** *West African.* The spokesman of a chief, especially in Ghana. [Latin *lingua,* tongue, language.]

lin·guis·tic (ling-gwístik) *adj.* Of or pertaining to language or linguistics. —**lin·guis·ti·cal·ly** *adv.*

linguistic form *n.* Any meaningful unit of speech, such as an affix, word, phrase, or sentence. Also called "form".

lin·guis·tic·ian (líng-gwiss-tísh'n) *n.* A specialist in linguistics. Usually used derogatorily.

lin·guis·tics (ling-gwístiks) *n. Used with a singular verb. Abbr.* **ling.** The science of language; the study of the nature and structure of human speech.

lin·gu·late (líng-gew-layt) *adj.* Tongue-shaped. [Latin *lingulātus,* from *lingula,* diminutive of *lingua,* tongue.]

lin·i·ment (línnimənt) *n.* A medicinal fluid applied to the skin by rubbing as an anodyne or to relieve stiffness. [Middle English *lynyment,* from Late Latin *linīmentum,* from Latin *linere,* to anoint.]

li·nin (līnin) *n.* The filamentous, achromatic material in the nucleus of a cell that interconnects the chromatin granules. [Latin *līnum,* flax + -IN.]

lin·ing (līning) *n.* **1. a.** An interior covering or coating. **b.** Material that may be used for such covering or coating. **2.** The act or process of applying a lining to something.

link[1] (lingk) *n.* **1.** Any of the rings or loops forming a chain. **2.** Anything resembling a chain link in its physical arrangement or its connecting function, such as a cuff link or a loop in crochet. **3.** Anything that connects or provides a connection, such as: **a.** Something constituting a causal relation: *the link between stress and heart disease.* **b.** A system of transport or communications, as between two or more points: *a satellite link; the Heathrow to Gatwick helicopter link.* **c.** A single unit or element in such a system: *the islanders' only link with the outside world.* **d.** A passage, continuity, or progression, as in music, prose, or a broadcast. **4.** A unit of length used in surveying, equal to 0.01 chain or 20.1 centimetres (7.92 inches). **5.** A rod or lever transmitting motion in a machine.
~*v.* **linked, linking, links.** —*tr.* **1.** To connect or couple with or as if with links. **2.** To intertwine: *link arms.* —*intr.* To become connected with or as with links. —See Synonyms at **join.** [Middle English, from Old Norse *hlenkr* (unattested), variant of *hlekkr,* link, ring.]

link[2] *n.* A torch formerly used at night for lighting one's way in the streets. [Perhaps from Medieval Latin *linchinus,* variant of *lichinus,* from Latin *lychnus,* from Greek *lukhnos,* lamp.]

link·age (língkij) *n.* **1.** The act or process of linking. **2.** The state or condition of being linked. **3.** A system of interconnected machine elements, such as rods, springs, and pivots, used to transmit power or motion. **4.** *Electricity.* A measure of the induced voltage in a circuit caused by a magnetic flux, and equal to the flux multiplied by the number of turns in the coil that surrounds it. **5.** *Genetics.* The occurrence of genes together on the same chromosome such that they are likely, in proportion to their proximity, to be inherited together rather than independently. **6.** In international relations, a bargaining tactic whereby apparently diverse issues are combined so that agreement on one is dependent on agreement on another or others.

linked (lingkt) *adj.* **1.** Connected, especially by or as if by links. **2.** Intertwined: *linked arms.* **3.** *Genetics.* Exhibiting linkage.

linking verb *n.* A verb, such as *appear, be, feel, grow,* or *seem,* that connects a subject and a predicate adjective or predicate nominative; a copula.

Link·lat·er (língk-laytər), **Eric** (1899–1974). Scottish writer. He wrote many novels, including *Private Angelo* (1946).

link·man (língk-man) *n., pl.* **-men** (-men). **1.** A person responsible for providing continuity between different items in a radio or television broadcast. **2.** In games such as football and hockey, a player who acts as a link between the forwards and the backs.

Lin·kö·ping (*Swedish* línt-khöping). Ancient city in southern Sweden, capital of Östergötland county.

links (lingks) *pl.n.* **1.** A golf course, especially one along a seashore. **2.** *Chiefly Scottish.* Relatively flat or undulating ground, sandy and turf-covered, along a seashore. [Middle English, from Old English *hlincas,* plural of *hlinc,* ridge.]

Link trainer *n. Aeronautics.* A trademark for a device used to train aircrew in reading flight instruments.

Lin·lith·gow (lin-líthgō). Ancient burgh in Lothian Region, Scotland. James V and his daughter Mary, Queen of Scots, were born at the now ruined Linlithgow Palace.

linn (lin) *n. Chiefly Scottish.* **1.** A waterfall. **2.** A steep ravine. [Scottish Gaelic *linne.*]

Lin·nae·us (li-née-əss, -náy-), **Carolus,** also known as Karl Linné (after 1761 von Linné) (1707–78). Swedish biologist. He created the system of classification of plants and animals used today. In his *Systema Naturae* (1735) and *Species Plantarum* (1753), animals and plants were described by genus and species. —**Lin·ne·an, Lin·nae·an** (-née-ən, -náy-) *adj.*

lin·net (línnit) *n.* **1.** A small Old World songbird, *Acanthis cannabina,* having brownish plumage. **2.** A similar bird, *Carpodacus mexicanus,* of western North America. [Old French dialectal *linette,* from *lin,* flax (the bird feeds on linseed), from Latin *līnum.*]

linnet *Though linseed is the linnet's favourite food, it feeds on other plants as well. But its numbers are declining as the increasing use of weedkillers depletes its food supply. The linnet is native to Eurasia and Africa.*

li·no (līnō) *n., pl.* **-nos.** Linoleum.

li·no·cut (līnō-kut) *n.* **1.** A print taken from a block of linoleum on which a design has been carved with a gouging tool. **2.** The technique of producing such prints.

lin·o·le·ic acid (lín-ō-lée-ik, -ə-, -láy-) *n.* A clear to straw-coloured liquid, $C_{18}H_{32}O_2$, an important component of drying oils and an essential fatty acid in the human diet, being obtained from vegetable seed oils and some animal fats. [Greek *linon,* flax + OLEIC ACID (so called because found in linseed oil).]

lin·o·len·ic acid (lín-ō-lénnik, -ə-) *n.* A colourless liquid, $C_{18}H_{30}O_2$, an important component of natural drying oils and an essential fatty acid in the human diet, being obtained from vegetable oils. [Arbitrarily from LINOLEIC ACID.]

li·no·le·um (li-nōli-əm) *n.* A durable, washable material made in sheets by pressing a mixture of heated linseed oil, rosin, powdered cork, and pigments onto a burlap or canvas backing, used chiefly as a floor covering. Also called "lino". [Latin *līnum,* flax + *oleum,* OIL.]

Li·no·type (līnə-tīp) *n.* A trademark for a machine that can set an entire line of type on a single metal slug and that is operated by a keyboard similar to that of a typewriter. —**Li·no·type** *v.* —**Li·no·typ·er, Li·no·typ·ist** *n.*

Lin Piao. See **Lin Biao.**

lin·sang (lín-sang) *n.* Any of several Asian or African catlike carnivorous mammals of the genera *Poiana* and *Prionodon,* having a spotted coat and a long striped tail. [Malay.]

lin·seed (lín-seed) *n.* The seed of flax, especially when used as the source of linseed oil. [Middle English, Old English *līnsǣd* : Old English *līn,* flax, from Latin *līnum* + SEED.]

linseed oil *n.* A golden-yellow, amber, or brown oil that thickens and hardens on exposure to air, extracted from the seeds of flax, and used as a drying oil in paints and varnishes, and in linoleum, printing inks, and synthetic resins.

lintel *A massive lintel above the shoulder-high main entrance to the Church of the Nativity, Bethlehem.*

lin·sey-wool·sey (línzi-wóolzi) *n., pl.* **-seys.** A coarse fabric of cotton or linen woven with wool. [Middle English *lynsy-wolsye* : probably after *Lindsey,* village in Suffolk (where it was originally manufactured) + WOOL.]

lin·stock (lín-stok) *n.* A long forked stick for holding a match, formerly used to fire cannon. [Dutch *lontstok* : *lont,* match, wick, akin to Middle Low German *lunte*† + *stok,* stick.]

lint (lint) *n.* **1.** Downy material obtained by scraping linen cloth and used for dressing wounds. **2.** The mass of soft fibres surrounding the seeds of unginned cotton. **3.** Clinging bits of fibre and fluff; fuzz. [Middle English *lynet,* from Latin *linteum,* linen cloth, from *linteus,* made of linen, from *līnum,* flax.]

lin·tel (línt'l) *n.* The horizontal beam that forms the upper member of a window or door frame and supports part of the structure above it. [Middle English, from Old French *lintel, lintier,* from Vulgar Latin *līmitāris* (unattested), alteration (influenced by Latin *līmes,* stem *līmit-,* boundary, LIMIT) of Latin *līminaris,* of a threshold, from *līmen,* threshold, LIMEN.]

lint·er (líntər) *n. U.S.* **1.** A machine that removes the short fibres that cling to cotton seeds after the first ginning. **2.** *Plural.* The fibres thus removed.

lion *Unlike most wild cats, which are solitary animals, the lion lives in groups, known as prides. It spends up to 20 hours a day asleep and may feed only once or twice a week. Once found all over Asia, Africa, and Europe, lions are now largely confined to eastern and southern Africa.*

PRONUNCIATION KEY

a, trap; aa, father; ai, fair; ar, star; aw, lawn; ay, play; b, bb, stab; rubber; ch, church; ck, ticket; d, dd, dead; ladder; e, dress; ee, bee; er, defer; ew, few; ewr, pure; ə, about; ər, letter; f, ff, fife; differ; g, gg, giggle; h, hat; i, kit; ī, price; īr, fire; j, judge; k, kick; l, ll, let; 'l, needle; m, mm, man; n, nn, no; 'n, sudden; ng, thing; o, lot; ō, no; ŏŏ, foot; ōō, shoe; oor, poor; ow, cow; owr, hour; oy, boy; p, pp, pepper; r, rr, red; s, ss, sauce; sh, ship; t, tt, totter; th, thick; th, this; smooth; u, cut; ur, turn; v, vv, valve; w, wet; y, yes; z, zz, zebra; zh, vision; pleasure

IN FOREIGN WORDS:

aN, oN, Saint-Saëns; hl, Llanelli; Hluhluwe; kh, loch; lough; Khaled

STRESS MARK:

ín-sīt, insight; in-sít, incite

lint·white (lint-wīt, -hwīt) *n. Poetic & Regional.* A linnet. [Middle English *lynkwhyte,* Old English *līnetwige,* "linseed eater" : *līn,* flax + *-twige,* "plucker", "eater", from West Germanic *twig-* (unattested), to pluck.]

Linz (lints). Capital of Upper Austria, situated on the river Danube. It is an iron and steel centre.

li·on (lī-ən) *n., pl.* **lions** or collectively (senses 1, 2) **lion. 1.** A large, carnivorous feline mammal, *Panthera leo,* of Africa and India, having a short tawny coat and a long, heavy mane around the neck and shoulders in the male. **2.** Any of several related animals considered to resemble a lion in some way. **3.** A person resembling a lion, as in bravery or ferocity. **4.** One whose eminence, as in arts and letters, has led to social prestige; a sought-after celebrity. **5.** A heraldic representation of a lion, the national emblem of Great Britain. **6.** *Capital* **L.** A member of the British international Rugby Union team. **7.** *Capital* **L.** *Astronomy.* The constellation and sign of the zodiac, **Leo** *(see).* Preceded by *the.* **—beard the lion in his den.** To face or defy the opposition in its own territory or home. **—twist the lion's tail.** To irritate or insult the nation or government of Great Britain. [Middle English *li(o)un, leoun,* from Anglo-French *liun* and Old French *lion,* both from Latin *leō* (stem *leōn-*), from Greek *leōn,* perhaps from Semitic.]

li·on·ess (lī-ən-ess, -iss, -éss) *n.* A female lion. [Middle English *leonesse,* from Old French *lionnesse,* from *lion,* LION.]

li·on-heart·ed (lī-ən-haartid, -hártid) *adj.* Extraordinarily courageous.

lionise, li·on·ize (lī-ən-īz) *tr.v.* **-ised, -ising, -ises.** To look upon or treat (a person) as a celebrity. **—li·on·i·sa·tion** (-ī-záysh'n ‖ *U.S.* -i-) *n.* **—li·on·is·er** *n.*

lion's share *n.* The largest or best part of a whole.

lip (lip) *n.* **1.** *Anatomy.* Either of two fleshy, muscular folds that together surround the opening of the mouth. **2.** Any structure or part that similarly encircles or bounds an orifice, as: **a.** *Anatomy.* A labium. **b.** The margin of flesh around a wound. **c.** Either of the margins of the aperture of a gastropod shell. **d.** The rim of a vessel, bell, crater, or the like. **3.** *Botany.* Any of the protruding divisions of an irregular corolla or calyx, either paired, as in the snapdragon, or single, as in an orchid. **4.** The tip of a pouring spout. **5.** *Slang.* Insolent talk. **6.** *Music.* The ability to shape the lips properly in playing a brass instrument; embouchure. **—bite (one's) lip. 1.** To hold back one's anger or other feeling. **2.** To show vexation.

~*tr.v.* **lipped, lipping, lips. 1. a.** To touch the lips to. **b.** *Poetic.* To kiss. **2.** To utter; especially, to whisper or murmur. **3.** *Literary.* To lap. Used of water. **4.** To serve as a lip or rim to. **5.** *Golf.* To hit the ball so that it stops just at the edge of (the hole). [Middle English *lip(pe),* Old English *lippa.*]

Li·pa·ri Islands (líppəri; *Italian* lée-paa-ree). Formerly **Aeolian Islands.** Italian islands lying north of Sicily. They are volcanic, and include Lipari, Vulcano, Stromboli, and Salina.

lip·ase (līp-ayz, líp-, -ayss) *n.* An enzyme that hydrolyses fats to form glycerol and fatty acids. [LIP(O)- + -ASE.]

lip gloss *n.* A clear or coloured cosmetic grease used to add shine to the lips.

lip·id (líp-īd) *n.* Also **lip·ide** (lī-pīd). Any of numerous fats and fatlike materials that are generally insoluble in water but soluble in common organic solvents, that are related to the fatty-acid esters, and that together with carbohydrates and proteins constitute the principal structural material of living cells. [French *lipide* : LIP(O)- + -ID.]

Lip·iz·za·ner, Lip·pi·zan·er *n.* Any of a breed of nearly white horses, used by the Spanish Riding School in Vienna and trained in feats of dressage. [German, after *Lippiza,* Yugoslavia, where the breed was developed.]

Lip·mann (lípmən), **Fritz Albert** (1899–). U.S. biochemist, born in Germany. He discovered coenzyme A, which is necessary for the oxidation of carbohydrate during metabolism, and shared the 1953 Nobel prize in physiology and medicine with H.A. Krebs.

lipo–, lip– *comb. form.* Indicates fat or fatty; for example, **lipolysis, lipoma.** [New Latin, from Greek *lipos,* fat.]

li·po·gen·e·sis (lipō-jénnə-siss) *n.* The synthesis of fatty acids in living cells. [LIPO- + -GENESIS.]

lip·oid (líp-oyd, līp-) *adj.* Also **lip·oi·dal** (li-póyd'l). Resembling fat; fatty. [LIP(O)- + -OID.] **—lip·oid** *n.*

li·pol·y·sis (li-pólla-siss, lī-) *n.* The hydrolysis of fats or lipids. [LIPO- + -LYSIS.]

li·po·ma (li-pōmə) *n., pl.* **-mata** (-tə) or **-mas.** A benign tumour of fatty cells. [LIP(O)- + -OMA.] **—li·pom·a·tous** (-pómmətəss) *adj.*

lip·o·pro·tein (líppō-prō-teen, līpō-, -tee-in) *n.* A conjugated protein consisting of a simple protein combined with a lipid group.

lip·o·some (líp-ō-sōm, līp-, -ə-) *n.* A small sac consisting of a synthetic membrane made of phospholipid, used to convey relatively toxic drugs to target organs or cancerous tumours. [LIPO- + -SOME.]

lip·o·trop·ic (líppō-tróppik, līpō-) *adj.* Preventing abnormal or excessive accumulation of fat in the liver. [LIPO- + -TROPIC.] **—li·pot·ro·pism, li·pot·ro·py** (li-póttrəpi, lī-) *n.*

Lip·pe (lipp-e). Former independent state of Germany, now part of Nordrhein-Westfalen, West Germany.

lipped (lipt) *adj.* **1.** Having a lip or lips. **2.** Having a specified number or kind of lips: *thick-lipped.*

Lip·per·shey (líppər-shay), **Hans,** also called Jan or Hans Lippersheim (líppərss-hīm) (*c.*1570–*c.*1619). German-born Dutch inventor of the telescope.

Lip·pi (líppi), **Filippino** (*c.*1457–1504). Florentine painter, son of Fra Filippo. He completed (*c.*1480) Masaccio's frescoes in the Brancacci chapel, Florence. He also painted the *Vision of St. Bernard* (*c.*1486), and the *Madonna Enthroned.*

Lippi, Fra Filippo, also known as Fra Lippo (*c.*1406–69). Florentine painter, father of Filippino. He left the Carmelite order to become a pupil of Masaccio. His paintings, such as the *Annunciation* (*c.*1438) and the *Coronation of the Virgin* (*c.*1441), display a bold three-dimensional style.

Lippizaner. Variant of **Lipizzaner.**

lip-read (líp-reed) *v.* **-read** (-red), **-reading, -reads.** *—tr.* To interpret (another's utterance) by lip-reading. *—intr.* To use lip-reading. **—lip-read·er** *n.*

lip-read·ing (líp-reeding) *n.* A technique used, especially by the deaf, to understand inaudible speech by interpreting lip and facial movements.

lip service *n.* Superficial respect or agreement.

lip·stick (líp-stik) *n.* A stick of waxy or creamy lip colouring enclosed in a small cylindrical case.

liq. **1.** liquid. **2.** liquor.

li·quate (lī-kwáyt ‖ lī-kwayt) *tr.v.* **-quated, -quating, -quates.** To separate (the metals in an alloy) by melting some constituents while leaving others solid. [Latin *liquāre,* to melt, dissolve.] **—li·qua·tion** (-kwáysh'n) *n.*

liq·ue·fac·tion (líkwi-fáksh'n) *n.* **1.** The process of liquefying. **2.** The state of being liquefied.

liq·ue·fi·er (líkwi-fī-ər) *n.* A device that liquefies; especially, an apparatus for liquefying gases.

liq·ue·fy, liq·ui·fy (líkwi-fī) *v.* **-fied, -fying, -fies.** *—tr.* To cause to become liquid, especially: **1.** To melt (a solid) by heating. **2.** To condense (a gas) by cooling. *—intr.* To become liquid. **—**See Synonyms at **melt.** [Old French *liquefier,* from Latin *liquefacere* : *liquēre,* to be liquid + *facere,* to make.] **—liq·ue·fa·cient** (-fáysh'nt) *n.*

li·ques·cent (li-kwéss'nt) *adj.* Becoming or tending to become liquid; melting. [Latin *liquescēns* (stem *liquescent-*), present participle of *liquescere,* to become liquid, from *liquēre,* to be liquid.] **—li·ques·cence, li·ques·cen·cy** *n.*

li·queur (li-kéwr, -kér, -kōr) *n.* **1.** A sweet syrupy alcoholic beverage, often with a brandy base, usually drunk in small quantities at the end of a meal. **2.** A mixture of sugar and wine used for inducing the second fermentation in the making of champagne. [French, from Old French *licour,* liquid, LIQUOR.]

liq·uid (líkwid) *n. Abbr.* **liq. 1.** The state of matter in which a substance exhibits a characteristic readiness to flow, little or no tendency to disperse, and relatively high incompressibility. **2.** Matter or a specific body of matter in this state. **3.** *Phonetics.* A liquid consonant.

~*adj.* **1.** Of or being a liquid. **2.** Liquefied, especially: **a.** Melted by heating: *liquid wax.* **b.** Condensed by cooling: *liquid oxygen.* **3.** Clear; shining: *liquid eyes.* **4.** Flowing and clear; musical: *a liquid voice.* **5.** *Phonetics.* Designating a consonant, especially (l) or (r), that is produced without friction and can be prolonged like a vowel. **6.** Flowing gracefully in motion. **7.** Readily converted into cash: *liquid assets.* [Middle English *liquide* (adjective), from Old French, from Latin *liquidus,* from *liquēre,* to be liquid.] **—liq·uid·ly** *adv.*

liquid air *n.* Air in the liquid state, condensed from the gas by cooling and sometimes pressure, and used as a refrigerant.

liq·uid·am·bar (líkwid-ámbər) *n.* A tree of the genus *Liquidambar,* such as the sweet gum. [New Latin *Liquidambar,* "liquid amber" (from its aromatic resin) : LIQUID + Medieval Latin *ambar,* ambergris, AMBER.]

liq·ui·date (líkwi-dayt) *v.* **-dated, -dating, -dates.** *—tr.* **1.** To pay off or settle (a debt, claim, or obligation). **2.** To wind up the affairs of (a business, a bankrupt estate, or the like) by determining the liabilities and applying the assets to their discharge. **3.** To convert (assets) into cash. **4.** To abolish. **5.** To dispose of; kill, especially by impersonal means: *The double agent was liquidated.* *—intr.* To go into liquidation. [Late Latin *liquidāre,* to make clear, melt, from Latin *liquidus,* LIQUID.] **—liq·ui·dat·or** *n.*

liq·ui·da·tion (líkwi-dáysh'n) *n.* **1.** The action or process of liquidating. **2.** The state of being liquidated.

liquid crystal *n.* Any of various liquids in which the atoms or molecules have partial order and are regularly arrayed in either one dimension or two dimensions, the order giving rise to optical properties, such as anisotropic scattering, associated with the crystals.

liquid-crystal display (líkwid-kríst'l) *n.* See **LCD.**

liquid glass *n.* **Sodium silicate** *(see).*

liq·uid·ise, liq·uid·ize (líkwi-dīz) *v.* **-ised, -ising, -ises.** *—tr.* **1.** To make liquid. **2.** To process (food) in a blender so as to reduce it to a liquid. *—intr.* To become liquid.

liq·uid·ise·r (líkwi-dīzər) *n. Chiefly British.* A **blender** *(see).*

li·quid·i·ty (li-kwíddəti) *n., pl.* **-ties. 1.** The condition or quality of being liquid. **2.** The condition of having sufficient cash or liquid assets to pay debts or assume obligations.

liquidity preference *n. Economics.* A preference, influenced by factors such as income level and interest rates, for keeping one's assets in the form of money rather than investing them.

liquid measure *n.* **1.** A unit or system of units of liquid capacity. **2.** A measure for liquids.

liquid oxygen *n.* A pale blue liquid produced by distilling liquid air and used as a rocket fuel. Boiling point −182.9°C. Also called "lox".

liquid paraffin *n.* A clear oily liquid obtained by distillation of petroleum and used as a laxative. Also *chiefly U.S.* "mineral oil".

liq·uor (lĭckər) *n. Abbr.* **liq.** **1. a.** Alcoholic drink made by distillation or fermentation. **b.** *U.S.* Alcoholic spirits. **2.** A liquid substance, such as broth or juice, which has been used in cooking. **3.** *Pharmacy.* An aqueous solution of a nonvolatile substance. **4.** A solution, emulsion, or suspension for industrial use. **5.** Warm water used in brewing.
~*tr.v.* **liquored, -uoring, -uors.** **1. a.** To treat (leather) with grease. **b.** To steep (malt, for example) in warm water. **2.** *Chiefly U.S. Slang.* To cause to become drunk with alcoholic spirits. Used with *up.* [Middle English *lic(o)ur,* liquid, beverage, from Old French, from Latin *liquor,* from *liquēre,* to be liquid.]

li·quo·rice, *U.S.* **li·co·rice** (lĭckə-riss, -rish) *n.* Also **li·quo·rish** (-rish). **1.** A plant, *Glycyrrhiza glabra,* of the Mediterranean region, having blue flowers and a sweet, distinctively flavoured root. **2.** The root of this plant, used as a flavouring in sweets, drinks, tobacco, and medicines. **3.** A sweet made from or flavoured with this root. **4.** Any of various plants resembling or tasting like liquorice, especially the wild liquorice, *Astragalus glycyphyllos.* [Middle English *licoris, licorice,* from Anglo-French *lycorys* and Old French *licoresse, licorece,* from Late Latin *liquirītia,* alteration (influenced by Latin *liquor,* LIQUOR) of Greek *glukurrhiza,* "sweetroot": *glukus,* sweet + *rhiza,* root.]

liquorice all-sort (áwl-sort) *n.* Any of a number of variously coloured and shaped sweets, typically made from liquorice and sugar icing.

liquorish. **1.** Variant of **lickerish.** **2.** Variant of **liquorice.**

li·ra (léer-ə) *n., pl.* **lire** (-ay) or **-ras.** *Abbr.* **l.** **1.** The standard monetary unit of Italy. **2.** The standard monetary unit of Turkey, equal to 100 kurus. **3.** A coin or note worth one lira. [Italian, from Latin *lībra,* balance, measure.]

lir·i·o·den·dron (lirri-ə-déndrən) *n., pl.* **-drons** or **-dra.** Any of various trees of the genus *Liriodendron* in the family Magnoliaceae, especially the tulip tree, *L. tulipifera,* from North America, or *L. chinense* from China. [New Latin, from greek *leirion,* lily + *dendron,* tree.]

Lis·bon (lízbən). *Portuguese* **Lis·bo·a** (lizh-bŏ-ə). Capital and chief port of Portugal lying on the Tagus estuary. It exports wine, cork, and tinned fish, and produces textiles, chemicals, and paper. Voyages of discovery in the 15th and 16th centuries made it one of Europe's wealthiest cities. The city was rebuilt after an earthquake destroyed it in 1755.

Lis·burn (líz-burn, -bərn). Town in Co. Antrim, Northern Ireland. It was formerly noted for linen products, but now produces linen thread only.

lisle (līl) *n.* **1.** A fine, smooth, tightly twisted cotton thread used especially for hosiery and underwear. Also called "lisle thread". **2.** Fabric knitted of lisle. [From *Lisle,* earlier form of LILLE, where it was originally made.]

lisp (lisp) *n.* **1.** A speech defect or mannerism characterised by the failure to produce normal sibilants, especially by the substitution of the sounds (th) and (<u>th</u>) for the sibilants (s) and (z). **2.** A sound suggestive of a lisp, such as the rustling of leaves.
~*v.* **lisped, lisping, lisps.** —*intr.* **1.** To speak with a lisp. **2.** To speak imperfectly, as a child does. —*tr.* To pronounce or express with a lisp. [Middle English *(w)lispen,* Old English *wlispian* (attested only in compound *awlispian*), from *wlisp,* a lisping, akin to Old High German *lisp* (imitative).] **—lisp·er** *n.*

lis pen·dens (liss péndenz) *n., pl.* **lites pendentes.** *Law.* A pending suit, usually concerning property, notice of which may be officially registered so that a prospective purchaser will be aware that litigation is in progress. [Latin, "pending lawsuit".]

Lis·sa·jous figure (lée-sə-zhŏŏ, -zhŏŏ) *n.* A type of curve: the locus of a point that moves with two simple harmonic motions in mutually perpendicular directions, the shape depending on the frequencies and relative phase of the motions. Lissajous figures can be formed from two electrical signals on an oscilloscope and used to measure frequency and phase. [After Jules *Lissajous* (1822-80), French physicist.]

lis·som, lis·some (líss'm) *adj.* **1.** Lithe; supple. **2.** Capable of moving with ease; limber; nimble. [Variant of LITHESOME.] **—lis·som·ly** *adv.* **—lis·som·ness** *n.*

list¹ (list) *n.* An item-by-item printed or written entry of persons or things, often arranged in a particular order, and usually of a specified nature or category: *a guest list; a shopping list.*
~*v.* **listed, listing, lists.** —*tr.* **1.** To make a list of; itemise. **2.** To enter in a list or register, especially: **a.** To register (a security) as officially approved for trading on the stock exchange. **b.** *British.* To classify as a listed building. **3.** *Archaic.* To enlist. —*intr. Archaic.* To enlist in the armed forces. [Old French *liste,* band, border, strip of paper, list, from Old Italian *lista,* from Germanic.]

list² *n.* **1.** A border or selvage of cloth, usually of a different material from the cloth it is bordering. **2.** A stripe or band of colour. **3.** *Obsolete.* A boundary; a border. **4.** *Plural.* **a.** An arena for tournaments or other contests. **b.** Any scene of combat. **5.** *U.S.* A ridge thrown up between two furrows in ploughing. [Middle English *liste,* border, edge, strip, Old English *līste.*]

list³ *n.* An inclination to one side, as of a ship; a tilt.
~*v.* **listed, listing, lists.** *Nautical.* —*intr.* To lean or tilt to the side. —*tr.* To cause (a ship) to list. [Origin unknown.]

list⁴ *v.* **listed, listing, lists.** *Poetic.* —*tr.* To listen to. —*intr.* To listen. [Middle English *listen, lusten,* Old English *hlystan.*]

liquid-crystal display

EASY-TO-READ FACES FOR CLOCKS AND CALCULATORS
How a well-known theory of bending light was put to practical use

Liquid-crystal displays (LCDs) are used for showing the numbers on pocket calculators and digital watches and clocks. The numbers show up dark against a light background. Although the unusual properties of liquid crystals were known almost a century ago, it was not until the 1960s that anyone thought of using them for display panels.

A liquid crystal is one of a range of complex chemicals that share certain of the properties of a crystal – the molecules, for example, are arranged in an ordered, repeating pattern. But they also share a property of liquids – their molecular arrangement can easily change. A liquid crystal rearranges its molecules when an electric voltage is applied to it.

When a minute amount of power is applied to certain parts of an LCD, the liquid crystals in those parts change formation and alter the path of light passing through them. The parts no longer reflect light and their sections of the display panel appear dark.

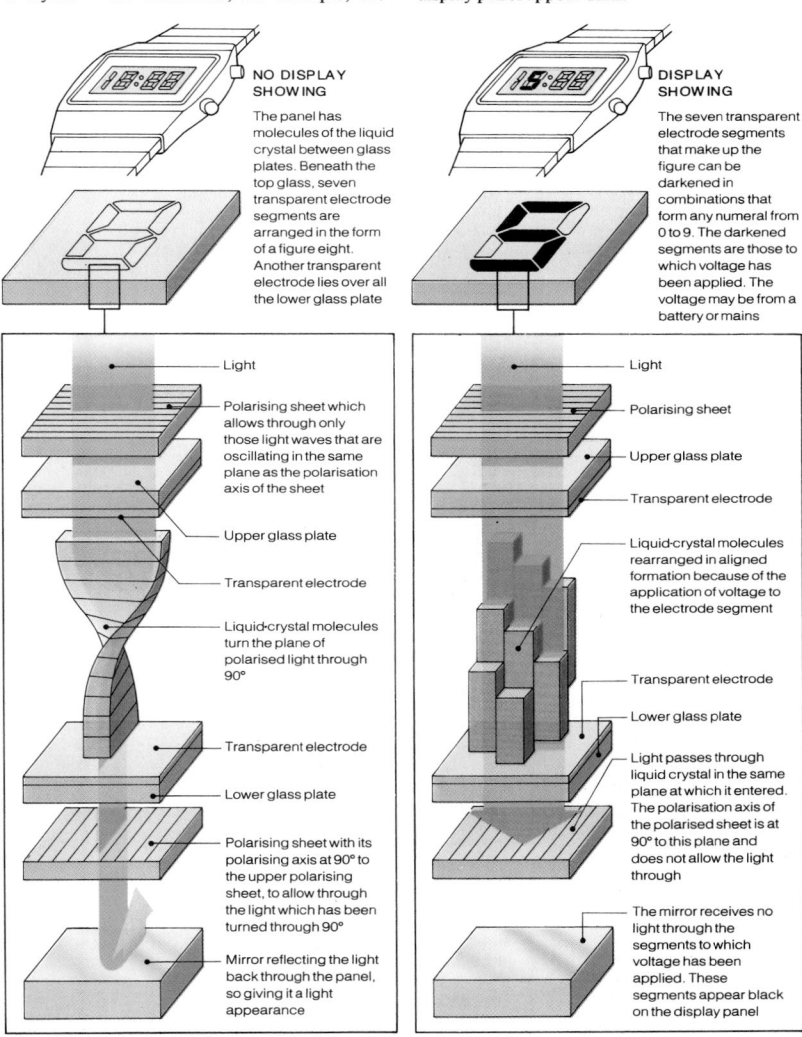

NO DISPLAY SHOWING
The panel has molecules of the liquid crystal between glass plates. Beneath the top glass, seven transparent electrode segments are arranged in the form of a figure eight. Another transparent electrode lies over all the lower glass plate

DISPLAY SHOWING
The seven transparent electrode segments that make up the figure can be darkened in combinations that form any numeral from 0 to 9. The darkened segments are those to which voltage has been applied. The voltage may be from a battery or mains

Light
Polarising sheet which allows through only those light waves that are oscillating in the same plane as the polarisation axis of the sheet
Upper glass plate
Transparent electrode
Liquid-crystal molecules turn the plane of polarised light through 90°
Transparent electrode
Lower glass plate
Polarising sheet with its polarising axis at 90° to the upper polarising sheet, to allow through the light which has been turned through 90°
Mirror reflecting the light back through the panel, so giving it a light appearance

Light
Polarising sheet
Upper glass plate
Transparent electrode
Liquid-crystal molecules rearranged in aligned formation because of the application of voltage to the electrode segment
Transparent electrode
Lower glass plate
Light passes through liquid crystal in the same plane at which it entered. The polarisation axis of the polarised sheet is at 90° to this plane and does not allow the light through
The mirror receives no light through the segments to which voltage has been applied. These segments appear black on the display panel

HOW A WATCH USES LIQUID CRYSTALS *In a digital watch, a liquid-crystal display shows the time in dark numbers. Each numeral is made up from seven electrode segments, which darken in many combinations to show any numeral required. The segments are activated by electrodes controlled by oscillations of the watch's quartz crystal.*

list⁵ *v.* **listed, listing, lists.** *Archaic.* —*tr.* To be pleasing to; satisfy; please. —*intr.* To be disposed; choose.
~*n. Archaic.* A desire or inclination. [Middle English *listen,* Old English *lystan.*]

list·ed building (lĭstid) *n. British.* A building designated as being of particular historical or architectural interest and therefore subject to restrictions regarding to its alteration or demolition.

lis·tel (lĭst'l) *n. Architecture.* A narrow border, moulding, or fillet. [Old French, from Old Italian *listello,* diminutive of *lista,* band, border, LIST.]

lis·ten (líss'n) *intr.v.* **-tened, -tening, -tens.** **1.** To apply oneself to hearing something. **2.** To take notice; heed: *begged her to reconsider, but she wouldn't listen.* **3.** To be alert so as to hear. Used with *for.* —**listen in.** **1.** To tune in and listen to a broadcast. **2.** To listen to a conversation, sometimes surreptitiously. [Middle English *listnen,* Old English *hlysnan.*] **—lis·ten·er** *n.*

Lis·ter (lístər), **Joseph, 1st Baron** (1827–1912). British surgeon. He demonstrated in 1865 that carbolic acid was an effective antiseptic agent, showing that hygiene could save lives during surgery.

list·ing (lísting) *n.* **1.** An entry in a list. **2.** A list. **3.** *Computing.* A series of records on a file. **4.** *Plural.* Information, such as details of forthcoming events, presented in the form of lists. Also used adjectivally: *listings magazines.*

list·less (líst-ləss, -liss) *adj.* Marked by a lack of energy or enthusiasm; disinclined towards any effort; indifferent; languid. [Middle English *listles* : *list,* desire, from *listen,* to be pleasing, to LIST + -LESS.] **—list·less·ly** *adv.* **—list·less·ness** *n.*

list price *n.* A basic published or advertised price, often subject to discount.

Liszt (list), **Franz** (1811–86). Hungarian composer. In his lifetime he was more famous for his virtuoso piano playing than his compositions. His popular works include 20 *Hungarian Rhapsodies,* 6 Paganini *Études,* and 2 piano concertos.

lit[1]. **1.** Alternative past tense and past participle of **light** (to illuminate). **2.** Alternative past tense and past participle of **light** (to descend).

lit[2]. **1.** literal; literally. **2.** literary; literature.

lit·a·ny (líttəni, lítt'n-i) *n., pl.* **-nies. 1.** A liturgical prayer consisting of phrases recited by a leader alternating with responses by the congregation. **2.** *Capital* **L.** The set of prayers in this form in the Book of Common Prayer. **3.** Any repetitive or incantatory recital. [Middle English *letanie,* from Old French, from Late Latin *litanīa,* from Greek *litaneia,* entreaty, from *litanuein,* to entreat, from *litanos,* entreating, from *litē*†, supplication.]

litchi. Variant of **lychee.**

lit. crit. (lit krít) *n. Informal.* Literary criticism.

-lite *n. comb. form.* Indicates stone. Used in names of minerals; for example, **cryolite, actinolite.** [French *-lite* and German *-lit,* variants of *-lithe* and *-lith,* from Greek *lithos,* stone.]

liter. *U.S.* Variant of **litre.**

lit·er·a·cy (líttrə-si, líttərə-) *n.* **1.** The condition or quality of being literate; especially, the ability to read, write, and use language. **2.** A basic understanding of or ability in a specified discipline.

lit·e·rae hu·man·i·o·res (líttər-ee hew-mánni-áwr-eez; *also* -ī -ayz) *n. Used with a singular verb.* The faculty of classics, philosophy, and ancient history at Oxford University. [Latin, "the more humane studies".]

lit·er·al (líttrəl, líttərəl) *adj. Abbr.* **lit. 1.** In accordance with, conforming to, or upholding the explicit or primary meaning of a word or the words of a text. **2.** Word for word; verbatim: *a literal translation.* **3.** Matter-of-fact; prosaic: *a literal mind.* **4.** Avoiding exaggeration, metaphor, or embellishment; plain: *a literal statement.* **5.** Consisting of, using, or expressed by letters: *literal notation.*
~n. A misspelling or misprint. Also called "literal error". [Middle English *lit(t)eral,* of letters, written, from Old French *literal,* from Late Latin *litterālis,* from Latin *littera,* letter.] **—lit·er·al·ness** *n.*

lit·er·al·ise, lit·er·al·ize (líttrəl-īz, líttərəl-) *tr.v.* **-ised, -ising, -ises.** To make literal.

lit·er·al·ism (líttrəl-iz'm, líttərəl-) *n.* **1.** Adherence to the explicit sense of a given text or doctrine. **2.** Literal portrayal; realism. **—lit·er·al·ist** *n.* **—lit·er·al·is·tic** (-ístik) *adj.*

lit·er·al·ly (líttrəli, líttərəli) *adv. Abbr.* **lit. 1.** In a literal or strict sense. **2.** Really; actually: *She literally works 12 hours a day.* **3.** *Nonstandard.* Used as an intensive: *The company is literally bleeding to death.*

lit·er·ar·y (líttrəri, líttə-rəri || -rerri. *Note: the pronunciation* líttri *is nonstandard*) *adj. Abbr.* **lit. 1.** Of, pertaining to, or dealing with literature. **2. a.** Found in or appropriate to literature: *a literary style.* **b.** Employed chiefly in writing rather than speaking: *a literary language.* **3.** Versed in or fond of literature or learning: *a literary woman.* **4.** Of or pertaining to writers or the profession of literature: *literary circles.* [French *littéraire,* from Latin *litterārius,* of writing, from *litterae,* epistle, writing, plural of *littera,* letter.] **—lit·er·ar·i·ly** *adv.* **—lit·er·ar·i·ness** *n.*

literary agent *n.* A person who handles an author's business affairs, especially in dealing with publishers. **—literary agency** *n.*

lit·er·ate (líttrət, líttər-ət, -it) *adj.* **1. a.** Able to read and write. **b.** Able to write well. **2.** Knowledgeable; educated. **3.** Familiar with literature; literary.
~n. **1.** A literate person. **2.** One admitted to holy orders in the Church of England without having a university degree. [Middle English *litterate,* from Latin *lit(t)erātus,* acquainted with writings, learned, from *litterae,* epistle, writing, plural of *littera,* letter.]

lit·e·ra·ti (líttə-raáti, *old-fashioned* -ráytī) *pl.n.* The literary intelligentsia. [Italian, from Latin *litterātī,* plural of *litterātus,* LITERATE.]

lit·e·ra·tim (líttə-raátim, -ráytim) *adv.* Literally; letter for letter. [Medieval Latin, from *lit(t)era,* letter.]

lit·er·a·ture (líttri-chər, líttrə-, líttəri-, -tewr) *n. Abbr.* **lit. 1.** A body of writings in prose or verse. **2.** Writings of particular excellence or artistic value. **3.** The art or occupation of a writer of artistic or critical works. **4.** The body of written work produced by scholars or researchers in a given field: *medical literature.* **5.** Printed material of any kind, as for a political or publicity campaign. **6.** *Archaic.* Literary culture; learning. [Middle English *litterature,* from Old French, from Latin *litterātūra,* writing, learning, from *litterātus,* learned, LITERATE.]

-lith *n. comb. form.* Indicates stone or rock; for example, **monolith, palaeolith.** [Greek *lithos,* stone.]

lith. lithograph; lithographic; lithography.

lith·arge (líthaarj || *U.S. also* li-thárj) *n.* A yellow lead oxide, PbO, used in storage batteries, glass, and as a pigment. Also called "lead monoxide". Compare **massicot.** [Middle English *lit(h)arge,* from Old French, from Latin *lithargyrus,* from Greek *litharguros,* "silver stone" : LITH(O)- + *arguros,* silver.]

lithe (lī<u>th</u>) *adj.* **1.** Supple; limber. **2.** Marked by effortless grace. [Middle English *lith(e), lythe,* meek, mild, flexible, Old English *līthe.*] **—lithe·ly** *adv.* **—lithe·ness** *n.*

lithe·some (lī<u>th</u>-s'm) *adj.* Lithe; lissom.

li·thi·a·sis (li-thī-ə-siss) *n. Pathology.* The formation of stones in the body. [New Latin, from Greek : LITH(O)- + -IASIS.]

lithia water *n.* Mineral water containing some lithium salts.

lith·ic (líthik) *adj.* **1.** Pertaining to stone. **2.** Pertaining to lithium. [Greek *lithikos,* from *lithos,* stone.] **—lith·ic·al·ly** *adv.*

-lithic *adj. comb. form.* Indicates the use of stone; for example, **Neolithic.**

lith·i·um (líthi-əm) *n. Symbol* **Li** A soft, silvery, highly reactive metallic element that is used as a heat-transfer medium, in thermonuclear weapons, and in various alloys, ceramics, and optical forms of glass. Atomic number 3, atomic weight 6.939, melting point 179°C, boiling point 1317°C, relative density 0.534, valency 1. [New Latin : LITH(O)- (from its mineral origin) + -IUM.]

lithium carbonate *n.* A white crystalline solid, Li_2CO_3, used in the ceramic and glass industries and as a drug in the treatment and prevention of schizophrenia and some depressive conditions.

lithium oxide *n.* A strongly alkaline white powder, Li_2O, used in ceramics and glass. Also called "lithia".

litho-, lith- *comb. form.* Indicates stone; for example, **lithosphere, lithia.** [Latin, from Greek, from *lithos*†, stone.]

litho., lithog. lithograph; lithographic; lithography.

lith·o·graph (líth-ə-graaf, -ō-, -graf; *in technical usage often* līth-) *n. Abbr.* **lith., litho., lithog.** A print produced by lithography.
~tr.v. **lithographed, -graphing, -graphs.** To produce by lithography. [Back-formation from LITHOGRAPHY.] **—li·thog·raph·er** (li-thóggrəfər, lī-) *n.* **—lith·o·graph·ic** (-gráffik), **lith·o·graph·i·cal** *adj.* **—lith·o·graph·i·cal·ly** *adv.*

li·thog·ra·phy (li-thóggrəfi, lī-) *n. Abbr.* **lith., litho., lithog.** A printing process in which the image to be printed is rendered on a flat surface, as on stone or now chiefly on sheet zinc or aluminium, and treated so that it will retain ink while the nonimage areas are treated to repel ink. [German *Lithographie* : LITHO- + -GRAPHY.]

li·thol·o·gy (li-thólləji) *n.* **1.** The physical character of a rock or rock formation. **2.** The study, description, and classification of rock, generally in handheld specimens and outcrops. [New Latin *lithologia* : LITHO- + -LOGY.] **—lith·o·log·ic** (lithə-lójik), **lith·o·log·i·cal** *adj.* **—lith·o·log·i·cal·ly** *adv.* **—li·thol·o·gist** (li-thólləjist) *n.*

lith·o·marge (líthə-maarj) *n.* A white, reddish, or mottled clay, having a greasy feel. [New Latin *lithomarga* : LITHO- + *marge,* marl.]

lith·o·phyte (líthə-fīt) *n.* **1.** *Botany.* A plant that grows on a rocky surface. **2.** An organism, such as coral, having a stony structure. [French : LITHO- + -PHYTE.] **—lith·o·phyt·ic** (-fíttik) *adj.*

lith·o·pone (líth-ə-pōn, -ō-) *n.* A white pigment consisting of a mixture of zinc sulphide, zinc oxide, and barium sulphate. [LITHO- + Greek *ponos,* artefact, product.]

lith·o·sphere (líth-ə-sfeer, -ō-) *n.* The solid outer layer of the Earth. It lies above the semifluid asthenosphere, and includes the crust and the solid upper part of the mantle down to about 75 kilometres (47 miles).

lith·o·stra·tig·ra·phy (líth-ə-stra-tíggrəfi, -ō-, -strə-) *n.* **1.** Stratigraphy based on the physical and petrographic properties of rocks. **2.** The interpretation of the physical characters of sedimentary rocks. **—lith·o·strat·i·graph·ic** (-strátti-gráffik) *adj.*

li·thot·o·my (li-thóttəmi) *n., pl.* **-mies.** A surgical operation to remove stones from the urinary tract. [Late Latin *lithotomia,* from Greek : LITHO- + -TOMY.]

li·thot·ri·ty (li-thóttrəti) *n., pl.* **-ties.** A surgical operation to pulverise stones in the bladder or urethra. [Irregularly from Greek *lithōn thrutika,* "stone-crushing (drug)" : *lithōn,* genitive plural of *lithos,* stone + *thrutikos,* crushing, from *thruptein,* to crush.]

Lith·u·a·ni·an (lithew-áyni-ən, lithōō-) *adj.* Of or pertaining to Lithuania, its people, or their language.
~n. **1.** An inhabitant or native of Lithuania. **2.** The Baltic language of the Lithuanian S.S.R.

Lithuanian Soviet Socialist Republic. *Lithuanian* **Lie·tu·va** (lye-tōō-vaá); *Russian* **Li·tov·ska·ya S.S.R.** (lee-táwfskə-yə). Also **Lith·u·a·ni·a** (-ə). One of the U.S.S.R.'s 15 republics, bordering on the Baltic Sea. Once a flourishing state, Lithuania was a province of the Russian empire from 1795, but became an independent republic in 1918. It was incorporated into the U.S.S.R. in 1940. Vilnius is the capital.

lit·i·ga·ble (líttigəb'l) *adj.* Capable of being litigated.

lit·i·gant (líttigənt) *n.* One who is engaged in a lawsuit.
~adj. Engaged in a lawsuit. [Latin *lītigāns* (stem *lītigant-*), present participle of *lītigāre,* LITIGATE.]

lit·i·gate (lítti-gayt) *v.* **-gated, -gating, -gates.** *—tr.* To subject (something) to legal proceedings; contest. *—intr.* To engage in legal proceedings. [Latin *lītigāre,* to dispute, quarrel, sue : *līs*† (stem *līt-*), lawsuit + *agere,* to drive, lead, act.] **—lit·i·ga·tor** (-gaytər) *n.*

lit·i·ga·tion (lítti-gáysh'n) *n.* Legal action or process.

PRONUNCIATION KEY

a, trap; aa, father; ai, fair; ar, star; aw, lawn; ay, play; b, bb, stab; rubber; ch, church; ck, ticket; d, dd, dead; ladder; e, dress; ee, bee; er, defer; ew, few; ewr, pure; ə, about; ər, letter; f, ff, fife; differ; g, gg, giggle; h, hat; i, kit; ī, price; īr, fire; j, judge; k, kick; l, ll, let; 'l, needle; m, mm, man; n, nn, no; 'n, sudden; ng, thing; o, lot; ō, no; ŏŏ, foot; ōō, shoe; oor, poor; ow, cow; owr, hour; oy, boy; p, pp, pepper; r, rr, red; s, ss, sauce; sh, ship; t, tt, totter; th, thick; <u>th</u>, this; smooth; u, cut; ur, turn; v, vv, valve; w, wet; y, yes; z, zz, zebra; <u>zh</u>, vision; pleasure

IN FOREIGN WORDS:

aN, oN, Saint-Saëns; <u>hl</u>, Llanelli; Hluhluwe; <u>kh</u>, loch; lough; Khaled

STRESS MARK:

ín-sīt, insight; in-sít, incite

li·ti·gious (li-tíjəss) *adj.* **1.** Given to or fond of litigation. **2.** Disputable at law; litigable. **—li·ti·gious·ly** *adv.* **—li·ti·gious·ness** *n.*

lit·mus (lít-məss) *n.* A blue, amorphous powder derived from certain lichens, that takes on a red colour in acid solutions and a blue in alkaline solutions. [Perhaps from Old Norse *litmosi,* "dye moss" : *litr,* a dye, colour + *mosi,* moss.]

litmus paper *n.* An unsized white paper impregnated with litmus and used as an acid-base indicator.

litmus test *n.* **1.** A test to determine alkalinity or acidity using litmus paper. **2.** Any decisive test: *The strike will be a litmus test of the government's industrial relations policy.*

li·to·tes (lī́-tō-teez, lī́-tō-, -tə- || *U.S. also* líttə-) *n.* A figure of speech consisting of an understatement in which an affirmative is expressed by the negation of its opposite, as in *This is no small problem.* [Greek *litotēs,* from *lītos,* simple, plain, unadorned.]

li·tre, *U.S.* **li·ter** (léetər) *n. Abbr.* **l.** **1.** A unit of volume equal to one cubic decimetre (0.22 gallon). **2.** Formerly, a unit of volume equal to the volume of one kilogram of pure water at its temperature of maximum density (4° C) and at standard pressure (760mmHg); it is equivalent to 1.000 028 cubic decimetres. ***Note:*** The first definition is a special name for the cubic decimetre in SI units. The second definition, based on a volume of water, is still applicable for purposes of the British 1963 Weights and Measures Act. Because of the small difference between the two defined volumes, use of the term *litre* is not recommended for expressing precise measurements. [French, from *litron,* (an obsolete measure of capacity), from Medieval Latin, from Greek, a monetary unit of Sicily.]

Litt. B., Lit. B. Bachelor of Letters [Latin *Litterarum Baccalaureus.*]

Litt.D., Lit.D. Doctor of Letters [Latin *Litterarum Doctor.*]

lit·ter (líttər) *n.* **1.** A disorderly accumulation of objects; especially, carelessly discarded rubbish, paper, and the like. **2.** The young produced at one birth by a multiparous mammal. **3. a.** Straw or other material used as bedding for livestock. **b.** Granules of a porous material based on fuller's earth or sawdust, kept in a tray so that pets may excrete indoors. Also called "cat litter". **4.** A conveyance carried by people or animals, typically consisting of an enclosed couch mounted on shafts. **5.** A stretcher for the sick or wounded. **6.** The uppermost layer of a forest floor, consisting chiefly of decaying leaves.

~v. **littered, -tering, -ters.** *—tr.* **1.** To give birth to (young). **2. a.** To make untidy by discarding rubbish carelessly. **b.** To lie scattered untidily about (a place): *discarded cans and bottles littering the streets.* **3.** To scatter about. **4.** To supply (animals) with litter for bedding. *—intr.* **1.** To give birth to a litter. **2.** To scatter litter. [Middle English *litere,* bed, offspring at birth, from Anglo-French, variant of Old French *litiere,* from Medieval Latin *lectāria,* from Latin *lectus,* bed.]

lit·tér·a·teur, lit·ter·a·teur (líttə-rə-tér, -ra-, -tóor, -tőr) *n.* A literary person, especially a writer. [French, from Latin *litterātor,* elementary teacher, grammarian, from *littera,* LETTER.]

lit·ter·lout (líttər-lowt) *n. Informal.* One who litters public areas with discarded rubbish. Also *U.S.* "litterbug".

lit·tle (lítt'l) *adj.* **littler** or **less** (less) (especially for senses 2, 3, 4), **littlest** or **least** (leest) (especially for senses 2, 3, 4). **1.** Small, or smaller by comparison. **2.** Short in extent or duration; brief: *in a little while.* **3. a.** Small in quantity or degree; not as much as needed or desired: *little hope of a recovery; speaks little English.* **b.** Small, but not too small, in quantity or degree. Preceded by *a*: *speaks a little English; Would you like a little sugar?* **4.** Unimportant; trivial; insignificant: *life's little troubles.* **5.** Without much force; weak. **6.** Narrow; petty. **7.** Without much power or influence; of minor status. **8. a.** Being at an early stage of growth. Said of children and animals. **b.** Younger: *my little sister.* **c.** Smaller or smallest of a set: *little toe.* **9.** Operating on a relatively small scale: *the little man who mends radios.* **10.** Resembling the specified person, place, or thing, but on a smaller scale: *Little Venice.* **11.** Appealing; endearing: *the little rascal; a pretty little cottage.* —See Synonyms at **small.**

~adv. **less, least.** **1.** Not much; scarcely: *He sleeps little.* Often used in combination: *little-known; little-loved.* **2.** Rarely: *I see her very little.* **3.** Not at all; not in the least. Used before a verb: *I little thought I'd see you here; little did she know .*

~n. **1.** A small quantity: *Give me a little.* **2.** An insignificant amount. **3.** A short distance or time: *a little down the road; a little past four o'clock.* **—in little.** On a small scale. **—little by little.** By small degrees or increments; gradually. **—make little of.** To regard or treat as not very important; dismiss. **—think little of. 1.** To have no hesitation about (some course of action). **2.** To think of as relatively unimportant or valueless. [Middle English *litel, lutel,* Old English *lȳtel.*] **—lit·tle·ness** *n.*

little auk *n.* A small, short-billed, stout-bodied diving bird, *Plautus alle,* with a black and white plumage. It is found in northern oceans. Also called "dovekie".

Little Bear *n.* **Ursa Minor** *(see).* Also *U.S.* "Little Dipper".

little bird *n.* An informant whose name is supposedly not known. Used humorously or ironically. [From the traditional phrase refusing to name one's informant, "A little bird told me".]

little end *n. Mechanics.* **1.** The smaller end of a connecting rod. **2.** The bearing between this and the gudgeon pin.

little Eng·land·er (íng-gləndər) *n.* One who advocates a self-sufficient British foreign policy, as: **1.** In the 19th century, an opponent of imperialist expansion. **2.** An opponent of involvement in the European Economic Community.

little finger *n.* The smallest finger on the hand, the fifth and last as counted from the thumb.

little grebe *n.* A small Old World grebe, *Podiceps ruficollis,* having a chestnut throat.

little hours *pl.n. Roman Catholic Church.* The canonical hours of prime, terce, sext, and nones, and sometimes including vespers and compline.

little magazine *n.* A literary magazine specialising in experimental writings and appealing to a limited readership.

little owl *n.* A small Old World owl, *Athene noctua,* having speckled brownish plumage.

little people *pl.n. Chiefly Irish.* Fairies, pixies, and the like; especially, leprechauns.

little slam *n.* See **slam.**

Lit·tle·wood (lítt'l-wŏŏd), **Joan (Maud)** (1914–). British theatre director. In 1945 she founded the Theatre Workshop in Manchester and in 1953 moved it to the Theatre Royal, Stratford, in London's East End. It specialised in plays about contemporary social issues.

lit·to·ral (líttərəl) *adj.* Of or existing on a shore.

~n. A shore or coastal region, especially the zone between the high- and low-tide marks of spring tides. [Latin *littorālis, lītorālis,* from *lītus* (stem *lītor-*), shore.]

li·tur·gics (li-túrjiks) *n. Used with a singular verb.* The study of liturgies. Also called "liturgiology".

lit·ur·gist (líttərjist) *n.* **1.** One who uses or advocates the use of liturgical forms. **2.** A scholar in liturgics.

lit·ur·gy (líttərji) *n., pl.* **-gies.** **1.** The rite of the Eucharist. **2. a.** A system of public worship in the Christian church. **b.** The Book of Common Prayer. [Late Latin *lītūrgia,* from Greek *leitourgia,* public service, service of a priest, from *leitourgos,* public servant, minister, priest : *leōs* (stem *leit-*), variant of *laos,* people, multitude + *ergon,* work.] **—li·tur·gi·cal** (li-túrjik'l) *adj.* **—li·tur·gi·cal·ly** *adv.*

Lit·vi·nov (lit-vée-noff; *Russian* -nəf), **Maxim Maximovich,** born Maxim Maximovich Wallach (1876–1951). Soviet politician. He was Soviet Foreign Minister (1930–39) and ambassador to the United States (1941–43).

Liu Shao-qi or **Liu Shao-ch'i** (lyő shów-chée) (*c.* 1898–1973). Chinese Communist leader. He was Chairman of the People's Republic of China from 1959 until he was purged in 1966 during the Cultural Revolution. He was officially rehabilitated in 1980.

liv·a·ble, live·a·ble (lívvəb'l) *adj.* **1.** Fit to live in; habitable. **2.** Worth living.

live[1] (liv) *v.* **lived, living, lives.** *—intr.* **1.** To exhibit the characteristic signs of life. **2.** To continue to remain alive: *lived to a great age.* **3.** To subsist; be maintained: *living on rice and fish; lived on inherited income.* **4. a.** To have one's usual dwelling in a particular place; reside. **b.** *Informal.* To be usually kept: *Where do these knives live?* **5.** To conduct one's existence in a particular manner: *lived by the old code of personal honour; lives for her work.* **6.** To enjoy life and experience it to the full: *They really know how to live.* **7. a.** To remain in human memory: *She lives in the minds of us all.* Often used with *on.* **b.** To remain in existence; escape destruction. Often used with *on*: *Despite persecution, the faith lived on.* *—tr.* **1.** To go through (a particular form of existence or experience): *lived a nightmare.* **2.** To embody in one's manner of existence: *We lived our beliefs.* **—live and let live.** To be tolerant. **—live down.** *Informal.* To live sufficiently long, or sufficiently blamelessly, to overcome the effects of (a scandal, for example). **—live it up.** *Informal.* To have fun, especially in an extravagant way. **—live out. 1.** To reside away from the place where one works or studies. **2.** To live through (a period); live beyond (a time limit): *The injured butterfly lived out the day.* **—live together.** To reside together, especially in sexual intimacy. **—live up to. 1.** To succeed in guiding one's life by: *live up to religious ideals.* **2.** To show oneself to be as good as: *live up to a great reputation.* **—live with. 1.** To reside with, especially in sexual intimacy. **2.** To put up with (a continuing adverse factor). [Middle English *liven,* Old English *libban, lifian.*]

live[2] (līv) *adj.* **1.** Having life. **2.** Characteristic of life. **3.** Of current interest: *a live topic.* **4.** Actual, as opposed to pretended or imitation: *a real live princess.* **5.** Glowing; burning: *a live coal.* **6.** Brilliant; vivid. **7. a.** Explosible: *a live bomb.* **b.** Charged with a bullet or shell; not blank: *live ammunition.* **8.** *Electricity.* Carrying current or electric potential. **9.** Native; not mined or quarried. Said of rocks and ores. **10. a.** Designating or participating in a programme broadcast at the time of filming rather than recorded in advance. **b.** Involving actual performers rather than recorded material: *a party with live music.* **11.** *Printing.* **a.** Not yet set into type: *live copy.* **b.** Set and still in use. Said of type. **12.** *Sports.* Being or capable of being in play: *a live ball.*

~adv. As, participating in, or during a live broadcast, performance, or the like: *a rock band playing live.* [Shortened from ALIVE.]

live-bear·er (līv-báir-ər, -bair-) *n.* An ovoviviparous fish, such as a guppy. **—live-bear·ing** *adj.*

live in *intr.v.* To reside in the place where one works or studies.

live-in (lív-ín) *adj.* **1.** Living in the place where one works: *a live-in barmaid.* **2.** Living with another person without being married: *her live-in companion.*

live·li·hood (līvli-hŏŏd) *n.* Means of support; subsistence. [Variant (influenced by LIVELY and -HOOD) of Middle English *liv(e)lode,* course of life, sustenance, Old English *līflād* : *līf,* LIFE + *lād,* course.]

Synonyms: *livelihood, living, subsistence, maintenance, keep.*

live load (līv) *n.* A moving, variable weight added to the dead load

little auk *The little auk (above), which lives around the Arctic Ocean, is a member of the auk family of seabirds. The family also includes razorbills, guillemots, and puffins.*

or intrinsic weight of a structure or vehicle. Compare **dead load**.

live·long (lív-long || lív-, *U.S. also* -lawng) *adj.* **1.** Long or seemingly long in passing. **2.** Complete; whole. Used chiefly in the phrase *the livelong day*. **3.** *British*. A plant, the **orpine** (*see*). [Middle English *lefe longe*, "dear long" : *lef*, "dear" (here used as an intensive), Old English *lēof* + LONG.]

live·ly (lívli) *adj.* **-lier, -liest. 1.** Full of life; vigorous; energetic. **2.** Full of activity, interest, or excitement. **3.** Exhibiting or characterised by intense intellectual or emotional activity; keen: *a lively debate*. **4.** Exhibiting or inspiring liveliness; gay; cheerful. **5.** Effervescent; sparkling. **6.** Invigorating; brisk. **7.** Bouncing readily upon impact; resilient, as a ball is. **8.** *Nautical*. Buoyant; rising lightly with the sea swell. **9.** Lifelike. —See Synonyms at **active**. ~*adv.* In a vigorous, energetic, or spirited manner. —**look lively**. To hurry up; make haste. Usually used in the imperative. [Middle English *lifliche*, Old English *līflic*, living, vital, from *līf*, life.] —**live·li·ly** *adv.* —**live·li·ness** *n.*

li·ven (lív'n) *v.* **-vened, -vening, -vens.** —*tr.* To cause to become lively. Often used with *up.* —*intr.* To become lively. Often used with *up.*

live oak (lív) *n.* Any of several evergreen North American oaks, such as *Quercus virginiana*, of the southeastern United States.

liv·er¹ (lívvər) *n.* **1.** *Anatomy*. A large, reddish-brown, multilobed, vertebrate gland situated in the top right hand part of the abdominal cavity. It secretes bile and acts in the formation of blood and in the metabolism of carbohydrates, fats, proteins, minerals, and vitamins. **2.** A similar invertebrate organ. **3.** The liver of an animal, used as food. [Middle English *liver*, Old English *lifer*.]

liver² *n.* One who lives in a specified manner: *a loose liver.*

liver extract *n.* A dry, brownish powder containing vitamin B_{12}, which is prepared from mammalian livers and is capable of increasing the number of healthy red blood corpuscles in persons suffering from pernicious anaemia.

liver fluke *n.* **1.** Any of several parasitic trematode worms, such as *Fasciola hepatica* or *Opisthorchis sinensis* (or *Clonorchis sinensis*), that infest the liver of various animals, including human beings. **2.** Infestation with such parasites. Also called "liver rot".

liv·er·ied (lívvə-rid || -reed) *adj.* Wearing livery, especially as a servant.

liv·er·ish (lívvərish) *adj.* **1.** Resembling liver, particularly in colour. **2.** Having a liver disorder; bilious. **3.** Having a disagreeable disposition; irritable.

Liv·er·pool (lívvər-pool). City and port on the river Mersey in Merseyside, England, Britain's second largest port after London. The city's Anglican cathedral, begun in 1904 and completed in 1978, is the largest Anglican cathedral in the world. The modernist Roman Catholic cathedral, designed by Frederick Gibberd, was opened in 1968. Liverpool's industries include chemicals and engineering.

Liverpool, Robert Banks Jenkinson, 2nd Earl of (1770–1828). English Tory politician. He was prime minister (1812–27), occupying that office longer than any other politician, except Walpole and the younger Pitt.

Liv·er·pud·li·an (lívvər-púddli-ən) *n.* A native or inhabitant of Liverpool. ~*adj.* Of or pertaining to Liverpool, its inhabitants, or its characteristic speech. [From *Liverpool,* with humorous substitution of *puddle* for *pool*.]

liver salts *pl.n.* A mixture of mineral salts taken to relieve indigestion or biliousness.

liver sausage *n.* A type of sausage made of or containing liver. Also *chiefly U.S.* "liverwurst".

liver spot *n.* A localised brown discoloration of the skin occurring especially in old age; a lentigo.

liver starch *n.* A carbohydrate, **glycogen** (*see*).

liv·er·wort (lívvər-wurt || -wawrt) *n.* Any of numerous green non-flowering plants of the class Hepaticae within the division Bryophyta, found in moist habitats and lacking true roots. Also called "hepatic". [Referring to its liver-shaped leaves.]

liv·er·y (lívvəri) *n., pl.* **-ies. 1.** The distinctive uniform or insignia worn by a person's servants or retainers. **2.** The distinctive dress or garb worn by the members of a particular organisation or group. **3.** Any distinctive dress or outward marking. **4.** Persons collectively who wear such costumes or uniforms, such as the members of a livery company. **5.** *Archaic*. **a.** The provision of food or clothing to servants. **b.** The boarding and care of horses for a fee. **6.** *U.S.* A livery stable. **7.** *Archaic. Law.* The official transfer of property, especially land, to a new owner. [Middle English *livere, liverye,* from Anglo-French *livere,* variant of Old French *livree,* "something delivered or given", allowance (later clothes) granted to servants, from the feminine past participle of *livrer,* to deliver, relieve, from Latin *līberāre,* to set free, from *līber,* free.]

livery company *n.* Any of various associations in the City of London that originated from the early trade guilds. Their members are no longer necessarily connected with the trades after which the companies are named, but they retain considerable influence over the election of the Lord Mayor and other City officers.

liv·er·y·man (lívvəri-mən) *n., pl.* **-men** (-mən, -men). **1.** A keeper or employee of a livery stable. **2.** A member of a livery company.

livery stable *n.* A stable that boards horses and keeps horses and carriages for hire.

lives. Plural of **life**.

live steam (lív) *n.* Steam coming from a boiler at full pressure.

live·stock (lív-stok) *n.* Used with a singular or plural verb. Domestic

THE VITAL WORK OF THE LIVER
The body's complex chemical factory

The liver is the largest organ in the body – a wedge-shaped gland weighing about 1.4 kilograms (3 pounds). In the liver, millions of cells process, store, and distribute the products of digestion that have been absorbed by the blood. They transform some into forms that the body can use; they break down poisons, such as alcohol, for removal as waste; and they build up and store the sugars that are needed for short-term energy. The liver also removes worn-out cells from the blood and reprocesses their red pigment haemoglobin. Another function of the liver is to secrete bile – a bitter liquid which facilitates digestion of food in the duodenum.

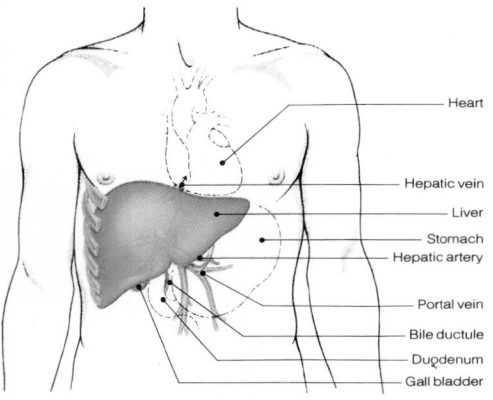

THE LIVER'S ROLE *Chemicals, such as sugars, amino acids, and vitamins, enter the bloodstream during digestion. The blood then passes from the stomach and intestines to the liver through the portal vein. When it has been filtered, the hepatic vein returns it to the heart. The bile ductule takes bile to the gall bladder, from where it passes to the duodenum. The hepatic artery supplies the liver with oxygenated blood.*

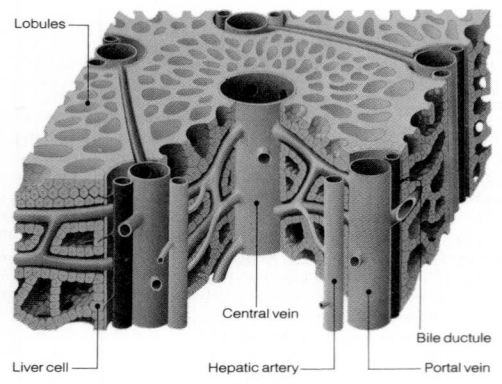

ANATOMY OF THE LIVER *Blood enters the liver and diffuses through thousands of minute lobules where the liver cells process the products of digestion.*

animals, such as cattle, sheep, or goats, raised for home use or for profit, especially on a farm.

live·ware (lív-wair) *n.* Programmers and other operating personnel working in a computer installation. [By analogy with **hardware, software**.]

live wire (lív) *n.* **1.** A wire carrying electric current. **2.** *Slang*. An extremely vivacious, alert, or energetic person.

liv·id (lívvid) *adj.* **1.** Having a bluish discoloration of the skin, as from a bruise. **2.** Ashen or pallid, as with illness or rage. **3.** Extremely angry; furious. [French *livide,* from Latin *līvidus,* from *līvēre,* to be bluish.] —**li·vid·i·ty** (li-víddəti), **liv·id·ness** *n.* —**liv·id·ly** *adv.*

liv·ing (lívving) *adj.* **1.** Possessing life; alive. **2. a.** Still alive; not yet dead. **b.** In active function or use. **c.** Still in existence as a species; extant. **3.** Of or pertaining to persons who are alive. **4. a.** Of, pertaining to, or characteristic of daily life: *living standards.* **b.** Of or pertaining to the maintenance of existence: *living costs.* **5.** True to life; real: *the living image of her mother.* **6.** Experienced while still alive: *a living hell.*

~n. **1.** The state or condition of being alive. **2.** A manner or style of life: *plain living.* **3.** A manner or means of maintaining life; a livelihood. **4.** *British.* A church benefice, including the revenue attached to it. —See Synonyms at **livelihood.**

Synonyms: *living, alive, extant.*

living fossil *n.* An extant organism, such as a coelacanth, that belongs to a taxonomic group whose other members are extinct.

living memory *n.* The collective experience or memory of all those currently alive: *the worst winter in living memory.*

living room, living-room (lívving-ro͝om, -ro͞om) *n.* A room in a private residence intended for the general use of the members of the household and for the reception and entertainment of guests.

Livingstone. See **Maramba.**

Liv·ing·stone (lívving-stən || -stōn), **David** (1813–73). Scottish missionary and explorer. He discovered the Zambezi river in 1851 and Victoria Falls in 1855. While searching for the source of the Nile (from 1866), he discovered Lake Mweru and Lake Bangweulu. Sickness forced him to return to Ujiji, on Lake Tanganyika, where Stanley found him in 1871.

living wage *n.* A wage sufficient to provide minimally satisfactory living conditions.

Li·vor·no (li-vórnō). *English* **Leg·horn** (lég-hawrn, -hórn). Seaport and capital of Livorno province, Tuscany, Italy.

li·vre (léevrə; *French* leevr) *n. Abbr.* **lv.** A former French unit of account originally worth a pound of silver. [French, from Latin *lībra,* a pound.]

Liv·y (lívvi). Latin name Titus Livius (*c.*59 B.C.–A.D. 17). Roman historian, born in Padua. His history of Rome originally consisted of 142 books, of which only 35 survive.

lix·iv·i·ate (lik-sívvi-ayt) *tr.v.* **-ated, -ating, -ates.** To wash or percolate the soluble matter from. [Late Latin *lixīvium,* lye, from the neuter of Latin *lixīvius,* of lye, from *lixa,* lye.] **—lix·iv·i·al** *adj.* **—lix·iv·i·a·tion** (-áysh'n) *n.*

lix·iv·i·um (lik-sívvi-əm) *n., pl.* **-ums** or **-ivia** (-ivvi-ə). A solution obtained by lixiviation; especially, the lye obtained by leaching wood ash. [Late Latin, from *lixivius,* of lye, from *lix,* lye.]

liz·ard (lízzərd) *n.* **1.** Any of numerous reptiles of the suborder Sauria (or Lacertilia), characteristically having an elongated, scaly body, four legs, and a tapering tail. **2.** Broadly, any reptile or amphibian resembling a lizard. **3.** Leather made from the skin of a lizard. [Middle English *liserd, lesard(e),* from Old French *lesard, laisarde,* from Latin *lacertus, lacerta*†.]

lizard fish *n.* Any of various bottom-dwelling fishes of the family Synodontidae, of warm seas, having a lizard-like head.

Liz·ard Point (lízzərd). The most southerly point of England, at the end of the Lizard peninsula in Cornwall.

Ljub·lja·na (léwbli-áanə, lóobli-, lóobli-). Capital of the republic of Slovenia, northwest Yugoslavia.

ll. lines.

lla·ma (laámə; *Spanish* yaámə) *n.* **1.** A South American ruminant mammal, *Lama peruana* (or *L. glana*), domesticated as a beast of burden and for its soft, fleecy wool. **2.** Any other animal of the genus *Lama,* such as the guanaco. [Spanish, from Quechua.]

Llanbedr Pont Steffan. See **Lampeter.**

Llan·daff (lán-dəf, hlán-, -dáf). *Welsh* **Llan·daf** (hlan-daáv). City now forming part of the city of Cardiff, South Glamorgan, Wales.

Llan·dud·no (hlan-díd-nō, lan-, -dúd-). Holiday resort on the coast of Gwynedd, Wales.

Llan·elli (hla-néhli, lə-néthli, la-). Town on the Burry estuary, Dyfed, Wales. Its port was closed in 1951, and tin-plate manufacturing and petrochemicals are now the main industry.

Llan·fair PG (lán-fair pée jée; *Welsh* hlán-vīr). Also **Llan·fair·pwll** (-po͞ohl) or **Llan·fair·pwll·gwyn·gyll** (-po͞ohl-gwín-gihl). Village in Anglesey, Gwynedd, Wales, with the longest place name in Britain: Llanfairpwllgwyngyllgogerychwyrndrobwllllantysiliogogogoch.

Llan·goll·en (hlan-góhlen, lan-góthlən). Market town in central Clwyd, north Wales, where the International Eisteddfod, an annual festival of traditional music, poetry, and dance, is held.

lla·no (laánō || *U.S. also* lánnō) *n., pl.* **-nos.** A large, grassy, almost treeless plain, as in Latin America; savannah. [Spanish, from Latin *plānum,* a plain, from the neuter of *plānus,* level.]

LL.B. Bachelor of Laws [Latin *Legum Baccalaureus*].

LL.D. Doctor of Laws [Latin *Legum Doctor*].

Lle·well·yn (hlə-wéllin, lə-, loo-éllin), **Sir Harry,** also known as Lieutenant-Colonel Sir Henry Morton Llewellyn (1911–). British show-jumper. He won many prizes with his horse Foxhunter.

LLewellyn, Richard, pen name of Richard Dafydd Vivian Llewellyn Lloyd (1907–). British novelist, born in Wales. He wrote *How Green Was My Valley* (1939), a portrait of life in a South Wales mining village.

LL.M. Master of Laws [Latin *Legum Magister*].

Lloyd (loyd), **Chris(tine) Evert,** born Christine Evert (1954–). U.S. tennis player. She was U.S. women's singles champion (1975–78, 1982) and won the Wimbledon title in 1974, 1976, and 1981.

Lloyd, Harold (1893–1971). U.S. comedian of the silent screen. His stunts included hanging from a clockface high above a street in *Safety Last* (1923).

Lloyd, Marie, stage name of Matilda Wood (1870–1922). British music-hall artiste, famous for such songs as *Oh, I Do Like to be Beside the Seaside.* Her Cockney humour won her great popularity.

Lloyd George, David, 1st Earl of Dwyfor (1863–1945). British prime minister (1916–22). He was elected a Liberal M.P. in 1890, and as Chancellor of the Exchequer (1908–15) initiated the welfare state, introducing old-age pensions, unemployment benefit, and national health insurance. In 1916 he succeeded Asquith as prime minister. His postwar coalition government set up the Irish Free State. Lloyd George remained Liberal party leader until 1931, and was an M.P. until his death.

Lloyd's (loydz) *n.* An association of underwriters founded in London in 1688, originally specialising in marine insurance and shipping information and now noted for the variety of insurance dealt with. [After *Lloyd's* Coffee House in London, a gathering place of marine underwriters.]

Lloyd's List *n.* A daily newssheet concerned with shipping matters, published by Lloyd's.

Lloyd's Register *n.* A compilation of data about oceangoing vessels of all nations, published annually by Lloyd's.

Lly·wel·yn ap Gru·ffudd (hlə-wéllin ap griffith), also called Llywelyn II (died 1282). Native-born Prince of Wales (1258–82), known as Llywelyn the Last. His death in a war with the English king Edward I marked the end of Welsh independence.

Llywelyn ap Ior·werth (ap yór-wairth), also called Llywelyn I (1173–1240). Welsh Prince of Gwynedd (1194–1238), known as Llywelyn the Great. He paid homage to King John of England, but commanded the allegiance of lesser princes in Wales. In 1238 he became a monk, handing over the succession to his son.

lm lumen.

LM lunar module.

LMT local mean time.

ln natural logarithm.

lo (lō) *interj.* Used to attract attention or to show surprise. Now archaic except in the phrase *lo and behold.* [Middle English *lo, la,* Old English *lā.*]

loach (lōch) *n.* Any of various Eurasian and African freshwater fishes of the family Cobitidae, having barbels around the mouth. [Middle English *loch(e),* from Old French *loche*†.]

load (lōd) *n. Abbr.* **ld.** **1. a.** A supported weight or mass. **b.** The overall force to which a structure is subjected in supporting a weight or mass, or in resisting externally applied forces. **2. a.** Anything that is transported by a motor vehicle, ship, or aircraft, or carried by a person or pack animal. **b.** The quantity so transported or capable of being so transported: *a full load.* Often used in combination: *a busload of football supporters.* **3. a.** The share of work allocated to or required of an individual, machine, group, or organisation: *has a fairly light teaching load.* **b.** The demand for services or performance made on a machine or system. **4.** The amount that can be loaded into a machine or device at one time. **5.** A single charge of ammunition for a firearm. **6.** A source of stress or anxiety, regarded as a depressing weight on the mind; a burden. **7.** The external mechanical resistance against which a machine acts. **8. a.** The power output of a generator or power plant. **b.** A device, or the resistance of a device, to which power is delivered. **9.** *Geology.* Material carried by a river, stream, sea, glacier, or wind during the process of denudation. **10.** *Usually plural. Informal.* Any large amount or quantity. **—get a load of.** *Chiefly U.S. Slang.* To look at or pay attention to: *Get a load of that!* **—shed** or **shoot (one's) load.** *Vulgar Slang.* To ejaculate semen.

~v. **loaded, loading, loads.** *—tr.* **1.** To put or place (a load) in or on a structure, device, or conveyance. **2.** To put or place in or on (a structure, device, or conveyance). **3.** To provide with an abundant or excessive supply. **4.** To weigh down; burden; oppress. **5.** To charge (a firearm) with ammunition. **6. a.** To insert (film or tape, for example) into a holder or magazine. **b.** To insert film or tape, for example, into (a magazine, camera, or similar device). **7.** To tamper with; especially, to make (dice) heavier on one side by adding weight. **8. a.** To twist or bias (evidence). **b.** To charge (a question) with broader implications that may not be immediately obvious, especially so as to trap the person being questioned. **9.** To dilute, adulterate, or doctor. **10.** To increase (an insurance premium) by adding a loading. **11.** *Electricity.* **a.** To raise the power demand in (a circuit), as by adding resistance. **b.** To draw power from (a generator). **12.** To raise the power output of (an engine). **13.** *Physics.* To add a material such as barium to (concrete, for example) in order to increase radiation-shielding efficiency. *—intr.* **1.** To receive a load; take on cargo. **2.** To be charged with ammunition. **3.** To insert ammunition, film, or tape, for example. [Middle English *lode* (influenced in sense by Middle English *laden,* to load, LADE), Old English *lād,* way, course, conveyance.]

Usage: The past tense and past participle of this verb are both *loaded*: *We loaded the goods; The goods were loaded. Laden* is an adjective, generally used after the verb unless premodified itself: *The table was laden with good things to eat; a heavily laden table.* In contexts where either word could be used, there is usually a difference in meaning: *The ship was loaded with ammunition* (i.e. ammunition was put on board by someone or something), but *The ship was laden with ammunition* (it was weighed down with ammunition).

load displacement *n. Nautical.* The displacement of a fully loaded ship.

load·ed (lódid) *adj. Slang.* **1.** Extremely wealthy. **2.** Drunk. **3.** *Chiefly U.S.* Drugged.

load·er (lódər) *n.* **1.** One that loads. **2.** *Computing.* A program that transfers data from an off-line memory to an on-line memory by means of an input or storage device. **3.** An apparatus, such as a

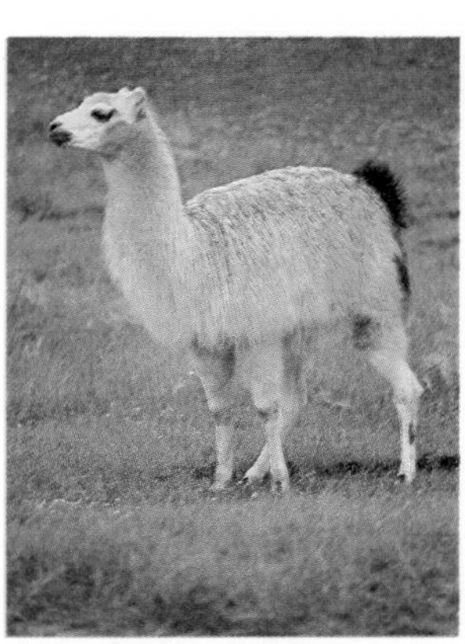

llama *The llama, which is a member of the camel family, is one of the few animals apart from dogs to have been domesticated in the Americas. Horses, cattle, and sheep were unknown until the Spanish Conquest. Indian peoples in the Andes rely upon the llama still as a pack animal and for its meat, milk, and fleece. Its droppings are also dried and burnt to provide heat in the mountains. The vicuña, alpaca, and guanaco (wild llama) are close relatives.*

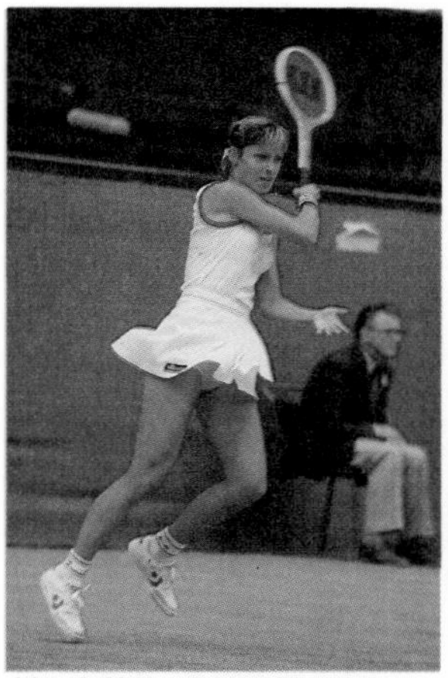

Lloyd, Chris *Born in Florida in December 1954, American tennis player Chris Lloyd won the women's singles championship at Wimbledon in 1974, 1976, and 1981. She married the British tennis player John Lloyd in 1979.*

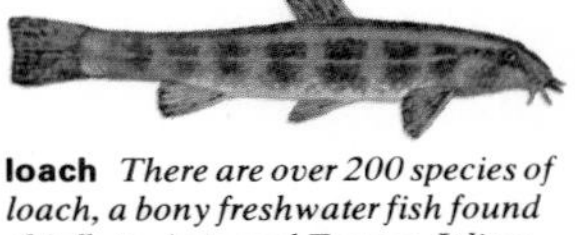

loach *There are over 200 species of loach, a bony freshwater fish found chiefly in Asia and Europe. It lives and feeds on muddy riverbeds. The stone loach (above) lives in fast-flowing streams.*

washing machine or firearm, that is loaded in the specified way. Used in combination: *top-loader; breechloader.*

load factor *n.* **1.** A measure of the load on an electrical supply system, equal to the ratio of average load to peak load. **2. a.** The ratio of the load of an aircraft to its unloaded weight. **b.** The ratio of the load carried by an aircraft to its maximum load, often expressed as a percentage.

load·ing (lṓding) *n. Abbr.* **ldg. 1.** A weight, stress, or burden. **2.** The act of supplying a load. **3.** A substance added to something; a filler. **4.** An addition to an insurance premium taking account of special circumstances: *an extra loading for those with hazardous occupations.* **5.** *Electricity.* The addition of inductance to a transmission line to improve its transmission characteristics. **6.** *Aeronautics.* The ratio of the weight of an aircraft to its power (the *power loading*), to its wing span (the *span loading*), or to its wing area (the *wing loading*). **7.** *Psychology.* The correlation or degree of correlation between a specific factor or variable, such as a test score, and a broad condition or constant, such as a personality trait. **8.** A contractually agreed bonus or extra payment added to basic wages or salary in certain conditions; a weighting.

loading program *n. Computing.* A sequence of computer instructions that starts the processing of a program entered by means of an automatic input device.

load line *n. Nautical.* A Plimsoll line *(see).*

load shedding *n.* Temporary reduction of the electric power supply in an area to avoid overloading the generators.

loadstar. Variant of **lodestar.**

loadstone. Variant of **lodestone.**

loaf[1] (lōf) *n., pl.* **loaves** (lōvz). **1.** A shaped mass of bread baked in one piece. **2.** Any shaped, typically oblong mass of food: *nut loaf.* **3.** *British Slang.* The head; the brains: *Use your loaf.* [Middle English *lo(o)f, laf,* Old English *hlāf,* loaf, bread, from Germanic *hlaibaz* (unattested). See also **lord, lady.** Sense 3, rhyming slang, *loaf of bread, head.*]

loaf[2] *v.* **loafed, loafing, loafs.** *—intr.* **1.** To spend time lazily or aimlessly. Used with *around* or *about.* **2.** To waste time on a job; dawdle. *—tr.* To spend (time) lazily or idly. Usually used with *away.* [Probably back-formation from **LOAFER.**]

loaf·er (lṓfər) *n.* **1.** One who loafs. **2.** *Chiefly U.S.* A casual or informal moccasin-like shoe. [Perhaps from German *Landläufer,* wanderer, vagabond.]

loam (lōm) *n.* **1.** Fertile soil consisting of sand, clay, silt, and organic matter. **2.** A mixture of moist clay and sand, together with straw, used principally in making bricks and foundry moulds. [Middle English *lome, lame,* Old English *lām.*] **—loam·y** *adj.*

loan[1] (lōn) *n.* **1.** A sum of money lent at interest. **2.** Anything lent for temporary use. **3.** An act of lending or permission to borrow: *gave me the loan of her bike.* **4.** A loanword. **—on loan. 1.** Borrowed: *She has my coat on loan.* **2.** Transferred temporarily to some duty or place away from a regular position or location. *~tr.v.* **loaned, loaning, loans.** To lend; grant a loan of. [Middle English *lone, lane,* from Old Norse *lān.*]

Usage: The use of *loan* as a verb is increasingly common, especially in American English, where it is encountered in formal as well as informal contexts: *Can you loan me 50 dollars?* Many people prefer to restrict *loan* to its use as a noun, especially in British English, using *lend* as the analogous verb. But *loan* is now often used in the sense of "making a formal act of lending, especially as an instruction" in British English: *She has loaned her collection to a museum.*

loan[2] *n.* Also **loan·ing** (lṓning). *Chiefly Scottish.* **1.** A lane. **2.** An open space where cows are milked. [Middle English, variant of **LANE.**]

loan translation *n.* The process or an instance of verbal borrowing from one language to another, whereby the semantic components or morphemes of a given term are literally translated into their equivalents in the borrowing language; for example, *superman* is a loan translation of the German *Übermensch* (*über,* over = *super-*; *Mensch,* man = *man*). Also called "calque".

loan word *n.* A word adopted from another language that has become at least partly naturalised; for example, *angst, hors d'oeuvre.*

loath, loth (lōth ‖ lōth) *adj.* Unwilling; reluctant; disinclined. Usually used with an infinitive: *loath to go.* **—nothing loath.** Willing; willingly. [Middle English *loth(e), lath,* Old English *lāth,* hateful, loathsome.]

loathe (lōth) *tr.v.* **loathed, loathing, loathes.** To detest greatly; abhor. [Middle English *lothen,* Old English *lāthian.*] **—loath·er** *n.* **—loath·ing·ly** *adv.*

loath·ing (lṓthing) *n.* Abhorrence.

loath·some (lōth-səm, lōth-) *adj.* Also *archaic* **loath·ly** (-li). Repulsive; disgusting. [Middle English *lothsum : loth,* hatred, Old English *lāth,* from adjective (see **loath**) + **-SOME.**] **—loath·some·ly** *adv.*

loaves. Plural of **loaf.**

lob (lob) *v.* **lobbed, lobbing, lobs.** *—tr.* **1.** To hit, toss, or propel slowly in or as if in a high arc. **2.** *Informal.* To throw casually; toss. *—intr.* To hit a ball in a high arc. *~n.* **1.** A ball hit, bowled, or thrown in a high arc. **2.** An act of lobbing a ball. [Probably of Low German origin, akin to Low German *lubbe,* awkward person. [Middle Low German *lobbe†,* hanging lip, thus extended to anything clumsy, pendulous, or slow.]

Lo·ba·chev·ski (lóbbə-chéfski; *Russian* ləbá-), **Nikolai Ivanovich** (1793–1856). Russian mathematician. His revolutionary system of

geometry, published in 1829, challenged the accepted Euclidean theory.

lo·bar (lṓb-ər ‖ -aar) *adj.* Of or pertaining to a lobe, such as one of those in the lungs: *lobar pneumonia.*

lo·bate (lṓbayt) *adj.* Also **lo·bat·ed** (lō-báytid ‖ *chiefly U.S.* lṓ-baytid) **1.** Having lobes. **2.** Resembling a lobe. **3.** Having separate toes, each bordered with a weblike lobe. Said of certain birds. **—lo·bate·ly** *adv.*

lo·ba·tion (lō-báysh'n) *n.* **1.** The state of being lobed. **2.** A lobe or part resembling a lobe.

lob·by (lóbbi) *n., pl.* **-bies. 1. a.** An entrance hall or corridor. **b.** A foyer, waiting room, or reception area in a hotel, theatre, or other public building. **2. a.** A public room next to the assembly chamber of a legislative body, where legislators and members of the public can meet. **b.** Any of three anterooms in the British Houses of Parliament, the *members' lobby* for members of the House of Commons, the *peers' lobby* for members of the House of Lords, and the *central lobby* for all members of Parliament and members of the public. **3.** *Chiefly British.* Either of the two corridors attached to a legislative chamber to which the members go to register their votes. In this sense, also called "division lobby". **4.** A group of people, usually representing a particular interest, who seek to influence legislation: *the environmental lobby.* **5.** *Often capital* **L.** A group of British political journalists having access to cabinet ministers and senior civil servants, from whom they acquire confidential information on *lobby terms,* allowing the information to be reported without the source being identified. *~v.* **lobbied, -bying, -bies.** *—intr.* To seek to influence legislators in favour of some special interest. *—tr.* **1.** To seek to influence or gain the support of (legislators or public opinion, for example). **2.** To seek to influence legislators to pass (legislation). [Medieval Latin *lobium, lobia, laubia,* a monastic cloister, from Germanic.] **—lob·bi·er, lob·by·er** *n.*

lob·by·ist (lóbbi-ist) *n.* One employed to influence legislators to introduce or vote for measures favourable to the interest he represents. **—lob·by·ism** *n.*

lobe (lōb) *n.* **1.** A rounded projection; especially, a rounded, projecting anatomical part such as the **ear lobe** *(see).* **2.** A subdivision of an organ or part bounded by fissures, connective tissue, or other structural boundaries. **3.** A loop forming part of a curve or graph. [Late Latin *lobus,* from Greek *lobos,* lobe (of the ear or liver).]

lo·bec·to·my (lṓb-éktəmi) *n., pl.* **-mies.** A surgical operation for the excision of a lobe. [**LOB(E)** + **-ECTOMY.**]

lobed (lōbd) *adj.* Having lobes: *lobed leaves.*

lobe-fin (lṓb-fin) *n.* Any of various mostly extinct bony fishes of the subclass Sarcopterygii, of which the coelacanth is a living representative.

lo·be·li·a (lō-béel-i-ə, lə-, -yə) *n.* Any of numerous plants of the genus *Lobelia,* having terminal clusters of variously coloured, often blue, flowers. It is widely grown as an ornamental border plant. [New Latin, after Matthias de *Lobel* (1538–1616), Flemish botanist.]

Lo·ben·gu·la (lō-ben-gṓ-lə, -géw-) (c.1836–94). King of the Ndebele (1870–94), ruling in Bulawayo. In 1888 he granted mineral concessions to Cecil Rhodes's British South Africa Company, which later subjugated his kingdom (1893), forcing him into exile.

lo·bo (lṓ-bō) *n., pl.* **-bos.** *U.S.* The grey or timber wolf, *Canis lupus.* [Spanish, from Latin *lupus,* wolf.]

lo·bo·la (lō-bṓ-lə, law-báw-) *n.* Also **lo·bo·lo** (-lō). *South African.* **1.** A wedding gift, comparable to a dowry, among black African peoples, consisting of a payment in cash or cattle made by the bridegroom or his family to the family of his prospective wife. **2.** The amount involved in such a transaction; the bride price. [Zulu.]

lo·bot·o·my (lō-bóttə-mi, lə-) *n., pl.* **-mies. 1.** A surgical division of one or more cerebral nerve tracts in the frontal lobe of the brain. See **leucotomy. 2.** Surgical incision into a lobe. [**LOB(E)** + **-TOMY.**] **—lob·ot·o·mise** (-mīz) *tr.v.*

lob·scouse (lób-skowss) *n.* A seaman's stew made of meat, vegetables, and hardtack. [Perhaps dialectal *lob,* to bubble, boil + *scouse†,* broth.]

lob·ster (lób-stər) *n., pl.* **-sters** or collectively **lobster. 1.** Any of several relatively large marine crustaceans of the genus *Homarus,* having five pairs of legs, the first pair modified into large claws. **2.** Any of several related crustaceans, such as the **spiny lobster** *(see).* **3.** The flesh of any of these crustaceans, used as food. **4.** A bright orange-red, the colour of cooked lobster. [Middle English *lobster, lopster,* Old English *loppestre, lopystre,* from Latin *locusta,* locust, lobster (influenced by Old English *loppe,* spider).] **—lob·ster** *adj.*

lobster pot *n.* A slatted cage with an opening covered by a funnel-shaped net, used for trapping lobsters underwater. Also called "lobster trap".

lob·u·late (lóbbew-lət, -lit, -layt) *adj.* Also **lob·u·lat·ed** (-laytid) Having or consisting of lobules. **—lob·u·la·tion** (-láysh'n) *n.*

lob·ule (lóbbewl) *n.* **1.** A small lobe. **2.** A section or subdivision of a lobe. [French, from New Latin *lobulus,* diminutive of Late Latin *lobus,* **LOBE.**] **—lob·u·lar** (-ər), **lob·u·lose** (-ōz, -ōss) *adj.* **—lob·u·lar·ly** *adv.*

lob·worm (lób-wurm) *n.* A lugworm *(see).* [**LOB** (obsolete sense "lump") + **WORM.**]

lo·cal (lṓk'l) *adj.* **1.** Of or pertaining to a place. **2.** Pertaining to, existing in, of interest to, peculiar to, or serving a certain locality: *local government.* **3.** Not broad or general; confined: *a little local difficulty.* **4.** *Medicine.* Of or affecting a limited part of the body;

not systemic: *a local disease.* **5.** Making many stops; not express: *a local train.*

~*n.* **1.** A local person; a native inhabitant. **2.** A public conveyance that makes all possible or scheduled stops. **3.** *British Informal.* A pub close to one's work or home. **4.** *Informal.* A local anaesthetic. **5.** *U.S.* A local branch of an organisation, especially of a trade union. [Middle English, from Old French, from Late Latin *locālis,* from Latin *locus,* place, LOCUS.]

local anaesthetic *n. Medicine.* An injected or topically applied anaesthetic that induces loss of sensation in a particular region of the body. Compare **general anaesthetic.**

local area network *n. Abbr.* **LAN** A network of word processors or computers connected together, for example in an office building, so that information can be transferred from one to another or accessed from a main store.

local authority *n. British.* A local council and its officials, responsible for administering the services of an area; the organ of local government.

local colour *n.* The atmosphere or flavour of a locality imparted by the presentation, as in a novel, of the customs and sights peculiar to that locality.

lo·cale (lō-kaál || *chiefly U.S.* -kál) *n.* **1.** A locality, with reference to some event. **2.** The scene or setting, as of a novel. [French *local,* locality, from Old French, LOCAL.]

lo·cal·ise, lo·cal·ize (lṓkə-līz) *v.* **-ised, -ising, -ises. 1.** To make local. **2.** To confine or restrict to a particular area or part. **3.** To assign to a locality or determine more precisely the origin or source of: *localise a dialect.* **—lo·cal·is·a·tion** (-lī-záysh'n || *U.S.* -li-) *n.*

lo·cal·ism (lṓk'l-iz'm) *n.* **1.** An idiom, mannerism, custom, or the like peculiar to a locality. **2.** Provincialism.

lo·cal·i·ty (lə-kál-əti, lō-) *n., pl.* **-ties. 1.** A neighbourhood, place, or district. **2.** A site, as of an event. **3.** The fact or quality of having position in space. **—**See Synonyms at **area.** [French *localité,* from Late Latin *locālitās* (stem *locālitāt-*), from *locālis,* LOCAL.]

lo·cal·ly (lṓkəli) *adv.* At or near a particular location: *lives locally.*

local option *n.* An option granted usually by a central or regional government to a community or a local government, allowing it discretion, sometimes subject to a referendum, in such issues as whether to keep shops open or to sell spirits on Sundays.

local solar time *n.* Local time.

local time *n.* The time of day at any point on Earth indicated by the apparent movement of the sun, as shown on a sundial. Also called "apparent time", "local solar time". Compare **mean solar time.**

Lo·car·no (lə-kárnō, lō-, lo-). Resort on Lake Maggiore in the south of canton Ticino, Switzerland. It was here in 1925 that representatives of Belgium, Czechoslovakia, France, Germany, Great Britain, Italy, and Poland drew up the *Locarno Pact.* Among other things this resolved the status of the Rhineland and guaranteed the French-German and Belgian-German borders.

lo·cate (lō-káyt, lə- || *chiefly U.S.* lṓ-kayt) *v.* **-cated, -cating, -cates.** —*tr.* **1.** To determine or specify the position and boundaries of: *locate Timbuktu on the map.* **2.** To find by searching, examining, or experimenting: *locate the source of error.* **3.** To station, situate, or place: *locate an agent in Manchester.* —*intr. U.S.* To become established in some spot; settle. [Latin *locāre,* to place, from *locus,* place, LOCUS.]

lo·ca·tion (lə-káysh'n, lō-) *n.* **1.** The act or process of locating. **2.** The fact of being located or settled. **3.** A place or position where something is or might be located. **4.** In television or film production, a site away from the studio grounds, where a scene is shot: *That safari film was made on location.* **5.** *South African.* A small township for black or Coloured residents. [Latin *locātio* (stem *locātiōn-*), a placing, from *locāre,* to place, LOCATE.]

loc·a·tive (lóckətiv) *n. Grammar.* **1.** The noun case in certain Indo-European languages, such as Sanskrit or Old Church Slavonic, that denotes the place where. **2.** A form or construction in this case. ~*adj.* Designating, pertaining to, or inflected in the locative. [French *locatif,* from Old French, from Latin *locāre,* to LOCATE.]

loc. cit. *adv.* In the place cited. [Latin *locō citātō.*]

loch (lok͟h, lok) *n.* In Scotland: **1.** A lake. **2.** A sea loch. [Middle English (Scottish) *louch,* from Scottish Gaelic *loch,* probably from Old Irish.]

loch·an *n.* In Scotland, a small lake. [LOCH and Gaelic diminutive suffix *-an.*]

lo·chi·a (lócki-ə || lṓki-ə) *pl.n.* The normal discharge of blood, tissue, and mucus from the vagina after childbirth. [New Latin, from Greek *lokhia,* from neuter plural of *lokhios,* of childbirth, from *lokhos,* childbirth.] **—lo·chi·al** *adj.*

lo·ci. Plural of **locus.**

lock¹ (lok) *n.* **1.** A device used to provide restraint; especially, a key- or combination-operated mechanism used to fasten shut a door, lid, or the like. **2.** Such a device used to prevent unauthorised operation of a machine: *a telephone lock.* **3.** A section of a canal closed off by gates, within which a vessel may be raised or lowered by the raising or lowering of the section's water level. **4.** A mechanism in a firearm for exploding its charge of ammunition. Usually used in combination: *a flintlock.* **5.** A jamming or locking together of elements or parts. **6.** Any of several holds in wrestling. **7.** In Rugby football: **a.** Either of the two forwards who form the second row of the scrum. **b.** The position of such a player. In both senses, also called "lock forward". **8.** *British.* The degree of turn of which a motor vehicle is capable; the turning base. **9.** A gas bubble or pocket preventing the flow of liquid through a pipe. **—lock, stock, and barrel.** Completely; totally. **—under lock and key.** In complete security or safety.

~*v.* **locked, locking, locks.** —*tr.* **1.** To fasten with a lock, as: **a.** To secure against passage or entry: *lock a door.* **b.** To secure against loss or theft: *lock a bicycle.* **2. a.** To confine or safeguard by putting behind a lock. Used with *in* or *up*: *lock the dog in for the night.* **3.** To engage and fix together securely; intertwine. **4.** To clasp or embrace tightly. **5.** To entangle in struggle or battle. **6.** To jam or force together so as to make unmovable. **7.** To pass (a vessel) through a lock. **8.** To provide or section off (a waterway) with locks. —*intr.* **1. a.** To become fastened by or as if by a lock. **b.** To admit of being locked: *Does this drawer lock?* **2.** To become entangled; interlock. **3.** To become rigid or unmovable. **4.** To pass or flow through a lock. **5.** To find, fasten onto, and automatically follow a target, especially with radar. Used with *on* or *onto.* [Middle English *lo(c)k,* Old English *loc.*] **—lock·a·ble** *adj.*

lock² *n.* **1.** A strand or curl of hair; a tress. **2.** *Plural.* The hair of the head. **3.** A small wisp or tuft, as of wool or cotton. [Middle English *lock, lok(k),* Old English *locc.*]

lock·age (lóckij) *n. Nautical.* **1.** The passage of a vessel through a lock by operation of the lock. **2.** The toll for the use of a lock. **3. a.** A system of locks. **b.** The works of a lock. **4.** The amount of the rise and fall effected by a lock or system of locks.

Locke (lok), **John** (1632–1704). English empiricist philosopher, author of *An Essay Concerning Human Understanding* (1690). His *Two Treatises of Government* (1690) justified the English Revolution of 1688, opposing the notion of the divine right of kings.

lock·er (lóckər) *n.* **1.** One that locks. **2.** A small metal cupboard or enclosure that may be locked; especially, one of many provided at a sporting centre or school for the safekeeping of clothing and valuables. **3.** A flat storage trunk.

locker room *n.* **1.** A room in a gymnasium, school, clubhouse, or the like, furnished with rows of lockers. **2.** A room for changing one's clothes, as at public swimming baths.

lock·et (lóckit) *n.* A small ornamental metal case for a picture or keepsake, such as a lock of hair, usually worn as a pendant. [Old French *locquet,* latch, small lock, diminutive of *loc,* lock, probably from Old English *loc,* lock.]

lock·jaw (lók-jaw) *n. Pathology.* **1. Tetanus** *(see).* **2.** A symptom of tetanus, in which the jaws are clamped shut because of a tonic spasm of the muscles of mastication. Also called "trismus".

lock·nut (lók-nut) *n.* **1.** A usually thin nut screwed down on a primary nut to keep the latter from loosening. **2.** A self-locking nut.

lock out *tr.v.* **1.** To bar or shut out by locking a door. **2.** To refuse work to (employees) during a dispute.

lock·out (lók-owt) *n.* The closing down of a place of employment by an employer to coerce the workers into meeting his terms or modifying theirs. Also called "shutout".

lock·smith (lók-smith) *n.* One who makes or repairs locks.

lock step *n.* A marching technique in which the marchers follow each other as closely as possible.

lock stitch *n.* A stitch made on a sewing machine by the interlocking of the upper thread and the bobbin thread.

lock up *tr.v.* **1.** To shut and make secure by fastening all locks: *lock up a house.* **2.** To put in jail or some other place of confinement. **3.** *Printing.* **a.** To secure (letterpress type) in a chase or press bed by tightening the quoins. **b.** To fasten (a curved plate) to the cylinder of a rotary press. **4.** To invest (funds) in such a way that they cannot easily be converted back into cash.

~*intr.v.* To shut and make secure a house or other premises, as when going out in the evening.

lock·up (lók-up) *n.* **1.** An act of locking up or the state of being locked up. **2.** *Informal.* A jail, especially a local one in which offenders are held while awaiting a court hearing. **3.** *British.* A small shop or other business premises where the manager or proprietor does not live. Also used adjectivally: *a lockup shop.* **4.** *British.* A garage or row of garages, often at some distance from the owner's home or place of work.

lo·co¹ (lṓkō) *n. Informal.* A railway train or engine. [Shortened from LOCOMOTIVE.]

loco² *adj. Chiefly U.S. Slang.* Mad; insane. [Spanish *loco*†, crazy, insane.]

lo·co·mo·tion (lṓkə-mṓsh'n) *n.* **1.** The act of moving or ability to move from place to place. **2.** Movement from place to place; travel. [Latin *locō,* ablative of *locus,* place, LOCUS + MOTION.]

lo·co·mo·tive (lṓkə-mōtiv, -mṓtiv) *n.* A self-propelled engine, now usually electric or diesel-powered, that pulls or pushes trains along railway tracks.

~*adj.* **1.** Of or involved in locomotion. **2.** Able to move independently from place to place. **3.** Of or pertaining to travel. [Latin *locō* (see **locomotion**) + MOTIVE.]

lo·co·mo·tor (lṓkə-mṓtər, -mōtər) *adj.* Locomotive. [Latin *locō* (see **locomotion**) + *mōtor,* mover, MOTOR.]

locomotor ataxia *n. Pathology.* **Tabes dorsalis** *(see).*

lo·co·weed (lṓkō-weed) *n.* Any of several plants of the genera *Oxytropis* and *Astragalus,* of the western and central United States, causing severe poisoning when eaten by livestock. [Mexican Spanish *loco,* locoweed, from Spanish, LOCO (referring to the effects of the poison, which seems to drive livestock mad).]

loc·u·lar (lóckew-lər) *adj.* Also **loc·u·late** (-layt, -lat, -lit), **loc·u·lat·ed** (-laytid). *Biology.* Having, formed of, or divided into small cells or cavities. **—loc·u·la·tion** (-láysh'n) *n.*

loc·ule (lóckewl) *n.* Also **loc·u·lus** (-əss) *pl.* **-li** (-ī). A small cavity or

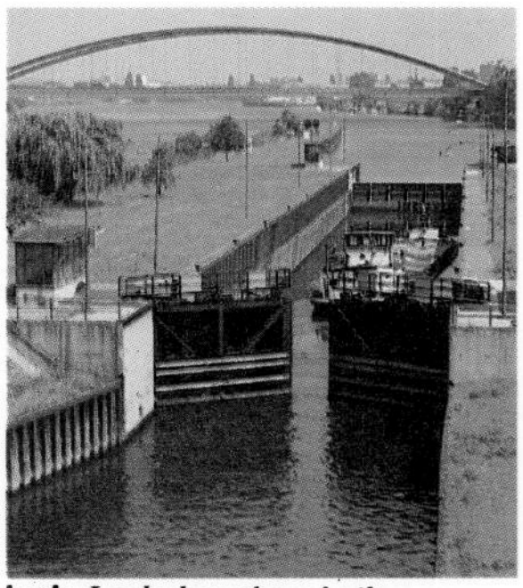

lock *Locks have been built on navigable waterways for at least 2,000 years. This one is at Offenbach in West Germany, on the River Main.*

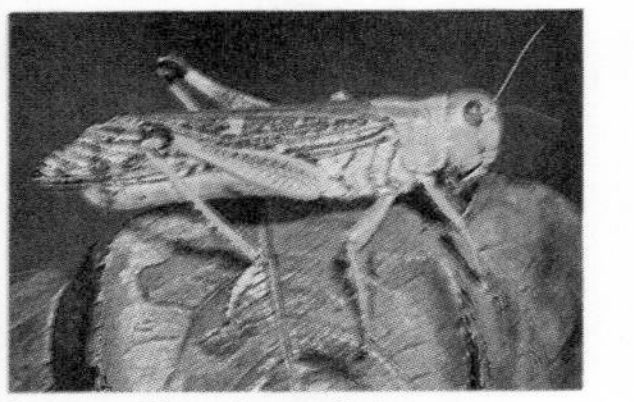

locust *These large, flying grasshoppers migrate periodically – sometimes over hundreds of kilometres – when the population outgrows its food supplies; they can devastate crops along the way.*

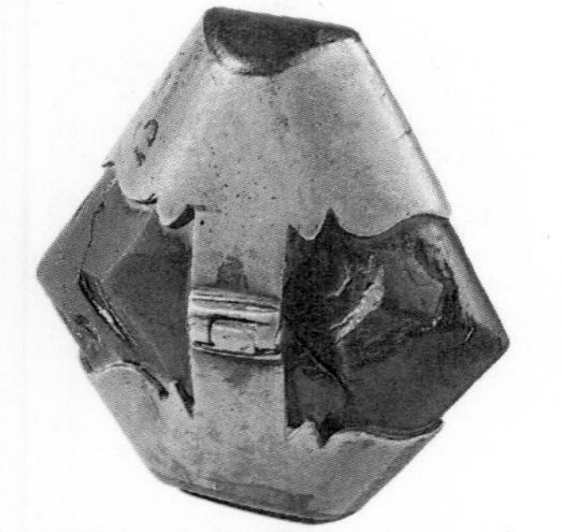

lodestone *The Chinese discovered the magnetic properties of lodestone – a naturally occurring type of iron oxide known as magnetite – about 2,500 years ago. However, the discovery was not applied to direction-finding until the invention of the compass in about the 11th century* A.D. *This brass-bound lodestone, dating from the 17th century, was used to magnetise iron compass needles.*

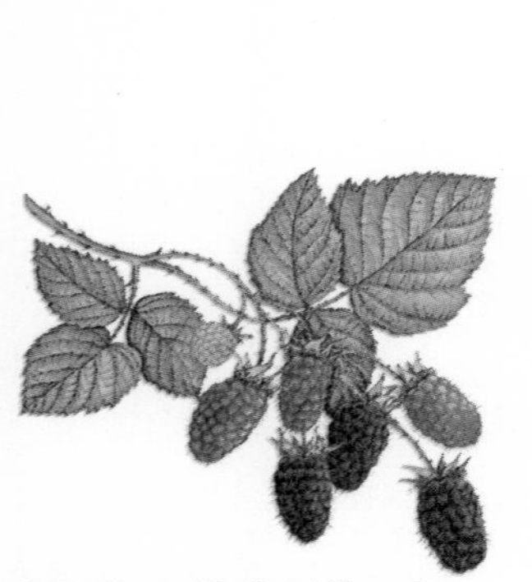

loganberry *The hybrid loganberry is said to have been created in California, in the United States, by the accidental crossing of a blackberry and a raspberry.*

compartment within an organ or part, such as any of the cavities within a plant ovary. [Latin, diminutive of *locus,* place, LOCUS.]

lo·cum (lōkəm) *n. Chiefly British.* A clergyman, chemist, or, especially, a doctor, temporarily replacing another. Also called "locum tenens". [Medieval Latin *locum tenēns,* "(one) holding the place".]

lo·cus (lṓkəss, lóckəss) *n., pl.* **-ci** (lō-sī, lóckee). **1.** A place, especially when considered as the site of a particular activity. **2.** *Mathematics.* The set or configuration of all points satisfying given conditions. **3.** *Genetics.* The position that a gene occupies on a chromosome. [Latin *locus*†, place.]

locus clas·si·cus (klássi-kəss) *n., pl.* **loci classici** (-sī, -kee). A passage from a classic or standard work that is often cited as an authoritative illustration or instance. [Latin, "classical place".]

locus stan·di (stán-dī, -dee) *n.* **1.** *Law.* The right of a party to be heard in court. **2.** Any recognised right or official status, such as the right to participate in meetings. [Latin, "place of standing".]

lo·cust[1] (lṓkəst) *n.* **1.** Any of numerous grasshoppers of the family Locustidae, often travelling in swarms and devouring vegetation in huge quantities. **2.** A cicada such as the **seventeen-year locust** *(see).* [Middle English, from Old French *locuste,* from Latin *lōcusta,* locust, lobster.]

locust[2] *n.* **1.** *British.* A tree, the **carob** *(see).* **2.** *U.S.* A tree, the **false acacia** *(see).* [From the locust-shaped pods of some species.]

locust bird *n.* Any of the African pratincoles, such as *Glareola pratincola,* that feed on swarms of locusts.

lo·cu·tion (lə-kéwsh'n, lo-, lō-) *n.* **1.** A particular word, phrase, or expression considered from the point of view of style. **2.** Style of speaking; phraseology. [Middle English *locucion,* from Latin *locūtiō* (stem *locūtiōn-*), speech, utterance, from *loquī* (past participle *locūtus*), to speak.]

Lod (lod). Also **Lyd·da** (líddə). Ancient Hebrew city, southeast of Tel Aviv, Israel, the site of Israel's main international airport.

lode (lōd) *n.* **1.** A mineral deposit contained in hard rock, usually in the form of a group of veins. **2.** A rich source or supply. **3.** In East Anglia, an artificial watercourse. [Middle English *lode, lade,* course, way, Old English *lād.*]

lo·den (lṓd'n) *n.* **1.** A thick, waterproof, woollen fabric, used in making coats. **2.** A dark green colour. [German, from Old High German *lodo,* heavy cloth.]

lode·star, load·star (lṓd-staar) *n.* **1.** A star that is used as a point of reference; especially, the North Star. **2.** A guiding principle, interest, or ambition: *Nuclear disarmament was her constant lodestar.* [Middle English *lo(o)de sterre,* "guiding star" : *lode, lade,* course, guidance (see **lode**) + STAR.]

lode·stone, load·stone (lṓd-stōn) *n.* **1.** A magnetised piece of magnetite. **2.** One that attracts or magnetises. [From its former use by sailors as a compass to guide their course.]

lodge (loj) *n.* **1.** A small house on the grounds of an estate or park for a caretaker, gatekeeper, or the like. **2.** A cottage or hut, often located in an isolated place, used as temporary accomodation or shelter by huntsmen, climbers, or the like: *a skiing lodge.* **3.** The room or rooms near the entrance of a university, college, or similar building which house the porter's office, the notice boards, and the students' pigeon holes. **4.** At Cambridge university, the residence of the head of a college. **5. a.** A local chapter of certain fraternal organisations. **b.** The members of such a chapter considered collectively. **c.** The meeting hall of such a society. **6.** The den of certain animals, such as otters. **7.** *Chiefly U.S.* The central building in a camping ground or nature park. **8. a.** A North American Indian living unit such as a hogan, wigwam, or long house. **b.** The group living in such a unit.

~v. **lodged, lodging, lodges.** *—tr.* **1.** To provide with temporary quarters. **2.** To rent a room or rooms to; take in as a paying guest. **3.** To place or establish in quarters: *lodge children with relatives.* **4.** To serve as a depository for; harbour. **5.** To place, leave, or deposit for safety. **6.** To fix, embed, or implant. **7.** To register (a charge) in court or with an appropriate authority or official: *lodge a complaint.* **8.** To vest (authority or power, for example). Used with *in* or *with.* **9.** To beat down (crops). Used of wind or rain: *"If rye or wheat be lodged, cut it though it be not ripe."* (Robert Browning). *—intr.* **1.** To reside temporarily. **2.** To rent living accommodation; be a lodger. **3.** To be or become embedded. [Middle English *log(g)e,* from Old French *loge,* shed, small house, from Frankish *laubja* (unattested).]

lodg·er (lójər) *n.* A person who rents and lives in a furnished room or rooms in the landlord's home.

lodg·ings (lójing) *pl.n.* **1.** Rented rooms. **2.** *Sometimes singular.* Sleeping accommodation. **3.** *Sometimes singular.* At Oxford university, the residence of the head of a college.

lodg·ment, lodge·ment (lójmənt) *n.* **1. a.** The act of lodging. **b.** The state of being lodged. **2.** A place for lodging. **3.** An accumulation or deposit. **4.** *Military.* A foothold, beach-head, or salient gained in enemy or neutral territory.

lod·i·cule (lóddi-kewl || lṓdi-) *n. Botany.* Any of the small scales at the base of the ovary in grasses. [Late Latin *lōdīcula,* diminutive of *lōdīx* (stem *lōdīc-*), covering, perhaps from Celtic.]

Łódź (loj; *Polish* wŏoch). Second largest city in Poland, renowned for its textiles.

lo·ess, löss (lṓ-iss, lerss, löss || *U.S. also* less) *n.* A fine-grained, friable, porous, yellowish to grey silt or dust, generally thought to have been initially worn away and then deposited by the wind. [German *Löss,* from Swiss German *Lösch,* from *lösch,* loose.]

loft (loft || lawft) *n.* **1.** An open space under a roof; an attic. **2.** A gallery or balcony, as in a church: *a choir loft.* **3.** *U.S.* The top floor, usually unpartitioned, as of a factory or warehouse. **4.** A **hayloft** *(see).* **5. a.** A coop in which pigeons are kept. **b.** A flock of pigeons kept in such a coop. **6.** In golf: **a.** The backward slant of the face of a club head, designed to drive the ball in a high arc. **b.** A golf stroke that lofts the ball. **c.** The upward course of a lofted ball.

~v. **lofted, lofting, lofts.** *—tr.* **1.** To put, store, or keep in a loft. **2.** To send (a ball) in a high arc. **3.** To give a loft to (a golf club). *—intr.* To loft a golf ball. [Middle English *lofte,* upper room, sky, Old English *loft,* sky, air, from Old Norse *lopt,* air, attic.]

loft·er (lóftər || láwftər) *n.* A golf club designed to loft the ball. Also called "lofting iron".

loft·y (lófti || láwfti) *adj.* **-ier, -iest.** **1.** Of imposing height; towering. **2.** Elevated in character; exalted; noble. **3.** High-flown; affecting grandness; pompous. **4.** Arrogant; haughty. —See Synonyms at **high.** [Middle English, from *lofte,* raised, elevated, from *lofte,* sky, LOFT.] **—loft·i·ly** *adv.* **—loft·i·ness** *n.*

log[1] (log || *chiefly U.S.* lawg) *n.* **1. a.** The trunk of a large fallen or felled tree. **b.** A thick section of trimmed but unhewn timber. **2.** *Nautical.* A device trailed from a ship to determine its speed through the water. **3. a.** A record of a ship's speed, progress, and shipboard events of navigational importance. **b.** The book in which this record is kept. Also called "logbook". **c.** Any record of performance, such as the flight record of an aircraft. **d.** Any record of events or experiences, such as the journal of an expedition. **4.** A record of radio transmissions, frequencies, and the like. **—sleep like a log.** To sleep soundly.

~v. **logged, logging, logs.** *—tr.* **1. a.** To cut down the timber of (a section of land). **b.** To cut (trees) into logs. **2.** To achieve and record (a specified time, distance, or speed, for example) in a ship's or other log. **3.** *Informal.* To achieve: *She's logged 25 years with her company.* *—intr.* To cut down, trim, and haul timber. **—log on.** To register, especially with a computer as an authorised user. [Middle English *logge*†.]

log[2] *n. Informal.* **1.** A logarithm. **2.** *Plural.* Logarithmic tables.

Lo·gan, Mount (lṓgən). Canada's highest peak at 6 050 metres (19,850 feet). It lies in the St. Elias Mountains in southwest Yukon Territory and was first climbed in 1925.

lo·gan·ber·ry (lṓgən-bri, -bəri || -berri) *n., pl.* **-ries.** **1.** A trailing, prickly plant, *Rubus loganobaccus,* cultivated for its raspberry-like edible fruit. **2.** The dark red fruit of this plant. [First grown by James H. *Logan* (1841–1928), U.S. judge and horticulturist.]

log·a·oe·dic (lóggə-éedik) *adj.* Of, pertaining to, or designating a form of verse in which different metrical units occur within a single line.

~n. A line of such verse. [Late Latin, from Greek *logaoidikos,* (of verse) like natural (prose) speech : *logos,* speech + *aoidē,* poetry.]

log·a·rithm (lóggə-rith'm, *rarely* -rith'm || *U.S. also* láwgə-) *n.* The exponent indicating the power to which a fixed number, the base, must be raised to produce a given number. For example, if $n^x = a$, the logarithm of *a,* with *n* as the base, is *x*; symbolically, $\log_n a = x$. See **common logarithm, natural logarithm.** [New Latin *logarithmus* : Greek *logos,* reckoning, reason, ratio + *arithmos,* number.]

log·a·rith·mic (lóggə-ríthmik, -ríthmik) *adj.* **1.** Of or pertaining to logarithms. **2.** Involving a logarithmic function. Said of a scale in which successive distances are proportional to logarithms, as in certain measuring instruments, slide rules, and graph paper, for example. **—log·a·rith·mi·cal** *adj.* **—log·a·rith·mi·cal·ly** *adv.*

logarithmic function *n. Mathematics.* A function containing an expression of the form log *x.*

log·book (lóg-bŏŏk || láwg-, -bŏŏk) *n.* **1.** The official record book of a ship, aircraft, or expedition, for example. **2.** *British.* Formerly, the identifying document of a motor vehicle, listing its specifications, registration number, and owner. Also called "log".

loge (lōzh) *n.* **1.** A small compartment; especially, a box in a theatre. **2.** The front rows of the upper block of seating in a theatre, especially in Europe or the United States. [French, from Old French, shed, small house. See **lodge.**]

log·ger (lóggər || láwgər) *n.* **1.** A lumberjack. **2.** A tractor, crane, or other machine used for hauling or loading logs.

log·ger·head (lóggər-hed || láwgər-) *n.* **1.** A marine turtle, *Caretta caretta,* having a large, beaked head. **2.** An iron tool consisting of a long handle with a bulbous end, used when heated to melt tar or to warm liquids. **3.** *Nautical.* A post on a whaleboat used to help secure a rope holding a harpooned whale. **4.** *Archaic & Regional.* **a.** A blockhead; a dolt. **b.** A disproportionately large head. **5.** A loggerhead shrike. **—at loggerheads.** Engaged in a dispute. [Dialectal *logger,* wooden block, from LOG + HEAD.]

loggerhead shrike *n.* A North American bird, *Lanius ludovicianus,* having grey and white plumage and a hooked beak. Also called "loggerhead".

log·gi·a (lṓj-ə, lój-, -i-ə) *n., pl.* **-gias** or **-gie** (-ay). **1.** A roofed but open gallery or arcade along the front or side of a building, often at an upper level. **2.** An open balcony in a theatre. [Italian, from French *loge,* LOGE.]

log·ging (lógging || láwging) *n.* The work or business of felling and trimming trees and transporting the logs to a mill.

log·ic (lójik) *n.* **1.** *Philosophy.* The study of the principles of reasoning, especially of the structure of propositions as distinguished from their content and of method and validity in deductive reasoning. **2. a.** A system of reasoning. **b.** A mode of reasoning. **c.** The formal, guiding principles of a discipline, school, or science. **3.** Valid reasoning as distinguished from invalid or irrational argument. **4.** The relationship of elements to one another and to the whole in a set of objects, individuals, principles, or events. **5.** *Computing.* The way in which signals are combined in a circuit to perform logical operations. **6.** The apparently irresistible force which brings about or holds together a sequence of events: *the logic of circumstances.* **7.** *Informal.* Reasonableness; good sense: *What's the logic of trying to do it before you're ready?* [Middle English *logik,* from Old French *logique,* from Late Latin *logica,* from Greek *logikē (tekhnē),* "(art) of reasoning", from the feminine of *logikos,* of speech, of reasoning, from *logos,* speech, reason.]

log·i·cal (lójik'l) *adj.* **1.** Pertaining to, in accordance with, or of the nature of logic. **2.** Showing consistency of reasoning. **3.** Reasonable on the basis of earlier statements or events: *a logical development; a logical choice.* **4.** Able to reason clearly: *a logical thinker.* **—log·i·cal·i·ty** (lóji-kál-əti), **log·i·cal·ness** *n.* **—log·i·cal·ly** *adv.*

logical positivism *n. Philosophy.* A doctrine, developed in the 20th century, asserting the primacy of observation in assessing the truth of statements of fact and holding that metaphysical and subjective arguments not based on observable data are meaningless, meaningful statements being either a priori and analytic or a posteriori and synthetic.

logic gate *n. Computing.* An electronic gate that gives an output signal for certain combinations of two or more input signals, used for performing logical operations. Also called "logic circuit".

lo·gi·cian (lə-jísh'n, lo-, lō-) *n.* A person who is trained in or expert at logic.

lo·gi·on (lóggi-on || *chiefly U.S.* lōgi-) *n., pl.* **-gia** (-ə || -aa). Any of the sayings of Jesus not recorded in the Gospels but supposed to have belonged to the source material from which they were compiled. [Greek, "saying".]

lo·gis·tic (lə-jístik, lo-, lō-) *adj.* Also **lo·gis·tic·al** (for sense 1). **1.** Of or pertaining to logistics. In this sense, also "logistical". **2.** *Rare.* Of or skilled in arithmetical calculation. [French *logistique,* from Late Latin *logisticus,* of reason, from Greek *logistikos,* skilled in calculation, from *logistēs,* calculator, from *logizein,* to calculate, from *logos,* reckoning.] **—lo·gis·tic·al·ly** *adv.* **—lo·gis·ti·cian** (-jís-s-tísh'n, lójiss-) *n.*

lo·gis·tics (lə-jístiks, lo-, lō-) *n.* **1.** *Used with a singular verb. Military.* The science or study of the procurement, distribution, maintenance, and replacement of equipment and personnel. **2.** *Used with a plural verb.* The planning and control of any complex operation, as for example in finance or transport.

log jam *n. Chiefly U.S.* **1.** A mass of floating logs crowded immovably together. **2.** *Informal.* A deadlock in the progress of negotiations, debates, or the like.

log·log (lóg-lóg || *U.S. also* láwg-láwg) *n.* The logarithm of a logarithm. Also used adjectivally: *a loglog scale.*

lo·go (lōgō, lóggō || *U.S. also* láwgō) *n., pl.* **-gos.** A logotype.

logo- *comb. form.* Indicates word or speech; for example, **logogram.** [Greek, from *logos,* speech, word, reason, account.]

log·o·gram (lóggə-gram, lóggō- || *U.S. also* láwgə-) *n.* Also **log·o·graph** (-graaf, -graf). A symbol or letter representing an entire word, such as £ for pounds or *e* for energy (in physics). [LOGO- + -GRAM.] **—log·o·gram·mat·ic** (-grə-máttik) *adj.* **—log·o·gram·mat·i·cal·ly** *adv.*

log·o·graph·ic (loggə-gráffik) *adj.* Of or pertaining to logography or logograms. **—log·o·graph·i·cal·ly** *adv.*

lo·gog·ra·phy (lə-góggrəfi, lo-, lō-) *n.* The use of logotypes in design and printing. Also called "logotypy". [LOGO- + -GRAPHY.]

log·o·griph (lóggə-grif || *U.S. also* láwgə-) *n.* A word puzzle, such as an anagram or one in which clues are given in a set of verses. [French *logogriphe* : LOGO- + Greek *griphos*†, fishing basket.]

lo·gom·a·chy (lə-gómməki, lo-, lō-) *n.* **1.** An argument about words or their meanings. **2.** An argument apparently about something substantial but in fact turning merely on different definitions of the terms involved. [Greek *logomakhia* : LOGO- + -MACHY.]

log·o·pae·dics (lóg-ə-péediks, -ō- || *U.S. also* láwg-) *n.* *Usually used with a singular verb.* **Speech therapy** *(see).* [LOGO- + Greek *paideia,* education (see **paedo-**) + -ICS.]

log·or·rhoe·a (lóg-ə-rée-ə, -ō-, -réer || *U.S. also* láwg-) *n.* A compulsive tendency to talk, often incoherently, as in mental illness; excessive talkativeness. [LOGO- + -RRHOEA.]

Log·os (lóggoss || lōgōss) *n.* **1.** *Often small* **l.** **a.** Cosmic reason, regarded in ancient Greek philosophy as the source of world order and intelligibility. **b.** Reason or an expression of reason in words or things. **2.** The self-revealing thought and will of God, as set forth in the Gospel of St. John, often associated with the second person of the Trinity. In this sense, also called the "Word". [Greek *logos,* speech, word, reason.]

lo·go·type (lóg-ō-tīp, -ə- || *U.S. also* láwg-) *n. Printing.* **1.** A single piece of type bearing two or more usually separate elements. **2. a.** The name, trademark, or, especially, the identifying symbol of an organisation or publication. In this sense, also called "logo". **b.** A piece of type bearing this. [LOGO- + TYPE.]

log·roll (lóg-rōl || láwg-, -rol) *v.* **-rolled, -rolling, -rolls.** *Chiefly U.S.* *—tr.* To work towards the passage of (legislation) by logrolling. *—intr.* To engage in political logrolling.

log·roll·ing (lóg-rōlling || láwg-, -rolling) *n.* **1. Birling** *(see).* **2.** The transportation of logs by water. **3.** *Chiefly U.S.* The exchanging of political favours; especially, the swapping of influence or votes between legislators to their mutual advantage. **—log·roll·er** *n.*

-logue, *U.S.* **-log** *n. comb. form.* Indicates speech, discourse, recitation, or description; for example, **monologue, travelogue.** [Greek *-logos,* from *legein,* to speak.]

log·wood (lóg-wŏŏd || láwg-) *n.* **1.** A tropical American tree, *Haematoxylon campechianum,* having dark heartwood from which a dyestuff is obtained. **2.** The wood of this tree. **3.** The blackish or brownish dye, haematoxylin, obtained from this wood.

-logy *n. comb. form.* Indicates: **1.** Discourse or expression; for example, **phraseology.** **2.** The science, theory, or study of; for example, **palaeontology.** [Middle English *-logie,* from Old French, from Latin *-logia,* from Greek, from *logos,* word, speech.] **—-logist** *n. comb. form.* **—-logistic, -logistical** *adj. comb. form.*

Lo·hen·grin (lṓ-ən-grin, -in-; *German* -green). In Germanic legend, a son of Parsifal and knight of the Holy Grail.

loin (loyn) *n.* **1.** *Usually plural. Anatomy.* The part of the side and back between the ribs and the pelvis. **2.** A cut of meat taken from this part of an animal. **3.** *Plural.* **a.** The pelvic region, including the thighs and groin. **b.** *Literary.* The reproductive organs. **—gird up (one's) loins.** To prepare oneself for strenuous effort. [Middle English *loyne,* from Old French *loigne,* dialectal form for *longe,* from Vulgar Latin *lumbia* (unattested), from feminine of *lumbeus* (unattested), of the loin, from Latin *lumbus,* loin.]

loin·cloth (lóyn-kloth || -klawth) *n., pl.* **-cloths** (-kloths || -klawths, -klawthz). A strip of cloth worn around the loins.

Loire (lwaar). France's longest river. It flows some 1 015 kilometres (630 miles) from the Cévennes Mountains in the southeast roughly northwards to Orléans, and then westwards through Tours and Nantes to the Bay of Biscay at St. Nazaire. The middle and lower Loire valley is noted for its fine chateaux.

loi·ter (lóytər) *intr. v.* **-tered, -tering, -ters. 1. a.** To stand idly about; linger aimlessly. **b.** To linger or wait somewhere with the intention of committing a crime. **2.** To proceed slowly or with many stops. **3.** To dawdle: *loiter over a job.* [Middle English *loyteren,* perhaps from Middle Dutch *loteren,* to shake, totter.] **—loi·ter·er** *n.*

Lo·ki (lṓki). *Norse Mythology.* The god who creates discord, especially among his fellow gods. [Old Norse, probably related to *logi,* flame, fire.]

Lo·li·ta (lə-léetə, lo-, lō-) *n.* A pubescent girl considered sexually precocious and attractive to adult men. [After Vladimir Nabokov's novel *Lolita* (1955).]

loll (lol) *v.* **lolled, lolling, lolls.** *—intr.* **1.** To move, stand, or recline in an indolent or relaxed manner. **2.** To hang or droop loosely. *—tr.* To allow to hang or droop loosely.
~n. Archaic. An act or attitude of lolling. [Middle English *lollen,* probably of Low German origin, akin to Middle Dutch *lollen,* to lull to sleep.] **—loll·er** *n.* **—loll·ing·ly** *adv.*

Lol·lard (lól-əd, -aard) *n.* A member of a sect of reformers who were followers of John Wycliffe in the 14th, 15th, and 16th centuries. [Middle English, from Middle Dutch *lollaerd,* "mumbler (of prayers)", from *lollen,* to mutter.] **—Lol·lard·ism, Lol·lard·ry** *n.*

lol·li·pop, lol·ly·pop (lólli-pop) *n.* **1.** A piece of hard sweet attached to a narrow stick. **2.** The sign held by a lollipop man. **3.** *Informal.* A short piece of light orchestral music, suitable for playing as an encore. [Perhaps northern English dialect *lolly,* the tongue, from LOLL, to hang out (the tongue) + POP.]

lollipop lady *n.* A female lollipop man.

lollipop man *n. British.* A man employed to assist schoolchildren in crossing roads by stopping traffic with a large portable traffic sign consisting of a pole and brightly coloured disc.

lol·lop (lólləp) *intr.v.* **-loped, -loping, -lops.** *British Informal.* **1.** To walk or run in an ungainly way. **2.** To loll. [From LOLL + *-op,* perhaps from GALLOP.]

lol·ly (lólli) *n., pl.* **-lies. 1.** *Informal.* A lollipop. **2.** *British.* An **ice lolly** *(see).* **3.** *British Slang.* Money. **4.** *Australian Informal.* A boiled sweet.

Lo·lo (lṓlō) *n.* **1.** A member of a Tibeto-Burman people living in the mountains between Sichuan and Yunnan provinces, southwest China. **2.** The language of this people. **—Lo·lo** *adj.*

Lom·bard (lóm-bərd, lúm-, -baard) *n.* **1.** A member of a Germanic people that invaded northern Italy in A.D. 568 and established a kingdom in the Po Valley. Also called "Langobard", "Longobard". **2.** A native of Lombardy. **3.** *Archaic.* A banker or pawnbroker.
~adj. Also **Lom·bar·dic** (lom-bárdik, lum-). Of or pertaining to the Lombards or to Lombardy.

Lombard Street *n.* The British banking and financial world. [After the moneychangers and bankers from LOMBARDY who once occupied this street in the City of London.]

Lom·bar·dy (lóm-bərdi, lúm-). *Italian* **Lom·bar·di·a** (lom-bárdi-ə). Region in north Italy bounded by the Alps and the river Po. It is the most densely populated region in Italy. The Po valley is a rich agricultural area, while Milan, the capital, lies at the centre of an industrial region.

Lombardy poplar *n.* A tree, *Populus nigra italica,* having upward-pointing branches that form a slender, columnar outline.

Lo·mé (lṓ-may || lō-máy). Capital city of the republic of Togo, West Africa. Its deepwater port exports phosphates, cocoa, and coffee.

Lomé Convention *n.* Either of two trade and economic cooperation agreements signed in Lomé by members of the European Economic Community and certain ACP states (less developed countries in Africa, the Caribbean, and Pacific). *Lomé I* signed in 1975 to run from April 1976 to February 1980, involved 46 ACP states. *Lomé II,* signed in 1979 to run from March 1980 to Febrary 1985, involved 57 ACP states.

lo·ment (lṓ-ment) *n.* A pod, as of the tick trefoil or similar legumi-

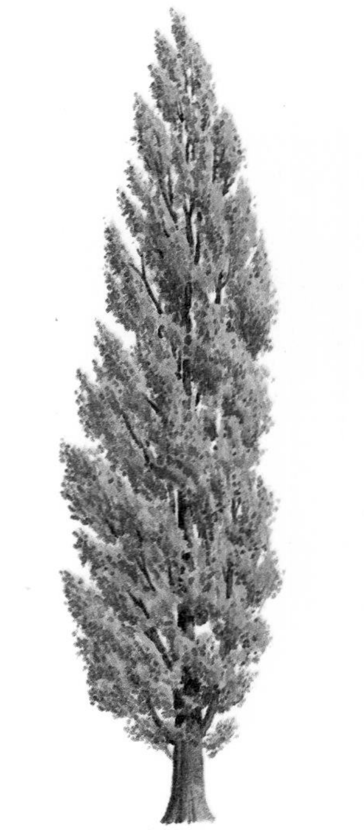

Lombardy poplar *This tree, now thought to be a native of Asia, acquired its common English name after cuttings were introduced to Britain from Lombardy in northern Italy during the 18th century.*

PRONUNCIATION KEY

a, trap; aa, father; ai, fair; ar, star; aw, lawn; ay, play; b, bb, stab; rubber; ch, church; ck, ticket; d, dd, dead; ladder; e, dress; ee, bee; er, defer; ew, few; ewr, pure; ə, about; ər, letter; f, ff, fife; differ; g, gg, giggle; h, hat; i, kit; ī, price; īr, fire; j, judge; k, kick; l, ll, let; 'l, needle; m, mm, man; n, nn, no; 'n, sudden; ng, thing; o, lot; ō, no; ŏŏ, foot; ōō, shoe; oor, poor; ow, cow; owr, hour; oy, boy; p, pp, pepper; r, rr, red; s, ss, sauce; sh, ship; t, tt, totter; th, thick; th, this; smooth; u, cut; ur, turn; v, vv, valve; w, wet; y, yes; z, zz, zebra; zh, vision; pleasure

IN FOREIGN WORDS:

aN, oN, Saint-Saëns; hl, Llanelli; Hluhluwe; kh, loch; lough; Khaled

STRESS MARK:

ín-sīt, insight; in-sīt, incite

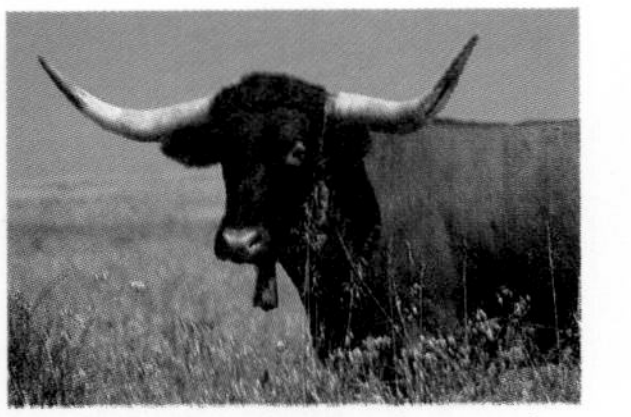

longhorn *Modern longhorn cattle were developed by the pioneering livestock breeder Robert Bakewell (1725–95) as beef animals.*

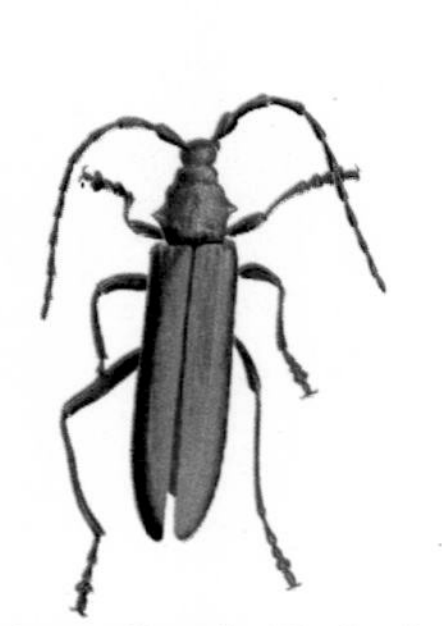

long-horned beetle *The longhorn is a shiny green insect with long curved antennae. Found in woodlands in Britain and Europe, it has a pleasant musklike scent.*

PRONUNCIATION KEY

a, trap; aa, father; ai, fair; ar, star; aw, lawn; ay, play; b, bb, stab; rubber; ch, church; ck, ticket; d, dd, dead; ladder; e, dress; ee, bee; er, defer; ew, few; ewr, pure; ə, about; ər, letter; f, ff, fife; differ; g, gg, giggle; h, hat; i, kit; ī, price; īr, fire; j, judge; k, kick; l, ll, let; 'l, needle; m, mm, man; n, nn, no; 'n, sudden; ng, thing; o, lot; ō, no; o͝o, foot; o͞o, shoe; oor, poor; ow, cow; owr, hour; oy, boy; p, pp, pepper; r, rr, red; s, ss, sauce; sh, ship; t, tt, totter; th, thick; th, this; smooth; u, cut; ur, turn; v, vv, valve; w, wet; y, yes; z, zz, zebra; zh, vision; pleasure

IN FOREIGN WORDS:

aN, oN, Saint-Saëns; hl, Llanelli; Hluhluwe; kh, loch; lough; Khaled

STRESS MARK:

ín-sīt, insight; in-sít, incite

nous plants, having constrictions separating the individual seeds, such that it divides into one-seeded portions when ripe. [New Latin *lomentum,* from Latin *lōmentum, lōvimentum,* a bean meal used by Roman women as a wash or cosmetic, from *lavāre,* to wash.]

Lo·mond, Loch (lṓmənd). Largest natural freshwater lake in Britain, 39 kilometres (24 miles) long and 8 kilometres (5 miles) wide at its broadest, in Strathclyde Region, Scotland.

Lon·don (lúndən). Capital city of the United Kingdom and one of the largest cities in the world, covering 1 580 square kilometres (610 square miles) north and south of the river Thames. The City (of London), about one square mile in area and occupying the site of a Roman settlement, is surrounded by Greater London, which consists of 32 boroughs. One of these, the City of Westminster, contains the Houses of Parliament, Westminster Abbey, the governmental ministries, and Buckingham Palace. Much of the City was destroyed by the Great Fire of 1666, after which Sir Christopher Wren rebuilt St. Paul's Cathedral and many other buildings. London is one of the world's most important banking and insurance centres, and Britain's largest port. It is also a major industrial area, its products ranging from machinery, chemicals, and motor vehicles to films, clothing, and luxury goods. London is also one of the world's major cultural and tourist centres.

London, Jack, pen name of John Griffith London (1876–1916). U.S. writer. He was a tramp and a prospector in the Klondike Gold Rush (1897). His tales include *The Call of the Wild* (1903) and *The People of the Abyss* (1903).

London Bridge. First recorded bridge to span the river Thames in London, England. The first London Bridge of stone, which replaced a wooden one, was completed in 1209 and was lined with houses and a chapel. It was demolished after a new bridge, designed by John Rennie, was built to its west in 1824–31. In 1973, a 32-metre (105-foot) wide bridge replaced the Rennie bridge, which was re-erected at the resort of Lake Havasu City, in Arizona, United States.

Lon·don·der·ry[1] (lúndən-dérri, -derri, -dəri). Also **Der·ry** (dérri). Hilly county in Northern Ireland. It is mostly agricultural, with coastal and inland fishing and some light industries. In the 17th century much of the land was confiscated from its Irish owners (the O'Neill family) and granted to City Companies of London.

Londonderry[2]**.** Also **Derry.** Second largest city of Northern Ireland, on the river Foyle, Co. Londonderry. Derry dates from 546 when St. Columba founded a monastery there. In 1613 the city was granted to the Corporation of the City of London (hence the name Londonderry).

Lon·don·er (lúndənər) *n.* A native or inhabitant of London.

London plane *n.* A hybrid plane tree, *Platanus hybrida,* often planted in cities, having a bark which flakes off, making it resistant to smoke and fumes.

London pride *n.* An alpine garden plant that is a hybrid between *Saxifraga spathularis* and *S. umbrosa.* It has a basal rosette of leaves and a cluster of small pink flowers borne on a long stem.

lone (lōn) *adj.* **1.** Single; solitary: *a lone spectator.* **2.** Isolated; set apart: *a lone cottage.* **3.** *Poetic.* Lonely. **4.** *Rare.* Unmarried or widowed. [Shortened from ALONE (*a-* being taken for the indefinite article).]

lone hand *n.* **1.** In some card games, a hand played without help from a partner's hand. **2.** A cardplayer without a partner.

lone·ly (lṓnli) *adj.* **-lier, -liest. 1. a.** Without companions; lone. **b.** Characterised by aloneness; solitary: *a lonely existence.* **2.** Unfrequented; empty of people; desolate: *a lonely crossroads.* **3. a.** Dejected by the awareness of being alone. **b.** Producing such dejection: *the loneliest night of the week.* [From LONE.] **—lone·li·ly** *adv.* **—lone·li·ness** *n.*

lonely hearts *pl.n.* People who are distressed by lack of emotional companionship, especially those who seek it through advertisements in newspapers or periodicals. Also used adjectivally: *a lonely hearts club.*

lon·er (lṓnər) *n. Informal.* One who prefers to be or work alone.

lone·some (lṓn-səm) *adj. Chiefly U.S.* Lonely. **—by** or **on (one's) lonesome.** *Chiefly U.S. Informal.* Alone; by oneself.

lone wolf *n.* A person who likes to live or work alone.

long[1] (long || *U.S. also* lawng) *adj.* **longer** (-gər), **longest** (-gist). **1. a.** Having great length. **b.** *Rare.* Tall. **2.** Of relatively great duration: *a long time.* **3. a.** Of a specified linear extent or duration; in length: *a mile long; an hour long.* **b.** Lengthways: *two inches long, and one inch wide.* **4.** Extending beyond an average or a standard: *a long game; a long memory.* **5.** Tediously protracted; lengthy: *a long speech.* **6.** Concerned with distant issues; far-reaching: *the long view.* **7.** Risky; chancy: *long odds.* **8.** Having an abundance or an excess of. Used with *on*: *long on hope.* **9.** *Finance.* Having an unsold holding of a security or commodity in expectation of a rise in price: *long in steel.* **10.** *Phonetics.* Having a comparatively protracted sound: *a long vowel.* **11.** In verse: **a.** Designating a vowel sound of relatively great duration, as *feed* compared with *feet.* **b.** Bearing stress: *a long syllable.* **12.** In cricket, designating a fielding position near to the boundary: *long leg.*
~*adv.* **1.** During or for an extended period of time: *The promotion was long due.* Often used in combination: *long-lasting; long-lost.* **2.** Far: *He read long into the night.* **3.** For or throughout a specified period: *They talked all night long.* **4.** At a point of time distant from that referred to: *long before we were born.* **—as** or **so long as. 1.** Since; inasmuch as. **2.** During or only during the time that. **3.** Provided that; on condition that. **—no longer.** Not now as formerly; no more: *He no longer smokes.*
~*n.* **1.** A long time. **2.** A relatively long sound, such as a vowel or a signal in Morse code. **3.** *Finance.* **a.** One who acquires large holdings of a security expecting a rise in price or commodity. **b.** *Plural.* Long-dated gilt-edged securities. **4.** A clothing size for a tall person. **—before long.** Soon. **—the long and the short of.** The essential details; the substance: *The long and short of it is they won.* [Middle English *long, lang,* Old English *long, lang.*] **—long·ish** *adj.*

long[2] (long || lawng) *intr.v.* **longed, longing** (-ing), **longs.** To yearn; wish earnestly; desire greatly: *He longed to go home.* See Synonyms at **yearn.** [Middle English *longen,* Old English *langian,* "to seem long (to some)", to yearn for.]

long. longitude.

lon·gan (lóng-gən || láwng-) *n.* **1.** A Chinese tree, *Euphoria longana.* **2.** The edible fruit of this tree, which is similar to but smaller than a lychee. [Chinese *lóng yǎn,* dragon's eye.]

long-and-short work (lóng-ən-shórt || láwng-) *n. Architecture.* The alternation of vertical and horizontal stone slabs at the corner of an Anglo-Saxon or Early English building.

Long Beach. Coastal resort south of Los Angeles, California, United States. It has a large harbour, naval shipyard, dry dock, and refineries for oil, discovered nearby in the 1920s.

long·boat (lóng-bōt || láwng-) *n.* **1.** The longest boat carried by a sailing ship. **2.** A **longship** *(see).*

long·bow (lóng-bō || láwng-) *n.* **1.** A wooden bow roughly 1.5 to 1.8 metres (five to six feet) long. **2.** A powerful hand-drawn bow, sometimes as much as two metres (over six feet) in length, much used in medieval England.

long·case clock (lóng-kayss || láwng-) *n.* A **grandfather clock** *(see).*

long-chain *adj.* Designating a molecule whose constituent atoms are arranged in an extended chainlike structure.

long-dat·ed (lóng-dáytid || láwng-) *adj. Finance.* Designating gilt-edged securities redeemable after a time more than 15 years away. Compare **medium-dated, short-dated.**

long-day (lóng-dáy) *adj.* Of or designating plants that will flower only when exposed to periods of daylight in excess of ten hours. Compare **short-day.**

long-dis·tance (lóng-dístənss || láwng-) *adj.* **1.** Located or from far away. **2.** Covering a long distance. **3.** Of or designating telephone communications to a distant place. **—long-distance** *adv.*

long division *n.* A process of division in arithmetic, usually used when the divisor has more than one digit, in which the remainders leading to succeeding steps of the procedure are recorded in a determinate pattern.

long dozen *n.* Thirteen; a baker's dozen.

long-drawn-out (lóng-dráwn-owt || láwng-) *adj.* Unduly prolonged.

long drink *n.* A thirst-quenching drink, usually served chilled in a tall glass, having little or no alcohol and often diluted with water, soda water, or a soft drink.

lon·ge·ron (lónjə-rən || *U.S. also* -ron) *n.* A structural member that runs from front to rear of an aircraft's fuselage. [French, from *longer,* to pass along, extend along, from Late Latin *longāre,* to lengthen, from Latin *longus,* long.]

longeur. Variant of **longueur.**

lon·gev·i·ty (lon-jévvəti, *also* long-) *n.* **1.** A long duration of life. **2.** Long duration, as in an occupation or political office. [Late Latin *longevitās* (stem *longevitāt-,* from Latin *longaevus,* living to a great age : *longus,* long + *aevum,* age.] **—lon·ge·vous** (-jéevəss) *adj.*

long face *n.* A discontented or sullen facial expression.

Long·fel·low (lóng-fellō || láwng-), **Henry Wadsworth** (1807–82). U.S. poet. He wrote *The Wreck of the Hesperus* (1841), *Paul Revere's Ride* (1863), and *The Song of Hiawatha* (1855), an epic of Indian life written in the metrical pattern of a Norse saga.

Long·ford (lóng-fərd || láwng-). Inland county in Leinster province, Republic of Ireland. The rearing of beef cattle and butter-making are its main industries.

long·hair (lóng-hair || láwng-) *n.* **1.** A man with long hair who is considered to be a social misfit. **2.** *Chiefly U.S.* **a.** One dedicated to the arts and especially to classical music. **b.** One whose taste in the arts is held to be overrefined. In all senses, usually used derogatorily. **—long·hair, long·haired** *adj.*

long·hand (lóng-hand || láwng-) *n.* Handwriting as distinct from shorthand, typing, or printing.
~*adj.* Handwritten. **—long·hand** *adv.*

long haul *n.* **1.** A journey covering a great distance or taking a long time. **2.** Any task or project that takes a long time to carry out.

long-haul (lóng-hawl || láwng-) *adj.* Designating flights or other journeys over a long distance.

long·head·ed (lóng-héddid || láwng-) *adj.* **1.** Dolichocephalic. **2.** Possessing foresight; shrewd; astute; cunning.

long·horn (lóng-hawrn || láwng-) *n.* A member of any of several breeds of beef cattle having long horns.

long-horned beetle (lóng-hawrnd || láwng-) *n.* Any of numerous beetles of the family Cerambycidae, having long legs and long antennae. Also called "longicorn", "longicorn beetle".

long house *n.* A long, often communal, wooden dwelling used by various peoples, as in North America, Borneo, and New Guinea.

longi- *n. comb. form.* Indicates long; for example, **longicorn.** [Latin, from *longus,* long.]

lon·gi·corn (lónji-kawrn)
~*adj.* Having long antennae.
~*n.* A long-horned beetle. Also called "longicorn beetle". [New

Latin *Longicornia* (former classification) : LONGI- + Latin *cornū,* horn.]

long·ing (lóng-ing || láwng-) *n.* A persistent, unfulfilled yearning or desire.
~*adj.* Affected by or expressing such a yearning: *look with longing eyes.* **—long·ing·ly** *adv.*

Long Island. Island in New York state, United States, separated from Connecticut by Long Island Sound and including part of New York City.

lon·gi·tude (lónji-tewd, lóng-gi- || -to͞od) *n. Abbr.* **long. 1.** The angular distance east or west of the prime meridian at Greenwich, England, to the point on the earth's surface for which the longitude is being ascertained, expressed either in degrees or in hours, minutes, and seconds. **2.** *Astronomy.* The angular distance, measured in degrees eastward along the ecliptic from the vernal equinox to the great circle passing through the pole of the ecliptic and the celestial point being measured. Also called "celestial longitude". [Middle English, from Latin *longitūdō,* from *longus,* LONG.]

lon·gi·tu·di·nal (lónji-téwd-in'l, lóng-gi- || -to͞od-) *adj.* **1.** Of or pertaining to length. **2.** Placed or running lengthways. **3.** Pertaining to longitude. **—lon·gi·tu·di·nal·ly** *adv.*

longitudinal wave *n.* A wave propagated in the same direction as the displacement of the transmitting medium. Compare **transverse wave.**

long johns (jonz) *pl.n. Informal.* Long, warm underpants reaching to the ankle.

long jump *n.* In athletics, an event in which the participants compete to cover the greatest distance by jumping, after a sprinting run, from a fixed mark into a flat pit of sand. Also U.S. "broad jump".

long·leaf pine (lóng-leef || láwng-) *n.* An evergreen coniferous tree, *Pinus australis* (or *P. palustris*), of the southeastern United States, having long needles and heavy, tough, resinous wood valued as timber and as a source of turpentine.

Long·leat (lóng-leet). Historic house, near Warminster, Wiltshire, in England. It was begun in 1568 and is owned by the Marquess of Bath. It has a safari park.

long-lived (lóng-livd || láwng-, -līvd) *adj.* **1.** Having a long life. **2.** Persistent: *a long-lived rumour.* **—long-lived·ness** *n.*

Long March *n.* The hazardous journey to safety undertaken (1934–35) by an army of about 100,000 Communist Chinese soldiers and officials, of whom a third at most survived. Their route led northwest across China from Jiangxi to Shaanxi, a distance of about 10 000 kilometres (6,000 miles).

long measure *n.* **Linear measure** *(see).*

long multiplication *n.* A method for obtaining the product of two numbers, especially when both numbers consist of several digits. The multiplicand is multiplied by each digit of the multiplier in turn, the partial products so obtained being set out in an array that takes account of the position of their decimal points; the final product is the sum of the partial products.

Lon·go·bard (lóng-gō-baard || láwng-) *n., pl.* **-bards** or **-bardi** (-bárdee). An early **Lombard** *(see).* **—Lon·go·bar·di·an** (-bárdi-ən), **Lon·go·bar·dic** (-bárdik) *adj.*

Long Parliament *n.* The English Parliament that was convened by Charles I in 1640, dismissed by Oliver Cromwell in 1653, and reconvened in 1659–1660. See **Rump Parliament.**

long pig *n.* A human being used for meat by cannibals.

long-play·ing (lóng-pláy-ing || láwng-) *adj. Abbr.* **LP** Pertaining to or designating a microgroove gramophone record, especially one turning at 33¹/₃ revolutions per minute.

long-range (lóng-ráynj || láwng-) *adj.* **1.** Requiring or involving a span of years; not immediate: *long-range planning.* **2.** Of, suitable for, or equipped to travel long distances: *long-range aircraft.*

long·ship (lóng-ship || láwng-) *n.* A narrow uncovered vessel powered by oars and sail, used by the Vikings and other peoples in Europe during the early Middle Ages. Also called "longboat".

long·shore (lóng-shawr || láwng-, -sháwr, -shōr, -shṓr) *adj.* Occurring, living, or working along a seacoast. [Short for ALONGSHORE.]

long·shore·man (lóng-shawr-mən || láwng-, -sháwr-, -shōr-, -shṓr), *n., pl.* **-men** (-mən, -men). *U.S.* A **docker** *(see).*

long shot *n.* **1. a.** An entry, as in a horse race, with only a slight chance of winning. **b.** A bet made at and against great odds. **2. a.** A risky venture that will pay off handsomely if successful. **b.** An attempt or guess that has only a slight chance of proving successful. **3.** A film scene shot at some distance from the subject. **—not by a long shot.** Not by any means; nor nearly.

long-sight·ed (lóng-sītid || láwng-) *adj.* **1.** Suffering from **hypermetropia** *(see);* able to see only distant objects clearly. **2.** Possessing foresight; planning for the future. **—long-sight·ed·ness** *n.*

long-stand·ing (lóng-stánding || láwng-) Having been in existence or force for a long time.

long·stop (lóng-stop || láwng-) *n.* **1. a.** In cricket, the fielding position behind the wicketkeeper and near the boundary. **b.** The fielder in this position, whose function is to stop balls that the wicketkeeper has missed. **2.** *British.* A secondary or supplementary safeguard: *The second check is a longstop to catch minor errors.*

long-suf·fer·ing (lóng-súffər-ing, -súffring || láwng-) *adj.* Patiently enduring wrongs or difficulties.
~*n.* Also **long-suf·fer·ance** (-ənss). Patient endurance. **—long-suf·fer·ing·ly** *adv.*

long suit *n.* **1.** In card games, a suit containing more cards than any of the other suits in a hand. **2.** *Informal.* The personal quality or talent that is one's strongest asset.

long-tailed tit (lóng-tayld || láwng-) *n.* A small Eurasian songbird, *Aegisthalos caudatus,* with a black, pink, and white plumage and a long, black and white tail.

long-term (lóng-térm || láwng-) *adj.* In effect for, involving, or maturing after a number of years: *a long-term investment.*

long-time (lóng-tīm || láwng-) *adj.* Having existed or persisted for a long time: *a long-time acquaintance.*

long tom *n. Sometimes capital* **L,** *capital* **T. 1.** A long pivoted cannon formerly used on warships. **2.** A similar long-range gun used on land. **3.** A trough in which gold-bearing sand is washed.

long ton *n.* A **ton** *(see).*

lon·gueur, lon·geur (long-gér, loɴ-, -gṓr) *n. Often plural.* **1.** A boring or tedious period of time. **2.** A tedious, overlong passage, as in a book or film. [French, "length".]

long vacation *n.* The summer vacation at the end of an academic year.

long-waisted (lóng-waystid) *adj.* Having or being of more than average length between shoulders and waist.

long wave *n.* A radio waveband in which the wavelength exceeds 1 000 metres (frequency less than 300 kilohertz).

long·ways (lóng-wayz || láwng-) *adj.* Also *chiefly U.S.* **long·wise** (-wīz). Lengthways.

long-wind·ed (lóng-wíndid || láwng-) *adj.* **1.** Wearisomely verbose: *a long-winded bore.* **2.** Not subject to quick loss of breath. **—long·wind·ed·ly** *adv.* **—long·wind·ed·ness** *n.*

Lons·dale (lonz-dayl), **Dame Kathleen,** born Kathleen Yardley (1903–71). British physicist. She worked on the structure and growth of crystals and in 1945 she became one of the first two women to be elected to the Royal Society.

loo¹ (lo͞o) *n., pl.* **loos.** *British Informal.* A lavatory. [Perhaps from French *lieux* (*d'aisances*), privy.]

Usage: Words for lavatory constitute one of the most changeable areas of vocabulary, as people search for the most polite or neutral expressions. *Loo* is a recent development in British English, used widely but only informally. *Lavatory* and *toilet* are both acceptable in middle-class usage, but the latter is more frequently used. There are several euphemisms (*powder room, men's room, rest room,* and the like) available for formal use, and several colloquial and semijocular expressions (*gents, ladies,* and so on) available for informal use. The use of *bathroom* in the sense of "toilet" has a different range of usage in British and American English. In British English, a bathroom has to contain a bath, and it may contain a toilet; in American English, the reference would be to a room which contains a toilet, and which may not contain a bath.

loo² *n., pl.* **loos.** A card game in which each player contributes stakes to a pool. [Shortened from *lanterloo,* from French *lanturlu,* originally the refrain of a popular song.]

loo·by (lo͞obi) *n., pl.* **-bies.** *Chiefly U.S. Informal.* A stupid or clumsy person. [Middle English *loby,* probably of Low German origin, akin to Middle Low German *lobbe,* loose-hanging lip, bumpkin. See **lob.**]

loo·fah (lo͞ofə) *n.* Also *chiefly U.S.* **loo·fa, luf·fa** (lúffə). **1.** The dried, fibrous, spongelike interior of the fruit of the dishcloth gourd, used as a washing sponge or as a filter. **2.** The **dishcloth gourd** *(see).* [New Latin *Luffa,* from Arabic *lūf, lūfah.*]

look (lo͝ok || lo͞ok) *v.* **looked, looking, looks.** *—intr.* **1.** To employ one's eyes in seeing. **2. a.** To turn one's glance. **b.** To turn one's attention. Often used with *at.* **3.** To seem or appear to be: *look morose.* **4.** To face in a specified direction. Often used with *onto* or *out onto: The cottage looks onto the river.* **5.** *Informal.* To hope or expect. Used with an infinitive: *He looked to hear from her.* *—tr.* **1.** To turn one's eyes on. **2.** To express by one's appearance: *She looked her joy.* **3.** To have an appearance in conformity with: *look one's age.* **—look after.** To take care of. **—look as if.** To seem likely that. **—look back.** To reflect on the past; remember. **—look down on** or **upon.** To regard with contempt or condescension. **—look for. 1.** To search for. **2.** To expect. **—look forward to.** To anticipate eagerly. **—look into.** To investigate. **—look like.** To indicate as a likely possibility: *It looks like war.* **—look on. 1.** To be a spectator. **2.** To consider; regard: *look on the accident as a stroke of luck.* **—look over.** To inspect; especially, to inspect casually. **—look sharp** or **lively.** To hurry up, or respond quickly. Usually used as an imperative. **—look through. 1.** To inspect briefly: *look through a report.* **2.** To pretend to be unacquainted with (a person); ignore; snub. **—look to. 1.** To expect. **2.** To attend to. **3.** To rely upon. **4.** To resort to: *If you won't agree, I must look to force.* **—look towards.** To be a pointer to; herald; prefigure: *His poetry looks towards the modernist revolution.* **—look up. 1.** To search for and find, as in a reference book. **2.** To locate and call upon; visit. **3.** *Informal.* To improve: *Things are looking up.* **—look up and down. 1.** To inspect critically, coldly, or disdainfully. **2.** To search everywhere. **—look up to.** To admire. **—never look back.** To make uninterrupted progress. **—not look at.** To refuse to have anything to do with: *He won't look at Spanish wines.*
~*n.* **1.** The action or an instance of looking; a gaze or glance. **2.** An appearance or aspect. **3.** *Plural.* Physical appearance, especially when pleasing. **—by the look of.** Taking appearances as a guide or indication: *by the look of her, she's ill.*
~*interj.* Used to request attention, preface an objection, or express impatience or insistence. [Middle English *loken,* to look, have the appearance, Old English *lōcian,* to look, from West Germanic *lokōn* (unattested).]

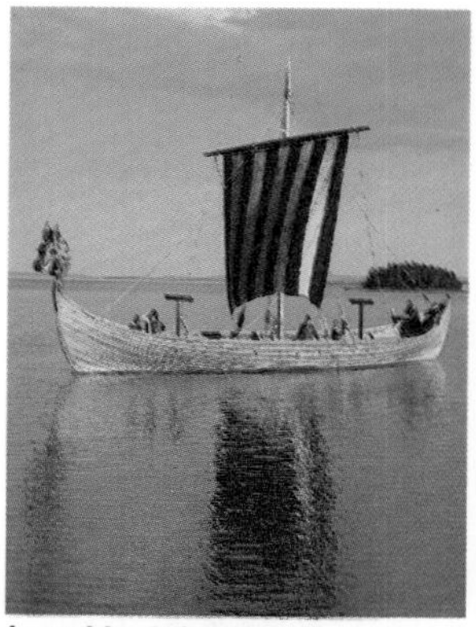

longship *Viking longships were used to attack coastal villages all over northern Europe during the early Middle Ages. This is a modern Norwegian replica.*

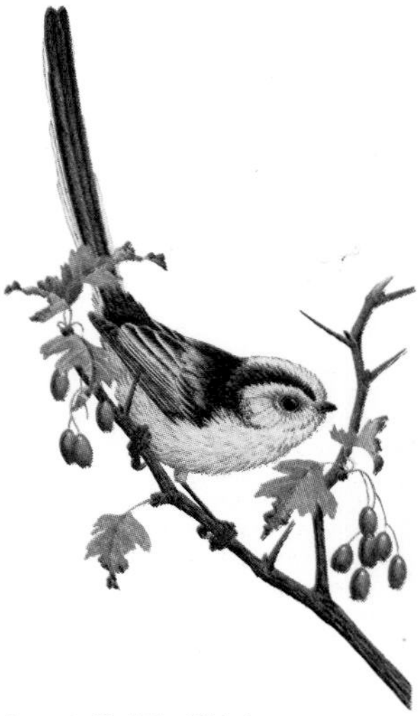

long-tailed tit *This insect-eater uses lichen, animal hair, and cobwebs to build a complex, domed nest. It is found throughout Europe and across Asia to China and Japan.*

loosestrife *Yellow loosestrife, once tied in bunches around the necks of draught animals in Britain, was used to keep away irritating flies and insects and to keep the animals calm.*

–look *adj. comb. form.* Indicates resemblance to or imitation of something specified; for example, *a leather-look handbag.*

look·a·like (lŏŏk-ə-līk ‖ lŏŏk-) *n.* One that closely resembles another; especially, one bearing a close resemblance to a celebrity. **—look·a·like** *adj.*

look·er (lŏŏkər ‖ lŏŏkər) *n.* 1. One that looks. 2. *Chiefly U.S. Informal.* A very pretty woman or a very handsome man.

look·er-on (lŏŏkər-ón ‖ lŏŏkər-, -áwn) *n., pl.* **lookers-on.** A spectator.

look in *intr.v.* To drop in; make a brief visit. Often used with *on.*

look-in (lŏŏk-in ‖ lŏŏk-) *n.* 1. A short visit. 2. *Informal.* An opportunity to take part, prove oneself, or achieve something: *His opponent never gave him a look-in.*

looking glass *n.* A mirror.

look·ing-glass (lŏŏk-ing-glaass ‖ lŏŏk-, -glass) *adj.* Topsy-turvy; disconcertingly unfamiliar: *Travelling in the East, she felt herself to be in a looking-glass world.* [After the fantastic logic of Lewis Carroll's *Through the Looking-Glass.*]

look out *intr.v.* 1. To be careful or protective: *looking out for one's interests.* 2. To be careful to notice some hazard: *Look out for the step!* 3. To watch in the hope of finding something: *looking out for bargains.* ~*tr.* To make some effort to find: *I'll look out that book for you.*

look-out (lŏŏk-owt ‖ lŏŏk-) *n.* 1. The act of observing or keeping watch. 2. A high place or structure commanding a wide view for observation. 3. One who keeps watch. 4. An outlook; prospects. 5. *Informal.* An unfortunate prospect: *If they don't work, that's their lookout!* **—on the lookout.** Watching out, as for a hazard or something needed.

look-see (lŏŏk-see ‖ lŏŏk-) *n. Informal.* A quick survey or glance.

loom¹ (lŏŏm) *intr.v.* **loomed, looming, looms.** 1. To come into view as a massive, distorted, or indistinct image. 2. To appear to the mind in a magnified and threatening form. 3. To seem imminent; impend. 4. To tower above; overhang. Used with *over: The crag looms over the house.* **—loom large.** 1. To be a preoccupation. 2. To be a significant element: *Beethoven's influence looms large in his earlier works.* ~*n.* A distorted, threatening appearance of something, as through fog or darkness. [Probably of Low German origin; akin to East Frisian *lōmen,* to move slowly, *lōm,* lame, crippled.]

loom² *n.* 1. A machine or device from which a textile is produced by interweaving thread or yarn at right angles. 2. *Nautical.* The shaft of an oar. [Middle English *lome,* Old English *gelōma,* utensil, tool : *ge-* (collective prefix) + *-lōma,* akin to Middle Dutch *allame†,* tool.]

loon¹ (lŏŏn) *n. Chiefly U.S.* Any of several northern diving birds of the genus *Gavia,* a **diver** *(see).* [Probably from Old Norse *lomr.*]

loon² *n. Informal.* A simple-minded or mad person. [Middle English *loun, lown†.*]

loon·y, loon·ey (lŏŏni) *adj.* **-ier, -iest.** *Informal.* 1. So odd as to appear demented; mad; crazy. 2. Foolish; senseless. ~*n., pl.* **loonies.** *Informal.* A loony person.

loony bin *n. Slang.* A mental hospital. Often considered offensive.

loop¹ (lŏŏp) *n.* 1. A length of line, as of wire, thread, rope, or ribbon, that is folded over and joined at the ends. 2. The opening formed by such a doubled line. 3. Any roughly oval, closed, or nearly closed turn or figure. 4. Something having such a turn or figure. 5. *Electricity.* A closed circuit. 6. A flight manoeuvre in which an aircraft flies a circular path in a vertical plane with the lateral axis of the aircraft remaining horizontal. 7. The commonest of the basic patters of ridges making up the human fingerprint. Compare **arch, whorl.** 8. *Anatomy.* A bend in a tubular organ, such as *Henle's loop* in a kidney tubule. 9. An intrauterine contraceptive consisting of a small device in the shape of a loop. 10. *Mathematics.* A closed curve on a graph. 11. *Computing.* A series of program instructions that are performed repeatedly untils one specific condition is fulfilled. 12. A loop aerial. 13. A loopline. 14. A tape-loop *(see).* 15. A figure executed by an ice-skater by describing a figure of eight on one edge and doubling back into and out of the eight at the top and bottom. ~*v.* **looped, looping, loops.** —*tr.* 1. To form (thread, for example) into a loop or loops. 2. To fasten, join, or encircle with a loop or loops. 3. To fly (an aircraft) in a loop. 4. *Electricity.* To join (conductors) so as to complete a circuit. —*intr.* 1. To form a loop or loops. 2. In aviation, to make a loop or loops. 3. To progress by looping the body. Used of measuring worms. **—loop the loop.** To make a vertical loop or loops in the air. Used of an aircraft. [Middle English *loupe†.*]

loop² *n. Archaic.* A small opening in a wall; a loophole. [Middle English *loupe†.*]

loop aerial *n.* A radio aerial consisting of one or more coils of wire wound on a frame. Also called "frame aerial", "loop".

loop·er (lŏŏpər) *n.* 1. One that makes loops. 2. The caterpillar of a geometrid moth; a **measuring worm** *(see).*

loop·hole (lŏŏp-hōl) *n.* 1. A small hole or slit in a wall, especially one through which small arms may be fired. 2. A way of escaping a difficulty; especially, an omission or an ambiguity, as in the wording of a contract or law, that provides a means of evasion. [LOOP (opening) + HOLE.]

loop·line (lŏŏp-līn) *n.* A railway line that leaves and later rejoins a main line.

loop·y (lŏŏpi) *adj.* 1. Containing, resembling, or pertaining to loops: curly. 2. *Informal.* Eccentric; crazy.

loose (lŏŏss) *adj.* **looser, loosest.** 1. a. Not fastened or restrained; unbound. b. Not tightly anchored or secured: *a loose tooth.* 2. Not taut or drawn up tightly; slack. 3. Free from confinement or imprisonment; unfettered. 4. Not tight-fitting or tightly fitted. 5. Allowing some latitude; not rigidly arranged: *a loose association.* 6. Not bound, bundled, packed, stapled, or gathered together. 7. Not compact or dense. 8. Not fast: *a loose dye.* 9. Lacking a sense of restraint or responsibility; idle: *loose talk.* 10. Licentious; unchaste; immoral: *a loose woman; a loose way of life.* 11. Not precise or exact: *a loose translation.* 12. Not strict or totally correct: *a loose use of the term.* 13. Readily available; not committed: *loose cash.* 14. *Chiefly U.S. Informal.* Calm; unruffled. 15. Designating bowels that empty easily or overactively. 16. Designating a cough that produces or results from an excess of phlegm in the throat. ~*n.* In Rugby football, the period of play when possession of the ball is being disputed in a ruck. **—on the loose.** *Informal.* 1. At large; free from confinement. 2. Acting in an uninhibited or licentious fashion. ~*adv.* In a loose manner. ~*v.* **loosed, loosing, looses.** —*tr.* 1. To let loose; set free; release. 2. To undo, untie, or unwrap. 3. To release pressure on; make less tight, firm, or compact. 4. To relax (rules or regulations); make less strict. 5. To let fly (a projectile). —*intr.* 1. To become loose. 2. To discharge a projectile; fire. [Middle English *lous(e), lo(o)s,* from Old Norse *lauss, louss.*] **—loose·ly** *adv.* **—loose·ness** *n.*

loose box *n.* A covered stall in which a horse is kept without having to be tied up.

loose cover *n.* A fitted, removable cover of cloth or other material for a piece of upholstered furniture.

loose-joint·ed (lŏŏss-jóyntid) *adj.* 1. Having freely articulated joints. 2. Supple in movement. **—loose-joint·ed·ness** *n.*

loose-leaf (lŏŏss-léef) *adj.* Designating a binder or folder that allows the insertion and removal of pages.

loose-limbed (lŏŏss-límd) *adj.* Having supple limbs.

loos·en (lŏŏss'n) *v.* **-ened, -ening, -ens.** —*tr.* 1. To make looser. 2. To untie. 3. To free from restraint, pressure, or strictness. 4. To free (the bowels) from constipation. —*intr.* To become loose or looser. [Middle English *lo(o)snen,* from *lo(o)s,* LOOSE.]

loose-strife (lŏŏss-strīf) *n.* 1. Any of various plants of the genus *Lysimachia,* having typically yellow flowers. 2. Any of various plants of the genus *Lythrum.* See **purple loosestrife.** 3. Any of various related or similar plants. [LOOSE + STRIFE (literal translation of Latin *lysimachia,* from Greek *lusimakheion.*]

loot (lŏŏt) *n.* 1. Valuables that have been looted; spoils. 2. *Informal.* Goods illicitly obtained, as by theft or bribery. 3. *Informal.* Money. ~*v.* **looted, looting, loots.** —*tr.* 1. To steal from in the process of war or civil disturbance. 2. To take as spoils. —*intr.* To loot property. **—See Synonyms at rob.** [Hindi *lūṭ,* from Sanskrit *lō(p)tra,* booty.]

lop¹ (lop) *tr.v.* **lopped, lopping, lops.** 1. To cut off branches or twigs from; trim. 2. To cut off (branches) from a tree or shrub. 3. To cut off (a part), especially with a single swift blow. Usually used with *off.* 4. To eliminate or excise as superfluous. Used with *off.* ~*n.* 1. The trimmings of a felled tree; twigs and branches. 2. Anything lopped off. [Middle English, Old English *loppian* (unattested), to prune.] **—lop·per** *n.*

lop² *v.* **lopped, lopping, lops.** —*intr.* 1. To hang loosely; droop. 2. To slouch; dawdle; loiter. 3. To lope. —*tr.* To allow or cause to hang loosely. [Akin to LOB.]

lope (lōp) *intr.v.* **loped, loping, lopes.** To run or ride with a steady, easy gait. ~*n.* A steady, easy stride or movement. [Middle English *lo(u)pen,* from Old Norse *hlaupa,* to leap.] **—lop·er** *n.*

lop-eared (lóp-éerd) *adj.* Having bent or drooping ears. Said of animals: *lop-eared beagles.*

Lope de Vega. See **Vega (Carpio), Lope Felix de.**

lopho- *comb. form.* Indicates a crested or tufted part; for example, **lophobranch.** [From Greek *lophos,* crest.]

lo·pho·branch (lŏfə-brangk, lóffə-) *n.* Any fish of the suborder Lophobranchii, having gills arranged in tufts, and including the sea horses. [LOPHO- + -BRANCH.] **—lo·pho·branch** *adj.*

lo·pho·phore (lŏfə-fawr, lóffə- ‖ -fōr) *n.* The filter-feeding organ of certain small, aquatic, invertebrate animals, such as brachiopods, consisting of a circular or horseshoe-shaped ring of tentacles around the mouth. [LOPHO- + -PHORE.] **—lo·pho·phor·ate** (-fáwr-ayt, -ət, -it ‖ -fōr-) *adj.*

Lop Nur or **Lop Nor** (lóp nóor). Also **Lo-pu p'o, Luo Bu Po.** Largely dried-up salt lake in the Tarim Basin, Xinjiang Uygur Autonomous Region, Western China. Since 1964 it has been the country's nuclear research and testing site.

lop·o·lith (lóppo-lith) *n.* A saucer-shaped body of intrusive igneous rock. [Greek *lopos,* shell + -LITH.]

lop·py (lóppi) *adj.* **-pier, -piest.** Hanging limp; pendulous.

lop·sid·ed (lóp-sídid) *adj.* 1. Heavier, larger, or higher on one side than on the other; not symmetrical. 2. Sagging or leaning to one side. 3. Not showing proper balance. **—lop·sid·ed·ly** *adv.* **—lop·sid·ed·ness** *n.*

loq. loquitur.

lo·qua·cious (lə-kwáyshəss, lō-, lō-) *adj.* Very talkative. See Synonyms at **talkative.** [Latin *loquāx* (stem *loquāc-*), from *loquī,* to speak.] **—lo·qua·cious·ly** *adv.* **—lo·qua·cious·ness, lo·quac·i·ty** (-kwássəti) *n.*

lo·quat (lō-kwot, -kwət) *n.* 1. A small tree, *Eriobotrya japonica,* native to eastern Asia, having white flowers and yellow, pear-shaped fruit. **2.** The edible fruit of this tree. [Cantonese *lō kwat, lō kat.*]

lo·qui·tur (lókwi-tər, -toor || lŏkwi-). *Abbr.* **loq.** He or she speaks or begins to speak. Used as a stage direction. [Latin.]

lo·ran (láwr-ən, -an || lōr-) *n.* A long-range navigational system based on pulsed radio signals from two or more pairs of ground stations of known position, with which a navigator can establish his own position by an analysis involving the time intervals between pulses. [*Lo*ng-*ra*nge *n*avigation.]

Lor·ca (lórkə), **Federico García** (*c.* 1899–1936). Spanish poet and playwright. His work, notably *Gipsy Ballads* (1928), draws on Andalusian culture. He was shot by Falangists in the Civil war.

lord (lord) *n.* **1.** A man of high rank in a feudal society or in one that retains feudal forms and institutions, as: **a.** A king. **b.** A territorial magnate. **c.** The proprietor of a manor. **2.** *Capital* **L.** *British. Abbr.* **Ld.** The general masculine title of nobility and other rank, used: **a.** Semiformally for any peer other than a duke: *Lord Cardigan* (the Earl of Cardigan). **b.** As the usual style for a baron: *Lord Morrison* (titularly, Baron Morrison of Lambeth). **c.** As a courtesy title for a younger son of a duke or marquis: *Lord Randolph Churchill* (third son of the Duke of Marlborough). **d.** As part of the titles of certain high officials and dignitaries, as *the Lord Mayor of London, the Lord Chancellor, the Lords of the Admiralty.* **e.** As a nominal title for a bishop. ***Note:*** In direct address, *my lord* and *your lordship* are deferential appellations for any of the above. *My lord,* usually pronounced (mə-lúd), is also used in addressing a British judge in court. In direct address and in informal reference, **c** may be shortened to *Lord Randolph,* but it may never be given as *Lord Churchill,* while **a** and **b** may never be used with Christian names. With **b** and **c,** the formal usage (as in addressing a letter) is *The Lord Morrison.* **3. a.** *Capital* **L.** God or Jesus. **b.** *Archaic.* The head of a household. **c.** A husband. **d.** A man of renowned power. **e.** A man who has mastery in some field or activity. **—the Lords.** The House of Lords.
~*interj.* Used to express surprise, distress, and the like. Often used in phrases such as *Lord knows!* and *Good Lord!*
~*intr.v.* **lorded, lording, lords.** To play the lord; domineer. Used with *it*: *lording it over the newcomers.* [Middle English *lord, loverd,* Old English *hlāford, hlāfweard,* "keeper of the bread" : *hlāf,* LOAF + *weard,* WARD.]

Lord Advocate *n.* In Scotland, the senior **law officer** *(see).*

Lord Chamberlain *n.* The senior member of the British royal household, responsible especially for the ceremonial aspects of royal activities.

Lord Chancellor *n., pl.* **Lords Chancellor.** The presiding officer and speaker of the House of Lords, Keeper of the Great Seal, Head of the judiciary in England and Wales, and usually a senior cabinet minister. Also called "Lord High Chancellor".

Lord Chief Justice *n. Abbr.* **L.C.J.** A senior English judge, the highest judicial officer after the Lord Chancellor, head of the Queen's Bench Division of the High Court of Justice, and President of the Criminal Division of the Court of Appeal.

lord·ing (lórding) *n. Archaic & Poetic.* Lord; sir. Used chiefly as a form of address.

Lord Lieutenant *n., pl.* **Lords Lieutenant. 1.** In Britain, a representative officer of the Crown in a county or in some Scottish burghs, performing largely ceremonial duties and nominally responsible for the proper administration of justice. **2.** Formerly, the British viceroy in Ireland.

lord·ling (lórdling) *n.* A young or unimportant lord.

lord·ly (lórdli) *adj.* **-lier, -liest. 1.** Of or pertaining to a lord. **2.** Dignified; noble. **3.** Arrogant; overbearing; haughty.
~*adv. Archaic.* In a lordly fashion. **—lord·li·ness** *n.*

Lord Mayor *n.* The mayor in certain cities such as London.

Lord of Appeal *n.* Any of several judges appointed to hear appeal cases in the House of Lords. Also called "Lord of Appeal in Ordinary".

Lord of Hosts *n.* Jehovah; God.

Lord of Misrule *n.* The master of traditional Christmas revelry in England during the 15th and 16th centuries.

lor·do·sis (lawr-dṓ-siss) *n. Pathology.* An abnormal forward curvature of the spine in the lumbar region. [New Latin, from Greek *lordōsis* : *lordos,* bent backwards + -OSIS.] **—lor·dot·ic** (-dóttik) *adj.*

Lord Privy Seal *n.* The official who is Keeper of the Privy Seal, usually a senior cabinet member with some other ministerial responsibility.

Lord Provost *n.* The provost in any of the six major Scottish burghs.

Lord's (lordz). A cricket ground in northwest London, the headquarters of the M.C.C. and Test and County Cricket Board.

lords-and-la·dies (lórdz'n-láydiz) *n. Used with a singular verb.* A plant, the **cuckoopint** *(see).* [From its dark (for lords) and light (for ladies) spadices.]

Lord's Day, Lord's day *n.* The Christian Sabbath; Sunday.

lord·ship (lórd-ship) *n.* **1.** *Usually capital* **L.** A title of or form of address for a British nobleman, judge, or bishop. Used with *Your, His,* or *Their.* See Note at **lord. 2.** The position or authority of a lord. **3.** The territorial fief of a feudal lord.

Lord's Prayer *n.* The prayer taught by Jesus to his disciples. Matthew 6:9–13. Also called "Our Father", "paternoster".

Lords Spiritual *pl.n.* Those members of the House of Lords who are Anglican bishops.

Lord's Supper *n.* **1.** The **Last Supper** *(see).* **2.** The Eucharist.

Lord's Table *n.* The Communion table.

Lords Temporal *pl.n.* Those members of the House of Lords who are not Anglican bishops.

Lord Steward *n.* An officer of the British royal household ranking between the Lord Chamberlain and the Master of the House, whose main duties are to supervise the servants.

lore[1] (lor || lōr) *n.* **1.** Accumulated fact, tradition, or belief about a particular subject: *country lore.* **2.** Knowledge acquired through education or experience. —See Synonyms at **knowledge.** [Middle English *lore,* Old English *lār.*]

lore[2] *n.* The area between a bird's eye and the base of the bill. [New Latin *lorum,* from Latin *lōrum*†, thong.]

Lo·re·lei (láwrə-lī, lórrə- || lṓrə-) *n. Germanic Mythology.* A siren of the Rhine whose singing lures sailors to shipwreck.

Lo·ren (láwr-ən, -en, lə-rén), **Sophia,** born Sophia Scicoloni (1934–). Italian film actress. Her films include *Two Women* (1961), for which she won an Academy Award, *Yesterday, Today, and Tomorrow* (1963), and *Man of La Mancha* (1972). In 1957, she married the film producer Carlo Ponti (1913–).

Lo·rentz (láw-rənts, ló- || lṓ-), **Hendrik Antoon** (1853–1928). Dutch physicist. His studies of the influence of magnetism on radiation won him and his pupil, Zeeman, the 1902 Nobel prize in physics.

Lorentz contraction *n.* The contraction in length of a moving body, as measured by an observer at rest with respect to the body, by the factor $(1-v^2/c^2)^{1/2}$, where *v* is the relative speed of the moving body and *c* the speed of light. Also called "Lorentz-Fitzgerald contraction". [After Hendrik LORENTZ.]

Lo·renz (láw-rents, ló-, -rənts || lṓ-), **Konrad (Zacharias)** (1903–). Austrian zoologist. He was the first to describe imprinting, the learning process which occurs during the first hours of life. His book *On Aggression* (1963) describes the ritualisation of aggressive impulses in animals. He was awarded a Nobel prize in physiology and medicine (1973) jointly with Frisch and Tinbergen.

Lo·re·to (lə-réttō, lo-, -ráytō). Town in Ancona, Italy. The Virgin Mary's house was reputed to have been miraculously transported there in 1295 from Nazareth.

lor·gnette (lawrn-yét) *n.* A pair of spectacles or opera glasses with a short handle. Also called "lorgnon". [French, from *lorgner,* to leer at, from Old French, from *lorgne*†, squinting.]

lo·ri·ca (lo-rī́-kə, lə-, law- || lō-) *n., pl.* **-cae** (-see, -kee). **1.** *Zoology.* A protective external shell or case, as of a rotifer. **2.** A cuirass or body armour, usually of leather and metal, worn by soldiers in ancient Rome. [Latin *lōrīca,* leather cuirass, from *lōrum,* thong.] **—lor·i·cate** (lórri-kayt, -kət, -kit || láwri-), **lor·i·ca·ted** (-kaytid) *adj.*

lor·i·keet (lórri-keet, -keét || láwri-) *n.* Any of several small Australasian parrots of the subfamily Loriinae; a small lory. [LOR(Y) + (PARA)KEET.]

lor·i·mer (lórrimər) *n.* One who made spurs, bits, and similar metal accessories for horse riders in former times. [Middle English, from Old French *loremier, lorenier,* from *lorain,* harness strap, from Vulgar Latin *loranum* (unattested), from Latin *lōrum,* thong, strap.]

lo·ris (láw-riss || lṓ-) *n., pl.* **lorises.** Any of several slow-moving, nocturnal, arboreal, prosimian primates of the genera *Loris* and *Nycticebus,* of tropical Asia, having dense, woolly fur, large eyes, and a vestigial tail. [French, probably from obsolete Dutch *loeris*†, simpleton, clown.]

lorn (lorn) *adj. Poetic.* Forlorn; desolate. [Middle English *lorn, loren,* lost, Old English *-loren,* past participle of *-lēosan,* to lose.]

Lorrain, Claude. See **Claude Lorrain.**

Lor·raine (lo-ráyn, lə-). *German* **Loth·ring·en** (lṓtring-ən). Former province in northeast France, now comprising the départements of Vosges, Moselle, Meurthe-et-Moselle, and Meuse. It was originally part of the kingdom of Lotharingia, belonging to Charlemagne's grandson Lothair I. Lorraine, with its neighbour Alsace, disputed between France and Germany for many years, was returned to France after World War I. The area contains deposits of iron ore. The main industrial towns are Metz and Nancy.

lor·ry (lórri || lúrri, láwri) *n., pl.* **-ries. 1.** A large road vehicle designed to carry goods. Also *chiefly U.S.* "truck". **2.** Any of various flat carts or vehicles that run on rails and are used for carrying goods. [19th century (northern dialect) : perhaps akin to dialect *lurry,* to tug, pull.]

lo·ry (láwri || lōri) *n., pl.* **-ries.** Any of various brightly coloured Australasian parrots of the subfamily Loriinae, having a tongue with a brushlike tip for feeding on pollen and nectar. [Malay *luri, nuri.*]

Los An·ge·les (loss ánji-leez, áng-gi-, -liss || *U.S. also* lawss, lōss). Commercial, industrial, and tourist city in southern California, United States. It is the third largest city in the United States, and its greater metropolitan area, including independent cities such as Long Beach, Santa Monica, and Beverly Hills, stretches 80 kilometres (50 miles). Los Angeles harbour handles oil and petrol, and the city's main industries include the manufacture of cars, planes, textiles, and electrical equipment. It also produces films for cinema and television in Hollywood, now a suburb of the city.

lose (lōōz) *v.* **lost** (lost || lawst) **losing, loses.** —*tr.* **1.** To experience the disappearance of (a possession, for example); be unable to find; mislay. **2. a.** To be unable to maintain, sustain, or keep: *lose one's balance.* **b.** To cease to feel: *lose hope.* **3. a.** To be deprived of: *lose a friend.* **b.** To be deprived of through death. **4.** To fail to win: *lose the game.* **5.** To fail to use or take advantage of: *lose a chance.* **6.** To fail to hear, see, or understand: *lose the thread of an argument.* **7.** To remove (oneself), as from everyday reality into a fantasy world; engross. Often used in the passive: *lost in thought.* **8.** To rid

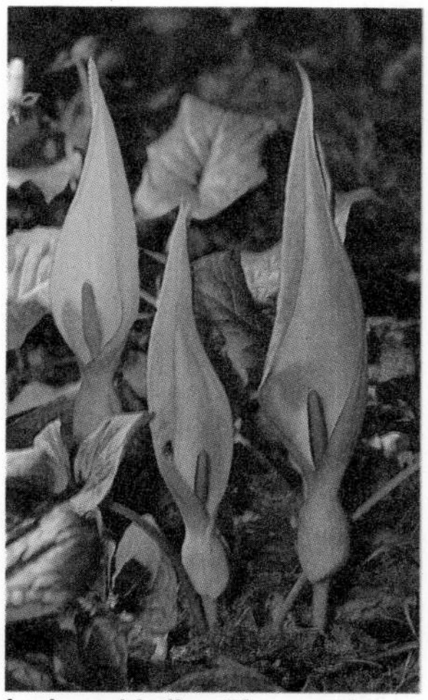

lords-and-ladies *The roots of lords-and-ladies,* Arum maculatum *(above), have a very high starch content and were used in Elizabethan Britain for stiffening the high, pleated, linen ruffs that were then fashionable. Arum grows in the hedgerows of the Northern Hemisphere and has many local names such as Adam and Eve and cuckoopint.*

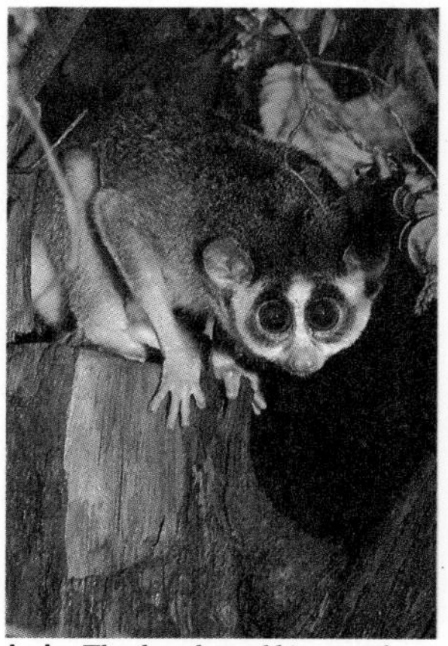

loris *The thumbs and big toes of these tree-dwelling primates are set at right-angles to their other fingers and toes so that they can grip branches. Lorises, which are native to Asia, are meat-eaters and hunt at night.*

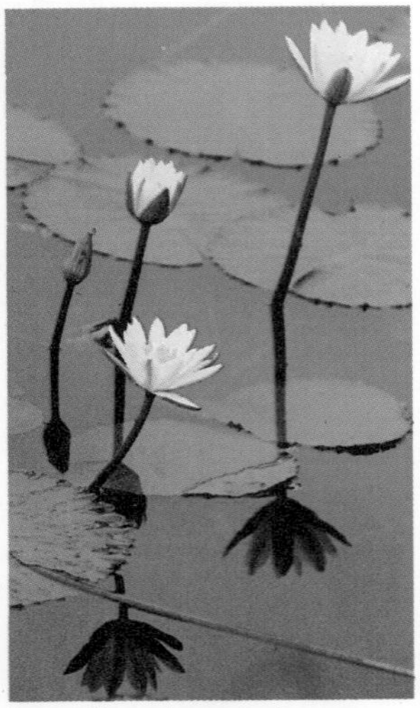

lotus *Several aquatic plants are known as lotuses. This is a Sri Lankan species which is related to the white waterlily of Europe.*

oneself of: *lose ten pounds.* **9.** To stray or wander from: *lose one's way.* **10.** To allow to disappear or fade from view: *We lost him in the crowd.* **11.** To elude or outdistance: *lose one's pursuers.* **12.** To cause or result in the loss of: *Failure to reply lost her a job.* **13.** To cause to die or be destroyed. Used in the passive: *Both planes were lost in the crash.* **14.** To fail to keep alive or resuscitate: *The surgeon lost his patient on the operating table.* **15.** To fail to give birth to (a living baby), as through miscarriage. *—intr.* **1.** To suffer loss. **2.** To be defeated. **3.** To run slow. Used of a timepiece. **4.** To suffer a reduction in impact or value: *The play lost slightly in translation.* **—lose out.** To be defeated. **—lose out on.** To fail to benefit from: *lose out on the sponsorship scheme.* [*Lose, lost, lost*; Middle English *losen, lost, loste,* Old English *lōsian, lōsode, gelōsod,* from *los,* loss, perdition, destruction.]

lo·sel (lṓz'l, lṓōz'l) *n. Archaic.* One that is worthless. [Middle English, profligate, "lost one", from *losen,* alternative past participle of *losen,* to lose, Old English *-lēosan.*]

los·er (lṓōzər) *n.* **1.** One that loses or seems fated to lose. **2.** One who accepts defeat in a specified way: *a good loser.* **3.** One who fails repeatedly, or is always being taken advantage of: *a born loser.*

Lo·sey (lṓ-si, -zi), **Joseph** (1909–). U.S. film director. In 1952, he was blacklisted in Hollywood because of alleged Communist sympathies. He made several films in Britain, including *The Servant* (1963), and *The Go-Between* (1970).

los·ing (lṓōzing) *adj.* **1.** Unprofitable: *sell off the losing parts of the company.* **2.** Being defeated: *the losing team.*

loss (loss ‖ lawss) *n.* **1.** The act or an instance of losing. **2.** Something or someone that is lost. **3.** The harm or suffering caused by losing or by being lost. **4.** *Plural.* The number of people killed in war or an accident. **5.** *Electricity.* The power decrease in a circuit, circuit element, or device caused by resistance. **6. a.** A failure to make a profit on a commercial transaction. **b.** The amount of money lost on an unprofitable transaction. **c.** *Often plural.* The amount by which a business enterprise's spending exceeds its income. **7.** *Insurance.* **a.** An instance of theft, damage by fire, or the like, as a result of which a policyholder may make a claim. **b.** The amount of such a claim by an insured. **—at a loss.** Reduced to a state of helplessness or perplexity: *at a loss for words.* **—cut (one's) losses.** To withdraw from a situation so that losses or damage are kept to a minimum. [Middle English *los,* probably back-formation from *loste,* past participle of *losen,* to lose, Old English *lōsian,* to perish, be destroyed or ruined, from *los,* destruction, loss.]

löss. Variant of **loess.**

loss leader *n.* An item of merchandise offered by a retailer at cost price or less to attract customers. Also called "leader".

loss ratio *n.* The ratio between the premiums paid to an insurance company and the claims settled by the company.

los·sy (lóssi ‖ láwssi) *adj.* Designating a transmission line, dielectric material, or the like that has a high attenuation. [From LOSS.]

lost (lost ‖ lawst) *adj.* **1.** Strayed; unable to find one's way. **2.** Misplaced; missing. **3.** Gone in time; passed away: *lost youth.* **4.** Gone morally astray; fallen: *a lost woman.* **5.** Bewildered or bemused. **6.** No longer possessed or practised: *a lost art.* **7.** Not appreciated or made use of. Used with *on*: *His hints were lost on her.* **8.** Dead or destroyed: *his lost comrades.* **9.** Unavailable; forfeited: *That opportunity is now lost to you.* **10.** Unconscious; not susceptible. Used with *to*: *lost to reason.* **11.** Absorbed; engrossed: *lost in her book.* **12.** Damned: *lost souls.* **—get lost.** *Informal.* To go away. Usually used in the imperative. [From the past participle of LOSE.]

lost cause *n.* A case that seems hopeless or bound for failure.

Lost Generation *n.* The generation of promising young men who died as soldiers in World War I.

lost wax process *n.* A technique of casting bronze, in which a wax model is used to form a mould and is then melted and drained off. Also called "cire perdue". [Translation of French *cire perdue.*]

lot (lot) *n.* **1.** Any of a group of nearly identical objects used in making a determination or choice by chance. **2.** The use of such objects for selection. **3.** The selections made. **4.** That which befalls an individual as a result of such a selection. **5. a.** A share; an allotted portion. **b.** One's fortune in life; one's fate. **6.** A number or group of people or things: *Let's get rid of that lot.* **7.** Kind, type, or sort: *him and his lot.* **8. a.** A **job lot** *(see).* **b.** An item or group of items sold at an auction. **9.** *Sometimes plural.* A large amount or number. **10. a.** *Chiefly U.S.* A piece of land: *a parking lot.* **b.** A piece of land having fixed boundaries. **c.** A film studio. **—a lot.** A great deal: *I like him a lot.* **—draw** or **cast lots.** To arrive at a decision or selection by means of lots. **—the lot.** All of a specific collection, quantity, or group. **—throw** or **cast in (one's) lot with.** To join with voluntarily.
~v. **lotted, lotting, lots.** *—tr.* **1.** To apportion by lots; allot. **2.** To draw lots for. **3.** To divide (land) into lots. *—intr.* To draw lots. [Middle English *lot(te),* Old English *hlot.*]
Usage: *Lot* is frequently criticised as inelegant in expressions such as *a lot of money* and *lots of people.* The alternative would be to use such phrases as *a variety of, a great deal of, a great many,* and these are often preferred in formal speech and writing.

Lot (lot). Abraham's nephew, whose wife was turned into a pillar of salt when she looked back as they fled from Sodom. Genesis 19:1–26. [Hebrew *lōṭ,* "covering".]

loth. Variant of **loath.**

Lo·thar·i·o (lə-tháar-i-ō, lō-, -tháir-) *n., pl.* **-os.** A seducer; a sexually promiscuous man. [Name of a seducer in *The Fair Penitent* (1703) by Nicholas Rowe.]

Lo·thi·an (lṓthi-ən). Region in southeast Scotland, stretching along the south shore of the Firth of Forth. It comprises the former counties of East Lothian, Midlothian, and West Lothian. Edinburgh is the administrative centre.

Lothringen. See **Lorraine.**

loti (lṓti) *n., pl.* **maloti** (mə-lṓti). The basic monetary unit of Lesotho, equal to 100 lisente.

lo·tic (lṓtik) *adj.* Of, pertaining to, or designating ecological communities living in fast-flowing rivers or streams. Compare **lentic.** [Latin *lotus,* past participle of *lavāre,* to wash.]

lo·tion (lṓsh'n) *n.* **1.** A medicated liquid for external application, especially one containing a substance in suspension, having a soothing or antiseptic effect. **2.** Any of various externally applied cosmetic liquids. [Middle English *loscion,* from Old French *lotion,* from Latin *lōtiō* (stem *lōtiōn-*), washing, from *lavere* (past participle *lautus, lōtus*), to wash.]

lots (lots) *adv. Informal.* A great deal; very much: *She's lots prettier than she used to be.*

lot·ter·y (lóttəri) *n., pl.* **-ies.** **1.** A game of chance offering money or prizes in which tickets are distributed or sold, the winning ticket or tickets being secretly predetermined or ultimately selected in a chance drawing. **2.** An activity or event regarded as having an outcome depending on fate. [Old French *loterie,* from Middle Dutch *loterije,* from *lot,* lot.]

lot·to (lóttō) *n.* A game of chance resembling bingo, played mainly by children. [French *loto,* from Italian *lotto,* from Old French *lot,* lot, from Frankish *lot* (unattested).]

lo·tus, lo·tos (lṓtəss) *n.* **1. a.** An aquatic plant, *Nelumbo nucifera,* native to southern Asia and widely regarded as sacred there, having large leaves, fragrant, pinkish flowers, and a broad, rounded, perforated seed pod. **b.** Any of several similar or related plants, such as certain water lilies of the genus *Nymphaea*; especially, *N. lotus,* a white-flowered species regarded as sacred in ancient Egypt. **2.** A representation of such a plant in sculpture, architecture, and art. **3.** Any of several leguminous plants of the genus *Lotus.* **4. a.** A plant in Greek legend whose fruit was eaten by the lotus-eaters. **b.** The fruit of this tree. [Latin *lōtus,* from Greek *lōtos,* fruit eaten by the lotus-eaters, of Semitic origin; akin to Hebrew *lōṭ,* myrrh.]

lo·tus-eat·er (lṓtəss-eetər) *n.* **1.** A member of a North African people described in the *Odyssey* who lived on the lotus, in a drugged, indolent state. **2.** One who defers the tasks of life in favour of self-indulgent pleasure; an indolent sybarite.

lotus position *n.* A sitting position in which the legs are crossed with the feet resting on opposite thighs and the hands resting on the knees, used in yoga and meditation.

louche (lōōsh) *adj.* Dubious; appearing unsavoury or shady. [French, "squinting".]

loud (lowd) *adj.* **louder, loudest.** **1.** Characterised by high volume and intensity of sound: *a loud crash.* **2.** Producing or capable of producing a sound of high volume and intensity. **3.** Clamorous and insistent: *loud denials.* **4. a.** Having offensively bright colours: *a loud tie.* **b.** Brash and vulgar in manner.
~adv. **louder, loudest.** In a loud manner. **—out loud.** Audibly. [Middle English *l(o)ud, lowde,* Old English *hlūd.*] **—loud·ly** *adv.* **—loud·ness** *n.*
Usage: *Loud* and *loudly* are often interchangeable: *Don't shout so loud(ly)! Loudly* is, however, somewhat more formal, and is the usual form found in writing, and when the meaning is not simply "intensity of the sound", but "clamorous and insistent": *They aired their grievances loudly.*

loud·en (lówd'n) *v.* **-ened, -ening, -ens.** *—tr.* To make louder. *—intr.* To become louder.

loud·hail·er (lówd-háylər ‖ -haylər) *n.* A portable megaphone with a built-in microphone, amplifier, and loudspeaker.

loud·mouth (lówd-mowth) *n.* One whose speech is loud and irritating or indiscreet. **—loud·mouthed** (-mowthd, -mowtht) *adj.*

loud pedal *n. Music.* A **sustaining pedal** *(see).*

loudspeak·er (lówd-spéekər ‖ *chiefly U.S.* -speekər) *n.* A device that converts electric signals to audible sound. Also called "speaker".

lough (lokh, lok) *n.* In Ireland: **1.** A lake. **2.** A bay or inlet of the sea. [Middle English *lough, lowe,* perhaps from Old English *luh,* from Old Irish *loch.*]

Lough·bor·ough (lúf-brə, -bərə ‖ -burrə). Industrial and market town in Leicestershire, England. It has a bell foundry and engineering works and produces knitwear and hosiery.

Lou·is XIV (lōō-i), also known as the Sun King (1638–1715). King of France (1643–1715), the greatest of the Bourbon monarchs. After the death of Cardinal Mazarin in 1661, Louis asserted his authority, insisting on the divine right of kings. He waged three major wars: The Dutch War (1672–78), the War of the Grand Alliance (1688–97), and the War of the Spanish Succession (1701–13). Louis presided over a brilliant court at Versailles, but the unity of France which he sought was foiled by his own persecution of the Huguenots, after his revocation of the Edict of Nantes (1685).

Louis XV (1710–74). King of France (1715–74). Louis was a weak ruler much influenced by his mistresses, Madame de Pompadour and Madame du Barry. He led France into the War of the Austrian Succession (1740–48), and the Seven Years' War (1756–63), which led to the loss of the French territories in India, Canada, and the West Indies.

Louis XVI (lōō-i) (1754–93). King of France (1774–93), whose reign ended in the turmoil of the French Revolution. In the French economic crisis following the American War of Independence, Louis summoned the States General (1789), but was reluctant to grant the wide-ranging reforms demanded. Revolution followed. Louis and his queen Marie Antoinette fled but were arrested at Varennes (1791) and brought back to Paris. In 1792, the monarchy was abolished. Louis was guillotined the following year.

Lou·is (lōō-iss), **Joe**, born Joseph Louis Barrow (1914–81). U.S. boxer, known as the Brown Bomber. He held the world heavyweight title for nearly 12 years (1937–49), successfully defending it for a record 25 times.

lou·is d'or (lōō-i-dór) n., pl. **louis d'or** (pronounced as singular). **1.** A gold coin of France from 1640 until the Revolution. **2.** A 20-franc gold coin of post-Revolutionary France. Also called "louis". [French, "gold Louis", first minted in the reign of Louis XIII.]

Lou·i·si·an·a (lōō-éezi-ánnə, lōō-izi-, -áanə ‖ lōōzi-). State in the southern United States, on the Gulf of Mexico. It is dominated by the marshy valley of the river Mississippi. Louisiana is the United States' main source of salt and sulphur, and a major producer of oil and natural gas, cotton, sugar cane, and rice. It was part of a French province, named after Louis XIV, and was sold to the United States (1803). It became a state in 1812. Baton Rouge is the state capital and New Orleans the largest city.

Louisiana French n. French as spoken by descendants of the original French settlers of Louisiana.

Louisiana Purchase. The purchase in 1803 by the United States from France of a vast area of land between the Mississippi and the Rocky Mountains. This area, extending over some 2 144 500 square kilometres (about 828,000 square miles), doubled the national territory of the United States at a cost of $15 million.

Louis Napoleon. See Napoleon III.

Louis Phi·lippe (lōō-i fi-léep) (1773–1850). King of France (1830–48), son of the Duke of Orléans. When the Bourbons were overthrown in the July Revolution (1830), Louis succeeded to the throne. He was known as the Citizen King. He abdicated during the revolution of 1848, and retired to England.

Louis Qua·torze (ka-tórz) adj. Pertaining to the baroque style of architecture, furniture, and decoration of the reign of Louis XIV. [French, "Louis XIV".]

Louis Quinze (kánz) adj. Pertaining to the rococo style in architecture, furniture, and decoration of the reign of Louis XV. [French, "Louis XV".]

Louis Seize (séz, sáyz) adj. Pertaining to the neoclassical style in architecture, furniture, and decoration of the reign of Louis XVI. [French, "Louis XVI".]

Louis Treize (tráyz, tréz) adj. Pertaining to the heavy late-Renaissance style in architecture, furniture, and decoration of the reign of Louis XIII. [French, "Louis XIII".]

Lou·is·ville (lōō-i-vil). Industrial city and port on the Ohio river in Kentucky, United States. It makes cars, electrical equipment, and whiskey.

lounge (lownj) v. **lounged, lounging, lounges.** —intr. **1.** To stand, lean, sit, or lie in a lazy, relaxed way; loll. **2.** To walk in a leisurely way. **3.** To pass time idly. —tr. To pass (time) in lounging. ~n. **1.** The act of lounging. **2.** A period of lounging. **3.** A lounging walk or gait. **4. a.** A public waiting room with seats, as in a theatre, or air terminal. **b.** A lounge bar. **5. a.** A living room in a house. **b.** A sitting room in a hotel: a TV lounge. **6.** Chiefly U.S. A long couch, especially one having no back and a headrest at one end. [16th century : origin obscure.] —**loung·er** n.

lounge bar n. A bar in a hotel, or a **saloon bar** (see).

lounge chair n. A deep, comfortable chair.

lounge lizard n. Informal. A man who does nothing but frequent social gatherings; a hanger-on in fashionable society.

lounge suit n. A man's ordinary two-piece suit.

loupe (lōōp) n. A small magnifying glass usually set in an eyepiece and used chiefly by watchmakers and jewellers. [French, from Old French loupe†, imperfect gem.]

loup-ga·rou (lōō-ga-rōō) n., pl. **loups-garous** (-rōōz, -rōō). A werewolf. [French, from Old French leu garoul : leu, wolf, from Latin lupus + garoul, garulf, werewolf, from Frankish werwulf (unattested), "man wolf".]

loup·ing ill (lówp-ing, lōōp-) n. A disease of sheep caused by a virus and transmitted by ticks, characterised by partial paralysis and twitching. Also called "trembles". [From earlier loup, to leap, Middle English loupen, to LOPE.]

lour. Variant of **lower** (scowl).

Lourdes (loord, often loordz). Town at the foot of the Pyrenees in the département of Hautes-Pyrénées, France. The Virgin Mary is said to have appeared in a grotto there to a peasant girl, Marie Bernarde Soubirous (St. Bernadette), several times in 1858. Since that time, pilgrims have flocked there, many seeking cures.

Lourenço Marques. See Maputo.

louse (lowss) n., pl. **lice** (līss) or **louses** (for sense 4). **1.** Any of numerous small, flat-bodied, wingless, bloodsucking insects of the order Anoplura, many of which are external parasites on various animals, including man. Common species are the head louse, Pediculus capitis, and the body louse, Pediculus corporis. **2.** Any of numerous small, wingless, biting insects of the order Mallophaga, which are external parasites on birds. In this sense, also called "biting louse", "bird louse". **3.** Any of various similar insects, such as the book louse. **4.** Slang. A mean or despicable person. ~tr.v. **loused, lousing, louses. 1.** Slang. To bungle. Often used

with up: louse up a deal. **2.** To remove lice from; delouse. [Louse, lice; Middle English lous, lys, Old English lūs, lȳs.]

louse·wort (lówss-wurt ‖ -wawrt) n. Any of numerous plants of the genus Pedicularis, having clusters of irregular, variously coloured flowers. [Sheep feeding on it were believed to be subject to vermin.]

lous·y (lówzi) adj. **-ier, -iest. 1.** Infested with lice. **2.** Slang. Mean; nasty; contemptible: a lousy trick. **3.** Slang. **a.** Painful; unpleasant: a lousy headache. **b.** Unwell; sick: feel lousy. **c.** Paltry; mere: a lousy £5. **4.** Slang. Inferior; worthless. **5.** Slang. Abundantly supplied; having a surfeit of. Used with with: lousy with money. —**lous·i·ly** adv. —**lous·i·ness** n.

lout¹ (lowt) n. An awkward or ill-mannered man or youth; a boor. [Perhaps ultimately from Old Norse lútr, bent low, from lúta, to bend down, bow.] —**lout·ish** adj.

lout² intr.v. **louted, louting, louts.** Archaic. **1.** To bow or curtsy. **2.** To bend or stoop. [Middle English l(o)uten, Old English lūtan, to bend down, bow.]

Louth (lowth; also lowth). Smallest county in the Republic of Ireland, on the northeast coast. Cattle rearing, fishing, crop raising, brewing, food processing, and textile manufacturing are its main industries. Dundalk is the county town.

Lou·vain (lōō-ván). Flemish **Leu·ven** (lővən). Market town in north Brabant, Belgium, with a 15th-century university.

lou·var (lōō-vaar) n. A widely distributed, silvery whalelike fish, Louvaris imperialis, that feeds on plankton. [Italian (Calabrian and Sicilian dialect) luvaru, perhaps akin to Latin ruber, red.]

L'Ouverture, Toussaint. See Toussaint L'Ouverture.

*****lou·vre, lou·ver** (lōōvər) n. **1. a.** A framed opening, as in a wall, fitted with fixed or movable slanted slats. **b.** Such a slatted frame. **c.** A structure, such as a door or window, incorporating a slatted frame. **2.** Any of the slats used in a louvre. Also called "louvre board". **3.** Architecture. A lantern-shaped cupola on the roof of many medieval buildings to admit air and provide for the escape of smoke. **4.** Any slatted ventilating opening. [Middle English luver, lover, from Old French lov(i)er†.] —**lou·vered** adj.

lov·a·ble, love·a·ble (lúvvəb'l) adj. Having characteristics that attract love or affection; endearing. —**lov·a·bil·i·ty** (lúvvə-billəti), **lov·a·ble·ness** n. —**lov·a·bly** adv.

lov·age (lúvvij) n. **1.** A European plant, Levisticum officinale, having small, aromatic seeds used as seasoning. **2.** A similar and related plant, L. scoticum. [Middle English lov(e)ache, from Old French luvesche, levesche, from Late Latin levisticum (apium), from "Ligurian (parsley)", variant of ligusticum, neuter of ligusticus, of LIGURIA.]

love (luv) n. **1.** An intense affectionate concern for another person. **2.** An intense sexual desire and overwhelming affection for another person. **3.** A beloved person. Often used as a term of endearment. **4.** A strong fondness or enthusiasm for something: a love of the woods. **5. a.** Capital L. Eros or Cupid, the god of sexual love in classical mythology. **b.** Sexual love as a force, as a literary subject or personified. **6.** Theology. **a.** God's benevolence and mercy towards man. **b.** Man's devotion to or adoration of God. **c.** The benevolence, kindness, or brotherhood that human beings should rightfully feel towards others. **7.** An expression of one's warm feelings: give them my love. **8.** One that is liked or thought of as sweet and endearing: he's a love. **9.** British Informal. Used as a term of address, especially in northern England. **10.** A zero score in tennis. —**fall in love.** To become enamoured of or feel strong affection and sexual desire for someone. —**for love.** As a favour; out of fondness; without payment. —**for love or money.** Under any circumstances. Usually used in the negative: He would not do that for love or money. —**for the love of. 1.** For the sake of. **2.** Used in expressions of impatience or surprise: for the love of Mike! —**in love.** Feeling love for someone or something; enamoured. —**make love. 1.** To have sexual intercourse. **2.** To embrace and caress. **3.** Archaic. To court; pay amorous attention to a person. ~v. **loved, loving, loves.** —tr. **1.** To feel love for. **2.** To make love to. **3.** To like or desire enthusiastically; delight in. **4.** To thrive on: The cactus loves hot, dry air. —intr. **1.** To experience loving tenderness for another. **2.** To be in love. —See Synonyms at **like.** [Middle English love, Old English lufu.]

Synonyms: love, affection, devotion, fondness, infatuation.

love affair n. **1.** An intimate sexual episode between lovers. **2.** An episode characterised by an enthusiastic liking or desire.

love apple n. Archaic. A tomato.

love·bird (lúv-burd) n. **1.** Any of various small African parrots, chiefly the genus Agapornis, often kept as a cage bird. **2.** Plural. Informal. Sweethearts; lovers.

love-bomb·ing (lúv-bomming) n. A technique of demonstrating strong concern and affection for a person in order to convert him to the views or beliefs of an organisation.

love child n. An illegitimate child. Used euphemistically.

love feast n. **1.** Among early Christians, a meal eaten with others as a symbol of love. **2.** A similar symbolic meal among certain modern Christians.

love game n. In tennis, a game in which the winner loses no points.

love-hate (lúv-háyt) adj. Characterised by alternating feelings of love and hatred or approval and disapproval: a love-hate relationship.

love-in-a-mist (lúv-in-ə-míst) n. A plant, Nigella damascena, native to Europe, having blue or whitish flowers surrounded by numerous threadlike bracts.

lousewort Named because it was once thought to infest sheep with lice, lousewort probably does transmit the parasitic liver fluke. Sheep infested with liver fluke almost always have lice, hence the mistaken belief. The species shown here is the common lousewort, Pedicularis sylvatica.

love-in-i·dle·ness (lúv-in-íd'l-nəss, -niss) *n. Archaic.* A plant, **heartsease** *(see).*
love knot *n.* A stylised knot, generally in the form of a bow, regarded as a symbol of the constancy of two lovers or as an emblem of love. Also called "true lover's knot".
Love·lace (lúv-layss, -ləss, -liss), **Richard** (1618–57). English poet. He supported the Royalists during the English Civil War and was twice imprisoned. He wrote "To Althea, from Prison" (1642).
love·less (lúv-ləss, -liss) *adj.* **1.** Characterised by an absence of love. **2.** Feeling no love; unloving. **3.** Receiving no love; unloved.
love-lies-bleed·ing (lúv-līz-bléeding) *n.* A tropical plant, *Amaranthus caudatus,* having clusters of small red flowers.
Lov·ell (lúvv'l), **Sir (Alfred Charles) Bernard** (1913-). British astronomer, director of Jodrell Bank Experimental Station (now Nuffield Radio Astronomy Laboratories) (1951–81). His written works include *The Exploration of Outer Space* (1961).
love·lock (lúv-lok) *n.* **1.** A lock of hair, often curled and tied with ribbon, worn over the shoulder by men of fashion during the 17th and 18th centuries. **2.** A lock of hair curled over the forehead.
love·lorn (lúv-lawrn) *adj.* Suffering because of love; feeling unrequited love or bereft of love or one's lover.
love·ly (lúvli) *adj.* **-lier, -liest. 1. a.** Having pleasing or attractive qualities: *a lovely landscape.* **b.** Beautiful; graceful: *a lovely girl.* **2.** Enjoyable; delightful: *a lovely party.* **3.** Inspiring love or affection. **4.** *Rare.* Full of love; loving. **—lovely and.** *Informal.* Pleasingly: *lovely and hot.* —See Synonyms at **beautiful.**
~n., pl. **lovelies.** *Informal.* **1.** A beautiful woman, especially an entertainer or model. **2.** Used as a term of endearment or address. **—love·li·ness** *n.* **—love·ly** *adv.*
love·mak·ing (lúv-mayking) *n.* **1.** Sexual activity between lovers; especially, sexual intercourse. **2.** *Archaic.* Courtship.
love match *n.* A marriage based on love, rather than on financial, dynastic, or other considerations.
love nest *n.* A place, such as a house or flat, used by lovers, especially in an illicit love affair. Often used euphemistically.
lov·er (lúvvər) *n.* **1.** Someone who loves another; especially, a man in love with a woman. **2.** *Plural.* A couple having a love affair. **3. a.** Someone engaged in an extramarital love affair. **b.** A sexual partner. **4.** One who is fond of or devoted to something. Usually used in combination: *a dog-lover.* **—lov·er·ly** *adj. & adv.*
love seat *n.* A small sofa or double chair that seats two people.
love set *n. Tennis.* A set in which the winner loses no games.
love·sick (lúv-sik) *adj.* **1.** Stricken, as if with illness, by love. **2.** Exhibiting unhappiness because of love. **—love·sick·ness** *n.*
lov·ey (lúvvi) *n. British Informal.* Used as an affectionate form of address.
lov·ey-dov·ey (lúvvi-dúvvi) *adj. Informal.* Exhibiting excessive sentimentality and affection towards a loved one.
lov·ing (lúvving) *adj.* **1.** Feeling love; affectionate; tenderly devoted. **2.** Indicative of or exhibiting love.
loving cup *n.* **1.** A large, ornamental wine vessel, usually made of silver and having two or more handles, from which each person drinks in turn, as at a ceremonial banquet. **2.** A similar cup given as an award in modern sporting events and similar contests.
lov·ing-kind·ness (lúvving-kīnd-nəss, -niss) *n.* Affection or tenderness stemming from sincere love for someone.
low¹ (lō) *adj.* **lower, lowest. 1. a.** Having little relative height; not tall. **b.** Rising only slightly above surrounding surfaces: *a low hill.* **c.** Situated or placed below normal height: *a low lighting fixture.* **d.** Situated below the surrounding surfaces, especially below sea level: *water standing in low spots.* **e.** Dead or prostrate. **f.** Cut to show the wearer's chest, back, and neck; décolleté. **2.** Near or at the horizon: *The sun is low in the sky.* **3.** *Phonetics.* Sounded with all or part of the tongue depressed. Said of a vowel, for example (aa) in *large.* **4.** Of less than usual or average depth; shallow: *The river is low.* **5. a.** Of inferior quality or character: *low intelligence.* **b.** Of relatively simple structure in the scale of living organisms. **c.** Inferior in rank or scale: *a low priority.* **6. a.** Morally base. **b.** Having inferior social, moral, or cultural status. **c.** Vulgar; coarse: *low jokes.* **7. a.** Wanting vigour; weak. **b.** Emotionally or mentally depressed. **c.** Giving little nourishment. **8. a.** Below average in quantity, degree, or intensity: *a low temperature.* **b.** Below an average or standard figure: *low wages.* **c.** Pertaining to or designating latitudes nearest to the equator. **d.** Of relatively small price: *The cost is low.* **e.** Involving or having a small amount: *low in fat.* **9. a.** *Music.* Being a sound produced by a relatively small frequency of vibrations: *a low note.* **b.** Hushed; not loud: *a low voice.* **10.** Being almost without money: *low in funds.* **11.** Not well supplied with; not adequately provided with or equipped for. **12.** Of small value or quality; depreciatory; disparaging: *a low opinion of his qualities.* **13.** Brought down or reduced in health or wealth. **14.** Overthrown; defeated. **15.** Designating a gear designed to produce power and slow speed. **16.** *Often capital* **L.** Low-Church. **17.** *Meteorology.* A **depression** *(see).* —See Synonyms at **mean** (ignoble).
~adv. **1. a.** In a low position, level, or space. **b.** In a low condition or rank; humbly: *You value yourself too low.* **2.** In or to a reduced, humbled, or degraded condition: *"A woman too brought Parnell low."* (James Joyce). **3.** Softly; quietly: *speak low.* **4.** With a deep pitch. **5.** At a small price: *bought low, sold high.* **6.** In hiding; biding one's time: *keep low; lie low.*
~n. **1.** A low level, position, or degree: *The stock market fell to a new low.* **2.** *Meteorology.* A region of depressed barometric pressure. Also called "depression", "atmospheric low". **3.** The gear configuration or setting that produces the lowest range of output speeds, as in the transmission of a motor vehicle. **4.** In some card games, the lowest trump. **5.** In some other games, the lowest score. [Middle English *low(e), lah,* from Old Norse *lāgr.*] **—low·ness** *n.*
low² *n.* The characteristic sound uttered by cattle; a moo.
~v. **lowed, lowing, lows.** *—intr.* To emit a low. *—tr.* To utter by means of a low. [Middle English *loowen,* Old English *hlōwan.*]
Low, Sir David (Alexander Cecil) (1891–1963). British cartoonist, born in New Zealand. He created a character called Colonel Blimp, a pompous and diehard reactionary.
low·born (lō-bórn) *adj. Rare.* Of humble birth.
low·bred (lō-bréd) *adj.* **1.** Lowborn. **2.** Coarse; vulgar.
low·brow (lō-brow) *n. Informal.* One having uncultivated tastes. Compare **highbrow, middlebrow. —low·brow, low·browed** *adj.*
Low Church *n.* A movement or faction in the Anglican Church that is opposed to excessive ritualism and favours a more evangelical doctrine. Compare **Broad Church, High Church. —Low-Church** (lō-chúrch) *adj.* **—Low-Church·man** (-mən) *n.*
low comedy *n.* Comedy characterised by slapstick, visual, and physical humour.
Low Countries. Region in northwest Europe comprising Belgium, the Netherlands, and Luxembourg.
low-down (lō-dówn || *West Indies also* -dúng) *adj.* Mean; unfair; despicable.
low·down *n. Informal.* All the facts; the relevant information from an informed source. Preceded by *the.*
Low Dutch *n.* The language of the Netherlands, **Dutch** *(see).*
Low·ell (lō-əl), **Amy** (1874–1925). U.S. poet. She was a leading imagist writer. Her works include *Men, Women, and Ghosts* (1916).
Lowell, Robert (Trail Spence) (1917–77). U.S. poet. He was imprisoned as a conscientious objector in World War II. His works include *Lord Weary's Castle* (1946), and *For the Union Dead* (1964).
low·er¹ (low-ər, lowr) *intr.v.* **-ered, -ering, -ers.** Also **lour, loured, louring, lours. 1.** To look angry, sullen, or threatening; scowl. **2.** To appear dark or threatening. Said especially of the sky or weather.
~n. Also **lour. 1.** A threatening, sullen, or angry look. **2.** A dark and ominous look. [Middle English *l(o)uren*†.] **—low·er·ing·ly** *adv.*
low·er² (lō-ər). Comparative of **low.**
~adj. **1.** Below someone or something in rank, position, or authority. **2.** Below a similar or comparable thing: *a lower shelf.* **3.** *Capital* **L.** *Geology & Archaeology.* Being an earlier division of.
~n. One that is beneath another; especially, a lower berth.
~v. **lowered, -ering, -ers.** *—tr.* **1.** To let, bring, or move something down to a lower level. **2.** To reduce in value, degree, intensity, or quality. **3.** To weaken; undermine: *lower one's energy.* **4.** To reduce in standing or respect. *—intr.* To diminish; become less.
Lower Austria. *German* **Nie·der·öster·reich** (needər-ōstərīkh). Formerly (1938–1945) **Lower Danube.** *German* **Nie·der·do·nau** (needər-dónnow). State in northeast Austria. It is a largely agricultural region, crossed by the Danube. Vienna is the capital.
lower bound *n. Mathematics.* A number that is not greater than any number in a set.
Lower California. *Spanish* **Ba·ja California** (baákhə). Mountainous peninsula in western Mexico separated from the mainland by the Gulf of California. It is mainly desert with limited agriculture. However, it has pearl and deep-sea fisheries, and considerable mineral resources, including gold, silver, copper and iron.
lower case *n. Abbr.* **l.c. 1.** Small letters, as opposed to capitals. **2.** The case of printing type containing the small letters.
low·er-case (lō-ər-káyss, -kayss) *adj. Abbr.* **l.c.** *Printing.* Pertaining to or designating small letters as distinguished from capitals: *a, b, and c are lower-case letters.*
~tr.v. **lower-cased, -casing, -cases.** To print in lower-case letters.
lower class *n. Often plural.* The class of lower than middle rank in a society; the working class. **—low·er-class** *adj.*
lower criticism *n.* Textual criticism and verbal examination of Biblical texts. Compare **higher criticism.**
lower deck *n.* **1.** The deck of a ship immediately above the hold. **2.** *Informal.* The petty officers and seamen of a navy, or of a ship, collectively.
Lower House *n.* The branch of a bicameral legislative body that is larger and more representative of the population, such as the House of Commons in the British Parliament. Also called "Lower Chamber". Compare **Upper House.**
low·er·most (lō-ər-mōst) *adj.* Lowest.
Lower Saxony. *German* **Nied·er·sach·sen** (neédər-zaks'n). State in northern West Germany comprising the former province of Hanover and the states of Brunswick, Oldenburg, and Schaumburg-Lippe. It is mainly agricultural, but has several manufacturing centres, including Brunswick and Hanover (the state capital).
lower world *n.* **1.** The realm of the dead, considered in ancient times to be beneath the surface of the earth; hell. Also called "lower regions". **2.** The earth.
low·er·y (lówəri, lówr-i) *adj.* Overcast; threatening: *a lowery sky.*
lowest common denominator *n. Abbr.* **l.c.d., L.C.D. 1.** The least common multiple of the denominators of a set of fractions. Also called "least common denominator". **2. a.** The most basic, least sophisticated level of taste, sensibility, or opinion among a group of people. **b.** A group reacting at such a level.
lowest common multiple *n. Abbr.* **l.c.m., L.C.M.** The least quantity that is exactly divisible by each of two or more specified quantities;

for example, 12 is the lowest common multiple of 2, 3, 4, and 6. Also called "least common multiple".

Lowes·toft (lṓ-stoft, lṓ-i-, -stəft; *locally* lṓ-stəf). Fishing port and resort in Suffolk, England, the most easterly town in England.

low explosive *n.* An explosive, as used in firearms, that has relatively low power.

low frequency *n. Abbr.* **lf** A **radio frequency** *(see)* in the range from 30 to 300 kilohertz.

Low German *n. Abbr.* **LG, L.G.** 1. Any of several German dialects spoken in northern Germany. 2. All of the West Germanic languages except High German. See **High German**.

low-key (lṓ-kée) *adj.* 1. Having low intensity; restrained, as in style or quality. 2. In photography, having or producing uniformly dark tones with little contrast.

low-keyed (lṓ-kéed) *adj.* Restrained; low-key.

low·land (lṓ-lənd) *n.* 1. Low-lying ground. **b.** *Plural.* A flat low-lying region of a country.
~*adj.* Pertaining to or characteristic of low, usually level, land.

Low·land (lṓ-lənd) *n.* The English dialect of the Scottish Lowlands; Lallans.
~*adj.* Of or from the Scottish Lowlands.

low·land·er (lṓ-ləndər) *n.* 1. A native or inhabitant of a lowland. 2. *Capital* **L.** An inhabitant of the Scottish Lowlands.

Low·lands, The (lṓ-ləndz). Scotland south of the Highlands.

Low Latin *n.* Loosely, late or medieval latin.

low-level language (lṓ-levv'l) *n.* A computer language that bears more resemblance to a machine language than to human language. Compare **high-level language**.

low life *n.* Life among the less respectable sections of society. —**low-life** *adj.*

low·ly (lṓ-li) *adj.* **-lier, -liest.** 1. Having or suited for a low rank or position. 2. Humble; meek. 3. Plain; simple; undistinguished.
~*adv.* 1. In a low manner, condition, or position. 2. Humbly; meekly. —**low·li·ness** *n.*

Low Mass *n.* A Mass without singing or ceremonial.

low-mind·ed (lṓ-míndid) *adj.* Exhibiting a coarse, vulgar character. —**low-mind·ed·ly** *adv.* —**low-mind·ed·ness** *n.*

low-necked (lṓ-nékt) *adj.* Also **low-neck** (-nék). Having a low-cut neckline; décolleté.

low-pass filter (lṓ-paass ‖ -pass) *n.* An electronic filter that allows frequencies below a specific value to pass but substantially attenuates frequencies above this value.

low-pitched (lṓ-pícht) *adj.* 1. Low in tone or tonal range. 2. Having a moderate slope: *a low-pitched roof.*

low-pres·sure (lṓ-préshər) *adj.* 1. Having, working under, or exerting little pressure. 2. Relaxed; calm; easy-going.

low profile *n.* An unobtrusive, restrained behaviour or stance; especially, an avoidance of militancy, publicity, or intervention.

low relief *n.* **Bas-relief** *(see).* [Translation of French *bas-relief.*]

low-rise (lṓ-ríz) *adj.* Of or designating a building or buildings having few storeys: *a low-rise development.* Compare **high-rise**.

Low·ry (lówr-i), **(Clarence) Malcolm** (1909–57). British novelist. His best-known work is *Under the Volcano* (1947), a partly autobiographical novel about an alcoholic ex-consul in Mexico.

Lowry, L(awrence) S(tephen) (1887–1976). British painter. He mirrored working-class life as a clerk in Lancashire, filling his canvasses with matchstick figures in dark industrial towns.

low season *n.* The time of year, for example winter at seaside resorts, when there is least demand for a service or product.

low-spir·it·ed (lṓ-spírritid) *adj.* In low spirits; depressed.

Low Sunday *n.* The Sunday following Easter.

low-ten·sion (lṓ-ténsh'n) *adj. Abbr.* **LT** Having, carrying, or operating at a low voltage.

low-test (lṓ-tést) *adj.* Having low volatility and a high boiling point. Said of petrol.

low tide *n.* 1. The tide at its lowest ebb. 2. The time of this ebb.

Low·veld (lṓ-felt). In South Africa, the savannah of the African plateau below 900 metres (about 3,000 feet).

low water *n. Abbr.* **L.W.** 1. Low tide. 2. The lowest level of water in a body of water, such as a river, lake, or reservoir.

low-wa·ter mark (lṓ-wáwtər ‖ *U.S. also* -wóttər) *n.* 1. A mark that indicates the lowest level reached by a river or sea water at low tide or on some other regular occasion. 2. The lowest point in something, when there seems the least prospect of success: *the low-water mark in her career.*

lox¹ (loks) *n. U.S.* Smoked salmon. [Yiddish *laks,* from Middle High German *lahs,* salmon, from Old High German.]

lox² *n.* Liquid oxygen *(see).*

lox·o·drome *n.* A **rhumb line** *(see).* Also called "loxodromic curve".

lox·o·drom·ic (lóksə-drómmik) *adj.* Also **lox·o·drom·i·cal** (-'l). *Nautical.* Pertaining to sailing on a rhumb line. [Greek *loxos†,* slanting + *dromos,* a running, course.] —**lox·o·drom·i·cal·ly** *adv.*

loy·al (lóy-əl) *adj.* 1. Steadfast in support and devotion to and never betraying the interests of one's homeland, government, or sovereign. 2. Faithful to a person, ideal, or custom; constantly supporting or following. 3. Of or professing loyalty. —See Synonyms at **faithful**. [French, from Old French *loyal, loial, leial,* faithful to obligations, legal, from Latin *legālis,* legal, from *lēx* (stem *lēg-*), law.] —**loy·al·ism** *n.* —**loy·al·ly** *adv.*

loy·al·ist (lóy-əl-ist) *n.* 1. One who maintains loyalty to a lawful government, political party, or sovereign, especially during war or revolutionary change. 2. *Capital* **L.** A Northern Irish Protestant wishing to keep Northern Ireland as part of the United Kingdom

and strongly opposed to the unification of Ireland. 3. *Capital* **L.** One who supported the lawful government of Spain during the Spanish Civil War; a Republican.

loyal toast *n. British.* A toast to the monarch drunk during a formal dinner.

loy·al·ty (lóy-əlti) *n., pl.* **-ties.** 1. The state or quality of being loyal. 2. *Plural.* Feelings of devoted attachment, affection, or duty: *divided loyalties.* —See Synonyms at **fidelity**.

Loyalty Islands. *French* **Îles Loy·au·té** (eel lwa-yō-táy). Group of coral islands in the southwest Pacific Ocean, forming part of the French Overseas Territory of New Caledonia. It comprises Maré, Lifou, Uvéa, and numerous islets, and exports copra and rubber.

Lo-yang. See Luoyang.

Loyola, Saint Ignatius. See Saint Ignatius Loyola.

loz·enge (lózzinj) *n.* 1. **a.** A four-sided planar figure with a diamond-like shape; a rhombus that is not a square. **b.** Something with this shape, especially a heraldic device. 2. **a.** A medicated drop that dissolves slowly in the mouth for local medication of the mouth or throat. **b.** A sugary tablet like this, eaten as a sweet. [Middle English *losenge,* from Old French, originally a diamond-shaped figure in heraldic design, from Gaulish *lausa* (unattested), flat stone.]

LP *adj.* Long-playing.
~*n., pl.* **LP's** or **LPs.** A long-playing gramophone record.

LPG liquefied petroleum gas.

L-plate (él-playt) *n.* In Britain, a white plate bearing a capital L in red that must be displayed on a vehicle driven by a learner-driver.

Lr The symbol for the element lawrencium.

L.S. the place of the seal [Latin *locus sigilli.*]

LSD Lysergic *a*cid *d*iethylamide: a crystalline compound, $C_{20}H_{25}N_3O$, prepared from lysergic acid, used illegally as a hallucinogenic drug. Also called "acid".

L.S.D., £.s.d. pounds, shillings, and pence [Latin *Librae, solidi, denarii.*]
~*n. British Informal.* Money.

L.S.E. London School of Economics.

lt. light.

Lt. lieutenant.

l.t. *Chiefly U.S.* local time.

LT low tension.

Lt. Col. lieutenant-colonel.

Lt. Comdr. lieutenant-commander.

ltd, ltd., Ltd. limited.

Lt. Gen. lieutenant-general.

Lt. Gov. lieutenant governor.

Lu The symbol for the element lutetium.

Lu·an·da (loo-án-də). Capital and port of Angola, on the Atlantic coast of Africa. It was founded as São Paulo de Loanda by the Portuguese in 1575. The city has a fine natural harbour, an oil refinery, and chemical, cement, and textile industries.

lu·au (loo-ow) *n.* An elaborate Hawaiian feast. [Hawaiian *lu'au.*]

lub. lubricant; lubrication.

Lu·ba (loobə) *n., pl.* Luba. 1. A member of a Negroid people of the southeastern Congo. 2. The language of this people. —**Lu·ba** *adj.*

lub·ber (lúbbər) *n.* 1. A clumsy fellow. 2. An inexperienced sailor; a landlubber. [Middle English *lobur, lobre†.*] —**lub·ber·ly** *adj. & adv.*

lubber line *n.* Also **lubber's line.** A line or mark on a compass or cathode-ray indicator that represents the heading of a ship or aircraft.

lubber's hole *n.* A hole through the platform surrounding the upper part of a ship's mast, through which one may climb to go aloft.

Lub·bock (lúbbək). City in northwest Texas, United States. It is the major distribution centre for the southern Great Plains.

Lü·beck (loo-bek, léw-; *German* lǘ-). Commercial city and river port in Schleswig-Holstein, West Germany. A major Baltic port and industrial centre, it has foundries and shipyards, and is connected to the river Elbe by canal. The present city, dating from 1143, was the leading town of the Hanseatic League. It remained a free city until 1937, when it was included in Schleswig-Holstein, a province of the Prussian state.

Lu·bitsch (loo-bich), **Ernst** (1892–1947). U.S. film director, born in Germany. His Hollywood productions include *Design For Living* (1933), *Ninotchka* (1939), and *Heaven Can Wait* (1943).

Lub·lin (loobleen). *Russian* **Lyu·blin** (lew-blín). Industrial and agricultural marketing city of central Poland. It is also a regional capital and cultural centre. A council of workers and peasants proclaimed Poland's independence from Russia there in 1918. There also, a Soviet-sponsored liberation group proclaimed itself the provisional government of Poland in December 1944, and this was recognised by the Allies at the Potsdam Conference (August 1945).

lu·bri·cant (loo-bri-kənt, léw-) *n. Abbr.* **lub.** 1. Any of various usually oily liquids or solids, such as grease, machine oil, or graphite, that reduce friction, heat, and wear when applied as a surface coating to moving parts. 2. *Informal.* Something or someone that helps to reduce difficulty or conflict. [Latin *lūbricāns* (stem *lūbricant-*), present participle of *lūbricāre,* to LUBRICATE.] —**lu·bri·cant** *adj.*

lu·bri·cate (loo-bri-kayt, léw-) *v.* **-cated, -cating, -cates.** —*tr.* 1. To apply a lubricant to. 2. To make slippery. 3. *Informal.* To reduce friction or difficulty in. —*intr.* To act as a lubricant. [Latin *lūbricāre,* from *lūbricus,* slippery.] —**lu·bri·ca·tion** (-káysh'n) *n.* —**lu·bri·ca·tive** (-kaytiv, -kətiv) *adj.* —**lu·bri·ca·tor** *n.*

lu·bric·i·ty (loo-bríssəti, lew-) *n.* 1. Lewdness; salaciousness.

2. Shiftiness; trickiness. **3.** Slipperiness. [Late Latin *lŭbricĭtās* (stem *lŭbricĭtāt-*), slipperiness, from Latin *lŭbricus*, slippery.]

lu·bri·cous (lóō-bri-kəss, léw-) *adj.* Also **lu·bri·cious** (lóō-bríshəss, lew-) **1.** Characterised by lewdness. **2.** Elusive. **3.** Slippery. [Latin *lŭbricus*, slippery.]

Lu·bum·bash·i (loo-bóōm-báshi). Formerly **E·liz·a·beth·ville** (ilízzə-bəth-vil). Capital of Shaba province, southern Zaire. It is a copper mining and smelting centre, and also a marketing point. The city was the capital of the secessionist state of Katanga (the former name of Shaba province) in Zaire's civil war (1960–63).

Lu·can (lóō-kən, lew-) *adj.* Pertaining to those parts of the New Testament attributed to St. Luke. [Ecclesiastical Latin *Lucas*, from Greek *Loukas*, Luke.]

lu·carne (lóō-kárn, lew-) *n.* A dormer window. [Variant (influenced by French *lucarne*) of earlier *lucane*, Old French *lucanne*, from Frankish *lukinna* (unattested), from *lūk* (unattested), something that closes.]

lu·cent (lóōss'nt, léwss'nt) *adj. Literary.* **1.** Giving off light; luminous. **2.** Translucent. [Latin *lūcēns* (stem *lūcent-*), present participle of *lūcēre*, to shine.] **—lu·cen·cy** *n.* **—lu·cent·ly** *adv.*

lu·cerne (lóō-sérn, lew-, lóō-, lóō-sern) *n. Chiefly British.* A plant, **alfalfa** (see). [French *luzerne*, from Provençal *luzerno*, special use of *luzerno*, glowworm (from its shiny seeds), perhaps from Latin *lucerna*, lamp.]

Lu·cerne (lóō-sérn, lew-; *French* lü-saírn). *German* **Lu·zern** (lóō-tsaírn). Canton in central Switzerland, noted for dairy and forest products. The city of Lucerne, on Lake Lucerne, is the capital and one of Switzerland's leading resorts.

Lucerne, Lake. *German* **Vier·wald·stät·ter·see** (feer-vaált-shtettər-zay). Resort lake in central Switzerland, its German name meaning "Lake of the Four Forest Cantons" (Lucerne, Schwyz, Unterwalden, and Uri).

lu·cid (lóō-sid, lew-) *adj.* **1.** Easily understood; clear: *a lucid speech.* **2.** Sane; rational: *a lucid moment.* **3.** *Poetic.* Shining. [French *lucide* and Italian *lucido*, from Latin *lūcidus*, from *lūcēre*, to shine.] **—lu·cid·i·ty** (lóō-síddəti, lew-), **lu·cid·ness** *n.* **—lu·cid·ly** *adv.*

lu·ci·fer (lóō-si-fər, léw-) *n.* A friction match. Not in current usage. [After LUCIFER.]

Lu·ci·fer¹ (lóō-si-fər, lew-) **1.** (The archangel cast from Heaven for leading a revolt of the angels; Satan. [Middle English *Lucifer*, Old English *Lucifer*, from Latin *Lūcifer*, "light-bearer" : *lūx* (stem *lūc-*), light + -FER.]

Lucifer² *n.* The planet Venus in its appearance as the morning star.

lu·cif·er·ase (lóō-siffər-ayz, lew-, -ayss) *n.* An enzyme that catalyses the oxidation of luciferin. [LUCIFER(IN) + -ASE.]

lu·cif·er·in (lóō-siffərin, lew-) *n.* A pigment in bioluminescent animals, such as fireflies or certain marine crustaceans, that produces an almost heatless, bluish-green light when oxidised. [Latin *lūcifer*, "light-bearer". See Lucifer.]

luck (luk) *n.* **1.** The fortuitous happening of fortunate or adverse events; fortune. **2.** One's (often specified) fate or lot. **3.** Good fortune; prosperity or success that comes by chance: *I wish you luck.* **—down on (one's) luck.** Afflicted by misfortune. **—in luck.** Fortunate; enjoying success. **—out of luck.** Unsuccessful; not having good fortune. **—push (one's) luck.** To take a risk, often by acting overconfidently and relying on luck. **—try (one's) luck.** To attempt something without knowing if one will be successful. [Middle English *lucke*, perhaps from Low German *luk* or Middle Dutch *luc*, akin to Middle High German *gelücke†*.]

luck·i·ly (lúckili) *adv.* With or by favourable chance.

luck·less (lúck-ləss, -liss) *adj.* Unlucky; having poor luck.

Luck·now (lúk-now; *also* lŏŏk-). Capital city and rail centre in Uttar Pradesh, north India, once the capital of the kings of Oudh (1775–1856). The city was besieged for five months during the Indian Mutiny (1857).

luck·y (lúcki) *adj.* **-ier, -iest. 1.** Having or resulting in good luck. **2.** Occurring by fortunate chance. **3.** Believed to bring good luck: *a lucky number.* —See Usage note at **fortuitous**. **—luck·i·ness** *n.*

lucky dip *n. British.* **1.** A large barrel or box containing concealed prizes which are selected at random. **2.** *Informal.* Any undertaking whose outcome is uncertain.

lu·cra·tive (lóō-krətiv, léw-) *adj.* Producing wealth; profitable. [Middle English *lucratif*, from Old French, from Latin *lucrātīvus*, from *lucrārī*, to profit, from *lucrum*, gain, LUCRE.]

lu·cre (lóō-kər, lew-) *n.* Money; profits. Often used humorously in the phrase *filthy lucre.* [Middle English, from Latin *lucrum*, gain, profit.]

Lu·cre·ti·us (lóō-kréesh-əss, lew-, -yəss). Latin name Titus Lucretius Carus (c. 95–c. 55 B.C.). Roman poet. He wrote *De rerum natura*, a philosophical poem on the teachings of Democritus and Epicurus, which tried to explain the universe without a divinity.

lu·cu·brate (lóō-kew-brayt, léw-) *intr.v.* **-brated, -brating, -brates.** To write in a scholarly fashion. [Latin *lūcubrāre*, to work at night by lamplight.]

lu·cu·bra·tion (lóō-kew-bráysh'n, léw-) *n.* **1. a.** Laborious study or writing. **b.** A product of such study, such as a treatise. **2.** Pedantry in speech or writing.

lu·cu·lent (lóō-kew-lənt, léw-) *adj. Archaic.* Easily understood; clear; lucid. [Middle English, full of light, clear, from Latin *lūculentus*, from *lūx* (stem *lūc-*), light.]

Lu·cul·lan (lóō-kúllən, lew-) *adj.* Lavish; luxurious. [After Lucius Lucullus, first-century B.C. Roman general noted for his luxurious banquets.]

lud (lud) *n.* Lord. Used when addressing a judge, in the phrase *m'lud* (my lord).

Lü·da or **Lü·ta** (lú-daa). Also **Dai·ren** (dí-ren), **Da·lian** (daa-lyen), or **Ta·lien** (daa-lyen). Industrial conurbation and rail terminus in southern Liaoning province, northeast China. It now includes the city of Lüshun (Lü-shun or Port Arthur), northeast China's chief port and also a major naval station. Lüda's industries include shipbuilding, heavy engineering, coalmining, chemicals, and food processing.

Lud·dite (lúddīt) *n.* **1.** Any of a group of British workmen who, between 1811 and 1816, rioted and destroyed textile machinery in the belief that mechanisation would diminish employment. **2.** One who aggressively opposes technical or technological progress. [Probably after Ned *Lud(d)*, an insane person who destroyed some stocking frames about 1779.]

Lu·den·dorff (lóōd'n-dawrff), **Erich** (1865–1937). German general and politician. He was Hindenburg's chief of staff in the east during World War I, and won the battle of Tannenberg (1916). He was defeated as a Nazi candidate for the presidency in 1925.

lu·dic (lóō-dik, léw-) *adj.* Pertaining to play. [Latin *lūdus*, game, and *lūdere*, to play.]

lu·di·crous (lóō-di-krəss, léw-) *adj.* Laughable or hilarious through obvious absurdity or incongruity. See Synonyms at **foolish.** [Latin *lūdicrus*, done playfully, from *lūdus*, game.] **—lu·di·crous·ly** *adv.* **—lu·di·crous·ness** *n.*

Lud·low (lúd-lō). Market town in Shropshire, England, dominated by ruins of its massive 11th–16th century castle.

lu·do (lóō-dō ‖ léw-) *n.* A children's board game played with counters that are moved according to the throw of a dice. [Latin, "I play".]

lu·es (lóō-eez, léw-) *n., pl.* **lues.** *Pathology.* **1.** Syphilis. **2.** A plague; a pestilence. [New Latin, from Latin *luēs*, plague.] **—lu·et·ic** (lóō-éttik, lew-) *adj.* **—lu·et·i·cal·ly** *adv.*

luff (luf) *n.* **1.** The forward side of a fore-and-aft sail. **2.** The fullest part of the bow of a ship.
~*v.* **luffed, luffing, luffs.** *—intr.* **1.** To steer a sailing vessel nearer into the wind, especially with the sails flapping. **2.** To flap while losing wind. Used of a sail. **3.** To sail closer to the wind than, or to come between the wind and, an opponent's yacht during a race. **4.** To move the jib of a crane or the boom of a derrick. *—tr.* To cause (a ship, for example) to sail closer to the wind. [Earlier *loufe*, Middle English *luff, lof*, from Old French *lof*, perhaps from Middle Dutch *loef* (unattested).]

luffa. *Chiefly U.S.* Variant of **loofah.**

Luft·waf·fe (lóōft-vaafə) *n.* The German air force before and during World War II. [German, "air weapon".]

lug¹ (lug) *n.* **1.** An earlike handle or projection on a vessel or machine, used as a hold or support. **2.** In machinery, a nut, especially one that is closed at one end to serve as a cap. **3.** A loop, usually of leather, at the side of the saddle of a harness rig through which one of the shafts of a cart or other conveyance passes. **4.** A projection from a battery plate to which an electrical connection can be made. **5.** *Chiefly Scottish.* An ear. **6.** A lugsail. [Middle English (Scottish) *lugge*, flap, ear, perhaps from *luggen*, to LUG (to pull, as the ear).]

lug² *v.* **lugged, lugging, lugs.** *—tr.* **1.** To drag or haul (something) laboriously. **2.** To introduce or include (something irrelevant) in a forced manner. *—intr.* To pull with difficulty; tug.
~*n.* **1.** The act or an instance of lugging. **2.** Something that is lugged. [Middle English *luggen*, to pull, perhaps from Scandinavian, akin to Swedish *lugga†*, to pull one's hair.]

lug³ *n.* The lugworm.

Lu·gan·da (lóō-gándə, lew-) *n.* The Bantu language of the Ganda, a people of Uganda. **—Lu·gan·da** *adj.*

luge (lóōzh) *n.* A light, short toboggan for one person.
~*intr.v.* **luged, luging, luges.** To ride or travel on a luge. [French.]

Lu·ger (lóōgər) *n.* A trademark for a German automatic pistol.

lug·gage (lúggij) *n.* The suitcases, trunks, bags, and the like of a traveller; baggage. [Probably LUG (to drag) + (BAG)GAGE.]

luggage van *n.* A railway van (see).

lug·ger (lúggər) *n.* A small boat used for fishing, sailing, or coasting and having two or three masts, each with a lugsail, and two or three jibs set on the bowsprit. [From LUG(SAIL).]

lug·hole (lúg-hōl) *n. British Slang.* An ear.

lug·sail (lúg-sayl, *nautical* -s'l) *n.* A quadrilateral sail lacking a boom and having the foot larger than the head, bent to a yard hanging obliquely on the mast. Also called "lug". [Perhaps from LUG "ear".]

lu·gu·bri·ous (lóō-góōbri-əss, lə-, lóō-, lew-) *adj.* Mournful or doleful, especially to an excessive degree. [Latin *lūgubris*, mournful, from *lūgēre*, to mourn.] **—lu·gu·bri·ous·ly** *adv.* **—lu·gu·bri·ous·ness** *n.*

lug·worm (lúg-wurm) *n.* Any of various segmented, burrowing marine worms of the genus *Arenicola*; especially, *A. marina*, often used as fishing bait. Also called "lug", "lobworm". [17th century : origin obscure.]

Luik. See **Liège.**

Luke (lóōk, lewk) *n.* A book of the New Testament, the third Gospel, attributed to St. Luke.

Luke, Saint. A companion of the Apostle Paul, traditionally regarded as author of the third Gospel and The Acts of the Apostles.

luke·warm (lóōk-wáwrm, léwk-, -wawrm) *adj.* **1.** Mildly warm; tepid. **2.** Lacking in enthusiasm; indifferent. [Middle English : *luke*, perhaps from *lew*, tepid, Old English *hlēow*, warm + WARM.] **—luke·warm·ly** *adv.* **—luke·warm·ness** *n.*

lucerne *A plant from the Mediterranean, also known as alfalfa. Its sprouting seeds can be grown in jars on a windowsill and used to garnish salads.*

lull (lul) *v.* **lulled, lulling, lulls.** —*tr.* **1.** To cause to sleep or rest; soothe; calm. **2.** To dispel or quieten (fears or suspicions). **3.** To deceive into trustfulness. —*intr.* To become calm.
∼*n.* **1.** A relatively calm interval in a storm or other turbulence. **2.** An interval of lessened activity: *a lull in sales.* [Middle English *lullen,* perhaps of German origin; akin to Middle Low German *lollen.*]

lull·a·by (lúllə-bī) *n., pl.* **-bies.** A soothing song with which to lull a child to sleep.
∼*tr.v.* **lullabied, -bying, -bies.** To quieten with or as if with a lullaby. [Perhaps LULL + good*bye.*]

Lul·ly (lo͞o-lée; *French* lü-), **Jean Baptiste,** born Giovanni Battista Lulli (1632–87). Italian-born French composer. He was court composer to Louis XIV of France, founding French opera and producing court ballets for Molière's plays.

lu·lu (lo͞o-lo͞o) *n. Chiefly U.S. Slang.* An object, action, or idea that is remarkable. [Perhaps from *Lulu,* pet form of the name *Louise.*]

lum·ba·go (lum-báygō) *n.* Pain in the region of the lower back, resulting from various causes. [Latin *lumbāgo,* from *lumbus,* loin.]

lum·bar (lúm-bər ‖ -baar) *adj.* Of, near, or situated in the part of the back and sides between the lowest ribs and the pelvis. [New Latin *lumbaris,* from Latin *lumbus,* loin.]

lumbar puncture *n.* The insertion of a hollow needle into the lumbar region of the spinal cord in order to withdraw cerebrospinal fluid for diagnostic examination or inject drugs.

lum·ber¹ (lúmbər) *n.* **1.** *Chiefly British.* Miscellaneous stored articles. **2.** Anything useless or cumbersome. **3.** *U.S. & Canadian.* Timber.
∼*v.* **lumbered, -bering, -bers.** —*tr.* **1.** *Chiefly British.* To clutter with or as if with unused articles. **2.** To jumble or heap together. **3.** *Informal.* To burden or encumber, as with difficulties or responsibilities. **4.** *Chiefly U.S.* To cut or saw into timber. —*intr. Chiefly U.S.* To cut and prepare timber for the market. [Perhaps from LUMBER (to move clumsily, hence something clumsy).] —**lum·ber** *adj.* —**lum·ber·er, lum·ber·man** (-mən) *n.*

lum·ber² *intr.v.* **-bered, -bering, -bers.** To walk or move with heavy clumsiness. [Middle English *lomeren,* perhaps from Scandinavian; akin to Swedish dialectal *loma,* to move heavily.]

lum·ber·jack (lúmbər-jak) *n.* One who fells trees and transports the timber to a mill; a logger. [LUMBER (wood) + JACK (man).]

lum·ber·jack·et (lúmbər-jackit) *n.* A heavy, waist-length jacket worn especially by outdoor workers.

lum·bri·coid (lúmbri-koyd) *adj.* Resembling or pertaining to an earthworm.
∼*n.* A parasitic roundworm, *Ascaris lumbricoides,* that infests the human intestine. [New Latin *lumbricoides* : Latin *lumbrīcus,* earthworm + -OID.]

lu·men (lo͞o-min, léw-, -men, -mən) *n., pl.* **-mens** or **-mina** (-mi-nə). **1.** *Anatomy.* The inner open space of a tubular organ, as of a blood vessel or an intestine. **2.** *Botany.* The space enclosed by the cell walls of a plant cell that has lost its living contents. **3.** *Abbr.* **lm** *Physics.* The SI unit of luminous flux, equal to the luminous flux emitted in a solid angle of one steradian by a uniform point source having an intensity of one candela. [New Latin, from Latin *lūmen,* light, eye, opening.] —**lu·men·al, lu·min·al** *adj.*

Lu·mière (lo͞omi-áir; *French* lüm-yáir), **Auguste** (1862–1954). French photographer. Auguste and his brother Louis Jean Lumière (1864–1948) gave the first public showing of a projected cinematic film in Paris (1895).

lu·mi·nance (lo͞o-mi-nənss, léw-) *n.* **1.** The condition or quality of being luminous. **2.** *Physics.* The luminous intensity in a given direction of a small element of surface area divided by the orthogonal projection of this area onto a plane at right angles to the direction. Formerly called "brightness". [Latin *lūmen* (stem *lūmin-*), light + -ANCE.]

lu·mi·nar·y (lo͞o-mi-nəri, léw- ‖ -nerri) *n., pl.* **-ies. 1.** An object, as a celestial body, that gives light. **2.** A source of intellectual or spiritual enlightenment. **3.** A notable person in a given field. [Middle English *luminarye,* from Old French *luminarie,* from Late Latin *lūmināre,* lamp, heavenly body, from Latin *lūmen* (stem *lūmin-*), light.] —**lu·mi·nar·y** *adj.*

lu·mi·nesce (lo͞o-mi-néss, léw-) *intr.v.* **-nesced, -nescing, -nesces.** To be or become luminescent. [Back-formation from LUMINESCENT.]

lu·mi·nes·cence (lo͞o-mi-néss'nss, léw-) *n.* **1.** The emission of light, as in phosphorescence, fluorescence, and bioluminescence, by processes that derive energy from essentially nonthermal sources such as chemical, biochemical, or crystallographic changes, the motion of subatomic particles, or the excitation of an atomic system by radiation; especially, such emission distinguished from incandescence. **2.** The light so emitted.

lu·mi·nes·cent (lo͞o-mi-néss'nt, léw-) *adj.* Capable of, exhibiting, or suitable for the emission of luminescence. [Latin *lūmen* (stem *lūmin-*), light + -ESCENT.]

lu·mi·nif·er·ous (lo͞o-mi-níffərəss, léw-) *adj.* Generating, yielding, or transmitting light. [Latin *lūmen* (stem *lūmin-*), light (see **luminous**) + -FEROUS.]

lu·mi·nos·i·ty (lo͞o-mi-nóssəti, léw-) *n.* **1.** The condition or quality of being luminous. **2.** Something luminous. **3.** The attribute of an object or colour that enables the observation of the extent to which an object emits light. **4.** *Astronomy.* A measure of the absolute brightness of a star, equal to the total power radiated.

lu·mi·nous (lo͞o-mi-nəss, léw-) *adj.* **1.** Emitting light; especially, emitting self-generated light. **2.** Full of light; illuminated. **3.** Designating a photometric physical quantity that is evaluated on the basis of the visual sensation it produces in the observer. Compare **radiant. 4.** Intelligible; clear. —See Synonyms at **bright.** [Middle English, from Old French *lumineux,* from Latin *lūminōsus,* full of light, from *lūmen* (stem *lūmin-*), light.] —**lu·min·ous·ly** *adv.* —**lu·min·ous·ness** *n.*

luminous efficacy *n.* **1.** The ratio of the total luminous flux to the total radiant flux of an emitting source. **2.** The ratio of the luminous flux emitted by a source of radiation to the power it consumes, usually expressed in lumens per watt.

luminous efficiency *n.* The efficiency of polychromatic radiation in producing a visual sensation measured as the ratio of the radiant flux, weighed according to the spectral luminous efficiencies of its constituent wavelengths, to the corresponding radiant flux.

luminous energy *n.* Energy in the form of light, expressed as luminous flux multiplied by its duration and measured in lumen seconds.

luminous exitance *n.* The ability of a surface to emit light, equal to the luminous flux per unit area at a specific position on the surface.

luminous flux *n.* The rate of flow of luminous energy evaluated on the basis of its ability to produce a visual sensation. For monochromatic light it is the radiant flux multiplied by the spectral luminous efficiency and is measured in lumens.

luminous intensity *n.* The amount of light radiated by a point source in a given direction expressed as the luminous flux in that direction per unit of solid angle. It is measured in candelas.

luminous paint *n.* A paint containing a phosphorescent or fluorescent substance that makes it glow in the dark.

lum·me, lum·my (lúmmi) *interj. Informal.* Used to express surprise or mild dismay. [Pronunciation of *(Lord) love me.*]

lump¹ (lump) *n.* **1.** An irregularly shaped mass or piece. **2.** A small cube or cuboid of sugar. Also used adjectivally: *lump sugar.* **3.** *Pathology.* A swelling or small, palpable tumour. **4.** An aggregate; a collection; a totality. **5.** An ungainly, heavy or lazy person. **6.** A piece of coal or coke suitable for use in a stove or fireplace. —**a lump in the throat.** A feeling of constriction in the throat caused by emotion. —**the lump.** *British.* Casual workers in the building trade operating as self-employed, often to avoid paying tax or national insurance contributions.
∼*v.* **lumped, lumping, lumps.** —*tr.* **1.** To put together or amass in a single group or pile. **2.** To treat as a single group; fail to differentiate. Often used with *together.* **3.** To make lumpy. —*intr.* **1.** To become lumpy. **2.** To move heavily. [Middle English, perhaps of Low German origin; Low German *lump,* coarse.]

lump² *tr.v.* **lumped, lumping, lumps.** *Informal.* To tolerate (what must be endured): *like it or lump it.* [16th century : origin obscure.]

lump·ec·tomy (lúmp-éktəmi) *n., pl.* **-mies.** A surgical operation for the removal of a tumour from the breast. [LUMP + -ECTOMY.]

lump·en (lúmpən) *adj.* Ignorant or stupid. Used derogatorily or humorously. [German *Lumpen,* rag, vagabond.]

lum·pen·pro·le·tar·i·at (lúmpən-prōli-táir-i-ət, -at) *n.* **1.** According to Marxist analysis, a social grouping consisting of outcasts such as tramps and thieves, considered to be below the proletariat. **2.** The unthinking, ignorant lower classes, uninterested in advancement or social change. Used derogatorily. [German, "ragged proletariat".]

lump·fish (lúmp-fish) *n., pl.* **-fishes** or collectively **lumpfish.** Any of various fishes of the family Cyclopteridae; especially, *Cyclopterus lumpus,* of Atlantic waters, having a body covered with tuberous excrescences, a ventral sucker formed from fused pelvic fins, and an edible roe resembling caviar. Also called "lumpsucker". [Obsolete *lump,* lumpfish, from Middle Dutch *lumpe* + FISH.]

lump·ish (lúmpish) *adj.* **1.** Stupid; dull. **2.** Clumsy; heavy; cumbersome. —**lump·ish·ly** *adv.* —**lump·ish·ness** *n.*

lump sum *n.* A sum of money as an inclusive payment.

lump·y (lúmpi) *adj.* **-ier, -iest. 1.** Covered with lumps. **2.** Full of lumps. **3.** Thickset or cumbersome in appearance. **4.** Characterised by short, choppy waves. Said of a windblown sea.

lumpy jaw *n. Pathology.* **Actinomycosis** *(see).*

Lu·mum·ba (lo͞o-mo͝ombə), **Patrice** (1925–61). First prime minister (1960–61) of the Congo (now Zaire). He fought to form a united Congo, but was ousted in 1961, and murdered by Katanga secessionists.

lu·na (lo͞o-nə, léw-) *n.* In alchemy, silver. [Middle English, from Medieval Latin *lūna,* from Latin, moon (from its colour).]

Lu·na (lo͞o-nə, léw-). The Roman goddess of the moon. [Latin.]

lu·na·cy (lo͞o-nə-si, léw-) *n., pl.* **-cies. 1.** Insanity. Not in technical usage. **2.** Foolish and irresponsible conduct. **3.** *Archaic.* Mental derangement associated with certain phases of the moon. —See Synonyms at **insanity.** [From LUNATIC.]

luna moth *n.* A large, pale green North American moth, *Actias luna,* having a long projection on each hind wing. [Latin *lūna,* moon (from the yellow rings on its wings).]

lu·nar (lo͞o-nər, léw-) *adj.* **1.** Of, involving, caused by, or affecting the moon. **2.** Measured by or based on the revolution of the moon: *a lunar month; a lunar calendar.* **3.** Of or pertaining to silver. [Latin *lūnāris,* from *lūna,* moon.]

lunar caustic *n.* Silver nitrate in the form of sticks, formerly used in cauterisation.

lunar excursion module *n. Abbr.* **LEM** A spacecraft designed to transport astronauts from a command module orbiting the Moon to the lunar surface and back. Also called "lunar module".

lunar month *n.* A **month** *(see).*

PRONUNCIATION KEY

a, **trap**; aa, **father**; ai, **fair**; ar, **star**; aw, **lawn**; ay, **play**; b, bb, **stab**; **rubber**; ch, **church**; ck, **ticket**; d, dd, **dead**; **ladder**; e, **dress**; ee, **bee**; er, **defer**; ew, **few**; ewr, **pure**; ə, **about**; ər, **letter**; f, ff, **fife**; **differ**; g, gg, **giggle**; h, **hat**; i, **kit**; ī, **price**; īr, **fire**; j, **judge**; k, **kick**; l, ll, **let**; 'l, **needle**; m, mm, **man**; n, nn, **no**; 'n, **sudden**; ng, **thing**; o, **lot**; ō, **no**; o͝o, **foot**; o͞o, **shoe**; oor, **poor**; ow, **cow**; owr, **hour**; oy, **boy**; p, pp, **pepper**; r, rr, **red**; s, ss, **sauce**; sh, **ship**; t, tt, **totter**; th, **thick**; t͟h, **this**; **smooth**; u, **cut**; ur, **turn**; v, vv, **valve**; w, **wet**; y, **yes**; z, zz, **zebra**; z͟h, **vision**; **pleasure**

IN FOREIGN WORDS:

aɴ, oɴ, **Saint-Saëns**; h͟l, **Llanelli**; **Hluhluwe**; k͟h, **loch**; **lough**; **Khaled**

STRESS MARK:

ín-sīt, **insight**; in-sít, **incite**

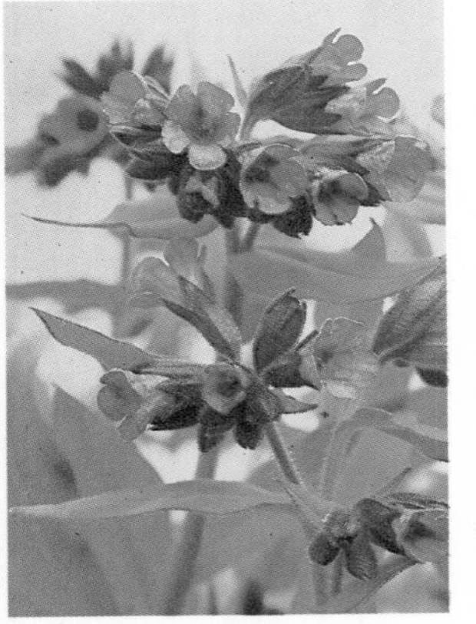

lungwort *Lungworts – a group of spring-flowering European plants with coarse leaves – were so named because they were once thought to be a cure for lung diseases. This species is* Pulmonaria officinalis.

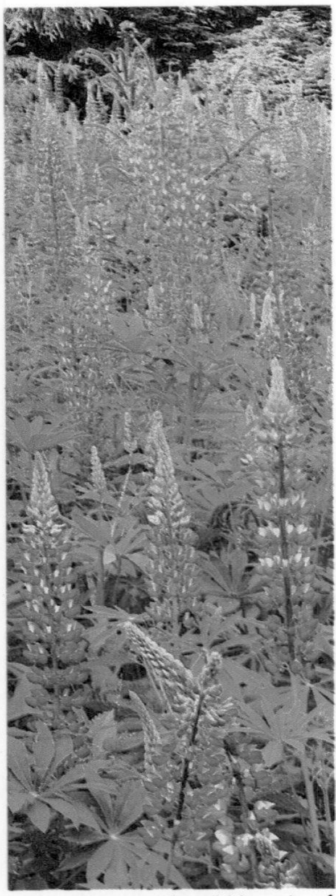

lupin *There are about 200 species of lupin, a plant native to the Americas and the Mediterranean. Most garden varieties – like the ones shown here – are hybrids of the North American species* Lupinus polyphyllus, *and are commonly known as Russell lupins after one of the breeders who developed the strain.*

lunar year *n.* An interval of 12 lunar months.

lu·nate (lōō-nayt, léw-, -nət, -nit) *adj.* Also **lu·nat·ed** (lōō-náytid, lew-) Crescent-shaped. [Latin *lūnātus,* from *lūnāre,* to form into a crescent, from *lūna,* moon.]

lunate bone *n.* The second of three bones forming the upper row of bones in the wrist. Also called "semilunar bone".

lu·na·tic (lōō-nətik, léw-) *adj.* **1.** Suffering from lunacy; insane. Not in technical usage. **2.** Of or for the insane: *a lunatic asylum.* Not in technical usage. **3.** Wildly or absurdly foolish: *a lunatic decision.* [Middle English *lunatik,* from Old French *lunatique,* from Latin *lūnāticus,* "moonstruck", crazy, from *lūna,* moon.] **—lu·na·tic** *n.*

lunatic fringe *n.* The fanatical, extreme, or irrational members of a society or group.

lu·na·tion (lōō-náysh'n, lew-) *n.* A lunar **month** *(see).* [Middle English *lunacioun,* from Medieval Latin *lūnātiō* (stem *lūnātiōn-*), from Latin *lūna,* moon.]

lunch (lunch) *n.* **1.** A meal eaten at midday. **2.** The food provided for this meal. See Usage note at **dinner. —out to lunch.** *Slang.* Crazy; mad.
~*v.* **lunched, lunching, lunches.** To take (a prospective client, for example) to lunch, especially to discuss business.
~*intr.* **1.** To have one's lunch. **2.** To lunch clients or others. [Shortened from LUNCHEON.] **—lunch·er** *n.*

lunch·eon (lúnchən) *n.* **1.** A lunch, especially a formal one. **2.** An early afternoon party at which a light meal is served. [17th century : origin obscure.]

luncheon meat *n.* Meat, often pork, processed and pressed into a small loaf shape and usually tinned.

luncheon voucher *n. Abbr.* **L.V.** A trademark for a voucher, given by an employer to an employee, that can be exchanged for food in certain shops and restaurants.

Lund (lōōnd). A market and industrial city north of Malmö, Sweden. It was the largest town in Scandinavia during the Middle Ages, and is now an educational centre with a university (founded in 1666) and technical institute (1961).

Lun·dy (lúndi). Island in the Bristol Channel off Hartland Point, Devon, England, preserved by the National Trust as a sanctuary for wild flowers, seals, and birds, particularly puffins.

lune (lōōn, lewn) *n.* A portion of a sphere enclosed between two semicircles having their common end points at opposite poles. [Latin *lūna,* moon.]

Lü·ne·burg (lōōnə-burg; *German* lǘnə-boork). City and river port in Lower Saxony, West Germany. It is also a spa. On Lüneburg Heath (Lüneburger Heide) to the south, the Nazi forces in the West surrendered to the Allies in May 1945.

lu·nette (lōō-nét, lew-) *n.* **1.** *Architecture.* **a.** A small, circular or crescent-shaped opening in a vaulted roof. **b.** A crescent-shaped or semicircular space, usually over a door or window, that may contain another window, a sculpture, or a mural. **2.** *Military.* A type of fieldwork fortification that has two projecting faces and two parallel flanks. **3.** A flattened, glass covering for a watch. **4.** *Roman Catholic Church.* A flat, round case with a hinged glass lid used for holding the consecrated host in a monstrance. [French, diminutive of *lune,* from Latin *lūna,* moon.]

lung (lung) *n.* **1.** Either of two spongy, saclike respiratory organs in air-breathing vertebrates, occupying the chest cavity together with the heart, and functioning to remove carbon dioxide from the blood and provide it with oxygen. **2.** A comparable invertebrate structure. [Middle English *lunge,* from Old English *lungen.*]

lunge¹ (lunj) *n.* **1.** A sudden thrust or pass, as with a sword or rapier. **2.** Any sudden forward movement or plunge.
~*v.* **lunged, lunging, lunges.** *—intr.* **1.** To make a thrust or pass. **2.** To move with a lunge. *—tr.* To thrust forward suddenly. [Earlier *allonge, elonge,* from French *allonger, alongier,* to lengthen, extend, from Vulgar Latin *allongāre* (unattested) : Latin *ad-* (towards) + *longus,* long.] **—lung·er** *n.*

lunge² *n.* A long rope or leather rein used for schooling or exercising a horse by someone on foot. Also called "lunging rein".
~*tr.v.* **lunged, lunging, lunges.** To school or exercise (a horse) by means of a lunge. [French *longe,* "long (rein)", from Latin *longus,* long.]

lung·fish (lúng-fish) *n., pl.* **-fishes** or collectively **lungfish.** Any of several elongated tropical freshwater fishes of the order Dipnoi (or Dipneusti), having lungs as well as gills, and in certain species constructing a mucus-lined mud covering in which to withstand an extended drought.

lun·gi, lun·gee (lōōng-gee) *n.* **1.** A loincloth, turban, or scarf, as worn by Indian men. **2.** The long piece of fabric used to form this. [Hindi, from Persian *lungī*†.]

Lungki. See **Zhangzhou.**

lung·worm (lúng-wurm) *n.* Any of various parasitic nematode worms that are parasites of the lungs of mammals, such as any of the family Metastrongylidae.

lung·wort (lúng-wurt || -wawrt) *n.* **1.** Any of several plants of the genus *Pulmonaria,* native to Europe, with long-stalked leaves and coiled clusters of blue or purple flowers. **2.** Any of various plants of the genus *Mertensia,* having drooping clusters of tubular, usually blue flowers. [Formerly used to treat lung diseases.]

lu·ni·so·lar (lōō-ni-sōlər, léw-) *adj.* Of, caused or measured by both the Sun and the Moon. [Latin *lūna,* moon + SOLAR.]

lu·ni·ti·dal (lōō-ni-tīd'l, léw-) *adj.* Of or pertaining to tidal phenomena caused by the Moon. [Latin *lūna,* moon + TIDAL.]

lunitidal interval *n.* The time elapsing between the Moon's transit at a place and the next high tide there.

lu·nu·la (lōō-new-lə, léw-) *n., pl.* **-lae** (-lee). Also **lu·nule** (-newl). A small crescent-shaped structure or marking; especially, the white crescent-shaped area at the base of a fingernail. [Latin *lūnula,* crescent-shaped ornament, "little moon", from *lūna,* moon.]

lu·nu·lar (lōō-new-lər, léw-) *adj.* Crescent-shaped.

lu·nu·late (lōō-new-lət, léw-, -lit, -layt) *adj.* Also **lu·nu·lat·ed** (-laytid). **1.** Small and lunular. **2.** Having lunular markings.

Luo·yang or **Lo·yang** (lwō-yáng). Formerly **Ho·nan** (ĥ-nán). Industrial city in Henan province, north central China. It is the market centre of an agricultural and coalmining region. An ancient city, it was a Chinese capital under the Han, Tang, and Song dynasties.

Lu·per·ca·li·a (lōō-pər-káyli-ə, léw-) *n.* A fertility festival in ancient Rome, celebrated on February 15 in honour of the pastoral god Lupercus. **—Lu·per·ca·li·an** *adj.*

lu·pin, *U.S.* **lu·pine** (lōō-pin, léw-) *n.* Any of various plants of the genus *Lupinus,* having tall spikes of brightly coloured flowers. [Middle English, from Latin *lupīnum,* from *lupīnus,* LUPINE (wolflike), from the ancient belief that it destroyed the soil.]

lu·pine (lōō-pīn, léw-) *adj.* **1.** Wolflike. **2.** Rapacious; ravenous. [Latin *lupīnus,* from *lupus,* wolf.]

lu·pu·lin (lōō-pew-lin, léw-) *n.* Minute yellowish-brown hairs from the female flowers of the hop plant, formerly used as a sedative. [New Latin *lupulus,* hop plant, diminutive of Latin *lupus,* wolf, hop plant + -IN.]

lu·pus (lōō-pəss, léw-) *n.* Any of several diseases of the skin and mucous membranes, many causing disfiguring lesions, especially: **1.** *Lupus vulgaris,* tuberculosis of the skin characterised by ulcerating, nodular facial lesions, especially around the nose and ears. **2.** *Lupus erythematosus,* a chronic inflammatory disease affecting the skin and internal organs characterised by a scaly red rash on the face. [New Latin, from Latin, wolf.]

Lupus *n.* A constellation in the Southern Hemisphere near Centaurus and Scorpius. [Latin *lupus,* wolf. See **lupine.**]

lurch¹ (lurch) *intr.v.* **lurched, lurching, lurches. 1.** To stagger. **2.** To roll or pitch suddenly or erratically, as a ship during a storm.
~*n.* **1.** A staggering or tottering movement or gait. **2.** An abrupt rolling or pitching. [From *lee-lurch,* variant of *lee-latch,* drifting to leeward.]

lurch² *n.* **1.** A position of difficulty or discomfort. Now used only in the phrase *to leave (someone) in the lurch.* **2.** In the game of cribbage, the losing position of a player who scores 30 points or less to the winner's 61. [French *lourche,* a game resembling backgammon, also a defeat or bad score in this game, probably from Middle High German *lurz,* left, wrong, "defeat".]

lurch·er (lúrchər) *n.* **1.** *Chiefly British.* A crossbred hunting dog, especially one formerly used by poachers. **2.** *Archaic.* A lurker; a sneak thief. [From obsolete *lurch,* to lurk, Middle English *lorchen,* variant of *lurken,* to LURK.]

lure (lewr, loor) *n.* **1. a.** Anything that entices, tempts, or attracts with the promise of gaining a pleasure or reward. **b.** An attraction or appeal. **2.** Any decoy used in catching animals; especially, an artificial bait used in catching fish. **3.** A bunch of feathers attached to a long cord, used in falconry to recall the hawk.
~*tr.v.* **lured, luring, lures. 1.** To attract by wiles or temptation; entice. **2.** To recall (a falcon) with a lure. [Middle English, from Old French *loirre,* bait, from Germanic *lōthr* (unattested).]
Synonyms: *lure, entice, inveigle, decoy, tempt, seduce, beguile.*

Lu·rex (léwr-eks, lóor-) *n.* A trademark for a shiny plastic-coated thread, or for a fabric made from this thread.

lur·gy, lurg·i (lúrgi) *n. Informal.* A disease or illness. Used humorously, often in the phrase *the dreaded lurgy.* [Phrase invented and popularised by the Goons (radio show).]

lu·rid (léwr-id, lóor-) *adj.* **1.** Causing shock or horror. **2.** Vivid; glaring; unnaturally bright. **3.** Glowing or glaring through a haze. **4.** *Rare.* Sallow in colour; pallid. —See Synonyms at **ghastly.** [Latin *lūridus,* pallid, ghastly, from *lūror*†, pale yellow, ghastliness.] **—lu·rid·ly** *adv.* **—lu·rid·ness** *n.*

lurk (lurk) *intr.v.* **lurked, lurking, lurks. 1.** To lie in wait, as in ambush or for some other evil purpose. **2.** To move furtively; sneak; slink. **3.** To exist unobserved or unsuspected. [Middle English *lurken,* probably frequentative of *luren,* LOWER (to frown).]

lurk·ing (lúrking) *adj.* Concealed; hitherto unacknowledged or unsuspected: *a lurking suspicion; lurking sympathy.*

Lu·sa·ka (lōō-saákə). Capital city and industrial centre of Zambia, central Africa. It replaced Livingstone (Maramba) as the capital of the then British colony of Northern Rhodesia in 1935.

Lu·sa·tia (loo-sáyshə, lew-). *German* **Lau·sitz** (lów-zits). Home of the Sorbs, an ancient Slav people. The area successively part of Brandenburg, Bohemia, Saxony, and Prussia, is now confined between the rivers Elbe and Oder in East Germany.

Lu·sa·tian (lōō-sáysh'n, -sáysh-yən || lew-) *n.* **1.** A native of Lusatia. **2.** A language, **Wendish** *(see).* **—Lu·sa·tian** *adj.*

lus·cious (lúshəss) *adj.* **1.** Sweet and pleasant to taste or smell; delicious: *a luscious melon.* **2.** Having strong sensory appeal; voluptuous. **3.** *Archaic.* Excessively rich or sweet; cloying. [Perhaps from Middle English *lucius,* possibly shortened from DELICIOUS.]

lush¹ (lush) *adj.* **lusher, lushest. 1.** Having or characterised by luxuriant growth or vegetation. **2.** Luxurious; opulent: *lush carpets.* **3.** Succulent; juicy. [Middle English *lusch,* lax, soft, perhaps variant of *lasche,* soft, watery, from Old French, lax, slack, from Latin *laxus,* spacious, loose.]

lung

THE BREATH OF LIFE FOR HUMAN BEINGS
How the lungs provide the body with oxygen to burn its fuel

Just as the furnace of a boiler needs air to burn its fuel and produce heat and power, so every living animal needs constant supplies of oxygen to burn up its intake of food and produce energy from it. In human beings, these oxygen needs are supplied by the lungs, two spongy organs in the chest that contain air sacs called alveoli. It is in the alveoli that carbon dioxide, the exhaust gas of the body's energy system, is exchanged for oxygen drawn from the air. The human body has some 750 million alveoli; laid out flat they would cover more than 40 square metres (50 square yards).

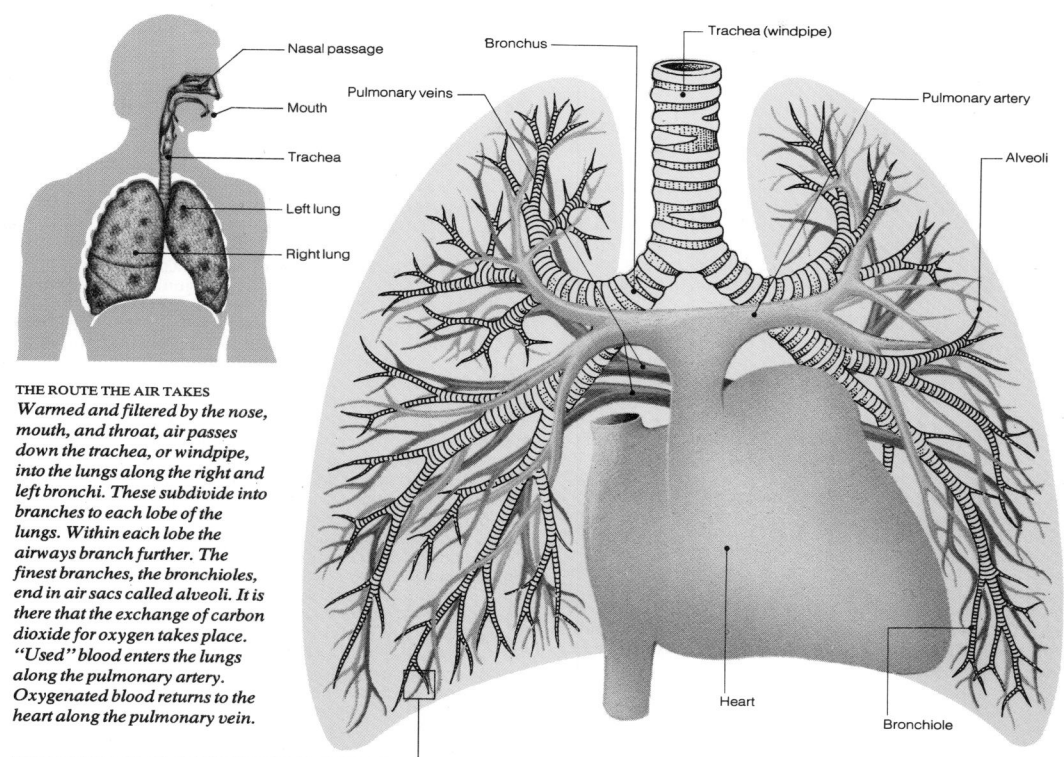

THE ROUTE THE AIR TAKES
Warmed and filtered by the nose, mouth, and throat, air passes down the trachea, or windpipe, into the lungs along the right and left bronchi. These subdivide into branches to each lobe of the lungs. Within each lobe the airways branch further. The finest branches, the bronchioles, end in air sacs called alveoli. It is there that the exchange of carbon dioxide for oxygen takes place. "Used" blood enters the lungs along the pulmonary artery. Oxygenated blood returns to the heart along the pulmonary vein.

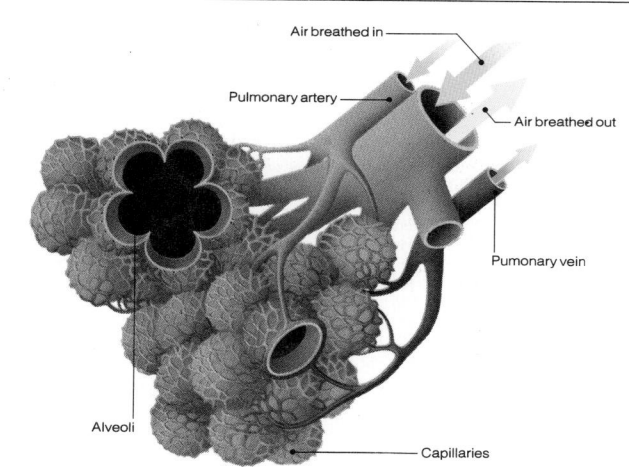

WHERE THE EXCHANGE TAKES PLACE

The airways of the lungs, branching and ever-branching, end in some 750 million alveoli, or air sacs, each surrounded by a network of minute, thin-walled blood vessels called capillaries. Carbon dioxide, a waste product of bodily processes, is carried to the alveoli in the bloodstream. It passes through the walls of the capillaries to be breathed out from the lungs. Molecules of haemoglobin capture oxygen from the air in the alveoli, and freshly oxygenated blood is returned to the heart, to be pumped on another circuit of the body. The entire exchange takes less than a second. The lungs can hold 4–5.5 litres (7–10 pints) of air, but someone at rest may take in only 0.4 litre (¾ pint) at a time, and breathe in and out less than 6 litres (10¼ pints) in a minute. During strenuous exercise, when the body needs more oxygen, this can increase nearly 25-fold to more than 140 litres (250 pints) a minute. Respiratory systems of other animals are similar.

---

lush² *n. Chiefly U.S. Slang.* **1.** A drunkard. **2.** Intoxicating drink. [18th century : perhaps humorous use of LUSH, opulent, delicious.]
Lushün. See **Lüda.**
Lusitania. See **Portugal.**
lust (lust) *n.* **1.** Sexual desire, especially excessive or unrestrained. **2.** Any overwhelming desire or craving: *a lust for power.* ~*intr.v.* **lusted, lusting, lusts.** To have or feel lust. Usually used with *after* or *for.* [Middle English *lust,* Old English *lust.*]
lust·ful (lúst-f'l) *adj.* **1.** Excited by lust. **2.** *Archaic.* Vigorous.
lus·tral (lústrəl) *adj.* **1.** Of, pertaining to, or used in a rite of purification. **2.** Pertaining to a lustrum. [Latin *lustrālis,* from LUSTRUM.]
lus·trate (luss-tráyt ‖ *U.S.* lúss-trayt) *tr.v.* **-trated, -trating, -trates.** To purify ceremonially. [Latin *lustrāre,* to purify, from LUSTRUM.]
—**lus·tra·tion** (luss-tráysh'n) *n.* —**lus·tra·tive** (lústrə-tiv) *adj.*
lus·tre, *U.S.* **lus·ter** (lústər) *n.* **1.** Soft reflected light; sheen; gloss. **2.** Brilliance or radiance of light; brightness. **3. a.** Brilliant or radiant quality. **b.** Glory; distinction. **4.** A glass pendant, especially on a chandelier. **5.** A decorative object, such as a chandelier having glass pendants. **6.** Any of various substances, such as wax, used to give an object a gloss or polish. **7.** An opalescent, shiny glaze on pottery and porcelain. Also used adjectivally: *lustre* ware. **8.** *Mineralogy.* The appearance of a mineral surface judged by its brilliance and ability to reflect light in comparison with metals, glasses, diamonds, and other materials regarded as standards.

lychee *The warty-skinned fruits of the lychee tree,* Nephelium chinensis, *contain a pale and jelly-like edible flesh. The tree is native to southern China but is now grown commercially in warm regions around the world.*

~*v.* lustred *or U.S.* -tered, -tring *or U.S.* -tering, -tres *or U.S.* -ters. —*tr.* To give a gloss or sheen to. —*intr.* To become or be lustrous. [French *lustre*, from Italian *lustro*, from *lustrare*, to brighten, from Latin *lūstrāre*, to purify, make bright, from *lūstrum*, purification.]

lus·trous (lústrəss) *adj.* 1. Having a sheen. 2. Radiant; bright: *a lustrous gaze.* —See Synonyms at **bright.** —**lus·trous·ly** *adv.* —**lus·trous·ness** *n.*

lus·trum (lústrəm) *n., pl.* -trums *or* -tra. 1. A ceremonial purification of the entire ancient Roman population after the census every five years. 2. A period of five years. [Latin *lustrum.*]

lust·y (lústi) *adj.* -ier, -iest. 1. Full of vigour; robust. 2. Powerful; strong: *a lusty drink.* 3. Lustful. 4. *Archaic.* Merry; joyous. —**lust·i·ly** *adv.* —**lust·i·ness** *n.*

lu·su na·tu·rae (lōō-səss nə-téwr-ee, léw-, na-, -ī) *n.* A freak of nature. [Latin *lūsus nātūrae,* "a joke of nature".]

Luta. See **Lüda.**

lu·ta·nist, lu·te·nist (lōō-tən-ist, léw-, -t'n-) *n.* A lute player. [Medieval Latin *lūtānista,* from *lūtāna,* from Old French *lut,* LUTE.]

lute¹ (lōot, lewt) *n.* A musical stringed instrument having a body shaped like a pear halved lengthways and usually a bent neck with a fretted fingerboard with pegs for tuning it. [Middle English, from Old French *lut,* earlier *leut,* from Arabic *al-'ud,* "the wood".]

lute² *n.* A substance, such as dried clay or cement; used to pack and seal joints and other connections or seal a porous surface. ~*tr.v.* **luted, luting, lutes.** 1. To apply lute to. 2. To seal with lute. [Middle English, from Old French *lut,* from Latin *lutum,* mud, clay.]

lute-, luteo- *comb. form.* Indicates corpus luteum; for example, *lu-teal.* [New Latin (corpus) *luteum,* from Latin, neuter of *luteus,* yellow.]

lu·te·al (lōō-ti-əl, léw-) *adj.* Of or pertaining to the **corpus luteum** *(see)* or to the phase of the oestrous cycle during which it develops.

lu·te·in (lōō-ti-in, léw-, -teen) *n.* 1. A yellow pigment isolated from the corpus luteum and found in body fats and egg yolk. 2. A photosynthetic pigment found in green leaves and certain algae. [LUTEO- + -IN.]

lu·te·in·is·ing hormone (lōō-ti-in-īzing, léw-, -teen-) *n. Abbr.* **LH** A hormone, secreted by the anterior lobe of the pituitary gland, that stimulates ovulation and corpus luteum formation in female mammals and androgen synthesis by the interstitial cells of the testis in male mammals. Also called "interstitial-cell-stimulating hormone".

lu·te·o·tro·phic hormone (lōō-ti-ə-tróffik, léw-, -ō-, -trōfik) *n.* **Pro·lactin** *(see).* [LUTEO- + -TROPHIC.]

lu·te·ous (lōō-ti-əss, léw-) *adj.* Of a light or moderate greenish yellow. [Latin *lūteus,* yellow, from *lūtum†,* yellow weed.]

lu·te·ti·um, lu·te·ci·um (lōō-tée-shi-əm, lew-, -shəm) *n. Symbol* **Lu** A silvery-white rare-earth element that is exceptionally difficult to separate from the other rare-earth elements, used in nuclear technology. Atomic number 71, atomic weight 174.97, melting point 1 652°C, boiling point 3 327°C, relative density 9.872, valency 3. [New Latin, from *Lūtētia,* Latin name for Paris, native city of its discoverer, Georges Urbains (1872–1938), French chemist.]

Lu·ther (lōō-thər, léw-; *German* lōōtər), **Martin** (1483–1546). German leader of the Reformation. Luther, an Augustinian monk, visited Rome in 1510–11 and was shocked by the wealth and corruption of the papacy. In 1517 he nailed to the chapel door at Wittenberg castle 95 theses attacking the sale of papal indulgences. In 1520, Luther launched the Protestant Reformation, publicly burning a papal bull of condemnation against him, and was excommunicated in 1521. He refused to recant at the Diet of Worms (1521), and was sheltered by the Elector of Saxony. He translated the New Testament into German and married in 1525, breaking the rule of celibacy. Luther confirmed the Augsburg Confession (1530), which effectively established the Lutheran churches.

Lu·ther·an (lōō-thərən, léw-) *adj.* 1. Of or pertaining to Martin Luther or his religious teachings and especially to the doctrine of justification by faith alone. 2. Of, pertaining to, or designating the branch of the Protestant Church adhering to the views of Martin Luther. ~*n.* A member of the Lutheran Church. —**Lu·ther·an·ism** *n.*

Lutheran Church *n.* The Protestant denomination founded in Germany in the 16th century by Martin Luther.

Lu·thu·li (lōō-tōōli), **Albert (John)** (c. 1898–1967). Black South African political leader. As president of the African National Congress, he came into conflict with the government of white-ruled South Africa. He advocated universal suffrage, but rejected the use of violence as a means of attaining it. He was awarded the Nobel Peace prize in 1960.

Lu·tine bell (lōō-téen) *n.* A bell kept at Lloyd's and rung to announce news of a missing ship insured at Lloyd's, once for bad news and twice for good. [Bell salvaged from the *Lutine,* ship wrecked in 1799.]

Lu·ton (lōōt'n). Manufacturing town in Bedfordshire, England, which expanded rapidly in the 19th century with the straw hat industry. It now manufactures vehicles and aircraft components.

Lut·yens (lúchənz, lút-yənz), **Sir Edwin (Landseer)** (1869–1944). British architect. He combined traditional and modern influences in his work, which includes the Whitehall Cenotaph. He was chief architect of New Delhi (1912–30).

Lutyens, (Agnes) Elizabeth (1906–83). British composer, daughter of Sir Edwin. She has written many chamber and orchestral works, often using a 12-tone technique, as well as music for films.

lutz (lōōts) *n., pl.* **lutzes.** A jump by an ice-skater, performed by taking off from the back off one blade, making a complete spin in the air, and landing on the rear of the other blade. [Probably after Gustave *Lussi* (born 1898), Swiss figure skater.]

lux (luks) *n., pl.* **lux.** *Abbr.* **lx** The SI unit of illumination, equal to one lumen per square metre. [Latin *lūx,* light.]

lux·ate (luk-sáyt, lúksayt) *tr.v.* -ated, -ating, -ates. To put out of joint; dislocate. [Latin *luxāre,* from *luxus,* dislocated.] —**lux·a·tion** (luk-sáysh'n) *n.*

luxe *n.* See **de luxe.**

Lux·em·bourg (Ville) (lúksəm-burg; *French* lükso̅N-bo̅or (veel). *German* **Lux·em·burg** (lōōks'm-bo̅ork). Capital of the Grand Duchy of Luxembourg, on the river Alzette. The city has several offices of the European Economic Community, the European Court of Justice, and the European Parliament, and a commercial radio station transmitting in six languages.

Luxembourg, Grand Duchy of. *French* **Grand-Duché de Luxembourg.** Small independent state in northwest Europe. The north is part of the Ardennes, the south being a continuation of Lorraine. From 1443 to 1839 it was ruled in turn by Burgundians, Spaniards, Austrians, French, and Dutch. Its neutrality was guaranteed in 1867. Luxembourg joined with Belgium and the Netherlands in the Benelux Customs Union in 1948. Area, 2 586 square kilometres (998 square miles). Population, 400,000. Capital, Luxembourg (Ville). See map at **Belgium.**

Lux·em·burg (lúksəm-burg; *German* lōōks'm-bo̅ork), **Rosa** (c. 1870–1919). German socialist leader, born in Poland. She took part in the revolution of 1905 while in Russian Poland. With Karl Liebknecht she led the antiwar Spartacus party (1916), which became the German Communist Party after the war. She was arrested and killed by soldiers during the Spartacist revolt in Berlin.

Lux·or (lúk-sawr || lóok-). *Arabic* **Al Uqsor.** Town on the east bank of the river Nile in central Egypt. It covers part of the site of the ancient city of Thebes, with the great Temple of Luxor.

lux·u·ri·ant (lug-zéwr-i-ənt, ləg-, -zhóor-) *adj.* 1. Growing abundantly, vigorously, or lushly. 2. Exuberantly elaborate; ornate; florid. 3. Abundantly fertile or productive. [Latin *luxuriāns (stem luxuriant-),* present participle of *luxuriāre,* to grow profusely, LUXURIATE.] —**lux·u·ri·ance** *n.* —**lux·u·ri·ant·ly** *adv.*

Usage: There is a slight tendency in modern English to use *luxuriant* where one would expect *luxurious* (a luxuriant meal), but this should be avoided. *Luxury* is being increasingly used as an adjective in place of *luxurious* (luxury hotel, luxury goods) to refer to something of exceptional quality or comfort.

lux·u·ri·ate (lug-zéwr-i-ayt, ləg-, -zhóor-) *intr.v.* -ated, -ating, -ates. 1. To take luxurious pleasure; indulge oneself. Used with *in.* 2. To proliferate. 3. To grow profusely. [Latin *luxuriāre,* to grow profusely, from *luxuria,* excess, LUXURY.]

lux·u·ri·ous (lug-zéwr-i-əss, ləg-, -zhóor-). 1. Sensuously comfortable: *a luxurious hot bath.* 2. Characterised by or contributing to luxury. 3. Fond of or given to luxury. —See Synonyms at **sensuous.** —**lux·u·ri·ous·ly** *adv.* —**lux·u·ri·ous·ness** *n.*

lux·u·ry (lúkshəri || lúgzhəri) *n., pl.* -ries. 1. Rich or sumptuous comfort. 2. An item or activity that is expensive, pleasurable, and unnecessary: *I can't afford luxuries.* 3. Anything conducive to physical comfort. 4. The enjoyment of sumptuous living. ~*adj.* 1. Providing sumptious comfort: *a luxury hotel.* 2. Of high quality, and usually expensive: *luxury goods.* [Middle English *luxurie,* from Old French, from Latin *luxuria,* excess, rankness, from *luxus,* excess, extravagance.]

Luzern. See **Lucerne.**

Lu·zon (lōō-zón). Main island of the Philippines. It has fertile volcanic soils and many fine natural harbours, including Manila Bay, on which the country's capital, Manila, is situated.

lv. livre.

L.V. luncheon voucher.

Lvov (lə-vóv; *Russian* lvawf). *Polish* **Lwów** (lvo̅of); *Ukrainian* **Lviv** (lviv); *German* **Lem·berg** (lém-bairk). Capital of the Lvov Region of the Ukraine, U.S.S.R. It is a centre of communications, learning, trade, and industry. The city was founded by Ukrainians in the 13th century and captured by the Poles a century later. From 1772 it was the capital of Galicia, an Austrian province. The Poles regained the city in 1919, but formally ceded it to the U.S.S.R. in 1945.

Lvov, Georgi Yevgenyevich, Prince (1861–1925). Russian prime minister (1917). He headed the first provisional government after the February Revolution of 1917.

Lw The former symbol for the element lawrencium (now Lr).

L.W. low water.

lwei (lway) *n.* A unit of currency equal to 1/100 of the kwanza of Angola.

lx lux.

LXX Septuagint.

–ly¹ *adj. suffix.* Indicates: 1. Having the characteristics of or resembling; for example, **sisterly.** 2. Appearing or occurring at specified intervals; for example, **weekly, monthly.** [Middle English *-li, -lich,* Old English *-lic,* "having the form of".]

–ly² *adv. suffix.* Indicates: 1. In a specified manner or degree; for example, **gradually, partly.** 2. From a specified point of view; for example, **politically.** 3. At every specified interval; for example, **hourly, daily.** 4. The event or statement in question is viewed as specified; for example, **regrettably, ironically.** 5. Speaking in a specified way; for example, **frankly, honestly.** [Middle English *-li, -liche,* Old English *-lice,* from *-lic,* -LY (adjectival suffix).]

ly·ase (lí-ayz, -ayss) *n.* Any of a group of enzymes that catalyse the formation of double bonds or the addition of groups to double bonds. [LYO- + -ASE.]

ly·can·thrope (lī́kən-thrōp, lī-kán-) *n.* **1.** A werewolf. **2.** A person suffering from the delusion that he is a wolf. [New Latin *lycanthropus,* from Greek *lukanthrōpos,* werewolf : *lukos,* wolf + *anthrōpos,* man.]

ly·can·thro·py (lī-kánthrəpi) *n.* **1.** The mythical, supernatural ability to assume the form and characteristics of a wolf. **2.** A psychological illness in which someone believes himself to be a wolf.

ly·cée (lée-say) *n. pl.* **lycées.** A state secondary school in France or a French-speaking country. [French, "lyceum".]

ly·ce·um (lī-sée-əm) *n.* A large public building or hall. Now used chiefly in place names. [Latin *Lyceum,* garden near temple of Apollo where Aristotle taught, from Greek *Lukeion,* neuter of *Lukeios* (epithet of Apollo).]

ly·chee, li·chee, li·chi, li·tchi (lī-chee, -chée ‖ lée-, lichi) *n.* **1.** A Chinese tree, *Nephelium chinensis,* bearing edible fruit. **2.** The small, round fruit of this tree, consisting of a thin, brown, scaly shell enclosing a white fleshy interior with a seed at the centre. [Cantonese *lai ji.*]

lych gate. Variant of **lich gate.**

lych·nis (lík-niss) *n.* Any of various plants of the genus *Lychnis,* which includes the campions and ragged robin. [New Latin *Lychnis,* from Latin, a kind of rose of fiery colour, from Greek *lukhnis,* from *lukhnos,* lamp.]

Lyc·i·a (líssi-ə, líshi-ə ‖ líshə). Ancient country and later a Roman province on the southwestern coast of Asia Minor.

Lyc·i·an (líssi-ən, líshi-ən ‖ líshən) *n.* **1.** An inhabitant of ancient Lycia. **2.** The Anatolian language of the Lycians. —**Lyc·i·an** *adj.*

ly·co·pod (lík-ə-pod, -ō-) *n.* Any pteridophyte plant of the order Lycopodiales; especially, any of the genus *Lycopodium.*

ly·co·po·di·um (lī̄kə-pṓdi-əm) *n.* **1.** Any plant of the genus *Lycopodium;* a **club moss** (see). **2.** The yellowish powdery spores of certain club mosses, especially *Lycopodium clavatum,* used in fireworks and explosives, and as a covering for pills. [New Latin *Lycopodium,* "wolf foot" (from its claw-shaped roots) : Greek *lukos,* wolf + *pous* (stem *pod-*), foot.]

Lydda. See **Lod.**

lyd·dite (líddīt) *n.* An explosive consisting chiefly of picric acid. [From *Lydd,* town in Kent where it was first tested.]

Lyd·i·a (líddi-ə, líd-yə). Ancient country which in 546 B.C. covered all Asia Minor west of the river Halys, excluding Lycia. The Lydians probably coined the first money.

Lyd·i·an (líddi-ən, líd-yən) *n.* **1.** A member of a people of ancient Lydia. **2.** The Anatolian language of this people. —**Lyd·i·an** *adj.*

Lydian mode *n. Music.* A church mode with F as final and C as dominant. [After an ancient Greek mode associated with Lydia.]

lye (lī) *n.* **1.** The alkaline liquid containing potassium hydroxide obtained by leaching wood ashes. **2. Potassium hydroxide** *(see).* **3. Sodium hydroxide** *(see).* [Middle English *lye, ley(e),* Old English *lēag.*]

Ly·ell (lī́-əl), **Sir Charles** (1797–1875). British geologist. He established the theory of uniformitarianism. His *Principles of Geology* (1830–33) made him the most influential geologist of the 19th century.

ly·ing (lī́-ing) *adj.* Untruthful; false. See Synonyms at **dishonest.**

ly·ing-in (lī́-ing-in) *n., pl.* **lyings-in** or **lying-ins.** The confinement of a woman in childbirth.

lyme grass (līm) *n.* A perennial grass, *Elymus arenarius,* with bluish-green leaves, that grows on sand dunes in north temperate regions. [Perhaps from LIME (respelling influenced by genus name, *Elymus*), alluding to its binding effect (as lime in mortar).]

Lymeswold *n.* A trademark for a mild, soft, blue-veined English cheese.

lymph (limf) *n.* **1.** A clear, transparent, watery, sometimes faintly yellowish liquid, derived from body tissues, that contains mainly white blood cells and travels through the lymphatic system to return to the venous blood stream through the thoracic duct. It acts to remove bacteria and certain proteins from the tissues, to transport fat from the intestines, and to supply lymphocytes to the blood. **2.** *Archaic.* A spring or stream of pure, clear water. [Latin *lympha,* earlier *lumpa, limpa,* water.]

lym·phad·e·ni·tis (limf-addi-nī́-tiss, lim-fáddi-) *n.* Inflammation of the lymph nodes. [New Latin : *lympha,* LYMPH + Greek *adēn,* gland + -ITIS.]

lym·phan·gi·tis (límfan-jī́-tiss) *n.* Inflammation of the lymphatic vessels, most commonly occurring during a streptococcal infection. [LYMPH + ANGIO- + -ITIS.]

lym·phat·ic (lim-fáttik) *adj.* **1.** Of or pertaining to lymph, a lymph vessel, or a lymph node. **2.** Sluggish; indifferent; phlegmatic. ~*n.* A vessel that conveys lymph. [New Latin *lymphaticus,* from *lympha,* LYMPH.]

lymphatic system *n.* The interconnected system of spaces and vessels between tissues and organs by which lymph is circulated throughout the body and returned to the venous system.

lym·pha·tism (límfə-tiz'm) *n.* A pathological condition of infancy and childhood characterised by overgrowth of the lymphatic structures, spleen, and bone marrow.

lym·pha·ti·tis (límfə-tī́tiss) *n.* Inflammation of lymph nodes or vessels. [LYMPHAT(IC) + -ITIS.]

lymph node *n.* Any of numerous oval or round bodies, located along the lymphatic vessels, that supply lymphocytes to the circula-

lymphatic system

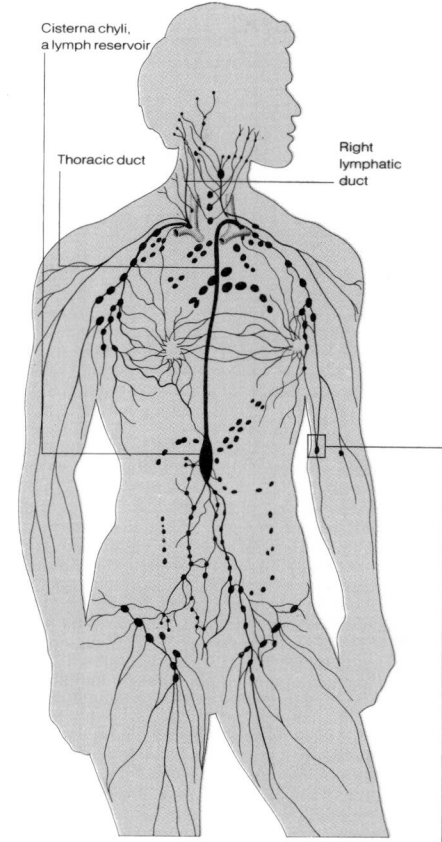

THE FLUID THAT FIGHTS DISEASE
How the body strikes back at bacteria

Cisterna chyli, a lymph reservoir

Thoracic duct

Right lymphatic duct

A painful, swollen throat is a sign that your lymphatic system is doing its job of protecting the body against infection. For the swelling is the result of a "battle" between bacteria and white blood cells in the lymph nodes.

These white cells, known as lymphocytes, seek out, surround, and ingest bacteria and other foreign proteins. The lymph nodes also act as filters against bacteria and foreign particles such as tiny bits of dead tissue; and they produce antibodies that give immunity against specific diseases.

Lymph is a colourless fluid that flows through a network of vessels and joins the bloodstream where the lymph system drains into veins at the base of the neck.

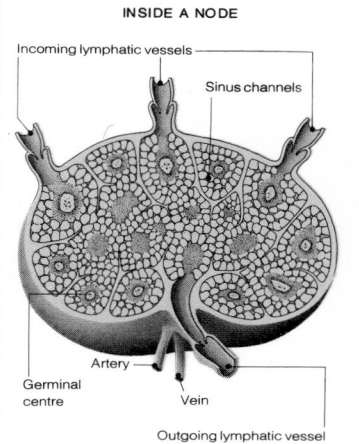

INSIDE A NODE

Incoming lymphatic vessels

Sinus channels

Artery

Germinal centre

Vein

Outgoing lymphatic vessel

NETWORK OF PROTECTION *Bean-sized lymph glands, or nodes, are situated throughout the body, with concentrations in the neck, armpits, chest, abdomen, and groin.*

Infection-fighting white blood cells, the lymphocytes, are produced in the germinal centres. Sinus channels filter out bacteria and foreign particles.

tory system and remove bacteria and foreign particles from the lymph. Also called "lymph gland".

lympho-, lymph– *comb. form.* Indicates lymph or lymphatic system; for example, **lymphocyte, lymphoma.** [From LYMPH.]

lym·pho·blast (limf-ō-blaast, -ə-, -blast) *n.* An abnormal cell found in the blood in a type of leukaemia, formerly believed to be an immature lymphocyte. [LYMPHO- + -BLAST.] —**lym·pho·blas·tic** (-blástik) *adj.*

lym·pho·cyte (límf-ō-sīt, -ə-) *n.* A white blood cell formed in lymphoid tissue, as in the lymph nodes, spleen, thymus, and tonsils, and constituting between 22 to 28 per cent of all leucocytes in the normal adult human's blood. Also called "lymph cell". [LYMPHO- + -CYTE.] —**lym·pho·cyt·ic** (-sittik) *adj.*

lym·pho·cy·to·sis (límf-ō-sī-tṓ-siss, -ə-) *n. Pathology.* A form of leucocytosis in which lymphocytes are greatly increased in number. —**lym·pho·cy·tot·ic** (-tóttik) *adj.*

lym·phoid (límfoyd) *adj.* Of or pertaining to lymph or the lymphatic system. [LYMPH(O)- + -OID.]

lymphoid tissue *n.* Tissue responsible for the production of lymphocytes, which includes the lymph nodes, tonsils, thymus, and spleen.

lym·pho·ma (lim-fṓmə) *n., pl.* **-mata** (-tə) or **-mas.** Any of various malignant tumours of lymph nodes or lymphoid tissue. —**lym·pho·ma·toid, lym·phom·a·tous** (-fṓmətəss, -fómmətəss) *adj.*

lym·pho·poi·e·sis (límf-ō-poy-ée-siss, -ə-) *n., pl.* **-ses** (-seez). The formation of lymphocytes. [New Latin : LYMPHO- + -POIESIS.] —**lym·pho·poi·et·ic** (-éttik) *adj.*

lyn·ce·an (lin-sée-ən) *adj.* **1.** Of or resembling a lynx. **2.** *Rare.* Sharp-sighted. [Latin *lyncēus,* from Greek *Lunkeios,* pertaining to Lynceus (an Argonaut noted for his keenness of sight), from *Lunkeos,* Lynceus.]

lynch (linch) *tr.v.* **lynched, lynching, lynches.** To kill (a person suspected of a crime), especially by hanging, without due process of law. [After Charles *Lynch* (1736–96), Virginia planter and justice of the peace.]

Lynch (linch), **Jack,** born John Lynch (1917–). Prime minister of the Republic of Ireland (1966–73, 1977–79). He was a Fianna Fáil M.P. from 1948, and tried to moderate his party's demands for a united Ireland.

lynch·et (linchit) *n.* A man-made terrace on a hillside resulting from culturation, probably in the Iron Age. [From dialect *linch,* from Old English *hlinc,* ridge.]

lynch law *n.* The punishment of persons suspected of crime without due process of law.

lynch mob *n.* A group or crowd of people wishing to kill or succeeding in killing a person they suspect of a crime.

lynchpin. Variant of **linchpin.**

lynx (lingks) *n.* Any of several wild cats of the genus *Lynx;* especially, *L. lynx* (or *canadensis*), of Eurasia and northern North America, having thick, soft fur, a short tail, and tufted ears. [Latin, from Greek *lunx.*]

Lynx *n.* A constellation in the Northern Hemisphere near Ursa Major and Auriga.

lynx-eyed (lingks-īd) *adj.* Keen of vision; sharp-sighted.

lyo– *comb. form.* Indicates dispersion or dissolution; for example, **lyophilic.** [Green *luein,* to loosen, dissolve.]

Lyon (lée-ON; *French* lyón). English **Ly·ons** (lī-ənz). Administrative centre of the Rhône département in east central France, and the country's second metropolis after Paris. A communications, cultural, and financial centre, the city grew after Italians introduced silk manufacturing in the 15th century. It now specialises in artificial fibres, and also makes cars, clothing, chemicals, and machinery.

ly·on·naise (lée-ə-náyz, lī-, *French* -néz) *adj.* Cooked, usually fried, with onions: *potatoes lyonnaise.* [French *à la Lyonnaise,* in the manner of LYON.]

ly·o·phil·ic (lī-ō-fíllik, -ə-) *adj. Chemistry.* Of, pertaining to, or exhibiting a strong affinity between the dispersed phase and the dispersing medium of a colloid. [LYO- + -PHILIC.]

ly·o·pho·bic (lī-ō-fóbik, -ə-) *adj. Chemistry.* Of, pertaining to, or exhibiting a lack of strong affinity between the dispersed phase and the dispersing medium of a colloid. [LYO- + PHOBIC.]

Ly·ra (lī̄r-ə) *n.* A constellation in the Northern Hemisphere near Cygnus and Hercules containing the star Vega. [Latin *lyra,* LYRE.]

ly·rate (lī̄r-ət, -it, -ayt) *adj.* 1. Having a form or curvature suggestive of a lyre. 2. Designating leaves having a large terminal lobe and smaller lateral lobes. [New Latin *lyratus,* from Latin *lyra,* LYRE.]

lyre (līr) *n.* A stringed instrument of the harp family used to accompany a singer or reader of poetry, especially in ancient Greece. [Middle English *lire,* Old French, from Latin *lyra,* from Greek *lura†.*]

lyre-bird (līr-burd) *n.* Either of two Australian birds, *Menura superba* (or *M. novaehollandae*) or *M. alberti,* the male of which has a long tail spread during courtship in a lyre-shaped display.

lyr·ic (lírrik) *adj.* 1. a. Of or pertaining to a category of poetry or verse that is distinguished from the narrative and dramatic, is typically lucid and simple or direct, with smooth, regular rhythms, and is often considered representational of music in its sound patterns. b. Writing this type of verse. 2. a. Of or pertaining to the lyre or harp. b. Appropriate for accompaniment by the lyre. 3. *Music.* a. Having a singing voice of a light, rather than dramatic quality. b. Pertaining to or designating opera or musical drama, especially of the lighter kind.
~*n.* 1. A lyric poem. 2. *Often plural.* The words of a song, especially a popular song. [Old French *lyrique,* of a lyre, from Latin *lyricus,* from Greek *lurikos,* from *lura,* LYRE.]

lyr·i·cal (lírrik'l) *adj.* 1. Highly enthusiastic or emotional; exuberant. 2. Romantic and poetic. 3. Lyric.

lyr·i·cism (lírri-siz'm) *n.* 1. The character or quality of subjectivism and sensuality of expression, especially in the arts. 2. An intense outpouring of exuberant emotion.

lyr·i·cist (lírri-sist) *n.* A writer of lyrics for a popular song or musical.

lyr·ism (lírriz'm) *n.* Lyricism. [French *lyrisme,* from Greek *lurismos,* played on the lyre, from *lura,* LYRE.]

lynx *A short-tailed wild cat found in the coniferous forests of North America, Europe, and Asia, the lynx lives alone or in small groups and hunts at night. It is a good climber and strong jumper and generally feeds on small mammals.*

lyr·ist (lírrist *for sense 1;* līr-ist *for sense 2*) *n.* 1. *Rare.* A lyricist. 2. One who plays a lyre. [Latin *lyristês,* one who plays a lyre, from Greek *luristês,* from *lura,* LYRE.]

lyse (līz, līss) *v.* **lysed, lysing, lyses.** —*tr.* To cause (something) to undergo lysis. —*intr.* To undergo lysis. [From LYSIS.]

–lyse, *U.S.* **–lyze** *v. comb. form.* Indicates the causing of chemical decomposition; for example, **pyrolyse.** [From -LYSIS.]

Ly·sen·ko (li-séng-kō; *Russian* -kə), **Trofim Denisovich** (1898–1976). Soviet biologist. Stalin backed his belief that acquired characteristics could be inherited. This seriously hampered Soviet research into chromosomes and the mechanics of inheritance. —**Ly·sen·ko·ism** *n.*

ly·ser·gic acid (lī-sérjik, li-) *n.* A crystalline alkaloid, $C_{16}H_{16}N_2O_2$, derived from ergot and used in medical research. [From LYS(O)- + ERG(OT) + -IC.]

lysergic acid di·eth·yl·am·ide (dī-ethil-ámmīd) *n.* See **LSD.**

ly·sin (lī-sin) *n.* A specific antibody that acts to destroy blood cells, tissues, or microorganisms. [LYS(O)- + -IN.]

ly·sine (lī-seen, -sin) *n.* An essential, crystalline amino acid, $C_6H_{14}N_2O_2$, used in nutrition studies, in culture media, and to fortify foods and feeds. [LYS(O)- + -INE.]

ly·sis (lī-siss) *n.* 1. *Biochemistry.* The dissolution or destruction of red blood cells, bacteria, or other antigens by a specific lysin. 2. *Medicine.* The gradual subsiding of the symptoms of an acute disease. [New Latin, from Greek *lusis,* a loosing, deliverance, from *luein,* to loosen, unbind.]

–lysis *n. comb. form.* Indicates dissolving or decomposition; for example, **hydrolysis.** [New Latin, from Greek *lusis.* See **lysis.**]

lyso–, lys– *comb. form.* Indicates loosening, dissolving, or freeing; for example, **lysin, lysogenesis.** [Greek *lusis,* a loosening. See **lysis.**]

ly·so·gen·e·sis (lī-sō-jénnə-siss) *n.* The production of lysins. [New Latin : LYSO- + -GENESIS.]

Ly·sol (lī-sol ‖ -sōl) *n.* A trademark for a liquid antiseptic and disinfectant. [LYS(O)- + -OL (phenol).]

ly·so·some (lī-sō-sōm, -sə-) *n.* Any of a number of particles in the cytoplasm of cells that contain enzymes capable of breaking down substances in the cell. [LYSO- + -SOME (body).]

ly·so·zyme (lī-sō-zīm, -sə-) *n.* An enzyme occurring naturally in tears, capable of destroying the cell walls of certain bacteria, thereby acting as a mild antiseptic. [LYSO- + -ZYME.]

–lyte *n. comb. form.* Indicates a substance that can be decomposed by a specified process; for example, **electrolyte.** [Greek *lutos,* soluble, from *luein,* to loosen.]

lyt·ic (líttik) *adj.* 1. Of, pertaining to, or causing lysis. 2. Of or pertaining to a lysin. [Greek *lutikos,* able to loosen, laxative, from *lutos,* capable of being untied, from *luein,* to untie, loosen. See **lysis.**]

–lytic *adj. comb. form.* Indicates a loosening or dissolving; for example, **hydrolytic.** [Greek *lutikos,* able to loose. See **lytic.**]

lyt·ta (líttə) *n., pl.* **lyttae** (líttee). A thin cartilaginous strip on the underside of the tongue of certain carnivorous mammals, such as dogs. [Latin, "worm under a dog's tongue" (believed to cause madness), from Greek *lutta, lussa,* madness, frenzy.]

Lyt·tle·ton (litt'l-tən), **Humphrey** (1921–). British jazz trumpeter. His *Bad Penny Blues* (1955) was the first jazz record to get into the Top Twenty in Britain.

Lyt·ton (litt'n), **Edward George Earle Bulwer-Lytton, 1st Baron,** also known as Owen Meredith (1803–73). British novelist. He wrote *Pelham* (1828) and *The Last Days of Pompeii* (1834), a historical romance. He sat as a Liberal, then a Tory, M.P., and was Secretary for the colonies (1858–59).

Lytton (Edward) Robert Bulwer-Lytton, 1st Earl of Lytton. (1831–91). British colonial administrator and poet, the son of the novelist, Bulwer-Lytton. He was viceroy of India (1876–80) and instigated the second Afghan War (1878–80) in which the British occupied Kabul. He was ambassador to France (1887–91).

Lyublin. See **Lublin.**

M

m, M (em) *n., pl.* **m's** or *rare* **ms, Ms** or **M's**. **1.** The 13th letter of the modern English alphabet. **2.** Any of the speech sounds represented by the letter **M**.

m, M, m., M. *Note:* As an abbreviation or symbol, *m* may be a small or a capital letter, with or without a full stop. Established forms or those generally preferred precede the definition. When no form is given, all four forms are in general use in that sense. **1. m, M** *Printing.* **a.** em. **b.** pica em. **2. M** *Physics.* Mach number. **3. M.** majesty (in titles). **4.** male; masculine. **5. M.** mark (currency). **6. m, M** *Physics.* mass. **7. M.** master (in titles). **8. M.** medieval. **9.** medium. **10. M** mega-. **11. M.** member (in titles). **12. m., M.** meridian. **13. M** *Chemistry.* metal. **14. m** metre (measure). **15. M** *Logic.* middle term of a syllogism. **16. m.** mile. **17. m** milli-. **18. m, M.** million. **19. M.** minim (liquid measure). **20. m, M** *Physics.* modulus. **21. M** *Chemistry.* molar. **22. M** *Physics.* moment. **23. M.** Monday. **24. M.** *French.* Monsieur. **25.** month. **26. M** motorway. **27. M** *Physics.* mutual inductance. **28. m., M.** noon [Latin *meridies.*] **29. M** Roman numeral for 1,000 [Latin *mille.*] **30.** The 13th in a series; 12th when *J* is omitted.

M1 *n. Economics.* See **money supply**.

M2 *n. Economics.* See **money supply**.

M3 *n. Economics.* See **money supply**.

ma (maa ‖ *U.S. also* maw) *n. Informal.* Mother. [Shortened form of MAMMA.]

mA milliampere.

M.A. **1.** Master of Arts [Latin *Magister Artium.*] **2.** mental age.

Ma'am (mam, maam, məm). Contraction of *Madam.*

maar (mar) *n.* A flat-bottomed, roughly circular volcanic crater of explosive origin, often filled with water. [Dialectal North German *maar,* from Middle Low German *mare,* lake.]

Maas. See **Meuse**.

Maas·tricht or **Maes·tricht** (maȧ-strik̲h̲t, *Dutch* maa-strík̲h̲t). Industrial city in southeast Netherlands, capital of Limburg province. Its cathedral of St. Servatius, founded in the sixth century, is the country's oldest church.

Maa·zel (maa-zél), **Lorin** (1930–). U.S. conductor, born in France. He has worked with the German Opera, Berlin (1965–71), and is director of the Vienna State Opera.

Mab·i·nog·ion (mábbi-nóggi-on) *n.* A collection of medieval Welsh folk tales translated by Lady Charlotte Guest in 1838–49. [Welsh, plural of *mabinogi,* "tales of youth", from *mab,* youth, son, from Old Welsh *map,* from Common Celtic *makwos* (unattested), son.]

mac, mack (mak) *n. Chiefly British Informal.* A mackintosh.

Mac (mak) *n. U.S. Slang.* Used as a familiar term of address. [Abstracted from (especially Scottish) surnames (*Macdonald, Macleod,* and so on).]

Mac-, M'-, Mc- *prefix.* Indicates son of. Used in surnames. [Gaelic *Mac-,* from Common Celtic *makkos* (unattested), son.]

Mac. Maccabees (books of the Apocrypha).

ma·ca·bre (mə-kaȧ-brə, ma-, -bər) *adj.* **1.** Suggesting the horror of death and decay; gruesome; ghastly. **2.** Associated with or suggestive of the *danse macabre,* in which an allegorical figure of death summons those about him to dance with him to their deaths. —See Synonyms at **ghastly**. [French, ghastly, from Old French *Danse Macabre,* the Dance of Death, probably originally *Danse Macabé,* "the Maccabean Dance", translation of Medieval Latin *Chorea Maccabaeorum,* probably referring to a representation of the slaughter of the Maccabees in a miracle play.] —**ma·ca·bre·ly** *adv.*

ma·ca·co (mə-kaȧ-kō, -káy-) *n. pl.* **-cos.** Any of various lemurs; especially, the species *Lemur macaco.* [French *mococo†.*]

mac·ad·am (mə-káddəm) *n.* **1.** A surface, especially of a road, made of layers of compacted small stones, now usually bound with tar or asphalt. **2.** The material used to make this surface. [After John L. McADAM.]

mac·a·da·mi·a (máckə-dáymi-ə) *n.* Any of five trees of the genus *Macadamia,* native to eastern Australia; especially, *M. tetraphylla* which has edible, nutlike seeds called macadamia nuts. [New Latin, after John Macadam (1827–1865), Australian chemist.]

mac·ad·am·ise, mac·ad·am·ize (mə-káddə-mīz) *tr.v.* **-ised, -ising,**

-ises. To construct or pave (a road) with macadam. —**mac·ad·am·i·sa·tion** (-mī-záysh'n ‖ *U.S.* -mi-) *n.* —**mac·ad·am·is·er** *n.*

Macao. See **Macau**.

ma·caque (mə-kaȧk, -kák) *n.* Any of several short-tailed monkeys of the genus *Macaca,* of southeast Asia, Japan, Gibraltar, and north Africa. See **Barbary ape, rhesus monkey**. [French, from Portuguese *macaco,* from Fiot *makaku,* "some monkeys" : *ma,* numerical sign + *kaku,* monkey.]

mac·a·ro·ni, mac·ca·ro·ni (máckə-rŏ́ni) *n., pl.* **-roni** (for senses 1 and 2), **-nis** or **-nies** (for all senses). **1.** A pasta of wheat flour in the form of hollow tubes or other shapes, dried, and prepared for eating by boiling. **2.** A dish containing or consisting of macaroni. **3.** A fashionable fop of the 18th century. [Italian (Neapolitan dialect), plural of *maccarone,* from Late Greek *makaria,* food made from barley.]

mac·a·ron·ic (máckə-rónnik) *adj.* **1.** Of or pertaining to a literary composition containing a mixture of vernacular words with Latin words or with non-Latin words that are humorously given Latin endings: *macaronic verse.* **2.** Of or involving a mixture of two or more languages.
~*n. Usually plural.* A macaronic composition. [New Latin *macaronicus,* "like macaroni" (i.e., a crude rustic mixture), from Italian *maccaroni,* MACARONI.]

macaroni cheese *n.* A dish consisting of macaroni coated in a cheese sauce and baked.

mac·a·roon (máckə-rŏ́on) *n.* A chewy biscuit made with sugar, egg whites, and ground almonds or coconut. [French *macaron,* from Italian *maccarone,* MACARONI.]

Mac·Ar·thur (mə-kárthər), **Douglas** (1880–1964). U.S. general. Much-decorated in World War I, he rose to become U.S. Chief of Staff (1935–37). He was recalled from retirement by the Army in 1941, but failed to prevent the invasion of the Philippines by the Japanese. He regained the Philippines (1944–45), and with the surrender of Japan became Supreme Commander of the Allied Forces in Japan (1945–51). He was Commander (1950–51) of the United Nations Forces in the Korean War, until President Truman relieved him of his U.S. command for insubordination.

Ma·cas·sar oil (mə-kássər) *n.* A perfumed oil used, especially in the 19th century, for the hair. [After *Macassar* (Makassar), port and region in Celebes (Sulawesi), Indonesia, which was claimed to be the source of the ingredients.]

Ma·cau or **Ma·cao** (mə-ków). Portuguese overseas province in southeast China. The Portuguese founded a trading post between the Xi Jiang and Zhu Jiang (Pearl river) estuaries in 1557, and paid China tribute for it until 1849, when it became a free port. In 1887 China formally leased Macau to Portugal, but the colony declined following the rise of Hong Kong. It is now a gambling, tourist, and transit trade centre. Area, 16 square kilometres (6 square miles). Capital, Macau Town. —**Mac·a·nese** (máckə-néez ‖ -néess) *n.*

Ma·cau·lay (mə-káwli), **Dame (Emilie) Rose** (1881–1958). English writer. Her books include *Potterism* (1920), *Some Religious Elements in English Literature* (1931), and *The Towers of Trebizond* (1956). She was made a D.B.E. (1958).

Ma·cau·lay, Thomas Babington, 1st Baron (1800–59). English historian, politician, and poet. He was elected an M.P. (1830), then after a period in India, became Secretary for War (1839–41). He was made a peer in 1857. Besides his essays for the Edinburgh Review, he wrote the uncompleted *History of England* (1849–61) and *Lays of Ancient Rome* (1842).

ma·caw (mə-káw) *n.* Any of various tropical and subtropical American parrots of the genera *Ara* and *Anodorhynchus,* including the largest parrots, characterised by long sabre-shaped tails, curved powerful bills, and usually brilliant plumage. [Portuguese *macaú,* perhaps from *macaúba,* a kind of palm (on whose fruit the parrot feeds), from Tupi *macahuba, macahiba* : probably *maca-,* thorn (of African origin) + *-yba,* tree.]

Mac·beth (mək-béth, mak-) (died 1057). King of Scotland (1040–57). In pursuit of a tenuous claim to the throne, he killed Duncan in battle (1040) to become king. He was later killed by

macaque *Macaca mulatta, the Indian rhesus monkey (above), is one of a dozen species of this Asian primate. It is widely used in medical research because of its biological similarity to humans.*

macaw *The macaw parrot probably gets its name because it feeds chiefly on the large nuts of the macaw palm, cracking them open with its large hooked beak. The blue and yellow macaw (above) is native to South America.*

Malcolm, son of Duncan. Shakespeare loosely based *Macbeth* on his life.

Macc. Maccabees (books of the Apocrypha).

Mac·ca·be·an (máckə-beé-ən) *adj.* Of or pertaining to Judas Maccabeus or to the Maccabees.

Mac·ca·bees (máckə-beez) *pl.n.* **1.** A Jewish dynasty of patriots, high priests, and kings of the second and first centuries B.C. See Judas **Maccabeus.** **2.** *Abbr.* **Mac., Macc.** Four books in the Old Testament Apocrypha, the first two of which tell about the feats of this family. In the Protestant churches, all four books are apocryphal; in the Roman Catholic and Eastern Orthodox churches, the first two are canonical. Also called in the Douay Bible "Machabees".

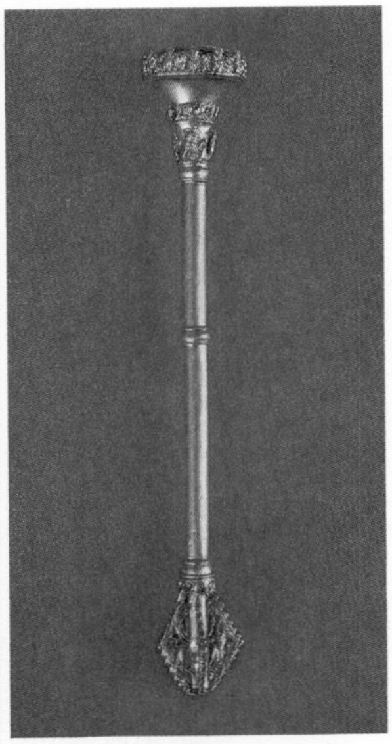

mace *These heavy metal clubs, often fearsomely spiked, were developed as weapons in the Middle Ages after the adoption of plate armour made knights almost invulnerable to sword thrusts. This ceremonial mace was probably made in the 15th century; it is now a symbol of office carried on formal occasions by the mayor of Newtown in the Isle of Wight, England.*

Mac·ca·be·us (máckə-beé-əss), **Judas** (died 160 B.C.). Jewish patriot, most famous of the Maccabees; leader of a Jewish revolt against Syria in 166 B.C. His rededication of the Temple at Jerusalem (164 B.C.) is commemorated by the Feast of Chanukkah.

mac·ca·boy (máckə-boy) *n.* A perfumed snuff made in Martinique. [French *macouba,* after *Macouba,* district of Martinique.]

maccaroni. Variant of **macaroni.**

Mac·cles·field (máck'lz-feeld). Market town in Cheshire, northwest England. It is the silk-milling centre of England.

Mac·Diar·mid (mək-dúr-mid || mak-), **Hugh,** born Christopher Murray Grieve (1892–1978). Scottish poet, Marxist, and founder member of the Scottish Nationalist Party. He wrote in Scots dialect, his early work including *Sangschaw* (1925) and *Penny Wheep* (1926). *A Drunk Man Looks at the Thistle* (1926), giving his views on Scottish independence, was a landmark in modern Scots poetry.

Mac·Don·ald (mək-dónn'ld || mak-), **Flora** (1722–90). Scottish Jacobite heroine. On the Isle of Benbecula, she met Prince Charles Edward Stuart, the Young Pretender, who was in hiding after Culloden (1746). She took him, disguised as a maid, to Skye, and he escaped to France. She was imprisoned briefly in the Tower.

MacDonald, (James) Ramsay (1866–1937). Britain's first Labour prime minister, born in Scotland. He became an M.P. (1906) and prime minister and Secretary of State for foreign affairs (1924). He was out of parliament (1924–29), but returned as prime minister of a minority government until he lost the support of his own party (1931). He then formed a coalition government made up mainly of Conservatives and resigned in 1935.

Macdonald, Sir John Alexander (1815–91). Scottish-born Canadian politician, the first prime minister (1867–73, 1878–91) of the Dominion of Canada. He was a powerful advocate of the movement which led to Canadian confederation in 1867.

Mac·don·nell Ranges (mák-də-nél, mək-dónn'l). A group of mountain ranges in southern Northern Territory, Australia. The highest point is Mount Ziel (1 510 metres; 4,955 feet).

mace[1] (mayss) *n.* **1.** A heavy medieval war club, usually with a spiked or flanged metal head, used to crush armour. **2.** A ceremonial staff borne or displayed as the symbol of authority of a legislative body. **3.** A macebearer. [Middle English, from Old French *mace, masse,* from Vulgar Latin *mattea*† (unattested), club.]

mace[2] *n.* An aromatic spice made from the dried, waxy, scarlet or yellowish covering that partly encloses the kernel of the nutmeg. [Middle English, formed as singular of *macis* (wrongly taken to be plural), from Medieval Latin, misreading of Latin *macir,* from Greek *makir,* an Indian spice.]

Mace (mayss) *n.* **Chemical Mace** *(see).*

~*tr.v.* **Maced, Macing, Maced.** *Often small* **m.** To spray with Chemical Mace.

mace·bear·er (máyss-bair-ər) *n.* An official who carries a mace of office. Also called "mace", "macer".

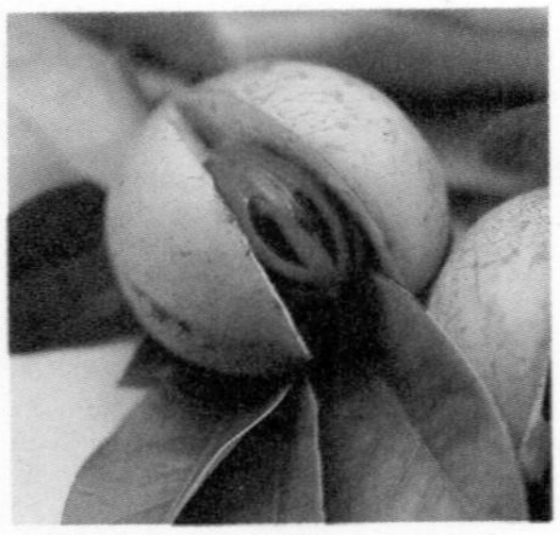

mace *The waxy red coating on the seed of the nutmeg tree (above) is dried and powdered to produce mace, which is used to scent perfumes and soaps as well as in cooking.*

Maced. Macedonia; Macedonian.

mac·é·doine (mássi-dwaán, -dwaan) *n.* **1.** A mixture of finely cut or diced vegetables or fruits, sometimes jellied, served as a salad, dessert, or appetiser. **2.** Any mixture; a medley; a hotchpotch. [French *macédoine,* "Macedonian" (the population of Macedonia is a mixture of various peoples).]

Mac·e·do·ni·a (mássi-dṓni-ə). *Abbr.* **Maced.** Region in the Balkans, in southeast Europe. Largely mountainous, it was peopled by Slavs in the sixth century A.D. and is now divided between Bulgaria, Greece, and Yugoslavia. A powerful empire under Philip II and his son Alexander the Great (fourth century B.C.), Macedonia was later ruled by the Romans, Byzantine Greeks, Bulgars, Serbs, and Turks. The present division resulted largely from the Second Balkan War (1913).

Mac·e·do·ni·an (mássi-dṓni-ən) *adj. Abbr.* **Maced.** Of or pertaining to ancient or modern Macedonia, or the people or languages of these regions.

~*n. Abbr.* **Maced.** **1.** A native or inhabitant of ancient or modern Macedonia. **2.** The language of ancient Macedonia, having characteristics regarded as Indo-European. **3.** The Slavonic language of modern Macedonia.

mac·er (máy-sər) *n.* **1.** A macebearer. **2.** A Scottish usher in a law court.

mac·er·ate (mássə-rayt) *v.* **-ated, -ating, -ates.** —*tr.* **1.** To soften (a solid substance) by soaking or steeping in a liquid, sometimes using heat. **2.** To separate (a solid substance) into constituents by soaking. **3.** To cause to become lean; emaciate, usually by starvation. —*intr.* To become macerated; undergo macerating. [Latin *mācerāre,* to soften.] **—mac·er·a·tion** (-ráysh'n) *n.* **—mac·er·a·tor, mac·er·a·ter** *n.*

Mac·gil·li·cud·dy's Reeks (mə-gílli-kuddiz reeks). Mountain range in County Kerry, Republic of Ireland. It lies between the Lakes of Killarney and Lough Caragh and rises to 1 041 metres (3,414 feet) at Carrantuohill, the highest mountain in Ireland.

Mach, mach (mak, maak) *n.* **Mach number** *(see).*

Mach (maakh, maak; *German* makh), **Ernst** (1838–1916). Austrian physicist and philosopher. He gave his name to the **Mach number,** and contributed to the philosophy of scientific positivism.

mach. machine; machinery; machinist.

Mach·a·bees (máckə-beez). In the Douay Bible, **Maccabees** *(see).*

mach·air (mákhər) *n.* **1.** A whitish, almost entirely calcareous sand forming undulating lowlands along the coasts of western Scotland and the Hebrides, and providing light, arable soils. **2.** A coastal lowland formed from such sand. [Gaelic *machair(e).*]

Ma·chel (ma-shél, mə-), **Samora (Moïsés)** (1933–). Mozambique politician. As leader of the Mozambique Liberation Front (FRELIMO), he led the movement against Portuguese rule (1966–74). He became the first president of independent Mozambique (1975).

ma·chet·e (mə-chétti, -shétti, -cháyti) *n.* Also **ma·tchet** (máchit). A large, heavy knife with a broad blade, used for cutting vegetation and as a weapon. [American Spanish, from Spanish, diminutive of *macho,* axe, club, hammer, from Late Latin *marcus*†, hammer.]

Mach·i·a·vel·li (mácki-ə-vélli), **Niccolò** (1469–1527). Italian statesman and writer. As diplomat and statesman, he served the Florentine Republic (1498–1512). His book, *The Prince* (published 1532), describes the achievement and maintenance of power by a determined ruler indifferent to moral considerations.

Mach·i·a·vel·li·an (mácki-ə-vélli-ən) *adj.* **1.** Of or pertaining to Niccolò Machiavelli. **2.** Of or pertaining to Machiavellianism. **3.** *Often small* **m.** Devious; cunning.

~*n.* One who believes in or practises Machiavellianism.

Mach·i·a·vel·li·an·ism (mácki-ə-vélli-ə-niz'm) *n.* Also **Mach·i·a·vel·lism** (-véll-iz'm). The political doctrine of Machiavelli, which denies the relevance of morality in political affairs and holds that craft and deceit are justified in pursuing and maintaining political power; political opportunism.

ma·chic·o·late (mə-chíckō-layt, ma-, -chíckə-) *tr.v.* **-lated, -lating, -lates.** To build or furnish with machicolations. [Old French *machicoler,* from Anglo-Latin *machicollāre,* from Provençal *machacol* : *macar,* crush + *col,* neck.] **—ma·chic·o·la·ted** *adj.*

ma·chic·o·la·tion (mə-chíckō-láysh'n, ma-, -chíckə-) *n.* **1. a.** A projecting gallery at the top of a castle wall or above an entrance, supported by a row of corbelled arches, having openings in the floor through which stones and boiling liquids could be dropped on attackers. **b.** Any of these openings. **c.** Any of these corbelled arches. **2.** *Usually plural.* A row of small corbelled arches used as an ornamental architectural feature.

mach·i·nate (mácki-nayt, -máshi-) *v.* **-nated, -nating, -nates.** —*tr.* To devise (a plot). —*intr.* To plot. [Latin *māchinārī,* from *māchina,* contrivance, MACHINE.] **—mach·i·na·tor** *n.*

mach·i·na·tion (mácki-náysh'n, máshi-) *n.* **1.** The act of plotting. **2.** *Usually plural.* A hostile intrigue. —See Synonyms at **conspiracy.**

ma·chine (mə-sheén) *n. Abbr.* **mach.** **1. a.** Any system or device formed and connected to alter, transmit, and direct applied forces in a predetermined manner to accomplish a specific objective, such as the performance of useful work. **b.** Any of a number of simple devices, such as the lever, the pulley, the wedge, the screw, or the inclined plane, that alters the magnitude or direction, or both, of an applied force. In this sense, also called "simple machine". **2.** Any such system or device together with its power source and auxiliary equipment, for example, a car, aircraft, or jackhammer. **3. a.** Any system or device, such as an electronic computer, that performs or assists in the performance of a human task. **b.** Any automated device, such as a slot machine. **4.** *Archaic.* **a.** An intricate natural system or organism, such as the human body. **b.** A functional unit of such a system, for example, an organ such as the heart or kidney. **5.** A person who acts in a rigid, mechanical, or unfeeling manner. **6. a.** Any complex system, organisation, or agency of people that functions in what appears to be an inexorable manner: *the military machine; a propaganda machine.* **b.** Any established group of people controlling a political or other organisation. Often used derogatorily: *the party machine.* **7.** A **deus ex machina** *(see).*

~*v.* **machined, -chining, -chines.** —*tr.* To make, cut, shape, or finish using a machine, for example a sewing machine. —*intr.* To undergo machining: *This metal machines easily.* [French, from Old French, from Latin *māchina,* engine, contrivance, from Doric Greek *makhana,* from *makhos,* contrivance, means.] **—ma·chin·a·ble** *adj.*

machine bolt *n.* A bolt with a square or hexagonal head.

machine finish *n.* A finish on paper surfaces, **mill finish** *(see).*

machine gun *n.* An automatic gun, usually mounted, that fires rapidly and repeatedly. Compare **submachine gun.**

ma·chine-gun (mə-sheén-gun) *tr.v.* **-gunned, -gunning, -guns.** To fire at or kill with a machine gun.

~*adj.* Fast and staccato.

machine language *n.* Any of various systems of symbols used to code information that is to be fed into a computer. Also called "machine code".

ma·chine-read·a·ble (mə-sheén-reédəb'l) *adj.* Able to be fed directly into a computer. Said of data stored magnetically or on punched cards or punched tape.

ma·chin·er·y (mə-sheénəri) *n., pl.* **-ies.** *Abbr.* **mach.** **1.** Machines or machine parts collectively. **2.** The working parts of a particular machine. **3. a.** An organised, highly interdependent system, often

machine gun

"THE DEVIL'S SPRINKLER"

How sustained firing comes from "waste" energy

A machine gun will fire a continuous stream of bullets as long as the trigger is pressed and ammunition fed in by belt or magazine. The automatic mechanism for cartridge ejection and reloading is powered by the gun's "waste" energy – the force of the recoil or the gas generated by the explosion of the cartridge. Because of its deadly fire power, the weapon became known as "The Devil's sprinkler".

The earliest machine guns had multiple barrels; the first practical one was the hand-cranked Gatling gun invented by an American, Richard Gatling, in 1862. A five-barrelled Gatling gun could fire 700 rounds a minute, but it had to be mounted on a field carriage and was heavy and awkward to use.

The first automatic machine gun was the recoil-operated Maxim gun produced in 1884 by another American, Hiram Maxim (who was later knighted in Britain). It was single-barrelled and weighed about 27 kilograms (60 pounds). The British army used it in the Sudan in 1896, and it was used throughout World War I by both sides. Development trends were towards lighter weapons, and the gas-operated Lewis light machine gun, weighing about 12 kilograms (26 pounds), was also extensively used from 1915.

The Bren gun, first manufactured by Skoda in Czechoslovakia and weighing 9.5 kilograms (21 pounds), was the standard British infantry machine gun of World War II. It could be fired by one man at up to 500 rounds a minute. Lighter but less powerful submachine guns for firing from the hip or shoulder were also in use. The best known were the Sten gun, and the Thompson (or Tommy) gun invented in the 1920s by a retired U.S. Ordnance officer to combat gangsters. In the 1982 Falklands War, British infantry used the gas-operated General Purpose Machine Gun capable of firing 750-1,000 rounds a minute.

Machine guns proved ideal for using in aircraft, and in 1940 Battle of Britain Spitfires were armed with wing-mounted Browning guns with a fire power of 1,200 rounds a minute. Later developments for aircraft and armoured vehicles included cannon guns that could fire both rifle ammunition and small shells, and the multibarrelled Vulcan MiniGun powered by an electric motor and capable of 6,000 rounds a minute; this was used in Vietnam.

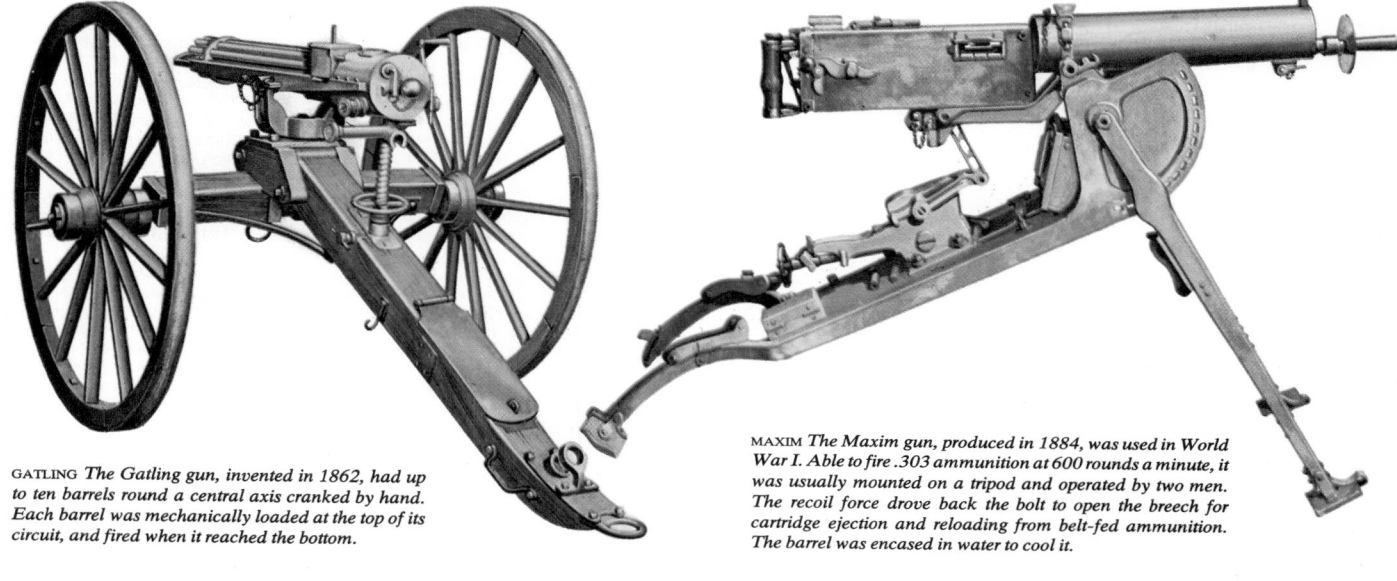

GATLING *The Gatling gun, invented in 1862, had up to ten barrels round a central axis cranked by hand. Each barrel was mechanically loaded at the top of its circuit, and fired when it reached the bottom.*

MAXIM *The Maxim gun, produced in 1884, was used in World War I. Able to fire .303 ammunition at 600 rounds a minute, it was usually mounted on a tripod and operated by two men. The recoil force drove back the bolt to open the breech for cartridge ejection and reloading from belt-fed ammunition. The barrel was encased in water to cool it.*

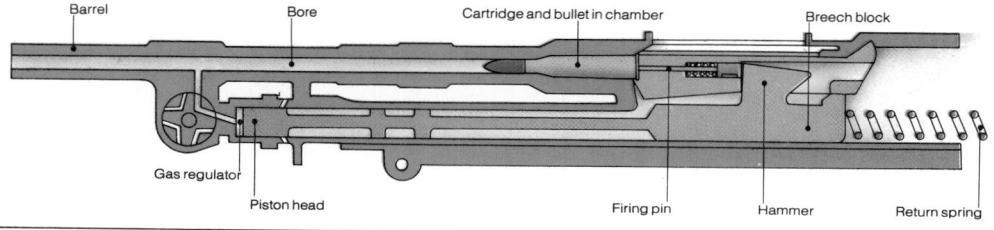

Barrel   Bore   Cartridge and bullet in chamber   Breech block
Gas regulator   Piston head   Firing pin   Hammer   Return spring

BREN *The Bren light machine gun took its name from Brno (Czechoslovakia) and Enfield, where it was developed in Britain. Gas from each cartridge explosion was channelled through a regulator to operate a piston that drove back the breech for cartridge ejection. A spring returned the breech, which picked up a new round on the way.*

---

exerting power: *bureaucratic machinery; the machinery of government.* **b.** Any system of related elements that operates in a definable manner: *the machinery of grammar.* **4.** A generally unsubtle device in literature, for example the introduction of a new character or an unlikely event, for bringing about a calculated effect such as a happy ending. See **deus ex machina.**

machine screw *n.* A screw with a thread along the whole length of its shank.

machine shop *n.* A workshop where power-driven tools are used for making, finishing, or repairing machines or machine parts.

machine tool *n.* A power-driven tool for machining, such as a lathe or milling machine.

ma·chine-wash (mə-shéen-wósh) *v.* **-washed, -washing,-washes.**
—*tr.* To wash (clothing, material, or the like) in a washing machine. —*intr.* To undergo washing in a washing machine without damage: *Wool doesn't machine-wash easily.* **—ma·chine-wash·able** *adj.*

ma·chin·ist (mə-shéenist) *n. Abbr.* **mach. 1.** One who operates and makes objects with a machine, for example a sewing machine, for a living. **2.** One skilled in operating machine tools. **3.** One who makes, operates, or repairs machines.

ma·chis·mo (ma-chíz-mō, mə-, -kíz- ‖ *U.S. also* maa-, -chéez-) *n.* An exaggerated sense of masculinity stressing such attributes as physical courage, virility, domination of women, and aggressiveness or violence. [Spanish : MACHO + -*ismo*, -ISM.]

Mach·me·ter (mák-meetər, maák-) *n. Sometimes small* **m.** An aircraft instrument that indicates speed in Mach numbers.

Mach number, mach number *n. Abbr.* **M** The ratio of the speed of an object to the speed of sound in the surrounding medium. For example, an aircraft moving twice as fast as sound is said to be travelling at Mach 2. [After Ernst MACH.]

ma·cho (máchō, maá-chō) *adj.* Characterised by machismo. ~*n., pl.* **machos.** *Chiefly U.S.* **1.** Machismo. **2.** A macho man. [Spanish, male, virile, from Latin *masculus,* MALE.]

ma·chree (mə-krée) *n. Irish.* A dear; a darling. Used as a term of endearment. [Irish *mo chroidhe,* "my heart".]

Mach's principle *n. Physics.* The principle that inertia is not an intrinsic property of a body but results from the presence of other matter in the universe. [After Ernst MACH.]

Ma·chu Pic·chu (maáchōo peék-chōo). Inca city northwest of Cuzco, Peru. Built on a mountain overlooking the Urubamba valley, it lay forgotten after the Spanish conquest in the 16th century until discovered almost intact in 1911.

mach·zor, mah·zor (maak-zór, maakh-) *n., pl.* **machzorim** or **-zors.** A Jewish prayer book containing rituals prescribed for holidays and festivals. Compare **siddur.** [Hebrew, "cycle".]

Maciás Nguema. See **Bioko.**

macintosh. Variant of **mackintosh.**

Mac·in·tosh (máckin-tosh), **Charles** (1766–1843). British chemist and inventor. He produced a waterproof material (patented 1823) by dissolving rubber in naphtha, a by-product of tar, and sandwiching it between layers of cloth.

mack¹. Variant of **mac** (mackintosh).

mack² (mak) *n. Slang.* A pimp. [Shortening of obsolete *mackerel*, from Old French *maquerel*, from Middle Dutch *makelaer*, broker.]

Mac·kay (mə-kī). Seaport of eastern Queensland, Australia. Built on the Pioneer river, it processes and exports sugar.

Mac·ken·zie¹ (mə-kénzi). District in Canada's Northwest Territories. It is rich in gold, oil, zinc, and uranium, and is peopled mainly by Eskimos and North American Indians. Yellowknife is the capital.

Mackenzie². River in Northwest Territories, Canada. It flows from Great Slave Lake to the Arctic Ocean and is navigable from June to October. The Finlay-Peace-Mackenzie system is Canada's longest river (4 212 kilometres; 2,635 miles).

Mackenzie, Alexander¹ (1822–92). First Liberal prime minister (1873–78) of the Dominion of Canada. He left Scotland to settle in Canada in 1842 and was elected to the Canada assembly in 1861.

Mackenzie, Sir Alexander² (c. 1755–1820). Canadian fur-trader and explorer, born in Scotland. He charted the Mackenzie river (1789) and was the first man to cross the North American continent north of Mexico.

Mackenzie, Sir (Edward Montague) Compton (1883–1972). British novelist. His books include *Sinister Street* (1914) and *Whisky Galore* (1947, filmed 1949).

mack·er·el (máckrəl, máckərəl) *n., pl.* **-els** or collectively **mackerel**. 1. Any of several marine fishes of the family Scombridae, found worldwide. Some species are important food fishes, especially the Atlantic mackerel, *Scomber scombrus*, which has dark, wavy bars on the back and a silvery belly. 2. Any of the smaller fishes of the suborder Scombroidea, such as the **Spanish mackerel** *(see).* 3. Any of various fishes resembling mackerel. [Middle English *makerel*, from Anglo-French, from Old French *maquerel†*.]

mackerel shark *n.* The **porbeagle** *(see).*

mackerel sky *n.* A striped formation of high, white cirrocumulus or altocumulus clouds suggesting the bars on a mackerel's back.

Mac·ker·ras (mə-kérrəss), **Sir (Alan) Charles** (1925–). Australian conductor and oboist. Born in the United States, he directed the Hamburg State Opera (1966–69) and the English National Opera (1970–77). He is noted for his interpretations of Janáček.

mack·i·naw (mácki-naw) *n. U.S.* 1. A short, double-breasted coat of heavy woollen material, usually plaid. 2. The cloth from which such a coat is made, usually of wool, often with a heavy nap. [After *Mackinac*, island in Lake Huron, Michigan, a 19th-century entrepôt where the cloth and the coat were traded.]

mack·in·tosh, mac·in·tosh (máckin-tosh) *n. Chiefly British.* 1. **a.** A raincoat of patented rubberised cloth. **b.** This cloth. 2. Any raincoat. Also informally called "mac", "mack". [After Charles MacINTOSH.]

Mack·in·tosh (máckin-tosh), **Charles Rennie** (1868–1928). Scottish architect and artist in the Art Nouveau style. He redesigned Glasgow School of Art (completed 1909).

mack·le (máck'l) *n.* Also **mac·ule** (máckewl). *Printing.* A spot, especially a blurred or double impression caused by a slipping of the type or a wrinkle in the paper.
~*v.* **mackled, -ling, -les.** Also **mac·ule, -uled, -uling, -ules.** —*tr.* To blur or double (a printed impression). —*intr.* To become blurred. [French *macule*, from Latin *macula*, spot.]

Mac·Lau·rin series (mə-kláwrin, -klórrin) *n. Mathematics.* An infinite series by which a function can be expressed in terms of the values of its derivatives when the independent variable is zero. It has the form $f(x) = f(0) + f'(0)/1! + f''(0)/2! + f'''(0)/3! + \ldots$. [After Colin *MacLaurin* (1698–1746), Scottish doctor and mathematician.]

mac·le (máck'l) *n.* 1. A mineral, **chiastolite** *(see).* 2. A crystalline form, **twin** *(see).* 3. A spot or discoloration in a mineral. [French, double crystal, from Old French *macle*, heraldic term for a "voided lozenge" (one diamond shape within another), originally a stylised mesh of a net, from Latin *macula*, mesh, hole in a net, spot.]

Mac·leish (mə-kléesh), **Archibald** (1892–1982). U.S. poet and playwright. He was Librarian of Congress (1939–44). His works include *Streets in the Moon* (1926), and he won Pulitzer prizes for *Conquistador* (1932), *Collected Poems 1917–52* (1952), and *J.B.* (1958).

Mac·leod (mə-klówd), **Iain (Norman)** (1913–70). British Conservative politician. He entered Parliament in 1950 and was Minister of Health (1952–55) and Minister of Labour (1955–59). As Colonial Secretary (1959–61) he encouraged the independence of Britain's African colonies, to the dismay of his party's right wing. He was Chairman of the Conservative Party (1961–63).

Mac·lise (mə-kléess), **Daniel** (1806–70). Irish painter and illustrator. He decorated the Royal Gallery of the House of Lords, and painted *Wellington and Blücher at Waterloo* (1859–61) and *The Death of Nelson* (1863–64).

Mac·Mil·lan (mək-míllən ‖ mak-), **Kenneth** (1929–). British choreographer. Beginning as a ballet dancer, he turned to choreography in 1953, directing the Royal Ballet, Covent Garden (1970–77) and becoming its principal choreographer (1977). His many creations include *Romeo and Juliet, Song of the Earth, Manon,* and *Isadora.*

MacMillan, (Maurice) Harold (1894–). British prime minister (1957–63). He became an M.P. in 1924, and during the 1930s he backed Churchill in condemning British appeasement of Hitler. After the re-election of the Conservatives (1951), he was in turn minister of Housing (1951–54), of Defence (1954–55), of Foreign Affairs (1955), and Chancellor of the Exchequer (1955–57).

Mac·Neice (mək-néess ‖ mak-), **(Frederick) Louis** (1907–63). British poet and playwright, born in Northern Ireland. He wrote satirical poetry in colloquial style in a literary group with Christopher Isherwood, Cecil Day-Lewis, and W.H. Auden. His works include *Blind Fireworks* (1929), *Autumn Journal* (1939), *Holes in the Sky* (1948), and *The Strings are False* (published 1965).

Mâ·con¹ (má-koɴ, máa-, -kon, -kən). French town, capital of the Saône-et-Loire département. Built on the river Saône, it is noted for its fine Burgundy wines.

Mâcon² *n.* A red or white Burgundy wine produced in the area around Mâcon.

Mac·on·chy (mə-kóngki), **Elizabeth** (1907–). British composer, who studied with Vaughan Williams. She has composed chamber music and twelve string quartets as well as choral and ballet music.

Mac·quar·ie (mə-kwórri). River of New South Wales, Australia, flowing 950 kilometres (590 miles) from the Blue Mountains to the Darling river.

Macquarie, Lachlan (1761–1824). Scottish colonial administrator. He was governor of New South Wales (1809–21), where he encouraged the convicts to learn trades, and extended the road system.

mac·ra·mé (mə-kráami, máckrə-may, -máy) *n.* 1. Ornamental lacework made by weaving and knotting cords, especially string, into a pattern. 2. The art of making this kind of lacework. [French, from Italian *macramè*, from Turkish *makrama*, napkin, towel, from Arabic *miqramah*, striped cloth.]

mac·ren·ceph·a·ly (mák-rən-séffəli, -ren-) *n.* Also **mac·ren·ce·pha·li·a** (-sə-fáyli-ə). *Pathology.* Abnormal enlargement of the brain. [MACR(O)- + ENCEPHAL(O)- + -Y.]

mac·ro (máckrō) *n., pl.* **-ros.** *Informal.* A macrocode.

macro-, macr- *comb. form.* Indicates: 1. Largeness in extent, duration, or size; for example, **macrocosm**. 2. Abnormal largeness or overdevelopment, especially in some part; for example, **macrencephaly**. Compare **micro-**. [Greek *makros*, large, long.]

mac·ro·bi·o·sis (máckrō-bī-ō-siss) *n.* Longevity. [Late Greek *makrobiōsis* : MACRO- + -BIOSIS.]

mac·ro·bi·o·ta (máckrō-bī-ōtə) *n.* The macroscopic plant and animal life of a particular region. [New Latin : MACRO- + Greek *biotos*, life.]

mac·ro·bi·ot·ics (máckrō-bī-óttiks) *n. Used with a singular verb.* The theory or practice of promoting longevity, especially by means of a diet consisting of completely unprocessed cereals and vegetables grown without chemical additives. [Greek *makrobiotos*, long-lived : MACRO- + *biotos*, life + -ICS.] —**mac·ro·bi·ot·ic** *adj.*

mac·ro·ceph·a·ly (máckrō-séffəli) *n.* Also **mac·ro·ce·pha·li·a** (-sə-fáyli-ə). *Pathology.* Abnormally large cranial capacity, often observed in the mentally handicapped. Also called "megacephaly", "megalocephaly". [French *macrocéphalie*, from *macrocéphale*, having a long head, from Greek *makrokephalos* : MACRO- + -CEPHALOUS.] —**mac·ro·ce·phal·ic** (-sə-fál-ik), **mac·ro·ceph·a·lous** (-séffələss) *adj.*

mac·ro·chem·is·try (máckrō-kémmiss-tri, -kemmiss-) *n.* Chemistry requiring neither microscopy nor microanalysis. Compare **microchemistry**. —**mac·ro·chem·i·cal** (-kémmik'l) *adj.*

mac·ro·cli·mate (máckrō-klī-mət, -mit) *n. Meteorology.* The climate of a large geographical area. Compare **microclimate**. —**mac·ro·cli·mat·ic** (-klī-máttik) *adj.*

mac·ro·code (máckrō-kōd) *n.* 1. A coding system that assembles sets of computer instructions. 2. A single code representing a set of computer instructions. Also informally called "macro".

ma·cro·con·sum·er (máckrō-kən-sewmər) *n.* An organism in an ecological community that feeds on other organisms or organic matter.

mac·ro·cosm (máckrō-koz'm, máckrə-) *n.* 1. The universe itself, or the concept of universe. 2. A system regarded as an entity containing subsystems. Compare **microcosm**. [French *macrocosme*, from Medieval Latin *macrocosmus*, from Late Greek *makros kosmos*, great world : MACRO- + *kosmos*, world.] —**mac·ro·cos·mic** (-kózmik) *adj.*

mac·ro·cyte (máckrō-sīt) *n. Pathology.* An abnormally large red blood cell associated with some forms of anaemia. [MACRO- + (ERYTHRO)CYTE.] —**mac·ro·cyt·ic** (-sittik) *adj.*

mac·ro·cy·to·sis (máckrō-sī-tō-siss) *n. Pathology.* A condition in which the blood contains macrocytes. —**mac·ro·cy·tot·ic** (-tóttik) *adj.*

mac·ro·e·co·nom·ics (máckrō-éekə-nómmiks, -éckə-) *n. Used with a singular verb.* The study of the economics of large-scale systems or aggregates, such as the economy of a country. Compare **microeconomics**. —**mac·ro·e·co·nom·ic** *adj.*

mac·ro·ev·o·lu·tion (máckrō-éevə-lóosh'n, -évvə-, -léwsh'n) *n.* Evolution involving whole genera, or larger groups, of organisms. —**mac·ro·ev·o·lu·tion·ar·y** *adj.*

mac·ro·ga·mete (máckrō-ga-méet, -gə-, -gámmeet) *n.* Also **meg·a·ga·mete** (méggə-). *Biology.* The larger of two conjugating cells, usually female, in protozoans. Compare **microgamete**.

mac·ro·glob·u·lin (máckrō-glóbbew-lin) *n.* A plasma globulin that has an unusually large molecular weight.

mac·ro·glob·u·lin·ae·mi·a (máckrō-glóbbew-li-néemi-ə) *n.* The presence in the blood of an abnormal form of macroglobulin.

mac·ro·graph (máckrō-graaf, -graf) *n.* A representation of an object which is at least as large as the object. [MACRO- + -GRAPH.]

ma·crog·ra·phy (mə-króggrəfi, ma-) *n.* 1. Examination of objects with the unaided eye. Compare **micrography. 2.** Abnormally large handwriting, sometimes indicating a nervous disorder. [MACRO- + -GRAPHY.] —**mac·ro·gra·phic** (máckrō-gráffik) *adj.*

mac·ro·mol·e·cule (máckrō-mólli-kewl) *n.* **1.** A very large molecule, especially in a natural or synthetic polymer, such as a protein or synthetic resin. **2.** A covalent or ionic crystal, such as diamond or salt, in which individual atoms or molecules cannot be distinguished. —**mac·ro·mo·lec·u·lar** (-mə-léckewlər, -mo-, -mō-) *adj.*

ma·cron (máckron ‖ *U.S. also* máy-kron, -krən) *n.* A diacritical mark placed above a vowel to indicate a long sound or phonetic value in pronunciation, such as the mark in (ō). Compare **breve.** [Greek *makron,* neuter of *makros,* long.]

mac·ro·nu·cle·us (máckrō-néw-kli-əss ‖ -nóo-) *n., pl.* **-clei** (-ī) or *rare* **-cleuses.** The larger of the two nuclei in ciliate protozoans, which is involved in the nonreproductive functions of the cell. Compare **micronucleus.**

mac·ro·nu·tri·ent (máckrō-néw-tri-ənt ‖ -nóo-) *n.* An element, such as carbon, hydrogen, oxygen, or nitrogen, required in relatively large proportion for growth and development.

mac·ro·phage (máckrō-fayj, máckrə-) *n.* A large phagocytic cell present in connective tissue, bone marrow, lymph nodes, and the like. [MACRO- + -PHAGE.] —**mac·ro·phag·ic** (-fájik) *adj.*

mac·ro·phys·ics (máckrō-fízziks) *n. Used with a singular verb.* The physics of macroscopic phenomena.

ma·crop·ter·ous (ma-króptərəss, mə-) *adj. Zoology.* Having unusually large wings. [Greek *makropteros* : MACRO- + -PTEROUS.]

mac·ro·scop·ic (máckrō-skóppik, máckrə-) *adj.* Also **mac·ro·scop·i·cal** (-'l). **1.** Large enough to be perceived or examined without instruments, especially as by the naked eye. **2.** Pertaining to observations made without magnifying instruments, especially by the naked eye; megascopic. **3.** *Physics.* Of or pertaining to systems or properties that depend on large numbers of atoms rather than individual atoms or molecules. **4.** Of, pertaining to, or concerned with large units or wide issues; large-scale. [MACRO- + -SCOP(Y) + -IC.] —**mac·ro·scop·i·cal·ly** *adv.*

mac·ro·spo·ran·gi·um (máckrō-spawr-ánji-əm, -spər-) *n., pl.* **-gia** (-ji-ə). *Botany.* A **megasporangium** (*see*).

mac·ro·spore (máckrō-spawr, máckrə- ‖ -spōr) *n. Botany.* A **megaspore** (*see*).

mac·u·la (máckew-lə) *n., pl.* **-lae** (-lee). Also **macule** (for sense 2). **1.** A spot, stain, blemish, or pit; especially, a discoloration of the skin caused by excess or lack of pigment. **2.** *Anatomy.* A small area distinguishable from surrounding tissue, such as the macula lutea. **3.** A sunspot. [Latin *macula,* spot, blemish.] —**mac·u·lar** (-lər) *adj.*

macula lu·te·a (lōō-ti-ə, léw-) *n., pl.* **maculae luteae** (-ee). *Anatomy.* An area in the eye near the centre of the retina at which visual perception is most acute. [New Latin, "yellow spot".]

mac·u·late (máckew-layt) *tr.v.* **-lated, -lating, -lates.** To spot, blemish, or pollute.
~*adj.* (-lət, -lit). **1.** Spotted or blotched. **2.** Stained; impure. [Middle English *maculaten,* to stain, from Latin *maculāre,* from *macula,* spot, blemish.]

mac·u·la·tion (máckew-láysh'n) *n.* **1.** The act of spotting or staining. **2.** A spotted or stained condition. **3.** The spotted markings collectively of a plant or animal, such as the spots of the leopard.

mac·ule (máckewl) *v.* **-uled, -uling, -ules.** —*tr.* To blur; mackle. —*intr.* To become blurred or mackled.
~*n.* **1.** *Printing.* Variant of **mackle. 2.** *Anatomy.* Variant of **macula.** [Middle English, from Old French, from Latin *macula,* spot, blemish.]

mad (mad) *adj.* **madder, maddest. 1.** Suffering from a disorder of the mind; insane. **2.** As if insane; temporarily or apparently deranged by violent sensations, emotions, or ideas: *mad with pain; mad with love.* **3.** *Informal.* Feeling or showing strong liking or enthusiasm. Used with *about, on,* or *over: mad about golf.* Sometimes used in combination: *golf-mad.* **4.** *Informal.* Angry; resentful. **5.** Lacking restraint or reason; wildly foolish; senseless. **6.** Marked by extreme excitement, confusion, or agitation; frantic. **7.** Boisterously gay; hilarious: *to have a mad time.* **8.** Affected by rabies; rabid. —**like mad.** *Slang.* Wildly; impetuously: *He drove like mad.* —**mad keen.** Wildly enthusiastic.
~*v.* **madded, madding, mads.** *Archaic.* —*tr.* To madden or make mad. —*intr.* To act, be, or become mad. [Middle English *madd,* Old English *gemǣdd,* past participle of *gemǣdan,* to madden, from *gemād,* mad.]

MAD mutually assured destruction.

Madagascan periwinkle *n.* A plant, *Catharanthus roseus* (or *Vinca rosea*), native to Madagascar, having pink or white flowers. It is a source of various alkaloids used in treating leukaemia.

Mad·a·gas·car (máddə-gáskər), **Democratic Republic of.** Island state off southeast Africa. Its coastal plains in the east and west rise to a central plateau. Rice-growing and livestock-rearing are the main occupations, and exports include chrome ore, coffee, vanilla, cloves, and meat. Made a French colony in 1896, it was granted self-rule as the Malagasy Republic in 1958 and full independence in 1960. It became a democratic republic in 1975. The island separated from Africa 150 million years ago and is noted for its unique wildlife. Area, 587 041 square kilometres (226,658 square miles). Population, 9,200,000. Capital, Antananarivo (Tananarive). —**Mad·a·gas·can** (-gáskən) *n.* & *adj.*

mad·am (máddəm) *n., pl.* **mesdames** (may-dám, -daám, máy-dam) (for sense 1) or **madams** (for senses 3 and 4). **1.** *Capital* **M. a.** A title of courtesy used as a form of address, originally to a woman of

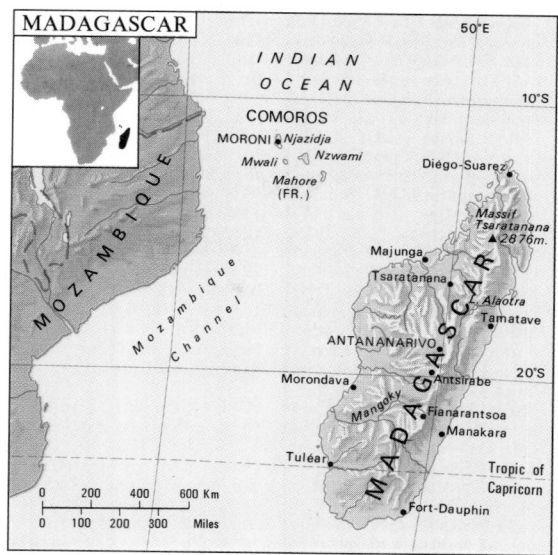

MADAGASCAR

rank, now to any woman. **b.** A conventional form of address used instead of a woman's name at the opening of a letter. **2.** A respectful form of address used before a woman's surname or the title of her office: *Madam Chairwoman.* **3.** *Informal.* A bossy or impudent girl. Used chiefly in the phrase *a little madam.* **4.** A woman who manages a brothel. [Middle English, from MADAME.]

mad·ame (máddəm, mə-dám) *n., pl.* **mesdames** (may-dám, máy-dam). *Abbr.* **Mme., Mme 1.** The French title of courtesy for a married woman, equivalent to the English *Mrs.;* sometimes used of older unmarried women. **2.** A title of courtesy prefixed to the surname of certain foreign women, especially heads of state or the wives of heads of state and artists in the opera or ballet. [Middle English, from Old French *ma dame,* my lady.]

mad·cap (mád-kap) *n.* A rash or impulsive person.
~*adj.* Rash; impulsive; wild. [MAD + CAP (head).]

mad·den (mádd'n) *v.* **-dened, -dening, -dens.** —*tr.* **1.** To make mad; drive insane. **2.** *Informal.* To make angry; excite or irritate. —*intr.* To become infuriated.

mad·den·ing (mádd'n-ing) *adj.* **1.** Causing madness or serving to drive mad. **2.** *Informal.* Extremely irritating; infuriating. —**mad·den·ing·ly** *adv.*

mad·der[1] (máddər) *n.* **1.** Any of various plants of the genus *Rubia;* especially, a Eurasian species, *R. tinctoria,* having small, yellow flowers and a red, fleshy root. **2.** The root of this plant, formerly an important source of dye. **3.** A red dye obtained from the madder root. **4.** Medium to strong red or reddish orange. [Middle English *mader,* Old English *mædere.*]

madder[2]. Comparative of **mad.**

mad·ding (mádding) *adj. Archaic.* Acting as if mad; frenzied.

made (mayd). The past tense and past participle of **make.**
~*adj.* **1.** Produced or manufactured by constructing, shaping, forming, or the like. Used in combination: *handmade.* **2.** Produced or created artificially; not found naturally. **3.** Having a packed, smooth surface; sealed. Said of a road. **4.** Invented; designed; contrived. **5.** Assured of success or fortune: *a made man.* —**have (got) it made.** *Informal.* To be assured in advance of success. —**made for.** Perfectly suited for: *made for each other.*

Ma·dei·ra[1] (mə-déer-ə) *n.* A fortified white dessert wine from the island of Madeira.

Madeira[2]. River in Brazil, the most important tributary of the Amazon. It forms on the Bolivian border and flows 3 315 kilometres (2,060 miles) to the Amazon below Manaus.

Madeira cake *n.* A rich, pale yellow, densely textured sponge cake. [Eaten with Madeira wine.]

Madeira Islands. Also **Fun·chal Islands** (fōon-sháal). Archipelago off northwest Africa, forming the Funchal overseas district of Portugal. Only two of the volcanic islands are inhabited, Madeira being the larger. The main industries are tourism, fishing, agriculture, and the production of Madeira wine. See map at **Atlantic Ocean.** —**Ma·dei·ran** *adj.* & *n.*

mad·e·leine (mádd'l-in, -ayn, -én) *n.* A small, rich cake, usually coated with jam or coconut. [French, perhaps after *Madeleine* Paulmier, 19th-century French pastry cook.]

mad·e·moi·selle (máddəm-wə-zél, -ə-, mam-zél; *French* mad-mwa-zél ‖ mam-zél) *n., pl.* **mesdemoiselles** (máyd-mwə-zél). *Abbr.* **Mlle., Mlle 1.** The French title of courtesy for a young girl or unmarried woman, equivalent to the English *Miss.* It may be used separately or prefixed to either a first or last name. **2.** A French governess or teacher. [French, from Old French *ma demoiselle* : *ma,* my, from Latin *mea,* + *demoiselle,* young lady, from Gallo-Roman *dom(i)nicella* (unattested), diminutive of Latin *domina,* lady, feminine of *dominus,* lord.]

made-to-meas·ure (máyd-tə-mézhər) *adj.* **1.** Made to fit certain measurements, as of a person. **2.** Made-to-order.

made-to-or·der (máyd-too-órdər ‖ -tə-) *adj.* **1.** Made in accordance with particular instructions to fill the requirements of a customer. Compare **ready-made**. **2.** Highly appropriate; just right.

made-up (máyd-úp) *adj.* **1.** Fabricated; fictitious; imaginary; invented: *a made-up story*. **2.** Wearing cosmetics or make-up: *a made-up actress*. **3. a.** Complete; finished: *a made-up package*. **b.** Put together; assembled; arranged: *a made-up page of type*.

mad·house (mád-howss) *n. Informal.* **1.** A mental hospital. Not in technical usage. **2.** A place of uproar or great disorder.

Madison, James (1751–1836). Fourth president of the United States (1809–17). As a member of the Philadelphia Convention (1787) he helped to frame the U.S. constitution and the Bill of Rights. As president he instigated a war with Britain (1812–15) known as "Mr. Madison's War".

Madison Avenue *n.* **1.** A street in Manhattan, New York City, the centre of the American advertising business. **2.** The principles, attitudes, ideas, and methods of advertising and mass communications. Often used derogatorily.

mad·ly (mádli) *adv.* **1.** Insanely. **2.** Wildly; furiously; frantically. **3.** Foolishly; rashly. **4.** *Informal.* To an extreme or excessive degree; very much: *madly in love*.

mad·man (mád-mən) *n., pl.* **-men** (-mən, -men). An insane man; especially, a maniac or lunatic, or a person who behaves like one. Not in technical usage.

mad·ness (mád-nəss, -niss) *n.* **1.** Insanity. **2.** Great folly. **3.** Fury; rage. **4.** Wild enthusiasm; excitement. —See Synonyms at **insanity**.

ma·don·na (mə-dónnə) *n.* **1.** *Capital* **M. a.** The Virgin Mary. Usually preceded by *the*. **b.** An artistic representation of the Virgin Mary. **2.** A woman having qualities of purity, serenity, gentleness, or steadfast love that suggest the Madonna. **3.** Formerly, an Italian title for a married woman, equivalent to *madam*. It has been replaced in current usage by *signora*. [Italian : *ma*, my, from Latin *mea* + *donna*, lady, from Latin *domina*, feminine of *dominus*, lord.]

Madonna lily *n.* A plant, *Lilium candidum*, native to Eurasia and widely cultivated for its white, trumpet-shaped flowers. Also called "Annunciation lily".

ma·dras (mə-dráss, -dráass, máddrəss) *n.* **1.** A fine cotton cloth, usually with a plaid, striped, or checked pattern. **2.** A light cloth, usually of cotton, used for curtains. **3.** A large kerchief of brightly coloured silk or cotton. [Originally produced in MADRAS, India.]

Ma·dras¹ (mə-dráass, -dráss). Indian seaport and capital of Tamil Nadu State, regarded as the traditional burial place of St. Thomas. It was founded as Fort St. George on the Cooum estuary by the British East India Company in 1639. Its chief manufacturing products are bicycles, cars, cement, textiles, and leather products.

Madras² *adj.* Served with a very hot, spicy curry sauce: *chicken Madras*.

Madras hemp *n.* A plant, **sunn** (*see*), or its fibre.

mad·re·pore (máddri-pór, -pawr ‖ -pốr, -pōr) *n.* Any of various corals of the genus *Madrepora*, including the reef builders of tropical seas. [French, from Italian *madrepora*, "mother-stone", referring to the manner in which polyps produce coral : *madre*, mother, from Latin *māter* + Latin *pōrus*, tufa, from Greek *pōros†*.] —**mad·re·por·ic** (-pórrik) *adj.*

mad·re·por·ite (máddri-pawr-īt ‖ -pốr-) *n.* A sievelike structure that forms the inlet of the water vascular system in echinoderms. [MADREPOR(E) + -ITE.]

Ma·drid (mə-drid; *Spanish* ma-thréeth). Capital city of Spain and of Madrid province. Built on the Castile plateau overlooking the river Manzanares, it is a cultural, commercial, and industrial centre, producing leather, textiles, and chemicals. Begun on the site of a Moorish fortress in the tenth century, it became capital under Philip II in 1561, and was a Republican stronghold during the Spanish Civil War (1936–39). Its fine buildings include the Prado art gallery.

mad·ri·gal (máddrig'l) *n.* **1.** An unaccompanied vocal composition for two or three voices in simple harmony, following a strict poetic form, developed in Italy in the early 14th century. **2.** A contrapuntal part song, typically unaccompanied and with parts for five or six voices, using a secular text. This form was developed in Italy in the 16th century, and was popular in England in the 16th and early 17th centuries. **3.** A lyric poem with a pastoral, idyllic, or amatory subject, developed from the lyrics of the 14th-century Italian madrigal. **4.** Any part song. [Italian *madrigale*, earlier *madriale*, "(piece) without accompaniment", probably from Medieval Latin *mātrīcālis*, "of the womb", newly sprung from the womb, simple, from *mātrix*, womb, from *māter*, mother.] —**mad·ri·gal·ist** *n.*

ma·dri·lène, ma·dri·lene (máddri-len, -layn) *n.* A consommé flavoured with tomato, generally chilled. [Abbreviation of French *consommé madrilène*, from Spanish *madrileño*, of MADRID.]

Ma·du·rai (mád-yŏŏrī). Formerly **Ma·thu·rai** (mát-yŏŏrī). City on the river Vaigai in Tamil Nadu State, south India. Known as the "city of festivals and temples", it is a centre of Hindu pilgrimage, with the great temple complex of Sundareswara and Meenakshi, which has 1,000 exquisitely carved columns. The city is a cultural, craft, and market centre. It was the capital of the Pandya kingdom (5th century B.C. to 11th century A.D.) and part of the Hindu Vijayanagar kingdom (1378 to *c.* 1550).

Mad·u·rese (máddwr-éez ‖ -éess) *n., pl.* **Madurese**. **1.** A member of a Malayan people inhabiting the Indonesian island of Madura. **2.** The Austronesian language of the Malayans of Madura and eastern Java. —**Mad·u·rese** *adj.*

ma·du·ro (mə-dóor-ō) *n., pl.* **-ros**. A strong-flavoured cigar with a dark wrapper. [Spanish, MATURE.] —**ma·du·ro** *adj.*

mad·wo·man (mád-wŏŏmən) *n., pl.* **-women** (-wimmin). An insane woman; especially, a maniac or lunatic or a woman who behaves like one. Not in technical usage.

mad·wort (mád-wurt ‖ -wawrt) *n.* **1.** A low-growing plant, *Asperugo procumbens*, native to Eurasia, having rough stems and small blue flowers. **2.** Any of several plants of the genus *Alyssum*. [Formerly believed to cure madness.]

Mae·an·der (mee-ándər). Now known as **Büyük Menderes**. Turkish river, flowing about 400 kilometres (250 miles) from the west of Afyonkarahisar into the Aegean Sea.

Mae·ce·nas (mī-sée-nass, mi-, mee-, -nəss) *n.* A patron, especially one generous to artists. [Gaius *Maecenas*, 1st-century B.C. Roman statesman, patron of Horace and Virgil.]

mael·strom (máyl-strom, -strŏm) *n.* **1.** A whirlpool. **2.** A strong eddy in a tidal current in a restricted, irregular channel. **3.** A state of great confusion or turbulence that resembles such a whirlpool in violence or power to engulf. [Early Modern Dutch *maelstrom*, "whirlstream" : *malen*, to whirl, grind + *stroom*, stream.]

Mael·strom (máyl-strŏm) *n.* A notoriously dangerous tidewater whirlpool, between the Lofoten Islands off the northwest coast of Norway. Preceded by *the*.

mae·nad, me·nad (mée-nad) *n., pl.* **-nads** or **-nades** (ménnə-deez). **1.** *Greek Mythology.* A woman member of the orgiastic cult of Dionysus. **2.** A frenzied woman. [Latin *maenas* (stem *maenad-*), from Greek *mainas*, "she who is mad", from *mainesthai*, to be mad.] —**mae·nad·ic** (mee-náddik) *adj.*

maes·to·so (mī-stố-sō, máa-e-, -zō) *adv. Music.* In a majestic and stately manner. Used as a direction. [Italian, majestic, from *maestà*, majesty, from Latin *mājestās*.] —**maes·to·so** *n. & adj.*

Maestricht. See **Maastricht.**

maes·tro (mīss-trō; *Italian* ma-éss-trō) *n., pl.* **-tros** or **-tri** (-tree). A master in any art, especially a composer, conductor, or teacher of music. Often used as a term of address. [Italian, from Latin *magister*, master.]

Mae·ter·linck (máytər-lingk; *French* méttair-lánk, *Dutch* máatər-lingk), **Count Maurice (Polydore Marie Bernard)** (1862–1949). Belgian poet and playwright, and a leading member of the Symbolist movement. Among his plays were *Pelléas et Mélisande* (1892), on which Debussy based his opera (1902), and *The Blue Bird* (1909). He received the Nobel prize for literature (1911).

Mae West (máy wést) *n.* An inflatable life jacket. [After *Mae* WEST, whose generous figure it was thought to be reminiscent of.]

Mafeking. See **Mafikeng.**

maf·fick (máffik) *intr.v.* **-ficked, -ficking, -ficks**. *British.* To rejoice or celebrate with boisterous public demonstrations. No longer in current usage. [Back-formation from *Mafeking*, MAFIKENG, referring to the celebration of the raising of the siege there (1900).]

Ma·fi·a, Maf·fi·a (máffi-ə ‖ máafi-) *n.* **1.** An international criminal organisation active, especially in Italy and the United States, since the late 19th century. Preceded by *the*. Compare **Black Hand, Camorra, Cosa Nostra**. **2.** A secret terrorist organisation in Sicily, operating since the early 19th century in opposition to legal authority. Preceded by *the*. **3.** Any organisation using terrorist methods to control an activity. **4.** *Often small* **m**. Any exclusive group or clique, especially an influential one. [Italian (Sicilian dialect) *mafia*, boldness, "boasting", from Arabic *mahyah*, boasting.]

Ma·fi·keng (máffi-keng, -king). Formerly **Ma·fe·king** (-king). A town in the Republic of Bophuthatswana, formerly included in the Cape Province of South Africa. The 217-day siege and relief of Mafeking (October 1899–May 1900) was one of the celebrated events of the Boer War.

Ma·fi·o·so (máffi-ố-sō ‖ máafi-) *n., pl.* **-si** (-see). A member of the Mafia. [Italian.]

mag (mag) *n. British Informal.* A magazine or periodical.

mag. **1.** magnetism. **2.** magnitude.

mag·a·zine (mággə-zéen, -zeen) *n. Abbr.* **mag. 1. a.** A place where goods are stored; especially, a building (as in a fort) or storeroom (as on a warship) where ammunition is stored. **b.** The contents of a storehouse; a stock of ammunition. **2.** A publication appearing at regular intervals, containing articles, stories, photographs, or other features. **3. a.** A compartment in some types of firearms, often a small, detachable box, in which cartridges are held to be fed into the firing chamber. **b.** A compartment in a camera in which rolls or cartridges of film are held for feeding through the exposure mechanism. **c.** Any of various other compartments attached to machines, for storing or supplying necessary material. [Old French *magazin*, storehouse, from Italian *magazzino*, from Arabic *makhāzin*, plural of *makhzan*, storehouse, from *khazana*, to store up.]

mag·da·len (mágdə-lin) *n.* Also **mag·da·lene** (-leen). *Rare.* **1.** A reformed prostitute. **2.** A reformatory for prostitutes. [From MARY MAGDALENE.]

Mag·da·le·ni·an (mágdə-léeni-ən) *adj. Archaeology.* Of, belonging to, or designating the last upper Palaeolithic culture of Europe, and characterised by cave art and decorative work in bone and ivory. [French *magdalénien*, La Madeleine, village in Dordogne, France, near which artefacts were found.]

Mag·de·burg (mágdə-burg; *German* mákdə-boork). Capital of Magdeburg district in East Germany, built on the river Elbe. It became self-governing (13th century) and was a leader of the Hanseatic League. It is a major river port and rail and canal centre, and makes steel and metal goods, petroleum products, sugar, textiles, and chemicals.

mage (mayj) *n. Archaic.* **1.** A magician. **2.** One of the Magi. [Middle English, from Latin *magus,* sorcerer. See **Magi.**]

Ma·gel·lan (mə-géllən, -jéllən), **Ferdinand** (*c.* 1480–1521). Portuguese navigator. He was financed by Charles V of Spain (1519) to find a westward route to the Moluccas. Magellan crossed the Atlantic without charts and was blown by storms into the strait that carries his name (1520). He crossed the ocean, which he named the Pacific, reaching the Marianas and the Philippines, where he was killed fighting for the King of Cebu. One of his ships arrived back in Sanlúcar (1522), completing the world's first circumnavigation.

Magellan, Strait of A passage between the Atlantic and Pacific Oceans, between mainland South America and Tierra del Fuego. It is some 530 kilometres (330 miles) long and a maximum of only 24 kilometres (15 miles) wide. Magellan discovered it in 1520.

Mag·el·lan·ic cloud (mággi-lánnik, máji-) *n.* Either of two small companion galaxies of the Milky Way, faintly visible near the south celestial pole. They are the *Large Magellanic Cloud* (Nubecula Major) and the *Small Magellanic Cloud* (Nubecula Minor). [After Ferdinand MAGELLAN.]

Ma·gen Da·vid, Mo·gen Da·vid (máwgən dáyvid, máagən, daávid, dáwvid) *n.* The Star of David *(see).* [Hebrew *māgen Dāwid,* shield of (King) David.]

ma·gen·ta (mə-jéntə) *n.* **1.** A coal-tar dye, **fuchsine** *(see).* **2.** Moderate to vivid purplish red, or strong reddish purple; one of the subtractive primaries. See **primary colour.** [After the bloodshed of the battle of MAGENTA : the dye was discovered that same year (1859).]

Magenta. North Italian town, to the west of Milan, in Lombardy. The nearby river Ticino was the scene of the decisive French-Sardinian victory over the Austrians in 1859.

mag·gie (mággi) *n. Australian Informal.* A magpie.

Mag·gi·o·re, Lake (máji-áwri, maj-). *Italian* **Lago Maggiore** or **Ver·ba·no** (vair-baáanō). Italy's second largest lake, on the Swiss border. Lying in the Alpine foothills, it is a tourist area with resorts such as Locarno and Stresa.

mag·got (mággət) *n.* **1.** The legless, soft-bodied larva of any of various insects of the order Diptera, especially of the housefly and the bluebottle, usually found in decaying matter or as a parasite. **2.** *Rare.* An extravagant notion; a whim. [Middle English *magot, maked,* earlier *maddock, madhek,* from Old Norse *mathkr.*]

mag·got·y (mággəti) *adj.* **1.** Infested with maggots. **2.** *Rare.* Full of strange whims. **3.** *Australian Informal.* Angry.

Ma·ghreb or **Ma·ghrib** (mág-reb, -rib, múggrəb). *Arabic* **Djezira el Maghreb.** Region of northwest Africa comprising the coastlands and Atlas ranges of Algeria, Morocco, and Tunisia. Its Arabic name means "the western island", the island of land between the Sahara and the Mediterranean. —**Ma·ghre·bi, Ma·ghri·bi** *(-ee) adj. & n.*

Ma·gi (máy-jī) *pl.n. Singular* **Ma·gus** (máygəss). **1.** *Sometimes small* **m.** The Zoroastrian priestly caste of the Medes and Persians. **2.** The "wise men from the East", traditionally three in number, who travelled to Bethlehem to pay homage to the infant Jesus. Matthew 2:1–12. According to St. Augustine their names were Balthasar, Caspar, and Melchior. [Middle English, from Latin, plural of *magus,* sorcerer, from Greek *magos,* from Old Persian *maguš.*] —**Ma·gi·an** (máyji-ən) *adj. & n.*

mag·ic (májik) *n.* **1.** The art that purports to control or forecast natural events, effects, or forces by invoking the supernatural. **2.** The practice of using charms, spells, or rituals to attempt to produce supernatural effects or to control events in nature. **3.** The exercise of sleight of hand for entertainment; the use of deception to produce baffling effects. **4.** Any mysterious and overpowering quality that lends singular distinction and enchantment.
~*adj.* **1.** Pertaining to the supernatural; having to do with magic and its practice. **2.** Possessing distinctive qualities that produce unaccountable or baffling effects: *a magic wand.* **3.** *British Slang.* Wonderful; marvellous: *His new car is really magic.*
~*tr.v.* **magicked, -gicking, -gics.** To produce or make by or as if by magic. [Middle English, from Old French *magique,* from Late Latin *magica,* from Greek *magikē (tekhnē),* the sorcerer's art, from *magikos,* pertaining to sorcery, from *magos,* sorcerer, from Old Persian *maguš.*]

Synonyms: magic, black magic, sorcery, voodoo, witchcraft, necromancy, alchemy.

mag·i·cal (májik'l) *adj.* **1.** Of or produced by or as if by magic. **2.** Having a mysteriously captivating quality. —**mag·i·cal·ly** *adv.*

magic carpet *n.* A mythical carpet possessing magical powers that enable it to transport a person through the air.

magic eye *n.* A **photoelectric cell** *(see).*

ma·gi·cian (mə-jísh'n) *n.* **1.** A sorcerer; a wizard. **2.** A person who performs magic for entertainment or diversion. **3.** One whose skill or art seems to be magical: *a magician with words.*

magic lantern *n.* An early type of slide projector used to project the enlarged image of a picture. Also called "lantern".

magic mushroom *n.* A hallucinogenic mushroom, *Psilocybe semilanceata,* having a conical pileus with a sharply pointed umbo. Also called "liberty cap".

magic number *n. Physics.* Any of the numbers 2, 8, 20, 28, 50, 82, 126, that represent the number of neutrons, protons, or both, in strongly bound, exceptionally stable, and abundant atomic nuclei.

magic square *n.* A square arrangement of numbers such that the numbers in any row, column, or diagonal all add up to the same sum.

magilp. Variant of **megilp.**

Ma·gi·not Line (mázhi-nō) *n.* A 320-kilometre (200-mile) line of fortifications built by France along its border with Germany before World War II. It was thought to be impregnable but fell to the Germans in 1940 after they had bypassed it through Belgium. [After André *Maginot* (1877–1932), French minister of war.]

mag·is·te·ri·al (máji-stéer-i-əl) *adj.* **1.** Pertaining to a master, teacher, or person in a similar position of authority. **2. a.** Characteristic of a master; authoritative; commanding. **b.** Dictatorial; dogmatic; overbearing: *offended by his magisterial manner of giving advice.* **3.** Of or pertaining to a magistrate or his official functions. [Latin *magisterius,* from *magister,* master.] —**mag·is·te·ri·al·ly** *adv.*

mag·is·te·ri·um (máji-stéer-i-əm) *n.* The teaching authority of the Roman Catholic Church. [Late Latin, from Latin *magister,* teacher, MASTER.]

mag·is·ter·y (máji-stəri, -stri ‖ *U.S.* -sterri) *n., pl.* **-ies.** Also **ma·gis·ter** (mə-jístər). A substance or power in nature supposed by alchemists to be capable of effecting transmutation, such as the philosopher's stone. [Medieval Latin *magisterium,* from Latin, position of a master, from *magister,* MASTER.]

mag·is·tra·cy (máji-strə-si) *n., pl.* **-cies. 1.** The position, function, or term of office of a magistrate. **2.** A body of magistrates. **3.** The district under the jurisdiction of a magistrate.

mag·is·tral (mə-jístrəl, máji-strəl) *adj.* **1.** Magisterial. **2.** In pharmacology, prepared or prescribed for a specific occasion. Compare **officinal. 3.** Principal; main: *the magistral line of fortifications.* [Latin *magistrālis,* masterful, from *magister,* MASTER.]

mag·is·trate (máji-strayt, -strət, -strit) *n.* **1.** A civil officer with power to administer and enforce law. **2.** A person conducting a magistrate's court, such as a justice of the peace. [Latin *magistrātus,* magistracy, magistrate, from *magister,* MASTER.]

magistrate's court *n.* In England, a minor court with summary jurisdiction presided over by a minimum of two justices of the peace or a stipendiary magistrate, that deals with minor crimes and local civil matters, and holds preliminary criminal hearings.

mag·is·tra·ture (máji-strə-tewr, -chər) *n.* A magistracy.

Ma·gle·mo·si·an (mágglə-mōzi-ən) *adj. Archaeology.* Of, designating, or pertaining to an early Mesolithic forest culture of northern Europe, characterised by wood-working tools and dugout canoes. [After *Maglemose,* Denmark, where evidence was found.]

mag·ma (mág-mə) *n., pl.* **magmata** (-mətə, -maátə) or **-mas. 1.** A mixture of finely divided solids with enough liquid to produce a pasty mass. **2.** *Geology.* Molten matter formed within the earth's crust or upper mantle, which may consolidate on cooling to form igneous rock. **3.** In pharmacology, a suspension of particles in a liquid. [Middle English, dregs of a liquid, from Latin, sediment, from Greek *magma,* unguent.] —**mag·mat·ic** (-máttik) *adj.*

Mag·na Car·ta, Mag·na Char·ta (mág-nə kártə) *n.* **1.** The great charter of English political and civil liberties granted by King John at Runnymede on June 15, 1215. Preceded by *the.* **2.** Any document or piece of legislation that serves as a guarantee of basic rights. [Medieval Latin, "Great Charter".]

mag·na cum lau·de (mág-nə kŏŏm lów-day ‖ maág-, láw-, -də) *adv. Chiefly U.S.* With great praise. Used on university and college diplomas to designate the second-highest degree of academic distinction. Compare **cum laude, summa cum laude.** [Latin.]

Mag·na Grae·ci·a (mág-nə grée-shi-ə, -shə). The colonies of ancient Greece in southern Italy and Sicily in the eighth to fourth centuries B.C. [Latin, "Great Greece".]

mag·nan·i·mous (mag-nánniməss) *adj.* Noble of mind and heart; generous in forgiving; above revenge or resentment. [Latin *magnanimus,* "great-souled" : *magnus,* great + *animus,* soul.] —**mag·nan·i·mous·ly** *adv.* —**mag·na·nim·i·ty** (mág-nə-nímməti), **mag·nan·i·mous·ness** *n.*

mag·na op·er·a. Plural of **magnum opus.**

mag·nate (mág-nayt, -nit) *n.* A powerful or influential man, especially in business or industry: *a steel magnate.* [Middle English *magnates* (plural only), from Late Latin *magnātēs,* plural of *magnās,* "great man", from Latin *magnus,* great.]

mag·ne·sia (mag-née-shə, məg-, -zi-ə, -zhə) *n.* **Magnesium oxide** *(see),* especially when processed for purity. [Middle English, from Medieval Latin, from Late Greek *magnēsia,* name of various minerals, from *Magnēsia,* name of a metalliferous region of Thessaly.] —**mag·ne·sian** (-shən, -zi-ən, -zhən) *adj.*

magnesian limestone *n. Geology.* Dolomite *(see).*

mag·ne·site (mág-ni-sīt) *n.* **1.** A white, yellowish, or brown, mineral composed of magnesium carbonate, $MgCO_3$. It is used in the manufacture of refractory bricks. **2.** Any of several grades of magnesium oxide obtained from this material. [MAGNES(IUM) + -ITE.]

mag·ne·si·um (mag-née-zi-əm, məg-, -si-əm, -shi-əm, -zhəm) *n. Symbol* **Mg** A light, silvery, moderately hard, metallic element that in ribbon or powder form burns with a brilliant white flame. It is used in structural alloys, pyrotechnics, flash photography, and incendiary bombs. Atomic number 12, atomic weight 24.312, melting point 651°C, boiling point 1,107°C, relative density 1.74, valency 2. [New Latin, from MAGNESIA.]

magnesium carbonate *n.* A very light, odourless, white powdery compound, $MgCO_3$, used in a wide variety of manufactured products including inks, glass, dentifrices, and cosmetics.

magnesium hydroxide *n.* A white powder, $Mg(OH)_2$, used as an antacid and laxative, especially in milk of magnesia.

magnesium oxide *n.* A white, powdery compound, MgO, having a high melting point (2,800°C), and used in high-temperature refractories, electric insulation, semiconductor devices and in medicine as a mild antacid and laxative. Also called "magnesia".

magnesium sulphate *n.* A colourless, crystalline compound, $MgSO_4$, used in fireproofing, ceramics, matches, explosives, and fertilisers. The hydrate, $MgSO_4 \cdot 7H_2O$, is **Epsom salts** (see).

mag·net (mág-nit) *n.* **1.** A body that attracts iron and certain other materials by virtue of a surrounding field of force produced by the motion of its atomic electrons and the alignment of its atoms. **2.** An **electromagnet** (see). **3.** A person, place, object, or situation that exerts attraction, especially irresistible attraction. [Middle English *magnete,* from Old French, from Latin *magnēs* (stem *magnēt-*), from Greek *magnēs,* short for *Magnēs lithos,* "the Magnesian stone", from *Magnēs,* pertaining to *Magnēsia.* See **magnesia.**]

mag·net·ic (mag-néttik, məg-) *adj.* **1.** Of or relating to magnetism or magnets. **2.** Having the properties of a magnet; exhibiting magnetism. **3.** Relating to the magnetic poles of the earth: *a magnetic compass bearing.* **4.** Capable of being magnetised or of being attracted by a magnet. **5.** Operating by means of magnetism: *a magnetic recorder.* **6.** Exerting great powers of attraction: *a magnetic personality.* —**mag·net·i·cal·ly** *adv.*

magnetic bearing *n.* The angular direction from magnetic north.

magnetic bottle *n.* An arrangement of magnetic fields used to confine the plasma in a controlled thermonuclear reaction.

magnetic bubble *n.* A small, nonvolatile, cylindrical region of magnetisation in a thin film of material that can be manipulated by an external magnetic field and used to represent data in the memory of a computer.

magnetic character recognition *n.* A method of introducing printed or written information into a computer. The information is printed using magnetic ink and the resulting text is scanned with a *magnetic character reader,* which recognises each character by its magnetic outline.

magnetic circuit *n.* A closed path through which a magnetic flux can pass, analogous to a circuit through which a current flows.

magnetic compass *n.* An instrument using a **magnetic needle** (see) to show direction relative to the earth's magnetic field.

magnetic constant *n.* The permeability of free space. It has the value $4\pi \times 10^{-7}$ henry per metre. Also called "absolute permeability".

magnetic core *n. Computing.* A **core** (see).

magnetic declination *n.* The angle between the geographical meridian and the local magnetic meridian, in navigation expressed as degrees plus (+) to the east, or degrees minus (–) to the west, of the geographical meridian. Also called "declination", "magnetic variation".

magnetic dip *n.* The angle that the earth's magnetic field makes with the horizontal plane at any specific location. Also called "dip", "magnetic inclination".

magnetic dipole moment *n.* A measure of the strength of a magnet or coil expressed as the torque produced when the magnet or coil is set with its axis perpendicular to unit magnetic field. Also called "magnetic moment".

magnetic disk *n.* **1.** A computer storage device consisting of a stack of plates coated with a magnetic layer arranged so that they can be rotated at high speed as one unit. A read-write head can move radially on concentric tracks to enter or remove data from the store. **2.** A **floppy disk** (see).

magnetic domain *n. Physics.* A **domain** (see).

magnetic drum *n.* A computer storage device consisting of a rotating cylinder covered with magnetic material.

magnetic equator *n.* A line connecting all points on the earth's surface at which there is no magnetic dip. Also called "aclinic line". Compare **geomagnetic equator.**

magnetic field *n.* A condition in a region of space, established by the presence of a magnet, or of an electric current, and characterised by the existence of a detectable magnetic force at every point in the region.

magnetic field strength *n.* **1.** Magnetic intensity. **2.** Magnetic induction.

magnetic flux *n.* The total number of magnetic lines of force passing through a bounded area in a magnetic field.

magnetic flux density *n.* Magnetic induction.

magnetic force *n.* **1.** The force on a **magnetic pole** (see) in a magnetic field. **2.** The force on an electrically charged particle, or on an electric current, in a magnetic field.

magnetic head *n.* A device, as in a tape recorder, that converts electric impulses into variations in the magnetism of a surface for storage and subsequent retrieval. See **magnetic recording.**

magnetic hysteresis *n.* The failure of the **magnetisation** (see) in a body to return to its original value when the external field is reduced.

magnetic inclination *n.* **Magnetic dip** (see).

magnetic induction *n.* **1.** A vector quantity that specifies the direction and magnitude of magnetic force at every point in a magnetic field. Also called "magnetic field strength", "magnetic flux density". **2.** The temporary conversion of a piece of iron or of certain other materials into a magnet by a magnetic field.

magnetic ink *n.* Ink that contains particles of a magnetic material to enable it to be used in **magnetic character recognition** (see).

magnetic intensity *n.* That part of a magnetic field related solely to external currents as a cause, without reference to the presence of matter.

magnetic lens *n.* An arrangement of magnets, usually electromag-

nets, used to focus a beam of particles in such devices as an electron microscope or particle accelerator.

magnetic line of force *n.* A curve whose tangent at any point is along the direction of magnetic force at that point. The number of lines of force per unit area in the neighbourhood of a point is proportional to the magnetic induction at that point.

magnetic meridian *n.* A meridian passing through the earth's magnetic poles.

magnetic mine *n.* A marine mine detonated by a mechanism that responds to magnetic material, such as the steel hull of a ship.

magnetic mirror *n.* An arrangement of magnetic fields that can reflect charged particles, used to contain the plasma in thermonuclear reactors.

magnetic moment *n.* **Magnetic dipole moment** (see).

magnetic monopole *n.* A hypothetical elementary particle that has a single north or south magnetic pole, predicted theoretically but so far undiscovered.

magnetic needle *n.* A needle-shaped bar magnet usually suspended on a low-friction mounting and used in various instruments, especially in the magnetic compass, to indicate the alignment of a local magnetic field.

magnetic north *n.* The direction of the earth's magnetic pole, to which the north-seeking pole of a magnetic needle points when free from local magnetic influence. See **magnetic declination.**

magnetic permeability *n.* A characteristic of a medium in a magnetic field, that is equal to the ratio of magnetic induction to magnetic intensity. Also called "permeability".

magnetic pick-up *n.* A type of gramophone pick-up that utilises a coil in a magnetic field to receive vibrations from the stylus and convert them into electric impulses. Compare **crystal pick-up.**

magnetic pole *n.* **1.** Either of two limited regions in a magnet at which the magnet's field is most intense, each of which is designated by the approximate geographical direction to which it is attracted: *a north, or north-seeking pole; a south, or south-seeking pole.* **2.** Either of two variable points on the earth, close to but not coinciding with the North and South Poles, corresponding to the poles of the earth's magnetic field.

magnetic pole strength *n.* A measure of the effectiveness of a magnet, equal to the magnetic moment divided by the magnetic induction.

magnetic pyrites *n.* A mineral, **pyrrhotite** (see).

magnetic recording *n.* **1.** A recording of a signal, such as sound or computer instructions, in the form of a magnetic pattern on a magnetisable surface for storage and subsequent retrieval. **2.** A surface containing such a magnetic pattern. —**magnetic recorder** *n.*

magnetic storm *n.* A severe but short-lived disturbance in the earth's magnetosphere field believed to be produced by currents of charged particles and gamma rays, resulting from abnormal solar activity and fluctuations in the earth's magnetic field.

magnetic susceptibility *n.* The ratio of the magnetic permeability of a medium to that of a vacuum, minus one. It is positive for a paramagnetic or ferromagnetic medium, negative for a diamagnetic medium. Also called "susceptibility".

magnetic tape *n.* A plastic tape coated with a magnetisable material such as iron oxide for use in magnetic recording.

magnetic variation *n.* **Magnetic declination** (see).

mag·net·i·sa·tion (mág-ni-tī-záysh'n ‖ *U.S.* -ti-) *n.* **1.** The process of making a substance temporarily or permanently magnetic, as by insertion in a magnetic field. **2.** The magnetic moment per unit volume induced in a body by an external field. **3.** The property of being magnetic.

mag·net·ise, mag·net·ize (mág-ni-tīz) *tr.v.* **-ised, -ising, -ises. 1.** To make magnetic. **2. a.** To exert a strong influence on. **b.** To attract strongly. —**mag·net·is·able** *adj.* —**mag·net·is·er** *n.*

mag·net·ism (mág-ni-tiz'm) *n. Abbr.* **mag. 1.** The class of phenomena exhibited by the field of force produced by a magnet or by an electric current. **2.** The study of magnets and their effects. **3.** The force exerted by a magnetic field. **4.** Unusual power to attract, fascinate, or influence: *the magnetism of money.* **5. Animal magnetism** (see).

mag·net·ite (mág-ni-tīt) *n.* A black mineral of iron oxide, Fe_3O_4, often occurring with titanium or magnesium, and an important ore of iron. A magnetically polarised piece of this mineral is called a **lodestone** (see).

mag·ne·to (mag-néetō, məg-) *n., pl.* **-tos.** A small generator of alternating current using permanent magnets, used in the ignition systems of some internal-combustion engines. [Short for *magnetoelectric machine.*]

magneto– *comb. form.* Indicates magnetic properties; for example, **magnetometer, magnetohydrodynamics.**

mag·ne·to·chem·is·try (mag-néetō-kémmistri) *n.* The study of the interrelation of magnetic and chemical phenomena. —**mag·ne·to·chem·i·cal** *adj.*

mag·ne·to·elec·tric (mag-néetō-i-léktrik) *adj.* Pertaining to both magnetism and electricity, especially to electricity produced using magnetic fields. —**mag·ne·to·elec·tric·i·ty** *n.*

mag·ne·to·graph (mag-néetō-graaf, -graf) *n.* A magnetometer with three variometers that are equipped for recording three perpendicular components of a magnetic field. [MAGNETO- + -GRAPH.]

mag·ne·to·hy·dro·dy·nam·ics (mag-néetō-hídrō-dī-námmiks, -néttō-, -di-) *n. Abbr.* **MHD.** *Used with a singular verb.* **1.** The study of electrically conducting fluids, such as molten metal or plasma, in electric and magnetic fields. **2.** A method of generating electricity by subjecting a plasma to a magnetic field so that the flow of free electrons constitutes a current. Also called "hydromagnetics", "magnetoplasmadynamics". —**mag·ne·to·hy·dro·dy·nam·ic** adj.

mag·ne·tom·e·ter (mág-ni-tómmitər) n. An instrument for comparing the magnitude and direction of magnetic fields. [MAGNETO- + -METER.]

mag·ne·to·mo·tive force (mag-néetō-mótiv, -néttō-) n. Abbr. **mmf**, **m.m.f.** 1. The agency that produces **magnetic flux** (see) in a magnetic circuit. 2. The strength of such an agency, equal to the work required to carry a hypothetical isolated magnetic pole of unit strength completely round the circuit.

mag·ne·ton (mág-ni-ton, mag-néeton) n. A unit of magnetic moment applied to atoms, molecules, and subatomic particles, equal to $eh/4\pi mc$, where e is the particle's electric charge, m its mass, h Planck's constant, and c the speed of light; especially: 1. The *Bohr magneton*, calculated using the mass and charge of the electron. 2. The *nuclear magneton*, calculated using the mass of the nucleon. [French *magnéton* : MAGNET + -ON.]

mag·ne·to·plas·ma·dy·nam·ics (mag-néetō-plázmə-dī-námmiks, -néttō- -di-) n. Used with a singular verb. Magnetohydrodynamics. —**mag·ne·to·plas·ma·dy·na·mic** adj.

mag·ne·to·sphere (mag-néetō-sfeer, -néttō-) n. An asymmetric region surrounding the earth, extending from about 400 to several thousand miles above the surface, in which charged particles are trapped and their behaviour dominated by the earth's magnetic field. [MAGNETO- + -SPHERE.] —**mag·ne·to·spher·ic** (-sférrik) adj.

mag·ne·to·stric·tion (mag-néetō-stríksh'n, -néttō-) n. The deformation of a ferromagnetic material subjected to a magnetic field. —**mag·ne·to·stric·tive** adj.

mag·ne·tron (mág-ni-tron) n. A thermionic valve in which the electron beam is controlled by electromagnetic fields and generates high-power microwaves. [MAGNE(T) + -TRON.]

mag·nif·ic (mag-níffik) adj. Also **mag·nif·ic·al** (-'l). Archaic. Magnificent; grand. [Middle English *magnifyque*, from Old French *magnifique*, from Latin *magnificus*, "great in deeds" : *magnus*, great + -FIC.] —**mag·nif·i·cal·ly** adv.

Mag·nif·i·cat (mag-níffi-kat, məg- ‖ -kaat) n. 1. The canticle beginning *Magnificat anima mea Dominum* ("My soul doth magnify the Lord"). The text is Luke 1:46-55. 2. A musical setting of this text. 3. *Small* **m.** Any hymn or song of praise.

mag·ni·fi·ca·tion (mág-ni-fi-káysh'n) n. 1. **a.** The act of magnifying or the state of being magnified. **b.** The process of enlarging the size of something, such as an optical image. **c.** Something that has been magnified; an enlarged representation, image, or model. **d.** The degree to which something is magnified. 2. In optics, the ratio of image size to object size.

mag·nif·i·cence (mag-níffi-sənss, məg-) n. 1. Greatness or lavishness of surroundings or ornament; splendour; sumptuousness. 2. Grand or imposing beauty: *the magnificence of the scenery*.

mag·nif·i·cent (mag-níffi-sənt, məg-) adj. 1. **a.** Splendid; stately; grand. **b.** Lavishly decorated; sumptuous. 2. Grand or imposing to the mind; marked by nobility of thought or deed; exalted. 3. Outstanding of its kind; superlative: *a magnificent sunset*. See Synonyms at **grand**. [Latin *magnificent-*, variant stem of *magnificus*, MAGNIFIC.] —**mag·nif·i·cent·ly** adv.

mag·nif·i·co (mag-níffi-kō) n., pl. **-coes**. 1. A person of distinguished rank, importance, or appearance. Often used humorously. 2. A nobleman of the Venetian Republic. [Italian, from *magnifico*, magnificent, from Latin *magnificus*, MAGNIFIC.]

mag·ni·fi·er (mág-ni-fī-ər) n. 1. **a.** A magnifying glass. **b.** Broadly, any system of optical components that magnifies. 2. A person who magnifies.

mag·ni·fy (mág-ni-fī) v. **-fied**, **-fying**, **-fies**. —tr. 1. To make greater in size; enlarge, amplify, or intensify: *Our problems are magnified by lack of time.* 2. To cause to appear greater or seem more important; exaggerate. 3. To increase the apparent size of, especially by means of a lens. 4. Archaic. To glorify. —intr. To increase or have the power to increase the size or volume of an image or sound. —See Synonyms at **increase**. [Middle English *magnifien*, from Old French *magnifier*, from Latin *magnificāre*, to make great, from *magnificus*, MAGNIFIC.]

magnifying glass n. A converging lens that enlarges the image of an object. Also called "magnifier".

mag·nil·o·quent (mag-níllə-kwənt) adj. Lofty and extravagant in speech; grandiloquent. [Latin *magniloquus* : *magnus*, great + *loquī*, to speak.] —**mag·nil·o·quence** n. —**mag·nil·o·quent·ly** adv.

mag·ni·tude (mág-ni-tewd ‖ -tōod) n. Abbr. **mag**. 1. **a.** Greatness of rank or position. **b.** Greatness in size or extent. **c.** Greatness in significance or influence: *the magnitude of the achievement*. 2. Astronomy. The relative brightness of a celestial body designated on a numerical scale, originally integers from 1 (brightest) to 6 (faintest visible), now extended to include negative integers, integers above 6, and decimals, with the scale rule that a decrease of 1 unit represents an increase in apparent brightness by a factor of 2.512. Also called "apparent magnitude". 3. Mathematics. A property that can be quantitatively described, such as the volume of a sphere or the length of a vector. 4. The force of an earthquake as measured on the **Richter scale**. [Middle English, from Latin *magnitūdō*, greatness, from *magnus*, great.]

mag·no·lia (mag-nŏli-ə, məg-) n. 1. Any of various evergreen or deciduous trees and shrubs of the genus *Magnolia*, of the Western Hemisphere and Asia, many of which are cultivated for their showy white, pink, purple, or yellow flowers. 2. The flower of any of these

trees or shrubs. 3. A creamy white tinged with pink. [New Latin, after Pierre *Magnol* (1638–1715), French botanist.]

mag·num (mág-nəm) n. 1. A bottle holding the equivalent of two normal-sized wine bottles. 2. The amount of liquid contained in such a bottle. 3. An extremely powerful .44 calibre handgun. [Latin, "a big one", neuter of *magnus*, great.]

magnum opus n., pl. **magna opera**. 1. A great work; especially, a literary or artistic masterpiece. 2. The greatest single work of an artist, writer, or composer. [Latin, "great work".]

mag·nus hitch (mág-nəss) n. A knot, a clove hitch with one extra turn. [Probably from Latin *magnus*, "large".]

Magog. See **Gog and Magog.**

ma·got (maa-gō, mággot) n. A Chinese or Japanese figurine, usually grotesque and rendered in a crouching position. [French *magot*, *magog*, a monstrous figure, after the Biblical giant Magog.]

mag·pie (mág-pī) n. 1. Any of various birds of the genus *Pica*, found throughout the Northern Hemisphere and noted for their chattering call. *P. pica*, the black-billed magpie, has black plumage with prominent white markings. 2. Any of various birds resembling the magpie. 3. Any of several piping crows and bell magpies of the genus *Gymnorhina*, of Australia. 4. A person who chatters. 5. *British*. A person who compulsively collects miscellaneous small objects. 6. **a.** The outermost ring but one of a target. **b.** A shot that hits this ring. [*Mag*, a dialectal name for a chatterbox (probably from *Mag*, pet form of *Margaret*) + PIE (magpie).]

magpie lark n. A distinctively marked black and white bird, *Grallina cyanoleuca*, found throughout Australia and parts of New Zealand. Also called "mudlark".

Ma·gritte (ma-gréet, mə-), **René** (1898-1967). Belgian surrealist painter. From 1922, he produced dreamlike paintings showing ordinary objects in impossible situations.

ma·guey (mág-way, mə-gáy) n. 1. Any of various plants of the genus *Agave*, native to tropical America; especially, any yielding a fibre or beverage. Also called "mescal". 2. Any plant of the related genus *Furcraea*. 3. The fibre obtained from any of these plants. [Spanish, from Taino.]

Ma·gus (máy-gəss) n., pl. **-gi** (-jī, -gī). 1. A member of the Zoroastrian caste, the **Magi** (see). 2. A wizard or sorcerer, especially in ancient times. 3. Any of the **Magi** (see).

Mag·yar (mág-yaar, máag-; Hungarian mód-yaar) n. 1. A member of the principal ethnic group of Hungary. 2. The Finno-Ugric language of the Magyars, the official language of Hungary; Hungarian. ~adj. 1. Of or pertaining to the Magyars or their language. 2. Designating a loose-fitting sleeve or a blouse with sleeves that is cut as one whole with the bodice. [Hungarian *Magyar†*.]

Magyarország. See **Hungary**.

Ma·ha·bha·ra·ta (mə-háa-báarə-tə) n. Also **Ma·ha·bha·ra·tam** (-təm). A great epic poem of ancient India, written in Sanskrit and containing the Bhagavad-Gita. Compare **Ramayana**. [Sanskrit *Mahābhārata*, "the great story" : *mahā*, great + *bhārata*, story.]

ma·ha·ra·jah, ma·ha·ra·ja (máa-hə-ráa-jə, máa-ə-, -zhə) n. A king or prince in India, especially the sovereign of any of the former States. [Hindi *mahārājā*, from Sanskrit : *mahā*, great + *rājā*, king.]

ma·ha·ra·ni, ma·ha·ra·nee (máa-hə-ráa-nee) n. 1. The wife of a maharajah. 2. A queen or princess in India, especially the sovereign ruler of any of the former States. [Hindi *mahārānī*, from Sanskrit *mahārājñī* : *mahā*, great + *rājñī*, queen.]

Ma·ha·rash·tra (máa-haa-rásh-trə, -hə-, -raash-). Western state of India bordering the Arabian Sea. Its rice-producing coastlands rise to the Western Ghats, beyond which lies the Deccan plateau, where cotton is grown. Mostly peopled by Marathas, the state was created when the former Bombay state was divided between its Marathi and Gujarati inhabitants. Bombay is the capital.

ma·ha·ri·shi (máa-hə-rishi, -réeshi, mə-háar-i-shi) n. Hinduism. 1. A great sage or spiritual leader. 2. *Capital* **M.** A title of or form of address for a guru or spiritual leader, preceding the person's name. [Sanskrit *māha*, great + *rishi*, sage.]

ma·hat·ma (mə-háat-mə, -hát-) n. 1. In India and Tibet, any of a class of persons venerated for great knowledge and love of humanity. 2. *Capital* **M.** A Hindu title of respect for a man renowned for spirituality and thought to possess extraordinary powers. [Sanskrit *mahātman* : *mahā*, great + *ātman*, soul.]

Ma·ha·ya·na (máa-hə-yáanə) n. One of the major schools of Buddhism, active in Japan, Korea, Nepal, Tibet, Mongolia, and China. Compare **Hinayana**. [Sanskrit *mahāyāna*, "the great vehicle" : *mahā*, great + *yāna*, vehicle.]

Mah·di (maadi) n. 1. The Islamic messiah who it is believed will appear at the end of the world and establish a reign of peace and righteousness. 2. A title assumed by various Islamic religious leaders; especially, Mohammed Ahmed (1844-1885), Sudanese leader of a religious war against the British and Egyptians. [Arabic *mahdīy*, "rightly guided (one)", past participle of *madā*, to lead rightly.] —**Mah·dism** n. —**Mah·dist** adj. & n.

Ma·hi·can (mə-héekən) n., pl. **-cans** or collectively **Mahican**. Also **Mo·hi·can** (mố-i-kən, mō-héekən, mə-). A member of a group or confederacy of Algonquian-speaking North American Indians that formerly lived between the upper Hudson River Valley and Lake Champlain.

mah-jong, mah-jongg (máa-jóng, -zhóng) n. A game of Chinese origin usually played by four persons. Tiles bearing various designs, are drawn and discarded until one player wins with a hand of four combinations of three tiles each and a pair of matching tiles. [Chi-

magnolia *There are about 80 species of magnolia. All are trees and shrubs native to North and Central America and Asia.*

nese *má jiàng,* possibly from *máquè,* sparrow (from the figure of a sparrow on a leading piece of one of the suits).]

Mah·ler (maa'lər), **Gustav** (1860–1911). Austrian composer and conductor. He was conductor at the Vienna State Opera House (1897–1907). He completed nine symphonies, some with voices, and the song cycles *Das Lied von der Erde* (1908) and *Kindertotenlieder* (1902). —**Mah·ler·i·an** (maa-léer-i-ən) *adj. & n.*

mahlstick. Variant of **maulstick.**

ma·ho·e (maa-hō-i) *n.* A New Zealand tree, *Melicytus ramiflorus,* yielding a useful fibre and a wood from which charcoal is produced. [Maori.]

ma·hog·a·ny (mə-hóggəni) *n., pl.* **-nies. 1. a.** Any of various tropical American trees of the genus *Swietenia,* valued for their hard, reddish-brown wood. **b.** The wood of any of these trees; especially, that of *S. mahogani,* much used for making furniture. **2. a.** Any of several trees having wood resembling true mahogany. **b.** The wood of any of these trees. See **African mahogany, Philippine mahogany. 3.** Moderate reddish brown. [17th century : origin obscure.]

Mahomet. Variant of **Muhammad.**

Mahometan. Variant of **Muhammadan.**

Mahometanism. Variant of **Muhammadanism.**

ma·ho·ni·a (mə-hōni-ə) *n.* An evergreen plant of the genus *Mahonia,* certain of which are cultivated as ornamental shrubs. [New Latin, after Bernard *McMahon* (1775–1816), U.S. botanist.]

Ma·hore (mə-hór, ma-ór). Formerly **Ma·yotte** (ma-yót). An island in the Indian Ocean, the southeasternmost of the Comoros group. When the Comoros government declared its independence from France in 1975, the Mayottes refused to join them, and the following year voted overwhelmingly (80 per cent) to become an overseas département of France. Area, 373 square kilometres (144 square miles). Dzaoudzi is the capital.

Ma·hound (mə-hównd, -hoónd). *Archaic.* Muhammad.

ma·hout (mə-hówt) *n.* In India and the East Indies, the keeper and driver of an elephant. [Hindi *mahāut, mahāwat,* from Sanskrit *mahāmātra,* "of great measure", originally an honorific title : *mahā,* great + *mātra,* measure.]

Mahrati, Mahratti. Variants of **Marathi.**

Mahratta. Variant of **Maratha.**

Mähren. See **Moravia.**

mah·seer (máa-seer) *n.* Any of several large Indian freshwater fishes of the carp family, such as *Barbus tor.* [Hindi, probably from Sanskrit *mahāciras,* "big-head".]

mahzor. Variant of **machzor.**

Mai·a¹ (mí-ə, máy-ə). *Greek Mythology.* A goddess, the eldest of the **Pleiades** *(see).* [Greek, from *maia,* mother, nurse.]

Maia² *n.* The brightest star in the **Pleiades** *(see).*

maid (mayd) *n.* **1.** A female servant. **2.** A spinster. Used chiefly in the phrase *old maid.* **3.** *Archaic & Literary.* **a.** A girl or young woman. **b.** A virgin. [Middle English *maide,* shortening of MAIDEN.]

mai·dan (mī-da'an, ma-) *n.* In India and Southeast Asia, an open space in or near a town, used for parades, sports, or the like. [Urdu, from Arabic.]

maid·en (máyd'n) *n.* **1.** *Archaic & Literary.* **a.** An unmarried girl or woman. **b.** A virgin. **2.** A machine resembling the guillotine, used for executions in the 16th and 17th centuries in Scotland. **3.** A racehorse that has never won a race. **4.** In cricket, a maiden over. —*adj.* **1.** Of, pertaining to, or befitting a maiden: *a maiden blush.* **2.** Unmarried. Said only of women: *a maiden aunt.* **3.** Inexperienced; untried. Said especially of a soldier or weapons. **4.** Designating a racehorse that has never won a race. **5.** First or earliest: *a maiden voyage.* **6.** Designating territory that has never been explored or captured. [Middle English *maiden,* Old English *mægden,* diminutive of *mægeth,* maid, from Germanic.]

maid·en·hair (máyd'n-hair) *n.* Any of various ferns of the genus *Adiantum,* having dark stems and light green, feathery fronds with fan-shaped leaflets. Also called "maidenhair fern". [From the fineness of the stems.]

maidenhair tree *n.* The **ginkgo** *(see).*

maid·en·head (máyd'n-hed) *n.* **1.** The hymen. Not in technical usage. **2.** *Poetic.* Virginity.

maid·en·hood (máyd'n-hoód) *n.* The condition or time of being a maiden or virgin.

maid·en·ly (máyd'n-li) *adj.* Pertaining to or suitable for a maiden. —**maid·en·li·ness** *n.*

maiden name *n.* A woman's family name before marriage.

maiden over *n.* In cricket, an over during which no runs are scored. Also called "maiden".

maid in waiting *n., pl.* **maids in waiting.** An unmarried woman attending a queen or princess.

Maid Mar·i·an (márri-ən) *n.* The Queen of the May in morris dances and May Day games.

maid of honour *n., pl.* **maids of honour. 1.** An unmarried noblewoman attending upon a queen or princess. **2.** *U.S.* The chief unmarried female attendant of a bride. Compare **bridesmaid, matron of honour. 3.** *British.* An almond-flavoured custard tart.

Maid of Orléans. See **Joan of Arc.**

maid·ser·vant (máyd-servənt) *n.* A female servant.

Maid·stone (máyd-stən, -stōn). County town of Kent, southeast England, on the river Medway. Its main industries are paper-making and brewing, and it is a major market for hops and grain.

mai·eu·tic (may-oótik, mī-) *adj.* Also **mai·eu·ti·cal** (-'l). Pertaining to the Socratic method of bringing forth latent ideas through a logical sequence of questions and answers. [Greek *maieutikos,* obstetric, "bringing ideas to birth", from *maieuesthai,* to act as midwife, from *maia,* midwife, nurse.]

mai·gre (máygər) *adj.* **1.** Not containing meat or its juices: *a maigre diet.* **2.** *Roman Catholic Church.* Formerly, of or designating a day of abstinence on which any maigre food was permitted. [French, thin, from Old French, from Latin *macer,* thin.]

mail¹ (mayl) *n.* **1. a.** Letters, packages, and other material handled in a postal system; post. **b.** *Chiefly U.S.* Postal material for a specific person or organisation: *I received my mail today.* **c.** *Chiefly U.S.* Material collected or processed for distribution from a post office at a specified time: *the morning mail.* **2.** The postal system; the post. **3.** A train, ship, or aircraft by which mail is transported: *The ship is a fast mail.* **4.** *Capital* **M.** Used as part of the title of certain newspapers: *Daily Mail.* ~*adj.* Of, pertaining to, carrying, or used in the handling of mail: *mail delivery.* ~*tr.v.* **mailed, mailing, mails.** *Chiefly U.S.* To send by mail; post. [Middle English *male,* mailbag, from Old French *male,* pouch, bag, from Old High German *malha.*] —**mail·a·ble** *adj.*

mail² *n.* **1.** Flexible body armour composed of small overlapping metal rings, interlocking loops of chain, or scales. See **chain mail, coat of mail. 2.** The protective shell or covering of certain animals, such as the turtle. ~*tr.v.* **mailed, mailing, mails.** To cover or armour with mail. [Middle English *maille,* from Old French, from Latin *macula,* spot, mesh.]

mail·bag (máyl-bag) *n.* **1.** A large canvas sack used for transporting mail. **2.** A leather or canvas bag suspended from the shoulder, used by postmen. Also called "postbag".

mail·box (máyl-boks) *n.* *Chiefly U.S.* A **letter box** *(see).*

mail carrier *n.* *Chiefly U.S.* A postman.

mail coach *n.* A railway wagon designed to carry mail.

mail drop *n.* *U.S.* **1.** Any receptacle for holding mail at the address of delivery. **2.** A slot for the insertion of mail. **3.** An address at which a person receives mail but does not reside.

mailed (mayld) *adj.* **1.** Covered with or made of plates of mail. **2.** Having a hard covering of scales, spines, or horny plate. Said, for example, of an armadillo or lobster.

mailed fist *n.* The threat of the use of force, as between nations.

mail·er (máylər) *n.* A person or device that addresses, stamps, or otherwise prepares mail.

Mail·er (máylər), **Norman** (1923–). U.S. author. Concerned with political, moral, and social questions, he rose to prominence with a World War II novel, *The Naked and the Dead* (1948). His other books include *Why Are We In Vietnam?* (1967), *The Armies of the Night* (1968), which won a Pulitzer prize, and *The Executioner's Song* (1979).

mail·ing list (máyling) *n.* A list of persons to whom advertising leaflets, brochures, or the like are to be posted.

mail·lot (mī-ō̄, maa-yō̄) *n.* **1.** A coarsely knitted, stretchable jersey fabric. **2. a.** A pair of tights or a leotard made of this material and worn for ballet or gymnastics. **b.** A bathing suit of this material, usually of one piece. [French, tight garment, originally a child's swaddling bands, from Old French, from *maille,* band of cloth, mail, from Latin *macula,* spot, mesh.]

mail·man (máyl-man) *n., pl.* **-men** (-men) *Chiefly U.S.* A postman.

mail order *n. Abbr.* **m.o., M.O. 1.** A request for goods or services that is received, and usually dealt with, through the post. **2.** The system of ordering and receiving goods through the post.

mail-or·der firm (máyl-awrdər, -órdər) *n.* A business establishment that is primarily organised to promote, receive, and deal with requests for goods or services through the post.

mail·ship (máyl-ship) *n.* A ship carrying mail, and often passengers, regularly between two ports or countries; especially, that between South Africa and Britain.

maim (maym) *tr.v.* **maimed, maiming, maims. 1.** To deprive (a person) of, or of the use of, a limb or bodily part; mutilate; disable; cripple. **2.** To make imperfect or defective; impair. [Middle English *maymen,* to wound, from Old French *mahaignier†.*]

Mai·mon·i·des (mī-mónni-deez), **Moses ben Maimon,** also known as Rambam (1135–1204). Jewish doctor, rabbi, and philosopher. He codified Jewish laws and philosophy in the such works as *The Mishneh Torah* and *The Guide of the Perplexed.*

main¹ (mayn) *adj.* **1. a.** Most important; principal; major. **b.** Being the largest or greatest in size, extent, or degree: *the main road.* **2.** Exerted to the utmost; sheer; utter. **3.** Of or pertaining to a continuous area or stretch, as of land or water: *the main ocean.* **4.** *Archaic.* **a.** Very great or considerable of its kind; remarkable: *"I am a main bungler at a long story."* (R.B. Sheridan). **b.** Highly important; momentous. **5.** *Grammar.* Designating the principal clause, verb, or phrase referring to the subject in a complex sentence. **6.** *Nautical.* Connected to or located near the mainmast: *a main skysail.* ~*n.* **1.** The principal, most important, or largest part or point: *"The main of life is composed of small incidents."* (Samuel Johnson). **2. a.** The principal pipe or conduit in a system for conveying water, gas, oil, or other utility. **b.** *Plural.* The place from which switches, valves, or the like can be operated to control the supply of electricity, water, or gas to an entire building or area. **3.** Physical strength. Used chiefly in the phrase *might and main.* **4.** *Rare.* The mainland, as distinguished from islands. See **Spanish Main. 5.** *Poetic.* The open ocean. **6.** *Nautical.* **a.** The **mainsail** *(see).* **b.** The **mainmast**

(see). **—in the main.** Mostly; on the whole; chiefly. —See Synonyms at **chief.** [Middle English, from Old English *mægen,* strength, and *mægn-* (used in compounds), strong, great.]

main² *n.* **1.** In dice playing, a throw of the dice. **2.** A series of cockfights consisting of an odd number of matches. [16th century : perhaps from the phrase MAIN CHANCE.]

main•brace (máyn-brayss) *n.* A rope that controls the movement of the main yard on a sailing ship.

main chance *n.* One's most advantageous opportunity.

main clause *n. Grammar.* A clause in a complex sentence, containing a subject, verb and sometimes an object and modifiers, capable of standing alone syntactically as a complete sentence.

main course *n.* The largest and usually most substantial course of a meal that consists of more than one course.

main deck *n.* The principal deck of a ship or other large vessel.

main drag *n. Chiefly U.S. Slang.* The principal street of a city or town.

Maine¹ (mayn; *French* men). Former province of northwest France, largely corresponding with the départements of Mayenne and Sarthe. Le Mans was its capital. The region is noted for its cattle.

Maine² (mayn). Largest state in New England, United States. The north and west are mountainous, the east hilly with a fragmented coast. There are more than 2,200 lakes. Maine is four-fifths forested. Tourism, timber, dairying, market gardening, fishing, and the making of paper and wood products are its chief industries. It has considerable mineral wealth. Augusta is the capital.

main•frame (máyn-fraym) *n.* **1.** A high-speed computer with a large memory store. Also called "mainframe computer". Compare **minicomputer. 2.** The central processing unit of a computer exclusive of peripheral and remote devices.

main•land (máyn-lənd, -land) *n.* The principal land mass of a country, area, or continent, as distinguished from an island or peninsula.

Main•land¹ (máyn-land). Also **Po•mo•na** (pə-mṓnə). Largest of the 65 Orkney Islands. It has Stone Age and other prehistoric remains. The main town is Kirkwall.

Mainland². Largest of the Shetland Islands. The main town is Lerwick.

main line *n.* **1.** A principal section of a railway line. Compare **branch line. 2.** *Slang.* A principal and easily accessible vein, usually in the arm or leg, into which narcotics can be injected.

main•line (máyn-līn) *v.* **-lined, -lining, -lines.** *Slang.* —*tr.* To inject (narcotics) directly into a major vein. —*intr.* To take drugs in this way. **—main•lin•er** *n.*

main•ly (máynli) *adv.* Most importantly; for the most part.

main•mast (máyn-maast, *nautical* -məst || -mast) *n.* **1.** The principal mast of a vessel. **2.** The taller mast, whether forward or aft, of any two-masted sailing vessel. **3.** The second mast aft of any sailing ship with three or more masts.

main•plane (máyn-playn) *n.* **1.** Either of the wings of an aircraft. **2.** The principal supporting surfaces of an aircraft, including both wings.

main•sail (máyn-sayl, *nautical* -s'l) *n.* **1.** The principal sail of a vessel. **2.** A quadrilateral or triangular sail set from the after part of the mainmast on a fore-and-aft rigged vessel. **3.** A square sail set from the main yard on a square-rigged vessel.

main sequence *n.* A major grouping of stars, containing the Sun and 90 per cent of the known stars, characterised by an approximately uniform average increase of luminosity with surface temperature as represented by a single band on the **Hertzsprung-Russell diagram** *(see).*

main•sheet (máyn-sheet) *n.* The rope that controls the angle at which the mainsail is adjusted to take advantage of the wind.

main•spring (máyn-spring) *n.* **1.** The principal spring in a mechanical device, especially in a watch or clock, that drives the mechanism by uncoiling. **2.** A motivating force; an impelling cause: *He was the mainspring of the reform movement.*

main•stay (máyn-stay) *n.* **1.** A strong rope that serves to steady and support the mainmast of a sailing vessel. **2.** A principal support: *Agriculture is a mainstay of the economy.*

main•stream (máyn-streem) *n.* The prevailing current or direction of a movement, activity, or influence: *writers in the mainstream of 18th-century thought.*

~adj. Avoiding extremes; neither traditional nor avant-garde: *mainstream jazz.*

main street *n.* **1.** The principal street of an American town or city. **2.** *U.S. Capital* **M,** *capital* **S.** The culture of smug, materialistic, and provincial small towns. [Sense 2, influenced by *Main Street* (1920), novel by Sinclair LEWIS.]

main•tain (mayn-táyn, mən-, men-) *tr.v.* **-tained, -taining, -tains. 1.** To continue; carry on; keep up: *maintain good relations; maintain a custom.* **2.** To preserve or retain: *tried to maintain her composure.* **3.** To keep in a condition of good repair or efficiency: *maintain public roads.* **4. a.** To provide for; bear the expenses of: *maintain a family.* **b.** To keep in existence; sustain: *food to maintain life.* **5.** To defend or sustain; hold against attack. **6. a.** To declare to be true; defend against dispute: *The defendant maintains his innocence.* **b.** To assert in or as if in an argument; state; declare: *He maintained that he was innocent.* —See Synonyms at **keep, support.** [Middle English *mainteine,* from Old French *maintenir,* from Medieval Latin *manūtenēre,* from Latin *manū tenēre,* "to hold in the hand", support, know : *manū,* ablative of *manus,* hand + *tenēre,* to hold.] **—main•tain•a•ble** *adj.* **—main•tain•er** *n.*

maintained school *n.* In Britain, a school maintained by funds from the local authority, rather than by private money.

main•te•nance (máyntə-nənss, máynt- || mayn-táynənss) *n.* **1.** The action of maintaining or the state of being maintained: *the maintenance of tribal custom.* **2.** *Law.* An interference in a lawsuit by someone who is a disinterested party. **3.** The act or work of keeping something in proper condition. Also used adjectivally: *a maintenance man.* **4. a.** The provision or means of support or livelihood: *maintenance of serfs by a lord.* **b.** *Law.* Financial support ordered by a court to be given by one person to another, as in the case of a divorced couple. In this sense, also *U.S.* "alimony". —See Synonyms at **livelihood.** [Middle English *maintenaunce,* from Old French *maintenance,* from *maintenir,* to MAINTAIN.]

Main•te•non (máN-tə-noN; *French* maNt-nóN), **Marquise de,** born Françoise d'Aubigné (1635–1719). Second wife of Louis XIV. Her first husband, Paul Scarron, died in 1660. She married Louis in secret in 1684 after the death of the Queen.

main•top (máyn-top) *n.* A platform at the head of the mainmast on a square-rigged vessel.

main topgallant *n.* A sail or yard set from the topgallant section of a mainmast.

main topgallantmast *n.* The section of the mainmast immediately above the main topmast on a square-rigged vessel.

main topmast *n.* The section of the mainmast on a square-rigged sailing vessel between the lower mast and the main topgallantmast.

main topsail *n.* The sail that is set above the mainsail.

main yard *n.* The lower yard on a mainmast.

Mainz (mīnts). *French* **Ma•yence** (ma-yoNs). River port and capital of Rhineland-Palatinate, West Germany. At the confluence of the rivers Rhine and Main, it grew on an early Roman camp site (*c.* 13 B.C.), was the seat of the first German archbishopric (8th century), and was made Europe's first printing centre by Johannes Gutenberg (15th century). An industrial and communications centre, it is also important in the wine trade.

mai•ol•i•ca (mī-óllikə, mə-yóllikə) *n.* A type of richly coloured and decorated pottery that is enamelled and glazed, especially as produced in Italy in the 16th century. [From *Majolica,* medieval form of MALLORCA where the ceramic style originated.]

mai•son•ette, mai•son•nette (máyzə-nét, máysə-) *n.* A self-contained unit of living accommodation, especially that occupying two or more floors of a larger building and having its own outside front door. [Diminutive of French *maison,* house.]

maî•tre d'hô•tel (méttrə-dō-tél, máytrə-) *n., pl.* **maîtres d'hôtel** *(pronounced as singular).* **1.** A head steward or butler, a **major-domo** *(see).* **2.** A **head waiter** *(see).* **3.** A sauce of melted butter, chopped parsley, lemon juice, salt, and pepper. [French, "master of hotel".]

maize (mayz) *n.* **1.** A New World grass, *Zea mays,* widely cultivated for animal feed and for its yellow cob, which may be cooked and eaten as a vegetable. Also called "Indian corn", "corn". **2.** Light yellow to moderate orange yellow. [Spanish *maíz,* or French *maïs,* probably from Taino *mahiz.*] **—maize** *adj.*

Maj. major.

ma•jes•tic (mə-jéstik) *adj.* Also **ma•jes•ti•cal** (-'l). Having or exhibiting stateliness or great dignity; royal; dignified: *a majestic gesture.* See Synonyms at **grand. —ma•jes•ti•cal•ly** *adv.*

maj•es•ty (májə-sti) *n., pl.* **-ties. 1. a.** The greatness and dignity of a sovereign. **b.** The sovereignty and power of God. **2. a.** A royal personage. **b.** *Capital* **M.** *Abbr.* **M.** A title of or form of address for a sovereign monarch. Used with *His, Her,* or *Your*: *His Majesty's wish; Your Majesty.* **3. a.** Royal dignity of bearing or aspect; grandeur. **b.** Stateliness, splendour, or magnificence, as of appearance, style, or character; imposing quality. [Middle English *maieste, mageste,* from Old French *majeste,* from Latin *mājestās* (stem *mājestāt-*), authority, grandeur.]

Maj. Gen. major general.

ma•jol•i•ca (mə-yólli-kə, -jólli-) *n.* **1.** A type of pottery made, chiefly in the 19th century, in imitation of maiolica. **2.** Loosely, maiolica. [Alteration of MAIOLICA.]

ma•jor (máyjər) *adj.* **1.** Great in importance, rank, or stature: *a major writer; a major scientific discovery.* **2.** Serious or dangerous; requiring great attention or concern: *major difficulties; a major illness.* **3.** *Law.* Having attained full legal age. **4.** Designating the senior or older of two pupils with the same surname. Used especially in some British schools. **5.** *Chiefly U.S.* Designating or pertaining to the principal field of academic specialisation chosen by students in a college or university. **6.** *Logic.* More inclusive in scope; broader, as are the **major premise** and **major term** *(both of which see).* **7.** *Music.* **a.** Designating a scale or mode having semitones between the third and fourth and the seventh and eighth degrees. **b.** Equivalent to the distance between the tonic note and the second or third or sixth or seventh degrees of a major scale or mode: *a major interval.* **c.** Based on a major scale: *major key.* Compare **minor.**

~n. **1.** *Abbr.* **Maj.** *Military.* **a.** An officer of the British Army or Royal Marines ranking between a lieutenant colonel and a captain, equivalent in rank to lieutenant-commander in the Royal Navy and squadron leader in the Royal Air Force. **b.** An officer of corresponding rank in the U.S. and certain other armies. **2.** *Law.* One who has reached full legal age. **3.** *Chiefly U.S.* **a.** The principal field of academic specialisation of a student in a college or university: *His major is chemistry.* **b.** A student specialising in such a field: *a history major.* **4.** A **major premise** or **major term** *(both of which see).* **5.** *Music.* A major scale, key, interval, or mode.

~intr.v. **majored, -joring, -jors.** *Chiefly U.S.* To pursue academic

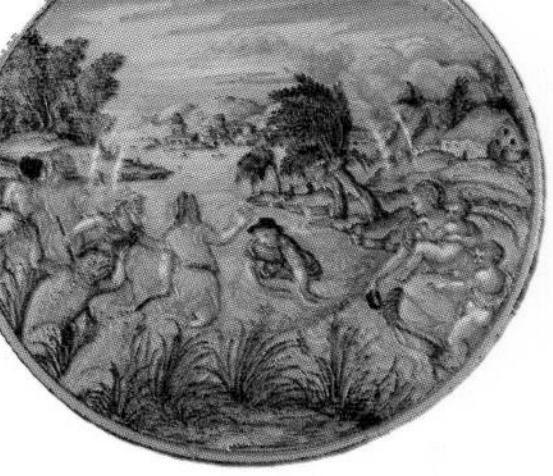

maiolica *A tin-glazed earthenware plate painted by Alfonso Patanazzi near the end of the 16th century. The plate is entitled:* Latona changing peasants into frogs.

studies in a major field. Used with *in.* [As adjective, Middle English, from Latin *mājor,* greater. As noun (in military sense), from French, shortened from SERGEANT MAJOR.]

major axis *n.* In geometry: **1.** The line intersecting an ellipse and passing through both its focuses. **2.** The longest axis of an ellipsoid.

Majorca. See **Mallorca.** —**Majorcan** *adj. & n.*

ma·jor-do·mo (máyjər-dṓmō) *n., pl.* **-mos.** **1.** The head steward or butler in the household of a sovereign or great nobleman. Also called "maître d'hôtel". **2.** Broadly, any steward or butler. [Italian *maggiordomo* and Spanish *mayordomo,* from Medieval Latin *mājor domūs,* "head of the house", "mayor of the palace" : *mājor,* noun use of Latin *mājor,* greater + *domūs,* genitive of *domus,* house.]

ma·jor·ette (máyjə-rét) *n.* A **drum majorette** *(see).*

major general *n. Abbr.* **Maj. Gen.** *Military.* **1.** An officer of the British Army or Royal Marines ranking between a lieutenant-general and a brigadier, and equivalent in rank to a rear admiral in the Royal Navy and an air vice marshal in the Royal Air Force. **2.** An officer of corresponding rank in the U.S. and certain other armies. [French *major-général* : MAJOR (officer) + *général* (adjective), "of general rank".] —**major generalcy, major generalship** *n.*

ma·jor·i·ty (mə-jórrəti) *n., pl.* **-ties.** **1.** The greater number or part: *the majority of the consumers.* **2.** The number of votes cast in any election above the total number obtained by the runner-up or all other votes cast. See **absolute majority, relative majority.** **3.** The political party, group, or faction having the most power by virtue of its larger representation or electoral strength. **4.** The status of legal age when full civil and personal rights may be exercised legally, in Britain at 18, in various other countries at 21. **5.** The military rank, commission, or office of a major. [French *majorité,* from Medieval Latin *mājōritās* (stem *mājōritāt-*), the state of being greater, greater number, from Latin *mājor,* greater.]

Usage: *Majority* is used only with reference to estimates of number, and not for general statements of quantity: thus one may say *The majority of the strikers have decided to go back to work,* but not *The majority of the strike action has been unsuccessful.* In precise contexts, *majority* can apply to anything over 50 per cent, but it is more commonly used to mean "most", and often "almost all", where it is frequently preceded by an intensive, such as *vast* or *great.* The construction *greater majority* is used only with reference to a comparison of two specific numbers (i.e. two majorities) in careful English, but loosely it can be heard as an equivalent of *great majority* (i.e. "most of").

When *majority* signifies a specific number, it takes a singular verb: *His majority was five votes.* When it signifies the larger of two groups it (like such other collective nouns as *committee* or *jury*) may be singular or plural, depending on the sense: *The majority is determined* stresses the unity of the group in question, whereas *The majority are of different minds* stresses the individuality of the group's members. When discussing politics, speakers of British English can use *majority* to mean either the difference between the number of votes for the winner and the number of votes for the runner-up, or the difference between the number of votes for the winner and the number of votes for all other candidates combined. Speakers of American English tend to use *majority* for the latter sense and *plurality* for the former.

majority carrier *n.* The electrons in n-type semiconductors and the holes in p-type semiconductors that carry the majority of the current. Compare **minority carrier.**

majority leader *n. U.S.* The leader of the majority party in a legislative body. Compare **minority leader.**

majority rule *n.* A political doctrine and practice by which a numerical majority of the voters holds the power to make decisions binding on all the voters.

major league *n.* **1.** In the United States, either of the two principal groups of professional baseball teams: the **American League** or the **National League** *(both of which see).* **2.** Any league of principal importance in other professional sports, such as basketball or football. —**major-league** *adj.*

major orders *pl.n.* See **holy orders.**

major planet *n.* Any of the four planets, Jupiter, Saturn, Uranus, or Neptune, that are larger than Earth. Compare **terrestrial planet.**

major premise *n. Logic.* In a **syllogism** *(see),* the premise containing the major term.

Major Prophets *pl.n.* **1.** The Hebrew prophets Isaiah, Jeremiah, and Ezekiel. **2.** In the Old Testament, the books of these prophets.

major scale *n. Music.* A diatonic scale having semitones between the third and fourth and the seventh and eighth notes. Compare **minor scale.**

major suit *n.* In the game of bridge, a suit, either spades or hearts, of superior scoring value.

major term *n. Logic.* A term of a **syllogism** *(see)* that forms the predicate of the conclusion and the subject or predicate of the major premise.

Ma·ju·ba Hill (mə-jo͞obə). Also **A·ma·ju·ba** (ámmə-). A mountain in the Drakensberg range, South Africa. It was the scene in 1881 of the rout of 554 British soldiers by 150 Boers.

ma·jus·cule (májə-skewl || *U.S. also* mə-júss-kewl) *n.* A large letter, either capital or uncial, used in writing or printing. Compare **minuscule.**

~*adj.* **1.** Of or pertaining to such a letter. **2.** Written in such letters. [French *majuscule,* from Medieval Latin *(littera) mājuscula,* largish (script), from *mājusculus,* somewhat larger, diminutive of *mājor,* larger.] —**ma·jus·cu·lar** (mə-júss-kewlər) *adj.*

Ma·ka·lu (máckə-lo͞o). Also **Chomo Lonzo.** The world's fifth highest mountain, lying in the Himalayas of Nepal. Its higher peak, rising to 8 481 metres (27,825 feet), was first climbed in 1955.

Ma·kar·i·os III (mə-kaári-oss), **Archbishop,** born Mikhail Christodoulou Mouskos (1913–77). Primate of the Orthodox Church of Cyprus. He was deported by the British (1956) for alleged support of the Eoka terrorists. He returned in 1959 to become president. He fled in 1974 after a coup by Greek extremists and a subsequent invasion by Turkey, but returned later that year to resume his presidency.

make (mayk. *Note: the pronunciation* (mek) *is not considered standard.*) *v.* **made** (mayd), **making, makes.** —*tr.* **1.** To create; construct; form; shape: *make a statue.* **2.** To give a new form or use to: *make a stone into a weapon.* **3.** To cause to become: *That'll make him sorry.* **4.** To cause to acquire a specified characteristic or property: *make a stone sharp.* **5. a.** To cause to behave in a specified manner: *Heat makes a gas expand.* **b.** To compel: *make him obey.* **6.** To use or adopt for a specified purpose: *make Perth one's home.* **7.** To bring about; cause: *make trouble; make a noise.* **8.** To engage in: *make war.* **9.** To perform: *make a phone call.* **10.** To arrive at; come round to: *make a decision.* **11.** To form as one's own; acquire: *make a friend.* **12. a.** To score; achieve: *make a run in cricket; make two tricks in bridge.* **b.** To earn: *make money.* **c.** To manage to come within reach of; attain: *make the grade.* **13.** To confer rank upon: *made him president.* **14. a.** To put into proper condition; prepare: *make the bed.* **b.** *South African.* To cook or prepare: *making chicken for dinner.* **15.** To prepare and start: *make a fire.* **16.** To regard as the nature or meaning of something. Used with *of*: *What do you make of his behaviour?* **17.** To allow provision for; provide: *make room.* **18.** To be suitable for; serve as: *Oak makes good building material.* **19. a.** To constitute: *Twenty members make a quorum.* **b.** To add up to: *One and one makes two.* **c.** To amount to: *It makes no difference.* **20.** To be the completion or satisfaction of: *That makes my day.* **21.** To succeed in becoming a member of: *He didn't make the cricket team.* **22.** To calculate as being; estimate: *We make the distance 20 miles.* **23.** To reach or arrive at: *made Salisbury by sunset; made the train in time.* **24.** To develop into: *She will make a fine doctor.* **25.** To cause to be or seem: *The beard makes him quite distinguished.* **26.** To close an electrical circuit. **27.** *Slang.* To have sexual intercourse with. **28.** In some card games: **a.** To name (the trump). **b.** To win a trick with (a card). **c.** To shuffle (the cards). —*intr.* **1. a.** To give an appearance of doing something: *She made as if to shake my hand.* **b.** To behave or act in a specified manner: *make merry.* **2.** To head in a specified direction; set out: *a ship making for shore.* —**make after.** To chase or pursue. —**make away with.** To carry off; especially, to steal. —**make for. 1.** To move towards with haste. **2.** To attack or assail: *made for his throat.* **3.** To lead to; be conducive to: *Champagne makes for a good time.* —**make it. 1.** To arrange or come to a meeting: *Let's make it tomorrow; I can't make it on Friday.* **2.** *Informal.* To become successful: *Made it as a dancer.* **3.** *Slang.* To have sexual intercourse. Often used with *with*: *made it with a girl.* —**make it up.** To satisfy a grievance or debt. —**make like.** *U.S. Slang.* To imitate: *make like a bird.* —**make off.** To leave or run away in a hurry. —**make off with.** *Informal.* To take away; steal. —**make out. 1. a.** To discern or see, especially with difficulty. **b.** To decipher: *I can't make out her handwriting.* **2.** To understand or comprehend: *I can't make out what he is saying.* **3. a.** To write out or draw up: *She made out the invoices.* **b.** To fill in by writing: *make out an application.* **4.** To attempt to prove, show, or imply: *He makes me out to be a liar.* **5.** To get along; manage: *How is he making out in his new job?* —**make over. 1.** To change or redo; renovate: *We made over the cellar into a playroom.* **2.** To change or transfer the ownership of, usually by means of a legal document: *He made over the property to his son.* —**make with.** *U.S. Slang.* To perform; produce. Usually followed by *the*: *Start making with the hard work.*

~*n.* **1.** The act or process of making. **2.** The style or manner in which a thing is made: *I dislike the make of this coat.* **3. a.** A manufacturing style. **b.** A specific line of manufactured goods, identified by the maker's name or the registered trademark: *a famous make of shirt.* **4.** The physical or moral nature of a person: *Let's see what make of man you are.* **5.** *Rare.* The amount produced; the yield or output, especially of a factory. **6.** In cards: **a.** The act of naming trumps. **b.** The act of shuffling the cards. —**on the make. 1.** Applying oneself brashly to social or financial advancement. **2.** *Slang.* Seeking out a sexual partner. [Make (infinitive), made (past tense), made (past participle); Middle English *maken, mad, mad,* Old English *macian, macode, macod,* from Germanic.]

make believe *tr.v.* To feign; pretend.

make-be·lieve (máyk-bi-leev, -bə-) *n.* Playful pretence or fanciful belief, as in the conscious suspension of reality in a child's game. —**make-be·lieve** *adj.* —**make-be·liev·er** *n.*

make-or-break (máyk-awr-bráyk) *adj.* Liable to end in either complete success or complete failure: *a make-or-break policy.*

mak·er (máykər) *n.* **1.** One that makes. **2.** *Law.* An individual who signs a promissory note. **3.** *Archaic.* A poet.

Mak·er (máykər) *n. Capital* **M.** God. Usually used with a possessive pronoun: *our Maker.* —**go to meet (one's) Maker.** To die.

make-read·y (máyk-reddi) *n. Printing.* The operation of preparing a forme for printing by adjusting and levelling the plates to ensure a clear impression.

make·shift (máyk-shift) *adj.* Used or assembled as a temporary or expedient substitute. —**make·shift** *n.*

PRONUNCIATION KEY

a, trap; aa, father; ai, fair; ar, star; aw, lawn; ay, play; b, bb, stab; rubber; ch, church; ck, ticket; d, dd, dead; ladder; e, dress; ee, bee; er, defer; ew, few; ewr, pure; ə, about; ər, letter; f, ff, fife; differ; g, gg, giggle; h, hat; i, kit; ī, price; īr, fire; j, judge; k, kick; l, ll, let; 'l, needle; m, mm, man; n, nn, no; 'n, sudden; ng, thing; o, lot; ō, no; o͝o, foot; o͞o, shoe; oor, poor; ow, cow; owr, hour; oy, boy; p, pp, pepper; r, rr, red; s, ss, sauce; sh, ship; t, tt, totter; th, thick; th, this; smooth; u, cut; ur, turn; v, vv, valve; w, wet; y, yes; z, zz, zebra; zh, vision; pleasure

IN FOREIGN WORDS:

aN, oN, Saint-Saëns; hl, Llanelli; Hluhluwe; kh, loch; lough; Khaled

STRESS MARK:

ín-sīt, insight; in-sít, incite

make up *tr.v.* **1.** To create or put together by assembling parts or ingredients: *make up a prescription.* **2.** To prepare or organise for use: *make up the beds.* **3.** To apply cosmetics to (the face). **4.** To devise as a fiction or falsehood; invent: *make up an excuse.* **5.** *Printing.* To arrange (type in columns or pages) ready for printing. **6. a.** To add up to or constitute. **b.** To make complete: *make up a foursome at golf.* **7. a.** To make good (a deficit or lack): *make up the difference.* **b.** To resolve (a personal difference or quarrel). *—intr.v.* **1. a.** To apply cosmetics to the face. **b.** To apply theatrical make-up. **2.** To be reconciled after a personal difference: *Let's kiss and make up.* **—make up for.** To compensate for: *make up for lost time.* **—make up to. 1.** To act in a friendly or ingratiating manner towards. **2.** To make amorous overtures to.

make-up (máyk-up) *n.* **1.** The way in which something is composed or arranged; construction: *the complex make-up of UNESCO.* **2.** *Printing.* The arrangement or composition, as of type or illustrations, on a page or in a book. **3.** The qualities or temperament that constitute a personality; disposition: *Lying is not in her make-up.* **4.** Cosmetics applied especially to the face. **5.** The cosmetics, costumes, wigs, and the like, that an actor uses in playing a role.

make·weight (máyk-wayt) *n.* **1.** Something added on a scale in order to meet a required weight. **2.** A person or thing added to make good a deficiency or lack.

mak·ing (máyking) *n.* **1.** The act of one that makes or the process of being made. Often used in combination: *matchmaking.* **2.** A means of gaining success or realising potential: *The job will be the making of him.* **3. a.** Something made. **b.** The amount or quantity of something made at one time: *the largest making of pastry for the week.* **4.** *Often plural.* The materials or substances necessary for making or achieving something: *We have the makings of a fine team.* **5.** *Often plural.* Earnings or profits. **6.** *Plural. Chiefly U.S. Slang.* The paper and tobacco for rolling a cigarette. **—in the making.** In the process of being realised; potential: *a politician in the making.*

-making *adj. comb. form. Chiefly British Informal.* Indicates causing or producing a specified emotional reaction or condition; for example, **anxious-making, sick-making.**

ma·ko (ma'akō) *n., pl.* **-kos.** Any shark of the genus *Isurus,* such as *I. oxyrinchus.* [Maori.]

ma·ko-ma·ko (ma'akō-ma'akō) *n., pl.* **-kos.** A small evergreen tree *Arisfotelia serrata,* native to New Zealand, having large racemes of reddish flowers. [Maori.]

ma·ku·ta. Plural of **likuta.**

mal– *comb. form.* Indicates: bad, badly, not, or wrongly; for example, **maladminister, malodorous.** [Middle English, from Old French *mal-* (prefix) and *mal* (adverb and adjective), from Latin *mal-, male-* (prefix), *male* (adverb), ill, and *malus* (adjective), bad.]

Mal. 1. Malachi (Old Testament). **2.** Malay; Malayan.

Mal·a·bar Coast (mál-ə-bár). The southwest coast of India. It stretches from Goa in the north to Cape Comorin, and produces coconuts, rice, spices, and hardwoods.

Mal·a·bo (ma-la'a-bō). Formerly **Santa Isabel.** Capital of Equatorial Guinea, and the chief town of the island of Bioko.

Ma·lac·ca[1] or **Me·la·ka** (mə-láckə). Seaport of Peninsular Malaysia and capital of Malacca state. Founded on the Strait of Malacca in about 1400, the city became one of the chief trading centres of the Far East. It was later colonised in turn by the Portuguese, Dutch, and British (1824), and its commercial importance declined with the expansion of Singapore.

Malacca[2] or **Melaka.** State of Peninsular Malaysia. Formerly one of the Straits Settlements, it consists mainly of swampy plains on the southwest coast of the Malay Peninsula, rising to low hills inland. Its main products are rubber, tin, rice, and copra.

Malacca, Strait of. Sea channel in Southeast Asia, between Sumatra and the Malay Peninsula. It is a major world shipping route and has been claimed by both Indonesia and Malaysia.

Malacca cane *n.* The stem of the rattan palm of Asia, used for walking sticks. Also called "Malacca". [After MALACCA.]

Mal·a·chi[1] (mál-ə-kī). A Hebrew prophet of the fifth century B.C., the last of the **Minor Prophets** *(see).*

Malachi[2] *n. Abbr.* **Mal.** A prophetic book of the Old Testament attributed to Malachi.

mal·a·chite (mál-ə-kīt) *n.* A green mineral, copper carbonate, $CuCO_3 \cdot Cu(OH)_2$, used as a source of copper and for ornamental stoneware. [French, from Old French *melochite,* from Latin *molochītēs,* from Greek *molokhitis,* malachite, "the mallow-green stone", from *molokhē,* variant of *malakhē,* mallow.]

Mal·a·chy (mál-əki), **Saint,** born Mael Maedoc ua Morgair (1095–1148). Irish churchman. He became Bishop of Connor (1124) and Archbishop of Armagh (1134–37), and founded the first Cistercian abbey in Ireland (1142). The "Prophesies of St. Malachy" are incorrectly attributed to him. His feast day is November 3.

mal·a·col·o·gy (mál-ə-kólləji) *n.* The scientific study of molluscs. [French *malacologie,* abbreviation of *malacozoologie*; New Latin *Malacozoa,* molluscs : Greek *malakos,* soft + -ZOA + -LOGY.] **—mal·a·col·o·gist** *n.*

mal·a·cop·te·ryg·i·an (mál-ə-kóptə-ríji-ən) *adj.* Of or pertaining to the Malacopterygii, a group of soft-finned fishes including the herring and salmon.
~n. A malacopterygian fish. Compare **acanthopterygian.** [Greek *malakos,* soft + *pterux* (stem *pterug-*), wing, fin + -IAN.]

mal·ad·just·ment (mál-ə-jústmənt) *n.* **1.** Faulty adjustment, as in a machine. **2.** *Psychology.* Inability to adjust one's personality to the demands of one's social environment. **—mal·ad·just·ed** *adj.*

mal·ad·min·is·ter (mál-əd-mínni-stər || -ad-) *tr.v.* **-tered, -tering, -ters.** To administer inefficiently or dishonestly. **—mal·ad·min·is·tra·tion** (-stráysh'n) *n.* **—mal·ad·min·is·tra·tor** (-straytər) *n.*

mal·a·droit (mál-ə-dróyt) *adj.* Lacking dexterity; clumsy; awkward. —See Synonyms at **awkward.** [French, from Old French : MAL- + ADROIT.] **—mal·a·droit·ly** *adv.* **—mal·a·droit·ness** *n.*

mal·a·dy (mál-ədi) *n., pl.* **-dies. 1.** A disease, disorder, or ailment. **2.** Broadly, any unwholesome condition. [Middle English *maladie,* from Old French, from *malade,* sick, from Latin *male habitus,* "ill-kept", "in poor condition" : *male,* ill, from *malus,* bad + *habitus,* past participle of *habēre,* to have, keep.]

ma·la fi·de (mál-ə fídi, ma'alə) *adv. Latin.* In bad faith. Compare **bona fide. —ma·la fi·de** *adj.*

Mal·a·ga (mál-əgə) *n.* A sweet white wine originally from Málaga.

Mál·ag·a (mál-əgə). Seaport and capital of Málaga province, Spain. Founded in the 12th century B.C. by the Phoenicians on the coast of Andalusia, it became a Moorish city (711–1487) and is now a major resort of the Costa del Sol. It exports wine, almonds, dried fruits, and olives. Pablo Picasso was born here.

Mal·a·gas·y (mál-ə-gássi, -ga'azi) *n., pl.* **-gasies** or collectively **Malagasy. 1.** A native of the Malagasy Republic. **2.** The Austronesian language spoken in the Madagascar. **—Mal·a·gas·y** *adj.*

Malagasy Republic. See **Madagascar, Democratic Republic of.**

ma·la·gue·ña (mál-ə-gáyn-yə) *n.* **1.** A dance native to Málaga, a variety of the fandango. **2.** The music for such a dance. [Spanish, feminine of *malagueño,* of MÁLAGA.]

mal·aise (ma-láyz, mə-) *n.* **1.** A feeling of illness or depression. **2.** A vague feeling of unease. **3.** An unwholesome or undesirable condition or state of affairs: *Violence is a symptom of a malaise in society.* [French, from Old French : MAL- + *aise,* EASE.]

ma·la·mute, ma·le·mute (mál-ə-mōōt, -mewt) *n.* A powerful dog of a breed developed in Alaska as a sledge dog, having a thick grey, black, or white coat. Also called "Alaskan malamute". [Inuit Eskimo *Mahlemut,* name of the Alaskan tribe that bred the dog.]

Ma·lan (mə-lán, -la'an), **Daniel (François)** (1874–1959). South African politician. Formerly a preacher in the Dutch Reformed Church (1905–15), he became an M.P. (1918), Nationalist Party leader (1934–54), and prime minister (1948–54). He introduced the country's first apartheid laws.

mal·a·pert (mál-ə-pert, -pért) *adj. Archaic.* Impudent in speech or manner; saucy; bold.
~n. Archaic. An impudent, saucy person. [Middle English, from Old French : MAL- + *apert,* clever, from Latin *apertus,* open, from past participle of *aperīre,* to open.] **—mal·a·pert·ly** *adv.* **—mal·a·pert·ness** *n.*

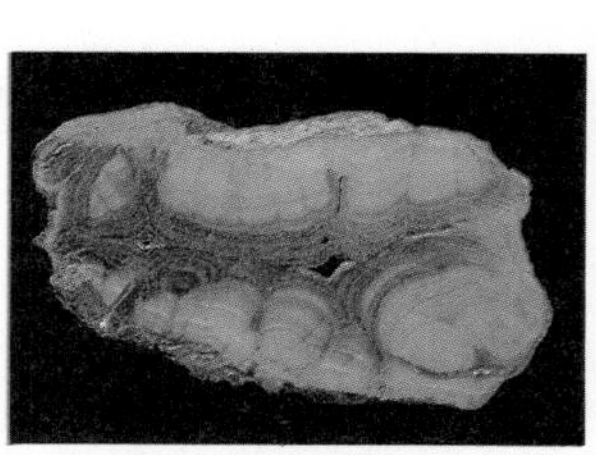

malachite *A naturally occurring copper carbonate. The vivid green pigment produced from powdered malachite was used by the ancient Egyptians for eye make-up.*

mal·a·prop·ism (mál-ə-prop-iz'm) *n.* **1.** A humorous misuse of a word by confusing it with one of similar sound; for example, "a shrewd awakening" instead of "a rude awakening". **2.** A word so misused. [After *Mrs. Malaprop* in Sheridan's play *The Rivals* (1775), from MALAPROPOS.] **—mal·a·prop·i·an** (-própi-ən) *adj.*

mal·a·pro·pos (mál-áppro-pō) *adj.* Inappropriate; out of place.
~adv. In an inappropriate or inopportune manner. [French *mal à propos,* "not to the purpose".]

ma·lar (máy-lər || -laar) *adj. Anatomy.* Of or pertaining to the cheekbone or the cheek.
~n. Anatomy. The cheekbone, the **zygomatic bone** *(see).* [Latin *mālāris,* from *māla*†, cheekbone, upper jaw. See **maxilla.**]

ma·lar·i·a (mə-láir-i-ə) *n.* **1.** An infectious disease characterised by cycles of chills, fever, and sweating, transmitted by the bite of a female anopheles mosquito infected with a protozoan parasite of the genus *Plasmodium.* Also called "paludism", "marsh fever". **2.** *Rare.* Bad or foul air. [Italian *mal'aria,* foul air (hence, also the fever once erroneously associated with it) : *mal(a),* bad + *aria,* air.] **—ma·lar·i·al, ma·lar·i·an, ma·lar·i·ous** *adj.*

ma·lar·i·ol·o·gy (mə-láir-i-ólləji) *n.* The medical study and treatment of malaria. **—ma·lar·i·o·l·o·gist** *n.*

ma·lar·key, ma·lar·ky (mə-lárki) *n. Slang.* Exaggerated or meaningless talk; nonsense. [20th century : origin obscure.]

mal·as·sim·i·la·tion (mál-ə-símmi-láysh'n) *n. Pathology.* Incomplete assimilation of food.

mal·ate (mál-ayt, máyl-) *n.* A salt or an ester of malic acid. [MAL(IC ACID) + -ATE.]

Mal·a·thi·on (mál-ə-thí-on) *n.* A trademark for an organic compound, $C_{10}H_{19}O_6PS_2$, similar to but less toxic than parathion and used as a garden insecticide.

Ma·la·wi (mə-la'a-wi). Formerly **Nyasaland** (nī-ássə-land). Small, landlocked country in east central Africa. Mostly highland, it depends on agriculture, exporting sugar, tobacco, tea, and groundnuts. However, it has untapped deposits of bauxite and coal and considerable hydroelectric potential. A British protectorate from 1891, the country joined Northern and Southern Rhodesia (now Zambia and Zimbabwe) in a federation (1953–63). Led by Dr. Hastings Banda, it became independent as Malawi in 1964 and a republic in 1966. Area, 118 484 square kilometres (45,747 square miles). Population, 6,600,000. Capital, Lilongwe. See map, next page.

Malawi, Lake. Also **Lake Nyasa** (nī-ássə). Lake of east central Africa, at the southern end of the Great Rift Valley. With an area of some 30 040 square kilometres (11,600 square miles), it is the third largest of Africa's lakes, and drains southwards via the river Shiré to the Zambezi. David Livingstone reached the lake in 1859.

Ma·lay (mə-láy || máy-lay) *n. Abbr.* **Mal. 1.** A member of a people inhabiting much of Malaysia and Indonesia, and some adjacent

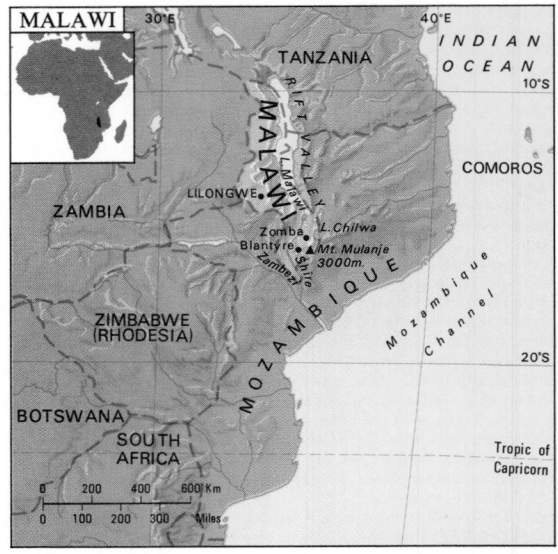

areas. **2.** The Austronesian language of this people. **3.** In South Africa, a Muslim of Malay or Indonesian descent.

~*adj.* **1.** Of or pertaining to the Malays or their language. **2.** Of or pertaining to Malaya or Malaysia. —**Ma·lay·an** *adj. & n.*

Ma·lay·a, Federation of (mə-láy-ə). Former state in Southeast Asia. The British established trading centres on Penang (now Pinang) Island (1786) and Singapore (1819). In 1824 they formally acquired Malacca from the Dutch. The three territories were joined as the Straits Settlements (1926). By 1930 the British controlled the entire Malay Peninsula, and the independent Federation of Malaya was formed in 1957. See **Malaysia, Federation of.**

Mal·a·ya·lam (mál-i-aáləm, -ay-) *n.* A Dravidian language spoken on the Malabar coast in Kerala, in southwestern India.

Ma·lay Archipelago. Chain of islands off Southeast Asia separating the Indian and Pacific Oceans. Extending some 6 100 kilometres (about 3,800 miles) from Sumatra to Timor, it includes the Indonesian, Malaysian, and Philippine islands. The island of New Guinea (without the Bismarck Archipelago) is sometimes included.

Ma·lay·o·Pol·y·ne·sian (mə-láy-ō-pólli-néezh'n, -néesh'n) *n.* **Aus·tronesian** *(see).* —**Ma·lay·o·Pol·y·ne·sian** *adj.*

Ma·lay Peninsula. Also **Kra Peninsula** (kraa) or **Malaya.** Peninsula of Southeast Asia. Extending south between the Andaman Sea and the South China Sea, it includes part of Thailand in the north, Peninsular Malaysia in the south, and the island of Singapore.

Ma·lay·si·a, Federation of (mə-láy-zi-ə, -zhi-, -zhə). State in Southeast Asia. Formed in 1963, it comprised West Malaysia (the former **Federation of Malaya** and now called Peninsular Malaysia) and East Malaysia, the former British colonies of Sabah (North Borneo) and Sarawak on the northwest coast of Borneo, now called by their original names. Singapore seceded in 1965. Generally mountainous, with much tropical rain forest, Malaysia is the world's leading producer of tin and natural rubber, and Sabah and Sarawak have valuable oilfields. Tension between the Malay (44 per cent) and Chinese (36 per cent) populations has contributed to a history of political unrest. Area, 329 749 square kilometres (127,317 square miles). Population, 14,700,000. Capital, Kuala Lumpur.

Mal·colm III (mál-kəm), also known as Malcolm Canmore (1031–93). King of Scotland (1057–93). He was the son of Duncan, and became king on the death of Macbeth (1057). He was killed at Alnwick while raiding England.

Malcolm X, born Malcolm Little; also known as El Hajj Malik El-Shabass (1925–65). U.S. black militant leader. Joining the Black Muslims (1952), he preached that Western society was inherently racist and that black people must create a separate society, by violence if necessary. Suspended from the Black Muslims (1963), he

founded the Organisation of Afro-American Unity (1964) and was assassinated in Harlem while addressing a rally.

mal·con·tent (mál-kən-tent ‖ -tént) *adj.* Discontented with or in rebellion against established conditions.

~*n.* A discontented or rebellious person. [French : MAL- + CONTENT.]

mal de mer (mál də maír) *n.* Seasickness. [French.]

Mal·dives (máwl-divz ‖ mól-, -dīvz), **Republic of.** Formerly **Maldive Islands.** *Divehi* **Divehi Raajje.** South Asian state comprising a group of some 2,000 coral islands in the Indian Ocean, 220 of which are inhabited. It was a sultanate (1100–1965), and from 1887 was under British protection. The sultanate gained full independence in 1965 and became a republic in 1968. Fishing and coconuts are the mainstay of the economy. The R.A.F. staging post on Gan, given to the republic in 1976, is to be a major airport. Area, 298 square kilometres (115 square miles). Capital, Malé. See map at **Indian Ocean.** —**Mal·div·i·an** *adj. & n.*

male (mayl) *adj. Abbr.* **m, M, m., M. 1. a.** Of, pertaining to, or designating the sex that has organs to produce spermatozoa for fertilising ova. **b.** Capable of fertilising ova. Said of gametes. **2.** Of or characteristic of the male sex; masculine: *male aggression.* **3.** Virile; manly. **4.** Composed of men or boys, or both: *a male choir.* **5.** *Botany.* Bearing stamens but not pistils; staminate: *male flowers.* **6.** Designating the projecting part of a machine, plug, or the like designed for insertion into a corresponding hollow part or socket.

~*n. Abbr.* **m, M, m., M. 1.** A male human or animal. **2.** A plant having only staminate flowers. [Middle English, from Old French *male, masle,* from Latin *masculus,* diminutive of *mas,* male.] —**male·ness** *n.*

ma·le·ate (máli-ayt) *n.* A salt or an ester of maleic acid. [MALEIC + -ATE.]

Male·branche (mal-brónsh), **Nicolas de** (1638–1715). French philosopher. He attempted to reconcile the philosophy of Descartes with religion.

male chauvinist *n.* A man who regards women as being innately inferior to men. —**male chauvinism** *n.*

male chauvinist pig *n. Abbr.* **M.C.P.** A male chauvinist. Used derogatorily.

mal·e·dict (mál-i-dikt, -díkt) *adj. Archaic.* Accursed.

~*tr.v.* **maledicted, -dicting, -dicts.** *Archaic.* To pronounce a curse against. [Middle English, from Latin *maledictus,* past participle of *maledīcere,* to speak ill of, curse : *male,* ill, from *malus,* bad + *dīcere,* to say.]

mal·e·dic·tion (mál-i-díksh'n) *n.* **1. a.** The utterance of a curse. **b.** A curse. **2.** Slander. —**mal·e·dic·tor·y** (-dík-təri, -tri) *adj.*

mal·e·fac·tor (mál-i-faktər) *n.* **1.** One who has committed a crime; a criminal. **2.** An evildoer. [Middle English, from Latin *malefactor,* from *malefacere,* to do wrong : *male,* ill, from *malus,* bad + *facere,* to do.] —**mal·e·fac·tion** (-fáksh'n) *n.*

male fern *n.* A fern, *Dryopteris filix-mas,* that yields the drug used to treat tapeworm infestation.

ma·lef·ic (mə-léffik) *adj. Literary.* Producing or causing evil; causing disaster: *malefic arts.* [Latin *maleficus,* doing wrong : *male,* ill, from *malus,* bad + -FIC.]

ma·lef·i·cence (mə-léffi-sənss) *n. Literary.* **1.** Evil or harm; evildoing. **2.** Harmful or evil nature or quality. [Latin *maleficentia,* from *maleficus,* MALEFIC.] —**ma·lef·i·cent** *adj.*

ma·le·ic ac·id (mə-láy-ik, -lée-) *n.* A colourless crystalline acid, HOOCCH:CHCOOH, used in the synthesis of resins and as an oil and fat preservative. [French *maléique,* variant of *malique,* MALIC (ACID).]

malemute. Variant of **malamute.**

Ma·len·kov (mál-ən-kof, -kov; *Russian* mullin-káwf), **Georgi Maximilianovich** (1901–). Soviet Communist leader. He became a trusted aide of Stalin and deputy premier (1946), succeeding him as premier in 1953. He was also briefly first secretary of the Communist Party. He resigned in 1955 because of the failure of the government's agricultural policy.

ma·lev·o·lent (mə-lévvələnt) *adj.* **1.** Having or exhibiting ill will; wishing harm to others; malicious. **2.** *Obsolete.* Having an evil influence: *malevolent stars.* [Latin *malevolēns* (stem *malevolent-*) : *male,* ill, from *malus,* bad + *volēns,* present participle of *velle,* to will, wish.] —**ma·lev·o·lence** *n.* —**ma·lev·o·lent·ly** *adv.*

mal·fea·sance (mal-féez'nss) *n. Law.* Misconduct or wrongdoing; especially, wrongdoing that is committed by one who has official obligations. Compare **misfeasance, nonfeasance.** [MAL- + Old French *faisance,* doing, from Medieval Latin *faciēntia,* from Latin *facere,* to do.] —**mal·fea·sant** *adj. & n.*

mal·for·ma·tion (mál-fawr-máysh'n) *n.* **1.** The condition of being malformed. **2.** An abnormal structure or form, especially a deformity present at birth.

mal·formed (mál-fórmd) *adj.* Abnormally or faultily formed.

mal·func·tion (mál-fúngksh'n) *intr.v.* **-tioned, -tioning, -tions. 1.** To fail to function. **2.** To function abnormally; perform imperfectly.

~*n.* The act or an instance of malfunctioning.

Mal·herbe (ma-laírb), **François de** (1555–1628). French poet. He helped to formulate the norms of the French classical style.

Ma·li (maáli), **Republic of.** A landlocked West African state. The Sahara covers the north and savannah the south. The country's agricultural economy has been ravaged by drought, and its exports of cotton and groundnuts have to be supplemented by foreign aid, especially from France. The seat of several ancient empires, Mali was conquered by the French (1893) and as French Sudan became

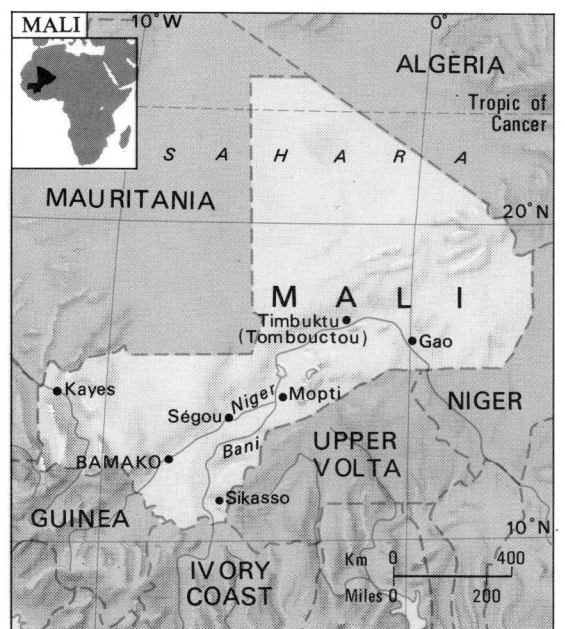

part of French West Africa. In 1959 it joined Senegal in the Mali Federation, but broke away to full independence the next year. Area, 1 240 000 square kilometres (478,767 square miles). Capital, Bamako.

mal·ic acid (mál-ik, máyl-) n. A colourless, crystalline compound, $COOHCH_2CH(OH)COOH$, that occurs naturally in a wide variety of unripe fruit, including apples, cherries, and tomatoes, and is used as a flavouring and an aid in ageing wine. [French *acide malique; malique* from Latin *mālum,* apple, from Doric Greek *malon,* variant of Attic *mēlon.*]

mal·ice (mál-iss) n. 1. The desire to harm others, or to see others suffer; ill will; spite: *Her eyes glittered with malice.* 2. *Law.* The intent, without just cause or reason, to commit an unlawful act that will result in harm to another or others. Often used in the phrases *malice aforethought* and *malice prepense.* [Middle English, from Old French, from Latin *malitia,* from *malus,* bad.]

ma·li·cious (mə-líshəss) adj. 1. Resulting from or having the nature of malice: *malicious rumours.* 2. *Law.* Motivated by or experiencing malice. —**ma·li·cious·ly** adv. —**ma·li·cious·ness** n.

ma·lign (mə-līn) tr.v. -ligned, -ligning, -ligns. To speak evil of; slander; defame. ~adj. 1. Evil in nature or intent. 2. Evil in influence; injurious; baleful. [Middle English *maligne,* evil, from Old French, from Latin *malignus,* from *malus,* bad.] —**ma·lign·er** n. —**ma·lign·ly** adv.

    Synonyms: malign, defame, traduce, vilify, revile, vituperate, slander, calumniate, libel.

ma·lig·nan·cy (mə-lígnən-si) n., pl. -cies. Also **ma·lig·nance** (-lígnənss). 1. The state or quality of being malignant. 2. A malignant tumour.

ma·lig·nant (mə-líg-nənt) adj. 1. Showing great malevolence; actively evil in nature. 2. Highly injurious; pernicious. 3. *Pathology.* a. Designating an abnormal growth that tends to metastasise. Compare **benign.** b. Threatening to life or health; virulent: *a malignant disease.* —**ma·lig·nant·ly** adv.

ma·lig·ni·ty (mə-líg-nəti) n., pl. -ties. 1. a. Intense ill will or hatred; great malice. b. An act or feeling of great malice. 2. The condition or quality of being highly dangerous or injurious; deadliness.

ma·li·hi·ni (maáli-héeni) n. A newcomer, foreigner, or stranger among the natives of Hawaii. [Hawaiian.]

ma·lines, ma·line (mə-léen) n., pl. **malines.** 1. A thin, stiff, gauzy material woven in a hexagonal pattern. 2. A fine lace, **Mechlin** (see). [French, from *Malines* (MECHELEN), Belgium, where the lace was made.]

Malines. See **Mechelen.**

ma·lin·ger (mə-líng-gər) intr.v. -gered, -gering, -gers. To pretend to be ill or injured in order to avoid duty or work. [French *malingre,* sickly, from Old French *malingre†* : perhaps MAL- + *haingre,* weak.] —**ma·lin·ger·er** n.

Ma·lin·ke (mə-língki) n., pl. -kes or collectively **Malinke.** 1. A member of a people of west Africa related to the Mandingos. 2. The language of the Malinke.

Ma·li·now·ski (mál-i-nófski), **Bronislaw** (1884–1942). Polish-born anthropologist. He believed that customs and beliefs have specific social functions. His works, based on his research in New Guinea and the Trobriand Islands, include *Crime and Custom in Savage Society* (1926) and *The Sexual Life of Savages in Northwestern Melanesia* (1929).

mal·i·son (mál-i-sən, -zən) n. *Archaic.* A curse. [Middle English

malisoun, from Old French *maleison,* from Latin *maledictiō* (stem *malediction-*), from *maledīcere,* MALEDICT.]

mal·kin (máw-kin, máwl- ‖ mál-) n. *British Regional.* 1. A slovenly woman. 2. A cat. 3. A hare. [Middle English, diminutive of *Maalde,* Matilda.]

mall (mawl; *in sense 3, and in the names of certain thoroughfares,* mal) n. 1. A shady public walk or promenade. 2. *Chiefly U.S.* A street lined with shops and closed to vehicles. 3. A game, **pall-mall** (see). [After The *Mall* in London, originally a pall-mall lane, shortened from PALL-MALL.]

mal·lard (mál-aard, -ərd) n., pl. -lards or collectively **mallard.** A wild duck, *Anas platyrhynchos,* the male of which has a green head and neck. It is the ancestor of most domestic ducks. [Middle English, from Old French *mallart,* probably from *maslart* (unattested) : *masle,* MALE + -art, -ARD.]

Mal·lar·mé (mál-aar-máy), **Stéphane** (1842–98). French poet, founder with Verlaine of the Symbolist school. He developed a deliberately obscure style, using allegory and unconventional construction and vocabulary. His works include *L'Après-midi d'un faune* (1876) (which inspired Debussy) and *Un coup de dés jamais n'abolira le hasard* (1897).

mal·le·a·ble (mál-i-əb'l) adj. 1. Capable of being shaped or formed, as by hammering or pressure: *a malleable metal.* 2. Designating a form of iron that has been toughened by gradual heating or slow cooling. 3. Capable of being altered or influenced; tractable; pliable. —See Synonyms at **flexible.** [Middle English *malliable,* from Old French *malleable,* from Medieval Latin *malleābilis,* from *malleāre,* to hammer, from *malleus,* a hammer.] —**mal·le·a·bil·i·ty** (-ə-bílləti), **mal·le·a·ble·ness** n. —**mal·le·a·bly** adv.

mal·lee (mál-ee) n. 1. Any of several low, scrubby, evergreen trees of the genus *Eucalyptus,* of western Australia. 2. Scrub formed by these trees. 3. *Australian.* The bush; the outback. Preceded by *the.* [Native Australian name.]

mallee fowl n. An Australian ground-living bird, *Leipoa ocellata,* that places its eggs to incubate in a sandy mound. Also called "mallee bird", "mallee hen". [From MALLEE.]

mal·le·muck (mál-i-muk) n. Any of several sea birds, such as the fulmar, the petrel, or the shearwater. [Dutch *mallemok,* fulmar : Middle Dutch *mal,* silly + *mocke,* thing.]

mal·le·o·lus (mə-lée-ə-ləss) n., pl. -li (-lī). *Anatomy.* Either of the two rounded protuberances on each side of the ankle, formed by a projection of the tibia or fibula. [New Latin, diminutive of Latin *malleus,* hammer (from the resemblance to a hammerhead).]

mal·let (mál-it) n. 1. a. A short-handled hammer, usually with a wooden head, used chiefly to drive a chisel or wedge. b. Any of various specialised forms of this tool. 2. *Sports.* A longer handled, similar implement used to strike the ball, as in croquet and polo. 3. A light hammer with a spherical, often padded head, used to play instruments such as the vibraphone or xylophone. [Middle English *maillet,* from Old French, from *mailler,* to hammer, from *mail,* a hammer, from Latin *malleus,* hammer.]

mal·le·us (mál-i-əss) n., pl. **mallei** (-i-ī). The largest of three small bones in the middle ear. Also called "hammer". Compare **incus, stapes.** See **ear.** [Latin, hammer.]

Ma·llor·ca (ma-yáwr-kə, mə-). *English* **Ma·jor·ca** (mə-jáwr-kə, -yáwr-). Largest of the Balearic Islands, Baleares province, Spain. Its northern mountains give it a mild climate and tourism is the economy's mainstay, together with agriculture, fishing, and mining. Palma is the capital and chief port. —**Ma·llor·can** adj. & n.

mal·low (mál-ō) n. 1. Any plant of the widely distributed genus *Malva,* typically having pink flowers. 2. Any of various related plants, such as the marsh mallow or musk mallow. [Middle English *malwe,* Old English *mealuwe, mealwe,* from Latin *malva.*]

malm (maam) n. 1. a. A soft, easily crumbled limestone. b. Loam formed by the disintegration of such limestone. 2. A mixture of clay and chalk used in making bricks. [Middle English *malme,* Old English *mealm-* (only in compounds).]

Mal·mö (mál-mö; *Swedish* -mö). Seaport in Sweden, situated on the Öresund opposite Copenhagen. It is a naval port and a shipbuilding and textile centre.

malm·sey (maʹamzi) n., pl. -seys. A sweet fortified white wine originally made in Greece, but now also produced in Madeira, the Canary Islands, the Azores, and Spain. [Middle English, from Medieval Latin *Malmasia,* alteration of Greek *Monembasia,* Greek seaport from which it was shipped.]

mal·nour·ished (mál-núrrisht) adj. Suffering from improper nutrition or insufficient food.

mal·nu·tri·tion (mál-new-trísh'n ‖ -nōō-) n. A lack of, or condition resulting from a lack of, adequate nutrition. It is caused by an insufficient or ill-balanced diet or by defective digestion or utilisation of food.

mal·oc·clu·sion (mal-ə-klōō-zh'n ‖ -kléw-) n. Failure of the upper and lower teeth to meet when the mouth is closed.

mal·o·dor·ous (mal-ōdərəss) adj. Having a bad odour; ill-smelling. —**mal·o·dor·ous·ly** adv. —**mal·o·dor·ous·ness** n.

ma·lo·nic acid (mə-lŏnik, -lónnik) n. *Propanedioic acid* (see).

Mal·o·ry (mál-əri), **Sir Thomas** (died 1471). English writer. He was the author of *Le Morte Darthur* (published by Caxton, 1485), a collection of Arthurian romances adapted from French sources.

Mal·pi·ghi (mal-péegi), **Marcello** (1628–94). Italian physiologist. He was the first to use a microscope in the study of anatomy. He became physician to Pope Innocent XII (1691).

Mal·pigh·i·an body (mal-píggi-ən, -péegi-) n. *Anatomy.* A mass of

mallard *Found throughout the Northern Hemisphere, the mallard is Britain's commonest duck, living on reservoirs, lakes, and ponds. It is the ancestor of most domestic duck breeds.*

arterial capillaries enveloped in a capsule and attached to a tubule in the kidney. Also called "Malpighian corpuscle". [Discovered by Marcello Malpighi.]

Malpighian layer *n. Anatomy.* The deepest layer of the epidermis, from which the outer layers develop.

Malpighian tubule *n.* Any of the excretory tubes leading into the rear part of the gut of arthropods. Also called "Malpighian tube".

mal·po·si·tion (mál-pə-zísh'n) *n.* An abnormal position, especially of a foetus or of a bodily part.

mal·prac·tice (mal-práktiss) *n.* **1.** Improper or negligent treatment of a patient by a doctor or surgeon, for example, resulting in damage or injury. **2.** Improper or unethical conduct by the holder of an official or professional position. **3.** An improper practice. **—mal·prac·ti·tion·er** (mál-prak-tísh'n-ər) *n.*

Mal·raux (mal-rố), **André** (1901–76). French writer and political figure. Under de Gaulle's Fifth Republic he served as Minister of Information (1945–46) and Minister for Culture (1959–69). His books include *la Condition humaine* (1933), *le Temps du mépris* (1935), and an autobiography, *Antimémoires* (1967).

malt (mawlt ‖ molt) *n.* **1.** Grain, usually barley, that has been allowed to sprout, used chiefly in brewing and distilling. **2.** Malt liquor *(see).* **3.** A whisky that is made from malt and not blended with grain spirit. **4.** *Informal.* Malted milk.
~*v.* **malted, malting, malts.** *—tr.* **1.** To process (grain) into malt. **2.** To treat or to mix with malt or a malt extract. *—intr.* To become malt. [Middle English, Old English *mealt.*] **—malt·y** *adj.*

Mal·ta (máwltə ‖ móltə), **Republic of.** Mediterranean state comprising the islands of Malta, Gozo, and Comino, and two uninhabited islets. Its strategic value led to a series of foreign invasions, starting with that of the Phoenicians before 1000 B.C., and it became a British colony (1814). A naval base was built on Grand Harbour, and during World War II the Maltese people were awarded the George Cross for gallantry under bombardment. Malta became an independent Commonwealth republic in 1974 and in 1979 the naval base closed. The economy now depends on shipping, tourism, and light industries. Area, 316 square kilometres (122 square miles). Capital, Valletta.

Malta fever *n.* **Brucellosis** *(see).*

mal·tase (máwl-tayz, -tayss ‖ mól-) *n.* An enzyme that hydrolyses maltose to glucose.

mal·ted milk (máwltid ‖ móltid) *n.* **1.** A soluble powder made of dried milk, malted barley, and wheat flour. **2.** A beverage made by mixing milk with this powder. In this sense, also called "malt", "malted".

Mal·tese (máwl-téez ‖ mól-, -téess) *adj.* Of or pertaining to Malta, its inhabitants, or the language spoken in Malta.
~*n., pl.* **Maltese. 1.** A native or inhabitant of Malta. **2.** The language spoken in Malta, a dialect of North Arabic with elements of Italian. **3.** A Maltese dog. **4.** A Maltese cat.

Maltese cat *n.* A North American domestic cat with short, silky, bluish-grey fur.

Maltese cross *n.* A cross having the form of four triangles, often with the outer edges indented, placed with their points towards the centre of a circle.

Maltese dog *n.* A dog of a toy breed, probably originating in Malta, having a long, silky, white coat, short legs, and a tail arched over the back. Also called "Maltese", "Maltese poodle", "Maltese terrier".

mal·tha (mál-thə) *n.* **1.** A black, viscous natural bitumen. **2.** Any of certain mineral waxes composed of mixtures of hydrocarbons. [Latin, from Greek *maltha*, a mixture of wax and pitch.]

malt house *n.* A building where malt is made or stored. Also called "malting".

Mal·thus (mál-thəss), **Thomas Robert** (1766–1834). British economist. He wrote *Essay on the Principle of Population* (1798), arguing that a population without planning increased faster than food production. His ideas were used to justify birth control. **—Mal·thu·si·an** (mal-théw-zi-ən, -thoo-) *n. & adj.* **—Mal·thu·si·an·ism** *n.*

malt liquor *n.* Any alcoholic drink, such as beer, brewed from malt.

mal·tose (máwl-tōz ‖ mól-, -tōss) *n.* A sugar, $C_{12}H_{22}O_{11}$, formed during the digestion of starch and also occurring in germinating cereal grains. Also called "malt sugar".

mal·treat (mál-tréet) *tr.v.* **-treated, -treating, -treats.** To treat cruelly; handle roughly. See Synonyms at **abuse.** [French *maltraiter* : MAL- + *traiter*, to TREAT.] **—mal·treat·ment** *n.*

malt·ster (máwlt-stər ‖ mólt-) *n.* One employed to make malt. [Middle English : MALT + -STER.]

mal·va·ceous (mal-váyshəss) *adj.* Of or pertaining to the Malvaceae, a family of flowering plants that includes the mallow, cotton, and hollyhock. [Latin *malvaceus*, from *malva*, MALLOW.]

mal·va·si·a (mál-və-sée-ə) *n.* **1.** A grape from which malmsey wine is made. **2.** Malmsey wine. Also called "malvoisie". [Italian, from Medieval Greek *Monemvasia*, MALMSEY.] **—mal·va·si·an** *adj.*

Mal·vern (máwl-vərn ‖ mól-, -vern, *locally also* máw-). Spa in west central England, in the Malvern Hills, in Hereford and Worcester. It is the site of an important annual drama and music festival.

mal·ver·sa·tion (mál-vər-sáysh'n) *n.* Misconduct committed while in public office. [Old French, from *malverser*, to misbehave, from Latin *male versārī* : *male*, ill, from *malus*, bad + *versārī*, to behave.]

Malvinas, Islas. See **Falkland Islands.**

mal·voi·sie (mál-voy-zi, -və-) *n.* Malmsey wine, or a type of grape from which it is made; malvasia. [Middle English *malvesie*, from Old French, from Medieval Greek *Monemvasia*, MALVASIA.]

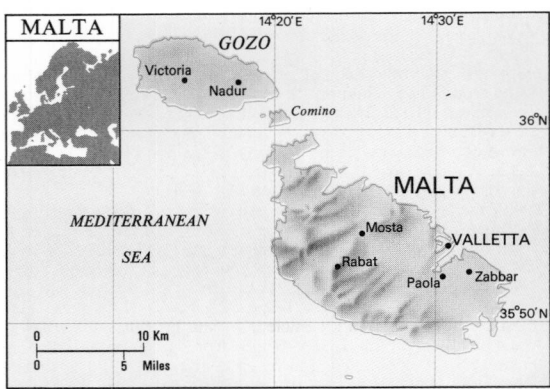

mam (mam) *n. British Regional.* Mother. Used familiarly, especially by children.

mama. *Chiefly U.S.* Variant of **mamma.**

mam·ba (mámbə) *n.* Any of several venomous arboreal snakes of the genus *Dendroaspis*, found in equatorial and southern Africa; especially, *D. angusticeps*, a green tree snake. [Zulu *im-amba.*]

mam·bo (mámbō) *n., pl.* **-bos. 1.** A dance of Latin American origin, resembling the rumba. **2.** The music for this dance, in 4/4 time.
~*intr.v.* **mamboed, -boing, -boes.** To dance the mambo. [American Spanish, from Haitian Creole *mambo*, a voodoo priestess.]

mam·e·lon (mámm'l-ən) *n.* A small, rounded hill. [French, "nipple", from *mamelle*, breast. See **mamilla.**]

Mam·e·luke (mámmi-loōk ‖ -lewk) *n.* A member of a former military caste, originally composed of slaves from Turkey, that held the Egyptian throne from about 1250 until 1517 and remained powerful until 1811. [Arabic *mamlūk*, slave.]

mamey. Variant of **mammee.**

mam·il·la (ma-míl-ə) *n., pl.* **-illae** (-ee). Also *chiefly U.S.* **mam·mil·la. 1.** A nipple or teat. **2.** Any nipple-shaped protuberance. [Latin, diminutive of *mamma*, breast.] **—mam·il·lar·y** (mə-mílləri, mámmi-ləri ‖ *U.S.* -lerri) *adj.*

mam·il·late (mámmi-layt) *adj.* Also **mam·il·lat·ed** (-laytid). **1.** Having nipples or mamillae. **2.** Shaped like a nipple or mamilla. **—mam·il·la·tion** (-láysh'n) *n.*

mam·ma¹ (mə-máa ‖ mámmə) *n.* Also *chiefly U.S.* **ma·ma.** Mother. Used familiarly, as by children. [Reduplication of baby-talk *ma.*]

mam·ma² (mámmə) *n., pl.* **mammae** (mámmee). An organ of female mammals that contains milk-producing glands; a breast or udder. [Latin.]

mam·mal (mámm'l) *n.* A member of the class Mammalia. [New Latin MAMMALIA.] **—mam·mal·i·an** (ma-máyli-ən, mə-) *adj. & n.*

Mam·ma·li·a (ma-máyli-ə, mə-) *pl.n.* A class of vertebrate animals of more than 15,000 species, including humans, distinguished by self-regulating body temperature, separation of oxygenated and deoxygenated blood in the heart, and, in the females, milk-producing mammae. [New Latin, from Latin *mammalis*, of the breast, from *mamma*, breast.]

mam·mal·o·gy (ma-mál-əji, mə-, -mól-) *n.* The branch of zoology dealing with the study of the Mammalia. [MAMMAL + -LOGY.] **—mam·ma·log·i·cal** (mámmə-lójik'l) *adj.* **—mam·mal·o·gist** (ma-mál-əjist, mə-, -mól-) *n.*

mam·ma·ry (mámməri) *adj.* Of or pertaining to a mamma.

mammary gland *n.* **1.** A milk-producing organ in female mammals, consisting of clusters of alveoli or small cavities with ducts terminating in a nipple or teat. **2.** A woman's breast. Used humorously.

mam·mee (ma-mée) *n.* Also **ma·mey** *pl.* **-meys. 1.** A tropical American tree, *Mammea americana*, bearing edible fruits. **2.** The large, red-rinded fruit of this tree, having a yellow, pulpy centre. In this sense, also called "mammee apple". [Spanish *mamey, mamei*, from Haitian.]

mam·mif·er·ous (ma-míffərəss) *adj.* Having mammary glands. [French *mammifère* : MAMMA (breast) + -FEROUS.]

mammilla. *Chiefly U.S.* Variant of **mamilla.** **—mammillate** *adj.*

mam·mo·gram (mámmə-gram) *n.* An X-ray photograph or radiograph of the breast. [MAMMA (breast) + -GRAM.]

mam·mog·ra·phy (ma-móggrəfi, mə-) *n.* Examination of the breast by X-rays, used for the early detection of abnormal growths. [MAMMA (breast) + -GRAPHY.]

Mam·mon (mámmən) *n.* **1.** In the New Testament, riches, avarice, and worldly gain personified as a false god. Matthew 6:24; Luke 16:9,11,13. **2.** *Often small* **m.** Riches regarded as a worldly goal or an evil influence. [Middle English *Mammona*, from Medieval Latin *mammōna*, from Greek *mamōnas*, from Aramaic *māmōnā*, riches.] **—mam·mon·ism** *n.* **—mam·mon·ist** *n.*

mam·mo·plas·ty (mámmō-plasti) *n., pl.* **-ties.** The altering of the shape or size of the breast by plastic surgery. [MAMMA (breast) + -PLASTY.]

mam·moth (mámməth) *n.* **1.** An extinct elephant of the genus *Mammuthus*, once found throughout the Northern Hemisphere. The best-known species is the woolly mammoth, *M. primigenius*, of northern Eurasia and North America. **2.** Something of great size.
~*adj.* Of enormous size, scale, or importance; gigantic. See Syn-

onyms at **enormous**. [Obsolete Russian *mammot*, from Tartar *mamont*, "earth" (because the first mammoth remains were dug out of the earth in Siberia).]

mam·my, mam·mie (mámmi) *n., pl.* **-mies**. **1.** Mother. Used familiarly, especially by children. **2.** *Chiefly southern U.S.* A black nurse for white children. Often considered offensive. [Baby talk, variant of MAMMA.]

mam·poer (mam-po͞or) *n.* In South Africa, a brandy, usually homemade, distilled from the juice of peaches or other soft fruits. [Afrikaans, possibly after *Mampura*, a Sotho chieftain.]

man (man) *n., pl.* **men** (men). **1.** An adult male human being, as distinguished from a female. Sometimes used in combination: *milkman; he-man*. **2.** Loosely, any human being, as distinguished from an animal or deity; a member of the human race; a person. Sometimes used in combination: *draughtsman; workmanlike; man-day*. See Usage note at **-person**. **3.** *Often capital* **M**. The human race; mankind. Used without an article: *the family of man*. **4.** *Zoology*. A member of the genus *Homo*, family Hominidae, order Primates, class Mammalia, characterised by erect posture and an opposable thumb; especially, a member of the only extant species, *Homo sapiens*, distinguished by the ability to communicate by means of organised speech and to record information in a variety of symbolic systems. **5.** A male human being endowed with such qualities as courage, strength, and fortitude, considered characteristic of manhood: *Stop snivelling and be a man!* **6.** A husband, lover, or boyfriend. Now used chiefly informally, except in the phrase *man and wife*. **7.** A member of the armed forces, especially one who is not an officer: *officers and men*. **8.** Any workman, servant, or subordinate, as opposed to an employer or master. **9.** A valet; a male servant. **10.** *Informal*. Fellow: *Look here, my good man!* **11.** One who swore allegiance to a lord in the Middle Ages; a liegeman; a vassal. **12.** Any of the pieces used in chess, draughts, backgammon, and other board games. **13.** *Nautical*. A ship. Used in combination: *merchantman; man-of-war*. **14.** A representative of a government, large company, or the like in a specified town or country: *our man in Paris*. **—as one man**. Unanimously: *They answered him as one man*. **—be (one's) own man**. To be independent in judgment and action. **—man and boy**. From boyhood on: *Man and boy, I've lived here 40 years*. **—the Man**. *U.S. Slang*. **1.** The police. **2.** A white man. Used derogatorily, especially by blacks. **—the man on the Clapham omnibus**. The ordinary citizen regarded as the embodiment of common sense. **—to a man**. Including everyone; without exceptions. See Usage note at **gentleman**. ~*tr.v.* **manned, manning, mans**. **1.** To supply or furnish with men for defence, support, or service: *manning a ship*. **2.** To be stationed at in order to defend, care for, or operate: *man the guns*. ~*interj. Chiefly U.S. Slang*. Used as an expletive to indicate strong feeling or to draw attention: *Man! it's hot in here*. [Middle English *man* (plural *men*), Old English *mann* (plural *menn*), from Germanic *mann-* (unattested).]

Man (man), **Isle of**. Island in the Irish Sea, an autonomous possession of the British Crown. Its parliament, the Court of Tynwald, is one of the oldest legislative assemblies in the world. The island depends on tourism, and is famous for the annual T.T. motorcycle racing. Douglas is the capital. See map at **United Kingdom**.

ma·na (má̈anə) *n.* **1.** In the native religions of Oceania, an impersonal supernatural force inherent in gods and sacred objects. **2.** Broadly, any power, prestige, or influence. [Maori.]

man-about-town (mán-əbówt-tówn) *n., pl.* **men-about-town** (mén-). A worldly and sophisticated man, especially one who frequents fashionable places.

man·a·cle (mánnək'l) *n.* **1.** A device for confining the hands, usually consisting of two metal rings that are fastened about the wrists and joined by a metal chain. **2.** Anything that confines or restrains. ~*tr.v.* **manacled, -cling, -cles**. **1.** To restrain with manacles. **2.** To confine or restrain as if with manacles; shackle; fetter. [Middle English *manicle*, from Old French, from Latin *manicula*, little hand, handle, diminutive of *manus*, hand.]

man·age (mánnij) *v.* **-aged, -aging, -ages**. —*tr.* **1.** To direct or control the use of; handle, wield, or use (a tool, machine, or weapon, for example). **2.** To exert control over; make submissive to one's authority, discipline, or persuasion: *Her mother can't manage her*. **3.** To direct or administer the affairs of (an organisation, estate, or the like): *He manages a football team*. **4. a.** To contrive or arrange; succeed in doing or accomplishing, especially with difficulty: *I'll manage to come on Friday*. **b.** To deal or cope with: *She couldn't manage any more food*. —*intr.* **1.** To direct, supervise, or carry on business affairs; perform the duties of a manager. **2.** To carry on or get along, especially in financial matters: *They can't manage without her*. —See Synonyms at **conduct**. [Italian *maneggiare*, to handle (a horse), probably from Vulgar Latin *manidiāre* (unattested), to handle, from Latin *manus*, hand.] **—man·age·a·bil·i·ty** (-bíllǝti), **man·age·a·ble·ness** *n.* **—man·age·a·ble** *adj.* **—man·age·a·bly** *adv.*

managed currency *n.* A monetary system in which the money supply and its buying power are controlled by government, rather than automatically regulated by the gold standard.

man·age·ment (mánnijmǝnt) *n.* **1.** The act, manner, or practice of managing, handling, or controlling something. **2.** The person or persons who manage a business establishment, organisation, or institution. **3.** Skill in managing; executive ability.

man·ag·er (mánnijǝr) *n. Abbr.* **mgr., Mgr. 1.** A person who manages a business or other enterprise. **2.** A person who is in charge of the business affairs of an entertainer or group of entertainers. **3.** *Sports*.

A person in charge of the training and performance of an athlete or team. **4.** In Britain, any of a number of members of either of the Houses of Parliament appointed to arrange business matters in which both Houses are involved. **5.** *Law*. One who is appointed by a court to run a business while it is in the hands of the receiver. **—man·ag·er·ship** *n.*

man·ag·er·ess (mánnijǝ-réss ‖ -ress, -rǝss) *n.* A female manager; especially, a woman in charge of a restaurant, shop, or the like.

man·a·ger·i·al (mánnǝ-jéer-i-ǝl) *adj.* Of, pertaining to, or characteristic of a manager or management. **—man·a·ge·ri·al·ly** *adv.*

man·ag·ing (mánnijing) *adj.* Having administrative power or control: *managing director; managing editor*.

Ma·na·gua (mǝ-nág-wǝ, -ná̈ag-). Capital of Nicaragua since 1855. It lies on the south shore of Lake Managua, and is a centre for industry, trade, and administration. It was badly damaged by earthquakes (1931 and 1972) and in the civil war (1979).

man·a·kin (mánnǝkin) *n.* **1.** Any of various small, colourful birds of the family Pipridae, found in forests of Central and South America. **2.** Variant of **manikin**.

Ma·na·ma (mǝ-ná̈amǝ). *Arabic* **Al Ma·na·mah**. Capital of Bahrain since 1971. Formerly a pearl fishing centre, its newer activities include oil-refining, fishing, petrochemicals, and (at Mina Sulman) marine industries. It is also the free transit port for the southern (Persian) Gulf.

ma·ña·na (man-yá̈anǝ) *adv.* **1.** Tomorrow. **2.** At some unspecified future time. ~*n.* Some indefinite time in the future. [Spanish, tomorrow, from Vulgar Latin (*cras*) *māneāna* (unattested), "early tomorrow" : *crās*, tomorrow (see **procrastinate**) + *māneāna*, early, from Latin *māne*, in the morning.]

Ma·nas·seh[1] (mǝ-nássi, -nássǝ). The elder son of Joseph. Genesis 41:51.

Manasseh[2]. A king of Judah in the seventh century B.C. II Kings 21:1–18.

Manasseh[3] *n.* A tribe of Israel descended from Manasseh, son of Joseph.

man-at-arms (mán-ǝt-ármz) *n., pl.* **men-at-arms** (mén-). A soldier; especially, a medieval cavalryman supplied with heavy arms.

man·a·tee (mánnǝ-tée) *n.* Any whalelike mammal of the genus *Trichechus*, found in Atlantic coastal waters of the tropical Americas and Africa. Each has paddle-like forelimbs and a horizontally flattened tail. [Spanish *manati*, from Carib *manattouï*.]

Ma·náus or **Ma·náos** (mǝ-nówss). Capital of Amazonas state, Brazil. Situated on the Rio Negro, near the Amazon, it is a free port, accessible to ocean-going ships, and the commercial centre for the upper Amazon basin. Around 1900 it was the centre of a rubber boom. With the opening up of Amazonas and the discovery of oil nearby, it is booming again.

Man·cha, La (mánchə). Region and former province of central Spain. A bleak plateau notable for its windmills, it was the setting for Cervantes' novel, *Don Quixote de la Mancha*.

Man·ches·ter (mán-chistǝr, -chestǝr, -chǝstǝr). City in the metropolitan county of Greater Manchester, northwest England. It began as a Roman camp, Mancunium, and its people are still known as Mancunians. A medieval wool town, it became the country's main cotton centre during the Industrial Revolution. England's first passenger railway linked it with Liverpool in 1830, and with the completion of the Manchester Ship Canal (1894) the city became a major port and financial centre.

Manchester terrier *n.* A short-haired, black-and-tan dog of a breed that originated in Manchester. Formerly called "black-and-tan terrier".

man·chi·neel (mánchi-néel) *n.* A tropical American tree, *Hippomane mancinella*, having poisonous sap and fruit. [French *mancenille*, from Spanish *manzanilla*, "small apple", MANZANILLA.]

Man·chu (mán-cho͞o) *n., pl.* **-chus** or collectively **Manchu. 1.** A member of a nomadic Mongoloid people, native to Manchuria, who conquered China in 1644 and established the **Ch'ing** (see) dynasty that was overthrown by revolution in 1911. **2.** The Tungusic language of the Manchu. ~*adj.* **1.** Of or pertaining to the Manchu, their dynasty, language, or culture. **2.** Of or pertaining to Manchuria. [Manchu, "pure".]

Man·chu·guo, Man·chu·kuo (mán-cho͞o-gwáw). Also **Man·zhou·guo** (-jo͞o-gwáw). See **Manchuria**.

Man·chu·ri·a (man-cho͞or-i-ǝ). Region of northeast China, composed of the modern provinces of Heilongjiang, Jilin, and Liaoning. It was the home of the Manchu conquerors of China in the 17th century. Of great strategic value, it was subsequently seized by the Russians, then the Japanese, who in 1932 set up their protégé state of Manchuguo plus the former province of Jehol, now mostly in the Inner Mongolian Autonomous Region). China regained this territory in 1946. **—Man·chu·ri·an** *adj. & n.*

man·ci·ple (mán-sip'l) *n.* In Britain, a steward responsible for purchasing the provisions of a college, an Inn of Court, or similar institution. [Middle English, from Anglo-French, from Latin *mancipium*, purchase : *manus*, hand + *cip-*, from *capere*, to take.]

Man·cu·ni·an (man-kéwni-ǝn) *n.* A native or inhabitant of Manchester. [Medieval Latin *Mancunium*, MANCHESTER.] **—Man·cu·ni·an** *adj.*

-mancy *n. comb. form.* Indicates divination by a specified means or in a specified manner; for example, **chiromancy, necromancy**. [Middle English, from Old French *-mancie*, from Late Latin *-man-*

tīa, from Greek *manteia,* divination, from *manteuesthai,* to prophesy, from *mantis,* a prophet.]

Man·dae·an, Man·de·an (man-dée-ən). *n.* **1.** A member of an ancient Gnostic sect still surviving in Iraq. **2.** A form of the Aramaic language used by the Mandaeans. [Aramaic *mandaiia,* Gnostics, from *manda,* knowledge.]
~adj. Of or pertaining to the Mandaeans or their language.

man·da·la (mándələ, man-daálə) *n.* In Oriental art and religion, any of various usually circular designs symbolic of the universe. [Sanskrit *maṇḍala,* circle, probably from Tamil *muṭalai.*]

mandala *This symbolic map of the Buddhist universe was painted in the 19th century. The mandala's central circle contains the eight-armed figure of Avolokitesvara, a compassionate deity revered in Nepal.*

Man·da·lay (mándə-láy, -lay). Last capital of the Burman kingdom, annexed by the British in 1885. Situated on the Irrawaddy river, it is a major port and commercial centre of Upper Burma.

man·da·mus (man-dáyməss) *n., pl.* **-muses.** *Law.* An order issued by a higher court ordering a public official or body or a lower court to perform a specific duty.
~tr.v. Law. **mandamused, -musing, -muses.** To serve with a mandamus. [Latin *mandāmus,* "we order", from *mandāre,* to order.]

man·da·rin[1] (mándə-rin || -rín) *n.* **1.** In imperial China, a member of any of the nine ranks of high public officials. **2. a.** A high civil servant thought to exercise wide undefined powers outside political control. **b.** A member of any influential intellectual or highbrow circle, especially when conservative or elderly. **3.** *Capital* **M.** Mandarin Chinese. **4.** *Capital* **M.** In imperial China, the dialect used by mandarins and other officials of the empire.
~adj. **1.** Of or resembling a mandarin. **2.** Marked by elaborate and intricate language or literary style. [Portuguese, from Malay *mēntēri,* from Hindi *mantrī,* from Sanskrit *mantrin,* counsellor, from *mantra,* counsel.]

man·da·rin[2] (mándə-rin) *n.* Also **man·da·rine** (-réen). **1.** A small citrus tree, *Citrus nobilis* or *C. deliciosa,* cultivated for its edible, orange-like fruit. **2.** The small, loose-skinned fruit of this tree. Also called "mandarin orange". [French *mandarine,* perhaps from MANDARIN (Chinese public official), comparing the colour of the fruit to the yellow robes worn by mandarins.]

Mandarin Chinese *n. Chinese* **guo yu** (gwó yǘ) or **pu·tong·hua** (pŏŏ-tŏŏng-hwá). The national language of the People's Republic of China and of Taiwan, based on the principal dialect spoken in the area around Beijing (Peking).

mandarin collar *n.* A narrow, stiff collar that stands up around the neck and does not quite meet at the front.

mandarin duck *n.* A perching duck, *Aix galericulata,* of Asia, having brightly coloured plumage and a crested head in the male.

mandarin *The damp woodlands of China are the natural habitat of the mandarin duck, but it is also kept as an ornamental bird in the West. Mandarin ducks usually nest in holes in trees.*

man·da·tar·y, man·da·to·ry (mándə-təri, -tri || *U.S.* -terri) *n., pl.* **-ies.** A person or nation that receives a mandate. [Late Latin *mandātārius* : MANDATE + -ARY.]

man·date (mándayt) *n.* **1.** An authoritative command or instruction. **2.** An instruction or authorisation to a government to follow a particular policy, supposedly expressed in election results. **3. a.** Formerly, a commission from the League of Nations authorising a nation to administer a territory. **b.** Formerly, a region under such administration. Compare **trusteeship, trust territory. 4.** In Roman and Scots law, a contract by which an individual agrees to perform services for another without payment.
~tr.v. (*also* man-dáyt) **mandated, -dating, -dates. 1.** To assign (a colony or territory) to a particular nation under a mandate. **2.** To give authority to by means of a mandate. [Latin *mandātum,* a command, from *mandāre,* to command.]

man·da·tor (mán-daytər, man-dáytər) *n.* One who gives a mandate.

man·da·to·ry (mándə-tri, -təri, man-dáytəri) *adj.* **1.** Of, pertaining to, having the nature of, or containing a mandate. **2.** Required as if by mandate; obligatory. **3.** Holding a mandate over some region. Said of a nation.
~n., pl. **mandatories.** Variant of **mandatary.**

man-day (mán-dáy) *n., pl.* **man-days.** The work performed by one person during one day.

Man·de (mán-day, maán-) *n., pl.* **-des** or collectively **Mande. 1.** A Mandingo. **2.** A branch of the Niger-Congo language family, spoken chiefly in Mali, Liberia, and Sierra Leone. [Mandingo : *ma-,* "mother" + *-nde,* diminutive suffix. See **Mandingo.**]

Mandean. Variant of **Mandaean.**

Man·de·la (man-déllə, -dáylə), **Nelson (Rolihlahla)** (1918–). South African black political leader. While a practising lawyer in Johannesburg, he became the national organiser of the banned African National Congress. He was tried for treason and acquitted (1956–61), retried (1963–64), and sentenced to life imprisonment. His publications include *No Easy Walk to Freedom* (1965).

man·di·ble (mándib'l) *n.* A jaw, especially: **1.** The lower jaw in vertebrates. **2.** Either the upper or lower part of the beak in birds. **3.** Any of various mouth-parts in insects. [Middle English, from Old French, from Latin *mandibula,* from *mandere,* to chew.] **—man·dib·u·lar** (man-díbbewlər) *adj.*

man·dib·u·late (mən-díbbew-lət, -lit, -layt) *n.* An animal having mandibles. **—man·dib·u·late** *adj.*

Man·din·go (man-díng-gō) *n., pl.* **-gos, -goes,** or collectively **Mandingo. 1.** A member of any of various Negroid peoples inhabiting the region of the upper Niger river valley of west Africa. **2.** Any language or dialect of the Mandingo. [Mandingo : *ma-,* "mother" + *-ndi, -nde,* diminutive suffix + *-ngo,* variant of *-ko,* suffix of nationality or tribe.] **—Man·din·go** *adj.*

man·do·la (mán-dələ) *n.* Also **man·dor·a** (-dawrə). An early, larger form of mandolin. [Italian.]

man·do·lin, man·do·line (mándə-lín, -léen, -lin, -leen) *n.* **1.** A musical instrument with a usually pear-shaped wooden body and a fretted neck over which several pairs of metal strings are stretched. **2.** A utensil for slicing vegetables finely, consisting of a wooden board fitted with an adjustable metal blade. [French *mandoline,* from Italian *mandolino,* diminutive of *mandola, mandora,* lute, from Greek *pandoura.*] **—man·do·lin·ist** *n.*

man·dor·la (man-dórlə) *n.* An oval aureole used especially in medieval painting and sculpture. [Italian, almond.]

man·drag·o·ra (man-drággərə) *n. Chiefly Poetic.* The mandrake, or a narcotic drug prepared from it. [Old English. See **mandrake.**]

man·drake (mándrayk) *n.* **1.** A Eurasian plant, *Mandragora officinarum,* having purplish flowers and a branched root thought to resemble the human body, from which a narcotic drug was formerly prepared. This plant was once widely believed to have magical powers and to shriek when pulled up by the roots. **2.** A North American plant, the **May apple** *(see).* [Middle English *mandragge, mandrake* (probably influenced by DRAKE, dragon), from Middle Dutch *mandragre* and Old English *mandragora,* both from Latin *mandragoras,* from Greek *mandragoras*†.]

man·drel, man·dril (mándrəl) *n.* **1.** A spindle or axle used to secure or support material being machined or milled. **2.** A metal core around which wood and other materials may be shaped. **3.** A shaft on which a working tool is mounted, as in a dental drill. **4.** A miner's pick with a large flattish blade on one side of the head. [16th century : perhaps akin to French *madrin,* lathe.]

man·drill (mándril) *n.* A large, fierce baboon, *Mandrillus sphinx,* of west Africa, having a beard, a crest, and a mane, with brilliant blue, purple, and scarlet markings on the face, and scarlet markings on the hindquarters in the adult male. [MAN + DRILL (baboon).]

mane (mayn) *n.* **1. a.** The long hair along the top and sides of the neck of such mammals as the horse and the male lion. **b.** The feathers on the back of the neck and head of some pigeons. **2.** A long, thick growth of hair on a person's head. [Middle English, Old English *manu.*] **—maned** *adj.*

man-eat·er (mán-eetər) *n.* **1.** An animal or fish that eats or is reputed to eat human flesh. **2.** A cannibal. **3.** *Informal.* A type of woman seen as habitually dominating and discarding male lovers. **—man-eat·ing** *adj.*

ma·nège, ma·nege (ma-náyzh, -nézh) *n.* **1.** The art and practice of training a horse in the more difficult exercises of riding. **2.** A riding academy. [French *manège,* from Italian *maneggio,* from *maneggiare,* to MANAGE.]

ma·nes (maánaynz, máyneez) *pl.n. Sometimes capital* **M.** In ancient Rome: **1.** The spirits of the dead, especially ancestors, deified as minor gods. **2.** *Used with a singular verb.* Any revered spirit of one who has died. Compare **lemures.** [Latin *mānēs,* probably "the good ones", from *mānis,* good.]

Ma·net (mánnay, ma-náy), **Edouard** (1832–83). French painter. His *Déjeuner sur l'herbe* (1863), showing a nude woman at a picnic, was rejected by the Paris Salon and caused a scandal. He had a considerable influence on the impressionists.

maneuver. *U.S.* Variant of **manoeuvre.**

man Friday *n.* Any devoted male servant, aide, or employee, especially one having a high degree of responsibility. [After *Friday,* the devoted native servant in Defoe's novel *Robinson Crusoe* (1719).]

man·ful (mánf'l) *adj.* Having or displaying qualities considered as befitting a man; brave and resolute. **—man·ful·ly** *adv.* **—man·ful·ness** *n.*

man·ga·bey (máng-gə-bay) *n., pl.* **-beys.** Any monkey of the genus *Cercocebus,* of equatorial Africa, having a long tail and a relatively long muzzle. [After *Mangaby,* a region of Madagascar.]

man·ga·nate (máng-gə-nayt) *n.* Any salt containing manganese in its anion, especially a salt containing the MnO_4^{2-} ion. [MANGAN(ESE) + -ATE (salt).]

man·ga·nese (máng-gə-néez, -neez || -néess, -neess) *n. Symbol* **Mn** A grey-white or silvery, brittle metallic element, occurring in several allotropic forms, found worldwide, especially in the ore pyrolusite. Manganese is alloyed with steel to increase hardness, resistance, and other properties, and with other metals to form highly-ferromagnetic materials. Atomic number 25, atomic weight 54.9380, melting point 1,244°C, boiling point 2,097°C, relative density 7.21 to 7.44, valencies 2,3,4,6,7. [French *manganèse,* from Italian *manganese,* probably alteration of Medieval Latin *magnēsia,* manganese, magnesia, from Late Greek *magnēsia.* See **magnesia.**]

manganese dioxide *n.* A black crystalline compound, MnO_2, used as a depolariser for electric cells and in textile dyeing.

manganese nodule *n.* An irregular fragment of rock found on the deep ocean floor, and containing on average 20 per cent manganese, 6 per cent iron, and also nickel and copper. The nodules will probably prove an important commercial resource in future.

manganese spar *n.* A mineral, **rhodonite** *(see).*

man·gan·ic (mang-gánnik) *adj.* Pertaining to or containing manganese. Used especially to designate compounds of manganese with a valency of 3 or 6. [MANGAN(ESE) + -IC.]

Man·gan·in (máng-gə-nin) *n.* A trademark for an alloy of copper, manganese, and nickel used for making electrical resistors that do not vary much with changes in temperature.

man·ga·nite (máng-gə-nīt) *n.* A steel-grey to black mineral form of manganese oxide, MnO(OH), found in North America and Europe. It is an important ore of manganese. [MANGAN(ESE) + -ITE.]

man·ga·nous (máng-gə-nəss, mang-gánnəss) *adj.* Pertaining to or containing manganese. Used especially to designate compounds of manganese with a valency of 2. [MANGAN(ESE) + -OUS.]

mange (maynj) *n.* A contagious skin disease of many mammals, occasionally affecting humans. It is caused by parasitic mites and characterised by itching and loss of hair. [Middle English *maniewe,* from Old French *manjue,* "eating", itch, from *mangier,* to eat, from Latin *mandūcāre,* to eat, chew, from *mandūcō,* glutton, from *mandere,* to chew.]

man·gel-wur·zel (máng-g'l-wurz'l) *n.* A variety of the common beet having a large yellowish root, used chiefly as cattle fodder. Also called "mangel", "mangold". [German, (properly) *Mangold-wurzel,* "beet-root" : *Mangold,* beet, from Old High German *mānegolt*† + *Wurzel,* root, from Old High German *wurzala.*]

man·ger (máynjər) *n.* **1.** A trough or open box in which feed for horses or cattle is placed. **2.** *Nautical.* A small basin-like device in the bows of a ship for catching any water entering through the hawseholes. [Middle English *maniure, ma(w)nger,* from Old French *mangeoire, manjeure,* from Vulgar Latin *mandūcātōria* (unattested), feeding place, from *mandūcāre,* to chew. See **mange.**]

mange·tout (móNzh-tōō, -tōō) *n., pl.* **mange·tout.** **1.** A variety of pea, *Pisum sativum* or *P. saccharatum,* the pods of which are picked when fairly young and eaten entire. **2.** The pod of this plant. Also called "sugar pea". [French, "eat all".]

man·gle¹ (máng-g'l) *tr.v.* **-gled, -gling, -gles.** **1.** To mutilate or disfigure by battering, hacking, cutting, or tearing. **2.** To ruin or spoil through ineptitude or ignorance: *mangle a speech.* [Middle English *manglen,* from Anglo-French *mangler, mahangler,* probably frequentative of Old French *mahaignier,* to MAIM.] **—man·gler** *n.*

mangle² *n.* **1.** A laundry machine for wringing out or pressing fabrics. **2.** *Chiefly British.* A clothes wringer.
~*tr.v.* **mangled, -gling, -gles.** To wring out or press with a mangle. [Dutch *mangel,* from German, diminutive of Middle High German *mange,* mangle, from Late Latin *manganum,* MANGONEL.]

man·go (máng-gō) *n., pl.* **-goes** or **-gos.** **1.** A tropical evergreen tree, *Mangifera indica,* native to Asia, cultivated for its edible fruit. **2.** The ovoid fruit of this tree, having a smooth rind and sweet, juicy, yellow-orange flesh. **3.** Any of various types of pickle; especially, mango chutney. [Portuguese *manga,* from Malay *manggā,* from Tamil *mānkāy* : *mān,* mango tree + *kāy,* fruit.]

man·go·nel (máng-gə-nel) *n.* A military machine used during the Middle Ages for hurling stones and other missiles. [Middle English, from Old French, from Medieval Latin *mangonellus, manganellus,* diminutive of Late Latin *manganum,* mangonel, from Greek *manganon,* enchantment, contrivance, war machine.]

man·go·steen (máng-gō-steen, -gə-) *n.* **1.** A tropical tree, *Garcinia mangostana,* having thick, leathery leaves and edible fruit. **2.** The fruit of this tree, having a hard rind and segmented, sweet, juicy pulp. [From obsolete Malay *manggustan.*]

man·grove (máng-grōv) *n.* **1.** Any of various tropical evergreen trees or shrubs of the genus *Rhizophora,* having stiltlike, aerial roots and forming dense thickets along tidal shores. **2.** Any of various similar shrubs or trees, especially any of the genus *Avicennia.* [Portuguese *mangue* (influenced by GROVE), from Taino *mangle.*]

man·gy, man·gey (máynji) *adj.* **-gier, -giest.** **1.** Having, resembling, or caused by mange. **2.** Having many bare spots; shabby: *a mangy old mink coat.* **3.** Having a squalid appearance; wretched: *mangy tenements.* **—man·gi·ly** *adv.* **—man·gi·ness** *n.*

man·han·dle (mán-hánd'l, -hand'l) *tr.v.* **-dled, -dling, -dles.** **1.** To handle roughly. **2.** To move by manpower, without machinery.

Man·hat·tan¹ (man-hátt'n, mən-) *n., pl.* **-tans** or collectively **Manhattan.** A member of an Algonquian-speaking North American Indian people, formerly inhabiting the area that is now roughly New York City. **—Man·hat·tan** *adj.*

Manhattan². Borough of New York City, New York state, United States. Most of it lies on Manhattan Island, the original nucleus of the city, bounded by the Hudson, East, and Harlem rivers and New York Bay. The financial, business, and cultural heart of the city, it includes Broadway, Wall Street, and Greenwich Village.

Manhattan³ *n. Sometimes small* **m.** A cocktail made from vermouth, rye whiskey or bourbon, and angostura bitters. [After MANHATTAN, New York.]

Manhattan District *n.* In World War II, the name given to a unit of the U.S. Army Corps of Engineers established in 1942 to administer the nuclear energy project that produced the atomic bomb. Also unofficially called "Manhattan Project".

man·hole (mán-hōl) *n.* A hole through which a person may enter a boiler, pipe, conduit, or drain. Also called "inspection chamber".

man·hood (mánhŏŏd) *n.* **1.** The state or condition of being an adult male as distinguished from being a boy or a woman: *Green youths grow to manhood.* **2.** The composite of qualities, such as courage, determination, and vigour, considered desirable in an adult male. **3.** Men collectively. **4.** Loosely, the state or condition of being part of or endowed with humanity.

man-hour (mán-owr) *n., pl.* **man-hours.** An industrial unit of production equal to the work a person can produce in one hour.

man·hunt (mán-hunt) *n., pl.* **manhunts.** An organised and extensive search for a man, usually a fugitive criminal.

ma·ni·a (máyni-ə) *n.* **1.** *Psychology.* A state of mind characterised by profuse and rapidly changing ideas, exaggerated gaiety that may quickly change to irritability or violence, and physical overactivity. **2.** *Informal.* An inordinately intense desire or enthusiasm for something; a craze. **3.** Any violent abnormal behaviour. [Middle English, madness, from Late Latin, from Greek.]

-mania *n. comb. form.* Indicates an exaggerated desire for or pleasure in, or a pathological excitement induced by something; for example, **monomania, pyromania.** — **-maniac** *n. & adj. comb. form.*

ma·ni·ac (máyni-ak) *n.* **1.** An insane person; a lunatic. **2.** *Informal.* A person who has excessive enthusiasm or desire for something: *a bridge maniac.* **3.** A person who behaves in a wild, irresponsible way: *Look out for maniacs on the motorway.*
~*adj.* Maniacal. [Greek *maniakos,* from *mania,* madness.]

ma·ni·a·cal (mə-nī-ək'l) *adj.* Also **maniac.** **1.** Insane: *a maniacal killer.* **2.** *Informal.* Characterised by excessive enthusiasm: *a maniacal fondness for gambling.* **—ma·ni·a·cal·ly** *adv.*

man·ic (mánnik) *adj.* **1.** Of, pertaining to, or afflicted with mania; hyperactive. **2.** Loosely, crazy; apparently insane, especially in a frenetic way: *manic humour.*
~*n.* A person afflicted with mania. [MANIA + -IC.]

man·ic-de·pres·sive (mánnik-di-préssiv) *adj. Psychology.* Designating, displaying, or suffering from a psychosis in which periods of manic excitation alternate with melancholic depressions.
~*n. Psychology.* A manic-depressive person. **—man·ic-de·pres·sion** *n.*

Man·i·chae·an, Man·i·che·an (mánni-keé-ən) *n.* Also **Man·i·chee** (-kee). A believer in Manichaeism.
~*adj.* Of or pertaining to Manichaeism. [Middle English, from Medieval Latin *Manichaeus,* from Late Greek *Manikhaios,* a follower of *Manikhaios* or *Manes,* the Persian founder of the sect.]

Man·i·chae·ism, Man·i·che·ism (mánni-kee-iz'm) *n.* Also **Man·i·chae·an·ism, Man·i·che·an·ism** (-keé-ən-iz'm). **1.** The syncretic, dualistic religious philosophy taught by the Persian prophet Manes about the third century A.D., according to which God and Satan reigned as equals. It combined elements of Zoroastrian, Christian, and Gnostic thought. **2.** Any similar dualistic philosophy holding that there is an evil deity who exists in opposition to God, especially any considered a heresy by the Roman Catholic Church.

man·i·cot·ti (mánni-kótti) *n.* An Italian dish consisting of pasta with a filling of chopped ham and ricotta cheese, usually served hot with a tomato sauce. [Italian, "sleeves", plural of *manicotto,* augmentative of *manica,* sleeve, from Latin *manica,* from *manus,* hand.]

man·i·cure (mánni-kewr) *n.* A cosmetic treatment of the hands and fingernails, including shaping, cleaning, and polishing of the nails. Also used adjectivally: *a manicure set.*
~*tr.v.* **manicured, -curing, -cures.** **1.** To care for (the hands and fingernails) by shaping, cleaning, and polishing, or other treatment. **2.** To clip or trim evenly and closely: *manicured lawns.* [French *manicure,* "hand-care" : Latin *manus,* hand + *cūra,* care.] **—man·i·cur·ist** *n.*

man·i·fest (mánni-fest) *adj.* **1.** Clearly apparent to the sight or understanding; obvious. **2.** *Psychology.* Of or pertaining to impulses which appear to be conscious but which may hide unconscious ones. —See Synonyms at **evident.**
~*v.* **manifested, -festing, -fests.** —*tr.* **1.** To show or demonstrate plainly; reveal. **2.** To be evidence of; prove. **3. a.** To record or list in a ship's manifest. **b.** To display or present a manifest of (cargo). —*intr.* To appear. Used of a spirit.
~*n.* **1. a.** A list of cargo or passengers; especially one for use by customs. **b.** *U.S.* A list of railway trucks, according to owner and location. **2.** *U.S.* A fast freight train, usually one that carries perishable goods. [Middle English, from Latin *manifestus, manufestus,* palpable, "grasped by hand" : *manus,* hand + *-festus,* "gripped".] **—man·i·fest·a·ble** *adj.* **—man·i·fest·ly** *adv.*

man·i·fes·ta·tion (mánnifess-táysh'n) *n.* **1. a.** The act of manifesting or the state of being manifested. **b.** The demonstration of the existence, reality, or presence of a person, object, or quality: *a manifestation of ill will.* **c.** Any of the forms in which someone or something, such as an individual, a divine being, or an idea, is revealed. **2.** A public demonstration, usually of a political nature.

Manifest Destiny *n.* The 19th-century doctrine that the United States had the right and duty to expand throughout the North American continent.

man·i·fes·to (mánni-féstō) *n., pl.* **-toes** or **-tos.** A public declaration of principles, policies, or intentions, especially of a political party.
~*intr.v. Rare.* **manifestoed, -toing, -toes.** To issue a manifesto. [Italian, "manifestation", from adjective, manifest, from Latin *manifestus,* MANIFEST.]

man·i·fold (mánnifōld) *adj.* **1.** Of many kinds; varied; multiple: *our manifold failings.* **2.** Having many features or forms: *manifold intelligence.* **3.** Consisting of or operating several of one kind.
~*n.* **1.** A whole composed of diverse elements. **2.** Any one of many copies; a copy made by manifolding. **3.** A pipe so fitted that it has several apertures for making multiple connections. **4.** *Mathematics.* A topological space consisting of matched, overlapping open sets in which each point is homeomorphic to an open subset of Euclidean space.
~*tr.v.* **manifolded, -folding, -folds.** **1.** To make several copies of. **2.** To make manifold; multiply. [Middle English, Old English *manig-feald* : MANY + -FOLD.] **—man·i·fold·ly** *adv.* **—man·i·fold·ness** *n.*

man·i·fold·er (mánni-fōldər) *n.* A machine for making manifold copies of documents or other writings.

man·i·kin, man·ni·kin (mánni-kin) *n.* Also **man·a·kin** (mánnə-) (for sense 1). **1. a.** A dwarf or pixie. **b.** A little boy. **2.** An anatomical model of the human body, used primarily for study in art and medical schools. **3.** Variants of **mannequin.** [Middle Dutch *mannekīn,* diminutive of *man,* MAN.]

ma·nil·a, ma·nil·la (mə-nillə) *n. Often capital* **M.** **1.** A cigar or che-

mandrill *This member of the baboon family is found in the coastal forests of West Africa. It lives mainly on the ground in small groups led by a male and feeds on insects and plants.*

mangrove Rhizophora mangle, *a mangrove species which grows in Florida, U.S.A. The trunk grows above ground, supported by roots anchored in the mud below. The wood is so dense that it sinks in water.*

root of a type made in Manila. **2.** A fibre, Manila hemp. **3.** Manila paper. **4.** Light yellowish brown.

Ma·nil·a (mə-níllə). Capital and main seaport of the Philippines. It was founded (1571) by the Spanish on Manila Bay, Luzon Island, and is the country's industrial centre.

Manila hemp *n.* The fibre of a tropical plant, the **abaca** *(see)*, used for making rope, cordage, and paper. Also called "Manila".

Manila paper *n.* Strong paper or thin cardboard with a smooth finish, usually buff in colour, made from Manila hemp or wood fibres similar to it. Also called "manila".

ma·nil·la (mə-níllə) *n.* A metal bracelet worn by certain West African peoples, formerly used as currency. [Spanish, bracelet, probably diminutive of *mano*, hand.]

ma·nille (ma-níl) *n.* The second-best trump in the card games quadrille and ombre. [French, from Spanish *malilla,* diminutive of *mala,* bad.]

man in the moon *n.* The face or shape of a man in the light and dark areas of the Moon's surface, as apparently visible from the earth. Preceded by *the.*

man in the street *n.* The ordinary citizen; the common man. Preceded by *the.*

man·i·oc (mánni-ok) *n.* Also **man·i·o·ca** (-ṓkə). A tropical plant, the **cassava** *(see).* [French, from Tupi *mandioca.*]

man·i·ple (mánnip'l) *n.* **1.** A former ecclesiastical vestment, a coloured band on the left arm near the wrist. **2.** A subdivision of an ancient Roman legion, containing 60 or 120 men. [Sense 1, Middle English, from Old French, handkerchief, from Latin *manipulus,* handful. Sense 2, direct from Latin *manipulus,* handful, hence, a bundle of hay on a pole used as a standard, hence a detachment of troops : *manus,* hand + *-pulus†.*]

ma·nip·u·lar (mə-níppewlər) *adj.* **1.** Of or pertaining to an ancient Roman maniple. **2.** Of or pertaining to manipulation.
~*n.* A Roman soldier in a maniple.

ma·nip·u·late (mə-níppew-layt) *tr.v.* **-lated, -lating, -lates. 1.** To operate or control by skilled use of the hands; handle. **2. a.** To influence or manage shrewdly or deviously: *She manipulated public opinion in her favour.* **b.** To control the will or emotions of (another person) by exploiting guilt or affection, for example, to one's own ends: *His parents quite openly manipulate him.* **3.** To tamper with or falsify (financial records) for personal gain. **4.** *Medicine.* To handle and move (a limb, for example), either in an examination or for therapeutic purposes. —See Synonyms at **handle.** [Back-formation from MANIPULATION.] —**ma·nip·u·la·bil·i·ty** (-lə-bílləti) *n.* —**ma·nip·u·la·ble** *adj.* —**ma·nip·u·lat·ive** (-lətiv ‖ -laytiv), **ma·nip·u·la·to·ry** (-lə-təri, -tri) *adj.* —**ma·nip·u·la·tor** *n.*

ma·nip·u·la·tion (mə-níppew-láysh'n) *n.* **1.** The act of manipulating. **2.** The state of being manipulated. **3.** Shrewd or devious effort to manage or influence for one's own purposes: *manipulation of popular feeling.* **4.** The therapeutic movement of bones or other tissue, as by an osteopath or physiotherapist, to restore normal action. [Latin *manipulus,* handful. See **maniple.**]

ma·ni·pu·ri (mánni-póori, múnni-) *n., pl.* **-ris.** One of the four classical Hindu dance forms, presenting episodes from the life of the god Krishna. [After *Manipur,* region of India, where the dance originated.]

Man·i·to·ba (mánni-tṓbə). Province of central Canada, the most easterly of the Prairie Provinces. The southwest produces vast amounts of wheat, and the northern tundra, furs. There are large reserves of timber, oil, and metal ores. Winnipeg is the capital.

man·i·tou, man·i·tu (mánni-tṓ) *n., pl.* **-tous, -tus** or **-tou, -tu.** Also **man·i·to** (-tṓ) *pl.* **-tos** or **-to. 1.** A spirit or force of nature, either good or bad, deified in the religion of the Algonquian Indians. **2.** A representation or image of such a spirit. [French, from Ojibwa *manitu,* "he has surpassed".]

man jack *n. Informal.* A single individual. Used in the phrase *every man jack (of them).* [MAN + JACK (fellow, chap).]

man·kind (man-kínd *for sense 1;* mán-kínd *for sense 2*) *n.* **1.** The human race. **2.** *Rare.* Men as distinguished from women.

mank·y (mángki) *adj.* **-ier, -iest. 1.** *Scottish.* Decaying; dirty. **2.** *Northwest English.* Spoilt; naughty. [From obsolete (Scottish) *mank,* maimed, defective, from Old French *manc,* from Latin *mancus,* maimed; current sense perhaps influenced by French *manqué,* failed, missed, miscarried.]

Man·ley (mánli), **Michael (Norman)** (1923–). Jamaican politician. He worked as a journalist before entering politics, leading the People's National Party in opposition (1969–72) and as prime minister (1972–80). A socialist, he strengthened his country's links with Cuba, spoke out for Third World interests, and gave the state a majority holding in the bauxite industry.

man·like (mán-līk) *adj.* **1.** Resembling a man. **2.** Pertaining to or befitting a man.

man·ly (mánli) *adj.* **-lier, -liest. 1.** Having qualities generally considered desirable in a man: *manly courage.* **2.** Suited to or befitting a man; masculine: *manly clothes.*
~*adv. Rare.* In a manly manner. —**man·li·ness** *n.*

man-made (mán-máyd) *adj.* Made by people; manufactured; not of natural origin.

Mann (man), **Thomas** (1875–1955). German novelist. Concerned with the artist's role in society, his works include *Death in Venice* (1912), *The Magic Mountain* (1924), and *Dr. Faustus* (1947). He was awarded the Nobel prize in 1929.

man·na (mánnə) *n.* **1.** The food miraculously provided for the Israelites in the wilderness during their flight from Egypt. Exodus 16:14–36. **2.** Any spiritual nourishment of divine origin, especially the Eucharist. **3.** Something of value that a person receives unexpectedly when in need. **4.** The dried exudate of certain plants; especially, that of a Eurasian ash tree, *Fraxinus ornus,* formerly used as a laxative. [Aramaic *mannā,* from Hebrew *mān.*]

manned (mand) *adj.* **1.** Having the personnel required for operation. **2.** Involving a human crew or having humans on board as well as or instead of machinery: *a manned space capsule.*

man·ne·quin (mánnikin) *n.* Also **manikin, mannikin** (for sense 1). **1.** A life-size, full or partial representation of the human body, used for the fitting or displaying of clothes; a dummy. **2.** A lay figure *(see).* **3.** A woman who models clothes; a model. [French, from Middle Dutch *mannekīn,* MANIKIN.]

man·ner (mánnər) *n.* **1.** A way of doing something, or the way in which a thing is done or happens: *boasting in their usual manner.* **2.** A way of acting; a person's bearing or behaviour: *a very flirtatious manner.* **3.** *Plural.* **a.** The socially correct way of acting; polite bearing or behaviour; etiquette. **b.** The prevailing systems or modes of social conduct of a specific society, period, or group. **4.** Practice, style, execution, or method in the arts: *This fresco is typical of the painter's early manner.* **5.** Exaggerated style; a mannerism. **6.** *Archaic.* Kind or sort: *What manner of man is that?* —See Synonyms at **bearing, method.** —**by all manner of means.** Of course; surely. —**in a manner of speaking.** In a way; so to speak. —**not by any manner of means.** In no way whatever. —**to the manner born. 1.** Born to follow or obey usual practices or customs. **2. a.** Fitted by birth, education, or experience to occupy a specific position, usually one of leadership. **b.** As if naturally equipped for an activity. [Middle English *manere,* from Anglo-French, from Old French *maniere,* from Vulgar Latin *manuāria* (unattested), "way of handling", manner, from Latin *manuārius,* of the hand, from *manus,* hand.]

man·nered (mánnərd) *adj.* **1.** Having a manner or manners of a specified kind. Often used in combination: *ill-mannered.* **2.** Artificial or affected: *His mannered speech irks me.* **3.** Of, pertaining to, or exhibiting mannerisms. Said of art or literature.

man·ner·ism (mánnə-riz'm) *n.* **1.** A distinctive behavioural trait; an idiosyncrasy. **2.** An exaggerated or affected style or habit, as in dress, speech, or art. **3.** *Capital* M. An artistic style of the late 16th century characterised by distortion of such elements as scale and perspective. —**man·ner·ist** *n.*

man·ner·ly (mánnərli) *adj.* Having good manners; polite.
~*adv.* With good manners; politely. —**man·ner·li·ness** *n.*

mannikin. Variant of **manikin.**

Man·ning (mánning), **Henry Edward, Cardinal** (1808–92). British cardinal. Educated at Oxford and an adherent of the Oxford Movement, he entered the Anglican ministry and became archdeacon of Chichester (1841) before his conversion to Roman Catholicism (1851). He was archbishop of Westminster (1865) and became a cardinal (1875). He was a staunch defender of papal infallibility.

man·nish (mánnish) *adj.* **1.** Of or befitting a man. **2.** Resembling a man in appearance or bearing. Said of a woman. —**man·nish·ly** *adv.* —**man·nish·ness** *n.*

man·ni·tol (mánni-tol ‖ -tōl) *n.* Also **man·nite** (mánnīt). An alcohol, $C_6H_8(OH)_6$, used as a nutrient, a dietary supplement, and as the basis of dietetic sweets. [MANN(A) + -IT(E) + -OL.]

man·nose (mán-ōz, -ōss) *n.* A sugar, $C_6H_{12}O_6$, occurring in various polysaccharides. [MANN(A) + -OSE.]

ma·noeu·vre, *U.S.* **ma·neu·ver** (mə-nṓō-vər ‖ -néw-) *n.* **1. a.** A strategic or tactical military movement. **b.** *Often plural.* A large-scale military training exercise simulating combat. **2.** A movement or way of doing something generally requiring skill and dexterity; especially: **a.** An act of changing direction in a car, boat, or other transport. **b.** A controlled change in the flight path of an aircraft, rocket, or space vehicle. **3.** A calculated procedure intended to further personal or partisan interests: *devious political manoeuvres.* See Synonyms at **artifice.**
~*v.* **manoeuvred** or *U.S.* **maneuvered, -vring** or *U.S.* **-vering, -vres** or *U.S.* **-vers.** —*intr.* **1.** To perform or carry out a military manoeuvre. **2.** To make a change, or a series of changes, in position or direction for some desired end. **3.** To make tactical changes, as in debate or negotiation: *The opposition had no room in which to manoeuvre.* **4.** To attempt to bring about something by planning or scheming. —*tr.* **1.** To alter the tactical placement of (troops or warships, for example). **2.** To move into a desired position. **3.** To manipulate (people, for example) for one's own ends: *manoeuvred her into signing the contract.* [French, from Medieval Latin *man(u)operārī,* from Latin *manus,* hand + *operārī,* to work.] —**man·oeu·vra·bil·i·ty** (-vrə-bílləti, -vərə-) *n.* —**man·oeu·vra·ble** *adj.*

man of God *n.* **1.** A man who is notably holy. **2.** A clergyman.

man of straw *n.* **1.** A person without financial substance. **2.** A person who is nominally, but not actually responsible, especially one involved in a dubious enterprise. Also *U.S.* "straw man". **3.** A spurious argument, put forward only to be refuted immediately. Also *U.S.* "straw man".

man of the world *n.* A sophisticated or worldly-wise man.

man-of-war (mán-ə-wáwr, -əv-) *n., pl.* **men-of-war** (mén-). **1.** A warship. **2.** A jellyfish, the **Portuguese man-of-war** *(see).*

ma·nom·e·ter (mə-nómmitər) *n.* **1.** Any of various instruments for measuring the pressure of liquids and gases. **2.** An instrument for measuring blood pressure, a **sphygmomanometer** *(see).* [French *manomètre:* Greek *manos,* sparse (here used of gaseous conditions) + -METER.] —**man·o·met·ric** (mánnə-méttrik), **man·o·met·ri·cal** *adj.* —**man·o·met·ri·cal·ly** *adv.* —**ma·nom·e·try** (mə-nómmitri) *n.*

man·or (mánnər) n. **1. a.** The district over which a lord had domain in medieval western Europe. **b.** The lord's residence in such a district. **2.** Any landed estate. **3.** The main house on any estate; a mansion. In this sense, also "manor house". **4.** In certain North American colonies, a tract of land with hereditary rights granted by royal charter. **5.** *British Slang.* **a.** A police district. **b.** The area of operations or pitch of a criminal or gang. **c.** An area that one lives in and knows well: *South London's my manor.* [Middle English *maner*, from Anglo-French *manere*, Old French *maneir*, "dwelling place", from *maneir*, to dwell, remain.]
—ma·no·ri·al (mə-náwr-i-əl ‖ -nór-) *adj.*
man·o'-war bird n. The **frigate bird** *(see).*
man·pow·er (mán-powr) n. **1.** The power of human physical strength. **2.** Power in terms of the people available to a particular group, or required for a particular task.
man·qué (móng-kay, MON-káy) *adj.* Unsuccessful or frustrated; unfulfilled. Used after the noun: *an artist manqué.* [French, from *manquer*, to fail, lack, from Italian *mancare*, from *manco*, lacking, defective, from Latin *mancus*, maimed.]
man·rope (mán-rōp) n. *Nautical.* A rope rigged as a handrail on a gangplank or ladder.
man·sard (mán-saard, -sərd) n. **1.** A roof having two slopes on all four sides, the lower slope almost vertical, and the upper almost horizontal. Also called "mansard roof". **2.** The upper storey formed by the lower slope of such a roof. [French *(toit en) mansarde*, "mansard (roof)"; originally designed by François MANSART.]
Man·sart (MON-saár), **François** (1598–1666). French classical architect. He adapted the Baroque style and developed the mansard roof for the château of Blois (1635–38). His works include the Hôtel de la Vrillière (1635–38), the Church of Val-de-Grâce (1645), and the château of Maisons-Laffitte (1642–51).
manse (manss) n. **1. a.** *Chiefly Scottish.* A Church of Scotland clergyman's house and land. **b.** A Methodist or Nonconformist clergyman's house. **2.** *Rare.* A mansion. [Medieval Latin *mansa, mansus, mansum*, dwelling place, from Latin *manēre*, to dwell, remain.]
man·ser·vant (mán-serv'nt) n., pl. **menservants** (mén-serv'nts). A male servant, especially a valet.
Mans·field (mánss-feeld, mánz-), **Katherine**, born Kathleen Mansfield Beauchamp (1888–1923). New Zealand short-story writer. Educated in London, she settled in Europe (1908) and wrote chiefly short stories in a style reminiscent of Chekhov's. Her works include *Bliss* (1920) and *The Garden Party* (1922).
-manship n. comb. form. Indicates: **1.** Skill in a specified field; for example, **horsemanship**. **2.** Manoeuvring to gain advantage; for example, **gamesmanship**. [Abstracted from terms such as *workmanship* (*workman* + *-ship*) and used to create new terms such as *one-upmanship* (*one up* + *-manship*).]
man·sion (mánsh'n) n. **1.** A large, stately house. **2.** A manor house. **3.** *Archaic.* A dwelling; an abode. **4.** *Plural. British.* Used as part of the name of certain blocks of flats: *Gresham Mansions.* **5.** *Astrology.* **a.** A **house** *(see).* **b.** Any one of the 28 divisions of the moon's monthly path. [Middle English, house, from Old French, from Latin *mānsiō* (stem *mānsiōn*-), dwelling, from *manēre*, to dwell, remain.]
Mansion House n. The official residence of the Lord Mayor of London. Preceded by *the.*
man-sized (mán-sīzd) *adj. Informal.* Large enough for a man; hefty: *a man-sized piece of cheese.*
man·slaugh·ter (mán-slawtər) n. **1.** The taking of human life without premeditation. **2.** *Law.* The unlawful killing of one human being by another without express or implied intent to take life. Compare **murder**.
man·sue·tude (mán-swi-tewd ‖ -tōōd) n. *Archaic.* Gentleness of manner; mildness. [Middle English, from Latin *mānsuētūdō*, from *mānsuēscere*, to tame, "to accustom to the hand" : *manus*, hand + *suēscere*, to accustom.]
man·ta (mántə) n. **1.** A rough-textured cotton fabric or blanket made and used in Latin America and the southwestern United States. **2.** Any of several fishes of the family Mobulidae, having large, flattened bodies with winglike pectoral fins. Also called "devilfish", "manta ray". [Spanish, cape, blanket, hence (in American Spanish) fish trap shaped like a blanket, manta ray (caught with such a trap), from Vulgar Latin *manta* (unattested), cloak, variant of Latin *mantus*, shortened from *mantellum†*, MANTLE.]
man·teau (mán-tō; *French* MON-tṓ) n., pl. **-teaus** (-tōz) or **-teaux** (-tṓ). A loose cloak or mantle. [French, from Old French *mantel*, from Latin *mantellum†*, MANTLE.]
Man·teg·na (man-tén-ya), **Andrea** (c. 1431–1506). Italian painter and engraver. Influenced by Donatello, his works reflect an interest in the classical period, and include a Pietà and the nine paintings of the Triumph of Caesar.
man·tel, man·tle (mánt'l) n. **1.** An ornamental facing around a fireplace. **2.** The protruding shelf over a fireplace. Also called "mantelpiece". [Middle English *mantel*, cloak, covering, from Old French, from Latin *mantellum†*, MANTLE.]
man·tel·et (mánt'l-et, mántlit) n. Also **mant·let** (mántlit) (for sense 2). **1.** A short cape worn by women in the mid-19th century. **2.** A mobile screen or shield formerly used to protect soldiers. [Middle English, from Old French, diminutive of *mantel*, mantle, from Latin *mantellum†*, MANTLE.]
man·tel·let·ta (mánti-létta) n. A knee-length, sleeveless vestment worn by Roman Catholic prelates. [Italian, from Old French *mantelet*, MANTELET.]

man·tel·piece (mánt'l-peess) n. The shelf over a fireplace, a mantel.
man·tel·tree (mánt'l-tree) n. A beam, stone, or arch that functions as a lintel over a fireplace, supporting the masonry above. [Middle English : MANTEL + TREE (beam).]
man·tic (mántik) *adj.* Of, pertaining to, or having the power of divination; prophetic. [Greek *mantikos*, from *mantis*, prophet.]
man·ti·core (mánti-kor ‖ -kōr) n. A fabulous monster having the head of a man, the body of a lion, and the tail of a dragon or scorpion. [Middle English, from Latin *mantichora*, from Greek *mantikhōras*, a misreading of *martikhoras*, a fabulous Oriental beast, from an unattested Old Iranian word meaning "man-eater" : represented by Old Persian *martīya-*, man + Avestan *khvar-*, to eat.]
man·til·la (man-tíllə) n. **1.** A scarf, usually of lace, worn over the head and shoulders, often over a high comb, by women in Spain and Latin America. **2.** A shawl or a short veil, as worn by Roman Catholic women in church. [Spanish, diminutive of *manta*, cape, MANTA.]
man·tis (mán-tiss) n., pl. **-tises** or **-tes** (-teez). Any of various carnivorous insects of the family Mantidae, primarily tropical but including a few Temperate Zone species. They are usually pale green and have two pairs of walking legs and powerful forelimbs that are often folded in a praying position. See **praying mantis.** [New Latin, from Greek *mantis*, prophet, diviner, hence (from its praying appearance) mantis.]
man·tis·sa (man-tíssə) n. *Mathematics.* The decimal part of a common logarithm when the logarithm is written as the sum of an integer and a decimal. In 1.7041 the mantissa is .7041. [Latin, makeweight, probably from Etruscan.]
mantis shrimp n. A burrowing crustacean, the **squilla** *(see).*
man·tle (mánt'l) n. **1.** A loose, sleeveless cloak worn over outer garments. **2.** Anything that covers, envelops, or conceals: *a mantle of ivy.* **3.** Variant of **mantel.** **4.** A zone of hot gases around a flame. **5.** A device in lamps consisting of a conical or cylindrical gauze, impregnated with certain salts, that gives off brilliant illumination when heated by the flame. **6.** *Anatomy.* The outer part of the brain, the **cerebral cortex** *(see).* **7.** *Geology.* The layer of the earth between the crust and the core. See **Mohorovičić discontinuity. 8.** *Zoology.* The wings, shoulder feathers, and back of a bird, when differently coloured from the rest of the body. **9.** *Zoology.* In molluscs and brachiopods, a membrane that covers most of the body and secretes the substance forming the shell. **10.** A clay mould placed around a wax model and used for making a cast.
~v. **mantled, -tling, -tles.** —tr. To cover with or as if with a mantle; cloak; conceal: *mountains mantled in snow.* —intr. **1.** To spread or become extended over a surface. **2.** To become covered with a coating, such as scum or froth on the surface of a liquid. **3.** To be or become covered or overspread by blushes or colours: *Her face mantled.* **4.** To spread the wings over food. Used of hawks. [Middle English, from Old French, from Latin *mantellum†*, cloak.]
mantle rock n. *Geology.* **Regolith** *(see).*
mantlet. Variant of **mantelet.**
mant·ling (mántling) n. *Heraldry.* The ornamental drapery or scrollwork around an achievement. [MANTLE + -ING.]
man-to-man (mán-tə-mán) *adj.* **1.** Characterised by forthrightness and candour between two participants, usually male: *man-to-man talks.* **2.** *Sports.* Involving or designating a strategy in which each defending player deals with one particular player on the attacking team: *man-to-man marking.* **—man to man** *adv.*
Man·toux test (man-tōō; *French* mon-) n. A test to determine whether a person has developed any immunity to tuberculosis. Some tuberculin is injected below the skin and the appearance of inflammation during the next 24 hours indicates a certain degree of immunity. Also called "tuberculin test". [After C. *Mantoux* (1877–1947), French doctor.]
man·tra (mántrə, múntrə) n. **1.** *Hinduism.* A sacred formula believed to embody the divinity invoked and to possess magical power. It is used in prayer and incantation. **2.** A similar formula or word repeated, often in one's head, to induce a contemplative state in some techniques of meditation. **3.** A Vedic psalm of praise. [Sanskrit, "prayer", "hymn".]
man·tu·a (mántew-ə) n. A loose gown, caught open in front to reveal an underskirt, worn in the 17th and 18th centuries. [French *manteau*, mantle (influenced by MANTUA, formerly famous for silks), from Old French *mantel*, from Latin *mantellum*, MANTLE.]
Man·tu·a (mántew-ə). *Italian* **Man·to·va** (mántōva). City on the river Mincio, Lombardy, Italy. It is the capital of Mantova province, and is a tourist, manufacturing, and agricultural centre.
—Man·tu·an *adj. & n.*
man·u·al (mánnew-əl) *adj.* **1. a.** Of, pertaining to, or done by the hands. **b.** Used by or operated with the hands, as a weapon, tool, or simple machine may be: *manual controls.* **c.** Employing human rather than mechanical energy: *manual labour.* **d.** Pertaining to unskilled work done with the hands, as opposed to clerical or administrative work, for example: *manual workers.* **2.** Of, pertaining to, or resembling a manual or guidebook.
~n. **1.** Any small reference book, especially one giving instructions; a guidebook; a handbook. **2.** The keyboard of an organ. **3.** *Military.* A set of prescribed movements in the handling of a weapon, especially a rifle. **4.** Manual control: *on manual.* [Middle English *manuel*, from Old French, from Latin *manuālis*, of the hand, from *manus*, hand.] **—man·u·al·ly** *adv.*

mantis *There are about 1,800 species of mantis – all members of the insect family* Mantidae *and often known as praying mantises. They feed on live insects, including others of their own kind. The female often eats the male after they mate; the young nymphs often eat each other.*

maple

THE FIERY FOLIAGE OF THE MAPLE FAMILY
Trees used for garden ornament, building timber – and sweet syrup

Maple wood was used to make spears in prehistoric times – hence its botanical name *Acer,* the Latin for sharp. In the past 2,000 years, maple wood has been used in cabinetwork and to make musical instruments – for example, the sycamore is also called the fiddle-back maple.

The giant maples from the temperate regions of Europe and North America, which grow to more than 33 metres (100 feet), are the most valued for timber.

Most forest species, such as America's red maple, have brilliant autumn foliage and some – for example, the Chinese paperbark maple – have decorative bark. The Norway maple also bears flowers in spring, which is unusual for a forest tree. The more delicate Japanese maples are the most highly prized as garden trees.

Among the maple family's 200 or more members at least one is edible. The extraction of the sugar maple's rich sap, and its preservation as syrup or sugar, was a secret given to the 18th-century settlers of Canada by the native Indians.

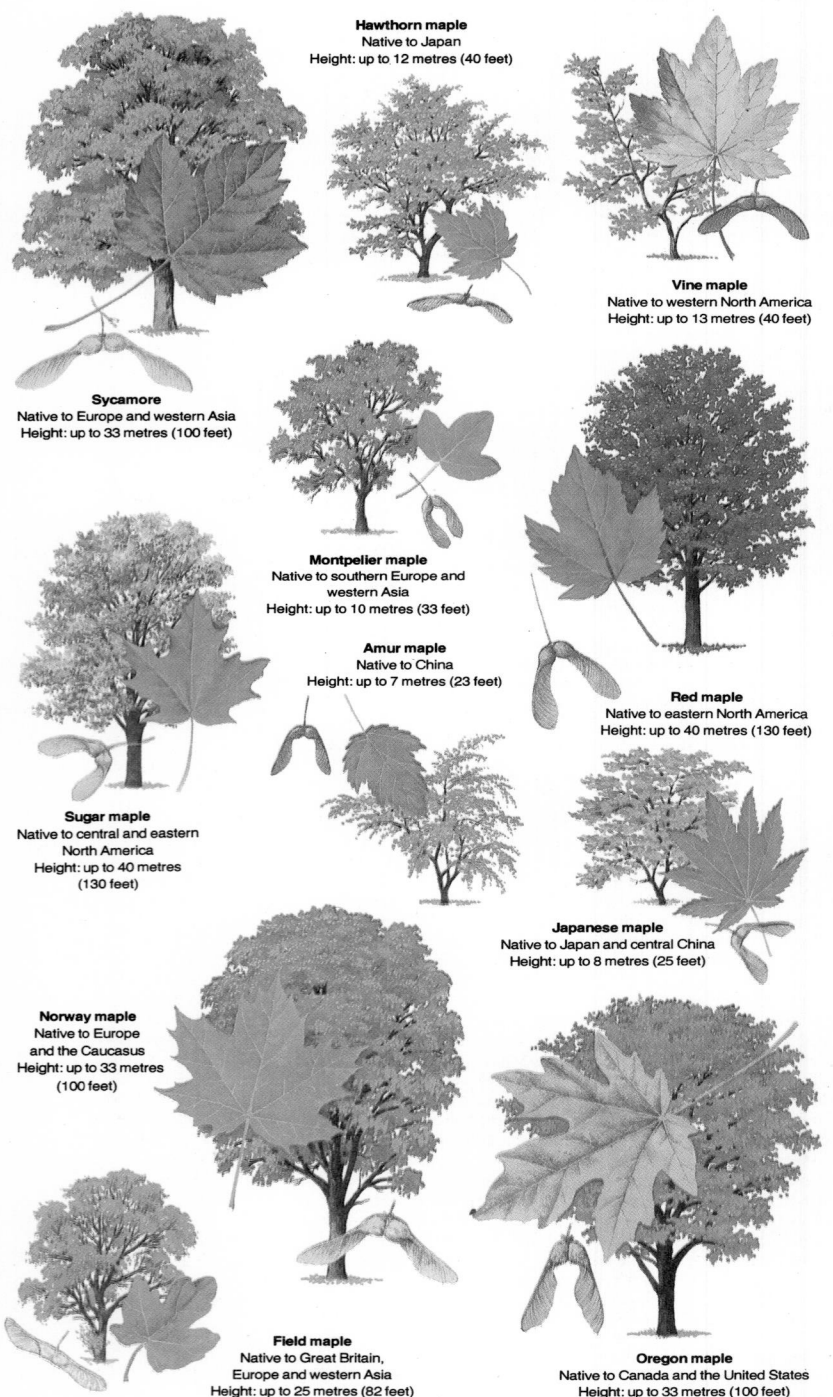

Hawthorn maple
Native to Japan
Height: up to 12 metres (40 feet)

Vine maple
Native to western North America
Height: up to 13 metres (40 feet)

Sycamore
Native to Europe and western Asia
Height: up to 33 metres (100 feet)

Montpelier maple
Native to southern Europe and western Asia
Height: up to 10 metres (33 feet)

Amur maple
Native to China
Height: up to 7 metres (23 feet)

Red maple
Native to eastern North America
Height: up to 40 metres (130 feet)

Sugar maple
Native to central and eastern North America
Height: up to 40 metres (130 feet)

Japanese maple
Native to Japan and central China
Height: up to 8 metres (25 feet)

Norway maple
Native to Europe and the Caucasus
Height: up to 33 metres (100 feet)

Field maple
Native to Great Britain, Europe and western Asia
Height: up to 25 metres (82 feet)

Oregon maple
Native to Canada and the United States
Height: up to 33 metres (100 feet)

manual alphabet *n.* An alphabet of hand signals used for communication with or between deaf people.

ma·nu·bri·um (mə-néw-bri-əm ‖ -nŏŏ-) *n., pl.* **-bria** (-bri-ə). *Anatomy.* **1.** The upper part of the breastbone. **2.** The handle-shaped projection of the malleus in the ear. [New Latin, from Latin *manubrium,* handle : *manus,* hand + an obscure second element.]

Manucci. See **Manutius.**

Ma·nu·el I (mánnew-el, -əl; *Portuguese* man-wél), also called Emmanuel; also known as Manuel the Great or the Fortunate (1469–1521). King of Portugal (1495–1521). He presided over the golden age of Portugal's overseas exploration, including the discovery of the sea route to India by Vasco da Gama.

man·u·fac·to·ry (mánnew-fák-təri, -tri) *n., pl.* **-ries.** *Archaic.* A factory. [MANUFACT(URE) + (FACT)ORY.]

man·u·fac·ture (mánnew-fákchər ‖ mánnə-) *v.* **-tured, -turing, -tures.** —*tr.* **1. a.** To make or process (a raw material) into a finished product, especially by means of a large-scale industrial operation. **b.** To make or process (a product), especially by industrial machines. **2.** To create, produce, or turn out in a mechanical manner: *A street artist manufacturing portraits to order.* **3.** To concoct or invent; fabricate. —*intr.* To make or process goods, especially in large quantities and by means of industrial machines. —*n. Abbr.* **manuf., manufac., mfg., mfr. 1.** The act, craft, or process of manufacturing. **2.** A product that is manufactured. [French, a making by hand, handiwork, from Late Latin *manūfactus,* handmade : Latin *manus,* hand + *factus,* from *facere,* to make.] —**man·u·fac·tur·a·ble** *adj.*

man·u·fac·tured gas (mánnew-fákchərd ‖ mánnə-) *n.* A gaseous fuel made from various petroleum products or from soft coal.

man·u·fac·tur·er (mánnew-fákchərər ‖ mánnə-) *n. Abbr.* **mfr.** A person or enterprise that manufactures; especially, the owner or operator of a factory.

ma·nu·ka (máanəkə, mə-nŏŏkə) *n.* An ornamental tree or shrub, *Leptospermum scoparium,* native to New Zealand, with aromatic leaves and hard timber. [Maori.]

man·u·mit (mánnew-mít) *tr.v.* **-mitted, -mitting, -mits.** To free from slavery or bondage; emancipate. [Middle English *manumitten,* from Old French *manumitter,* from Latin *manumittere,* from *manū ēmittere,* to liberate, release from one's hand : *manū,* ablative of *manus,* hand + *ēmittere,* to EMIT.] —**man·u·mis·sion** (-mísh'n) *n.* —**man·u·mit·ter** *n.*

ma·nure (mə-néwr ‖ -nŏŏr) *n.* Animal dung, compost, or other material used to fertilise soil. —*tr.v.* **manured, -nuring, -nures.** To apply manure to. [Middle English *manour,* cultivation of soil, from *manouren,* to till, from Anglo-French *mainoverer,* from Old French *manoeuvrer,* to till, "work by hand", from Medieval Latin *manuoperārī* : Latin *manus,* hand + *operārī,* to work.] —**ma·nur·er** *n.*

ma·nus (máynəss) *n., pl.* **manus. 1.** *Zoology.* The end of the forelimb in vertebrates, such as the hand, claw, or hoof. **2.** In Roman law, the authority of a husband over his wife. [Latin, hand.]

man·u·script (mánnew-skript) *n. Abbr.* **ms, MS, ms., MS. 1.** A book, document, or other composition written by hand. **2.** A typewritten or handwritten version of a book, article, document, or other work, prepared and submitted for publication in print. **3.** Handwriting, as opposed to printing. —*adj.* Handwritten or typewritten. [Medieval Latin *manūscrīptus,* handwritten : Latin *manus,* hand + *scrīptus,* from *scrībere,* to write.]

Ma·nu·ti·us (mə-néw-shi-əss, -shəss ‖ -nŏŏ-), also called Manucci. Family of Italian printers. Aldus Manutius (1450–1518) established the Aldine Press in Venice (c. 1498) to publish Greek and Latin classics. Paulus Manutius (1512–74) and Aldus Manutius the Younger (1547–97) directed the papal press.

Manx (mangks) *adj.* Of or pertaining to the Isle of Man or Manx (the language). —*n., pl.* **Manx. 1.** A native or resident of the Isle of Man. **2.** The nearly extinct Goidelic Celtic language spoken on the Isle of Man. **3.** A Manx cat.

Manx cat *n. Sometimes small* **m.** A domestic cat of a breed having short hair and an internal vestigial tail. Also called "Manx". [Originally bred on the Isle of MAN.]

Manx shearwater *n.* A small European oceanic bird, *Puffinus puffinus,* that shows remarkably accurate homing ability.

man·y (ménni ‖ *Irish also* mánni) *adj.* **more, most. 1.** Amounting to or consisting of a large or indefinite number: *many friends; as many eggs as you can eat.* **2.** Designating each of a large number of persons or things. Used with *a, an,* or *another: many a woman; many another day.* —*pl.n.* **1.** A large, indefinite number of persons or things. Often used with *of: Many of the children were ill.* **2.** The great body of the people; the masses. Usually preceded by *the: "The many fail; the one succeeds."* (Alfred, Lord Tennyson). —*pl. pron.* A large number of persons or things: *"Many are called, but few are chosen."* (Matthew 22:14). —**as many.** The same number of: *had six cars in as many years.* —**many's the time.** Often. —**one too many.** One more than is necessary or desirable: *drank one too many.* [Middle English, Old English *manig, mænig.*]

man·y·plies (ménni-plīz) *n.* The third stomach of a cud-chewing mammal, the **omasum** (*see*). [MANY + *plies,* plural of PLY (modelled by analogy on *manifolds.*)]

man·y·sid·ed (ménni-sīdid) *adj.* Having a variety of aspects or qualities: *a many-sided book.* —**man·y·sid·ed·ness** *n.*

man·za·ni·lla (mánzə-níllə) *n.* A pale dry sherry from Spain. [Spanish, small apple, hence (from its aromatic bouquet) manzanilla sherry, diminutive of *manzana,* apple, from Old Spanish, from Latin *(māla) Matiāna,* "(apples) of *Matius*", a particular kind of apple, probably named after Caius *Matius* Calvena, Roman author of a cookery book (first century B.C.).]

Man·zo·ni (man-dzṓni), **Alessandro** (1785–1873). Italian novelist and poet. He was the leader of the Italian romantic school and is best known for his romantic-historical novel *I Promessi Sposi* (*The Betrothed,* 1825–27). The refined Florentine dialect which he used as a literary language set the standard for modern Italian prose.

Mao (mow) *adj.* Being of a plain, uniform-like style characteristic of clothing worn in China under Mao Ze-dong: *a Mao jacket.*

MAO monoamine oxidase.

Mao·ism (mów-iz'm) *n.* The Communist political philosophy and practice developed in China chiefly by Mao Ze-dong, emphasising the peasantry's role in a revolution. **—Mao·ist** *n. & adj.*

Ma·o·ri (mówr-i, mów-ri) *n., pl.* **-ris** or collectively **Maori. 1.** A member of the aboriginal people of New Zealand, of Polynesian-Melanesian descent. **2.** The Austronesian language of this people. **—Ma·o·ri** *adj.*

mao-tai, mao tai (mów-tī́) *n.* A potent, colourless Chinese alcoholic drink distilled from a mixture of Chinese sorghum and millet. [Chinese, after *Maotai,* town in southwest China where it is produced.]

Mao Ze-dong or **Mao Tse-t'ung** (mów-dzə-dŏŏng), also known as Chairman Mao (1893–1976). Chinese Communist leader. In 1921 he helped to form the Chinese Communist Party, and with its split from the Guomindang Nationalist Party (1927) became a leader of the Chinese Soviet Republic in southeast China (1931). He led the Long March (1934–35) to Yan'an where, after the collapse of the Japanese, he defeated the Nationalists and proclaimed the People's Republic of China (1949). As Chairman of the People's Republic (1949–59), he instituted the Great Leap Forward and the founding of the communes. He continued as party chairman after 1959 and instituted the Cultural Revolution (1966–69) to re-establish the revolutionary spirit. His writings have had great influence on revolutionary thinking throughout the world.

map (map) *n.* **1. a.** A representation, usually on a plane surface, of a region of the earth showing geographical, political, or other features. **b.** A similar representation of stars, planets, and other heavenly bodies. **2.** Something suggesting a map, as in comprehensiveness or clarity of representation. **3.** *Mathematics.* A mapping. **4.** *Slang.* The face. **5.** The arrangement of genes on a chromosome. **—put on the map.** To make famous or known. **—wipe off the map.** To destroy completely; annihilate.
~*tr.v.* **mapped, mapping, maps. 1.** To make a map of. **2.** To explore or make a survey of (a region) for the purpose of making a map. **3.** To plan or delineate, especially in detail; arrange. Often used with *out: mapping out holiday plans.* **4.** *Mathematics.* To establish a mapping of (a set or aggregate). **5.** To locate (a gene) on a chromosome. [Medieval Latin *mappa (mundī),* map (of the world), from *mappa,* napkin, sheet, cloth.] **—map·per** *n.*

ma·ple (mayp'l) *n.* **1.** Any tree or shrub of the genus *Acer,* found in the North Temperate Zone. Most are deciduous trees, having lobed leaves and winged seeds borne in pairs. **2.** The wood of a maple, especially the hard, close-grained wood of the **sugar maple** *(see).* **3.** The flavour of the concentrated sap of the sugar maple. [Middle English, Old English *mapel(treow),* maple (tree).]

maple sugar *n.* A sugar made by boiling down maple syrup.

maple syrup *n.* **1.** A sweet syrup made from the sap of maple trees, especially the **sugar maple** *(see).* **2.** Syrup made from other sugars and flavoured with maple syrup or artificial maple flavouring.

map·ping (mápping) *n. Mathematics.* A rule of correspondence established between two sets that associates each member of the first set with one or more members of the second; a function. Also called "map".

map projection *n.* A representation of the earth's parallels of latitude and meridians of longitude as a network, or graticule, on a plane surface.

Ma·pu·to (mə-pṓōtō). Formerly **Lou·ren·ço Mar·ques** (lə-rén-sō márks; *Portuguese* lō-ráN-su márkish). Capital of Mozambique, situated on Maputo Bay. It is a resort and a major seaport, exporting metal ores and coal from southern Africa.

maq·uette (ma-két) *n.* A preliminary model or sketch made by a sculptor. [French, from Italian *machietta,* diminutive of *macchia,* spot, ultimately from Latin *macula,* spot.]

ma·quill·age (mákee-aázh) *n.* **1.** Cosmetics; make-up. **2.** The application of cosmetics. [French, from *maquiller,* to make up, from Old French *masquiller,* to stain.]

ma·quis (mákee, maákee, ma-kée) *n., pl.* **maquis.** In the Mediterranean area, a shrubby vegetation made up of mainly evergreen small trees and bushes. [French (via Corsica), from Italian *macchia,* thicket, "spot", from Latin *macula,* spot.]

Ma·quis (ma-kée) *n., pl.* **Maquis. 1.** The French underground organisation that fought against German occupation forces during World War II; the resistance. **2.** A member of this organisation. [French, from *maquis,* MAQUIS, "bush" (referring to undergrowth as a hiding place).]

mar (mar) *tr.v.* **marred, marring, mars. 1.** To damage or deface. **2.** To spoil the quality of: *"Mend your speech lest it mar your fortunes."* (Shakespeare). **—**See Synonyms at **injure.**
~*n.* A mark that disfigures; a blemish. [Middle English *marren, merran,* Old English *merran, mierran.*]

mar. maritime.

Mar. March.

mar·a·bou, mar·a·bout (márrə-bōō) *n.* **1.** A large Old World stork, *Leptoptilus crumeniferus.* Also called "adjutant", "adjutant stork". **2.** A neckpiece, hat, dress, or coat trimmed with the down of the marabou. **3. a.** A raw silk that can be dyed without being separated from the gum. **b.** A fabric or an article of clothing made from such silk. [French *marabout,* from Portuguese *marabuto,* from Arabic *murābit,* holy man, hermit, hence stork (the stork is a sacred bird in Islam). See **marabout.**]

mar·a·bout[1] (márrə-bōō, -bōōt) *n.* **1.** A Muslim hermit or saint, especially in north Africa. **2.** The tomb of a marabout or a shrine to his memory. [French, from Portuguese *marabuto,* from Arabic *murābit,* hermit, holy man, "(one) stationed (at a frontier post)", from *ribāt,* frontier post (those stationed there fought against infidels and were thus considered holy).]

marabout[2]. Variant of **marabou.**

ma·ra·bun·ta (márrə-buntə) *n. West Indian.* **1.** Any of several social wasps. **2.** *Slang.* A bad-tempered, nagging woman. [Probably of West African origin.]

ma·rac·a (mə-ráckə || -raákə) *n.* A percussion instrument consisting of a hollow gourd rattle containing pebbles or beans. Maracas are often played in pairs. [Brazilian Portuguese *maracá,* from Tupi.]

ma·rae (mə-rī́) *n.* A Maori meeting place.

mar·ag·ing (maár-ayjing) *n. Metallurgy.* The process of heating a martensite steel at around 500°C followed by cooling in air without quenching. It is used to modify the martensite structure and produce strong low-carbon steels. [MAR(TENSITE) + AG(E)ING.]

Ma·ram·ba (mə-rámbə). Formerly **Liv·ing·stone** (lívving-stən || -stōn). City of southern Zambia, situated on the Zambezi river. Founded in 1905, and named at first after the explorer David Livingstone, it was the capital of Northern Rhodesia from 1911 to 1935, when Lusaka replaced it.

ma·ran·ta (mə-rántə) *n.* **1.** Any plant of the tropical American genus *Maranta,* one species of which, *M. arundinacea,* yields arrowroot. Several species are cultivated for their ornamental foliage. **2.** A starch made from arrowroot. [New Latin, after Bartolomeo *Maranta,* 16th-century Italian herbalist.]

ma·ras·ca (mə-ráskə) *n.* A European cherry tree, *Prunus cerasus marasca,* bearing bitter red fruit from which maraschino is made. [Italian, shortened from *amarasca (ciliegia),* bitter (cherry), from *amaro,* bitter, from Latin *amārus,* bitter.]

mar·a·schi·no (márrə-skéenō, *also* -shéenō) *n.* A liqueur made from the fermented juice and crushed kernels of the marasca cherry. [Italian, from MARASCA.]

maraschino cherry *n.* A maraschino-flavoured preserved cherry.

ma·ras·mus (mə-rázməss) *n. Pathology.* A wasting away of the body, especially of infants, associated with inadequate or inadequately assimilated food. [Late Latin, from Greek *marasmos,* from *marainein,* to waste away.] **—ma·ras·mic** *adj.*

Ma·rat (márraa; *French* ma-rá), **Jean Paul** (1743–93). French journalist, and Revolutionary politician. He was trained as a doctor and wrote scientific works before founding (1789) and editing *l'Ami du peuple* which supported the French Revolution. Hero of the working classes, he was elected to the National Convention (1792) and struggled against the Girondins, one of whose supporters, Charlotte Corday, murdered him in his bath.

Ma·ra·tha (mə-raátə) *n., pl.* **-thas** or collectively **Maratha.** Also **Mah·rat·ta** (-ráttə). A member of a Scytho-Dravidian people of southwest India.

Ma·ra·thi (mə-raáti) *adj.* Also **Mah·rat·i, Mah·rat·ti** (-rátti). Of or pertaining to the state of Maharashtra, India.
~*n.* Also **Mahrati, Mahratti.** The major Indic language in Maharashtra.

mar·a·thon (márrə-th'n || -thon) *n.* **1.** A race on foot of 42.195 kilometres (26 miles 385 yards). It is an event in the Olympic games. **2.** Any long-distance race: *a swimming marathon.* **3.** A contest of endurance: *a dance marathon.* **4.** A task or action that requires endurance: *a letter-writing marathon.* [Named in commemoration of the messenger who ran to Athens to report the news of the Greek victory over the Persians at *Marathon* (490 B.C.).] **—mar·a·thon** *adj.*

ma·raud (mə-ráwd) *v.* **-rauded, -rauding, -rauds.** *—intr.* To rove in search of booty; raid for plunder. *—tr.* To invade for loot; raid or pillage.
~*n. Archaic.* A raid. [French *marauder,* from *maraud,* vagabond, rogue, perhaps from dialectal *maraud,* tomcat (imitative of purring).] **—ma·raud·er** *n.*

mar·ble (márb'l) *n.* **1.** A metamorphic rock, chiefly calcium carbonate, $CaCO_3$, often irregularly coloured by impurities. It is used for architectural and ornamental purposes. **2.** A piece of marble. **3.** A sculpture of marble: *the Elgin marbles.* **4.** A small hard ball made of stone or glass, used in children's games. See **marbles. —lose (one's) marbles.** *Slang.* **1.** To take leave of one's senses; go mad. **2.** To become senile. **—make (one's) marble good with.** *Australian Slang.* To make oneself popular with; win the approval of.
~*tr.v.* **marbled, -bling, -bles.** To mottle and streak with colours and veins in imitation of marble: *marbled paper.*
~*adj.* **1.** Consisting of or constructed with marble: *marble halls.* **2.** Resembling marble in consistency, texture, venation, colour, or coldness: *a marble heart.* [Middle English *marbel,* from Old French *marbre,* from Latin *marmor,* from Greek *marmaros*†, marble, originally any hard stone.] **—mar·bly** *adj.*

marble cake *n.* A sponge cake with a marbled appearance, made

Manx cat *A tailless cat probably first bred on the Isle of Man. Its long hind legs give it a curious hopping gait.*

marabou *The African adjutant, or marabou, is the world's largest species of stork, growing to a height of 1.5 metres (5 feet). Native to central and parts of southern Africa, it feeds on fish, frogs, and carrion.*

PRONUNCIATION KEY

a, trap; aa, father; ai, fair; ar, star; aw, lawn; ay, play; b, bb, stab; rubber; ch, church; ck, ticket; d, dd, dead; ladder; e, dress; ee, bee; er, defer; ew, few; ewr, pure; ə, about; ər, letter; f, ff, fife; differ; g, gg, giggle; h, hat; i, kit; ī, price; īr, fire; j, judge; k, kick; l, ll, let; 'l, needle; m, mm, man; n, nn, no; 'n, sudden; ng, thing; o, lot; ō, no; ŏŏ, foot; ōō, shoe; oor, poor; ow, cow; owr, hour; oy, boy; p, pp, pepper; r, rr, red; s, ss, sauce; sh, ship; t, tt, totter; th, thick; th, this; smooth; u, cut; ur, turn; v, vv, valve; w, wet; y, yes; z, zz, zebra; zh, vision; pleasure

IN FOREIGN WORDS:

aN, oN, Saint-Saëns; hl, Llanelli; Hluhluwe; kh, loch; lough; Khaled

STRESS MARK:

ín-sīt, insight; in-sī́t, incite

MAPPING THE WORLD

Every type of map projection distorts the world in some way

The Age of Discovery, when European mariners explored the world in the late 15th and 16th centuries, saw the work of the first great modern mapmaker, Gerardus Mercator (1512–94).

As maps became more accurate and as it became widely understood that the Earth was round, it became apparent that no large-scale map could be drawn on a flat surface without distortion in some way – whether in areas, angles, or distances. Since then many methods of map projection have been devised, but it is possible only to minimise distortion. More accuracy in one way will mean that there is distortion in the others.

Mercator's projection is probably the most familiar. It is based on an imaginary cylinder of paper wrapped round the Earth and touching it at the equator. An imaginary light from inside the Earth "projects" the continents onto the cylinder. When the cylinder is flattened out, the lines of latitude and longitude are straight, but the length along them is greatly exaggerated. The land areas near the Poles, such as Greenland and Antarctica, are greatly exaggerated, but the angles are correct. In marine navigation, this allows a course to be plotted by drawing a straight line from point to point.

For aircraft navigation, however, different problems arise. The shortest distance between London and Tokyo is not a straight line across Europe and Asia, as the map projection suggests, but a route across the North Pole. A special map is produced for each airport, using a zenithal projection. On it any route from that airport is shown as a straight line, with lines of latitude and longitude curved.

Another type of map, called a conical projection, involves an imaginary cone placed over the Earth so that a line parallel with the equator is touched by the cone. The tip of the cone is directly over the North (or South) Pole. By varying the size of the cone, almost any spot on a hemisphere can be made to touch it. An imaginary light from the centre of the Earth would show up the projection on the cone. If the area to be mapped is small, the distortion is negligible.

Numerous types of map projection have been devised mathematically, and atlases usually carry the name of the projection under each map.

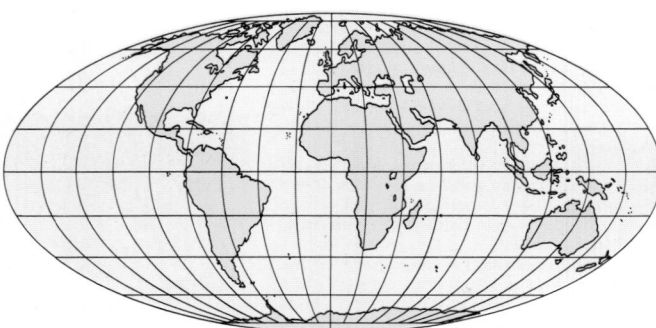

MOLLWEIDE'S HOMOLOGRAPHIC PROJECTION *An equal-area projection on which each land mass corresponds to the real one in relative size. However, angles are distorted and navigation would have to be plotted on curved lines.*

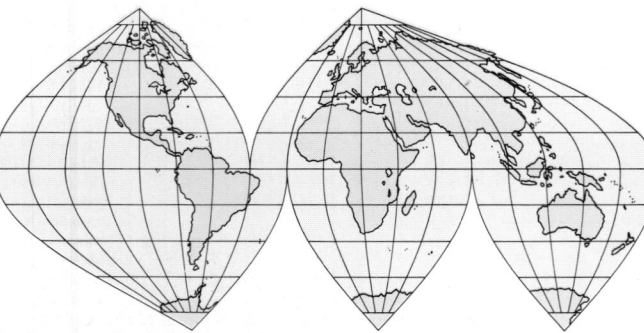

INTERRUPTED PROJECTION *A map with three points of view. This evens out the distortion of angles across the map and represents shapes fairly accurately. Despite its appearance, it could not be cut out and wrapped round a sphere.*

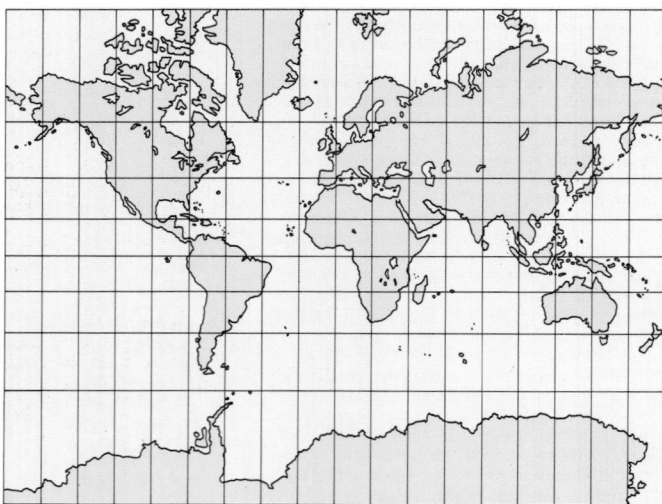

MERCATOR PROJECTION *A correct-angle projection, suitable for marine navigation. The lines of longitude run parallel rather than converging. Consequently Antarctica and Greenland are shown about ten times their relative size.*

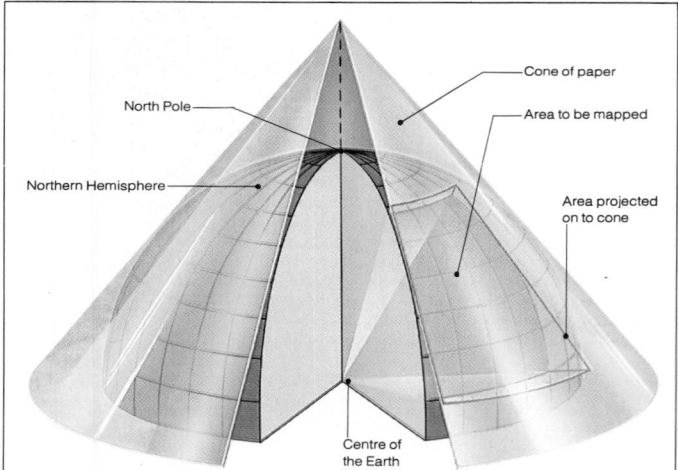

CONICAL PROJECTION *Suitable for small areas as well as for much of a hemisphere. An imaginary cone is placed over the Earth so that it touches the area to be mapped. The point of projection is the centre of the Earth, the tip of the cone is above a Pole.*

with a light and a dark mixture of ingredients, swirled together slightly just before cooking.

mar·bled white (márb'ld) *n.* A widely distributed butterfly, *Melariargia galathea,* with distinctive black and cream marking.

mar·ble·ise, mar·ble·ize (márb'l-īz) *tr.v.* **-ised, -ising, -ises.** To give a veined or mottled appearance to.

mar·bles (márb'lz) *n. Used with a singular verb.* Any of various children's games played with marbles, the object usually being to strike a marble or group of marbles belonging to one's opponent by throwing at it a marble of one's own.

mar·bling (márbling) *n.* **1.** A mottling or streaking that resembles marble. **2.** The process or operation of giving something the surface appearance of marble. **3.** The decorative imitation of marble patterns printed on page edges and endpapers of books. **4.** The streaks of fat found in beef of good quality.

Mar·burg[1] (már-burg; *German* -bŏork). City in Hessen, West Germany. It is the site of Germany's first Protestant university (1527) and the 13th- to 14th-century castle where Luther and Zwingli held their famous religious debate (1529). It produces precision machinery, pharmaceuticals, and pottery.

Marburg[2]. See **Maribor.**

Marburg disease *n.* A fatal virus disease that is transmitted to humans from the vervet or green monkey by contact with infected tissue in a laboratory. Also called "green monkey disease". [After MARBURG, West Germany, where laboratory technicians contracted the disease in 1967.]

marc (mark, mar) *n.* **1.** The pulpy residue left after the juice has been pressed from grapes, apples, or other fruit. **2.** Brandy distilled from grape residue. [French, from Old French *marcher,* to trample (grapes), MARCH.]

Marc·an (márkən) *adj.* Pertaining to or designating St. Mark's Gospel. [Latin *Marcus,* Mark + -AN.]
mar·ca·site (márkə-sīt || -zīt) *n.* **1.** A mineral form of iron disulphide, FeS_2, having the same composition as pyrite but differing in crystalline structure. Also called "white iron pyrites". **2.** An ornament of pyrite, polished steel, or white metal. [Middle English *marchasite,* from Medieval Latin *marcasīta,* from Arabic *marqashīṭā,* probably from Persian.]
Mar·ceau (maar-sṓ), **Marcel** (1923–). French mime, trained as a conventional actor. His most famous character is the clown-harlequin Bip. His films include *Un Jardin public* (1955).
mar·cel (már-sél) *n.* A once fashionable hairstyle characterised by regular waves. Also called "marcel wave".
~*tr.v.* **marcelled, -celling, -cels.** To style (the hair) in a marcel. [After *Marcel* Grateau (1852–1936), French hairdresser.]
mar·ces·cent (maar-séss'nt) *adj. Botany.* Withering but not falling off. Said especially of a blossom that persists on a twig after flowering. [Latin *marcēscēns* (stem *marcēscent-*), present participle of *marcēscere,* inceptive of *marcēre,* to wither.]
march¹ (march) *v.* **marched, marching, marches.** —*intr.* **1. a.** To walk in a formal military manner with measured steps at a steady rate. **b.** To begin to move in such a manner: *The troops will march at dawn.* **2.** To advance or proceed assertively or belligerently: *marched up to the shop assistant to make a complaint.* —*tr.* **1.** To cause to march: *soldiers being marched into battle.* **2.** To traverse by marching: *They marched the route in a day.*
~*n.* **1. a.** The act of marching. **b.** The steady forward movement of a body of troops. **2.** A long tiring journey on foot. **3.** Forward movement; advancement; progression: *the march of time.* **4.** A regulated pace: *quick march.* **5.** The distance covered by marching: *a week's march away.* **6.** A procession held as a form of public demonstration. **7.** *Music.* A musical composition in regularly accented, usually duple, time with a rhythm suitable for accompanying marching. **—on the march.** Advancing; progressing: *Science is on the march.* **—steal a march on.** To get ahead of, especially by quiet enterprise. [French *marcher,* to walk, tramp, trample, from Frankish *markôn* (unattested), to mark out with footprints.] **—march·er** *n.*
march² *n.* **1.** The border or boundary of a country or area of land. **2.** A tract of land bordering on two countries: *the Welsh Marches.* ~*intr.v.* **marched, marching, marches.** To border upon a country or have a common boundary. Used with *with*: *England marches with Scotland.* [Middle English *marche,* from Old French, *marche, marc,* borderland, from Germanic.]
March (march) *n. Abbr.* **Mar.** The third month of the Gregorian calendar. March has 31 days. [Middle English, from Old French *Marche, Marz,* from Latin *Mārtius (mēnsis),* (month) of Mars, from *Mārs* (stem *Mārt-*), MARS (god).]
March. marchioness.
Mar·che (márkay). Also **the Marches.** Coastal region of central Italy, covered largely by Apennine ranges and foothills. It produces cereals, fruit, wine, tobacco, cattle, and fish. It is so called because it lay on the southern border (or march) of the Holy Roman Empire. Ancona is the capital.
Mär·chen (máirkhən) *n., pl.* **Märchen.** *German.* A folk tale or fairy story.
March·es, the (márchiz). The areas along the English-Welsh and English-Scottish borders. In medieval times, the lords of these areas were given wide-ranging powers to defend the borders.
mar·che·sa (mar-káy-za, -sa, -zə, -sə) *n., pl.* **-se** (-ze, -se). A wife or widow of a marchese. [Italian, feminine of MARCHESE.]
mar·che·se (mar-kay-zə) *n., pl.* **-si** (-zee). An Italian nobleman ranking between a prince and a count. [Italian, from Late Latin *marcēnsis,* "ruler of a march", from *marca,* borderland, MARCH.]
Marcheshvan. Variant of **Cheshvan.**
marching orders *pl.n.* **1. a.** Orders to move on or depart. **b.** Official instructions to proceed. **2.** *Informal.* A warning that one is no longer wanted: *was given her marching orders by her lover.*
mar·chion·ess (mársh'n-iss, -éss) *n., pl.* **-esses.** *Abbr.* **March. 1.** The wife or widow of a marquis. **2.** A peeress of the rank of marquis in her own right. In certain countries, also called "marquise". [Medieval Latin *marchionissa,* feminine of *marchiō,* marquis, "ruler of the march", from *marca,* borderland, MARCH.]
march·land (márch-land, -lənd) *n.* A borderland; a march.
march·pane (márch-payn) *n. Archaic.* A confection, **marzipan** *(see).*
march past *n.* The ceremonial marching of troops or other uniformed personnel past a saluting base during a review.
Mar·cio·nism (mársh'n-izm) *n.* A Gnostic movement of the second and third centuries A.D. that rejected the Old Testament and emphasised the teachings of St. Paul. [After *Marcion* of Sinope (*c.* 100–160), who founded the sect.]
Mar·co·ni (maar-kṓni), **Guglielmo** (1874–1937). Italian physicist and electrical engineer. He developed the equipment for converting radio waves into electrical signals: in 1895 he successfully transmitted long-wave radio signals, and in 1901 sent signals across the Atlantic. He shared the Nobel prize for physics (1909).
Marconi rig *n.* A **Bermuda rig** *(see).* [After Guglielmo MARCONI, since the rig resembles an early radio transmitting aerial.]
Mar·cos (már-koss), **Ferdinand (Edralin)** (1917–). President of the Philippines (1965–). He declared martial law (1972), and has suppressed political opposition.
Mar·cus (Ae·li·us) Au·re·li·us (An·to·ni·nus) (márkəss éeli-əss aw-réeli-əss ántə-nīnəss), born Marcus Annius Verus (121–180 A.D.). Roman emperor (161–180) and Stoic philosopher. An active emperor, he ruled with Lucius Verus until 169 A.D., afterwards ruling alone. Sometimes called the Philosopher Emperor, he wrote the *Meditations,* 12 volumes of aphorisms, illustrating his Stoic ideals.
Mar·cus·e (maar-kóozə), **Herbert** (1898–1979). U.S. Marxist philosopher. A Jewish refugee from Nazi Germany, he criticised both orthodox Marxism and western positivism, and advocated using the tolerance of contemporary society to overthrow that very society. His works include *Eros and Civilisation* (1954), *One Dimensional Man* (1965), and *Counter-Revolution and Revolt* (1972).
Mar·di gras (márdi graá) *n.* Shrove Tuesday, the last day before Lent. It is celebrated in some places, such as New Orleans, United States, by carnivals, masquerade balls, and parades of costumed merrymakers. [French, "fat Tuesday".]
Mar·duk (márdŏŏk). The chief god of ancient Babylon.
mar·dy (márdi) *adj. British Regional.* **1.** Spoilt. **2.** Naughty; sulky. Said of a child. [From *marred,* past participle of MAR.]
mare¹ (mair) *n.* A female horse or the female of other equine species. [Middle English *mare, mere,* Old English *mēre* (unattested).]
ma·re² (maá-ray, -ri, márray, márri) *n., pl.* **-ria** (maári-ə, márri-ə). *Astronomy.* Any of the large dark areas on the moon or Mars, originally thought to be seas. [New Latin, from Latin, sea.]
mare clau·sum (klów-səm, -sŏŏm) *n. Law.* A sea under the jurisdiction of one nation and closed to all others. [Latin, "closed sea".]
mare li·be·rum (léebə-rəm, -rŏŏm) *n. Law.* A sea open to navigation by all nations. [Latin, "free sea".]
ma·rem·ma (mə-rémmə) *n.* Low, unhealthy coastal marshland, especially in Italy. [Italian, from Latin *maritima.* See **maritime.**]
Ma·ren·go (mə-réng-gō) *adj.* Browned in oil and sautéed in a sauce of tomatoes, mushrooms, garlic or onion, and white wine. Used after the noun: *veal Marengo.* [Said to be from the chicken dish served to Napoleon after the battle of *Marengo* (1800).]
mare's nest (mairz) *n.* **1.** A hoax or fraud. **2.** An extraordinarily complicated situation. [From the proverbial expression "to find a mare's nest" (that is, an impossible fantasy).]
mare's-tail (maírz-tayl) *n.* **1.** An aquatic plant, *Hippuris vulgaris,* of the North Temperate Zone, having minute flowers and whorls of tapering leaves. **2.** *Usually plural.* A drawn out, wispy cirrus cloud.
marg. Variant of **marge.**
Mar·ga·ret (márg-rit, márgə-, -rət), **Maid of Norway** (1283–90). Queen of Scotland (1286–90). Daughter of Eric II, King of Norway, and Princess Margaret of Scotland, she became queen on the death of her grandfather Alexander III. Betrothed to the future Edward II of England, she died in the Orkneys on her way to Scotland, thereby causing a war of succession.
Margaret (Rose), H.R.H. Princess, Countess of Snowdon (1930–). A princess of the United Kingdom, the younger daughter of George VI and sister of Queen Elizabeth II. She was married (1960–78) to Anthony Armstrong-Jones, later Lord Snowdon.
Margaret of Anjou (1430–82). Queen of England. Daughter of René of Anjou, she was married to Henry VI of England (1445) in an attempt to establish peace between France and England. The incompetent rule of Henry led to the Wars of the Roses (1455–85) during which Margaret led the Lancastrian faction, hoping to secure the succession of her son Edward (1453–71). Defeated and captured at the Battle of Tewkesbury (1471), she was ransomed to France (1476), where she died in poverty.
Margaret of Scotland (*c.* 1045–93). Queen of Scotland. The granddaughter of the English king Edmund Ironside, she married Malcolm III of Scotland (1067). She reformed the Scottish Church, and was canonised (1250).
Margaret of Valois (1553–1615). Queen of Navarre and France. She was the daughter of Henry II of France and Catherine de' Medici. Her marriage to Henry of Navarre (later Henry IV of France) in 1572 was annulled in 1599. Remembered for her *Mémoires,* she formed a literary circle during her stay at Usson (1587–1605).
Margaret Tudor (1489–1541). Regent of Scotland (1513–14). Daughter of Henry VII of England, she married James IV of Scotland (1503), after whose death she was regent for her son James V. Her marriage to Archibald Douglas, Earl of Angus (1514), lost her the regency.
mar·gar·ic (maar-gárrik). *adj.* Also **mar·ga·rit·ic** (márgə-ríttik). Resembling pearl; pearly. [French *margarique,* from Greek *margaron,* pearl.]
margaric acid *n.* A synthetic crystalline fatty acid, $C_{16}H_{33}COOH$. Also called "heptadecanoic acid". [French *margarique,* "pearly" (referring to its colour), from Greek *margaron,* pearl.]
mar·ga·rine (márjə-réen, *occasionally* márgə- || -reen) *n.* Also **mar·ga·rin** (-rin). A fatty solid consisting of a blend of hydrogenated vegetable or animal oils mixed with emulsifiers, vitamins, colouring matter, and other ingredients. It is used as a butter substitute. Also called "marge", "oleomargarine". [French, from *margarique,* MARGARIC (ACID).]
mar·ga·ri·ta (márga-réetə) *n.* A cocktail made with tequila, orange liqueur, and lemon or lime juice, usually served in a salt-rimmed glass. [Mexican Spanish, probably from *Margarita,* a feminine name.]
mar·ga·rite (márgə-rīt) *n.* **1.** A mineral, $CaAl_2(Si_2Al_2)O_{10}(OH)_2$, with a pearly, translucent lustre, formed in sheets of monoclinic crystals and related to mica. **2.** *Archaic.* A pearl. **3.** A rock formation that resembles beads. [Sense 1, from German *Margarit,* from Greek *margaritēs,* pearl. Sense 2, Middle English, from Old French,

Marduk *A detail from a boundary stone carrying the serpent symbol of the ancient Babylonian god Marduk. The stone was carved in about 1120 B.C.*

mare *A female horse, or mare, normally has a single foal at a time after a gestation period of 11 months.*

marionette *Strings attached to the marionette's limbs, and operated from above, make it possible to reproduce even complicated movements such as dancing. A simple marionette may have nine strings, but others can have three times as many.*

from Latin *margarīta,* from Greek *margaritēs,* pearl. Sense 3, from sense 2.]

Mar·gate (márgayt, márgit). Popular seaside resort of Kent, south-east England. It includes Westgate-on-Sea and Cliftonville.

marge (marj) *n.* Also **marg** (marg). *Informal.* Margarine.

mar·gin (márjin) *n.* **1.** An edge and the area adjacent to it; a border; a rim; a verge. **2. a.** The blank space bordering the written or printed area on a page. **b.** A vertical line drawn usually on the left-hand side of a page marking off such blank space. **3.** A limit of a state or process: *the margins of reality.* **4.** An amount allowed beyond what is strictly necessary; a surplus measure or amount: *a margin of safety.* **5.** A measure, quantity, or degree of difference: *a margin of 500 votes.* **6.** *Economics.* **a.** The minimum return that an enterprise may earn and still pay for itself. **b.** The difference between the cost and the selling price of securities or commodities. **7.** *Finance.* An amount in money, or represented by securities, deposited by a customer with a broker as a provision against loss on transactions made on account. **8.** *Australian.* An additional or bonus payment made to an employee, especially for extra responsibilities. **9.** *Botany.* The border of a leaf. **10.** *Zoology.* The boundary area of an insect's wing. —See Synonyms at **border.**

~*tr.v.* **margined, -gining, -gins. 1.** To provide with a margin. **2.** *Finance.* To deposit a margin upon. [Middle English, from Latin *margō* (stem *margin-*).]

mar·gin·al (márjin'l) *adj.* **1.** Of, pertaining to, or constituting a margin: *the marginal strip of beach.* **2.** Geographically adjacent: *counties marginal to Wales.* **3.** Written or printed in the margin of a book: *marginal notes.* **4. a.** Barely within a lower standard or limit of quality: *marginal writing ability.* **b.** Amounting to mere subsistence: *a marginal existence.* **c.** Barely noticeable; very small: *a marginal difference.* **5.** *Economics.* **a.** Designating enterprises that produce goods or are capable of producing goods at a rate that barely covers production costs. **b.** Pertaining to commodities thus manufactured and sold. **6.** *Psychology.* Pertaining to the fringe of consciousness. **7.** Lying next to more fertile agricultural land and yielding only a small crop. **8.** Only loosely associated with a main body; fringe: *marginal social groups.* **9.** *British.* Designating an electoral district where the majority of the elected councillor or Member of Parliament is so small that it may easily be won by an opposing candidate at a subsequent election. [Medieval Latin *marginālis,* from Latin *margō* (stem *margin-*), margin.] **—mar·gin·al·i·ty** (márji-nál-əti) *n.* **—mar·gin·al·ly** *adv.*

mar·gi·na·li·a (márji-náyli-ə) *pl.n.* Notes in the margin of a book or other printed matter. [New Latin, neuter plural of Medieval Latin *marginālis,* MARGINAL.]

mar·gin·ate (márji-nayt) *tr.v.* **-ated, -ating, -ates.** To provide with margins or a margin.

~*adj.* Also **mar·gin·at·ed** (-naytid). *Biology.* Having a border or edge of distinctive colour or pattern. **—mar·gin·a·tion** (-náysh'n) *n.*

mar·grave (már-grayv) *n.* **1.** The lord or military governor of a medieval German border province. **2.** A hereditary title of certain princes in the Holy Roman Empire. [Middle Dutch *markgrave,* "count of the march" : *mark,* border, MARCH + *grave,* count.]

mar·gra·vi·ate (maar-gráyvi-ət, -ayt) *n.* Also **mar·gra·vate** (márgrəv-ət, -ayt). The territory governed by a margrave.

mar·gra·vine (márgrə-veen) *n.* The wife or widow of a margrave. [Middle Dutch *markgravin,* feminine of *markgrave,* MARGRAVE.]

Mar·gre·the II (maar-gráy-tə, -də) (1940–). Queen of Denmark. She inherited the throne from her father Frederick IX (1972) after alterations in the constitution to permit the accession of women.

mar·gue·rite (márgə-réet) *n.* **1.** A garden plant, *Chrysanthemum frutescens,* native to the Canary Islands, having white or pale yellow flowers. **2.** Any of several similar or related plants having daisy-like flowers. [French, from Old French *margarite,* daisy, from Latin *margarīta,* pearl, from Greek *margaritēs,* pearl.]

Ma·ri (maári). Ancient Amorite city of Mesopotamia (now Tel Hariri, Syria), on the Euphrates river. Excavations began in 1933 and the royal palace yielded over 20,000 cuneiform tablets, mostly letters and historical accounts.

ma·ri·a. *Astronomy.* Plural of **mare.**

Mar·i·an (maíri-i-ən) *n.* **1.** A devotee of the Virgin Mary. **2. a.** A supporter of Queen Mary I of England. **b.** An adherent of Mary, Queen of Scots.

~*adj.* Of or pertaining to the Virgin Mary, Queen Mary I of England, or Mary, Queen of Scots.

Mar·i·a·nas, Northern (márri-aánəz). Also **Mariana Islands, Marianas.** A commonwealth of the United States in the northwest Pacific. The Mariana Islands, from 1947 part of the United Nations Trust Territory of the Pacific Islands administered by the United States, voted for their present status in 1978, with the exception of **Guam.** They rely heavily on tourism and exports of copra. Saipan is the largest island, with most inhabitants. Their area is 471 square kilometres (182 square miles), and their capital is Saipan. See map at **Pacific Ocean.**

Marianas Trench. Ocean trench just east of the Mariana Islands in the northwest Pacific. It includes Challenger Deep, the deepest point of any ocean in the world (11 033 metres; 36,197 feet).

Ma·ri·án·ské Láz·ně (márri-aanske laázn-ye). *German* **Ma·ri·en·bad** (mə-rée-ən-bad, *German* -baat). A spa in Bohemia, west Czechoslovakia. Popular since the late 18th century, it was visited by such notables as King Edward VII and Richard Wagner.

Ma·ri Autonomous Soviet Socialist Republic (maári). Republic in R.S.F.S.R., U.S.S.R, lying on the east bank of the Volga between Gorky and Kazan. About half is forested and most industries are timber-related. Grain, flax, and potatoes are grown. The Mari people, who now make up some 40 per cent of the population, were conquered by Ivan the Terrible in 1552.

Ma·ri·bor (márribawr). *German* **Mar·burg** (már-boork). City in Yugoslavia, lying on the river Drava. It is one of the principal industrial centres of Slovenia, producing aeroplanes, cars, armaments, and machinery.

Ma·rie An·toi·nette (márri óN-twə-nét, mə-rée, maá-ri, -twa-) (1755–1793). Austrian princess and wife of Louis XVI of France. Her origins, extravagances, and political intrigue made her highly unpopular. She attempted to influence French policy in favour of Austria and resisted the post-revolutionary settlement for the monarchy proposed by Mirabeau. She was tried for treason by the Revolutionary Tribunal and guillotined.

Ma·rie de Mé·di·cis (márri də may-di-seéss, mə-rée, maá-ri, méd-di-chi) (1573–1642). Queen of France. Married to Henry IV of France from 1600 to 1610, she was regent, after his murder, for her son Louis XIII (1610–1617). She was banished by Louis (1617), but they were reconciled in 1622. She encourgaged the rise of Richelieu to chief minister, but then lost all influence. She fled to the Netherlands (1631) and died in poverty.

Marienbad. See **Mariánské Lázně.**

mar·i·gold (márri-gōld) *n.* **1.** Any plant of the genus *Tagetes,* native to tropical America. Several species are widely cultivated for their showy yellow or orange flowers. **2.** Any of several plants having similar flowers, such as the **corn marigold** and the **marsh marigold** *(both of which see).* [Middle English *marygould* : *Mary* (with some reference to the Virgin Mary) + dialect *gold,* a marigold, Old English *gold,* probably from GOLD.]

mar·i·jua·na, mar·i·hua·na (márri-hwaánə, -waánə, -yoo-aánə) *n.* The dried flower clusters and leaves of the hemp plant, especially when taken as a drug to induce euphoria. Slang equivalents include "pot", "grass", "weed", and as a cigarette, "joint", "reefer". See **hashish.** [Mexican Spanish *mariguana, marihuana*†.]

ma·rim·ba (mə-rímbə) *n.* Any of various xylophones with resonators. [Bantu : *ma-,* plural prefix + *rimba, limba,* musical note.]

ma·ri·na (mə-réenə) *n.* A boat basin that has docks, moorings, supplies, and other facilities for small boats. [Italian, feminine of *marino,* MARINE.]

mar·i·nade (márri-náyd) *n.* A pickling liquid of vinegar or wine and oil, with various spices and herbs, in which meat and fish are soaked before cooking.

~*tr.v.* **marinaded, -nading, -nades.** To marinate. [French, from Spanish *marinada,* from *marinar,* to marinate, from *marino,* "briny", MARINE.]

mar·i·nate (márri-nayt) *tr.v.* **-nated, -nating, -nates.** To soak (meat or fish) in a marinade. [French *mariner* or Italian *marinare* + -ATE.]

ma·rine (mə-réen) *adj.* **1. a.** Of or pertaining to the sea: *marine exploration.* **b.** Native to or formed by the sea: *marine plant life.* **2.** Of or pertaining to shipping or maritime affairs: *marine insurance.* **3.** Of or pertaining to sea navigation; nautical: *a marine chart.* **4.** Designating or pertaining to troops that serve at sea as well as on land.

~*n.* **1.** Shipping in general; maritime interests as represented by ships. Now rare except in the phrase *merchant marine.* **2. a.** A soldier serving on a ship or at a naval installation. **b.** *Capital* **M.** A member of the Marine Corps or similar military grouping. **3.** In some nations, the government department in charge of naval affairs. **4.** A painting or photograph of the sea. **—tell it to the marines.** *U.S. Informal.* Used to express scepticism. [Middle English, from Old French *marin,* from Latin *marīnus,* from *mare,* sea.]

Marine Corps *n. Abbr.* **MC, USMC, U.S.M.C.** A branch of the U.S. Armed Forces composed chiefly of amphibious troops under the authority of the Secretary of the Navy. Also officially called "United States Marine Corps".

mar·i·ner (márrinər) *n.* A person who navigates or serves on a ship; a sailor or seaman. [Middle English, from Old French *marinier,* from *marin,* MARINE.]

Mar·i·ol·a·try (maíri-óllətri, márri-) *n.* Excessive veneration of the Virgin Mary. Used derogatorily. [Latin *Maria,* Mary + -LATRY (by analogy with *idolatry*).]

Mar·i·ol·o·gy (maíri-ólləji, márri-) *n.* Also **Mar·y·ol·o·gy.** The body of belief pertaining to the Virgin Mary. [MARY + -LOGY.]

mar·i·o·nette (márri-ə-nét) *n.* A jointed puppet manipulated by strings or wires attached to its limbs. [French, diminutive of the feminine name *Marion.*]

mar·i·po·sa lily (márri-pṓ-zə, -sə) *n.* Any of several bulbous plants of the genus *Calochortus,* of the southwestern United States and Mexico, having variously coloured, tulip-like flowers. Sometimes called "mariposa tulip". [Spanish *mariposa,* butterfly : probably *Maria,* Mary + *posar,* to perch, alight.]

mar·ish (márrish) *adj. Archaic & British Regional.* Marshy.

~*n.* A marsh. [Middle English *mareis,* Old English *merisc,* ultimately from West Germanic *marisk-* (unattested), MARSH.]

Mar·ist (maír-ist) *n.* **1.** A member of the Society of Mary, a congregation of Roman Catholic missionary priests founded in 1824. **2.** A member of the Little Brothers of Mary, a Roman Catholic teaching order founded in 1817. **—Mar·ist** *adj.*

Ma·ri·tain (marri-táN), **Jacques** (1882–1973). French Catholic philosopher. He abandoned the philosophy of Bergson to become a neo-Thomist, applying the medieval techniques of St. Thomas

Aquinas to modern social problems. His works include *les Degrés du savoir* (1932) and *la Philosophie morale* (1960).

mar·i·tal (márrit'l, *rarely* mə-rīt'l) *adj.* **1.** Of, pertaining to, or required by marriage. **2.** *Rare.* Of or pertaining to a husband. [Latin *marītālis,* from *marītus,* married, husband.] **—mar·i·tal·ly** *adv.*

mar·i·time (márri-tīm) *adj. Abbr.* **mar. 1.** Located on or near the sea. **2.** Of or concerned with shipping or navigation. **3.** Designating a climate characteristic of coastal areas, with relatively small seasonal and daily temperature changes. [French, from Latin *maritimus,* from *mare,* sea.]

Mar·i·time Alps (márri-tīm). *French* **Alpes Mar·i·times** (álp marri-téem). A branch of the western Alps along the French-Italian border, extending to the Mediterranean. They give their name to the French département of Alpes Maritimes, whose resorts include Cannes, Nice, and Grasse. Punta Argentera (3 297 metres; 10,817 feet) is the highest peak.

maritime pine *n.* A tree, the **pinaster** *(see).*

Maritime Provinces. Atlantic region of Canada, comprising the provinces of New Brunswick, Nova Scotia, and Prince Edward Island. It covers most of the area of the former Acadia (Acadie), French Canada (1605–1713).

Ma·ri·vaux (marri-vṓ), **Pierre Carlet de Chamblain de** (1688–1763). French dramatist, a writer of sophisticated romantic comedies. His works include *le Jeu de l'amour et du hasard* (1730) and the unfinished *la Vie de Marianne* (1731–41).

mar·jo·ram (márjərəm) *n.* **1.** An aromatic plant, *Origanum marjorana,* having small purplish or white flowers and leaves used as seasoning. Also called "sweet marjoram". **2.** A similar plant, *Origanum vulgare,* having spikes of pinkish flowers, and leaves used in cooking. Also called "oregano", "wild marjoram". **3.** A similar plant, *Origanum onites,* having white or pinkish flowers, of the Mediterranean region. In this sense, also called "pot marjoram". [Middle English *majorane,* from Old French, from Medieval Latin *majorāna*†.]

mark¹ (mark) *n. Abbr.* **mk. 1.** A visible trace or impression on something, such as a spot, dent, or line. **2.** A cross or other sign made in lieu of a signature by an illiterate person. **3. a.** A written or printed symbol used for punctuation; a punctuation mark. **b.** A written or printed symbol used to give information or instructions: *proofreaders' marks.* **4. a.** A number, letter, or point awarded to indicate the quality of academic work: *high marks in History.* **b.** *Plural.* An indication of how strongly one approves of a person's actions: *I give her full marks for initiative.* **5. a.** A name, stamp, label, seal, or inscription placed on an article to signify ownership, quality, manufacture, or origin. See **trademark, hallmark. b.** A notch in an animal's ear or hide indicating ownership. **6.** *Nautical.* A knot or piece of material placed at various measured lengths on a lead line to indicate the depth of the water. **7.** Something that indicates a position; a marker. **8. a.** A sign or indication of some quality, property, or feature: *bore all the marks of dejection; as a mark of my respect.* **b.** A visible sign or symbol, such as a badge or brand adopted by or imposed on a person: *Trouble had set its mark on her.* **c.** *Capital* **M.** A particular type or version, especially of machines or vehicles under development. Usually followed by a designation such as a numeral, and also used adjectivally: *the Mark 3 model.* **9.** Quality; note; importance. Usually preceded by *of: "A fellow of no mark nor likelihood."* (Shakespeare). **10.** Notice; attention; heed. Usually preceded by *of*: *Little worthy of mark happened.* **11.** A target: *The arrow hit the mark.* **12.** That which one wishes to achieve; a goal. **13.** An object or point that serves as a guide. **14.** *Slang.* A person who is an easy target for a swindler; a dupe. **15.** *Usually plural.* The place from which competitors in a race begin and sometimes end their contest: *on your marks.* **16.** A stationary ball in bowls; the jack. **17.** In Rugby and Australian Rules football, a mark deliberately made in the ground with the heel by a player who has caught the ball. **18.** The middle of a boxer's stomach, just above the waistband of his shorts. **19.** A boundary between countries. **20.** In medieval England and Germany, a tract of land held in common by a community. **21.** *Statistics.* A **class mark** *(see).* —See Synonyms at **sign. —beside the mark.** Beside the point; irrelevant. **—God** or **Heaven save** or **bless the mark!** *Archaic.* Used to express ironic deprecation. **—make (one's) mark.** To achieve recognition; be successful.

~interj. Used by a Rugby football player on catching the ball, whereupon he is entitled to a free kick.

~v. **marked, marking, marks.** *—tr.* **1.** To make a visible impression on, as with a spot, line, or dent. **2.** To form, make, or depict by making a visible impression on, as with a spot, line, or dent: *She marked a square on the board.* **3. a.** To distinguish or indicate by making a visible impression: *She marked the spot where the treasure is buried.* **b.** To distinguish, indicate, or characterise: *This year marks the tenth anniversary.* **c.** To show (an emotion, for example): *marked her anger by leaving the room.* **4. a.** To set off by or separate as if by a mark. **b.** To limit or demarcate (a boundary, for example). **5. a.** To attach price tags, maker's labels, or other identification to (articles for sale). **b.** To write or print (a price, for example), as on a label. **6.** To correct and assess (scholastic work) by evaluating it according to a scale of letters or numbers. **7. a.** To give attention to; notice: *"Mark what radiant state she spreads".* (John Milton). **b.** To take note of in writing; write down. **8.** To consider; study; observe: *Mark my word.* **9.** To keep (score) in various games. **10.** *Sports. British.* To keep close to (an opponent) so as to hamper him. In Australian Rules football, to catch (the ball). *—intr.* **1.** To make a visible impression: *This pen will still mark under water.* **2.** To receive a visible impression: *The floor marks easily.* **3.** *Archaic & Poetic.* To notice; pay attention: *"Pray you, mark."* (Shakespeare). **4.** To keep score. Used of various games. **5.** To determine scholastic grades: *Our teacher marks strictly.* [Middle English, Old English *mearc,* boundary, hence landmark, sign, trace, from Germanic *markō* (unattested), boundary.]

mark² *n. Abbr.* **M. 1.** A former English and Scottish monetary unit equal to 13 shillings and 4 pence. **2.** *Capital* **M. a.** A former German monetary unit, the **Reichsmark** *(see).* **b.** The **Deutsche mark** *(see).* **c.** The basic monetary unit of East Germany, divided into 100 pfennings. Formerly called "Ostmark". **3.** Any of several former European units of weight equal to about 225 grams (eight ounces), used especially for weighing gold and silver. **4.** A Finnish monetary unit, a **markka** *(see).* [Sense 1, Middle English *mark,* Old English *marc.* Sense 2, German *Mark,* from Middle High German *marke.* The word exists in all Germanic and Romance languages; the source is probably identical with that of MARK (sign), in a sense such as "a mark on a bar of metal".]

Mark¹ (mark). In Arthurian legend, the king of Cornwall who was the husband of Iseult and the uncle of Tristan.

Mark² *n.* A book of the New Testament, the second Gospel, attributed to St. Mark.

Mark, Saint. A disciple of St. Peter, reputedly the author of the second Gospel of the New Testament.

Mark An·to·ny (ántəni), Latin name Marcus Antonius (*c.* 83–30 B.C.). Roman soldier and statesman. Dissolute in his youth, he fought under Julius Caesar in Gaul (54–50 B.C.) and after Caesar's assassination (44 B.C.) formed a triumvirate with Octavius and Lepidus, which defeated Cassius and Brutus at Philippi (42 B.C.). He met and fell in love with Cleopatra (41 B.C.) while in Egypt, gaining her territory in his division of the empire. When the senate declared war on Egypt, Antony was defeated at the naval battle of Actium (31 B.C.) and committed suicide, as did Cleopatra.

mark down *tr.v.* **1.** To reduce (goods) in price. **2.** To single out, usually for an undesirable end. **3.** To note down; record.

mark-down (márk-down) *n.* A reduction in price.

marked (markt) *adj.* **1.** Having a mark or marks. **2.** Having a noticeable character or trait; distinctive; clearly defined: *"certain strongly marked variations, which no one would rank as mere individual differences"* (Charles Darwin). **3.** Singled out, especially for an exceptional fate: *a marked man.* **4.** *Linguistics.* Of or pertaining to that one of a closely connected pair of words or other linguistic units which has some feature held to distinguish it from the other more neutral or general form; for example, in the pairs *dog/dogs* and *dog/bitch, dogs* and *bitch* are the marked forms. **—mark·ed·ly** (márkidli) *adv.* **—mark·ed·ness** (márkid-nəss, -niss) *n.*

marked cheque *n. British.* A cheque guaranteed by a bank as being covered by sufficient funds on deposit. Also *U.S.* "certified cheque".

mark·er (márkər) *n.* **1.** Something that marks or distinguishes, such as a bookmark, tombstone, milestone, or buoy. **2.** A person who marks objects, especially for industrial purposes. **3.** A person who corrects examination papers. **4.** *Sports.* **a.** A line, stake, flag, or other device on a playing field that shows the playing or scoring position. **b.** One who marks another player. **5. a.** A person or device that keeps score in various games. **b.** A score in a game. **6.** A pen or other writing instrument used for making marks on objects, as for identification or pricing. **7.** *Chiefly U.S. Slang.* A written, signed promissory note; an IOU.

mar·ket (márkit) *n. Abbr.* **mkt. 1.** A public gathering held at regular intervals for buying and selling merchandise. **2.** An open place or building where goods are offered for sale. Also called "marketplace". **3.** A store or shop that sells a particular type of merchandise: *a meat market.* **4. a.** The business of buying and selling a specified commodity. **b.** Market price. **c.** Commercial activity; trading: *a brisk market.* **5. a.** The opportunity to buy or sell; demand for or availability of merchandise. **b.** An area in which sales may be made: *one of our biggest export markets.* **6. a.** An exchange for buying and selling stocks or commodities: *securities sold on the London market.* **b.** The entire enterprise of buying and selling commodities and securities. Usually preceded by *the.* **—at the market.** At the price prevailing when a customer's order to buy or sell is placed. **—be in the market for.** To desire to acquire or buy. **—play the market.** To speculate on the stock exchange. **—price out of the market.** To price so highly as to remove demand. **—put on the market.** To put up for sale.

~v. **marketed, -keting, -kets.** *—tr.* **1.** To offer for sale. **2.** To sell. **3.** To promote the sale of (a product) by means of marketing techniques. *—intr.* **1.** To deal in a market. **2.** To buy household supplies: *He marketed for Sunday dinner.* [Middle English, Old English, from Vulgar Latin *marcātus* (unattested), variant of Latin *mercātus,* from the past participle of *mercārī,* to trade, from *merx,* merchandise.] **—mar·ket·er** *n.*

mar·ket·a·ble (márkitə-b'l) *adj.* **1.** Fit to be offered for sale. **2.** Salable. **3.** Pertaining to selling or buying. **—mar·ket·a·bil·i·ty** (-bíllәti) *n.*

market economy *n.* An economy in which the principles of free enterprise apply and there is no government intervention.

Mark·e·teer (márki-téer) *n.* In Britain, one who has a specified attitude to Britain's membership of the European Economic Community. Used in the combinations *anti-Marketeer* and *pro-Marketeer.*

PRONUNCIATION KEY

a, trap; aa, father; ai, fair; ar, star; aw, lawn; ay, play; b, bb, stab; rubber; ch, church; ck, ticket; d, dd, dead; ladder; e, dress; ee, bee; er, defer; ew, few; ewr, pure; ə, about; ər, letter; f, ff, fife; differ; g, gg, giggle; h, hat; i, kit; ī, price; īr, fire; j, judge; k, kick; l, ll, let; 'l, needle; m, mm, man; n, nn, no; 'n, sudden; ng, thing; o, lot; ō, no; o͝o, foot; o͞o, shoe; oor, poor; ow, cow; owr, hour; oy, boy; p, pp, pepper; r, rr, red; s, ss, sauce; sh, ship; t, tt, totter; th, thick; th, this; smooth; u, cut; ur, turn; v, vv, valve; w, wet; y, yes; z, zz, zebra; zh, vision; pleasure

IN FOREIGN WORDS:

aN, oN, Saint-Saëns; hl, Llanelli; Hluhluwe; kh, loch; lough; Khaled

STRESS MARK:

ín-sīt, insight; in-sít, incite

market forces *pl.n. Economics.* The effects on an economy of supply and demand, unmodified by government intervention.

market garden *n. Chiefly British.* An establishment, larger than a smallholding but smaller than a farm, where fruit and vegetables are cultivated on a commercial scale. Also *U.S.* "truck farm". —**market gardener** *n.* —**market gardening** *n.*

mark·et·ing (márkiting) *n.* The act or business of promoting sales of a product, as by market research, advertising, and packaging.

market order *n.* An order to buy or sell stocks or commodities at the prevailing market price.

mar·ket·place, market place (márkit-playss) *n.* **1.** A public square or other place in which a market is set up. In this sense, also called "market". **2.** The processes of buying and selling goods or services: *prices determined by the marketplace.* **3.** A forum, such as a journal or a conference, where views or information can be exchanged.

market price *n.* The prevailing price at which merchandise, securities, or commodities are sold. Also called "market".

market research *n.* The study of how a product or service is likely to sell or is already selling, usually carried out by asking questions of a cross-section of the population in order to determine consumers' reactions.

market value *n.* The amount that a seller may expect to obtain for merchandise, services, or securities in the open market.

mar·khor (márkawr) *n.* A Himalayan goat, *Capra falconeri,* having a red-brown coat and large, spirally curved horns. [Persian, "snake-eater" : *mār,* snake + *-khōr,* -eating.]

Mar·kie·wicz (márk-yevich), **Constance (Georgine), Countess,** born Constance Gore-Booth (1868–1927). Irish nationalist, married to a Polish count. She was imprisoned and sentenced to death for fighting in the Easter Rebellion of 1916. Her sentence commuted, she was released in 1917, and as a Sinn Fein candidate became the first woman M.P. elected to the British parliament (1918), although she did not take her seat.

mark·ing (márking) *n.* **1.** The act of making a mark or marks. **2.** A mark or marks. **3.** The arrangement or pattern of characteristic coloration of a plant or animal.

marking ink *n.* An indelible ink used for marking clothes, linen, and the like.

mark·ka (már-kə) *n., pl.* **-kaa** (-kaa). *Abbr.* **mk.** The basic monetary unit of Finland, equal to 100 penniä. Also called "mark". [Finnish, from Swedish *mark.* See **mark** (money).]

mark of mouth *n.* A depression in the incisor tooth of a horse that indicates the animal's age.

Mar·ko·va (maar-kṓva), **Dame Alicia,** born Lilian Alicia Marks (1910–). British ballet dancer. She studied with Pavlova and Astafieva and worked with Diaghilev's company; she was noted for her delicacy and graceful lightness in works which included *Swan Lake* and *Giselle.*

Mar·kov chain (márkof) *n. Statistics.* A sequence of events in which the probability of each event's taking place depends on the event immediately preceding it. [After Andrei *Markov* (1856–1922), Russian mathematician.]

marks·man (márks-mən) *n., pl.* **-men** (-mən, -men). A person skilled at shooting a gun or other weapon, especially one who has reached a certain standard of proficiency. [*Mark's man,* from MARK (target).] —**marks·man·ship** *n.*

mark up *tr.v.* To raise the price of.

mark·up, mark-up (márk-up) *n.* **1.** An increase in price. **2.** The amount added to the cost of an item when calculating the selling price.

marl[1] (marl) *n.* **1.** A fine-grained mixture of clay, calcium carbonate (including shell fragments), and magnesium carbonate, forming a loam used as a fertiliser. **2.** Any friable clay soil.
~*tr.v.* **marling, marled, marls.** To fertilise with marl. [Middle English, Old English *marle,* from Late Latin *margila,* diminutive of *marga†.*]

marl[2] *tr.v.* To bind with a marline. [Back-formation from MARLINE.]

Marl·bor·ough (mórl-brə, márl-, -bərə). Town in Wiltshire, England. A dairy and tanning centre, it lies on the river Kennet. Marlborough College, a public school, was founded here in 1843.

Marlborough, John Churchill, 1st Duke of (1650–1722). English soldier and statesman. He served under James II at the defeat of Monmouth and was made a baron (1685), but supported William of Orange against James in the revolution of 1688, receiving an earldom. He served in the War of the Spanish Succession with victories at Blenheim (1704), Ramillies (1706), Oudenarde (1708), and Malplaquet (1709). Dismissed for alleged corruption in 1711, he fled to Holland, returning to England in 1714.

mar·lin (márlin) *n.* Any of several large game fish of the family Istiophoridae, of the Atlantic and Pacific oceans, having a long upper jaw. Also called "spearfish". [Short for MARLINESPIKE (from the pointed shape of the snout).]

mar·line, mar·lin (már-lin) *n.* Also **mar·ling** (-ling). *Nautical.* A light rope made of two loosely twisted strands. [Middle English, from Middle Dutch *marlijn,* "tie-line" : *marren,* to tie + *lijn,* LINE.]

mar·line·spike, mar·lin·spike (már-lin-spīk) *n.* Also **mar·ling·spike** (-ling-). *Nautical.* A pointed metal spike, used to separate strands of rope in splicing and for similar purposes.

mar·lite (márlīt) *n.* A marl containing 25 to 75 per cent clay, the remainder being calcium carbonate, that is resistant to decomposition in air. Also called "marlstone". [MARL (loam) + -ITE.] —**mar·lit·ic** (maar-líttik) *adj.*

Mar·lowe (márlō), **Christopher** (1564–93). English playwright and

marmot *There are about 16 species of this ground-dwelling burrowing squirrel, found in North America, the European Alps, and in mountainous parts of Asia. This is* Marmota flaviventus, *the yellow-bellied marmot, which is native to the western United States and Canada.*

poet. His development of blank verse influenced Shakespeare. Among his plays are *Tamburlaine the Great* (c. 1587), *Dr. Faustus* (c. 1588), and *Edward II* (1592). While awaiting trial for atheism, he was killed in a tavern brawl in Deptford.

mar·ma·lade (mármə-layd) *n.* A preserve made from the pulp and rind of citrus fruits, especially oranges. [French *marmelade,* from Portuguese *marmelada,* "quince jam", from *marmelo,* quince, from Latin *melimēlum,* from Greek *melimēlon,* "honey-apple", the fruit of an apple tree grafted on a quince : *meli,* honey + *mēlon,* apple, fruit.]

marmalade box *n.* A tree, the **genipap** (see).

marmalade cat *n.* A domestic cat with orange-coloured stripes.

Mar·ma·ra, Sea of (mármərə). Small sea in northwest Turkey between Asia and Europe. It is connected to the Aegean Sea by the Dardanelles, and to the Black Sea by the Bosporus.

mar·mite (már-mīt; *in senses 1 and 2, also* -meet) *n.* **1. a.** A large covered pot, usually made of earthenware or metal. **b.** A small, covered earthenware casserole designed to hold an individual serving. **2.** The broth made in such a pot or served in such a casserole. **3.** *Capital M.* A trademark for a savoury spread made from yeast extract. [French, kettle, pot.]

mar·mo·re·al (maar-máwr-i-əl ‖ -mór-) *adj.* Also **mar·mo·re·an** (-ən). **1.** Of or pertaining to marble. **2.** Resembling marble, as in being cold, smooth, white, or hard: *a complexion of marmoreal lustre.* [Latin *marmoreus,* from *marmor,* MARBLE.]

mar·mo·set (mármə-zet ‖ -set) *n.* Any of various small monkeys of the genera *Callithrix, Cebuella, Saguinus,* and *Leontideus,* found in tropical forests of the Americas. They have soft, dense fur, tufted ears, and long tails. [Middle English, from Old French *marmoset†,* grotesque figure.]

mar·mot (mármət) *n.* Any of various stocky, coarse-furred rodents of the genus *Marmota,* having short legs and bushy tails, found throughout the Northern Hemisphere. [French *marmotte,* from earlier *marmottaine,* from Medieval Latin *mormotāna,* "mountain mouse" : Latin *mūs* (stem *mūr-*), mouse + *montānus,* mountain.]

Marne (marn). River of northern France. Flowing 525 kilometres (326 miles) from the Plateau de Langres to the Seine at Paris, it forms, with the Marne-Rhine and the Marne-Saône canals, a major inland waterway network. The two Battles of the Marne (1914, 1918) ended in decisive victories for the Allies.

mar·o·cain (márrə-kayn) *n.* **1.** A crepe dress fabric, especially one made of silk. **2.** A garment made of this fabric. [French, "Moroccan", from *Maroc,* Morocco.]

Mar·o·nite (márrə-nīt) *n.* A member of a Christian sect established in Syria in the fifth century, and now found mainly in Lebanon. [Medieval Latin *Marōnīta,* from *Maro,* 5th-century Syrian monk and founder of the sect.] —**Mar·o·nite** *adj.*

ma·roon[1] (mə-rṓon) *v.* **-rooned, -rooning, -roons.** —*tr.* **1.** To put (a person) ashore on a deserted island or coast. **2.** To abandon or isolate (a person) with little hope of rescue or escape. —*intr.* To wander or wait around in an idle manner.
~*n.* **1. a.** A fugitive slave in the West Indies in the 17th and 18th centuries. **b.** A descendant of such a slave. **2.** A person who is marooned. [French *marron,* alteration of American Spanish *cimarrón,* fugitive slave, originally, "living on the mountain tops", possibly from *cima,* summit, from Latin *cȳma,* sprout, from Greek *kuma.*]

ma·roon[2] *n.* **1.** Dark reddish brown to dark purplish red. **2.** An explosive device; especially, one used as a warning signal. [Originally "chestnut", from French *marron†.*] —**ma·roon** *adj.*

mar·plot (már-plot) *n. Literary.* A stupid and officious meddler whose interference compromises the success of any undertaking. [After *Marplot* ("to spoil plots"), character in *The Busybody* (1709), a comic play by Susanna Centlivre (c. 1667–1723), English author.]

marque (mark) *n.* **1.** A make of car or other product. **2.** An emblem or nameplate used to identify such a make. [French, mark.]

marque, letters of *pl.n.* See **letters of marque.**

mar·quee (maar-kée) *n.* **1.** A large tent, sometimes with open sides, used chiefly for outdoor entertainment or for serving refreshments. **2.** *U.S.* A rooflike structure, often made of canvas and bearing a signboard, projecting over an entrance to a building. In this sense, also called "marquise". [French *marquise* (taken as a plural), a linen tent pitched above an officer's tent to distinguish it from others, from *marquis,* MARQUIS (disparagingly).]

Már·ques (már-kess), **Gabriel Garcia** (1928–). Colombian novelist and short-story writer. His most famous work is the novel *One Hundred Years of Solitude* (1967). He was awarded the Nobel prize (1982).

Mar·que·san (maar-káy-z'n, -s'n) *n.* **1.** An inhabitant of the Marquesas Islands. **2.** The Austronesian language of the Marquesans.
~*adj.* Of or pertaining to the Marquesas Islands, their inhabitants, or their language.

Mar·que·sas Islands (maar-káy-səss, -sass, -zass). *French* Îles Marquises (eel maar-kéez). Group of 11 volcanic islands in the east Pacific, part of French Polynesia. They were annexed by France in 1842, and now export copra, vanilla, cotton, and tobacco. Gauguin is buried on Hiva Oa, near the capital, Atuona. See map at **Pacific Ocean.**

mar·que·try, mar·que·terie (márkətri) *n.* Inlaid work in wood, ivory, or the like, used chiefly in decorating furniture. [French *marqueterie,* from *marqueter,* to checker, from MARQUE.]

mar·quis (márkwiss; *French* maar-kée) *n., pl.* **marquis** or **-quises.** Also *chiefly British* **mar·quess** (márkwiss). A nobleman ranking below a duke and above an earl or count. [Middle English *marchis, markis,* from Old French *marquis, marchis,* "count of the march (frontier)", from *marche,* MARCH.]

mar·quis·ate (márkwi-zət, -zayt, -zit ‖ -sət, -sit) *n.* The rank or territory of a marquis.

mar·quise (már-kéez) *n.* **1.** A **marchioness** (*see*). **2.** *U.S.* A **marquee** (*see*). **3. a.** A finger ring set with a pointed oval stone or cluster of pointed oval stones. **b.** A pointed oval shape in diamonds or other gems. [French, feminine of *marquis,* MARQUIS.]

mar·qui·sette (már-ki-zét, -kwi-) *n.* A sheer fabric of cotton, rayon, silk, or nylon, used for clothing, curtains, and mosquito nets. [From MARQUISE (marquee).]

Marquis of Queensberry Rules *pl.n.* See **Queensberry Rules.**

Mar·ra·kesh (márrə-késh, *rarely* mə-ráckesh). *French* **Mar·ra·kech** (márrə-késh). Former capital of Morocco. A major Islamic, commercial, and tourist centre, it is best known for its leatherwork.

mar·ram (márrəm) *n.* **1.** A beach grass, *Ammophila arenaria,* widely planted to stabilise shifting dunes. **2.** Any of several other grasses of the genus *Ammophila.* Also called "marram grass". [East Anglian dialect, from Old Norse *maralmr : marr,* sea + *halmr,* grass.]

mar·riage (márrij) *n.* **1. a.** The state of being wife and husband; wedlock. **b.** The legal union of a woman and man as wife and husband. **2.** The act of marrying or the ceremony of being married; a wedding. **3.** Any close union: *a true marriage of minds.* **4.** In some card games, such as pinochle, the combination of the king and queen of the same suit. [Middle English *mariage,* from Old French, from *marier,* to MARRY.]

   Synonyms: marriage, matrimony, wedlock, wedding, nuptials.

mar·riage·a·ble (márrijə-b'l) *adj.* Suitable or ready for marriage. **—mar·riage·a·bil·i·ty** (-bílləti), **mar·riage·a·ble·ness** *n.*

marriage guidance *n.* Counsel given to help couples with their marital problems.

marriage of convenience *n.* A marriage contracted for financial, social, or similar reasons, rather than out of love.

mar·ried (márrid) **1. a.** Having a spouse: *a married man.* **b.** United in matrimony: *a married couple.* **2.** Of or pertaining to the state of marriage: *married bliss.* ~*n. Often plural.* A married person: *young marrieds.*

mar·ron (márrən; *French* ma-rón) *n.* The fruit of the sweet chestnut. [French. See **maroon** (colour).]

mar·rons gla·cés (*French* ma-rón gla-sáy) *pl.n. French.* Sweet chestnuts preserved in or coated with sugar.

mar·row (márrō) *n.* **1.** The soft material that fills bone cavities, consisting, in varying proportions, of fat cells and maturing blood cells, together with supporting connective tissue and numerous blood vessels. **2.** Spinal marrow; the spinal cord. **3.** A cucurbitaceous plant, *Cucurbita peop,* cultivated for its large, white-fleshed, green-skinned gourd which is eaten as a vegetable. Also called "vegetable marrow". **4. a.** The inmost, choicest, or essential part; the pith: *chilled to the marrow.* **b.** Strength or vigour; vitality. [Middle English *marowe, margh,* Old English *mærg, mærh.*]

mar·row·bone (márrō-bōn) *n.* A bone containing marrow, used for example for flavouring soup.

mar·row·fat (márrō-fat) *n.* **1.** Any of several varieties of pea that produce large seeds. **2.** The seed of such a plant. Also called "marrow pea".

mar·ry¹ (márri) *v.* **-ried, -rying, -ries.** —*tr.* **1. a.** To become united with in matrimony: *They married each other in June.* **b.** To take as a husband or wife: *She married her sweetheart.* **c.** To give in marriage. **2.** To obtain by marriage: *marry wealth.* **3.** To join together (a couple) in marriage. **4.** To join together or unite closely: *a woman in whom wisdom and love were married.* **5.** To manoeuvre into a matching or locking position. Used with *up: marry up the two edges before gluing.* **6.** *Nautical.* To join (two ropes) end to end by interweaving their strands. —*intr.* **1.** To take a wife or husband; wed. **2. a.** To match; join easily. **b.** To enter into a close relationship; unite. **—marry into. 1.** To become a member of (a family) by marriage. **2.** To obtain or become involved in through marriage: *married into money.* **—marry off.** To find an appropriate spouse for. Often used derogatorily. [Middle English *marien,* from Old French *marier,* from Latin *marītāre,* from *marītus,* husband.]

marry² *interj. Archaic.* Used to express surprise, indignation, or emphasis. [Middle English *Marie,* "Mary!" (the Virgin).]

Mar·ry·at (márri-ət), **Captain Frederick** (1792–1848). British naval officer and author. He used the experiences of his naval career (1806–30) as a source for novels such as *Mr. Midshipman Easy* (1934–36). His children's books include *The Children of the New Forest* (1847) and *Masterman Ready* (1841).

Mars¹ (marz). *Roman Mythology.* The god of war; identified with the Greek god Ares.

Mars² *n.* The fourth planet from the Sun, having a sidereal period of revolution around the sun of 687 days at a mean distance of 227.9 million kilometres (141.6 million miles), a mean radius of approximately 3 363 kilometres (2,090 miles), and a mass approximately 0.11 that of Earth.

Mar·sa·la¹ (maar-sáálə). Ancient name **Lil·y·bae·um** (lílli-bée-əm). Seaport and major fishing centre in west Sicily, Italy. Founded by the Carthaginians (397 B.C.), it exports Marsala wine, salt, and grain. Garibaldi landed here in 1860 for his campaign against the Kingdom of the Two Sicilies.

Marsala² *n.* A pale brown, sweet dessert wine, originally exported from Marsala, Sicily.

Mar·seil·laise (már-say-áyz, -éz, -sə-láyz) *n.* The French national

---

Mars

MARS: A BARREN PLANET WITH AN ACTIVE PAST
Pink skies overhang an icy, windswept, rock-strewn terrain

Mars is smaller than the Earth, only about half the diameter, and is roughly half as far again from the Sun. In some ways it is more Earth-like than any other planet, with a day that lasts 24 hours 37 minutes and 23 seconds, and similar seasons to those on Earth – although they are much longer because Mars takes 687 days to orbit the Sun.

Viewed from Earth, Mars shows white polar caps, dark patches, and red areas usually called deserts. The Mariner and Viking spacecraft probes of the 1960s and 1970s have shown that the dark areas are not, as once thought, old seabeds filled with vegetation. Some are plateaux, differing from the "deserts" in colour only.

The Martian landscape is harsh – cratered and rock-strewn and subject to violent dust storms. There are giant volcanoes – Olympus Mons is three times as high as Everest – and gigantic canyons such as Valles Marineris, four times as deep as the Grand Canyon. Mars has no oceans, but the pear-shaped islands around some craters were formed by massive floods. Because of the freezing temperatures and thin atmosphere, there are icy fogs and clouds that vaporise in the day's heat and freeze again towards night.

As recently as the mid-20th century, it was believed that Mars might support advanced forms of life. Some astronomers even believed there were irrigation canals. But the 1976 Viking spacecraft programmed to search for life found no evidence of it.

Two dwarf satellites, Phobos and Deimos, orbit Mars. Each is less than 30 kilometres (19 miles) across, and unlikely to light up the Martian night.

APPROACH TO MARS *The spacecraft camera reveals the planet's craters, massive volcanoes (including Olympus Mons), ground frost or fog (bottom left), and thin white cloud patches.*

RED DESERT *The red-coloured landscape around Viking Lander 2 justifies Mars's ancient nickname: the Red Planet. The salty whiteness on the soil is a thin coating of ice.*

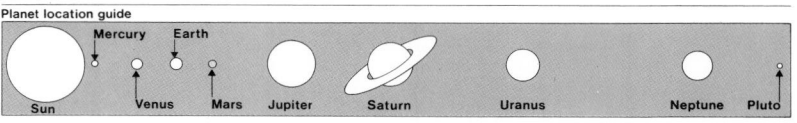

Planet location guide

Sun | Mercury | Venus | Earth | Mars | Jupiter | Saturn | Uranus | Neptune | Pluto

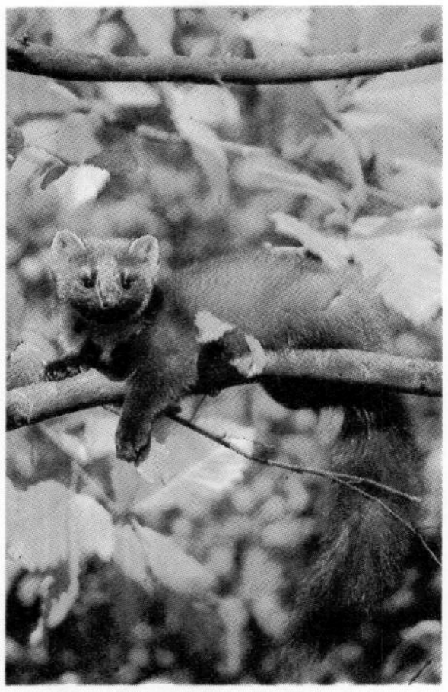

marten *These tree-dwelling members of the weasel family live in the forests of the Northern Hemisphere, feeding largely on rodents and small birds. This is the pine marten,* Martes martes.

anthem, written in 1792 by Claude Joseph Rouget de Lisle. [French *(chanson) Marseillaise,* (song) of Marseilles.]

mar·seille (maar-sáyl) *n.* Also **mar·seilles** (-sáylz). A heavy cotton fabric with a raised pattern of stripes or figures, used for bedspreads, curtains, or the like. [Shortened from *Marseille quilting,* originally made in MARSEILLE.]

Mar·seille (maar-sáy). *English* **Mar·seilles** (-sáylz). Principal seaport of France and capital of Bouches-du-Rhône département, founded on the Mediterranean by the Greeks (*c.* 600 B.C.). It is linked to the Rhône by canal, and its industries include oil-refining, ore-smelting, chemicals, shipbuilding, and food processing.

marsh (marsh) *n.* **1.** An area of temporarily flooded land beside a river or lake, characterised by water-loving plants such as reeds, and often silty. **2.** Loosely, any area of low-lying, wet land; a fen, swamp, or bog. **3.** A **salt marsh** *(see).* [Middle English *mersh,* Old English *mersc, merisc.*] **—marsh·i·ness** *n.* **—marsh·y** *adj.*

Marsh (marsh), **Dame Ngaio (Edith)** (1899–1982). New Zealand author. She wrote many detective novels which include *A Man Lay Dead* (1934), *Death in a White Tie* (1938), and *Last Ditch* (1977).

mar·shal (márshʼl) *n.* **1.** In some countries, a military officer of the highest rank. See **field marshal. 2.** In the United States: **a.** A Federal officer who carries out court orders. **b.** A city officer who carries out court orders. **c.** The head of a police or fire department. **3.** A person in charge of a ceremony, parade, or the like. **4.** Formerly in England, a high official in the royal court, especially one aiding the sovereign in judicial matters. Also called "knight marshal". **5.** In England, a clerical assistant accompanying a judge on circuit.

~v. **marshalled** or *U.S.* **marshaled, -shalling** or *U.S.* **-shaling, -shals.** *—tr.* **1.** To arrange or place (soldiers) in line for a parade, manoeuvre, or review. **2.** To arrange, place, or set in methodical order: *marshalled facts; marshalled her thoughts.* **3.** To enlist and organise. **4.** To guide (a person) ceremoniously; conduct or usher. **5.** *Heraldry.* To join together (two or more coats of arms) on one shield. *—intr.* To take form or order; especially, to take up positions in or as if in a military formation. —See Synonyms at **gather.** [Middle English *mareschal,* from Old French, from Late Latin *mariscalcus,* from Germanic *marhas kalkaz* (unattested), "keeper of the horses" : *marhaz,* horse + *skalkaz,* servant.] **—mar·shal·cy, mar·shal·ship** *n.*

Mar·shall (márshəl), **George C(atlett)** (1880–1959). U.S. soldier and statesman. While secretary of state (1947–49) he initiated the European Recovery Programme, known as the Marshall Plan, which gave economic aid to Europe. He served briefly as secretary of defence (1950–51) and received the Nobel prize for peace (1953).

mar·shall·ing yard (márshʼl-ing) *n.* An area in which railway rolling stock is kept and in which locomotives, carriages, goods wagons, and the like, are made up into trains.

Marshall Islands, Republic of the. State in the central Pacific Ocean, comprising some 1,259 islets and atolls. The economy depends on exports of copra, and U.S. payments for a military base. Fishing is also important. Germany bought the islands from Spain (1899), and they became a Japanese mandate (1920). From 1947 they were part of the U.S. Trust Territory of the Pacific Islands, but became self-governing in 1979. Area, 118 square kilometres (70 square miles). Population, 12,000. Capital, Majuro. See map at **Pacific Ocean.**

Marshall Plan *n.* See **European Recovery Program.**

marsh andromeda *n.* A plant, **bog rosemary** *(see).*

marsh crocodile *n.* A crocodile, the **mugger** *(see).*

marsh fever *n.* **Malaria** *(see).*

marsh gas *n.* Methane produced by rotting vegetation in marshes.

marsh harrier *n.* A Eurasian hawk, *Circus aeruginosus,* that frequents reedbeds and marshes. It has a dark brown plumage with paler markings.

marsh hawk *n. U.S.* The **hen harrier** *(see).*

marsh hen *n.* Any of various marsh birds of the family Rallidae, which includes the gallinules, coots, and rails.

marsh·land (márshland, -lənd) *n.* Land consisting of marshes.

marsh mallow *n.* A plant, *Althaea officinalis,* native to Europe, having showy pink flowers and a mucilaginous root used as a demulcent and in confectionery.

marsh·mal·low (mársh-mál-ō) *n.* **1.** A confection of sweetened paste, formerly made from the root of the marsh mallow. **2.** A soft confection made of gelatine, sugar, and starch, and dusted with powdered sugar. [From MARSH MALLOW.] **—marsh·mal·low** *adj.*

marsh marigold *n.* Any plant of the genus *Caltha;* especially, *C. palustris,* growing in swampy places and having bright yellow flowers. Also called "king-cup".

marsh samphire *n.* A plant, the **glasswort** *(see).*

marsh tit *n.* A small European songbird, *Parus palustris,* having a greyish body and a black head.

Mars·ton (már-stən), **John** (1576–1634). English dramatist. His literary career began with satirical and frequently licentious poetry, such as *The Scourge of Villainy* (1598), and declined after he took holy orders (1609). His plays include *The Malcontent* (1604) and *What You Will* (1607).

Marston Moor. The site in Yorkshire of the first decisive battle of the English Civil War (July 2, 1644), won by the Parliamentarians.

mar·su·pi·al (maar-séw-pi-əl, -sŏŏ-) *n.* Any mammal of the order Marsupialia, including kangaroos, opossums, bandicoots, and wombats, found principally in the Australian region and South and Central America. The female of most species lacks a placenta and possesses a marsupium.

~adj. **1.** Of or pertaining to the Marsupialia. **2.** Of or pertaining to a marsupium. [New Latin *marsupialis,* from MARSUPIUM.]

marsupial mole *n.* **1.** An Australian marsupial, *Notoryctes typhlops,* that resembles the mole. **2.** Any of several related animals.

mar·su·pi·um (maar-séw-pi-əm, -sŏŏ-) *n., pl.* **-pia** (-pi-ə). **1.** An external abdominal pouch in female marsupials that contains mammary glands and that shelters the young. **2.** A temporary egg pouch in various animals. [Latin *marsupium,* pouch, from Greek *marsupion, marsipion,* diminutive of *marsipos,* purse, probably from Avestan *maršu†,* belly.]

mart (mart) *n.* **1.** A market; a trading or auction centre. **2.** *Archaic.* A fair. [Middle English, shortened from MARKET.]

mar·ta·gon (mártəgən) *n.* A Eurasian lily, *Lilium martagon,* having pinkish-purple, spotted flowers. Also called "martagon lily". See **Turk's-cap lily.** [Middle English, from Old French, from Spanish *martagón,* from Turkish *martağan,* a kind of turban.]

Mar·tel·lo tower (maar-téllō) *n.* A small circular fort, formerly used in Europe for coastal defence. Also called "martello". [Alteration from Cape *Mortella,* Corsica, where a tower of this type had proved effective in a battle in 1794.]

mar·ten (mártin) *n., pl.* **-tens** or collectively **marten. 1.** Any carnivore of the genus *Martes,* similar to the weasel, and found in northern wooded areas. See **pine marten. 2.** The fur of the marten. See **sable.** [Middle English *martren,* marten, marten's fur, from Old French *martrine,* marten's fur, from *martre,* marten, from Germanic *marthuz* (unattested).]

mar·ten·site (mártin-zīt) *n.* A solid solution of iron and up to one per cent of carbon, the chief constituent of hardened carbon tool steels. [After Adolf *Marten* (1914–), German metallurgist.] **—mar·ten·sit·ic** (-zíttik) *adj.*

Mar·tha (márthə). A sister of Lazarus and Mary, and friend of Jesus, who busied herself with household chores while her sister listened to Jesus. Luke 10:38–41.

mar·tial (márshʼl) *adj.* **1.** Of, pertaining to, or suggesting war. **2.** Pertaining to or connected with the armed forces or the military profession: *court martial.* **3.** Resembling, characteristic of, or befitting a warrior: *a martial roar of indignation.* [Middle English, from Latin *mārtiālis,* from *Mārs* (stem *Mārt-*), MARS.] **—mar·tial·ism** *n.* **—mar·tial·ist** *n.* **—mar·tial·ly** *adv.*

Mar·tial (márshəl), born Marcus Valerius Martialis (A.D. 40–104). Latin poet. Spanish-born, he came to Rome (A.D. 64), gaining patronage through the Senecas. His 12 books of epigrams are keen, witty observations of contemporary Roman life.

martial art *n.* Any of several methods of fighting or self-defence, such as judo or karate, originating in the East.

martial law *n.* Rule by military authorities imposed upon a civilian population in time of war or when civil authority is considered to be functioning inadequately. Compare **military law.**

Mar·tian (márshʼn) *adj.* Of or pertaining to the planet Mars.

~n. An inhabitant of the planet Mars, especially as a stock fictional character. [Middle English, from Latin *mārtius,* from *Mārs* (stem *Mārt-*), MARS.]

mar·tin (már-tin || -tʼn) *n.* Any of several birds resembling and closely related to the swallows, such as the **house martin** *(see).* [Middle English, after St. *Martin* (the birds migrate from England near the time of Martinmas).]

Mar·ti·neau (márti-nō), **Harriet** (1802–76). British writer. Her work dealt with economic and religious themes based on the ideas of Ricardo and Mill. Her works include *Illustrations of Political Economy* (1832–34) and the children's story *The Play Fellow* (1841).

mar·ti·net (márti-nét) *n.* **1.** A rigid military disciplinarian. **2.** A person who demands absolute adherence to standards or rules. [After Jean *Martinet,* 17th-century French general.]

mar·tin·gale (mártin-gayl) *n.* Also **mar·tin·gal** (-gal). **1.** A part of a harness designed to prevent a horse from throwing back its head. **2.** *Nautical.* Any of several parts of standing rigging strengthening the bowsprit and jib boom against the force of the head stays. **3.** A method of gambling in which one doubles the stakes after each loss. [16th century : from French *martingale†.*]

mar·ti·ni (maar-téeni) *n., pl.* **-nis.** A cocktail usually made of three or more parts of gin to one part of dry vermouth, sometimes with a dash of angostura bitters. [Supposedly after a New York barman, *Martinez,* who invented the drink; the name was quickly confused with that of the Italian vermouth firm.]

Mar·ti·ni (maar-téeni) *n.* A trademark for an Italian vermouth.

Mar·ti·nique (márti-néek). Overseas département of France in the Caribbean, settled by the French in 1635. The small volcanic island is dominated by Mont Pelée, which erupted in 1902, killing more than 30,000 people and destroying the town of Saint Pierre. The economy depends on bananas, sugar, pineapple canning, and rum. Fort-de-France is the capital. See map at **Latin America.**

Mar·tin·mas (már-tin-məss, -mass || -tʼn-) *n.* A Christian festival celebrated annually on St. Martin's Day, November 11. It is one of the Scottish quarter days.

Mar·ti·nů (márti-nŏŏ), **Bohuslav** (1890–1959). Czech composer. He studied in Prague and Paris, and fled to the United States in 1941. His works include the ballet *Ishtar* (1920), the opera *Julietta* (1938), symphonies, and chamber music.

mart·let (márt-lət, -lit) *n.* **1.** *Archaic.* A martin. **2.** *Heraldry.* A representation of a bird without feet, used as a crest or bearing to indicate a fourth son. [French *martelet,* probably an alteration of *martinet,* diminutive of MARTIN.]

mar·tyr (mártər) *n.* 1. One who suffers death through refusing to renounce religious or political principles. 2. One who sacrifices something very important to him in order to further a belief, cause, or principle. 3. A person who endures great suffering: *a martyr to migraine.* 4. A person who makes a great show of suffering in order to arouse sympathy.
~*tr.v.* **martyred, -tyring, -tyrs.** 1. To make a martyr of (a person). 2. To inflict great pain upon; torment: *martyred by toothache.* [Middle English *martir,* Old English *martyr,* from Late Latin *martyr,* from Greek *martus†,* witness (of Christ).]

mar·tyr·dom (mártər-dəm) *n.* 1. The state of being a martyr; the suffering of death by a martyr. 2. Extreme suffering.

mar·tyr·ise, mar·tyr·ize (mártər-īz) *tr.v.* **-ised, -ising, -ises.** To martyr.

mar·tyr·ol·o·gy (mártə-róllǝji) *n.* 1. An official catalogue of saints and martyrs. 2. A list of those who have suffered or died for their beliefs: *Islamic martyrology.*

mar·tyr·y (mártǝri) *n.* A monument, such as a shrine or chapel, erected in honour of a martyr. [Middle English, from Medieval Latin *martyrium,* from Latin *marturion,* martyrdom.]

mar·vel (márv'l) *n.* 1. Something that evokes surprise, admiration, or wonder. 2. *Archaic.* A sense of wonder or astonishment.
~*v.* **marvelled** or *U.S.* **marveled, -velling** or *U.S.* **-veling, -vels.** —*intr.* To be or become filled with wonder or astonishment. —*tr. Archaic.* To wonder at or about. [Middle English *marveile,* from Old French *merveille,* from Vulgar Latin *mīrābilia* (unattested), marvel, originally "wonderful things", Latin neuter plural of *mīrābilis,* wonderful, from *mīrārī,* to wonder, from *mīrus,* wonderful.]

Mar·vell (márvǝl), **Andrew** (1621–1678). English Metaphysical poet. His frequently satirical work includes the poems *To His Coy Mistress* and *The Definition of Love,* and pamphlets attacking the monarchy and political corruption.

mar·vel·lous, *U.S.* **mar·vel·ous** (márv-lǝss, -'l-ǝss) *adj.* 1. Causing wonder or astonishment: *a marvellous cure.* 2. Of the highest or best kind or quality: *a marvellous recipe.* 3. *Archaic.* Miraculous; supernatural. —**mar·vel·lous·ly** *adv.* —**mar·vel·lous·ness** *n.*

mar·vel-of-Pe·ru (márv'l-ǝv-pǝ-rōō) *n.* A plant, the **four-o'clock** *(see).* [Originally found in Peru.]

Marx (marks), **Karl (Heinrich)** (1818–83). German journalist and philosopher. He edited the *Rheinische Zeitung* (1842–43) before working with Friedrich Engels, producing the *Communist Manifesto* in 1848. Expelled from Prussia (1849), he settled in London. He adapted Hegel's ideas to produce a theory of social change, dialectical materialism, and believed that violent revolution by the proletariat is necessary to create a classless society. *Das Kapital* (1867) greatly influenced subsequent socialism and communism.

Marx Brothers. U.S. family of comedians. Touring from early childhood in vaudeville, they later starred in films full of irreverent and anarchic humour, both verbal and visual, including *Duck Soup* (1933), *A Night at the Opera* (1935), and *A Day At the Races* (1937). Julius (Groucho) (1895–1977), with his comic moustache, cigar, and biting sarcasm, Arthur (Harpo) (1893–1964), the dumb clown and harpist, and Leonard (Chico) (1891–1961), the piano-playing confidence trickster, contrasted with Herbert (Zeppo) (1901–79), who played the straight man before retiring from films. Milton (Gummo) (1894–1977) followed his own career.

Marx·i·an (márks-i-ǝn, -yǝn) *n.* One who studies or makes use of Karl Marx's philosophical or other concepts as a method of analysis and interpretation, as in political economy or in historical or literary criticism. —**Marx·i·an** *adj.* —**Marx·i·an·ism** *n.*

Marx·ism (márks-iz'm) *n.* The political and economic ideas of Karl Marx and Friedrich Engels; specifically, a system of thought in which the concept of class struggle plays a primary role both in analysing Western society in general, and in understanding its allegedly inevitable development from bourgeois oppression under capitalism to a socialist society and thence to communism.

Marx·ism-Len·in·ism (márks-iz'm-lénnin-iz'm) *n.* Marxism as developed to include Lenin's concept of imperialism as the final form of capitalism, and a shift in the focus of struggle from the developed to the underdeveloped countries. —**Marx·ist-Lenin·ist** *n. & adj.*

Marx·ist (márks-ist) *n.* 1. One who believes in or follows the ideas of Marx and Engels. 2. Loosely, any militant Communist.
~*adj.* Of or pertaining to Marxism.

Mar·y (maír-i). The mother of Jesus. Matthew 1:18–25. Also called the "Virgin Mary", "Our Lady".

Mary I, also known as Mary Tudor (1516–58). Queen of England (1553–58). Daughter of Henry VIII and Catherine of Aragon, she came to the throne on the death of her half-brother, Edward VI. She married Philip II of Spain (1554) and restored papal supremacy in England: the persecution of the Protestants followed, including the burning of bishops Cranmer, Latimer, and Ridley, thus earning her the nickname of "Bloody Mary".

Mary II, (1662–94). Queen of England, Scotland, and Ireland (1689–94). Daughter of James II, she married her cousin William of Orange (1677), ruling jointly with him after the "Glorious Revolution" (1688) which forced her father's abdication.

Mary, Queen of Scots, also known as Mary Stuart (1542–87). Queen of Scotland (1542–67). The daughter of James V and Mary of Guise, she was brought up as a Catholic in France, where she married the dauphin (later Francis II). She returned to Scotland after the death of her husband (1561). She married her cousin, the

Earl of Darnley (1565), by whom she had a son, later to be James VI of Scotland and James I of England. Darnley was murdered by the Earl of Bothwell (1567), whom she married three months later. Forced to abdicate by the nobles in favour of her son, she fled to England (1568) and was imprisoned by Elizabeth I. Catholic supporters plotted to place her on the throne of England, and this resulted in her trial and execution.

Mar·y·land (maír-i-lǝnd, -land, *also* mérri- *in imitation of U.S. pronunciation*). Atlantic state of the United States. One of the original 13 states, it had been founded (1634) by Lord Baltimore as a refuge for English Roman Catholics. Its Atlantic plain, divided by Chesapeake Bay, rises in the northwest to the Blue Ridge Mountains (Appalachians). Although livestock, cereal, and tobacco farming are important, the economy rests mainly on manufacturing, particularly of steel, metal products, and machinery. Annapolis is the capital.

Mary Mag·da·len·e (mágdǝ-léeni, -leen, -lin). Also **Mary Mag·da·len** (-lin). A woman in the New Testament (Luke 8:2) whom Jesus cured of evil spirits. She is usually considered identical with the repentant prostitute in Luke 7:36–50. Also called the "Magdalene".

Maryology. Variant of **Mariology.**

mar·zi·pan (márzi-pan, -pán || *U.S. also* mártsǝ-, -paan) *n.* A confection in the form of a paste, made from ground almonds and sugar, often moulded into decorative forms or used in icing cakes. [German *Marzipan,* from Italian *marzapane,* fine box for confections, originally a box containing a tenth of a load, from Venetian *matapan,* coin bearing a seated Christ figure, originally a ten per cent tax, from Arabic *mawthabān,* "seated king", name given to similar coins in circulation since the Crusades.]

-mas *n. comb. form.* Indicates a Christian festival; for example, **Christmas.** [Middle English *-masse,* MASS.]

Ma·sac·cio (ma-záchō), born Tommaso di Giovanni di Simone Guidi (1401–28). Early Italian Renaissance painter. His revolutionary use of linear perspective and mastery of light and shade are illustrated in his fresco series in the Brancacci Chapel at Santa Maria del Carmine, Florence.

Ma·sa·da (ma-saádǝ, mǝ-). Mountain fortress in the Judaean Desert, Israel, overlooking the Dead Sea. In A.D. 73, after a two-year siege, the Zealots, a Jewish sect who were defending the fortress, committed mass suicide rather than surrender to the Romans.

Ma·sai (maá-sī, maa-sí) *n., pl.* **-sais** or collectively **Masai.** 1. A member of a nomadic people of Kenya and parts of Tanzania. 2. The Nilotic language of this people. —**Ma·sai** *adj.*

Masandam, Ras. See **Musandam, Ras.**

Ma·sa·ryk (mázzǝ-rik, mássǝ-), **Tomáš (Garrigue)** (1850–1937). Czech statesman. He became first president of the independent Czech Republic (1918), retiring in 1935. His son, Jan Masaryk (1886–1948), entered the Czech diplomatic service (1918), was minister to Britain (1925–38), and foreign minister in the exiled Czech government in London (1940–45) and in Czechoslovakia itself (1945–48). After the Communist takeover, he is alleged to have committed suicide.

masc. masculine.

Mas·ca·gni (ma-skaán-yee), **Pietro** (1863–1945). Italian composer. He wrote several operas, none of which equalled the success of his one-act work *Cavalleria Rusticana* (1890).

mascanonge. Variant of **muskellunge.**

mas·car·a (mass-kaárǝ || *U.S.* -kárrǝ) *n.* A cosmetic applied to darken or thicken the eyelashes. [Italian *mascara, maschera,* MASK, probably from Arabic *maskharah,* "buffoon".]

mas·cle (mássk'l, maásk'l) *n. Heraldry.* A charge consisting of a lozenge with the inner area also shaped like a lozenge. [Middle English, from Anglo-French, from Anglo-Latin *mascula,* from Latin *macula,* spot.]

mas·con (máss-kon) *n.* Any of several areas of high-density mass below the surface of the Moon causing an exceptionally high gravitational attraction in that vicinity. [From *mass concentration.*]

mas·cot (máss-kǝt, -kot) *n.* A person, animal, or object believed to bring good luck: *She took a toy bear into her exam as a mascot.* [French *mascotte,* from Provençal *mascotto,* diminutive of *masco,* sorcerer, from Late Latin *masca,* witch, from Langobard.]

mas·cu·line (máss-kew-lin, maáss-) *adj. Abbr.* **masc.** 1. **a.** Of or pertaining to men or boys; male. **b.** Manly or virile. 2. Mannish; unwomanly: *She had a masculine face.* 3. *Grammar.* Belonging or pertaining to a category of words or forms which in some languages, such as French or German, are assigned a grammatical gender associated with maleness, and in others, such as English, actually refer to males.
~*n. Abbr.* **masc.** 1. The masculine gender. 2. A word or word form of the masculine gender. [Middle English *masculin,* from Old French, from Latin *masculīnus,* from *masculus,* male, diminutive of *mas,* male.] —**mas·cu·line·ly** *adv.* —**mas·cu·line·ness, mas·cu·lin·i·ty** (-línnǝti) *n.*

masculine ending *n.* The ending of a line of verse with a stress on the last syllable. Compare **feminine ending.**

masculine rhyme *n.* A rhyme of only a single syllable, terminal and stressed, as in *cat, hat* and *annoy, enjoy.* Compare **feminine rhyme.**

mas·cu·lin·ise, mas·cu·lin·ize (máss-kew-lin-īz, maáss-) *v.* **-nised, -nising, -nises.** —*tr.* To make masculine. —*intr.* To become masculine. Used especially of a woman who has developed masculine characteristics owing to hormonal imbalance or male hormone therapy. —**mas·cu·lin·i·sa·tion** (-ī-záysh'n || *U.S.* -i-) *n.*

mask

FACES TRANSFIGURED IN CEREMONY, ENTERTAINMENT, AND DEATH

Masks vary in style as much as the cultures that produced them

Masks – which disguise, transform, or define the beings behind them – have been vital in primitive rituals and in drama for many hundreds, even thousands, of years.

They are used by tribes the world over to impersonate supernatural beings or animals, for numerous reasons. A mask may be a totem to represent a protective spirit, like the 6 metre (20 foot) masks of the Papuans in New Guinea.

In many places, shamans (or medicine-men) don grotesque demon masks to scare off evil spirits, a task also performed by the so-called False Face society of the Iroquois Indians, whose long-haired, grimacing masks were used to exorcise demons. The golden masks of Andean tribes were sometimes purely formal (for burial) or practical (for ceremonial use) or both.

In Greek theatre, masks were worn to represent fixed characteristics, like grief or rage. The tradition was preserved in Roman theatre and inherited much later, in the 16th century, by the Italian *commedia dell'arte*, masked comedies with stock characters that found their way into modern pantomime, Punch and Judy, and clowning traditions.

Masks are integral as well to Japanese and Chinese theatrical traditions. The Japanese *Noh* plays of the 14th century and onwards use in rigidly formal terms no less than 125 types of wooden mask, each with its own fixed role.

BURIAL MASK *Made in the 12th–13th centuries by the Chimu of Peru, this mask has emerald eyes, red paint, and large ear-spools that indicate the high status of its wearer.*

DEMONIC MASK *Ornate masks, like this demonic wooden one from the Baron tribe of Indonesia, are – with shields and baskets – important forms of artistic expression among many Indonesian peoples.*

BADGE OF SECRECY *In Liberia, masks are worn by members of the Poro secret society, which regulates male behaviour.*

PROTECTIVE TOTEM *Papuan tribesmen make wood and bark-cloth masks, some of them enormously large, as totems to protect members of a tribe.*

Mase·field (máyss-feeld, máyz-), **John (Edward)** (1878–1967). British poet and novelist. His poetry includes the colloquial *Everlasting Mercy* (1911), *Dauber* (1913), and the Chaucerian *Reynard the Fox* (1919), while his novels include *Sard Harker* (1924) and *Basilissa* (1940). He became Poet Laureate (1930).

ma·ser (máyzər) *n. Physics.* Any of several devices that convert incident electromagnetic radiation from a wide range of frequencies to one or more discrete frequencies of highly amplified and coherent microwave radiation. Compare **laser.** [*M*icrowave *a*mplification by *s*timulated *e*mission of *r*adiation.]

Ma·se·ru (ma-sáir-ōō, mə-). Capital of Lesotho.

mash (mash) *n.* **1.** Any fermentable, starchy mixture from which alcohol or spirits can be distilled. **2.** A mixture of ground grain and nutrients fed to livestock and poultry. **3. a.** Any soft, pulpy mixture or mass. **b.** *British Informal.* Mashed potatoes.
~*v.* **mashed, mashing, mashes.** —*tr.* **1.** To convert (malt or grain) into mash. **2.** To convert (something) into a soft, pulpy mixture resembling mash: *to mash potatoes.* **3.** To crush or grind. **4.** *Northern English.* To brew (tea). **5.** *Archaic Slang.* To flirt with. —*intr. Northern English.* To brew: *Leave the tea to mash.* [Middle English, Old English *māsc.*]

mash·er (máshər) *n.* **1.** A kitchen utensil for mashing vegetables or fruit. **2.** *U.S. Slang.* A man who attempts to force his sexual attentions upon a woman. [Sense 2 originally "a flirt", from *mash* (verb), to flirt, make advances, from obsolete *mash* (noun), a "crush".]

Mash·had or **Me·shed.** Ancient city of northeast Iran at the junction of major caravan routes. It is a provincial capital, and centre of a rich agricultural region.

mash·ie, mash·y (máshi) *n., pl.* **-ies.** A golf club of medium loft. [Perhaps from French *massue,* club.]

Mashona. Variant of **Shona.**

Ma·sho·na·land (mə-shónnə-land, -shōnə-). Region of northeast Zimbabwe, now divided into the provinces of Northern Mashonaland and Southern Mashonaland. Inhabited by the Shona people (or Mashona), it includes the country's capital, Harare (Salisbury).

mas·jid (múss-jid) *n.* A **mosque** *(see).*

mask (maask ‖ mask) *n.* **1.** A covering worn on the face to conceal one's identity; especially: **a.** A cloth, plastic, or paper covering that has openings for the eyes, entirely or partly conceals the face, and is worn especially at a masquerade ball, fancy-dress dance, or the like. **b.** A representation of a grotesque face: *a horror mask.* **c.** A facial covering worn for a parade, carnival, ritual, or the like. **d.** A complete facial covering and headdress, usually made of plaster or wood, worn by actors in Greek and Roman drama to emphasise a single character trait. **2. a.** A protective covering for the face or head, as worn in fencing and some other sports. **b.** A facial covering worn to prevent infection, especially during surgery. **3. a.** A **gas mask** *(see).* **b.** A device fitting over the mouth and nose through which oxygen or an anaesthetic gas may be supplied. **4.** A representation of a face or head: **a.** A **death mask** *(see).* **b.** An often grotesque representation of a head and face, used for ornamentation. **5.** The face or facial markings of certain animals, such as a fox or dog. **6.** A face having a blank, fixed, or enigmatic expression: *She* *displayed an impenetrable mask to the world.* **7.** Something, often a trait, that disguises or conceals: *hid his shyness under a mask of confidence.* **8.** A natural or artificial feature of terrain that conceals and protects military forces or installations. **9. a.** An opaque border or pattern placed between a source of light and a photosensitive surface to prevent exposure of specific portions of the surface. **b.** The translucent border framing a television picture tube and screen. **10.** See **face mask. 11.** A **masque** *(see).* **12.** *Archaic.* A person wearing a mask. **13.** *Electronics.* A thin sheet of material with a pattern cut into it to enable a semiconducting chip to be made into an integrated circuit.

~*tr.v.* **masked, masking, masks. 1.** To cover (the face, for example) with a decorative or protective mask. **2.** To disguise; especially, to make indistinct or blurred to the senses: *The spice masks the strong flavour of the meat.* **3.** To cover up for concealment or protection: *They masked their guns with branches.* **4.** To block the view of: *Undergrowth masked the entrance.* **5.** To cover (a part of a photographic film) by the application of an opaque border. **6.** To apply masking paper or masking tape to (an area not to be painted). **7.** *Chemistry.* To inhibit (a compound or radical) with a reagent more active in a specific reaction. [French *masque,* from Italian *maschera,* perhaps from Arabic *maskharah,* "buffoon".]

maskalonge. Variant of **muskellunge.**

masked (maaskt || maskt) *adj.* **1.** Wearing a mask. **2.** Disguised; concealed: *masked intentions.* **3.** Latent or hidden, as a symptom or disease may be. **4.** *Botany.* Resembling a mask; personate. **5.** *Zoology.* Having masklike markings on the head or face.

maskeg. Variant of **muskeg.**

mask•er, mas•quer (maáskər, máskər) *n.* A participant in a masquerade or masque.

mas•o•chism (mássə-kiz'm || mázzə-) *n.* **1.** The deriving of pleasure, especially sexual arousal, from having physical or emotional pain inflicted on one. **2.** Loosely, the practice of deliberately undergoing unpleasant experiences, usually in the pursuit of some higher satisfaction: *the sheer masochism of entering a marathon.* [After Leopold von Sacher-*Masoch* (1836–95), Austrian novelist who wrote on the theme of sexual masochism.] **—mas•o•chist** *n.* **—mas•o•chis•tic** (-kístik) *adj.* **—mas•o•chis•ti•cal•ly** *adv.*

ma•son (máyss'n) *n.* **1. a.** A person who builds with stone. **b.** A person who dresses stone. **c.** *South African.* A bricklayer. **2.** *Capital* **M.** A **Freemason** *(see).*

~*tr.v.* **masoned, -soning, -sons.** To build or strengthen with masonry. [Middle English *masoun, machoun,* from Anglo-French *machun,* from Old French *masson,* from Frankish *makjo* (unattested), from *makōn,* to make (unattested).]

mason bee *n.* Any of various solitary bees of the family Megachilidae which build nests of sand or clay under stones or in cavities.

Ma•son-Dix•on Line (máyss'n-díks'n). Former political boundary between Pennsylvania and Maryland, United States. Drawn up (1763–67) by the astronomers Charles Mason and Jeremiah Dixon, it was extended (1779) as the boundary between Pennsylvania and Virginia (now West Virginia). The line became a cultural boundary between the Northern and Southern states.

Ma•son•ic (mə-sónnik) *adj.* Of or pertaining to Freemasons or Freemasonry.

ma•son•ry (máyss'n-ri) *n., pl.* **-ries. 1.** The trade of a mason. **2.** Stonework or brickwork. **3.** *Capital* **M. Freemasonry** *(see).*

masonry cement *n.* A kind of cement especially prepared to be used in the mortar of block and brick masonry.

Ma•so•ra, Ma•so•rah (mə-sáwrə || -sṓrə) *n.* **1.** The body of tradition pertaining to correct textual reading of the Old Testament. **2.** The critical notes in which this tradition is embodied, made by Jewish scholars before the tenth century A.D. [Middle Hebrew *māsōrāh,* "tradition", from Hebrew *māsar,* root of *limsor,* to hand over, transmit.] **—Mas•o•ret•ic** (mássə-réttik) *adj.*

masque, mask (maask, mask) *n.* **1.** A dramatic entertainment, usually based on a mythological or allegorical theme, popular in England in the 16th and early 17th centuries. **2.** A dramatic verse composition written for a masque production. **3.** A masquerade. [Variant of MASK.]

masquer. Variant of **masker.**

mas•quer•ade (máss-kə-ráyd, maáss-) *n.* **1.** A costume ball or party at which masks are worn; a masked ball. Also called "masque". **2.** The costume for such a party or ball. **3.** Any disguise or false outward show; a pretence: *a masquerade of humility.*

~*intr.v.* **masqueraded, -ading, -ades. 1.** To wear a mask or disguise, as at a masquerade: *She masqueraded as a shepherdess.* **2.** To pretend to be something one is not: *He masqueraded as the ship's surgeon.* [French *mascarade,* from Italian *mascherata* or Spanish *mascarada,* from Italian *maschera,* MASK.] **—mas•quer•ad•er** *n.*

mass (mas) *n.* **1.** A unified body of matter with no specific shape. **2.** A grouping of individual parts or elements that compose a unified body of unspecified size or quantity: *A mass of people poured into the streets.* **3.** Any large but nonspecific amount or number: *a mass of bruises.* **4.** The major part of something; the majority. **5.** The bulk of a solid body. **6.** *Physics. Abbr.* **m, M** The measure of a body's resistance to acceleration. The mass of a body is different from but proportional to its **weight** *(see),* is independent of the body's position but dependent on its velocity relative to other bodies, and may be expressed in mass units, such as kilograms or slugs, or corresponding energy units, by means of the mass-energy relationship of the special theory of relativity. **7.** In painting, an area of unified light, shade, or colour. **8.** In pharmacology, a thick, pasty mixture of drugs used to form pills. **9.** In mining, a mineral deposit with no specific shape. Compare **bed, vein. —in the mass.** Considered as a whole. **—the masses.** The body of common people; the many; the proletariat.

~*v.* **massed, massing, masses.** —*tr.* To gather or form into a mass. —*intr.* To assemble in a mass.

~*adj.* **1.** Of, pertaining to, characteristic of, or involving a large number of people: *mass education; mass destruction.* **2.** Done on a large scale; involving great numbers or large amounts: *mass production.* [Middle English, from Old French *masse,* from Latin *massa,* from Greek *maza,* barley cake, lump, mass.]

Mass (mass, maass) *n. Sometimes small* **m. 1.** In the Roman Catholic and some Protestant churches, such as the Lutheran, the celebration of the Eucharist. See **High Mass, Low Mass. 2.** A musical setting of certain parts of the Mass, especially the Kyrie, Gloria, Credo, Sanctus, Benedictus, and Agnus Dei. [Middle English *masse,* Old English *mæsse, messe,* from Late Latin *missa,* eucharist, perhaps deriving from the final words, *Ite, missa est,* "Go, it is the dismissal", from *mittere* (past participial stem *miss-*), to send away.]

Mass. Massachusetts.

Mas•sa•chu•set (mássə-chṓō-sit, -zit) *n., pl.* **-sets** or collectively **Massachuset.** Also **Mas•sa•chu•sett. 1.** A member of an Algonquian-speaking Indian people who lived on or near Massachusetts Bay. **2.** The Algonquian language of these Indians.

Mas•sa•chu•setts (mássə-chṓō-sits, -zits). State in New England, United States. It was the destination of the *Mayflower* (1620), and became one of the 13 original states. Massachusetts is largely a manufacturing state with shipping, machinery, paper, printing, textile, and leather industries. Boston is the capital.

mas•sa•cre (mássə-kər) *n.* **1.** An act of savage and indiscriminate killing, especially of large numbers of people. **2.** *Informal.* A severe defeat, as in a sports event. **3.** *Informal.* An act of wanton destruction: *the massacre of our hopes.*

~*tr.v.* **massacred** (-kərd), **-cring** (-kring, -kər-ing), **-cres. 1.** To kill indiscriminately and wantonly; slaughter. **2.** *Informal.* To defeat decisively, as in a sports event. [French, from Old French *maçacre†,* slaughterhouse.] **—mas•sa•crer** (-kər-ər, -krər) *n.*

mas•sage (máss-aazh, -aaj || *chiefly U.S.* mə-saázh, -saáj) *n.* The rubbing or kneading of parts of the body, as to aid circulation or relax the muscles.

~*tr.v.* **massaged, -saging, -sages. 1.** To give a massage to. **2.** To treat by or as if by means of a massage: *massaged her ego.* **3.** *Informal.* To mould or adjust to suit a preconceived interpretation: *massage statistics.* [French, from *masser,* to massage, probably from Portuguese *amassar,* to knead, from *massa,* dough, MASS.]

Mas•sa•wa or **Ma•sau•a** (mə-saáwə). Ancient Red Sea port in Ethiopia. It is the commercial port for the north of the country, and also a fishing and industrial centre.

mass defect *n. Physics.* The amount by which the mass of an atomic nucleus is less than the sum of the masses of its constituent particles. It is equivalent to the **binding energy** *(see)* of the nucleus. Also called "mass deficiency".

mas•sé (mássi) *n.* In billiards, a stroke made by hitting the cue ball on its side with the cue held nearly perpendicular to the table, such that the cue ball will curve around a ball that is immediately obstructing it. [French, from *masser,* to cue, from *masse,* cue, MACE.]

mass-energy equivalence *n. Physics.* The principle that a measured quantity of energy is equivalent to a measured quantity of mass. The equivalence is expressed by Einstein's equation, $E = mc^2$, where E represents energy, m the equivalent mass, and c the speed of light.

Mas•se•net (mássə-nay; *French* mass-náy), **Jules (Émile Frédéric).** (1842–1912). French composer. Both a student and professor at the Paris Conservatoire, he composed over 20 operas, including *Manon Lescaut* (1884) and *Thaïs* (1894).

mas•se•ter (ma-seétər, mə-) *n.* A large muscle in the cheek that acts to close the jaws and is therefore important in chewing. [Greek *masētēr,* one who chews, from *masasthai,* to chew.] **—mas•se•ter•ic** (mássi-térrik) *adj.*

mas•seur (ma-súr || -séwr, -sóor) *n. Feminine* **mas•seuse** (-súrz || -séwz, -sóoz, -sṓz). A person who gives massages professionally. [French, from *masser,* to MASSAGE.]

mas•si•cot (mássi-kot, -kō) *n.* **1.** A rare mineral, the yellow crystalline mineral form of lead monoxide, PbO. Compare **litharge. 2.** A yellow pigment, lead monoxide. [Middle English *masticot,* from Old French, akin to Italian *marzacotto,* ointment.]

mas•sif (ma-seéf, másseef) *n.* **1.** A large plateau-like region with marked edges, often formed by faults. **2.** A compact group of connected mountains forming a distinct portion of a mountain range. [French, from *massif,* MASSIVE.]

Mas•sif Cen•tral (ma-seéf SON-traál). The "central upland" of France, covering nearly a sixth of the country. It is a mountainous plateau: its highest point is the Puy de Sancy (1 886 metres; 6,186 feet). Stock rearing and dairying are the chief occupations, but peripheral coal and kaolin deposits support industrial centres such as Limoges and Clermont-Ferrand.

Mas•sine (ma-seén), **Léonide** (1896–1979). Russian ballet dancer and choreographer. He worked with Diaghilev's Ballets Russes. He created the first cubist ballet, *Parade* (1917), *La Boutique Fantasque* (1919) and *Les Présages* (1933).

mas•sive (mássiv) *adj.* **1.** Consisting of or making up a large mass; bulky; heavy; solid: *a massive piece of furniture.* **2.** Unusually large or imposing: *a massive head.* **3.** Large or impressive in quantity,

PRONUNCIATION KEY

a, trap; aa, father; ai, **fair**; ar, **star**; aw, **lawn**; ay, **play**; b, bb, **stab**; **rubber**; ch, **church**; ck, **ticket**; d, dd, **dead**; **ladder**; e, dress; ee, **bee**; er, **defer**; ew, **few**; ewr, **pure**; ə, **about**; ər, **letter**; f, ff, **fife**; **differ**; g, gg, **giggle**; h, **hat**; i, **kit**; ī, **price**; īr, **fire**; j, **judge**; k, **kick**; l, ll, **let**; 'l, **needle**; m, mm, **man**; n, nn, **no**; 'n, **sudden**; ng, **thing**; o, **lot**; ō, **no**; ŏŏ, **foot**; ōō, **shoe**; oor, **poor**; ow, **cow**; owr, **hour**; oy, **boy**; p, pp, **pepper**; r, rr, **red**; s, ss, **sauce**; sh, **ship**; t, tt, **totter**; th, **thick**; th, **this**; **smooth**; u, **cut**; ur, **turn**; v, vv, **valve**; w, **wet**; y, **yes**; z, zz, **zebra**; zh, **vision**; **pleasure**

IN FOREIGN WORDS:

aN, oN, **Saint-Saëns**; hl, **Llanelli**; **Hluhluwe**; kh, **loch**; **lough**; **Khaled**

STRESS MARK:

in-sīt, **insight**; in-sít, **incite**

scope, or scale: *a massive work of the finest scholarship.* **4.** *Medicine.* Large in comparison with the usual amount. Said of dosage. **5.** *Pathology.* Affecting a large area of bodily tissue; widespread and severe: *massive gangrene.* **6.** *Physics.* Having mass: *a massive particle.* **7.** *Geology.* Lacking obvious layering, banding, or foliation, or having very thick layers. Said of rock or rocks. **8.** *Mineralogy.* Lacking externally observable crystalline form. —See Synonyms at **heavy.** [Middle English, from Old French *massif*, from Vulgar Latin *massīceus* (unattested), from Latin *massa*, MASS (amount).] —**mas·sive·ly** *adv.* —**mas·sive·ness** *n.*

mass·less (máss-ləss, -liss) *adj.* Having no mass: *a massless particle.* —**mass·less·ness** *n.*

mass media *pl.n. Singular* **mass medium.** The means of communication, such as television, radio, or sometimes newspapers, that can reach large numbers of people over a widespread area, in a relatively short time.

mass noun *n.* A **noncountable** *(see)* noun. Compare **count noun.**

mass number *n.* The total number of neutrons and protons in an atomic nucleus. Also called "nucleon number". See **atomic number, atomic mass.**

mass production *n.* The manufacture of goods in large quantities, using assembly-line techniques. —**mass-pro·duce** (máss-prə-déwss || -doōss) *tr.v.* —**mass-pro·duced** *adj.*

mass ratio *n.* The mass of a rocket loaded with fuel at liftoff divided by the mass of the rocket without fuel.

mass spectrograph *n. Physics.* An instrument used to separate charged particles in a prepared beam by means of an electromagnetic field and to photograph the resulting distribution or spectrum of masses.

mass spectrometer *n.* An instrument used to separate charged particles in a prepared beam by means of an electromagnetic field according to their charge to mass ratio. An electrical detector moves across the beam, recording the relative amounts of the various types of ion present.

mass spectrum *n.* The record produced by a mass spectrometer or mass spectrograph, characteristic of the compound analysed.

mass·y (mássi) *adj.* **-ier, -iest.** *Archaic.* Massive; solid; having great mass or bulk. [Middle English, perhaps from Old French *massiz*, variant of *massif*, MASSIVE.] —**mass·i·ness** *n.*

mast¹ (maast || mast) *n.* **1.** A tall vertical spar, sometimes sectioned, that rises from the keel of a sailing vessel to support the sails and running rigging. **2.** Any tall, narrow pole or structure: *a radio mast.* —**before the mast.** Serving as an ordinary seaman. ~*tr.v.* **masted, masting, masts.** To fit out (a ship) with masts. [Middle English *maste*, Old English *mæst*.]

mast² *n.* The nuts of forest trees, such as beech and oak, accumulated on the ground, used especially as food for pigs. [Middle English *maste*, Old English *mæst*.]

mas·ta·ba, mas·ta·bah (mástəbə) *n.* An ancient Egyptian tomb with a rectangular base and sloping sides. [Arabic *maṣṭabah*, stone bench.]

mast cell *n.* A cell present in connective tissue that releases histamine and other chemicals during inflammatory conditions. [Partial translation of German *Mastzelle* : *Mast*, food MAST (referring to the cell's appearance) + *Zelle*, CELL.]

mas·tec·to·my (mast-éktəmi) *n., pl.* **-mies.** Surgical removal of a breast, usually as a treatment for cancer. [MAST(O)- + -ECTOMY.]

mas·ter (maˊastər || mástər) *n.* **1.** A man having control over the action of another or others. **2.** The captain of a merchant ship. Also called "master mariner". **3.** An employer. **4.** The owner of a slave or an animal. **5.** The male head of a household: *Who is the master of the house?* **6. a.** One who has complete mastery over something requiring skill, such as the playing of a game or a musical instrument: *a master of the backhand pass.* **b.** One who has the ability to control or deal with something: *master of his emotions; master of the situation.* **7.** One who defeats another; a victor. **8.** A male teacher; a schoolmaster. **9. a.** A person whose teachings or doctrines are accepted by followers. **b.** *Capital* **M.** Jesus. Preceded by *our* or *the.* **10.** A person holding a master's degree such as a Master of Arts or Master of Science. **11.** A skilled craftsman, especially one qualified to teach apprentices. Also used adjectivally: *a master engraver.* **12.** An **old master** *(see).* **13.** A former title for a naval officer just below a lieutenant and in charge of navigation on a warship. **14.** The title of the head or presiding officer of certain societies, clubs, orders, university colleges, or other institutions. **15.** *Chiefly British.* The title of any of various law court officers, such as the chief clerks in Chancery. **16.** A master of foxhounds. **17.** *Capital* **M.** A title prefixed to the name of a boy or youth not considered old enough to be addressed as Mr. **18.** An **International Master** *(see).* **19. a.** An original from which copies can be made. Also called "master copy". **b.** The machine playing a video-tape master from which **slave** *(see)* machines can copy. ~*adj.* **1.** Of, pertaining to, or characteristic of a master. **2.** Chief; principal: *the master bedroom.* **3.** Highly skilled, masterful: *a master thief.* **4.** Being a part of a mechanism that controls all other parts: *a master switch.* **5.** Being an original from which copies are made. ~*tr.v.* **mastered, -tering, -ters. 1.** To make oneself a master of (an art, craft, or science). **2.** To overcome or defeat: *mastered the tyranny of gambling.* **3.** To reduce to subjugation; break or tame (a person or animal). [Middle English, from Old English *mægister*, *magister* and Old French *maistre*, both from Latin *magister*.] —**mas·ter·dom** *n.* —**mas·ter·hood** *n.* —**mas·ter·ship** *n.*

mas·ter-at-arms (maˊastər-ət-ármz || mástər-) *n., pl.* **masters-at-arms.** A naval petty officer assigned to maintain discipline.

master cylinder *n.* A large cylinder in a hydraulic system, in which a fluid is compressed by a piston so that the compressed fluid will operate the pistons in smaller slave cylinders.

mas·ter·ful (maˊastər-fˊl || mástər-) *adj.* **1.** Revealing an inclination to play the master; imperious; domineering. **2.** Revealing mastery; expert; skilful: *a masterful rendition of Othello.* See Usage note below. —**mas·ter·ful·ly** *adv.* —**mas·ter·ful·ness** *n.*

Usage: Masterful generally means "domineering or powerful"; *masterly* means "showing the knowledge or skill of a master". Thus one would expect *a masterful woman* but *a masterly argument.* Occasionally, *masterful* is used in contexts where *masterly* would normally be expected *(masterful Spanish, a masterful speech),* but this use has been criticised and is best avoided.

master key *n.* A key that opens several locks which each usually have different keys. Also called "passkey".

mas·ter·ly (maˊastər-li || mástər-) *adj.* Like a master; indicating the knowledge or skill of a master. See Usage note at **masterful.** ~*adv.* With the skill of a master. —**mas·ter·li·ness** *n.*

master mason *n.* **1.** An expert mason. **2.** *Capital* **M,** capital **M.** One who has achieved the third degree of Freemasonry.

mas·ter·mind (maˊastər-mīnd || mástər-) *n.* **1.** A highly intelligent person. **2.** Such a person who plans and directs a project. ~*tr.v.* **masterminded, -minding, -minds.** To direct, plan, or supervise (a project, often one of a criminal nature).

Master of Arts *n. Abbr.* **M.A. 1.** A degree granted by a university or other institution of higher education, normally to a person who has completed at least one year of postgraduate study, or at Scottish universities to a person completing an undergraduate course, especially in nonscientific subjects. **2.** A person holding such a degree. Compare **Bachelor of Arts, Doctor of Philosophy.**

master of ceremonies *n. Abbr.* **M.C. 1.** A person who acts as host at a formal event, making the welcoming speech and introducing other speakers. **2.** A performer who acts as the host of a variety show; a compere. Also called "emcee".

master of foxhounds *n. Abbr.* **M.F.H.** The chief officer of a hunt, who is responsible for the hounds and for organising the hunting programme. Also called "master".

Master of Science *n. Abbr.* **M.Sc. 1.** A degree granted by a university or other institution of higher education to a person who has completed at least one year of postgraduate study in the sciences. **2.** A person holding such a degree. Compare **Bachelor of Science, Doctor of Philosophy.**

Master of the Horse *n.* An officer of the British royal household, ranking below the Lord Chamberlain and the Lord Steward, whose main duty is to attend the sovereign on State occasions.

Master of the Rolls *n.* One who keeps the roll of solicitors in England and Wales and is one of the judges of the Court of Appeal, Keeper of the Records at the Public Records Office, and President of the Civil Division of the Court of Appeal.

mas·ter·piece (maˊastər-peess || mástər-) *n.* **1. a.** An outstanding work of art or craft. **b.** An artist's greatest work: *"Paradise Lost" was Milton's masterpiece.* **2.** Any superlative achievement: *a masterpiece of public speaking.* [Probably translation of Dutch *meesterstuk* or German *Meisterstück*, the piece of work presented to a guild by a craftsman for admission to the rank of master.]

master race *n. Sometimes capital* **M,** *capital* **R.** A people who consider themselves endowed with the right to dominate and exploit other supposedly inferior peoples; especially, the German nation viewed as such a master race in the ideology of German imperialism (about 1890–1945). Also called "Herrenvolk".

master sergeant *n. Abbr.* **MSgt, M. Sgt.** A noncommissioned officer of the next to highest rating in the U.S. Army, Air Force, and Marine Corps.

mas·ter·sing·er (maˊastər-sing-ər || mástər-) *n.* A **Meistersinger** *(see).*

mas·ter·stroke (maˊastər-strōk || mástər-) *n.* A masterly achievement or manoeuvre: *a masterstroke of statesmanship.*

mas·ter·work (maˊastər-wurk || mástər-) *n.* A masterpiece.

mas·ter·y (maˊastəri || mástəri) *n., pl.* **-ies. 1.** Possession of consummate skill: *displayed mastery in handling the situation.* **2.** The state or condition of having power or control: *mastery of the seas.* **3.** Full command of some subject of study: *a poet's mastery of the language.*

mast·head (maˊast-hed || mást-) *n.* **1.** The top of a ship's mast. **2.** The listing in a newspaper, magazine, or other publication of information about its staff and operation.

mas·tic (mástik) *n.* **1.** The aromatic resin of the mastic tree, used in varnishes and lacquers and as an astringent. **2.** A pastelike cement, especially one made with powdered lime or brick and tar. [Middle English *mastyk*, from Old French *mastic*, from Late Latin *mastichum*, variant of *mastichē*, from Greek *mastikhē*, mastic, "chewing gum", from *mastikhān*, to grind the teeth.]

mas·ti·cate (másti-kayt) *tr.v.* **-cated, -cating, -cates. 1.** To chew. **2.** To grind and knead. [Late Latin *masticāre*, from Greek *mastikhān*, to grind the teeth.] —**mas·ti·ca·tion** (-káysh'n) *n.* —**mas·ti·ca·tor** (-kaytər) *n.*

mas·ti·ca·to·ry (másti-kə-tri, -təri, -káytəri) *adj.* **1.** Of, pertaining to, or used in mastication. **2.** Being adapted for chewing. ~*n., pl.* **masticatories.** A substance chewed to increase salivation.

mastic tree *n.* A small evergreen tree, *Pistacia lentiscus,* of the Mediterranean region, that yields mastic. Also called "lentisk".

mas·tiff (mástif, maˊastif) *n.* A large dog of an ancient breed, probably originating in Asia, having a short fawn-coloured coat. [Middle English *mastif*, from Old French *mastin*, from Vulgar Latin *mānsuētīnus* (unattested), "tame", from Latin *mānsuētus*, tamed, "accustomed to the hand" : *manus*, hand + *suēscere*, to accustom.]

mastiff bat *n.* Any of various bats of the family Molossidae, found in the tropics, having narrow wings and brown, grey, or black fur. [So called because of its apparently doglike ears.]

mas·ti·goph·o·ran (másti-góffərən) *n.* Any member of the class Mastigophora, which includes protozoans with one or more flagella. [New Latin *Mastigophora*, "whip bearers" : Greek *mastix*† (stem *mastig-*), whip, lash + -*phora*, -PHORE.] —**mas·ti·goph·o·ran** *adj.*

mas·ti·tis (mass-tí-tiss) *n.* Inflammation of the breast or udder. [MAST(O)- + -ITIS.]

masto-, mast- *comb. form.* Indicates the breast or protuberances resembling a breast or nipple; for example, **mastitis, mastodon.** [New Latin, from Greek *mastos*†, breast.]

mas·to·don (másta-don, -dən) *n.* Any of several extinct mammals of the genus *Mammut* (sometimes called *Mastodon*), resembling the elephant. [New Latin, "breast-tooth" : MAST(O)- + -ODON; from the nipple-shaped protuberances on the teeth.] —**mas·to·don·tic** (-dóntik) *adj.*

mas·toid (mástoyd) *n.* The mastoid process. ~*adj.* Pertaining to the mastoid process. [New Latin *mastoides*, "breast-shaped" : MAST(O)- + -OID.]

mas·toid·ec·to·my (mástoyd-éktəmi) *n., pl.* -mies. *Surgery.* Removal of part or all of the mastoid process.

mas·toid·i·tis (mástoyd-í-tiss) *n. Pathology.* Inflammation of part or all of the mastoid process.

mastoid process *n. Anatomy.* The nipple-shaped rear portion of the temporal bone on each side of the head behind the ear in humans and many other vertebrates. Also called "mastoid", "mastoid bone".

mas·tur·bate (mástər-bayt, maʹastər-) *v.* -bated, -bating, -bates. —*intr.* To perform an act of masturbation. —*tr.* To perform an act of masturbation on. [Latin *masturbārī*†.]

mas·tur·ba·tion (mástər-báysh'n, maʹastər-) *n.* 1. Excitation of the genital organs, especially one's own, and usually to orgasm, by means other than sexual intercourse. 2. Loosely, any act of blatant self-indulgence. Used derogatorily: *He regards his fantasising as poetry, but it's just mental masturbation.* —**mas·tur·ba·tion·al, mas·tur·ba·to·ry** (-baytəri, -báytəri) *adj.* —**mas·tur·ba·tor** (-baytər) *n.*

ma·su·ri·um (mə-séwri-əm, -zéwr-, -sóor-, -zóor-) *n.* A chemical element, **technetium** (*see*). Not in current technical usage. [New Latin, after *Masuria*, region of north-east Poland (formerly East Prussia), where it was discovered.]

mat¹ (mat) *n.* 1. A flat piece of fabric or other material used for wiping one's shoes or feet, or as a floor covering. 2. A small, flat piece of decorated material, such as cloth or cork, placed under a lamp, dish of food, or other object, to protect a surface or for ornament. 3. A thick floor pad to protect athletes, as in wrestling or gymnastics. 4. Any densely woven or thickly tangled mass: *a mat of hair.* 5. A heavy, woven net of rope or wire cable placed over a blasting site to keep debris from scattering. ~*v.* matted, matting, mats. —*tr.* 1. To cover, protect, or decorate with a mat or mats. 2. To interweave into or cover with a thick mass: *A heavy growth of vines matted the tree.* —*intr.* To be interwoven into a thick mass; become entangled. [Middle English, Old English *matt(e)*, from Late Latin *matta*†, mat.]

mat² *n.* 1. A decorative border of cardboard or similar material placed around a picture to serve as a frame or act as a contrast between the picture and the frame. 2. Variant of **matt.** ~*v.* matted, matting, mats. 1. To put a mat around (a picture). 2. Variant of **matt.** ~*adj.* Variant of **matt.** [French, Old French, "dead". See **checkmate.**]

mat³ *n. Printing.* A matrix (*see*).

mat. matinee.

Mat·a·be·le (máttə-béeli, -bélli) *n., pl.* -les or collectively **Matabele.** 1. An Ndebele (*see*). 2. A language, **Ndebele** (*see*). [Sotho, from *letebele*, "the disappearing ones"; so called because the warriors of this people would sink down (*teba*) behind their huge shields during battle.]

Mat·a·be·le·land (máttə-béeli-land, -bélli-). Region of southwest Zimbabwe. Inhabited by the Ndebele people (or Matabele), it has important gold deposits. Bulawayo is the chief town.

mat·a·dor (máttə-dawr) *n.* 1. A bullfighter who performs the **faena** (*see*) and kills the bull. 2. One of the highest trumps in certain card games, such as ombre. [Spanish, "killer", from *matar*, to kill, from Latin *mactāre*, to sacrifice, from *mactus*, sacred.]

Ma·ta Ha·ri (maʹatə haʹari), born Margaretha Geertruida Zelle; also known as Lady MacLeod (1876–1917). Dutch spy. Married to a Dutch army officer, she became a professional "oriental" dancer in Paris (1905) and adopted her stage name. During World War I she worked for both the French and the Germans and was finally shot by the French for espionage.

Mat·a·pan, Cape (máttə-pan, -pán). *Greek* **Ak·ra Taí·na·ron** (áckra ténnə-ron). The southernmost tip of the Greek mainland. It gave its name to a sea battle (1941), in which an Italian fleet was heavily defeated by the British.

match¹ (mach) *n.* 1. a. A person or thing that is exactly like another; a counterpart. b. A person or thing that is similar to another in some specified quality: *He is John's match for bravery.* 2. a. A person or thing that closely resembles or harmonises with another.

b. A pair made up of two things or persons that resemble or harmonise with each other: *The colours were a close match.* 3. A person or thing equal in qualities or able to compete with another of the same class or type: *The boxer had met his match.* 4. a. An organised athletic contest or game in which individuals or teams oppose and compete with each other: *a boxing match; a football match.* b. A tennis contest decided on the basis of victory in a certain number of sets, usually two out of three or three out of five. 5. a. A marriage or an arrangement of marriage: *Her parents tried to arrange a match for her.* b. A person viewed as a prospective marriage partner. ~*v.* matched, matching, matches. —*tr.* 1. a. To be exactly like; correspond exactly to. b. To be equal or comparable to (another) with respect to some specified quality: *The new model doesn't match the old one for speed.* c. To equal; rival: *beauty that could never be matched.* 2. To resemble or harmonise with: *The coat matches the dress.* 3. To adapt or suit so that a balanced or harmonious result is achieved; cause to correspond: *matching skill with speed.* 4. To fit together or cause to fit together. 5. To join or give in marriage; find a suitable match for. 6. To place in opposition or competition with; pit: *The only way to ensure peace is to match strength with strength.* 7. To provide with an adversary or competitor, especially one of equivalent worth: *well-matched contestants.* 8. To couple (electric circuits) by means of a transformer. —*intr.* To be a close counterpart; correspond. [Middle English *macche*, match, mate, Old English *gemæcca*, mate.] —**match·a·ble** *adj.* —**match·er** *n.*

match² *n.* 1. A narrow strip of wood, cardboard, or wax coated on one end with a compound that ignites easily by friction. See **safety match.** 2. An easily ignited cord or wick, formerly used for detonating powder charges or firing cannons and muzzle-loading firearms. [Middle English *macche, mecche*, lamp wick, candle, from Old French *meiche*, from Medieval Latin *myxa*, lamp wick, from Latin, nozzle of a lamp.]

match·board (mách-bawrd ‖ -bórd) *n.* A board cut with a tongue on one side and a matching groove on the other to fit with other boards of identical cut.

match·book (mách-book ‖ -book) *n.* A small folded piece of card containing rows of detachable matches, and a rough strip for striking them against.

match·box (mách-boks) *n.* A box for holding matches, edged on one or two sides with a strip of rough card or treated paper for striking the matches against.

matchet. Variant of **machete.**

match·less (mách-ləss, -liss) *adj.* Having no match or equal; peerless; unsurpassed: *matchless beauty.* —**match·less·ly** *adv.* —**match·less·ness** *n.*

match·lock (mách-lok) *n.* 1. A gunlock in which powder is ignited by a match. 2. A musket having such a gunlock.

match·mak·er (mách-maykər) *n.* One who attempts to arrange marriages by bringing unmarried people together, either for personal satisfaction or, in some societies, as a profession. —**match·mak·ing** *n. & adj.*

match·mark (mách-maark) *n.* Any of several marks made on the mating components of a machine or engine to ensure that the components are assembled in the correct relative positions. ~*tr.v.* -marked, -marking, -marks. To stamp such marks on (components).

match play *n.* The form of competition in golf in which the basis of the score is the number of holes won by each side rather than the number of strokes taken. Compare **medal play.**

match point *n.* The final point needed to win certain sports games, such as tennis or squash.

match·wood (mách-wood) *n.* 1. Wood in small pieces or splinters, suitable especially for making matches. 2. Splinters.

mate¹ (mayt) *n.* 1. a. Either of a conjugal pair of animals or birds. b. Either of a pair of animals brought together for breeding. 2. A spouse. 3. A person with whom one is in close association. Often used in combination: *flatmate; teammate.* 4. Either of a matched pair: *the mate to this glove.* 5. Chiefly British. a. Slang. A friend. b. An informal form of address used to men. 6. A deck officer on a merchant ship ranking below the master. 7. In some professions, an assistant: *a plumber's mate.* ~*v.* mated, mating, mates. —*tr.* 1. To pair (animals) for breeding. 2. To unite in marriage. 3. To join closely; pair; couple. 4. To connect (gear wheels, machine parts, or the like) together so that parts interlock. —*intr.* 1. To pair for reproduction; breed. 2. To become mated; join together. 3. To become joined in marriage. 4. To fit or interlock exactly. Used of gears, machine parts, and the like. [Middle English, from Middle Low German *mate, gemate*, companion.]

mate² *n.* In chess, a **checkmate** (*see*). ~*v.* mated, mating, mates. —*tr.* To checkmate. —*intr.* To achieve a checkmate: *White mated in 20 moves.* [Middle English *mat*, from Old French, short for *eschec mat*, CHECKMATE.]

ma·té (máttay, maʹa-tay) *n.* 1. An evergreen tree, *Ilex paraguayensis*, of South America, where it is widely cultivated. 2. A mildly stimulant beverage, popular in South America, made from the dried leaves of this tree. Also called "Paraguay tea", "yerba maté". [American Spanish *maté*, alteration (influenced by *té*, tea) of *mate* (with initial stress), from Quechua.]

mate·lot (mát-lō) *n. Chiefly British Slang.* A sailor. [French.]

mat·e·lote (máttə-lōt ‖ *U.S. also* -lŏt) *n.* 1. A wine sauce for fish. 2. Fish stewed in such a sauce. [French (*sauce*) *matelote*, "sailor (sauce)".]

Matisse

"A PAINTING ON A WALL SHOULD BE LIKE A BOUQUET OF FLOWERS"
The artist whose use of colour and simple shapes influenced the course of 20th-century art

Matisse's use of pure colour and simple shapes, and his exquisite sense of design, made him a dominant influence on 20th-century art. He believed that colour should parallel light in nature. A painting on a wall, he said, should be like a bouquet of flowers in an interior.

With Andre Derain he led the Fauvist movement (1904–8), from whose bold use of colours he developed his characteristic simplified style in which figures, objects, and background all form part of a flat, brightly coloured, decorative pattern. In his *Notes of a Painter* (1908), he wrote that he was seeking an art of balance, purity, and serenity "devoid of troubling or depressing subject matter".

Matisse's style evolved from the contrast of patterns in *Odalisque with Raised Hand* (1920), through simplified interiors with plants and women, to its final extreme of large coloured-paper collage works, the most notable of which are *Jazz: Cavalier and Clown* (1947), and *The Snail* (1953).

Among his other works are *Open Window, Collioure* (Fauvist period, 1905), *Bonheur de Vivre* (1906), *Bathers with a Turtle* (1908), *The Dance* (1909), and the *Red Room* (1948). In 1949 he designed the stained-glass windows and murals for the Dominican Chapel of the Rosary in Vence, a work which he considered to be the summation of his career as an artist. But he will be chiefly remembered for his brilliant use of colour, and line drawings of the human figure, which he perfected by shifting the emphasis from powerful muscles to the body's pure outlines.

THE DANCE I *In these murals (1930–32), which are now in the Museum of Modern Art in Paris, Henri Matisse refined his art until he had reduced it to its simplest and purest state.*

---

ma·ter (máytər) *n. British Slang.* Mother. Now used only humorously. [Latin *māter.*]

ma·ter·fa·mil·i·as (máytər-fə-mílli-ass, -əss) *n., pl.* **matresfamilias** (máytreez-). The mother of a family. [Latin : *māter,* mother + *familias,* archaic genitive of *familia,* FAMILY.]

ma·te·ri·al (mə-téer-i-əl) *n.* 1. The substance or substances out of which a thing is or may be constructed: *raw material; building material.* 2. The basic elements, such as factual data, plans, and ideas, to be refined and made or incorporated into a finished effort: *material for a novel.* 3. *Plural.* Tools or apparatus for the performance of a given task: *writing materials.* 4. Fabric or cloth. 5. A person having sufficient qualities for a specified job or level of achievement: *a competent athlete, but not world record material.*
~adj. 1. Composed of or pertaining to physical substances; relating to matter; corporeal. 2. Of, pertaining to, or affecting the enjoyment of physical well-being: *material comfort.* 3. Of or concerned with the physical as distinct from the intellectual or spiritual. 4. Of substantial or crucial importance: *a material part of the plan.* 5. *Law.* Relevant to or having significant bearing upon the case: *a material witness.* 6. *Philosophy.* Of or pertaining to the matter of reasoning, rather than the form. —See Synonyms at **relevant.** [Middle English, from Old French *materiel,* from Late Latin *māteriālis,* from *māteria,* matter.] —**ma·te·ri·al·ness** *n.*

ma·te·ri·al·ise, ma·te·ri·al·ize (mə-téer-i-əl-īz) *v.* **-ised, -ising, -ises.** —*tr.* 1. To invest with material or physical characteristics; cause to become real or actual: *By building the house, he materialised his dream.* 2. To cause to adopt materialistic values. —*intr.* 1. To assume material or effective form: *The promised reinforcements did not materialise.* 2. To take form or shape. 3. To take bodily form or shape. Used of a ghost, spirit, or the like. —**ma·te·ri·al·i·sa·tion** (-ī-záysh'n || *U.S.* -i-) *n.* —**ma·te·ri·al·is·er** *n.*
Usage: The intransitive use of this verb to mean "happen" or "occur" (as in *Nothing has yet materialised*) still attracts criticism as being unnecessarily complicated. However, it is frequently used in all styles of spoken and written English. See **transpire.**

ma·te·ri·al·ism (mə-téer-i-əl-iz'm) *n.* 1. *Philosophy.* **a.** The theory or doctrine that physical matter in its movements and modifications is the only reality and that everything in the universe, including thought, feeling, mind, and will, can be explained in terms of physical laws. Compare **idealism. b.** The theory or doctrine that physical well-being constitutes the greatest good and highest value in life. 2. An excessive devotion to worldly rather than spiritual concerns, and especially to the acquisition of material possessions. —**ma·te·ri·al·ist** *adj. & n.* —**ma·te·ri·al·is·tic** (-ístik) *adj.* —**ma·te·ri·al·is·ti·cal·ly** *adv.*

ma·te·ri·al·i·ty (mə-téer-i-ál-əti) *n., pl.* **-ties.** 1. The state or quality of being material. 2. Matter; physical substance.

ma·te·ri·al·ly (mə-téer-i-əli) *adv.* 1. *Philosophy.* With regard to matter as distinguished from form. 2. To a significant extent or degree; importantly. 3. With regard to the physical world.

ma·te·ri·a med·i·ca (mə-téer-i-ə méddikə) *n. Medicine.* 1. The study of medicinal drugs and their sources, preparation, and use. 2. A substance used in preparing medicinal drugs or as a medicine. [Latin, "medical material".]

ma·te·ri·el, ma·té·ri·el (mə-téer-i-él, ma-) *n.* 1. The equipment, apparatus, and supplies, such as guns and ammunition, of a military force. 2. The equipment, apparatus, and supplies of any organisation. [French, from *matériel,* MATERIAL (adjective).]

ma·ter·nal (mə-térn'l) *adj.* 1. Pertaining to or characteristic of a mother or motherhood; motherly: *maternal instinct.* 2. Received or inherited from one's mother: *a maternal trait.* 3. Related through one's mother: *my maternal uncle.* [Middle English, from Old French *maternel,* from Latin *māternus,* from *māter,* mother.] —**ma·ter·nal·ly** *adv.*

ma·ter·ni·ty (mə-térnəti) *n.* 1. The state of being a mother; motherhood. 2. The feelings or characteristics associated with being a mother; motherliness.
~adj. Associated with or adapted for pregnancy and childbirth: *a maternity dress.* [French *maternité,* from Medieval Latin *māternitās* (stem *māternitāt-*), from *māternus,* MATERNAL.]

ma·tey (máyti) *adj. Chiefly British Informal.* Sociable; friendly. See Synonyms at **familiar.** —**ma·tey·ness, ma·ti·ness** *n.* —**ma·ti·ly** *adv.*

math (math) *n. U.S.* Mathematics.

math·e·mat·i·cal (máthə-máttik'l, máth-, máthi-, math-) *adj.* Also **math·e·mat·ic** (-máttik). 1. Of or pertaining to mathematics. 2. Precise; rigorous; exact. [Old French *mathematique,* from Latin *mathēmaticus,* from Greek *mathēmatikos,* from *mathēma,* science, from *manthanein* (stem *math-*), to learn.] —**math·e·mat·i·cal·ly** *adv.*

mathematical induction *n.* A principle and method of proof in mathematics. See **induction.**

mathematical logic *n.* **Symbolic logic** (see).

math·e·ma·ti·cian (máthə-mə-tísh'n, máth-, máthi-) *n.* A person skilled or learned in mathematics.

math·e·mat·ics (máthə-máttiks, máth-, máthi-, math-) *n.* 1. *Used with a singular verb.* The study of number, form, arrangement, and associated relationships, using rigorously defined literal, numerical, and operational symbols. 2. *Used with a plural verb.* The application of mathematics to a calculation or problem. [Probably from French *(les) mathématiques,* from Latin *mathēmatica* (neuter plural), from Greek *(ta) mathēmatika.* See **mathematical.**]
Usage: In the sense of the academic subject, *mathematics* takes a singular verb: *Mathematics is an enormous field.* In the sense of "performing calculations", it takes a plural verb (*Your mathematics are wrong*). In American English, the contraction is *math,* not *maths: He failed math.*

maths (maths) *n.* Mathematics.

Ma·thu·ra (múttoor-ə, mu-thoor-ə). Also **Mut·tra** (múttrə). City in Uttar Pradesh, northern India. Lying on the river Jumna, it is the region's commercial centre, and, as the traditional birthplace of Krishna, a place of pilgrimage for Hindus. It was the centre of the Mathura school of Indian art (second to fifth century A.D.).

Mathurai. See **Madurai.**

ma·til·da (mə-tíldə) *n. Australian Informal.* A bushman's pack or bundle. [From *Matilda,* woman's name.]

Ma·til·da (mə-tíldə), also known as the Empress Maud (1102–67). Queen of England (1141–53). The daughter of Henry I, she married Emperor Henry V (1114) and, after his death, Geoffrey of Anjou (1128), by whom she bore Henry II. When her cousin Stephen was elected king, she waged civil war against him and was crowned queen in 1141, establishing the succession of her son after Stephen by the Treaty of Wallingford (1153).

mat·in (máttin || mátt'n) *adj.* Also **mat·in·al** (-'l). **1.** Of or pertaining to matins. **2.** *Literary.* Of or pertaining to the early morning. [From MATINS.]

mat·i·née, matinee (máttin-ay, -áy || mátt'n-) *n. Abbr.* **mat.** A concert, theatrical performance, or showing of a film given in the daytime, usually in the afternoon. [French *matinée,* "morning", early performance, from Old French *matinee,* from *matin,* morning, from Latin *(tempus) mātūtīnum,* morning (time), from *mātūtīnus,* of the morning, from *Mātūta,* goddess of dawn.]

matinée jacket *n.* A baby's short coat, usually knitted. Also called "matinée coat".

mat·ins (máttinz || mátt'nz) *n. Used with a singular or plural verb.* Also *chiefly British* **mat·tins. 1.** In the Roman Catholic Church, the office that, together with lauds, constitutes the first of the seven **canonical hours** *(see).* **2.** In the Anglican Church, **Morning Prayer** *(see).* **3.** *Poetic.* The morning song of a bird. [Middle English *matines,* from Old French, from Medieval Latin *(vigiliae) mātūtīnae,* morning (watches, vigils). See **matinée.**]

Ma·tisse (ma-téess), **Henri** (1869–1954). French painter and sculptor. Having studied under Gustave Moreau, he led the artistic group Les Fauves from 1905, with colourful, strongly patterned, and often distorted portraits, still lifes and nudes. He was also influenced by impressionist, cubist, and Islamic art. His works include *The Pink Nude* and *Woman With the Hat.*

Ma·to Gros·so (máttō grṓssō; *Portuguese* maàtōō grṓssōō). A state in west central Brazil, comprising the plateau of Mato Grosso. Its name means "thick forest", but this is largely confined to its great river valleys, with extensive wooded savannas between. The state is being opened up, with new roads, development of a beef industry and exploitation of its rich mineral deposits. Cuiabá is the capital.

mat·rass, mat·trass (máttrəss) *n.* A glass vessel with a long neck, formerly used in chemistry for distilling. [French *matras*†.]

mat·res·fa·mil·i·as. Plural of **materfamilias.**

matri– *comb. form.* Indicates mother; for example, **matriclinous.** [Latin *māter,* mother.]

ma·tri·arch (máytri-aark) *n.* **1.** A woman who rules a family, clan, or tribe. **2.** A woman who dominates any group or activity. [MATRI- + -ARCH.] **—ma·tri·ar·chal** (-árk'l), **ma·tri·ar·chic** (-árkik) *adj.* **—ma·tri·ar·chal·ism** *n.*

ma·tri·ar·chate (máytri-aar-kət, -kit, -kayt) *n.* **1.** A matriarchy. **2.** A hypothetical stage in the evolution of primitive society in which authority is held by matriarchs.

ma·tri·ar·chy (máytri-aarki) *n., pl.* **-chies.** A social system in which women are dominant and descent is traced through the mother of the family.

ma·tric (mə-trík) *n.* Matriculation.

mat·ri·cide (máytri-sīd || máttri-) *n.* **1.** The act of killing one's mother. **2.** One who kills his mother. [Latin *mātricīda* (person), and *mātricīdium* (act) : MATRI- + -CIDE.] **—mat·ri·ci·dal** (-sīd'l) *adj.*

mat·ri·cli·nous (máttri-klīnəss, máytri-) *adj.* Having predominantly maternal hereditary traits. Said of plants and animals. Compare **patriclinous.** [MATRI- + *-clinous,* from Greek *-klinēs,* "leaning", from *klinein,* to lean.]

ma·tric·u·lant (mə-tríckew-lənt) *n.* A person who matriculates or is a candidate for matriculation.

ma·tric·u·late (mə-tríckew-layt) *v.* **-lated, -lating, -lates.** *—tr.* To admit formally to membership of a college, university, or the like. *—intr.* To be so admitted.

~n. One who has matriculated. [Medieval Latin *mātriculāre,* to enrol, from *mātricula,* list, roll, from *mātrīx,* list, originally, womb, source. See **matrix.**]

ma·tric·u·la·tion (mə-tríckew-láysh'n) *n.* **1.** The act or process of matriculating. **2.** The qualification acquired by matriculating. **3.** In South Africa, the final set of high-school examinations, the successful completion of which entitles the candidate to undertake university studies. Also called "matric".

mat·ri·lin·e·al (máttri-línni-əl, máytri-) *adj.* Pertaining to, based upon, or tracing ancestral descent through the maternal line rather than through the paternal. Compare **patrilineal.**

mat·ri·lo·cal (máttri-lṓk'l, máytri-) *adj.* Designating or following a system of marriage in primitive societies, whereby the couple go to live in the home territory of the wife's kin group or clan. Compare **patrilocal. —mat·ri·lo·cal·ly** *adv.*

mat·ri·mo·ny (máttri-məni || *U.S.* -mōni) *n., pl.* **-nies. 1.** The state of being married. **2.** The sacrament or rite of marriage. **3. a.** A card game in which the combination of a king and queen is needed to win. **b.** Such a winning combination. —See Synonyms at **marriage.** [Middle English, from Anglo-French *matrimonie,* from Latin *mātrimōnium,* marriage, "motherhood" : MATRI- + *-mōnium,* abstract noun suffix.] **—mat·ri·mo·ni·al** (-mṓni-əl, -mṓn-yəl) *adj.* **—mat·ri·mo·ni·al·ly** *adv.*

ma·trix (máytriks; *for sense 10 also* máttriks) *n., pl.* **matrices** (máytri-seez, máttri-) or **-trixes. 1.** The environment or surrounding substance within which something originates, develops, or is contained: *contented children nurtured in the matrix of parental love.* **2.** The womb. No longer in technical usage. **3.** *Anatomy.* **a.** The formative cells of a tooth, fingernail, or toenail. **b.** The substance between the cells of animal or plant tissue. **4.** *Geology.* The fine-grained rock material in which a fossil or crystal is embedded. **5.** A mould or die. **6.** The principal metal in an alloy, such as the iron in steel. **7.** A binding substance, such as cement in concrete. **8.** *Mathematics.* A rectangular array of numerical or algebraic quantities treated as an algebraic entity. **9.** The network of intersections between input and output leads in a computer, functioning as an encoder or decoder. **10.** *Printing.* **a.** A metal plate used for casting type faces. **b.** A mould used in stereotyping and designed to receive positive impressions of type or illustrations from which metal plates can be cast. In this sense, also called "mat". [Latin *mātrix,* womb, originally, pregnant animal, from *māter,* mother.]

matrix mechanics *n. Used with a singular verb. Physics.* A formulation of quantum mechanics developed by Heisenberg using matrix algebra to determine the behaviour of physical systems, mathematically equivalent to **wave mechanics** *(see).* Physical quantities are represented by operators in matrix element form.

ma·tron (máytrən) *n.* **1.** A married woman; especially, a mother of mature age with established dignity and social position. **2.** A woman who supervises the medical and domestic arrangements of a boarding school or other institution. **3.** A woman in charge of the nursing staff of a hospital. In this sense, now called "senior nursing officer". [Middle English, from Old French *matrone,* from Latin *mātrōna,* matron, wife, from *māter,* mother.] **—ma·tron·al** (-'l, mə-trṓn'l) *adj.* **—ma·tron·li·ness** *n.* **—ma·tron·ly** *adj. & adv.*

matron of honour *n., pl.* **matrons of honour** *n.* A married woman serving as chief attendant of the bride at a wedding. Compare **bridesmaid, maid of honour.**

matronymic. Variant of **metronymic.**

matt, mat, matte (mat) *n.* A dull, often rough finish, as on glass, metal, or paper.

~tr.v. **matted, matting, matts.** To produce a dull finish on.

~adj. Having a dull surface; not shiny. [French *mat,* "dead". See **checkmate.**]

Matt. Matthew (New Testament).

matte[1] (mat) *n. Metallurgy.* A mixture of a metal with its oxides and sulphides, produced by smelting certain sulphide ores. Also called "regulus". [French, from dialectal *mate*†, a lump.]

matte[2]**.** Variant of **matt.**

mat·ted (máttid) *adj.* **1.** Covered with or made from mats. **2.** Tangled in a dense mass: *matted hair.* **—mat·ted·ly** *adv.*

mat·ter (máttər) *n.* **1. a.** That which occupies space, can be perceived by one or more senses, and constitutes any physical body or the universe as a whole; that which is corporeal as distinguished from that which is spiritual or intellectual. **b.** *Physics.* Any entity displaying gravitation and inertia when at rest as well as when in motion. **2.** A specified type of substance: *inorganic matter.* **3.** Discharge or waste from a living organism, such as pus or faeces. **4.** The actual substance of thought or expression; the theme of what is expressed as distinguished from the manner in which it is stated or conveyed. **5.** *Philosophy.* In Aristotelian and scholastic use, that which is in itself undifferentiated and formless and which, as the subject of change and development, receives form and becomes substance and experience. **6.** *Law.* **a.** That which must be proved or is the subject of litigation. **b.** Statements, allegations, or the like brought before the court. **7.** Something that is the subject of consideration or attention; a concern or affair, especially of a specified kind: *a personal matter; In matters of finance, his advice is usually reliable.* **8. a.** A circumstance tending to evoke a specified response: *a matter for regret.* **b.** Something largely dependent on or likely to be determined by a specified factor: *a matter of luck.* **c.** A situation presenting a choice that depends on the application of a specified faculty: *a matter of conscience; a matter of opinion.* **9.** A particular factor adversely affecting a person or thing; a trouble or difficulty. Preceded by *the: What's the matter with the car?* **10.** An indefinite or approximate quantity, amount, or extent: *a matter of a few hours.* **11.** Something that is printed or otherwise set down in writing: *reading matter.* **12.** *Printing.* **a.** Composed, or set, type. **b.** Material to be set in type. **—for that matter.** With regard to that: *For that matter, we didn't know when to come.* **—no matter.** Irrespective or regardless of: *No matter what the time is, come!*

~intr.v. **mattered, -tering, -ters. 1.** To be of importance: *It matters very much.* **2.** To suppurate. [Middle English *matere,* from Anglo-French, from Latin *māteria,* matter.]

Mat·ter·horn (máttər-hawrn). *French* **Mont Cer·vin** (sair-váɴ), *Italian* **Monte Cer·vino** (chair-véenō). Mountain (4 477 metres; 14,688 feet) in the Pennine Alps, on the Swiss-Italian border near Zermatt. Its distinctive pyramidal crest was first climbed (1865) by the Englishman Edward Whymper.

matter of course *n.* An expected, natural, or logical outcome. **—mat·ter-of-course** (máttər-əv-kórss || -kṓrss) *adj.*

matter of fact *n.* That which pertains to fact as opposed to opinion; especially, the establishing of the truth of certain alleged facts in the course of a judicial inquiry.

mat·ter-of-fact (máttər-əv-fákt) *adj.* Adhering to or solely concerned with facts; prosaic, unemotional, or unimaginative: *discussed her divorce in a very matter-of-fact way.* **—mat·ter-of-fact·ly** *adv.* **—mat·ter-of-fact·ness** *n.*

Mat·the·an (mə-thée-ən, ma-) *adj.* Of, pertaining to, or designating the Gospel of Saint Matthew. [MATTHE(W) + -AN.]

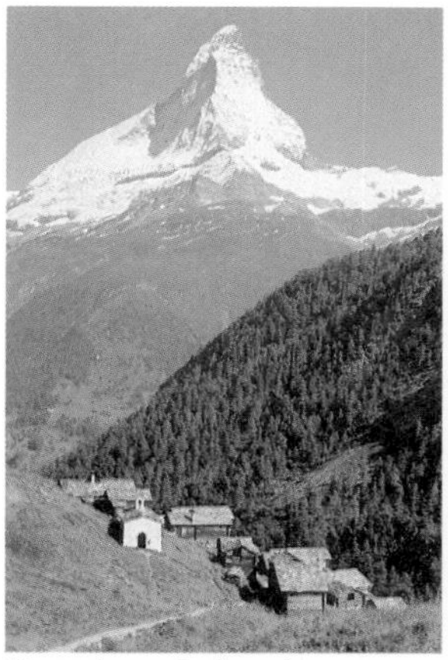

Matterhorn *Perhaps the most spectacular of the Alps, this pyramidal peak on the Swiss-Italian border was first climbed by the British explorer Edward Whymper in 1865.*

PRONUNCIATION KEY

a, trap; aa, father; ai, fair; ar, star; aw, lawn; ay, play; b, bb, stab; rubber; ch, church; ck, ticket; d, dd, dead; ladder; e, dress; ee, bee; er, defer; ew, few; ewr, pure; ə, about; ər, letter; f, ff, fife; differ; g, gg, giggle; h, hat; i, kit; ī, price; īr, fire; j, judge; k, kick; l, ll, let; 'l, needle; m, mm, man; n, nn, no; 'n, sudden; ng, thing; o, lot; ō, no; ōō, foot; ōō, shoe; oor, poor; ow, cow; owr, hour; oy, boy; p, pp, pepper; r, rr, red; s, ss, sauce; sh, ship; t, tt, totter; th, thick; th, this; smooth; u, cut; ur, turn; v, vv, valve; w, wet; y, yes; z, zz, zebra; zh, vision; pleasure

IN FOREIGN WORDS:

aɴ, oɴ, Saint-Saëns; hl, Llanelli; Hluhluwe; kh, loch; lough; Khaled

STRESS MARK:

ín-sīt, insight; in-sít, incite

Mat·thew (máthew) n. Abbr. **Matt.** A book of the New Testament, the first Gospel, attributed to Saint Matthew.

Matthew, Saint. One of the Apostles of Christ and traditionally the author of the first Gospel.

Matthew Paris (c. 1200–59). English chronicler. He was a monk in the Benedictine monastery at St. Albans. His major work was the *Chronica Majora*, a history of the world from the Creation to 1259.

Mat·thews (máthewz), **Sir Stanley** (1915–). English soccer-player. He played for Stoke City (1931–47, 1961–65) and Blackpool (1947–61) and 56 times for England. He was knighted in 1965.

Mat·thi·as (mə-thí-əss), **Saint.** One of the Apostles of Jesus, chosen by lot to take the place of Judas Iscariot. Acts 1:23–26.

mat·ting[1] (mátting) n. **1.** A coarsely woven fabric used for covering floors and similar purposes. **2.** Mat-making.

matting[2] n. **1.** A dull surface or finish. **2.** A border or mat used for framing a picture.

mattins. Chiefly British. Variant of **matins**.

mat·tock (máttək) n. A digging tool with a blade set at right angles to the handle and used with a downward motion. [Middle English *mattok*, Old English *mattuc*†.]

mat·tress (máttrəss, máttriss) n. **1.** A rectangular pad of heavy cloth enclosing soft material, such as foam rubber, and sometimes coiled springs, used as or on a bed. **2.** A closely woven mat of brush and poles used to protect an embankment, dyke, or dam from erosion. **3.** A raft or slab, made of concrete or metal, used as a foundation. **4.** A network of reinforcing rods or expanded metal forming the basis of reinforced concrete. [Middle English *materas*, from Old French, from Italian *materasso*, from Arabic *maṭraḥ*, place where something is thrown, from *ṭaraḥa*, to throw, fling.]

mat·u·rate (máttewr-ayt, máchər-) v. **-rated, -rating, -rates.** —intr. **1.** Archaic. To mature, ripen, or develop. **2.** To suppurate. —tr. To cause to suppurate. [Latin *mātūrāre*, to mature, from *mātūrus*, MATURE.] —**mat·u·ra·tive** (-ətiv, -aytiv) adj.

mat·u·ra·tion (máttewr-áysh'n) n. **1.** The process of becoming mature; development or ripening: *the maturation of the personality*. **2.** Biology. **a.** Formation of a sex cell, **gametogenesis** (see). **b.** The final differentiation processes in biological systems, such as the final ripening of a seed. **3.** Discharge of pus, **suppuration** (see).

ma·ture (mə-téwr, -choor ‖ -toor) adj. **-turer, -turest. 1. a.** Complete and finished in natural growth or development: *a mature cell*. **b.** Fully developed; ripe: *a mature cheese*. **c.** Fully established: *a mature garden*. **2. a.** Having reached a stage of intellectual and emotional development usually associated with adulthood: *mature for her age*. **b.** Characteristic of one who has reached such a stage. **3.** Worked out fully by the mind; carefully considered: *a mature piece of criticism*. **4.** Finance. At the limit of its time; payable; due: *a mature bond*. **5.** Geology. Designating a landscape in which hills and valleys predominate over flat areas as a result of erosion. ~v. **matured, -turing, -tures.** —tr. **1.** To bring to full development; ripen. **2.** To work out fully in the mind: *to mature one's views*. —intr. **1.** To evolve towards or attain full development: *Judgement matures with age*. **2.** Finance. To become due. Used of notes, bonds, or the like. [Middle English, from Latin *mātūrus*, timely.] —**ma·ture·ly** adv. —**ma·ture·ness** n.

mature student n. **1.** A college or university student who is above a specific age, usually 25, and is or has been financially self-supporting. **2.** Any student who is older than average.

ma·tur·i·ty (mə-téwr-əti, -choor- ‖ -toor-) n., pl. **-ties. 1.** The state or quality of being fully grown or fully developed. **2. a.** The time at which a note, bill, or bond is due. **b.** The state of being due, as of a note, bill, or bond. **3.** Geology. The state of being mature. [Middle English *maturite*, from Latin *mātūritās* (stem *mātūritāt-*), from *mātūrus*, MATURE.]

ma·tu·ti·nal (máttew-tín'l, mə-téwtin'l ‖ -toòtin'l) adj. Of, pertaining to, or occurring in the morning; early. [Late Latin *mātūtīnālis*, from Latin *mātūtīnus*, from *Mātūta*, goddess of dawn.] —**ma·tu·ti·nal·ly** adv.

mat·zo (mát-sō, mót-, -sə) n., pl. **-zoth** (-sōt, -sŏt) or **-zos** (-sōz, -səz) or **-zot** (-sŏt). A brittle, flat piece of unleavened bread, eaten especially during the Passover. [Yiddish *matse*, from Hebrew *maṣṣah*.]

maud (mawd) n. In Scotland, a grey woollen plaid, used as a shawl, rug, or the like. [18th century : origin obscure.]

maud·lin (máwdlin) adj. **1.** Effusively sentimental. **2.** Tearfully emotional, especially because of drunkenness. [From *Maudlin*, MARY MAGDALENE (who was depicted as a weeping penitent).] —**maud·lin·ly** adv.

Maugham (mawm), **(William) Somerset** (1874–1965). British novelist and dramatist. Born in Paris and trained as a doctor, he wrote such realistic novels as *Liza of Lambeth* (1897), *Of Human Bondage* (1915), and *Cakes and Ale* (1930). He was a popular dramatist too and is most famous of all perhaps for his short stories.

mau·gre (máwgər) prep. Archaic. In spite of; notwithstanding. [Middle English, in spite of, "to the displeasure of", from noun, "ill will", from Old French *maugré* (whence French *malgré*) : *mal*, bad, from Latin *malus* + *gré*, pleasure, from Latin *gratus*, pleasing.]

maul (mawl) n. **1.** A heavy, long-handled hammer used to drive stakes, piles, or wedges. **2.** In Rugby football, a loose scrum. ~tr.v. **mauled, mauling, mauls. 1.** To handle roughly; bruise or mangle: *a hunter mauled by a bear*. **2.** To injure by or as if by beating: *badly mauled by his critics*. [Middle English *meall, mal*, from Old French *mail*, from Latin *malleus*, hammer.] —**maul·er** n.

maul·stick (máwl-stik) n. Also **mahl·stick** (máwl-, maàl-). A long wooden stick used by painters to support the hand that holds the brush. [Partial translation and alteration of Dutch *maalstok* : *maalen*, to paint, from Middle Dutch *malen* + *stok*, STICK.]

Mau Mau (mów-mow, -mów) n., pl. **Mau Maus** or collectively **Mau Mau. 1.** A secret organisation of Kikuyu tribesmen in Kenya that used terrorism during the 1950s with the aim of driving out white settlers and ending colonial rule. **2.** A member of this organisation. [Origin obscure.]

Mau·na Lo·a (máwnə lṓ-ə). Volcano lying in Hawaii Volcanoes National Park, United States. It is the world's largest volcano, rising to 4 170 metres (13,681 feet).

maund (mawnd) n. Any of several Asian units of weight of varying amounts; especially, the official maund in India, equivalent to about 37 kilograms (82 pounds). [Hindi *mān*, from Persian, from Akkadian *manū*, designating a unit of weight. See **mina.**]

maun·der (máwndər) intr.v. **-dered, -dering, -ders. 1.** To talk incoherently or aimlessly. **2.** To move or act aimlessly or vaguely; wander. [Perhaps from obsolete *maunder*†, to beg.] —**maun·der·er** n.

Maun·dy (máwndi) n. Sometimes small **m. 1. a.** The distribution of specially minted coins by the British sovereign to a selected group of poor people on Maundy Thursday. **b.** The coins so distributed. Also called "Maundy money". **2.** In the Roman Catholic Church, the ceremony of washing the feet of twelve people on Maundy Thursday, in commemoration of Jesus' washing of his apostles' feet at the Last Supper. [Middle English, from Old French *mandé*, a thing commanded, from Medieval Latin *mandātum*, the ceremony, "command", from the words of Christ in the first antiphon of Maundy Thursday, *Mandātum novum dō vōbis*, "A new commandment give I unto you" (John 13).]

Maundy Thursday n.. The Thursday before Easter, commemorating Jesus' Last Supper.

Mau·pas·sant, (mō-pa-SON, -paa-), **(Henri René Albert) Guy de** (1850–93). French novelist and short-story writer. While a civil servant, he was encouraged to write by Flaubert, and produced his first success with *Boule de Suif* (1880). His works, mainly realistic short stories, examine the themes of hypocrisy, madness, the social world of Paris, and peasant life in Normandy.

Mau·re·ta·ni·a (mórri-táyni-ə, máwri-). North African district of the Roman Empire, comprising the Atlas Mountains of Morocco and western Algeria and land to the north. Settled before 2000 B.C. by Maures (Moors), a Berber people, it fell to Rome in about 100 B.C. Arabs overran the area in the seventh century A.D., and by 1000 the Moors, fanatical Muslims, had spread into Spain and southwestwards in Africa. Their Arab-Berber descendants now form the majority in Algeria, Mauritania, and Morocco.

Mau·riac (mórri-ak ‖ máwri-, móri-, -ák; French mō-ryák), **François** (1885–1970). French novelist. His works include *le Baiser au lépreux* (1922), *le Noeud de vipères* (1932), and his play *Asmodée* (1938). He was awarded the Nobel prize for literature (1952).

Mau·ri·ta·ni·a, Islamic Republic of (mórri-táyni-ə, máwri-). Arabic **Muritaniyah**, French **Republique Islamique de Mauritanie.** A large, sparsely populated, mostly desert country of northwest Africa. Its only major fertile area is along the Senegal river, and most people live by stock rearing. The country, badly hit by the Sahel droughts of the 1970s, depends on exports of iron ore. Fish is also exported. The area was settled by Berbers from the north in about A.D. 1000, and their Arab-Berber descendants, the Maures (Moors), make up 75 per cent of the population. The rest, mostly in the south, are black Africans. European traders plied the coast from the 15th century. The French took over the country (1860–1903) and governed it until it became fully independent in 1960. In 1964 it became a one-party state, and has been under military rule since 1979, the

same year in which it renounced its claim to southern Western Sahara (Tiris al Gharbia). Area, 1 030 700 square kilometres (397,956 square miles). Population, 1,700,000. Capital, Nouakchott. **—Mau·ri·ta·ni·an** *adj. & n.*

Mau·ri·tius (mə-ríshəss, mo-, maw-). Formerly **Île de France**. State in the Indian Ocean, comprising the mountainous island of Mauritius and several tiny dependencies. The economy rests on the growing and processing of sugar cane, but tea and tobacco growing, small-scale manufacturing, fishing, and tourism are increasingly important. The first European settlers were Dutch (1598–1710). During French occupation (1715–1810), black African slaves were imported to work the sugar plantations. Creoles (of French-African descent) now make up about one third of the population. The British captured the islands (1810), abolished slavery, and brought in Indian contract labourers, whose descendants now account for some two thirds of Mauritians. Tension between the two groups and high unemployment are major problems for the country, independent within the Commonwealth since 1968. Area, 2 045 square kilometres (790 square miles). Population, 1,000,000. Capital, Port Louis. **—Mau·ri·tian** (-ríshən) *n. & adj.*

Mau·rois (máw-rwaa || mō̃-, -rwàa), **André**, born Emile Herzog (1885–1967). French biographer and novelist. Having served with the British army during World War I, he produced two perceptive portrayals of the British character with *les Silences du Colonel Bramble* (1918) and *les Discours du Docteur O'Grady* (1921).

Mau·ser (mów-zər) *n.* A trademark for a repeating rifle or pistol. [After Paul *Mauser* (1838–1914), German arms manufacturer, who invented it.]

mau·so·le·um (máw-sə-lée-əm || -zə-) *n., pl.* **-leums** or **-lea** (-ə). A large and stately tomb, or a building housing such a tomb or tombs. [Latin *mausōlēum,* from Greek *mausōleion,* originally, the tomb of *Mausōlos,* satrap of Caria (377–353 B.C.), at Halicarnassus.] **—mau·so·le·an** *adj.*

mau·vais quart d'heure (mō̃-vay kaar dér, -váy, dőr) *n.* A short-lived but unpleasant experience. [French, bad quarter of an hour.]

mauve (mōv) *n.* **1.** Brilliant violet to strong or brilliant purple to moderate reddish purple. **2. a.** A mauve dye. **b.** Mauveine. [French *mauve,* "mallow(-coloured)", from Latin *malva,* mallow.] **—mauve** *adj.*

mau·veine (mō̃-veen, -vin) *n.* A purple dye made from aniline; the first synthetic dye. Also called "mauve", "Perkin's mauve". [MAUVE + -INE.]

mav·er·ick (mávvərik, mávvrik) *n.* **1.** *U.S.* An unbranded calf or colt that has strayed from the herd, traditionally considered the property of the first person who brands it. **2. a.** One who refuses to abide by the dictates of his group; a dissenter. **b.** One who resists adherence to or affiliation with any single organised group or faction; an independent. Often used adjectivally: *maverick politicians.* [After Samuel A. *Maverick* (1803–1870), Texas cattleman who did not brand his calves.]

ma·vis (máyviss) *n.* A bird, the **song thrush** *(see).* [Middle English *mavys,* from Old French *mauvis*†.]

ma·vour·neen, ma·vour·nin (mə-vóor-neen) *n. Irish.* My darling. [Irish *mo mhuirnín* : *mo,* my + *muirnín,* darling, diminutive of *muirn,* delight, from Old Irish, revels, banquet, tumult.]

maw (maw) *n.* **1.** The stomach, mouth, jaws, or gullet of a voracious carnivore. **2.** Something suggestive of a gaping opening or the appetite of a voracious animal. [Middle English *mawe,* Old English *maga.*]

mawk·ish (máwkish) *adj.* **1.** Excessively and objectionably sentimental. **2.** *Archaic.* Sickly; nauseating. [Earlier senses "nauseating", "nauseous", from obsolete *mawk,* maggot, whim, fastidious person, from Middle English *mathek,* MAGGOT.] **—mawk·ish·ly** *adv.* **—mawk·ish·ness** *n.*

max. maximum.

max·i (máksi) *n.* **1.** An ankle- or floor-length skirt or coat. **2.** Something larger or longer than other members of its class. Often used adjectivally and in combination: *a maxicoat.* [Short for MAXIMUM.]

max·il·la (mak-síl-ə) *n., pl.* **-lae** (-ee) or **-las**. **1.** *Anatomy.* Either of a pair of bones forming part of the upper jaw. See **skull**. **2.** *Zoology.* Either of two laterally moving appendages behind the mandibles in insects and most other arthropods, used in feeding. [Latin, "lower jaw", akin to *māla*†, upper jaw. See also **malar**.] **—max·il·lar, max·il·lar·y** (-əri || *U.S.* máksə-lerri) *adj.*

max·il·li·ped (mak-sílli-ped) *n.* The first pair or first three pairs of appendages in crustaceans, situated behind the maxillae and used for feeding. [MAXILL(A) + -PED.]

max·im (máksim) *n.* A succinct formulation of some fundamental principle or rule of conduct. —See Synonyms at **saying**. [Middle English, from Old French *maxime,* from Medieval Latin *(prōpositiō) maxima,* "greatest proposition", philosophical term for a fundamental axiom, from *maximus,* greatest.]

max·i·mal (máksim'l) *adj.* **1.** Of, pertaining to, or consisting of a maximum. **2.** The greatest or highest possible. **3.** *Mathematics.* Designating an element, in an ordered set, that is followed by no other.

~*n. Mathematics.* A maximal element. **—max·i·mal·ly** *adv.*

max·i·mal·ist (máksim'l-ist) *n.* **1.** *Sometimes capital* **M.** One who advocates direct revolutionary action to secure social and political gains. **2.** One who rejects all compromise and insists on all his demands being met. [French *maximaliste* (probably from English MAXIMAL).]

Max·im gun (máksim) *n.* The first automatic repeating gun. [After Sir Hiram *Maxim* (1840–1916), British engineer, who invented it.]

Max·i·mil·i·an (máksi-míl-yən, -i-ən), **(Ferdinand Joseph)** (1832–67). Emperor of Mexico (1864–67). The younger brother of Francis Joseph I of Austria, he accepted the title of Emperor of Mexico from the French, who had recently captured the country. Lacking popular support, he was captured and shot by the republicans when the French withdrew under American pressure.

max·i·min (máksi-min) *n.* **1.** *Mathematics.* The highest of a set of minimum values. **2.** In games theory, the selection of a strategy for a member of the group that gives the maximum value for the member's minimum gains. Compare **minimax**. [*Max*imum + *mini*mum.]

max·i·mise, max·i·mize (máksi-mīz) *tr.v.* **-mised, -mising, -mises.** **1.** To make as great as possible; increase to a maximum. **2.** To represent as having the greatest degree of importance or value; magnify. **3.** *Mathematics.* To find a maximum value of (a function). **—max·i·mi·sa·tion** (-mī-záysh'n || *U.S.* -mi-) *n.* **—max·i·mis·er** *n.*

max·i·mum (máksi-məm) *n., pl.* **-mums** or **-ma** (-mə). *Abbr.* **max.** **1. a.** The greatest possible quantity, degree, or number. **b.** The time or period during which the highest point or degree is attained. **2.** An upper limit stipulated by law or otherwise fixed or agreed: *a price maximum; a wage increase maximum.* **3.** *Astronomy.* **a.** The moment when a variable star is most brilliant. **b.** The magnitude of the star at such a moment. **4.** *Mathematics.* **a.** The value of a function that is not exceeded by neighbouring values. **b.** The greatest value assumed by a function within some subset of its domain of definition. **c.** The largest number in a set.

~*adj. Abbr.* **max.** **1.** Having, being, or showing the greatest quantity or the highest degree that has been or can be attained: *maximum temperature.* **2.** Of, pertaining to, or making up a maximum or maximums: *a maximum number in a series.* [Latin *maximum,* "greatest (quantity)", neuter of *maximus,* greatest.]

maximum permissible dose. *Physics.* A **dose** *(see).*

max·i·sin·gle (máksi-sing-g'l) *n.* **1.** A record the size of an LP but designed to be played at 45 r.p.m. **2.** An EP.

ma·xi·xe (mə-shée-shay, -shə, -shéesh) *n.* A Brazilian dance similar to the two-step. [Brazilian Portuguese *maxixe*†.]

max·well (máks-wəl, -wel) *n. Abbr.* **Mx** A unit of magnetic flux in the centimetre-gram-second electromagnetic system, equal to the flux perpendicularly intersecting an area of one square centimetre in a region where the magnetic induction is one gauss. [After James Clerk MAXWELL.]

Max·well (máks-wəl, *also* -wel), **James Clerk** (1831–79). British physicist. Educated at Edinburgh and Cambridge, he published in 1873 the *Treatise on Electricity and Magnetism,* expounding a set of four equations which were applicable to electricity, magnetism, and light. He predicted the existence of radio waves and worked on the kinetic theory of gases and the study of colour perception.

may[1] (may) *v.* Past **might** (mīt), present **may** or *archaic* **mayest** (mayst, máy-ist) or **mayst** (mayst) (for second person singular). Used as an auxiliary, followed by an infinitive without *to,* or with the infinitive understood, to indicate: **1.** A requesting or granting of permission: *May I take a swim? You may.* See Usage note at **can**. **2.** Possibility: *It may rain this afternoon.* **3.** Ability or capacity, with the force of *can: If I may be of service.* **4.** Obligation or function, with the force of *must* or *shall,* in statutes, deeds, and other legal documents. **5.** Desire or fervent wish. Used chiefly in exclamatory phrases: *Long may he live!* **6.** Purpose or result, in clauses introduced by *that* or *so that*: *expressing ideas so that the average person may understand.* **7.** Contingent or conditional: *Whatever you may think, I still believe he's innocent.* **8.** Less abrupt or pointed questioning: *How old may this little boy be?* **—be that as it may.** Nevertheless; despite that. **—come what may.** Whatever happens. **—may as well.** To have no compelling reason not to. **—may well.** To be very likely. [Middle English *may,* past *mighte, moghte,* Old English *maeg* (first and third person singular), past *mighte, moghte,* infinitive *magan,* to be strong, be able, have permission.]

Usage: *Might* and *may*: *might* functions in context as a past form and subjunctive *(She said she might leave early; so that the average person might understand).* It is often interchangeable with *may,* however, thought it tends to emphasise the hypothesis more strongly: *Might I take a swim?; It might rain this afternoon.*

may[2] *n. British.* The **hawthorn** *(see).* Also called "may tree". [From MAY (month).]

May (may) *n.* **1.** The fifth month of the year according to the Gregorian calendar. May has 31 days. **2.** *Poetic.* The springtime of life; youth. **3.** The festivities of May Day. [Middle English, from Old French *Mai,* from Latin *Maius (mēnsis),* (the month) of *Maia,* Italic goddess.]

ma·ya (mī-ə, maa-yə) *n. Hinduism.* Illusion; especially, the visible material world conceived of as being purely illusory. [Sanskrit *māyā*†.]

Ma·ya (mī-ə, maa-yə) *n., pl.* **Mayas** or collectively **Maya**. **1.** A member of an Indian people of southern Mexico and Central America whose civilization reached its height in about A.D. 300–900. **2.** The language spoken by the Maya; Mayan. **—Ma·ya** *adj.*

Ma·ya·kov·sky (mī-ə-kóf-ski; *Russian* mə-yi-káwf-), **Vladimir** (1893–1930). Soviet poet and playwright. He combined experimental poetic techniques with Bolshevik propaganda, and was a leading member of the futurist movement. His works include the poems *150 Million* (1920) and *Mystery-Bouffe* (1918), and the plays *The Bedbug* (1928) and *The Bath-House* (1929). He committed suicide.

PRONUNCIATION KEY

a, trap; aa, father; ai, fair; ar, star; aw, lawn; ay, play; b, bb, stab; rubber; ch, church; ck, ticket; d, dd, dead; ladder; e, dress; ee, bee; er, defer; ew, few; ewr, pure; ə, about; ər, letter; f, ff, fife; differ; g, gg, giggle; h, hat; i, kit; ī, price; īr, fire; j, judge; k, kick; l, ll, let; 'l, needle; m, mm, man; n, nn, no; 'n, sudden; ng, thing; o, lot; ō, no; ŏŏ, foot; ōō, shoe; oor, poor; ow, cow; owr, hour; oy, boy; p, pp, pepper; r, rr, red; s, ss, sauce; sh, ship; t, tt, totter; th, thick; th, this; smooth; u, cut; ur, turn; v, vv, valve; w, wet; y, yes; z, zz, zebra; zh, vision; pleasure

IN FOREIGN WORDS:

aN, oN, Saint-Saëns; hl, Llanelli; Hluhluwe; kh, loch; lough; Khaled

STRESS MARK:

ín-sīt, insight; in-sīt, incite

Maya

LOST CITIES IN THE CENTRAL AMERICAN JUNGLE

A civilisation that excelled in mathematics, astronomy, and architecture

Nineteenth-century explorers in the lowland jungles of Mexico and Guatemala were amazed to find massive stone ruins swamped by vegetation. They were remains of the Maya civilisation, which began to emerge about 2000 B.C. and reached a peak in the period A.D. 300–900.

The three million Mayas, living in hamlets surrounding the large temple-cities, were ruled by hereditary chiefs and priests skilled in the arts, astronomy, and mathematics. Their mathematics – not equalled by Europe for several centuries – was based on a unit of 20 and incorporated the concept of zero, unknown to the Greeks and Romans. They calculated the solar year and lunar months accurately enough to predict eclipses. Their writing, however, remains mysterious.

Despite the Mayans' failure to invent the true arch, their stone cities, with pyramids 60 metres (200 feet) high and huge palaces,

were masterpieces of architecture. They also built great courts, some more than 80 metres (over 250 feet) long, used for a ritual ball game, *pok-ta-pok*.

Their standards of beauty now seem odd. Their artists' ideas of perspective give the figures in wall paintings and sculptures a cross-eyed look. Some figures have flattened, egg-shaped heads with receding chins and teeth filed down flat. Some have nose plugs and decorative fillings in the teeth.

In about 900, perhaps as a result of peasant revolts, the old cities were abandoned. The centre of civilisation moved north to the Yucatan peninsula and Chichen Itza was made the capital. In the 16th and 17th centuries, the Mayas were conquered by the Spanish, but they still number about two million and have mixed many of their old traditions with the Christianity taught them by their conquerors.

DIFFERENT CONSTRUCTION *Like all Mayan buildings, the Pyramid of the Soothsayer at Uxmal (above) had mortar used in its construction – unique on that continent then.*

MAYA WRITING *The symbols round the pictures in this astrological text (left) are ideograms. Each symbol represents an idea. They are largely undeciphered.*

Ma·yan (mī́-ən, maá-yən) *adj.* Of or pertaining to the Maya, their culture, their language or the language group to which it belongs. ~*n.* **1.** A Maya. **2.** A family of Central American languages, including the language of the Maya.

May apple *n.* **1.** A North American plant, *Podophyllum peltatum,* having a single, nodding white flower and oval edible fruit. **2.** The fruit of this plant.

may·be (máy-bee, -bi; *occasionally* -bée) *adv.* Perhaps; possibly.

Usage: Written as a single word, it has the meaning "perhaps" and tends, especially in British English, to be restricted to informal usage *(Maybe they'll attack tomorrow),* except in certain cases where it occurs in rather formal British English in final position and has stress on the second syllable *(They will attack tomorrow maybe, but we shall be ready to repel them).* Written as two words, it functions as a verb phrase *(It may be that they will attack).*

May bug *n.* The **cockchafer** *(see).*

May Day *n.* **1.** The first day of May, traditionally marked by the celebration of spring. **2.** May 1, or the first working day of May, widely observed as a public holiday in honour of workers.

may·day (máy-day) *n.* An international radio-telephone signal word used by aircraft and ships in distress. [Phonetic rendering of French *m'aider,* help me.]

Mayence. See **Mainz.**

May·er (máy-ər), **Sir Robert** (1879–). British music patron, born in Germany. In 1923 he organised the Robert Mayer Children's Concert, which has continued every year since. In 1954 he founded the Youth and Music scheme. He was knighted in 1939.

May·fair (máy-fair). A district of the City of Wesminster, Greater London. A wealthy residential, recreational, and commercial area of London's West End, it takes its name from the annual fair held there until the end of the 18th century.

may·flow·er (máy-flowr, -flow-ər) *n.* Any of a wide variety of plants that bloom in May, such as the hawthorn and cowslip.

May·flow·er (máy-flowr, -flow-ər). The name of the ship on which the Pilgrims sailed to America in 1620.

may·fly (máy-flī) *n., pl.* **-flies.** Any of various fragile, winged insects of the order Ephemeroptera that develop from aquatic nymphs and live in the adult stage for a few days at most. Also called "dayfly". [So named because it swarms in May.]

may·hap (máy-hap, -háp) *adv. Archaic.* Perhaps; perchance. [From the phrase *it may hap.*]

may·hem (máy-hem || -əm) *n.* **1.** The infliction of violent injury upon a person or thing; wanton destruction: *children committing mayhem in the flower beds.* **2.** A state of violent disorder or riotous confusion; havoc. **3.** *Law.* Formerly, the offence of wilfully maiming or crippling a person. [Middle English, from Anglo-French *maihem, mahaym,* injury, from Old French *mahaignier,* MAIM.]

May·hew (máy-hew), **Henry** (1812–87). English journalist and sociologist. He pioneered a study of London's poor for the *Morning Chronicle,* which were published in three volumes (1851). A fourth, *London Labour and the London Poor,* appeared in 1862.

may·ing (máy-ing) *n. Poetic.* The celebration of or participation in traditional May Day festivities. [From MAY (month).]

may·n't (maynt, máy-ənt). Contraction of *may not.*

May·o¹ (máy-ō || *Irish also* may-ŏ). Family of U.S. physicians and surgeons. William Worrall (1819–1911), born in England, went to the United States in 1845 and concentrated on gynaecological surgery. A clinic he started in Rochester, Minnesota, grew into the renowned Mayo Clinic under the supervision of his sons, William James (1861–1939) and Charles Horace (1865–1939).

Mayo². *Irish* **Muigheo.** Atlantic county in Connacht province, in the west of the Republic of Ireland. It is mountainous and barren in the west, but more fertile in the east, producing oats, potatoes, and livestock. It has many lakes and a fragmented coastline. The county town is Castlebar.

may·on·naise (máy-ə-náyz, -nayz) *n.* **1.** A creamy salad dressing made of beaten raw egg yolk, oil, vinegar or lemon juice, and seasonings. **2.** A dish of a specified food incorporating this dressing: *salmon mayonnaise; egg mayonnaise.* [French, perhaps named in commemoration of the capture in 1756 of Port *Mahon,* capital of Minorca, by the Duke of Richelieu.]

mayor (mair ‖ máy-ər) *n.* The chief officer of a city, town, or (in large cities) a local borough, usually elected annually by the local council. [Middle English *mair,* from Old French *maire,* from Medieval Latin *mājor,* title of various officials, from Latin *mājor,* "greater".] —**mayor·al** (mair-əl ‖ máy-ərəl, may-áwrəl) *adj.* —**mayor·ship** *n.*

mayor·al·ty (mair-əlti ‖ máy-ər-) *n., pl.* -**ties. 1.** The office of a mayor. **2.** The term of office of a mayor. [Middle English, from Old French *mairalté,* from *maire,* MAYOR.]

mayor·ess (mair-iss, -ess, -éss ‖ máy-ər-) *n.* **1.** A woman holding the office of mayor. **2.** The wife of a mayor or (when the mayor is a woman, for example) a woman, such as the mayor's daughter, fulfilling the same official function.

Mayotte. See **Mahore.**

May·pole (máy-pōl) *n. Sometimes small* **m.** A pole decorated with streamers that May Day celebrants hold while dancing round it.

May queen *n.* A young woman or girl who is crowned with a ring of flowers and presides over the traditional May Day celebrations. Also called "Queen of the May".

may tree *n. British.* The **hawthorn** *(see).*

may·weed (máy-weed) *n.* A widespread weed, *Anthemis cotula,* having unpleasant-smelling leaves and white flowers. Also called "dog fennel", "stinking mayweed".

Ma·za·rin (mázzərin; *French* ma-za-ráN), **Jules,** born Giulio Mazarini (1602–61). French statesman, born in Italy. He became advisor to Louis XIII's chief minister, Richelieu. After the death of Louis (1643), he was the chief minister of the regent, Anne of Austria, and after 1653 was all-powerful in the French government. He was never ordained a priest, but was made a cardinal on the recommendation of Louis XIII in 1641.

Maz·da·ism (máz-dər-iz'm, -də-) *n.* A religion, **Zoroastrianism** *(see).* [Avestan *mazda,* the good principle in Zoroastrianism + -ISM.]

maze (mayz) *n.* **1. a.** An intricate, usually confusing, network of walled or hedged pathways; a labyrinth. **b.** Any physical situation resembling such a network, in which it is easy to get lost. **c.** Any elaborate, confusing, or impenetrable network: *a maze of regulations.* **2.** A puzzle consisting of a graphic representation of a maze. **3.** *Archaic.* A state of confusion or perplexity.
~*tr.v.* **mazed, mazing, mazes.** *Archaic.* To daze, bewilder, or perplex. [Middle English, a maze, earlier, "delusion", from *mazen,* to bewilder, amaze. See **amaze.**] —**ma·zy** *adj.*

ma·zer (máyzər) *n.* A large, often elaborately ornamented, drinking bowl made of hard wood or metal. [Middle English *mazer,* originally, "an outgrowth of maple wood" (from which a mazer was made), from Germanic.]

ma·zu·ma (mə-zōomə) *n. U.S. Slang.* Money; cash. [Yiddish *mezumen,* "ready" (i.e., ready cash), from Hebrew *məzumān.*]

ma·zur·ka, ma·zour·ka (mə-zúr-kə, -zóor-) *n.* **1.** A lively Polish dance resembling the polka. **2.** A piece of music for such a dance. [French, from Polish *Mazurka,* oblique form of *mazurek,* diminutive of *mazur,* one from *Mazovia* province.]

maz·zard (máz-ərd, -aard) *n.* A wild sweet cherry, *Prunus avium,* often used as grafting stock. [Perhaps akin to MAZER.]

Maz·zi·ni (mat-séeni), **Giuseppe** (1805–72). Italian revolutionary nationalist. He was exiled in 1830 for joining a secret society, the Carbonari, and lived mainly in London after 1837. In 1849 he was a leader of the Roman republic, and after its fall he organised an unsuccessful uprising in Milan (1853). In 1858, in London, he began the revolutionary paper *Thought and Action,* stirring Italian nationalist opinion.

M.B. Bachelor of Medicine [Latin *Medicinae Baccalaureus.*]

M.B.A. Master of Business Administration.

Mba·ba·ne (m-baa-báani). Capital of Swaziland, situated in the Mdimba Mountains. It is also a commercial centre.

M.B.E. Member of the Order of the British Empire.

M·bo·ya (m-bóy-ə), **Thomas Joseph,** known as Tom (1930–69). Kenyan politician. In 1957 he was one of the first eight Africans elected to the legislative council. A year later he was elected president of the All-African People's Conference at Accra. After independence in 1963 he served in Jomo Kenyatta's government as minister of justice (1963–64) and minister of economic planning (1964–69). He was assassinated in 1969.

m.c. master of ceremonies.

M.C. 1. Master of Ceremonies. **2.** *U.S.* Member of Congress. **3.** *British.* Military Cross.

M.C.C. Marylebone Cricket Club.

Mc·Ad·am (mə-káddəm), **John Loudon** (1756–1836). British engineer. He developed the technique of improving roads by raising their level and covering them with graded stones. He became surveyor general of Britain's roads (1827).

Mc·Car·thy (mə-kárthi), **Joseph Raymond,** known as Joe (1908–57). U.S. politician. He was elected to the U.S. Senate (1947). As chairman of the permanent subcommittee on investigations, he began public hearings, accusing army officials, media employees, and public personalities of communism. His charges were never proved and he was censured by the Senate (1954).

McCarthy, Mary (Therese) (1912–). U.S. writer. She has satirised

urban American life in novels such as *The Company She Keeps* (1942), *The Group* (1963), and *Birds of America* (1971).

Mc·Car·thy·ism (mə-kárthi-iz'm) *n.* **1.** A political stance, especially prevalent in the United States in the 1950s, of intense anticommunism, characterised by the practice of driving suspected communists from government office by means of well-publicised but often unsubstantiated allegations. **2.** The use of underhand methods or unsupported allegations in order to suppress opposition. [Coined by opponents of Joseph R. MCCARTHY.] —**Mc·Car·thy·ist, Mc·Car·thy·ite** *n. & adj.*

Mc·Cart·ney (mə-kártni), **(James) Paul** (1942–). British rock musician and composer. As a member of the Beatles group (1960–71), he wrote with John Lennon many memorable songs, including *She Loves You* and *Yesterday.* Since the disbandment of the Beatles, he has worked as a solo artist and with the group Wings.

Mc·Coy (mə-kóy) *n. Slang.* The authentic thing or quality; something that is not an imitation or substitute. Used in the phrase *the real McCoy.* [After Kid *McCoy,* professional name of Norman Selby (1873–1940), American boxer.]

Mc·Cul·lers (mə-kúllərz), **Carson (Smith)** (1917–67). U.S. novelist. Her books, set in the South, are compassionate studies of the macabre and grotesque. They include *The Heart is a Lonely Hunter* (1940) and *The Member of the Wedding* (1946).

Mc·En·roe (máckən-rō), **John (Patrick)** (1959–). U.S. tennis player. He was U.S. singles champion (1979–81) and Wimbledon champion (men's doubles 1979, 1981; singles 1981).

Mc·Gon·a·gall (mə-gónnəg'l) **William** (1830–1902). Scottish writer. He is often called "the world's worst poet": his poems, such as *The Tay Bridge Disaster* and *Attempted Assassination of the Queen,* frequently fail to rhyme or scan and are full of unintentional bathos.

Mc·Kin·ley, Mount (mə-kínli). The highest mountain in North America. It lies in Mount McKinley National Park, in the Alaska Range, Alaska, United States, and rises to 6 194 metres (20,322 feet). It is named after William **McKinley.**

McKinley, William (1843–1901). 25th President of the United States (1897–1901). He was elected to Congress as a Republican in 1876, where he introduced the protectionist McKinley Tariff Act (1890). His presidency was imperialist, with the destruction of the Spanish fleet in the Spanish-American war (1898) to gain Cuba, and the annexation of the Philippines. He was shot by an assassin.

Mc·Lu·han (mə-klóo-ən), **(Herbert) Marshall** (1911–80). Canadian literary critic and communications sociologist. He argued that the media, such as print or television, affect or overshadow the message they convey. His books include *Understanding Media* (1964) and *The Medium is the Message* (1967).

Mc·Mil·lan (mək-millən), **Edwin Mattison** (1907–). U.S. physicist. He discovered the first transuranic element, neptunium, in 1940 by bombarding uranium with neutrons. Together with Glenn Seaborg, he was awarded the Nobel Prize for chemistry (1951).

M.C.P. male chauvinist pig.

Md The symbol for the element mendelevium.

M.D. 1. Doctor of Medicine [Latin *Medicinae Doctor.*] **2.** Managing Director.

M.D.S. Master of Dental Surgery.

mdse. merchandise.

me¹ (mee, *weak form* mi) *pron.* The objective case of the first person pronoun *I.* It is used: **1.** As the direct object of a verb: *He assisted me.* **2.** As the indirect object of a verb: *They offered me a lift.* **3.** As the object of a preposition: *This letter is addressed to me.* **4.** After *than* or *as* in comparisons in which the first term is in the objective case: *The judges praised you more than me.* **5.** *U.S. Informal.* In place of the reflexive pronoun *myself,* as the indirect object of a verb: *I'm going to get me a gun.* **6.** In various elliptical, absolute, or interjectional phrases in which it is neither subject nor object: *Goodness me! Unlucky me. Who, me?*
~*n.* The speaker's image or personality: *This dress isn't really me; the real me.* [Middle English, Old English *mē, mě.*]

Usage: Until about thirty years ago, grammarians taught that the correct answer to the question *"Who is there?"* is *"It is I",* not *"It's me".* They pointed out that the verb "to be" has no object, so that any pronoun following it should be in the subjective form. Today, however, *It is I* sounds overcareful to the point of being pedantic, and objective forms of the pronouns *(me, him, her, us, them)* are acceptable even in formal contexts, unless there is a following construction (as in *It was he who told the vicar*). In such cases, formal speech requires the subjective form, informal speech the objective. Similarly, following *than* or *as,* subjective forms of the pronoun are used in formal writing *(John is bigger than I),* objective forms in other styles. If the construction continues, the subjective form must be used in standard English whether written or spoken, formal or informal *(John is bigger than I am).* The choice of an objective as opposed to a possessive form of these pronouns is an issue when an *-ing* form of a verb follows. Purists insist on the possessive form, in such sentences as *I remember your doing that.* But the objective form has become normal in informal usage, and is often heard in all but the most formal contexts. Sometimes a subtle distinction of meaning is involved: *I remember you acting in Macbeth* means "I remember the fact that you acted in that play"; whereas *I remember your acting in Macbeth* may additionally mean "I remember the quality of your acting".

me², mi (mee) *n. Music.* In tonic sol-fa, a syllable representing the third note of a diatonic scale. [Originally *mi,* Medieval Latin, from Latin *mīra,* "wonders", a word sung to this note in a hymn to St.

mayfly *In their nymph stage, mayflies live in ponds and streams for a period of from several months to three years. Then the nymphs moult to become a subimago and a second time to become a true adult (above) – the only insects to undergo this two-stage transformation. Adult mayflies do not eat; they live for only a few hours, just long enough to mate and lay eggs.*

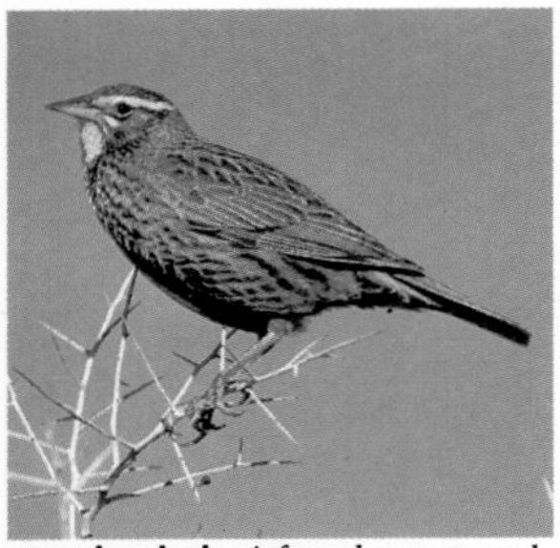

meadowlark *A female greater red-breasted meadowlark of South America. The species gets its name from the colouring of the male bird. All meadowlarks are songbirds, living in fields and meadows in South, Central, and North America.*

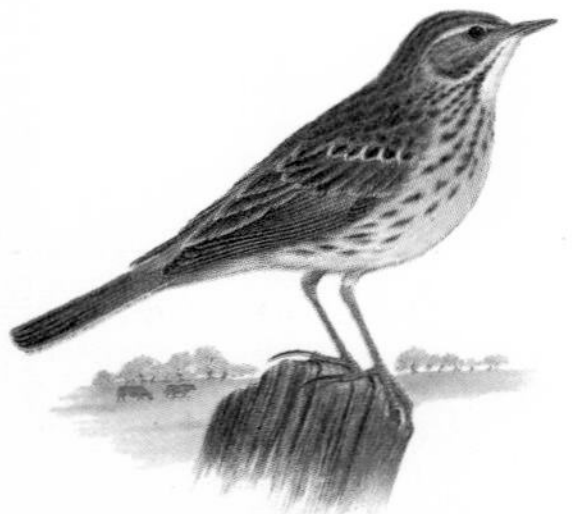

meadow pipit *This small songbird, which grows to about 145 millimetres (5¾ inches) is something of a victim among birds. It is the chief prey of the merlin, and a favourite host for the cuckoo, whose fostered young grow so large that the meadow pipit sometimes stands on the nestling's back to feed it. Meadow pipits nest in open country – often on the edge of meadows – in northern Europe, and migrate in winter to southwestern Europe and around the Mediterranean.*

John the Baptist (see **gamut**), from Latin *mīrārī,* to be amazed at, from *mīrus,* wonderful.]

Me methyl group (CH_3–).

ME Middle English.

M.E. **1.** mechanical engineer; mechanical engineering. **2.** Middle English. **3.** mining engineer.

me·a cul·pa (máy-ə kŏol-pə, mée-, kúl-) *n. Latin.* An admission of fault or error. Often used interjectionally. [Literally, my fault.]

mead¹ (meed) *n.* An alcoholic drink made from fermented honey and water. [Middle English *mede,* Old English *medu, meodu.*]

mead² *n. Archaic.* A meadow. [Middle English *mede,* Old English *mǣd.*]

Mead (meed), **Margaret** (1901–78). U.S. anthropologist. She was a curator of ethnology at the American Museum of Natural History in New York (1926–69). She wrote *Coming of Age in Samoa* (1928) and *Growing Up in New Guinea* (1930).

Meade (meed), **Richard** (1938–). British equestrian. He rode in the British Olympic gold medal team (1968, 1972) and won an individual Olympic gold (1972).

mead·ow (méddō) *n.* **1.** A tract of grassland mown for hay, as opposed to pasture, which is grazed by animals. **2.** A **water meadow** *(see).* [Middle English *medwe,* Old English *mǣdwe,* oblique case of *mǣd,* MEAD.] **—mead·ow·y** *adj.*

meadow fescue *n.* A grass, *Festuca pratensis* (or *eliator*), native to Eurasia and introduced in North America.

meadow grass *n.* A perennial grass, *Poa pratensis,* widely distributed in meadows and fields in northern temperate regions.

mead·ow·lark (méddō-laark) *n.* **1.** Either of two North American songbirds, *Sturnella magna* or *S. neglecta,* related to the Baltimore oriole. **2.** Any of various other birds of the genus *Sturnella,* of North, Central, and South America.

meadow mushroom *n.* A **field mushroom** *(see).*

meadow pipit *n.* A European songbird, *Anthus pratensis,* with a brown and white speckled plumage.

meadow rue *n.* Any of various plants of the genus *Thalictrum,* having clusters of small white, yellowish, or purplish flowers.

meadow saffron *n.* A plant, the **autumn crocus** *(see).*

mead·ow·sweet (méddō-sweet) *n.* Any of several plants of the genera *Filipendula* or *Spiraea;* especially, *F. ulmaria,* of Eurasia, having clusters of small, creamy white, fragrant flowers.

Meads (meedz), **Colin (Earl)** (1935–). New Zealand Rugby football player. He played lock forward for the All Blacks a record 100 times, and appeared in 55 test matches.

mea·gre, *U.S.* **mea·ger** (méegər) *adj.* **1.** Having little flesh; thin; lean. **2.** Markedly deficient in quantity, fullness, or extent; scanty. **3.** Markedly deficient in richness, fertility, or vigour; barren or feeble. [Middle English *megre,* from Anglo-French *megre* and Old French *maigre,* from Latin *macer* (stem *macr-*), thin.] **—mea·gre·ly** *adv.* **—mea·gre·ness** *n.*

Synonyms: *meagre, spare, sparse, skimpy, scanty, scant.*

meal¹ (meel) *n.* **1.** The edible seed or other edible part of a pulse or grain, usually excluding wheat, coarsely ground. **2.** *Scottish.* Oatmeal. **3.** Any granular substance produced by grinding. [Middle English *mele,* Old English *melu,* flour.]

meal² *n.* **1.** An amount of food served and eaten, often as several courses, in one sitting. **2.** A customary time or occasion of eating food. **—make a meal of.** To devote unnecessary effort or attention to (a task, for example). [Middle English *meel,* Old English *mǣl,* "mark", "measure", fixed time, mealtime.]

meal·ie (méeli) *n. South African.* **1.** An ear of maize. **2.** *Plural.* Maize. [Afrikaans *mielie,* from Portuguese *milho,* millet, from Latin *milium.*]

meals on wheels *n. Used with a singular verb.* A service, usually funded by a local authority, providing hot meals to elderly or disabled people in their own homes.

meal ticket *n.* **1.** *Chiefly U.S.* A card or ticket entitling the holder to a meal or meals. **2.** *Slang.* A person or thing depended on as a source of financial support.

meal·time (méel-tīm) *n.* The usual time for eating a meal.

meal·worm (méel-wurm) *n.* The larva of any of several beetles of the genus *Tenebrio.* Mealworms infest flour and other grain products and are raised for bird feed.

meal·y (méeli) *adj.* **-ier, -iest. 1.** Resembling meal in texture or consistency; granular: *mealy potatoes.* **2. a.** Made of or containing meal. **b.** Sprinkled or covered with meal or a similar granular substance. **3.** Flecked with spots; mottled. **4.** Unhealthily pale. Said of the complexion. **5.** Mealy-mouthed. **—meal·i·ness** *n.*

meal·y·bug (méeli-bug) *n.* Any insect of the genus *Pseudococcus* and related genera. Some species, such as *P. citri,* are destructive to plants, especially citrus trees. [So named because they are covered with a white powdery substance.]

meal·y-mouthed (méeli-mówthd, -mowthd || -mowtht) *adj.* Unwilling to state facts or opinions simply and directly.

mean¹ (meen) *v.* **meant** (ment), **meaning, means.** *—tr.* **1. a.** To be defined or described as; refer to; denote: *The word "dog" means a certain species of mammal.* **b.** To convey the same sense as; refer to the same thing as: *The French word "chien" means "dog".* **c.** To act as a symbol of; represent. **d.** To signify; serve as a sign. Used with a clause: *The flashing light means that you can cross.* **2. a.** To intend to convey or indicate: *What do you mean by that look?* **b.** To have in mind as one's true meaning or intention: *said £12 but meant 12 pence; said she would resign, and meant it.* **3.** To have as a purpose, aim, or intention; want: *I mean to get to the bottom of this.* **4.** To design or intend for a certain purpose, person, or end: *a building meant for storage; Was this letter meant for me?* **5.** To have as a consequence; entail; imply: *This decision means another 20% on the rates.* **6.** To have as its full implications and true character: *He doesn't know what hard work means.* **7.** To require or oblige. Used in the passive: *You're meant to knock before you go into his office.* *—intr.* **1.** To be of a specified importance or significance; matter: *The opinions of critics meant little to him.* **2.** To have intentions of a specified kind; be disposed. Followed by *well* or *ill: She means well, despite her blunders.* [Middle English *menen,* Old English *mǣnan,* to intend, tell, signify.]

Synonyms: *mean, signify, import, denote, represent, purport.*

Usage: In clauses conveying the idea of intention or purpose, the following construction is introduced by *that* in standard English: *I did not mean that you should leave.* British English can also use the infinitive: *I didn't mean you to leave.* A construction using *for* is sometimes encountered in American English: *I didn't mean for you to leave.*

mean² *adj.* **meaner, meanest. 1.** Ignoble; small-minded; petty: *a mean motive.* **2.** Lacking elevating human qualities, such as kindness, generosity, and goodwill: **a.** Reluctant to help or oblige; selfish. **b.** Cruel; malicious; spiteful. **c.** Reluctant to give; stingy. See Synonyms at **stingy. 3.** Low in quality or grade; inferior. **4.** Low in social status; of humble origin or rank. **5.** Common or poor in appearance; shabby. **6.** *U.S. Informal.* Ill-tempered. Said often of animals. **7.** *Chiefly U.S. Informal.* In poor health; out of sorts; ill. **8.** *Slang.* Skilful; hard to beat: *She plays a mean game of bridge.* **—no mean.** Very good: *He's no mean cook.* [Middle English *mene, imene,* Old English *gemǣne,* "common".] **—mean·ly** *adv.* **—mean·ness** *n.*

Synonyms: *mean, low, base, abject, infamous, ignoble.*

mean³ *n.* **1.** That which lies between two extremes; a middle point, condition, quality, or course of action. See **golden mean. 2.** *Mathematics.* **a.** A number that represents a set of numbers in any of several ways determined by a rule involving all members of the set; an average. **b.** The **arithmetic mean** *(see).* Compare **geometric mean. 3.** *Logic.* The middle term in a syllogism. **—See means.** *~adj.* **1.** Occupying a middle or intermediate position between two extremes. **2.** Intermediate in size, extent, quality, time, or degree; medium. **3.** Constituting a mean; average. [Middle English *mene,* from Anglo-French *meen* and Old French *meien,* from Latin *mediānus,* median, from *medius,* middle.]

me·an·der (mee-ándər, mi-) *intr.v.* **-dered, -dering, -ders. 1.** To follow a winding and turning course: *Streams tend to meander through level land.* **2.** To wander aimlessly and idly without fixed direction: *vagabonds meandering through life.* —See Synonyms at **wander.** *~n.* **1.** *Plural.* Circuitous, sinuous windings, as of a stream or path. **2.** A circuitous journey or excursion; a ramble. **3.** An ornamental pattern of intertwining lines, used in art and architecture; a fret. [Originally as a noun, from Latin *maeander,* from Greek *maiandros,* from *Maiandros,* the river MAEANDER, noted for its windings.] **—me·an·der·er** *n.* **—me·an·der·ing·ly** *adv.* **—me·an·drous** (-ándrəss) *adj.*

mean deviation *n. Statistics.* The arithmetic mean of the absolute values of deviations from the arithmetic mean, or from the median, in a statistical distribution.

mean distance *n.* The average distance between two bodies; especially, the average of the greatest and the least distances between an orbiting body and the body about which it is orbiting.

mean free path *n.* The average distance covered by a particle, molecule, ion, or the like, between collisions.

mean free time *n.* The average time that elapses between collisions of a particle, molecule, ion, or the like.

meanie. Variant of **meany.**

mean·ing (méening) *n.* **1.** That which is signified or denoted by a linguistic expression such as a word or phrase; sense; semantic content: *a word with several different meanings.* **2.** That which one wishes to convey by words or actions; import: *I listened carefully to grasp his meaning.* **3.** The full implications or true character of something: *doesn't know the meaning of pain.* **4.** That which is felt to be the inner significance of something: *the meaning of dreams.* **5.** Functional value; efficacy; significance.
~adj. **1.** Full of meaning; expressive: *a meaning look.* **2.** Intentioned or disposed in a specified manner. Used in the combinations *ill-meaning* and *well-meaning.*

Synonyms: *meaning, sense, significance, signification, import, purport.*

mean·ing·ful (méening-f'l) *adj.* Having meaning, function, value, or purpose; significant. **—mean·ing·ful·ly** *adv.*

mean·ing·less (méening-ləss, -liss) *adj.* Having no meaning or significance; senseless. **—mean·ing·less·ly** *adv.*

mean life *n.* The average time for which an unstable or reactive particle, ion, or the like, can exist; a lifetime.

means (meenz) *pl.n.* **1.** *Sometimes used with a singular verb.* A method, instrument, or course of action by which some act or end can be accomplished: *The fastest means of communication is the telephone.* **2.** Material resources; income, wealth, or property: *a man of means.* **—by all means.** Without fail; certainly. **—by means of.** With the use of; owing to: *They succeeded by means of patience and sacrifice.* **—by no means** or **not by any means.** In no sense; certainly not: *by no means an easy opponent.*

Usage: *Means,* in the sense of "resources" (of money or property, for example), takes a plural verb: *His means are sufficient to* *keep him alive. Means,* in the sense of "way to an end", takes either a singular or a plural verb, depending on the type of construction in which it occurs. Used with *a, any, each* and so on, it takes a singular verb *(A means of transport is essential);* used with *all, several, such,* and the like, it takes a plural verb *(Several means of transport are available).* Used with *the,* it takes a verb that may be singular or plural, depending on whether or not a collective sense of the noun is intended: *The means of transport is for you to decide* (collective), but *The means of transport are many and various* (individualised).

mean sea level *n.* The average level of the sea, used in geography as a basis from which to measure height.

mean solar day *n.* The average period between successive transits of the Sun, equal to 24 hours, and now measured from midnight to midnight. It is used because the apparent solar day, the actual period between successive transits of the Sun, varies. Also called "civil day".

mean solar time *n.* Time based on the mean solar day. Also called "civil time", loosely "mean time".

mean square *n. Mathematics.* The arithmetic mean of the squares of a set of numbers.

means test *n.* An official examination of a person's material resources to establish eligibility for social security or other benefits. **—means-test** (méenz-test) *tr.v.*

mean sun *n.* A hypothetical sun defined as moving at a uniform rate along the celestial equator so that it completes its orbit in the same period as the apparent sun. It is used in computing the mean solar day.

meant. Past tense and past participle of **mean.**

mean time *n.* Loosely, mean solar time.

mean·time (méen-tīm, -tīm) *n.* The time between one occurrence and another; an interval.
~adv. During a period of intervening time; meanwhile.

Usage: *Meantime* is used principally as a noun, usually in the phrase *in the meantime. Meanwhile* is used principally as an adverb: *Meanwhile, we were waiting in the shop.* But some speakers, in Scotland for example, do use *meantime* as an adverb, and *meanwhile* as a noun, without any change of meaning.

mean·tone system (méen-tōn) *n. Music.* A former system for tuning keyboard instruments. It has now been replaced by **equal temperament** *(see).*

mean·while (méen-wīl, -wīl, -hwīl, -hwīl) *adv.* **1.** During or in the intervening time: *Meanwhile, life goes on.* **2.** At the same time: *The court is deliberating; meanwhile, we must be patient.*
~n. The intervening time. See Usage note at **meantime.**

mean·y, mean·ie (méeni) *n., pl.* **-nies.** *Informal.* **1.** A miserly, ungenerous person. **2.** A malicious, spiteful person.

meas. measurable; measure.

mea·sles (méez'lz) *n. Used with a singular verb.* **1.** An acute, contagious virus disease, usually occurring in childhood. Its symptoms include those of the common cold and the eruption of red spots. Also called "rubeola". See **German measles. 2.** A disease of cattle and pigs, caused by tapeworm larvae. **3.** A plant disease, usually caused by fungi, and producing minute spots on leaves and stems. [Middle English *maseles,* plural of *masel,* from Middle Dutch *māsel,* blemish.]

mea·sly (méez-li, -'l-i) *adj.* **-slier, -sliest. 1.** Infected or spotted with measles; measled. **2.** Infected with larval tapeworms. Said of meat. **3.** *Slang.* Contemptibly small; meagre: *a measly tip.*

meas·ur·a·ble (mézh-rəb'l, mézhə-) *adj. Abbr.* **meas. 1.** Capable of being measured. **2.** Important; significant: *a measurable feat.*

meas·ure (mézhər) *n. Abbr.* **meas. 1.** The dimensions, quantity, or capacity of anything as ascertained by measuring: *Length, area, volume, and mass are basic measures of material properties.* **2.** A reference standard or sample used for the quantitative comparison of properties: *The standard kilogram is maintained as a measure of mass.* **3.** A unit specified by a scale, such as an inch, or by variable conditions, such as a day's march. **4.** A system of measurement, such as the metric system. **5.** A device, such as a marked tape or a graduated container, used for measuring. **6.** An act of measurement. **7.** A basis for evaluation or comparison: *the measure of an achievement.* **8.** An amount taken or prescribed as a standard: *a good measure of oats; short measure.* **9.** A specified extent, degree, or amount: *achieved some measure of success; hasn't yet grasped the full measure of the calamity.* **10.** An implied extent, degree or amount, such as: **a.** A fitting amount: *a measure of recognition.* **b.** A limited amount: *a measure of happiness.* **11.** Limit; bounds: *a generosity knowing no measure.* **12.** Appropriate restraint; moderation: *criticism in measure.* **13.** An action taken as a means to an end; an expedient: *desperate measures.* **14.** A legislative bill or enactment: *"I have opposed measures, not men."* (Lord Chesterfield). **15. a.** Poetic metre. **b.** Poetic rhythm or cadence. **16. a.** *Archaic.* A dance. **b.** *Poetic.* A tune. **17.** *Music.* **a.** The time of a piece of music. **b.** *Chiefly U.S.* The metrical unit between two bars on the staff; a **bar** *(see).* **18.** *Printing.* The width of a page or column of type. **—for good measure.** In addition to the required amount.
~v. **measured, -uring, -ures.** *—tr.* **1.** To ascertain the dimensions, quantity, or capacity of. **2.** To mark, lay out, or establish dimensions for by measuring. Often followed by *off: measure off an area.* **3.** To evaluate, especially by comparison with something else: *an encouraging result when measured against last year's figures.* **4.** To bring into opposition: *She measured her power with that of a dangerous adversary.* **5.** To serve as a measure of: *The inch measures length.* **6.** To mark off or separate, usually with reference to some unit of measurement. Often followed by *out: measure out a pint of milk.* **7.** To have a measurement of: *The room measures 10 by 12 metres.* **8.** To allot or distribute as if by measuring; mete. Often followed by *out: The revolutionary tribunal measured out harsh justice.* **9.** To consider or choose with care; weigh: *She measures her words with pedantic caution.* **10.** *Archaic.* To travel over or through. *—intr.* To take measurements; work out the dimensions of something. **—measure up.** To have the right qualifications. **—measure up to.** To match (expectations, standards, or the like). [Middle English *mesure,* from Old French *mesure,* from Latin *mēnsūra,* a measure, from *mētīrī* (past participial stem *mēns-*), to measure.] **—meas·ur·er** *n.*

meas·ured (mézhərd) *adj.* **1.** Regular in rhythm. **2.** Carefully weighed; calculated; deliberate: *with measured irony.* **3.** Written in metre. **—meas·ured·ly** *adv.* **—meas·ured·ness** *n.*

meas·ure·less (mézhər-ləss, -liss) *adj.* Limitless; immeasurable; infinite: *"Through caverns measureless to man"* (S.T. Coleridge). See Synonyms at **infinite. —meas·ure·less·ly** *adv.*

meas·ure·ment (mézhərmənt) *n.* **1.** The act of measuring or the process of being measured. **2.** A system of measuring: *measurement in miles.* **3.** The dimensions, quantity, or capacity determined by measuring: *room measurements.* See feature, next page.

meas·ur·ing jug (mézhəring) *n.* A transparent or semitransparent jug marked with a graduated scale and used in cookery to measure dry or liquid ingredients.

measuring worm *n.* The caterpillar of a geometrid moth, which moves in alternate contractions and expansions suggestive of measuring. Also called "inchworm", "looper".

meat (meet) *n.* **1.** The edible flesh of mammals, as distinguished from that of fish or poultry. **2.** Edible flesh including poultry and some fish and shellfish: *crab meat.* **3.** The edible portions of eggs, fruits, or nuts. **4. a.** The essence or principal part of something: *the meat of the editorial.* **b.** Valuable or significant content; substance: *a witty book, but without much meat in it.* **5.** *Archaic & Regional.* Food in general, especially solid food. [Middle English *mete,* "food", meat, Old English *mete,* food.]

meat and drink *n.* Something from which one derives great satisfaction or enjoyment.

meat·ball (méet-bawl) *n.* **1.** A small ball of minced meat variously prepared and cooked. **2.** *U.S. Slang.* A stupid person; especially, a stupid boy or man.

Meath (meeth; *locally always* meeth). *Irish* **Mhidhe.** County in Leinster province, Republic of Ireland, on the Irish Sea. It is mainly fertile, producing grain, potatoes, cattle, and horses. Its many historical sites include Newgrange, Tara, Kells, and the Boyne valley. Trim is the county town.

meat·less (méet-ləss, -liss) *adj.* **1.** Lacking meat or food. **2.** When meat is not to be eaten: *meatless days.*

meat loaf *n.* A dish of meat and other ingredients shaped into a loaf and usually baked.

meat-safe (méet-sayf) *n.* A cupboard for storing meat, usually consisting of a boxlike frame covered with wire netting or gauze.

me·a·tus (mi-áytəss, mee-) *n., pl.* **-tuses** or **meatus.** A body canal or opening, such as the opening of the ear or the urethral canal. [Latin *meātus,* passage, from *meāre* (past participial stem *meāt-*), to pass.]

meat·y (méeti) *adj.* **-ier, -iest. 1.** Of, resembling, or full of meat. **2.** Supplying ample food for thought; substantial: *a meaty theme for study and debate.* **—meat·i·ness** *n.*

mec·a·myl·a·mine (méckə-míllə-meen) *n.* A drug, $C_{11}H_{21}N.HCL$, taken orally to treat high blood pressure.

mec·ca (méckə) *n. Sometimes capital* **M. 1.** A place that is the centre of an activity or the goal to which adherents of a faith or practice aspire. **2.** Any place visited by many people. [After MECCA, as a goal of pilgrims.]

Mec·ca (méckə). *Arabic* **Mak·kah** (máck-kə). Holiest city of Islam. Capital of Hejaz province, western Saudi Arabia, it is circled by hills. The birthplace of Muhammad (*c.* A.D. 570) and site of the **Kaaba,** Mecca is a pilgrimage centre which all Muslims hope to visit at least once in their lives.

Mec·ca·no (mi-kaánō, me-, mə-) *n.* A trademark for any of various miniature construction sets consisting of metal or plastic parts that may be bolted together to make mechanical models.

mech. 1. mechanical; mechanics. **2.** mechanism.

me·chan·ic (mi-kánnik, mə-) *n.* **1.** A worker skilled in making, using, or repairing machines and tools. **2.** *Archaic.* A craftsman; an artisan. [Earlier form of MECHANICAL.] **—me·chan·ic** *adj.*

me·chan·i·cal (mi-kánnik'l, mə-) *adj. Abbr.* **mech. 1.** Of or pertaining to machines or tools. **2.** Operated or produced by a machine. **3.** Of or pertaining to mechanics. **4.** Acting like a machine or performed as if by a machine; automatic: *The speaker's delivery was mechanical.* **5.** Pertaining to, produced by, or dominated by physical forces. **6.** Interpreting and explaining the phenomena of the universe by reference to causally determined material forces; mechanistic. **7.** *Archaic.* Of or pertaining to manual labour, its tools, and its skills.
~n. U.S. Printing. A **paste-up** *(see).* [Middle English, pertaining to manual labour, earlier *mechanic,* from Latin *mēchanicus,* from Greek *mēkhanikos,* from *mēkhanē,* MACHINE.] **—me·chan·i·cal·ly** *adv.* **—me·chan·i·cal·ness** *n.*

mechanical advantage *n.* The ratio of the output force of a machine to the input force.

mechanical drawing *n.* **1.** Any drawing to scale of a machine, engine, building, or the like, from which measurements can be taken.

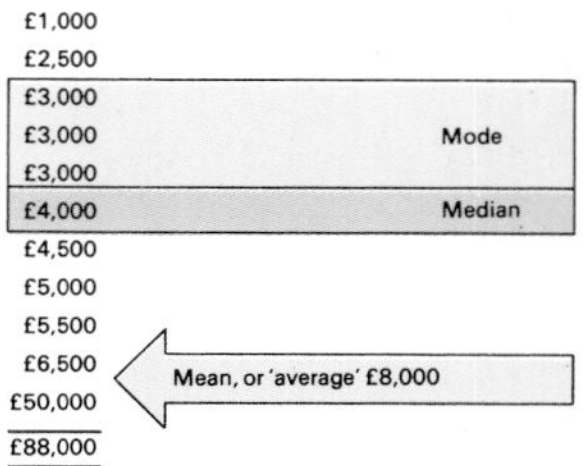
£1,000
£2,500
£3,000
£3,000
£3,000
Mode
£4,000
Median
£4,500
£5,000
£5,500
£6,500
£50,000
£88,000
Mean, or 'average' £8,000

mean³ *In this table of 11 incomes, the mean, or average, is the result of dividing the total equally; the mode is the most common income; and the median is the middle number in the set.*

PRONUNCIATION KEY

a, trap; aa, father; ai, fair; ar, star; aw, lawn; ay, play; b, bb, stab; rubber; ch, church; ck, ticket; d, dd, dead; ladder; e, dress; ee, bee; er, defer; ew, few; ewr, pure; ə, about; ər, letter; f, ff, fife; differ; g, gg, giggle; h, hat; i, kit; ī, price; īr, fire; j, judge; k, kick; l, ll, let; 'l, needle; m, mm, man; n, nn, no; 'n, sudden; ng, thing; o, lot; ō, no; ŏŏ, foot; ōō, shoe; oor, poor; ow, cow; owr, hour; oy, boy; p, pp, pepper; r, rr, red; s, ss, sauce; sh, ship; t, tt, totter; th, thick; th, this; smooth; u, cut; ur, turn; v, vv, valve; w, wet; y, yes; z, zz, zebra; zh, vision; pleasure

IN FOREIGN WORDS:

aN, oN, Saint-Saëns; hl, Llanelli; Hluhluwe; kh, loch; lough; Khaled

STRESS MARK:

in-sīt, insight; in-sīt, incite

TWO SYSTEMS OF WEIGHTS AND MEASURES
How the imperial and metric forms of measurement were established

By an order of Elizabeth I in 1588 the pound weight and the yard were defined by a bronze weight and a bronze bar. The word "pound" came from the Latin *pondo*, "by weight". A yard was made up of three feet, and a foot was the length of a man's foot. It was divided into 12 inches—from the Latin *uncia*, "a twelfth".

In 1824 Parliament set up the "imperial" system. A new standard yard and pound weight were stored in the House of Commons, but were destroyed with the building in 1834.

New standards were made and authorised in 1855. They were designed to be affected as little as possible by variations in atmosphere, temperature, air pressure, and humidity. The yard was defined as the distance between lines engraved in gold studs set into a gun-metal bar. The pound was defined as the weight of a cylinder of platinum-iridium alloy, 1.15 inches in diameter and 1.35 inches high. The standards were stipulated to be correct at 62°F and an atmospheric pressure of 30 inches of mercury.

The metric system was devised in France in the 1790s, and named after its basic unit of length, the metre—from the Greek for "measure". The metre was defined as one ten-millionth of the distance from the North Pole to the equator. Latin and Greek prefixes were given to divisions and multiples of the metre: "centimetre" for one-hundredth of a metre; "millimetre" for one-thousandth; "kilometre" for 1000 metres, and so on. The new unit of weight was the gram, the weight of one cubic centimetre of water at 4°C, when at its densest. The unit of capacity was the litre, defined as 100 cubic centimetres.

The metric system was gradually expanded to incorporate units of electricity, magnetism, temperature, and other quantities. In 1960, all these units were formalised in a single, world-wide system called the *Système Internationale*.

IMPERIAL UNITS

LENGTH
		Metric equivalent
	1 inch	2.54 centimetres
12 inches	1 foot	30.48 centimetres
3 feet	1 yard	0.9144 metres
1,760 yards	1 mile	1.6093 kilometres

AREA
	1 square inch	6.45 sq. centimetres
144 square inches	1 square foot	0.0929 sq. metres
9 square feet	1 square yard	0.836 sq. metres
4,840 sq. yards	1 acre	0.405 hectares
640 acres	1 square mile	259.00 hectares

VOLUME
	1 cubic inch	16.3871 cu. centimetres
1,728 cubic inches	1 cubic foot	0.028 cu. metres
27 cubic feet	1 cubic yard	0.765 cu. metres
	1 pint	0.57 litre
2 pints	1 quart	1.14 litres
4 quarts	1 gallon	4.55 litres

WEIGHT
	1 ounce	28.3495 grams
16 ounces	1 pound	0.4536 kilograms
14 pounds	1 stone	6.35 kilograms
8 stones	1 hundredweight	50.8 kilograms
20 hundredweight	1 ton	1.016 tonnes

HOW TO CONVERT FROM IMPERIAL TO METRIC
To convert	into	multiply by
LENGTH		
inches	millimetres	25.4
inches	centimetres	2.54
feet	metres	0.3048
yards	metres	0.9144
miles	kilometres	1.6093
AREA		
square inches	sq. centimetres	6.4516
square feet	square metres	0.093
square yards	square metres	0.836
acres	hectares	0.405
square miles	square kilometres	2.58999
VOLUME		
cubic inches	cubic centimetres	16.387
cubic feet	cubic metres	0.0283
cubic yards	cubic metres	0.7646
fluid ounces	millilitres	28.41
pints	litres	0.568
gallons	litres	4.55
WEIGHT		
ounces	grams	28.35
pounds	kilograms	0.45359
tons	tonnes	1.016

METRIC UNITS

LENGTH
		Imperial equivalent
	1 millimetre	0.03937 inches
10 millimetres	1 centimetre	0.39 inches
10 centimetres	1 decimetre	3.94 inches
100 centimetres	1 metre	39.37 inches
1000 metres	1 kilometre	0.62 mile

AREA
	1 sq. millimetre	0.0016 sq. inches
	1 sq. centimetre	0.155 sq. inches
100 sq. centimetres	1 sq. decimetre	15.50 sq. inches
10 000 square cm.	1 square metre	10.76 square feet
10 000 sq. metres	1 hectare	2.47 acres

VOLUME
	1 cubic centimetre	0.061 cubic inch
1000 cu. centimetres	1 cubic decimetre	61.024 cu. inches
1000 cu. decimetres	1 cubic metre	35.31 cubic feet
		1.308 cu. yards
	1 litre	1.76 pints
100 litres	1 hectolitre	22 gallons

WEIGHT
	1 gram	0.035 ounces
1000 grams	1 kilogram	2.2046 pounds
1000 kilograms	1 tonne	0.9842 ton

HOW TO CONVERT METRIC TO IMPERIAL
To convert	into	multiply by
LENGTH		
millimetres	inches	0.0394
centimetres	inches	0.3937
metres	feet	3.2808
metres	yards	1.0936
kilometres	miles	0.6214
AREA		
sq. centimetres	square inches	0.155
square metres	square feet	10.764
square metres	square yards	1.196
hectares	acres	2.471
square kilometres	square miles	0.386
VOLUME		
cubic centimetres	cubic inches	0.061
cubic metres	cubic feet	35.315
cubic metres	cubic yards	1.308
litres	pints	1.760
litres	gallons	0.220
WEIGHT		
grams	ounces	0.0353
kilograms	pounds	2.2046
tonnes	tons	0.984

sq. = square   cu. = cubic   cm. = centimetre

2. The art or skill of producing such drawings; draughtsmanship.

mechanical engineering *n. Abbr.* **M.E.** The branch of engineering that encompasses the generation and application of heat and mechanical power and the design, production, and use of machines and tools. —**mechanical engineer** *n.*

me·chan·ics (mi-kánniks, mə-) *n. Abbr.* **mech. 1.** *Used with a singular verb.* The analysis of the action of forces on matter or material systems. See **dynamics, statics, quantum mechanics, statistical mechanics. 2.** *Used with a singular verb.* The design, construction, operation, and application of machinery or mechanical structures. **3.** *Used with a plural verb.* The process by or way in which something operates, is constructed, or is carried out; the technical or procedural aspects of something: *grasps the mechanics of music but has no feel for it; the mechanics of getting a bill through Parliament.*

mech·a·nise, mech·a·nize (méckə-nīz) *tr.v.* **-nised, -nising, -nises. 1.** To equip with or perform by means of machinery: *mechanise a factory; mechanised farming.* **2.** To equip (a military unit) with motor vehicles, such as tanks and trucks. **3.** To make (something) mechanical, automatic, or unspontaneous. [MECHAN(ICAL) + -ISE.] —**mech·a·ni·sa·tion** (-nī-záysh'n ‖ *U.S.* -ni-) *n.*

mech·a·nism (méckə-niz'm) *n.* **1.** *Abbr.* **mech. a.** A machine or mechanical appliance. **b.** The arrangement of connected parts in a machine. **2.** Any system of parts that operate or interact like those of a machine: *the mechanism of the Solar System.* **3.** An instrument or process, physical or mental, by which something is done or comes into being: *The mechanism of learning includes studying.* **4.** *Psychology.* **a.** The automatic and consistent response of an organism to various stimuli. **b.** A usually unconscious mental and emotional pattern that influences behaviour: *a defence mechanism.* **5.** *Philosophy.* The doctrine that all natural phenomena are explicable by material causes and mechanical principles. [Late Latin *mēchanisma*, from Greek *mēkhanē*, machine.]

mech·a·nist (méckə-nist) *n.* One who subscribes to the philosophical doctrine of mechanism.

mech·a·nis·tic (méckə-nístik) *adj.* **1.** Of or pertaining to mechanics as a branch of physics. **2.** Of or pertaining to the philosophy of mechanism; specifically, tending to explain phenomena only by reference to physical or biological causes. —**mech·a·nis·ti·cal·ly** *adv.*

mech·a·no·chem·i·cal coupling (méckənō-kémmik'l) *n. Biochemistry.* The reversible conversion of chemical energy into mechanical work, as in the control of muscle·contraction and relaxation by ATP.

mech·a·no·ther·a·py (méckənō-thérrəpi) *n.* Physiotherapy using mechanical methods to improve the functioning of joints and muscles by producing repeated movements.

Me·chel·en (mékhə-lən) *French* **Ma·lines** (ma-léen). City on the Dijle river, Antwerp province, north central Belgium. Once a famous lace-making centre, it is now an important commercial and industrial city and a transport centre.

Mech·lin (mécklin) *n.* A delicate lace in which the pattern details are defined by a flat thread. Also called "malines". [After MECHELEN, where it was made.]

Meck·len·burg (mécklən-burg; *German* -boork). Former north German state. A much forested lowland along the Baltic with many lakes, it produces potatoes, rye, and sugar beet.

M.Econ. Master of Economics.

me·co·ni·um (mi-kóni-əm) *n.* Excrement in the foetal intestinal tract that is discharged after birth. [New Latin, from Latin, from Greek *mēkōnion*, "poppy juice", from *mēkōn*, poppy; from a fancied resemblance.]

Med (med) *n. Informal.* The Mediterranean Sea and its coastal regions. Preceded by *the.*

med. 1. medical; medicine. **2.** medieval. **3.** medium.

M. Ed. Master of Education.

med·al (médd'l) *n.* A piece of metal, stamped with a design or inscription commemorating an event or person, often given as an award.
~*tr.v.* **medalled** or *U.S.* **medaled, -alling** or *U.S.* **-aling, -als.** To honour or decorate with a medal. [French *médaille*, from Italian *medaglia*, from Common Romance *medallia* (unattested), from Vulgar Latin *metallea* (unattested), from Latin *metallum*, METAL.]

me·dal·lion (mi-dál-yən, me-, mə-) *n.* **1.** A large medal. **2.** Something resembling a large medal, such as an oval or circular panel or tablet bearing a design or portrait. [French *médaillon*, from Italian *medaglione*, augmentative of *medaglia*, MEDAL.]

med·al·list, *U.S.* **med·al·ist** (médd'l-ist) *n.* **1.** One who designs, makes, or collects medals. **2.** One who receives a medal.

Medal of Honour *n. Abbr.* **MH** The highest U.S. military decoration, awarded for bravery beyond the call of duty in action against the enemy. Also called "Congressional Medal of Honour".

medal play *n.* A form of competition in golf in which the total number of strokes taken is the basis of the score. Also called "stroke play". Compare **match play.**

Med·a·war (méddə-wər), **Sir Peter (Brian).** (1915–). British zoologist and anatomist. He developed techniques of joining the ends of severed nerves. He was awarded, with Sir Macfarlane Burnet, the Nobel prize in physiology and medicine (1960) for work on tissue transplants.

med·dle (médd'l) *intr.v.* **-dled, -dling, -dles. 1.** To intrude in other people's affairs or business; interfere. Used with *in* or *with.* **2.** To handle idly or ignorantly; tamper. Used with *with.* —See Synonyms at **interfere.** [Middle English *medlen*, "to mix", meddle, from Old French *medler*, variant of *mesler*, from Vulgar

Latin *misculāre* (unattested), frequentative of Latin *miscēre*, to mix.] —**med·dler** (médd'l-ər, méddlər) *n.*

med·dle·some (médd'l-səm) *adj.* Inclined to meddle or interfere. —**med·dle·some·ly** *adv.* —**med·dle·some·ness** *n.*

Mede (meed) *n.* A native or inhabitant of ancient Media.

Me·de·a (mi-déer, -dée-ə). *Greek Mythology.* A princess and sorceress of Colchis who helped Jason to obtain the Golden Fleece, lived as his consort, and killed their children as revenge for his infidelity.

Me·de·llín (medde-lín, -yín). Major industrial city of Colombia, and capital of Antioquia department in the northwest of the country. It has an important coffee market, a mint, and three universities.

me·di·a[1] (méedi-ə) *n., pl.* **-diae** (-ee). **1.** The middle layer of the wall of an artery or vein. **2.** The middle layer of various other parts or organs. **3.** Any of the main veins in an insect's wing. [Latin, feminine of *medius*, middle.]

media[2]. Alternative plural of **medium.**
~*pl.n. Informal.* The mass media as a whole. Preceded by *the.* Also used adjectivally: *a media personality.*
   Usage: In the sense "means of mass communication", *media* is a plural noun, derived from *medium.* The incorrect use of *media* as a singular is sometimes heard *(Television is an unpredictable media).* A new plural form is sometimes used *(medias),* but it is still considered unacceptable. The phrase *the mass media* is more commonly encountered as a singular, and attracts less criticism.

Me·di·a (méedi-ə). Ancient country of western Asia, in what is now northern Iran. —**Me·di·an** *adj. & n.*

me·di·a·cy (méedi-ə-si) *n.* The state or quality of being mediate.

mediaeval. Variant of **medieval.**

me·di·al (méedi-əl) *adj.* **1.** Pertaining to, situated in, or extending towards the middle; median. **2.** *Phonetics.* Designating a sound, syllable, or letter occurring between the initial and final positions in a word or morpheme. **3.** Designating or pertaining to a mathematical average or mean. **4.** Of average or ordinary size. [Late Latin *mediālis*, from Latin *medius*, middle.] —**me·di·al·ly** *adv.*

me·di·an (méedi-ən) *adj.* **1.** Pertaining to, located in, or directed towards the middle; medial. **2.** *Anatomy & Zoology.* Of, pertaining to, or lying in the plane that divides a bilaterally symmetrical animal into right and left halves; mesial. **3.** *Statistics.* Pertaining to or constituting the middle value in a distribution.
~*n.* **1.** A median point, plane, line, or part. **2.** *Statistics.* The middle value in a distribution, above and below which lie an equal number of values. **3.** In geometry: **a.** The line that joins a vertex of a triangle to the midpoint of the opposite side. **b.** The line that joins the midpoints of the nonparallel sides of a trapezoid. [Latin *mediānus*, from *medius*, middle.] —**me·di·an·ly** *adv.*

median plane *n.* A plane dividing a bilaterally symmetrical animal into right and left halves.

median point *n.* The intersection of the medians of a triangle.

me·di·ant (méedi-ənt) *n.* The third note in a diatonic musical scale between the tonic and the dominant, traditionally related harmonically to them.

me·di·as·ti·num (méedi-ə-stí-nəm, -ə-) *n., pl.* **-na** (-nə). **1.** The space between the pleural sacs in mammals, containing all the thoracic viscera except the lungs. **2.** A membrane between two parts of a cavity or organ. [New Latin, from neuter of Latin *mediastīnus*, median, from *medius*, middle.] —**me·di·as·ti·nal** *adj.*

me·di·ate (méedi-ayt) *v.* **-ated, -ating, -ates.** —*tr.* **1.** To resolve or settle (differences) by acting as an intermediary agent between two or more conflicting parties. **2.** To bring about (a settlement, agreement, or compromise) by action as an intermediary. **3.** To serve as a vehicle for bringing about (a result) or for transmitting (information, for example) to others. —*intr.* **1.** To occupy an intermediate or middle position. **2.** To intervene between parties in a dispute in order to effect an agreement, settlement, or compromise.
~*adj.* (-ət, -it). Acting through, involving, or dependent upon some intervening agency. [Latin *mediāre*, to be in the middle, from *medius*, middle.] —**me·di·ate·ly** *adv.* —**me·di·a·tive** (-ətiv, -aytiv) *adj.*

me·di·a·tion (méedi-áysh'n) *n.* **1.** The act of mediating; intervention. **2.** The intervention of a neutral power in an attempt to bring about a peaceful settlement between disputing nations.
   Synonyms: mediation, conciliation, arbitration.

me·di·a·tise, me·di·a·tize (méedi-ə-tīz) *tr.v.* **-tised, -tising, -tises.** To annex (a small state) to a large one, leaving the ruler of the smaller power with his title and a share of authority. [German *mediatisieren*, from *mediat*, mediate, from Latin *mediāre*, to be in the middle, MEDIATE.] —**me·di·a·ti·sa·tion** (-tī-záysh'n ‖ *U.S.* -ti-) *n.*

me·di·a·tor (méedi-aytər) *n.* One that mediates; especially, a person who serves as an intermediary to reconcile differences. —**me·di·a·tor·y** (-ətri, -ətəri, -áytəri) *adj.*

medic[1]. *U.S.* Variant of **medick.**

med·ic[2] (méddik) *n. Informal.* A doctor, medical orderly, or medical student. [Latin *medicus*, doctor.]

medic-. Variant of **medico-.**

med·i·ca·ble (méddikəb'l) *adj.* Potentially responsive to treatment with medicine; curable.

Med·i·caid (méddi-kayd) *n.* In the United States, a publicly-funded scheme providing medical aid for people who fall below a certain income level. [MEDIC(AL) + AID.]

med·i·cal (méddik'l) *adj. Abbr.* **med. 1.** Of or pertaining to the study or practice of medicine. **2.** Requiring or concerned with treatment by medicine as distinct from surgery. **3.** Medicinal; curative.
~*n. Informal.* A thorough physical examination. [French *médical,*

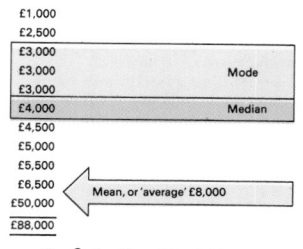

£1,000	
£2,500	
£3,000	
£3,000	Mode
£3,000	
£4,000	Median
£4,500	
£5,000	
£5,500	
£6,500	Mean, or 'average' £8,000
£50,000	
£88,000	

median[2] *In this table of 11 incomes, the median is the middle number in the set; the mean, or average, is the result of dividing the total equally; and the mode is the most common income.*

medicine man *This North American Indian witch doctor was painted by John White, a 17th-century artist and Virginia colonist.*

from Medieval Latin *medicālis,* from Latin *medicus,* doctor, from *medērī,* to heal.]

medical card *n.* In the United Kingdom, a card issued by the National Health Service and bearing the name of the card holder's doctor and general information about medical services.

medical certificate *n.* A certificate given by a medical practitioner after a medical examination, stating a person's fitness or unfitness, as for work, military service, or the like.

medical examiner *n.* In the United States, a public official responsible for determining the cause of death in cases of death by crime or violence. Compare **coroner.**

medical jurisprudence *n.* **Forensic medicine** *(see).*

medical social worker *n.* In Britain, a social worker attached to a hospital and responsible for the general welfare of patients. Formerly called "almoner".

me·dic·a·ment (me-díkkə-mənt, mi-, mə-, méddikə-) *n.* An agent that promotes recovery from injury or ailment; a medicine. [Latin *medicāmentum,* from *medicārī,* to MEDICATE.]

Med·i·care (méddi-kair) *n.* **1.** In the United States, a government health scheme providing medical care for the elderly. **2.** In Canada, a government health insurance scheme. [MEDI(CAL) + CARE.]

med·i·cate (méddi-kayt) *tr.v.* **-cated, -cating, -cates. 1.** To treat medicinally. **2.** To tincture or permeate with a medicinal substance. [Latin *medicārī,* from *medicus,* a doctor, from *medērī,* to heal.] **—med·i·ca·tive** (-kətiv, -kaytiv) *adj.*

med·i·ca·tion (méddi-káysh'n) *n.* **1.** A medicine. **2.** The act or process of being medicated. **3.** The administration of medicine.

Me·di·ci (méddi-chee, -chi, me-dée-; *Italian* méddee-chee). Italian noble and banking family, which produced three popes (Leo X, Clement VII, and Leo XI) and two queens of France (Catherine de Médicis and Marie de Médicis). The family's lavish patronage of the arts helped to make Florence one of the richest storehouses of European culture. The first of the family to rule Florence was Cosimo (1389–1464), who became Grand Duke of Tuscany in 1569. The most outstanding patron of learning and the arts was Lorenzo the Magnificent (1449–92), whose artists included Michelangelo and Botticelli. The line ended with Gian Gastone's death in 1737. **—Me·di·ce·an** (méddi-chéeən) *adj.*

me·dic·i·nal (me-díssin'l, mi-, mə-) *adj.* Pertaining to or having the properties of medicine; healing; curative.
~*n.* A medicinal substance. **—me·dic·i·nal·ly** *adv.*

med·i·cine (méd-s'n, méddi-, -sin) *n.* **1.** *Abbr.* **med.** The science of diagnosing, treating, alleviating, or preventing disease and other damage to the body or mind. **2.** The branch of this science encompassing treatment by drugs, diet, exercise, and other nonsurgical means. **3.** The practice of medicine. **4.** Any drug or other agent used to treat disease or injury. **5.** Among various tribal peoples, something believed to control natural or supernatural powers and to serve as a preventive or remedy. **—(someone's) own medicine.** Treatment, especially unkind or unfriendly treatment, given to a person who usually gives it to others. Used chiefly in the phrases *give someone a taste* or *dose of his own medicine.* **—take (one's) medicine.** To endure deserved punishment. [Middle English, from Old French, from Latin *medicīna,* the art of a physician, from *medicus,* doctor, from *medērī,* to heal.]

medicine ball *n.* A large, heavy ball used for exercise.

medicine chest *n.* A cabinet, chest, or cupboard containing medicines, bandages, and the like.

medicine lodge *n.* A large wooden structure used by some North American Indian peoples for various ritualistic ceremonies.

medicine man *n.* A person believed, especially among North American Indians, to possess supernatural powers for healing, invoking spirits, and other purposes; a sorcerer; a shaman.

medicine show *n.* A travelling show, popular especially in 19th-century America, that offered various entertainments and acts, between which medicines were peddled.

med·ick, *U.S.* **med·ic** (méddik) *n.* Any of several plants of the genus *Medicago,* native to the Old World and having clusters of small, usually yellow or purple flowers and compound leaves with three leaflets. [Middle English, from Latin *mēdica,* from Greek *Mēdikē (poa),* Median (grass).]

med·i·co (méddikō) *n., pl.* **-cos.** *Informal.* A doctor or medical student. [Italian and Spanish, from Latin *medicus,* doctor, from *medērī,* to heal.]

medico-, medic- *comb. form.* Indicates medical; for example, **medicodental.** [Latin *medicus,* doctor.]

me·di·e·val, me·di·ae·val (méddi-éev'l, med-, méedi- || meed-) *adj. Abbr.* **M., med. 1.** Of, pertaining to, or characteristic of the Middle Ages. **2.** *Informal.* Old-fashioned or out-of-date. [New Latin *Medium Aevum,* the Middle Age : Latin *medium,* neuter of *medius,* middle + *aevum,* age.] **—me·di·e·val·ly** *adv.*

Medieval Greek *n. Abbr.* **Med. Gr.** Greek as used from about A.D. 700 to 1500. Also called "Middle Greek".

me·di·e·val·ism, me·di·ae·val·ism (méddi-éev'l-iz'm, med-, méedi- || meed-) *n.* **1.** The spirit, beliefs, or practices of the Middle Ages. **2.** Devotion to or acceptance of the ideas of the Middle Ages. **3.** Scholarly study of the Middle Ages. **—me·di·e·val·ist** *n.*

Medieval Latin *n. Abbr.* **ML, M.L.** Latin as used throughout Europe in the Middle Ages, from about A.D. 700 to 1500.

me·di·na (me-déenə, mi-) *n.* The ancient native quarter of various North African towns. [Native name in North Africa.]

Me·di·na (me-déenə, mi-). *Arabic* **Al Madinah.** Second most holy city of Islam, in western Saudi Arabia. It lies in a fertile date-producing oasis, some 355 kilometres (220 miles) north of Mecca. Muhammad lived in the city after fleeing from Mecca (A.D. 622) and died there. The Mosque of the Prophet contains his tomb.

me·di·o·cre (méedi-ṓkər, méddi-, -ōkər) *adj.* Neither good nor very bad; lacking in commendable qualities; very ordinary. See Synonyms at **average.** [Latin *mediocris,* "halfway up the mountain", in a middle state : *medius,* middle + *ocris,* mountain, peak.]

me·di·oc·ri·ty (méedi-óckrəti, méddi-) *n., pl.* **-ties. 1.** The state or quality of being mediocre. **2.** Mediocre ability, achievement, or performance. **3.** A person who displays mediocre qualities.

Medit. Mediterranean Sea.

med·i·tate (méddi-tayt) *v.* **-tated, -tating, -tates.** *—tr.* **1.** To plan or intend in the mind: *He meditated revenge.* **2.** *Archaic.* To reflect upon; ponder; contemplate. *—intr.* **1.** To direct one's thoughts; reflect. Used with *on* or *upon*: *He meditated upon his loss.* **2.** To engage in deep, contemplative thought, or to concentrate on one thing or nothing, having emptied the mind of all thoughts, especially as a religious exercise or a means of achieving spiritual enlightenment. [Latin *meditārī.*] **—med·i·ta·tor** (-taytər) *n.*

med·i·ta·tion (méddi-táysh'n) *n.* **1. a.** The act of meditating. **b.** A devotional exercise of contemplation. **2.** A contemplative discourse, usually on a religious or philosophical subject. —See **transcendental meditation.**

med·i·ta·tive (méddi-tətiv, -taytiv) *adj.* Devoted to, characterised by, or expressing meditation. See Synonyms at **pensive. —med·i·ta·tive·ly** *adv.* **—med·i·ta·tive·ness** *n.*

Med·i·ter·ra·ne·an (médditə-ráyni-ən) *adj.* **1.** Designating a subgroup of the Caucasian race, characterised by dark hair and complexion, and relatively short stature. **2.** Of, pertaining to, or characteristic of the Mediterranean Sea or the countries bordering it and their inhabitants: *a lazy, Mediterranean life-style.* **3.** *Meteorology.* Having or pertaining to a type of climate with hot dry summers and warm, wet winters. **4.** *Small* **m.** Surrounded or almost surrounded by land. Said of large bodies of water.
~*n.* **1.** The Mediterranean Sea. **2.** A member of the Mediterranean racial subgroup. **3.** A native or inhabitant of the Mediterranean region. [Latin *mediterrāneus* : *medius,* middle + *terra,* land.]

Mediterranean fever *n.* A disease, **brucellosis** *(see).*

Mediterranean Sea. *Abbr.* **Medit.** Almost landlocked body of water lying between Europe, North Africa, and Asia. It connects with the Atlantic through the Strait of Gibraltar, with the Black Sea through the Dardanelles, the Sea of Marmara, and the Bosporus, and with the Red Sea through the Suez Canal. Its larger islands include Crete, Cyprus, Sardinia, Corsica, and Sicily, and its shores have cradled many civilisations. Commercial developments have caused severe pollution which is aggravated by the Sea's nearly tideless nature; nevertheless, tourism remains a major industry.

me·di·um (méedi-əm, méed-yəm) *n., pl.* **-dia** (méedi-ə, méed-yə) or **-ums** (the only form for sense 5). *Abbr.* **m, M, m., M., med. 1.** Something occupying a position or having a condition midway between extremes; a mean; a compromise. **2.** *Physics.* An intervening substance through which something is transmitted or carried, such as an agency for transmitting energy. **3.** An agency, such as a person, object, or quality, by means of which something is accomplished, conveyed, or transferred: *Money is used as a medium of exchange.* **4.** A means of mass communication, such as newspapers, magazines, or television. See Usage note at **media. 5.** A person thought to have powers of communicating with the spirits of the dead. **6.** A surrounding environment in which something functions and thrives; especially: **a.** The substance in which a specific organism lives and thrives. **b.** A substance in which microorganisms are cultivated for scientific purposes; a culture medium. **7. a.** A specific type of artistic technique or means of expression as determined by the materials used or the creative methods involved. **b.** The materials used. **8.** Any solvent with which paint is thinned to the proper consistency. **9.** *Chemistry.* A filtering substance, such as filter paper. **10.** A size of paper, usually 46 × 58 centimetres (18 × 23 inches). —See Synonyms at **average.**
~*adj. Abbr.* **m, M, m., M., med. 1.** Occurring or being between two degrees, positions, amounts, or quantities; intermediate: *a medium steak.* **2.** Average; mean: *a medium-grade ore.* [Latin *medium,* the middle, from *medius,* middle.]

me·di·um-dat·ed (méedi-əm-dáytid, méed-yəm-) *adj. Finance.* Designating gilt-edged securities that are redeemable at any time between 5 and 15 years after the date of purchase. Compare **long-dated, short-dated.**

medium frequency *n. Abbr.* **MF, M.F.** A radio frequency or radio-frequency band in the range 3,000 to 300 kilohertz.

medium of exchange *n.* Anything that is commonly used in a specific area or among a certain group of people as money. See **circulating medium, money.**

medium wave *n. Abbr.* **MW, M.W.** A radio wave or band of radio waves with wavelengths between 100 and 1 000 metres.

med·lar (méddlər) *n.* **1.** A tree, *Mespilus germanica,* cultivated for its fruit. **2.** The fruit of this tree, similar in appearance to a crab apple but eaten when soft. [Middle English, from Old French *medler,* from *medle* (unattested), variant of *mesle,* a medlar fruit, from Latin *mespila,* from Greek *mespilē†.*]

med·ley (méddli) *n., pl.* **-leys. 1.** A jumbled assortment; a mixture: *a medley of grating noises.* **2.** A musical arrangement made up of a series of melodies from various sources. **3.** A swimming race in which each participant swims lengths using various different, pre-

PRONUNCIATION KEY

a, trap; aa, father; ai, **fair**;
ar, **star**; aw, **lawn**; ay, **play**;
b, bb, stab; **rubber**;
ch, **church**; ck, **ticket**;
d, dd, **dead**; **ladder**; e, **dress**;
ee, **bee**; er, **defer**; ew, **few**;
ewr, **pure**; ə, about;
ər, **letter**; f, ff, **fife**; **differ**;
g, gg, **giggle**; h, **hat**; i, **kit**;
ī, price; īr, **fire**; j, **judge**;
k, **kick**; l, ll, **let**; 'l, **needle**;
m, mm, **man**; n, nn, **no**;
'n, sudden; ng, **thing**; o, **lot**;
ō, **no**; o͝o, **foot**; o͞o, **shoe**;
oor, **poor**; ow, **cow**;
owr, **hour**; oy, **boy**;
p, pp, **pepper**; r, rr, **red**;
s, ss, **sauce**; sh, **ship**;
t, tt, **totter**; th, **thick**; <u>th</u>, **this**;
smooth; u, **cut**; ur, **turn**;
v, vv, **valve**; w, **wet**; y, **yes**;
z, zz, **zebra**; <u>zh</u>, vision;
pleasure

IN FOREIGN WORDS:

aɴ, oɴ, Saint-Saëns;
<u>hl</u>, **Llanelli**; **Hluhluwe**;
<u>kh</u>, loch; **lough**; **Khaled**

STRESS MARK:

ín-sīt, insight; in-sī́t, incite

scribed strokes (in individual races) or in which each member of a team swims using a different stroke (in relay races).
~*adj.* 1. Made up of a jumbled mixture of elements. 2. Of or pertaining to a swimming medley: *a medley relay.* [Middle English *medlee,* from Old French, variant of *meslee,* from Vulgar Latin *misculāta* (unattested), from Late Latin *misculāre,* to mix up, frequentative of *miscēre,* to mix.]

Mé·doc[1] (máy-dok, méddok, may-dók). A region of southwest France, north of Bordeaux, between the Gironde estuary and the Bay of Biscay. It is particularly famous for its red wines, its vineyards including those of Château Lafite and Château Latour.

Médoc[2] *n.* A red Bordeaux wine made in Médoc.

me·dul·la (me-dúllə, mi-) *n., pl.* **-las** or **-lae** (-dúllee). 1. *Anatomy.* The inner core of certain animal body structures where this differs in form or function from the outer zone; for example, the marrow of bone. 2. The medulla oblongata. 3. *Botany.* The **pith** *(see)* or central tissue in stems of certain plants. [Latin *medulla,* marrow.] **—me·dul·lar** (-dúllər), **med·ul·lar·y** (-dúlləri || *U.S. also* méd-də-lerri) *adj.*

medulla ob·lon·ga·ta (ób-long-gaá-tə, -gáy-) *n., pl.* **medulla oblongatas** or **medullae oblongatae** (-tee). The nervous tissue at the bottom of the brain that controls respiration, circulation, and certain other bodily functions. [New Latin, "elongated marrow".]

medullary ray *n. Botany.* The undifferentiated tissue between the vascular bundles in young plants and in plants not undergoing secondary thickening.

medullary sheath *n.* 1. *Anatomy.* **Myelin** *(see).* 2. *Botany.* A layer of thick-walled cells surrounding the pith in the stems of various plants.

med·ul·lat·ed (me-dúl-aytid, mi-, méddəl- || *U.S. also* méjəl-) *adj.* 1. *Anatomy.* Myelinated. 2. Having a medulla. [Late Latin *medullātus,* having a marrow, from Latin *medulla,* MEDULLA.] **—med·ul·la·tion** (-áysh'n) *n.*

med·ul·li·sa·tion (me-dúl-ī-záysh'n, mi-, méddəl- || *U.S.* -i-, *also* méjəl-) *n.* Replacement of bone tissue by marrow, as in inflammatory bone disease.

me·du·sa (mi-déw-zə, me-, -sə || -dóō-) *n., pl.* **-sas** or **-sae** (-zee, -see). The tentacled, free-swimming sexual stage in the life cycle of a coelenterate of the class Scyphozoa or Hydrozoa; a jellyfish. Compare **polyp.** [New Latin.] **—me·du·san** *adj.*

Me·du·sa (mi-déw-zə, me-, -sə || -dóō-) *Greek Mythology.* One of the three Gorgons, slain by Perseus.

me·du·soid (mi-déw-zoyd, -soyd, me- || -dóō-) *n.* A jellyfish or a shape resembling a jellyfish. **—me·du·soid** *adj.*

Med·way (méd-way). River of southeast England, rising in Sussex to flow some 113 kilometres (70 miles) through Kent to join the Thames estuary at Sheerness. It divides the "Kentish Men", born west of the river, from the "Men of Kent", born to the east.

meed (meed) *n. Archaic.* A merited gift or reward. [Middle English *mede,* Old English *mēd.*]

meek (meek) *adj.* **meeker, meekest.** 1. a. Showing patience and humility; long-suffering. b. Easily imposed upon; submissive. 2. *Archaic.* Kind; merciful: *"that I am meek and gentle with these butchers."* (Shakespeare). —See Synonyms at **humble.** [Middle English *mēk, mēoc,* from Old Norse *mjūkr,* gentle, soft.] **—meek·ly** *adv.*

meer·kat (méer-kat) *n.* Any of several small South African mammals similar to the mongoose; especially, *Suricata suricatta.* [Afrikaans, from Dutch, "sea-cat", originally a type of monkey, so called because imported from overseas.]

meer·schaum (méer-shəm, -showm || -shawm) *n.* 1. A compact, usually white mineral of hydrous magnesium silicate, $Mg_4[Si_6O_{15}](OH)_2{\cdot}6H_2O$, found chiefly in the Mediterranean area and used in fashioning tobacco pipes and as a building stone. Also called "sepiolite". 2. A tobacco pipe with a bowl of meerschaum. [German, "sea-foam", translation of Persian *kef-i-daryā,* referring to its frothy appearance.]

Mee·rut (méer-ət). City of Uttar Pradesh, north central India, where the Indian Mutiny began (1857).

meet[1] (meet) *v.* **met** (met), **meeting, meets.** —*tr.* 1. To come into the presence or company of, by chance or by arrangement: *met her on the stairs.* 2. To come into the presence or company of, for the purpose of conferring: *meeting the directors at 11.* 3. To be present at the arrival of: *I plan to meet the train.* 4. To be introduced to; make the acquaintance of: *We'd like to meet your sister.* 5. To come into association or conjunction with; join: *where the sea meets the sky.* 6. To come to the notice of (the senses): *more than meets the eye.* 7. To experience; undergo; suffer: *to meet one's fate.* 8. To encounter in conflict or competition; oppose: *Spurs will meet Leeds in the final.* 9. To cope or contend effectively with: *met every accusation with a satisfactory explanation.* 10. To come into conformity with the views, wishes, or opinions of: *The firm must meet us on that point.* 11. To satisfy (a demand, obligation, or the like); fulfil: *meet a need.* 12. To pay; settle: *enough money to meet the expenses.* —*intr.* 1. To come together by chance or by arrangement. Often used with *up* or *up with: met up with an old friend; Let's meet for a drink.* 2. To come into conjunction or contact; be joined: *"East is East, and West is West, and never the twain shall meet"* (Rudyard Kipling). 3. To come together as opponents; contend. 4. To be introduced or become acquainted. 5. To assemble, as for a meeting or other common purpose. **—meet with.** 1. To experience or encounter: *The housing bill met with approval.* 2. To suffer or undergo: *meet with an accident.*
~*n.* 1. A meeting or contest, especially an athletic competition. 2. The gathering of hounds and riders for a hunt. [Middle English *meten,* Old English *mētan.*]

meet[2] *adj. Archaic.* Fitting; proper; suitable. [Middle English *mete, y-mete,* Old English *gemǣte.*] **—meet·ly** *adv.*

meet·ing (méeting) *n. Abbr.* **mtg.** 1. a. A coming together of people for a common purpose; an assembly. b. The persons so assembled. 2. A place or point where things meet; a conjunction. 3. A hostile or competitive encounter. 4. A programme of horse-racing or dog-racing at a particular racecourse.

meeting house *n.* 1. A place of worship, especially one used by Quakers. 2. In New Zealand, the central large building on a Maori marae where gatherings of the community take place.

meet·ing-point (méeting-poynt) *n.* 1. A place of assembly. 2. An area where different cultures, ideas, or the like converge: *a meeting-point between East and West.*

mega– *comb. form.* Indicates: 1. *Abbr.* **M** One million (10^6); for example, **megahertz.** 2. a. Large; for example, **megalith.** b. Large in comparison with others of its kind; for example, **megatanker.** 3. *Informal.* Great or exaggeratedly large; for example **megastar, megahype.** [Greek, from *megas,* great.]

meg·a·ceph·a·ly (méggə-kéffəli, -séffəli) *n.* Enlargement of the head, **macrocephaly** *(see).* [MEGA- + -CEPHALY.] **—meg·a·ce·phal·ic** (-kə-fál-ik, -si-), **meg·a·ceph·a·lous** (-kéffə-ləss, -séffə-) *adj.*

meg·a·cy·cle (méggə-sīk'l) *n. Physics.* One million cycles per second; a megahertz. Not in current technical usage.

meg·a·death (méggə-deth) *n.* 1. The death of one million people, especially as the result of a war. 2. Loosely, the death of a very large number of people.

Me·gae·ra (mi-jéer-ə). *Greek Mythology.* One of the **Furies** *(see).*

megagamete. Variant of **macrogamete.**

meg·a·hertz (méggə-herts, -hairts) *n., pl.* **megahertz.** *Abbr.* **MHz** *Physics.* One million cycles per second, used especially as a radio-frequency unit.

meg·a·lith (méggə-lith) *n.* A very large stone used in various prehistoric architectures or monumental styles, notably in western Europe during the second millennium B.C. See **dolmen, menhir.** [MEGA- + -LITH.] **—meg·a·lith·ic** (-líthik) *adj.*

megalo–, megal– *comb. form.* Indicates largeness, greatness, or exaggerated size; for example, **megalocephaly, megalomania.** [Greek, from *megas* (extended stem *megal-*), great.]

meg·a·lo·blast (méggəlō-blast, -blaast) *n.* A large blood cell that is an abnormal form of a red-blood-cell precursor. It occurs in certain types of anaemia *(megaloblastic anaemias).* [MEGALO- + -BLAST.] **—meg·a·lo·blas·tic** (-blástik) *adj.*

meg·a·lo·car·di·a (méggəlō-kárdi-ə) *n. Pathology.* Enlargement of the heart. Also called "cardiomegaly". [MEGALO- + Greek *kardia,* heart.]

meg·a·lo·ceph·a·ly (méggəlō-séffəli) *n.* Enlargement of the head, **macrocephaly** *(see).* [MEGALO- + -CEPHALY.] **—meg·a·lo·ce·phal·ic** (-si-fál-ik), **meg·a·lo·ceph·a·lous** (-séffələss) *adj.*

meg·a·lo·ma·ni·a (méggəlō-máyni-ə) *n.* A psychopathological condition involving fantasies of wealth or power. **—meg·a·lo·ma·ni·ac** *adj.* & *n.* **—meg·a·lo·ma·ni·a·cal** (-mə-nī-ək'l) *adj.*

meg·a·lop·o·lis (méggə-lóppə-liss) *n.* A region made up of several large cities and their surrounding areas in sufficiently close proximity to be considered a single urban complex. [MEGALO- + Greek *polis,* city.] **—meg·a·lo·pol·i·tan** (-lə-póllit'n, -lō-) *adj.*

meg·a·lo·saur (méggə-lō-sawr, -lə-) *n.* Also **meg·a·lo·sau·rus** (-sáwrəss). An extinct gigantic carnivorous dinosaur, genus *Megalosaurus,* of the Jurassic period. [New Latin *Megalosaurus* : MEGALO- + -SAURUS.] **—meg·a·lo·saur·i·an** (-sáwri-ən) *n.* & *adj.*

meg·a·phone (méggə-fōn) *n.* A funnel-shaped device used to direct and amplify the voice. Compare **loud-hailer. —meg·a·phon·ic** (-fónnik) *adj.* **—meg·a·phon·i·cal·ly** *adv.*

meg·a·pode (méggə-pōd) *n.* Any bird of the family Megapodiidae, found in Australia and many South Pacific islands, that incubates its eggs by natural heat from mounds of rotting vegetation, sand, and the like. Also called "scrub fowl", "scrub turkey". [New Latin *Megapodius* : MEGA- + -PODE.]

Még·a·ra (méggə-rə). The capital of Megaris, a small Dorian state. It was a wealthy centre of sea trade (eighth to fifth century B.C.), and its people founded many colonies, including Byzantium.

meg·a·ron (méggə-ron) *n., pl.* **-ra** (-rə). The main hall or central room of an ancient Greek house, having a hearth. [Greek, from *megas,* large.]

meg·a·scop·ic (méggə-skóppik) *adj.* Visible to the naked eye; macroscopic. **—meg·a·scop·i·cal·ly** *adv.*

meg·a·spo·ran·gi·um (méggə-spaw-ránji-əm, -spə-) *n., pl.* **-gia** (-ránji-ə). *Botany.* A structure that encloses a megaspore. Sometimes called "macrosporangium".

meg·a·spore (méggə-spawr || -spōr) *n. Botany.* 1. The larger of two types of spores formed by heterosporous plants, such as certain ferns, giving rise to the female gametophyte. Compare **microspore.** 2. A spore that forms the embryo sac in seed plants. Sometimes called "macrospore". **—meg·a·spor·ic** *adj.*

meg·a·spo·ro·phyll (méggə-spáwr-ə-fil || -spṓr-) *n. Botany.* A leaf-like structure that bears megasporangia.

meg·a·there (méggə-theer) *n.* A member of the extinct family Megatheriidae, composed of large ground sloths of the Miocene and Pleistocene epochs. [New Latin *Megatherium* : MEGA- + -THERE.] **—meg·a·ther·i·an** (-théer-i-ən) *adj.*

Medusa *In Greek mythology, anyone who looked at the face of this snake-haired monster was turned to stone. Medusa was killed eventually by the hero Perseus, who avoided looking at her directly by watching her reflection in his polished shield. This representation of her is on the handle of a krater – a vessel used for diluting wine – and dates from about 520 B.C.*

megalith *A prehistoric standing stone, or megalith, in Brittany, France. Megaliths, which were usually of undressed stone, are thought to have had religious significance for their builders, and this one has been converted into a Christian shrine.*

meg·a·ton (méggə-tun) *n.* A unit of explosive force equal to one million tons of TNT. —**meg·a·ton·nage** *n.*

me generation *n.* People collectively, especially in the United States, who lived or live by the self-preoccupied and self-advancing values of the *me decade,* the 1970s. [Coined by Tom WOLFE, probably influenced by earlier phrase, *now generation* (1960s).]

Me·gid·do (mə-gíddō). Ancient fortress town of north Israel. Strategically situated in the valley of Esdraelon, on the route between Mesopotamia and Egypt, it was the site of many battles, and it may be the Armageddon of the Bible (Revelation 16:16), where the last battle on earth will be fought.

me·gil·lah (mə-gíllə) *n.* **1.** The Judaic scroll containing the Biblical narrative of the Book of Esther, traditionally read in synagogues to celebrate the festival of Purim. **2.** *Small m. Informal.* A prolix, tediously detailed narrative or explanation. [Hebrew *məgillāh,* "scroll", from *gālal,* to roll.]

me·gilp, ma·gilp (mə-gílp) *n.* A base used for oil colours, usually linseed oil and mastic varnish. [18th century : origin obscure.]

meg·ohm (méggōm) *n. Symbol* **M** Ω. One million ohms. [MEGA- + OHM.]

me·grim (mée-grim) *n.* **1.** A severe headache, a **migraine** *(see).* **2.** *Often plural.* A caprice or fancy: *"Can't one work for sober truth as well as for megrims?"* (George Eliot). **3.** *Plural.* Depression or unhappiness: *"If these megrims are the effect of Love, thank Heaven, I never knew what it was."* (Samuel Richardson). **4.** *Plural.* A disease of cattle and horses. In this sense, also called "blind staggers". [Middle English *mygreyn,* from Old French, MIGRAINE.]

Me·hem·et A·li (mi-hémmit a'ali), also called Mohammed Ali (*c.* 1769–1849). Turkish soldier, pasha of Egypt (1805–49). He rose from common soldier to command the Turkish army in Egypt and became pasha of Egypt, then an Ottoman province. In the late 1830s he attacked Turkey. The European powers forced a peace which made Mehemet's line hereditary in Egypt.

Mei·ji (máy-jée), also known as Mutsuhito (1852–1912). Emperor of Japan (1867–1912). He took the throne, aged 15, in the Meiji Restoration of 1867, and presided over the transformation of Japan from a feudal state into a modern constitutional one. His name means "enlightened government".

mei·o·sis (mī-ō-siss) *n., pl.* **-ses** (-seez). **1.** *Biology.* The cell division in sexually reproducing organisms that reduces the number of chromosomes in reproductive cells to half that found in the somatic cells, leading to the production of gametes in animals and spores in plants. Also called "reduction division". Compare **mitosis.** **2.** Rhetorical understatement; litotes. [New Latin, from Greek *meiōsis,* diminution, from *meioun,* to diminish, from *meiōn,* less.] —**mei·ot·ic** (-óttik) *adj.* —**mei·ot·i·cal·ly** *adv.*

Me·ir (may-éer), **Golda,** born Golda Mabovitch (1898–1978). Russian-born Israeli stateswoman, prime minister of Israel (1969–74). She lived in the United States from 1906 and settled in Palestine in 1921. After Israel was created (1948) she became minister of labour (1949–56) and foreign minister (1956–66). In 1966 she became leader of the Mapai (later Labour) Party and succeeded Levi Eshkol as prime minister in 1969. She resigned in April, 1974.

Meis·sen (míss'n). City in Dresden district, East Germany, on the river Elbe. It is famous for its porcelain, known as Meissen ware or Dresden china, made from local kaolin. Production moved here from Dresden in 1710.

Meissen ware *n.* A delicate porcelain ware made in Meissen, East Germany. Also called "Dresden china".

Meis·ter·sing·er (míe-stər-sing-ər; *German* -zing-) *n., pl.* **-ers** or **Meistersinger.** *German.* A member of any of the guilds organised in the principal cities of Germany in the 14th, 15th, and 16th centuries for the purpose of establishing competitive standards for the composition and performance of music and poetry. Also called "mastersinger". [German, mastersinger.]

Meit·ner (mītnər), **Lise** (1878–1968). Austrian-born physicist. She worked in Berlin with Otto Hahn, and in 1918 they discovered the element protactinium. Her analysis of Hahn's experiments on uranium nuclei marks the discovery of nuclear fission (1939). Meitner became a Swedish citizen in 1949, and worked on subatomic physics at the Nobel Institute at Stockholm.

Méjico. See **Mexico.**

Me·kong (mée-kóng, máy-). *Chinese* **Lancang Jiang** or **Lan-ts'ang Chiang.** Major river of southeast Asia, 4 184 kilometres (2,600 miles) long. Rising in Tibet, China, it flows mainly south through China, Laos, Kampuchea, and Vietnam to join the South China Sea. Its delta is a major rice-growing area, and its last 550 kilometres (340 miles) can take moderate-sized ships. The United Nations Mekong Scheme to develop the lower Mekong valley includes the hydroelectric power station at Khône Rapids, South Laos.

mel (mel) *n.* A constituent of certain pharmaceutical preparations, consisting of a pure form of honey. [Latin, honey.]

mel·a·mine resin (méllə-meen) *n.* A thermosetting resin produced from melamine, $C_3H_6N_6$, used for moulded products, adhesives, and surface coatings. [German *Melamin* : *Melam* (arbitrary term for distillate of ammonium thiocyanate) + AMINE.]

mel·an·cho·li·a (méllən-kōli-ə) *n.* A mental disorder characterised by feelings of dejection and usually by withdrawal. It is often a phase of manic-depressive psychosis. [New Latin, MELANCHOLY.] —**mel·an·cho·li·ac** *adj.* & *n.*

mel·an·chol·ic (méllən-kóllik) *adj.* **1.** Suffering from or subject to melancholy; depressed. **2.** Pertaining to, subject to, or suffering from melancholia. —**mel·an·chol·ic** *n.* —**mel·an·chol·i·cal·ly** *adv.*

mel·an·chol·y (méllən-kəli, -kolli) *n.* **1.** Sadness or depression of the spirits; gloom. **2.** Pensive reflection or contemplation. **3.** *Archaic.* **a.** Black bile, one of the four humours of ancient or medieval physiology. **b.** An emotional state characterised by sullenness and outbreaks of violent anger, believed to arise from the bile.
~*adj.* **1.** Sad; depressed; gloomy. **2. a.** Tending to cause sadness or gloom. **b.** Expressive of gloom or sadness: *a melancholy sigh.* **3.** Pensive; thoughtful: *"He had a pleasing face and a melancholy air."* (Jane Austen). —See Synonyms at **sad.** [Middle English *malencolie, melancholye,* from Old French *melancolie,* from Late Latin *melancholia,* from Greek *melankholia,* sadness, "(an excess of) black bile" : *melas* (stem *melan-*), black + *kholē,* bile.] —**mel·an·chol·i·ly** *adv.* —**mel·an·chol·i·ness** *n.*

Me·lanch·thon (mə-lángk-thən, me-, -thon, me-lánkh-ton), **Philip,** born Philip Schwarzerd (1497–1560). German theologian and a leader of the German Reformation. He was a friend of Luther, and wrote *Loci communes* (1521), outlining Lutheran doctrine.

Mel·a·ne·si·a (méllə-née-zi-ə, -zhi-ə, -zhə, -si-ə, -shi-ə, -shə). A division of the Pacific islands, including Papua New Guinea, the Solomons, Vanuatu, New Caledonia, the Bismarck Archipelago, Fiji, and other islands in the southwest. The name comes from the Greek word *melas* (black), referring to the dark skin of the dominant race of inhabitants. See **Micronesia, Polynesia.**

Mel·a·ne·sian (méllə-née-zi-ən, -zhi-ən, -zhən, -si-ən, -shi-ən, -shən) *adj.* Of or pertaining to Melanesia, its people, or their languages. ~*n.* **1.** An indigenous inhabitant of Melanesia. **2.** A subfamily of Austronesian languages spoken in Melanesia.

mé·lange, me·lange (may-lónzh) *n.* **1.** A mixture. **2.** *Geology.* A mixture of different rock types, of diverse origin and age. [French, from Old French, from *mesler,* to mix, from Vulgar Latin *misculāre* (unattested), from Latin *miscēre,* to mix.]

me·lan·ic (me-lánnik) *adj.* **1.** Of, pertaining to, or exhibiting melanism. **2.** Suffering from melanosis.

mel·a·nin (méllənin) *n.* A dark pigment found in the skin, retina, and hair. [MELAN(O)- + -IN.]

mel·a·nism (méllə-niz'm) *n.* **1.** Dark coloration of skin, hair, fur, feathers, or the like, due to excessive production of melanin. It occurs, for example, among populations of moths in regions blackened by pollution *(industrial melanism),* where dark coloration provides camouflage. **2.** *Pathology.* Melanosis. [MELAN(O)- + -ISM.] —**mel·a·nist** *n.* —**mel·a·nis·tic** (-nístik) *adj.*

mel·a·nite (méllə-nīt) *n.* A black variety of garnet. [German *Melanit* : MELAN(O)- + -ITE.] —**mel·a·nit·ic** (-níttik) *adj.*

melano-, melan- *comb. form.* Indicates blackness or darkness; for example, **melanocyte, melanoma.** [New Latin, from Greek, from *melas* (stem *melan-*), black.]

Mel·a·noch·ro·i (méllə-nóckrō-ī, -nóck-roy) *pl.n.* The members of a subdivision of Caucasians, having dark hair and light skin. [New Latin, "the dark-pale (people)" : MELAN(O)- + Greek *ōkhroi,* plural of *ōkhros,* pale.] —**Mel·a·noch·roid** (-nóck-royd) *adj.*

mel·a·no·cyte (méllə-nō-sīt) *n. Biology.* An epidermal cell capable of synthesising the black pigment melanin, and responsible for colour variations in the skin of many animals including humans. [MELANO- + -CYTE.]

mel·a·noid (méllə-noyd) *adj.* **1.** Black-pigmented; dark in colour. **2.** Suffering from or resembling melanosis. [Greek *melanoeidēs,* black-looking : MELAN(O)- + -OID.] —**mel·a·noid** *n.*

mel·a·no·ma (méllə-nō-mə) *n., pl.* **-mas** or **-mata** (-mətə). A dark-pigmented malignant tumour. [New Latin : MELAN(O)- + -OMA.]

mel·a·no·sis (méllə-nō-siss) *n. Pathology.* Abnormally dark pigmentation of the skin or other tissues, resulting from sunburn and various dermatoses. [New Latin : MELAN(O)- + -OSIS.] —**mel·a·not·ic** (-nóttik) *adj.*

mel·a·nous (méllə-nəss) *adj.* Having a swarthy or black complexion and black hair. Compare **xanthous.** [MELAN(O)- + -OUS.] —**mel·a·nos·i·ty** (-nóssəti) *n.*

mel·a·to·nin (méllə-tōnin) *n.* A hormone secreted by the pineal gland that causes lightening of the skin in certain animals. [*Mel*anocyte + serotonin (referring to its ability to lighten melanocytes).]

Mel·ba (mélbə), **Dame Nellie,** stage name of Helen Porter Mitchell (1859–1931). Australian soprano. She made her debut in Brussels (1887), and sang regularly at Covent Garden (1888–1926) and the Metropolitan Opera (1893–1910).

Melba toast *n.* Very thin crisp toast. [After Dame Nellie MELBA.]

Mel·bourne (mél-bərn, -bawrn; *locally* -'bərn). Capital of Victoria, southeast Australia, and the country's second largest city. It was founded (1835) at the mouth of the Yarra river on Port Phillip Bay, and after the gold rush of 1851 developed into a financial and market centre. Its industries include engineering, vehicle and textile production, and food processing. Melbourne was the national capital (1901–27) and the venue for the 1956 Olympic Games.

Mel·bourne (mél-bərn, -bawrn), **William Lamb, 2nd Viscount** (1779–1848). British prime minister (1834 and 1835–41). He was home secretary in Lord Grey's government (1830–34) and succeeded Grey as prime minister. As home secretary he was responsible for the deportation of the Tolpuddle martyrs (1834).

Mel·chi·or (mélki-awr). One of the three **Magi** *(see)* who travelled to see the infant Jesus.

Mel·chite (mélkīt) *n.* A member of the Uniat Greek Catholic Church, concentrated in the Middle East. [Medieval Latin *Melchita,* from Greek *Melkhitēs,* "royalist", from Syriac *malkā,* king.] —**Mel·chite** *adj.*

Mel·chiz·e·dek, Mel·chis·e·dec (mel-kízzə-dek). The king of Salem and high priest who blessed Abraham. Genesis 14:18.

meld[1] (meld) v. **melded, melding, melds.** —tr. To declare or display (a card or combination of cards) for inclusion in one's score in a game such as canasta or rummy. —intr. To present a meld. ~n. 1. An act of melding. 2. A combination of cards to be declared for a score. [German melden, to declare, from Old High German meldōn.]

meld[2] v. **melded, melding, melds.** —tr. To cause to unite, blend, or combine. —intr. To become blended or combined. [Perhaps MELT + WELD.]

me·lee, mê·lée (méllay, máy-lay, me-láy) n. 1. a. A confused, hand-to-hand fight. b. Any riotous skirmish or brawl. 2. Any confused and tumultuous mingling, as of a crowd: the rush-hour melee. 3. An argumentative or noisy debate between several people. —See Synonyms at **conflict.** [French mêlée, a mixture, from Old French mes-lee, MEDLEY.]

mel·ic (méllik) adj. Designating poetry intended to be sung, especially ancient Greek lyric poems. [Latin melicus, from Greek melikos, from melos, song.]

mel·i·lot (mélli-lot) n. Any of several plants of the genus Melilotus, native to the Old World, having compound leaves and narrow clusters of small, fragrant, white or yellow flowers. Also called "sweet clover". [Middle English mellilot, from French melilot, from Latin melilōtus, from Greek melilōtos, sweet clover, "honey-lotus" : meli, honey + lōtos, LOTUS.]

mel·i·nite (mélli-nīt) n. A high explosive made with picric acid. [French mélinite, from Greek mēlinos, quince-yellow, pertaining to quinces or apples, from mēlon, fruit, apple.]

me·li·o·rate (méeli-ə-rayt) v. **-rated, -rating, -rates.** —tr. To make better; improve. —intr. To grow better; evolve towards higher forms. [Latin meliorāre, from melior, better.] —**me·li·o·ra·ble** (-rəb'l) adj. —**me·li·o·ra·tive** (-rətiv, -raytiv) adj. & n. —**me·li·o·ra·tor** (-raytər) n.

me·li·o·ra·tion (méeli-ə-ráysh'n) n. 1. a. The act or process of improving something or the state of being improved. b. A specific instance of this; an improvement. 2. Linguistics. Amelioration (see).

me·li·o·rism (méeli-ə-riz'm) n. The belief that society has an innate tendency towards improvement and that this tendency may be furthered through deliberate human effort. [Latin melior, better.] —**me·li·o·rist** adj. & n. —**me·li·o·ris·tic** (-rístik) adj.

me·lis·ma (me-líz-mə) n., pl. **-mas** or **-mata** (-mətə). Music. 1. A passage of several notes sung to one syllable of text, as in Gregorian chant. 2. Any elaborate vocal passage. [Greek, from melizein, to sing, from melos, song.] —**me·lis·mat·ic** (mélliz-máttik) adj.

mel·lif·er·ous (mə-lífferəss, me-) adj. Also **mel·lif·ic** (-liffik). Forming or bearing honey. [Latin mellifer : mel, honey + -FER.]

mel·lif·lu·ous (mə-lifflooəss, me-) adj. Also **mel·lif·lu·ent** (-ənt). 1. Flowing with honey or sweetness. 2. Smooth and sweet; rich and harmonious. Said especially of sounds and utterances. [Latin mellifluus : mel, honey + -fluus, flowing.] —**mel·lif·lu·ous·ly** adv. —**mel·lif·lu·ous·ness** n.

mel·lo·phone (méllə-fōn, méllō-) n. A brass musical wind instrument, sometimes used as a substitute for the French horn, which it resembles in tone. [MELLO(W) + -PHONE.]

mel·lo·tron (méllə-tron) n. An electronic keyboard instrument that uses prerecorded tape loops to imitate the individual sounds of an orchestra. [Mellow + electronic.]

mel·low (méllō) adj. **-lower, -lowest.** 1. a. Soft, sweet, juicy, and full-flavoured because of ripeness. Said of fruit. b. Suggesting any of these qualities. 2. Rich and soft in quality; not harsh: a mellow sound. 3. Having the gentleness, wisdom, or dignity often characteristic of maturity. 4. Informal. Relaxed and at ease; genial. 5. Informal. Slightly and pleasantly intoxicated. 6. Moist, rich, soft, and loamy. Said of soil. 7. Fully matured and free from acidity. Said of wine. ~v. **mellowed, -lowing, -lows.** —tr. To bring to maturity; ripen. —intr. 1. To become ripe; mature. 2. To become gentle and sympathetic: He mellowed as he aged. [Middle English mel(o)we, probably from an attributive use of Old English melu, meal, "soft and rich, like meal".] —**mel·low·ly** adv. —**mel·low·ness** n.

me·lo·de·on (mi-lṓdi-ən, me-) n. A small reed organ, similar to the harmonium. [Alteration of earlier melodium, from MELODY (by analogy with HARMONIUM).]

me·lod·ic (mi-lóddik, me-) adj. Pertaining to or containing melody. —**me·lod·i·cal·ly** adv.

me·lod·i·ca (mi-lóddikə) n. A small instrument like a harmonica but with a small keyboard on top that is played with the fingers. [Melodeon + harmonica.]

melodic minor scale n. Music. A minor scale that has the sixth and seventh notes sharpened in its ascending form. Compare **harmonic minor scale.**

me·lo·di·ous (mi-lṓdi-əss, me-) adj. 1. Containing or pertaining to a pleasing succession of sounds; tuneful. 2. Agreeable or pleasant to the ear. —**me·lo·di·ous·ly** adv. —**me·lo·di·ous·ness** n.

mel·o·dise, mel·o·dize (méllə-dīz) v. **-dised, -dising, -dises.** —tr. 1. To write a melody for (a song lyric). 2. To make melodious. —intr. 1. To make melody; play on a musical instrument. Often used humorously. 2. Poetic. To mingle or blend melodiously: "To murmur through the . . . groves, and melodise with man's blest nature there." (P.B. Shelley). —**mel·o·dis·er, -diz·er** n.

mel·o·dra·ma (méllə-draamə, méllō- || -drammə) n. 1. A dramatic presentation characterised by use of suspense, sensational episodes, romantic sentiment, and usually a happy ending. 2. The dramatic genre characterised by this treatment. 3. Behaviour or occurrences, in fiction or real life, having melodramatic characteristics. 4. Music. Spoken words with a musical accompaniment, especially as part of an opera. [French mélodrame, originally "musical drama" : Greek melos, song + French drame, DRAMA.]

mel·o·dra·mat·ic (méllə-drə-máttik) adj. 1. Having the excitement and emotional appeal of melodrama: a melodramatic account of her arrest by the police. 2. Exaggeratedly sensational, emotional, or sentimental; histrionic. ~n. Plural. Melodramatic behaviour. —**mel·o·dra·mat·i·cal·ly** adv.

mel·o·dram·a·tise, mel·o·dram·a·tize (méllō-drámmə-tīz, méllə-, -draámə-) tr.v. **-tised, -tising, -tises.** To create a melodrama out of; make melodramatic. —**mel·o·dram·a·ti·sa·tion** (-tī-záysh'n || U.S. -ti-) n.

mel·o·dy (méllədi) n., pl. **-dies.** 1. A pleasing succession or arrangement of sounds. 2. Musical quality: the melody of verse. 3. Music. a. A rhythmically organised sequence of single notes so related to one another as to make up a particular musical phrase or idea; a tune. b. The structure of music with respect to the arrangement of single notes in succession. Together with harmony and rhythm, melody is one of the three basic elements of traditional Western music. c. The leading part or the air in a harmonic composition. [Middle English melodie, from Old French, from Late Latin melōdia, from Greek melōidia, choral song : melos, tune + -ōidia, "singing", from aoidein, to sing.]

mel·oid (mélloyd) n. Any beetle of the family Meloidae, which includes the oil beetles and blister beetles. ~adj. Of or pertaining to such beetles. [New Latin meloidae (family), from Meloe† (genus name).]

mel·on (méllən) n. 1. Any of several varieties of two related vines, Cucumis melo or Citrullus vulgaris, widely cultivated for their edible fruit. 2. The fruit of any of these vines, characteristically having a hard rind and juicy flesh. See cantaloupe, honeydew melon, muskmelon, watermelon. [Middle English, from Old French, from Late Latin mēlo (stem mēlōn-), shortening of mēlopepōn from Greek, melon, "apple-gourd", from mēlon, apple.]

Me·los (mée-loss). Greek Mílos. Greek island in the Cyclades group in the Aegean Sea. It was a thriving centre of early Aegean civilisation, but later declined and was conquered by the Athenians (416 B.C.). Excavations on the island have unearthed many treasures, including (1820) the Venus de Milo, a marble statue of the second or first century B.C., now in the Louvre, Paris.

Mel·pom·e·ne (mel-pómmini). Greek Mythology. The Muse of tragedy. [Latin Melpomenē, from Greek, "the singing one", from the feminine present participle of melpesthai, to sing, sing of, from melpein†, to sing.]

melt (melt) v. **melted, melted** or archaic **molten** (mṓltən), **melting, melts.** —intr. 1. To be changed from a solid to a liquid state, as by the application of heat. 2. To become liquid; dissolve: Icing melts in the mouth. 3. To disappear or vanish gradually as if by melting. Often used with away: The crowd melted away. 4. To pass or merge imperceptibly into something else; blend gradually. Used with into: Sea melted into sky. 5. To become softened in feeling, as by compassion; be made gentle: Her heart melted at the child's tears. 6. Informal. To be extremely hot; perspire from heat. —tr. 1. a. To reduce from a solid to a liquid state, as by the application of heat. b. To reduce (manufactured metal articles) to the state of raw material, usually for making other metal articles. Used with down: They melted everything down, from statues to spoons, for shell casings. 2. To dissolve: She melted some honey in hot milk. 3. To cause to disappear gradually; disperse: The sun melted the fog. 4. To cause to pass or merge imperceptibly; blend (colours or outlines, for example): "This effect is produced by melting . . . the shadows in a ground still darker." (Sir Joshua Reynolds). 5. To soften (someone's feelings); make gentle or tender: "O ye critics! will nothing melt you?" (Laurence Sterne). ~n. 1. a. A melted solid. b. A blended or fused mass. 2. The state of being melted. 3. a. The act or operation of melting. b. The quantity melted in one period or operation. [Melt (infinitive), molten (past participle); Middle English melten, molten, Old English meltan, gemolten, from Germanic maltjan (unattested), dissolve.] —**melt·a·bil·i·ty** (méltə-bílləti) n. —**melt·a·ble** adj. —**melt·er** n.

Synonyms: melt, liquefy, thaw, dissolve, deliquesce.
Usage: The standard past tense form is melted (The sun melted the ice), but melt is often heard in casual use, and is a common alternative in regional speech. Molten can be used only as an adjective; it differs from the adjectival use of melted in that it refers only to substances that melt at a very high temperature. Thus one may refer to molten rock, but to melted ice cream.

melt·age (méltij) n. 1. The quantity or substance produced by a melting process. 2. The process or act of melting.

melt·down (mélt-down) n. Severe overheating of the core of a nuclear reactor causing melting of the core and supporting base, so that molten radioactive material flows into the space below the reactor.

melting point n. Abbr. **mp, m.p.** 1. The temperature at which a solid becomes a liquid at standard atmospheric pressure. 2. The temperature at which a solid and its liquid are in equilibrium, at any fixed pressure.

melting pot n. A place where much change or mixing occurs, as of people, ideas, or cultures. —**in the melting pot.** Under consideration and therefore uncertain and likely to change.

melon A member of the Cucurbitaceae family, which includes gourds, cucumbers, and pumpkins. This is a tiger melon, a type of cantaloupe.

mel·ton (mélton) *n.* A heavy, woollen cloth used chiefly for making overcoats and hunting jackets. [After *Melton* Mowbray, town in Leicestershire.]

melt·wa·ter (mélt-wawtər ‖ *U.S. also* -wottər) *n.* Water produced by the melting of snow or ice.

Mel·ville (mélvil), **Herman** (1819–91). U.S. novelist. Many of his works, such as his allegorical masterpiece *Moby Dick* (1851), draw on his experiences as a crewman on a whaler. He also wrote *Redburn* (1849) and the story *Billy Budd* (published 1924).

mem (mem) *n.* The thirteenth letter of the Hebrew alphabet. [Hebrew, perhaps from *mayim*, water.]

mem. 1. member. 2. memoir. 3. memorandum. 4. memorial.

mem·ber (mémbər) *n.* 1. *Abbr.* **M., mem.** An individual belonging to a group or organisation. 2. *Abbr.* **M., mem.** *Often capital* **M.** One who serves on or is elected to a political body such as Parliament. 3. A distinct part of a whole, such as an architectural support in a building or a proposition of a syllogism. 4. A part or organ of a human or animal body; especially: **a.** A limb, such as an arm or leg. **b.** The penis. 5. A part of a plant. 6. *Biology.* Any individual organism belonging to a taxonomic group. 7. *Mathematics.* The expression on either side of an equality sign. **b.** An element of a set. [Middle English, from Old French *membre*, from Latin *membrum*.]

Member of Parliament *n. Abbr.* **M.P.** A person who has been elected to the House of Commons or a similar legislative body, as in many Commonwealth countries.

mem·ber·ship (mémbər-ship) *n.* 1. The state of being a member. 2. The total number of members of a group or organisation.

mem·brane (mém-brayn) *n.* 1. *Biology.* A thin, pliable layer of tissue covering surfaces or separating or connecting regions, structures, or organs of an animal or plant. 2. A piece of parchment. 3. *Chemistry.* A thin sheet of natural or synthetic material that is permeable to substances in solution. 4. A thin piece of skin or plastic stretched over a drumhead. [Latin *membrāna*, membrane, "skin covering an organ or member of the body", from *membrum*, member.]

membrane bone *n.* A bone formed directly in the connective tissue, as some cranial bones are. Compare **cartilage bone.**

mem·bra·nous (mémbrə-nəss, mem-bráy-) *adj.* Also **mem·bra·na·ceous** (mémbrə-náyshəss). Made of or similar to a membrane.

Memel. See **Klaipeda.**

me·men·to (mi-méntō, me-) *n., pl.* **-tos** or **-toes.** Any reminder of the past; a keepsake, souvenir, or relic. [Middle English, from Latin *mementō*, "remember", imperative of *meminisse*, to remember.]

memento mo·ri (mórree, máwree) *n.* Any reminder of death or mortality, such as a skull or an ornament bearing symbols of death. [Latin, "remember that you must die".]

Mem·ling (mémling), **Hans** (*c.* 1430–94). Flemish painter of religious works and portraits, born in Germany. Among his paintings are *Tomaso Portinari and his Wife* (*c.* 1468) and the *Diptych of Martin van Nieuwenhoven* (1487).

Mem·non[1] (mém-non). *Greek Mythology.* An Ethiopian king killed by Achilles in the Trojan War and made immortal by Zeus.

Memnon[2] *n.* A huge statue of the Egyptian Pharaoh Amenhotep III at Thebes.

mem·o (mémmō) *n., pl.* **-os.** A memorandum.

mem·oir (mém-waar, -wawr) *n. Abbr.* **mem.** 1. **a.** A narrative of one's experiences or a historical account based on personal experience. **b.** *Usually plural.* An autobiography. **c.** A biography or biographical sketch. 2. A monograph: *a memoir on anthills.* 3. *Plural.* The report or a collection of reports of the proceedings of a learned society. [French *mémoire*, MEMORY.]

mem·o·ra·bil·i·a (mémmərə-billi-ə) *pl.n.* Things worthy of remembrance. [Latin *memorābilia*, from *memorābilis*, MEMORABLE.]

mem·o·ra·ble (mémmə-rə-b'l, mémmrə-) *adj.* Worth being remembered; notable. [Middle English, from Latin *memorābilis*, from *memorāre*, to remember, from *memor*, mindful.] **—mem·o·ra·bil·i·ty** (-billəti), **mem·o·ra·ble·ness** *n.* **—mem·o·ra·bly** *adv.*

mem·o·ran·dum (mémmə-rán-dəm) *n., pl.* **-dums** or **-da** (-də). *Abbr.* **mem.** 1. A short note written as a reminder. 2. A written record or communication, as in a business office. 3. *Law.* A short, written statement outlining the terms of an agreement, transaction, or contract. 4. A brief, unsigned diplomatic communication. [Middle English, from Latin, "let it be remembered", neuter singular gerundive of *memorāre*, to remember, from *memor*, mindful.]

me·mo·ri·al (mi-máwri-əl ‖ -móri-) *n. Abbr.* **mem.** 1. Something, such as a monument or a public holiday, designed or established to serve as a remembrance of a person or an event. 2. *Plural.* A historical record. 3. A written statement of facts or a petition presented to a legislative body or an executive.
~*adj.* 1. Serving as a remembrance of a person or event; commemorative. 2. Of, pertaining to, or in memory. [Middle English, from Latin *memoriālis*, belonging to memory, from *memoria*, MEMORY.] **—me·mo·ri·al·ly** *adv.*

me·mo·ri·a·lise, me·mo·ri·a·lize (mi-máwri-ə-līz) *tr.v.* **-ised, -ising, -ises.** 1. To commemorate. 2. To present a memorial to; petition. **—me·mo·ri·a·li·sa·tion** (-lī-záysh'n ‖ *U.S.* -li-) *n.* **—me·mo·ri·a·li·ser** *n.*

me·mo·ri·al·ist (mi-máwri-ə-list ‖ -móri-) *n.* 1. A person who writes memoirs. 2. A person who writes or signs a memorial.

me·mo·ri·a tech·ni·ca (mi-máwri-ə téknikə) *n.* A device or system that is used to aid the memory, such as a mnemonic. [New Latin, artificial memory.]

mem·o·rise, mem·o·rize (mémmə-rīz) *tr.v.* **-rised, -rising, -rises.** To commit to memory; learn by heart. **—mem·o·ris·a·ble** *adj.* **—mem·o·ri·sa·tion** (-rī-záysh'n ‖ *U.S.* -ri-) *n.* **—mem·o·ris·er** *n.*

mem·o·ry (mémməri, mémmri) *n., pl.* **-ries.** 1. The mental faculty of retaining and recalling past experience; the ability to remember. 2. An act or instance of remembrance; a recollection: *pleasant memories of his childhood.* 3. All that a person can remember, or all that is retained in the mind. 4. Something remembered of a person, thing, or event: *He has no memory of that occasion.* 5. **a.** The fact of being remembered, as after death. **b.** Remembrance; recollection: *in memory of our loved ones.* 6. The period of time covered by the remembrance or recollection of a person or group of persons: *within the memory of man.* 7. *Physics.* The property of a substance or system that depends on past treatment or states of the substance or system. 8. **a.** A unit, such as one in or attachable to a computer, calculator, or word processor, that preserves data for retrieval. Also called "memory store", "store". **b.** The capacity of such a unit. 9. *Statistics.* The set of past events affecting a given event in a stochastic process. [Middle English *memorie*, from Old French, from Latin *memoria*, from *memor*, mindful.]
Synonyms: *memory, remembrance, recollection, reminiscence.*

memory span *n.* The length of time that a person is able to retain something in his short-term memory.

memory trace *n.* A hypothetical change to a brain cell or to structures of brain cells as a result of learning.

Mem·phis[1] (mémfiss). Ruined city on the river Nile 18 kilometres (12 miles) south of Cairo, Egypt. Reputedly founded by the pharaoh Menes, it was the capital of the Old Kingdom (*c.* 3100 – *c.* 2258 B.C.), the first united Egyptian state, and was the centre for the worship of Ptah. The city declined with the rise of Thebes, but temporarily revived under the Persians, Ptolemies, and Romans. Its remains include the temple of Ptah.

Memphis[2]. City of southwest Tennessee, United States, at the confluence of the Mississippi and Wolf rivers.

mem·sa·hib (mém-saa-ib, -hib, -saab) *n.* Formerly, a title of respect or form of address for a European woman in India. [MA'AM + SAHIB.]

men. Plural of **man.**

men·ace (ménnəss, ménniss) *n.* 1. *Literary.* **a.** A threat: *menace of the gun.* **b.** The act of threatening. 2. A dangerous or potentially dangerous person or thing. 3. *Informal.* A troublesome or annoying person: *She has become a menace by her gossip.*
~*v.* **menaced, -acing, -aces.** *—tr.* To threaten in a hostile or nasty manner. *—intr.* To make threats; indicate danger or coming harm. —See Synonyms at **threaten.** [Middle English *manace*, from Old French, from Latin *minācia*, menace, originally "threatening things", neuter plural of *mināx* (stem *mināc*-), threatening, from *minārī*, to threaten, from *minae*, threats.] **—men·ac·er** *n.* **—men·ac·ing·ly** *adv.*

men·a·di·one (ménnə-dī-ōn, -dī-ón) *n.* A yellow crystalline powder, $C_{11}H_8O_2$, having physiological effects similar to vitamin K. It is used as a medicine and as a fungicide. [methyl + naphtha + DI- + -ONE.]

mé·nage, me·nage (may-naázh, me-) *n.* 1. A group of people living together as a unit; a household. 2. The management of a household. [French, from Old French *menage*, from Vulgar Latin *mansiōnāticum* (unattested), household, from *mansiō* (stem *mansiōn*-), house, dwelling, from *manēre*, to dwell.]

ménage à trois (aa trwáa) *n., pl.* **ménages à trois** (*pronounced as singular*). A sexual relationship involving three people who live together, such as a married couple and the lover of one of them. [French, household of three.]

me·nag·er·ie (mi-nájəri, me-, -naázhəri) *n.* 1. A collection of live wild animals on exhibition. 2. The enclosure in which such animals are kept. [French *ménagerie*, originally "the management of domestic animals", from *ménage*, MÉNAGE.]

Men·ai Strait (ménnī). Channel of the Irish Sea separating the island of Anglesey from the mainland, in Gwynedd, Wales. It is 23 kilometres (14 miles) long and is crossed by the famous road suspension bridge of Thomas Telford (built 1819–26) and the tubular rail bridge of Robert Stevenson (1850).

Me·nan·der (me-nándər, mi-) (*c.* 342 B.C.–*c.* 290 B.C.). Greek dramatist, who wrote tangled love plays. Only one, *The Curmudgeon,* discovered at Cairo in 1957, survives complete.

men·a·qui·none (ménnə-kwi-nōn) *n.* A form of **vitamin K** (see). [methylnaphthoquinone.]

me·nar·che (me-nárki, mə-, ménnaarki) *n.* The first occurrence of menstruation in young women. [New Latin : Greek *mēn*, month + *arkhē*, beginning.] **—me·nar·che·al** *adj.*

Menck·en (méngkən), **H(enry) L(ouis)** (1880–1956). U.S. journalist and literary critic. He founded the magazine *American Mercury* with George Nathan in 1924. His essays are collected in six volumes, *Prejudices* (1919–27). He also wrote a four-volume work on philology, *The American Language* (1919).

mend (mend) *v.* **mended, mending, mends.** *—tr.* 1. To make right or correct; repair. 2. To reform or improve. Used chiefly in the phrases *mend one's ways* or *manners.* *—intr.* 1. To undergo a moral improvement; reform. 2. **a.** To improve in health: *He is mending well.* **b.** To heal: *The bone mended in a month.*
~*n.* 1. The act of mending. 2. A part or place mended or repaired after breaking or coming apart. 3. A place on a piece of material that has been mended, as by a patch or darning. **—on the mend.** Improving, especially in health; recuperating. [Middle English

menden, shortening of *amenden,* to AMEND.] —**mend·a·ble** *adj.* —**mend·er** *n.*

men·da·cious (men-dáyshəss) *adj. Formal.* **1.** Lying; untruthful: *a mendacious child.* **2.** False; untrue: *a mendacious statement.* —See Synonyms at **dishonest.** [Latin *mendāx* (stem *mendāc-*).] —**men·da·cious·ly** *adv.* —**men·dac·i·ty** (-dássəti) *n.*

Men·del (ménd'l), **Gregor (Johann)** (1822–84). Moravian (Austrian) monk and founder of the science of genetics. He entered the Augustinian monastery at Brno in 1843 and for 25 years experimented with plants, chiefly garden peas. He discovered the principle of the inheritance of characteristics through the combination of genes from parent cells. His conclusions, published in 1866 and ignored during his lifetime, form the basis of scientific genetics.

men·de·le·vi·um (méndi-léevi-əm, *also* -láyvi-) *n.* Symbol **Md** A radioactive transuranic element of the actinide series. Atomic number 101, half-life of the most stable isotope (Md258) 60 days. Also called "unnilunium". [New Latin, after Dmitri MENDELEYEV.]

Men·de·le·yev (méndə-láy-ef, -ev; *Russian* mindi-láy-əf), **Dmitri Ivanovich** (1834–1907). Russian chemist. He formulated the periodic table of the elements noting the regular recurrence of their chemical and physical properties when they are arranged by their atomic numbers. Other scientists, notably Lothar Meyer, independently reached the same conclusions, but Mendeleyev was the first to draw attention to gaps in the periodic arrangement and to postulate the existence of undiscovered elements to fill them.

Men·de·li·an (men-déeli-ən) *adj.* Of or pertaining to Gregor Mendel or his theories of genetics.

Men·del·ism (méndə-liz'm) *n.* Also **Men·de·li·an·ism** (men-déeli-ə-niz'm). The theoretical principles of heredity formulated by Gregor Mendel. See **Mendel's laws.**

Mendel's laws *pl.n.* The principles of heredity of sexually reproducing organisms formulated by Gregor Mendel, now usually summarised in two laws: **1.** *Law of Segregation:* Certain paired characteristics, one from each parent, do not blend with or alter each other in the offspring, thus accounting for contrasting traits in successive generations. **2.** *Law of Independent Assortment:* The genes determining such pairs of traits combine in the offspring according to the laws of chance.

Men·dels·sohn (ménd'l-s'n; *German* ménd'l-zōn), **Felix,** born Jacob Ludwig Felix Mendelssohn-Bartholdy (1809–47). German composer. Mendelssohn was a child prodigy; his overture to *A Midsummer Night's Dream* and his *Octet* for strings were both written by the time he was 17. He wrote five symphonies, the oratorios *St. Paul* (1836) and *Elijah* (1846), the violin concerto in E Minor (1844), and six string quartets.

Men·de·res (méndə-réss), **Adnan** (1889–1961). Turkish prime minister (1950–60). During his period of office, Turkey joined NATO (1952) and the Baghdad Pact (1955). He was ousted in a military coup led by General Gürsel and executed.

Men·dès-France (mén-dess fráanss; *French* maN-dess-frónss), **Pierre** (1907–82). French prime minister (1954–55). He was economic minister in de Gaulle's government (1944–45). As prime minister he negotiated France's withdrawal from Indochina, but he resigned when his liberal policies on the North African colonies were rejected. He led the Radical Socialist Party until 1957.

men·di·cant (méndi-kənt) *adj.* **1.** Depending upon alms for a living; practising begging. **2.** Characteristic of a beggar or begging. ~*n.* **1.** *Rare.* A beggar. **2.** A member of a mendicant order of friars. [Latin *mendicāns* (stem *mendicānt-*), present participle of *mendicāre,* to beg, from *mendicus,* beggar, poor man, originally "injured", from *mendum,* physical defect.] —**men·di·can·cy, men·dic·i·ty** (men-díssəti) *n.*

mend·ing (ménding) *n.* Articles, especially clothes, that are to be or have been mended.

Men·dip Hills (méndip). Limestone range in Somerset, southwest England. The range runs northwest from the Frome valley, reaching 325 metres (1,068 feet) at Blackdown.

Men·e·la·us (ménni-láy-əss). *Greek Mythology.* The king of Sparta, brother of Agamemnon, and husband of Helen whose abduction gave rise to the Trojan War.

me·ne, me·ne, tek·el, u·phar·sin (méeni méeni téck'l yŏŏ-fár-sin). *Aramaic.* Numbered, numbered, weighed, divided. The phrase appeared on the wall at Belshazzar's feast, and was interpreted by Daniel to mean that God had doomed Belshazzar's kingdom. Daniel 5:25–28.

men·folk (mén-fōk) *pl.n.* **1.** Men collectively. **2.** A particular group of men, as in a family: *They lost their menfolk.*

men·ha·den (men-háyd'n, mən-) *n., pl.* -**dens** or collectively **menha·den.** An abundant inedible fish, *Brevoortia tyrannus,* of American Atlantic and Gulf waters, used as a source of fish oil, fish meal, fertiliser, and bait. Also *U.S.* "mossbunker", "oldwife". [Algonquian; akin to Natick *munnohquohteau,* "he fertilises" (menhaden were used by the Algonquins as fertiliser for maize).]

men·hir (mén-heer) *n.* A prehistoric monument consisting of a single tall, upright megalith. Compare **dolmen.** [French, from Breton *men hir,* "long stone" : *men,* stone + *hir,* long.]

me·ni·al (méeni-əl) *adj.* **1.** Of, pertaining to, or appropriate for a servant. **2.** Of or pertaining to work or a job regarded as servile or degrading. **3.** Of, pertaining to, or involving work, such as cleaning, that is routine, boring, and requires little skill. ~*n.* **1.** A servant, especially a domestic servant. **2.** A person who has a servile or low nature. [Middle English *meynial,* from Anglo-French *menial,* Old French *meinie, mesne,* servant, from Vulgar

Latin *mānsiōnātā* (unattested), household, from *mānsiō,* house dwelling. See mansion.] —**me·ni·al·ly** *adv.*

Mé·nière's disease (ménni-airz, mayn-yáirz) *n.* A disorder of the inner ear involving progressive deafness, loss of balance, ringing in the ear, and nausea. Also called "Ménière's syndrome". [After Prosper *Ménière* (1799–1862), French physician.]

me·nin·ge·al (mə-nínji-əl, ménnin-jée-əl) *adj.* Of, pertaining to, or concerned with a meninx or meninges.

men·in·gi·tis (ménnin-jítiss) *n. Pathology.* Inflammation of any meninx or all of the meninges of the brain and the spinal cord, usually caused by a bacterial infection. [New Latin : *meninges* + -ITIS.] —**men·in·git·ic** (-jíttik) *adj.*

me·ninx (mée-ningks, ménningks) *n., pl.* **meninges** (mə-nín-jeez, me-). Any of the three membranes enclosing the brain and spinal cord in vertebrates. [New Latin, from Greek *mēninx* (stem *mēning-*), membrane.]

me·nis·cus (mi-níss-kəss, me-) *n., pl.* -**cuses** or **menisci** (-níssī). **1.** A crescent-shaped body. **2.** A concavo-convex lens. **3.** The curved upper surface of a stationary liquid in a container. It is concave if the liquid wets the container walls and convex if it does not. **4.** *Anatomy.* A cartilage disc that cushions the ends of bones in a joint. [New Latin, from Greek *mēniskos,* crescent, diminutive of *mēnē,* moon.] —**me·nis·cal** (-k'l), **me·nis·cate** (-kayt), **me·nis·coid** (-koyd), **men·is·coi·dal** (ménniss-kóyd'l) *adj.*

Men·non·ite (ménnə-nīt) *n.* A member of a Protestant Christian sect opposed to baptism, taking oaths, holding public office, or performing military service. [German *Mennonit,* after *Menno* Simons (1492–1559), religious reformer.]

me·nol·o·gy (mi-nólləji) *n., pl.* -**gies.** **1.** An ecclesiastical calendar of the months with important religious events recorded. **2.** In the Eastern Orthodox Church, a collection of short biographies of the lives of the saints arranged in the form of a calendar. [Medieval Greek *mēnologion,* "list of months" : Greek *mēn,* month + -LOGY.]

me·no mos·so (ménnō móssō, máynō, móss-sō) *adv. Music.* With less speed. Used as a direction. [Italian, "less rapid".]

Men·on (ménnən), **(Vengalil Krishnan) Krishna** (1897–1974). Indian politician. After independence (1947) he became High Commissioner to the United Kingdom. In 1952 he headed the Indian delegation to the United Nations, and in 1957 became defence minister. He resigned in 1962, after China's border attacks.

men·o·pause (ménnə-pawz, ménnō-) *n.* The period of cessation of menstruation in a woman, occurring typically between the ages of 45 and 50. Also called "change of life", "climacteric". [New Latin *menopausis* : *meno-,* from Greek *mēn,* month + *pausis,* PAUSE.] —**men·o·paus·al** (-páwz'l) *adj.*

me·no·rah (mi-náwrə ‖ -nôrə) *n.* **1.** A ceremonial seven-branched candelabrum of the Jewish Temple symbolising the seven days of the Creation. Exodus 37:17–24. **2.** A nine-branched candelabrum used in the celebration of Chanukkah. [Hebrew *mənorāh,* candlestick.]

Me·nor·ca (me-nórkə). *English* **Mi·nor·ca** (mi-). Second largest of the Balearic islands, Spain. Situated in the Mediterranean Sea, it is predominantly low-lying; agriculture, fishing, and tourism are its main industries. Mahón is the chief town and port. —**Me·nor·can** *adj. & n.*

men·or·rha·gi·a (ménnə-ráy-ji-ə, ménnaw-, -jə ‖ -ráa-, -zhə) *n. Pathology.* Abnormally heavy menstrual flow. [New Latin : Greek *mēn,* month + -RRHAGIA.]

Me·not·ti (mə-nótti, me-), **Gian-Carlo** (1911–). Italian composer, who has lived chiefly in the United States since 1927. He has written his own English libretti for most of his operas, which include *The Medium* (1946) and *The Consul* (1950).

Men·sa1 (mén-sə) *n.* A southern constellation between Hydrus and Carina. [Latin *mēnsa,* table.]

Mensa2 *n.* An international society established in 1946 for the stimulation of and exchange of ideas among its members. Membership is restricted to those with an I.Q. in the top two percent in each member country.

men·sal1 (mén-s'l) *adj. Rare.* Belonging to or used at the table. [Late Latin *mēnsālis,* from *mēnsa†,* table.]

mensal2 *adj. Rare.* Monthly. [Latin *mēnsis,* month.]

mensch (mensh) *n. U.S. Informal.* A person having admirable characteristics, such as fortitude and firmness of purpose. [Yiddish *mens(c)h,* from Middle High German *mensch,* man, from Old High German *mennisco.*]

men·ses (mén-seez) *pl.n.* **1.** *Physiology.* Blood and dead cell debris that is discharged from the uterus through the vagina by nonpregnant adolescent girls and women at approximately monthly intervals between puberty and menopause. **2.** Menstruation. [Latin *mēnsēs,* months, hence also "monthly periods", plural of *mēnsis,* month.]

Men·she·vik (ménshə-vik) *n., pl.* -**viks** or -**viki** (-véekee). **1. a.** A member of the liberal minority faction of the Russian Social Democratic Party, which struggled against the more radical majority element, the Bolsheviks, from 1903 until the Russian Revolution in 1917. Also called "Minimalist". **b.** A member of a liberal socialist group established after the Russian Revolution to oppose the Bolshevik Party. **2.** A person having views in accord with the Menshevik faction. Compare **Bolshevik.** [Russian *men'shevik,* a member of the smaller (faction), from *men'she,* less, from Old Church Slavonic *mĭnĭshĭī,* less.] —**Men·she·vism** *n.* —**Men·she·vist** *adj.*

mens re·a (ménz ráy-ə, rée-) *n. Law.* Criminal intent, the essential mental element that in theory has to be proved for all crimes, although in practice some statutory offences are crimes of absolute liability, regardless of criminal intent. [Latin, guilty mind.]

men·stru·al (mén-stroo-əl) *adj.* Also **men·stru·ous** (-əss). Pertaining to menstruation. [Middle English *menstruall*, from Latin *mēnstruālis*, from *mēnstruus*, menstrual, monthly, from *mēnsis*, month.]

men·stru·ate (mén-stroo-ayt) *intr.v.* **-ated, -ating, -ates.** To undergo menstruation. [Latin *mēnstruāre*, from *mēnstruus*, MENSTRUAL.]

men·stru·a·tion (mén-stroo-áysh'n) *n.* **1.** *Physiology.* The process or an instance of discharging the menses. **2.** The period of time during which this occurs. Also called "menses".

men·stru·um (mén-stroo-əm) *n., pl.* **-ums** or **-strua** (-stroo-ə). A solvent, especially one used in extracting and preparing drugs. [Middle English, from Medieval Latin *mēnstruum*, solvent, originally "menstrual blood" (alchemists regarded the gold-transmuting solvent as similar to menstrual blood, which they believed transformed sperm in the womb into an embryo), from Latin *mēnstruus*, MENSTRUAL.]

men·su·ra·ble (mén-shər-əb'l, -sewr-) *adj.* **1.** Capable of being measured. **2.** Having fixed rhythm and measure, as in music; mensural. —**men·su·ra·bil·i·ty** (-ə-bílləti) *n.*

men·su·ral (mén-shər-əl, -sewr-) *adj.* **1.** Of or pertaining to measure. **2.** *Music.* Of, pertaining to, or designating music having notes of fixed rhythmic value. [Latin *mēnsurālis*, from *mēnsūra*, MEASURE.]

men·su·ra·tion (mén-shə-ráysh'n, -sewr-) *n.* **1.** The process, act, or art of measuring. **2.** The measurement of geometric quantities. —**men·su·ra·tive** (-rətiv, -raytiv) *adj.*

mens·wear (ménz-wair) *n.* Clothing and accessories for men.

-ment *n. suffix.* Indicates: **1.** Product or result; for example, **pavement, statement. 2.** Means, action, or process; for example, **appeasement, measurement. 3.** State or condition; for example, **amazement, merriment.** [Middle English, from Old French, from Latin *-mentum*, abstract noun suffix originally added only to verbs.]

men·tal[1] (mént'l) *adj.* **1.** Of or pertaining to the mind; intellectual. **2.** Done or performed by the mind; existing in the mind: *a mental image; mental arithmetic.* **3.** Concerning, involving, or dealing with disorders of the mind: *mental illness; mental institutions.* **4.** Suffering from a disorder or illness of the mind: *a mental patient.* **5.** *Informal.* Very stupid or crazy. [Middle English, from Old French, from Latin *mentālis*, from *mēns* (stem *ment*-), mind.] —**men·tal·ly** *adv.*

mental[2] *adj. Rare.* Of or pertaining to the chin. [French, from Latin *mentum*, chin.]

mental age *n. Abbr.* **MA, M.A.** A measure of mental development, as determined by intelligence tests, generally restricted to children and expressed as the age at which the level achieved is considered to be average.

mental block *n.* A temporary inability to think, remember, or concentrate.

mental cruelty *n.* Cruel behaviour towards or ill-treatment of another person that causes emotional and psychological distress but does not involve physical violence. It is sometimes cited as grounds for divorce in the United States.

mental deficiency *n.* Subnormal intellectual development, either congenital or induced by brain injury or disease, characterised broadly by deficiencies ranging in severity from impaired learning ability through social and vocational inadequacy to inability to learn connected speech or guard against common dangers. Also called "amentia", "mental retardation", "subnormality".

mental hospital *n.* A hospital or institution that provides care and treatment for the mentally ill. Also called "mental institution".

men·tal·ism (mént'l-iz'm) *n.* **1.** *Philosophy.* The doctrine that the mind is the only true reality and that the material world exists only on a subjective level as aspects of the individual's mind. **2.** *Philosophy & Linguistics.* The doctrine that mental processes exist independently of, and can account for, their manifestations in observable behaviour. —**men·tal·ist** *n. & adj.* —**men·tal·is·tic** (-ístik) *adj.*

men·tal·i·ty (men-tál-əti) *n., pl.* **-ties. 1.** The sum of a person's intellectual capabilities or endowments; mental capacity; intelligence. **2.** Cast or turn of mind; mental make-up or inclination: *She has a very conservative mentality.* —See Synonyms at **mind.**

mental retardation *n.* Mental deficiency.

mental telepathy *n.* Telepathy (see).

men·thol (mén-thol ‖ -thōl) *n.* A white, crystalline, organic compound, $C_{10}H_{20}O$, obtained from peppermint oil or synthesised. It is used in perfumes, as a mild anaesthetic, and as a flavouring. [German *Menthol* : Latin *mentha*, MINT + -OL.] —**men·tho·lat·ed** (-thə-laytid) *adj.*

men·tion (ménsh'n) *tr.v.* **-tioned, -tioning, -tions. 1.** To cite or refer to incidentally. **2.** To refer to by name, especially as an acknowledgement or to show appreciation. —**don't mention it.** A formula of courtesy used as a self-deprecating reply to proffered thanks or apologies. —**not to mention.** Used to draw attention to or emphasise the importance of: *Our thanks to all those who helped with the cooking, not to mention the chef herself, who planned the entire meal.* —*n.* **1. a.** The act of briefly or casually referring to something. **b.** An incidental reference or allusion. **2.** A reference to a person by name, especially in order to acknowledge or honour him. [Middle English *mencioun*, from Old French *mention*, from Latin *mentiō* (stem *mentiōn*-), remembrance, mention.] —**men·tion·a·ble** *adj.* —**men·tion·er** *n.*

men·tor (mén-tawr ‖ -tər) *n.* A wise and trusted counsellor or teacher. [French, after *Mentor*, a character in Fénelon's *Télémaque* (1699), based on Homer's MENTOR.]

Men·tor (mén-tawr ‖ -tər). *Greek Mythology.* Odysseus' trusted counsellor who became the guardian and teacher of Telemachus. [Greek *Mentōr*, name probably meaning "adviser", "wise man", from *men-* (unattested), to think.]

men·u (ménnew ‖ méenew, *U.S. also* máynew) *n.* **1.** A list of the dishes that are served or that can be ordered, as in a restaurant. **2.** The dishes served or available. **3.** *Computing.* A list of available options, usually displayed on a VDU, from which a user can select and access a particular program, function, or file. [French, menu, list, from *menu*, detailed, small, from Latin *minūtus*, minute, diminished, past participle of *minuere*, to diminish.]

Me·nu·hin (ménnew-in), **Yehudi** (1916-). U.S. violinist. He made his professional debut in San Francisco in 1924. Bartok's sonata for solo violin (1945) was written for him. Resident in England since 1959, he was director of the Bath music festival (1959–68), and in 1963 founded a school for musically gifted children.

Men·zies (ménziz), **Sir Robert (Gordon)** (1894–1978). Australian prime minister (1939–41; 1949–66). He was attorney-general in Joseph Lyons's government (1935–39), and succeeded Lyons as prime minister. His second period as prime minister was as the head of a Liberal/Country Party coalition.

me·ow, mi·aou, mi·aow (mee-ów) *n.* **1.** The characteristic high-pitched crying sound of a cat. **2.** Any similar sound. —*v.* **meowed, -owing, -ows.** —*intr.* To emit a meow. —*tr.* To express by means of a meow. [Imitative.]

mep, m.e.p. mean effective pressure.

M.E.P. Member of the European Parliament.

mep·a·crine (méppəkrin) *n.* A drug, $C_{23}H_{30}ClN_3O$, formerly used in the treatment of malaria.

me·per·i·dine hydrochloride (me-pérri-deen, mə-, -din) *n.* An organic compound, $C_{15}H_{21}NO_2$·HCl, used as an analgesic and sedative. Also called "meperidine".

meph·i·stoph·e·les (méffi-stóffə-leez) *n.* **1.** The part of a beard directly below the lower lip. **2.** A beard consisting solely of the hairs between the lower lip and the chin, often waxed and shaped in an upward curve. [19th century : after MEPHISTOPHELES, represented in medieval and Renaissance painting as having a pronounced beard or part of a beard of this type.]

Meph·i·stoph·e·les (méffi-stóffə-leez). The devil in the Faust legend to whom Faust sold his soul. —**Me·phis·to·phe·le·an, Me·phis·to·phe·li·an** (méffi-stə-féeli-ən, mə-fístə-) *adj.*

me·phi·tis (me-fítiss, mi-) *n.* **1.** An offensive smell; a stench. **2.** A poisonous or foul-smelling gas emitted from the earth. [Latin *mefitis*†, stench.] —**me·phit·ic** (me-fíttik, mi-), **me·phit·i·cal** *adj.* —**me·phit·i·cal·ly** *adv.*

me·pro·ba·mate (mə-próbə-mayt, me-, mépprō-bámmayt) *n.* A bitter white powder, $CH_3(C_3H_7)C(CH_2OOCNH_2)_2$, used as a tranquilliser.

mer. meridian.

-mer. Variant of **-mere.**

mer·bro·min (mər-brómin) *n.* A green, crystalline, organic compound, $C_{20}H_8Br_2HgNa_2O_6$, that forms a red aqueous solution. It is used as a germicide and antiseptic under the trademark Mercurochrome.

mer·can·tile (mérkən-tīl ‖ *U.S. also* -teel, -til) *adj.* **1.** Of or pertaining to merchants, trade, or commerce. **2.** Of or pertaining to mercantilism. [French, from Italian, from *mercante*, MERCHANT.]

mer·can·til·ism (mérkən-ti-liz'm, -tī- ‖ -tee-, mər-kánti-) *n.* The theory and system of political economy prevailing in Europe after the decline of feudalism, based on national policies of accumulating bullion, establishing colonies and a merchant navy, and developing industry and mining to attain a favourable balance of trade. Also called "mercantile system". [French *mercantilisme*, from MERCANTILE.] —**mer·can·til·ist** *n. & adj.*

mer·cap·tan (mer-káp-tan, mər-) *n.* Any sulphur-containing organic compound with the general formula RSH, R being any radical; for example, ethyl mercaptan, C_2H_5SH. Also called "thiol". [German, from Danish, from Medieval Latin *(corpus) mercurium captans*, "(substance) seizing mercury" : *mercurium*, MERCURY + *captāns*, present participle of *captāre*, frequentative of *capere*, to take.]

mer·cap·tide (mer-káp-tīd, mər-) *n.* A salt of a mercaptan containing the ion RS⁻, where R is an alkyl or aryl group.

mercapto- *comb. form.* Indicates an HS- group in a chemical compound; for example, **mercaptopurine.** [From MERCAPTAN.]

Mer·ca·tor (mer-káy-tawr, -tər), **Gerardus**, born Gerhard Kremer (1512–94). Flemish inventor of the map projection (1569) which bears his name. He produced his first world map in 1538 and his first globe in 1541. His great atlas, started in 1585, was completed by his son (1594).

Mercator projection *n.* Also **Mercator's projection.** A map projection in which the globe is projected onto a cylinder, the meridians and parallels appearing as straight lines crossing at right angles. Lines of constant direction are straight lines, so it is used widely for navigation, despite increasing expansion and distortion of areas the further they are from the equator.

mer·ce·nar·y (mér-sinnəri, -sinri ‖ *U.S.* -si-nerri) *adj.* **1. a.** Motivated solely by a desire for monetary or material gain. **b.** Greedy; venal. **2.** Hired for service in a foreign army. —*n., pl.* **mercenaries. 1.** A professional soldier who is hired by a foreign country or organisation. **2.** A person who serves or works merely for monetary gain; a hireling. [Middle English *mercenarie*, from Latin *mercēnārius*, from *mercēs*, pay.] —**mer·ce·nar·i·ly** (*also* -si·nérri·li) *adv.* —**mer·ce·nar·i·ness** *n.*

mer·cer (mér-sər) *n. British.* A dealer in textiles, especially in expensive fabrics such as silks. [Middle English, from Old French *mercier*, trader, from Vulgar Latin *merciārius* (unattested), from Latin *merx* (stem *merc-*), merchandise.]

mer·cer·ise, mer·cer·ize (mér-sə-rīz) *tr.v.* -**ised**, -**ising**, -**ises**. To treat (cotton thread) with sodium hydroxide in order to shrink the fibre and increase its colour absorption and lustre. [After John Mercer (1791–1866), English textile maker.] —**mer·cer·i·sa·tion** (-rī-záysh'n ‖ *U.S.* -ri-) *n.*

mer·chan·dise (mérchən-dīz, -dīss) *n. Abbr.* **mdse.** Commodities of commerce; goods that may be bought or sold.
~*v.* (-dīz) **merchandised**, -**dising**, -**dises**. —*tr.* 1. To buy and sell (commodities). 2. To promote the sale of, as by advertising or display. —*intr.* To trade commercially. [Middle English, from Old French, from *marcheant*, MERCHANT.] —**mer·chan·dis·er** *n.*

mer·chant (mérchənt) *n.* 1. A person whose occupation is the wholesale purchase and retail sale of goods for profit; a trader. 2. *Chiefly U.S.* A person who runs a retail business; a shopkeeper. 3. Someone fond of or involved with something specified that is generally thought undesirable: *a speed merchant.*
~*adj.* 1. Of or pertaining to a merchant, merchandise, or commercial trade; dealing in commerce: *a merchant guild.* 2. Of or pertaining to the merchant navy. [Middle English, from Old French *marcheant*, trader, from Vulgar Latin *mercātāns* (unattested), present participle of *mercātāre* (unattested), to trade, from Latin *mercārī*, to trade, from *merx* (stem *merc-*), merchandise.]

mer·chant·a·ble (mérchənt-əb'l) *adj.* Suitable for buying and selling; marketable.

merchant bank *n. British.* An institution engaged in a number of financial activities, such as accepting foreign bills of exchange, dealing in loans and securities, and supervising the issue of new securities. —**merchant banker** *n.* —**merchant banking** *n.*

mer·chant·man (mérchənt-mən) *n., pl.* -**men** (-mən, -men). 1. A ship used in commerce. 2. *Archaic.* A merchant.

merchant navy *n.* 1. A nation's ships that are engaged in commerce. 2. The personnel of such ships. Also called "mercantile marine", *U.S.* "merchant marine".

Mer·ci·a (mér-si-ə, -shi-ə, -shə). Anglo-Saxon kingdom of England, roughly corresponding with the Midlands. It became a major power under Penda (c. 632–54), overlord of all England south of the Humber: East Anglia, Kent, Mercia, Sussex, and Wessex. Offa (757–96) extended this power, controlling Northumberland too. Mercia came under Wessex overlordship (825), and the east was incorporated into the Danelaw (886).

Mer·ci·an (mér-si-ən, -shi-, -shən) *n.* 1. A native or inhabitant of Mercia. 2. The dialect of Old English used in Mercia. —**Mer·ci·an** *adj.*

mer·ci·ful (mér-sif'l) *adj.* Full of mercy; compassionate; lenient. —**mer·ci·ful·ness** *n.*

mer·ci·ful·ly (mér-sif'l-i, -si-fli) *adv.* 1. In a merciful manner. 2. It is a mercy that: *The climber fell, but mercifully landed in a tree.*

mer·ci·less (mér-si-ləss, -liss) *adj.* Having no mercy; pitiless; cruel. —**mer·ci·less·ly** *adv.* —**mer·ci·less·ness** *n.*

Merckx (mairks), **Eddy** (1945–). Belgian racing cyclist. He was world amateur champion (1964) and equalled the record of Jacques Anquetil by winning the Tour de France five times between 1969 and 1974.

Mer·cou·ri (mer-kóor-i, mər-), **Melina** (1925–). Greek film actress. She starred in *Never on Sunday* (1959). In 1981 she was elected to the Greek parliament and appointed Minister of Culture and Sciences.

mer·cu·rate (mér-kewr-ayt) *tr.v.* -**curated**, -**curating**, -**curates**. To treat or mix with mercury. —**mer·cu·ra·tion** (-áysh'n) *n.*

mer·cu·ri·al (mər-kéwr-i-əl) *n.* A medical or chemical preparation containing mercury.
~*adj.* 1. *Usually capital* **M.** Of or pertaining to the Roman god Mercury or the planet Mercury. 2. Having the characteristics of eloquence, shrewdness, swiftness, and thievishness attributed to the god Mercury in Roman mythology. 3. Containing or caused by the action of the element mercury. 4. Being quick and changeable in character: *a mercurial temperament.* [Latin *mercuriālis*, from *Mercurius*, the god MERCURY.] —**mer·cu·ri·al·ly** *adv.*

mer·cu·ri·al·ism (mər-kéwr-i-ə-liz'm) *n.* Poisoning caused by mercury or its compounds. Also called "hydrargyria", "hydrargyrism".

mer·cu·ric (mər-kéwr-ik) *adj. Chemistry.* Pertaining to or containing bivalent mercury.

mercuric chloride *n.* A poisonous white crystalline compound; $HgCl_2$, used as an antiseptic and disinfectant and in insecticides, preservatives, and batteries, and in metallurgy and photography. Also called "corrosive sublimate".

mercuric oxide *n.* A poisonous compound, HgO, existing as red and yellow crystals and used as a pigment.

mercuric sulphide *n.* A poisonous compound, HgS, having two forms: 1. *Black mercuric sulphide*, a black powder obtained from mercury salts or by the reaction of mercury with sulphur, used as a pigment. Also called "metacinnabarite". 2. *Red mercuric sulphide*, a bright scarlet powder derived from heating mercury with sulphur, used as a pigment. In this form, also called "artificial cinnabar", "vermilion".

Mer·cu·ro·chrome (mər-kéwr-ə-krōm) *n.* A trademark for a solution of **merbromin** (*see*), used as an antiseptic.

mer·cu·rous (mér-kewr-əss ‖ mər-kéwr-əss) *adj. Chemistry.* Pertaining to or containing monovalent mercury.

mercurous chloride *n.* A white powder, Hg_2Cl_2, used as a fungicide and formerly used in medicine as a cathartic.

mer·cu·ry (mérkewr-i) *n., pl.* -**ries**. 1. Symbol **Hg** A silvery-white poisonous metallic element, liquid at room temperature. It is used in thermometers, barometers, vapour lamps, and batteries, and in the preparation of chemical pesticides. Atomic number 80, atomic weight 200.59, melting point –38.87°C, boiling point 356.58°C, relative density 13.546, valencies 1, 2. Also called "quicksilver". 2. Temperature. 3. Any of several weedy plants of the genera *Mercurialis* or *Acalypha*. See **dog's mercury.** 4. *Archaic.* A messenger or guide. Now used only in the titles of some newspapers. [Middle English *Mercurie*, god, planet, metal, and plant (after Greek *Hermou poa*, "herb of Hermes"), from Latin *Mercurius*, MERCURY.]

Mer·cu·ry¹ (mérkewr-i) *Roman Mythology.* A god, often identified with the Greek god **Hermes** (*see*), serving as messenger to the other gods and being the god of commerce, travel, and thievery.

Mercury² *n.* The smallest of the planets (with the possible exception of Pluto) and the one nearest the Sun. It has a sidereal period of revolution around the Sun of 88 days at a mean distance of 58 million kilometres (36 million miles), a mean radius of approximately 2 420 kilometres (1,500 miles), and a mass 0.05 that of Earth. [Latin *Mercurius*, the god, the planet.] See feature, next page.

mercury arc *n.* A bluish discharge containing some ultraviolet radiation produced by passing a high current through ionised mercury vapour.

mercury barometer *n.* A type of **barometer** (*see*) in which pressure is measured by the height of a column of mercury.

mer·cu·ry-va·pour lamp (mérkewr-i-váypər) *n.* A lamp in which ultraviolet and yellowish-green to blue visible light is produced by an electric discharge through mercury vapour. It is used as a source of ultraviolet light and for outdoor lighting.

mer·cy (mér-si) *n., pl.* -**cies**. 1. Kind and compassionate treatment of an offender, enemy, prisoner, or other person under one's power who might deserve harsh treatment; clemency. Also used ironically in the phrase *tender mercies: He was left to the tender mercies of the Inquisition.* 2. A possible disposition to be kind and forgiving: *I threw myself on her mercy.* 3. Something for which to be thankful; a fortunate occurrence. 4. Alleviation of distress; relief: *Her death was a mercy.* —**at the mercy of.** Totally in the power of.
~*adj.* Of or involving an emergency or the alleviation of critical distress: *a mercy dash; a mercy flight.* [Middle English *merci*, from Old French, compassion, forbearance (to someone in one's power), from Late Latin *mercēs*, reward, God's gratuitous compassion, from Latin, pay, reward.]
Synonyms: mercy, leniency, clemency, forbearance.

mercy killing *n.* Euthanasia (*see*).

mercy seat *n.* 1. The golden covering of the ark of the covenant regarded as the resting place of God. Exodus 25:12–22. Also called "propitiatory". 2. The throne of God.

mere¹ (meer) *adj.* Superlative **merest.** 1. Being nothing more than what is specified: *Her fee was a mere ten pounds.* 2. *Archaic.* Pure; unadulterated. [Latin *merus*, clear, pure, unmixed.]

mere² (meer) *n.* A small, usually circular lake or pond. [Middle English, Old English, sea, lake.]

mere³ (meer) *n. Archaic.* A boundary. [Middle English, Old English *mǣre, gemǣre*, boundary.]

–mere, –mer *n. comb. form. Zoology.* Indicates a part or segment; for example, **blastomere, elastomer.** [French, from Greek *meros*, a part.]

Mer·e·dith (mérrədith), **George** (1828-1909). British novelist and poet. His novels include *The Ordeal of Richard Feverel* (1859), *The Adventures of Harry Richmond* (1871), *The Egoist* (1879), and *Diana of the Crossways* (1885).

Meredith, Owen. See **Lytton, (Edward) Robert Bulwer-Lytton, 1st Earl Lytton.**

mere·ly (méerli) *adv.* 1. Nothing more than what is specified; only: *"Although he seems so firm to us / He is merely flesh and blood."* (T.S. Eliot). 2. *Archaic.* Purely. 3. *Obsolete.* Absolutely; completely.

mer·e·tri·cious (mérri-tríshəss) *adj.* 1. **a.** Superficially attractive. **b.** Attracting attention in a vulgar manner: *meretricious ornamentation.* 2. Lacking sincerity: *a meretricious argument.* 3. *Archaic.* Pertaining to or resembling a prostitute. [Latin *meritricius*, from *meretrix*, a prostitute, from *merere*, to earn pay.] —**mer·e·tri·cious·ly** *adv.* —**mer·e·tri·cious·ness** *n.*

mer·gan·ser (mər-gán-sər, -zər) *n., pl.* -**sers** or collectively **merganser.** Any marine fish-eating duck of the genus *Mergus*, having a slim, hooked, serrated bill. Also called "sawbill". [New Latin, "diver-goose" : Latin *mergus*, diver (bird) + *anser*, goose.]

merge (merj) *v.* **merged**, **merging**, **merges.** —*tr.* To cause to blend, fuse, or be absorbed so as to lose identity. —*intr.* To blend together so as to lose identity. —See Synonyms at **mix.** [Latin *mergere*, to dive, plunge.] —**mer·gence** *n.*

merg·er (mérjər) *n.* 1. The union of two or more commercial interests or companies. 2. *Law.* The absorption of a lesser estate, liability, right, action, or offence into a greater one.

me·rid·i·an (mə-riddi-ən) *n. Abbr.* **m., M., mer.** 1. *Geography.* **a.** Half of any of the imaginary great circles on the Earth's surface passing through both geographical poles. **b.** A representation of such a half-circle; a line of longitude on a map. 2. *Astronomy.* A

Mercury

A SCORCHED (AND FROZEN) WORLD
Mercury, the Sun's neighbour, scarred by ancient craters

Mercury, the closest planet to the Sun, is an arid, airless world with a cratered surface baked above 350°C (662°F) at midday and cooled to −150°C (about −240°F) at night. Mercury orbits at about 58 million kilometres (about 36 million miles) from the Sun and takes 88 Earth days to complete an orbit.

It is difficult to observe Mercury from Earth. For one thing, it is small – about half as large again as the Moon; for another, the Sun's glare washes out almost all detail.

For almost a century, astronomers believed that Mercury kept one face permanently pointed towards the Sun, as the Moon does towards the Earth. Not until 1965 did radar waves reflected from the surface reveal that the planet rotates on its axis, with a rotation period that is a fraction under 59 Earth days.

In 1974–75, the U.S. spacecraft Mariner 10 flew past Mercury three times, and the obscure little planet suddenly became very well known. Mariner's photographs revealed a lunar-like surface scarred with ancient craters made by meteorites early in the history of the solar system. Though it looks like the Moon, and is as lifeless, it lacks the Moon's large "seas" of volcanic basalt; Mercury seems to have been geologically inactive for more than 4,000 million years.

The planet has two unique types of feature. Massive scarps hundreds of kilometres long slice across its surface. And on one side there is an area of strangely jumbled rock. It lies on the opposite side of the planet to a huge crater, the Caloris Basin. Possibly the impact that made the crater produced shock waves that met precisely on the opposite side of the planet, throwing the ground into convulsions.

FEWER METEORITE STRIKES *This crescent of Mercury, with north at the right, is a photo-mosaic built up from Mariner 10 pictures. The inset shows a bright, small crater, Kuiper, 40 kilometres (25 miles) across, formed on the wall of a more ancient crater, Murasaki. After its formation, Murasaki was partly eroded by minor meteorite strikes, but Kuiper was not, evidence that the level of bombardment fell with time.*

Planet location guide
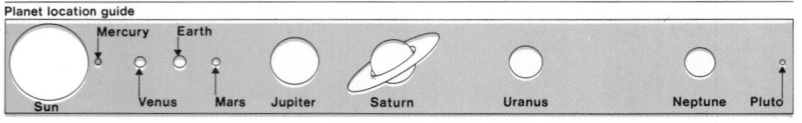

---

great circle passing through the two poles of the celestial sphere and the observer's zenith; the celestial meridian. **3.** *Mathematics.* **a.** A curve on a surface of revolution, formed by the intersection of a plane containing the axis of revolution with the surface. **b.** A plane section of a surface of revolution containing the axis of revolution. **4.** The highest point or stage of development of anything; a zenith: *"Men come to their meridian at various periods of their lives."* (J.H. Newman). **5.** *Obsolete.* Noon. [Middle English *meridien,* noon, meridian circle, from Old French, from Latin *merīdiānus,* from *merīdiēs,* midday, dissimulated variant of *medidiēs : medius,* middle + *diēs,* day.] **—me·rid·i·an** *adj.*

meridian circle *n.* **1.** *Geography.* Any of the imaginary great circles on the Earth's surface passing through both geographical poles, and consisting of a meridian and its complementary meridian, such as 0° and 180°. **2.** An astronomical instrument consisting of a telescope mounted on a graduated circle, used to determine the declination and right ascension of stars.

me·rid·i·o·nal (mə-ríddi-ən'l) *adj.* **1.** Of or pertaining to a meridian. **2.** Characteristic of southern areas or people. **3.** Located in the south; southerly. *~n.* An inhabitant of a southern region, especially of France. [Middle English, from Old French *meridionel,* from Late Latin *merīdiōnālis,* variant extension of Latin *merīdiānus,* MERIDIAN.]

Mé·ri·mée (mérri-may; *French* may-ree-máy), **Prosper** (1803–70). French writer. His work includes *The Chronicle of the Reign of Charles IX* (1829), a historical novel, and *Carmen* (1845), on which Bizet's opera is based.

me·ringue (mə-ráng) *n.* **1.** Beaten egg whites mixed with sugar and baked, used as a topping for puddings or pies. **2.** A small, crisp shell or cake made of meringue, often eaten with whipped cream. [French *méringue†.*] **—me·ringue** *adj.*

me·ri·no (mə-rēenδ) *n., pl.* **-nos.** **1. a.** A sheep of a breed originally from Spain. **b.** The fine wool of this sheep. **2.** A soft, lightweight fabric made originally of merino wool but now of any fine wool. **3. a.** A type of fine wool and cotton yarn used for knitting underwear, hosiery, and other articles of clothing. **b.** A knitted fabric made from merino yarn. *~adj.* Made of merino wool, yarn, or cloth. [Spanish, perhaps from Berber *Benī Merīn,* a people that developed the breed.]

Mer·i·on·eth·shire (mérri-ónnith-sheer, -shər). Former county of Wales, since 1974 part of Gwynedd. It borders Cardigan Bay and its fine mountain scenery, with Cader Idris (892 metres; 2,927 feet), attracts many tourists. Dolgellau was the county town.

mer·i·stem (mérri-stem) *n. Botany.* The growing point or area of rapidly dividing cells in the cambium or at the tip of a stem, root, or branch. [Greek *meristos,* divided, divisible, from *merizein,* to divide, from *meris,* a division, part + *-em,* by analogy with *xylem.*] **—mer·i·ste·mat·ic** (-sti-máttik) *adj.*

me·ris·tic (mə-rístik) *adj. Biology.* **1.** Made up of segments, as some worms are. **2.** Modified by changes in the number or placement of entire body parts, as contrasted with modification by gradual change of the entire organism. [Greek *meristos,* divided, divisible. See **meristem.**]

mer·it (mérrit) *n.* **1.** Value, excellence, or superior quality: *a play of some merit.* **2.** An aspect of a person's character or behaviour deserving approval or disapproval: *to each according to his merits.* **3.** *Theology.* Spiritual credit granted for good works. **4.** *Plural. Law.* **a.** A party's strict legal rights, excluding jurisdictional or technical aspects. **b.** The factual substance of a case as distinguished from its form and procedural aspects. **5.** *Plural.* **a.** The intrinsic right or wrong of any matter. **b.** The actual facts of a matter. *~tr.v.* **merited, -iting, -its.** To earn; deserve; warrant: *"How can the unknown merit reverence?"* (Harold Pinter). [Middle English, from Old French *merite,* that which is deserved, from Latin *meritum,* recompense, desert, from *merēre* (past participle *meritus*), to earn, deserve.] **—mer·it·ed·ly** *adv.*

mer·i·toc·ra·cy (mérri-tóckrə-si) *n., pl.* **-cies.** **1.** A system in which advancement is based on ability or achievement. **2. a.** An elite composed of talented people who have achieved success through their own efforts. **b.** Leadership by such an elite. [MERIT + -CRACY.] **—mer·it·o·crat** (-tə-krat) *n.* **—mer·it·o·crat·ic** (-tə-kráttik) *adj.*

mer·i·to·ri·ous (mérri-táwri-əss ‖ -tōri-) *adj.* Deserving reward or praise; having merit. [Latin *meritōrius,* earning money, from *merēre* (past participle *meritus*), to earn, MERIT.] **—mer·i·to·ri·ous·ly** *adv.*

merle, merl (merl) *n.* The European blackbird, *Turdus merula.* See **blackbird.** [Middle English, from Old French, from Latin *merulus, merula,* blackbird.]

mer·lin (mérlin) *n.* A small falcon, *Falco columbarius,* which has dark plumage and a black-striped tail. [Middle English *meriloun,* from Anglo-French *merilun,* from Old French *esmerillon, esmeril,* merlin, from Frankish *smeril†* (unattested).]

Mer·lin (mérlin). In Arthurian legend, a wizard and prophet serving as mentor and counsellor to King Arthur.

mer·lon (mérlən) *n.* The solid portion of a crenellated wall between two open spaces. [French, from Italian *merlone,* from *merlo,* blackbird, battlement (probably from ranks of blackbirds perched on castle walls), from Latin *merulus, merula,* blackbird.]

mer·maid (mér-mayd) *n.* A fabled creature of the sea with the head and upper body of a woman and the tail of a fish. [Middle English : MERE (sea) + MAID.]

mermaid's purse *n.* A flat, rectangular envelope containing fertilised eggs, produced by certain sharks and skates such as the dogfish. Also called "sea purse".

mer·man (mér-man, -mən) *n., pl.* **-men** (-men, -mən). A male mermaid. [By analogy with MERMAID.]

mero– *comb. form.* Indicates parts or segments; for example, **meroblastic, merocrine**. [New Latin, from Greek *meros*, part, division.]

mer·o·blas·tic (mérrō-blástik, mérrə-) *adj. Biology.* Undergoing partial cleavage. Said of an egg with a large yolk. Compare **holoblastic**. [MERO- + -BLAST + -IC.] —**mer·o·blas·ti·cal·ly** *adv.*

mer·o·crine (mérrə-krīn, -krin, -kreen) *adj.* Of or pertaining to a gland the cells of which remain intact during secretion; eccrine. Compare **holocrine**. [Literally, "partly separating" (referring to the cells) : MERO- + Greek *krinein*, to separate.]

Meroë. See **Merowe**.

Mer·o·pe[1] (mérrəpi, mer-ŏpi). *Greek Mythology.* One of the **Pleiades** *(see)*, who, after marrying a mortal, hid her face in shame.

Merope[2] *n.* The seventh star in the Pleiades cluster and the only one not visible to the naked eye.

me·ro·pi·a (mə-rŏpi-ə) *n.* Partial blindness. [New Latin : MER(O)- + -OPIA.] —**me·ro·pic** (mə-rŏpik, -rŏpik) *adj.*

-merous *adj. comb. form. Biology.* Having a specified number or kind of parts; for example, **pentamerous**. [New Latin *-merus,* from Greek *-meres,* from *meros,* a part.]

Mer·o·vin·gi·an (mérrō-vin-ji-ən, mérrə-, -jən) *adj.* Of or pertaining to the first dynasty of Frankish kings that ruled over Gaul from about A.D. 500 until 751.
~*n.* A member of this dynasty. [French *mérovingien,* from Medieval Latin *Merovingī,* "the descendants of Merovaeus", from Frankish *Merowig,* the eponymous ancestor.]

Mer·o·we or **Me·ro·ë** (mérrō-ee). Ruined capital of Cush (ancient Ethiopia) on the Nile north of Khartoum, Sudan.

mer·o·zo·ite (mérrō-zŏ-īt, mérrə-) *n.* A cell produced by fission of a sporozoan. [MERO- + ZO(O)- + -ITE.]

mer·ri·ment (mérrimənt) *n.* Gay conviviality; hilarity. See Synonyms at **mirth**.

mer·ry (mérri) *adj.* **-rier, -riest. 1.** Full of spirited gaiety; jolly. **2.** Marked by or affording humour and fun; festive. **3.** *Informal.* Slightly drunk. —See Synonyms at **jolly**. [Middle English *merie,* Old English *mirige,* pleasant.] —**mer·ri·ly** *adv.* —**mer·ri·ness** *n.*

mer·ry-an·drew (mérri-án-drōō) *n.* A prankster, jester, or clown. [17th century : reference to the name *Andrew* unexplained.]

mer·ry-go-round (mérri-gō-rownd) *n.* **1. a.** A circular platform fitted with seats, often in the form of wooden animals, revolved mechanically, usually to music, and ridden for amusement. **b.** A piece of playground equipment consisting of a small circular platform that revolves when pushed or pedalled. In both senses, also called "roundabout". **2.** Any whirl or swift round: *a merry-go-round of parties.*

merry hell *n. Informal.* Great disruption or disturbance. Often used in the phrase *to play merry hell.*

mer·ry·mak·ing (mérri-mayking) *n.* **1.** Participation in a party or revel. **2.** A festivity; revelry. —**mer·ry·mak·er** *n.*

mer·ry·thought (mérri-thawt) *n. Rare.* A wishbone.

Mer·sey (mérzi). River of northwest England. Formed by the confluence of the rivers Tame and Goyt, it flows 113 kilometres (70 miles) from Stockport to the Irish Sea where its estuary, 26 kilometres (16 miles) long, can be used by ocean-going ships. The river connects with the Manchester Ship Canal.

Mer·sey·side (mérzi-sīd). County of northwest England, created in 1974 from northwest Cheshire and southwest Lancashire. It includes Liverpool, the administrative capital, its suburbs, the coast northwards to Southport, St. Helens, and the Wirral.

Mer·thyr Tyd·fil (mérthər tídvil). Town of Mid Glamorgan, South Wales. Situated on the river Taff in the South Wales Coalfield, it was once an iron and steel town of great importance. It now relies on light industries, including engineering, textiles, and clothing.

Mer·ton (múrt'n). Borough of southwest Greater London, incorporating the former boroughs of Mitcham and Wimbledon.

mes–. Variant of **meso–**.

me·sa (máy-sə) *n.* A flat-topped elevation with one or more clifflike sides, common in the southwestern United States. [Spanish, from Old Spanish, from Latin *mēnsa†,* table.]

mé·sal·li·ance (me-zál-i-ənss, may-; *French* may-zal-yónss) *n.* A marriage with a person of inferior social position. [French : *més-,* MIS- + *alliance,* ALLIANCE.]

mes·cal (me-skál) *n.* **1.** A spineless, globe-shaped cactus, *Lophophora williamsii,* of Mexico and the southwestern United States, having button-like tubercles (*mescal buttons*) that are dried and chewed as a drug. Also called "peyote". See **mescaline. 2.** A Mexican alcoholic drink distilled from the fermented juice of certain species of **agave** *(see).* **3.** A plant, the **maguey** *(see).* [Spanish *mescal, mezcal, mexcal,* from Nahuatl *mexcalli.*]

mes·ca·line, mes·ca·lin (méskə-leen, -lin) *n.* An alkaloid drug, $(CH_3O)_3C_6H_2(CH_2CH_2NH_2)$, that produces hallucinations and other psychedelic effects.

Mes·dames. *Abbr.* **Mmes**. Plural of **Madame** or **Madam**.

Mes·de·moi·selles. *Abbr.* **Miles**. Plural of **Mademoiselle**.

mes·em·bry·an·the·mum (mi-zémbri-ánthə-məm) *n.* Any of various succulent plants of the chiefly South African genus *Mesembryanthemum,* having showy, daisy-like flowers. They are widely grown as ornamentals. See **ice plant**. [New Latin : Greek *mesēmbria,* noon + *anthemon,* flower.]

mes·en·ceph·a·lon (méss-en-séffə-lon, mézz-, mée-sen-, -zen-, -lən) *n.* Also **mes·o·ceph·a·lon** (méssō-). The region of the brain that develops from the middle section of the embryonic brain. Also called "midbrain". See **brain**. [New Latin : MES(O)- + ENCEPHALON.] —**mes·en·ce·phal·ic** (-si-fál-ik) *adj.*

mes·en·chyme (méss-eng-kīm, mézz-, mée-seng-, -zeng-) *n.* Also **mes·en·chy·ma** (me-séng-kimə, -zéng-). The part of the embryonic mesoderm from which develop connective tissue, cartilage, and the circulatory and lymphatic systems. [German *Mesenchym* : MESO- + ENCHYMA.] —**mes·en·chy·mal** (me-séng-kim'l, -zéng-), **mes·en·chym·a·tous** (mésseng-kímmətəss, mézzeng-, mée-seng-, -zeng-) *adj.*

mes·en·ter·i·tis (me-séntə-rītiss, mee-, -zéntə-) *n.* Inflammation of the mesentery. [New Latin : *mesenterium,* MESENTERY + -ITIS.]

mes·en·ter·on (me-séntə-ron, mee-, -zéntə-) *n. Biology.* **1.** The middle part of the intestinal cavity, the **midgut** *(see).* **2.** The middle part of the gastrovascular cavity in sea anemones and corals. [New Latin : MES(O)- + ENTERON.] —**mes·en·ter·on·ic** (-rónnik) *adj.*

mes·en·ter·y (méssən-təri, mézzən-‖ -terri) *n., pl.* **-ies**. Also **mes·en·ter·i·um** (méssən-tóri-əm, mézzən-) *pl.* **-ia** (-i-ə). Any of several peritoneal folds that connect the intestines to the dorsal abdominal wall. [New Latin *mesenterium* : MES(O)- + ENTERON.] —**mes·en·ter·ic** (-térrik) *adj.*

mesh (mesh) *n.* **1.** Any of the open spaces in a cord, thread, or wire network. **2.** *Often plural.* The cords, threads, or wires surrounding these spaces. **3.** A net or network. **4.** Either of two measures of the fineness of a net, according to the frequency of strands or the distance between strands. **5.** Something that snares or entraps: *entangled in the meshes of politics.* **6.** The engagement of gear teeth. —**in mesh.** In gear.
~*v.* **meshed, meshing, meshes.** —*tr.* **1.** To entangle or ensnare. **2.** To cause (gear teeth) to become engaged. **3.** To cause to work closely together or harmoniously. —*intr.* **1.** To be or become entangled. **2.** To be or become engaged or interlocked, as gear teeth might. **3. a.** To coordinate or fit harmoniously and effectively: *mesh with the boss's idiosyncratic methods.* **b.** To accord with another; harmonise. [Earlier *meash, mash,* from Middle Dutch *masche, maesche.*] —**mesh·ing** *n.* —**mesh·y** *adj.*

Me·shach (mée-shak). A Hebrew captive who, with Shadrach and Abednego, miraculously escaped death in Nebuchadnezzar's fiery furnace. Daniel 3.

Meshed. See **Mashhad**.

me·shu·ga, me·shug·ga (mi-shŏŏgə, mə-) *adj. Informal.* Mad; crazy. [Yiddish, from Hebrew.]

mesh·work (mésh-wurk) *n.* Meshes; network.

me·si·al (mée-zi-əl, -si-) *adj.* Of, in, near, or towards the middle; medial. [MES(O)- + -IAL.] —**me·si·al·ly** *adv.*

me·si·tes (mə-sīteez) *n.* A flightless, rail-like bird, *Monias benschi,* found in the forests and brushlands of Madagascar.

me·sit·y·lene (mə-sítti-leen, méssi-ti-) *n.* A hydrocarbon, $(CH_3)_3C_6H_3$, occurring in petroleum and coal tar and synthesised from acetone; 1,3,5-trimethylbenzene.

mes·i·tyl oxide (méssi-til) *n.* An oily liquid, $(CH_3)_2C:CHCOCH_3$, obtained from acetones and used as a solvent and insect repellent. [Greek *mesitēs,* mediator, from *mesos,* middle + -YL.]

Mes·mer (méz-mər; *German* méss-), **Franz Anton**, also known as **Friedrich Anton Mesmer** (1734–1815). German medical practitioner who pioneered hypnotism and psychoanalysis in medicine. He first used magnets in treatment, then treated patients by psychological suggestion. He settled in Paris in 1778, and although denounced by the French Academy of Medicine, his methods, known as "mesmerism", led to the development of therapeutic medicine.

mes·mer·ise, mes·mer·ize (méz-mə-rīz, méss-) *tr.v.* **-ised, -ising, -ises. 1.** To hypnotise. **2.** To enthral: *She mesmerised the audience.* —**mes·mer·ic** (mez-mérrik, mess-) *adj.*

mes·mer·ism (méz-mə-riz'm, méss-) *n.* Hypnotism or a theory concerning it. Not in technical usage. See **animal magnetism**. [After Franz Anton MESMER.]

mesne (meen) *adj. Law.* Intermediate; intervening. [Middle English, from Anglo-French *mesne, meen,* from Old French *meien,* from Latin *mediānus,* median, from *medius,* middle.]

mesne lord *n.* A feudal lord intermediate between a superior lord and his own vassals or tenants.

meso–, mes– *comb. form.* Indicates centre or intermediate; for example, **mesoblast, mesoderm**. [Greek, from *mesos,* middle.]

mes·o·blast (méss-ō-blast, mézz-, méess-, méez-, -ə-, -blaast) *n.* The middle germinal layer of the embryo; the mesoderm in its early stage of development. [MESO- + -BLAST.] —**mes·o·blas·tic** (-blástik) *adj.*

mes·o·carp (méss-ō-kaarp, mézz-, méess-, méez-, -ə-) *n. Botany.* The middle, usually fleshy layer of a **pericarp** *(see).* [MESO- + -CARP.]

mes·o·ceph·al·ic (méss-ō-séff'l-ik, mézz-, méess-, méez-, -ə-) *n.* **1.** Having a head form intermediate between **brochycephalic** and **dolichocephalic** *(both of which see).* **2.** A medium cranial capacity. [MESO- + -CEPHALIC.]

mesocephalon. Variant of **mesencephalon**.

mes·o·derm (méss-ō-derm, mézz-, méess-, méez-, -ə-) *n.* The embryonic germ layer, lying between the ectoderm and the endoderm, from which develop connective tissue, muscles, and the urogenital and vascular systems. [MESO- + -DERM.] —**mes·o·der·mal** (-dérm'l), **mes·o·der·mic** (-dérmik) *adj.*

mes·o·gle·a, mes·o·gloe·a (méss-ō-glée-ə, mézz-, méess-, méez-, -ə-) *n.* The layer of jelly-like material that separates the inner and outer cell layers in coelenterates. [New Latin : MESO- + Greek *gloia,* glue.]

Mes·o·lith·ic (méss-ō-líthik, mézz-, méess-, méez-, -ə-) *adj.* Archae-

merlin *The merlin, which is a small falcon, little larger than a thrush, flies fast and low to catch small birds in flight. The male takes its prey to a "plucking post", a rock outcrop or stone wall, where it plucks the kill before presenting the carcass to its mate.*

Mesopotamia *A king of southern Mesopotamia relaxes on his throne with a drink in a detail from a mosaic known as the Standard of Ur, made in about 2500* B.C. *Ur – a city which is identified with the biblical Ur of the Chaldees and which is reputed to have been the early home of Abraham – was one of the principal city-states of ancient Mesopotamia, now part of Iraq. Founded on the banks of the Euphrates some time before 3000* B.C.*, Ur was abandoned in about 316* B.C. *after the river changed its course.*

ology. Designating the cultural period between the Palaeolithic and Neolithic Ages, marked by the appearance of microlithic cutting tools, and the introduction of boats and fishing.
~*n. Archaeology.* The Mesolithic Age. Preceded by *the.* Also called "Middle Stone Age". [MESO- + -LITHIC.]

mes·o·morph (méss-ō-mawrf, mézz-, méess-, méez-, -ə-) *n.* A human build characterised by powerful musculature and a predominantly bony framework. Compare **ectomorph, endomorph.** [MESO- + -MORPH.]

mes·o·mor·phic (méss-ō-mór-fik, mézz-, méess-, méez-, -ə-) *adj.* Also **mes·o·mor·phous** (-fəss) (for sense 1). **1.** *Chemistry.* Of, pertaining to, or existing in a state of matter intermediate between liquid and crystal. **2.** *Anatomy.* Of or pertaining to a mesomorph. **—mes·o·mor·phy** (-mawrfi) *n.*

mes·on (méé-zon, -son, mésson, mézzon) *n. Physics.* Any of several elementary particles, having integral spins and masses generally intermediate between those of leptons and baryons. Formerly called "mesotron". [MES(O)- + -ON.] **—me·son·ic** (mi-zónnik, mee-, -sónnik) *adj.*

mes·o·neph·ros (méss-ō-néff-ross, mézz-, méess-, méez-, -ə-, -rəss) *n.* The middle part of the embryonic excretory system in vertebrates that becomes the functioning kidney in fish and amphibians and the epididymis in reptiles, birds, and mammals. Also called "Wolffian body". [New Latin : MESO- + Greek *nephros,* kidney.] **—mes·o·neph·ric** *adj.*

mes·o·pause (méss-ō-pawz, mézz-, méess-, méez-, -ə-) *n.* The atmospheric zone, about 80 kilometres (50 miles) above the Earth, forming the upper limit of the mesosphere.

mes·o·phil·ic (méss-ō-fíllik, mézz-, méess-, méez-, -ə-) *adj.* Pertaining to or designating an organism, usually a bacterium, thriving at moderate temperatures, between 20°C and 40°C. Compare **psychrophilic, thermophilic.** [MESO- + -PHIL(E) + -IC.]

mes·o·phyll (méss-ō-fil, mézz-, méess-, méez-, -ə-) *n.* The soft tissue of a leaf, between the upper and lower epidermis, that contains the chloroplasts and is involved in photosynthesis. [New Latin *mesophyllum* : MESO- + -PHYLL.] **—mes·o·phyl·lic** (-fillik), **mes·o·phyl·lous** (-fílləss) *adj.*

mes·o·phyte (méss-ō-fīt, mézz-, méess-, méez-, -ə-) *n.* A land plant that grows in a temperate environment having a moderate amount of moisture. Compare **xerophyte, hydrophyte.** [MESO- + -PHYTE.] **—mes·o·phyt·ic** (-fíttik) *adj.*

Mes·o·po·ta·mi·a (méssəpə-táymi-ə). Ancient region of southwest Asia, between the Euphrates and Tigris rivers. Its name is derived from the Greek for "between rivers". Most of it lies in modern Iraq. The site of some of the earliest human settlements, such as Jarmo (*c.* 7000 B.C.), it saw the rise of early civilisations: Sumer (*c.* 3100 B.C.), Akade (*c.* 2370 B.C.), and Babylon (*c.* 1800 B.C.).

mes·o·sphere (méss-ō-sfeer, mézz-, méess-, méez-, -ə-) *n.* **1.** The portion of the atmosphere from about 50 to 80 kilometres (30 to 50 miles) above the Earth, characterised by a temperature range that decreases from 10°C to –90°C with increasing altitude. See **atmosphere. 2.** The solid part of the Earth's mantle, lying between the semi-fluid asthenosphere and the fluid outer core. [MESO- + -SPHERE.] **—mes·o·spher·ic** (-sférrik, -sféer-ik) *adj.*

mes·o·spor·i·um (méss-ō-spáwri-əm, mézz-, méess-, méez-, -ə-) *n. Botany.* The **exo-intine** *(see).*

mes·o·the·li·um (méss-ō-théé-li-əm, mézz-, méess-, méez-, -ə-) *n., pl.* **-lia** (-li-ə). A layer of squamous cells of the epithelium lining the peritoneum, pericardium, and pleura, derived from the mesoderm. [New Latin : MESO- + (EPI)THELIUM.] **—mes·o·the·li·al** *adj.*

mes·o·tho·rax (méss-ō-tháwr-aks, mézz-, méess-, méez-, -ə- || -thṓr-) *n., pl.* **-raxes** or **-races** (-ə-seez). The middle section of an insect's thoracic region, bearing the middle legs and the front wings.

mes·o·tho·ri·um (méssō-tháwr-i-əm, mézz-, méess-, méez-, -ə- || -thṓr-) *n. Abbr.* **Ms-Th.** Either of two decay products of thorium: **1.** Mesothorium I, now called radium-228. **2.** Mesothorium II, now called actinium-228. Not in technical usage.

mes·o·tron (méss-ə-tron, mézz-, méess-, méez-) *n. Physics.* A **meson** *(see).* No longer in technical usage. [MESO- + (ELEC)TRON.]

Mes·o·zo·ic (méss-ō-zṓ-ik, mézz-, méess-, méez-, -ə-) *adj.* Of, belonging to, or designating the third era of geological time, which includes the Cretaceous, Jurassic, and Triassic periods, and is characterised by the predominance of reptilian life forms.
~*n.* The Mesozoic era. Preceded by *the.* [MESO- + -ZOIC.]

mes·quite, mes·quit (me-skéét, mə-, méss-keet) *n.* Any of several shrubs or small trees of the genus *Prosopis*; especially, *P. juliflora,* of the southwestern United States and Mexico. Its pods are used as forage. Also called "algarroba", "honey locust". [Spanish *mezquite,* from Nahuatl *mizquitl.*]

mess (mess) *n.* **1.** A disorderly accumulation of items. **2. a.** A cluttered, untidy, usually dirty state or condition. **b.** *Informal.* An untidy or dirty person or thing. **3. a.** A disturbing, confusing, and troublesome state of affairs; a muddle. **b.** *Informal.* A confused, muddled, or disturbed person or thing. **4.** *Archaic.* An amount of food for a meal, course, or dish: *"at their savoury dinner set / Of herbs, and other country messes"* (John Milton). **5.** *Archaic.* A serving of soft, semiliquid food: *a mess of gruel.* **6.** A distasteful and unappetising concoction. **7.** An animal's faeces, especially those of a pet: *The cat's made a mess on the carpet again.* **8. a.** A group of persons, usually in the military, who regularly eat meals together. **b.** A meal eaten in such a group. **c.** The place where such meals are served, and, in the armed forces, where there are facilities for recreation, entertainment, and accommodation: *the officers' mess.* **—make a mess of.** To bungle or ruin.
~*v.* **messed, messing, messes.** *—tr.* **1.** To make disorderly and soiled; clutter. Often used with *up: messed up the kitchen with pots and pans.* **2.** To bungle, mismanage, or botch. Usually used with *up: She messed up the test.* **3.** *Slang.* To be rough with; manhandle. Usually used with *up: a mugger messing up his victim.* *—intr.* **1.** To take a meal in a military mess. **2.** To cause or make a mess. **3.** To interfere; meddle. Usually used with *with* or *about with.* **—mess about** or **around.** *Informal.* **1.** To occupy time by pottering or tinkering; work aimlessly: *"there is nothing . . . half so much worth doing as simply messing about in boats"* (Kenneth Grahame). **2.** To waste time; procrastinate. **3.** To treat (someone) inconsiderately or badly. [Middle English *mes,* course of a meal, dish of food, group of messmates, from Old French, from Latin *missus,* "placement", course of a meal, from *mittere* (past participle *missus*), to send, place, put.]

mes·sage (méssij) *n. Abbr.* **msg. 1.** A communication transmitted by spoken or written words, by signals, or by other means from one person or group to another. **2.** A formal diplomatic communication. **3.** A statement made or read before a gathering: *a farewell message.* **4.** An apparent communication from God, delivered by a prophet. **5.** A moral or religious point or theme. **6.** The basic theme, inspiration, or significance of something: *"the life of Britain, her message, and her glory"* (Winston Churchill). **7.** *Regional.* An errand: *run a message.* **—get the message.** *Informal.* To understand; learn the truth. [Middle English, from Old French, from Vulgar Latin *missāticum* (unattested), "something sent", communication, from Latin *mittere* (past participle *missus*), to send.]

mes·sa·line (méssə-léén, -leen) *n.* A lightweight, soft, shiny silk cloth with a twilled or satin weave. [French *messaline*†.]

Mes·sei·gneurs. Plural of **Monseigneur.**

mes·sen·ger (méssinjər) *n.* **1.** One charged with transmitting messages or performing errands; especially: **a.** One employed to carry telegrams, letters, or parcels. **b.** A military or official dispatch bearer; a courier. **2.** A bearer of news. Also used in the titles of some newspapers. **3.** *Archaic.* A forerunner or prophet; a harbinger. **4.** *Nautical.* A chain or rope used for hauling in a cable. [Middle English *messager, messanger,* from Old French *messagier,* from MESSAGE.]

messenger RNA *n.* A **ribonucleic acid** *(see)* that carries the genetic information required for protein synthesis in cells from DNA to the ribosomes. Also called "messenger ribonucleic acid", "mRNA".

Mes·ser·schmitt (méssər-shmit), **Wilhelm,** known as Willy (1898–1978). German aircraft designer. He designed the Messerschmitt 109 (1937), which set a world speed record; the Messerschmitt 163 Komet, the first aircraft to be powered by a liquid-fuel rocket; and the Messerschmitt 262, the first jet aeroplane used in combat (1944).

Mes·siaen (méss-yoN, mess-yóN), **Olivier-Eugène-Prosper-Charles** (1908–). French organist and composer. His organ works include *La Nativité du Seigneur* (1935) and *Les Corps glorieux* (1939), and a mammoth symphony in ten movements, *Turangalîla* (1946–48). He made use of bird songs in *Réveil des oiseaux* (1953) and *Oiseaux exotiques* (1955).

Mes·si·ah (mi-sī́-ə, me-) *n.* Also **Mes·si·as** (-əss, me-). **1.** *Judaism.* The anticipated deliverer and king of the Jews. **2.** Jesus Christ. **3.** *Small* **m.** Any expected or supposed deliverer or liberator. [Middle English, from Old French *Messie,* from Late Latin, from Greek *Messias,* from Aramaic *məshīḥa,* Hebrew *māshiaḥ,* "the anointed", the Messiah.]

mes·si·an·ic (méssi-ánnik) *adj. Also capital* **M.** Of or pertaining to a messiah or the salvation and ideal state he is expected to produce.

Mes·sieurs. *Abbr.* **Messrs., M.M.** Plural of **Monsieur.**

Mes·si·na (me-séénə, mə-). Port of northeast Sicily, Italy, on the Strait of Messina. It exports wine, fruit, and olive oil and manufactures chemicals and pasta. It was founded by the Greeks (late eighth century B.C.). Its many occupiers included the Carthaginians, Romans, and Spaniards. Garibaldi took the city in 1860–61. It was destroyed by earthquakes in 1783 and 1908.

Messina, Strait of. Channel of the Mediterranean Sea between Sicily and mainland Italy. Linking the Ionian and Tyrrhenian seas, it is 32 kilometres (20 miles) long and at its narrowest 3 kilometres (2 miles) wide. Its rocks, currents, and whirlpools may have given rise to the legend of Scylla and Charybdis.

mess jacket *n.* An officer's fitted, waist-length jacket, often worn in the mess on formal occasions. Also called "monkey jacket".

mess kit *n.* **1.** *British.* A military officer's formal evening wear. **2.** Special cooking and eating utensils for soldiers in the field.

mess·mate (méss-mayt) *n.* A person with whom one eats regularly, as in a military or naval mess.

Messrs. 1. Messieurs. **2.** Plural of **Mr.**

mes·suage (méss-wij, méssew-ij) *n. Law.* A dwelling house with its outbuildings and adjoining lands. [Middle English, from Anglo-French, household, probably based on a misreading of Old French *me(s)nage,* MÉNAGE.]

mess·y (méssi) *adj.* **-ier, -iest.** Resembling, being in, or causing a mess; untidy; dirty; disordered. **—mess·i·ly** *adv.* **—mess·i·ness** *n.*

mestee. Variant of **mustee.**

mes·ti·zo (me-stéé-zō, mə-) *n., pl.* **-zos** or **-zoes.** *Feminine* **mes·ti·za** (-zə). In Latin America, a person of mixed European and American Indian ancestry. [Spanish, from *mestizo,* mixed, from Old Spanish, from Vulgar Latin *mixtīcius* (unattested), of mixed race, from Latin *mixtus*, from the past participle of *miscēre*, to mix.]

mes·tra·nol (méss-trə-nol ‖ -nōl) *n.* A synthetic oestrogen, $C_{21}H_{26}O_2$, used as an oral contraceptive in combination with progestogens. [*Methyl* o*estrogen* pregn*ane* + -OL.]

met. Past tense and past participle of **meet**.

met. 1. metaphor. 2. metaphysics. 3. meteorological; meteorology. 4. metropolitan.

me·ta (métta) *adj. Chemistry.* 1. Of, pertaining to, or designating positions in a benzene ring separated by one carbon atom. Used in combination: *metadichlorobenzene*. Compare **ortho, para, pyro**. 2. Of, pertaining to, or designating the least hydrated form of an acid. Used in combination: *metaphosphoric acid*. 3. Of, pertaining to, or designating a polymer of an organic compound. Used in combination: *metaldehyde*. [Independent use of META-.]

meta–, met– *prefix.* Indicates: 1. *Anatomy.* Situated behind; for example, **metacarpus**. 2. Occurring later; for example, **metazoan**. 3. **a.** Going beyond or transcending; for example, **metalanguage**. **b.** A discipline concerned with the analysis of a specified and related discipline; for example, **metalinguistics**. 4. Changed or involving change; for example, **metachromatism**. 5. Alternating; for example, **metagenesis**. 6. *Geology.* Having undergone metamorphic change. [In borrowed Greek compounds, *meta*- indicates: 1. Between, as in **metope**. 2. After, following, as in **method**. 3. Behind, backward, hence reversed, changed, as in **metathesis, metamorphosis**. 4. Intensified action, as in **meteor**. *Meta*- is the preverbal form of the preposition *meta*, between, with, beside, after.]

met·a·bol·ic (métta-bóllik) *adj. Biology.* Of, pertaining to, or exhibiting metabolism. [Greek *metabolikos*, changeable, from *metabolē*, change. See **metabolism**.] —**met·a·bol·i·cal·ly** *adv.*

metabolic pathway *n.* Any of the chains or cycles of reactions occurring in living cells, during which materials are broken down or built up with accompanying release or expenditure of energy.

me·tab·o·lise, me·tab·o·lize (mi-tábbə-līz, me-) *v.* -lised, -lising, -lises. —*tr.* To subject (a substance) to metabolism or produce (a substance) by metabolism. —*intr.* To undergo change or be produced by metabolism.

me·tab·o·lism (mi-tábbə-liz'm, me-) *n. Biology.* 1. **a.** The complex of physical and chemical processes involved in the maintenance of life. See **anabolism, catabolism**. **b.** The rate at which such processes function: *a slow metabolism.* 2. The functioning of any specified substance within the living body: *water metabolism; iodine metabolism.* [Greek *metabolē*, change, from *metaballein*, to change : *meta* (denoting change) + *ballein*, to throw.]

me·tab·o·lite (mi-tábbə-līt, me-) *n.* Any of various organic compounds produced by or taking part in metabolism. [METABOL(ISM) + -ITE.]

met·a·car·pal (métta-kárp'l) *adj. Anatomy.* Pertaining to the metacarpus.
~*n. Anatomy.* Any of the bones of the metacarpus.

met·a·car·pus (métta-kárpəss) *n. Anatomy.* The part of the hand or forefoot in mammals that includes the five bones between the fingers and the wrist. [New Latin : META- (behind) + CARPUS.]

met·a·cen·tre (métta-sentər) *n.* The intersection of the verticals through the centre of buoyancy of a floating body when in equilibrium and when tilted. This point must be above the centre of gravity for stability. —**met·a·cen·tric** (-séntrik) *adj.*

met·a·chro·mat·ic (métta-krō-máttik) *adj.* 1. Changing to a different colour from that of the dye used for staining. Said of cells and tissues stained for microscopic examination. 2. Designating a dye that is able to stain cells or tissues a different colour from its own. 3. Characteristic of or pertaining to metachromatism.

met·a·chro·ma·tism (métta-krōmə-tiz'm) *n.* A change in colour caused by variation of the physical conditions to which a body is subjected, as in heating. [META- (denoting change) + CHROMAT(O)- + -ISM.]

met·a·cin·na·bar (métta-sínnə-bar) *n.* The black form of **mercuric sulphide** (*see*).

met·a·gal·ax·y (métta-gál-ək-si, -gal-) *n., pl.* -ies. The entire collection of all galaxies, considered as the total physical universe.

met·age (méetij) *n.* 1. The official measurement of weight or contents. 2. The fee charged for metage. [From METE (to measure).]

met·a·gen·e·sis (métta-jénni-siss) *n. Biology.* **Alternation of generations** (*see*). —**met·a·ge·net·ic** (-ji-néttik) *adj.* —**met·a·ge·net·ic·al·ly** *adv.*

me·tag·na·thous (mi-tág-nə-thəss) *adj.* Having a beak in which the tips of the mandibles cross, as the crossbill does. [META- + -GNATHOUS.] —**me·tag·na·thism** *n.*

met·al (métt'l) *n.* 1. *Symbol* **M** Any of a category of electropositive elements that are usually silvery-white, lustrous, good conductors of electricity and heat, and, in the transition metals, typically ductile and malleable with high tensile strength. Typical metals form salts with nonmetals, basic oxides with oxygen, and alloys with one another. 2. An alloy of two or more metallic elements. 3. An object made of metal. 4. Basic character; mettle. 5. Broken stones used to form the surface of a macadamised road. In this sense, also called "road metal". 6. Molten glass, especially when used in glassmaking. 7. Molten cast iron. 8. *Printing.* Type made of metal. 9. *Plural.* Railway-line rails. 10. The total weight, number, or power of a warship's guns. 11. *Heraldry.* Either of the tinctures *or* (gold) and *argent* (silver), as distinguished from the colours and the furs.
~*tr.v.* **metalled** or *U.S.* **metaled, -alled** or *U.S.* **-aling, -als.** 1. To cover or equip with metal. 2. To make (a road) with broken stones.

[Middle English, from Old French, from Latin *metallum*, from Greek *metallon*†, a mine, mineral, metal.]

metal. metallurgical; metallurgy.

met·a·lan·guage (métta-lang-gwij) *n.* The natural language, formal language, or logical system used to discuss or analyse another language, the **object language** (*see*).

met·a·lin·guis·tics (métta-ling-gwístiks) *n. Used with a singular verb.* The study of the interrelationship between language and other cultural or behavioural phenomena.

metall. metallurgical; metallurgy.

me·tal·lic (mi-tál-ik) *adj.* 1. Of, pertaining to, or having the characteristics of a metal. 2. Containing a metal: *a metallic compound.* 3. Having a quality characteristic of metal: *a metallic tinkle.* [French *métallique*, from Latin, from Greek *metallikos*. See **metal**.] —**me·tal·li·cal·ly** *adv.*

metallic bond *n.* The chemical bond characteristic of metals, produced by the sharing of valency electrons between atoms in a usually stable crystalline structure.

metallic soap *n.* A soft, waxlike organic compound composed of a metal and a fatty acid, used as a drier or lubricant.

met·al·lif·er·ous (métt'l-íffərəss) *adj.* Containing metal. [Latin *metallifer* : *metallum*, METAL + -FEROUS.]

met·al·line (métt'l-īn) *adj.* 1. Of, resembling, or having the properties of a metal. 2. Containing metal ions. [METAL + -INE.]

met·al·lise, met·al·lize, *U.S.* **met·al·ize** (métt'l-īz) *tr.v.* -ised, -ising, -ises. To make metallic; coat with metal. —**met·al·li·sa·tion** (-ī-záysh'n ‖ *U.S.* -i-) *n.*

met·al·list, *U.S.* **met·al·ist** (métt'l-ist) *n.* 1. One who works with metals; especially, a craftsman producing fine metal objects. 2. One who has an expert knowledge of metals. 3. One who advocates metal money instead of paper currency.

met·al·log·ra·phy (métt'l-óggrəfi) *n.* 1. The study of the structure of metals and their compounds, especially with a microscope. 2. A printing process, **lithography** (*see*), in which metal plates are used. [METAL + -GRAPHY.] —**met·al·log·ra·pher** *n.* —**me·tal·lo·graph·ic** (mi-tál-ə-gráffik) *adj.* —**me·tal·lo·graph·i·cal·ly** *adv.*

met·al·loid (métt'l-oyd) *n.* A nonmetallic element, such as arsenic, that has some of the chemical properties of a metal, or one, such as carbon, that can form an alloy with metals.
~*adj.* Also **met·al·loi·dal** (-óyd'l). 1. Pertaining to or having the properties of a metalloid. 2. Having the appearance of a metal. [METAL + -OID.]

met·al·lo·phone (me-tál-ə-fōn) *n.* 1. Any of various musical instruments resembling the xylophone but having metal bars. 2. A musical instrument resembling a piano but having metal bars rather than strings. [METAL + -PHONE.]

met·al·lur·gy (mi-tál-ər-ji, me-, métt'l-urji) *n. Abbr.* **metal., metall.** 1. The science or procedures of extracting metals from their ores, of purifying metals, and of creating useful objects from metals. 2. The knowledge and study of metals and their properties in bulk and at the atomic level. [New Latin *metallurgia*, from Greek *metallourgos*, a miner : *metallon*†, a mine + -*ourgos*, agent suffix of *ergon*, work.] —**met·al·lur·gic** (métt'l-úrjik), **met·al·lur·gi·cal** *adj.* —**met·al·lur·gi·cal·ly** *adv.* —**met·al·lur·gist** (métt'l-urjist, mi-tál-ər-jist) *n.*

met·al·work (métt'l-wurk) *n.* 1. The craft of working in or making objects from metal. 2. Articles of or work done in metal.

met·al·work·ing (métt'l-wurking) *n.* 1. The craft or process of shaping things out of metal. 2. The processing of metal to prepare it for industrial use, as by rolling or flattening it. —**met·al·work·er** *n.*

met·a·math·e·mat·ics (métta-máthi-máttiks) *n.* The study of the principles, conceptual elements, consistency, and other aspects of logical systems, especially of mathematical systems. —**met·a·math·e·mat·i·cal** *adj.* —**met·a·math·e·ma·ti·cian** (-mə-tísh'n) *n.*

met·a·mer (métta-mər) *n.* Any pair or larger group of isomeric compounds that exhibit metamerism. [META- + -MER.]

met·a·mere (métta-meer) *n.* Any of a series of similar body segments, as in worms and lobsters. Also called "somite". [META- + -MERE.]

met·a·mer·ic (métta-mérrik, -méer-ik) *adj.* 1. *Zoology.* Of, pertaining to, or having metameres. 2. *Chemistry.* Of, pertaining to, or exhibiting metamerism. —**met·a·mer·i·cal·ly** *adv.*

metameric segmentation *n.* The repetition of similar body segments along the length of an animal, as seen in the earthworm. In most animals such segmentation is confined to embryonic stages. Also called "metamerism", "segmentation".

me·tam·er·ism (mi-támmə-riz'm, me-) 1. *Chemistry.* A form of isomerism in which different organic radicals form compounds (metamers) by attachment to the same central atom or group. 2. *Zoology.* Metameric segmentation.

met·a·mor·phic (métta-mórfik) *adj.* Also **met·a·mor·phous** (métta-mórfəss). 1. Of or pertaining to metamorphosis. 2. *Geology.* Characteristic of, pertaining to, or changed by metamorphism. [From METAMORPHOSIS.]

met·a·mor·phism (métta-mór-fiz'm) *n.* 1. *Geology.* Any alteration in composition, texture, or structure of rock masses, caused by great heat or pressure or both. 2. Metamorphosis (of an insect). [META- MORPH(OSIS) + -ISM.]

met·a·mor·phose (métta-mór-fōz, -fōss) *v.* -phosed, -phosing, -phoses. —*tr.* 1. To transform, as by sorcery: *"His eyes turned bloodshot, and he was metamorphosed into a raging fiend."* (Jack London). 2. To cause to change in form, structure, or character; subject to metamorphosis or metamorphism. —*intr.* To be changed or transformed by or as if by metamorphosis or metamorphism. [French *metamorphoser,* from *metamorphose,* transformation, from METAMORPHOSIS.]

met·a·mor·pho·sis (méttə-mórfə-siss, -mawr-fő-siss) *n., pl.* **-ses** (-seez). **1.** A transformation, as by magic or sorcery. **2.** A marked change in appearance, character, condition, or function. **3.** One that has been transformed or changed in this way. **4.** *Biology.* Change in the structure and habits of an animal during normal growth, usually in the postembryonic stage. Metamorphosis includes, in insects, the emerging of an adult fly from a maggot or of a butterfly from a caterpillar, and, in amphibians, the changing of a tadpole into a frog. **5.** *Physiology.* Transformation of one kind of tissue into another; especially, degeneration; metaplasia. [Latin *metamorphōsis,* from Greek : *meta-* (involving change) + MOR-PHOSIS.]

met·a·neph·ros (méttə-néff-ross, -rəss) *n.* The section of the embryonic kidney that is the third and last stage to be formed in reptiles, birds, and mammals. It develops into the adult kidney. [New Latin : META- + Greek *nephros,* kidney.]

metaph. **1.** metaphor; metaphorical. **2.** metaphysics.

met·a·phase (méttə-fayz) *n. Biology.* The stage of mitosis or meiosis during which the chromosomes are aligned along the equator of the nuclear spindle.

met·a·phor (méttə-fər, -fawr) *n.* **1.** *Abbr.* **met., metaph.** A figure of speech in which a term is transferred from the object it ordinarily designates to an object it may designate only by implicit comparison or analogy, as in the phrase *evening of life.* Compare **simile.** **2.** Figurative language: *the effective use of metaphor in her poetry.* [Old French *metaphore,* from Latin *metaphora,* from Greek, transference, from *metapherein,* to transfer : *meta-* (involving change) + *pherein,* to bear.] **—met·a·phor·ic** (-fórrik ‖ -fáwrik), **met·a·phor·i·cal** *adj.* **—met·a·phor·i·cal·ly** *adv.*

met·a·phos·phate (méttə-fóss-fayt) *n.* The inorganic anion PO$_3^-$, or a compound containing it.

met·a·phos·phor·ic acid (méttə-foss-fórrik ‖ -fáwrik, -fóss-fər-ik) *n.* A polymeric inorganic compound, $(HPO_3)_n$, used as a dehydrating agent and in dental cements.

met·a·phrase (méttə-frayz) *n.* A word-for-word translation. **—*tr.v.* metaphrased, -phrasing, -phrases. 1.** To manipulate the wording of (a text), especially as a means of subtly altering the sense. **2.** To make a word-for-word translation of. [New Latin *metaphrasis,* from Greek, from *metaphrazein,* to translate : *meta-* (involving change) + *phrazein,* to relate, tell.] **—met·a·phras·tic** (-frástik) *adj.*

met·a·phrast (méttə-frast) *n.* One who changes a text into a different form, as by recasting prose into verse. [Middle Greek *metaphrastēs,* from Greek *metaphrazein,* to METAPHRASE.]

met·a·phys·i·cal (méttə-fízzik'l) *adj.* Also *rare* **met·a·phys·ic** (-fízzik). **1.** Of or pertaining to metaphysics. **2.** Based on speculative or abstract reasoning. **3.** Too abstract; excessively subtle: *metaphysical speculations.* **4. a.** Immaterial; incorporeal. **b.** Supernatural. **5.** *Usually capital* **M.** Of or designating a group of 17th-century English poets, such as John Donne, whose verse is characterised by scholarly imagery and elaborate metaphors. **—*n. Usually capital* M.** Any of the Metaphysical poets or their imitators. [Middle English, from Medieval Latin *metaphysicālis,* from *metaphysica,* METAPHYSICS.] **—met·a·phys·i·cal·ly** *adv.*

met·a·phy·si·cian (méttə-fi-zísh'n) *n.* One who specialises or is skilled in metaphysics.

met·a·phys·ics (méttə-fízziks) *n. Used with a singular verb.* Also *rare* **met·a·phys·ic** (-fízzik). **1.** *Abbr.* **met., metaph.** The branch of philosophy that systematically investigates the nature of first principles and problems of ultimate reality. Metaphysics includes the study of being (ontology) and, often, the study of the structure of the universe (cosmology). See **epistemology. 2.** Speculative or critical philosophy in general. **3.** Excessively subtle, abstract, or speculative reasoning. Used derogatorily. [Medieval Latin *metaphysica,* metaphysics, from Greek *Ta meta ta phusika,* "the (works) after the *Physics*", Aristotle's treatise on transcendental philosophy, so called because it followed his work on physics.]

met·a·pla·sia (méttə-pláyzi-ə ‖ U.S. -pláyzhi-, -pláyzhə) *n.* The change of cells from a normal to an abnormal state. [New Latin : META- + -PLASIA.]

met·a·plasm (méttə-plaz'm) *n.* **1.** *Biology.* Inert material in the protoplasm of a cell, such as the yolk of an egg. **2.** *Grammar.* The changing of a word by adding, subtracting, or transposing letters or syllables, or the changing of the word order of a sentence. [Sense 1, META- + PLASM; sense 2, Latin *metaplasmus,* transformation, from Greek *metaplasmos,* from *metaplassein,* to remould : *meta-* (change) + *plassein,* to mould.] **—met·a·plas·mic** (-plázmik) *adj.*

met·a·pro·tein (méttə-prő-teen, -tee-in) *n.* Any of various organic compounds resulting from a reaction between an acid or alkali and a protein. Metaproteins are soluble in weak acids or alkalis, and insoluble in neutral solutions.

met·a·psy·chol·o·gy (méttə-sī-kóllə̇ji) *n.* **1.** Philosophical speculation on the origin, structure, and function of the mind, and on the relationship between the mind and objective reality. **2.** The philosophical analysis of the foundations or laws of psychology. **—met·a·psy·cho·log·i·cal** (sĭk'l-ójik'l) *adj.*

met·a·so·ma·tism (méttə-sőmə-tiz'm) *n.* Also **met·a·so·ma·to·sis** (-tő-siss). *Geology.* Metamorphism in which chemical as well as physical changes occur as a result of reaction with external material. [META- + SOMAT(O)- + -ISM.]

met·a·sta·ble (méttə-stáyb'l) *adj.* Designating a relatively unstable, transient, but significant state or condition of a chemical or physical system, as of a supersaturated solution or an energetically excited atom. **—met·a·sta·bil·i·ty** (-stə-bílləti) *n.*

me·tas·ta·sis (mi-tássə-siss, me-) *n., pl.* **-ses** (-seez). **1.** *Pathology.* Transmission of disease from an original site to one or more sites elsewhere in the body, as in tuberculosis or cancer. **2.** *Rhetoric.* A sudden transition from one point to another. **3.** A geological process, **paramorphism** *(see).* [New Latin, from Late Latin, transition, from Greek, from *methistanai,* to change : *meta-* (involving change) + *histanai,* to cause to stand.] **—met·a·stat·ic** (-státtik) *adj.*

me·tas·ta·sise, me·tas·ta·size (mi-tássə-sīz, me-) *intr.v.* **-sised, -sising, -sises.** To be transmitted, transferred, or transformed by metastasis.

met·a·tar·sal (méttə-tár-s'l) *adj.* Of or pertaining to the metatarsus. **—*n.*** Any of the bones of the metatarsus.

met·a·tar·sus (méttə-tár-səss) *n., pl.* **-si** (-sī). **1.** The middle part of the foot in humans, composed of the five bones between the toes and the tarsus, that forms the instep. **2.** A corresponding part of the hind foot in four-legged animals, or of the foot in birds.

met·a·the·ri·an (méttə-théer-i-ən) *adj.* Of or pertaining to the Metatheria, a group of mammals consisting of the marsupials. **—*n.*** A metatherian mammal; a marsupial.

me·tath·e·sis (mi-táthə-siss, me-) *n., pl.* **-ses** (-seez). **1.** Transposition within a word of letters, sounds, or syllables, as in the change from Old English *brid* to modern English *bird,* or in the confused use of *revelant* for *relevant.* **2.** *Chemistry.* **Double decomposition** *(see).* [Late Latin, from Greek, from *metatithenai,* to transpose : *meta-* (involving change) + *tithenai,* to place.] **—met·a·thet·ic** (méttə-théttik), **met·a·thet·i·cal** *adj.*

me·tath·e·sise, me·tath·e·size (mi-táthə-sīz) *v.* **-sised, -sising, -sises. —*tr.*** To subject to metathesis. **—*intr.*** To undergo metathesis.

met·a·tho·rax (méttə-tháwr-aks ‖ -thór-) *n., pl.* **-raxes** or **-thoraces** (-tháwr-ə-seez ‖ -thór-). The hindmost of the three thoracic segments of an insect, which bears the third pair of legs and the hind wings.

met·a·xy·lem (méttə-zí-lem, -ləm) *n. Botany.* Xylem that is differentiated after the protoxylem is distinguished by wider vessels and thickening of supporting cells. Compare **protoxylem.**

met·a·zo·an (méttə-ző-ən) *n.* A member of a division of the animal kingdom, the Metazoa, which includes all animals more complex than protozoans and sponges. [New Latin *Metazoa* : META- + -ZOA.] **—met·a·zo·al, met·a·zo·an, met·a·zo·ic** *adj.*

mete¹ (meet) *tr.v.* **meted, meting, metes. 1.** To distribute by or as if by measure; deal out; allot. Often used with *out: a judge meting out justice.* **2.** *Archaic.* To measure. **—*n. Archaic.* A measure.** [Middle English *meten,* Old English *metan.*]

mete² *n. Rare.* A boundary line or limit. Used chiefly in the phrase *metes and bounds.* [Middle English, from Old French, from Latin *meta,* boundary.]

me·tem·psy·cho·sis (méttem-sī-kő-siss, méttemp-, -si- ‖ mətém-si-) *n., pl.* **-ses** (-seez). The passing of a soul into another body or form of existence, after bodily death; the transmigration of souls. [Greek *metempsukhōsis,* from *metempsukhousthai,* (of the soul) to transmigrate : *meta-* (involving transfer) + *empsukhos,* animate : *en-,* in + *psukhē,* soul.]

met·en·ceph·a·lon (métten-séffə-lon, -lən) *n., pl.* **-la** (-lə). The part of the embryonic hindbrain from which the cerebellum and the pons develop. [New Latin : MET(A)- + ENCEPHALON.] **—met·en·ce·phal·ic** (-si-fál-ik) *adj.*

me·te·or (méeti-ər, -awr) *n.* **1.** The luminous trail or streak that appears in the sky when a meteoroid, usually no larger than a grain of sand, is made incandescent by friction with the earth's atmosphere. Also called "shooting star". **2.** A meteoroid. **3.** *Obsolete.* Any atmospheric phenomenon, such as a rainbow or lightning. [Middle English, from Old French *meteore,* from Medieval Latin *meteōrum,* from Greek *meteōron,* astronomical phenomenon, from *meteōros,* high in the air : *meta-* (intensifier) + *aeirein,* to raise.]

meteor. meteorological; meteorology.

me·te·or·ic (méeti-órrik ‖ -áwrik) *adj.* **1.** Of, pertaining to, or formed by a meteor or meteors. **2.** Resembling a meteor in speed and brilliance: *a meteoric rise to fame.* **3.** Of or pertaining to the earth's atmosphere. **—me·te·or·i·cal·ly** *adv.*

me·te·or·ite (méeti-ə-rīt) *n.* The stony or metallic object consisting of the material of a meteoroid that is large enough to survive the passage through the atmosphere and reach the Earth's surface. **—me·te·or·it·ic** (-ríttik) *adj.*

me·te·or·o·graph (méeti-ərə-graaf, -graf ‖ U.S. -áwrə-, -órrə-) *n.* An instrument that records simultaneously several meteorological conditions, such as temperature, barometric pressure, and moisture. [French *météorographe* : METEOR + -GRAPH.]

me·te·or·oid (méeti-ə-royd) *n.* Any of numerous celestial bodies, ranging in size from specks of dust to asteroids weighing thousands of tons, which appear as meteors when entering the earth's atmosphere.

me·te·or·ol·o·gy (méeti-ə-róllə̇ji) *n. Abbr.* **met., meteor., meteorol.** The science dealing with the phenomena of the atmosphere, especially weather and weather conditions. [Greek *meteōrologia,* discussion of astronomical phenomena : *meteōron,* METEOR + -LOGY.] **—me·te·or·o·log·i·cal** (-ərə-lójik'l), **me·te·or·o·log·ic** *adj.* **—me·te·or·o·log·i·cal·ly** *adv.* **—me·te·or·ol·o·gist** (-róllə̇jist) *n.*

meteor shower *n.* Any group of meteors that appear together and have an apparent common origin.

me·ter¹ (méetər) *n.* Any of various devices designed to measure time, distance, speed, or intensity, or to indicate and record or regulate the amount or volume of something, such as a flow of fluid or an electric current, or the passage of time, as in a coin-operated parking meter. ~*tr.v.* **metered**, **-tering**, **-ters**. **1.** To measure or regulate with a metering device. **2.** To imprint with postage or other revenue stamps by means of a postage meter or similar device: *metered mail*. [From -METER.]

meter². *U.S.* Variant of **metre**.

-meter *n. comb. form.* Indicates: **1.** A measuring device; for example, **barometer**, **speedometer**. **2.** A line of verse having a specified number of feet; for example, **hexameter**. [New Latin *-metrum*, or French *-mètre*, both from Greek *metron*, meter, measure.]

meter maid *n. Informal.* A female traffic warden.

metestrus. *U.S.* Variant of **metoestrus**.

Meth. Methodist.

meth– *comb. form.* Indicates chemical compounds containing methyl; for example, **methacrylate**. [From METHYL.]

meth·ac·ry·late (meth-áckri-layt) *n.* **1.** An ester of methacrylic acid, $CH_2:C(CH_3)COOR$, R being an organic radical. It is used in the manufacture of plastics. **2.** A resin derived from methacrylic acid.

meth·a·cryl·ic acid (métha-kríllik) *n.* A colourless liquid, $CH_2:C(CH_3)COOH$, used in the manufacture of resins and plastics.

meth·a·done hydrochloride (métha-dōn) *n.* A synthetic organic compound, $C_{21}H_{27}NO \cdot HCl$, used as an analgesic and in treating morphine addiction.

met·hae·mo·glo·bin (met-héema-glóbin, me-théema- ‖ -glóbin) *n.* A brownish-red, crystalline, organic compound formed by oxidation of haemoglobin and found in the blood after poisoning by chlorates, nitrates, ferricyanides, or after ingestion of oxidising drugs. [MET(A)- + HAEMOGLOBIN.]

meth·ane (mée-thayn ‖ *chiefly U.S.* méth-ayn) *n.* An odourless, colourless, flammable gas, CH_4, that is the major constituent of natural gas. It is used as a fuel and is an important source of hydrogen and a wide variety of organic compounds. See **marsh gas**. [METH- + -ANE.]

methane series *n.* A group of hydrocarbons of similar structure, the **alkanes** *(see)*.

meth·a·nol (métha-nol ‖ -nōl) *n.* A colourless, flammable, poisonous liquid, CH_3OH, used as an antifreeze, general solvent, fuel, and denaturant for ethanol. Also called "methyl alcohol", "wood alcohol", "wood spirit". [METHAN(E) + -OL.]

me·theg·lin (me-thégglin) *n.* A kind of spiced mead. [Welsh *meddyglyn* : *meddyg*, medicinal, from Latin *medicus*, MEDICAL + *llyn*, alcoholic liquor.]

me·the·na·mine (me-théena-meen, -mīn, -min) *n. Chemistry.* **Hexamine** *(see)*.

me·thinks (mi-thíngks) *v.* Past tense **me·thought** (mi-tháwt). *Archaic.* It seems to me. [Middle English *me thinketh*, Old English *mē thyncth* (impersonal) : *mē*, ME + *thyncth*, third person singular present of *thyncan*, to seem.]

me·thi·o·nine (me-thī́-a-neen, mə-, -nīn) *n.* An essential amino acid, $C_5H_{11}NO_2S$, used as a dietary supplement and in pharmaceuticals.

meth·od (méthəd) *n.* **1.** A means or manner of procedure; especially, a regular and systematic way of accomplishing anything. **2.** Orderly and systematic arrangement; orderliness. **3.** *Often plural.* The procedures and techniques characteristic of a particular discipline or field of knowledge. **—the Method.** A system of acting formulated by Stanislavsky, in which the actor recalls emotion and reactions from his past experience and utilises them in the role he is playing. Also used adjectivally: *a Method actor*. [French *méthode*, from Latin *methodus*, from Greek *methodos*, "a going after", pursuit (as of knowledge) : *met(a)-*, after + *hodos*, road, journey.]

Synonyms: **method**, system, routine, manner, mode, way.

me·thod·i·cal (mi-thóddik'l, me-, mə-) *adj.* Also **me·thod·ic** (-thóddik). **1.** Arranged or proceeding in regular, systematic order. **2.** Characterised by ordered and systematic habits or behaviour. **—See Synonyms at orderly. —me·thod·i·cal·ly** *adv.* **—me·thod·i·cal·ness** *n.*

meth·od·ise, **meth·od·ize** (métha-dīz) *tr.v.* **-ised**, **-ising**, **-ises**. To reduce to or organise according to a method; systematise. **—meth·od·i·sa·tion** (-dī-záysh'n ‖ *U.S.* -di-) *n.* **—meth·od·is·er** *n.*

Meth·od·ism (métha-diz'm) *n.* The beliefs, worship, and system of organisation of the Methodists.

Meth·od·ist (métha-dist) *n. Abbr.* **Meth.** A member of any of various Nonconformist Protestant Christian denominations having an evangelical theology based on the teachings of John and Charles Wesley and others in the early 18th century, and characterised by an emphasis on the doctrines of free grace and individual responsibility. [From METHOD; Wesley's early followers at Oxford were apparently contemptuously described as methodical in their devotions.] **—Meth·od·ist, Meth·od·is·tic** (-dístik), **Meth·od·is·ti·cal** *adj.*

meth·od·ol·o·gy (métha-dólləji) *n., pl.* **-gies. 1.** The system of principles, practices, and procedures applied to any specific branch of knowledge. **2.** The philosophical study of scientific method; the branch of logic dealing with the general principles of the formation of knowledge. **—meth·od·o·log·i·cal** (-da-lójik'l) *adj.* **—meth·od·o·log·i·cal·ly** *adv.*

methought. Past tense of **methinks**.

meth·ox·ide (meth-óksīd) *n.* A methylate.

meths (meths) *n. Informal.* Methylated spirits.

me·thu·se·lah (mə-théw-zə-lə, mi-, -thŏó-) *n.* **1.** A champagne bottle holding the equivalent of eight standard bottles. **2.** An extremely old man. [After METHUSELAH.]

Methuselah. A Biblical patriarch said to have lived for 969 years, Genesis 5:27.

meth·yl (méthil, mée-thīl) *n.* The univalent organic radical CH_3, derived from methane, and occurring in many important organic compounds. [French *méthyle*, back-formation from *méthylène*, METHYLENE.] **—me·thyl·ic** (mə-thíllik) *adj.*

methyl acetate *n.* An organic compound, CH_3COOCH_3, used as a paint remover, general solvent, and in the manufacture of perfumes.

meth·yl·al (méthi-lal) *n.* A colourless flammable liquid, $CH_2(OCH_3)_2$, used in the manufacture of perfumes, adhesives, and protective coatings.

methyl alcohol *n.* **Methanol** *(see)*.

meth·yl·a·mine (mee-thī́-lə-meen, mə-thílla-, méthi-lə-méen) *n.* A flammable gas, CH_3NH_2, produced by the decomposition of organic matter, and synthesised for use as a solvent and in the manufacture of many products, such as dyes and insecticides.

meth·yl·ate (méthi-layt) *n.* An organic compound in which the hydrogen of the hydroxyl group (OH) of methanol is replaced by a metal. Also called "methoxide". ~*tr.v.* **methylated**, **-lating**, **-lates. 1.** To mix or combine with methanol. **2.** To combine with the methyl radical. **—meth·yl·a·tion** (-láysh'n) *n.*

meth·yl·at·ed spirits (méthi-laytid) *pl.n. Sometimes singular.* A denatured form of ethanol containing methanol, pyridine, and a violet dye. Also informally called "meths".

methyl chloride *n.* An explosive gas, CH_3Cl, used in organic synthesis and polymerisation, as a refrigerant, and as an anaesthetic.

meth·yl·ene (méthi-leen) *n.* A bivalent organic radical, CH_2, a component of unsaturated hydrocarbons. [French *méthylène* : Greek *methu*, wine, mead + *hulē*, wood + -ENE.]

methylene blue *n.* An organic compound, $C_{16}H_{18}ClN_3S \cdot 23H_2O$, the dark green crystals or powder of which forms a deep-blue solution when dissolved in water. It is used to treat the accumulation of methaemoglobin induced by drugs and as a bacteriological stain.

methyl ethyl ketone *n. Chemistry.* **Butanone** *(see)*.

methyl methacrylate *n.* A colourless liquid, $CH_2:C(CH_3)COOCH_3$, that is used as a monomer in plastics.

meth·yl·naph·tha·lene (mée-thīl-náp-thə-leen, méthil-, -náf-) *n.* An organic compound, $C_{10}H_7CH_3$, obtained from coal tar in two isomeric forms, one a liquid, the other a solid. The liquid is used to standardise diesel fuels, the solid for insecticides, and both are used in organic synthesis.

me·thyl·pro·pane (mée-thīl-prṓ-payn, méthil-) *n.* A gaseous hydrocarbon, $CH_3C_3H_7$; an isomer of **butane** *(see)*.

met·ic (méttik) *n.* In ancient Greece, an alien enjoying certain rights of citizenship in the city where he resided. [Greek *metoikos* : META- + *oikos*, house.]

me·tic·u·lous (mi-tíckew-ləss, me-) *adj.* **1.** Extremely careful and precise. **2.** Excessively concerned with details; overscrupulous. [Latin *meticulōsus*, over concerned, fearful : *metus†*, fear + *(per)ī-culōsus*, perilous, from *perīculum*, PERIL.] **—me·tic·u·los·i·ty** (-lóssəti), **me·tic·u·lous·ness** *n.*

Synonyms: meticulous, conscientious, scrupulous, fastidious, punctilious.

mé·ti·er (máyti-ay, métti-; *French* mayt-yáy) *n.* **1.** An occupation, trade, or profession; especially, the work for which one is especially suited. **2.** One's special interest, talent, or strong point; a speciality. [French, from Old French *mestier*, from Vulgar Latin *misterium* (unattested), from Latin *ministerium*, trade, service.]

mé·tis (may-téess, me-) *n., pl.* **métis** *(pronounced as singular).* Feminine **mé·tisse** (-téess). *Sometimes capital* **M. 1.** A person of mixed American Indian and French-Canadian ancestry. **2.** Any person of mixed descent. [Canadian French, from Old French *metis*, mongrel, from Vulgar Latin *mixtīcius* (unattested). See **mestizo**.]

met·oes·trus (met-éess-trəss ‖ *U.S.* -éss-) *n.* The period of sexual inactivity that follows oestrus in the female of most mammals apart from higher primates and humans. [META- (after) + OESTRUS.]

Met Office (met) *n.* The Meteorological Office: a government department that records and studies the weather and issues weather forecasts and reports.

me·tol (mée-tol ‖ -tōl) *n.* A colourless substance, $CH_3(NH_2)C_6H_3OH$, used in photographic developers.

Me·ton·ic cycle (mi-tónnik) *n.* A period of 235 lunar months or about 19 Julian years, at the end of which the phases of the moon recur in the same order and on the same days as in the preceding cycle. [Discovered by *Meton*, Athenian astronomer of the fifth century B.C.]

met·o·nym (métta-nim) *n.* A word or phrase used in metonymy. [Back-formation from METONYMY, after *synonym*.]

me·ton·y·my (mi-tónnimi, me-) *n., pl.* **-mies.** A figure of speech in which an idea is evoked or named by means of a term designating some associated notion, for example the use of the *Law* for the *Police*. [Late Latin *metōnymia*, from Greek *metōnumia*, "substitute naming" : *meta-* (involving transfer) + *onoma*, name.] **—met·o·nym·i·cal** (métta-nímmik'l) *adj.*

met·o·pe (méttōp, méttəpi) *n. Architecture.* The space between any two triglyphs on a Doric frieze. [Latin *metopa*, from Greek *metopē*, area between two beam-ends : *meta*, between + *opē*, opening.]

me·top·ic (mi-tóppik) adj. Anatomy. Of or pertaining to the forehead. [Greek metōpikos, from metōpon, forehead.]

me·tre¹, U.S. **me·ter** (méetər) n. Abbr. **m.** The fundamental unit of length (equivalent to 39.37 inches) in the metric system. It is defined (1960) as the length equal to 1,650,763.73 wavelengths in a vacuum of the orange-red light emitted by krypton-86 in a discharge tube. [French mètre, from Greek metron, measure.]

metre², U.S. **meter** n. **1. a.** The measured rhythm characteristic of verse. **b.** A specified rhythmic pattern of verse, usually determined by the number and kinds of metric units in a typical line. See **foot** (prosody). **2.** Music. Chiefly U.S. Time. See Synonyms at **rhythm.** [Middle English meter, metre, from Old English meter and Old French metre, from Latin metrum, measure, from Greek metron.]

Usage: British English uses the spelling metre for the senses "rhythm" and "unit of length", but meter for any of the instruments which measure (gas meter, speedometer, and so on) and for the types of poetic line (pentameter, for example). American English uses the spelling meter in all senses.

me·tre-kil·o·gram-sec·ond-am·pere system (méetər-kíllə-gram-séckənd-ám-pair) n. Abbr. **MKSA.** A coherent system of units for mechanics, electricity, and magnetism, using the metre, the kilogram, the second, and the ampere as basic units for length, mass, time, and current intensity. See **SI units.**

me·tre-kil·o·gram-sec·ond system (méetər-kíllə-gram-séckənd) n. Abbr. **mks.** A coherent system of units for mechanics, using the metre, the kilogram, and the second as basic units of length, mass, and time. See **centimetre-gram-second system.**

met·ric¹ (méttrik) adj. Designating, pertaining to, or using the metric system. [French métrique, from mètre, METRE (unit of length).]

met·ric² n. **1.** A standard of measurement. **2.** In geometry, a function defined for a coordinate system such that the distance between any two points in that system may be determined from their coordinates.

met·ri·cal (méttrik'l) adj. **1.** Of, pertaining to, or composed in rhythmic metre. **2.** Of, or pertaining to measurement. [From Latin metricus, from Greek metrikos, from metron, measure, meter.] —**met·ri·cal·ly** adv.

met·ri·cate (méttri-kayt) v. -cated, -cating, -cates. —tr. To convert to the metric system. —intr. To adopt the metric system.

met·ri·ca·tion (méttri-káysh'n) n. Conversion to the metric system of weights and measures; metrification.

metric centner n. A unit of mass equal to 100 kilograms.

metric grain n. A unit of weight, a **grain** (see).

metric hundredweight n. A unit of mass equal to 50 kilograms.

met·rics (méttriks) n. Used with a singular verb. The branch of prosody dealing with measure and metrical structures; the use of poetic metre: Greek metrics.

metric system n. A decimal system of weights and measures based on the metre as a unit length and the kilogram as a unit mass. Derived units include the litre for liquid volume, the stere for solid volume, and the are for area. See **SI units.**

metric ton n. Abbr. **m.t., M.T.** A unit of mass equal to 1 000 kilograms.

met·ri·fi·ca·tion (méttri-fi-káysh'n) n. Metrication.

me·tri·tis (mi-trītiss) n. Inflammation of the uterus. [New Latin : METR(O)- + -ITIS.]

met·ro, Mét·ro (méttrō; French may-tró) n. The underground railway system in various cities, especially that of Paris. [French, short for (chemin de fer) métropolitain, "metropolitan (railway)".]

metro-, metr- comb. form. Indicates the uterus or things pertaining to the uterus; for example, metritis. [New Latin, from Greek mētro-, mētr-, from mētra, womb, uterus, from mētēr, mother.]

me·trol·o·gy (me-trólləji, mi-) n., pl. -gies. **1.** The science that deals with measurement. **2.** A system of measurement. [French métrologie, from Greek metrologia, theory of measurements : metron, measure + -LOGY.]

met·ro·nome (méttrə-nōm) n. A device to mark time at a steady beat in adjustable intervals, used especially as an aid to keeping time when practising music. [Greek metron, measure + nomos, rule, law.] —**met·ro·nom·ic** (-nómmik) adj.

met·ro·nym·ic (mét-rō-nímmik, méet-, rə-) n. Also **mat·ro·nym·ic** (mát-) A name derived from the name of one's mother or a female ancestor. [Medieval Greek mētronumikos : Greek mētēr, mother + onoma, name.] —**me·tro·nym·ic, ma·tro·nym·ic** adj.

me·trop·o·lis (mi-tróppəliss, me-) n., pl. -lises. **1.** A major city; especially, the capital, largest, or most important city of a particular country, state, or region. **2.** A large urban centre of culture, trade, or other activity. **3.** The chief see of a metropolitan bishop; especially, the main diocese of a specific ecclesiastical province. **4.** The mother city of a state or colony in ancient Greece. —**the Metropolis.** British Informal. London. [Late Latin mētropolis, from Greek : mētēr, mother + polis, city.]

met·ro·pol·i·tan (méttrə-póllitən) adj. Abbr. **met. 1. a.** Of, pertaining to, or characteristic of a metropolis. **b.** Making up a metropolis. **2.** Pertaining to or constituting the home territory of a sovereign state, as distinguished from its dependencies, protectorates, or overseas territories and provinces: metropolitan France. **3.** Of or pertaining to a metropolitan. **4.** Often capital **M.** Of or pertaining to London: the Metropolitan Police.

—n. **1.** In the Roman Catholic and other episcopal churches, an archbishop who has authority over bishops. **2.** In the Eastern Orthodox Church, a bishop ranking just below the patriarch who serves as the head of an ecclesiastical province. [Middle English,

from Late Latin mētropolītānus, from Greek mētropolitēs, a citizen of a METROPOLIS.]

metropolitan county n. Any of the six urban areas established in England in 1974 as units of local government on a par with counties. They are: Greater Manchester, Merseyside, South Yorkshire, Tyne and Wear, West Midlands, and West Yorkshire.

me·tror·rha·gi·a (méet-raw-ráyji-ə, mét-, -rə-) n. An abnormal haemorrhage of the uterus, especially between menstrual flows. [New Latin : METRO- + -RRHAGIA.]

-metry n. comb. form. Indicates the science or process of measuring; for example, **calorimetry, photometry.** [Middle English -metrie, from Old French, from Latin -metria, from Greek, from metron, meter, measure.]

Met·ter·nich (méttər-nikh), **Klemens Wenzel Nepomuk Lothar, Fürst von** (1773–1859). Austrian statesman. In 1809 he became the Austrian foreign minister and helped form the Quadruple Alliance which ultimately defeated Napoleon. For the next 30 years he upheld Austrian rule in Italy.

met·tle (métt'l) n. **1.** Inherent quality of character and temperament. **2.** Courage and fortitude; spirit: show one's mettle in combat. —See Synonyms at **courage.** —**on (one's) mettle.** Ready to put one's spirit, courage, or energy to the test. [Middle English metel, fortitude, metal, variant of metal, METAL.]

met·tled (métt'ld) adj. Mettlesome; full of mettle.

met·tle·some (métt'l-səm) adj. Full of mettle; high-spirited; plucky. See Synonyms at **brave.**

Metz (mets; French mess). Capital of Moselle département, northeast France. Situated on the river Moselle, it is a cultural and market centre in a fertile agricultural and wine-producing area and at the heart of the Lorraine iron and steel region.

meu·niè·re (mən-yáir, mön-) adj. Designating a fish dish, or a style of cooking fish, in which the fish is lightly coated with flour and fried in butter, and served with melted butter, lemon juice, and parsley. [French (à la) meunière, (in the manner of the) miller's wife.]

Meuse (merz ‖ mewz; French möz). Dutch **Maas** (maass). River of western Europe. Rising in the Plateau de Langres, northeast France, it flows through Belgium and The Netherlands, entering the North Sea by the Rhine delta.

MeV mega electronvolts.

mew¹ (mew) n. **1.** A cage for hawks, especially when moulting. **2.** A secret place; a hideaway.

~v. **mewed, mewing, mews.** —tr. To confine in a cage or as if in a cage. Often followed by up. —intr. Archaic. To moult. Used of a hawk. [Middle English mewe, hawk cage, from Old French mue, a moulting, from muer, to moult, from Latin mūtāre, to change.]

mew² n. **1.** The crying sound of a cat; a meow. **2.** Any similar sound.

~v. **mewed, mewing, mews.** —intr. To emit a mew. —tr. To express by means of a mew. [Middle English mewen (imitative).]

mew³ n. A sea bird, Larus canus, one of the gulls. It is found in northern Eurasia and western North America. [Middle English mew, Old English mǣw, from Germanic mai(g)wiz (unattested).]

mewl (mewl) n. A whimper or weak cry.

~v. **mewled, mewling, mewls.** —intr. To cry weakly; emit a mewl. —tr. To express by means of a mewl. [Imitative.]

mews (mewz) n. Used with a singular verb. **1.** A small street behind a residential street, formerly containing private stables for town houses, now mostly converted into small houses and flats. **2.** Such a house or flat, or a row of such houses or flats. [After the Mews at Charing Cross, London, medieval royal stables built on a site previously used for hawk cages, plural of MEW (cage).]

Mex. Mexican; Mexico.

Mex·i·can (méksikən) n. A native or inhabitant of Mexico.

—adj. Abbr. **Mex.** Of or pertaining to Mexico or to its inhabitants, their language, or their culture.

Mexican hairless n. A small dog of a breed of unknown origin, found in Mexico, having a smooth almost hairless body.

Mexican War n. A war between the United States and Mexico (1846–48) settled by the Treaty of Guadalupe Hidalgo.

Mex·i·co, United States of (méksi-kō). Spanish **Estados Unidos Mexicanos** or **Méjico** (mekhi-kô). Central American republic. Three quarters of it lies above 500 metres (1,640 feet), the Sierra Madre ranges flanking a central plateau. Half the land is too dry for crops, but farming is the chief occupation, with maize the main crop. Tourism and fishing are also important. Large mineral deposits, including iron ore, oil, natural gas, and some coal, give Mexico great industrial potential, and it has established iron and steel, vehicle, engineering, textile, and fertiliser plants. In 1979, crude oil, cotton, sugar, coffee, shrimps, zinc, lead, and copper were the chief exports, but the country has been badly hit by the slump in world demand for oil. Mexico's Indian civilisations included the Maya, Toltec, and finally the Aztec, conquered by Hernán Cortés (1521). Mexico, the nucleus of New Spain (Nueva España), achieved independence only after a struggle (1810–20). It lost its territory north of the Rio Grande to the United States after the war of 1846–48. Internal strife finally erupted in revolution (1910–17), and the present constitution was adopted. Since 1930 the republic has been one of Latin America's most stable countries. Area, 1 972 547 square kilometres (761,605 square miles). Population, 71,300,000. Capital, Mexico City.

Mexico City Spanish **Ciudad de México.** The capital and largest city of Mexico. It lies on the southern edge of the earthquake-prone central plateau at about 2 380 metres (7,800 feet), on the site of the Aztec city of Tenochtitlán, destroyed by Cortés (1521). It is a centre of commerce and finance, and an industrial centre. A cultural centre, with much Spanish colonial and modern architecture, and the national university (founded in 1551), the city is a major tourist attraction. The 1968 Olympic Games were held there.

Mey·er·beer (mī́-ər-beer, -bair), **Giacomo**, born Jakob Liebmann Beer (1791–1864). German composer. He worked mainly in France, and wrote operas such as *Les Huguenots* (1836).

Mey·er·hof (mī́-ər-hōf), **Otto** (1884–1951). German physiologist. He studied oxygen consumption in muscle tissues, and was awarded the Nobel prize in physiology and medicine, with A.V. Hill, in 1922.

Mey·nell (ménn'l, máyn'l), **Alice (Christiana Gertrude)**, born Alice Thompson (1847–1922). English poet, whose work includes *Preludes* (1875) and the essays *The Second Person Singular* (1921).

MEZ **1.** Central European Time [German *Mitteleuropäische Zeit*]. **2.** Maritime Exclusion Zone.

me·ze·re·on (mə-zéer-i-ən) *n.* **1.** A shrub, *Daphne mezereum*, native to Eurasia, having fragrant lilac-purple flowers and small scarlet fruit. **2.** A bark, mezereum. [Middle English *mizerion*, from Medieval Latin *mezereon*, from Arabic *māzaryūn*.]

me·ze·re·um (mə-zéer-i-əm) *n.* **1.** A shrub, the mezereon. **2.** The dried bark of certain shrubs of the genus *Daphne*, once used externally as a vesicant (blistering agent) and internally for arthritis. [New Latin, variant of Medieval Latin *mezereon*, MEZEREON.]

me·zu·zah, **me·zu·za** (mə-zŏŏ-zə, -zŏŏ-) *n.*, *pl.* **mezuzoth** (-zot, -zəss) or **-zahs**. *Judaism*. A small piece of parchment inscribed with the Biblical passages Deuteronomy 6:4–9 and 11:13–21 and marked with the word "Shaddai", a name for God. The parchment is rolled up in a container and affixed to a door frame as a sign that a Jewish family lives within. It may also be carried as an amulet. [Hebrew *məzūzāh*, "doorpost".]

mez·za·nine (mét-sə-neen, mézzə-, -néen) *n.* **1.** A partial storey situated between two main storeys of a building, especially one between the ground and first floors. **2.** *British*. A floor beneath a theatre stage. **3.** *U.S.* The lowest balcony in a theatre or its first few rows. [French, from Italian *mezzanino*, from *mezzano*, middle, from Latin *mediānus*, MEDIAN.]

mez·zo (mét-sō, méd-zō) *n.*, *pl.* **-zos**. A mezzo-soprano.

mez·zo-re·lie·vo (mét-sō-ri-léevō, méd-zō-) *n.*, *pl.* **-vos**. Also Italian **mez·zo·ri·lie·vo** (mét-sō-ril-yáyvō, méd-zō-) *pl.* **-vi** (-vee). Sculptural relief in which the modelled forms project about halfway from the background. Also called "demirelief", "half relief". [Italian *mezzorilievo* : *mezzo*, half + *rilievo*, relief, from *rilevare*, to raise.]

mez·zo-so·pran·o (mét-sō-sə-práanō, méd-zō- ‖ -pránnō) *n.*, *pl.* **-os** or **-prani** (-práanee ‖ -pránnee). **1.** A voice or voice part having a range between soprano and contralto. **2.** A woman having such a voice. [Italian : *mezzo*, half + SOPRANO.]

mez·zo·tint (mét-sō-tint, méd-zō-) *n.* **1.** A method of engraving a copper plate by scraping and burnishing areas to produce effects of light and shadow. **2.** A print made from a plate so treated. ~*tr.v.* **mezzotinted**, **-tinting**, **-tints**. To engrave (a metal plate) using the method of mezzotint. [Italian *mezzotinto* : *mezzo*, half + *tinto*, tint, from Latin *tingere* (past participle stem *tinctus*), to TINT.]

mF millifarad.

MF, M.F. medium frequency.

m.f. *Music*. mezzo-forte.

mfg. manufacture; manufactured; manufacturing.

MFH Master of Foxhounds.

mfr. manufacture; manufacturer.

mg milligram.

Mg The symbol for the element magnesium.

mgr. manager.

Mgr. **1.** manager. **2.** Monseigneur; Monsignor.

mH millihenry.

MHA Member of the House of Assembly (in Australia).

MHD magnetohydrodynamics.

MHG Middle High German.

mho (mō) *n.*, *pl.* **mhos**. *Electricity*. A unit of conductance; a **siemens** *(see)*. [Backward spelling of OHM.]

MHR Member of the House of Representatives (in Australia).

MHz megahertz.

mi. *Music*. Variant of **me**.

MI Military Intelligence.

mi. **1.** mile. **2.** mill (monetary unit).

Mi·am·i[1] (mī-ámmi ‖ *U.S. also* -ámmə) *n.*, *pl.* **-is** or collectively **Miami**. A member of an Algonquian North American Indian people who lived in what is now Ohio, Indiana, Illinois, and Wisconsin. **—Mi·am·i** *adj.*

Miami[2] A city and port in southeast Florida, United States. It grew in the 1920s land boom and is now a famous holiday resort and cruise centre for the Caribbean.

miaou, miaow. Variants of **meow**.

mi·as·ma (mi-áz-mə, mī-) *n.*, *pl.* **-mas** or **-mata** (-mətə). **1. a.** A poisonous atmosphere formerly thought to rise from swamps and putrid matter and cause disease. **b.** A thick, vaporous atmosphere: *a miasma around the factory*. **2.** Any noxious atmosphere or influence: *a miasma of evil*. [New Latin, from Greek *miainein*, to pollute.] **—mi·as·mal** (-məl), **mi·as·mat·ic** (mée-əz-máttik, mī-), **mi·as·mic** *adj.*

Mic. Micah (Old Testament).

mi·ca (mī́kə) *n.* Any of a group of chemically and physically related

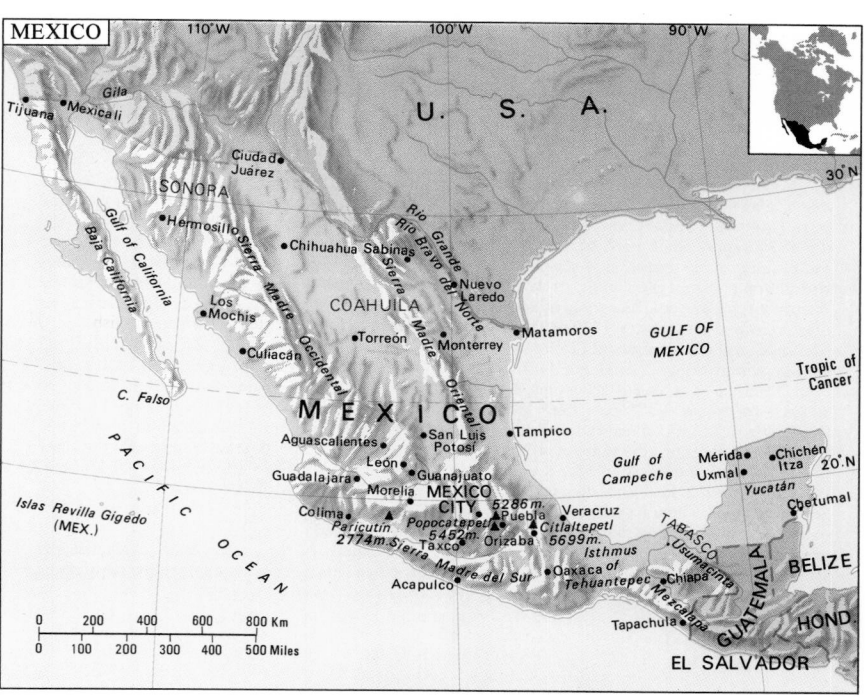

complex mineral silicates, common in igneous and metamorphic rocks, occurring as thin flaky sheets. The two main members of the group are muscovite and biotite. [New Latin (meaning influenced by Latin *micāre*, to shine), from Latin *mīca*, grain.] **—mi·ca·ceous** (mī-káyshəss) *adj.*

Mi·cah[1] (mī́kə). Also **Mi·che·as** (mī-kée-əss). A Hebrew prophet of the eighth century B.C.

Micah[2] *n.* Also **Micheas** *Abbr.* **Mic.** The sixth of the Old Testament books of the Minor Prophets.

mi·caw·ber (mi-káwbər) *n.* An improvident person who, despite constant adversity, remains doggedly optimistic about a change in his luck. [After Wilkins *Micawber*, a character in Charles Dickens' novel *David Copperfield* (1849–50).] **—mi·caw·ber·ish** *adj.*

mice. Plural of **mouse**.

mi·celle, **mi·cell** (mi-sél, mī-) *n.* Also **mi·cel·la** (mi-séllə, mī-) *pl.* **-cellae** (-séllee). **1.** A submicroscopic aggregation of molecules such as a droplet in a colloidal system. **2.** A coherent strand or structure in natural or synthetic fibres. **3.** A submicroscopic structural unit of protoplasm. [New Latin *micella*, from Latin *mīca*, grain, MICA.] **—mi·cel·lar** (mi-séllər, mī-) *adj.*

Mich. Michigan.

Mi·chael[1] (mī́k'l). The guardian archangel of the Jews in the Old Testament. Daniel 10:13; Revelation 12:7–9.

Michael[2], born Mikhail Fyodorovich Romanov (1596–1645). Tsar of Russia (1613–45) and founder of the Romanov dynasty.

Michael I (1921–). King of Romania (1927–30 and 1940–47). He became king on the death of his grandfather, King Ferdinand, but was reduced to Crown Prince when his father, Carol II, returned from exile in 1930. On his father's abdication, he became king again in 1940. He was forced into exile by the communist government.

Mich·ael·mas (míck'l-məss) *n.* A church festival celebrated on September 29 in honour of the archangel Michael. It is one of the four quarter days in England, Wales, and Ireland. [Middle English *mychelmesse*, Old English *Michaeles mæsse* : *Michaeles*, genitive of *Michael* + *mæsse*, MASS.]

Michaelmas daisy *n.* Any of several hybrid asters derived primarily from North American species such as *A. novi-belgii*, having clusters of small, variously coloured, daisy-like flowers.

Michaelmas term *n.* In some universities, schools, or the like, the term beginning near Michaelmas; the autumn term.

Micheas. Variant of **Micah**.

Mi·chel·an·ge·lo Buo·nar·ro·ti (mík'l-ánjə-lō bwónnə-rótti, míck'l-) (1475–1564). Italian sculptor, painter, and architect. He created some of the greatest masterpieces of world art: the marble sculpture *David*, commissioned in 1501 by the council of Florence, the paintings which decorate the ceiling of the Sistine Chapel (1508–12), and the plans for much of St. Peter's, Rome. See feature, next page.

Mi·chel·son (mík'l-sən), **Albert Abraham** (1852–1931). U.S. physicist, born in Prussia. He accurately measured the speed of light. He was awarded the Nobel prize for physics (1907).

Mi·chel·son-Mor·ley experiment (mík'l-sən-mórli) *n.* An experiment performed (1887) in an attempt to detect the motion of the earth through the ether by measuring the difference in velocity of two perpendicular beams of light; no such difference was detected. This important result led to disbelief in the existence of the ether and was later explained by the theory of relativity. [After Albert

Michelangelo

CREATOR OF THE SISTINE CHAPEL'S MASTERPIECE
Michelangelo endowed his works with a unique spiritual quality

Although he regarded himself chiefly as a sculptor, Michelangelo (1475–1564) was an artist of many talents – painter, sculptor, architect, and poet. He studied under Ghirlandaio and Bertoldo in Florence, then went to Rome (1496), establishing a reputation as a sculptor (1499) with his magnificent pietà in St. Peter's, Rome. Returning to Florence, he carved another great masterpiece, the 4.8 metres (16 feet) high statue of *David*, and also completed (1504) one of his best-known paintings, *The Holy Family*.

In 1505 he was called to Rome by Pope Julius II to design the Pope's tomb, which he finished in 1545, in a much reduced form from the original intention; the tomb is in San Pietro in Vincoli, with the statue of *Moses* as the main element. In 1508 he began the ceiling of the Sistine Chapel, which he painted, virtually unaided, in four years. This masterpiece, one of the greatest achievements in the history of art, consists of a profusion of Biblical scenes, from the Creation to the aftermath of the Flood.

From 1520 to 1534, Michelangelo worked in Florence as architect and sculptor on the Medici chapel, where his impressive sculptures include the figures of *Dawn, Evening, Night,* and *Day*. He returned once more to Rome (1534) and was commissioned (1536) by Pope Paul III to paint the vast fresco of the *Last Judgment* behind the high altar of the Sistine Chapel, which he finished in 1541.

In his declining years, Michelangelo carved another pietà for his own tomb; at present (1982) it is in Florence cathedral museum. He also finished the Palazzo Farnese, laid out the plan of the Capitoline Hill, designed the dome of St. Peter's, Rome, painted frescoes for the Cappella Paolina in the Vatican, and began his final, unfinished, pietà (in the Castello, Milan). His literary works include letters and some 200 poems, mostly sonnets.

A master of the human form, Michelangelo endowed his works with a spiritual quality never before achieved by an artist.

MASTERPIECE IN MARBLE *After Michelangelo had finished the pietà in St. Peter's, Rome, critics commented that the Virgin Mary appeared too young in relation to Christ's age. Michelangelo replied to the effect that a chaste woman long retains her youth and beauty.*

Abraham MICHELSON and Edward Williams Morley (1838–1923), U.S. chemist.]

Mich·i·gan (míshi-gən). Northern state of the United States, comprising two peninsulas divided by Lake Michigan, and linked by a bridge across the Straits of Mackinac since 1957. The state is predominantly industrial, with motor manufacture, centred on Detroit, the largest city, the chief industry. Other products include iron ore, and oil and gas. French explorers reached the area in the early 17th century. It was occupied by the British (1763–96), became a territory (1805), and was admitted to the Union (1837). Lansing is the capital. —**Mich·i·gan·der** (-gándər) n. —**Mich·i·gan·ite** (-gənīt) n.

Michigan, Lake. The largest freshwater lake in the United States, with an area of 57 757 square kilometres (22,300 square miles). It is

the largest of the Great Lakes, and the only one of them wholly within the country. Lake Michigan is a major trade artery, linked via the Illinois Waterway with the Mississippi and Gulf of Mexico. Ocean-going ships from the Atlantic reach it via the St. Lawrence Seaway. The ports of Gary, Chicago, and Milwaukee constitute a major industrial region.

mick (mik) n. Also **Mick**. *Slang*. **1.** An Irishman. **2.** A Roman Catholic. In both senses, used derogatorily. [From *Mick*, nickname for *Michael*.]

mick·ey (míckí) n. —**take the mickey**. To tease; poke fun at. [20th century : origin obscure.]

Mickey Finn n. *Slang*. **1.** An alcoholic drink that is surreptitiously drugged to stupefy, render unconscious, or otherwise incapacitate the drinker. **2.** The drug used for this purpose. Also called "Mickey". [20th century : origin obscure.]

mickey mouse adj. **1.** Not serious; childish. **2.** Insubstantial; of little worth: *mickey mouse money*. [After a mouse character in the cartoons of Walt Disney.]

mick·le (míck'l) adj. Also **muck·le** (múck'l). *Scottish*. Great. ~adv. Also **muck·le**. *Scottish*. Greatly. ~n. *Chiefly Scottish*. Also **muckle** (for sense 2). **1.** A small amount. Used chiefly in the proverb *Many a mickle makes a muckle*. **2.** A large amount: *Many a pickle makes a mickle*. [Middle English *mikell*, from Old Norse *mikill*, replacing Old English *micel*, MUCH.]

Mic·mac (mík-mak) n., pl. **-macs** or collectively **Micmac**. **1.** A member of an Algonquian North American Indian people formerly inhabiting the areas that are now Nova Scotia and New Brunswick. **2.** The Algonquian language of this people.

mi·cra. Alternative plural of **micron**.

micro– comb. form. Indicates: **1.** The smaller, inner, or more detailed of two contrasting things; for example, **microcosm**. Compare **macro–**. **2.** An instrument or technique for working with small quantities; for example, **microchemistry**. **3.** Use of a microscope and related tools; for example, **microscopy**. **4.** Abnormally small size; for example, **microcephaly**. **5.** Amplification or enlargement; for example, **microphone**. **6.** *Symbol* μ One-millionth (10^{-6}) part of a unit in the metric or related measurement systems; for example, **microampere**. *Note:* Many compounds other than those entered here may be formed with *micro-*. In forming compounds, *micro-* is normally joined to the following word or element without space or hyphen: *micrometer*. However, if the second element begins with a capital letter, it is separated with a hyphen: *micro-America*. If the second element begins with *o*, a hyphen is normally used, but as the compound grows widely familiar, the hyphen may be dropped. An example is the word *microorganism*, which the usage of scientists has established in that form. This prefix is usually pronounced (míkrō); there is a less frequent variant (míckrō), which is not shown below. [Middle English, from Latin *micro-*, from Greek *mikro-, mikr-*, from *mikros*, small.]

mi·cro·a·nal·y·sis (míkrō-ə-nál-ə-siss) n. *Chemistry*. The analysis of quantities weighing one milligram or less. —**mi·cro·an·a·lyst** (-ánnə-list) n. —**mi·cro·an·a·lyt·ic** (-ánnə-líttik), **mi·cro·an·a·lyt·i·cal** (-ánnə-líttik'l) adj.

mi·cro·bal·ance (míkrō-bal-ənss) n. A very accurate balance capable of weighing quantities of between a milligram and a microgram.

mi·crobe (mí-krōb) n. A minute life form; a microorganism, especially one that causes disease. Not in technical usage. See Usage note at **germ**. [MICRO- + Greek *bios*, life.] —**mi·cro·bi·al** (mī-krōbi-əl), **mi·cro·bic** (mī-krōbik) adj.

mi·cro·bi·ol·o·gy (míkrō-bī-ólləji) n. The science that deals with microorganisms, and especially their effects on other forms of life. —**mi·cro·bi·o·log·i·cal** (-bī-ə-lójik'l) adj. —**mi·cro·bi·o·log·i·cal·ly** adv. —**mi·cro·bi·ol·o·gist** (-bī-ólləjist) n.

mi·cro·ceph·a·ly (míkrō-séffəli) n. Abnormal smallness of the head, often associated with pathological mental conditions. [Greek *mikrokephalos*, small-headed : MICRO- + -CEPHALOUS.] —**mi·cro·ce·phal·ic** (-si-fál-ik) n. & adj. —**mi·cro·ceph·a·lous** (-séffələss) adj.

mi·cro·chem·is·try (míkrō-kémmi-stri) n. Chemistry that deals with minute quantities of materials, weighing one milligram or less. Compare **macrochemistry**. —**mi·cro·chem·i·cal** adj.

mi·cro·chip (míkrō-chip) n. A chip of semiconductor material carrying integrated circuits, especially one having logic circuits for computing. —**mi·cro·chipped** (-chipt) adj.

mi·cro·cir·cuit (míkrō-surkit) n. A very small electronic circuit, especially one using small integrated circuits on semiconductor chips. —**mi·cro·cir·cuit·ry** (-súrkitri) n.

mi·cro·cli·mate (míkrō-klī-mit, -mət) n. The climate of a specific place within an area, rather than that of the area as a whole. Compare **macroclimate**. —**mi·cro·cli·mat·ic** (-klī-máttik) adj.

mi·cro·cli·ma·tol·o·gy (míkrō-klīmə-tólləji) n. The scientific study of microclimates. —**mi·cro·cli·ma·to·log·ic** (-tə-lójik) **mi·cro·cli·ma·to·log·i·cal** adj.

mi·cro·cline (míkrō-klīn) n. A mineral of the feldspar group, potassium aluminium silicate $KAlSi_3O_8$, used in making pottery. [German *Mikroklin* : MICRO- + CLINE.]

mi·cro·coc·cus (míkrō-kóckəss) n., pl. **-cocci** (-kók-sī, -kóckī). A bacterium of any of several species of the genus *Micrococcus*, containing gram positive, spherical cells that occur in irregular clusters.

mi·cro·com·pu·ter (míkrō-kəm-pewtər ‖ -kom-) n. A small computer consisting of a microprocessor and input and output devices such as a visual display unit, usually with external memory.

mi·cro·cop·y (míkrō-koppi) n., pl. **-ies**. A greatly reduced photographic copy, usually reproduced by projection.

SAVING SPACE WITH PHOTOGRAPHIC FILES OF DOCUMENTS AND PUBLICATIONS

The process that fitted Queen Victoria's family into a finger-ring

The principles and practice of microfilming are almost as old as photography itself. In the 1850s, an Englishman, John Dancer, produced minute film slides. One series was of Queen Victoria's family mounted in a ring with a built-in magnifying glass. The first commercial process, Kodak's Recordak, used for reducing cheques onto 16 millimetre film, was launched in 1928. Techniques have since been much refined. Reductions, now ranging from 10 to 60 times, are stored on film or on cards (microfiches). Microfilms are indispensable for long-term, compact storage of official records, books, documents, and newspapers.

SIZE BEFORE REDUCTION *Printed above at their actual size, three headline letters from the magazine on the right occupy about the same space as ten pages reduced onto microfilm.*

FILES IN MINIATURE *A 98 page magazine, such as the American Business Week shown here, can be recorded on a single microfilm card about 140 × 90 millimetres (5¼ × 3¼ inches) – about the same size as a postcard.*

mi·cro·cosm (mĭkrō-koz'm, mĭkrə-) *n.* **1.** A diminutive, representative system more or less analogous to a much larger system in constitution, configuration, or development: *The council meeting is a microcosm of British democracy.* **2.** The human race or any specific person, community, or the like regarded as the epitome of the universe. Compare **macrocosm.** [Middle English *microcosme,* from Medieval Latin *mīcro(s)cosmus,* from Greek *mikros kosmos,* small world : MICRO- + COSMOS.] —**mi·cro·cos·mic** (-kózmik), **mi·cro·cos·mi·cal** (-kózmik'l) *adj.*

microcosmic salt *n.* A white solid, ammonium sodium hydrogen phosphate, obtained from human urine and used in bead tests on metal oxides.

mi·cro·crys·tal·line (mĭkrō-krĭst'l-īn, -in, -een) *adj.* Designating a solid substance that consists of microscopic crystals.

mi·cro·cyte (mĭkrō-sīt, mĭkrə-) *n.* An abnormally small red blood cell, less than five microns in diameter. [MICRO- + (ERYTHRO)-CYTE.]

mi·cro·dot (mĭkrō-dot) *n.* A piece of text reduced in size to a small dot, typically used for secret messages.

mi·cro·e·co·nom·ics (mĭkrō-éekə-nómmiks, -éckə-) *n. Used with a singular verb.* The study of the economics of small-scale systems such as individuals, families, companies, and the production and selling of particular commodities. Compare **macroeconomics.**

mi·cro·e·lec·tron·ics (mĭkrō-i-lek-trónniks, -ee-, -e-) *n. Used with a singular verb.* The branch of electronics that deals with components of miniature size. —**mi·cro·e·lec·tron·ic** *adj.*

mi·cro·fiche (mĭkrō-feesh, -fish) *n., pl.* **-fiches** or **microfiche.** A sheet of microfilm, usually measuring 10 by 15 centimetres (4 by 6 inches), capable of accommodating and preserving a considerable number of book pages in reduced form. Also called "fiche". ~*tr.v.* **microfiched, -fiching, -fiches.** To record on microfiche. [French : MICRO- + *fiche,* slip of paper.]

mi·cro·fil·ar·i·a (mĭkrō-fi-laír-i-ə) *n., pl.* **-ariae** (-i-ee) A slender larval form of a filaria, often found in the blood of people infected with filariae.

mi·cro·film (mĭkrə-film, mĭkrō-) *n.* **1.** A film upon which documents are photographed greatly reduced in size. **2.** A reproduction on microfilm. ~*tr.v.* **microfilmed, -filming, -films.** To reproduce (documents or other materials) on microfilm.

mi·cro·form (mĭkrə-fawrm, mĭkrō-) *n.* Any arrangement of images reduced in size, as on microfilm or microfiche.

mi·cro·ga·mete (mĭkrō-gámmeet, -gə-méet) *n. Biology.* The smaller of a pair of conjugating gametes in protozoans; the male gamete. Compare **macrogamete.**

mi·cro·ga·met·o·cyte (mĭkrō-gə-méetə-sīt) *n.* A cell that divides to produce microgametes in protozoa.

mi·cro·graph (mĭkrō-graaf, -graf) *n.* **1.** A photograph or drawing of an object enlarged by a microscope. **2.** A device for producing very small writing or engraving. [MICRO- + -GRAPH.]

mi·crog·ra·phy (mī-króggrəfi) *n.* **1.** The representation, study, or description of microscopic objects. **2.** The writing or engraving of very small characters. Compare **macrography.** [MICRO- + -GRAPHY.] —**mi·cro·graph·ic** (mĭkrō-gráffik, mĭkrə-) *adj.*

mi·cro·groove (mĭkrō-grōov) *n.* A narrow groove of the type used on long-playing records.

mi·cro·hab·i·tat (mĭkrō-hábbi-tat) *n.* The smallest unit of a habitat, as in a clump of grass or a space between rocks.

mi·cro·light (mĭkro-līt) *n.* A light motorised aircraft, consisting essentially of à wing structure similar to that of a hang-glider with a suspended frame to carry one or two people.

mi·cro·lith (mĭkrō-lith, mĭkrə-) *n. Archaeology.* A small flint that is the remnant of a Stone Age tool or weapon. [MICRO- + -LITH.]

mi·cro·man·ip·u·la·tion (mĭkrō-mə-níppew-láysh'n) *n.* The manipulation of extremely small instruments under a microscope, as in microsurgery. —**mi·cro·man·ip·u·la·tor** (-laytər) *n.*

mi·cro·me·te·or·ite (mĭkrō-méeti-ə-rīt) *n.* A very small meteorite, typically having a diameter of a few micrometres.

mi·cro·me·te·or·ol·o·gy (mĭkrō-méeti-ə-rólləji) *n.* The study of meteorological conditions in a small region, usually a shallow layer up to about 100 metres (110 yards) above ground in which temperature and humidity extremes are found. —**mi·cro·me·te·or·o·log·i·cal** (-rə-lójik'l) *adj.* —**mi·cro·me·te·or·o·lo·gist** (-rólləjist) *n.*

mi·crom·e·ter (mī-krómmitər) *n.* Any device for measuring minute distances, especially an instrument (*micrometer gauge*) based on the rotation of a finely threaded screw. [French *micromètre* : MICRO- + -METER.]

micrometer screw *n.* A screw that has a fine, accurately cut thread, used in a micrometer.

mi·cro·me·tre (mĭkrō-meetər) *n.* A unit of length equal to one-millionth (10⁻⁶) of a metre. Also called "micron".

microscope

SEEING FURTHER INTO MINIATURE WORLDS DURING 400 YEARS OF IMPROVING MICROSCOPES

How combinations of lenses reveal the minute structure of materials

Without the microscope, there could have been no proper understanding of the nature of living things. Mankind would still be largely ignorant of (among other things) the nature of germs, chromosomes and the mechanisms of heredity, the manner in which muscles contract, and how malaria is transmitted.

The first compound microscope was pioneered (*c.* 1590) by Dutch spectacle-makers Zacharias and Hans Janssen. It is called "compound" because it has more than one lens – an objective lens, which magnifies the object, and an eyepiece lens, which enlarges the magnified image. Since then, microscopes have been progressively refined: magnifications have been increased and distortions eliminated by adding extra lenses. By the 1880s, magnifications of 2,000 times had been achieved, the limit for compound microscopes dictated by the nature of light itself.

The first electron microscope was made in Germany in 1931. It uses electron beams instead of light rays to reveal detail. Today electron microscopes can magnify specimens by up to 1,000,000 times. They have extended our ability to view matter to the level of the infinitesimal molecule.

Microscopes have proved invaluable not only in medicine and biology, but also for metallurgists, geologists, forensic scientists, and other specialists interested in the minute structure of materials.

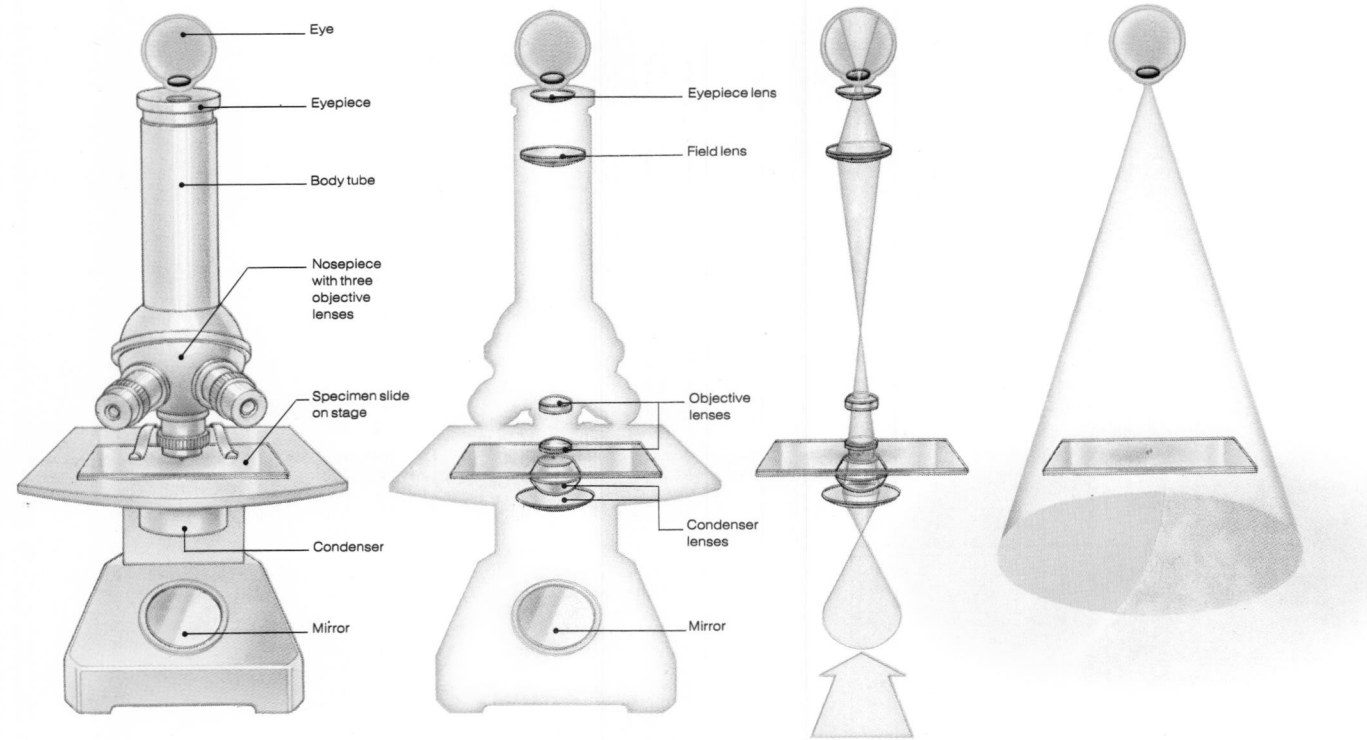

THE STRUCTURE *The slide is seen under a basic compound microscope, which has a single body tube. The eye sees an image formed by one of three objective lenses of different powers in the rotating nosepiece. The image is magnified by lenses in the eyepiece. The whole microscope can be tilted for convenience, the slide moving with the body tube and nosepiece to keep the objective lens that is in use in the same plane as the slide.*

THE LENSES *To form the image, three systems of lenses are used. Under the stage is the condenser, made of two or three separate lenses. Above the stage is the objective lens, made of up to 18 separate lenses. At the top of the microscope is the eyepiece, consisting of a field lens and an eye lens. If a high-powered objective lens is lowered into a drop of oil on the glass that covers the specimen, magnification up to × 2,000 can be obtained.*

FORMING THE IMAGE *Artificial light reaches the eye of the observer through the three lens systems. The light, generated by a lamp, is reflected by a mirror through the condenser, which concentrates light on the specimen on the stage. The objective lenses and the eyepiece lenses together form a reversed image of the specimen. This is what is seen by an observer looking into the microscope.*

MAGNIFICATION *The eye sees an image of part of the specimen in fine detail. Careful lens design and manufacture correct distortion in the image, giving it clarity and sharpness – called high resolution. To help to achieve this, the lenses are made of two kinds of glass – crown and flint – and sometimes of a transparent mineral, fluorite, which is necessary for the very best image. Objective and eyepiece lenses of different magnifications give a range of powers, usually between × 40 and × 1,500.*

mi·crom·e·try (mī-krómmətri) *n.* Measurement with a micrometer. —**mi·cro·met·ric** (mīkrō-méttrik), **mi·cro·met·ri·cal** *adj.* —**mi·cro·met·ri·cal·ly** *adv.*

mi·cro·min·ia·tur·ise, mi·cro·min·ia·tur·ize (mīkrō-mínnəchər-īz, -mín-yəchər-) *tr.v.* **-ised, -ising, -ises.** To construct or produce very small (electronic circuits) using integrated circuits. —**mi·cro·min·ia·tur·i·sa·tion** (-ī-záysh'n ‖ *U.S.* -i-) *n.*

mi·cron (mī-kron) *n., pl.* **-crons** or **-cra** (-krə). Also **mi·kron.** *Symbol* **μ** A micrometre. Note that in technical usage *micrometre* is preferred. [New Latin, from Greek, from *mikros*, small.]

Mi·cro·ne·si·a (mīkrō-née-zi-ə, -zhi-ə, -zhə, -si-ə, -shi-ə, -shə). A division of the Pacific islands, including Kiribati, the Caroline, Mariana, and Marshall groups and other islands. The Micronesians are of Australoid and Polynesian stock, with light to dark brown skins and straight or slightly wavy hair. See **Melanesia, Polynesia.**

Micronesia, Federated States of. A country of the west Pacific comprising the Caroline Islands excluding **Palau.** The federation's 600 or so coral or volcanic islands export copra, fish products, and handicrafts, and tourism is increasing. However, most islanders, of Australoid and Polynesian origin, are subsistence farmers. The Spaniards discovered the islands (16th century). They were seized by Japan (1914), and were part of the U.N. Trust Territory of the Pacific Islands administered by the United States (1947–81). The federation is in "free association" with the United States: it is self-governing at home and in foreign affairs, but the United States is responsible for its defence and has rights to military facilities (until 1996). Area, 701 square kilometres (271 square miles). Population, 81,700. Capital, Kolonia (on Ponape). See map at **Pacific Ocean.**

Mi·cro·ne·sian (mīkrō-née-zi-ən, -zhən, -shən) *adj.* Of or pertaining to Micronesia, its inhabitants, their languages, or their culture. ~*n.* **1.** A native or inhabitant of Micronesia. **2.** A subfamily of Austronesian languages spoken in Micronesia.

mi·cro·nu·cle·us (mīkrō-néw-kli-əss ‖ -noo-) *n., pl.* **-clei** (-kli-ī) or **-uses.** The smaller nuclear mass in protozoans, distinguished from the macronucleus in such animals and functioning in sexual reproduction. Compare **macronucleus.**

mi·cro·nu·tri·ent (mĭkrō-néw-tri-ənt ‖ -nŏo-) *n.* A substance, such as a vitamin, that in minute amounts is essential to life.

mi·cro·or·gan·ism, mi·cro·or·gan·ism (mĭkrō-órgə-niz'm) *n.* An animal or plant of microscopic size, especially a bacterium or a protozoan.

mi·cro·pa·lae·on·tol·o·gy (mĭkrō-pál-i-on-tóllŏji, -ən-) *n.* The scientific study of microscopic fossils. —**mi·cro·pa·lae·on·to·log·ic** (-tə-lójik), **mi·cro·pa·lae·on·to·log·i·cal** *adj.* —**mi·cro·pa·lae·on·tol·o·gist** (-tóllŏjist) *n.*

mi·cro·pas·cal (mĭkrō-pass-káa) *n. Symbol* **mPa** A unit of pressure equal to one thousandth of a pascal.

mi·cro·phone (mĭkrə-fōn) *n.* An instrument that converts sound waves into an electric current or voltage, usually fed into an amplifier, recorder, or broadcast transmitter. [MICRO- + -PHONE.] —**mi·cro·phon·ic** (-fónnik) *adj.*

mi·cro·pho·to·graph (mĭkrō-fótə-graaf, -graf) *n.* **1.** A photograph requiring magnification for viewing. **2.** A photograph on microfilm. **3.** A photomicrograph. —**mi·cro·pho·to·graph·ic** (-gráffik) *adj.* —**mi·cro·pho·tog·ra·phy** (-fə-tóggrəfi) *n.*

mi·cro·phys·ics (mĭkrō-fizziks) *n. Used with a singular verb.* The physics of molecular, atomic, nuclear, and subnuclear systems. —**mi·cro·phys·i·cal** *adj.*

mi·cro·phyte (mĭkrō-fīt, mĭkrə-) *n.* Any plant of microscopic size. [MICRO- + -PHYTE.] —**mi·cro·phyt·ic** (-fíttik) *adj.*

mi·cro·print (mĭkrō-print, mĭkrə-) *n.* The printed or positive reproduction of a microphotograph.

mi·cro·pro·ces·sor (mĭkrō-prŏ-sessər ‖ -prŏ-) *n.* A small integrated circuit used as the processor in a minicomputer or microcomputer.

mi·cro·pyle (mĭkrō-pīl, mĭkrə-) *n.* **1.** *Botany.* A minute opening in the ovule of a plant, through which the pollen tube usually enters. **2.** *Zoology.* A pore in the membrane of the ova of some animals, through which the spermatozoon enters. [MICRO- + Greek *pulē,* gate.] —**mi·cro·py·lar** (-pílər) *adj.*

mi·cro·read·er (mĭkrō-reedər) *n.* An optical device for producing an enlarged image of microfilm, microfiche, or the like.

mi·cro·scope (mĭkrə-skōp) *n.* An optical instrument that uses a combination of lenses to produce magnified images of small objects, especially of objects too small to be seen by the unaided eye. See **simple microscope, compound microscope, electron microscope, X-ray microscope.** [New Latin *microscopium* : MICRO- + -SCOPE.]

mi·cro·scop·ic (mĭkrə-skóppik) *adj.* Also **mi·cro·scop·i·cal** (-skóppik'l). **1.** Too small to be seen by the unaided eye but large enough to be studied under a microscope. **2.** Exceedingly small; minute. **3.** Characterised by or done with extreme attention to detail: *conducted a microscopic investigation.* **4.** Of, pertaining to, or concerned with a microscope. **5.** Like or resembling a microscope; having the ability to observe very small objects. **6.** *Physics.* Involving or pertaining to the properties of individual atoms or molecules, rather than collections of atoms. In this sense, compare **macroscopic.** —**mi·cro·scop·i·cal·ly** *adv.*

Mi·cro·sco·pi·um (mĭkrə-skŏpi-əm) *n.* A constellation in the Southern Hemisphere. [New Latin, MICROSCOPE.]

mi·cros·co·py (mī-króskəpi) *n.* **1.** Investigation employing a microscope. **2.** The study or use of microscopes. —**mi·cros·co·pist** *n.*

mi·cro·seism (mĭkrō-sīz'm, mĭkrə-) *n.* A faint, recurrent tremor of the earth's crust. —**mi·cro·seis·mic** (-sízmik, sísss), **mi·cro·seismi·cal** (-sīz-mik'l, -sīsss-) *adj.*

mi·cro·some (mĭkrō-sōm, mĭkrə-) *n.* A cell particle of the smallest size, typically consisting of a piece of endoplasmic reticulum to which ribosomes are attached. [German *Mikrosom* : MICRO- + -SOME.] —**mi·cro·so·mal** (-sōm'l), **mi·cro·so·mic** (-sómmik) *adj.*

mi·cro·spo·ran·gi·um (mĭkrō-spaw-rán-ji-əm, -spə-) *n., pl.* **-gia** (-ji-ə) A structure or receptacle in which microspores are formed.

mi·cro·spore (mĭkrō-spawr, mĭkrə- ‖ -spōr) *n. Botany.* **1.** The smaller of two types of spores produced by heterosporous plants, such as ferns, giving rise to the male gametophyte. Compare **megaspore. 2.** A pollen grain. —**mi·cro·spor·ic** (-spórrik, -spáwrik ‖ -spórik), **mi·cro·spo·rous** (-spáwrəss ‖ -spórəss, mī-króspərəss) *adj.*

mi·cro·spo·ro·phyll (mĭkrō-spáwr-ə-fil, mĭkrə- ‖ -spōr-) *n.* The structure in ferns and similar plants that bears the microsporangia.

mi·cro·struc·ture (mĭkrō-strukchər) *n.* Microscopic structure; especially, the structure of a material as viewed under a microscope.

mi·cro·sur·ger·y (mĭkrō-súrjəri) *n.* Surgery involving intricate operations on relatively inaccessible parts of the body, performed through a microscope using minute instruments. —**mi·cro·sur·geon** *n.* —**mi·cro·sur·gi·cal** *adj.*

mi·cro·tome (mĭkrō-tōm, mĭkrə-) *n.* An instrument used to cut samples into very thin sections for microscopic examination.

mi·crot·o·my (mī-króttəmi) *n.* The preparation of specimens by use of a microtome. —**mi·cro·tom·ic** (mĭkrō-tómmik, mĭkrə-) *adj.*

mi·cro·tone (mĭkrō-tōn, mĭkrə-) *n. Music.* An interval smaller than a half tone.

mi·cro·vil·lus (mĭkrō-villəss) *n., pl.* **-vil·li** (-víllī) Any of the minute, hairlike structures that project from the surface of absorptive or secretory epithelial cells, such as those of the intestinal tract.

mi·cro·wave (mĭkrə-wayv, mĭkrə-) *n.* **1.** Electromagnetic radiation having a wavelength in the approximate range from one millimetre to one metre, the region between infrared and short-wave radio wavelengths. Also used adjectivally: *microwave radiation.* **2.** A microwave oven.

microwave background *n.* Background microwave radiation throughout the universe; corresponding to black-body radiation at

a temperature of 2.7K and thought to be a remnant of the big-bang origin of the universe. Also called "cosmic background".

microwave oven *n.* An oven which heats food by means of microwaves: food is heated as water molecules dissipate the energy they have absorbed from the microwaves. Also called "microwave".

mic·tu·rate (mík-tewr-ayt) *intr.v.* **-rated, -rating, -rates.** To urinate. [Latin *micturīre,* from *mingere* (past participial stem *mict-*), to urinate.] —**mic·tu·ri·tion** (-ísh'n) *n.*

mid¹ (mid) *adj.* **1.** Middle; central. **2.** Being the part in the middle or centre: *in the mid Pacific.* **3.** *Phonetics.* Pronounced with the tongue approximately intermediate between high and low, as in the (u) in *cut* or the (e) in *pet.* Said of vowel sounds. ~*n. Archaic.* The middle. [Middle English *mid, midde,* Old English *midd.*]

mid² *prep. Chiefly Poetic.* Amid: *mid smoke and flame.*

mid– *prefix.* Indicates a middle part, time, or location; for example, **midship, midway.** *Note:* Many compounds other than those entered here may be formed with *mid-.* In this dictionary, in forming compounds, *mid-* is normally joined to the following word or element without space or hyphen: *midday.* However, many users prefer the hyphenated form, especially in less standardised compounds: *mid-season.* If the second element begins with a capital letter, it is always separated with a hyphen: *mid-May.* It is always advisable to separate the elements with a hyphen to avoid possible confusion with another form; for example, *mid-den* (the middle of a den) as distinct from the word *midden.* Note that the adjective *mid¹* above is a separate word, though, as with any adjective, it may be joined to another word with a hyphen when used as a unit modifier: *in the mid Pacific,* but *a mid-Pacific island.* [From MID (middle).]

mid. middle.

mid·air (mid-áir, mĭd-) *n.* A point or region in the middle of the air; space: *floating in midair.*

Mi·das (mī-dass, -dəss). The legendary king of Phrygia to whom Dionysus gave the power of turning to gold all that he touched.

mid-At·lan·tic (mid-ət-lántik) *adj.* **1.** Pertaining to the middle of the Atlantic Ocean. **2.** Adopting U.S. speech mannerisms in an attempt to impress a British or European audience: *a mid-Atlantic accent.* **3.** Compromising between styles or tastes prevalent in the United States and Britain.

Mid Atlantic Ridge. Mountain range on the floor of the Atlantic Ocean, stretching from Iceland to the Antarctic Circle. Some of its peaks rise above sea level, forming islands such as the Azores group, Ascension, Iceland, and Tristan da Cunha. See **sea floor spreading, plate tectonics.**

mid·brain (mĭd-brayn) *n.* **1.** The middle region of the embryonic vertebrate brain, the **mesencephalon** *(see).* **2.** The parts that develop from this region.

mid·course (mid-kórss ‖ -kórss) *n.* The part of a spacecraft's flight between burnout and the point where final guidance is made.

mid·day (mĭd-day, -dáy) *n.* The middle of the day; noon. ~*adj.* Of, pertaining to, or occurring in the middle of the day or at noon: *a midday snack.* [Middle English *midday,* Old English *middæg* : MID (middle) + *dæg,* DAY.]

mid·den (mídd'n) *n.* **1.** A dunghill or refuse heap, especially one near a dwelling. **2.** A kitchen midden *(see).* [Middle English *myddung,* from Old Norse *myki-dyngja* (unattested) : *myki-,* muck + *dyngja,* heap (see **dung**).]

mid·dle (mídd'l) *adj. Abbr.* **mid. 1. a.** Equally distant from extremes or limits; central; mean: *the middle point on a line.* **b.** Approximately halfway between two limits: *the middle ground.* **2.** Intermediate; in-between: *the middle piece of cake.* **3.** Medium; moderate: *"He was about the middle height."* (Charles Dickens). **4.** Intervening between an earlier and later period of time; part of a sequence or series: *the middle years.* **5.** *Capital* M. Designating a stage in the development of a language or literature between earlier and later stages: *Middle English.* **6.** *Logic.* Designating a term that appears in both premises of a syllogism but not in the conclusion. **7.** *Grammar.* Intermediate between active and passive voice. Said of verb forms in Sanskrit and Greek in which the subject is represented as acting on, for, or with reference to itself. ~*n.* **1.** An area or point equidistant between extremes; the centre: *the middle of a circle.* **2.** Something intermediate between extremes; a mean. **3.** The interior portion: *the middle of the chain.* **4.** The middle part of the human body; the waist. **5.** *Logic.* The **middle term** *(see).* **6.** *Grammar.* The middle voice. ~*tr.v.* **middled, -dling, -dles. 1.** To place in the middle. **2.** In cricket, to hit (the ball) with the middle of the bat. **3.** *Nautical.* To fold in the middle: *middle the sail.* [Old English *middel.*]

middle age *n.* The time of human life between youth and old age, usually reckoned as the years between 40 and 60.

mid·dle-age spread (mídd'l-áyj) *n.* Also **middle-aged spread.** Thickening of the waistline and a general gain in weight that often takes place in middle age.

mid·dle-aged (mídd'l-áyjd) *adj.* Of or pertaining to middle age.

Middle Ages *n.* **1.** The period in European history between Antiquity and the Renaissance, often dated from A.D. 476, when the last emperor of the Western Roman Empire was deposed, to A.D. 1453, when Constantinople was conquered by the Turks. **2.** The period from about A.D. 1000 to A.D. 1400. Compare **Dark Ages.**

Middle America *n.* **1.** That part of the U.S. middle class thought of as being average in income and education and conservative in values and attitudes. **2.** The American heartland, thought of as being made up of small towns, small cities, and suburbs. **3.** A division of the **Americas.** —**Middle American** *adj.*

mid·dle·brow (mídd'l-brow) *n. Informal.* A person of some education and culture, but whose interests may be considered artistically and intellectually limited or conventional. Compare **highbrow,** **lowbrow.** —**mid·dle·brow** *adj.*

middle C *n. Music.* The musical note represented by the first ledger line below the treble clef or the first ledger line above the bass clef. It is near the middle of a piano keyboard.

middle class *n. Often plural.* The members of society occupying an intermediate social and economic position between the working classes and the aristocracy.

mid·dle-class (midd'l-kláass ‖ -kláss) *adj.* Of, pertaining to, or characteristic of the middle class.

middle common room *n.* In various British universities and colleges, a common room for postgraduate students.

middle distance *n.* **1.** The area between the foreground and background in a painting, drawing, or photograph. **2.** In athletics, a division of competition in racing with events usually ranging from 800 metres to 1500 metres. —**middle-distance** *adj.*

Middle Dutch *n.* Dutch from the mid-12th century to the 15th.

middle ear *n.* The space between the tympanic membrane and the internal ear. It contains the auditory ossicles that convey vibrations to the internal ear. Also called "tympanic cavity", "tympanum". See **ear.**

Middle East *n.* Also **West Asia.** The western subcontinent of Asia. It includes only 5 per cent of the world's land and 4 per cent of its people. The region's northern mountains, enclosing high plateaus, are part of the Alpine-Himalayan system, subject to frequent earthquakes. The stabler tablelands of Arabia and Egypt are slashed by the Great Rift Valley.

The Middle East is the driest of the world's major regions by far. More than 75 per cent of it has less than 250 millimetres (about 10 inches) of rain a year, and is covered by desert, semidesert, or mountain steppe, yet some 60 per cent of its inhabitants rely on farming for a living.

Economically, oil dominates the region, which has half the world's known reserves. It produces more than 30 per cent of world crude oil. The oil states are using their vast wealth to industrialise and diversify their economies against the day when the oil wells run dry. They spend much on irrigation, welfare, and education schemes, interregional aid, and aid to other Third World countries; the Middle East shows the greatest disparity between rich and poor nations.

Middle Empire *n.* The Middle Kingdom of Egypt.

Middle English *n. Abbr.* **M.E., ME., ME** English from the 12th century to the 15th. The five main dialects of Middle English were: Kentish (southeastern), Southern (southwestern), East Midland, West Midland, and Northern. See **Midland.**

Middle French *n.* French from the mid-15th century to the mid-16th.

Middle Greek *n.* **Medieval Greek** *(see).*

Middle High German *n.* High German from the 11th century to the 16th.

Middle Irish *n.* Irish Gaelic from the 10th century to over the 15th.

Middle Island. See **South Island.**

Middle Kingdom *n.* **1.** A kingdom of ancient Egypt lasting from about 2100 to about 1600 B.C. Capitals, Heracleopolis, later Thebes. Also called "Middle Empire". **2. a.** The former Chinese empire, considered by its inhabitants to be the centre of the world. **b.** The original 18 provinces of China. Often called "China Proper".

Middle Low German *n.* Low German from the middle of the 13th century to the 16th.

mid·dle·man (mídd'l-man) *n., pl.* **-men** (-men). **1.** A trader who buys from producers and sells to retailers or consumers. **2.** An intermediary or go-between.

middle management *n.* Middle-ranking executives responsible for day-to-day running of a department.

mid·dle·most (mídd'l-mōst) *adj.* Midmost. [Middle English *middelmast : middel,* MIDDLE + *-mast,* -MOST.]

middle name *n.* **1.** A name that comes between a person's first or Christian name and surname. **2.** *Informal.* A person's most significant character trait: *Carefulness is his middle name.*

mid·dle-of-the-road (mídd'l-əv-thə-rŏd) *adj. Abbr.* **M.O.R. 1.** Moderate; not extreme, as in tastes or views. **2.** Designating a type of popular music that is conventional, usually melodic, and has a wide popular appeal.

middle passage *n.* The passage of slave ships from Africa to the West Indies and America during the 16th to the 19th centuries.

Middle Persian *n.* The language of the Sassanians, from the third century A.D. to the seventh.

Mid·dles·brough (mídd'lzbrə). Industrial town and port on the south side of the Tees estuary in Cleveland, northeast England. Its chief products are chemicals, iron and steel, and ships.

Mid·dle·sex (mídd'l-seks). Former county of southeast England. It was absorbed mainly by Greater London in 1965, with small areas passing to Surrey and Hertfordshire.

Middle South Asia. Also **South Asia.** The subcontinent of India. It covers only 3 per cent of the world's land, but has 20 per cent of its people, and is the world's most densely peopled region of comparable size. Its fertile Indus and Ganges plains comprise a vast alluvium-filled trough. To the south, the stable tableland of the Deccan has fertile volcanic soils, but generally, soils are poor. The

rising fold mountains of Baluchistan, and the Himalayas, have the highest peaks in the world—more than 30 over 8 600 metres (28,200 feet).

The region is dominated by its monsoon climate, all but parts of the west having a wet season from June to October. Rainfall varies greatly from year to year, much of the region having periodic floods and droughts. Even so, farming is still the majority occupation. Rice is the major food crop, the region producing (and consuming) 25 percent of the world's output. Important commercial crops include tea, cotton, hemp, and jute. Although less than 7 per cent of the region remains forested, it provides 10 per cent of the world's hardwoods.

The subcontinent has rich mineral resources, including iron ore, bauxite, mica, and chrome, but they are mostly in peninsular India. Pakistan and Bangladesh have sizable gas deposits, and India has oil. However, Middle South Asia will be hard pressed to sustain its population, which could reach nearly 1,400 million by A.D. 2000. Already the region has some of the world's largest cities—more than 15 with well over a million inhabitants. See map at **Asia.**

Middle Stone Age *n.* The **Mesolithic** Age *(see).*

Middle Temple *n.* One of the four legal societies forming the **Inns of Court** *(see)* in England.

middle term *n. Logic. Abbr.* **M** The term in a syllogism presented in both premises but not appearing in the conclusion.

Mid·dle·ton (mídd'l-tən), **Thomas** (1580–1627). English playwright. His comedies, written between 1604 and 1611, include *A Chaste Maid in Cheapside,* a mirror of contemporary corruption.

mid·dle·weight (mídd'l-wayt) *n.* **1.** A professional boxer weighing between 147 and 160 pounds (66.8 and 72.6 kilograms). **2.** An amateur boxer weighing between 71 and 75 kilograms (157 and 165 pounds).

Middle West. See **Midwest.** —**Middle Western** *n.* —**Middle Westerner** *n.*

mid·dling (míd-ling, mídd'l-ing) *adj.* Of medium size, quality, or state; mediocre; ordinary. See Synonyms at **average.**
~*adv. Informal.* Fairly; moderately. [Middle English (Scottish) *mydlyn : midde,* MID (middle) + -LING (small).] —**mid·dling·ly** *adv.*

mid·dlings (míd-lingz) *pl.n.* **1.** Products that are intermediate in quality, size, price, or grade. **2.** Coarsely ground flour.

Middx Middlesex.

mid·dy¹ (míddi) *n., pl.* **-dies. 1.** *Informal.* A midshipman. **2.** A middy blouse.

middy² *n. Australian.* A medium-sized beer glass.

middy blouse *n.* A woman's or child's loose blouse with a sailor collar. Also called "middy".

mid·field (míd-féeld, -feeld) *n.* In soccer, the area approximately midway between two goalmouths. Also used adjectivally: *a midfield player.*

Mid·gard (míd-gaard). Also **Mid·garth** (míd-gaarth), **Mith·gar·thr** (míth-gaarthər). *Norse Mythology.* The part of the world inhabited by men, imagined as a fortress encircled by a huge serpent, built by the gods around the middle region of the universe. [Old Norse *Midhgardhr.* See **mid, yard.**]

midge (mij) *n.* **1.** Any of various widely distributed gnatlike flies of the family Chironomidae, particularly common near water, where they form large swarms. **2.** Any of various similar insects, such as any member of the family Ceratopogonidae *(biting midges),* which suck the blood of mammals and birds. **3.** *Informal.* Any small person. [Middle English *migge,* Old English *mycg.*]

midg·et (mijit) *n.* **1.** An extremely small person who is otherwise normally proportioned. **2.** A small or miniature version of something.
~*adj.* **1.** Miniature; diminutive; dwarfed. **2.** Belonging to a type or class much smaller than what is considered standard: *a midget car.* [Diminutive of MIDGE.]

Mid Gla·mor·gan (míd glə-mórgən). County of south Wales, comprising the central region of the former county of Glamorganshire, plus the Rhymney valley, formerly in Monmouthshire, and a few villages from south Breconshire. The new county (1974), part of the South Wales Coalfield, has mines and industries concentrated in its deep valleys, including the Rhondda. The steel industry is being replaced by light industries, with Aberdare, Bridgend, and Merthyr Tydfil the main centres.

mid·gut (míd-gut) *n.* **1.** The middle section of the digestive tract of vertebrates, which is lined with endoderm and includes the small intestine. Also called "mesenteron". **2.** The middle section of the digestive tract of anthropods.

mid·i (míddi) *n.* A skirt or coat of mid-calf length. [From MIDDLE.] —**mid·i** *adj.*

Mi·di (mée-dee, mee-dée) *n. French.* The south of France.

Mid·i·an·ite (mídi-ə-nīt) *n.* A member of the ancient Arabian tribe of Midian claiming descent from *Midian,* a son of Abraham. Exodus 2:15–22; Judges 6–8. —**Mid·i·an·ite** *adj.*

mid·i·ron (míd-ī-ərn) *n.* An iron golf club that has more loft than a driver and less than a mashie, used for medium fairway shots and long approach shots.

mid·land (míd-lənd) *n.* The middle or interior part of a country or region. —**mid·land** *adj.*

Midland *n.* The dialect of Middle English spoken in the Midlands, which formed the basis of Modern English.

Mid·lands (míd-ləndz). A region of central England. Imprecisely defined, it roughly corresponds with the Anglo-Saxon kingdom of Mercia, which originally included the present counties of Derbyshire, Nottinghamshire, Staffordshire, West Midlands, northern Leicestershire, and northern Warwickshire. Mercia expanded to include all Leicestershire and Warwickshire, and Northamptonshire and east Hereford and Worcester. In the broadest sense, the Midlands include Shropshire, all Hereford and Worcester, and parts of Bedfordshire, Buckinghamshire, and Oxfordshire.

mid·life crisis (míd-līf) n. A stage in a life, especially a man's life, when the realisation of the approach of middle or old age may lead to emotional upheaval. Sometimes used humorously.

Mid·lo·thi·an (mid-lṓthi-ən). Former county of southeast Scotland, now part of Lothian region. It lay south of the Firth of Forth and the county town was Edinburgh.

mid·most (míd-mōst) adj. 1. Situated in the exact middle; middlemost. 2. Situated nearest the middle.
~adv. In the middle. [Middle English midmest, Old English midmest : midd, MID + -mest, -MOST.]

mid·night (míd-nīt) n. 1. The middle of the night; specifically, twelve o'clock at night. 2. a. Intense darkness or gloom. b. A period of darkness and gloom.
~adj. 1. Of or pertaining to the middle of the night. 2. Resembling the middle of the night; dark; gloomy; dreary. —**burn the midnight oil.** To work or study very late at night. [Middle English midnight, Old English midniht : midd, MID + niht, NIGHT.]

mid·night blue n. A very deep blue. —**midnight-blue** adj.

midnight sun n. The sun as seen at midnight during the summer within the Arctic or Antarctic Circle.

mid-off (míd-óff, -áwf) n. In cricket: 1. A fielding position nearest the bowler on the off side. 2. A fielder in this position.

mid-on (míd-ón) n. In cricket: 1. A fielding position nearest the bowler on the on side. 2. A fielder in this position.

mid·point (míd-poynt) n. 1. The point of a line segment or curvilinear arc that divides it into two parts of the same length. 2. A position midway between two extremes.

Mid·rash (míd-rash, -raash) n., pl. **Midrashim** (mid-ráshim, -raáshim, -róshim), **Midrashoth** (míd-rash-ót, -raásh-). Any of a group of Jewish commentaries on the Hebrew Scriptures, written between A.D. 400 and 1200. [Late Hebrew midhrāsh, commentary.]

mid·rib (míd-rib) n. The central or principal vein of a leaf.

mid·riff (míd-rif) n. 1. A part of the body, the **diaphragm** (see). 2. The middle, outer portion of the front of the human body, extending roughly from just below the breast to the waistline. [Middle English midrif, Old English midhrif : midd, MID + hrif, belly.]

mid·ship (míd-ship) adj. Pertaining to the middle of a ship.

mid·ship·man (míd-ship-mən ‖ mid-shíp-) n., pl. **-men** (-mən). 1. Formerly a naval cadet on British ships of war whose battle station was amidships or abreast of the mainmast. 2. A noncommissioned officer ranking below sublieutenant in the Royal and British Commonwealth navies. 3. Any of various American fishes of the genus Porichthys, having several rows of light-producing organs along their bodies. [From earlier midshipsman : MIDSHIPS + MAN.]

mid·ships (míd-shipss) adv. Nautical. 1. Amidships. 2. In the centre position. Said of the helm.
~n. The middle part of a ship.

midst (midst, mitst) n. 1. Archaic. The middle position or part; the centre. 2. The condition of being in the interior of, surrounded by, or enveloped in something. Used chiefly in the phrases in the midst of and in our (their, your) midst: in the midst of nature.
~prep. Archaic. Among. [Middle English middest, variant of middes, from phrases such as in middes, variant of in middan, dative of midde, MID.]

mid·stream (míd-streem, -stréem) n. The middle of a stream or river.

mid·sum·mer (míd-súmmər, -summər) n. 1. The middle of the summer. 2. The **summer solstice** (see). —**mid·sum·mer** adj.

Midsummer's Day n. Also **Midsummer Day**. June 24, one of the quarter days in England, Ireland, and Wales, and the feast of Saint John the Baptist.

mid·term (míd-term, -térm) n. 1. The middle of an academic term or a political term of office or a pregnancy. 2. a. An examination given at the middle of an academic term. b. Plural. A series of such examinations. —**mid·term** adj.

mid-Vic·to·ri·an (mid-vik-táwri-ən ‖ -tóri-) adj. Pertaining to, occurring in, or characteristic of the middle period of the reign of Queen Victoria in Great Britain (1837–1901), a period known for rigid social standards.
~n. 1. A person living in the mid-Victorian period. 2. A person having mid-Victorian ideas.

mid·way (míd-way) n. 1. U.S. The area of any fair, carnival, circus, or exposition where side shows and other amusements are located. 2. Obsolete. a. The middle of a way or distance. b. A middle way or course of action or thought.
~adv. (also -wáy) 1. In the middle of a way or distance; halfway. 2. In an intermediate position: midway between thrift and meanness. —**mid·way** adj.

Midway Islands. Two small islands surrounded by an atoll in the north Pacific Ocean, annexed by the United States in 1867. There is no indigenous population, but some 2,200 personnel man the U.S. military base there. In the Battle of Midway during World War II (June 1942), U.S. forces, despite heavy losses, won a decisive victory over the Japanese, the turning point of the war in the Pacific.

mid·week (míd-week, -wéek) n. The middle of the week.
~adj. Happening in the middle of the week. —**mid·week** adv. —**mid·week·ly** adj. & adv.

Mid·west (míd-wést) n. Also **Middle West**. A region of north central United States, around the Great Lakes and upper Mississippi valley. Although its limits are ill-defined, it is generally considered to comprise the prairie states of Indiana, Iowa, Ohio, Illinois, Michigan, Minnesota, Missouri, Wisconsin, and Nebraska. Kansas is usually included, and sometimes Ontario peninsula of Canada. A rich farming region, its chief products are maize and pigs. —**Mid·west**, **Mid·west·ern** adj. —**Mid·west·ern·er** n.

mid·wick·et (míd-wickit) n. In cricket: 1. A fielding position towards the boundary on the on side, and between the two batting creases. 2. A player fielding in this position.

mid·wife (míd-wīf) n., pl. **-wives** (-wīvz). One qualified to assist women in childbirth. [Middle English midwif : mid, with, Old English mid + wif, WIFE.]

mid·wife·ry (míd-wiffəri, -wiffri, mid-wiffəri, -wiffri ‖ U.S. also míd-wīfəri, -wīfri) n. The practice of a midwife.

midwife toad n. A European toad, Alytes obstetricans, the male of which carries the fertilised eggs on its hind legs until they hatch.

mid·win·ter (míd-wintər) n. 1. The middle of the winter. 2. The **winter solstice** (see).

mid·year (míd-yeer, -yéer, -yer, -yér) n. 1. The middle of the calendar or academic year. 2. a. An examination in the middle of the academic year. b. Plural. A series of such examinations. —**mid·year** adj.

mien (meen) n. Literary. 1. One's bearing or manner; expression: a person of noble mien. 2. An appearance or aspect: of fearsome mien. See Synonyms at **bearing**. [From earlier meane, mine (influenced by French mine, appearance); short for DEMEAN.]

Mies van der Ro·he (méess ván dər rṓ-ə, méez, vaán), **Ludwig** (1886–1969). German-born U.S. architect. His steel-frame and glass buildings include the Seagram Building, New York (with Philip Johnson, 1956–59) and the Chicago Federal Center (1963–68).

miff (mif) n. Informal. 1. A petulant, bad-tempered mood; a huff. 2. A petty quarrel or argument; a tiff.
~tr.v. **miffed, miffing, miffs.** To cause (a person) to become offended or annoyed. [Perhaps imitative of an expression of disgust.]

mif·fy (míffi) adj. **-fier, -fiest.** Informal. Easily offended; over-sensitive. —**mif·fi·ness** n.

might¹ (mīt) n. 1. a. Tremendous power held by an individual or group: the whole might of the superpowers. b. Supreme power attributed to a divine being: the might of God. 2. Physical or bodily strength. —See Synonyms at **strength**. —**with might and main.** With all one's strength; with the utmost effort. [Middle English might, Old English miht.]

might². Past tense of **may**.

might·i·ly (mítili, mít'l-i) adv. 1. In a mighty manner; forcefully; powerfully. 2. To a great degree; greatly.

might·y (míti) adj. **-ier, -iest.** 1. a. Having might; powerful; strong. b. Having great emotional or intellectual power: a mighty intelligence. 2. a. Exerting great force; violent: a mighty blow of his axe. b. Very strong or urgent: a mighty clamour. 3. Awesomely huge: "the city stood on a mighty hill" (John Bunyan).
~adv. Chiefly U.S. Informal. In a great degree; very; extremely. —**might·i·ness** n.

mi·gnon·ette (mín-yə-nét) n. 1. A plant of the genus Reseda; especially R. odorata, native to the Mediterranean region but widely cultivated for its clusters of fragrant but inconspicuous greenish flowers. 2. A light, fine pillow lace. [French, feminine of obsolete mignonnet, diminutive of mignon, dainty, small, MINION.]

mi·graine (mée-grayn, mí-). 1. Severe, recurrent headache, usually affecting only one side of the head, characterised by sharp pain and often accompanied by nausea. 2. An attack of such a headache. [French, from Old French, from Late Latin hēmicrānia, pain in half of the head, from Greek hēmikrania : HEMI- + kranion, CRANIUM.] —**mi·grain·oid** (-oyd), **mi·grain·ous** (-əss) adj.

mi·grant (mígrənt) n. 1. A person, animal, bird, or fish that moves from one region to another by chance, instinct, or plan. 2. An itinerant worker who travels from one area to another in search of work. 3. Australian. An immigrant.
~adj. Moving from one place to another; migratory. [Latin migrāns (stem migrant-), present participle of migrāre, to MIGRATE.]

mi·grate (mī-gráyt, mī-grayt) intr.v. **-grated, -grating, -grates.** 1. To move from one country or region and settle in another. 2. To change location periodically; move seasonally from one region to another. Used of such animals as birds and fish. 3. Physics & Chemistry. To move from one position to another. Used of atoms, molecules, ions, or groups of atoms. [Latin migrāre.]

Usage: Migrate, emigrate, and immigrate are sometimes confused. Migrate is the neutral term: it can be used with reference to both the place of departure and the destination (migrate from. . .migrate to), and can be said of persons, animals, or birds. It often implies a lack of permanent settlement, especially due to seasonal movement. Emigrate specifically refers to the place of departure, emphasising movement from that place, and is thus usually followed by from (He has emigrated from England), but it is increasingly being used with to with the emphasis on the place of destination (He has emigrated to Australia). It is said only of persons, and implies a single move, usually of a permanent character. Immigrate specifically refers to the destination, emphasising movement to that place, and is thus usually followed by to, but the verb is less commonly used in British English than emigrate. It too is said only of persons, and implies a single, and usually permanent move. A complication arises from the use of the noun, immigrant, which is

milk vetch *Goats that ate* Astragalus glycyphyllos *were thought to give more milk: hence its common name. It is sometimes difficult to identify because the creamy-green flowers blend with surrounding foliage.*

milkweed *Floss from the seed pods of this genus of American herbs has been used as a stuffing in life-jackets and upholstery. The milkweed species shown here is* Asclepias speciosa.

frequently followed by *from (They're immigrants from India),* and is now probably more common than *emigrant.*

mi·gra·tion (mī-gráysh'n) *n.* **1.** The action or an act of migrating. **2.** A group migrating together. **—mi·gra·tion·al** *adj.*

mi·gra·to·ry (mī-grə-təri, -tri, mī-gráytəri) *adj.* **1.** Characterised by migration; migrating periodically: *migratory birds.* **2.** Of or relating to a migration. **3.** Roving; nomadic.

mih·rab (mée-rab, -rəb, -raab) *n. Islam.* A niche or similar indication in a mosque used to show the direction of Mecca. [Arabic.]

mi·ka·do (mi-ka'adō) *n., pl.* **-dos.** *Often capital* **M.** The emperor of Japan. The title is not used by Japanese people, who use "Tenno". [Japanese, "exalted gate" : *mi* (honorific prefix) + *kado,* gate. Probably originally said of the imperial court.]

mike[1] (mīk) *n. Informal.* A microphone.

~tr.v. **miked, miking, mikes.** *Informal.* **1.** To amplify the sound of by means of a microphone. **2.** To attach a microphone to. In both senses, often used with *up.*

mike[2] *intr.v.* **miked, miking, mikes.** *British Informal.* To avoid work; shirk. [19th century : origin obscure.]

mikron. Variant of **micron.**

mil[1] (mil) *n.* **1.** A unit of length equal to one-thousandth (10^{-3}) of an inch. Used chiefly to specify the diameter of wire. **2.** A millilitre. **3.** A unit of angular measurement used in artillery and equal to $1/6400$ of a complete revolution. [Short for Latin *millēsimus,* thousandth, from *mīlle,* thousand.]

mil. military; militia.

mi·la·dy (mi-láydi) *n., pl.* **-dies.** Also **mi·la·di** *pl.* **-dis.** **1.** My lady. A title or form of address formerly used in Europe of an English noblewoman or gentlewoman. **2.** A chic or fashionable woman. [French, from English *my lady.*]

milage. Variant of **mileage.**

Mi·lan (mi-lán) *Italian* **Mi·la·no** (mee-la'anō). Capital of Milan province and of Lombardy region, northern Italy. At a strategic crossing of the river Olona, it has been a market, industrial, financial, and cultural centre since medieval times. It is now Italy's second city and chief manufacturing centre, its products including textiles, motor vehicles, machinery, aircraft, and clothing. Printing and publishing are also important. The city has three universities, and numerous historic buildings including the cathedral (1386–1813) and La Scala opera house (1778).

Mil·an·ese (millə-néez || -néess) *n., pl.* **Milanese.** **1.** A native or inhabitant of Milan. **2.** The dialect spoken in Milan. **3.** A fine fabric of silk or rayon.

~adj. **1.** Of or pertaining to Milan or its people, dialect, culture, or products. **2.** Coated with bread crumbs or flour and fried in oil or butter.

milch (milch) *adj.* Giving milk: *a milch cow.* [Middle English *milche,* Old English *-milce.*]

milch cow *n.* **1.** A cow that produces milk for human consumption. **2.** A source of money or other resources, such as a person or fund, especially one that can be taken for granted: *treated his family as a milch cow.*

mild (mīld) *adj.* **milder, mildest.** **1.** Gentle or kind in disposition, manners, or behaviour: *a strong but mild man.* **2.** Moderate in type, degree, effect, or force: *a mild punishment.* **3.** Not very harmful; light: *a mild fever.* **4.** Having no extremes in temperature; temperate: *a mild climate.* **5.** Not sharp, bitter, or strong in taste or smell: *a mild cheese; mild tobacco.*

~n. British. A dark draught beer with a low hop content. **—draw it mild.** To moderate one's speech or act calmly. Usually used in the imperative. [Middle English *mild,* Old English *milde.*] **—mild·ly** *adv.* **—mild·ness** *n.*

Mil·den·hall (mildən-hawl). Market town in Suffolk, eastern England, situated on the river Lark. Nearby was found (1942) the "Mildenhall treasure", a hoard of fourth-century Roman silverware, now in the British Museum.

mil·dew (mil-dew || -dōō) *n.* **1.** Any of various plant diseases in which a fungus forms a superficial growth on the plant. See **downy mildew, powdery mildew.** **2.** A superficial coating or discolouring of organic materials, such as paint, paper, cloth, leather, and the like, caused by fungi, especially under damp conditions. Compare **mould.**

~v. **mildewed, -dewing, -dews.** *—tr.* To affect with mildew. *—intr.* To become affected with mildew. [Middle English *mildew,* Old English *mildēaw,* from Germanic *melith* (unattested), honey + *dawwaz* (unattested), DEW.] **—mil·dew·y** *adj.*

mild steel *n.* A type of steel containing a low amount of carbon (up to 0.25 per cent).

mile (mīl) *n. Abbr.* **m., mi.** **1.** A unit of length, equal to 5,280 feet, 1,760 yards, or 1.60934 kilometres, used in most English-speaking countries. Also called "statute mile". **2.** A **nautical mile** *(see).* **3.** Any of various similar units of distance. **4.** A race of a mile. **5. a.** *Informal.* Any relatively great distance. **b.** *Plural.* By a great amount or extent. Used as an intensive: *She's miles better at golf than I am.* **—by a mile.** By a wide margin: *He won by a mile.* [Middle English *mile,* Old English *mīl,* from West Germanic *mīlja* (unattested), from Latin *mīlia, mīllia,* plural of *mīle, mīlle,* thousand.]

mile·age, mil·age (mīlij) *n.* **1.** Total length, extent, or distance measured or expressed in miles. **2.** Total miles covered or travelled in a given time. **3.** The amount of service, use, or wear estimated by miles used or travelled: *This tyre will give very good mileage.* **4.** The number of miles travelled by a motor vehicle on a certain quantity, usually a gallon, of fuel. **5.** *Informal.* The amount of service something has yielded or may yield in the future; usefulness; benefit; advantage: *get full mileage out of a typewriter.* **6.** An allowance for travel expenses established at a specified rate per mile. **7.** Expense per mile, as for the use of a car.

mile·om·e·ter (mī-lómmitər) *n.* A device for indicating the number of miles travelled by a vehicle.

mile·post (mīl-pōst) *n.* **1.** A post on a racetrack marking a point one mile before the winning post. **2.** *Chiefly U.S.* A post set up to indicate distance in miles, as along a road.

mil·er (mīlər) *n.* One trained to or specialising in racing a mile.

mi·les glo·ri·o·sus (mée-layz gláwri-ō-səss || glōri-) *n.,pl.* **milites gloriosi** (mée-li-tayz, -ō-see, -sī) *Latin.* A bragging, swaggering soldier, especially as a stock character in comedy. [After *Miles Gloriosus* ("braggart soldier"), a comedy (*c.* 206 B.C.) by Plautus.]

Mi·le·sian[1] (mī-lée-zi-ən, -zhi-ən, -zhən, -shən) *adj.* Of or pertaining to Miletus or its inhabitants.

~n. A native or inhabitant of Miletus.

Milesian[2] *n. Formal.* A native of Ireland; an Irishman.

~adj. Of or pertaining to Ireland or its people; Irish. [After *Milesius,* legendary Spanish king whose sons were supposed to have conquered Ireland in about 1300 B.C.]

Miles of Blackfriars (mīlz), **Bernard, Baron** (1907–). British actor and director. He founded the Mermaid Theatre, London, in 1950. He was awarded a life peerage in 1979.

mile·stone (mīl-stōn) *n.* **1.** A stone marker set up on a roadside to indicate the distance in miles to or from a given point. **2.** An important event or turning point in a person's history or career.

Mi·le·tus (mi-léetəss). Ancient Greek seaport of Ionia, west Asia Minor (now Turkey). A centre of learning, Miletus produced the philosophers Thales (*c.* 634–546 B.C.) and Anaximander (*c.* 611–547 B.C.). St. Paul visited it twice (Acts 20, 15; 2 Timothy 4, 20).

mil·foil (mil-foyl) *n.* **1.** A plant, the **yarrow** *(see).* **2.** See **water milfoil.** [Middle English, from Old French, from Latin *millefolium,* "thousand-leafed" (from the fine divisions of the leaves) : *mille,* thousand + *folium,* leaf.]

Mil·ford Ha·ven (milfərd háyvən). Seaport of Dyfed, southwest Wales. Oil refining and fishing are its main industries.

Milford Haven, 1st Baron. See **Mountbatten, Louis Alexander.**

Mil·haud (mée-ō, mee-ṓ), **Darius** (1892–1974). French composer. He composed chiefly ballet scores and chamber works, including *le pauvre Matelot* and *le Boeuf sur le toit.*

mil·i·ar·i·a (milli-áir-i-ə) *n. Pathology.* A skin disease caused by an inflammation of the sweat glands and characterised by blebs, redness, and a prickling or burning sensation. Also called "prickly heat", "heat rash". [New Latin *(fēbris) miliaria,* "miliary (fever)", from Latin *mīliārius,* MILIARY.]

mil·i·ar·y (milli-əri || *U.S.* -erri) *adj.* **1.** Designating a lesion or growth that is very small. **2.** Designating a disease marked by small skin lesions that look like millet seeds. [Latin *mīliārius,* of millet, like millet seeds (as lesions may be), from *milium,* MILLET.]

miliary tuberculosis *n.* An acute form of tuberculosis characterised by very small tubercles in various body organs, caused by the spread of tubercle bacilli through the blood stream.

mi·lieu (méel-yer, meel-yér, -yṓ) *n., pl.* **-lieus** or **-lieux.** Environment or surroundings. [French, environment, midst, from Old French, midst, centre : *mi,* middle, from Latin *medius* + *lieu,* place, from Latin *locus,* place, LOCUS.]

mil·i·tant (milli-tənt) *adj.* **1.** Fighting or warring. **2.** Aggressive or combative: *a militant mood.* **3.** Vigorously pursuing some cause, especially through a course of confrontation: *militant trade unions.*

~n. A militant person; especially, a political activist. [Middle English, from Old French, from Latin *militāns* (stem *militānt-*), present participle of *militāre,* to MILITATE.] **—mil·i·tan·cy** (-tən-si) *n.* **—mil·i·tant·ly** *adv.*

mil·i·tar·i·a (milli-táir-i-ə) *n. Used with a singular or plural verb.* Items of military equipment and uniform considered as antiques or collectors' pieces. [Latin, neuter plural of *mīlitāris,* MILITARY.]

mil·i·ta·rise, mil·i·ta·rize (millitə-rīz) *tr.v.* **-rised, -rising, -rises.** **1.** To make military; equip or train for war. **2.** To imbue with militarism. **—mil·i·ta·ri·sa·tion** (rī-záysh'n) *n.*

mil·i·ta·rism (millitə-riz'm) *n.* **1.** The glorification of the ideals of a professional military class. **2.** Predominance of the armed forces in the administration or policy of the state.

mil·i·ta·rist (millitə-rist) *n.* **1.** One who supports or advocates militarism or warlike policies. **2.** One who studies or is skilled in military science. **—mil·i·ta·ris·tic** (-ristik) *adj.* **—mil·i·ta·ris·ti·cal·ly** *adv.*

mil·i·tar·y (milli-təri, -tri || *U.S.* -terri) *adj. Abbr.* **mil.** **1.** Of, pertaining to, characteristic of, or performed by a soldier or soldiers; soldierly: *military swagger.* **2.** Characteristic of or befitting the armed forces. **3.** Of or pertaining to war.

~n., pl. **military** or **-ies.** *Abbr.* **mil.** Soldiers generally; the armed forces. Preceded by *the*: *ruled by the military.* [French *militaire,* from Latin *mīlitāris,* from *mīles*† (stem *mīlit-*), soldier.] **—mil·i·tar·i·ly** (-tərili, -trili || *U.S.* -térrili) *adv.*

military academy *n.* A college for young trainee officers belonging to, or about to join, the armed forces.

military attaché *n.* An army officer on the official staff of an ambassador, consul general, or minister to a foreign country.

military honours *pl.n.* The ceremonial procedures performed by soldiers on such occasions as state funerals.

military intelligence *n.* **1.** Any information important for its military value. **2.** The branch of the army that procures, analyses, and uses information of military value.

military law *n.* Regulations and rules pertaining to the discipline and administration of the armed forces. Compare **martial law.**

military orchid *n.* A pinkish-purple orchid, *Orchis militaris,* found in Europe and southern England. Also called "soldier orchid".

military police *n. Abbr.* **MP, M.P.** Members of the armed forces assigned to perform internal police duties. —**military policeman** *n.*

mil·i·tate (míli-tayt) *intr.v.* **-tated, -tating, -tates. 1.** To have force as evidence or influence. Used with *against* or, rarely, *for: The facts available to us militate against this interpretation.* **2.** To make less likely or feasible: *factors militating against industrial recovery.* [Latin *mīlitāre,* to serve as a soldier, from *mīlest,* soldier.]

Usage: Militate and *mitigate* are not interchangeable in standard English. *Militate* means "provide forceful evidence": *The findings militate against the view that he is innocent. Mitigate* means "lessen in force or intensity": *His apology should mitigate the President's anger.* The words are sometimes confused and *mitigate* is used in the sense of *militate: This ought not to mitigate against the decision,* but this is not an acceptable standard usage.

mi·li·tia (mi-líshə) *n. Abbr.* **mil. 1. a.** A citizen army, as distinct from a body of professional soldiers. **b.** The armed citizenry, as distinct from the regular army. **2.** The able-bodied male citizens in a state who are not members of regular armed forces, but who are called to military service in cases of emergency. **3.** The whole body of physically fit male civilians eligible by law for military service. [Original sense, "military organisation", from Latin *mīlitia,* warfare, from *mīlest,* soldier.] —**mi·li·tia·man** (-iə) *n.*

mil·i·um (míl-i-əm) *n., pl.* **-ia** (-i-ə). *Pathology.* A small, hard, white or yellowish mass just below the surface of the skin, caused by blockage of the secretion of a sebaceous gland. [Middle English, from Latin, millet (the lesions resemble millet seeds).]

milk (milk) *n.* **1. a.** A whitish liquid that is produced by the mammary glands of all mature female mammals after they have given birth and is used for feeding their young until weaned. **b.** The milk of cows, goats, or other animals, used as food by man, or as the principal ingredient of other foods such as butter and cheese. **2.** Any liquid similar to milk in appearance, such as coconut milk, milkweed sap, or plant latex. **3.** Any of various medicinal emulsions or suspensions. —**cry over spilt milk.** To lament what is already past and beyond remedying.

~*v.* **milked, milking, milks.** —*tr.* **1.** To draw milk from the teat or udder of (a female mammal). **2.** To press out, drain off, or remove by or as if by milking: *He milked the information out of him.* **3.** To draw out or extract something from as if by milking: *milk the snake of its venom.* **4.** To obtain money or benefits from for personal gain; exploit: *corrupt officials milking the company's treasury.* —*intr.* **1.** To yield or supply milk. **2.** To draw milk from a female mammal. [Middle English *milk,* Old English *milc, meolc,* from Germanic *meluks* (unattested).] —**milk·er** *n.*

milk-and-wa·ter (milk-ən-wáwtər ‖ *U.S. also* -wóttər) *adj.* Lacking forcefulness; insipid; feeble.

milk bar *n.* A café, or a counter in a café, serving ice cream, nonalcoholic drinks, and light snacks.

milk chocolate *n.* Sweetened chocolate made with milk and other ingredients to give it a creamy taste or appearance.

milk fever *n.* **1.** A mild fever, usually occurring at the beginning of lactation, associated with infection following childbirth. **2.** A disease affecting dairy cows and occasionally sheep or goats, especially soon after giving birth.

milk·fish (mílk-fish) *n., pl.* **-fishes** or collectively **milkfish.** A large fish, *Chanos chanos,* of the South Pacific and Indian oceans, widely used for food. [From its milky colour.]

milk float *n. British.* A small motor vehicle, usually battery-powered, used in delivering milk to houses.

milk glass *n.* An opaque or translucent whitish glass.

milk·ing machine (mílking) *n.* An apparatus fitted with suction devices, used for milking cows mechanically.

milking stool *n.* A low stool with three legs.

milk leg *n. Pathology.* A painful swelling of the leg, occurring in women after childbirth as a result of clotting and inflammation in the femoral veins. Also called "white leg".

milk·maid (mílk-mayd) *n.* A girl or woman who milks cows.

milk·man (mílk-mən, -man) *n., pl.* **-men** (-mən, -men). A man who sells or delivers milk to customers.

milk of magnesia *n.* A trademark for a liquid suspension of magnesium hydroxide, $Mg(OH)_2$, used as an antacid and laxative.

milk pudding *n.* A pudding prepared by cooking rice, semolina, or other grains in sweetened milk.

milk run *n. Informal.* A military aerial mission that is either of short duration or lacking in danger. [From the suggestion that it is as monotonous as the daily delivery of milk.]

milk shake *n.* A beverage made of milk, flavouring, and usually ice cream, shaken or beaten until frothy.

milk·sop (mílk-sop) *n.* A boy or man lacking in courage and manliness; a weakling. [Middle English, sop dipped in milk, hence child fed on this, weakling.] —**milk·sop·py, milk·sop·ping** *adj.*

milk sugar *n.* A constituent of milk, **lactose** (see).

milk thistle *n.* **1.** An annual or biennial herb, *Silybum marianum,* common in lowlands of Britain and Europe, which has an erect grooved stem and red or purple flowers. **2.** Any of a group of plants of the genus *Sonchus;* especially, *S. oleraceus.* In this sense, also called "sow thistle".

Milky Way

EARTH'S OWN GALAXY
A band of hazy light stretching across the night sky

The hazy belt of stars stretching across the night sky is known as the Milky Way. It goes from horizon to horizon, passing within about 30° of the Pole Star and through the constellations of Perseus, Cassiopeia, Scorpio, Sagittarius, and the Southern Cross in the Southern Hemisphere. The hazy appearance of the Milky Way results from the combined light of stars too far away to be seen by the naked eye.

In the Milky Way there are 100,000 million stars that make up the Galaxy to which our Solar System belongs. The Galaxy is just one of millions of galaxies that make up the Universe. It is a disc-shaped collection of stars with the Earth about a third of the way out from the centre. An observer looking at the Milky Way from Earth is actually looking edge on into the Galaxy.

The Galaxy, which started to form more than 14,000 million years ago, is about 100,000 light-years in diameter. It is called a spiral galaxy because it has a dense central region with several arms coiling around it in the same plane.

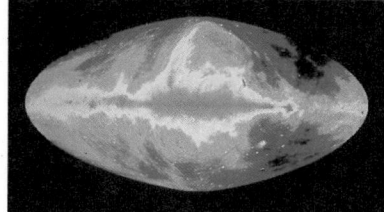

RADIO REVELATION *Seen by the naked eye or through an ordinary telescope, the Milky Way (above) appears to be shaped like a flattish box, with the stars concentrated more in one section – the centre – than anywhere else. But studies made with radio telescopes show that it is shaped like a disc with a central bulge (as seen in the radio map, left). When we look up at the sky at night, we are observing at right-angles to the disc. We see far fewer stars than there really are, as our eyes cannot penetrate the Galaxy as radio can.*

milk tooth *n.* Any of the temporary first teeth of a young mammal. Also called "baby tooth".

milk vetch *n.* Any of various plants of the genus *Astragalus,* having compound leaves and clusters of purple, white, or yellowish flowers. [From its supposed ability to increase a goat's yield of milk.]

milk·weed (mílk-weed) *n.* **1.** Any plant of the chiefly North American genus *Asclepias,* most of which have milky juice and pointed pods that split open to release seeds with downy tufts. **2.** Loosely, any of various other plants having milklike juice.

milkweed butterfly *n.* A butterfly, the **monarch** *(see).*

milk·wort (mílk-wurt ‖ -wawrt) *n.* Any plant of the genus *Polygala,* having variously coloured, usually small flowers. [From its supposed ability to increase human lactation.]

milk·y (mílki) *adj.* **-ier, -iest. 1.** Like milk in colour or consistency; opaque-white: *milky glass.* **2.** Filled with, consisting of, or yielding milk or a fluid resembling milk: *a milky kernel of corn.* **3.** Subdued: *a milky character.* —**milk·i·ness** *n.*

Milky Way *n.* **1.** The faint luminous band sometimes observed across the sky, consisting of very large numbers of faint stars visible when the observer looks towards the centre of the Galaxy. **2.** The Galaxy itself, containing the Earth and Solar System. Also called "Galaxy", "Milky Way Galaxy". [Middle English, translation of Latin *Via lactea.*]

mill¹ (mil) *n.* **1.** A building or establishment equipped with machinery for grinding grain into flour or meal. **2.** A device or mechanism, such as rotating millstones, that grinds grain. **3.** A mechanical appliance or machine that reduces a solid or coarse substance into a pulp or minute grains by crushing, grinding, or pressing: *a pepper mill.* **4.** A machine that releases the juice of fruits and vegetables by pressing or grinding: *a cider mill.* **5. a.** Any machine that produces something by the repetition of a simple process, such as a machine for stamping coins. **b.** Any of various machines for shaping, cutting, polishing, or dressing metal surfaces. **6. a.** A building or group of buildings equipped with machinery for processing materials such as wood, hay, textile fibres, and iron ore into finished products, such as paper, fodder, cloth, and steel: *a textile mill.* **b.** Any building or collection of buildings that has machinery for manufacture; a factory. **7.** An agency, institution, or process that operates in a routine way or turns out products in the manner of a factory: *Don't treat university like a degree mill.* **8.** A slow or laborious process: *It took three years for the bill to get through the legislative mill.* **9.** A steel roller bearing a raised design, such as one used for making a die or a banknote printing plate by pressure. **10.** *Slang.* A fist fight. **—go through the mill. 1.** To go through some process, such as training, that is routine and monotonous but necessary. **2.** To go through a difficult experience, usually having a definite effect on personality or character. **~v. milled, milling, mills. —tr. 1.** To grind, pulverise, or break down into smaller particles in a mill. **2.** To transform or process mechanically in a mill. **3.** To shape, polish, dress, or finish in a mill or with a milling tool. **4. a.** To produce a ridge around the edge of (a coin, for example). **b.** To groove or flute the rim of (a coin, for example). **5.** To agitate or stir until foamy. **—intr. 1.** To move around in churning confusion: *milling around the stage door.* **2.** *Slang.* To fight with the fists; box. **3.** To undergo milling. [Middle English *mille,* Old English *mylen,* from West Germanic *mulīna* (unattested), from Late Latin *molīna,* from *molīnus,* of a mill, from Latin *mola,* millstone.]

mill² *n. Abbr.* **M., mi.** A notional monetary unit equal to ¹/₁₀₀₀ of the dollar of the United States. [Short for Latin *millēsimus,* thousandth.]

Mill (mil), **James** (1773–1836). British philosopher and historian. He published a three volume *History of India* (1818), the *Essay on Government* (1820), and *Elements of Political Economy* (1821).

Mill, John Stuart (1806–73). British philosopher. He wrote *A System of Logic* (1843) and *Principles of Political Economy* (1848). He expressed his utilitarian views in *On Liberty* (1859) and *Utilitarianism* (1863). Mill was a Liberal M.P. (1865–68).

Mil·lais (míllay, mi-láy), **Sir John Everett** (1829–96). English painter, and a founder of the Pre-Raphaelite Brotherhood (1848). His work includes *Christ in the Carpenter's Shop* (1850) and *Order of Release* (1853).

Mil·lay (mi-láy), **Edna St. Vincent** (1892–1950). U.S. poet. Her first volume of verse was *Renascence* (1917). *The Ballad of the Harp Weaver* won her the Pulitzer Prize (1922).

mill·board (míl-bawrd || -bōrd) *n.* A stiff, heavy pasteboard used mainly for book covers. [Alteration of *milled board.*]

mill·dam (mil-dam) *n.* A dam constructed across a stream to raise the water level so the overflow will have sufficient power to turn a mill wheel.

milled (mild) *adj.* **1.** Processed or manufactured in a mill. **2.** Fluted or grooved around the edge, as certain coins are.

mille-feuille (méel-fő-i) *n.* A small rectangular pastry consisting of iced layers of puff pastry filled with confectioners' custard or cream. [French, "thousand-leaf".]

mil·le·nar·i·an (mílli-naír-i-ən) *adj.* **1.** Of or pertaining to a thousand, especially to a thousand years. **2.** Of, pertaining to, or believing in millenarianism.
~n. One who believes the millennium will occur; an adherent of millenarianism. [Late Latin *millēnārius,* MILLENARY.]

mil·le·nar·i·an·ism (mílli-naír-i-ə-niz'm) *n.* **1.** In Christianity, the belief in the holy millennium. **2.** Any belief in, doctrine of, or movement aimed at a perfect period or society in the future.

mil·le·nar·y (mi-lénnəri, mílli-nəri || -nerri) *adj.* **1.** Of or pertaining to a thousand; millenarian. **2.** Of or pertaining to millenarianism or the millenarians.
~n., pl. millenaries. 1. a. A sum or total of one thousand, especially a thousand years. **b.** A thousandth anniversary. **2.** A millenarian. [Late Latin *millēnārius,* of a thousand, from *millēnī,* a thousand each, from *mille,* thousand.]

mil·len·ni·um (mi-lénni-əm) *n., pl.* **-ums** or **-lennia** (-lénni-ə). **1. a.** A span of one thousand years; a millenary. **b.** A thousandth anniversary. **2.** A thousand-year period of holiness either following or preceding the Second Coming of Christ. Revelation 20:1–5. **3.** A hoped-for period of joy, prosperity, and justice. [New Latin (influenced by BIENNIUM) : Latin *mille,* thousand + *annus,* year.] **—mil·len·ni·al** (-əl) *adj.* **—mil·len·ni·al·ist** *n.* **—mil·len·ni·al·ly** *adv.*

milleped, millepede. Variants of millipede.

mil·le·pore (mílli-pawr || -pōr) *n.* Any of various reef-building hydrocorals of the genus *Millepora,* of tropical marine waters, forming white or yellowish calcareous formations, and resembling the true corals of the class Anthozoa. [New Latin *Millepora* (genus), "thousand-pored" : Latin *mille,* thousand + *porus,* PORE.]

mill·er (míllər) *n.* **1.** One who works in, operates, or owns a mill for grinding grain. **2.** A milling machine (see). **3.** Any of various moths having wings and bodies covered with a powdery substance.

Mil·ler (míllər), **Arthur** (1915–). U.S. playwright. *Death of a Salesman* won the Pulitzer Prize (1949). Other works include *A View*

from the Bridge (1955), *The Crucible* (1953), and *After the Fall* (1964).

Miller, Henry (1891–1980). U.S. novelist. His two early novels, *Tropic of Cancer* (1931) and *Tropic of Capricorn* (1935), were published in Paris but banned from the United States until the 1960s because of their frank sexual themes. He also wrote *The Colossus of Maroussi* (1941), and a trilogy, *The Rosy Crucifixion* (1949–60).

mil·ler·ite (míllə-rīt) *n.* A mineral, nickel sulphide, NiS, usually occurring in long slender crystals, and used as a nickel ore. [German *Millerit,* after William *Miller* (1801–80), British mineralogist.]

miller's thumb *n, pl.* **miller's thumbs.** Any of several freshwater fishes of the genus *Cottus,* found in Europe and North America. They have spiny heads and fins, and are mainly bottom dwellers. Also called "bullhead". [Middle English (because of its stocky, thumblike shape). The phrase "miller's thumb" originally referred to the proverbial dishonesty of millers, who gave short weight by tipping the scales with their thumbs.]

mil·les·i·mal (mi-léssim'l) *adj.* **1.** Thousandth. **2.** Consisting of a thousandth, or pertaining to thousandths.
~n. A thousandth. [From Latin *millēsimus,* from *mille,* thousand.]

mil·let (míllit) *n.* **1.** A grass, *Panicum miliaceum,* cultivated in Asia and Africa for its seed and in Europe and North America for hay. **2.** The white seeds of this plant, widely used as a food grain in Africa and Asia. **3.** Any of several milletlike grasses, such as *Setaria italica,* Italian millet, or their seeds. **4.** A sorghum (see). [Middle English *milet,* from Old French, from *mil,* millet, from Latin *milium.*]

Mil·let (mée-ay, -lay, mee-áy, -láy), **Jean François** (1814–75). French painter, whose pictures concentrated on themes of peasant life, as in *The Gleaners* (1857) and *The Angelus* (1859).

mill finish *n.* A smooth surface on various papers, made by machine. Also called "machine finish".

milli– *comb. form. Abbr.* **m** Indicates one-thousandth (10⁻³) of a unit; for example, **millibar, millimetre.** [French, from Latin *milli-,* from *mille,* thousand.]

mil·li·ard (mílli-aard) *n. British.* One thousand million; 10⁹. [French, from Old French *miliart,* from *milion,* MILLION.]

mil·li·ar·y (mílli-əri || *U.S.* -erri) *adj.* Pertaining to or marking the distance of an ancient Roman mile, which equalled 1,000 paces. [Latin *milliārius,* consisting of a thousand, one mile long, from *mille,* thousand.]

mil·li·bar (mílli-baar) *n. Abbr.* **mb.** A unit of pressure, used especially for measuring the pressure of the atmosphere, equal to one thousandth of a bar. It is equivalent to 100 newtons per square metre.

mil·li·gram, mil·li·gramme (mílli-gram) *n. Abbr.* **mg.** A unit of mass equal to one thousandth of a gram.

Mil·li·kan (míllikən), **Robert Andrews** (1868–1953). U.S. physicist. He was awarded the Nobel prize in physics (1923) for his measurement of the charge of the electron.

mil·li·li·tre (mílli-leetər) *n. Abbr.* **ml.** A unit of volume equal to one thousandth of a litre, or one cubic centimetre.

mil·lime (meel-éem, mee-) *n.* A coin equal to ¹/₁₀₀₀ of the dinar of Tunisia. [Perhaps from French *millième,* a thousandth.]

mil·li·me·tre (mílli-meetər) *n. Abbr.* **mm.** A unit of length equal to one-thousandth (10⁻³) of a metre or 0.0394 inch.

mil·li·ner (míllinər) *n.* **1.** A person who makes, trims, designs, or sells women's hats. **2.** *Obsolete.* A seller of ribbons, laces, and other trimmings. [Variant of obsolete *Milaner,* importer of goods, such as women's finery, from MILAN.]

mil·li·ner·y (mílli-nəri, -nri || *U.S.* -nerri) *n.* **1.** Articles, especially women's hats, sold by a milliner. **2.** The profession, business, or shop of a milliner.

mill·ing (milling) *n.* **1.** The act or process of grinding, especially grain into flour or meal. **2.** The operation of cutting, shaping, finishing, or working metal, cloth, or any other product manufactured in a mill. **3.** The ridges cut on the edges of coins.

milling machine *n.* A machine tool with a rotating cutter acting on a metal workpiece held on a movable table. Also called "miller".

mil·lion (mil-yən) *n., pl.* **million** (for senses 1, 2) or **-lions** (chiefly for sense 3). **1.** The cardinal number written 1,000,000 or 10⁶. **2.** A million monetary units, as of pounds: *He made a million on the stock market.* **3.** *Often plural.* An indefinitely large number: *millions of ants.* **—the millions.** The masses; the common people. [Middle English *milioun,* from Old French *milion,* from Italian *milione,* augmentative of *mille,* thousand, from Latin *mille.*] **—mil·lion** *adj.*

mil·lion·aire, mil·lion·naire (míl-yə-naír) *n.* **1.** A person whose wealth amounts to a million or more pounds or dollars, or the equivalent in some other currency. **2.** A very wealthy person. [French *millionnaire,* from MILLION.]

mil·lion·air·ess, mil·lion·nair·ess (míl-yə-naír-iss, -ess, -nair-éss) *n.* A female millionaire.

mil·lionth (míl-yənth) *n.* **1.** The ordinal number one million in a series. **2.** Any of a million equal parts. **—mil·lionth** *adj.*

mil·li·pede, mil·le·pede (mílli-peed) *n.* Also **mil·li·ped, mil·le·ped** (-ped). Any crawling, herbivorous arthropod of the class Diplopoda, found throughout the world. They have wormlike bodies with two pairs of legs on each body segment. Compare **centipede.** [Latin *millepeda,* woodlouse, "thousand-feet" : *mille,* thousand + *pēs* (stem *ped*-), foot.]

mil·li·sec·ond (mílli-sekənd) *n. Abbr.* **ms.** A unit of time equal to one thousandth of a second.

---

mill·pond (míl-pond) *n.* **1.** The pond or dam from which water is channelled to drive a mill. **2.** Any still stretch of water.
mill·race (míl-rayss) *n.* The fast-moving stream of water that drives a millwheel. Also called "millrun".
mill·run (míl-run) *n.* **1.** A millrace. **2.** The output of a sawmill. **3. a.** A test of the mineral quality or content of a rock or ore by the process of milling. **b.** The mineral yielded by this test.
Mills (milz), **Sir John,** born Lewis Ernest Watts (1908–). British actor. He has had a distinguished career in the theatre, besides giving many noted screen performances, as in *Tunes of Glory* (1960), and *Ryan's Daughter* (1971), which won him an Academy Award. He is married to the playwright Mary Hayley Bell, and his two daughters, Hayley and Juliet, have followed acting careers.
Mills bomb *n. Military.* A high-explosive, oval hand grenade. Also called "Mills grenade". [After Sir William *Mills* (1856–1932), British inventor.]
mill·stone (míl-stōn) *n.* **1.** Either of a pair of cylindrical stones used in a mill for grinding grain. **2.** A heavy weight; a burden, especially a mental burden, such as a responsibility or debt.
mill·stream (míl-streem) *n.* **1.** The water flowing in a millrace. **2.** A stream whose flow is used to run a mill.
mill·wheel (míl-weel, -hweel) *n.* A large wheel, especially one turned by a stream of water, used to work a mill.
mill·wright (míl-rīt) *n.* A person who designs, builds, or repairs mills or mill machinery.
Milne (miln, mil), **A(lan) A(lexander)** (1882–1956). British writer. He wrote for the magazine *Punch* before turning to children's books. His tales of Christopher Robin and his animal friends are told in *Winnie-the-Pooh* (1926) and *The House at Pooh Corner* (1928).
mi·lo (mílō) *n., pl.* **-los.** An early-growing grain sorghum. Some varieties are drought-resistant. Compare **durra, feterita, kaffir corn.** [Sotho *maili.*]
mi·lord (mi-lórd) *n.* My lord. A title or form of address formerly used in Europe of an English nobleman or gentleman. [French, from English *my lord.*]
milque·toast (milk-tōst) *n. U.S.* A person with a meek, timid, and retiring nature. [After Caspar *Milquetoast,* a character in the newspaper cartoon *The Timid Soul,* by H(arold) T(ucker) Webster (1885–1952), from *milk toast,* a bland dish of hot buttered toast in warm milk, often associated with frail persons.]
mil·reis (míl-rayss, mil-ráysh) *n., pl.* **milreis.** A former coin and monetary unit of Portugal and Brazil, worth 1,000 reis. [Portuguese *milréis* : *mil,* thousand, from Latin *mīlle* + *réis,* plural of *real,* royal, from Latin *rēgālis,* REGAL.]
milt (milt) *n.* **1.** Fish sperm, including the seminal fluid. **2.** The reproductive glands of male fishes when filled with this fluid. **3.** *Zoology.* The **spleen** *(see).*
~*tr.v.* **milted, milting, milts.** To fertilise (fish roe) with milt. [Sense 1: probably from Middle Dutch *milte,* milt, spleen. Sense 3: Middle English *milte,* Old English *milte.* Both from Germanic *miltjaz* (unattested).]
milt·er (míltər) *n.* A male fish that is ready to breed.
Mil·ton (míltən), **John** (1608–74). English poet. In the Civil War he supported Parliament, and wrote a poem in defence of a free press, *Areopagitica* (1644). The essay, *The Tenure of Kings and Magistrates* (1649), in defence of the regicides, gained him a post as Cromwell's Latin secretary for foreign affairs. Shortly afterwards he became totally blind. The epic poem, *Paradise Lost,* was published in 10 books in 1667 and in 12-book form in 1674. *Paradise Regained* and *Samson Agonistes* were published in 1671. **—Mil·ton·ic, Mil·to·ni·an** *adj.*
Milton Keynes (keénz). New town of Buckinghamshire, south central England. It was designated a new town to relieve Greater London in 1967. It is the site of the Open University.
Mil·wau·kee (mil-wáwki). The port and largest city of Wisconsin, United States, situated on Lake Michigan. It exports coal and grain from the Midwest via the St. Lawrence Seaway, and produces heavy machinery, electrical equipment, tractors, internal-combustion engines, beer, and tinned meat.
mim (mim) *n. British Regional.* Old-fashioned in appearance or behaviour; prim. [Perhaps imitative of pursing of the lips.]
mim·bar (mím-baar) *n.* A pulpit in a mosque, with steps on which the preacher stands. [Arabic *minbar.*]
mime (mīm) *n.* **1. a.** A performing art in which characters are mimicked or ideas and moods conveyed by means of facial expressions, gestures, and the like, without the use of words. **b.** A performance or act of mime. **c.** A performer of mime. **2.** *Archaic.* An actor or comedian who specialises in comic mimicry; a buffoon; a clown. **3. a.** A form of ancient Greek and Roman drama in which realistic characters and situations were farcically portrayed and actual persons were mimicked on the stage. **b.** A performance of, or dialogue for, such a comic drama. **c.** An actor in such a drama.
~*v.* **mimed, miming, mimes.** *—tr.* **1.** To portray in mime; act out with gestures and facial expressions. **2.** To ridicule by imitation; mimic. *—intr.* **1.** To act as a mimic. **2.** To portray characters and situations by wordless gesture, facial expression, and body movement. [Latin *mīmus,* from Greek *mimos,* imitator.] **—mim·er** *n.*
mim·e·o·graph (mímmi-ə-graf, -graaf) *n. Sometimes capital* **M. 1.** A duplicating machine that makes copies of written, drawn, or typed material from a stencil that is fitted around an inked drum. **2.** A copy made by such a machine.
~*v.* **mimeographed, -graphing, -graphs.** *—tr.* To make copies of (a stencil or text) on a mimeograph. **2.** To make (copies) on a mimeograph. *—intr.* To use a mimeograph. [Originally a trademark : from Greek *mimeomai,* first person singular of *mimeisthai,* to imitate + -GRAPH.]
mi·me·sis (mi-meé-siss, mī-) *n.* **1. a.** The imitation or representation of nature or human nature, especially in art and literature. **b.** An instance of such imitation or representation. **2.** *Biology.* Mimicry. **3.** *Medicine.* The appearance, often due to hysteria, of symptoms of a disease not actually present. [Greek *mimēsis,* from *mimeisthai,* to imitate, from *mimos,* imitator.]
mi·met·ic (mi-méttik, mī-) *adj.* **1.** Pertaining to, characteristic of, or showing mimicry. **2. a.** Of or pertaining to an imitation; imitative. **b.** Using imitative means of representation: *a mimetic dance*; *mimetic gesture.* [Greek *mimētikos,* from *mimeisthai,* to imitate.] **—mi·met·i·cal·ly** *adv.*
mim·ic (mímmik) *tr.v.* **-icked, -icking, -ics. 1.** To copy or imitate closely, especially by reproducing external characteristics such as speech, expression, and gesture; ape. **2.** To copy or imitate so as to ridicule; mock. **3.** To resemble closely; simulate: *an insect mimicking a twig.* **—**See Synonyms at **imitate.**
~*n.* **1.** One who imitates: **a.** A performer skilled in mimicking. **b.** A person or trained animal that copies or mimics others, especially for entertainment. **c.** An animal that resembles another. **2.** A copy or imitation of some person or object.
~*adj.* **1.** Pertaining to, acting as, resembling, or characteristic of a mimic or mimicry; imitative. **2.** *Literary.* Imitating a person or object, often for amusement; make-believe. [Latin *mīmicus,* imitative, from Greek *mimikos,* from *mimos,* imitator.] **—mim·ick·er** *n.*
mim·ic·ry (mímmikri) *n., pl.* **-ries. 1. a.** The act, practice, or art of mimicking. **b.** An instance of mimicking. **2.** *Biology.* The resemblance, through natural selection, of one organism to another or to a natural object, as a natural aid in concealment. Also called "mimesis".
Mi·mir (meé-meer) *Norse Mythology.* A giant who dwelt by the roots of Yggdrasil, where he guarded the well of wisdom.
mi·mo·sa (mi-mṓ-zə ‖ -sə) *n.* **1.** Any of various mostly tropical plants, shrubs, and trees of the genus *Mimosa,* having ball-like clusters of small flowers, and compound leaves that are often sensitive to touch or light. See **sensitive plant. 2.** Loosely, any of several similar or related plants or trees, such as species of acacia used by florists. [New Latin, from Latin *mīmus,* MIME, from its imitation of animal sensitivity.]
min minute (unit of time).
min. 1. mineralogical; mineralogy. **2.** minimum. **3.** mining.
Min. Minister; Ministry.
mi·na¹ (mī́-nə) *n., pl.* **-nas** or **-nae** (-nee). A varying unit of weight or money, used in ancient Greece and Asia Minor. [Latin, from Greek *mna,* from Akkadian *manū,* designating a unit of weight, from Sumerian *mana.*]
mina². Variant of **myna.**
mi·na·cious (mi-náyshəss) *adj. Formal.* Of a menacing or threatening nature. [Latin *minax* (stem *mināc-*), from *minārī,* to menace, from *minae,* threats.] **—mi·na·cious·ness, mi·nac·i·ty** (-nássəti) *n.*
Min·a·mo·to Yor·i·to·mo (mínna-mṓtō yórri-tṓmō) (1148–99). Japanese warrior landlord, the founder of the Shogunate, or *bakufu,* the feudal system by which Japan was ruled until 1867. In 1185, he put down a rebellion by his cousin, Minamoto Yoshinaka, against the emperor, then set up a rival government. He appointed *shugo,* or constables, throughout Japan, and in 1192 he assumed supreme authority as *shogun,* with his capital at Kamakura.
min·a·ret (mínnə-rét, -ret) *n.* A tall, slender tower on a mosque, with one or more projecting balconies from which a muezzin summons the people to prayer. [French, from Spanish *minarete,* from Turkish *minārat,* from Arabic *manārat,* lamp.]
min·a·to·ry (mínnə-təri, mī́nə-, -tri) *adj.* Also **min·a·to·ri·al** (-táwri-əl ‖ -tṓri-əl) *Formal.* Menacing; threatening. [French *minatoire,* from Late Latin *minātōrius,* from Latin *minārī,* to menace. See **minacious.**] **—min·a·to·ri·ly** *adv.*
mince (minss) *v.* **minced, mincing, minces.** *—tr.* **1.** To cut or chop into very small pieces. **2.** To pronounce in an affected way, as with forced elegance and refinement: *He minced his phrases in the presence of his employer.* **3.** To moderate or restrain for the sake of politeness and decorum. Used chiefly in the phrase *not to mince one's words.* *—intr.* **1.** To walk with very short steps or with excessive primness. **2.** To speak in an affected way, as with forced elegance and refinement.
~*n.* Food, especially meat, that is finely chopped; mincemeat. [Middle English *mincen,* from Old French *mincier,* to diminish, from Vulgar Latin *minūtiāre* (unattested), from Late Latin *minūtia,* minutia, from Latin *minuere,* to diminish.] **—minc·er** *n.*
mince·meat (mínss-meet) *n.* **1.** Finely chopped meat. **2.** A mixture of finely chopped dried fruit, spices, and other ingredients, used especially as a pie filling. **—make mincemeat of.** *Slang.* To defeat or destroy utterly, as if by cutting into little pieces.
mince pie *n.* A sweet pie filled with mincemeat.
minc·ing (mín-sing) *adj.* Affectedly refined or dainty. **—minc·ing·ly** *adv.*
mind (mīnd) *n.* **1.** Consciousness considered as residing in the human brain, manifested especially in thought, perception, feeling, will, memory, or imagination. **2.** The totality of conscious and unconscious processes of the brain and central nervous system that directs mental and physical activity. **3. a.** In some philosophical systems a principle of intelligence or consciousness held to pervade

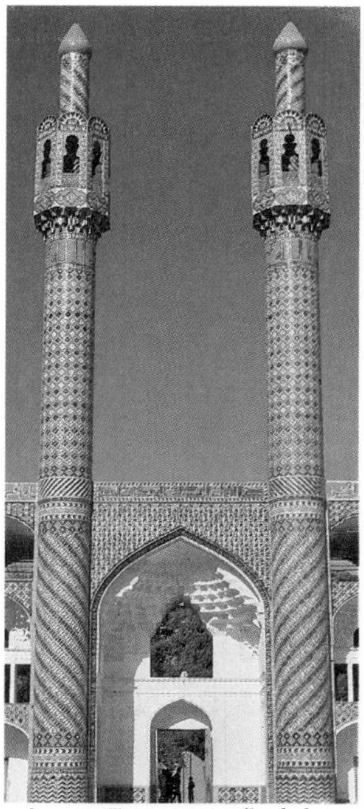

minaret *Two minarets flank the entrance to a mosque at Mahan, in Iran. In the seventh century the Prophet Muhammad said that the call to prayer five times a day should be made from the highest roof near a mosque. Minarets were eventually added to the mosques themselves.*

reality. **b.** Intelligence or the nonmaterial aspect of being, in contrast to the material: *mind over matter.* **4.** A person's ability to reason as distinguished from emotion or will: *Follow your mind, not your heart.* **5. a.** Intellectual power or ability. **b.** A person considered with reference to intellect: *the greatest mind of the century.* **6. a.** A person's awareness of and attitude to the external world, as shaped by remembered experience: *To my mind, it's impossible.* **b.** Collective memory or attitudes: *the British mind.* **7.** An attitude or emotional state: *left him in a very different mind.* **8.** Opinion or sentiment: *I may change my mind when I hear the facts.* **9.** A desire or purpose. Often used with *good: I have a good mind to leave.* **10. a.** Focus of thought; attention; concentration. **b.** Processes of thought and feeling: *preying on her mind.* **11.** Mental balance; sanity: *losing one's mind.* **—blow (someone's) mind.** *Informal.* **1.** To astonish, especially in a pleasurable way. **2.** To give or produce a psychedelic experience to or in. **—bring to mind. 1.** To remember; recollect. **2.** To produce the memory or thought of (a past experience, for example). **—in (one's) mind's eye.** Visualised within one's imagination. **—in** or **of two minds.** Unable to choose; undecided. **—make up (one's) mind.** To decide between alternatives; come to a definite decision or opinion. **—on (one's) mind.** In one's thoughts; especially, worrying one. **—piece of (one's) mind.** *Informal.* One's bluntly expressed opinion; especially, a strongly worded rebuke or condemnation. **—put (one) in mind.** *Informal.* To fill with memories; remind: *The novel put her in mind of her youth.* **—put** or **set (someone's) mind at rest.** To reassure (someone). **—put (someone) in mind of.** To cause to remember or think about; remind of. **—speak (one's) mind.** To speak frankly and in a forthright way.

~*v.* **minded, minding, minds.** —*tr.* **1. a.** To object to; dislike: *Of course I mind your smoking.* **b.** Used in the negative to express willingness or desire: *We don't mind sleeping on the floor.* **c.** Used to express polite requests: *Would you mind asking her?* **2.** To care or be concerned about: *I don't mind who wins.* **3.** To pay attention to the advice or instructions of: *The children minded their mother.* **4.** To make sure: *"And before you let the sun in, mind it wipes its shoes."* (Dylan Thomas). **5. a.** To attend to; heed: *Mind closely what I tell you.* **b.** Used in negative commands to express reassurance: *Don't mind his shouting.* **6.** To be careful about; take heed of or watch out for. **7.** To take care or take charge of; look after. **8.** *Regional.* **a.** To remember or reflect on. **b.** To cause (a person) to remember or reflect on. —*intr.* **1.** To find something objectionable: *Do you mind if I leave now?* **2.** To be concerned or troubled; care: *Nobody minds about what happens to him.* **4.** To be cautious or careful: *Mind as you go down the stairs.* **5.** To get out of the way; shift one's position so as to cease being an obstruction. Usually used in the imperative. **—mind out.** To be careful; beware; pay attention. Usually used in the imperative. **—mind you.** Come to think of it; on the other hand. Used as a mild qualification of a statement: *He seems suitable for the job. Mind you, he's had very little experience.* **—never mind.** *Informal.* Disregard it; it doesn't matter. [Middle English *minde,* Old English *gemynd,* memory, mind, from Germanic *gamundhiz* (unattested).]

Synonyms: *mind, intellect, intelligence, mentality, brains, wits, sense, reason.*

Min·da·nao (míndə-nów). Second largest island of the Republic of the Philippines. Its volcanic, heavily forested mountains include Mount Apo, an active volcano and the country's highest point (2 954 metres; 9,692 feet). The rich volcanic soils produce pineapples, hemp, coffee, rice, and timber. Iron, gold, and coal are mined. The Muslim Moros, the minority since the 1960s, seek self-rule and have resorted to terrorism. Davao is the chief port and city.

mind-bend·ing (mīnd-bending) *adj. Informal.* **1. a.** Hallucinogenic. **b.** Producing distortions of perception or thought. **2.** Mind-boggling.

mind-bog·gling (mīnd-boggling) *adj. Informal.* Beyond one's usual experience or mental grasp; overwhelming; stunning.

mind·blow·ing (mīnd-blō-ing) *adj. Slang.* **1.** Hallucinogenic. **2.** Extremely surprising or exciting.

mind·ed (mīndid) *adj.* **1.** Having an intention; disposed; inclined: *I am not minded to answer any of your questions.* **2.** Having a specified kind of mind or tendency. Often used in combination: *evil-minded.* **3.** Having an interest in a specified field. Often used in combination: *arts-minded; ecologically minded.*

mind·er (mīndər) *n.* **1.** A childminder. **2.** *U.S.* A babysitter. **3.** *Slang.* A bodyguard or henchman hired by a criminal.

mind-ex·pand·ing (mīnd-ik-spanding, -ek-) *adj.* Producing intensified or distorted perceptions; psychedelic; hallucinogenic. Said especially of drugs.

mind·ful (mīndf'l) *adj.* Attentive; heedful. Used with *of: mindful of her responsibilities.* **—mind·ful·ly** *adv.* **—mind·ful·ness** *n.*

mind·less (mīnd-ləss, -liss) *adj.* **1. a.** Lacking intelligence or good sense; foolish. **b.** Without the need of much mental effort: *a mindless job.* **c.** Without intelligent purpose, meaning, or direction: *mindless violence.* **2.** Giving or showing little attention or care; heedless. Usually used with *of: They proceeded, mindless of the dangers.* **—mind·less·ly** *adv.* **—mind·less·ness** *n.*

mind-read·ing (mīnd-reeding) *n.* **1.** The guessing of what someone is thinking by observing facial expressions and other signs. **2.** The supposed faculty of discerning another's thoughts through extrasensory means of communication; telepathy. **—mind-read·er** *n.*

Mind·szen·ty (mínd-senti), **József** (1892–1975). Hungarian prelate, who became Archbishop of Esztergom and Primate of Hungary after World War II. In 1946 he was made a cardinal. He opposed the Communist regime and in 1948 was jailed for life on a charge of treason. He was freed in 1955, but after suppression of the 1956 uprising he took refuge in the American legation in Budapest. In 1971, the Hungarian government let him go to the Vatican.

mind-your-own-busi·ness (mīnd-yər-ōn-bíz-nəss, -niss) *n.* A plant, **mother-of-thousands** *(see).*

mine[1] (mīn) *n.* **1. a.** An excavation in the earth for the purpose of extracting free metals, coal, salt, or other minerals. **b.** The site of such an excavation, with its surface buildings, shafts, and equipment. **2.** Any deposit of ore or minerals in the earth or on its surface. **3.** An abundant supply or source of something valuable: *a mine of information.* **4.** *Military.* **a.** A tunnel dug under an enemy emplacement to gain an avenue of attack or to lay explosives. **b.** An explosive device used to destroy enemy personnel, ships, vehicles, or equipment, usually placed just beneath the surface of the ground or sea and designed to be detonated by contact or by a time fuse. **5.** A burrow, tunnel, or gallery made by an insect.

~*v.* **mined, mining, mines.** —*tr.* **1. a.** To extract (ores or minerals) from the earth. **b.** To dig a mine or mines in (the earth) to obtain ores or minerals. **2. a.** To dig under (the earth, or a surface feature); tunnel under. **b.** To make (a tunnel) by digging. **3.** *Military.* To lay explosive mines in or under. **4.** To attack, damage, or destroy by underhand means; undermine; subvert. **5.** To delve into and make use of; exploit: *mine the archives for information.* —*intr.* **1.** To excavate the earth for the purpose of extracting minerals or ores; work in a mine. **2.** To dig a tunnel or tunnels under the earth; especially, to dig under an enemy emplacement or fortification. **3.** *Military.* To lay explosive mines. [Middle English, from Old French, from Vulgar Latin *mina* (unattested), perhaps from Celtic *meini-*† (unattested), ore.] **—min·a·ble, mine·a·ble** *adj.*

mine[2] *pron.* Absolute form of *my. Used with a singular or plural verb.* **1.** Belonging to me; my own. Used after a verb: *The green boots are mine.* **2.** The one or ones belonging or pertaining to me: *Mine is the one in the corner.* **3.** *Archaic.* Used to modify: **a.** A following noun beginning with a vowel or *h: mine host.* **b.** A preceding noun: *Mother mine.* **—of mine.** Belonging or pertaining to me: *a friend of mine.* [Middle English *min,* Old English *mīn.*]

mine detector *n.* Any of various electromagnetic devices used to locate explosive mines. **—mine detection** *n.*

mine·field (mīn-feeld) *n.* **1.** An area in which explosive mines have been anchored or sunk in water or buried on land. **2.** Anything which is full of hidden dangers: *These negotiations are a minefield.*

mine·lay·er (mīn-lay-ər) *n.* A ship or aircraft equipped for laying explosive underwater mines.

min·er (mīnər) *n.* **1. a.** One who works in a mine. **b.** One who makes his living from extracting minerals from the earth. **2.** A machine for the automatic extraction of minerals, especially of coal. **3.** A member of a military unit engaged in laying explosive mines. **4.** Any of various insects that burrow in leaves, a **leaf miner** *(see).*

min·er·al (mínnərəl, mínrəl) *n.* **1.** Any naturally occurring, homogeneous inorganic substance having a definite chemical composition and characteristic crystalline structure, colour, and hardness. **2.** Any of various natural substances: **a.** An element, such as gold or silver. **b.** A mixture of inorganic compounds, such as bauxite. **c.** An organic derivative, such as coal or petroleum. **3.** Any substance that is neither animal nor vegetable; inorganic matter. **4.** An ore. **5.** *British Informal.* **a.** *Often plural.* Mineral water. **b.** A nonalcoholic carbonated drink, usually with a sweet flavouring.

~*adj.* **1.** Of or pertaining to minerals: *a mineral deposit; mineral salts.* **2.** Impregnated with minerals: *mineral water.* [Middle English, from Medieval Latin *minerāle* (noun), from *minerālis* (adjective), from Old French *miniere,* from *mine,* MINE.]

min·er·al·ise, min·er·al·ize (mínnərə-līz, mínrə-) *v.* **-ised, -ising, -ises.** —*tr.* **1.** To convert to a mineral substance; petrify. **2.** To transform a metal into a mineral by oxidation. **3.** To impregnate with minerals. —*intr.* To develop or hasten mineral formation. **—min·er·al·i·sa·tion** (-lī-záysh'n || *U.S.* -li-) *n.* **—min·er·al·is·er** *n.*

mineral jelly *n.* **Petrolatum** *(see).*

mineral kingdom *n.* The group of objects and substances that are composed only of inorganic matter. Compare **animal kingdom, plant kingdom.**

min·er·al·o·cor·ti·coid (mínnərəlō-kórti-koyd) *n.* Any corticosteroid hormone that regulates ionic balance and, indirectly, fluid absorption. The main mineralocorticoid is **aldosterone** *(see).*

min·er·al·o·gy (mínnə-rál-əji || -rŏl-) *n. Abbr.* **min.** The study of minerals, including their distribution, identification, and properties. [MINERA(L) + -LOGY.] **—min·er·a·log·i·cal** (-rə-lójik'l) *adj.* **—min·er·a·log·i·cal·ly** *adv.* **—min·er·al·o·gist** (-ə-jist) *n.*

mineral oil *n.* **1.** Any of various light hydrocarbon oils, especially a distillate of petroleum. **2.** *Chiefly U.S.* **Liquid paraffin** *(see).*

mineral pitch *n.* A bituminous material, **asphalt** *(see).*

mineral tar *n.* A form of bitumen, **maltha** *(see).*

mineral water *n.* Naturally occurring or prepared water that contains dissolved minerals or gases, often used therapeutically.

mineral wax *n.* A hydrocarbon wax, **ozocerite** *(see).*

mineral wool *n.* Any inorganic fibrous material produced by steam blasting and cooling molten silicate or a similar substance. It is used chiefly as an insulator.

Mi·ner·va (mi-nérvə) *Roman Mythology.* The goddess of wisdom, invention, the arts, and martial prowess, identified with the Greek Athena. [Latin.]

min·e·stro·ne (mínni-strṓni || *U.S. also* -strṓn) *n.* A soup of Italian

PRONUNCIATION KEY

a, trap; aa, father; ai, fair; ar, star; aw, lawn; ay, play; b, bb, stab; rubber; ch, church; ck, ticket; d, dd, dead; ladder; e, dress; ee, bee; er, defer; ew, few; ewr, pure; ə, about; ər, letter; f, ff, fife; differ; g, gg, giggle; h, hat; i, kit; ī, price; īr, fire; j, judge; k, kick; l, ll, let; 'l, needle; m, mm, man; n, nn, no; 'n, sudden; ng, thing; o, lot; ō, no; ŏŏ, foot; ōō, shoe; oor, poor; ow, cow; owr, hour; oy, boy; p, pp, pepper; r, rr, red; s, ss, sauce; sh, ship; t, tt, totter; th, thick; th, this; smooth; u, cut; ur, turn; v, vv, valve; w, wet; y, yes; z, zz, zebra; zh, vision; pleasure

IN FOREIGN WORDS:

aN, oN, Saint-Saëns; hl, Llanelli; Hluhluwe; kh, loch; lough; Khaled

STRESS MARK:

ín-sīt, insight; in-sī́t, incite

origin containing assorted vegetables, vermicelli, and herbs in a meat or vegetable broth. [Italian, augmentative of *minestra*, from *minestrare*, to serve, dish out, from Latin *ministrāre*, to serve.]

mine·sweep·er (mīn-sweepər) *n.* A ship equipped for destroying, removing, or neutralising explosive marine mines.

Ming (ming). A dynasty which ruled China from 1368 until the Manchu Conquest of 1644. It was founded by a rebel Buddhist monk, Zhu Yuan-zhang who proclaimed himself emperor in 1368. By 1382 he had unified most of China. The arts flourished and periods of foreign trade made the distinctive blue and white porcelain famous abroad. [Mandarin Chinese *míng*, "luminous", "enlightened".] **—Ming** *adj.*

min·gle (míng-g'l) *v.* **-gled, -gling, -gles.** *—tr.* **1.** To mix or bring together (two or more different elements) in close association; combine. **2.** To mix (things) so that the components become united; merge: *"I desired my dust to be mingled with yours"* (Ezra Pound). *—intr.* **1.** To be or become mixed or united. **2.** To mix or pass freely among: *Servants mingled with guests.* **—**See Synonyms at **mix.** [Middle English *menglen*, frequentative of *mengen*, to mix, Old English *mengan*.] **—min·gler** *n.*

Min·gus, Charles (míng-gəss), (1922–79). U.S. black jazz musician, composer, and bandleader. Although a virtuoso on the string bass, he has been more influential as a composer. His many compositions include *Conversation* (1957) and *Folk Forms No. 1* (*c.*1959).

min·gy (mínji) *adj.* **-gier, -giest.** *British Informal.* **1.** Miserly, stingy; mean: *a mingy father.* **2.** Paltry; inadequate: *a mingy helping of dessert.* [Perhaps MEAN + STINGY.]

min·i (mínni) *n. Informal.* Something distinctively smaller or shorter than other members of its class, especially **1.** A miniskirt. **2.** *Capital* **M.** A trademark for a compact motor car. **—min·i** *adj.*

mini– *comb. form.* Indicates something distinctively smaller or shorter than other members of its class; for example, **minibus, miniskirt.** ***Note:*** Compounds with *mini-* can be formed at will, many such formations being humorous. It is usual to hyphenate less standardised compounds: *a mini-lecture.* [Shortening of MINIATURE.]

min·i·a·ture (mínni-chər, mín-yə-, -tewr) *n.* **1.** A copy or model that represents or reproduces something in a greatly reduced size. **2. a.** A small painting executed with great detail, often on a surface of ivory or vellum. **b.** A small portrait, picture, or decorative letter on an illuminated manuscript. **c.** The art of making such paintings, portraits, or letters. **3.** Any extremely small representative or example of a class: *These goldfish are miniatures.* **—in miniature.** On a small scale: *The classroom is the real world in miniature.*
~adj. On a small or greatly reduced scale: *miniature furniture.* [Italian *miniatura*, painting (especially the miniature illuminations in medieval manuscripts), from *miniare*, to illuminate, from Latin *miniāre*, to colour with red lead, from *minium*, MINIUM.]

min·i·a·tur·ise, min·i·a·tur·ize (mínni-chər-īz, mín-yə-, -tewr-) *tr.v.* **-ised, -ising, -ises.** To plan or make on a greatly reduced scale; especially, to make (compact electronic equipment) by using integrated circuits. **—min·i·a·tur·i·sa·tion** (-ī-záysh'n || *U.S.* -i-) *n.*

min·i·a·tur·ist (mínni-chər-ist, mín-yə-, -tewr-) *n.* An artist who paints miniatures.

mini·i·bus (mínni-buss) *n.* A high motorised van with rows of seats in the back, capable of transporting small groups of passengers.

min·i·cab (mínni-kab) *n. Chiefly British.* A small motor car used as a taxi.

min·i·com·put·er (mínni-kəm-péwtər, -pewtər || -kom-) *n.* A relatively small digital computer. Compare **mainframe.**

Mi·ni·coy Island (mínni-koy). See **Lakshadweep.**

min·i·é ball (mínni-ay) *n. Often capital* **M.** A conical rifle bullet made in the 19th century and designed with a hollow base that expands when fired to fit the spiral grooves of the bore. [After Captain Claude *Minié* (1814–79), French Army officer, who invented it.]

min·i·fy (mínni-fī) *tr.v.* **-fied, -fying, -fies.** *Rare.* To make smaller or less significant; reduce. [From MINIMUM, after *magnify*.] **—min·i·fi·ca·tion** (-fi-káysh'n) *n.*

min·i·kin (mínnikin) *n. Rare.* A very small or delicate creature.
~adj. **1.** *Obsolete.* Diminutive. **2.** Affectedly dainty; mincing. [Middle Dutch *minneken*, darling, diminutive of *minne*, love.]

min·im (mínnim) *n.* **1.** *Abbr.* **M.** A unit of fluid measure: **a.** In Great Britain, $^1/_{20}$ of a scruple or 0.00361 cubic inch. **b.** In the United States, $^1/_{60}$ of a fluid dram or 0.00376 cubic inch. **2.** *Music.* A note with a time value of a half a semibreve. Also *U.S.* "half note". **3.** An insignificantly small portion, thing, or person; a jot. **4.** A downward vertical stroke in handwriting. [In music, Middle English *mynym*, from Medieval Latin *minimus*, from Latin, least; other senses, from Latin *minimus*, least. See **minimum.**]

min·i·mal (mínnim'l) *adj.* **1.** Smallest in amount or degree; least possible. **2.** Insignificant or negligible.
~n. Mathematics. In an ordered set, a member that precedes all others. **—min·i·mal·ly** *adv.*

minimal art *n.* A style of abstract painting and sculpture that seeks to obtain an effect of impersonality and restraint by the use of simple geometric shapes and primary colours.

min·i·mal·ist (mínnimə-list) *n.* **1.** A person who champions or produces minimal art. **2. a.** A person who advocates restraint in or the least possible use of something, for example, ornamentation in art or policing in society. **b.** A person who agrees to accept a minimum as a temporary measure. **3.** *Capital* **M. a.** A member of a revolutionary group in Russia during the early 20th century whose policy was the immediate implementation of democracy. **b.** A **Menshevik** *(see).* **—min·i·mal·ist** *adj.*

minimal pair *n. Linguistics.* A pair of words or sounds differing in only one very small respect and thereby serving to isolate and identify the phonemes, morphemes, and other minimal linguistic units of a given language. For example, *bang* and *pang* together make up a minimal pair in English.

min·i·max (mínni-maks) *adj. Mathematics.* Of or pertaining to the strategic principle in game theory by which a player selects the strategy to minimise an opponent's greatest possible gain and maximise his own. Compare **maximin.** [*mini*mum + *max*imum.]

min·i·mise, min·i·mize (mínni-mīz) *tr.v.* **-mised, -mising, -mises.** **1.** To reduce to the smallest possible amount, extent, size, or degree. **2.** To represent as having the least degree of importance, value, or size; depreciate. [From MINIMUM.] **—min·i·mi·sa·tion** (-mī-záysh'n || *U.S.* -mi-) *n.* **—min·i·mis·er** *n.*

Usage: Because the traditional senses of this verb relate to an absolute value (the least possible, or lowest), the use of qualifications such as *greatly, somewhat, very much* is criticised. When a qualification needs to be made, an alternative verb, such as *reduce* or *lessen* is preferred, but such usage indicates a continuing shift towards this meaning.

min·i·mum (mínni-məm) *n., pl.* **-mums** or **-ma** (-mə). *Abbr.* **min.** **1.** The least possible quantity or degree. **2.** The lowest quantity, degree, or number reached or recorded; the lower limit of variation. **3.** *Mathematics.* **a.** A number not greater than any other in a finite set of numbers. **b.** A value of a function that is exceeded for any sufficiently small increase or decrease in the function's variables.
~adj. Abbr. **min.** Of, consisting of, or representing the lowest possible amount or degree permissible or attainable. [Latin, from *minimus*, least, superlative of *minor*, minor.]

minimum lending rate *n.* Until 1981, the lowest rate at which the Bank of England would discount approved bills of exchange.

minimum wage *n.* The lowest wage, determined by law or contract, that an employer may pay an employee.

min·ing (mīning) *n. Abbr.* **min.** **1.** The process or business of extracting coal, minerals, or ore from a mine. **2.** The process of laying explosive mines.

min·ion (mín-yən) *n.* **1.** One who is esteemed; a favourite. **2. a.** An obsequious follower or dependant; a sycophant. **b.** A subordinate of an individual or organisation: *Civil Service minions.* **3.** *Printing.* A size of type, 7-point.
~adj. Rare. Endearingly dainty; delicate. [French *mignon*, darling, from Old French *mignot*, from Gaulish; akin to Old High German *minna*, love.]

min·i·pill (mínni-pil) *n.* An oral contraceptive that contains only progesterone.

min·i·skirt (mínni-skurt) *n.* A short skirt hemmed several inches above the knees. **—min·i·skirt·ed** *adj.*

min·is·ter (mínnistər) *n.* **1.** A person serving as an agent for another by carrying out specified orders or functions. **2. a.** A person authorised to perform religious functions in a church, especially in a non-Catholic church; a clergyman. **b.** A clergyman officiating at a religious service. **3.** A member of a government appointed to head an executive or administrative department of government, in Britain, usually under the direction of a Secretary of State. **4.** In some countries, a person authorised to represent his government in diplomatic dealings with other governments, usually ranking next below an ambassador.
~v. **ministered, -tering, -ters.** *—intr.* **1.** To attend to the wants and needs of others. Usually followed by *to: Volunteers ministered to the injured.* **2.** To exercise clerical functions. *—tr. Archaic.* **1.** To administer or dispense: *ministered the Sacrament.* **2.** To furnish or provide. [Middle English *ministre*, from Old French, from Latin *minister*, attendant, servant, from *minus*, less.]

min·is·te·ri·al (mínni-stéer-i-əl) *adj.* **1.** Of, pertaining to, or characteristic of a minister of religion or of the ministry. **2. a.** Of or pertaining to a government minister or department. **b.** Of, pertaining to, or representing the government when challenged by the opposition. **3.** *Law.* Of or designating a mandatory act or delegated duty admitting of no personal discretion or judgment or requiring no special expertise in its performance. Compare **judicial.** **4.** Acting or serving as an agent; instrumental. **—min·is·te·ri·al·ly** *adv.*

minister of state *n.* **1.** A government minister who is not head of a department and usually not in the cabinet, who works as an assistant to a senior minister. **2.** Any government minister.

Minister of the Crown *n. British.* Any of the senior government ministers, usually but not necessarily in the cabinet, appointed by the Crown on the recommendation of the Prime Minister.

minister plenipotentiary *n.* A diplomatic representative with full authority to speak and act for his government, though lower in rank than an ambassador; a plenipotentiary.

minister resident *n.* A diplomatic agent ranking below a minister plenipotentiary.

min·is·trant (mínnistrənt) *adj.* Serving as a minister.
~n. One who ministers. [Latin *ministrāns* (stem *ministrant-*), present participle of *ministrāre*, to serve, from *minister*, MINISTER.]

min·is·tra·tion (mínni-stráysh'n) *n.* **1.** An act or process of serving or aiding. **2.** The act of performing the duties of a minister of religion. [Latin *ministrātiō* (stem *ministrātiōn-*), from *ministrāre*, to serve, from *minister*, MINISTER.] **—min·is·tra·tive** (-strətiv) *adj.*

min·is·try (mínnistri) *n., pl.* **-tries.** **1.** The act of serving; ministration. **2. a.** The profession, duties, and services of a minister of reli-

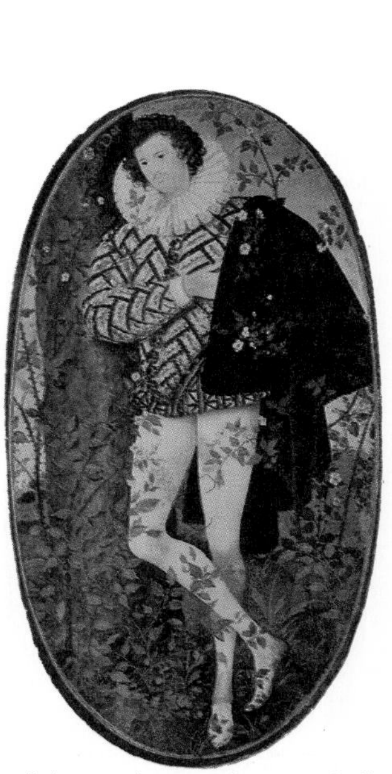

miniature *A watercolour portrait of a young man, by the English artist Nicholas Hilliard (1547–1619). The painting is only 13.5 centimetres ($5\frac{3}{8}$ inches) high and 7 centimetres ($2\frac{3}{4}$ inches) wide.*

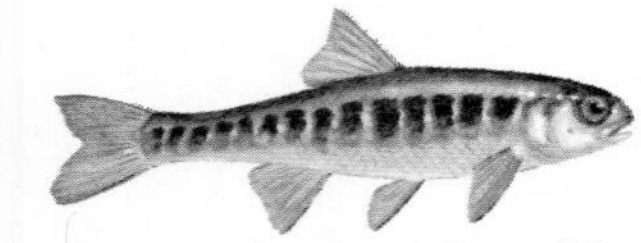

minnow *These inconspicuous fish rarely grow to more than 80 millimetres (about 3 inches) long. They are particularly common in upland streams with gravel bottoms, but are also found in ponds and lakes.*

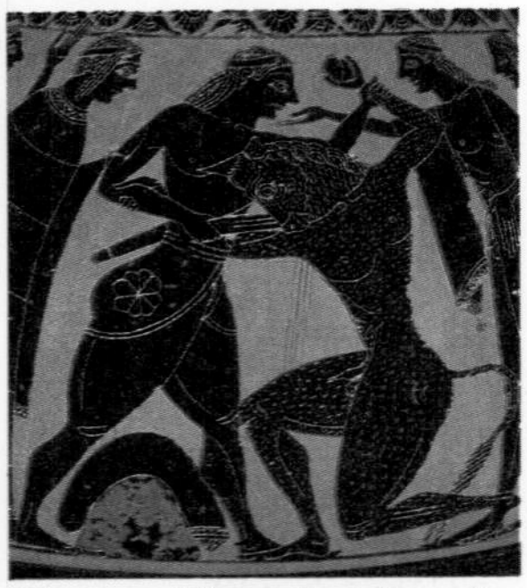

Minotaur *Minos, a legendary ruler of Crete, demanded periodic sacrifices of Athenian youths and girls to the bull-headed Minotaur. This Athenian vase, from the sixth century* B.C., *depicts the monster's death at the hands of the Greek hero Theseus.*

gion. **b.** Ministers of religion as a group; the clergy. **c.** The period of service of a minister of religion. **3. a.** A government department presided over by a minister. **b.** The building in which such a department is housed. **c.** The duties, functions, or term of a government minister and his staff. **d.** *Often capital* **M.** Government ministers as a group. [Middle English *ministerie,* from Latin *ministerium,* functions of a MINISTER.]

Min·i·track (mínni-trak) *n.* A trademark for an electronic measuring system designed to follow the course of satellites and rockets and to correlate radio signals received by a network of ground stations.

min·i·um (mínni-əm) *n. Chemistry.* A lead oxide, **red lead** *(see).* [Middle English, from Latin, cinnabar, red lead, probably of Iberian origin; akin to Basque *arminea,* cinnabar.]

min·i·ver (mínnivər) *n.* **1.** A white or light-grey fur of uncertain origin, used as a rich trim on medieval robes. **2.** The ermine used in the ceremonial robes of peers. [Middle English, from Anglo-French *menuver,* Old French *menu vair,* small vair : *menu,* small, from Latin *minūtus,* small, MINUTE + *vair,* VAIR.]

min·i·vet (mínni-vet) *n.* Any tropical Asian songbird of the genus *Pericrocotus,* related to the cuckoo shrikes and having a brightly coloured plumage. [19th century : origin obscure.]

mink (mingk) *n., pl.* **minks** or collectively **mink. 1.** Any of various semiaquatic carnivores of the genus *Mustela,* especially *M. vison* of North America, resembling the weasel and having short ears, a pointed snout, short legs, and partly webbed toes. **2.** The soft, thick, lustrous fur of this animal. **3.** A coat or stole made of this fur. [Middle English *mynk,* from Scandinavian; akin to Danish *mink*†.]

Min·ne·ap·o·lis (mínni-áppəliss). A city of Minnesota, United States, at the head of navigation on the Mississippi. Adjacent to, and twinned with, St. Paul, it lies in a rich agricultural area, and meat-packaging and flour-milling are its main industries.

Min·nel·li, Liza (mi-nélli) (1946–). U.S. singer and actress. Daughter of Judy Garland, the Hollywood film actress, and Vincente Minnelli, the film director. She has been hailed for her performances in the films *Cabaret* (1972) and *New York, New York* (1977).

min·ne·sing·er (mínni-sing-ər, -zing-) *n.* Any of the German lyric poets and singers in the troubadour tradition who flourished from the 12th to the 14th centuries. [German, "love singer".]

Min·ne·so·ta (mínni-sṓtə). Northernmost state of United States, outside Alaska. Its southern two thirds are prairieland, producing dairy products, meat, and grain. To the north lie reafforested hills, the basis of the state's timber industry. In the eastern mountains beside Lake Superior, exploitation of nickel and copper reserves has superseded the mining of iron ore. Manufacturing is the state's chief activity, yielding processed foods, paper products, machinery, and electronic equipment. With more than 11,000 lakes, tourism is also important. The state was admitted to the Union in 1858. St. Paul on the Mississippi is its capital. **—Min·ne·so·tan** *adj. & n.*

min·now (mínnō) *n., pl.* **minnows** or collectively **-now. 1.** Any of a large number of small, freshwater fishes of the family Cyprinidae; especially, the European species *Phoxinus phoxinus,* widely used as live bait. **2.** Any other small, silver-coloured fish. **3. a.** A small or unimpressive person. **b.** Someone or something that is relatively small in size or status: *The firm was then just a minnow in the car trade.* [Middle English *menow,* Old English *mynwe* (unattested).]

Mi·ño or **Mi·nho** (méen-yō). A river of the Iberian peninsula. Rising in Galicia in northwest Spain, it flows generally southwest to the Atlantic. Its lower course forms Portugal's northern boundary with Spain.

Mi·no·an (mi-nṓ-ən, mī-) *adj.* **1.** Of, pertaining to, or designating the advanced Bronze Age culture that flourished in Crete from about 3000 to 1100 B.C. **2.** Of, pertaining to, or designating either of two writing systems, **Linear A** and **Linear B** *(both of which see).*
~n. A person living in this Bronze Age culture. [From Greek *Minōs,* MINOS.]

mi·nor (mī́nər) *adj.* **1.** Lesser or smaller in amount, extent, quantity, or size. **2.** Lesser or relatively low in importance, rank, or stature: *a minor essayist.* **3.** Lesser or relatively small in seriousness or danger; requiring comparatively little attention or concern: *minor difficulties; a minor injury.* **4.** *Law.* Under legal age; not yet a legal adult. **5.** *British.* Designating the junior or younger of two pupils, especially brothers, with the same surname. Used especially in British public schools. **6.** *U.S.* Designating or pertaining to an academic subject taken as a subsidiary course. **7.** *Logic.* Dealing with a more restricted category; narrower in scope. **8.** *Music.* **a.** Designating a **minor scale** *(see).* **b.** Less in distance by a semitone than the corresponding major interval. **c.** Based on a minor scale: *minor key.* **9.** Of or pertaining to the minority.
~n. **1.** A person or thing that is lesser in comparison with others of the same class. **2.** *Law.* One who has not reached full legal age (in Britain, 18; in some other countries, 21). **3. a.** *U.S.* An area of specialised study of a degree candidate in a college or university that requires fewer class hours or credits than his major. **b.** One studying a minor: *a chemistry minor.* **4.** *Logic.* A **minor premise** or **minor term** *(both of which see).* **5.** *Music.* A minor key, scale, or interval. **6.** In bell-ringing, a change rung on six bells. **7.** *U.S. Sports.* **a.** A **minor league** *(see).* **b.** *Plural.* The minor leagues of a sport, as a group. **8.** *Capital* **M.** A Minorite.
~intr.v. **minored, -noring, -nors.** *U.S.* To pursue academic studies in a minor subject. Used with *in.* [Middle English, from Latin *minor,* less.]

Minorca[1] See **Menorca. —Minorcan** *adj. & n.*

Mi·nor·ca[2] (mi-nórkə) *n.* A domestic fowl of a breed originating in the Mediterranean region, having white or black plumage.

minor canon *n.* An Anglican clergyman who helps to conduct the daily service at a cathedral but is not a member of its chapter.

Mi·nor·ite (mī́nə-rīt) *n.* Also **Mi·nor·ist** (-rist) A Franciscan friar, especially one belonging to the order of *Friars Minor.* [From *Friars Minor* (Medieval Latin *Frātrēs Minōrēs*), name given to the order by its founder, Saint Francis of Assisi, as a title of humility.]

mi·nor·i·ty (mī-nórrəti, mi- || -náwrəti) *n., pl.* **-ties. 1.** The smaller in number of two groups which together form a whole; a group of persons or things numbering less than half of a total. Compare **majority. 2.** A racial, religious, political, national, or other group regarded as different from the larger group of which it is part. Also used adjectivally: *minority parties.* **3.** The state or period of being under legal age: *an heir still in his minority.* [French *minorité,* from Medieval Latin *minōritās* (stem *minoritāt-*), from Latin *minor,* MINOR.]

minority carrier *n. Electronics.* The carrier that transports the smaller fraction of the current in a semiconductor. Compare **majority carrier.**

minority leader *n. U.S.* The head of the minority party in a legislative body. Compare **majority leader.**

minor league *n. Chiefly U.S.* Any league of professional sports clubs, especially baseball, not belonging to the major leagues.

minor-league (mī́nər-léeg) *adj.* **1.** *Chiefly U.S.* Pertaining or belonging to a minor sports league. **2.** Being of subordinate position or secondary importance: *a minor-league politician.* **—mi·nor-lea·guer** *n.*

minor orders *pl.n. Roman Catholic Church.* The former orders of acolyte, exorcist, reader or lector, and doorkeeper.

minor planet *n.* An **asteroid** *(see).*

minor premise *n. Logic.* The premise in a syllogism containing the minor term, which will form the subject of the conclusion.

Minor Prophets *pl.n.* **1.** The Hebrew prophets Hosea, Joel, Amos, Obadiah, Jonah, Micah, Nahum, Habakkuk, Zephaniah, Haggai, Zechariah, and Malachi. **2.** In the Old Testament, the group of books containing their prophecies.

minor scale *n. Music.* A diatonic scale having a minor third between the first and third notes. It has several forms with different intervals above the fifth. Compare **major scale.**

minor suit *n.* In bridge, the suit of clubs or of diamonds, so called because of their lower scoring value.

minor term *n. Logic.* The term in a syllogism that is stated in the minor premise and forms the subject of the conclusion.

Mi·nos (mī́-noss, -nəss) *Greek Mythology.* A king of Crete, the son of Zeus and Europa, who ordered the building of the Labyrinth.

Mi·no·taur (mī́nə-tawr, mínnə-) *Greek Mythology.* The son of Pasiphaë by a sacred bull, having a man's body and a bull's head, slain by Theseus in the Labyrinth. [Middle English, ultimately from Greek *Minōtauros* : MINOS (husband of Pasiphaë) + *tauros,* bull.]

Minsk (minsk). The capital of Belorussian S.S.R., U.S.S.R. It is a communications, market, and cultural and industrial centre. Its substantial Jewish population (40 per cent) was virtually exterminated by the Germans in World War II.

min·ster (mín-stər) *n. British.* **1.** A monastery church. **2.** Any of certain abbeys or cathedrals, such as those of Beverley or York. [Middle English *minster,* Old English *mynster,* from Vulgar Latin *monisterium* (unattested), variant of Late Latin *monastērium,* MONASTERY.]

min·strel (mín-strəl) *n.* **1.** A medieval musician who travelled from place to place singing and reciting poetry. **2.** *Archaic.* Any lyric poet or musician. **3.** A performer in a minstrel show. [Middle English *ministral,* from Old French *menestral,* entertainer, servant, from Late Latin *ministeriālis,* household officer, from Latin *ministerium,* MINISTRY.]

minstrel show *n.* A variety show in which performers, some with blackened faces, sing, dance, and tell jokes.

min·strel·sy (mín-strəl-si) *n., pl.* **-sies. 1.** The art or profession of a minstrel. **2.** A troupe of minstrels. **3.** A group of ballads and lyrics sung by minstrels.

mint[1] (mint) *n.* **1.** A place where the coins of a country are manufactured by authority of the government. **2.** An abundant amount or repository, especially of money: *He is worth a mint.* **3.** Anything that may be exploited as a source of money or ideas: *a mint of useful ideas.*
~tr.v. **minted, minting, mints. 1.** To produce (money) by stamping metal; coin. **2.** To invent or fabricate (a word, for example).
~adj. As if freshly minted; unused: *in mint condition; a mint stamp.* [Middle English *mynt,* Old English *mynet,* money, from West Germanic *munita* (unattested), from Latin *monēta,* money, mint, after the temple of Juno *Monēta* in Rome, where money was minted.]

mint[2] *n.* **1.** Any of various plants of the genus *Mentha,* characteristically having aromatic foliage and spiked flowers. Many species are cultivated for their leaves, used for flavouring. See **peppermint, spearmint. 2.** Any of various similar or related plants. **3.** A sweet flavoured with mint. [Middle English *minte,* Old English *minte,* from West Germanic *minta* (unattested), from Latin *menta, mentha,* from Greek *minthē,* of Mediterranean origin.] **—mint·y** *adj.*

mint·age (míntij) *n.* **1.** The act or process of minting coins. **2.** Money manufactured in a mint. **3.** The fee paid to a mint by the government. **4.** The impression stamped on a coin.

mint jelly *n.* A clear green jelly, usually made with apples or crab apples, chopped mint, and green vegetable colouring.

mint julep *n.* A tall, frosted drink, popular in the United States, made of bourbon, sugar, crushed mint leaves, and shaved ice.

Min·toff (míntof), **Dom(inic)** (1916–). Maltese prime minister (1955–8 and 1971–). He helped to reorganise the Maltese Labour Party 1944 and was elected to the legislative assembly in 1947.

mint sauce *n.* A sauce, traditionally served with roast lamb, made of chopped mint leaves with vinegar and sugar.

min·u·end (mínnew-end) *n.* The quantity or number from which another, the subtrahend, is to be subtracted. [Latin *minuendum*, something to be diminished, neuter gerundive of *minuere*, to lessen.]

min·u·et (mínnew-ét) *n.* 1. A slow, stately, pattern dance for groups of couples, that originated in 17th-century France. 2. A piece of music for or in the rhythm of this dance, in ³/₄ time. [French, from obsolete *menuet*, dainty, small, from Old French *menu*, small, from Latin *minūtus*, small, MINUTE.]

mi·nus (mínəss) *prep.* 1. *Mathematics.* Reduced by the subtraction of; less: *Seven minus four equals three.* 2. *Informal.* Lacking; deprived of; without.
~*adj.* 1. Negative or on the negative part of a scale: *a minus value; minus five degrees.* 2. Designating one subdivision of a grade less than; slightly less than: *a mark of B minus.* 3. Of, pertaining to, or involving a loss, deficiency, or disadvantage: *a minus consideration.* 4. Having a negative electric charge.
~*n.* 1. A minus sign (–). 2. A negative quantity. 3. A loss, deficiency, or disadvantage. 4. A negative electric charge. [Middle English *mynus*, from Latin *minus*, less, from *minor*, less, minor.]

min·us·cule (mínnə-skewl ‖ mín-yə-, mi-núss-, mī-) *n.* 1. A small, cursive script developed from uncial between the seventh and ninth centuries A.D. and used in medieval manuscripts. 2. A letter written in this script. 3. A lower-case letter. Compare **majuscule**.
~*adj.* 1. **a.** Of, pertaining to, or written in minuscule. **b.** Of, pertaining to, or written in lower-case letters. 2. Lower-case. Said of letters of the alphabet. 3. Very small; tiny; minute. —See Synonyms at **small.** [French, from Latin *minuscula (littera)*, minuscule (letter), from *minusculus*, diminutive of *minor* (stem *minus-*), less, minor.] —**mi·nus·cu·lar** (mi-núskew-lər) *adj.*

minus sign *n. Mathematics.* The symbol (–) as in 4–2=2. It is used to indicate subtraction or a negative quantity. Also called "minus". Compare **plus sign.**

min·ute¹ (mínnit) *n.* 1. *Abbr.* **min** *Symbol* **'** **a.** A unit or period of time equal to one-sixtieth of an hour; or to 60 seconds. **b.** A unit of angular measurement equal to one-sixtieth of a degree, or to 60 seconds. Also called "minute of arc". 2. Any short interval of time; a moment. 3. A specific point in time. 4. *Informal.* A distance that can be covered in a minute: *ten minutes from here.* 5. A note or summary covering points to be remembered; a memorandum. 6. *Plural.* An official record of proceedings at the meeting of an organisation. —See Synonyms at **moment.**
~*tr.v.* **minuted, -uting, -utes.** 1. To record (a meeting, for example) exactly, as it proceeds. 2. To record in a memorandum or other notation. 3. To send a minute to (a person). 4. To record in the minutes of a meeting. [Middle English, from Old French, from Medieval Latin *minūta*, minute, small note, from Late Latin, from *minūtus*, small, MINUTE.]

mi·nute² (mī-néwt ‖ mi-, -nóot) *adj.* 1. Exceptionally small; tiny: *minute spores carried by the wind.* 2. Beneath notice; insignificant; trifling. 3. Characterised by careful scrutiny and close examination: *her minute and accurate researches.* —See Synonyms at **small.** [Latin *minūtus*, small, from the past participle of *minuere*, to lessen.] —**mi·nute·ness** *n.*

minute hand (mínnit) *n.* The long hand on a clock or watch that indicates the minutes.

min·ute·ly¹ (mínnitli) *adj.* At intervals of one minute.
~*adv.* Every minute.

mi·nute·ly² (mī-néwt-li ‖ mi-, -nóot-) *adv.* 1. With attention to minutiae. 2. On a very small scale.

min·ute·man (mínnit-man) *n., pl.* **-men** (-men). *Sometimes Capital* M. 1. An American militiaman or armed civilian pledged during the War of American Independence to be ready to fight at a minute's notice. 2. *U.S.* Any militiaman or civilian keen to take up arms. 3. A U.S. intercontinental ballistic missile.

minute mark *n.* The symbol **'** used to indicate the measurement minutes of arc and also the measurement feet.

minute of arc *n.* A minute (unit of angular measurement).

minute steak *n.* A small, thin steak that can be cooked quickly.

mi·nu·ti·a (mī-néw-shi-ə, mi-, -nóo-, -shə) *n., pl.* **-tiae** (-shi-ee). A small, exact, or trivial detail: *pedantic minutiae.* [Latin *minūtia*, smallness, from *minūtus*, small, MINUTE.]

minx (mingks) *n., pl.* **minxes.** 1. A pert, impudent, or flirtatious woman or girl. 2. *Archaic.* A prostitute or promiscuous woman. [16th century : origin obscure.]

min·yan (mín-yən, min-ya'an) *n., pl.* **-yans** or **minyanim** (-im). The quorum of ten male Jews aged 13 or older required according to orthodox Jewish law before a religious service can take place. [Hebrew, "number".]

Mi·o·cene (mí-ə-seen, -ō-) *adj. Geology.* Of, belonging to, or characteristic of the geological time and rock series of the fourth epoch of the Tertiary period, characterised by the appearance of primitive apes, whales, and grazing animals.
~*n. Geology.* 1. The Miocene epoch. Preceded by *the.* 2. The deposits of this epoch. [Greek *meiōn*, less + -CENE.]

mi·o·sis, my·o·sis (mī-ō-siss) *n., pl.* **-ses** (-seez). *Pathology.* An ex-cessive contraction of the pupil of the eye, often due to the action of drugs. [New Latin : Greek *muein*, to close the eyes + -OSIS.]

mi·ot·ic (mī-óttik) *adj.* An agent that causes contraction of the pupil of the eye. [From MIOSIS.] —**mi·ot·ic** *adj.*

Miquelon Island. See **St. Pierre and Miquelon Islands.**

mir (meer) *n.* A prerevolutionary Russian peasant commune. [Russian, commune, peace, world, from Old Church Slavonic *miru*, joy, peace.]

Mi·ra·beau (mírrə-bō, *French* mee-raa-bō), **Honoré Gabriel Riquetti, Comte de** (1749–91). French revolutionary leader. In 1789, he was a delegate to the States-General, where his oratory made him spokesman for the Third Estate. His policy of a constitutional monarchy weakened his influence and in 1790 he entered into secret negotiations with the court.

mi·ra·bi·le dic·tu (mi-ráabi-li dík-tew, -lay, -tōō). *Latin.* Wonderful to relate.

mi·ra·cid·i·um (mír-ə-síddi-əm) *n., pl.* **-ia** (-ə). A ciliated larva of a parasitic fluke in the form in which it hatches from the egg. [New Latin, from Late Latin *miracidion*, diminutive of Greek *meirax* (stem *meirac-*), offspring.]

mir·a·cle (mírrək'l) *n.* 1. An event that appears unexplainable by the laws of nature and so is held to be supernatural in origin or an act of God. 2. Broadly, any event that seems exceptionally fortunate: *It was a miracle she escaped unhurt.* 3. A person, thing, or event that excites admiring awe. 4. A miracle play. [Middle English, from Old French, from Latin *mīrāculum*, from *mīrārī*, to wonder at, from *mīrus*, wonderful.]

miracle play *n.* A form of religious drama of the Middle Ages in which scenes and events of the Bible or the lives of saints and martyrs were represented. Compare **mystery play.**

mi·rac·u·lous (mi-ráckew-ləss) *adj.* 1. Of the nature of a miracle. 2. Caused by or as if by a miracle: *a miraculous cure.* 3. Having the power to work miracles. [French *miraculeux*, from Medieval Latin *mīrāculōsus*, from Latin *mīrāculum*, MIRACLE.] —**mi·rac·u·lous·ly** *adv.* —**mi·rac·u·lous·ness** *n.*

mir·a·dor (mírrə-dawr, -dór) *n.* A balcony, window, or turret affording a wide view. [Spanish, from *mirar*, to look.]

mi·rage (mírraazh ‖ *chiefly U.S.* mi-raázh) *n.* 1. An optical phenomenon in which an image, often inverted, is produced as a result of refraction of light by layers of air with differing densities. The commonest form involves an image of the sky, producing the illusion of water. 2. Something that is illusory or insubstantial like a mirage. [French, from *mirer*, to look at, from Latin *mīrārī*, to wonder at, from *mīrus*, wonder.]

MIRAS. mortgage interest relief at source.

mire (mīr) *n.* 1. An area of wet, soggy, and muddy ground; a bog. 2. Deep, slimy soil or mud. 3. A difficult or unpleasant position.
~*v.* **mired, miring, mires.** —*tr.* 1. To cause to sink or become stuck in mire. 2. To soil with mud. 3. To trap or entangle as if in mire. —*intr.* To sink or become stuck in mire. [Middle English, from Old Norse *mȳrr*, a bog, from Germanic; akin to MOSS.] —**mir·i·ness** *n.* —**mir·y** *adj.*

mire·poix (meer-pwaá) *n.* A mixture of finely diced vegetables fried in butter, sometimes used as a base for brown sauces and stews. [French, probably in honour of C.P.G.F. de Lévis, Duc de *Mirepoix*, 18th-century French general.]

Mir·i·am (mírri-əm). The sister of Moses. Exodus 15:20.

mirk. Variant of **murk.**

mirky. Variant of **murky.**

Mi·ró (mi-rō), **Joan** (1893–). Spanish surrealist painter, born in Catalonia. His style is distinguished by naïve, free-floating forms. He painted a mural at Harvard University and made the ceramic decorations for the UNESCO headquarters in Paris. He has donated much of his work to the Joan Miró museum of contemporary art in Barcelona.

mir·ror (mírrər) *n.* 1. Any surface capable of reflecting sufficient undiffused light to form an image of an object placed in front of it; especially, one of coated glass or polished metal, often mounted in a frame. 2. Anything that faithfully reflects or gives a true picture of something else: *a mirror of society.* 3. A **speculum** (see) on a bird's wing.
~*tr.v.* **mirrored, -roring, -rors.** To reflect in or as if in a mirror: *mirroring contemporary problems.* [Middle English *mirour*, from Old French *miroir, mirour*, from *mirer*, to look at, from Latin *mīrārī*, to wonder at, from *mīrus*, wonderful.]

mirror carp *n.* A variety of the common carp that has a smooth, shiny body.

mirror image *n.* 1. An image in or as if in a mirror, showing left and right reversed but otherwise identical to the original. 2. Something that has the same constituent parts as something else, but has them in reverse order or with inverted values: *Is fascism the mirror image of communism?*

mirror plane *n.* A plane that divides an object or system into two halves that are mirror images of each other.

mirror symmetry *n.* Symmetry such that one half of an object or system is identical to the mirror image of the other half.

mirror twins *pl.n.* Twins whose bodies, including internal organs, are mirror images of each other, such that the heart of one, for example, is located on the right-hand side.

mirror writing *n.* Writing in which both letters and words are reversed, that appears as normal when seen reflected in a mirror.

mirth (murth) *n.* Merriment, gaiety, or enjoyment, especially when

minstrel *Strolling players portrayed in a 15th-century Flemish* Book of Hours.

expressed in laughter. [Middle English *mirthe,* Old English *myrgth.* See **merry, -th.**] **—mirth·ful** *adj.* **—mirth·less** *adj.*

Synonyms: *mirth, merriment, hilarity, glee.*

MIRV (murv) *n.* An offensive ballistic-missile system in which a number of warheads aimed at independent targets can be launched by a single booster rocket. [*M*ultiple *I*ndependently targeted *R*e-entry *V*ehicles.]

mir·za (múrzə, meer-zaá) *n.* In Iran, a respectful title used: **1.** After the name of a prince. **2.** Before the name of a hero, scholar, or high official. [Persian *mīrzā,* short for *mīrzād,* "son of a lord" : *mīr,* prince, from Arabic, *amīr,* prince, EMIR + *zād,* born, from *zādan,* to be born.]

mis-[1] *prefix.* Indicates: **1.** Error or wrongness; for example, **misspell. 2.** Badness or impropriety; for example, **misbehave, misdeed. 3.** Unsuitableness; for example, **misalliance. 4.** Opposite or lack of; for example, **mistrust. 5.** Failure; for example, **misfire.** [There are two separate developments of *mis-* that became confused in Modern English: 1. Middle English *mis-,* wrong, Old English *mis-,* from Germanic *missa-* (unattested), amiss, divergent, mutual. 2. Middle English *mes-,* bad, wrong, from Old French, from Vulgar Latin *minus-* (unattested), from Latin *minus,* MINUS.]

mis-[2] Variant of **miso-.**

mis·ad·ven·ture (míss-əd-vénchər || -ad-) *n.* **1.** An instance of great misfortune; a disaster. **2.** *Law.* Death as a result of an accident, rather than negligence or crime. —See Synonyms at **misfortune.** [Middle English *misaventure,* from Old French *mesaventure,* from *mesavenir,* to result in misfortune : *mes-,* badly, MIS- + *avenir,* to turn out, from Latin *advenīre,* to come to : *ad,* to + *venīre,* to come.]

mis·ad·vise (míss-əd-vī́z || -ad-) *tr.v.* **-vised, -vising, -vises.** To advise wrongly.

mis·al·li·ance (míssə-lī́-ənss) *n.* An unsuitable alliance, especially in marriage. [French *mésalliance* : *més-,* improper, MIS- + ALLIANCE.]

mis·al·ly (míssə-lī́) *tr.v.* **-lied, -lying, -lies.** To ally or unite badly.

mis·an·dry (mi-sándri, -zándri) *n.* Hatred of or hostility towards men; man-hating. [MIS(O) + *-andry,* from Greek *anēr* (stem *andr-*); man.] **—mis·andr·ist** *n.* & *adj.*

mis·an·thrope (míss'n-thrōp, mízz'n-) *n.* Also **mis·an·thro·pist** (miss-ánthrəpist, miz-). A person who hates or distrusts humankind. [Greek *misanthrōpos,* hating humankind : MISO- + *anthrōpos,* human.] **—mis·an·throp·ic** (-thróppik) *adj.* **—mis·an·throp·i·cal·ly** *adv.* **—mis·an·thro·py** (miss-ánthrəpi, miz-) *n.*

mis·ap·ply (míssə-plī́) *tr.v.* **-plied, -plying, -plies. 1.** To apply wrongly. **2.** To make wrong use of; especially, to misappropriate (funds). **—mis·ap·pli·ca·tion** (míss-áppli-káysh'n) *n.*

mis·ap·pre·hend (míss-áppri-hénd) *tr.v.* **-hended, -hending, -hends.** To fail to interpret correctly; misunderstand. **—mis·ap·pre·hen·sion** (-hénsh'n) *n.*

mis·ap·pro·pri·ate (míssə-prṓpri-ayt) *tr.v.* **-ated, -ating, -ates. 1.** To appropriate (money, funds, or the like) wrongly or dishonestly, especially for one's own use. **2.** To use illegally or wrongly.

mis·be·come (míss-bi-kúm, -bə-) *tr.v.* **-came** (-káym), **-come, -coming, -comes.** To be unsuitable or inappropriate for: *"what I have done that misbecame my place"* (Shakespeare).

mis·be·got·ten (míss-bi-gótt'n, -bə-) *adj.* Also **mis·be·got** (-gót). Begotten in an illegal or disreputable way; especially, illegitimate.

mis·be·have (míss-bi-háyv, -bə-) *v.* **-haved, -having, -haves.** *—intr.* To behave badly. *—tr.* To conduct (oneself) badly.

mis·be·lief (míss-bi-léef, -bə-) *n.* **1.** A wrong or faulty belief; an erroneous opinion. **2.** A heretical or unorthodox religious belief.

mis·be·lieve (míss-bi-léev, -bə-) *intr.v.* **-lieved, -lieving, -lieves.** *Obsolete.* To believe wrongly; hold a false or erroneous opinion.

misc. miscellaneous.

mis·cal·cu·late (míss-kálkew-layt) *v.* **-lated, -lating, -lates.** *—tr.* To calculate wrongly; make a wrong estimate of. *—intr.* To make an error in calculation or judgment. **—mis·cal·cu·la·tion** (-láysh'n) *n.*

mis·call (míss-káwl) *tr.v.* **-called, -calling, -calls. 1.** To call by a wrong or inappropriate name. **2.** *Regional.* To call by a bad name; revile.

mis·car·riage (míss-kárrij, *for sense 2* míss-karrij) *n.* **1. a.** Mismanagement; bad administration: *a miscarriage of justice.* **b.** Failure to attain the right or desired end: *the miscarriage of a hope; a miscarriage of a cargo.* **2.** Premature expulsion of a nonviable foetus from the uterus. In this sense, also called "spontaneous abortion".

mis·car·ry (míss-kárri) *intr.v.* **-ried, -rying, -ries. 1.** To go astray; be lost in transit: *the freight miscarried.* **2.** To go wrong; fail: *a good idea that miscarried.* **3.** To bring forth a foetus prematurely so that it does not survive; abort.

mis·cast (míss-kaást || -kást) *tr.v.* **-cast, -casting, -casts. 1.** To cast in an unsuitable role. **2.** To cast (a role or a theatrical production) inappropriately.

mis·ce·ge·na·tion (míssiji-náysh'n || mi-séji-) *n.* Intermarriage or interbreeding between different races; especially, marriage between white and nonwhite persons. [Latin *miscēre,* to mix + *genus,* race.] **—mis·ce·ge·net·ic** (-néttik) *adj.*

mis·cel·la·ne·a (míssə-láyni-ə) *pl.n.* A conglomeration of various items; especially, a collection of diverse literary works. [Latin *miscellānea,* from the neuter plural of *miscellāneus,* MISCELLANEOUS.]

mis·cel·la·ne·ous (míssə-láyn-i-əss, -yəss) *adj. Abbr.* **misc. 1.** Made up of a variety of parts or ingredients: *a miscellaneous collection.* **2.** Having a variety of characteristics, abilities, or appearances: *miscellaneous opinions.* **3.** Concerned with diverse subjects or aspects: *"various miscellaneous objections . . . against my views"* (Charles Darwin). [Latin *miscellāneus,* from *miscellus,* mixed, from *miscēre,* to mix.] **—mis·cel·la·ne·ous·ly** *adv.* **—mis·cel·la·ne·ous·ness** *n.*

Synonyms: *miscellaneous, heterogeneous, motley, mixed, varied, assorted.*

mis·cel·la·nist (mi-séllənist || *U.S.* míssə-laynist) *n.* One who compiles or edits a miscellany; a writer of miscellanies.

mis·cel·la·ny (mi-sélləni, *rarely* miss'l-əni || *U.S.* miss'l-ayni) *n., pl.* **-nies. 1.** A collection of various items, parts, or ingredients, especially one composed of diverse literary works. **2.** *Often plural.* A book or other publication containing writings of differing types or on different subjects. [Latin *miscellānea,* MISCELLANEA.]

mis·chance (míss-chaánss, -chaanss || -chánss, -chanss) *n.* **1.** An unfortunate occurrence; an unlucky incident. **2.** Bad luck. —See Synonyms at **misfortune.** [Middle English *mischaunce,* from Old French *mescheaunce* : *mes-,* ill, MIS- + *cheaunce,* CHANCE.]

mis·chief (míss-chif || -cheef) *n.* **1.** An act or behaviour that causes discomfiture or annoyance in another: *She's up to some mischief or other again.* **2.** An inclination or tendency to play pranks or cause embarrassment: *full of mischief.* **3.** One that causes minor trouble or a disturbance: *The child was a mischief in school.* **4.** Damage, destruction, or injury caused by a specified person or thing: *Wind wreaked untold mischief upon the crops.* [Middle English *meschief,* from Old French *meschief, meschef,* from *meschever,* to meet with misfortune : *mes-,* amiss, ill, MIS- + *chever,* to "come to a head", happen, from Common Romance *capāre* (unattested), from Latin *caput,* head.]

mis·chie·vous (míss-chivəss || -chéevəss) *adj.* **1.** Causing mischief. **2.** Playfully naughty; teasing: *a mischievous smile.* **3.** Troublesome; irritating: *a mischievous prank.* **4.** Causing harm, injury, or damage: *mischievous lies.* —See Synonyms at **playful.** [MISCHIEF + -OUS.] **—mis·chie·vous·ly** *adv.* **—mis·chie·vous·ness** *n.*

misch metal (mish) *n.* An alloy of cerium and several rare-earth elements. It produces sparks when struck and is used in lighter flints. [Partial translation of German *Mischmetall,* from *mischen,* to mix.]

mis·ci·ble (míssi-b'l) *adj. Chemistry.* Capable of being mixed in all proportions. Said especially of liquids. [Medieval Latin *miscībilis,* from Latin *miscēre,* to mix.] **—mis·ci·bil·i·ty** (-bílləti) *n.*

mis·con·ceive (míss-kən-séev || -kon-) *tr.v.* **-ceived, -ceiving, -ceives.** To interpret in the wrong way; misunderstand. **—mis·con·ceiv·er** *n.*

mis·con·ceived (míss-kən-séevd || -kon-) *adj.* Based on a false understanding; badly thought out.

mis·con·cep·tion (míss-kən-sépsh'n || -kon-) *n.* An incorrect interpretation or understanding; a delusion.

mis·con·duct (míss-kón-dukt, -dəkt) *n.* **1.** Behaviour not conforming to prevailing standards or laws; impropriety; immorality: *professional misconduct.* **2.** Dishonest or bad management, especially by persons entrusted to act on another's behalf; malfeasance.

~tr.v. (míss-kən-dúkt || -kon-) **misconducted, -ducting, -ducts. 1.** To behave (oneself) improperly. **2.** To administer or manage poorly or dishonestly.

mis·con·struc·tion (míss-kən-strúksh'n || -kon-) *n.* **1.** An inaccurate explanation, interpretation, or report; a misunderstanding. **2.** A faulty construction, especially of a sentence or clause.

mis·con·strue (míss-kən-stróo || -kon-, -stréw) *tr.v.* **-strued, -struing, -strues.** To mistake the meaning of; misinterpret; misunderstand.

mis·count (míss-kównt || *West Indies also* -kúngt) *v.* **-counted, -counting, -counts.** *—tr.* To count or estimate incorrectly; miscalculate. *—intr.* To err in counting.

~n. (míss-kownt || -kungt). An inaccurate count.

mis·cre·ant (mískri-ənt) *n.* **1.** An evildoer or villain. **2.** *Archaic.* An infidel or heretic. [Middle English *miscreaunt,* heretical, unbelieving, from Old French *mescreant,* present participle of *mescroire,* to disbelieve : *mes-,* MIS- + *croire,* to believe, from Latin *crēdere.*] **—mis·cre·ant** *adj.*

mis·cre·ate (míss-kri-áyt) *tr.v.* **-ated, -ating, -ates.** To make or shape badly.

~adj. (-ayt, -ət, -it). *Rare.* Formed unnaturally; deformed. **—mis·cre·a·tion** (-áysh'n) *n.*

mis·cue (míss-kéw) *n.* **1.** In billiards, a stroke that misses or just brushes the ball due to a slip of the cue. **2.** A blunder or mistake.

~intr.v. **miscued, -cuing, -cues. 1.** To make a miscue. **2.** In acting, to miss one's own cue or mistake someone else's cue for one's own.

mis·date (míss-dáyt) *tr.v.* **-dated, -dating, -dates.** To date wrongly or incorrectly.

mis·deal (míss-déel) *v.* **-dealt** (-délt), **-dealing, -deals.** *—tr.* To deal (playing cards) in the wrong order or incorrectly. *—intr.* To deal cards incorrectly. **—mis·deal** *n.* **—mis·deal·er** *n.*

mis·deed (míss-déed, -deed) *n.* A wicked, immoral, or illegal deed.

mis·de·mean·ant (míss-di-méenənt) *n.* One who is guilty of, or has been convicted and sentenced for, a misdemeanour.

mis·de·mean·our, *U.S.* **mis·de·mean·or** (míss-di-méenər) *n.* **1.** A wrong action; a misdeed. **2.** *Law.* Formerly in Britain, an offence of lesser gravity than a felony. Compare **crime, felony.**

mis·di·ag·nose (míss-dī́-əg-nṓz, -nōss) *tr.v.* **-nosed, -nosing, -noses.** To diagnose incorrectly. **—mis·di·ag·no·sis** *n.*

mis·di·al (míss-dī́-əl, -dī́l) *tr.v.* **-dialled** or *U.S.* **-dialed, -dialling** or *U.S.* **-dialing, -dials.** To dial (a telephone number) incorrectly.

mis·di·rect (míss-di-rékt, -də-, -dīr-) *tr.v.* **-rected, -recting, -rects. 1.** To instruct incorrectly: *The judge misdirected the jury.* **2. a.** To put a wrong address on. **b.** To give incorrect directions to (someone seeking a location or address). **3.** To direct (energy or an emotion) mistakenly or misguidedly. **—mis·di·rec·tion** (-rék·sh'n) *n.*

mis·do (míss-dōō) *v.* **-did** (-díd), **-done** (-dún), **-doing, -does** (-dúz). **—***tr.* To do wrongly or awkwardly; botch. **—***intr. Obsolete.* To do wrong or harm. **—mis·do·er** *n.*

mis·doubt (míss-dówt) *v.* **-doubted, -doubting, -doubts.** *Archaic.* **—***tr.* To suspect; fear; feel wary of. **—***intr.* To have doubts or be fearful.

mis·em·ploy (míss-im-plóy || -em-) *tr.v.* **-ployed, -ploying, -ploys.** To put to a wrong use; abuse. **—mis·em·ploy·ment** *n.*

mise en scène (méez-on-sáyn, -ON-, -sén) *n.* **1. a.** The properties, scenery, and the like, used to stage a play or a scene in a play. **b.** The arrangement of the performers and of such properties. **2.** An environment; surroundings. [French, "placing on stage".]

mi·ser (mízər) *n.* **1.** One who deprives himself of all but the barest essentials in order to hoard money. **2.** A greedy, stingy, or avaricious person. [Originally, "wretch", from Latin *miser*, wretched.]

mis·er·a·ble (míz-rəb'l, mízzə- || mízh-) *adj.* **1.** Very unhappy; wretched. **2.** Causing or accompanied by wretchedness or other discomfort: *a miserable climate.* **3.** Gloomy; dismal: *a miserable film.* **4.** Unworthy; contemptible: *a miserable fellow.* **—See Synonyms at sad.** [Middle English, from Old French *miserable*, from Latin *miserābilis*, pitiable, from *miserārī*, to have pity, from *miser*, wretched, unfortunate.] **—mis·er·a·ble·ness** *n.* **—mis·er·a·bly** *adv.*

mi·sère (mi-záir) *n.* In some card games, such as solo whist, an undertaking that a hand will win no tricks. [French, poverty.]

mis·e·re·re (mízzə-ráir-i, -réer-i) *n.* **1.** Part of a church seat, a misericord. **2.** A prayer for mercy. [From MISERERE.]

Mis·e·re·re (mízzə-ráir-i, -réer-i) *n.* **1.** The 51st Psalm, which opens with *"Miserere mei Deus"* (Have mercy upon me, O God). **2.** A musical setting of this Psalm. [Latin, imperative of *miserērī*, to have pity, from *miser*, wretched.]

mis·er·i·cord, mis·er·i·corde (mi-zérri-kawrd, *rarely* mízzəri- || U.S. *also* -sérri-) *n.* **1.** In a monastery: **a.** The relaxation of a rule, such as a dispensation from fasting. **b.** A room used by monks granted such a dispensation. **2.** A bracket, sometimes in the form of a carved figure, attached to the underside of a hinged seat in a church stall, against which a standing person may lean. Also called "miserere". **4.** A narrow dagger used in medieval times to deliver the death stroke to one who was seriously wounded, especially a knight. [Middle English, pity, mercy, dagger, from Old French, from Latin *misericordia*, from *misericors*, pitiful : *miserērī*, to have pity + *cors* (stem *cord*-), heart.]

mis·er·ly (mízərli) *adj.* Characteristic of a miser; tending to hoard money or possessions; extremely mean: *too miserly to leave a tip.* See Synonyms at **stingy. —mis·er·li·ness** *n.*

mis·er·y (mízzəri) *n., pl.* **-ies. 1.** Prolonged or extreme suffering; a state of great mental, emotional, or physical pain; wretchedness. **2.** A cause or source of suffering or pain, such as an affliction or deprivation. **3.** *British Informal.* One who is constantly depressed or gloomy. [Middle English *miserie*, from Anglo-French, from Latin *miseria*, from *miser*, wretched.]

mis·es·teem (míss-i-stéem, -e-) *tr.v.* **-teemed, -teeming, -teems.** *Formal.* To fail to regard with deserved esteem; disrespect.

mis·es·ti·mate (míss-ésti-mayt) *tr.v.* **-mated, -mating, -mates.** To estimate or appraise inaccurately or wrongly. **~***n.* (-mət, -mit || -mayt). An inaccurate estimate or appraisal.

mis·fea·sance (miss-féez'nss) *n. Law. Rare.* The improper and unlawful execution of some act that in itself is lawful and proper. Compare **malfeasance, nonfeasance.** [Old French *mesfaisance*, from *mesfaire*, to misdo : *mes-*, wrongly, MIS- + *faire*, to do, from Latin *facere*.]

mis·fea·sor (miss-féezər) *n. Law.* One guilty of misfeasance.

mis·fire (miss-fír) *intr.v.* **-fired, -firing, -fires. 1.** To fail to explode or ignite when expected, as a gun or internal-combustion engine may. **2.** To fail to achieve the anticipated result: *a scheme that misfired.* **—mis·fire** (-fír) *n.*

mis·fit (míss-fit, *rarely* -fít) *n.* **1.** Something of the wrong size or shape for its purpose. **2.** A person who is maladjusted or finds it difficult to fit in with people or the immediate environment. **~***v.* (-fit) misfitted, -fitting, -fits. *Rare.* **—***tr.* To fit poorly. **—***intr.* To be of the wrong size or shape.

mis·for·tune (miss-fór-chən, miss-, -chōon, -tewn) *n.* **1.** Bad fortune or ill luck. **2.** An instance of this; a distressing occurrence.
Synonyms: misfortune, adversity, mishap, mischance, misadventure.

mis·give (miss-gív) *v.* **-gave** (-gáyv), **-given** (-gívv'n), **-giving, -gives.** **—***tr.* To arouse suspicion or apprehension in. **—***intr.* To be suspicious, apprehensive, or doubtful. [Originally, to suggest doubt (used of the mind) : MIS- (wrongly) + GIVE (in the Middle English sense "to suggest").]

mis·giv·ing (miss-gívving) *n. Often plural.* A feeling of uncertainty or apprehension: *approached the empty house with some misgivings.* See Synonyms at **apprehension, qualm.**

mis·gov·ern (míss-gúvvərn) *tr.v.* **-erned, -erning, -erns.** To govern or administrate inefficiently or badly. **—mis·gov·ern·ment** *n.* **—mis·gov·er·nor** *n.*

mis·guide (miss-gíd) *tr.v.* **-guided, -guiding, -guides.** To give wrong or misleading directions to; lead astray; misdirect. **—mis·guid·ance** *n.* **—mis·guid·er** *n.*

mis·guid·ed (míss-gídid) *adj.* Confused or erring in thought or action; foolish: *a misguided comment.* **—mis·guid·ed·ly** *adv.*

mis·han·dle (miss-hánd'l) *tr.v.* **-dled, -dling, -dles.** To treat or deal with clumsily or inefficiently.

mis·hap (míss-hap, *rarely* -háp) *n.* **1.** Bad luck or misfortune. **2.** An unfortunate accident.

mis·hear (miss-héer) *tr.v.* **-heard** (-hérd), **-hearing, -hears.** To hear wrongly or badly.

Mi·shi·ma (míshimə), **Yukio,** born Kimitake Hiraoka (1925–70). Japanese writer and one of a samurai family. His stories are often evocations of the imperial past. His novels include *Confessions of a Mask* (1949) and *The Sailor who Fell from Grace with the Sea* (1963).

mis·hit (míss-hit) *n.* In certain games, such as tennis or squash, a faulty or bad hit: *mishits that came off the handle and not the strings.* **~***tr.v.* (-hít) **mishit, -hitting, -hits.** To hit (a ball) faultily or badly.

mish·mash (mísh-mash || U.S. *also* -mosh) *n.* A collection or mixture of unrelated things; a hotchpotch. [Reduplication of MASH.]

Mish·nah, Mish·na (mísh-nə, -náa) *n., pl.* **Mish·na·yoth** (-náa-yōt, -nə-yōth). **1.** The first section of the Talmud, consisting of a collection of early oral interpretations of the scriptures as compiled about A.D. 200. **2.** A paragraph from this collection. [Rabbinical Hebrew *mishnāh*, repetition, instruction, from *shānāh*, to repeat.] **—Mish·na·ic** (-náy-ik), **Mish·nic** (mísh-nik), **Mish·ni·cal** *adj.*

mis·in·form (miss-in-fórm) *tr.v.* **-formed, -forming, -forms.** To give wrong or inaccurate information to. **—mis·in·form·ant** (-ənt), **mis·in·form·er** *n.* **—mis·in·for·ma·tion** (-fər-máysh'n) *n.*

mis·in·ter·pret (míss-in-térprit) *tr.v.* **-preted, -preting, -prets. 1.** To infer inaccurately. **2.** To err in understanding. **—mis·in·ter·pre·ta·tion** (-térpri-táysh'n) *n.* **—mis·in·ter·pret·er** *n.*

mis·join·der (miss-jóyndər, míss-) *n. Law.* Improper joining of different causes of action or different parties in a suit. Compare **nonjoinder.**

mis·judge (míss-júj) *v.* **-judged, -judging, -judges.** **—***tr.* To make a mistake in one's judgment of. **—***intr.* To be wrong in judging. **—mis·judg·ment** *n.*

Miskito. Variant of **Mosquito.**

mis·lay (míss-láy) *tr.v.* **-laid** (-láyd), **-laying, -lays. 1.** To put in a place that is afterwards forgotten; lose. **2.** *Rare.* To place or put down incorrectly: *mislay linoleum.* **—mis·lay·er** *n.*

mis·lead (míss-léed) *tr.v.* **-led** (-léd), **-leading, -leads. 1.** To lead or guide in the wrong direction. **2.** To lead into error or wrongdoing, whether by accident or design. **—See Synonyms at deceive.**

mis·lead·ing (míss-léeding, miss-) *adj.* Tending to mislead; deceptive. **—mis·lead·ing·ly** *adv.*

mis·like (miss-lík) *tr.v.* **-liked, -liking, -likes. 1.** To disapprove of; dislike. **2.** *Archaic.* To be displeasing to. **~***n. Rare.* Dislike; disapproval. [Middle English *misliken*, Old English *mislīcian* : *mis-*, ill + *līcian*, to LIKE.]

mis·man·age (míss-mánnij) *tr.v.* **-aged, -aging, -ages.** To manage badly or carelessly. **—mis·man·age·ment** *n.*

mis·match (míss-mách) *tr.v.* **-matched, -matching, -matches.** To match unsuitably or inaccurately, especially in marriage. **—mis·match** (míss-mach) *n.*

mis·mate (míss-máyt) *tr.v.* **-mated, -mating, -mates.** *Literary.* To mate or match unsuitably: *Fate mismated them.*

mis·name (míss-náym) *tr.v.* **-named, -naming, -names.** To call by a wrong or inappropriate name.

mis·no·mer (míss-nómər) *n.* **1.** An error in naming a person or place. **2.** A name wrongly or unsuitably applied to a person or object. [Middle English, from Anglo-French, from Old French *mesnommer*, to misname : *mes-*, wrongly, MIS- + *nommer*, to name, from Latin *nōmināre*, from *nōmen*, name.]

miso–, mis– *comb. form.* Indicates hating, hatred, or hostility; for example, **misogyny, misandry.** [Greek, from *misein*, to hate, and *misos†*, hatred.]

mi·sog·a·my (mī-sóggəmi, mi-) *n.* Hatred of marriage. [MISO- + -GAMY.] **—mi·sog·a·mist** (-sóggəmist) *n. & adj.*

mi·sog·y·ny (mi-sójəni, mī-) *n.* Hatred of or hostility towards women. [Greek *misogunia* : MISO- + -GYNY.] **—mi·sog·y·nist** (-sójinist) *n. & adj.* **—mi·sog·y·nis·tic** (-sójinístik), **mi·sog·y·nous** (-sójinəss) *adj.*

mi·sol·o·gy (mī-sólləji, mi-) *n.* Hatred of reason, argument, or enlightenment. [Greek *misologia* : MISO- + -LOGY.] **—mi·sol·o·gist** *n.*

mis·o·ne·ism (mísō-née-iz'm, míssō-) *n.* Hatred of change or innovation. [Italian *misoneismo* : MISO- + Greek *neos*, new.] **—mis·o·ne·ist** *n. & adj.*

mis·pick·el (míss-pick'l) *n.* A mineral, **arsenopyrite** (see). [German, variant of earlier *Mispūtl, Mispilt†*.]

mis·place (míss-pláyss) *tr.v.* **-placed, -placing, -places. 1. a.** To put in a wrong place. **b.** To lose; mislay. **2.** To bestow (faith, affection, or confidence, for example) wrongly, as on an improper, unsuitable, or unworthy person or thing: *Your loyalty to that firm is quite misplaced.* **—mis·place·ment** *n.*

mis·play (míss-play) *n.* A mistaken action in a game. **~***tr.v.* (-pláy) **misplayed, -playing, -plays.** To make a misplay of.

mis·plead·ing (miss-pléeding, míss-) *n. Law.* An error in pleading.

mis·print (míss-prínt) *tr.v.* **-printed, -printing, -prints.** To print incorrectly. **~***n.* (míss-print, *rarely* -prínt). An error in printing.

mis·prise, mis·prize (míss-príz) *tr.v.* **-prised, -prising, -prises.** To undervalue; disparage.

mis·pri·sion (míss-prízh'n) *n. Law.* **1.** Maladministration of public office. **2.** Neglect in reporting a crime: *misprision of treason.* [Middle English, from Anglo-French *mesprisioun*, from *mesprendre* :

mes-, wrongly, MIS- + *prendre*, to take, from Latin *praehendere*, to grasp, seize.]

mis·pro·nounce (míss-prə-nównss || *West Indies also* -núngss) *tr.v.* **-nounced, -nouncing, -nounces.** To pronounce badly or incorrectly. **—mis·pro·nun·ci·a·tion** (-núnsi-áysh'n.) *n.*

mis·quote (míss-kwṓt) *tr.v.* **-quoted, -quoting, -quotes.** To quote incorrectly. **—mis·quo·ta·tion** (-kwō-táysh'n) *n.*

mis·read (míss-réed) *tr.v.* **-read** (-réd), **-reading, -reads. 1.** To read inaccurately. **2.** To misinterpret: *misread her intentions.*

mis·re·lat·ed participle (míss-ri-láytid, -rə-) *n. Grammar.* A participle that lacks clear connection with the word it modifies. In the sentence *Working at my desk, the sudden noise startled me,* the participle *working* is misrelated because it modifies *me,* not *noise.* Also called "dangling participle".

mis·re·mem·ber (míss-ri-mémbər, -rə-) *tr.v.* **-bered, -bering, -bers. 1.** To recollect incorrectly. **2.** *Regional.* To forget.

mis·re·port (míss-ri-pórt, -rə- || -pṓrt) *tr.v.* **-ported, -porting, -ports.** To report mistakenly or falsely.
~n. An inaccurate or wrong report. **—mis·re·port·er** *n.*

mis·rep·re·sent (míss-réppri-zént) *tr.v.* **-sented, -senting, -sents. 1.** To give an incorrect or misleading representation of: *misrepresented the facts of the case.* **2.** To serve incorrectly or dishonestly as an official representative of. **—mis·rep·re·sen·ta·tion** (-zen-táysh'n, -z'n-) *n.* **—mis·rep·re·sen·ta·tive** (-zéntətiv) *adj.* **—mis·rep·re·sent·er** *n.*

mis·rule (míss-rṓol || -réwl) *tr.v.* **-ruled, -ruling, -rules.** To rule wrongly, unjustly, or unwisely; misgovern.
~n. **1.** Misgovernment. **2.** Disorder or lawless confusion.

miss¹ (miss) *v.* **missed, missing, misses.** *—tr.* **1.** To fail to hit, reach, attain, catch, meet, or otherwise make contact with: *miss the target; missed the bus.* **2.** To fail to perceive, understand, or otherwise experience: *missed the subtlety of the argument.* **3.** To fail to accomplish or achieve: *You missed catching her by ten minutes; my heart missed a beat.* **4.** To fail to be present for or perform: *We don't want to miss a day of work.* **5. a.** To leave out or omit. Often used with *out*: *You missed out a name in typing the list.* **b.** To overlook or let go by; let slip: *miss a chance.* **6.** To escape or avoid: *missed death by inches.* **7. a.** To discover the absence or loss of: *I was halfway home before I missed my gloves.* **b.** To feel the lack or loss of; yearn for (what is past or absent): *I miss the good old days.* *—intr.* **1.** To fail to hit or otherwise make contact with something: *She fired her final shot and missed again.* **2.** To misfire. **—miss out.** *Informal.* To fail to benefit from or achieve something desirable. Often used with *on*: *She missed out on getting a promotion.*
~n. A failure to hit, succeed, or find. **—give (something) a miss.** *Informal.* To pass over something, as by not visiting or attending: *gave the party a miss.* [Middle English *missen,* Old English *missan,* from Germanic *missjan* (unattested); akin to MIS-.]

miss² *n., pl.* **misses. 1.** *Capital* **M.** A title or form of address used when speaking to or of an unmarried woman or girl: **a.** Used before her surname. **b.** Used before her first name, as formerly by servants. **2.** A title used in speaking to an unmarried woman or girl, used without her name. **3.** An unmarried woman or girl. **4.** A title or form of address used by schoolchildren when speaking of or to a schoolmistress. **5.** *Capital* **M.** A title given to a young woman representing a town, country, institution, or the like at certain events, especially beauty contests: *Miss Sweden.* **6.** *Capital* **M. a.** A title or form of address given to some women who have achieved fame or prominence in certain spheres of activity and who retain their maiden name after marriage. **b.** *Southern U.S.* A respectful title or form of address used with a first name, given to married women. [Short for MISTRESS.]

Usage: In recent years, criticism has been directed, largely from feminist sources, at the twofold titular classification of women into *Miss* and *Mrs.* — a distinction which, unlike the male *Master* and *Mr.,* is not restricted in terms of age. Since *Miss* and *Mrs.* may be seen as defining women solely in terms of their relationship to men, the use of *Ms* has been advocated as a neutral alternative, to be used for or by any woman, regardless of marital status. *Ms* has become increasingly common in written English, especially in letter-writing, where the writer is unsure of the married status of the addressee. In speech, the word has had less success, because of its uncertain pronunciation (miz, although some prefer məz), and is generally only used in a self-conscious or jocular manner.

mis·sal (míss'l) *n.* **1.** A book containing all the prayers and responses necessary for celebrating the Roman Catholic Mass throughout the year. **2.** Loosely, any prayer book. [Middle English *messel,* from Medieval Latin *missāle,* from *missālis,* pertaining to the mass, from Late Latin *missa,* MASS.]

missel thrush. Variant of **mistle thrush.**

mis·shape (míss-sháyp, mísh-) *tr.v.* **-shaped, -shaped** or **-shapen** (-sháypən), **-shaping, -shapes.** To shape badly; deform. **—mis·shap·en** *adj.*

mis·sile (míssīl || *chiefly U.S.* míss'l) *n.* **1.** Any object or weapon that is fired, thrown, dropped, or otherwise projected at a target; a projectile. **2.** A **guided missile** *(see).* **3.** A **ballistic missile** *(see).* [Latin *missilis,* from *mittere* (past participle *missus*), to let go, send.]

mis·sile·ry (míssīl-ri || míss'l-) *n.* Also **mis·sil·ry** (míss'l-). **1.** The science of making and using guided or ballistic missiles. **2.** Missiles collectively.

miss·ing (míssing) *adj.* **1.** Not present; absent; lost; lacking. **2.** *Military.* Unaccounted for after combat or manoeuvres, and possibly killed or injured.

missing link *n.* **1.** A theoretical primate postulated to bridge the evolutionary gap between the anthropoid apes and humans. **2.** Something needed to complete a series or solve a mystery.

mis·sion (mísh'n) *n.* **1. a.** A body of persons sent to a foreign country, especially to conduct negotiations or establish relations. **b.** The business with which such a body of persons is charged. **2. a.** A body of persons sent to do missionary work in a foreign land. **b.** An establishment of missionaries abroad. **c.** The district assigned to a missionary. **d.** Missionary duty or work. **e.** A missionary building or compound. **f.** An organisation for carrying on missionary work in any territory. **3.** *Chiefly U.S.* A permanent diplomatic office in a foreign country. **4. a.** A journey undertaken to perform an assigned task, such as espionage or exploration. **b.** *Military.* A combat operation assigned to an individual or unit; especially, an air operation against an enemy. **5.** A church welfare establishment, especially in a large city: *a seaman's mission.* **6.** A church or congregation, especially of a Protestant church, without a resident minister. **7.** A series of special religious services to deepen or spread religious faith. **8.** An impelling task or duty; a vocation: *a woman with a mission.*
~adj. **1.** Of or pertaining to a mission. **2.** *U.S.* In the style of early Spanish missions of the southwestern United States: *mission furniture.*
~v. **missioned, -sioning, -sions.** *—tr.* **1.** To send on a mission. **2.** To organise or establish a mission among (a people) or in (a territory). *—intr.* To conduct a religious mission. [French, from Latin *missiō* (stem *missiōn-*), from *mittere* (past participle *missus*), to let go, send.] **—mis·sion·er** *n.*

mis·sion·ar·y (mísh'n-ri, -əri, mísh-nəri || *U.S.* míshə-nerri) *n., pl.* **-ies.** One who is sent on a mission; especially, a person sent to do religious or charitable work in some territory or foreign country.
~adj. **1.** Of or pertaining to missions or missionaries. **2.** Engaged in the activities of a mission or missionary. **3.** Tending to propagandise or use insistent persuasion: *missionary fervour.*

missionary position *n.* A conventional position used in heterosexual intercourse in which the partners lie facing one another with the woman underneath. [19th-century British missionaries are supposed to have introduced this position to Polynesian natives.]

missis. Variant of **missus.**

Mis·sis·sip·pi¹ (míssi-síppi). State of the southern United States on the Gulf of Mexico, bounded by the Mississippi river in the west. All of it is below 250 metres (820 feet), with swamplands along the Mississippi river. Mississippi is the leading state in cotton production, and soya beans, rice, maize, and hay are also important. The state has vast reserves of oil and natural gas, and its manufactures include wood products, clothing, processed foods (including seafood), and chemicals. The first settlers were French (1699), and the area became part of Louisiana. It was British (1763–79), then Spanish, until ceded to the United States (1783). It was admitted to the Union in 1817. Jackson is the capital and largest city.

Mississippi². Chief river of the United States. Rising in the lake region of north Minnesota, it flows 3 780 kilometres (2,348 miles) to the Gulf of Mexico through a delta in south Louisiana. Its many tributaries include the Missouri, Ohio, Arkansas, and Red rivers. The Mississippi-Missouri, 6 212 kilometres (3,860 miles) long, is the world's third longest river after the Nile and Amazon. Its vast basin stretches into Canada and includes or touches 31 U.S. states. St. Louis, Memphis, and New Orleans are its chief ports.

Mis·sis·sip·pi·an (míssi-síppi-ən) *adj.* **1.** *Geology. U.S.* Of, belonging to, or designating the **Lower Carboniferous period** *(see).* **2.** Of or concerned with the state of Mississippi.
~n. **1.** *U.S. Geology.* The Mississippian period. Preceded by *the.* **2.** A native or inhabitant of Mississippi.

mis·sive (míssiv) *n. Formal.* A letter or message, especially a formal or official one. Sometimes used humorously.
~adj. Sent or dispatched; intended for sending: *letters missive.* [Noun, Middle English phrase *letter missive,* letter sent by superior authority, from Medieval Latin *litterae missīvae* (plural); adjective, Medieval Latin *missīvus,* from Latin *mittere* (past participle *missus*), to let go, send.]

Mis·so·lon·ghi (míssə-lóng-gi). *Greek* **Mesolóngion.** Port of west central Greece. Situated on the north shore of the Gulf of Pátrai (Patras), it withstood two sieges by the Turks during the Greek War of Independence (1822–23, 1825–26). It was the place of Lord Byron's death (1824).

Missouri¹ (mi-zṓor-i). State of the central United States, bounded in the east by the Mississippi river. Prairies lie north of the Missouri, with the Great Plains to the west, the rolling hills of the Ozark plateau in the south, and the Mississippi cotton lands to the southeast. The state produces lead, zinc, coal, iron ore, cattle, pigs, maize, soya beans, wheat, and cotton, but is a predominantly manufacturing state, with major transport equipment and food processing industries. The area was under Spanish control (1762–1800), and passed to the United States with the Louisiana Purchase (1803). The Missouri valley became a major pioneer route, St. Louis being known as the "Gateway to the Far West". Missouri became a state in 1821. Jefferson City is its capital.

Missouri². Longest river of the United States. It rises in the Rocky Mountains of Montana and flows 4 130 kilometres (2,565 miles) across the Great Plains to join the Mississippi near St. Louis. Omaha and Kansas City are on its banks. French explorers reached the river in the late 17th century.

PRONUNCIATION KEY

a, trap; aa, father; ai, fair; ar, star; aw, lawn; ay, play; b, bb, stab; rubber; ch, church; ck, ticket; d, dd, dead; ladder; e, dress; ee, bee; er, defer; ew, few; ewr, pure; ə, about; ər, letter; f, ff, fife; differ; g, gg, giggle; h, hat; i, kit; ī, price; īr, fire; j, judge; k, kick; l, ll, let; 'l, needle; m, mm, man; n, nn, no; 'n, sudden; ng, thing; o, lot; ō, no; ŏŏ, foot; ōō, shoe; oor, poor; ow, cow; owr, hour; oy, boy; p, pp, pepper; r, rr, red; s, ss, sauce; sh, ship; t, tt, totter; th, thick; th, this; smooth; u, cut; ur, turn; v, vv, valve; w, wet; y, yes; z, zz, zebra; zh, vision; pleasure

IN FOREIGN WORDS:

aN, oN, Saint-Saëns; hl, Llanelli; Hluhluwe; kh, loch; lough; Khaled

STRESS MARK:

ín-sīt, insight; in-sī́t, incite

mis·spell (miss-spél) *tr.v.* **-spelt** or **-spelled, -spelling, -spells.** To spell incorrectly. **—mis·spell·ing** *n.*
mis·spend (miss-spénd) *tr.v.* **-spent** (-spént), **-spending, -spends.** To spend improperly or extravagantly; squander.
mis·state (miss-stáyt) *tr.v.* **-stated, -stating, -states.** To state wrongly or falsely. **—mis·state·ment** *n.*
mis·step (miss-stép) *n.* **1.** A misplaced or awkward step. **2.** An instance of wrong or improper conduct.
mis·sus (missiz || missəss) *n. Informal.* **1.** The mistress of a household. Usually preceded by *the.* **2.** A wife. Usually preceded by *the.*
miss·y (míssi) *n., pl.* **-ies.** *Often capital* **M.** A familiar form of address to a young girl, especially a pert one.
mist (mist) *n.* **1.** A mass of fine droplets of water in the atmosphere, impairing visibility near the ground. Technically, visibility is 1–2 kilometres. **2.** Water vapour condensed on and clouding the appearance of a surface. **3.** Fine drops of any liquid, such as perfume, sprayed into the air. **4.** A colloidal suspension of a liquid in a gas. **5.** Something that dims or conceals sight or judgment. **6.** Something that produces or gives the impression of dimness or obscurity: *lost in the mists of time.*
~*v.* **misted, misting, mists.** —*intr.* To be or become obscured or misty; be blurred or concealed by or as if by a mist. Often used with *up.* —*tr.* To conceal or veil as if with a mist. [Middle English, Old English *mist,* from Germanic.]
mis·tak·a·ble (mi-stáykəb'l) *adj.* Capable of being mistaken or misunderstood. **—mis·tak·a·bly** *adv.*
mis·take (mi-stáyk) *n.* **1.** An error or fault. **2.** A misconception or misunderstanding.
~*v.* **mistook** (-stóok), **-taken** (-stáykən), **-taking, -takes.** —*tr.* **1.** To understand wrongly; misinterpret: *"Aziz overrated hospitality, mistaking it for intimacy"* (E.M. Forster). **2.** To recognise or identify incorrectly: *We mistook her for her sister.* **3.** To judge incorrectly: *mistook her own talent.* —*intr.* To make a mistake. [Middle English *mistaken,* from Old Norse *mistaka,* to take in error : *miss-,* wrongly + *taka,* to TAKE.]
mis·tak·en (mi-stáykən) *adj.* **1.** Wrong or incorrect in opinion, understanding, or perception. **2.** Based on error; wrong: *a mistaken view of the situation.* **—mis·tak·en·ly** *adv.* **—mis·tak·en·ness** *n.*
Mis·ter (místər) *n.* **1.** *Abbr.* **Mr.** A title or form of address used when speaking to or of a man. It is usually written in its abbreviated form and placed before a man's surname: *Mr. Jones.* **2.** *Abbr.* **Mr.** A form of address used before the title of a male office-holder: *Mr. Speaker.* **3.** The official term of address for certain naval personnel: **a.** A warrant officer. **b.** In the merchant navy, any officer except for the captain. **4.** *British.* A title or form of address for a male surgeon or consultant, used in preference to *Doctor.* **5.** *Small* **m.** *Informal.* A form of address, without a name, used when speaking to a man. [Weakened form of MASTER.]
mis·ti·gris (místi-gree) *n.* **1.** A blank card that is used in a type of poker. **2.** The type of poker in which this card is used. [French *mistigri†,* jack of clubs, game in which this card is wild.]
mis·time (miss-tím) *tr.v.* **-timed, -timing, -times.** To time (a stroke or remark, for example) wrongly or inappropriately.
Mis·tin·guett (miss-tang-gét, meess-, -taN-), stage name of Jeanne Bourgeois (1875–1956). French comedienne. She took her name from Miss Tinguett in the musical comedy, *Miss Helyett.*
mis·tle thrush, mis·sel thrush (miss'l) *n.* A European thrush, *Turdus viscivorus,* with a spotted breast. [Referring to its feeding on mistletoe berries.]
mis·tle·toe (miss'l-tō) *n.* **1.** A Eurasian parasitic shrub, *Viscum album,* having leathery evergreen leaves and waxy white berries. **2.** A mistletoe sprig, used as a Christmas decoration, under which kissing is traditionally permitted. [Middle English *mistilto,* Old English *misteltān* : *mistel,* mistletoe + *tān,* twig, from Germanic *tainaz* (unattested).]
mis·took. Past tense of **mistake.**
mis·tral (místrəl, miss-traál; *French* meess-) *n.* A dry, cold, northerly wind that blows in squalls through the Rhône Valley and nearby areas towards the Mediterranean coast of southern France. [French, from Provençal, from Latin *magistrālis (ventus),* "master (wind)", from *magistrālis,* MAGISTRAL.]
mis·trans·late (miss-traanz-láyt, -tranz-, -traanss-, -transs-) *tr.v.* **-lated, -lating, -lates.** To translate (material, especially in a foreign language) wrongly. **—mis·trans·la·tion** (-láysh'n) *n.*
mis·treat (miss-tréet) *tr.v.* **-treated, -treating, -treats.** To handle or treat roughly or wrongly; abuse. See Synonyms at **abuse.** **—mis·treat·ment** *n.*
mis·tress (miss-triss, -trəss) *n.* **1.** A woman in a position of authority, such as the head of a college, household, or estate: *"Thirteen years had seen her mistress of Kellynch Hall"* (Jane Austen). **2.** A woman owning an animal or, formerly, a slave. **3.** A woman who has strong control over something: *mistress of the situation.* **4.** *Often capital* **M.** Any idea or object personified as a woman having control or authority over something: *Britain was once mistress of the seas.* **5.** A woman who has mastered a skill: *a mistress of mechanical engineering.* **6. a.** Especially formerly, a woman who has a continuing sexual relationship with a man to whom she is not married and who often receives financial support from the man. **b.** *Archaic.* A woman loved by a man. **7.** *Capital* **M.** A title or form of address used with a woman's name. Now archaic except in parts of Scotland. **8.** *British.* A female schoolteacher. [Middle English, from Old French *maistresse,* from *maistre,* MASTER.]
mis·tri·al (miss-trí-əl, -tríl) *n. Law.* **1.** A trial that becomes invalid because of a basic error in procedure. **2.** *U.S.* An inconclusive trial, such as one in which the jurors fail to agree on a verdict.
mis·trust (miss-trúst) *n.* Lack of trust; suspicion; doubt.
~*v.* **mistrusted, -trusting, -trusts.** —*tr.* To regard without confidence; be wary or suspicious of. —*intr.* To be wary or doubtful. —See Synonyms at **uncertainty.** —See Usage note at **distrust.** **—mis·trust·ful** *adj.* **—mis·trust·ing·ly** *adv.*
mist·y (místi) *adj.* **-ier, -iest.** **1.** Consisting of or resembling mist: *a misty rain.* **2.** Obscured or clouded by or as if by mist. **3.** Lacking in clarity; vague: *misty ideas.* **—mist·i·ly** *adv.* **—mist·i·ness** *n.*
mis·un·der·stand (miss-undər-stánd) *tr.v.* **-stood** (-stóod), **-standing, -stands.** To understand incorrectly; misinterpret.
mis·un·der·stand·ing (miss-undər-stánding) *n.* **1.** A failure to understand correctly. **2.** A disagreement or quarrel.
mis·un·der·stood (miss-undər-stóod) *adj.* **1.** Understood wrongly or incorrectly. **2.** Not appreciated or given sympathetic understanding: *Is she a misunderstood genius or merely a crank?*
mis·use (miss-yóoss) *n.* Also **mis·us·age** (-ij). Improper or wrong use; misapplication.
~*tr.v.* (-yóoz) **-used, -using, -uses.** **1.** To use wrongly or incorrectly. **2.** To mistreat or abuse. —See Synonyms at **abuse.** **—mis·us·er** *n.*
mis·val·ue (miss-vál-yoo) *tr.v.* **-ued, -uing, -ues.** To value or estimate incorrectly.
mis·word (miss-wúrd) *tr.v.* **-worded, -wording, -words.** To express incorrectly; word inaccurately.
M.I.T. Massachusetts Institute of Technology.
Mitch·ell (míchəl), **Margaret** (1900–49). U.S. writer. Her only novel, *Gone with the Wind* (1936), won the Pulitzer prize. The film of the same name, a Hollywood epic, was first released in 1939.
mite[1] (mīt) *n.* Any of various small arachnids of the order Acarina (or Acari), some of which are parasitic. They may infest foods and carry disease. [Middle English *mite,* Old English *mīte,* from Germanic *mītōn* (unattested).]
mite[2] *n.* **1. a.** A very small amount of money or contribution. **b.** A **widow's mite** *(see).* **2.** A coin of very small value, especially a former Flemish coin. **3.** The smallest bit or slightest thing: *not a mite of sympathy.* **4.** Any very small object or creature, especially a child: *Poor wee mite!* [Middle English (originally in the phrase "not worth a mite"), from Middle Dutch *mīte,* probably of same origin as MITE (arachnid).]
miter. *U.S.* Variant of **mitre.**
Mithgarthr. *Norse Mythology.* Variant of **Midgard.**
Mith·ra·ism (míth-ray-iz'm || -rə-) *n.* A Persian religious cult that flourished in the late Roman Empire, in the first three centuries A.D., rivalling Christianity. See **Mithras.** **—Mith·ra·ic** (-ráy-ik) *adj.* **—Mith·ra·ist** (míth-ray-ist, -ráy- || -rə-) *n. & adj.*
mith·ra·my·cin (míthrə-mī-sin) *n.* An antibiotic that prevents the growth of cancer cells and is used mainly in the treatment of cancer of the testicle.
Mith·ras (míth-rass || -rəss). Also **Mith·ra** (-rə). *Persian Mythology.* The god of light and guardian against evil, often identified with the sun. [Latin, from Greek, from Old Persian *mithra-,* from Sanskrit *Mitra,* Vedic god.]
mith·ri·date (míthrə-dayt) *n.* Formerly, a substance thought to be an antidote against any poison.
mith·ri·da·tism (míthrə-dáyt-iz'm) *n.* Tolerance of a poison, acquired by taking gradually larger doses of it. [After *Mithradates* VI, King of Pontus (died 63 B.C.), said to have immunised himself in this manner.] **—mith·ri·dat·ic** (-dáttik, -dáytik) *adj.* [Medieval Latin *mithridatum,* from Late Latin, antidote, from Latin, dogtooth violet (used an antidote). See **mithridatism.**]
mit·i·cide (mítti-sīd) *n.* An agent that kills mites. **—mit·i·cid·al** (-sīd'l) *adj.*
mit·i·gate (mítti-gayt) *v.* **-gated, -gating, -gates.** —*tr.* **1.** To moderate (a quality or condition) in force or intensity; alleviate: *mitigate anger; mitigate heat.* **2.** To serve to lessen the gravity of (an offence); extenuate. —*intr.* To serve to lessen the gravity of something: *mitigating circumstances.* —See Synonyms at **relieve.** —See Usage note at **militate.** [Middle English *mitigaten,* from Latin *mītigāre,* from *mītis,* gentle, mild.] **—mit·i·ga·ble** (-gəb'l) *adj.* **—mit·i·ga·tion** (-gáysh'n) *n.* **—mit·i·ga·tive** (-gətiv, -gaytiv), **mit·i·ga·to·ry** (-gə-tri, -təri, -gáytəri) *adj.* **—mit·i·ga·tor** (-gaytər) *n.*
Mitilíni. See **Mytilene.**
mi·to·chon·dri·on (mīt-ō-kóndri-ən, -ə-) *n., pl.* **-dria.** *Biology.* A microscopic body or organelle found in the cytoplasm of eukaryotic cells, consisting of two sets of membranes. The inner membrane is invaginated, and is the site of energy production by the process of cellular respiration. Also called "chondriosome". [New Latin : Greek *mitos,* thread + *khondrion,* small grain, diminutive of *khondros.*] **—mi·to·chon·dri·al** *adj.*
mit·o·gen (míttə-jen, mī-tō-, -tə-) *n.* An agent that induces mitosis in cells. [MITOSIS + -GEN.] **—mit·o·gen·ic** (-jénnik) *adj.* **—mit·o·gen·ic·it·y** (-jə-nissəti, -je-) *n.*
mi·to·sis (mī-tō-siss, mi-) *n. Biology.* A type of cell division in which the nucleus divides to produce two daughter cells, each with the same number of chromosomes as the parent cell. Compare **meiosis.** See **anaphase, metaphase, prophase, telophase.** [New Latin : Greek *mitos,* a thread + -OSIS.] **—mi·tot·ic** (-tóttik) *adj.* **—mi·tot·i·cal·ly** *adv.*
mit·rail·leuse (mittrī-érz || méetrə-, -yőz) *n.* An obsolete type of breech-loading machine gun with several barrels. [French, feminine

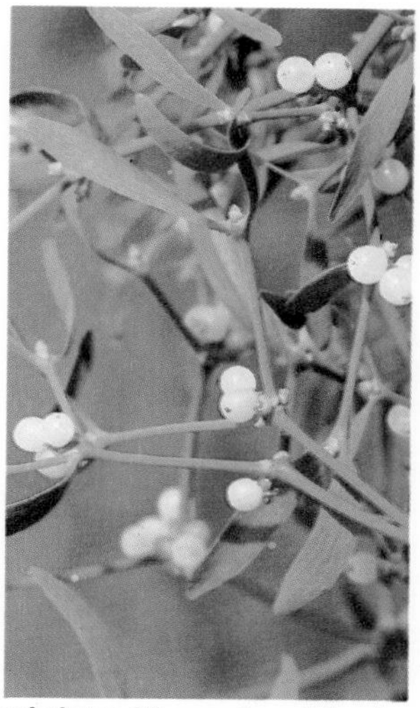

mistletoe *Viscum album (above) is one of several species of this parasitic plant which grows on trees. The berries are poisonous to humans, but are eaten safely by birds. The seeds – in the centre of the fruit – are spread to new trees through the birds' droppings.*

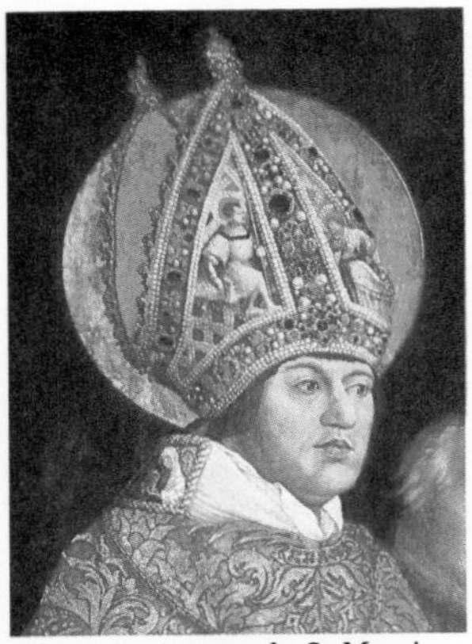

mitre *A mitre worn by St. Maurice in a painting by the 16th-century German artist Matthias Grünewald. Mitres, which first came into use in the 11th century, were modelled originally on the papal crown.*

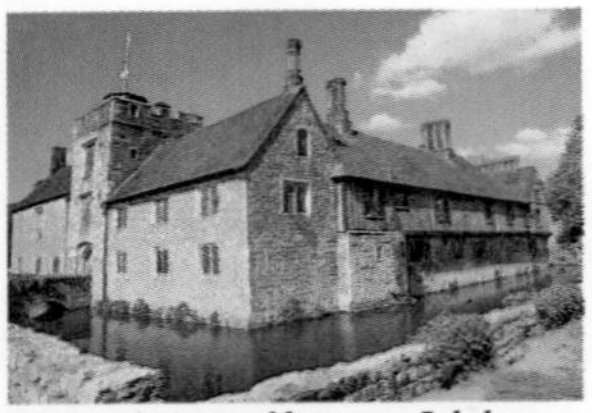

moat *A moated house at Ightham in Kent, England. Medieval castles usually had an initial defence of one or more moats or ditches with drawbridges.*

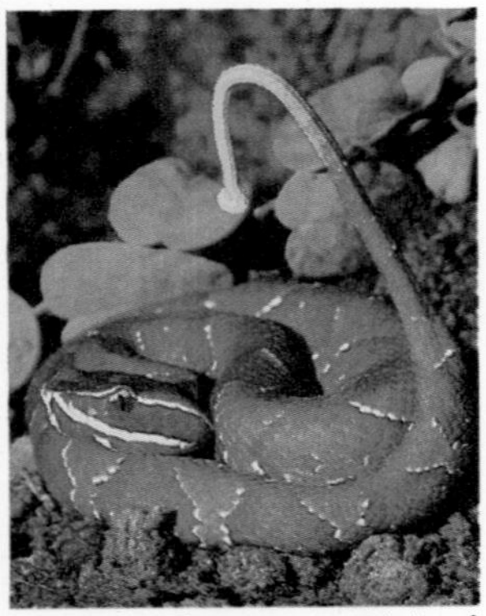

moccasin *There are two varieties of this poisonous New World pit viper: the water moccasin and the Mexican moccasin. The Mexican one shown here, of the species* Agkistrodon bilineatus, *is young; the yellow tip on the tail disappears in the adult.*

agent-noun from *mitraille,* small shot, from Old French *mistraille,* small money, from *mite,* MITE.]

mi·tral (mī́trəl) *adj.* **1.** Of or resembling a mitre. **2.** Pertaining to a mitral valve. [New Latin *mitrālis,* from Latin *mitra,* MITRE.]

mitral valve *n.* The heart valve between the left atrium and the left ventricle that regulates blood flow from the atrium to the ventricle. Also called "bicuspid valve".

mi·tre, *U.S.* **mi·ter** (mī́tər) *n.* **1.** A tall, pointed hat with two lappets at the back, worn by bishops and abbots. **2. a.** See **mitre joint. b.** The edge of a piece of material to be joined in a mitre joint. **c.** See **mitre square.**
~*v.* **mitred** or *U.S.* **mitered, mitring** or *U.S.* **mitering, mitres** or *U.S.* **miters.** —*tr.* **1.** To appoint as bishop or abbot. **2.** To make join in a mitre joint. **3.** To cut a mitre in. —*intr.* To meet in a mitre joint. [Middle English, from Old French, from Latin *mitra,* from Greek, headband, turban, (in the Septuagint) headdress of the high priest.]

mitre box *n.* **1.** A box open at the ends with sides slotted to guide a saw in cutting mitre joints. **2.** A device for handsaws that may be set to guide cuts at various degrees.

mitre joint *n.* A joint made by bevelling each of two surfaces to be joined, usually at a 45° angle to form a 90° corner.

mitre square *n.* A carpenter's square with a blade set at 45° or at an adjustable angle.

mitt (mit) *n.* **1.** A type of glove that extends over the hand but only partially covers the fingers. **2.** A mitten. **3.** In baseball, a large leather padded mitten worn by catchers. **4.** *Slang.* The hand. [Short for MITTEN.]

mit·ten (mítt'n) *n.* **1.** A covering for the hand that encases the thumb separately and the four fingers together. Also called "mitt". **2.** *Slang.* A boxing glove. [Middle English *mytayne,* from Old French *mitaine,* from Vulgar Latin *medietāna* (unattested), "skin-lined glove cut off at the middle", from Latin *medietās,* half, from *medius,* middle.]

Mit·ter·rand (méetə-rON), **François (Maurice Marie)** (1916–). French president (1981–). A World War II Resistance fighter, he was elected to the Chamber of Deputies (1946), where he has sat ever since except for four years (1959–62) in the Senate. In 1965, as the candidate of the Left, he lost the presidential election to Charles de Gaulle. He lost again to Giscard d'Estaing in 1974, and was finally elected in 1981.

mit·ti·mus (mítti-məss) *n., pl.* **-muses. 1.** *Law.* A writ committing a person to prison. **2.** *British Archaic.* A dismissal. [Latin, "we send", the first word of such a writ, from *mittere,* to send.]

mitz·vah (míts-və, -vaa) *n., pl.* **mitzvoth** (-vōth, -váwt) or **-vahs.** *Judaism.* **1.** A command enjoined by the Scriptures. **2.** A meritorious act. [Hebrew *miṣwāh,* "(divine) commandment", from *ṣiwwāh,* to command.]

mix (miks) *v.* **mixed, mixing, mixes.** —*tr.* **1. a.** To combine or blend (ingredients or elements) into one mass or mixture so that the constituent parts are indistinguishable: *mix sugar and egg yolks.* **b.** To create or form by adding ingredients together: *mix a cake; mixing purple from red and blue.* **c.** To add (an ingredient or element) to another: *mix flour into the batter.* **2.** To combine; bring together: *mix business and pleasure.* **3.** To consume (different types of drink or food) in succession: *mixed gin and wine and was sick.* **4.** To crossbreed. **5.** To combine (two or more sounds) for broadcasting or recording. —*intr.* **1. a.** To become mixed or blended together. **b.** To be capable of being blended together: *Oil and water do not mix.* **2. a.** To join in socially or get along easily with others: *She does not mix well at parties.* **b.** To associate oneself with a group of people: *mixed with the jet set.* **3.** To be crossbred. —**mix it.** *Slang.* **1.** To start to fight. **2.** To cause trouble.
~*n.* **1.** An act of mixing. **2. a.** A product of mixing; a mixture: *a good mix of people at the party.* **b.** A mixture of ingredients packaged and sold commercially: *a cake mix.* [Back-formation from *mixed, mixt,* from Middle English, from Old French *mixte,* from Latin *miscēre* (past participle *mixtus*), to mix.] —**mix·a·ble** *adj.*
Synonyms: *mix, blend, mingle, coalesce, merge, amalgamate, combine, compound, fuse.*

mixed (mikst) *adj.* **1.** Composed of or involving a variety of differing, sometimes conflicting, entities or elements: *mixed feelings; got a mixed reception from the critics; mixed-ability classes.* **2.** Composed of or involving people of different sex, race, or social class: *Is your school single-sex or mixed?* —See Synonyms at **miscellaneous.**

mixed bag *n. Informal.* An assortment or collection of diverse elements.

mixed blessing *n.* An event or situation that has disadvantages as well as its more obvious advantages.

mixed crystal *n. Chemistry.* A crystalline material composed of two or more compounds that have crystallised in a single lattice but have retained their chemical identity.

mixed doubles *n.* A doubles game, as in tennis or badminton, with each team consisting of a male and a female.

mixed farming *n.* The farming of both crops and livestock on the same farm.

mixed grill *n.* A dish consisting of a variety of grilled meats, such as lamb chops and bacon.

mixed marriage *n.* A marriage between persons of different races or religions.

mixed metaphor *n.* **1.** A succession of metaphors that produce an incongruous or ludicrous effect, for example: *Her mounting ambition was soon bridled by a wave of opposition.* **2.** The use of such metaphors.

mixed nerve *n.* A nerve containing both sensory and motor nerve fibres.

mixed number *n.* A number, such as 7¼, made up of an integer and a fraction.

mixed-up (míkst-úp) *adj. Informal.* Emotionally confused: *a mixed-up kid.*

mix·er (míksər) *n.* **1.** One that mixes. **2.** A person who mixes socially: *She was a good mixer with people of all ages.* **3.** Any device, especially mechanical or electrical, that blends or mixes substances or ingredients. Often used in combination: *a cement-mixer.* **4.** A non-alcoholic drink, such as soda water or ginger ale, used in diluting alcoholic drinks. **5.** *Electronics.* A circuit or device for combining two or more signals or sounds into a single output.

mix·o·lyd·i·an (míksō-líddi-ən) *adj. Music.* Of or designating a mode represented by the white notes of the scale of G on the piano keyboard. [Greek *mixoludios,* half-Lydian : *mixo-,* half + *ludios,* Lydian.]

Mix·tec (méess-tek, méesh-, mísh-) *n., pl.* **-tecs** or collectively **Mixtec. 1.** A member of an American Indian people inhabiting Mexico. **2.** The language of this people. —**Mix·tec** *adj.*

mix·ture (míks-chər, *sometimes* -tewr) *n.* **1.** Something produced by mixing. **2.** Anything consisting of diverse elements. **3.** A fabric made of different kinds of thread or yarn. **4.** The act or process of mixing or of being mixed. **5.** *Chemistry.* Any composition of two or more substances that are not chemically bound to each other. **6.** A liquid medicine containing a combination of different drugs, such as a suspension of a solid in a liquid. **7.** The mixture of air and petrol produced in the carburettor of an internal-combustion engine. **8.** *Plural.* Any of variously coloured and flavoured selections of sweets: *dolly mixtures.* [French, from Latin *mixtūra,* from *miscēre* (past participle *mixtus*), to mix.]

mix up *tr.v.* **1.** To confuse: *I always mix her up with her sister.* **2.** To put into disorder. **3.** To cause to become associated with a group or activity of a usually undesirable nature. Used in the passive with *with*: *got mixed up with a bad crowd.*

mix-up (míks-up) *n.* **1.** A state of confusion; a muddle. **2.** *Informal.* A fight or melee.

Mi·zar (mī́-zaar, -zər) *n.* One of the seven stars in the constellation **Ursa Major** *(see).* [Arabic *mi'zar,* veil, cloak.]

Mi·zo·gu·chi (méezō-gōōchi), **Kenji** (1898–1956). Japanese film director. His films, examining the conflict between traditional Japanese values and a modern industrial society, include *Street Sketches* (1925) and *Metropolitan Symphony* (1929). After 1945, he filmed love stories, including *The Love of Actress Sumaku* (1947) and *Red-light District* (1956).

miz·zen, miz·en (mízz'n) *n.* **1.** A fore-and-aft sail set on the mizzenmast. **2.** A mizzenmast. [Middle English *mesan, meseyn,* from Old French *misaine,* from Italian *mezzana,* mizzen sail, from *mezzano,* middle, from Latin *mediānus,* MEDIAN.] —**miz·zen** *adj.*

miz·zen·mast (mízz'n-maast; *nautical* -məst || -mast) *n.* **1.** The third mast aft on sailing ships carrying three or more masts. **2.** A **jigger mast** *(see).*

miz·zle[1] (mízz'l) *intr.v.* **-zled, -zling, -zles.** *Regional.* To rain in fine, mistlike droplets; drizzle. [Late Middle English *misellen,* perhaps from Middle Dutch *miezelen.*] —**miz·zle** *n.*

mizzle[2] *intr.v.* **-zled, -zling, -zles.** *British Slang.* To leave suddenly; vanish; decamp. [18th century : origin obscure.]

mk. 1. mark. **2.** markka.

mks metre-kilogram-second (system of units).

MKSA metre-kilogram-second-ampere (system of units).

mkt. market.

ml millilitre.

ML, M.L. Medieval Latin.

MLD *n.* Minimum lethal dose: the smallest quantity of a drug or other compound that will cause death.

MLF multilateral force (nuclear force).

M.Litt. Master of letters. [Latin *Magister Litterarum.*]

Mlle. Mademoiselle.

Mlles. Mesdemoiselles.

mm millimetre; millimetres.

MM. Messieurs.

m.m. with the necessary changes having been made. [Latin *mutatis mutandis.*]

M.M. Military Medal (in Britain).

Mma·ba·tho (m-mə-baátō). Capital of Bophuthatswana.

Mme. Madame.

Mmes. Mesdames.

mmf, m.m.f. magnetomotive force.

mmHg millimetre of mercury (unit of pressure).

M.Mus. Master of Music.

Mn The symbol for the element manganese.

M.N. Merchant Navy (in Britain).

MND *n.* See **motor neurone.**

mne·mon·ic (ni-mónnik, mni-, nee-) *adj.* Pertaining to, assisting, or designed to assist the memory.
~*n.* A device, such as a formula or rhyme, used as an aid in remembering. [Medieval Latin *mnēmonicus,* from Greek *mnēmonikos,* from *mnēmōn,* mindful.] —**mne·mon·i·cal·ly** *adv.*

mne·mon·ics (ni-mónniks, mni-, nee-) *n. Used with a singular verb.* The art or system of improving or developing the memory.

Mne·mos·y·ne (ni-mózzi-nee, mni-, nee-, -móssi-, -ni). *Greek Mythology.* The goddess of memory, mother of the Muses. [Latin, from Greek *mnēmosunē,* memory, from *mnasthai,* to remember.]

Mngr. Monseigneur; Monsignor.

-mo *n. comb. form.* Indicates the specified number of leaves formed by folding a larger sheet of paper; used after numerals or the names of numerals; for example, **duodecimo**, which is generally written "12 mo" and called by printers "twelvemo". [Latin ablative ending of ordinals, after the preposition *in*, in, as in *duodecimo*, from *duodecimus*, twelfth.]

Mo The symbol for the element molybdenum.

MΩ megohm.

mo. month.

m:o., M.O. 1. mail order. 2. medical officer. 3. money order.

mo·a (mṓ-ə) *n.* Any of various large, long-necked, flightless birds of the family Dinorthidae, native to New Zealand and now extinct for over a century. [Maori.]

Mo·ab (mṓ-ăb). Ancient kingdom east of the Dead Sea, in an area that is now part of Jordan.

Mo·ab·ite (mṓ-ə-bīt) *n.* 1. A descendant of Moab, the son of Lot. Genesis 19:37. 2. An inhabitant or native of Moab. **—Mo·ab·ite** *adj.*

moan (mōn) *n.* 1. A low, sustained, mournful sound, usually indicative of sorrow or pain. 2. Any similar sound: *the moan of the wind.* 3. *Informal.* A complaint or grievance.
~*v.* **moaned, moaning, moans.** *—intr.* 1. To utter a moan or moans. 2. To make a sound resembling a moan: *The wind moaned through the trees.* 3. *Informal.* To grumble; complain. Often used with *at.* *—tr.* 1. To complain about; bewail: *She moaned her misfortunes to anyone who would listen.* 2. To utter with a moan or moans. —See Synonyms at **cry.** [Middle English *mone*, complaint, from Old English *mān* (unattested), complaint, from Germanic.]

moat (mōt) *n.* 1. A wide, deep ditch, usually filled with water, surrounding a medieval town, fortress, or castle as a protection against assault. 2. A similar, though often smaller, ditch surrounding a more modern building, such as a zoo enclosure.
~*tr.v.* **moated, moating, moats.** To surround with or as if with a moat. [Middle English *mote*, originally, "mound", "embankment", from Old French *mote, motte*, clod, hill, mound, probably from (unattested) Gaulish *mutt(a)†*.]

mob (mŏb) *n.* 1. A large, disorderly crowd or throng; a rabble. 2. The common people, regarded as ignorant, brutish, or fickle; the masses. Preceded by *the.* 3. *Informal.* An organised gang of criminals. 4. *Informal.* Any indiscriminate or loosely associated group of persons or things. 5. *Australian.* A flock or herd of animals. 6. *U.S. Slang.* The Mafia. Preceded by *the.*
~*tr.v.* **mobbed, mobbing, mobs.** 1. To crowd around and jostle or annoy, especially in anger or excessive enthusiasm: *The fans mobbed the singer.* 2. To crowd into (a place): *Crowds mobbed the fairgrounds.* 3. To attack violently, usually in a crowd or mob; specifically, to surround and attack (a wounded member of one's own species or a member of another species). Used of birds, for example. [Shortening of earlier *mobile*, from Latin *mōbile (vulgus)*, "the fickle (crowd)", neuter of *mōbilis*, MOBILE.]

mob·cap (mŏb'-kăp) *n.* A large, indoor cap trimmed with frills and ribbons, originally worn by women in the 18th and early 19th centuries. [From earlier *mob*, "negligee", "informal attire", earlier, "slattern", variant of *mab*, short for the name *Mabel*.]

mo·bile (mṓ-bīl; *rarely* -beel || *chiefly U.S.* -b'l) *adj.* 1. Capable of moving or of being moved from place to place. See Usage note at **movable.** 2. Moving quickly from one state to another: *a mobile face.* 3. Changing or capable of changing one's social status: *This area of London is upwardly mobile.* 4. Flowing freely; not viscous: *a mobile liquid.* 5. a. *Military.* Equipped with transport and capable of rapid deployment: *a mobile unit.* b. *Informal.* Having one's own means of transport: *no longer mobile since she lost her licence.* c. Incorporated in a vehicle and therefore capable of being driven from place to place: *a mobile library.*
~*n.* An ornament or type of sculpture that is suspended and consists of parts that move, especially in response to air currents. [Old French *mobile*, from Latin *mōbilis*, from the root of *movēre*, to move.] **—mo·bil·i·ty** (mō-bĭl'ə-tĭ, mə-) *n.*

-mobile *n. comb. form.* Indicates a specialised kind of vehicle; for example, **snowmobile.** [From AUTOMOBILE.]

mo·bi·lise, mo·bi·lize (mṓbi-līz) *v.* **-lised, -lising, -lises.** *—tr.* 1. a. To make mobile or capable of movement. b. To put into circulation. 2. To assemble, prepare, or put into operation for war or a similar emergency: *mobilise troops.* 3. To organise or gather together for a purpose. *—intr.* To become prepared for war or a similar emergency. [French *mobiliser*.] **—mo·bi·li·sa·tion** (-lī-záy-sh'n || *U.S.* -li-) *n.*

Mö·bi·us strip (mérbi-əss, mṓbi-, mṓbi-) *n.* A one-sided surface that can be formed from a rectangular strip by rotating one end 180° and attaching it to the other end. Also called "Möbius band". Compare **Klein bottle.** [After its inventor August *Möbius* (1790–1868), German mathematician.]

mob·oc·ra·cy (mob-ŏckrə-si) *n., pl.* **-cies.** Political control by a mob. **—mob·o·crat** (mŏbbə-krăt) *n.* **—mob·o·crat·ic** (-krättik), **mob·o·crat·i·cal** *adj.*

mob·ster (mŏb-stər) *n. Chiefly U.S.* A gangster.

Mo·bu·tu Sese Seko (mə-bōō-tōō, mō-, sésse séckô), born Joseph Désiré Mobutu; also known as Mobutu. (1930–). President of Zaire. In September 1960, he took control of the Congo in a coup supported by the army. In 1967 he became president of the Congo (now Zaire).

Mobutu (Sese Seko) Lake. Formerly **Lake Albert.** A shallow body of water 160 kilometres (100 miles) long and 30 kilometres (18 miles) wide, lying above sea level in the Great Rift Valley on the border between Zaire and Uganda. Its high salinity is caused by rapid evaporation.

M.O.C. *n. British.* Mother of the chapel: the female leader of the members of a trade union in a particular newspaper office, printing firm, or the like. Compare **F.O.C.**

Moçambique. See **Mozambique.**

moc·ca·sin (mŏckə-sin) *n.* 1. A soft flat-soled leather slipper worn by American Indians. 2. A shoe or slipper resembling an Indian moccasin. 3. A snake, the **water moccasin** *(see).* [Natick *mohkussin*, from Proto-Algonquian *maxkeseni* (unattested).]

moccasin flower *n.* Any of several orchids of the genus *Cypripedium.* See **lady's slipper.**

mo·cha (mŏckə || *chiefly U.S.* mṓkə) *n.* 1. A rich, pungent Arabian coffee. 2. Coffee of high quality. 3. A flavouring made of coffee often mixed with chocolate. 4. A soft, thin glove leather made from goatskin or sheepskin. 5. Dark olive brown. [Originally exported from *Mocha*, a port of Yemen.] **—mo·cha** *adj.*

mock (mŏk) *v.* **mocked, mocking, mocks.** *—tr.* 1. To treat with scorn or contempt; deride; ridicule. 2. a. To mimic, as when teasing or in derision. b. To imitate; counterfeit. 3. To delude; disappoint. 4. To defy successfully; thwart: *A small band of defenders mocked the enemy's superior forces.* *—intr.* To express scorn or ridicule. Often used with *at*: *They mocked at the idea.* —See Synonyms at **ridicule.**
~*n.* 1. a. An act of mocking. b. Mockery; derision. 2. Something deserving of derision. 3. Something simulated; an imitation or counterfeit. **—put the mock** or **mocks on.** *Australian Slang.* To thwart the chances of.
~*adj.* Simulated; false; imitation: *a mock battle; mock cream.* [Middle English *mokken, mocquen*, from Old French *mocquer*, to deride, from Vulgar Latin *moccāre* (unattested), probably from a root *mokk-*, imitative of laughter.] **—mock·ing·ly** *adv.*

mock·er (mŏckər) *n.* One that mocks. **—put the mockers on.** *Slang.* To thwart the chances of; stymie.

mock·er·y (mŏckə-ri) *n., pl.* **-ies.** 1. Scornful contempt; ridicule; derision. 2. A derisive or contemptuous act or remark. 3. An object of scorn or ridicule. 4. A contemptible, shameful, or impudent imitation; a travesty: *The trial was a mockery of justice.* 5. Something that is ludicrously futile or unsuitable: *made a mockery of our principles.*

mock-he·ro·ic (mŏk-hi-rṓ-ĭk) *n., pl.* **mock-heroics.** A satirical imitation or burlesque of the heroic manner or style. **—mock-he·ro·ic** *adj.* **—mock-he·ro·i·cal·ly** *adv.*

mock·ing·bird (mŏcking-bûrd) *n.* Any of several New World birds of the family Mimidae that are noted for their ability to mimic other birds; especially, *Mimus polyglottus*, a grey and white bird of the southern United States.

mock moon *n.* A paraselene *(see).*

mock orange *n.* 1. Any of several deciduous shrubs of the genus *Philadelphus*, having white, usually fragrant, flowers. Also called "syringa". 2. Any of various other shrubs or trees having flowers or fruit resembling those of the orange.

mock sun *n.* A parhelion *(see).*

mock turtle soup *n.* Soup made from calf's head or veal and spiced to taste like real turtle soup.

mock up *tr.v.* To make a mock-up of.

mock-up (mŏk-ŭp) *n.* 1. A usually full-sized model of a building, machine, or structure, used for demonstration, study, or testing. 2. A layout of printed matter.

Moctezuma. See **Montezuma II.**

mod¹ (mŏd) *n. Sometimes capital* **M.** A member of a group of teenagers which originated in England in the 1960s, noted for their tidy and uniform style of dress, motorscooters, and for its opposition to the **rockers** *(see).*
~*adj.* Characteristic of or pertaining to the mods, especially to their style of dress. [From MODERN.]

mod² *Sometimes capital* **M.** An annual Gaelic meeting for the holding of literary and musical competitions. [Gaelic *mōd*, assembly, from Old Norse; akin to MOOT.]

mod³ *Mathematics.* modulus.

MOD, MoD Ministry of Defence (in Britain).

mod. 1. moderate. 2. *Music.* moderato. 3. modern.

mo·dal (mṓd'l) *adj.* 1. Of, pertaining to, or characteristic of a mode. 2. *Grammar.* Of, pertaining to, or expressing the mood of a verb. 3. *Music.* Of, pertaining to, characteristic of, or composed in a mode, especially any of the modes typical of medieval church music. 4. *Philosophy.* Of or pertaining to mode or form as opposed to substance or attributes. 5. *Logic.* Expressing or characterised by modality. 6. *Statistics.* Of or pertaining to a statistical mode; most frequent, common, or typical.
~*n.* A modal auxiliary. [Medieval Latin *modālis*, from Latin *modus*, measure, mode.] **—mo·dal·ly** *adv.*

modal auxiliary *n. Grammar.* Any of a set of English verbs, including *can, may, must, ought, shall, should, will,* and *would*, that are characteristically used with other verbs to express mood or tense. Also called "modal verb".

mo·dal·i·ty (mō-dál-ə-ti, mə-) *n., pl.* **-ties.** 1. The fact, state, or quality of being modal. 2. A modal quality or attribute of something; a mode. 3. *Logic.* The classification of propositions on the basis of whether they assert or deny the possibility, impossibility, contingency, or necessity of their content. 4. *Medicine.* a. A method of

mockingbird *The mockingbird is so called because of its habit of imitating the calls of other birds. It is found throughout North and South America and feeds on fruit and insects.*

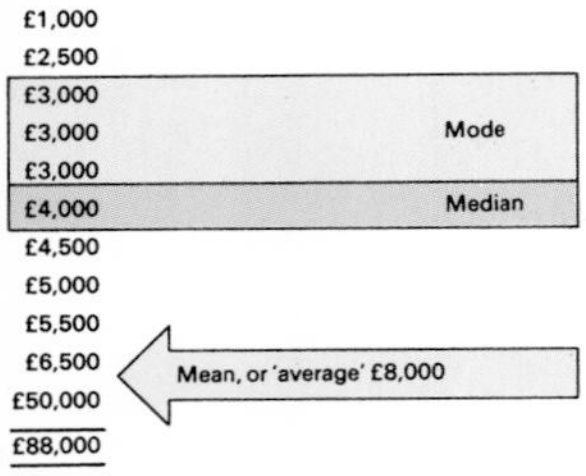
£1,000
£2,500
£3,000
£3,000
£3,000
£4,000
£4,500
£5,000
£5,500
£6,500
£50,000
£88,000
Mode
Median
Mean, or 'average' £8,000

mode[6] *In this table of 11 incomes, the mode is the most common income; the mean, or average, is the result of dividing the total equally; and the median is the middle number in the set.*

therapy, usually physical, such as massage. **b.** An apparatus for such a therapy. **5.** Any of the five senses, such as smell or hearing.

modal logic *n.* The logical study of the formal properties of concepts such as necessity, contingency, possibility, or impossibility and the study of the modality of propositions.

mod cons (mód kónz) *pl.n.* Modern conveniences in the home, such as a washing machine, a telephone, or central heating.

mode (mōd) *n.* **1. a.** Manner, way, or method of doing or acting: *"The modern mode of travelling cannot compare with the old mail-coach system in grandeur and power."* (Thomas De Quincey). **b.** A particular form, variety, or manner: *a mode of communication.* **c.** A condition in which a specified operation may be performed: *switched the tape machine to the record mode.* **2.** The current or customary fashion or style. **3.** *Music.* **a.** Any of certain arrangements of the diatonic notes of an octave. The two chief modes in Western music have been the **major** and **minor** *(both of which see).* **b.** Any of several patterned arrangements characteristic of classical Greek and medieval church music. **4.** *Philosophy.* The particular form or manner in which an underlying substance, or some permanent aspect or attribute of it, is manifested. **5.** *Logic.* **a.** The arrangement or order of the propositions in a syllogism according to both quality and quantity. **b.** The modality of a proposition. **6.** *Statistics.* The value or item occurring most frequently in a series of observations or set of statistical data. Also called "norm". **7.** *Geology.* The mineral composition of a specific sample of igneous rock expressed in percentages of weight. **8.** *Physics.* Any of numerous patterns of vibration or wave motion, as of acoustic or electromagnetic waves, corresponding to resonant frequencies of physical systems. —See Synonyms at **fashion, method.** [French *mode,* fashion, from Latin *modus,* measure, manner, size, harmony, melody.]

mod·el (módd'l) *n.* **1.** A representation, usually smaller but built to scale, of a building or other structure. **2.** A preliminary pattern or representation of an item not yet constructed, serving as the plan from which the finished work, usually larger, will be produced. **3.** A tentative framework of ideas describing something intangible and used as a testing device: *"two conflicting models of generative grammar"* (Noam Chomsky). **4.** A style or design of a product, especially one of a series: *Her car is last year's model.* **5. a.** A person or quality regarded as an example to be imitated or compared: *"in her temper, manners, mind, a model of female excellence"* (Jane Austen). **b.** A pattern, design, or arrangement serving as a basis for imitation: *a constitution on the American model.* **6.** A person or object serving as the subject for an artist or photographer. **7.** A person employed to display clothing, cosmetics, or the like, for prospective buyers or in advertisements. **8.** A figure or object made in clay or wax, for example, especially as used by a sculptor as a preliminary work to copy in a more durable or precious material, such as marble or bronze. **9.** An original garment by a well-known designer. —See Synonyms at **ideal.**
~*v.* **modelled** or *U.S.* **modeled, -elling** or *U.S.* **-eling, -els.** —*tr.* **1.** To make or construct a model of. **2.** To plan, form, or construct according to a particular model or standard. **3. a.** To manipulate or work (a plastic substance): *model clay.* **b.** To make by shaping a plastic substance: *modelled animals in clay.* **4.** To display by wearing or posing with. **5.** In painting and drawing, to give a three-dimensional appearance to, as by shading. —*intr.* **1.** To make a model. **2.** To work as a model: *He models for a living.*
~*adj.* **1.** Serving as or used as a model. **2.** Serving as a standard of excellence; worthy of imitation: *a model husband.* [Obsolete French *modelle,* from Italian *modello,* from Vulgar Latin *modellus* (unattested), from Latin *modulus,* little measure, diminutive of *modus,* measure, rhythm, harmony.] —**mod·el·ler** *n.*

mo·del·lo (mə-déllō, mo-) *n., pl.* **-li** (-lee) or **-los.** A sketch of a proposed larger painting, or a model for a proposed sculpture. [Italian, model.]

mo·dem (mṓ-dem) *n.* A device used in transmitting data between computers along a telephone line. It converts signals from a computer into audio signals and vice versa. [From *mo*dulator *dem*odulator.]

Mo·de·na (mo-dáynə, mə-, móddinə). Capital of Modena province, Emilia-Romagna, north Italy. It is a commercial and industrial centre in a rich agricultural region, and motor vehicles, agricultural machinery and shoes are made there. An Etruscan town, colonised by the Romans (2nd century B.C.) who called it Mutina, it was ruled by the Este family from 1288 to 1859 and has many fine buildings.

mod·er·ate (móddrət, móddrit, móddər-ət, -it) *adj. Abbr.* **mod. 1.** Keeping or kept within reasonable limits; not excessive or extreme: *moderate drinking.* **2.** Not violent; mild; calm: *a moderate climate.* **3. a.** Of medium or average quantity, quality, or extent: *a moderate increase in living standards.* **b.** Of relatively low or below average quantity, quality, or extent: *very moderate prices.* **4.** Opposed to radical or extreme views or measures, especially in politics.
~*n.* One who holds moderate opinions, especially in politics.
~*v.* (móddə-rayt) **moderated, -ating, -ates.** —*tr.* **1.** To make less violent, severe, or extreme. **2.** *Physics.* To reduce the energy of (neutrons), especially by use of a moderator. —*intr.* **1.** To become less violent, severe, or extreme; abate. **2.** To act as a moderator. [Latin *moderātus,* past participle of *moderārī, moderāre,* to reduce, regulate, control; akin to *modus,* MODE.] —**mod·er·ate·ly** *adv.* —**mod·er·ate·ness** *n.* —**mod·er·at·ism** *n.*

moderate breeze *n.* A wind whose speed is 5.5 to 7.9 metres per second (13 to 18 miles per hour); force 4 on the Beaufort scale.

moderate gale *n.* A wind whose speed is 13.9 to 17.1 metres per second (32 to 38 miles per hour); force 7 on the Beaufort Scale.

mod·er·a·tion (móddə-ráysh'n) *n.* **1.** An instance or act of moderating or being moderate. **2.** Freedom from excess or extremes; temperance. —**in moderation.** In moderate amounts or degrees; within reasonable limits.

mod·e·ra·to (móddə-raátō) *adv. Abbr.* **mod.** *Music.* At a moderate tempo; slower than allegretto but faster than andante. Used as a direction. —**mod·e·ra·to** *adj.* & *n.* [Italian, from Latin *moderātus,* MODERATE.]

mod·er·a·tor (móddə-raytər) *n.* **1. a.** An arbitrator or mediator. **b.** One who presides over a meeting or assembly. **2.** The officer who presides over a synod or general assembly of the Presbyterian Church. **3.** *Physics.* A substance, such as water or graphite, that is used in a nuclear reactor to decrease the speed of fast neutrons, increase the likelihood of fission, and sustain a chain reaction.

mod·ern (módd'n, móddərn) *adj. Abbr.* **mod. 1.** Of, pertaining to, or characteristic of recent times or the present: *modern science; modern dress.* **2.** Up-to-date; modish: *a very modern flat with white walls and high-tech furniture.* **3.** Designating the period of history from about 1450 until the present day. **4.** Characteristic of or done in the style of contemporary art, music, drama, or the like; especially, avant-garde or experimental. **5.** *Capital* **M.** Designating the form of a language that is in current use.
~*n.* **1.** One who lives in modern times. **2.** One who has modern ideas, standards, or beliefs; especially, an artist, writer, or the like who works in an avant-garde or experimental style. **3.** *Printing.* Any of various typefaces characterised by strongly contrasted heavy and thin parts. [French *moderne,* from Late Latin *modernus,* from *modō,* "just now", originally "to the measure", from *modus,* measure.] —**mod·ern·i·ty** (mo-dérnəti, mə-) *n.* —**mod·ern·ly** *adv.*

modern dance *n.* A style of contemporary dance based on ballet but using much freer and often more expressive bodily movements.

Modern English *n.* English since the early 16th century.

Modern Greek *n.* Greek since the early 16th century, divided into **Dhimotiki** and **Katharevusa** *(both of which see).*

Modern Hebrew *n.* The form of Hebrew, revived from ancient Hebrew, that is now in current use in Israel.

mod·ern·ise, mod·ern·ize (módd'n-īz, móddərn-) *v.* **-ised, -ising, -ises.** —*tr.* To make modern; bring up to date in respect of technology, appearance, style, or character. —*intr.* To accept or adopt modern ways, views, procedures, or styles. —**mod·ern·i·sa·tion** (-ī-záysh'n || *U.S.* -i-) *n.* —**mod·ern·i·ser** *n.*

mod·ern·ism (módd'n-iz'm, móddərn-) *n.* **1. a.** Modern thought, character, or practice. **b.** Sympathy with modern ideas, practices, or standards. **2.** Something, such as a peculiarity of usage or style, that is characteristic of modern times. **3.** *Often capital* **M.** In Christian Churches, any of various movements that attempt to adapt church teachings to take account of modern scientific and philosophical thought; especially, such a movement in the Roman Catholic Church in the late 19th and early 20th centuries. **4.** The theory or practice of modern art, literature, or the like. —**mod·ern·ist** *n.* & *adj.* —**mod·ern·ist·ic** (-ístik) *adj.*

modern jazz *n.* Any style of jazz developed since the 1940s that is avant-garde or experimental in style, for example bop and free jazz.

modern pentathlon *n.* A **pentathlon** *(see).*

mod·est (móddist) *adj.* **1.** Having or showing a moderate estimation of one's own talents, abilities, and value. **2.** Having a shy and retiring nature; reserved. **3.** Having a regard for decencies of behaviour or dress. **4.** Quiet and humble in appearance; unpretentious: *a modest house.* **5.** Moderate; not extreme or excessive: *a modest charge.* —See Synonyms at **humble, shy.** [French *modeste,* from Latin *modestus,* "keeping due measure"; akin to *modus,* MODE.] —**mod·est·ly** *adv.*

mod·es·ty (móddisti) *n., pl.* **-ties.** The state or quality of being modest, especially: **1.** Lack of vanity or pretentiousness. **2.** Reserve or propriety in speech, dress, or behaviour.

mod·i·cum (móddi-kəm || *U.S. also* mṓdi-) *n., pl.* **-cums** or **-ca** (-kə). A small or moderate amount or quantity. [Latin, short way, short time, from *modicus,* moderate, from *modus,* (due) measure.]

mod·i·fi·ca·tion (móddifi-káysh'n) *n.* **1.** The act of modifying or the condition of being modified. **2.** The result of modifying; a modified form. **3.** A small alteration, adjustment, or limitation. **4.** *Biology.* A physical change in an organism due to environment or activity, but not transmitted to the organism's descendants. —**mod·i·fi·ca·tive** (-kaytiv), **mod·i·fi·ca·to·ry** (-kaytəri, -káytəri) *adj.* —**mod·i·fi·ca·tor** (-kaytər) *n.*

mod·i·fi·er (móddi-fī-ər) *n.* **1.** One that modifies. **2.** *Grammar.* A word, phrase, or clause that limits or qualifies the sense of another word or phrase. Also called "qualifier".

mod·i·fy (móddi-fī) *v.* **-fied, -fying, -fies.** —*tr.* **1.** To change in form or character, usually without fundamental transformation: *"the first tools must have been natural objects only slightly modified"* (V. Gordon Childe). **2.** To make less extreme, severe, or strong: *cannot be persuaded to modify her position in any way.* **3.** *Grammar.* To qualify or limit the meaning of. For example, *"wet"* modifies *"day"* in the phrase *a wet day.* **4.** *Linguistics.* To change (a vowel) by umlaut. —*intr.* To be or become modified. —See Synonyms at **change.** [Middle English *modifien,* to limit, moderate, from Old French *modifier,* from Latin *modificāre* : *modus,* a measure + *facere,* to do, make.] —**mod·i·fi·a·ble** (-əb'l, -fī-əb'l) *adj.*

Mo·di·glia·ni (mō-dil-yaáni, mó-), **Amedeo** (1884–1920). Italian painter and sculptor who settled in Paris (1906), where he concentrated on chiselling heads in stone and painting portraits, mostly of women, in a characteristic elongated style.

mo·dil·lion (mə-dil-yən, mō-) *n. Architecture.* An ornamental bracket used in series under the cornice of the Corinthian, Composite, or Roman Ionic orders. [French *modillon,* from Italian *modiglione,* from Vulgar Latin *mutellio* (stem *mutellion-*), from *mutellus* (unattested), alteration of Latin *mutulus,* projecting block under cornice (Doric order).]

mo·di·o·lus (mə-dī́-ə-ləss, mō-) *n., pl.* **-li** (-lī). *Anatomy.* The central, conical, bony shaft of the cochlea. [New Latin, from Latin, hub of a wheel, bucket of a water wheel, diminutive of *modius,* a measure for grain.]

mod·ish (mṓdish) *adj.* Being in or conforming to the prevailing or current fashion; stylish. [From MODE (fashion).] **—mod·ish·ly** *adv.* **—mod·ish·ness** *n.*

mo·diste (mō-de͞est) *n.* One who produces, designs, or deals in ladies' fashions. [French, from *mode,* MODE (fashion).]

Mo·dred (mṓ-drid, -dred). Also **Mor·dred** (mór-). In Arthurian legend, a knight of the Round Table who led a rebellion against his uncle, King Arthur, and mortally wounded him.

mod·u·lar (móddewlər) *adj.* **1.** Pertaining to, based on, or made up of modules: *a modular training scheme; a modular hotel.* **2.** Of or pertaining to a modulus.

mod·u·late (móddew-layt) *v.* **-lated, -lating, -lates.** *—tr.* **1.** To adjust or adapt to a certain measure or proportion; regulate; temper. **2.** To change or vary the pitch, intensity, or tone of: *modulated his voice to a confidential murmur.* **3.** *Electronics.* To vary the frequency, amplitude, phase, or some other characteristic of (a carrier wave). *—intr.* **1.** *Music.* To pass from one key or pitch to another by means of a regular melodic or chord progression. **2.** *Electronics.* To alter the frequency, amplitude, phase, or some other characteristic of a carrier wave. See **modulation.** [Latin *modulārī,* to measure off, set to a measure, play music, from *modulus,* diminutive of *modus,* measure, rhythm.] **—mod·u·la·tive** (-laytiv, -lətiv), **mod·u·la·to·ry** (-lətri, -lətəri, -láytəri) *adj.*

mod·u·la·tion (móddew-láysh'n) *n.* **1.** The act or process of modulating. **2.** *Music.* A passing from one key to another by means of a regular melodic or chord progression. **3. a.** A change in pitch or loudness of the voice; an inflection of the voice. **b.** The use of a particular intonation or inflection of the voice to convey meaning. **4.** *Electronics.* The variation of a property of an electromagnetic wave or signal, such as its amplitude, frequency, or phase, in a manner determined by another wave or signal, especially for the purpose of transferring information from an audible signal, such as the human voice, to a carrier wave suitable for radio or telephonic transmission.

mod·u·la·tor (móddew-laytər) *n.* **1.** One that modulates. **2.** *Electronics.* A device or electric circuit used to modulate a carrier wave. See **modulation. 3.** *Anatomy.* A receptive sensory end organ, found in light-adapted eyes, which is thought to be related to the discrimination of colour.

mod·ule (móddewl) *n.* **1.** A standard or unit of measurement. **2. a.** *Architecture.* The part of a construction used as a standard to which the rest is proportioned. **b.** A standardised structural component used as a unit in a building or item of furniture. **3.** *Electronics.* A self-contained assembly of electronic components and circuitry. **4.** Any of the self-contained, often separable, units that make up a spacecraft. **5.** Any of a set of distinct learning units that make up a course of education or training. [Latin *modulus,* MODULUS.]

mod·u·lus (móddew-ləss) *n., pl.* **-li** (-lī). *Abbr.* **m, M 1.** *Physics.* A constant or coefficient that expresses the degree to which a substance possesses some property; especially, a ratio of the stress on a solid to the strain produced, measuring the elastic properties of the material. See **bulk modulus, rigidity modulus, Young's modulus. 2.** *Mathematics.* **a.** The **absolute value** *(see)* of a complex number, a negative quantity, or a vector. **b.** *Abbr.* **mod** A number or quantity that produces the same remainder when divided into each of two quantities. **c.** The number by which a logarithm in one system must be multiplied to obtain the corresponding logarithm in another system. [New Latin, from Latin, diminutive of *modus,* measure.]

mo·dus op·er·an·di (mṓd-əss óppə-rán-dī, mód-, -dee) *n., pl.* **modi operandi** (-ī, -ee). **1.** The manner in which something operates. **2.** A person's manner of working. [Latin.]

modus vi·ven·di (vi-vén-dī, -dee) *n., pl.* **modi vivendi** (-ī, -ee). **1.** A way of living. **2.** A practical compromise enabling contending parties to coexist peacefully, either indefinitely or pending a final settlement of their differences. [Latin.]

Moe·so·goth, Moe·so·Goth (me͞e-sō-goth, -zō-) *n.* A Goth of Moesia, an ancient region corresponding approximately to modern Bulgaria and Serbia.

Moe·so·goth·ic, Moe·so·Goth·ic (me͞e-sō-góthik, -zō-) *n.* The language of the Moesogoths, the only documented form of **Gothic** *(see).* **—Moe·so·goth·ic** *adj.*

mo·fette (mō-fét, mo-) *n.* **1.** An opening in the earth from which carbon dioxide and other gases escape, usually marking the last stage of volcanic activity. **2.** The gases escaping from such a fissure. [French, "fetid exhalation", from Italian (Neapolitan dialect) *mofetta,* from *muffa,* mustiness, probably of imitative origin.]

mog (mog) *n.* Also **mog·gy** (móggi) *pl.* **-gies.** *British Informal.* A cat. [20th century : of dialect origin, originally a pet name for a cow.]

Mog·a·dish·u (móggə-díshoo). *Italian* **Mo·ga·di·scio;** *Arabic* **Muqdisho.** Capital and main port of Somalia, on the Indian Ocean. A commercial and financial centre, it exports fruit, livestock, hides, and skins. Founded by the Arabs in the 9th or 10th century, it was taken by the Sultan of Zanzibar (1871), was sold to Italy (1905), and became the capital of Italian Somaliland.

Mog·a·don (móggə-don) *n.* A trademark for nitrazepam, a hypnotic drug used in the form of pills, usually to treat insomnia.

Mogen David. Variant of **Magen David.**

mo·gul¹ (mṓg'l) *n.* A small mound on a ski slope. [Perhaps from German dialect (Austro-Bavarian) *Mugl.*]

mo·gul² (mṓg'l) *n.* **1.** A very rich or powerful person: *an oil mogul.* **2.** A kind of heavy steam locomotive. [From MONGOL.]

Mo·gul (mṓg'l, mō-gul, -gúl, -gōol). Also **Mo·ghul, Mu·ghal** (mōo-gúl) (for sense 1). **1. a.** One of the followers of Baber, who conquered India in 1526 and founded a Muslim empire that lasted formally until 1857. See **Great Mogul. b.** A descendant of a follower of Baber. **2.** A Mongol or Mongolian. [Persian and Arabic *mughūl,* MONGOL.] **—Mo·gul** *adj.*

Mo·hács (mṓ-hach). Small industrial town, and important Danube port in southern Hungary near the Yugoslav border. There the annihilation of a Hungarian army by the Ottoman Turks (1526) resulted in their domination of Hungary for more than 150 years, and paved the way for the Turkish sieges of Vienna. The retreating Turks were defeated at the Second Battle of Mohács (1687).

mo·hair (mṓ-hair) *n.* **1.** The hair of the Angora goat. Also called "angora". **2.** A shiny, heavy, shaggy yarn or fabric made of this hair, often with a mixture of cotton or wool. [Variant (influenced by HAIR) of earlier *moochary, mocayare,* from Italian *moccaiaro,* from Arabic *mukhayyar,* "select", "choice", cloth of goat's hair, from *khayyara,* to choose.] **—mo·hair** *adj.*

Mohammed. See **Muhammad.**

Mohammedan. Variant of **Muhammadan.**

Moharram. Variant of **Muharram.**

Mo·ha·ve (mo-ha͞avi, mō-) *n., pl.* **-ves** or collectively **Mohave.** Also **Mo·ja·ve** (-ha͞avi). A member of a Yuman-speaking North American Indian people, formerly living along the Gila and Colorado rivers. **—Mo·ha·ve** *adj.*

Mo·hawk (mṓ-hawk) *n., pl.* **-hawks** or collectively **Mohawk. 1.** A member of the Iroquoian-speaking North American Indian people that occupied the territory from the Mohawk river to the St. Lawrence. **2.** The language of this people. **—Mo·hawk** *adj.*

Mo·he·gan (mō-he͞egən) *n., pl.* **-gans** or collectively **Mohegan.** A member of an Algonquian-speaking North American Indian people, formerly living in Connecticut. **—Mo·he·gan** *adj.*

Mo·hen·jo-Da·ro (mō-hénjō-da͞arō). Ruined ancient city on the Indus river in the Sind province of Pakistan, dating from about 2500 to 1500 B.C.

mo·hi·can (mō-he͞e-kən, mṓ-i-) *n.* An unconventional type of hairstyle in which the sides of the head are completely shaved, leaving a central growth of hair from forehead to nape, which may be stiffened into spikes or dyed a different colour. [After the American Indian people.]

Mohican. Variant of **Mahican.**

Mo·ho (mṓhō) *n.* The Mohorovičić discontinuity.

Mo·hock (mṓ-hok) *n.* A member of a band of young aristocrats who terrorised London in the early 18th century. [Variant of MOHAWK.]

Mo·hole (mṓ-hōl) *n.* A research project, now abandoned, to drill a hole through the ocean floor, through the Mohorovičić discontinuity and into the mantle, to obtain samples of rocks.

Mo·holy-Nagy (mṓ-hoy-nój), **Laszlo** (1895–1946). Hungarian painter and photographer, and a founder of constructivism. He made "photograms" and "space modulators" out of plastic at the Bauhaus in the 1920s. In 1937, he settled in the United States, where his ideas influenced commercial and industrial design.

Mo·ho·ro·vi·čić discontinuity (mṓ-hə-rṓvi-chich) *n.* The boundary between the earth's crust and mantle, ranging in depth from about 5 kilometres (3 miles) under ocean basins to 30-35 kilometres (19-22 miles) under continents. Also called "Moho". [After Andrija *Mohorovičić* (1857–1936), Yugoslav geophysicist.]

Mohs scale (mōz) *n.* A scale for determining the relative hardness of a mineral according to its resistance to scratching by one of the following minerals, arranged in order of increasing hardness: 1. talc; 2. gypsum; 3. calcite; 4. fluorite; 5. apatite; 6. orthoclase; 7. quartz; 8. topaz; 9. corundum; 10. diamond. [After Friedrich *Mohs* (1773–1839), German mineralogist who devised it.]

mo·hur (mṓ-hər || mə-hōor) *n.* **1.** A currency unit of Nepal, equal to ½ rupee. **2.** A gold coin, formerly used in India, equal to 15 rupees. [Hindi *muhur, muhr,* from Persian *muhr,* a seal.]

moider. Variant of **moither.**

moi·dore (móy-dawr, -dór || -dōr, -dṓr) *n.* A former Portuguese gold coin. [Earlier *moyodore,* from Portuguese *moeda d'ouro,* "coin of gold" : *moeda,* from Latin *monēta,* MONEY + *d'ouro,* "of gold".]

moi·e·ty (móy-əti) *n., pl.* **-ties. 1.** A half. **2.** A part, portion, or share of indefinite size. **3.** *Anthropology.* Either of two basic social divisions that make up a people on the basis of unilateral descent. [Middle English *moite, moitie,* from Old French *moite,* from Latin *medietās* (stem *medietāt-*), half, from *medius,* middle.]

moil (moyl) *intr.v.* **moiled, moiling, moils.** To toil or slave. Used chiefly in the phrase *toil and moil.*
~*n. Archaic.* **1.** Toil; drudgery. **2.** Confusion; turmoil. [Middle English *moillen,* to moisten, smear, from Old French *moillier,* to moisten, paddle in mud, from Vulgar Latin *molliāre* (unattested), from Latin *mollis,* soft.]

Moirae (móyr-ī, -ee) *pl.n.* See **Fates.** [Greek.]

moi·ré (mwa͞a-ray || mwáw-, *U.S.* -ráy) *n.* Also **moire** (mwaar ||

PRONUNCIATION KEY

a, trap; aa, father; ai, fair; ar, star; aw, lawn; ay, play; b, bb, stab; rubber; ch, church; ck, ticket; d, dd, dead; ladder; e, dress; ee, bee; er, defer; ew, few; ewr, pure; ə, about; ər, letter; f, ff, fife; differ; g, gg, giggle; h, hat; i, kit; ī, price; īr, fire; j, judge; k, kick; l, ll, let; 'l, needle; m, mm, man; n, nn, no; 'n, sudden; ng, thing; o, lot; ō, no; ŏŏ, foot; ōō, shoe; oor, poor; ow, cow; owr, hour; oy, boy; p, pp, pepper; r, rr, red; s, ss, sauce; sh, ship; t, tt, totter; th, thick; th, this; smooth; u, cut; ur, turn; v, vv, valve; w, wet; y, yes; z, zz, zebra; zh, vision; pleasure

IN FOREIGN WORDS:

aN, oN, Saint-Saëns; hl, Llanelli; Hluhluwe; kh, loch; lough; Khaled

STRESS MARK:

ín-sīt, insight; in-sī́t, incite

mwawr). **1.** Cloth, especially silk, that has a watered or wavy pattern. **2.** A watered pattern produced on cloth by engraved rollers. [French, from *moire, mouaire,* from MOHAIR (the fabric originally used for this pattern).] —**moi·ré** *adj.*

moiré pattern *n.* A pattern produced by superimposing a repetitive design, such as a grid, on a slightly displaced design, either the same or different, in order to produce a pattern distinct from its components.

moist (moyst) *adj.* **moister, moistest. 1.** Slightly wet or damp. **2.** Filled with moisture. **3.** Humid. —See Synonyms at **wet.** [Middle English, from Old French *moiste,* probably from Vulgar Latin *muscidus* (unattested), mouldy, wet, alteration of Latin *mūcidus,* from *mūcus,* mucus.] —**moist·ly** *adv.* —**moist·ness** *n.*

mois·ten (móyss'n ‖ móystǝn) *v.* **-tened, -tening, -tens.** —*tr.* To make moist. —*intr.* To become moist. —**mois·ten·er** *n.*

mois·ture (móyss-chǝr) *n.* Diffuse wetness that can be felt as vapour in the atmosphere or as condensed liquid on the surfaces of objects; dampness. [Middle English, from Old French *moistour,* from *moiste,* MOIST.]

mois·tur·ise, mois·tur·ize (móyss-chǝrīz) *tr.v.* **-ised, -ising, -ises.** To remove dryness from (the skin, for example); add moisture to.

mois·tur·is·er (móyss-chǝr-īzǝr) *n.* A cosmetic lotion or cream applied to the skin to soften it and counter dryness.

moi·ther (móythǝr ‖ mĭthǝr) *tr.v.* **-thered, -thering, -thers.** Also **moi·der** (móydǝr), **-dered, -dering, -ders.** *British Regional.* To confuse, baffle, or bewilder. Usually used in the passive. [17th century : origin obscure.]

Mojave. Variant of **Mohave.**

Mo·ja·ve Desert (mō-háavi, mǝ-). Arid region of southern California, United States. Part of the Great Basin, it has low mountains and broad valleys. Its mineral reserves include iron, potash, gold, and silver. Death Valley National Monument is included in the region.

moke (mōk) *n. Slang.* **1.** *British.* A donkey. **2.** *Australian & N.Z.* An old, broken-down horse. [19th century : origin obscure.]

mo·ko (mókō) *n., pl.* **-kos.** A Maori pattern of tattoos. [Maori.]

mol *Chemistry.* The symbol for **mole.**

mol. molecular; molecule.

mo·lal (mólǝl) *adj. Chemistry.* Of or designating a solution containing one mole of solute in 1 000 grams of solvent, usually water. Compare **molar.** [From MOLE (chemistry) + -AL.]

mo·lal·i·ty (mō-lál-ǝti) *n., pl.* **-ties.** *Chemistry.* The molal concentration of a solute, usually expressed as the number of moles of solute per 1 000 grams of solvent. See **molal.**

mo·lar¹ (mólǝr) *adj. Chemistry.* **1.** Designating a physical property that is measured for unit amount of substance, usually for one mole: *molar enthalpy.* **2.** Of or designating a solution that contains one mole of solute per litre of solution. Compare **molal.** [From MOLE (quantity).]

molar² *n.* A tooth with a broad crown for grinding food, located behind the premolars. A human being has twelve molars, three in each side of the upper and lower jaws.
~*adj.* **1.** Of or pertaining to the molar teeth. **2.** Capable of grinding. [Latin *molāris* (adjective), from *mola,* millstone.]

mo·lar·i·ty (mō-lárrǝti) *n., pl.* **-ties.** *Chemistry.* The molar concentration of a solute, usually expressed as the number of moles of solute per litre of solution. See **molar¹.**

mo·las·ses (mǝ-lássiz, mō-) *n., pl.* **molasses. 1.** A thick uncrystallised syrup produced when raw sugar cane is cut. **2.** *U.S.* Black treacle. [Earlier *melasus, malassos,* from Portuguese *melaço,* from Late Latin *mellāceum,* must, from Latin *mel,* honey.]

mold. *U.S.* Variant of **mould.**

Mold (mōld) *Welsh* **Yr Wydd·grug** (ǝr ōo-ĭth-grig). Market town in northeast Wales, on the river Alyn; county town of Clwyd.

Mol·da·vi·a (mol-dáyvi-ǝ). *Romanian* **Mol·do·va.** The major grain-producing province of Romania, lying between the river Prut and the Carpathian mountains. Founded as a principality in the 14th century, it included Bukovina and Bessarabia, but lost the former to Austria (1775), and the latter to Russia (1812). Following the Crimean War, it united with Walachia (1859) to form modern Romania. See map at **Romania.**

Mol·da·vi·an (mol-dáyvi-ǝn) *n.* **1.** A native or inhabitant of Moldavia or the Moldavian S.S.R. **2.** The language of Moldavia, a form of Romanian. —**Mol·da·vi·an** *adj.*

Moldavian Soviet Socialist Republic. *Russian* **Mol·dav·ska·ya S.S.R.** (mal-dǎafskǝyǝ). Landlocked republic of the southwest U.S.S.R. between the rivers Prut and Dnestr. It was created (1940) from the Moldavian A.S.S.R. in the Ukraine and part of Bessarabia, the Moldavian territory gained by Russia in 1812 and held by Romania (1918–40). Its economy rests on sturgeon fisheries. Kishinev is the capital.

mole¹ (mōl) *n.* A small, pigmented growth on the human skin, usually slightly raised and brown, and sometimes hairy. It is a type of **naevus** (see). [Middle English *mool, mole,* Old English *māl.*]

mole² *n.* **1.** Any of various small, insectivorous, burrowing mammals of the family Talpidae, having thickset bodies with silky light brown to dark grey fur, rudimentary eyes, tough muzzles, and strong forefeet for digging. Most live underground. See **desman, shrew mole. 2.** The pelt of the mole, **moleskin** (see). **3.** *British.* **a.** An intelligence agent who establishes a cover by working as a legitimate member of a foreign organisation for a period of years, until assigned a mission. **b.** Loosely, any person who works under cover within an organisation, and gives away secret or classified

mole cricket *The brown mole cricket, which grows to more than 6 centimetres long (about 2¼ inches), spends most of its life in underground burrows. The male's burrow has a double entrance which acts like a loudspeaker. When the cricket "sings" – by rubbing its forewings together – the horn-shaped entrances amplify the sound so that it can be heard more readily by any passing females.*

mole-rat *Animals from several different families of rodents are given the name mole-rat because of their resemblance to the mole and their similar burrowing habits. This is an African mole-rat, a member of the family* Bathyergidae, *which lives and feeds almost entirely underground in the dry earth of the African plains.*

---

mollusc

WIDE DIVERSITY, UNDERLYING UNITY
Ancient and successful life forms

Molluscs include creatures as superficially different as slugs, snails, periwinkles, oysters, and squids. They do, however, have several features in common; they have soft, unsegmented bodies consisting of a head, muscular foot, and humped back – all covered by a tentlike mantle of skin. In most species, this mantle secretes a shell. Molluscs, which inhabit watery environments from deep oceans to moist places on land, are one of the most ancient of life forms. Some 35,000 extinct species are known, dating back nearly 600 million years.

Living molluscs can be divided into three main classes: gastropods, bivalves, and cephalopods. Gastropods, or "belly-footed" molluscs, such as slugs and snails, have sensory tentacles and generally a coiled shell, but in some the shell is reduced or absent. Bivalves, such as cockles, mussels, and oysters, have a shell in two hinged halves, or valves. Cephalopods, or "head-footed" molluscs, include squids and octopuses. These are the most highly evolved molluscs, with a well-developed nervous system.

There are also three lesser classes of mollusc: amphineura – some with cross-bands of shell, some wormlike and without shells; monoplacophora – with one-piece, cap-shaped shells; and scaphopods – tiny, burrowing, tubular-shelled creatures.

SNAIL *The thousands of species of snail are typical gastropods, with a conical shell, eyes on stalks, and a large foot on which they move.*

OCTOPUS *The common octopus grows to a width of 3 metres (almost 10 feet). Other cephalopods range from about 50 millimetres (2 inches) across to about 9 metres (30 feet) in the case of the Pacific giant octopus.*

MUSSEL *Bivalves, which include the mussel, feed and breathe by filtering some 45 litres (10 gallons) of water a day. Mussels move very little; most bivalves move by extending a foot outside the hinged shell.*

---

information. [Middle English *molle, mulle, mole,* from Middle Dutch *mol* and Medieval Latin *mulus,* both from an unknown Germanic source.]

mole³ *n.* **1.** A massive stone wall used as a breakwater or jetty. **2.** The harbour enclosed by such a barrier. [French *môle,* from Medieval Greek *môlos,* from Latin *mōlēs,* pier, dam, massive structure, mass.]

mole⁴ *n.* A mass or tumour in the uterus, caused by the degeneration or abortive development of a fertilised ovum. [French *môle,* from Latin *mola,* "millstone" (since it is a hardened mass), MOLE (wall, harbour).]

mole⁵ *n. Chemistry. Symbol* **mol.** The basic unit of amount of substance. It is equal to the amount of substance that contains the same number of entities (atoms, ions, molecules, photons, or the like) as there are atoms in 0.012 kilogram of the isotope of carbon with mass number 12. [German *Mol,* short for *Molekulargewicht,* molecular weight.]

mole cricket *n.* Any of various burrowing crickets of the family Gryllotalpidae, with short wings and front legs well adapted for digging and shearing.

mo·lec·u·lar (mǝ-léckew-lǝr, mō-, mo-) *adj. Abbr.* **mol.** Pertaining to, consisting of, caused by, or existing between molecules.

molecular beam *n. Physics.* A parallel stream of atoms or molecules, having a low pressure such that the number of collisions between molecules within the beam is negligible. It is used to study atomic and nuclear properties and chemical reactions.

molecular biology n. The field of biology in which the structure and development of biological systems are analysed in terms of the physics and chemistry of their molecular constituents, particularly nucleic acids and proteins.

molecular film n. A surface film of thickness comparable to that of a single molecule.

molecular formula n. A type of chemical formula that indicates the number of each type of atom in each molecule of a compound. Compare **empirical formula, structural formula.**

molecular sieve n. A crystalline substance, such as a zeolite, that can absorb large amounts of certain compounds. Molecular sieves are used for producing high vacua, purifying gases, and separating mixtures.

molecular weight n. Abbr. **mol. wt.** Chemistry. The sum of the atomic weights of a molecule's constituent atoms. Also called "relative molecular mass".

mol·e·cule (mólli-kewl) n. Abbr. **mol.** 1. A stable configuration of atomic nuclei and electrons bound together by electrostatic and electromagnetic forces. It is the simplest structural unit that displays the characteristic physical and chemical properties of a compound. 2. A small particle; a very tiny bit. [French molécule, from New Latin molecula, diminutive of Latin mōlēs, mass, bulk.]

mole·hill (mōl-hil) n. A small mound of loose earth thrown up by a burrowing mole. —**make a mountain out of a molehill.** To exaggerate a minor problem.

mole rat n. 1. Any of various burrowing rodents resembling moles, found in Africa and Eurasia. 2. A rodent, the **bandicoot** (see).

mole·skin (mōl-skin) n. 1. The short, soft, silky, dark grey fur of the mole. Also called "mole". 2. a. A heavy-napped cotton twill fabric. b. Plural. Clothing, especially trousers, of this fabric.

mo·lest (mə-lést, mō-) tr.v. **-lested, -lesting, -lests.** 1. To disturb, torment, or annoy. 2. a. To accost and harass sexually. b. To abuse or assault sexually: He not only accosted her verbally, but molested her as well. [Middle English molesten, to vex, molest, from Old French molester, from Latin molestāre, to annoy, from molestus, troublesome.] —**mo·les·ta·tion** (mō-less-táysh'n, mō-) n. —**mo·lest·er** n.

Mo·lière (mólli-air ‖ U.S. mōl-yaír; French mawl-yaír), born Jean-Baptiste Poquelin (1622–73). French dramatist, and founder of high French comedy. His plays include Les Précieuses ridicules (1659), Tartuffe (1664), Le Misanthrope (1666), L'Avare (1668), Le Bourgeois Gentilhomme (1670), and his last play, Le Malade imaginaire (1673). Molière died while performing on stage.

mo·line (mə-lín, mo-, mō-) adj. Heraldry. Designating a cross that has arms of equal length with the ends of each slightly broadened and curved back. [Probably from Anglo-French moliné, from molin, MILL (referring to the curved arms, which resemble those of a windmill).]

moll (mol) n. Slang. 1. A female companion of a thief or gangster. 2. A prostitute. [From Moll, pet form for the name Mary.]

mol·li·fy (mólli-fī) tr.v. **-fied, -fying, -fies.** 1. To allay (the anger of); placate; calm. 2. To make gentler; soften or ease: "with a countenance greatly mollified by the softening influence of tobacco" (Charles Dickens). —See Synonyms at **pacify.** [Middle English mollifien, from Old French mollifier, from Latin mollificāre, to make soft : mollis, soft + facere, to make, do.] —**mol·li·fi·a·ble** adj. —**mol·li·fi·ca·tion** (-fi-káysh'n) n. —**mol·li·fi·er** n. —**mol·li·fy·ing·ly** adv.

mol·lusc, U.S. **mol·lusk** (mól-əsk; rarely -usk) n. Any invertebrate animal of the phylum Mollusca, having a soft body typically protected by a shell. The group includes the snails and slugs, the clams and other bivalves, and the octopuses and squids. [French mollusque, from New Latin Mollusca, "the soft ones", from Latin molluscus, extension of mollis, soft.] —**mol·lus·cous** (mo-lúskəss, mə-) adj.

mol·lus·can (mo-lúskən, mə-) adj. Of or pertaining to the molluscs. ~n. A mollusc.

Moll·wei·de projection (mól-vídə) n. An equal-area map projection using an ellipsoidal shape and having straight lines for parallels of latitude and for the central meridian, other meridians being curved. It is used for representing the whole Earth and often split into sections, with continental areas having their own central meridians. [After Karl Mollweide (died 1825), German mathematician and astronomer.]

mol·ly, mol·lie (mólli) n., pl. **-lies.** Any of several tropical and subtropical fishes of the genus Mollienesia. The males of some species have sail-like dorsal fins and are bred in aquaria. [New Latin Mollienesia, after Comte François N. Mollien (1758–1850), French statesman.]

mol·ly·cod·dle (mólli-kodd'l) n. A person of weak character who seeks to be pampered and protected. ~tr.v. **mollycoddled, -dling, -dles.** To be overprotective and indulgent towards; spoil by pampering and coddling. See Synonyms at **pamper.** [Slang molly, milksop, from Molly, pet form of Mary + CODDLE.] —**mol·ly·cod·dler** n.

Molly Ma·guire (mə-gwír) n. 1. A member of a secret society in Ireland that terrorised law officers attempting to evict tenants in the 1840s. 2. A member of a secret society of Pennsylvania miners who terrorised mine owners from about 1865 to 1877 in order to secure better working conditions and better pay. [The name refers to the female disguise adopted by members.]

mo·loch (mō-lok) n. An Australian ant-eating desert lizard, Moloch horridus, with a spiny, yellow and brown body. [After MOLOCH (alluding to its grotesque appearance).]

Mo·loch (mō-lok ‖ U.S. also mōllák) n. 1. In the Old Testament, a god of the Ammonites and Phoenicians to whom children were sacrificed by burning. 2. Anything regarded as demanding a terrible sacrifice. [Late Latin Moloch, from Greek Molokh, from Hebrew Molekh.]

Mol·o·tov (mólla-tov, -tof ‖ U.S. also mōla-; Russian -təf), **Vyacheslav Mikhailovich,** born Vyacheslav Mikhailovich Skriabin (1890–). Soviet politician. He joined the Bolsheviks in 1906 and took the surname Molotov, meaning "the hammer". He helped to found Pravda in 1912 and became its acting editor. In 1939 he was made Foreign Secretary and cosigned, with Ribbentrop, the Hitler-Stalin pact. He remained Foreign Minister until 1949 and held office again from 1953 to 1956. In July 1957, he was expelled with Malenkov from the Central Committee for allegedly having formed an anti-party group.

Molotov cocktail n. A makeshift incendiary bomb made of a breakable container filled with inflammable liquid and provided with a rag wick. [After V.M. MOLOTOV.]

molt U.S. Variant of **moult.**

mol·ten (mōltən). Archaic past participle of **melt.** ~adj. 1. Made liquid by heat; melted. Said chiefly of substances, such as metal or rock, that melt at extremely high temperatures. 2. Brilliantly glowing.

mol·to (mól-tō ‖ U.S. mōl-) adv. Music. Very; much. Used with directions: molto sostenuto. [Italian, from Latin multum, much (adverb), from multus, much (adjective).]

Mo·luc·cas (mə-lúckəz) Bahasa Indonesian. **Ma·lu·ku; Mo·luk·ken.** Formerly **Spice Islands.** Group of islands in eastern Indonesia. They are hot, humid, and fertile and their cloves, nutmeg, and other spices attracted traders and colonisers. They gained independence from the Dutch (1949) as a province of Indonesia, but the South Moluccans resent rule by Indonesia, and have taken urban guerrilla action. Ambon is the capital. —**Mo·luc·can** n. & adj.

mol. wt. molecular weight.

mo·ly (mōli) n., pl. **-lies.** 1. In the Odyssey, a magic herb with black roots and white flowers, given to Odysseus by Hermes to nullify the spells of Circe. 2. A plant, the **lily leek** (see). [Latin mōly, from Greek mōlu, akin to Sanskrit mūlam, root.]

mo·lyb·de·nite (mo-líbdən-īt, mə-, mō-) n. A mineral form of molybdenum sulphide, MoS_2, that is the principal ore of molybdenum.

mo·lyb·de·num (mo-líbdən-əm, mə-, mō-) n. Symbol **Mo** A hard, grey, metallic element used to toughen alloy steels and soften tungsten alloy. It is also used in fertilisers, dyes, enamels, and reagents. Atomic number 42, atomic weight 95.94, melting point 2,620°C, boiling point 4,800°C, relative density 10.2, valencies 2, 3, 4, 5. [New Latin, from obsolete molybdena, from Latin molybdaena, galena, from Greek molubdaina, a lead (of a plumb line), from molubdos, lead.]

mo·lyb·dic (mo-líbdik, mə-, mō-) adj. Of or containing molybdenum. Said especially of a compound containing molybdenum with a high valency.

mo·lyb·dous (mo-líbdəss, mə-, mō-) adj. Of or containing molybdenum. Said especially of a compound containing molybdenum with a low valency.

mom (mom) n. U.S. Informal. A mother; a mum. [Short for momma, from baby talk.]

Mom·ba·sa (mom-bássə, -báʹsə). Seaport and industrial centre of southeast Kenya. It is the country's chief port, and also handles trade for Uganda and Tanzania.

mo·ment (mōmənt) n. 1. A brief, indefinite interval of time: She'll join you in a moment. 2. a. A specific point in time: at that moment. b. The present time: out at the moment. 3. The appropriate or right point in time: This is the moment to act. 4. a. A particular period or event of importance, significance, excellence, enjoyment, or the like: "Swinburne's entry was for me a great moment." (Max Beerbohm). b. Such a period or event occurring in something that is otherwise unexceptional: a dull play, but it has its moments. 5. Outstanding significance or value; importance: Your views are of no great moment. 6. Philosophy. A phase or aspect of a logically developing process; a momentum. 7. Physics. Abbr. **M a.** The product of a quantity, especially a force, and its perpendicular distance from a reference point. **b.** The rotation produced in a body when a force is applied; torque. See **moment of inertia.** 8. Statistics. The expected value of a positive integral power of a random variable. The first moment is the mean of the distribution. —See Synonyms at **importance.** [Middle English, from Old French, from Latin mōmentum, movement, MOMENTUM.]

Synonyms: moment, minute, instant, second, trice, jiffy, flash.

mo·men·tar·i·ly (mōmən-trə-li, -tərə- ‖ U.S. -térrə-) adv. 1. For only an instant or moment. 2. Rare. Momently. 3. U.S. Informal. Very soon; in just a moment.

mo·men·tar·y (mōmən-tri, -təri ‖ -terri) adj. 1. Lasting only a brief time. 2. Occurring or present at every moment: in momentary fear of being exposed. 3. Short-lived; ephemeral. Said of a living creature. —See Synonyms at **transient.** [Latin mōmentārius, from mōmentum, MOMENT.] —**mo·men·tar·i·ness** n.

Usage: Momentary and momentous are sometimes confused. Momentary refers to shortness of time; momentous to level of significance. A momentary decision would be one made on the spur of the moment; a momentous decision would be a very important one.

mo·ment·ly (mōmənt-li) adv. 1. Every moment; from moment to

PRONUNCIATION KEY

a, trap; aa, father; ai, fair; ar, star; aw, lawn; ay, play; b, bb, stab; rubber; ch, church; ck, ticket; d, dd, dead; ladder; e, dress; ee, bee; er, defer; ew, few; ewr, pure; ə, about; ər, letter; f, ff, fife; differ; g, gg, giggle; h, hat; i, kit; ī, price; īr, fire; j, judge; k, kick; l, ll, let; 'l, needle; m, mm, man; n, nn, no; 'n, sudden; ng, thing; o, lot; ō, no; ŏŏ, foot; ōō, shoe; oor, poor; ow, cow; owr, hour; oy, toy; p, pp, pepper; r, rr, red; s, ss, sauce; sh, ship; t, tt, totter; th, thick; th, this; smooth; u, cut; ur, turn; v, vv, valve; w, wet; y, yes; z, zz, zebra; zh, vision; pleasure

IN FOREIGN WORDS:

aN, oN, Saint-Saëns; hl, Llanelli; Hluhluwe; kh, loch; lough; Khaled

STRESS MARK:

ín-sīt, insight; in-sít, incite

moment: *"The throng momently increased."* (Edgar Allan Poe). **2.** For a moment.

moment of inertia *n. Physics.* **1.** A measure of a body's resistance to angular acceleration, equal to: **a.** The product of the mass of a particle and the square of its distance from a reference point or line. **b.** The sum of the products of each mass element of a body multiplied by the square of its distance from an axis. **2.** The sum of the products of each element of an area multiplied by the square of its distance from a coplanar axis.

moment of momentum *n.* **Angular momentum** *(see).*

moment of truth *n.* **1.** A time of crisis or testing, especially one in which the true nature or capabilities of a person or thing are revealed. **2.** In bullfighting, the moment when the matador makes his final sword-thrust.

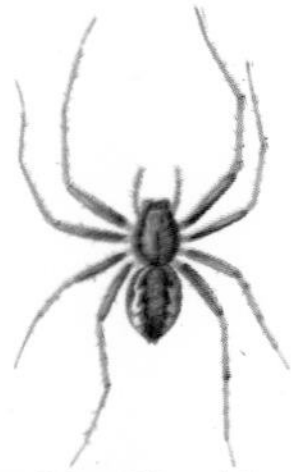

money spider Linyphia triangularis, *shown here about 1½ times life size, is one of some 250 British species called money spiders, from old popular superstitions associating them with wealth. On warm mornings following cool nights, they spin long gossamer threads which they use as parachutes. Rising warm air currents carry threads and spiders aloft. Cooler air brings them down again, sometimes hundreds of kilometres from their starting point.*

mo·men·tous (mə-méntəss, mō-) *adj.* Of utmost importance or outstanding significance; having grave implications or consequences: *a momentous decision affecting our future.* See Usage note at **momentary.** —**mo·men·tous·ly** *adv.* —**mo·men·tous·ness** *n.*

mo·men·tum (mə-mén-təm, mō-) *n., pl.* **-ta** (-tə) or **-tums. 1.** *Physics. Symbol* **p a.** The product of a body's mass and linear velocity. Also called "linear momentum". **b.** See **angular momentum. 2.** The force of motion, **impetus** *(see).* **3.** Impetus or force gained through movement or progression: *the campaign's momentum.* **4.** *Philosophy.* A moment. [Latin *mōmentum,* motion, movement, from *movimentum* (unattested), from *movēre,* to move.]

mom·ma (mómmə) *n.* Also **mom·mie, mom·my** (mómmi) (for sense 1) *pl.* **-mies.** *Informal.* **1.** *U.S.* A mother; a mummy. **2.** A woman; especially, a large, earthy, usually black, singer. Sometimes considered offensive. [Variant of MAMMA.]

Mo·mus (mṓməss) *n., pl.* **-muses. 1.** *Greek Mythology.* The god of blame and ridicule. **2.** A fault-finder; a critic of petty details.

Mon (mōn) *n., pl.* **Mons** or collectively **Mon. 1.** A member of the principal native people of the Pegu region in Burma. **2.** The Mon-Khmer language of this people. —**Mon** *adj.*

Môn. See **Anglesey.**

mon. 1. monastery. **2.** monetary.

Mon. Monday.

mon-. Variant of **mono-.**

mo·na (mṓnə) *n.* An African monkey, *Cercopithecus monas,* with a dark back and pale underparts. It is a type of guenon. [Portuguese or Spanish, monkey.]

mon·a·chism (mónnəkiz'm) *n.* Monasticism. [Middle English, from Medieval Latin *monachismus,* from Late Greek *monakhismos,* from *monakhos,* MONK.] —**mon·a·chal** (monnək'l) *adj.*

monacid, monacidic. Variants of **monoacid.**

Mon·a·co, Principality of (mónnəkō, mə-na̋akō). Small, independent principality on France's south coast. Business interests, centred at La Condamine, gambling at the Casino at Monte Carlo, and tourism are the main sources of revenue, and spare the Monégasques (who are excluded from the gambling tables) taxation. The Genoese family of Grimaldi have ruled the principality since 1297. At various times under the protection of Spain, Sardinia, and France, its sovereignty was restored in 1861. Area, 1 square kilometre (0.4 square mile). Population, 28,000. Capital, Monaco-Ville. See map at **France.** —**Mon·a·can** *adj. & n.*

mo·nad (mónnad, mṓ-nad) *n.* **1.** An independent, indivisible, and impenetrable unit of substance viewed as the basic constituent element of physical reality, as in the philosophy of Leibniz. **2.** *Biology.* Any single-celled microscopic organism, especially a flagellate protozoan. Also called "monas". **3.** *Chemistry.* An atom or radical with a valency of 1. [Late Latin *monas* (stem *monad-*), unit, from Greek, from *monos,* single.] —**mo·nad·i·cal** *adj.* —**mo·nad·i·cal·ly** *adv.*

mon·a·del·phous (mónnə-délfəss) *adj. Botany.* **1.** United by the filaments into a single tubelike group. Said of stamens. **2.** Having stamens thus united. Compare **diadelphous.** [MON(O)- + -ADELPHOUS.]

mo·nad·ic (mo-náddik, mə-, mō-) *adj.* **1.** Considered or dealt with singly, not comparatively. **2.** *Biology & Chemistry.* Of or pertaining to a monad.

mon·ad·ism (mónnə-diz'm, mṓnə-) *n. Philosophy.* The doctrine, as in the philosophy of Leibniz, that monads are the basic constituent elements of physical reality.

mo·nad·nock (mə-nád-nok) *n.* A mountain or rocky mass that is more resistant and stands isolated above the general level of erosion (peneplain). [After Mt. *Monadnock* in New Hampshire, United States.]

Mon·a·ghan (mónnə-hən, *rarely* -k͟hən, -gən). *Irish* **Contae Mhuineachain.** County in the Republic of Ireland. It lies in the ancient province of Ulster, and is largely agricultural, producing beef and dairy cattle. The county town, Monaghan, produces footwear.

mo·nan·drous (món-ándrəss, mən-) *adj.* **1.** *Botany.* Of, pertaining to, or characterised by monandry. **2. a.** Designating flowers having a single stamen. **b.** Having flowers bearing a single stamen. [MON(O)- + -ANDROUS.]

mo·nan·dry (món-ándri, mən-, món-andri) *n.* **1.** The custom of having one husband at a time. Compare **polyandry. 2.** *Botany.* The condition of being monandrous. [MON(O)- + -ANDRY.]

mo·nan·thous (món-ánthəss, mən-) *adj. Botany.* Bearing a single flower. [MON(O)- + Greek *anthos,* flower.]

mon·arch (mónnərk. *Note: a spelling pronunciation* mónnaark *is sometimes heard*). *n.* **1.** A person, such as a king or emperor, who is a head of state, usually by hereditary right and for life, and whose powers vary from those of an absolute ruler to the constitutionally limited powers of a figurehead. **2.** One that surpasses others in power or pre-eminence: *"Mont Blanc is the monarch of the mountains."* (Lord Byron). **3.** A large orange and black butterfly, *Danaus plexippus,* having a wingspread of up to 110 millimetres (4 inches). Also called "milkweed butterfly". [Late Latin *monarcha,* from Greek *monarkhēs* : *mono-,* sole + *-arkhes,* -ARCH.] —**mo·nar·chal** (mo-nárk'l, mə-), **mo·nar·chi·al** (-nárki-əl), **mon·ar·chic** (-nárkik), **mon·ar·chi·cal** (-nárkik'l) *adj.* —**mo·nar·chal·ly, mon·ar·chi·cal·ly** *adv.*

mo·nar·chi·an·ism (mo-nárki-ən-iz'm, mə-) *n.* A Christian heresy of the second and third centuries that denied the doctrine of the Trinity. [Late Latin *monarchiānī,* "the monarchians," from *monarchia,* MONARCHY.] —**mo·nar·chi·an** (mə-nárki-ən) *n. & adj.*

mon·ar·chism (món-ər-kiz'm || -aar-) *n.* **1.** The principles of monarchy. **2.** Belief in or advocacy of monarchy. —**mon·ar·chist** (-kist) *n. & adj.* —**mon·ar·chis·tic** (-kístik) *adj.*

mon·ar·chy (món-ər-ki || -aar-) *n., pl.* **-chies. 1.** Government by a monarch. **2.** A state that is ruled by or has a monarch. [Middle English *monarchie,* from Old French, from Late Latin *monarchia,* from Greek *monarkhia,* from *monarkhēs,* MONARCH.]

mo·nas (mónnass, mṓ-nass) *n., pl.* **monades** (mónnə-deez). *Biology.* A **monad** *(see).* [Late Latin *monas* (stem *monad-*), MONAD.]

mon·as·ter·y (mónnə-stri, -stəri || -sterri) *n., pl.* **-ies.** *Abbr.* **mon.** The residence of a community of persons, especially monks, living under religious vows and usually in seclusion. [Middle English *monasterie,* from Late Latin *monastērium,* from Late Greek *monastērion,* from Greek *monazein,* to live alone, from *monos,* alone.] —**mon·as·te·ri·al** (-stéer-i-əl || -stérri-əl) *adj.*

mo·nas·tic (mə-nástik, mo-) *adj.* Also **mo·nas·ti·cal** (-nástik'l). **1.** Pertaining to or characteristic of monasteries or persons living in religious or contemplative seclusion. **2.** Loosely, leading an ascetic or celibate life.

~*n.* A person who lives a monastic life; especially, a monk. [Late Latin *monasticus,* from Late Greek *monastikos,* from Greek *monazein,* to live alone. See **monastery.**] —**mo·nas·ti·cal·ly** *adv.*

mo·nas·ti·cism (mə-násti-siz'm, mo-) *n.* The monastic life or system.

mon·a·tom·ic (mónnə-tómmik) *adj.* **1.** Occurring as single atoms, as, for example, does helium. **2.** Having one replaceable atom or radical. **3.** Univalent. [MON(O)- + ATOMIC.]

mon·au·ral (món-áwrəl, *sometimes* -ówr-əl) *adj.* **1.** Designating sound reception by one ear. **2.** *Electronics.* Monophonic. [MON(O)- + AURAL.] —**mon·au·ral·ly** *adv.*

mon·ax·i·al (món-áksi-əl) *adj.* **Uniaxial** *(see).*

mon·a·zite (mónnə-zīt) *n.* A pale yellow to reddish-brown mineral phosphate of rare-earth metals, chiefly cerium, yttrium, and lanthanum, usually together with thorium. [German *Monazit,* from Greek *monazein,* to live alone (because it is rare). See **monastery.**]

Monck or **Monk** (mungk), **George, 1st Duke of Albemarle** (1608–70). English military commander. Having earlier fought for Charles I, he was commissioned by Cromwell to put down rebellion in Ireland and Scotland in 1652, but in 1660 he led his forces successfully in support of the royalist cause.

Mon·day (mún-di, -day) *n. Abbr.* **Mon., M.** The day of the week following Sunday; the first day of the working week. [Middle English *monday,* Old English *mōnan dæg,* moon's day (translation of Late Latin *lūnae diēs*) : *mōna,* MOON + *dæg,* DAY.]

Monday Club *n.* In Britain, an extreme right-wing grouping within the Conservative Party whose members try to influence official party policy. [From the Club's custom of meeting for lunch on Mondays.]

mon·di·al (móndi-əl) *adj.* Of, pertaining to, or involving the whole world. [French, from ecclesiastical Latin *mundiālis,* from *mundus,* world.]

Mond process *n.* An industrial process for producing nickel by heating the ore in carbon monoxide and decomposing, at a higher temperature, the nickel carbonyl vapour that is produced, in order to yield the metal. [After Ludwig *Mond* (1839–1909), German-born British chemist and industrialist who developed the process.]

Mon·dri·an (móndri-ən, -aan), **Piet** (1872–1944). Dutch painter, influenced by cubism in Paris after 1910. He painted compositions in primary colours of space enclosed by lines and rectangles. He outlined his theories in a book, *Neo-Plasticism* (1920).

monecious. Variant of **monoecious.**

Mo·né·gasque (mónni-gásk, mónnay-) *n.* A citizen of Monaco; a Monacan. [French, from Provençal *Mounegasc,* from *Mounegue,* MONACO.] —**Mo·né·gasque** *adj.*

Mo·nel metal (mo-nél || *U.S.* mō-) *n.* A corrosion-resistant alloy of nickel, copper, iron, and manganese. [After Ambrose *Monel,* president of International Nickel Co. (1873–1921).]

Mo·net (mónnay, mo-náy), **Claude** (1840–1926). French painter, and a founder of impressionism. He began to experiment with depicting variations of light and atmosphere from the outset of his career. It was his painting, *Impression: Sunrise* (1872), which gave the impressionists their name.

mon·e·tar·ist (múnni-tə-rist, mónni-) *n.* One who advocates the regulation of the money supply as a method of controlling and stabilising the economy. —**mon·e·tar·ism** *n.* —**mon·e·tar·ist** *adj.*

mon·e·tar·y (múnni-tri, mónni-, -təri || -terri) *adj. Abbr.* **mon. 1.** Of or pertaining to money. **2.** Of or pertaining to a nation's money supply, interest rates, or the like. —See Synonyms at **financial.**

PRONUNCIATION KEY

a, trap; aa, father; ai, fair; ar, star; aw, lawn; ay, play; b, bb, stab; rubber; ch, church; ck, ticket; d, dd, dead; ladder; e, dress; ee, bee; er, defer; ew, few; ewr, pure; ə, about; ər, letter; f, ff, fife; differ; g, gg, giggle; h, hat; i, kit; ī, price; īr, fire; j, judge; k, kick; l, ll, let; 'l, needle; m, mm, man; n, nn, no; 'n, sudden; ng, thing; o, lot; ō, no; o͝o, foot; o͞o, shoe; oor, poor; ow, cow; owr, hour; oy, boy; p, pp, pepper; r, rr, red; s, ss, sauce; sh, ship; t, tt, totter; th, thick; t͟h, this; smooth; u, cut; ur, turn; v, vv, valve; w, wet; y, yes; z, zz, zebra; z͟h, vision; pleasure

IN FOREIGN WORDS:

aɴ, oɴ, Saint-Saëns; h͟l, Llanelli; Hluhluwe; k͟h, loch; lough; Khaled

STRESS MARK:

ín-sīt, insight; in-sī́t, incite

[Late Latin *monētārius,* from Latin *monēta,* MONEY.] —**mon·e·tar·i·ly** *adv.*

mon·e·tise, mon·e·tize (múnni-tīz, mónni-) *tr.v.* **-tised, -tising, -tises. 1.** To make legal tender. **2.** To make into money; mint. [Latin *monēta,* MONEY.] —**mon·e·ti·sa·tion** (-tī-záysh'n ‖ *U.S.* -ti-) *n.*

mon·ey (múnni) *n., pl.* **-eys** or **-ies. 1.** A commodity such as gold or silver that is legally established as an exchangeable equivalent of all other commodities and is used as a measure of their comparative values on the market. **2.** The official currency, as in coins and negotiable paper notes, issued by a government. **3. a.** Assets and property that may be converted into actual currency; wealth: *made her money in the property boom of the 70s.* **b.** *Informal.* Opportunities to acquire wealth: *There's no money in writing.* **c.** Those who own wealth: *married into money.* **4.** Any pecuniary amount of indefinite extent: *put a lot of money into the business; the company is still losing money.* **5.** *Plural. Chiefly Law.* Sums of money: *sued for the return of all monies paid into the fund.* **6.** Any unspecified amount of currency: *money for groceries.* —**in the money.** *Informal.* **1.** Having won money. **2.** Having plenty of money; rich. —**money for jam** or **old rope.** *Informal.* Profit made with little or no effort; something for nothing. —**put money on.** To place a bet or place one's confidence in. [Middle English *moneye,* from Old French *moneie,* from Latin *monēta,* money, mint, from *Monēta,* epithet of Juno, whose temple in Rome housed the mint.]

Usage: Moneys is the preferred plural form, though *monies* is also to be found. It is used only in referring to the mediums of exchange of different countries, or to forms of currency or particular sums of money in a country.

mon·ey·bags (múnni-bagz) *n. Used with a singular verb. Informal.* A rich or miserly person.

mon·ey·chang·er (múnni-chaynjər) *n.* **1.** A person who exchanges money, as from one currency to another. **2.** *Chiefly U.S.* A machine that holds and dispenses coins.

money cowry *n.* A small shell used as money in certain parts of Africa and the South Pacific. See **cowry.**

mon·ey·eyed, mon·ied (múnnid ‖ múnneed) *adj.* **1.** Having a great deal of money. **2.** Representing or arising from the possession of money: *the triumph of moneyed interests over landed interests.*

mon·ey·er (múnni-ər) *n.* Formerly, a person authorised to coin or mint money. [Middle English *monyer,* from Old French *monier,* from Late Latin *monētārius,* minter, from *monēta,* MONEY.]

mon·ey·grub·ber (múnni-grubbər) *n. Informal.* A person who is intent on accumulating money at every opportunity. —**mon·ey·grub·bing** *adj.*

mon·ey·lend·er (múnni-lendər) *n.* One whose business is lending money at an interest rate. —**mon·ey·lend·ing** *n.*

mon·ey·mak·er (múnni-maykər) *n.* **1.** One who accumulates wealth. **2.** An enterprise or product that is actually or potentially profitable. —**mon·ey·mak·ing** *n. & adj.*

money market *n.* The sphere of the financial market dealing in short-term securities and loans, gold, and foreign exchange. Compare **capital market.**

money of account *n. Chiefly U.S.* **Unit of account** (see).

money order *n. Abbr.* **m.o., M.O.** An order for the payment of a specific amount of money, usually issued and payable at a bank or post office.

money spider *n.* Any of various spiders of the family Linyphiidae, having a small reddish or black body. [From the belief that the tiny spider brings good luck.]

mon·ey·spin·ner (múnni-spinnər) *n. Informal.* Something, such as an idea, project, or business, that is or will be very successful and profitable. [Originally, a name of the money spider, extended to promising or profitable business.] —**mon·ey·spin·ning** *n. & adj.*

money supply *n. Economics.* The total amount of money held by individuals and organisations in a country at a given time, as measured by any of several indicators, specifically (in Britain): **1.** M_1, based on actual currency in circulation plus readily transferrable money in private current or deposit accounts. **2.** M_2, similar to M_1 but including longer-term deposits. **3.** M_3, the most comprehensive, based on all the above plus nonsterling deposits and public-sector deposits.

mon·ey·wort (múnni-wurt ‖ -wawrt) *n.* Any of several plants with rounded, coinlike leaves, such as the Cornish moneywort, *Sibthorpia europaea.*

mon·ger (múng-gər ‖ móng-) *n.* **1.** A dealer in a specified commodity. Usually used in combination: *ironmonger.* **2.** A person promoting something specified and usually undesirable. Used in combination: *scandalmonger, warmonger.*

~*tr.v.* **mongered, -gering, -gers.** To peddle or deal in. [Middle English *mongere,* Old English *mangere,* from *mangian,* to traffic, from Germanic *mangōjan* (unattested), from Latin *mangō,* (fraudulent) dealer.]

mon·go (móng-gō) *n., pl.* **mongo** (mőng-gő). A monetary unit, ¹⁄₁₀₀ of the Mongolian tugrik.

mon·gol (móng-g'l, -gol) *n.* A person affected with **Down's syndrome** (see). Not in technical usage. See Usage note at **mongolism.**

Mon·gol (móng-g'l, -gol ‖ -gōl) *n.* **1.** A member of one of the nomadic peoples of Mongolia or a native of Mongolia. **2.** A member of the Mongoloid ethnic group. **3.** The language of Mongolia. **4.** Loosely, the Yuan dynasty of China. [Mongol *Mongol,* perhaps from *mong,* brave.] —**Mon·gol** *adj.*

Mon·go·li·a (mong-gōl-i-ə, mon-, -yə). Ancient region inhabited by

---

THE MEANS OF BUYING AND SELLING
From internal bartering to international credit cards

Ancient civilisations such as the Egyptians and Babylonians traded by barter – a farmer, for instance, would trade livestock for its equivalent in other goods. This was a clumsy way of doing business. Transactions speeded up when the first coins appeared in Asia Minor in about 700 B.C., and their use later spread throughout the Mediterranean world, the Greeks minting large numbers of coins bearing artistic designs. The Chinese were using a form of coin (a miniature of a knife or spade with the exchange value of the real thing) by the 7th century B.C.

Although paper money had been used in China in the 7th century A.D., it was not until the 11th century that it was issued in bulk – when the Mongol emperor Kublai Khan paid his soldiers in paper currency. In 1661 the first European banknotes were issued in Stockholm, and the first Bank of England notes – redeemable in gold – appeared in London in the 1690s.

Today, coins have little intrinsic value and banknotes can no longer be converted into gold. Even this "token" money has been partly replaced by the use of cheques for large payments. The cheque, in turn, is being replaced by the credit card.

SHELL MONEY *Early settlers in North America commonly used as money Indian wampum – tubular white and mauve shells threaded into strings or belts. Wampum was made legal tender in Massachusetts in 1641.*

SILVER DOWRY *A bride of a hill tribe in North Vietnam wears silver coins in her bridal headdress. The headdress and silver necklets are part of her dowry, which is handed down from generation to generation.*

U.S. BANKNOTE *The world's first decimal currency, with 100 cents to the dollar, appeared in the American colonies in 1729. Present-day U.S. banknotes are authorised by the U.S. Treasury.*

---

the Mongols, and now comprising the Mongolian People's Republic, and the Inner Mongolian Autonomous Region of China. In the 13th century, the Mongols under Genghis Khan built one of the world's greatest empires, stretching from China to the Danube, and into Persia. This broke up, his successors establishing the khanate of the Golden Horde in Russia, and the Yuan dynasty in China. See also **Mongolian People's Republic.**

Mongolia, Inner See **Inner Mongolian Autonomous Region.**

mon·go·li·an (mong-gōl-i-ən, mon-, -yən) *adj.* Of, pertaining to, or exhibiting **Down's syndrome** (see). Not in technical usage.

Mon·go·li·an (mong-gōl-i-ən, mon-, -yən) *n.* **1.** A Mongol. **2.** The Mongolic language of Mongolia. —**Mon·go·li·an** *adj.*

Mongolian People's Republic Also **Mon·go·li·a, Outer Mongolia.** Republic of east central Asia. It consists of a high plateau, with

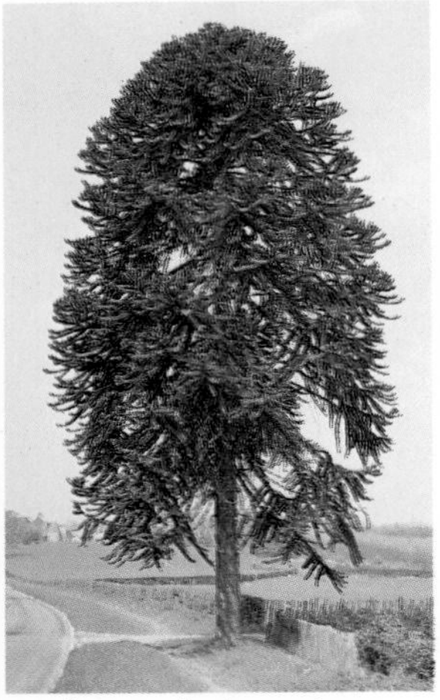

monkey puzzle Araucaria araucana, *which is native to Chile and Argentina, is thought to be the most ancient and primitive conifer in the world. It acquired its common English name because its branches were said to be so tangled that they would baffle a monkey wanting to climb it.*

mountains in the centre, west and north and the Gobi (desert) in the south and east. Much of the terrain is used for pasture, livestock herding (now largely collectivised) being the principal occupation of the seminomadic people. Once the centre of the Mongol empire (1206), it was a province of China (1691–1911 and 1919–21), and then an independent republic, under the protection of the U.S.S.R. See map at **China.** Area, 1 565 000 square kilometres (604,250 square miles). Population, 1,800,000. Capital, Ulan Bator.

Mon·gol·ic (mong-góllik, mon-) *n.* The Altaic subfamily that includes Mongolian and Kalmuck. **—Mon·gol·ic** *adj.*

mon·gol·ism (móng-gə-liz'm) *n. Also capital* **M.** A congenital condition, **Down's syndrome** *(see).* Not in technical usage. [From a supposed resemblance to the features of ethnic Mongoloids.]

Usage: The terms *mongolism* and *mongol* have been replaced in medical usage by *Down's syndrome* and *Down's baby* (or *child*) respectively, and should be avoided as they may give offence.

mon·gol·oid (móng-gə-loyd) *adj.* Characterised by or pertaining to **Down's syndrome** *(see).* Not in technical usage.

Mon·gol·oid (móng-gə-loyd) *adj. Anthropology.* **1.** Of, pertaining to, or designating a major ethnic division of the human species whose members are characterised by yellowish-brown to white skin pigmentation, coarse straight black hair, dark eyes with pronounced epicanthic folds, and prominent cheekbones. This division is considered to include the Chinese, Japanese, Malayans, Mongolians, Siberians, Eskimos, and American Indians. **2.** Characteristic of or like a Mongol.

~n. A member of the Mongoloid ethnic division of the human species.

mon·goose (móng-gōōss, múng-, gōōss || *U.S. also* món-) *n., pl.* **-gooses.** Any of various Old World carnivorous mammals of the genus *Herpestes* and related genera, having a slender body and a long tail and notable for the ability to kill poisonous snakes. [Marathi *mangūs,* from Dravidian, akin to Telugu *mangisu.*]

mon·grel (múng-grəl || móng-) *n.* **1.** An animal or plant resulting from various interbreedings; especially, a dog of mixed breed or no definable breed. **2.** A person of mixed racial stock. Used derogatorily or facetiously. **3.** A cross between one thing and another. Also used adjectivally: *a mongrel language, half English, half Spanish.* [Probably diminutive of Middle English *mong,* Old English *gemang,* mixture.] **—mon·grel·ism** *n.* **—mon·grel·ly** (-grəli) *adj.*

mon·grel·ise, mon·grel·ize (múng-grəl-īz, móng-) *tr.v.* **-ised, -ising, -ises.** To make mongrel in race, nature, or character. Usually used derogatorily when applied to human beings.

'mongst (mung-st, -kst || mong-) *prep. Poetic.* Amongst.

monied. Variant of **moneyed.**

mon·ies. Alternative plural of **money.**

mon·i·ker, mon·ick·er (mónnikər) *n. Informal.* A personal name or nickname. [19th century : origin obscure.]

mon·i·li·a·sis (mónni-lī-ə-siss, mōni-) *n.* **Candidiasis** *(see).* [New Latin : *Monilia* (genus), from Latin *monile,* necklace (referring to the chain of spores) + -IASIS.]

mo·nil·i·form (mo-nílli-fawrm, mə-, mō-) *adj. Biology.* Resembling a string of beads, as do various fungi, the antennae of certain insects, and the nuclei of some members of the Ciliata. [Latin *monīle,* necklace + -FORM.]

mon·ish (mónnish) *tr.v.* **-ished, -ishing, -ishes.** *Archaic.* To admonish. [Middle English *monisshen,* variant of *monesten,* from Old French *monester,* from Vulgar Latin *monestāre* (unattested), extension of Latin *monēre,* to warn.]

mon·ism (món-iz'm || mōn-) *n. Philosophy.* A metaphysical theory according to which reality is conceived as consisting of only one basic substance. Compare **dualism, pluralism.** [German *Monismus* : MON(O)- + -ISM.] **—mon·ist** *n. & adj.* **—mo·nis·tic** (mo-nístik, mə- || mō-) *adj.* **—mo·nis·ti·cal·ly** *adv.*

mo·ni·tion (mə-nísh'n, mo-, mō-) *n.* **1.** A warning or intimation of some impending danger. **2. a.** Admonition. **b.** A piece of advice. **3.** A formal order from a bishop or ecclesiastical court to refrain from some particular offence. [Middle English *monicioun,* from Old French *monition,* from Latin *monitiō* (stem *monitiōn-*), from *monēre,* to warn.]

mon·i·tor (mónnitər) *n.* **1.** *Archaic.* One that admonishes, cautions, or reminds. **2. a.** A pupil who assists a teacher in routine duties. **b.** A senior pupil with various responsibilities such as keeping order in class. **3. a.** Any device used to record, check, or control a process. **b.** A television set in a studio showing images for transmission. **4.** An articulated device holding the rotating nozzle of a water jet, used in mining and fire-fighting. **5.** A heavily ironclad warship of the 19th century with a low, flat deck and one or more gun turrets. **6.** Any carnivorous lizard of the family Varanidae, of tropical and subtropical regions, ranging in length from about 20 centimetres to 3 metres (8 inches to 10 feet). See **Komodo dragon.**

~v. **monitored, -toring, -tors.** *—tr.* **1.** To check (the transmission quality of a signal) by means of a receiver or monitor. **2.** To test (a surface) for radiation intensity. **3.** To keep track of by means of an electronic device. **4.** To check by means of a receiver for significant content: *monitor foreign radio broadcasts.* **5.** To scrutinise or check systematically: *carefully monitored the experiment at every stage.* **6.** To keep watch over; supervise: *monitor an examination.* **7.** To direct as a monitor. *—intr.* To act as a monitor. [Latin, one who warns, from *monēre,* to warn.] **—mon·i·tor·i·al** (mónni-táwri-əl || -tōri-) *adj.* **—mon·i·tress** (-trəss, -triss, -tress) *n.*

mon·i·to·ry (mónni-tri, -təri) *adj.* Conveying an admonition or warning: *a monitory glance.*

~n., pl. **monitories.** A letter containing the admonition of a bishop or ecclesiastical court. [Latin *monitōrius,* from *monitor,* MONITOR.]

monk (mungk) *n.* A member of a religious brotherhood living in a monastery, bound by vows such as those of poverty, chastity, and obedience, and devoted to a discipline prescribed by a religious order. [Middle English *munk,* Old English *munuc,* from Late Latin *monachus,* from Late Greek *monakhos,* solitary, monk, from Greek *monos,* alone.]

Monk, Thelonius (1920–82). U.S. black jazz pianist and composer. His spare piano style and unusual harmonic sense made him one of the most influential of modern jazz musicians. His notable compositions include *Round About Midnight* (*c.* 1947).

monk·er·y (múngkəri) *n., pl.* **-ies. 1.** Monks or monastic life or practices. Used derogatorily. **2.** A monastery. Used derogatorily.

mon·key (múngki) *n., pl.* **-keys. 1. a.** Any long-tailed primate, including the Old and New World monkeys and the marmosets, but excluding the anthropoid apes and the lemurs, lorises, tree shrews, and tarsiers. **b.** Loosely, any member of the order Primates, apart from the human race. **2.** A mischievous, playful child or young person. Used familiarly: *you cheeky monkey!* **3.** The iron block or ram of a pile driver. **4.** *Slang.* £500. **5.** *Slang.* A person who is mocked, duped, or made to appear a fool. Used chiefly in the phrase *make a monkey out of.* **6.** *Slang.* Drug addiction, regarded as a burdensome affliction: *have a monkey on one's back.* **7.** *Australian Informal.* A sheep.

~v. **monkeyed, -keying, -keys.** *—intr. Informal.* To play or fiddle with something idly: *Don't monkey around with my watch.* *—tr.* To imitate or mimic; ape. [16th century : origin obscure.]

monkey bread *n.* The fruit of the **baobab** *(see).*

monkey business *n. Informal.* Mischievous or deceitful behaviour.

mon·key-flow·er (múngki-flowr) *n.* Any of various plants of the genus *Mimulus,* especially *M. luteus,* which has yellow, two-lipped flowers, and is widely cultivated. [From the supposed resemblance of the flower to a monkey's face.]

monkey jacket *n.* **1.** A short, tight-fitting jacket, formerly worn by sailors. **2.** A **mess jacket** *(see).* [From its similarity to the jackets worn by performing monkeys.]

monkey nut *n. British Informal.* A peanut.

monkey pot *n.* **1.** The large, urn-shaped lidded pod of tropical trees of the genus *Lecythis.* **2.** Any tree bearing this type of pod.

monkey puzzle *n.* A coniferous tree, *Araucaria araucana,* native to Chile, having intricately ramifying branches covered with broad, stiff, prickle-tipped leaves. Also called "Chile pine". [Because its branches supposedly make it difficult for a monkey to climb.]

mon·key·shine (múngki-shīn) *n. Usually plural. U.S. Slang.* A playful, mischievous trick. [MONKEY + SHINE (prank).]

monkey suit *n. Slang.* A man's formal dress suit or a full-dress military uniform. [Probably extended from **monkey jacket.**]

monkey wrench *n.* A large wrench with adjustable jaws for turning nuts of varying sizes.

monk·fish (múngk-fish) *n., pl.* **-fishes** or collectively **monkfish. 1.** Any of several raylike sharks of the genus Squatina, having a broad, flat head and body. Also called "angel shark", "angelfish". **2.** Any of various angler fishes of the genus *Lophius.* Also *U.S.* "goosefish". [From the cowled appearance of the head.]

Mon-Khmer (mōn-kmáir) *n.* A family of languages, including Khmer, spoken in Southeast Asia. **—Mon-Khmer** *adj.*

monk·hood (múngk-hōōd) *n.* **1.** The state or profession of a monk; monasticism. **2.** Monks collectively.

monk·ish (múngkish) *adj.* Of, pertaining to, or characteristic of monks or monasticism. Often used derogatorily.

monk's cloth *n.* A heavy cotton cloth in a coarse basket weave. [Originally used for the habits of monks.]

monk seal *n.* A seal of the nearly extinct genus *Monachus,* formerly much hunted in Mediterranean and Caribbean waters for its fur, which may be grey or yellow with black spots or uniformly brown. [From the cowled appearance of its head.]

monks·hood (múngks-hōōd) *n.* Any of various plants of the genus *Aconitum,* having hooded flowers; especially, *A. napellus,* with purplish flowers. Most species are poisonous. Also called "acōnite", "wolfsbane".

Mon·mouth (món-məth, mún-). *Welsh* **Tre·fyn·wy** (tre-vún-wi). Market town in Gwent, southeast Wales, formerly the county town of Monmouthshire. It is an agricultural and tourist centre.

Monmouth, James Scott, 1st Duke of (1649–85). English pretender to the throne, bastard son of Charles II by Lucy Walter. After 1662 he lived at court, and Charles acknowledged him as his son, creating him duke in 1663. When the Catholic James II succeeded (1685), Monmouth led a rebellion. He was defeated at Sedgmoor, captured, and beheaded.

Mon·mouth·shire (món-məth-shər, mún-, -sheer). *Welsh* **Myn·wy, Sir Fyn·wy** (mún-wi, sheer vún-wi). Former county of western England, for some purposes, such as censuses, included in Wales. Most of it is now incorporated in the Welsh county of Gwent, the far west now being in Mid Glamorgan and South Glamorgan.

Mon·net (mónnay, mo-náy), **Jean (Omer Marie Gabriel)** (1888–1979). French statesman, called the "father of Europe". He was the first president (1952–55) of the European Coal and Steel Community, and laid the plans for the European Economic Community.

mon·o (mónnō) *adj. Electronics.* Monophonic.

~n., pl. **monos.** Monophonic sound reproduction.

mono–, mon– *comb. form.* Indicates: **1.** One; single; alone; for example, **monogamy. 2.** The presence of a single atom, radical, or group in a compound; for example, **monohydric.** [Middle English, from Old French, from Latin, from Greek, from *monos*, single, sole, alone.]

mon·o·ac·id (mónnō-ássid) *adj.* Also **mon·o·a·cid·ic** (-ə-síddik, -a-), **mon·ac·id** (món-), **mon·a·cid·ic.** *Chemistry.* Having only one hydroxyl group to react with acids. Said of bases.

mon·o·a·mine (mónnō-ámmin, -ə-méen) *n. Chemistry.* An amine that has only one functional (-NH₂) group per molecule.

monoamine oxidase *n. Abbr.* **MAO.** An enzyme that catalyses the oxidation of adrenaline, noradrenaline, and other monoamines. Drugs that inhibit its action are used in the treatment of depression.

mon·o·ba·sic (món-ō-báysik, -ə-) *adj. Chemistry.* **1.** Monoprotic. **2.** Having only one metal ion or positive radical.

mon·o·carp (món-ō-kaarp, -ə-) *n. Botany.* A monocarpic plant. [MONO- + -CARP.]

mon·o·car·pel·lar·y (món-ō-kárpi-ləri, -ə- ǁ -lerri) *adj. Botany.* Consisting of or having only one carpel.

mon·o·car·pic (món-ō-kárpik, -ə-) *adj.* Also **mon·o·car·pous** (-kárpəss). *Botany.* Flowering and bearing fruit only once.

mon·o·cha·si·um (món-ō-káyz-i-əm, -ə- ǁ -káyzh-əm) *n., pl.* **-sia** (-ə). *Botany.* A **cyme** *(see)* in which each flowering branch gives rise to one other branch only. Compare **dichasium. —mon·o·cha·si·al** *adj.* [MONO- + (DI)CHASIUM.]

mon·o·chord (món-ə-kawrd, -ō-) *n.* A musical instrument consisting of a sounding box with one string and a movable bridge, used to study musical notes and intervals. [Middle English *monocorde*, from Old French, from Medieval Latin *monochordum*, from Greek *monokhordon* : MONO- + *khordē*, CHORD.]

mon·o·chro·mat (món-ō-krṓ-mat, -ə-) *n.* A person who is completely colourblind, perceiving all colours as a single hue. [Back-formation from MONOCHROMATIC.] **—mon·o·chro·ma·tism** (-mə-tiz'm) *n.*

mon·o·chro·mat·ic (món-ō-krə-máttik, -ō-, -krō-) *adj.* Also **mon·o·chro·ic** (-krṓ-ik). **1.** Having or being in only one colour or shades of one colour. **2.** Having or producing electromagnetic radiation of only one wavelength. **3.** Having a single kinetic energy. Said of a beam of particles. [Greek *monokhrōmatos* : MONO- + *khrōma*, -CHROME.] **—mon·o·chro·mat·i·cal·ly** *adv.*

mon·o·chrome (mónnə-krōm) *n.* **1.** A painting done in different shades of one colour. **2.** The technique of executing such paintings. **3.** A black-and-white photograph.
~*adj.* **1.** Black-and-white. **2.** Having or being in only one colour or shades of one colour. [Medieval Latin *monochroma*, from Greek *monokhrōmos*, of one colour : MONO- + *khrōma*, -CHROME.] **—mon·o·chro·mic** (-krṓmik) *adj.*

mon·o·cle (mónnək'l) *n.* A single lens correcting the vision for one eye. [French, from Late Latin *monoculus*, one-eyed : MONO- + *oculus*, eye.] **—mon·o·cled** (mónnək'ld) *adj.*

mon·o·cline (món-ə-klīn, -ō-) *n.* A geological formation in which all strata are inclined in the same direction. Compare **isocline.** **—mon·o·cli·nal** (-klīn'l) *adj.*

mon·o·clin·ic (món-ə-klínnik, -ō-) *adj. Crystallography.* Having three unequal axes, two of which intersect obliquely and are perpendicular to the third. Said of crystals. [MONO- + Greek *-klinēs*, leaning, from *klinein*, to lean.]

mon·o·cli·nous (món-ə-klīnəss, -ō-) *adj. Botany.* Having pistils and stamens in the same flower. [New Latin *monoclinus*, monoclinous, "hermaphroditic" : MONO- + Greek *klinē*, couch.]

mon·o·coque (món-ə-kok, -ō- ǁ *U.S. also* -kōk) *n.* A metal structure, as of an aircraft or racing car, in which the covering absorbs a large part of the stresses to which the body is subjected. [French : MONO- + *coque*, shell, from Latin *coccum*, berry.]

mon·o·cot·y·le·don (món-ə-kótti-léed'n, -ō-) *n.* Also **mon·o·cot** (-kot). *Botany.* Any plant of the Monocotyledonae, one of the two major divisions of angiosperms, characterised by a single embryonic seed leaf that appears at germination. Included among the monocotyledons are such plants as grasses, orchids, and lilies. Compare **dicotyledon. —mon·o·cot·y·le·don·ous** (-əss) *adj.*

mo·noc·ra·cy (mo-nóckrə-si, mə-) *n.* Government or rule by a single person; autocracy. [MONO- + -CRACY.]

mon·o·crat (món-ə-krat, -ō-) *n.* One who favours autocracy or monarchy. **—mon·o·crat·ic·al·ly** *adv.*

mo·noc·u·lar (mo-nóckew-lər, mə-) *adj.* **1.** Having or pertaining to one eye. **2.** Adapted for the use of only one eye. [Late Latin *monoculus*, one-eyed. See **monocle.**]

mon·o·cy·cle (món-ə-sīk'l, -ō-) *n.* A vehicle having a single wheel, a **unicycle** *(see).*

mon·o·cyte (món-ə-sīt, -ō-) *n.* A large white blood cell, having an oval nucleus. It engulfs foreign particles, such as bacteria. [MONO- + -CYTE.] **—mon·o·cyt·ic** (-síttik), **mon·o·cy·toid** (-sítoyd) *adj.*

Mo·nod (mónnō, mo-nṓ), **Jacques** (1910–76). French molecular biologist, director of the Pasteur Institute in Paris from 1971. He described the process of synthesis of protein in cells, for which he and his collaborators, François Jacob and André Lwoff, were awarded the Nobel prize in medicine and physiology (1965).

mon·o·dac·tyl (món-ə-dák-til, -ō-, -dak-) *n.* An animal having only one claw on each limb. [French *monodactyle*, from Greek *monodaktulos*, one-toed, one-fingered : MONO- + *daktulos*, DACTYL.] **—mon·o·dac·ty·lous** (-dáktiləss) *adj.*

mon·o·dra·ma (món-ə-draamə, -ō- ǁ -drammə) *n.* A dramatic composition for one performer. **—mon·o·dra·mat·ic** (-drə-máttik) *adj.*

mon·o·dy (mónnədi) *n., pl.* **-dies. 1.** In Greek tragedy, an ode for one voice or actor. **2.** An elegiac verse expressing personal lament. **3.** *Music.* **a.** A style of composition in which one vocal part or melodic line predominates. **b.** A composition in this style. [Late Latin *monōdia*, from Greek *monōidia* : MONO- + *ōidē*, song.] **—mo·nod·ic** (mə-nóddik, mo-), **mo·nod·i·cal** *adj.* **—mon·o·dist** (mónnədist) *n.*

mo·noe·cious, mo·ne·cious (mo-néeshəss, mə-) *adj.* Also **mo·noi·cous** (-nóykəss). **1.** *Botany.* Having male and female reproductive organs in separate flowers on a single plant. Compare **dioecious. 2.** *Zoology.* Hermaphroditic. [New Latin *Monoecia* : MON(O)- + Greek *oikia*, dwelling, from *oikos*, house.] **—mo·noe·cious·ly** *adv.*

mon·o·fil·a·ment (món-ə-fílləmənt, -ō-) *n.* A single filament of yarn or plastic, for example. Also called "monofil."

mo·nog·a·my (mə-nógga-mi, mo-) *n.* **1. a.** The custom or condition of being married to or having a sexual relationship with only one person at a time. **b.** *Archaic.* The custom of marrying only once during one's lifetime. **2.** *Zoology.* The habit of having only one mate. [French *monogamie*, from Late Latin *monogamia*, from Greek : MONO- + -GAMY.] **—mo·nog·a·mist** *n.* **—mo·nog·a·mous** (-məss) *adj.* **—mo·nog·a·mous·ly** *adv.*

mon·o·gen·e·sis (món-ō-jénnə-siss, -ə-) *n.* **1.** The theory that all living organisms are descended from a single cell. Compare **polygenesis. 2.** Asexual reproduction, as by sporulation. **3.** The development of an ovum into an organism resembling the parent, without metamorphosis. [New Latin : MONO- + -GENESIS.] **—mon·o·gen·ous** (mo-nójənəss, mə-) *adj.* **—mon·o·gen·ous·ly** *adv.*

mon·o·ge·net·ic (món-ō-jə-néttik, -ə-, -je-) *adj.* **1.** Pertaining to or showing monogenesis. **2.** Asexual. **3.** *Geology.* Formed by a single process or from a single source: *a monogenetic range.*

mon·o·gen·ic (món-ō-jénnik, -ə-) *adj.* **1.** Of or regulated by one gene or one of a pair of allelic genes. **2.** Producing offspring mostly of one sex. **3.** Of or pertaining to monogenism. [MONO- + -GENIC.] **—mon·o·gen·i·cal·ly** *adv.*

mo·nog·e·nism (mo-nójən-iz'm, mə-) *n.* The theory that humankind has descended from a single pair of ancestors. Compare **polygenism.** [MONO- + -GEN- + -ISM.] **—mo·nog·e·nist** *n.* **—mo·nog·e·nis·tic** (-ístik) *adj.*

mon·o·glot (món-ō-glot, -ə-) *adj.* Monolingual. **—mon·o·glot** *n.*

mon·o·gram (mónnə-gram) *n.* A design composed of one or more letters, usually the initials of a name, as put on letter paper or linen, for example. [Late Latin *monogramma* : MONO- + -GRAM.] **—mon·o·grammed** (-gramd) *adj.* **—mon·o·gram·mat·ic** (-grə-máttik) *adj.*

mon·o·graph (mónnə-graaf, -graf) *n.* A scholarly book, article, or pamphlet on a specific and usually narrowly limited subject.
~*tr.v.* **monographed, -graphing, -graphs.** To write a monograph on. [MONO- + -GRAPH.] **—mo·nog·ra·pher** (mə-nóggrəfər, mo-) *n.* **—mon·o·graph·ic** (-gráffik) *adj.* **—mon·o·graph·i·cal·ly** *adv.*

mo·nog·y·ny (mo-nójəni, mə-) *n.* The practice or condition of having only one wife at a time. [MONO- + -GYNY.] **—mo·nog·y·nist** *n.* & *adj.* **—mo·nog·y·nous** *adj.*

mon·o·hy·brid (món-ō-hī-brid, -ə-, -hī-) *n.* Hybrid offspring of parents differing in a single characteristic or genetic factor.

mon·o·hy·drate (món-ō-hídrayt, -ə-) *n. Chemistry.* A compound, especially a crystalline salt, that contains one molecule of water per molecule of compound. **—mon·o·hy·drat·ed** (-hī-dráytid, -hídraytid) *adj.*

mon·o·hy·dric (món-ō-hídrik, -ə-) *adj. Chemistry.* Containing one hydroxyl radical. [MONO- + HYDRO- + -IC.]

monoicous. Variant of **monoecious.**

mon·o·ki·ni (món-ō-kéeni, -ə-) *n.* A woman's topless swimsuit. [MONO- + *-kini* (from humorous analysis of *bikini* as BI- (two, two-piece) + *kini*).]

mo·nol·a·try (mo-nóllətri, mə-) *n.* The worship of one god to the exclusion of the others but without denying the existence of others. [MONO- + -LATRY.]

mon·o·lay·er (món-ō-lay-ər, -ə-) *n.* **1.** A film of a compound one molecule thick; a monomolecular layer. **2.** A layer one atom thick; a monatomic layer.

mon·o·lin·gual (món-ə-líng-gwəl, -ō- ǁ -gew-əl) *adj.* Speaking, knowing, using, or expressed in only one language.

mon·o·lith (món-ə-lith, -ō-) *n.* **1.** A large block of stone, especially a natural rock buttress or one used in architecture or sculpture. **2.** A column, monument, or the like made from one large block of stone. **3.** Something resembling or suggestive of a monolith, especially in being large, uniform, impersonal, or immovable. [French *monolithe*, from Greek *monolithos* : MONO- + -LITH.]

mon·o·lith·ic (món-ə-líthik, -ō-) *adj.* **1.** Consisting of a monolith or monoliths. **2.** Like a monolith; massive, solid, impersonal, or uniform: *a monolithic bureaucracy.*

monolithic circuit *n. Electronics.* A type of integrated circuit in which all the components are formed in the surface of the chip, with no added connections. Compare **hybrid circuit.**

mon·o·logue, *U.S.* **mon·o·log** (mónnə-log, *rarely* -lōg) *n.* **1.** A long speech or talk made by one person, often monopolising a conversation. **2. a.** A long speech delivered by an actor; a soliloquy. **b.** Any literary composition in the form of a soliloquy: *dramatic monologue.* [French : MONO- + (DIA)LOGUE.] **—mon·o·log·ic** (-lójik), **mon·o·log·i·cal** *adj.* **—mo·nol·o·gist** (mo-nóllajist, mə- ǁ mónnə-log-ist, -lawg-) *n.*

mon·o·ma·ni·a (món-ə-máyn-i-ə, -ō-, -yə) *n.* **1.** Pathological obsession with one idea. Not in technical usage. See **paranoia. 2.** Intent concentration on, or exaggerated enthusiasm for, a subject or an

monolith *A prehistoric monolith at Carnac, in Brittany, France.*

idea. [New Latin : MONO- + -MANIA.] —**mon·o·ma·ni·ac** (-i-ak, -yak) n. —**mon·o·ma·ni·a·cal** (-mə-nī′-ək′l) adj.

mon·o·mer (mónnə-mər) n. Any molecule, usually of a simple structure and of low molecular weight, that can be chemically bound as a unit of a **polymer** (see): *Ethylene is a monomer of polyethylene.* [MONO- + Greek *meros*, part.] —**mon·o·mer·ic** (-mérrik) adj.

mon·o·me·tal·lic (món-ō-mə-tál-ik, -ə-, -mi-) adj. 1. Consisting of or containing one metal. 2. Pertaining to monometallism.

mon·o·met·al·lism (món-ō-métt′l-iz'm, -ə-) n. 1. The use of only one metal, usually gold or silver, as a standard of money. 2. The economic theory supporting the use of one metallic monetary standard. —**mon·o·met·al·list** n.

mo·nom·e·ter (mo-nómmitər, mə-) n. A line of verse that consists of only one metrical foot. —**mon·o·met·ric** (món-ō-méttrik, -ə-), **mon·o·met·ri·cal** adj.

mo·no·mi·al (mo-nóm-i-əl, mə-) n. 1. Algebra. An expression consisting of only one term. 2. Biology. A taxonomic name consisting of a single word. [MON(O)- + (BIN)OMIAL.] —**mo·no·mi·al** adj.

mon·o·mo·lec·u·lar (món-ō-mə-léckew-lər, -ə-, -mō-, -mo-) adj. 1. Of or pertaining to a single molecule. 2. Of or consisting of a layer one molecule thick.

mon·o·mor·phic (món-ə-mór-fik, -ə-) adj. Also **monomorphous**. Zoology. Having a basic structure remaining unchanged through a series of developmental changes. —**mon·o·mor·phism** n.

mon·o·mor·phous (món-ō-mór-fəss, -ə-) adj. 1. Chemistry. Existing in only one crystalline form. 2. Monomorphic.

mon·o·nu·cle·ar (món-ō-néwklə-ər, -ə- || -nóōkli-) adj. Having only one nucleus. Said of cells.

mon·o·nu·cle·o·sis (món-ō-néwkli-ó-siss || -nóōkli-) n. 1. The presence of an abnormally large number of monocytes in the bloodstream. 2. **Glandular fever** (see). [New Latin : MONO- + NUCLE(US) + -OSIS.]

mon·o·nu·cle·o·tide (món-ō-néw-kli-ə-tīd, -ə-, -ō- || -nōō-) n. Biochemistry. A compound consisting of one molecule each of a pentose sugar, phosphoric acid, and a purine or pyrimidine base.

mon·o·pet·al·ous (món-ə-pétt′l-əss, -ə-) adj. Having petals united to form one corolla; gamopetalous.

mo·noph·a·gous (mo-nóffəgəss, mə-) adj. Eating only one kind of food. Said especially of insects. [MONO- + -PHAGOUS.]

mon·o·pho·bi·a (món-ō-fṓb-i-ə, -ə-) n. Excessive fear of solitude. [New Latin : MONO- + -PHOBIA.] —**mon·o·pho·bic** (-fṓbik) adj.

mon·o·phon·ic (món-ə-fónnik, -ō-) adj. 1. Music. Of the nature of monophony; having a single melodic line; monodic. 2. Electronics. Designating a system of transmitting, recording, or reproducing sound that uses only one channel to carry or reproduce the sound; monaural.

mo·noph·o·ny (mo-nóffəni, mə-) n. Music consisting of a single melodic line, as for example in plainsong. Compare **homophony**, **polyphony**. [MONO- + -PHONY.]

mon·oph·thong (món-əf-thong || -əp-, -ə) n. 1. A single vowel sound made while the supraglottal speech organs are in a fixed position. 2. Two written letters representing a single vowel sound; for example, *ea* in *plead* is a monophthong. [Late Greek *monophthongos* : MONO- + *phthongos†*, vowel.] —**mon·oph·thon·gal** (-thóng-g′l) adj. —**mon·oph·thon·gal·ly** adv.

mon·oph·thong·ise,   **mon·oph·thong·ize**   (món-əf-thong-gīz, mə-nóf- || -əp-, -ə-) v. -**ised**, -**ising**, -**ises**. —tr. To make into a monophthong. —intr. To become a monophthong. —**mon·oph·thong·i·sa·tion** (-gī-záysh'n || U.S. -gi-) n.

mon·o·phy·let·ic (món-ō-fī-léttik, -ə-) adj. 1. Of or descended from a single ancestral group of plants or animals. 2. Belonging to one stock.

Mo·noph·y·site (mo-nóffi-sīt, mə-) n. Theology. An adherent of the doctrine, held by Coptic and Syrian Christians, that in the person of Christ there was only one single, divine nature. [Medieval Latin *monophysīta*, from Medieval Greek *monophusitēs* : MONO- + *phusis*, nature.] —**Mo·noph·y·sit·ic** (-síttik) adj. —**Mo·noph·y·sit·ism** n.

mon·o·plane (món-ə-playn, -ō-) n. An aircraft with only one pair of wings. Compare **biplane**.

mon·o·ple·gi·a (món-ə-plée-ji-ə, -ō-, -jə) n. Paralysis of a single limb or part of the body, such as one side of the face. [MONO- + -PLEGIA.] —**mon·o·ple·gic** (-pléejik || -pléjik) adj. & n.

mon·o·ploid (món-ə-ployd, -ō-) adj. Having a single set of chromosomes; haploid.
~n. A monoploid individual or cell. [MONO- + -*ploid*, as in HAPLOID.]

mon·o·pod (món-ə-pod, -ō-) n. An adjustable single-legged support for a camera, used in situations where a tripod would be too cumbersome. [MONO- + -POD.]

mon·o·po·di·um (món-ə-pṓdi-əm, -ō-) n., pl. -**dia** (-ə). Also **mon·o·pode** (-pōd). Botany. A main axis of a plant, such as the trunk of certain conifers, that maintains a single line of growth, giving off lateral branches. Compare **sympodium**. [New Latin, from Late Latin *monopodius*, one-footed, from Greek *monopous* (stem *monopod-*) : MONO- + *pous*, foot.] —**mon·o·po·di·al** (-əl) adj.

Monopolies and Mergers Commission n. In Britain, a public body responsible for determining whether a particular supplier or group of suppliers constitutes a monopoly, and making appropriate recommendations to the government, especially in the case of proposed mergers.

mo·nop·o·lise, **mo·nop·o·lize** (mə-nóppə-līz) tr.v. -**lised**, -**lising**, -**lises**. 1. To acquire or maintain a monopoly of. 2. To dominate or

take complete possession of, to the exclusion of others. —**mo·nop·o·li·sa·tion** (-lī-záysh'n || U.S. -li-) n. —**mo·nop·o·lis·er** n.

monopolistic competition n. Economics. A situation in commerce that exists when a large number of competitive firms produce products that are similar but are not perfect substitutes, so that one firm can afford to raise its prices relative to the others without necessarily jeopardising its sales. Also called "imperfect competition".

mo·nop·o·ly (mə-nóppə-li) n., pl. -**lies**. 1. Economics. **a.** Exclusive control by one person, group, or company of the means of producing or selling a commodity or service. Compare **oligopoly**. **b.** Such control that is not exclusive but is sufficient to allow the person or company to control prices. 2. Law. A right granted by a government, giving exclusive control over a specified commercial activity to a single party. 3. **a.** A company or group having exclusive control over a commercial activity. **b.** A commodity or service controlled exclusively by one company or group. 4. Exclusive possession of or control over anything: *You haven't got a monopoly on hardship, you know.* [Latin *monopōlium*, from Greek *monopōlion*, sole selling rights : MONO- + *pōlein*, to sell.] —**mo·nop·o·lism** (-liz'm) n. —**mo·nop·o·list** n. & adj. —**mo·nop·o·lis·tic** (-lístik) adj.

Mo·nop·o·ly (mə-nóppəli) n. A trademark for a board game in which two to six players advance by throws of dice and attempt to acquire the property marked on the board and put the other players out of business.

monopoly money n. Informal. Money, especially in banknotes, that seems like toy money, as, for example, an unfamiliar foreign currency or a currency that has been devalued so as to be almost worthless. [Referring to toy banknotes used in MONOPOLY.]

mon·o·pro·pel·lant (món-ō-prə-péllənt, -ə-) n. A rocket propellant in which fuel and oxidiser are combined prior to combustion, such as a mixture of hydrogen peroxide and alcohol.

mon·o·pro·tic (món-ō-prṓtik, -ə-) adj. Chemistry. Having only one hydrogen ion to donate to a base in an acid-base reaction; monobasic. [MONO- + PROT(ON) + -IC.]

mo·nop·so·ny (mo-nópsəni, mə-) n., pl. -**nies**. A situation in commerce in which the product or service of several sellers is sought by only one buyer. Compare **oligopsony**. [MON(O)- + Greek *opsōnia*, a buying, from *opsōnein*, to buy food (see **opsonin**).]

mon·o·rail (món-ə-rayl, -ō-) n. 1. A railway system in which trains run on a single rail, often an elevated one from which they are suspended. 2. The track used in such a system.

mon·o·sac·cha·ride (món-ō-sáckə-rīd, -ə-, -rid) n. A simple sugar, such as glucose or fructose, that cannot be decomposed by hydrolysis, having the general formula $C_nH_{2n}O_n$. Also called "simple sugar".

mon·o·sep·al·ous (món-ō-séppələss, -ə-) adj. Botany. Having sepals united to form a single calyx; gamosepalous.

mon·o·so·di·um glu·ta·mate (món-ə-sṓdi-əm glṓo-tə-mayt, -ō- glêw-) n. Abbr. **MSG**. A white crystalline salt, $NaC_5H_8O_4$, with a taste like meat, used extensively as a food additive. Also called "glutamate", "sodium glutamate".

mon·o·some (món-ə-sōm, -ō-) n. An unpaired chromosome, particularly an X chromosome, in an otherwise diploid cell or organism. [MONO- + -SOME (body).] —**mon·o·so·mic** (-sṓmik, rarely -sómmik) adj. —**mon·o·so·my** (-sṓmi) n.

mon·o·sper·mous (món-ō-spérm-əss, -ə-) adj. Also **mon·o·sper·mal** (-spérm′l). Having a single seed. Said of certain plants. [MONO- + -SPERMOUS.]

mon·o·stome (món-ə-stōm, -ō-) adj. Also **mo·nos·to·mous** (mo-nóstəməss, mə-). 1. Having one oral sucker only, as do certain flatworms. 2. Having one mouth or similar opening. [Greek *monostomos*, having one mouth : MONO- + *stoma*, -STOME.]

mon·o·strophe (món-ə-strōf, -ō-; mo-nóstrəfi, mə-) n. A poem in which all the stanzas or strophes have the same metrical form. —**mon·o·stroph·ic** (-stróffik) adj.

mon·o·sty·lous (món-ō-stīləss, -ə-) adj. Botany. Having one style.

mon·o·syl·lab·ic (món-ō-si-lábbik, -ə-) adj. 1. Having only one syllable. 2. Characterised by or consisting of monosyllables; terse or laconic. —**mon·o·syl·lab·ic·al·ly** adv.

mon·o·syl·la·ble (món-ō-sílləb'l, -ə-) n. A word or utterance of one syllable. [Late Latin *monosyllabum*, from Greek *monosullabon* : MONO- + *sullabē*, SYLLABLE.]

mon·o·the·ism (món-ō-thee-iz'm, -ə-) n. The doctrine or belief that there is only one God. Compare **henotheism**. —**mon·o·the·ist** n. & adj. —**mon·o·the·is·tic** (-ístik) adj. —**mon·o·the·is·ti·cal·ly** adv.

mon·o·tint (món-ə-tint, -ō-) n. A picture, a **monochrome** (see).

mon·o·tone (mónnə-tōn) n. 1. A succession of sounds or words uttered without changing the pitch of the voice. 2. Music. **a.** A single note that is continuously repeated with different words or time values, as in plainsong. **b.** A chant on a single note. 3. Sameness, dull repetition, or lack of variety in sound, style, manner, or colour. ~adj. Also **mon·o·ton·ic** (-tónnik) (for sense 2). 1. Of, pertaining to, or characteristic of sounds emitted at a single pitch. 2. Mathematics. Designating sequences of which the successive members either consistently increase or decrease but do not oscillate in relative value. Each member of a *monotone increasing* sequence is greater than or equal to the preceding member; each member of a *monotone decreasing* sequence is less than or equal to the preceding member. See **sequence**. [Greek *monotonos*, having one tone : MONO-, single + *tonos*, TONE.] —**mon·o·ton·i·cal·ly** (-tónni-kli, -k'l-i) adv.

mo·not·o·nous (mə-nótt'n-əss) adj. 1. Unvarying in vocal inflection or pitch; sounded in one persistent tone: *a monotonous drone.* 2. Without variation or variety; boringly dull: *monotonous work.*

monorail *The monorail train at Disneyland in California, U.S.A. The car rides on a single rail of concrete and is supported by rubber wheels on top and at the sides.*

—See Synonyms at **boring**. [Greek *monotonos* : MONO-, single + *tonos*, TONE.] —**mo·not·o·nous·ly** *adv.* —**mo·not·o·nous·ness** *n.*

mo·not·o·ny (mə-nótt'n-i) *n.* **1.** Uniformity or lack of variation in pitch, intonation, or inflection. **2.** Wearisome sameness; lack of variety. [Greek *monotonia*, from *monotonos*, MONOTONOUS.]

mon·o·treme (món-ō-treem, -ə-) *n.* A member of the Monotremata, an order of egg-laying mammals restricted to Australia and New Guinea, and including the platypus and the echidna. [New Latin *Monotremata* : MONO- + Greek *trēma* (stem *trēmat-*), hole.] —**mon·o·tre·ma·tous** (-treéma-təss, -trémmə-) *adj.*

mo·not·ri·chous (mo-nóttrikəss, mə-) *adj.* Also **mon·o·trich·ic** (món-ō-tríckik, -ə-). Having one flagellum at only one pole or end. Said of certain bacteria. [MONO- + TRICH(O)- + -OUS.]

mon·o·troph·ic (món-ō-tróffik, -ə-, -trŏfik) *adj.* Requiring only one kind of food; monophagous.

mon·o·type (món-ə-tīp, -ō-) *n.* **1.** *Printing.* A single impression from a metal or glass plate of a design or picture. **2.** *Biology.* The sole member of its group, such as a species that also constitutes a genus. —**mon·o·typ·ic** (-típpik) *adj.*

Mon·o·type (món-ə-tīp, -ō-) *n.* A trademark for a typesetting machine operated from a keyboard which activates a unit that casts individual letters from matrices and assembles them.

mon·o·va·lent (món-ō-váylənt, -ə-) *adj.* *Chemistry.* Possessing a valency of one; univalent. —**mon·o·va·lence, mon·o·va·len·cy** *n.*

mon·ox·ide (mo-nóksīd, mə-) *n.* A compound having only one atom of oxygen. [MON(O)- + OXIDE.]

mon·o·zy·got·ic twin (món-ō-zī-góttik, -ə-) *n.* An **identical twin** (*see*).

Mon·roe (mən-rṓ, mun- ‖ mon-), **James** (1758–1831). U.S. president (1817–25), after whom the **Monroe Doctrine** is named.

Monroe, Marilyn, born Norma Jean Mortenson, also known as Norma Jean Baker (1926–62). U.S. film star. She first came to attention in *The Asphalt Jungle* (1950), and revealed her talent for comedy in *Gentlemen Prefer Blondes* (1953) and *How to Marry a Millionaire* (1953). Her other most notable films were *The Seven Year Itch* (1955), *Bus Stop* (1956), *Some Like It Hot* (1959), and her last film, *The Misfits* (1961), written by her husband Arthur Miller. She died from an overdose of sleeping pills.

Monroe Doctrine *n.* The U.S. policy of opposition to outside interference by Europe in the Americas. [After a foreign policy statement (1823) by President MONROE.]

Mon·ro·vi·a (mən-rṓvi-ə). Capital of Liberia. The country's chief port and industrial centre, it was founded (1822) as a settlement for freed U.S. slaves, and was named after President Monroe.

mons (monz) *n., pl.* **montes** (mónteez). A protuberance of the human body; especially, the mons pubis (or mons veneris), situated over the junctions of the pubic bones at the front of the body. [New Latin, from Latin *mōns* (stem *mont-*), mountain.]

Mons (monz; *French* mawNss). Flemish **Ber·gen** (baírkhə). Capital of Hainaut province, Belgium. It has been much fought over, and British forces fought their first major action of World War I here (1914).

Mon·sar·rat (món-sə-rát, -rat), **Nicholas (John Turney)** (1910–79). English novelist. He served in the Royal Navy (1940–6) on convoy runs in the Atlantic, and from his experiences wrote the best seller, *The Cruel Sea* (1951).

Mon·sei·gneur (món-sen-yér, -yŏr) *n., pl.* **Messeigneurs** (máy-). *Abbr.* **Mgr., Mngr., Msgr.** *French.* A title of or form of address for princes and prelates. [French, "my lord".]

Mon·sieur (məss-yér, -yŏ, *weak form* məss-yə ‖ mə-séwr) *n., pl.* **Messieurs** (mayss-, mess-; *also* mèssərz). *Abbr.* **M. 1.** A title of courtesy prefixed to the name or nobiliary or professional title of a Frenchman, equivalent to the English "Mr", "Sir", or "my Lord", according to the rank of the man. **2.** A respectful form of address for a Frenchman, used instead of the man's name. [French, "my lord".]

Mon·si·gnor (mon-seén-yər) *n., pl.* **-gnors.** *Italian* **Mon·si·gno·re** (món-seen-yáw-ray) *pl.* **-ri** (-ree). *Abbr.* **Mgr., Mngr., Monsig., Msgr.** A title of or form of address for certain officials of the Roman Catholic Church. [Italian, from French *monseigneur*, MONSEIGNEUR.]

mon·soon (món-sṓon, mən-) *n.* **1.** A pressure and wind system that influences large climatic regions and reverses seasonally; specifically, the Asiatic monsoon that produces dry and wet seasons in southern and southeastern Asia. **2.** The rain brought by such a system. [Obsolete Dutch *monssoen*, from Portuguese *monção*, from Arabic *mausim*, season, monsoon season.]

mons pu·bis (péwbiss) *n.* See **mons**.

mon·ster (món-stər) *n.* **1.** An imaginary being, such as a cyclops or dragon, made up of elements from various human or animal forms. **2.** An animal or plant having structural defects or deformities. **3.** *Pathology.* A foetus or infant that is grotesquely malformed. **4.** Any very large animal, plant, or object. **5.** One who inspires horror or disgust: *a monster of wickedness.* **6.** *Chiefly U.S. Slang.* One that is highly successful or exercises great influence, especially in a specified field: *The Beatles are monsters of rock music.* ~*adj.* Gigantic; huge. [Middle English *monstre*, from Old French, from Latin *mōnstrum*, prodigy, portent, from *monēre*, to warn.]

mon·ste·ra (món-steér-ə) *n.* Any plant of the tropical American genus *Monstera*, such as *M. deliciosa*, the Swiss cheese plant, often grown as a house plant for its glossy foliage. [New Latin, perhaps irregularly from Latin *monstrum*, MONSTER.]

mon·strance (món-strənss) *n. Roman Catholic Church.* A receptacle in which the Host is held and exhibited to the congregation. [Mid-

dle English, from Old French, from Medieval Latin *mōnstrantia*, from Latin *mōnstrāre*, to show.]

mon·stros·i·ty (món-stróssəti) *n., pl.* **-ties. 1.** One that is monstrous. **2.** The quality or character of being monstrous.

mon·strous (món-strəss) *adj.* **1.** Deviating excessively from the norm in appearance or structure; grotesquely unnatural. **2.** Exceptionally large; enormous: *"Just then flew down a monstrous crow"* (Lewis Carroll). **3.** Hideous; shocking; loathsome: *a monstrous crime.* **4.** Outrageous; disgraceful; indefensible: *a monstrous waste of money.* **5.** Of, pertaining to, or like a fabulous monster: *"Harpies and Hydras, or all the monstrous forms / 'Twixt Africa and Ind"* (Milton). —See Synonyms at **outrageous**. [Middle English from Old French *monstruex*, from Latin *mōnstruōsus*, from *mōnstrum*, MONSTER.] —**mon·strous·ly** *adv.* —**mon·strous·ness** *n.*

mons ve·ne·ris (vénnəriss) *n.* See **mons**.

mon·tage (món-taazh, mon-taázh, mon-) *n.* **1. a.** The art, style, or process of making one pictorial composition from many pictures or designs, closely arranged or superimposed upon each other. **b.** A picture so made. **2.** In films and television: **a.** The technique of producing a rapid sequence of thematically related short scenes or images exhibiting different aspects of the same idea or situation. **b.** A portion of a film or television programme employing such a special effect. **3.** In various other art forms, a sequence using different sensory elements presented at short intervals. [French, "mounting", from *monter*, to MOUNT.]

Mon·taigne (mon-táyn; *French* moN-téñ), **Michel Eyquem, Seigneur de** (1533–92). French essayist. His essays, sceptical, discursive, witty, and lively, are held to be the highest expression of 16th-century French prose.

Mon·tan·a (mon-tánnə, *rarely* -taánə). The fourth largest state of the United States lying in the northwest of the country. The Rockies rely on forestry, tourism, and mining, while the Great Plains to the east produce cattle, oil, gas and coal. Part of the Louisiana Purchase (1803), Montana was admitted to the Union in 1889. The capital is Helena. —**Mon·ta·nan** *adj. & n.*

mon·tane (món-tayn ‖ -táyn) *adj.* Of, growing in, or inhabiting mountain areas. [Latin *montānus*, from *mōns*. See **mons**.]

mon·tan wax (món-tan, -tən) *n.* A hard, white wax obtained from lignite and used in the manufacture of polishes, candles, and insulators. [Latin *montānus*, MONTANE.]

Mont Blanc (món blón). Mountain in France, near the French-Italian border. It is the highest peak (4 807 metres; 15,771 feet) in Europe outside the U.S.S.R. Beneath it runs a road tunnel (12 kilometres; 7.5 miles) opened in 1965.

mont·bre·tia (mon-brèesh-ə, mom-, mont-, -yə) *n.* **1.** A South African plant, *Crocosmia crocosmiiflora*, widely grown as a garden ornamental for its orange-red, funnel-shaped flowers. **2.** Any South African plant of the similar and related genus *Montbretia*. [New Latin, after A.F.E. Coquebert de *Montbret* (died 1801), French botanist.]

mon·te (mónti) *n.* **1.** A game of Spanish origin in which each player bets that one of two cards will be matched by the dealer before the other one. Also called "monte bank". See **three-card monte**. **2.** *Australian Informal.* A certainty; a sure thing. [Spanish, "mountain", referring to the pile of unplayed cards, from Latin *mōns* (stem *mont-*), mountain.]

Mon·te Al·ban (mónti al-bán ‖ -ay, *U.S.* aal-baán). A ruined Zapotec city in southwestern Mexico.

Monte Bel·lo Islands (béllō). A formation of uninhabited atolls off Western Australia, used for British nuclear tests (1952, 1956).

Monte Car·lo (kárlō). Seaside resort of Monaco, famous for its casinos, annual motor-car rally, and the Monaco Grand Prix race.

Monte Carlo method *n. Mathematics.* A method of obtaining approximate solutions to problems by statistical sampling. [After a method applied to roulette at the casino in MONTE CARLO.]

Monte Cas·si·no (kə-séenō, ka-). A hill overlooking the town of Cassino, central Italy. Its monastery, founded (*c.* 529) by St. Benedict, was used in World War II by the Nazis as a fortress, and was consequently destroyed by the Allies. It has since been restored and rededicated (1964).

Mon·te·go Bay (mon-téego). Seaport and tourist centre in Jamaica. The island's second city and second seaport, it exports agricultural produce.

Mon·te·ne·gro (mónti-néegrō). *Serbo-Croat* **Crna Gora** (chórna gáwra). The smallest constituent republic of Yugoslavia. Lying on the Adriatic, it is predominantly mountainous and agricultural, but does have considerable mineral resources. An ancient state of the Balkans, it was an independent kingdom from 1910 until 1918, when it joined the new Kingdom of Serbs, Croats, and Slovenes, which became Yugoslavia in 1929.

mon·te·ro (mon-taír-ō) *n., pl.* **-ros.** A huntsman's cap with side flaps. [Spanish, "hunter", from *monte*, forest region, mountain. See **monte**.]

Mon·ter·rey (mónta-ráy). Capital of Nuevo León state, northeast Mexico. The country's third city, it is an important industrial centre with iron and steel and lead works, and textile, glass, and chemical industries. It is also a resort with hot springs.

mon·tes. Plural of **mons**.

Mon·tes·quieu (món-te-skéw, -skew, -skyúr, -skyṓ), **Charles Louis de Secondat, Baron de la Brède et de** (1689–1755). French jurist and political philosopher, one of the outstanding figures of the early French Enlightenment. He is famous chiefly for two books, the *Persian Letters* (1721), a veiled attack on the monarchy and

monstera *A genus of plants cultivated for their ornamental leaves. This is the fruit of* Monstera tuberculata.

Moon

A DEAD AND BATTERED WORLD
Over craters large and small lies a blanket of dust

The Moon is the Earth's only natural satellite, and is exceptionally large compared to satellites of other planets. Its obvious features have long been known – that it creates tides, that its phases mark its monthly orbit, that it is scarred with craters and dark areas known as "seas" (*maria*), and that it keeps one side permanently towards the Earth.

It is no longer believed that the Earth and the Moon were originally one body. The Moon has always been separate from the Earth and is about as old. The Moon was formed 4,600 million years ago. Many astronomers believe that its craters were formed by meteorite impacts more than 3,000 million years ago. Very large strikes caused molten rock to flow and form the *maria*. However, other astronomers consider that volcanic activity has played a major role in the moulding of the lunar surface. A rain of tiny particles has eroded the surface into a thin layer of dust. Space research between 1960 and 1975 revealed much detail about the Moon.

METEORITE-MADE "SEAS" *The Moon's disc as seen from an approaching spacecraft clearly reveals the huge, dark maria, and also shows their roughly circular shapes. They may be the result of massive meteorite impacts in the early stages of the formation of the Earth, Moon, and Solar System. One such feature is the Mare Imbrium, about 676 kilometres (420 miles) across and produced by the impact of a meteorite 128 kilometres (80 miles) across. It scattered rocks for over 1600 kilometres (1,000 miles). The basins were filled with dark lava welling up from the Moon's interior. The lava was later pitted with secondary impacts. Generally, the larger the crater, the older it is. Apparently, larger meteorites ceased to exist soon after the Solar System formed.*

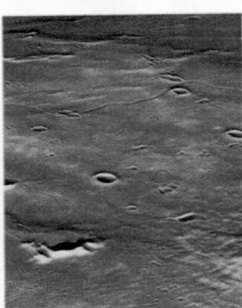

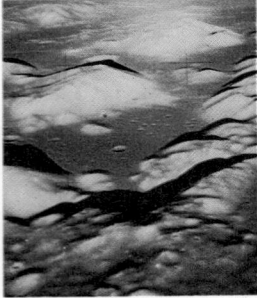

MEN ON THE MOON *The site where Apollo 11, the first manned mission to the Moon, landed was here, in the Sea of Tranquillity. It is typical of the floors of the maria – a smooth lava base that filled in the impact crater, a scattering of younger smaller craters, and a light covering of dust formed by the rain of micro-meteorites. It was on July 21, 1969 that Neil Armstrong took what he called "one small step for a man, one giant leap for mankind" as he stepped onto the Moon.*

GLASS AT HIS FEET *Apollo 17, the last of the U.S. lunar missions, landed on this rough area on the edge of the Sea of Serenity in December 1972. One of the crew was geologist Harrison Schmitt, the first scientist on the Moon. Lunar soil and rocks had been returned to Earth on previous missions, but Schmitt caused excitement when he kicked up some "orange soil" – tiny glass beads formed by intense heat. This type of information made the Apollo missions very valuable to science.*

A YOUNG CRATER *A steep, crisply outlined young crater overlapping the heavily eroded ridge of a much older crater clearly shows its meteoric origins. Although some craters on the Moon may be the result of volcanic activity, this one is not. The floor of the crater is below that of the surrounding rock, whereas in a volcano the crater is created on the top of a mound of ejected lava. The nearly circular rim is the result of the explosion of compressed, hot rock that took place at impact.*

institutions of the ancien régime, and *The Spirit of the Laws* (1748), a lengthy disquisition on the forms of government.

Mon·tes·so·ri method (món-ti-sáw-ri ‖ -te-, -sŏ́-) *n.* A method of educating young children that stresses development of a child's own initiative and natural abilities, especially through practical play and individual guidance rather than through strict control. Also called "Montessori system". [After Maria *Montessori* (died 1952), Italian educationalist.]

Mon·te·ver·di (mónti-vaírdi), **Claudio (Giovanni Antonio)** (1567–1643). Italian composer. Throughout his life he wrote madrigals and sacred music, but his great importance is as one of the founders of opera. His operas are remarkable for the rich texture of the orchestral scoring and the dramatic effectiveness of the recitative passages. They include *Orfeo* (1607), *Il ritorno di Ulisse in Patria* (1641), and *L'incoronazione di Poppea* (1642).

Mon·te·vi·de·o (mónti-vi-dáy-ŏ ‖ -víddi-). Capital of Uruguay since 1828. An important seaport, fishing centre, resort, and railway junction, it was founded (1726) by the Spanish on the Rio de la Plata. The country's only important industrial centre, it has footwear, textiles, soap, food processing, and tanning industries.

Mon·tez (món-tez), **Lola**, born Marie Dolores Eliza Rosanna Gilbert (*c.* 1818–61). Irish dancer, famous for her beauty. She adopted the name Lola Montez when she began to dance, claiming Spanish descent. She had brief affairs with Liszt and Dumas *père* and also, most notoriously, with Ludvig of Bavaria, from 1846 to 1848.

Mon·te·zu·ma II (mónti-zŏŏ-mə, -zéw-), also known as Moctezuma (*c.* 1480–1520). Aztec emperor (*c.* 1502–20), known as Montezuma II to distinguish him from the mid-15th-century ruler of the same name. The Spanish explorer **Cortés** tried to govern through him, but during an Aztec insurrection Montezuma was killed, though whether by the Spanish or the Aztecs it is not certain.

Montezuma's revenge *n.* An attack of diarrhoea experienced by a tourist visiting a tropical country. Used humorously.

Mont·fort (mónt-fərt, -fawrt), **Simon de, Earl of Leicester** (*c.* 1208–65). English baron, born in France, leader of the baronial opposition to Henry III. He and other barons forced Henry to sign the Provisions of Oxford (1258), and after his victory over the king at Lewes (1264) he was the effective ruler of England. He called a parliament in 1265 which included representatives from the boroughs, and is therefore often taken as the first modern parliament.

Mont·gol·fi·er (mont-gólfi-ay, moN-, -ər), **Joseph Michel** (1740–1810) and **Jacques Étienne** (1745–99). French brothers who invented the hot-air balloon in which the first manned flight took place in November 1783.

Mont·gom·er·y (mənt-gúm-ri, mont-, mən-, mon-, -góm-, -əri). Capital of Alabama, United States. It is a market and industrial centre on the Alabama river. It became the first capital of the Confederate States of America (1861). In the 1950s and 60s it was the centre of the black civil rights movement.

Montgomery, Lucy Maud (1874–1942). Canadian novelist. Her best-known book is *Anne of Green Gables* (1908).

Montgomery of Alamein, 1st Viscount, born Bernard Law Montgomery (1887–1976). British soldier. He served in India and World War I and was awarded the D.S.O. In 1939 he commanded the Third Division in France; he was made leader of the Fifth Corps after Dunkirk, and at the end of 1941 was given command of the South Eastern Army in England. In command of the Eighth Army in North Africa he halted Rommel's Africa Corps at Alam el-Haifa in August 1942, and in October won victory at El Alamein. Knighted and promoted to general, he led the Allied assault through Normandy in 1944 and in 1945 he became a field marshal and Commander in Chief of the British Army in Germany. From 1951–58 he was Deputy Supreme Allied Commander in Europe.

Mont·gom·er·y·shire (mənt-gúm-ri-shər, mont-, -góm-, -əri-, -sheer). *Welsh* **Sir Dre·fald·wyn, Mald·wyn** (sheer dre-vál-dwin; máld-dwin). Former county of central Wales, now part of Powys.

month (munth) *n. Abbr.* **m, M, m., M., mo.** **1.** Any of the 12 divisions of a year as determined by the Gregorian calendar. Also called "calendar month". **2.** Any period extending from a date in one calendar month to the corresponding date in the following month. **3.** The average period of revolution of the Moon around the Earth determined by using a fixed star as a reference point and equal to 27 days 7 hours 43 minutes 12 seconds. Also called "sidereal month". **4.** The average time between successive new, or full, moons; equal to 29 days 12 hours 44 minutes. Also called "lunar month", "synodic month", "lunation". **5.** One twelfth of a tropical year, totalling 27 days 7 hours 43 minutes 5 seconds. Also called "solar month". **—month of Sundays.** *Informal.* An indefinitely long period of time. [Middle English *moneth*, Old English *mōnath*, from Germanic; akin to MOON.]

Usage: When used before a noun, the singular form is used along with a hyphen: *a three-month stay in France.* Alternatively, the slightly more formal possessive form may be used, but in this case the hyphen is omitted: *a three months' stay in France.*

Mon·ther·lant (moN-tair-lóN), **Henry de** (1896–1972). French novelist and dramatist. His works portray masculine, aristocratic pride in a feminised and democratic society. His plays include *Malatesta* (1946) and *Port-Royal* (1954).

month·ly (múnthli) *adj.* **1.** Occurring, appearing, or coming due every month. **2.** Continuing or lasting for a month.
~*adv.* Once a month; by the month; every month.
~*n., pl.* **monthlies. 1.** A periodical publication appearing once each month. **2.** *Informal.* A menstrual period.

mon·ti·cule (mónti-kewl) *n.* **1.** A small hill. **2.** A small mound produced by volcanic eruption. [French, from Late Latin *monticulus*, diminutive of Latin *mōns* (stem *mont-*), mountain.]

Mont·martre (moN-mártrə). See **Paris**.

Mont·par·nasse (món-paar-náss). See **Paris**.

Mont·pel·lier (moN-pélli-ay, mont-, -ər). Capital of Hérault département, southern France. It is a centre of the wine trade, and famous for its university (constituted 1289), incorporating a tenth-century medical school.

Mon·tre·al (móntri-áwl || múntri-). *French* **Mont·ré·al** (mon-ray-ál). City in Quebec, southeast Canada. Sited on Montreal island at the confluence of the St. Lawrence and Ottawa rivers, it was founded (1642) as the French settlement of Ville Marie de Montréal, at the foot of Mont Royal. Today it is Canada's largest city and most important port (it lies on the St. Lawrence Seaway), the world's second largest French-speaking city, and an important communications, industrial, trade, and cultural centre.

Mon·treux (mon-trér, -trő). Town in Vaud canton, Switzerland, at the eastern end of Lake Geneva. An important tourist centre, it has an annual television festival. The 13th-century Château de Chillon nearby figures in Byron's *Prisoner of Chillon.*

Mont·ser·rat (mónt-sə-rát, -se-, -rat). British island colony, in the Caribbean Sea. It was discovered by Columbus (1493), and settled by the British Tourism and agriculture are important, and exports include cotton and bananas. Plymouth is the capital.

Mont St. Mi·chel (món-san-mee-shél; *French* mon-san-). Rocky islet in Manche département, northwest France. Its principal feature is a Benedictine abbey (708–9), which was used as a prison from the French Revolution until 1863. It is connected to the mainland by a causeway.

mon·u·ment (mónnew-mənt) *n.* **1.** A structure, such as a building, tower, or sculpture, erected as a memorial. **2.** An inscribed stone or other marker placed at a grave or tomb; a tombstone. **3.** A site or building of special historical or archaeological importance, preserved by the government. See **ancient monument, national monument.** **4.** A written legal document. **5. a.** An outstanding and enduring achievement viewed as a model for later generations and worthy of lasting fame. **b.** An exceptional example of something: *Her attitude was a monument of selfishness and insensitivity.* [Middle English, from Latin *monumentum,* from *monēre,* to remind, warn.]

mon·u·men·tal (mónnew-mént'l) *adj.* **1.** Of, resembling, or serving as a monument. **2.** Impressively large, sturdy, and enduring. **3.** Of outstanding and lasting significance: *her monumental contribution to the theatre.* **4.** Enormous and astounding: *her monumental stupidity.* **5.** *Fine Arts.* Larger than life-size. **—mon·u·men·tal·ly** *adv.*

Mon·za (mónzə; *Italian* móntsa). City in Lombardy, northern Italy. A centre of the textile industry, it was an important medieval commercial centre. It has a famous motor-racing circuit.

mon·zo·nite (mónzə-nīt, mon-zṓ-) *n.* A coarse-grained igneous rock composed chiefly of plagioclase and orthoclase in approximately equal proportions, with small amounts of other minerals. [French, after Mount *Monzoni* in northeast Italy, where it was discovered.]

moo (mo͞o) *n., pl.* **moos.** **1.** The characteristic deep, bellowing sound made by a cow. **2.** Any similar sound.
~*intr.v.* **mooed, mooing, moos.** To make a moo. [Imitative.]

mooch (mo͞och) *v.* **mooched, mooching, mooches.** Also *chiefly British* **mouch** (mo͞och). *Slang.* —*intr.* **1.** To dawdle or loiter aimlessly. Often used with *along.* **2.** To sit or wander about in a depressed or apathetic fashion. Often used with *about.* —*tr. Chiefly U.S.* **1.** To obtain by cajolery or begging. **2.** To steal or filch. [Middle English *mowche,* from Old French *muchier,* to hide.] **—mooch·er** *n.*

mood¹ (mo͞od) *n.* **1.** A temporary state of mind or feeling, as evidenced by one's behaviour or the tendency of one's thoughts: *a gloomy mood.* **2.** A prevailing spirit, disposition, or set of attitudes: *The book captures the mood of the Edwardian period.* **3.** A pervading impression on the feelings of an observer: *the sombre mood of the painting.* **4.** A spell of sulking or morose behaviour: *He's in one of his moods.* **—in the mood.** Inclined; disposed. [Middle English *mod,* Old English *mōd,* mind, thought, from Germanic.]
Synonyms: *mood, humour, temper.*

mood² *n.* **1.** *Grammar.* A class of verb forms used to indicate the speaker's attitude towards either the utterance or the addressee, concerning for example the factuality or likelihood of the action or condition expressed, or types of address such as requests or orders. In English, the indicative mood is usually used for factual statements, the subjunctive mood to indicate doubt, unlikelihood, or wish, and the imperative mood to express a command. Compare **aspect.** **2.** *Logic.* Any of the various ways in which a proposition may be constructed. [Alteration (influenced by MOOD¹) of MODE.]

mood·y (mo͞odi) *adj.* **-ier, -iest.** **1.** Given to changeable emotional states; temperamental. **2.** Gloomy; glum; grumpy: *a moody silence.* **—mood·i·ly** *adv.* **—mood·i·ness** *n.*

Moog synthesiser (mo͞og, mōg) *n.* A trademark for an electronic keyboard instrument that is capable of generating a large variety of sounds. Also called "Moog", "synthesiser". [After R.A. *Moog,* U.S. engineer who invented it.]

moo·lah (mo͞olə) *n. Slang.* Money. [Origin unknown.]

mool·vi, mool·vie (mo͞ol-vi, -vee) *n.* A Muslim who is very learned or a doctor of the law. Used especially in India as a title of respect. [Urdu *Mulvī,* from Arabic *mawlawīyah,* judicial.]

moon (mo͞on) *n.* **1.** *Capital* **M.** The natural satellite of the Earth, visible by reflection of sunlight, having a slightly elliptical orbit, approximately 356 500 kilometres (221,600 miles) distant at perigee and 407 000 kilometres (252,900 miles) at apogee. Its mean diameter is 3 475 kilometres (2,160 miles), its mass approximately one eightieth that of the Earth, and its average period of revolution around the Earth 29 days 12 hours 44 minutes calculated with respect to the Sun. **2.** Any natural satellite orbiting a planet. **3.** The moon as it appears at a particular time in its cycle of phases: *the full moon; a half moon.* **4.** A month, especially a lunar month. **5.** Any disc, globe, or crescent resembling the moon. **6.** Moonlight. **—crying for the moon.** Striving or yearning for something unattainable. **—once in a blue moon.** Never or hardly ever.
~*v.* **mooned, mooning, moons.** —*intr.* **1.** To wander about or pass time languidly and aimlessly. Usually used with *about* or *around.* **2.** To exhibit infatuation by being inattentive or listless. Usually used with *over.* **3.** *Slang.* To expose the buttocks, especially in a public place, with the aim of shocking passers-by. —*tr.* To pass (time) idly. Used with *away.* [Middle English *moone, mon,* Old English *mōna,* from Germanic; akin to MONTH.]

moon·beam (mo͞on-beem) *n.* A ray of moonlight.

moon blindness *n.* Recurrent inflammation of horses' eyes, often resulting in blindness. Also called "mooneye". **—moon·blind** *adj.*

moon·calf (mo͞on-kaaf || *chiefly U.S.* -kaf) *n.* **1.** A fool from birth; a stupid creature. **2.** An inattentive, daydreaming person. **3.** *Archaic.* A freak. [From the supposed maleficent influence of the Moon on the unborn.]

moon dog *n.* A bright spot on a lunar halo, a **paraselene** *(see).*

moon·eye (mo͞on-ī) *n.* **1.** A silvery freshwater fish, *Hiodon tergisus,* of northern North America. **2.** Moon blindness.

moon-faced (mo͞on-fayst) *adj.* Having a round face.

moon·fish (mo͞on-fish) *n., pl.* **-fishes** or collectively **moonfish.** **1.** Any of various fishes of the family Carangidae, having rounded bodies that are silver to yellowish in colour. Also called "dollarfish". **2.** A large marine fish, the **opah** *(see).*

moon·flow·er (mo͞on-flowr) *n.* Any of various white-flowered, often night-blooming plants, such as *Ipomaea alba,* a morning glory.

Moon·ie (mo͞oni) *n.* A member of a religious sect, the Unification Church, founded by Sun Myung Moon. It combines elements of Christian fundamentalism and Buddhism, demands absolute obedience, and has become controversial because of brainwashing techniques it is alleged to use and the way in which it cuts members off from their friends and families. [After S.M. *Moon.*]

moon·light (mo͞on-līt) *n.* The light reflected from the surface of the Moon, principally that originating at the Sun.
~*adj.* **1.** Of moonlight. **2.** Under moonlight.
~*intr.v.* **moonlighted, -lighting, -lights.** *Informal.* To work at a spare-time job, often at night, in addition to one's full-time job. **—moon·light·er** *n.* **—moon·light·ing** *n.*

moonlight flit *n. British Informal.* A hurried departure, usually made at night and with one's possessions, to avoid creditors.

moon·lit (mo͞on-lit) *adj.* Illuminated by the Moon.

moon rat *n.* A large, ratlike, nocturnal, insectivorous mammal, *Echinosorex gymnurus,* of southeast Asia, having greyish fur and a long snout.

moon·scape (mo͞on-skayp) *n.* **1.** A view or picture of the surface of the moon. **2.** Loosely, any desolate landscape. [MOON + -SCAPE.]

moon·seed (mo͞on-seed) *n.* Any of several climbing vines of the genus *Menispermum* or related genera, having red or blackish fruit with crescent-shaped or ring-shaped seeds.

moon·shine (mo͞on-shīn) *n.* **1.** Moonlight. **2.** *Informal.* Foolish or nonsensical talk, thought, or action. **3.** *U.S. Slang.* Illegally distilled whiskey.
~*v.* **moonshined, -shining, -shines.** *U.S.* —*tr.* To distil (alcoholic liquor) illegally. —*intr.* To operate an illegal still. **—moon·shine** *adj.* **—moon·shin·er** *n.*

moon·shot (mo͞on-shot) *n.* A launching of a spacecraft or rocket to the Moon.

moon·stone (mo͞on-stōn) *n.* A mineral valued as a gem for its pearly translucence, commonly **albite, labradorite,** or **orthoclase** *(all of which see).* It is found worldwide.

moon·struck (mo͞on-struk) *adj.* **1.** Dazed or distracted with romantic sentiment; lovelorn. **2.** Afflicted with insanity; crazed; deranged. [From the belief that moonlight inspires romantic love and causes insanity.]

Moon type *n.* A system of printing for the blind that uses embossed letters instead of the raised dots of Braille, requiring less sensitivity of the fingers. [After William *Moon* (1819–94), British inventor.]

moon·wort (mo͞on-wurt || -wawrt) *n.* Any of various ferns of the genus *Botrychium;* especially, *B. lunaria,* having crescent-shaped leaflets. [The leaflets being shaped like the crescent Moon.]

moon·y (mo͞oni) *adj.* **-ier, -iest.** **1.** Of or resembling the moon. **2.** Dreamy in mood or nature; absent-minded. **—moon·i·ly** *adj.*

moor¹ (moor, mor) *v.* **moored, mooring, moors.** —*tr.* **1.** To secure or make fast (a boat, for example) by means of cables, anchors, or other contrivances. **2.** To fix in place; secure. —*intr.* **1.** To secure a vessel or aircraft. **2.** To be secured, as is a vessel or hot-air balloon. [Middle English *moren,* from Middle Low German *mōren.*]

moor² *n.* A broad tract of open land, often high but poorly drained, often having patches of heath and peat bogs. [Middle English *mor,* Old English *mōr,* from Germanic.]

Moor (moor, mor) *n.* **1.** A member of a Muslim people of mixed Berber and Arab descent, now living chiefly in North Africa. **2.** Any of the Muslims who invaded Spain in the eighth century A.D. and established a civilisation there which lasted until 1492. [Middle English *More,* from Old French, from Latin *Maurus,* from Greek *Mauros,* probably of North African origin.]

moor·age (mo͝or-ij, máwrij) *n.* **1.** A place where a vessel may be moored. **2.** The act of mooring or state of being moored. **3.** A charge for the use of mooring facilities.

moor·cock (mo͝or-kok, mór-) *n.* A male red grouse.

Moore, Bobby, born Robert Frederick Moore (1941–). English footballer. He played for West Ham United (1958–74). He won a record 108 caps, 90 of them as captain, in full internationals. He

Montezuma *The Aztec emperor Montezuma is carried in state on his way to meet Cortés (detail of a painting on mother of pearl by Miguel Gonzales in the Museo de America, Madrid).*

moonstone *This semi-precious stone, found in Sri Lanka and India, appears to shimmer like moonlight when it is cut "en cabuchon" – with a domed top and flat bottom. In folklore, it is said to have magic properties which change with the phases of the moon: during a waxing moon it is a love charm; during a waning moon it is an aid to clairvoyance.*

Moore

SCULPTURES WHOSE BEAUTY IS THEIR VITALITY

The natural forms of bones, shells, and rocks inspire Britain's most original sculptor

Born the seventh son of a Yorkshire coal miner in 1898, Henry Moore began his working life at 18 as a schoolteacher in his home town of Castleford. After serving in the latter part of World War I, he studied sculpture in Leeds and London, and became attracted by Egyptian, African, Etruscan, and Mexican art forms. They had a profound influence on his future work.

Moore exhibited his first concrete sculptures – of reclining female figures – in 1926 in London. He obtained his first public commission in 1928; it was for a relief carving, *North Wind*, to be placed on the façade of the new London Underground station, St. James's Park.

During the 1930s he concentrated on stone and wood carvings, both figurative and abstract. In September 1940, during the German blitz on London, he made an evocative set of drawings of people sheltering in the Underground from the bombs, and became an official war artist. He made a series of drawings of miners working at the coal face at Castleford, then in 1942 resumed his drawings for sculpture.

In sculpting human forms, he strove to make the spaces they contained as meaningful as the figures themselves. He rejected traditional ideas

of beauty in sculpture. "A work of art must have a vitality of its own," he stated. "When a work has this powerful vitality we do not connect the word 'beauty' with it."

After his early work, Moore's sculptures became less abstract. He examined bones, shells, rocks, and hills to find what he called "nature's principles of form and rhythm", and he tried to use these natural forms, rather than geometric shapes, in his work. He separated the shapes that make up the human body, but they remained powerful human figures, expressing intense emotions.

In 1943–44 Moore carved a tender *Madonna and Child* for St. Matthew's Church, Northampton. His later works include forms for outdoor settings – among them the striking, two-piece reclining figure set in a pool at New York's Lincoln Centre (1963–64).

Henry Moore has been internationally hailed as Britain's most original sculptor, and was awarded the Order of Merit in 1963. In New York in May, 1982, an elmwood figure carved by him fetched a price higher than any previously paid at auction for a work by a living artist: £705,915.

FAMILY GROUP *Moore became a father in 1946 when he was 47. He celebrated the birth of his only child, Mary, with this casting in bronze, now at Barclay School, Stevenage, Hertfordshire.*

was captain when the English team won the World Cup in 1966.

Moore, G(eorge) E(dward) (1873–1958). English philosopher. From 1925 to 1939 he was professor of philosophy at Cambridge University and from 1921 to 1947 he edited the journal *Mind*. His *Principia Ethica* (1903), laid the foundations of much of 20th-century development in epistemology and linguistic analysis.

Moore, Henry (1898–). English sculptor. He established his international reputation with his one-man retrospective show at the Museum of Modern Art, New York, in 1946. Moore carves abstract figures in many media.

Moore, Sir John (1761–1809). British general and M.P. (1784–90). A good strategist, he was attempting to cut off a French army in Spain when he had to lead a retreat from Madrid to La Coruña. He was killed in action as his men repulsed a French attack.

Moore, Thomas (1779–1852). Irish-born poet. His Irish lyrics included *Believe Me If All Those Endearing Young Charms*.

moor·fowl (moor-fowl, mór-) *n. Archaic*. The **red grouse** (*see*).

moor·hen (moor-hen, mór-) *n.* **1.** A common, widely distributed water bird, *Gallinula chloropus*, having dark plumage and a red bill and found in ponds and marshes. **2.** A female red grouse.

moor·ing (moor-ing, mór-) *n.* **1. a.** *Usually plural*. Equipment, such as anchors, chains, or lines, for holding fast a vessel. **b.** A permanent anchor for mooring a vessel, with a buoy attached. **2.** A place at which a vessel can be moored. **3.** *Usually plural*. An element providing stability or security: *lost her emotional moorings*.

Moor·ish (moor-ish, mór-) *adj.* **1.** Of or pertaining to the Moors or their culture. **2.** Designating a style of Spanish architecture of the 13th to 16th centuries, characterised by the horseshoe arch and ornate decoration.

Moorish idol *n.* A tropical marine fish, *Zanclus canescens*, with a deeply compressed body marked with black and yellow stripes, a beaklike mouth, and an enlarged dorsal fin.

moor·land (moor-lənd, mór-, *rarely* -land) *n. British*. A tract of moors.

moor·wort (moor-wurt ‖ -wawrt) *n.* A plant, the **bog rosemary** (*see*). [MOOR + WORT.]

moose (mooss) *n., pl.* **moose**. A hoofed mammal, *Alces alces* (or *A. americana*), of the deer family, found in forests of northern North America, and also in Eurasia, where it is called "elk". It has a broad, pendulous muzzle, and the male has large, flat antlers. [Natick *moos*, from Proto-Algonquian *mooswa* (unattested).]

moot (moot) *n.* **1.** In early medieval England, a meeting; especially, a representative meeting of the freemen of a shire. **2.** An imaginary case argued by law students as an exercise.

~*tr.v.* **mooted, mooting, moots**. **1. a.** To offer as a subject for debate; bring up for discussion. **b.** To discuss or debate. **2.** To plead or argue (a case) in a moot court.

~*adj.* Subject to debate; arguable; unresolved: *a moot point*. [Middle English *mot*, *moot*, Old English *mōtian* (verb), to converse, *(ge)mōt* moot, assembly, from Germanic; akin to MEET.]

moot court *n.* A mock court where hypothetical cases are tried for the training of law students.

mop[1] (mop) *n.* **1.** A household implement made of absorbent material attached to a handle and used for polishing or washing floors or dishes, for example. **2.** Any loosely tangled bunch or mass: *a mop of hair*.

~*tr.v.* **mopped, mopping, mops**. To wash, scrub, or wipe with, or as if with, a mop. Often used with *up*. [Middle English *mappe*, perhaps from *mappel*, from Medieval Latin *mappula*, towel, cloth, diminutive of Latin *mappa*, cloth.]

mop[2] *intr.v.* **mopped, mopping, mops**. *Archaic*. To grimace. Used chiefly in the phrase *mop and mow*.

~*n. Archaic*. A grimace or dejected expression. [Perhaps imitative of a pout.]

mop·board (móp-bawrd ‖ -bōrd) *n. U.S.* A skirting board.

mope (mōp) *intr.v.* **moped, moping, mopes**. **1.** To be gloomy or dejected. **2.** To give oneself up to brooding or sulking.

~*n.* **1.** A person given to gloomy or dejected moods. **2.** *Plural*. Low spirits; the blues. [Originally, to move as in a daze, perhaps from Middle Dutch *mopen*.] —**mop·er** *n.* —**mop·ing·ly** *adv.* —**mop·ish** *adj.* —**mop·ish·ly** *adv.*

mo·ped (mō-ped) *n.* A light cycle powered by pedals and by a small motor. [Swedish *mo*(tor) *ped*(aler), motor pedals.]

mo·poke (mō-pōk) *n.* Also **more·pork** (mór-pawrk ‖ mōr-pōrk). A small owl, *Ninox novaeseelandiae*, of Australia and New Zealand, having a spotted plumage.

mop·pet (móppit) *n.* A young child; especially, a little girl. [Diminutive of obsolete *moppe*, child, fool, probably of Low German origin, akin to Low German *mops*, fool.]

mop up *tr.v. Military*. To destroy (remaining enemy resistance) after an initial victory. —*intr.v.* To complete a task; finish. —**mop-up** (móp-up) *n.*

mo·quette (mo-két, mō-) *n.* **1.** A heavy fabric with a thick nap, used for upholstery. **2.** A type of carpet with a deep, tufted pile. [French, variant of obsolete *moucade*†.]

Moqui. Variant of **Moki.**

mor. morocco (leather).

MOR (ém-ō-aár) *n.* See **middle-of-the-road**. —**MOR** *adj.*

mo·ra (máwr-ə ‖ mōr-ə) *n., pl.* **morae** (-ee) or **-ras**. **1.** In quantitative verse, the unit of metrical time equal to the short syllable. **2.** A phonological unit equal to one short-vowelled syllable or half of a long-vowelled syllable. [Latin, "pause".]

mo·raine (mə-ráyn, mo-) *n.* An accumulation of rocks, stones, or other debris carried and deposited by a glacier or ice sheet. *Ground moraine* is taken up by the base of the ice, and deposited over wide areas. *Terminal moraine* is material carried forward by the ice, and deposited as a hummocky ridge at the tip or edge. *Lateral moraine*, carried on the side of a valley glacier, is mostly derived from the valley wall, and is deposited at the sides. *Medial moraine* is the combined adjacent lateral moraines of two valley glaciers below their confluence. [French, from Italian dialect *morena*†.] **—mo·rain·al, mo·rain·ic** *adj.*

mor·al (mórrəl || máwrəl) *adj.* **1.** Of or concerned with the judgment of the goodness or badness of human action and character; pertaining to the discernment of good and evil: *moral philosophy.* **2.** Designed to teach goodness or correctness of character and behaviour; instructive of what is good and bad: *"the highest precepts and the strongest examples of moral and religious endurances"* (Jane Austen). **3.** Being or acting in accordance with standards and precepts of goodness or with established codes of behaviour, especially with regard to sexual conduct. **4.** Arising from conscience or the sense of right and wrong: *a moral obligation.* **5.** Having psychological rather than physical or tangible effects; concerning morale: *moral support.* **6.** Based upon strong likelihood or firm conviction, rather than upon the actual evidence or demonstration: *a moral certainty.*
~*n.* **1. a.** The lesson or principle contained in or taught by a fable, story, or event. **b.** This lesson as encapsulated in the concluding sentence of a fable: *Moral: Look before you leap.* **2.** A concisely expressed precept or general truth; a maxim. **3.** *Plural.* Rules or habits of conduct, especially sexual conduct, with reference to standards of right and wrong: *loose morals.* [Middle English, from Old French, from Latin *mōrālis,* from *mōs* (stem *mōr-*), custom.]
Synonyms: *moral, ethical, virtuous, righteous.*
Usage: *Moral* and *morale* are sometimes confused in their noun uses. *Moral* has the sense of "lesson, precept", and has a plural form, referring to "rules of proper conduct". *Morale* refers to the degree of confidence or optimism of a person or group, as shown in their behaviour; it has no plural form.

mo·rale (mə-raál, mo-) *n.* The state of mind or optimistic spirits of an individual or group, as shown in confidence, cheerfulness, and discipline. [French, feminine of MORAL.]

moral hazard *n. Insurance.* A risk to the insurer resulting from uncertainty about the insured's honesty or discretion.

mor·al·ise, mor·al·ize (mórrəl-īz || máwrəl-) *v.* **-ised, -ising, -ises.** —*tr.* **1.** To derive a moral lesson from (a story, for example); explain in moral terms. **2.** To improve the morals of; reform. —*intr.* **1.** To think about or discuss moral or ethical issues. **2.** To make moral judgements or statements, often in a priggish way. **—mor·al·i·sa·tion** (-ī-záysh'n || *U.S.* -i-) *n.* **—mor·al·is·er** *n.*

mor·al·ism (mórrəl-iz'm || máwrəl-) *n.* **1.** A conventional moral maxim or attitude. **2.** The act or practice of moralising. **3.** The practice of or belief in a system of principles governing conduct, as distinct from a religion.

mor·al·ist (mórrəl-ist || máwrəl-) *n.* **1.** A teacher or student of ethics. **2.** A person who follows a system of moral principles as distinct from an established religion.

mor·al·is·tic (mórrə-lístik || máwrə-) *adj.* Characterised by or given to moralising, especially in a priggish way. **—mor·al·is·ti·cal·ly** *adv.*

mo·ral·i·ty (mə-rál-əti, mo-) *n., pl.* **-ties.** **1.** The quality of being moral. **2.** The evaluation of or means of evaluating human conduct, especially: **a.** A set of ideas of right and wrong: *Christian morality.* **b.** A set of customs of a given society, class, or social group which regulate personal and social relationships and prescribe modes of behaviour to facilitate the group's existence or ensure its survival: *middle-class morality.* **3.** Virtuous conduct, especially in compliance with approved codes for sexual behaviour. **4.** A rule or lesson in moral conduct; a moral. **5.** A morality play.

morality play *n.* A play in a genre of the 15th and 16th centuries in which moral instruction was conveyed through allegorically personifying virtues and vices in stories drawn from popular legend.

mor·al·ly (mórrəli || máwrəli) *adv.* **1.** In accordance with accepted rules of conduct; virtuously. **2.** With reference to moral law; ethically. **3.** In all probability; virtually: *morally certain.*

moral philosophy *n.* In philosophy, **ethics** *(see).*

Moral Rearmament *n.* An international movement advocating spiritual revival and the consolidation of morality on conservative Christian principles. It was established in 1938 by Frank Buchman. Also called "Buchmanism", "Oxford Group".

mo·rass (mə-ráss, mo-) *n.* **1.** An area of low-lying, soggy ground; a bog or marsh. **2.** Any difficult or perplexing situation, especially one from which it is difficult to escape. [Dutch *moeras,* variant (influenced by *moer,* moorland) of Middle Dutch *marasch,* from Old French *marasc,* from Germanic; akin to MARSH.]

mor·a·to·ri·um (mórrə-táwri-əm || máwrə-, -tōri-) *n., pl.* **-ums** or **-toria** (-ə). **1.** *Law.* An authorisation to a debtor, such as a bank or nation, permitting temporary suspension of payments. **2.** A deferment or delay of any action. [New Latin, from Late Latin *morātōrius,* MORATORY.]

mor·a·to·ry (mórrə-tri, -təri || máwrə-) *adj.* Authorising delay in payment; postponing: *a moratory contract.* [French *moratoire,* from Late Latin *morātōrius,* from Latin *morārī,* to delay, from *mora,* delay.]

Mo·ra·vi·a (mə-ráyv-yə, mo-, -i-ə). *Czech* **Mo·ra·va** (mórrava); *German* **Mäh·ren** (máir-ən). Central region of Czechoslovakia. It is a fertile agricultural area, with major mineral resources and industries. A great Slav empire in the 9th century, Moravia eventually passed to the Habsburgs of Austria (1526), under whom most of its towns became German-speaking. It became part of Czechoslovakia in 1918. In 1938, because of their high proportion of Germans, Hitler annexed parts of Moravia, later making the whole a German "protectorate". After World War II, most of its German-speaking people were expelled. Brno (Brünn) is the chief town.

Mo·ra·via (mo-raáv-yə), **Alberto,** born Alberto Pincherle (1907–). Italian novelist. His first novel, *The Indifferent Ones* (1929), introduced the continuing theme of his works, the despair and alienation of contemporary human life. His best-known works are *The Woman of Rome* (1947), *The Conformist* (1951), and *Two Women* (1957).

Mo·ra·vi·an (mə-ráyvi-ən) *n.* **1.** A native or inhabitant of Moravia. **2.** The Czech dialect spoken in Moravia. **3.** A member of the Moravian Church, a Protestant denomination founded in Saxony in 1722 by Hussite emigrants from Moravia. **—Mo·ra·vi·an** *adj.*

mo·ray (máwray, mo-ráy, mə- || mōray) *n.* Any of various often voracious, brightly coloured marine eels of the family Muraenidae, of chiefly tropical coastal waters. Also called "moray eel". [Portuguese *moreia,* from Latin *mūrēna,* from Greek *muraina*†.]

Mor·ay (múrri) or **Mor·ay·shire** (-shər, -sheer || -shīr). Former county of northeast Scotland, divided between the Highland and Grampian Region (1975). Elgin was the county town.

Moray, James Stewart or **Stuart, Earl of** (*c.* 1531–70). Regent of Scotland (1567–70), bastard son of King James V, one of the first Scottish noblemen to embrace Protestantism. When Mary married Darnley in 1565, he opposed the marriage and fled to England; in 1566 he returned to Scotland and after Mary's overthrow was appointed regent for James VI. In 1568–69 he gave evidence against Mary, accusing her of complicity in Darnley's murder. He was assassinated by James Hamilton at Linlithgow.

Moray Firth. An arm of the North Sea between Highland and Grampian Regions, east Scotland, containing valuable oil fields. Inverness lies at its head.

mor·bid (mórbid) *adj.* **1. a.** Of, pertaining to, or caused by disease. **b.** Psychologically unhealthy: *a morbid fear of dogs.* **2.** Susceptible to or characterised by preoccupation with unwholesome matters: *a morbid imagination.* **3.** Gruesome; grisly. **4.** *Informal.* Sad; melancholy. [Latin *morbidus,* diseased, from *morbus,* disease.] **—mor·bid·ly** *adv.* **—mor·bid·ness** *n.*

morbid anatomy *n.* The branch of medicine concerned with the anatomy of diseased organs and tissues.

mor·bi·dez·za (mórbi-détsə) *n. Art.* Great delicacy, especially in the painting of flesh tints. [Italian, from *morbido,* delicate, tender. See **morbid.**]

mor·bid·i·ty (mawr-biddəti) *n., pl.* **-ties.** **1.** The state or quality of being diseased. **2.** The number of cases of a particular disease occurring in a given number of a population. In this sense, also called "morbidity rate". **3.** A concern with morbid matters.

mor·bif·ic (mawr-bíffik) *adj.* Causing or producing disease; pathogenic. [New Latin *morbificus* : Latin *morbus,* disease + *-ficus,* -FIC.]

mor·bil·li (mawr-billī) *n.* A disease, **measles** *(see).* [Latin, plural of *morbillus,* pustule, from *morbus,* disease.]

mor·ceau (máwr-sō, -sṓ) *n., pl.* **-ceaux** (-sṓ). A short literary or musical composition. [French, "morsel".]

mor·da·cious (mawr-dáyshəss) *adj.* **1.** Given to biting; biting. **2.** Caustic; sarcastic. [Latin *mordāx* (stem *mordāc-*), caustic, biting, from *mordēre,* to bite.] **—mor·da·cious·ly** *adv.* **—mor·dac·i·ty** (-dássəti) *n.*

mor·dant (mórd'nt) *adj.* **1. a.** Bitingly sarcastic. **b.** Incisive and trenchant. **2.** Bitingly painful. **3.** Serving to fix colours in dyeing.
~*n.* **1.** A reagent, such as alumina or tannic acid, used to fix colouring matter in textiles, leather, or other materials. **2.** A corrosive substance, such as an acid, used to etch treated areas on a metal or other surface, especially a printing plate. —See Synonyms at **incisive.**
~*tr.v.* **mordanted, -danting, -dants.** To treat with a mordant. [French, from Old French, from the present participle of *mordre,* to bite, from Latin *mordēre.*] **—mor·dan·cy** *n.* **—mor·dant·ly** *adv.*

mor·dent (mórd'nt || *U.S. also* mawr-dént) *n. Music.* A melodic ornament in which a principal note is rapidly interrupted, usually only once, by a note a semitone or full tone above *(upper mordent)* or below *(lower mordent).* [German, from Italian *mordente,* a grace note, from *mordere,* to bite (in allusion to the sharpness of attack with which it is executed), from Latin *mordēre.*]

Mordred. Variant of **Modred.**

more (mor || mōr). **1.** Comparative of **many.** **2.** Comparative of **much.**
~*adj.* **1. a.** Greater in number. **b.** Greater in size, amount, extent, or degree. **2.** Additional; extra: *They need more food.*
~*n.* **1.** A greater or additional quantity, number, degree, or amount. Used with *of* and a plural verb: *More of them are coming.* **2.** Something that exceeds or surpasses expectation: *more than necessary.*
~*adv.* **1. a.** To a greater extent or degree: *His insults upset her more than his blows did.* **b.** Used to form the comparative of many adjectives and adverbs, especially those of two or more syllables: *more difficult; more intelligently.* **2.** In addition; besides; further; again; longer: *I can't eat a mouthful more.* **—more or less.** **1.** About; approximately. **2.** To an undetermined degree. [Middle English *more,* Old English *māra* (adjective), *māre* (adverb and noun).]

More (mor || mōr), **Sir Thomas** (1478–1535). English statesman, humanist scholar, writer, and saint. His essay *Utopia* (1516) described an ideal form of Commonwealth. He was knighted (1521)

moorhen *The moorhen, which is found in most parts of the world except Australia, has no connection with moors; it nests beside freshwater ponds, lakes, and rivers, and its name is derived from the word "mere", meaning lake. When alarmed, it can sink below the surface, leaving only its bill protruding like a snorkel.*

moose *The elk of Europe and Asia and the moose of North America are the same species,* Alces alces. *The largest of the deer family, growing to 2 metres (6½ feet) tall, they use their mobile lips to gather water plants and browse on trees and bushes.*

and made Lord Chancellor by Henry VIII (1529). After resigning (1532), he refused to subscribe to the Act of Supremacy which made Henry, not the pope, head of the English Church. He was imprisoned in the Tower and beheaded. He was canonised in 1935.

Morea. See **Peloponnese.**

mo·reen (mə-réen, maw-) n. A sturdy ribbed fabric of wool or cotton, often with an embossed finish, used for clothing and upholstery. [Perhaps blend of MOIRE and VELVETEEN or SATEEN.]

more·ish, mor·ish (máwrish ‖ mŏrish) adj. Informal. Causing one to want more; appetising. Said of food.

mo·rel¹ (mo-rél, mo- ‖ maw-) n. Any of various edible mushrooms of the genus *Morchella* and related genera, characterised by a brownish, spongelike cap. [French *morille*, from Dutch *morilje†*.]

morel² n. A nightshade; especially, the black nightshade. [Middle English, from Old French *morele*, feminine noun from *morel*, dark brown, from Vulgar Latin *maurellus* (unattested), from Latin *Maurus*, MOOR.]

mo·rel·lo (mə-réllō, mo-) n., pl. **-los.** A variety of the sour cherry, *Prunus cerasus austera*, having fruit with dark red skin. Also called "morello cherry". [Italian, "dark", from Medieval Latin *morellus*, from Latin *Maurus*, MOOR.]

more·o·ver (mawr-ōvər, máwr- ‖ mōr-, mór-) adv. Beyond what has been stated; furthermore; besides. See Synonyms at **also.**

morepork. Variant of **mopoke.**

mo·res (máwr-eez, -ayz ‖ mór-) pl.n. The accepted traditional customs and usages of a particular social group that come to be regarded as essential to its survival and welfare, thence often becoming, through general observance, part of a formalised legal code. [Latin *mōrēs*, plural of *mōs*, custom.]

Moresco. Variant of **Morisco.**

Mo·resque (maw-résk, mə-, mo-) adj. Moorish. Said of decoration and architecture.
~n. An ornament or decoration in Moorish style. [French, from Spanish *Morisco*, MORISCO.]

Mor·gan (mórgən) n. A small saddle horse or trotting horse of an American breed. [After Justin *Morgan* (1747–98), owner of the stallion from which the breed is descended.]

Morgan, Sir Henry (c.1635–88). Welsh buccaneer and colonial administrator. As commander of the British pirates in the Caribbean, he sacked Puerto Bello (1688) and captured Maracaibo (1669) and Panama (1671). In 1672 he was sent to England as a prisoner for his acts of piracy, but was received as a hero and knighted (1673). He went back to Jamaica as governor.

Morgan, John Pierpont (1837–1913). U.S. industrialist and financier. He founded (1901) the U.S. Steel Corporation, the first billion-dollar corporation in the world.

mor·ga·nat·ic (mórgə-náttik) adj. Of, pertaining to, or designating a legal marriage between a woman or man of royal or noble birth and a partner of lower rank, in which agreement is made that any titles or estates of the royal or noble partner will not be shared by the commoner or by any of their offspring. [French or German, from Medieval Latin *matrimonium ad morganaticam*, "marriage for (no dowry but) the morning-gift" (i.e., the husband's token gift to the wife on the morning after the wedding night), from Old High German *morgan*, morning.] —**mor·ga·nat·i·cal·ly** adv.

mor·gan·ite (mórgən-īt) n. A rosy-pink variety of beryl, valued as a semiprecious gem. [Named in honour of J.P. MORGAN.]

Mor·gan le Fay (mór-gən-lə-fáy, -li-). Also **Mor·gain le Fay** (-gən-, -gayn-). A sorceress, the half sister and enemy of King Arthur.

mor·gen (mórgən, mórkhən) n., pl. **morgen** or **-gens. 1.** A former Dutch and South African unit of land area equal to 0.86 hectare

morel *Morchella esculenta is one of about 15 edible species of this genus of fungus; it is found in temperate climates, often growing on rotting wood.*

(2.116 acres). **2.** A unit of land area formerly used in Norway, Denmark, and Prussia, equal to about two thirds of an acre. [Dutch, from Middle Dutch *morghen*, morning, that is, "a morning's ploughing".]

morgue (morg) n. **1.** A mortuary (see). **2.** U.S. Informal. A reference file or storage room containing old newspapers, clippings, notebooks, and the like, in a newspaper or magazine office. [French, from *le Morgue†*, the mortuary building in Paris.]

mor·i·bund (mórri-bund) adj. **1.** At the point of death; about to die. **2.** Approaching an end; obsolescent: *moribund ideas.* [Latin *moribundus*, from *morī*, to die.] —**mor·i·bun·di·ty** (-búnditi) n. —**mor·i·bund·ly** adv.

mo·ri·on¹ (máwri-ən ‖ mŏri-, -on) n. A crested metal helmet with curved peaks in front and behind, worn by soldiers in the 16th and 17th centuries. [French, from Spanish *morrion*, from *morro*, crown of the head, from Vulgar Latin *murrum†* (unattested), round thing.]

morion² n. A variety of smoky quartz, often nearly black. [Manuscript error for Latin *mormorion†*.]

Mo·ris·co (mə-rískō) n., pl. **-cos** or **-coes.** Also **Moresco** (-réskō). **1.** A Spanish Moor. **2.** A morris dance.
~adj. Also **Moresco.** Moorish. Said of a style of architecture. [Spanish, from *Moro*, Moor, from Latin *Maurus*, MOOR.]

morish. Variant of **moreish.**

Mo·ri·sot (mórri-sō), **Berthe** (1841–95). French painter in the impressionist style. A student of Corot, she is most admired for her graceful paintings of women and children.

mo·ri·tu·ri te sa·lu·ta·mus (mórri-téwr-ī tee sál-yōō-táyməss, -tóor-, -ee, tay, -ōō-, -táaməss) Latin. We who are about to die salute you. The gladiators' salutation to the Roman emperor.

Mor·mon¹ (mórmən). In the Mormon Church, an American prophet, warrior, and historian of the fourth century A.D., who was revealed to Joseph Smith as the author of a sacred history of the Americas, which Smith translated as the Book of Mormon.

Mormon² n. **1.** A member of the Church of Jesus Christ of Latter-day Saints, founded by Joseph Smith in 1830. **2.** A member of any of various sects deriving from Smith's original church that accept the Book of Mormon as the word of God.
~adj. Of or pertaining to the Mormons, their religion, or their church. —**Mor·mon·ism** n. —**Mor·mon·ist** adj.

morn (morn) n. Poetic. The morning. —**the morn.** Scottish. Tomorrow. [Middle English *morwen, morn*, Old English *morgen.*]

Mor·nay (mor-náy, mór-nay) n. Sometimes small **m.** A white sauce flavoured with grated cheese.
~adj. Designating a dish prepared with this sauce: *eggs Mornay.* [20th century : origin obscure.]

morn·ing (mórning) n. **1.** The first or early part of the day, lasting from midnight to noon or from sunrise to noon. **2.** The hour from daybreak to sunrise; dawn. **3.** The first or early part of anything. [Middle English *morwening*, from *morwen*, MORN (by analogy with EVENING).] —**morn·ing** adj.

morning after n., pl. **mornings after.** Informal. The morning following a night of dissipation, especially drunkenness. Also called the "morning after the night before".

morning-after pill (mórning-áaftər ‖ -áftər) n. An oral contraceptive that prevents the implantation of a fertilised egg in the uterus.

morning coat n. A tailcoat, usually grey in colour, worn as part of a morning suit.

morning glory n., pl. **-ries.** Any of various, usually twining vines of the genus *Ipomoea*, having funnel-shaped, variously coloured flowers that close late in the day.

Morning Prayer n. In the Anglican Church; the service of morning worship. Also called "matins".

morn·ings (mórningz) adv. Informal. In the mornings; every morning.

morning sickness n. Nausea and vomiting upon rising in the morning, often one of the early symptoms of pregnancy. Not in technical usage.

morning star n. A planet visible in the east just before sunrise, especially Venus. Compare **evening star.**

morning suit n. A suit for a man, worn on formal occasions during the day, such as at weddings, and consisting of a morning coat and grey striped trousers, worn with a top hat.

Mo·ro (máw-rō ‖ mŏ-) n., pl. **-ros** or collectively **Moro. 1.** A member of any of various Muslim Malay peoples of the southern Philippines. **2.** The language of these peoples, of the Malayo-Polynesian family of languages. [Spanish, from Latin *Maurus*, MOOR.] —**Moro** adj.

Moro, Aldo (1916–78). Italian Christian Democratic politician. He was Prime Minister from 1963 to 1968. In 1978 he was kidnapped and murdered by the Red Brigade.

mo·roc·co (mə-róckō) n., pl. **-cos.** Abbr. **mor. 1.** A soft, fine leather of goatskin tanned with sumac, made originally in Morocco. It is used chiefly for bookbindings and shoes. **2.** Any imitation of this. Also called "morocco leather".

Mo·roc·co (mə-róckō). Arabic **Al Mam·la·ka al Magh·re·bi·a.** Country of northwest Africa, comprising the Atlas mountain ranges, with a fertile plain along the Atlantic, and the Sahara to the southeast. Most of the people are Arab-speaking Muslims, but a third are Muslim Berbers. European penetration begun by Portugal and Spain (15th century) increased in the 19th century, and by 1912 virtually all Morocco was administered by France or Spain, with an international zone at Tangier. Independence came in 1956. In 1976 Morocco occupied the northern two-thirds of the phosphate-rich

Spanish Sahara, and the rest in 1979. A border dispute with Algeria from 1963, and from 1976, war against the Polisario Front, fighting for an independent Sahara, drained Morocco's resources. The economy now relies on agriculture and mining, especially of phosphates, with fishing and tourism. Its area is some 659 970 square kilometres (254,748 square miles), but the southern borders are not defined. Population, 22,300,000. Capital, Rabat. —**Mo·roc·can** *adj. & n.*

mo·ron (máw-ron ‖ mŏ́-) *n.* **1.** *Informal.* A remarkably stupid or oafish person. **2.** A mentally subnormal person, having a mental age between 7 and 12 years or an intelligence quotient between 50 and 75. Not in current technical usage. [Greek *mōron*, neuter of *mōros*, foolish.] —**mo·ron·ic** (mə-rónnik, mo-, maw-) *adj.* —**mo·ron·i·cal·ly** *adv.* —**mo·ron·ism, mo·ron·i·ty** (mə-rónnəti, mo-, maw-) *n.*

mo·rose (mə-rŏ́ss ‖ maw-) *adj.* Sullenly melancholy; gloomy; ill-humoured. See Synonyms at **glum**. [Latin *mōrōsus*, captious, fretful, from *mōs* (stem *mōr-*), custom, manner, humour, caprice.] —**mo·rose·ly** *adv.* —**mo·rose·ness** *n.*

morph (morf) *n. Linguistics.* A morpheme, or the phonological representation of a morpheme. [Back-formation from *morpheme.*]

morph-. Variant of **morpho-**.

morph., morphol. morphological; morphology.

-morph *n. comb. form.* Indicates: **1.** A specified form, shape, or structure; for example, **endomorph**. **2.** A morpheme; for example, **allomorph**. [Greek *-morphos*, from *morphē*, shape, form.]

morph·ac·tin (mawrf-áktin) *n.* Any of a group of substances that regulate plant growth, usually by inhibiting elongation of shoots.

mor·phal·lax·is (mórfə-lák-siss) *n., pl.* **-laxes** (-seez). *Biology.* The regeneration of a part by means of structural reorganisation of existing cells with only limited production of new cells, a process observed primarily in invertebrate organisms, such as certain lobsters. [New Latin, "structure exchange" : MORPH(O)- + Greek *allaxis*, exchange, from *allassein*, to exchange, from *allos*, other.]

mor·pheme (mórfeem) *n.* A linguistic unit of relatively stable meaning that cannot be divided into smaller meaningful parts, such as whole words like *god*, word-forming elements like *-ly* as found in *godly*, or grammatical inflections like the plural ending *-s* in *gods*. Morphemes may be abstract units, as when the *-en* in *oxen*, the *-i-* in *mice*, and the *-s* in *girls* are all considered to be identical. [French *morphème*, from Greek *morphē*, form (by analogy with PHONEME).] —**mor·phem·ic** (mor-féemik) *adj.* —**mor·phem·i·cal·ly** *adv.*

mor·phe·mics (mawr-féemiks) *n. Linguistics.* The study of morphemes, their forms, and their functions.

Mor·phe·us (mór-fi-əss, -fewss). The god or personification of sleep: *in the arms of Morpheus.* —**Mor·phe·an** *adj.*

mor·phi·a (mórfi-ə) *n.* Morphine. Not in current technical usage. [New Latin : obsolete *morphium*, from MORPHEUS + -IA.]

mor·phic (mórfik) *adj.* Pertaining to form; morphological. [MORPH(O)- + -IC.] —**mor·phi·cal·ly** *adv.*

-morphic, -morphous *adj. comb. form.* Indicates possession of a specified shape or form; for example, **polymorphic, amorphous.** [From -MORPH.]

mor·phine (mórfeen) *n.* A narcotic drug extracted from opium, $C_{17}H_{19}NO_3$, the soluble salts of which are used in medicine to relieve severe and persistent pain. Repeated dosage causes addiction. [French, from MORPHEUS.]

mor·phin·ism (mór-fi-niz'm, -fee-) *n.* **1.** Morphine addiction. **2.** A chronic condition of poisoning caused by sustained or immoderate dosage of morphine.

morpho-, morph- *comb. form.* Indicates: **1.** A shape, form, or structure; for example, **morphogenesis, morphology. 2.** A morpheme; for example, **morphophonemics.** [German, from Greek, from *morphē*, shape.]

mor·pho·gen·e·sis (mórfō-jénnə-siss) *n.* **1.** Evolutionary development of the structure of an organism or part. **2.** Embryological development of the structure of an organism or part. —**mor·pho·ge·net·ic** (-ji-néttik), **mor·pho·gen·ic** (-jénnik) *adj.*

mor·phol·o·gy (mawr-fóllaji) *n. Abbr.* **morph., morphol. 1.** The biological study of the form and structure of living organisms. **2.** The structure and form of an organism, excluding its functions. **3.** *Linguistics.* **a.** The form and structure of words in any given language; especially, the consistent and classifiable forms and changes of inflections and derivations. **b.** The study of such form and structure. **4.** *Geology.* The study of the structure of earth features, geomorphology *(see).* [German *Morphologie* : MORPHO- + -LOGY.] —**mor·pho·log·ic, mor·pho·log·i·cal** (mórfə-lójik'l) *adj.* —**mor·pho·log·i·cal·ly** *adv.* —**mor·phol·o·gist** (-fóllajist) *n.*

mor·pho·pho·neme (mórf-ə-fōneem, -ō-) *n. Linguistics.* A member of the set of variant phonemes which may be used as part of a given morpheme according to phonological context. For example, the morpheme *electric-* has as its final constituent a morphophoneme consisting of three phonemes, (k), (s), and (sh), as in the words *electrical, electricity, electrician.*

mor·pho·pho·ne·mics (mórfō-fə-néemiks, -fō-) *n. Used with a singular verb. Linguistics.* The study of phonological variations within morphemes; the study of morphophonemes. Also called "morphophonology". —**mor·pho·pho·ne·mic** *adj.*

mor·pho·sis (mawr-fō-siss) *n., pl.* **-ses** (-seez). The manner in which an organism or one of its parts changes form or the manner or order of its development. [New Latin, from Greek *morphōsis*, formation, from *morphoun*, to form, from *morphē*, form.]

Mor·ris (mórriss), **William** (1834–96). British craftsman, poet, painter, and political activist. He first made his name in the 1850s

---

Morse code

SAMUEL MORSE'S SIMPLE SYSTEM

Dots and dashes to be flashed, bleeped, or written

Samuel Morse devised his code, in which letters are represented by combinations of long and short signals, in about 1838. It simplified the transmission of telegraphic messages and required only a single-wire machine. The code can also be written in dots and dashes or signalled with flash lamps or radio bleeps. In 1912, the easily memorised letters SOS were chosen to be the international distress signal. "*Save Our Souls*" was a catchphrase devised later.

Letter	Code	Letter	Code
A	·—	N	—·
B	—···	O	———
C	—·—·	P	·——·
D	—··	Q	——·—
E	·	R	·—·
F	··—·	S	···
G	——·	T	—
H	····	U	··—
I	··	V	···—
J	·———	W	·——
K	—·—	X	—··—
L	·—··	Y	—·——
M	——	Z	——··

SIMPLIFIED VERSION *The International Morse code is a form of Morse's original code, simplified for use in radio telegraphy. It differs from the American Morse adaptation in 11 letters and in all numerals except 4.*

---

as a painter attached to the Pre-Raphaelites, and as a poet, with *The Defence of Guenevere and other Poems*, which appeared in 1858. In 1861 he founded a firm of decorators, dedicated to combating the mass-produced art of the industrial system by producing handmade goods. In 1884 he helped to found the Socialist League.

Morris chair *n.* A large armchair with an adjustable back and removable cushions. [Designed by William MORRIS.]

mor·ris column (mórris ‖ *U.S. also* máwriss) *n.* A round pillar on a pavement, on which advertisements are displayed.

morris dance *n.* An English country dance traditionally performed by men *(morris men)* wearing bright costumes, handkerchiefs, and bells, and often representing a folk tale. Also called "morris". [Middle English *Moreys*, Moorish, from *More*, MOOR.]

Mor·ri·son of Lambeth (mórri-s'n), **Herbert Stanley, Baron** (1888–1965). English politician. He was secretary of the London Labour Party (1915–47) and a member of the London County Council (1922–45). In 1945 he was unofficially deputy prime minister under Attlee and leader of the House of Commons, a post he held until he was appointed Foreign Secretary in 1951. He was awarded a life peerage in 1959.

mor·row (mórrō) *n. Archaic.* **1.** The day following some particular day. Preceded by *the.* **2.** The time immediately subsequent to some particular event. **3.** The morning: *Good morrow!* [Middle English *morwe*, Old English *morgen.*]

morse (morss) *n.* The clasp or fastening, often of gold or silver, on a cope. [Middle English, from Old French *mors*, from Latin *morsus*, bite, clasp, from *mordēre* (past participial stem *mors-*), to bite.]

Morse (morss), **Samuel (Finley Breese)** (1791–1872). U.S. painter and inventor. He is most famous for his refinement of the electric telegraph and earlier telegraph codes (1838).

Morse code *n.* A system of communication in which letters of the alphabet and numbers are represented by patterns of short and long signals, which may be conveyed as sounds, flashes of light, written

---

dots and dashes, or the waving of flags. Also called "Morse", "Morse alphabet". [Invented by Samuel MORSE.]

mor·sel (mórss'l) n. **1.** A small piece or bite of food. **2.** A light meal; a snack. **3.** A small piece or amount of anything. [Middle English, from Old French *mors*, a bite, from Latin *morsum*, past participle of *mordēre*, to bite.]

mort[1] (mort) n. The note sounded on a hunting horn to announce the death of the hunted animal. [Middle English, from Old French, from Latin *mors* (stem *mort-*), death.]

mort[2] n. British Regional. A great number or quantity: *a mort of money*. [Perhaps from northern dialect *murth* (influenced by MORTAL, "extremely"), from Old Norse *mergth*, multitude.]

mort[3] n. A salmon two to three years old. [16th century : origin obscure.]

mor·tal (mórt'l) adj. **1.** Liable or subject to death. **2.** Of or pertaining to humans as beings who must die. **3.** Of, pertaining to, or accompanying death: *mortal throes*. **4.** Causing death; fatal; deadly: *a mortal wound*. **5.** Fought to the death: *"with victorious Germany and Italy engaged in mortal attack upon us"* (Sir Winston Churchill). **6.** Unrelenting; implacable: *one's mortal enemy*. **7.** Of or like the fear of death; dire; grievous: *in mortal terror*. **8.** Slang. Very great; extreme: *"I go there a mortal sight of times"* (Charles Dickens). **9.** Slang. Used as an intensive: *There is no mortal reason for us to go.*
~n. A human being.
~adv. Regional. Extremely; very: *mortal angry*. [Middle English, from Old French *mortal, mortel*, from Latin *mortālis*, from *mors* (stem *mort-*), death.] —**mor·tal·ly** adv.

mor·tal·i·ty (mawr-tál-əti) n., pl. **-ties. 1.** The condition of being subject to death. **2. a.** Archaic. Death. **b.** The loss of a great many lives. **3.** The frequency or number of deaths in proportion to a population in a given period. Also called "death rate", "mortality rate". **4.** Deadliness. **5.** The quality of being mortal. Said of a sin. **6.** Humankind.

mortality table n. Insurance. A table which lists the life expectancies of people according to their age, sex, occupation, and other considerations.

mortal sin n. **1.** Theology. A sin which totally estranges the soul from the grace of God. Compare **venial sin**. **2.** Informal. Any major miscalculation or common error.

mor·tar (mórtər) n. **1.** A receptacle made of a hard material in which substances are crushed or ground with a pestle. **2.** Any machine in which materials are ground and blended or crushed. **3.** Military. A muzzle-loading cannon used to fire shells at low velocities, short ranges, and great angular elevation. Also called "trench mortar". **4.** Any of several similar devices used for various purposes, such as shooting lifelines across a stretch of water. **5.** A mixture of cement or lime with sand and water that is used in building.
~v. **mortared, -taring, -tars.** —tr. **1.** To plaster or join with mortar. **2.** To bombard with a mortar; hit with mortar shells. —intr. To fire mortars. [Middle English *morter*, partly from Old English *mortere* and partly from Old French *mortier*, both from Latin *mortārium*, a mortar and the substance made in it.]

mor·tar·board (mórtər-bawrd ‖ -bōrd) n. **1.** A square board with a handle, for holding and carrying mortar. **2.** An academic cap topped by a flat square covered with cloth, usually black and having a tassel on top. Also called "square", "trencher", "trencher cap".

Morte d'Ar·thur, Le (lə mórt dárthər) n. A collection of Arthurian stories compiled and translated from Old French by Sir Thomas Malory, and printed by William Caxton in 1485.

mort·gage (mórgij) n. Abbr. **mtg.** Law. **1.** A temporary and conditional pledge or conveyance of property to a creditor as security against a debt. **2.** A contract or deed specifying the terms of such a conveyance. **3.** The claim that the mortgagee or creditor has upon property pledged in this manner.
~tr.v. **mortgaged, -gaging, -gages. 1.** To pledge (property) by mortgage. **2.** Informal. To pledge or stake against future success or failure; place an advance liability upon. [Middle English *morgage*, from Old French *mortgage*, "dead pledge" : *mort*, dead, from Latin *mortuus*, from *mors* (stem *mort-*), death + *gage*, GAGE (pledge).]

mort·ga·gee (mórgi-jée) n. The holder of a mortgage, usually as security against a loan.

mort·ga·gor (mórgi-jər, -jór) n. Also **mort·gag·er** (-jər). A person who mortgages property.

mor·ti·cian (mawr-tísh'n) n. U.S. A funeral director; an undertaker. [MORT(UARY) + -ICIAN.]

mor·ti·fi·ca·tion (mórtifi-káysh'n) n. **1.** A feeling of shame, humiliation, or wounded pride. **2.** The cause of such a feeling: *Her sister's imprisonment was a mortification to her.* **3.** The mortifying of the body and appetites. **4.** The death or decay of one part of a living body; necrosis; gangrene.

mor·ti·fy (mórti-fī) v. **-fied, -fying, -fies.** —tr. **1.** To cause to experience shame, humiliation, or wounded pride; humiliate. **2.** To discipline (one's body and appetites) by self-denial and austerity: *mortify the flesh.* **3.** To cause (a bodily part) to die, as by gangrene. —intr. **1.** To practise ascetic discipline or punishment of the body. **2.** To become gangrenous or necrosed, as a part of the body might. —See Synonyms at **degrade.** [Middle English *mortifien*, from Old French *mortifier*, from Late Latin *mortificāre*, to cause to die : *mors* (stem *mort-*), death + *facere*, -FY.] —**mor·ti·fy·ing·ly** adv.

Mor·ti·mer (mórtimər), **Roger de, 1st Earl of March** (c.

1287–1330). English nobleman. He was the lover of Edward II's wife, Isabella, with whom he raised a force to invade England from France (1326). They deposed Edward (1327) and together ruled England until 1330, when Edward III seized power and had Mortimer put to death after trial and conviction by Parliament.

mor·tise, mor·tice (mórtiss) n. **1.** A cavity, usually rectangular, in a piece of wood, stone, or other material, cut to receive a similarly shaped projection or **tenon** (see) of another piece, to hold the two together. **2.** Printing. A hole cut in a plate for the insertion of type.
~tr.v. **mortised** or **morticed, -tising** or **-ticing, -tises** or **-tices. 1.** To join or fasten securely, as with a mortise and tenon. **2.** To cut or make a mortise in. **3.** Printing. **a.** To cut a hole in (a plate) for the insertion of type. **b.** To cut such a hole and insert (type). [Middle English *mortays*, from Old French *mortoise*, from Arabic *murtazz*, fixed in.]

mortise lock n. A lock fixed into a mortise in the edge of a door, such that the body of the lock is enclosed. Compare **deadlock, Yale lock.**

mort·main (mórt-mayn) n. Law. Perpetual ownership of land by institutions such as churches that cannot transfer or sell them. Also called "dead hand". [Middle English *mortemayne*, from Old French *mortemain*, "dead hand" (that is, institutional possession) : *morte*, feminine of *mort*, dead, from Latin *mortuus*, from *mors* (stem *mort-*), death + *main*, hand, from Latin *manus*.]

Mor·ton (mórt'n), **James Douglas, 4th Earl of** (1516–81). Scottish nobleman. He was appointed Lord High Chancellor to Mary, Queen of Scots (1563). He played a leading role in the murder of David Riccio (1566) and conspired in the plot to murder Darnley. He became Regent after the death of the Earl of Mar (1572). He was removed from power by the Earl of Argyll (1578) and was executed for his part in the murder of Darnley.

mor·tu·ar·y (mór-tew-əri, -choo- ‖ -erri) n., pl. **-ies.** A place where dead bodies are prepared or kept prior to burial or cremation. Also called "morgue".
~adj. Of or pertaining to death or to the burial of the dead. [Middle English *mortuarie*, from Anglo-French, from Late Latin *mortuārium*, from *mortuārius*, of burial, from Latin *mortuus*, dead, from *mors* (stem *mort-*), death.]

mor·u·la (mórrew-lə ‖ mórrə-) n., pl. **-lae** (-lee) or **-las.** Biology. **1.** The spherical mass of embryonic cells formed by cleavage of a fertilised ovum before blastulation. Compare **gastrula. 2.** A spherical mass of developing male gametes occurring especially in certain annelid worms. [New Latin, diminutive of Latin *mōrum*, mulberry.] —**mor·u·lar** (-lər) adj.

mor·wong (mór-wong) n. An Australasian food fish of the family Cheilodactylidae. [From a native Australian language.]

mos. months.

mo·sa·ic (mə-záy-ik, mō-) n. **1. a.** A picture or decorative design made by setting small coloured pieces of glass, stone, or tile in mortar. **b.** The art of process of making such designs. **2.** Anything that resembles a piece of mosaic work: *The stained-glass windows cast light in a mosaic on the church floor.* **3.** Any of several virus diseases of plants, resulting in light and dark areas in the leaves, which often become shrivelled and dwarfed. **4.** A set of overlapping photographs, usually aerial, assembled into a composite picture. **5.** A photosensitive surface in a television camera, consisting of a large number of small sensitive patches on an insulating base. **6.** Genetics. An organism containing genetically different types of tissue; a chimera.
~tr.v. **mosaicked, -icking, -ics.** Rare. **1.** To make by mosaic or as if by mosaic. **2.** To adorn with mosaic or as if with mosaic. [Middle English, from Old French *mosaique*, from Italian *mosaico*, from Medieval Latin *mosaicus, musaicus*, irregularly from Late Greek *mouseion*, a mosaic, from *mouseios*, belonging to the Muses, from *Mousa*, Muse.] —**mo·sa·ic** adj. —**mo·sa·i·cist** (-i-sist) n.

Mo·sa·ic (mō-záy-ik, mə-) adj. Also **Mo·sa·i·cal** (mō-záy-ik'l, mə-). Of or pertaining to Moses or the laws and writings attributed to him. [New Latin *Mosaicus*, from MOSES.]

mosaic gold n. An alloy resembling gold, **ormolu** (see).

mo·sa·i·cism (mō-záy-i-siz'm, mə-) n. Genetics. The condition in which tissues of genetically different types occur in the same organism. [From MOSAIC.]

Mosaic Law n. The ancient law of the Hebrews, traditionally attributed to Moses and contained mainly in the Pentateuch. Also called "Law of Moses".

mo·sa·saur (mó-sə-sawr) n. Any of various extinct marine lizards of the genus *Mosasaurus* and related genera, which attained a very large size and had paddle-like limbs. [New Latin : *Mosa*, river Meuse (near which fossil remains were found) + *-saurus*, -SAUR.]

mos·cha·tel (móskə-tél) n. A plant, *Adoxa moschatellina*, of northern regions, having greenish-white, musk-scented flowers. [French *moscatelle*, from Italian *moscatella*, from *moscato*, MUSK.]

Mos·cow (móss-kō ‖ U.S. also -kow). Russian **Mos·kva** (mass-kváa). Capital of the U.S.S.R. and of the R.S.F.S.R. Lying on the Moskva river, it is also the communications, economic, and cultural centre of the country, and accounts for a sixth of the national industrial output, with metal-working, oil-refining, aircraft, publishing, vehicle, chemical, textile, and clothing plants. Founded in the 12th century, the minor principality of Moscow gradually assumed sovereignty over its neighbors by virtue of its strategic importance at the crossing of major trade routes and as bulwark against the Tatars. By the 15th century it was the capital of the Russian state, and its Grand Duke Ivan IV took the title of tsar in 1547. The

mosaic *A fish portrayed in a Roman mosaic from North Africa.*

mosque

THE MUSLIM PLACE OF WORSHIP
Ancient desert building traditions embodied in the monuments of Islam

The Muslim enclosure for prayer, the mosque (from the Arabic word *masjid*, "place of worship") was the first Islamic architectural form. The earliest mosque to have survived intact, the Great Mosque built in Damascus in 707, is roofed and domed, but many early mosques consisted of a large rectangular open courtyard surrounded by roofed or vaulted colonnades. Typical of the building traditions of the desert, they were featureless from the outside like fortified desert villages built round their wells. During the 13th century, cruciform mosques were introduced into Egypt by Suleiman, an Ottoman ruler from Turkey.

Every mosque has a niche called the *mihrab* built into the wall facing Mecca to indicate the direction for worshippers to face when praying. There may be a space in front of it, enclosed by a screen, for the caliph, sultan, or governor. Near by is a raised pulpit, often canopied, called the *minbar*. Most mosques have at least one high minaret, from which the *muezzin* or crier calls the faithful to prayer five times a day. Most have running water for ritual ablution – often a fountain or well set in the centre of the colonnaded courtyard.

Walls, gates, minarets, roofs, and domes may be ornately decorated with abstract designs and inscriptions from the Koran. The *Haddith*, the Islamic Traditions, forbid the representation of living human figures in art, because man is a work of God. The decoration may take the form of patterned brickwork (often found in Turkish mosques); of painted and gilded stucco (seen in early Egyptian mosques); of precious marbles or mosaics (used in Syria and other areas which once formed part of the Byzantine Empire); or ceramic tiles (which face many Persian mosques).

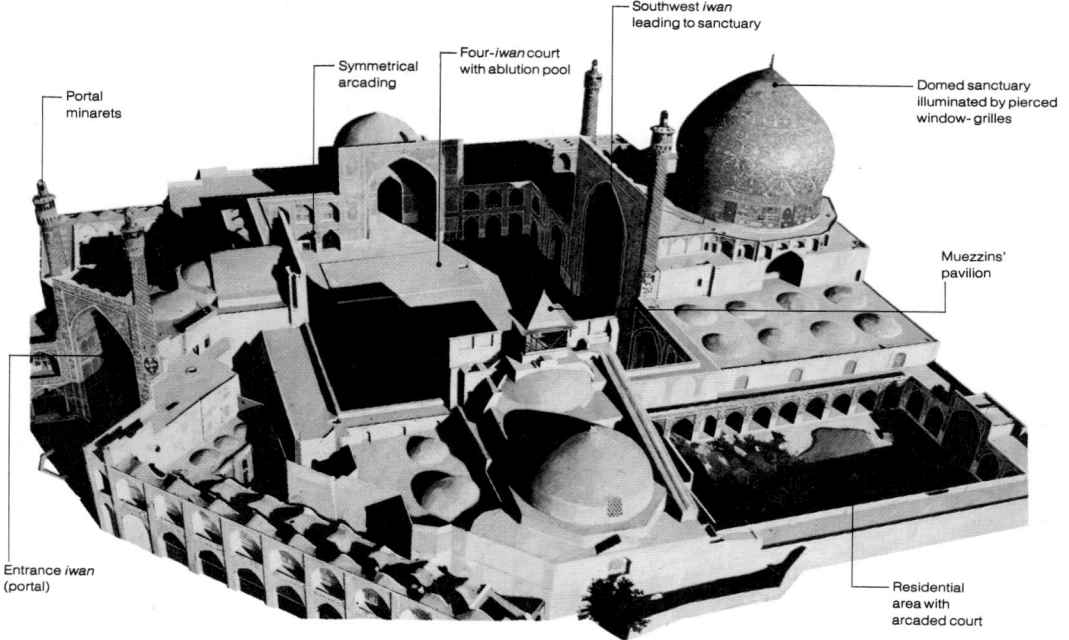

PERSIAN MOSQUE *Lavish ornamentation marks the Persian (Iranian) mosque. In early mosques the square court surrounded by arcades was built in traditional decorative brick and stucco. The later mosques, such as the 17th-century Masjid-i-Shah or Imperial Mosque in Isfahān (above), were large complexes of buildings entirely covered in lustrous polychrome tiles. The ceremonial portal, called the* iwan, *is characteristically Persian, inherited from the building traditions of the ancient Persian Empire.*

capital was transferred to St. Petersburg (1712), but Moscow was reinstated (1918) after the Revolution. It is the site of the Kremlin (citadel) with its many cathedrals, and Red Square with the Lenin Mausoleum and 16th-century cathedral of St. Vassily (Basil). Many times destroyed by fire, as during the French occupation (1812), and rebuilt, the city was heroically defended against the Nazis in World War II (1941). It was the venue for the 1980 Summer Olympics.

Mose·ley (mōzli), **Henry Gwyn-Jeffreys** (1887–1915). English physicist. His research on radioactivity demonstrated the relationship betwen X-ray spectra and the atomic number of an element and enabled him to formulate (1913) the law that established the atomic number of elements.

Mo·selle¹ (mō-zél, mə-). *German* **Mo·sel** (mōz'l). River of northwest Europe, flowing 547 kilometres (340 miles) from the Vosges in France to join the Rhine at Koblenz in West Germany.

Moselle² *n. Also small* **m.** A light, dry white wine produced in the valley of the Moselle river.

Mo·ses (mōz-iz ‖ -iss). The lawgiver who led the Israelites out of Egypt.

mo·sey (mōzi) *intr.v.* **-seyed, -seying, -seys.** *Chiefly U.S. Informal.* To walk in a leisurely manner; stroll. Often used with *along, down,* or *on down.* [19th century : origin obscure.]

mo·shav (mō-shaáv) *n., pl.* **-shavim** (-sha-véem). An agricultural cooperative settlement in Israel. [Hebrew *moshāb,* "dwelling".]

Mo·shesh (mō-shésh), (1795–1870). *Also* **Mo·shoe·shoe** (-shŏō-shŏō) or **M·shwe·shwe** (m-shwéshwi). Founder of the Basuto (Sotho) nation, and its undisputed chief through many wars with South Africa's white settlers. He was noted especially for his diplomatic skill.

Moslem. Variant of **Muslim.**

Mos·ley (mōzli), **Sir Oswald (Ernald)** (1896–1980). English politician, founder of the British Union of Fascists. He entered the House of Commons as a Conservative in 1918 and switched to the Labour Party in 1924. In 1929 he became a junior minister in the Labour government. He resigned from the government in 1930 when his economic policies to overcome the Depression were rejected. In 1932 he founded the New Party, and a year later the British Union of Fascists. He married his second wife, Diana Mitford, then Diana Guinness, in 1936 and they were both interned (1940–43) during World War II. Mosley failed in his attempts at a political comeback after the war.

Mo·so·tho (mŏō-sŏōtŏō) *n., pl.* **-thos** or collectively **Mosotho.** A member of the Sotho people of Southern Africa, or a citizen of **Lesotho** *(see).* Also called "Basotho", formerly "Basuto".

mosque (mosk) *n.* A Muslim house of worship. Also called "masjid", "musjid". [French *mosquée,* from Italian *moschea,* from Arabic *masjid,* a place of worship, from *sajada,* to worship.]

mos·qui·to (mə-skéetō, mo-) *n., pl.* **-toes** or **-tos.** Any of various winged insects of the family Culicidae, in which the female of most species is distinguished by a long proboscis for sucking blood. Some species are vectors of diseases such as malaria and yellow fever. [Spanish, diminutive of *mosca,* fly, from Latin *musca.*]

Mos·qui·to (mə-skéetō) *n., pl.* **-tos** or collectively **Mosquito.** *Also* **Mis·ki·to** (mi-). **1.** A member of a Central American people of mixed native Indian and Negro descent, living on the Atlantic coast

Image labels:
Portal minarets
Symmetrical arcading
Four-*iwan* court with ablution pool
Southwest *iwan* leading to sanctuary
Domed sanctuary illuminated by pierced window-grilles
Muezzins' pavilion
Residential area with arcaded court
Entrance *iwan* (portal)

of Nicaragua and Honduras. **2.** The language of this people. —**Mos·qui·to** *adj.*

mosquito boat *n.* A motor torpedo boat. [Referring to its speed and small size.]

Mosquito Coast. Also **Miskito Coast** or **Mos·qui·tia** (mi-skéeshə). Sparsely populated banana-growing plain on the Caribbean coast of Nicaragua and Honduras, named after its indigenous Indians. It was discovered (1502) by Columbus, and later became a British protectorate (1678–1860).

mosquito hawk *n.* A bird, the **nighthawk** (*see*).

mosquito net *n.* A fine net used for covering windows and beds to keep out mosquitoes.

moss (moss ‖ mawss) *n.* **1.** Any of various green, usually small bryophyte plants of the class Musci, typically growing in clumps on moist ground or trees, for example. **2.** A patch or covering of such plants. **3.** Any of various other plants that are similar in appearance or manner of growth, such as **club moss, Irish moss,** or **Spanish moss** (*all of which see*). **4.** *Chiefly Scottish.* A peat bog or moor. [Middle English *moss, mos,* Old English *mos.*]

Moss, Stirling (1929–). British racing driver. He was the British champion in 1955 and became the number one driver in the Maserati team in 1954. His career lasted from 1947 to 1962, during which time he won 33 Grand Prix races.

moss agate *n.* A semiprecious stone with greenish-brown markings. It is a type of chalcedony.

Mössbauer effect (móss-bow-ər; *German* möss-) *n. Physics.* The emission of gamma rays by excited nuclei in some solids such that the recoil momentum is taken up by the whole lattice rather than by the emitting atom. The resulting gamma rays have a very narrow frequency range and can be used in studying the corresponding gamma-ray absorption in a sample material (*Mössbauer spectroscopy*), giving information about the energies of nuclei and the molecular structure of the sample. [After Rudolf *Mössbauer* (born 1929), German physicist.]

moss·bunk·er (móss-bungkər ‖ máwss-) *n.* Also **moss·bank·er** (-bangkər). *U.S.* A fish, the **menhaden** (*see*). [Dutch *marsbanker*†.]

moss campion *n.* A low-growing plant, *Silene acaulis,* of cool regions, having purplish-red flowers and forming dense, cushion-like mats.

moss green *n.* Moderate yellowish to greyish green. —**moss-green** *adj.*

moss-grown (móss-grōn ‖ máwss-) *adj.* **1.** Overgrown with moss. **2.** *Informal.* Old-fashioned; antiquated.

moss-hag, moss-hagg (móss-hag ‖ máwss-) *n. Scottish.* **1.** Ground from which peat has been removed. **2.** A pit in a bog. [MOSS + dialect and Scottish *hag,* gap, pit, from Scandinavian; akin to Old Norse *hogg,* gap, cut, from *hoggva,* to strike, hack, HEW.]

mos·sie¹ (móssi) *n. Chiefly South African.* A **Cape sparrow** (*see*). [Afrikaans, from Dutch *mosje,* diminutive of *mos,* sparrow.]

mos·sie² (mózzi) *n. Informal.* A mosquito. [By shortening.]

mos·so (mósso ‖ *U.S.* mô-sō) *adv. Music.* With motion or animation. Used as a direction. [Italian, from the past participle of *muovere,* to move, from Latin *movēre.*]

moss pink *n.* A low-growing plant, *Phlox subulata,* forming dense, mosslike mats. It is widely cultivated for its profuse pink or white flowers. Also called "ground pink".

moss rose *n.* A variety of rose, *Rosa centifolia muscosa,* having fragrant pink flowers with a mossy flower stalk and calyx.

moss stitch *n.* A pattern or stitch in knitting consisting of alternate plain and purl stitches on one row, and alternate purl and plain stitches on the next row, giving a minutely chequered fabric with the nubbly texture of moss.

moss·troop·er (móss-trōopər ‖ máwss-) *n.* **1.** A member of a band of raiders operating in the marshy lands on the borders of England and Scotland during the 17th century. **2.** A raider or marauder.

moss·y (móssi ‖ máwssi) *adj.* **-ier, -iest. 1.** Covered with moss or anything resembling moss. **2.** Resembling moss. —**moss·i·ness** *n.*

most (mōst). **1.** Superlative of **many. 2.** Superlative of **much.** —*adj.* **1.** Greatest in number or quantity. **2.** Largest or greatest in amount, size, or degree. **3.** In the greatest number of instances: *Most fish have fins.* —*n.* **1.** The greatest amount, quantity, or degree; the largest part: *Most of the land was fertile.* **2.** The greatest number (of a group or classification); the majority. Used with a plural verb: *Most of her novels have been well received.* —**at (the) most.** Not over; at the absolute limit: *It's four miles at most.* —**make the most of.** To use as advantageously as possible. —**the most.** *Chiefly U.S. Slang.* A person or thing that produces great excitement or satisfaction. —*adv.* **1.** In the highest degree, quantity, or extent. Used with many adjectives and adverbs to form the superlative degree: *most honest; most impatiently.* **2.** Very: *a most impressive piece of writing.* **3.** *U.S. Informal & Regional.* Almost: *Most everyone agrees.* [Middle English *most, mest, mast,* Old English *mǣst.*]

Usage: Most has attracted attention on three counts. As an alternative to the adverb *almost,* it is unacceptable in writing or formal speech (*Most everyone agrees*), and is largely restricted to informal American English. As an alternative to the intensifier *very,* it is widely used (*a most amusing experience*), though some stylists object to it, especially in writing, on the grounds that no explicit comparison is involved. As an adverb of degree, it has a standard use (*Those most affected are farmers*), but it is frequently replaced by *mostly* in informal speech.

-most *adj. & adv. suffix.* Indicates the superlative degree; for example, **foremost, innermost.** [Middle English *-most, -mast,* Old English *-mǣst, -mest,* originally an independent superlative suffix, later erroneously regarded as being from the adverb *mǣst,* most.]

most·ly (mōstli) *adv.* **1.** For the most part; almost entirely. **2.** Usually; as a rule. See Usage note at **most.**

mot (mō) *n.* A witticism or short, clever saying; a bon mot. [French, from Old French, from Vulgar Latin *mottum* (unattested), from Latin *muttum,* grunt, from *muttīre,* to mutter.]

M.O.T.¹ Ministry of Transport.

M.O.T.² (ém-ō-tée) *n.* **1.** An **M.O.T. test** (*see*). **2.** A certificate awarded after a successful M.O.T. test. ~*tr.v.* **M.O.T.d, M.O.T.ing, M.O.T.s. 1.** To give (a motor vehicle) an M.O.T. test. **2.** To cause (a motor vehicle) to be given an M.O.T.

mote¹ (mōt) *n.* A speck, especially of dust. [Middle English *mot, moot,* Old English *mot.*]

mote² *intr.v. Archaic.* May; might. [Middle English *moten,* Old English *mōtan,* to be allowed.]

mo·tel (mō-tél, mō-) *n.* A hotel for motorists, usually with blocks of rooms opening directly onto a parking area. [Blend of *motor* + *hotel.*]

mo·tet (mō-tét) *n.* A polyphonic musical composition based on a text of a sacred nature and usually sung without accompaniment. [Middle English, from Old French, from *mot,* phrase, word, MOT.]

moth (moth ‖ mawth) *n., pl.* **moths** (mothss ‖ mothz, *U.S. also* mawthz). **1.** Any of numerous insects of the order Lepidoptera, generally distinguished from butterflies by their nocturnal activity, hairlike or feathery antennae, and stout bodies. **2.** The **clothes moth** (*see*). **3.** The damage caused by the clothes moth. Preceded by *the.* [Middle English *motthe,* Old English *moththe.*]

moth·ball (móth-bawl ‖ máwth-) *n.* **1.** A small disc or ball, originally of camphor but now of naphthalene, stored with clothes to repel moths. **2.** *Plural.* A condition of long storage. Used chiefly in the phrase *put in* or *into mothballs.* ~*tr.v.* **-balled, -balling, -balls. 1.** To preserve with or as if with mothballs: *mothball a battleship.* **2.** To defer (a project) indefinitely; shelve.

moth-eat·en (móth-eet'n ‖ máwth-) *adj.* **1.** Eaten away by moths. **2.** Old and decayed; timeworn: *a moth-eaten phrase.*

moth·er¹ (múthər) *n.* **1.** A female that has borne offspring. **2.** One's own female parent. Often used as a term of address. **3.** A female who has adopted a child or otherwise established a maternal relationship with another person. **4.** A pregnant woman: *When a foetus quickens, the mother begins to feel its movements.* **5.** A woman having some of the responsibilities of a mother: *a house mother; a mother of the chapel.* **6.** Qualities attributed to a mother, such as the capacity to love selflessly: *a man who appealed to the mother in her.* **7.** *Archaic.* An affectionate or familiar form of address for an elderly woman. **8.** *Sometimes capital* **M.** A title of, or form of address for, certain senior nuns: *Mother Abbess.* **9.** A creative or environmental source: *Necessity is the mother of invention.* ~*adj.* **1.** Being or resembling a mother: *a mother duck.* **2.** Characteristic of a mother: *mother love.* **3.** Having a maternal relationship: *the mother church.* **4.** Derived from or as if from one's mother; native: *one's mother language.* ~*tr.v.* **mothered, -ering, -ers. 1.** To give birth to; be the mother of. **2.** To create and care for; instigate and carry through. **3.** To watch over, nourish, and protect. **4.** *Informal.* To behave in an overprotective manner towards; coddle: *Stop mothering me — I'm a grown woman!* [Middle English *moder,* Old English *mōdor.*]

mother² *n.* A stringy slime composed of yeast cells and bacteria that forms on the surface of fermenting liquids. It is added to wine or cider to start the production of vinegar. Also called "mother of vinegar". [From MOTHER, partly by association with afterbirth.]

Mother Car·ey's chicken (káir-iz) *n.* Any of various petrels, especially the **storm petrel** (*see*). [Perhaps from Latin *Mater Cara,* "Dear Mother", title of the Virgin Mary as patroness of seamen.]

mother country *n.* The country from which the settlers or colonists, or their forebears, of a distant territory or dominion originally came, and to which they still feel a sense of allegiance.

Mother Goose *n.* The imaginary story-teller in *Mother Goose's Tales* or *Melody,* a traditional collection of the main bulk of English nursery rhymes, first published in the 18th century.

mother hen *n.* A person, especially a woman, who is fussy and overprotective.

moth·er·hood (múthər-hŏŏd) *n.* **1.** The state or condition of being a mother. **2.** The feelings or qualities considered characteristic of a mother. **3.** Mothers collectively.

Mother Hub·bard (húbbərd) *n.* Also *small* **m,** *small* **h.** A woman's long, loose, unbelted dress. [After a character in a nursery rhyme.]

Mothering Sunday *n. British.* The fourth Sunday in Lent, on which mothers traditionally receive posies and other gifts from their children. Also called "Mother's Day". [From the custom of "going a-mothering", visiting parents, on this day.]

moth·er-in-law (múthər-in-law) *n., pl.* **mothers-in-law.** The mother of one's wife or husband.

mother-in-law's tongue *n.* A plant, **sansevieria** (*see*).

moth·er·land (múthər-land) *n.* **1.** The land or country of one's birth. **2.** The native land of one's ancestors.

moth·er·less (múthər-ləss, -liss) *adj.* Without a mother. ~*adv. Australian Informal.* Absolutely; completely.

mother liquor *n. Chemistry.* The liquid remaining after crystals have separated out of a solution.

mother lode *n.* The main lode in a source of ore.

moth·er·ly (múthərli) *adj.* Of, befitting, resembling, or characteristic of a mother; maternal. —**moth·er·li·ness** *n.*

Mother of Parliaments *n.* The British Parliament, which initiated and provided the model for a number of other national parliaments.

moth·er-of-pearl (múthər-əv-pérl) *n.* The pearly, iridescent internal layer of certain mollusc shells, used to make decorative objects. Also called "nacre". —**moth·er-of-pearl** *adj.*

mother-of-thousands (múthər-əv-thówz'ndz) *n.* A European perennial plant, *Helxine soleirolii*, forming dense evergreen mats on walls, for example. Also called "mind-your-own-business", "mother-of-millions".

Mother's Day *n.* **1.** Mothering Sunday. **2.** An annual day of commemoration of mothers and motherhood observed on the second Sunday in May.

mother superior *n., pl.* **mothers superior** or **mother-superiors.** A woman in charge of a female religious community.

mother tongue *n.* **1.** One's native language. **2.** The language from which another has developed.

mother wit *n.* Innate intelligence; common sense.

moth·er·wort (múthər-wurt ‖ -wawrt) *n.* Any of several plants of the genus *Leonurus*; especially, *L. cardiaca*, a weed having clusters of small purple or pink flowers. [Middle English *moderwort* : MOTHER (from its once reputed power to cure diseases of the uterus) + WORT.]

moth mullein *n.* A plant, *Verbascum blattaria*, native to Eurasia, having spikelike clusters of yellow or white flowers.

moth·proof (móth-proof ‖ máwth-, -proof) *adj.* Resistant to damage by moths.
~*tr.v.* **mothproofed, -proofing, -proofs.** To make resistant to damage by moths.

moth·y (móthi ‖ máwthi) *adj.* **-ier, -iest. 1.** Infested with moths. **2.** Shabby or moth-eaten.

mo·tif (mō-téef) *n.* Also **mo·tive** (mótiv, mō-téev). **1.** A recurrent thematic element used in the development of an artistic or literary work. **2.** A short significant phrase in a musical composition. **3.** A repeated figure or design in architecture or decoration. [French, from Old French, MOTIVE.]

mo·tile (mō-tīl ‖ *U.S. also* mót'l) *adj.* Moving or having the power to move spontaneously, as certain spores and microorganisms do. ~*n. Psychology.* A person whose mental imagery chiefly consists of his own bodily motion. [Latin *motus*, motion + -ILE.] —**mo·til·i·ty** (mō-tílləti) *n.*

mo·tion (mósh'n) *n.* **1.** The action or process of change of position. **2.** A meaningful or expressive change in the position of the body or a part of the body; a gesture. **3.** The way in which a body moves; gait. **4.** The ability or power to move. **5.** A prompting from within; an impulse. **6.** *Music.* Melodic ascent or descent of pitch. **7.** *Law.* An application to a court for a ruling. **8.** A formal proposal put to the vote in Parliament or at a meeting or conference. **9.** *Chiefly British.* **a.** The act or process of evacuating the bowels. **b.** Faeces. **10. a.** A mechanical device or piece of machinery that moves or causes motion, as in a watch. **b.** The movement or action of such a device. —**go through the motions of.** To attempt the performance of (a task) without making a serious effort to accomplish it.
~*v.* **motioned, -tioning, -tions.** —*tr.* To signal to or direct by making a gesture. —*intr.* To make a gesture signifying something, such as agreement. [Middle English *mocioun*, from Old French *motion*, from Latin *mōtiō* (stem *mōtiōn-*), from *movēre*, to move.]

mo·tion·less (mósh'n-ləss, -liss) *adj.* Not moving. —**mo·tion·less·ly** *adv.* —**mo·tion·less·ness** *n.*

motion picture *n. Chiefly U.S.* A film (see).

motion sickness *n.* Travel sickness (see).

motion study *n.* A time and motion study (see).

mo·tion-work (mósh'n-wúrk) *n.* The mechanism for moving the hands of a watch or clock.

mo·ti·vate (móti-vayt) *tr.v.* **-vated, -vating, -vates.** To stimulate to action; provide with an incentive. [From MOTIVE.]

mo·ti·va·tion (móti-váysh'n) *n.* **1.** The act or process of motivating. **2.** An incentive, inducement, or motive, especially for an act. **3.** *Psychology.* The mental process, function, or instinct that produces and sustains incentive or drive in human and animal behaviour. —**mo·ti·va·tion·al** *adj.*

motivational research *n.* The use of certain techniques borrowed from psychology and sociology, especially by advertisers and marketers, to assess consumer attitudes towards products and services. Also called "motivation research".

mo·tive (mótiv; *also* mō-téev *for sense 2) n.* **1.** An emotion, desire, physiological need, or similar impulse acting as an incitement to action. **2.** A motif (see).
~*adj.* **1.** Causing or able to cause motion: *motive power.* **2.** Of, pertaining to, or constituting a motive.
~*tr.v.* **motived, -tiving, -tives.** To provide with an incentive; motivate. [Middle English, from Old French *motif*, from adjective, "causing to move", from Late Latin *mōtīvus*, from Latin *movēre* (past participle *mōtus*), to move.] —**mo·tiv·i·ty** (mō-tívvəti) *n.*

mot juste (mō zhũst) *n., pl.* **mots justes** (*pronounced as singular*). The most suitable word or expression. [French, "exact word".]

mot·ley (mótli) *adj.* **1.** Having components of great variety; heterogeneous: *a motley bunch.* **2.** Exhibiting or having many colours; multicoloured. —See Synonyms at **miscellaneous.**
~*n.* **1.** The particoloured professional attire of a court jester. **2.** A heterogeneous mixture or assemblage. **3.** *Obsolete.* A professional jester or clown. —**wear motley. 1.** To play the fool; jest in a frivolous manner. **2.** To be a fool. [Middle English *motteley*, perhaps from Anglo-French *motelé* (unattested), from MOTE (speck).]

mot·mot (mót-mot) *n.* Any of several tropical American birds of the family Momotidae, usually having green and blue plumage. [American Spanish *mot-mot* (imitative).]

mo·to·cross (mōt-ō-kross, -ə- ‖ -krawss) *n.* Motorcycle racing, or scrambling, over a hazardous cross-country course. [Alteration of *motor* + *cross*-country.]

mo·to·neu·ron (mōtō-néwr-on ‖ -noor-) *n. Anatomy. U.S.* A **motor neurone** (see). [Motor + *neuron.*]

mo·tor (mótər) *n.* **1.** Something that imparts or produces motion, such as a machine or engine. **2.** A device that converts any form of energy into mechanical energy, especially an **internal-combustion engine** (see), or an arrangement of coils and magnets that converts electrical energy into mechanical power. **3.** *Informal.* A motorised conveyance; especially, a car.
~*adj.* **1.** Causing or producing motion: *motor power.* **2.** Driven by or having a motor: *motor scooter.* **3.** Of, pertaining to, or for motor vehicles: *motor oil.* **4.** *Physiology.* **a.** Of, pertaining to, or designating nerves carrying impulses from the nerve centres to the muscles. **b.** Of or pertaining to movements of the muscles: *motor coordination.*
~*v.* **motored, -toring, -tors.** —*intr.* To drive or travel in a motor vehicle. —*tr.* To carry by motor vehicle. [Latin *mōtor*, agent-noun of *movēre* (past participle *mōtus*), to move.]

mo·tor·bike (mótər-bīk) *n.* A motorcycle.

mo·tor·boat (mótər-bōt) *n.* A boat with a propeller driven by an internal-combustion engine.

mo·tor·bus (mótər-buss) *n., pl.* **-buses** or **-busses.** A bus that is powered by an internal-combustion engine or other type of engine.

mo·tor·cade (mótər-kayd) *n. Chiefly U.S.* A procession of cars or other motor vehicles. [*Motor* + *cavalcade.*]

motor car *n.* A car.

motor caravan *n.* A motor vehicle having a large caravan-like living-space behind the driver's cab, equipped with beds, a cooker, and other domestic facilities.

mo·tor·cy·cle (mótər-sīk'l) *n.* A vehicle with two wheels in tandem propelled by an internal-combustion engine.
~*intr.v.* **motorcycled, -cycling, -cycles.** To ride on or drive a motorcycle. —**mo·tor·cy·clist** *n.*

motor drive *n.* A system consisting of an electric motor and accessory parts, used to power machinery.

mo·tor·ise, mo·tor·ize (mótər-īz) *tr.v.* **-ised, -ising, -ises. 1.** To equip with a motor or motors. **2.** To supply with motor-driven vehicles in substitution for ones drawn by horses or other animals. **3.** To provide motor-vehicle transport for. —**mo·tor·i·sa·tion** (-ī-záysh'n ‖ *U.S.* -i-) *n.*

mo·tor·ist (mótərist) *n.* One who drives a car.

mo·tor·man (mótər-mən) *n., pl.* **-men** (-mən, -men). *Chiefly U.S.* One who drives an electrically powered train.

motor neuron *n.* A nerve cell that conveys impulses away from the brain and spinal cord to muscles or other effector organs. Also *U.S.* "motorneurone". **2.** A disease that causes progressive spinal muscular atrophy.

motor scooter *n.* A two-wheeled vehicle with small wheels and a low-powered enclosed engine geared to the rear wheel.

motor vehicle *n.* Any self-propelled, wheeled conveyance that does not run on rails, especially one driven by an internal-combustion engine.

mo·tor·way (mótər-way) *n. British.* A main road designed for fast-moving traffic, usually having two or three lanes in each direction, and uninterrupted by junctions or traffic lights.

Mo·town (mó-town) *n. Sometimes small* **m.** A style of black popular music. [After the trade name of a U.S. record company that specialised in this style from Detroit ("Motortown"), Michigan.]

motte (mot) *n.* A mound on which a castle or fortification is or was sited. [Middle English, from Old French *mote*, mound, MOAT.]

M.O.T. test *n. British.* An annual test of roadworthiness for motor vehicles over a certain age. usually conducted by garages. Also called "M.O.T.". [Ministry of Transport.]

mot·tle (mótt'l) *tr.v.* **-tled, -tling, -tles.** To cover (a surface) with spots or streaks of different shades or colours.
~*n.* **1.** A spot of colour or shading contrasting with the rest of the surface on which it is found. **2.** A variegated pattern, as on marble. [Probably back-formation from MOTLEY.]

mot·to (móttō) *n., pl.* **-toes** or **-tos. 1.** A brief sentence, phrase, or single word used to express a principle, goal, or ideal, especially when accompanying a coat of arms. **2.** A maxim adopted as a guide to one's conduct. **3.** A quotation prefacing a book or chapter. **4.** A briefly stated sentiment of appropriate character inscribed on or attached to an object. **5.** A proverb or joke contained inside a paper cracker. **6.** *Music.* A recurring theme or motif. —See Synonyms at **saying.** [Italian, "a word", from Gallo-Roman *mottum* (unattested), a sound uttered, from Latin *muttum*, a mutter, grunt, from *muttīre*, to mutter.]

mo·tu pro·pri·o (mōtoo própri-ō) *n., pl.* **motu proprios.** An administrative papal bull. [Latin, of (our) own accord.]

mouch. *Chiefly British.* Variant of **mooch.**

moue (moo) *n.* A sulky or disdainful expression; a pout. [French, from Old French, from Germanic, akin to Middle Dutch *mouwe*, pouting lip.]

mou·flon, mouf·flon (moo-flon) *n., pl.* **-flons** or collectively **mouf-**

mountain

HOW MOUNTAINS ARE MADE

The growth of mountains shows that the Earth's surface is mobile

Mountains are made in four main ways: by volcanoes, faulting, folding, and doming. Folding generally also involves one or more of the other three methods.

Folding is a by-product of the forces of continental drift. In the last two decades, the Earth's surface has come to be seen as a collection of plates of lightweight rock resting on denser material that moves in response to heat in the Earth's interior. The plates, some of which bear the continents, move about the Earth's surface at the rate of about an inch a year. The edges at which they meet crumple, forming mountain ranges. Mountains are continuously eroded. Old ranges like the Urals, remnants of an ancient clash between Europe and Asia, are worn down almost flat, but younger ranges like the Alps retain their youthful ruggedness.

VOLCANIC *Volcanoes form mountains by erupting lava, which creates several different shapes, from conical strato-volcanoes like Mt. Fuji to low shield volcanoes like Hawaii's Mauna Loa.*

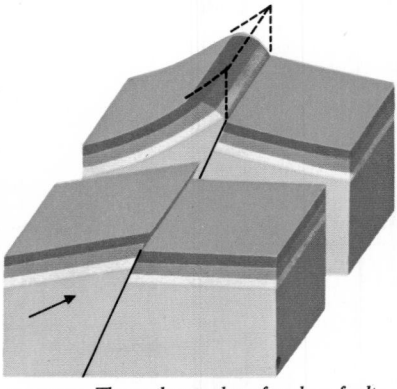

FAULTING *The upthrust edge of a deep fault – caused by subterranean forces cracking the Earth's crust – is weathered to form a block mountain. Streams may carve out peaks.*

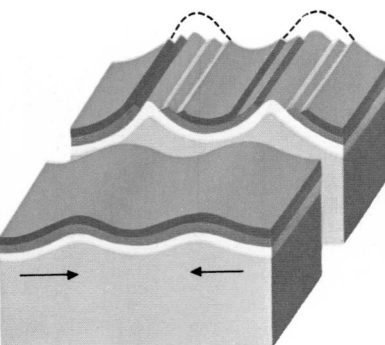

FOLDING *Rocks are folded by lateral pressure that compresses the strata. Often the folding is made more complex by other layers of rock thrusting underneath the raised area.*

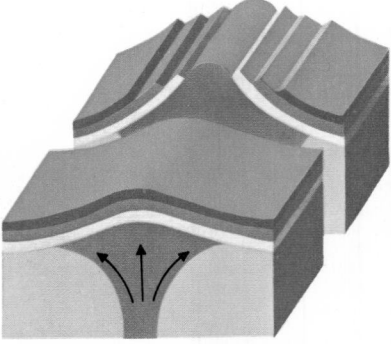

DOMING *A dome mountain is formed when an upsurge of molten rock from below does not break the Earth's surface, but instead causes it to swell like a giant blister.*

lon. A wild sheep, *Ovis musimon*, of Sardinia and Corsica. [French, from Italian *muflone*, from Vulgar Latin *mufro†*, sheep.]

moujik. Variant of **muzhik.**

mou·lage (moo-laäzh) *n.* **1.** The making of a mould from a mark, such as a footprint, especially for identification. **2.** A mould of this kind. [French, from Old French, from *mouler*, to mould, from *moule, modle*, a mould, from Latin *modulus*, diminutive of *modus*, a measure, manner.]

mould¹, *U.S.* **mold** (mōld) *n.* **1.** A form or matrix for shaping a fluid or plastic substance: *a jelly mould.* **2.** A frame or model around or on which something is formed or shaped. **3.** Something that is made in or shaped on a mould. **4.** The pattern of a mould. **5.** General shape or form: *the oval mould of her face.* **6.** Distinctive shape, character, or type: *in the mould of her ancestors.* **7.** *Architecture.* A moulding.
~*tr.v.* **moulded, moulding, moulds. 1.** To shape in or on a mould. **2.** To form into a desired shape. **3.** To guide or determine the growth or development of; influence: *mould public opinion.* **4.** To make a mould of or from (sand, for example) prior to casting metal. [Middle English, probably from Old French *modle*, from Latin *modulus*, MODULE.] **—mould·a·bil·i·ty** (mōldə-bílləti) *n.* **—mould·a·ble** *adj.* **—moul·der** *n.*

mould², *U.S.* **mold** *n.* **1.** A rough, variously coloured coating that forms on decaying food, for example, owing to the action of sapro-

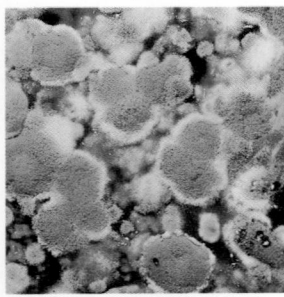

mould *A mould growing on fermenting elderberry wine.*

phytic fungi. **2.** Any fungus that causes this growth. Compare **mildew.**
~*v.* **moulded, moulding, moulds.** —*intr.* To become mouldy. —*tr.* To cause to become mouldy. [Middle English, probably from obsolete adjective *mould*, past participle of *moul*, to become mouldy, from Old Norse *mugla* (unattested).]

mould³, *U.S.* **mold** *n.* **1.** Loose, friable soil that is rich in humus. **2.** *Poetic.* **a.** The earth; the ground. **b.** The earth of the grave, or the grave itself. [Middle English, Old English *molde*, from Germanic *moldō* (unattested); akin to MEAL.]

mould-board, *U.S.* **mold-board** (mōld-bawrd ‖ -bōrd) *n.* The curved plate of a plough that turns over the furrow.

mould·er, *U.S.* **mold·er** (mōldər) *v.* **-ered, -ering, -ers.** —*intr.* To become dust gradually, by natural decay; crumble. Often used with *away.* —*tr.* To cause to decay or crumble. Often used with *away.* See Synonyms at **decay.** [Perhaps from MOULD (soil).]

mould·ing, *U.S.* **mold·ing** (mōlding) *n.* **1.** *Architecture.* A strip of stone, wood, plaster, or other material, with a shaped section, used as an embellishment on a building, wall, or other surface. Also called "mould". **2.** An object that has been moulded.

moulding board *n.* A board on which dough is kneaded.

mould·y, *U.S.* **mold·y** (mōldi) *adj.* **-ier, -iest. 1.** Covered with or containing mould: *mouldy bread.* **2.** Musty or stale, as from age or decay. **3.** *Slang.* **a.** Unfair. **b.** Boring. **c.** Of poor quality; second-rate. **—mould·i·ness** *n.*

mould·y·warp (mōldi-wawrp) *n.* Also **mold·warp** (mōld-wawrp). *Archaic & Regional.* A mole. [Middle English *moldwarp*, Old English *moldweorp*, "earth-thrower" : MOULD (soil) + *weorpan*, to throw.]

mou·lin (moolin, moo-láN) *n.* A vertical shaft in a glacier, kept open by falling water and rock debris. [French, "mill", from Old French, from Late Latin *molīnum*, from Latin *molīnus*, of a mill, from *mola*, mill, millstone.]

moult, *U.S.* **molt** (mōlt ‖ molt) *v.* **moulted, moulting, moults.** —*intr.* To shed part or all of an outer covering, such as feathers, fur, or skin, which is replaced periodically by a new growth. —*tr.* To shed or cast off by moulting.
~*n.* **1.** The process of moulting, which occurs in certain mammals, birds, and reptiles. See **ecdysis. 2.** The material cast off during moulting. [Middle English *moute*, Old English *mutian* (unattested), ultimately from Latin *mutāre*, to change; present spelling influenced by *-lt* words such as *fault.*] **—moult·er** *n.*

mound¹ (mownd) *n.* **1.** A pile of earth, gravel, sand, rocks, or debris heaped for protection or concealment. **2.** A natural elevation, such as a small hill. **3.** Any raised mass, as of hay. **4.** *Archaeology.* A **barrow** *(see).* **5.** In baseball, the small elevation where the pitcher stands when pitching.
~*tr.v.* **mounded, mounding, mounds. 1.** To fortify or conceal with a mound. **2.** To heap in a mound. [Originally "enclosing hedge or fence", perhaps from Dutch *mond*, protection, or Old Norse *mund.*]

mound² *n.* *Heraldry.* An orb or ball of gold representing the earth. [Middle English, from Old French *monde*, from Latin *mundus*, world.]

Mound Builder *n.* A member of one of the prehistoric North American Indian peoples who built burial and effigy mounds, mainly in the Mississippi valley.

mound-builder (mównd-bildər) *n.* A bird, the **megapode** *(see).*

mount¹ (mownt) *v.* **mounted, mounting, mounts.** —*tr.* **1.** To climb or ascend. **2.** To get up on; place oneself upon: *mount a horse.* **3.** To get up on in order to copulate. Used of male animals. **4.** To provide with a horse or horses for riding: *The stable mounted all the riders.* **5.** To prepare, place, or fix on or in an appropriate or convenient setting, as for display, study, or use: *mount pictures on cardboard.* **6.** To prepare for display, production, or public viewing: *mount a theatrical performance.* **7.** To place (a specimen) on a microscope slide in preparation for microscopical examination. **8.** *Military.* **a.** To set (guns) in position. **b.** To put in readiness and start to carry out: *mount an attack.* **c.** To be furnished with or carry: *The warship mounted ten guns.* **d.** To post (a guard): *mount sentries.* —*intr.v.* **1.** To go or move upwards. **2.** To get or climb up on a horse or vehicle. **3.** To increase, as in amount, degree, extent, intensity, or number. Often used with *up.* —See Synonyms at **rise.**
~*n.* **1. a.** A horse, other animal, or vehicle on which to ride. **b.** The opportunity to ride a horse, especially in a race. **2.** An object to which another is affixed, such as a piece of cardboard, or on which another is placed for accessibility, display, or use, such as a stamp hinge. **3.** A glass slide on which specimens are placed for microscopy. [Middle English *mounten*, from Old French *monter*, from Vulgar Latin *montāre* (unattested), "to climb a mountain", from Latin *mōns* (stem *mont-*), mountain.] **—mount·a·ble** *adj.* **—mount·ing·ly** *adv.*

mount² *n.* **1.** *Abbr.* **mt., Mt.** A mountain or hill. Used chiefly as part of a proper name or in poetry. **2.** In palmistry, any of the seven fleshy cushions around the edges of the palm of the hand. [Middle English *mont, munt*, from Old French *mont* and Old English *munt*, both from Latin *mōns* (stem *mont-*), mountain.]

moun·tain (mówn-tin, -tən ‖ *West Indies also* múng-) *n. Abbr.* **mt., Mt., mtn. 1.** A natural elevation of the earth's surface having considerable mass, generally steep sides, and a height greater than that of a hill. **2. a.** A large heap: *a mountain of ironing.* **b.** A huge quantity. **3.** *Capital M.* The extreme revolutionary party of the French Revolution, so called because its members occupied the uppermost seats in the National Convention Hall in 1793. Preceded by *the.* [Middle English *mountaine*, from Old French *montaigne*, from Vulgar Latin *montānea* (unattested), from Latin *montānus*, mountainous, from *mōns* (stem *mont-*), mountain.] **—moun·tain** *adj.*

mountain ash *n.* **1.** Any of various deciduous trees of the genus *Sorbus*, such as *S. aucuparia*, the European mountain ash, having clusters of small white flowers and bright orange-red berries. This species is also called "rowan". **2.** Any of several Australian eucalyptus trees.

mountain devil *n.* A lizard, the **moloch** *(see)*.

mountain dew *n. Chiefly U.S. Slang.* Illegally distilled spirits.

moun·tain·eer (mówn-tin-éer, -tən-) *n.* **1.** One who climbs mountains as a sport or hobby. **2.** An inhabitant of a mountainous area. *~intr.v.* **mountaineered, -eering, -eers.** To climb mountains as a hobby or sport. **—moun·tain·eer·ing** *n.*

mountain goat *n.* Any wild goat of mountainous regions.

mountain laurel *n.* An evergreen shrub, *Kalmia latifolia*, of eastern North America, having leathery, poisonous leaves and clusters of pink or white flowers. Also called "calico bush".

mountain lion *n.* A **puma** *(see)*.

moun·tain·ous (mówn-tin-əss, -tən-) *adj.* **1.** Of, pertaining to, or designating a region having many mountains. **2.** Of impressive size or height.

mountain ringlet *n.* Any of several brown butterflies of the genus *Erebia*, found in mountains and northern regions of Eurasia and North America.

mountain sheep *n.* Any wild sheep native to a mountainous area.

mountain sickness *n.* **Altitude sickness** *(see)*.

Mountain Standard Time *n. Abbr.* **MST, M.S.T.** Local time in one of the standard time zones of North America, based on the 105th meridian west of Greenwich, seven hours behind Greenwich Mean Time.

Mount·bat·ten, Louis Alexander (mownt-bátt'n), born Prince Louis Alexander of Battenberg; also known as 1st Marquess of Milford Haven (1854–1921). British admiral and first sea lord (1912–14). He became a naturalised British subject when he joined the Royal Navy (1868), and married a granddaughter of Queen Victoria (1884). He subsequently gave up his German titles, changed his surname, and was created a marquess by George V.

Mountbatten of Burma, Louis, 1st Earl (1900–79). English naval officer, great-grandson of Queen Victoria. In 1943 he was appointed Supreme Allied Commander in southeast Asia. He was made a viscount in 1946 and an earl in 1947, when he was appointed Viceroy of India, presiding over the transfer of power to independent India in that year. He stayed in India as Governor-General until 1948. From 1959 to 1965 he was chief of the United Kingdom Defence Staff. He was killed by the Provisional I.R.A. when a bomb detonated by remote control exploded on his yacht.

moun·te·bank (mównti-bangk) *n.* **1.** A hawker of quack medicines and nostrums who attracts customers with stories, jokes, or tricks. **2.** Any charlatan or trickster. [Italian *montambanco, montimbanco*, "one who climbs on a bench" : *montare*, to mount, (see **mount**[1]) + *in*, in, on, from Latin + *banco, banca*, bench.]

mount·ed (mówntid) *adj.* **1.** Seated upon or riding on a horse, bicycle, or other means of conveyance. **2.** Serving on horseback, or equipped with a horse or horses: *a mounted policeman.* **3.** Fitted into or set in a backing or support: *mounted photographs.*

mount·ing (mównting) *n.* **1.** The act of rising or getting up on something. **2.** That which provides a backing, support, or setting for something else: *a mounting for a gem; a telescope mounting.*

mounting block *n.* A block of stone used as an aid in mounting a horse.

Mount Rush·more National Memorial (rúsh-mawr || -mōr). A tract in the Black Hills, South Dakota, United States. It includes the northeastern side of Mount Rushmore, from which Gutzon Borglum and his son carved (1927–41) gigantic busts of Presidents Washington, Jefferson, Lincoln, and Theodore Roosevelt.

Mount·y, Mount·ie (mównti) *n., pl.* **-ies.** *Informal.* A Royal Canadian Mounted Policeman.

mourn (morn, *rarely* moorn || mōrn) *v.* **mourned, mourning, mourns.** *—intr.* **1.** To express or feel grief or sorrow, especially for someone who has died. **2.** To express public grief for a death by conventional signs; be in mourning. *—tr.* **1. a.** To feel grief for (a dead person, for example). **b.** To show public signs of grief for (a dead person, for example). **2.** To feel or express regret over; lament: *mourned the abolition of the death penalty.* [Middle English *mournen*, Old English *murnan*.]

Mourne Mountains (morn || mōrn). Mountain range in County Down, southeast Northern Ireland. Slieve Donard (852 metres; 2,796 feet) is the highest point in the province.

mourn·er (mórnər || mórnər) *n.* One who mourns, especially: **1.** A person attending a funeral out of grief or respect. **2.** Formerly, a person hired to attend a funeral.

mourn·ful (mórn-f'l || mōrn-) *adj.* **1.** Feeling or expressing sorrow or grief. **2.** Arousing or suggesting sorrow or grief: *the mournful sound of the train whistle.* —See Synonyms at **glum. —mourn·ful·ly** *adv.* **—mourn·ful·ness** *n.*

mourn·ing (mórn-ing, móorn- || mōrn-) *n.* **1.** The actions or expressions of one who has suffered a bereavement. **2.** The symbols or conventional outward signs of grief for the dead. **3.** The period during which a death is mourned. **—in mourning. 1.** Wearing clothes conventionally expressive of mourning, such as a black tie or armband, or entirely black clothes. **2.** Abiding by appropriate conduct during a period of mourning: *I can't remarry yet—I'm still in mourning for my last husband.* **—mourn·ing·ly** *adv.*

mourning cloak *n. U.S.* A butterfly, the **Camberwell beauty** *(see)*.

mourning dove *n.* A wild dove, *Zenaidura macroura*, of North America, noted for its plaintive call and its ability to survive in deserts.

mouse (mowss) *n., pl.* **mice** (mīss). **1. a.** Any of numerous small rodents of the families Muridae and Cricetidae, such as the **house mouse** or the **harvest mouse** *(both of which see)*, characteristically having a long, naked or almost hairless tail. **b.** Any of various similar or related animals, such as the **jumping mouse** or the **pocket mouse** *(both of which see)*. **2.** *Informal.* **a.** A cowardly or timid person. **b.** *Chiefly U.S.* An affectionate term for a little girl or young woman. **3.** *Slang.* A black eye. **4.** A mousing on a hook. **5.** A **hair mouse** *(see)*.
~intr.v. (*usually* mouz) **moused, mousing, mouses. 1.** To hunt, stalk, or catch mice. **2.** To search furtively for something; prowl. Often used with *about.* [Mouse, mice; Middle English *mous, mys*, Old English *mūs, mȳs*.]

mouse-bird (mówss-burd) *n.* The **coly** *(see)*.

mouse deer *n.* A **chevrotain** *(see)*.

mouse-ear (mówss-eer) *n.* Any of various weedy plants of the genus *Cerastium*, having small white flowers. Also called "mouse-ear chickweed".

mous·er (mówzər, mów-sər) *n.* An animal that catches mice, especially a cat.

mouse-tail (mówss-tayl) *n.* Any plant of the genus *Myosurus*, especially *M. minimus*, having a tail-like flower spike.

mouse·trap (mówss-trap) *n.* **1.** A trap for catching mice. **2.** *British. Informal.* Cheese of poor quality. [Sense 2, as used in such traps.]

mous·ing (mówzing) *n. Nautical.* **1.** A binding around the point and shank of a hook to prevent it from slipping from an eye. **2.** A metal shackle used for the same purpose. [From its mouselike shape.]

mous·sa·ka, mous·a·ka (mōō-saákə; *Greek* -sa-kaá) *n.* A Greek dish consisting of minced meat, aubergines, and tomatoes covered in cheese sauce. [Greek or Turkish.]

mousse (mōōss) *n.* **1.** Any of various chilled desserts made with cream, separated and whipped eggs or gelatine, and flavouring. **2.** A similar dish made from a purée of meat, fish, or shellfish with whipped cream. [French *mousse*†, "froth".]

mousse·line (mōōss-léen) *n.* A fine cotton or silk fabric originally made in Mosul, Iraq. [French, MUSLIN.]

Moussorgsky. See **Mussorgsky.**

mous·tache, *U.S.* **mus·tache** (mə-staásh || -stásh, -stósh, *U.S. also* mústash) *n.* **1.** *Sometimes plural.* The hair growing on the upper lip, especially when it is cultivated and groomed. **2.** Something similar to a moustache in appearance and position, especially: **a.** A group of bristles or hairs around the mouth of an animal. **b.** Distinctive colouring or feathers near the beak of a bird. [French, from Italian *mostaccio*, from Greek *mustax* (stem *mustak-*).]

Mous·te·ri·an, Mous·tie·ri·an (mōō-stéer-i-ən) *adj. Archaeology.* Designating or belonging to a Middle Palaeolithic culture following the Acheulian, characterised by the use of flint implements. [French *moustérien, moustiérien*, from *Le Moustier*, village in southwestern France near which archaeological specimens were found.]

mous·y, mous·ey (mów-si || -zi) *adj.* **-ier, -iest. 1.** Of a dull, pale brown colour. Said of hair. **2.** Resembling a mouse in appearance: *a mousy face.* **3.** Shy; retiring; unassertive.

mouth (mowth) *n., pl.* **mouths** (mowthz). **1.** *Anatomy.* **a.** The body opening through which an animal takes in food; the oral cavity. **b.** The system of related organs including the lips, teeth, tongue, and associated parts, with which food is chewed and swallowed and sounds and speech are articulated. **2.** The part of the lips visible on the human face. **3.** A person viewed as a consumer of food: *I've got three mouths to feed at home.* **4.** A pout, grimace, or similar expression. **5. a.** The capacity of speech; a propensity for speaking: *"A fool's mouth is his destruction."* (Proverbs 18:7). **b.** A manner of speech, especially when considered as inappropriate: *a foul mouth.* **c.** *Informal.* Impudent or vulgar talk. **6.** The part of the inner lip of a horse, donkey, or similar animal on which the bit presses, and varying in sensitivity to the bit: *a hard mouth.* **7.** A natural opening, such as the part of a stream or river that empties into a larger body of water, or the entrance to a harbour, canyon, valley, or cave. **8.** The opening through which any container is filled or emptied. **9.** An opening in tools and devices whose function is to hold or grip. **10. a.** An opening in the pipe of an organ. **b.** The opening in the mouthpiece of a flute across which the player blows. **—down in the mouth.** *Informal.* Crestfallen; unhappy. **—give mouth.** To bark. Used of a dog. **—shoot (one's) mouth off.** To speak forcibly but unreliably on a particular subject or issue. **—shut (one's) mouth.** *Informal.* To desist from speaking. Usually used in the imperative.
~v. (mowth). **mouthed, mouthing, mouths.** *—tr.* **1.** To utter in a meaninglessly declamatory manner: *mouthing empty compliments.* **2.** To put, take, or move around in the mouth. **3.** To train the mouth of (a horse). *—intr.* **1.** To orate affectedly; declaim; rant. **2.** To grimace. [Middle English *mouth*, Old English *mūth*.]

mouth·brood·er (mówth-brōōdər) *n.* Also **mouth·breed·er** (-breedər). Any of various African cichlid fishes that carry their eggs and young in the mouth.

mouth·ful (mówthfōōl) *n., pl.* **mouthfuls. 1.** The amount of food or other material that can be placed or held in the mouth at one time. **2.** A small amount to be tasted or eaten. **3.** *Informal.* Anything,

mountaineer *A modern mountaineer wearing an oxygen mask, used on high-altitude climbs.*

mountain ringlet *A brown European butterfly that lives in rough, often boggy, moorland and among fir trees at altitudes of between 500 metres (1,650 feet) and 2600 metres (8,000 feet). The illustrations show the top and the underside of its wings.*

Mount Rushmore National Memorial *These rock portraits of four American presidents – from the left, Washington, Jefferson, Theodore Roosevelt, and Lincoln – are about 28 metres (60 feet) high, and can be seen for nearly 100 kilometres (60 miles). Their sculptor, Gutzon Borglum, died in 1941 when they were nearly complete, and his son finished them.*

such as a long name, that is complicated or difficult to pronounce.

mouth organ *n.* Either of two musical instruments, a **harmonica** or a **panpipe** (both of which see).

mouth-part, mouth·part (mówth-paart) *n.* Any of the appendages situated around the mouth in arthropods and adapted for feeding; for example, the maxillae and mandibles.

mouth·piece (mówth-peess) *n.* **1.** A part, as of a musical instrument or a telephone, that functions in or near the mouth. **2.** A protective rubber device worn over the teeth by boxers; a gumshield. **3.** *Informal.* One through whom views are expressed, such as a spokesman or newspaper. **4.** *Chiefly U.S. Slang.* A lawyer.

mouth-to-mouth (mówth-tə-mówth) *adj.* Designating a method of artificial respiration in which air is blown forcefully into the lungs of the patient by one whose mouth is placed firmly over the patient's mouth: *mouth-to-mouth resuscitation.*

mouth·wash (mówth-wosh ‖ -wawsh) *n.* An aqueous solution containing an antiseptic or astringent, used for gargling and for cleansing the mouth and teeth.

mouth·wat·er·ing (mówth-wawtəring) *adj.* Appetising; delicious.

mouth·y (mów-<u>thi</u>, -thi) *adj.* **-ier, -iest.** Given to ranting; grandiloquent; bombastic. **—mouth·i·ly** *adv.* **—mouth·i·ness** *n.*

mou·ton (mōóton) *n.* Sheepskin sheared and processed to resemble beaver or seal, and used for garments. [French, "sheep", from Old French *mo(u)ton*, MUTTON.]

mou·ton·née (mōó-to-nay, -tə-, -náy) *adj.* Also **mou·ton·néed** (-náyd). *Geology.* Rounded by glacial action to a shape likened to a sheep's back. Said of a rock formation. See **roche moutonnée.** [French, from *mouton*, sheep.]

mov·a·ble, move·a·ble (mōōvə-b'l) *adj.* **1.** Capable of being moved. **2.** Varying in date from year to year: *a movable holiday.* **3.** *Law.* Of or pertaining to personal property that can be moved, as opposed to real property such as land. **4.** *Printing.* Cast with each character on a separate piece of type.
　~*n. Usually plural.* **1.** Something that can be moved, especially furniture, as opposed to permanent fixtures. **2.** *Law.* Personal property, as distinguished from real property such as land. **—mov·a·bil·i·ty** (-billəti), **mov·a·ble·ness** *n.* **—mov·a·bly** *adv.*
　Usage: Movable and mobile are usually not interchangeable. *Movable* denotes something that has the capability of being moved, usually by some external force (the furniture in a room is *movable*); *mobile* denotes something that can move, usually on account of its own internal characteristics (as with a *mobile crane* or *mobile library*). Occasionally, something may be referred to by either word (as when the tongue is said to be a very *movable* or *mobile* organ), and here the different implications reflect the above distinction.

movable feast *n.* **1.** A religious feast, such as Easter, which varies in date from year to year. **2.** Any event which occurs erratically. Used humorously: *The fire drill is something of a movable feast.*

move (mōōv) *v.* **moved, moving, moves.** **—***intr.* **1.** To change in position from one point to another. **2.** To march, as an army or procession does. **3.** To progress in sequence, as in the development of a literary or musical composition. **4.** To follow some specified course: *The Earth moves in orbit around the Sun.* **5. a.** To be transferred from one position to another in a board game. **b.** To transfer a piece in a board game. **6.** To change to or settle in a new place of residence or business. Often used with *in, out,* or *away.* **7.** To be disposed of commercially: *Furs move slowly in summer.* **8.** To change posture or position; stir. **9.** To be disturbed or displaced: *The foliage moved in the breeze; When you kissed me, the earth moved!* **10.** To be put into motion or to turn according to a prescribed motion. Used of machinery. **11.** *Informal.* **a.** To hum with activity; be busy. **b.** To become interesting and exciting. **12.** To initiate some action: *Wait for the election results before we move.* **13. a.** To behave, progress, or proceed as specified: *move towards a solution.* **b.** To change: *the situation hasn't moved.* **14.** To live or be active in a specified environment: *move in diplomatic circles.* **15.** To make a legal submission or a formal motion in parliamentary procedure: *move for an adjournment.* **16.** To evacuate; void. Used of the bowels. **—***tr.* **1. a.** To change the place of; shift; remove; displace. **b.** To change the position of: *move one's head.* **c.** To cause to change position: *moved the spectators on.* **d.** To change the course of: *moved the discussion on to more general topics.* **2.** To dislodge from a fixed point of view, especially by persuasion. **3.** To prompt (someone) to some action; actuate: *She was moved to intercede on his behalf.* **4.** To set or maintain in motion. **5.** To set astir; agitate; shake: *The wind moved the blossoms.* **6.** To excite or provoke the expression of some feeling: *moved to tears.* **7.** To affect deeply. **8.** *Archaic.* To arouse (someone's feelings). **9.** To propose or request in formal parliamentary procedure: *move an adjournment.* **10.** To cause (the bowels) to evacuate. **—**See Synonyms at **affect.**
　~*n.* **1.** An act of moving: *Nobody dared make a move.* **2.** A change of residence or place of business. **3.** In board games: **a.** An act of transferring a piece from one position to another. **b.** The prescribed manner in which a piece may be manoeuvred. **c.** A player's turn to manoeuvre a piece. **4.** One of a series of calculated actions undertaken to achieve some end. **—**See Synonyms at **affect.** **—get a move on.** *Informal.* To get started; get going; hurry up. Usually used in the imperative. **—on the move.** **1.** In the process of moving about; travelling. **2.** Making progress; advancing; changing. [Middle English *moven,* from Anglo-French *mover,* variant of Old French *moveir,* from Latin *movēre,* to move.]

move·ment (mōōvmənt) *n.* **1. a.** The act or an instance of moving; a change in position. **b.** *Military.* A change in the location of

MOZAMBIQUE

troops, ships, or aircraft for tactical or strategic purposes; a manoeuvre. **2. a.** The activities of a group of people to achieve a specific goal: *the Peace movement.* **b.** A group of people associated through some common aim: *the Labour movement.* **c.** A tendency or trend. **3.** Activity, especially: **a.** Commercial trading. **b.** A change in price of a security or commodity. **4. a.** An evacuation of the bowels. **b.** The faeces so evacuated. **5.** *Fine Arts.* The impression or illusion of motion. **6.** The progression of events in the development of a literary plot. **7.** The rhythmical or metrical structure of a poetic composition. **8.** *Music.* A self-contained component section of a composition. **9.** A mechanism that produces or transmits motion, as do the works of a watch. [Middle English, from Old French, from Medieval Latin *movimentum,* from Latin *movēre,* to move.]

mov·er (mōōvər) *n.* **1.** One that moves: *a beautiful mover on the dance floor.* **2.** One who proposes a motion in a debate.

mov·ie (mōōvi) *n. Chiefly U.S. Informal.* **1.** A cinematic film. **2.** A cinema. **3.** *Plural.* **a.** A showing of a film. Preceded by *the.* **b.** The film industry. [Shortened from MOVING PICTURE.]

mov·ing (mōōving) *adj.* **1.** Changing or capable of changing position. **2.** Causing or producing motion. **3.** Pertaining to house or furniture removals: *moving day.* **4.** Affecting the emotions, especially those of sympathy and sorrow: *a moving tale.* **—mov·ing·ly** *adv.* **—mov·ing·ness** *n.*
　Synonyms: moving, stirring, poignant, touching, pathetic, affecting.

moving average *n.* A form of statistical average obtained by replacing one item in the numerator but keeping the denominator unchanged. It therefore has several successive values.

moving pavement *n.* A device similar to an escalator but running horizontally, used, for example, at airports to help those carrying heavy luggage. Also called "travelator", "walkway".

moving picture *n. U.S.* A cinematic film.

moving staircase *n.* An **escalator** (see).

mow¹ (mō) *v.* **mowed, mowed** or **mown** (mōn ‖ mō-ən), **mowing, mows.** **—***tr.* **1.** To cut down (crops, grass, or similar growth) with a scythe or a mechanical device such as a lawn mower or mowing machine. **2.** To cut such growth from: *mow the lawn.* **—***intr.* To mow crops or grass, for example. **—mow down.** To fell in great numbers, as in battle: *mown down by the enemy's guns.* [Mow, mown; Middle English *mowen, mowen,* Old English *māwan, māwen,* from Germanic.] **—mow·er** (mō-ər) *n.*
　Usage: Mowed is the traditionally recommended past participle from, but *mown* is frequently heard in British English (*I have mown the lawn*), less often in American English. *Mown* is the standard form when used before a noun (*A mown lawn looks very nice*) and in compounds (*new-mown*).

mow² *n.* **1.** A place for storing hay or crops. **2.** Feed so stored. [Middle English *mough, mow,* stack of hay, Old English *mūga, mūha, mūwa,* from Scandinavian; akin to Old Norse *mūgi,* crowd.]

mow³ *Archaic.* A grimace.
~*intr.v.* **mowed, mowing, mows.** *Archaic.* To grimace. Used chiefly in the phrase *mop and mow.* [Middle English *mouwe,* from old French. See **moue.**]

mowing machine *n.* A machine for cutting hay, grass, or crops.

mox·i·bus·tion (móksi-bús-chən) *n.* An Asian method of treating skin irritation and various other disorders by placing down from the leaves of *Artemisia moxa* on the skin and igniting it. [Blend of (*Artemisia*) *moxa* + com*bustion.*]

Mo·zam·bique, People's Republic of (mō-zəm-béek, -zam-). *Portuguese* **Mo·çam·bi·que** (moo-sum-béeka). Formerly **Portuguese East Africa.** Country of southeast Africa, consisting in the centre and south of a broad coastal plain crossed by the Zambezi, Save, and Limpopo rivers, and plateaus and highlands elsewhere. Some 80 per cent of the people are subsistence farmers producing cassava and maize, but the country is the world's leading exporter of cashew nuts. Transit trade is a vital economic factor, since Mozambique acts as a port for South Africa and Zaire, and landlocked Swaziland, Zambia, Malawi, and Zimbabwe. Portuguese colonisation began in 1505. After World War II, African nationalists demanded independence, and set up the Mozambique Liberation Front (Frelimo), which began guerrilla activity in 1964. Led by Samora Machel, it achieved independence as a Marxist one-party state in 1975. Frelimo also aided African nationalists in neighbouring Zimbabwe/Rhodesia (1973–80). Area, 783 030 square kilometres (302,330 square miles). Capital, Maputo (formerly Lourenço Marques). —**Mo·zam·biqu·an** *n. & adj.*

Mozambique Current *n.* A warm ocean current flowing southwards down the east coast of Southern Africa.

Moz·ar·ab (mō-zárrəb) *n.* A member of a group of Spanish Christians who practised a modified form of their religion under the Muslims. [Spanish *Mozárabe,* from Arabic *Musta'rib,* "a would-be Arab", from *'arab,* ARAB.] —**Moz·ar·a·bic** *adj.*

Mo·zart (mōt-saart), **Wolfgang Amadeus** (1756–91). Austrian composer, one of the most highly gifted and prolific composers in history. Although he began as a child prodigy, both as performer and composer, he had irregular patronage and was often destitute. He wrote most of his greatest works in the last five years of his short life, including his last three symphonies (1788) and the operas *Don Giovanni* (1787) and *Die Zauberflöte* (*The Magic Flute,* 1791). —**Mo·zart·i·an, Mozart·e·an** (mōt-sárti-ən) *adj. & n.*

mo·zet·ta, Moz·zet·ta (mō-zéttə, mə- ‖ *Italian* mo-tsétta) *n. Roman Catholic Church.* A short, hooded cape worn by bishops. [Italian, short for *almozzetta,* irregular diminutive formed from Medieval Latin *almūtia,* ALMUCE.]

moz·za·rel·la (mótsə-réllə) *n.* A soft, white Italian curd cheese, formerly made from buffalo milk and often used melted in cookery. [Italian, diminutive of *mozza,* "slice", (sliced) cheese, from *mozzare,* to cut off, perhaps from Vulgar Latin *mutiāre* (unattested), from Latin *mutilāre,* to mutilate, cut up, from *mutilus,* cut short.]

mp, m.p. 1. melting point. 2. *Music.* mezzo-piano.

MP military police; military policeman.

M.P. 1. Member of Parliament. 2. Metropolitan Police. 3. military police; military policeman. 4. mounted police; mounted policeman.

mpg, m.p.g. miles per gallon.

mph, m.p.h. miles per hour.

M. Phil, M.Ph. Master of Philosophy.

M.P.S. Member of the Pharmaceutical Society.

Mr. (místər) *n., pl.* **Messrs** (méssərz). A title of courtesy used when speaking to or of a man, preceding the man's surname or office. [Abbreviation of **Mister.**]

M.R. 1. Master of the Rolls. 2. motivational research.

M.R.A., MRA Moral Rearmament.

M.R.C. Medical Research Council.

mRNA. messenger RNA.

Mrs. (míssiz) *n., pl.* **Mrs.** A title of courtesy used in speaking to or of a married woman, preceding the woman's surname or office. [Abbreviation of **mistress.**]

ms 1. manuscript. 2. millisecond.

MS 1. manuscript. 2. multiple sclerosis.

ms., MS. manuscript.

Ms, Ms. (miz, məz) *n., pl.* **Mses** or **Mss.** A title of courtesy used before a woman's surname or before her first name and surname, without regard to her marital status. See Usage note at **Miss.** [Coined to combine MISS and MRS.]

M.S. 1. Master of Surgery. 2. memorial sacrum.

M.Sc. Master of Science.

MSG monosodium glutamate.

msg. message.

m.s.l., M.S.L. mean sea level.

mss, MSS, mss., MSS. manuscripts.

MST, M.S.T. Mountain Standard Time.

Mt., mt. mount; mountain.

m.t., M.T. metric ton.

M.T.B., MTB *British.* motor torpedo boat.

M.Tech. Master of Technology.

mtg. 1. meeting. 2. mortgage.

mtn. mountain.

mu (mew ‖ moo) *n.* The 12th letter in the Greek alphabet, written M, μ. Transliterated in English as *M, m.*

muc-. Variant of **muco-.**

much (much) *adj.* **more, most.** Great in quantity, degree, or extent: *Was there much rain?* —**a bit much.** *Informal.* Difficult to accept.

~*pron.* 1. A large quantity or amount. 2. Anything remarkable or important: *As a leader, she is not much.* —**make much of.** To pay great attention to. —**think much of.** To esteem highly.
~*adv.* **more** (mor ‖ mōr), **most** (mōst). 1. To a great degree; to a large extent: *much impressed.* Often used in combination: *much-maligned.* 2. Often. Used especially in negative sentences: *She doesn't come much these days.* 3. Just about; almost: *much the same.* —**as much.** Whatever is indicated or implied: *I expected as much.* [Middle English *muche, miche,* shortened from *muchel, michel,* Old English *mycel, micel,* great, large, greatly, much.]

much·ness (múch-nəss, -niss) *n.* 1. Magnitude; bulk. 2. Greatness in quantity, number, or degree. —**much of a muchness.** *British.* Barely distinguishable; showing no great variation.

mu·cic acid (méw-sik) *n.* An organic acid, $HOOC(CHOH)_4COOH$, often derived from milk sugar. [From MUCUS.]

mu·ci·lage (méwssi-lij) *n.* 1. A sticky substance used as an adhesive. 2. A gummy substance obtained from certain plants. [Middle English *muscilage,* from Old French *mucilage,* from Late Latin *mūcilāgō,* musty juice, from Latin *mūcus,* MUCUS.] —**mu·ci·lag·i·nous** (-lájinəss) *adj.*

mu·cin (méw-sin) *n.* Any of a group of glycoproteins produced by mucous membranes. [MUC(O)- + -IN.]

muck (muk) *n.* 1. A moist, sticky mixture, especially of mud or filth. 2. Moist animal dung, especially when mixed with decayed vegetable matter and used as a fertiliser; manure. 3. Dark, fertile soil containing putrid vegetable matter. 4. Anything regarded as inferior, filthy, or disgusting. 5. Earth, rocks, or clay excavated in mining. —**make a muck of.** *Informal.* To botch or mismanage.
~*tr.v.* **mucked, mucking, mucks.** 1. To fertilise with manure or compost. 2. *Informal.* To soil or make dirty with or as if with muck. 3. **a.** To remove muck or dirt from (a mine or site). **b.** To remove muck from (a stable, for example). Used with **out.** —**muck about.** *Informal.* 1. To behave badly or in a silly way. 2. To potter about; do nothing in particular. 3. To prevaricate. 4. To cause inconvenience to. —**muck in.** *British Informal.* To participate in a task; do one's share. —**muck up.** *Informal.* To make dirty or untidy. 2. To mismanage or interfere with (a plan or project). [Middle English *muk,* from Old Norse *mykr.*] —**muck·i·ly** *adv.* —**muck·y** *adj.*

muck·a·muck (múckə-muck) *n.* Also **muck·et·y·muck** (múckəti-). *U.S. Slang.* A self-important person. Also called "high muckamuck".

muck·er (múckər) *n.* 1. A person who moves waste material in a mine. 2. *British Slang.* A heavy fall. 3. *British Slang.* A friend. 4. *U.S. Slang.* A coarse, vulgar person.

muckle. Variant of **mickle.**

muck·rake (múck-rayk) *intr.v.* **-raked, -raking, -rakes.** To search for and expose scandalous conduct, especially personal, political, or commercial misconduct in public affairs, usually in a sensational manner.
~*n.* A rake used for gathering and spreading muck. [Backformation from *muckraker,* used in 1906 by Theodore Roosevelt in allusion to the "man with a Muck-rake" in Bunyan's *Pilgrim's Progress.*] —**muck·rak·er** *n.*

muck sweat, muck·sweat (múk-swét, -swet) *n. British Informal.* A state of profuse sweating. [MUCK (soil) + SWEAT.]

muck·worm (múk-wurm) *n.* Any worm or larva found in mud and animal droppings.

muco-, muc– *comb. form.* Indicates mucus or something pertaining to the mucous membrane; for example, **mucoprotein, mucin.** [Latin *mūcus.*]

mu·coid (méw-koyd) *n.* Any of a group of glycoproteins similar to the mucins and found in connective tissue. [MUC(O)- + -OID.] —**mu·coid, mu·coi·dal** (mew-kóyd'l) *adj.*

mu·co·pol·y·sac·cha·ride (méwko-pólli-sáckə-rīd) *n.* Any of the polysaccharides that form chemical bonds with water to produce mucilaginous and lubricating fluids and which contain sugar derivatives such as amino acids.

mu·co·pro·tein (méwko-prṓ-teen, -tee-in) *n.* Any of a group of organic compounds, such as the mucins, that contain proteins and mucopolysaccharides.

mu·co·sa (mew-kṓ-sə, -zə) *n., pl.* **-sae** (-see, -zee) or **-sas.** A mucous membrane. [New Latin *mūcōsa (membrana),* from *mūcōsus,* MUCOUS.] —**mu·co·sal** *adj.*

mu·cous (méw-kəss) *adj.* Also **mu·cose** (-kōss, -kōz). 1. Producing or secreting mucus. 2. Pertaining to, consisting of, or resembling mucus. [Latin *mūcōsus,* from *mūcus,* MUCUS.]

mucous membrane *n.* The membrane lining all bodily channels that communicate with the air, such as the respiratory and alimentary tracts, the glands of which secrete mucus.

mu·cro (méwkrō) *n., pl.* **mucrones** (mew-krṓneez). *Biology.* A sharp tip of certain plant and animal organs. [New Latin, from Latin *mucrō†,* a sharp point, sword's point.]

mu·cro·nate (méwkrə-nət, -nit, -nayt) *adj. Biology.* Having a mucro. [Latin *mucronātus,* from *mucrō,* a point, MUCRO.] —**mu·cro·na·tion** (-náysh'n) *n.*

mu·cus (méwkəss) *n.* The viscous suspension of mucin, water, cells, and inorganic salts secreted as a protective, lubricant coating by glands in the mucous membrane, or by the external body surface of many animals. [Latin *mūcus, muccus.*]

mud (mud) *n.* 1. Wet, sticky, soft earth. 2. *Informal.* Slanderous or defamatory charges: *threw mud at her opponents.* 3. **a.** That which is degrading: *My name was dragged in the mud.* **b.** *Informal.* That

mulberry *There are about 15 species of this ornamental fruit-bearing tree, native to Asia and North America.* Morus alba, *the Asian species shown here, is now grown widely around the world.*

mule *A cross between a donkey and a horse, a mule is larger and stronger than a donkey, and more sure-footed on rough ground than a horse. Every generation of mules has to be bred afresh from the parent animals because the hybrid is always sterile.*

mullein *The flowers of mullein plants – the white mullein is shown here – were once used to make a medicine for the relief of coughs and chills.*

which is disreputable: *Her name was mud.* **—clear as mud.** Very unclear; confusing.
~tr.v. **mudded, mudding, muds.** To soil or bury with or as if with mud. [Middle English *mudde, mode*†.]

mud bath *n.* **1.** An immersion in heated mud, usually rich in supposedly medicinal minerals, for the purpose of curing certain ailments such as rheumatism. **2.** A muddy event or experience, such as a game of Rugby football played in the rain.

mud dauber *n.* Any of several wasps, including those of the genus *Sceliphron,* having long hind legs and a slender abdomen terminating in a bulb. The female lays eggs in paralysed insect larvae, which are placed in a nest of mud.

mud·dle (múdd'l) *v.* **-dled, -dling, -dles.** *—tr.* **1.** To mix confusedly; jumble: *muddled up the two names.* **2.** To mix up (the mind), as with alcohol; confuse or befuddle. **3.** To mismanage or bungle. **4.** To make turbid; muddy. **5.** *U.S.* To stir or mix (a drink) gently. *—intr.* **1.** To act or think in a confused manner. **2.** *Chiefly British.* To progress in an ineffective or disorganised way. Used with *on* or *along.* **—muddle through.** *Chiefly British.* To push on to a successful conclusion in a disorganised way.
~n. A confusion, jumble, or mess. [Perhaps from Middle Dutch *moddelen,* to make muddy, from *modde*†, mud.] **—mud·dler** *n.*

mud·dle-head·ed (múdd'l-héddid) *adj.* Mentally confused; stupid; dull. **—mud·dle-head·ed·ness** *n.*

mud·dy (múddi) *adj.* **-dier, -diest. 1.** Covered in, full of, or spattered with mud. **2. a.** Not bright or pure: *muddy blue.* **b.** Not clear; cloudy: *This beer is rather muddy.* **3.** Confused, vague, or obscure, as in expression or meaning: *a muddy style of writing.*
~tr.v. **muddied, -dying, -dies. 1.** To make muddy or dirty. **2.** To make dull or cloudy. **3.** To make obscure or confused. **—mud·di·ly** *adv.* **—mud·di·ness** *n.*

Mu·dé·jar, mu·dé·jar (*Spanish* mōō-thékhaar) *n., pl.* **-jares.** Any of the Christianised Moors permitted to remain in Spain after it had been restored to Christian control in the Middle Ages.
~adj. Of or pertaining to a type of Moorish architecture of the Middle Ages. [Spanish, from Arabic *mudajjan,* permitted to stay.]

mud·fish (múd-fish) *n., pl.* **-fishes** or collectively **mudfish.** Any of various fishes found in muddy water, such as the **bowfin** *(see).*

mud flat *n.* Land covered at high tide and exposed at low tide.

mud·guard (múd-gaard) *n.* The part of a bicycle, motorbike, or the like, that fits over the back of the wheels as a shield against thrown-up water and mud. Also *U.S.* "fender".

mud·lark (múd-laark) *n.* **1.** A bird, the **magpie lark** *(see).* **2.** *British Slang.* **a.** Formerly, one who scavenged in mudflats. **b.** A street urchin.

mud·pack (múd-pak) *n.* A paste made from a type of mud, spread thickly, especially over the face, for cosmetic purposes.

mud puppy *n.* Any of various aquatic salamanders of the genus *Necturus,* especially *N. maculosus,* of North America, having conspicuous clusters of external gills.

mu·dra (mə-dráa) *n.* In Hindu classical dancing, a series of body postures and hand movements enacting a narrative. [Hindi.]

mud·skip·per (múd-skippər) *n.* Any of several species of fishes of the family Gobiidae that are found along the coast of tropical Africa and in the Indo-Pacific region and are noted for their ability to manoeuvre on land and withstand drought.

mud·sling·er (múd-sling-ər) *n. Informal.* One who makes malicious charges against an opponent. **—mud·sling·ing** *n.*

mud·stone (múd-stōn) *n.* A fine-grained, nonfissile rock similar to shale that decomposes into mud when exposed to moisture.

mud·wort (múd-wurt || -wawrt) *n.* Any of various waterweeds of the genus *Limosella,* having creeping runners and small flowers.

muenster. Variant of **münster.**

mues·li (méwzli; *German* müssli) *n.* A food consisting of a mixture of nuts, cereal, dried fruit, honey, and the like, eaten with milk. [Swiss German.]

mu·ez·zin (mōō-ézzin, mew-) *n. Islam.* The crier who calls the faithful to prayer five times a day, usually from a minaret. [Arabic *mu'adhdhin,* active participle of *adhana,* to cause to listen, from *adhina,* to listen.]

muff[1] (muf) *tr.v.* **muffed, muffing, muffs.** *Informal.* **1.** To perform (an act) clumsily; bungle: *muffed the job.* **2.** *Sports.* To fail to execute (a kick, catch, or the like).
~n. Informal. **1.** A clumsy or bungling person. **2.** A clumsy or bungled act. [19th century : origin obscure.]

muff[2] *n.* A small cylindrical fur or cloth cover, open at both ends, in which the hands are placed to keep them warm. [Dutch *mof,* from Middle Dutch *moffel,* from Medieval Latin *muffula*†.]

muf·fin (múffin) *n.* **1.** *British.* A small, round, thick, doughy tea cake, usually toasted and served with butter. **2.** A small, cup-shaped bread roll, often sweetened and usually served hot. [Probably from Low German *muffen,* plural of *muffe*†, cake.]

muf·fle[1] (múff'l) *tr.v.* **-fled, -fling, -fles. 1.** To wrap up in a blanket, shawl, or scarf for warmth, protection, or secrecy. **2.** To wrap or pad in order to deaden a sound: *muffled drums.* **3.** To deaden (a sound): *Their hoofbeats were muffled by the sand.* **4.** To make vague or obscure: *a message muffled by excess of detail.*
~n. **1.** Anything that muffles. **2.** A kiln or part of a kiln in which pottery can be fired without being exposed to direct flame. [Middle English *muflen,* from Old French *enmoufler,* to "put on a muff or mittens", from *moufle,* mitten, from Medieval Latin *muffula*†.]

muffle[2] *n.* The hairless snout of ruminants and rodents. [French *mufle*†.]

muf·fler (múfflər) *n.* **1.** A heavy scarf worn round the neck for warmth. **2.** Any device that absorbs noise.

muf·ti, Muf·ti[1] (múfti, mŏŏfti) *n., pl.* **-tis.** A judge who interprets Muslim religious law. [Arabic *muftī,* "one who decides", from *aftā,* to decide (by legal opinion).]

muf·ti[2] (múfti) *n.* Civilian dress, especially when worn by one whose regular clothing is a military or other uniform. [Slang use of MUFTI (judge).]

mug[1] (mug) *n.* **1.** A cylindrical drinking vessel, usually having a handle. **2.** The liquid contained in such a vessel. **3.** The quantity that such a vessel is capable of containing. In this sense, also called "mugful". [Probably from Scandinavian.]

mug[2] *n. Slang.* **1.** The face of a person. **2.** The area of the mouth, chin, and jaw. **3.** A grimace. **4.** *British.* A person who is easily deceived or duped. **5.** *U.S.* A hoodlum; a ruffian. **—a mug's game.** *British Slang.* A foolish and unprofitable activity.
~v. **mugged, mugging, mugs.** *Slang. —tr.* To waylay and sometimes beat severely, usually with intent to rob. *—intr.* **1.** To grimace; especially, to overact as a performer by means of exaggerated facial expressions. **2.** *British.* To study books, notes, or the like, intensely. **—mug up.** *British Slang.* To study (a subject) intensely. Sometimes used with *on.* [Probably from MUG (vessel), from tankards shaped like grotesque human faces. Sense of "attack" from old slang sense of noun "hoodlum".]

Mu·ga·be (mōō-gáabi), **Robert (Gabriel)** (1924–). Zimbabwian politician. He entered black nationalist politics in Rhodesia (1960) and helped to found the Zimbabwe African National Union (ZANU) in 1963. From 1964 to 1974 he was detained by the Rhodesian government. In 1976 he became president of ZANU and co-leader, with Joshua Nkomo, of the Patriotic Front which waged war against the ruling white minority in Rhodesia. He became prime minister in April, 1980, after the first one-man-one-vote elections under the new constitution.

mug·ger[1] (múggər) *n.* One who commits a mugging.

mug·ger[2], **mug·gar, mug·gur** (múggər) *n.* A large crocodile, *Crocodylus palustris,* of southwestern Asia, having an exceptionally broad, wrinkled snout. Also called "marsh crocodile". [Hindi *magar,* from Sanskrit *makara,* a crocodile, from Dravidian.]

mug·ging (múgging) *n. Informal.* An assault, sometimes violent and usually by surprise and with intent to rob.

mug·gins (mugginz) *n. British Slang.* A fool or simpleton.
~pron. Oneself. Used in humorous self-deprecation: *Muggins will have to pay, as usual.* [Perhaps from surname *Muggins,* with allusion to MUG (simpleton).]

mug·gy (múggi) *adj.* **-gier, -giest.** Warm and extremely humid. [From dialectal *mug,* fine rain, from Middle English *muggen,* to drizzle, from Old Norse *mugga.*] **—mug·gi·ness** *n.*

Mughal, Mughul. Variants of **Mogul.**

mug·shot (múg-shot) *n.* A photograph of a person's face, especially one of a criminal used for purposes of identification.

mug·wort (múg-wurt || -wawrt) *n.* Any of several plants of the genus *Artemisia;* especially, *A. vulgaris,* native to Eurasia, having clusters of small yellowish-brown flowers. [Middle English *mugwort,* Old English *mucgwyrt* : *mucg-,* a midge, fly + *wyrt,* WORT.]

mug·wump (múg-wump) *n. U.S. Informal.* A person who acts independently or neutrally, especially in politics. [Natick *mugquomp, mugwomp,* "captain".] **—mug·wump·er·y** *n.*

Mu·ham·mad (mōō-hám-əd). Also **Mo·ham·med** (mō-, mə-, -ed) or **Ma·hom·et** (mə-hómmit) (*c.* 570–632). The prophet and founder of Islam, the son of Abdallah ibn Abd-al-Mutalib of the ruling tribe of Mecca. He was a rich merchant who had a vision in the cave of Mt. Hira telling him to preach true religion. In 622 he fled Mecca, where he made few converts, and set up a theocracy at Yathrib, which was renamed Medina, meaning "city of the prophet". In 630 Muhammad conquered Mecca without a struggle and began to win Arabia to Islam. His teachings are recorded in the Koran.

Mu·ham·ma·dan, Mo·ham·me·dan (mōō-hámmid'n) *adj.* Also **Mo·ham·me·dan** (mō-, mə-), **Ma·hom·e·tan** (mə-hómmitən). Of or pertaining to Muhammad or Islam; Muslim.
~n. A follower of Muhammad or believer in Islam; a Muslim.

Mu·ham·ma·dan·ism (mōō-hámmid'n-iz'm) *n.* Also **Mo·ham·me·dan·ism** (mō-, mə-), **Ma·hom·e·tan·ism** (-hómmitən-). The Muhammadan religion, **Islam** *(see).*

Mu·ham·mad Re·za Pah·la·vi (mō-hámməd ráyzə páaləvi) (1919–80). Shah of Iran (1941–79). His attempts to modernise Iranian society, together with the growth of corruption and the activities of the secret police under his regime, provoked the Islamic reaction culminating in the revolution of 1979 by which he was overthrown.

Mu·har·ram, Mu·har·rum (mōō-hárrəm) *n.* Also **Mo·har·ram** (mō-). **1.** The first month of the Muslim calendar. **2.** A festival held during the first ten days of this month.

Muir (mewr), **Edwin** (1887–1959). British poet, novelist, and literary critic. He was little recognised as a poet until the publication of the *Collected Poems* (1960). By then he had established his reputation more as a critic by the publication of studies such as *The Structure of the Novel* (1928) and *Essays on Literature and Society* (1949).

Muj·i·bur Rah·man (mŏŏjiboor ráamən), also known as Sheik Mujib (1920–75). Bengali politician, the first president of Bangladesh. He was elected to the East Pakistan Provincial assembly in 1954 and twice between 1958 and 1966 was imprisoned by General Ayub Khan for conspiring with the Indian government to secure the independence of East Pakistan. He led the Awami League in its campaign for independence, and after winning the provincial election of 1970, he proclaimed East Pakistan's independence, was arrested, and convicted of treason in 1971. When Indian intervention gained Bangladesh its independence he became prime minister of the provisional government in 1972. He was killed in a coup in 1975, soon after having named himself president with dictatorial powers.

mujik. Variant of **muzhik.**

Mukden. See **Shenyang.**

muk·luk (múk-luk) *n.* **1.** A soft Eskimo boot made of reindeer skin or sealskin. **2.** A boot resembling this. [Eskimo *muklok,* "large seal".]

mu·lat·to (mə-láttō, moō- ‖ mew-, moō-) *n., pl.* **-tos** or **-toes.** **1.** A person having one white and one black parent. **2.** Broadly, any person of mixed Caucasian and Negro ancestry.
~*adj.* Of the tawny colour of a mulatto. [Spanish *mulato,* young mule, mulatto, from *mulo,* mule, from Latin *mūlus,* MULE.]

mul·ber·ry (múl-bəri, -bri ‖ *U.S.* also -berri) *n., pl.* **-ries. 1.** Any of several trees of the genus *Morus,* especially the black mulberry, *M. nigra,* having edible fruit and leaves that are used to feed silkworms. **2.** The sweet, berry-like fruit of any of these trees. **3.** Any of several related or similar trees, such as the **paper mulberry** (see). **4.** *Archaic.* Greyish to dark purple. [Middle English *mulberrie, murberie,* Old English *mōrberie : mōr-,* a Germanic borrowing, from Latin *mōrum,* mulberry + Old English *berie,* BERRY.] —**mul·ber·ry** *adj.*

mulch (mulch) *n.* A mixture of straw, earth, leaves, peat, and the like, placed around plants to prevent evaporation of moisture and freezing of roots and to fertilise the soil.
~*tr.v.* **mulched, mulching, mulches.** To cover with a mulch. [Originally "rotten hay", probably extended use of Middle English *mulsh,* soft, yielding, variant of *melsh,* Old English *mel(i)sc, mylsc,* mild, mellow.]

mulct (mulkt) *n.* A fine or similar penalty.
~*tr.v.* **mulcted, mulcting, mulcts. 1.** To penalise by fining or demanding forfeiture. **2.** To cheat or swindle. [Latin *mulcta, multa,* a fine, of Italic origin.]

Mul·doon (mul-doōn), **Robert David** (1921–). New Zealand politician. He became leader of the National Party in 1974, after serving for five years (1967–72) as Minister of Finance. He became prime minister in 1975.

mule[1] (mewl) *n.* **1.** A sterile hybrid of a male ass and a female horse. Compare **hinny. 2.** Any sterile hybrid, as between a canary and other finches. **3.** *Informal.* A stubborn person. **4.** A type of spinning machine that makes thread or yarn from fibres. Also called "spinning mule". [Middle English *mul,* from Old English *mūl* and Old French *mul,* both from Latin *mūlus,* mule, probably from Mediterranean; akin to Albanian *mušk,* mule.]

mule[2] *n.* A slipper that has no counter or strap to fit around the heel of the foot. [French, from Latin *mulleus (calceus),* "red (shoe)".]

mu·le·ta (mew-léttə) *n.* A short red cape, suspended from a hollow staff, that is used by the matador to manoeuvre the bull during the **faena** (see). [Spanish, crutch, support, "small mule", from *mula,* "she-mule", from Latin *mūlus,* MULE.]

mu·le·teer (mēwli-téer) *n.* A mule driver. [French *muletier,* from *mulet,* diminutive of Old French *mul,* MULE.]

mu·ley (mēwli ‖ moŏolli, moŏoli) *adj.* Hornless. Said of cattle.
~*n., pl.* **muleys.** A hornless animal. [Variant of dialectal *moiley,* from *moil,* hornless, a hornless cow, from Irish *maol,* from Old Irish *máel,* bald, hornless.]

mul·ga (múlgə) *n. Australian.* **1.** Any of various Australian acacias, especially *Acacia aneura,* which grow in the desert. **2.** Scrub consisting of dense growth of acacia. [From a native Australian language.]

mu·li·eb·ri·ty (mēwli-ébbrəti) *n. Formal.* **1.** The state or condition of being a woman. **2.** The qualities characteristic of women. [Late Latin *muliebritās,* from Latin *muliebris,* womanly, from *mulier†,* a woman.]

mul·ish (mēwlish) *adj.* Characteristic of a mule; stubborn. See Synonyms at **obstinate.** —**mul·ish·ly** *adv.* —**mul·ish·ness** *n.*

mull[1] (mul) *tr.v.* **mulled, mulling, mulls.** To heat and spice (an alcoholic drink such as wine or ale). [17th century : origin obscure.]

mull[2] *v.* **mulled, mulling, mulls.** —*tr.* To reflect on or consider (a problem) deeply. Often used with *over.* [Middle English *mullen,* to grind, pulverise, from *mul,* dust, from Middle Dutch *mol, mul.*]

mull[3] *n.* A soft, thin muslin used in dresses and for trimmings. [Short for *mulmull,* from Hindi *malmal,* from Persian *malmal†.*]

mull[4] *n.* In Scotland, a promontory. [Middle English; Gaelic *maol.*]

mull[5] *n.* A moist type of humus that is formed under non-acid conditions and found mingled with mineral soil rather than as a distinct layer. [German, from Danish *muld.*]

Mull (mul). The largest of the Inner Hebrides, western Scotland, and since 1975 part of Strathclyde Region. The island is mountainous, rising to 966 metres (3,169 feet) at Ben More. Tobermory, the chief town, is also a summer resort.

mul·lah, mul·la (múllə, moŏollə) *n.* A Muslim religious teacher or leader. Sometimes used as a title. [Turkish *mulla* and Persian *mullā,* from Arabic *mawlā,* "master".]

mul·lein (múllin) *n.* Any plant of the genus *Verbascum,* having leaves covered with white, woolly down, and yellow flowers. See **Aaron's rod.** [Middle English *moleyne,* from Old French *moleine,* from Gaulish *melena* (unattested).]

mul·ler (múllər) *n.* **1.** Any of several manual or mechanical devices used for grinding. **2.** A device with a stone or other hard base, used

manually or mechanically to grind paints or drugs. [Middle English *molour,* probably from *mullen,* to grind, pulverise. See **mull**[2].]

Mül·ler·i·an duct (mew-léer-i-ən) *n.* The oviduct of all vertebrates except the jawless fish, which in mammals is differentiated into the Fallopian tubes, womb, and vagina. [After Johannes *Müller* (1801–58), German anatomist.]

mul·let[1] (múllit) *n., pl.* **-lets** or collectively **mullet.** Any of various edible fishes of the families Mugilidae or Mullidae found worldwide in tropical and temperate coastal waters and some freshwater streams; especially, the grey mullets of the genus *Mugil.* See **red mullet.** [Middle English *molet,* from Old French *mulet,* from Latin *mullus,* red mullet, from Greek *mollos.*]

mul·let[2] (múllət) *n. Heraldry.* A star having five straight points. [Old French *molette,* rowel on a spur.]

mul·li·gan (múlligən) *n. U.S.* A stew of various meats and vegetables. Also called "mulligan stew". [Probably from the Irish surname *Mulligan.*]

mul·li·ga·taw·ny (múlligə-táwni) *n.* An Indian soup with meat and strongly flavoured with curry. [Tamil *milagutaṇṇī(r),* "pepper-water".]

mul·li·grubs (múlli-grubz) *pl.n. Informal.* **1.** A stomach ache; griping of the intestines; colic. **2.** Ill temper or depression. Often used humorously. [Alteration of earlier *mulligrums,* perhaps alteration of MEGRIM.]

mul·li·on (múlli-ən) *n.* A vertical strip dividing the panes of a window or panels of screen. [Perhaps variant of Middle English *monial,* from Old French *moinel,* from *moien,* MEAN.] —**mul·li·oned** *adj.*

mul·lo·way (múllə-way) *n.* A large Australian marine food fish, *Sciaena antarctica.* [19th century : origin obscure.]

multi– *comb. form.* Indicates: **1.** Many or much; for example, **multicoloured. 2.** More than one; for example, **multiparous.** *Note:* Many compounds other than those entered here may be formed with *multi-.* In this dictionary, in forming compounds, *multi-* is normally joined to the following word or element without space or hyphen: *multiangular.* However, many users prefer the hyphenated form, especially in less standardised compounds: *multi-company.* The hyphenated form is also used if the second element begins with *i: multi-infection.* In American English the prefix is sometimes pronounced (múltī-); this is not shown in the entries below. [Middle English, from Latin, from *multus,* much.]

mul·ti·ad·dress (múlti-ə-dréss ‖ *U.S.* -áddress) *adj.* Designating a storage system of data-processing computers in which it is possible to store instructions or quantities in more than one position.

mul·ti·cel·lu·lar (múlti-séllewlər) *adj.* Consisting of more than one cell. Said chiefly of metazoans.

mul·ti·col·oured (múlti-kúllərd, -kullərd) *adj.* Having many colours.

mul·ti·cul·tur·al (múlti-kúlchərəl) *adj.* Of or pertaining to a society that includes several different cultures: *a multicultural city.*

mul·ti·dis·ci·pli·nar·y (múlti-díssi-plin-əri, -plín-, -plín- ‖ *U.S.* -erri) *adj.* Embracing, or involving contributions from, several distinct academic or other disciplines: *a multidisciplinary approach.*

mul·ti·fac·to·ri·al (múlti-fak-táwr-i-əl ‖ -tōr-) *adj. Genetics.* Designating inheritance or a characteristic, such as height, that is controlled by two or more genes. See **multiple factor.**

mul·ti·far·i·ous (múlti-fáir-i-əss) *adj.* Having great variety; made up of many parts or kinds. [Latin *multifārius,* MULTI- + *-fārius,* doing.] —**mul·ti·far·i·ous·ly** *adv.* —**mul·ti·far·i·ous·ness** *n.*

mul·ti·fid (múlti-fid) *adj. Biology.* Having many clefts forming lobes: *multifid leaves.* [Latin *multifidus :* MULTI- + -FID.]

mul·ti·flo·ra rose (múlti-fláwrə ‖ -flōrə) *n.* A climbing or sprawling shrub, *Rosa multiflora,* native to Asia, having clusters of small, fragrant flowers. It is the origin of many horticultural varieties. [New Latin *Rosa multiflōra,* "many-flowered rose".]

mul·ti·foil (múlti-foyl) *adj. Architecture.* Having many foils.
~*n.* Any design or object having many foils or scalloped edges.

mul·ti·fold (múlti-fōld) *adj.* Many times doubled; manifold.

mul·ti·form (múlti-fawrm) *adj.* Occurring in or having many forms, shapes, or appearances. [Latin *multiformis :* MULTI- + -FORM.] —**mul·ti·for·mi·ty** (-fórməti) *n.*

mul·ti·grav·i·da (múlti-grávvidə) *n., pl.* **-dae** (-grávvidee). A pregnant woman who has had at least two previous pregnancies. [New Latin : MULTI- + *gravida,* pregnant woman. See **gravid.**]

mul·ti·lat·er·al (múlti-láttrəl, -láttərəl) *adj.* **1.** Having many sides. **2.** Involving more than two nations or groups: *multilateral disarmament.* —**mul·ti·lat·er·al·ly** *adv.*

mul·ti·lat·er·al·ist (múlti-láttrəl-ist, -láttərəl-) *n.* One who favours multilateral action, especially multilateral nuclear disarmament. Compare **unilateralist.** —**mul·ti·lat·er·al·ist** *adj.*

mul·ti·lin·gual (múlti-líng-gwəl ‖ -gew-əl) *adj.* **1.** Capable of speaking or writing in many languages. **2.** Written in many languages. **3.** Designating a society composed of various different language groups.

mul·ti·me·di·a (múlti-méedi-ə) *adj.* Including or involving the use of several media of communication, such as films, records, or the like, for the purpose of education or entertainment.

mul·ti·mil·lion·aire (múlti-míl-yə-naír) *n.* A person whose financial assets equal many millions of pounds, dollars, or other currency.

mul·ti·na·tion·al (múlti-násh-ənəl, -nəl) *adj.* **1.** Having operations, subsidiaries, or investments in more than one country: *a multinational corporation.* **2.** Of, in, or involving several or many countries.
~*n.* A multinational company.

mullion *Wooden mullions divide the window panes in the 15th-century Little Hall, at Lavenham, in Suffolk, England.*

mul·ti·no·mi·al (múlti-nṓmi-əl) n. Mathematics. A polynomial (see). [MULTI- + binomial.] —**mul·ti·no·mi·al** adj.

multinomial theorem n. Mathematics. The theorem that establishes the rule for forming the terms of a polynomial expansion. See **binomial theorem, expansion, polynomial.**

mul·tip·a·ra (mul-típpərə) n., pl. **-rae** (-ree). A pregnant woman who has borne at least one child; especially, one who is in labour for the second time. [New Latin, feminine of multiparus, MULTIPAROUS.]

mul·tip·a·rous (mul-típpərəss) adj. 1. Having borne more than one child. 2. Giving birth to more than one offspring at one time. [New Latin multiparus : MULTI- + -PAROUS.]

mul·ti·par·tite (múlti-pártīt) adj. 1. Having many parts. 2. Multilateral. [Latin multipartītus : MULTI- + PARTITE.]

mul·ti·ple (múltip'l) adj. Having, pertaining to, or consisting of more than one individual, element, part, or other component; manifold; multiplicate.

~n. Mathematics. A quantity into which another quantity may be divided with zero remainder: 4, 6, and 12 are multiples of 2. A common multiple is a quantity into which each of two or more other quantities may be divided with zero remainder: 6, 12, and 24 are common multiples of 2 and 3. A lowest common multiple is the least quantity into which two or more other quantities may be divided with zero remainder: 6 is the lowest common multiple of all common multiples of 2 and 3. [Old French, from Late Latin multiplus : MULTI- + -plus, -fold.]

multiple allele n. Genetics. A set of three or more alternative forms of a gene at a single locus. Also called "multiple allelomorph".

mul·ti·ple-choice (múltip'l-chóyss) adj. Offering a number of solutions from which one correct one is to be chosen: multiple-choice exam questions.

multiple factor n. Genetics. A combination of genes having a joint or cumulative effect.

multiple fruit n. A fruit, such as a pineapple or mulberry, in which the fruits of several flowers are combined into a single structure. Also called "aggregate fruit", "collective fruit".

multiple root n. Mathematics. A root a of the polynomial equation $f(x) = 0$ in which $(x - a)$ occurs at least twice as a factor of $f(x)$. Also called "root".

multiple sclerosis n. Abbr. **MS** A degenerative disease of the central nervous system, in which the sheaths surrounding individual nerve cells of the brain or spinal cord, or both, are damaged causing disorders of speech, vision, and muscle coordination, and partial paralysis.

multiple star n. Three or more stars, usually with a common gravitational centre, that appear very close together as one system to the naked eye.

multiple store n. Any of a number of shops in different locations owned by the same company, such as a branch of a chain store. Also called "multiple shop".

mul·ti·plet (múlti-plət, -plet, -plit) n. Physics. 1. A spectral line having more than one component representing slight variations in energy states characteristic of an atom. 2. Any of several classes or groupings of subatomic particles, such as the nucleon, each member of which has the same set of **quantum numbers** (see) except for electric charge. [From MULTIPLE.]

mul·ti·plex (múlti-pleks) adj. 1. Multiple; manifold. 2. Designating a simultaneous communication of two or more messages on the same wire or radio channel. Compare **duplex, simplex.** 3. Designating a method of making topographic maps with three cameras arranged to employ stereoscopic principles.

~v. **multiplexed, -plexing, -plexes.** —intr. To send messages or signals in a multiplex system. —tr. To send simultaneously (more than one signal) using one radio frequency. [Latin : MULTI- + -plex, -fold.] —**mul·ti·plex·er** n.

mul·ti·pli·a·ble (múlti-plī̄-əb'l ‖ -plĭ-) adj. Also **mul·ti·plic·a·ble** (-plik-, -plík-). Capable of being multiplied.

mul·ti·pli·cand (múltipli-kánd) n. The number that is or is to be multiplied by another. [Latin multiplicandum, neuter of multiplicandus, gerundive of multiplicāre, to MULTIPLY.]

mul·tip·li·cate (mul-típli-kət, -kit) adj. Rare. Manifold; multiple. [Middle English, from Latin multiplicātus, past participle of multiplicāre, to MULTIPLY.]

mul·ti·pli·ca·tion (múltipli-káysh'n) n. 1. The act of multiplying or the process of being multiplied. 2. The propagation of plants and animals. 3. Mathematics. **a.** An operation in which an integer, the multiplicand, is added to itself a specific integral number of times. **b.** The extension of this process to the combination of two real numbers by using laws valid for integers. **c.** Any of certain analogous operations combining expressions other than real numbers. Compare **division.** 4. An increase or build-up achieved by adding. —**mul·ti·pli·ca·tion·al** adj.

multiplication sign n. Mathematics. Any of various signs, especially (×), placed between multiplicand and multiplier, or operand and operator, as in a × b.

multiplication table n. A table listing the products of certain numbers multiplied together, usually the numbers 1 to 12.

mul·ti·pli·ca·tive (múlti-plíckətiv, -pli-káytiv) adj. 1. Tending to multiply or capable of multiplying or increasing. 2. Pertaining to multiplication. —**mul·ti·pli·ca·tive·ly** adv.

mul·ti·plic·i·ty (múlti-plíssəti) n., pl. **-ties.** 1. The state of being various or manifold. 2. A large number: a multiplicity of ideas. 3. Physics. **a.** The number of subatomic particles in a **multiplet** (see). **b.** The number of levels into which the energy of an atom,

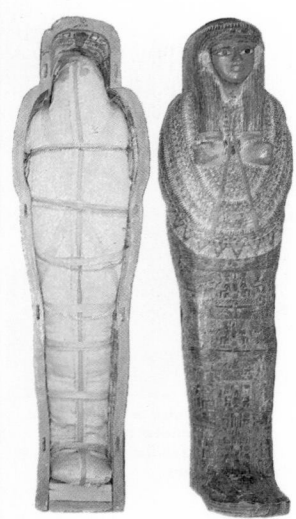

mummy The mummy and case of an ancient Egyptian priestess from Thebes, who died in the 11th century B.C.

molecule, nucleus, or the like can split as a result of coupling between spin angular momentum and orbital angular momentum. [French multiplicité, from Latin multiplicitās, from multiplex (stem multiplic-), having many folds, MULTIPLEX.]

mul·ti·pli·er (múlti-plī̄-ər) n. 1. One that multiplies. 2. Mathematics. The number by which the multiplicand is multiplied. If 3 is multiplied by 2, 3 is the multiplicand, 2 is the multiplier, and 6 is the product. 3. Physics. Any device, such as a phototube, used to enhance or increase an effect. 4. Economics. The ratio between an initial increase in investment expenditure and the total income amassed from that first expenditure.

mul·ti·ply (múlti-plī̄) v. **-plied, -plying, -plies.** —tr. 1. To increase the amount, number, or degree of; make more numerous. 2. Mathematics. To perform multiplication on. —intr. 1. To become more in number, amount, or degree. 2. To breed; propagate. 3. Mathematics. To perform multiplication. [Middle English multiplien, from Old French multiplier, from Latin multiplicāre, from multiplex (stem multiplic-), having many folds, MULTIPLEX.]

mul·ti·pur·pose (múlti-púrpəss) adj. Having several different purposes: a multipurpose machine.

mul·ti·ra·cial (múlti-ráysh'l) adj. Of, pertaining to, or composed of people of different races: a multiracial community.

mul·ti·se·ri·ate (múlti-séer-i-ət, -ayt) adj. Botany. Borne in many whorls or rows. Said of flower parts.

mul·ti·stage (múlti-stayj) adj. 1. Functioning by stages. 2. Designating a device, such as a turbine, compressor, or supercharger, that has more than one rotating section.

multistage rocket n. A rocket composed of two or more stages, each stage firing in succession. Also called "step rocket".

mul·ti·sto·rey (múlti-stáw-ri ‖ -stṓ-) adj. Of or designating a building that has several storeys: a multistorey car park.

mul·ti·tude (múlti-tewd ‖ -tōōd) n. 1. The condition or quality of being numerous. 2. **a.** A great, indefinite number: a multitude of sins. **b.** A huge gathering of people. 3. The masses; the populace. Preceded by the. [Middle English, from Old French, from Latin multitūdō, a great number, from multus, many.]

   Synonyms: multitude, host, legion, army, array.

mul·ti·tu·di·nous (múlti-téw-dinəss ‖ -tōō-) adj. 1. Very numerous; existing in great numbers. 2. Consisting of many parts. 3. Poetic. Crowded. —**mul·ti·tu·di·nous·ly** adv.

mul·ti·va·lent (múlti-váylənt) adj. 1. Chemistry. Polyvalent. 2. Biology. Of or pertaining to homologous chromosomes during meiosis. 3. Having various meanings or values. —**mul·ti·va·lency** n.

mul·tum in par·vo (mōol-tōom in párvō, múl-, -təm) n. Latin. A large amount within a small space or range.

mul·ture (múlchər) n. British. Formerly, a fee, usually in the form of a quantity of flour, paid to a miller for grinding one's grain at his mill. [Middle English, from Old French mo(u)lture, from Medieval Latin molitura, from molere (past participial stem molit-), to grind.]

mum¹ (mum) adj. Not talking; silent: Keep mum about my mistake. —**mum's the word.** Used to enjoin or promise silence: Remember our secret—mum's the word! [Middle English mum, mom, probably from Low German (imitative of closed lips).]

mum² n. Chiefly British Informal. A mother. Used chiefly as a term of address.

mum³ intr.v. **mummed, mumming, mums.** To act or play in a masque; especially, to act as a mummer. [Middle English mummen, mommen, from Old French momer.]

mum·ble (múmb'l) v. **-bled, -bling, -bles.** —tr. 1. To utter indistinctly by lowering the voice or partially closing the mouth. 2. Rare. To chew (food) slowly or painfully without or as if without teeth. —intr. 1. To speak indistinctly, as by lowering the voice or partially closing the mouth. 2. Rare. To chew food slowly or painfully, as if without teeth. —See Synonyms at **mutter.**

~n. A low, indistinct sound or speech. [Middle English momelen, frequentative of mum, inarticulate sound, MUM¹.] —**mum·bler** n.

mum·bo jum·bo (múmbō júmbō) n. 1. Confusing or meaningless words or actions. 2. Unintelligible or obscure ritual. 3. An object believed to have supernatural powers; a fetish. [Perhaps from the name of a Mandingo idol.]

mum·chance (múm-chaanss ‖ -chanss) adj. Archaic. Not speaking; silent. [Originally noun, "dumb show", from Middle Low German mummenschanze, masked serenade : mummen, from Old French momer, from MUM³ + schanze, from Old French, CHANCE.]

mu meson n. Physics. A particle, the **muon** (see). Not in current technical usage.

mum·mer (múmmər) n. 1. One who acts or plays in a traditional masque, mime, or the like. 2. Slang. An actor. [Middle English mummar, from Middle Dutch mommer, from Old French mommeur, from momer, to MUM³.]

mum·mer·y (múmməri) n., pl. **-ies.** 1. A performance by mummers. 2. A pretentious or hypocritical show or ceremony.

mum·mi·fy (múmmi-fī̄) v. **-fied, -fying, -fies.** —tr. 1. To make into a mummy by embalming and drying. 2. To invest with the appearance or qualities of a mummy: mummified ideas. —intr. To shrivel or dry up like a mummy. —**mum·mi·fi·ca·tion** (-fi-káysh'n) n.

mum·my¹ (múmmi) n., pl. **-ies.** 1. The body of a human being or animal embalmed after death, as found in ancient Egyptian tombs. 2. Any withered or shrunken body, living or dead, that resembles a preserved mummy. 3. British Regional. A pulp or formless mass. Used in the phrase beat to a mummy. 4. A rich brown pigment. [Middle English mummie, from Old French momie, embalming ointment, mummy, from Medieval Latin *mumia,* from Arabic *mūmiyā,* mummy, bitumen, from *mūm,* wax.]

mummy² *n., pl.* **-ies.** *Informal.* A mother. [Alteration of MAMMY.]

mump¹ (mump) *intr.v.* **mumped, mumping, mumps.** To be silent and moody: *always mumping and moaning.* [Imitative (of closed mouth).]

mump² *v.* **mumped, mumping, mumps.** *Archaic.* —*intr.* To beg. —*tr.* To get by begging. [Perhaps from obsolete Dutch *mompen,* to cheat.]

mumps (mumps) *n.* *Used with a singular verb.* An acute, contagious viral infection of the salivary glands, especially the parotids, which may spread to the pancreas, brain, or testicles. It is common in children and is characterised by swelling of the area under the lower jaw. [Plural of dialect *mump,* grimace; akin to MUMP (be silent).] **—mump·ish** *adj.*

munch (munch) *v.* **munched, munching, munches.** —*tr.* **1.** To chew (food) steadily with a crunching sound. **2.** *Slang.* To eat. —*intr.* **1.** To chew steadily. Sometimes used with *away, at,* or *on.* **2.** *Slang.* To eat. [Middle English *monchen* (imitative).]

Munch (mo͝ongk), **Edvard** (1863–1944). Norwegian painter, etcher, and lithographer. In the 1890s he painted the best-known of his works, the cycle called *Frieze of Life,* which included what has become by far his most famous painting (also produced as a woodcut and a lithograph), *The Scream.*

mun·dane (múndayn, mún-dáyn) *adj.* **1.** Unidealised or unelevated; bodily or worldly: *Mundane pleasures undermined those of the spirit.* **2.** Ordinary; dull; banal: *lived a dull, mundane existence.* [Middle English *mondeyne,* from Old French *mondain,* from Late Latin *mundānus,* from Latin *mundus,* the world.] **—mun·dane·ly** *adv.* **—mun·dane·ness, mun·dan·i·ty** (mun-dánnəti) *n.*

mung bean (mung, mo͝ongh) *n.* A bean, *Phaseolus aureus,* of eastern Asia. It is the source of bean sprouts used in cookery. [*Mung,* shortened form *mungo,* from Tamil mūngu, from Sanskrit *mudga.*]

mun·go (múng-gō) *n.* **1.** Recycled wool used for cheap cloth. **2.** The cloth produced from such wool. See **shoddy.** [Perhaps from Yorkshire dialect *mong*†, mixture, and Scottish *Mungo,* male forename.]

Mu·nich (méwnik). *German* **Mün·chen** (mǖnkhən). Capital of Bavaria, West Germany. It is the cultural, industrial, and commercial focus of south Germany and a major tourist centre. Its products include machinery, chemicals, instruments, and beer. Founded on the river Isar (1158), Munich became the home of the Wittelsbach family (1255). They made it their capital (1506), from which they ruled Bavaria until 1918, from 1806 as kings. Hitler founded the National Socialist (Nazi) movement in Munich (*c.* 1919). There he attempted his "beer-hall putsch" (1923) and signed the Munich Agreement (1938). The city was the venue of the 1972 summer Olympic Games. Munich's Oktoberfest, an annual beer festival, is world famous. See map at **Germany.**

mu·nic·i·pal (mew-níssip'l ‖ méwni-sípp'l) *adj. Abbr.* **mun. 1. a.** Of or pertaining to a city or its government. **b.** Having local self-government: *a municipal borough.* **2.** Of or pertaining to the internal affairs of a nation, as distinguished from its international affairs. [Latin *mūnicipālis,* from *mūnicipium,* a franchised city, from *mūniceps,* citizen of a *mūnicipium* (who could perform public offices but not hold magistracies) : *mūnus,* public office + *-ceps,* "-taker", from *capere,* to take.] **—mu·nic·i·pal·ly** *adv.*

mu·nic·i·pal·ise, mu·nic·i·pal·ize (mew-níssip'l-īz) *tr.v.* **-ised, -ising, -ises. 1.** To place under municipal ownership. **2.** To make a municipality of. **—mu·nic·i·pal·i·sa·tion** (-ī-záysh'n ‖ *U.S.* -i-) *n.*

mu·nic·i·pal·i·ty (mew-níssi-pál-əti) *n., pl.* **-ties.** *Abbr.* **mun. 1.** A city, town, village, borough, or other district having local self-government. **2.** A body of officials appointed or elected to manage the affairs of such a community.

mu·nif·i·cence (mew-níffi-sənss) *n.* **1.** A disposition to bestow lavish benefits; a generous nature. **2.** The lavish bestowal of gifts, entertainment, hospitality, or other benefits.

mu·nif·i·cent (mew-níffi-sənt) *adj.* **1.** Extremely liberal in giving; very generous. **2.** Showing great generosity: *a munificent gift.* [Latin *mūnificens* (stem *mūnificent-*), from *mūnificus,* "present-making", generous, bountiful : *mūnus,* office, duty, gift + *-ficus,* -FIC.] **—mu·nif·i·cent·ly** *adv.*

mu·ni·ment (méwnimənt) *n.* **1.** *Plural. Law.* Documentary evidence of ownership; written proof by which a person defends ownership of property or maintains rights. **2.** *Rare.* A means of defence or protection. [Middle English, from Old French, Medieval Latin *mūnīmentum,* from Latin, defence, from *mūnīre,* to defend.]

mu·ni·tion (mew-nísh'n) *n.* *Usually plural.* War material, especially weapons and ammunition.
~*tr.v.* **munitioned, -tioning, -tions.** To supply with munitions. [Originally, "fortification", from French, from Latin *mūnītiō* (stem *mūnītiōn-*), from *mūnīre,* to defend, fortify.] **—mu·ni·tion·er** *n.*

Mun·ro (mun-rṓ), **H(ector) H(ugh),** known as Saki (1870–1916). English short-story writer, born in Burma. His highly original short stories are written in a mordant, witty style and often bitter in tone. The first collection of these, *Reginald,* appeared in 1904. It was followed by *Reginald in Russia* (1910), *The Chronicles of Clovis* (1911), and *Beasts and Super-beasts* (1914).

Mun·sell scale (múnss'l) *n.* A scale used in specifying colour, based on equal changes in visual hue. [After A.H. *Munsell* (1858–1918), U.S. scientist.]

Mun·ster¹ (múnstər). Province in the southwest Republic of Ireland. A former kingdom, it is the largest Irish province, covering the counties of Clare, Cork, Kerry, Limerick, Tipperary, and Waterford.

Munster². Variant of **Muenster.**

mün·ster, mun·ster, muen·ster (mún-stər, mo͝on-, *German* mǖn-) *n.* A semisoft, creamy, yellow Alsatian cheese of mild flavour. [After *Münster,* port and industrial centre in North Rhine-Westphalia, West Germany.]

munt (mo͝ont) *n.* Also **mun·tu** (mo͝ontōō). *South African Slang.* A black African. Used derogatorily by whites. [Afrikaans, from Bantu *umuntu,* singular of *abantu,* person, black person.]

munt·jac, munt·jak (múntjak) *n.* Any of several small deer of the genus *Muntiacus,* of southeastern Asia and the East Indies. *M. muntjak* is now widespread in the woods of south central England. Also called "barking deer". [Malay *menjangan,* deer.]

muntjac *Even when fully grown, this small deer is only about 50 centimetres (20 inches) tall. It is native to the forests of India, southern China, and Southeast Asia, but has also been introduced to European woods.*

Muntz metal (munts) *n.* A form of brass used for costings and extrusions, consisting of three parts copper and two parts zinc. [After G.F. *Muntz* (died 1857), English manufacturer.]

mu·on (méw-on) *n.* *Symbol* μ *Physics.* A subatomic particle in the lepton family, having a mass 207 times that of the electron, a negative electric charge, and a mean lifetime of 2.2×10^{-6} second. Formerly called "mu meson". [From *mu* (Greek letter) + -ON.] **—mu·on·ic** (mew-ónnik) *adj.*

mu·o·ni·um (mew-ṓni-əm) *n.* *Physics.* A short-lived entity formed by a muon and its antiparticle attracted together and revolving about a common centre.

mu·rage (méwr-ij) *n.* Formerly, a tax levied to finance the building or repairing of city walls. [Middle English, from Old French, from *mur,* from Latin *murus,* wall.]

mu·ral (méwr-əl) *n.* A picture or decoration, usually a very large one, applied directly to a wall or ceiling.
~*adj.* **1.** Of, pertaining to, or resembling a wall. **2.** On or affixed to a wall: *a mural painting.* [Old French, from Latin *mūrālis,* from *mūrus,* a wall.] **—mu·ral·ist** *n.*

mur·der (múrdər) *n.* Also *obsolete* **mur·ther** (múrthər). **1.** The unlawful, usually premeditated, killing of one human being by another. Compare **homicide, manslaughter. 2.** *Slang.* Something that is very difficult or hazardous or that causes extreme discomfort: *This heat is murder.* **—cry** or **scream blue murder.** *Informal.* To make a loud cry, as in protest or anger. **—get away with murder.** *Informal.* To escape punishment for or detection of a blameworthy act.
~*v.* **murdered, -dering, -ders.** Also *obsolete* **mur·ther.** —*tr.* **1.** To kill (a human being) unlawfully. **2.** To kill (one or more human beings) brutally or inhumanly. **3.** To destroy or put an end to. **4.** To mar or spoil by ineptness: *murdering the English language with sloppy speech.* **5.** *Slang.* To defeat decisively; trounce: *The new magazine was murdering the competition.* **6.** *British Slang.* To consume ravenously: *I could murder a pint.* —*intr.* To commit murder. [Middle English *murther, mordre,* Old English *morthor.*] **—mur·der·er** (-ər), **mur·der·ess** (-ess, -riss) *n.*

mur·der·ous (múrdərəss) *adj.* **1.** Capable of, guilty of, or intending murder: *a murderous rage.* **2.** Characteristic of or involving murder: *a murderous ambush.* **3.** *Informal.* Very difficult or dangerous: *a murderous exam.* **—mur·der·ous·ly** *adv.* **—mur·der·ous·ness** *n.*

Mur·doch (múr-dok), **(Jean) Iris** (1919–). Irish-born British novelist. She was trained as a philosopher and in 1948 was appointed lecturer in philosophy at Oxford University. Her first novel, *Under the Net,* was published in 1954. Among the most popular of her later novels are *The Flight from the Enchanter* (1955), *A Severed Head* (1961), *The Unicorn* (1963), and *The Sea, the Sea* (1978), for which she was awarded the Booker Prize.

mure (mewr) *tr.v.* **mured, muring, mures.** *Rare.* To immure; confine; wall in. [Middle English *muren,* from Old French *murer,* from Late Latin *mūrāre,* to wall in, from Latin *mūrus,* a wall.]

mu·rex (méwr-eks) *n., pl.* **murices** (méwr-i-seez) or **-rexes.** Any of various marine gastropods of the genus *Murex,* with rough, spiny shells, common in warm seas. One species, *M. trunculus,* was the source of the royal dye, Tyrian purple. [New Latin, from Latin *mūrex,* of Mediterranean origin.]

Murillo painting *Murillo's* The Immaculate Conception, *in the Prado, Madrid.*

mu·ri·ate (méwr-i-ət, -it, -ayt) *n.* A **chloride** *(see).* Not in current technical usage. [Latin *muria,* brine.]

mu·ri·at·ic acid (méwr-i-áttik) *n.* **Hydrochloric acid** *(see).* Not in current technical usage. [Latin *muriāticus,* from *muria,* brine.]

mu·ri·cate (méwr-i-kayt) *adj.* Also **mu·ri·cat·ed** (-kaytid). Having a roughened surface because of many short spines. [Latin *mūricātus,* murex-shaped, pointed, from MUREX.]

Mu·ri·llo (mewr-ríllō, -ríl-yō; *Spanish* moo-rée-yō), **Bartolomé Esteban** (1617–82). Spanish painter. He painted chiefly religious subjects, genre paintings (especially of street arabs and peasant boys), and portraits. In 1660 he helped to found the academy of painting and drawing at Seville and he served as its first president.

mu·rine (méwr-īn, -in, -een) *adj.* **1.** Of or pertaining to a member of the rodent family Muridae, including rats and mice. **2.** Caused, transmitted, or affected by rodents of the family Muridae: *a murine plague.* **3.** Resembling a rat or mouse.
~*n.* A murine rodent. [Latin *mūrinus,* from *mūs* (stem *mūr-*), mouse.]

murk, mirk (murk) *n.* Darkness; gloom.
~*adj. Archaic.* Dark; gloomy. [Middle English *mirke,* from an oblique case of Old English *mirce,* darkness.]

murk·y, mirk·y (múrki) *adj.* **-ier, -iest. 1.** Dark or gloomy: *the murky recesses of the deserted chapel.* **2.** Heavy and thick with, or as if

SERVANTS OF THE BRAIN
How body movement is controlled by contracting tissues

A muscle is tissue that moves by contracting and relaxing. Most muscles work in pairs – one contracts to move a bone or organ at the same time as its paired muscle relaxes. To reverse the movement, the second muscle contracts and the first relaxes.

There are about 640 muscles in the body and they are of three different types: striated, smooth, and cardiac. Striated (or striped, or skeletal) muscles are made up of parallel bundles of fibres attached to bones by connective tissue known as tendons. Many of them move under the conscious control of the brain and are known as voluntary muscles.

Smooth (or visceral) muscles are found in the walls of the tubes and cavities of the body, such as the intestines, the stomach, and the blood vessels. One type of smooth muscle, found in the digestive tract, produces slow waves of contraction (a process called peristalsis) that propel food along. Another type of smooth muscle moves rapidly; it is found in the iris and internal muscles of the eye.

Because the nerves stimulating the visceral muscles are part of the autonomic nervous system, these muscles work without conscious effort and are therefore known as involuntary muscles. There is no sensation of movement as they work.

Some organs of the body have a mixture of muscle types. For example, the top of the oesophagus, or gullet, is operated by voluntary muscle, but the lower part is moved by involuntary muscle. When food is swallowed, sensation of its passage ends as it reaches the lower end of the oesophagus. The bladder also has a combination of voluntary and involuntary muscles.

Cardiac muscle is found only in the heart. It resembles skeletal muscle in its structure, but it is not under conscious control.

Muscles need two types of nerve – sensory nerves to carry information from the muscles to the brain, and motor nerves to carry from the brain to the muscles the impulses that make them move.

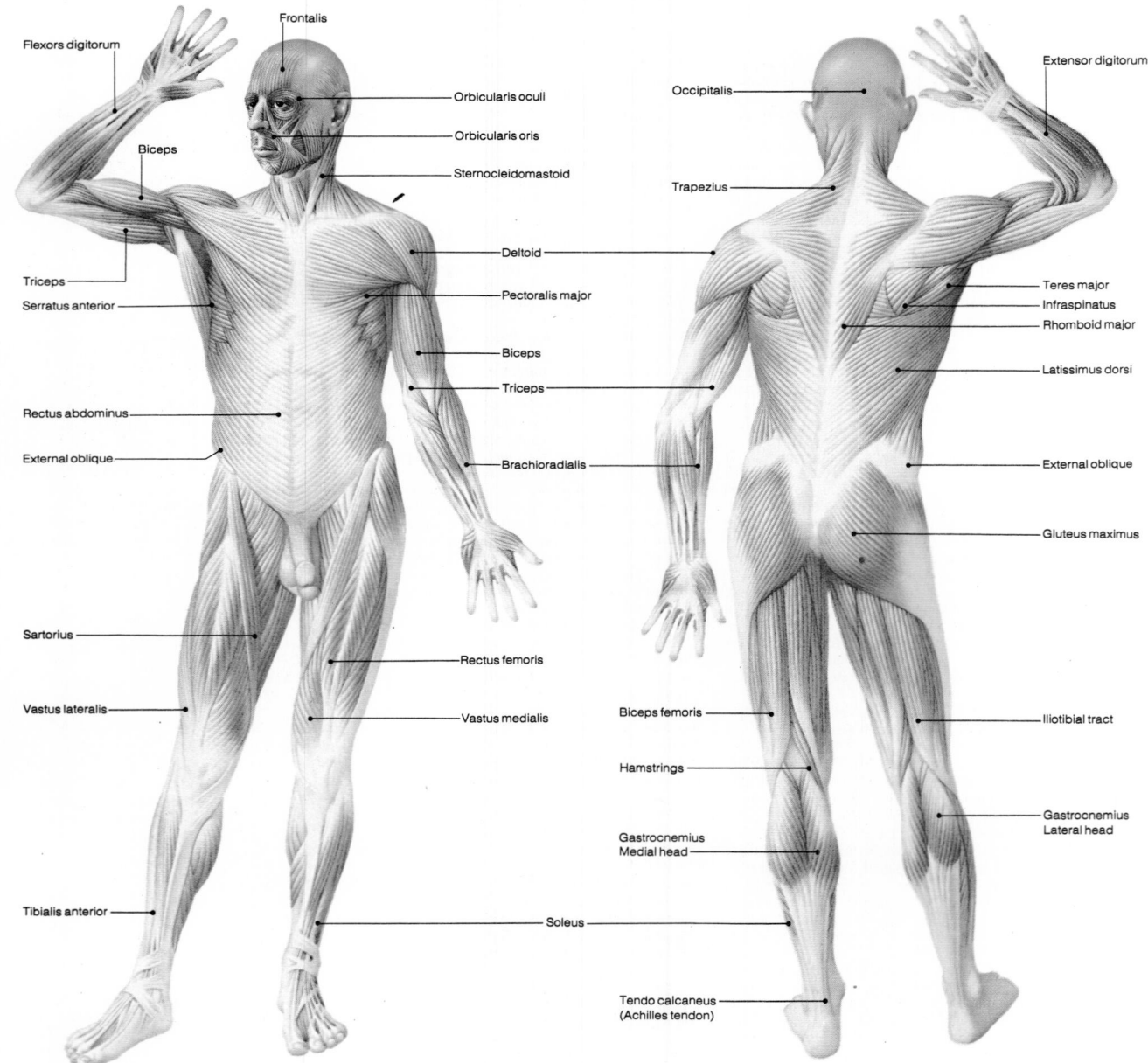

BODY SHAPERS WORKING IN PAIRS *The shape of the body is defined largely by the striated muscles, which form by far the greatest part of the body's muscle tissue. These muscles, of which the major ones are shown above, vary greatly in size – from the gluteus maximus, or buttock muscle, which extends the thigh, to the tiny stapedius, 1.27 millimetres (1/20 inch) long, which controls the stirrup bone of the inner ear. Muscles consume four or five times as much energy as they produce. Their efficiency can increase with training. Because muscles cannot push – they can work only by contraction – most striated muscles are in pairs to move arms, legs, spine, and head. In the upper arm, for example, the biceps contracts to raise the forearm, then relaxes while the triceps contracts to lower the forearm again.*

with, smoke, fog, or mist, for example. —See Synonyms at **dark.** **—murk·i·ly** *adv.* **—murk·i·ness** *n.*

mur·mur (múrmər) *n.* **1.** A low, indistinct, and continuous sound or succession of sounds: *the murmur of the waves.* **2.** An indistinct or muttered complaint. **3.** A low utterance: *a murmur of approval.* **4.** *Medicine.* An abnormal sound, usually in the thoracic cavity, originating from the heart or lungs and detectable by the ear or a device such as a stethoscope.
~*v.* **murmured, -muring, -murs.** —*intr.* **1.** To make a low, continuous, and indistinct sound or succession of sounds. **2.** To complain in low mumbling tones; grumble. —*tr.* To say in a low indistinct voice; utter indistinctly. —See Synonyms at **mutter.** [Middle English *murmure,* from Old French, from Latin *murmur,* rumble, murmur.] **—mur·mur·er** *n.* **—mur·mur·ing·ly** *adv.* **—mur·mur·ous** (-əss) *adj.* **—mur·mur·ous·ly** *adv.*

mur·phy (múrfi) *n., pl.* **-phies.** *Slang.* A potato. [From the Irish surname *Murphy* (the potato was a staple Irish food).]

Murphy's Law *n.* An axiom of engineers and scientists: "If anything can go wrong, it will". [20th century : origin obscure.]

mur·ra, mur·rah (múrrə) *n.* A precious substance, variously conjectured to have been jade, fluorite, or porcelain, obtained by the Romans from Parthia to make cups and bowls. [Latin *murr(h)a,* from Late Greek *morria†.*] **—mur·rine, mur·rhine** (múrrīn, múrrin) *adj.*

mur·rain (múrrin, múrrayn) *n.* **1.** Any highly infectious and malignant disease of cattle, such as anthrax. **2.** *Archaic.* Any pestilence or dire disease. [Middle English *moreyne,* from Old French *morine,* from *morir,* to die, from Vulgar Latin *morīre* (unattested), variant of Latin *morī,* to die.]

Mur·ray (múrri). River of southeast Australia. Flowing from the Australian Alps to Lake Alexandrina, it forms, with its tributaries, the country's main river system.

Murray, Sir James (Augustus Henry) (1837–1915). British philologist and lexicographer. He established his reputation by his article on the English language for the *Encyclopedia Britannica.* His most important work was establishing the general framework of the Oxford English Dictionary, of which he was appointed the editor in 1879.

Murray, Sir Lionel (Len) (1922–). British trade unionist. After studying at the Universities of London and Oxford, he joined the economic department of the Trade Union Congress in 1947, serving as its head from 1954 to 1969. He was Assistant General Secretary of the T.U.C. (1969–73), until he was chosen as its General Secretary. He was knighted in 1981.

mur·rey (múrri) *n. Archaic.* A colour, **mulberry** *(see).* [Middle English *morreye,* from Old French *more,* from Medieval Latin *morātum,* from *morātus,* mulberry-coloured, from Latin *morum,* mulberry.] **—mur·rey** *adj.*

murrhine glass, murrine glass *n.* **1.** Glassware believed to resemble ancient Roman vessels of murra. **2.** Glassware embedded with precious stones, or with coloured metals and glass. [Latin *murr(h)inus,* from *murr(h)a,* MURRA.]

Mur·ry (múrri), **John Middleton** (1889–1957). British literary critic, husband of Katherine Mansfield. He was editor of the *Athenaeum* and founded his own literary review, the *Adelphi* (1923). During World War II he also edited the pacifist journal, *Peace News.* His volumes of criticism include *The Problem of Style* (1922) and *Keats and Shakespeare* (1925).

murther. *Obsolete.* Variant of **murder.**

mus. 1. museum. **2.** music; musical; musician.

Mus. B., Mus. Bac. Bachelor of Music. [Latin *Musicae Baccalaureus.*]

Mus·ca (múskə) *n.* A constellation in the polar region of the Southern Hemisphere near Apus and Carina. [Latin, "the fly".]

mus·ca·dine (múskə-din, -dīn) *n.* **1.** A musk-flavoured grape used to make wine. Also called "scuppernong". [Variant of MUSCATEL.]

mus·cae vo·li·tan·tes (mússee vólli-tánteez, múskee) *pl.n.* Small motes and threads that seem to move about the field of vision, due to the presence of cell fragments or other defects in the vitreous humour and the lens of the eye. [Latin, "fluttering flies".]

mus·ca·rine (múskə-rin, -reen) *n.* A highly toxic organic compound, $C_8H_{19}O_3N$, related to the cholines, and derived from the mushroom *Amanita muscaria.* [New Latin *(Amanita) muscaria,* from Latin *muscārius,* of a fly, from *musca,* a fly.]

mus·cat (múss-kət, -kat) *n.* **1.** Any of various sweet white grapes used for making wine or raisins. **2.** Muscatel. [French, from Provençal *muscat,* "musky" (flavour), from *musc,* MUSK.]

Mus·cat or **Mas·kat** or **Mas·qut** (múss-kət, máss-, -kat). Capital of Oman. Lying on a fine harbour, it was an important port, but it has lately been eclipsed by neighbouring Matrah. Exports include dates, mother-of-pearl, and dried fish, and it has an oil terminal.

Muscat and Oman. See **Oman, Sultanate of.**

mus·ca·tel (múskə-tél) *n.* Also **mus·ca·del** (-dél). **1.** A rich, sweet wine made from muscat grapes. **2.** A muscat grape or raisin. [Middle English *muscadelle,* from Old French *muscadel,* diminutive of MUSCAT.]

mus·cle (múss'l) *n.* **1.** A tissue composed of fibres capable of contracting and relaxing to effect bodily movement. The principal types are **striated muscle** and **smooth muscle,** with **cardiac muscle** *(all of which see)* intermediate between them. **2.** A contractile organ consisting of muscle tissue. **3.** Strength or powerful authority: *Her credentials added muscle to her argument.*
~*v.* **muscled, -cling, -cles.** —*intr. Informal.* To force one's way into a place or situation where one is not wanted. Usually used with *in.* —*tr.* To push (one's way) into a crowded or restricted place or situation: *She muscled her way into the debating chamber.* [French, from Latin *mūsculus,* "little mouse", muscle (from the shape of certain muscles, for example the biceps), from *mūs,* mouse.]

mus·cle-bound (múss'l-bownd) *adj.* **1.** Having stiff, overdeveloped muscles, usually as the result of excessive exercise. **2.** Unable to act flexibly; rigid: *an army too muscle-bound to be effective in a crisis.*

muscle fibre *n.* An elongated, contractile cell having highly striated cytoplasm.

mus·cle·man (múss'l-man) *n., pl.* **-men** (-men). A man with large, highly developed muscles; especially, an aggressive, powerful, or intimidating man.

muscle sense *n.* **Kinaesthesia** *(see).*

mus·co·va·do, mus·ca·va·do (múskə-vaádō) *n.* Unrefined sugar obtained from the juice of sugar cane by evaporation and extraction of the molasses. [Portuguese *(açúcar) mascavado,* unrefined or low quality (sugar), from *mascavar,* to adulterate, depreciate, from Vulgar Latin *minuscapāre* (unattested) : *minus,* less, from *minor,* smaller + *capāre* (unattested), to "bring to a head", cause, from Latin *caput,* head.]

mus·co·vite (múss-kə-vīt, -kō-) *n.* A mineral, the most common form of mica, consisting essentially of hydrous potassium aluminium silicate with hydroxyl and fluorine, $KAl_2(AlSi_3O_{10})(OH,F)_2$. It ranges from colourless or pale yellow to grey and brown, has a pearly lustre, and is used as an insulator. Also called "isinglass", "white mica". [Formerly called *Muscovy* glass.]

Mus·co·vite (múss-kə-vīt, -kō-) *n.* **1.** A native or resident of Moscow or of Muscovy. **2.** *Archaic.* A native or resident of Russia. **—Mus·co·vite** *adj.*

Mus·co·vy (múss-kə-vi, -kō-). **1.** The principality of Moscow (12th–16th centuries). **2.** *Archaic.* Russia.

Muscovy duck *n.* A waterfowl, *Cairina moschata,* found wild from Mexico to Brazil, but domesticated around the world for its succulent flesh. It is greenish-black with heavy red wattles. Also called "Muscovy", "musk duck". [Folk etymology from *musk duck* (by mistaken association with MUSCOVY).]

mus·cu·lar (múskew-lər) *adj.* **1.** Pertaining to or consisting of muscle or muscles. **2.** Accomplished with or involving the use of muscle or muscles: *muscular effort.* **3.** Having strong muscles. [Latin *mūsculus,* MUSCLE.] **—mus·cu·lar·i·ty** (-lárrəti) *n.* **—mus·cu·lar·ly** *adv.*

muscular dystrophy *n.* A chronic, noncontagious, congenital disease, in which complete incapacitation follows gradual but irreversible muscular deterioration.

mus·cu·la·ture (múskewlə-chər, -tewr) *n.* The system of muscles of an animal or a body part. [French, from Latin *mūsculus,* MUSCLE.]

Mus. D., Mus. Doc. Doctor of Music. [Latin *Musicae Doctor.*]

muse (mewz) *v.* **mused, musing, muses.** —*intr.* To ponder or meditate, usually in silence; consider or deliberate at length. Often followed by *over, on,* or *upon*: *She gazed into the distance, musing on human existence.* —*tr. Archaic.* **1.** To meditate on; consider reflectively: *muse the problem.* **2.** To wonder: *"The maiden paused, musing what this might mean."* (S.T. Coleridge).
~*n. Archaic.* A state of musing or deep meditation. [Middle English *musen,* from Old French *muser,* to muse, dawdle, "sniff around", from *mus,* snout, from Medieval Latin *mūsum.*] **—muse·ful** *adj.* **—muse·ful·ly** *adv.*

Muse (mewz) *n.* **1.** *Greek Mythology.* Any of the nine daughters of Mnemosyne and Zeus, each of whom presided over a different art or science. The Muses are Calliope, Clio, Erato, Euterpe, Melpomene, Polyhymnia, Terpsichore, Thalia, and Urania. **2.** *Small* **m.** The spirit or power regarded as inspiring poets, musicians, and artists; a source of inspiration. Often preceded by *the.* [Middle English, from Old French, from Latin *Mūsa,* from Greek *Mousa.*]

mu·sette (mew-zét) *n.* **1.** A small French bagpipe with a soft sound. **2.** A soft, pastoral tune that imitates the sound of a bagpipe. **3.** A kind of dance performed to such a tune. [Middle English, from Old French, from *muser,* to MUSE, dawdle, play the musette.]

mu·se·um (mew-zée-əm) *n. Abbr.* **mus.** A place or building in which works of artistic, historical, and scientific value are cared for and exhibited. [Latin *mūsēum,* library, study, museum, from Greek *mouseion,* "place of the Muses", from *mouseios,* of the Muses, from *Mousa,* a Muse.]

museum piece *n.* **1.** An object of sufficient artistic or historical interest to warrant its inclusion in a museum. **2.** *Informal.* Someone or something considered to be old-fashioned.

Mus·grave (múz-grayv), **Thea** (1928–). British composer. She studied with Nadia Boulanger at the Paris Conservatoire. She has written music of almost every kind, including operas such as *Mary, Queen of Scots* (1976–77).

Musgrave Ranges. Highland along the border of South Australia with Northern Territory, the highest point being Mount Woodroffe (1 514 metres; 4,970 feet). It is a traditional site of Aborigine reservations.

mush[1] (mush) *n.* **1.** Anything thick, soft, and pulpy in texture. **2.** *Informal.* Maudlin sentimentality. [Probably alteration of MASH.]

mush[2] (mōōsh, mush) *interj.* A command given to a team of sledge dogs to start or go faster.
~*intr.v.* **mushed, mushing, mushes.** To travel with a dog sledge.
~*n.* A journey by dog sledge. [Canadian French *mouche!* "run", from *moucher,* to fly, hasten, from French *mouche,* a fly, from Latin *musca.*] **—mush·er** *n.*

mush[3] (mōōsh) *n. British Slang.* A human face. [From MUSH[1].]

mush·room (músh-rōōm, -rōōm) *n.* **1.** Any of various fleshy fruit-

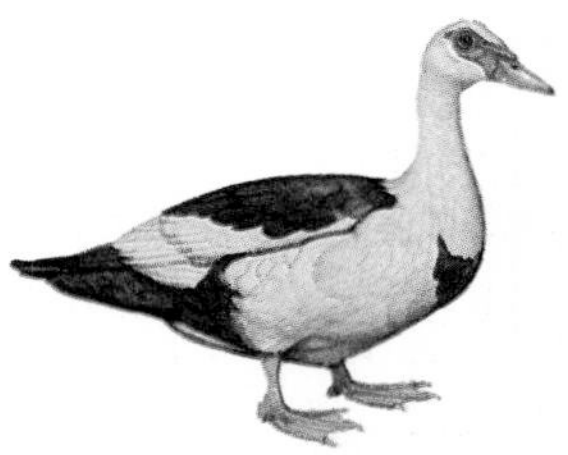

Muscovy duck *Wild flocks of Muscovy ducks flourish along the inland waterways of Brazil. Muscovies are also common ducks in the farmyards and on the tables of Europe.*

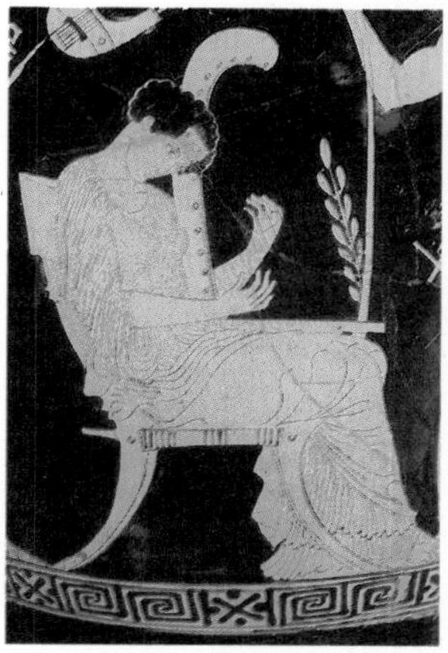

muse *In classical mythology, the muses were deities who gave inspiration to artists, philosophers, and scientists. Terpsichore, the patron muse of dance and song, is shown here on a Greek vase made in about 440* B.C.

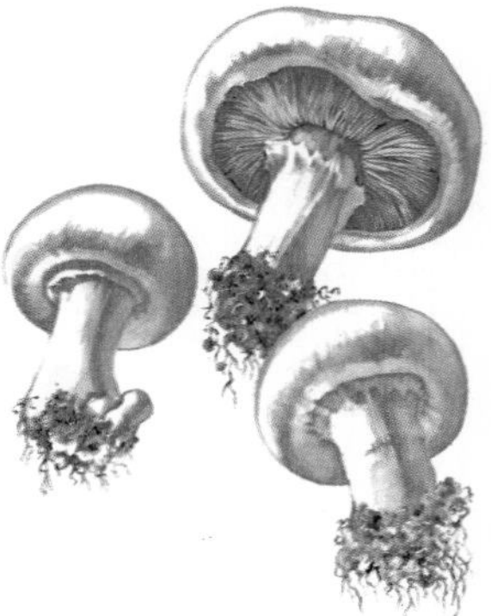

mushroom *The common name for a number of types of wild, edible fungi. They are often abundant in pasture where cattle or horses have grazed. This species is the common field mushroom,* Agaricus campestris.

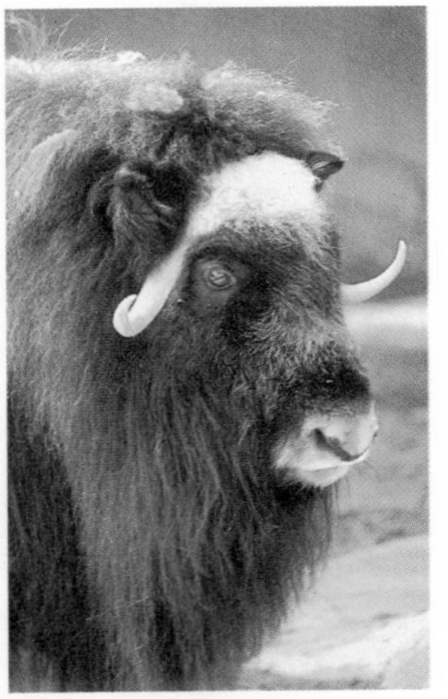

musk ox *Herds of musk oxen roam the northern regions of Canada and Greenland. Both sexes have horns and when the herd is attacked – by wolves, for example – the adults bunch together in a ring around the calves, forming a defensive barricade with their horns. Musk oxen are so called because they have a musky scent; the musk used in perfumes, however, comes from the musk deer.*

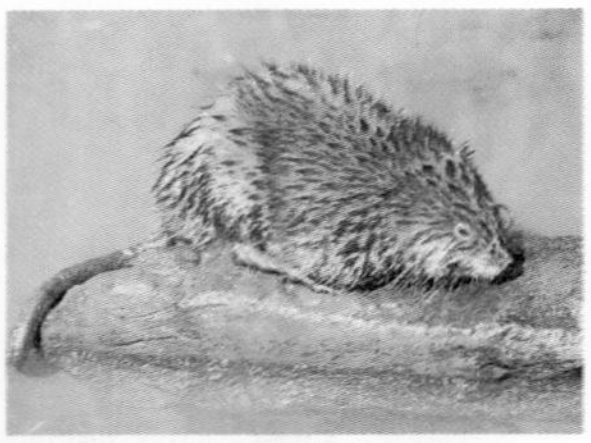

muskrat *This North American rodent lives in marshes, streams, and shallow lakes. Its partially webbed hind feet and its flattened rudder-like tail make it a strong swimmer, and it can remain submerged for up to ten minutes to avoid danger.*

ing bodies produced by fungi of the class Basidiomycetes, characteristically having an umbrella-shaped cap borne on a stalk; especially, any of the edible varieties. **2.** Any of the fungi producing such structures. **3.** Something resembling a mushroom in shape. ~*intr.v.* **mushroomed, -rooming, -rooms. 1.** To multiply, grow, or expand rapidly: *The demonstration mushroomed into a riot.* **2.** To spread out, flatten, or swell into a mushroom-like shape. **3.** To search for and gather mushrooms. [Middle English *musseroun, muscheron,* from Old French *mousseron, moisseron,* from Gallo-Roman *mussiro*† (unattested), agaric.]

mushroom cloud *n.* The cloud of gas, dust, and the like, rising in the shape of a mushroom, following a nuclear explosion.

mush·y (múshi) *adj.* **-ier, -iest. 1.** Like mush; soft and pulpy. **2.** *Informal.* Excessively sentimental. **—mush·i·ly** *adv.* **—mush·i·ness** *n.*

mu·sic (méwzik) *n. Abbr.* **mus. 1.** An art or art form consisting of organised tones that produce a coherent sequence of sounds intended to elicit a pleasurable response in a listener. **2.** Vocal or instrumental sounds having some degree of rhythm, melody, and harmony. **3. a.** A musical composition. **b.** A body of such compositions: *the music of Béla Bartók; French music.* **c.** The written or printed score for a musical composition. **d.** Such scores collectively. **4.** A musical accompaniment. **5.** The study of musicology. **6.** Any aesthetically pleasing or harmonious sound or combination of sounds: *the music of your voice; the music of the wind in the trees.* **7.** *Rare.* A group of musicians: *The Queen's music.* **—face the music.** *Informal.* To accept the consequences, especially of one's own actions. **—music to (someone's) ears.** That which is received with pleasure: *News of her promotion was music to our ears.* [Middle English *musik,* from Old French *musique,* from Latin *mūsica,* from Greek *mousikē (tekhnē),* (art) of the Muses, that is, poetry, literature, and music, for example, from *mousikos,* of the Muses, from *Mousa,* Muse.]

mu·si·cal (méwzik'l) *adj. Abbr.* **mus. 1.** Of, pertaining to, or capable of producing music: *a musical instrument.* **2.** Characteristic of or resembling music; melodious: *a musical tone of voice.* **3.** Set to or accompanied by music: *a musical revue.* **4.** Devoted to or skilled in music.
~*n.* A musical comedy. **—mu·si·cal·ly** *adv.*

musical chairs *n.* A game in which the players walk to music around a row of chairs containing one chair fewer than the number of players. When the music stops, the players rush to sit down, and the one left without a chair is ruled out of the game.

musical comedy *n.* **1.** A play or film in which dialogue is interspersed with songs and dances, usually based upon a rather sketchy plot. **2.** Such plays or films collectively.

musical glasses *pl.n.* An instrument, the **glass harmonica** *(see).*

mu·si·cal·i·ty (méwzi-kál-əti) *n.* **1.** Musical quality. **2.** Skill in the performance of, ability to respond to, or talent for music.

music box *n.* Also **musical box.** A box containing a device, activated by clockwork, which plays tunes when the box is opened.

music centre *n.* A record player, radio, and cassette player combined into one high-fidelity domestic unit.

music drama *n.* **1.** An opera in which the musical and dramatic continuity is sustained, without being interrupted by arias, recitatives, or ensembles, while its text is set to continuously expressive music often based extensively on leitmotifs. **2.** Such operas collectively. See **opera.**

music hall *n. Chiefly British.* **1. a.** Stage entertainment, especially popular in the early 20th century, offering a variety of short acts such as song-and-dance routines, impersonations, and the like. **b.** A theatrical performance of this kind. Also *chiefly U.S.* "vaudeville". **2.** A theatre for such entertainment. **—music-hall** *adj.*

mu·si·cian (mew-zísh'n) *n. Abbr.* **mus.** A person skilled in composing or performing music, especially professionally. [Middle English *musicien,* from Old French, from Latin *mūsica,* MUSIC.] **—mu·si·cian·ly** *adj.*

mu·si·cian·ship (mew-zísh'n-ship) *n.* Skill, taste, and artistry in performing or composing music.

music of the spheres *n.* An inaudible harmony thought by Pythagoras to be produced by the movements of celestial bodies.

mu·si·col·o·gy (méwzi-kólləji) *n.* The historical and scientific study of music. **—mu·si·co·log·i·cal** (-kə-lójik'l) *adj.* **—mu·si·co·log·i·cal·ly** *adv.* **—mu·si·col·o·gist** (-kólləjist) *n.*

music paper *n.* Paper, printed with staves, on which music may be written.

music roll *n.* A roll of paper that is perforated and used in certain mechanical keyboard instruments, such as the player piano.

music stand *n.* A stand that can be raised or lowered, used for holding a musical score.

mus·jid (múss-jid) *n.* A **mosque** *(see).*

musk (musk) *n.* **1.** A greasy secretion with a powerful odour, produced in a glandular sac beneath the skin of the abdomen of the male musk deer. It is used in the manufacture of perfumes. **2.** Any similar secretion of certain other vertebrates, such as the otter or civet. **3.** Any synthetic chemical resembling natural musk in odour or use. **4.** The odour of musk or an odour resembling it. **5.** A plant, *Mimulus moschatus,* which resembles a small **monkey flower** *(see),* formerly cultivated for its musky scent. [Middle English *muske,* from Old French *musc,* from Late Latin *muscus,* from Greek *moskhos,* from Persian *mushk,* probably from Sanskrit *muṣka,* testicle, scrotum (from the scrotum-shaped musk bag of a musk deer), "little mouse", from *mūṣ,* mouse.] **—musk, musk·y** *adj.* **—musk·i·ness** *n.*

musk deer *n.* A small, hornless deer, *Moschus moschiferus,* of central and northeastern Asia. The male secretes musk.

musk duck *n.* **1.** A waterfowl, the **Muscovy duck** *(see).* **2.** A waterfowl, *Biziura lobata,* of Australia. The male has a leathery chin lobe, and emits a musky odour during the breeding season.

mus·keg (múss-keg) *n.* Also **mas·keg** (máss-). In Canada, a swamp or bog formed by an accumulation of sphagnum moss, leaves, and decayed matter resembling peat. [Cree *maskeek,* from Proto-Algonquian *maškyeekwi* (unattested), swamp.]

mus·kel·lunge (músskə-lunj) *n., pl.* **-lunges** or collectively **muskellunge.** Also **mas·ka·longe** (másskə-lonj), **mas·ca·nonge** (másskə-nonj). A large game fish, *Esox masquinongy,* similar to the pike, found in the cooler fresh waters of North America. Also informally called "muskie". [Of Algonquian origin; akin to Algonquian *maskinonge,* "big pike".]

mus·ket (múskit) *n.* A smoothbore shoulder gun used from the late 16th to the 18th century. [French *mousquet,* from Italian *moschetto,* crossbolt, later musket, diminutive of *mosca,* a fly, from Latin *musca.*]

mus·ket·eer (múski-téer) *n.* **1.** Formerly, a soldier armed with a musket; specifically, a member of the French royal household bodyguard in the 17th and 18th centuries. [French *mousquetaire,* from *mousquet,* MUSKET.]

mus·ket·ry (múskitri) *n.* **1.** Muskets collectively. **2.** Musketeers collectively. **3.** The technique of using small arms.

Mus·kho·ge·an, Mus·ko·ge·an (muss-kṓgi-ən) *n.* A North American Indian language family, including Chickasaw, Choctaw, Creek, and Seminole. **—Mus·kho·ge·an, Mus·ko·ge·an** *adj.*

musk mallow *n.* **1.** A plant, *Malva moschata,* native to Europe, having finely divided leaves and pink flowers with a faint scent of musk. **2.** A plant, the **abelmosk** *(see).*

musk·mel·on (músk-mellən) *n.* **1.** Any of several varieties of the melon *Cucumis melo,* such as the cantaloupe, having fruit characterised by a netted rind and flesh with a musky aroma. **2.** The fruit of any of these plants.

musk ox *n.* A large, hoofed mammal, *Ovibos moschatus,* of northern Canada and Greenland, that emits a musky odour. It has a long, dark, shaggy, coat and downward-curving horns.

musk·rat (músk-rat) *n., pl.* **-rats** or collectively **muskrat. 1.** An aquatic rodent, *Ondatra zibethica,* native to North America, having a brown coat that is widely used as a fur. It has partly webbed hind feet, and musk glands under a broad, flat tail. Also called "musquash". **2.** The fur of this rodent. [MUSK + RAT (possibly influenced by Algonquian (Natick) *musquash,* MUSQUASH).]

musk rose *n.* A prickly shrub, *Rosa moschata,* native to the Mediterranean region, having musk-scented white flowers.

musk thistle *n.* A plant, *Carduus nutans,* that has purple, nodding, brushlike flowers which emit a musky fragrance.

musk tree *n.* Any of various small Australasian trees, especially of the genus *Olearia,* having a musky fragrance.

Mus·lim (mo͝oz-lim, múz-, mo͝oss-) *n.* Also **Mus·lem, Mos·lem** (móz-, *also* -lem). **1.** A believer in or adherent of Islam. **2.** A member of the **Nation of Islam** *(see).*
~*adj.* **1.** Of or pertaining to Islam, its adherents, culture, or the like. **2.** Pertaining or belonging to the Nation of Islam. [Arabic *muslim,* "one who surrenders (to God)", active participle of *salama,* to surrender.]

Usage: *Moslem* is the form generally preferred in popular journalism and in popular usage. *Muslim* is preferred by scholars, and by English-speaking adherents of Islam. It is considered the only correct form by members of the Nation of Islam (or "Black Muslims"). *Mohammedan* is offensive to many Muslims, because of the implication of worship of the Prophet, which is forbidden by Islam.

Muslim calendar *n.* The lunar calendar used in Muslim countries reckoning time from July 16, A.D. 622, the day after the Hegira, based on a cycle of 30 years, 19 of which have 354 days each and 11 of which are leap years, having 355 days each.

mus·lin (múzlin) *n.* Any of various fine, diaphanous, plain-weave cotton fabrics, used for dresses, or curtains, for example. [French *mousseline,* from Italian *mussolina,* "cloth of Mosul", from Arabic *mūṣlin,* originally made in *Al-Mawṣil,* in Iraq.]

Mus. M. Master of Music. [Latin *Magister Musicae.*]

mus·quash (múss-kwosh || *U.S. also* -kwawsh) *n.* A muskrat. [Algonquian (Natick).]

muss (muss) *tr.v.* **mussed, mussing, musses.** *Chiefly U.S. Informal.* To make messy or untidy; rumple. Often used with *up.*
~*n.* A state of disorder; a mess. [Perhaps variant of MESS.] **—muss·i·ly** *adv.* **—muss·y** *adj.*

mus·sel (múss'l) *n.* **1. a.** Any of several marine bivalve molluscs, especially *Mytilus edulis,* having a blue-black shell. **b.** The edible flesh of any of these molluscs. **2.** Any of several freshwater bivalve molluscs of the genera *Anodonta,* and *Unio,* whose shells provide mother-of-pearl. [Middle English, Old English *mus(c)le,* from West Germanic *muskul,* from Latin *mūsculus,* "little mouse", muscle, mussel (from its mouselike shape), from *mūs,* mouse.]

Mus·set (mű-sáy), **(Louis Charles) Alfred de** (1810–57). French poet and dramatist, one of the leading poets of the French Romantic movement. He is most famous for the four poems, *Les Nuits* (1835–37), and for his plays, such as *On ne badine pas avec l'amour* and *Lorenzaccio* (1834).

Mus·so·li·ni (mo͝ossə-léeni || *Italian* mo͝ossō-), **Benito** (1883–1945). Italian politician, founder of the Fascist movement and prime minister and dictator of Italy (1922–45). He founded the first *fascio di* *combattimento* at Milan (1919) and two years later, when he was elected to parliament, the National Fascist party was formally established. He was invited by King Victor Emmanuel III to form a government in October, 1922. Opposition parties were suppressed and parliamentary government ended by 1928. In the 1930s Mussolini conducted an expansionist foreign policy, invading Ethiopia (1935) and annexing Albania (1939). The Rome-Berlin axis forged during the Spanish Civil War was confirmed by a formal alliance (1939). He brought Italy into World War II on the side of the Axis powers in June, 1940. He was dismissed by the king and arrested in July, 1943, escaped, and headed a puppet Nazi government in north Italy until April, 1945, when he was captured and executed by Italian partisans.

Mus·sorg·sky or **Mous·sorg·sky** (mŏŏ-sórg-ski; *Russian* mŏŏ-sərk-ski), **Modest Petrovich** (1839–81). Russian composer. His works include the opera *Boris Godunov* (first produced 1874), the piano suite *Pictures at an Exhibition* (1874), and many songs.

Mus·sul·man (múss'l-mən) *n., pl.* **-men** (-mən) or **-mans.** *Archaic.* A Muslim. [Turkish *musulmān,* probably from Arabic *mushmūn,* plural of *muslim,* MUSLIM.]

must[1] (must; *weak form* məst) *v.* Used as an auxiliary followed by an infinitive without *to,* or, in reply to a question or suggestion, with the infinitive understood. It can indicate: **1.** Compulsion or obligation: *When duty calls, you must answer.* **2.** Requirement or prerequisite: *You must register in order to vote.* **3.** Probability, expectation, or supposition: *It must be nearly midnight.* **4.** Inevitability or certainty: *To each of us, death must come.* **5. a.** In the first person, insistence or fixed resolve: *I must finish this tonight.* **b.** In the second and third persons, insistence imputed by the speaker to others: *Have another drink, if you must.* **6.** Unpleasant inevitability. Used as a past or historical present: *The rain was coming down and I must lose my umbrella!* **7.** Imminent departure. Used with *away*: *We must away!*

~n. **1.** A requirement or necessity: *In teaching, patience is a must.* **2.** Something that should without fail be done, seen, or otherwise acted upon: *If you visit Rome, the Vatican is a must.* [Middle English *moste* (past tense), Old English *mōste,* past tense of *mōtan,* to be allowed, from Germanic.]

Usage: The meanings of *must* are traditionally divided into two major groups: "obligation" and "firm likelihood", or "assumption".

When *must* refers to obligation, it can often be paraphrased with *have (got) to,* especially if the obligation is being reported rather than imposed: *Passengers must surrender their tickets at the barrier; The notice says that passengers have (got) to give in their tickets to the person at the barrier.* When *must* refers to assumption (*If you haven't eaten since breakfast, you must be hungry*), it cannot usually be so paraphrased, although there is a tendency in this direction, especially in American English: *Surely you don't mean that! You must be joking/you have to be joking/you've got to be joking.* When *must* refers to obligation, it has two types of negation, which differ in meaning. The contradictory of *I must stop work early* (="I am obliged to stop work early") is *I must not stop work early* (="I am obliged not to stop work early"), which means, in effect, *I must work late.* The contrary of *I must stop work early* is *I don't have to/needn't stop work early* (="I am not obliged to stop work early").

When *must* refers to assumption, its negative form is expressed in standard English with *cannot*: *If you've just eaten a steak, you can't be very hungry.* But in American English, *must not* is frequently used here, too.

must[2] (must) *n.* Mould; mustiness. [Back-formation from MUSTY.]

must[3] (must) *n.* The unfermented or fermenting juice being processed for wine; new wine. [Middle English *must,* Old English *must, moste,* from Latin *mustum,* "new wine", from neuter of *mustus,* new, newborn.]

must[4]. Variant of **musth.**

mustache. *U.S.* Variant of **moustache.**

mus·ta·chi·o (mə-staáshi-ō || -stásh-) *n., pl.* **-chios.** *Often plural.* A moustache, especially a luxuriant one. Usually used humorously. [Spanish *mostaccho* and Italian *mustaccio,* MOUSTACHE.] **—mus·ta·chi·oed** (-ōd) *adj.*

mus·tang (múss-tang) *n.* A wild horse of the North American plains, descended from Spanish stock. [Mexican Spanish *mesten(g)o,* from Spanish, stray (animal), from *mesta,* meeting of owners of stray animals, from Medieval Latin *(animalia) mixta,* wild or stray animals that mixed with and became attached to a grazier's herd, "mixed animals", from Latin *mixtus,* past participle of *miscēre,* to mix.]

mus·tard (mústərd) *n.* **1.** Any of various plants of the genus *Brassica* native to Eurasia, having four-petalled yellow flowers and slender pods. Some species, especially *B. nigra* and *B. alba,* are cultivated for their pungent seeds. **2.** Any of various other plants of the family Cruciferae (or Brassicaceae), such as garlic mustard. **3. a.** Powdered mustard seeds used medicinally, as in mustard plaster. **b.** A condiment consisting of a paste made from powdered mustard seeds mixed with wine, vinegar, or water, and various spices, such as turmeric. **3.** Dark yellow to light olive brown. [Middle English *mustarde,* condiment, later also plant, from Old French *mo(u)starde,* from Common Romance *mosto,* from Latin *mustum,* MUST, "new wine" (because mustard paste was originally made by mixing grape juice with mustard powder).] **—mus·tard** *adj.*

mustard and cress *n.* Seedlings of white mustard and garden cress, eaten together in salads or as a garnish.

mustard gas *n.* An oily, volatile liquid, $(ClCH_2CH_2)_2S$, used in warfare as a gaseous blistering agent. [From its mustard-like odour.]

mustard oil *n.* Any oil obtained from mustard seeds.

mustard plaster *n.* A pastelike mixture of powdered mustard, flour, and water, spread on cloth or paper, and applied in poultice as a counterirritant. Also called "mustard flour", "plaster".

mus·tee (mu-stée, mústee) *n.* Also **mes·tee** (me-stée). **1.** A person one of whose parents is white and the other a quadroon. **2.** Loosely, any person of mixed racial descent. [Spanish *mestizo,* person of mixed parentage.]

mus·ter (mústər) *v.* **-tered, -tering, -ters.** *—tr.* **1.** To summon or assemble (troops, for example). **2.** To collect or gather. Sometimes used with *up*: *to muster arguments; muster up courage.* *—intr.* To assemble or gather: *mustering for inspection.*

~n. **1. a.** A gathering, especially of troops, for service, inspection, review, or roll call. **b.** The persons assembled for such a gathering. **2.** The official roll of men in a military or naval unit. Also called "muster roll". **3.** Any gathering or collection. **4.** A flock of peacocks. **—pass muster.** To be acceptable. [Middle English *mostren,* from Old French *mo(u)strer,* from Latin *monstrāre,* to show, indicate (originally by an omen), from *mōnstrum,* an omen, prodigy, probably from *monēre,* to warn.]

musth, must (must) *n.* A condition of frenzied sexual excitement occurring in the males of certain mammals such as the elephant and camel.

~adj. Designating a mammal in musth. [Urdu, from Persian *mast,* drunk.]

must·y (músti) *adj.* **-ier, -iest.** **1.** Having a stale or mouldy odour or taste. **2.** Hackneyed; dull; antiquated; stale: *musty views on life.* [Variant (influenced by MUST, juice) of obsolete *moisty,* from MOIST.] **—must·i·ly** *adv.* **—must·i·ness** *n.*

mu·ta·ble (méwtə-b'l) *adj.* **1.** Subject to change or alteration. **2.** Prone to frequent change; inconstant; fickle. [Latin *mūtābilis,* from *mūtāre,* to change, MUTATE.] **—mu·ta·bil·i·ty** (-bílləti), **mu·ta·ble·ness** *n.* **—mu·ta·bly** *adv.*

mu·ta·gen (méwtə-jən) *n.* Any agent, including radioactive elements, ultraviolet radiation, and certain chemicals, that causes biological mutation. [MUTA(TION) + -GEN.] **—mu·ta·gen·ic** (-jénnik) *adj.* **—mu·ta·gen·i·cal·ly** *adv.*

mu·tant (méwt'nt) *n. Biology.* **1.** An individual or organism differing from the parental strain or strains as a result of mutation. **2.** A gene that has undergone mutation. [Latin *mūtans* (stem *mūtant-*), changing, participle of *mūtāre,* to change, MUTATE.] **—mu·tant** *adj.*

mu·tate (mew-táyt || méw-tayt) *v.* **-tated, -tating, -tates.** *—tr.* To cause to undergo alteration, especially by mutation. *—intr.* To undergo change by mutation. [Latin *mūtāre* (past stem *mutat-*).] **—mu·ta·tive** (méwtətiv, mew-táytiv) *adj.*

mu·ta·tion (mew-táysh'n) *n.* **1.** The act or process of being altered or changed. **2.** An alteration or change, as in nature, form, or quality. **3.** *Biology.* **a.** Any heritable alteration of the genes or chromosomes of an organism. **b.** A mutant. **4.** *Linguistics.* **a.** The change that is caused in the sound of one vowel by its assimilation to another vowel; especially, **umlaut** *(see).* **b.** In Celtic languages, a change in the initial consonant of a word or morpheme based upon the phonetic nature of the word preceding it or upon its gender or syntactic function. [Middle English *mutacioun,* from Old French *mutation,* from Latin *mūtātiō* (stem *mūtātiōn-*), from *mūtāre,* to change, MUTATE.] **—mu·ta·tion·al** *adj.* **—mu·ta·tion·al·ly** *adv.*

mu·ta·tis mu·tan·dis (mew-taátiss məw-tándiss, mŏŏ-, -táytiss) *Abbr.* **m.m.** *Latin.* The necessary changes having been made; substituting new terms.

mutch (much) *n.* In Scotland, a linen cap worn by children or women. [Middle English, from Middle Dutch *mutse,* from Medieval Latin *almucia,* AMICE.]

mutch·kin (múchkin) *n. Scottish.* A unit of liquid measure equal to approximately one pint. [Middle English (Scottish) *muchekyn,* from obsolete Dutch *mudseken,* diminutive of *mudde,* bushel, from Latin *modius.*]

mute (mewt) *adj.* **muter, mutest.** **1. a.** Refraining from producing speech or vocal sound. **b.** Not expressed in speech in speech or vocal sound: *a mute agreement.* **2. a.** Unable to speak; dumb. **b.** Unable to vocalise, as certain animals are. **3.** *Law.* Refusing, as a defendant, to plead either guilty or not guilty when under arraignment. Used chiefly in the phrase *stand mute.* **4.** *Phonetics.* Not pronounced; silent, as is the *e* in *house.* —See Synonyms at **dumb.**

~n. **1.** A person incapable of speech; especially, one both deaf and mute. **2.** *Law.* A defendant who refuses to plead either guilty or not guilty when under arraignment. **3.** *Music.* Any of various devices used to muffle or soften the tone of a musical instrument. **4.** *Phonetics.* **a.** A silent or unpronounced letter. **b.** A plosive; a stop. **5.** One who acts in a dumb show. **6.** Formerly, one hired to mourn at a funeral.

~tr.v. **muted, muting, mutes.** **1.** To muffle or soften the sound of (a musical instrument, for example). **2.** To soften the tone, colour, shade, or hue of. **3.** To lessen the intensity of: *muted criticism.* [Middle English *muet,* from Old French, diminutive of *mu,* mute, from Latin *mūtus,* silent, dumb.] **—mute·ly** *adv.* **—mute·ness** *n.*

mute[2] *v.* **muted, muting, mutes.** *—tr.* To discharge (faeces). Used of a bird. *—intr.* To discharge faeces. Used of a bird. [Middle English, from Old French *meutir, esmeutir,* from Frankish *smeltjan* (unattested), to SMELT.]

mute swan *n.* A white Eurasian swan, *Cygnus olor,* with an orange bill and a curved neck.

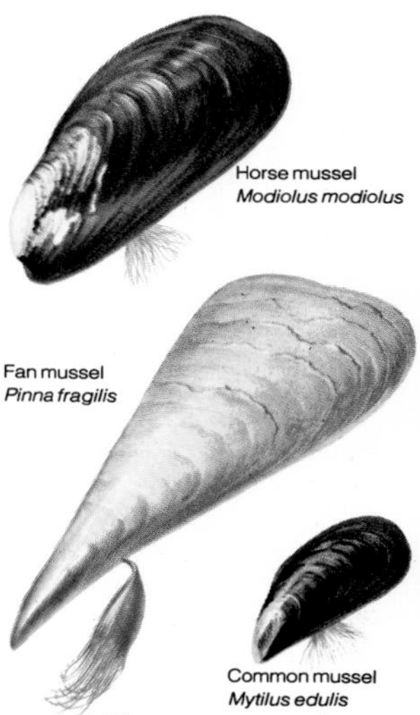
Horse mussel
Modiolus modiolus
Fan mussel
Pinna fragilis
Common mussel
Mytilus edulis

mussel *The common mussel is found along the shores and estuaries of the northern Atlantic. It may grow as long as 100 millimetres (4 inches). Mussels are usually edible but may be unsafe in polluted areas because chemicals can build up in their bodies as they filter food particles from the water. The horse mussel and the fan mussel are found in deeper waters of the northern Atlantic and are larger than the common type.*

PRONUNCIATION KEY

a, trap; aa, father; ai, fair; ar, star; aw, lawn; ay, play; b, bb, stab; rubber; ch, church; ck, ticket; d, dd, dead; ladder; e, dress; ee, bee; er, defer; ew, few; ewr, pure; ə, about; ər, letter; f, ff, fife; differ; g, gg, giggle; h, hat; i, kit; ī, price; īr, fire; j, judge; k, kick; l, ll, let; 'l, needle; m, mm, man; n, nn, no; 'n, sudden; ng, thing; o, lot; ō, no; ŏŏ, foot; ōō, shoe; oor, poor; ow, cow; owr, hour; oy, boy; p, pp, pepper; r, rr, red; s, ss, sauce; sh, ship; t, tt, totter; th, thick; th, this; smooth; u, cut; ur, turn; v, vv, valve; w, wet; y, yes; z, zz, zebra; zh, vision; pleasure

IN FOREIGN WORDS:

aN, oN, Saint-Saëns; hl, Llanelli; Hluhluwe; kh, loch; lough; Khaled

STRESS MARK:

ín-sīt, insight; in-sít, incite

mu·ti·late (méwti-layt) *tr.v.* **-lated, -lating, -lates. 1.** To deprive (a person or animal) of a limb or other essential part. **2.** To render imperfect by damaging or excising a part: *to mutilate books.* [Latin *mutilāre*, to cut off, from *mutilus*, maimed.] —**mu·ti·la·tion** (-láysh'n) *n.* —**mu·ti·la·tive** (-laytiv, -lōtiv) *adj.* —**mu·ti·la·tor** *n.*

mu·ti·neer (méwti-neér) *n.* A person, especially a soldier or sailor, who takes part in a mutiny. [Obsolete French *mutinier*, from Old French *mutin*, MUTINY.]

mu·ti·nous (méwtinəss) *adj.* **1.** Pertaining to, engaged in, or disposed towards mutiny. **2.** Rebellious; unruly; disaffected. —See Synonyms at **insubordinate.** [From obsolete *mutine*, MUTINY.] —**mu·ti·nous·ly** *adv.* —**mu·ti·nous·ness** *n.*

mu·ti·ny (méwtini) *n., pl.* **-nies.** Open rebellion against constituted authority; especially, rebellion of sailors or soldiers against superior officers. See Synonyms at **rebellion.**
~*intr.v.* **mutinied, -nying, -nies.** To rebel by engaging in or as if in a mutiny. [From obsolete *mutine*, mutiny, from Old French *mutin*, rebellious, rebellion, from *muete*, revolt, "movement", from Vulgar Latin *movita* (unattested), from Latin *movēre*, to move.]

mut·ism (méwtiz'm) *n.* **1.** The condition of being unable to speak. **2.** *Psychology.* A condition resulting in a refusal to speak.

mutt (mut) *n. Chiefly U.S. Slang.* **1.** A mongrel dog. **2.** A fool. [Shortened from MUTTONHEAD.]

mut·ter (múttər) *v.* **-tered, -tering, -ters.** —*intr.* **1.** To speak indistinctly in low tones. **2.** To complain or grumble morosely. —*tr.* To utter or say in low, indistinct tones.
~*n.* A low, indistinct uttering or utterance, often of discontent. [Middle English *muteren*, akin to Old Norse *mudhla*.] —**mut·ter·er** *n.* —**mut·ter·ing** *n.*
　　Synonyms: *mutter, mumble, murmur.*

mut·ton (mútt'n) *n.* The flesh of fully grown sheep. —**dead as mutton.** Absolutely dead. —**mutton dressed as lamb.** An old or older person attempting to look young, usually by dressing in an inappropriately youthful style. [Middle English *moto(u)n*, from Old French *moton*, sheep, from Medieval Latin *multō* (stem *multōn-*).]

mutton bird *n. Australian.* Any of various petrels with dark plumage and greyish underparts.

mutton chop *n.* **1.** A thick chop cut from the loin section of mutton. **2.** *Plural.* Side whiskers shaped like chops of meat. Also called "mutton-chop whiskers".

mut·ton·head (mútt'n-hed) *n. Slang.* A stupid person. [From the stupidity of sheep.] —**mut·ton·head·ed** (-heddid) *adj.*

mu·tu·al (méw-choo-əl, -tew-) *adj.* **1.** Having the same relationship each to the other: *mutual friends.* **2.** Directed and received in equal amount. **3.** Possessed in common: *mutual interests.* [Middle English *mutuall*, from Old French *mutuel*, from Latin *mūtuus*, exchanged, reciprocal, mutual.] —**mu·tu·al·i·ty** (-ál-əti) *n.* —**mu·tu·al·ly** *adv.*
　　Usage: *Mutual* is often used in the general sense of "common" (*We all had a mutual interest in getting a decision made*), but this usage is criticised by purists, who feel that the word should be restricted to what only two people do, feel, or represent to each other. Thus, when two people have a *mutual distrust*, each distrusts the other in like manner. As a consequence, in strict usage a phrase such as *a mutual distrust of each other* is felt to be repetitive.

mutual fund *n. U.S.* **A unit trust** (see).

mutual inductance *n. Abbr.* **M** *Physics.* **1.** The ratio expressed by the flux linking one circuit with a neighbouring circuit divided by the current in the neighbouring circuit. **2.** The ratio expressed by the electromotive force induced in a circuit by a neighbouring circuit divided by the corresponding change of current in the neighbouring circuit. See **inductance.**

mutual induction *n. Physics.* Electromagnetic induction in which electromotive force in one circuit is produced by a changing current in a neighbouring circuit.

mutual insurance *n.* An insurance system in which the insured persons become company members, each paying specific amounts into a common fund from which members are entitled to protection and compensation in case of loss.

mu·tu·al·ise, mu·tu·al·ize (méw-choo-ə-līz, -tew-) *tr.v.* **-ised, -ising, -ises. 1.** To make mutual. **2.** To set up or reorganise (a business) as a cooperative.

mu·tu·al·ism (méw-choo-ə-liz'm, -tew-) *n. Biology.* Any association between two or more organisms, in which all benefit. See **symbiosis.**

muu·muu (mṓo-mṓo) *n.* A long, loose dress that hangs free from the shoulders. [Hawaiian *mu'u mu'u*.]

Muy·bridge (míbrij), **Eadweard,** born Edward James Muggeridge (1830–1904). English photographer. His reputation rests on his experiments in photographing moving objects, especially horses. His *zoöpraxiscope*, patented in 1881, projected animated figures onto a screen and was the forerunner of cinematic photography.

Mu·zak (méwzak) *n.* **1.** A trademark for a system of recorded light music played as a soothing or pleasant background in factories, shops, or airports, for example. **2.** *Small* **m.** Any bland, mediocre background music. Usually used derogatorily.

mu·zhik, mou·jik, mu·jik (mṓozhik; *Russian* mōo‑zhéek) *n.* A peasant in tsarist Russia. [Russian *muzhik*, a peasant, diminutive of *muzh*, man, from Old Church Slavonic *mǫzhi*.]

Mu·zo·re·wa (mṓozzə-ráy-wə), **Bishop Abel (Tendekayi)** (1925–). Black Zimbabwean (formerly Rhodesian) politician, generally considered a moderate voice during the black-white conflict

of the 1970s. He was prime minister for some months before the transfer of power to the black majority.

muz·zle (múzz'l) *n.* **1.** The forward, projecting part of the head, including the jaws and nose, of certain animals. **2.** A leather or wire device fitted over an animal's snout to prevent biting and eating. **3.** The forward, discharging end of the barrel of a firearm.
~*tr.v.* **muzzled, -zling, -zles. 1.** To put a muzzle on (an animal). **2. a.** To restrain (a person) from expressing opinions. **b.** To prevent (views, for example) from being expressed. [Middle English *mosel, musell,* from Old French *musel,* from Gallo-Roman *mūsellum* (unattested), diminutive of Late Latin *mūsum,* snout.] —**muz·zler** *n.*

muz·zle·load·er (múzz'l-lōdər) *n.* A firearm loaded through the muzzle. —**muz·zle·load·ing** *adj.*

muz·zy (múzzi) *adj.* **-zier, -ziest.** *Informal.* **1.** Muddled; confused. **2.** Blurred; indistinct. [18th century : origin obscure.] —**muz·zi·ly** *adv.* —**muz·zi·ness** *n.*

mV millivolt.

MV 1. megavolt. **2.** motor vessel.

M.V. 1. motor vessel. **2.** muzzle velocity.

MVD, M.V.D. 1. Ministry of Internal Affairs (Russian *Ministyerstvo Vnutryennikh Dyel*), a former administrative branch of the Soviet government functioning, from 1946, as a successor to the NKVD. In 1954 the KGB took over the secret police functions of the MVD, and it was disbanded in 1960.

mW milliwatt.

MW, M.W. 1. medium wave. **2.** megawatt.

Mx *Physics.* maxwell.

my (mī. *There is a weak form* mi, mə, *used in standard speech only in a few set phrases.*) The possessive form of the pronoun I. **1.** Used attributively to indicate possession, agency, or reception of an action by the speaker: *my wallet; pursuing my tasks; suffered my first rebuff.* See Usage note at **me. 2.** Used preceding various forms of polite, affectionate, or familiar address: *my lady; my dear Dr. Mitchell; my good man.* **3.** Used in various interjectional phrases: *My word! My goodness!*
~*interj.* Used as an exclamation of surprise, pleasure, or dismay. [Middle English *my, mi, min,* Old English *mīn.*]

my–. Variant of **myo-.**

my·al·gi·a (mī-ál-ji-ə) *n. Pathology.* Muscular pain. [New Latin : MY(O)- + -ALGIA.]

my·all¹ (mí-awl) *n.* Any of various Australian acacias with hard wood, used for fences. [From *maiāl*, native Australian name.]

myall² *n. Australian.* An Aborigine living in a traditional way, outside white civilisation. [From a native Australian language.]

myasis. Variant of **myiasis.**

my·as·the·ni·a (mí-əss-théeni-ə, -ass-) *n.* Abnormal muscular weakness or fatigue. [New Latin : MY(O)- + ASTHENIA.] —**my·as·then·ic** (-thénnik) *adj.*

myc. mycological; mycology.

my·ce·li·um (mī-sée-li-əm) *n., pl.* **-lia** (-li-ə). The vegetative part of a fungus, consisting of a mass of branching, threadlike filaments called hyphae. [New Latin, from Greek *mukēs,* fungus + *-elium,* as in *epithelium.*] —**my·ce·li·al, my·ce·loid** (mí-si-loyd) *adj.*

My·ce·nae (mī-séenee, -séeni). City of ancient Greece, in the northeast Peloponnese. It flourished from *c.* 1600 to 1200 B.C., as a centre of Mycenaean civilisation, and was the seat of king Agamemnon. Excavations begun by Heinrich Schliemann in the late 19th century revealed the noted Lion Gate and treasure-filled tombs.

My·ce·nae·an (mí-si-née-ən) *adj.* Of, pertaining to, or designating the Aegean civilisation that spread its influence from Mycenae to many parts of the Mediterranean region from about 1400 B.C. to 1150 B.C. —**My·ce·nae·an** *n.*

Mycenaean Greek *n.* The early East Greek dialect of the Mycenaeans, attested in documents in Linear B script.

—**mycete** *n. comb. form.* Indicates a member of a specified class of fungi; for example, **basidiomycete.** [New Latin *-mycetes* (class), from Greek *mukētes,* plural of *mukēs,* fungus.]

my·ce·to·ma (mí-si-tṓ-mə) *n., pl.* **-mas** or **-mata** (-mətə). **1.** A chronic fungous infection usually affecting the foot, characterised by nodules that discharge oily pus. **2.** A mycetoma nodule. [New Latin : Greek *mukētes,* fungi (see **-mycete**) + -OMA.] —**my·ce·tom·a·tous** (-tómmətəss, -tṓmə-) *adj.*

my·ce·to·zo·an (mī-séetə-zṓ-ən) *n.* **A slime mould** (see).
~*adj.* Of or pertaining to slime moulds. [New Latin *Mycetozoa,* "fungus-animals" (formerly classed in the animal kingdom) : Greek *mukētes,* fungi (see **-mycete**) + -ZOA.]

—**mycin** *n. comb. form.* Indicates derivation of a substance from bacteria or fungi; for example, **streptomycin.** [MYC(O)- + -IN.]

myco-, myc– *comb. form.* Indicates fungus; for example, **mycelium, mycology.** [New Latin, from Greek *mukēs,* fungus.]

my·co·bac·te·ri·um (mí-kōbak-téer-i-əm) *n., pl.* **-teria** (-téer-i-ə). Any slender, rod-shaped bacterium of the genus *Mycobacterium,* which includes the bacterium that causes tuberculosis.

mycol. mycological; mycology.

my·col·o·gy (mī-kóllə̣ji) *n. Abbr.* **myc., mycol. 1.** The branch of botany that deals with fungi. **2.** The fungi native to a region. [New Latin *mycologia* : MYCO- + -LOGY.] —**my·co·log·ic** (míkə-lójik), **my·co·log·i·cal** *adj.* —**my·col·o·gist** (-kóllə̣jist) *n.*

my·cor·rhi·za, my·co·rhi·za (míkə-rízə) *n., pl.* **-zae** (-zee) or **-zas.** *Botany.* The symbiotic association of the mycelium of a fungus with the roots of certain plants, such as conifers or orchids. [New Latin : MYCO- + Greek *rhiza,* a root.] —**my·cor·rhi·zal** *adj.*

my·co·sis (mī-kṓ-siss) *n., pl.* **-ses** (-seez). **1.** A fungous growth in the body. **2.** A disease caused by a fungous growth. [New Latin : MYC(O)- + -OSIS.]

my·co·tox·in (mī̆kō-tóksin) *n.* Any poisonous substance produced by a fungus.

my·dri·a·sis (mi-drī́-ə-siss, mī-) *n.* Prolonged and abnormal dilatation of the pupil of the eye as a result of disease or a drug. [Latin, from Greek *mudriasis†.*]

myd·ri·at·ic (míddri-áttik) *n.* A drug that produces dilatation of the pupils. [From MYDRIASIS.] —**myd·ri·at·ic** *adj.*

myel–, myelo– *comb. form.* Indicates the spinal cord or bone marrow; for example, **myelencephalon, myelitis.** [New Latin, from Greek *muelos,* marrow, from *mus,* muscle.]

my·e·len·ceph·a·lon (mī̆-ilen-séffə-lon) *n.* The rear part of the embryonic hindbrain from which the medulla oblongata develops. —**my·e·len·ce·phal·ic** (-sə-fál-ik) *adj.*

my·e·lin (mī́-i-lin) *n.* Also **my·e·line** (-lin, -leen). **1.** A white, fatty material encasing some nerve fibres. Also called "medullary sheath". **2.** One of several fatlike substances found in body tissues. [MYEL- + -IN.] —**my·e·lin·ic** (-línnik) *adj.*

my·e·li·nat·ed (mī́-ili-naytid) *adj.* Having a myelin sheath; medullated. Said of nerves.

my·e·li·tis (mī́-i-lītiss) *n.* Inflammation of the spinal column or bone marrow. [New Latin : MYEL- + -ITIS.]

my·e·loid (mī́-i-loyd) *adj.* **1.** Of, related to, or derived from bone marrow. **2.** Of or pertaining to the spinal cord. [MYEL- + -OID.]

my·e·lo·ma (mī́-i-lṓ-mə) *n., pl.* **-mas** or **-mata** (-mətə). A malignant tumour of the bone marrow. [New Latin : MYEL- + -OMA.] —**my·e·lo·ma·toid** *adj.*

my·ia·sis (mī́-ə-siss, mī-í-ə-siss) *n.* Also **my·a·sis** (mī́-ə-siss). *Pathology.* Infestation of human tissue by fly maggots or a disease resulting from it. [New Latin : Greek *muia, mua,* fly + -IASIS.]

my·lo·nite (mílə-nīt) *n.* A fine-grained laminated rock formed along zones of extensive crustal dislocation. [Greek *mulōn,* mill, from *mulē, mulos,* mill, millstone + -ITE.]

my·na, my·nah, mi·na (mī́nə) *n.* Any of various birds of the family Sturnidae, of southeastern Asia. They are blue-black to dark brown with yellow bills. Certain species can mimic human speech. Also called "myna bird". [Hindi *mainā,* from Sanskrit *madana.*]

myn·heer (mə-neér) *n.* **1.** *Often capital* **M.** The Dutch title of courtesy and respect equivalent to the English *sir* or *Mr.* **2.** *Informal.* A Dutchman. [Dutch *mynheer,* obsolete variant of *mijnheer,* "my lord" : *mijn,* my, from Middle Dutch *mijni* + *heer,* lord, sir, master, from Middle Dutch.]

myo–, my– *comb. form.* Indicates muscle; for example, **myograph, myasthenia.** [New Latin, from Greek *mus,* muscle.]

my·o·car·di·al infarction (mī́-ō-kárdi-əl) *n.* Death of a section of heart muscle that occurs when its blood supply is obstructed by coronary thrombosis, characterised by severe pain in the chest.

my·o·car·di·o·graph (mī́-ō-kárdi-ō-graaf, -ə-, -graf) *n.* An instrument for recording graphically the movement of the heart muscle.

my·o·car·di·tis (mī́-ō-kaar-dítiss) *n.* Inflammation of the myocardium. [MYOCARD(IUM) + -ITIS.]

my·o·car·di·um (mī́-ō-kárdi-əm) *n.* The muscle tissue of the heart. [New Latin : MYO- + Greek *kardia,* heart.] —**my·o·car·di·al** *adj.*

my·o·gen·ic (mī́-ō-jénnik) *adj.* Also **my·o·ge·net·ic** (-jə-néttik). **1.** Giving rise to muscle tissue. **2.** Of muscular origin. [MYO- + -GENIC.]

my·o·glo·bin (mī́-ō-glṓbin) *n.* The form of haemoglobin found in muscle fibres, having a greater affinity for oxygen than blood haemoglobin.

my·o·graph (mī́-ō-graaf, -ə-, -graf) *n.* An instrument that records muscular contractions by means of tracings *(myograms).* [MYO- + -GRAPH.]

my·ol·o·gy (mī-óllǝji) *n.* The scientific study of muscles. —**my·o·log·ic** (mī-ə-lójik) *adj.* —**my·ol·o·gist** (mī-óllǝjist) *n.*

my·o·ma (mī́-ō-mə) *n., pl.* **-mas** or **-mata** (-mətə). A benign tumour composed of muscle tissue. [MY(O)- + -OMA.] —**my·om·a·tous** (-ómmətəss, -ṓmǝtəss) *adj.*

my·ope (mī́-ōp) *n.* One who has myopia. [French, from Late Latin *myops,* myopic, from Greek *muōps.* See myopia.]

my·o·pi·a (mī-ṓpi-ə) *n.* **1.** *Pathology.* A visual defect in which distant objects appear blurred because their images are focussed in front of the retina rather than on it; shortsightedness. Compare **hypermetropia. 2.** Mental shortsightedness or lack of discernment in thinking or planning. [New Latin, from Greek *muōpia,* from *muōps,* myopic, "closing or contracting the eyes" : *muein,* to close + *ōps,* eye.] —**my·op·ic** (mī-óppik) *adj.* —**my·op·i·cal·ly** *adv.*

my·o·sin (mī́-ə-sin) *n.* A common protein in muscle; with **actin** it forms **actomyosin** *(both of which see).* [Greek *muos,* genitive of *mus,* muscle + -IN.]

myosis. *Pathology.* Variant of **miosis.**

my·o·so·tis (mī́-ə-sṓtiss) *n.* Any plant of the genus *Myosotis,* such as the forget-me-not. [New Latin, from Latin *myosotis,* from Greek *muosōtis,* "mouse-ear" (from its furry leaves) : *muos,* genitive of *mus,* mouse + *ous* (stem *ōt-*), ear.]

my·o·to·ni·a (mī́-ə-tṓni-ə) *n. Pathology.* Tonic spasm or temporary muscular rigidity. [MYO- + -TONIA.] —**my·o·ton·ic** (-tónnik) *adj.*

Myr·dal (mūr-daal), **Gunnar** (1898–). Swedish economist and sociologist. He is chiefly famous for *Rich Lands and Poor Lands* (1957), *Asian Drama* (1968), and *The Challenge of World Poverty* (1970). He was awarded the Nobel prize in economics in 1974.

myria– *comb. form.* Indicates: A very large or countless number;

for example, **myriapod.** [Greek *murios,* countless, and its plural *murioi,* ten thousand.]

myr·i·ad (mírri-əd) *adj.* **1.** Amounting to a very large, indefinite number. **2.** Highly varied. ~*n.* **1.** *Archaic.* Ten thousand. **2.** A vast number; a great multitude. [Late Latin *mȳrias* (stem *mȳriad-*), from Greek *murias,* from *murios,* countless, and its plural *murioi,* ten thousand.]

myr·i·a·pod (mírri-ə-pod) *n.* Any of a class of arthropods, such as the centipedes, having a distinct head, one pair of antennae, and many segments bearing legs. [New Latin *myriapoda* : MYRIA- + -POD.] —**myr·i·ap·o·dan** (-áppədən) *adj. & n.* —**myr·i·ap·o·dous** (-áppədəss) *adj.*

my·ris·tic acid (mi-rístik, mī-) *n.* An organic compound, $CH_3(CH_2)_{12}COOH$, occurring in animal and vegetable fats. It is used in cosmetics and flavourings. [Greek *muristikos,* fragrant, from *muron,* perfume.]

myrmeco– *comb. form.* Indicates ant; for example, **myrmecophile.** [Greek, from *murmēx,* ant.]

myr·me·col·o·gy (múrmi-kóllǝji) *n.* The study of ants. [MYRMECO- + -LOGY.] —**myr·me·co·log·i·cal** (-kǝ-lójik'l) *adj.* —**myr·me·col·o·gist** (-kóllǝjist) *n.*

myr·me·coph·a·gous (múrmi-kóffǝgǝss) *adj.* **1.** Feeding on ants. **2.** Adapted for eating ants. Said, for example, of jaws. [MYRMECO- + -PHAGOUS.]

myr·me·co·phile (múrmi-kō-fīl) *n.* Any organism that habitually shares the nest of an ant colony. [MYRMECO- + -PHILE.] —**myr·me·coph·i·lous** (-kóffilǝss) *adj.* —**myr·me·coph·i·ly** (-kóffili) *n.*

myr·mi·don (múrmi-don, -dən) *n.* A faithful follower who carries out orders without question. [After MYRMIDON.]

Myr·mi·don (múrmi-don, -dən) *n.* One of a legendary Greek warrior people of ancient Thessaly who followed their king Achilles on the expedition against Troy. —**Myr·mi·don** *adj.*

my·rob·a·lan (mī-róbbǝlǝn, mi-) *n.* **1.** A tree, *Prunus cerasifera,* native to Asia, bearing edible red or yellow fruit. Also called "cherry plum". **2.** A tree, the **Indian almond** *(see).* **3.** The fruit of either of these trees. [Old French *mirobolan,* from Latin, from Greek *murobalanos* : *muron,* perfume, unguent + *balanos,* acorn, date.]

myrrh (mur) *n.* **1.** An aromatic gum resin obtained from several trees and shrubs of the genus *Commiphora,* of India, Arabia, and eastern Africa. It is used in perfume and incense, and was one of the gifts of the Magi to the infant Jesus. **2.** Any shrub or tree that exudes such a gum resin. **3.** A plant, **sweet cicely** *(see).* [Middle English *myrre,* Old English *myrrha,* from Common Germanic *murra* (unattested), from Latin *myrrha,* from Greek *murrha,* perhaps from Semitic, akin to Arabic *murr.*]

myr·tle (múrt'l) *n.* **1.** Any of several evergreen shrubs or trees of the genus *Myrtus;* especially, *M. communis,* an aromatic shrub native to the Mediterranean region. **2.** Any of various other plants or shrubs, such as the **crape myrtle** and the **bog myrtle** *(both of which see).* **3.** *U.S.* A plant, the **periwinkle** *(see).* [Middle English *mirtille,* from Old French, from Medieval Latin *myrtillus,* diminutive of Latin *myrtus,* from Greek *murtos†.*]

my·self (mī-sélf, *also* mi-, mə-) *pron.* A specialised form of the first person singular pronoun. It is used: **1.** As a reflexive pronoun, forming the direct or indirect object of a verb or the object of a preposition: *hurt myself; give myself time; talk to myself.* **2.** For emphasis, after *I: I myself wasn't certain.* **3.** As an emphasising substitute: *Myself in debt, I could offer her no assistance.* **4.** Used as an indication of one's real, normal, or healthy condition or identity: *I have not been myself lately.* [Middle English *miself,* alteration of *meself,* Old English *mē selfum* (dative), *mē selfne* (accusative) : *mē, me* + *selfum, selfne,* dative and accusative of *self,* SELF.]

Usage: Myself is often heard in everyday speech as part of a compound subject or object, especially in some regional speech (Irish English, for example): *She asked Jane and myself to go to the meeting.* But the usage has attracted criticism, and in formal speech and in writing, the basic form of the pronoun should be used: *She asked Jane and me to go to the meeting.*

my·so·pho·bi·a (mī-sō-fṓbi-ə) *n.* A pathological fear of dirt, contamination, or faeces. [New Latin : Greek *musos,* uncleanness, defilement + -PHOBIA.] —**my·so·pho·bic** *adj.*

My·sore (mī-sór ‖ -sōr). Former name of Karnataka state, southwest India.

mys·ta·gogue (místə-gog) *n.* **1.** In Mediterranean mystery religions, one who prepared candidates for initiation into the mysteries. **2.** A teacher of religious mysteries; a hierophant. **3.** One who holds or spreads mystical doctrines. [Old French, from Latin *mystagogus,* from Greek *mustagōgos* : *mustēs,* an initiate (see **mystery**) + *agōgos,* leader, from *agein,* to lead.] —**mys·ta·gog·ic** (-gójik) *adj.* —**mys·ta·go·gy** (místə-goji, -gōji) *n.*

mys·te·ri·ous (mi-steéri-əs) *adj.* **1.** Full of mystery; difficult to explain or account for; of obscure origin: *a mysterious light in the sky.* **2.** Beyond human understanding. Used especially in religious contexts: *the mysterious love of God.* **3.** Implying a mystery. **4.** Enigmatic in manner: *She was given to mysterious silences.* [Old French *mystérieux,* from *mystère,* mystery, from Latin *mystērium,* MYSTERY (riddle).] —**mys·te·ri·ous·ly** *adv.* —**mys·te·ri·ous·ness** *n.*

mys·ter·y¹ (místri, místəri) *n., pl.* **-ies. 1.** Anything that arouses curiosity because it is unexplained, inexplicable, or secret. **2.** The quality or air of being unexplained, secret, or unknown. **3.** A piece of fiction dealing with a mystery, especially a puzzling crime. **4.** The behaviour of someone given to secrecy and intrigue: *"He professed to despise all mystery . . . either in a prince or a minister."*

(Jonathan Swift). **5.** *Theology.* A religious truth divinely revealed and unknowable through reason. **6. a.** A Christian rite, such as the Eucharist. **b.** *Often plural.* The elements of the Eucharist. **7.** Any of 15 incidents in the lives of Christ and the Virgin Mary, as commemorated in the 15 divisions of the rosary and considered as subjects of meditation. **8.** A mystery play. **9.** *Often plural.* **a.** Among some ancient Mediterranean peoples, any of certain cults and secret rites to which only initiates were admitted. **b.** The secrets of Freemasonry. [Middle English *misterie, mysterie,* from Latin *mystērium,* from Greek *mustērion,* "secret rites", from *mustēs,* one initiated into secret rites, from *muein,* to initiate, from *muein,* to close the eyes or mouth, hence to keep secret (as in religious initiation).]

mystery² *n., pl.* **-ies.** *Archaic.* A trade or occupation. [Middle English *mysterie, misterie,* from Late Latin *misterium,* variant (by association with *mystērium,* secret rites, mystery) of Latin *ministerium,* service, work, occupation, from *minister,* servant.]

mystery play *n.* A medieval drama based on episodes in the life of Christ. Compare **miracle play.** [Old French *mistere, mystere,* from Latin *mystērium,* religious symbol, MYSTERY.]

mystery tour *n.* A pleasurable excursion, such as a coach trip or train journey, to an unknown destination.

mys·tic (místik) *adj.* **1.** Of or pertaining to the religious mysteries of Greece and Rome or to other occult rites. **2.** Mysteriously symbolic; inspiring a sense of mystery and wonder. **3.** Mystical. *~n.* One who practises or believes in mysticism or a specified form of mysticism. [Middle English *mistik,* from Latin *mysticus,* from Greek *mustikos,* from *mustēs,* an initiated person. See **mystery¹.**]

mys·ti·cal (místik'l) *adj.* **1.** Characteristic of mystics or of the nature of mysticism. **2.** Believing in or practising mysticism. **3.** Mysterious; enigmatic; symbolic. **4.** *Theology.* **a.** Of a nature or import that by virtue of its divinity surpasses understanding: *the mystical vision of God.* **b.** Spiritually symbolic: *a mystical emblem of the Trinity.* **—mys·ti·cal·ly** *adv.* **—mys·ti·cal·ness** *n.*

mys·ti·cete (místtə-seet) *n.* A whalebone whale *(see).* [New Latin *mysticetus,* from Greek *mustikētos,* some kind of whale, supposedly a corruption of *ho mus to kētos,* "the mouse, the whale", that is "that whale which is called 'the mouse' " (the semantic development is obscure) : *mus,* mouse + *kētos,* whale (see **cetacean**).]

mys·ti·cism (místi-siz'm) *n.* **1. a.** A spiritual discipline aiming at union with the divine through deep meditation or trancelike contemplation. **b.** The experience of such communion, as described by mystics. **2.** Any belief in the existence of realities beyond perceptual or intellectual apprehension but central to being and directly accessible by intuition. **—mys·ti·cist** *n. & adj.*

mys·ti·fi·ca·tion (místifi-káysh'n) *n.* **1.** The act or an instance of deliberately or wilfully making something obscure or mysterious. **2.** The fact or condition of being mystified; bafflement.

mys·ti·fy (místi-fī) *tr.v.* **-fied, -fying, -fies. 1.** To awe or perplex; bewilder. **2.** To make obscure or difficult to comprehend. **—See Synonyms at puzzle.** [French *mystifier,* irregularly from *mystère,* mystery, from Latin *mystērium,* MYSTERY.] **—mys·ti·fi·er** *n.* **—mys·ti·fy·ing·ly** *adv.*

mys·tique (mi-stéek) *n.* **1.** An attitude of mystical veneration conferring upon an occupation, person, or thing an awesome and mythical status; the special cult of anything: *the mystique of Eastern music.* **2.** A mystical or philosophical conception used as a guide, especially for a doctrine or cult: *Hegelian mystique.* **3.** A rarefied quality that sets a person or thing apart and apparently beyond the understanding of an outsider. [French, from adjective, "mystic", from Latin *mysticus,* MYSTIC.]

myth (mith) *n.* **1. a.** A traditional story originating in a preliterate society, dealing with supernatural beings, ancestors, or heroes that serve as primordial types in a primitive view of the world. **b.** A body of such stories told among a given people; a mythology: *in Norse myth.* **c.** All such stories collectively. **2.** Any real or fictional story, recurring theme, or character type that appeals to the consciousness of a people by embodying its cultural ideals or by expressing commonly felt emotions: *the myth of rebirth.* **3.** An allegorical story. **4.** Any of the fictions or half-truths forming part of the ideology of a society; a notion based more on tradition or convenience than on fact: *the myth of male superiority.* **5.** Any fictitious or imaginary story, explanation, person, or thing. [New Latin *mythus,* from Late Latin *mythos,* tale, myth, from Greek *muthos†.*]

myth. mythological; mythology.

myth·i·cal (míthik'l) *adj.* Also **myth·ic** (míthik). **1.** Having the nature of a myth. **2.** Existing only in myth: *the mythical unicorn.* **3.** Imaginary; fictitious; fancied. **—myth·i·cal·ly** *adv.*

myth·i·cise, myth·i·cize (míthi-sīz) *tr.v.* **-cised, -cising, -cises. 1.** To turn (a person or event) into myth. **2.** To interpret as a myth. **—myth·i·cism** *n.* **—myth·i·cis·er, myth·i·cist** *n.*

myth·mak·er (míth-maykər) *n.* **1.** One who creates a myth. **2.** One who produces false stories or doctrines, especially as propaganda. Used derogatorily: *combating the inventions of the mythmakers.* **—myth·mak·ing** *n. & adj.*

mytho– *comb. form.* Indicates myth; for example, **mythogenesis.**

my·thog·ra·pher (mi-thóggrəfər) *n.* A recorder or narrator of myths. [Greek *muthographos* : MYTH + -GRAPHER.]

my·thoi. Plural of **mythos.**

mythol. mythological; mythology.

myth·o·log·i·cal (mítha-lójik'l) *adj.* Abbr. **myth., mythol.** Also **myth·o·log·ic** (-lójik). **1.** Of, pertaining to, or celebrated in mythology. **2.** Fabulous; imaginary; mythical. **3.** Story-telling. **—myth·o·log·i·cal·ly** *adv.*

my·thol·o·gise, my·thol·o·gize (mi-thóllə-jīz) *v.* **-gised, -gising, -gises.** *—tr.* To convert into myth; mythicise. *—intr.* **1.** To construct or relate a myth. **2.** To interpret or write about myths or mythology. **—my·thol·o·gis·er** *n.*

my·thol·o·gist (mi-thóllajist) *n.* **1.** A student of mythology. **2.** A writer of myths.

my·thol·o·gy (mi-thóllaji) *n., pl.* **-gies.** Abbr. **myth., mythol. 1. a.** A collection of myths, especially about the origin and history of a people and their deities, ancestors, and heroes. **b.** A body of myths, especially mistaken beliefs, concerning some individual, event, or institution. **2.** The field of scholarship dealing with the systematic collection and study of myths. [French *mythologie,* from Late Latin *mȳthologia,* from Greek *muthologia* : *muthos,* MYTH + *-logia,* -LOGY.]

myth·o·ma·ni·a (míth-ō-máyni-ə, -ə-) *n.* A compulsion to embroider the truth, exaggerate, or tell lies. [MYTH + -MANIA.] **—myth·o·ma·ni·ac** (-máyni-ak) *n. & adj.*

myth·o·poe·ic (míth-ō-pée-ik, -ə-) *adj.* Productive of myths; mythmaking. [Greek *muthopoios,* mythmaker, from *muthopoiein,* to make a myth : *muthos,* MYTH + *poiein,* to make, create.] **—myth·o·poe·ia** (-pée-ə), **myth·o·po·e·sis** (-pō-ée-siss) *n.*

my·thos (míthoss, míthoss) *n., pl.* **mythoi** (míthoy, míthoy). **1.** Myth. **2.** Mythology. **3.** The pattern of basic values and historical experiences of a people, characteristically transmitted through the arts. **4.** A deliberately fostered cult; a mystique. [Greek *muthos†,* MYTH.]

Myt·i·le·ne (mítti-léeni). *Modern Greek* **Mit·i·li·ni.** **1.** Ancient port on the island of Lesbos in Greece. **2.** A former name for **Lesbos.**

myxo–, myx– *comb. form.* Indicates mucus or mucus-like material; for example, **myxomycete, myxoma, myxocyte.** [New Latin, from Greek *muxa,* mucus, slime.]

myx·o·cyte (mík-sō-sīt, -sə-) *n.* A cell found in mucous tissue. [MYXO- + -CYTE.]

myx·oe·de·ma (mík-si-déemə) *n.* A disease caused by decreased activity of the thyroid gland in adults, and characterised by dry skin, swellings around the lips and nose, mental deterioration, and a subnormal basal metabolic rate. [MYX(O)- + OEDEMA.]

myx·o·ma (mik-sō-mə) *n., pl.* **-mas** or **-mata** (-mətə). A benign tumour composed of connective tissue and mucous elements. [New Latin : MYX(O)- + -OMA.] **—myx·om·a·tous** (-sómmətəss) *adj.*

myx·o·ma·to·sis (míksəmə-tō-siss) *n., pl.* **-ses** (-seez). A highly infectious, usually fatal, viral disease of rabbits characterised by many skin tumours similar to myxomas. [New Latin : MYXOMA + -OSIS.]

myx·o·my·cete (mík-sō-mī-séet, -sə-) *n.* A **slime mould** *(see).* [New Latin *Myxomycetes* (class) : MYXO- + -MYCETE.]

myx·o·vir·us (mík-sō-vīr-əss, -sə-) *n.* Any of a group of RNA-containing viruses that cause such diseases as influenza and mumps.

M·zi·li·ka·zi (m-zílli-gáazi, -káazi) (c. 1800-68). Also **Moselekatze** or **Silkaats.** Founder and chief of the Matabele nation, an offshoot of the Zulu. For nearly half a century his warriors harassed the peoples living in what are now the Transvaal and Zimbabwe.

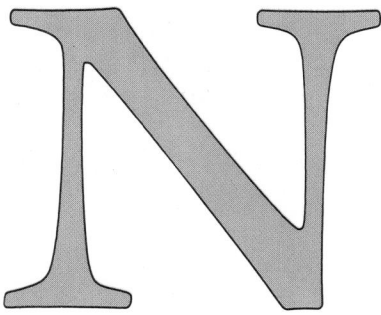

n, N (en) *n., pl.* **n's** or *rare* **ns, N's** or **Ns.** 1. The 14th letter of the modern English alphabet. 2. Any of the speech sounds represented by this letter.

n, N, n., N. *Note:* As an abbreviation or symbol, *n* may be a small or a capital letter, with or without a full stop. Established forms or those generally preferred precede the definition. When no form is given, all four forms are in general use in that sense. 1. **N** Avogadro number. 2. **n.** born [Latin *nātus*]. 3. **n,** *Printing.* en. 4. **n** nano-. 5. **n., N.** *Grammar.* neuter. 6. **n.** neutron. 7. **N** neutron number. 8. **N** newton. 9. **N** The symbol for the element nitrogen. 10. **n, N, n-** *Chemistry.* normal; normality. 11. north; northern. 12. **n.** note. 13. **n.** noun. 14. **N.** November. 15. **n.** number. 16. **n** *Mathematics.* The symbol for an indefinite number.

Na The symbol for the element sodium [Latin *natrium*].

N.A. North America.

NAACP, N.A.A.C.P. National Association for the Advancement of Colored People (in the United States).

NAA·FI, N.A.A.F.I. (náffi) *n. British.* Navy, Army, and Air Force Institutes: 1. An organisation that runs canteens and shops for service personnel and their families. 2. A canteen or shop run by the NAAFI.

naar·tjie, nar·tjie (nárchi, nártzi) *n. South African.* A tangerine or mandarin orange. [Afrikaans, from Tamil *nartei;* akin to Arabic *naranj,* Spanish *naranja.*]

nab (nab) *tr.v.* **nabbed, nabbing, nabs.** *Slang.* 1. To catch in the act of wrongdoing; arrest. 2. To grab; snatch. [Variant of dialectal *nap,* to seize, probably from Scandinavian; akin to KIDNAP.]

Nab·a·tae·an, Nab·a·te·an (nábbə-tée-ən) *n.* 1. A member of a northwestern Arab people whose kingdom, centred on Petra, flourished from the fourth century B.C. to the first century A.D. 2. The Aramaic dialect of this people. —**Nab·a·tae·an** *adj.*

nab·la (náb-lə) *Mathematics.* Del *(see).*

Nab·lus (naáb-ləss, náb-). A city in Samaria, West Bank, under Israeli administration since 1967. It lies near the site of Schechem, a capital of ancient Samaria and an ancient Canaanite city.

na·bob (náy-bob) *n.* 1. A governor in India under the Mogul Empire. 2. In the 18th century, an Englishman who returned from India having acquired a fortune. 3. A man of wealth and prominence. [Portuguese *nababo,* from Urdu, NAWAB.] —**na·bob·er·y** (-əri, nay-bóbbəri), **na·bob·ism** *n.*

Na·bo·kov (nə-bŏkof, nábbə-kof), **Vladimir** (1899–1977). Russian-born U.S. novelist. He is best known for his novel *Lolita* (1958). His later novels include *Pale Fire* (1962) and *Ada* (1969).

na·celle (nə-sél) *n.* A separate streamlined enclosure on some aircraft for sheltering the crew or cargo or housing an engine. [French, "small boat", from Late Latin *nāvicella,* diminutive of *nāvis,* ship.]

na·cre (náykər) *n.* Mother-of-pearl *(see).* [French, from Old Italian *naccara,* mother-of-pearl, from Arabic *naqqārah,* shell.]

na·cre·ous (náykri-əss) *adj.* 1. Consisting of mother-of-pearl. 2. Like mother-of-pearl; pearly.

NAD *n. Biochemistry.* Nicotinamide adenine dinucleotide: a coenzyme that carries hydrogen atoms in electron-transfer reactions.

Na·dar (na-dár, náddaar), **Gaspard Félix Tournachon** (1820–1910). French photographer. Known during his lifetime as a novelist and caricaturist, he is best remembered as a pioneer of photography. He took aerial photographs (1858) from a balloon.

Na-De·ne, Na-Déné (naá-dénnay) *n.* A phylum of North American Indian languages that includes Athapascan, Haida, and Tlingit. [Coined by E. Sapir : Haida *na,* "to dwell", "house" + Athapascan *dene* (unattested), "people".]

Na·der (náydər), **Ralph** (1934–). U.S. lawyer. A pioneer in the field of consumer protection, he founded the Center for the Study of Responsive Law (1969).

NADH *n. Biochemistry.* NAD chemically reduced by the addition of hydrogen.

na·dir (náy-deer, náddeer ‖ -dər) *n.* 1. A point on the celestial sphere diametrically opposite the zenith. 2. The point or time of deepest depression, greatest misfortune, or the like; the lowest point. [Middle English, from Old French, from Arabic *naẓīr as-samt : naẓīr,* opposite + *as-samt,* the ZENITH.]

NADP *n. Biochemistry.* Nicotinamide adenine dinucleotide phosphate: a coenzyme similar in action to NAD.

nae (nay) *adj. Scottish.* No.
~*adv. Scottish.* Not.

nae·vus (née-vəss) *n., pl.* **-vi** (-vī). Also *chiefly U.S.* **nevus.** Any malformation of the skin that is present at birth, such as a strawberry mark or mole; a birthmark. [Latin, birthmark; akin to *(g)natus,* born.]

naff (naff) *Slang. adj.* Of poor or disappointing quality: *a naff present.*
~*intr.v.* **naffed, naffing, naffs.** *Slang.* To go away or cease being an annoyance. Used in the imperative with *off.*

nag¹ (nag) *v.* **nagged, nagging, nags.** —*tr.* 1. To pester or annoy by constant scolding, complaining, or urging. 2. To torment with anxiety, discomfort, or doubt: *nagged by worries.* —*intr.* 1. To scold, complain, or find fault constantly. 2. To be a continuing source of discomfort, anxiety, or annoyance. Often followed by *at: The problem nagged at his mind.* —See Synonyms at **scold.**
~*n.* A person who habitually nags. [From northern dialect *nag, naeg,* to bite, worry at, nag, perhaps from Old Norse *gnaga,* to bite.] —**nag·ger** *n.* —**nag·ging·ly** *adv.*

nag² *n.* 1. **a.** An old or worn-out horse. **b.** *Informal.* Any horse, especially a racehorse, regarded with contempt. 2. *Archaic.* A small saddle horse or pony. [Middle English *nagge†.*]

na·ga·na (nə-gáanə) *n.* Also **n'ga·na.** An often fatal disease of African livestock transmitted by the bite of the tsetse or other flies. [Zulu *u-nakane.*]

Na·ga·sa·ki (naáagə-saáki, nággə-sácki). A port in west Kyushu, Japan. The city was devastated (August 1945) by an atomic bomb at the end of World War II. Rebuilt, it is now a shipbuilding and steel-making centre.

na·gor (náygawr) *n.* The **reedbuck** *(see).* [French, name arbitrarily invented by Buffon, based on earlier *nanguer.*]

Nagy (noj), **Imre** (1896–1958). Hungarian politician. Taken prisoner in World War I by the Russians, he later became a Soviet citizen, and when Hungary was overrun by the U.S.S.R., he was installed as a member of the new government. While prime minister (1953–55), he implemented agrarian reforms that won him popularity. In the uprising of 1956 he was again proclaimed prime minister, but was seized by Russian troops and later executed.

Na·hua·tl (naá-waat'l, -waát'l) *n., pl.* **-tls** or collectively **Nahuatl.** 1. A member of a group of Mexican and Central American Indian tribes, including the Aztecs. 2. The Uto-Aztecan language of the Nahuatl. [Spanish, from Nahuatl, singular of *Nahua,* the Nahuatl people.] —**Na·hua·tl** *adj.*

Na·hum¹ (náy-həm, -əm). A Hebrew prophet of the seventh century B.C. who predicted the fall of Nineveh.

Na·hum² *n.* The book of the Old Testament containing the prophecies of Nahum.

NAI, N.A.I. non-accidental injury.

nai·ad (nī-ad ‖ náy-, -əd) *n., pl.* **-ades** (-ə-deez) or **-ads.** 1. *Greek Mythology.* Any of the nymphs living in and presiding over brooks, springs, and fountains. 2. The aquatic nymph of certain insects, such as the mayfly. 3. An aquatic plant of the genus *Naias.* [Greek *Naias* (stem *Naiad-*), from *naein,* to flow.]

naif, naïf. Variants of **naive.**

nail (nayl) *n.* 1. A slim piece of metal, pointed at one end and usually having a flat head at the other, hammered into wood or other materials as a fastener. 2. **a.** A fingernail or toenail. **b.** A claw or talon. 3. Anything resembling a nail in shape, sharpness, or use. 4. A former measure of length for cloth, equal to 2¼ inches. —**hard as nails.** 1. Callous; harsh; pitiless. 2. In rugged physical condition; tough. —**hit the nail on the head.** To grasp and express the sense of something exactly and concisely. —**on the nail.** Immediately; without any delay: *paid cash on the nail.*
~*tr.v.* **nailed, nailing, nails.** 1. To fasten, join, or attach with or as if with nails. 2. To cover or shut by fastening with nails. Often used

with *down* or *up*. **3.** To keep fixed, motionless, or intent: *Fear nailed him to his seat.* **4.** To secure or make sure of, especially by prompt action or concentrated effort; clinch. Often used with *down*: *nail down the facts.* **5.** To bind to an agreement, promise, or the like. Often used with *down*: *tried to nail her down to a date.* **6.** *Informal.* To detect and expose: *nail a lie.* **7.** *Informal.* To strike or bring down, especially with something shot or hurled: *nail a bird in flight.* [Middle English *nail*, Old English *nægl*.] —**nail·er** *n.*

nail·bit·ing (náyl-bīting) *n.* Biting of the fingernails, usually as a sign of nervousness or as a habit.

~*adj.* Causing anxiety or a feeling of suspense: *a nail-biting climax.*

nail bomb *n.* A bomb, usually of gelignite, filled with nails that are flung out when the bomb explodes.

nail·brush (náyl-brush) *n.* A small brush with short, stiff bristles for cleaning the fingernails or sometimes the toenails.

nail file *n.* A small, flat metal file, or piece of emery board, used for shaping the fingernails or toenails.

nail·head (náyl-hed) *n.* **1.** The broadened or flattened, often circular, end of a nail opposite the point. **2.** An ornamental device resembling the head of a nail.

nail polish *n.* A clear or coloured cosmetic lacquer applied to the fingernails or toenails. Also *chiefly British* "nail varnish", *chiefly U.S.* "nail enamel", "nail lacquer".

nail scissors *pl.n.* Small scissors with short, curved blades for trimming and shaping fingernails or toenails.

nail·set (náyl-set) *n.* A tool for driving a nail into material so that its head is beneath or flush with the surface. Also called "nail-punch".

nain·sook (náyn-sŏŏk, nán-) *n.* A soft, light cotton material, often with a woven stripe. [Hindi *nainsukh*, "pleasure to the eye" : *nain*, eye + *sukh*, pleasure.]

Nai·paul (nī-pawl), **V(idiadhar) S(urajprasad)** (1932–). West Indian novelist. His novels and reportage concentrate on the subtly destructive effects of Western culture on the Third World, as in *A Bend in the River* (1979). His earlier, more comic novels included *The Suffrage of Elvira* (1958) and *A House for Mr. Biswas* (1961).

nai·ra (nír-ə) *n., pl.* **naira.** The basic monetary unit of Nigeria, equal to 100 kobo. [Alteration of Nigeria.]

Nairn (nairn). County town of Nairn, a former county in northeast Scotland, now part of Highland Region.

Nai·ro·bi (nī-rṓbi). The capital of Kenya. Founded (1899) on the Mombasa-Uganda railway, it lies in Kenya's eastern highlands. Nairobi is a major industrial and commercial centre, and is also one of Africa's chief tourist centres, attracting visitors to the Nairobi National Park, a wildlife reserve on the city's outskirts.

na·ive, na·ïve (naa-éev, nī-) *adj.* Also **na·if, na·ïf** (-éef). **1. a.** Lacking worldliness and sophistication; artless; inexperienced. **b.** Simple and credulous as a child; ingenuous. **2.** Lacking critical ability or analytical insight; not subtle or learned. **3.** Untrained or employing unsophisticated or primitive techniques, especially in art. **4.** Not previously exposed to particular experiences, conditions, or information. Said, for example, of a subject in a psychology experiment who has not taken part in one before.

~*n.* Also **na·if, na·ïf.** A naive person. [French, feminine of *naïf*, from Old French, ingenuous, natural, from Latin *nātīvus*, NATIVE.] —**na·ive·ly** *adv.* —**na·ive·ness** *n.*

Synonyms: *naive, simple, innocent, ingenuous, unsophisticated, natural, unaffected, guileless, artless.*

na·ive·té, na·ïve·té (naa-éev-tay, nī-, -ti) *n.* Also **na·ive·ty** (-éev-ti, -éevə-), **na·ive·ty** *pl.* **-ties. 1.** The quality of being naive; natural simplicity or artlessness; ingenuousness. **2.** A naive statement or action. [French, ingenuousness, from *naïf*, NAIVE.]

Na·ka·so·ne (náckə-sṓnay), **Yasuhiro** (1917–). Japanese politician. He was Minister of Transport (1967–68), Minister of Trade (1972–74), and became prime minister of Japan in 1982.

na·ked (náykid) *adj.* **1.** Without clothing or covering on the body; nude. **2.** Without covering; especially, without the usual covering: *a naked flame.* **3.** Devoid of vegetation, trees, or foliage. **4.** Without addition, concealment, disguise, or embellishment: *the naked truth; naked aggression.* **5.** Stripped or bare of something specified; destitute. Used with *of*: *a room naked of furniture.* **6.** Inadequately armed or protected; defenceless; vulnerable: *naked before his enemies.* **7.** *Botany.* **a.** Not encased in ovaries. Said of seeds. **b.** Unprotected by scales. Said of buds. **c.** Lacking a perianth. Said of flowers. **d.** Without leaves or pubescence. Said of branches or stalks. **8.** Lacking protective covering such as scales, fur, feathers, or a shell. **9.** *Physics.* Designating a quark flavour, especially charm or bottom, which is present in an elementary particle unaccompanied by its antiquark. **10.** Unsupported or uncorroborated by authority, evidence, or proof. Chiefly used in legal contexts. [Middle English *naked*, Old English *nacod*, from Germanic.] —**na·ked·ly** *adv.* —**na·ked·ness** *n.*

naked eye *n.* The eye unassisted by an optical instrument.

naked singularity *n. Astronomy.* A **singularity** *(see)* that is not surrounded by an event horizon, regarded as a point at which matter may be created and ejected.

N.A.L.G.O. National and Local Government Officers' Association.

Na·ma·qua·land (na-maákwə-land, nə-). Large relatively arid northwestern district of South Africa, noted for its spectacular display of spring wildflowers following the winter rains.

nam·by-pam·by (námbi-pámbi) *adj.* **1.** Weakly sentimental; insipidly affected. **2.** Lacking vigour or decisiveness; spineless.

~*n., pl.* **namby-pambies. 1.** Insipid, mawkish language or style.

2. A namby-pamby person. [From *Namby-Pamby*, a satire on the sentimental pastorals of *Ambrose* Philips, by Henry Carey (died 1743).]

name (naym) *n.* **1.** A word or words by which any person or thing is designated and distinguished from others. **2.** A word or words used to describe or evaluate, often disparagingly: *Names will never hurt me.* **3.** Verbal representation or repute as opposed to effective reality: *a democracy in name, a police state in fact.* **4. a.** General reputation: *a bad name.* **b.** A distinguished reputation; renown. **5.** *Informal.* A famous or outstanding person: *a big name in local government.* —**in the name of. 1.** On behalf of; for the sake of. **2.** By the authority of. —**know (someone) by name.** To have heard of someone but not met him. —**name names.** To reveal the identity of people involved in criminal or otherwise dubious activities. —**the name of the game.** The essential or indispensable part or quality of some activity: *If you're job-hunting, persistence is the name of the game.* —**to (one's) name.** Belonging to one: *not a penny to his name.* —**under the name of.** Using as a name.

~*tr.v.* **named, naming, names. 1.** To attach a name to. **2.** To identify by name; call by the right name: *name the Stuart Kings of England.* **3.** To mention, specify, or cite by name. **4.** To call by some epithet: *He named them all cowards.* **5.** To nominate or appoint to some duty, office, or honour. **6.** To specify or fix: *name a price.* **7.** *British.* To indicate that (a Member of Parliament) has behaved in an unacceptable way and is required to leave the chamber. Used of the Speaker of the House of Commons. —**name the day.** To arrange to get married, and, usually, to specify a date for the ceremony. —**you name it.** *Informal.* Whatever you can think, say, or imagine: *Writing, acting, selling encyclopedias —you name it, he's done it.*

~*adj. Informal.* Well-known by a name: *name brands.* [Middle English *name*, Old English *nama*.] —**nam·a·ble, name·a·ble** *adj.*

Usage: In British English, a child is named *after* someone. In American English, it is also possible to use *for*: *He was named Fred, for his grandfather.*

name-call·ing (náym-kawling) *n.* Abuse; insulting language.

name day *n. Roman Catholic Church.* The feast day of the saint after whom one is named.

name-drop (náym-drop) *intr.v.* **-dropped, -dropping, -drops.** To show off by implying that one is on intimate terms with famous people, especially by mentioning their names in a familiar fashion. —**name-drop·per** *n.* —**name-drop·ping** *n.*

name·less (náym-ləss, -liss) *adj.* **1.** Having or bearing no name: *nameless stars.* **2.** Unknown by name; obscure: *the nameless dead.* **3. a.** Not designated by name; anonymous: *a nameless benefactor.* **b.** Intentionally left unnamed: *a certain person who shall be nameless.* **4.** Inexpressible; indescribable: *nameless horror.* —**name·less·ly** *adv.* —**name·less·ness** *n.*

name part *n.* A title role *(see).*

name·plate (náym-playt) *n.* A small sign, such as a brass plate, fastened to a door or wall of an office or building and showing the occupant's name and sometimes profession.

name·ly (náymli) *adv.* That is to say; to wit; specifically.

name·sake (náym-sayk) *n.* A person or thing with the same name as or deliberately named after another. [From *for the name's sake*.]

name-tape (náym-tayp) *n.* A small strip of cloth sewn or glued to a garment and showing the owner's name.

Na·mib Desert (naá-mib). Extremely dry region running along the coast of Namibia, considered by some authorities to be the oldest of the world's present desert regions. It is noted for its population of plant and animal species adapted to survive in desert conditions.

Na·mib·i·a (nə-míbbi-ə, naa-). Formerly **South West Africa.** Country of southwest Africa. Rich in minerals, including diamonds, uranium, and copper, it is sparsely populated and mostly too dry for crops. The Namib desert along the Atlantic is one of the harshest in the world, and the Kalahari covers much of the northeast. A German protectorate from 1884, it was occupied by South Africa (1915), which governed it under a League of Nations mandate (1920–46), but refused to accept the U.N. trusteeship that replaced it. In 1971, the International Court of Justice ruled South Africa's presence in Namibia to be illegal. The South West African People's Organisation (SWAPO), recognised by the U.N. as the lawful representative of the Namibian people, began guerrilla activity in 1966. Area, 826 269 square kilometres (318,252 square miles). Population, 1,100,000. Capital, Windhoek. —**Namibian** *adj. & n.*

Na·mur (na-méwr, nə-; *French* -múr). Flemish **Na·men** (naámə). The capital of Namur province, south central Belgium. Owing to its strategic position at the confluence of the Sambre and Meuse rivers, it has been fought over many times, and it was severely damaged in World Wars I and II.

nan (nan) *n.* Also **nan·na** (nánnə). A grandmother. Used especially by and to children. [From baby talk.]

na·na (naánə) *n. British Informal.* A fool. —**do (one's) nana.** *Australian Informal.* To become extremely angry; lose one's temper. [Probably from BANANA (compare *bananas*, crazy).]

Na·nak (naánək) (1469–1538). Indian spiritual teacher and first Sikh guru. Under Islamic influence he broke away from orthodox Hinduism to preach a monotheistic faith.

Na·na Sahib (naánə), born Dandu Panth (c. 1820–60). Indian prince. During the Indian Mutiny (1857) he led a force of rebel sepoys against Delhi, and was responsible for the Cawnpore massacre. Following his defeat (1859), he disappeared into the Himalayan foothills.

nan·cy (nán-si) *n., pl.* **-cies.** *Slang.* **1.** An effeminate man. **2.** A male homosexual. Also called "nancy boy". [From *Nancy* (woman's name).]

Nan·cy (nán-si; *French* noN-sée). The capital of the Meurthe-et-Moselle *département*, northeast France. The former seat of the Dukes of Lorraine, it passed to France in 1766. The city is still the economic and cultural focus of Lorraine. Its products include iron and steel, machinery, and textiles.

NAND gate (nand) *n.* A logic gate used in computers in which the output signal is high if any one or more of the input signals is low, and low if all the input signals are high. Also called "NAND circuit". [From *not* AND (that is, the reverse of an AND GATE).]

Nan·jing or **Nan·ching** (nán-jíng). Also **Nan·king** (nán-kíng). The capital of Jiangsu province, east China. Lying on the Chang Jiang (Yangtze) river, it is a former national capital (1368–1421, 1928–37). The Japanese took the city in 1937, and it was here that they formally surrendered to the Chinese (1945). It is an important cultural and industrial centre.

nan·keen (nang-kéen) *n.* Also **nan·kin** (nán-kin, -kín). **1.** A sturdy yellow or buff cotton cloth. **2.** A yellow or buff colour. **3.** *Plural.* Trousers made of nankeen cloth, worn especially in the 19th century. **4.** *Capital* N. A kind of Chinese porcelain with a blue-and-white pattern. [Originally imported from NANJING.]

nan·ny (nánni) *n., pl.* **-nies.** A woman employed to look after a child or children in a family; a children's nurse. [From baby talk *nana*.]

nanny goat *n., pl.* **nanny goats.** A female goat. Compare **billy goat.** [From *Nanny,* pet form for *Ann.*]

nano– *comb. form. Abbr.* **n** Indicates: **1.** Extreme smallness; for example, **nanoplankton. 2.** One thousand-millionth (10^{-9}) of a specified unit; for example, **nanosecond.** [Latin *nānus,* dwarf, from Greek *nan(n)os.*]

na·no·me·tre (nánnõ-meetər, nánnə-) *n.* One thousand-millionth (10^{-9}) of a metre.

na·no·plank·ton, nan·no·plank·ton (nánnõ-plangk-tən, nánnə- ‖ -ton) *n.* Aquatic animal and plant organisms of microscopic size comprising the smallest of the **plankton** *(see).*

na·no·sec·ond (nánnõ-sekənd, nánnə-) *n.* One thousand-millionth (10^{-9}) of a second.

Nan·sen (nán-sən), **Fridtjof** (1861–1930). Norwegian explorer and politician. He helped to negotiate Norwegian independence (1905), and was awarded the Nobel Peace prize (1922) for his League of Nations work for refugees, used in Russian famine relief. He took part in Polar and North Atlantic expeditions (1882–1914).

Nansen passport *n.* A passport issued after World War I by the League of Nations to individuals who were stateless. [After Fridtjof NANSEN who, as High Commissioner for Refugees, introduced it.]

Nantes, Edict of (noNt) *n.* A decree issued in 1598 by Henry IV of France, granting restricted religious and civil liberties to Huguenots; revoked in 1685 by Louis XIV.

Nan·tuck·et (nan-túckit). A resort island off southeast Massachusetts, northeast United States. It was settled in 1659 and was an Atlantic whaling centre until the 1850s.

Naoi·se (néeshi). *Irish Mythology.* The husband of **Deirdre** *(see).*

nap¹ (nap) *n.* A brief sleep, often during a period other than one's regular sleeping hours.

~*intr.v.* **napped, napping, naps. 1.** To doze or sleep for a brief period. **2.** *Informal.* To be unaware of imminent danger or trouble. Used chiefly in such phrases as *to be caught napping.* [Middle English *nappen,* to doze, Old English *hnappian.*]

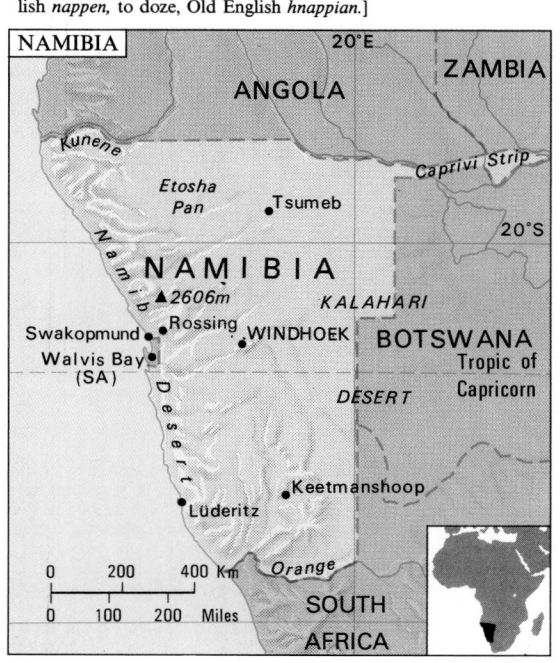

nap² *n.* A dense, soft or fuzzy surface on certain textiles or leathers, usually formed by raising fibres from the underlying material. Compare **pile.**

~*tr.v.* **napped, napping, naps.** To form or raise a nap on (fabric or leather). [Middle English *noppe,* from Middle Dutch *noppe.*]

nap³ *n.* **1. a.** A card game played for money and resembling whist. Also called "napoleon". **b.** A bid in this game, announcing the intention to win the maximum number (five) of tricks in a hand. **2.** A selection by a tipster of a horse or greyhound that is strongly fancied to win. **—go nap. 1.** To attempt to win all the tricks at nap. **2.** To risk everything on one chance or bet.

~*tr.v.* **napped, napping, naps.** To tip (a horse or greyhound) as a certain winner in a race. [Shortened from *napoleon.*]

na·palm (náy-paam, -paalm, náppaam) *n.* **1.** An aluminium soap of various fatty acids that when mixed with petrol makes a firm jelly used in flame throwers and incendiary bombs. **2.** The jelly so used in flame throwers and bombs. **3.** A similar incendiary mixture of polystyrene, benzene, and petrol. Also called "napalm-B".

~*tr.v.* **napalmed, -palming, -palms.** To bombard with napalm. [*Naphthenic* (see **naphthene**) + *palmitic acid.*]

nape (nayp) *n.* The back of the neck. [Middle English, probably akin to Old Frisian *(hals)knap*†, nape.]

Naph·ta·li¹ (náftə-lī). A son of Jacob. Genesis 30:7, 8.

Naphtali² *n.* A tribe of Israel descended from Naphtali. Numbers 1:15, 43.

naph·tha (náf-thə, náp-) *n.* **1.** A colourless flammable liquid, obtained from crude petroleum and used as a solvent and cleaning fluid, and as a raw material for petrol. **2.** Any of several volatile hydrocarbon liquids derived from coal tar and other materials and used as solvents. **3.** Petroleum. In this sense, not in current technical usage. [Greek *naphtha*†.]

naph·tha·lene (náf-thə-leen, náp-) *n.* A white crystalline compound, $C_{10}H_8$, derived from coal tar or petroleum, and used to manufacture dyes, moth repellents, explosives, and solvents. [NAPHTHA + *al*cohol + -ENE.]

naph·thene (náf-theen, náp-) *n.* Any of several cycloalkanes and their alkyl derivatives having the general formula C_nH_{2n}, found in various petroleums. [*Naphtha* + -ENE.]

naph·thol (náf-thol, náp- ‖ -thõl) *n.* An organic compound, $C_{10}H_7OH$, occurring in two isomeric forms: **1.** *alpha-naphthol,* colourless or yellow prisms or powder, used in dyes, organic synthesis, and perfumes. **b.** *beta-naphthol,* white lustrous leaflets or powder, used in dyes, insecticides, and in the manufacture of rubber. [*Naphth*alene + -OL (hydroxyl group).]

naph·thyl (náf-thīl, náp-, -thil) *n.* Either of the two forms of the univalent organic radical $C_{10}H_7$-, derived from naphthalene. [*Naphtha* + -YL.]

Napier (náypi-ər), **John** (1550–1617). Scottish mathematician. He is best known for his discovery of natural logarithms (published 1614), and his work on spherical trigonometry.

Na·pier·i·an logarithm (nə-péer-i-ən, nay-) *n.* A **natural logarithm** *(see).*

Napier's bones *n.* A device consisting of a set of graduated rods formerly used for carrying out multiplication and division. [After John NAPIER, who invented the method on which it is based.]

na·pi·form (náypi-fawrm) *adj.* Shaped like a turnip. Said of a root. [Latin *nāpus,* turnip (probably of Mediterranean origin) + -FORM.]

nap·kin (nápkin) *n.* **1.** A square piece of fabric, such as cotton or linen, or a similar piece of soft, absorbent paper, used at table to protect one's clothes or wipe one's lips and fingers. Also called "table napkin". **2.** Any similar cloth or towel. **3.** *Chiefly British.* A nappy. **4.** *U.S.* A **sanitary towel** *(see).* [Middle English *nappekin,* diminutive of *nappe,* tablecloth, from Old French, from Latin *mappa,* napkin, towel.]

Na·ples (náyp'lz). *Italian* **Na·po·li** (naáapo-li). The capital of Campania, south central Italy. Founded by Greeks in the sixth century B.C. below Mount Vesuvius, on the Bay of Naples, it became the capital of the kingdom of Naples (1270–1860). Naples is now a major seaport and a cultural, tourist, and industrial centre. It suffered severe earthquake damage in 1980.

Naples yellow *n.* **1.** A permanent yellow pigment consisting of lead antimonate. **2.** A similar pigment consisting of zinc oxide mixed with a yellow colouring matter. **3.** The colour of either of these pigments. [After NAPLES, where it was originally manufactured.]

na·po·le·on (nə-põli-ən) *n.* **1.** A rectangular piece of pastry, iced on top, with crisp, flaky layers filled with custard cream. **2.** A former 20-franc gold coin of France. **3.** A card game, nap *(see).* [After NAPOLEON I.]

Na·po·le·on I (nə-põli-ən), born Napoleon Bonaparte or Buonaparte (1769–1821). Emperor of the French and King of Italy. His victories as French Revolutionary commander in Italy (1796–97) established him as the most brilliant general of his time, and as a skilled politician. Following an abortive attempt to conquer Egypt (1798–99), he deposed the Directory and proclaimed himself First Consul (1799), and later Emperor (1804). His military ascendancy in Europe over the next decade was insufficient to combat the commercial and maritime power of Britain despite his attempted trade embargo, known as the Continental System. After the disastrous Russian campaign (1812–13) an alliance of hostile powers forced him to abdicate (1814). After a brief exile on the island of Elba, he regained power (1815), but was finally defeated at Waterloo, and exiled to St. Helena. His grasp of military technique remains unsurpassed, and his codification of laws, the *Code Napoléon,* still forms the basis of French civil law. —**Na·po·le·on·ic** *adj.*

Napoleon III, born Louis Napoleon Bonaparte (1808–73). Emperor of the French (1852–70). The nephew of Napoleon I, he led Bonapartist opposition to Louis-Philippe, became President of the Second Republic (1848), and later (1852) proclaimed himself Emperor. He instituted reforms and rebuilt Paris. His imperialist adventures in the Crimea (1854–56) and Italy (1859) were successful, but his lack of judgment was shown in the Mexican campaign (1861–67) and culminated in the disastrous Franco-Prussian War and his abdication (1870).

nappe (nap) *n.* **1.** A sheet of water flowing over a dam or similar structure. **2.** *Geology.* A folded sheetlike formation that has been moved from its site of origin by tectonic forces which caused the folding. **3.** *Geometry.* Either of the two parts into which a cone is divided by the vertex. [French *nappe (d'eau),* sheet (of water), from Old French *nappe,* tablecloth, from Latin *mappa,* napkin, towel.]

nap·py¹ (náppi) *n., pl.* **-pies.** A folded piece of towelling or other absorbent or disposable material, worn around a baby's waist and between the legs and used to absorb excreta. Also called "napkin", *U.S* "diaper". [From NAPKIN.]

nap·py² *adj.* **-pier, -piest.** Having a nap; shaggy; fuzzy.

Nar·bonne (naar-bón). Latin name **Narbo Martius.** City of southern France. The first Roman colony in Transalpine Gaul, it was later a port until its harbour silted up in the 14th century. It is the commercial centre for a wine-producing area.

narc, nark (nark) *n. Chiefly U.S. Slang.* A police officer dealing with crimes concerning illegal drugs; a narcotics agent. [Perhaps from Romany *nāk,* nose (influenced by NARCOTIC).]

nar·ce·ine (nár-seen, -si-een) *n.* Also **nar·ce·in** (-sin, -si-in). A white crystalline narcotic, $C_{23}H_{27}O_8N \cdot 3H_2O$, obtained from opium. [French *narcéine* : Greek *narkē,* numbness + -INE.]

nar·cis·sism (naar-síss-iz'm, nár-si-) *n.* Also **nar·cism** (nár-siz'm). **1.** Excessive admiration of oneself. **2.** *Psychoanalysis.* An arresting of development at, or a regression to, the infantile stage of development in which one's own body is the object of erotic interest. [After NARCISSUS.] —**nar·cis·sist** (-sist) *n.* —**nar·cis·sis·tic** (-sístik) *adj.*

nar·cis·sus (naar-síssəs) *n., pl.* **-suses** or **-cissi** (-síssī, -síssee). **1.** Any of several widely cultivated plants of the genus *Narcissus,* having narrow, grasslike leaves, and usually white or yellow flowers characterised by a cup-shaped or trumpet-shaped central crown. See **daffodil, jonquil, Chinese sacred lily. 2.** Pheasant's eye *(see).* [Latin, from Greek *narkissos,* probably of Mediterranean origin.]

Narcissus. *Greek Mythology.* A youth who, having spurned the love of Echo, pined away in love for his own reflection in a pool of water and was transformed into a flower, the narcissus.

narco– *comb. form.* Indicates: **1.** Numbness, sluggishness, or stupor; for example, **narcolepsy. 2.** A narcotic drug; for example, **narcotine.** [Greek *narko-,* from *narkoun,* to benumb, from *narkē,* numbness.]

nar·co·a·nal·y·sis (nárkō-ə-nál-ə-siss) *n.* Psychoanalysis conducted while the patient is in a drug-induced drowsy state.

nar·co·lep·sy (nárkə-lep-si) *n. Pathology.* A condition characterised by sudden and uncontrollable attacks of deep sleep. [NARCO- + -LEPSY.] —**nar·co·lep·tic** (-léptik) *adj.*

nar·co·sis (naar-kṓ-siss) *n.* Diminished consciousness or complete unconsciousness produced by a drug. Also called "narcotism". [Greek *narkōsis,* a numbing, from *narkoun,* to make numb, from *narkē,* numbness.]

nar·co·syn·the·sis (nárkō-síntha-siss) *n.* Narcoanalysis directed towards making the patient recall suppressed memories and emotional traumas for later interpretation.

nar·cot·ic (naar-kóttik) *n.* **1. a.** Any drug that dulls the senses, induces sleep, and with prolonged use becomes addictive. **b.** Broadly, any illegal drug. **2.** Something that numbs, soothes, or induces a dreamlike or insensitive state.

~*adj.* **1.** Inducing sleep or stupor. **2.** Of or pertaining to narcotics, their effects, or their use. **3.** Of or pertaining to one addicted to a narcotic drug. [Middle English *narkotike,* from Old French *narcotique* (originally an adjective), from Medieval Latin *narcōticus,* from Greek *narkōtikos,* numbing, narcotic, from *narkoun,* to make numb, from *narkē,* numbness.] —**nar·cot·i·cal·ly** *adv.*

nar·co·tine (nárkə-teen, -tin) *n.* An alkaloid, $C_{22}H_{23}NO_7$, obtained from opium and used to relieve coughing, fever, and spasms. [French : *narcotique,* NARCOT(IC) + -INE.]

nar·co·tise, nar·co·tize (nárkə-tīz) *tr.v.* **-tised, -tising, -tises. 1.** To place under the influence of a narcotic. **2.** To lull or induce sleep in. **3.** To dull; deaden. —**nar·co·ti·sa·tion** (-tī-záysh'n ‖ *U.S.* -ti-) *n.*

nar·co·tism (nárkə-tiz'm) *n.* **1.** Addiction to narcotics such as opium, heroin, or morphine. **2.** A drugged state; narcosis. [French *narcotisme,* from *narcotique,* NARCOTIC.]

nard (nard) *n.* **1.** A plant, **spikenard** *(see).* **2.** A balm made from spikenard. [Middle English *narde,* from Latin *nardus,* from Greek *nardos,* from Semitic.]

nar·doo (naar-dṓo) *n.* **1.** An Australian clover-like fern, *Marsilea drummondii,* found growing in swamps. **2.** The spores of this plant, used as a food by the Aborigines. [From a native language.]

nar·es (náir-eez) *pl.n. Singular* **-is** (-iss). The openings in the nasal cavities of vertebrates; nostrils. [Latin *nārēs,* plural of *nāris,* nostril.] —**nar·i·al** (-i-əl) *adj.*

nar·ghi·le, nar·gi·le (nárgi-li, -lay) *n.* An Oriental tobacco pipe, a **hookah** *(see).* [French *narguilé,* from Persian *nārgīleh,* a pipe

(whose bowl was originally made of coconut shell), from *nārgīl,* coconut, from Sanskrit *nārikela†,* coconut.]

nark¹ (nark) *n. British Slang.* An informer, especially one working for the police.

~*v.* **narked, narking, narks.** *British Slang.* —*tr.* To irritate or annoy. —*intr.* To complain; grumble. [Thieves' slang, from Romany *nāk,* nose.]

'nark². Variant of **narc.**

Nar·ra·gan·set (nárrə-gán-sit) *n., pl.* **-sets** or collectively **Narraganset. 1.** A member of an Algonquian-speaking North American Indian people that formerly inhabited the area of Rhode Island. **2.** The language of this tribe. —**Nar·ra·gan·set** *adj.*

Narragansett Bay. An inlet of the Atlantic Ocean in Rhode Island state, United States. It is known for its resorts and fishing centres.

nar·rate (nə-ráyt, na- ‖ *U.S.* also nárrayt) *v.* **-rated, -rating, -rates.** —*tr.* To give an oral or written account of; tell (a story). —*intr.* To give an account or description; especially, to supply a commentary for a film, television programme, or the like. [Latin *narrāre,* from *gnārus,* knowing.] —**nar·ra·tor** (-ər ‖ nárrətər) *n.*

nar·ra·tion (nə-ráysh'n, na-) *n.* **1.** The act or an instance of narrating. **2.** Something narrated; a narrative.

nar·ra·tive (nárrətiv) *n.* **1.** A story or description of actual or fictional events; a narrated account. **2.** The part of a piece of writing that is concerned with the narration of events. **3.** The act, technique, or process of narrating.

~*adj.* **1.** Consisting of or characterised by the telling of a story or the description of events without analysis: *narrative poetry.* **2.** Of or pertaining to narration: *narrative skill.* —**nar·ra·tive·ly** *adv.*

nar·row (nárrō) *adj.* **-rower, -rowest. 1.** Of small or limited width, especially in comparison with length: *a narrow corridor.* **2. a.** Limited in area; cramped; confined. **b.** Limited in scope; restricted: *the enquiry's narrow terms of reference.* **3.** Lacking flexibility; rigid in adherence to an idea or way: *narrow principles; a narrow outlook.* **4.** *Rare.* Straitened; pinched: *narrow circumstances.* **5.** Barely sufficient or successful; precarious: *a narrow margin of victory.* **6.** Painstakingly thorough or attentive: *a narrow scrutiny.* **7.** *Regional.* Miserly; stingy. **8.** *Phonetics.* Tense.

~*v.* **narrowed, -rowing, -rows.** —*tr.* **1.** To make narrow or narrower; reduce in width or extent. **2.** To limit or restrict. Often used with *down: That narrowed down the possibilities.* —*intr.* To grow less in width or extent; contract.

~*n.* **1.** A narrow place or part, such as a pass through mountains or a valley. **2.** *Plural.* Any narrow body of water, especially connecting two larger ones. [Middle English *nearwe, narow,* Old English *nearu,* from Germanic.] —**nar·row·ly** *adv.* —**nar·row·ness** *n.*

narrow gauge *n.* A distance between the rails of a railway track that is less than the standard width of 56½ inches. —**nar·row-gauge** (nárrō-gáyj) *adj.*

nar·row-mind·ed (nárrō-míndid) *adj.* Lacking breadth of view, tolerance, or sympathy; bigoted; prejudiced. —**nar·row-mind·ed·ly** *adv.* —**nar·row-mind·ed·ness** *n.*

nar·thex (nár-theks) *n.* **1.** A portico or lobby of an early Christian church or basilica, separated from the nave by a railing or screen. **2.** Any church entrance hall leading to the nave. [Medieval Greek *narthēx,* "enclosure", originally "casket", "box" (made of hollow stems of giant fennel), from Greek *narthēx,* giant fennel.]

nartjie. Variant of **naartjie.**

Nar·vik (nár-vik, -veek). Ice-free port and tourist centre within the Arctic Circle, Norway.

nar·whal (nár-wəl, -hwəl) *n.* An arctic aquatic mammal, *Monodon monoceros,* having a spotted pelt and (in the male) a spiral tusk several feet long. It is hunted for ivory and oil. [Dutch *narwal,* from Danish *narhval,* from Old Norse *nāhvalr,* "corpse-whale" (so called because with its whitish colour it resembles a floating corpse) : *nār,* corpse + *hvalr,* whale.]

na·ry (naír-i) *adj. Regional.* Not one; no. Usually followed by *a* or *an: Nary a woman remained.* [From *ne'er a,* "never a".]

NAS·A (nássə) *n.* In the United States, the National Aeronautics and Space Administration.

na·sal (náyz'l) *adj.* **1.** Of or pertaining to the nose. **2.** *Phonetics.* Formed by lowering the soft palate so that most of the air is exhaled through the nose rather than the mouth, as in sounding *m, n,* and *ng* in English or *un, on,* or *en* in French. **3.** Characterised by or resembling sounds so formed: *a nasal whine.*

~*n.* **1.** *Phonetics.* A nasal sound. **2.** A nasal part or bone. **3.** The nosepiece of a helmet. [French, from New Latin *nāsālis,* from Latin *nāsus,* nose.] —**na·sal·i·ty** (nay-zál-əti, nə-) *n.* —**na·sal·ly** *adv.*

nasal index *n.* The ratio of the width to the length of the nose, multiplied by 100. It is used in anthropological measurements.

na·sal·ise, na·sal·ize (náyzə-līz) *v.* **-ised, -ising, -ises.** —*tr.* To render nasal. —*intr.* To produce nasal sounds. —**na·sal·i·sa·tion** (-lī-záysh'n ‖ *U.S.* -li-) *n.*

nas·cent (náss'nt, náy-sənt) *adj.* **1.** Coming into existence; in the process of emerging. **2.** *Chemistry.* Designating or pertaining to a substance that is produced in a highly active form in the reaction mixture: *nascent hydrogen.* [Latin *nāscēns* (stem *nāscent-*), present participle of *nāscī,* to be born.] —**nas·cence** *n.*

nase·ber·ry (náyz-berri, -bəri, -bri) *n., pl.* **-ries.** A tropical tree, the **sapodilla** *(see),* or its fruit. [Spanish *néspera* (influenced by BERRY), from Latin *mespila,* MEDLAR.]

Nash (nash), **John** (1752–1835). English architect. He designed much of the area around Regent's Park, as well as Regent Street, and Brighton Pavilion, and remodelled Buckingham Palace. He is also responsible for many of England's finest country houses.

Nash, Ogden (1902–71). U.S. humorist. A regular contributor to the *New Yorker*, he is best known for his epigrammatic verse.

Nash, Paul (1889–1946). British painter. A war artist in both World Wars, he painted many striking war scenes, such as *The Menin Road* (1918) and *Totes Meer* (1941).

Nashe (nash), **Thomas** (1567–1601). English writer. His witty, colourful works include several anti-Puritan pamphlets, a lost dramatic collaboration with Ben Jonson, *The Isle of Dogs* (1597), for which he was imprisoned, and possibly the best of all Elizabethan narrative works, *The Unfortunate Traveller* (1594).

Nash·ville (násh-vil). The capital of Tennessee, United States. Lying on the Cumberland river, it is an important communications, industrial, and commercial centre, with publishing and music industries, and is the home of country-and-western music.

na·si go·reng (naa-si gáw-reng) *n.* A Dutch-Indonesian dish of fried rice mixed with cooked pork, ham, chicken, or seafood, and served with strips of omelette. [Malay, cooked rice (with pork).]

na·si·on (náyzi-ən) *n.* The point at the top of the nose marking the boundary between the nasal bone and the frontal bone of the forehead. [French, from Latin *násus*, nose.]

naso– *comb. form.* Indicates nose; for example, **nasofrontal.** [New Latin, from Latin *nāsus*, nose.]

na·so·fron·tal (náyzō-frúnt'l) *adj.* Of or pertaining to the nasal and frontal bones.

na·so·phar·ynx (náyzō-fárringks) *n.*, *pl.* **-pharynges** (-fə-rín-jeez) or **-ynxes.** The portion of the pharynx directly behind the nasal cavity and above the soft palate. **—na·so·pha·ryn·ge·al** (-fə-rín-ji-əl, -jəl, fárrin-jée-əl, -jéel) *adj.*

Nas·sau[1] (nássaw). The capital of the Bahamas, on New Providence Island. Tourism, fundamental to the country's economy, is centred here.

Nas·sau[2] (nássow). Former duchy in West Germany, now incorporated in Hessen and Rhineland Palatinate. Its capital was Wiesbaden. The area is fertile and known for its wines and mineral springs. Branches of the house of Nassau still rule the Netherlands and Luxembourg.

Nas·ser (naá-sər, nássər), **Gamal Abdul** (1918–70). Egyptian soldier and statesman. He was President of Egypt (1956–58) and of the United Arab Republic (1958–70). After the war with Israel (1948–49), he led the revolt (1952) under General Neguib that deposed King Farouk. In 1954 he supplanted Neguib as premier. His nationalisation of the Suez Canal (1956) provoked Anglo-French intervention and precipitated an international crisis. He subsequently formed close ties with the U.S.S.R. Despite unsuccessful attempts to form an Arab federation, he did much for Egyptian prosperity.

Nasser, Lake. See **Aswan High Dam.**

nas·tic (nástik) *adj.* Of, pertaining to, or characterised by a tendency in plants to move in a direction determined by an internal stimulus, such as growth movement, rather than an external stimulus. [From Greek *nastos*, pressed down, from *nassein†*, to press.]

na·stur·tium (nə-stúrshəm ‖ na-) *n.* Any of various trailing plants of the genus *Tropaeolum*, having flowers with five broad petals that are usually yellow, orange, or red. Their round pungent leaves and seeds are sometimes used as seasoning. [Latin *nāsturtium*, a kind of cress, originally *nāsitortium* (unattested), "nose-pain" (so called because cress plants such as mustard when eaten cause burning sensations in the nose) : *nāsus*, nose + *tort-*, past stem of *torquēre*, to twist, torture.]

nas·ty (naʼasti ‖ nɑ́sti) *adj.* **-tier, -tiest. 1.** Disgusting to see, smell, or touch; filthy; foul. **2.** Morally offensive; indecent. **3.** Malicious; spiteful; mean: *saying nasty things about us.* **4.** Causing discomfort or annoyance; unpleasant; disagreeable: *nasty weather.* **5.** Painful or dangerous; grave: *a nasty accident.*
~*n.*, *pl.* **-nasties.** One that is evil, unpleasant, or offensive: *a new law to control the spread of video nasties.* —See Synonyms at **dirty.** [Middle English, *nasty, naxty*, probably akin to Dutch *nestig*, earlier *nistich*, perhaps originally meaning "fouled like a dirty bird's nest", from *nest*, nest.] **—nas·ti·ly** *adv.* **—nas·ti·ness** *n.*

-nasty *n. comb. form.* Indicates a specified kind of nastic response or change; for example, **epinasty.** [From NASTIC.] **—-nastic** *adj. comb. form.*

nat. 1. national. **2.** native. **3.** natural.

na·tal (náyt'l) *adj.* **1.** Of or relating to birth; accompanying birth: *natal injuries.* **2.** Of or pertaining to the time or place of one's birth: *a natal star.* [Middle English, from Latin *nātālis*, from *nāscī* (past participle *nātus*), to be born.]

Na·tal (nə-tál ‖ -táal). The smallest province of South Africa. Inland uplands rise to the Drakensberg Mountains. Industries, dominated by sugar refining, are concentrated around Durban and the capital, Pietermaritzburg. A Boer republic (1838), Natal was annexed by the British (1843), and it absorbed Zululand in 1897.

na·tal·i·ty (nay-tál-əti, nə-) *n.*, *pl.* **-ties. Birth rate** (see).

Natal plum *n.* A South African shrub, *Carissa grandiflora*, having forked spines, white flowers, and an edible scarlet berry. [From NATAL, South Africa.]

na·tant (náyt'nt) *adj.* Swimming or floating; especially, floating on the surface. Said, for example, of an aquatic plant. [Latin *natāns* (stem *natant-*), from *natāre*, to swim.]

na·ta·tion (nə-táysh'n, nay-, na-) *n. Formal.* The action or art of swimming. [Latin *natātiō* (stem *natātiōn-*), from *natāre*, to swim.]

na·ta·to·ri·al (náytə-táwri-əl, náttə- ‖ -tóri-) *adj.* Also **na·ta·to·ry** (-tri, -təri, nə-táytəri). Of, pertaining to, or adapted for swimming. [Late Latin *natātōrius*, from Latin *natāre*, to swim.]

Natch·ez (náchiz) *n.*, *pl.* **Natchez. 1.** A member of a Muskhogean-speaking North American Indian people, formerly living in the area of Mississippi. **2.** The language of this tribe. **—Natch·ez** *adj.*

na·tes (náy-teez) *pl.n. Anatomy.* The **buttocks** (see). [Latin *natēs*, plural of *natis*, buttock.]

Na·than (náy-thən, -than). A prophet during the reigns of David and Solomon. II Samuel 12:1–15.

Na·than·ael (nə-thán-yəl). One of the 12 Apostles, usually identified as **Bartholomew.**

nathe·less (náyth-ləss, -liss) *adv.* Also **nath·less** (náth-). *Archaic.* Nevertheless; notwithstanding. [Middle English *nathles*, Old English *nā thē lǣs*, "not less by that" : *nā*, NO + *thē*, by that, instrumental case of *sē*, that + *lǣs*, LESS.]

na·tion (náysh'n) *n.* **1.** A people, usually the inhabitants of a specific territory, who share common customs, origins, history, and frequently language or related languages. **2. a.** An aggregation of people organised under a single government; a country. **b.** The entire people of a country, as distinct from any of the various groups and classes composing it. Preceded by *the: The nation responded in a wonderful show of solidarity.* **3.** The government of a sovereign state: *The Western nations have reacted favourably to the proposal.* **4. a.** A federation or tribe of people, as of black South Africans or North American Indians. **b.** The territory occupied by such a federation or tribe. **—the nations.** In Biblical use, the gentile or heathen peoples: *"And the Lord shall scatter you among the nations."* (Deuteronomy 4:27). [Middle English *nacioun*, from Old French *nacion*, from Latin *nātiō* (stem *nātiōn-*), "race", "breed", from *nāscī* (past participle *nātus*), to be born.]

Usage: nation, state, country, people, race. Nation primarily signifies a political body rather than a physical territory—the citizens united under one independent government, without close regard for their origins. *State* even more specifically indicates political organisation, generally on a sovereign basis and pertaining to a well-defined area. *Country*, in strict usage, is a geographical term signifying the territory of one nation, but it is often used in the extended sense of *nation. People*, in this context, signifies a group united over a long period by common cultural and social ties, although not necessarily by racial and national bonds. *Race* refers to those recognisable physical traits, stemming from common ancestry, that succeeding generations have in common.

na·tion·al (násh'n'l, násh-n'l) *adj. Abbr.* **nat., natl. 1.** Of, pertaining to, or belonging to a nation as an organised whole. **2.** Characteristic of or peculiar to the people of a nation: *a national trait.* **3.** Occurring, distributed, or recognised nationwide: *a national figure.* **4.** Of or maintained by the government of a nation: *a national park.* **5.** Devoted to one's own nation or its interests; patriotic.
~*n.* **1.** A citizen of a particular nation. **2.** A newspaper distributed to all parts of a nation. **—na·tion·al·ly** *adv.*

national anthem *n.* A hymn or song adopted by a nation and sung or played as an expression of national pride and unity, as on state occasions.

National Assembly *n.* A national legislative body in various countries; especially, the first of the Revolutionary assemblies in France (1789–91).

national assistance *n. British.* The social security benefits that preceded **supplementary benefit** (see).

national bank *n.* **1.** A bank associated with national finances and usually owned or controlled by a government. **2.** In the United States, any in a system of Federally chartered, privately owned banks, each required by law to be an investing member of its district Federal Reserve Bank.

national debt *n.* The total amount of money borrowed by a national government.

National Economic Development Council *n. Abbr.* **N.E.D.C.** A British organisation advising government and industry on how to increase economic growth and efficiency.

National Front *n. Abbr.* **N.F.** In Britain, an extreme right-wing political party, best known for its racist policies regarding non-white ethnic minorities.

National Girobank *n.* In Britain, the official registered name of the Post Office banking system, **Giro** (see).

National Guard *n.* **1.** In the United States, the military reserve units controlled by each state. **2.** Formerly in France, an armed national force operating intermittently from 1789 to 1871.

National Health Service *n. Abbr.* **NHS.** A comprehensive service providing medical care in the United Kingdom, financed by national insurance and from taxation, in operation since 1948.

national income *n.* The total net value of all goods and services produced within a nation over a specific period of time, usually a year, and representing the sum of wages, profits, rents, interest, and pension payments to residents of the nation. Compare **gross national product.**

national insurance *n.* In the United Kingdom, the insurance system used to help to finance state welfare provisions such as pensions and medical care through regular contributions required from employers and employees.

na·tion·al·ise, na·tion·al·ize (násh'n-ə-līz, náshnə-) *tr.v.* **-ised, -ising, -ises. 1.** To convert (a sector of industry, agriculture, commerce, or public service, together with associated means of production) from private to governmental ownership and control. **2.** To

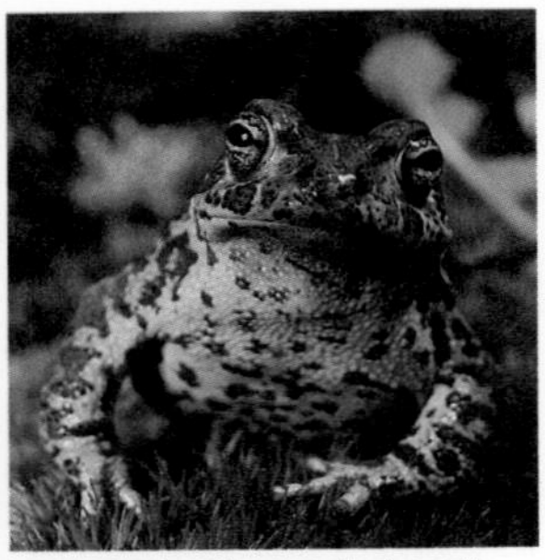

natterjack *The natterjack toad,* Bufo calamita, *adopts a peculiar stance when threatened, with its body inflated, front legs tucked under, and hind legs extended on tiptoe.*

make national in character. **3.** To accept as a citizen or national; naturalise. **—na·tion·al·i·sa·tion** (-lī-záysh'n || *U.S.* -li-) *n.*

na·tion·al·ism (násh'n-ə-liz'm, náshnə-) *n.* **1.** Pride in and devotion to one's own nation and its interests, especially when excessive. **2.** A strong sense of national identity, often associated with aspirations for national independence or separatism. **—na·tion·al·ist** *adj.* & *n.* **—na·tion·al·is·tic** (-lístik) *adj.* **—na·tion·al·is·ti·cal·ly** *adv.*

na·tion·al·i·ty (násh'n-ál-əti) *n., pl.* **-ties. 1.** The status of belonging to a particular nation by origin, birth, or naturalisation. **2.** A people having common origins or traditions and constituting or being considered to constitute a nation. **3.** Existence as a politically autonomous entity; the status of a nation. **4.** National character. **5.** A nation or country: *people of different nationalities.*

national monument *n. Chiefly U.S.* A natural landmark or a structure or site of historic interest set aside by a national government and maintained for enjoyment or study by the public.

national park *n.* A tract of land administered by a government-appointed body to preserve its natural character and wildlife.

National Savings Bank. See **Savings Bank.**

national service *n.* In various countries, compulsory military service for a limited period of time.

National Socialism *n.* **Nazism** *(see).*

National Trust *n.* In the United Kingdom, an organisation that aims to preserve places and buildings of aesthetic, cultural, and historical value, for the benefit of the public.

na·tion·hood (náysh'n-hŏŏd) *n.* The state of being a nation.

Nation of Islam *n.* An organisation of black Americans who follow the religious practices of Islam and propose segregation of blacks and whites, with a view to the establishment of a new black nation. Members are known as "Black Muslims".

na·tion-state (náysh'n-stáyt, -stayt) *n.* A state whose people have a sense of national identity based on a common cultural heritage.

na·tion·wide (náysh'n-wíd, -wīd) *adj.* Throughout a whole nation. **—na·tion·wide** *adv.*

na·tive (náytiv) *adj. Abbr.* **nat. 1.** Belonging to one by nature; inborn; innate: *native ability.* **2.** Belonging by birth or origin to a specified country or place: *a native Englishman.* **3.** One's own because of the place or circumstances of one's birth: *our native land.* **4.** Originating, growing, or produced in a certain place; indigenous as opposed to exotic or foreign: *native products.* **5.** Belonging to or characteristic of the original inhabitants of a particular place, especially those of primitive culture: *native customs of Borneo.* **6.** Occurring in nature pure or uncombined with other substances. Said of metallic or other solid elements: *native copper.* **7.** In a natural state; unaffected by artificial influences: *native beauty.* **8.** *Archaic.* Closely related, as by birth or race.
~*n. Abbr.* **nat. 1.** One who is connected with a place by birth or origin. **2.** An established local resident, as distinguished from a visitor or newcomer. **3.** One who is an original inhabitant of a place; especially one belonging to a people of primitive culture originally occupying a country, as distinguished from an invader or settler. **4.** *South African.* Formerly, a black South African. Now considered offensive. **5.** Something, especially an animal or a plant, that originated in a particular place. [Middle English *natif,* from Old French, from Latin *nātīvus,* born, native, from *nāscī* (past participle *nātus*), to be born.] **—na·tive·ly** *adv.* **—na·tive·ness** *n.*

native bear *n. Australian.* The **koala** *(see).*

na·tive-born (náytiv-bórn) *adj.* Belonging to a place by birth.

native peach *n.* A tree, the **quandong** *(see).*

native speaker *n.* One who speaks a particular native language as a first language.

na·tiv·ism (náytiv-iz'm) *n.* **1.** *Philosophy.* The doctrine that the mind produces ideas that are not derived from external sources; the doctrine of innate ideas. **2.** The re-establishment or perpetuation of native cultural traits, especially in opposition to acculturation. **—na·tiv·ist** *n.* **—na·tiv·is·tic** (-ístik) *adj.*

na·tiv·i·ty (nə-tívvəti || *U.S. also* nay-) *n., pl.* **-ties. 1.** Birth, especially the place, conditions, or circumstances of one's birth. **2.** *Capital* **N. a.** The birth of Jesus. **b.** A representation, such as a painting or a play, of this. **c.** Christmas. **3.** *Astrology.* A horoscope based on the time of one's birth. [Middle English *nativite,* from Old French, from Latin *nātīvitās,* from *nātīvus,* born, NATIVE.]

nativity play *n.* A play, especially a short one performed by schoolchildren, based on the gospel accounts of the birth of Christ.

natl. national.

NA·TO (náytō) *n.* The **North Atlantic Treaty Organisation** *(see).*

na·tro·lite (náttrə-līt, náytrə-) *n.* A white zeolite mineral, $Na_2(Al_2Si_3O_{10})\cdot 2H_2O$. [German *Natrolith* : NATRO(N) + -LITE.]

na·tron (náy-trən, -tron) *n.* A mineral form of hydrous sodium carbonate, $Na_2CO_3\cdot 10H_2O$, often found crystallised with other salts. [French, from Spanish *natrón,* from Arabic *naṭrūn,* from Greek *nitron,* NITRE.]

Nat·so·pa, NAT·SO·PA (nát-sṓpə) National Society of Operative Printers Graphical and Media Personnel (in Britain).

nat·ter (náttər) *intr.v.* **-tered, -tering, -ters.** *Chiefly British Informal.* To talk idly about trivial subjects; chatter; gossip.
~*n.* An aimless or trivial conversation; a chat. [19th century (Scottish) : imitative.]

nat·ter·jack (náttər-jak) *n.* A European toad, *Bufo calamita,* with short legs and a yellow stripe down its back. It inflates its body when alarmed. [Perhaps from NATTER (referring to its loud croak) + JACK (chap).]

nat·ty (nátti) *adj.* **-tier, -tiest.** *Informal.* Neat, trim, and smart; spruce; dapper. [Perhaps variant of obsolete *netty,* from Middle English *net,* trim, neat, from Old French *net,* NEAT (tidy).]

nat·u·ral (náchrəl, náchə-) *adj. Abbr.* **nat. 1.** Present in or produced by nature; not artificial or man-made: *a natural reservoir; natural dyes.* **2.** Pertaining to or concerning physical reality, as opposed to a spiritual, intellectual, or imagined reality: *natural science.* **3.** Pertaining to or produced solely by nature or the expected order of things: *a natural event; natural causes.* **4. a.** Pertaining to or resulting from inherent nature; not acquired empirically: *Self-preservation is an instinct natural to man.* **b.** Distinguished by innate qualities or aptitudes: *a natural leader.* **5.** Free from affectation or artificiality; spontaneous: *She is natural even in awkward company.* **6.** Not altered, treated, or disguised: *natural colouring; a natural landscape.* **7.** Consonant with particular circumstances; expected and accepted: *She saw children as a natural consequence of marriage.* **8.** Based on or in accordance with a supposedly innate sense of what is right and fair: *natural justice.* **9.** In a primitive, unenlightened, or unregenerate state. **10. a.** Illegitimate. Said of offspring. **b.** Related by blood: *They were his natural parents.* **11.** *Music.* **a.** Neither sharp nor flat: *a natural note.* **b.** Having no sharps or flats: *a natural key.* —See Synonyms at **naive, normal, sincere.**
~*n.* **1.** One seeming to have the qualifications necessary for success: *a natural for the job.* **2.** *Music.* **a.** The sign (♮) placed before a note to cancel a preceding sharp or flat. Also *U.S.* "cancel". **b.** A note so affected. **3.** In certain card and dice games, such as pontoon and craps, a combination that wins immediately it is dealt or thrown. [Middle English, from Old French, from Latin *nātūrālis,* from *nātūra,* NATURE.] **—nat·u·ral·ness** *n.*

Usage: There are two ways of forming the opposite of *natural.* The general antonym is *unnatural,* which has a range of applications all to do with being "outside the expected order of things". *Supernatural* and *preternatural* are restricted to contexts where the contrast is between this world and some other miraculous one.

natural childbirth *n.* An approach to childbirth that seeks to avoid the use of anaesthesia and surgical intervention and to ensure the psychological and physiological well-being of the mother through preparation in the form of exercises and relaxation techniques, for example.

natural classification *n.* Classification of animals and plants according to similarities based on supposed descent from a common ancestor.

natural frequency *n. Physics.* The frequency at which a given system will vibrate or oscillate freely.

natural gas *n.* A mixture of hydrocarbon gases found within the Earth, often with petroleum deposits, principally methane together with varying quantities of ethane, propane, butane, and other gases. It is used as a fuel and in the manufacture of organic compounds.

natural gender *n. Grammar.* Gender based upon actual sex or absence of sex of the referent of a noun. Compare **common gender, grammatical gender.**

natural history *n.* **1.** The study of natural objects and organisms, their origins, evolution, interrelationships, and description. **2.** The natural phenomena of a particular region or time.

nat·u·ral·ise, nat·u·ral·ize (náchrə-līz, náchə-) *v.* **-ised, -ising, -ises.** —*tr.* **1.** To grant full citizenship to (one of foreign birth). **2.** To adopt (something foreign, such as a word or custom) into general use. **3.** To adapt (a plant or animal) to life in a new environment. **4.** To cause to conform to nature; make natural or lifelike. **5.** To explain or account for (a phenomenon) in terms of natural, rather than supernatural causes. —*intr.* To become naturalised or acclimatised; adapt. **—nat·u·ral·i·sa·tion** (-lī-záysh'n || *U.S.* -li-) *n.*

nat·u·ral·ism (náchrə-liz'm, náchə-) *n.* **1.** Conformity to nature; factual or realistic representation, especially: **a.** In literature, the practice of and belief in presenting a detailed and lifelike account of the circumstances of human life, rather than a conventionalised, fantastic, or symbolic account. **b.** In the visual arts, the practice of and belief in reproducing subjects as exactly as possible. **c.** A movement or school advocating such a practice or belief. **2.** *Philosophy.* The system of thought holding that all phenomena can be explained in terms of natural causes and laws, without attributing moral, spiritual, or supernatural significance to them. **3.** *Theology.* The doctrine that all religious truths are derived from nature and natural causes and not from revelation. **4.** Conduct or thought prompted by natural desires or instincts.

nat·u·ral·ist (náchrə-list, náchə-) *n.* **1.** One versed in natural history, especially in zoology or botany. **2.** One who believes in and follows the tenets of naturalism.

nat·u·ral·is·tic (náchrə-lístik, náchə-) *adj.* **1.** Imitating or producing the effect or appearance of nature. **2.** Of, pertaining to, or in accordance with the doctrines of naturalism. **3.** Of or pertaining to natural history.

natural law *n.* **1.** A law of morality thought to derive from an instinctive sense of right and wrong rather than from the legislation of society, for example. **2.** A law of science that ascribes order and regularity to natural phenomena such as tides, for example.

natural logarithm *n. Symbol* **ln** *Mathematics.* A logarithm to the base e (=2.71828 . . .). For example, in 10 = $\log_e$ 10 = 2.30258. Also called "Napierian logarithm".

nat·u·ral·ly (náchrə-li, náchə-) *adv.* **1.** In a natural manner. **2.** By nature; inherently. **3. a.** As might be expected in the circumstances. **b.** Without a doubt; of course.

natural number *n. Mathematics.* One of the set of positive whole numbers; a positive integer.

natural philosophy *n.* The study of nature and the physical universe, especially studies that led historically to the modern science of physics.

natural resources *pl.n.* Material sources of wealth that occur in a natural state, such as forests or minerals.

natural science *n.* A science, such as biology, chemistry, or physics, based on the study of the physical world and its phenomena. **2.** These sciences collectively.

natural selection *n.* The phenomenon that individuals possessing characteristics advantageous for survival in a specific environment constitute an increasing proportion of the population in that environment with each succeeding generation. See **Darwinism.**

natural theology *n.* A theology in which knowledge of God is based on reasoning from natural phenomena, not divine revelation.

natural varnish *n.* **Varnish** *(see).*

natural virtues *pl.n.* The **cardinal virtues** *(see).*

natural wastage *n.* A gradual reduction in the personnel of a company or organisation through retirement, resignation, or death, rather than through enforced redundancies, for example. Also *chiefly U.S.* "attrition".

na·ture (náychər) *n.* **1.** The intrinsic characteristics and qualities of a person or thing: *the essential nature of poetry.* **2.** The order, disposition, and essence of all entities composing the physical universe. **3.** The physical world, usually the outdoors, including all living things and natural phenomena such as fire, snow, and thunder. **4.** Natural scenery: *gaze upon nature.* **5.** *Often capital* **N.** The forces or processes of the physical world, sometimes personified as a female being: *leave it to Mother Nature.* **6.** The primitive state of existence, untouched and uninfluenced by civilisation or artificiality. **7.** *Theology.* Man's natural state, as distinguished from the state of grace. **8.** Kind; type: *something of that nature.* **9.** The aggregate of a person's instincts, and preferences. **10. a.** A particular kind of individual character or disposition; temperament: *a sweet nature.* **b.** *Literary.* A person or thing characterised by some particular disposition: *"Strange natures made a brotherhood of ill."* (P.B. Shelley). **11.** The natural or real aspect of a person, place, or thing: *her true nature.* **12.** Generally accepted standards of morality or conduct: *thought homosexuality to be against nature.* **13.** Bodily processes and functions, such as urination. Often used euphemistically in the phrase *a call of nature.* —See Synonyms at **disposition, type.** —**by nature.** Because of natural qualities; inherently. —**in** or **of the nature of.** Belonging to the type or category of. [Middle English, from Old French, from Latin *nātūra,* nature, "birth", from *nāscī* (past participle *nātus*), to be born.]

nature study *n.* The observation and study of plants, animals, and natural phenomena, usually nontechnical and informal.

nature trail *n.* A path through a park or in the countryside allowing people to study the flora and fauna as they walk along it.

na·tur·ism (náychə-riz'm) *n.* **Nudism** *(see).*

na·tur·op·a·thy (náychə-róppəthi) *n.* A system of therapy that relies exclusively on natural remedies, such as sunlight, organically grown foods, fresh air, and massage, to treat the sick. [From NATURE + -PATHY.] —**na·tur·o·path** (náychə-rə-path, nə-téwr-ə- || -tóor-) *n.* —**na·tur·o·path·ic** (-páthik) *adj.*

naught (nawt) *n.* **1.** *Archaic.* Nothing. **2.** *Chiefly U.S.* Variant of **nought.** —**set at naught.** To consider as being of little importance. ~*adj.* Worthless; of no value. [Middle English *nauht,* Old English *nāwiht* : *nā,* NO + *wiht,* creature, thing.]

naugh·ty (náwti) *adj.* **-tier, -tiest.** **1.** Disobedient; mischievous. Usually said of a child or a child's misdeeds. **2.** Indecent or suggestive of indecency. **3.** *Archaic.* Wicked; evil. [Middle English *nauhty,* from *nauht,* "worthless", NAUGHT.] —**naugh·ti·ly** *adv.* —**naugh·ti·ness** *n.*

Nau·pli·a (náwpli-ə). *Greek* **Návplion** (naáf-pli-on). A seaport and capital of Argolís prefecture, Peloponnese, southeast Greece. It was the first capital of independent Greece (1830–34).

nau·pli·us (náw-pli-əss) *n., pl.* **-plii** (-pli-ī). *Zoology.* The microscopic, free-swimming larva of certain crustaceans, having an oval body and three pairs of limbs. [Latin, from Greek *nauplios,* sailor, perhaps variant of *nautilos,* sailor, NAUTILUS.]

Na·u·ru, Republic of (naa-róo, *properly* -óo-róo). Formerly **Pleasant Island.** A state of the central Pacific. Consisting of one coral island, its sole product is phosphates, reserves of which will run out in about 2000. It is a member of the Commonwealth. Area, 21 square kilometres (8 square miles). Population, 7,000. Capital, Yaren. See map at **Pacific Ocean.**

nau·se·a (náw-zi-ə, -si-, -zhi-, -shi- || -zhə, -shə) *n.* **1.** The sensation characterised by a feeling of the need to vomit. **2.** Strong aversion; repugnance; disgust. [Latin, from Greek *nausia,* seasickness, from *naus,* ship.]

nau·se·ate (náw-zi-ayt, -si-, -zhi-, -shi-) *v.* **-ated, -ating, -ates.** —*tr.* **1.** To cause to feel nausea; make queasy. **2.** To cause to feel loathing or disgust; sicken. —*intr.* To feel nausea or queasiness; be queasy. [Latin *nauseāre,* from *nausea,* NAUSEA.] —**nau·se·at·ing·ly** *adv.* —**nau·se·a·tion** (-áysh'n) *n.*

nau·se·ous (náw-zi-əss, -si-, -zhi-, -shi- || -shəss) *adj.* **1.** Causing nausea; sickening. **2.** Repulsive to the mind or senses; very offensive. **3.** Suffering from nausea. —**nau·seous·ly** *adv.* —**nau·se·ous·ness** *n.*

naut. nautical.

nautch (nawch) *n.* A dance form of northern India for girl dancers *(nautch-girls)* accompanied by several musicians and sometimes by a singer. [Hindi *nāc,* from Prakrit *nacca,* dance, from Sanskrit *nṛtya,* from *nṛtyati,* he dances.] —**nautch** *adj.*

nau·ti·cal (náw-tik'l) *adj. Abbr.* **naut.** Of, pertaining to, or characteristic of ships, shipping, seamen, or navigation. [From Latin *nauticus,* from Greek *nautikos,* from *nautēs,* seaman, from *naus,* ship.] —**nau·ti·cal·ly** *adv.*

Usage: *Nautical* is a general term pertaining to sailors, ships, and navigation *nautical miles. Naval* now pertains specifically to the personnel and ships of a navy, or a military sea force.

nautical mile *n. Abbr.* **nm, n.m.** A unit of length used in sea and air navigation: **1.** An international unit equal to 1 852 metres (6,076.103 feet). In this sense, also called "air mile". **2.** A British unit equal to 6,080 feet (1 853 metres). In this sense, formerly called "geographical mile". Compare **sea mile.**

nau·ti·loid (náw-ti-loyd) *n.* A mollusc of the subclass Nautiloidea, which includes the nautiluses and numerous extinct species known only as fossils. [From New Latin *Nautiloidea* : NAUTIL(US) + *-oidea,* from Latin *-oīdēs,* -OID.] —**nau·ti·loid** *adj.*

nau·ti·lus (náw-ti-ləss) *n., pl.* **-luses** or **-li** (-lī). **1.** Any cephalopod mollusc of the genus *Nautilus,* found in the Indian and Pacific oceans, and having a spiral shell with a series of air-filled chambers. See **chambered nautilus. 2.** The **paper nautilus** *(see).* [Latin, from Greek *nautilos,* sailor, from *naus,* ship.]

nav. **1.** naval. **2.** navigable. **3.** navigation.

Nav·a·ho (návvə-hō, naávə-) *n., pl.* **-hos** or collectively **Navaho.** Also **Nav·a·jo** (-hō). **1.** A member of a group of Athapascan-speaking North American Indians occupying an extensive reservation in parts of New Mexico, Arizona, and Utah. **2.** The language of this group. [From Spanish, pueblo.] —**Nav·a·ho** *adj.*

na·val (náyv'l) *adj. Abbr.* **nav. 1.** Of or pertaining to the equipment, operations, personnel, or customs of a navy: *a naval officer.* **2.** Having a navy: *a great naval power.* —See Usage note at **nautical.** [Latin *nāvālis,* from *nāvis,* ship.]

naval architect *n.* One who designs ships. —**naval architecture** *n.*

naval dockyard *n.* A dockyard owned by the government for the repair, equipping, or docking of naval ships.

nav·ar (návvaar) *n.* A method of air navigation in which traffic in a pilot's vicinity is observed by ground radar and relayed to the pilot's radarscope. [*Nav*igational + rad*ar.*]

nav·ar·in (návvə-rin, -raN) *n.* A lamb or mutton stew with vegetables. [French.]

Na·varre (nə-vár). *Spanish* **Na·var·ra** (na-bárra). Former kingdom astride the Pyrenees, southwest Europe. Ruled by a Basque dynasty (9th–13th century), it was absorbed by Spain and France (1589). Today, much of it forms the Spanish province of Navarra. —**Na·var·rese** (naávə-réez, návvə-, -réess) *adj.*

nave[1] (nayv) *n.* The central part of a church, extending from the narthex to the chancel and flanked by aisles. [Medieval Latin *nāvis,* "ship" (referring to the general shape) from Latin.]

nave[2] *n.* The hub of a wheel. [Middle English *nave,* Old English *nafu.*]

na·vel (náyv'l) *n.* **1.** The mark on the abdomen of mammals, where the umbilical cord was attached during gestation; the umbilicus. **2.** A central point; the middle. —**contemplate (one's) navel.** To indulge in introspection. Used humorously. [Middle English *navel,* Old English *nafela.*]

navel orange *n.* A sweet, usually seedless orange having at its apex a navel-like formation enclosing an underdeveloped fruit.

na·vel·wort (náyv'l-wurt || -wawrt) *n.* **1.** A plant, **pennywort** *(see).* **2.** Any plant of the genus *Omphalodes,* having one-sided clusters of usually blue flowers. [From the navel-like depression on its leaves.]

na·vic·u·lar (nə-víckew-lər) *n. Anatomy.* **1.** A comma-shaped bone of the wrist. **2.** The concave bone in front of the anklebone on the instep of the foot. Also called "scaphoid".
~*adj.* Shaped like a boat. [Late Latin *nāviculāris,* "boat-shaped", from Latin *nāvicula,* boat, diminutive of *nāvis,* ship.]

nav·i·ga·ble (návvi-gəb'l) *adj. Abbr.* **nav. 1.** Sufficiently deep or wide to provide passage for ships or boats. **2.** Capable of being steered. Said of sea vessels or aircraft. —**nav·i·ga·bil·i·ty** (-gə-bílləti), **nav·i·ga·ble·ness** *n.* —**nav·i·ga·bly** *adv.*

nav·i·gate (návvi-gayt) *v.* **-gated, -gating, -gates.** —*tr.* **1.** To plan, record, and control the course and position of (a ship or aircraft). **2.** To follow a planned course on, across, or through: *navigate a stream.* **3.** *Informal.* To direct the course of (someone or something) towards some destination. —*intr.* **1.** To control the course of a ship or aircraft. **2.** To voyage over water in a boat or ship; sail. **3.** To guide the driver of a vehicle to a destination, often with the use of maps. [Latin *nāvigāre,* to manage a ship : *nāvis,* ship + *agere,* to drive, conduct.]

nav·i·ga·tion (návvi-gáysh'n) *n. Abbr.* **nav. 1.** The theory and skill of navigating, especially the charting of a course for a ship or aircraft. **2.** The act and practice of navigating. —**nav·i·ga·tion·al** *adj.*

nav·i·ga·tor (návvi-gaytər) *n.* **1.** One who navigates, especially: **a.** One who explores by ship. **b.** A crew member who plots the course of a ship or aircraft. **c.** A person guiding a driver in a car rally. **2.** A device that directs the course of an aircraft or missile.

Nav·ra·ti·lo·va (návrəti-lṓvə; *Czech* -lo-vaá), **Martina** (1956–). U.S. lawn tennis player, born in Czechoslovakia. She defected to the United States in 1975. She was Wimbledon singles champion in 1978, 1979, and 1982.

nav·vy (návvi) *n., pl.* **-vies.** *British Informal.* A labourer, especially one employed in construction or excavation projects. [Slang short-

PRONUNCIATION KEY

a, trap; aa, father; ai, fair;
ar, star; aw, lawn; ay, play;
b, bb, stab; rubber;
ch, church; ck, ticket;
d, dd, dead; ladder; e, dress;
ee, bee; er, defer; ew, few;
ewr, pure; ə, about;
ər, letter; f, ff, fife; differ;
g, gg, giggle; h, hat; i, kit;
ī, price; īr, fire; j, judge;
k, kick; l, ll, let; 'l, needle;
m, mm, man; n, nn, no;
'n, sudden; ng, thing; o, lot;
ō, no; ŏo, foot; ōo, shoe;
oor, poor; ow, cow;
owr, hour; oy, boy;
p, pp, pepper; r, rr, red;
s, ss, sauce; sh, ship;
t, tt, totter; th, thick; th, this;
smooth; u, cut; ur, turn;
v, vv, valve; w, wet; y, yes;
z, zz, zebra; zh, vision;
pleasure

IN FOREIGN WORDS:

aN, oN, Saint-Saëns;
hl, Llanelli; Hluhluwe;
kh, loch; lough; Khaled

STRESS MARK:

ín-sīt, insight; in-sīt, incite

Neanderthal man *An artist's impression shows how archaeologists visualise Neanderthal man, a Stone Age hunter who lived in Europe 35–70,000 years ago. The hunters were named after the site where their skeletal remains were first discovered: the Neander Valley near Düsseldorf in West Germany.*

ening of NAVIGATOR, humorously applied to labourers who built the navigation canals of England in the 18th and 19th centuries.]

na·vy (náyvi) *n., pl.* **-vies. 1.** All of a nation's warships. **2.** *Often capital* **N.** A nation's entire military organisation for sea warfare and defence, including vessels, personnel, and shore establishments. **3.** *Archaic.* A group of ships; a fleet. **4.** Navy blue. [Middle English *navie*, from Old French, from Vulgar Latin *nāvia* (unattested), fleet, from Latin *nāvis*, ship.] —**na·vy** *adj.*

navy blue *n.* Dark greyish blue. [From the colour of the British naval uniform.] —**na·vy-blue** *adj.*

navy yard *n. U.S.* A naval dockyard (*see*).

na·wab (nə-wáab) *n.* **1.** A governor or ruler in India under the Mogul empire. **2.** A title given to eminent Muslims in India. [Urdu *nawwāb*, from Arabic *nuwwāb*, originally plural of *nā'ib*, deputy.]

Nax·os (nák-soss, -sŏss). The largest island of the Cyclades, in the Aegean Sea, Greece. It was associated, through its wine trade, with Dionysiac cults in ancient times.

nay (nay) *adv.* **1.** No. Now archaic or regional except in recording or expressing a vote. **2.** And moreover. Used to introduce a further, more precise or emphatic expression: *He was ugly, nay, hideous.* ~*n.* **1.** A denial or refusal. **2.** A negative or dissenting vote or voter. —**say (someone) nay.** To deny, refuse, or forbid someone. [Middle English *nay, nei*, from Old Norse *nei* : *ne*, not + *ei*, ever.]

na·ya pai·sa (ní-ə pí-sə), *pl.* **naye paise** (-ay -say). A monetary unit of India, the **paisa** (*see*). [Hindi *nayā paisā*, "new pice".]

Naz·a·rene (názzə-réen, -reen) *n.* **1. a.** A native or inhabitant of Nazareth. **b.** Jesus. Preceded by *the.* **2.** A member of a sect of early Christians of Jewish origin who retained many of the prescribed Jewish observances. [Middle English *Nazaren*, from Late Latin *Nazarēnus*, from Greek *Nazarēnos*, from *Nazarat*, NAZARETH.] —**Naz·a·rene** *adj.*

Naz·a·reth (názzə-rəth). Market town in Galilee, northern Israel. Through its links with Jesus Christ, it has become a place of pilgrimage for Christians and Muslims.

Na·zi (naát-si ‖ nát-) *n., pl.* **-zis. 1.** A member of the National Socialist German Workers' Party, founded in Germany in 1919 and brought to power in 1933 under Adolf Hitler. **2.** *Often small* **n.** An adherent or advocate of policies characteristic of this party; a fascist. [German, phonetic shortening of *Nationalsozialist* National Socialist.] —**Na·zi** *adj.* —**Na·zi·fy** *tr.v.*

Naz·i·rite, Naz·a·rite (názzə-rīt) *n.* In Biblical times, a person, usually a man, who had made a vow to God and was bound to abstain from strong drink and ritual defilement. [From Late Latin *Nazaraeus*, from Hebrew *nāzīr*, from *nāzar*, to consecrate oneself.]

Na·zism (naát-siz'm ‖ nát-) *n.* Also **Na·zi·ism** (naát-si-iz'm ‖ nát-). The ideology and practice of the Nazis; especially, the policy of state control of the economy, racist nationalism, and national expansion. Also called "National Socialism".

Nb The symbol for the element niobium.

n.b. 1. *Cricket.* no ball. **2.** nota bene.

N.B. 1. New Brunswick. **2.** nota bene.

N.B.C. National Broadcasting Corporation (in the United States).

NbE north by east.

N.B.G. *British Informal.* No bloody good.

n-bod·y problem (én-bóddi) *n. Physics.* The problem of determining the motions of *n* bodies moving under the influence of mutual interactions that depend on their distances apart; for example, determining the paths of bodies interacting by gravitational forces. For more than two bodies, there is no complete solution to the problem.

n-butane *n.* A gaseous hydrocarbon, **butane** (*see*).

NbW north by west.

N.C.B. National Coal Board (in Britain).

N.C.C.L. National Council for Civil Liberties (in Britain).

NCO, N.C.O. noncommissioned officer.

Nd The symbol for the element neodymium.

n.d. No date.

Nde·be·le (əndə-béle) *n., pl.* **-les** or collectively **Ndebele. 1.** A member of a Zulu people of southern Africa, now living chiefly in northern Transvaal and Matabeleland. **2.** The Bantu language of this people. Also called "Matabele". [See **Matabele**.] —**Nde·be·le** *adj.*

N'dja·me·na (ən-jaa-máynə). Formerly **Fort La·my** (fór-lə-mée). The capital of Chad. At the confluence of the Chari and Longone rivers, it is a river port on a main caravan route.

né (nay) *adj.* Born. Used after a man's name to indicate an original name: *Michael Caine, né Maurice Micklewhite.* [French, masculine past participle of *naître*, be born.]

Ne The symbol for the element neon.

NE northeast.

Neagh, Lough (nay). Lake in Northern Ireland. With an area of 396 square kilometres (153 square miles), it is the largest freshwater lake in the British Isles.

Ne·an·der·thal (ni-ándər-taal, nay-, -aándər- ‖ -thawl) *adj.* **1.** Of or pertaining to Neanderthal man. **2.** *Informal.* Crude or reactionary: *a Neanderthal mentality.* —**Ne·an·der·thal** *n.*

Neanderthal man *n.* An extinct species or race of man, *Homo sapiens neanderthalensis*, living during the late Pleistocene age in the Old World, and associated with Middle Palaeolithic tools. [After *Neanderthal*, valley near Düsseldorf, West Germany, where remains were found.]

neap (neep) *adj.* Of or pertaining to a neap tide. ~*n.* A neap tide. [Old English *nēp-*†, as in *nēpflōd*, "neap flood".]

Ne·a·pol·i·tan (née-ə-póllitən) *adj.* Of, belonging to, or characteristic of Naples. ~*n.* A native or resident of Naples.

Neapolitan ice cream *n.* Ice cream in brick form, with layers of different colours and flavours.

neap tide *n.* A tide of lowest range, occurring when the sun and moon are in quadrature. Compare **spring tide**.

near (neer) *adv.* **nearer, nearest. 1.** To, at, or within a short distance or interval in space or time: *The day was drawing near.* **2.** Almost; nearly. Now rare except when followed by *to*, in the informal phrase *damn near*, or in combination: *came near to winning; damn near killed him; near-extinct.* **3.** With or in a close relationship. —**near as dammit.** *Informal.* Varying only in insignificant detail; almost: *It cost £80, near as dammit.* ~*adj.* **nearer, nearest. 1.** Close in time, space, position, or degree: *near neighbours; near equals; the near future.* **2.** Closely related by kinship or association; intimate: *near and dear friends.* **3. a.** Accomplished by a small margin; close; narrow: *a near escape.* **b.** Missed or avoided by a small margin: *a near disaster.* **4.** Closely corresponding to or resembling an original: *a near likeness.* **5. a.** Closer or shorter of two or more. **b.** On the left side, as of a vehicle, animal, or draught team: *the near front wheel; the near hind leg.* **6.** *Archaic.* Strictly economical; stingy; parsimonious. ~*prep. Abbr.* **nr.** Close to; within a short distance or time of. ~*v.* **neared, nearing, nears.** —*tr.* To come close or closer to. —*intr.* To draw near or nearer. [Middle English *nere*, Old English *nēar*, comparative adverb of *nēah*, "near".] —**near·ness** *n.*

near·by (néer-bī, -bī) *adj.* Located a short distance away; close at hand; adjacent. —**near·by** *adj.*

Ne·arc·tic (nee-árk-tik ‖ -ár-) *adj.* Of or designating the zoogeographical region that includes the Arctic and temperate areas of North America and also includes Greenland. Compare **Palaearctic**. [NE(O)- + ARCTIC.]

Near East 1. A region including the countries of the eastern Mediterranean, the Arabian Peninsula, and, sometimes, northeastern Africa. **2.** Formerly, the Balkan Peninsula and Turkey.

near·ly (néerli) *adv.* **1.** Almost but not quite. **2.** Closely; intimately: *a matter nearly affecting our interests.* —**not nearly.** Deficient by a long way: *not nearly good enough.*

near point *n.* The closest point to the eye at which an object can be focused without strain. The distance of this point increases with age; for the normal eye it is about 25 centimetres (10 inches).

near·sight·ed (néer-sītid) *adj.* Afflicted with **myopia** (*see*); shortsighted. —**near·sight·ed·ly** *adv.* —**near·sight·ed·ness** *n.*

near thing *n. Informal.* An outcome, such as a victory or disaster, decided by a narrow margin.

neat¹ (neet) *adj.* **1.** In good order or clean condition; tidy. **2.** Orderly and precise in appearance or procedure; not careless or messy. **3.** Skilfully executed; deft; adroit: *a neat turn of phrase.* **4.** Simply, precisely, or cleverly worked out or arranged: *a neat idea.* **5.** Not diluted or mixed with other substances. Said chiefly of alcoholic drinks. **6.** *Rare.* Obtained after all deductions; net: *neat profit.* **7.** *Chiefly U.S. Slang.* Appealing: *It would be really neat to go to Paris.* [Old French *net*, from Latin *nitidus*, elegant, shiny, from *nitēre*, to shine.] —**neat·ly** *adv.* —**neat·ness** *n.*

neat² *n., pl.* **neat.** *Archaic.* A domestic bovine animal. [Middle English *nete*, Old English *nēat*.]

neath, 'neath (neeth) *prep. Poetic.* Beneath.

neat·herd (néet-herd) *n. Archaic.* A cowherd.

neat's-foot oil (néets-fŏŏt) *n.* A light, yellow oil obtained from the feet and shinbones of cattle, used chiefly to dress leather.

neb (neb) *n. Chiefly Scottish.* **1. a.** A beak of a bird. **b.** A nose or snout. **2.** A projecting part, especially a nib. [Middle English *neb(b)*, Old English *neb(b).*]

N.E.B. New English Bible.

Ne·bras·ka (ni-brásko). State in central United States. Rising from the Missouri prairie lands in the east to the Great Plains and foothills of the Rocky Mountains in the west, it is predominantly agricultural, producing cattle, maize, pigs, and wheat. The state also has large oil reserves. Part of the Louisiana Purchase, it was admitted to the Union in 1867. Lincoln is the capital. —**Ne·bras·kan** *adj. & n.*

Neb·u·chad·nez·zar (nébbew-kəd-nézzər, -kad-) *n.* An extremely large wine bottle, equivalent in capacity to 20 standard bottles. [After NEBUCHADNEZZAR II (from the custom of naming very large wine bottles after Old Testament characters).]

Nebuchadnezzar II (*c.*630–562 B.C.). Chaldean King of Babylon. He extended Chaldean power throughout the old Assyrian empire; sacking Jerusalem (586 B.C.), he deported its inhabitants to Babylon.

neb·u·la (nébbew-lə) *n., pl.* **-lae** (-lee) or **-las. 1.** *Astronomy.* **a.** Any diffuse mass of interstellar dust, gas, or both, visible as luminous patches or areas of darkness depending on the way the mass absorbs, scatters, or emits electromagnetic radiation. There are two types: bright nebulae, which include emission and reflection nebulae, and dark nebulae, which are also called absorption nebulae. **b.** A galactic nebula (*see*). **2.** *Pathology.* **a.** A cloudy spot on the cornea. **b.** Cloudiness in the urine. **3.** *Medicine.* A liquid medication applied by spraying. [New Latin, from Latin, cloud.] —**neb·u·lar** (-lər) *adj.*

nebular hypothesis *n.* A hypothesis put forward by Laplace in 1796 to account for the origin of the Solar System, according to which a rotating nebula cooled and contracted, throwing off rings of matter that contracted into the planets and their moons, while the greater mass of the condensing nebula became the Sun. Compare **planetesimal hypothesis, presolar nebular hypothesis.**

neb·u·lise, neb·u·lize (nébbew-līz) *tr.v.* **-lised, -lising, -lises. 1.** To convert (a liquid) to a fine spray; atomise. **2.** To treat with a medicated spray. [From NEBULA.] **—neb·u·li·sa·tion** (-lī-záysh'n ‖ *U.S.* -li-) *n.* **—neb·u·lis·er** *n.*

neb·u·los·i·ty (nébbew-lóssəti) *n., pl.* **-ties. 1.** The quality or condition of being nebulous. **2.** A nebula or a mass of material constituting a nebula.

neb·u·lous (nébbew-ləss) *adj.* **1.** Cloudy, misty, or hazy. **2.** Lacking definite form or limits; unclearly identified or established; vague: *gave an evasive, nebulous answer.* **3.** Of or characteristic of a nebula. [Latin *nebulōsus,* from *nebula,* cloud, NEBULA.] **—neb·u·lous·ly** *adv.* **—neb·u·lous·ness** *n.*

nec·es·sar·i·ly (néssə-sərəli, néssi-, -serrəli, -sérrəli) *adv.* **1.** As dictated by necessity; of necessity. **2.** As a necessary or inevitable consequence: *He isn't necessarily angry just because he won't come.*

nec·es·sar·y (néssə-səri, néssi-, -sri, -serri) *adj.* **1.** Needed for the continuing existence or functioning of something; essential; indispensable: *Oxygen is necessary to most living organisms.* **2.** Needed to achieve a certain result or effect; requisite: *the necessary tools.* **3.** Following unavoidably from conditions, circumstances, or premises; inevitable: *the necessary results of overindulgence.* **4.** Required by obligation, compulsion, or convention: *making the necessary apologies.* **5.** *Logic.* **a.** Designating a proposition whose denial would be a self-contradiction. **b.** Designating an argument or inference whose denial would lead to a contradiction.
~*n., pl.* **necessaries. 1.** *Often plural.* That which is needed; especially, money or provisions: *the necessaries for the trip.* **2.** *Plural. Law.* Whatever is needed for the maintenance of a dependant, in keeping with his economic and social status. **—the necessary.** *Informal.* Money. [Middle English *necessarie,* from Latin *necessārius,* extension of *necesse,* necessary.]

Synonyms: necessary, essential, vital, indispensable, requisite, required, prerequisite.

Usage: In its plural form, a distinction needs to be made between *necessaries* and *necessities. Necessaries* are those things which we need, but which are not absolutely essential. *Necessities* is a much stronger term, referring to those things which are essential - for example, to survive. For some people, the *necessaries* of modern life include the possession of a television set, but few people would consider it a *necessity* of the same order as food or heating.

necessary condition *n. Logic.* A condition for the truth of a proposition or state of affairs that must hold if the proposition is true, but that does not guarantee its truth; for example, it is a necessary condition for my car to start that it has not run out of petrol: it is not a **sufficient condition** (see) since many other things may be wrong with the car.

ne·ces·si·tar·i·an·ism (ni-séssi-taír-i-ə-niz'm) *n.* Also **nec·es·sar·i·an·ism** (néssə-saír-i-ə-niz'm) The doctrine that events are inevitably determined by preceding causes. **—ne·ces·si·tar·i·an** *adj. & n.*

ne·ces·si·tate (ni-séssi-tayt) *tr.v.* **-tated, -tating, -tates. 1.** To make necessary or unavoidable: *The emergency necessitated a change in plans.* **2.** *Chiefly U.S.* To require or compel (someone). Used chiefly in the passive: *He was necessitated to back down.* **—See Synonyms at force.** [Medieval Latin *necessitāre* (past participle *necessitātus*), from Latin *necessitās,* NECESSITY.] **—ne·ces·si·ta·tion** (-táysh'n) *n.*

ne·ces·si·tous (ni-séssitəss) *adj.* Needy; destitute; indigent. [French *nécessiteux,* from Old French *necessite,* NECESSITY.] **—ne·ces·si·tous·ly** *adv.*

ne·ces·si·ty (ni-séssəti) *n., pl.* **-ties. 1.** Something needed for the existence, effectiveness, or success of something; an essential requirement. **2.** Something that must inevitably exist or occur, as: **a.** That which is dictated by invariable physical laws or strict social requirements. **b.** That which is dictated by constraining circumstances: *the grim necessities of war.* **3.** The state or fact of being indispensable or unavoidable. **4.** Pressing or urgent need, such as that arising from poverty, misfortune, or emergency: *Necessity drove him to desperation.* **—of necessity.** As an inevitable consequence; necessarily. **—See Usage note at necessary.** [Middle English *necessite,* from Old French, from Latin *necessitas* (stem *necessitāt-*), from *necesse,* be NECESSARY.]

neck (nek) *n.* **1.** The part of the body joining the head to the trunk. **2. a.** The part of a garment around or near the neck of the wearer. **b.** The neckline of a dress, blouse, or other garment. **3.** *Anatomy.* Any relatively narrow portion of a structure, as of a bone or organ, that joins its parts. **4.** The part of a tooth between the crown and the root. **5.** Any relatively narrow elongation, projection, or connecting part, as: **a.** A peninsula. **b.** A strait. **c.** A pass. **d.** The narrow top part of a bottle, jug, or the like. **6.** *Music.* The narrow part along which the strings of a stringed instrument extend to the pegs. **7.** *Architecture.* The narrow, upper part of a column, just below the capital. **8.** *Geology.* Solidified lava filling the vent of an extinct volcano. **9.** *Botany.* The upper, tubular section of an archegonium. **10. a.** The length of the head and neck of a horse: *winning a race by a neck.* **b.** *Informal.* Any narrow margin by which a competition is won or lost. **11.** *Informal.* One's life or personal safety: *risk one's neck; save one's neck.* **—break (one's) neck.** *Informal.* **1.** To incur serious physical injury. **2.** To make a great effort to accomplish something. **—get it in the neck.** *Informal.* To undergo severe punishment, rebuke, or penalty. **—neck and neck.** Even in a race or contest. **—stick (one's) neck out.** *Informal.* To act boldly, despite the risk of criticism, trouble, or danger.

nebula

CLOUDS OF STARDUST AND GAS
The birthplace of the stars

Nebulae are huge, wispy patches of dust and gas (mainly hydrogen), and are the material from which new stars are produced. A nebula starts to form into stars when it becomes dense enough to collapse under the inward pull of its own gravity. As the nebula collapses, it separates into clumps, each of which will form a star. Eventually the pressure and temperature at the centre of the clump rise sufficiently for nuclear reactions to begin, and the star is born.

When stars form in the nebula their light makes the gas in the surrounding cloud glow, creating a bright (or emission) nebula. Some, however, do not emit light, but reflect it from nearby stars (reflection nebulae).

Dark (or absorption) nebulae have not yet begun to create stars, and form a dark cloud in space, obscuring other stars beyond them.

The Crab Nebula in the constellation Taurus is not a nebula but a remnant of a supernova (a huge stellar explosion) in which a massive star blew itself to pieces. It left a gas cloud within which is a small, dense pulsar (a flashing object made up of particles called neutrons).

TRIFID NEBULA *Dark clefts in the cloud mass seem to split the Trifid Nebula in Sagittarius into three. A bright (emission) nebula, it was discovered in the 18th century by the French astronomer Legentil de la Galaisière, but was named in the 19th century by Sir John Herschel.*

~*intr.v.* **necked, necking, necks.** *Slang.* To kiss and caress. [Middle English *necke,* Old English *hnecca.*]

necked (nekt) *adj.* Having a neck or neckline of the specified kind. Used in combination: *a low-necked dress.*

Neck·er (néckər, ne-kaír), **Jacques** (1732–1804). French financier and politician. As a director of of the French East India Company (1768), and director of general finance (1777), he introduced reforms and fought corruption. He resigned (1781), was reappointed (1788), and then dismissed and imprisoned. He was subsequently reappointed, but soon resigned and retired to Switzerland (1790).

neck·er·chief (néckər-chif, -cheef) *n.* **1.** A kerchief worn around the neck. **2.** A triangular piece of coloured cloth worn round the neck as part of a Scout's uniform.

neck·ing (nécking) *n. Architecture.* A moulding or mouldings between the upper part of the shaft of a column and the projecting part of the capital.

neck·lace (néck-ləss, -liss) *n.* An ornament, such as a string of beads or a flexible metal chain or band, worn around the neck.

neck·let (néck-lət, -lit) *n.* **1.** A close-fitting necklace. **2.** Something worn about the neck for ornamentation, such as a fur piece.

neck·line (néck-līn) *n.* The line formed by the edge of a garment at or near the neck: *a plunging neckline.*

neck microphone *n.* A small microphone on a loop worn round the neck. Also *U.S.* "lavaliere".

neck of the woods *n. Informal.* A district; a neighbourhood.

neck·tie (nék-tī) *n. Chiefly U.S.* A tie (sense 3).

neck·wear (nék-wair) *n.* Articles of dress worn around the neck, such as ties, scarves, and collars.

necro–, necr– *comb. form.* Indicates: **1.** Death or the dead; for

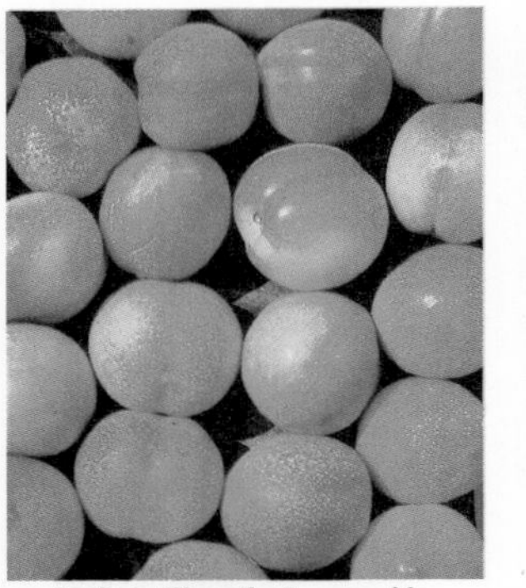

nectarine *These fruits resemble plums with their smooth skin, but they are, in fact, a type of peach.*

example, **necrology.** **2.** A dead body or dead tissue; for example, **necrobiosis, necropsy.** [New Latin, from Greek *nekros,* corpse.]

nec·ro·bi·o·sis (néckrō-bī-ṓ-siss) *n.* The natural degeneration and death of cells and tissues, as opposed to death from injury or disease and distinguished from death of the entire organism. Compare **gangrene, necrosis.** [New Latin : NECRO- + -BIOSIS.] **—nec·ro·bi·ot·ic** (-óttik) *adj.*

ne·crol·a·try (ne-króllə-tri, ni-) Worship of the dead. [NECRO- + -LATRY.]

ne·crol·o·gy (ne-króllәji, ni-) *n., pl.* **-gies. 1.** A list or record of people who have died. **2.** The study of the phenomena associated with death. **3.** An obituary. [New Latin *necrologium* : NECRO- + -LOGY.] **—nec·ro·log·i·cal** (néckrə-lójik'l) *adj.* **—ne·crol·o·gist** (-króllәjist) *n.*

nec·ro·man·cy (néckrō-man-si-, néckrə-) *n.* **1.** The art that professes to conjure up the spirits of the dead and commune with them in order to predict the future. **2.** Magic, especially black magic or sorcery. See Synonyms at **magic.** [Confusion of: **a.** Late Latin *necromantīa,* from Greek *nekromanteia,* divination by corpses : NECRO- + -MANCY; **b.** Middle English *nigromancie,* from Old French, from Medieval Latin *nigromantia,* black magic : *niger,* black + -MANCY.] **—nec·ro·man·cer** *n.* **—nec·ro·man·tic** (-mántik) *adj.*

ne·croph·a·gous (ne-króffәgәss, ni-) *adj.* Feeding on carrion or corpses. [Greek *nekrophagos* : NECRO- + -PHAGOUS.]

nec·ro·phil·i·a (néckrō-fílli-ə, néckrə-) *n.* Also **ne·croph·i·lism** (ne-króffiliz'm). Sexual attraction to corpses. [NECRO- + -PHILIA.] **—nec·ro·phil·i·ac** (-ak), **nec·ro·phile** (néckrō-fīl, néckrə-) *n.* **—nec·ro·phil·ic** (-fíllik) *adj.*

nec·ro·pho·bi·a (néckrō-fṓbi-ə, néckrə-) *n.* **1.** A morbid fear of death. **2.** A morbid horror of corpses. [New Latin : NECRO- + -PHOBIA.] **—nec·ro·pho·bic** *adj.*

ne·crop·o·lis (ne-króppə-liss, ni-) *n., pl.* **-lises** or **-leis** (-layss). A cemetery; especially, a large and elaborate one belonging to an ancient city. [Greek *nekropolis* : NECRO- + *polis,* city.]

nec·rop·sy (néck-rop-si) *n., pl.* **-sies.** Also **ne·cros·co·py** (ne-króskəpi, ni-) *pl.* **-pies.** An **autopsy** *(see).* [NECR(O)- + -OPSY.]

ne·crose (ne-krṓss, -krṓz, néckrōss) *v.* **-crosed, -crosing, -croses.** Also **nec·ro·tise** (néckrə-tīz), **-tised, -tising, -tises.** *—intr.* To be affected with necrosis. *—tr.* To affect with necrosis. [Back-formation from NECROSIS.]

ne·cro·sis (ne-krṓ-siss, ni-) *n., pl.* **-ses** (-seez). **1.** The death of living tissue due to disease, injury, or interruption of the blood supply. **2.** The death of plant tissue due to injury, frost, or the like. Compare **necrobiosis.** [Late Latin *necrōsis,* from Greek *nekrōsis,* mortification, from *nekroun,* to mortify, from *nekros,* corpse.] **—ne·crot·ic** (-króttik) *adj.*

ne·crot·o·my (ne-króttəmi, ni-) *n., pl.* **-mies. 1.** The dissection of a dead body. **2.** Surgical removal of a piece of dead tissue, especially bone. [NECRO- + -TOMY.]

nec·tar (néktər) *n.* **1.** A sweet liquid secreted by flowers of various plants and gathered by bees for making honey. **2. a.** *Greek & Roman Mythology.* The drink of the gods. Compare **ambrosia. b.** Any delicious or invigorating drink. [Latin, from Greek *nektar.*] **—nec·tar·ous** *adj.*

nec·tar·ine (néktə-reen, -rin, -réen) *n.* A variety of peach, *Prunus persica nectarina,* having a smooth, waxy skin. [Short for *nectarine peach,* from obsolete *nectarine,* "sweet as nectar", from NECTAR.]

nec·ta·ry (néktəri) *n., pl.* **-ries. 1.** *Botany.* **a.** A glandlike organ, usually at the base of a flower, that secretes nectar. **b.** The part of a flower in which such an organ is contained. **2.** *Entomology. A* **siphuncle** *(see).* Not in current technical usage. [New Latin *nectarium,* from NECTAR.] **—nec·tar·i·al** (nek-táiri-əl) *adj.*

N.E.D.C. National Economic Development Council.

Ned·dy (néddi) **1.** A name for a donkey. **2.** *Informal.* See **National Economic Development Council.**

Nederland. See **Netherlands.**

née, nee (nay) *adj.* Born. Used when identifying a married woman by her maiden name: *Mrs. Brown neé Jones.* [French, feminine past participle of *naître,* to be born.]

need (need) *n.* **1.** A condition or situation in which something necessary or desirable is required or wanted: *in need of water.* **2.** A wish or strong desire for something that is lacking: *a need for affection.* **3.** Necessity; obligation: *There is no need for you to go.* **4.** Something required or wanted; a requisite: *Our needs are modest.* **5.** A condition of poverty, emergency, or misfortune.
~*v.* **needed, needing, needs.** Used as an uninflected auxiliary followed by an infinitive without *to,* indicating obligation or necessity: *He need not come. Need you have been so rude?* *—tr.* **1.** To have need of; require; want urgently. **2.** To be obliged or required; have to: *You will need to leave now.* *—intr.* **1.** To be in need or want. **2.** *Archaic.* To be necessary. —See Synonyms at **lack.** [Middle English *nede,* Old English *nēd, nēod,* necessity, distress.]

Usage: *Need* is used in two different constructions in standard English. It can be a full verb, taking an *-s* ending in the third person, being followed by an infinitive with *to,* and having a past tense: *He needs to go; he needed to go.* It can also be an auxiliary verb, in which case it has no ending or past tense, and takes an infinitive without *to: He need do it only once, He needn't go just yet, Need they have done it so fast?* The full verb construction is more frequent than the auxiliary use, which tends to be restricted to negative and interrogative sentences: even *He need do it only once* can be interpreted to mean the negative: *He needn't do it more than once.* The auxiliary construction is more commonly used in British than in American English. As always when two closely related constructions are available, there is some uncertainty of usage. Thus, alongside *no-one need go* and *no one needs to go,* you may sometimes hear *no-one needs go;* alongside *need we go* and *do we need to go,* you may hear *do we need go.* See also **dare** and **use.**

need·ful (néedf'l) *adj. Literary.* Necessary; required.
~*n.* Whatever is needed, especially money. Preceded by *the: Have you got the needful?* **—need·ful·ly** *adv.* **—need·ful·ness** *n.*

nee·dle (néed'l) *n.* **1.** A small, slender sewing implement, now usually of polished steel, pointed at one end, and having an eye at the other through which a length of thread is passed and held. **2.** Any of various implements similar in appearance and use: **a.** A short, sharp instrument with an eye near the pointed end, used in sewing machines. **b.** A slender, pointed rod used in knitting. **c.** A similar implement, usually shorter, and with a hook at one end, used in crocheting. **3.** A gramophone stylus. **4. a.** Any slender pointer or indicator on a dial, scale, or similar part of a mechanical device. **b.** A **magnetic needle** *(see).* **5.** *Medicine.* **a.** A **hypodermic needle** *(see).* **b.** A slender, sharp-pointed surgical instrument used for sewing up tissues during operations. **6.** A stiff, narrow leaf, as on a conifer. **7.** Any fine, sharp projection, such as a spine of a sea urchin or a crystal. **8.** A sharp, pointed instrument used in engraving. **9.** A beam passed through or under a wall and serving as a usually temporary support. **10.** *Informal.* Hostility or animosity, especially as a result of rivalry: *a lot of needle between the teams.* Also used adjectivally: *a needle match.* **—give (someone) the needle.** *Informal.* To goad or provoke so as to rouse to action.
~*v.* **needled, -dling, -dles.** *—tr.* **1.** To prick, pierce, or stitch with or as if with a needle. **2.** *Informal.* To goad, provoke, or tease. *—intr.* To sew or do similar work with a needle. [Middle English *nedle,* Old English *nǣdl,* from Germanic.]

nee·dle-bath (néed'l-baath || -bath) *n.* A shower with very fine jets of water which produce a stinging sensation.

needle bearing. A type of roller bearing with long rollers about two to four millimetres in diameter, which bear directly on the shaft.

nee·dle·cord (néed'l-kawrd) *n.* A finely ribbed corduroy fabric.

nee·dle·fish (néed'l-fish) *n., pl.* **-fishes** or collectively **needlefish. 1.** Any of several marine carnivorous fishes of the family Belonidae, having slender bodies and narrow jaws with sharp teeth. **2.** Any of various fishes with projecting jaws, such as the **pipefish** *(see).*

nee·dle·point (néed'l-poynt) *n.* **1.** Decorative needlework on canvas, usually in a diagonal stitch covering the entire surface of the material. See **gros point, petit point. 2.** A type of lace worked on paper patterns with a needle, as distinguished from bobbin lace. Also called "point lace". **—nee·dle·point** *adj.*

need·less (néedliss) *adj.* Not needed or wished for; unnecessary. **—need·less·ly** *adv.* **—need·less·ness** *n.*

needle valve *n.* A valve having a slender point fitting into a conical seat, for accurately regulating the flow of a liquid or gas.

nee·dle·wom·an (néed'l-wŏŏmən) *n., pl.* **-women** (-wimmin). A woman who does needlework, especially a seamstress.

needlewood *n.* An Australian tree, *Hakea leucoptera,* with needle-like leaves and soft wood used mainly for veneers.

nee·dle·work (néed'l-wurk) *n.* Work done with a needle, such as sewing or embroidery. **—nee·dle·work·er** *n.*

need·n't (néed'nt). Contraction of *need not.*

needs (needz) *adv.* Of necessity; necessarily. Used following *must* and preceding a simple infinitive: *He must needs go;* or preceding *must,* with an infinitive understood: *"She shall go, if needs must."* (Robert Browning). [Middle English *nedes,* Old English *nēdes,* "of need", genitive of *nēd,* NEED.]

need·y (néedi) *adj.* **-ier, -iest.** Being in need; impoverished. **—need·i·ness** *n.*

Né·el temperature (náy-el, -él) *n. Physics.* The characteristic temperature above which a given material changes from an antiferromagnetic state to a ferromagnetic state. Also called "Néel point". [After L. E. F. *Néel* (born 1904), French physicist.]

ne'er (nair). *Poetic.* Contraction of **never.**

ne'er-do-well (náir-dŏŏ-wel) *n.* A worthless, good-for-nothing person; especially, an irresponsible person who never succeeds in any enterprise. **—ne'er-do-well** *adj.*

ne·far·i·ous (ni-fáir-i-əss) *adj.* Evil; infamous: *a nefarious plot.* [Latin *nefārius,* from *nefās,* sin : *ne-,* not + *fās,* divine law, right.] **—ne·far·i·ous·ly** *adv.* **—ne·far·i·ous·ness** *n.*

Nef·er·ti·ti (néffər-téeti), (*c.* 1372–50 B.C.). Queen of Egypt. She was the chief wife of Akhenaton. The exquisite limestone bust of Nefertiti (now in the Berlin Museum) has given rise to the tradition that she was one of the most beautiful women in antiquity.

neg. negative.

ne·gate (ni-gáyt, ne-) *tr.v.* **-gated, -gating, -gates. 1.** To render ineffective or invalid; nullify. **2.** To rule out; deny. —See Synonyms at **nullify, neutralise.** [Latin *negāre,* to deny.]

ne·ga·tion (ni-gáysh'n, ne-) *n.* **1.** The act or process of negating. **2.** A denial, contradiction, or negative statement. **3.** The opposite or absence of something regarded as actual, positive, or affirmative: *"Death is nothing more than the negation of life."* (Henry Fielding).

neg·a·tive (néggə-tiv) *adj. Abbr.* **neg. 1.** Expressing, containing, or consisting of a negation, refusal, or denial: *a negative answer.* **2. a.** Lacking the quality of being positive or affirmative: *negative indications of their guilt.* **b.** Being of an opposite nature to that expected or intended: *a negative return on my investments.* **3.** Indicating opposition, indifference, or resistance: *a negative response to* *an advertising campaign.* **4.** Tending to oppose or disagree with that which is considered positive or constructive: *a negative attitude.* **5.** *Medicine.* Not indicative of the presence of microorganisms, disease, or a specific condition. **6.** *Logic.* Denying agreement between the subject and its predicate. Said of a proposition. **7.** *Mathematics.* Pertaining to or designating: **a.** A quantity less than zero. **b.** The sign (-). **c.** A quantity to be subtracted from another. **d.** A quantity, number, angle, velocity, or direction, in a sense opposite to another of the same magnitude indicated or understood to be positive. **8.** *Physics.* Pertaining to or designating: **a.** Electric charge of the same sign as that of an electron, designated by the symbol (-). **b.** Any body having an excess of electrons. **9.** *Chemistry.* Pertaining to or designating an ion, the anion, that is attracted to a positive electrode. **10.** *Biology.* Indicating resistance to, opposition to, or motion away from a stimulus: *a negative tropism.* **11.** *Optics.* Producing divergent rays. Said of a lens. **12.** Of or pertaining to a photographic negative. Compare **positive.**

~n. **1.** A statement or act indicating or expressing a contradiction, denial, or refusal. **2.** A thing or concept considered to be the counterpart or negation of something positive. **3.** *Grammar.* A word or part of a word, such as *no, not,* or *non-,* that indicates negation. **4.** *Archaic.* The right to veto something. **5.** In photography: **a.** An image in which the light areas of the object rendered appear dark and the dark areas appear light. **b.** A film, plate, or other photographic material containing such an image. **6.** *Mathematics.* A negative quantity. **—in the negative.** In a sense or manner indicating a refusal or denial: *answer in the negative.*

~interj. Chiefly U.S. Used, especially in a military context, to express negation or refusal. Compare **affirmative.**

~tr.v. **negatived, -tiving, -tives. 1.** To refuse to approve or accept; veto or reject. **2. a.** To deny; contradict. **b.** To give a negative sense to. **3.** To demonstrate to be false. **4.** To counteract or neutralise. [Late Latin *negātīvus,* from Latin *negāre,* to NEGATE.] **—neg·a·tive·ly** *adv.* **—neg·a·tive·ness, neg·a·tiv·i·ty** (-tivvəti) *n.*

negative feedback *n.* **1.** A type of **feedback** *(see)* in which an increase in output causes a decrease in input. **2.** Critical or discouraging reactions.

negative prescription *n. Law.* **Prescription** *(see).*

neg·a·tiv·ism (néggəti-viz'm) *n.* **1.** An attitude or system of thought marked by the questioning or denial of traditional beliefs with no attempt to propose alternatives. **2.** The state or tendency of being negative and unconstructive. **3.** *Psychology.* Behaviour characterised by stubborn and unfounded resistance to suggestions, orders, or instructions of others. **—neg·a·tiv·ist** *n. & adj.* **—neg·a·tiv·is·tic** (-vístik) *adj.*

ne·ga·tor (ni-gáytər) *n.* A logic gate, a **NOT gate** *(see).*

Neg·ev (néggev) or **Neg·eb** (néggeb). A desert covering the southern half of Israel, bounded in the north by the hills of Judaea. Irrigation projects support numerous agricultural settlements. There are valuable deposits of natural gas and phosphates.

ne·glect (ni-glékt) *tr.v.* **-glected, -glecting, -glects. 1.** To ignore or pay no attention to; disregard: *They neglected his warning.* **2.** To fail to care for or give proper attention to: *She neglected her appearance.* **3.** To fail to do or carry out through carelessness or oversight: *He neglected to make his point.*

~n. **1.** The act or an instance of neglecting something. **2.** The state of being neglected. **3.** Habitual lack of care. [Latin *negligere, neglegere* (past participle stem *neglect-*), "not to choose", not to heed : *neg-,* not + *legere,* to choose.] **—ne·glect·er, ne·glec·tor** *n.*

ne·glect·ful (ni-gléktf'l) *adj.* Tending to neglect; careless; heedless. Often followed by *of*: *neglectful of responsibilities.* **—ne·glect·ful·ly** *adv.* **—ne·glect·ful·ness** *n.*

neg·li·gee, neg·li·gée, neg·li·gé (néggli-zhay || *U.S.* -zháy) *n.* **1.** A woman's loose dressing gown, often of soft, delicate fabric. **2.** Loosely, any informal or skimpy attire. [French, "casual", "neglected", from *négliger,* to neglect, from Latin *negligere,* NEGLECT.]

neg·li·gence (négglijənss) *n.* **1.** The state or quality of being negligent. **2.** Any negligent act or failure to act. **3.** *Law.* The omission or neglect of any reasonable precaution, care, or action, resulting in accident, injury, or the like.

neg·li·gent (néggli-jənt) *adj.* **1.** Habitually guilty of neglect; lacking in due care or concern. **2.** Careless, especially in a nonchalant or easygoing way. —See Synonyms at **careless.** [Middle English, from Old French, from Latin *negligens* (stem *negligent-*), present participle of *negligere,* to NEGLECT.] **—neg·li·gent·ly** *adv.*

neg·li·gi·ble (négglijə-b'l) *adj.* Not worth considering; trifling: *a negligible amount.* [From Latin *negligere,* to NEGLECT.] **—neg·li·gi·bil·i·ty** (-bílləti), **neg·li·gi·ble·ness** *n.* **—neg·li·gi·bly** *adv.*

ne·go·tia·ble (ni-gṓshə-b'l, -shi-ə-, -si-ə-) *adj.* **1.** Capable of being negotiated. **2.** Capable of being legally transferred from one person to another, sometimes after endorsement: *a negotiable document.* **—ne·go·tia·bil·i·ty** (-bílləti) *n.*

ne·go·ti·ant (ni-gṓshi-ənt, -si-shənt) *n.* One that negotiates.

ne·go·ti·ate (ni-gṓshi-ayt, -si-) *v.* **-ated, -ating, -ates.** *—intr.* To confer with another or others in order to come to terms or reach an agreement. *—tr.* **1.** To arrange, settle, or bring about by conferring or discussing: *negotiate a contract.* **2.** *Finance.* **a.** To transfer title to or ownership of (notes, funds, documents, or similar property) to another person or party in return for value received. **b.** To sell or discount (assets or securities, for example). **3.** To succeed in passing over, accomplishing, or coping with: *negotiate a sharp curve.* [Latin *negōtiārī,* to transact business, from *negōtium,* business, "lack of leisure" : *neg-,* not + *ōtium*†, leisure.] **—ne·go·ti·a·tor** *n.*

ne·go·ti·a·tion (ni-gṓshi-áysh'n, -si-) *n.* An act or the procedure of negotiating.

Ne·gress (née-griss, -gress) *n.* A female Negro. Sometimes considered offensive.

Ne·gril·lo (ni-gríllō, ne-, -grée-ō) *n., pl.* **-los** or **-loes.** A member of a group of diminutive Negroid peoples of Africa, including the Bushmen and the Pygmies. Also called "Negrito". [Spanish, diminutive of NEGRO.]

Ne·gri·to (ni-gréetō, ne-) *n., pl.* **-tos** or **-toes. 1.** A Negrillo. **2.** Any of various groups of diminutive Negroid people inhabiting parts of Malaysia, the Philippines, and southeastern Asia. [Spanish, diminutive of NEGRO.]

ne·gri·tude (néegri-tewd, néggri- || -tōōd) *n.* **1.** The fact or quality of being a Negro. **2.** An aesthetic and ideological concept affirming the independent validity of black culture. [French *négritude* (coined by Léopold Senghor), from *nègre,* NEGRO.]

Ne·gro (néegrō) *n., pl.* **-groes. 1.** A member of the Negroid ethnic division of the human species, especially any of various peoples of central and southern Africa. —See Usage note at **black. 2.** A descendant of these or other Negroid peoples. See **Negroid.** [Spanish and Portuguese *negro,* black, from Latin *niger,* black.] **—Ne·gro** *adj.*

Neg·ro, Rio (náy-grō, néggrō). River of South America. Rising in eastern Colombia (where it is known as the Guainía), it flows some 2 250 kilometres (1,400 miles) across Brazil to join the Amazon near Manaus.

Ne·groid (née-groyd) *adj. Anthropology.* Of, pertaining to, characteristic of, or designating a major ethnic division of the human species whose members are characterised by brown to black pigmentation, and often by tightly curled hair, broad nose, and thick lips. This division includes the Negro and other peoples, such as the **Andamanese** and **Melanesian** *(both of which see).* [NEGR(O)- + -OID.] **—Ne·groid** *n.*

ne·gro·phile, ne·gro·phil (néegrō-fīl, néegrə-, -fil) *n. Often capital* **N.** One friendly to blacks and their interests.

ne·gro·pho·bi·a (néegrō-fṓbi-ə, néegrə-) *n. Often capital* **N.** Intense aversion to or fear of blacks. **—ne·gro·phobe** (-fōb) *n.*

ne·gus (néegəss) *n.* A beverage made of wine, hot water, lemon juice, sugar, and nutmeg. [After Colonel Francis *Negus* (died 1732), English soldier who invented it.]

Ne·gus (néegəss) *n.* The title of the emperor of Ethiopia. [Amharic *negūs,* king.]

Neh. Nehemiah.

Ne·he·mi·ah[1] (née-i-mī́-ə, -hi-, -hə-) A Jewish leader and governor of Judah during the Babylonian Captivity (fifth century B.C.).

Nehemiah[2] *n. Abbr.* **Neh.** A book of the Old Testament describing the moral, political, and religious reforms of Nehemiah, and the rebuilding of Jerusalem under his leadership. Also called "Esdras".

Neh·ru (náir-ōō), **Jawaharlal** (1889–1964), also known as Pandit Nehru. Indian politician. Succeeding his father, Pandit Motilal Nehru, as president of the Indian Congress (1929), he took part in the campaign for independence from Britain, and was frequently imprisoned. He became India's first prime minister (1947). The political dynasty was continued by his daughter, Indira Gandhi.

neigh (nay) *intr.v.* **neighed, neighing, neighs. 1.** To utter the cry of a horse. **2.** To utter a sound similar to a horse's cry.

~n. The cry of a horse. [Middle English *neien,* Old English *hnǣgan,* from Germanic (imitative).]

neigh·bour, *U.S.* **neigh·bor** (náybər) *n.* **1.** One who lives near or next to another. **2.** A person or thing adjacent to or located near another. **3.** A person like oneself; a fellow human being.

~adj. Living or situated near another.

~v. **neighboured** or *U.S.* **neighbored, -bouring** or *U.S.* **boring, -bours** or *U.S.* **-bors.** *—tr.* To lie close to; border upon; adjoin. *—intr.* To live or be situated close by. [Middle English *neigh(e)bor,* Old English *nēahgebūr* : *nēah,* near + *gebūr,* dweller.]

neigh·bour·hood (náybər-hŏŏd) *n.* **1.** A district, especially one comprising a distinct community in a town or city, often considered in regard to its inhabitants or distinctive characteristics: *a chic neighbourhood.* **2.** The people who live in a particular vicinity. **3.** A range of numbers, prices, or other quantities: *in the neighbourhood of a million dollars.* **4.** *Mathematics.* The set of points surrounding a given point, each of which is at a distance from the given point less than an arbitrary bound.

neigh·bour·ing (náybəring) *adj.* Living or situated close by.

neigh·bour·ly (náybərli) *adj.* Appropriate to, characteristic of, or showing the feelings of a friendly neighbour. **—neigh·bour·li·ness** *n.*

Neis·se (nī́-sə). *Polish* **Nysa** (níssə); *Czech* **Nisa.** River of eastern Europe. Rising in Czechoslovakia, it flows 225 kilometres (140 miles) northwards to the Oder river, forming part of the Polish-German border. It is known as the Lusatian Neisse to distinguish it from the Glatzer Neisse, another Oder tributary to the east.

nei·ther (nī́-thər, née-) *adj.* Not either; not one and not the other: *Neither shoe fits comfortably.*

~pron. Not either one; not the one nor the other: *Neither of them fits.*

~conj. **1.** Not either; not in either case. Used with the correlative conjunction *nor: Neither we nor they want it.* **2.** *Archaic.* Nor yet; nor: *"They toil not, neither do they spin."* (Matthew 6:28).

~adv. **1.** Also not; not either: *John couldn't understand it, and neither could I.* **2.** *Nonstandard.* In any case; either. Forms a double negative when used for *either* following a negative statement: *I don't*

PRONUNCIATION KEY

a, trap; aa, father; ai, fair;
ar, star; aw, lawn; ay, play;
b, bb, stab; rubber;
ch, church; ck, ticket;
d, dd, dead; ladder; e, dress;
ee, bee; er, defer; ew, few;
ewr, pure; ə, about;
ər, letter; f, ff, fife; differ;
g, gg, giggle; h, hat; i, kit;
ī, price; īr, fire; j, judge;
k, kick; l, ll, let; 'l, needle;
m, mm, man; n, nn, no;
'n, sudden; ng, thing; o, lot;
ō, no; ŏŏ, foot; ōō, shoe;
oor, poor; ow, cow;
owr, hour; oy, boy;
p, pp, pepper; r, rr, red;
s, ss, sauce; sh, ship;
t, tt, totter; th, thick; th, this;
smooth; u, cut; ur, turn;
v, vv, valve; w, wet; y, yes;
z, zz, zebra; zh, vision;
pleasure

IN FOREIGN WORDS:

aN, oN, Saint-Saëns;
hl, Llanelli; Hluhluwe;
kh, loch; lough; Khaled

STRESS MARK:

ín-sīt, insight; in-sī́t, incite

like it, neither. **—neither here nor there.** Of no immediate concern; immaterial. [Middle English *neither, nauther,* Old English *nāhwæther, nōhwæther* : *nā,* no, not + *hwæther,* which of two.]

Usage: *Neither* is restricted to a choice of two items, when reference is being made to a preceding list: *Painting and drawing have been suggested, but he is interested in neither.* If the list contains more than two items, *none* is the required form: *Painting, drawing, and sculpture have been suggested, but he is interested in none of them.*

Neither takes a singular verb, even when it is accompanied by plural nouns or pronouns: *Neither motor car has arrived, Neither of them has come, Neither of the houses has been built.* The plural noun or pronoun preceding the verb nonetheless exercises a strong influence, and in informal speech and writing a plural form of the verb is often used loosely: *Neither of the cars have been fixed.*

In the *neither . . . nor* construction, when both elements are singular, the verb is in the singular *(Neither John nor Jim has arrived).* When both are plural, the verb is in the plural *(Neither the cars nor the buses have been fixed).* Purists often insist on a singular verb even in a strongly plural context, but this has come to sound pedantic and stilted.

When the second element in a *neither-nor* construction is a pronoun, the verb agrees with the pronoun: *Neither the boys nor I am interested.* When both elements are pronouns, the agreement is with the one nearer the verb: *Neither he nor I am interested.*

When the construction follows a verb, there is a tendency in informal speech to allow *neither* to precede the verb *(He was neither able to think nor speak),* the lack of stress on the verb making ambiguity unlikely: but this usage is open to criticism in writing, and in formal speech. *He was able neither to think nor to speak* is preferred. See also Usage note at **nor.**

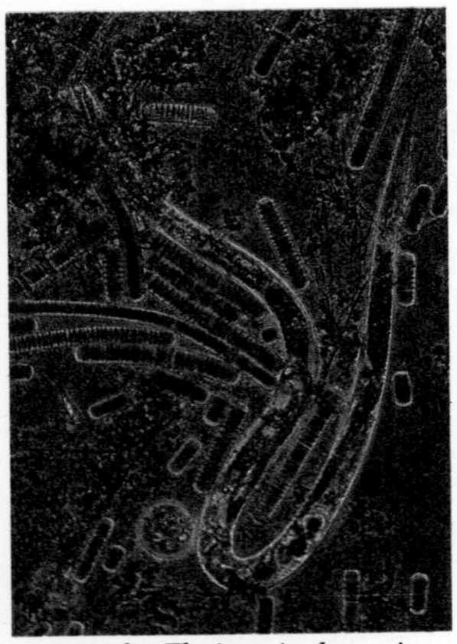

nematode *The intestinal parasites known as pinworms and roundworms, which live in the digestive tracts of humans, are both nematodes – a group of threadlike worms which range in length from 1 to 200 millimetres (0.04 to 8 inches). Here the lighter outline of a nematode curls through a logjam of smaller organisms.*

nek (nek) *n. South African.* A narrow ridge connecting two mountains. [Dutch, "neck".]

nek·ton (nék-ton, -tən) *n.* The total population of actively swimming aquatic animals in a sea or lake, including fish, turtles, and whales. Compare **plankton.** [German, from Greek *nēkton,* "swimming thing", neuter of *nēktos,* swimming, from *nēkhein,* to swim.] **—nek·ton·ic** (nek-tónnik) *adj.*

nel·ly (nélli) *n.* **—not on your nelly.** *British Slang.* Emphatically not; absolutely not. [Perhaps from *Nelly* (woman's name).]

nel·son (nél-sən) *n.* In wrestling, any of a variety of holds in which the user places an arm under the opponent's arm and applies pressure with the palm of the hand against the opponent's neck. See also **full nelson, half nelson.** [Probably from surname *Nelson.*]

Nelson¹ (nél-sən). City of South Island, New Zealand. On Tasman Bay, it is the terminus of a ferry service to North Island, and the centre of the country's only hop-growing district.

Nelson². River in central Manitoba, Canada, flowing from Lake Winnipeg for 640 kilometres (400 miles) into Hudson Bay.

Nelson (nélsən), **Horatio, 1st Viscount** (1758–1805). British admiral. Despite the loss of an eye at Calvi (1794), and an arm at Santa Cruz (1797), he was the most successful naval commander of his age. He fought with distinction at Cape St. Vincent (1797) and Copenhagen (1801), and destroyed French power in the eastern Mediterranean at the Battle of the Nile (Aboukir 1798). His destruction of the French fleet, with its Spanish allies, at Trafalgar (1805), secured Britain from invasion.

ne·lum·bo (ni-lúmbō) *n., pl.* **-bos.** An aquatic plant of the genus *Nelumbo,* having large, variously coloured flowers. See **lotus.** [New Latin, from Sinhalese *neḷumbu,* lotus, probably of Dravidian origin.]

Ne·man (nyémmən). *Polish* **Nie·man;** *German* **Me·mel** (máym'l). River of the western U.S.S.R. It was formerly the western border of the Russian empire.

ne·mat·ic (ni-máttik) *adj. Chemistry.* Pertaining to one of the two types of anisotropic melts characteristic of a liquid crystal in which the molecules are linearly oriented but are not in a planar arrangement. Compare **smectic.** [NEMATO- (referring to the threadlike chains of molecules) + -IC.]

nemato– *comb. form.* Indicates threadlike form; for example, **nematocyst.** [New Latin, from Greek *nēma* (stem *nēmat-*), thread.]

nem·a·to·cyst (némmə-tō-sist, -tə-, ni-máttə-) *n. Zoology.* A stinging organ in various coelenterates, such as jellyfish, which when stimulated puts out a coiled tube that injects the victim with a paralysing poison. [NEMAT(O)- + CYST.] **—nem·a·to·cys·tic** (-sístik) *adj.*

nem·a·tode (némmə-tōd) *n.* Any worm of the phylum Nematoda, having unsegmented, threadlike bodies, many of which, including the hookworm, are parasitic. Also called "nematode worm", "roundworm". [New Latin *Nematoda,* "the threadlike ones" : NEMAT(O)- + -ODE (like).]

Nem·bu·tal (némbew-taal || *U.S.* -tawl) *n.* A trademark for the drug **pentobarbitone sodium** *(see).*

nem con (ném kón) *adv.* Unanimously; without any opposition: *The proposal was adopted nem con.* [Abbreviation of Latin *nemine contradicente,* with no one opposing.]

ne·mer·te·an, ne·mer·ti·an (ni-mérti-ən) *adj.* Also **nem·er·tine** (némmər-tīn). Of, pertaining to, or belonging to the phylum Nemertea (or Nemertina), consisting chiefly of marine worms having soft, cylindrical or flattened bodies, usually brightly coloured, and an evertible proboscis used for catching prey.
~*n.* A worm of this phylum. Also called "proboscis worm", "ribbon worm". [New Latin *Nemertea,* "the Nemertes group", from *Nemertēs,* name of one of the genera in the group, from Greek *Nēmertēs,* name of a Nereid.]

ne·me·sia (ni-méezhə) *n.* Any plant of the genus *Nemesia,* native to southern Africa, several species of which are cultivated as ornamental garden plants for their brightly coloured flowers. [New Latin, from Greek *nemesion,* name of a plant resembling nemesia.]

nem·e·sis (némmi-siss, némmə-) *n., pl.* **-ses** (-seez). **1.** One that inflicts relentless vengeance or destruction. **2.** Retributive justice in its execution or outcome: *invite nemesis.* [From NEMESIS.]

Nemesis *Greek Mythology.* The goddess of retributive justice or vengeance. [Greek, "retribution", from *nemein,* to allot.]

nen·u·phar (nénnew-faar) *n.* A water lily. [From Medieval Latin, from Arabic and Persian *nīnūfar, nīlūfar,* from Sanskrit *nīlōtpala* : *nīla,* blue + *utpala,* lotus.]

ne·ne (náy-nay) *n.* A goose, *Branta sandvicensis,* of the Hawaiian Islands, now very rare. [Hawaiian *nēnē.*]

neo– *comb. form.* Indicates: **1.** A new, revived, or recent form, development, or type; for example, **neologism, neomycin. 2.** A recent formation, modification, or abnormal change; for example, **neoplasm. 3.** The most recent subdivision of a series of geological periods; for example, **Neolithic.** ***Note:*** Many compounds other than those entered here may be formed with *neo-.* In this dictionary, in forming compounds, *neo-* is joined to the following word without space or hyphen: *neocolonialism.* Many users, however, prefer the hyphenated form, which should be used if the second element begins with a capital letter, the *N* of *Neo-* being also capitalised: *Neo-Platonism.* (The *N* may be capitalised in other words too: *Neolithic.*) If the second element begins with *o,* again it is separated by a hyphen: *neo-orthodoxy.* [Greek, from *neos,* new.]

ne·o·ars·phen·a·mine (nee-ō-aarss-fénnə-meen, -fi-námmin) *n. Medicine.* A yellow powder, $C_{13}H_{13}As_2N_2NaO_4S$, containing arsenic, formerly used in the treatment of syphilis and yaws.

ne·o·clas·si·cism (nee-ō-klássi-siz'm) *n.* **1.** A revival of classical aesthetics and forms in art, architecture, music, and literature. **2.** *Usually capital* **N. a.** Such a revival as that which occurred in the 18th and 19th centuries in architecture and art, especially the decorative arts, characterised by order, symmetry, and simplicity of style. **b.** A similar revival that occurred in literature in the late 17th and 18th centuries, characterised by a regard for the classical ideals of reason, form, and restraint. **c.** A movement in music of the late 19th and early 20th centuries that sought to avoid subjective emotionalism and return to the style of the pre-Romantic composers. **—ne·o·clas·sic, ne·o·clas·si·cal** *adj.* **—ne·o·clas·si·cist** *n.*

ne·o·col·on·i·al·ism (nee-ō-kə-lṓni-ə-liz'm) *n.* The use by a major power of economic constraints as a means of perpetuating or extending its effective control over a less powerful nation, especially a former colony. **—ne·o·col·on·i·al** *adj.* **—ne·o·col·on·i·al·ist** *n. & adj.*

ne·o·cor·tex (nee-ō-kór-teks) *n.* The **neopallium** *(see).*

Ne·o-Dar·win·ism (nee-ō-dárwin-iz'm) *n.* The theory that incorporates Darwin's theory of evolution by **natural selection** *(see)* with subsequent discoveries concerning the inheritance and source of genetic variation. See **Darwinism.** Compare **Neo-Lamarckism. —Ne·o-Dar·win·i·an** (-daar-wínni-ən) *adj. & n.*

ne·o·dym·i·um (nee-ō-dímmi-əm) *n. Symbol* **Nd** A bright, silvery, rare-earth metal element of the lanthanide group found in the minerals monazite and bastnaesite, and used for colouring glass and for doping some glass lasers. Atomic number 60, atomic weight 144.24, melting point 1,024°C, boiling point 3,027°C, relative density 6.80 or 7.004 (depending on allotropic form), valency 3. [New Latin : NEO- + (DI)DYMIUM.]

Ne·o·gae·a (nee-ō-jée-ə, -ə-) *n.* An area that is coextensive with the Neotropical region and is considered one of the primary zoogeographic regions. See **Neotropical.** [New Latin : NEO- + Greek *gaia,* earth.] **—Ne·o·gae·an** *adj.*

ne·o·gen·e·sis (nee-ō-jénnə-siss) *n. Medicine.* The regeneration of tissue.

ne·o·im·pres·sion·ism, Ne·o-Im·pres·sion·ism (nee-ō-im-présh'n-iz'm) *n.* A movement in 19th-century painting that was led by Georges Seurat and characterised by strict and formal composition and meticulous execution using **pointillism** *(see).* **—ne·o·im·pres·sion·ist** *n. & adj.*

Ne·o-La·marck·ism (nee-ō-lə-márkiz'm) *n.* The theory that acquired characteristics can be inherited, but that natural selection is also a valid evolutionary principle. See **Lamarckism.** Compare **Neo-Darwinism. —Ne·o-La·marck·i·an** (-márki-ən) *adj. & n.*

ne·o·lith (nee-ə-lith, -ō-) *n.* A stone implement of the Neolithic Age. [Back-formation from NEOLITHIC.]

Ne·o·lith·ic (nee-ə-líthik, -ō-) *adj. Sometimes small* **n.** *Archaeology.* Of or designating the cultural period beginning around 10,000 B.C. in the Middle East and later elsewhere, and characterised by the development of farming and the making of technically advanced, polished, stone implements.
~*n. Archaeology.* The Neolithic period. Preceded by *the.* [NEO- + -LITHIC.]

ne·ol·o·gise, ne·ol·o·gize (nee-óllə-jīz) *intr.v.* **-gised, -gising, -gises.** To coin or use neologisms.

ne·ol·o·gism (nee-óllə-jiz'm) *n.* **1.** A newly coined word, phrase, or expression, or a new meaning for an old word. **2.** The use or formation of new words, phrases, or expressions or of new meanings for old words. [French *néologisme* : NEO- + LOG(O)- + -ISM.] **—ne·ol·o·gist** *n.* **—ne·ol·o·gis·tic** (-jístik), **ne·ol·o·gis·ti·cal** *adj.*

ne·ol·o·gy (nee-ólləji) *n., pl.* **-gies.** Neologism or an instance of it. [French *néologie* : NEO- + -LOGY.] **—ne·o·log·i·cal** (nee-ə-lójik'l) *adj.* **—ne·o·log·i·cal·ly** *adv.*

THE ROMANTIC REVIVAL OF NEOCLASSICISM

A rebirth of ancient Greek and Roman art in 18th and 19th-century Europe

Neoclassicism was developed by European artists in the 18th and 19th centuries as a reaction against the extravagance of the Rococo style. The neoclassical movement was an attempt to revive the artistic rules and values of ancient Greece and Rome and came about after the discovery and excavation of classical sites in Italy, Greece, and Asia Minor. The style is characterised by its principles of order, simplicity, and dignity. Leading exponents included the French painter Jacques-Louis David (1748–1825), whose paintings were inspired by Roman history, and the Italian sculptor Antonio Canova (1757–1822).

The architectural movement was often self-conscious and pedantic. During the second half of the 18th century, however, designs by Scottish architect Robert Adam (1728–92) dominated British architecture because he was able to combine precision with skilful delicacy.

The term neoclassicism can be used in a general sense; it is used to describe the style of 17th and 18th-century writers such as Dryden, Johnson, La Fontaine, and Racine. In music it has been used to describe, for example, the reaction against excessive romanticism that led Stravinsky to adopt a simpler, purer style in such works as the opera-oratorio *Oedipus Rex* (1927), and the ballet *Apollon musagète* (1928).

DEATH OF SOCRATES
A favourite subject of neoclassical artists, the death of the famous Greek philosopher was painted by Jacques-Louis David in 1787. Socrates, who lived in the last part of the 5th century B.C., was accused of impiety – corruption of the young and neglect of the gods – because of his teachings, and condemned to drink a bowl of the deadly poison hemlock.

BEECHWOOD CHAIR *One of a set of decorative chairs made by Thomas Chippendale for the Adam-designed Harewood House.*

WEDGWOOD JASPERWARE *John Flaxman designed a relief showing Apollo and the Nine Muses for this neoclassical vase.*

GREEK GODDESS *In Greek mythology Hebe is the goddess of eternal youth. This statue of her carved by Thorvaldsen in 1806 shows the neoclassical ideals of purity, proportion, and repose.*

ne·o·morph (née-ō-mawrf, -ə-) *n.* A biological structure that has not evolved from a similar structure in an ancestor. [NEO- + -MORPH.] —**ne·o·morph·ic** (-mórfik) *adj.*

ne·o·my·cin (née-ō-mī-sin) *n.* An antibiotic drug, $C_{12}H_{26}N_4O_6$, used to treat a wide range of infections, especially those affecting the skin and eyes. [NEO- + -MYCIN.]

ne·on (née-on, -ən) *n. Symbol* **Ne** A rare, inert, gaseous element occurring in the atmosphere to the extent of 18 parts per million, and obtained by fractional distillation of liquid air. It is colourless but glows reddish-orange in an electrical discharge and is used in fluorescent tubes. Atomic number 10, atomic weight 20.183, melting point -248.67°C, boiling point -245.95°C, valency 0.
~*adj.* Illuminated by a tube with neon in it: *a neon sign.* [Greek, "the new (gas)", neuter of *neos*, new.]

ne·o·nate (née-ō-nayt, -ə-) *n.* A newborn child. [New Latin *neonātus* : NEO- + Latin *nātus*, born, from *nascī*, to be born.] —**ne·o·na·tal** (-náyt'l) *adj.*

ne·o·or·tho·dox·y (née-ō-órthə-doksi) *n.* A Protestant movement of the 20th century that aims to revive adherence to certain Reformation doctrines. —**ne·o·or·tho·dox** *adj.*

ne·o·pal·li·um (née-ō-pál-i-əm) *n.* The tissue that makes up most of the cerebral cortex in the brain of mammals. Also called "neocortex".

ne·o·phyte (née-ō-fīt, -ə-) *n.* **1.** A recent convert to a religion. **2. a.** A newly ordained Roman Catholic priest. **b.** A novice of a religious order. **3.** A beginner or novice. [Late Latin *neophytus*, from New Testament Greek *neophutos*, "newly planted" : NEO- + *phutos*, "grown", from *phuein*, to bring forth, produce.]

ne·o·plasm (née-ō-plaz'm, -ə-) *n.* Any abnormal new growth of tissue in animals or plants; a benign or malignant tumour. [NEO- + -PLASM.] —**ne·o·plas·tic** *adj.*

Ne·o·Pla·to·nism, Ne·o·pla·to·nism (née-ō-pláyt'n-iz'm) *n.* **1.** A philosophical and religious system developed in Alexandria in the third century A.D., based on the doctrines of Plato and other Greek philosophers, and modified with elements of Oriental mysticism and some Judaic and Christian concepts. **2.** A revival of this system, as in the Middle Ages and Renaissance. —**Ne·o·Pla·ton·ic** (-plə-tónnik) *adj.* —**Ne·o·Pla·to·nist** *n.*

ne·o·prene (née-ō-preen, -ə-) *n.* A synthetic rubber produced by polymerisation of chloroprene and used in waterproof products, adhesives, paints, and rocket fuels. [NEO- + PR(OPYL) + -ENE.]

Ne·o·scho·las·ti·cism (née-ō-skə-lásti-siz'm, -sko-) *n.* A movement to revive the scholasticism of Aquinas by infusing it with modern concepts. —**Ne·o·scho·las·tic** *adj.*

ne·ot·e·ny (ni-óttəni *also* née-ə-teeni) *n.* The retention of larval features in the adult form of an animal. It occurs, for example, in the axolotl, which retains the external gills of the larva. [From German *Neotenie* : NEO- + Greek *teinein*, to extend.]

ne·o·ter·ic (née-ō-térrik, -ə-) *adj.* Of recent origin; new; modern. ~*n.* A modern writer or philosopher. [Late Latin *neōtericus*, from

Greek *neōterikos*, "youthful", modern, from *neōteros,* younger, comparative of *neos,* new.]

Ne·o·trop·i·cal (née-ō-tróppik'l) *adj.* Of or designating the zoogeographic region stretching southwards from the tropic of Cancer and including southern Mexico, Central and South America, and the West Indies.
~*n.* The Neotropical region.

ne·o·type (née-ō-tīp) *n.* A plant or animal specimen selected to replace the original **holotype** *(see)* when this has been lost or destroyed.

Ne·o·zo·ic (née-ō-zṓ-ik, -ə-) *adj.* Of or formed in any geological period after the end of the Mesozoic era.

Ne·pal, Kingdom of (ni-páwl, ne-, -paál). State of south central Asia. Lying in the Himalayas, it is a predominantly agricultural country, exporting jute and rice. With massive foreign aid, roads, hydroelectric power, and light industry are being developed. Tourism is important. It is ruled by a hereditary Hindu monarchy. It has been an ally of the United Kingdom since 1850; Nepalese Gurkha battalions still serve in the British army. Area, 140 797 square kilometres (54,348 square miles). Population, 14,500,000. Capital, Kathmandu. See map at **India**. —**Nep·al·ese** (néppə-leéz, néppaw- ‖ -leéss) *adj. & n.*

Nep·al·i (ni-páwli, ne-, -paáli) *n., pl.* **-is** or collectively **Nepali**. 1. A native or inhabitant of Nepal. 2. The central Indic language of Nepal. —**Nep·al·i** *adj.*

ne·pen·the (ni-pénthi) *n.* 1. A drug, perhaps opium, mentioned in the *Odyssey* as a remedy for grief. 2. Anything that induces oblivion of sorrow or eases pain. [Greek *nēpenthes (pharmakon),* "grief-banishing (drug)" : *nē-,* not + *penthos,* grief.] —**ne·pen·the·an** (ni-pénthi-ən) *adj.*

ne·per (néepər, náypər) *n.* **Symbol Np.** A unit used for comparing quantities, used especially for telecommunication signal amplitudes. The natural logarithm of the ratio of the quantities is the value in nepers.

neph·e·line (néffi-lin, -leen) *n.* A sodium or potassium aluminium silicate mineral, occurring in igneous rocks, and used in the manufacture of ceramics and enamels. Also called "nephelite". [French *néphéline,* from Greek *nephelē,* cloud (because it becomes cloudy when placed in acid).]

neph·e·lin·ite (néffili-nīt) *n.* An igneous rock consisting chiefly of pyroxene and nepheline.

neph·e·lom·e·ter (néffi-lómmitər) *n.* Any apparatus used to measure the size or concentration of particles in a suspension by the amount of light scattered by the particles. [Greek *nephelē,* cloud + -METER.] —**neph·e·lo·met·ric** (-lō-méttrik) *adj.* —**neph·e·lom·e·try** (-lómmətri) *n.*

neph·ew (névvew, néffew) *n.* The son of one's brother or sister, or of one's brother-in-law or sister-in-law. [Middle English *neveu,* nephew, grandson, from Old French *neveu,* from Latin *nepōs,* nephew, grandson.]

neph·o·graph (néffō-graaf, néffə-, -graf) *n. Meteorology.* A device used for producing photographic records *(nephograms)* of clouds.

ne·phol·o·gy (ni-fólləji, ne-) *n.* The science of clouds. [Greek *nephos,* cloud + -LOGY.] —**neph·o·log·i·cal** (néffə-lójik'l) *adj.* —**ne·phol·o·gist** (-fólləjist) *n.*

neph·o·scope (néffō-skōp, néffə-) *n. Meteorology.* An instrument for observing clouds and measuring their height, speed, and direction of movement.

ne·phral·gi·a (ni-frál-ji-ə, ne-, -jə) *n.* Pain in the kidney, caused by any of various kidney disorders. —**ne·phral·gic** *adj.*

ne·phrec·to·my (ni-fréktəmi, ne-) *n., pl.* **-mies.** The surgical removal of a kidney. [NEPHR(O)- + -ECTOMY.]

ne·phrid·i·um (ni-fríd-i-əm, ne-) *n., pl.* **-ia** (-i-ə). An excretory organ in many invertebrates, consisting basically of a tube through which waste products pass to the exterior. [New Latin : NEPHR(O)- + -IDIUM.] —**ne·phrid·i·al** *adj.*

neph·rite (néffrīt) *n.* A white to dark green variety of jade. [German *Nephrit,* "kidney mineral" (from its supposed power to cure kidney diseases) : NEPHR(O)- + -ITE.]

ne·phrit·ic (ne-fríttik, ni-) *adj.* 1. Pertaining to the kidneys. 2. *Pathology.* Of, pertaining to, or affected by nephritis.

ne·phri·tis (ne-frítiss, ni-) *n. Pathology.* Any of various acute or chronic inflammations of the kidneys. Also called "Bright's disease" when chronic. [Late Latin, from Greek : NEPHR(O)- + -ITIS.]

nephro-, nephr- *comb. form.* Indicates the kidney; for example, **nephrogenous, nephritis.** [Greek, from *nephros,* kidney.]

ne·phrog·e·nous (ne-frójinəss, ni-) *adj.* Also **neph·ro·gen·ic** (néffrə-jénnik) Originating in the kidney. [NEPHRO- + -GENOUS.]

neph·ron (néffron) *n.* Any of the excretory units of the kidney, consisting of a tiny, coiled tubule into which urine is filtered from the blood. [German *Nephron,* from Greek *nephros,* kidney.]

ne·phro·sis (ne-frṓ-siss, ni-) *n.* Any disease of the kidneys, especially when marked by degenerative changes in the renal tubules, as opposed to the inflammation characteristic of nephritis. [New Latin : NEPHR(O)- + -OSIS.] —**ne·phrot·ic** (-fróttik) *adj.*

neph·ros·to·my (ne-fróstəmi, ni-) *n., pl.* **-mies** A surgical operation in which a tube is inserted into a kidney from the skin surface in order to drain the urine from the kidney. [NEPHRO- + -STOMY.]

ne·phrot·o·my (ne-fróttəmi, -ni-) *n., pl.* **-mies.** Surgical incision into the kidney. [New Latin *nephrotomia* : NEPHRO- + -TOMY.]

ne plus ul·tra (née pluss últrə, náy plōoss ōoltraa) *n.* The extreme or utmost point; especially, the point of highest achievement.

[Latin, "(sail) no more beyond (this point)", a warning to mariners allegedly inscribed on the Pillars of Hercules.]

nep·o·tism (néppə-tiz'm) *n.* Favouritism shown or patronage granted by persons in high office to relatives. [French *népotisme,* from Italian *nepotismo,* "favouring of nephews" (by 16th-century prelates), from *nepote,* nephew, from Latin *nepōs.*] —**nep·o·tist** *n.* —**nep·o·tis·ti·cal** (-tístik'l) *adj.*

Nep·tune[1] (nép-tewn ‖ -tōon). *Roman Mythology.* The god of the sea, corresponding to the Greek Poseidon. [Latin *Neptūnus†.*]

Neptune[2] *n. Poetic.* The ocean or sea.

Neptune[3] *n.* The eighth planet from the sun, having a sidereal period of revolution around the sun of 164.8 years at a mean distance of 4.5×10^9 kilometres (2.8×10^9 miles), a mean radius of 24 500 kilometres (14,000 miles), and a density 17.2 times that of Earth. —**Nep·tu·ni·an** *adj.*

nep·tu·ni·um (nep-téwni-əm ‖ -tōoni-) *n.* **Symbol Np** A silvery, metallic, naturally radioactive element, atomic number 93, the first of the transuranium elements, having a number of isotopes with mass numbers from 231 to 241 and half-lives ranging from 7.3 minutes to 2.2 million years. It is found in trace quantities in uranium ores and is produced synthetically by nuclear reactions. [After *Neptune* (planet), since neptunium follows uranium in the periodic table, as Neptune is the next planet after Uranus.]

N.E.R.C. National Environment Research Council (in Britain).

nerd, nurd (nerd) *n. Chiefly U.S. Slang.* An idiotic, foolish, or very unattractive person. [Perhaps from earlier *nert,* alteration of *nut.*]

Ne·re·id[1] (néer-i-id) *n., pl.* **Nereides** (nə-rée-i-deez, ni-). *Greek Mythology.* Any of the 50 daughters of Nereus; a sea nymph. [Greek *Nēreis,* from *Nēreus,* NEREUS.]

Nereid[2] *n.* The smaller of the two satellites of the planet Neptune. [From NEREID (nymph); the Nereids were attendants on Neptune.]

ne·re·is (néer-i-iss) *n., pl.* **nereides** (ni-rée-i-deez) Any of several marine worms of the genus *Nereis,* having a long, flat, segmented body and a pair of paddles on each segment. See **ragworm.** [New Latin, from Latin *Nēreis,* NEREID.]

Ne·re·us (néer-i-ōoss, -əss) *Greek Mythology.* A sea god, father of the Nereids.

ne·rit·ic (ne-rittik, nə-) *adj.* Pertaining to or designating the waters and deposits of a shoreline. See **continental shelf.** [Probably from Latin *nērīta,* sea snail, from Greek *Nēreus,* NEREUS.]

Nernst (nairnst), **Walther Hermann** (1864–1941). German physicist. Best known for his discovery of the third law of thermodynamics, he also carried out important research into free radicals. He received a Nobel prize for chemistry (1920).

Nernst heat theorem *n.* The principle in thermodynamics that changes in entropy tend to zero as the temperature tends to absolute zero. It was an earlier form of the third law of thermodynamics.

Ne·ro (Claudius Caesar) (néer-ō), born Lucius Domitius Ahenobarbus (A.D. 37–68). Roman emperor (A.D. 54–68). He was adopted by the Emperor Claudius, but his early reign was dominated by his mother, Agrippa. He murdered his mother and wife and was rumoured to have started the Great Fire of Rome (A.D. 64) for which the Christians were blamed. His cruelty and irresponsibility provoked revolts throughout the empire which led to his suicide.

ner·o·li (néer-ə-li, nérrə-) *n.* An essential oil distilled from orange flowers and used in perfumery. Also called "neroli oil", "orange flower oil". [Perhaps after Anna Maria de la Trémoille, princess of *Neroli,* who is said to have introduced it into France.]

Ne·ro·ni·an (ni-rṓni-ən) *adj.* 1. Marked by the cruelty, tyranny, or depravity characteristic of the emperor Nero. 2. Of or pertaining to Nero or his times.

Ne·ru·da (ni-rṓo-də), **Pablo,** pen name of Neftalí Ricardo Reyes Basoalto (1904–73). Chilean poet and diplomat. Though his early works were nihilistic, his later poems reflected the socialist commitment of the Allende government, which he served as ambassador. He was awarded a Nobel prize for literature (1971).

ner·vate (nér-vayt) *adj. Botany.* Having veins. Said of leaves.

ner·va·tion (ner-váysh'n) *n.* A pattern of veins or nerves; venation.

nerve (nérv) *n.* 1. Any of the bundles of fibres interconnecting the central nervous system and the organs or parts of the body, capable of transmitting both sensory stimuli and motor impulses from one part of the body to another. 2. A tendon or muscle. Now rare except in the phrase *to strain every nerve.* 3. The source from which feeling, energy, or dynamic action emanates. 4. *Usually plural.* The nervous system considered as imparting certain characteristics, such as courage, determination, or endurance. 5. a. Forcefulness; stamina. b. Courage and composure; firm self-control: *lost his nerve at the last minute.* c. *Informal.* Brazenness; effrontery: *What a nerve!* 6. *Plural.* An agitated condition induced by anxiety: *an attack of nerves.* 7. *Biology.* A vein in an insect's wing. 8. *Botany.* The midrib or any of the larger veins in a leaf. —See Synonyms at **temerity.** —**get on (someone's) nerves.** To exasperate or irritate someone. ~*tr.v.* **nerved, nerving, nerves.** To give strength or courage to (someone, especially oneself). [Latin *nervus,* sinew, nerve.]

nerve block *n.* A method of producing local anaesthesia in a particular part of the body by injecting a local anaesthetic into another part of the body some distance away, in order to block the passage of pain impulses.

nerve cell *n.* Any of the cells of nerve tissue. It consists of a nucleated cell body and cytoplasmic extensions (the dendrites and axons). Also called "neurone".

nerve centre *n.* 1. A group of nerve cells that perform a specific function. 2. A source or focus of power or control.

Neptune *A 17th-century work by the Italian sculptor Bernini depicts the Roman god of the sea, Neptune, and Triton, the Greek demigod who was half man half fish.*

nervous system

THE CONTROLLER OF THE BODY
How the brain receives information and organises movement

The central nervous system consists of the brain and the spinal cord. Major peripheral nerves branch out from the cord to serve every organ and part of the body. By sending and receiving impulses along the nerves, the brain exercises voluntary control over muscular movements.

Sensation begins in specialised nerve endings, called receptors. There are light-sensitive receptors in the eye and others in the ear which respond to vibrations caused by sound as well as others in the skin which convey the senses of touch, pain, and temperature. Impulses from the receptors travel along the nerves to the brain carrying their information.

To control movement the brain transmits commands along motor nerves to the muscles, which are then stimulated into response. These commands may be a reaction to information received from the receptors or they may be originated independently within the brain, which can store memory and generate emotions such as fear, anger, shame, or delight.

Besides sending and receiving impulses, the brain exerts a ceaseless automatic control by means of a self-regulating nervous system that is known as the autonomic system. Through these nerves the brain can alter the pace of the heart, influence the rate of breathing, and control the processes of digestion and excretion.

The nerves themselves, which provide this web of communication through the body, are made of specialised tissue through which tiny impulses can pass back and forth. They consist of long nerve fibres, or neurones, bound by connective tissue and each capable of transmitting 1,000 separate impulses a second.

A typical neurone consists of a central body, a long threadlike extension called an axon, and a number of shorter branches called dendrites. There are millions of neurones in the body, all of which are formed before birth. This huge number provides a safety margin and the nervous system still functions very efficiently even if some neurones are diseased or destroyed.

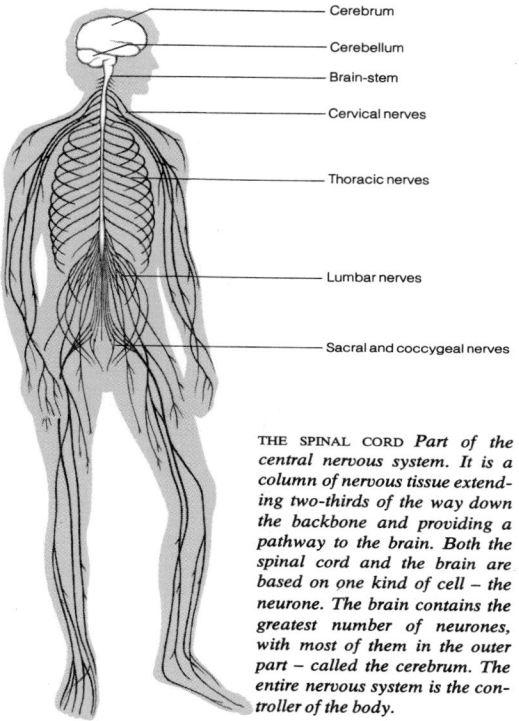

THE SPINAL CORD *Part of the central nervous system. It is a column of nervous tissue extending two-thirds of the way down the backbone and providing a pathway to the brain. Both the spinal cord and the brain are based on one kind of cell – the neurone. The brain contains the greatest number of neurones, with most of them in the outer part – called the cerebrum. The entire nervous system is the controller of the body.*

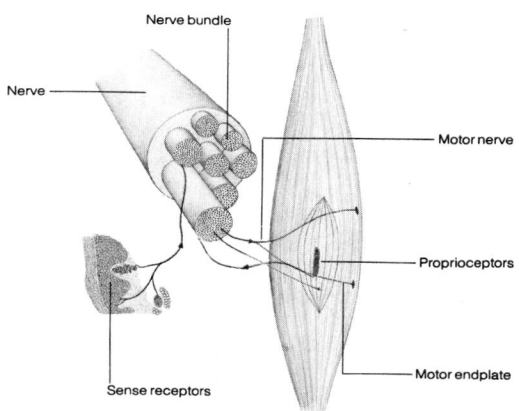

A NERVE *Thousands of nerve fibres are bound together in bundles. Each bundle has sensory fibres and motor fibres. The sensory fibres carry information to the brain from sense receptors and the nerve endings known as proprioceptors which provide information about the changes in muscle tone. Motor nerves carry instructions from the brain to the muscles. Nerve impulses are generated by tiny chemical changes that produce electrical pulses which pass along the bigger nerves at 100 metres (110 yards) a second and along the smallest at about 0.3 metres (1 foot) a second. When the impulse reaches the end of the nerve it releases a chemical that passes the "message" across a junction, or synapse, to another nerve; or, when the nerve ends at a motor endplate in a muscle, the released chemical will generate a response from that muscle causing it to contract or relax.*

---

nerve fibre *n.* A threadlike process that is part of a nerve cell; an axon.

nerve gas *n.* Any gas used in chemical warfare that affects the normal functioning of nerves and thereby paralyses the muscles they supply.

nerve impulse *n.* The wavelike progression of electrical activity that marks the transmission of information along a stimulated nerve fibre.

nerve·less (nérv-ləss, -liss) *adj.* **1.** Lacking courage or energy; listless; spiritless. **2.** Undisturbed by danger or upsetting circumstances; confident, courageous, and self-controlled. —**nerve·less·ly** *adv.* —**nerve·less·ness** *n.*

nerve-rack·ing, nerve-wrack·ing (nérv-racking) *adj.* Intensely distressing, irritating, or exhausting.

Ner·vi (naírvi), **Pier Luigi** (1891–1979). Italian architect. His public buildings, such as the UNESCO building in Paris (1953–57), pioneered the decorative use of reinforced concrete.

nerv·ine (nér-veen, -vīn) *adj.* Affecting the nerves; especially, calming nervous excitement. ~*n.* A tonic for nervous disorders.

nerv·ous (nérvəss) *adj.* **1. a.** Agitated, or liable to become agitated, as a result of anxiety; jittery. **b.** Indicating an anxious or agitated condition: *a nervous stammer*. **2.** Spirited or vigorous, especially in style, feeling, or thought: *a nervous, vibrant prose*. **3.** Strung with nerves; containing many delicate nerves. **4. a.** Of or pertaining to the nerves or nervous system. **b.** Stemming from or affecting the nerves or nervous system: *a nervous disorder*. **5. a.** Anxious or afraid: *nervous of heights*. **b.** Producing anxiety; uneasy: *the nervous moments before takeoff*. [Middle English, from Latin *nervōsus*, from *nervus*, sinew, NERVE.] —**nerv·ous·ly** *adv.* —**nerv·ous·ness** *n.*

nervous breakdown *n.* **1.** Neurasthenia (*see*). **2.** Any severe or incapacitating emotional disorder.

nervous exhaustion *n.* Neurasthenia (*see*).

nervous system *n. Anatomy.* A coordinating mechanism in all multicellular animals, except sponges, that regulates internal body functions and responses to external stimuli. In vertebrates it consists of the brain, spinal cord, nerves, ganglia, and parts of receptor and effector organs. See **autonomic nervous system, central nervous system, peripheral nervous system.**

ner·vure (nérvewr, nérv-yər) *n.* **1.** *Botany.* Any of the vascular ridges that form the framework of a leaf. **2.** *Biology.* Any of the thickened ribs of tissue that form the framework of an insect's wing. [French, from Latin *nervus*, NERVE.]

nerv·y (nérvi) *adj.* **-ier, -iest. 1.** *Chiefly British Informal.* Having bad nerves; jumpy; nervous. **2.** *Archaic.* Full of muscular force; sinewy. **3.** Showing or requiring fortitude, energy, or endurance. **4.** *U.S. Informal.* Impudently confident; brazen.

nes·ci·ence (néssi-ənss ‖ *U.S. also* nésh-, néshi-, néesh-) *n.* **1.** *Formal.* Absence of knowledge or awareness; ignorance. **2.** *Rare.* Agnosticism. [Late Latin *nesciēntia*, from *nesciens* (stem *nescient-*), ignorant, from *nescīre*, to be ignorant : *ne-*, not + *scīre*, to know.] —**nes·ci·ent** *adj. & n.*

–ness *n. suffix.* Indicates: **1.** State, quality, or condition of being; for example, **quietness. 2.** An instance or example of a state, quality, or condition; for example, **kindness.** [Middle English, from Old English *-ness, -niss,* of Germanic origin.]

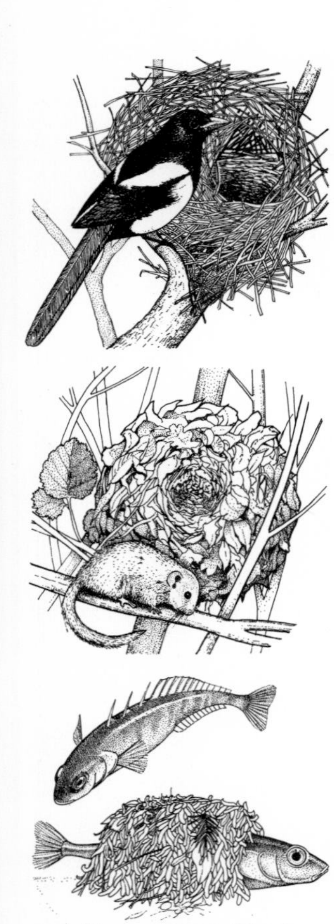

nest *Many creatures build nests, either as a place to rear their young or as a protective home. Seen here are: a magpie's nest (top) built of twigs; the nest of a dormouse (centre) built of leaves and moss; and a nest of weeds where the stickleback lays its eggs.*

PRONUNCIATION KEY

a, trap; aa, father; ai, fair; ar, star; aw, lawn; ay, play; b, bb, stab; rubber; ch, church; ck, ticket; d, dd, dead; ladder; e, dress; ee, bee; er, defer; ew, few; ewr, pure; ə, about; ər, letter; f, ff, fife; differ; g, gg, giggle; h, hat; i, kit; ī, price; īr, fire; j, judge; k, kick; l, ll, let; 'l, needle; m, mm, man; n, nn, no; 'n, sudden; ng, thing; o, lot; ō, no; o͝o, foot; o͞o, shoe; oor, poor; ow, cow; owr, hour; oy, boy; p, pp, pepper; r, rr, red; s, ss, sauce; sh, ship; t, tt, totter; th, thick; th, this; smooth; u, cut; ur, turn; v, vv, valve; w, wet; y, yes; z, zz, zebra; zh, vision; pleasure

IN FOREIGN WORDS:

aN, oN, Saint-Saëns; hl, Llanelli; Hluhluwe; kh, loch; lough; Khaled

STRESS MARK:

ín-sīt, insight; in-sīt, incite

Ness, Loch (ness). A lake of north Scotland. It lies in Glen More, on the Caledonian Canal between Lochend and Fort Augustus. Its depths are supposed to contain the Loch Ness Monster.

Nes·sel·rode (néss'l-rōd) *n.* A frozen dessert, often rum-flavoured, made with chestnuts, preserved oranges, cherries, dried fruits, and cream. [After Count Karl NESSELRODE, whose chef invented it.]

Nesselrode, Karl (Robert), Count (1780–1862). Russian foreign minister (from 1816). He pursued a belligerent policy in the Balkans.

nest (nest) *n.* **1. a.** The structure made by a bird for holding its eggs and young. **b.** The structure or place in which fishes or insects deposit eggs or shelter their young. **c.** Any place where young are reared; a lair. **d.** A number of insects, birds, or other animals occupying such a place; a swarm, brood, or colony: *a nest of hornets.* **2.** A place affording snug seclusion or lodging. **3. a.** A place or environment favouring rapid growth or development of something bad or dangerous; a hotbed: *a nest of rebellion.* **b.** The persons occupying or frequenting such a place. **4.** A set of objects, such as small tables, of graduated size, that can be stacked together, each fitting within the one immediately larger. **5.** A group of weapons in a prepared position: *a nest of missiles.* **—feather (one's) nest.** To exploit one's position in order to procure benefits, especially financial benefits, for oneself.
~*v.* **nested, nesting, nests.** —*intr.* **1.** To build or occupy a nest. **2.** To hunt for birds' nests, especially in order to collect the eggs. **3.** To fit together in a stack. —*tr.* **1.** To place in or as if in a nest. **2.** To place within or arrange into a hierarchy, as of mathematical operations. [Middle English *nest,* Old English *nest.*]

nest egg *n.* **1.** An artificial or natural egg placed in a nest to induce a bird to lay. **2.** A sum of money put by as a reserve.

nes·tle (néss'l) *v.* **-tled, -tling, -tles.** —*intr.* **1. a.** To settle snugly and comfortably: *The kittens nestled down lazily among the cushions.* **b.** To lie or be situated in a sheltered or snug position: *The cottage nestled in the wood.* **2.** To draw or press close, especially in an affectionate manner. Often used with *up: She nestled up to him.* **3.** *Archaic.* To nest. —*tr.* **1.** To place or settle as if in a nest: *nestled the baby in my arms.* **2.** To snuggle or press affectionately or contentedly: *nestled his head into her shoulder.* [Middle English *nestlen,* Old English *nestlian,* to make a nest.] **—nes·tler** *n.*

nest·ling (nést-ling, néss-) *n.* **1.** A bird too young and frail to leave its nest. **2.** A young child.

Nes·tor (néss-tawr, -tər). In the Homeric poems, a hero celebrated for his age and wisdom.

Nes·to·ri·an (ne-stáwri-ən) *adj.* Of or designating a church of the East that adheres to the doctrines of Nestorius, a fifth-century Patriarch of Constantinople, asserting that Christ had two distinct natures, divine and human, and that the Virgin Mary should not be called the Mother of God.
~*n.* A member of this church. **—Nes·to·ri·an·ism** *n.*

net¹ (net) *n.* **1. a.** An openwork material of fibres, cords, wire, or the like, with the threads woven, knotted, or twisted together at regular intervals, forming meshes of varying sizes. **b.** A light mesh fabric, used especially as a curtain or dress material. **2.** Something made of net: **a.** A device for capturing birds, fish, butterflies, or other animals. **b.** A device for excluding birds or insects, especially a **mosquito net** *(see).* **c.** A mesh for holding the hair in place. **3.** *Sports.* **a.** In racket games, a barrier of meshwork cord or rope strung between two posts to divide the playing area in half. **b.** A ball that is hit into such a net. Also called "net ball". **c.** Either of the goals in soccer, hockey, and some other games. **4.** In cricket: **a.** *Usually plural.* A practice area enclosed by netting. **b.** A practice session in such an area. **5.** A meshed network of lines, figures, or fibres. **6.** A situation or circumstance that entraps or is intended to trap.
~*tr.v.* **netted, netting, nets. 1.** To catch or entangle in or as if in a net. **2.** To cover, protect, or surround with or as if with a net. **3.** To hit (a ball) into a net. [Middle English, Old English *net(t).*]

net², nett *adj.* **1.** *Abbr.* **n. a.** Remaining after all necessary deductions have been made or all losses accounted for: *net profit.* Compare **gross. b.** Designating the weight remaining after tare is deducted. **2.** Ultimate; final: *net result; net conclusion.*
~*n. Abbr.* **n.** Total gain; the net amount, as of profit, income, price, or weight.
~*tr.v.* **netted, netting, nets.** To bring in as profit or as a final total. [Middle English *net,* neat, clear, plain, from Old French *net,* neat, elegant, from Latin *nitidus,* bright, clear, from *nitēre,* to shine.]

net·ball (nét-bawl) *n.* A team game, usually played by women, similar to basketball but in which a player is not allowed to move while holding the ball or to let it touch the ground.

neth·er (néthər) *adj.* Located beneath or below. [Middle English *nether,* Old English *nithera,* lower, from *nither,* down, downwards.]

Neth·er·lands, Kingdom of (néthərləndz). *Dutch* **Ne·der·land** (náydər-laant) A kingdom of northwest Europe, often known as Holland. A low-lying area, much of it reclaimed from the sea, with 40 per cent of the land below sea-level, it is a heavily agricultural state, but its economy has come to depend increasingly on industry and commerce. Dominated through its history by various European powers, it was, in the 16th century, a leader in European culture, commerce, and colonialism. The Hague is the seat of government. Area, 33 812 square kilometres (13,055 square miles). Population, 14,300,000. Capital, Amsterdam.

Netherlands Antilles. Dutch-administered islands in the Caribbean, in two groups of islands more than 800 kilometres (500 miles) apart. The main group comprises Curaçao (the largest island), Aruba, and Bonaire, off the coast of Venezuela; to the northeast are Saba, St. Eustatius, and the southern half of Sint Maarten (the northern half is French-owned). The islands' autonomy within the Dutch state is guaranteed. The chief economic activity is the refining of petroleum from Venezuela. Area, 996 square kilometres (385 square miles). Capital, Willemstad (on Curaçao).

neth·er·most (néthər-mōst) *adj.* Farthest down; deepest.

nether world *n.* **1.** The world of the dead; Hades. **2.** Hell. **3.** A place or situation likened to hell. Also called "nether regions".

Ne·to (néttō), **Antonio Agostinho** (1922–79). Angolan politician. After Angola's liberation from Portugal (1975), he became its first president.

net·su·ke (nét-so͝oki, -so͝okay) *n.* A small toggle of wood or ivory, usually elaborately carved, used in Japan to fasten a purse or other article to a kimono sash. [Japanese.]

nett. Variant of **net** (remaining after deductions).

net·ting (nétting) *n.* **1.** Any openwork fabric or structure of string, wire, or the like. **2.** A piece of this fabric.

net·tle (nétt'l) *n.* **1.** Any plant of the genus *Urtica,* such as *U. dioica,* the stinging nettle, having toothed leaves often covered with hairs that secrete a stinging fluid that affects the skin on contact. **2.** Any of various other stinging or prickly plants. **—grasp the nettle.** To approach a difficulty or task decisively.
~*tr.v.* **nettled, -tling, -tles. 1.** To sting with or as if with a nettle. **2.** To irritate; vex. [Middle English *nettle,* Old English *netle, netel(e),* from Germanic.]

nettle rash *n.* **Urticaria** *(see).*

net ton *n.* A short **ton** *(see).*

net·work (nét-wurk) *n.* **1.** An openwork fabric or other structure in which rope, thread, wires, or other materials cross at regular intervals. **2.** Something resembling a net in concept or form, such as: **a.** A system of intersecting lines of communication: *a network of railways.* **b.** Any complex, interconnected group or system: *an espionage network.* **3.** A chain of interconnected radio or television broadcasting stations. **4.** A group or system of electrical components and connecting circuitry designed to function as a unit.
~*tr.v.* **networked, -working, -works.** To broadcast over a radio or television network.

net·work·ing (nét-wurking) *n.* The establishing of professional contacts, especially among feminists, at many levels of industry and business for such purposes as disseminating information about jobs or promotions, or offering mutual guidance.

Neu·châ·tel (núr-sha-tél, nő-) A city in northwest Switzerland, capital of the canton of the same name. It lies on the north shore of Lake Neuchâtel. The town is noted for its manufacture of watches, jewellery, and chocolate.

Neu·mann (nóy-man), **(Johann) Balthasar** (1687–1753). Bohemian architect. He designed ornate buildings such as the Vierzehnheiligen church, completed almost 20 years after his death.

Neu·mann (néw-mən), **Johannes von,** known as John (1903–57). Hungarian-born U.S. mathematician. He developed the **game theory** *(see),* and contributed to the mathematical analysis of quantum physics.

neumes, neums (newmz || no͞omz) *pl.n.* The signs used in the notation of plainsong during the Middle Ages, surviving today in transcriptions of Gregorian chant. [Middle English, musical phrase sung to a single syllable, from Old French, from Medieval Latin *neuma, neupma,* from Greek *pneuma,* breath.] **—neu·mat·ic** (new-máttik || no͞o-) *adj.*

neur. neurological; neurology.

neu·ral (néwr-əl || no͝or-) *adj.* **1.** Of or pertaining to the nerves or nervous system. **2.** Of, pertaining to, or located on the same side of the body as the spinal cord; dorsal. [NEUR(O)- + -AL.]

neu·ral·gia (newr-álјə || noor-) *n.* Paroxysmal pain along a nerve. [New Latin : NEUR(O)- + -ALGIA.] **—neu·ral·gic** *adj.*

neu·ras·the·ni·a (néwr-əss-théeni-ə || no͝or-) *n.* A condition marked by fatigue, loss of energy and memory, and feelings of inadequacy, once thought to result from exhaustion of the nervous system. Now rare in scientific usage. Also called "nervous breakdown", "nervous exhaustion". [NEUR(O)- + ASTHENIA.] **—neu·ras·then·ic** (-thénnik) *adj.* **—neu·ras·then·i·cal·ly** *adv.*

neu·rax·on (newr-ák-son || noor-) *n.* A part of a nerve cell, the **axon** *(see).* [New Latin : NEUR(O)- + AXON.]

neu·rec·to·my (newr-éktəmi || noor-) *n., pl.* **-mies.** Surgical removal of a nerve or part of a nerve. [NEUR(O)- + -ECTOMY.]

neu·ri·lem·ma, neu·ri·lem·a (néwr-i-lémmə || no͝or-) *n.* The outer covering of a nerve fibre. [New Latin : NEUR(O)- + Greek *eilēma,* veil, covering, from *eilein,* to wind.] **—neu·ri·lem·mal, neu·ri·lem·ma·tous** (-lémmətəss) *adj.*

neu·ri·tis (newr-ítiss || noor-) *n.* Inflammation of a nerve, causing pain, loss of reflexes, and muscular atrophy. [New Latin : NEUR(O)- + -ITIS.] **—neu·rit·ic** (-íttik) *adj.*

neuro–, neur– *comb. form.* Indicates nerve or nervous system; for example, **neuroblast, neurectomy.** [New Latin, from Greek *neuron,* tendon, nerve.]

neu·ro·blast (néwr-ō-blast, -ə- || no͝or-) *n.* An embryonic cell from which a nerve cell develops. [NEURO- + -BLAST.]

neu·ro·cyte (néwr-ō-sīt, -ə- || nóor-) *n.* A nerve cell.

neu·ro·en·do·crine system (néwr-ō-éndə-krin, -krīn, -kreen || no͝or-) *n.* The system of nerves and hormones that function together to control certain activities of the body.

neu·ro·fib·ril (néwr-ō-fíbril || no͝or-) *n.* Any of the cytoplasmic threads in the cell body of a neurone, extending into the axon in peripheral nerves.

neu·ro·gen·ic (newr-ō-jénnik, -ə- ‖ noor-) *adj.* **1.** Originating in the nervous system. **2.** Caused by stimulation of the nerves. **3.** Caused by disease of the nervous system. **—neu·ro·gen·i·cal·ly** *adv.*

neu·rog·li·a (newr-óggli-ə, newr-ō-glī-ə ‖ noor-) *n.* The network of branched cells and fibres that supports the nerve cells of the central nervous system. Also called "glia". [New Latin : NEURO- + Medieval Greek *glia*, "glue", tissue.] **—neu·rog·li·al** *adj.*

neu·ro·gram (newr-ō-gram, -ə- ‖ noor-) *n.* An **engram** *(see)*. [NEURO- + -GRAM.]

neu·ro·hor·mone (newr-ō-hór-mōn ‖ noor-) *n.* A hormone that is produced within nervous tissue and secreted by specialised nerve cells. An example is oxytocin, produced in the hypothalamus and secreted by the pituitary gland.

neu·ro·hy·po·phy·sis (newr-ō-hī-póffi-siss ‖ noor-) *n.* The posterior part of the pituitary gland. Compare **adenohypophysis**.

neurol. neurological; neurology.

neu·rol·o·gy (newr-óllәji ‖ noor-) *n. Abbr.* **neur., neurol.** The branch of medical science concerned with the nervous system and its disorders. [New Latin *neurologia* : NEURO- + -LOGY.] **—neu·ro·log·i·cal** (newr-ə-lójik'l ‖ noor-) *adj.* **—neu·rol·o·gist** (-óllәjist) *n.*

neu·ro·ma (newr-ō-mə ‖ noor-) *n., pl.* **-mata** (-mətə). A tumour made of nerve tissue. [New Latin : NEUR(O)- + -OMA.]

neu·ro·mus·cu·lar (newr-ō-mús-kewlәr ‖ noor-) *adj.* Of, pertaining to, or affecting both nerves and muscles.

neu·rone (newr-ōn ‖ noor-) *n.* Also **neu·ron** (-on). A **nerve cell** *(see)*. [Greek *neuron*, sinew, nerve.] **—neu·ron·ic** (newr-ónnik ‖ noor-) *adj.* **—neu·ron·i·cal·ly** *adv.*

neu·ro·pa·thol·o·gy (newr-ō-pə-thóllәji ‖ noor-) *n.* The medical study of diseases of the nervous system. **—neu·ro·path·o·log·i·cal** (-pátho-lójik'l) *adj.* **—neu·ro·pa·thol·o·gist** (-pə-thóllәjist) *n.*

neu·rop·a·thy (newr-óppәthi ‖ noor-) *n.* Any disease or abnormality of the nervous system. [NEURO- + -PATHY.]

neu·ro·phys·i·ol·o·gy (newr-ō-fízzi-óllәji ‖ noor-) *n.* The study of the physical and chemical changes associated with the functioning of the nervous system. **—neu·ro·phys·i·o·log·i·cal** (-ə-lójik'l) *adj.* **—neu·ro·phys·i·ol·o·gist** (-óllәjist) *n.*

neu·ro·psy·chi·a·try (newr-ō-sī-kī́-әtri, -sə- ‖ noor-) *n. Abbr.* **NP** The integrated medical study of both neurological and psychiatric disorders. **—neu·ro·psy·chi·at·ric** (-sī́ki-áttrik) *adj.* **—neu·ro·psy·chi·a·trist** (-kī́-әtrist) *n.*

neu·rop·ter·an (newr-óptәrәn ‖ noor-) *n.* Any insect of the order Neuroptera, having four net-veined wings, such as the **ant lion, dobson fly,** or **lacewing** *(all of which see).* ~*adj.* Of or belonging to the Neuroptera. [New Latin *Neuroptera*, "nerve-winged" : NEURO- + -PTER.] **—neu·rop·ter·ous** *adj.*

neu·ro·sis (newr-ṓ-siss ‖ noor-) *n., pl.* **-ses** (-seez). Any of various illnesses affecting the mind or emotions, without obvious organic lesion or change, and involving anxiety, depression, phobia, hysteria, or other abnormal patterns of behaviour. Also called "psychoneurosis". Compare **psychosis**. [New Latin : NEUR(O)- + -OSIS.]

neu·ro·sur·ger·y (newr-ō-súrjәri ‖ noor-) *n.* Surgery of any part of the nervous system. **—neu·ro·sur·geon** *n.* **—neu·ro·sur·gi·cal** *adj.*

neu·rot·ic (newr-óttik ‖ noor-) *adj.* **1.** Of or pertaining to a neurosis: *a neurotic disorder.* **2.** Suffering from neurosis: *a neurotic patient.* **3.** *Informal.* Showing an exaggerated, distorted, or obsessional attitude to the real world: *neurotic about hygiene.* ~*n.* A person suffering from a neurosis. **—neu·rot·i·cal·ly** *adv.*

neu·rot·i·cism (newr-ótti-siz'm ‖ noor-) *n.* A quality of personality characterised by anxiety and a tendency to become neurotic.

neu·rot·o·my (newr-óttәmi ‖ noor-) *n., pl.* **-mies**. The surgical cutting or stretching of a nerve, usually to relieve pain. [NEURO- + -TOMY.]

neu·ro·trans·mit·ter (newr-ō-transs-míttәr, -tranz-, -traanz- ‖ noor-) *n.* A chemical substance, such as acetylcholine, released from nerve endings and transmitting impulses across a synapse to nerve, muscle, or other cells. Also called "transmitter".

Neus·tri·a (new-stri-ə ‖ nóō-). The western part of the Frankish kingdom during the Merovingian period (sixth to eighth century). It consisted of the Loire and Seine country and land farther to the north; the chief towns were Soissons and Paris. **—Neus·tri·an** *n. & adj.*

neut. 1. neuter. **2.** neutral.

neu·ter (new-tәr ‖ nóō-) *adj. Abbr.* **neut. 1.** *Grammar.* Neither masculine nor feminine in gender. **2.** Lacking sexual organs or having only nonfunctional ones; specifically: **a.** *Botany.* Having no pistils or stamens; asexual. **b.** *Zoology.* Sexually undeveloped. **3.** Taking no side; neutral. ~*n.* **1.** *Grammar.* **a.** The neuter gender. **b.** A neuter word. **2. a.** A castrated animal. **b.** A sexually undeveloped or imperfectly developed female insect; a worker. **c.** A plant without stamens or pistils. **3.** A neutral person. ~*tr.v.* **neutered, -tering, -ters.** To castrate (an animal). [Middle English *neutre*, from Old French, from Latin *neuter*, neither : *ne-*, not + *uter*, either of two.]

neu·tral (new-trәl ‖ nóō-) *adj. Abbr.* **neut. 1.** Not inclining towards or actively taking either side, as in a war or other dispute. **2.** Belonging to neither side or party: *on neutral ground.* **3.** Occupying a middle position; not one thing or the other; indifferent. **4.** Of no sex; sexless; neuter. **5.** *Chemistry.* Of or designating a compound that is neither acidic nor alkaline. **6.** *Physics.* **a.** Of or designating a particle, object, or system that has neither positive nor negative

electric charge. **b.** Of or designating a particle, object, or system that has a net electric charge of zero. **7.** Of or pertaining to the state of a mechanical system in which gears are not engaged for transmission of power. **8. Achromatic** *(see).* **9.** *Phonetics.* Designating a vowel that is pronounced with the tongue in a relaxed, middle position, such as the *a* in *around*. ~*n.* **1.** One who takes no side in a dispute. **2. a.** A neutral nation. **b.** A citizen of a neutral nation. **3.** An achromatic colour. **4.** The position of gears in a power system when power cannot be transmitted: *The car is in neutral.* [Latin *neutrālis*, neuter (grammatically), from NEUTER.] **—neu·tral·ly** *adv.*

neu·tral·i·sa·tion (néw-trә-lī-záysh'n ‖ nóō-; *U.S.* -li-) *n.* **1.** The act of neutralising. **2.** *Chemistry.* A reaction between an acid and a base that yields a salt and water.

neu·tral·ise, neu·tral·ize (néw-trә-līz ‖ nóō-) *v.* **-ised, -ising, -ises.** *—tr.* **1.** To make neutral. **2.** To counterbalance or counteract and so render ineffective. **3.** To prohibit warfare in (an area) by signed agreement. **4.** *Chemistry.* **a.** To make (a solution) chemically neutral. **b.** To cause (an acid or base) to undergo neutralisation. *—intr.* To become neutral. **—neu·tral·is·er** *n.*

Synonyms: neutralise, counteract, negate, nullify.

neu·tral·ism (néw-trә-liz'm ‖ nóō-) *n.* A political attitude of nonalignment or non-involvement with conflicting alliances. **—neu·tral·ist** *adj. & n.*

neu·tral·i·ty (new-trál-әti ‖ nóō-) *n.* The state or policy of being neutral; especially, nonparticipation in war.

neutral spirits *pl.n. U.S.* Ethanol distilled at or above 190° proof and used frequently in alcoholic beverage blends.

neu·tri·no (new-tréenō ‖ nóō-) *n., pl.* **-nos**. *Physics.* Any of various electrically neutral particles, thought to be massless, belonging to the lepton family. Each is associated with a specific massive lepton; for example, the *electron-type neutrino* or the *muon-type neutrino*. [Italian, diminutive of *neutrone*, neutron, from English NEUTRON.]

neu·tron (néw-tron, *rarely* -trәn ‖ nóō-) *n. Symbol* **n** *Physics.* An elementary particle of the baryon family, having almost the same mass as the proton but no electric charge. It is stable when bound in an atomic nucleus, but has a mean lifetime of approximately 15.5 minutes as a free particle. It is present in any atomic nucleus with mass number greater than one. [NEUTR(AL) + -ON.]

neutron bomb *n.* A nuclear weapon that produces a large number of high-energy neutrons but relatively little blast or long-term radioactivity. It is designed to kill people without causing excessive damage or contamination in the target area. Also called "enhanced radiation bomb".

neutron number *n. Symbol* **N** The number of neutrons in the nucleus of a given isotope.

neutron star *n.* A celestial body of great density, formed by the

netsuke *Between the 17th and 19th centuries these ornamental toggles, usually made of wood or ivory, and used to secure the silk cord of a purse, became miniature works of art. This one depicts Hotei, one of the seven gods of luck in Japanese mythology.*

collapse of a star under its own gravity and consisting almost entirely of neutrons. A neutron star has a mass of between 1.5 and 3 times that of the Sun, but might have a radius as small as 100 kilometres.

neu·tro·phil (néw-trə-fil ‖ nŏŏ-) *adj.* Also **neu·tro·phile** (-fīl). Easily stained by neutral dyes. Said of such cells as leucocytes.
~n. A phagocytic leucocyte of a type having a lobed nucleus and granular cytoplasm that stains with neutral dyes. [NEUTR(AL) + -PHIL(E).]

Ne·va·da (ni-va̋adə, nə-, ne- ‖ -váddə). State in the western United States, lying between California on the west and Utah on the east. Most of the state lies within the desert region known as the Great Basin. Carson City is the capital, but the largest city is Las Vegas. Nevada is a leading supplier of copper, gold, iron ore, and mercury, and oil was discovered there in 1954. The state was admitted to the Union in 1864. **—Ne·vad·an** *adj. & n.*

né·vé (névvay, náy-vay) *n.* **1.** The upper part of a glacier, where the snow turns into ice. **2.** A field of snow at the head of a glacier. **3.** The granular snow typically found in such a field. See **firm.** [French dialect (Valais), from Latin *nix* (stem *niv-*), snow.]

nev·er (névvər) *adv.* **1. a.** Not ever; on no occasion: *never tasted venison.* **b.** At no time and under no circumstances whatsoever. Used emphatically: *Do such a thing? Never!* **2. a.** Not at all; in no way: *Never fear; This will never do!* **b.** *Nonstandard.* Not: *I waited but you never arrived.* **—never so.** *Archaic.* Very.
~interj. Also **well I never.** Used to express disbelief or amazement. [Middle English *never,* Old English *nǣfre* : *ne,* not + *ǣfre,* ever.]

nev·er·more (névvər-mór ‖ -môr) *adv.* Never again.

nev·er-nev·er (névvər-névvər) *n. British Informal.* The hire-purchase system. Used with *the.*

nev·er-nev·er land *n.* An imaginary and wonderful place; a fantasy land. [After the country in J.M. Barrie's play *Peter Pan* (1904).]

nev·er·the·less (névvər-thə-léss) *adv.* None the less; however.

Nevis. See **St. Kitts-Nevis-Anguilla.**

nevus. *Chiefly U.S.* Variant of **naevus.**

new (new ‖ nŏŏ) *adj.* **newer, newest. 1.** Of recent origin; having existed only a short time; lately made, produced, or grown: *a new television series.* **2. a.** Not yet old; fresh; recent. **b.** Used for the first time; not secondhand. **3. a.** Previously existing but recognised, discovered, or encountered lately for the first time: *a new galaxy.* **b.** Not belonging to one's own previous experience: *visiting new places.* **4.** Freshly introduced; unfamiliar; unaccustomed. Used with *to* or *at: I'm new at it.* **5.** Being the latest in a sequence: *the new edition.* **6. a.** Newly entered into a state or position; being so for the first time: *the new rich.* **b.** Changed for the better; refreshed; rejuvenated: *A nap made a new man of him.* **7.** Different and distinct from a former one of the same type: *new neighbours.* **8. a.** Modern; current; fashionable: *a new dance.* **b.** In the most recent form, period, or development of something: *New Latin.* **9.** Novel; unconventional: *a new concept in bathroom accessories.* **10.** Designating crops that are harvested early: *new potatoes.* **11.** Additional; more: *send him some new work.*
~adv. Freshly; recently. Used in combination: *new-cut grass.* [Middle English *newe,* Old English *nēowe, nīwe.*] **—new·ness** *n.*
Usage: new, novel, original. *New* is a general term referring to both time and condition. *Novel,* which emphasises condition, is applied to that which is both new and strikingly unusual: *His symphony is not only new* (chronologically), *but novel in its treatment of folk songs. Original* also emphasises state rather than time, and is said of that which is the first of its kind.

New·ark (new-ark ‖ nŏŏ-). City in New Jersey, in the northeast United States, lying on the river Passaic and Newark Bay. It is a major industrial and commercial centre.

new arrival *n. Informal.* A newborn baby.

new-born, new-born (new-bawrn ‖ nŏŏ-) *adj.* Just born; very recently born: *a newborn baby.*

New Britain. Volcanic island in the southwest Pacific, belonging to Papua New Guinea. It is the largest island in the Bismarck Archipelago. The chief town and port is Rabaul. The island is mountainous with many active volcanoes and hot springs. It was named by the English explorer, William Dampier, who discovered it in 1700.

new broom *n.* A new and enthusiastic person in charge of a job, who attempts to reorganise it and institute changes. [From the proverbial saying *a new broom sweeps clean.*]

New Brunswick. Province in east Canada, lying to the south of Quebec and east of Maine (in the United States) and connected to Nova Scotia by the Chignecto Isthmus. The capital is Fredericton; the two largest cities are Saint John and Moncton. Three-quarters of the province is forested, and timber is the chief industry. About 40 per cent of the population is French-speaking.

New·burg (new-burg ‖ nŏŏ-) *adj.* **1.** Designating a sauce used for seafood, made from cream, egg yolks, butter, wine, and usually nutmeg. **2.** Cooked or served in this sauce: *lobster Newburg.* [Alteration of *Wenburg,* name of patron for whom sauce was created.]

New Caledonia. Large island in the southwest Pacific Ocean, lying about 1 200 kilometres (750 miles) east of Australia. It has a number of smaller islands as dependencies and is itself an overseas territory belonging to France. Coffee is the main cash crop, but the economic value of the island lies in its rich mineral deposits. It was annexed by France in 1853. See map at **Pacific Ocean.**

New·cas·tle¹ (new-kaass'l ‖ nŏŏ-, -kass'l). Coastal city and port of New South Wales, in southeast Australia, lying at the mouth of the Hunter River. It is a leading steel-manufacturing centre.

newel *A central stone newel supports the steps of a spiral stairway at Dover Castle, built in the 12th century.*

Newcastle disease *n.* Fowl pest *(see).* [After NEWCASTLE UPON TYNE, where there was an outbreak of it in 1926.]

New·cas·tle-un·der-Lyme (new-kaass'l-úndər-līm ‖ nŏŏ-, -kass'l-). Industrial town in Staffordshire, west central England, on the river Lyme. It is important for textiles, bricks, and coalmining.

New·cas·tle up·on Tyne (new-kaass'l-ə-pón-tīn ‖ nŏŏ-, -kass'l-; *locally* new-káss'l-). City in the metropolitan county of Tyne and Wear, northeast England, situated on the north bank of the river Tyne. It is the centre of the industrial region known as Tyneside, and one of the world's largest shipbuilding centres. It is set among the Northumberland and Durham coalfields.

new chum *n. Australian & N.Z. Informal.* A recent immigrant.

New Church *n.* The **New Jerusalem Church** *(see).*

New·combe (new-kəm ‖ nŏŏ-), **John** (1944–). Australian tennis player. He was Wimbledon singles champion (1967, 1970, and 1971), and five times doubles champion (between 1965 and 1974).

new·com·er (new-kummər ‖ nŏŏ-) *n.* One who has lately come to a place or situation.

New Commonwealth *n.* Those countries belonging to the British Commonwealth that have gained independence since 1945.
~adj. Of, pertaining to, or coming from these countries. Sometimes used euphemistically to refer to nonwhites.

New Criticism *n.* A form of literary criticism established in the early 1940s chiefly in the United States, involving a detailed analysis of the literary text's verbal organisation and imagery, and a corresponding rejection of biographical and historical considerations surrounding the composition of the text. **—New Critic** *n.*

New Deal *n.* **1.** The programmes and policies for economic recovery and reform, relief, and social security, introduced in the United States during the 1930s by President Franklin D. Roosevelt and his administration. **2.** The period between 1933 and 1940 during which these programmes and policies were developed.

New Delhi. See **Delhi.**

New Economic Policy *n.* The programme in the U.S.S.R. between 1921 and 1928 whereby concessions were made to capitalism in small industry, the retail trade, and agriculture.

new·el (new-əl, newl ‖ nŏŏ-) *n.* **1.** The vertical support at the centre of a winding staircase. **2.** Any of the posts supporting a handrail at the bottom or on the landings of a staircase. Also called "newel post." [Middle English *nowell,* from Old French *nouel,* "kernel", newel, from Latin *nucālis,* nut-shaped, from *nux,* nut.]

New England. The extreme northeasterly states of the United States, settled during the colonial era: Maine, New Hampshire, Vermont, Massachusetts, Rhode Island, and Connecticut.

New English Bible *n. Abbr.* **N.E.B.** A Modern English translation of the Bible and Apocrypha, prepared by an interdenominational panel and published in full in 1970.

new-fan·gled (new-fáng-g'ld, -fang- ‖ nŏŏ-) *adj.* **1.** Excessively or needlessly novel: *newfangled ideas.* **2.** *Archaic.* Excessively fond of novelty. Used derogatorily in both senses. [Middle English *newe fangled,* alteration of *newefangel,* fond of new things : NEW + *-fangel,* from Old English *fangol* (unattested), "ready to seize", from *fangen,* past participle of *fōn,* to seize.]

new-fash·ioned (new-fásh'nd ‖ nŏŏ-) *adj.* Made according to or following a current fashion.

New Forest. A thickly wooded area, mostly of oak and beech, interspersed with heathland in Hampshire, in south England. The woods were made a royal forest by William I in 1079. Much of its 36 500 hectares (90,000 acres) is open to the public.

New·found·land¹ (new-fənd-lənd, -land, -lánd, new-fównd-lənd ‖ nŏŏ-; *locally* new-fənd-land). *Abbr.* **N.F., Nfld.** Province in east Canada, comprising the island of Newfoundland (north of the Gulf of St. Lawrence) and the mainland region of Labrador. The capital and largest city is St. John's. For centuries the island has been important for the fishing, but is now the leading industry and Newfoundland is Canada's largest supplier of iron.

Newfoundland² *n.* A dog of a large breed, growing to 71 centimetres (28 inches) at the shoulder, with a broad head and square muzzle, a powerful body, and a dense, usually black coat. [Believed bred in NEWFOUNDLAND, Canada.]

New France. The French possessions in Canada in the colonial era. The name derived from the fur-trading Company of New France, but the region was formally proclaimed the royal province of New France by Louis XIV in 1663. Although French rule in Canada ended with the Peace of Paris in 1763, the feudal, or seigneurial, system instituted in the province by the French monarchy was not abolished formally until 1854.

New·gate (new-git, -gayt ‖ nŏŏ-). A famous prison in London, demolished in 1902.

New Greek *n. Abbr.* **NGk., N.Gr.** Modern Greek *(see).*

New Guinea. See **Papua New Guinea.**

New·ham (new-əm, *sometimes* -ham ‖ nŏŏ-). Borough of Greater London, England, lying north of the river Thames in the eastern part of the city.

New Hampshire. State in the northeast United States, lying between Vermont to the west and Maine to the east. The capital is Concord; the largest cities are Manchester and Nashua. The northern part of the state is noted for the scenic beauty of its lakes and mountains. The industrial centres to the south make the state one of the most heavily industrialised in the Union. One of the original Thirteen Colonies, New Hampshire was a founding member of the United States (1788).

New Haven. City and port in Connecticut, United States. It is famous as the site both of Yale University (since 1716) and of the world's first commercial telephone exchange (1879).

New Hebrides. See **Vanuatu.**

New High German n. Abbr. **N.H.G. German** (see).

Ne Win (náy wín), **U,** born Maung Shu Maung (1911–). Burmese politician. After independence from the United Kingdom, he served as commander in chief (1948–58), then as defence minister and prime minister (1958–60, 1962–74). In 1974 he suspended the constitution and proclaimed himself President. He retired in 1981.

New Ireland. An island in Papua New Guinea.

new·ish (néwish ‖ nōo-) adj. Of fairly recent origin; fairly new.

New Jersey. State in the northeast United States, lying on the coast to the south of New York state and to the east of Pennsylvania. The capital is Trenton. The largest city is Newark. It is one of the most heavily populated and industrialised states. New Jersey was one of the original Thirteen Colonies and a founding member of the United States (1788).

New Jerusalem n. The celestial city; heaven. [From the Apocalypse (Revelation), chapter 21.]

New Jerusalem Church n. The church, founded in 1787, based on the philosophy and teachings of Swedenborg. Also called "New Church". See **Swedenborgianism.**

New Latin n. Abbr. **NL, NL., N.L.** The form of Latin in use, especially for scientific nomenclature, since the early Renaissance.

New Learning n. The revived study of the Bible and Greek and Latin classics in the original occurring in the 15th and 16th centuries in Renaissance Europe.

New Left n. A diffuse left-wing movement, especially amongst radical students, that began in many countries in the 1960s. **—New Left·ist** n.

New Look n. **1.** A fashion in women's clothing of the late 1940s characterised by long, full skirts. Preceded by the. **2.** Small **n,** small **l.** Informal. Any up-to-date fashion.

new·ly (néw-li ‖ nōo-) adv. **1.** Lately; recently: newly baked bread. **2.** In a new or different way: an old idea newly phrased.

new·ly·wed (néw-li-wed ‖ nōo-) n. A person recently married.

New·man (néw-mən ‖ nōo-), **John Henry** (1801–90). English poet and priest. As an Anglican he helped to found the Oxford Movement (1833); he later joined the Roman Catholic church (1845), and was made a cardinal (1879). His best known works are Apologia pro Vita Sua (1864) and The Dream of Gerontius (1866).

Newman, Paul (1925–). U.S. film actor. Among his many successful films are Butch Cassidy and The Sundance Kid (1969) and The Sting (1973). He has also produced and directed films of his own.

New·mar·ket[1] (néw-maarkit ‖ nōo-) n. Sometimes small **n.** **1.** British. A long, close-fitting coat for men and women, worn especially in the late 19th century. Also called "Newmarket coat". **2.** A card game in which players gamble on their chances of duplicating cards on the table. [After NEWMARKET, Suffolk.]

Newmarket[2]. Market town in Suffolk, in east England. It has been a famous racing town since the reign of James I. The four main races held annually are the One Thousand Guineas, the Two Thousand Guineas, the Cambridgeshire, and the Cesarewitch.

new mathematics n. Used with a singular verb. A form of mathematics introduced in schools and making use of set theory. Also called "new maths".

New Mexico. State in the southwest United States, lying to the south of Colorado and to the east of Arizona. The capital is Santa Fe; the largest city is Albuquerque. Most of the state consists of arid desert and forested mountain wilderness. New Mexico is the United States' leading supplier of uranium ore and a major supplier of manganese, potash, salt, and copper. Strong traces of Spanish culture remain: about a third of the population is of mixed Spanish descent, and Spanish is still the dominant language in many parts. New Mexico entered the Union in 1912.

New Model Army n. The British army as reorganised by the Parliamentarians in 1645 during the Civil War.

new moon n. **1.** The phase of the moon occurring when it passes between the earth and the sun and is invisible, or visible only as a narrow crescent at sunset. **2.** The crescent moon.

New Neth·er·land (néthərland). An area of land in the Hudson River Valley granted by Holland to the Dutch West India Company in 1621. The area included New Amsterdam, founded in 1624 on Manhattan Island (later New York City). The region was seized by England in 1664, when it was divided into the two colonies of New York and New Jersey.

New Or·le·ans (órli-ənz, ór-léenz). City in Louisiana, in the southern United States, on the banks of the Mississippi river. It is the largest city in Louisiana and a major port. It is famous for the surviving French flavour of its streetlife and nightlife, for its annual Mardi Gras carnival, and for its jazz and blues tradition, dating from the late 19th century. Andrew Jackson's forces defeated the British at the Battle of New Orleans in 1815.

New Orleans jazz n. The jazz played in New Orleans from 1900 to 1925, characterised by collective improvisation on simple harmonies by a front line of clarinet, trumpet, and trombone.

new penny n., pl. **new pence.** A coin of the United Kingdom, a penny (see).

New Plymouth. City on the west coast of North Island, New Zealand. It was founded by the New Plymouth Company in 1841 and for some years served as the landing point for settlers to New Zealand. It is now a busy commercial port and the distributing centre for the surrounding dairy-farming region.

---

new mathematics

SETS AND THEIR SYMBOLS

A new language to help children understand relationships

Set theory explains the logical relationship between sets of objects, and is the cornerstone of the new mathematics. A set is a collection of distinct objects, which may be concrete (for example, playing cards) or abstract (for example, numbers). A range of traditional and new mathematical symbols is used to express the concept mathematically; Venn diagrams use geometrical figures such as squares and circles to represent sets and the relations between them. Set theory notation is a useful language for expressing complex mathematical ideas.

NOTATION	MEANING	EXAMPLE	VENN DIAGRAM
$=$	is equal to	$2+2=4$	
$\neq$	is not equal to	$2+3\neq4$	
$<$	is less than	$2+1<4$	
$>$	is greater than	$2+3>4$	
$S=\{1,3,5\}$	the set of numbers 1, 3, 5 (a listed set).	If $S=$ the suits in a pack of cards, then: $S=\{♣ ♦ ♥ ♠\}$	or
S is $\{x: x$ is odd and $x<7\}$	the set of numbers x such that x is odd and is less than 7 (a defined set)		
ε	is a member of	If $S=$ the suits in a pack of cards, then: $♣\,\varepsilon\,S$	or
$\mathcal{E}$ or U	the universal set	The set of aces is contained in $\mathcal{E}$, the universal set of a pack of cards	
$\varnothing$	the empty set: a set having no members (see $A\cap B=\varnothing$ below)	The set of black hearts and diamonds is the empty set, which is contained in every set　$S=\varnothing$ (there are no black hearts and diamonds)	
$A\subset B$	A is a subset of B	The set of vowels is a subset of the set of the letters of the alphabet Vowels $\subset$ Alphabet $=\{a,e,i,o,u\}$	
$A\cup B$	union of sets A and B	$A=\{3,4,6,8\}$ $B=\{6,8,12,16\}$ $A\cup B=\{3,4,6,8,12,16\}$	
$A\cap B$	intersection of sets A and B	$A\cap B=\{6,8\}$	
$A\cap B=\varnothing$	A and B are disjoint; they have no members in common and their intersection is therefore empty	$A=$ even numbers $=\{2,4,8,16\}$ $B=$ odd numbers $=\{3,5,7,9\}$	or $A\cap B$ (empty)
A'	complement of A	if $\mathcal{E}=\{1,2,3,4,5,6,7,8,9\}$ and $A=\{$ all numbers that 6 can be divided evenly by $\}$ then $A=\{1,2,3,6\}$ and $A'=\{4,5,7,8,9\}$ The complement of set A is everything not in A	

New·port[1] (néw-pawrt ‖ nōo-, -pórt) Welsh **Cas·new·ydd-ar-Wysg** (kass-né-with-aar-wisk). City in the county of Gwent, Wales, lying on the Bristol Channel at the mouth of the river Usk (Wysg). Long an important port serving the west Monmouthshire coalfield, it is now a leading centre for the manufacture of steel.

Newport[2]. Market town on the Isle of Wight, off the coast of southern England. It is situated at the navigable head of the river Medina, and is the island's administrative centre.

Newport News. City in Virginia, in the eastern United States, one of the world's largest shipbuilding and ship-repairing centres.

New·ry (néwr-i ‖ nóor-i). Town in southeastern Northern Ireland, in county Down, lying on the river Clanrye and the Newry Canal.

news (newz ‖ nōoz) n. Used with a singular verb. **1. a.** Information about recent events of general interest, especially as reported by the

newt *These lizard-like amphibians are a type of salamander. They are widely distributed and sometimes kept as pets. Like all amphibians, they need a wet environment, absorbing water through their skin. Triturus alpestris (above) is found mostly in central and eastern Europe.*

mass media. Often used in combination: *newsdesk*. **b.** A presentation or broadcast of such information. Also used adjectively: *news bulletin.* **2.** New information about a subject: *What's the news about John's operation?* **3. a.** A person, event, or the like that is a source of interest or provides scope for conversation. **b.** A subject that is given a great deal of coverage by the press, radio, and television: *The government's policies are still news after two years.* **4.** *Capital* **N.** Used as part of the title of certain newspapers: *News of the World.* —**good** (or **bad**) **news.** Something or someone regarded as highly desirable (or undesirable).

news agency *n.* An organisation that provides news coverage or collects news reports for subscribers, such as newspapers. Also called "press agency".

news·a·gent (newz-ayjənt ‖ nōōz-) *n. British.* A person with a shop that sells newspapers, magazines, stationery, and the like.

news·boy (newz-boy ‖ nōōz-) *n.* A boy who sells or delivers newspapers.

news·cast (newz-kaast ‖ nōōz-, -kast) *n.* A radio or television broadcast, often with commentary, of events in the news. [NEWS + (BROAD)CAST.] —**news·cast·er** *n.* —**news·cast·ing** *n.*

New Scotland Yard. The official name for **Scotland Yard** (*see*).

news·flash (newz-flash) *n.* A short, usually unscheduled, announcement of news, a **flash** (*see*).

news·girl (newz-gurl ‖ nōōz-) *n.* A female newsboy.

news·let·ter (newz-lettər ‖ nōōz-) *n.* A printed periodical report devoted to news for members of a group such as a society or firm, or for subscribers with a particular common interest.

news·mong·er (newz-mung-gər ‖ nōōz-, -mong-) *n.* A person who spreads news; a gossip.

New South *n.* Those U.S. states of the South that were members of the Confederate States of America but were not among the 13 original colonies; especially, Alabama, Arkansas, Mississippi, Tennessee, and Texas.

New South Wales. State in southeastern Australia, bounded on the east by the Pacific Ocean. The capital and largest city is Sydney. The state is economically the most important in Australia, the Sydney-Newcastle-Wollongong complex being the industrial heartland of the country. The leading product is steel.

New Spain. The former Spanish possessions governed from Mexico City, including islands in the West Indies, Central America north of Panama, Mexico, the southwestern United States, and the Philippine Islands.

news·pa·per (newss-paypər, newz- ‖ nōōz-) *n.* **1.** A publication, typically issued daily or weekly, printed on folded sheets of paper, and containing news and opinion of current events, feature articles, and usually advertising. Also called "paper". **2.** A newspaper-publishing company. **3.** The paper on which a newspaper has been printed: *wrapped in newspaper.*

news·pa·per·man (newss-paypər-man, newz- ‖ nōōz-) *n., pl.* -**men** (-men). *Chiefly U.S.* **1.** The owner or publisher of a newspaper. **2.** A journalist or editor employed by a newspaper.

news·pa·per·wo·man (newss-paypər-wŏŏmən, newz- ‖ nōōz-) *n., pl.* -**women** (-wimmin). A female newspaperman.

new·speak (new-speek ‖ nōō-) *n.* Language that consists of or is full of jargon, propaganda, and ambiguities, especially as used by politicians or bureaucrats. [After the bureaucratic language in George Orwell's novel, *1984.*]

news·print (newz-print ‖ nōōz-) *n.* **1.** Inexpensive paper made from wood pulp, used chiefly for printing newspapers. **2.** Printing ink: *hands covered in newsprint after reading the paper.*

news·read·er (newz-reedər ‖ nōōz-) *n.* A person who reads the news on television or the radio; a newscaster.

news·reel (newz-reel ‖ nōōz-) *n.* A short film that presents current events.

news·room (newz-rōōm, -rŏŏm ‖ nōōz-) *n.* A room in a newspaper office or radio or television station where news stories are researched, written, and edited.

news·stand (newz-stand ‖ nōōz-) *n.* An open booth or stand at which newspapers are sold.

New Style *n. Abbr.* **N.S.** The current method of reckoning the months and days of the year, according to the Gregorian calendar, as distinct from the former style of reckoning according to the Julian calendar.

news vendor *n. Chiefly U.S.* A person who sells newspapers, especially at a newsstand.

news·wor·thy (newz-wurthi ‖ nōōz-) *adj.* Of sufficient interest or importance to be reported as news.

news·y (newzi ‖ nōōzi) *adj.* -**ier**, -**iest.** *Informal.* Full of news; informative.

newt (newt ‖ nōōt) *n.* Any small amphibian of the genus *Triturus* or related genera, having a long, slender body and tail and short legs. [Middle English, from the phrase *a newt(e)*, originally *an ewt(e)* : *an* (indefinite article) + *ewt(e), evete,* EFT.]

new technology *n.* Technology and technological products developed during and since the 1970s and chiefly characterised by the use of microprocessors.

New Territories. The portion of Hong Kong colony leased by Great Britain from China in 1898 for 99 years. The area includes most of the colony's islands and the greater part of its mainland north of Kowloon.

New Test. New Testament.

New Testament *n. Abbr.* **NT, N.T., New Test.** The Gospels, Acts, Pauline and other Epistles, and the Book of Revelation, which to-gether have been viewed by Christians as forming the record of the new dispensation belonging to the Church, as distinct from the Old Testament dispensation shared with Judaism. Together with the Old Testament it makes up the Christian Bible. [Translation of Latin *Novum Testāmentum,* translation of Greek *Kainē Diathēkē,* "new dispensation, covenant, or testament" (Mark 14:24).

new·ton (newt'n ‖ nōōt'n) *n. Abbr.* **N** *Physics.* The SI unit of force, equal to the force required to accelerate a mass of one kilogram one metre per second per second. It is equal to 100,000 dynes. [After Sir Isaac NEWTON.]

New·ton (newt'n ‖ nōōt'n), **Sir Isaac** (1642–1727). English mathematician and physicist. He devised calculus independently of Leibniz, and made important discoveries about light. His greatest work, however, is his treatise on gravitation (supposedly inspired by the sight of a falling apple), *Principia Mathematica* (1687).

New·to·ni·an (new-tōni-ən ‖ nōō-) *adj.* Pertaining to or in accordance with the work of Newton, especially that in mechanics and gravitation: *Newtonian physics; a Newtonian explanation.*

Newtonian telescope *n.* A type of telescope in which light from a distant object is reflected by a large concave mirror onto an angled plane mirror, which directs the light into an eyepiece.

Newton's law of gravitation *n.* The principle that two bodies attract each other with a force that is directly proportional to the product of the masses and inversely proportional to the square of their distance apart. It is often written in the form $F = G m_1 m_2 / d^2$, where G is the gravitational constant.

Newton's laws of motion *pl.n.* Three laws describing motion, used as the basis for Newtonian mechanics. They are: a body continues in a state of rest or of uniform motion in a straight line unless it is acted on by external forces; the rate of change of momentum of a body is proportional to the external force; any force (*action*) on a system gives rise to an equal and opposite force (*reaction*).

new town *n.* Any of a number of towns built in Britain since 1946, planned and partly financed by central government as new areas of growth.

new wave *n. Often capital* **N,** *capital* **W. 1.** A movement in the French cinema in the 1960s, led by such directors as Godard and Resnais, that abandoned traditional narrative techniques in favour of greater use of symbolism and abstraction. Also called "Nouvelle Vague". **2.** A form of rock music developed from punk rock in the late 1970s, showing a more sophisticated and commercial approach. **3.** Any cultural movement that is considered to be avant-garde or in reaction against traditional methods, styles, or techniques. [Originally, translation of French *nouvelle vague.*]

New World *n.* The countries of the Western Hemisphere; North and South America, and adjacent islands.

new year *n.* **1.** The year about to begin or just begun. **2.** *Capital* **N,** *capital* **Y.** The first day or days of the calendar year. **3. Rosh Hashanah** (*see*).

New Year's Day *n.* The first day of the year, as reckoned according to the Gregorian calendar; January 1.

New Year's Eve *n.* The eve of New Year's Day; December 31.

New York[1]. State in the northeast United States, bordering on Canada to the west and north and on Pennsylvania and New Jersey to the south. The capital is Albany; the largest city is New York. The other major cities, Buffalo, Rochester, and Syracuse, lie near the New York State Barge Canal which crosses the central region of the state from east to west. In the regions between New York's many industrial and commercial towns and cities lie rich mixed farming land. The state's origins can be traced to 1664, when England seized from the Dutch the land around the Hudson river known as New Netherland and divided it into the colonies of New York and New Jersey. New York was thus one of the original 13 colonies and was also a founding member of the United States (1787).

New York[2]. Largest city in the United States, lying on the northeast coast, at the mouth of the Hudson river on New York bay. It consists of five boroughs: Manhattan (an island), Queens and Brooklyn (both on Long Island), Richmond (on Staten Island), and the Bronx (on the mainland). The metropolitan area of the city spills over into New Jersey and Connecticut. New York is one of the world's busiest ports. Since the end of World War II the city has gradually replaced London as the world's financial centre, and is the artistic and publishing centre of the United States. Many of its streets, such as Wall Street (finance), Broadway (the theatre), Madison Avenue (advertising), and Fifth Avenue (shopping) have become world famous. New York's population, including large numbers of blacks, Puerto Ricans, and European immigrants, is the most ethnically varied of any American city. It dates from the establishment of New Amsterdam on Manhattan Island in 1624.

New Zea·land (zēelənd). Independent dominion within the Commonwealth, consisting of two main islands, North Island and South Island, and some smaller islands, lying in the southwest Pacific Ocean southeast of Australia. The islands are poor in natural resources and the mainstay of the country's economy is the export of agricultural products, especially meat and dairy products. The population is predominantly of British stock; the indigenous Maoris make up less than ten per cent of the total. The islands were first settled by Polynesians in the 9th or 10th century. New Zealand became a British colony in 1840, received a large measure of self-government in 1852, and was granted dominion status in 1907. Area, 269 057 square kilometres (167,192 square miles). Population, 3,100,000. Capital, Wellington. —**New Zea·land·er** *n.*

New Zealand flax *n.* See **phormium.**

Nex·ø (nég-sö), **Martin Andersen** (1869–1954). Danish novelist. One of Denmark's greatest literary figures, he did not begin his formal education until he was 20. Among his novels are *Pelle the Conqueror* (4 volumes, 1906–10) and *Ditte, the Daughter of Man* (5 volumes, 1917–21), which, like his other works, reflect a Marxist philosophy influenced by a childhood in the slums of Copenhagen.

next (nekst) *adj.* **1.** Nearest in space; adjacent: *the next room.* **2.** Coming directly after in time or sequence; immediately succeeding: *next Monday; the next person on the list.* ~*adv.* **1.** In the time, order, or place immediately following. **2.** On the first subsequent occasion: *when next I write.* —**next to. 1.** Adjacent to; in the closest place to: *the car next to yours.* **2.** Following in order or degree: *Next to drinking he likes sleeping best.* **3.** *Informal.* Almost; practically: *next to impossible.* ~*prep. Archaic.* Next to: *next my skin.* ~*n.* The next person or thing: *The next will be better.* [Middle English *nexte,* Old English *nēahst, nēhst,* superlative of *nēah,* near.]

Usage: In the sense "coming directly after in time or sequence", *next* is generally unambiguous. For example, there is no ambiguity about referring to *next Friday,* if said on Tuesday; but if said on Thursday, a time reference of eight days hence would usually be intended; and if said on Wednesday, there would often be uncertainty as to which of the two Fridays was in question. The use of *this* as a way out of the problem (*this Friday:* the Friday of this week) is thus very common. *Next* and *nearest* are sometimes interchangeable, but not always. *Next* always indicates direct succession in a series. *Nearest,* which does not necessarily imply a sequence, is employed more generally to indicate the closest proximity, as in time, space, or kinship.

next door *adv.* To or in the adjacent house or building. —**next·door** (nékst-dór ‖ -dôr) *adj.*

next friend *n. Law.* One who is admitted to court to sue as the representative of a minor or other person under legal disability.

next of kin *n., pl.* **next of kin. 1.** The person most nearly related to one by blood. **2.** *Law.* **a.** The closest relative of a deceased person. **b.** *Used with a plural verb.* Those relatives entitled to the estate of a deceased person in accordance with the statutes of distribution.

nex·us (néksəss) *n., pl.* **nexus** or **-uses. 1.** The bond, link, or tie existing between members of a group or series; a means of connection between things. **2.** A connected series or group. **3.** *Anatomy.* A connection or link. [Latin, from *nectere* (past participle *nexus*), to bind, connect.]

Ney (nay), **Michel, Duc d'Elchingen et Prince de la Moskowa** (1769–1815). French marshal. His command of the rearguard in the retreat from Moscow (1812) saved Napoleon's army from annihilation. He deserted Louis XVIII to rejoin Napoleon in the Waterloo campaign. He was shot for treason by the restored monarchy.

Nez Percé (néz pérss, néss, páírss; *French* nay pair-sáy) *n., pl.* **Nez Percés** (-iz) or collectively **Nez Percé. 1.** A member of an American Indian people formerly occupying much of the Pacific Northwest. **2.** The language of this people, of the Sahaptin family of languages. [Canadian French, "pierced nose", either translation of Salish *Chopunnish,* "Nez Percé", or from the pierced nose sign whereby the tribe was designated in Salishan sign language, presumably with reference to the custom of wearing ornamental seashells on pierced noses.]

N.F. 1. National Front (in Britain). **2.** Newfoundland. **3.** Norman French.

Nfld. Newfoundland.

N.F.U. National Farmers' Union (in Britain).

N.G.A. National Graphical Association (in Britain).

ngai·o (nī-ō) *n.* A small tree, *Myoporum laetum,* of New Zealand, producing a useful timber. [Maori.]

n'gana. Variant of **nagana.**

NGC *New General Catalogue of Nebulae and Clusters of Stars:* a catalogue of over 8,000 entries.

NGk., N.Gr. New Greek.

NGO *n., pl.* **NGOs.** *Nongovernmental organisation:* an organisation not under direct government control that is concerned with human welfare in such fields as health, the environment, or economics.

ngul·trum (əng-gúltrəm) *n.* The monetary unit of Bhutan, introduced in 1974, equivalent in value to an Indian rupee. [Bhutanese.]

Ngu·ni (əng-gŏoni) *n.* A group of languages of the Bantu family, including Swazi, Xhosa, and Zulu, spoken chiefly in southern Africa.

ngwee (əng-gwáy) *n.* A coin equal to ¹/₁₀₀ of the kwacha of Zambia. [Chibemba, "bright".]

Nha Trang (nyáa tráng). City and port in southern Vietnam, lying on the South China Sea. It is an important centre for the fishing industry, and during the Vietnam war was used by the United States as a major military base.

N.H.G. New High German.

NHS National Health Service (in Britain).

Ni The symbol for the element nickel.

N.I. 1. National Insurance (in Britain). **2.** Northern Ireland.

ni·a·cin (nī-ə-sin) *n.* One of the B vitamins, **nicotinic acid** (see). [NI(COTINIC) AC(ID) + -IN.]

Ni·ag·a·ra Falls (nī-ággərə, -ággrə). Spectacular cataract on the border between Canada and the United States, situated on the Niagara river between Lake Erie and Lake Ontario. The cataract consists of two main falls, the American Falls (51 metres; 167 feet) in New York state and the Canadian, or Horseshoe, Falls (48 metres;

158 feet) in the province of Ontario. The Falls are a popular tourist attraction and a major supplier of hydroelectric energy.

Nia·mey (nyaa-máy). Capital of Niger, lying on the river Niger in the southwest of the country. It is Niger's largest city and chief port. It has been the capital since 1926.

nib (nib) *n.* **1. a.** The point of a quill pen, especially when sharpened. **b.** A tapered penpoint designed to be inserted into a penholder or fountain pen. **2.** A beak or bill, as of a bird; a neb. **3.** Any small, sharp, projecting part. **4.** *Plural.* Crushed cocoa beans. [Probably of Low German origin, variant of NEB.]

nib·ble (nibb'l) *v.* **-bled, -bling, -bles.** —*tr.* **1.** To bite at gently and repeatedly. **2. a.** To eat with small, quick bites, in the manner of a mouse or other small creature. **b.** To eat in small morsels: *nibble a biscuit.* —*intr.* **1.** To take small or hesitant bites: *The fish nibbled at the bait.* **2.** To raise petty objections or criticisms; carp. Used with *at.* **3.** To show cautious interest. Used with *at.* ~*n.* **1.** A small quantity, especially of food; a bite; a morsel. **2.** An act or instance of nibbling. **3.** *Computing.* Half a **byte** (see). [Probably from Low German *nibbeln, knibbeln,* to gnaw, nibble.]

Ni·be·lung (néebə-lŏong) *n., pl.* **-lungs** or **-lungen** (-ən). *Germanic Mythology.* **1.** Any of a race of subterranean dwarfs who possessed a hoard of riches and a magic ring, taken from them by Siegfried. **2.** Any of the followers of Siegfried. **3.** Any of the Burgundian kings in the *Nibelungenlied.* [German, from Middle High German *Nibelungen,* probably corresponding to a tribal name *Nebulones,* perhaps from Old High German *nebul,* mist.]

Ni·be·lung·en·lied (néebə-lŏong-ən-leet) *n.* A Middle High German epic poem written in the early 13th century by an unknown author, based on the legends of Siegfried and the Burgundian kings.

nib·lick (níbblik) *n.* A golf club, a **nine iron** (see). [19th century : origin obscure.]

nibs (nibz) *n. Used with a singular verb. Informal.* A person who is in authority or who is self-important. Used humorously in the expression *his nibs.* [19th century : akin to earlier (cant) *nabs†* (as in *his nabs,* himself).]

Nic·a·rag·u·a (níckə-rággew-ə, -raágwə). Largest republic on the Central American mainland. It is sparsely populated, and the mainstay of the economy is agriculture—cotton, coffee, rice, sugar, and tobacco. Nicaragua was a Spanish possession until it gained its independence in 1821. Area, 130 000 square kilometres (50,193

niche *A niche in the tomb of Pope Julius II, at the church of St Peter in Chains (San Pietro in Vincoli), in Rome. The niche contains a statue of Leah, attributed to Michelangelo. He was commissioned by Julius to build the tomb, which was to have had 40 statues, but in the end Michelangelo sculpted only a statue of Moses, and possibly Leah and Rachel flanking Moses in their niches.*

PRONUNCIATION KEY

a, trap; aa, father; ai, fair; ar, star; aw, lawn; ay, play; b, bb, stab; rubber; ch, church; ck, ticket; d, dd, dead; ladder; e, dress; ee, bee; er, defer; ew, few; ewr, pure; ə, about; ər, letter; f, ff, fife; differ; g, gg, giggle; h, hat; i, kit; ī, price; īr, fire; j, judge; k, kick; l, ll, let; 'l, needle; m, mm, man; n, nn, no; 'n, sudden; ng, thing; o, lot; ō, no; o͝o, foot; o͞o, shoe; oor, poor; ow, cow; owr, hour; oy, boy; p, pp, pepper; r, rr, red; s, ss, sauce; sh, ship; t, tt, totter; th, thick; th, this; smooth; u, cut; ur, turn; v, vv, valve; w, wet; y, yes; z, zz, zebra; zh, vision; pleasure

IN FOREIGN WORDS:

aN, oN, Saint-Saëns; hl, Llanelli; Hluhluwe; kh, loch; lough; Khaled

STRESS MARK:

ín-sīt, insight; in-sít, incite

square miles). Population, 2,600,000. Capital, Managua. See map at **Central American States.** —**Nic·a·ra·guan** *adj. & n.*

Nicaragua, Lake. Largest lake in Central America, lying in south Nicaragua. It is a freshwater lake, but supports a number of salt-water fish, especially tuna and sharks, which have adapted themselves to its water. See map at **Central American States.**

nic·co·lite (níckə-līt) *n.* A nickel ore, essentially nickel arsenide, NiAs, found in America and Europe. Also called "arsenical nickel", "copper nickel", "kupfernickel". [New Latin *niccolum,* nickel, probably from Swedish *nickel,* NICKEL + -ITE.]

nice (nīss) *adj.* **nicer, nicest. 1.** Pleasing to the mind or the senses; attractive; appealing: *a nice dress.* **2.** Kind; considerate; well-mannered: *a nice person.* Sometimes used ironically: *That's a nice thing to say!* **3.** Morally upright; virtuous: *a nice girl, careful of her reputation.* **4.** Showing refinement or delicacy; proper; seemly: *a nice way of putting it.* Sometimes used ironically: *You have some nice friends!* **5.** *Archaic.* Difficult to please; fastidious; exacting: *"Good company requires only birth, education, and manners, and with regard to education is not very nice."* (Jane Austen). **6. a.** Showing or requiring sensitive critical discernment; subtle: *a nice distinction.* **b.** Done with precision and skill; deft: *a nice bit of craftsmanship.* **7.** *Obsolete.* **a.** Wanton; profligate. **b.** Affectedly modest; coy. **c.** Silly. —**nice and.** Pleasingly: *nice and cosy.* [Middle English, foolish, wanton, shy, from Old French, silly, from Latin *nescius,* ignorant, from *nescīre,* to be ignorant : *ne-,* not + *scīre,* to know.] —**nice·ness** *n.*

Usage: *Nice* has long been criticised by stylists as a "lazy" word in writing — used as a general-purpose term of praise where more precise adjectives could have been used.

Nice (neess). Capital of the département of Alpes-Maritimes, France, on the Mediterranean Sea. It is a famous tourist resort and important as a commercial port and industrial city.

nice·ly (nīss-li) *adv.* **1.** In a pleasing manner. **2.** With precision; exactly: *nicely balanced.* **3.** Satisfactorily; acceptably: *That'll do nicely.*

Ni·cene Creed (nī-seén) *n.* **1.** A formal statement of the tenets of Christian faith, and chiefly of the doctrine of the Trinity, set forth by the Council of Nicaea in A.D. 325. **2.** Any of several modifications of this statement, now used in the services of various Christian churches.

ni·ce·ty (nī-səti) *n., pl.* **-ties. 1.** The quality of showing or requiring careful and precise treatment; delicacy; subtlety: *the nicety of a diplomatic exchange.* **2.** Delicacy of character or feeling; scrupulousness; fastidiousness. **3.** A subtle point, detail, or distinction: *He left the niceties of spelling to his secretary.* **4.** An elegant or refined characteristic or feature; an amenity: *niceties of dress.* —**to a nicety.** With the utmost care and precision; exactly. [Middle English *nicete,* nicety, foolishness, from Old French *nicete,* foolishness, from *nice,* silly, NICE.]

niche (nich, neesh) *n.* **1.** A recess in a wall for holding a statue or other ornament. **2.** Any steep, shallow recess or concavity, as in a rock or hill. **3.** A situation or activity specially suited to a person's abilities or character. **4.** *Ecology.* **a.** The role and status of an organism within the community it occupies. **b.** The area within a habitat occupied by an organism.
~*tr.v.* **niched, niching, niches.** To place in a niche. [French, from Old French *niche,* "nest", from *nichier,* to nest, from Vulgar Latin *nīdicāre* (unattested), from Latin *nīdus,* nest.]

Nich·o·las I (níckələss) (1796–1855). Russian Tsar (1825–55). A reactionary, he suppressed the reformist Decembrist movement and strengthened the autocracy with the aid of censorship and secret police. His willingness to assist Turkey's Christians against the sultan involved him in the humiliations of the Crimean War (1853–56). The outstanding achievement of his reign was the codification of all existing laws.

Nicholas II (1868–1918). The last Russian Tsar (1894–1917). He pursued a policy of expansionism in the Balkans and Asia. This culminated in Russia's humiliating defeat in the Russo-Japanese War (1904–05), and the 1905 Revolution. Internal difficulties, reverses during World War I, the unpopularity of the court under Rasputin and the Tsarina, and governmental incompetence all helped to precipitate the 1917 Revolution. Forced to abdicate, he and his family were shot by Bolsheviks at Ekaterinburg (Sverdlovsk).

Nicholas, Saint (fourth century A.D.). Patron saint of children, sailors, and Russia. Believed to have been Bishop of Myra, he is attributed with charitable works and miracles; the practice of giving presents on his feast day (6th December) has been transferred to Christmas. He has passed into folklore as "Father Christmas" or "Santa Claus".

Nich·ol·son (níck'l-sən), **Ben** (1894–1982). British painter. He began by specialising in the still life, and progressed to more abstract works.

Nicholson, Jack (1937–). U.S. actor. His films include *Chinatown* (1974) and *One Flew Over the Cuckoo's Nest* (1976), for which he won an Academy Award.

Ni·chrome (nī-krōm) *n.* A trademark for an alloy of nickel, iron, and chromium. It has a high resistance and is used in electrical heating elements.

nick (nik) *n.* **1.** A shallow notch, cut, or indentation on a surface. **2.** *Printing.* A groove down the side of a piece of type used to ensure that it is correctly placed. **3.** *British Slang.* A prison or police station. —**in good (or bad) nick.** *Informal.* In good (or bad) working order or condition. —**in the nick of time.** Just at the critical moment; just in time.
~*v.* **nicked, nicking, nicks.** —*tr.* **1.** To cut a nick or notch in. **2. a.** To make an incision into (a horse's tail) at the root and reset certain muscles to make the horse carry it higher. **b.** To do this to (a horse). **3.** *British Slang.* **a.** To steal. **b.** To arrest. **4.** *U.S. Slang.* To cheat, especially by overcharging. —*intr.* **1.** To mingle or mate together successfully. Used of breeding stock. **2.** *Australian Informal.* To make a hurried or quick departure. Used with *off.* [Middle English *nyke*† (noun).]

nick·el (níck'l) *n.* **1.** *Symbol* **Ni** A silvery, hard, ductile, ferromagnetic metallic element. It is used in alloys, in corrosion-resistant surfaces and batteries, and for electroplating. Atomic number 28, atomic weight 58.71, melting point 1,555°C, boiling point 2,837°C, relative density 8.902, principal valency 2. **2.** A U.S. coin worth five cents, made of a nickel and copper alloy.
~*tr.v.* **nickelled, -elling, els.** To coat with nickel. [Shortened from German *Kupfernickel,* "copper-demon", an old mining term for niccolite, from which nickel was first extracted (so called because it appeared to contain copper but did not) : *Kupfer,* copper, from Old High German *kupfar,* from Late Latin *cuprum, cyprum,* COPPER + *nickel,* demon, dwarf, from *Nickel,* familiar form of the name *Nikolaus,* NICHOLAS (probably by association with *Nix,* sprite, NIX).]

nickel bloom *n.* A rare mineral, **annabergite** *(see).*

nick·el·ic (ni-kéllik) *adj.* Of or containing nickel. Said especially of compounds containing nickel with a valency of 3.

nick·el·if·er·ous (níckə-líffərəss) *adj.* Bearing or containing nickel. Said of ores.

nick·el·o·de·on (níckə-lṓdi-ən) *n. U.S.* **1.** In the early 20th century, a cinema charging an admission price of five cents. **2.** A juke box or player piano. [NICKEL + (MEL)ODEON.]

nick·el·ous (níckələss) *adj.* Of or containing nickel. Said especially of compounds containing nickel with a valency of 2.

nickel plate *n.* **1.** A thin layer of nickel on a metal surface, usually formed by electrolysis. **2.** Material or articles with such a layer.

nick·el-plate (níck'l-pláyt) *tr.v.* **-plated, -plating, -plates.** To deposit a thin, even layer of nickel on (a surface of metal or other conducting material), as by the electrolysis of a solution containing nickel.

nickel silver *n.* A silvery, hard, corrosion-resistant, malleable alloy of copper, zinc, and nickel, used in tableware. Also called "albata" and formerly "German silver".

nick·er¹ (níckər) *intr.v.* **-ered, -ering, -ers.** To neigh quietly. Used of a horse. [Perhaps from NEIGH.] —**nick·er** *n.*

nicker² *n. British Slang.* One pound sterling. [20th century : origin obscure.]

Nick·laus (ník-lowss), **Jack (William)** (1940–). U.S. golfer. He has won 17 major international titles, including five Masters' championships.

nick·nack. Variant of **knick-knack.**

nick·name (ník-naym) *n.* **1.** A name added to or replacing the actual name of a person, place, or thing, often used humorously or affectionately and referring to some notable characteristic. **2.** A familiar or shortened form of a proper name.
~*tr.v.* **nicknamed, -naming, -names.** To give a nickname to; call by a nickname. [Middle English *a nekename,* originally *an ekename,* an additional name : *eke,* an addition, Old English *ēaca* + NAME.]

nick point. *U.S.* Variant of **knickpoint.**

Nicobar Islands. See **Andaman and Nicobar Islands.**

Nic·o·de·mus (níckə-deéməss). A Pharisee and member of the Sanhedrin who was a secret disciple of Christ and provided his tomb.

Nic·ol prism (níck'l) *n. Physics.* A device for producing or analysing plane-polarised light, consisting of a piece of calcite cut at suitable angles and cemented with Canada balsam. It is used especially in microscopes to identify minerals within a thin slice of rock. Also called "polariser", "polaroid". [After William *Nicol* (1768–1851), Scottish physicist who invented it.]

Nic·ol·son (níck'l-sən), **Sir Harold (George)** (1886–1968). British diplomat, critic, and biographer. An M.P., (1935–45), he published studies of poets, a biography of George V, and volumes of his diaries and letters. He married the novelist Vita Sackville-West.

Nic·o·si·a (níckə-seé-ə). Capital city of Cyprus, lying in the north central part of the island on the flat, arid Mesaoria Plain. It is the country's largest city and the chief trading centre. Since the Turkish invasion of 1974, it has been in Turkish hands.

ni·co·ti·an·a (ni-kṓshi-áanə, -áynə || -ánnə) *n.* Any of various flowering plants of the genus *Nicotiana,* native to the Americas and Australia, and including ornamental species with fragrant flowers as well as the tobacco plant. [New Latin *herba nicotiana,* "herb of Nicot", after Jean *Nicot,* French ambassador at Lisbon, who, in 1560, sent some tobacco to Catherine de Médicis.]

nic·o·tin·a·mide (níckə-tínnə-mīd, -teénə-) *n.* The amide of nicotinic acid, having similar vitamin activity. [NICOTIN(E) + AMIDE.]

nicotinamide adenine dinucleotide *n.* **NAD** *(see).*

nicotinamide adenine dinucleotide phosphate *n.* **NADP** *(see).*

nic·o·tine (níckə-teen, -teén) *n.* A poisonous alkaloid, $C_5H_4NC_4H_7NCH_3$, derived from the tobacco plant, used as an insecticide. [French, earlier *nicotiane,* from NICOTIANA.]

nic·o·tin·ic (níckə-tínnik) *adj.* **1.** Of or pertaining to nicotine. **2.** Of or pertaining to nicotinic acid.

nicotinic acid *n.* A member of the vitamin B complex, C_5H_4NCOOH, essential for growth and synthesised for use in treating pellagra. Dietary sources include milk, yeast, and liver. Also called "niacin". [Often obtained by the oxidation of NICOTINE.]

nic·o·tin·ism (nickə-teen-iz'm) *n.* Nicotine poisoning.

nic·ti·tate (níkti-tayt) *intr.v.* **-tated, -tating, -tates.** Also **nic·tate** (nik-tayt, nik-táyt). To wink or blink. Used in technical contexts. **—nic·ti·ta·tion** (-táysh'n) *n.*

nictitating membrane *n.* Also **nictating membrane.** An inner eyelid in birds, reptiles, and some mammals that helps to keep the eye clean.

Nidaros. See **Trondheim.**

nid·er·ing, nid·er·ing (níddəring) *n. Rare.* A cowardly person; a wretch.
~*adj.* Base; cowardly; vile. [Earlier *nidering*, 16th-century misreading of Middle English *nithing*, Old English *nīthing*, wretch, coward, villain, from Old Norse *nīdhingr*, from *nīdh*, scorn.]

nid·dle-nod·dle (nídd'l-nodd'l) *intr.v.* **-dled, -dling, -dles.** To nod repeatedly or in a trembling way.
~*adj.* Nodding; unsteady. [Reduplication of NOD.]

nide (nīd) *n.* A nest or brood of pheasants. [Latin *nīdus*, nest.]

ni·dic·o·lous (ni-díckələss) *adj.* Born blind and helpless and therefore requiring a relatively long stay in the nest and protracted parental care for some time. Said of certain birds. [Latin *nīdus*, nest + *colere*, to inhabit.]

ni·dif·u·gous (ni-diffew-gəss) *adj.* Born in a relatively well-developed state and soon able to leave the nest. Said of certain birds. [Latin *nīdus*, nest + *fugere*, to leave, flee.]

nid·i·fy (níddi-fī) *intr.v.* **-fied, -fying, -fies.** Also **nid·i·fi·cate** (níddi-fi-kayt) **-cated, -cating, -cates.** To make a nest. Used of birds. [Latin *nīdificāre : nīdus*, nest + *facere*, to make.] **—nid·i·fi·cant** (-kənt) *adj.* **—nid·i·fi·ca·tion** (-fi-káysh'n) *n.*

nid-nod (níd-nod) *v.* **-nodded, -nodding, -nods.** *—intr.* To nod repeatedly. *—tr.* To nod (one's head) repeatedly. [Reduplication of NOD.]

ni·dus (ní-dəss) *n., pl.* **-duses** or **-di** (-dī). **1.** A nest; especially one for the eggs of insects or spiders. **2.** A cavity where spores develop. **3.** *Pathology.* The seat of bacterial growth in a living organism; a focus of infection. [Latin *nīdus*, nest.]

niece (neess) *n.* The daughter of one's brother or sister, or of one's brother-in-law or sister-in-law. [Middle English *nece*, from Anglo-French, Old French *nięce*, from Vulgar Latin *neptia* (unattested), from Latin *neptis*, granddaughter, niece.]

Niedersachsen. See **Lower Saxony.**

ni·el·lo (ni-éllō) *n., pl.* **-elli** (-éllee) or **-los. 1.** Any of several black compounds of sulphur with copper, silver, or lead, used to fill an incised design on the surface of another metal. **2.** A surface or object decorated with niello. **3.** The art or process of ornamenting metal surfaces with niello.
~*tr.v.* **nielloed, -loing, -los.** To decorate or inlay with niello. [Italian, from Medieval Latin *nigellum*, from Latin *nigellus*, blackish, diminutive of *niger*, black.] **—ni·el·list** *n.*

Niel·sen (néel-sən), **Carl (August)** (1865–1931). Danish composer and conductor. His work (especially his six symphonies) experimented with tonality, harmony, and form.

Nie·mey·er (née-mī-ər), **Oscar** (1907–). Brazilian architect. He has had a major influence on South American architecture. His work can be seen in Rio de Janeiro and Brasilia.

Nie·möl·ler (née-möllər), **Martin** (1892–). German churchman. A U-boat captain in World War I, he became a Lutheran pastor (1924), and was later sent to a concentration camp (1937) for denouncing Nazism. In 1961 was appointed one of the six presidents of the World Council of Churches.

Nier·stein·er (néer-shtīnər, -stīnər) *n.* A white Rhine wine. [After *Nierstein*, city in central West Germany.]

Nie·tzsche (néechə), **Friedrich (Wilhelm)** (1844–1900). German philosopher. Rejecting the "slave morality" and values of Christianity in works such as *Also Sprach Zarathustra* (1883–91), he proposed a philosophy asserting the self and the "will to power".

Nie·tzsche·an·ism (née-chi-ə-niz'm) *n.* Also **Nie·tzsche·ism** (née-chi-iz'm). **1.** The philosophy of Nietzsche, based upon a distinction between thought and emotion, and emphasising the value of intense emotion in art and life. **2.** Nietzsche's doctrine of the **superman** (*see*). **—Nie·tzsche·an** *adj. & n.*

nieve (neev) *n. Scottish.* A fist. [Middle English, from Old Norse *hnefi*†.]

niff (nif) *n. British Slang.* A nasty or distasteful smell.
~*intr.v.* **niffed, niffing, niffs.** To have an unpleasant smell; stink. [Of dialect origin; perhaps akin to SNIFF.] **—niff·y** *adj.*

Nif·l·heim, Nif·el·heim (nívv'l-haym) *n. Norse Mythology.* The realm of the dead. [Old Norse *niflheim*, "home of mist" : *nifl*, mist + *heimr*, home.]

nif·ty (nífti) *adj.* **-tier, -tiest.** *Informal.* **1.** Stylish or pleasing. **2.** *British.* Nimble; agile. [Perhaps from MAGNIFICENT.]

Ni·ger¹ (níjər; *French* nee-zhaír). Independent African republic. The largest nation in West Africa, it is landlocked. Its economy is based on livestock breeding and the export of cotton and groundnuts. Formerly a French possession, it became an independent republic in 1960. Area, 1 267 000 square kilometres (489,191 square miles). Population, 5,800,000. Capital, Niamey.

Niger². Third longest river in Africa (4 180 kilometres; 2,600 miles) rising in southwest Guinea on the Fouta Djalion plateau. It follows a roughly semicircular course through Mali, Niger, and Nigeria to the Gulf of Guinea. In Mali it forms a huge inland delta, comprising hundreds of channels and shallow lakes, used for irrigation, especially for rice production. The delta at its mouth, which is the

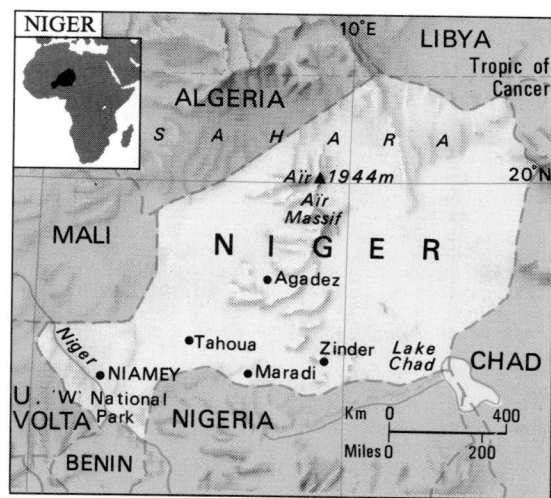

largest in Africa, is an important source of petroleum and palm oil. Most of the Niger is navigable the year round.

Ni·ger-Con·go (níjər-kóng-gō) *n.* A large language family of Africa that includes the Mande, Gur, Kwa, and Bantu languages.

Ni·ge·ri·a (nī-jéer-i-ə), **Federal Republic of.** Independent republic in West Africa, by size the fourteenth largest, but by population the largest, country in Africa. The capital is Lagos, but a new capital district is being developed near Abuja in the central region of the country. Nigeria is self-sufficient in food and is also Africa's leading petroleum producer. Nigeria gained its independence from Great Britain in 1960, and became a member of the Commonwealth in that year. Area, 923 768 square kilometres (356,669 square miles). Population, 82,800,000. **—Ni·geri·an** *adj. & n.*

Niger seed *n.* The seed of the African plant **ramtil** (*see*), used as birdseed. [Probably first found near the NIGER River.]

nig·gard (níggərd) *n.* A stingy, grasping person; a miser.
~*adj.* Parsimonious; niggardly. [Middle English *nigart, niggard*, earlier *nigon*, from *nig*, a miser, from Scandinavian; akin to Swedish dialect *nygg*, from Old Norse *hnöggr*, miserly.]

nig·gard·ly (níggərdli) *adj.* **1.** Unwilling to part with anything; stingy. **2.** Meagre; insufficient. **—See** Synonyms at **stingy. —nig·gard·li·ness** *n.* **—nig·gard·ly** *adv.*

nig·ger (níggər) *n. Slang.* A Negro or member of any dark-skinned people. Used derogatorily. **—a nigger in the woodpile.** *Informal.* Something hidden that obstructs or upsets. [Earlier English dialectal *neeger, neger,* from French *nègre,* from Spanish *negro,* NEGRO.]

nig·gle (nígg'l) *v.* **-gled, -gling, -gles.** *—intr.v.* **1.** To be preoccupied with trifles; worry over petty details; fret. **2.** To keep finding fault; complain trivially; carp. *—tr.v.* To annoy or irritate. [Probably from Scandinavian and akin to NIGGARD.] **—nig·gler** *n.*

nig·gling (níggling, nígg'l-ing) *adj.* **1.** Excessively concerned with

night heron *The black-crowned night heron,* Nycticorax nycticorax, *is one of three species in this genus which is found worldwide near lakes, streams, and rivers. Night herons feed by night on fish, and spend the day in thick cover.*

details; fussy. **2.** Persistently nagging; petty. **3.** Showing or requiring close attention to details; exacting: *niggling paperwork.* **—nig·gling·ly** *adv.*

nigh (nī) *adj.* **nigher, nighest** or **next.** *Archaic, Poetic, & Regional.* Close at hand; near.
~*adv. Archaic, Poetic, & Regional.* **1.** Near in time or location: *Night is drawing nigh.* **2.** Nearly; almost. Used with *on* or *onto: nigh on two hours.*
~*prep. Archaic & Regional.* Not far from; near to. [Middle English *neigh,* Old English *nēah.*]

night (nīt) *n.* **1. a.** The period between sunset and sunrise; especially, the hours of darkness. **b.** This period considered as a unit of time: *two nights running.* **c.** This period considered from the viewpoint of its conditions or events: *a starry night.* **2. a.** The period between evening and bedtime: *Tuesday night.* **b.** This period considered from the viewpoint of its activities or events: *a night at the opera.* **c.** This period set aside for a specific purpose or occasion: *Ladies' Night at the club.* **3. a.** The period between bedtime and morning: *spent the night at a friend's.* **b.** One's sleep during this period: *had a bad night.* **4. a.** Darkness: *vanished into the night.* **b.** The onset of darkness. **5.** Any time or condition of gloom, obscurity, ignorance, or sorrow. **—make a night of it.** To spend the evening or most of a night celebrating or in festivity. **—night and day.** Continuously; without stopping.
~*adj.* **1.** Pertaining to the night. **2.** Intended for use at night: *a night key.* **3.** Working or occurring during the night: *night shift; night porter.* [Middle English *niht, night,* Old English *niht, neaht.*]

night blindness *n.* Poor vision in the dark, **nyctalopia** *(see).* **—night·blind** (nīt-blīnd) *adj.*

night-bloom·ing cereus (nīt-blōōming) *n.* Any of several flowering cacti of the genus *Salenicereus* and related genera, having large, fragrant flowers that open at night.

night·cap (nīt-kap) *n.* **1.** A cloth head-covering worn especially in bed. **2.** A drink taken just before bedtime; especially: **a.** A milk drink. **b.** An alcoholic drink.

night·clothes (nīt-klōthz, -klōz) *pl.n.* Clothes, such as pyjamas or a nightdress, worn in bed.

night·club (nīt-klub) *n.* An establishment that stays open late at night and usually provides food, drink, dancing, and entertainment.

night·dress (nīt-dress) *n.* **1.** A loose dress, often long, worn in bed by women. **2.** Nightclothes.

night·fall (nīt-fawl) *n.* The approach of darkness; close of day.

night·gown (nīt-gown) *n.* **1.** A nightdress. **2.** A man's nightshirt.

night·hawk (nīt-hawk) *n.* **1.** Any of several American nightjars of the genus *Chordeiles,* having buff to black mottled feathers. Also called "bullbat", "mosquito hawk". **2.** *Informal.* A night owl.

night heron *n.* Any of several nocturnal herons of the genus *Nycticorax*; especially, *N. nycticorax,* which has black and white plumage and short legs, neck, and bill.

night·ie, night·y (nīti) *n., pl.* **-ies.** *Informal.* A nightdress.

night·in·gale (nīting-gayl) *n.* **1.** A European songbird, *Luscinia megarhyncha,* with brownish plumage, noted for its nocturnal song. **2.** Any of various similar songbirds. [Middle English *nihtyngale,* Old English *nihtegale,* "night-singer" : *niht,* NIGHT + *galan,* to sing.]

Night·in·gale (nīting-gayl), **Florence** (1820–1910). British nurse. Although nursing was not an accepted occupation for upper-class women of her day, she became superintendent of a London hospital (1853). In 1854 she attached herself to the army in the Crimea, and despite strong opposition reformed the medical services. On her return, she became a leading figure in the campaign for improved nursing care. She was the first woman to receive the Order of Merit (1907).

night·jar (nīt-jaar) *n.* Any of various nocturnal birds of the family Caprimulgidae; especially, the common European nightjar, *Caprimulgus europaeus,* having a dull-coloured, mottled plumage. [NIGHT + JAR (make a harsh sound).]

night latch *n.* A spring lock that may be opened from the inside by turning a knob, but from the outside only with a key.

night letter *n. U.S.* A telegram sent at night at a reduced rate.

night·life (nīt-līf) *n.* The entertainment or social activities, as in theatres or clubs, to be found in the evening or at night, especially in a particular area: *the London nightlife.*

night·light (nīt-līt) *n.* A dim light that is left on all night, especially for children or invalids.

night·long (nīt-lóng, -long) *adj.* Lasting through the whole night.
~*adv.* Through the night; all night.

night·ly (nītli) *adj.* **1.** Of or occurring during the night; nocturnal: *nightly prowlings.* **2.** Happening or done every night: *nightly rounds.*
~*adv.* Every night: *He visited her nightly.*

night·mare (nīt-mair) *n.* **1.** A dream arousing feelings of acute fear, dread, or anguish. **2.** An event or condition that evokes feelings of acute anguish or dread: *the nightmare of urban loneliness.* **3.** A demon or spirit formerly thought to plague sleeping people.
~*adj.* Like something in a nightmare; appalling: *a nightmare journey into the unknown.* [Middle English *nihtmare,* female incubus : NIGHT + *mare,* incubus, Old English *mare, mære,* goblin.] **—night·mar·ish** *adj.* **—night·mar·ish·ly** *adv.* **—night·mar·ish·ness** *n.*

night-night (nīt-nīt) *interj. Informal.* Goodnight.

night owl *n.* A person who habitually stays up late and is active at night.

night·rid·er (nīt-rīdər) *n.* Any of a band of mounted and usually masked white men who engaged in nocturnal terrorism in the southern United States after the Civil War. **—night·rid·ing** *n.*

nights (nīts) *adv. Informal.* At night: *He works nights.* [Middle English *nightes,* Old English *nihtes,* adverbial genitive of *niht,* NIGHT.]

night-scent·ed stock (nīt-sentid) *n.* An annual plant, *Matthiola bicornis,* native to Eurasia, whose purple flowers open at night and give out a heavy scent.

night school *n.* Classes or courses, especially of a vocational nature, held in the evening for people who are busy during the day.

night·shade (nīt-shayd) *n.* Any of several plants of the family Solanaceae, many of them having a poisonous juice; especially, the **deadly nightshade** and the **bittersweet** *(both of which see).* See **enchanter's nightshade.** [Middle English *nighteschede,* Old English *nihtscada* : probably NIGHT + SHADE (since it was used in folk medicine as a soporific).]

night·shirt (nīt-shurt) *n.* A long, loose shirt worn in bed, especially by men.

night soil *n.* Human faeces collected for use as fertiliser.

night·spot (nīt-spot) *n. Informal.* A nightclub.

night·stick (nīt-stik) *n. U.S.* A policeman's truncheon.

night table *n.* A small table or stand placed at a bedside.

night-tide (nīt-tīd) *n. Chiefly Poetic.* Night-time.

night-time (nīt-tīm) *n.* The time between sunset and sunrise.

night watch *n.* **1.** A guard or watch kept during the night, as on a ship or encampment. **2.** A person who keeps watch at night. **3.** Any of the periods of a watch kept at night.

night watchman *n.* **1.** One who acts as guard during the night. **2.** An inferior batsman in cricket sent in to play out remaining time near the close of day, in order to prevent a better player from being dismissed.

nighty. Variant of **nightie.**

nig·nog (níg-nog) *n. Slang.* A stupid person. [From obsolete dialect *nigmenog†,* fool.]

ni·gres·cence (nī-gréss'nss, ni-) *n.* **1.** The process of becoming black or dark. **2.** Blackness or darkness of hair, eyes, or skin. [Latin *nigrescens* (stem *nigrescent-*), from *nigrescere,* to become black, from *niger,* black.] **—ni·gres·cent** *adj.*

nig·ri·fy (níggri-fī) *tr.v.* **-fied, -fying, -fies.** *Rare.* To make black; blacken. [Late Latin *nigrificāre* : *niger,* black + *facere,* to make.]

nig·ri·tude (níggri-tewd, nīgri- || -tōōd) *n. Rare.* Blackness. [Late Latin *nigritūdō,* from *niger,* black.]

ni·gro·sine (níggrə-seen, nīgrə-, -sin) *n.* Any of a class of dyes, varying from blue to black, used in the manufacture of inks and for dyeing wood and textiles. [Latin *niger,* black + -OS(E) + -INE.]

ni·hil (nī-hil, née-, ní-) *n.* **1.** Nothing. **2.** A thing of no value. [Latin.]
shortened from *nihilum,* nothing.]

ni·hil·ism (nī-i-liz'm, née-, -hi-, ní-hi-) *n.* **1.** A metaphysical doctrine that nothing exists, is knowable, or can be communicated. **2.** *Philosophy.* The rejection of all distinctions in moral value, and a willingness to repudiate all previous theories of morality. **3.** The belief that destruction of existing political or social institutions is necessary to ensure future improvement. **4.** A doctrine among the Russian intelligentsia of the 1860s and 1870s, advocating terrorism and denying all authority in favour of individualism. [Latin *nihil,* nothing.] **—ni·hil·ist** *n.* **—ni·hil·is·tic** (-lístik) *adj.*

ni·hil·i·ty (nī-hílləti, nee-, ni-) *n.* Non-existence; nothingness. [French *nihilité,* from Old French, from Medieval Latin *nihilitās* (stem *nihilitāt-*), from *nihil,* nothing.]

nihil ob·stat (ób-stat) *n.* **1.** An attestation by a Roman Catholic censor that a book contains nothing damaging to faith or morals. **2.** Official approval, especially of an artistic work. [Latin, "nothing hinders".]

Nihon. See **Japan.** [Japanese, "Land of the Rising Sun" : *ni,* the sun + *hon,* source, origin.]

Ni·jin·sky (ni-jín-ski, -zhín-), **Vaslav** (1890–1950). Russian ballet dancer. Starting his career with the Imperial Ballet School, St. Petersburg, he later joined Diaghilev's company in Paris, where he performed in such works as *Petrushka* (1911), and choreographed many ballets, including *Le Sacre du Printemps* (*The Rite of Spring*) (1913). Schizophrenia forced him to retire (1919).

Nij·me·gen (nī-maygən; *Dutch* náy-maykhə). *German* **Nim·we·gen.** City in the east Netherlands, lying on the river Waal near the border with West Germany. It is one of the oldest cities in the Netherlands, having been founded by the Romans.

-nik *n. suffix. Informal.* Indicates: **1.** A person involved with something specified; for example, **computernik.** **2.** A person who has undergone a specified experience; for example, **refusenik.** **3.** A person promoting a specified aim or cause; for example, **peacenik.** [Russian *-nik* (as in SPUTNIK) and Yiddish *-nik* (agent suffix).]

Ni·ke (nīkee). The Greek goddess of victory.

nil (nil) *n.* Nothing; 0. Used especially in scoring certain games. [Latin, contraction of NIHIL.]

Nile (nīl). River in northeast Africa, the longest in the world, about 6 700 kilometres (4,150 miles) from its remotest source in the highlands south of the equator to the Mediterranean Sea. It drains an area of about 2 850 000 square kilometres (1,000,000 square miles), or about one tenth of Africa. The trunk stream of the Nile is formed at Khartoum by the confluence of the Blue Nile and the White Nile. Only after Aswan, Egypt, site of the last of the river's cataracts, does the floodplain begin to widen. Since 4000 B.C., when the river spawned the rise of the early Egyptian civilisation, the waters of the Nile have supported, by irrigation, almost all of Egypt's agriculture and much of Sudan's.

Nile blue *n.* Light greenish blue.

Nile green *n.* Light bluish green.

nil·gai (nílgī) *n.* A large Indian antelope, *Boselaphus tragocamelus,* the male of which has a blue-grey coat with white underparts and short horns. The female is tawny brown and lacks horns. [Hindi *nīlgāi,* "blue cow" : Sanskrit *nīla,* blue + *gāi, go,* cow.]

nill (nil) *v.* **nilled, nilling, nills.** *Archaic.* —*tr.* Not to will; refuse. —*intr.* To be unwilling. [Middle English *nilen,* Old English *nyllan* : *ne,* not + *wyllan,* to wish.]

Ni·lo-Ham·ite (nīlō-hámmīt) *n.* A member of a group of Negroid peoples of eastern Africa.

Ni·lo-Ham·it·ic (nīlō-ha-míttik) *n.* A former designation for a number of languages that are now considered part of the Nilotic group.

Ni·lo-Sa·har·an (nīlō-sə-háar-ən) *n.* A large language family of Africa, including Chari-Nile and a number of smaller groups. **—Ni·lo-Sa·har·an** *adj.*

Ni·lot·ic (nī-lóttik) *adj.* **1.** Belonging to the Nile or the Nile Valley. **2.** Pertaining to a group of peoples in eastern Africa who constitute a distinctive Negroid race, characterised especially by their extreme height. **3.** Pertaining to the languages of these peoples.
~*n.* A group of languages, including Dinka and Masai, considered as a family or as a branch of the Chari-Nile family. [Latin *Nīlōticus,* from Greek *Neilōtikos,* from *Neilos,* the NILE.]

nim¹ (nim) *v.* **nimmed, nimming, nims.** *Archaic.* —*tr.* **1.** To take. **2.** To steal; filch. [Middle English *nimen,* Old English *niman.*]

nim² *n.* A game in which two players alternately remove small objects from a collection, usually matchsticks arranged in rows, and attempt to take, or avoid taking, the last one. [20th century : probably special use of archaic NIM.]

nim·ble (nímb'l) *adj.* **-bler, -blest.** **1.** Quick and agile in movement or action; deft: *nimble fingers.* **2. a.** Quick at devising or understanding: *a nimble mind.* **b.** Cleverly contrived: *a nimble trick.* —See Synonyms at **dexterous.** [Middle English *nemel, nym(b)yl,* agile, Old English *nǣmel,* quick to seize or understand, quick-witted, and *numol,* seizing.] **—nim·ble·ness** *n.* **—nim·bly** *adv.*

Synonyms: *nimble, agile, quick, brisk, spry, sprightly.*

nim·bo·stra·tus (nímbō-stráytəss, -stráatəss || -stráttəss) *n.* A low, grey cloud, often dark, that precipitates rain, snow, or sleet. [NIMB(US) + STRATUS.]

nim·bus (ním-bəss) *n., pl.* **-bi** (-bī) or **-buses.** **1.** In art: **a.** A cloudy luminescence surrounding a classical deity when depicted visiting mortals. **b.** Any of various pictorial devices symbolising sanctity, usually a radiance or a bright circle, appearing behind or above the heads of saints and of the Deity. **2.** A favourable or splendid aura about someone or something. **3.** A rain cloud, a nimbostratus. [Latin *nimbus,* heavy rain, rain cloud.]

Ni·meir·y (ni-mīr-i), **Gaafar Muhammad al** (1930–). Sudanese politician. Taking power after a military coup (1969), he reformed the constitution to end a 17-year revolt in the south of the country (1972). He was re-elected president in 1977.

Nîmes (neem). Town in south France, capital of the Gard département. An ancient Roman town, it was a Huguenot centre before the revocation of the Edict of Nantes (1685). It is notable for its Roman remains, including a temple, the Pont du Gard, and an arena which is still in use. Denim is named after it (French *de Nîmes).*

ni·mi·e·ty (ni-mī-əti) *n. Literary.* Excess; redundancy. [Late Latin *nimietās* (stem *nimietāt-*), from Latin *nimius,* excessive, from *nimis,* excessively.]

nim·i·ny-pim·i·ny (nímmini-pímmini) *adj.* Affectedly delicate or refined; mincing. [Perhaps variant of NAMBY-PAMBY.]

Nim·itz (nímmits), **Chester (William)** (1885–1966). U.S. fleet admiral. Appointed commander in chief of the Pacific Fleet after the Japanese attack on Pearl Harbour (1941), he contained Japanese expansion, and eventually destroyed their battle fleets. His success owed much to his appreciation of aircraft carrier strategy.

Nim·rod¹ (ním-rod). A mighty hunter and king. Genesis 10:8–9.

Nimrod² *n. Sometimes small* **n.** A skilled hunter.

nin·com·poop (nín-kəm-pōōp) *n.* A fool; a blockhead. [17th century *nicompoop* : origin obscure.] **—nin·com·poop·er·y** (-əri) *n.*

nine (nīn) *n.* **1. a.** The cardinal number that is one more than eight. **b.** A symbol representing this, such as 9 or IX. **2.** A set made up of nine persons or things. **3. a.** The ninth in a series. **b.** A playing card marked with nine pips. **4.** Nine parts; the components of a whole that has been divided into nine. **5.** A size, as in clothing, designated as nine. **6.** Nine hours after midnight or midday. **—dressed (up) to the nines.** Dressed in one's most formal clothes or very elaborately. [Middle English *ni(gh)en, nyne,* Old English *nigon.*] **—nine** *adj.* **—nine·fold** (nīn-fōld) *adj. & adv.*

nine days' wonder *n.* Something that creates brief interest or excitement.

nine iron *n.* In golf, an iron-headed club with a face slanted at a greater angle than any other iron. Also called "niblick".

nine·pin (nīn-pin) *n.* A skittle.

nine·pins (nīn-pinz) *n. Used with a singular verb.* The game of **skittles** *(see).*

nine·teen (nīn-téen) *n.* **1. a.** The cardinal number that is one more than 18. **b.** A symbol representing this, such as 19 or XIX. **2.** A set made up of 19 persons or things. **3.** The 19th in a series. **4.** A size, as in clothing, designated as 19. **—talk nineteen to the dozen.** To talk very quickly and at length; babble. **—nine·teen** *adj.*

1984, nineteen eight·y-four (nīn-teen áyti-fór || -áyt-ti-, -fōr) *n.* A totalitarian society in which government propaganda and control suppress free speech and create a dehumanised and regimented state. [From the title of George Orwell's novel *1984,* which depicts a hypothetical totalitarian state.]

nine·teenth (nīn-téenth) *n.* **1.** The ordinal number 19 in a series. **2.** Any of 19 equal parts. **—nine·teenth** *adj. & adv.*

nineteenth hole *n.* A place, especially the club bar, where golfers gather for relaxation after a game. Used humorously.

nine·ti·eth (nīnti-ith, -əth) *n.* **1.** The ordinal number 90 in a series. **2.** Any of 90 equal parts. **—nine·ti·eth** *adj. & adv.*

nine to five *n. Chiefly British.* Usual office hours; working hours. **—nine-to-five** *adj. & adv.*

nine·ty (nīnti) *n., pl.* **-ties.** **1. a.** The cardinal number that is 10 more than 80. **b.** A symbol representing this, such as 90 or XC. **2.** A set made up of 90 persons or things. **3.** The 90th in a series. **4.** A size, as in clothing, designated as 90. **5.** *Plural.* **a.** The range of numbers from 90 to 99, considered as a range of age, price, temperature, or the like. **b.** *Often capital* **N.** The years numbered 90 to 99 in a century. Also used adjectivally: *nineties fashions.* **—nine·ty** *adj.*

Nin·e·veh (nínnivə). Capital of the ancient empire of the Assyrians, lying on the east bank of the river Tigris, opposite the modern Iraqi town of Mosul. It was at the height of its glory during the reigns of Sennacherib (705–681 B.C.) and Assurbanipal (699–626 B.C.). It fell to the combined forces of the Babylonians, Medes, and Scythians in 612 B.C. Excavation has uncovered magnificent remains.

nin·ny (nínni) *n., pl.* **-nies.** A fool; a simpleton. [Perhaps from *innocent* (simple, foolish), on analogy with *Ninny,* familiar form for the Christian name *Innocent.*]

ni·non (née-non, nī-; *French* nee-nóN) *n.* A sheer fabric of silk, rayon, or nylon made in a variety of tight, smooth weaves or open lacy patterns. [Probably from French *Ninon,* a nickname for *Anne.*]

ninth (nīnth) *n.* **1.** The ordinal number nine in a series. **2.** Any of nine equal parts. **3.** *Music.* **a.** A harmonic or melodic interval of an octave and a second. **b.** The note at the upper limit of such an interval. **c.** A chord consisting of a triad and its seventh and ninth. [Middle English *nynthe,* Old English *nigotha,* from *nigon,* NINE.] **—ninth** *adj. & adv.*

Ni·o·be (nī-ə-bi, -ō-) *Greek Mythology.* The daughter of Tantalus; she was turned to stone while bewailing the loss of her children.

ni·o·bic (nī-ōbik, -óbbik) *adj. Chemistry.* Of or containing niobium. Said especially of compounds that contain niobium with a valency of 5.

ni·o·bi·um (nī-ōbi-əm) *n. Symbol* **Nb** A silvery, soft, ductile, metallic element. It occurs chiefly in columbite-tantalite, and is used in steel alloys, arc welding, and superconductivity research. Atomic number 41, atomic weight 92.906, melting point 2,468°C, boiling point 4,927°C, relative density 8.57, valencies 2, 3, 4, and 5. Formerly called "columbium". [New Latin, after NIOBE (because obtained from tantalite, which is named after Tantalus, father of Niobe).]

ni·o·bous (nī-ōbəss) *adj. Chemistry.* Of or containing niobium. Said especially of compounds that contain niobium with a valency of 3.

nip¹ (nip) *v.* **nipped, nipping, nips.** —*tr.* **1. a.** To catch, pinch, or press between two surfaces or points, such as the fingers. **b.** To give a small, sharp bite to. Used of animals. **2.** To remove or sever by pinching, biting, or snipping. Usually used with *off.* **3.** To have a stinging or biting effect on: *nipped by the cold.* **4.** To check in growth or cut off the development of: *nip the scandal before it spreads.* **5.** *Slang.* To steal. Not in current usage. —*intr.* **1.** To give small, sharp bites. Used of animals. **2.** *British Informal.* To go or move quickly and nimbly: *nipped out to the shops.*
~*n.* **1.** The act of catching, pressing, or pinching between two surfaces; a bite or pinch. **2. a.** A pinch or snip that cuts off or removes a part: *He gave a nip to each corner.* **b.** The small piece removed in this manner. **3. a.** A sharp, stinging quality, as of frosty air. **b.** Severely sharp cold or frost. **4.** *Archaic.* A cutting or stinging remark. **5.** A pungent or sharp flavour; a tang: *the nip of Mexican cooking.* **—nip and tuck.** *U.S.* Neck and neck. [Middle English *nippen, nīpen,* perhaps from Old Norse *hnippa.*]

nip² *n.* A small quantity or sip of spirits: *a nip of brandy.*
~*v.* **nipped, nipping, nips.** —*tr.* To drink (spirits) in small doses: *He had been nipping brandy.* —*intr.* To take a nip or nips of spirits: *He nips all day.* [Short for *nipperkin,* probably from Dutch *nippertje,* a dram, from *nippen,* to sip.] **—nip·per** *n.*

ni·pa (née-pə, nī-) *n.* **1.** A large, distinctive palm, *Nypa fruticans,* of the Philippines and Australia, having long leaves much used for thatching. Also called "nipa palm". **2.** An alcoholic beverage made from the sap of this palm. [Spanish and Portuguese, from Malay *nipah.*]

nip·per (níppər) *n.* **1.** One that nips. **2.** *Plural.* Any of various devices for squeezing or snipping; especially, a small pair of pliers used for electrical work. **3.** The large claw of a crustacean. **4.** *Chiefly British Informal.* A young child.

nip·ping (nípping) *adj.* **1.** Sharp and biting, as cold air might be. **2.** Sarcastic. **—nip·ping·ly** *adv.*

nip·ple (nípp'l) *n.* **1. a.** The small conical protuberance near the centre of the mammary gland in females containing the outlets of the milk ducts. Also called "mamilla". **b.** A corresponding vestigial protuberance on the male chest. **2. a.** A teat on a nursing bottle. **b.** *U.S.* A baby's dummy. **3.** Any of various devices resembling a nipple in appearance or function: **a.** A regulated opening for discharging a liquid, as in a small stopcock. **b.** A pipe coupling threaded at both ends. **c.** A short extension of pipe to which a nozzle can be attached. **4.** A drilled bush screwed into a bearing to enable grease to be forced into the bearing from a grease gun. Also

PRONUNCIATION KEY

a, trap; aa, father; ai, fair;
ar, star; aw, lawn; ay, play;
b, bb, stab; rubber;
ch, church; ck, ticket;
d, dd, dead; ladder; e, dress;
ee, bee; er, defer; ew, few;
ewr, pure; ə, about;
ər, letter; f, ff, fife; differ;
g, gg, giggle; h, hat; i, kit;
ī, price; īr, fire; j, judge;
k, kick; l, ll, let; 'l, needle;
m, mm, man; n, nn, no;
'n, sudden; ng, thing; o, lot;
ō, no; ŏŏ, foot; ōō, shoe;
oor, poor; ow, cow;
owr, hour; oy, boy;
p, pp, pepper; r, rr, red;
s, ss, sauce; sh, ship;
t, tt, totter; th, thick; th, this;
smooth; u, cut; ur, turn;
v, vv, valve; w, wet; y, yes;
z, zz, zebra; zh, vision;
pleasure

IN FOREIGN WORDS:

aN, oN, Saint-Saëns;
hl, Llanelli; Hluhluwe;
kh, loch; lough; Khaled

STRESS MARK:

ín-sīt, insight; in-sīt, incite

nitrogen cycle

AN ELEMENT ESSENTIAL TO LIFE
How nitrogen circulates through nature

All life on Earth needs nitrogen because it is an essential ingredient of every protein. Plants and animals cannot, however, absorb nitrogen directly from the air. The element circulates in nature through various organisms whose life processes depend on it, a progression known as the nitrogen cycle.

Some atmospheric nitrogen is fixed, or combined, by the action of bacteria in the roots of leguminous plants, such as clover, and by the action of atmospheric electricity. Fertilisers and

other inorganic nitrogen compounds in the soil are used by plants, which combine them with other elements to form nucleic acids and proteins. These proteins are part of the food used by grazing animals. The decay of plant and animal matter (brought about by microorganisms that include bacteria) releases nitrogen into the soil as ammonium compounds, which are converted by other bacteria into nitrogen salts usable by plants, and nitrogen gas. Some combined nitrogen is also set free by denitrifying bacteria.

KEY:

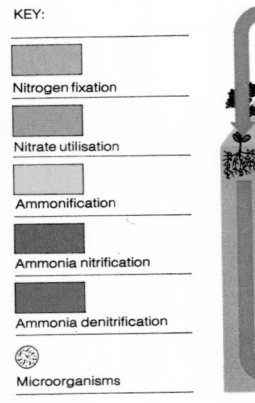

Nitrogen fixation

Nitrate utilisation

Ammonification

Ammonia nitrification

Ammonia denitrification

Microorganisms

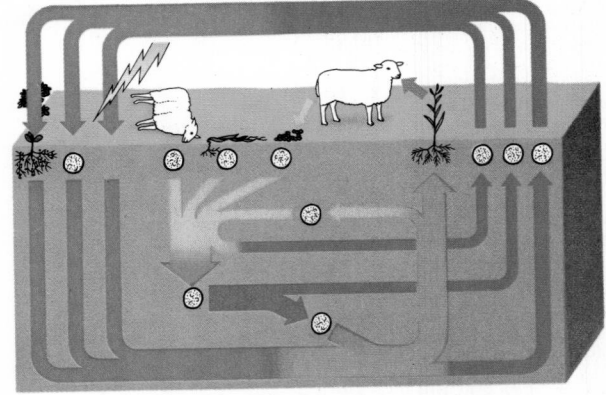

called "grease nipple". **5.** Any natural or geographic body or projection resembling a nipple, such as a mountain crest. [From earlier *neble, nible,* perhaps diminutives of *neb, nib,* a point, beak, NEB.]

nip·ple·wort (níppʼl-wurt ‖ -wawrt) *n.* A plant, *Lapsana communis,* having a milky juice and small, yellow flower heads. [Formerly used in folk medicine to treat breast tumours.]

Nippon. See **Japan.** [Short for *Nippon-koku,* "land of the origin of the sun".] **—Nip·pon·ese** (níppə-néez, -néess) *adj. & n.*

nip·py (níppi) *adj.* **-pier, -piest. 1.** Sharp or biting; nipping. **2.** *British Informal.* **a.** Active; vigorous; sharp; quick. **b.** Small but having a relatively powerful engine. Said of a motor vehicle. **—nip·pi·ly** *adv.* **—nip·pi·ness** *n.*

nir·va·na (neer-vaʹanə, nur-) *n.* **1.** *Often capital* **N. a.** *Buddhism.* The state of absolute blessedness, characterised by release from the cycle of reincarnations and attained through the extinction of the self. **b.** *Hinduism.* A similar state in which reunion with Brahma is attained through the suppression of individual existence. **2.** Freedom from the pain and care of the external world; bliss. [Sanskrit *nirvāna,* "extinction (of individual existence)", from *nirvā,* to be extinguished, be blown out : *nir-, nis-†,* out + *vātī,* he blows.]

Ni·san, Nis·san (níʹ-san, níssʹn, nee-saʹan) *n.* In the Hebrew calendar, the seventh month of the civil year and the first of the religious year. Formerly called "Abib". [Hebrew *Nīsān,* from Akkadian *Nissanu,* "the first month".]

ni·si (níʹ-sī) *adj. Law.* Coming into effect at a given date unless cause is shown for modification or nullification: *a decree nisi.* [Latin *nisi,* unless.]

nisi pri·us (príʹəss) *n. Abbr.* **n.p.** *Law.* **1.** In Britain: **a.** A trial of a civil cause before a single judge and a jury in Crown Court. **b.** Formerly, a trial before an assize court. **2.** In the United States: **a.** The court in which a civil action is tried before a judge and jury, as distinguished from an appellate court. **b.** The trial of a civil action before such a court: *cause of nisi prius.* [Medieval Latin, "unless before" (originally the first two words of a writ ordering a sheriff to provide a jury at the Westminster court on a fixed day, *unless* the judges of assize come to the county *before* this day).]

Nis·sen hut (níssʹn) *n.* A prefabricated building of corrugated steel in the shape of half a cylinder, used as a military shelter. [After Lieutenant-Colonel Peter N. *Nissen* (1871–1930), British mining engineer.]

ni·sus (níʹ-səss) *n., pl.* **nisus.** Effort; endeavour; exertion; impulse. [Latin *nīsus,* from the past participle of *nītī,* to strive, endeavour.]

nit¹ (nit) *n.* **1.** The egg of a parasitic insect, such as that of a head louse or body louse. **2.** The young insect. **3.** *Plural.* Infestation with head lice. [Middle English *nite,* Old English *hnitu,* louse egg.] **—nit·ty** *adj.*

nit² *n. Chiefly British Informal.* A nitwit.

nit³ *n.* A unit of luminance equal to 1 candela per square metre. [Latin *nitor,* brightness.]

nit⁴ *n. Computing.* A unit of information equal to 1.44 bits. [From Napierian dig*it*.]

nit⁵ *n. Australian Informal.* Watch; a lookout: *to keep nit.* [Origin obscure; perhaps akin to NIX (interjection).]

nit-pick·ing (nít-piking) *n. Informal.* Finding fault or arguing over insignificant details. **—nit-pick·ing** *adj.* **—nit-pick·er** *n.*

ni·tra·mine (níʹtrə-meen) *n.* Tetryl *(see).* [NITRO- + AMINE.]

ni·trate (níʹtrayt) *n.* **1.** The radical NO_3^- or any compound containing it, as a salt or ester of nitric acid. **2.** Fertiliser consisting of sodium nitrate or potassium nitrate.
~*tr.v.* (*usually* níʹtráyt) **nitrated, -trating, -trates.** To treat with nitric acid or with a nitrate, usually to change an organic compound into a nitrate. [French : NITR(O)- + -ATE.] **—ni·tra·tion** (nī-tráy-shʹn) *n.*

ni·traz·e·pam (nī-trázzə-pam) *n.* A hypnotic drug sold in the form of pills to induce sleep. A common trademark is Mogadon.

ni·tre, *U.S.* **niter** (níʹtər) *n.* **1.** Potassium nitrate *(see).* **2.** Sodium nitrate *(see).* [Middle English, from Old French, from Latin *nitrum,* from Greek *nitron,* of Semitic origin.]

ni·tric (níʹtrik) *adj.* Of, derived from, or containing nitrogen, especially in a valency state higher than that in a comparable nitrous compound. [French *nitrique* : NITR(O)- + -IC.]

nitric acid *n.* A transparent, colourless to yellowish, fuming, corrosive liquid, HNO_3, a highly reactive oxidising agent, used in the production of fertilisers, explosives, and rocket fuels. Formerly called "aqua fortis".

nitric oxide *n.* A colourless, poisonous gas, NO, produced as an intermediate during the manufacture of nitric acid from ammonia or atmospheric nitrogen.

ni·tride (níʹ-trīd) *n.* A compound containing nitrogen with another, more electropositive element. [NITR(O)- + -IDE.]

ni·trid·ing (níʹ-trīding) *n. Metallurgy.* The case-hardening of a ferrous alloy, such as steel, by heating it in ammonia.

ni·tri·fi·ca·tion (níʹtri-fi-káysh'n) *n.* **1.** The attachment of a nitro group to an organic compound either as an addition or substitution. **2.** The oxidation of ammonium compounds in the soil by nitrifying bacteria, which convert them into nitrates and nitrites.

ni·tri·fy (níʹtri-fī) *tr.v.* **-fied, -fying, -fies. 1.** To oxidise into nitric acid, nitrous acid, or any nitrate or nitrite, as by the action of nitrifying bacteria. **2.** To treat or combine with nitrogen or compounds containing nitrogen. [French *nitrifier* : NITR(O)- + -FY.] **—ni·tri·fi·er** *n.*

ni·tri·fy·ing bacteria (níʹtri-fī-ing) *pl.n.* Any of various soil bacteria, such as *Nitrosomonas* and *Nitrobacter,* that oxidise ammonia to nitrite or nitrite to nitrate.

ni·trile (níʹ-tril, -trīl) *n.* Also **ni·tril** (-tril) *n.* Any compound containing trivalent nitrogen, N^{-3}, in a cyanogen group. [NITR(O)- + -ILE.]

ni·trite (níʹ-trīt) *n.* Any salt or ester of nitrous acid. [NITR(O)- + -ITE.]

nitro-, nitr- *comb. form.* Indicates a compound containing the univalent group NO_2; for example, **nitrobenzene** ($C_6H_5NO_2$), **nitride.** [New Latin, from Latin *nitrum,* from Greek *nitron,* NITRE.]

ni·tro·ben·zene (níʹtrō-bén-zeen, -ben-zéen) *n.* A poisonous organic compound, $C_6H_5NO_2$, occurring either as bright yellow crystals or as an oily liquid, having the odour of almonds, and used in the manufacture of aniline, insulating compounds, and polishes.

ni·tro·cel·lu·lose (níʹtrō-séllew-lōss, -lōz) *n.* Cellulose nitrate *(see).* Not in technical usage.

ni·tro·chlo·ro·form (níʹtrō-klórrə-fawrm, -kláwrə- ‖ -klórə-) *n.* A poison gas, **chloropicrin** *(see).*

ni·tro·gen (níʹtrəjən) *n. Symbol* **N** A nonmetallic element constituting nearly four-fifths of the air by volume, occurring as a colourless, odourless, almost inert diatomic gas, N_2, in various minerals and in all proteins. It is used in the manufacture of a wide variety of important compounds, including ammonia, nitric acid, TNT, and fertilisers. Atomic number 7, atomic weight 14.0067, melting point -209.86°C, boiling point -195°C, valencies 3, 5. [French *nitrogène* : NITR(O)- + -GEN.] **—ni·trog·e·nous** (nī-trójinəss) *adj.*

ni·tro·ge·nase (níʹtrəjə-nayz, -nayss) *n.* An enzyme that takes part in the fixation of atmospheric nitrogen.

nitrogen balance *n.* The difference between the amounts of nitrogen taken into and lost by the body or the soil.

nitrogen cycle *n.* **1.** The cyclic progression of natural chemical reactions to atmospheric nitrogen: the nitrogen either forms organic compounds in rainwater, or is fixed by nitrogen-fixing bacteria; it is then assimilated and metabolised by plants and animals, and returned by decomposition to the soil; here some is recycled as organic compounds by bacteria and fungi, and the remainder is returned to the atmosphere. **2.** The **carbon-nitrogen cycle** *(see).*

nitrogen dioxide *n.* A mildly poisonous brown gas, NO_2, often found in smog and internal-combustion engine exhaust fumes, and synthesised for use as a nitrating agent, catalyst, and oxidising agent. Also called "nitrogen peroxide".

nitrogen fixation *n.* **1.** The conversion of atmospheric nitrogen into nitrogenous compounds by natural agencies or by various industrial processes. **2.** The conversion by certain fungi and soil bacteria of atmospheric nitrogen or inorganic nitrogen compounds into organic compounds assimilable by plants. **—ni·tro·gen-fix·ing** (níʹtrə-jən-fik-sing) *adj.*

ni·trog·en·ise, ni·trog·en·ize (nī-tróji-nīz, níʹtrəjə-) *tr.v.* **-ising, -ises, -ised.** To combine or treat with nitrogen.

nitrogen mustard *n.* Any of a group of organic compounds resembling mustard gas and having the general formula, RN

(CH₂CH₂CL)₂, where R is an organic group. They are used in the chemotherapy of cancer.

nitrogen peroxide n. 1. Nitrogen dioxide. 2. The equilibrium mixture of nitrogen dioxide and dinitrogen tetroxide.

nitrogen tetroxide n. A brown liquid, formed by freezing or pressurising nitrogen dioxide, and used as an oxidising, nitrating, and bleaching agent. Also called "dinitrogen tetroxide".

ni·tro·glyc·er·in, ni·tro·glyc·er·ine (nītrō-glíssa-reen, -rin) n. A thick, pale yellow liquid, CH₂NO₃CHNO₃CH₂NO₃, explosive on concussion or exposure to sudden heat. It is used in the production of dynamite and blasting gelatine, and as a vasodilator in medicine. Also called "trinitroglycerin".

nitro group n. Chemistry. The group of atoms –NO₂, present in certain types of organic compounds (nitro compounds).

ni·tro·hy·dro·chlo·ric acid (nītrō-hīdra-kláwrik, -klórrik ‖ -klórik) n. A mixture of acids, **aqua regia** (see).

ni·trom·e·ter (nī-trómmitar) n. Any device or instrument for measuring the amount of nitrogen in a substance. [NITRO- + METER.]

ni·tro·meth·ane (nītrō-mée-thayn, -méthayn) n. An oily, colourless liquid, CH₃NO₂, used in making dyes and resins, in organic synthesis, and as a rocket propellant.

ni·tro·par·af·fin (nītrō-párra-fin, -feen) n. Any of a group of organic compounds formed by replacing one or more of the hydrogen atoms of a paraffin hydrocarbon with the nitro group, NO₂⁻, as in nitromethane, CH₃NO₂.

ni·tros·a·mine (nī-trózameen, nītrō-sa-méen, -sámmeen) n. Any of a group of oily, yellow compounds that contain the divalent group –NNO. [Latin nitrōsus, full of nitre + AMINE.]

ni·tro·so (nī-trṓ-sō) adj. Designating an organic compound that contains the monovalent group –NO. Compare **nitrosyl**. [Latin nitrōsus, full of nitre.]

ni·tro·syl (nītra-sil, nītrō-, -sīl) adj. Designating an inorganic compound that contains the monovalent group –NO. Compare **nitroso**. [Latin nitrōsus (see nitroso) + -YL.]

ni·trous (nītrass) adj. Of, derived from, or containing nitrogen, especially in a valency state lower than that in a comparable nitric compound. [New Latin nitrosus, from Latin nitrōsus, full of nitre, from nitrum, from Greek nitron, NITRE.]

nitrous acid n. An unstable inorganic acid, HNO₂, existing in solution only.

nitrous oxide n. A colourless inorganic gas, N₂O, used as a mild anaesthetic. Also called "laughing gas".

nit·ty-grit·ty (nítti-grítti) n. Slang. The core of a matter; the fundamental truth: Let's get down to the nitty-gritty. [Probably based on a reduplication of grit in various senses.]

nit·wit (nít-wit) n. Informal. A stupid or silly person. [Perhaps NIT + WIT.]

ni·val (nīv'l) adj. Botany. Of or growing in or under snow. [Latin nivālis, from nix (stem niv-), snow.]

ni·va·tion (nī-váysh'n) n. The weathering of rocks as a result of the alternate freezing and thawing of surrounding snow. [Latin nix (stem niv-), snow.]

Niv·en (nívv'n), **(James) David (Graham)** (1910–). British actor, known chiefly for his portrayals of easy-going, upper-class Englishmen. His racy, anecdotal volumes of autobiography, beginning with The Moon's a Balloon (1971), have been popular bestsellers.

niv·e·ous (nívvi-ass) adj. Like snow; snow-white. [Latin niveus, from nix (stem niv-), snow.]

nix¹ (niks) n. Germanic Mythology. A water sprite, usually in human form or half-human and half-fish. [German Nix, from Middle High German nickes, from Old High German nihhus.]

nix² n. Chiefly U.S. Informal. Nothing. ~adv. Chiefly U.S. Informal. No. ~interj. Chiefly U.S. Informal. Stop! Watch out! ~tr.v. nixed, nixing, nixes. U.S. Informal. To forbid; veto; ·deny. [German, dialect and colloquial variant of nichts, nothing, from Old High German niwiht, nothing : ni, ne, no + wiht, thing, man.]

Nix·ie tube (níksi) n. A trademark for a **digitron** (see).

Nix·on (níks'n), **Richard (Milhous)** (1913–). U.S. politician and 37th president. Vice-president from 1953 to 1960, he served as Republican president from 1969 to 1974, during which term he established close ties with China and a measure of détente with the U.S.S.R. Although he increased U.S. commitment in Southeast Asia, he was responsible for the eventual withdrawal of U.S. forces from the area. He became the first U.S. president to resign, when the Watergate scandal linked him with electoral malpractices.

ni·zam (nī-zám, -za'am, ni-) n., pl. **nizam.** A Turkish soldier, especially in the 19th century. [Turkish, from Arabic niẓām, government, NIZAM.]

Ni·zam (nī-zám, -za'am ‖ ni-) n. The title of the former rulers of Hyderabad, India. [Hindi nizām(-al-mulk), "governor (of the empire)", from Arabic niẓām, government.]

Nizhny Novgorod. See Gorky.

Nko·mo (ang-kṓma), **Joshua** (1917–). Zimbabwean politician. A trade unionist, he became leader of the ZAPU guerrilla organisation (1961) which, as part of the Patriotic Front, was instrumental in the defeat of the Rhodesian government. In 1980 he became a minister under Robert Mugabe, the former head of the rival ZANU.

Nkru·mah (ang-krṓma), **Kwame** (1909–72). Ghanaian statesman. His country's first premier (1952-1960), he was instrumental in achieving Ghana's independence from the United Kingdom (1957).

He became president (1960), but was deposed and exiled after a military coup (1966).

NKVD, N.K.V.D. n. People's Commissariat for Internal Affairs (Russian Narodny Kommisariat Vnutrennikh Del): a former administrative branch of the Soviet government corresponding to the later **KGB** (see).

NL, NL., N.L. New Latin.

N.L.F. National Liberation Front.

n.m., nm 1. nautical mile. 2. nanometre.

NMR nuclear magnetic resonance.

NNE, N.N.E. north-northeast.

NNW, N.N.W. north-northwest.

no¹ (nō) adv. 1. Not so; opposed to "yes". Used in expressing refusal, denial, disagreement, or disbelief. 2. Not at all; not by any degree. Used with the comparative: no better; no more. 3. Archaic. Not. ~n., pl. **noes.** 1. A negative response; a denial or refusal: The proposal produced only noes. 2. A negative vote or voter. [Middle English no, na, Old English nā : ne, not + ā, ever.]

no² adj. 1. Not any; not one; not a: No biscuits are left. Also used in the imperative: No smoking. 2. Not at all; not close to being: He is no child. 3. Hardly any: got there in no time. [Middle English no, na, Old English nā, reduced form of nān, NONE.]

No The symbol for the element nobelium.

Nō. Variant of **Noh.**

no. number.

No. 1. northern. 2. number.

n.o. Not out (in cricket).

no-ac·count (nṓ-a-kownt) adj. Also **no-count** (nṓ-kownt). U.S. Regional. Worthless; good-for-nothing. —**no-ac·count** n.

No·a·chi·an (nō-áyki-an) adj. Also **No·ach·ic** (-áckik, -áykik). Of or relating to Noah or his time: the Noachian flood.

No·ah (nṓ-a ‖ naw) n. The patriarch chosen by God to build the ark in which he, his family, and many animals were saved from the Flood. Genesis 5-9. [Hebrew Nóah, "rest".]

nob¹ (nob) n. Slang. 1. The head. 2. In cribbage, the jack of the suit turned up by the dealer, scoring one point for the holder: one for his nob. [Slang variant of KNOB.]

nob² n. Chiefly British Slang. A person of wealth or social standing. [18th century (Scottish knabb, nab) : origin obscure.] —**nob·bi·ly** adv. —**nob·by** adj.

no-ball (nō-báwl) n. Sports. Abbr. **n.b.** 1. In cricket, a ball rendered invalid, as by a bowler overstepping the popping crease, and for which the batting side receives one run. 2. In rounders, a ball not delivered according to the rules, as by not being bowled in a continuous underarm action or being bowled too high or too low. ~interj. Used by the umpire to indicate a no-ball. —**no-ball** intr.v.

nob·ble (nóbb'l) tr.v. -bled, -bling, -bles. British Slang. 1. To disable (a racehorse), especially with drugs. 2. To win over, outdo, or get the better of by devious means. 3. To filch or steal. 4. To kidnap. [Perhaps from dialect knobble, to knock, beat : KNOB + -LE.] —**nob·bler** n.

nob·but (nóbbat) adv. British Regional. No more than; only. [NO + BUT.]

No·bel (nṓ-bél), **Alfred (Bernhard)** (1833-96). Swedish chemist, entrepreneur, and philanthropist. The inventor of dynamite, and developer of nitroglycerin as a high explosive, he was so appalled at the use of explosives in war that he bequeathed the considerable fortune he had amassed to institute the Nobel prizes.

No·bel·ist (nṓ-béllist) n. One who receives a Nobel prize.

no·bel·i·um (nō-béeli-am, -bélli-) n. Symbol **No** A radioactive transuranic element in the actinide series, artificially produced in trace amounts. Atomic number 102, isotopic masses 251-259, of which 259 has the longest half-life. Also called "unnilbium". [After the Nobel Institute at Stockholm, where it was discovered.]

Nobel prize n. Any of the six prizes awarded annually (since 1901) by the Nobel Foundation for outstanding achievements in the fields of physics, chemistry, physiology or medicine, literature, and (since 1969) economics, and for the promotion of world peace.

No·bi·le (no-béele), **Umberto** (1885-1978). Italian aeronautical engineer and explorer. He designed several airships, including the semirigid dirigibles, Roma, Italia, and Norge, in the last of which he flew over the North Pole with Roald Amundsen (1926).

no·bil·i·ar·y (nō-bílli-ari ‖ U.S. -erri) adj. Of or pertaining to the nobility. [French nobiliaire, from Latin nōbilis, NOBLE.]

nobiliary particle n. A preposition occurring as a mark of noble rank before a title or surname; for example, the German von and French de in Ulrich von Bertele and Guy de Maupassant.

no·bil·i·ty (nō-bílləti) n., pl. -ties. 1. a. The class comprising nobles, which in Britain consists of dukes, marquesses, earls, viscounts, and barons, together with their female counterparts. b. The state of being a noble. 2. The state or quality of being exalted in character or being morally noble. [Middle English nobilite, from Old French, from Latin nōbilitās (stem nōbilitāt-), from nōbilis, NOBLE.]

no·ble (nōb'l) adj. -bler, -blest. 1. Possessing hereditary rank in a political system or social class usually derived directly or indirectly from a feudalistic stage of a country's development. 2. a. Lofty and exalted in character. b. Proceeding from such a character; showing greatness and magnanimity. 3. Grand, stately, and magnificent in appearance. 4. Of superior quality. 5. Designating an especially corrosion-resistant metal, such as gold. ~n. 1. A person of high birth, rank, or title; a nobleman. 2. A former English gold coin. [Middle English, from Old French, from

Latin *nōbilis,* knowable, known, famous, noble.] **—no·ble·ness** *n.* **—no·bly** *adv.*

noble art *n. Sports. Chiefly British.* Boxing. Preceded by *the.*

noble gas *n. Chemistry.* An **inert gas** *(see).*

no·ble·man (nṓb'l-mən) *n., pl.* **-men** (-mən). A man of noble rank.

noble rot *n.* A fungus, *Botrytis cinerea,* which coats the skins of grapes, resulting in a grape of increased sweetness that is used for making Sauternes and certain Rhine wines. [Translation of German *Edelfäule.*]

noble savage *n.* Primitive man portrayed in Romantic literature as uncorrupted by civilisation.

no·blesse (nṓ-bléss, nə-) *n.* **1.** Noble birth or condition. **2.** The nobility; the aristocracy. [Middle English *noblesce, noblesse,* from Old French *noblesse,* from *noble,* NOBLE.]

noblesse o·blige (ō-bleézh) *n.* Benevolent and honourable behaviour considered to be the responsibility of persons of high birth or rank. [French, "nobility obliges".]

no·ble·wom·an (nṓb'l-wŏŏmən) *n., pl.* **-women** (-wimmin). A woman of noble rank.

no·bod·y (nṓ-bədi, -boddi) *pron.* No person; no one: *Nobody told him what to do.*

~*n., pl.* **nobodies.** A person of no importance, influence, or social position.

Usage: *Nobody* and *no one* take singular verbs and pronominal forms: *Nobody has arrived yet, No one likes his time to be wasted.* Plural pronominal forms are quite often heard in casual speech, but a sentence such as *No one likes their time to be wasted* presents an inappropriate contrast between singular *likes* and plural *their.* However, when short questions (so-called "tag questions") are added to sentences containing *nobody* or *no one,* the use of plural forms is hard to avoid: *Nobody's left me a message, have they?*

noctule *The largest British bat is a noctule,* Nyctalus noctula *(above), which has a 38 centimetre (15 inch) wingspan. It usually roosts in hollow trees, emerging at daybreak and dusk to hunt insects which it catches on the wing.*

no·cent (nṓ-sənt) *adj. Archaic.* **1.** Causing injury; harmful. **2.** Guilty of a crime. [Middle English, from Latin *nocēns* (stem *nocent-*), from the present participle of *nocēre,* to harm.]

no·ci·cep·tive (nṓ-si-séptiv) *adj.* Concerned with or causing pain.

nock (nok) *n.* **1.** The groove at either end of a bow for holding the bowstring. **2.** The notch in the end of an arrow that fits on the bowstring.

~*tr.v.* **nocked, nocking, nocks. 1.** To put a notch in (a bow or arrow). **2.** To fit (an arrow) to a bowstring. [Middle English *nocke, nokke,* from Middle Dutch *nocke.*]

no-claim discount *n.* A reduction in an insurance premium, especially one on a motor vehicle, in cases where no claims have been made on the policy for a stipulated period. Also called "no-claim bonus", "no-claims bonus".

no-count. *U.S. Regional.* Variant of **no-account.**

noc·tam·bu·la·tion (nok-támbew-láysh'n) *n.* Also **noc·tam·bu·lism** (-liz'm). **Somnambulism** *(see).* [NOCT(I)- + AMBULATION.] **—noc·tam·bu·lant** *adj.* **—noc·tam·bu·list** *n.*

nocti-, noct- *comb. form.* Indicates night; for example, **noctambulism.** [New Latin, from Latin *nox* (stem *noct-*), night.]

noc·ti·lu·ca (nókti-lŏŏ-kə, -léw-) *n., pl.* **-cae** (-see). Any of various plantlike, bioluminescent marine organisms of the genus *Noctiluca* which, when grouped in large numbers, make the seas phosphorescent. [New Latin, from Latin *noctilūca,* moon, lantern : NOCTI- + *lūcere,* to shine.]

noc·ti·lu·cent (nókti-lŏŏ-sənt, -léw-) *adj.* Luminous at night. Said especially of certain high clouds. **—noc·ti·lu·cence** *n.*

noc·tu·id (nóktew-id) *n.* Any night-flying moth of the family Noctuidae, the larvae of which are destructive pests. [New Latin *Noctuidae* (family name) : *Noctua,* generic name, from Latin *noctua,* night owl + -IDAE.] **—noctuid** *adj.*

noc·tule (nóktewl) *n.* Any large, reddish-brown, insectivorous bat of the genus *Nyctalus,* found in Eurasia, Indonesia, and the Philippines. Also called "noctule bat". [French, from Italian *nottola,* from Late Latin *noctula,* diminutive of Latin *noctua,* night owl.]

noc·turn (nókturn) *n. Roman Catholic Church.* Any of the three canonical divisions of the office of **matins** *(see).* [Middle English *nocturne,* from Old French, from Medieval Latin *nocturna,* from the feminine of Latin *nocturnus,* NOCTURNAL.]

noc·tur·nal (nok-túrn'l) *adj.* **1.** Of, suitable to, or occurring at night. **2.** *Botany.* Having flowers that open during the night. **3.** *Zoology.* Active by night, as certain animals are. Compare **diurnal.** [Late Latin *nocturnālis,* from Latin *nocturnus,* of night, at night, from *nox* (stem *noct-*), night.] **—noc·tur·nal·i·ty** (nóktur-nál-əti) *n.* **—noc·tur·nal·ly** *adv.*

nocturnal emission *n.* An emission of semen during a **wet dream** *(see).*

noc·turne (nókturn, nok-túrn) *n.* **1.** *Music.* A romantic composition intended to embody sentiments appropriate to the evening or night; a pensive melody. **2.** A painting of a night scene. [French, "nocturnal", from Latin *nocturnus,* NOCTURNAL.]

noc·u·ous (nóckew-əss) *adj. Rare.* Harmful; noxious. [Latin *nocuus,* from *nocēre,* to harm.]

nod (nod) *v.* **nodded, nodding, nods.** *—intr.* **1.** To lower and raise the head quickly in a gesture of agreement or acknowledgment. **2.** To let the head fall forward when sleepy; doze momentarily. Often used with *off.* **3.** To be careless or momentarily inattentive as if sleepy; lapse: *Even Homer nods.* **4.** To sway, move up and down, or bend, as flowers do in the wind. *—tr.* **1.** To lower and raise (the head) quickly in agreement or acknowledgment. **2.** To express (greetings or approval, for example) by lowering and raising the head: *He nodded his agreement.* **3.** To summon, guide, send, or the like by nodding the head: *He nodded her into the room.*

~*n.* **1.** A forward or up-and-down inclination of the head, usually expressive of affirmation or drowsiness. **2.** The nodding motion of anything. **—on the nod.** *Informal.* **1.** Without formal deliberation. **2.** On credit. [Middle English *nodden,* perhaps of Low German origin; akin to Middle High German *notten.*] **—nod·der** *n.*

Nod, Land of. See **Land of Nod.**

no·dal (nṓd'l) *adj.* Of, resembling, or located at a node. **—no·dal·i·ty** (nō-dál-əti) *n.*

nod·ding *adj. Botany.* Designating flowers that droop from their stalks, as in the bluebell.

nodding acquaintance *n.* A slight acquaintance with a person or subject.

nod·dle[1] (nódd'l) *n. Informal.* The head. Used humorously: *not an idea in his noddle.* [Middle English *nodle*†, back of the head.]

noddle[2] *v.* **-dled, -dling, -dles.** *—intr.* To nod frequently. *—tr.* To nod (the head) briefly. [Frequentative of NOD (verb).]

nod·dy[1] (nóddi) *n., pl.* **-dies. 1.** A dunce or fool; a simpleton. **2.** Any tern of the genus *Anous,* that is found in tropical waters and is dark brown with a white head. [From obsolete adjective *noddy,* foolish, "sleepy", "drowsy", probably from NOD (verb). The tern is so named because it is fearless of man and therefore seems stupid.]

noddy[2] *n., pl.* **-dies.** A shot taken during the filming of television interviews, consisting of individual head movements which will be incorporated during editing to provide continuity in the main body of the film. Also called "noddy shot". [From NOD (noun).]

node (nōd) *n.* **1.** A knob, knot, protuberance, or swelling: *a lymph node.* **2.** *Botany.* The often enlarged point on a stem where a leaf, bud, or other organ diverges from the stem to which it is attached; a joint. **3.** *Physics.* A point or region of minimum or zero amplitude in a periodic system. Compare **antinode. 4. a.** *Mathematics.* The point at which a continuous curve crosses itself; the **crunode** *(see).* **b.** The point where lines branch or intersect. **5.** *Astronomy.* **a.** Either of two diametrically opposite points at which the orbit of a planet intersects the ecliptic. The *ascending node* is the point at which the planet moves from the south of the ecliptic to the north, the opposite point being the *descending node.* **b.** Either of two points at which the orbit of a satellite intersects the orbital plane of a planet. **6.** Any central point. [Latin *nōdus,* a knob, knot.]

node of Ran·vi·er (rónvee-ay) *n.* Any of the regions of exposed axon that occur along a myelinated nerve fibre at regular intervals. [After Louis Antoine *Ranvier* (1835–1922), French histologist.]

no·di·cal (nṓdi-k'l, nóddi-) *adj. Astronomy.* Of or pertaining to the nodes of a heavenly body. [NOD(E) + -ICAL.]

no·dose (nṓ-dōss, -dṓss, -dōz) *adj.* Also **no·dous** (nṓ-dəss). Having nodes or knots: *a nodose branch.* [Latin *nodōsus,* from *nodus,* NODE.] **—no·dos·i·ty** (nō-dóssəti) *n.*

nod·ule (nóddewl) *n.* **1.** A small, knotlike protuberance; a node. **2.** *Anatomy.* A localised swelling. **3.** *Botany.* A small, knoblike outgrowth, such as any of those found on the roots of most leguminous plants. **4.** A small lump of a mineral. [Latin *nōdulus,* diminutive of *nōdus,* a knob, NODE.] **—nod·u·lar** (-ər), **nod·u·lose** (-ōss, -ōz), **nod·u·lous** (-əss) *adj.*

no·dus (nṓ-dəss) *n., pl.* **-di** (-dī). A knotty situation, problem, or point; a complication. [Latin *nōdus,* "knot", NODE.]

No·ël (nō-él) *n.* **1.** Christmas. **2.** *Small* **n.** A Christmas carol. [French, from Old French *no(u)el, nael,* from Latin *nātālis (dies),* "birth(day of Christ)", from *nātālis,* of birth, from *nāscī* (past participle *nātus*), to be born.]

No·el-Bak·er (nṓ-əl-báykər), **Philip John, Baron** (1889–1982). British politician. One of the founders of the League of Nations, and subsequently the United Nations Organisation, he was awarded the Nobel peace prize (1959).

no·e·sis (nō-eé-siss) *n.* **1.** *Psychology.* The cognitive process; the mental process by which knowledge is gained. **2.** *Philosophy.* The highest knowledge, as of universal forms. [Greek *noēsis,* intelligence, understanding, from *noein,* to perceive, from *nous,* the mind.]

no·et·ic (nō-éttik) *adj.* **1.** Of, pertaining to, originating in, or comprehended by the intellect. **2.** Of cognition or rational thought that is comprehended by the intellect alone. [Greek *noētikos,* from *noēsis,* NOESIS.]

no-fault (nṓ-fáwlt || -fólt) *adj.* **1.** Of, pertaining to, or designating a legal action of a type in which blame is not assigned to either party. **2.** *Chiefly U.S.* Of or designating a system of motor-vehicle insurance in which accident victims are compensated by their insurance companies without any assignment of blame.

nog[1] (nog) *n.* **1.** A wooden block built into a masonry wall to hold nails that support joinery structures. **2.** A wooden peg or pin. [17th century : origin obscure.]

nog[2] *n.* **1. Eggnog** *(see).* **2.** *British Regional.* A strong beer of a type brewed in East Anglia. [17th century : origin obscure.]

nog·gin (nóggin) *n.* **1.** A small mug or cup. **2.** A unit of liquid measure equal to one quarter of a pint. **3.** *Informal.* The head. [17th century : origin obscure.]

nog·ging (nógging) *n.* **1.** Brickwork used to fill in the boards of a wooden framework. **2.** A short horizontal wooden beam used to strengthen upright posts in the framework of a wall. Also called "nogging piece". [From NOG (wooden block, peg).]

no-go area (nṓ-gō) *n.* An area, as in a town, entry to which is barred to certain persons or groups, such as the police or the army.

no-good (nṓ-gŏŏd) *adj. Slang.* Good-for-nothing; contemptible.

Noh, Nō *n. Sometimes small* **n.** The classical drama of Japan, performed with music and dancing in a highly stylised manner by elaborately dressed actors on an almost bare stage. [Japanese *nō*, "talent", "ability", from Chinese *néng*.]

no-hoper (nō-hṓpər) *n. Informal.* **1.** *British.* A person who appears doomed to failure; a loser. **2.** Anything that appears extremely unpromising, such as a bet, plan, or racehorse. **3. a.** *Chiefly Australian.* An ineffectual or shiftless person. **b.** A socially incompetent or ostracised person.

no-how (nō-how) *adv. Nonstandard.* In no way; not at all.

noil (noyl) *n.* A short fibre combed from the long fibres during the preparation of textile yarns. [Probably from Old French *noel*, "small knot (of wool)", from Medieval Latin *nōdellus*, diminutive of Latin *nōdus*, knot, NODE.]

noise (noyz) *n.* **1.** A sound of any kind, especially when loud, confused, indistinct, or disagreeable. **2.** An outcry or clamour: *the noise of the mob.* **3.** General interest or commotion; a stir. **4.** *Physics.* Any electrical disturbance, especially a random and persistent disturbance, that obscures or reduces the clarity or quality of a signal. **5.** *Plural. Informal.* Superficial remarks conveying a specified impression: *made approving noises.*
~*v.* **noised, noising, noises.** —*tr.* To spread the rumour or report of. Usually used with *about* or *abroad.* —*intr.* **1.** To talk much or volubly. **2.** *Archaic.* To be noisy; make noise. [Middle English, from Old French *noise, noyse,* from Latin *nausea,* seasickness (with extended senses in popular use, such as "unpleasant situation", "noisy confusion"), from Greek *nausia,* from *naus,* a ship.]
Synonyms: noise, din, racket, uproar, pandemonium, hullabaloo, hubbub, clamour, babel.

noise-less (nóyz-ləss, -liss) *adj.* Creating no noise; silent; quiet. See Synonyms at **still.** —**noise-less-ly** *adv.* —**noise-less-ness** *n.*

noise pollution *n.* Environmental noise of sufficient loudness to be annoying, distracting, or physically harmful.

noi-sette (nwaa-zét, nwə-) *n.* A small round piece of meat, especially loin or fillet of lamb, veal, or pork.
~*adj.* Made or flavoured with hazelnuts. [French, diminutive of *noix,* nut.]

noi-some (nóy-səm) *adj. Literary.* **1.** Offensive to the point of arousing disgust; foul and filthy: *a noisome smell.* **2.** Harmful or dangerous. [Middle English *noyesum* : *(a)noy,* vexation, annoyance, from *anoien,* ANNOY + -SOME.] —**noi-some-ly** *adv.* —**noi-some-ness** *n.*

nois-y (nóyzi) *adj.* **-ier, -iest. 1.** Making a loud noise. **2.** Characterised by noise. —**nois-i-ly** *adv.* —**nois-i-ness** *n.*

No-lan (nṓlən), **Sir Sidney (Robert)** (1917–). Australian painter. He began his career as an abstract painter, but it was through his landscapes of the Australian outback and figures from Australia's history that he achieved recognition.

no-lens vo-lens (nṓlenz vṓlenz) *adv. Latin.* Willing or not; willy-nilly.

no-li-me-tan-ge-re (nṓli-máy-táng-gəri, -mée-tánjəri) *n.* **1.** A warning or prohibition against meddling, touching, or interfering. **2.** A picture representing Christ appearing to Mary Magdalene after the Resurrection. [Latin, "do not touch me", Christ's warning to Mary Magdalene (Vulgate, John 20:17).]

nol-le pros-e-qui (nólli próssikwī) *n. Law.* A declaration entered in court records that the plaintiff in a civil case or the prosecutor in a criminal case will drop prosecution of all or part of a suit or indictment. [Latin, "to be unwilling to pursue".]

no-lo con-ten-de-re (nṓlō kən-téndəri) *n. Law. U.S.* A plea made by the defendant in a criminal action, equivalent to an admission of guilt and subjecting him to punishment but leaving it open to him to deny the alleged facts in other proceedings. [Latin, "I do not wish to contend".]

nom. nominative.

no-ma (nṓmə) *n.* A severe, often gangrenous inflammation of the mouth, occurring especially in a young child after a debilitating disease. [Latin *nomē,* "eating ulcer", from Greek *nomē,* spreading ulcer, "a feeding", "a pasturage".]

no-mad (nṓ-mad, -məd) *n.* **1.** Any of a group of pastoral people having no fixed abode and usually moving from place to place in a search for food and water. **2.** One who has no permanent domicile; a wanderer.
~*adj.* Nomadic. [French *nomade,* from Latin *nomas* (stem *nomad-*), from Greek *nomas,* one that wanders about for pasture; related to *nemein,* to feed or pasture animals.] —**no-mad-ism** *n.*

no-mad-ic (nō-máddik) *adj.* Also **no-mad-i-cal** (-'l). Leading the life of a nomad; wandering; roving. —**no-mad-i-cal-ly** *adv.*

no-man's-land (nō-manz-land) *n.* **1.** Land under dispute by two opposing parties; especially, the field of battle between two opposing entrenched armies. **2.** An unclaimed or unowned piece of land. **3.** Any area of indefiniteness or ambiguity.

nom-arch (nómmaark) *n.* A governor, especially of a nome or nomarchy. [Greek *nomarkhēs* : NOME + -ARCH.]

nom-ar-chy (nómm-aarki, -ərki) *n., pl.* **-ies.** Any of the administrative provinces of modern Greece. [Greek *nomarkhia* : NOME + -ARCHY.]

nom-bril (nómbril) *n. Heraldry.* The point on an escutcheon between the fess point and the base point; the midpoint in the lower half of an escutcheon. [Old French *nombril,* navel, probably alteration of *l'ombril,* the navel.]

nom de guerre (nóm də gáir; *French* noN) *n.* A fictitious name adopted for a particular course of action; a pseudonym. [French, "war name".]

nom de plume (nóm də plōōm; *French* noN də plúm) *n.* A pseudonym adopted by a writer. [French, "pen name".]

nome (nōm) *n.* **1.** A province in ancient Egypt. **2.** A nomarchy. [Greek *nomos,* division, district.]

no-men (nōmen) *n., pl.* **-mina** (nómmina, nómina). The second name of a citizen of ancient Rome, designating gens or patrilinear clan. Compare **cognomen, praenomen.** [Latin, name.]

no-men-cla-tor (nō-mən-klaytər, -men-) *n.* One who assigns names, as in scientific classification. [Latin *nōmenclātor,* "name-caller", a slave who accompanied his master to tell him the names of people he met : *nōmen,* name + *-clātor,* caller, from *calāre,* to call.]

no-men-cla-ture (nō-méngkləchər, nə-, nō-mən-klaychər, -men-) *n.* A system of names or terms; a systematic naming in any art, science, or area of activity. [Latin *nōmenclātūra,* from *nōmenclātor,* NOMENCLATOR.] —**no-men-cla-tur-al** (-kláychərəl) *adj.*

nom-i-nal (nómminəl) *adj.* **1. a.** Of, like, or consisting of a name or names. **b.** Bearing a person's name: *nominal shares.* **2.** Existing in name only; not real or actual; theoretical: *the nominal head of the firm.* **3.** Minimal in comparison to the real value: *a nominal sum.* **4.** *Grammar.* Of, like, or functioning as a noun or nouns.
~*n.* A word or phrase that functions as a noun. [Latin *nōminālis,* from *nōmen* (stem *nōmin-*), name.] —**nom-i-nal-ly** *adv.*

nom-i-nal-ism (nómmin'l-izm) *n. Philosophy.* The doctrine that abstract concepts, general terms, or universals have no objective reference but exist only as names. Compare **realism.** —**nom-i-nal-ist** *adj. & n.* —**nom-i-nal-is-tic** (-ístik) *adj.*

nominal value *n.* The stated or par value of a share certificate or bond, as opposed to the actual or market value.

nom-i-nate (nómminayt) *tr.v.* **-nated, -nating, -nates. 1.** To propose by name as a candidate. **2.** To designate or appoint to some office, responsibility, or honour. **3.** To designate; name.
~*adj.* (-ət, -it, -ayt). Having a particular name. [Latin *nōmināre,* to name, from *nōmen* (stem *nōmin-*), name.] —**nom-i-na-tor** *n.*

nom-i-na-tion (nómmi-náysh'n) *n.* **1.** The act or an instance of nominating. **2.** The state of being nominated.

nom-i-na-tive (nómmi-nətiv, nóm- || U.S. for senses 2 and 3 also -naytiv) *adj. Abbr.* **nom. 1.** *Grammar.* Of or designating the case of the subject of a finite verb (as *We* in *We awoke at dawn*) and of words identified with the subject, such as *women* in *These are the women.* **2.** Having or bearing a person's name. **3. a.** Appointed to office. **b.** Nominated as a candidate to office.
~*n. Abbr.* **nom.** *Grammar.* **1.** The nominative case. **2.** A form or construction in this case. [Noun, Middle English *nominatif (case),* from Old French *(cas) nominatif,* from Latin *nōminātīvus (cāsus),* from *nōmināre,* to NOMINATE.]

nom-i-nee (nómmi-née) *n.* One who is nominated to an office or as a candidate. [NOMIN(ATE) + -EE.]

nomo– *comb. form.* Indicates law, usage, or custom; for example, **nomology.** [Greek *nomos,* usage, law.]

nom-o-gram (nómmə-gram, nṓmə-) *n.* Also **nom-o-graph** (-graf). A graph consisting of three coplanar curves, usually parallel straight lines, each graduated for a different variable so that a straight line cutting all three curves intersects the related values of each variable. It is used to represent an equation containing three variables. Also called "alignment chart". [NOMO- + -GRAM.]

no-mog-ra-phy (no-móggrəfi, nō-, nə-) *n.* The science of constructing nomograms.

no-mol-o-gy (nō-mólləji, no-) *n.* The science of physical and logical laws. [NOMO- + -LOGY.] —**no-mo-log-i-cal** (nōmə-lójik'l, nómmə-) *adj.* —**no-mo-log-ist** (-móllə jist) *n.*

nom-o-thet-ic (nómmə-théttik, nṓmə-) *adj.* Also **nom-o-thet-ic-al** ('l). **1.** Lawmaking; legislative. **2.** Of or concerned with the formulation of general or scientific laws. [From obsolete *nomothete,* from Greek *nomothetēs,* legislator : *nomos,* law + *tithēnai,* to put.]

–nomy *n. comb. form.* Indicates the systematisation of knowledge about, or laws governing, a specified field; for example, **astronomy.** [Latin *-nomia,* from Greek; either from agent nouns or adjectives in *-nomos,* from *nemein,* to distribute, manage, or from *nomos,* distribution, law.]

non– *prefix.* Indicates: **1.** Failure or lack; for example, **noncommunication. 2.** Absence of the qualities or characteristics typically associated with; for example, **nonperson. 3.** Not; for example, **nonviable.** *Note:* Many compounds other than those entered here may be formed with non-. In forming compounds, *non-* in this dictionary is normally joined with the following element without space or hyphen. However, many users prefer the hyphenated form, which is used here only if the second element begins with a vowel, an *n,* or a capital letter: *non-iron, non-nutritive, non-French.* The prefix is pronounced (nón), or occasionally (nún); the latter variant is ignored in the entries below. [Middle English *non-,* from Old French *non-,* from Latin *nōn,* not.] See also **un-.**

nona– *comb. form.* Indicates nine or ninth; for example, **nonagon.** [From Latin *nōnus,* ninth.]

non-ac-ci-dent-al injury (nón-aksi-dént'l) *n. Abbr.* **NAI, N.A.I.** An injury inflicted deliberately; specifically, a cut, bruise, burn, or fracture inflicted on a child at home, detected by authorities such as health visitors or social workers, and deemed to call for outside investigation or intervention.

non-ad-di-tive (nón-áddi-tiv) *adj. Mathematics.* Having a numerical value that is not equal to the sum of its component parts. —**non-ad-di-tiv-i-ty** (-tívvəti) *n.*

no-nage (nṓnij || nónnij) *n.* **1.** The period during which one is legally under age. **2.** A stage of immaturity: *"the bravest achievements*

Nolan painting *"The Dog and Duck Hotel" – a heat-laden Australian scene, typical of the paintings which made Sidney Nolan famous.*

were always accomplished in the nonage of a nation" (Thomas Paine). [Middle English, from Old French : NON- + AGE.]

non·a·ge·nar·i·an (nŏnə-ji-náir-i-ən, nónnə-, -jə-) *adj.* **1.** Being ninety years old or between ninety and one hundred years old. **2.** Of or like someone of this age.
~*n.* A person of ninety or between ninety and one hundred years of age. [Latin *nōnāgēnārius*, from *nōnāgēnī*, ninety each, from *nōnāginta*, ninety : *novem*, nine + *-gintā*, ten times.]

non·ag·gres·sion (nónnə-grésh'n) *n.* The avoidance of aggression or hostilities, as between nations. Also used adjectivally: *a non-aggression pact.*

non·a·gon (nónnə-gən, nŏnə-, -gon) *n.* A polygon having nine sides and nine angles. [NONA- + -GON.]

non·ag·o·nal (non-ággən'l, nōn-) *adj.* **1.** Having nine sides and nine angles. **2.** Of, pertaining to, or formed in nonagons. —**non·a·gon·al·ly** *adv.*

non·al·co·hol·ic (nón-al-kə-hóllik) *adj.* Containing no alcohol.

non·a·ligned (nón-ə-lĭnd) *adj.* Not in alliance with any power bloc; neutral: *a non-aligned nation.* —**non·a·lign·ment** *n.*

non·a·no·ic acid (nónnə-nŏ-ik) *n.* A chemical, **pelargonic acid** *(see).* [From *nonane*, a paraffin : NONA- + -ANE (because it is the ninth in the methane series).]

non·ap·pear·ance (nónnə-péer-ənss) *n.* Failure to appear, as in a court of law.

non·bel·lig·er·ent (nón-bə-líjərənt) *n.* A person or a country that takes no part in a war. —**nonbelligerent** *adj.*

nonce[1] (nónss) *n.* The present or particular time or occasion. Used in the phrase *for the nonce.* [Middle English *for the nones, for the nanes*, originally *for then anes*, "for the one (purpose or occasion)" : FOR + *then*, dative singular neuter of THE + *anes*, ONCE.]

nonce[2] *n. Slang.* An imprisoned sex offender. [20th century : origin obscure.]

nonce word *n.* A word invented and used only once, to meet a particular requirement; an example is the word *mileconsuming* in *"the wagon beginning to fall into its slow and mileconsuming clatter"* (William Faulkner).

non·cha·lant (nónshələnt) *adj.* Appearing casually unconcerned; indifferent. See Synonyms at **cool.** [French, from Old French, from *nonchaloir*, to be unconcerned : NON- + *chaloir*, to be interested or concerned, from Latin *calēre*, to be warm.] —**non·cha·lance** *n.* —**non·cha·lant·ly** *adv.*

non·com (nón-kóm) *n. Informal.* A noncommissioned officer.

non·com·bat·ant (nón-kóm-bətənt, -kúm- ‖ *U.S. also* -kəm-bátt'nt) *n.* **1.** A person connected with the armed forces whose duties are other than fighting, such as a chaplain. **2.** A civilian in wartime.

non·com·mis·sioned officer (nón-kə-mísh'nd) *n. Abbr.* **NCO, N.C.O.** A member of the armed forces, such as a sergeant or corporal, appointed to a rank conferring leadership over other men but not holding a commission. Compare **commissioned officer, warrant officer.**

non·com·mit·tal (nón-kə-mítt'l) *adj.* Refusing commitment to any particular course of action or opinion; revealing no preference or purpose. —**non·com·mit·tal·ly** *adv.*

non·com·pli·ance (nón-kəm-plí-ənss ‖ -kom-) *n.* Failure or refusal to comply with something. —**non·com·pli·ant** *adj. & n.*

non com·pos men·tis (nón kóm-poss méntiss, -pəss) *adj.* Not of sound mind, and therefore not responsible for one's actions. [Latin, "not having control of the mind."]

non·con·duc·tor (nón-kən-dúktər ‖ -kon-) *n.* A substance that conducts little or no electricity or heat. —**non·con·duct·ing** *adj.*

non·con·form·ist (nón-kən-fórmist ‖ -kon-) *n.* **1.** One who refuses to be bound by the accepted rules, beliefs, or practices of a group. **2.** *Capital N.* A member of a Protestant church that dissents from the Church of England. —**non·con·form·ism** *n.* —**non·con·form·ist** *adj.* —**non·con·form·i·ty** *n.*

non·con·trib·u·to·ry (nón-kən-tríb-bew-təri, -tri ‖ -kóntri-béwtəri) *adj.* **1.** Not requiring contributions. **2.** Designating a pension or insurance scheme in which employees' contributions are paid by the employer. **3.** Not contributing; not making contributions.

non·co·op·er·a·tion (nón-kō-óppə-ráysh'n) *n.* **1.** Failure or refusal to cooperate. **2.** Resistance to government through civil disobedience or refusal to perform civil duties, such as paying taxes. —**non·co·op·er·a·tion·ist** *n. & adj.* —**non·co·op·er·a·tive** (-óppə-rətiv, -óp- ‖ -raytiv) *adj.* —**non·co·op·er·a·tor** (-raytər) *n.*

non·count·a·ble (nón-kówntəb'l) *adj. Grammar.* Of or designating a noun that refers to an object lacking clearly standardised or defined limits and that is not preceded by the indefinite article; for example, *earth* and *soil* are noncountable nouns, whereas *clod* and *boulder* are not. Some nouns, such as *speed* or *fear*, have both countable and noncountable senses. Compare **countable.**

non·de·nom·i·na·tion·al (nón-di-nómmi-náysh'n'l) *adj.* Not restricted to or associated with a particular religious denomination.

non·de·script (nón-di-skript) *adj.* Lacking in distinctive qualities; without any individual character or form.
~*n.* A person or thing with no outstanding or distinguishing features. [NON- + Latin *dēscrīptus*, past participle of *dēscrībere*, DESCRIBE.]

non·dis·junc·tion (nón-diss-júngksh'n) *n. Biology.* The failure of homologous chromosomes to move to separate poles during meiosis.

non·dis·tinc·tive (nón-diss-tíngktiv) *adj.* **1.** Not distinctive. **2.** *Phonetics.* Not helping to distinguish meaning: *The vowel in the words*

"on" *and* "off" *is nondistinctive; only the consonants are differentiated.*

none (nun ‖ *Northern English also* non) *pron.* **1.** No one; not one; nobody: *None dared to do it.* **2.** Not any; no persons or things of a specified group: *None of my cardigans will go with this new dress.* **3.** No part; not any: *none of my business; none of his concern.*
~*adj. Archaic.* Not one; no. Now used only before vowels: *There is none other available.*
~*adv.* In no way; not at all: *We were none the wiser.* [Middle English *nan, none*, Old English *nān : ne*, no + *ān*, one.]
Usage: None may be used with either a singular or a plural verb, depending on the construction in which it appears. Thus when *none* precedes or refers back to a singular noun, the verb is also in the singular: *None of the laundry is clean; Where's the orange juice?* — *There is none* (which is a more formal version of *There isn't any*). A singular verb is also used when *none* can be interpreted as "not one" or "no one": *None of us is to blame.* A plural verb is used when *none* refers back to a plural noun: *Where are the sugar lumps?* — *There are none.* The plural verb is also generally used when the meaning of *none* is "not any of a group of persons or things": *None have been more in need of a pay rise than the nurses.* Problems of usage arise when *none* can be interpreted as either singular or plural: *None of these books is/are helpful.* Purists insist on the singular form in such contexts, but the plural is often used in all styles, when no individualising sense is intended. See also **neither.**

non·e·go (nón-éego, -éggō) *n., pl.* **-gos.** *Philosophy.* All that is not part of the ego or the conscious self.

non·e·lec·tro·lyte (nón-i-léktrə-līt) *n.* A substance that does not ionise in solution or in liquid form and therefore forms solutions or liquids of low conductivity.

non·emp·ty (nón-émpti) *Mathematics.* Designating a set that has at least one member.

non·en·ti·ty (nón-éntəti, nən-) *n., pl.* **-ties. 1.** An insignificant person or thing. **2.** Non-existence. **3.** Something that does not exist, or that exists only in the imagination.

nones (nōnz) *pl.n.* **1.** In the ancient Roman calendar, the ninth day before the ides of a month; the seventh of March, May, July, or October, and the fifth day of the other months. **2.** *Ecclesiastical.* **a.** The fifth of the seven **canonical hours** *(see).* **b.** The time of day set aside for this prayer, usually the ninth hour after sunrise. [In sense 1, Middle English *nonys, nonas*, from Old French *nones*, from Latin *nōnae*, feminine plural of *nōnus*, ninth. In sense 2, plural of *none*, from Old French *none*, from Late Latin *nōna (hōra)*, the ninth hour, from the feminine of Latin *nōnus*, ninth.]

non·es·sen·tial (nón-i-sénsh'l) *adj.* **1.** Not essential. **2.** *Biochemistry.* Designating amino acids that a particular organism is able to synthesise and that are therefore not essential to its diet.

none·such, non·such (nún-such ‖ nón-) *n.* **1.** *Archaic.* A person or thing without equal: *a nonesuch among athletes.* **2.** A plant, the **black medick** *(see).* —**none·such** *adj.*

non·et (nó-nét) *n. Music.* **1.** A composition for nine instruments or voices. **2.** A group of nine musicians or performers. [Italian *nonetto*, from *nono*, ninth, from Latin *nōnus*.]

none·the·less, nonetheless (núnthə-léss ‖ nón-) *adv.* No less; nevertheless; however.
Usage: Nonetheless is now usually written as a single word, especially in American English, but traditionalists generally recommend the form *none the less.*

non-Eu·clid·e·an (nón-yōō-klíddi-ən) *adj.* Designating any of several modern geometries that change or discard one or more of the axioms of Euclid.

non-e·vent (nón-i-vént) *n.* An occurrence which is expected to be interesting or exciting but which fails to take place or to live up to expectations.

non-ex·ist·ence (nón-ig-zístənss ‖ -eg-, -ik-) *n.* **1.** The condition of not existing. **2.** A thing that does not exist. —**non-ex·ist·ent** *adj.*

non·fea·sance (nón-féez'nss) *n. Law.* Failure to perform some act that is either an official duty or a legal requirement. Compare **malfeasance, misfeasance.** [NON- + obsolete *feasance*, a doing, from Old French *faisance* (see **malfeasance**).]

non·fer·rous (nón-férrəss) *adj.* **1.** Not composed of or containing iron. **2.** Of or pertaining to metals other than iron.

non·fic·tion (nón-fíksh'n) *n.* Prose works other than fiction. —**non·fic·tion·al** *adj.*

non·flam·ma·ble (nón-flámməb'l) *adj.* Not flammable; not easily set alight. See Usage note at **flammable.**

nong (nong) *n. Australian Slang.* A stupid person; a fool. [Perhaps shortened from earlier *ningnong*, fool. See **nignog.**]

non·gov·ern·men·tal organisation (nón-guvvərn-mént'l) *n.* See **NGO.**

non·har·mon·ic (nón-haar-mónnik) *adj.* Of or designating a note, such as a grace note, that is not part of the chord with which it is played.

no·nil·lion (nō-níl-yən) *n.* **1.** In Britain, the cardinal number represented by the figure 1 followed by 54 zeros; usually written 10^{54}. **2.** In the United States and France, the cardinal number represented by the figure 1 followed by 30 zeros; usually written 10^{30}. In this sense, also *British* "quintillion". [French, from Old French, "the ninth power of a million" : *non-*, nine, ninth + *(m)ilion, (m)illion*, (M)ILLION.] —**no·nil·lion** *adj.*

no·nil·lionth (nō-níl-yənth) *n.* **1.** The ordinal number nonillion in a series. **2.** Any of a nonillion equal parts. —**no·nil·lionth** *adj.*

non·in·duc·tive (nón-in-dúktiv) *adj. Electricity.* Having low inductance.

non·in·ter·ven·tion (nón-intər-vénsh'n) *n.* Failure or refusal to interfere or intervene in the affairs of another; especially, a deliberate refusal of one nation to intervene in the affairs of another nation or one of its own subdivisions. —**non·in·ter·ven·tion·ist** *n. & adj.*

non-iron (nón-í-ərn ‖ -íron) *adj. Chiefly British.* Requiring little or no ironing. Said of garments or fabrics.

non·join·der (nón-jóyndər) *n. Law.* The omission of a party, plaintiff, defendant, or cause of action that should have been included as a necessary part of an action or suit. Compare **misjoinder**.

non·ju·ror (non-jōor-ər ‖ -awr) *n.* 1. One who refuses to take an oath, as of allegiance. 2. *Capital* N. An Anglican clergyman who refused to swear allegiance to William and Mary in 1689.

non li·cet (nón lí-sit) *adj. Law.* Not allowed; unlawful. [Latin.]

non·lin·e·ar (nón-línni-ər) *adj.* 1. Not in a straight line. 2. *Mathematics.* Occurring as a result of a non-additive operation. —**non·lin·e·ar·i·ty** (-árrəti) *n.*

non li·quet (nón líkwit) *adj. Law.* Unclear. Said of evidence. [Latin.]

non·met·al (nón-métt'l) *n. Chemistry.* Any of a number of elements, such as oxygen or sulphur, that generally occur as negatively charged ions or radicals, form oxides that produce acids, and are poor conductors of heat and of electricity when solid.

non·me·tal·lic (nón-mi-tál-ik) *adj.* 1. Not of metal. 2. *Chemistry.* Of or pertaining to a nonmetal.

non·met·ro·pol·i·tan (nón-méttrə-póllit'n) *adj.* Of or designating an English county that is not one of the six metropolitan counties.

non·mor·al (nón-mórrəl ‖ -máwrəl) *adj.* Unrelated to morals or to ethical considerations; neither moral nor immoral.

non-New·ton·i·an fluid (nón-new-tóni-ən ‖ -nōō-) *n.* A fluid with a flow behaviour such that the rate of shear is not proportional to the corresponding stress.

non·nu·cle·ar (nón-néw-kli-ər ‖ -nōō-) *adj.* Not possessing, producing, or powered by nuclear energy or nuclear weapons.

no-no (nṓ-nō̄) *n., pl.* **-noes.** *Slang.* 1. Something that is forbidden or unacceptable. 2. Something or someone that is useless or doomed to failure.

non·ob·jec·tive (nón-əb-jéktiv ‖ -ob-) *adj.* Designating a style of art that does not represent objects; abstract.

non ob·stan·te (nón ob-stánti ‖ *U.S. also* -stáantay) *prep. Abbr.* **non obs., non obst.** *Latin.* Notwithstanding.

no-non·sense (nō̄-nón-sənss ‖ -senss) *adj.* 1. Not tolerating extremes of behaviour or taste. 2. Practical; down-to-earth.

non·pa·reil (nón-pə-rəl, -prəl, -ráyl ‖ *U.S.* -rél) *adj.* Without rival; matchless; peerless; unequalled.
~*n.* 1. A person or thing that is unmatched or unequalled; a paragon or nonesuch. 2. *Printing.* Especially formerly, a size of type, 6-point type. [Middle English *nonparaille,* from Old French *nonpareil :* NON- + *pareil,* equal, like, from Vulgar Latin *pariculus* (unattested), diminutive of Latin *pār,* equal.]

non·par·tic·i·pat·ing (nón-paar-tissi-payting) *adj.* 1. Not participating. 2. *Insurance.* Not giving the right to participate in the profits of a company. —**non·par·tic·i·pa·tor** *n.*

non·par·ti·san (nón-párti-zán, -zan ‖ *U.S.* -zən, -sən) *adj.* 1. Not partisan. 2. Not influenced by, affiliated with, or supporting the interests or policies of any one political party.

non·per·son (nón-pérss'n) *n.* An insipid or unimpressive person. Also called "unperson".

non pla·cet (nón pláss-et, plák) *n.* A negative vote in a church or university assembly, especially at Oxford or Cambridge University. [Latin, "it is not pleasing".]

non·plus (nón-plúss) *n.* A state of perplexity or bafflement preventing action, speech, or thought: *never at a nonplus; reduced to a perfect nonplus.*
~*tr.v.* **nonplussed** or *U.S.* **-plused, nonplussing** or *U.S.* **-plusing, nonplusses** or *U.S.* **-pluses.** To perplex; baffle. [Latin *nōn plūs,* "no more (can be said)" : *nōn,* not + *plūs,* more.]

non pos·su·mus (nón póssew-məss ‖ póssə-) *n. Latin.* A statement indicating an inability to take action on a matter.

non·pro·duc·tive (nón-prə-dúktiv) *adj.* 1. Of or belonging to that part of the labour force that does not directly produce goods, such as clerical personnel. 2. Not yielding what was expected; unproductive. —**non·pro·duc·tive·ly** *adv.* —**non·pro·duc·tive·ness** *n.*

non-prof·it-mak·ing (nón-próffit-mayking) *adj.* Not set up with the aim of making a profit; not making a profit.

non·pro·lif·er·a·tion (nón-prə-liffə-ráysh'n, -prō-) *n.* Limitation of the production or spread of something, especially nuclear weapons. Also used adjectivally: *a nonproliferation agreement.*

non·pros (nón-próss) *tr.v.* **-prossed, -prossing, -prosses.** *Law.* To enter a judgment of non prosequitur against (a plaintiff).

non pro·se·qui·tur (nón prō-sékwitər) *n. Abbr.* **non pros.** *Law.* The judgment entered against a plaintiff who fails to appear in court to prosecute a suit. [Latin, "he does not prosecute".]

non·re·new·a·ble (nón-ri-néw-əb'l, -rə- ‖ -nōō-) *adj.* 1. Unable to be renewed or extended. 2. Of or designating fuels, especially fossil fuels, that cannot be replaced once exhausted.

non·rep·re·sen·ta·tion·al (nón-réprizen-táysh'n'l) *adj.* Not representational; especially in art, abstract.

non·res·i·dent (nón-rézzidənt) *n.* 1. One who does not live or stay at a particular place. 2. One who does not live in the place where he works. —**non·res·i·dence, non·res·i·den·cy** *n.* —**non·res·i·dent** *adj.*

non·re·sis·tant (nón-ri-zístənt, -rə-) *adj.* 1. Not resistant; submissively obedient. 2. Unable to resist illness or infection.
~*n.* 1. One who believes in complete obedience to authority, even though it may be unjust or arbitrary. 2. One who will not resort to force, even in self-defence. —**non·re·sis·tance** *n.*

non·re·stric·tive (nón-ri-stríktiv, -rə-) *adj.* 1. Not restrictive. 2. *Grammar.* Designating a word, clause, or phrase that is descriptive of but does not limit the basic application of the element it modifies. Compare **restrictive**.

non·re·turn·a·ble (nón-ri-túrnəb'l, -rə-) *adj.* Designating a bottle or other container on which no returnable deposit is paid when it is purchased.

non·rig·id (nón-ríjid) *adj.* 1. Not rigid. 2. Designating a lighter-than-air aircraft that holds its shape by gas pressure.

non·se·cre·tor (nón-si-kréetər) *n.* A person in whose saliva and other body fluids the A, B, or O antigens determining blood group cannot be detected. Compare **secretor**.

non·sched·uled (nón-shéddewld ‖ *U.S.* -skéjōold) *adj.* 1. Operating without fixed flying schedules. Said of certain airlines. 2. Not according to a schedule or plan: *a nonscheduled stop at Manchester.*

non·sec·tar·i·an (nón-sek-taír-i-ən) *adj.* Not limited to or associated with any particular religious denomination.

non·sense (nón-sənss ‖ -senss) *n.* 1. Something that does not make or have sense; especially, behaviour or language that is meaningless or absurd. Also used adjectivally: *a nonsense poem.* 2. Extravagant foolishness or frivolity. 3. Things of little or no importance or usefulness; trifles: *ribbons, laces, and other nonsense.* 4. *Genetics.* A sequence of DNA that is not used as a template for the synthesis of messenger RNA during transcription.
~*interj.* Used to express rejection or dismissal of an idea or statement. [NON- (not) + SENSE.] —**non·sen·si·cal** (-sén-sik'l) *adj.* —**non·sen·si·cal·ly** *adv.*

nonsense verse *n.* A form of verse dealing with illogical and absurd ideas or characters, and usually employing words invented for humorous effect.

non se·qui·tur (nón sékwitər) *n. Abbr.* **non seq.** 1. *Logic.* An inference or conclusion that does not follow from established premises or evidence. 2. A statement that appears to have no relevance to what has just been said. [Latin, "it does not follow".]

non·skid (nón-skíd) *adj.* Having a ridged tread or specially treated surface designed to prevent or inhibit skidding. Said of tyres or flooring, for example.

non·smok·er (nón-smōkər) *n.* 1. A person who does not smoke. 2. A carriage or compartment, as in a train, in which smoking is forbidden.

non·spe·ci·fic urethritis (nón-spi-síffik, -spə-) *n. Abbr.* **NSU.** Inflammation of the urethra, a sexually transmitted infection not caused by gonococcal or other specific infectious agents.

non·stan·dard (nón-stándərd) *adj.* 1. Varying from or not adhering to a standard. 2. *Linguistics.* Of or pertaining to usages or varieties of a language that do not conform to those approved by educated native users of the language.

non·start·er (nón-stártər) *n.* 1. A horse, racing car, or the like that does not compete in a race for which it was entered. 2. *Informal.* A person, idea, or project regarded as unlikely to succeed and hence not worthy of consideration.

non·stick (nón-stík) *adj.* Coated with a substance that prevents food adhering during cooking: *a nonstick frying pan.*

non·stop (nón-stóp) *adj.* 1. Making or having made no stops: *a nonstop flight.* 2. *Informal.* Not relieved by any pause; unceasing. —**non·stop** *adv.*

non·stri·at·ed (nón-strī-áytid) *adj.* Having no striations. Said chiefly of certain muscle fibres.

non·strik·er (nón-strīkər) *n.* 1. *Sports.* In cricket, the batsman who is not receiving the bowling. 2. A person who does not strike.

nonsuch. Variant of **nonesuch**.

non·suit (nón-séwt, -sōōt) *n. Law.* A judgment given against a plaintiff when he fails to prosecute his case or to introduce sufficient evidence.
~*tr.v.* **nonsuited, -suiting, -suits.** To dismiss the lawsuit of. [Middle English, from Anglo-French *no(u)nsuyte :* NON- + Old French *suite, sieute,* SUIT.]

non·sup·port (nón-sə-pórt ‖ -pórt) *n. Law.* Failure to provide for the maintenance of one's legal dependants.

non·triv·i·al (nón-trívvi-əl) *adj.* 1. Not trivial. 2. *Mathematics.* Designating a relationship or expression in which at least one variable is not equal to zero.

non trop·po (nón tróppō, nón) *adv. Music.* Moderately. Used to modify a direction: *adagio non troppo.* [Italian, "not too much".]

non-U (nón-yōō) *adj. British Informal.* Not belonging or appropriate to upper-class custom, especially in language. Compare **U**.

non-un·ion (nón-yōōn-yən) *adj.* 1. **a.** Not belonging to a trade union. **b.** Not unionised: *a non-union shop.* 2. Not manufactured or serviced by union labour.
~*n. Medicine.* Failure of a bone fracture to heal.

non·u·ple (nónnew-p'l) *adj.* 1. Consisting of nine members; having nine parts or elements; ninefold. 2. Multiplied by nine.
~*n.* A number or total that is nine times as great as another. [Old French *nonuple : non-,* nine + *-ple,* -fold, from Latin *-plus.*]

non-user (nón-yōōzər) *n.* One who does not make use of or take something, especially narcotic drugs.

non·vi·a·ble (nón-ví-əb'l) *adj.* 1. Not capable of living independently after birth. 2. Not workable or practicable.

Norman *Norman architecture is characterised by round-arched doors and windows and heavy buttresses. Roofs are usually steeply pitched; towers are squat and square.*

PRONUNCIATION KEY

a, trap; aa, father; ai, fair; ar, star; aw, lawn; ay, play; b, bb, stab; rubber; ch, church; ck, ticket; d, dd, dead; ladder; e, dress; ee, bee; er, defer; ew, few; ewr, pure; ə, about; ər, letter; f, ff, fife; differ; g, gg, giggle; h, hat; i, kit; ī, price; īr, fire; j, judge; k, kick; l, ll, let; 'l, needle; m, mm, man; n, nn, no; 'n, sudden; ng, thing; o, lot; ō, no; ŏŏ, foot; ōō, shoe; oor, poor; ow, cow; owr, hour; oy, boy; p, pp, pepper; r, rr, red; s, ss, sauce; sh, ship; t, tt, totter; th, thick; th, this; smooth; u, cut; ur, turn; v, vv, valve; w, wet; y, yes; z, zz, zebra; zh, vision; pleasure

IN FOREIGN WORDS:

aN, oN, Saint-Saëns; hl, Llanelli; Hluhluwe; kh, loch; lough; Khaled

STRESS MARK:

ín-sīt, insight; in-sī́t, incite

non·vi·o·lence (nón-vī́-ələnss) *n.* Lack of violence; specifically, a social philosophy based on the rejection of violent means to gain objectives. **—non·vi·o·lent** *adj.* **—non·vi·o·lent·ly** *adv.*

non·vol·a·tile (nón-vóllə-tīl || -t'l) *adj.* Designating or pertaining to a computer memory in which information is retained when the power is switched off.

non·vot·er (nón-vṓtər) *n.* A person who does not vote or who has no right to vote. **—non·vot·ing** *adj.*

non·white, non-white (nón-wī́t, -hwī́t) *n.* **1.** A person not of the white race. **2.** *South African.* A person not of European descent or not classified as white. **—non·white** *adj.*

noodle[1] (nṓōd'l) *n.* A thin, usually flat strip of pasta. [German *Nudel*†.]

noodle[2] *n.* **1.** A fool; a simpleton. **2.** *Chiefly U.S. Slang.* The head. [In sense 1, perhaps blend of NODDLE (head) and NOODLE (food).]

nook (nŏŏk || nōōk) *n.* **1.** A corner, especially in a room; a recess: *They searched for it in every nook and cranny.* **2.** A quiet, narrow, or secluded spot outdoors. [Middle English *noke, nok,* perhaps from Scandinavian; akin to Norwegian (dialectal) *nok,* hook.]

nook·y, nook·ie (nŏŏki) *n. Vulgar Slang.* Sexual intercourse. [Perhaps from NOOK (alluding to the pudendum).]

noon (nōōn) *n.* **1. a.** Twelve o'clock in the daytime; midday. **b.** The time or the point in the Sun's path when it is on the local meridian. **2.** The highest point or zenith; the best or brightest part. **3.** *Archaic.* The midpoint: *the noon of night.* [Middle English *none, noon,* midday, the hour of the nones (originally 3 p.m.), Old English *nōn,* "the ninth hour (after sunrise)", from Late Latin *nōna (hōra),* from the feminine of Latin *nōnus,* ninth.] **—noon** *adj.*

noon·day (nōōn-day) *n.* Noon. **—noon·day** *adj.*

no one, no-one (nṓ-wun || *Northern England also* -won) *pron.* No person; nobody. See Usage note at **nobody.**

noon·tide (nōōn-tīd) *n.* Noon. [Middle English *nonetyde,* Old English *nōntīd* : *nōn,* NOON + *tīd,* TIDE (time).] **—noon·tide** *adj.*

noose (nōōss) *n.* **1.** A loose loop secured in a rope or cord by means of a slipknot which slides along to tighten it if pulled. **2.** A snare or trap. **3.** Death by hanging. Preceded by *the.*

~tr.v. **noosed, noosing, nooses. 1.** To capture or to hold by or as if by a noose. **2.** To make a noose of or in. [Middle English *nose,* from Old French *nos, nous,* from Latin *nōdus,* a knot.]

no·pal (nṓp'l, nō-pál, -paál) *n.* **1.** Any cactus of the genus *Nopalea,* found chiefly in Mexico; especially, *N. coccinellifera,* having erect petals and scarlet flowers. **2.** A prickly pear of the genus *Opuntia,* having yellow or red flowers and purple fruit. [Spanish, from Nahuatl *nopalli.*]

no-par (nṓ-pár) *adj.* Without face value; having no par value. Said of share certificates.

nope (nōp) *adv. Informal.* No. [Alteration of NO (adverb).]

nor[1] (nor; *occasional weak form* nər) *conj.* **1.** And not; or not; likewise not; not either. Used as a correlative to give continuing negative force: *She neither worked nor offered to help.* **2.** *Archaic.* Used in place of *neither,* as the first correlative of a negative pair: *Nor grey his beard, nor shambling his gait.* [Middle English *nor,* contraction of *nother, nauther,* NEITHER.]

Usage: *Neither* is followed by *nor,* not by *or.* When other negative forms are used early in a sentence, the continuation of the negative meaning requires *nor* when separate clauses are involved *(I have no experience of chemistry, nor does the subject interest me). Or* may be used when the constructions are within a single clause *(I have no experience or interest in chemistry),* or share one or more elements (such as *she* in *She will not permit the change, or even consider it),* but *nor* is also available as a more emphatic form in such cases. The use of *and* with *nor* is common in informal British English speech *(Many didn't go to the cinema, and nor did Joan),* but is rare elsewhere. *And neither* prevails in American English.

nor[2] *conj. Regional.* Than. [Middle English *nor*†.]

nor– *comb. form. Chemistry.* Indicates an unaltered parent compound; for example, **noradrenaline.** [From NORMAL.]

Nor. 1. Norman. 2. north. 3. Norway; Norwegian.

nor·a·dren·a·line, nor·a·dren·a·lin (náwrə-drénnəlin) *n.* A hormone, $(OH)_2C_6H_3{\cdot}CHOH{\cdot}CH_2NH_2$, secreted by the adrenal medulla and the endings of sympathetic nerves. It is a vasoconstrictor and acts as a transmitter of nerve impulses. Also *U.S.* "norepinephrine". [NOR- + ADRENALINE.]

Nord·hau·sen acid (nórd-howz'n) *n.* **Fuming sulphuric acid** *(see).* [After *Nordhausen,* a town in Prussian Saxony where it was made.]

Nor·dic (nórdik) *adj. Anthropology.* **1.** Of, pertaining to, or belonging to a subdivision of the Caucasoid ethnic group most predominant in Scandinavia. The typical Nordic person is tall, long-headed, blonde, and blue-eyed. **2.** Of or pertaining to cross-country skiing and ski-jumping. Compare **Alpine.**

~n. A member of a Nordic people. [French *nordique,* from Old French *nord,* north, from Old English *north.*]

Nord-Ostsee Kanal. See **Kiel Canal.**

nor'easter. *Nautical.* Variant of **northeaster.**

Nor·folk[1] (nór-fək). County in eastern England, bordering on the North Sea. The county town is Norwich. It is a chiefly agricultural county. The eastern portion is notable for the series of shallow lakes and channels known as the Broads.

Norfolk[2]. Largest city in Virginia, eastern United States, lying on the Elizabeth river. It is a major industrial and commercial port and an important military centre.

Norfolk, Thomas Howard, 3rd Duke of (1473–1554). English soldier and politician. He fought at Flodden (1513), and was president of Henry VIII's privy council. He fell from power following the execution of Catherine Howard, his niece and Henry's fifth wife.

Norfolk Island pine *n.* An evergreen tree, *Araucaria excelsa,* native to Norfolk Island in the South Pacific.

Norfolk jacket *n.* A single-breasted men's jacket with a belt, a pocket on each side, and two box pleats in front and back. [Formerly worn for duck hunting in NORFOLK.]

Norfolk plover *n.* A bird, the **stone curlew** *(see).*

NOR gate (nor) *n. Computing.* A logic gate having one output wire and two or more input wires in which there is an output signal only if all the input signals are low. Also called "NOR circuit". Compare **AND gate.** [From NOR, since the gate has a function comparable to the operation of the conjunction *nor* in logic.]

no·ri·a (náwri-ə || nṓri-) *n.* A waterwheel with buckets attached to its rim that are used to raise water from a stream, especially for transferral to an irrigation trough. [Spanish, from Arabic *nā'ūrah,* "creaking device", from *na'ara,* to grunt, creak.]

nor·ite (náwrīt) *n.* See **gabbro.** [Norwegian *norit,* "Norwegian rock", from *Norge,* Norway.] **—nor·it·ic** (naw-rittik) *adj.*

norks (norks) *pl. n. Australian Slang.* A woman's breasts. [Perhaps from *Norco* Co-operative Ltd., a butter manufacturer in New South Wales (alluding to a cow's udders).]

nor·land (nórlənd) *n. Often capital* **N.** *Poetic.* Northland.

norm (norm) *n.* **1.** A standard, model, or pattern regarded as typical for a specific group. **2.** *Mathematics.* **a.** A **mode** *(see).* **b.** An average. **c.** The length of a vector. **3.** *Geology.* The theoretical composition of a standard igneous rock. [Latin *norma,* carpenter's square, pattern.]

norm. normal.

Nor·ma (nórmə) *n.* A constellation in the Southern Hemisphere within the Milky Way near Lupus and Ara.

nor·mal (nórm'l) *adj.* **1.** Conforming, adhering to, or constituting a usual or typical pattern, standard, level, or type; usual; typical: *"Almost all normal people want to be rich without great effort"* (F. Scott Fitzgerald). **2.** *Abbr.* **norm.** *Biology.* **a.** Not affected, immunised, or changed by experimentation. **b.** Functioning or occurring in a natural way. **3.** *Chemistry.* **a.** *Abbr.* **n, N** Designating a solution having one gram equivalent weight of solute per litre of solution. **b.** *Abbr.* **n-** Designating an aliphatic hydrocarbon having a straight and unbranched chain of carbon atoms. **4.** *Abbr.* **norm.** *Geometry.* At right angles; perpendicular. **5.** *Abbr.* **norm.** *Psychology.* Considered average in intelligence, ability, emotional traits, or personality.

~n. Abbr. **norm. 1.** Anything that is normal; the standard. **2.** The usual or expected state, form, amount, or degree. **3. a.** Correspondence to a norm. **b.** An average. **4.** *Geometry.* A perpendicular; especially, a perpendicular to a line tangent to a plane curve or to a plane tangent to a space curve. [French, or Late Latin *normālis,* from Latin, made according to the carpenter's square, rectangular, from *norma,* NORM.] **—nor·mal·ly** *adv.*

Synonyms: *normal, regular, standard, natural.*

nor·mal·cy (nórm'l-si) *n. Chiefly U.S.* Normality.

Usage: This alternative to *normality* is now frequently encountered in formal speech and writing, especially of a technical or semi-technical kind; it continues to attract criticism when used in everyday contexts, where *normality* would be considered the more natural form. *Normalcy* is more common in American English than in British English, but is criticised even in the United States.

normal decane *n. Chemistry.* A **decane** *(see).*

normal distribution *n. Statistics.* A theoretical frequency distribution for a set of variable data, usually represented by a bell-shaped curve symmetrical about the mean. Also called "Gaussian distribution".

nor·mal·ise, nor·mal·ize (nórm'l-īz) *tr.v.* **-ised, -ising, -ises. 1.** To make normal; cause to conform to a standard or norm. **2.** *Metallurgy.* To remove strains and reduce coarse crystalline structures in (steel) by applying heat. **3.** *Mathematics.* To introduce a numerical factor into (an equation) in order to make the area under the graph of the function equal to one, as in quantum mechanics and probability calculations. **—nor·mal·i·sa·tion** (-ī-záysh'n || *U.S.* -i-) *n.* **—nor·mal·is·er** *n.*

nor·mal·i·ty (nawr-mál-əti) *n.* **1.** The state or fact of being normal. See Usage note at **normalcy. 2.** *Symbol* **N** *Chemistry.* An obsolescent measure of the concentration of a solution equal to the number of gram equivalents of the solute per litre of the solution.

normal pentane *n.* A **pentane** *(see).*

normal school *n.* A school that trains teachers, chiefly of younger children, in countries such as France, the United States, and Canada. [Translation of French *école normale,* originally the name of a school founded as a model for other teacher-training colleges, from Late Latin *normālis,* NORMAL.]

Nor·man (nórmən) *n. Abbr.* **Nor. 1.** A member of a Scandinavian people who conquered Normandy in the tenth century. **2.** A member of the people of Normandy who conquered England in 1066. **3.** A native or inhabitant of Normandy. **4.** A language, Norman French.

~adj. **1.** Of or pertaining to Normandy, the Normans, their culture, or their language. **2.** *Architecture.* Designating a variety of Romanesque architecture that was introduced from Normandy into England before the Norman Conquest and flourished until about 1200. [Middle English *Norman,* from Anglo-French, from Old Norse *Northmathr* (stem *Northmann-*), Northman, Scandinavian.]

Norman Conquest *n.* The conquest of England by the Normans

under William the Conqueror, beginning in 1066 with the Battle of Hastings.

Nor·man·dy (nórməndi). *French* **Nor·man·die**. Region and former province of northern France, on the English Channel. Major industries include agriculture, cheesemaking (Camembert, Brie), iron ore (at Caen), textiles, shipbuilding, and oil refining. Its major ports are Cherbourg and Le Havre. Viking raids on Normandy began in the ninth century, and it was finally ceded to the Norsemen or Normans (911). After their conquest of England, Normandy passed to England (1106), but was finally recognised to be French territory in 1450. The historic capital of the region is Rouen, where Joan of Arc was burnt at the stake in 1431.

Norman French *n. Abbr.* **N.F.** The dialect of Old French used in medieval Normandy and England. See **Anglo-French.**

nor·ma·tive (nórmətiv) *adj.* **1.** Based upon or prescribing a norm, especially one regarded as a standard of usage in speech and writing: *normative grammar.* **2.** Pertaining to, implying, or establishing a norm or standard: *normative laws.* [French *normatif*, from *norme*, NORM.] —**nor·ma·tive·ly** *adv.* —**nor·ma·tive·ness** *n.*

nor·mo·blast (nórmō-blast) *n.* An immature red blood cell, characterised by abundant haemoglobin and a small nucleus.

nor·mo·ten·sive (nórmō-tén-siv) *adj.* Having, pertaining to, or designating blood pressure that is within the normal range.

Norn¹ (norn) *n., pl.* **Nornir** (nórneer) or **Norns.** *Norse Mythology.* Any of the Fates, Skuld (the Future), Verdandi (the Present), and Urd (the Past). [Old Norse.]

Norn² *n.* An extinct Norse dialect formerly spoken in Orkney and Shetland. [Old Norse *Norrænn*, Norse, from *nordhr*, north.] —**Norn** *adj.*

Norse (norss) *adj. Abbr.* **N.** **1.** Of or pertaining to ancient Scandinavia, its people, or their language. **2. a.** Of or pertaining to West Scandinavia (Norway, Iceland, and the Faeroe Islands) or the languages of its inhabitants. **b.** Of or pertaining to Norway, its people, or their language.

~*n., pl.* **Norse.** *Abbr.* **N.** **1.** *Used with a plural verb.* **a.** The people of Scandinavia; the Scandinavians. **b.** The people of West Scandinavia; especially, the Norwegians. **c.** The ancient Norwegians. **2.** The Scandinavian or North Germanic branch of Germanic languages; especially, Norwegian. **3.** Any of the West Scandinavian languages

or dialects. [Dutch *noor(d)sch*, from *noord*, north, from Middle Dutch *nort.*]

Norse·man (nórss-mən) *n., pl.* **-men** (-mən, -men). Any of the ancient Scandinavians.

north (north) *n. Abbr.* **n, N, n., N., No., Nor. 1. a.** The direction along a meridian to the left of an observer facing in the direction of the earth's rotation; the direction to the left as one faces the rising sun. **b.** The cardinal point on the mariner's compass, located at 0°. **2.** Any area or region lying in this direction. **3.** *Often capital* **N. a.** One of four positions at 90° intervals, that lies in the north, points south, and stands at right angles to east and west. **b.** In games such as bridge or mah-jong, a player who occupies or is said to occupy this position. **4.** *Poetic.* The north wind. **—the North. 1.** The northern or Arctic part of the earth. **2.** The northern part of any country or region, as: **a.** In England, that part of the country lying approximately north of the Humber. **b.** Northern Ireland as distinguished from the Republic of Ireland. **c.** In the United States, the states lying north of Maryland, the Ohio river, and Missouri, and including those that fought for the Union against the Confederacy (or the South) in the Civil War. **3.** The industrialised and technologically advanced nations of the world. Compare **South.**

~*adj.* **1.** To, towards, of, facing, or in the north. **2.** Coming from or originating in the north. Said of a wind. **3.** *Capital* **N.** Officially or conventionally designating the northern part of a country, continent, or other geographical area: *North Korea.*

~*adv.* In, from, or towards the north. [Middle English *north*, Old English *north.*]

North, Frederick, Lord (1732–92). British statesman. A Tory M.P., he became Chancellor of the Exchequer (1767), and, as a favourite of George III, was appointed prime minister (1770). Britain's loss of the American colonies, for which he bore the ultimate responsibility, led to his resignation.

North, Sir Thomas (*c.*1535–1601). English translator. His best-known work, a vivid, poetic translation of Plutarch's *Lives of the Noble Grecians and Romans* (1579), was extensively used as source material by Shakespeare.

North America. A division of the **Americas.** It is the world's third largest continent, and it covers about 13 per cent of the earth's land surface and contains about 6 per cent of the world's population.

North·amp·ton (nawr-thámptən, nər-, nórth-hámptən). County

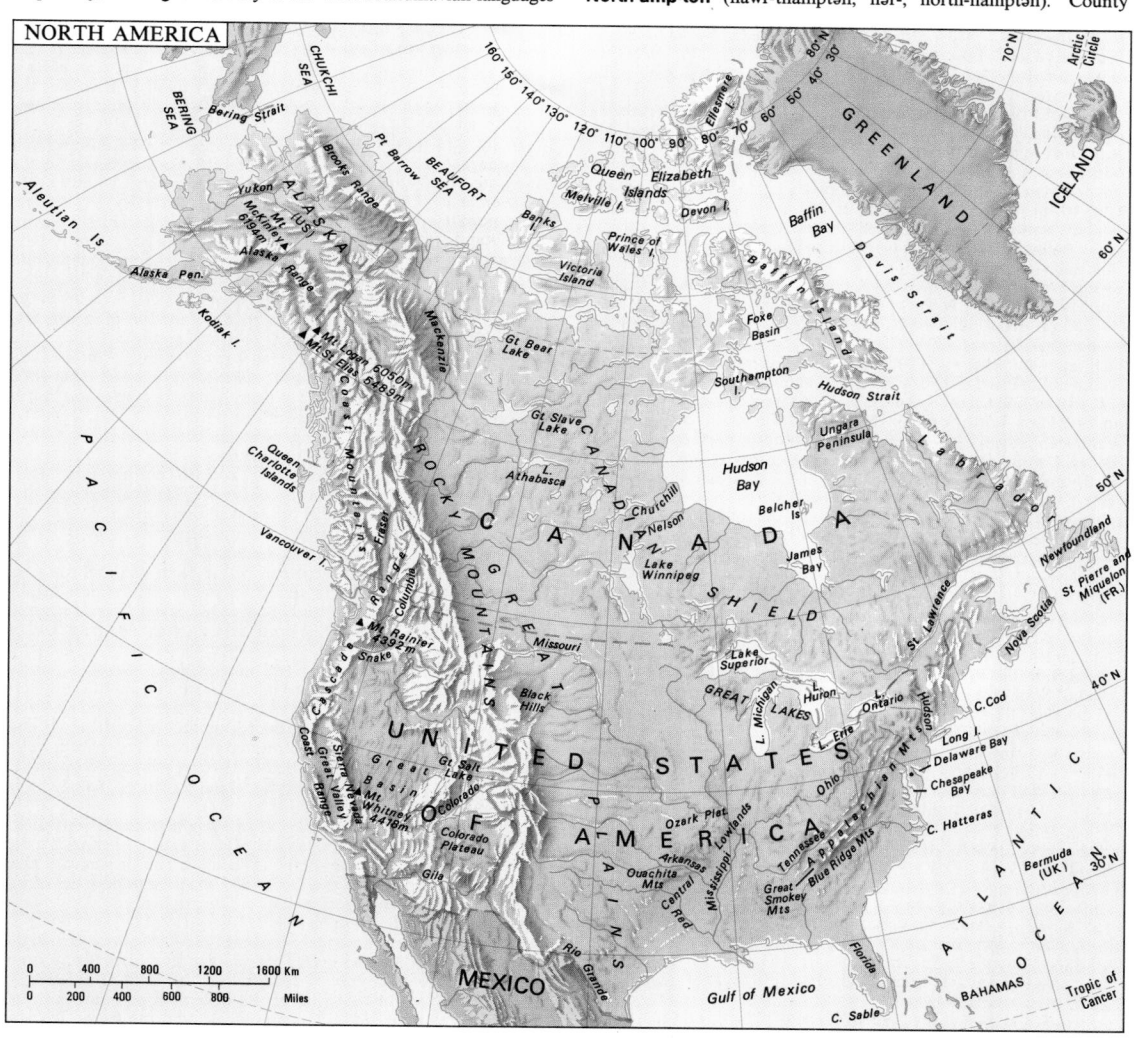

town of Northamptonshire, central England, lying on the river Nene. It has long been one of the country's shoemaking centres and today there is also considerable manufacture of machinery.

North·amp·ton·shire (nawr-thámptən-shər, nər-, nórth-hámptən-, -sheer). County in central England. Most of it consists of gently rolling pasture and woods. Iron ore deposits, now largely worked out, led to the siting of iron and steel works at Corby. The county town is Northampton.

North Atlantic Current n. An ocean current or drift formed southeast of Newfoundland by the junction of the Gulf Stream and the Labrador Current, and flowing generally northeast across the Atlantic. Also called "North Atlantic Drift".

North Atlantic Treaty Organisation n. Abbr. **NATO** (náytō). An alliance for military and naval defence established on April 4, 1949, by countries situated on or near the Atlantic Ocean. The original membership was: Belgium, Canada, Denmark, France (withdrew from some military aspects in 1966, and now has an independent nuclear deterrent), Iceland, Italy, Luxembourg, the Netherlands, Norway, Portugal, the United Kingdom, and the United States. Greece and Turkey joined in 1952 and West Germany in 1955. The headquarters of the organisation is in Brussels.

North Borneo. See **Sabah.**

north·bound (nórth-bownd) adj. Heading towards or leading towards the north.

north by east n. Abbr. **NbE** The direction, or point on a compass, halfway between due north and north-northeast. It is 11° 15' east of due north. —**north by east** adv. & adj.

north by west n. Abbr. **NbW** The direction, or point on a compass, halfway between due north and north-northwest. It is 11° 15' west of due north. —**north by west** adv. & adj.

North Carolina. State on the Atlantic coast of the eastern United States. Since colonial times it has been a tobacco-producing state and it still leads the nation in the production of tobacco, as well as of textiles and furniture. The capital is Raleigh.

north celestial pole n. Astronomy. The **North Pole** (see).

North·cliffe (nórth-klif), **Alfred Charles William Harmsworth, 1st Viscount** (1865–1922). Irish-born British newspaper proprietor. A pioneer of popular journalism in the United Kingdom, he founded the Daily Mirror (1903), and with his brother, Viscount Rothermere, founded the Daily Mail (1896), the first daily paper to achieve a circulation of one million.

North Country n. The north of England. Preceded by the. —**North· coun·try·man** (nórth-kúntrimən) n.

North Dakota. State in the north central United States, lying on the border with Canada. One of the most rural states in the Union, its only industries of importance are connected with food processing. The leading products are wheat, cattle, oil, and natural gas. The capital is Bismarck.

north·east (nórth-éest; nautical nór-) n. Abbr. **NE 1.** The direction, or point on a compass, halfway between north and east. It is 45° east of due north. **2.** Any area or region lying in this direction. —**the Northeast.** In England, that part of the country approximately comprising Northumberland, Durham, and neighbouring areas.

~adj. **1.** Situated towards, facing, or in the northeast. **2.** Coming from or originating in the northeast. Said of a wind.

~adv. In, from, or towards the northeast. —**north·east·ern** adj. —**north·east·ern·er** n.

northeast by east n. Abbr. **NEbE** The direction, or point on a compass, halfway between northeast and east-northeast. It is 56° 15' east of due north. —**northeast by east** adv. & adj.

northeast by north n. Abbr. **NEbN** The direction, or point on a compass, halfway between northeast and north-northeast. It is 33° 45' east of due north. —**northeast by north** adv. & adj.

north·east·er (nórth-éestər; nautical nór-) n. Also **nor'east·er** (nor-e-'éstər). A storm or gale from the northeast.

north·east·er·ly (nórth-éestərli; nautical nór-) adj. **1.** Towards or in the northeast. **2.** From the northeast.

~n., pl. **easterlies.** A storm or wind from the northeast. —**north·east·er·ly** adv.

Northeast Passage. Sea route between the Atlantic and Pacific oceans along the northern coast of Europe and Asia. It was first traversed by Nils Nordenskjöld of Sweden (1878–79). Since the establishment of the Northern Sea Route (a shipping lane) by the U.S.S.R. in the 1930s, the passage has largely been controlled by a fleet of Soviet ice-breakers which keep the passage open from June to October.

north·east·ward (nórth-éestwərd; nautical nór-) adj. Situated towards or facing the northeast.

~n. **1.** A direction or point towards the northeast. **2.** A region or part situated in or towards the northeast.

~adv. Chiefly U.S. Variant of **northeastwards.** —**north·east·ward· ly** adj. & adv.

north·east·wards (nórth-éestwərdz) adv. Also chiefly U.S. **northeastward.** Towards the northeast.

north·er (nórthər) n. U.S. A sudden, cold gale from the north, especially around the Gulf of Mexico. The norther may reach a speed of 100 kilometres (about 60 miles) per hour.

north·er·ly (nórthərli) adj. **1.** Situated in or towards the north. **2.** From the north. Said of a wind.

~n., pl. **northerlies.** A storm or wind from the north. —**north·er·ly** adv.

north·ern (nórthərn) adj. Abbr. **n, n., N, N. 1.** Situated towards, in,

or facing the north. **2.** Coming from the north. Said of a wind. **3.** Growing in the north. **4.** Often capital **N.** Of, pertaining to, or characteristic of northern regions or the North. **5.** Astronomy. North of the celestial equator. [Middle English northerne, Old English northerne.]

Northern Cross n. A cross formed by six stars in the constellation **Cygnus** (see).

Northern Crown n. A constellation, **Corona Borealis** (see).

north·ern·er (nórthərnər) n. **1.** A native or inhabitant of the north. **2.** Often capital **N.** A native or inhabitant of the north of England or of the northeastern United States.

Northern Hemisphere n. The half of the earth lying north of the equator.

Northern Ireland. Province of the United Kingdom consisting of 6 of the counties in the ancient Irish province of Ulster, by which name it is often inaccurately known. Mostly low-lying, it rises to the Sperrin Mountains in the northwest, and the Mourne Mountains in the southeast. Lough Neagh, Ireland's largest lake, is in the centre of the province. Its traditional industries, shipbuilding and linen, have been in decline since World War II. Attempts by successive British governments to revive its economy have been hampered by the state of near civil war that has existed since 1969 between Protestant and Roman Catholic extremists. Its unemployment rate is the highest in the United Kingdom. Until 1972, when all powers were transferred to Westminster, the province had its own semiautonomous parliament which sat at Stormont near Belfast, the capital and chief port.

northern lights pl.n. The **aurora borealis** (see).

north·ern·most (nórthərn-mōst) adj. Farthest north.

Northern Rhodesia. See **Zambia.**

Northern Territory. Territory in north central Australia, with a coastline along the Timor Sea, the Arafura Sea, and the Gulf of Carpentaria. The chief economic activity is stock-breeding, although exploitation of the region's mineral resources—gold, uranium, bauxite, iron, lead, and zinc—is increasing. The territory was formerly part of New South Wales (1825–63) and South Australia (1863–1911), but since 1911 it has been ruled directly by the Commonwealth of Australia and is now in the process of becoming a fully fledged state. The capital and largest town is Darwin.

North Germanic n. A branch of the Germanic group of languages, which includes Danish, Faeroese, Icelandic, Norwegian, and Swedish. See **Germanic.** —**North Germanic** adj.

North Holland. Province of the Netherlands, occupying the peninsula between the North Sea and the IJsselmeer. It also includes a number of the West Frisian islands. The capital is Haarlem, the largest city, Amsterdam. A region of low-lying fenland, it is now largely a manufacturing area.

north·ing (nór-thing, -thing) n. In navigation: **1.** The difference in latitude between two positions as a result of a movement to the north. **2.** Progress towards the north. **3.** Astronomy. A north declination.

North Island. The northern of the two main islands which make up New Zealand. It is the smaller of the two, but the more heavily populated. The main cities are Wellington, the national capital, and Auckland. Most of New Zealand's dairy farming is carried out here.

north·land (nórth-lənd ‖ -land) n. **1.** Often capital **N.** A region in the north, such as the northern part of the earth or of a country. **2.** Capital **N.** Norway and Sweden. —**north·land·er** n.

North·man (nórth-mən) n., pl. -**men** (-mən, -men). A Norseman.

north-north-east (nórth-nórth-éest; nautical nór-nór-). n. Abbr. **NNE** The direction, or point on a compass, halfway between due north and northeast. It is 22° 30' east of due north.

~adj. Situated towards, facing, or in this direction.

~adv. In, from, or towards this direction.

north-north-west (nórth-nórth-wést; nautical nór-nór-) n. Abbr. **NNW** The direction, or point on a compass, halfway between due north and northwest. It is 22° 30' west of due north.

~adj. Situated towards, facing, or in this direction.

~adv. In, from, or towards this direction.

North Pole n. **1.** The northern end of the earth's axis of rotation. **2.** The celestial zenith of this terrestrial point, slightly more than 1 degree from Polaris, the North Star. Also called "north celestial pole". **3.** Small n, small p. The north-seeking **magnetic pole** (see) of a magnet.

North Rhine-West·pha·li·a (rín-wést-fáyli-ə). German **Nord·rhein-West·fa·len** (nórt-rīn-vest-faʼalən). State in western West Germany, lying in the lower Rhine basin. It is a densely populated and extensively industrialised state, the region known as the Ruhr district being the most highly concentrated industrial complex in western Europe. The state was created in 1946 by merging Westphalia, Lippe, and the northern part of the Rhine province. The capital is Düsseldorf.

North Sea. Arm of the Atlantic Ocean, lying between Great Britain and northwest Europe, connected to the English Channel by the Strait of Dover. Long the source of valuable fish, it gained a new economic importance in the late 1960s when large deposits of oil and natural gas were discovered under its sea bed.

North Star n. A star, **Polaris** (see).

North·um·ber·land (nawr-thúmbərlənd, nər-). County in northeastern England, bordering on Scotland and the North Sea. It is an almost entirely rural county, having lost Newcastle (formerly the county town) and Tynemouth to the new metropolitan county of Tyne and Wear in 1974. The county includes the Farne Islands, with their large bird sanctuary. Sheep-farming is the predominant agricultural activity. The county is especially rich in remains of medieval military architecture and the Roman wall is well preserved from Heddon-on-the-Wall to the Cumbria border.

Northumberland, John Dudley, Earl of Warwick and Duke of (1502–53). English politician. He was regent to Edward VI, and tried to prevent the accession of the Catholic Mary Tudor by persuading Edward to name his daughter-in-law, Lady Jane Grey, his heir. The strategy failed however, and after Mary's accession (1553), he and Lady Jane were executed for treason.

North·um·bri·a (nawr-thúmbri-ə). Kingdom of Anglo-Saxon England, extending from eastern Scotland to the east riding of Yorkshire. It was settled by Angles early in the sixth century and originally consisted of two kingdoms, Bernicia and Deira, which were separated by the river Tees. The two kingdoms were united by Aethelfrith of Bernicia early in the seventh century and shortly thereafter Northumbria became the most powerful kingdom in the country. During the late seventh century the power of Northumbria waned as that of Mercia grew.

North·um·bri·an (nawr-thúmbri-ən) *adj.* **1.** Of or pertaining to Northumbria or its dialect. **2.** Of or pertaining to Northumberland. ~*n.* **1.** A native of Northumbria or Northumberland. **2. a.** The Old English dialect of Northumbria. **b.** The Modern English dialect of Northumberland.

north·ward (nórthwərd; *nautical* nórthərd) *adj.* Situated towards, facing, or in the north. ~*n.* **1.** A direction or point towards the north. **2.** A region situated in or towards the north. ~*adv. Chiefly U.S.* Variant of **northwards.** —**north·ward·ly** *adj.* & *adv.*

north·wards (nórth-wərdz) *adv. Also chiefly U.S.* **northward.** Towards the north.

north·west (nórth-wést; *Nautical* nór-) *n. Abbr.* **NW 1.** The direction, or point on a compass, halfway between north and west. It is 45° of due north. **2.** Any area or region lying in this direction. —**the Northwest.** The northwestern part of England, especially the Lake District and Lancashire. ~*adj.* **1.** To, towards, of, facing, or in the northwest. **2.** Coming from or originating in the northwest. Said of a wind. ~*adv.* In, from, or towards the northwest. —**north·west·ern** *adj.*

northwest by north *n. Abbr.* **NWbN** The direction, or point on a compass, halfway between northwest and north-northwest. It is 33° 45′ west of due north. —**northwest by north** *adv.* & *adj.*

northwest by west *n. Abbr.* **NWbW** The direction, or point on a compass, halfway between northwest and west-northwest. It is 56° 15′ west of due north. —**northwest by west** *adv.* & *adj.*

north·west·er (nórth-wéstər; *nautical* nór-) *n.* Also **nor'west·er** (nor-wéstər). A storm or gale from the north west.

north·west·er·ly (nórth-wéstərli; *nautical* nór-) *adj.* **1.** Towards or in the northwest. **2.** From the northwest. ~*n., pl.* **westerlies.** A storm or wind from the northwest. —**north·west·er·ly** *adv.*

North-West Frontier Province. Province of northwest Pakistan, bordering on Afghanistan to the north and west. It is a largely mountainous area, with agriculture practised in the fertile valleys. The chief product is wheat. Historically of great importance because of its proximity to the Khyber Pass, the region came under British control in 1849; it remained British until 1947 when the people of the province voted to become part of newly independent Pakistan. The capital is Peshawar.

Northwest Passage. Northern sea route joining the Atlantic and Pacific oceans, through the Canadian Arctic Archipelago and the waters north of Alaska. The first explorations were undertaken by Sir Martin Frobisher (1576–78); proof of the existence of the passage was obtained by the early 19th century, but the first expedition actually to navigate the whole of the route was led by Roald Amundsen (1903–06). The first commercial ship to cross the passage was the U.S. oil tanker, the S.S. *Manhattan* (1969).

Northwest Semitic *n.* A subgroup of the Semitic family of languages, consisting of Canaanite and Aramaic.

Northwest Territories. Territory in northwest Canada, lying between the Yukon to the west and Hudson Bay to the east, and extending north from the borders of the Prairie Provinces to include the Arctic Archipelago. In all, the Territories occupy one third of Canada's area. Only the extreme south is outside the permafrost area and the region is sparsely populated, mostly by Indians, Eskimos, and Metis. Fur-trading and fishing are the traditional economic activities of the region, but mining is now by far the most important source of wealth. The capital is Yellowknife.

north·west·ward (nórth-wéstwərd; *nautical* nór-) *adj.* Situated towards, facing, or in the northwest. ~*n.* **1.** A direction or point towards the northwest. **2.** A region or part situated in or towards the northwest. ~*adv. Chiefly U.S.* Variant of **northwestwards.** —**north·west·ward·ly** *adj.* & *adv.*

north·west·wards (nórth-wést-wərdz) *adv. Also chiefly U.S.* **northwestward.** Towards the northwest.

North Yorkshire. County in northeastern England, created in 1974 from the rural parts of the North Riding of the former county of Yorkshire. It also includes some parts of the former East and West Ridings. The major towns in the county are York, Harrogate, and Scarborough.

Norw. Norway; Norwegian.

Nor·way, Kingdom of (nór-way). *Norwegian* **Nor·ge** (-gə). Independent kingdom of northern Europe, occupying the western coastland of the Scandinavian peninsula. Most of the country consists of a mountainous plateau unsuited to agriculture; only about three per cent of the land is cultivated. Fishing, timber, and shipbuilding have traditionally been the mainstays of the economy. Now an industrial country, Norway relies on exports of natural gas and petroleum (discovered in the North Sea in the 1960s), aluminium, iron and steel, chemicals, wood products, and fish, and on shipping. At various times united with Sweden and Denmark from the 14th century, Norway finally gained its independence in 1905. Area, 324 219 square kilometres (125,182 square miles). Population, 4,100,000. Capital, Oslo.

Norway lobster *n.* A slender, edible, European lobster of the genus *Nephrops.*

Norway maple *n.* A tall Eurasian tree, *Acer platanoides,* with pale green, palmately lobed leaves. [First cultivated in NORWAY.]

Norway pout *n.* A small greenish fish, *Trisopterus esmarkii,* found in the northeast Atlantic. It is important in the diet of several food fish, such as cod and haddock. Also called "pout".

Norway rat *n.* The **brown rat** *(see).*

Norway spruce *n.* A tall evergreen tree, *Picea abies,* of northern regions, growing up to 46 metres (150 feet) in height and having long, dark green needles. It is commonly used as a Christmas tree.

Nor·we·gian (nawr-wéejən) *n. Abbr.* **Nor., Norw. 1.** A native or inhabitant of Norway. **2.** The North Germanic language of the Norwegians. See **Bokmål, Nynorsk.** —**Nor·we·gian** *adj.*

Norwegian elkhound *n.* An **elkhound** *(see).*

nor'west·er (nór-wéstər) *n.* **1.** Variant of **northwester. 2.** A drink of strong spirits. **3.** An oilskin hat, a **sou'wester** *(see).*

Nor·wich (nórrij, nórrich). County town of Norfolk, east central England, lying on the river Wensum just above its confluence with the Yare. An important provincial centre since the rise of the wool trade in the high Middle Ages, Norwich is now a market city and the site of the University of East Anglia (founded 1963).

nos., Nos. numbers.

nose

THE TWO FUNCTIONS OF THE NOSE
Protecting the lungs and picking up scents

The nose has a dual function. It is both the organ of smell and one of the entrances to the respiratory tract. Its purpose is to warm, moisten, and filter air passing through it, in order to protect the lungs. Bones and cartilage form it, and the septum that divides it into two nostrils. In the skull behind the nose are a number of cavities, called paranasal cavities, which are linked and open into the nasal cavity. Like the nasal passages themselves, they are lined with a mucous membrane in which cells secrete mucus – a lubricating and moistening fluid.

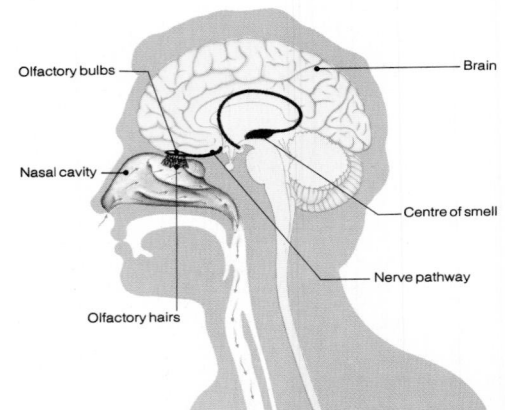

Olfactory bulbs — Brain

Nasal cavity — Centre of smell

Nerve pathway

Olfactory hairs

DETECTING SMELL *Sense of smell begins in a patch of tissue at the top of the nasal passage. Thousands of brush-shaped receptors are located there on olfactory bulbs. Nerve fibres lead directly from the olfactory bulbs, carrying the impulses about scent along a pathway to the centre in the brain where they are interpreted as different odours.*

nose (nōz) *n.* **1.** In humans and other primates, the part of the face bearing the nostrils and containing the organ of smell and the beginning of the respiratory tract. **2.** In many other animals, a similar feature or organ in the face, muzzle, snout, or front end. **3. a.** The sense of smell: *a dog with a good nose.* **b.** The ability to detect or discover, as if by smell: *a nose for a good story.* **4.** An aroma or bouquet, as of wine or tea, for example. **5.** *Informal.* The nose as a symbol of prying: *Keep your nose out of my business.* **6.** Anything that resembles a nose because of shape or position, such as the forward part of an aircraft. **7.** *Slang.* A police informer. **—by a nose.** In horse racing, by the length of a horse's nose, considered as a narrow margin of victory. **—follow (one's) nose. 1.** To go straight ahead. **2.** To be guided by instinct. **—keep (one's) nose clean.** *Informal.* To keep out of trouble. **—lead by the nose.** To control (someone) completely, often humiliatingly, without his perceiving it. **—look down (one's) nose at.** *Informal.* To treat haughtily. **—on the nose.** *Slang.* **1.** *U.S.* Designating a bet on a horse to win. **2.** *Chiefly U.S.* Exactly; precisely. **3.** *Australian.* Bad; foul-smelling. **—pay through the nose.** *Informal.* To pay an exorbitant price. **—put (someone's) nose out of joint.** To displease by supplanting. **—turn up (one's) nose at.** To treat with contempt. **~v. nosed, nosing, noses. —tr. 1.** To find out by or as if by smell. **2.** To touch or examine with the nose; nuzzle. **3.** To steer (a vehicle or one's way) with care to avoid a collision. **~intr. 1.** To smell or sniff. **2.** *Informal.* To pry from curiosity or in a meddlesome way. Followed by *around*, *about*, or *into*. **3.** To move forward slowly and carefully. **—nose out. 1.** To find by persistent searching. **2.** To defeat by a very narrow margin. [Middle English *nose*, Old English *nosu.*]

nose-bag (nōz-bag) *n.* A bag containing feed that fits over a horse's muzzle. Also *U.S.* "feedbag".

nose-band (nōz-band) *n.* The part of a bridle or halter that passes over the animal's nose. Also called "nosepiece".

nose-bleed (nōz-bleed) *n.* A nasal haemorrhage; bleeding from the nose. Also called "epistaxis".

nose cone *n.* The front, usually separable, section of a rocket or guided missile, shaped to offer minimum aerodynamic resistance and often bearing a heat-resistant cladding.

nose dive *n.* **1.** A sudden plunge of an aircraft with its nose towards the earth. **2.** Any sudden, swift, downward plunge or drop.

nose-dive (nōz-dīv) *intr.v.* **-dived** or *U.S.* **-dove** (-dōv), **-diving, -dives.** To perform a nose dive.

nose-gay (nōz-gay) *n.* A small bunch of flowers. [Middle English : NOSE (fragrance) + *gay,* toy, ornament, from GAY (adjective).]

nose-piece (nōz-peess) *n.* **1.** A piece of armour forming part of a helmet and serving as a guard for the nose. **2.** The bridge of a pair of glasses. **3.** Part of a bridle, a noseband. **4.** The part of a microscope, often rotatable, to which one or more objective lenses are attached.

nose wheel *n.* The landing wheel fitted below the nose of an aircraft.

nosh (nosh) *n.* *Informal.* Food; a snack or meal.
~intr.v. noshed, noshing, noshes. *Informal.* To eat. [Yiddish, from *nosherai,* titbits, from Old High German *(h)nascōn,* to gnaw, nibble.]

no-show (nō-shō) *n.* *U.S. Slang.* A traveller who reserves a place, especially on an aircraft, but neither claims nor cancels the reservation before the time of departure.

nosh-up (nosh-up) *n. British Slang.* A large, hearty meal.

no side *n.* In Rugby football, the signal or announcement by the referee that the game has finished.

nos-ing (nōzing) *n.* **1.** The horizontally projecting edge of a stair tread. **2.** A shield covering this edge. **3.** A projecting edge of a moulding.

noso- *comb. form.* Indicates disease; for example, **nosology.** [Greek, from *nosos†,* a disease.]

no-sog-ra-phy (no-sóggrəfi, nō-) *n.* The written systematisation and description of diseases. [New Latin *nosographia* : NOSO- + -GRAPHY.] **—no-sog-ra-pher** *n.* **—no-so-graph-ic** (nóssə-gráffik, nō-sə-), **no-so-graph-i-cal** *adj.*

no-sol-o-gy (no-sólləji, nō-) *n.* The branch of medicine that deals with the naming and classification of diseases. [New Latin *nosologia* : NOSO- + -LOGY.] **—no-so-log-i-cal** (nóssə-lójik'l, nō-sə-) *adj.* **—no-so-log-i-cal-ly** *adv.* **—no-sol-o-gist** (-sólləjist) *n.*

nos-tal-gi-a (no-stál-jə, -ji-ə ‖ nə-; *U.S. also* nō-, -staál-) *n.* **1.** A wistful or sentimental longing for things, persons, or situations that are past and irrevocable. **2.** Homesickness. [New Latin (translation of German *Heimweh,* homesickness) : Greek *nostos,* a return + -ALGIA.] **—nos-tal-gic** *adj.* **—nos-tal-gic-al-ly** *adv.*

nos-toc (nóstok) *n.* Any freshwater blue-green alga of the genus *Nostoc,* forming colonies of filaments with a gelatinous covering. [New Latin; coined by Paracelsus as a name for algae that he believed were derived from starlight.]

Nos-tra-da-mus (nóstrə-daáməss, -dáyməss), born Michel de Nostre-Dame (1503–66). French astrologer and physician. He was court physician to Charles IX, but is best known for his book of prophecies, *Centuries* (1555), written in quatrains.

nos-tril (nóss-trəl, -tril) *n.* Either of the external openings of the nose. [Middle English *nostrill,* Old English *nosthyrl* : *nosu,* NOSE + *thyrl, thyrel,* hole.]

nos-trum (nóstrəm) *n., pl.* **-trums. 1.** A patent medicine, or one in which the ingredients are kept secret; especially, a quack remedy. **2.** A pet scheme for the solution of some problem. [New Latin *nostrum,* "our own" (that is, invented and made by the seller), from Latin, neuter of *noster,* ours.]

nos-y, nos-ey (nōzi) *adj.* **-ier, -iest.** *Informal.* Prying; inquisitive. See Synonyms at **curious.** [From NOSE.] **—nos-i-ly** *adv.* **—nos-i-ness** *n.*

nosy parker *n.* *Chiefly British Informal.* A person who pries into other people's affairs. [Arbitrary use of surname *Parker.*]

not (not) *adv.* In no way; to no degree. Used to express negation, denial, refusal, disbelief, or prohibition: *Definitely not; I will not go; You may not have any.* In informal speech and writing, *not* is often contracted and suffixed to auxiliary verbs, for example, *aren't, don't.* **—not at all.** You do not need to thank me. Used as a polite reply when one has been thanked. **—not that.** Although it is not to be supposed that: *She denies everything—not that I believe her.* [Middle English *not,* reduced form of *nought,* nothing, not, Old English *nōwiht, nāwiht* : *nō, nā,* no + *wiht,* a man, thing.]

not-. Variant of **noto-.**

no-ta be-ne (nōtə bénni, béeni; *also* nōtaa báynay). *Abbr.* **n.b., N.B.** *Latin.* Note well.

no-ta-bil-i-ty (nōtə-bílləti) *n., pl.* **-ties. 1.** The state or quality of being notable. **2.** A notable or prominent person.

no-ta-ble (nōtəb'l) *adj.* **1.** Worthy of notice; remarkable; striking: *a notable beauty.* **2.** *Archaic & Regional.* Diligent, especially in household management.
~n. 1. A person of note or distinction. **2.** *Often capital* **N.** Any of a council of prominent persons, before the French Revolution, called into assembly by the king at times of emergency. [Middle English, from Old French, from Latin *notābilis,* from *notāre,* to note, from *nota,* a NOTE.] **—no-ta-ble-ness** *n.* **—no-ta-bly** *adv.*

no-tar-i-al (nō-taúr-i-əl) *adj.* **1.** Of or pertaining to a notary. **2.** Executed or drawn up by a notary. **—no-tar-i-al-ly** *adv.*

no-ta-rise, no-ta-rize (nōtə-rīz) *tr.v.* **-rised, -rising, -rises.** *Chiefly U.S.* To authenticate or attest as a notary. [From NOTARY.] **—no-ta-ri-sa-tion** (-rī-záysh'n ‖ *U.S.* -ri-) *n.*

no-ta-ry (nōtəri) *n., pl.* **-ries. 1.** A notary public. **2.** *Obsolete.* A clerk; especially, one licensed to draft legal documents. [Middle English *notarie,* "clerk", from Latin *notārius,* "stenographer", from *notārius,* cipher, shorthand character, from *nota,* mark, NOTE.]

notary public *n., pl.* **notaries public.** *Abbr.* **N.P.** A public officer authorised by law to certify documents, take affidavits, and administer oaths. Also called "notary".

no-tate (nō-táyt ‖ *chiefly U.S.* nō-tayt) *tr.v.* **-tated, -tating, -tates.** To represent (music, for example) in notation. [Back-formation from NOTATION.]

no·ta·tion (nō-táysh'n) *n.* **1.** A system of figures or symbols used in specialised fields to represent numbers, quantities, or other facts or values: *musical notation.* **2.** The act or process of using such a system. **3.** *U.S.* A jotting or annotation; a note: *a notation in the margin.* [Latin *notātiō* (stem *notātiōn-*), from *notāre,* to note, from *nota,* a NOTE.] **—no·ta·tion·al** *adj.*

notch (noch) *n.* **1.** A V-shaped cut, especially one used for keeping count. **2.** *U.S.* A narrow pass between mountains. **3.** *Informal.* A level or degree: *She is a notch better than her brother.* **4.** The undercutting of a cliff at high-water level, producing an indentation at its base.

~*tr.v.* **notched, notching, notches. 1.** To cut a notch or notches in. **2.** To record by or as if by making notches: *notched the score on a stick.* **3.** *Informal.* To score. Often used with *up*: *She notched up three wins in succession.* [Anglo-French *noche*†.]

note (nōt) *n. Abbr.* **n. 1.** *Often plural.* A brief record of something, written down to aid the memory. **2.** A brief written communication. **3.** A formal written diplomatic or official communication. **4.** A commentary to or explanation of a passage in a text, printed in the margin, at the foot of the page, or at the end of the text. **5. a.** A piece of paper currency. **b.** A certificate issued by a government or a bank and sometimes negotiable as money. **c.** A **promissory note** *(see).* **6.** *Music.* **a.** A musical sound of definite pitch. **b.** The symbol of such a note in musical notation, indicating the pitch by its position on the staff and the duration by details of its appearance such as shape. **c.** A key of a piano or similar instrument. **7. a.** The musical call of a bird. **b.** Any expressive vocal sound, such as the cry or call of an animal. **8.** A tone, sign, or suggestion that reveals or characterises a quality, mood, or atmosphere; a mark: *a note of gaiety.* **9.** Importance or consequence: *Nothing of note happened.* **10.** Notice or observation: *We took note of what had happened.* **11.** *Poetic.* A song, melody, or tune. **—compare notes.** To exchange ideas, views, or opinions.

~*tr.v.* **noted, noting, notes. 1.** To observe carefully; notice; perceive. **2.** To write down; make a note of. **3.** To show; indicate. **4.** To make particular mention of; remark. [Middle English *note,* from Old French, from Latin *nota,* mark, sign, cipher, shorthand character.] **—not·er** *n.*

note·book (nōt-bo͝ok || -bo͝ok) *n.* A small book for writing notes in.

note·case (nōt-kayss) *n.* A slim flat wallet designed to hold paper money.

not·ed (nōtid) *adj.* Distinguished by reputation; notable; eminent: *a noted author.* **—not·ed·ly** *adv.* **—not·ed·ness** *n.*

note·let (nōt-lət, -lit) *n.* A folded card, usually with decorative illustration, for writing short informal letters.

note of hand *n.* A **promissory note** *(see).*

note·pap·er (nōt-paypər) *n.* Paper for writing letters on; writing paper.

note row *n. Music.* A **tone row** *(see).*

note·wor·thy (nōt-wurthi) *adj.* Deserving recognition; worthy of notice; remarkable: *a noteworthy young talent.* **—note·wor·thi·ly** *adv.* **—note·wor·thi·ness** *n.*

NOT gate (not) *n. Computing.* A logic gate that provides an output signal if the input signal is low and vice versa. Also called "inverter", "negator", "NOT circuit". [From NOT, since the gate's function is comparable to the operation of *not* in logic.]

noth·ing (núth-ing || *Northern England also* nóth-). *n.* **1.** No thing; not anything. **2.** No significant or notable thing: *There is nothing on television tonight.* **3.** No part; no portion: *Nothing remains of its former glory.* **4.** Insignificance; obscurity: *rising from nothing.* **5.** Absence of anything perceptible; non-existence: *The sound faded into nothing.* **6.** That which has no qualitative value or positive effect: *amount to nothing.* **7.** A zero; a nought. **8.** A person or thing of no consequence or significance. **9.** *Plural.* An affectionate word or remark: *sweet nothings.* **—for nothing.** Free of charge; gratis. **—have (got) nothing on. 1.** To be naked. **2.** To have no social engagements or obligations. **3.** To be markedly inferior in comparison to. **—have (got) nothing on (one).** To have no money on one's person. **—have (got) nothing on (someone).** To have no incriminatory evidence against. **—look like nothing on earth.** To appear ugly or outlandish. **—make nothing of.** To be unable to understand or cope with. **—nothing but.** Only; no other than. **—nothing doing.** *Informal.* **1.** Certainly not. Used as an emphatic refusal. **2.** Nothing of interest happening; not a thing going on. **—nothing for it.** No other course of action is possible. **—nothing like. 1.** Not at all like: *She's nothing like her sister.* **2.** Not nearly: *The blizzard here was nothing like as heavy as it was up north.* **—nothing short of.** No less than; tantamount to. **—nothing to it.** It is quite straightforward.

~*adj. Slang.* Insignificant or unimportant: *a nothing job.*

~*adv.* In no way or degree; not at all: *nothing daunted.* [Middle English *nathing, nothing,* Old English *nāthing, nān thing* : *nān,* NONE + THING.]

noth·ing·ness (núth-ing-nəss, -niss || *Northern England also* nóth-) *n.* **1.** The condition or quality of being nothing; non-existence. **2.** Empty or featureless space; the void. **3.** Lack of consequence; insignificance. **4.** Something inconsequential or insignificant.

no·tice (nōtiss) *n.* **1.** The act of observing or regarding with the senses; perception; attention: *That detail escaped my notice.* **2.** Heed or attention paid to another person or thing; especially, respectful attention or consideration: *grateful for the notice you took.* **3.** A formal written announcement, published or displayed for all to see: *a notice of sale.* **4. a.** A formal announcement of purpose, especially of intention to withdraw from an agreement or leave a job: *give two weeks' notice.* **b.** Notification of dismissal from a job. **5.** A printed critical review of a play, book, or other cultural work. **6.** Any announcement of some present or coming event.

~*v.* **noticed, -ticing, -tices.** —*tr.* **1.** To observe; perceive; be aware of: *She did not notice the child in the doorway.* **2.** To consider; take note of; mark: *notice the discrepancy.* **3.** To comment on; mention in passing: *She began her speech by noticing the size of the audience.* **4.** To treat with courteous attention. —*intr. Nonstandard.* To show; be evident: *The stain won't notice.* [Middle English *notyce,* from Old French *notice,* from Latin *nōtitia,* knowledge, acquaintance, from *nōtus,* known, from the past participle of *nōscere,* to get acquainted with.]

no·tice·a·ble (nōtissəb'l) *adj.* **1.** Readily observed or detected; evident. **2.** Worth noticing; significant. **—no·tice·a·bly** *adv.*

notice board *n. British.* A board on which notices, advertisements, and the like are displayed.

notifiable disease *n.* Any of certain infectious diseases, such as cholera, diphtheria, and tuberculosis, cases of which must be reported to the health authorities.

no·ti·fi·ca·tion (nōtifi-káysh'n) *n.* **1.** The act or an instance of notifying. **2.** The sign, letter, or other form by which notice is given.

no·ti·fy (nōti-fī) *tr.v.* **-fied, -fying, -fies. 1.** To give formal notice to; inform. **2.** *Chiefly British.* To give notice or information of (something); make known; proclaim. [Middle English *notifien,* from Old French *notifier,* from Latin *nōtificāre,* to make known : *nōtus,* known, from *nōscere,* to get acquainted with + *facere,* to make.] **—not·i·fi·a·ble** (-fī-əb'l, -fī-) *adj.* **—no·ti·fi·er** *n.*

no·tion (nōsh'n) *n.* **1.** A general impression or feeling. **2.** A view; a concept; a theory, especially if subjective or mistaken. **3.** *Rare.* Intention or inclination: *"Men's notion was, not for abolishing punishments, but for making laws just"* (Thomas Carlyle). **4.** *Plural. Chiefly U.S.* Small items for household and clothing use, such as needles, buttons, thread, and ribbons. **—See Synonyms at caprice, idea.** [Latin *nōtiō* (stem *nōtiōn-*), "a becoming acquainted", from *nōscere* (past participle *nōtus*), to get acquainted.]

no·tion·al (nōsh'n'l) *adj.* **1.** Of, containing, or being a notion or notions; conceived in the mind rather than actual. **2.** *Linguistics.* **a.** Having full lexical meaning, as distinguished from relational meaning. In the phrase *we did the work,* the verb *did* refers to a real activity (*doing* work), and is therefore notional; in the phrase *we did not agree, did* serves merely as a grammatical marker, and is therefore relational. **b.** Conveying an idea directly to the mind; nonsymbolic. **—no·tion·al·ly** *adv.*

noto-, not-[1] *comb. form.* Indicates south or southern; for example, **notornis.** [New Latin, from Greek *notos,* south, south wind.]

noto-, not-[2] *comb. form.* Indicates back or back part; for example, **notochord.** [Greek *nōton,* the back.]

no·to·chord (nōtə-kawrd) *n.* **1.** A flexible rodlike structure in some lower vertebrates that provides dorsal support; the primitive backbone. **2.** A similar structure in embryos of higher vertebrates, from which the spine develops. [Greek *nōtos,* back + CHORD (cord).]

No·to·gae·a (nōtə-jée-ə) *n.* A zoogeographical region that includes Australia, New Zealand, and the southwestern Pacific islands. Compare **Arctogaea.** [New Latin, "south realm" : NOTO- + Greek *gaia,* land, earth.] **—No·to·gae·al, No·to·gae·an** *adj.*

no·to·ri·e·ty (nōtə-rī-əti) *n.* The quality or condition of being notorious. See Synonyms at **fame.**

no·to·ri·ous (nō-táwri-əs, nə- || -tōri-) *adj.* **1.** Known widely and regarded unfavourably; infamous: *A notorious highwayman.* **2.** Generally known and discussed: *notorious facts.* [Medieval Latin *nōtōrius,* from Late Latin, causing to be known, from *nōtus,* known, from the past participle of *nōscere,* to get acquainted.] **—no·to·ri·ous·ly** *adv.* **—no·to·ri·ous·ness** *n.*

no·tor·nis (nō-tórniss) *n.* Any flightless bird, now rare, of the genus *Notornis,* found in New Zealand. See **takahe.** [New Latin, "bird of the south" (that is, New Zealand) : NOT(O)- + Greek *ornis,* bird.]

no·tour bankrupt (nōtər) *n.* In Scots law, one who has not discharged his debts in the time allowed by the court. [*Notour,* short for NOTORIOUS.]

not proven *adj.* Designating a verdict in Scots law that is returned when there is insufficient evidence available to convict a defendant.

no-trump (nō-trúmp) *n.* Also **no-trumps** (-trúmps). **1.** In bridge and other card games, a declaration to play a hand without a trump suit. **2.** A hand played without a trump suit. **—no-trump** *adj.*

Not·ting·ham (nótting-əm || -həm). Largest city in Nottinghamshire, central England, lying on the river Trent. It has long been a centre for the manufacture of lace and hosiery.

Not·ting·ham·shire (nótting-əm-shər, -sheer || -həm-). County in central England. Most of the land is low-lying and fertile. The rich Nottinghamshire coalfields lie in the west. There are also small oilfields. The county town is Nottingham.

Notts. Nottinghamshire.

not·with·stand·ing (nót-with-stánding, -with-) *prep.* In spite of; regardless of hindrance by: *She left notwithstanding her father's opposition. Her father's opposition notwithstanding, she left.*

~*adv.* All the same; nevertheless: *We proceeded, notwithstanding.*

~*conj.* In spite of the fact that; although. [Middle English *notwithstonding* : NOT + present participle of *withstonden,* to WITHSTAND.]

nou·gat (no͞o-gaa || -gət, núggət) *n.* A confection made from a sweet sugar or honey paste into which nuts, almonds, cherries, and the like are mixed. [French *nougat,* from Provençal, from Old Proven-

PRONUNCIATION KEY

a, trap; aa, father; ai, fair; ar, star; aw, lawn; ay, play; b, bb, stab; rubber; ch, church; ck, ticket; d, dd, dead; ladder; e, dress; ee, bee; er, defer; ew, few; ewr, pure; ə, about; ər, letter; f, ff, fife; differ; g, gg, giggle; h, hat; i, kit; ī, price; īr, fire; j, judge; k, kick; l, ll, let; 'l, needle; m, mm, man; n, nn, no; 'n, sudden; ng, thing; o, lot; ō, no; o͝o, foot; o͞o, shoe; oor, poor; ow, cow; owr, hour; oy, boy; p, pp, pepper; r, rr, red; s, ss, sauce; sh, ship; t, tt, totter; th, thick; th, this; smooth; u, cut; ur, turn; v, vv, valve; w, wet; y, yes; z, zz, zebra; zh, vision; pleasure

IN FOREIGN WORDS:

aN, oN, Saint-Saëns; hl, Llanelli; Hluhluwe; kh, loch; lough; Khaled

STRESS MARK:

ín-sīt, insight; in-sít, incite

çal *nogat*, confection of nuts, from Vulgar Latin *nucātum* (unattested), from Latin *nux* (stem *nuc-*), nut.]

nought (nawt) *n.* Also *chiefly U.S.* **naught.** A zero; the figure 0.

noughts and crosses *n. Used with a singular verb.* A game in which two players fill in a figure of nine squares with alternate noughts or crosses. Also *U.S.* "crisscross", "tick-tack-toe".

nou·me·non (nōō-mi-nən, nów-, -mə-, -non) *n., pl.* **-na** (-nə). In the philosophy of Kant: **1.** An object of purely intellectual intuition, as opposed to an object perceived by the senses. **2.** A thing in itself, independent of sensory or intellectual perception of it. Compare **phenomenon.** [German *Noumenon*, from Greek *noumenon*, concept, thought, from *nouein*, to think, apprehend, from *nous*, mind.] **—nou·me·nal** *adj.* **—nou·me·nal·ism** *n.* **—nou·me·nal·ist** *n.* **—nou·me·nal·ly** *adv.*

noun (nown) *n. Abbr.* **n. 1.** A word used to denote or name a person, place, thing, quality, or act. **2. a.** The part of speech of a word that is the subject or object of a verb, object of a preposition, or an appositive. **b.** Any word, phrase, or clause used in this way. [Middle English *nowne*, from Anglo-French *noun*, Old French *non*, *nom*, from Latin *nōmen*, name.] **—noun, noun·al** *adj.* **—noun·al·ly** *adv.*

nour·ish (núrrish) *tr.v.* **-ished, -ishing, -ishes. 1.** To provide with food or other substances necessary for life and growth. **2.** To foster the development of; promote and sustain: *Freedom nourishes self-respect.* [Middle English *nurishen*, *norishen*, from Old French *norrir* (stem *norriss-*), from Latin *nūtrīre*, to feed.] **—nour·ish·a·ble** *adj.* **—nour·ish·er** *n.* **—nour·ish·ing·ly** *adv.*

nour·ish·ment (núrrishmənt) *n.* **1. a.** The act of nourishing. **b.** The state of being nourished. **2.** That which supports life and growth in a living organism; food; sustenance. **3.** That which promotes the development or vitality of something.

nous (nowss; *for sense 1 also* nōōss) *n.* **1.** *Philosophy.* Mind; reason; specifically, the principle of divine reason. **2.** *British Informal.* Common sense. [Greek.]

nou·veau riche (nōōvō réesh) *n., pl.* **nouveaux riches** (*pronounced as singular*). One who has lately become ostentatiously rich. Usually used derogatorily. [French, "new rich".]

nou·velle vague (nōōvel vaág) *n.* The **New Wave** *(see).* [French.]

Nov. November.

no·va (nṓ-və) *n., pl.* **-vae** (-vee) or **-vas.** *Astronomy.* A variable star that suddenly increases in brightness to several times its normal magnitude, and returns to its original appearance over a period from a few weeks to several months or years. Compare **supernova.** [New Latin (*stella*) *nova*, "new (star)", from Latin *novus*, new.]

no·vac·u·lite (nō-váckew-līt) *n.* A very hard, dense, silica-bearing rock used in whetstones. [Latin *novācula*, razor + -ITE.]

No·va Sco·tia (nṓ-və skṓsha). Easternmost province of mainland Canada, connected to New Brunswick by the Chignecto Isthmus. It also includes Cape Breton Island. Coalmining and fishing are the chief industries, but the Annapolis Valley is also famous for its apple orchards. It was one of the four original provinces in the Canadian confederation (1867). The capital and largest city is Halifax. **—Nova Sco·tian** *adj. & n.*

no·va·tion (nō-váysh'n) *n. Law.* The substitution of a new obligation for an old one; especially, the transference of a debt. [Late Latin *novātiō* (stem *novātiōn-*), a making new, from Latin *novāre*, to make new, from *novus*, new.]

No·va·ya Zem·lya (nṓvə-yə zémli-ə; *Russian* zim-lyá). Largest group of islands in the Eurasian Arctic, lying off the Arctic coast of the U.S.S.R. and belonging to the U.S.S.R. It consists mainly of two large islands, which are continuations of the Ural and Pai-Khoy mountain systems.

nov·el¹ (nóvv'l) *n.* **1.** A fictional prose narrative of considerable length, typically having a plot that is unfolded by the actions, speech, and thoughts of the characters. **2.** The literary genre represented by this form of narrative. [Italian (*storia*) *novella*, a short tale, "new story", from feminine of *novello*, new, from Latin *novellus*, NOVEL.]

novel² *adj.* Strikingly new, unusual, or different. See Usage note at **new.** [Middle English *novel*, from Old French, from Latin *novellus*, from *novus*, new.] **—nov·el·ly** *adv.*

nov·el·ette (nóvv'l-ét) *n.* **1.** A short novel. **2.** A light romantic or trivial novel, usually short and of little literary merit. **3.** A short, lyrical, instrumental piece. **—nov·el·et·tish** (-éttish) *adj.*

nov·el·ise, nov·el·ize (nóvv'l-īz) *tr.v.* **-ised, -ising, -ises. 1.** To turn (facts or a film script, for example) into a novel. **2.** To make novel or new. **—nov·el·i·sa·tion** (-ī-záysh'n ‖ *U.S.* -i-) *n.*

nov·el·ist (nóvv'l-ist) *n.* A writer of novels.

nov·el·is·tic (nóvv'l-ístik) *adj.* Of, pertaining to, or characteristic of novels. **—nov·el·is·ti·cal·ly** *adv.*

no·vel·la (nō-vélla, no-) *n., pl.* **-las** or **-le** (-vélláy). **1.** A short prose tale of the type developed by Boccaccio, characterised by epigrammatic terseness. **2.** A short novel. [Italian. See **novel** (narrative).]

No·vel·lo (nə-véllō), **Ivor,** born David Ivor Davies (1893–1951). Welsh composer, actor-manager, and dramatist. He wrote comedies and musical comedies such as *Glamorous Night* (1935) and *The Dancing Years* (1939), and the patriotic World War I song "Keep the Home Fires Burning".

No·vels (nóvv'lz) *pl., n. Roman Law.* Amendments made by the Emperor Justinian and his successors to the Justinian Code. [New Latin *novella*, singular of Late Latin *novellae* (*constitutiōnes*), "new (statutes)", from Latin *novellus*, new, from *novus*, new.]

nov·el·ty (nóvv'lti) *n., pl.* **-ties. 1.** The quality of being novel; newness; originality. **2.** Something that is novel; a new or unusual

thing; an innovation. **3.** *Plural.* Small mass-produced articles, such as toys or trinkets. [Middle English *noveltee*, from Old French *novelte*, from *novel*, new, NOVEL.]

No·vem·ber (nō-vémbər, nə-) *n. Abbr.* **Nov., N.** The 11th month of the Gregorian calendar. November has 30 days. [Middle English *Novembre*, from Old French, from Latin *Novembris* (*mēnsis*), the ninth (month) (of the Roman calendar), from *novem*, nine.]

no·ve·na (nō-vée-nə) *n., pl.* **-nas** or **-nae** (-nee). *Roman Catholic Church.* A recitation of prayers and devotions over a period of time, usually nine consecutive days. [Medieval Latin *novēna*, from Latin *novēnus*, nine each, from *novem*, nine.]

no·ver·cal (nō-vérk'l) *adj. Rare.* Of, pertaining to, or characteristic of a stepmother. [Latin *novercālis*, from *noverca*, a stepmother.]

Nov·go·rod (nóv-gə-rod; *Russian* -rət). City in the northwestern U.S.S.R., lying on the river Volkhov. It is one of the oldest Russian cities, and during the Middle Ages rose to commercial prosperity owing to its position on one of the major trade routes of eastern Europe. The city's rich architectural heritage was largely destroyed by bombing in World War II, but much has since been restored.

nov·ice (nóvviss) *n.* **1.** A person new to any field or activity; a beginner. **2.** A person who has entered a religious order, but who is on probation before taking final vows. Compare **postulant. 3.** *Sports.* **a.** A competitor who has not previously won a race or reached a certain standard. **b.** A racehorse that has yet to win a certain number of races. [Middle English *novyce*, from Old French *novice*, from Medieval Latin *novīcius*, from Latin *novīcius*, extension of *novus*, new.]

no·vi·ti·ate, no·vi·ci·ate (nō-víshi-ət, nə-, -it, -ayt) *n.* **1.** *Ecclesiastical.* **a.** The period of time served by a novice. **b.** A place where novices live. **c.** A novice. **2.** The state or time of being a beginner. **3.** A beginner. [French *noviciat*, from Medieval Latin *novīciātus*, from *novīcius*, NOVICE.]

No·vo·caine (nṓ-və-kayn, -vō-) *n.* A trademark for the anaesthetic **procaine hydrochloride** *(see).*

No·vo·cas·tri·an (nō-vō-kástri-ən, -və-) *n.* A native or inhabitant of Newcastle. **—No·vo·cas·tri·an** *adj.*

now (now) *adv.* **1.** At the present time. **2.** At once; immediately: *Stop now.* **3.** In the immediate past; very recently. Often preceded by *just: She left just now.* **4.** At this point in a series of events; then: *The ship was now listing to port.* **5.** Nowadays. **6.** In these circumstances; as things are: *Now we won't be able to stay.* **7. a.** Used to introduce a statement or question: *Now, what do you think?* **b.** Used in commands to add emphasis: *Now be a good boy. Hurry up, now!* **—now and again** or **then.** Occasionally. ~*conj.* Since. Often followed by *that: Now that we have eaten, let's go.* ~*n.* The present time or moment: *Now is the time to act.* ~*adj.* **1.** *Informal.* Of the present time; current: *the now generation.* **2.** *Slang.* In tune with the latest trends; with-it. ~*interj.* Used: **1.** To express mild rebuke. **2.** To soothe or placate. [Middle English *nu, now*, Old English *nū.*]

now·a·days (nów-ə-dayz) *adv.* In these days; at the present time. [Middle English *now a dayes*, "on this day" : NOW + *a dayes*, Old English *on dæges* (adverbial genitive) : ON + DAY.]

no way *adv. Informal.* Not at all; absolutely not. ~*interj. Informal.* Used to express emphatic refusal.

no·way (nṓ-way) *adv.* Also *chiefly U.S.* **noways** (nṓ-wayz). Nowise; certainly not.

no·where (nṓ-wair, -hwair) *adv.* In, to, or at no place; not anywhere. ~*n.* **1.** No place; a non-existent or insignificant place. **2.** An insignificant or obscure position: *came from nowhere to win the election.*

no·wise (nṓ-wīz) *adv.* In no way, manner, or degree; not at all. [Middle English *nawyse* : NO + WISE (way).]

now-now (nów-now) *adv. South African Informal.* Very soon; right away. [Afrikaans *nou-nou.*]

nowt (nowt, nōt) *n. British Regional.* Nothing. [Variant of NOUGHT.]

nox·ious (nókshəss) *adj.* Injurious or harmful to health or morals. [Latin *noxius*, from *noxa*, injury, damage.] **—nox·ious·ly** *adv.* **—nox·ious·ness** *n.*

no·yade (nwaa-yaád) *n.* Execution by drowning; especially, that carried out on a large scale at Nantes in France in 1794. [French, from *noyer*, to drown, from Latin *necāre*, from *nex* (stem *nec-*), slaughter.]

noy·au (nwī́-ō) *n.* A liqueur consisting of brandy flavoured with the kernels of fruit stones or nuts. [French, kernel, from Vulgar Latin *nucale* (unattested), neuter noun from Late Latin *nucālis*, nutty, from Latin *nux* (stem *nuc-*), nut.]

noz·zle (nózz'l) *n.* A projecting, often adjustable, spout through which gas or liquid is discharged, such as the end of a hose or the pipe in a jet engine or rocket outlet. [Earlier *nosel, nosle*, diminutive of NOSE.]

Np 1. The symbol for the element neptunium. **2.** neper.

NP 1. neuropsychiatric; neuropsychiatry. **2.** new penny; new pence. **3.** noun phrase.

n.p. 1. new paragraph. **2.** *Law.* nisi prius. **3.** no place of publication.

N.P. notary public.

N.P.A. Newspaper Publishers' Association.

NPN, N.P.N. nonprotein nitrogen.

nr. near.

N.S. 1. New Style. 2. not satisfactory or sufficient. 3. Nova Scotia. 4. nuclear ship.

N.S.B. National Savings Bank (in Britain).

n.s.f., N.S.F. not sufficient funds.

N.S.P.C.C. National Society for the Prevention of Cruelty to Children (in Britain).

NSU nonspecific urethritis.

N.S.W. New South Wales.

–n't *comb. form.* Not.

NT, N.T. 1. National Trust. 2. New Testament. 3. Northern Territory. 4. no trumps.

nth (enth) *adj.* 1. Pertaining to an indefinitely large ordinal number: *ten to the nth power.* 2. Infinitely or indefinitely large or small; most extreme; utmost: *exaggerated to the nth degree.*

n.t.p., N.T.P. normal temperature and pressure (a temperature of 0°C and a pressure of 101.325 kPa).

n-type (én-tīp) *adj. Electronics.* Of or designating a semiconductor or its type of conductivity, in which the bulk of the electric current is carried by electrons. Compare **p-type.** [*Negative type.*]

nu (new ‖ nōō) *n.* The thirteenth letter of the Greek alphabet (N, ν), corresponding to the English *N, n.* Transliterated in English as *N, n.* [Greek *nu,* from a Phoenician word meaning "fish", from a Semitic root *nyn* meaning "to increase" or "to endure".]

nu·ance (new-ónss, néw-ónss; *French* nü- ‖ nōō-, nōō-) *n.* A subtle or slight variation, as in meaning, colour, or quality; a gradation of meaning. [French *nuance,* from Old French, from *nuer,* to show shades of colour (as in clouds), from *nue,* cloud, from Vulgar Latin *nūbe* (unattested), from Latin *nūbēs.*]

nub (nub) *n.* 1. A protuberance or knob. 2. A small lump or piece. 3. The gist or point: *the nub of a story.* [Variant of *knub,* from Middle Low German *knubbe,* knot on a tree, variant of *knobbe,* KNOB.]

Nu·ba (néwbə ‖ nōōbə) *n., pl.* **Nuba.** 1. A Nubian. 2. A member of any of several Nilotic peoples of southern Sudan. 3. The language spoken by these peoples. —**Nu·ba** *adj.*

nub·bin (núbbin) *n. U.S.* 1. A small, stunted ear of corn. 2. Anything stunted or imperfectly developed. [Diminutive of NUB.]

nub·ble (núbb'l) *n.* A small protuberance or lump. [Diminutive of NUB.] —**nub·bly** *adj.*

Nu·bi·a (néw-bi-ə ‖ nōō-). Ancient state of northeastern Africa,

---

nuclear energy

MASTERING THE MIGHTY ATOM

How man controls nuclear energy

In 1942, an Italian physicist, Enrico Fermi, working at the University of Chicago, withdrew some cadmium rods from a pile he had built of graphite with uranium inserts – and began a chain reaction in the uranium atoms that created a new and mighty power – nuclear energy. In so doing he controlled the reaction that occurs when the nucleus of an unstable atom, such as uranium, splits or undergoes fission.

When fission occurs, enormous energy is released, together with several neutrons. These neutrons will be captured by other uranium nuclei which will become unstable and, in turn, undergo fission. This chain reaction, if unchecked, will, in fractions of a second, set off the gigantic explosion of a nuclear blast. When the reaction is controlled, energy can be released as a steady flow of heat, which can be used to generate electricity.

Fermi's experiment is the basis on which nuclear-powered electricity generating stations work. The flow of heat is controlled by the cadmium rods. The heat is extracted by water, gas, or sodium, and used to raise steam to drive the generator. Nuclear reactors pose problems. If they break down, they may release dangerous radioactivity, and their fuel, even when expended, remains radioactive probably for centuries (making it difficult to dispose of).

The answer may lie in nuclear fusion – as yet unmastered by man. It is the harnessing of the energy created when two nuclei join, or fuse, together – a process that does not have such a great waste-disposal problem.

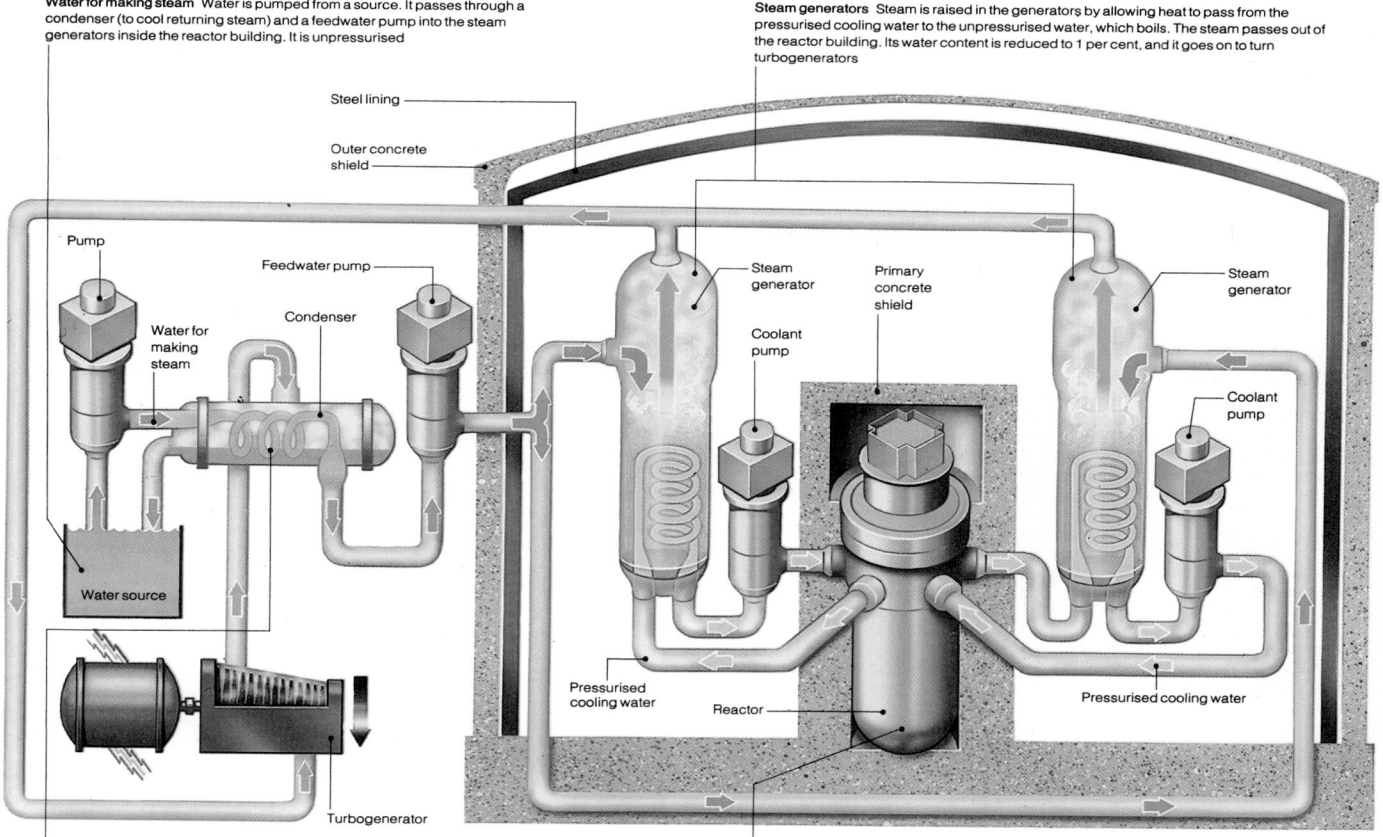

Water for making steam Water is pumped from a source. It passes through a condenser (to cool returning steam) and a feedwater pump into the steam generators inside the reactor building. It is unpressurised

Steam generators Steam is raised in the generators by allowing heat to pass from the pressurised cooling water to the unpressurised water, which boils. The steam passes out of the reactor building. Its water content is reduced to 1 per cent, and it goes on to turn turbogenerators

Steel lining

Outer concrete shield

Pump

Feedwater pump

Condenser

Water for making steam

Steam generator

Primary concrete shield

Steam generator

Coolant pump

Coolant pump

Water source

Pressurised cooling water

Reactor

Pressurised cooling water

Turbogenerator

Condenser The steam passes on to the condenser, where it is turned back into water by the coldness of the water coming in from source. It is then returned to the source

Reactor Water for cooling the reactor is maintained at a constant pressure, to prevent it from boiling in the reactor. Impelled by coolant pumps, the cooling water circulates between the reactor core and the steam generators

POWER FROM A REACTOR *Pressurised cooling water is driven round the reactor core to draw off the heat. It is then passed through steam generators, in which it turns other water into steam. The steam is siphoned off to drive a turbogenerator, which produces* *electricity. The steam is then cooled into water in a condenser and sent off round the system to be used again. This type of pressurised water reactor is cheap and simple to build, but it uses fuel less economically than later, gas-cooled reactors.*

extending at its height from Aswan to Khartoum. By the 20th century B.C. it had come completely under the sway of the Egyptians, although in the 8th and 7th centuries B.C. an independent kingdom of Nubia again asserted itself and Nubian kings conquered Egypt, establishing the Dynasty XXV in 712 B.C. In the 6th century A.D. Nubia was joined to Ethiopia, then a Christian kingdom. After Ethiopia fell to the Muslims in the 14th century, Nubia ceased to have a distinctive existence.

Nu·bi·an (néw-bi-ən ‖ nōō-) n. 1. A native or inhabitant of Nubia. 2. Any of the languages of Nubia. —**Nu·bi·an** adj.

Nubian Desert. An arid wilderness in northeastern Sudan, lying between the river Nile and the Red Sea and merging into the Arabian Desert of eastern Egypt. The desert is largely uninhabited.

nu·bile (néw-bīl ‖ nōō-, U.S. also -b'l) adj. 1. Young and physically attractive. Said of a girl or young woman: a nubile young girl. 2. Ready for marriage; of a marriageable age. Said of a woman. [French nubile, from Latin nūbilis, marriageable, from nūbere, to take a husband.] —**nu·bil·i·ty** (new-bíllǝti ‖ nōō-) n.

nu·cel·lus (new-séllǝss ‖ nōō-) n., pl. -**celli** (-séllī). Botany. The centre of the ovule of a plant, containing the embryo sac. [New Latin, irregularly from Latin nucella, diminutive of nux (stem nuc-), nut.] —**nu·cel·lar** adj.

nu·cha (néw-kǝ ‖ nōō-) n. The nape of the neck. [Middle English nucha, nuca, from Medieval Latin nucha, from Arabic nukhā', spinal marrow.] —**nu·chal** adj.

nucle-. Variant of **nucleo-**.

nu·cle·ar (néw-kli-ǝr ‖ nōō-) adj. 1. Biology. Of, pertaining to, or forming a nucleus: a nuclear membrane. 2. Physics. Of or concerning atomic nuclei: nuclear physics. 3. Using, armed with, or derived from the energy of atomic nuclei; atomic: nuclear power plants. 4. Of, involving, or possessing atomic or hydrogen bombs: nuclear war; nuclear nations. [From NUCLEUS.]

nuclear bomb n. 1. An explosive weapon of great destructive power derived from the rapid release of energy in the fission of heavy atomic nuclei, as of uranium-235. 2. Any bomb deriving its destructive power from the release of nuclear energy. Also called "A-bomb", "atom bomb", "atomic bomb". See **hydrogen bomb**.

nuclear emulsion n. Physics. Any of several photographic emulsions used to detect and display the paths of charged elementary particles, especially of charged cosmic-ray particles.

nuclear energy n. Physics. 1. The energy released by a nuclear reaction, especially by fission, fusion, or radioactive decay. 2. This energy regarded as a source of industrial, commercial, or military power. Also called "atomic energy". See feature, previous page.

nuclear family n. A self-contained family unit consisting of a mother and father and their children. Compare **extended family**.

nuclear fission n. Physics. See **fission**.

nu·cle·ar-free zone (néw-kli-ǝr-frée, -free ‖ nōō-) n. An area in which the siting of nuclear reactors or missiles is banned.

nuclear fuel n. A fuel used to provide nuclear power in a nuclear reactor.

nuclear fusion n. Physics. See **fusion**.

nuclear isomer n. Physics. A type of **isomer** (see).

nuclear magnetic resonance n. Abbr. **NMR** A technique for measuring the nuclear **magnetic moment** (see) of a substance by exposing a sample to a strong magnetic field and high-frequency electromagnetic radiation. It is used, as in spectroscopy, for providing information on the molecular structure of the substance.

nuclear magneton n. Physics. Symbol μ_N A unit of the magnetic moment of the nucleon. See **magneton**.

nuclear physics n. Used with a singular verb. The scientific study of the forces, reactions, and internal structures of atomic nuclei.

nuclear power n. 1. The electric or motive power produced by a nuclear reactor. 2. A state that possesses nuclear weapons. Also called "atomic power".

nuclear reaction n. Physics. A reaction that alters the energy, composition, or structure of an atomic nucleus. Also called "reaction".

nuclear reactor n. Any of several devices in which a **chain reaction** (see) is initiated and controlled, with the consequent production of heat, typically used for the generation of power. Neutrons and fusion products are also produced, and reactors are also used for a variety of experimental and medical purposes. Also called "atomic pile", "atomic reactor", "pile", "reactor".

nu·cle·ase (néw-kli-ayz, -ayss ‖ nōō-) n. Any of several enzymes that hydrolise nucleic acids. [NUCLE(O)- + -ASE.]

nu·cle·ate (newkli-ǝt, -it, -ayt ‖ nōō) adj. Having a nucleus or nuclei. ~v. (néw-kli-ayt ‖ nōō-) **nucleated, -ating, -ates.** —tr. To bring together into a nucleus. —intr. To form a nucleus. [NUCLE(US) + -ATE.] —**nu·cle·a·tion** (-áysh'n) n.

nu·cle·i. Plural of **nucleus**.

nu·cle·ic acid (new-klée-ik, -kláy- ‖ nōō-) n. Any member of either of two groups of complex compounds found in all living cells, and composed of purines, pyrimidines, sugars, and phosphoric acid. See **DNA, RNA.** [NUCLE(O)- + -IC (because found in nucleoproteins).]

nucleo-, nucle- comb. form. Indicates: 1. A nucleus; for example, **nucleon.** 2. Nucleic acid; for example, **nucleoprotein, nucleoside.** [From NUCLEUS.]

nu·cle·o·late (néw-kli-ǝ-layt ‖ nōō-) adj. Also **nu·cle·o·lat·ed** (-lay-tid). Having a nucleolus or nucleoli. [NUCLEOL(US) + -ATE.]

nu·cle·o·lus (néw-kli-ṓ-lǝss, -klée-ǝ- ‖ nōō-), n., pl. -**li** (-lī). Also **nu·cle·ole** (-ṓl). Biology. A small, usually round body composed of protein and RNA in the nucleus of a cell. Also called "plasmo-

some". 2. Any discrete, cellular particle resembling a nucleolus, other than a chromosome. [New Latin, from Latin, diminutive of nucleus, a kernel, NUCLEUS.] —**nu·cle·o·lar** (-lǝr) adj.

nu·cle·on (néw-kli-on ‖ nōō-) n. A proton or a neutron, especially as part of an atomic nucleus. [NUCLE(O)- + -ON.] —**nu·cle·on·ic** (-ónnik) adj.

nu·cle·on·ics (néw-kli-ónniks ‖ nōō-) n. Used with a singular verb. The technology of nuclear energy. [From NUCLEON.]

nucleon number n. Physics. **Mass number** (see).

nu·cle·o·phile (néw-kli-ṓ-fīl, -ǝ- ‖ nōō-) n. A substance whose atoms or molecules behave as an electron pair donor in combining with other atoms or molecules. [NUCLEO- + -PHILE.] —**nu·cle·o·phile**, **nu·cle·o·phil·ic** (-fíllik) adj.

nu·cle·o·plasm (néw-kli-ǝ-plaz'm, -ō- ‖ nōō-) n. The protoplasm of a cell nucleus. Also called "karyoplasm". [NUCLEO- + -PLASM.] —**nu·cle·o·plas·ma·tic** (-plaz-máttik), **nu·cle·o·plas·mic** adj.

nu·cle·o·pro·tein (néw-kli-ō-prṓ-teen, -tee-in ‖ nōō-) n. Any of a group of substances found in all living cells and viruses, and composed of a protein and a nucleic acid.

nu·cle·o·side (néw-kli-ǝ-sīd ‖ nōō-) n. Any compound made of a sugar and a purine or pyrimidine base without a phosphate group. [NUCLE(O) + -OS(E) + -IDE.]

nu·cle·o·some (néw-kli-ō-sōm, -ǝ- ‖ nōō-) n. Any of the basic globular subunits of chromatin consisting of DNA and histone. [NUCLEO- + -SOME.] —**nu·cle·o·som·al** (-sōm'l) adj.

nu·cle·o·tide (néw-kli-ǝ-tīd ‖ nōō-) n. Any of various organic compounds consisting of a nucleoside combined with phosphoric acid. [Irregularly from NUCLEO- + -IDE.]

nu·cle·us (néw-kli-ǝss ‖ nōō-) n., pl. -**clei** (-kli-ī) or rare -**cleuses**. 1. A central thing or part around which other things are grouped; a core: the nucleus of a city. 2. Anything regarded as a basis for future development and growth; a kernel: the nucleus of a stamp collection. 3. Biology. A complex, usually spherical, protoplasmic body within a living cell that contains the cell's hereditary material and that controls its metabolism, growth, and reproduction. 4. Botany. The central point of a starch granule. 5. Anatomy. A group of nerve cells or localised mass of grey matter in the brain, where nerve fibres interconnect. 6. Physics. The positively charged central region of an atom, composed of protons and neutrons, and containing almost all of the mass of the atom. See **atomic number, mass number.** 7. Chemistry. A group of atoms chemically bound in a structure resistant to alteration in chemical reactions. 8. Astronomy. **a.** The central portion of the head of a comet. **b.** The central or brightest part of a nebula or of a galaxy. 9. Meteorology. A minute solid particle upon which water vapour molecules accumulate to form a droplet or ice crystal. 10. Phonetics. The most sonorous part of a syllable; especially, a vowel. [Latin, "a nut", "kernel", from nux (stem nuc-), a nut.]

nu·clide (néw-klīd ‖ nōō-) n. Physics. Any atomic nucleus specified by its atomic number, atomic mass, and energy state. Compare **isotope.** [NUCLE(O)- + -IDE.] —**nu·clid·ic** (new-klíddik ‖ nōō-) adj.

nud·dy (núddi) Chiefly British Informal. n. Nudeness; a state of undress. Used in the phrase in the nuddy. [From NUDE.]

nude (newd ‖ nōōd) adj. 1. **a.** Without clothing; naked. **b.** Without covering; exposed. 2. Law. Lacking any of various legal requisites, such as evidence: a nude contract. ~n. 1. A nude human figure or a representation of it. 2. The condition of being nude: in the nude. [Latin nūdus, nude, bare.] —**nude·ly** adv. —**nude·ness** n.

nudge (nuj) tr.v. **nudged, nudging, nudges.** 1. To push or prod (a person) gently, especially with the elbow and in order to gain attention or give a signal. 2. To push against (an object) lightly: The car tyre just nudged the pavement. 3. To encourage or compel gradually: Slowly they nudged her into joining the conspiracy. ~n. 1. A gentle push. 2. An encouragement or incentive. [Perhaps from a Scandinavian word akin to Norwegian dialectal nugga, nyggja†, to push, rub.]

nudge-nudge, wink-wink (núj-nuj wink-wink) n. Informal. Sly sexual innuendo, or a gesture or expression conveying this: There was a bit of the old nudge-nudge, wink-wink going on in the office after Sarah kissed her boss at the Christmas party. ~adj. Informal. Of or designating a leering, smutty, suggestive attitude or reaction: "Rape is often regarded in a nudge-nudge, wink-wink way" (The Guardian). ~interj. Informal. Used to show prurience or hint gleefully at sexual matters: Nudge-nudge, wink-wink, know what I mean? [Alluding to gestures made when conveying sexual innuendo.]

nudi- comb. form. Indicates nakedness or bareness; for example, **nudibranch, nudicaul.** [Latin nūdus, NUDE.]

nu·di·branch (néwdi-brangk ‖ nōōdi-) n. Any mollusc of the order Nudibranchia; the **sea slug** (see). [New Latin Nudibranchia, "ones having naked gills" : NUDI- + BRANCHIA.] —**nu·di·bran·chi·an** (-brángki-ǝn) **nu·di·bran·chi·ate** (-brángki-ǝt, -it, -ayt) adj. & n.

nu·di·caul (néw-di-kawl ‖ nōō-) adj. Also **nu·di·cau·lous** (-káwlǝss). Botany. Having no leaves on the stem. [NUDI- + Latin caulis, stalk, stem.]

nu·die (néw-di ‖ nōō-) n. Slang. 1. A **skinflick** (see). 2. A magazine containing pornographic photographs of nudes. ~adj. Slang. Characterised by or featuring pornographic nudity: a nudie film. [From NUDE.]

nud·ism (néw-diz'm ‖ nōō-) n. The doctrine or practice of living in the nude. Also called "naturism". —**nud·ist** adj. & n.

nu·di·ty (néw-dǝti ‖ nōō-) n., pl. -**ties.** 1. The quality or state of

HOW THE POWER OF THE ATOM BECAME A WEAPON OF WAR

The growth of nuclear weapons from the atomic bomb to the neutron bomb

There are two main kinds of bomb that release the energy of the atomic nucleus; those that split nuclei (atomic, or fission bombs), and those that fuse nuclei (hydrogen, or thermonuclear bombs). An atomic-bomb explosion is a vast release of energy caused by a chain reaction in which some two million million million atoms (of uranium or plutonium) are split in a millionth of a second. The first detailed plans for an atomic bomb were produced in England in 1940 by two refugee German scientists, Otto Frisch and Rudolph Peierls. Parallel research was going on in the U.S.A. and in 1941 British and American scientists joined forces in the "Manhattan Project" led by J. R. Oppenheimer.

The first atomic explosion took place on July 16, 1945, at Alamogordo, New Mexico. In August, President Truman decided to use the world's only two atom bombs against Japan.

One was dropped on Hiroshima on August 6, the other on Nagasaki three days later. The Hiroshima bomb had an explosive force of 20 kilotons (equivalent to 20,000 tons of TNT) and killed 80,000 people outright.

The first hydrogen bomb, or H-bomb, was exploded by the United States on November 1, 1952, over Eniwetok Atoll in the Pacific. Its explosive force was about 10 megatons (10 million tons of TNT) – 500 times that of the Hiroshima bomb. By 1982, six countries were known to possess nuclear bombs: the United States, Russia, Britain, France, China, and India. In 1982, the United States began stockpiling the neutron bomb, which is designed to destroy people rather than buildings. It has a limited blast range but long radiation range. The present stock of such weapons could wipe out life on Earth.

 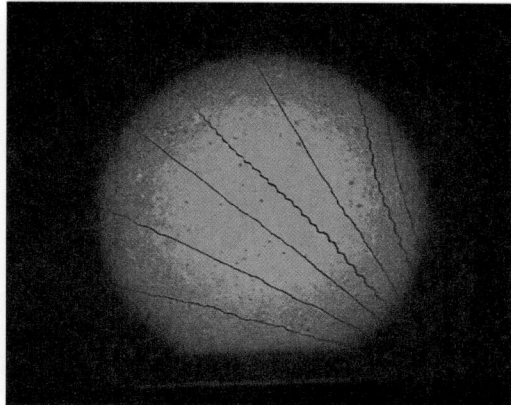

 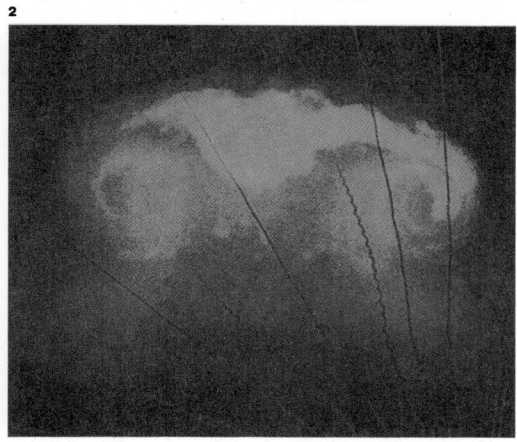

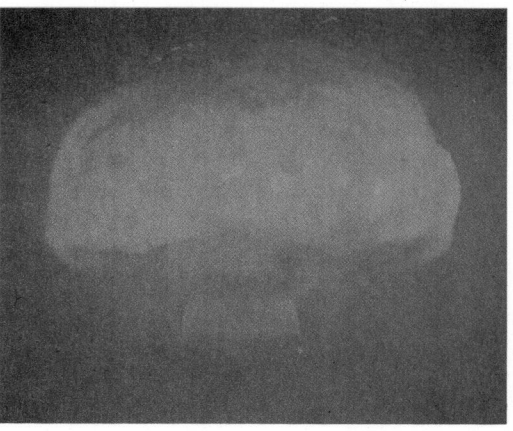

H-BOMB OVER THE PACIFIC *On November 1, 1952, the United States exploded the first hydrogen bomb 450 metres (1,476 feet) over Eniwetok Atoll in the Pacific Ocean. This colour film sequence shows stages of the thermonuclear explosion from shortly after detonation to the final "flourishing" of the fireball. 1 Vapour trails left by instrumentation rockets are silhouetted against the fireball. 2 The fireball's surface is dotted with light and dark spots. The exact nature of the spots is not known, but they are thought to be connected with the shock wave caused by the bomb. 3 The shock wave is reflected from the surface of the ocean and this flattens the bottom of the fireball. 4 The rising fireball starts to leave the vapour trails beneath it as it assumes the shape of a rotating doughnut. 5 The fireball takes the shape of a giant mushroom as it rises higher over the atoll. Brown metal oxides from the bomb debris gather on the fireball rim. The explosion formed a crater almost 1.5 kilometres (1 mile) across.*

Less than a year after the explosion at Eniwetok Atoll, the Russians tested a hydrogen bomb, and Britain followed in May, 1956. The 1950s saw the start of a nuclear arms race as Russia, the United States, Britain, and France tested ever more powerful bombs and strove to outstrip one another in delivery systems.

being nude; bareness; nakedness. **2.** *Rare.* A nude figure as represented in painting or sculpture.

nud·nik, nud·nick (nŏŏd-nik) *n. Chiefly U.S. Slang.* **1.** A boring or bothersome person; a pest. **2.** A stupid person; a fool. [Yiddish : Russian *nudny,* boring, wearisome + -NIK.]

nuff (nuf) *n. Nonstandard.* Enough. Used chiefly in the phrase *nuff said.*

nu·ée ar·dente (néw-ay aar-dóNt; *French* nü-) *n.* A turbulent, incandescent cloud of gas, ash, and rock fragments which flows rapidly over the ground after a violent volcanic eruption, destroying all forms of life in its path within seconds. [French, "burning cloud".]

Nuf·field (núffeeld), **William Richard Morris, 1st Viscount** (1877–1963). British motor-car manufacturer. At his Morris Motor works, in Oxford, he helped to pioneer mass-produced vehicles in Britain from 1912. His philanthropic activities include endowing Nuffield College, Oxford, and the Nuffield Trust and Nuffield Foundation medical and educational bodies.

nu·ga·to·ry (néw-gə-tri, -təri, new-gáytəri ‖ nŏŏ-) *adj.* **1.** Of no value; worthless; trifling: *a nugatory objection.* **2.** Having no power; invalid; inoperative: *a nugatory statute.* [Latin *nūgātōrius,* trifling, from *nūgārī,* to jest, trifle, from *nūgae†,* jokes.]

nug·gar (núggər) *n.* A broad-beamed sailing boat used for carrying cargo on the upper Nile. [Arabic *nukkār.*]

nug·get (núggit) *n.* **1.** A small lump, especially one of natural gold. **2.** A small but valuable portion or unit: *nuggets of information.* [Probably diminutive of dialect *nug†,* lump.] —**nug·get·y** *adj.*

nui·sance (néw-s'nss ‖ nŏŏ-) *n.* **1.** A source of inconvenience, annoyance, or vexation; a bother. **2.** *Law.* A use of property or course of conduct that interferes with the legal rights of others by causing damage, annoyance, or inconvenience. [Middle English *nusaunce,* injury, harmful thing, from Old French *nuisance,* from *nuire* (stem *nuis-*), to harm, injure, from Latin *nocēre.*]

nuisance value *n.* The capacity to annoy or frustrate, considered as a useful asset.

Nuits-Saint-Georges (nwée-saN-zhórzh) *n.* A fine red Burgundy wine. [After the town *Nuits-Saint-Georges.*]

N.U.J. National Union of Journalists.

Nu·jo·ma (nŏŏ-jômə), **Sam (Daniel)** (1929–). Black Namibian (South West African) revolutionary leader, founder and president of SWAPO (South West Africa People's Organisation).

nuke (newk ‖ nook) *n. Slang.* A nuclear bomb. ~*tr.v.* **nuked, nuking, nukes.** *Slang.* To attack or destroy with a nuclear bomb.

null (nul) *adj.* **1.** Having no legal force; invalid. Often used in the phrase *null and void.* **2. a.** Of no consequence, effect, or value; insignificant. **b.** Lacking distinctive personality; colourless: *a null face.* **3.** Amounting to nothing; lacking; absent; non-existent. **4.** *Mathematics.* Of or pertaining to zero magnitude or a set having no members. ~*n.* **1.** Zero. **2.** An instrumental reading of zero. **3.** A letter which has no meaning in a code or cipher. [French *nul, nulle,* "none", from Latin *nūllus* : *ne,* not + *ūllus,* any.]

nul·lah (núllə) *n.* In India, a ravine or watercourse. [Hindi *nālā,* rivulet, ravine, probably from Dravidian.]

nul·la-nul·la (núllə-nullə) *n. Australian.* A hardwood club used by Aborigines. [From a native Australian language.]

Nul·lar·bor Plain (núllər-bawr). Extensive plateau stretching along the Great Australian Bight in southern Australia from Ooldea to the lake district of Western Australia and extending north to the Great Victoria Desert. It is generally flat, with occasional peaks rising 400 metres above sea level.

null hypothesis *n. Statistics.* A hypothesis that is tested against another but is nullified in favour of the alternative, subject to a given level of error.

nul·li·fi·ca·tion (núllifi-káysh'n) *n.* **1.** The action of nullifying. **2.** *U.S.* The refusal or failure of a U.S. state to recognise or enforce Federal laws within its boundaries. —**nul·li·fi·ca·tion·ist** *n. & adj.*

nul·li·fid·i·an (núlli-fíddi-ən) *n.* A person having no beliefs, especially in religious matters; a sceptic. ~*adj.* Having or characterised by a lack of faith or belief. [Medieval Latin *nullifidius* : Latin *nullus,* no, none + *fidēs,* faith.]

nul·li·fy (núlli-fī) *tr.v.* **-fied, -fying, -fies.** **1.** To deprive of legal force; annul; make void: *The court nullified the contract.* **2.** To make ineffective or useless. See Synonyms at **neutralise.** [Late Latin *nūllificāre,* to make light of, despise : *nūllus,* none, NULL + *facere,* to make.] —**nul·li·fi·er** *n.*

Synonyms: nullify, negate, abolish, annul, void, invalidate, abrogate, cancel, repeal, revoke, rescind.

nul·lip·a·ra (nu-líppərə) *n.* A woman who has never given birth. [New Latin : Latin *nullus,* no, none + *-para,* from *parere,* to give birth.] —**nul·li·pa·ri·ty** (núlli-párrəti) *n.* —**nul·lip·a·rous** (nu-líppərəss) *adj.*

nul·li·pore (núlli-pawr ‖ -pōr) *n.* Any of several small red seaweeds that secrete calcium carbonate and form encrustations on rocks. [Latin *nullus,* no, none + PORE.]

nul·li·ty (núlləti) *n., pl.* **-ties.** **1.** The state or quality of being null: *the nullity of third parties in a two-party parliamentary system.* **2.** *Law.* **a.** The fact of being null and void. **b.** An act having no legal validity. **3.** A nonentity.

num. **1.** number. **2.** numeral.

Num. Numbers (Old Testament).

N.U.M. National Union of Mineworkers.

numb (num) *adj.* **number** (númmər), **numbest** (númmist). **1.** Insensible, as from excessive chill; benumbed: *toes numb with cold.* **2.** Stunned or paralysed, as from shock or strong emotion: *numb with grief.* **3.** Insensitive or inept. **4.** Resembling or of the nature of loss of sensation: *a numb feeling.* ~*v.* **numbed, numbing, numbs.** —*tr.* To make numb; deaden. —*intr.* To become numb. [Middle English *nome(n),* originally "seized with palsy, paralysed", past participle of *nimen,* to take, seize, Old English *niman.*] —**numb·ly** *adv.* —**numb·ness** *n.*

num·bat (núm-bat) *n.* Either of two marsupial mammals, *Myrmecobius fasciatus* or *M. rufus,* native to southern Australia, having a long snout and an extensile tongue for catching termites. [From a native Australian language.]

num·ber (númbər) *n. Abbr.* **n., no., No., num. 1.** *Mathematics.* **a.** A member of the set of positive integers; a member of a series of symbols of unique meaning in a fixed order which may be derived by counting. See **cardinal number, ordinal number.** **b.** A member of any of the further sets of mathematical objects that may be derived from the positive integers by mathematical induction. See **induction.** Thus, given the positive integers and zero, the operation of addition makes it possible to define the negative integers (those which added to the positive integers produce zero). The integers together with the fractions (of the form *m/n,* where *m* and *n* are integers and *n* is not zero) form the set of *rational numbers.* The rational numbers together with the *irrational numbers* (those not expressible as quotients of integers, such as $\sqrt{2}$) form the set of *real numbers.* Numbers of the form $a + bi,$ where a and b are real numbers and $i^2 = -1,$ form the set of *complex numbers,* which is the broadest set commonly used in mathematics. Numbers such as π (pi), that are not expressible as roots of any algebraic equation with rational coefficients, form the set of *transcendental numbers.* See **transfinite number. c.** A symbol used to represent a number; a numeral. **2.** *Plural.* The study or processes of arithmetic. **3. a.** A numeral or series of numerals assigned to or designating a specific person or thing: *a telephone number.* **b.** The person or thing thus

---

WAYS OF REPRESENTING QUANTITY
Using position to extend a symbol's meaning

A number describes a quantity; it evaluates an amount from one to millions by a symbol or a group of symbols. The oldest known writing, from Sumer in Mesopotamia, was an account – a 5,000-year-old record of supplies. Ancient Egyptians, Chinese, Greeks, Mayas, and Hindus all developed numbering systems – and all counted in tens, probably because they used their fingers. Some Brazilian Indians, however, use the joints of one finger, and thus all their counting is based on three numbers. The system most often used today is based on the original Hindu and was brought to Europe by Arab traders. Its place-value system, in which the position of a numeral determines its value, made it easier to work than the Roman system. Each move to the left makes the number's value ten times greater. Only a small range of symbols is needed no matter how large the number, and calculations are therefore less cumbersome.

Babylonian										
Egyptian										
Greek	A	B	Γ	Δ	E	F	Z	H	Θ	I
Roman	I	II	III	IV	V	VI	VII	VIII	IX	X
Ancient Chinese	一	二	三	四	五	六	七	八	九	十
Maya										
Hindu										0
Arabic/European 15th century	1	2	3	ϩ	4	6	∧	8	9	10	0
Modern Arabic/European	1	2	3	4	5	6	7	8	9	10	0
Digits designed for computer printing	1	2	3	4	5	6	7	8	9	10	0

designated: *Come in, number three, your time is up.* **4.** A specific quantity composed of equal units: *The number of apples in the bowl is ten.* **5.** Quantity of units or individuals: *The crowd was small in number.* **6.** *Plural.* A large quantity or collection: *Numbers of people visited the fair.* **7.** One item in a group or series, as of a journal, considered to be in numerical order: *I saw her article in the latest number of the Herald.* **8. a.** One of the separate offerings in a programme of music. **b.** *Informal.* A song or piece of instrumental music. **c.** Any self-contained item within a larger piece of music, such as an aria in an opera. **9.** *Informal.* A person or thing singled out for some notable characteristic; especially: **a.** A pretty woman. Often considered offensive. **b.** A well-designed garment. **c.** A fast car. **10.** *Informal.* A means or circumstance that allows one to gain profit or advantage: *has a nice little number with a generous expense account.* **11.** A usually exclusive group of people: *She is one of the duchess's number.* **12.** *Usually plural.* Strength or superiority based on quantity: *There's safety in numbers.* **13.** *Grammar.* The indication, as by inflection, of the singularity, duality, or plurality of a linguistic form. **14. a.** *Plural.* Metrical periods or feet; verses: *the melodious numbers of our old poets.* **b.** Measured rhythm in verse. **15.** *Plural.* Musical periods or measures. —**a number of.** A considerable, indefinite quantity of. See Usage note below. —**any number of.** A large, indefinite quantity of; numerous. —**by numbers.** **1.** *Military.* Step by step, as consecutive numbers are called out. **2.** In a mechanical or excessively regulated manner, as when children follow a number code to colour in picture books. —**get or have (someone's) number.** *Chiefly U.S. Informal.* To determine (or know) someone's real character or motives. —**(someone's) number is up.** *British Informal.* Used to describe a person who is, or is soon to be, defeated or dead. —**without** or **beyond number.** In a quantity too great to be counted.
~*v.* **numbered, -bering, -bers.** —*tr.* **1.** To total in number or amount; add up to. **2.** To count or determine the number or amount of. **3.** To include in a group or category: *She was numbered among the lost.* **4.** To mention one by one; enumerate. **5.** To assign a number to. Sometimes used with *off.* **6.** To limit or restrict in number: *The days of her life are numbered.* —*intr.* **1.** To count or call out numbers: *numbering to ten.* **2.** To constitute a group or number: *The applicants numbered in the thousands.* [Middle English *n(o)umbre,* from Old French *nombre,* from Latin *numerus.*] —**number·er** *n.*

Usage: When preceded by *the, number* takes a singular verb: *The number of people now out of work has reached. . .* When preceded by *a,* it takes a plural verb: *A number of people have left the area.*

number crunching *n. Informal.* Complex arithmetical calculations, especially as done by computers.

num·ber·less (númbər-ləss, -liss) *adj.* **1.** Innumerable; countless. **2.** Not consisting of or concerned with numbers; lacking a number. See Synonyms at **infinite.**

number one *n. Informal.* **1.** Oneself: *You think only of number one.* **2.** The first or most important. —**num·ber-one** (númbər-wún, wón) *adj.*

number plate *n.* Either of the rectangular metal plates displayed at the front and back of a motor vehicle that bear its registration number. Also called "registration plate".

Num·bers (númbərz) *n. Used with a singular verb. Abbr.* **Num.** The fourth book of the Old Testament, containing the two censuses of the Israelites after the Exodus.

Number Ten *n.* 10 Downing Street, the official London residence of the British prime minister.

number theory *n. Mathematics.* The study of integers and the relationships between them.

numb·fish (núm-fish) *n., pl.* **-fishes** or collectively **numbfish.** A fish, the **electric ray** (see).

num·bles (númb'lz) *pl.n. British Archaic.* Entrails, especially of a deer, used for food. Also called "umbles". [Middle English, from Old French *nomble(s),* thigh muscle of deer or other game, from Latin *lumbulus,* diminutive of *lumbus,* loin.]

numbskull. Variant of **numskull.**

num·dah (núm-də, -daa) *n.* Also **num·nah** (-nə). **1.** A coarse felt made in India. **2.** An article made from this felt, especially an embroidered rug. [Urdu *namdā,* from Persian *namad,* carpet.]

nu·men (néw-men ‖ noō-) *n., pl.* **numina** (-minə). **1.** The presiding divinity or spirit of a place. **2.** The spirit believed by animists to inhabit certain natural objects. **3.** Creative energy regarded as a guiding genius or demon dwelling within one. [Latin *nūmen,* "a nod", hence "command", divine power, deity.]

nu·mer·a·cy (néw-mərə-si ‖ noō-) *n.* The condition or quality of being numerate. Compare **literacy.** [NUMER(ATE) + -CY.]

nu·mer·al (néw-mərəl ‖ noō-) *n. Abbr.* **num.** A symbol, such as a letter, figure, or word used alone or in a group to represent a number. See **Arabic numeral, Roman numeral.**
~*adj.* Of, pertaining to, or expressing numbers. [Old French *numeral,* from Latin *numerālis,* from Latin *numerus,* NUMBER.] —**nu·mer·al·ly** *adv.*

nu·mer·ar·y (néw-mə-rəri ‖ noō-, -rerri) *adj.* Of or pertaining to a number or numbers. [Medieval Latin *numerārius,* from Latin *numerus,* NUMBER.]

nu·mer·ate (néw-mə-rət, -rit ‖ noō-) *adj.* Familiar with the basic principles of mathematics, especially arithmetic.
~*tr.v.* (-rayt) **numerated, -ating, -ates.** **1.** To enumerate; number; reckon. **2.** To read (numerals). [Latin *numerāre,* to number, count, from *numerus,* NUMBER.] —**nu·mer·a·ble** *adj.*

nu·mer·a·tion (néw-mə-ráysh'n ‖ noō-) *n.* **1.** The act or process of counting by means of reading, writing, or naming numbers. **2.** A system of numbering or of reading numbers. —**nu·mer·a·tive** (-rətiv ‖ -raytiv) *adj.*

nu·mer·a·tor (néw-mə-raytər ‖ noō-) *n.* **1.** *Mathematics.* **a.** The expression written above the line in a common fraction. Compare **denominator.** **b.** An expression to be divided by another; the dividend. **2.** One that numbers; an enumerator.

nu·mer·ic (new-mérrik ‖ noō-) *n.* A number or numeral.
~*adj.* Variant of **numerical.** [Medieval Latin *numericus,* from Latin *numerus,* NUMBER.]

nu·mer·i·cal (new-mérrik'l ‖ noō-) *adj.* Also **numeric.** **1.** Of or pertaining to a number or series of numbers: *numerical order.* **2.** Designating number or a number: *a numerical symbol.* **3.** Expressed in numbers: *numerical strength.* **4.** Represented by a number or numbers rather than by letter or symbol. [Medieval Latin *numericus,* from Latin *numerus,* NUMBER.] —**nu·mer·i·cal·ly** *adv.*

numerical taxonomy *n.* The branch of taxonomy that assesses quantitatively the relationships between organisms.

numerical value *n. Mathematics.* The absolute value of a number, regardless of sign: *The numerical values of* −9 *and* +9 *are equal.*

nu·mer·ol·o·gy (néw-mə-róllǝji ‖ noō-) *n.* The study of the occult meanings of numbers and of their supposed influence on human fate. [Latin *numerus,* NUMBER + -LOGY.] —**nu·mer·o·log·i·cal** (-rə-lójik'l) *adj.* —**nu·mer·ol·o·gist** (-róllǝjist) *n.*

nu·mer·ous (néw-mərəss ‖ noō-) *adj.* **1.** Consisting of many persons or things: *a numerous collection.* **2.** Many: *numerous books.* [Latin *numerōsus,* from *numerus,* NUMBER.] —**nu·mer·ous·ly** *adv.* —**nu·mer·ous·ness** *n.*

Nu·mid·i·a (new-míddi-ə ‖ noō-). Ancient country of north Africa, roughly corresponding to modern Algeria. It was part of the Carthaginian empire before the Punic Wars, but with the peace of 201 B.C., Numidia emerged as a separate kingdom under the rule of Masinissa. Its independence lasted until Juba I sided with Pompey in the Roman civil war; after Julius Caesar's victory (46 B.C.), it was absorbed into the Roman empire. —**Nu·mid·i·an** *adj. & n.*

nu·mi·na. Plural of **numen.**

nu·mi·nous (néw-minəss ‖ noō-) *adj.* **1.** Of or pertaining to a numen. **2.** Spiritually elevated or elevating; mysterious and awe-inspiring.
~*n.* The presence or revelation of a numen. Used with *the.* [Latin *nūmen* (stem *nūmin-*), NUMEN.]

nu·mis·mat·ics (néw-miz-máttiks ‖ noō-, -miss-) *n. Used with a singular verb.* The study and collection of money and medals. Also called "numismatology". [From *numismatic* (adjective), from French *numismatique,* from Latin *numisma,* a coin, from Greek *nomisma,* usage, current coin, from *nomizein,* to have in use, from *nomos,* custom.] —**nu·mis·mat·ic** *adj.* —**nu·mis·ma·tist** (new-míz-mətist ‖ noō-, -miss-) *n.*

num·ma·ry (númməri) *adj.* Of or pertaining to coins. [Latin *nummārius,* from *nummus,* coin.]

num·mu·lar (númmewlər) *adj.* Shaped like a coin; circular. [French *nummulaire,* from Latin *nummulus,* diminutive of *nummus,* a coin, "currency", probably from Greek *nomimos,* customary, legal, from *nomos,* custom.]

num·mu·lite (númmew-līt) *n.* Any extinct protozoan of the family Nummulitidae. They were chiefly marine foraminifers characterised by a coin-shaped shell closely coiled and divided into chambers. [New Latin *Nummulites* (genus name) : Latin *nummulus,* coin (see **nummular**) + -*ites,* -ITE.] —**num·mu·lit·ic** (-líttik) *adj.*

num·nah. Variant of **numdah.**

num·skull, numb·skull (núm-skul) *n.* A stupid person; a blockhead. [NUMB + SKULL.]

nun[1] (nun) *n.* **1.** A woman who belongs to a religious order devoted to religious service or meditation, usually under vows of poverty, chastity, and obedience, as in the Roman Catholic, Anglican, and Orthodox Churches. **2.** Any of various birds, especially a pigeon of a domestic breed, having a tuft of feathers on its head. [Middle English *nunne, nun, nonne,* from Old English *nunne* and Old French *nonne,* both from Medieval Latin *nonna,* nun (originally a respectful form of address to old women).]

nun[2] (noōn, noōn) *n.* **1.** The 14th letter of the Hebrew alphabet. **2.** The 25th letter of the Arabic alphabet. The consonant sound represented by either of these letters. [Hebrew and Arabic *nūn,* akin to NU.]

nun·a·tak (núnnə-tak) *n.* An isolated mountain peak or hill that projects through the surface of surrounding glacial ice or snow. [Eskimo.]

nun buoy (nun) *n.* A conical buoy, painted red, marking the right side of a channel leading into a harbour. [From obsolete *nun,* child's spinning top.]

Nunc Di·mit·tis (núngk di-míttiss, noōngk) *n.* **1.** The canticle of Simeon, beginning *"Nunc dimittis servum tuum"* ("Now lettest thou thy servant depart"). Luke 2:29-32. **2.** A musical setting of this. **3.** *Small* n, *small* d. Permission to depart; a dismissal. [Latin.]

nun·ci·a·ture (nún-si-ə-chər, -shi-, -tewr) *n.* The office or term of a nuncio. [Italian *nunciatura,* from *nuncio,* NUNCIO.]

nun·ci·o (nún-si-ō, -shi-) *n., pl.* -**os.** An ambassador from the pope. [Italian, from Latin *nūntius,* messenger.]

nun·cle (núngk'l) *n. Archaic & Regional.* An uncle. [From *an uncle.*]

nun·cu·pa·tive (núng-kew-paytiv, -kéwpətiv) *adj. Law.* Designating a will delivered orally to witnesses rather than written. [Medieval

nuthatch Sitta europaea, *the nuthatch, is one of the few birds which regularly climb down trees head first. It gets its name from its habit of wedging nuts in the bark of a tree and using its bill as a hatchet to split them open and get at the kernel.*

nutmeg *The aromatic spice used in cooking is made from the fruit of the nutmeg tree,* Myristica fragrans, *which is native to the Moluccas islands of Indonesia. The nutmeg is the kernel of the tree's red and black seeds, and the seeds are contained in the fleshy fruit which splits open naturally when ripe (above). The seeds' waxy red coating is dried to produce another spice, mace.*

Latin *nūncupātīvus,* from Latin *nūncupāre,* to call by name, name one's heirs : *nōmen,* name + *capere,* to take.]

Nun·ea·ton (nun-éet'n). Manufacturing town in Warwickshire, central England. It was the birthplace of the novelist George Eliot. It derives its name from the local 12th-century nunnery.

nun·ner·y (núnnəri) *n., pl.* **-ies.** A community of nuns or the building or buildings in which they live.

N.U.P.E. (néwpi || nóopi) National Union of Public Employees.

nup·tial (núp-sh'l, -ch'l. *Note: the pronunciations* -tew-əl, -tewl *are nonstandard.*) *adj.* **1.** Of or pertaining to marriage or the wedding ceremony. **2.** *Zoology.* Of or at the time of mating: *the nuptial flight of ants.*
~*n. Formal. Usually plural.* A wedding ceremony. Often used humorously. See Synonyms at **marriage.** [Latin *nuptiālis,* from *nuptiae,* wedding, from *nūbere* (past participle *nuptus*), to take a husband.] **—nup·tial·ly** *adv.*

N.U.R. National Union of Railwaymen.

nurd. Variant of **nerd.**

Nu·rem·berg (néwr-əm-berg || nóor-). *German* **Nürn·berg** (nŭrn-bairk). City in Bavaria, southern West Germany, lying on the river Pegnitz. It dates from the 11th century. From 1933–38 the Nazis held their annual party congresses there and in 1945–46 it was the site of the trials of the Nazi war criminals.

Nu·re·yev (newr-ráy-ef, néwr-ay-; *Russian* noo-ryáy-if), **Rudolf (Hametovich)** (1938–). Russian-born ballet dancer and choreographer. With the Kirov Ballet of Leningrad until his defection to the United Kingdom (1961), he joined the Royal Ballet and became the most celebrated male dancer of his generation. His association with Margot Fonteyn is remembered as one of the great partnerships of classical ballet. He took Austrian citizenship in 1982.

nurse (nurss) *n.* **1.** A person trained to care for the sick or disabled. **2.** Especially formerly, a woman employed to take care of another's children; a nursemaid. **3.** A woman employed to suckle children other than her own; a wet nurse. **4.** The state of being nursed: *the baby was put out to nurse.* **5.** That which fosters some quality or condition: *Leisure is the nurse of culture.* **6.** A worker ant or bee that cares for the young in the insect colony. **7.** A mature tree that shields a younger or newly planted tree from the elements.
~*v.* **nursed, nursing, nurses.** —*tr.* **1.** To feed (a baby or young offspring) at the breast; suckle. **2.** To care for or tend (a child or invalid). **3.** To try to cure or treat: *to nurse a cough.* **4.** To take special care of; foster; cultivate: *She nursed her business through the depression.* **5.** To keep in touch and foster relations with for one's own advantage. **6.** To harbour or bear privately in the mind: *nursing a grudge.* **7.** To hold or clasp carefully or soothingly: *He nursed his bruised knee.* **8.** To sit near, as if taking care of (a fire). **9.** To drink (usually an alcoholic drink) slowly. **10.** In billiards, to keep (the balls) together so as to make a series of cannons. —*intr.* **1.** To take nourishment from the breast; suckle. **2.** To serve as a nurse. [Middle English *norse, nurse,* from Old French *norrice,* from Late Latin *nūtrīcia,* from *nūtrīcius,* adjective of *nūtrix,* a nurse.] **—nurs·er** *n.*

nurse hound *n.* A type of dogfish.

nurse·maid (núrss-mayd) *n.* Also **nurs·er·y·maid** (-ri-, -əri-). A girl or woman employed to take care of children.

nurs·er·y (núrss-ri, -əri) *n., pl.* **-ies.** **1.** A building, room, or area set apart for the use of young children. **2.** A nursery school. **3.** A place where plants are grown for sale, transplanting, or experimentation. **4.** Any place in which something is produced or developed. **5.** In billiards, a series of cannons, or any one of the series, made when the three balls are adjacent to a cushion. In this sense, also called "nursery cannon". [Middle English *norserie,* from *norse,* NURSE.]

nurs·er·y·man (núrss-ri-mən, -əri-) *n., pl.* **-men** (-mən). A man who owns or works in a nursery for plants.

nursery rhyme *n.* A short, traditional rhymed poem or song for children.

nursery school *n.* A school for very young children. Also called "nursery".

nursery slopes *pl.n.* The lower, gentle ski-slopes used by those still learning to ski.

nursery stakes *pl.n. Used with a singular or plural verb.* A horse race for two-year-olds.

nurse shark *n.* Any of various large sharks of the family Orectolobidae, such as *Ginglymostoma cirratum,* a scavenging shark found in the Atlantic. [Middle English *nusse fisshe* (later altered through influence of *nurse*), perhaps from mistaken division of *a nuss* for *an huss* (fish), from *huss*†, shark, dogfish.]

nurs·ing home (núrssing) *n.* **1.** A private hospital or home for convalescent or aged people. **2.** A private maternity hospital.

nursing mother *n.* **1.** A woman who is breastfeeding her child. **2.** A foster mother.

nurs·ling, nurse·ling (núrssling) *n.* **1.** A nursing infant or young animal. **2.** A carefully nurtured person or thing.

nur·ture (núrchər) *n.* **1.** Anything that nourishes; sustenance; food. **2.** The act of promoting development or growth. **3.** *Biology.* The sum of environmental influences and conditions acting upon an organism, and partly determining its structure or behaviour.
~*tr.v.* **nurtured, -turing, -tures.** **1.** To nourish. **2.** To educate or train. **3.** To foster the development of. [Middle English *norture, nurture,* from Old French *nour(e)ture,* from Late Latin *nūtrītūra,* a feeding, from Latin *nūtrīre,* to feed.] **—nur·tur·er** *n.*

N.U.S. **1.** National Union of Seamen. **2.** National Union of Students.

nut (nut) *n.* **1. a.** A hard-shelled, solid-textured, one-seeded fruit that does not split open, such as an acorn or a hazelnut. **b.** Any seed borne in a fruit having a hard shell, such as the peanut or almond. **c.** The kernel of any of these. **2.** *Informal.* Any difficult person, endeavour, or problem. Used chiefly in the phrase *a hard* or *tough nut to crack.* **3.** *Slang.* The head. **4.** *Slang.* An eccentric, fanciful, or deranged person. **5.** *Slang.* An enthusiast; a buff. **6. a.** A ridge of wood at the top of the fingerboard or neck of stringed instruments, over which the strings pass. **b.** A device at the lower end of the bow of a violin or similar instrument, used for adjusting the hairs. **7.** A small block of metal or wood having a central, threaded hole, designed to fit round and secure a bolt or screw. **8.** Any small piece of a substance, as of coal or butter. **9.** A flat, sweet, round biscuit, usually flavoured with ginger. **10.** *Printing.* An **en** *(see).* **—do (one's) nut.** *British Slang.* To become very angry. **—off (one's) nut.** *Slang.* Crazy; mad. See **nuts.**
~*intr.v.* **nutted, nutting, nuts.** To gather or search for nuts. [Middle English *note, nute,* Old English *hnutu.*]

N.U.T. National Union of Teachers.

nu·tant (néw-t'nt || nóo-) *adj. Botany.* Pointing downwards; drooping. Said of flowers. [Latin *nutāns* (stem *nutant-*), present participle of *nutāre,* to nod.]

nu·ta·tion (new-táysh'n || nóo-) *n.* **1.** A nodding of the head. **2.** *Astronomy.* A small periodic motion of the celestial pole of the Earth with respect to the pole of the ecliptic. **3.** *Botany.* A spiral growth movement in the stems of certain plants, especially climbers, caused by differential growth rates in the stem. [Latin *nūtātiō* (stem *nūtātiōn-*), from *nūtāre,* frequentative of *nuere* (unattested), to nod.] **—nu·ta·tion·al** *adj.*

nut-brown (nút-brówn) *n.* Rich reddish brown. **—nut-brown** *adj.*

nut·case (nút-kayss) *n. Slang.* A deranged or very stupid person.

nut·crack·er (nút-krackər) *n.* **1.** *Usually plural.* An implement, typically consisting of two levers, used to crack nuts. **2. a.** A bird, *Nucifraga caryocatactes,* of northern Eurasia. **b.** A bird, the nuthatch.

nut·gall (nút-gawl) *n.* A nutlike swelling produced on an oak or other tree by certain parasitic wasps. Also called "gallnut".

nut·hatch (nút-hach) *n.* Any of several small birds of the family Sittidae, having long, sharp bills, and noted for their ability to manoeuvre on tree trunks and branches. Also called "nutcracker". [Middle English *notehache, nuthak,* "nut hatchet" (named from its habit of wedging nuts in bark and hacking them open) : *nute,* NUT + *hache,* axe, hatchet, from Old French, from Medieval Latin *hapia,* from Germanic *hapja* (unattested).]

nut·house (nút-howss) *n. Slang.* A mental hospital. Often considered offensive.

nut·let (nút-lət, -lit) *n.* **1.** A small nut. **2.** The stone in certain fruits, such as the peach or cherry. **3.** A hard, one-seeded portion of a schizocarpic fruit, such as the four parts making up fruits of the dead nettle family.

nut·meat (nút-meet) *n.* **1.** A vegetarian food made from nuts. **2.** *U.S.* The edible kernel of a nut.

nut·meg (nút-meg) *n.* **1.** An evergreen tree, *Myristica fragrans,* native to the East Indies and cultivated elsewhere in the tropics. **2.** The hard, aromatic seed of this tree, much used as a spice when grated or ground. See **mace.** **3.** Greyish to moderate brown. [Middle English *notemugge, nutemuge,* from Old French *nois muscade,* from Vulgar Latin *nuce muscāta* (unattested), "musky nut" : Latin *nux,* nut + *muscus,* MUSK.] **—nut·meg** *adj.*

nut oil *n.* Oil obtained from nuts such as walnuts and hazelnuts and used in paints and varnishes.

nu·tri·a (néw-tri-ə || nóo-) *n.* **1.** A rodent, the **coypu** *(see).* **2.** The fur of the coypu, often dyed to resemble beaver. **3.** Olive grey. [Spanish *nutr(i)a,* nasalised variant of *lutra,* otter, from Latin *lutra.*] **—nu·tri·a** *adj.*

nu·tri·ent (néw-tri-ənt || nóo-) *n.* Something that nourishes; especially, a nourishing ingredient in a food, or the mineral substances absorbed by the roots of plants.
~*adj.* Having nutritive value, as certain body fluids do. [Latin *nūtriēns* (stem *nūtrient-*), present participle of *nūtrīre,* to nourish.]

nu·tri·ment (néw-tri-mənt || nóo-) *n.* **1.** Anything that nourishes; food. **2.** Anything that aids growth or development. [Latin *nūtrīmentum,* from *nūtrīre,* to nourish.] **—nu·tri·men·tal** (-mént'l) *adj.*

nu·tri·tion (new-trísh'n || nóo-) *n.* **1.** The process of nourishing or being nourished; especially, the interrelated steps by which a living organism assimilates food and uses it for growth and for replacement of tissues. **2.** The study of food value, food intake, and the like. [Old French, from Late Latin *nūtrītiō* (stem *nūtrītiōn-*), from Latin *nūtrīre,* to nourish.] **—nu·tri·tion·al** *adj.* **—nu·tri·tion·al·ly** *adv.*

nu·tri·tion·ist (new-trísh'n-ist || nóo-) *n.* A person who specialises in the study of nutrition.

nu·tri·tious (new-tríshəss || nóo-) *adj.* **1.** Nourishing. **2.** Aiding the growth and development of a living organism. [Latin *nūtrītius,* from *nūtrix,* a nurse.] **—nu·tri·tious·ly** *adv.* **—nu·tri·tious·ness** *n.*

nu·tri·tive (néw-trə-tiv, -tri- || nóo-) *adj.* Promoting nutrition; nourishing.
~*n.* A nutritious food. [Middle English *nutritif,* from Old French, from Late Latin *nūtrītīvus,* from Latin *nūtrīre,* to feed, nourish.] **—nu·tri·tive·ly** *adv.*

nuts (nuts) *pl.n. Vulgar Slang.* The testicles.
~*adj. Slang.* **1.** Crazy; insane. **2.** Extremely fond or enthusiastic: *She's nuts about opera.*

~*interj. Slang.* Used to express contempt, disappointment, defiance, or emphatic refusal. See **nut**. [From NUT. Noun, by comparison in shape; adjective, from phrases such as *off one's nut* (head); interjection, from noun.]

nuts and bolts *pl. n. Informal.* The practical, basic details.

nut·shell (nút-shel) *n.* The shell enclosing the kernel of a nut. —**in a nutshell.** In concise or brief form; epitomised.

nut·ter¹ (núttər) *n.* A person who goes nutting.

nutter² *n. British Slang.* A deranged or eccentric person. [From NUT (mad person).]

nut·ty (nútti) *adj.* **-tier, -tiest. 1.** Containing or producing many nuts. **2.** Having a flavour or texture like that of nuts. **3.** *Informal.* Deranged; crazy. —**nut·ti·ly** *adv.* —**nut·ti·ness** *n.*

Nuuk (nōōk). Formerly **Godt·håb** (gód-hawb). Capital of Greenland, a port situated on the southwest coast of the country. Founded by the Danes (1721), it is a centre for the fishing of cod and halibut.

nux vom·i·ca (núks vómmikə) *n.* **1.** A tree, *Strychnos nux-vomica*, native to southeastern Asia, having poisonous seeds that are the source of strychnine, brucine, and a medicinal preparation. **2.** A seed of this tree. [Medieval Latin, "emetic nut" : Latin *nux*, nut + *vomica*, from Latin *vomere*, to VOMIT.]

nuz·zle (núzz'l) *v.* **-zled, -zling, -zles.** —*tr.* **1.** To rub or push against gently with or as if with the nose or snout. **2.** To uproot with the snout. —*intr.* **1.** To make rubbing or pressing motions with the nose or snout. **2.** To nestle or cuddle. [Earlier *nousle*, Middle English *noselen*, from *nose*, NOSE.]

NW northwest; northwestern.

NWbN northwest by north.

NWbW northwest by west.

N.W.T. Northwest Territories.

N.Y. New York.

nyaff (nyaf) *n. Scottish Slang.* A boorish or stupid person. [Perhaps akin to dialect *gonoph*, thief, ultimately from Hebrew *gannābh*, thief.]

nya·la (nyaálə) *n., pl.* **-las** or collectively **nyala.** A large spiral-horned antelope, *Tragelaphus angasi*, native to southern Africa. Also called "inyala". [Venda, from Zulu *inxala*.]

Nyan·ja (nyánjə) *n., pl.* **-jas** or collectively **Nyanja. 1.** A member of a central African people living mainly in Malawi. **2.** The Bantu language of this people, of the Niger-Congo family of languages. —**Nyan·ja** *adj.*

Nyasa, Lake. See **Lake Malawi.**

Nyasaland. See **Malawi.**

nyct–, nycti–, nycto– *comb. form.* Indicates night or darkness; for example, **nyctophobia.**

nyc·ta·lo·pi·a (níktə-lṓpi-ə) *n.* **1.** Vision that is normal in daylight but abnormally weak when the light is dim. In this sense, also called "night blindness". Compare **hemeralopia. 2.** The inability to see clearly except when the light is dim. Not in technical usage. [Late Latin *nyctalōpia*, from Latin *nyctalops*, night-blind, from Greek *nuktalōps* : *nux* (stem *nukt-*), night + *alaos†*, blind + *ōps*, eye.] —**nyc·ta·lo·pic** (-lṓpik, -lóppik) *adj.*

nyc·ti·nas·ty (níkti-nasti) *n.* The opening and closing of leaves and petals in response to changes of light and temperature. [Greek *nux* (stem *nukt-*), night + -NASTY.] —**nyc·ti·nas·tic** (-nástik) *adj.*

nyc·tit·ro·pism (nik-títtrə-piz'm) *n.* The tendency of the leaves or other parts of some plants to change their position at nightfall.

[Greek *nux* (stem *nukt-*), night + -TROPISM.] —**nyc·ti·tro·pic** (níkti-tróppik) *adj.*

nyc·to·pho·bi·a (ník-tō-fṓbi-ə, -tə-) *n.* An abnormal fear of the dark or of night. —**nyc·to·pho·bic** *adj.*

Nye·re·re (nye-ráir-i. *Note: not* nī-), **Dr. Julius (Kambarage)** (1922–). Tanzanian politician. After campaigning for Tanganyika's independence from the United Kingdom, he became its premier (1961) before taking office as president (1962) of the new independent republic. In 1964, he negotiated union with Zanzibar to form the state of Tanzania.

ny·lon (nī-lon, *rarely* -lən) *n.* **1.** Any of a family of high-strength, resilient, synthetic materials, the long-chain molecules of which contain the recurring amide group CONH. **2.** Cloth or thread made from nylon. **3.** *Plural.* Women's stockings made of nylon or a similar synthetic fabric. [Coined by the inventors, with *-on* by analogy with forms such as *rayon.*]

nymph (nimf) *n.* **1.** *Greek & Roman Mythology.* Any of numerous female nature spirits, inhabiting and animistically representing features of nature. **2.** *Poetic.* A beautiful young woman. **3.** *Zoology.* Any of the young of insects, such as the mayfly or dragonfly, that undergoes incomplete metamorphosis. Compare **pupa.** [Middle English *nimphe*, from Latin *nympha*, nymph, pupa, from Greek *numphē*, nymph, bride.] —**nymph·al, nym·phe·an** (nímfi-ən ‖ *U.S.* also nim-fée-ən) *adj.*

nym·phae (ním-fee) *pl.n. Singular* **nym·pha** (-fə). *Anatomy.* The **la·bia minora** *(see).* [New Latin, from Latin, NYMPH.]

nym·pha·lid (nímfəlid) *n.* Any of various medium to large butterflies of the family Nymphalidae. The family includes the admirals, fritillaries, and tortoiseshells. [New Latin *Nymphalidae* (family) : *Nymphalis* (genus), from Latin *nymphālis*, "nymphal", from *nympha*, NYMPH + -IDAE.] —**nym·pha·lid** *adj.*

nym·phet (nímfit, nim-fét) *n.* **1.** A young nymph. **2.** A pubescent or prepubescent girl regarded as sexually desirable to adult men. [Old French *nymphette*, diminutive of *nymphe*, NYMPH.]

nym·pho (nímfō) *n., pl.* **-phos.** *Slang.* A nymphomaniac.

nym·pho·lep·sy (nímfə-lep-si) *n., pl.* **-sies.** A frenzy induced by an obsession for something unattainable. [From NYMPHOLEPT.]

nym·pho·lept (nímfə-lept) *n.* One in a state of nympholepsy. [Greek *numpholēptos*, "caught by nymphs" : *numphē*, NYMPH + *lēptos*, seized.] —**nym·pho·lept, nym·pho·lep·tic** (-léptik) *adj.*

nym·pho·ma·ni·a (nímfə-máyni-ə) *n.* Abnormally strong sexual desire in a heterosexual woman, especially when directed at a large number of men. Compare **satyriasis.** [New Latin : NYMPH + -MANIA.] —**nym·pho·ma·ni·ac** (-ak) *n. & adj.*

Ny·norsk (née-nawrsk, néw-; *Norwegian* nū́-) *n.* One of the two officially recognised and mutually intelligible forms of Norwegian, incorporating various dialects. Formerly called "Landsmål". Compare **Bokmål.** [Norwegian, "new Norwegian".]

NYP not yet published.

Nysa. See **Neisse.**

nys·tag·mus (ni-stágməss) *n. Pathology.* A spasmodic, involuntary movement of the eyeball. [New Latin, from Greek *nustagmos*, drowsiness, from *nustazein*, to be sleepy.] —**nys·tag·mic** *adj.*

nys·ta·tin (nísstətin) *n. Medicine.* An antibiotic derived from the bacterium *Streptomyces noursei*, used to treat various fungal infections, especially thrush. [From *New York State* (where it was developed) + -IN.]

N.Z. New Zealand.

PRONUNCIATION KEY

a, trap; aa, father; ai, fair; ar, star; aw, lawn; ay, play; b, bb, stab; rubber; ch, church; ck, ticket; d, dd, dead; ladder; e, dress; ee, bee; er, defer; ew, few; ewr, pure; ə, about; ər, letter; f, ff, fife; differ; g, gg, giggle; h, hat; i, kit; ī, price; īr, fire; j, judge; k, kick; l, ll, let; 'l, needle; m, mm, man; n, nn, no; 'n, sudden; ng, thing; o, lot; ō, no; ōō, foot; ōō, shoe; oor, poor; ow, cow; owr, hour; oy, boy; p, pp, pepper; r, rr, red; s, ss, sauce; sh, ship; t, tt, totter; th, thick; th, this; smooth; u, cut; ur, turn; v, vv, valve; w, wet; y, yes; z, zz, zebra; zh, vision; pleasure

IN FOREIGN WORDS:

aN, oN, Saint-Saëns; hl, Llanelli; Hluhluwe; kh, loch; lough; Khaled

STRESS MARK:

ín-sīt, insight; in-sīt, incite

o, O (ō) *n., pl.* **o's** or *rare* **os, Os** or **O's. 1.** The 15th letter of the modern English alphabet. **2.** Any of the speech sounds represented by this letter. **3.** A zero: *a phone number with three O's.* **4.** Anything shaped like the letter **O**; a circle.

o, O, o., O. *Note:* As an abbreviation or symbol, *o* may be a small or a capital letter, with or without a full stop. Established forms or those generally preferred precede the definition. When no form is given, all four forms are in general use in that sense. **1. O, O.** ocean. **2. o., O.** octavo. **3. O.** October (unofficial). **4. O, O.** old. **5. o.** only. **6. O, O.** order. **7. O** The symbol for the element oxygen. **8. o.** pint. [Latin *octarius.*] **9. O** A human blood type of the **ABO** group. See **ABO. 10.** The 15th in a series, or the 14th when *J* is omitted.

O (ō) *interj.* **1.** Used before the noun or noun phrase in direct address, especially, as in poetry or prayer, to express earnestness or solemnity: *O my people, what have I done unto thee?* (Micah 6:3). **2.** Variant of **oh.**

, **Usage:** *O* is used to introduce an invocation, entreaty, or the like, in literary and religious contexts: *O God; O mighty ocean!* It is never followed immediately by a punctuation mark, and it is always capitalised. *Oh* is used to express a reflective pause or a degree of emotion: *Oh, I see.* It is capitalised only when it is the first word in a sentence, and is followed by a comma, or, when the emphasis is strong, by an exclamation mark. It may be part of a written sentence, or stand alone. In a few phrases, *Oh* can be replaced by *O,* especially in American English: *O my!; Oh/O dear!*

o' (ə, ō) *prep.* A reduced form of the preposition *of.* Used especially in the phrase *o'clock,* but also found in such terms as *will-o'-the-wisp,* and *man-o'-war,* and in numerous dialects.

O' (ō, ə) *prefix.* Indicates a descendant of. Used in various Irish surnames, for example *O'Connor, O'Malley, O'Reilly.* [Irish *ō,* grandson, descendant, from Old Irish *aue.*]

-o *n., adj., & adv. suffix.* Used to form an informal, abbreviated, or slang variant or word; for example, *ammo, blotto, wino.* [Perhaps from *oh* (interjection), used as humorous suffix.]

-o- *infix.* Used to connect the elements of a compound word, either in the sense of "and", or for the sake of euphony; for example, **Anglo-American; meritocracy.**

oaf (ōf) *n., pl.* **oafs** or *rare* **oaves. 1.** A stupid or clumsy person. **2.** *Obsolete.* A deformed child supposedly substituted for a human one by elves; a changeling. [Earlier *ouph, aufe,* elf, goblin, from Old Norse *alfr.*] —**oaf·ish** *adj.* —**oaf·ish·ly** *adv.* —**oaf·ish·ness** *n.*

O·a·hu (ō-a'a-hōō). Third largest island of the U.S. state of Hawaii in the north Pacific. It is the most populous, and highly developed with an economy based on sugar and pineapple plantations and tourism. The important U.S. military installations on the island include Pearl Harbor, attacked by the Japanese (1941). Honolulu is the chief port and state capital.

oak (ōk) *n.* **1.** Any of various deciduous or evergreen trees or shrubs of the genus *Quercus,* having lobed leaves and bearing acorns as fruit. See **cork oak, durmast oak, holm oak. 2.** The durable wood of any of these trees. **3.** Any of various trees or shrubs resembling the oak in some feature, such as the **poison oak** (see). **4.** Something made of oak wood, especially a heavy outer door to a set of rooms in an Oxford or Cambridge college. **5.** Any of various brown shades resembling that of oak wood. [Middle English *ok, ook,* Old English *āc,* from Germanic *aik-* (unattested).] —**oak** *adj.*

oak apple *n.* A harmless gall on oak trees, caused by the larva of a type of wasp. Also called "oak gall".

oak·en (ōkən) *adj.* Made of oak wood or a material resembling it.

oak fern *n.* Any of various ferns, especially *Dryopteris linnaeana,* having lobed fronds resembling oak leaves.

Oak·ley (ōkli), **Annie,** born Phoebe Anne Oakley Mozee (1860–1926). U.S. sharpshooter. She was a star attraction of Buffalo Bill's Wild West Show.

Oak Ridge. City in Tennessee, United States. It was founded (1943) by the U.S. government around the plants set up to produce uranium and plutonium for nuclear bombs.

Oaks (ōks) *n. Used with a singular verb.* A horse race held annually at Epsom for three-year-old fillies. Preceded by *the.* [From the name of an estate near Epsom.]

oa·kum (ōkəm) *n.* Loose hemp or jute fibre, sometimes treated with tar, creosote, or asphalt. It is used for caulking seams in wooden ships and packing pipe joints. [Middle English *okum,* Old English *ācumba,* "off-combings" : *ā-,* off, away + *-cumba,* from *cemban,* to comb.]

O. & M. organisation and method.

O.A.P. old-age pension; old-age pensioner.

oar (or ‖ ōr) *n.* **1.** A long, thin pole, usually wooden, with a blade at one end, used to row and, occasionally, to steer a boat. **2.** A person using an oar; a rower. **3.** An implement for stirring; especially, one used in brewing. —**put (one's) oar in.** To intrude impertinently; meddle. —**rest on (one's) oars.** To stop trying or working; take a rest.

~*v.* **oared, oaring, oars.** —*tr.* **1.** To propel with or as if with oars. **2.** To traverse with or as if with oars: *an hour to oar the strait.* —*intr.* To move forwards by or as if by rowing. [Middle English *oor, or,* Old English *ār,* from Common Germanic *airo* (unattested).] —**oared** *adj.*

oar·fish (or-fish ‖ ōr-) *n., pl.* **-fishes** or collectively **oarfish.** A marine fish, *Regalecus glesne,* having a slender body up to 8 metres (26 feet) long and a dorsal fin extending the entire body length.

oar·lock (or-lok ‖ ōr-) *n. U.S.* A **rowlock** (see).

oars·man (orz-mən ‖ ōrz-) *n., pl.* **-men** (-mən). A person who rows, especially an expert in rowing; a rower. [*Oar's,* possessive of OAR + MAN.]

oar·weed (or-weed ‖ ōr-) *n.* Any of various seaweeds of the family Laminariaceae, such as **kelp** (see). [From dialect *oare, ore,* seaweed (from Middle English *ware,* Old English *wār*) + WEED.]

OAS 1. Organisation de L'Armée Secrète: a terrorist organisation of French settlers in Algeria opposed to Algerian independence. **2.** Organisation of American States.

o·a·sis (ō-áy-siss) *n., pl.* **-ses** (-seez). **1.** A fertile or green area in a desert, resulting from the presence of water. **2.** A place or situation preserved from surrounding unpleasantness; a refuge: *The library was an oasis of calm in the noisy building.* [Late Latin *oasis,* from Greek, probably from an Egyptian word akin to Coptic *ouahe,* oasis, "dwelling area".]

oast (ōst) *n.* **1.** A kiln for drying hops or malt, or for drying and curing tobacco. **2.** An oast-house. [Middle English *ost,* Old English *āst.*]

oast-house (ōst-howss) *n.* A building containing hop-drying kilns, usually having a conical roof.

Oast·ler (ōstlər), **Richard** (1789–1861). British reformer. His campaigning against the exploitation of child labour in factories was instrumental in the introduction of a legal maximum of ten hours work a day for minors (1847).

oat. See **oats.**

oat·cake (ōt-kayk) *n.* A biscuit of baked oatmeal, eaten especially in Scotland and northern England.

oat·en (ōt'n) *adj.* Of, made of, or containing oats, oatmeal, or oat straw: *oaten fodder.*

Oates (ōts), **Joyce Carol** (1938–). U.S. novelist, short-story writer, and poet. Her third novel, *Them,* was awarded the U.S. National Book Award in 1969.

Oates, Titus (1649–1705). English clergyman and agitator. His allegations of a Roman Catholic conspiracy (the Popish Plot, 1678) to murder Charles II aroused anti-Catholic public hysteria, and led to the arrest and execution of many Catholics and the passing of the 1678 Test Act excluding Catholics from Parliament. Oates was later discredited and imprisoned.

oat grass *n.* **1.** Any grass of the genus *Arrhenatherum*; especially, *A. elatius,* common in meadows. **2.** Any of several oatlike grasses.

oath (ōth) *n., pl.* **oaths** (ōthz, ōths). **1.** A formal statement declaring the truth of a claim or promising to fulfil a pledge, often calling upon God or a sacred object as witness. **2.** The words or formula of such a declaration or promise. **3.** That which is promised or declared. **4.** An irreverent or blasphemous use of the name of God or anything held sacred. **5.** Any act or instance of cursing or swearing. **—on** or **under oath. 1.** Bound by an oath. **2.** *Law.* Sworn to tell the truth. [Middle English *ooth,* Old English *āth,* from Germanic *aithaz* (unattested).]

oat·meal (ōt-meel) *n.* **1.** Meal made from oats; ground oats. **2.** A porridge made from rolled or ground oats. **3.** Greyish yellow to fawn. **—oat·meal** *adj.*

oats (ōts) *pl.n.* **1.** Any of several grasses of the genus *Avena;* especially, *A. sativa,* widely cultivated for its edible seeds. **2.** The seeds of *Avena sativa* used as a food and fodder. **3.** *Singular. Archaic.* A shepherd's musical pipe made of an oat straw. **—feel (one's) oats.** *U.S. Informal.* **1.** To be joyous or frisky. **2.** To feel self-satisfied and important, or to act in a way suggesting this. **—get (one's) oats.** *Slang.* To have sexual intercourse. **—off (one's) oats.** *Informal.* To have no appetite for food. **—sow (one's) oats** or **wild oats.** To indulge in adventures and licentiousness during one's youth. [Old English *āte*† (plural *ātan*).] **—oat** *adj.*

O.A.U. Organisation of African Unity.

Ob (ob). River of Siberia, U.S.S.R., formed by the meeting of the Biya and Katun rivers, which rise in the Altai mountains. It flows north to the Arctic Ocean via the Gulf of Ob and Kara Sea.

ob– *prefix.* Indicates inverse shape or attachment; for example, **obcordate, obovate.** [In borrowed Latin compounds, *ob-* becomes *o-* before *m,* as in *omit, oc-* before *c,* as in *occlude, of-* before *f,* as in *offend, op-* before *p,* as in *oppose. Ob-* indicates: **1.** To, towards, as in **offer, obvert. 2.** Directed towards in a negative way, against, in opposition to, as in **opponent, obstacle. 3.** Opposite to, before, on, in front of, as in **obsess, obstetric. 4.** On account of, for, as in **obsecrate. 5.** In a certain direction, down, down upon, over, behind, as in **occasion, omit. 6.** Out of, away from, as in **obliterate. 7.** Intensified action, as in **obdurate, obtain.** Latin *ob-,* from the preposition *ob,* to, towards, in front of, on account of, against.]

ob. 1. incidentally [Latin *obiter*]. **2.** obiit. **3.** oboe.

O.B. *British.* **1.** old boy. **2.** outside broadcast.

Obad. Obadiah (Old Testament).

O·ba·di·ah[1] (ōbə-dī-ə). A Hebrew prophet.

Obadiah[2] *n. Abbr.* **Obad.** The book in the Old Testament written by Obadiah. Also, in the Douay Bible, "Abdias".

ob·bli·ga·to, ob·li·ga·to (òbbli-gáa-tō) *adj. Music.* Not to be left out; indispensable. Said of an accompaniment that is an integral part of a piece. Compare **ad libitum.**

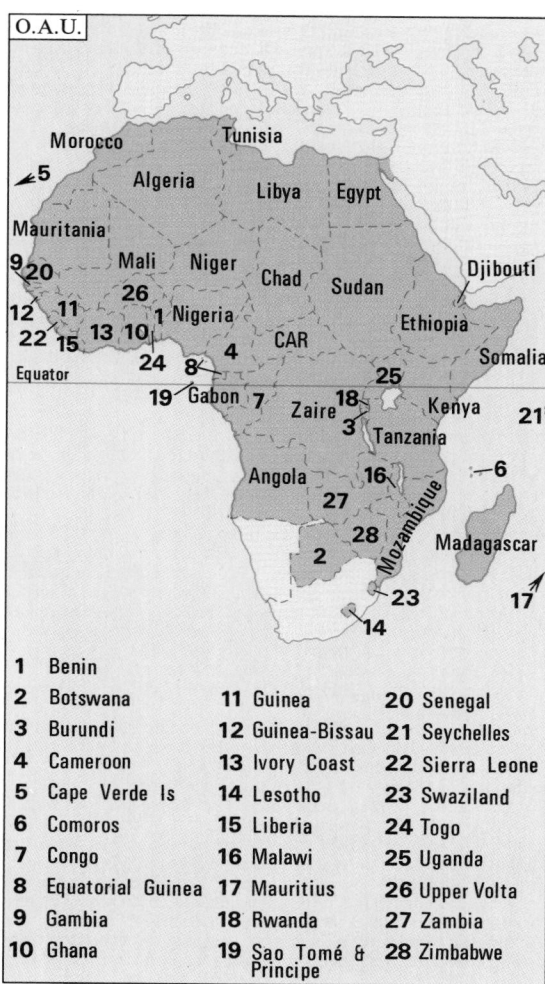

O.A.U.		
1	Benin	
2	Botswana	11 Guinea
3	Burundi	12 Guinea-Bissau
4	Cameroon	13 Ivory Coast
5	Cape Verde Is	14 Lesotho
6	Comoros	15 Liberia
7	Congo	16 Malawi
8	Equatorial Guinea	17 Mauritius
9	Gambia	18 Rwanda
10	Ghana	19 Sao Tomé & Principe

20	Senegal	
21	Seychelles	
22	Sierra Leone	
23	Swaziland	
24	Togo	
25	Uganda	
26	Upper Volta	
27	Zambia	
28	Zimbabwe	

~n., pl. **obbligatos** or **-ti** (-tee). *Music.* An obbligato musical accompaniment. [Italian, past participle of *obbligare,* to obligate, from Latin *obligāre,* to OBLIGE.]

ob·con·ic (ob-kónnik) *adj. Botany.* Also **ob·con·i·cal** (-'l). Cone-shaped, with the tapering end at the point of attachment: *an obconic fruit.*

ob·cor·date (ob-kórdayt) *adj. Botany.* Heart-shaped, with the tapering end at the point of attachment: *an obcordate leaf.*

ob·du·ra·cy (ob-dewr-ə-si ‖ -door-) *n.* The state or quality of being obdurate.

ob·du·rate (ob-dewr-ət, -it, -ayt; -dewr- ‖ -door-) *adj.* **1.** Hardened against persuasion or feeling; unyielding; hardhearted: *an obdurate judge.* **2.** Hardened against good or moral influence; stubbornly impenitent: *"obdurate conscience of the old sinner"* (Sir Walter Scott). **—See** Synonyms at **inflexible.** [Middle English *obdurat,* from Latin *obdūrātus,* past participle of *obdūrāre,* to harden : *ob-* (intensive) + *dūrāre,* to harden, from *dūrus,* hard.] **—ob·du·rate·ly** *adv.* **—ob·du·rate·ness** *n.*

O.B.E. 1. Officer (of the Order) of the British Empire. **2.** Order of the British Empire.

o·be·ah (ōbi-ə) *n.* Also **o·bi** (ōbi). **1.** A form of religious belief, probably of African origin, involving witchcraft or sorcery, and practised especially in the West Indies. **2.** A fetish or object used in the practice of obeah. [Of West African origin.]

o·be·di·ence (ō-beedi-ənss, ə-) *n.* **1. a.** The quality or condition of being obedient. **b.** The act of obeying. **2.** A sphere of ecclesiastical authority. **3.** A group of persons under such authority. **4.** An office or duty in a convent or monastery.

o·be·di·ent (ō-beedi-ənt, ə-) *adj.* **1.** Obeying or carrying out a request, command, or the like. **2.** Submissive to control; dutiful. [Middle English, from Old French, from Latin *oboediēns* (stem *oboedient-*), present participle of *oboedīre,* to OBEY.] **—o·be·di·ent·ly** *adv.*

Synonyms: *obedient, compliant, acquiescent, submissive, docile, amenable, servile, tractable, dutiful.*

o·be·di·en·tia·ry (ō-beedi-énshi-əri, ə- ‖ -erri) *n., pl.* **-ries.** A holder of any office subordinate to that of the superior in a convent or monastery. [Medieval Latin *obedientiarius.* See **obedient, -ary.**]

o·bei·sance (ō-báyss'nss, ə- ‖ -beess'nss) *n.* **1.** A gesture or movement of the body expressing reverence or respect, such as a bow or curtsy. **2.** An attitude associated with this gesture, such as deference or homage. [Middle English *obeisaunce,* from Old French *obeissance,* from *obeissant,* present participle of *obeir,* to OBEY.] **—o·bei·sant** *adj.*

o·be·lise, o·be·lize (òbbə-līz) *tr.v.* **-lised, -lising, -lises.** To mark or annotate with an obelus. [Greek *obelizein,* from *obelos,* OBELUS.]

o·be·lisk (òbbə-lisk, *rarely* ōbə-) *n.* **1.** A tall, four-sided shaft of stone, usually monolithic and tapering, that rises to a pyramidal point. **2.** A monument in this shape, especially one in ancient Egypt. **3.** Anything else in this shape, such as a mountain. **4.** *Printing.* The dagger sign (†) used especially as a reference mark. In this dictionary it refers to an etymological footnote indicating that the word or form so marked is of obscure origin. In this sense, also called "obelus", "dagger". [Old French *obelisque,* from Latin *obeliscus,* from Greek *obeliskos,* diminutive of *obelos,* spit, OBELUS.] **—ob·e·lis·cal** (-lísk'l) *adj.* **—ob·e·lis·koid** (-lískoyd) *adj.*

ob·e·lus (òbbə-ləss) *n., pl.* **-li** (-lī). **1.** A mark (— or ÷) used in ancient manuscripts to indicate a doubtful or spurious passage. **2.** *Printing.* An obelisk. [Late Latin *obelus,* from Greek *obelos*†, spit, obelisk, obelus.]

O·ber·am·mer·gau (ōbər-ámmər-gow). Town in Bavaria, West Germany. It is the site of passion plays, held every 10 years since 1634 in thanksgiving for deliverance from the Black Death (1633).

O·ber·on (ōbər-ən, -on). In medieval folklore, the king of the fairies, husband of Titania. [French, from Old French *Auberon,* of Frankish origin; akin to Old High German *Alberich.*]

o·bese (ō-beess, ə-) *adj.* Extremely fat; unpleasantly overweight. See Synonyms at **fat.** [Latin *obēsus,* "grown fat by eating", from past participle of *obedere,* to eat away : *ob-,* away + *edere,* to eat.] **—o·be·si·ty** (ō-béessəti, ə-), **o·bese·ness** *n.*

o·bey (ō-báy, ə-) *v.* **obeyed, obeying, obeys. —tr. 1.** To carry out or fulfil the command, order, or instruction of. **2.** To carry out or comply with (a command or request). **3.** To act in accordance with (one's own instincts or feelings). **—intr.** To behave obediently. [Middle English *obeien,* from Old French *obeir,* from Latin *oboedīre,* "to listen to" : *ob-,* to, towards + *audīre,* to hear.] **—o·bey·er** *n.*

ob·fus·cate (ob-fəss-kayt, -fuss- ‖ obb-fúss-) *tr.v.* **-cated, -cating, -cates. 1.** To confuse or make obscure; cloud: *His emotions obfuscated his judgment.* **2.** To bewilder or stupefy. **3.** To render indistinct or dim; darken: *The fog obfuscated the shore.* [Late Latin *obfuscāre,* to darken : *ob-* (intensive) + Latin *fuscāre,* to darken, from *fuscus,* dark.] **—ob·fus·ca·tion** (-káysh'n) *n.*

o·bi[1] (ōbi) *n., pl.* **obis** or **obi.** A wide sash fastened at the back with a large flat bow, worn by women and men in Japan as a part of the traditional dress. [Japanese, "belt", "band", "sash".]

obi[2]. Variant of **obeah.**

o·bi·it (ōbi-it). *Abbr.* **ob.** *Latin.* He (or she) died. Usually followed by the date of death.

o·bit (ōbit, ō-bít) *n. Informal.* **1.** An obituary. **2.** A memorial service.

o·bi·ter dic·tum (òbbitər dík-təm, ōbitər) *n., pl.* **obiter dicta** (-tə). **1.** *Law.* An opinion voiced by a judge that has only incidental bearing on the case in question and is therefore not binding. **2.** Any

oasis *Palm trees and lush vegetation in an otherwise arid desert appear where underground water comes to the surface. Oases can be much larger than this one in Nigeria, and the water may be fed from hundreds of kilometres away.*

incidental remark or observation; a passing comment. [Latin, "a statement in passing".]

o·bit·u·ar·y (ō-bíttew-əri, ə-, o- || -erri) *n., pl.* **-ies.** *Abbr.* **obit.** A notice of a death, usually with a brief biography of the deceased. [Medieval Latin *obituārius,* (report) of death, from Latin *obitus,* death, from the past participle of *obīre,* to fall, die : *ob-,* down + *īre,* to go.] **—o·bit·u·ar·y** *adj.*

obj. **1.** *Grammar.* object; objective. **2.** objection.

ob·ject[1] (əb-jékt || ob-) *v.* **-jected, -jecting, -jects.** *—intr.* **1.** To present a dissenting or opposing argument; raise an objection. Usually followed by *to*: *object to the testimony of a witness.* **2.** To feel adverse to or express disapproval of something. Usually followed by *to*: *object to modern fashion.* *—tr.* To put forward in, or as a reason for, opposition; offer as criticism: *They objected that discipline was lacking.* [Middle English *objecten,* from Latin *objicere, obicere* (past participle *objectus*), to throw against, oppose : *ob-,* towards + *jacere,* to throw.] **—ob·jec·tor** (-ər) *n.*

Synonyms: *object, protest, complain, dissent, demur, remonstrate, expostulate.*

ob·ject[2] (ób-jikt, -jekt) *n.* **1.** Anything perceptible by one or more of the senses, especially something that can be seen and felt; a material thing. **2.** *Philosophy.* Anything intelligible or perceptible by the mind. **3.** A person or thing serving as a focus of attention, curiosity, discussion, feeling, thought, or action; especially, one that evokes ridicule or pity: *an object of contempt.* **4.** The purpose, aim, or goal of a specific action or effort: *the object of the game.* **5.** *Abbr.* **obj.** *Grammar.* **a.** A noun, pronoun, or noun phrase that receives or is affected by the action of a verb within a sentence. In *Mary hit Julia, Julia* is the object of the verb *hit.* **b.** A noun, pronoun, or noun phrase governed by a preposition. In *on television,* the noun *television* is the object of the preposition *on.* —See Synonyms at **intention.** **—no object.** *Informal.* Not an obstacle or hindrance: *Cost is no object.* [Middle English, from Latin *objectus,* "something thrown before or presented to (the mind)", from the past participle of *obicere,* to throw before or against, OBJECT (verb).]

object ball *n.* In billiards and similar games, the ball that the striker hits or intends to hit first with the cue ball.

object glass *n.* A lens in an optical instrument, the objective.

ob·jec·ti·fy (əb-jékti-fī || ob-) *tr.v.* **-fied, -fying, -fies.** **1.** To present (someone) as an object; depersonalise: *Pornography objectifies women.* **2.** To impart reality to; externalise or make objective. [From OBJECT (noun).] **—ob·jec·ti·fi·ca·tion** (-fi-káysh'n) *n.*

ob·jec·tion (əb-jéksh'n || ob-) *n. Abbr.* **obj.** **1.** An act of objecting. **2.** A statement or other expression offered in opposition. **3.** A reason or cause for expressing opposition or disagreement.

ob·jec·tion·a·ble (əb-jéksh'n-əb'l || ob-) *adj.* Arousing disapproval; offensive: *objectionable behaviour.* See Synonyms at **offensive.** **—ob·jec·tion·a·bil·i·ty** (-ə-bílləti) *n.* **—ob·jec·tion·a·bly** *adv.*

ob·jec·tive (əb-jéktiv || ob-) *adj.* **1.** Of or having to do with a material object as distinguished from a mental concept, idea, or belief. **2.** Having actual existence or reality. **3. a.** Not influenced by emotion, surmise, or personal prejudice. **b.** Based on observable phenomena; presented factually: *an objective appraisal.* **4.** *Medicine.* Designating a symptom or condition perceived as a sign of disease by someone other than the person afflicted. **5.** *Grammar.* **a.** Designating the case of a noun or pronoun serving as the object of a verb or preposition, and sometimes having various other grammatical functions. **b.** Pertaining to a noun or pronoun used in such a case. **6.** Serving as a goal; being the object of a course of action: *an objective point.* —Compare **subjective.** —See Synonyms at **fair.** *~n.* **1.** Anything that actually exists, as distinguished from something thought or felt to exist. **2.** Something worked towards or striven for; a goal. **3.** *Abbr.* **obj.** *Grammar.* **a.** The objective case. **b.** A noun or pronoun in the objective case. **4. a.** The lens or lens system in a microscope or telescope that is closest to the object being viewed. **b.** A lens or lens system in a camera or projector that forms the image of the object. Also called "object glass", "object lens". —See Synonyms at **intention.** [Medieval Latin *objectīvus,* from Latin *objectus,* an OBJECT.] **—ob·jec·tive·ly** *adv.* **—ob·jec·tive·ness** *n.*

objective case *n. Grammar.* The case of a noun or pronoun when it is the object of a verb or preposition, or serves various other grammatical functions.

objective complement *n. Grammar.* A noun, noun phrase, or adjective serving as a complement to a verb and qualifying its direct object. In *They elected me president, president* is an objective complement.

objective genitive *n. Grammar.* **1.** The genitive case as indicating the object of a specified action. In the noun phrase *my wounds,* meaning "the wounds inflicted on me", the object *me* is transferred to the genitive case *my.* Compare **subjective genitive.** **2.** A noun or pronoun in this case. **—objective genitive** *adj.*

ob·jec·tiv·ism (əb-jéktiv-iz'm, ob-) *n.* **1.** *Philosophy.* Any of several doctrines holding that all reality is objective and external to the mind, and that our perceptions correspond with it. Compare **solipsism.** **2.** In art and literature, an emphasis on objective themes or subjects. **—ob·jec·tiv·ist** *n.* **—ob·jec·tiv·is·tic** (-ístik) *adj.*

ob·jec·tiv·i·ty (ób-jek-tívvəti) *n.* **1.** The state, condition, or quality of being objective. **2.** External or material reality.

object language *n.* **1.** A language that is under discussion or being analysed, especially when being discussed in another language, the **metalanguage** *(see).* **2.** A **target language** *(see).*

object lens *n.* A lens in an optical instrument, the objective.

object lesson *n.* A practical illustration of a moral or principle.

object program *n.* A computer program transcribed into machine language by the compiler or assembler from the equivalent source program.

ob·jet d'art (ób-zhay dár) *n., pl.* **objets d'art** *(pronounced as singular).* A usually small artefact valued for its artistic merit. [French, "object of art".]

objet trou·vé (ób-zhay tróo-vay, tróo-váy) *n., pl.* **objets trouvés** *(pronounced as singular).* An ordinary or commonplace object considered or presented as a work of art. [French, "found object".]

ob·jur·gate (ób-jur-gayt, -jər-) *tr.v.* **-gated, -gating, -gates.** *Rare.* To scold or rebuke sharply; berate. [Latin *objurgāre,* "to bring a lawsuit against", chide : *ob-,* against + *jurgāre,* "to bring a lawsuit", rebuke, from *jūs* (stem *jūr-*), law + *agere,* to act, perform.] **—ob·jur·ga·tion** (-gáysh'n) *n.* **—ob·jur·ga·to·ri·ly** (əb-júrgə-trə-li, ob-, -təri-; ób-jur-gaytərəli) *adv.* **—ob·jur·ga·to·ry** (əb-júrgə-tri, ob-, -təri; óbjur-gaytəri) *adj.*

obl. **1.** oblique. **2.** oblong.

ob·lan·ce·o·late (ób-laán-si-ə-lət, -lit, -layt || -lán-) *adj. Botany.* Broader and rounded at the apex, and tapering at the base: *an oblanceolate leaf.*

o·blast (ób-laast, -ləst || -last) *n.* In the U.S.S.R., a local administrative division. [Russian *oblast',* from Old Church Slavonic : *ob-,* on + *vlast',* power, administration.]

ob·late[1] (óbblayt, ob-láyt, ōb-) *adj.* Designating a spheroid having an equatorial diameter greater than the distance between poles; compressed along or flattened at the poles. Compare **prolate.** [New Latin *oblatus,* "carried towards", stretched, from Latin *oblātus* (past participle of *obferre,* to bring to, offer) : *ob,* to, towards + *-lātus,* "carried".] **—ob·late·ly** *adv.* **—ob·late·ness** *n.*

ob·late[2] (óbblayt) *n.* **1.** A person dedicated to a religious life, but who has not taken formal vows. **2.** *Capital* **O.** *Roman Catholic Church.* A member of any of various religious communities. [Medieval Latin *oblātus,* "one offered (to God)", from Latin, past participle of *obferre,* to offer. See **oblate**[1].] **—ob·late** *adj.*

ob·la·tion (ō-bláysh'n, ə-, o-) *n.* **1.** The act of offering something, such as worship or thanksgiving, to a deity. **2.** *Capital* **O. a.** The act of offering the bread and wine of the Eucharist. **b.** The bread and wine of the Eucharist. **3.** Any charitable offering or gift. [Middle English *oblacioun,* from Old French *oblation,* from Medieval Latin *oblātiō* (stem *oblātiōn-*), from *oblātus,* OBLATE (noun).] **—ob·la·tion·al, ob·la·to·ry** (óbblə-tri, -təri) *adj.*

ob·li·gate (óbbli-gayt) *tr.v.* **-gated, -gating, -gates.** To bind, compel, or constrain by a legal, moral, or social tie.

~adj. **1.** *Biology.* Able to survive in only one kind of environment; obligatory. Said of parasites that cannot live independently of their hosts. Compare **facultative.** **2.** Absolutely indispensable; essential. **3.** *Archaic.* Bound or constrained; obliged. [Latin *obligāre,* to OBLIGE.] **—ob·li·ga·ble** (-gəb'l) *adj.* **—ob·li·ga·tor** (-gaytər) *n.*

ob·li·ga·tion (óbbli-gáysh'n) *n.* **1.** The act of binding oneself or being bound by a legal, moral, or social tie. **2. a.** A duty, contract, promise, or any other legal, moral, or social requirement that compels one to follow or avoid a certain course of action. **b.** A course of action imposed by law, society, or conscience by which one is bound or restricted. **3.** The constraining power of a law, promise, contract, or sense of duty. **4.** *Law.* **a.** A legal agreement stipulating a specified payment or action, especially if the agreement also specifies the penalty for failure to comply. **b.** The document containing the terms of such an agreement. **5. a.** Something owed as payment or in return for a special service or favour. **b.** The service or favour for which one is indebted to another. **6.** The state, fact, or condition of being indebted to another for a special service or favour received.

obligato. Variant of **obbligato.**

o·blig·a·to·ry (ə-blíggə-tri, o-, óbbligə-, -təri) *adj.* **1.** Legally or morally constraining; binding. **2.** Of the nature of an obligation; compulsory: *Attendance is obligatory.* **3.** Imposing or recording an obligation: *a bill obligatory.* **4.** *Biology.* Restricted to one mode of life; obligate. **—o·blig·a·to·ri·ly** *adv.*

o·blige (ə-blīj || ō-) *v.* **obliged, obliging, obliges.** *—tr.* **1.** To force or cause to do or refrain from doing something; constrain by physical, legal, social, or moral means. **2.** To make indebted or grateful. Usually used in the passive and with *to*: *They were obliged to him for his hospitality.* **3.** To gratify the wishes of; do a service or favour for: *He obliged us by arriving early.* *—intr.* To do a service or favour; perform a courtesy: *The pianist will oblige with an encore.* —See Synonyms at **force.** [Middle English *obligen,* from Old French *obliger,* from Latin *obligāre,* to tie to : *ob-,* to + *ligāre,* to bind.] **—o·blig·er** *n.*

ob·li·gee (óbbli-jée) *n.* **1.** A person who is under obligation to another. **2.** *Law.* A person to whom another is bound by contract or legal agreement; a creditor. Compare **obligor.**

o·blig·ing (ə-blījing || ō-) *adj.* Ready to do favours for others; accommodating; helpful; considerate. See Synonyms at **amiable.** **—o·blig·ing·ly** *adv.* **—o·blig·ing·ness** *n.*

ob·li·gor (óbbli-gór, -jór) *n. Law.* A person who binds himself to another by contract or legal agreement; a debtor. Compare **obligee.**

o·blique (ō-bléek, ə-, o-) *adj. Abbr.* **obl.** **1. a.** Having a slanting or sloping direction, course, or position; inclined. **b.** In geometry, designating lines or planes that are neither parallel nor perpendicular. **2.** Indirect or evasive in execution, meaning, or expression; not straightforward. **3.** Devious, misleading, or dishonest: *oblique answers.* **4.** Not direct in descent; collateral. **5.** *Botany.* Having sides

of unequal length or form: *an oblique leaf.* **6.** *Anatomy.* Inclined at an angle; not perpendicular or horizontal: *oblique muscles.* **7.** *Grammar.* Designating any noun case except the nominative or the vocative. **8.** In rhetoric, indirect.
~*n.* **1.** Something that is oblique, such as a line, direction, or muscle. **2.** *Nautical.* The act of changing course by less than 90°. [Middle English *oblike,* from Latin *oblīquus*†.] **—o·blique·ly** *adv.* **—o·blique·ness** *n.*

oblique angle *n.* An angle that is not a right angle; an acute or obtuse angle. **—o·blique-an·gled** (ə-bleék-áng-g'ld) *adj.*

oblique triangle *n.* A triangle having no right angle.

o·bliq·ui·ty (ō-blíkwəti, ə-, o-) *n., pl.* **-ties. 1.** The state, quality, or condition of being oblique. **2. a.** A deviation from a vertical or horizontal line, plane, position, or direction. **b.** The angle or extent of such a deviation. **3. a.** A mental deviation or aberration. **b.** Immoral conduct. **4.** *Symbol* ε *Astronomy.* The angle at which the Earth's axis is tilted from the vertical, equal to the angle between the ecliptic and the celestial equator. It varies regularly between extreme values and the average value also changes with time; at present, it is about 23°27′. [Middle English *obliquitee,* from Old French *obliquite,* from Latin *oblīquitas,* from *oblīquus,* OBLIQUE.] **—o·bliq·ui·tous** *adj.*

o·blit·er·ate (ə-blíttə-rayt, o- || ō-) *tr.v.* **-ated, -ating, -ates. 1.** To do away with completely; destroy so as to leave no trace: *The forest was obliterated by the building of the new town.* **2.** To wipe out, rub off, or obscure (writing or other markings). —See Synonyms at **erase.** [Latin *obliterāre,* "to strike out words", erase : *ob-,* away from + *littera,* letter.] **—o·blit·er·a·tion** (-ráysh'n) *n.* **—o·blit·er·a·tive** (-rətiv, -raytiv) *adj.* **—o·blit·er·a·tor** (-ər) *n.*

o·bliv·i·on (ə-blívvi-ən, o- || ō-) *n.* **1.** The state or condition of being completely forgotten. **2.** Forgetfulness or an instance of forgetting or overlooking. **3.** The state of being completely unaware of oneself or one's surroundings: *drink myself into oblivion.* **4.** *Law.* An official forgetting of offences, or remission of punishment for them; an amnesty. [Middle English, from Old French, from Latin *oblīviō* (stem *oblīviōn-*), from *oblīvīscī,* to forget.]

o·bliv·i·ous (ə-blívvi-əss, o- || ō-) *adj.* **1.** Lacking all memory of something; forgetful. **2.** Unaware or unmindful. —See Synonyms at **forgetful. —o·bliv·i·ous·ly** *adv.* **—o·bliv·i·ous·ness** *n.*

Usage: The usual preposition following this word is *of (oblivious of the people around her),* though *to* is sometimes used, especially with inanimate nouns *(oblivious to the difficulties).* Purists have objected to the use of *oblivious* to mean "unaware", but this sense is now both common and widely accepted.

ob·long (ób-long) *adj. Abbr.* **obl. 1.** Having a long dimension, especially having one of two perpendicular dimensions, such as length or width, greater than the other; elongated. **2.** Having the shape of or resembling a rectangle or an ellipse.
~*n.* An object or figure, such as a rectangle, with an elongated shape. [Middle English *oblonge,* from Latin *oblongus* : *ob-* (intensive) + *longus,* long.]

ob·lo·quy (óbbləkwi) *n., pl.* **-quies. 1.** Abusively detractive language or utterance; condemnation. **2.** Ill repute or discredit suffered by one subjected to such abuse. —See Synonyms at **disgrace.** [Middle English *obloqui, from* Late Latin *obloquium,* from Latin *obloquī,* to speak against, contradict : *ob-,* against + *loquī,* to speak.]

ob·nox·ious (əb-nókshəss, ob-) *adj.* **1.** Highly disagreeable or offensive; odious. **2.** *Obsolete.* Exposed to harm, injury, or evil. **3.** *Obsolete.* Deserving of or liable to censure or punishment; reprehensible. —See Synonyms at **hateful, offensive.** [Latin *obnoxiōsus,* injurious, from *obnoxius,* subject to harm : *ob-,* to + *noxa,* a hurt.] **—ob·nox·ious·ly** *adv.* **—ob·nox·ious·ness** *n.*

ob·nu·bil·ate (ob-néwbi-layt) *tr.v.* **-ated, -ating, -ates.** *Literary.* To darken with or as if with clouds or fog; obscure. [Latin *obnūbilare,* from *nubes,* cloud.] **—ob·nu·bil·ation** (-láysh'n) *n.*

o·boe (ṓbō) *n. Abbr.* **ob. 1.** A slender woodwind musical instrument with a conical tube and a double-reed mouthpiece. It has a range of three octaves, and a penetrating, poignant sound. **2.** A performer on this instrument in an orchestra. **3.** A reed stop in an organ that produces a sound similar to that of an oboe. [Italian, from French *hautbois,* HAUTBOY.] **—o·bo·ist** *n.*

ob·ol (óbb'l, óbbol || ṓb'l) *n.* Also **ob·o·lus** (óbbə-ləss) *pl.* **-li** (-lī). **1.** A silver coin or unit of weight of ancient Greece equal to one sixth of a drachma. **2. a.** Any of various coins, mostly of small value, circulated in medieval Europe. **b.** Any small coin. [Latin, from Greek *obolos,* variant of *obelos,* OBELUS.]

O·bo·te (ō-bṓ-tay, o-, -ti), **(Apollo) Milton** (1924–). Ugandan statesman, the country's first premier (1962), later president of Uganda. He was deeply opposed to the Bugandan monarchy which he dismantled (1966). He was ousted by a military coup while attending the Commonwealth Conference (1971). A counter coup (1980) prepared the way for his re-election as president.

ob·o·vate (ob-ṓvayt, ób-) *adj. Botany.* Egg-shaped in outline, with the narrow end attached to the stalk: *an obovate leaf.*

ob·o·void (ob-ṓvoyd, ób-) *adj. Botany.* Egg-shaped, with the narrow end attached to the stem: *an obovoid fruit.*

O'Bri·en (ō-brī́-ən, ə-), **Conor Cruise** (1917–). Irish politician and journalist. He served as a Labour member of the Irish parliament from 1969 to 1977, when he became a senator until 1979. From 1977 to 1981 he was editor of the *Observer* newspaper.

O'Brien, Edna (1936–). Irish novelist and short-story writer. Her first novel, *The Country Girls,* was published in 1960. Her other works include *A Pagan Place* (1970) and a play, *Virginia* (1979).

O'Brien, Flann, pen name of Brian O'Nuallain (1911–66). Irish novelist and humorist. His novels in the English language include *At Swim-Two-Birds* (1939) and *The Third Policeman* (U.K. 1967).

O'Brien, William (1852–1928). Irish politician and journalist. As editor of *United Ireland,* and, from 1883 as an M.P. for the Home Rule party, he was an eloquent advocate of Irish Independence.

O'Brien, William Smith (1803–64). Irish politician and insurgent. Elected to Parliament (1828), he became an active member of the Young Ireland movement, and led the unsuccessful revolution of 1848. He was subsequently arrested and transported to Tasmania.

obs. 1. obscure. **2.** observation. **3.** observatory. **4.** obsolete. **5.** obstetrics.

Obs. observatory.

ob·scene (əb-seén, ob-) *adj.* **1.** Offensive to accepted standards of decency or modesty. **2.** Intended to incite lustful feelings; indecent; lewd. **3.** *Law.* Liable to deprave or corrupt. Said of a publication. **4. a.** Morally repulsive. **b.** Offensive or repulsive to the senses; loathsome. —See Synonyms at **coarse.** [French *obscène* or Latin *obscēnus, obscaenus*†, inauspicious, repulsive.] **—ob·scene·ly** *adv.*

ob·scen·i·ty (əb-sénnəti, ob-) *n., pl.* **-ties. 1.** The quality of being obscene. **2.** Indecency, lewdness, or offensiveness in behaviour, expression, or appearance. **3.** Something obscene, such as a word, act, or expression.

ob·scur·ant (ob-skéwr-ənt, əb-) *n.* **1.** One who opposes intellectual advancement and political reform; an enemy of rationalism. **2.** In German history, an opponent of the Enlightenment in the 18th century. **3.** One who deliberately obscures the truth or fails to give a full explanation. [Latin *obscūrāns* (stem *obscūrant-*), present participle of *obscūrāre,* to darken, from *obscūrus,* dark, OBSCURE.] **—ob·scur·ant** *adj.*

ob·scur·ant·ism (ób-skewr-ránt-iz'm, ob-skéwr-ənt-, əb-) *n.* The principles or practice of obscurants; opposition to enlightenment. **—ob·scur·ant·ist** *n. & adj.*

ob·scure (əb-skéwr, ob-) *adj.* **-scurer, -scurest.** *Abbr.* **obs. 1.** Not clearly expressed; vague or cryptic; difficult: *an obscure text.* **2.** Imperfectly known or understood: *the obscure workings of nature.* **3.** Of undistinguished or humble descent, status, or reputation. **4.** Inconspicuous; unnoticed: *the obscure beginnings of mighty things.* **5.** Out of sight; hidden: *an obscure retreat.* **6. a.** So faintly perceptible as to lack clear delineation; indistinct. **b.** Hardly audible; faint. **c.** *Phonetics.* Having an unstressed neutral sound as represented by the schwa (ə). Said of a vowel. **7. a.** Of sombre hue; dark. **b.** Dingy; dull. **8.** Partially or wholly deficient in light; gloomy. **9.** *Archaic.* Belonging to or inhabiting darkness. —See Synonyms at **dark.**
~*tr.v.* **obscured, -scuring, -scures. 1.** To darken. **2.** To lessen the glory of; overshadow. **3.** *Phonetics.* To reduce (a vowel) to the neutral unstressed sound represented by the schwa (ə). **4.** To conceal from view; hide. **5.** To obstruct; hinder. **6.** To render unintelligible.
~*n. Poetic.* Darkness; obscurity. [Middle English, from Old French *obscur,* from Latin *obscūrus.*] **—ob·scure·ly** *adv.* **—ob·scure·ness** *n.*

ob·scu·ri·ty (əb-skéwr-əti, ob-) *n., pl.* **-ties. 1.** Deficiency or absence of light; darkness: *"We wait for light, but behold obscurity."* (Isaiah 59:9). **2. a.** The condition of being unknown: *from obscurity to fame.* **b.** An unknown person. **3. a.** The condition or quality of being imperfectly known or of being difficult to understand: *The origin of the race is lost in obscurity.* **b.** An instance of this. [Old French *obscurité,* from Latin *obscūritās,* from *obscūrus,* OBSCURE.]

ob·se·crate (ób-si-krayt, -se-) *tr.v.* **-crated, -crating, -crates.** *Rare.* To beg for (something) solemnly. [Latin *obsecrāre* (past participle *obsecrātus*), "to entreat in the name of something sacred" : *ob-,* for the sake of + *sacer,* sacred.] **—ob·se·cra·tion** (-kráysh'n) *n.*

ob·se·quent (ób-sikwənt) *adj.* Flowing into another (subsequent) river in the opposite direction from the original (consequent) river. Said of a stream or river. Compare **consequent, subsequent.** [Latin *obsequens* (stem *obsequent-*), present participle of *obsequī,* to yield to : *ob-,* towards, over + *sequī,* to follow.]

ob·se·qui·ous (əb-seékwi-əss, ob-) *adj.* **1.** Displaying ingratiating servility. **2.** *Archaic.* Submissive and obedient; dutiful. [Middle English, from Latin *obsequiōsus,* from *obsequium,* compliance, from *obsequī,* to comply with : *ob-,* to + *sequī,* to follow.] **—ob·se·qui·ous·ly** *adv.* **—ob·se·qui·ous·ness** *n.*

ob·se·quy (ób-si-kwi, -sə-) *n., pl.* **-quies.** *Usually plural.* A funeral rite or ceremony. [Middle English *obsequy,* from Anglo-French *obsequie,* Old French *obseque,* from Medieval Latin *obsequiae* (influenced by *exsequiae,* exequy), from Latin *obsequia,* plural of *obsequium,* compliance, service. See **obsequious.**] **—ob·se·qui·al** (ob-seékwi-əl, əb-) *adj.*

ob·serv·a·ble (əb-zérvəb'l || ob-) *adj.* **1.** Capable of being observed; noticeable; discernible: *observable improvement.* **2.** Deserving or worthy of notice or mention; noteworthy. **3.** Requiring or deserving special notice or observance: *an observable religious holiday.*
~*n. Physics.* A physical property, such as mass or temperature, that can be observed or measured directly, as distinguished from a quantity, such as work or entropy, that must be derived from observed quantities. **—ob·serv·a·ble·ness** *n.* **—ob·serv·a·bly** *adv.*

ob·ser·vance (əb-zérv'nss || ob-) *n.* **1.** The act or practice of observing or complying with a law, custom, command, or other prescribed duty. **2.** The act or custom of keeping or celebrating a holiday or other ritual occasion. **3.** A customary rite or ceremony. **4.** The action of watching; observation: *"Consider how much intellect was*

PRONUNCIATION KEY

a, trap; aa, father; ai, fair; ar, star; aw, lawn; ay, play; b, bb, stab; rubber; ch, church; ck, ticket; d, dd, dead; ladder; e, dress; ee, bee; er, defer; ew, few; ewr, pure; ə, about; ər, letter; f, ff, fife; differ; g, gg, giggle; h, hat; i, kit; ī, price; īr, fire; j, judge; k, kick; l, ll, let; 'l, needle; m, mm, man; n, nn, no; 'n, sudden; ng, thing; o, lot; ō, no; ŏŏ, foot; ōō, shoe; oor, poor; ow, cow; owr, hour; oy, boy; p, pp, pepper; r, rr, red; s, ss, sauce; sh, ship; t, tt, totter; th, thick; th, this; smooth; u, cut; ur, turn; v, vv, valve; w, wet; y, yes; z, zz, zebra; zh, vision; pleasure

IN FOREIGN WORDS:

aN, oN, Saint-Saëns; hl, Llanelli; Hluhluwe; kh, loch; lough; Khaled

STRESS MARK:

ín-sīt, insight; in-sī́t, incite

needed in the architect, and how much observance of nature." (John Ruskin). **5.** *Roman Catholic Church.* **a.** The rule governing a religious order. **b.** The order itself or the house of such an order. **6.** *Archaic.* Respectful attention: *"He compassed her with sweet observances and worship."* (Alfred Lord Tennyson).

Usage: Both *observance* and *observation* derive from *observe. Observance* is the practice of paying attention to laws, customs, holidays, duties, or the like, whereas *observation* is the act of seeing or noticing something.

ob·ser·vant (əb-zérv'nt || ob-) *adj.* **1.** Characterised by or demonstrating an ability to perceive or apprehend quickly and accurately; alert. **2.** Diligent in observing a law, duty, or principle. Usually followed by *of.* [French, from Latin *observāns* (stem *observant-*), present participle of *observāre,* to OBSERVE.] **—ob·ser·vant·ly** *adv.*

ob·ser·va·tion (ób-zər-váysh'n || -sər-) *n. Abbr.* **obs. 1.** The act or faculty of paying attention or noticing, or the fact of being observed; notice. **2.** The act of noting a phenomenon, often with instruments, and recording it for scientific or other purposes. **3.** The result or record of such noting: *a meteorological observation.* **4.** A comment or remark. **5.** *Archaic.* That which is acquired from or based on observing, such as a conclusion or rule. **6.** *Archaic.* Observance. —See Usage note at **observance.** [Middle English, from Latin *observātiō* (stem *observātiōn-*), from *observāre,* to OBSERVE.] **—ob·ser·va·tion·al** *adj.* **—ob·ser·va·tion·al·ly** *adv.*

observation car *n. U.S.* A railway carriage with large windows providing passengers with extensive views of the countryside.

observation post *n. Military.* A position from which observations of enemy movements can be made or guns fired.

ob·ser·va·to·ry (əb-zérvə-tri, -təri || ob-) *n., pl.* **-ries.** *Abbr.* **Obs., obs. 1.** A building designed and equipped for making observations of astronomical, meteorological, or other natural phenomena. **2.** *Chiefly U.S.* A structure overlooking an extensive view. [New Latin *observatorium,* from Latin *observāre,* to OBSERVE.]

ob·serve (əb-zérv || ob-) *v.* **-served, -serving, -serves.** *—tr.* **1.** To perceive; notice; see. **2.** To watch attentively: *observe a child's behaviour.* **3.** To make a systematic or scientific observation of (a natural or other phenomenon): *observe the Moon's orbit.* **4.** To say by way of comment or remark. **5.** To adhere to or abide by (a law, duty, custom, decision, or the like): *observe the terms of a contract.* **6.** To keep or pay tribute to (a holiday, custom, rite, or the like) by celebration, solemnity, or other procedure: *observe an anniversary. —intr.* **1.** To take notice. **2.** To say something; make a comment or remark. **3.** To watch or be present without participating actively: *I was invited to the conference to observe.* —See Synonyms at **see.** [Middle English *observen,* from Old French *observer,* from Latin *observāre,* to pay attention to, look to : *ob-,* to + *servāre,* to keep, watch, pay attention.] **—ob·serv·ing·ly** *adv.*

Synonyms: *observe, keep, celebrate, solemnise, commemorate.*

ob·serv·er (əb-zérvər || ob-) *n.* **1.** One that observes. **2. a.** A delegate sent to observe and report on the proceedings of an assembly or meeting, but not to vote or otherwise participate. **b.** One sent to observe and report on the military, political, or administrative conditions in a country or area: *U.N. observers monitored the ceasefire.* **3.** *Military.* **a.** An aircraft crew member who makes observations. **b.** A soldier watching and reporting from an observation post. **4.** *Physics.* One whose observations are made in or referred to a completely specified frame of reference. **5.** *Capital* **O.** Used as part of the title of certain newspapers: *The Surrey Observer.*

ob·sess (əb-séss, ob-) *tr.v.* **-sessed, -sessing, -sesses.** To preoccupy totally; interest to the exclusion of any other object; haunt as a fixed idea. Often used in the passive. [Latin *obsidēre* (past participle *obsessus*), to sit down before, besiege, beset : *ob-,* on + *sedēre,* to sit.]

ob·ses·sion (əb-sésh'n, ob-) *n.* **1. a.** Compulsive preoccupation with a fixed idea or an unwanted feeling or emotion, often with symptoms of anxiety. **b.** A compulsive, often unreasonable, idea or emotion causing such preoccupation. **2.** The act of obsessing or the state of being obsessed. **3.** *Archaic.* The state of being beset or actuated by the devil or an evil spirit. **—ob·ses·sion·al** *adj.*

ob·ses·sive (əb-séss-iv; ob-) *adj.* Characterised by or suffering from obsession: *obsessive gambling.*

~n. One suffering from an obsession or obsessions.

ob·sid·i·an (ob-síddi-ən) *n.* An acid-resistant, lustrous volcanic glass, usually black or banded and displaying curved, shiny surfaces when fractured. [Latin *obsidiānus,* manuscript error for *obsiānus,* from *Obsius,* mentioned by Pliny as the discoverer of a stone similar to obsidian.]

ob·so·lesce (ób-sə-léss, -sō-) *intr.v.* **-lesced, -lescing, -lesced.** To become gradually obsolete. [Back-formation from OBSOLESCENT.]

ob·so·les·cent (ób-sə-léss'nt, -sō-) *adj.* In the process of passing out of use or usefulness; becoming obsolete. See Synonyms at **old.** [Latin *obsolēscēns* (stem *obsolēscent-*), present participle of *obsolēscere,* to grow old, from *obsolēre* (unattested), to be old or in disuse. See **obsolete.**] **—ob·so·les·cence** *n.* **—ob·so·les·cent·ly** *adv.*

ob·so·lete (ób-sə-leet, -léet, -sleet) *adj.* **1.** *Abbr.* **obs.** No longer in use or practice: *an obsolete word.* **2.** No longer used or useful, because of outmoded design or construction, or because of hard wear. **3.** *Biology.* Increasingly vestigial or disappearing in succeeding generations. Said of plant or animal characteristics or organs. —See Synonyms at **old.** [Latin *obsolētus,* from *obsolēre* (unattested), to be old or in use : *ob-,* away from + *solēre*†, to use, be accustomed.] **—ob·so·lete·ly** *adv.* **—ob·so·lete·ness** *n.* **—ob·so·let·ism** *n.*

ob·sta·cle (ób-stək'l) *n.* A person or thing that opposes, stands in the way of, or holds up progress towards some goal. [Middle English, from Old French, from Latin *obstāculum,* from *obstāre,* to hinder : *ob-,* against + *stāre,* to stand.]

Synonyms: *obstacle, obstruction, bar, barrier, block, impediment, hindrance, encumbrance, snag.*

obstacle course *n.* **1.** A series of physical obstacles, such as ladders and water jumps, to be negotiated at speed by soldiers undergoing training or by participants in an obstacle race. **2.** Any unduly demanding or complex activity.

obstacle race *n.* A race in which the participants have to go through, under, or over a number of obstacles.

obstet. obstetric; obstetrics.

ob·stet·ric (ob-stéttrik, əb-) *adj.* Also **ob·stet·ri·cal** (-'l). *Abbr.* **obstet.** Of or pertaining to the profession of obstetrics or to the care of women during and after pregnancy. [New Latin *obstetricus,* from Latin *obstetrīcius,* from *obstetrīx,* midwife, "she who is present", from *obstāre,* to stand before : *ob-,* before + *stāre,* to stand.] **—ob·stet·ri·cal·ly** *adv.*

ob·ste·tri·cian (ób-ste-trísh'n, -stə-, -sti-) *n.* A medical practitioner specialising in obstetrics.

ob·stet·rics (ob-stéttriks, əb-) *n. Used with a singular verb. Abbr.* **obs., obstet.** The branch of medicine concerned with the care of women during pregnancy and childbirth.

ob·sti·na·cy (ób-stinə-si) *n., pl.* **-cies. 1.** The state or quality of being obstinate. **2.** An act or instance of stubbornness.

ob·sti·nate (ób-sti-nət, -nit) *adj.* **1.** Inflexibly and immovably adhering to an attitude, opinion, or course of action; resistant to argument or entreaty. **2.** Difficult to manage, control, or subdue; refractory. **3.** Difficult to alleviate or cure: *an obstinate headache.* —See Synonyms at **contrary.** [Middle English *obstinat,* from Latin *obstinātus,* past participle of *obstināre,* to persist, from *stāre,* to stand.] **—ob·sti·nate·ly** *adv.* **—ob·sti·nate·ness** *n.*

Synonyms: *obstinate, stubborn, headstrong, stiff-necked, pigheaded, mulish, dogged, pertinacious.*

ob·strep·er·ous (əb-stréppərəss, ob-) *adj.* Noisily defiant; unruly; boisterously unmanageable. [Latin *obstreperus,* from *obstrepere,* to make noise against : *ob-,* against + *strepere,* to make noise.] **—ob·strep·er·ous·ly** *adv.* **—ob·strep·er·ous·ness** *n.*

ob·struct (əb-strúkt || ob-) *tr.v.* **-structed, -structing, -structs. 1.** To block or fill (a way or passage) with obstacles; make impassable. **2.** To interfere with, impede, or retard. **3.** To hide from view. —See Synonyms at **hinder.** [Latin *obstruere* (past participle *obstructus*) : *ob-,* against + *struere,* to pile up.] **—ob·struct·er, ob·struc·tor** *n.* **—ob·struc·tive** *adj. & n.* **—ob·struc·tive·ly** *adv.* **—ob·struc·tive·ness** *n.*

ob·struc·tion (əb-strúksh'n || ob-) *n.* **1.** A person or thing that gets in the way; an obstacle. **2.** An act or instance of obstructing, or the state of being obstructed. **3.** The causing of delay, or an attempt to cause a delay, in the conduct of business, especially in a legislative body. **4.** *Sports.* The act of impeding another player or competitor in a match or race. **5.** *Medicine.* A blockage in a bodily organ or passage, especially the intestine. —See Synonyms at **obstacle.**

ob·struc·tion·ist (əb-strúksh'n-ist || ob-) *n.* One who systematically obstructs or interrupts a process; especially, one who impedes the passage of legislation by delaying tactics, such as making long speeches. **—ob·struc·tion·ism** *n.* **—ob·struc·tion·ist** *adj.*

ob·tain (əb-táyn || ob-) *v.* **-tained, -taining, -tains.** *—tr.* **1.** To succeed in gaining possession of (something) as the result of planning or endeavour; get or acquire. **2.** *Archaic.* To reach or arrive at: *"obtain the age of manhood"* (Sir Walter Scott). *—intr.* **1.** To be established, accepted, or customary: *Certain formal customs still obtain today.* **2.** *Archaic.* To win victory; prevail; succeed: *"This, though it failed at present, yet afterwards obtained."* (Jonathan Swift). [Middle English *obteinen,* from Old French *obtenir,* from Latin *obtinēre,* attain : *ob-* (intensive) + *tenēre,* to hold.] **—ob·tain·a·ble** *adj.* **—ob·tain·er** *n.*

ob·tect (əb-tékt, ob-) *adj.* Also **ob·tect·ed** (-id). *Zoology.* Enclosed or covered by a hardened secretion. Said especially of pupae having wings, antennae, and legs enclosed and sealed against the body surface in this way. [Latin *obtectus,* past participle of *obtegere,* to cover up, conceal : *ob-,* down upon, over + *tegere,* to cover.]

ob·test (əb-tést, ob-) *v.* **-tested, -testing, -tests.** *Archaic. —tr.* **1.** To supplicate; entreat. **2.** To call (a spirit or power) to witness. **3.** To object or protest. *—intr.* To protest. Sometimes used with *against* or *with.* [Latin *obtestārī,* to call as a witness to, entreat : *ob-,* to + *testārī,* to call as a witness, from *testis,* witness.] **—ob·tes·ta·tion** (ób-tess-táysh'n) *n.*

ob·trude (əb-trōōd, ob- || -tréwd) *v.* **-truded, -truding, -trudes.** *—tr.* **1.** To force (oneself or one's ideas) upon others with undue insistence or without invitation. **2.** To thrust out; push forward; eject. *—intr.* To force oneself upon others or upon their attention. See Synonyms at **intrude.** [Latin *obtrūdere* : *ob-,* against + *trūdere,* to thrust.] **—ob·trud·er** *n.* **—ob·tru·sion** (-trōōzh'n || -tréwzh'n) *n.*

ob·tru·sive (əb-trōō-siv, ob- || -tréw-, -ziv) *adj.* **1.** Projecting; protruding: *an obtrusive rock formation.* **2.** Tending to push self-assertively forward; brashly intrusive. **3.** Undesirably noticeable; unattractively showy. [Latin *obtrūs-,* past participle stem of *obtrūdere,* OBTRUDE.] **—ob·tru·sive·ly** *adv.* **—ob·tru·sive·ness** *n.*

ob·tund (əb-túnd, ob-) *tr.v.* **-tunded, -tunding, -tunds.** *Rare.* To dull or deaden; make less intense. [Middle English *obtunden,* from Latin *obtundere,* to strike against, blunt : *ob-,* against + *tundere,* to beat.] **—ob·tund·ent** *adj. & n.*

ob·tu·rate (ób-tewr-ayt || -tə-) *tr.v.* **-rated, -rating, -rates. 1.** To close

PRONUNCIATION KEY

a, trap; aa, father; ai, **fair**; ar, **star**; aw, **lawn**; ay, **play**; b, bb, stab; **rubber**; ch, **church**; ck, ticket; d, dd, **dead**; **ladder**; e, dress; ee, bee; er, defer; ew, **few**; ewr, **pure**; ə, about; ər, letter; f, ff, **fife**; differ; g, gg, **giggle**; h, **hat**; i, **kit**; ī, price; īr, **fire**; j, **judge**; k, **kick**; l, ll, let; 'l, needle; m, mm, **man**; n, nn, **no**; 'n, sudden; ng, **thing**; o, **lot**; ō, **no**; ŏŏ, **foot**; ōō, **shoe**; oor, **poor**; ow, **cow**; owr, **hour**; oy, **boy**; p, pp, **pepper**; r, rr, red; s, ss, **sauce**; sh, **ship**; t, tt, totter; th, **thick**; th, **this**; smooth; u, **cut**; ur, **turn**; v, vv, **valve**; w, **wet**; y, **yes**; z, zz, zebra; zh, vision; pleasure

IN FOREIGN WORDS:

aN, oN, **Saint-Saëns**; hl, **Llanelli**; **Hluhluwe**; kh, **loch**; **lough**; **Khaled**

STRESS MARK:

ín-sīt, insight; in-sī́t, incite

by obstructing or stopping up. **2.** To seal (a gun breech) in order to prevent gas from escaping on firing. [Latin *obturāre*†.] —**ob·tu·ra·tion** (-áysh'n) *n.*

ob·tu·ra·tor (ób-tewr-aytər || -tə-) *n.* **1.** A prosthetic device that closes an opening in the body, especially a denture that closes a defect in the palate. **2.** A device for sealing a gun breech to prevent gas from escaping on firing.

ob·tuse (əb-téwss, ob- || -tōōss) *adj.* **1.** Lacking astuteness or discernment; slow to understand or perceive. **2. a.** Not sharp, pointed, or acute in form; blunt. **b.** Not acute or intense; indistinctly perceived; dull: *an obtuse pain.* **3.** *Botany.* Having a blunt or rounded tip: *an obtuse leaf.* —See Synonyms at **dull, stupid.** [Latin *obtūsus,* past participle of *obtundere,* to blunt, OBTUND.] —**ob·tuse·ly** *adv.* —**ob·tuse·ness** *n.*

obtuse angle *n.* An angle greater than 90° and less than 180°.

ob·verse (ób-verss, -vérss) *adj.* **1.** Facing or turned towards the observer: *the obverse side of a statue.* **2.** *Botany.* Having a narrower base than top; inverse. Said of certain leaves. **3.** Serving as a counterpart or complement.
~*n.* **1.** The side of a coin, medal, badge, or the like that bears the principal stamp or design; in most coinages, the side bearing the head. Compare **reverse. 2.** A counterpart or complement. **3.** *Logic.* The counterpart of a proposition obtained by exchanging the affirmative for the negative quality of the whole proposition and then negating the predicate. The obverse of *every act is predictable* is *no act is unpredictable.* [Latin *obversus,* past participle of *obvertere,* to turn towards, OBVERT.] —**ob·verse·ly** *adv.*

ob·ver·sion (əb-vérsh'n, ob-, -vérzh'n) *n.* **1.** The process of or condition resulting from obverting something. **2.** *Logic.* Inference of the obverse of a proposition.

ob·vert (ob-vért) *tr.v.* **-verted, -verting, -verts. 1.** *Rare.* To turn so as to present another side or aspect to view. **2.** *Logic.* To subject to obversion, or deduce the obverse of. [Latin *obvertere,* to turn towards : *ob-,* towards + *vertere,* to turn.]

ob·vi·ate (óbvi-ayt) *tr.v.* **-ated, -ating, -ates.** To prevent or dispose of effectively; anticipate so as to render unnecessary. See Synonyms at **prevent.** [Late Latin *obviāre,* "to meet in the way", prevent, from Latin *ob viam,* in the way. See **obvious.**] —**ob·vi·a·tion** (-áysh'n) *n.* —**ob·vi·a·tor** (-ər) *n.*

ob·vi·ous (óbvi-əss) *adj.* **1.** Easily perceived or understood; quite apparent. **2.** *Informal.* Lacking subtlety. **3.** *Archaic.* Standing in the way or in front. —See Synonyms at **evident.** [Latin *obvius,* from *ob viam,* in the way : *ob,* against + *viam,* accusative of *via,* way.] —**ob·vi·ous·ness** *n.*

ob·vi·ous·ly (óbvi-əssli) *adv.* **1.** In an obvious manner. **2.** It is obvious; as is obvious: *He is obviously extremely stupid.*

ob·vo·lute (ób-və-lōōt, -lōōt, -lewt, -léwt) *adj. Botany.* Folded together with overlapping edges. Said of leaves and petals in a bud. [Latin *obvolutus,* past participle of *obvolvere,* to wrap around, surround : *ob-,* over + *volvere,* to roll, wrap.] —**ob·vo·lu·tion** (-lōōsh'n, -léwsh'n) *n.* —**ob·vo·lu·tive** *adj.*

OC Officer Commanding.

oc., Oc. ocean.

o.c. in the work cited [Latin *opere citato*].

O.C. 1. Officer Commanding. **2.** Old Catholic.

o/c overcharge.

oc·a·ri·na (óckə-réenə) *n. Music.* A small terracotta or plastic wind instrument, used especially in Inca music, with a mouthpiece, finger holes, and an ovoid shape. [Italian, "little goose" (from its shape), diminutive of *oca,* goose, from Vulgar Latin *avica* (unattested), from Latin *avicula,* diminutive of *avis,* bird.]

O'Ca·sey (ō-káyssi, ə-), **Sean** (1884–1964). Irish playwright. Drawing on a childhood spent in the slums of Dublin and on his experiences in the Irish fight for independence he produced three early works: *The Shadow of a Gunman* (1923), *Juno and the Paycock* (1924), and *The Plough and the Stars* (1926). His six volumes of autobiography were published under the title *Mirror in My House* (1956).

occ. 1. occident; occidental. **2.** occupation.

Occam's razor. Variant of **Ockham's razor.**

occas. occasional; occasionally.

oc·ca·sion (ə-káyzh'n || ō-) *n.* **1. a.** An event or happening. **b.** The time at which an event or happening occurs. **2.** A significant or special event, happening, or celebration. **3.** An appropriate or favourable time; an opportunity. **4.** That which brings on or precipitates an action or event; the immediate cause. **5.** A reason; grounds. **6.** A requirement; a need; a necessity: *"He must buy what he has little occasion for"* (Laurence Sterne). **7.** *Plural. Archaic.* Personal requirements or necessities. **8.** *Plural. Archaic.* Personal affairs or business matters. —See Usage note at **cause.** —**on occasion.** From time to time; now and then. —**rise to the occasion.** To have the resources to cope with a particular situation.
~*tr.v.* **occasioned, -sioning, -sions.** To provide occasion for; cause. [Middle English *occasioun,* from Old French *occasion,* from Latin *occāsiō* (stem *occāsiōn-*), "a falling down, happening", from *occīdere* (past participle *occāsus*), to fall down : *ob-,* down + *cadere,* to fall.]

Usage: *Occasion* is followed by different prepositions or particles, depending on its sense. When it means "reason" or "grounds", it is followed by *for* or *to*: *This is an occasion for rejoicing; You have no occasion to object.* When it means "opportunity", it is followed by *to*: *He took the occasion to ask me for advice.* When it means "time of occurrence", it is followed by *of*: *On the occasion of your visit.*

oc·ca·sion·al (ə-káyzh'n'l || ō-) *adj. Abbr.* **occas. 1. a.** Coming irregularly; occurring from time to time: *an occasional visit.* **b.** Infrequent; not habitual: *took an occasional drink.* **2.** Occurring on or created for a special occasion: *occasional verse.* **3.** Designating a cause that is secondary or incidental. **4.** Designed not as part of a set but for use as the occasion requires: *an occasional chair for unexpected guests.* —See Synonyms at **periodic.**

oc·ca·sion·al·ism (ə-káyzh'n'l-iz'm || ō-) *n. Philosophy.* The theory that the connection between mental and bodily processes is the result of divine agency. —**oc·ca·sion·al·ist** *adj. & n.*

oc·ca·sion·al·ly (ə-káyzh'n'l-i, -nəli || ō-) *adv. Abbr.* **occas.** Now and then; from time to time; sometimes.

oc·ci·dent (óksi-dənt || -dent) *n. Abbr.* **occ. 1.** *Literary.* The west; western lands or regions. **2.** *Capital* **O. a.** The Western Hemisphere. **b.** The countries of Europe and the Western Hemisphere. Usually preceded by *the.* Compare **Orient.** [Middle English, from Old French, from Latin *occīdēns* (stem *occīdent-*), "quarter of the setting sun", west, from present participle of *occīdere,* to fall down, set (of the sun). See **occasion.**]

oc·ci·den·tal (óksi-dént'l) *adj. Abbr.* **occ.** *Often capital* **O.** Of or pertaining to the countries of the Occident, their peoples, or their culture; western.
~*n. Usually capital* **O.** A native or inhabitant of a western country. —**oc·ci·den·tal·ism** *n.* —**oc·ci·den·tal·ist** *n.*

oc·ci·den·tal·ise, oc·ci·den·tal·ize (óksi-dént'l-īz) *v.* **-ised, -ising, -ises.** *Often capital* **O.** —*tr.* To make occidental in character, outlook, or way of life. —*intr.* To become occidental; adopt occidental ways. —**oc·ci·den·tal·i·sa·tion** (-ī-záysh'n || *U.S.* -i-) *n.*

oc·cip·i·tal (ok-síppit'l) *adj.* Of or pertaining to the back of the head or to the occipital bone: *an occipital fracture.*
~*n.* The occipital bone. [Old French, from Medieval Latin *occipitālis,* from Latin *occiput* (stem *occipit-*), OCCIPUT.]

occipital bone *n.* A curved, compound bone that forms the lower posterior part of the skull.

occipital lobe *n.* The posterior portion of each cerebral hemisphere, functional in the interpretation of sensory impulses from the eyes.

oc·ci·put (óksi-put, -pət) *n., pl.* **-puts** or **occipita** (ok-síppitə). The back of the skull, especially the occipital area. [Middle English, from Latin : *ob-,* back of + *caput,* head.]

oc·clude (ə-klōōd, o- || -kléwd) *v.* **-cluded, -cluding, -cludes.** —*tr.* **1.** To cause to become closed; obstruct: *occlude a larynx.* **2.** To prevent the passage of; shut in, out, or off: *occlude light.* **3.** *Chemistry.* To absorb or adsorb (a substance) in great quantity. **4.** *Meteorology.* To force (air) upwards from the earth's surface, as when a cold front overtakes and undercuts a warm front. **5.** In dentistry, to bring together (the upper and lower teeth) in proper alignment for chewing. —*intr.* In dentistry, to close so that the cusps fit together. Used of the teeth of the upper and lower jaws. [Latin *occlūdere* : *ob-* (intensive) + *claudere,* to close.] —**oc·clud·ent** *adj.*

occluded front *n. Meteorology.* The air front established when a cold front occludes a warm front. Also called "occlusion".

oc·clu·sion (ə-klōōzh'n, o- || -kléwzh'n) *n.* **1. a.** An act or the process of occluding. **b.** The state of being occluded. **c.** That which occludes or blocks. **2.** *Meteorology.* **a.** The process of occluding air masses. **b.** An occluded front. **3.** In dentistry, the normal fit of the teeth when brought together. **4.** *Phonetics.* **a.** The complete closure of the vocal tract at some point. **b.** A speech sound involving occlusion; a plosive. —**oc·clu·sal** (-klōō-z'l, -s'l || -kléw-) *adj.*

oc·clu·sive (ə-klōō-siv, o- || -kléw-, -ziv) *adj.* Occluding or tending to occlude.
~*n. Phonetics.* **1.** A closing of the breath passage; a stop. **2.** A nasal consonant.

oc·cult (o-kúlt, ə-, óckult) *adj.* **1.** Of, pertaining to, dealing with, or knowledgeable in supernatural influences, agencies, or phenomena. **2.** Beyond the realm of human comprehension; mysterious; inscrutable. **3.** Available only to the initiated; not divulged; secret: *occult lore.* **4.** *Rare.* Hidden from view; concealed. **5.** *Medicine.* Not immediately obvious.
~*n.* Occult practices or techniques. Usually preceded by *the.*
~*v.* (o-kúlt, ə-) **occulted, -culting, -cults.** —*tr.* **1.** To conceal or cause to disappear from view. **2.** *Astronomy.* To conceal by occultation: *The Moon occulted Mars.* —*intr.* To become concealed or extinguished at regular intervals: *a lighthouse beacon that occults every 45 seconds.* [Latin *occultus,* past participle of *occulere,* to conceal; akin to *celāre,* to hide.] —**oc·cult·ly** *adv.* —**oc·cult·ness** *n.*

oc·cul·ta·tion (óckul-táysh'n, óck'l-) *n.* **1.** *Astronomy.* **a.** The passage of a celestial body across a line between an observer and another celestial object, as when the Moon moves between Earth and Sun in a solar eclipse. **b.** The disappearance of the further celestial object, or the progressive blocking of light, radio waves, or other radiation from a celestial source during such a passage. **c.** An observational technique for determining the position or radiant structure of a celestial source so occulted: *a lunar occultation of a quasar.* **2.** The act of occulting or the state of being occulted. [Middle English *occultacion,* concealment, from Latin *occultātiō* (stem *occultātiōn-*), from *occultāre,* frequentative of *occulere,* to conceal. See **occult.**]

oc·cult·ism (óckul-tiz'm, óck'l-, o-kúl-, ə-) *n.* **1.** The study of the supernatural. **2.** A belief in occult powers and the possibility of bringing them under human control. —**oc·cult·ist** *n. & adj.*

obverse *A golden aureus of the Roman emperor Septimius Severus (A.D. 146–211) showing his head (left), with that of his son Caracalla (186–217).*

oc·cu·pan·cy (óckewpən-si) *n., pl.* **-cies.** **1. a.** The act of taking or holding possession; the act of occupying. **b.** The condition of being occupied. **2.** The period during which one owns, rents, or uses certain premises or land. **3.** The state of being an occupant or tenant. **4.** *Law.* The taking possession of previously unowned property with the intent of obtaining the right to own it.

oc·cu·pant (óckewpənt) *n.* **1.** One who holds a position or place. **2.** One who has certain legal rights to or control over the premises he occupies; a tenant or owner. **3.** *Law.* One who is the first to take possession of something previously unowned. [French, from the present participle of *occuper*, to OCCUPY.]

oc·cu·pa·tion (óckew-páysh'n) *n. Abbr.* **occ.** **1. a.** An activity that serves as one's regular source of livelihood, such as a profession or a vocation. **b.** An activity engaged in, especially as a means of passing time. **2. a.** The act or process of holding or possessing a place. **b.** The state of being held or possessed. **3. a.** The invasion, conquest, and control of a nation or territory by a foreign military force. **b.** The military government exercising such control. **c.** The period during which such control is in force. [Middle English *occu*-*pacioun*, from Old French *occupation*, from Latin *occupātiō* (stem *occupātiōn*-), from *occupāre*, to OCCUPY.]

oc·cu·pa·tion·al (óckew-páysh'n'l) *adj.* Of, pertaining to, or caused by engagement in a particular occupation: *occupational disease.* —**oc·cu·pa·tion·al·ly** *adv.*

occupational psychology *n.* The study of human behaviour in relation to work, including such aspects as stress and job satisfaction. —**occupational psychologist** *n.*

occupational therapy *n.* Therapy for the physically and mentally ill in which the principal element is some form of productive or creative activity, such as pottery or basket-weaving. —**occupational therapist** *n.*

oc·cu·pi·er (óckew-pī-ər) *n.* **1.** One that occupies. **2.** *British.* A person who occupies or has possession of a building or piece of land. Usually used in combination: *owner-occupier.*

oc·cu·py (óckew-pī) *tr.v.* **-pied, -pying, -pies.** **1.** To seize possession of and maintain control over (a place or region), as by military conquest or a sit-in, for example. **2.** To fill up; take (time or space): *a lecture that occupied three hours.* **3.** To live in or on, or be a tenant in or of (premises or land). **4.** To hold or fill (an office or position).

---

ocean

THE ELEMENT THAT COVERS SEVEN-TENTHS OF THE EARTH'S CRUST
Mountains, valleys, and canyons of the ocean deeps

The Earth is the only watery planet in our Solar System. Although its waters are divided by the continents into the Atlantic, Pacific, Indian, Arctic, and Antarctic oceans, they are all connected, forming a single world ocean which covers some 70 per cent of the surface of the Earth.

The continental shelves are the oceans' shallows. These regions are richest in fish and other food resources and in gas and oil deposits. They slope down from the coasts to the 200 metres (656 feet) depth contour, then slope down much more steeply to form the continental rises. Winding submarine canyons scored into the continental rises may have been worn away by underwater currents or gouged out by sediment-laden waters gushing from large estuaries.

The ocean bottoms level out at around 4000 metres (13,123 feet) below the surface into vast, shallow basins with sea mounts edging them and scattered over them. They are floored

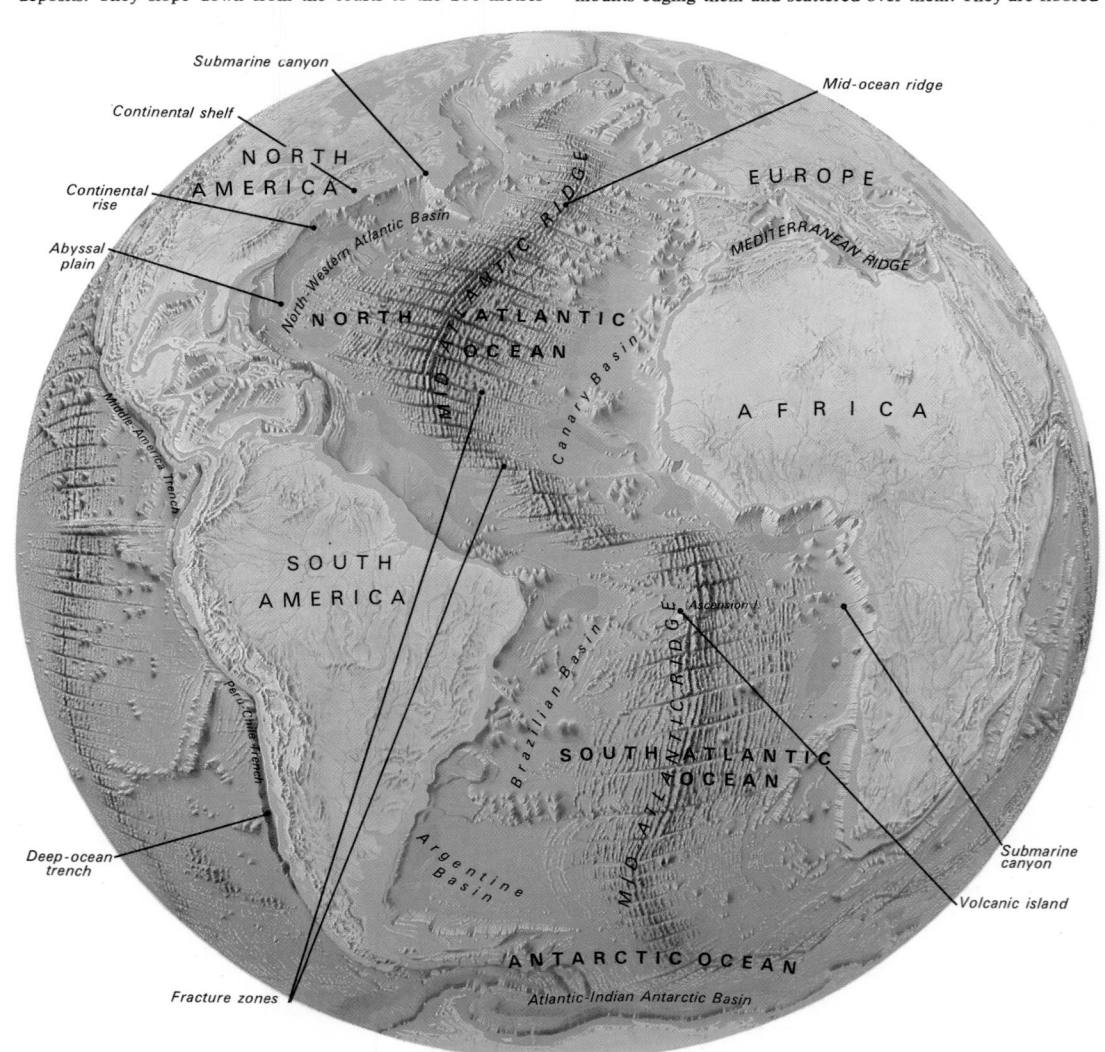

5. To engage, employ, or keep busy (a person or animal). [Middle English *occupien,* from Old French *occuper,* from Latin *occupāre,* to seize : *ob-* (intensive) + *capere,* to take.]

oc·cur (ə-kúr ‖ ŏ-) *intr.v.* **-curred, -curring, -curs. 1.** To take place; come about. **2.** To be found to exist or appear. **3.** To come to mind; suggest itself: *It occurred to me.* —See Synonyms at **happen.** [Latin *occurrere,* to run to meet : *ob-,* towards + *currere,* to run.]

oc·cur·rence (ə-kúrrənss ‖ ŏ-) *n.* **1.** An act or instance of occurring. **2.** Something that takes place; an incident. —**oc·cur·rent** *adj.*

    Synonyms: occurrence, happening, event, incident, episode, circumstance.

o·cean (ŏsh'n) *n.* **1.** *Abbr.* **O, O., oc., Oc.** The entire body of salt water that covers about 70 per cent of the earth's surface. **2.** *Often capital* **O.** *Abbr.* **O, O., oc., Oc.** Any of the principal divisions of this body of water, including the Atlantic, Pacific, and Indian oceans, their southern extensions in Antarctica, and the Arctic Ocean. **3.** *Usually plural.* Any great expanse or amount: *oceans of money.* **4.** In classical mythology, the sea encircling the earth. [Middle English *ocean,* from Old French, from Latin *ōceanus,* from Greek *ōkeanos,* OCEANUS.]

o·cean·ar·i·um (ŏsh'n-aír-i-əm) *n., pl.* **-iums** or **-ia** (-i-ə). A large aquarium for the study or display of marine life.

ocean basin *n.* A **basin** (sense 6) *(see).*

O·ce·an·i·a (ŏ-shi-áyni-ə, -si-, -aáni-ə ‖ -ánni-ə). Also **O·ce·an·i·ca** (-ánnikə). The islands of the central, western, and southern Pacific Ocean, taken customarily to include Australia and New Zealand. —**O·ce·an·i·an** *adj.* & *n.*

o·ce·an·ic (ŏ-shi-ánnik, -si-) *adj.* **1.** Of or pertaining to the ocean. **2.** Produced by or living in an ocean, especially in the open sea rather than in shallow coastal waters. **3.** Like an ocean in expanse; wide; huge; sweeping.

O·ce·an·ic (ŏ-shi-ánnik, -si-) *adj.* **1.** Pertaining to a subfamily of the Austronesian language family, comprising Melanesian and Polynesian. **2.** Pertaining to the cultures of the peoples speaking languages in this subfamily. —**O·ce·an·ic** *n.*

O·ce·a·nid (ō-sée-ə-nid) *n., pl.* **-nids** or **Oceanides** (ŏ-si-ánni-deez). *Greek Mythology.* Any of the ocean nymphs held to be the daughters of Oceanus and Tethys. [Greek *ōkeanis* (stem *ōkeanid-*), from *Ōkeanos,* OCEANUS.]

Ocean Island. Also **Ba·na·ba** (bə-naábə). One of the Gilbert is-

---

with abyssal plains, soft carpets of oozes formed from the perpetual rain of dead organisms from above and clayey debris washed down from the continents. Nodules of manganese, nickel, copper, and cobalt, looking like flintstones, accumulate on parts of the abyssal plains. The nodules take millennia to build up in concentric layers around fragments of shell.

    Underwater mountain ranges, the mid-ocean ridges, run like spines down the centres of the oceans, often rising to within 1000 metres (3,280 feet) of the surface. The highest peaks break the surface as islands. Geologists now accept that these ridges mark the paths of faults along which the continental plates are being forced apart by convection currents from deep within the Earth's mantle. Volcanic material is constantly rising out of the mantle to the Earth's surface and solidifying along the edges of the plates, causing the sea floors to spread. V-shaped trenches, cutting deep into the ocean floors, and arcs of volcanic islands, mark the zones where the sea floor is being subducted, or thrust down, beneath the continental plates and absorbed back into the mantle. Such trenches almost encircle the Pacific. They are thousands of kilometres long, hundreds of kilometres wide, and the deepest, the Marianas Trench east of Philippines, reaches 11 033 metres (36,197 feet) below sea level.

lands (now Kiribati) in the west Pacific. Vast quantities of its valuable phosphate deposits (discovered 1900) were exported before supplies ran out (late 1970s). The Banabans were deported by the Japanese (1942) and accepted resettlement on Rambi, a Fijian island. Accused of gross exploitation, the British Phosphate Commissioners offered them £6.5 million in 1977.

oceanog. oceanography.

o·cean·og·ra·phy (ōsh'n-óggrəfi) *n. Abbr.* **oceanog.** The exploration and scientific study of the ocean and its phenomena. [OCEAN + -GRAPHY.] **—o·cean·og·ra·pher** *n.* **—o·cean·o·graph·ic** (-ə-gráf-fik) **—o·cean·o·graph·i·cal** *adj.*

ocean sunfish *n.* The **sunfish** (*see*).

O·ce·a·nus (ō-si-áynəss, ō-sée-ə-nəss). *Greek Mythology.* A Titan, the god of the outer sea encircling the earth, and father of the Oceanides and of the river gods.

oc·el·lat·ed (óssil-aytid, ō-síl-, ō-sél-) *adj.* Also **oc·el·late** (-ayt). **1.** Having an ocellus or ocelli. **2.** Resembling an ocellus. **3.** Marked with spots. [Latin *ocellātus*, having little eyes, from *ocellus*, little eye, OCELLUS.] **—oc·el·la·tion** (-áysh'n) *n.*

o·cel·lus (ō-sél-əss) *n., pl.* **-li** (-ī). **1.** A small simple eye, found in many invertebrates. **2.** A marking that resembles an eye. [New Latin, from Latin, diminutive of *oculus*, eye.] **—o·cel·lar** (-ər) *adj.*

oc·e·lot (ó-si-lot, ó-, -lət) *n.* A brush- and forest-dwelling cat, *Felis pardalis*, of the southwestern United States and Central and South America, having a tawny-greyish or yellow coat with black-bordered brown spots. [French, from Nahuatl *ocelotl*.]

och (okh) *interj. Scottish & Irish.* Used to express surprise, regret, or disagreement. [Gaelic, "oh".]

och·e (ocki) *n.* **1.** The line behind which a darts player stands to throw darts at the board. **2.** The place from which a darts player throws darts at the board. **—on the oche.** Standing ready to throw.

och·loc·ra·cy (ok-lóckrə-si) *n., pl.* **-cies.** Government by the masses; mob rule. [French *ochlocratie*, from Greek *okhlokratia* : *okhlos*, mob + *-kratia*, -CRACY.] **—och·lo·crat** (ócklə-krat) *n.* **—och·lo·crat·ic** (-kráttik), **och·lo·crat·i·cal** *adj.* **—och·lo·crat·i·cal·ly** *adv.*

och·lo·pho·bi·a (ócklə-fóbi-ə) *n. Psychology.* Abnormal dread of crowds. [New Latin : Greek *okhlos*, crowd + -PHOBIA.] **—och·lo·pho·bic** *adj. & n.*

och·one (o-khṓn) *interj. Scottish & Irish.* Used to express regret or grief. [Gaelic *ochóin*, "oh, alas".]

o·chre, *U.S.* **o·cher** (ōkər) *n.* **1.** Any of several earthy mineral oxides of iron mingled with varying amounts of clay and sand, occurring in yellow, brown, or red, and used either untreated or processed as pigments. **2.** Moderate orange yellow, from moderate or deep orange to moderate or strong yellow.

~tr.v. ochred or *U.S.* **ochered, ochring** or *U.S.* **ochering, ochres** or *U.S.* **ochers.** To colour or mark with ochre. [Middle English *oker*, from Old French *ocre*, from Latin *lochra*, from Greek *ōkhra*, from *ōkhros†*, yellow, pale yellow.] **—o·chre** *adj.* **—o·chre·ous** (ōkər-əss, ōkri-), **o·chre·y** (ōkəri, ōkri) *adj.*

-ock *n. suffix.* Indicates smallness; for example, **hillock.** [Middle English *-oc*, Old English *-oc, -uc.*]

ock·er (ókər) *n. Australian Slang.* An ill-mannered, uncultivated Australian. Compare **Alf, Roy.**
~adj. Australian Slang. Rude, uncultivated. [Informal variant of *Oscar*; from the name of such a character in an Australian television series (1973).]

Ock·ham's razor, Oc·cam's razor (óckəmz) *n.* A principle of scientific and philosophical discussion urging the use of the most economical and least complex assumptions, terms, and theories. It is usually formulated as "Entities should not be multiplied unnecessarily". [After William of *Ockham* (died *c.* 1350), English philosopher, + RAZOR (figuratively, as a sharp instrument for cutting away inessentials).]

o'clock (ə-klók ‖ ō-) *adv.* **1.** Of or according to the clock. Used to indicate the time: *three o'clock.* **2.** According to an imaginary clock dial with the observer at the centre and 12 o'clock considered as straight ahead in horizontal position or straight up in vertical position. Used to indicate relative position: *enemy planes at 11 o'clock.* [Reduced from *of the clock.*]

O'Con·nell (ō-kónn'l, ə-), **Daniel** (1775–1847). Irish politician. He battled (within the constitution) to repeal the laws excluding Roman Catholics from Parliament. Eventually he took his seat (1829), as a Roman Catholic, in the House of Commons. His subsequent campaign for Irish independence was unsuccessful and cost him his legal practice, his fortune, and his health.

o·co·ti·llo (ōkə-téel-yō, ócka- ‖ *U.S.* -tée-yō) *n., pl.* **-llos.** A succulent, spiny shrub or tree, *Fouquieria splendens*, of Mexico and the southwestern United States, having clusters of tubular scarlet flowers. Also called "candlewood". [Mexican Spanish, diminutive of *ocote*, a Mexican pine, from Nahuatl *ocotl*, torch.]

OCR 1. optical character reader. **2.** optical character recognition.

oc·re·a, och·re·a (óckri-ə) *n., pl.* **-reae** (-ee). *Botany.* A sheath composed of one or more stipules that enclose the base of a leaf, as in some members of the Polygonaceae. [Latin *ocrea†*, greave, legging.] **—oc·re·ate** (-ət, -it, -ayt) *adj.*

oct. octavo.

Oct. October.

octa-, oct-. Variants of **octo-.**

oc·ta·chord (óktə-kawrd) *n. Music.* **1.** An eight-stringed instrument.

ocelot *Native to the forests of the southwestern United States, and Central and South America, the ocelot is a large cat which feeds on reptiles and small mammals such as opossums and deer. It is a good climber, and often sleeps in the branches of trees.*

2. A sequence of eight notes, especially a scale. [Latin *octachordus*, from Greek *oktakhordos* : OCTA- + CHORD.]

oc·tad (óktad) *n.* A group or series of eight. [Greek *oktas* (stem *oktad-*), number eight, from *oktō*, eight.] **—oc·tad·ic** (ok-táddik) *adj.*

oc·ta·gon (ókta-gən ‖ *U.S.* -gon) *n.* A polygon with eight sides and eight angles. [Latin *octagōnum*, from Greek *oktagōnon*, from neuter of *oktagōnos*, having eight angles : OCTO- + -GON.]

oc·tag·o·nal (ok-tággən'l) *adj.* **1.** Having eight sides and eight angles. **2.** Of, relating to, or formed in octagons. **—oc·tag·o·nal·ly** *adv.*

oc·ta·he·dral (óktə-héedrəl) *adj.* **1.** Having eight plane surfaces. **2.** Of, relating to, or formed in octahedrons. **—oc·ta·hed·ral·ly** *adv.*

oc·ta·he·drite (óktə-héedrīt) *n.* A mineral, **anatase** (*see*). Not in current technical usage. [French *octaédrite*, from *octaèdre*, octahedron (with reference to its octahedral crystals), from Greek *oktaedron*, OCTAHEDRON.]

oc·ta·he·dron (óktə-hée-drən) *n., pl.* **-drons** or **-dra** (-drə). A polyhedron with eight plane surfaces. [Greek *oktaedron* : OCTO- + -HEDRON.]

oc·tal (óktəl) *n.* A number system using the number eight as a base, which is used in computing. Also called "octal notation". [OCTA- + -AL.]

oc·tam·er·ous (ok-támmə-rəss) *adj.* Also **oc·tom·er·ous** (-tómmə-). *Biology.* Having or consisting of parts arranged in sets of eight. Said especially of flowers having sepals, petals, or other parts arranged in sets of eight. [Greek *oktameres* : OCTO- + -MEROUS.] **—oc·tam·er·ism** (-riz'm) *n.*

oc·tam·e·ter (ok-támmitər) *n.* A line of verse consisting of eight metrical feet. [OCTO- + METER (after *hexameter*).] **—oc·tam·e·ter** *adj.*

oc·tane (óktayn) *n.* **1.** Any of various isomeric alkanes with the formula C_8H_{18}. **2.** A colourless, inflammable hydrocarbon, $CH_3(CH_2)_6CH_3$, found in petroleum, and used as a solvent. **3.** Octane number. [OCT(O)- + -ANE.]

oc·tane·di·o·ic acid (óktayn-dī-ō-ik) *n.* A colourless crystalline dicarboxylic derivative of octane, $HOOC(CH_2)_6COOH$, used in the manufacture of synthetic resins and occurring in castor oil and suberin. Also called "suberic acid".

octane number *n.* A numerical measure of the antiknock properties of petrol, based on the percentage by volume of isooctane in a standard reference fuel. For example, a petrol that produces the same degree of knocking as a standard reference fuel containing 80 per cent isooctane has an octane number of 80. Also called "octane rating". Compare **cetane number.**

oc·tan·gu·lar *adj.* Octagonal.

Oc·tans (ok-tanz) *n.* The constellation that includes the south celestial pole. Also called "Octant". [New Latin, from Latin *octāns*, half-quadrant. See **octant.**]

oc·tant (óktənt) *n.* **1.** One eighth of a circle: **a.** A 45° arc. **b.** The area enclosed by two radii at a 45° angle and the intersected arc. **2.** An instrument based on the principle of the sextant, but employing only a 45° angle, used as an aid in navigation. **3.** *Astronomy.* The position of a celestial body when it is separated from another by a 45° angle. **4.** Any one of eight parts into which three-dimensional space is divided by three, usually perpendicular, coordinate planes. **5.** *Capital* **O.** Octans. [Latin *octans* (stem *octant-*), half-quadrant, from *octō*, eight.] **—oc·tan·tal** (ok-tánt'l) *adj.*

octaroon. Variant of **octoroon.**

oc·ta·va·lent (óktə-váylənt) *adj. Chemistry.* Having a valency of eight.

oc·tave (ók-tiv; *also usually for sense 2 but rarely for other senses,* -tayv) *n.* **1.** *Music.* **a.** The interval of eight diatonic degrees between two notes, one of which has twice as many vibrations per second as the other. **b.** A note that is eight full tones above or below another given note. **c.** Two notes, eight diatonic degrees apart, sounded together, or the consonance that results. **d.** A series of notes included within this interval, or the keys of an instrument that produce such a series. **e.** An organ stop that produces notes an octave above those usually produced by the keys played. **2.** *Ecclesiastical.* **a.** The eighth day after a feast day, counting the feast day as one. **b.** The entire period between a feast day and the eighth day following it. **3.** Any group or series of eight. **4. a.** A stanza of eight lines. **b.** An octet in a sonnet. **5.** *Fencing.* A rotating parry.
~adj. **1.** Composed of eight elements or parts. **2.** *Music.* Producing tones one octave higher, as an organ stop may. [Middle English, the eighth day (after a festival), from Medieval Latin *octāva (diēs)*, from Latin, feminine of *octāvus*, eighth, from *octō*, eight.] **—oc·ta·val** (ok-táyv'l, óktiv'l) *adj.*

octave coupler *n.* A mechanical device on an organ that automatically enables notes an octave apart to be played simultaneously by pressing the key or pedal for just one note.

Oc·ta·vi·a (ok-táyvi-ə) (64–11 B.C.). Sister of the Roman emperor Augustus. At her brother's behest, she married (40 B.C.) Mark Antony. Though she raised an army and finance for his Armenian campaign, he divorced her (32 B.C.) for Cleopatra. The Porticus Octaviae in Rome was erected to commemorate her.

Octavian. See **Augustus.**

oc·ta·vo (ok-táy-vō ‖ -táʿa-) *n., pl.* **-vos.** *Abbr.* **o., O., oct. 1.** The page size of a book composed of printer's sheets folded into eight leaves, originally printed on one side of each sheet. **2.** A book composed of pages of this size. Also called "eightvo". Also written *8vo, 8°.*

[Latin *(in) octāvō,* "in eighth", ablative of *octāvus,* eighth. See **octave.**] **—oc·ta·vo** *adj.*

oc·ten·ni·al (ok-ténni-əl) *adj.* **1.** Happening or recurring every eight years. **2.** Lasting eight years. [Late Latin *octennium,* period of eight years : OCT(O)- + Latin *annus,* a year.] **—oc·ten·ni·al·ly** *adv.*

oc·tet (ok-tét, ók-) *n.* Also **oc·tette** (for senses 1, 2, 3, 5). **1.** A musical composition written for eight voices or eight instruments. **2.** A group of eight singers or eight instrumentalists. **3.** Any group of eight. **4.** *Chemistry.* A group of eight electrons in the orbital shell of an atom, necessary for stability in the formation of many molecules. **5.** The first eight lines of an Italian sonnet. In this sense, also called "octave". Compare **sestet.** [Italian *ottetto* (influenced by *duet*), from *otto,* eight, from Latin *octō.*]

oc·til·lion (ók-tíl-yən) *n.* **1.** In Great Britain, the cardinal number represented by the figure 1 followed by 48 zeros; usually written 10^{48}. **2.** In the United States, the cardinal number represented by the figure 1 followed by 27 zeros; usually written 10^{27}. [French : OCT(O)- + (M)ILLION.]

oc·til·lionth (ók-tíl-yənth) *n.* **1.** The ordinal number octillion in a series. **2.** Any of an octillion equal parts. **—oc·til·lionth** *adj.*

octo–, octa-, oct– *comb. form.* Indicates eight parts or elements; for example, **octopus, octameter, octane.** [Latin *octō-,* from *octō,* eight; Greek *okta-,* from *oktō,* eight.]

Oc·to·ber (ok-tōbər) *n. Abbr.* **Oct. 1.** The tenth month of the Gregorian calendar. October has 31 days. **2.** *British Archaic.* Ale brewed in this month. [Middle English *octobre,* from Old French, from Latin *Octōber,* "eighth month", from *octō,* eight.]

October Revolution *n.* A part of the **Russian Revolution** *(see).*

Oc·to·brist (ok-tōbrist) *n.* A member of a moderate Russian political party that accepted the reforms outlined in the Imperial Constitutional Manifesto issued by Nicholas II in October, 1905. **—Oc·to·brist** *adj.*

oc·to·dec·i·mo (ók-tō-déssi-mō || -tə-) *n., pl.* **-mos. 1.** The page size of a book composed of printer's sheets folded into 18 leaves or 36 pages. **2.** A book composed of pages of this size. Also called "eighteenmo". Also written *18mo, 18°.* [Latin *octōdecimō,* ablative of *octōdecimus,* eighteenth, from *octōdecim,* eighteen: OCTO- + *decem,* ten.] **—oc·to·dec·i·mo** *adj.*

oc·to·ge·nar·i·an (ók-tōji-naír-i-ən, -tə-) *adj.* **1.** Being eighty years old or between eighty and ninety years old. **2.** Of or like someone of this age.
~*n.* A person eighty years old or between eighty and ninety years old. [Latin *octōgēnārius,* containing eighty, from *octōgēnī,* eighty each, from *octōgintā,* eighty : *octō,* OCTO- + *-gintā,* "ten times".]

octomerous. Variant of **octamerous.**

oc·to·nar·y (óktə-nəri || -nerri) *adj.* **1.** Of or pertaining to the number eight. **2.** Consisting of eight members or of groups containing eight.
~*n., pl.* **octonaries.** A group or set of eight. [Latin *octōnārius,* containing eight, from *octōnī,* eight at a time, from *octō,* eight.]

oc·to·ploid (óktə-ployd) *adj. Genetics.* Having eight times the number of haploid chromosomes in a somatic cell nucleus. [OCTO- + -PLOID.]

oc·to·pod (óktə-pod) *n.* Any mollusc of the order Octopoda, such as an octopus, having eight arms and no internal shell. [New Latin *Octopoda,* from Greek *oktōpoda,* neuter plural of *oktōpous* (stem *oktōpod-*), OCTOPUS.]

oc·to·pus (óktə-pəss) *n., pl.* **-puses** or **octopi** (-pī). **1.** Any of numerous carnivorous, marine molluscs of the genus *Octopus* or related genera, found worldwide. It has a saclike body, eight tentacles, each bearing two rows of suckers, a large distinct head, and a strong beaklike mouth. Compare **squid. 2.** *Informal.* Any powerful and far-reaching organisation or person. [New Latin, from Greek *oktōpous,* eight-footed : OCTO- + *pous,* foot.]

oc·to·roon, oc·ta·roon (óktə-rōōn) *n.* The offspring of a white person and a quadroon; one who is one-eighth black. [OCTO- + (QUAD)ROON.]

oc·to·syl·la·ble (ók-tō-sílləb'l, -tə-) *n.* **1.** In poetry: **a.** A line of verse containing eight syllables. **b.** A verse with eight syllables in each line. **2.** A word of eight syllables. [Late Latin *octosyllabus,* having eight syllables : OCTO- + *syllaba,* SYLLABLE.] **—oc·to·syl·lab·ic** (-si-lábbik) *adj.*

oc·troi (ók-trwaa || -troy) *n., pl.* **-trois** (-trwaa || -troyz). **1.** A local tax levied on certain items brought into some European cities. **2.** The officials responsible for collecting this tax. **3.** The place where the tax is collected. [French, from Old French, a tax which a city is authorised to levy, from *octroyer,* to grant as a privilege, authorise, from Gallo-Roman *auctōricāre* (unattested), to authorise, from Latin *auctor,* author, originator, from *augēre,* to originate, increase.]

oc·tu·ple (ók-tewp'l || -tōōp'l, ok-téwp'l, -tōōp'l) *adj.* **1.** Consisting of or having eight parts, members, or copies. **2.** Multiplied by eight; eight times as much, as many, or as large.
~*n.* An eightfold amount or number.
~*v.* **octupled, -pling, -ples.** *—tr.* To multiply or increase by eight. *—intr.* To be multiplied eightfold. [Latin *octuplus* : OCTO- + *-plus,* -fold.]

oc·u·lar (óckewlər) *adj.* **1.** Of or pertaining to the eye: *ocular exercises.* **2.** Of or pertaining to the sense of sight: *an ocular aberration.* **3.** Seen by the eye; visual: *ocular proof.*
~*n.* The eyepiece of an optical instrument. [Late Latin *oculāris,* of the eyes, from Latin *oculus,* eye.]

oc·u·lar·ist (óckewlərist) *n.* One who makes artificial eyes.

oc·u·list (óckewlist) *n.* A medical practitioner who treats diseases of the eyes; an ophthalmologist. [French *oculiste,* from Latin *oculus,* eye.]

oc·u·lo·mo·tor (óckew-lō-mōtər, -lə-) *adj.* **1.** Pertaining to movements of the eyeball. **2.** Pertaining to the oculomotor nerve. [Latin *oculus,* eye + MOTOR.]

oculomotor nerve *n. Anatomy.* The third cranial nerve, which controls the muscles of the eyeballs.

Od, 'Od, Odd (od) *interj. Archaic.* Used in oaths as a euphemism for "God".

OD (ō dée) *n. Slang.* A drug overdose.
~*intr. v.* **OD'd** or **ODd, OD'ing** or **ODing, OD's** or **ODs.** *Slang.* To take an overdose of a drug: *He OD'd on barbiturates.*

o.d. on demand.

O.D. 1. officer of the day. **2.** on demand. **3.** overdraft. **4.** overdrawn.

o·da·lisque, o·da·lisk (ōdə-lisk, óddə-) *n.* A female slave or concubine in a harem. [French, from Turkish *ōdalik,* chambermaid : *ōdah,* room + *-lik,* noun suffix.]

odd (od) *adj.* **odder, oddest. 1. a.** Strange, unusual, or peculiar. **b.** Queer or eccentric in conduct. **2. a.** In excess; left over: *odd change.* **b.** Greater than a specified number by a relatively small amount: *twenty odd years ago.* **3. a.** Being one of an incomplete pair or set: *an odd shoe.* **b.** Not matching: *odd socks.* **c.** Remaining after others are paired or grouped: *the odd one out.* **4.** Occasional; irregular; chance: *odd jobs.* **5.** Designating a number or something bearing a number not divisible by two: *1, 3, and 5 are odd numbers.* Compare **even.** —See Synonyms at **strange.** [Middle English *odde,* from Old Norse *oddi,* triangle, point, third, odd number.] **—odd·ly** *adv.* **—odd·ness** *n.*

Usage: *Odd* is used to express an indefinite, usually small, amount in excess of a specified round number: *60 odd books.* It is not used with precise numbers (as in *63 odd books*), and the hyphen should be used whenever there is a possible ambiguity (as in *60-odd people/60 odd people*). *60 odd* never means more than 61–69.

odd·ball (ód-bawl) *n. Informal.* A person marked by eccentric behaviour or attitudes. Also *chiefly British* "odd fish". **—odd·ball** *adj.*

Odd·fel·low (ód-fellō) *n.* A member of the Independent Order of Odd Fellows, a fraternal and benevolent society in Britain.

odd·ish (óddish) *adj.* Somewhat odd; rather peculiar.

odd·i·ty (óddəti) *n., pl.* **-ties. 1.** A person or thing that is odd. **2.** An odd quality, trait, or characteristic; an eccentricity. **3.** The state or quality of being odd; strangeness.

odd-job man (ód-jób-man) *n.* A man who does casual or occasional work for a living, especially odd domestic jobs. Also called "odd-jobber".

odd lot *n.* A quantity that differs from a standard trading unit, especially an amount of stock of fewer than 100 shares.

odd·ment (ód-mənt) *n.* **1.** *Usually plural.* Something left over; a fragment, scrap, or remnant. **2.** An oddity.

odd-pin·nate (ód-pínnayt) *adj. Botany.* Pinnate with a single, unpaired leaflet at the end of the leafstalk.

odds (odz) *pl.n.* **1.** A certain number of points given beforehand to a weaker side in a contest to equalise the chances of all participants. **2.** A ratio expressing the probability of an event or outcome. Used especially of sports contests: *The odds on the champion winning are three to two.* **3.** A ratio expressing the amount by which the stake of one better differs from that of his opposing better: *The bookmaker gave odds of ten to one.* **4.** The likelihood of one thing occurring, rather than another, in any contest or issue of indefinite outcome: *The odds are that she will get the leadership on the first ballot.* **5.** Favourable chance; advantage: *The odds are with me.* **6.** Unfavourable conditions; adversity: *overcame the odds.* **7.** *Chiefly British Informal.* Difference or significance. Used chiefly in phrases such as *it makes no odds* or *what's the odds?* **—at odds.** In disagreement; in conflict. **—over the odds. 1.** More than is agreed on or expected. **2.** Too much; excessive. [Plural of ODD.]

odds and ends *pl.n.* Miscellaneous items, remnants, or pieces.

odds and sods *pl.n. Chiefly British Informal.* Miscellaneous items or people. [ODD (noun) + SOD (person, thing).]

Odd's bodikins. Variant of **Od's bodkins.**

odds-on (ódz-ón || -áwn) *adj.* More likely to win than not; having a good chance of success.

ode (ōd) *n.* **1.** In classical literature, a poem intended to be sung by a chorus at a public festival or as part of a drama. **2.** A lengthy lyrical poem, usually rhymed, often addressed to some praised object, person, or quality, and often characterised by a lofty style. See **Horatian ode, Pindaric ode.** [French, from Old French, from Late Latin *ōda, ōdē,* from Greek *ōidē, aoidē,* song.] **—od·ic** *adj.*

-ode¹ *comb. form.* Indicates a way or path; for example, **electrode.** [Greek *-odos,* from *hodos,* a way.]

-ode² *comb. form.* Indicates resemblance or characteristic nature; for example, **nematode.** [Greek *-ōdēs,* from *eidos,* form, shape.]

O·dels·ting, O·dels·thing (ōd'lss-ting) *n.* The lower house of the Norwegian parliament. Compare **Lagting.** [Norwegian, from *odel, oda,* from Old Norse *ōthal,* property + *ting,* assembly (see **thing**).]

O·der (ōdər). *Polish & Czech* **Od·ra** (ódra). River in eastern Europe. Rising in the east Sudeten mountains, Czechoslovakia, it flows northwards to the Baltic Sea near Szczecin. It is a major trading route, navigable from Ratibor, and north of its confluence with the Neisse, it forms part of the German-Polish border.

O·der-Neis·se Line (ōdər-nī-sə) *n.* The border between Poland and East Germany, running along the Oder and Neisse rivers. Adopted

octagon *This eight-sided figure in the ceiling of Ely Cathedral, Cambridgeshire, England, is made of wood. It is 21 metres (70 feet) across, and was finished in 1346.*

PRONUNCIATION KEY

a, **trap**; aa, **father**; ai, **fair**; ar, **star**; aw, **lawn**; ay, **play**; b, bb, **stab**; **rubber**; ch, **church**; ck, **ticket**; d, dd, **dead**; **ladder**; e, **dress**; ee, **bee**; er, **defer**; ew, **few**; ewr, **pure**; ə, **about**; ər, **letter**; f, ff, **fife**; **differ**; g, gg, **giggle**; h, **hat**; i, **kit**; ī, **price**; īr, **fire**; j, **judge**; k, **kick**; l, ll, **let**; 'l, **needle**; m, mm, **man**; n, nn, **no**; 'n, **sudden**; ng, **thing**; o, **lot**; ō, **no**; ŏŏ, **foot**; ōō, **shoe**; oor, **poor**; ow, **cow**; owr, **hour**; oy, **boy**; p, pp, **pepper**; r, rr, **red**; s, ss, **sauce**; sh, **ship**; t, tt, **totter**; th, **thick**; th, **this**; **smooth**; u, **cut**; ur, **turn**; v, vv, **valve**; w, **wet**; y, **yes**; z, zz, **zebra**; zh, **vision**; **pleasure**

IN FOREIGN WORDS:

aɴ, oɴ, **Saint-Saëns**; hl, **Llanelli**; **Hluhluwe**; kh, **loch**; **lough**; **Khaled**

STRESS MARK:

ín-sīt, insight; in-sīt, incite

at the Potsdam conference (August 1945) it was recognised by Poland and East Germany in 1950, and by West Germany in 1970.

O·des·sa (ō-déssǝ). Black Sea port in the Ukrainian S.S.R. It is a major administrative, industrial, cultural, and tourist centre. Kept open all year by icebreakers, it has a major naval base and fishing and whaling fleets. Founded (14th century) as a Tatar fortress, it was claimed by Lithuanians and Turks, and finally ceded to Russia.

o·de·um (ō-dée-ǝm, ódi-) n., pl. **odea**. Also **o·de·on** (ódi-ǝn ‖ U.S. -on) pl. **-ons**. A building, especially in ancient Greece and Rome, used for public performances of music and poetry. [Latin ōdēum, from Greek ōideion, from ōidē, song, ODE.]

O·din (ódin). Norse Mythology. The supreme deity and creator of the cosmos and humankind; the god of wisdom, war, art, culture, and the dead, often identified with the Teutonic god Woden. [Old Norse Ōdhinn.]

o·di·ous (ódi-ǝss) adj. Exciting hatred or repugnance; abhorrent; offensive. See Synonyms at **hateful**. [Middle English, from Old French, from Latin odiōsus, from odium, ODIUM.] —**o·di·ous·ly** adv. —**o·di·ous·ness** n.

o·di·um (ódi-ǝm) n. **1.** Strong dislike; contempt or aversion. **2.** The disgrace resulting from hateful conduct. —See Synonyms at **disgrace**. [Latin, hatred, from ōdī, I hate.]

O·do of Bayeux (ódō). (c. 1036–97). Bishop of Bayeux. The half-brother of William the Conqueror, he was co-regent of England while William was in Normandy. He was banished (1088) for conspiring against William II, his nephew.

o·dom·e·ter (ō-dómmitǝr, o-) n. An instrument that indicates distance travelled by a vehicle; a mileometer. [French odomètre, from Greek hodometron : hodos, road, journey + metron, measure, METER.] —**o·dom·e·try** (-dómmǝtri) n.

-odon comb. form. Indicates an animal having teeth of a specified type; for example, **mastodon**. [New Latin, from Greek odous (stem odont-), tooth.]

-odont comb. form. Indicates: **1.** A tooth or teeth of a specified type; for example, **acrodont**. **2.** Having a tooth or teeth of a specified type; for example **diphyodont**. [Greek odous (stem odont-), tooth.]

odonto- comb. form. Indicates tooth or teeth; for example, **odontoblast, odontology**. [Greek, from odous (stem odont-), tooth.]

o·don·to·blast (o-dóntǝ-blast ‖ ō-) n. A tooth cell in the outer surface of dental pulp that produces dentine. [ODONTO- + -BLAST.] —**o·don·to·blas·tic** (-blástik) adj.

o·don·to·glos·sum (o-dóntǝ-glóssǝm, ō-) n. Any orchid of the genus Odontoglossum, having large colourful flowers with a toothlike projection on the lip. [New Latin, "tooth-tongue" : ODONTO- + glossum, from Greek glossa, tongue.]

o·don·toid (o-dóntoyd ‖ ō-) adj. **1.** Resembling a tooth. **2.** Of or pertaining to the odontoid process. [Greek odontoeidēs : ODONT(O)- + -OID.]

odontoid process n. Anatomy. A small, toothlike projection from the second vertebra of the neck, around which the first vertebra rotates.

o·don·tol·o·gy (ód-on-tóllǝji ‖ ōd-) n. The study of the anatomy, growth, and diseases of the teeth. [French odontologie : ODONTO- + -LOGY.] —**o·don·to·log·i·cal** (o-dóntǝ-lójik'l ‖ ō-) adj. —**o·don·to·log·i·cal·ly** adv. —**o·don·tol·o·gist** (-tóllǝjist) n.

o·don·to·phore (o-dóntǝ-fawr ‖ ō-, -fōr) n. A protrusile structure at the base of the mouth of most molluscs, supporting the radula. [ODONTO- + -PHORE.] —**o·don·toph·o·ral** (ód-on-tóffǝrǝl ‖ ōd-), **o·don·toph·o·rine** (-tóffǝ-rīn, -rin), **o·don·toph·o·rous** (-tóffǝrǝss) adj.

o·dor·if·er·ous (ódǝ-ríffǝrǝss) adj. Having or giving off an odour. [Latin odōrifer : ODOUR + -FER.] —**o·dor·if·er·ous·ly** adv. —**o·dor·if·er·ous·ness** n.

o·dor·im·e·ter (ódǝ-rímmitǝr) n. Also **o·dor·om·e·ter** (-rómmitǝr). An instrument for measuring the intensity of odours.

o·dor·ous (ódǝrǝss) adj. Having a distinctive odour, usually, but not necessarily, an unpleasant odour. —**o·dor·ous·ly** adv. —**o·dor·ous·ness** n.

o·dour, U.S. **o·dor** (ódǝr) n. **1.** The property or quality of a thing that affects, stimulates, or is perceived by the sense of smell; its scent. **2.** Any sensation, stimulation, or perception of the sense of smell; a smell. **3.** A strong, pervasive quality. **4.** Esteem; repute. Used chiefly in the phrases in good odour and in bad odour. —See Synonyms at **smell**. [Middle English, from Anglo-French odour, Old French odor, from Latin odor.] —**o·dour·less** adj.

Od's bod·kins (ódz bód-kinz) interj. Also **Odd's bod·i·kins** (bóddi-). Archaic. Used as an oath. [Euphemism for "(by) God's body".]

O·dys·seus (ǝ-díss-yōóss, o-, ō-, -i-ǝss). Latin name **U·lys·ses** (yōō-li-seez, yōō-lisseez). Greek Mythology. The cunning king of Ithaca, a leader of the Greeks in the Trojan War, whose return home was for ten years frustrated by the god Poseidon.

od·ys·sey (óddi-si) n. An extended adventurous wandering. [After ODYSSEY.]

Od·ys·sey (óddi-si) n. The second epic of Homer, recounting the wanderings and adventures of Odysseus after the fall of Troy and his eventual return home. [French Odyssée, from Latin Odysséa, from Greek Odusseia, from Odusseus, ODYSSEUS.] —**Od·ys·sey·an** (-sée-ǝn, -sáy-) adj.

Oe oersted.

Oea. See Tripoli.

OE, OE., O.E. Old English.

O.E.C.D. n. Organisation for Economic Cooperation and Development: an international organisation formed in 1961 to supersede the O.E.E.C., whose aims include the promotion of trade and economic growth and aid to developing countries. The member countries are Australia, Austria, Belgium, Canada, Denmark, West Germany, Finland, France, Greece, Iceland, the Republic of Ireland, Italy, Japan, Luxembourg, the Netherlands, New Zealand, Norway, Portugal, Spain, Sweden, Switzerland, Turkey, the United Kingdom and the United States. Yugoslavia is also a participant with special status.

OED, O.E.D. Oxford English Dictionary.

oe·de·ma, U.S. **e·de·ma** (ee-déemǝ, i-) n., pl. **-mas** or **-mata** (-tǝ). Pathology. An excessive accumulation of serous fluid in the tissues. [Late Latin, from Greek oidēma, swelling, from oidein, to swell.]

oed·i·pal (éedi-p'l ‖ U.S. also éddi-) adj. Also **oed·i·pe·an** (-pée-ǝn). Sometimes capital **O**. Of, relating to, or characteristic of the Oedipus complex.

Oed·i·pus (éedi-pǝss ‖ U.S. also éddi-). Greek Mythology. A son of Laius and Jocasta, who was abandoned at birth and who unwittingly killed his father and married his mother.

Oedipus complex n. In Freudian psychology, a boy's feelings, often unconscious, of sexual desire for his mother, usually accompanied by hostility to his father and generally first manifesting itself between the ages of three and five. Compare **Electra complex**.

oeil-de-boeuf (úr-dǝ-búrf, í-, ō-i-, -bőf) n., pl. **oeils-de-boeuf** (pronounced as singular). A small round or oval window. [French, "bull's eye".]

oe·nol·o·gy, U.S. **e·nol·o·gy** (ee-nóllǝji) n. Also **oi·nol·o·gy** (oy-). The study of wine. [Greek oinos, wine + -LOGY.] —**oe·nol·og·i·cal** (éenǝ-lójik'l) adj. —**oe·nol·o·gist** (-nóllǝjist) n.

oe·no·mel (éen-ō-mel, -ǝ-) n. **1.** A beverage of ancient Greece, consisting of wine and honey. **2.** Poetic. A source of strength and sweetness. [Greek oinomeli : oinos, wine + meli, honey.]

o'er. Poetic. Contraction of **over**.

oer·sted (ér-sted) n. Abbr. **Oe** The centimetre-gram-second electromagnetic unit of magnetic field strength, equal to the magnetic field strength that would cause a unit magnetic pole to experience a force of one dyne in a vacuum. [After Hans Christian OERSTED.]

Oer·sted or **Ör·sted** (ér-sted, -stǝd), **Hans Christian** (1777–1851). Danish physicist. Though his discoveries include metallic aluminium and the compressibility of water, he is best known for discovering the magnetic field generated by an electric current.

oe·soph·a·gus, U.S. **e·soph·a·gus** (ee-sóffǝ-gǝss, i-) n., pl. **-gi** (-gī, -jī). A muscular tube for the passage of food from the pharynx to the stomach; the gullet. [New Latin, from Greek oisophagos, of obscure origin; -phagos, perhaps from phagein, to eat.]

oestr-, oestro-, U.S. **estr-, estro-** comb. form. Indicates oestrus; for example, **oestrogen**.

oes·tra·di·ol (éestrǝ-dí-ol ‖ éstrǝ-, -ōl) n. A naturally occurring oestrogen, $C_{18}H_{24}O_2$, produced by the ovarian follicle that can now be made synthetically for treatment of menstrual disorders, menopausal problems, and cancer of the prostate in men. [Irregularly from OESTRIN + DI- + -OL.]

oes·tri·ol (éestri-ol ‖ éstri-, -ōl) n. An oestrogenic hormone, $C_{18}H_{24}O_3$, found in the ovaries of mammals, obtained commercially from the urine of pregnant animals and used in treating oestrogen deficiency. [OESTRIN + TRI- + -OL.]

oes·tro·gen (éestrǝ-jǝn, éestrō-, -jen ‖ U.S. also éstrǝ-) n. Any of several steroid hormones produced chiefly by the ovary and responsible for promoting oestrus and the development and maintenance of female secondary sex characteristics. Compare **androgen**. [OESTRUS + -GEN.] —**oes·tro·gen·ic** (-jénnik) adj.

oes·trone (éestrōn ‖ U.S. also éstrōn) n. An oestrogenic hormone, $C_{18}H_{22}O_2$, found in the mammalian ovary and isolated commercially from the urine of pregnant females for use in treating oestrogen deficiency. Also called "theelin". [OESTRUS + -ONE.]

oes·trous (éestrǝss ‖ U.S. also éstrǝss) adj. **1.** Of or pertaining to oestrus. **2.** In heat. Said of an animal.

oestrous cycle n. The series of chemical and physiological changes in female mammals from one period of oestrus to the next.

oes·trus (éestrǝss ‖ U.S. also éstrǝss) n. A regularly recurrent period of ovulation and sexual excitement in female mammals other than humans. Also called "heat". [New Latin, from Latin oestrus, gadfly, frenzy, from Greek oistros.]

oeu·vre (érv-rǝ, őv-,-r) n., pl. **oeuvres** (pronounced as singular). French. **1.** A work of art. **2.** The sum of an artist's work.

of (ov, weak form ǝv ‖ chiefly U.S. uv; nonstandard weak form, before consonants only, ǝ) prep. **1.** Derived or coming from; originating at or from: Jesus of Nazareth; men of the north. **2. a.** Caused by; resulting from: of her own free will. **b.** Owing to; through: died of tuberculosis. **3.** Away from; at a distance from: a mile east of here. **4.** Used to indicate: **a.** Lack or absence: free of prejudice. **b.** Separateness: regardless of race. **c.** Removal: robbed of his dignity; cured of distemper. **5.** From the total or group comprising; from among: give of one's time; two of his friends; most of the cases; the third week of March. **6. a.** Composed or made from: a dress of silk. **b.** Constituted by: a field of three acres. **7.** Associated with or adhering to: a man of your religion. **8.** Belonging or connected to: the coughing of a smoker; the houses of my friends; the rungs of a ladder. **9.** Possessing; having: a man of honour. **10.** Containing or carrying: a basket of groceries. **11. a.** That is: the subject of philosophy. **b.** Specified as; named or called: a depth of ten feet; the Garden of Eden; the town of Brighton. **12.** Centring upon (some object); directed towards: a love of horses; in search of the escaped prisoner. **13.** Produced by; issuing from: *the novels of Ernest Hemingway; products of the vine.* **14.** Characterised or identified by: *a year of famine; a painter of distinction.* **15.** Concerning; with reference to; about: *think highly of his proposals; speak of it later.* **16.** Set aside for; having as a purpose; taken up by: *a hall of residence; a day of rest.* **17. a.** *U.S.* Before; until. Used in telling the time: *five minutes of two.* **b.** Used in dates: *third of May.* **18.** During or on (a specified time): *of recent years; of an evening.* **19.** As specified: *smelling of lavender.* **20.** *Rare.* By: *beloved of his family.* **21.** Used after an adjective to express a personal judgment on the following noun or noun phrase: *How rude of him to leave!* **22.** Used to indicate a particular relationship, for example: **a.** Between an adjective and a noun or noun phrase, similar to that between a verb and its object: *sure of the facts; capable of stealing.* **b.** A verb and a noun or noun phrase: *She tired of waiting; reminded him of the date.* **c.** A noun and a noun or noun phrase: *made a good job of the car; that rogue of a solicitor.* **d.** An adverb and a noun or noun phrase: *upwind of the smoke.* [Middle English *of,* Old English *of* (preposition and adverb).]

Usage: The normal use of *of* following a noun, to express possession or close relationship, is seen in such phrases as *the crew of the ship; a friend of my mother.* In certain circumstances it is also possible to use the *s* apostrophe forms of the noun following *of*: *a friend of my mother's.* However, the noun in the *of*-phrase must be definite and human. One cannot say *a friend of a mother's,* or *the crew of the ship's.* The noun before the *of*-phrase is usually indefinite *(a friend. . .)*: one is unlikely to hear *the friend of my mother's,* though, in informal English, the use of a demonstrative such as *this* or *that* is common: *I was talking to that friend of my mother's.* The preposition *of* is also used after such verbs as *speak, inform,* and *talk,* as a more formal literary variant of *about*: *I spoke of that to the committee.* After the verb *think,* however, two senses are involved: *think of* means "bring to mind", *think about* means "consider".

o·fay (ō-fay) *n. U.S. Slang.* A white person. Used derogatorily by blacks. [Perhaps Pig Latin, for FOE.]

off (off, awf) *adv.* **1.** At or to a distance from a nearer place; so as to be away: *drive off.* **2.** Distant or away in space or time: *The station is a mile off; The party is a week off.* **3.** So as to be no longer on, attached, or connected: *The electricity was cut off.* **4.** So as to be no longer continuing, operating, or functioning: *turn off the radio.* **5. a.** So as to be completely removed: *Take your clothes off.* **b.** So as to finish, eliminate, or be rid of: *write off a report; kill off the mice.* **6.** So as to be smaller, fewer, or less: *Sales dropped off.* **7.** So as to be away from work or duty: *They took a day off.* **8.** Off-stage. **9.** *Informal.* So as no longer to like: *went right off her.* **10.** Used without a definite independent meaning in many phrasal verbs: *show off; tell off.* **—off and on.** Intermittently: *He slept off and on.* **—off with.** Remove. Used as an imperative interjection: *Off with his head! Off with all of you!*

~*adj.* **1.** Sour, rotten, bad, or stale. Said of food: *this mince is off.* **2.** Not on, attached, or connected; removed: *with my shoes off.* **3. a.** Not continuing, operating, or functioning: *The oven is off.* **b.** Effecting a disconnection: *the off switch.* **4.** No longer existing or effective; cancelled: *The wedding is off.* **5.** No longer available or on the menu: *Ham is off.* **6. a.** Not up to standard; below a normal or satisfactory level: *Your bowling is off today.* **b.** Characterised by mediocrity or low standards: *an off day.* **7.** In a specified; circumstance or condition: *You are better off staying home.* **8. a.** *Informal.* Impolite or unfair; unacceptable: *Arriving so late is a bit off.* **b.** Inconsistent with accuracy or truth; in error: *My guess was slightly off.* **9.** Started on the way; going: *The runners were off.* **10.** Absent or away from work or duty: *He's off every Tuesday.* **11.** On the right-hand side of a vehicle, horse, or team of horses: *The off horse is lame.* **12.** *Nautical.* Seaward; farthest from the shore. **13.** Designating or placed on the off of a cricket field: *the off stump.*

~*prep.* **1. a.** So as to be removed or distant from (a position of rest or support): *The bird hopped off the branch.* **b.** Taken or subtracted from: *a slice off the joint.* **2.** Away or relieved from: *off duty.* **3. a.** By consuming: *living off locusts and honey.* **b.** With the means provided by: *living off her pension.* **4. a.** Extending or branching out from: *an artery off the heart.* **b.** Near but not on; slightly away: *off the Market Square.* **5. a.** Deviating from: *off course.* **b.** Not up to the standard of: *off my usual form.* **6. a.** Abstaining from: *He is off the booze.* **b.** *Informal.* No longer liking: *She's right off him.* **7.** Seaward of: *a mile off Land's End.*

~*n.* **1.** In cricket, the side of the field that is on the right of or behind the right shoulder of a right-handed batsman who is facing the bowling, or on the left of or behind the left shoulder of a left-handed batsman. **2.** The beginning of a horse race. [Middle English *of, off,* of, off, from Old English *of.*]

Usage: The use of *off,* followed by *of* and sometimes by *from, (He stepped off of the pavement; leave off from doing that)* is unacceptable in formal speech and writing, and open to criticism even in informal speech. The use of *off* for *from,* in indicating the notion of "source", should be restricted to informal contexts *(He took the book off me).*

off. office; officer; official.

Of·fa (óffə) (died 796). Anglo-Saxon king of Mercia. Seizing power (757) from his cousin, he dominated much of England south of the Humber. He issued the first Anglo-Saxon coinage, established commercial and diplomatic links with the Frankish empire of Charlemagne, and accepted greater papal control of the English church. After repelling a Welsh invasion, he established the Welsh-Mercian border at the huge earthwork known as Offa's Dyke.

of·fal (óff'l || áwf'l) *n.* **1.** The edible internal organs, such as the heart, liver, or kidneys, of a dead animal. **2.** Dead or decaying matter; putrid flesh. **3.** Refuse; rubbish. [Middle English *offal, ofall,* from Middle Dutch *afval,* "that which falls off", giblets, refuse : *af,* off + *vallen,* to fall.]

Of·fa·ly (óffəli). *Irish* **Uabh Fáilghe.** County of the Republic of Ireland, in the province of Leinster. Tullamore is the county town.

off·bal·ance (óff-bál-ənss, áwf-) *adj.* **1.** Unsteady. **2.** Unprepared: *the remark caught her off-balance.* **—off-bal·ance** *adv.*

off·beat (óff-beet, áwf-) *n. Music.* An unaccented beat in a bar. ~*adj.* (-béet). *Slang.* Not conforming to an ordinary type or pattern; unconventional: *offbeat humour.*

off-break *n.* In cricket, a ball bowled so that it moves from off to leg when it bounces.

off-Broad·way (óff-bráwdway, áwf-) *adj. U.S.* Designating or pertaining to theatrical activity, often experimental and low-cost, presented in theatres outside the Broadway entertainment district of New York City; fringe.

~*n. U.S.* Theatrical productions presented outside the Broadway entertainment district; fringe theatre. Compare **Broadway.**

off-cen·tre (óff-séntər, áwf-) *adj.* **1.** Not quite central; slightly away from the centre. **2.** Offbeat; eccentric. **—off-cen·tre** *adv.*

off·chance, off chance (óff-chaans) *n.* A remote or slight chance; a hope: *I approached him on the off chance of a loan.*

off-col·our, off colour (óff-kúllər, áwf-) *adj.* **1.** Varying from the usual, expected, or required colour. **2.** Improper; in bad taste: *an off-colour joke.* **3.** *Chiefly British.* Not in good health or spirits.

off-course (óff-kórss, áwf- || -kŏrss) *adj.* Pertaining to or designating betting not taking place at a racecourse. **—off course** *adv.*

off·cut (óff-kut, áwf-) *n.* A remnant of a piece of material, such as carpet or wood, left after removing larger pieces of the material for selling.

Of·fen·bach (óff'n-baak), **Jacques (Levy)** (1819–80). German-born French composer and cellist. He composed more than 90 pieces, including *Orpheus in the Underworld* (1858).

of·fence, *U.S.* **of·fense** (ə-fénss || ō-; *for sense 4, U.S.* óffenss) *n.* **1.** The act of offending or causing anger, resentment, or displeasure. **2. a.** Any violation or infraction of a moral or social code; a transgression or sin. **b.** A transgression of law; a crime. **3.** Something that offends. **4.** The act of attacking or assaulting. **—give offence.** To cause anger, displeasure, or resentment. **—no offence.** Used to excuse a possibly offensive remark. **—take offence.** To become angered, displeased, or resentful; feel hurt. [Middle English, from Old French, from Latin *offensa,* from the feminine past participle of *offendere,* to OFFEND.]

of·fend (ə-fénd || ō-) *v.* **-fended, -fending, -fends.** *—tr.* **1.** To create or excite anger, resentment, or annoyance in; hurt the feelings of; affront: *Her brusqueness offends many people.* **2.** To be displeasing or disagreeable to: *Onions offend his sense of smell.* **3.** *Obsolete.* **a.** To transgress; violate: *"He hath offended the law"* (Shakespeare). **b.** To cause to sin: *"If thy right eye offend thee, pluck it out."* (Matthew 5:29). *—intr.* **1.** To cause displeasure. **2.** *Archaic.* **a.** To break the law. **b.** To violate a moral or divine law; sin. [Middle English *offenden,* from Old French *offendre,* from Latin *offendere,* to strike against: *of-, ob-,* against + *fendere,* to strike.]

Synonyms: *offend, insult, affront, outrage.*

of·fend·er (ə-féndər || ō-) *n.* **1.** A person who has committed some minor misdemeanour: *sent the offenders to bed early.* **2.** A person who has committed a crime: *a sex offender.*

of·fend·ing (ə-fénding || ō-) *adj.* **1.** Causing offence. **2.** Responsible for some fault or inconvenience: *removed the offending splinter.*

of·fen·sive (ə-fén-siv || ō-) *adj.* **1.** Disagreeable to the senses: *an offensive odour.* **2.** Causing anger, displeasure, or resentment; giving offence; affronting. **3.** Of, pertaining to, or characteristic of an attack; aggressive. —See Synonyms at **hateful.**

~*n.* **1.** An attitude of attack. Often used with *the.* **2.** An attack or assault, especially a military one. **3.** An aggressive campaign or initiative: *an electoral offensive.* **—of·fen·sive·ly** *adv.* **—of·fen·sive·ness** *n.*

Synonyms: *offensive, insulting, objectionable, obnoxious.*

of·fer (óffər || *chiefly U.S.* áwfər) *v.* **-fered, -fering, -fers.** *—tr.* **1.** To present for acceptance or rejection; proffer. **2.** To put forward for consideration or examination; propose: *offer an opinion.* **3.** To present for sale. **4.** To propose as payment; bid. **5.** To present as an act of worship. Often followed by *up*: *offer up prayers.* **6.** To exhibit readiness or desire to do; volunteer: *offered to help me.* **7.** To exhibit an intention; attempt: *"ready to shoot me if I should offer to stir"* (Jonathan Swift). **8.** To try to inflict upon: *"He was not afraid of their offering him any harm."* (Herman Melville). **9.** To provide; furnish; afford. **10.** To produce or present (an artistic work): *The theatre offered one new play that season.* **11.** To present; reveal. *—intr.* **1.** To present an offering in worship or devotion. **2.** To make an offer or proposal; especially formerly, to make an offer of marriage. **3.** To present itself; appear; arise: *"This plan was dropped, because of its risk, and because a better offered."* (T.E. Lawrence).

~*n.* **1.** The act of offering. **2.** Something offered, such as a suggestion, proposal, bid, or recommendation. **3.** *Law.* A proposal which, if accepted, constitutes a legally binding contract. **4.** *Informal.* **a.** A reduction on the normal price of retail goods: *a special offer.* **b.** Goods whose price is thus reduced. **5.** Especially formerly, a pro-

ogee *Each side of an ogee arch is formed from an S-shaped curve. This 14th-century example is at Ely Cathedral, in Cambridgeshire, England.*

posal of marriage. **6.** *Archaic.* **a.** An attempt; a try: *"imperfect offers and essays"* (Francis Bacon). **b.** A show of intention. **—on offer.** For sale or available. **—under offer.** Having been the object of an offer or bid. Said of property. [Middle English *offeren, offren,* partly (in the sense "to sacrifice") from Old English *offrian,* and partly (in other senses) from Old French *offrir;* both from Latin *offerre* : *ob-,* to + *ferre,* to bring, carry.] **—of·fer·er, of·fer·or** (-ər) *n.*
Synonyms: *offer, proffer, tender, present.*

of·fer·ing (óffər-ing ‖ áwfər-) *n.* **1.** The act of making an offer. **2.** Something that is offered. **3.** A presentation made to a deity as an act of religious worship or sacrifice. **4.** A contribution or gift, especially one made at a religious service. [Middle English *offring,* Old English *offrung,* from *offrian,* to sacrifice, OFFER.]

Of·fer·to·ry (óffər-tri, -təri ‖ áwfər-) *n., pl.* **-ries. 1. a.** One of the principal parts of the Eucharistic liturgy at which bread and wine are offered to God by the celebrant. **b.** A musical setting of the Offertory. **2.** *Small* **o.** A collection of offerings of the congregation. [Old French *offertoire,* from Medieval Latin *offertōrium,* from Latin *offerre,* to OFFER.]

off·hand (óff-hánd, áwf-) *adv.* Without preparation or forethought.
~adj. Also **off·hand·ed** (-hándid). **1.** Said or done offhand. **2.** Inconsiderate; impolite; abrupt. **—off·hand·ed·ly** *adv.* **—off·hand·ed·ness** *n.*

of·fice (óffiss ‖ *chiefly U.S.* áwfiss) *n. Abbr.* **off. 1. a.** A place, such as a building, room, or suite, in which services, clerical work, or professional duties are carried out: *the manager's office; booking office.* **b.** The administrative personnel, executives, or entire staff working in such a place. **2.** A duty or function assigned to or assumed by someone: *"the maternal office was supplied by my aunt"* (Edward Gibbon). **3.** A position of authority, duty, or trust given to a person, as in a government, business, or other organisation: *the office of president.* **4.** *Capital* **O,** *when part of a title.* **a.** A major executive division of the British government, often headed by a cabinet minister. **b.** Any of the branches of the Federal government of the United States ranking just below the departments. **5.** A public position: *take office.* **6.** *Plural. Chiefly British.* Formerly, the parts of a house, such as the laundry and kitchen, in which the servants carried out household work, and often including outbuildings such as the barn. **7.** *Often plural.* An act, usually beneficial, performed for another; a favour: *through the offices of friends.* **8.** *Ecclesiastical.* A ceremony, rite, or service, usually prescribed by liturgy: **a.** *Roman Catholic Church.* The canonical hours. **b.** *Anglican Church.* A prayer service, such as Morning or Evening Prayer. **c.** Any ceremony or service for a special purpose; especially, a rite for the dead. **—in** (or **out of**) **office.** In (or out of) government; in (or out of) power. [Middle English, from Old French, from Latin *officium,* performance of duty, from *opificium* (unattested) : *opus,* work + *-ficium,* from *facere,* to do.]

office block *n.* A large, usually modern, building housing a number of offices.

office boy *n.* A boy employed to do minor tasks and to run errands in an office.

of·fice·hold·er (óffiss-hōldər ‖ áwfiss-) *n.* One who holds public office.

office hours *n.* The usual period or periods of the day during which business is conducted or work performed in an office.

of·fi·cer (óffi-sər ‖ *chiefly U.S.* áwfi-) *n. Abbr.* **off. 1. a.** One who holds an office of authority or trust in a business, government, or other institution. **b.** A public or government official: *medical officer; customs officer.* **2. a.** One in a position of authority in the armed forces. **b.** One holding a commission in the armed forces. **3.** One holding authority in the merchant navy, such as a captain, master, mate, chief engineer, or assistant engineer. **4.** A policeman. **5. a.** One elected to an office in a society or club. **b.** A rank above the lowest rank in some honorary societies. **6.** A member of the Order of the British Empire, in the grade below commander.
~tr.v. **officered, -cering, -cers. 1.** To provide with officers; allocate officers to. **2.** To direct or command; act as an officer over. [Middle English, from Anglo-French, Old French *officier,* from Medieval Latin *officiārius,* "officeholder", from Latin *officium,* OFFICE.]

officer of arms *n. Heraldry.* A herald or pursuivant.

officer of the day *n. Abbr.* **O.D.** A military officer who, for a given day, assumes responsibility for security, order, and the performance of the guard.

of·fi·cial (ə-físh'l ‖ ō-) *adj. Abbr.* **off. 1.** Of or pertaining to an office or post of authority: *official duties.* **2.** Authorised by a proper authority; authoritative: *official permission.* **3.** Holding office or serving in some public capacity; authorised to perform some special duty: *an official representative.* **4.** Characteristic of or befitting a person of authority: *official behaviour.* **5.** Formal or ceremonial: *an official banquet.* **6.** *Capital* **O.** Of, pertaining to, or designating the wing of both the IRA and Sinn Fein, formed by the split that occurred in those organisations in 1969, that emphasises peaceful political methods of achieving the unification of Ireland. Compare **Provisional. 7.** Designating pharmaceutical products that are recognised and identified in an official publication, such as (in the United Kingdom) the *British Pharmacopoeia.*
~n. Abbr. **off. 1.** One who holds an office or position; especially, one who acts in a subordinate capacity for an organisation, government department, or other institution. **2.** *Capital* **O.** A member of the official IRA or Sinn Fein. [Middle English, an authority, from Old French, from Late Latin *officiālis,* functionary, official, from Latin, of an office or duty, from *officium,* OFFICE.] **—of·fi·cial·ism** *n.* **—of·fi·cial·ly** *adv.*

of·fi·cial·dom (ə-físh'l-dəm ‖ ō-) *n.* Bureaucracy; officials or bureaucrats collectively, especially when considered as rigidly adhering to official regulations, forms, and procedures.

of·fi·cial·ese (ə-físh'l-éez ‖ ō-, -éess) *n.* Language characteristic of official documents or statements, often considered obscure, pretentiously wordy, or formal in style.

Official Receiver *n.* In Britain, a person appointed by the Department of Trade and Industry to act as a **receiver** *(see),* and to manage the estate of a bankrupt temporarily until the appointment of a trustee in bankruptcy.

Official Referee *n. Law.* In England until 1971, a judicial official to whom civil cases were referred, if both parties were willing, for a private trial followed by an award or report to the court. See **referee.**

of·fi·ci·ant (ə-físhi-ənt ‖ ō-) *n.* One who officiates at a religious service or ceremony; a celebrant.

of·fi·ci·ar·y (ə-físhi-əri ‖ ō-, -erri) *n., pl.* **-ies. 1.** A body of officials or officers. **2.** *Rare.* An official or officer.
~adj. **1.** Attached to or resulting from an office held. Said of a title. **2.** Having a title resulting from the holding of an office. Said of a dignitary.

of·fi·ci·ate (ə-físhi-ayt ‖ ō-) *intr.v.* **-ated, -ating, -ates. 1.** To perform the duties and functions of an office or position of authority. **2.** To serve as a priest or minister at a religious service. **3.** To take on a particular role, and perform the duties and functions associated with that role, as at a special occasion or ceremony: *officiated as host.* [Medieval Latin *officiāre,* to conduct a religious service, from Latin *officium,* OFFICE (in Late Latin, also "religious service").] **—of·fi·ci·a·tion** (-áysh'n) *n.* **—of·fi·ci·a·tor** (-ər) *n.*

of·fic·i·nal (óffi-sín'l, o-físsin'l ‖ ō-) *adj.* **1.** Designating a drug available without prescription. Compare **magistral. 2.** Designating a plant used in medicine.
~n. An officinal drug or plant. [Medieval Latin *officīnālis,* "used or kept in a workshop" (especially a medical laboratory), from Latin *officīna,* workshop, reduction of *opificīna,* workshop, from *opifex,* workman : *opus,* work + *facere,* to do.]

of·fi·cious (ə-físhəss ‖ ō-) *adj.* **1.** Excessively forward in offering one's services or advice to others; intrusive; meddling. **2.** In diplomacy, of a casual nature; not official; unauthorised. **3.** *Obsolete.* Eager to render services or help others. [Latin *officiōsus,* eager to oblige, from *officium,* duty, service, OFFICE.] **—of·fi·cious·ly** *adv.* **—of·fi·cious·ness** *n.*

off·ing (óff-ing, áwf-) *n.* **1.** The near immediate future. Used in the phrase *in the offing.* **2.** The part of the sea that is distant yet visible from the shore. **3.** A position at a distance from the shore. [Perhaps from OFF.]

off·ish (óff-ish, áwf-) *adj.* Inclined to be distant and reserved in manner; aloof. **—off·ish·ly** *adv.* **—off·ish·ness** *n.*

off-key, off key (óff-kée, áwf-) *adj.* **1.** Not played or sung in the correct key. **2.** Out of tune. **3.** Discordant; clashing. **—off key** *adv.*

off-licence (óff-līss'nss, áwf-) *n. British.* **1.** A shop or part of a shop or public house selling alcoholic drinks for consumption elsewhere (off the premises). **2.** A licence legally permitting such sales.

off line *adj.* **1.** Not in direct connection with a mainframe computer but controlled by a computer storage device. Said of part of a computer system or a peripheral device. **2.** Switched off. Said of a computer. Compare **on line.**

off-load (óff-lṓd, áwf-, -lōd) *tr.v.* **-loaded, -loading, -loads. 1.** *Aerospace.* To launch (a guided missile or rocket) with propellant tanks less than fully loaded, for altering the centre of gravity of the projectile. **2.** To unload (a vehicle, especially an aircraft). **3. a.** To shift or delegate (work, for example). **b.** To get rid of (something unwanted): *offloaded her problems onto me.*

off-peak (óff-péek, áwf-) *adj.* **1.** Designating periods of time in which there is least demand for a facility, service, or the like. **2.** Of or pertaining to something offered or existing during off-peak periods: *off-peak prices.*

off·print (óff-print, áwf-) *n.* A reproduction or excerpt of a printed article that was originally contained in a larger publication.
~tr.v. **offprinted, -printing, -prints.** To reproduce or reprint (an excerpt). [Translation of German *Abdruck.*]

off-putting (óff-pŏŏtting, áwf-) *adj. Chiefly British Informal.* **1.** Unpleasant; unappealing. **2.** Disconcerting; discouraging.

off-sales (óff-saylz, áwf-) *pl.n.* Sales of alcohol and other drinks at an off-licence.

off·scour·ing (óff-skowr-ing, áwf-) *n.* **1.** *Usually plural.* That which is scoured off; refuse. **2.** A social outcast or misfit.

off·screen (óff-skréen, áwf-) *adj.* **1.** On the soundtrack of a film or television programme only; not seen: *an offscreen commentator.* **2.** In real life; away from the television or cinema screen: *offscreen romances between stars.* **—off·screen** *adv.*

off-season (óff-seez'n, áwf-, -séez'n) *n.* The time of year when there is least demand for something, such as holiday accommodation or other services. **—off-season** *adj. & adv.*

off·set (óff-set, áwf-) *n.* **1.** Something that balances, counteracts, or compensates. **2.** Something deriving or originating but set off from something else. **3.** *Architecture.* A ledge or recess in a wall, formed by a reduction in thickness above. Also called "setoff". **4.** *Botany.* A shoot that develops laterally at the base of a plant, often rooting to form a new plant. **5.** *Geology.* A spur of a range of mountains or hills. **6.** A bend in a pipe or bar to allow it to pass around an

obstruction. **7.** *Mining.* A crosscut or drift from a main level. **8.** In surveying, a short distance measured perpendicularly from the main line, used to help in calculating the area of an irregular plot. **9.** *Printing.* **a.** A method of printing whereby the impression or image to be printed is transferred from the inked plate to an intermediate surface, usually a rubber-covered cylinder that transfers the image by rolling onto paper. Also used adjectivally: *offset lithography.* **b.** The unintentional or faulty transfer of ink not yet dry from a printed sheet to any surface, such as the next sheet, that is laid over it.
~*v.* (-sét) **offset, -setting, -sets.** —*tr.* **1.** To compensate or cause to compensate for: *offset the loss against tax.* **2.** *Printing.* **a.** To print by offset. **b.** To smear with an offset. **3.** To make or form an offset in (a wall, bar, or pipe). —*intr.* To develop as an offset. —**off·set** *adj.*

off·shoot (óff-shσot, áwf-) *n.* **1.** Something that branches out or derives its existence or origin from a particular source: *an offshoot of the parent company.* **2.** A branch, descendant, or member of a family or social group. **3.** A lateral shoot from the main stem of a plant.

off·shore (óff-shór, áwf- ‖ -shór) *adj.* **1.** Moving or directed away from the shore: *an offshore wind.* **2.** Located or occurring at a distance from the shore: *an offshore oil rig.*
~*adv.* **1.** Away from the shore: *The storm moved offshore.* **2.** At a distance from the shore: *a boat moored offshore.*

off·side (óff-síd, áwf-) *adj.* **1.** On the wrong side of the ball when it is played, according to the rules in certain games such as soccer, hockey, or Rugby football; usually, illegally ahead of the ball or puck in the opponent's half or an attacking zone. Said of a player, team, or play in various games. **2.** *Chiefly British.* On the right-hand side of a vehicle, horse, or team of horses.
~*n.* **1.** A situation in a game in which a player is offside. **2.** *Chiefly British.* The right-hand side of a vehicle, horse, or team of horses.

off·spring (óff-spring, áwf-) *n., pl.* **offspring** *or rare* **-springs. 1.** The progeny of a person, animal, or plant. **2.** A result; an outcome; a product. [Middle English *ofspring,* Old English *ofspring : of,* from + *springan,* to SPRING.]

off·stage (óff-stáyj, áwf-) *adj.* Located or occurring in the area of a stage not visible to the audience.
~*adv.* Away from the area of a stage visible to the audience.

off·street (óff-stréet, áwf-) *adj.* Away from or not on the street: *off-street parking.*

off-the-cuff (óff-thσ-kúf, áwf-) *adj.* Impromptu; not thought up in advance; unprepared. [Referring to notes written on a shirt cuff as reminders for someone delivering a speech.] —**off the cuff** *adv.*

off-the-peg, off the peg (óff-thσ-pég, áwf-) *adj. British.* Ready-made: *an off-the-peg dress; off-the-peg ideas.* —**off the peg** *adv.*

off-the-rec·ord, off the record (óff-thσ-rék-awrd, áwf- ‖ -σrd) *adj.* Not for publication; not to be repeated. —**off the record** *adv.*

off-the-wall, off the wall (óff-thσ-wáwl, áwf-) *adj. U.S. Informal.* Unusual or unconventional; crazy: *off-the-wall notions.* [Perhaps alluding to a ball off the wall in squash or handball, hence unexpected, surprising.] —**off the wall** *adv.*

off-white (óff-wít, áwf-, -hwít) *n.* Greyish or yellowish white. —**off-white** *adj.*

O.F.M. Order of Friars Minor (Franciscans).

O.F.S. Orange Free State.

oft (oft, awft) *adv. Poetic.* Often. Sometimes used in combination: *oft-repeated.* [Middle English, Old English *oft.*]

OFT Office of Fair Trading (in Britain).

of·ten (óff-'n, áwf-, -tσn) *adv.* **1.** Frequently; repeatedly; customarily; many times. **2.** Much of the time; in many instances. —**as often as. 1.** As many times as. **2.** Every time that. —**every so often.** Sometimes; fairly regularly. —**more often than not.** More than half the time; in most instances.
~*adj. Archaic.* Repeated; frequent. [Middle English *oftin, often,* variants (before vowels and *h*) of *ofte,* OFT.]
Usage: Many people believe that the *t* in *often* should be pronounced, because it is there in the spelling. The pronunciation (óff-tσn) is, however, far less commonly heard. The comparative and superlative forms *oftener* and *oftenest* have achieved some acceptability in standard English; but the compound forms *more often* and *most often* are more regularly used.

of·ten·times (óff-'n-tímz, áwf-, -tσn-) *adv. Archaic.* Also **oft·times** (óft-tímz, óft-, áwf-, áwft-). Frequently; repeatedly.

OG, O.G. 1. officer of the guard. **2.** *Philately.* original gum.

Og·a·den, the (óggσ-dén ‖ *U.S. also* ó-gáa-dayn). Arid wilderness in southeast Ethiopia, inhabited chiefly by Somali pastoral nomads. Intermittent border warfare between Ethiopia and Somalia culminated in an invasion by Somali forces (1978). Control was re-established by Ethiopia in 1978, but some fighting continues.

Og·den (óg-dσn), **C(harles) K(ay)** (1889–1957). British semanticist. From ideas presented in his book *The Meaning of Meaning* (1923), written in collaboration with I. A. Richards (1893–1979), he developed the concept of Basic English, an international language of 850 essential words and 150 scientific terms.

o·gee (ó-jee, *rarely* ó-jée) *n. Architecture.* **1.** A double curve with the shape of an elongated S. **2.** A moulding having in profile an S-shaped curve. **3.** An arch of two of these curves meeting at a point. In this sense, also called "ogee arch". [Alteration of OGIVE.]

og·ham, o·gam (óggσm ‖ *U.S. also* ó-σm, óg-) *n.* **1. a.** An Ancient British and Irish alphabet used for writing Irish from the fourth or fifth century A.D. to the early seventh century. **b.** A character of this alphabet. **2. a.** An inscription in the ogham alphabet. **b.** A

stone inscribed in the ogham alphabet. [Irish *ogham,* from Old Irish *ogom,* said to be named after its mythical inventor *Ogma*†.]

o·give (ó-jīv, *rarely* ó-jív) *n.* **1.** *Statistics.* **a.** The graphic representation of a frequency distribution, in which every ordinate represents the sum of frequencies in preceding intervals. **b.** A frequency distribution. **2.** *Architecture.* **a.** A diagonal rib of a Gothic vault. **b.** A pointed arch. Also called "ogive curve". [Middle English, from Old French *augive*†.] —**o·gi·val** (ō-jív'l) *adj.*

o·gle (óg'l ‖ *U.S. also* ógg'l) *v.* **ogled, ogling, ogles.** —*tr.* **1.** To stare at. **2.** To stare at lecherously. —*intr.* To stare in a lecherous manner. —See Synonyms at **gaze.**
~*n.* A stare, especially one that is lecherous. [From Low German *oegeln,* frequentative of *oegen,* to eye, from *oog,* eye.] —**o·gler** *n.*

OG·PU, O.G.P.U. (óg-pσo) *n.* Unified Government Political Administration (Russian *Obyedinyonnoye Gosudarstvyennoye Politicheskoye Upravlenie*): a former security branch of the Soviet government functioning as a successor to the **Cheka** and corresponding in broad outline to the later **KGB** *(both of which see).*

o·gre (ógσr) *n.* **1.** A legendary, man-eating giant or monster. **2.** Anyone who is especially cruel, brutish, or hideous. [French *ogre*† (first used by Perrault in *Contes de ma mère l'oye;* 1697).] —**o·gre·ish** (ógσr-ish) *adj.*

o·gress (ó-griss, -gress) *n.* A female ogre.

oh (ō) *interj.* Also *rare* **O.** Used to express strong emotion, such as surprise, fear, anger, or pain.
~*n., pl.* **oh's** *or* **ohs.** The exclamation *oh* or any occurrence of it. —See Usage note at **O.** [Middle English *o* (expressive formation). The spelling *oh* is not older than 1548.]

ohc, o.h.c. overhead camshaft.

O. Henry (ó-hénri), pen name of William Sydney Porter (1862–1910). U.S. short-story writer, famous for his stories with a "twist in the tail". He wrote more than 300 stories, as collected in *Cabbages and Kings* (1904) and *The Voice of the City* (1908).

OHG Old High German.

O'Higgins (ō-hígginz, σ-; *Spanish* ō-ée-geenss), **Bernardo** (c. 1778–1842). Chilean politician and soldier. The illegitimate son of an Irish soldier, he was commander of the Republican army which liberated Chile from Spain (1818). O'Higgins became president, but his social and economic reforms provoked unrest, and he was forced to resign (1823).

O·hi·o (ō-hí-ō). State in the Great Lakes Region of the Middle West, United States. Rich in mineral resources, it is a major coal producing area and one of the main industrial states. Agriculture is also extensive, and large amounts of corn, soya beans, wheat, and dairy goods are produced. Ohio was accepted into the Union in 1803. Capital, Columbus.

Ohio. River of the east central United States. Formed at Pittsburgh (Pennsylvania) by the confluence of the Monogahela and Allegheny rivers, it flows southwest to join the Mississippi at Cairo (Illinois). The river is important for the transportation of bulk cargoes such as coal and gravel.

ohm (ōm) *n. Symbol* Ω The SI unit of electrical resistance equal to that of a conductor in which a current of one ampere is produced by a potential of one volt across its terminals. [After Georg Simon OHM.]

Ohm (ōm), **Georg Simon** (1787–1854). German physicist. Though he made considerable contributions to mathematics and acoustics, he is best known for his work in the field of electrical resistance.

ohm·age (ómij) *n. Electricity.* Resistance expressed in ohms.

ohm·me·ter (óm-meetσr) *n. Electricity.* An instrument for the direct measurement of the resistance of a conductor in ohms.

OHMS, O.H.M.S. On Her (or His) Majesty's Service.

Ohm's law *n. Physics.* The law stating that the direct electrical current flowing in a conductor is directly proportional to the potential difference between its ends. It is usually formulated as: $V = IR$, where V is the applied voltage, I is the current, and R (the constant of proportionality) is the resistance of the conductor.

o·ho (ō-hó, σ-) *interj.* Used especially to express ironic surprise or mock astonishment. [Middle English : o + HO.]

-oholic. Variant of **-holic.**

o.h.v., ohv overhead valve.

oi (oy) *interj.* Used to attract attention or express indignation.
~*adj.* Pertaining to or designating a style of popular music of the early 1980s associated with the skinhead movement, and characterised by its aggressiveness, raucousness, and repetitive rhythm. [Variant of HOY.]

-oic *adj. suffix.* Indicates the presence of a carboxyl group or a derivative of it; for example, **decanoic acid.** [Lengthening of -IC (denoting acids).]

oick (oyk) *n. British Slang.* An uncultivated person. [Imitative of uncultivated speech.]

-oid *n. & adj. suffix.* Indicates: **1.** Likeness, resemblance, or similarity to; for example, **anthropoid, crystalloid, planetoid. 2.** A spurious likeness to; for example, **factoid.** [Latin *-oïdes,* from Greek *-oeidēs,* of or having the shape or nature of, from *eidos,* form, shape.]

-oidea *pl. n. comb. form.* Indicates an echinoderm belonging to a taxonomic class; for example, **Asteroidea, Crinoidea.** [New Latin, from Latin *-oïdēs,* -OID.]

o·id·i·um (ō-íddi-σm) *n., pl.* **-ia.** A spore produced by the fragmentation of a hypha in certain fungi. [New Latin, from Greek *ōïon,* egg + *-idion,* diminutive suffix.]

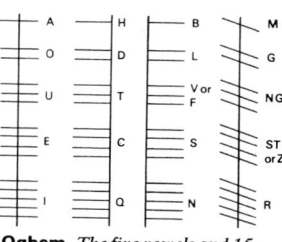

Ogham *The five vowels and 15 consonant sounds of this fourth-century Irish script were notched or drawn around the corners of objects such as stone monuments. Not many inscriptions have survived in legible form, because of weathering of the objects.*

oil (oyl) *n.* **1.** Any of numerous mineral, vegetable, and synthetic substances and animal and vegetable fats, that are generally slippery, combustible, viscous, liquid or liquefiable at room temperatures, soluble in various organic solvents, such as ether, but not in water, and used in a great variety of products, especially lubricants and fuels. **2. a.** Petroleum. **b.** A petroleum derivative, such as a machine oil or lubricant. **3.** Any substance with an oily consistency. **4.** Paraffin used as a domestic fuel. Also used adjectivally: *an oil lamp.* **5. a.** *Often plural.* An **oil paint** (see). **b.** An **oil painting** (see). **6.** *Informal.* Insincere flattery. **—burn the midnight oil.** To work hard or study late into the night. **—pour oil on troubled waters.** To bring calm to a difficult situation. **—strike oil. 1.** To discover crude oil by drilling in the ground for it. **2.** To gain sudden wealth or success. **—the good** or **dinkum oil.** *Australian & N.Z. Informal.* True and useful information.
~*v.* **oiled, oiling, oils.** —*tr.* **1.** To lubricate, supply, cover, or polish with oil. **2.** *Informal.* To bribe. Used chiefly in the phrase *oil someone's palm.* —*intr.* **1.** To load up with or take on fuel oil. **2.** To become oil by melting. [Middle English *oli, oil(e),* (olive) oil, from Old French, from Latin *oleum,* from Greek *elaion,* from *elaia,* olive.] **—oil** *adj.*

oil beetle *n.* Any of various insects of the family Meloidae, that, when disturbed, exude an oily yellow substance.

oil-bird (óyl-burd) *n.* A nocturnal bird, *Steatornis caripensis,* native to South America and Trinidad, that navigates by echo location and feeds on fruit detected by smell. Also called "guacharo".

oil burner *n.* **1.** A heating unit, furnace, or boiler that burns fuel oil. **2.** A device for spraying fine droplets of fuel oil into such a heating unit.

oil cake *n.* The solid residue left after certain oilseeds, such as cottonseed and linseed, have been pressed free of their oil. It is used after grinding as cattle feed or fertiliser.

oil-can (óyl-kan) *n.* A can with a spout for applying lubricating oil.

oil-cloth (óyl-kloth ‖ -klawth) *n.* A fabric treated with clay, oil, and pigments to make it waterproof. It is used as a cover for tables or shelving.

oil colour *n.* An oil paint.

oil-cup (óyl-kup) *n.* A small cup with a tube at the base that feeds oil continuously into a bearing.

oil drum *n.* A metal drum used to transport oil, oil products, or similar liquids.

oil-er (óylər) *n.* **1.** One that oils machinery and engines. **2.** An oil tanker. **3.** An oilcan. **4.** A well that produces oil. **5.** A ship that burns oil.

oil field *n.* An area with reserves of recoverable petroleum, especially one with several oil-producing wells.

oil-fired (óyl-fīrd) *adj.* Designating a furnace, boiler, or heating system that burns oil as a fuel.

oil gland *n.* **1.** Any gland that secretes oil. **2.** *Zoology.* The **uropygial gland** (see).

oil of cloves *n.* An oil derived from the flowers of the clove and used in microscopy, dentistry, and confectionery.

oil of turpentine *n.* Refined turpentine.

oil of vitriol *n. Chemistry.* **Sulphuric acid** (see).

oil paint *n.* A paint consisting of a pigment ground in a drying oil, usually linseed, and used in oil painting. Also called "oil", "oil colour".

oil painting *n.* **1.** A picture painted in oil paints. **2.** The art or practice of painting with oil paints.

oil palm *n.* **1.** A tall palm tree, *Elaeis guineensis,* native to tropical Africa, having nutlike fruits that yield a commercially valuable oil. **2.** Any of several other palms yielding oil.

oil-pa-per (óyl-paypər) *n.* Paper that is soaked in oil to make it transparent and water-resistant.

oil rig *n.* An installation at the head of an oil well for drilling for and extracting oil and natural gas from the earth or the sea bed.

oil sand *n. Geology.* **1.** Any stratum or rock formation containing oil. **2.** A stratum of porous sandstone from which petroleum can be extracted through drilled wells.

oil-seed (óyl-seed) *n.* Any seed, such as linseed or rapeseed, from which oil can be extracted in commercially viable quantities.

oil shale *n. Geology.* A black or dark brown shale containing hydrocarbons that yield petroleum by distillation.

oil-skin (óyl-skin) *n.* **1.** Cloth treated with oil so that it is waterproof. **2.** *Often plural.* An outer garment made of this material.

oil slick *n.* A thin film of oil on water; especially, a large patch of oil on the surface of the sea that has leaked from or been discharged by a ship.

oil-stone (óyl-stōn) *n.* A smooth whetstone lubricated with oil, used for fine sharpening.

oil sump *n.* The bottom of the crankcase of an internal-combustion engine that serves as an oil reservoir.

oil varnish *n.* A **varnish** (see).

oil well *n.* A hole dug or drilled in the earth or sea bed from which petroleum flows or is pumped.

oil-y (óyli) *adj.* **-ier, -iest. 1.** Of or pertaining to oil. **2.** Impregnated or smeared with oil; greasy. **3.** Excessively suave in action or behaviour; unctuous. **—oil-i-ly** *adv.* **—oil-i-ness** *n.*

oinology. Variant of **oenology.**

oint-ment (óynt-mənt) *n.* Any of numerous viscous or semisolid substances used on the skin as a cosmetic, a soothing agent, or a medicament; an unguent; a salve. [Middle English, variant (influenced by obsolete *oint,* to anoint) of *oinement,* from Old French *oignement,* from Vulgar Latin *unguimentum* (unattested), from Latin *unguentum,* from *unguens* (stem *unguent-*), present participle of *unguere,* to anoint.]

Oir-each-tas (érrəkh-thəss, érrək-) *n.* The parliament of the Republic of Ireland, consisting of the Dáil Eireann (the representative assembly) and the Seanad Eireann (the senate). [Irish, "assembly", "conference", from Old Irish *airech,* nobleman, free man.]

Oisin. See **Ossian.**

Oi-strakh (óy-straak; *Russian* -strəkh), **David (Feodorovich)** (1908–74). Russian violinist. Famous for his interpretations of Russian music, he gave many recitals with his son, Igor (1931–).

O-jib-wa (ō-jíb-way, ō-, ə-, -wə) *n., pl.* **-was** or collectively **Ojibwa.** Also **O-jib-way** (-way) *pl.* **-ways** or collectively **Ojibway. 1.** A member of an Algonquian-speaking North American Indian people inhabiting regions of the United States and Canada around Lake Superior. **2.** The Algonquian language spoken by this people. **—O-jib-wa** *adj.*

O.K., OK, o-kay (ō-káy) *n., pl.* **O.K.'s** or **OK's** or **okays.** *Informal.* Approval; endorsement; agreement.

THE PRIMITIVE LIFE FORMS THAT PRODUCE "BLACK GOLD"

How oil is formed beneath the oceans

Oil, the lifeblood of industrialised society, is a mixture of chemicals derived from the smallest and most primitive life forms. Microorganisms called plankton, which inhabit the oceans, are thought to be the basis of crude oil.

Dead organisms, trapped in the mud and clay carried out to the continental shelves by rivers, are attacked by bacteria that break down the fatty and waxy organic debris into simpler chemical compounds. Under the high temperature resulting from gradual burial beneath new deposits, these are converted into a bituminous substance called kerogen. Further burial and further increase of temperature converts this into oil and gas. Once formed, the oil migrates out of its bedrock and, being less dense, moves upwards. If it meets a ceiling of impermeable rock it will spread out in a thin film beneath it, but where folding of the Earth's crust has occurred, the oil and gas can accumulate in pockets.

Seepages to the surface, or "shows" of oil, such as those occurring in the Dead Sea and Mesopotamia, were exploited for caulking watercourses and ships, and have been used as building materials for houses and roads since the dawn of civilisation. The oil industry first developed in the 1850s in the United States, when oil discovered in brine wells was exploited for lighting. Oil could also be broken down or "refined" to produce gas, lubricating oil, and paraffin wax.

It was about 1910, with the development of the motor car, that the oil industry began on a large scale, and during the 1920s and 1930s refining processes were devised to improve the yield of petrol from oil. By-products could be converted into drugs, dyes, explosives, insecticides, plastics, detergents, and synthetic fibres. In little over a century the oil industry has become the world's biggest enterprise.

THE FORMATION OF AN OIL FIELD

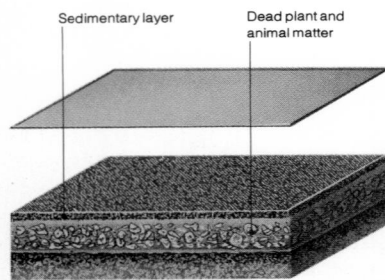

Sedimentary layer   Dead plant and animal matter

Dead marine organisms collect on the floor of the continental shelf and are broken down by bacteria. They are covered by muddy sediment washed down by the rivers.

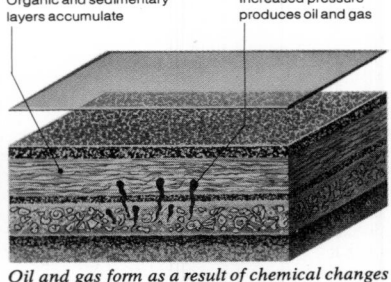

Organic and sedimentary layers accumulate   Increased pressure produces oil and gas

Oil and gas form as a result of chemical changes brought about by high temperatures to which the organic deposits are subjected beneath successive layers of sediment.

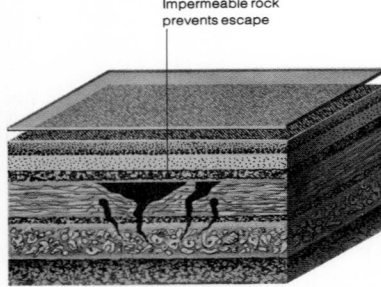

Impermeable rock prevents escape

Helped perhaps by water pressure, the oil and gas move up from their bed of shale. Where flat impermeable rock above prevents their escape, they spread out in a thin layer.

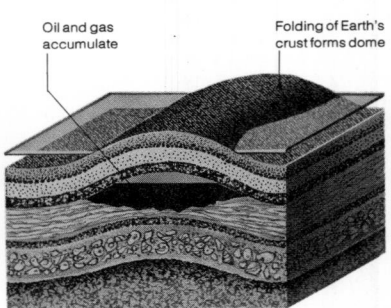

Oil and gas accumulate   Folding of Earth's crust forms dome

Where pressures in the Earth's crust have caused an impermeable layer to rise in a dome shape, the oil and gas rise into it, and are trapped there, forming a potential oil field.

~*tr.v.* **O.K.'d** or **OK'd** or **okayed, O.K.'ing** or **OK'ing** or **okaying, O.K.'s** or **OK's** or **okays.** *Informal.* To approve or endorse; agree to.
~*interj. Informal.* **1.** Used to express approval or agreement. **2.** Used to indicate that the speaker appreciates a point or objection made by another: *O.K. he's clever, but he's very slow.*
~*adj. Informal.* **1.** Satisfactory; all right. **2.** In good condition or health. **3.** *Chiefly U.S.* Used as a term of approval: *an O.K. guy.* [Popularised as a slogan of the O.K. Club, Democratic party political club of 1840; for *Old Kinderhook,* nickname of President Martin Van Buren, born at *Kinderhook,* New York.] **—O.K.** *adv.*
Usage: This word, used as a noun or verb (*he gave his O.K., he okayed the agreement*), is restricted to informal speech and writing, and to some forms of official correspondence, especially in business circles. The form *okay* is generally used when there is an inflectional ending, as in *okayed.*

o·ka·pi (ō-kaápi) *n., pl.* **-pis** or collectively **okapi.** A ruminant forest mammal, *Okapia johnstoni,* related to the giraffe, but smaller and having a short neck, found in the Congo region in Africa. [Central African name, from Mbuba.]

O'Keeffe (ō-keéf), **Georgia** (1887–). U.S. artist. Her first one-woman show was in 1917. She is well-known for her semi-abstract paintings of flowers and desert landscapes.

O·ke·fe·no·kee Swamp (ṓkəfi-nṓki). A swamp on the Georgia-Florida border in the southeast United States. It has rich and varied wildlife, and in Georgia is designated the Okefenokee National Wildlife Refuge.

O·kie (ṓki) *n. U.S. Informal.* An impoverished migrant farm worker; especially, one from Oklahoma forced to leave his farm during the depression of the 1930s. [From OKLAHOMA.]

O·ki·na·wa (ṓki-naáwə). *Japanese* **Okinawa Gunto.** An island of Japan. The main island of the Ryukyu group, it is 531 kilometres (330 miles) south of the main Japanese chain. Sugar cane, sweet potatoes, and rice are grown and fishing is important. It was occupied by the United States (1945–72). Naha is the capital.

Ok·la·ho·ma (ṓklə-hṓmə). State of south central United States drained by the Red and Arkansas rivers. Western Oklahoma is part of the Great Plains. The central and eastern regions are mostly prairie. Cotton was formerly the major crop but has been superseded by wheat. It is a major oil and gas producing state. Explored by the Spanish, it was bought by the United States as part of the Louisiana Purchase (1803) and the eastern section became Indian Territory. Oklahoma was admitted to the Union, as the forty-sixth state, in 1907. Adverse weather conditions and overuse of the land combined to make northwestern Oklahoma part of the Dust Bowl of the 1930s. State capital, Oklahoma City. **—Ok·la·ho·man** *adj. & n.*

Oklahoma City. State capital of Oklahoma, United States. Lying on the North Canadian river, it was founded (1889) during the Oklahoma Land Rush; it grew rapidly, becoming capital in 1910. It is an important livestock market and has grain mills, meat packing, and cotton processing plants. The city is the centre of a vast oil and natural gas field. It houses one of the nation's largest collections of Indian relics.

o·kra (ṓkrə) *n.* **1.** A tall tropical and semitropical plant, *Hibiscus esculentus,* having edible, mucilaginous green pods. Also called "bhindi", "lady's finger". **2.** The edible pods of this plant, used in soups and as a vegetable. **3.** A dish prepared with okra, **gumbo** *(see).* [West African native name *nkruma.*]

-ol[1] *n. suffix. Chemistry.* Indicates alcohol or phenol; for example, **glycerol, naphthol.** [From ALCOHOL.]

-ol[2]. Variant of **-ole.**

O·laf I (ṓləv), also known as Olav Tryggvassön (*c.* 969–1000). King of Norway. He was a Viking marauder of England until converted to Christianity. On his accession to the throne (995) he attempted to convert Norway, causing disaffection. He died at the battle of Svolder, leaping into the sea rather than surrender to the Danes.

Olaf II Haraldsson, Saint, also known as Olaf the Stout (*c.* 995–1030). King and patron saint of Norway. On ascending the throne (1015), he continued Olaf I's conversion of Norway to Christianity. Driven from his kingdom (1028) by Canute the Great, he died in battle at Stiklestad. He was canonised in 1031.

O·lav V (ō-ləv, -ləf; *Norwegian* ōō-lav) (1903–). King of Norway. Grandson of Edward VII of the United Kingdom, he succeeded Haakon VII to the throne in 1957.

old (ōld) *adj.* **older, oldest. 1. a.** Having lived or existed for a relatively long time; far advanced in years or life: *a feeble old woman.* See Usage note at **elder. 2. a.** Made long ago; in existence for many years; not new: *an old book.* **b.** No longer current or in use: *old magazines.* **c.** In existence long enough to lack freshness; stale: *This bread is a bit old; the same old answers.* **3.** Of or pertaining to a long life or to persons who have had a long life: *a ripe old age.* **4. a.** Having or exhibiting the physical characteristics of advanced life or an aged person: *She had an old face for her years.* **b.** Weak or infirm from, or as if from, age: *feeling very old.* **5.** Having or exhibiting the wisdom of age; mature; sensible: *That child is old for her years.* **6.** Having a specified age: *She was twelve years old.* **7. a.** Belonging to a remote or former period in history; ancient: *old manuscripts.* **b.** Belonging to or being of an earlier time: *his old classmates.* **c.** Previous; former: *his old job.* **8.** *Usually capital* **O.** *Abbr.* **O, O.** Being the earlier or earliest of two or more related objects, stages, versions, or periods: *the Old Testament; Old High German.* **9.** *Geology.* **a.** Having become slower in flow and less vigorous in action. Said of rivers. **b.** Having become simpler in form and of lower relief. Said of land forms. **10.** Worn or dilapidated through age or use; worn-out: *an old coat.* **11.** Known through long acquaintance or use; long familiar: *an old friend; the old routine.* **12. a.** Dear or cherished, as through long acquaintance. Used as a term of affection or cordiality: *good old Harry.* **b.** *Chiefly British Informal.* Used with certain nouns as a form of address: *Sorry, old chap! Look here, old thing!* **c.** *Chiefly British Informal.* Used with no definite independent meaning to imply some humorous familiarity: *a touch of the old rheumatism.* **13.** Skilled or able through long experience; practised: *He was an old hand at shipbuilding; an old campaigner.*
~*n.* **1.** Former times; yore: *in days of old.* **2.** An individual of a specified age. Used in combination: *a five-year-old.* [Middle English *old, ald,* Old English *eald, ald,* from West Germanic *aldha* (unattested).] **—old·ish** *adj.* **—old·ness** *n.*
Synonyms: *old, elderly, aged, venerable, superannuated, archaic, ancient, elder, obsolete, antique, antiquated.*

old age pension *n. British.* A **retirement pension** *(see).* **—old age pen·sion·er** *n.*

Old Bai·ley (báyli) *n.* Popular name for the Central Criminal Court, the Crown Court for the City of London. It is so called because it stands in the thoroughfare called Old Bailey.

old bird *n. British Informal.* One who is cunning, astute, or shrewd.

old boy *n. British.* **1.** A former pupil of a boys' school, especially a private one. **2.** *Informal.* **a.** An old man. **b.** A husband or senior male colleague. **c.** Used as a familiar term of address to a boy, man, or thing personified as a male.

old boy network *n. British.* An unofficial system of mutual help, especially in obtaining jobs, among men who have shared a usually privileged form of schooling, university background, or the like.

Old Bulgarian *n.* Old Church Slavonic. Not in technical usage. **—Old Bulgarian** *adj.*

Old Catholic *n. Abbr.* **O.C. 1.** A member of a Jansenist church originating in Utrecht in the 18th century. **2.** A member of an independent religious organisation formed by a group of German Roman Catholics who refused to accept the doctrine of papal infallibility proclaimed by the first Vatican Council of 1870. **—Old Catholic** *adj.*

Old Church Slavonic *n.* The literary Slavonic language into which the Bible was translated in the 10th or early 11th century. It is still used as the liturgical language of various Slavonic Eastern churches. **—Old Church Slavonic** *adj.*

old country *n.* The native country of an immigrant.

Old Dutch *n.* Dutch from the beginning of the 12th century to the middle of the 13th. **—Old Dutch** *adj.*

old·en (ṓldən) *adj. Archaic & Poetic.* Old; ancient: *in olden times.* See Synonyms at **old.** [Middle English, from *old,* OLD.]

Ol·den·burg (ṓldən-burg), **Claes (Thure)** (1929–). Swedish-born U.S. sculptor. A leading pop artist, he recreated "ordinary environments", as in *The Store* (1960–61), and "soft sculptures" of household objects made from stuffed vinyl and canvas.

Old English *n. Abbr.* **OE, OE., O.E. 1.** English from the beginning of the 8th century to the middle of the 12th. Also called "Anglo-Saxon". **2.** *Printing.* **Black letter** *(see).* **—Old English** *adj.*

Old English sheepdog *n.* A large sturdy dog of a breed having a thick, shaggy, bluish-grey and white coat, with hair that hangs over the eyes.

old-e·stab·lished (ṓld-i-stábblisht, -e-) *adj.* Established for a long time.

oldest profession *n.* Prostitution. Used euphemistically, preceded by *the.*

olde-worlde. Variant of **old-world** (quaint). [Pseudo-archaic spelling.]

old-fash·ioned (ṓld-fásh'nd) *adj.* **1.** Of a style or method formerly in vogue; outdated; antiquated. **2.** Attached to or favouring methods, ideas, or customs of an earlier time: *an old-fashioned girl.* **3.** Indicating dignified reproach. Used in the phrase *an old-fashioned look.* —See Synonyms at **old.**

Old French *n.* French from the 9th century to the middle of the 16th. **—Old French** *adj.*

Old Frisian *n.* Frisian from the beginning of the 13th century to the end of the 15th. **—Old Frisian** *adj.*

old girl *n. British.* **1.** A former female pupil of a school, especially a private one. **2.** *Informal.* **a.** An old woman. **b.** A wife, mother, or senior female colleague. **c.** Used as a familiar form of address to a girl, woman, or thing personified as a female.

Old Glory. A nickname for the flag of the United States.

old gold *n.* Dark yellow, from light olive or olive brown to deep or strong yellow. **—old-gold** *adj.*

old guard *n.* **1.** *Capital* **O,** *capital* **G.** The imperial guard of Napoleon I. **2.** A group of defenders of an existing or formerly existing cause or principle. **3.** The conservative, often reactionary element of a given class, society, or political group. **4.** Loosely, any group of people who are experienced in or veterans of a given field. [Translation of French *Vieille Garde.*]

old hand *n.* One who has had much practice or experience in a particular sphere of activity.

old hat *adj. Informal.* Behind the times; no longer new; old-fashioned.

Old High German *n. Abbr.* **OHG** High German from the middle of the 9th century to the end of the 11th. **—Old High German** *adj.*

Old Icelandic *n.* Icelandic from the middle of the 12th century to

oil beetle *This soft-bodied beetle has no hindwings and only short forewings which leave most of its abdomen exposed. When molested, it exudes an evil-tasting oily secretion from its joints. The species shown here is native to Europe, but there are numerous related species all over Europe and Asia.*

okapi *Native to the rain forests of central Africa, the okapi is a hoofed mammal related to the giraffe. It lives on leaves, twigs, and fruit and was unknown to science until 1900.*

okra *The gummy pods of this tropical and subtropical plant are used to thicken soups and stews. In the southern United States, the plant and the stew are known as gumbo.*

the middle of the 16th. Also called "Old Norse". —**Old Icelandic** *adj.*

Old Iranian *n.* Iranian before the Christian era, the principal attested forms being **Avestan** and **Old Persian** *(both of which see).* —**Old Iranian** *adj.*

Old Irish *n.* **Irish Gaelic** *(see),* from 725 A.D. to the mid-tenth century. —**Old Irish** *adj.*

Old Italian *n.* Italian before the middle of the 16th century. —**Old Italian** *adj.*

old lady *n.* **1.** *Informal* **a.** One's mother. **b.** One's wife. **2.** A moth, *Mormo maura,* having dark brown patterned wings.

Old Latin *n.* Latin from the first texts (sixth century B.C.) up to the second century B.C. —**Old Latin** *adj.*

old-line (ŏld-līn) *adj. U.S.* **1.** Adhering to conservative or reactionary principles. **2.** Long established; traditional. —**old-lin·er** *n.*

Old Low German *n.* Low German from the middle of the 9th century to the middle of the 13th. Also called "Old Saxon". —**Old Low German** *adj.*

old maid *n.* **1.** *Informal.* A woman who is not married, especially an older woman; a spinster. **2.** *Informal.* A primly fastidious person. **3.** A children's card game. —**old-maid·ish** (ŏld-máydish) *adj.*

old man *n.* **1.** *Informal.* **a.** One's father. **b.** One's husband. **c.** A man in authority. **2.** A plant, the **southernwood** *(see).* **3.** *Australian.* An adult male kangaroo.

old man's beard *n.* Any of various plants having parts suggestive of a beard, such as **traveller's joy** *(see).*

old master *n.* **1.** A distinguished European artist of the period from around 1500 to the early 1700s; especially, one of the great painters of this period. **2.** A work created by an old master.

old moon *n.* A phase of the waning moon; the last quarter.

Old Nick *n. Informal.* The devil; Satan.

Old Norse *n. Abbr.* **ON, O.N.** **1.** The North Germanic language from which the modern Scandinavian languages are descended. **2.** This language as represented in either of two national literatures: **a.** Old Icelandic *(see).* **b.** Old Norwegian. —**Old Norse** *adj.*

Old Norwegian *n.* Norwegian from the middle of the 12th century to the end of the 14th. Also called "Old Norse". —**Old Norwegian** *adj.*

Old Persian *n.* An ancient form of Persian, recorded in cuneiform inscriptions dating from the sixth to the fifth century B.C. —**Old Persian** *adj.*

Old Prussian *n.* The Baltic language of the original Prussians, that became extinct in the 18th century. —**Old Prussian** *adj.*

old rose *n.* Dark pink to greyish or moderate red. —**old-rose** *adj.*

Old Russian *n.* The Russian language from the 11th to the 16th century. It emerged both as a separate East Slavonic vernacular in private letters and as a liturgical and later literary language based on a South Slavonic dialect, **Old Church Slavonic** *(see).* —**Old Russian** *adj.*

Old Saxon *n.* **Old Low German** *(see).* —**Old Saxon** *adj.*

old school *n.* **1.** Any group committed to traditional ideas or practices. **2.** *British.* One's former school. —**old-school** *adj.*

old school tie *n. British.* **1.** A tie that bears the colours of a particular school, especially one that is prestigious. **2.** The unofficial system of mutual assistance found amongst old members of certain schools, especially British public schools.

Old Slavonic *n.* The language of those Slavonic texts of the 11th, 12th, and 13th centuries which are written in any of the regional versions of **Old Church Slavonic** *(see).* —**Old Slavonic** *adj.*

old soldier *n.* **1.** A long-serving or retired soldier. **2.** Loosely, one who has accumulated much experience; an old hand.

Old South *n.* The southern states of the original thirteen American colonies; especially, those that later joined the Confederate States of America: Virginia, North and South Carolina, and Georgia.

Old Spanish *n.* Spanish before the middle of the 16th century. —**Old Spanish** *adj.*

old squaw *n.* A marine duck, *Clangula hyemalis,* with black and white plumage and long upward-pointing tail feathers, that is found in Arctic and North Temperate regions.

old stager *n. Informal.* A person with great experience; an old hand.

old·ster (ŏld-stər) *n. Informal.* An old or elderly person.

Old Stone Age *n.* See **Palaeolithic.**

old style *n. Capital* O, *capital* S. *Abbr.* **O.S.** The old method of reckoning dates according to the Julian calendar.

Old Testament *n. Abbr.* **OT, O.T.** **1.** The first of the two main divisions of the Christian Bible, containing the Hebrew Scriptures. Compare **Hebrew Scriptures.** **2.** The covenant of God with Israel as distinguished in Christianity from the dispensation of Christ constituting the New Testament. [Middle English, translation of Late Latin *Vetus Testāmentum,* translation of Greek *Palaia Diathēkē,* "Old Covenant", designation based on the Pauline distinction between the covenant with Israel and the new covenant of Christ.]

old-time (ŏld-tīm) *adj.* Of or pertaining to a time in the past: *old-time dancing; old-time music.*

old-tim·er (ŏld-tīmər) *n. Informal.* **1.** One who has been a resident, member, employee, or the like for a long time. **2.** An old man.

Old Turkic *n.* Turkic from the seventh century A.D. to the tenth century, attested in documents from various places in Central Asia, and divided into two principal dialects, Turkut and Old Uighur. —**Old Turkic** *adj.*

Old Uighur *n.* See **Old Turkic.** —**Old Uighur** *adj.*

Ol·du·vai Gorge (ŏl-doo-vī, -də-). Gorge in northern Tanzania. It

contains archaeological sites rich in fossils and palaeolithic implements. Detailed study of the site began in 1931 by Mary and Louis Leakey. One of their most famous discoveries was *Homo habilis.* *Homo erectus* remains have also been found there.

Old Welsh *n.* Welsh before the 12th century. —**Old Welsh** *adj.*

old·wife (ŏld-wīf) *n., pl.* **-wives** (-wīvz). Any of several fishes, such as the **alewife** and the **menhaden** *(both of which see).*

old wives' tale *n.* An example of superstitious folklore, usually claiming to explain natural or medical phenomena.

old woman *n. Informal.* **1.** A wife or mother. **2.** A nervous or fussy person, especially a male.

Old World *n.* The countries of the Eastern Hemisphere, including Eurasia and Africa, with special reference to Europe.

old-world (ŏld-wŭrld) *adj.* Also **olde-worlde** (ŏldi-wŭrldi). **1.** Antique; old-fashioned; quaint. **2.** *Often capital* O, *capital* W. Native or pertaining to the Eastern Hemisphere, or Old World.

Old World monkey *n.* Any monkey of the family Cercopithecidae, which is widespread throughout the warmer zones of the Eastern Hemisphere and includes the baboons, macaques, and rhesus and colobus monkeys.

Old Year's Night, Auld Year's Night *n. Scottish.* New Year's Eve.

o·lé (ō-láy) *interj.* Used to express excited approval, especially in Spanish-speaking countries. —*n.* A cry of olé. [Spanish.]

-ole *n. suffix.* Indicates small, little; for example, **petiole.** [Latin *-olus, -ola, -olum,* diminutive suffixes.]

o·le·a·ceous (ŏli-áyshəss) *adj.* Of or pertaining to the Oleaceae, a family of trees and shrubs containing the olive, ash, and lilac.

o·le·ag·i·nous (ŏli-ájinəss) *adj.* **1.** Of or pertaining to oil. **2.** Oily; unctuous. [French *oléagineux,* from Latin *oleāginus,* belonging to the olive tree, from *olea,* olive, from Greek *elaia.*] —**o·le·ag·i·nous·ly** *adv.* —**o·le·ag·i·nous·ness** *n.*

o·le·an·der (ŏli-ándər || -ander) *n.* Any poisonous evergreen shrub of the genus *Nerium,* found in warm climates, especially *N. oleander,* having fragrant white, pink, or red flowers. [Medieval Latin, alteration of *arodandrum, lorandrum,* perhaps from a Vulgar Latin deformation of Latin *rhododendron,* RHODODENDRON.]

o·le·as·ter (ŏli-ástər || -astər) *n.* A small Eurasian tree, *Elaeagnus angustifolia,* having silvery leaves and flowers, and olive-like fruit. Also called "wild olive". [Latin, wild olive tree : *olea,* olive tree, olive, from Greek *elaia* + *-aster,* diminutive suffix.]

o·le·ate (ŏli-ayt) *n.* An ester or salt of oleic acid. [French *oléate* : OLE(O)- + -ATE.]

o·lec·ra·non (ō-léckrə-nən, ŏli-kráy- || -non) *n. Anatomy.* The large point on the upper end of the ulna that projects behind the elbow joint and forms the point of the elbow. Also informally called "funny bone". [New Latin, from Greek *ōlekranon,* "elbow-tip" : *ōlenē,* elbow + *kranion,* head, skull.] —**o·lec·ra·nal** (-n'l), **o·le·cra·ni·al** (-kráyni-əl), **o·le·cra·ni·an** (-kráyni-ən) *adj.*

o·le·fine (ŏli-feen, -fin) *n.* Also **o·le·fin** (-fin). An **alkene** *(see).* [French *(gaz) oléfiant,* "oil forming (gas)", ethylene (which forms an oily liquid with chlorine) : OLE(O)- + *-fiant,* making, from *-fier,* -FY + -IN.] —**o·le·fin·ic** (-fínnik) *adj.*

o·le·ic acid (ō-lée-ik) *n.* An oily liquid occurring in animal and vegetable oils, $CH_3(CH_2)_7CH{:}CH(CH_2)_7COOH$; *cis*-9-octadecanoic acid.

o·le·in (ŏli-in) *n.* Also **o·le·ine** (-een, -in). A yellow oily liquid, $(C_{17}H_{33}COO)_3C_3H_5$, occurring naturally in most fats and oils, including olive oil. It is used as a textile lubricant. Also called "triolein". [French *oléine* : OLE(O)- + -IN.]

oleo-, ole- *comb. form.* Indicates oil or pertaining to oil; for example, **oleoresin, oleomargarine, oleic.** [French *olé-, oléo-,* from Latin *oleo-,* from *oleum,* (olive) oil, from Greek *elaion,* from *elaia,* olive.]

o·le·o·graph (ŏli-ə-graaf, -ō-, -graf) *n.* **1.** A chromolithograph printed in imitation of an oil painting. **2.** The lacelike pattern formed by a drop of oil on the surface of water. [OLEO- + -GRAPH.] —**o·le·og·ra·pher** (-óggrəfər) *n.* —**o·le·o·graph·ic** (-gráffik) *adj.* —**o·le·og·ra·phy** (-óggrəfi) *n.*

o·le·o·mar·ga·rine (ŏli-ō-már-jə-rin, -gə-, -reen) *n.* Also **o·le·o·mar·ga·rin** (-rin). *U.S.* **Margarine** *(see).* Also called "oleo".

oleo oil *n.* An oil obtained from beef fat and used in the manufacture of certain types of margarine.

o·le·o·res·in (ŏli-ō-rézzin) *n.* **1.** A naturally occurring mixture of an oil and resin, such as the exudate from pine trees. **2.** An oil-resin mixture extracted from plants. —**o·le·o·res·in·ous** (-əss) *adj.*

o·le·um (ŏli-əm) *n., pl.* **-lea** (-ə) or **-ums.** A corrosive solution of sulphur trioxide in sulphuric acid. [Latin, OIL.]

ol·fac·tion (ol-fáksh'n || ŏl-) *n.* **1.** The sense of smell. **2.** The action of smelling. [Latin *olfacere,* to smell. See olfactory.]

ol·fac·to·ry (ol-fák-tri, -təri || ŏl-) *adj.* Of or contributing to the sense of smell: *olfactory organ.* —*n., pl.* **-ries.** A nerve or organ involved in the sense of smell. [Latin *olfactōrius* (unattested), from *olfacere,* to smell : *olēre,* to smell + *facere,* to make.]

olfactory nerve *n.* Either of two bundles of nerve fibres, one on each side of the nasal cavity, that conduct chemical indications of smell.

O level *n. British.* **1.** Ordinary level: the lower of the two standards of examination for the **GCE** *(see).* **2. a.** An examination at this level. **b.** A certificate awarded for passing such an examination. Compare **A level.**

o·lib·a·num (o-líbbənəm, ō-) *n.* A gum resin, **frankincense** *(see).* [Middle English, from Medieval Latin, from Arabic *al-lubān,* "the

frankincense", probably from Greek *libanos,* of Semitic origin, akin to Hebrew *lĕbōriā,* incense.]

ol·i·garch (ólli-gaark) *n.* A member of an oligarchy. [Greek *oligarkhēs* : OLIG(O)- + -*arkhēs,* -ARCH.]

ol·i·gar·chy (ólli-gaarki) *n., pl.* **-chies. 1. a.** Government by the few, especially by a small faction of persons or families. **b.** Those making up such a faction. **2.** A state governed by oligarchy: *"Greek oligarchies were based on . . . the notion that their members were superior to other men."* (Maurice Bowra). —**ol·i·gar·chal** (-gárk'l), **ol·i·gar·chic** (-gárkik), **ol·i·gar·chi·cal** *adj.*

oligo–, olig– *comb. form.* Indicates few; for example, **oligopoly, oligosaccharide.** [Greek, from *oligos,* few, little.]

Ol·i·go·cene (óllig-ō-seen, o-líg-, -ə-) *adj.* Of or designating the geological time and deposits of the epoch in the Tertiary period of the Cenozoic era that extended from the Eocene to the Miocene. ~*n.* **1.** The Oligocene epoch. Preceded by *the.* **2.** The deposits of this epoch. [OLIGO- + -CENE.]

ol·i·go·chaete (ólligō-keet) *n.* Any of various worms of the class Oligochaeta, including the earthworms. [New Latin *Oligochaeta* : OLIGO- + CHAETA.] —**ol·i·go·chaete** *adj.* —**ol·i·go·chae·tous** (-kéetəss) *adj.*

ol·i·go·clase (ólligō-klayz, -klayss) *n.* One of the plagioclase group of minerals. It is greyish green to yellowish white, and occurs mainly in acid to intermediate igneous rocks. [German *Oligoklas* : OLIGO- + -CLASE.]

o·li·go·mer (ólligə-mər) *n.* A molecule consisting of only two, three, or four monomers, that can combine with more monomers to form a polymer. [OLIGO- + -MER.]

ol·i·go·phre·ni·a (ólligō-fréeni-ə) *n.* Arrested mental development, **mental deficiency** (see). Not in technical usage. [New Latin : OLIGO- + -PHRENIA.] —**ol·i·go·phren·ic** (-frénnik) *adj.*

ol·i·gop·o·ly (ólli-góppə-li) *n., pl.* **-lies.** *Economics.* A market condition in which sellers are so few that the actions of any one of them will materially affect price and hence have a measurable impact upon competitors. Compare **monopoly.** [OLIGO- + (MONO)POLY.] —**ol·i·gop·o·lis·tic** (-lístik) *adj.*

ol·i·gop·so·ny (ólli-gópsə-ni) *n., pl.* **-nies.** *Economics.* A market condition in which purchasers are so few that the actions of any one of them can materially affect price and hence the costs that competitors must pay. Compare **monopsony.** [OLIG(O)- + (MON)OPSONY.] —**ol·i·gop·so·nis·tic** (-nístik) *adj.*

ol·i·go·sac·cha·ride (ólligō-sáckə-rīd, -rid) *n.* Any carbohydrate in which a few monosaccharide units are joined together.

ol·i·go·troph·ic (ólligō-tróffik) *adj.* Poor in plant nutrients and hence plant life, but rich in oxygen. Said of lakes and similar habitats.

ol·i·gu·ri·a (ólli-géwr-i-ə) *n.* Also **ol·i·gu·re·sis** (-gewr-ée-siss). The excretion of an abnormally small volume of urine in relation to fluid intake.

o·li·o (óli-ō) *n., pl.* **-os. 1.** A heavily spiced stew of meat, vegetables, and chickpeas. **2. a.** Any mixture or medley; a potpourri. **b.** A collection of various artistic or literary works or musical pieces; a miscellany. [Modification of Spanish *olla,* pot, OLLA.]

ol·i·va·ceous (ólli-váyshəss) *adj.* Olive-green. [OLIV(E) + -ACEOUS.]

ol·i·var·y (ólli-vəri ‖ -verri) *adj.* **1.** Shaped like an olive. **2.** *Anatomy.* Of or pertaining to one of the two oval bodies of nervous tissue (olivary bodies) found on either side of the medulla oblongata. In this sense, also called "olive". [Latin *olīvārius,* from *olīva,* OLIVE.]

ol·ive (ólliv) *n.* **1.** An Old World semitropical evergreen tree, *Olea europaea,* having an edible fruit, white flowers, and leathery leaves. **2.** The small ovoid fruit of this tree, an important food from the earliest historical times and a source of oil. **3.** An olivary. **4.** The wood of the olive tree. **5.** Yellowish to brownish green. [Middle English, from Old French, from Latin *olīva,* from Greek *elaia.*] —**ol·ive** *adj.*

olive branch *n.* **1.** A branch of an olive tree regarded as an emblem of peace. **2.** An offer of peace.

olive drab *n. U.S.* **1.** Greyish olive to dark olive brown or olive grey. **2. a.** Cloth of this colour. **b.** A U.S. army uniform made from such cloth. —**ol·ive-drab** (ólliv-dráb) *adj.*

olive green *n.* Greenish yellow. —**ol·ive-green** (ólliv-gréen) *adj.*

o·liv·e·nite (o-lívvə-nīt, ə- ‖ ō-) *n.* A basic arsenate of copper, $Cu_3As_2O_8 \cdot Cu(OH)_2$, brown, olive-green, or grey in colour, found in copper deposits. [German *Olivenit* : OLIVE + -ITE.]

olive oil *n.* Oil pressed from olives, used in salad dressings, for cooking, as an ingredient of soaps, and as a skin softener.

Ol·ives, Mount of (óllivz). Hill in west Jordan under Israeli Military Administration. Lying in east Jerusalem, it is the Biblical site of the Garden of Gethsemane and of Christ's ascension.

Olivier (ə-lívvi-ay, o- ‖ ō-), **Laurence (Kerr), Baron Olivier of Brighton** (1907-). British actor. Before World War II, he directed and starred in film adaptations of *Henry V, Hamlet,* and *Richard III.* In the decade following the war, he established himself as a great Shakespearian actor. He is a character actor of international repute in both films and television.

ol·i·vine (ólli-veen, -véen) *n.* **1.** Any of a group of mineral silicates, all members of which consist of compounds of iron silicate and magnesium silicate in various proportions. They occur in basic and ultrabasic igneous rocks and some metamorphic rocks. Also called "chrysolite". **2.** A transparent green variety valued as a gem. Also called "peridot". [German *Olivin,* chrysolite : OLIVE (because of its colour) + -IN.]

o·lla (óllə, Spanish ól-yə) *n.* **1.** An earthenware pot or jar with a

wide mouth. **2.** An olla podrida. [Spanish, from Old Spanish, from Latin *olla,* variant of *aulla,* jar, pot.]

o·lla po·dri·da (po-dréedə, pə-, Spanish -threétha) *n.* **1.** A stew of highly seasoned meat and vegetables. **2.** Any assorted mixture or miscellany. [Spanish, "rotten pot" : OLLA + *podrida,* rotten, from Latin *putridus,* to rot, from *puter,* decaying, rotten.]

olm (olm, ōlm) *n.* An unpigmented eel-like salamander, *Proteus anguinus,* found in underground caves in southeastern Europe. [German.]

ol·o·gy (ólləji) *n., pl.* **-gies.** *Informal.* Any of various studies or concepts designated by terms ending in -*logy* and thereby regarded as generically related. Usually used humorously.

ol·o·ro·so (óllə-rō-sō, ōlə-, -zō) *n.* A full-bodied, medium-sweet sherry. [Spanish, "fragrant".]

O·lym·pi·a (ə-límpi-ə, ō-). City of ancient Greece situated in the West Peloponnese. It was the scene of the Olympic Games and the site of the temple of Zeus, which contained the statue of Zeus by Phidias, one of the Seven Wonders of the World.

O·lym·pi·ad (ə-límpi-ad, ō-) *n.* **1.** The interval of four years between celebrations of the Olympic Games, by which the ancient Greeks reckoned dates. **2.** A celebration of the modern Olympic Games. **3.** A regularly held international competition in games such as chess or bridge. [Middle English *Olympiade,* from Latin *Olympias,* from Greek *Olumpias* (stem *Olumpiad-*), from *Olumpia,* OLYMPIA.]

O·lym·pi·an (ə-límpi-ən, ō-) *adj.* **1.** Of or pertaining to the greater gods of the ancient Greek pantheon, whose abode was Olympus. **2. a.** Majestic in manner. **b.** Superior to or aloof from mundane affairs. ~*n.* **1.** Any of the 12 major gods inhabiting Olympus. **2.** One who exhibits Olympian qualities. **3.** A contestant in the Olympic Games.

O·lym·pic (ə-límpik, ō-) *adj.* Of or belonging to the games held at Olympia or the modern international revival of them.

Olympic Games *pl.n.* **1.** In ancient Greece, a Pan-Hellenic festival of athletic games and contests of choral poetry and dance, first celebrated in 776 B.C., and held every four years on the plain of Olympia in honour of the Olympian Zeus. **2.** A modern international revival of athletic and sports contests on the model of these ancient games, held every four years. In this sense, also called the "Olympics".

O·lym·pus, Mount (ə-límpəss, ō-). Greek **Óros Ólimbos.** The highest mountain of Greece (2 917 metres; 9,570 feet). In Greek mythology it is the home of the gods.

Om (ōm) *n.* In Hindu theology, a sacred syllable that embodies the ultimate, divine principle and is used as a mantra in meditation. [Sanskrit.]

OM. ostmark.

O.M. Order of Merit.

–oma *n. comb. form.* Indicates tumour; for example, **fibroma, myoma.** [New Latin, from Greek -*ōma,* abstract nominal ending formed from -*o-* stem verbs.]

O·magh (ō-maá, ōmə). Town in Northern Ireland. Lying on the river Strule, it is the county town of Tyrone.

O·man, Sultanate of (ō-maán, -mán). Formerly **Muscat and Oman.** Sultanate located in the southeast of the Arabian peninsula. It is a fertile coastal plain backed by hill ranges and an interior desert

olivine *The gemstone peridot (above) is a crystalline form of the mineral olivine. The mineral is also used to line the inside of furnaces because of its ability to withstand intense heat.*

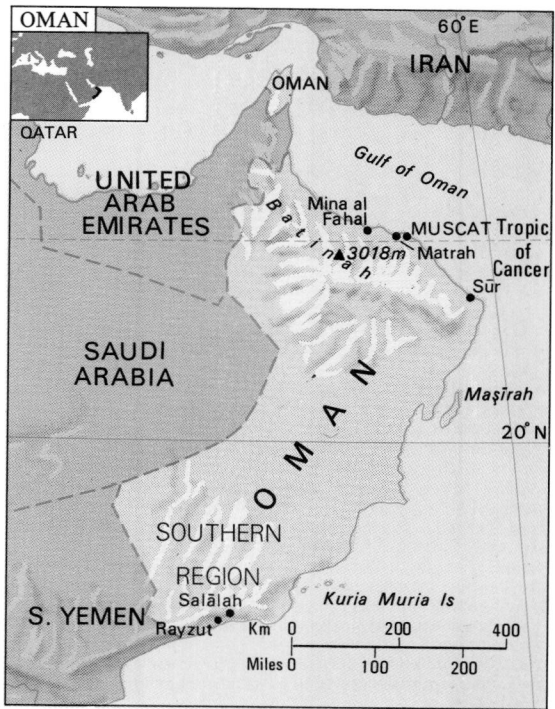

plateau. Dates, limes, sugar cane, and cattle are the chief products. Oil is the major source of revenue. Oman has had a close association with Britain since the late 18th century. Area, 212 457 square kilometres (82,030 square miles). Population, 900,000. Capital, Muscat.

O·mar Khay·yam (ṓmaar kī́-ám ‖ -áam) (*c.*1050–1123). Persian poet and mathematician. Though his astronomical observations were instrumental in the reform of the Islamic calendar, he is best known in the West for his *Ruba'iyat* of nearly 500 quatrains expressing wistful, agnostic hedonism, some of which were first translated into English (1859) by Edward Fitzgerald.

o·ma·sum (ō-máy-səm, ə-) *n., pl.* **-sa** (-sə). The third stomach of a ruminant animal, located between the **abomasum** and the **reticulum** *(both of which see).* Also called "manyplies", "psalterium". [Latin *omāsum,* pouch, bullock's tripe, probably from Gaulish.]

om·bre (ómbər) *n.* Also *chiefly U.S.* **om·ber.** A card game played by three players with forty cards, that was popular in Europe during the 17th and 18th centuries. [Spanish *hombre,* "man" (name given to the player who attempts to win the pool), from Latin *homo.*]

om·buds·man (óm-bŏŏdz-mən, -man ‖ -budz-) *n., pl.* **-men** (-men, -mən). In Britain, any of several officials who investigate citizens' complaints of maladministration by government departments (Parliamentary Commissioner for Administration), local authorities or local police authorities (Commissioner for Local Administration), or the National Health Service (Health Service Commissioner). [Swedish, from Old Norse *umbodhsmadhr,* "administration-man, king's representative" : *um,* about + *bodh,* command + *madhr,* (rarely) *mannr,* man.]

Om·dur·man (ómder-maán, -mán). City of the central Sudan. The nation's second city and former capital (1885–98), it is situated on the left bank of the White Nile, opposite Khartoum.

-ome *n. suffix. Biology.* Indicates mass, body, or group; for example, **biome, phyllome.** [Variant of -OMA.]

o·me·ga (ṓmi-gə, ṓmə- ‖ *chiefly U.S.* ō-máygə, -méggə, -méegə) *n.* **1.** The 24th and final letter in the Greek alphabet, written Ω, ω. Transliterated in English as *o* or sometimes as *ō.* **2.** The ending; the last of anything: *"I am Alpha and Omega, the beginning and the ending"* (Revelation 1:8). **3.** *Symbol* Ω- *Physics.* A fundamental particle in the baryon family, having a mass 3,276 times that of the electron, a negative electric charge, and a mean lifetime of 1.5 × 10^{-10} second. Also called "omega minus". See **particle.** [Greek *ō mega,* "large ō" : *ō* + *mega,* neuter of *megas,* large, great.]

om·e·lette (óm-lət, -lit, -let ‖ ómmə-) *n.* Also *chiefly U.S.* **om·e·let.** A dish prepared in a shallow pan, consisting of beaten egg cooked in fat until set, and often having a variety of savoury or sweet fillings. [French *omelette,* from Old French *amelette,* "thin plate", alteration of *alumette,* variant of *alumelle,* from *lemelle,* from Latin *lāmella,* thin metal plate, diminutive of *lāmina,* plate, layer.]

o·men (ṓ-men, -mən) *n.* **1.** Any phenomenon supposed to portend good or evil; a prophetic sign. **2.** Prognostication; portent.
~*tr.v.* **omened, omening, omens.** To be an omen of; portend; presage. [Latin *ōmen.*]

o·men·tum (ō-mén-təm, ə-) *n., pl.* **-ta** (-tə). *Anatomy.* Either of two pairs of peritoneal folds. The greater omentum consists of a double fold of peritoneum which covers the stomach and the intestine; the lesser omentum is doubled to link the stomach and duodenum to the liver. [Latin *ōmentum*†.] **—o·men·tal** *adj.*

om·i·cron (ō-mī́-krən, -kron ‖ *chiefly U.S.* ómmi-, ṓmi-) *n.* The 15th letter in the Greek alphabet, written O, o. Transliterated in English as *o.* [Greek *o mikron,* "small o" : *o* + *mikron,* neuter of *mikros,* small.]

om·i·nous (ómmi-nəss, *rarely* ṓmi-) *adj.* **1.** Menacing; threatening: *an ominous silence.* **2.** Being or pertaining to an evil omen; portentous. [Latin *ōminōsus,* from *ōmen* (stem *ōmin-*), OMEN.] **—om·i·nous·ly** *adv.* **—om·i·nous·ness** *n.*

o·mis·sion (ō-mísh'n, ə-) *n.* **1.** The act or an instance of omitting. **2.** The state of being omitted. **3.** Something that is omitted or neglected. [Middle English *omissioun,* from Late Latin *omissiō* (stem *omissiōn-*), from Latin *omittere* (past participle *omissus-*), to OMIT.] **—o·mis·sive** (-míssiv) *adj.*

o·mit (ō-mít, ə-) *tr.v.* **omitted, omitting, omits. 1.** To leave out; fail to include: *a name omitted from the list.* **2.** To pass over; neglect; fail to do: *omitted to tell her the message.* [Middle English *omitten,* from Latin *omittere* : *ob-,* away + *mittere,* to send.] **—o·mis·si·ble** (-míssəb'l) *adj.*

om·ma·tid·i·um (ómmə-tíddi-əm) *n., pl.* **-ia** (-ə). *Zoology.* One of the elements, resembling a single simplified eye, that make up the compound eye of arthropods. [New Latin, "small eye" : Greek *omma* (stem *ommat-*), eye + -IDIUM.] **—om·ma·tid·i·al** *adj.*

om·mat·o·phore (o-máttə-fawr, ə- ‖ ō-, -fōr) *n. Zoology.* A movable stalk ending with an eye, as found in snails. [Greek *omma* (stem *ommat-*), eye + -PHORE.] **—om·ma·toph·o·rous** (ómmə-tóffərəss) *adj.*

Ommiad. Variant of **Umayyad.**

omni- *comb. form.* Indicates all, everywhere; for example, **omnidirectional, omnirange.** [Latin, from *omnis,* all.]

om·ni·bus (óm-ni-bəss, -buss) *n., pl.* **-buses. 1.** A **bus** *(see).* **2.** A printed anthology of the works of one author or of writings on a related subject.
~*adj.* Including many things or classes; covering many things or situations at once. [French *(voiture) omnibus* "(vehicle) for all", and Latin *omnibus* "for all", dative plural of *omnis,* all.]

om·ni·com·pe·tent (óm-ni-kómpitənt) *adj.* Capable of judging or handling all matters. **—om·ni·com·pe·tence** *n.*

om·ni·di·rec·tion·al (óm-ni-di-réksh'n'l, -dīr-) *adj.* Capable of transmitting or receiving signals in all directions.

om·ni·far·i·ous (óm-ni-fáir-i-əss) *adj.* Of all sorts and kinds: *omnifarious knowledge.* [Late Latin *omnifarius* : OMNI- + *fārius,* "-doing"; akin to *facere,* to do.] **—om·ni·far·i·ous·ness** *n.*

om·nif·ic (om-níffik) *adj.* Also **om·nif·i·cent** (-níffiss'nt). *Rare.* All-creating. [Medieval Latin *omnificus* : OMNI- + -FIC.]

om·nip·o·tent (om-níppə-tənt) *adj.* **1.** Having a great amount of power, authority, or sway: *omnipotent police.* **2.** All-powerful: *an omnipotent god.*
~*n. Capital* **O.** God. Preceded by *the.* [Middle English, from Old French, from Latin *omnipotēns* : OMNI- + *potēns,* POTENT.] **—om·nip·o·tence** (-tənss), **om·nip·o·ten·cy** (-tən-si) *n.*

om·ni·pres·ence (óm-ni-prézz'nss) *n.* The fact of being present everywhere. [Medieval Latin *omnipraesentia,* from *omnipraesēns* : OMNI- + *praesēns,* PRESENT.] **—om·ni·pres·ent** *adj.*

om·ni·range (óm-ni-raynj) *n.* A radio network that provides complete bearing information for aircraft. Also called "omnidirectional radio range".

om·nis·cient (om-níssi-ənt, -níshi-, -nísh-) *adj.* **1.** Having total knowledge; knowing everything. **2.** Having great knowledge.
~*n. Capital* **O.** God. Preceded by *the.* [Latin *omnisciēns* : OMNI- + *sciēns* (stem *scient-*), present participle of *scīre,* to know.] **—om·nis·cience** (-ənss), **om·nis·cien·cy** *n.* **—om·nis·cient·ly** *adv.*

om·ni·um-gath·er·um (óm-ni-əm-gáthərəm) *n.* A miscellaneous collection; a hotchpotch. [Mock Latin formation : Latin *omnium,* of all, genitive plural of *omnis,* all + GATHER.]

om·ni·vore (óm-ni-vawr ‖ -vōr) *n.* An omnivorous animal. [Latin *omnivorus,* OMNIVOROUS.]

om·niv·o·rous (om-nívvərəss) *adj.* **1.** *Zoology.* Eating both animal and vegetable substances. **2.** Eating all kinds of food: *Pigs are omnivorous creatures.* **3.** Taking in everything available, as with the mind: *an omnivorous reader.* [Latin *omnivorus* : OMNI- + -VOROUS.] **—om·niv·o·rous·ly** *adv.* **—om·niv·o·rous·ness** *n.*

om·pha·los (ómfə-loss, -ləss) *n., pl.* **-li** (-lī). **1.** In Ancient Greece, a stone at Delphi thought to mark the centre of the earth. **2.** *Formal.* The navel. **3.** A centre. [Greek.]

Omsk (omsk). City of central U.S.S.R., founded (1716) at the confluence of the Om and Irtysh rivers. It is a major junction on the Trans-Siberian Railway, and an industrial centre.

on (on ‖ awn) *prep.* **1.** Used to indicate: **a.** Position upon and above the surface of; position in contact with and supported by the surface of: *The vase is on the table.* **b.** Contact, as between two surfaces: *mud on trousers; a ring on her finger.* **c.** Location at or along: *a house on the beach.* **d.** Proximity: *a town on the border; on the brink of extinction.* **e.** Attachment to or suspension from: *beads on a string.* **2.** Used to indicate: **a.** Motion towards, against, or onto: *jump on the table; the march on Moscow.* **b.** Direction or tendency as regards: *had a crush on her; an attack on the press.* **c.** Affecting: *hard on her parents; backed out on us.* **d.** A comparison or point of reference: *an improvement on last time.* **3.** Used to indicate: **a.** Occurrence during: *on the third of July.* **b.** The point of time of a specified action: *On entering the room, she saw me.* **c.** The exact moment or point of: *every hour on the hour.* **d.** After a specified process: *on reflection.* **e.** A current occupation: *on her rounds; on duty.* **4.** Used to indicate a connection between an object and a perceptible agent or agency: *I cut my foot on the broken glass; night fell on the town.* **5.** Used to indicate: **a.** A means of support or a sustaining source or agency: *live on bread and water; survives on a small income.* **b.** A means of progress or transmission: *on foot; on the radio.* **6.** Used to indicate: **a.** The state, condition, mode, or process of: *on record; on fire; on the increase.* **b.** The purpose of: *travel on business.* **c.** Availability by means of: *beer on tap; a nurse on call.* **d.** Association with; membership of: *a doctor on the hospital staff; on the board of directors.* **e.** The ground or basis for: *I refused it on principle.* **f.** Addition or repetition: *error on error; 10 per cent on the bill.* **7.** Concerning; about: *a book on astronomy.* **8.** In one's possession; with: *I haven't a penny on me.* **9.** At the expense of: *drinks on the house.* **10.** Indicates regular intake: *on drugs; back on the booze.* **11.** Indicates way or manner. Preceded by *the*: *on the quiet, on the sly.* **12.** Used preceded by an adjective indicating an attitude or characteristic: *keen on tennis; weak on dates.* **13.** *British Informal.* Earning: *You must be on a small fortune in that job.*
~*adv.* **1.** In or into a position of being attached to or covering something: *Put your clothes on.* **2.** In or into a state or condition of receiving a source of energy, such as electricity: *put the kettle on; turn the radio on.* **3. a.** In the direction of something visible: *looked on while the ship docked.* **b.** With a specified part forward or visible: *edge on.* **4. a.** Towards or at a point lying ahead in space or time; forward: *moved on to the next town.* **b.** At or to a specified point in time or space: *I'll do it later on.* **5.** In a continuous or persistent manner: *She worked on quietly.* **6.** In or at the present position: *stay on; hang on.* **—and so on.** And like the preceding; and so forth. **—on and off.** Intermittently. **—on and on.** Without stopping; continuously. **—on at.** *Informal.* Complaining to or nagging: *She's always on at me.* **—on to.** *Informal.* Having made a discovery about: *We're on to something big.*
~*adj.* **1. a.** Operating: *The radio is on.* **b.** Being supplied. Said especially of electricity, gas, and water. **2.** Taking place or due to take place: *There's a conference on now.* **3.** Onstage or about to go onstage: *You're on after the conjurer.* **4.** Ready to join in some ac-

tivity: *I'm on for a game.* **5.** Designating or placed on the legside of a cricket pitch: *an on drive.* **—not on.** *Informal.* **1.** Unable to be performed or accomplished: *a good idea, but it's not on.* **2.** Violating accepted standards: *His behaviour just wasn't on.*
~n. In cricket, the side of the cricket pitch that is on the **leg** *(see).* [Middle English *on,* preposition and adverb, Old English *on, an,* from Germanic.]

Usage: To indicate motion to a particular position, the prepositions *on* and *onto* are often interchangeable, though *onto* more strongly conveys movement towards the position: *He jumped on/onto the table. He jumped on the table* means he was already on it and started jumping — or that he jumped down on it from above. If he jumped up, you have to use *onto.* In such contexts, *onto* is written as a single word. When *on* is adverbial, however, it is written separately: *Let us move on to a new topic.* The same distinction applies to *on* and *upon*: *He jumped upon the table; He clambered up on the table.*

ON, O.N. Old Norse.

-on *n. suffix.* Indicates subatomic particle, unit, or quantum; for example, **electron, photon.** [From (I)ON.]

on·a·ger (ónnə-jər, -gər) *n., pl.* **-gers** or **-gri** (-grī). **1.** A wild ass, *Equus hemionus onager,* of central Asia. **2.** An ancient and medieval stone-propelling siege engine. [Middle English, from Latin *onager,* from Greek *onagros* : *onos,* ass + *agros,* field.]

o·nan·ism (ṓnan-iz'm, -nən-) *n.* **1.** Masturbation. **2.** Coitus interruptus. [After *Onan,* son of Judah (Genesis 38:9).] **—o·nan·ist** *n.* **—o·nan·is·tic** (-ístik) *adj.*

O·nas·sis (ō-nássiss, o-, ə-), **Aristotle (Socrates)** (1906–75). Greek entrepreneur. Owning one of the world's largest private commercial fleets, he pioneered the use of oil supertankers.

O.N.C. Ordinary National Certificate: an academic qualification in technical subjects in Britain.

once (wunss || *Northern England also* wonss. *The pronunciation* wunst *is not standard.*) *adv.* **1.** One time only: *once a day.* **2.** At one time in the past; formerly. **3.** At any time; ever: *Once known, never forgotten.* **4.** By one degree: *She is my first cousin once removed.* **—once and for all.** Finally; conclusively.
~n. A single occurrence; one time: *You can go this once.* **—all at once. 1.** All at the same time. **2.** Suddenly. **—at once. 1.** Without delay; immediately. **2.** All together; simultaneously.
~conj. As soon as; if ever; when: *Once he goes, I can clean up.*
~n. One time or occasion: *Once is enough; Please, just for once, be quiet.* [Middle English *ones, anes,* adverbial genitive of *on, an,* ONE.]

once-o·ver (wúnss-ōvər || wónss-) *n. Informal.* **1.** A quick but comprehensive glance or survey. Often preceded by *the.* **2.** A quick beating: *gave him the once-over.*

onc·er (wún-sər || wón-) *n. British Slang.* A one-pound note. [ONCE + -ER.]

onco- *comb. form.* Indicates tumour; for example, **oncogenic, oncology.** [Greek *onkos,* mass.]

on·co·gen·e·sis (óngkō-jénnə-siss) *n.* The formation and development of a tumour.

on·co·gen·ic (óngkō-jénnik) *adj.* Also **on·co·gen·ous** (ong-kójənəss, on-). Producing a tumour or tumours. [ONCO- + -GENIC.]

on·col·o·gy (ong-kólləji, on-) *n.* The scientific study of tumours. [ONCO- + -LOGY.] **—on·co·log·i·cal** (óngkə-lójik'l) *adj.* **—on·col·o·gist** (-kólləjist) *n.*

on·com·ing (ón-kumming || áwn-) *adj.* Coming nearer; approaching: *the oncoming storm.*
~n. An approach; an advance.

on·co·sphere (óngkō-sfeer) *n.* The six-hooked larva of a tapeworm, which, if ingested by an appropriate host, penetrates the intestine wall and invades muscle tissue. Also called "hexacanth". [Greek *onkos,* barb + SPHERE.]

on-cost (ón-kost || áwn-, -kawst) *n.* An overhead cost.

O.N.D. *n. British.* Ordinary National Diploma: an academic qualification in technical subjects in Britain.

ondes Mar·te·not (óɴd mártə-nō) *pl.n.* A musical instrument that uses electronic vibrations to produce characteristically eerie tones. [French, "Martenot waves", after Maurice *Martenot* (born 1898), who invented it.]

on dit (óɴ-dée) *n., pl.* **on dits** (-dée, -déez). *French.* A piece of gossip or hearsay. [Literally, it is said.]

on·do·graph (ón-dō-graaf, -də-, -graf) *n.* An instrument that produces a graphical trace representing an alternating current by measuring the charge imparted to a capacitor at different points in the cycle. [French, from *onde,* wave + -GRAPH.]

on·dom·e·ter (on-dómmitər) *n.* An instrument that measures the frequency of electromagnetic waves, especially in the radio-frequency band. [French *onde,* wave + METER.]

one (wun || *Northern England also* won) *adj.* **1.** Designating a single entity, unit, object, or being; single; individual. Sometimes used in combination: *one-eyed.* **2.** Characterised by unity; of a single kind or nature; undivided: *with one accord; one with my colleagues.* **3.** Designating a person or thing that is contrasted with another or others: *from one end to the other.* **4.** Designating a specified but indefinite thing or time: *He will come one day.* **5. a.** Designating a certain person, especially a person not previously known or mentioned: *One Mr. Jones called for you.* **b.** Designating an indefinite time or occasion: *One Tuesday, he returned.* **6.** *U.S.* A or an. Used informally as a substitute for the indefinite article for emphasis: *That is one fine dog.* **7.** Single in kind; alike or the same. **8.** Being unique in some specified respect: *The one man to leave.*
~n. **1. a.** The first cardinal number; the first positive whole number after zero. **b.** A symbol representing this, such as 1, I, or i. **2.** A size or thing designated as one. **3.** A single person or thing; a unit: *The one in the High street.* **4.** The first in a series. **5.** A banknote or coin having a denomination of one. **6.** One hour after midnight or midday. **7.** *British Informal.* A humorous or jocular person: *You are a one!* **—a right one.** *British Informal.* A fool or nuisance: *We've got a right one here!*
~pron. **1.** A certain person or thing; someone or something. **2.** Any person or thing; anyone or anything: *It's as good as one will get.* **3. a.** Any person representing the same, usually privileged, social class as the speaker: *One does meet intelligent people at Oxford.* **b.** The speaker: *One does so dislike package holidays.* **4.** A single person or thing among persons or things already known or mentioned: *one of the Elizabethans.* **—at one.** In accord or unity. **—in one.** At the first or in a single attempt: *got it in one; downed it in one.* **—one and all.** Everyone. **—one another.** Each other. Used to describe a reciprocal relation or action. **—one by one.** Individually and in succession. **—one up.** *Informal.* In a position of psychological superiority: *one up on the neighbours.* [Middle English *an, on,* Old English *ān.*]

Usage: *One* and *ones* should not be used immediately after a determiner such as *this, that,* or *many. Do you want to buy these books as well as those (books)?* is preferred to *Do you want to buy these books as well as those ones?* However, . . . *as well as those red/nice/inexpensive ones* is perfectly acceptable.

Formal British English is strict about maintaining the use of *one* as a generalising third person pronoun, and sequences such as *One should look after oneself, shouldn't one?* will be heard. American English is more likely to replace such sequences by forms of *he*: *One should ask himself . . . One* is particularly associated with extremely formal speech, where it is often used as a replacement for the first person form even in relation to mundane topics (*One fell off one's horse,* where the meaning is "I fell off my horse"). Because of these associations, the usage is frequently the butt of satire, and nowadays is often avoided, even in formal speech.

-one *n. suffix.* Indicates: **1.** An oxygen-containing or ketone compound; for example, **acetone. 2.** A chemical compound containing oxygen, especially in a carbonyl or similar group; for example, **lactone.** [Greek *-ōnē,* feminine patronymic suffix.]

one-armed bandit (wún-ármd-bándit || wón-) *n. Informal.* A fruit machine, especially one with an arm-like handle that is pulled to set the machine in motion.

one-di·men·sion·al (wún-dī-ménsh'n'l, -di- || wón-) *adj.* Having only one dimension; unidimensional.

O·ne·ga, Lake (on-yáygə). Lake of the northwest U.S.S.R. Europe's second largest lake, it is drained by the Onega river northwards to the White Sea, and connected by canal to the Baltic Sea and the river Volga. Petrozavodsk is the chief port.

one-horse (wún-hórss || wón-) *adj.* **1.** Drawn by or using only one horse: *a one-horse carriage.* **2.** Contemptibly small, limited, or insignificant: *a one-horse town.*

O·nei·da (ō-nī́də) *n., pl.* **-das** or collectively **Oneida. 1.** A member of one of the five peoples belonging to the league of the Iroquois. **2.** The Iroquoian language of this people. **—O·nei·da** *adj.*

O'Neill (ō-néel, ə-), **Eugene (Gladstone)** (1888-1953). U.S. playwright. His best-known works include *Mourning Becomes Electra* (1931), an adaptation of the trilogy of Aeschylus, and *Long Day's Journey Into Night* (1956). He was awarded the Nobel prize for literature (1936).

O'Neill, Terence Marne, Baron (1914–). Northern Irish politician. Becoming Unionist prime minister of the province in 1963, he was forced to resign (1969) over concessions granted to the Catholic Civil Rights campaign. He was made a life peer (1970).

o·nei·ric (o-nī́r-ik, ə-, ō-) *adj.* Of or pertaining to dreams. [Greek *oneiros,* dream.]

oneiro- *comb. form.* Indicates dreams; for example, **oneirocritic.** [Greek *oneiros,* dream.]

o·nei·ro·crit·ic (o-nī́r-ō-kríttik, ə-, ō-, -ə-) *n.* One who interprets dreams. [Greek *oneirokritikos* : ONEIRO- + CRITIC.] **—o·nei·ro·crit·i·cal** *adj.* **—o·nei·ro·crit·i·cism** (-krítti-siz'm) *n.*

on·ei·rol·o·gy (ón-īr-ólləji, ṓn-) *n.* The art of interpreting dreams. [ONEIRO- + -LOGY.]

o·nei·ro·man·cy (o-nī́r-ə-man-si, ə-, ō-, -ō-) *n.* Divination by dreams. [Greek *oneiros,* dream + -MANCY.] **—o·nei·ro·man·cer** *n.*

one-lin·er (wún-lī́nər || wón-) *n. Chiefly U.S. Informal.* A short, pithy joke or comment.

one-man (wún-mán || wón-) *adj.* Of, pertaining to, consisting of, or performed by one man: *a one-man show.*

one-man band *n.* **1.** A performer, usually a street musician, who plays a number of instruments at once, such as a drum, trumpet, and pair of cymbals, which are fastened to each other and to his body. **2.** A person who single-handedly performs various functions that are more usually performed by a number of people.

one-man, one-vote *adj.* Designating or pertaining to a voting system in which each member of a population or membership is entitled to an equal vote in an election.

one·ness (wún-nəss, -niss || wón-) *n.* **1.** The quality or state of being one; singleness: *the infinite oneness of God.* **2.** Singularity; uniqueness. **3.** Undividedness; wholeness. **4.** Sameness of character or nature: *the dull oneness of motorway landscapes.* **5.** Unison; agreement: *oneness of mind and purpose.*

one-night stand (wún-nī́t || wón-) *n.* **1.** A performance, by a theatre

PRONUNCIATION KEY

a, trap; aa, **father**; ai, **fair**; ar, **star**; aw, **lawn**; ay, **play**; b, bb, stab; **rubber**; ch, **church**; ck, **ticket**; d, dd, **dead**; **ladder**; e, dress; ee, **bee**; er, **defer**; ew, **few**; ewr, **pure**; ə, about; ər, letter; f, ff, fife; **differ**; g, gg, **giggle**; h, **hat**; i, kit; ī, price; īr, **fire**; j, **judge**; k, **kick**; l, ll, **let**; 'l, needle; m, mm, **man**; n, nn, **no**; 'n, **sudden**; ng, **thing**; o, **lot**; ō, **no**; ŏŏ, **foot**; ōō, **shoe**; oor, **poor**; ow, **cow**; owr, **hour**; oy, **boy**; p, pp, **pepper**; r, rr, red; s, ss, **sauce**; sh, **ship**; t, tt, **totter**; th, **thick**; th, **this**; **smooth**; u, **cut**; ur, **turn**; v, vv, **valve**; w, **wet**; y, **yes**; z, zz, **zebra**; zh, **vision**; **pleasure**

IN FOREIGN WORDS:

aɴ, oɴ, **Saint-Saëns**; hl, **Llanelli**; **Hluhluwe**; kh, **loch**; **lough**; **Khaled**

STRESS MARK:

ín-sīt, insight; in-sī́t, incite

onion *This vegetable has been cultivated since prehistoric times and is now unknown in the wild state. These are maincrop onions, used mostly for cooking; smaller varieties are used for pickling.*

PRONUNCIATION KEY

a, trap; aa, father; ai, fair; ar, star; aw, lawn; ay, play; b, bb, stab; rubber; ch, church; ck, ticket; d, dd, dead; ladder; e, dress; ee, bee; er, defer; ew, few; ewr, pure; ə, about; ər, letter; f, ff, fife; differ; g, gg, giggle; h, hat; i, kit; ī, price; īr, fire; j, judge; k, kick; l, ll, let; 'l, needle; m, mm, man; n, nn, no; 'n, sudden; ng, thing; o, lot; ō, no; o͝o, foot; o͞o, shoe; oor, poor; ow, cow; owr, hour; oy, boy; p, pp, pepper; r, rr, red; s, ss, sauce; sh, ship; t, tt, totter; th, thick; th, this; smooth; u, cut; ur, turn; v, vv, valve; w, wet; y, yes; z, zz, zebra; zh, vision; pleasure

IN FOREIGN WORDS:

aN, oN, Saint-Saëns; hl, Llanelli; Hluhluwe; kh, loch; lough; Khaled

STRESS MARK:

ín-sīt, insight; in-sít, incite

company for example, in one place on one night only. **2.** *Informal.* **a.** A sexual encounter lasting only one evening or night. **b.** The other person involved in such an encounter.

one-off (wún-óff, -áwf ‖ wón-) *n. British.* One who or that which is highly original or individual, or is not intended to be copied or repeated. Also used adjectivally: *a one-off performance.*

one-piece (wún-pe͞ess ‖ wón-) *adj.* Consisting of one piece: *a one-piece bathing costume.*

on•er•ous (ónnə-rəss, ṓnə-) *adj.* **1.** Troublesome or oppressive; burdensome. **2.** *Law.* Entailing obligations that exceed any advantage to the possessor. Said, for example, of a contract. —See Synonyms at **burdensome.** [Middle English, from Old French *onereus,* from Latin *onerōsus,* from *onus* (stem *oner-*), burden.] **—on•er•ous•ly** *adv.* **—on•er•ous•ness** *n.*

one•self (wun-sélf ‖ won-) *pron.* Also **one's self.** A specialised form of the third person singular pronoun **one.** It is used: **1.** As a reflexive pronoun, forming the direct or indirect object of a verb or the object of a preposition: *faith in oneself.* **2.** For emphasis, after *one*: *One must take a certain amount of initiative oneself.* **3.** As an emphasising substitute for *one*: *Oneself is usually to blame.* **4.** As an indication of one's real, normal, or healthy condition or identity: *come to oneself.* **5.** Euphemistically, to indicate one's genitals or private parts: *to expose oneself; to play with oneself.*

one-sid•ed (wún-sī́did ‖ wón-) *adj.* **1. a.** Favouring one side or group; partial; biased: *a one-sided view.* **b.** Laying obligation only on one of the parties: *a one-sided agreement.* **2.** Larger or more developed on one side: *a one-sided pattern.* **3.** With one side stronger or more powerful: *a one-sided contest.* **4.** Existing or occurring on one side only. **—one-sid•ed•ly** *adv.* **—one-sid•ed•ness** *n.*

one-step (wún-step ‖ wón-) *n.* **1.** A ballroom dance resembling the foxtrot and consisting of a series of unbroken rapid steps in 2/4 time. **2.** Music for such a dance.
~*intr.v.* **one-stepped, -stepping, -steps.** To dance the one-step.

one-time (wún-tīm ‖ wón-) *adj.* At or in some past time; former: *a one-time boxing champion.*

one-to-one (wún-tə-wún, -to͞o- ‖ wón-, -wón) *adj.* **1.** Allowing the pairing of each member of a class uniquely with a member of another class. **2.** Characterised by pairing and equality between two individuals or groups: *one-to-one discussions.* **3.** *Mathematics.* Pertaining to a correspondence that assigns to each member of one set a unique member of another set. **4.** Characterised by proportional amounts on both sides. **—one to one** *adv.*

one-track (wún-trák ‖ wón-) *adj.* Obsessively limited to a single idea or purpose: *a one-track mind.*

one-up•man•ship (wún-úpmənship ‖ wón-) *n. Informal.* The technique of maintaining a psychological superiority over one's associates or keeping one step ahead of a competitor. [From the phrase *be one up (on),* after GAMESMANSHIP.]

one-way (wún-wáy ‖ wón-) *adj.* **1.** Moving, operating, or permitting movement in one direction only: *a one-way street.* **2.** *U.S.* Providing for travel in one direction only: *a one-way ticket.*

one-woman (wún-wo͝o-man ‖ wón-) *adj.* Of, pertaining to, consisting of, or performed by one woman: *a one-woman show.*

on•go•ing (ón-gō-ing, -gṓ- ‖ áwn-) *adj.* Progressing or evolving.

ONI Office of Naval Intelligence.

on•ion (ún-yən) *n.* **1.** A bulbous plant, *Allium cepa,* cultivated worldwide as a vegetable. **2.** The rounded, edible bulb of the onion plant, composed of tight, concentric layers of succulent white leaf bases, having a pungent odour and taste. **3.** Any of several similar plants of the genus *Allium,* such as the **Welsh onion, shallot,** or **chive** *(all of which see).* **—know (one's) onions.** *British Informal.* To have a thorough and practical knowledge of a certain field.
~*adj.* Of, pertaining to, tasting of, or resembling an onion: *an onion dome; onion flavour.* [Middle English *unyon, oyn(y)oun,* from Anglo-French, Old French *oignon,* from Latin *uniō* (stem *union-*), a dialectal word for a kind of onion, perhaps from *ūniō,* oneness, unity, from *ūnus,* one (perhaps referring to the concentric unity of the layers of an onion).] **—on•ion•y** *adj.*

on•ion•skin (ún-yən-skin) *n.* A thin, strong, translucent paper.

on-line (ón-līn ‖ áwn-) *adj.* **1.** Connected to and controlled by a mainframe computer. Said of a part of a computer system or a peripheral device. **2.** Switched on. Said of a computer. Compare **off-line.**

on•look•er (ón-lo͝ok-ər ‖ áwn-, -lo͝ok-) *n.* One who looks on; a spectator. **—on•look•ing** *adj. & n.*

on•ly (ōnli ‖ ōni) *adj.* **1. a.** Alone in kind or class; sole. **b.** Having no brothers or sisters. Said of a child. **2.** Standing alone by reason of superiority or excellence: *the only place to be.*
~*adv.* **1.** Without anyone or anything else; alone: *Only three survived.* **2. a.** No more than: *He left only an hour ago.* **b.** At least; just: *If you would only come home.* **c.** Merely: *I only work here.* **3.** Exclusively; solely: *I work only here.* **4.** With the specified unexpected result. Used with an infinitive: *They went, only to be turned away.* **—only too.** Extremely: *only too ready to laugh.*
~*conj. Informal.* But; except (that): *I would have rung, only I couldn't remember the number.* [Middle English *only,* Old English *ānlīc* : *ān,* ONE + *-līc,* -LY.]

Usage: It is generally recommended that *only* should be placed before the words it limits, in written English: *I saw only Jane* (and no one else) rather than *I only saw Jane* (I did not speak to her). The tendency to use *only* apart from the limited word, putting it earlier in the sentence, usually before the verb, is widespread in speech: *I only saw Jane, not Jim.* Purists criticise this usage on logical grounds, maintaining that *only* should always go next to the word it limits, or else ambiguity will result. However this construction is rarely ambiguous in speech, because the stress pattern of the sentence indicates clearly which word goes with which: *I ONLY saw JANE* (not Jim) as opposed to *I only SAW Jane* (I didn't speak to her). Even in the written language, context usually makes it clear which is the intended meaning, but the weight of grammatical tradition, together with the risk of ambiguity, is enough to foster widespread observance of the adjacency rule in formal written English.
The form *not only . . . but also* is a special instance of the general problem affecting the placement of *only.* The two components should be placed before the same word classes in the two parts of the construction: *They recognise not only the theoretical issues but also the practical consequences.* In a speech-influenced style, however, *They not only recognise . . .* will be used.

o.n.o. *British.* or near offer.

on•o•mas•tic (ón-ə-mástik, -ō-) *adj.* **1.** Of or pertaining to a name or names. **2.** *Formal.* Designating the signature of the nominal author of a document that is copied out in another's handwriting. [Greek *onomastikos,* from *onomazein,* to name, from *onoma,* a name.]

on•o•mas•tics (ón-ə-mástiks, -ō-) *n. Used with a singular verb.* The study of the origins of names, especially the proper names of people and places.

on•o•mat•o•poe•ia (ón-ə-máttə-pe͞e-ə, -ō-, *rarely* o-nómmətə-, ə-) *n.* **1.** The formation of a word that sounds like that to which it refers, as *buzz, crack, cuckoo.* **2.** A word so formed. **3.** The use, especially as a literary device, of words whose sounds suggest a sound referred to or produce some other evocative effect. [Late Latin, from Greek *onomatopoiia,* from *onomatopoiein,* to coin names : *onoma* (stem *onomat-*), name + *poiein,* to make.] **—on•o•mat•o•poe•ic** (-ik), **on•o•mat•o•po•et•ic** (-pō-éttik) *adj.* **—on•o•mat•o•poe•ic•al•ly** *adv.*

On•on•da•ga (ónnən-da͞agə ‖ *U.S. also* -dáwgə) *n., pl.* **-gas** or collectively **Onondaga.** A member of a North American Iroquoian-speaking Indian people. **—On•on•da•gan** *adj.*

on•rush (ón-rush ‖ áwn-) *n.* A powerful, forward rush or flow: *the onrush of events.* **—on•rush•ing** (on-rúsh-ing ‖ awn-) *adj.*

on•set (ón-set ‖ áwn-) *n.* **1.** An onslaught; an assault. **2.** A beginning; a start: *the onset of a cold.*

on•shore (ón-shór ‖ áwn-, -shṓr) *adj.* **1.** Towards the shore: *an onshore gale.* **2.** Located or operating on the shore: *an onshore patrol.*
~*adv.* Towards the shore: *The wind shifted onshore.*

on•slaught (ón-slawt ‖ áwn-) *n.* A violent attack. [Earlier *anslaight* (influenced by obsolete English *slaught,* slaughter), from Middle Dutch *aenslag* : *aan,* on + *slag,* a striking.]

on•stage (ón-stáyj ‖ áwn-) *adj.* On the stage; in front of the audience: *onstage action.* **—on•stage** *adv.*

on stream *adj.* In operation or production. Said of industrial products, processes, or equipment.

On•tar•i•o (on-taír-i-ō). Province of eastern Canada. Lying between the Great Lakes in the south, and Hudson Bay and James Bay in the north, it is Canada's wealthiest and most populous province. Its industries include food processing, machinery, engineering, and timber. Hydroelectricity is exported to the United States. Ottawa and Toronto, are the chief cities. Area, 1 068 583 square kilometres (412,582 square miles). Provincial capital, Toronto.

Ontario, Lake. The smallest of the Great Lakes. Lying on the U.S.-Canadian border, it is the most easterly of the Lakes, and receives the entire drainage of the Great Lakes through the Niagara river; it is drained by the St. Lawrence. Its chief cities and ports include Toronto (in Canada), and Rochester (in the United States).

on•to (ón-to͞o, *before a word beginning with a consonant* -tə ‖ áwn-, -to͞o) *prep.* **1.** On top of; to a position on; upon: *The dog jumped onto the chair.* —See Usage note at **on.** **2.** *Informal.* Having made a discovery about: *I'm onto your schemes.* **3.** In contact with: *get onto the police.* [ON + TO.]

onto– *comb. form.* Indicates being or existence; for example, **ontogeny.** [Greek, from *ōn* (stem *ont-*), present participle of *einai,* to be.]

on•tog•e•ny (on-tójəni) *n., pl.* **-nies.** Also **on•to•ge•ne•sis** (ón-tə-jénnə-siss, -tō-). The course of development of an individual organism. Compare **phylogeny.** [ONTO- + -GENY.] **—on•to•ge•net•ic** (ón-tə-jə-néttik, -tō-) *adj.*

ontological argument *n. Philosophy.* An argument attempting to prove the existence of God through analysis of the nature of the concept of God, as by questioning the ultimate origin of the concept.

on•tol•o•gy (on-tólləji) *n.* The branch of philosophy that deals with the nature of being and first principles. [New Latin *ontologia* : ONTO- + -LOGY.] **—on•to•log•i•cal** (ón-tə-lójik'l, -tō-) *adj.* **—on•to•log•i•cal•ly** *adv.*

o•nus (ṓnəss) *n.* **1.** Anything that is burdensome, especially a responsibility or necessity. **2.** Loosely, stigma or blame. [Latin *onus,* burden.]

on•ward (ón-wərd ‖ áwn-) *adj.* Moving or tending forwards.

on•wards (ón-wərdz ‖ áwn-) *adv.* Also *chiefly U.S.* **onward.** In a direction or towards a position that is ahead in space or time.

-onym *comb. form.* Indicates word or name; for example, **acronym, tautonym.** [Latin *-onymum,* from Greek *-onumon,* from *onuma, onoma,* name.]

-onymy *n. comb. form.* Indicates a set of names or the study of a kind of name, for example, **toponymy.** [Greek *-ōnumia,* from *-ōnumos,* having a (specific) name, from *onuma, onoma,* name.]

on•yx (ónniks, *rarely* ṓ-niks) *n.* **1.** A type of chalcedony that occurs in bands of different colours, usually white with grey or brown. It is used as a gemstone, especially in cameos and intaglios. **2.** Onyx marble. [Middle English *onix*, from Old French, from Latin *onyx*, from Greek *onux*, claw, fingernail, hence onyx (which sometimes has a vein of white on a pink background, like the lunula in a fingernail).]

onyx marble *n.* A banded form of calcite used as an ornamental stone. Also called "onyx", "oriental alabaster".

oo– *comb. form.* Indicates egg or ovum; for example, **oogenesis, oology.** [Greek *ōio-*, from *ōion*, egg.]

o·o·cyst (ṓ-ə-sist) *n.* An encysted form of the zygote that develops in certain sporozoan protozoans, such as the malaria parasite *(Plasmodium).*

o·o·cyte (ṓ-ə-sīt, -ō-) *n.* **1.** A cell of the animal ovary, derived from an oogonium, that undergoes meiosis and produces an ovum. **2.** A female gamete in certain protozoa. [OO- + -CYTE.]

oo·dles (ṓod'lz) *pl.n. Informal.* A great amount; a lot; lashings. [19th century (U.S.): origin obscure.]

o·og·a·mous (ō-óggəməss) *adj.* **1.** Characterised by small male gametes and large, less mobile female gametes. **2.** Pertaining to reproduction by oogamy.

o·og·a·my (ō-óggəmi) *n., pl.* **-mies.** Reproduction between oogamous gametes. [OO- + -GAMY.]

o·o·gen·e·sis (ō-ə-jénnə-siss) *n. Biology.* The formation, development, and maturation of ova in the ovary from unspecialised precursor cells. [New Latin : OO- + -GENESIS.] **—o·o·ge·net·ic** (-jə-néttik) *adj.*

o·o·go·ni·um (ō-ə-gṓ-ni-əm) *n., pl.* **-nia** (-ni-ə) or **-ums. 1.** *Biology.* Any of the cells of the animal ovary that develop into oocytes during ovum formation. **2.** *Botany.* A female reproductive structure in certain algae and fungi, containing oospheres. [New Latin : OO- + -GONIUM.] **—o·o·go·ni·al** *adj.*

ooh (ōo) *interj.* Used to express a sudden thrill of excitement, pleasure, fear, or the like.
~*intr v.* **oohed, oohing, oohs.** To utter "ooh". Used chiefly in the phrase *ooh and ah.*

o·o·lite (ṓ-ə-līt) *n.* **1.** A sedimentary rock, usually a limestone, composed of tiny rounded grains embedded in a fine matrix. **2.** Any of the grains of which such rock is composed. [New Latin *oolites* (translation of German *Rogenstein,* "roe stone") : OO- + -LITE.] **—o·o·lit·ic** (ō-ə-líttik) *adj.*

o·ol·o·gy (ō-óllə ji) *n.* The study of eggs, especially birds' eggs. [OO- + -LOGY.] **—o·o·log·i·cal** (ō-ə-lójik'l) *adj.* **—o·o·log·i·cal·ly** *adv.* **—o·ol·o·gist** *n.*

oo·long (ōo-long ‖ -lawng) *n.* A dark Chinese tea, from Fujian that is partly fermented before drying. See **black tea.** [Mandarin Chinese *wū lóng,* black dragon.]

oomiak. Variant of **umiak.**

oom·pah (ṓom-paa, ṓom-) *n.* A sound made by a brass instrument, such as a tuba. [Imitative.]

oomph (ōomf) *n. Informal.* **1.** Enthusiasm; spirited vigour; drive. **2.** Sex appeal. [Expressive.]

o·o·pho·rec·to·my (ō-əfə-réktəmi) *n., pl.* **-mies.** The surgical removal of one or both ovaries. [Greek *ōophoron,* ovary (*ōion,* egg + *-phoros,* bearing) + -ECTOMY.]

o·o·pho·ri·tis (ō-əfə-rîtiss) *n.* Inflammation of an ovary. Also called "ovaritis". [New Latin : Greek *ōophoron,* ovary + -ITIS.]

o·o·phyte (ṓ-ə-fīt) *n. Botany.* The stage in the alternation of generations of lower plants when sexual organs are developed. [OO- + -PHYTE.] **—o·o·phyt·ic** (ō-ə-fíttik) *adj.*

oops (ōopss, ōopss, wōopss) *interj.* Used to express: **1.** Alarm or apology when dropping something. **2.** The sudden realisation of a mistake or blunder. [Expressive.]

o·o·sperm (ṓ-ə-sperm) *n. Biology.* A fertilised ovum.

o·o·sphere (ṓ-ə-sfeer) *n. Botany.* A nonmotile female gamete or egg, formed in an oogonium and ready for fertilisation. [OO- + -SPHERE.]

o·o·spore (ṓ-ə-spawr ‖ -spōr) *n. Botany.* A thick-walled spore in certain algae and fungi, developed from a fertilised oosphere. **—o·o·spor·ic** (-spórrik, -spáwrik ‖ -spṓrik), **o·os·po·rous** (-spáwrəss ‖ -spṓrəss) *adj.*

o·o·the·ca (ō-ə-théekə) *n., pl.* **-cae** (-see). *Zoology.* The capsule or egg case of certain insects and molluscs. **—o·o·the·cal** *adj.*

ooze¹ (ōoz) *v.* **oozed, oozing, oozes.** —*intr.* **1.** To flow or leak out slowly, as through small openings. **2.** To disappear or ebb slowly: *His courage oozed away.* **3.** To emit or exude moisture. —*tr.* **1.** To give out; exude. **2.** To emit or radiate in pervasive abundance: *The waiter oozed charm.*
~*n.* **1.** The act of oozing; a gradual flow or leak. **2.** Something that oozes. **3.** An infusion of vegetable matter, as from oak bark, used in tanning. [Middle English *wosen,* from *wose,* juice, Old English *wōs;* akin to Old Norse *vás.*]

ooze² *n.* **1.** Soft, thin mud, especially that found at the bottom of rivers and lakes. **2.** The layer of mudlike sediment covering the floor of oceans and lakes, composed chiefly of remains of microscopic sea animals. **3.** Muddy, boggy ground. [Middle English *wose,* Old English *wāse;* akin to Old Norse *veisa,* puddle.]

ooz·y¹ (ṓozi) *adj.* **-ier, -iest.** Slowly leaking; oozing; dripping: *an oozy packet of ice cream.* **—ooz·i·ly** *adv.* **—ooz·i·ness** *n.*

oozy² *adj.* **-ier, -iest.** Of, resembling, or containing ooze: *an oozy riverbed.* **—ooz·i·ness** *n.*

op. 1. operation. **2.** opposite. **3.** optical. **4.** opus. **5.** out of print.
Op. 1. operation. **2.** opus. **3.** out of print.
o.p. 1. opposite prompt (side). **2.** out of print.

O.P. 1. Order of Preachers (in the Dominican order). [Latin *Ordinis Praedicatorum.*] **2.** *Military.* Observation post.

o·pac·i·ty (ə-pássəti, ō-) *n., pl.* **-ties. 1.** The quality or state of being opaque. **2.** Something that is opaque. **3.** *Physics.* The ratio of the amount of light or other radiation falling on a surface to the amount that passes through the surface. [French *opacité,* from Latin *opācitās* from *opācus,* OPAQUE.]

o·pah (ṓpə) *n.* A large, vividly coloured marine fish, *Lampris guttatus,* found in all temperate and tropical seas. Also called "kingfish", "moonfish". [West African name; akin to Ibo *ubà.*]

o·pal (ṓp'l) *n.* A hydrated amorphous variety of silica, often used as a gem. See **fire opal.** [Latin *opalus,* from Greek *opallios,* from Sanskrit *úpala* (precious) stone, from *úpara,* lower, comparative of *úpa,* under.]

o·pal·esce (ṓp'l-éss) *intr.v.* **-esced, -escing, -esces.** To emit or show an iridescent shimmer of colours. [Back-formation from OPALESCENT.]

o·pal·es·cent (ṓp'l-éss'nt) *adj.* Having or exhibiting a milky iridescence like that of an opal. [OPAL + -ESCENT.] **—o·pal·es·cence** *n.*

o·pal·ine (ṓp'l-īn) *adj.* Opalescent.
~*n.* A whitish opalescent or opaque glass.

o·paque (ə-páyk, ō-) *adj.* **1. a.** Impenetrable by light; neither transparent nor translucent. **b.** Not reflecting light; without lustre; dull: *an opaque finish.* **2.** Impenetrable by any form of radiant energy other than visible light: *opaque to ultraviolet radiation.* **3. a.** Obscure or unintelligible: *an opaque remark.* **b.** Obtuse; dense.
~*n.* Something that is opaque; especially, an opaque pigment used to darken parts of a photographic print or negative. [Middle English *opake,* assimilated to French *opaque,* both from Latin *opācus†,* dark.] **—o·paque** *tr.v.* **—o·paque·ly** *adv.* **—o·paque·ness** *n.*

op art (op) *n.* Sometimes capital **O,** capital **A.** A form of abstract art that uses geometric shapes, lines, or the like, to create an optical illusion of movement. [*Op,* short for *optical.*]

op. cit. (óp sit) *adv.* In the work cited. [Latin *opere citato*]

O·PEC (ṓ-pek) Organisation of Petroleum Exporting Countries.

o·pen (ṓpən) *adj.* Also *poetic* **ope** (ōp). **1. a.** Affording unobstructed entrance and exit; not shut or closed: *His mouth was open; an open*

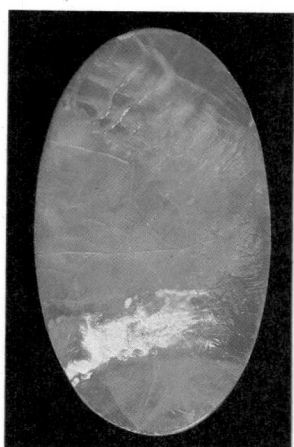

opal *The basic material of an opal is colourless – the vivid colours are produced by impurities, or by light catching on minute cracks in the stone. Opals range in colour from pearly white, through yellows and reds, to the most valuable black or blue gems.*

op art

THE ART OF ILLUSION
Paintings that deceive the eye

Op, or optical, art is a form of abstract art that became popular in the early 1960s. Based on geometric shapes, lines, stripes, or waves, it depends for its effects on deceiving the eye. The paintings create an illusion of movement. The French artist Victor Vasarély (1908–) and the British artist Bridget Riley (1931–) are well-known exponents.

MOVING PICTURE *A segment from* Fall, *which Bridget Riley painted in emulsion on board in 1963. The painting was constructed by using a template, or cut-out shape, of undulating curves as a drawing guide some 240 times across the board. Every alternate space was filled in with black.*

door. **b.** Affording unobstructed passage or view; spacious and unenclosed: *open countryside.* **2. a.** Having no protecting or concealing cover; exposed: *an open wound; an open sports car.* **b.** Unconcealed; undisguised; blatant: *an open disregard for manners.* **3.** Not sealed, tied, or folded: *an open package; an open newspaper.* **4. a.** Having small holes; porous. **b.** Having interspersed gaps, spaces, or intervals: *open columns; open fingers.* **c.** Widely spaced or leaded. Said of printed matter. **5. a.** Accessible to all; unrestricted: *an open meeting.* **b.** Having no restrictions with regard to the status or age of a person: *an open competition.* **6. a.** Ready or willing to entertain or consider; susceptible. Used with *to*: *open to persuasion.* **b.** Unprotected; vulnerable: *open to attack.* **7. a.** Available; obtainable: *The job is still open.* **b.** Available for use; active: *an open account.* **c.** *British.* Not crossed. Said of a cheque. **d.** Available as an option: *two courses open to us.* **8.** Ready to transact business; operating: *When is the zoo open?* **9.** To be considered further; without a definite conclusion: *an open question.* **10. a.** Characterised by lack of pretence; candid; undissembling: *an open nature.* **b.** Free of prejudice; receptive to new ideas and arguments: *an open mind.* **11.** *Music.* **a.** Not stopped by a finger. Said of a string of an instrument such as a guitar. **b.** Not stopped at either end. Said of an organ pipe. **c.** Produced by an unstopped string or hole, or without the use of slides, valves, or keys: *an open note on a trumpet.* **12.** *Phonetics.* **a.** Articulated with the tongue in a low position: *The vowel sound in the word "far" is open.* **b.** Ending in a vowel or diphthong: *an open syllable.* **13. a.** Not frosty; clement: *open weather.* **b.** Not frozen over so as to prevent passage: *open waters.* **14.** *Mathematics.* **a.** Designating or pertaining to an interval that does not contain the end points. **b.** Designating or pertaining to a set in which each point has points in its neighbourhood that also belong to the set. —See Synonyms at **frank.**

~*v.* **opened, opening, opens.** —*tr.* **1.** To cause to become open; release from a closed or fastened position. **2.** To remove obstructions from; clear. **3.** To make or force an opening in: *open an old wound.* **4.** To form spaces or gaps between; spread out: *soldiers opening ranks.* **5. a.** To remove the cover, cork, or lid from; expose: *Open the box.* **b.** To remove the wrapping from; unseal; undo: *opened the parcel.* **6.** To unfold so that the inner parts are displayed; spread out: *a newspaper opened at the sports page.* **7. a.** To begin; initiate; commence: *open a meeting.* **b.** To commence the operation of or start business in: *open an account; open a shop.* **c.** In certain games, such as cricket, or in some card games, to start (a specified action): *He opened the bowling; opened the bidding.* **8.** To permit the use of; make available; especially, to declare ceremonially to be ready for use or action: *The Queen opened Parliament.* **9.** To make more responsive or understanding. **10.** To reveal the secrets of; bare. —*intr.* **1.** To become open or unfastened. **2. a.** To draw apart; separate: *The wound opened under pressure.* **b.** To spread apart; separate. **3.** To extend; unfold: *The gardens opened out onto a stretch of woodland.* **4.** To come into view; become revealed: *The plain opened before us.* **5.** To become receptive or understanding. **6. a.** To begin; commence: *I opened with a bid.* **b.** To begin business or operation: *When does the shop open?* **c.** To give or have the first public performance: *The film opens in March.* **7.** To give access or view. Usually followed by *into* or *onto*: *The door opens into a passage.* **3.** *Law.* To make preliminary statements in court. Used of counsel. —**open up.** *Informal.* **1.** To speak or act freely and unrestrainedly. **2.** To begin shooting with guns. **3.** To accelerate. **4. a.** To make accessible: *The railway opened up remoter regions.* **b.** To make available (opportunities, for example). **5.** To transform from dull routine: *Amateur dramatics opened up her life.*

~*n.* **1. a.** An unobstructed area of land or water; an opening or clearing. **b.** The outdoors. Preceded by *the.* **2.** An undisguised or unconcealed state. Preceded by *the*: *The affair was brought into the open.* **3.** A tournament or contest in which both professional and amateur players may participate. [Middle English *open,* Old English *open,* from Germanic *upanaz* (unattested).] —**o·pen·a·ble** *adj.* —**o·pen·ly** *adv.* —**o·pen·ness** *n.*

o·pen-air (ṓpən-aír) *adj.* Outdoor: *an open-air concert.*

o·pen-and-shut (ṓpən-ənd-shút) *adj.* Presenting no difficulties; easily settled: *an open-and-shut case.*

open book *n.* A person whose mind, motives, or character are easily understood.

o·pen-cast mining (ṓpən-kaast || -kast) *n.* A method of mining by excavating the surface of the ground, rather than by sinking shafts underground. Also *U.S.* "strip mining".

open chain *n. Chemistry.* A linear arrangement of atoms in a molecule. Compare **closed chain.**

open circuit *n.* An electrical circuit in which there is no continuous loop, so that no current can flow. Compare **closed circuit.**

open city *n.* A city that is declared demilitarised during a war, thus, under international law, gaining immunity from attack.

open court *n.* A court that is open to the public.

open day *n.* An occasion when an institution, such as a school, may be inspected by the friends or relatives of its members, or by the general public. Also *U.S.* "open house".

open door *n.* **1.** An unhindered opportunity for progress; free access. **2.** Admission to all on equal terms. **3.** A policy whereby a nation opens its foreign and internal trade to nationals of all other nations on equal terms. —**o·pen-door** (ṓpən-dór || -dṓr) *adj.*

o·pen-end·ed (ṓpən-éndid) *adj.* **1.** Not restrained by definite limits, restrictions, or structure. **2.** Open or adaptable to change. **3.** Having no fixed repayment date: *an open-ended mortgage.* **4.** Inconclusive or indefinite. **5.** Allowing for a spontaneous, unstructured response: *an open-ended question.*

o·pen·er (ṓpənər, ṓpnər) *n.* **1.** One that opens; especially, a device used to cut open tins or prise off bottle caps. **2.** The player who starts the action in certain games, as: **a.** In cricket, either of a side's first two batsmen. **b.** In poker, one who begins the betting. **3.** *Plural.* In card games such as poker, cards of sufficient value for the holder to open the betting.

o·pen-eyed (ṓpən-īd) *adj.* **1.** Having the eyes wide open as in surprise. **2.** Watchful and alert.

o·pen-faced (ṓpən-fáyst) *adj.* Having an undisguised or sincere face or expression.

o·pen-hand·ed (ṓpən-hándid) *adj.* Giving freely; generous. —**open-hand·ed·ly** *adv.* —**o·pen-hand·ed·ness** *n.*

o·pen-heart (ṓpən-hárt) *adj.* Of, pertaining to, or designating surgery in which the heart is exposed while its normal functions in the circulatory system are assumed by external apparatus.

o·pen-heart·ed (ṓpən-hártid) *adj.* **1.** Frank. **2.** Kindly.

o·pen-hearth (ṓpən-hárth) *adj.* **1.** Designating or pertaining to a reverberatory furnace used in the production of high-quality steel. **2.** Designating steel produced in such a furnace.

open house *n.* **1.** A situation in which friends are always welcome to enjoy the hospitality offered at one's home: *keep open house.* **2.** The extending of hospitality or acceptance to all: *a policy of open house towards refugees.* **3.** *U.S.* An **open day** *(see).* —**o·pen-house** (ṓpən-hówss) *adj.*

o·pen·ing (ṓpəning, ṓpning) *n.* **1.** The act of becoming open or being made to open. **2.** An open space serving as a passage or gap. **3.** A hole or aperture. **4.** The first period or stage: *The opening of the book was dull.* **5.** The first occasion for or performance of something, such as a play. **6.** A specific pattern or series of initial moves in certain games, especially chess. **7.** A favourable opportunity or chance. **8.** An unfilled job or position; a vacancy. **9.** *Law.* Preliminary remarks made by counsel to the court or jury.

opening time *n.* In Britain, the time at which pubs or bars are open to serve drinks. Compare **closing time.**

open letter *n.* A letter on a subject of general interest, addressed to an individual but intended for general readership, as published in a newspaper for example.

open market *n.* A market in which supply and demand determine prices and where there is no external interference, as from a government.

open marriage *n.* A marriage in which both partners are free to pursue sexual relationships with others.

o·pen-mind·ed (ṓpən-mīndid) *adj.* Having a mind receptive to new ideas or to reason; free from prejudice or bias. —**o·pen-mind·ed·ly** *adv.* —**o·pen-mind·ed·ness** *n.*

o·pen-mouthed (ṓpən-mówthd || -mówtht) *adj.* Having an open mouth; especially, gaping in astonishment.

open order *n. Military.* A formation where there are open spaces between military or naval units; especially, in a ceremonial parade, a formation whereby easier access between ranks of troops is afforded to an inspecting officer.

o·pen-plan (ōpən-plán) *adj.* Having few or no walls or partitions.

open prison *n.* A prison reserved for certain categories of prisoner and designed to allow more freedom of movement than in a conventional prison.

open sandwich *n.* A slice of bread with meat, cheese, salad, or other garnish on top, eaten as a snack.

open season *n.* **1.** A period when hunting or fishing is permitted for a particular game animal or fish. Compare **close season. 2.** *Informal.* A situation in which criticism is unrestrained.

open secret *n.* Something purporting to be a secret that is in fact widely known.

open ses·a·me (séssəmi, sézzəmi) *n.* An unfailing means of gaining admittance or attaining success. [From the formula used by Ali Baba in the *Arabian Nights* to open the door of the robbers' cave.]

open shop *n.* A business establishment or factory in which workers are employed without regard to union membership. Compare **closed shop, union shop.**

Open University *n.* In Britain, a university whose courses are designed especially for mature students and conducted by such means as television, radio, and correspondence. Preceded by *the.*

open verdict *n.* A verdict of death given by a coroner's jury but with the cause unstated.

o·pen·work (ṓpən-wurk) *n.* Ornamental or structural work, as of metal or embroidery, containing numerous openings, usually in set patterns. —**o·pen·work** *adj.*

op·er·a[1] (óppərə, ópprə) *n.* **1.** A form of theatrical presentation in which a dramatic performance is set to music. See **grand opera, music drama, operetta. 2. a.** A presentation of this kind. **b.** A work of this kind. **3.** A theatre designed primarily for operas. [Italian, from Latin *opera,* works.]

opera[2]. Alternative plural of **opus.**

op·er·a·ble (óppərə-b'l, ópprə-) *adj.* **1.** Capable of being used or operated: *an outmoded but operable motor.* **2.** Capable of being put into practice; practicable: *an operable plan.* **3.** Capable of being treated by surgical operation: *an operable stage of cancer.* —**op·er·a·bil·i·ty** (-bílləti) *n.*

opera buf·fa (bṓōfə) *n., pl.* **opere buffe** (óppə-ray bṓō-fay). Also *French* **o·pé·ra bouffe** (bōōf). **1.** Comic opera, especially in the 18th century. **2.** A performance of such an opera. [Italian : OPERA + *buffa,* feminine of *buffo,* comic, BUFFO.]

opera cloak *n.* A cloak worn at a formal occasion such as a theatrical performance or a party.

o·pé·ra co·mique (óppərə ko-méek; French ō-pay-ráa) *n., pl.* **opéras comiques** (*pronounced as singular*). **1.** Opera that, in addition to musical solos and ensembles, has dialogue that is spoken rather than sung. **2.** An opera of this type or a performance of it. [French, "comic opera".]

opera glasses *pl. n.* Small, low-powered binoculars for use especially at a theatrical performance.

opera hat *n.* A collapsible top hat.

opera house *n.* A theatre designed chiefly for presenting operas.

op·er·and (óppə-rand ‖ -rənd) *n. Mathematics.* A quantity, variable, or function on which an operation is performed. For example, in d*y*/d*x*, *y* is the operand. See **operator**. [Latin *operandum*, something to be worked upon, neuter gerundive of *operāri*, to work.]

op·er·ant (óppərənt) *adj.* **1.** Operating to produce effects; effective. **2.** *Psychology.* Characterising, pertaining to, or designating a response or behaviour elicited, from a rat for example, by an environment rather than by a specific stimulus and reinforced by rewarding consequences in the environment.
~*n.* **1.** One that operates. **2.** *Psychology.* An instance of operant behaviour. [Latin *operāns* (stem *operānt*-), present participle of *operāri*, to OPERATE.]

opera se·ri·a (séer-i-ə) *n., pl.* **opere serie** (óppə-ray séer-i-ay). **1.** Italian opera of a type popular especially in the 17th and 18th centuries, having serious themes and elaborate formal arias. **2.** An opera of this type or a performance of it. [Italian.]

op·er·ate (óppə-rayt) *v.* **-ated, -ating, -ates.** —*intr.* **1.** To function effectively; work: *The system is operating well.* **2. a.** To have an effect or influence. **b.** To bring about a desired or proper effect: *The medicine took some time to operate.* **3.** To perform surgery. **3.** To carry on a military or naval action or campaign. —*tr.* **1.** To run or control the functioning of: *operate a machine.* **2.** To conduct the affairs of; manage: *operate a business.* **3.** To bring about; effect. [Latin *operāri*, to work, from *opus* (stem *oper*-), a work.]

op·er·at·ic (óppə-ráttik) *adj.* **1.** Of, pertaining to, or typical of the opera: *an operatic aria.* **2.** Histrionic or implausible in a way considered characteristic of grand opera. [From OPERA (influenced by DRAMATIC).] —**op·er·at·i·cal·ly** *adv.*

op·er·at·ics (óppə-ráttiks) *pl. n.* Histrionics.

operating table *n.* The table-like structure on which a patient lies during a surgical operation.

operating theatre *n.* The room in which surgical operations are carried out.

op·er·a·tion (óppə-ráysh'n) *n. Abbr.* **op., Op. 1.** The act, process, or way of operating. **2.** The state of being operative or functioning: *in operation.* **3.** A process or series of acts performed to effect a certain purpose or result. **4.** A process or method of productive activity: *the operation of writing.* **5.** *Medicine.* Any procedure for remedying an injury, ailment, or dysfunction in a living body, especially one performed with instruments. **6.** *Mathematics.* A process or action, such as addition, substitution, transposition, or differentiation, performed in a specific sequence and in accordance with specific rules of procedure. **7.** A military or naval action, campaign, or project: *a combined operation.* [Middle English *operacioun*, from Old French *operation*, from Latin *operātiō* (stem *operātiōn*-), from *operāri*, to OPERATE.]

op·er·a·tion·al (óppə-ráysh'n'l) *adj.* **1.** Of or pertaining to an operation or a series of operations. **2.** Of, for, or engaged in military operations. **3.** Serviced and declared fit for proper functioning: *an operational aircraft.* **4.** In use. —**op·er·a·tion·al·ly** *adv.*

op·er·a·tion·al·ism (óppə-ráysh'n'l-iz'm) *n. Philosophy.* The doctrine that the meanings of many scientific concepts are derived from or given by specific operations performed to investigate the phenomena to which the concepts allegedly refer. —**op·er·a·tion·al·ist** *n.*

operational research *n.* Mathematical or scientific analysis of the systematic efficiency and performance of manpower, machinery, equipment, and policies used in a government, military, or commercial operation, providing quantitative information which may be used in decision-making. Also called "operations research", "O.R.".

op·er·a·tive (óppə-rətiv, ópprətiv ‖ -raytiv) *adj.* **1.** Exerting influence or force: *operative laws.* **2.** Functioning effectively; efficient. **3.** Significant; relevant. **4.** Engaged in, concerned with, or related to physical or mechanical activity. **5.** Of, pertaining to, or resulting from a surgical operation.
~*n.* **1. a.** A skilled worker, especially in industry. **b.** Broadly, any worker. **2.** *U.S.* **a.** A secret or trusted agent. **b.** A private detective. —**op·er·a·tive·ly** *adv.*

op·er·a·tor (óppə-ráytər) *n.* **1.** A person who operates a mechanical device. **2.** A person employed at a telephone exchange or switchboard to connect calls or assist callers. **3.** The owner or director of a business or industrial concern. **4.** A dealer in stocks or commodities. **5.** *Mathematics.* A symbol or symbols standing for a mathematical operation, such as a plus sign representing addition or d/d*x* representing differentiation of the following term or function in an equation. See **operand**. **6.** *Informal.* A shrewd and sometimes unscrupulous person who gets what he wants by devious means: *a smooth operator.*

o·per·cu·late (ō-pérkew-lət, -lit, -layt) *adj.* Also **o·per·cu·lat·ed** (-laytid). Having an operculum.

o·per·cu·lum (ō-pérkew-ləm) *n., pl.* **-la** (-lə) or **-lums. 1.** *Biology.* A lid or flap covering an aperture, such as the gill cover in some fishes, the horny flap covering the shell opening in snails or other molluscs, or the lid of a moss capsule. **2. a.** *Anatomy.* Any flap or lid, such as the layer of tissue over an erupting tooth. **b.** A plug of mucus that fills the opening of the womb in a pregnant woman. [Latin, a lid, cover, diminutive formation from *operīre*, to cover.] —**o·per·cu·lar** *adj.* —**o·per·cu·lar·ly** *adv.*

o·pe·re buf·fe. Plural of **opera buffa.**

o·pe·re se·ri·e. Plural of **opera seria.**

op·e·ret·ta (óppə-réttə) *n.* A theatrical production that has many of the musical elements of opera, but is lighter and more popular in subject and style, and contains spoken dialogue. Also called "light opera". [Italian, diminutive of OPERA.]

op·er·on (óppə-ron) *n. Genetics.* A cluster of genes in physical proximity to one another, which act together, under the control of a regulator gene outside the operon, to determine the production of a set of functionally related enzymes. [From OPERATE.]

op·er·ose (óppə-rōss, -rōz) *adj. Archaic.* **1.** Involving great labour; laborious. **2.** Industrious; diligent. [Latin *operōsus*, from *opus* (stem *oper*-), work.] —**op·er·ose·ly** *adv.* —**op·er·ose·ness** *n.*

oph·i·cleide (óffi-klīd, ōfi-) *n.* A former musical wind instrument consisting of a long, tapering brass tube bent double and having keys. [French *ophicléide* : Greek *ophis*, snake (see **ophidian**) + *kleis* (stem *kleid*-), key.]

o·phid·i·an (ō-fíddi-ən) *adj.* Of or pertaining to snakes; snakelike.
~*n.* Any member of the suborder Ophidia or Serpentes; a snake; a serpent. [New Latin *Ophidia*, from Greek *ophis*, snake, serpent.]

oph·i·ol·o·gy (óffi-óllə̄ji, ōfi-) *n.* The scientific study of snakes. [Greek *ophis*, snake (see **ophidian**) + -LOGY.] —**oph·i·o·log·i·cal** (ə-lójik'l) *adj.* —**oph·i·ol·o·gist** (-óllə̄jist) *n.*

o·phite (ō-fīt, óffīt) *n.* **1.** A mottled-green rock composed of diabase. **2.** Any of various green rocks, such as serpentine. [Latin *ophītes*, from Greek *ophītēs*, serpentine (stone), from *ophis*, serpent.]

o·phit·ic (ō-fíttik, o-) *adj. Mineralogy.* **1.** Of or pertaining to ophite. **2.** Having a structure composed of laths of plagioclase crystals occurring within an individual anhedral pyroxene crystal.

Oph·iu·chus (o-féwkəss, óffi-ōōkəss) *n.* A constellation in the equatorial region near Hercules and Scorpius. [Latin *Ophiūchus*, from Greek *ophioukhos*, "serpent-holder" : *ophis*, snake + *ekhein*, to hold.]

oph·thal·mia (of-thál-mi-ə ‖ op-) *n.* Also **oph·thal·mi·tis** (óf-thal-mí-tiss ‖ óp-). Inflammation of the eye, especially of the conjunctiva. Now used chiefly in compounds. [Middle English *obtalmia*, from Late Latin *ophthalmia*, from Greek *ophthalmos*, eye.]

oph·thal·mic (of-thál-mik ‖ op-) *adj.* **1.** Of or pertaining to the eye or eyes; ocular. **2.** Affected by ophthalmia. [Greek *ophthalmikos*, from *ophthalmos*, eye.]

ophthalmo– *comb. form.* Indicates the eye or eyeball; for example, **ophthalmology, ophthalmoscope.** [Greek, from *ophthalmos*, eye.]

oph·thal·mol·o·gist (óf-thal-móllə̄jist ‖ óp-) *n. Abbr.* **ophthal.** A medical practitioner specialising in treatment of eye diseases.

oph·thal·mol·o·gy (óf-thal-móllə̄ji ‖ óp-) *n. Abbr.* **ophthal.** The branch of medical science dealing with the anatomy, functions, pathology, and treatment of the eye. [OPHTHALMO- + -LOGY.] —**oph·thal·mo·log·i·cal** (-thál-mə-lójik'l) *adj.* —**oph·thal·mo·log·i·cal·ly** *adv.*

oph·thal·mom·e·ter (óf-thal-mómmitər ‖ óp-) *n.* An optical instrument for measuring astigmatism. Also called "keratometer". [OPHTHALMO- + -METER.] —**oph·thal·mo·met·ric** (of-thál-mə-méttrik ‖ op-), **oph·thal·mo·met·ri·cal** *adj.*

oph·thal·mo·scope (of-thál-mə-skōp ‖ op-) *n.* An instrument consisting essentially of a mirror with a hole and fitted with lenses of different strengths, and used to examine the interior of the eye through the pupil. [OPHTHALMO- + -SCOPE.] —**oph·thal·mo·scop·ic** (-skóppik), **oph·thal·mo·scop·i·cal** *adj.* —**oph·thal·mos·co·py** (óf-thal-móskəpi ‖ op-) *n.*

O·phuls (ōfəlss; German óp-hülss), **Max,** born Max Oppenheimer (1902–57). German film director. Among his ornate, romantic films are *La Ronde* (1950) and *Lola Montes* (1955).

–opia *n. comb. form.* Indicates a specified visual condition or defect; for example, **diplopia, senopia.** [Greek *-ōpia*, from *ōps*, eye.]

o·pi·ate (ōpi-ət, -it, -ayt) *n.* **1.** Any of various sedative narcotic drugs containing opium or one or more of its derivatives. **2.** Any sedative or narcotic drug. **3.** Anything that relaxes or induces sleep or torpor.
~*adj.* **1.** Consisting of or containing opium. **2.** Causing or producing sleep or sedation.
~*tr.v.* (ōpi-ayt) **opiated, -ating, -ates. 1.** To subject to the action of an opiate. **2.** To dull or deaden as if with a narcotic drug. [Medieval Latin *opiātum*, an opiate, from *opiātus*, treated with opium, soporific, from Latin *opium*, OPIUM.]

o·pine (ō-pín, ə-) *tr.v.* **opined, opining, opines.** *Formal.* To hold or state as an opinion; think. [Old French *opiner*, from Latin *opīnāri*, to think.]

o·pin·ion (ə-pín-yən) *n.* **1.** A belief or conclusion held with confidence, but not substantiated by positive knowledge or proof. **2. a.** An evaluation or judgment based on special knowledge and given by an expert: *a medical opinion.* **b.** A formal statement given by a legal expert of his views on a particular case. **3.** A judgment or estimation of the worth or value of a person or thing: *In my opinion, he is a fool.* **4.** The common, usual, or prevailing feeling or sentiment: *public opinion.* **5.** *Law.* A formal statement by a judge or jury of the legal reasons and principles for the conclusions of the court. —**be of the opinion.** To hold the view. [Middle English, from Old

opium poppy *The seeds of this flower are used in cakes and bread and are crushed for oil. The drugs morphine, codeine, and heroin are derived from an Asian variety of the plant.*

opossum *There are more than 70 species of this marsupial in South America, but only one – the Virginian or common opossum pictured here – is found in North America as well. It hunts at night for insects and small animals, and when threatened, it feigns death – hence the term "playing possum".*

French, from Latin *opīniō* (stem *opiniōn-*), from *opīnārī*, to think.]
Synonyms: *opinion, view, sentiment, feeling, impression, belief, conviction, persuasion, judgment.*

o·pin·ion·at·ed (ə-pín-yə-naytid) *adj.* Holding stubbornly and often unreasonably to one's own opinions. **—o·pin·ion·at·ed·ly** *adv.* **—o·pin·ion·at·ed·ness** *n.*

o·pin·ion·a·tive (ə-pín-yə-naytiv) *adj. Rare.* **1.** Pertaining to or of the nature of an opinion; based on opinion. **2.** Opinionated. **—o·pin·ion·a·tive·ly** *adv.*

opinion poll *n.* **1. a.** A canvassing of a selected sample group of persons to analyse public opinion on a particular question. **b.** The result of this canvassing.

o·pis·tho·branch (ə-písthə-brangk) *n.* Any marine gastropod mollusc of the subclass Opisthobranchia, characterised by a shell that is reduced or absent. [New Latin, from Greek *opisthen*, behind + -BRANCH.]

op·is·thog·na·thous (óppiss-thógnəthəss) *adj.* Having receding jaws. [Greek *opisthen*, behind + -GNATHOUS.] **—op·is·thog·na·thism** *n.*

o·pi·um (ṓpi-əm) *n.* **1.** A bitter yellowish-brown drug prepared from the dried juice of unripe seed capsules of the opium poppy, containing many alkaloids such as morphine, noscapine, codeine, and papaverine. It may be chewed and smoked for its narcotic effects and is still used in medicine as an analgesic for severe pain. Habitual use induces strong addiction; excessive use is fatal. **2.** Something that numbs or stupefies. [Middle English, from Latin, from Greek *opion*, poppy juice, opium, diminutive of *opos*, juice.]

opium den *n.* A room or establishment where opium is sold and used.

opium poppy *n.* A poppy plant, *Papaver somniferum*, originally of Asia Minor, having greyish-green leaves and variously coloured flowers. The juice of its unripe seed capsules is the source of opium.

o·pos·sum (ə-póss'm) *n., pl.* **-sums** or collectively **opossum. 1.** Any of various nocturnal, arboreal marsupials of the family Didelphidae, especially *Didelphis marsupialis*, of the Americas. **2.** Any of several Australian marsupials of the family Phalangeridae, some of which have valuable fur. In both senses, also called **possum.** [Algonquian (Powhatan) *āpassūm*, from Proto-Algonquian *waap-a't-hemwa* (unattested), "white beast".]

opossum shrimp *n.* Any of various shrimplike crustaceans of the order Mysidacea, the females of which carry their eggs and young in a brood pouch.

opp. opposite.

Op·pen·hei·mer (óppən-hīmər), **J(ulius) Robert** (1904–67). U.S. physicist. He led the Los Alamos bomb project (1942–45), and was responsible for the building of the first nuclear bomb. He opposed the development of the hydrogen bomb and was eventually dismissed (1953) by the Atomic Energy Commission as a security risk. He won the Fermi award (1963) for his work on the peaceful application of nuclear energy.

op·pi·dan (óppidən) *adj.* Of or pertaining to a town.
~n. An inhabitant of a town. [Latin *oppidānus*, town-dweller (outside Rome), from *oppidum*, town.]

op·po·nent (ə-pṓnənt) *n.* One that opposes another or others in a battle, contest, controversy, debate, or game.
~adj. **1.** Acting against an antagonist or an opposing force. **2.** Opposite. **3.** *Anatomy.* Designating muscles that act to bring two parts into opposing positions. [Latin *oppōnēns* (stem *oppōnent-*), present participle of *oppōnere*, to OPPOSE.] **—op·po·nen·cy** *n.*
Synonyms: *opponent, adversary, antagonist, competitor, rival.*

op·por·tune (óppər-tewn, -téwn || -tōōn, -tōōn) *adj.* **1.** Suited or right for a particular purpose. **2.** Occurring at a time that is fitting or advantageous. [Middle English, from Old French *opportun*, from Latin *opportūnus*, seasonable, (originally of wind) "blowing towards the harbour" : *ob-*, to + *portus*, harbour.] **—op·por·tune·ly** *adv.* **—op·por·tune·ness** *n.*

op·por·tun·ist (óppər-téw-nist, -tew- || -tṓō-, -tōō-) *n.* A person who takes advantage of any opportunity to achieve an end, usually with little or no regard for moral principles. [French *opportuniste*, from *opportunisme*, from Italian *opportunismo*, from *opportuno*, opportune, from Latin *opportūnus*, OPPORTUNE.] **—op·por·tun·ism** *n.* **—op·por·tun·ist, op·por·tun·is·tic** (-nístik) *adj.*

op·por·tu·ni·ty (óppər-téw-nəti || -tṓō-) *n., pl.* **-ties. 1.** A favourable or advantageous combination of circumstances; a suitable occasion or time. **2.** A prospect; a chance: *job opportunities.* [Middle English *opportunite*, from Old French, from Latin *opportūnitās* (stem *opportūnitāt-*), from *opportūnus*, OPPORTUNE.]
Usage: *Opportunity* may be followed by an infinitve form of the verb, introduced by *to* (*She has the opportunity to leave now*); a participial form of the verb, introduced by *of* or *for* (*You have a wonderful opportunity for getting back your job*); or a noun phrase, introduced by *for* (*an opportunity for new ideas*).

op·pos·a·ble (ə-pṓzə-b'l) *adj.* **1.** Capable of being opposed. **2.** Capable of being placed opposite or in opposition to something. Said especially of the thumb, which can be placed opposite the other digits. **—op·pos·a·bil·i·ty** (-bílləti) *n.*

op·pose (ə-pṓz) *v.* **-posed, -posing, -poses.** *—tr.* **1.** To be in contention or conflict with; combat; resist: *oppose the enemy force.* **2.** To be against; be hostile to: *oppose new ideas.* **3.** To place in opposition, or be in opposition to; contrast or counterbalance by antithesis. **4.** To place so as to be opposite something else. *—intr.* To act or be in opposition to something. [French *opposer*, from Old French, from Latin *oppōnere* (past participial stem *opposit-*), to set against : *ob-*, against + *pōnere*, to put.] **—op·pos·er** *n.*
Synonyms: *oppose, resist, withstand, combat, contest.*

op·po·site (óppə-zit, -sit. *The pronunciations* -zīt, -sīt *are not standard.*) *adj. Abbr.* **op., opp. 1.** Placed or located directly across from something else or from each other; lying in corresponding positions in relation to an intervening space or object: *opposite sides of a building.* **2.** Facing the other way; moving or tending away from each other: *opposite directions.* **3.** Contrary or antithetical in nature or tendency; diametrically opposed; altogether different. **4.** *Botany.* Growing in pairs on either side of a stem. Said especially of leaves. Compare **alternate.**
~n. **1.** A person or thing that is opposite or contrary to another. **2.** A word that means the opposite of another; an **antonym** *(see).* **3.** *Archaic.* An opponent or antagonist.
~adv. In an opposite position or positions: *sat opposite at the table.*
~prep. **1.** Across from or facing: *opposite the bank.* **2.** In a complementary dramatic role to: *played opposite her.* [Middle English, from Old French, from Latin *oppositus*, from the past participle of *oppōnere*, to OPPOSE.] **—op·po·site·ly** *adv.* **—op·po·site·ness** *n.*
Synonyms: *opposite, contrary, antithetical, contradictory.*
Usage: As a noun, *opposite* is followed by *of* (*The opposite of good is bad*), though *to* is sometimes heard in casual speech. As an adjective, the normal preposition following is *to:* (*His ideas on the subject are opposite to mine*), though *from* is also acceptable. As a preposition, *opposite* can sometimes by followed by *to*: *the house opposite mine; the house opposite to mine.*

opposite number *n.* A person who holds a position which corresponds to that of a specified person, as in an organisation or team; a counterpart.

opposite sex *n.* Men considered in relation to women, or women considered in relation to men. Preceded by *the.*

op·po·si·tion (óppə-zísh'n) *n.* **1.** The act or condition of opposing or of being in conflict; resistance or antagonism. **2. a.** A position or location opposite to or facing another. **b.** Placement in such a position or location. **3.** That which is or serves as an obstacle. **4. a.** *Often capital* **O.** A political party or organised group opposed to the group, party, or government in power. Preceded by *the.* **b.** Any person or group hostile to the ideas of another. **5.** *Astronomy.* **a.** A geometric configuration in which the Earth lies on a straight line between the Sun and a planet. **b.** The position of the exterior planet in this configuration. **6.** *Logic.* The relation existing between two propositions having an identical subject and predicate but differing in quantity, quality, or both. **7.** *Linguistics.* Contrast between two phonemes or other elements of a language that have a relationship such that the contrast is significant. [Middle English *opposicioun* (only in the astronomical sense), from Old French *opposition*, from Medieval Latin *oppositiō* (stem *oppositiōn-*), from Latin, act of opposing, from *oppōnere* (past participial stem *opposit-*), to OPPOSE.] **—op·po·si·tion·al** *adj.* **—op·po·si·tion·ist** *n.*

op·press (ə-préss || ō-) *tr.v.* **-pressed, -pressing, -presses. 1.** To subjugate or persecute by unjust or tyrannical use of force or authority. **2.** To weigh heavily upon, especially so as to depress the mind or spirits: *Poverty oppressed me.* **3.** *Obsolete.* To overwhelm or crush. [Middle English *oppressen*, from Old French *oppresser*, from Medieval Latin *oppressāre*, frequentative of Latin *opprimere* (past participle *oppressus*), to press against : *ob-*, against + *premere*, to press.] **—op·pres·sor** *n.*

op·pres·sion (ə-présh'n || ō-) *n.* **1.** The act of oppressing, or the state of being oppressed. **2.** That which oppresses or burdens. **3.** A feeling of being heavily weighed down, either mentally or physically; depression; weariness.

op·pres·sive (ə-préssiv || ō-) *adj.* **1.** Harsh; tyrannical. **2.** Causing a state of physical or mental discomfort or weariness: *an oppressive afternoon.* —See Synonyms at **burdensome.** [Medieval Latin *oppressīvus*, from Latin *opprimere*, to OPPRESS.] **—op·pres·sive·ly** *adv.* **—op·pres·sive·ness** *n.*

op·pro·bri·ous (ə-prṓbri-əss) *adj.* **1.** Expressing or carrying a sense of disgrace or contemptuous scorn: *opprobrious epithets.* **2.** Shameful; infamous. [Middle English, from Old French *opprobreus*, from Late Latin *opprobriōsus*, from Latin *opprobrium*, OPPROBRIUM.] **—op·pro·bri·ous·ly** *adv.*

op·pro·bri·um (ə-prṓbri-əm) *n.* **1.** Disgrace inherent in or arising from shameful conduct; ignominy. **2.** Scornful reproach or contempt: *a term of opprobrium.* **3.** A cause of shame or disgrace. —See Synonyms at **disgrace.** [Latin, "a reproach against", dishonour : *ob-*, against + *probrum*, reproach, infamy.]

op·pugn (ə-péwn) *tr.v.* **-pugned, -pugning, -pugns.** To oppose, contradict, or call into question. [Middle English *oppugnen*, from Latin *oppugnāre*, to fight against : *ob-*, against + *pugnāre*, to fight.] **—op·pug·nant** (ə-púg-nənt) *adj.* **—op·pug·nant·ly** *adv.* **—op·pugn·er** *n.*

op·sin (óp-sin) *n.* The protein constituent of **rhodopsin** *(see).*

-opsis *n. comb. form.* Indicates view, appearance, or resemblance; for example, **coreopsis.** [Greek, from *opsis*, sight, appearance.]

op·son·ic (op-sónnik) *adj.* Of, pertaining to, or having the effect of opsonin. [OPSON(IN) + -IC.]

opsonic index *n.* The ratio of the number of bacteria per phagocyte in the blood of a test patient to the number in the blood of a normal individual. It is a measure of the power of a patient's serum to destroy invading bacteria.

op·son·i·fy (op-sónni-fī) *tr.v.* **-fied, -fying, -fies.** To make (invading bacteria) susceptible to phagocytosis by opsonic action; opsonise. [OPSON(IN) + -FY.] **—op·son·i·fi·ca·tion** (-fi-káysh'n) *n.*

op·so·nin (ópsənin) *n.* A substance naturally present in the blood that renders invading bacteria susceptible to phagocytosis. [Latin *opsōnium,* relish (opsonin being a "relish" enabling the body to "digest" bacteria), indirectly from Greek *opsōnein,* to buy food or delicacies, from *opson*†, relish, delicacy.]

op·so·nise, op·so·nize (ópsə-nīz) *tr.v.* **-nised, -nising, -nises. 1.** To form opsonins in. **2.** To opsonify. [From OPSONIN.] **—op·so·ni·sa·tion** (-nī-záysh'n || *U.S.* -ni-) *n.*

-opsy *n. comb. form.* Indicates an examination; for example, **biopsy.** [New Latin *-opsia,* condition of the eyes, examination, from Greek, from *opsis,* sight, appearance.]

opt (opt) *intr.v.* **opted, opting, opts.** To make a choice or decision; indicate a preference. Often used with *for.* **—opt out.** To withdraw; decide against participating; especially, to refuse to conform with conventional society. Often used with *of.* [French *opter,* from Latin *optāre.*]

opt. 1. optative. **2.** optical; optician; optics. **3.** optimum. **4.** optional.

op·ta·tive (op-táytiv, óptətiv) *adj.* **1.** Expressing a wish or choice. **2.** *Abbr.* **opt.** *Grammar.* **a.** Designating a mood of verbs in some languages, such as Greek, used to express a wish. **b.** Designating a statement using a verb in the subjunctive mood to indicate a wish or desire; for example, *Had I the means, I would do it.*
~*n.* *Abbr.* **opt.** *Grammar.* **1.** The optative mood. **2.** A verb or expression in this mood. [Middle English, from Old French *optatif,* from Late Latin *optātīvus,* from Latin *optāre,* to choose, wish.] **—op·ta·tive·ly** *adv.*

op·tic (óptik) *adj.* **1.** Of or pertaining to the eye or to vision. **2.** Of or pertaining to the science of optics.
~*n.* **1.** An eye. Not in technical usage. **2.** Any of the components of an optical instrument. **3.** *British. Capital* **O.** A trademark for a valved tap fitted to inverted bottles of spirits, especially in public houses, and releasing an exact measure into a glass when pressed. [Old French *optique,* from Medieval Latin *opticus,* from Greek *optikos,* from *optos,* visible.]

op·ti·cal (óptik'l) *adj. Abbr.* **opt. 1.** Of or pertaining to sight: *an optical illusion.* **2.** Designed to assist sight: *optical instruments.* **3.** Of or pertaining to optics. **4.** Using or depending on light: *an optical character reader.* **—op·ti·cal·ly** *adv.*

optical activity *n. Chemistry.* A property of a substance that enables it to rotate the plane of transmitted polarised light.

optical bench *n.* An adjustable arrangement of lenses, mirrors, and other components for experiments on optical systems.

optical character reader *n. Abbr.* **OCR** A device for converting printed characters into digital form by optical character recognition. See **optical scanner.**

optical character recognition *n. Abbr.* **OCR** A method of scanning printed characters with an optical device and transforming them into electrical signals, so that the data can be stored magnetically in a computer.

optical fibre *n.* A very thin, typically flexible, optically transparent fibre, as of glass or plastic, through which light can be transmitted by successive internal reflections.

optical glass *n.* Any of various types of clear glass, such as flint and crown glass, having known reproducible optical properties and used in lenses, prisms, and the like.

optical isomer *n. Chemistry.* A type of **isomer** *(see).*

optical maser *n. Physics.* A laser, especially one that produces visible radiation. No longer in technical usage.

optical rotation *n. Physics & Chemistry.* Rotation of the plane of polarisation of polarised light by a substance that shows optical activity.

optical scanner *n.* A device for converting printed or illustrated matter into digital form. See **optical character reader.**

optic axis *n.* An optical path through a crystal along which a ray of light can pass without undergoing double refraction.

optic chiasma *n.* The X-shaped structure formed by the two optic nerves when they cross each other on the undersurface of the brain.

optic disc *n.* An area of the retina, the **blind spot** *(see).*

op·ti·cian (op-tísh'n) *n. Abbr.* **opt. 1.** One who makes lenses and eyeglasses. **2.** One who sells lenses, glasses, and other optical instruments. Compare **optometrist.** [French *opticien,* from Medieval Latin *optica,* OPTICS.]

optic nerve *n.* A motor nerve that connects the retina of the eye with the brain.

op·tics (óptiks) *n. Used with a singular verb. Abbr.* **opt.** *Physics.* The scientific study of light and vision, chiefly of the generation, propagation, and detection of electromagnetic radiation having wavelengths greater than X-rays and shorter than microwaves. [Latin *optica,* from Greek *optika,* neuter plural of *optikos,* OPTIC.]

op·ti·mise, op·ti·mize (ópti-mīz) *tr.v.* **-mised, -mising, -mises.** To make the most effective use of. **—op·ti·mi·sa·tion** (-mī-záysh'n || *U.S.* -mi-) *n.*

op·ti·mism (ópti-miz'm) *n.* **1.** A tendency or disposition to expect the best possible outcome, or to dwell upon the most hopeful aspects of a situation. **2.** *Philosophy.* **a.** The doctrine, asserted by Leibniz, that our world is the best of all possible worlds. **b.** The belief that the universe is improving and that good will ultimately triumph over evil. [French, from Latin *optimum,* best, OPTIMUM.]

op·ti·mist (ópti-mist) *n.* **1.** One who habitually or in a particular case expects a favourable outcome. **2.** A believer in philosophical optimism. **—op·ti·mis·tic** (-místik) *adj.* **—op·ti·mis·ti·cal·ly** *adv.*

op·ti·mum (ópti-məm) *n., pl.* **-ma** (-mə) or **-mums.** *Abbr.* **opt.** The best or most favourable condition, degree, or amount for a particular situation.
~*adj.* Also **op·ti·mal** (-m'l). Most favourable or advantageous; best. [Latin, from neuter of *optimus,* best.] **—op·ti·mal·ly** *adv.*

op·tion (ópsh'n) *n.* **1.** The act or an instance of choosing; a choice. **2.** The power or right of choosing; freedom to choose. **3. a.** The exclusive right, usually obtained for a fee, to buy or sell property within a stated time and at a stated price. **b.** A right to buy or sell specific securities or commodities at a stated price within a stated time. **4.** Something chosen or available as a choice. **—keep** or **leave (one's) options open.** To withhold one's decision; remain uncommitted. —See Synonyms at **choice.** [French, from Latin *optiō* (stem *optiōn-*), choice.]

op·tion·al (ópsh'n'l) *adj. Abbr.* **opt.** Left to choice; not compulsory or automatic. **—op·tion·al·ly** *adv.*

op·tom·e·ter (op-tómmitər) *n.* An instrument used for measuring the refraction of the eye. [Greek *optos,* visible + METER.]

op·tom·e·trist (op-tómmətrist) *n.* One who specialises in optometry. Compare **optician.**

op·tom·e·try (op-tómmətri) *n.* The techniques or profession of examining, measuring, and treating certain visual defects by means of corrective lenses or other methods that do not require the supervision of a doctor. [Greek *optos,* visible.] **—op·to·met·ric** (óptə-méttrik), **op·to·met·ri·cal** *adj.*

op·u·lent (óppewlənt) *adj.* **1.** Having or characterised by great wealth; rich. **2.** Abundant; plentiful; lavish. [Latin *opulentus,* from *opēs,* wealth.] **—op·u·lent·ly** *adv.* **—op·u·lence, op·u·len·cy** *n.*

o·pun·ti·a (o-púnshi-ə, ō-) *n.* Any of various cacti of the genus *Opuntia*; especially, the **prickly pear** *(see).* [New Latin, from Latin, a herb, after *Opus* (stem *Opunt-*), city of Locris, in ancient Greece, where it grew abundantly.]

o·pus (ṓpəss, óppəss) *n., pl.* **opuses** or **opera** (óppərə, ṓpərə). *Abbr.* **op., Op.** A creative work; especially, a musical composition. Used with a number to designate the order of a composer's works. [Latin, work.]

o·pus·cule (o-púskewl, ō-) *n.* A small and minor work. [French, from Latin *opusculum,* diminutive of *opus,* work, OPUS.]

Op·us De·i (óppəss dáy-ee) *n.* An international organisation of Roman Catholic priests and laymen founded in 1928 to foster Christian ideals, especially among professional people. [Latin, God's work.]

or¹ (or; *occasional weak form* ər) *conj.* Used to indicate: **1. a.** An alternative, usually only before the last term of a series: *hot or cold; this, that, or the other.* **b.** The second of two alternatives, the first being preceded by *either* or *whether*: *Your answer is either ingenious or wrong*; *She didn't know whether to laugh or to cry.* **c.** *Archaic.* The first of two alternatives, with the force of *either* or *whether.* **2.** A synonymous or equivalent expression: *acrophobia, or fear of great heights.* **3.** Uncertainty or indefiniteness: *two or three.* [Middle English *or,* contraction of *other,* alteration (influenced by EITHER, WHETHER) of Old English *oththe,* from Common Germanic.]
Usage: When all of the elements connected by *or* are singular, the verb they govern must be singular: *Beer or wine is included in the price.* When all of the elements are plural, the verb is also plural: *Either the cars or the bikes are in need of recall.* When the elements are of different number, the verb generally agrees with the element closest to it: *Either the books or the newspaper is correct; Either the newspaper or the books are correct.* See also **either, neither, nor.**

or² *conj. Archaic.* Before. Followed by *ever* or *ere.*
~*prep. Archaic.* Before. [Middle English *ar, or,* Old English *ār,* early, before, from Old Norse.]

or³ *n. Heraldry.* The metal gold, represented by a white field sprinkled with small dots.
~*adj. Heraldry.* Of gold. Used after the noun: *a bezant or.* [Old French, from Latin *aurum.*]

-or¹ *n. suffix.* Indicates the person or thing performing the action expressed by the root verb; for example, **investor, percolator.** [Middle English *-our, -or,* from Anglo-French *-eour,* Old French *-eor, -eur,* partly from Latin *-or,* and partly from Latin *-ātor* (past participial stem *-āt-* + *-or*).]
Usage: The normal suffix for forming an agent or instrument noun from a verb is *-er (sing-singer),* but *-or* is often used, especially in words which have been borrowed from other languages or in forms derived from Latin: *actor, inspector, percolator.* Occasionally both forms are available, in which case the *-er* ending tends to be used for persons and the *-or* ending for things, as in *converter* ("someone who converts") and *convertor* ("a machine which converts"), but this is not a hard and fast distinction.

-or² *n. suffix.* **1.** Used to indicate a state, quality, or activity; for example, **horror, torpor. 2.** *U.S.* Variant of **-our.** [Middle English *-or, -our,* from Old French *-eur,* from Latin *-or,* abstract suffix.]

O.R. *n.* **Operational research** *(see).*

o·ra. Plural of **os** (mouth).

or·ache (órrich) *n.* Also *chiefly U.S.* **or·ach.** Any of various plants of the genus *Atriplex*; especially, *A. hortensis,* whose edible leaves resemble spinach. [Middle English *arage, orage,* from Anglo-French *arasche,* modification of Vulgar Latin *atrapica* (unattested), variant of Latin *atriplex,* from Greek *atraphaxus*†.]

or·a·cle (órrək'l, órrik'l) *n.* **1.** A shrine consecrated to the worship and consultation of a prophetic god, such as that of Apollo at Delphi. **2.** The priest or other transmitter of prophecies at such a shrine. **3.** A prophecy made known at such a shrine, often in the form of an enigmatic statement or allegory. **4.** Any person or

opuntia *A genus of cacti which takes its name from the ancient Greek city of Opus where it grew abundantly. The plants are sometimes grown for their juicy fruit, known as prickly pears.*

PRONUNCIATION KEY

a, trap; aa, father; ai, fair;
ar, star; aw, lawn; ay, play;
b, bb, stab; rubber;
ch, church; ck, ticket;
d, dd, dead; ladder; e, dress;
ee, bee; er, defer; ew, few;
ewr, pure; ə, about;
ər, letter; f, ff, fife; differ;
g, gg, giggle; h, hat; i, kit;
ī, price; īr, fire; j, judge;
k, kick; l, ll, let; 'l, needle;
m, mm, man; n, nn, no;
'n, sudden; ng, thing; o, lot;
ō, no; ŏŏ, foot; ōō, shoe;
oor, poor; ow, cow;
owr, hour; oy, boy;
p, pp, pepper; r, rr, red;
s, ss, sauce; sh, ship;
t, tt, totter; th, thick; th, this;
smooth; u, cut; ur, turn;
v, vv, valve; w, wet; y, yes;
z, zz, zebra; zh, vision;
pleasure

IN FOREIGN WORDS:

aN, oN, Saint-Saëns;
hl, Llanelli; Hluhluwe;
kh, loch; lough; Khaled

STRESS MARK:

ín-sīt, insight; in-sī́t, incite

agency considered to be a source of wise counsel or prophesy; an infallible authority or judge. **5.** Any pronouncement or claim considered to be infallible. **6.** *Theology.* A command or revelation from God. **7.** In the Old Testament, the sanctuary of the Temple; the holy of holies. I Kings 6:16, 19–23. **8.** *Capital* **O.** In Britain, a trademark for a viewdata service broadcast by the IBA, providing information on a wide variety of subjects. **—work the oracle.** To achieve one's ends by scheming or manoeuvring. [Middle English, from Old French, from Latin *ōrāculum,* from *ōrāre,* to speak.]

o·rac·u·lar (ə-ráckewlər, o-, ō-) *adj.* **1.** Of or pertaining to an oracle. **2.** Resembling or characteristic of an oracle: **a.** Solemnly prophetic: *an oracular warning.* **b.** Brief and enigmatic; mysterious. [Latin *ōrāculum,* ORACLE.] **—o·rac·u·lar·ly** *adv.*

or·a·cy (áwrə-si, órrə-) *n.* The ability to speak, hear, and understand language. [Latin *os* (stem *or-*), mouth + -ACY, by analogy with *literacy.*]

o·ral (áw-rəl || ṓ-, órrəl) *adj.* **1.** Spoken, rather than written. **2. a.** Of or pertaining to the mouth: *oral hygiene.* **b.** Designating the surface of an invertebrate animal, such as a jellyfish, on which the mouth is situated. **3.** Used in or taken through the mouth: *an oral thermometer; oral vaccine.* **4.** Consisting of or using speech: *oral instruction.* **5.** *Phonetics.* Designating a speech sound emitted through the mouth only, with the nasal passages closed. **6.** In psychoanalysis: **a.** Of, pertaining to, or designating the first stage of psychosexual development of the infant, when sexual gratification is derived chiefly from stimulation of the mouth parts. **b.** Designating a personality fixated at this state, characterised by such traits as greediness and dependence. Compare **anal, genital.**
~*n.* *Often plural.* An academic examination in which the questions and answers are spoken rather than written. [Late Latin *ōrālis,* from Latin *ōs* (stem *ōr-*), the mouth.] **—o·ral·ly** *adv.*

orang-utan *Found in the tropical rain forests of Borneo and Sumatra, the orang-utan has very long arms and is chiefly vegetarian. Its name comes from a Malay phrase meaning "man of the woods".*

oral contraceptive *n.* *Medicine.* Any of various hormone compounds in pill form, typically consisting of an oestrogen and a progestogen, used in specific sequence to prevent ovulation and conception. Also informally called the "Pill".

oral history *n.* **1.** The practice or technique of gathering historical information by interviewing, and usually tape-recording, eyewitnesses of or participants in historical events. **2.** The information so gathered, or a historical study based on it.

or·ange (órrinj, órrənj) *n.* **1.** Any of several evergreen trees of the genus *Citrus,* cultivated in tropical and subtropical regions, and having fragrant white flowers and round fruit with a yellowish-red rind and a sectioned, pulpy interior; especially, *C. sinensis,* the sweet orange, and *C. aurantium,* the Seville or sour orange. **2.** The fruit of these trees, having a sweetish, acid juice. **3.** Any of several plants or trees resembling the orange in some respect, such as the **mock orange** *(see).* **4.** Any of a group of colours between red and yellow in hue, of medium lightness and moderate saturation. **5.** Orange clothing. **6.** An orange object. [Middle English, from Old French *orenge, orange,* from Arabic *nāranj,* from Persian *nārang,* from Sanskrit *nārangaț†,* orange, orange tree.] **—or·ange** *adj.* **—or·ange·y, or·ange·ish** *adj.*

Or·ange¹ (órrinj) Also **Or·ange-Nas·sau** (-nássaw). A princely European family who have been rulers of the Netherlands since 1815.

Or·ange² (órrinj; *French* o-róNzh). Town in the Vaucluse département, southeast France. Founded by Charlemagne, it was the seat of the House of Orange, whose descendants still rule the Netherlands.

Orange³. South African river, the longest in southern Africa. Rising in the Drakensberg mountains of Lesotho, it flows 2 093 kilometres (1,300 miles) west to join the Atlantic at Alexander Bay.

or·ange·ade (órrinj-áyd) *n.* A drink, often carbonated, of orange flavoring, sugar, and water. [French : ORANGE + -ADE.]

orange flower oil *n.* An essential oil, **neroli** *(see).*

orange flower water *n.* A solution of neroli in water, used in pharmaceutical preparations and cooking.

Orange Free State. *Afrikaans* **Oranje Vrystaat.** A province of South Africa, lying on the plateau of the Highveld. The economy is chiefly agricultural. Mineral resources include gold, uranium, and coal. Boer farmers settled in the territory from the 1820s but it was annexed by Britain as the Orange River Sovereignty (1848). After conflicts with the Boers, Britain granted the territory independence as the Orange Free State (1854). The British again annexed the Free State as the Orange River Colony (1900), but it was granted self-government (1907) and became a founding province in the Union of South Africa (1910). Area, 129 152 square kilometres (49,866 square miles). Capital, Bloemfontein.

Or·ange·man (órrinj-mən, -man) *n., pl.* **-men** (-mən, -men). **1.** A member of a secret society founded in Northern Ireland in 1795 to maintain the political and religious ascendancy of Protestantism. **2.** Any Irish Protestant, especially of Northern Ireland. [After William, Prince of *Orange* (William III).]

Orangeman's Day *n.* July 12, a public holiday in Northern Ireland celebrated by Protestants as the anniversary of the battles of the Boyne (1690) and of Aughrim (1691). Also called "Orange Day".

orange pekoe *n.* A grade of black tea from Sri Lanka or India, consisting of the end buds and their surrounding small leaves.

or·ang·e·ry (órrinj-əri, -ri) *n., pl.* **-ries.** A glass-walled enclosure used, especially formerly, for growing oranges in cool climates, or more commonly nowadays as a greenhouse. [French *orangerie,* from *orange,* from Old French, ORANGE.]

orange stick *n.* A stick of orangewood with tapering ends, used to manicure the fingernails and cuticles.

or·ange-tip (órrinj-tip) *n.* A European butterfly, *Anthocharis cardamines,* having whitish wings tipped with orange.

or·ange·wood (órrinj-wŏŏd) *n.* The fine-grained wood of the orange tree, used in fine woodwork.

o·rang-u·tan (ə-ráng-ŏŏ-tán, aw-, o-, -taán, áw-rangŏŏ-taan, -tan) *n.* Also **o·rang-ou·tang** (-tang). An arboreal anthropoid ape, *Pongo pygmaeus,* of Borneo and Sumatra, having a shaggy reddish-brown coat and very long arms. [Malay *orang hutan* : *ōrang,* man + *hūtan,* forest.]

o·rate (ə-ráyt, aw-, o- || ō-) *intr.v.* **orated, orating, orates. 1.** To speak publicly in a pompous, oratorical manner. **2.** To deliver an oration. [Back-formation from ORATION.]

o·ra·tion (ə-ráysh'n, aw-, o- || ō-) *n.* **1.** A formal address or speech, especially one given on some special occasion such as an academic celebration or funeral. **2.** A speech, written out and memorised, as for debating contests. **3.** Any high-flown speech. [Latin *ōrātiō* (stem *ōrātiōn-*), from *ōrāre,* to speak.]

or·a·tor (órrətər, órritər) *n.* **1.** A person who delivers an oration. **2.** A person skilled in the art of public speaking. [Middle English *oratour,* from Old French *orateur,* from Latin *ōrātor,* from *ōrāre,* to speak.] **—or·a·tor·ship** *n.*

or·a·tor·i·cal (órrə-tórrik'l) *adj.* Of or pertaining to an orator, or to oratory. **—or·a·tor·i·cal·ly** *adv.*

or·a·to·ri·o (órrə-táwri-ō || -tṓri-) *n., pl.* **-os.** A musical composition for solo voices, choir, and orchestra, usually telling a sacred story. [Italian, from *Oratorio,* the Oratory of St. Philip Neri at Rome, where famous musical services were held in the 16th century, from Late Latin *ōrātōrium,* ORATORY (chapel).]

or·a·to·ry¹ (órrə-təri, -tri) *n.* **1.** The art of public speaking; rhetoric. **2.** Rhetorical style or skill, or an instance of it. [Old French *(art) oratoire,* from Latin *(ars) ōrātōria,* (the art) of public speaking, from *ōrātōrius,* of an orator, oratorical, from *ōrātor,* ORATOR.]

oratory² *n., pl.* **-ries. 1.** A place for prayer, such as a small private chapel. **2.** *Capital* **O.** A Roman Catholic religious society founded by Saint Philip Neri and consisting of secular priests *(Oratorians).* **3.** *Capital* **O.** Any branch or church of such a society. [Middle English *oratorie,* from Anglo-French, from Late Latin *ōrātōrium (templum),* (place) of prayer, from *ōrātōrius,* of praying, from Latin *ōrāre,* to pray, speak.]

orb (orb) *n.* **1.** A sphere or spherical object. **2.** An area of endeavour, influence, or activity; a sphere; a province: *the orb of reason.* **3. a.** A heavenly body. **b.** *Archaic.* The Earth. **4.** Any of a series of concentric transparent spheres revolving about the Earth, postulated by medieval astronomers as support for the stars and planets. **5.** A jewelled globe surmounted by a cross, part of the regalia of a sovereign. **6.** *Poetic.* An eye. **7.** *Archaic.* A circle or an object of circular form. **8.** The orbit of a planet or satellite.
~*v.* **orbed, orbing, orbs.** *—tr.* **1.** To shape into a circle or sphere. **2.** *Archaic.* To encircle; enclose. *—intr.* To move in an orbit. [Old French *orbe,* from Latin *orbis†,* orb, disc.]

or·bic·u·lar (awr-bíckew-lər) *adj.* Also **or·bic·u·late** (-lət, -lit), **or·bic·u·lat·ed** (-laytid). **1.** Orb-shaped; circular or spherical. **2.** *Botany.* Circular and flat. Said especially of leaves. **3.** Rounded out; complete: *"The household ruin was thus full and orbicular."* (Thomas De Quincey). [Middle English *orbiculer,* from Old French *orbiculaire,* from Late Latin *orbiculāris,* from Latin *orbiculus,* diminutive of *orbis,* ORB.] **—or·bic·u·lar·i·ty** (-lárrəti) *n.* **—or·bic·u·lar·ly** *adv.*

or·bit (órbit) *n.* **1.** The path of a celestial body or man-made satellite as it revolves around another body. **2.** The path of any body in a field of force surrounding another body; for example, the movement of an atomic electron in relation to a nucleus. **3. a.** A range of activity, experience, or knowledge. **b.** A range of control or influence. **4.** Either of two bony cavities in the skull containing an eye and its external structures; an eye socket. **5.** The circular area of tissue surrounding the eye of a bird or an insect.
~*v.* **orbited, -biting, -bits.** *—tr.* **1.** To put into or cause to move in an orbit: *The first man-made satellite was orbited in 1957.* **2.** To revolve around (a centre of attraction). *—intr.* To revolve or move in an orbit. [Latin *orbita,* from *orbitus,* circular, from *orbis,* ORB.]

or·bit·al (órbit'l) *adj.* Of or pertaining to an orbit.
~*n.* **1.** *Chemistry.* A region around the nucleus of an atom *(atomic orbital)* or surrounding nuclei in a molecule *(molecular orbital)* containing one electron or a pair of electrons and characterised by a fixed energy. **2.** A **ring road** *(see).* **—or·bit·al·ly** *adv.*

orbital decay *n.* The effect of atmospheric drag on an orbiting body, such as an Earth-orbiting satellite, causing eventual re-entry.

orbital velocity *n.* The minimum velocity required to maintain a satellite in orbit around a celestial body.

orc (ork) *n.* **1.** Any of several whales; especially, the **killer whale** *(see).* **2.** Any of various mythical or fictional monsters. [Old French *orque,* from Latin *orca,* whale, probably from Greek *oruga,* accusative of *orux,* a pickaxe, hence (from its horn), narwhal, from *oroussein,* to dig.]

Or·cad·i·an (awr-káydi-ən) *n.* A native or inhabitant of the Orkney Islands. [Latin *Orcades,* Orkney Islands.] **—Or·cad·i·an** *adj.*

or·ce·in (órsi-in) *n.* A reddish dye made by oxidising orcinol with hydrogen peroxide in the presence of ammonia and used also as a biological stain and a mild antiseptic.

or·chard (órchərd) *n.* **1.** An area of land devoted to the cultivation of fruit or nut trees. **2.** The trees cultivated in such an area. [Middle English *orchard,* Old English *ortceard, ortgeard* : Latin *hortus,* a garden + Old English *geard,* YARD.]

or·ches·tra (ór-ki-strə, -ke-, -kə- || awr-késtrə) *n. Abbr.* **orch. 1. a.** A

MAKE-UP OF THE MODERN SYMPHONY ORCHESTRA

Striking a balance through the skill of the conductor

The typical modern symphony orchestra, with 90–120 players, has gradually evolved since the late 18th century. Before that, the composition of an orchestra was dependent on the instruments available and their technical limitations. Handel composed his *Water Music* in 1717 for two oboes, two horns, a bassoon, strings, and a harpsichord. Beethoven had to use trumpets with fixed pitch (as valves had not then been invented) and included trombones only in his later symphonies. During the 19th century, the orchestra settled into its familiar modern shape with balanced groups of instruments.

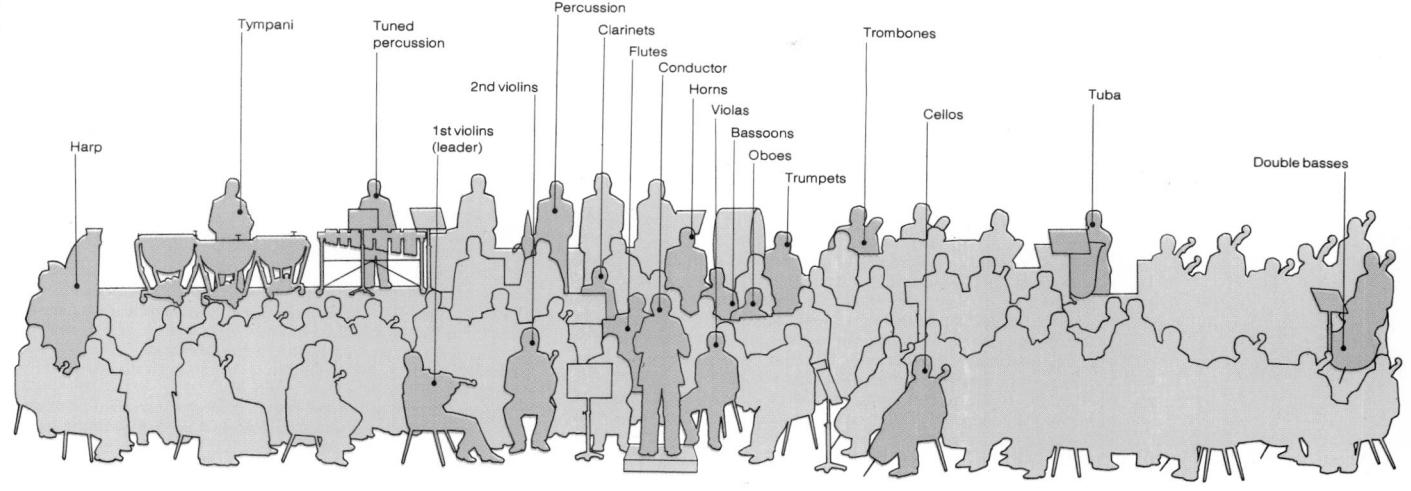

THE FOUR FAMILIES OF INSTRUMENT IN THE MODERN SYMPHONY ORCHESTRA

The woodwind section usually has two flutes, two oboes, two clarinets, two bassoons, and sometimes a piccolo. The percussion may include tympani, a xylophone, a glockenspiel, a marimba, chimes and gongs, drums, cymbals, tambourines, triangles, castanets, rattles, shakers, and clickers. The strings will have two groups of violins with the same number, usually 15, in each group. The other strings will be up to 12 violas, ten cellos, and eight double basses. The brass includes three trumpets, four French horns, and three trombones, and may include a bass tuba.

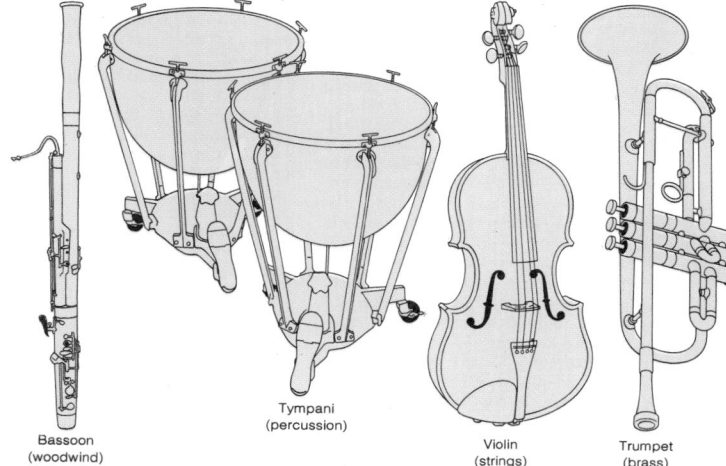

Bassoon (woodwind)

Tympani (percussion)

Violin (strings)

Trumpet (brass)

WHERE THE PLAYERS SIT *The conductor stands on a central rostrum, with the four groups of instruments – woodwind, percussion, brass, and strings – arranged in front of him.*

The principal first violinist – the "leader" of the orchestra – sits on the conductor's left. The other string players sit in groups to the left and right. The woodwind players sit in the centre, with the percussion at the back on the left and the brass at the back on the right.

Extra instruments such as the piano or the harp, shown on the left of the picture, are added when needed for a particular musical work. (The figures in darker shading indicate the principal players of each instrument.)

Before the performance begins, one instrument, usually the oboe, plays a sustained "A" note to which all the other instruments are tuned. The conductor sets the tempo and indicates the beat with his baton. He cues in the players and controls the loudness or softness of the playing. He conducts the music from a full score which shows him what each individual instrument should play. He is responsible for the overall interpretation of the music.

---

large group of musicians who play together on various musical instruments, usually including strings, woodwinds, brass instruments, and percussion instruments. **b.** A group of musicians all playing a specified instrument: *a gamelan orchestra.* **c.** The instruments played by such a group of musicians. **2.** An orchestra pit. **3.** *Chiefly U.S.* **a.** The front section of seats nearest the orchestra pit in a theatre; the stalls. **b.** The entire main floor of a theatre. Also called "parquet". **4.** In ancient Greek theatres, a semicircular space in front of the stage on which the chorus danced. [Latin *orchēstra,* from Greek *orkhēstra,* from *orkheisthai,* to dance.] —**or·ches·tral** (awr-kĕstrəl) *adj.* —**or·ches·tral·ly** *adv.*

orchestra pit *n.* In theatres and concert halls, the area where the musicians sit, immediately in front of and below the stage. Also called "orchestra", "pit".

or·ches·trate (ór-ki-stráyt, -ke-, -kə-) *tr.v.* -**trated,** -**trating,** -**trates.** **1. a.** To compose or arrange (music) for performance by an orchestra. **b.** To provide a musical arrangement for. **2.** To arrange, put together, or organise so as to achieve a desired overall effect. [French *orchestrer,* from *orchestre,* orchestra, from Latin *orchēstra,* ORCHESTRA.] —**or·ches·tra·tor** *n.*

or·ches·tra·tion (ór-ki-stráysh'n, -ke-, -kə-) *n. Abbr.* **orch. 1.** A musical composition that has been orchestrated. **2.** Arrangement of music for performance by an orchestra.

or·ches·tri·on (awr-kĕstri-ən) *n.* Also **or·ches·tri·na** (órki-stréenə). A large mechanical musical instrument, resembling a barrel organ and producing sound in imitation of an orchestra. [*Orchestra* + *melodion.*]

or·chid (órkid) *n.* **1.** Any of numerous epiphytic or terrestrial plants of the family Orchidaceae, found worldwide, though chiefly in the tropics, and often having brightly coloured flowers of unusual shapes. **2.** The flower of any of these plants, especially one cultivated for ornament or personal adornment. [Latin *orchis* (stem *orchid-*), from Greek *orkhis,* testicle, hence (from the shape of its root) orchid.]

or·chi·da·ceous (órki-dáyshəss) *adj.* **1.** Of, pertaining to, or characteristic of the orchid family of plants. **2.** Suggesting ostentatious luxury; showy. [New Latin *Orchidaceae* (family); *orchis,* ORCHID + -ACEOUS.]

or·chi·dec·to·my (órki-déktəmi) *n.* Surgical removal of a testicle. [Greek *orkhis* (stem *orkhid-*), testicle + -ECTOMY.]

or·chil (ór-kil, -chil) *n.* Also **ar·chil** (ár-). **1.** Any of several lichens, from which a dye is obtained. **2.** The violet-coloured dyestuff obtained from these lichens. Also called "cudbear". [Middle English, from Old French *orcheil,* perhaps ultimately from Latin *herba urceolāris,* plant used to polish pitchers, from *urceolus,* diminutive of *urceus,* pitcher.]

or·chis (órkiss) *n.* Any orchid of the genus *Orchis,* often having purple flowers. See **fringed orchis.** [New Latin *Orchis,* from Latin, ORCHID.]

or·chi·tis (awr-kítiss) *n.* Inflammation of one or both testicles. [New Latin, from Greek *orkhis,* testicle + -ITIS.]

or·ci·nol (ór-si-nol || -nōl) *n.* A white crystalline compound present in orchil and used as a source of the dye orcein.

OR circuit *n.* A computer logic gate, an **OR gate** *(see).*

Or·cus (órkəss). *Roman Mythology.* **1.** The world of the dead; Hades. **2.** The underworld god Pluto. [Latin *Orcus*†.]

ord. **1.** order. **2.** ordinal. **3.** ordinance. **4.** ordinary. **5.** ordnance.

or·dain (awr-dáyn) *tr.v.* **-dained, -daining, -dains.** **1. a.** To invest with ministerial or priestly authority; confer holy orders upon. **b.** To authorise as a rabbi. **2. a.** To order by virtue of superior authority. **b.** To decree as part of the order of nature or of the universe. **3.** To prearrange unalterably; predestine: *by fate ordained.* [Middle English *ordeinen,* from Anglo-French *ordeiner,* from Late Latin *ōrdināre,* from Latin, to arrange in order, from *ōrdō* (stem *ōrdin-*), order.] **—or·dain·er** *n.* **—or·dain·ment** *n.*

or·deal (awr-déel || órdeel) *n.* **1. a.** A severely difficult or painful experience that tests character or endurance. **b.** A trying experience. **2.** A former method of legal trial in which the accused was subjected to physically painful or dangerous tests by way of determining guilt or innocence, the result being regarded as a divine judgment. [Middle English *ordal,* Old English *ordāl, ordēl,* from Germanic *uzdailjam* (unattested), "a dealing out", judgment, trial : *uz-* (unattested), out + *dailjan* (unattested), to DEAL.]

ordeal bean *n.* The **Calabar bean** *(see).*

or·der (órdər) *n. Abbr.* **O, O., ord.** **1.** A condition of logical or comprehensible arrangement among the separate elements of a group. **2. a.** A condition of methodical or prescribed arrangement among component parts, such that proper functioning or appearance is achieved. **b.** The state, condition, or disposition of a thing: *in good order.* **3. a.** The structures of a given society and the relations defined among individuals and classes constituting it: *the old order.* **b.** The condition in which these structures and relations are maintained and preserved by the rule of law and the police power of the state: *Order was restored after the riot.* **c.** Discipline and good behaviour in any group. **4.** A sequence or arrangement of successive things in time or space. **5.** The established sequence; the customary procedure: *the order of operations.* **6.** A command or direction. **7.** *Military.* **a.** A command given by a superior officer requiring execution of a task or other obedience. **b.** *Plural.* Formal written instructions to report for duty at a stated time and place: *He received his orders to fly to Japan.* **8. a.** A commission or instruction to buy, sell, or supply something. **b.** That which is supplied, bought, or sold. **9. a.** A request for a portion of food by a customer at a restaurant. **b.** The food requested. **10.** *Law.* Any direction or command delivered by a court and entered into the court record, but not included in the final judgment or verdict. **11. a.** Any of several grades of the Christian ministry: *the order of priesthood.* **b.** *Plural.* The office and rank of an ordained minister or priest. **c.** *Plural.* **Holy orders** *(see).* **12.** A prescribed form of religious service for various occasions. **13.** Any of the nine grades or choirs of angels. See **angel.** **14.** An organisation of people united by some common fraternal bond or social aim: **a.** Any of various communities dedicated to a religious life, as through missionary work or monastic contemplation, and often bound by vows of poverty, chastity, and obedience: *the Order of St. Benedict.* **b.** An organisation of knights similarly united: *the Order of the Knights of St. John of Jerusalem.* **15. a.** A group of persons upon whom a government or sovereign has formally conferred honour for unusual service or merit, entitling such persons to wear a special insignia: *the Order of Merit.* **b.** The insignia worn by such persons. **16.** *Usually plural.* A social class: *the lower orders.* **17.** Degree of quality or importance; rank: *poetry of a high order.* **18.** *Architecture.* **a.** Any of several specific styles of classical architecture characterised by the type of column employed, such as **Composite order, Corinthian order, Doric order, Ionic order, Tuscan order** *(all of which see).* **b.** A specific style of architecture: *a cathedral of the Gothic order.* **19.** *Biology.* A taxonomic category of plants and animals ranking above the family and below the class. See **taxonomy.** **20.** *Mathematics.* **a.** An indicated number of successive differentiations to be performed on a function, or that have been performed on a derivative. **b.** The number of elements in a finite group. **c.** The number of rows or columns in a determinant or square matrix. Compare **degree.** **21.** Approximate size or magnitude: *costing somewhere in the order of a million pounds.* **—call to order.** **1.** To request to be quiet and attentive. **2.** To begin (a meeting). **—in order.** **1.** Well organised; under control; according to plan. **2.** Permitted or appropriate. **3.** In correct sequence. **—in order that.** So that. **—in order to.** For the purpose of; so that it is possible to. **—keep order.** To ensure the continuation of order or discipline. **—on order.** Requested but not yet delivered. **—out of order.** **1.** Not working; broken. **2.** Not following the correct sequence. **3.** Not according to rule or general procedure: *The objection is out of order.* **—to order.** According to the buyer's specifications.

~v. **ordered, -dering, -ders.** *—tr.* **1.** To issue a command or instruction to. **2.** To give a command or instruction that (something be done): *The judge ordered a retrial.* **3.** To give an order for; request to be supplied with. **4.** To instruct or force to move to or from a specified locality: *She ordered me out of the house.* **5.** To put in a methodical and systematic arrangement. **6.** To prearrange unalterably; predestine. **7.** *Rare.* To ordain: *He was ordered priest.* *—intr.* To give an order or orders; request that something be done or supplied: *Order now, before prices go up.* —See Synonyms at **command.** **—order about** or **around.** To treat in a domineering way; bully. [Middle English *ordre,* from Old French *ordre,* earlier *ord(e)ne,* from Latin *ōrdō.*] **—or·der·er** *n.*

or·der·ly (órdərli) *adj.* **1.** Having a methodical and systematic arrangement; tidy: *an orderly room.* **2.** Without violence or disruption; peaceful: *an orderly transition of governments.* **3.** *Military.* Of or pertaining to the transmission of military orders.

~n., pl. **orderlies.** **1.** A male attendant in a hospital. **2.** *Military.* A soldier assigned to attend upon a superior officer and carry orders or messages.

~adv. Systematically; regularly. **—or·der·li·ness** *n.*

Synonyms: *orderly, methodical, systematic.*

orderly room *n.* The office used for administration in the barracks of a military unit.

order of magnitude *n. Physics.* **1.** An estimate of size or magnitude expressed as a power of ten: *The Earth's mass is of the order of magnitude of 10^{22} tons, that of the Sun 10^{27} tons.* **2.** A range of values between a specified lower value and an upper value ten times as large: *The masses of the Earth and the Sun differ by five orders of magnitude.*

Order of Merit *n. Abbr.* **O.M.** An honour or title awarded in the United Kingdom for outstanding achievement in any field of endeavour.

Order of Prohibition *n. Law.* See **prohibition** (sense 3).

order of the day *n., pl.* **orders of the day.** **1.** The set of commands or instructions issued by a commanding officer to his men. **2.** The list of business to be discussed by a legislative body on a given day. **3.** The prevailing trend or state of affairs.

Order of the Garter *n.* The highest and most exclusive order of knighthood in the United Kingdom, consisting of members of the royal family and a limited number of knights companion who join the order at the specific behest of the sovereign.

order paper *n.* A list giving the order in which questions are to be raised, especially by a legislative body.

or·di·nal (órdin'l) *adj. Abbr.* **ord.** **1.** Having a specified position in a numbered series: *an ordinal rank of seventh.* **2.** Pertaining to a biological order.

~n. **1.** An ordinal number. **2.** In the Christian Church: **a.** A book of instructions for daily services. **b.** A book of forms for ordination. [Late Latin *ōrdinālis,* from Latin *ōrdō* (stem *ōrdin-*), ORDER.]

ordinal number *n.* A number indicating position in a series or order. The ordinal numbers are first (1st), second (2nd), third (3rd), and so on. Compare **cardinal number.**

or·di·nance (órdinənss) *n. Abbr.* **ord.** **1.** An authoritative command or order. **2.** A custom or practice established by long usage. **3.** A religious rite; especially, Holy Communion. **4.** A statute or regulation. [Middle English *ordinaunce,* from Old French *ordenance,* "the art of arranging", from Medieval Latin *ōrdinantia,* from Latin *ōrdinans,* present participle of *ōrdināre,* to put in order, from *ōrdō* (stem *ōrdin-*), ORDER.]

or·di·nand (órdi-nand) *n.* A prospective priest or minister; one about to be ordained. [Latin *ordinandus,* gerundive of *ordināre,* to ORDAIN.]

or·di·nar·i·ly (órd-'n-rə-li, -in-, -ri-, -ərə-, -əri- || -errəli, -érrəli) *adv.* **1.** As a general rule. **2.** In the regular or usual manner: *ordinarily dressed.* **3.** To the usual extent or degree: *ordinarily large profits.*

or·di·nar·y (órd-'n-ri, -in-, -əri || -erri) *adj.* **1.** Commonly encountered; usual: *"a man to be sought for on great emergencies, but ill adapted for ordinary services"* (Anthony Trollope). **2.** Occurring regularly or periodically; normal. **3.** Average in rank or merit; of no exceptional degree or quality; commonplace. **4.** Having immediate rather than delegated jurisdiction, as a judge might. **5.** *Mathematics.* Designating a differential equation containing no more than two variables and derivatives of one with respect to the other. **6.** Designating an academic degree (a pass degree) that is taken or awarded without honours; general. —See Synonyms at **common.**

~n., pl. **ordinaries.** **1.** A person, object, or situation that is common, normal, or average. **2.** *Law.* A judge or other official with immediate rather than delegated jurisdiction. **3.** In some states of the United States, the judge of a probate court. **4.** *Usually capital* **O.** In the Christian Church: **a.** The part of the Mass that remains unchanged from day to day. Compare **proper.** **b.** A division of the Divine Office containing the unchangeable parts of the office other than the Psalms. **c.** A cleric, such as the residential bishop of a diocese, with ordinary jurisdiction. **5.** *Heraldry.* Any of the simplest and commonest charges, such as the bend or the cross. **6.** Formerly, a priest or minister who visited condemned prisoners in jail. **—in ordinary.** *British.* Officially employed, especially by the monarchy; having regular rather than temporary or delegated responsibilities: *chaplain in ordinary to the sovereign.* **—out of the ordinary.** Extraordinary or exceptional; unusual; abnormal. [Middle English *ordinarie,* from Latin *ōrdinārius,* from *ōrdō* (stem *ōrdin-*), ORDER.] **—or·di·nar·i·ness** *n.*

Ordinary level. See **O level.**

ordinary ray *n. Physics.* The ray of light in double refraction that obeys the ordinary laws of refraction. Compare **extraordinary ray.**

ordinary seaman *n. Abbr.* **O.S.** A seaman of the lowest grade in the merchant navy.

ordinary shares *pl.n. Finance. British.* Capital shares in a company that have exclusive claim on the company's net assets and net income after all prior claims have been paid. Compare **preference shares.** Also *U.S.* "common stock", "equity stock".

or·di·nate (órdin-ət, -it) *adj.* Arranged in regular rows, as spots are on an insect's wings.

PRONUNCIATION KEY

a, trap; aa, father; ai, fair; ar, star; aw, lawn; ay, play; b, bb, stab; rubber; ch, church; ck, ticket; d, dd, dead; ladder; e, dress; ee, bee; er, defer; ew, few; ewr, pure; ə, about; ər, letter; f, ff, fife; differ; g, gg, giggle; h, hat; i, kit; ī, price; īr, fire; j, judge; k, kick; l, ll, let; 'l, needle; m, mm, man; n, nn, no; 'n, sudden; ng, thing; o, lot; ō, no; ŏŏ, foot; ōō, shoe; oor, poor; ow, cow; owr, hour; oy, boy; p, pp, pepper; r, rr, red; s, ss, sauce; sh, ship; t, tt, totter; th, thick; th, this; smooth; u, cut; ur, turn; v, vv, valve; w, wet; y, yes; z, zz, zebra; zh, vision; pleasure

IN FOREIGN WORDS:

aN, oN, Saint-Saëns; hl, Llanelli; Hluhluwe; kh, loch; lough; Khaled

STRESS MARK:

in-sīt, insight; in-sīt, incite

~*n. Symbol* **y** *Mathematics.* The plane Cartesian coordinate representing the distance from a given point to the *x*-axis, measured parallel to the *y*-axis. Compare **abscissa.** [Latin *ōrdināre,* to arrange in order, from *ōrdō* (stem *ōrdin-*), ORDER.]

or·di·na·tion (órdi-náysh'n) *n.* **1.** In the Christian Church: **a.** The ceremony during which a person is admitted to the ministry of a church. **b.** The admission itself. **2.** Any arrangement or ordering.

ord·nance (órdnənss) *n. Abbr.* **ord., ordn. 1.** Military weapons collectively, together with ammunition and the equipment to keep them in good repair. **2.** Heavy guns; artillery. **3.** The military or government department in charge of military equipment. [Middle English *ordinaunce,* ORDINANCE.]

Ordnance Survey *n. Abbr.* **O.S.** In Britain, the government agency in charge of making and checking maps of Scotland, England, and Wales. [After the *Ordnance* Department of the Army, which originally drew up the maps.]

or·do (ór-dō) *n., pl.* **-dines** (-di-neez). *Roman Catholic Church.* An annual calendar containing instructions for the Mass and office to be celebrated on each day of the year. [Medieval Latin *ōrdō,* from Latin, ORDER.]

or·don·nance (órdənənss; *French* awrdo-náNss) *n.* **1.** The arrangement of elements in a literary or artistic composition or architectural plan. **2.** In French history: **a.** A royal decree or body of laws on a specific subject. **b.** An order of a criminal court. [French, variant (influenced by *ordonner,* to order) of Old French *ordenance,* ORDINANCE.]

Or·do·vi·ci·an (órdō-víshi-ən) *adj. Geology.* Of, pertaining to, formed in, or designating the second period of the Palaeozoic era, characterised by the appearance of primitive types of fish.
~*n. Geology.* The Ordovician period. Preceded by *the.* [After the *Ordovices,* an ancient Celtic tribe of North Wales, by analogy with SILURIAN.]

or·dure (órdewr || órjər) *n.* **1.** Excrement; dung. **2.** Something considered to be morally offensive. [Middle English, from Old French, from *ord,* dirty, "disgusting", from Latin *horridus,* horrid, from *horrēre,* to shudder.]

ore (or || ōr) *n.* A mineral or aggregate of minerals from which a valuable constituent, especially a metal, can be profitably mined or extracted. [Middle English *oor, ǫr,* Old English *ār,* brass (in sense influenced by Old English *ora*†, unwrought metal, ore).]

ö·re (örə) *n., pl.* **öre.** A coin equal to $^1/_{100}$ of the krona of Sweden and the krone of Denmark and Norway. [Danish and Norwegian *øre* and Swedish *öre,* from Latin *aureus,* gold coin, from *aurum,* gold.]

o·re·ad (áwri-ad || ṓri-) *n. Greek Mythology.* A mountain nymph. [Greek *Oreias* (stem *Oreiad-*), from *oreios,* of a mountain, from *oros,* mountain. See **oro-.**]

o·rec·tic (o-réktik, ə-) *adj.* Of or pertaining to the appetites or desires. [Greek *orektikos,* from *oregein,* to desire.]

o·re·ga·no (órri-gáanō || *U.S.* ə-réggənō, aw-) *n.* A herb seasoning made from the dried leaves of a species of marjoram, *Origanum vulgare.* [Spanish, marjoram, from Latin *origanum,* Greek *origanon,* oregano, marjoram (probably from a North African language).]

Or·e·gon (órri-gən, -gon || áwri-). Pacific State of the northwest United States containing many areas of great natural beauty. The state is dominated by the Cascade Range, a rugged mountain chain running north to south some 160 kilometres (100 miles) inland. The region was jointly held by Britain and the United States (1818–46) and Oregon Territory was then created (1848). It was admitted to the Union as the 33rd state in 1859. Area, 251 180 square kilometres (96,981 square miles). Capital, Salem.

Oregon fir *n.* The **Douglas fir** *(see).*

Oregon grape *n.* **1.** An evergreen shrub, *Mahonia aquifolium,* of northwestern North America, having fragrant yellow flowers and small, edible, bluish berries. **2.** The berry of this shrub.

oreide. Variant of **oroide.**

O·res·tes (o-résteez, ə-, aw-). *Greek Mythology.* The son of Agamemnon and Clytemnestra, who, with his sister Electra, avenged his murdered father by slaying his mother and her lover Aegisthus.

Ø·re·sund (ö-rə-sŏŏnd). Strait in northern Europe, situated between Sweden and the Danish island of Sjaelland. Connecting the Kattegat with the Baltic Sea, it is an important shipping route.

orfe (orf) *n.* A European freshwater fish, *Idus idus,* with a blue-grey back and a silvery belly. A reddish-gold variety, the golden orfe, is often kept in garden ponds and aquariums. [German and French; akin to Latin *orphus,* Greek *orphos,* sea perch.]

Orff (orf), **Carl** (1895–1982). German composer. The inventor of a system of percussion instruments, he is best known for *Carmina Burana* (1937), a lively setting of medieval poems.

orfray. Variant of **orphrey.**

org. 1. organic. **2.** organisation; organised.

or·gan (órgən) *n.* **1.** A musical instrument consisting of a keyboard and a number of pipes supplied with wind by means of bellows. Sometimes also called "pipe organ". **2.** Any of various other instruments resembling the organ either in mechanism or sound, such as the electronic organ. **3.** *Biology.* A differentiated part of an organism, adapted for a specific function. **4.** The penis. Used euphemistically. **5.** An institution or medium through which or by means of which some action is performed. **6.** An instrument or vehicle of communication; especially, a periodical publication issued by a political party, business firm, or other group. [Middle English, from Old French *organe,* from Late Latin *organum,* church organ, from Latin, implement, instrument, from Greek *organon.*]

or·ga·na. 1. Alternative plural of **organon. 2.** Alternative plural of **organum.**

or·gan·die (órgəndi) *n.* **-dies.** Also *chiefly U.S.* **or·gan·dy.** A transparent crisp fabric of cotton or silk, used for trimming, curtains, and light clothing. [French *organdi*†.] **—or·gan·die** *adj.*

or·gan·elle (órgə-nél) *n. Biology.* A structure within a cell that is specialised for a particular function; for example, the nucleus and the mitochondria. [New Latin *organella,* diminutive of Latin *organum,* ORGAN.]

or·gan-grind·er (órgən-grīndər) *n.* A street musician who plays a barrel organ.

or·gan·ic (awr-gánnik) *adj. Abbr.* **org. 1.** Of, pertaining to, or affecting an organ of the body. **2.** Of, pertaining to, or derived from living organisms. **3. a.** Using or grown with fertilisers and mulches consisting only of animal or vegetable matter, with no use of chemical fertilisers or pesticides: *organic gardening; organic foods.* **b.** Free from chemical injections or additives: *organic meat.* **c.** Simple, basic, and close to nature: *an organic lifestyle.* **4.** Having properties associated with living organisms. **5.** Likened to an organism in organisation or development; interconnected: *society as an organic whole.* **6. a.** Of or constituting an integral part of something; fundamental; structural. **b.** *Law.* Designating or pertaining to the fundamental or constitutional laws and precepts of a government or organisation. **7.** *Chemistry.* Of or designating carbon compounds. Compare **inorganic.** [Old French *organique,* from Late Latin *organicus,* from Greek *organikos,* serving as an instrument, from *organon,* implement, ORGAN.] **—or·gan·i·cal·ly** *adv.*

organic chemistry *n.* The chemistry of carbon compounds. Compare **inorganic chemistry.**

organic disease *n.* Any disease associated with changes in the structure of an organ or tissue. Compare **functional disease.**

or·gan·i·cism (awr-gánni-siz'm) *n.* **1.** The theory that the total organisation of an organism, rather than the functioning of individual organs, is the principal or exclusive determinant of every life process; holism. **2.** The concept or doctrine that society is analogous to a biological organism, especially in its structure. **—or·gan·i·cist** *n. & adj.* **—or·gan·i·cist** *adj. & n.*

or·gan·i·sa·tion (órgə-nī-záysh'n || *U.S.* -ni-) *n. Abbr.* **org. 1.** The act of organising or the process of being organised. **2.** The state or manner of being organised: *a high degree of organisation.* **3.** Something that has been organised or made into an ordered whole. **4.** Something comprising elements with varied functions that contribute to the whole and to collective functions; an organism. **5.** A number of persons or groups having specific responsibilities and united for some purpose or work. **6.** A business, charity, international agency, or similar corporate concern. **—or·gan·i·sa·tion·al** *adj.* **—or·gan·i·sa·tion·al·ly** *adv.*

Organisation of African Unity *n. Abbr.* **OAU** An association formed (1963) by most independent African states to promote mutual help and cooperation.

Organisation of American States *n. Abbr.* **OAS** An association formed (1948) by the 21 American republics to promote mutual help and cooperation.

or·gan·ise, or·gan·ize (órgə-nīz) *v.* **-ised, -ising, -ises.** —*tr.* **1.** To pull or put together into an orderly, functional, structured whole. **2. a.** To arrange or systematise: *organise one's thoughts before speaking.* **b.** To arrange or compose in a desired pattern. **3.** To arrange systematically for harmonious or united action: *organise a strike.* **4.** To establish as an organisation. **5. a.** To cause (employees) to form or join a trade union. **b.** To induce the employees of (a business or industry) to form or join a union: *organise a department store.* —*intr.* **1.** To develop into or assume an organic structure. **2.** To join or form a trade union or other activist group. [Middle English *organysen,* from Old French *organiser,* from Medieval Latin *organizāre,* from Latin *organum,* instrument, ORGAN.]

or·gan·ised (órgənīzd) *adj.* **1.** Well-ordered and efficient; methodical: *Why can't you get organised?* **2.** Designating criminal activities planned in the manner of a commercial business: *organised crime.*

or·gan·is·er (órgə-nīzər) *n.* **1.** One who organises or is skilled at organising. **2.** A group of embryonic cells that releases a substance which stimulates differentiation in other embryonic cells.

or·gan·ism (órgə-niz'm) *n.* **1.** Any living individual; any plant or animal. **2.** Any system regarded as analogous to a living body: *the social organism.* **—or·gan·is·mal** (-nízm'l), **or·gan·is·mic** *adj.*

or·gan·ist (órgənist) *n.* One who plays the organ.

organo– *comb. form.* **1.** Indicates organ or organic; for example, **organology. 2.** Indicates carbon compounds; for example, **organometallic, organophosphorus.** [Middle English, from Medieval Latin *organum,* organ of the body, from Latin, implement, ORGAN.]

organ of Cor·ti (kórti) *n.* A sense organ situated on the inner surface of the cochlea in the inner ear that converts sound vibrations into nerve impulses which are then transmitted to the brain. [After Alfonso *Corti* (1822–88), Italian anatomist.]

or·gan·o·gen·e·sis (órgənō-jénni-siss, awr-gánnō-) *n., pl.* **-ses** (-seez). The origin and development of biological organs. [New Latin : ORGANO- + -GENESIS.] **—or·gan·o·ge·net·ic** (-jə-néttik) *adj.* **—or·gan·o·ge·net·i·cal·ly** *adv.*

or·gan·og·ra·phy (órgə-nóggrəfi) *n.* The scientific description of the organs of animals and plants.

or·gan·o·lep·tic (órgənō-léptik, awr-gánnō-) *adj.* Pertaining to, affecting, involving, or perceived by a sensory organ. [French *organoleptique* : ORGANO- + Greek *lēptikos,* receptive, from *lēptos,* to be

organ *The earliest organ of which there is any record was built in the third century* B.C. *A cathedral organ like this one at Ely Cathedral, Cambridgeshire, England, may have as many as 100 pipes for each note.*

apprehended (by the senses), from *lambanein,* to take, seize, apprehend.] —**or·gan·o·lep·ti·cal·ly** *adv.*

or·gan·ol·o·gy (órgə-nóllǝji) *n.* The study of plant and animal organs and their functions. [ORGANO- + -LOGY.] —**or·gan·o·log·i·cal** (-nǝ-lójik'l) *adj.*

or·gan·o·me·tal·lic (órgǝnō-mi-tál-ik, awr-gánnō-) *adj.* Of, pertaining to, or designating an organic chemical compound that also contains metal atoms.

~*n.* An organometallic chemical compound.

or·ga·non (órgǝ-non) *n., pl.* **-na** (-nǝ) or **-nons.** Also **or·ga·num** (-nǝm) *pl.* **-na** (-nǝ) or **-nums.** *Philosophy.* A set of logical requirements used in scientific investigation or demonstration. [Greek, tool (used as the title of Aristotle's writings on logic).]

or·gan·o·ther·a·py (órgǝnō-thérrǝpi, awr-gánnō-) *n.* The treatment of disease with animal organs or extracts such as insulin and thyroxine. —**or·gan·o·ther·a·peu·tic** (-thérrǝ-péwtik) *adj.*

or·gan·ot·ro·pism (órgǝ-nóttrǝpiz'm) *n.* Also **or·gan·ot·ro·py** (-nóttrǝpi). *Medicine.* The attraction of certain chemical compounds or microorganisms to specific tissues or organs of the body. [ORGANO- + -TROPISM.] —**or·gan·o·trop·ic** (órgǝnō-tróppik, awr-gánnō-) *adj.* —**or·gan·o·trop·i·cal·ly** *adv.*

or·gan-pipe cactus (órgǝn-pīp) *n.* A tall, branching cactus, *Pachycereus marginatus,* of Mexico and the southwestern United States.

or·ga·num[1] (órgǝ-nǝm) *n., pl.* **-na** (-nǝ) or **-nums.** Any of several types of vocal polyphonic music, in two, three, or four parts, of the 9th to the early 13th century. [Medieval Latin, from Late Latin, ORGAN.]

organum[2] Variant of **organon.**

or·gan·za (awr-gánzǝ) *n.* A sheer, stiff fabric of silk or synthetic material used for evening dresses or trimming. [Perhaps from *Lorganza,* a trademark.] —**or·gan·za** *adj.*

or·gan·zine (órgǝn-zeen, awr-gán-) *n.* 1. A thread of raw silk, usually used as a warp thread. 2. A fabric made of this thread. [French *organsin,* from Italian *organzino†.*]

or·gasm (ór-gaz'm) *n.* 1. The climax of sexual excitement, marked by ejaculation of semen in the male and by the release of tumescence in erectile organs of both sexes. 2. Loosely, any onrush of intense excitement. [French *orgasme,* from Greek *orgasmos,* from *organ,* to swell (with lust), be excited.] —**or·gas·mic** (awr-gázmik), **or·gas·tic** *adj.*

OR gate (or) *n. Electronics.* A computer logic gate that has one output and two or more inputs, and gives an output signal for any input signal or combination of input signals. Also called "OR circuit". [From its similarity to the function of the conjunction *or* in logic.]

or·geat (órzhaa) *n.* 1. A sweet flavouring of orange and almond used in cocktails and food. 2. A drink containing this flavouring. [French, from Old French, from Old Provençal *orjat,* from *orge,* barley, from Latin *hordeum.*]

or·gi·as·tic (órji-ástik) *adj.* Of, pertaining to, or characteristic of an orgy. [Greek *orgiastikos,* from *orgiazein,* to hold secret rites, from *orgia,* secret rites, ORGY.]

or·gy (órji) *n., pl.* **-gies.** 1. A revel involving unrestrained indulgence, especially sexual excesses. 2. Excessive indulgence in any specified activity: *an orgy of reading.* 3. *Often plural.* A secret rite in the cults of Demeter, Dionysus, or other Greek or Mediterranean deities, typically involving frenzied singing, dancing, drinking, and sexual activity. [Originally in the plural *orgies,* from Old French, from Latin *orgia,* from Greek.]

or·i·bi (órribi) *n., pl.* **-bis** or collectively **oribi.** Any of several small, brownish African antelopes of the genus *Ourebia,* especially *O. ourebia,* the male of which has straight, ridged horns. [Afrikaans, said to be from a Hottentot word meaning "antelope".]

o·ri·el (áwri-ǝl || órri-, óri-) *n.* A projecting bay window, usually in an upper storey, supported from below with corbels or brackets. Also called "oriel window". [Middle English *oriole, oriel,* from Old French *oriol,* from Medieval Latin *oriolum†,* upper chamber.]

o·ri·ent (áwri-ǝnt || órri-, -ent) *n.* 1. The east; eastern lands or regions. 2. *Capital* O. a. The Eastern Hemisphere. b. The countries of Asia, especially of eastern Asia, and the Eastern Hemisphere. Usually preceded by *the.* Compare **Occident.** c. In ancient times, the lands and regions east of the Mediterranean. 3. a. The lustre characteristic of a pearl of high quality. b. A pearl having this lustre.

~*adj.* Also **oriental** (for sense 2). 1. *Poetic.* Eastern; oriental. 2. Having exceptional quality and lustre. Said of pearls and gems. 3. *Archaic.* Rising; ascending: *"The orient moon"* (P.B. Shelley).

~*v.* (-ent) **oriented, -enting, -ents.** *Chiefly U.S.* To orientate. See Usage note at **orientate.** [Middle English, from Old French, from Latin *oriēns* (stem *orient-*), rising, rising sun, east, from *orīrī,* to rise.]

o·ri·en·tal (áwri-ént'l || órri-, óri-) *adj.* 1. Eastern. 2. *Usually capital* O. Pertaining to the countries or regions of the Orient or to their peoples, languages, or culture. 3. *Capital* O. *Ecology.* Of or designating the zoographical region that includes tropical Asia and the adjacent islands of the Malay Archipelago. 4. Variant of **orient** (sense 2). 5. Pertaining to or designating precious varieties of corundum: *an oriental ruby.*

~*n. Usually capital* O. An inhabitant or native of the Orient, or the descendant of one. —**o·ri·en·tal·ly** *adv.*

oriental alabaster *n.* A mineral, onyx marble *(see).*

oriental amethyst *n.* A type of amethyst *(see).*

o·ri·en·tal·ise, o·ri·en·tal·ize (áwri-ént'l-īz || órri-, óri-) *v.* **-ised, -ising, -ises.** *Often capital* O. —*tr.* To make oriental in character,

---

lifestyle, or appearance. —*intr.* To become oriental; adopt oriental qualities. —**o·ri·en·tal·i·sa·tion** (-ī-záysh'n || U.S. -i-).

O·ri·en·tal·ism (áwri-ént'l-iz'm || órri-, óri-) *n. Often small* o. 1. A quality, mannerism, or custom peculiar to or characteristic of the Orient. 2. Scholarly knowledge of eastern cultures, languages, and peoples. 3. A prejudiced or patronising attitude towards or a policy of discrimination against Eastern people and cultures. —**O·ri·en·tal·ist** *n. & adj.*

Oriental poppy *n.* A plant, *Papaver orientale,* native to western Asia and widely cultivated for its brilliant scarlet flowers.

Oriental rug *n.* A type of rug made by hand in the Orient.

o·ri·en·tate (áwri-en-tayt, -ǝn- || órri-, óri-, -én-) *v.* **-tated, -tating, -tates.** Also *chiefly U.S.* **orient.** —*tr.* 1. To place in a particular relation to the points of the compass: *orientate the swimming pool north and south.* 2. To cause (especially a church or grave) to face east; locate or place so as to face east. 3. To align or position with respect to a reference system. 4. To discover the bearings of. Often used reflexively: *She orientated herself by a familiar landmark.* 5. To cause to become familiar with or adjusted to facts or circumstances. —*intr.* 1. To turn towards the east. 2. To become adjusted or aligned.

Usage: There is some free variation between *orient* and *orientate* in modern English. *Orient* tends to be used much more in American English. *Orientate* is used more in British English, especially as an intransitive verb (*orientating towards the east*) and in forms that can function adjectivally (*It's orientated correctly; He is very work-orientated*). [Back-formation from ORIENTATION.]

o·ri·en·tat·ed (áwri-en-taytid, -ǝn- || órri-, óri-) *adj.* Directed or inclined towards; favouring. Used in combination: *career-orientated.*

o·ri·en·ta·tion (áwri-en-táysh'n, -ǝn- || órri-, óri-) *n.* 1. The act of orientating or the state of being orientated. 2. Location or position relative to the points of the compass. 3. *Architecture.* The location of a church so that its longitudinal axis is from west to east and its main altar at the eastern end. 4. The line or direction followed in the course of a trend, movement, or development. 5. An adjustment or adaptation to a new environment, situation, custom, or set of ideas. 6. *Psychology.* Individual awareness of the outside world in its relation to the self. 7. Introductory instruction concerning a new situation. [Probably ORIENT (verb) + -ATION.]

o·ri·en·teer·ing (áwri-en-téer-ing, -ǝn- || órri-, óri-) *n.* A cross-country race in which the competitors have to work out the route by means of a compass and map and report to checkpoints on the way. [Swedish *orientering,* orientation.]

or·i·fice (órri-fiss || áwri-) *n.* A mouth or vent; an aperture or cavity. [Old French, from Late Latin *ōrificium :* Latin *ōs* (stem *ōr-*), mouth + *facere,* to make.]

or·i·flamme, aur·i·flamme (órri-flam || áwri-) *n.* 1. The red flag of the Abbey of St. Denis, used as a standard by the early kings of France. 2. Any inspiring standard or symbol. [Middle English *oriflamble,* from Old French *oriflambe,* from Medieval Latin *auriflamma :* Latin *aurum,* gold + *flamma,* FLAME.]

orig. original; originally.

o·ri·ga·mi (órri-gáami, áwri-) *n.* 1. The art or process, originating in Japan, of folding paper into shapes resembling flowers, birds, or other objects. 2. A decorative object made in this way. Compare **kirigami.** [Japanese : *ori,* a folding + *-gami,* from *kami,* paper.]

o·ri·ga·num (órri-gáanǝm || U.S. ǝ-ríggǝnǝm) *n.* Also **o·ri·gan** (órrigǝn). Any plant of the genus *Origanum;* especially, wild marjoram. See **marjoram.** [Middle English, from Old French, from Latin *origanum,* from Greek *origanon.*]

Or·i·gen (órri-jen) (c. 185–c. 254). Christian writer and teacher, and one of the Greek Fathers of the Church. His many works include the *Hexapla* (interpretations of Old Testament texts), and *Contra Celsum,* a defence of Christianity against the attacks of the philosopher Celsus.

or·i·gin (órri-jin) *n.* 1. That from which anything derives its existence; a source or cause. 2. *Often plural.* Parentage; ancestry; derivation. 3. A coming into being. 4. *Anatomy.* a. The point of attachment of a muscle that remains fixed when the muscle contracts. b. The beginning of a nerve or blood vessel, especially when it arises from a larger nerve or blood vessel. 5. *Mathematics.* The point of intersection of coordinate axes, from which measurements are made. See **Cartesian coordinate system.** [Middle English *origyne,* from Latin *orīgō* (stem *orīgin-*), from *orīrī,* to rise.]

Synonyms: origin, inception, source, root.

o·rig·i·nal (ǝ-ríjin'l, o-) *adj. Abbr.* **orig.** 1. Of or pertaining to the beginning of something; initial; first. 2. Fresh and unusual; not imitative; strikingly new. 3. Able to think of and present new ideas; creative; inventive. 4. Designating that from which a copy, reproduction, or translation is made. —See Usage note at **new.**

~*n. Abbr.* **orig.** 1. The primary form of anything from which varieties arise: *Later models retained many features of the original.* 2. An authentic work of art, literature, or the like, as distinguished from a copy or reproduction. 3. One that is the model for an artistic or literary work. 4. One having an unusual turn of mind or pattern of behaviour. 5. *Informal.* A peculiar or eccentric person. [Middle English, from Old French, from Latin *orīginālis,* from *orīgō,* ORIGIN.]

o·rig·i·nal·i·ty (ǝ-ríji-nál-ǝti, o-) *n., pl.* **-ties.** 1. The quality of being original. 2. The capacity to act or think independently. 3. Something original.

o·rig·i·nal·ly (ǝ-ríj-inǝli, o-, -nǝli) *adv. Abbr.* **orig.** 1. With reference to origin. 2. At first. 3. In a highly distinctive manner.

oriel *An oriel window in a Tudor façade, at St. Osyth's Priory, Essex, England. Oriels were usually built over gateways and arches.*

original sin *n. Theology.* **1.** The tendency to evil inherent in human beings as a result of Adam's first act of disobedience. **2.** The state of deprivation from grace resulting from Adam's sinful disobedience.

o·rig·i·nate (ə-ríji-nayt, o-) *v.* **-nated, -nating, -nates.** *—tr.* To bring into being; create; invent. *—intr.* **1.** To come into being; start; spring. **2.** *Chiefly U.S.* To begin a journey from a specified starting point. Used of forms of transport. **—o·rig·i·na·tion** (-náysh'n) *n.* **—o·rig·i·na·tive** (-nətiv, -naytiv) *adj.* **—o·rig·i·na·tive·ly** *adv.* **—o·rig·i·na·tor** *n.*

o·ri·ole (áwri-ōl ‖ ṓri-) *n.* **1.** Any of various Old World birds of the family Oriolidae, of which the males are characteristically bright yellow and black. **2.** Any of various New World birds of the family Icteridae, of which the males are black and orange or yellow. See **Baltimore oriole.** [French *oriol,* from Old French, from Medieval Latin *oriolus,* "golden (bird)", variant of Latin *aureolus,* diminutive of *aureus,* golden, from *aurum,* gold.]

O·ri·on¹ (ə-rī́-ən, o-, aw-). *Greek Mythology.* A giant hunter, pursuer of the Pleiades and lover of Eos, killed by Artemis.

Orion² *n.* A constellation in the celestial equator near Gemini and Taurus, containing the stars Betelgeuse and Rigel.

or·i·son (órriz'n) *n. Poetic.* A prayer. [Middle English, from Old French, from Latin *ōrātiō* (stem *oration-*), ORATION.]

O·ri·ya (o-rée-ə) *n.* An Indic language, spoken chiefly in Orissa, in India. **—O·ri·ya** *adj.*

Ork·ney (órk-ni) *n.* A type of cheese resembling Cheddar but with a flakier texture, made in the Orkney Islands.

Orkney Islands. Also **Ork·neys** (órk-niz). Group of 70 islands off northern Scotland. The islands belonged to Norway until 1471. Formerly a county, now constituting a region, the islands are used as a base for the North Sea oil industry. Principal islands are Mainland (Pomona), Hoy, and Sanday; Kirkwall is the chief town.

Or·lan·do (awr-lándō), **Vittorio Emmanuele** (1860–1952). Italian politician. Elected prime minister (1917), he resigned (1919) after failing to convince the Allies of Italian claims to Austrian territory.

orle (orl) *n. Heraldry.* An inner border not quite touching the edge of a shield. [French *orle, ourle,* from *ourler,* to edge, hem, from Vulgar Latin *orulāre* (unattested), from *orula* (unattested), diminutive of Latin *ora,* edge, border.]

Or·le·an·ist (awr-lée-ənist, órli-) *n.* A supporter of the Orléans branch of the French royal family, descended from the Duke of Orléans, younger brother of Louis XIV.

Or·lé·ans (awr-lée-ənz, órli-; *French* -lay-ŏɴ). City in north central France. A royal residence since the seventh century, it is the capital of the Loiret département. Joan of Arc raised the English siege here (1429) in the Hundred Years' War; its cathedral was destroyed (1568) by the Huguenots, who were themselves massacred here on St. Bartholomew's Day, 1572.

Or·lé·ans (awrlay-ŏɴ), **Charles, Duc d'** (1391–1465). French general and poet. Captured by the English at Agincourt (1415), he spent the next quarter of a century as a prisoner in England and spent much of this time writing poetry in English. His son became Louis XII of France.

Orléans, Louis Philippe Joseph, Duc d', known as Philippe Égalité (1747–93). French politician. He was a radical revolutionary, despite being a member of the royal family. He voted for the execution of his cousin, Louis XVI, but was himself executed for treason. His son, Louis Philippe, became king.

Or·lon (ór-lon) *n.* A trademark for a synthetic acrylic fibre that is used alone or with other fibres in a variety of fabrics. **—or·lon** *adj.*

or·lop (ór-lop) *n. Nautical.* The lowest deck of a ship, especially a warship. Also called "orlop deck". [Middle English *overlop,* deck of a single-decker covering the hold, from Middle Low German *overlōp,* "a leaping over" : *over,* over + *lōpen,* to leap.]

Or·lov (awr-lóf; *Russian* aar-), **Grigory Grigoryevich, Count** (1734–83). Russian politician. A lover of Catherine the Great, he engineered, with his brother Alexei (1737–1808), the coup (1762) which brought Catherine to power. As adviser to the empress, he unsuccessfully supported reforms such as emancipation of the serfs.

Or·mazd, Or·muzd (órməzd). The chief deity of Zoroastrianism, the creator of the world, the source of light, and the embodiment of good. Also called "Ahura Mazda". Compare **Ahriman.** [Persian *Ormazd,* from Avestan *Ahura-Mazda,* "wise spirit" : *ahura,* spirit + *mazdā,* wise.]

or·mer (órmər) *n.* **1.** Any of various abalones; especially, an edible species, *Haliotis tuberculata,* found chiefly in the Channel Islands. **2.** The shell of this mollusc. Also called "sea ear". [Channel Islands French, from French *ormier,* short for *oreille-de-mer,* "sea-ear", from Latin *auris maris* : *auris,* ear + *maris,* genitive of *mare,* sea.]

or·mo·lu (ór-mə-lōō, -mō-, -lew, -lü) *n.* **1.** Any of several copper and tin or zinc alloys resembling gold in appearance and used to decorate furniture, mouldings, architectural ornamentations, and jewellery. Also called "mosaic gold". **2.** An imitation of gold. **3.** Formerly, gold or gold leaf used for gilding. [French *or moulu,* "ground gold" : *or,* gold, from Latin *aurum* + *moulu,* past participle of *moudre,* to grind, from Latin *molere.*]

Ormuz. See **Hormuz, Strait of.**

or·na·ment (órnə-mənt) *n.* **1.** Anything that decorates or adorns; an embellishment. **2.** Decorations or adornments collectively. **3.** A small object used as a decoration, such as a porcelain figure. **4.** A person considered as a source of pride, honour, or credit because of personality, talent, or skill: *He is an ornament to his profession.* **5.** *Music.* A group of notes that embellishes or decorates a melody.
~tr.v. (-mént) **ornamented, -menting, -ments.** **1.** To furnish with ornaments. **2.** To be an ornament to. [Middle English, from Old French *ornement,* from Latin *ōrnāmentum,* from *ōrnāre,* to adorn.] **—or·na·ment·er** (-mentər) *n.*

or·na·men·tal (órnə-mént'l) *adj.* Of, pertaining to, or serving as an ornament; especially, decorative but inessential.
~n. Something that is ornamental; especially, a plant grown for its beauty. **—or·na·men·tal·ly** *adv.*

or·na·men·ta·tion (órnə-men-táysh'n) *n.* **1. a.** The act, process, or result of ornamenting. **b.** The state of being ornamented. **2.** That which ornaments. **3.** Ornaments collectively.

or·nate (awr-náyt, ór-nayt) *adj.* **1.** Elaborately and heavily ornamented; excessively decorated. **2.** Showy or florid in style or manner; flowery. [Middle English *ornat,* from Latin *ōrnātus,* past participle of *ōrnāre,* to adorn.] **—or·nate·ly** *adv.* **—or·nate·ness** *n.*
Synonyms: *ornate, florid, flamboyant, lavish, gaudy, showy, ostentatious.*

or·ner·y (órnəri) *adj.* **-ier, -iest.** *U.S. Informal.* **1.** Having an ugly disposition; specifically, stubborn and mean-spirited. **2.** Deceitful; unfair; treacherous: *an ornery fraud.* **3.** Ordinary. [Variant of ORDINARY.] **—or·ner·i·ness** *n.*

ornith. ornithological; ornithology.

or·nith·ic (awr-níthik) *adj.* Of, pertaining to, or characteristic of birds. [Greek *ornithikos* : ORNITH(O)- + *-ikos,* -IC.]

or·ni·thine (órni-theen) *n.* An amino acid, $C_5H_{12}N_2O_{12}$, produced in the liver during the formation of urea. [ORNITH(O)- (representing *ornithuric acid,* secreted in urine of birds and reptiles) + -INE.]

ornitho-, ornith- *comb. form.* Indicates a bird or birds; for example, **ornithology.** [New Latin, from Greek, from *ornis* (stem *ornith-*), bird.]

or·ni·thol·o·gy (órni-thólləji) *n. Abbr.* **ornith., ornithol.** The scientific study of birds. [New Latin *ornithologia* : ORNITHO- + -LOGY.] **—or·ni·tho·log·i·cal** (-thə-lójik'l) *adj.* **—or·ni·tho·log·i·cal·ly** *adv.* **—or·ni·thol·o·gist** (-thólləjist) *n.*

or·ni·thop·ter (órni-thoptər) *n.* An aircraft supported in the air and propelled by wing movements. Also called "orthopter". [ORNITHO- + -PTER.]

or·ni·tho·rhyn·chus (órnithō-ríngkəss) *n.* The **duck-billed platypus** *(see).* [New Latin, from ORNITHO- + Greek *rhunkos,* bill.]

or·ni·tho·sis (órni-thṓ-siss) *n.* A contagious virus disease of the psittacosis group that infects poultry and other birds, and is transmissible to humans. [New Latin : ORNITH(O)- + -OSIS.] **—or·ni·thot·ic** (-thóttik) *adj.*

oro-¹ *comb. form.* Indicates a mountain; for example, **orology.** [Greek *oros*†, mountain.]

oro-² *comb. form.* Indicates a mouth; for example, **oropharynx.** [Latin *ōs* (stem *or-*), mouth.]

o·rog·e·ny (o-rójəni, aw-) *n.* The process of mountain formation, especially by folding and faulting of the earth's crust. Also called "orogenesis". [ORO- + -GENY.] **—or·o·gen·ic** (áw-rə-jénnik, ṓ-, -rō- ‖ ṓ-) *adj.* **—or·o·gen·i·cal·ly** *adv.*

o·rog·ra·phy (o-róggrəfi, aw- ‖ ō-) *n.* The study of the physical geography of mountains and mountain ranges. [ORO- + -GRAPHY.] **—or·o·graph·ic** (áw-rə-gráffik, ó-, -rō- ‖ ō-), **or·o·graph·i·cal** *adj.* **—or·o·graph·i·cal·ly** *adv.*

o·ro·ide (áw-rō-īd, ō- ‖ ṓ-) *n.* Also **o·re·ide** (-ri-). An inexpensive alloy of copper, zinc, and tin, used in imitation gold jewellery. [French *oréide* : *or,* gold, from Latin *aurum,* gold + *-éide,* -OID.] **—o·ro·ide, o·re·ide** *adj.*

o·rol·o·gy (o-rólləji, aw- ‖ ō-) *n.* The study of mountains. [ORO- + -LOGY.] **—o·ro·log·i·cal** (áw-rə-lójik'l, ó-, -rō- ‖ ṓ-) *adj.* **—o·ro·log·i·cal·ly** *adv.* **—o·rol·o·gist** *n.*

o·rom·e·ter (o-rómmitər, aw- ‖ ō-) *n.* An instrument that indicates height above sea level using barometric means.

O·ron·tes (o-rón-teez, ə-, aw-). River of southwestern Asia. Rising in the Lebanon, it flows 370 kilometres (230 miles) mainly northwards through Syria and Turkey to join the Mediterranean near Samandag. Though unnavigable, it is used extensively for irrigation.

o·ro·tund (ó-rō-tund, áw-, -rō- ‖ ṓ-) *adj.* **1.** Full in sound; sonorous: *spoke in orotund tones.* **2.** Pompous and bombastic: *orotund talk.* [Latin *ōre rotundō,* "with round mouth" : *ōs* (stem *ōr-*), mouth + *rotundus,* rounded, ROTUND.] **—o·ro·tun·di·ty** (-túndəti) *n.*

or·phan (órf'n) *n.* **1.** A child whose parents are dead. **2.** *Chiefly U.S.* A child who has lost one parent by death.
~adj. **1.** Being an orphan. **2.** For orphans: *an orphan home.*
~tr.v. **orphaned, -phaning, -phans.** To deprive (a child) as by the death of one or both parents. [Late Latin *orphanus,* from Greek *orphanos,* orphaned.] **—or·phan·hood** *n.*

or·phan·age (órf'n-ij) *n.* **1.** An institution for the care and protection of orphans and abandoned children. **2.** The state or condition of being an orphan.

or·phar·i·on (awr-fárri-on) *n.* A large, lutelike musical instrument popular in the 17th century. [Blend of *Orpheus* +*Arion* (legendary Greek musicians).]

Or·phe·an (awr-fée-ən ‖ órfi-ən) *adj.* **1.** Of or pertaining to Orpheus. **2.** Beautiful; entrancing. Said of sounds.

Or·pheus (ór-fewss ‖ -fi-əss). *Greek Mythology.* Poet and musician who ventured into Hades to retrieve his wife Eurydice. The poems on which Orphism is based were ascribed to him.

Or·phic (órfik) *adj.* **1.** Of or ascribed to Orpheus; Orphean: *the Orphic poems; Orphic mysteries.* **2.** Of, pertaining to, or characteristic of the dogmas, mysteries, and philosophical principles set forth in the poems ascribed to Orpheus. **3.** *Sometimes small* **o.** Mystic or

PRONUNCIATION KEY

a, trap; aa, father; ai, **fair**;
ar, **star**; aw, lawn; ay, play;
b, bb, stab; **rubber**;
ch, **church**; ck, ticket;
d, dd, **dead**; ladder; e, dress;
ee, bee; er, defer; ew, **few**;
ewr, **pure**; ə, about;
ər, letter; f, ff, fife; **differ**;
g, gg, giggle; h, hat; i, kit;
ī, price; īr, fire; j, **judge**;
k, **kick**; l, ll, let; 'l, **needle**;
m, mm, **man**; n, nn, **no**;
'n, sudden; ng, **thing**; o, lot;
ō, no; ŏŏ, **foot**; ōō, **shoe**;
oor, **poor**; ow, cow;
owr, **hour**; oy, boy;
p, pp, **pepper**; r, rr, **red**;
s, ss, **sauce**; sh, **ship**;
t, tt, totter; th, **thick**; th, **this**;
smooth; u, cut; ur, **turn**;
v, vv, valve; w, wet; y, yes;
z, zz, zebra; zh, vision;
pleasure

IN FOREIGN WORDS:

aɴ, oɴ, **Saint-Saëns**;
hl, **Llanelli**; **Hluhluwe**;
kh, loch; **lough**; **Khaled**

STRESS MARK:

in-sīt, insight; in-sī́t, incite

orrery *These mechanical planetariums are named after Charles Boyle, 4th Earl of Orrery, for whom the clockwork model shown here was made in 1716. When the model is operated, the Earth and Moon (on the left) revolve around the central Sun at the correct speed relative to each other. This model is now in the Science Museum, London.*

PRONUNCIATION KEY

a, trap; aa, father; ai, fair; ar, star; aw, lawn; ay, play; b, bb, stab; rubber; ch, church; ck, ticket; d, dd, dead; ladder; e, dress; ee, bee; er, defer; ew, few; ewr, pure; ə, about; ər, letter; f, ff, fife; differ; g, gg, giggle; h, hat; i, kit; ī, price; īr, fire; j, judge; k, kick; l, ll, let; 'l, needle; m, mm, man; n, nn, no; 'n, sudden; ng, thing; o, lot; ō, no; o͝o, foot; o͞o, shoe; oor, poor; ow, cow; owr, hour; oy, boy; p, pp, pepper; r, rr, red; s, ss, sauce; sh, ship; t, tt, totter; th, thick; th, this; smooth; u, cut; ur, turn; v, vv, valve; w, wet; y, yes; z, zz, zebra; zh, vision; pleasure

IN FOREIGN WORDS:

aN, oN, Saint-Saëns; hl, Llanelli; Hluhluwe; kh, loch; lough; Khaled

STRESS MARK:

in-sīt, insight; in-sī́t, incite

occult in nature; esoteric. [Latin *Orphicus,* from Greek *Orphikos,* from ORPHEUS.] **—Or·phi·cal·ly** *adv.*

Or·phism (órfiz'm) *n.* **1.** An ancient Greek mystery religion arising in the sixth century B.C. from a synthesis of pre-Hellenic beliefs with the cult of Dionysus **Zagreus** *(see).* **2.** An early form of cubism using geometric shapes and vivid colours. [French *orphisme,* from *Orphée,* from Greek *Orpheus,* ORPHEUS.] **—Or·phist** *n. & adj.*

or·phrey (órfri) *n., pl.* **-phreys.** Also **or·fray** *pl.* **-frays. 1.** A band of elaborate embroidery decorating the front of certain ecclesiastical vestments. **2.** Any elaborate embroidery, especially when worked in gold. [Middle English *orfrey, orphreis* (taken as plural), from Old French *orfreis,* from Medieval Latin *aurifrigium* : Latin *aurum,* + *Phrygium,* neuter of *Phrygius,* embroidered, PHRYGIAN.]

or·pi·ment (órpimənt) *n.* A mineral, arsenic trisulphide, As_2S_3, used as a lemon-yellow pigment in tanning and linoleum manufacture. [Middle English, from Old French, from Latin *auripigmentum* : *aurum,* gold + *pigmentum,* PIGMENT.]

or·pine (órpīn) *n.* Any of several plants of the genus *Sedum*; especially, *S. telephium,* native to Eurasia, having clusters of reddish-purple flowers. Also *British* "livelong". [Middle English *orpin,* from Old French *orpine,* short for *orpiment,* ORPIMENT, probably after the yellow flowers of one species.]

Or·ping·ton (órpingtən) *n.* A domestic fowl of a breed having a large body, a single comb, and unfeathered legs, such as the buff Orpington. [After *Orpington,* Kent, where the breed originated.]

or·re·ry (órrəri) *n., pl.* **-ries.** A mechanical model of the Solar System. [After Charles Boyle (1676–1731), 4th Earl of *Orrery,* for whom one was made.]

or·ris (órriss) *n.* **1.** Any of several species of iris having a fragrant rootstock; especially, *Iris florentina.* **2.** Orrisroot. [Probably unexplained variant of IRIS.]

or·ris·root (órriss-ro͞ot || -ro͝ot) *n.* The fragrant rootstock of the orris, used in perfumes and cosmetics.

Or·si·ni (awr-séeni). An aristocratic family of medieval Italy. Originating in Rome, they supported the Papal (or Guelph) faction against the Imperial (or Ghibelline) faction. The family included two popes—Celestine III (reigned 1191–98), and Nicholas III (reigned 1277–80).

or·tan·ique (órtə-néek) *n.* A fruit produced by crossing an orange with a tangerine. [From *or*ange + *tan*gerine + un*ique.*]

Or·te·ga y Gas·set (awr-táygə i ga-sét), **José** (1883–1955). Spanish philosopher. He is best known for his neo-Kantian doctrines of individualism and will-power, as expounded in such works as *The Revolt of the Masses* (1929).

Or·te·li·us (awr-táyli-əss), **Abraham** (1527–98). Flemish geographer. A careful scholar and an extensive traveller, he published his *Theatrum Orbis Terrarum* (1570), which appeared in 40 editions and is regarded as the first modern atlas. He was appointed Cartographer Royal of Spain (1575).

orth. orthopaedic; orthopaedics.

or·thi·con (órthi-kon) *n.* A television camera tube that uses a low-energy electron beam to scan a photoactive mosaic. Also called "image orthicon". [ORTH(O)- + ICON(OSCOPE).]

or·tho (órthō) *adj. Chemistry & Physics.* **1.** Of, pertaining to, or designating adjacent positions in a benzene ring. Used in combination, often italicised: *orthodichlorobenzene.* **2.** Of, pertaining to, or designating the most fully hydrated form of an acid. Used in combination: *orthophosphoric acid.* **3.** Of, pertaining to, or designating the form of a diatonic molecule in which the nuclear spins are parallel. Used in combination: *orthohydrogen.* Compare **meta, para, pyro.** [From ORTHO-.]

ortho–, orth– *comb. form.* Indicates: **1.** Straight or upright; for example, **orthotropic. 2.** *Mathematics.* Perpendicular to or at right angles; for example, **orthorhombic. 3.** Correct or standard; for example, **orthography. 4.** *Medicine.* Correction of maladjustments or deformities; for example, **orthopaedics.** [Middle English, from Old French, from Latin, from Greek *orthos,* straight, correct, right, upright.]

or·tho·bo·ric acid (órthō-báw-rik, -bó- || -bṓ-) *n. Chemistry.* **Boric acid** *(see).*

or·tho·cen·tre (órthō-sentər) *n.* The point of intersection of the three altitudes of a triangle.

or·tho·ce·phal·ic (órthō-si-fál-ik) *adj.* Also **or·tho·ceph·a·lous** (-séffələss). Having a ratio of skull height to skull length between 0.70 and 0.75. [ORTHO-, correct + -CEPHALIC.] **—or·tho·ceph·a·ly** (-séffəli) *n.*

or·tho·chro·mat·ic (ór-thō-krō-máttik-, -thə-, -krə-) *adj.* **1.** Of, having, or reproducing the colours of nature accurately. **2.** Of or pertaining to a film, plate, or emulsion that renders all colours, except red, in tones of grey approximating to the relative brilliance of these colours. Compare **panchromatic. —or·tho·chro·mat·ic·al·ly** *adv.* **—or·tho·chro·ma·tism** (-krṓmətiz'm) *n.*

or·tho·clase (órthō-klayss, -klayz) *n.* A **potassium feldspar** *(see),* essentially potassium aluminium silicate, $KAlSi_3O_8$, characterised by a monoclinic crystalline structure and found in igneous, metamorphic, and sedimentary rocks. [German *Orthoklas* : ORTHO- + -CLASE.]

or·tho·don·tics (ór-thō-dóntiks, -thə-) *n.* The dental speciality and practice of correcting abnormally aligned or positioned teeth. Also called "orthodontia". [ORTH(O)- + -ODONT + -ICS.] **—or·tho·don·tic** *adj.* **—or·tho·don·tist** *n.*

or·tho·dox (órthə-doks) *adj.* **1. a.** Adhering to a commonly accepted, customary, or traditional practice or belief. **b.** Broadly, conventional in outlook or behaviour. **2.** Adhering to the accepted or traditional and established faith, especially in religion. Compare **heterodox. 3.** Adhering to the Christian faith as expressed in the early Christian ecumenical creeds. **4.** *Capital* **O. a.** Of, pertaining to, or designating any of the churches of the Eastern Orthodox Church. **b.** Of, pertaining to, or designating Orthodox Judaism. [Old French *orthodoxe,* from Late Latin *orthodoxus,* from Greek *orthodoxos,* having the right opinion : ORTHO- + *doxa,* opinion, from *dokein,* to think.] **—or·tho·dox·ly** *adv.*

Orthodox Church *n.* The **Eastern Orthodox Church** *(see).*

Orthodox Judaism *n.* The branch of the Jewish faith that adheres to the Mosaic Law as interpreted in the Talmud, and considers it binding in modern as well as ancient times. Compare **Conservative Judaism, Reform Judaism.**

orthodox sleep *n.* The major part of sleep, during which no dreaming occurs and the body and brain are in a state of very low activity. Compare **paradoxical sleep.**

or·tho·dox·y (órthə-doksi) *n., pl.* **-ies. 1.** The quality or state of being orthodox. **2.** Orthodox practice, custom, or belief.

or·tho·e·py (órthō-eppi, -éppi, awr-thṓ-ipi) *n.* **1.** The study of the pronunciation of words. **2.** The customary pronunciation of words. [New Latin *orthoepia,* from Greek *orthoepeia* : ORTHO- + *epos,* word.] **—or·tho·ep·ic** (-éppik), **or·tho·ep·i·cal** *adj.* **—or·tho·e·pist** (órthō-eppist, -éppist, awr-thṓ-ipist) *n.*

or·tho·gen·e·sis (órthō-jénni-siss) *n.* **1.** *Biology.* The theory that evolutionary change is predetermined by the constitution of germ plasm and independent of external factors. **2.** *Anthropology.* The theory that all cultures pass through sequential periods in the same order. [New Latin : ORTHO- + -GENESIS.] **—or·tho·ge·net·ic** (jə-néttik) *adj.* **—or·tho·ge·net·i·cal·ly** *adv.*

or·tho·gen·ic (ór-thō-jénnik, -thə-) *adj.* **1.** In psychiatry, pertaining to the correction or treatment of mental and emotional abnormalities in children. **2.** Of or pertaining to orthogenesis. [ORTHO- + -GENIC.]

or·thog·na·thous (awr-thóg-nəthəss) *adj.* Also **or·thog·nath·ic** (órthəg-náthik). Having the lower jaw correctly aligned with the upper so that it does not protrude or recede. [ORTHO- + -GNATHOUS.] **—or·thog·na·thism** (-thóg-nəthiz'm), **or·thog·na·thy** *n.*

or·thog·o·nal (awr-thóggən'l) *adj. Mathematics.* **1.** Pertaining to or composed of right angles. **2. a.** Having a defined scalar product of zero. Said of two vectors. **b.** Having a defined product of zero. Said of two functions. **c.** Of or designating a matrix that is equal to the inverse of its transpose. [Greek *orthogōnios* : ORTHO- + *gōnia,* angle.] **—or·thog·o·nal·ly** *adv.*

orthogonal projection *n.* The two-dimensional graphic representation of an object formed by the perpendicular intersections of lines drawn from points on the object to a plane of projection. Also called "orthographic projection".

or·tho·graph·ic (órthə-gráffik) *adj.* Also **or·tho·graph·i·cal** (-gráffik'l). **1.** Of or pertaining to orthography. **2.** Spelt correctly. **3.** *Mathematics.* Having perpendicular lines. **—or·tho·graph·i·cal·ly** *adv.*

or·thog·ra·phy (awr-thóggrəfi) *n., pl.* **-phies. 1.** The art or study of correct spelling according to established usage. **2.** The aspect of language study concerned with letters and their sequences in words. **3.** Any method of representing the sounds of language by literal symbols. [Middle English *ortografie,* from Old French, from Latin *orthographia,* from Greek : ORTHO- + -GRAPHY.] **—or·thog·ra·pher, or·thog·ra·phist** *n.*

or·tho·hy·dro·gen (órthō-hī́drəjən) *n.* A form of hydrogen in which the two nuclei in each molecule have parallel spins; one of two possible forms of molecular hydrogen, constituting 75 per cent of hydrogen at room temperature. Compare **parahydrogen.**

or·tho·pae·dics, *U.S.* **or·tho·pe·dics** (ór-thə-péediks, -thō-) *n. Abbr.* **orth.** *Used with a singular verb.* The surgical or manipulative treatment of disorders of the skeletal system and associated muscles. [French *orthopédie* : ORTHO- + Greek *paideia,* education, from *pais* (stem *paid-*), child.] **—or·tho·pae·dic** *adj.* **—or·tho·pae·di·cal·ly** *adv.* **—or·tho·pae·dist** *n.*

or·tho·psy·chi·a·try (órthō-sī-kī́-ətri, -si-) *n.* The prevention and early treatment of mental disorders, especially in the young. **—or·tho·psy·chi·at·ric** (-sī-ki-áttrik), **or·tho·psy·chi·at·ri·cal** *adj.* **—or·tho·psy·chi·a·trist** (-sī-kī́-ətrist, -si-) *n.*

or·thop·ter (ór-thoptər) *n.* An aircraft, an **ornithopter** *(see).* [ORTHO- + -PTER.]

or·thop·ter·an (awr-thóptə-rən) *n.* Also **or·thop·ter·on** (-rən, -ron) *pl.* **-era.** Any insect of the order Orthoptera, characterised by membranous, folded hind wings covered by leathery, narrow fore wings, and including the locusts, cockroaches, crickets, and grasshoppers. [New Latin *Orthoptera* (order), "straight-wings" : ORTHO- + *-ptera,* from *-pterus,* -PTEROUS.] **—or·thop·ter·al, or·thop·ter·an, or·thop·ter·ous** *adj.*

or·thop·tics (awr-thóptiks) *n. Used with a singular verb.* The practice of using eye exercises and other nonsurgical methods to correct abnormalities of vision. [ORTH(O)- + OPTICS.] **—or·thop·tist** *n.*

or·tho·rhom·bic (órthō-rómbik) *adj.* Of, pertaining to, or designating a crystalline structure of three mutually perpendicular axes of different length.

or·tho·scope (ór-thō-skōp, -thə-) *n.* Formerly, an instrument for examining the eye through a layer of water that compensates for the curvature of the cornea. [ORTHO- + -SCOPE.]

or·tho·scop·ic (ór-thō-skóppik, -thə-) *adj.* **1.** Having or pertaining to normal vision. **2.** Pertaining to the use of the orthoscope.

or·thos·ti·chous (awr-thóstikəss) *adj. Biology.* Characterised by parallel arrangement in a vertical row. Said especially of leaves. [ORTHO- + Greek *stikhos,* a row.] —**or·thos·ti·chy** *n.*

or·thot·ics (awr-thóttiks) *n. Used with a singular verb.* The branch of orthopaedics concerned with the use of mechanical devices to support or correct weakened or deformed joints. [From *orthotic* : ORTH(O)- + -OTIC.] —**or·thot·ic** *adj.* —**or·tho·tist** *n.*

or·tho·trop·ic (ór-thō-tróppik, -thə-) *adj.* Tending to grow or form along a vertical axis. Said especially of plant parts. [ORTHO- + -TROPIC.] —**or·tho·trop·i·cal·ly** *adv.* —**or·thot·ro·pism** (awr-thóttrə-piz'm) *n.*

or·thot·ro·pous (awr-thóttrəpəss) *adj. Botany.* Growing straight, so that the micropyle is at the side opposite the stalk. Said of an ovule. [ORTHO- + -TROPOUS.]

or·to·lan (órtə-lən) *n.* **1.** A small, brownish bird, *Emberiza hortulana,* of Europe and Asia, eaten as a delicacy. **2.** Loosely, any of several American birds, such as the bobolink. [French, from Provençal, gardener, from Latin *hortolānus,* from *hortulus,* diminutive of *hortus,* garden.]

orts (orts) *n. Sometimes singular. Archaic & Regional.* Small scraps or leavings of food after a meal is completed. [Middle English, probably from Middle Dutch *orte,* contraction of *oor aete,* leftover, "out eat" : *oor-,* out + *eten,* to eat.]

Or·vie·to¹ (órvi-áytō). Town of west central Italy. Thought to be near the site of the Etruscan city of Volsinii, it has many Etruscan remains. Its most notable building is its cathedral.

Orvieto² *n.* A light, white Italian wine produced in the area around Orvieto.

Or·well (ór-wel, -wəl), **George,** pen name of Eric Arthur Blair (1903–50). British writer. Despite his prosperous background, he became a socialist and lived amongst low-paid workers and tramps as recorded in *Down and Out in Paris and London* (1933). Disillusioned with Communism while fighting the Nationalists in the Spanish Civil War, he attacked totalitarianism in novels such as *Animal Farm* (1946) and *1984* (1949). —**Or·well·i·an** (-wélli-ən) *adj.*

Or·well·ism (ór-wel-iz'm, -wəl-) *n.* The dubious use of propaganda; specifically, the distortion and manipulation of news or history by governments or official agencies in order to influence public opinion. [After George ORWELL, referring especially to the description of such practices in his novel *1984.*]

-ory¹ *n. suffix.* Indicates: **1.** A place for; for example, **conservatory, observatory. 2.** Something used as; for example, **accessory, directory.** [Middle English *-orie,* from Anglo-French *-orie* or Old French *-orie, -oire,* from Latin *-ōrium, -ōria,* from *-ōrius,* adjective suffix.]

-ory² *adj. suffix.* Indicates characterisation by, possession of the nature of, or tendency towards; for example, **compensatory.** [Middle English *-orie,* Anglo-French, Old French *-oire, -orie,* from Latin *-ōrius,* adjective suffix.]

o·ryx (órriks ‖ ṓ-riks, áw-) *n., pl.* **oryxes** or **oryx.** Any of several antelopes of the genus *Oryx,* of Africa and Arabia, having long, straight horns. [Latin, from Greek *orux,* pickaxe, spike, hence (from the sharp horns) gazelle, perhaps from *orussein,* to dig.]

os¹ (oss ‖ ōss) *n., pl.* **ora** (áwrə ‖ ṓrə). *Anatomy.* A mouth or opening. [Latin *ōs* (stem *ōr-*), mouth.]

os² (oss) *n., pl.* **ossa** (óssə). *Anatomy.* A bone. [Latin *os* (stem *oss-*), bone.]

os³ (ōss) *n., pl.* **osar** (ṓ-saar). *Geology.* An **esker** *(see).* [Swedish *ås,* ridge, from Old Norse *āss.*]

Os The symbol for the element osmium.

o.s., o/s out of stock.

O.S. 1. Old Series. **2.** Old Style. **3.** ordinary seaman. **4.** Ordnance Survey (in Britain).

OSA, O.S.A. Order of St. Augustine.

O·sage (ō-sáyj, ṓ-sayj) *n., pl.* **Osages** or collectively **Osage. 1.** A member of a Siouan-speaking North American Indian people, formerly inhabiting the region between the Missouri and Arkansas rivers. **2.** The Siouan language of this people. —**O·sage** *adj.*

O·sa·ka (ō-saákə). Port of southern Japan. Situated on the Yodo delta, it is the centre of the Osaka Bay conurbation of southwest Honshu, and the country's second most important industrial and commercial city. Among its historic buildings are Imperial palaces, and Buddhist temples dating from the 4th century.

OSB, O.S.B. Order of St. Benedict.

Os·borne (óz-bawrn, -bərn), **John (James)** (1929–). British playwright. His first major play, *Look Back in Anger* (1956), heralded a revolution in British postwar theatre, with naturalistic, politically and socially conscious plays coming to dominate serious drama.

Os·can (óskən) *n.* **1.** A member of an ancient people of Campania. **2.** The Italic language of this people.
~*adj.* Of or pertaining to the Oscans or their language.

Os·car (óskər) *n.* An **Academy Award** *(see).* [Apparently humorously named after a remark made by an official when he first saw it, that it looked like his uncle Oscar.]

os·cil·late (óssi-layt) *v.* **-lated, -lating, -lates.** —*intr.* **1.** To swing back and forth with a steady uninterrupted rhythm. **2.** To waver between two or more thoughts or courses of action; vacillate. **3.** *Physics.* To move or change between alternate extremes, usually in a regular way with a definable period. Said of vibrating objects, systems, waves, and the like. —*tr.* To cause to oscillate. —See Synonyms at **swing.** [Latin *ōscillāre,* from *ōscillum,* a swing, originally a mask of Bacchus hung from a tree in a vineyard to swing in the wind (as a charm), diminutive of *ōs,* face, mouth.] —**os·cil·la·tor** *n.* —**os·cil·la·to·ry** (óssi-lə-təri, -tri, -laytəri, -láytəri) *adj.*

os·cil·la·tion (óssi-láysh'n) *n.* **1.** The state or act of oscillating. **2.** A single cycle in which a system changes to one extreme state, then to the other extreme, and back to its original state; a period.

os·cil·lo·gram (o-síllə-gram, ə-) *n.* **1.** The graph traced by an oscillograph. **2.** An instantaneous oscilloscope trace or photograph of such a trace. [OSCILLO(GRAPH) + -GRAM.]

os·cil·lo·graph (o-síllə-graaf, ə-, -graf) *n.* A device that records oscillations as a continuous graph of variation in a quantity with time. [French *oscillographe* : OSCILL(ATION) + -GRAPH.] —**os·cil·log·ra·phy** (óssi-lóggrəfi) *n.*

os·cil·lo·scope (o-síllə-skōp, ə-) *n.* An electronic instrument that produces an almost instantaneous graph of the change of some quantity with time (or some other variable) by deflection of a narrow beam of electrons focused onto a fluorescent screen. The varying quantity is converted into an electrical signal used to deflect the electrons in a vertical direction, with repeated scanning in the horizontal direction by a periodic deflecting potential, thus producing a trace on the screen. [OSCILL(ATION) + -SCOPE (used especially for displaying oscillating signals).] —**os·cil·lo·scop·ic** (-skóppik) *adj.*

os·cine (óssīn, óssin) *adj.* Of or pertaining to the Oscines, a large suborder of the passerine birds that includes most songbirds. [New Latin *Oscines,* from Latin *oscinēs,* plural of *oscen,* a singing bird used for augury.] —**os·cine** *n.*

os·ci·tan·cy (óssi-tən-si) *n., pl.* **-cies.** Also **os·ci·tance** (-tənss). **1.** The act of yawning. **2.** The state of being drowsy or inattentive; dullness. [Latin *ōscitāns,* present participle of *ōscitāre,* to gape : *ōs,* mouth + *citāre,* to move.] —**os·ci·tant** *adj.*

Os·co-Um·bri·an (óskō-úmbri-ən) *n.* A subdivision of the Italic languages, including Oscan and Umbrian. —**Os·co-Um·bri·an** *adj.*

os·cu·lant (óskewlənt) *adj. Biology.* **1.** Intermediate in characteristics between two similar or related taxonomic groups. **2.** Closely adhering or joined; embracing. [Latin *ōsculāns* (stem *ōsculant-*), present participle of *ōsculārī,* to OSCULATE.]

os·cu·late (óskew-layt) *v.* **-lated, -lating, -lates.** —*tr.* To kiss. Usually used humorously. —*intr.* **1.** To kiss. Usually used humorously. **2.** *Biology.* To have characteristics intermediate between those of two similar or related taxonomic groups. **3.** In geometry, to touch at a single point without crossing. Used of two curves or surfaces. [Latin *ōsculārī,* from *ōsculum,* kiss, OSCULUM.]

os·cu·la·tion (óskew-láysh'n) *n.* **1. a.** The act of osculating. **b.** A kiss. **2.** In geometry: **a.** A point at which two figures touch. **b.** A **tacnode** *(see).* —**os·cu·la·to·ry** (-lə-təri, -tri, laytəri, -láytəri) *adj.*

os·cu·lum (óskew-ləm) *n., pl.* **-la** (-lə). Also **os·cule** (óskewl). *Zoology.* An opening; especially, the opening in a sponge for expelling water. [New Latin, from Latin *ōsculum,* little mouth, kiss, diminutive of *ōs,* mouth.] —**os·cu·lar** *adj.*

-ose¹ *adj. suffix.* Indicates possession of or similarity to; for example, **bellicose, grandiose.** [Middle English, from Latin *-ōsus.* See **-ous.**]

-ose² *n. suffix. Chemistry.* Indicates: **1.** A carbohydrate; for example, **fructose, lactose. 2.** A product of protein hydrolysis; for example, **proteose.** [From GLUCOSE.]

o·si·er (ṓ-zi-ər, -zhər, -zhi-ər) *n.* **1.** Any of several willows having long, rodlike twigs used in basketry; especially, *Salix viminalis* and *S. purpurea,* both native to Eurasia. **2.** A twig of such a willow. **3.** Any of various similar trees. [Middle English, from Old French, from Medieval Latin *auseria*†, willow bed.] —**o·si·er** *adj.*

O·si·ris (ō-sír-iss, o-). *Egyptian Mythology.* A god who was ruler and judge in the underworld, brother and consort of Isis. He is identified with the Nile, and his annual death and resurrection symbolised the self-renewing fertility of nature. —**O·si·ri·an** *adj.*

-osis *n. suffix.* Indicates: **1.** A condition or process; for example, **metamorphosis, osmosis. 2.** A diseased or abnormal condition; for example, **tuberculosis, neurosis. 3.** An increase or formation of; for example, **sclerosis, leucocytosis.** [Middle English, from Latin, from Greek *-ōsis,* abstract noun suffix formed from *o-*stem verbs.]

Os·lo (óz-lō, óss-; *Norwegian* ṓss-loō). Capital of Norway. An ice-free port at the head of Oslo Fjord, it was founded (1050) by Harald III and became the nation's capital in 1299. Following destruction by fire, it was rebuilt in 1624 when it was renamed Christiania, reverting to its former name in 1925.

Os·man I (oz-maán, oss-, ōss-, ózmən), also known as Othman I (1259–1326). Founder of the Ottoman dynasty that ruled Turkey after 1290. He raised a conquering army of Muslim Turks that held sway over most of northwestern Asia Minor.

Os·man·li (oz-mánli, oss-, -maánli) *n., pl.* **-lis. 1.** An Ottoman Turk. **2. Ottoman Turkish** *(see).* **3.** The Turkish language when written in Arabic script, as it was until 1930.
~*adj.* Ottoman. [Turkish : *Osman,* Osman I + *-li,* adjectival suffix.]

os·mat·ic (oz-máttik) *adj.* Also **os·mic** (ózmik). Having or characterised by a sense of smell. [Greek *osmē,* smell + -AT(E) + -IC.]

os·mic (ózmik) *adj.* Of, pertaining to, or containing osmium. Said especially of compounds containing osmium with a high valency. [From OSMIUM.]

os·mi·rid·i·um (ózmi-ríddi-əm) *n.* A natural alloy of osmium and iridium, used in needles, pen nibs, electric-switch contacts, and other small items subject to wear. Also called "iridosmine". [German : OSM(IUM)- + IRIDIUM.]

os·mi·um (ózmi-əm) *n. Symbol* **Os** A bluish-white, hard, metallic element, found in small amounts in osmiridium and platinum ores.

oryx *A long-horned antelope, the oryx is found in the deserts of Africa and Arabia. The points of its ringed horns are so sharp that they were once used by African peoples for the tips of spears. This is the Arabian oryx.*

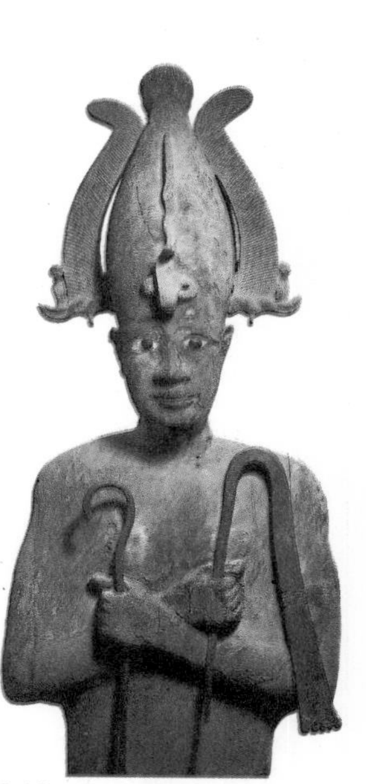

Osiris *The ancient Egyptian god of the underworld, Osiris was also the god of fertility, responsible for the annual flooding of the Nile. Horus, the god of the sky, was his son.*

osprey Pandion haliaetus, *the fish hawk or osprey, feeds largely on fish, diving in a long, looping plunge on to lakes and rivers to pluck trout and even pike from the water with its talons. The birds, which are found in most parts of the world, began nesting in Britain again in the 1950s after an absence of almost 50 years.*

PRONUNCIATION KEY

a, trap; aa, father; ai, fair; ar, star; aw, lawn; ay, play; b, bb, stab; rubber; ch, church; ck, ticket; d, dd, dead; ladder; e, dress; ee, bee; er, defer; ew, few; ewr, pure; ə, about; ər, letter; f, ff, fife; differ; g, gg, giggle; h, hat; i, kit; ī, price; īr, fire; j, judge; k, kick; l, ll, let; 'l, needle; m, mm, man; n, nn, no; 'n, sudden; ng, thing; o, lot; ō, no; o͝o, foot; o͞o, shoe; oor, poor; ow, cow; owr, hour; oy, boy; p, pp, pepper; r, rr, red; s, ss, sauce; sh, ship; t, tt, totter; th, thick; th, this; smooth; u, cut; ur, turn; v, vv, valve; w, wet; y, yes; z, zz, zebra; zh, vision; pleasure

IN FOREIGN WORDS:

aN, oN, Saint-Saëns; hl, Llanelli; Hluhluwe; kh, loch; lough; Khaled

STRESS MARK:

ín-sīt, insight; in-sī́t, incite

It has the highest measured density of any element. It is used as a platinum hardener, in making pen points and instrument pivots, and also as a catalyst in cortisone synthesis. Atomic number 76, atomic weight 190.2, melting point 3,000°C, boiling point 5,000°C, relative density 22.57, valencies 2, 3, 4, 8. [New Latin, from Greek *osmē*, smell (from the smell of osmium tetroxide).]

os·mom·e·ter (oz-mómmitər, oss-) *n.* Any of various instruments or pieces of apparatus used to measure osmotic pressures. [OSMO(SIS) + METER.] **—os·mo·met·ric** (óz-mə-méttrik, óss-) *adj.* **—os·mo·met·ri·cal·ly** *adv.* **—os·mom·e·try** (-mómmətri) *n.*

os·mo·reg·u·la·tion (óz-mō-réggew-láysh'n, óss-) *n.* The maintenance in the body of a living animal of the correct proportions of water and salts. [OSMO(SIS) + REGULATION.] **—os·mo·reg·u·la·to·ry** (-lə-tri, -təri, -láytəri) *adj.*

os·mose (óz-mōss, óss-, -mōz, -mṓz) *v.* **-mosed, -mosing, -moses.** *—intr.* To undergo or diffuse by osmosis. *—tr.* To subject to osmosis. [From OSMOSIS, taken to be the common element of *exosmose* and *endosmose,* obsolete forms of EXOSMOSIS and ENDOSMOSIS.]

os·mo·sis (oz-mṓ-siss, oss-) *n.* **1.** The diffusion of solvent through a semipermeable membrane until there is an equal concentration of solution on either side of the membrane. **2.** The tendency to diffuse in such a manner. **3.** *Informal.* Any gradual, often unconscious, process of assimilation or absorption that resembles this diffusion: *learning a language by osmosis.* [Earlier *osmose,* from Greek *ōsmos,* action of pushing, from *ōthein,* to push.] **—os·mot·ic** (-móttik) *adj.* **—os·mot·i·cal·ly** *adv.*

osmotic pressure *n. Symbol* **Π.** The pressure developed across a membrane as a result of osmosis. For a given solution it is the pressure required to prevent osmosis from the solution to a pure solvent, such as water. [Greek *ōsmos* (stem *ōsmot-*), OSMOSIS.]

os·mous (ózməss) *adj.* Also **os·mi·ous** (ózmi-əss). Of, pertaining to, or containing osmium. Said especially of compounds containing osmium with a low valency.

os·mun·da (oz-múndə) *n.* Also **os·mund** (ózmənd). Any fern of the genus *Osmunda,* having erect, compound fronds, and, in some species, fibrous roots used as a potting medium for cultivated plants. [Middle English, from Old French *osmunde*†.]

os·prey (óss-pri, -pray) *n., pl.* **-preys. 1.** A fish-eating hawk, *Pandion haliaetus,* having plumage that is dark on the back and white below. Also *chiefly U.S.* "fish eagle", "fish hawk", "ossifrage". **2.** A decorative feather formerly used to trim women's hats. [Middle English *ospray,* from Old French *ospreit* (unattested), from Vulgar Latin *avispreda* (unattested), from Latin *avis praedae,* "bird of prey" : *avis,* bird, + *praeda,* prey. The Old French form and meaning are influenced by Old French *osfraie,* from Latin *ossifraga,* OSSIFRAGE.]

os·sa. Plural of **os** (bone).

Os·sa, Mount (óssə). Mountain in the Duana range of central Tasmania, it is, at 1 617 metres (5,305 feet), the island's highest point.

os·se·in (óssi-in) *n.* The protein residue of bone after acid dissolution, used in gelatine and glue. [OSSE(OUS) + -IN.]

os·se·ous (óssi-əss) *adj.* Composed of, containing, or resembling bone; bony. [Latin *osseus,* from *os,* bone.] **—os·se·ous·ly** *adv.*

Os·set (óssit) *n.* Also **Os·sete** (ósseet). A member of a people of Iranian origin living in Ossetia, a region in the southwestern U.S.S.R., straddling the Caucasus mountains. **—Os·se·tian** (o-sée-sh'n) *n. & adj.*

Os·set·ic (o-séttik) *n.* The Iranian language of the Ossets. *~adj.* Of or pertaining to the Ossets, their country, or their languages.

os·si·a (óssi-ə) *conj. Music.* Or else. Used as a direction to the performer to designate an alternative section or passage. [Italian, from *o sia,* "or let it be".]

Os·si·an (óssi-ən || ósh'n) (*c.* third century A.D.). Legendary Irish warrior-poet. He occurs in the Fianna cycle of ballads under the name of Oisin. **—Os·si·an·ic** (-ánnik) *adj.*

os·si·cle (óssik'l) *n. Anatomy.* A small bone; especially, any of the three sound-conducting bones, malleus, incus, and stapes, of the inner ear. [Latin *ossiculum,* diminutive of *os,* bone.] **—os·sic·u·lar** (o-síckew-lər), **os·sic·u·late** (-lət, -lit) *adj.*

os·si·fi·ca·tion (óssifi-káysh'n) *n.* **1.** The natural process of bone formation. Also called "osteogenesis". **2. a.** The abnormal hardening or calcification of soft tissue into a bonelike material. **b.** A mass or deposit of such material. **3.** The process of becoming or state of being set in a rigidly conventional pattern, as of behaviour, habits, or beliefs. **—os·sif·i·ca·to·ry** (-káytəri, -kə-təri, -tri || o-síffikə-) *adj.*

os·si·frage (óssi-frij, -frayj) *n. Archaic.* Either of two hawks, the **osprey** or the **lammergeier** *(both of which see).* [Latin *(avis) ossifraga,* "bone-breaking (bird)", lammergeier (which is said to drop its prey from a height to break the bones), from *ossifragus,* bone-breaking : *os* (stem *oss-*), bone + *frangere,* to break.]

os·si·fy (óssi-fī) *v.* **-fied, -fying, -fies.** *—intr.* **1.** To change into bone; become bony. **2.** To become set in a rigidly conventional pattern of behaviour or attitude. *—tr.* **1.** To make or form bone in or of; convert (a membrane or cartilage, for example) into bone. **2.** To mould into a rigidly conventional pattern of behaviour or attitude. [Latin *os* (stem *oss-*), bone + -FY.] **—os·sif·ic** (o-síffik) *adj.*

os·so buc·co, os·so bu·co (óssō bo͝okō) *n.* A dish of Italian origin, consisting of shin of veal braised with tomatoes, wine, and spices. [Italian, marrow bone.]

os·su·ar·y (óssew-əri || *U.S.* -erri; *also* óshōo-) *n., pl.* **-ies.** A container or receptacle, such as an urn or vault, for holding the bones of the dead. [Late Latin *ossuārium,* from Latin, neuter of *ossuārius,* of bones, from *ossu,* variant of *os* (stem *oss-*), bone.]

os·te·al (ósti-əl) *adj.* **1.** Bony; osseous. **2.** Pertaining to bone or to the skeleton. [OSTE(O)- + -AL.]

os·te·ich·thy·es (ósti-íkthi-eez) *n.* A class of fish having an endoskeleton made of bone, an air bladder or lungs, and gills covered by an operculum. Also called "bony fish".

os·te·i·tis (ósti-ītiss) *n.* Inflammation of bone or bony tissue. [New Latin : OSTE(O)- + -ITIS.]

Os·tend (oss-ténd). *Flemish* **Oos·tende** (ōst-éndə); *French* **Os·tende** (-tóɴd). Seaport of northwest Belgium. Lying in the West Flanders province, it is the country's third port, the base of its fishing fleet, and the terminal of a ferry service across the English Channel to Dover.

os·ten·si·ble (o-sténsəb'l) *adj.* Given or appearing as such, especially in a false or pretended way; seeming; apparent: *His ostensible purpose was charity, his real goal popularity.* [French, from Medieval Latin *ostensībilis,* from Latin *ostendere,* to show : *ob-,* before + *tendere,* to stretch.] **—os·ten·si·bly** *adv.*

os·ten·sive (o-stén-siv) *adj.* **1. a.** Ostensible; apparent. **b.** Indicating meaning by a direct example of the term being defined. Said of a definition. **2.** Obviously or manifestly demonstrative. [Late Latin *ostensīvus,* from Latin *ostensus,* past participle of *ostendere,* to show. See **ostensible.**] **—os·ten·sive·ly** *adv.*

os·ten·so·ri·um (óss-tən-sáwri-əm, -ten- || -sṓri-) *n., pl.* **-soria** (-sáwri-ə || -sṓri-). Also **os·ten·so·ry** (o-stén-səri) *pl.* **-ries.** *Roman Catholic Church.* A receptacle in which the Host is exposed for adoration; a monstrance. [Medieval Latin *ostensōrium,* from Latin *ostendere,* to show. See **ostensible.**]

os·ten·ta·tion (óss-ten-táysh'n, -tən-) *n.* **1.** Pretentious, gaudy, or showy display, often meant to impress others. **2.** *Archaic.* An act of showing; an exhibition. [Middle English *ostentacioun,* from Old French *ostentation,* from Latin *ostentātiō* (stem *ostentātiōn-*), from *ostentāre,* frequentative of *ostendere,* to show. See **ostensible.**]

os·ten·ta·tious (óss-ten-táyshəss, -tən-) *adj.* Characterised by or given to ostentation; showy; pretentious. See Synonyms at **ornate.** **—os·ten·ta·tious·ly** *adv.*

osteo–, oste– *comb. form.* Indicates bone or bones; for example, **osteomyelitis, osteoid.** [Greek, from *osteon,* bone.]

osteo. osteopath; osteopathy.

os·te·o·ar·thri·tis (ósti-ō-aar-thrī́tiss) *n.* Degenerative joint disease due to destruction of joint cartilage, characterised by pain and impaired mobility of the affected joint.

os·te·o·blast (ósti-ō-blast, -ə-) *n.* A cell from which bone develops. [OSTEO- + -BLAST.] **—os·te·o·blas·tic** (-blástik) *adj.*

os·te·oc·la·sis (ósti-ócklәsiss) *n.* **1.** Surgical fracture of a bone, performed to correct a deformity. **2.** The dissolution and resorption of bony tissue. [New Latin : OSTEO- + Greek *klasis,* breakage (see **-clase**).]

os·te·o·clast (ósti-ō-klast, -ə-) *n.* **1.** An instrument used in surgical osteoclasis. **2.** A large multinuclear cell that resorbs bony tissue in osteoclasis. [OSTEO- + -CLAST.] **—os·te·o·clas·tic** (-klástik) *adj.*

os·te·o·cra·ni·um (ósti-ō-kráyni-əm) *n.* The ossified embryonic cranium, as distinguished from the **chondrocranium** *(see).* **—os·te·o·cra·ni·al** *adj.*

os·te·o·cyte (ósti-ə-sīt) *n.* A bone cell. [OSTEO- + -CYTE.]

os·te·o·gen·e·sis (ósti-ō-jénnəsiss) *n.* **Ossification** *(see).*

os·te·oid (ósti-oyd) *adj.* Resembling bone. [OSTE(O)- + -OID.]

os·te·ol·o·gy (ósti-ólləji) *n.* **1.** The anatomical study of bones. **2.** The bone structure or system of an animal. [Greek *osteologia* : OSTEO- + -LOGY.] **—os·te·o·log·i·cal** (-ə-lójik'l) *adj.* **—os·te·ol·o·gist** (-óllәjist) *n.*

os·te·o·ma (ósti-ṓ-mə) *n., pl.* **-mas** or **-mata** (-mətə). A benign bony tumour. [OSTE(O)- + -OMA.]

os·te·o·ma·la·ci·a (ósti-ō-mə-láyshi-ə, -láyshə) *n.* Softening of the bones because of a deficiency of vitamin D or of calcium. [New Latin : OSTEO- + *malacia,* softness, from Greek *malakia,* from *malakos,* soft.]

os·te·o·my·e·li·tis (ósti-ō-mī́-ə-lī́tiss) *n.* Inflammation of the bone marrow due to infection.

os·te·o·path (ósti-ə-path) *n.* Also *rare* **os·te·op·a·thist** (ósti-óppə-thist). *Abbr.* **osteo** (-ō). One who practises osteopathy.

os·te·op·a·thy (ósti-óppəthi) *n. Abbr.* **osteo.** A medical therapy relying on manipulative techniques, based on the theory that many diseases are caused or exacerbated by displacement of bones, especially those of the spine, from their correct positions. [OSTEO- + -PATHY.] **—os·te·o·path·ic** (ósti-ə-páthik) *adj.* **—os·te·o·path·i·cal·ly** *adv.*

os·te·o·phyte (ósti-ə-fīt) *n.* A small abnormal bony outgrowth, occurring, for example, in osteoarthritis. [OSTEO- + -PHYTE.] **—os·te·o·phyt·ic** (-fíttik) *adj.*

os·te·o·plas·tic (ósti-ə-plastik) *adj.* **1.** *Medicine.* Of or pertaining to osteoplasty. **2.** *Physiology.* Pertaining to or functioning in bone formation.

os·te·o·plas·ty (ósti-ə-plasti) *n., pl.* **-ties.** The surgical repair or alteration of bone. [OSTEO- + -PLASTY.]

os·te·o·por·o·sis (ósti-ō-pawr-ṓ-siss || -pōr-) *n.* Brittleness and porosity of the bones, resulting in a liability to fracture. It is common in the elderly.

os·te·o·sar·co·ma (ósti-ō-saar-kṓmə) *n.* A malignant bone tumour.

os·te·ot·o·my (ósti-óttəmi) *n., pl.* **-mies.** The surgical division or sectioning of bone. [OSTEO- + -TOMY.] **—os·te·ot·o·mist** *n.*

Österreich. See **Austria.**

os·ti·ar·y (ósti-əri || *U.S.* -erri) *n., pl.* **-ies.** *Archaic.* A doorkeeper at a church. [Latin *ōstiārius,* doorkeeper, from *ōstium,* an opening, from *ōs,* mouth.]
os·ti·na·to (ósti-naátō) *n., pl.* **-tos.** *Music.* A short melody or phrase that is constantly repeated in the same pitch. [Italian, "stubborn", from Latin *obstinātus,* OBSTINATE.]
os·ti·ole (ósti-ōl) *n. Biology.* A small opening or pore, such as that in the fruiting body of certain fungi. [Latin *ōstiolum,* diminutive of *ōstium,* OSTIUM.] **—os·ti·o·lar** (-ṓlər, -ələr) *adj.*
os·ti·um (óss-ti-əm) *n., pl.* **-tia** (-ti-ə). *Biology.* A small opening, such as any of the openings in a sponge, through which water enters the body of the organ or organism. [Latin *ōstium,* river mouth, opening, from *ōs,* mouth.]
os·tler, hos·tler (ósslə) *n.* One who takes charge of horses, as at an inn; a stableman. [16th century contraction of HOSTELLER.]
Ost·mark (óst-maark) *n. Abbr.* **OM.** See **mark²**.
Ost·po·li·tik (óst-polli-teek) *n.* **1.** A policy of the West German government designed to improve and ultimately normalise trade and diplomatic relations with the Communist countries of eastern Europe. **2.** A similar policy on the part of any other Western country. [German, East politics.]
os·tra·cise, os·tra·cize (óstrə-sīz) *tr.v.* **-cised, -cising, -cises. 1.** To banish or exclude from a group; shut out; shun. **2.** To banish by ostracism, as in ancient Greece. [Greek *ostrakizein,* from *ostrakon,* shell, shard (see **ostracon**).]
os·tra·cism (óstrə-siz'm) *n.* **1.** Banishment or exclusion from a group; disgrace. **2.** In Athens and other city states of ancient Greece, the temporary banishment by popular vote of a citizen considered dangerous to the state. **3.** The act of ostracising. **4.** The state or condition of being ostracised. [French *ostracisme,* from Greek *ostrakismos,* from *ostrakizein,* to OSTRACIZE.]
os·tra·cod (óstrə-kod) *n.* Any of various minute, chiefly freshwater crustaceans of the order Ostracoda, having a bivalved carapace. [New Latin *ostracoda,* from Greek *ostrakōdēs,* testaceous, from *ostrakon,* shell.]
os·tra·con (óstrə-kon) *n.* A fragment of pottery used in ancient Athens when voting for the ostracism of a citizen. [Greek *ostrakon,* potsherd.]
os·trich (óss-trich, -trij || áwss-) *n., pl.* **-triches** or collectively **ostrich. 1.** A large, flightless African bird, *Struthio camelus,* characterised by a long, bare neck and legs, two-toed feet, and plumage often used for decoration and brushes. **2.** *U.S.* A similar bird, the **rhea** *(see).* **3.** One who refuses to accept reality or heed a serious danger, and is therefore thought to emulate the ostrich's alleged habit of burying its head in the sand to escape danger. [Middle English *ostriche,* from Old French *ostrusce,* from Vulgar Latin *avistrūthius* (unattested) : Latin *avis,* bird + Late Latin *strūthiō,* ostrich, from Greek *struthiōn* (see **struthious**).]
ostrich fern *n.* A fern, *Matteuccia struthiopteris,* of northern temperate regions, having long, plumelike fronds.
Os·tro·goth (óss-trə-goth, -trō-) *n.* A member of a tribe of eastern Goths that conquered and ruled Italy from A.D. 493 to 555. [Late Latin *Ostrogothis* : *ostro-,* eastward + *Gothus,* GOTH.] **—Os·tro·goth·ic** (-góthik) *adj.*
Os·trov·sky (o-strófsk-yi), **Alexandr Nikolayevich** (1823–86). Russian dramatist. Often regarded in the U.S.S.R. as the greatest Russian playwright, he wrote more than 50 plays, of which the best known is *The Storm* (1860).
Os·ty·ak, Os·ti·ak (ósti-ak) *n.* **1.** A member of a Finno-Ugric people inhabiting western Siberia. **2.** The Ugric language spoken by this people. **—Os·ty·ak** *adj.*
OSU, O.S.U. Order of St. Ursula.
Oś·więcim (osh-fi-ént-shim). *German* **Ausch·witz** (ówsh-vits). Town of southern Poland. Situated at the confluence of the Iola and Vistula rivers, it lies near the site of the Auschwitz-Birkenau extermination camp, where, between 1942 and 1945, some 4,000 people, mostly German and east European Jews, were systematically put to death by the Nazis.
OT, O.T. Old Testament.
ot-. Variant of **oto-**.
o·tal·gi·a (ō-tál-ji-ə, -jə) *n. Medicine.* Earache. [OTO- + -ALGIA.]
OTC, O.T.C. 1. Officers' Training Corps. **2.** over-the-counter.
oth·er (ú*th*ər) *adj.* **1. a.** Being or designating the remaining one of two or more: *the other ear.* **b.** Being or designating the remaining ones of several. Used before a plural noun: *His other books are still in storage.* **2.** Different from that or those implied or specified: *Any other person would tell the truth; Call me some other time.* **3. a.** Of a different character or quality. Used with *than*: *other than meets the eye.* **b.** Besides; apart from. Used with *than*: *Nobody other than Peter could have got away with it.* **4.** Of a different time or era either future or past: *other centuries; other generations.* **5.** Additional; extra: *I have no other shoes.* **6.** Opposite; contrary; reverse: *the other side.* **7.** Alternate; second: *every other day.* **8.** Recent but unspecified. Used in phrases such as *the other day* and *the other morning.*
~pron. **1. a.** The remaining one of two or more: *One took a taxi, the other walked home.* **b.** *Plural.* The remaining ones of several: *After her departure the others resumed the discussion.* **2. a.** A different person or thing: *I don't want this toy, I want the other.* **b.** An additional person or thing: *How many others will come later?* **3.** *Plural.* People who do not share the attributes, experience, or views of the speaker or those he represents: *Others may disagree.* **—or other.** Used with *some* to refer to some unknown person or thing: *Some poet or other said that beauty is truth.*
~adv. **1.** Differently; in another way: *She never performs other than perfectly.* **2.** Otherwise; in other respects: *I felt a bit queasy, but other than that I was not carsick.* **—no other.** *Archaic.* No differently; nothing else: *She could do no other.* [Middle English *other,* Old English *ōther.*]
Usage: *Other than* may be used both in adjectival and adverbial constructions, as in *books other than fiction; perform other than efficiently.* It is also used as a conjunction (*I said nothing, other than to remark that...*), but many people prefer the use of *apart from* or (especially in American English) *aside from* in such constructions. In negative constructions, when *other* precedes the noun, *than* is recommended in formal usage, though *but* is more common informally: *I have no other shoes than/but these.* The same variation takes place in formal sentences such as *She could do no other than/but leave.*
o·ther-di·rect·ed (ú*th*ər-dī-réktid, -di-) *adj.* Guided by the values of one's peers or of society at large rather than by independent personal principles: *an other-directed personality.* Compare **inner-directed, tradition-directed. —o·ther-di·rect·ed·ness** *n.*
oth·er·ness (ú*th*ər-nəss, -niss) *n.* The quality or condition of being different, distinct, or unusual.
oth·er·wise (ú*th*ər-wīz) *adv.* **1.** In another way; differently: *She thought otherwise.* **2.** Under other circumstances: *Otherwise I might have helped.* **3.** In other respects: *an otherwise logical mind.*
~conj. If not: *Get going, otherwise they'll catch you.*
~adj. **1.** Other than supposed; different: *The evidence is otherwise.* **2.** Other: *be otherwise than happy.* [Middle English *otherwise,* Old English *(on) ōthre wīsan,* (in) another manner : *ōther,* OTHER + *wīse,* way, -WISE.]
oth·er·world·ly (ú*th*ər-wúrldli) *adj.* **1.** Of, pertaining to, or characteristic of another world, especially a mystical or transcendental world. **2.** Devoted to the world of the mind; concerned with intellectual or imaginative things, rather than with practical realities; absent-minded or impractical. **—oth·er·world·li·ness** *n.*
Othman¹. *Poetic.* Variant of **Ottoman.**
Othman². See **Osman I.**
o·tic (ṓtik, óttik) *adj.* Of, pertaining to, or located near the ear; auricular. [Greek *ōtikos,* from *ous* (stem *ōt-*), ear.]
-otic *adj. suffix.* Indicates: **1.** Affected with or by; for example, **sclerotic. 2.** Having a specific disease; for example, **epizootic. 3.** Producing or causing; for example, **narcotic.** [Old French *-otique* and Latin *-ōticus,* from Greek *-ōtikos,* adjectival suffix formed from *-o-* stem verbs and *-ōt-* stem nouns.]
o·ti·ose (ṓti-ōss, ṓshi-, -ōz) *adj.* **1.** Having no real use; purposeless. **2.** Having a lazy nature; indolent. [Latin *ōtiōsus,* from *ōtium*†, leisure. See also **negotiate.**] **—o·ti·ose·ly** *adv.* **—o·ti·os·i·ty** (-óssəti) *n.*
O·tis (ṓtiss), **Elisha Graves** (1811–61). U.S. inventor, best known for inventing the safety lift (1852), which he demonstrated (1854) by severing the cable of a lift in which he was travelling.
o·ti·tis (ō-tītiss) *n.* Inflammation of the ear; especially, *otitis media,* inflammation of the middle ear causing pain and impaired hearing. [New Latin : OT(O)- + -ITIS.] **—o·tit·ic** (ō-títtik) *adj.*
oto-, ot- *comb. form.* Indicates the ear; for example, **otology.** [New Latin, from Greek *ous* (stem *ōt-*), ear.]
o·to·cyst (ṓtō-sist, ṓtə-) *n.* **1.** The structure in the skull of a vertebrate embryo that develops into the inner ear in the adult. **2.** An organ of balance, the **statocyst** *(see).* **—o·to·cys·tic** (-sístik) *adj.*
otol. otology.
o·to·lar·yn·gol·o·gy (ṓtō-lárring-gólləji, ṓtə-) *n.* The branch of medicine concerned with diseases of the ear and throat. [OTO- + LARYNGO- + -LOGY.] **—o·to·lar·yn·go·log·i·cal** (-gə-lójik'l, -lə-ríng-) *adj.* **—o·to·lar·yn·gol·o·gist** (-góllәjist) *n.*
o·to·lith (ṓtō-lith, ṓtə-) *n.* Any of many minute calcareous particles found in the inner ear of certain vertebrates and in the statocysts of numerous invertebrates. [French *otolithe* : OTO- + -LITH.]
o·tol·o·gy (ō-tólləji) *n. Abbr.* **otol.** The anatomy, physiology, and pathology of the ear. **—o·to·log·i·cal** (ṓtə-lójik'l) *adj.* **—o·tol·o·gist** (ō-tólləjist) *n.* [OTO- + -LOGY.]
o·to·rhi·no·lar·yn·gol·o·gy (ṓtō-rīnō-lárring-gólləji, ṓtə-) *n.* The branch of medicine concerned with diseases of the ear, nose, and throat. [OTO- + RHINO- + LARYNGO- + -LOGY.] **—o·to·rhi·no·lar·yn·go·log·i·cal** (-gəlójik'l) *adj.* **—o·to·rhi·no·lar·yn·gol·o·gist** *n.*
o·to·scope (ṓtə-skōp, ṓtō-) *n.* An instrument for examining the eardrum and the passage in the outer ear leading to it. [OTO- + -SCOPE.] **—o·to·scop·ic** (-skóppik) *n.*
ottar. Variant of **attar.**
O.T.T. Over the top.
ot·ta·va (o-taávə, ō-) *n. Music.* An octave. [Italian.]
ottava ri·ma (reémə) *n.* A stanza form perfected by the poets Ariosto and Tasso, consisting of eight lines of eleven syllables each in iambic pentameter and having a rhyme pattern *abababcc.* [Italian, "eighth rhyme".]
Ot·ta·wa¹ (óttə-wə || -waa, -waw) *n., pl.* **-was** or collectively **Ottawa. 1.** A member of a North American Indian people, originally inhabiting the region of the Ottawa river in Ontario, Canada. **2.** The Ojibwa dialect of this people, of the Algonquian family of languages. **—Ot·ta·wa** *adj.*
Ottawa². Capital of Canada. Founded (1827) as Bytown on the Ottawa river, in the southeast of the country, it became the capital in 1867. The industrial development along the Ottawa valley, of which the city is the centre, rests mainly on sawmilling and timber. One third of the population is French-speaking.
Ottawa. River of eastern Canada. The principal tributary of the St.

ostrich *The world's largest living bird cannot fly, but it can run at up to 65 kilometres per hour (40 miles per hour). A male ostrich can be as much as 2.5 metres (8 feet) tall and can weigh up to 140 kilograms (300 pounds).*

Lawrence, it rises in the Laurentian plateau of western Quebec and flows 1 120 kilometres (696 miles) west to join the St. Lawrence west of Montreal.

ot·ter (óttər) *n., pl.* **-ters** or collectively **otter. 1.** Any of various aquatic, carnivorous mammals of the family Mustelidae, such as *Lutra lutra,* the Eurasian otter, having webbed feet and dense, dark brown fur. **2.** The fur of any of these animals. [Middle English *oter,* Old English *otor.*] —**ot·ter** *adj.*

ot·ter·hound (óttər-hownd) *n.* A dog of a breed formerly used to hunt otters. It is a good swimmer, strongly built with a large head and long drooping ears.

otter shrew *n.* Any of various small, otter-like, semiaquatic mammals of the family Potamogalidae, of west and central Africa.

otto. Variant of **attar.**

Ot·to I (óttō), also called Otto the Great (912–973). King of Germany (936–73); first Holy Roman Emperor (962–73).

Otto, Nikolaus August (1832–91). German engineer. His invention of the internal-combustion engine (1876) facilitated the development of the motor car.

Otto cycle *n.* A cycle of changes in a heat engine in which heat is produced and lost at constant volume, approximately applicable to a four-stroke petrol engine. [After N. A. OTTO.]

ot·to·man (óttə-mən, óttō-) *n., pl.* **-mans. 1. a.** An upholstered sofa or divan without arms or a back. **b.** An upholstered low seat or cushioned footstool. **2.** A heavy silk or rayon fabric with a corded texture, usually used for coats and trimmings. [French *ottomane,* feminine of OTTOMAN.]

Ot·to·man (óttə-mən, óttō-) *n., pl.* **-mans.** *Poetic* **Oth·man** (óth-mən, -maan). **1.** A Turk of the Ottoman Empire. **2.** A Turk belonging to the tribe or family of **Osman I** (*see*).

~*adj.* **1.** Of or pertaining to the Turks; Turkish. **2.** Of or pertaining to the Ottoman Empire and the dynasty founded by Osman I. [French, from Medieval Latin *Ottomānus,* from Arabic *Othmānī,* Turkish, from Turkish *Osman,* Osman I. See **Osmanli.**]

Ottoman Empire *n.* An empire of the east Mediterranean. Spanning over six hundred years (1300–1922), it started as a small enclave of Osmanli Turks, replaced the Byzantine Empire in Asia Minor, and during the 16th and 17th centuries included the Levant, Mesopotamia, much of North Africa, and southeast Europe to the borders of Austria. By the end of World War I it had lost all its possessions outside Turkey, where it was finally overthrown by revolution.

Ottoman Turkish *n.* The form of Turkish used by the Ottoman Turks. Also called "Osmanli". —**Ottoman Turkish** *adj.*

ou *n., pl.* **ous** (ōss, ōz). *South African Informal.* Any male person; a fellow; a guy. [Afrikaans, probably from Dutch *ouwe,* old person.]

O.U. 1. Open University. **2.** Oxford University.

oua·ba·in (waá-baa-in, -bayn, waa-báy-in) *n.* A white poisonous glucoside, $C_{29}H_{44}O_{12}$·$8H_2O$, extracted from the seeds of the African trees *Strophanthus gratus* and *Acokanthera ouabaio.* It is used as a heart stimulant, and by some African peoples as a dart poison. [French *ouaba(io),* from Somali *wabayo.*]

Oua·ga·dou·gou (waágə-dōō-gōō, wággə-). Capital of the republic of Upper Volta. Founded in the 11th century, in the heart of the country, it was once the centre of the Mossi empire.

ou·bli·ette (ōōbli-ét) *n.* A dungeon with a trapdoor in the ceiling as its only means of entrance or exit. [French, from *oublier,* to forget, from Old French *oblider,* from Vulgar Latin *oblītāre* (unattested), from Latin *oblīviscī* (past participle *oblītus*), to forget.]

ouch [1] (owch) *interj.* **1.** Used to express sudden pain. **2.** Used to express embarrassment, as on realising an error one has made. **3.** Used to express pretended distaste, as on hearing a poor joke.

ouch [2] *n. Archaic.* **1.** A setting for a precious stone. **2.** A brooch or ornament set with jewels. [Middle English *ouche,* from the phrase *an ouche,* mistaken division of *a nouche,* from Old French *nouche,* brooch, from Frankish *nuskja.*]

oud (ōōd) *n.* A musical instrument of northern Africa and southwest Asia resembling a lute. [Arabic *'ūd,* "wood".]

Ou·de·naar·de (ōōdə-naárdə). *French* **Au·de·narde** (ōdə-nárd). Town in East Flanders province, western Belgium. Here, in 1708, during the War of the Spanish Succession, an allied army led by Eugene of Savoy and Marlborough defeated the French.

ought [1] (awt) *v.* Used as an auxiliary followed by an infinitive with *to.* It can indicate: **1.** Obligation or duty: *You ought to work harder than that.* **2.** Expediency or prudence: *You ought to wear a raincoat in this weather.* **3.** Desirability: *You ought to have been there, it was great fun.* **4.** Probability or likelihood: *She ought to have it finished by next week.* [Middle English *aghten, oughten,* to be obliged to, owe, from *aghte, oughte,* possessed, owned, Old English *āhte,* first and third singular past indicative of *āgan,* to possess.]

Usage: As an auxiliary verb, *ought to* has no inflections, and may be negated using *not* or *n't: You ought not/oughtn't to go.* It does not itself take an auxiliary form, though in casual (and especially jocular) use such constructions as *You didn't ought to go* will be heard. An emphatic form, *did ought,* is also common in regional speech: *You did ought to go, you know.* In negative and question forms, *to* is sometimes omitted (*You oughtn't go; Ought she go?*), as it may be in cases where the main verb is not present, being understood from the context: *Are you going to visit her? We ought (to). Ought to* is often felt to be awkward in question forms, *should* being used instead. In negative questions, there are three possibilities: *Oughtn't we to go?, Ought we not to go?,* and the formal *Ought not we to go?*

ought [2]. Variant of **aught.**

ought [3] *n. Nonstandard.* Nothing; zero; nought. [Perhaps mistaken division (*an ought* for *a nought*).]

Oui·ja (wée-jə ‖ -ji) *n.* A trademark for a board with the alphabet and other symbols on it, and a planchette or movable pointer that is thought, when touched with the fingers of several people, to move in such a way as to spell out spiritualistic and telepathic messages on the board. [French *oui,* yes + German *ja,* yes.]

ounce [1] (ownss) *n. Abbr.* **oz 1. a.** A unit of mass or weight in avoirdupois measure equivalent to one sixteenth of a pound avoirdupois. It is equal to 28.349 grams. **b.** A unit of mass or weight in Troy measure equivalent to one twelfth of a Troy pound. It is equal to 31.103 grams. **c.** A unit of mass or weight in apothecaries' measure equal to one twelfth of an apothecaries' pound. It is identical to the Troy ounce. **2.** A **fluid ounce** (*see*). **3.** A very small quantity or portion. [Middle English *unce,* from Old French, from Latin *uncia,* a twelfth, ounce, from *ūnus,* unit, one.]

ounce [2] *n.* The snow leopard (*see*). [Middle English *once,* from Old French, variant of *lonce* (the *l* being taken as the definite article), from Latin *lynx* (stem *lync-*), lynx, from Greek *lunx.*]

our (owr, ar, ów-ər). The possessive form of the pronoun *we.* Used attributively to indicate possession, agency, or reception: *our house; our victory; our defeat.* [Middle English *ure, oure,* Old English *ūre.*]

-our, *U.S.* **-or** *n. suffix.* Indicates a state, quality, or activity; for example, **fervour, candour, behaviour.** [Old French *-or, -ur* or Latin *-or* (genitive *-oris*).]

Our Father *n.* The **Lord's Prayer** (*see*). [From the opening words.]

Our Lady. See **Mary.**

ours (owrz, arz, ów-ərz). Possessive pronoun, absolute form of *our.* **1.** Belonging to us; for us; our own: *The house is ours.* **2.** The one or ones belonging or pertaining to us: *They couldn't find their hats so they took ours; Ours is the best.* —**of ours.** Belonging or pertaining to us: *a friend of ours.* [Middle English *ures, oures,* from *ure, oure,* OUR.]

our·self (owr-sélf, aar-) *pron.* Myself or ourselves collectively. A specialised form corresponding to *ourselves,* but used only in regal or formal proclamations or editorial comments with the formal *we* understood as singular.

Ottoman Empire

THE TURKISH EMPIRE THAT LASTED 700 YEARS
Constantinople, capital of Byzantium, fell to Islamic invaders

The Ottoman Empire, largest and longest surviving of all Islamic states, was founded about 1300 by Osman, leader of a race of Turks who had migrated into Asia Minor from central Asia.

The Ottomans captured Constantinople in 1453 and ended the 1,000-year-old Byzantine Empire. In the next 150 years they overran much of eastern Europe and the Arab world, and most of North Africa.

The Ottoman Empire enlarged its civil service and its army by training and compulsorily converting to Islam, Christian slaves from their subject races. The elite corps of troops called Janissaries was made up of Christians.

In the 16th century the Ottomans were unable to match the technological progress of the European nations and their empire went into a long, slow decline. It finally came to an end after World War I; the Republic of Turkey was set up in 1923.

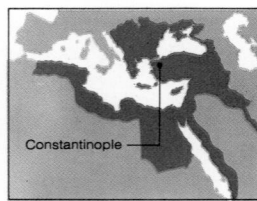

EXTENT OF THE EMPIRE *The dark area shows the Ottoman Empire at its peak, soon after 1600.*

OTTOMAN ART *This boldly coloured miniature is in a 16th-century manuscript telling of the victories of Suleiman the Magnificent. It shows the capture of Rhodes in 1522. Figures were forbidden in Islamic art, but Ottoman artists interpreted the ban loosely; manuscripts were not for public show and contain many human scenes.*

our·selves (owr-sélvz, aar-) *pron.* A specialised form of the first person plural pronoun. It is used: **1.** As a reflexive pronoun, forming the direct or indirect object of a verb, or the object of a preposition: *We injured ourselves; gave ourselves time; talked among ourselves.* **2.** For emphasis, after *we*: *We ourselves are excluded from the contract.* **3.** As an emphasising substitute: *The Smiths and ourselves are in trouble; She invited only Tom and ourselves; Ourselves in debt, we couldn't help you.* **4.** As an indication of (our) normal, real, or healthy condition or identity: *We have not been ourselves lately.*

-ous *adj. suffix.* Indicates: **1.** Possessing, having, or full of; for example, **cancerous, joyous.** **2.** *Chemistry.* Occurring with a valency that is lower than that in a comparable *-ic* system; for example, **ferrous, osmous.** Compare **-ic.** [Middle English, from Old French *-os, -us, -eus, -eux,* from Latin *-ōsus, -us,* adjectival suffixes.]

Ouse (ōōz). Any of four rivers of England: **1.** The **Great Ouse** *(see).* **2.** The **Yorkshire Ouse.** Formed by the rivers Swale and Ure, it flows 100 kilometres (60 miles) to join the river Trent, forming the Humber estuary on the northeast coast. **3.** The **Ouse.** Rising in the South Downs, it flows 48 kilometres 30 miles) across Sussex to enter the English Channel at Newhaven. **4.** The **Little Ouse.** Rising in the Gog Magog hills of Suffolk, it flows north and west across Norfolk to join the Great Ouse at the Cambridgeshire border.

ousel. Variant of **ouzel.**

Ou·spen·sky (ōō-spén-ski; *Russian* -spyén-), **Peter** (1878–1947). Russian philosopher and occultist. An associate of the mystic Gurdjieff (1873–1943), whose ideas he publicised, Ouspensky urged a form of mysticism on Europe and North America. *Tertium Organum* (1912) is one of his more readable books.

oust (owst) *tr.v.* **ousted, ousting, ousts.** **1.** To eject from a position or place; force out; displace. **2.** *Law.* To deprive of land or property. [Anglo-French *ouster,* from Latin *obstāre,* to hinder : *ob-,* off, against + *stāre,* to stand.]

oust·er (ówstər) *n.* **1.** One that ousts. **2.** *Law.* **a.** The act of forcing someone out of possession or occupancy of material property to which he is entitled. Also used adjectivally: *an ouster injunction.* **b.** Illegal or wrongful dispossession. **3.** *Chiefly U.S.* **a.** The act of ousting. **b.** The state of being ousted. [Anglo-French, substantive use of the infinitive *ouster,* to OUST.]

out (owt) *adv.* **1.** Away or forth from inside: *go out of the office.* **2. a.** Away from the centre or middle: *The troops fanned out.* **b.** Away from somewhere considered as central: *They live out at Harlow.* **3.** Away from a normal or usual place: *stepped out for a minute.* **4.** Away from the coast: *The tide goes out at three o'clock.* **5.** From inside a building or shelter into the open air; outside: *The girl went out to play.* **6.** From within a container or source: *drain the water out.* **7. a.** To exhaustion or depletion: *The supplies have run out.* **b.** Into extinction or imperceptibility: *The fire has gone out; rub out a mistake.* **8. a.** To a finish or conclusion: *Hear me out.* **b.** Completely: *We fitted out the kitchen.* **9.** Into being or evident existence: *The new car models have come out.* **10.** Into view: *The moon came out.* **11.** Without inhibition; boldly: *Speak out.* **12.** Into possession of another or others; into distribution: *giving out free passes.* **13.** Into disuse or an unfashionable status: *Knee-length hems have gone out.* **14.** So as to be unconscious or asleep: *went out like a light; knocked him out.* **15. a.** So as to be a rough representation: *sketch out.* **b.** So as to embellish or complete a rough representation or version: *type out; fill out the details.* **16.** So as to project: *Stuck out her tongue.* **17.** From a state of harmony to one of discord: *I was very put out; We fell out.* **18.** On strike: *The workers came out over pay and conditions.* **19.** *Informal.* Around; existing: *She's the best saxophone player out.* **20.** *Sports.* Incorrectly positioned, or beyond some limit as defined by the rules: *He kept serving out.* **21.** *British.* So as to be part of, or received into, adult society, especially high society: *a debutante coming out the year after next.* **—out of. 1.** From among: *one out of thousands.* **2.** Past the boundaries or limits of: *The eagle soared out of sight.* **3.** *Informal.* Based in or with headquarters in: *She works out of the branch office.* **4.** From: *made out of wood.* **5.** Because of; owing to: *They did it out of malice.* **6.** Born of; foaled by. **7.** In or into a condition of no longer having: *We're out of coffee; tricked out of her savings.* **8.** Away from a usual place, state, or condition: *moving out of publishing; getting out of control.* **—out of it.** Isolated; excluded; left out.

~adj. **1. a.** Outside: *She is out in the garden.* **b.** Away; not in the usual or expected place: *He is out at Harlow; I'm afraid she's out.* **2.** Exhausted; depleted: *Our supplies are out.* **3.** Extinct; extinguished; imperceptible: *The fire is out.* **4.** Finished; concluded: *before the week is out.* **5. a.** In existence: *My new book is out.* **b.** In view; evident: *The daffodils are out.* **6.** No longer fashionable or in use: *Those hairstyles are out.* **7.** Unconscious or asleep: *She's out for a good few hours.* **8.** Away from the courtroom, considering a verdict: *The jury is out.* **9.** On strike: *All our members are out.* **10.** *Sports.* Not in the correct position, or beyond some limit as defined by the rules: *That last ball was out.* **11.** No longer taking part in the game, or part of the game: *Yorkshire were out for 250.* **12.** Excluded, especially from power or control: *After the 1945 election, the Conservatives were out.* **13.** *Informal.* Not allowed; prohibited: *Smoking in here is out.* **14.** Inaccurate: *Your calculations were two millimetres out.* **15.** To be sent away: *out mail.* **16.** Determined and desirous: *out to get you; out for your blood.* **17.** *Chiefly U.S. Informal.* Without an amount (of money) possessed previously: *I am out ten dollars.* **18.** Not available for use or consideration: *Catching a taxi is out, because we haven't the money.* **19.** Bare or threadbare: *My jacket is out at the elbow.* **—out with it.** Used to demand that suppressed information be revealed. **—want out.** *Informal.* To wish to leave, escape, or be let out.

~prep. Through; forth from: *I fell out the window.*

~n. **1.** A means of escape: *The window was my only out.* **2.** In baseball: **a.** Any play in which a batter or base runner is dismissed. **b.** The player dismissed in such a play. **3.** *Chiefly U.S.* A person or thing that is out; especially, one who is out of power. **4.** *Printing.* A word or other part of a manuscript omitted from the printed copy.

~v. **outed, outing, outs.** *—intr.* To be disclosed or revealed; come out: *Truth will out.* *—tr.* **1.** To put (a person or thing) out. **2.** *British Slang.* To knock unconscious.

~interj. **1.** Used to demand the departure of a person or animal, as from a room or car, for example. **2.** Used by radio operators to indicate the end of transmission. **3.** Used in games such as tennis to declare a shot or ball out. [Middle English *out,* Old English *ūt.*]

out– *prefix.* Indicates: **1.** To a surpassing or greater degree; for example, **outplay, outshoot, outwork.** **2.** Situated outside or externally; for example, **outboard, outhouse.** **3.** Emerging or coming forth; for example, **outburst, outgrowth.** ***Note:*** Many compounds other than those entered here may be formed with *out-*. In forming compounds, *out-* is normally joined with the following element without space or hyphen: **outlive.** However, in formations (usually nonce words) in which the second element begins with a capital, the hyphen is used: *That jailbreaker could out-Houdini Houdini himself.* The separate word *out* also appears in a few phrases that are hyphenated. Those entered here are: **out-and-out, out-group, out-of-bounds, out-of-date, out-of-door(s), out-of-phase, out-of-pocket, out-of-the-way, out-relief,** and **out-tray.**

out·age (ówtij) *n. Chiefly U.S.* **1.** A quantity or portion of something lacking after delivery or storage. **2.** A temporary suspension of operation, especially of electric power. [OUT + -AGE.]

out-and-out (ówt'nd-ówt, ówt'n-) *adj.* Complete; thoroughgoing: *an out-and-out swindler.* **—out-and-out** *adv.*

out·back (ówt-bak) *n.* The remote and underdeveloped areas of a given country; especially, the inland bush country of Australia. Also used adjectivally: *outback life.* **—out·back·er** *n.*

out·bal·ance (ówt-bál-ənss) *tr.v.* **-anced, -ancing, -ances.** To be more important than; outweigh.

out·bid (ówt-bíd) *tr.v.* **-bid, -bidding, -bids.** To bid higher than: *She outbid her rivals at the auction.*

out·board (ówt-bawrd || -bōrd) *adj.* **1.** *Nautical.* **a.** Situated outside the hull of a vessel. **b.** Being away from the centre line of the hull of a ship. **2.** *Aeronautics.* Situated towards or nearer the end of a wing.

~n. **1.** An outboard motor. **2.** A boat with an outboard motor. **—out·board** *adv.*

outboard motor *n.* A detachable engine mounted on the stern of a boat, or on outboard brackets.

out·bound (ówt-bownd) *adj.* Outward bound; heading away.

out·brave (ówt-bráyv) *tr.v.* **-braved, -braving, -braves.** **1.** To be braver than. **2.** To face or stand up to defiantly.

out·break (ówt-brayk) *n.* A sudden occurrence; an eruption: *an outbreak of arrests; an outbreak of measles.*

out·breed (ówt-bréed, -breed) *v.* **-bred** (-bréd, -bred), **-breeding, -breeds.** *—tr.* To subject to outbreeding. *—intr.* To produce offspring by outbreeding.

out·breed·ing (ówt-bréeding, -breeding) *n.* **1.** The breeding of distantly related or unrelated stocks of animals. **2.** *Anthropology.* The bearing of children by parents from different groups, often as a consequence of taboos against marriage within the group.

out·build·ing (ówt-bilding) *n.* A smaller ancillary building detached from a main building.

out·burst (ówt-burst) *n.* A sudden, violent outpouring; an energetic display, as of activity or passion: *an outburst of spite.*

out·cast (ówt-kaast || -kast) *n.* One that has been excluded from a society or system; one that has been rejected. **—out·cast** *adj.*

out·caste (ówt-kaast || -kast) *n.* **1.** A Hindu who has been expelled from or has abandoned his caste. **2.** One who has no caste. **—out·caste** *adj.*

out·class (ówt-klaass || -kláss) *tr.v.* **-classed, -classing, -classes.** To surpass or defeat decisively, so as to appear of a higher class.

out·come (ówt-kum) *n.* A result or consequence. See Synonyms at **effect.**

out·crop (ówt-krop) *n. Geology.* **1.** A portion of bedrock or other stratum protruding through the soil level. **2.** An emergence or outbreak.

~intr.v. (-króp) **outcropped, -cropping, -crops.** *Geology.* To protrude above the soil. Used of rock formations.

out·cross (ówt-króss || -kráwss) *v.* **-crossed, -crossing, -crosses.** *—tr.* To breed (animals that belong to different strains of the same breed). *—intr.* To breed. Used of animals belonging to different strains of the same breed.

~n. (ówt-kross || -krawss). **1.** The process of outcrossing. **2.** An offspring produced by outcrossing.

out·cry (ówt-krī) *n., pl.* **-cries.** **1.** A strong protest or objection: *public outcry over the government cuts.* **2.** A loud cry or clamour.

out·date (ówt-dáyt) *tr.v.* **-dated, -dating, -dates.** To replace or make obsolete, antiquated, or old-fashioned.

out·dat·ed (ówt-dáytid) *adj.* Out-of-date; antiquated.

out·dis·tance (ówt-dístənss) *tr.v.* **-tanced, -tancing, -tances.** **1.** To outrun, especially in a long-distance race. **2.** To surpass by a wide margin, especially through superior skill or endurance.

out·do (ówt-dōō) *tr.v.* **-did** (-díd), **-done** (-dún), **-doing, -does** (-dúz). To exceed in performance; surpass. See Synonyms at **excel.**

outcrop *Monument Valley, in the U.S. state of Utah, is rich in sandstone outcrops. This handlike formation is one of a pair of outcrops known as The Mittens.*

PRONUNCIATION KEY

a, trap; aa, father; ai, fair; ar, star; aw, lawn; ay, play; b, bb, stab; rubber; ch, church; ck, ticket; d, dd, dead; ladder; e, dress; ee, bee; er, defer; ew, few; ewr, pure; ə, about; ər, letter; f, ff, fife; differ; g, gg, giggle; h, hat; i, kit; ī, price; īr, fire; j, judge; k, kick; l, ll, let; 'l, needle; m, mm, man; n, nn, no; 'n, sudden; ng, thing; o, lot; ō, no; ŏŏ, foot; ōō, shoe; oor, poor; ow, cow; owr, hour; oy, boy; p, pp, pepper; r, rr, red; s, ss, sauce; sh, ship; t, tt, totter; th, thick; th, this; smooth; u, cut; ur, turn; v, vv, valve; w, wet; y, yes; z, zz, zebra; zh, vision; pleasure

IN FOREIGN WORDS:

aN, oN, Saint-Saëns; hl, Llanelli; Hluhluwe; kh, loch; lough; Khaled

STRESS MARK:

ín-sīt, insight; in-sít, incite

out·door (ówt-dór ‖ -dŏr) *adj.* Also **out-of-door** (-əv-). Located in, done in, or suited to the open air.

out·doors (ówt-dórz ‖ -dŏrz) *adv.* Also **out-of-doors** (-əv-). In or into the open; outside a house or shelter: *go outdoors for fresh air.* ~*n.* Also **out-of-doors.** The open air; an area away from human habitation.

out·er (ówtər) *adj.* 1. Located on the outside; external. 2. Farther from the centre or middle.

outer ear *n.* The **external ear** *(see).*

Outer Hebrides. See **Hebrides.**

Outer Mongolia. See **Mongolian People's Republic.**

out·er·most (ówtər-mōst) *adj.* Most distant from the centre or inside; farthest out; outmost.

outer planet *n.* Any of the planets Jupiter, Saturn, Uranus, Neptune, or Pluto, whose orbit is beyond the asteroid belt. Compare **inner planet.**

outer space *n.* Space beyond the Earth's atmosphere. Not in technical usage.

out·face (ówt-fáyss) *tr.v.* **-faced, -facing, -faces.** 1. To overcome with a bold or self-assured look; stare down. 2. To defy; resist.

out·fall (ówt-fawl) *n.* The point where or mouth from which a sewer, drain, or stream discharges.

out·field (ówt-feeld) *n.* 1. The outer part of a cricket field; the part farthest from the wicket. Compare **infield.** 2. **a.** The grass-covered playing area extending outwards from a baseball diamond, divided into right, centre, and left fields. Compare **infield. b.** The members of a baseball team playing in the outfield. —**out·field·er** *n.*

out·fit (ówt-fit) *n.* 1. A set of tools or equipment for a specialised purpose: *a mountain-climber's outfit; a welder's outfit.* 2. A set of clothing: *appear at the dance in an elegant outfit.* 3. *Informal.* An association of persons, especially a military unit or a business organisation. 4. The act of equipping or fitting out. ~*v.* **outfitted, -fitting, -fits.** —*tr.* To provide with an outfit: *This shop outfits skiers.* —*intr.* To acquire an outfit: *We outfitted a week before departing.*

out·fit·ter (ówt-fittər) *n.* 1. A shop, often slightly old-fashioned, that sells men's clothes. 2. One who sells or provides outfits.

out·flank (ówt-flángk) *tr.v.* **-flanked, -flanking, -flanks.** 1. To manoeuvre around and behind the flank of (an opposing force). 2. To gain a tactical advantage over.

out·flow (ówt-flō) *n.* 1. The act of flowing out. 2. Something that flows out. 3. The amount flowing out.

out·fox (ówt-fóks) *tr.v.* **-foxed, -foxing, -foxes.** To outwit; be more cunning than.

out·gas (ówt-gáss, -gass) *v.* **-gassed, -gassing, -gasses.** *Physics.* —*tr.* To remove adsorbed gas from (a solid or liquid) by heating. —*intr.* To release gas.

out·go (ówt-gō) *tr.v.* **-went** (-wént), **-gone** (-gón ‖ -gáwn, -gáan), **-going, -goes** (-gōz). To exceed; surpass. ~*n.* (ówt-gō) *pl.* **outgoes.** 1. Something that goes out, especially expenditure or cost. 2. The act of going out.

out·go·ing (ówt-gō-ing, -gō-) *adj.* 1. **a.** Departing; going out: *an outgoing steamship.* **b.** Retiring or leaving: *the outgoing president.* 2. Friendly; sociable; extroverted: *an outgoing personality.*

out·go·ings (ówt-gō-ingz) *pl.n.* Regular and unavoidable expenses, such as payment of rent.

out·group (ówt-grōōp) *n.* A group of people excluded from or not belonging to an **in-group** *(see).*

out·grow (ówt-grō) *tr.v.* **-grew** (-grōō), **-grown** (-grōn), **-growing, -grows.** 1. To grow too large for: *She outgrew her new suit.* 2. To lose or discard in the course of maturation: *We outgrew our youthful idealism.* 3. To surpass in growth: *He has outgrown his father.*

out·growth (ówt-grōth) *n.* 1. That which grows out of something; an offshoot: *an outgrowth of new buds on a branch.* 2. The act or process of growing out. 3. A result or consequence: *Inflation is an outgrowth of war.*

out·guess (ówt-géss) *tr.v.* **-guessed, -guessing, -guesses.** 1. To anticipate correctly the actions of. 2. To gain the advantage over by cleverness or forethought; outwit.

out·gun (ówt-gún) *tr.v.* **-gunned, -gunning, -guns.** 1. To have more guns than. 2. To outshoot. 3. *Informal.* To outdo; surpass.

out·haul (ówt-hawl) *n. Nautical.* A rope used to extend a sail along a spar or boom.

out-Her·od (ówt-hérrəd) *tr.v.* **-oded, -oding, -ods.** To outdo in evil or surpass in cruelty. Used chiefly in the phrase *out-Herod Herod.* [The phrase *out-Herod Herod* is from Shakespeare's *Hamlet,* Act III, scene 2.]

out·house (ówt-howss) *n.* 1. An outbuilding. 2. *U.S.* An outside lavatory.

out·ing (ówting) *n.* 1. An excursion or pleasure trip: *an outing to the zoo.* 2. A walk outdoors; an airing. 3. An appearance in an outdoor competition, such as a horse race.

out·jock·ey (ówt-jócki) *tr.v.* **-eyed, -eying, -eys.** To get the better of, especially by trickery.

out·land (ówt-land, -lənd) *n.* 1. *Plural.* The outlying areas of a country; the provinces. 2. *Archaic.* A foreign land. [Middle English *outland,* Old English *ūtland : ūt,* OUT + *land,* LAND.] —**out·land** *adj.* —**out·land·er** *n.*

out·land·ish (owt-lándish) *adj.* 1. Conspicuously unconventional; bizarre; absurd. 2. Strikingly foreign; unfamiliar. 3. Geographically remote from the familiar world. 4. *Archaic.* Of foreign origin; not native. —See Synonyms at **strange.** [Middle English *outland-*

ish, Old English *ūtlandisc :* OUTLAND + -ISH.] —**out·land·ish·ly** *adv.* —**out·land·ish·ness** *n.*

out·last (ówt-laast ‖ -lást) *tr.v.* **-lasted, -lasting, -lasts.** To endure or live longer than.

out·law (ówt-law) *n.* 1. A habitual criminal. 2. *Law.* Formerly, a person excluded from normal legal protection and rights. 3. A wild or vicious animal. ~*tr.v.* **outlawed, -lawing, -laws.** 1. To declare illegal. 2. To ban. 3. To deprive of the protection of the law. [Middle English *outlawe, outlage,* Old English *ūtlaga,* from Old Norse *ūtlagi,* from *ūtlagr,* outlawed : *ūt,* out + *lög,* law.]

out·law·ry (ówt-lawri) *n., pl.* **-ries.** 1. The act or process of outlawing someone or something. 2. The state of being outlawed. 3. Defiance of the law. [Middle English *outlagerie,* from Anglo-French *utlagerie,* from Middle English *outlage,* an OUTLAW.]

out·lay (ówt-lay) *n.* 1. The spending or disbursing of money. 2. The amount spent. —See Synonyms at **price.** ~*tr.v.* (-láy) **outlaid** (-láyd), **-laying, -lays.** To spend (money).

out·let (ówt-let, -lit) *n.* 1. A passage for escape or exit, such as an air vent, drain, or river mouth. 2. **a.** A means of fulfilling potential or channelling energies or abilities: *"There is now scarcely any outlet for energy in this country except business."* (John Stuart Mill). **b.** A means of satisfying a drive, urge, or desire; emotional gratification. **c.** A means of achieving self-expression. 3. **a.** A commercial market for goods or services. **b.** A shop that sells the goods of a particular manufacturer or wholesaler. 4. A point at which an electric current is taken from a circuit; especially, a wall socket.

out·li·er (ówt-lī-ər) *n.* 1. A portion of anything that exists or lies apart from the main body or system to which it belongs. 2. One whose home lies at some appreciable distance from his place of work. 3. *Geology.* An area of younger rocks surrounded by older.

out·line (ówt-līn) *n.* 1. **a.** A line described in the plane of vision by the outer boundary of any object or figure. **b.** *Plural.* Contours delineating such a figure; lineaments. **c.** Contour; shape. 2. A drawing or style of drawing in which objects are delineated in contours without shading. 3. **a.** A general description or schematic summary. **b.** An abstract. **c.** A schematic synopsis of a written work. **d.** A preliminary draft or plan. 4. *Plural.* The salient characteristics or general principles of a given subject; the gist: *They agreed on the main outlines, but quibbled over particulars.* —See Synonyms at **form.** ~*tr.v.* **outlined, -lining, -lines.** 1. To draw the outline of. 2. To display or accentuate the outline of. 3. To give the main points of; summarise.

out·live (ówt-lív) *tr.v.* **-lived, -living, -lives.** 1. To live beyond or longer than; outlast. 2. To live through; survive.

out·look (ówt-lōōk ‖ -lŏōk) *n.* 1. A point of view or attitude. 2. Probable or expected outcome. 3. The act of looking out. 4. **a.** A place where something can be viewed. **b.** The view seen from such a place. —See Synonyms at **prospect.**

out·ly·ing (ówt-lī-ing) *adj.* Comparatively distant or remote from a centre or middle.

out·ma·noeu·vre (ówt-mə-nōōvər ‖ -néwvər) *tr.v.* **-vred, -vring, -vred.** To gain the advantage over by adroitness or skill.

out·mod·ed (ówt-mōdid) *adj.* 1. Not in fashion. 2. No longer usable or practical; obsolete: *an outmoded technique.* —**out·mod·ed·ly** *adv.* —**out·mod·ed·ness** *n.*

out·most (ówt-mōst) *adj.* Farthest out; outermost.

out·num·ber (ówt-númerór) *tr.v.* **-bered, -bering, -bers.** To exceed the number of; be more numerous than.

out of bounds, out-of-bounds (ówtəv-bównds) *adj.* Beyond certain prescribed limits; barred. —**out of bounds** *adv.*

out-of-date (ówtəv-dáyt) *adj.* Outmoded; old-fashioned.

out-of-door. Variant of **outdoor.**

out-of-doors. Variant of **outdoors.**

out-of-phase (ówtəv-fáyz) *adj.* Designating or pertaining to two or more waves, alternating signals, or other periodically varying quantities for which the maximum and minimum values of each quantity occur at different times.

out of pocket *adj.* Also **out-of-pocket** (ówtəv-póckit) (for sense 3). 1. Having suffered financial loss: *That deal left me out of pocket.* 2. Lacking readily available money. 3. Directly paid for in cash rather than charged to an expense account or bought on credit: *out-of-pocket expenses.*

out-of-the-way (ówtəv-thə-wáy) *adj.* 1. Distant; remote; secluded. 2. Out of the ordinary; unusual.

out·pa·tient (ówt-paysh'nt) *n.* A patient who receives treatment at a hospital or clinic without being hospitalised.

out·per·form (ówt-pər-fórm) *tr.v.* **-formed, -forming, -forms.** To do better than, usually in every respect.

out·play (ówt-pláy) *tr.v.* **-played, -playing, -plays.** To surpass (one's opponent) in playing some game.

out·point (ówt-póynt) *tr.v.* 1. To score a greater number of points than. 2. *Nautical.* To sail nearer to the direction of the wind than (another vessel).

out·post (ówt-pōst) *n.* 1. A detachment of troops stationed at a distance from a main unit of forces. 2. The station occupied by such troops. 3. **a.** Any outlying settlement. **b.** Anything regarded as an outlying settlement or representative: *The country club is the last outpost of 19th-century civilisation.*

out·pour (ówt-pór ‖ -pŏr) *tr.v.* **-poured, -pouring, -pours.** To pour out.

~*n.* (-pawr || -pōr). A rapid outflow; an outpouring. **—out·pour·er** *n.*

out·pour·ing (ówt-pawring || -pōring) *n.* **1.** The act or an instance of pouring out: *an outpouring of love.* **2.** Something that pours out or is poured out; an outflow: *an outpouring of lava.*

out·put (ówt-pŏŏt) *n.* **1.** The act of producing; production. **2.** The amount of something produced or manufactured during a given span of time. **3.** The material or substance produced in a process. **4.** The power or energy delivered by a motor or machine. **5.** The energy, power, or work produced by a technical system. **6.** *Computing.* **a.** The data produced by a computer from a specific input. **b.** The form in which the data is delivered: *paper-tape output.* **c.** A device used in producing output. **7.** *Electronics.* **a.** The voltage or current produced by a component or circuit. **b.** The terminal or point in a circuit from which this voltage or current is taken.
~*tr.v.* **output, -putting, -puts.** To produce (an output). Used of a factory, machine, or electronic device, for example.

out·rage (ówt-rayj, *rarely* -rij) *n.* **1.** An act of extreme violence or viciousness. **2.** Any act grossly offensive to decency, morality, or good taste. **3.** A severe insult or offence to one's integrity or pride: *"I have only had insults and outrage from her."* (W.M. Thackeray). **4.** A strong feeling of resentful anger.
~*tr.v.* **outraged, -raging, -rages. 1.** To offend or enrage. Often used in the passive. **2.** To commit an outrage upon. **3.** *Archaic.* To rape. —See Synonyms at **offend.** [Middle English, excess, from Old French, "excess", atrocity, from *outre,* beyond. See **outré.**]

out·ra·geous (ówt-ráyjəss, owt-) *adj.* **1. a.** Being an outrage; grossly offensive; heinous. **b.** Disgraceful; shameful. **2.** Having no regard for the conventions of morality, decency, or good taste; shocking. **3.** Extravagant; immoderate; extreme: *She spends an outrageous amount on clothes.* **4.** Violent or unrestrained in temperament or behaviour. **—out·ra·geous·ly** *adv.* **—out·ra·geous·ness** *n.*

out·rank (ówt-rángk) *tr.v.* **-ranked, -ranking, -ranked. 1.** To be of a higher rank than. **2.** To be more important than; take precedence over.

ou·tré (ōō-tray, ōō-tráy) *adj.* Deviating from what is usual or proper; eccentric. [French, past participle of *outrer,* to pass beyond, go to excess, from *outre,* beyond, from Old French, from Latin *ultrā,* beyond, further.]

out·reach (ówt-réech) *v.* **-reached, -reaching, -reaches.** —*tr.* **1.** To reach further than; surpass in reach. **2.** To go beyond; surpass. **3.** To extend (something) outward. —*intr.* To reach out.
~*n.* (-reech). **1.** An act of reaching out. **2.** The extent of a reach.

out-re·lief (ówt-ri-leef) *n. British.* Formerly, financial assistance given to the poor who were not living in the workhouse.

out·ride¹ (ówt-rīd) *tr.v.* **-rode** (-rṓd), **-ridden** (-rídd'n), **-riding, -rides.** To ride faster, farther, or better than; outstrip.

out·ride² (ówt-rīd) *n.* In verse, an unstressed syllable or cluster of syllables within a given metrical unit that is omitted from the scansion pattern in sprung rhythm. [Coined by the poet Gerard Manley Hopkins.]

out·rid·er (ówt-rīdər) *n.* **1.** A mounted attendant who rides in front of or beside a carriage. **2.** A person who precedes any procession or vehicle to clear the way and ensure easy progress. **3.** A person who patrols and reconnoitres ahead of a party of explorers, raiders, or the like; a scout. **4.** Any guide or escort. **5.** *U.S.* A herdsman or cowboy supervising cattle, usually at some distance from the farmhouse or central camp. **6.** Either of the two small balancing wheels attached by projecting spars to the back wheel of a child's bicycle.

out·rig·ger (ówt-riggər) *n.* **1. a.** In seagoing canoes of the South Pacific and Indian oceans and similar craft, a float attached to laterally projecting spars so as to ride parallel to the length of the craft on either side as a means of preventing it from capsizing. **b.** Any vessel fitted with such a float. **2.** Any frame extending laterally beyond the main structure of a vessel, vehicle, aircraft, building, or machine, to stabilise the structure or support an extending part. **3.** In rowing, a **rigger** *(see).* **—out·rigged** *adj.*

out·right (ówt-rīt) *adv.* **1.** Without reservation or qualification; openly. **2.** Entirely; utterly; wholly. **3.** Without delay; straightaway: *kill outright.*
~*adj.* (ówt-rīt). **1.** Without reservation; unqualified: *an outright gift.* **2. a.** Complete; total: *the outright cost.* **b.** Thoroughgoing; out-and-out: *outright cruelty.* **3.** Straightforward; forthright: *an outright speech.* **4.** *Archaic.* Directed straight on; moving straight onwards: *"an even, outright, but imperceptible speed"* (R.L. Stevenson).

out·run (ówt-rún) *tr.v.* **-ran** (-rán), **-run, -running, -runs. 1.** To run faster than. **2.** To escape from: *outrun one's creditors.* **3.** To go beyond or exceed (some limit): *Her ingenuity outran her intelligence.*

out·sell (ówt-sél) *tr.v.* **-sold** (-sṓld), **-selling, -sells. 1.** To surpass in amount sold. **2.** To outdo in selling.

out·set (ówt-set) *n.* **1.** The beginning; the start; the commencement. **2.** An initial stage, as of an activity.

out·shine (ówt-shīn) *v.* **-shone** (-shón || -shṓn), **-shining, -shines.** —*tr.* **1.** To shine more brightly than. **2.** To surpass (a rival). —*intr.* To shine forth.

out·shoot (ówt-shṓōt) *v.* **-shot** (-shót), **-shooting, -shoots.** —*tr.* **1.** To shoot better than. **2.** To extend beyond. —*intr.* To protrude or project.
~*n.* (-shōōt). **1.** A protuberance, projection, or outgrowth. **2.** A flowing or gushing forth.

out·side (ówt-sīd) *n.* **1.** The part or parts that face out; the outer surface; the exterior. **2. a.** The part or side of an object that is presented to the viewer; the external aspect. **b.** The superficial or obvious aspect of something. **3.** The space beyond a boundary or limit. **4. a.** An outer or external position: *The car door opens only from the outside.* **b.** Anything considered as external or most exposed; for example, the part of a pavement or path nearest the road. **5.** A player whose position is nearest the edge of the field. **—at the outside.** At the utmost limit; at the most: *We'll be leaving in ten days at the outside.* **—on the outside.** In society at large, as opposed to some enclosed community.
~*adj.* **1.** Acting, occurring, originating, or existing at a place beyond certain limits; outer; foreign: *outside assistance.* **2.** Of, restricted to, or situated on the outside of an enclosure or boundary; external: *outside environs; an outside door lock.* **3.** Extreme; uttermost: *The cost exceeded even my outside estimate.* **4.** Slight; slim: *an outside possibility.* **5.** Not part of a group; not a member: *an outside delegate.* **6.** *Sports.* Occupying a position near the specified edge of a playing field. Said of a player. **7.** Designating a curve that is less tight or that covers a greater distance than other concentric curves within it: *the outside track.*
~*adv.* **1.** On or into the outside. **2.** Outdoors. **3.** *Slang.* Out of prison. **—outside of.** *Chiefly U.S.* Outside: *She has few interests outside of her work.*
~*prep.* **1.** On or to the outer side of. **2.** Beyond the limits of. **3.** With the exception of; except: *no info outside the figures given.*
Usage: As a preposition, *outside* (like *inside*) is sometimes followed by *of,* but this is criticised in formal speech or writing: *Don't mention this outside of these four walls.* In writing, this usage is somewhat more common in American English.

outside broadcast *n. Abbr.* **O.B.** A radio or television broadcast made from outside a studio. Also used adjectivally: *outside-broadcast cameras.*

outside centre *n.* **1.** In Rugby football, a player occupying a position outside the scrum, just beyond the inside centre. **2.** The position of any such player.

outside half *n. British.* In Rugby football, a **stand-off half** *(see).*

out·sid·er (ówt-sīdər) *n.* **1. a.** A person who is excluded from some particular party, association, or set. **b.** One who is isolated or detached from the activities or concerns of the community in which he lives. **2.** A contestant in a race, especially a horse race, considered to have little chance of winning.

outside world *n.* Society at large as opposed to some private or enclosed community, such as that of an institution: *leaving prison for the outside world.*

out·size (ówt-sīz, -sīz) *n.* **1.** A very large size. **2.** A garment designed to fit a very large person. **—out·size, out·sized** *adj.*

out·skirts (ówt-skurts) *pl.n.* The parts or regions remote from a central district; peripheral areas: *the outskirts of the city.*

out·smart (ówt-smárt) *tr.v.* **-smarted, -smarting, -smarts.** To gain the advantage over by cunning; outwit.

out·span (ówt-spán) *v.* **-spanned, -spanning, -spans.** *South African.* —*intr.* **1.** To take off a yoke or harness from an animal. **2.** To pitch camp. Used especially of travellers by ox wagon. **3.** To interrupt a journey to rest. —*tr.* To unharness or unyoke (an animal).
~*n.* (-span). *South African.* **1.** An act of outspanning. **2.** A time or a place set aside for outspanning. **3.** Grazing land. [Partial translation of Afrikaans *uitspan* : *uit,* OUT + *spannen,* to stretch, hitch.]

out·spo·ken (ówt-spṓkən) *adj.* **1.** Spoken without reserve; candid. **2.** Frank and unsparing in speech. —See Synonyms at **frank.** **—out·spo·ken·ly** *adv.* **—out·spo·ken·ness** *n.*

out·spread (ówt-spréd) *v.* **-spread, -spreading, -spreads.** —*intr.* To spread out; stretch. —*tr.* To cause to spread out.
~*n.* (-spred). **1.** The act of spreading out. **2.** Extent.
~*adj.* (-spréd). Spread out; extended.

out·stand (ówt-stánd) *intr.v.* **-stood** (-stṓōd), **-standing, -stands. 1.** To stand out plainly; be outstanding. **2.** *Nautical.* To set sail; put out to sea.

out·stand·ing (ówt-stánding; *also, particularly in sense 1,* -standing) *adj.* **1.** Standing out; projecting upwards or outwards. **2.** Standing out among others of its kind; prominent; salient. **3.** Superior to others of its kind; distinguished; excellent. **4.** Still in existence; not settled or resolved: *outstanding debts; a long outstanding problem.*

out·stare (ówt-stáir) *tr.v.* **-stared, -staring, -stares.** To stare longer than (a person or animal staring back into one's eyes), such that one's adversary is the first to look away.

out·sta·tion (ówt-staysh'n) *n.* A remote station or post.

out·stay (ówt-stáy) *tr.v.* **-stayed, -staying, -stays. 1.** To stay longer than. **2.** To stay beyond (a certain limit); overstay: *We outstayed our welcome.*

out·stretch (ówt-stréch) *tr.v.* **-stretched, -stretching, -stretches. 1.** To stretch out; extend. **2.** To stretch beyond.

out·strip (ówt-stríp) *tr.v.* **-stripped, -stripping, -strips. 1.** To run faster than and leave behind; outrun. **2.** To exceed in growth, skill, or achievement; surpass. —See Synonyms at **excel.**

out·swing·er (ówt-swing-ər) *n.* In cricket, a bowled ball that moves in the air from leg to off. Compare **inswinger.**

out·take (ówt-tayk) *n.* A series of frames cut and discarded from the finished version of a film.

out-tray (ówt-tray) *n.* A tray or shallow basket usually on an office desk, in which are placed outgoing letters and messages and work that has been dealt with for filing. Compare **in-tray.**

out·turn (ówt-turn) *n. Rare.* **1.** Output. **2.** Outcome: *"But whether the outturn would have been very different is quite another question"* (The Guardian).

out·ward (ówt-wərd) *adj.* **1.** Of, pertaining to, or moving towards

PRONUNCIATION KEY

a, trap; aa, father; ai, fair;
ar, star; aw, lawn; ay, play;
b, bb, stab; rubber;
ch, church; ck, ticket;
d, dd, dead; ladder; e, dress;
ee, bee; er, defer; ew, few;
ewr, pure; ə, about;
ər, letter; f, ff, fife; differ;
g, gg, giggle; h, hat; i, kit;
ī, price; īr, fire; j, judge;
k, kick; l, ll, let; 'l, needle;
m, mm, man; n, nn, no;
'n, sudden; ng, thing; o, lot;
ō, no; ōō, foot; ōō, shoe;
oor, poor; ow, cow;
owr, hour; oy, boy;
p, pp, pepper; r, rr, red;
s, ss, sauce; sh, ship;
t, tt, totter; th, thick; th, this;
smooth; u, cut; ur, turn;
v, vv, valve; w, wet; y, yes;
z, zz, zebra; zh, vision;
pleasure

IN FOREIGN WORDS:

aN, oN, Saint-Saëns;
hl, Llanelli; Hluhluwe;
kh, loch; lough; Khaled

STRESS MARK:

in-sīt, insight; in-sīt, incite

the outside or exterior; outer. **2.** Pertaining to the physical self, as distinguished from the mind or spirit: *The ascetics have no interest in the outward being.* **3.** Easily perceptible, especially to sight; evident: *Her outward manner remained composed.* **4.** Purely external; superficial. **5.** Towards or sailing towards a destination away from home or a home port. Said of a voyage or a ship.
~*adv. Chiefly U.S.* Outwards.
~*n.* **1.** The outside; the exterior. **2.** Outward appearance. [Middle English *outward,* Old English *ūtanweard* : *ūtan,* outside, from *ūt,* OUT + *-weard,* -WARD.] **—out·ward·ness** *n.*

out·ward·ly (ówtwərdli) *adv.* **1.** According to external appearance, usually as distinct from the real state of affairs: *She remained outwardly composed at the news, but her mind was reeling.* **2.** From, to, or on the outside; externally.

out·wards (ówt-wərdz) *adv.* Also *chiefly U.S.* **outward.** Towards the outside; away from a central point.

out·wear (ówt-wáir) *tr.v.* **-wore** (-wór || -wōr), **-worn** (-wórn || -wōrn), **-wearing, -wears.** **1.** To wear out; exhaust by using. **2.** To last longer than; outlast. **3.** To outgrow or outlive: *ethics outworn by a changing society.*

out·weigh (ówt-wáy) *tr.v.* **-weighed, -weighing, -weighs.** **1.** To weigh more than. **2. a.** To be more significant, important, or influential than. **b.** To be preferred to; prevail over.

out·wit (owt-wít) *tr.v.* **-witted, -witting, -wits.** **1.** To surpass in cleverness or cunning; fool. **2.** *Archaic.* To surpass in intelligence. —See Synonyms at **deceive.**

out·with (ówt-wíth, -wi͟th) *prep. Scottish.* Outside.

out·work (ówt-wúrk) *tr.v.* **-worked, -working, -works.** **1.** To work better or faster than. **2.** To work out to a finish; complete.
~*n.* (-wurk). **1.** Work done outside a factory or shop; paid work done at home. **2.** *Often plural. Military.* A trench or fortification beyond the main defences. **—out·work·er** *n.*

ou·zel, ou·sel (o͞oz'l) *n.* **1.** A bird, the **ring ouzel** *(see).* **2.** *Archaic.* A blackbird. **3.** The water ouzel or **dipper** *(see).* [Middle English *ousel,* Old English *ōsle.*]

ou·zo (o͞ozō) *n., pl.* **-zos.** An aniseed-flavoured Greek liqueur. [Modern Greek *ouzon*†.]

o·va. Plural of **ovum.**

o·val (ṓv'l) *adj.* **1.** Resembling an ellipse in shape; ellipsoidal or elliptical. **2.** Resembling an egg in shape.
~*n.* **1.** An oval form or figure. **2.** An oval track or sports field, as for horse racing or athletic events. [Medieval Latin *ōvālis,* from Latin *ōvum,* egg.] **—o·val·ly** *adv.* **—o·val·ness** *n.*

O·val, The (ṓv'l). A cricket ground in south London. Second in importance only to Lords as a centre of the game, it is the headquarters of the Surrey County Cricket Club. Traditionally, the final test match of an English series is played here.

Oval Office *n.* The U.S. president: *a statement from the Oval Office.* [From the president's oval-shaped office in the White House.]

ovenbird *The South American ovenbird* Funarius rufus *perches on the curious clay nest from which it gets its name.*

O·vam·bo (ō-vámbō, -vaám-) *n., pl.* **-bos** or collectively **Ovambo.** **1.** A member of a southern African people of mixed Hottentot and Negroid descent, living chiefly in northern Namibia. **2.** The Bantu language of this people, of the Niger-Congo family of languages. **—O·vam·bo** *adj.*

o·va·ri·ec·to·my (ō-vaír-i-éktəmi) *n., pl.* **-mies.** Surgical excision of an ovary. [OVAR(Y) + -ECTOMY.]

o·va·ri·ot·o·my (ō-vaír-i-óttəmi) *n., pl.* **-mies.** **1.** Ovariectomy. **2.** Surgical incision into an ovary to remove a tumour. [New Latin *ovariotomia* : OVAR(Y) + *-tomia,* -TOMY.]

o·va·ri·tis (ōvə-rítiss) *n. Medicine.* **Oophoritis** *(see).* [New Latin : OVAR(Y) + -ITIS.]

o·va·ry (ṓvəri) *n., pl.* **-ries.** **1.** *Zoology.* Either of a pair of female reproductive glands that produce ova. **2.** *Botany.* The part of a pistil containing the ovules. [New Latin *ovarium,* from Latin *ōvum,* egg.] **—o·var·i·al** (ō-vaír-i-əl), **o·var·i·an** (ō-vaír-i-ən) *adj.*

o·vate (ṓ-vayt, -vət, -vit) *adj.* **1.** Oval; egg-shaped. **2.** *Botany.* Broad and rounded at the base and tapering towards the end: *an ovate leaf.* [Latin *ōvātus,* egg-shaped, from *ōvum,* egg.] **—o·vate·ly** *adv.*

o·va·tion (ō-váysh'n, ə-) *n.* **1.** Enthusiastic and prolonged applause. **2.** A show of public homage or welcome. **3.** An ancient Roman victory ceremony of lesser importance than a triumph. [Latin *ovātiō* (stem *ovātiōn-*), from *ovāre,* to rejoice, from imitative base *eu-.*]

ov·en (úvv'n || ṓv'n) *n.* **1.** A chamber or enclosed compartment in which food is heated, baked, or roasted. **2.** A similar device, usually refractory-lined, in which ceramics are fired, metals heat-treated, or objects dried. [Middle English *oven,* Old English *ofen.*]

ov·en·bird (úvv'n-burd) *n.* **1.** Any of various South American birds of the family Furnariidae that build intricate clay nests having a concealed entrance passage. **2.** A thrushlike North American warbler, *Seiurus aurocapillus,* having a shrill call, and characteristically building a domed nest on the ground. [From its nest, shaped like a Dutch oven.]

oven·proof (úvv'n-pro͞of || ṓv'n-, -pro͞of) *adj.* Not harmed by heating in an oven; able to withstand the heat of an oven without cracking. Compare **flameproof.**

oven-read·y (úvv'n-réddi) *adj.* Ready for immediate roasting or cooking in an oven; especially, plucked, gutted, and trussed: *an oven-ready chicken.*

oven·ware (úvv'n-wair) *n.* Plates, dishes, and pots made of ovenproof material.

o·ver (ṓvər) *prep.* Also *poetic* **o'er** (or, ṓ-ər || ōr). **1.** In or at a position above or higher than: *a sign over the door.* **2. a.** Above and across from one end or side to the other: *a leap over the fence.* **b.** Down the side of or across and down the other side: *jump over the cliff.* **3.** On the other side of: *a village over the border.* **4.** Upon the surface of: *a coat of varnish over the woodwork.* **5.** Covering all or various parts of; through the extent of: *The rash spread over her body.* **6.** So as to cover or close: *A rock slid over the cave entrance.* **7.** Up to the top of or higher than the level or height of: *water over one's knees.* **8.** Through the period or duration of: *records maintained over two years.* **9.** Until or beyond the end of: *stay over the holidays.* **10.** More than, in degree, quantity, or extent: *over ten miles.* **11.** In preference to: *respected over all others.* **12.** In a position to rule or control: *preside over the meeting.* **13.** Upon; directed towards: *her power over animals.* **14.** While occupied with, engaged in, or partaking of: *a chat over coffee.* **15.** With reference to; concerning: *an argument over methods.* **16.** By means of; by the agency of: *Don't tell me over the phone.* **17.** Recovered from; past the effects of: *over the worst.* **—be all over.** To be excessively affectionate towards or attentive to. **—over and above.** In addition to; besides.
~*adv.* Also *poetic* **o'er.** **1.** Above the top or surface. **2. a.** Across to another or opposite side. **b.** Across the edge or brim of a vessel: *The water boiled over.* **3. a.** Across a distance in a particular direction or place: *over in America.* **b.** To another specified place or position: *Move your chair over here.* **4.** Throughout an entire area or region: *wander all over.* **5.** To a different opinion or allegiance: *win someone over.* **6. a.** To a different person, condition, or title: *sign over land.* **b.** So as to be exchanged: *change over.* **7.** So as to be completely enclosed or covered: *The river froze over.* **8.** Through, from beginning to end: *Think the problem over; look this over.* **9. a.** From an upright position: *The book fell over.* **b.** From an upward position to an inverted or reversed position: *turn the book over.* **c.** Overleaf. **10.** *Chiefly U.S.* Another time; again: *Count your cards over.* **11.** In repetition: *ten times over.* **12.** In addition or excess; in surplus: *three pounds left over.* **13.** *Chiefly U.S.* Beyond or until a specified time: *stay a day over.* **—all over.** Typically; characteristically: *That's her all over.* **—over against.** **1.** As opposed to; contrasted with. **2.** Opposite; in front of.
~*adj.* **1.** Completely finished; done; past: *The war is over.* **2.** Having gone across or to the other side. **3. a.** Upper; higher. **b.** External; outer. **4.** In excess or addition; in surplus: *My estimate was fifty pounds over.*
~*n.* **1.** Something remaining or extra. **2.** In cricket: **a.** A series of six balls bowled from one end of the pitch. **b.** The play occurring during this spell of bowling.
~*tr.v.* **overed, overing, overs.** *Rare.* To go or pass over.
~*interj.* **1.** Used in radio conversations to mark the end of a transmission by one speaker. **2.** In cricket, used by an umpire to signal the change of bowling ends between overs. [Middle English *over,* Old English *ofer.*]

over– *prefix.* Indicates: **1.** Superiority of rank or power; for example, **overseer.** **2.** Location above, outside, or across, for example, **overhead.** **3.** Passage beyond or above a limit or boundary; for example, **overshoot.** **4.** Movement or transference to a lower or inferior position; for example, **overturn.** **5.** Quantity in excess of what is normal, agreed, or desirable; for example, **overheat.** ***Note:*** Many compounds other than those entered here may be formed with *over-.* In forming compounds, *over-* is joined with the following element without space or a hyphen: **overrule.** —See Usage note at **overly.** [Middle English *over-,* Old English *ofer-,* from *ofer,* OVER.]

o·ver·a·bun·dance (ṓvər-ə-búndənss) *n.* Prodigally lavish abundance; excessive profusion. **—o·ver·a·bun·dant** *adj.*

o·ver·a·chieve (ṓvər-ə-chéev) *intr.v.* **-achieved, -achieving, -achieves.** To perform better than expected or justified. **—o·ver·a·chiev·er** *n.* **—o·ver·a·chieve·ment** *n.*

o·ver·act (ṓvər-ákt) *v.* **-acted, -acting, -acts.** —*tr.* To act (a part) with unnecessary exaggeration. —*intr.* To exaggerate a role; overact a dramatic part.

o·ver·age (ṓvər-áyj) *adj.* Above the proper or required age.

o·ver·all (ṓvər-awl) *adj.* **1.** From one end to the other. **2.** Including everything; comprehensive.
~*adv.* (-áwl). **1.** From one end to the other: *it measures 12 metres overall.* **2.** Generally; on the whole.
~*n.* (-awl). *British.* A loose-fitting protective outer garment; a smock.

o·ver·alls (ṓvər-awlz) *pl.n.* Loose-fitting, coarse trousers with a bib front and shoulder straps, worn over clothing as protection from dirt and wear.

o·ver·arch (ṓvər-árch) *tr.v.* **-arched, -arching, -arches.** To form an arch over. **—o·ver·arch·ing** *adj.*

o·ver·arm (ṓvər-aarm) *adj. Sports.* Executed with the arm raised above the shoulder: *an overarm throw.* **—o·ver·arm** *adv.*

o·ver·awe (ṓvər-áw) *tr.v.* **-awed, -awing, -awes.** To subdue by inspiring awe; overcome with awe.

o·ver·bal·ance (ṓvər-bál-ənss) *v.* **-anced, -ancing, -ances.** —*tr.* **1.** To throw off balance. **2.** To have greater weight or importance than. —*intr.* To lose one's balance; tip over.
~*n.* (-bal-). Something that overbalances; an excess of weight or quantity.

o·ver·bear (ṓvər-baír) *v.* **-bore** (-bór || -bōr), **-borne** (-bórn || bōrn), **-bearing, -bears.** —*tr.* **1.** To crush or press down upon with physical force. **2.** To prevail over, as if by superior weight or force; dominate. —*intr.* To bear too much fruit or offspring.

o·ver·bear·ing (ṓvər-baír-ing) *adj.* **1.** Domineering; arrogant: *"the overbearing character and insulting manners of the English people"*

(Jawaharlal Nehru). **2.** Overwhelming in power or significance; predominant. —*See* Synonyms at **dictatorial.** —**o·ver·bear·ing·ly** *adv.*

o·ver·bid (ōvər-bíd) *v.* **-bid, -bid, -bidding, -bids.** —*tr.* **1.** To outbid (a person) for something. **2.** To bid unjustifiably high for (something). —*intr.* **1.** To bid higher than the actual value of something. **2.** In bridge and similar card games, to bid higher than is warranted by the value of one's hand.
~*n.* (ōvər-bid). **1.** A bid that is higher than another bid. **2.** A bid that is too high.

o·ver·bite (ōvər-bīt) *n.* In dentistry, the condition in which the front upper incisor and canine teeth project over the lower.

o·ver·blouse (ōvər-blowz) *n.* A blouse designed to be worn over a skirt or trousers, instead of tucked in.

o·ver·blow (ōvər-blō) *tr.v.* **-blew** (-blōō), **-blown** (-blōn), **-blowing, -blows.** To blow (a wind instrument) so as to produce a harmonic instead of a fundamental note.

o·ver·blown (ōvər-blōn) *adj.* **1.** Exaggerated; overdone. **2.** Pompous; conceited. **3.** Past the stage of full bloom. **4.** Blown past or over.

o·ver·board (ōvər-bawrd ‖ -bōrd) *adv.* Over the side of a boat or ship into the water. *Informal.* **1.** To show wild enthusiasm. **2.** To react in an exaggerated or extreme way. —**throw overboard.** To get rid of; abandon.

o·ver·book (ōvər-bŏŏk ‖ -bŏŏk) *v.* **-booked, -booking, -books.** —*tr.* To make more bookings for seats or accommodation on or in (an aeroplane or hotel, for example) than there are places available. —*intr.* To overbook places, as in an aeroplane or hotel.

o·ver·build (ōvər-bíld) *tr.v.* **-built, -building, -builds.** **1.** To build on top of. **2.** To build more buildings in (an area) than is justified or necessary. **3.** To build with excessive size or elaboration.

o·ver·bur·den (ōvər-búrd'n) *tr.v.* **-dened, -dening, -dens.** **1.** To burden with too much weight. **2.** To burden with too much work, worry, or responsibility.
~*n.* (-burd'n). **1.** *Geology.* **a.** Material overlying a useful mineral deposit. **b.** Unconsolidated material covering solid rock or bedrock. **2.** *Archaeology.* A sterile stratum overlying a stratum bearing traces of the culture being studied.

o·ver·buy (ōvər-bī) *v.* **-bought** (-báwt), **-buying, -buys.** —*tr.* **1.** To buy in excessive amounts. **2.** *Finance.* To buy (stocks and shares) on margin in excess of one's ability to provide further security if prices drop. —*intr.* To buy goods beyond one's means.

o·ver·call (ōvər-káwl) *tr.v.* **-called, -calling, -calls.** **1.** To overbid. **2.** In bridge, to bid higher than (one's opponent) when one's partner has not bid.
~*n.* (-kawl). **1.** An overbid. **2.** In bridge, an instance of overcalling.

o·ver·cap·i·tal·ise, o·ver·cap·i·tal·ize (ōvər-káppit'l-īz) *tr.v.* **-ised, -ising, -ises.** **1.** To provide an excess amount of capital for (a business enterprise). **2.** To estimate the value of (property) too highly. **3.** To place an unlawfully or unreasonably high value on the nominal capital of (a company). —**o·ver·cap·i·tal·i·sa·tion** (-ī-záysh'n ‖ U.S. -i-) *n.*

o·ver·cast (ōvər-kaast, -káast ‖ -kast, -kást) *adj.* **1. a.** Covered or obscured, as with clouds. **b.** *Meteorology.* Designating the sky when more than 95 per cent of it is covered with cloud. **2.** Gloomy; dark; melancholy. **3.** Sewn with long, overlying stitches in order to prevent unravelling, as at the edges of fabric.
~*n.* (ōvər-kaast ‖ -kast). **1.** A covering, as of clouds. **2.** In mining, an arch or support for a passage over another passage. **3.** A fishing cast falling beyond the point intended. **4.** An overcast stitch or seam. In this sense, also called "overcasting".
~*tr.v.* **overcasted, -casting, -casts.** **1.** To make cloudy or gloomy. **2.** In fishing, to cast beyond (the intended point). **3.** To sew with an overcast stitch.

o·ver·charge (ōvər-chárj) *v.* **-charged, -charging, -charges.** —*tr.* **1.** To charge (a customer) too high a price for something. **2.** To fill too full; overload. **3.** To supply (a battery) with too much charge or too high a current, so as to damage the electrodes. **4.** To exaggerate. —*intr.* To charge too high a price.
~*n.* (-chaarj). **1.** *Abbr.* **o/c** An excessive charge or price. **2.** A load or burden that is too full or heavy.

o·ver·cloud (ōvər-klówd) *v.* **-clouded, -clouding, -clouds.** —*tr.* **1.** To cover with clouds. **2.** To make dark and gloomy. —*intr.* To become cloudy.

o·ver·coat (ōvər-kōt) *n.* A heavy coat worn in cold weather.

o·ver·come (ōvər-kúm) *v.* **-came** (-káym), **-come, -coming, -comes.** —*tr.* **1.** To defeat in competition or conflict; conquer. **2.** To surmount; prevail over. **3.** To overpower, as with emotion; affect deeply; cause to break down. —*intr.* To surmount opposition; be victorious. —*See* Synonyms at **defeat.** [Middle English *overcomen*, Old English *ofercuman* : *ofer*, OVER + *cuman*, to COME.]

o·ver·com·pen·sate (ōvər-kóm-pen-sayt, -pen-) *v.* **-sated, -sating, -sates.** —*intr.* **1.** To pay or make excessive compensation. **2.** To show overcompensation. —*tr.* To compensate excessively. —**o·ver·com·pen·sa·to·ry** (-kóm-pən-sáy-təri, -pen-, -say-, -sə-, -tri) *adj.*

o·ver·com·pen·sa·tion (ōvər-kóm-pən-sáysh'n, -pen-) *n.* The exertion of effort in excess of that needed to compensate for a physical or psychological characteristic or defect.

o·ver·crop (ōvər-króp) *tr.v.* **-cropped, -cropping, -crops.** To exhaust the fertility of (land) by overcultivation.

o·ver·crowd (ōvər-krówd) *tr.v.* **-crowded, -crowding, -crowds.** To put too much or too many in (one place). —**o·ver·crowd·ed** *adj.*

o·ver·de·vel·op (ōvər-di-véləp) *tr.v.* **-oped, -oping, -ops.** **1.** To develop to excess: *muscles overdeveloped by weightlifting.* **2.** In photography, to process (a plate or film) too long or in too concentrated a solution. —**o·ver·de·vel·op·ment** *n.*

o·ver·do (ōvər-dōō) *tr.v.* **-did** (-díd), **-done** (-dún), **-doing, -does** (-dúz). **1.** To do, use, or stress to excess; carry too far. **2.** To wear out the strength of; overtax. **3.** To cook too much or too long.

o·ver·dose (ōvər-dōss) *v.* **-dosed, -dosing, -doses.** —*intr.* To commit or attempt to commit suicide by taking a lethal dose of a drug. —*tr.* To give too large a dose to.
~*n.* (-dōss). A lethal or excessive dose, especially of a drug or drugs.

o·ver·draft (ōvər-draaft ‖ -draft) *n.* **1.** The act of overdrawing an account. **2.** *Abbr.* **O.D.** The amount overdrawn.

o·ver·draught (ōvər-draaft ‖ -draft) *n.* **1.** A current of air made to pass over the fuel in a furnace. **2. a.** A series of flues in a kiln designed to force air down from the top. **b.** The air so forced.

o·ver·draw (ōvər-dráw) *v.* **-drew** (-drōō), **-drawn** (-dráwn), **-drawing, -draws.** —*tr.* **1.** To draw on (an account) in excess of credit. **2.** To pull back too far: *overdraw a bow.* **3.** To spoil the effect of by exaggeration in telling or describing. —*intr.* To draw on a bank account in excess of credit. —**be overdrawn.** To have drawn money from a bank account in excess of credit.

o·ver·dress (ōvər-dréss) *intr.v.* **-dressed, -dressing, -dresses.** To dress in a more formal or elaborate manner than is desirable in a given situation.
~*n.* A skirted garment, such as a pinafore, worn over other outer clothing.

o·ver·drive (ōvər-drīv) *n.* A gearing mechanism in a motor vehicle that reduces the power output required to maintain driving speed in a specific range by increasing the ratio of drive shaft to engine speed. —**go into overdrive.** To redouble one's energies or act with even greater speed or intensity, as if switching to the highest possible gear.
~*tr.v.* (-drīv) **overdrove** (-drōv), **-driven** (-drívv'n), **-driving, -drives.** **1.** To drive (a vehicle) too far or too long. **2.** To push (oneself) too far; overwork.

o·ver·dub (ōvər-dúb) *tr.v.* **-dubbed, -dubbing, -dubs.** **1.** To add the sound of (a voice or instrument) to a recording more than once, so that the sound is doubled, tripled, and so on. **2.** To add in (new sounds) to a recording.
~*n.* (-dub). An act or instance of overdubbing sounds.

o·ver·due (ōvər-déw ‖ -dōō) *adj.* **1.** Being unpaid after becoming due. **2.** Past the due time of arrival; expected or required but not yet come. —*See* Synonyms at **tardy.**

o·ver·es·ti·mate (ōvər-ésti-mayt) *tr.v.* **-mated, -mating, -mates.** **1.** To estimate too highly. **2.** To esteem too greatly.
~*n.* (-mət, -mit). An estimate or estimation that is excessively high. —**o·ver·es·ti·ma·tion** (-máysh'n) *n.*

o·ver·ex·ert (ōvər-ig-zért, -eg- ‖ -ik-) *tr.v.* **-erted, -erting, -erts.** To exert too much; overtax; strain. —**o·ver·ex·er·tion** *n.*

o·ver·ex·pose (ōvər-ik-spōz, -ek-) *tr.v.* **-posed, -posing, -poses.** **1.** To expose too long or too much. **2.** To expose (a photographic film or plate) too long or with too much light. —**o·ver·ex·po·sure** *n.*

o·ver·ex·tend (ōvər-ik-sténd, -ek-) *tr.v.* **-tended, -tending, -tends.** To expand or disperse (one's defences or finances, for example) beyond a safe or reasonable limit. —**o·ver·ex·ten·sion** *n.*

o·ver·fall (ōvər-fawl) *n.* **1.** A turbulent expanse of water caused by currents running over a submerged ridge or by the meeting of underwater currents. **2.** A device that releases or drains excess water from a canal, lock, or the like.

o·ver·flow (ōvər-flō) *v.* **-flowed, -flowing, -flows.** —*intr.* **1.** To flow or run over the top, brim, or banks. **2.** To be filled beyond capacity, as a container or waterway may be. **3.** To have a boundless supply; be superabundant: *overflowing with gratitude.* —*tr.* **1. a.** To flow over (the banks or a brim, for example). **b.** To flow over the top, brim, or banks of. **2.** To spread over or cover; flood. **3.** To cause to fill beyond capacity.
~*n.* (ōvər-flō). **1.** The act of overflowing. **2. a.** The liquid substance which flows over. **b.** The amount of such liquid. **3.** An outlet or vent through which excess liquid may escape.

o·ver·fly (ōvər-flī) *tr.v.* **-flew** (-flōō), **-flown** (-flōn), **-flying, -flies.** **1.** To fly over, or fly an aircraft over: *The helicopter accidentally overflew enemy territory.* **2.** To fly beyond, or fly an aircraft beyond: *The pilot overflew the runway.* —**over·flight** (-flīt) *n.*

o·ver·gar·ment (ōvər-gaarmənt) *n.* An outer garment.

o·ver·glaze (ōvər-glayz) *n.* A second coat of glaze on pottery.
~*adj.* Applied to a glazed surface. Said especially of a colour, design, or painting.
~*tr.v.* (-gláyz, -glayz) **overglazed, -glazing, -glazes.** To apply an overglaze to.

o·ver·graze (ōvər-gráyz) *v.* **-grazed, -grazing, -grazes.** —*tr.* To destroy or seriously damage (grass cover or pasture land) by allowing animals to graze for too long a period. —*intr.* To overgraze grass cover or pastureland.

o·ver·ground (ōvər-grownd, -grównd) *adj.* Above the surface of the ground: *an overground extension of the railway.*

o·ver·grow (ōvər-grō) *v.* **-grew** (-grōō), **-grown, -growing, -grows.** —*tr.* **1.** To grow and spread across (an area). Often used in the passive: *a pathway overgrown with weeds.* **2.** To cause the growth or spread of vegetation across: *We overgrew the old paddock with ferns.*

3. To choke and replace (a weaker plant). **4.** To grow too large for. —*intr.* To grow beyond normal size.

o·ver·grown (ṓvər-grṓn) *adj.* Grown too large for one's age; oversized: *That overgrown bully needs cutting down to size.*

o·ver·growth (ṓvər-grōth) *n.* **1.** A growth over or upon something. **2.** Excessively abundant or luxuriant growth.

o·ver·hand (ṓvər-hand) *adj.* **1.** Sewn with stitches drawing two edges together, with each stitch passing over the seam formed by the edges. **2.** *Chiefly U.S.* Thrown, struck, or executed with the hand above the level of the shoulder. ~*adv.* In an overhand manner. ~*n.* **1.** An overhand stitch or seam. **2.** *Chiefly U.S.* An overhand throw, stroke, or delivery. ~*tr.v.* **overhanded, -handing, -hands.** To sew with an overhand seam or stitches.

overhand knot *n.* A knot formed by making a loop in a piece of cord and pulling one end through it. Also called "single knot".

o·ver·hang (ṓvər-háng) *v.* **-hung** (-húng), **-hanging, -hangs.** —*tr.* **1.** To project or extend beyond. **2.** To hang over or above. **3.** To threaten or menace; loom over. **4.** To ornament with hangings. —*intr.* To hang or project over something. ~*n.* (-hang). **1.** A projecting part of something, such as an architectural structure or rock formation. **2.** The amount of projection: *an overhang of six inches.* **3.** The length of the wing of a biplane or other multiplane that projects beyond the tip of the wing above or below it.

o·ver·haul (ṓvər-háwl, -hawl) *tr.v.* **-hauled, -hauling, -hauls.** **1. a.** To examine or go over carefully, searching for defects to be repaired. **b.** To dismantle in order to make repairs. **c.** To make all needed repairs on; fix; renovate. **2.** *Nautical.* To slacken (a line) or release and separate the blocks of (a tackle). **3.** To catch up with; overtake. ~*n.* (-hawl). A comprehensive repair job; a renovation.

o·ver·head (ṓvər-hed, -héd) *adj.* **1.** Located, functioning, or performed above the level of the head: *an overhead light.* **2.** Of or pertaining to the operating expenses of a business concern. ~*n.* (-hed). **1.** *Usually plural.* The incidental operating expenses of a business, including the costs of rent, rates, electricity, and interior decoration, but excluding labour and materials. **2.** The top surface in an enclosed space of a ship. ~*adv.* (-héd). Over or above the level of the head: *look overhead.*

overhead camshaft *n. Abbr.* **ohc, o.h.c.** A camshaft in an internal-combustion engine that is situated above the valves and acts directly onto their stems or onto rocker arms.

overhead valve *n. Abbr.* **ohv, o.h.v.** An internal-combustion engine valve that is situated in the cylinder head above the piston. Also used adjectivally: *an overhead-valve engine.* Compare **side-valve.**

o·ver·hear (ṓvər-héer) *tr.v.* **-heard** (-hérd), **-hearing, -hears.** To happen to hear (something spoken or someone speaking) without being addressed intentionally by the speaker. —**o·ver·hear·er** *n.*

o·ver·heat (ṓvər-héet) *v.* **-heated, -heating, -heats.** —*tr.* **1.** To heat too much. **2.** To cause to become angry or excited: *overheated by a sharp exchange of insults.* **3.** *Economics.* To overstimulate (the economy), particularly by generating a level of demand so high that it cannot be met by the suppliers. —*intr.* To become overheated.

o·ver·in·dulge (ṓvər-in-dúlj) *v.* **-dulged, -dulging, -dulges.** —*tr.* To indulge excessively; gratify too much or unwisely. —*intr.* To indulge in something to excess. —**o·ver·in·dul·gence** *n.* —**o·ver·in·dul·gent** *adj.* —**o·ver·in·dul·gent·ly** *adv.*

o·ver·is·sue (ṓvər-íssew, -íshōō, -íssew, -íshōō) *tr.v.* **-sued, -suing, -sues.** To issue more than the necessary, sensible, or authorised amount of (shares or banknotes, for example). ~*n.* Shares, banknotes, or the like so issued.

o·ver·joyed (ṓvər-jóyd) *adj.* Filled with joy; delighted.

o·ver·kill (ṓvər-kil) *n. Informal.* **1.** Destructive capacity, especially that of nuclear weapons, exceeding the amount needed to defeat an enemy. **2.** Any greatly excessive action or response: *government overkill in dealing with dissent.*

o·ver·lad·en (ṓvər-láyd'n) *adj.* Overloaded; overburdened.

o·ver·land (ṓvər-land, -lánd) *adj.* **1.** Across land; proceeding over land: *an overland flight.* **2.** By land, rather than by sea or air: *an overland journey.* ~*v.* **overlanded, -landing, -lands.** *Australian.* —*tr.* To drive (livestock) overland for long distances, especially through remote areas such as the outback. —*intr.* To overland livestock. —**o·ver·land** *adv.* —**o·ver·land·er** *n.*

o·ver·lap (ṓvər-láp) *v.* **-lapped, -lapping, -laps.** —*tr.* **1.** To lie or extend adjacent to and partly over, partly covering part of. **2.** To have an area, time span, interest, or other dimension or aspect in common with; coincide partly with. —*intr.* **1.** To lie adjacent to and partly cover something. **2.** To coincide partly: *Their duties overlap.* ~*n.* (-lap). **1.** A part or portion that overlaps or is overlapped. **2.** The amount thus overlapping. **3.** An instance of overlapping.

o·ver·lay (ṓvər-láy) *tr.v.* **-laid, -laying, -lays.** **1.** To lay or spread over or upon. **2. a.** To cover or decorate the surface of: *overlay wood with silver.* **b.** To embellish superficially: *a simple tune overlaid with ornate harmonies.* **3.** *Printing.* To put an overlay upon. ~*n.* (-lay). **1.** Something that is laid over or covers something else. **2.** A layer of decoration, such as gold leaf or wood veneer, applied to a surface. **3.** *Printing.* A piece of paper or other material used on a press, cylinder, or plate to even out the pressure. **4.** A transparent sheet containing graphic matter, such as labels or coloured areas, placed on illustrative matter to be incorporated into it.

Usage: *Overlay* and *overlie* have similar senses, but are not usually interchangeable. *Overlay* applies mainly to the act of superimposing one thing on another, as when a carpenter *overlays* plywood with veneer. The past tense is *overlaid.* *Overlie* applies when one thing is seen to lie over or rest upon another, as when warm air *overlies* cold air. The past tense is *overlain.*

o·ver·leaf (ṓvər-léef) *adv.* On the other side of the page; especially, on the reverse side of a right-hand page.

o·ver·leap (ṓvər-léep) *tr.v.* **-leapt** (-lépt), or **-leaped, -leaping, -leaps.** **1.** To leap across or over. **2.** *Archaic & U.S.* To pass over; omit; ignore: *The report overleaps all but the most essential points.*

o·ver·lie (ṓvər-lí) *tr.v.* **-lay, -lain, -laying, -lies.** **1.** To lie over or upon. **2.** To smother by lying upon (an infant or other newborn creature). —See Usage note at **overlay.**

o·ver·load (ṓvər-lṓd) *tr.v.* **-loaded, -loading, -loads.** To load too heavily. ~*n.* (-lṓd). An excessive load.

o·ver·long (ṓvər-lóng ‖ -láwng) *adj.* Too long. —**o·ver·long** *adv.*

o·ver·look (ṓvər-lōōk ‖ -lṓōk) *tr.v.* **-looked, -looking, -looks.** **1.** To look over or at from a higher place. **2.** To rise above, especially so as to afford a view over: *The tower overlooks the sea.* **3.** To fail to notice or consider; miss. **4.** To ignore deliberately or indulgently; disregard. **5.** To look over; examine. **6.** To watch over; supervise; oversee. **7.** To cast a spell or the evil eye upon; bewitch. ~*n.* (-lōōk). *U.S.* **1.** An elevated place that affords an extensive view. **2.** An act or instance of overlooking something.

o·ver·lord (ṓvər-lawrd) *n.* **1.** A lord having power or sway over another or other lords. **2.** One who is in a position of supremacy or domination over others: *science overlords.* —**o·ver·lord·ship** *n.*

o·ver·ly (ṓvərli) *adv. Chiefly U.S.* To an excessive degree; too: *This hotel seems not to be overly clean.*

Usage: The use of this word as an intensifying adverb is common in American English (*She has been overly cautious about the problem*), but it has attracted criticism as an unnecessary development, the same sense already being expressed by the prefix *over-* (as in *overcautious*). The usage has as yet had little impact on British English.

o·ver·man (ṓvər-man, -mən) *n., pl.* **-men** (-men, -mən). **1.** A man having authority over others; especially, an overseer or foreman. **2.** The Nietzschean Superman. ~*tr.v.* (-mán). **overmanned, -manning, -mans.** To provide with more workers than are needed. —**o·ver·man·ning** *n.*

o·ver·mas·ter (ṓvər-máastər ‖ -mástər) *tr.v.* **-tered, -tering, -ters.** To overpower; overcome. —**o·ver·mas·ter·ing** *adj.* —**o·ver·mas·ter·ing·ly** *adv.*

o·ver·match (ṓvər-mách) *tr.v.* **-matched, -matching, -matches.** *Chiefly U.S.* **1.** To be more than the match of; exceed. **2.** To match with a superior opponent. ~*n.* (-mach). *Chiefly U.S.* A contest in which one opponent is distinctly superior.

o·ver·much (ṓvər-múch, -much) *adj.* Too much; excessive. ~*adv.* **1.** In too great a degree. **2.** Very much. Usually used in the negative: *I don't care for her overmuch.* ~*n.* An excessive amount.

o·ver·night (ṓvər-nít, -nít) *adj.* **1.** Lasting for, extending over, or remaining during a night: *an overnight journey.* **2.** For use over a single night or for a short journey. **3.** Sudden; meteoric: *an overnight success.* ~*adv.* **1.** During or for the length of the night. **2.** In or as if in the course of one night; suddenly: *The situation changed overnight.* **3.** On the preceding night or evening.

overnight bag *n.* A bag containing articles for an overnight stay, such as toilet articles and night clothes.

o·ver·pass (ṓvər-paass ‖ -pass) *n.* A passage, bridge, or flyover that crosses above another path or roadway. ~*tr.v.* (-pa'ass ‖ -pass) **overpassed, -passing, -passes.** **1.** To pass over or across; traverse. **2.** To go beyond; exceed; surpass. **3.** *Chiefly U.S.* To overlook; disregard.

o·ver·pay (ṓvər-páy) *v.* **-paid, -paying, -pays.** —*tr.* **1.** To pay (someone) too much. **2.** To pay (an amount) in excess of a sum due. —*intr.* To pay too much. —**o·ver·pay·ment** *n.*

o·ver·pitch (ṓvər-pích) *v.* **-pitched, -pitching, -pitched.** —*tr.* In cricket, to bowl (a ball) so that it pitches too close to the stumps making it relatively easy to hit. —*intr.* To overpitch a ball.

o·ver·play (ṓvər-pláy) *tr.v.* **-played, -playing, -plays.** **1.** To play (a dramatic role) in an exaggerated manner; overact. **2.** To overestimate the strength of (one's holding or position) and thus contribute to one's own defeat. Used chiefly in the phrase *overplay one's hand.* **3.** To exaggerate; invest with too much importance.

o·ver·plus (ṓvər-pluss) *n.* An amount in excess of need.

o·ver·pow·er (ṓvər-pówr, -pów-ər) *tr.v.* **-ered, -ering, -ers.** **1.** To overcome or vanquish by superior force; subdue. **2.** To affect so strongly as to make helpless or ineffective; overwhelm. **3.** To furnish with excessive mechanical power.

o·ver·pow·er·ing (ṓvər-pówr-ing, -pów-ər-) *adj.* So strong or intense as to overpower; overwhelming. —**o·ver·pow·er·ing·ly** *adv.*

o·ver·price (ṓvər-príss) *tr.v.* **-priced, -pricing, -prices.** To put too high a price on. —**o·ver·pric·ing** *n.*

o·ver·print (ṓvər-print, -print) *tr.v.* **-printed, -printing, -prints.** To imprint over something already printed; especially, to print over (printed images) with another colour.

~*n.* (-print). **1.** A mark or impression made by overprinting. **2. a.** A mark or words printed over a postage stamp. **b.** A stamp so marked.

o·ver·pro·duce (ŏvər-prə-déwss ‖ -dóoss) *v.* **-duced, -ducing, -duces.** —*tr.* To produce too much of; produce more than is needed or can be sold. —*intr.* To overproduce a commodity or article. —**o·ver·pro·duc·tion** (-dúksh'n) *n.*

o·ver·pro·tect (ŏvər-prə-tékt ‖ -prō-) *tr.v.* **-tected, -tecting, -tects. 1.** To protect more than is necessary or advisable. **2.** To shelter (someone, especially a child) excessively from the hard physical and social realities of the outside world, thereby distorting or stunting emotional development.

o·ver·rate (ŏvər-ráyt) *tr.v.* **-rated, -rating, -rates. 1.** To rate or assess too highly. **2.** To overestimate the merits of. —**o·ver·rat·ed** *adj.*

o·ver·reach (ŏvər-réech) *v.* **-reached, -reaching, -reaches.** —*tr.* **1.** To reach or extend over or beyond. **2.** To miss by reaching too far or attempting too much: *overreach a goal.* **3.** To defeat (oneself) by going too far, doing or trying to gain too much, or by being too cunning. **4.** *Chiefly U.S.* To get the better of; trick; outwit. —*intr.* **1.** To reach or go too far. **2.** To outwit others; cheat. **3.** To strike the front part of a hind foot against the rear or side part of a forefoot or foreleg. Used of horses. —**o·ver·reach·er** *n.*

o·ver·ride (ŏvər-rīd) *tr.v.* **-rode** (-rōd), **-ridden** (-rídd'n), **-riding, -rides. 1.** To declare null and void; set aside. **2.** To ride (a horse) too hard. **3.** To trample upon. **4.** To prevail over; conquer; supplant. **5.** To ride across. **6.** To extend over or overlap.

o·ver·rid·er (ŏvər-rīdər) *n.* Either of a pair of short, vertical, metal or rubber attachments to a motor-vehicle bumper that prevent the bumper interlocking with that of another vehicle.

o·ver·rid·ing (ŏvər-rīding) *adj.* Having the superior claim; prior to all others: *of overriding importance.* —**o·ver·rid·ing·ly** *adv.*

o·ver·ripe (ŏvər-rīp) *adj.* **1.** More than ripe; too ripe. **2.** Jaded; decadent. —**o·ver·ripe·ness** *n.*

o·ver·rule (ŏvər-rōol) *tr.v.* **-ruled, -ruling, -rules. 1. a.** To disallow the arguments of or rule against (a person), especially by virtue of higher authority. **b.** To decide or rule against (an argument, action, or decision). **c.** To declare null and void; invalidate; reverse. **2.** To dominate by strong influence; prevail over so as to change the opinion or course of action.

o·ver·run (ŏvər-rún) *v.* **-ran** (-rán), **-run, -running, -runs.** —*tr.* **1.** To attack and defeat conclusively: *The troops overran the town.* **2.** To spread or swarm over destructively: *Slugs overran the garden.* **3.** To spread swiftly throughout: *The new fashion overran the country.* **4.** To overflow: *The river overran its banks.* **5.** To run or extend beyond: *Her speech has overrun the time limit.* **6.** *Archaic.* To run faster than. **7.** *Printing.* **a.** To rearrange or move (set type or pictures) from one column, line, or page to another. **b.** To print (a job order) in a quantity larger than that ordered. —*intr.* **1.** To run over; overflow. **2.** To go beyond the normal or desired limit. **3.** To run with a closed throttle, as a motor vehicle engine does, such that the engine speed is controlled by the rotation of the wheels, and thus by such factors as the incline of the road. ~*n.* (-run). **1.** An instance or act of overrunning. **2.** The amount by which something overruns.

o·ver·score (ŏvər-skór ‖ -skór) *tr.v.* **-scored, -scoring, -scores.** To cross out by drawing a line or lines over or through.

o·ver·seas (ŏvər-séez) *adv.* Beyond the sea; abroad. ~*adj.* Also *rare* **o·ver·sea** (-sée). Pertaining to, originating in, or situated in areas across the sea: *overseas students; an overseas posting.* ~*n. Informal.* Used with a singular verb. Overseas countries collectively.

o·ver·see (ŏvər-sée) *tr.v.* **-saw** (-sáw), **-seen, -seeing, -sees. 1.** To watch over and direct; supervise. **2.** *Archaic.* To scrutinise; inspect. —See Synonyms at **conduct.**

o·ver·se·er (ŏvər-seer, -see-ər) *n.* **1.** One who keeps watch over and directs the work of others, especially labourers. **2.** A supervisor or superintendent.

o·ver·sell (ŏvər-sél) *tr.v.* **-sold** (-sóld), **-selling, -sells. 1.** To contract to sell more of (a commodity) than can be delivered within the terms of a contract. **2.** To be too aggressive in selling (something). **3.** To present with excessive or unwarranted enthusiasm.

o·ver·set (ŏvər-sét) *v.* **-set, -setting, -sets.** —*tr.* **1.** To tip over; overturn. **2.** To throw into a confused or disturbed state; upset. **3.** *Printing.* To set too much (printed matter) for a given space. ~*n.* (-set). **1.** *Printing.* An excess of set type. **2.** An upset.

o·ver·sew (ŏvər-sō, -sō) *tr.v.* **-sewed, -sewn** or **-sewed, -sewing, -sews.** To sew over (raw edges of fabric) to prevent fraying.

o·ver·sexed (ŏvər-sékst) *adj.* Having a sexual drive or interest that is judged to be excessive.

o·ver·shad·ow (ŏvər-sháddō) *tr.v.* **-owed, -owing, -ows. 1. a.** To cast a shadow over. **b.** To cast gloom and despondency on. **2.** To make insignificant by comparison; dominate.

o·ver·shoe (ŏvər-shōo) *n.* An article of footwear worn over shoes as protection from water, snow, or cold.

o·ver·shoot (ŏvər-shōot) *v.* **-shot** (-shót), **-shooting, -shoots.** —*tr.* **1.** To shoot or pass over or beyond. **2.** To miss by or as if by shooting, hitting, or propelling something too far. **3. a.** To fly beyond or past (a specific location): *The plane overshot the runway.* **b.** To fly (an aircraft) beyond or past a specific location. **4.** To go beyond; exceed. —*intr.* To shoot or go too far.

o·ver·shot (ŏvər-shot) *adj.* **1.** Having an upper part projecting beyond the lower, especially when excessive or abnormal: *an overshot*

jaw. **2.** Designating a water wheel or mill in which the flowing water feeds and drives the wheel from the top.

o·ver·side (ŏvər-sīd, -sīd) *adv.* Over the side of a ship into another boat or into the water.

o·ver·sight (ŏvər-sīt) *n.* **1.** An unintentional omission or mistake. **2.** Watchful care or management; supervision.

o·ver·sim·pli·fy (ŏvər-símpli-fī) *tr.v.* **-fied, -fying, -fies.** To distort by presenting in too simple a form. —**o·ver·sim·pli·fi·ca·tion** (fi-káysh'n) *n.*

o·ver·size (ŏvər-sīz, -sīz) *adj.* Also **o·ver·sized** (ŏvər-sīzd). Larger in size than usual or necessary. ~*n.* (ŏvər-sīz). **1.** An unusually large size. **2.** An article made in an unusually large size.

o·ver·skirt (ŏvər-skurt) *n.* An outer skirt, especially a shorter one worn draped over another skirt.

o·ver·sleep (ŏvər-sléep) *tr.v.* **-slept** (-slépt), **-sleeping, -sleeps.** To sleep beyond one's usual or planned time for waking.

o·ver·soul (ŏvər-sōl) *n.* In New England transcendentalism, a spiritual essence or vital force in the universe, in which all souls participate, and which therefore transcends individual consciousness.

o·ver·spend (ŏvər-spénd) *v.* **-spent** (-spént), **-spending, -spends.** —*intr.* To spend more than is prudent or necessary. —*tr.* **1.** To spend in excess of: *overspend one's income.* **2.** To exhaust. Used chiefly in the past participle: *overspent with worry.* ~*n.* The act or an instance of overspending.

o·ver·spill (ŏvər-spil) *n. British.* An overflow or excess; especially, an overflow of people from one area to another. Also used adjectivally: *an overspill estate.* ~*intr.v.* (-spil) **overspilt** (-spílt) or **-spilled, -spilling, -spills.** To overflow, especially as a growing town or a population might.

o·ver·state (ŏvər-stáyt) *tr.v.* **-stated, -stating, -states.** To state in exaggerated terms. —**o·ver·state·ment** *n.*

o·ver·stay (ŏvər-stáy) *tr.v.* **-stayed, -staying, -stays.** To stay beyond (set limits or expected duration): *She overstayed her welcome.*

o·ver·steer (ŏvər-steer) *intr.v.* **-steered, -steering, -steers.** To turn, or have a tendency to turn, more sharply than is usual or is intended by the driver turning the wheel. Used of a motor vehicle. ~*n.* (-steer). **1.** An instance of oversteering. **2.** A tendency to oversteer.

o·ver·step (ŏvər-stép) *tr.v.* **-stepped, -stepping, -steps.** To go beyond (a limit): *overstep the bounds of taste.*

o·ver·stock (ŏvər-stók) *tr.v.* **-stocked, -stocking, -stocks. 1.** To supply with too much of (a commodity). **2.** To stock too much of (a commodity). ~*n.* (-stok). An excessive supply.

o·ver·strung (ŏvər-strung *for sense 1; for sense 2,* -strúng) *adj.* **1.** Being or designating a piano having strings on two levels crossing diagonally. **2.** Tense and strained; highly strung.

o·ver·stuff (ŏvər-stúf) *tr.v.* **-stuffed, -stuffing, -stuffs. 1.** To stuff too much into. **2.** To upholster overall and thickly.

o·ver·sub·scribe (ŏvər-səb-skríb ‖ -sub-) *tr.v.* **-scribed, -scribing, -scribes.** To subscribe for (something) in excess of available supply or accommodation: *The opera season was oversubscribed.* —**o·ver·sub·scrip·tion** (-skrípsh'n) *n.*

o·ver·sup·ply (ŏvər-sə-plī, -plī) *n., pl.* **-plies.** A supply in excess of what is required. ~*tr.v.* (-plī) **oversupplied, -plying, -plies.** To supply in excess.

o·vert (ō-vert, ō-vért) *adj.* Open and observable; not concealed or hidden. [Middle English, from Old French, from the past participle of *ovrir,* to open, from Vulgar Latin *operīre* (unattested), from Latin *aperīre.*] —**o·vert·ly** *adv.*

o·ver·take (ŏvər-táyk) *tr.v.* **-took** (-tōók), **-taken** (-táykən), **-taking, -takes. 1. a.** To move past and take up a position in front of. **b.** To pass or surpass after catching up with. **2.** To catch up with; draw even or level with. **3.** To come upon unexpectedly; take by surprise: *Night overtook us.*

o·ver·task (ŏvər-taask ‖ -tásk) *tr.v.* **-tasked, -tasking, -tasks. 1.** To give too demanding a task to. **2.** To be too demanding a task for; strain to exhaustion.

o·ver·tax (ŏvər-táks) *tr.v.* **-taxed, -taxing, -taxes. 1.** To impose an excessive tax or taxes on. **2.** To subject to an excessive burden or strain. —**o·ver·tax·a·tion** (-tak-sáysh'n) *n.* —**o·ver·tax·ing** *adj.*

o·ver·the·count·er (ŏvər-thə-kówntər) *adj.* **1.** *Abbr.* **OTC, O.T.C.** Capable of being sold legally without a prescription. Said of certain drugs or medicines. **2.** Not listed or available on an officially recognised stock exchange but traded in direct negotiation between buyers and sellers. Said of securities. Compare **under-the-counter.** —**over the counter** *adv.*

o·ver·throw (ŏvər-thrō) *tr.v.* **-threw** (-thrōó ‖ -thréw), **-thrown** (-thrōn ‖ -thrō-ən), **-throwing, -throws. 1.** To throw over; overturn. **2.** To bring about the downfall or destruction of, especially by force or concerted action: *a plot to overthrow the government.* ~*n.* (-thrō). **1.** An instance of overthrowing. **2.** Downfall; destruction. **3.** In cricket: **a.** A throw by a fielder that goes beyond the wicket. **b.** A run made as a result of an overthrow.

o·ver·thrust (ŏvər-thrust) *n. Geology.* A fault caused by the movement of rocks on the upper surface of a gently inclined fault plane over the rocks on the lower surface. Compare **underthrust.**

o·ver·time (ŏvər-tīm) *n.* **1.** Time spent at a job in addition to regular working hours. Also used adjectively: *overtime payments.* **2.** Pay given for such extra work. **3.** *Sports. U.S.* Extra time. ~*adv.* Beyond the established time limit, especially that of the normal working day: *The staff worked overtime.*

owl *Sensitive sight and hearing enable owls to hunt at night, and their soft plumage allows them to swoop silently on their prey. The tawny owl (above) is native to Europe, North Africa, and parts of Asia. It roosts in trees by day, when its speckled body merges with the twigs and branches.*

PRONUNCIATION KEY

a, trap; aa, father; ai, fair; ar, star; aw, lawn; ay, play; b, bb, stab; rubber; ch, church; ck, ticket; d, dd, dead; ladder; e, dress; ee, bee; er, defer; ew, few; ewr, pure; ə, about; ər, letter; f, ff, fife; differ; g, gg, giggle; h, hat; i, kit; ī, price; īr, fire; j, judge; k, kick; l, ll, let; 'l, needle; m, mm, man; n, nn, no; 'n, sudden; ng, thing; o, lot; ō, no; ŏŏ, foot; ōō, shoe; oor, poor; ow, cow; owr, hour; oy, boy; p, pp, pepper; r, rr, red; s, ss, sauce; sh, ship; t, tt, totter; th, thick; th, this; smooth; u, cut; ur, turn; v, vv, valve; w, wet; y, yes; z, zz, zebra; zh, vision; pleasure

IN FOREIGN WORDS:

aN, oN, Saint-Saëns; hl, Llanelli; Hluhluwe; kh, loch; lough; Khaled

STRESS MARK:

ín-sīt, insight; in-sī́t, incite

~*tr.v.* (-tī́m) **overtimed, -timing, -times.** To exceed the desired time limit for: *overtime a photographic exposure.*

o·ver·tone (ṓvər-tōn) *n.* **1.** In music and acoustics, a **harmonic** *(see)* other than the fundamental. **2.** *Often plural.* An implication or hint: *praise with overtones of envy.* [Translation of German *Oberton.*]

o·ver·top (ṓvər-tóp) *tr.v.* **-topped, -topping, -tops. 1.** To extend or rise over or beyond the top of; tower above. **2.** To be superior to; surpass in importance; override.

o·ver·trick (ṓvər-trik) *n.* In card games, a trick won in excess of contract or game.

o·ver·trump (ṓvər-trúmp, -trump) *v.* **-trumped, -trumping, -trumps.** —*tr.* To trump with a higher trump card than any played on the same trick. —*intr.* To play a trump higher than one previously played on a trick.

o·ver·ture (ṓvər-tewr, -chər) *n.* **1.** *Music.* **a.** An instrumental composition intended especially as an introduction to an opera, oratorio, or other extended musical work. **b.** A similar orchestral work, such as one written as introductory music to a play, or as a concert piece. **2.** Any introductory section or part, as of a poem. **3.** *Often plural.* An act, offer, or proposal that indicates readiness to undertake a course of action or to open a relationship. Used chiefly in the phrase *make overtures to.* **4.** In the Presbyterian Church: **a.** The submitting of a proposal by the highest church court to the presbyteries for their judgment on it preceding formal decision by the court. **b.** A proposal thus submitted.
~*tr.v.* **overtured, -turing, -tures. 1.** To present as an overture or proposal. **2.** To present or offer an overture to. **3.** To introduce with an overture or prelude. [Middle English, from Old French, from Vulgar Latin *opertūra* (unattested), from Latin *apertūra,* an opening, from *aperīre* (past participle *apertus*), to open.]

o·ver·turn (ṓvər-túrn) *v.* **-turned, -turning, -turns.** —*tr.* **1.** To cause to turn over or capsize; upset. **2.** To overthrow; defeat. **3.** To negate; nullify: *overturn a decision.* —*intr.* To turn over or capsize; become upset. —**o·ver·turn** (ṓvər-turn) *n.*

o·ver·use (ṓvər-yṓōz) *tr.v.* **-used, -using, -uses.** To use to excess. ~*n.* (-yṓōss). Excessive use.

o·ver·val·ue (ṓvər-vál-yōō) *tr.v.* **-ued, -uing, -ues.** To place too high a value on.

o·ver·view (ṓvər-vew) *n.* **1.** A broad, comprehensive view. **2.** A general survey or inspection.

o·ver·ween·ing (ṓvər-wéening) *adj.* **1.** Presumptuously arrogant; overbearing. **2.** Excessive; immoderate: *overweening ambition.* [Middle English, "having an excessively high opinion of oneself" : OVER- + WEEN + -ING.] —**o·ver·ween·ing·ly** *adv.*

o·ver·weigh (ṓvər-wáy) *tr.v.* **-weighed, -weighing, -weighs. 1.** To weigh down excessively; overburden. **2.** To have more weight than; outweigh; overbalance.

o·ver·weight (ṓvər-wáyt) *adj.* Weighing more than is normal, necessary, or allowed.
~*n.* (-wayt). **1.** More weight than is normal, necessary, or allowed; an excess of weight. **2.** *Archaic.* Greater weight or importance; preponderance.
~*tr.v.* (-wáyt) **overweighted, -weighting, -weights. 1.** To weigh down too heavily; overload. **2.** To give too much emphasis, importance, or consideration to.

o·ver·whelm (ṓvər-wélm, -hwélm) *tr.v.* **-whelmed, -whelming, -whelms. 1.** To overcome completely, either physically or emotionally; overpower: *quite overwhelmed by all this praise.* **2.** To surge over and submerge; engulf. **3.** To turn over; upset; overthrow.

o·ver·whelm·ing (ṓvər-wélming, -hwélming) *adj.* Overpowering in effect or strength: *overwhelming news; an overwhelming majority.* —**o·ver·whelm·ing·ly** *adv.*

o·ver·wind (ṓvər-wī́nd) *tr.v.* **-wound, -winding, -winds.** To wind (a watch, for example) beyond the correct limit.

o·ver·win·ter (ṓvər-wíntər) *v.* **-wintered, -wintering, -winters.** —*intr.* **1.** To spend the winter in a specified place. **2.** To survive winter in a particular form or in a particular place. —*tr.* To preserve through the winter.

o·ver·work (ṓvər-wúrk) *v.* **-worked, -working, -works.** —*tr.* **1.** To force to work too hard or long. **2.** To use or rework too often or to excess: *overwork a metaphor.* —*intr.* To work too long or hard. ~*n.* Excessive work; work that is too hard or lasts too long.

o·ver·write (ṓvər-rī́t) *v.* **-wrote** (-rṓt), **-written** (-rítt'n), **-writing, -writes.** —*tr.* **1. a.** To write (something) over other writing. **b.** To write something over (other writing). **2.** To write (a text) or write about (a subject) in an excessively flowery, mannered, or prolix style. —*intr.* **1.** To write at unnecessarily great length. **2.** To write in an inappropriately ornate or fulsome style.

o·ver·wrought (ṓvər-ráwt) *adj.* **1.** Excessively nervous or excited; agitated; strained: *so overwrought that he fainted.* **2.** Extremely elaborate or ornate; overdone: *an overwrought prose style.*

ovi-, ovo- *comb. form.* Indicates egg or ovum; for example, **oviviparous, oviduct.** [Latin *ōvi-, ōvo-,* from *ōvum,* egg.]

Ov·id (óvvid, ṓvid), born Publius Ovidius Naso (43 B.C.–A.D. 18). Roman poet. His work includes *Metamorphoses,* an urbane treatment of several legends. He also wrote many love poems.

o·vi·duct (ṓvi-dukt, óvvi-) *n. Zoology.* A tube through which ova leave an ovary. In mammals it is called the **Fallopian tube** *(see).* [New Latin *oviductus* : OVI- + DUCT.] —**o·vi·duc·tal** (-dúkt'l) *adj.*

o·vif·er·ous (ō-víffərəss) *adj.* Bearing or producing ova or eggs. [OVI- + -FEROUS.]

o·vi·form (ṓvi-fawrm) *adj.* Egg-shaped. [OVI- + -FORM.]

o·vine (ṓ-vīn) *adj.* Of, pertaining to, or resembling a sheep; sheeplike. [Late Latin *ovīnus,* from Latin *ovis,* sheep.]

o·vip·a·rous (ō-vípparəss) *adj.* Producing eggs that hatch outside the body. Compare **ovoviviparous, viviparous.** [Latin *ōviparus* : OVI- + -PAROUS.] —**o·vi·par·i·ty** (ṓvi-párrəti) *n.* —**o·vip·a·rous·ly** *adv.*

o·vi·pos·it (ṓvi-pózzit) *intr.v.* **-ited, -iting, -its.** To lay eggs, especially with an ovipositor. —**o·vi·po·si·tion** (-pə-zísh'n) *n.*

o·vi·pos·i·tor (ṓvi-pózzitər) *n.* **1.** A tubular structure, consisting of a pair of valves extending near the rear of the abdomen, with which most insects lay eggs. **2.** An egg-laying organ in certain fish, which is an extension of the edge of the genital opening.

o·vi·sac (ṓvi-sak) *n. Biology.* An egg-containing capsule, such as a **Graafian follicle** or an **ootheca** *(both of which see).*

ovo-. Variant of **ovi-.**

o·void (ṓ-voyd) *adj.* Also **o·voi·dal** (ō-vóyd'l). **1.** Egg-shaped. **2.** *Botany.* Egg-shaped, and having the broader end nearest the point of attachment. Said of leaves or fruits, for example.
~*n.* Something egg-shaped. [French *ovoide* : OV(I)- + -OID.]

o·vo·lo (ṓvə-lō) *n., pl.* **-li** (-lee). *Architecture.* A rounded convex moulding, often a quarter section of a circle or ellipse. Also called "thumb". [Italian, diminutive of *ovo,* egg, from Latin *ōvum.*]

ov·on·ic (ō-vónnik) *adj.* Designating a phenomenon or device based on the Ovshinsky effect.
~*n.* An Ovshinsky device. [Blend of *Ov*shinsky + electr*onic.*]

o·vo·tes·tis (ṓvō-téss-tiss) *n., pl.* **-tes** (-teez). *Zoology.* The hermaphroditic reproductive organ of some gastropods.

o·vo·vi·vip·a·rous (ṓvō-vī-vípparəss, -vi-) *adj.* Producing eggs that hatch within the female's body, as do some fishes and reptiles. Compare **oviparous, viviparous.** [New Latin *ovoviviparus* : ovo- + *viviparus,* VIVIPAROUS.] —**o·vo·vi·vi·par·i·ty** (-vī-vi-párrəti), **o·vo·vi·vip·a·rous·ness** *n.* —**o·vo·vi·vip·a·rous·ly** *adv.*

Ov·shin·sky device (ov-shín-ski) *n.* An electronic device using the Ovshinsky effect. Also called "ovonic", "ovonic device".

Ovshinsky effect *n. Electronics.* An effect that occurs in certain glasses containing selenium and tellurium. When a suitable voltage is applied across a thin film of this material its resistance falls rapidly, enabling devices incorporating these glasses to be used as switches. [After S.R. Ovshinsky (born 1923), U.S. inventor.]

o·vu·late (óvvew-layt, ṓ-vew-) *intr.v.* **-lated, -lating, -lates.** *Biology.* **1.** To produce ova. **2.** To discharge ova. [New Latin *ovulum,* OVULE.] —**o·vu·la·tion** (-láysh'n) *n.*

o·vule (óvvewl, ṓ-vewl) *n.* **1.** *Botany.* A female reproductive structure consisting of the integuments, nucellus, and embryo sac which after fertilisation becomes a seed. **2.** *Zoology.* An immature ovum. [French, from New Latin *ovulum,* diminutive of Latin *ōvum,* egg.] —**o·vu·lar** (óvvew-lər, ṓ-vew-), **o·vu·lar·y** (óvvew-ləri, ṓ-vew- || *U.S.* -lerri) *adj.*

o·vum (ṓvəm) *n., pl.* **ova** (ṓvə). The unfertilised female reproductive cell of animals; an egg cell. [New Latin, from Latin *ōvum, egg.*]

owe (ō) *v.* **owed, owing, owes.** —*tr.* **1.** To be indebted to the amount of; have to pay or repay: *She owes me five pounds.* **2.** To be morally obliged to; have an obligation to render or offer: *I owe you an apology.* **3.** To be in debt to. **4. a.** To be indebted or obliged for: *I owe a lot to my friends.* **b.** To be indebted or obliged for being the cause of: *He owes his success to his mother.* **5.** To bear (a certain feeling) towards a person: *She owes them a grudge.* —*intr.* To be in debt: *She owes for everything she has.* [Middle English *owen,* to possess, owe, Old English *āgan,* to possess.]

Ow·en (ṓ-in), **Robert** (1771–1858). Welsh philanthropist. After establishing the mill community of New Lanark (where he was manager and later owner) as a cooperative (1800), he started similar ventures in the United States and Ireland.

Owen, Wilfred (1893–1918). British poet, who served in World War I. His poems describe the nightmarish conditions in which soldiers lived and died; among his most famous poems is "Anthem for Doomed Youth". He was killed a week before the armistice.

Owen Falls. Waterfall in southeast Uganda. Lying on the White Nile, 3.2 kilometres (2 miles) from Lake Victoria, it became (1954) the site of a dam which provides hydro-electric power for Uganda and Kenya, and irrigation for Sudan and Egypt.

Ow·ens (ṓ-inz), **Jesse,** born James Cleveland Owens (1913–80). U.S. athlete. In 1935/36 he broke six world records in sprinting, hurdling, and long jump; the new records stood for 20 years. His greatest triumph came at the 1936 Olympics in Germany, when his success as a black athlete embarrassed the Nazi government.

ow·ing (ṓ-ing) *adj.* Still to be paid; due; owed. —**owing to.** Because of; on account of. See Usage note at **due.**

owl (owl) *n.* **1.** Any of various often nocturnal birds of prey of the order Strigiformes, having hooked and feathered talons, short necks, large heads with short, hooked beaks, and large forward-facing eyes. **2.** Any of various breeds of domestic pigeon resembling owls. **3.** A solemn, wise-looking person. [Middle English *owle,* Old English *ūle.*]

owl·et (ów-lit, -let, -lət) *n.* A young owl.

owl·ish (ówlish) *adj.* Resembling an owl, especially in seeming solemn and wise. —**owl·ish·ly** *adv.* —**owl·ish·ness** *n.*

owl-light (ówl-līt) *n. Poetic.* Twilight; dusk.

own (ōn) *adj.* Of or belonging to oneself or itself; individual; particular. Used to intensify the fact of possession and usually preceded by a possessive pronoun: *My own book.* Sometimes used to indicate oneself as the sole agent of the action expressed by the verb: *She made her own bed while I made the rest.*

~n. That which belongs to one: *It is my own.* **—come into (one's) own. 1.** To obtain possession of what belongs to one. **2.** To reach one's deserved level; fulfil one's potential. **3.** To obtain rightful recognition. **—hold (one's) own.** To maintain one's place in spite of attack or criticism. **—of (one's) own.** Belonging completely to oneself alone. **—on (one's) own. 1.** Alone; without company; by oneself. **2.** Without help; through one's own unaided efforts. **3.** Completely independent; responsible for oneself.

~v. **owned, owning, owns.** —*tr.* **1.** To have or possess: *She owns the shop.* **2.** To acknowledge or admit: *"I own myself a debtor to the world for two items."* (Lawrence Sterne). —*intr.* To confess or acknowledge: *She owned to being annoyed.* **—See Synonyms at acknowledge. —own up.** To confess fully and openly. Sometimes used with *to.* [Middle English *owen,* Old English *āgen.*]

own·er (ṓnər) *n.* A person who owns or possesses; especially, the person having legal ownership.

own·er·ship (ṓnər-ship) *n.* **1.** The state or fact of being an owner. **2.** Legal right to possession; proprietorship; dominion.

owt. *Northern English.* Variant of **aught**[1].

ox (oks) *n., pl.* **oxen** (ŏks'n). **1.** An adult castrated bull of the genus *Bos.* **2.** Any bovine mammal. [Middle English *ox,* Old English *oxa.*]

ox-. 1. Variant of **oxa-.** **2.** Variant of **oxo-.**

oxa-, ox- *comb. form. Chemistry.* Indicates the presence of oxygen atoms, especially when replacing carbon; for example, **oxalic acid.** [From OXYGEN.]

ox·a·late (ŏksə-layt) *n.* Any salt or ester of oxalic acid.

~*tr.v.* **oxalated, -lating, -lates.** To treat (a specimen) with an oxalate or oxalic acid. [French: *oxalique,* OXALIC ACID + -ATE.]

ox·al·ic acid (ok-sál-ik) *n.* A poisonous, crystalline organic acid, HOOCCOOH·2H₂O, used as a cleansing agent for motor-vehicle radiators and for metals in general, as a laundry bleach, and in textile finishing and cleaning. Also called "ethanedioic acid". [French *oxalique,* from Latin *oxalis,* wood sorrel, OXALIS.]

ox·a·lis (ŏksəliss, ok-sál-iss) *n.* Any plant of the genus *Oxalis,* having clover-like leaves and pink, yellow, or white flowers. See **wood sorrel.** [New Latin, from Latin, from Greek, from *oxus,* "sharp", sour.]

ox·a·zine (ŏksə-zeen) *n.* A heterocyclic chemical compound, C₄H₅NO, that exists in 13 isomeric forms. [OXY- + AZINE.]

ox·blood red (ŏks-blud) *n.* Dark or deep red to medium reddish brown. Also called "oxblood". **—ox·blood red** *adj.*

ox·bow (ŏks-bō) *n.* **1.** A U-shaped piece of wood that fits under and around the neck of an ox, with its upper ends attached to the bar of the yoke. **2.** A U-shaped bend in a river. **3.** The land within such a bend of a river. **4.** A lake formed from a U-shaped bend in a river. In this sense, also called "oxbow lake". **—ox·bow** *adj.*

Ox·bridge (ŏks-brij) *n.* The universities of Oxford and Cambridge, especially considered as representing traditional academic and social excellence, privilege, and exclusiveness.

~*adj.* Of or pertaining to Oxbridge: *Oxbridge philosophers; Oxbridge snobbery.* [*Ox*ford + Cam*bridge.*]

ox·eye (ŏks-ī) *n.* **1.** Any of various Eurasian plants of the genus *Buphthalmum,* having daisy-like flowers with yellow rays and dark centres. **2.** A round or oval dormer window.

oxeye daisy *n.* A perennial plant, *Chrysanthemum leucanthemum,* having daisy-like flowers with white rays and yellow centres.

ox-fence (ŏks-fenss) *n.* **1.** A strong fence for containing cattle. **2.** A fence used as an obstacle in showjumping, steeplechasing, and the like, consisting of a hedge, a railing or railings, and usually a ditch. Also called "oxer".

Ox·ford[1] (ŏks-fərd). City in southern central England. The county town of Oxfordshire, it lies between the river Thames (known locally as the Isis) and its tributary, the Cherwell. Its university (1249) has been, and still is, one of the world's most important places of learning; its historic buildings dominate the city centre. Cowley, the industrial suburb, has grown around the Morris motor-car works since 1911.

Oxford[2] *n. Sometimes small* **o. 1.** A stout, low shoe that laces over the instep. **2.** A cotton cloth of a tight basket weave, used primarily for men's shirts. **3.** A sheep, the Oxford Down. [After OXFORD.]

Oxford bags *pl. n.* Trousers with extremely wide legs, originally fashionable in the 1920s.

Oxford blue *n.* **1.** Dark, deep blue. **2.** A sportswoman or sportsman who has been awarded a **blue** *(see)* by Oxford University. **—Oxford blue** *adj.*

Oxford Down *n.* A large sheep of an English breed, having a dark brown face and legs and short wool. Also called "Oxford".

Oxford English *n.* A style of English pronunciation, similar to **received pronunciation,** thought to be used at Oxford University and often considered to be affected. Also called "Oxford accent".

Oxford frame *n.* A picture frame whose sides cross and project outwards at the corners.

Oxford grey *n.* Dark grey. **—Oxford grey** *adj.*

Oxford Group *n.* See **Moral Rearmament.**

Oxford movement *n.* A movement within the Church of England that originated at Oxford University in 1833. It sought to link the Anglican Church more closely to the Roman Catholic Church. See **Tractarianism.**

Ox·ford·shire (ŏks-fərd-sheer, -shər) *Abbr.* **Oxon.** County of southern central England. An agricultural valley rising to the Cotswolds in the west and the Chilterns in the south, it is drained by the river

Thames. Dairy and sheep farming are important, and the major industrial centre is Cowley. The county town is Oxford.

ox·hide (ŏks-hīd) *n.* Leather made from the hide of an ox. **—ox·hide** *adj.*

ox·i·dant (ŏksidənt) *n.* A chemical reagent that oxidises. Also called "oxidiser".

ox·i·dase (ŏksi-dayz, -dayss) *n.* Any of various plant or animal enzymes that act as oxidants. [OXID(ATION) + -ASE.] **—ox·i·da·sic** (-dáy-zik, -sik) *adj.*

ox·i·da·tion (ŏksi-dáysh'n) *n. Chemistry.* The process of oxidising or a chemical reaction in which something is oxidised. Compare **reduction.** [French, from *oxyder,* to oxidise.] **—ox·i·da·tive** (-daytiv) *adj.* **—ox·i·da·tive·ly** *adv.*

ox·i·da·tion-re·duc·tion (ŏksi-dáysh'n-ri-dúksh'n) *n.* A chemical reaction in which an atom or molecule loses electrons to another atom or molecule. Also called "redox".

oxidative phosphorylation *n. Biochemistry.* A vital process of intracellular respiration, occurring within the mitochondria of the cell, and responsible for most **A.T.P.** *(see)* formation.

ox·ide (ŏks-īd) *n.* A binary compound of an element or radical with oxygen. [French, from *oxygène,* OXYGEN.] **—ox·id·ic** (ok-síddik) *adj.*

ox·i·dim·e·try (ŏksi-dímmətri) *n. Chemistry.* A form of volumetric analysis in which oxidising agents are used in titrations. [*Oxid*ation + -METRY.]

ox·i·dise, ox·i·dize (ŏksi-dīz) *v.* **-dised, -dising, -dises.** Also **ox·i·date** (-dayt). **-dated, -dating, -dates.** —*tr.* **1.** *Chemistry.* **2.** To add oxygen to (a compound), as in combustion reactions. **b.** To remove hydrogen from (a compound), as in dehydrogenation reactions. **c.** To remove electrons from (a compound, ion, or group), as in the change of ferrous ions (Fe²⁺) to ferric ions (Fe³⁺). **2.** To coat with oxide. —*intr.* **1.** *Chemistry.* To undergo oxidation; gain oxygen or lose hydrogen or electrons. Used of chemical compounds. **2.** To become coated with oxide. [From OXIDE.] **—ox·i·dis·a·ble** *adj.* **—ox·i·di·sa·tion** (-dī-záysh'n ‖ *U.S.* -di-) *n.*

ox·i·dis·er (ŏksi-dīzər) *n.* Any substance that oxidises or induces oxidisation; especially, the oxidant in a rocket fuel.

ox·i·dis·ing agent (ŏksi-dīzing) *n. Chemistry.* A substance, such as oxygen or hydrogen peroxide, that oxidises another substance and is itself reduced in doing so. Compare **reducing agent.**

ox·ime (ŏks-eem) *n.* Any of a group of chemical compounds, used in chemical analysis, that have the general formula RR′C:NOH. If R and R′ are both organic groups the compound is called a *ketoxime;* if R′ is an organic group and R is a hydrogen atom it is an *aldoxime.* [OXO- + -ime representing -IMIDE.]

ox·lip (ŏks-lip) *n.* **1.** A Eurasian plant, *Primula elatior,* very similar to the primrose with flowers borne in clusters. **2.** A hybrid plant, the *false oxlip,* a cross between primroses and cowslips and having darker yellow flowers than the true oxlip. [Old English *oxanslyppe : oxan,* genitive of *oxa,* OX + *slyppe, slypa,* sticky substance, dung.]

oxo-, ox- *comb. form. Chemistry.* Indicates a compound containing oxygen linked to another atom by a double bond; for example, **oxopropanoic acid.** [From OXYGEN.]

Oxon. 1. Of Oxford (University). Used in degree titles: *B.A.* Oxon. **2.** Oxfordshire.

Ox·o·ni·an (ok-sṓni-ən) *adj.* Of, pertaining to, or characteristic of Oxford or Oxford University.

~*n.* **1.** A student, graduate, or member of Oxford University. **2.** A native or inhabitant of Oxford. [Medieval Latin *Oxōnia,* Oxford, from Old English *Ox(e)naford,* OXFORD.]

ox·o·ni·um (ok-sṓni-əm) *adj.* **1.** Designating an ion with the general formula R₃O , where R is either a hydrogen atom or an organic group. **2.** Designating a compound formed from this ion: *an oxonium salt.* [OXO- + -ON(E) + -IUM.]

ox·peck·er (ŏks-peckər) *n.* Either of two African birds, *Buphagus africanus* or *B. erythrorhynchus,* that feed upon ticks on the hides of animals. Also called "rhinoceros bird", "tick bird".

ox·tail (ŏks-tayl) *n.* The tail of an ox, as used in soups and stews.

ox·ter (ŏkstər) *n. Northern British.* An armpit. [Old English *ōxta, ōhsta;* akin to Latin *axilla.*]

ox·tongue, ox-tongue (ŏks-tung ‖ -tong) *n.* **1.** The tongue of an ox used as food. **2.** Either of two plants, *Picris echioides* or *P. hieracioides,* having tongue-shaped, hairy leaves and yellow flowers.

Oxus. See **Amu Darya.**

ox·y (ŏksi) *adj.* **1.** Containing or mixed with oxygen. Often used in combination: *oxyhydrogen.* **2.** *Chemistry.* Combined with oxygen or containing oxygen in chemical combination. Used in combination: *oxyacide; oxyhaemoglobin.* See **oxo-.**

oxy- *comb. form.* Indicates something sharp; for example, **oxycephaly.** [Greek *oxus,* sharp.]

ox·y·a·cet·y·lene (ŏksi-ə-sétti-leen, -lin) *adj.* Containing a mixture of acetylene and oxygen, at a flame temperature of 3,300°C.

ox·y·ac·id (ŏksi-ássid) *n.* An acid, such as sulphuric acid or nitric acid, that contains oxygen in its molecule. Also called "oxygen acid".

ox·y·ceph·a·ly (ŏksi-séffəli) *n.* A congenital abnormality in which the skull assumes a conical shape. [OXY- (sharp) + -cephaly, from -CEPHALIC.] **—ox·y·ce·phal·ic** (-si-fál-ik), **ox·y·ceph·a·lous** (-séffələss) *adj.*

ox·y·gen (ŏksijən) *n. Symbol* **O** A colourless, odourless, tasteless gaseous element constituting 21 per cent of the earth's atmosphere by volume, from which the pure liquid form is obtained by fractional distillation. It combines with most elements, is essential for

oxeye daisy *A common flower of the British countryside, the oxeye daisy grows wild in meadows and on railway embankments.*

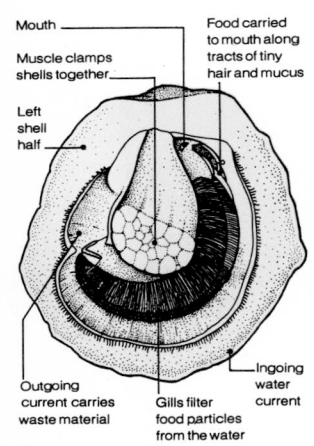

Labels on diagram:
Mouth
Food carried to mouth along tracts of tiny hair and mucus
Muscle clamps shells together
Left shell half
Outgoing current carries waste material
Gills filter food particles from the water
Ingoing water current

oyster *Edible oysters belong to one genus* (Ostrea), *pearl oysters to another* (Margaritifer). *This common edible oyster,* Ostrea edulis, *traps minute food particles on its gills and passes them on a sheet of mucus to its mouth. Some species of oyster change sex several times in the course of their lives.*

oystercatcher *Largely coastal birds, oystercatchers are waders which are found almost worldwide. They feed mainly on shellfish, using their long beaks to prise open the shell or to hammer a hole in it.*

plant and animal respiration, and is required for nearly all combustion and combustive processes. Atomic number 8, atomic weight 15.9994, melting point –218.4°C, boiling point –183.0°C, gas density at 0°C 1.429 kilograms per cubic metre, valency 2. [French *oxygène,* "acid-former" : OXY-, sharp (here, "acid") + -GEN.] —**ox·y·gen·ic** (óksi-jénnik), **ox·yg·e·nous** (ok-síjənəss) *adj.* —**ox·y·gen·i·cal·ly** *adv.*

oxygen acid *n.* An oxyacid.

ox·y·gen·ate (ók-sijə-nayt, ok-síjə-) *tr.v.* **-ated, -ating, -ates.** Also **ox·y·gen·ise** (-nīz), **-ised, -ising, -ises.** To treat, combine, or infuse with oxygen. —**ox·y·gen·a·tion** (-náysh'n) *n.*

oxygen debt *n.* The condition that exists in cells when insufficient oxygen is available for oxidation of foodstuffs to produce the energy required by the cells (for example, for strenuous exercise).

oxygen mask *n.* A device covering the mouth and nose of a patient through which oxygen is supplied from a tank or other source.

oxygen tent *n.* A transparent canopy placed over the head and shoulders of a patient for administering oxygen to aid respiration.

ox·y·hae·mo·glo·bin (óksi-héemə-glóbin, -glóbin) *n.* A bright red chemical complex of haemoglobin and oxygen, that transports oxygen from the lungs to the tissues via the blood.

ox·y·hy·dro·gen blowpipe (óksi-hídrəjən) *n.* A torch that burns a mixture of hydrogen and oxygen for welding. Also called "oxyhydrogen burner".

ox·y·mo·ron (óksi-máwr-on ‖ -mór-) *n., pl.* **-mora** (-máwr-ə ‖ -mór-) or **-morons.** A rhetorical figure in which an epigrammatic effect is created by the conjunction of incongruous or contradictory terms; for example, *a mournful optimist.* [Greek *oxumōron,* a clever remark, more pointedly witty for seeming stupid, neuter of *oxumōros,* "sharp-foolish" : OXY-, sharp, + *mōros,* stupid, foolish.]

oxy·salt (óksi-sawlt) *n.* A salt of an oxyacid.

ox·y·sul·phide (óksi-súl-fīd) *n. Chemistry.* A compound consisting of sulphur and oxygen, combined with a metal or positive radical, in which part of the sulphur has been replaced by oxygen.

ox·y·tet·ra·cy·cline (óksi-téttrə-sí-klin, -kleen) *n.* An antibiotic, $C_{22}H_{24}N_2O_9 \cdot 2H_2O$, derived from the mould *Streptomyces rimosus,* and used to treat bacterial infection in humans and animals. A trademark is "Terramycin".

ox·y·to·cic (óksi-tō-sik) *adj.* Hastening the process of childbirth, especially by inducing contraction of the uterine muscle.
~*n.* An oxytocic drug or agent. [OXY-, sharp + Greek *tokos,* childbirth, from *tiktein,* to bear + -IC.]

ox·y·to·cin (óksi-tō-sin) *n.* A pituitary hormone that increases contraction of the uterus during childbirth and stimulates the flow of milk. [See **oxytocic.**]

ox·y·tone (óksi-tōn) *adj.* In ancient Greek grammar, of or designating a word that has an acute accent on the last syllable.
~*n.* An oxytone word. [Greek *oxutonos* : OXY-, sharp, + *tonos,* TONE.] —**ox·y·ton·ic** (-tónnik) *adj.*

ox·y·u·ri·a·sis (ok-si-yoor-í-ə-siss) *n.* A disease, **enterobiasis** (see). [OXY- + URO- (urinary tract) + -IASIS.]

o·yez (ṓ-yess, -yez, ṓ-yéss, -yéz, -yáy) *interj.* Also **O·yes** (ṓ-yess, ṓ-yéss). Used three times in succession to order attention and silence, as by a public crier, or to open a court of law.
~*n.* Also **o·yes** *pl.* **oyesses** (ṓ-yessiz). *Archaic.* The cry "oyez": *"Fame with her loud'st Oyes cries 'This is he!' "* (Shakespeare). [Middle English *oyes!* from Anglo-French *oyez!,* hear ye!, imperative plural of *oyer,* Old French *oïr,* to hear, from Latin *audīre.*]

O·yo Empire (ṓ-yō) *n.* West African empire existing from the 17th to the 19th century. The modern city of Oyo is the capital of Oyo province, southwest Nigeria.

oys·ter (óystər) *n.* **1. a.** Any of several bivalve molluscs of the genus *Ostrea,* chiefly of shallow marine waters, having an irregularly shaped shell. **b.** The soft, edible flesh of any such mollusc, valued as a delicacy. **2.** Any of various similar or related bivalve molluscs, such as the **pearl oyster** *(see).* **3.** An oval-shaped piece of muscle, regarded as a delicacy, found in the hollow of the pelvic bone of a fowl. **4. a.** Any special delicacy. **b.** A source of complete fulfilment, affording every possible chance of personal advancement and satisfaction. Often used in the phrase *The world is (one's) oyster.* **5.** *Slang.* A quiet, reserved person. **6.** A colour, oyster white.
~*intr.v.* **oystered, -tering, -ters.** To gather, dredge for, or breed oysters. [Middle English *oistre,* from Old French, from Latin *ostrea,* from Greek *ostreon.*] —**oys·ter** *adj.*

oyster bed *n.* A place where oysters breed or are raised. Also called "oyster bank", "oyster park".

oys·ter·catch·er (óystər-kachər) *n.* Any of several shore birds of the genus *Haematopus,* especially *H. ostralogus,* having black and white plumage and a long orange-red bill.

oyster crab *n.* A small crab, *Pinnotheres ostreum,* that lives inside the shells of living oysters.

oyster mushroom *n.* A basidiomycete fungus, *Pleurotus ostreatus,* having a shell-shaped edible cap.

oyster pink *n.* Pale greyish pink. —**oyster pink** *adj.*

oyster plant *n.* **1.** A coastal plant, *Mertensia maritima,* having fleshy, blue-green, oyster-flavoured leaves and small blue flowers. **2.** A vegetable, **salsify** *(see).*

oyster white *n.* Pale yellowish green to light grey. Also called "oyster". —**oyster white** *adj.*

oz ounce; ounces.

Oz (oz.). *Informal.* Australia. [From the first syllable of *Australia.*]

O·zark Plateau (ṓ-zaark). Also **Ozark Mountains.** Highland of the south central United States. Lying between the Arkansas river to the south and west, the Missouri to the north and the Mississippi to the east.

o·zo·ce·rite (ṓzō-séer-īt) *n.* Also **o·zo·ke·rite** (-kéer-, ṓ-zṓkər-, o-, ə-, -it). A yellow-brown to black or green mineral hydrocarbon wax, used in making electrical insulation, lubricants, and inks. Also called "earth wax", "mineral wax". [German *Ozokerit* : Greek *ozein,* to smell + *kēros,* wax + -ITE.]

o·zone (ṓ-zōn, ṓ-zṓn) *n.* **1.** A blue, gaseous allotrope of oxygen, O_3, derived or formed naturally from diatomic oxygen by electric discharge or exposure to ultraviolet radiation. It is an unstable, powerfully bleaching, poisonous, oxidising agent, with a pungent, irritating odour, used to purify and deodorise air, to sterilise water, and as a bleach. **2.** *Informal.* Fresh, pure, invigorating air, especially that found at the seaside. [German *Ozon,* from Greek *ozōn,* present participle of *ozein,* to smell, reek.] —**o·zon·ic** (ṓ-zónnik, -zṓnik), **o·zo·nous** (ṓ-zṓnəss, ṓ-zṓnəss) *adj.*

ozone layer *n.* The ozonosphere.

o·zo·nide (ṓ-zṓ-nīd, ṓzṓ-) *n.* **1.** Any of various often explosive chemicals formed by attachment of ozone to the double bond of an unsaturated compound and used in analytical chemistry to locate such bonds.

o·zo·nise, o·zo·nize (ṓzṓ-nīz) *tr.v.* **-nised, -nising, -nises. 1.** To treat or impregnate with ozone. **2.** To convert (oxygen) to ozone. —**o·zo·ni·sa·tion** (-nī-záysh'n ‖ *U.S.* -ni-) *n.* —**o·zon·is·er** *n.*

o·zo·nol·y·sis (ṓzṓ-nóllə-siss) *n. Chemistry.* A method of treating an organic compound with ozone to locate a double bond by the formation of an ozonide. [OZONE + -LYSIS.]

o·zo·no·sphere (ṓ-zṓnə-sfeer, -zónnə-) *n.* **1.** A region of the upper atmosphere, between 15 and 30 kilometres (10 and 20 miles) in altitude, containing the greatest concentration of ozone, which absorbs solar ultraviolet radiation in a wavelength range not screened by other atmospheric components. **2.** A region of the atmosphere, between 10 and 50 kilometres (6 and 30 miles) in altitude, which contains a relatively high concentration of ozone. In both senses, also called "ozone layer". [OZON(E) + -SPHERE.] —**o·zo·no·spher·ic** (-sférrik ‖ -sféer-ik), **o·zo·no·spher·i·cal** *adj.*

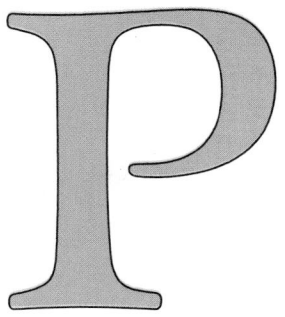

P

p, P (pee) *n., pl.* **p's,** or *rare* **ps, Ps** or **P's.** **1.** The sixteenth letter of the modern English alphabet. **2.** Any of the speech sounds represented by this letter. —**mind (one's) p's and q's.** To take care to observe polite social conventions in one's speech and manner.

p, P, p., P. *Note:* As an abbreviation or symbol, *p* may be a small or a capital letter, with or without a full stop. Established forms or those generally preferred precede the definition. When no form is given, all four forms are in general use in that sense. **1. p** *Physics.* momentum. **2. p.** page. **3. P** *Physics.* parity. **4. p.** part. **5. p.** participle. **6. p.** past. **7. P** *Chess.* pawn. **8. p.** penny; pence. See Usage note at **penny. 9. p.** per. **10. p.** peseta. **11. p.** peso. **12. P** The symbol for the element phosphorus. **13. p, p.** *Music.* piano (a direction). **14. p** *Physics.* pico-. **15. p.** pint. **16. p.** pipe. **17. p.** pole. **18. p.** population. **19. p., P.** president. **20. P** *Physics.* pressure. **21. P.** priest. **22. p., P.** prince. **23. p.** pro. **24. p** proton. **25. p.** purl. **26. P** The medieval Roman numeral for 400. **27.** The 16th in a series.

pa¹ (paa) *n. Informal.* Papa; father. [Short for PAPA.]

pa², pah (paa) *n.* A Maori village, originally a fortified village. [Maori *pà.*]

Pa The symbol for the element protactinium.

Pa. Pennsylvania.

p.a. per annum.

P.A. **1.** personal assistant. **2.** power of attorney. **3.** press agent. **4.** Press Association. **5.** public-address system. **6.** publicity agent. **7.** Publishers' Association. **8.** purchasing agent.

P/A power of attorney.

pab·u·lum (pábbewləm) *n., pl.* **-lums.** *Formal.* **1.** Any substance that gives nourishment; food. **2.** Insipid intellectual nourishment. [Latin *pābulum,* food, fodder.]

PABX private automatic branch (telephone) exchange.

Pac. Pacific.

pa·ca (paákə, páckə) *n.* Either of two species of tailless, nocturnal, tropical American rodent, especially *Cuniculus paca,* having a large head and brown fur with three to five lines of white spots running down each side. [Portuguese and Spanish, from Tupi *páca.*]

pace¹ (payss) *n.* **1.** A step made in walking; a stride. **2.** The distance spanned by a step or stride; specifically: **a.** A unit of length equal to 30 inches (76 centimetres). **b.** *Military.* 30 inches (76 centimetres) at quick time or 36 inches (91.5 centimetres) at double time. Called in full "regulation pace". **c.** A length measured from the point at which the heel of one foot is raised to the point at which it is set down again after an intervening step by the other foot; about 1.5 metres or 5 feet. **3. a.** The rate of speed at which a person, animal, or group walks or runs. **b.** The rate of speed at which any activity or movement proceeds. **c.** Great speed or intensity of activity: *couldn't keep up with the pace.* **d.** In Cricket, the fastest type of bowling. Also used adjectivally: *a pace bowler.* **4.** A manner of walking or running: *set out at a jaunty pace.* **5. a.** A gait of a horse in which both feet on one side leave and return to the ground together. **b.** Any of the gaits of a horse or other quadruped, such as the walk, trot, canter, or gallop. —**keep pace with.** To advance at the same speed as. —**put (someone) through his paces.** To test (someone's) abilities; require (someone) to demonstrate his skills. —**set the pace.** **1.** To go at a speed that other competitors attempt to match or surpass. **2.** To behave or perform in a way that others try to emulate. —**stand** or **stay the pace.** To be able to keep up with others. ~*v.* **paced, pacing, paces.** —*tr.* **1.** To walk or stride back and forth across, as in agitation or distress. **2.** To measure by counting the number of steps needed to cover a distance. Often used with *out.* **3.** To set or regulate the rate of speed for. **4.** To train (a horse) in a particular gait, especially the pace. —*intr.* **1.** To walk with long, deliberate steps. **2.** To go at the pace. Used of a horse or rider. [Middle English *pas,* from Old French, from Latin *passus,* a step, "a stretch of the leg", from *pandere* (past participle *passus*), to stretch.]

pa·ce² (paá-chay, páy-si) *prep.* With the permission of; with deference to. Used to express polite, or ironically polite, disagreement: *I have not, pace my detractors, entered into any "deals".* [Latin *pāce,* ablative of *pāx,* peace.] —**pa·ce** *adv.*

pace·mak·er (páyss-maykər) *n.* **1. a.** One who sets the pace in a race. **b.** A pacer. **2.** A leader in any field. **3. a.** *Physiology.* The sinoatrial node (*see*). **b.** *Medicine.* Any of several usually miniaturised and surgically implanted electronic devices used to regulate, or to aid in the regulation of, the heartbeat. —**pace·mak·ing** *n. & adj.*

pac·er (páy-sər) *n.* **1.** A horse trained to pace. **2.** A pacemaker.

pace·set·ter (páyss-settər) *n.* A pacemaker (senses 1 and 2). —**pace·set·ting** *adj.*

pace·way (páyss-way) *n. Australian.* A racecourse used for trotting and pacing races.

pacha. Variant of **pasha.**

pa·chi·si (pə-chéezi, paa-) *n.* **1.** An ancient game of India similar to backgammon but using cowry shells instead of dice. **2. Parcheesi** (*see*). [Hindi *pacīsī,* from *pacīs,* twenty-five (the highest throw) : Sanskrit *pañca,* five + *viṃsati,* twenty.]

pachouli. Variant of **patchouli.**

pach·y·derm (pácki-derm) *n.* Any of various large, thick-skinned, hoofed mammals, such as the elephant or hippopotamus. [French *pachyderme,* from Greek *pakhudermos,* thick-skinned : *pakhus,* thick + *derma,* skin, -DERM.] —**pach·y·der·ma·tous** (-dérmətəss), **pach·y·der·mous** (-dérməss) *adj.*

pach·y·tene (pácki-teen) *n. Biology.* The third stage of prophase in meiosis (*see*) during which the chromosomes coil up and shorten, the individual chromatids become visible, and crossing over may occur. [Greek *pakhus,* thick + *taina,* band.]

Pacif. Pacific.

pa·cif·ic (pə-siffik) *adj.* Also **pa·cif·i·cal** (-'l). **1.** Tending to diminish or put an end to conflict; appeasing; calming. **2.** Of a peaceful ·nature; tranquil; serene. [French *pacifique,* from Latin *pācificus* : *pāx* (stem *pāc-*), peace + *-ficus,* -FIC.] —**pa·cif·i·cal·ly** *adv.*

Pa·cif·ic (pə-siffik) *n. Abbr.* **Pac., Pacif.** The Pacific Ocean. Preceded by *the.* ~*adj. Abbr.* **Pac., Pacif.** Of or in the Pacific Ocean.

pac·i·fi·ca·tion (pássifi-káysh'n) *n.* **1.** Placation; appeasement. **2.** The act or process of pacifying or bringing about a state of peace. **3.** *Often capital P.* A peace treaty: *the Pacification of Ghent.* **4.** The reduction or elimination of insurgent or terrorist activity in an area. [French, from Latin *pācificātiō* (stem *pācification-*), "peace-making"; see **pacify.**] —**pac·i·fi·ca·tor** (-kaytər) *n.* —**pa·cif·i·ca·to·ry** (pə-siffi-kə-tri, -təri, -kaytəri, pássifi-kaytəri, -káytəri) *adj.*

Pacific Islands, Trust Territory of the. Area of the northwest Pacific Ocean including the Caroline, Marshall, and Mariana groups excluding Guam, with more than 2,000 islands overall. Captured from Germany by Japan (1914), it was made a Japanese mandate by the Treaty of Versailles (1919). The United States captured the islands (1944), and they were under U.S. administration as a United Nations Trust Territory (1947–78). Separate constitutional governments were then set up. The Caroline Islands, excluding Palau, form the Federated States of Micronesia, a republic in "free association" with the United States. The Republic of Belau (the island of Palau) has the same status, while the Marshall Islands form another republic. The Northern Marianas (the Mariana Islands except Guam) form a commonwealth of the United States. Guam remains an "unincorporated territory" of the United States, administered by the U.S. Interior Department.

Pacific Ocean. Largest of the world's oceans. It is larger than the world's entire land area and is deepest at Challenger Deep in the Marianas Trench (11 033 metres; 36,197 feet). To the south and west are coral and volcanic islands, while the ocean floor is scattered with volcanic mountains. See map, next page.

Pacific Standard Time *n. Abbr.* **PST, P.s.t., P.S.T.** Time in one of the standard time zones of North America, equal to the local time at the 120th meridian west of Greenwich, eight hours behind Greenwich Mean Time. Also called "Pacific Time".

pac·i·fi·er (pássi-fī-ər) *n.* **1.** One that pacifies. **2.** *U.S.* A baby's dummy or teething ring.

pac·i·fism (pássi-fiz'm) *n.* **1.** The belief that disputes between nations should and can be settled peacefully. **2. a.** Opposition to war or violence as a means of resolving disputes. **b.** Such opposition

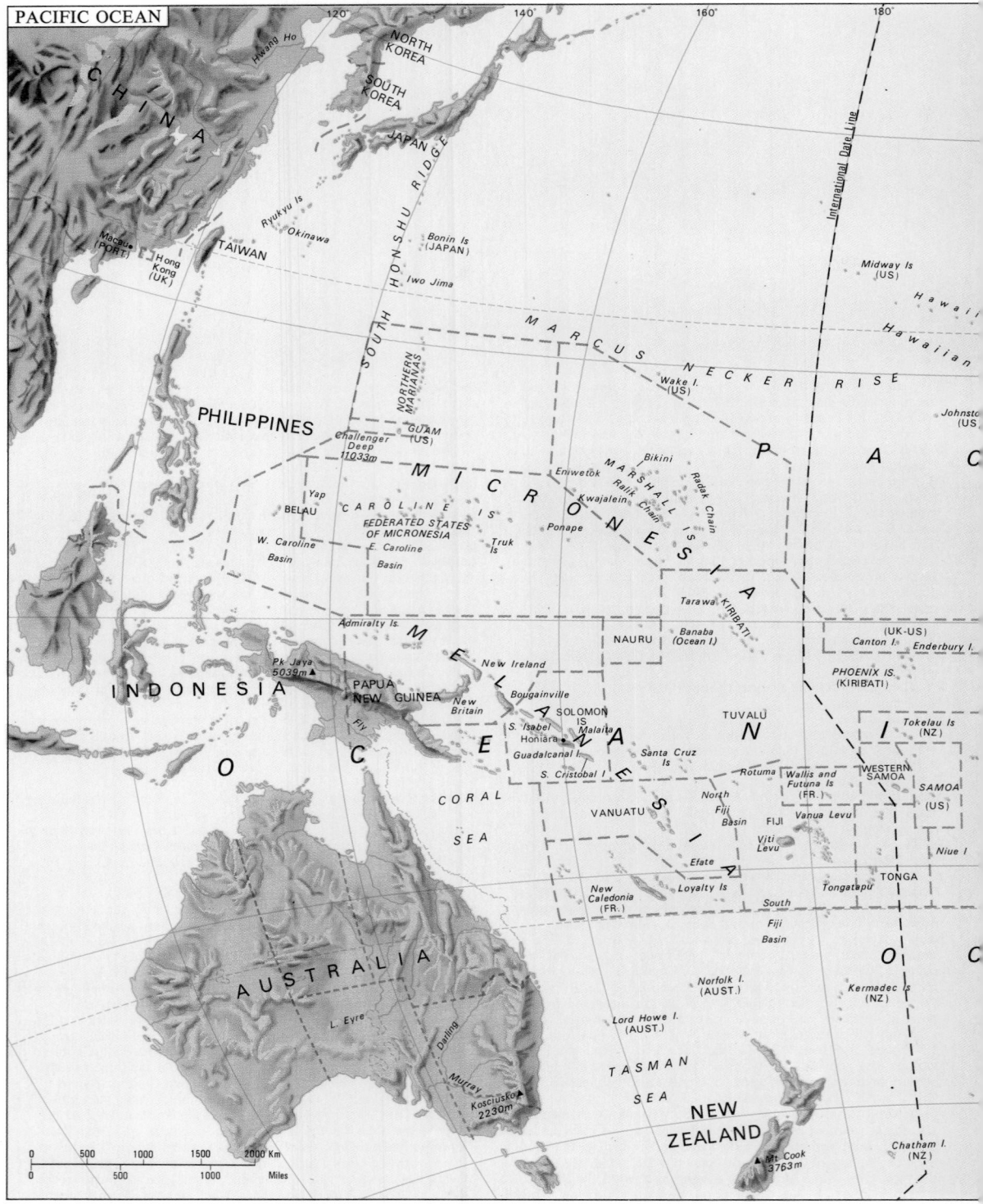

PACIFIC OCEAN

demonstrated by refusal to participate in military action. [French *pacificisme*, from *pacifique*, PACIFIC.] —**pac·i·fis·tic** (-fístik) *adj.*

pac·i·fist (pássifist) *n.* **1.** A person who supports or advocates pacifism. **2.** A person who refuses to do military service on the grounds of his belief in pacifism. —**pac·i·fist** *adj.*

pac·i·fy (pássi-fī) *tr.v.* **-fied, -fying, -fies. 1.** To ease the anger or agitation of; restore calm to; appease. **2.** To establish peace in; end war, fighting, or violence in. [Middle English *pacifien*, from Old French *pacifier*, from Latin *pācificāre* : *pax* (stem *pāc-*), peace + *facere*, to make.]

Synonyms: *pacify, placate, mollify, conciliate, appease, quieten.*

pack¹ (pak) *n. Abbr.* **pk. 1.** A collection of items tied up or wrapped; a bundle. **2.** A container made to be carried on the back of a person or an animal, such as: **a.** A knapsack or rucksack. **b.** A parachute prepared for use. **3.** The amount of something, such as food, that is processed and packaged at one time or in one season. **4.** *Chiefly*

U.S. A small package containing a standard number of identical or similar items: *a pack of matches.* Also used in combination: *a six-pack.* **5. a.** A complete set of related items: *a pack of cards.* **b.** A set of films to be inserted together into a camera. **c.** A large amount; a lot. Usually used derogatorily, chiefly in the phrase *a pack of lies.* **6. a.** A group of animals, such as dogs or wolves, that run and hunt together. **b.** A gang or band of people: *a pack of thugs.* **c.** A group of aircraft, ships, or vehicles moving in or as if in formation. **d.** An organised local unit of Cub Scouts or Brownies. **7.** In Rugby football, the forwards in a team. **8.** *Medicine.* **a.** The swathing of a patient in hot, cold, wet, or dry sheets or blankets. **b.** The sheets or blankets so used. **c.** A material, such as gauze, therapeutically inserted into a body cavity or wound. **9.** An **ice pack** (*see*). **10.** See **face pack. 11. Pack ice** (*see*). **12.** *Computing.* A pile of punched computer cards. —**go to the pack.** *Australian &*

~*v.* **packed, packing, packs.** —*tr.* **1.** To fold, roll, or combine into a bundle; wrap up. **2. a.** To put into a receptacle for transporting or storing: *pack one's belongings.* **b.** To fill up with items: *pack one's trunk.* **c.** To load (an animal) with a pack. **3.** To process and put into containers in order to preserve, transport, or sell. **4. a.** To bring together (persons or things) closely; crowd together. **b.** To fill up tight; cram. Often used with *out: The theatre was packed out.* **5.** *Medicine.* To wrap (a patient) in a pack. **6.** To wrap tightly for protection or insert packing into to prevent leakage: *pack a valve stem.* **7.** To press together; compact firmly: *clay and straw packed into bricks.* **8.** *Informal.* **a.** To be capable of delivering: *pack a hard punch.* **b.** *Chiefly U.S.* To carry: *pack a pistol.* **9.** To send away, especially peremptorily. Used with *off* or *away.* —*intr.* **1.** To place one's belongings in boxes, suitcases, or the like for transporting or storing. **2.** To be susceptible of compact storage: *Dishes pack more easily than glasses.* **3.** To crowd together; cram. **4.** To become compacted; form lumps or masses: *Rain caused the loose soil to pack.* **5.** To depart abruptly. Sometimes used with *off* or *away.* —**pack down.** In Rugby football, to form a scrum. —**pack in.** *Informal.* **1.** To stop doing or end (an activity); give up. **2.** To stop seeing or going out with (a girlfriend or boyfriend); give up. —**pack (one's) bags.** To prepare to depart. —**pack up.** *Informal.* **1.** To stop an activity; especially, to stop work. **2.** To break down; cease functioning. Used of a car or other machine, for example. —**send packing.** To dismiss (a person) abruptly.

~*adj.* Used or suitable for carrying loads: *a pack animal.* [Middle English *pak, pack,* from Middle Low German and Middle Dutch *pak†.*] —**pack·a·bil·i·ty** *n.* —**pack·a·ble** *adj.*

pack² *tr.v.* **packed, packing, packs.** To put one's own supporters on

paddle wheel *A steamboat on the Mississippi River in the United States. The flat-bottomed boat is driven by the paddle wheel at its stern.*

paddy *The cultivation of rice began at least 5,000 years ago in India. Seedlings 25 to 50 days old are transplanted to fields called paddies, which are enclosed by levees and submerged about 5 to 10 centimetres (2 to 4 inches) under water. These terraced paddy fields are on the Philippine island of Luzon.*

to (a jury or commitee, for example) in order to ensure decisions favourable to oneself.

pack·age (pákij) *n. Abbr.* **pkg.** **1.** A wrapped or boxed object; a parcel or bundle containing one or more objects. **2.** A container in which something is packed for storage or transporting. **3.** A package deal. **4.** A comprehensive arrangement; especially, an undertaking to provide together all the various goods, products, and services required by a customer. **5.** A set of programs designed to operate a computer for some specified purpose: *a bought-ledger package.*
~*tr.v.* **packaged, -aging, -ages.** **1.** To place in a package; make a package of. **2.** To design or make wrappers or containers for (goods). **3.** To put together or produce in a comprehensive package. [PACK (bundle) + -AGE.]

package deal *n.* A proposition or offer made up of several items, each of which must be accepted.

package holiday *n.* A holiday arranged by a company at a fixed price, including travel and accommodation.

pack·ag·er (pákijər) *n.* **1.** A person who makes up packages. **2.** A person or company producing finished products, especially books or television programmes, on another's behalf.

package store *n. U.S.* An off-licence.

pack·ag·ing (pákijing) *n.* **1.** The act, process, industry, art, or style of packing. **2.** Material used for making packages. **3.** The manner in which something, such as an idea or proposal, is presented. **4.** The occupation or activities of a packager.

packaging company *n.* A packager.

pack·drill (pák-dril) *n.* A military punishment that involves marching while carrying a full pack of equipment.

packed (pakt) *adj.* Also **packed-out** (pákt-ówt). *Informal.* Very crowded or full: *a packed auditorium.*

packed cell volume *n.* The volume of erythrocytes in the blood, given as a fraction of the blood's total volume. Also called "haematocrit".

packed lunch *n.* Food, such as sandwiches and fruit, packed and carried to be eaten at work or at school, for example.

pack·er (pákər) *n.* One that packs; specifically, one whose occupation is the processing and packing of wholesale goods, usually meat products.

Packer, Joy, born Joy Petersen (1905–77). South African author. Among her best-known works are *Valley of the Vines* (1955) and *Nor the Moon by Night* (1957).

pack·et (pákit) *n.* **1.** *Abbr.* **pkt.** **a.** A small container or a wrapping of cardboard, paper, or the like with or without its contents. **b.** A small package or bundle. **2.** *Slang.* A large sum of money: *It must have cost a packet.* **3.** A boat, usually a coastal or river steamer, that plies a regular route, carrying passengers, goods, and mail. In this sense, also called "packet boat". **—catch** or **cop** or **stop a packet.** *British Slang.* To undergo an injury, punishment, or other unpleasant experience. [PACK (bundle) + -ET.]

pack·horse (pák-hawrss) *n.* A horse used to carry loads.

pack ice *n.* Floating masses of ice on the sea, usually with channels *(leads)* between. Also called "pack".

pack·ing (pácking) *n.* **1.** The act or process of one that packs; especially, the processing and packaging of food products. **2.** Material used to cushion or fill gaps to protect fragile objects. **3.** A material used to prevent leakage or seepage, as around a pipe joint. **4. a.** The application of a medical pack. **b.** The material used to pack a wound.

packing box *n.* A **stuffing box** *(see).*

packing case *n.* A large wooden box or crate, used for moving large objects or a large number of objects.

packing fraction *n. Physics.* The quotient of the algebraic difference between the isotopic mass and the mass number of a nuclide, divided by its mass number, often interpreted as a measure of stability. For most nuclides, a negative or small positive value indicates relatively high stability. [From the presumed manner in which neutrons and protons are packed in the atomic nucleus.]

pack·ing-need·le (pácking-need'l) *n.* A large needle used for sewing up packages.

pack rat *n.* Any of various large western North American rodents of the genus *Neotoma,* that collect in their nests a great variety of small objects.

pack·sack (pák-sak) *n. U.S.* A rucksack.

pack·sad·dle (pák-sadd'l) *n.* A saddle for a pack animal on which loads can be secured.

pack·thread (pák-thred) *n.* A strong two-ply or three-ply twine for sewing or tying up packages or bundles.

pact (pakt) *n.* **1.** A formal agreement, as between nations; a treaty. **2.** A compact; a bargain. [Middle English, from Old French, from Latin *pactum,* from *pascisci* (past participle *pactus*), to agree.]

pad¹ (pad) *n.* **1. a.** A thin, cushion-like mass of soft material used as filling, to give shape, or for protection against jarring, scraping, or other injury. **b.** A piece of soft but resilient material worn in certain sports to protect various parts of the body. **2.** A flexible saddle made without a frame. **3.** An **ink pad** *(see).* **4.** A number of sheets of paper of the same size stacked one on top of the other and glued together at one end, such as a notepad or writing pad. **5.** The broad, floating leaf of an aquatic plant, such as the water lily. **6. a.** The cushion-like flesh on the underpart of the toes and feet of many animals. **b.** The foot of any of these animals. **7.** The fleshy underside of the end of a finger or toe: *the pad of the thumb.* **8.** A **launching pad** *(see).* **9.** *Slang.* **a.** *Chiefly U.S.* A home, apartment, or room. **b.** *U.S.* A bed.
~*tr.v.* **padded, padding, pads.** **1.** To line or stuff with soft material. **2.** To lengthen (something written or spoken) with extraneous material. Often used with *out.* [Dutch or Low German; akin to Flemish *pad,* probably to Lithuanian *pãdas,* "sole of the foot".]

pad² *v.* **padded, padding, pads.** *—intr.* **1.** To go about on foot, especially slowly. **2.** To move or walk about making a soft, dull sound: *padded barefoot over the rug.* *—tr.* To go along (a route) on foot, especially slowly and solemnly.
~*n.* **1.** A muffled sound resembling that of soft footsteps. **2.** *Archaic.* A horse with a plodding gait. **3.** *British Archaic.* A road or path. [16th century (noun) : cant, from Dutch or Low German *pad,* PATH, and *padden* (verb).]

pa·dauk (pə-dówk, -dáwk) *n.* Also **pa·douk** (-dŏŏk). **1.** Any of various tropical trees of the genus *Pterocarpus,* having reddish wood with a mottled or striped grain. **2.** The wood of any of these trees, used for decorative cabinetwork. See **amboyna.** [Native Burmese name.]

pad·ded cell (páddid) *n.* A room with soft, padded walls, as in a mental hospital, used for violent patients.

pad·ding (pádding) *n.* **1.** Any soft material used to pad something. **2.** Matter added to a speech or written work to make it longer.

pad·dle¹ (pádd'l) *n.* **1.** A wooden implement having a blade at one end, or sometimes at both ends, used without a rowlock to propel a canoe or small boat. **2.** Any of various implements resembling this, such as: **a.** An iron tool for stirring molten ore in a furnace. **b.** A tool with a shovel-like blade used to mix materials in glassmaking. **c.** A pallet with which to mix and shape clay. **d.** A narrow board used to beat clothes when washing them by hand. **e.** *U.S.* A flattened board used to administer corporal punishment. **f.** A light wooden racket used in playing table tennis. **3.** A board of a paddle wheel. **4.** *Usually plural.* A panel on the gate of a lock or on a sluice gate that controls the flow or level of water. **5.** A flipper or flattened appendage of certain animals. **6.** The act or an instance of paddling.
~*v.* **paddled, -dling, -dles.** *—intr.* **1.** To propel a boat, canoe, or the like with a paddle. **2.** To row slowly and gently. **3.** To move through water by means of repeated short strokes of the limbs. *—tr.* **1.** To propel (a canoe, for example) with a paddle or paddles. **2.** To convey, as in a boat or canoe propelled by paddles: *paddle the supplies across.* **3.** *U.S.* To beat with a paddle. **4.** To stir or shape (material) with a paddle. [Middle English *padell*†.] **—pad·dler** *n.*

paddle² *intr.v.* **-dled, -dling, -dles.** **1. a.** To walk in shallow water. **b.** To dabble about in shallow water; splash gently with the hands or feet. **2.** To move with a waddling motion; toddle.
~*n.* The act or an instance of paddling. [Of Dutch origin.]

paddle boat *n.* A steamship propelled through the water by paddle wheels on each side or by one paddle wheel astern.

pad·dle·fish (pádd'l-fish) *n., pl.* **-fishes** or collectively **paddlefish.** Any of various large fishes of the family Polyodontidae having an elongated, paddle-shaped snout.

paddle wheel *n.* A steam-driven wheel with boards or paddles affixed around its circumference, used to propel a ship.

pad·dock¹ (páddək) *n.* **1.** A fenced area, usually near a stable, used chiefly for grazing horses. **2. a.** An enclosure at a racecourse where the horses are assembled, saddled, and paraded before each race. **b.** In motor racing, an area near the racetrack where the cars assemble before a race. **3.** *Australian & N.Z.* Any piece of fenced-in land.
~*tr.v.* **paddocked, -docking, -docks.** To confine in a paddock. [Variant of dialectal *parrock,* Middle English *parrok,* Old English *pearruc,* from West Germanic *parruk* (unattested), perhaps from Medieval Latin *parricus*†. See also **park.**]

paddock² *n. Archaic & Regional.* A frog or toad. [Middle English *paddok,* from *pad, pade,* toad, from Old Norse *padda*†, toad.]

pad·dy¹ (páddi) *n., pl.* **-dies.** **1.** A specially irrigated or flooded field where rice is grown. Also called "paddy field". **2.** Rice, especially in the husk, whether gathered or still in the field. [Malay *pādi.*]

paddy² *n., pl.* **-dies.** *British Informal.* A display of bad temper; a paddywhack. [From PADDY. See **paddy whack.**]

Pad·dy (páddi) *n. Often small* **p.** *Informal.* An Irishman. Often considered offensive. [Pet form for *Patrick,* a common Irish name.]

paddy wagon *n. U.S. Slang.* A police van. [From PADDY.]

pad·dy·whack, pad·di·wack (páddi-wak, hwak) *n. British Informal.* **1.** A rage or display of bad temper. **2.** A beating or spanking. [PADDY (alluding to the supposedly hot temper of the Irish) + WHACK.]

pad·e·mel·on, pad·dy·mel·on (páddi-mellən) *n.* A small Australian wallaby of the genus *Thylogale,* inhabiting scrubland. Also called "scrub wallaby". [From a native Australian language.]

Pa·de·rew·ski (páddə-réfski), **Ignace Jan** (1860–1941). Polish pianist, composer, and politician. Famous for his interpretations of Chopin, he studied and taught at the Warsaw Conservatoire and taught at the Strasbourg Conservatoire before his performing debut in Vienna (1887). During World War I he organised the Polish Army in France and in 1919 became for 10 months the first prime minister of a newly independent Poland.

Pa·di·shah (paádi-shaa) *n.* **1.** Formerly, a title of a shah of Iran. **2.** Formerly, a title of the sultan of Turkey. [Persian *pādshāh,* from Middle Persian *pātakh-shāh* : *pati,* master + *shāh,* SHAH.]

pad·lock (pád-lok) *n.* A detachable lock, usually with a U-shaped bar hinged at one end, designed to be passed through the staple of a hasp or a link in a chain, and then snapped shut.

~*tr.v.* **padlocked, -locking, -locks.** To lock up with or as if with a padlock. [Middle English *padlok* : *pad*†, padlock + *lok*, LOCK.]

padouk. Variant of **padauk.**

pa·dre (paá-dri, -dray) *n.* **1.** Father. Used as a title of address for a priest in Italy, Spain, Portugal, and Latin America. **2.** *Informal.* A military chaplain. **3.** *Chiefly British Informal.* A clergyman. [Spanish, Portuguese, and Italian, father, from Latin *pater* (stem *patr-*).]

pa·dro·ne (pə-drṓ-ni, pa-, -nay) *n., pl.* **-nes** (-niz) or *Italian* **padroni** (-nee). **1.** *Italian.* **a.** A master or patron. **b.** An owner or manager of an inn; a proprietor. **2.** In the United States, a person who exploits Italian immigrant labour. [Italian, from Latin *patrōnus,* protector, PATRON.] **—pa·dro·nism** *n.*

pad·saw (pád-saw) *n.* A small narrow saw with a blade supported at one end only, used for cutting small curved holes. Also called "keyhole saw". [PAD, perhaps short for PADLOCK + SAW.]

Pad·u·a (páddew-ə, paádoo-ə). *Italian* **Pa·do·va** (paádova). Capital city of Padua province, Veneto region, northeast Italy. Situated on the river Bacchiglione, it became an important cultural centre during the late Middle Ages. It has superb architectural and artistic works by Giotto and Donatello, while Galileo taught at the university (*c.* 1600).

pad·u·a·soy (páddew-ə-soy) *n.* **1.** A rich, heavy silk fabric with a corded effect. **2.** A hanging or garment made of this fabric. [Variant (taken as *Padua say,* serge of Padua) of French *pou-de-soie,* from earlier *poult-de-soie*†.]

pae·an, *U.S.* **pe·an** (pée-ən) *n.* **1.** A song of joyful praise or exultation. **2.** Any fervent expression of joy or praise: *a paean to liberty.* **3.** An ancient Greek hymn of thanksgiving to a god, especially to Apollo. [Latin *paeān,* from Doric Greek *paian, paiōn,* war cry, hymn of praise to Apollo, from *Paian*†, title of Apollo as physician of the gods, ultimately from a cultic cry.]

paederast. Variant of **pederast.**

pae·di·a·trics (péedi-áttriks) *n.* *Used with a singular verb.* The branch of medicine that deals with the care of babies and children and their diseases. [PAEDO- + -IATRICS.] **—pae·di·a·tric** *adj.* **—pae·di·a·tri·cian** (-ə-trísh'n) *n.*

paedo-, paed- *comb. form.* Also *chiefly U.S.* **pedo-, ped-.** Indicates child; for example, **paed|iatrics, paedology.** [Greek *pais* (stem *paid-*), child.]

pae·do·gen·e·sis (péedō-jénni-siss) *n.* Reproduction of young during the larval or preadult stage, occurring chiefly in insects. **—pae·do·ge·net·ic** (-jə-néttik) *adj.*

pae·dol·o·gy (pee-dólləji) *n.* The study of the behaviour and development of children. [PAEDO- + -LOGY.] **—pae·do·log·ic** (péedə-lójik), **pae·do·log·i·cal** *adj.* **—pae·do·log·i·cal·ly** *adv.* **—pae·dol·o·gist** (pee-dólləjist) *n.*

pae·do·mor·pho·sis (pée-də-mórfə-siss, -dō-, -mawr-fṓ-siss) *n.* Evolutionary change in which primitive or embryonic structures appear in adult animals.

pae·do·phil·i·a (pée-də-fílli-ə, -dō-) *n.* Sexual attraction of adults, usually men, to children of either sex. [PAEDO- + -PHILIA.] **—pae·do·phile** (-fīl), **pae·do·phil·i·ac** (-fílli-ak) *n. & adj.*

pa·e·lla (pī-éllə; *Spanish* pa-él-ya) *n.* A saffron-flavoured Spanish dish made with varying combinations of rice, vegetables, chicken, and seafood. [Catalan, "frying pan", from Old French *paelle,* from Latin *patella,* diminutive of *patina,* pan, from Greek *patanē,* dish.]

pae·on (pée-ən) *n. Greek & Latin Prosody.* A metrical foot having one long syllable and three short syllables occurring in random order. [Latin *paeōn,* from Greek *paiōn,* variant of PAEAN.]

paeony. Variant of **peony.**

Pá·ez (paá-ess), **José Antonio** (1790–1873).Venezuelan revolutionary. With **Bolívar,** he overthrew Spanish rule (1823). Removing Venezuela from the confederation of Greater Colombia, he became its first president (1831–35, 1839–43) and dictator (1861–63).

pa·gan (páygən) *n.* **1.** A person who is not a Christian, Muslim, or Jew, although possibly having another faith; a heathen. **2.** One who has no religion. **3.** Formerly, any non-Christian.

~*adj.* **1.** Of or pertaining to pagans. **2.** Not religious; heathen. [Middle English, from Late Latin *pāgānus,* civilian ("heathen" in patristic writers), from Latin *pāgānus,* country-dweller, from *pāgus,* village, country.] **—pa·gan·dom** (-dəm) *n.* **—pa·gan·ish** *adj.* **—pa·gan·ism** *n.*

Pa·gan (paa-gaán). Ruined city on the Irrawaddy river, central Burma. Founded in *c.* A.D. 849, it was the capital of the Pagan dynasty (11th–13th century). Many of their 5,000 Buddhist temples, pagodas, and monasteries still exist, despite capture of the city by the Mongols (1287), sacking by the Shans (1299), and a severe earthquake (1975). The city remains a centre of pilgrimage, and an important architectural site.

Pa·ga·ni·ni (pággə-néeni), **Níccolo** (1782–1840). Italian violinist and composer. His works include six violin concertos and many other virtuoso violin pieces.

pa·gan·ise, pa·gan·ize (páygə-nīz) *v.* **-ised, -ising, -ises.** —*tr.* To make pagan. —*intr.* To become pagan. **—pa·gan·i·sa·tion** (-nī-záysh'n || *U.S.* -ni-) *n.*

page[1] (payj) *n.* **1.** In medieval times: **a.** A boy attending a knight, as the first stage of training for knighthood. **b.** A youth in ceremonial employment to a person of rank or in attendance at court. **2.** A boy employed to run errands, carry messages, or act as a guide, as in a hotel or club. Also called "pageboy". **3.** A boy who attends on the bride at a wedding. Also called "pageboy". **4.** *U.S.* A young person who acts as a messenger in Congress or certain other legislative bodies.

~*tr.v.* **paged, paging, pages. 1.** To summon or call (a person) by name, especially over a public address system or a signalling device. **2.** To attend as a page. [Middle English, from Old French, from Italian *paggio,* probably from Greek *paidion,* child, diminutive of *pais* (stem *paid-*), child, boy.]

page[2] *n. Abbr.* **p.,** *pl.* **pp. 1. a.** One side of a leaf of a book, letter, newspaper, manuscript, or the like. **b.** An entire leaf: *tear out a page.* **2.** The writing or printing on one side of a leaf. **3.** *Printing.* The type set for printing a page. **4.** A noteworthy or memorable event: *a new page in history.* **5.** *Plural.* **a.** A source or record of knowledge: *in the pages of science.* **b.** An extract or passage: *pages from Johnson.* **6.** An amount of viewdata displayed as a unit on a television or other screen. **7.** A unit of data in a computer memory that can be accessed or changed in a single operation.

~*tr.v.* **paged, paging, pages. 1.** To number the pages of; paginate. **2.** *Computing.* To call and connect to (a terminal). **3.** To call up and display a page of (viewdata) on a screen. [French, from Latin *pāgina,* page.]

pag·eant (pájənt) *n.* **1.** An elaborate public dramatic presentation, usually depicting some historical or traditional event. **2.** *Archaic.* **a.** A scene of a medieval mystery play. **b.** A portable platform on which mystery plays were presented. **3.** Any spectacular and colourful display or procession. **4.** Colourful display; pomp. [Middle English *pagyn,* from Medieval Latin *pāgina,* scene of a play, from Latin, PAGE.]

pag·eant·ry (pájəntri) *n., pl.* **-ries. 1.** Pageants and their presentation. **2.** Grand display; pomp. **3.** Empty or flashy display.

page·boy, page-boy (páyj-boy) *n.* **1.** A page who runs errands or attends a bride. **2.** A woman's hairstyle, reaching to the neck at the back and gradually curving up the sides to the forehead, with the ends curled under.

Pa·get's disease (pájits) *n.* **1.** A chronic disease affecting the elderly and characterised by thickening and deformation of the bones. **2.** An inflammatory condition of the nipple, associated with underlying cancer of the milk ducts. [After Sir James *Paget* (1814–99), British pathologist.]

pag·i·nal (pájin'l, páyjin'l) *adj.* **1.** Of, pertaining to, or consisting of pages. **2.** Page for page: *paginal facsimile.* [Late Latin *pāginālis,* from Latin *pāgina,* PAGE.]

pag·i·nate (páji-nayt, páyji-) *tr.v.* **-nated, -nating, -nates.** To number the pages of; page. Compare **foliate.** [Latin *pāgina,* PAGE.]

pag·i·na·tion (páji-náysh'n, páyji-) *n.* **1.** The system by which pages are numbered. **2.** The arrangement and number of pages in a book, as noted in a catalogue or bibliography.

pa·go·da (pə-gṓdə) *n.* **1.** A religious building of the Far East, typically: **a.** An ornate pyramidal Hindu temple. **b.** A many-storeyed Buddhist tower, erected as a memorial or shrine. **2.** A structure, such as a garden pavilion, built in imitation of an Eastern pagoda. [Portuguese *pagode,* probably from Persian *butkada* : *but,* idol + *kada,* temple; altered by association with Prakrit *bhagodī,* holy.]

pagoda tree *n.* A Chinese deciduous tree, *Sophora japonica,* having pinnate leaves and clusters of white, pealike flowers. [Referring to its shape.]

Pa·go Pa·go (paáng-gō paáng-gō). Formerly **Pan·go Pan·go.** Harbour and town of Tutuila Island, and the capital of American Samoa. It was a U.S. naval base (1878–1951), particularly important during World War II.

pah[1] *interj.* Used to express contempt.

pah[2]. Variant of **pa** (Maori village).

Pa·hang (pə-húng, háng). Longest river in Peninsular Malaysia. Navigable for most of its length (436 kilometres; 271 miles), it rises in the northwest, flows southwards, and then turns eastwards near Mengkarak through Pahang State to the South China Sea.

pah·la·vi (paáləvi) *n., pl.* **-vis.** A gold coin of Iran, not part of the official currency of the country. [Persian *pahlawī,* after MOHAMMED REZA PAHLAVI.]

Pah·la·vi (paáləvi) *n.* Also **Peh·le·vi** (páyləvi). The Iranian language used in Persia from the third to the ninth century. [Persian *pahlawī,* from *Pahlaw,* from Middle Persian, from Old Persian *Parthava,* PARTHIA.] **—Pah·la·vi** *adj.*

paid. Past tense and past participle of **pay.**

pail (payl) *n.* **1.** A bucket, especially one made of metal or wood. **2.** The amount contained in a pail. [Middle English *payle,* Old English *pægel*†, small measure, gill; Middle English form influenced by Old French *paelle,* pan; see **paella.**]

paillasse. *Chiefly U.S.* Variant of **palliasse.**

pail·lette (pal-yét, pálli-ét; *French* pa-yét) *n.* **1.** A small piece of metal or foil, used in enamel painting. **2.** A spangle used to ornament a dress or costume. [French, diminutive of *paille,* straw.]

pain (payn) *n.* **1.** An unpleasant sensation, occurring in varying degrees of severity, especially as a consequence of injury, disease, or emotional disorder. **2.** Suffering or distress. **3.** *Plural.* The physical distress accompanying certain physiological processes such as labour or teething. **4.** *Plural.* Great care or effort: *take pains with one's work.* **5.** *Informal.* An irritating or tiresome person or thing; a nuisance. In this sense, also called "pain in the neck". **—at pains.** Making great efforts: *at pains to be early.* **—on pain of.** Subject to the penalty of (some specified punishment, such as death).

~*v.* **pained, paining, pains.** —*tr.* **1.** To hurt or injure; cause pain to. **2.** To cause distress to or irritate. —*intr.* To hurt. [Middle English *paine,* from Old French *peine,* from Latin *poena,* penalty, from Greek *poinē,* penalty.]

Paine (payn), **Thomas** (1737–1809). British radical author. After

pagoda *Originally a religious building in the Far East, the pagoda became fashionable in the West in the mid-18th century as an ornament for parks and gardens. This 19th-century example is in Staffordshire, England.*

PRONUNCIATION KEY

a, trap; aa, father; ai, fair;
ar, star; aw, lawn; ay, play;
b, bb, stab; rubber;
ch, church; ck, ticket;
d, dd, dead; ladder; e, dress;
ee, bee; er, defer; ew, few;
ewr, pure; ə, about;
ər, letter; f, ff, fife; differ;
g, gg, giggle; h, hat; i, kit;
ī, price; īr, fire; j, judge;
k, kick; l, ll, let; 'l, needle;
m, mm, man; n, nn, no;
'n, sudden; ng, thing; o, lot;
ō, no; ŏŏ, foot; ōō, shoe;
oor, poor; ow, cow;
owr, hour; oy, boy;
p, pp, pepper; r, rr, red;
s, ss, sauce; sh, ship;
t, tt, totter; th, thick; th, this;
smooth; u, cut; ur, turn;
v, vv, valve; w, wet; y, yes;
z, zz, zebra; zh, vision;
pleasure

IN FOREIGN WORDS:

aN, oN, Saint-Saëns;
hl, Llanelli; Hluhluwe;
kh, loch; lough; Khaled

STRESS MARK:

ín-sīt, insight; in-sít, incite

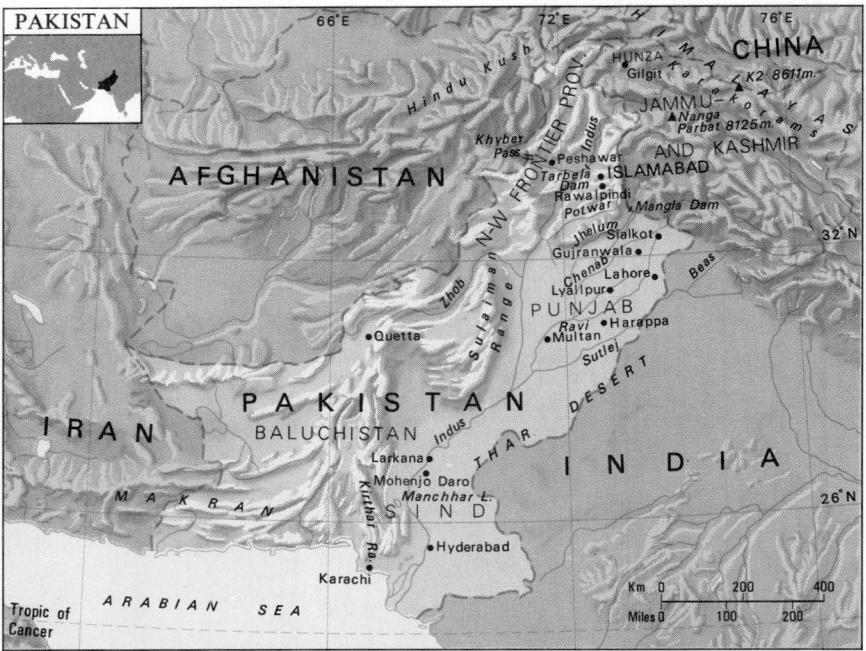

PAKISTAN

his arrival in America (1774), he wrote the pamphlet *Common Sense* (1776) arguing for American independence from Britain. After the War of Independence, he returned to Britain (1787) and published *The Rights of Man* (1791–92) defending the French Revolution. Accused of treason, he fled to France, but offended Robespierre and was imprisoned for 11 months (1793-94), during which time he continued writing his *Age of Reason,* a manifesto in favour of deism.

pained (paynd) *adj.* Showing or expressing irritation, boredom, or emotional distress.

pain·ful (páynf'l) *adj.* **1.** Causing pain; hurtful. **2.** Full of pain; distressing; hurting. **3.** Requiring care and labour; irksome: *a painful task.* **4.** *Informal.* Irritating; infuriating. **—pain·ful·ly** *adv.*

pain·kill·er (páyn-killər) *n.* Something, such as a drug, that relieves pain. **—pain·kill·ing** *adj.*

pain·less (páyn-ləss, -liss) *adj.* Free from pain, complication, or distress; not troublesome. **—pain·less·ly** *adv.* **—pain·less·ness** *n.*

pains·tak·ing (páynz-tayking) *adj.* Taking or involving great pains; careful and diligent. **—pains·tak·ing·ly** *adv.*

paint (paynt) *n.* **1. a.** A liquid mixture, usually of a solid pigment in a liquid vehicle such as oil or water, used as a decorative or protective coating. **b.** The thin dry film formed by such a mixture applied to a surface. **c.** The solid pigment before it is mixed with a liquid vehicle. **2. a.** A cosmetic, especially one that colours, such as rouge. **b.** Greasepaint *(see).* **3.** *Medicine.* A liquid containing analgesics, antiseptics, or other healing agents, applied to the skin or mucous membranes. **4.** An act or instance of painting. **5.** *U.S.* A piebald horse.

~*v.* **painted, painting, paints.** *—tr.* **1.** To make (a picture) with paints. **2. a.** To represent in a picture with paints. **b.** To portray vividly to the imagination, as with words or music. **3.** To coat or decorate with paint: *paint a house.* **4.** To apply cosmetics to. **5.** To apply medicine to; swab: *paint a wound.* *—intr.* **1.** To practise the art of painting pictures. **2.** To cover something with paint. **3.** To serve as a surface to be coated with paint: *These nonporous surfaces paint badly with a brush and should be sprayed.* [Middle English *peynten,* to paint, from Old French *peindre* (past participle *peint*), from Latin *pingere.*]

paint·box (páynt-boks) *n.* A box containing dry paints.

paint·brush (páynt-brush) *n.* A brush for applying paint.

paint·ed (páyntid) *adj.* **1.** Represented in paint. **2.** Covered or adorned with paint. **3.** Excessively made up with cosmetics. **4.** Having no reality; false; pretended: *painted expressions.*

painted lady *n.* A widely distributed butterfly, *Vanessa cardui,* having brown, black, and orange markings.

paint·er¹ (páyntər) *n.* A person who paints, either as an artist or as a workman.

painter² *n. Nautical.* A rope attached to the bow of a boat, used for tying up. [Middle English *paynter,* perhaps from Old French *pentoir,* clothesline, from *pendre,* to hang, from Latin *pendēre.*]

paint·er·ly (páyntərli) *adj.* **1.** Of, pertaining to, or characteristic of a painter; artistic. **2. a.** Having qualities unique to the art of painting as distinguished from other visual arts. **b.** Designating a style of painting marked by openness of form, with shapes distinguished by variations of colour rather than by outline or contour: *the painterly style of Titian.* Compare **linear.**

paint·ing (páynting) **1.** The process, art, or occupation of coating surfaces with paint, for either functional or artistic effect. **2.** An artistic composition, picture, or design done in paint.

painted lady *A common migratory butterfly which is found in Europe, North Africa, Asia, and North America. Painted ladies, whose caterpillars feed on thistles, cannot survive the British winter. Instead, new stocks fly across the English Channel each spring.*

pair (pair) *n., pl.* **pairs** or *informal* **pair.** *Abbr.* **pr. 1.** Two corresponding persons or items, similar in form or function and matched or associated: *a pair of shoes.* **2.** One object composed of two joined, similar parts, dependent upon each other: *a pair of pliers.* **3. a.** Two persons joined together in marriage, engagement, or a similar relationship. **b.** Two persons having something in common and considered together: *a pair of dancers.* **c.** Two mated animals. **d.** Two animals joined together in work. **4.** Two playing cards of the same denomination. **5. a.** Two members of a parliament or similar body with opposing opinions who agree to abstain from voting on some issues so as to allow for occasional absences at votes. **b.** A member taking part in such an arrangement. **6.** A member of a pair: *lost the pair to this earring.* **7.** A pair-oar. **8.** *Chemistry.* An **electron pair** *(see).* **—See Synonyms at couple.**

~*v.* **paired, pairing, pairs.** *—tr.* **1.** To arrange in sets of two; couple. **2.** To join in a pair; mate. Sometimes followed by *off.* **3.** To provide a partner for. *—intr.* **1.** To form a pair or pairs. Often followed by *off.* **2.** To join in marriage; mate. **3.** To form a pair in a voting body. [Middle English *paire,* from Old French, from Latin *paria,* equal things, from the neuter plural of *pār,* equal.]

Usage: Pair can be followed by a verb in the singular or the plural, depending on the intended meaning. The singular is used when *pair* emphasises the unity of the components: *This pair of shoes is not for sale.* The plural is used when the components are considered as individuals: *The pair are working together more harmoniously now.* When following a numeral (other than *one*), the plural is standard (*six pairs of shoes*), though the singular is used informally. See also Usage note at **couple.**

pair bond *n.* The mutual attraction that binds a female and a male animal of the same species. It occurs particularly among birds and may last for one or more breeding seasons or for a lifetime. **—pair-bond·ed** (páir-bóndid) *adj.* **—pair bonding** *n.*

paired (paird) *adj.* Existing in a pair; consisting of a linked pair, especially a left and right pair.

pair-oar (páir-awr) *n.* A boat rowed by two people, each with one oar, sitting one behind the other. Also called "pair".

pair production *n. Physics.* The simultaneous creation of a positron and electron from a high-energy gamma ray in a very strong electric field, especially in that of an atomic nucleus.

pair royal *n.* In some card games, three cards of the same denomination forming a set.

pai·sa (pí-sə, -saa) *n., pl.* **paise** (-say) (for sense 1) or **paisa** (for sense 2). **1.** A coin equal to ¹/₁₀₀ of the rupee of India. Also called "naya paisa". **2.** A coin equal to ¹/₁₀₀ of the rupee of Pakistan or ¹/₁₀₀ of the taka of Bangladesh. [Hindi *paisā,* PICE.]

pais·ley (páyzli) *adj. Sometimes capital* **P. 1.** Made of a soft wool fabric with a woven or printed, colourful, intricate pattern of abstract, curved shapes, ultimately derived from the palmette motif of Persian rugs. **2.** Marked with such a pattern.

~*n., pl.* **paisleys. 1.** A shawl or other article of clothing made of paisley fabric. **2.** A paisley pattern. [Originally popular in shawls made in PAISLEY.]

Pais·ley (páyzli). Industrial burgh and port of Stratchclyde region, Scotland. Situated on the White Cart Water west-southwest of Glasgow, it became famous in the 19th century for its shawls based on cashmere Indian designs, to which it has given its name.

Paisley, Ian (1926–). Ulster politician. As a minister of the Free Presbyterian Church of Ulster since 1946 and as an M.P. both in the Northern Irish Parliament (1970–72) and in the House of Commons, London (since 1970) he has adopted a militant Protestant and Unionist position.

Pais·ley·ite (páyzli-īt) *n.* A person who supports the ideas and methods of Ian Paisley.

Pai·ute, Pi·ute (pī-ōot, pī-yōot) *n., pl.* **-utes** or collectively **Paiute. 1.** A member of either of two distinct North American Indian peoples, the Northern Paiute and the Southern Paiute, belonging to the Shoshonean subfamily of the Uto-Aztecan language family. They formerly lived in the southwestern United States. **2.** The language of either of these peoples. **—Pai·ute** *adj.*

pajamas. *U.S.* Variant of **pyjamas.**

pak choi (pák chóy; *Chinese* baák) A plant, the **Chinese cabbage** *(see).* [Cantonese *paak ts'oi,* "white vegetable".]

pa·ke·ha (páaki-haa) *n. N.Z.* A white person as opposed to a Maori. [Maori.]

Pa·ki·stan, Islamic Republic of (páaki-staán, pácki-, -stán). Country of southern Asia, formerly West Pakistan. It was originally created from Indian territory as a Muslim state (1947) by the efforts of Jinah and the Muslim League. It was formerly in two separate parts, but East Pakistan separated in 1971 to become Bangladesh. Pakistan has suffered with the loss of East Pakistan, a source of jute (formerly the country's chief export), and relations with India are generally poor. Pakistan remains chiefly agricultural, rice, leather, and cotton being the main exports. However, industry is expanding, and cotton (yarn and cloth) and carpets account for a third of exports. Money sent home by expatriates is an important source of income. With considerable uranium reserves, Pakistan has an extensive nuclear programme. General Muhammad Zia al-Huq took power in a miltary coup (1977), deposing prime minister Zulfikar Ali Bhutto, and tightening martial law. In 1982 stricter Muslim laws were introduced. Some 2.7 million Afghan refugees in the country posed severe problems, and the United States promised economic and military aid. Area 803 943 square kilometres (310,322 square miles). Population, 93,000,000. Capital, Islamabad. **—Pa·ki·stan·i** *adj. & n.*

pal (pal) *n. Informal.* A friend; a chum.
~*intr.v.* **palled, palling, pals.** *Informal.* To associate as pals. **—pal up.** *Informal.* To make friends. [Romany (English) *pal, phal,* from *phrall* (continental), from Sanskrit *bhrātar-,* brother.] **—pal·ly** *adj.*

PAL *n.* Phase alternation line: a system of colour-television broadcasting used on the continent of Europe.

Pal. Palestine.

pal·ace (pál-iss, -əss) *n.* **1.** The official residence of royalty. **2.** The official residence of a high dignitary, such as a bishop or archbishop. **3. a.** Any large or splendid residence. **b.** Any large, often gaudy and ornate building used for entertainment, exhibitions, and the like. [Middle English *palais,* from Old French, from Latin *palātium,* from *Palātium,* the PALATINE Hill or the house built there by the emperor Augustus.]

palace revolution *n.* **1.** A usually peaceful overthrow of a sovereign or head of state effected by persons already in power. **2.** Any takeover of power or higher position in the hierarchy of an organisation.

pal·a·din (pál-ədin) *n.* **1.** Any of the 12 peers of Charlemagne's court. **2.** A paragon of chivalry; a heroic champion. [French, from Italian *paladino,* from Latin *palātīnus,* PALATINE.]

Pal·ae·arc·tic (pál-i-árktik, páyl-, -ártik) *adj.* Of or designating the zoogeographical region that covers the whole of Europe and Asia, Africa north of the Sahara, and the Himalayas. Compare **Nearctic.** [PALAE(O)- + ARCTIC.]

pal·ae·eth·nol·o·gy (pál-i-eth-nólləji, páyl-) *n.* The ethnology of early humankind. [PALAE(O)- + ETHNOLOGY.] **—pal·ae·eth·no·log·ic** (-éthnə-lójik), **pal·ae·eth·no·log·i·cal** *adj.* **—pal·ae·eth·nol·o·gist** (-nólləjist) *n.*

palaeo–, palae–, *U.S.* **paleo–, pale–** *comb. form.* Indicates ancient or prehistoric; for example, **palaeography, palae-ethnology.** [Greek *palaio-,* from *palaois,* ancient, from *palai,* long ago.]

pal·ae·o·an·thro·pol·o·gy (pál-i-ō-ánthrə-pólləji, páyl-) *n.* The study of humanlike creatures more primitive than *Homo sapiens.* **—pal·ae·o·an·thro·po·log·ic** (-ánthrəpə-lójik), **pal·ae·o·an·thro·po·log·i·cal** *adj.* **—pal·ae·o·an·thro·pol·o·gist** (-pólləjist) *n.*

pal·ae·o·bot·any (pál-i-ō-bóttən-i, páyl-) *n.* The study of plant fossils and ancient vegetation. **—pal·ae·o·bo·tan·ic** (-bə-tánnik, -bo-), **pal·ae·o·bo·tan·i·cal** *adj.* **—pal·ae·o·bot·a·nist** (-bóttənist) *n.*

Pal·ae·o·cene (pál-i-ə-seen, páyl-, -ō-) *adj. Geology.* Of, belonging to, or designating the geological time or rock series of the first epoch of the Tertiary period, preceding the Eocene and characterised by the appearance of placental mammals.
~*n. Geology.* **1.** The Palaeocene epoch. Preceded by *the.* **2.** The deposits of this epoch. Preceded by *the.* [PALAEO- + -CENE.]

pal·ae·og·ra·phy (pál-i-óggrəfi, páyl-) *n.* **1.** The study and scholarly interpretation of ancient written documents. Compare **epigraphy.** **2.** The documents so studied. **—pal·ae·og·ra·pher** *n.* **—pal·ae·o·graph·ic** (-ə-gráffik), **pal·ae·o·graph·i·cal** *adj.*

pal·ae·o·lith (pál-i-ə-lith, páyl-, -ō-) *n.* A stone implement of the Palaeolithic period. [PALAEO- + -LITH.]

Pal·ae·o·lith·ic (pál-i-ə-líthik, páyl-, -ō-) *adj. Sometimes small* **p.** Of, belonging to, or designating the cultural period beginning with the earliest chipped stone tools, about 2.5 to 3 million years ago, until the beginning of the Mesolithic, about 12,000 years ago.
~*n. Archaeology.* The Palaeolithic period. Preceded by *the.* Also called the "Old Stone Age".

pal·ae·o·mag·net·ism (pál-i-ō-mág-nit-iz'm, páyl-, -nət-) *n.* The study of the residual magnetism in rocks in order to try to reconstruct the configuration of the continents in the geological past.

pal·ae·on·tol·o·gy (pál-i-on-tólləji, páyl-) *n.* **1.** The study of fossils and ancient life forms. **2.** Palaeozoology. [PALAE(O)- + ONTO- + -LOGY.] **—pal·ae·on·to·log·ic** (-óntə-lójik), **pal·ae·on·to·log·i·cal** *adj.* **—pal·ae·on·tol·o·gist** (-tólləjist) *n.*

Pal·ae·o·zo·ic (pál-i-ə-zō-ik, páyl-, -ō-) *adj. Geology.* Of, belonging to, or designating the era of geological time between the Precambrian and Mesozoic eras, including the Cambrian, Ordovician, Silurian, Devonian, Carboniferous, and Permian periods, and which is characterised by the appearance of marine invertebrates, primitive fishes, land plants, and primitive reptiles.
~*n.* The Palaeozoic period. Preceded by *the.* [PALAEO- + -ZOIC.]

pal·ae·o·zo·ol·o·gy (pál-i-ō-zōō-ólləji, páyl-, -zō-) *n.* The study of animal fossils and ancient animal life. **—pal·ae·o·zo·o·log·i·cal** (-zōō-ə-lójik'l, -zō-) *adj.* **—pal·ae·o·zo·ol·o·gist** *n.*

pa·laes·tra, *U.S.* **pa·les·tra** (pə-léess-trə, -léss-) *n., pl.* **-trae** (-tree) or **-tras.** In ancient Greece, a public place for training in and practising wrestling and athletics. [Greek *palaistra,* from *palaein,* to wrestle.]

pal·ais (pál-ay) *n., pl.* **palais** (-ayz). A public dance hall. Also called "palais de danse". [French, "palace".]

pal·an·quin, pal·an·keen (pál-ən-kéen) *n.* An east Asian covered litter, carried on poles on the shoulders of four men. [Portuguese *palanquim,* from Javanese *pĕlangki,* from Sanskrit *palyaṅka, paryaṅka,* bed : *pari,* around + *añcati,* he bends.]

pal·at·a·ble (pál-ətə-b'l) *adj.* **1.** Acceptable to the taste; sufficiently agreeable in flavour to be eaten. **2.** Acceptable to the mind or sensibilities; agreeable: *a palatable suggestion.* [From PALATE.] **—pal·at·a·bil·i·ty** (-bílləti), **pal·at·a·ble·ness** *n.* **—pal·at·a·bly** *adv.*

pal·a·tal (pál-ət'l, pə-láyt'l) *adj.* **1.** Of or pertaining to the palate. **2.** *Phonetics.* Produced with the front of the tongue against the hard palate, as is the *y* in *young.*
~*n.* A palatal sound. **—pal·a·tal·ly** *adv.*

pal·a·tal·ise, pal·a·tal·ize (pál-ət'l-īz) *v.* **-ised, -ising, -ises.** *Phonetics.* —*tr.* To pronounce with a palatal quality. —*intr.* To develop a palatal quality. Said of a phoneme considered diachronically, for example. **—pal·a·tal·i·sa·tion** (-ī-záysh'n || *U.S.* -i-) *n.*

pal·ate (pál-ət, -it) *n.* **1.** The roof of the mouth in vertebrates which separates the mouth from the nasal cavity and consists of a bony front, the *hard palate,* backed by the fleshy *soft palate.* **2.** The projection from the lower lip of a lipped flower. **3.** The sense of taste: *delicacies pleasing to the most refined palate.* [Middle English, from Latin *palātum,* perhaps from Etruscan.]

pa·la·tial (pə-láysh'l) *adj.* **1.** Of or suitable for a palace: *the palatial gardens.* **2.** Of the nature of a palace; spacious and ornate. [Latin *palātium,* PALACE.] **—pa·la·tial·ly** *adv.*

pa·lat·i·nate (pə-látti-nayt, -nət, -nit) *n.* The territory or jurisdiction of a palatine, especially: **1.** The **Palatinate** *(see).* **2.** Any of the English counties palatine (Durham, Lancaster, Chester, and Ely), whose lords in the Middle Ages had royal powers. **3.** Any of the American palatine colonies (Maine, Maryland, and Carolina), whose proprietors had royal prerogatives. [Medieval Latin *palātīnātus,* from *palātīnus,* a PALATINE.]

Pa·lat·i·nate (pə-látti-nət, -nit). Either of two former regions of West Germany. *Lower* or *Rhineland* or *Rhenish Palatinate,* often called the "Palatinate", lay in what are now Rheinland-Pfalz, Hessen, and Baden-Württemberg. *Upper Palatinate* lay in what is now northeast Bavaria. They were ruled by counts palatine, who became electors of the Holy Roman Emperor (1356), and were then known as electors palatine.

pal·a·tine[1] (pál-ə-tīn) *n.* **1. a.** A soldier of the palace guard of the Roman emperors formed in the time of Diocletian. **b.** A soldier of a major division of the Roman army formed in the time of Constantine. **2.** Used as a title of various administrative officials of the late Roman and Byzantine Empires. **3.** A count delegated with royal powers, as: **a.** An imperial minister or emissary in the Carolingian Empire. **b.** A minor imperial official in the late Holy Roman Empire. **c.** A ruler of either of the German **Palatinates** *(see)*; an elector palatine. **d.** The lord of an English palatinate. **e.** The senior proprietor of a colonial American palatinate.
~*adj.* **1.** Belonging to or fit for a palace. **2.** Pertaining to or designating a palatine or palatinate. [Latin *palātīnus,* from *palātium,* a PALACE.]

pal·a·tine[2] (pálə-téen) *n.* A fur cape and hood worn by women. [French; introduced about 1676 by Anne de Gonzague, Princess *Palatine.*]

pal·a·tine[3] (pál-ə-tīn) *adj.* **1.** Of or pertaining to the palate. **2.** Designating either of the two bones that make up the hard palate.
~*n.* Either of these bones.

Pal·a·tine[1] (pál-ə-tīn) *adj.* Of or pertaining to the Palatinate.
~*n.* **1.** A ruler of the Palatinate (the Rhineland Palatinate); an Elector Palatine. **2.** A native or resident of the Palatinate.

Palatine. The chief of the seven hills of Rome.
~*adj.* Designating this hill or situated on it.

Palau. See **Belau, Republic of.**

pa·lav·er (pə-laavər || -lávvər) *n.* **1.** *Informal.* **a.** Confused or pointless chatter or fuss. **b.** A tiresome and lengthy procedure: *such a palaver to get through customs.* **c.** Talk intended to charm or beguile. **2.** Formerly, a parley between European explorers and representatives of local populations, especially in Africa.
~*v.* **palavered, -ering, -ers.** —*tr.* To flatter or cajole. —*intr. Informal.* To chatter confusedly and at length. [Portuguese *palavra,* word, speech, from Late Latin *parabola,* speech, PARABLE.]

pale[1] (payl) *n.* **1.** A stake or pointed stick; a picket. **2. a.** A boundary. **b.** *Archaic.* A fence enclosing an area. **3.** The area enclosed by a fence or boundary. **4.** *Heraldry.* A wide vertical stripe in the middle of a shield. **—beyond the pale.** Irrevocably unacceptable or unreasonable. **—the (English** or **Irish) Pale.** The medieval dominions of the English in Ireland.
~*tr.v.* **paled, paling, pales.** To enclose with pales; fence in. [Middle English, pointed stake, boundary, from Old French *pal,* stake, from Latin *pālus.*]

pale[2] *adj.* **paler, palest. 1.** Whitish in complexion; pallid; wan. **2.** Of a low intensity of colour; light. **3.** Designating a colour having high lightness and low saturation. Compare **deep. 4.** Of a low intensity of light; dim; faint. **5.** Feeble; weak; inferior.
~*v.* **paled, paling, pales.** —*tr.* To cause to turn pale. —*intr.* **1.** To become pale; blanch. **2.** To decrease in relative importance; be outshone; diminish. [Middle English, from Old French, from Latin *pallidus,* from *pallēre,* to be pale.] **—pale·ly** *adv.* **—pale·ness** *n.*

pa·le·a (páy-li-ə) *n., pl.* **-leae** (-li-ee). Also **pale** (payl). *Botany.* A small, chafflike bract partly enclosing the flower of a grass spikelet. [New Latin, from Latin, chaff.]

pale·face (páyl-fayss) *n.* A white person. A term said to have been used by North American Indians.

paleo–, pale–. *U.S.* Variant of **palaeo-.**

Pa·ler·mo (pə-láir-mō, -lér-). Capital of Sicily and Palermo province. Situated on the Tyrrhenian Sea at the foot of Mount Pellegrino, it is the chief port for Sicily.

Pal·es·tine (pál-ə-stīn, -i-, -e-). Historic region of southwest Asia, sometimes called the Holy Land. Situated on the eastern Mediterranean coast, it has at times included areas such as Bashan and Gilead to the east of the river Jordan, and now covers Israel and territories of Jordan and Egypt. Its many rulers have included the Hebrews, Egyptians, Romans, Byzantines, Arabs, and Turks. The area west of the Jordan was awarded to Britain under a League of

PRONUNCIATION KEY

a, trap; aa, father; ai, **fair**; ar, **star**; aw, **lawn**; ay, **play**; b, bb, stab; **rubber**; ch, **church**; ck, ticket; d, dd, **dead**; **ladder**; e, dress; ee, **bee**; er, **defer**; ew, **few**; ewr, **pure**; ə, about; ər, **letter**; f, ff, **fife**; **differ**; g, gg, **giggle**; h, **hat**; i, **kit**; ī, **price**; īr, **fire**; j, **judge**; k, **kick**; l, ll, let; 'l, **needle**; m, mm, **man**; n, nn, **no**; 'n, **sudden**; ng, **thing**; o, **lot**; ō, no; ŏŏ, **foot**; ōō, **shoe**; oor, **poor**; ow, **cow**; owr, **hour**; oy, **boy**; p, pp, **pepper**; r, rr, red; s, ss, **sauce**; sh, **ship**; t, tt, totter; th, **thick**; th, **this**; smooth; u, **cut**; ur, **turn**; v, vv, **valve**; w, **wet**; y, **yes**; z, zz, **zebra**; zh, vision; pleasure

IN FOREIGN WORDS:

aN, oN, **Saint-Saëns**; hl, **Llanelli**; **Hluhluwe**; kh, **loch**; **lough**; **Khaled**

STRESS MARK:

ín-sīt, insight; in-sít, incite

Palladian

INSPIRATION FROM ITALY
Palladio's classical designs reborn in England

Palladian architecture takes its name from the work of Andrea Palladio, a 16th-century Italian architect whose symmetrical designs were modelled on the temples and baths of ancient Rome. He designed elegant palaces and villas in Vicenza and the surrounding northern Italian countryside, and two churches in Venice. The Villa Rotonda outside Vicenza is the most famous of his villas.

Inigo Jones introduced the Palladian style to Britain with the Queen's House at Greenwich in the early 17th century; it did not become fashionable until a century later, when it dominated English domestic architecture for decades.

The revival was inspired partly by the work of Lord Burlington and of Colen Campbell, whose book *Vitruvius Britannicus* (1715–21) was the most influential architectural work of the period. It was also partly due to Palladio's own *Quattro Libri dell'Architettura* (Four books on Architecture) of 1570, translated into English in 1715. Textbook examples of the Palladian style are Mereworth Castle in Kent (1723) – almost an exact copy of Palladio's Rotonda; Chiswick House (1725; below), and Holkham Hall, Norfolk (1734). The city of Bath, planned from 1727 onwards, remains a monument to the overwhelming impact of the style.

CHISWICK HOUSE *Lord Burlington designed the house, built to display his art collection, on the lines of Palladio's Villa Capra near Vicenza in Italy. Its symmetrical design, central dome, and pedimented portico with Corinthian columns, are typical of the Palladian style.*

Nations mandate (1920). Britain supported Jewish claims to a separate homeland, and in 1948 it was divided by the United Nations between two separate states, Israel and Jordan. However, the Arabs refused to recognise the newly created Israel and immediately attacked it. Arab-Israeli military conflict has been frequent ever since. Israel occupied Jordanian territory west of the Jordan (1967), and the Palestine Liberation Organisation (formed 1964) has continued to fight for the creation of a Palestinian homeland for Arabs and the destruction of Israel. —**Pal·es·tin·i·an** (pál-ə-stínni-ən, -i-, -e-) *adj. & n.*

palestra. *U.S.* Variant of **palaestra**.

Pa·les·tri·na (pál-ess-tréenə, -iss-, -əss-), **Giovanni Pierluigi da** (*c.* 1525–94). Italian composer. His works include over 100 masses, 179 motets, and several magnificats, litanies, and madrigals. He was a master of polyphony and counterpoint.

pale·tot (pál-tō) *n.* 1. Especially formerly, a loose cloak or coat. 2. A 19th-century woman's fitted jacket. [French.]

pal·ette (pál-ət, -et, -it) *n.* Also **pallet** (senses 1, 2). 1. A board, typically with a hole for the thumb, upon which an artist mixes colours. 2. The range of colours used in a particular painting or class of paintings, or by a particular artist: *a limited palette.* 3. A **pallette** (*see*). [French, from Old French, flat board, diminutive of *pale*, shovel, from Latin *pāla*, spade, shovel.]

palette knife *n.* A knife with a thin, flexible blade, as used in cookery and by artists for mixing, scraping, or applying paint.

pal·frey (páwl-fri ‖ pól-) *n., pl.* **-freys**. *Archaic.* A woman's saddle horse. [Middle English, from Old French *palefrei*, from Medieval Latin *palafrēdus*, from Late Latin *paraverēdus*, extra post horse : Greek *para*, beside + Latin *verēdus*, post horse, of Gaulish origin.]

Pa·li (páali) *n.* An ancient Indic language, surviving in the scriptures of Theravada Buddhism. [Sanskrit *pāli-bhāsā* : *pāli*, canon (of scriptures) + *bhāsa*, language.] —**Pa·li** *adj.*

pal·i·kar (pál-i-kaar) *n.* A Greek soldier in the struggle for Greece's independence from Turkey (1821–28). [Modern Greek *palikari*, youth, from Late Greek *pallikarion*, page, diminutive of Greek *pallēx†*, a youth.]

pal·i·mon·y (pál-i-məni) *n. Informal.* Alimony or maintenance that

is demanded by a person who has lived with another person for some years without being married to her or him. [PAL + ALIMONY.]

pal·imp·sest (pál-imp-sest ‖ pə-limp-) *n.* A manuscript, typically of vellum or parchment, that has been written upon several times, often with remnants of earlier, imperfectly erased writing still visible. Remnants of this kind are a major source for the recovery of lost literary works of classical antiquity. [Latin *palimpsēstus*, from Greek *palimpsēstos*, rubbed again : *palin*, again + *-psēstos*, "scraped", from *psēn*, to rub, scrape.] —**pal·imp·sest** *adj.*

pal·in·drome (pál-in-drōm) *n.* A word or sequence of words which reads the same backwards or forwards, as *A man, a plan, a canal, Panama!* [Greek *palindromos*, running back again : *palin*, again + *dromos*, a running.] —**pal·in·drom·ic** (-drómmik, -drōmik) *adj.*

pal·ing (páyling) *n.* 1. Any of a row of upright, pointed sticks forming a fence; a pale; a picket. 2. Pointed sticks used in making fences; pales. 3. A fence made of pales or pickets.

pal·in·gen·e·sis (pál-in-jénni-siss) *n., pl.* **-ses** (-seez). 1. The doctrine of transmigration of souls; metempsychosis. 2. *Biology.* **Recapitulation** (*see*). [Greek *palin*, again + GENESIS.] —**pal·in·ge·net·ic** (-jə-néttik) *adj.* —**pal·in·ge·net·i·cal·ly** *adv.*

pal·i·node (pál-i-nōd) *n.* 1. A poem in which the poet recants something said in a previous poem. 2. Any formal statement of recantation. [Late Latin *palinōdia*, from Greek *palinōidia* : *palin*, again + *ōidē*, song.]

pal·i·sade (pál-i-sáyd) *n.* 1. A fence of pales forming a defence barrier or fortification. 2. Any of the pales of such a fence. 3. *Botany.* The upper part of the mesophyll tissue of a leaf consisting of closely packed cylindrical cells and forming the main photosynthesising area of the plant. 4. *Plural. U.S.* A line of lofty, steep cliffs, usually along a river.
~*tr.v.* **palisaded, -sading, -sades.** To equip or fortify with a palisade. [French *palissade*, from Provençal *palissada*, from *palissa*, a pale, from Vulgar Latin *pālicea*, from Latin *pālus*, stake.]

pall¹ (pawl) *n.* 1. A cover for a coffin, bier, or tomb, often made of black, purple, or white velvet. 2. A coffin, especially one being borne to a grave or tomb. 3. **a.** Any covering that darkens or obscures: *a pall of smoke over the city.* **b.** A gloomy or oppressive atmosphere: *Defeat cast a pall over the homecoming of the troops.* 4. *Ecclesiastical.* **a.** A linen cloth, or a square of cardboard faced with cloth, used to cover the chalice. **b.** A vestment, the **pallium** (*see*). 5. *Heraldry.* A Y-shaped charge on a shield.
~*tr.v.* **palled, palling, palls.** To cover with or as if with a pall. [Middle English *pal*, Old English *pæll*, from Latin *pallium*, a cover, cloak, PALLIUM.]

pall² *v.* **palled, palling, palls.** —*intr.* 1. To become insipid, boring, or wearisome. Often used with *on.* 2. To have a dulling, wearisome, or unpleasant effect. Often used with *on.* 3. To become cloyed or satiated. —*tr.* To cloy; satiate. [Middle English *pallen*, aphetic variant of *appallen*, to APPAL.]

Pal·la·di·an¹ (pə-láydi-ən) *adj.* 1. Of, pertaining to, or characteristic of Athena, the Greek goddess of wisdom. 2. *Literary.* Of, pertaining to, or characterised by wisdom or study. [Latin *palladius*, of Pallas, from Greek *palladios*, from *Pallas* (stem *Pallad-*), goddess of wisdom, PALLAS (Athena).]

Palladian² *adj. Architecture.* 1. In or designating the Renaissance style of Andrea Palladio. 2. In or designating a mid-18th-century style derived from that of Palladio, especially in Britain.

pal·lad·ic (pə-lád-ik, -láyd-) *adj. Chemistry.* Of or designating compounds containing trivalent or tetravalent palladium.

Pal·la·di·o (pə-laʹadi-ō; *Italian* pal-), **Andrea**, born Andrea di Pietro (1508–80). Italian architect. The founder of modern Italian architecture, he developed a style based on the classical style of ancient Rome, breaking with the ornate Italian Renaissance style. His works include the Villa Rotonda and the Palazzo Chiericati.

pal·la·di·um¹ (pə-láydi-əm) *n. Symbol* **Pd** A soft, ductile, steel-white, tarnish-resistant, metallic element occurring naturally with platinum, especially in gold, nickel, and copper ores. It is used as a catalyst in hydrogenation process, as a purification filtre for hydrogen, and is alloyed for use in electric contacts, jewellery, nonmagnetic watch parts, and surgical instruments. Atomic number 46, atomic weight 106.4, melting point 1 555°C, boiling point 3 167°C, relative density 12.02 (20°C), valency 2, 3, 4. [New Latin, from the asteroid PALLAS, discovered (1802) just before the element.]

pal·la·di·um² *n., pl.* **-dia** (-láydi-ə) or **-ums**. 1. A sacred object held to have the power to preserve a city or state possessing it. 2. A safeguard, especially one viewed as a guarantee of the integrity of social institutions: *the right to free speech, palladium of democracy.* [Latin, from Greek *Palladion*, the statue of Pallas Athena that assured the safety of Troy as long as it remained within the city, from *Pallas* (stem *Pallad-*), PALLAS (Athena).]

pal·la·dous (pə-láydəss, pál-ədəss) *adj. Chemistry.* Of, pertaining to, or containing palladium, especially bivalent palladium.

Pal·las (pál-əss, -ass) *n.* The second-largest asteroid of the Solar System, approximately 450 kilometres (300 miles) in diameter. [Discovered by Peter S. *Pallas* (died 1811), German naturalist.]

Pallas Athena, Pallas Athene. The goddess **Athena** (*see*).

pall·bear·er (páwl-bair-ər) *n.* Any of the persons carrying or attending the coffin at a funeral. [Originally, one who held up the corners of the pall covering the coffin.] —**pall·bear·ing** *n. & adj.*

pal·let¹ (pál-it, -ət) *n.* 1. A machine part that converts reciprocating motion to rotary motion, or vice versa, such as a click or pawl for controlling the motion of a ratchet wheel in a watch escapement. 2. The lip or projection of a pawl for engaging the teeth on a ratchet wheel. **3.** A wooden, paddle-like potter's tool for mixing and shaping clay. **4.** A tool used for printing or gilding letters on book bindings or taking up and applying gold leaf. **5.** A portable platform for storing or moving cargo or freight, especially by fork-lift truck. **6.** A painter's palette. **7.** A valve in the wind chest of an organ, connected to a key which when depressed admits air to a groove beneath the pipes corresponding to the key. [French PALETTE.]

pallet² *n.* A narrow, hard bed or straw-filled mattress. [Middle English *pailet,* from Anglo-French *paillete,* bundle of straw, from *paille,* straw, from Latin *palea,* chaff.]

pal·let·is·a·tion (pál-i-tī-záysh'n, -ə- || *U.S.* -ti-) *n.* The process of converting a warehouse, factory, or the like, to enable all goods to be moved on pallets by fork-lift truck.

pal·lette, pal·ette (pál-it, -ət, pə-lét) *n.* A plate that protects the armpit on a suit of armour. [Variant of PALETTE (thin board).]

pal·li·asse (pál-i-ass, -áss) *n.* Also *chiefly U.S.* **pail·lasse** (pal-yáss). A thin mattress filled usually with straw or sawdust. [French, from Italian *pagliaccio,* from Vulgar Latin *paleaceum* (unattested), from Latin *palea,* chaff, straw.]

pal·li·ate (pál-i-ayt) *tr.v.* **-ated, -ating, -ates. 1.** To make (an offence or crime) seem less serious; extenuate; excuse. **2.** To make less severe, without curing; reduce the pain or intensity of; mitigate; alleviate. [Late Latin *palliāre,* to cloak, from Latin *pallium,* cloak, PALLIUM.] **—pal·li·a·tion** (-i-áysh'n) *n.*

pal·li·a·tive (pál-i-ətiv || -aytiv) *adj.* Tending or serving to palliate. ~*n.* Something that palliates. **—pal·li·a·tive·ly** *adv.*

pal·lid (pál-id) *adj.* **1.** Having an abnormally pale or wan complexion. **2.** Lacking colour or brightness. **3.** Lacking in radiance or vitality; dull; lifeless: *a pallid performance.* [Latin *pallidus,* from *pallēre,* to be pale.] **—pal·lid·ly** *adv.* **—pal·lid·ness** *n.*

pal·li·um (pál-i-əm) *n., pl.* **-liums** or **-lia** (-i-ə). **1.** A large rectangular cloth worn as a cloak in ancient Rome. **2.** A woollen shoulder-band with two pendants hanging from it at the front and back, worn by the pope and conferred by him on archbishops and sometimes on bishops. Also called "pall". **3.** *Zoology.* An outer layer or covering, such as the mantle of a mollusc or the cerebral cortex. [Latin *pallium*†.]

pall-mall (pál-mál, pél-mél) *n.* **1.** A 17th-century game in which a boxwood ball was struck with a mallet to drive it through an iron ring suspended at the end of an alley. **2.** The alley in which this game was played. [Obsolete French *palle-maille,* from Italian *pallamaglio* : *palla, balla,* ball, from Middle High German *balle* + *maglio,* mallet, from Latin *malleus.*]

pal·lor (pál-ər) *n.* Extreme or unnatural paleness: *a ghostly pallor.* [Latin, from *pallēre,* to be pale.]

palm¹ (paam || polm, paalm) *n.* **1.** The inner surface of the hand, extending from the wrist to the base of the fingers. **2.** The similar part of the forefoot of a quadruped. **3.** A unit of length equal to either the width, about 75 to 100 millimetres (3 to 4 inches), or the length, about 175 to 200 centimetres (7 to 10 inches) of the hand. **4.** The part of a glove or mitten that covers the palm of the hand. **5.** A metal shield worn by sailmakers over the palm of the hand and used to force a needle through heavy canvas. **6.** The blade of an oar or paddle. **7.** The flattened part of the antlers of certain animals, such as the moose. **—cross (someone's) palm.** To pay, tip, or bribe (someone). **—grease the palm of.** To bribe. **—in the palm of (someone's) hand.** Completely subject to someone's will; ready to carry out someone's wishes.

~*tr.v.* **palmed, palming, palms. 1.** To conceal in the palm of the hand, as in cheating at dice or cards or in a sleight-of-hand trick. **2.** To pick up furtively. **—palm off. 1.** To dispose of or pass off by deception. **2.** To satisfy in a spurious or deceitful way: *tried to palm me off with some silly excuse.* **3.** To rid oneself of. Used with *on*: *palms off all his boring friends on her.* [Middle English *paume,* from Old French, from Latin *palma,* palm of the hand, palm tree.]

palm² *n.* **1.** Any of various chiefly tropical evergreen trees or shrubs of the family Palmae, characteristically having unbranched trunks with a crown of large pinnate or palmate leaves. **2.** A leaf or frond of a palm tree, carried as an emblem of victory, success, or joy. **3.** Triumph; victory. **4.** A small metallic representation of a palm leaf on certain military decorations indicating that they have been awarded a second time. **—bear** or **carry off the palm.** To win the prize in a given contest; be the victor. [Middle English *palme,* Old English *palm,* from Latin *palma,* PALM, hence (from the resemblance of its leaves to the outspread human hand) palm tree.]

Pal·ma (de Mallorca) (paámə, pál-mə; *Spanish* pál-ma). Capital and seaport of the Balearic Islands, Spain. Situated on the island of Majorca, it exports wine and agricultural produce and has become an important tourist and commercial centre.

pal·mar (pál-mər || paál-, pól-) *adj.* Of, pertaining to, or corresponding to the palm of the hand or an animal's paw: *palmar folds.* [New Latin *palmaris,* from Latin *palma,* PALM (hand).]

pal·ma·ry (pál-məri || paál-, pól-) *adj. Rare.* Worthy to receive the palm; outstanding; superior. [Latin *palmārius,* deserving of the palm of victory, from *palma,* PALM (tree).]

Palmas, Las. See **Las Palmas.**

pal·mate (pál-mayt, -mət, -mit || paál-, pól-) *adj.* Also **pal·mat·ed** (-máytid, -maytid). **1.** Resembling a hand with the fingers extended: *palmate antlers; palmate coral.* **2.** *Botany.* Having leaflets or lobes radiating or diverging from one point: *a palmate leaf.* **3.** *Zoology.* Having webbed toes, as on the feet of many water birds. [Latin *palmātus,* from *palma,* PALM (hand).] **—pal·mate·ly** *adv.*

pal·ma·tion (pal-máysh'n || paal-, pol-) *n.* **1.** The state of being palmate. **2. a.** A palmate structure or form. **b.** A division or part of a palmate structure.

Palm Beach. Seaside resort of southeast Florida, situated on a barrier beach between the Atlantic Ocean and Lake Worth.

palm civet *n.* Any of several arboreal mammals of the family Viverridae, of Africa and Asia, having long tails and grey or brown fur.

palm·er (paámər || pól-mər, paál-) *n.* In medieval Europe, a pilgrim who carried a palm branch as a token of having visited the Holy Land. [Middle English *palmere,* from Medieval Latin *palmārius,* from *palma,* PALM (branch).]

Palm·er·ston (paámər-stən), **Henry John Temple, 3rd Viscount** (1784–1865). British Whig statesman. Entering Parliament as a Tory (1807) he was secretary of war (1809–28) before joining the Whigs. As foreign secretary (1830–34, 1835–41, 1846–51) he helped to secure Belgian independence and worked against the increase of Russian influence in the east. As prime minister (1855–58, 1859–65), he nearly took Britain into the American Civil War on the side of the South, defeated the Sepoy revolt in the Indian Mutiny (1857–58), and spoke out for Italian nationalism. Popular with the people, he made many enemies among other ministers and abroad through his outspoken assertiveness.

palm·er·worm (paámər-wurm || pól-mər-, paál-) *n.* Any of several caterpillars that injure fruit trees by feeding upon their leaves.

pal·mette (pal-mét) *n.* A stylised palm leaf used as a decorative element, notably in Persian rugs and in classical mouldings, reliefs, frescoes, and vase paintings. [French, diminutive of *palme,* palm, from Latin *palma,* PALM.]

pal·met·to (pal-méttō) *n., pl.* **-tos** or **-toes.** Any of several small, mostly tropical palms having fan-shaped leaves; especially, *Sabal palmetto,* of the southern United States. This species is also called "cabbage palmetto". [Spanish *palmito,* diminutive of *palma,* palm, from Latin, PALM.]

palm·ist (paám-ist || pólm-, paálm-) *n.* Also **palm·is·ter** (-ər). One who practises palmistry. [Back-formation from PALMISTRY.]

palm·is·try (paá-mi-stri || pól-, paál-) *n.* The practice or art of telling fortunes from the lines, marks, and patterns on the palms of the hands; chiromancy. [Middle English *pawmestrie* : *paume,* PALM + an obscure element not corresponding to *-ist* + *-ry.*]

pal·mi·tate (pál-mi-tayt || pól-, paál-) *n. Chemistry.* An ester or salt of palmitic acid. [PALMIT(IN) + -ATE.]

pal·mit·ic acid (pal-míttik || pol-, paal-) A common saturated fatty acid, $CH_3(CH_2)_{14}COOH$, occurring in many natural oils and fats, and used in making soaps. [From PALMITIN.]

pal·mi·tin (pál-mitin || pól-, paál-) *n.* The glyceryl ester, $C_3H_5(OOCC_{15}H_{31})_3$, of palmitic acid, found in palm oil and animal fats, and used to manufacture soap. Also called "tripalmitin". [French *palmitine,* perhaps from *palmite,* pith of the palm tree, from *palme,* palm, from Latin *palma,* PALM.]

palm-kernel oil (paám-kern'l || pólm-, paálm-) *n.* **1.** A hard, white oil obtained from the kernel or endosperm of seeds of the West African palm, *Elaeis guineensis.* **2.** Any oil extracted from the kernels of other palms.

palm oil *n.* **1.** A yellowish fatty oil obtained from the pericarp of the fruits of the West African palm, *Elaeis guineensis,* and used in the manufacture of margarine, cooking fats, chocolates, and cosmetics. **2.** Oil obtained from the pericarp of any other palm fruits.

Palm Springs. Spa resort in California, United States, situated at the west end of the Coachella Valley.

palm sugar *n.* Sugar made from the sap of various palm trees.

Palm Sunday *n.* The Sunday before Easter, commemorating Christ's entry into Jerusalem, when palm branches were strewn before him.

palm wine *n.* An alcoholic drink made from the fermented sap of a palm and consumed especially in West Africa.

palm·y (paámi || pólmi, paálmi) *adj.* **-ier, -iest. 1.** Of or pertaining to palm trees. **2.** Covered with palm trees. **3.** Prosperous; flourishing: *palmy days.*

pal·my·ra (pal-mīr-ə) *n.* A tall palm, *Borassus flabellifer,* of tropical Asia, having large, fanlike leaves used for matting. Also called "palmyra palm". [Variant of earlier *palmeira,* from Portuguese, palm tree, from *palma,* palm, from Latin, PALM.]

Pal·my·ra (pal-mīr-ə). Biblical name **Tad·mor** (tád-mawr). City of ancient Syria. On the trade route between the Roman and Parthian Empires, in the third century A.D. it was capital of an empire that included Egypt, Syria, and Asia Minor. It was destroyed by the Romans (A.D. 273) and conquered by Muslims (A.D. 634).

pa·lo·lo worm (pə-lōlō) *n.* Any of several edible polychaete worms of the families Eunicidae and Vereidae living in reefs of the south Pacific, which come to the surface to reproduce twice a year. [Samoan and Tongan native name.]

Pal·o·mar, Mount (pál-ə-maar). Peak in California, United States. Rising to a height of 1 871 metres (6,140 feet), it is the site of an observatory, having one of the world's largest reflecting telescopes, 508 centimetres (200 inches) in diameter.

pal·o·mi·no (pál-ə-meénō) *n., pl.* **-nos.** A horse of a type having a golden or tan coat and a white or cream-coloured mane and tail. [American Spanish, from Spanish, dove-coloured, from Latin *palumbīnus,* pertaining to ring doves, from *palumbes,* ring dove.]

pa·loo·ka (pə-lo͞okə) *n. U.S. Slang.* An incompetent or easily defeated sports player, especially a boxer. [20th century origin.]

palp (palp) *n. Zoology.* **1.** Either of two elongated sensory organs, usually near the mouth, in invertebrate organisms such as crustaceans and insects. Also called "palpus". **2.** Either of two sensory

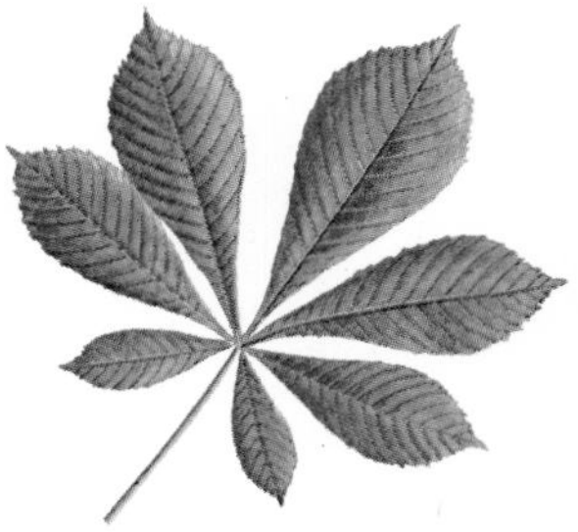

palmate *The hand-shaped, or palmate, leaf of the horse chestnut has seven leaflets stretching out like fingers.*

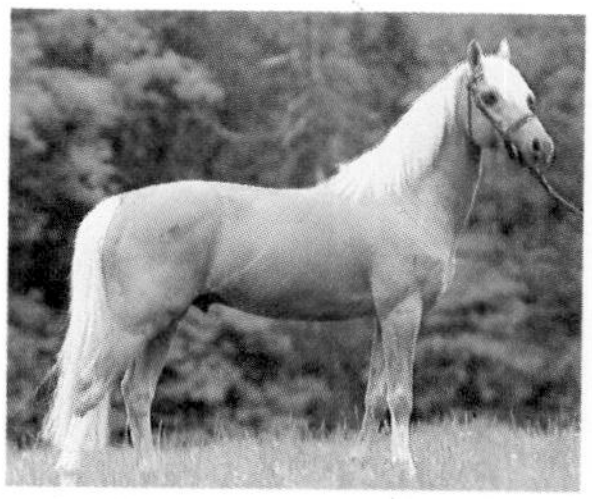

palomino *A golden-coloured type of horse. Its name comes from a Spanish-American word used to describe its pale mane and tail.*

PRONUNCIATION KEY

a, trap; aa, father; ai, fair; ar, star; aw, lawn; ay, play; b, bb, stab; rubber; ch, church; ck, ticket; d, dd, dead; ladder; e, dress; ee, bee; er, defer; ew, few; ewr, pure; ə, about; ər, letter; f, ff, fife; differ; g, gg, giggle; h, hat; i, kit; ī, price; īr, fire; j, judge; k, kick; l, ll, let; 'l, needle; m, mm, man; n, nn, no; 'n, sudden; ng, thing; o, lot; ō, no; o͝o, foot; o͞o, shoe; oor, poor; ow, cow; owr, hour; oy, boy; p, pp, pepper; r, rr, red; s, ss, sauce; sh, ship; t, tt, totter; th, thick; th, this; smooth; u, cut; ur, turn; v, vv, valve; w, wet; y, yes; z, zz, zebra; zh, vision; pleasure

IN FOREIGN WORDS:

aN, oN, Saint-Saëns; hl, Llanelli; Hluhluwe; kh, loch; lough; Khaled

STRESS MARK:

in-sīt, insight; in-sít, incite

organs extending from the heads of certain molluscs and annelids. **3.** A **pedipalp** (see). [French *palpe,* from Latin *palpus,* a touching.]
pal·pa·ble (pál-pəb'l) *adj.* **1.** Capable of being handled, touched, or felt; tangible. **2.** Easily perceived; obvious: *a palpable fraud.* **3.** *Medicine.* Perceptible by palpation: *a palpable tumour.* —See Synonyms at **perceptible.** [Middle English, from Late Latin *palpābilis,* from Latin *palpāre,* to touch.] —**pal·pa·bil·i·ty** (-pə-bíllətí) *n.* —**pal·pa·bly** *adv.*
pal·pate[1] (pal-páyt, pál-payt) *tr.v.* **-pated, -pating, -pates.** *Medicine.* To examine or explore by touching (an organ or area of the body) as a diagnostic aid. [Latin *palpāre,* to touch.] —**pal·pa·tion** (-páysh'n) *n.* —**pal·pa·tor** *n.*
pal·pate[2] (pál-payt) *adj. Zoology.* Having a palp or palps.
pal·pe·bral (pálpibrəl ‖ pal-péebrəl, -pébbrəl) *adj.* Of or pertaining to the eyelids. [Late Latin *palpebrālis,* from Latin *palpebra,* eyelid.]
pal·pe·brate (pál-pi-brayt ‖ pal-pée-, -pé-) *adj.* Having eyelids.
~*intr.v.* **palpebrated, -brating, -brates.** To blink or wink, especially rapidly and involuntarily.
pal·pi·tant (pálpitənt) *adj.* Palpitating; quivering. [Latin *palpitāns* (stem *palpitānt-*), present participle of *palpitāre,* to PALPITATE.]
pal·pi·tate (pál-pi-tayt) *intr.v.* **-tated, -tating, -tates.** **1.** To shake; quiver; flutter. **2.** To beat more quickly than normal; throb. Used especially of the heart. —See Synonyms at **pulsate.** [Latin *palpitāre,* to palpitate, frequentative of *palpāre,* to touch.] —**pal·pi·tat·ing·ly** *adv.*
pal·pi·ta·tion (pál-pi-táysh'n) *n.* **1.** A trembling or shaking. **2.** Irregular, rapid beating or pulsation of the heart.
pal·pus (pál-pəss) *n., pl.* **-pi** (-pī). *Zoology.* A palp.
pals·grave (páwlz-grayv) *n.* Formerly, a count palatine, especially one of the Counts Palatine of the Rhine or Electors Palatine. [Dutch *paltsgrave,* from Middle Dutch : *palts,* palatine, ultimately from Vulgar Latin *palāntius* (unattested), variant of *palātīnus,* PALATINE + *grave,* count, from Middle Dutch.]
pal·sied (páwl-zid ‖ pól-) *adj.* **1.** *Medicine.* Afflicted with palsy. **2.** Trembling; shaking.
pal·stave (páwl-stayv) *n. Archaeology.* A type of celt (axe), resembling a chisel, usually made of bronze with a tongue that slots into a handle. [From Danish *paalstav,* from Old Norse *pálstavr* : *páll,* hoe, from Latin *palus,* stake + *stafr,* STAFF.]
pal·sy (páwl-zi ‖ pól-) *n., pl.* **-sies.** **1.** Paralysis. **2.** A condition marked by loss of power to feel or to control movement in any part of the body. **3. a.** A weakening or debilitating influence. **b.** An enfeebled condition or debilitated state thought to result from such an influence. **4.** A fit of some strong emotion marked by an inability to act: *"a little palsy of indignation."* (Anthony Burgess).
~*tr.v.* **palsied, -sying, -sies.** **1. a.** To paralyse. **b.** To deprive of strength: *palsied blows.* **2.** To make helpless, as with fear. [Middle English *palesie,* from Old French *paralisie,* from Vulgar Latin *paralisia* (unattested), from Latin *paralysis,* PARALYSIS.]
pal·ter (páwl-tər ‖ pól-) *intr.v.* **-tered, -tering, -ters.** **1.** To talk or act insincerely; equivocate. **2.** To be capricious; trifle. **3.** To use trickery in bargaining. [16th century : origin obscure.]
pal·try (páwl-tri ‖ pól-) *adj.* **-trier, -triest.** **1.** Petty; trifling; insignificant. **2.** Worthless; contemptible. —See Synonyms at **trivial.** [Dialectal *paltry,* feeble, from *palt, pelt†,* rags, rubbish.] —**pal·tri·ly** *adv.* —**pal·tri·ness** *n.*
pa·lu·dal (pə-léw-d'l, -lóo-, pál-yŏod'l) *adj.* **1.** Of or pertaining to a swamp; marshy. **2.** Malarial. [From Latin *palūs* (stem *palūd-*), marsh.]
pal·u·dism (pál-yŏo-diz'm) *n.* A disease, **malaria** (see). [From Latin *palūs* (stem *palūd-*), marsh.]
pal·y[1] (páyli) *adj. Archaic.* Pale.
pal·y[2] *adj. Heraldry.* Designating a shield or heraldic charge that is vertically striped. [From Old French *palé,* from *pal,* PALE (stake).]
pal·y·nol·o·gy (pál-i-nólləji) *n.* The scientific study of living and fossil spores and pollen. Also called "pollen analysis". [From Greek *palunein,* to sprinkle + -LOGY.]
pam (pam) *n.* The jack of clubs and highest trump in certain variations of the card game **loo** (see). [Gamblers' slang, shortened from French *pamphile,* apparently from Latin name *Pamphilus,* from Greek *pamphilos,* "loved by all" : *pan,* all, PAN- + *philos,* beloved.]
pam. pamphlet.
pa·mir (pə-méer) *n.* Sparse grassland on the high plateaux of Central Asia.
Pa·mir (pə-méer) Also **Pamirs** (-meerz) or **Pamir Knot.** Mountain complex lying mainly in Tadzhik S.S.R., U.S.S.R., but also reaching into China, Jammu and Kashmir, Pakistan, and Afghanistan.
pam·pas (pám-pəz) *pl.n. Singular* **-pa** (-pə). A nearly treeless grassland area of South America, chiefly in east central Argentina and Uruguay. [Plural of American Spanish *pampa,* from Aymara and Quechua, plain.]
pam·pas grass (pámpəss) *n.* Any of several tall grasses of the genus *Cortaderia,* native to South America; especially, *C. argentea* which is widely cultivated for its creamy-white, long, fluffy panicles.
pam·pe·an (pámpi-ən, pam-pée-ən) *adj.* Of or pertaining to the pampas or the Indian people who inhabit them.
~*n. Capital* **P.** An Indian of the pampas.
pam·per (pámpər) *tr.v.* **-pered, -pering, -pers.** **1.** To treat with excessive indulgence; spoil; coddle. **2.** *Archaic.* To indulge with rich food; glut. [Middle English *pamperen,* frequentative of obsolete *pamp,* probably of Low German origin, akin to Flemish *pamperen.*] —**pam·per·er** *n.*
Synonyms: *pamper, indulge, spoil, coddle, mollycoddle, baby.*

pam·pe·ro (pam-paír-ō ‖ *U.S.* paam-) *n., pl.* **-ros.** A strong, cold, southwest wind that blows across the pampas. [American Spanish, "pampean", from *pampa,* PAMPAS.]
pam·phlet (pám-flit, -flət) *n. Abbr.* **pam., pamph., pph.** **1.** An unbound printed work, usually informative and with a paper cover. **2.** A short essay or treatise, usually on a current topic, published without a binding. [Middle English *pamflet,* from *Pamflet,* familiar name of *Pamphilus,* a popular short amatory Latin poem of the 12th century.] —**pam·phlet·ar·y** (-fli-təri, -tri ‖ *U.S.* -terri) *adj.*
pam·phlet·eer (pámf-li-téer, -lə-) *n.* A writer of pamphlets or other short works that take a partisan stand on an issue.
~*intr.v.* **pamphleteered, -eering, -eers.** To write, issue, or publish pamphlets.
Pam·phyl·i·a (pam-fílli-ə). An ancient region of southern Asia Minor that became a Roman province.
Pam·phyl·i·an (pam-fílli-ən) *n.* The Ancient Greek dialect of Pamphylia, belonging to Arcado-Cyprian.
Pam·plo·na (pam-plōnə). Capital of Navarra Province, northern Spain. Situated in the Basque region at the foot of the Pyrenees, it is famous for the Fiesta de San Fermin when bulls are let loose in the streets among crowds of revellers.
pan[1] (pan) *n.* **1. a.** A shallow, wide, open container, usually of metal and often without a lid, used for holding liquids, cooking, and other domestic purposes: *a milk pan.* **b.** The quantity a pan will hold. **2.** Any vessel similar in form, such as: **a.** An open, metal dish used to separate gold or other metal from gravel, earth, or other waste, by washing. **b.** Either of the receptacles on a balance or pair of scales. **c.** A vessel used for boiling and evaporating liquids. **d.** *British.* The bowl of a lavatory. **3.** See **dustpan.** **3. a.** A basin or depression in the earth, often containing mud or water. **b.** A natural or artificial basin used to obtain salt by evaporating brine. **4.** A piece of drift ice that has broken off a larger floe. **5.** A **hardpan** (see). **6.** In flintlocks, the small cavity in the lock used to hold powder. **7.** *Slang.* The face. **8.** The steel top of an oil drum used as a musical instrument in a steel band.
~*v.* **panned, panning, pans.** —*tr.* **1.** To wash (gravel, sand, or other sediments) in a pan for precious metal: **2.** *Informal.* To criticise harshly. **3.** *Slang.* To beat (someone) up. —*intr.* **1.** To wash gravel, sand, or other sediments in a pan. **2.** To yield gold as a result of washing in a pan. —**pan out.** *Informal.* To work out; turn out: *Let's see how things pan out.* [Middle English *panne,* Old English *panne,* from West Germanic *panna* (unattested), perhaps from Latin *patina,* from Greek *patanē,* pan, dish.]
pan[2] (pan, paan) *n.* **1.** The leaf of the betel palm. **2.** A preparation of this leaf with betel nuts and lime, used for chewing in Asia. [Hindi *pān,* from Sanskrit *parṇá,* feather, leaf.]
pan[3] (pan) *v.* **panned, panning, pans.** —*intr.* To move a film or television camera to follow a moving object or take in a larger scene. —*tr.* To move (a camera) in such a manner.
~*n.* An act or the process of panning with a camera. [Short for PANORAMA.]
Pan (pan). *Greek Mythology.* The god of woods, fields, and flocks, portrayed with a human torso with goat's legs, horns, and ears.
pan– *comb. form.* Indicates: **1.** All; entirely; for example, **panacea, panorama. 2.** *Capital* **P. a.** Of, involving, or comprising all; for example, **Pan-Arabism. b.** The aspiration for the political union of a specified group: **Pan-Africanism.** [Greek, from *pas* (neuter *pan*), all.]
pan·a·ce·a (pánnə-séer, -sée-ə). *n.* A remedy for all diseases, evils, or difficulties; a cure-all. [Latin *panacēa,* from Greek *panakeia,* from *panakēs,* all-healing : *pan-* + *akos,* cure.] —**pan·a·ce·an** *adj.*
pa·nache (pə-násh, pa-, -naásh) *n.* **1.** A dashing or stylish manner: *leapt upon the platform with panache.* **2.** A bunch of feathers or a plume, especially on a helmet. [French, from Italian *pennachio,* from Late Latin *pinnāculum,* diminutive of Latin *pinna,* feather.]
pa·na·da (pə-naádə) *n.* A thick mixture of flour or breadcrumbs combined with milk, stock, or water, used for soups, for thickening sauces, or as a base for souffles. [Spanish, from *pan,* bread, from Latin *pānis,* bread.]
Pan·a·ma, Isthmus of (pánnə-maá, -maa). Formerly **Isthmus of Darién.** Strip of land that joins North and South America. Situated between the Pacific Ocean and the Caribbean Sea, it is about 644 kilometres (400 miles) long and at its minimum 50 kilometres (30 miles) wide.
Panama, Republic of. Country of Central America. Situated in the Isthmus of Panama, it has central volcanic mountains and narrow coastal lowlands. Discovered by Columbus (1502), it was settled by the Spaniards, gaining independence from Spain as part of Colombia in 1819, and full independence in 1903. The **Panama Canal,** built in the Canal Zone by the United States, opened in 1914, and has dominated the country's economy. The country's chief foreign exchange earner is the canal, followed by petroleum products (made from imported oil), bananas, sugar, and shrimps. Area, 75 650 square kilometres (29,209 square miles). Population, 1,900,000. Capital, Panamá City. See map at **Central American States.** —**Pan·a·ma·ni·an** (-máyni-ən) *adj. & n.*
Panama Canal. Canal crossing the Isthmus of Panama, joining the Pacific and Atlantic Oceans. 82 kilometres (51 miles) long, it was begun by the French in 1881 but later abandoned (1889). In 1903, the United States backed a successful Panamanian revolt against Colombian rule and gained construction rights for the canal, which opened in 1914. A treaty ratified in 1978 provided for U.S. administration of the canal until the end of 1999.

Panama Canal Zone. Land, about 8 kilometres (5 miles) on each side of the Panama Canal, leased to the United States in 1903, when the canal was built. According to a treaty ratified in 1978, Panama assumed territorial jurisdiction in 1979.

Pa·na·má City (pánnə-máa). Capital of the Republic of Panama. Situated on the Pacific coast, it was founded in 1519, and became capital of Panama on independence (1903).

Panama hat n. Often small **p.** A natural-coloured, hand-plaited hat made from leaves of the jipijapa plant of South and Central America. Also called "panama".

Pan-A·mer·i·can (pánnə-mérrikən) adj. Of or pertaining to North, South, and Central America collectively.

pan·a·tel·la, pan·a·tel·a (pánnə-téllə) n. A long, slender cigar. [Spanish, from American Spanish, a long thin biscuit, from Italian *panatella*, from *panata*, PANADA.]

Pan·ath·e·nae·a (pán-áthi-née-ə) n. The main, annual civic and religious festival of ancient Athens, held in honour of Athena. [New Latin, from Greek *panathēnaia* : PAN- + *athēnaia*, from *Athēna*, Athena.] —**pan·ath·e·na·ic** (-náy-ik) adj.

Pan·a·vis·ion (pánnə-vizh'n) n. A trademark for a method of wide-screen film projection that superseded CinemaScope because of its improved anamorphic lens.

pan·broil (pán-broyl) tr.v. **-broiled, -broiling, -broils.** U.S. To fry in a heavy pan using little or no fat.

pan·cake (pán-kayk) n. **1.** A very thin flat cake made of batter that is fried on both sides until brown and usually rolled up with a savoury or sweet filling inside. **2.** U.S. A thin, fluffy cake made of sweetened batter, fried or baked on a griddle. Also called "griddle cake". **3.** A flat cake or a stick of compressed make-up. ~v. **pancaked, -caking, -cakes.** —intr. To make a pancake landing. —tr. To cause to make a pancake landing.

Pancake Day n. A day on which pancakes are traditionally eaten, Shrove Tuesday.

pancake landing n. An irregular or emergency landing in which an aircraft drops flat to the ground from a low altitude.

pan·chax (pán-chaks) n. Any of various small, brightly coloured Old World tropical fishes of the genus *Aplocheilus* and related genera, often kept in home aquariums. [New Latin *Panchax†*, former generic name.]

pan·cha·yat (pun-chí-ət) n. In India, a village council. [Hindi, from Sanskrit *pancha*, five (originally the number of members forming such a council).]

Pan·chen Lama (paánchən) n. One of Tibet's two Grand Lamas, the other being the Dalai Lama. See **Lamaism**. [From the Tibetan title *Pan-chen-rin-po-che*, "great jewel (among the) scholars".]

pan·chro·mat·ic (pán-krō-máttik, -krə-) adj. Sensitive to all colours: *panchromatic film.* —**pan·chro·ma·tism** (pan-krōmə-tiz'm) n.

pan·cre·as (páng-kri-əss, -ass) n. Anatomy. A long, soft, irregularly shaped gland lying near the stomach. It secretes pancreatic juice into the duodenum and contains the islets of Langerhans, which produce insulin. [Greek *pankreas*, "all-flesh", pancreas : PAN- + *kreas*, flesh.] —**pan·cre·at·ic** (-áttik) adj.

pancreatic juice n. A clear, alkaline secretion of the pancreas containing enzymes that aid in the digestion of proteins, carbohydrates, and fats.

pan·cre·a·tin (páng-kri-ətin ‖ pan-krée-) n. A mixture of enzymes extracted from the pancreases of cattle or pigs and used as a digestive aid. [From Greek *pankreas* (stem *pankreat-*), PANCREAS + -IN.]

pan·da (pándə) n. **1.** A chiefly herbivorous, bearlike mammal, *Ailuropoda melanoleuca*, of the bamboo forests in the mountains of China and Tibet, having woolly fur with distinctive black and white markings. Also called "giant panda". **2.** A small, raccoon-like mammal, *Ailurus fulgens*, of Nepal and China, having reddish fur and a long, ringed tail. Also called "lesser panda". [French, perhaps from a native Nepalese word.]

panda car n. In Britain, a police patrol car. [Alluding to the markings, similar to those of a panda.]

pan·da·nus (pan-dáynəss) n. Any of various palmlike trees and shrubs of the genus *Pandanus*, of southeastern Asia, having large buttress roots and a crown of narrow leaves. Also called "screw pine". [New Latin, from Malay *pandan*.] —**pan·da·na·ceous** (pándə-náyshəss) adj.

Pan·de·an pipe (pan-dée-ən). **Panpipes** (see).

pan·dect (pán-dekt) n. **1.** A comprehensive digest or complete treatise of a subject. **2.** Plural. Any complete body of laws; a legal code. **3.** Plural. Capital **P.** A digest of Roman civil law, compiled for the emperor Justinian in the sixth century A.D., and part of the **Corpus Juris Civilis** (see). Also called the "Digest". [Late Latin *Pandectēs*, the Corpus Juris Civilis, from Latin, book containing everything, from Greek *pandektēs*, all-receiving : PAN- + *dektēs*, receiver, from *dekheisthai*, to receive.]

pan·dem·ic (pan-démmik, pán-) adj. **1.** Widespread; general; universal. **2.** Epidemic over an especially wide geographical area. ~n. A pandemic disease. [From Late Latin *pandēmus*, from Greek *pandēmos*, of all the people : PAN- + *dēmos*, people.]

pan·de·mo·ni·um (pándi-mōni-əm) n. **1.** Any place characterised by great confusion, uproar, and noise. **2.** Wild uproar, noise, or chaos. —See Synonyms at **noise**. [From *Pandæmonium*, capital of Hell in Milton's *Paradise Lost* : PAN- + Greek *daimōn*, demon, spirit, deity.] —**pan·de·mo·ni·ac** (-ni·ac) adj.

pan·der (pándər) n. Also **pan·der·er** (pándərər) **1.** A go-between in sexual intrigues; a pimp; a procurer. **2.** One who caters to the lower tastes and desires of others or exploits their weaknesses.

~v. **pandered, -dering, -ders.** —tr. Archaic. To act as a pander for. —intr. To satisfy another's whims, tastes, or desires, especially when these are considered to be in some way inferior. Used with *to*. [From *Pandare*, character in Chaucer's *Troilus and Criseyde*, who procures Criseyde's love for Troilus; name taken from *Pandaro* (in Boccaccio's *Filostrata*), *Pandarus* (in the *Aeneid*), *Pandaros* (in the *Iliad*).] —**pan·der·ism** n.

pandit. Variant of **pundit.**

P & O Peninsular and Oriental (Steamship Company).

Pan·do·ra's box (pan-dáw-rəz ‖ -dŏ) n. **1.** Greek Mythology. The box that contained all the ills of mankind, opened by Pandora who was sent by Zeus as a punishment for Prometheus' theft of fire. Only hope was left in the box. **2.** Any source of great suffering or troubles, especially one that does not appear to be so at first.

pan·dore (pán-dawr ‖ -dŏr) n. An ancient musical instrument, a bandore (see). [From Italian *pandora*, from Late Latin, from Greek *pandoura*, three-stringed lute.]

pan·dow·dy (pan-dówdi) n., pl. **-dies.** U.S. Sliced apples baked with sugar and spices in a deep dish, with a thick crust on top. [19th century : origin obscure.]

p. & p. British. postage and packing.

pan·du·rate (pándewr-ayt) n. Also **pan·du·ri·form** (pan-déwr-i-fawrm ‖ -dŏor-). Botany. Resembling a violin in shape. Said of leaves. [New Latin *panduratus*, from Late Latin *pandūra*, three-stringed lute, PANDORE.]

pan·dy (pándi) n., pl. **-dies.** Archaic. A stroke on the hand with a leather strap, as a punishment. ~tr.v. **pandied, -dying, -dies.** Archaic. To slap on the hand. [Latin *pande (manum)*, extend (the hand), order given to a pupil about to be punished, from imperative of *pandere*, stretch out, extend.]

pan·dy·bat (pándi-bat) n. Chiefly Irish. A leather strap formerly used for hitting boys on the hand as a punishment in schools.

pane (payn) n. **1.** Any of the divisions of a window or door, filled with glass. **2.** A single sheet of glass used in such a division. **3.** A panel of a door, wall, or other surface. **4.** Any of the flat surfaces or facets of an object, such as a bolt, having many sides. **5. a.** A rectangular division of a sheet of stamps. **b.** A sheet of stamps with such divisions. [Middle English *pane, pan*, piece of cloth, section, from Old French *pan*, from Latin *pannus*, rag.]

pan·e·gyr·ic (pán-i-jirrik, -ə- ‖ -jír-ik) n. **1.** A formal eulogistic composition intended as a public compliment. **2.** Elaborate praise; an encomium. [French *panégyrique*, from Latin *panēgyricus*, from Greek *(logos) panēgurikos*, "(speech) for a public festival", from *panēguris*, general assembly, public festival : PAN- + *ēguris*, variant of *agora*, assembly.] —**pan·e·gyr·i·cal** adj. —**pan·e·gyr·i·cal·ly** adv.

pan·e·gy·rise, pan·e·gy·rize (pán-i-ji-rīz, -ə-) v. **-rised, -rising, -rises.** —tr. To eulogise. —intr. To compose or deliver a panegyric. [From Greek *panēgurizein*; see **panegyric, -ise**.] —**pan·e·gy·rist** (-jírrist, -jirrist ‖ -jír-ist) n.

pan·el (pánn'l) n. **1.** A flat, usually rectangular piece forming a part of a surface in which it is set, and being raised, recessed, or framed. **2.** A distinct section of the body of a motor vehicle. **3.** A vertical section of fabric, as in a skirt; a gore. **4. a.** A thin wooden board, used as a surface for oil painting. **b.** A painting on such a board. **5. a.** A board having switches to control parts of an electrical device. **b.** An **instrument panel** (see). **6. a.** Formerly in Britain, a list of patients entitled to medical treatment through the national health insurance scheme. **b.** A list of doctors available to such patients. **7. a.** The complete list of persons summoned for jury duty. **b.** Those persons selected from the list to compose a jury. **c.** A jury. **8. a.** A group of people gathered to plan or discuss an issue, answer questions, judge a contest, or to act as a team on a radio or television quiz programme. **b.** A discussion by such a group. **9.** Law. In Scotland, a person or persons standing trial.

~tr.v. **panelled** or U.S. **-eled, -elling** or U.S. **-eling, -els. 1.** To cover or furnish with panels. **2.** To decorate with panels. **3.** To separate into panels. **4.** To select or empanel (a jury). [Middle English, from Old French, piece of parchment on which names of a jury were written, from Vulgar Latin *panellus* (unattested), diminutive of Latin *pannus*, rag, cloth.]

panel beater n. One who beats out the panels of dented and crumpled motor-vehicle bodies.

panel heating n. A form of space heating in which heated panels are concealed in walls or ceilings. The panels are heated either by hot-water pipes or by electricity.

pan·el·ing (pánn'l-ing) n. **1.** A section of panels or a panelled wall. **2.** Panels collectively.

pan·el·list (pánn'l-ist) n. A member of a panel, especially a radio or television panel.

panel pin n. A small nail with a narrow head, used mainly for attaching plywood or hardboard panels to a frame.

panel saw n. A small handsaw used for cutting panelling.

pan·et·to·ne (pán-i-tŏ-ni, -e-, -ə-, -nay) n., pl. **-nes** or Italian **-ni** (-nee). An Italian yeast cake, made with candied fruit peels and raisins, and eaten especially at Christmas. [Italian, from *panetto*, diminutive of *pane*, bread, from Latin *panis*.]

pang (pang) n. **1.** A sudden, sharp spasm of pain. **2.** A sudden, sharp feeling of emotional distress. [16th century : variant of earlier *prange*, of Germanic origin; akin to Middle Low German *prange*, a pinching.]

pan·ga (páng-gə) n. A broad-bladed African knife, similar to a machete, used as a tool or weapon. [From an East African name.]

Pan·gae·a (pán-jée-ə) n. Geology. The single supercontinent into

panda *The giant panda, which is native to the mountains of China, feeds mainly on bamboo, but it also eats other plants, as well as small animals. It is very rare, and notoriously hard to breed in captivity.*

which all the world's landmass is thought to have been grouped before it began breaking up about 200 million years ago. [20th century : from Greek, "all earth" : PAN- + *gaia,* earth.]

pan·gen·e·sis (pán-jénni-siss) *n. Biology.* The discredited hypothesis that every somatic cell generates self-representative hereditary materials that enter the bloodstream and eventually coalesce in reproductive cells, making possible the inheritance of hereditary characteristics. [PAN- + -GENESIS.] **—pan·ge·net·ic** (-jə-néttik) *adj.* **—pan·ge·net·i·cal·ly** *adv.*

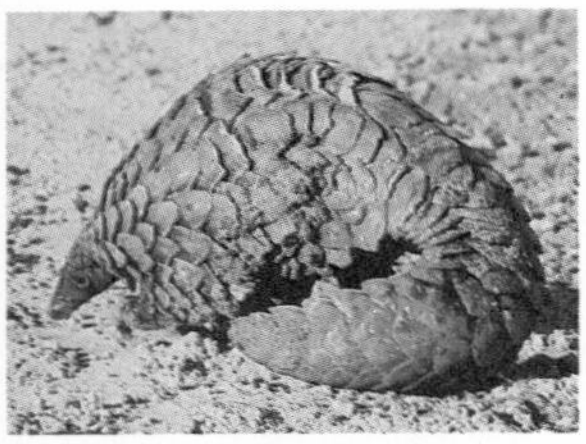

pangolin *There are seven species of this scaly anteater, which is native to Africa and Southeast Asia and which can grow to nearly 2 metres long (6 feet). This is the Cape pangolin. When attacked, pangolins roll themselves into a tight ball.*

Pan-Ger·man·ism (pán-jérməniz'm) *n.* A political movement, prominent especially in the 19th century, advocating the union of all German-speaking peoples. [French *Pangermanisme* (translation of German *Alldeutschtum*) : PAN- + *Germanisme,* Germanism.] **—Pan-Ger·man·ist** *n.*

pan·go·lin (pang-gṓlin, páng-gə-lin) *n.* Any of several long-tailed, scale-covered mammals of the genus *Manis,* of tropical Africa and Asia, having a long snout and a sticky tongue with which it catches and eats ants. Also called "scaly anteater". [Malay *pĕngguling,* from *guling,* to roll (referring to its habit of rolling itself up).]

Pango Pango. See **Pago Pago.**

pan·han·dle[1] (pán-hand'l) *intr.v.* **-dled, -dling, -dles.** *U.S. Informal.* To beg, especially on the streets. [Perhaps back-formation from *panhandler,* person who begs with a pan.] **—pan·han·dler** *n.*

pan·han·dle[2] *n.* **1.** The handle of a pan. **2.** *Often capital* **P.** *Chiefly U.S.* A narrow strip of territory projecting from a larger, broader area to which it belongs in such a way that its borders, as drawn on a map, appear to outline the handle of a pan.

Pan-Hel·len·ic, Pan·hel·len·ic (pán-he-lénnik, -hi-, -leénik) *adj.* Of or pertaining to all Greek peoples or a movement to unify them.

pan·ic (pánnik) *n.* **1.** A sudden, overpowering feeling of terror or anxiety. **2.** An outbreak of such a feeling, often affecting many people at once, usually leading to irrational or foolish behaviour. Also used adjectivally: *panic reactions.* —See Synonyms at **fear.** **—press** or **push the panic button.** *Informal.* To react to an emergency by taking hasty action.
~*v.* **panicked, -icking, -ics.** —*tr.* To affect with panic. —*intr.* To be affected with panic. —See Synonyms at **frighten.** [Originally adjectival, from French *panique,* from Greek *panikos,* of Pan (who would arouse terror in lonely places).] **—pan·ick·y** *adj.*

panic grass *n.* Any of numerous grasses of the genus *Panicum,* many of which are grown for grain and fodder. [Middle English *panyk,* from Latin *pānicum*†.]

pan·i·cle (pánnik'l) *n. Botany.* **1.** A branched raceme in which each branch bears a further raceme. **2.** Loosely, any branched racemose inflorescence. [Latin *pānicula,* diminutive of *pānus,* tuft, from Greek *pēnos,* web.] **—pan·i·cled** *adj.*

pan·ic-strick·en (pánnik-strickən) *adj.* Also **pan·ic-struck** (pánnik-struk). Overcome by panic; terrified.

pa·nic·u·late (pə-níckew-lət, -lit, -layt) *adj.* Also **pa·nic·u·lat·ed** (-laytid). *Botany.* Growing or arranged in a panicle. [New Latin *paniculatus,* from Latin *pānicula,* PANICLE.] **—pa·nic·u·late·ly** *adv.*

Panjabi. Variant of **Punjabi.**

pan·jan·drum (pan-jándrəm) *n.* A pompous and pretentious person who has an exaggerated idea of his own importance. Used humorously, often as a mock title. [From the *Grand Panjandrum,* character in a nonsense story by Samuel Foote (1720–1777), English playwright.]

Pank·hurst (pángk-hurst), **Emmeline Goulden** (1858–1928). British suffragette. Founder of the Women's Social and Political Union (1903) she fought, with violence when she considered it necessary, for women's suffrage. Frequently imprisoned, she went on hunger strikes and was force-fed. Her daughters, Dame Christabel (1880–1958) and Sylvia (1882–1960), supported her, the former becoming leader of the suffragette movement before turning to preaching and the latter becoming a pacifist, socialist, and internationalist.

pan·mix·is (pan-míksiss) *n. Genetics.* Random mating within an interbreeding population. [New Latin, from Greek : PAN- + *mixis,* act of mating.]

pan·nage (pánnij) *n. Archaic.* **1.** Food or pasturage for pigs, especially in a forest. **2.** The right to pasture pigs in a forest or a fee paid to obtain this right. [Middle English, from Old French *pannage, pasnage,* from Medieval Latin *pastionaticum,* from Latin *pastiō* (stem *pastiōn-*), pasture, from *pascere,* to feed.]

panne (pan) *n.* A velvet-like fabric with a flattened pile and a very high lustre. [French, from Old French, fur lining, from Latin *penna, pinna,* feather.]

pan·ni·er (pánni-ər) *n.* **1.** A large wicker basket, especially: **a.** Either of a pair of baskets carried on either side of a pack animal. **b.** A basket carried on a person's back. **2.** A container on the rear of a bicycle or motorcycle, often one of a pair. **3. a.** A framework of wire, bone, or other material formerly used to expand a woman's skirt at the hips. **b.** A part of a skirt or overskirt looped up around the hips so as to reveal the underskirt. [Middle English *panier,* from Old French, from Latin *pānārium,* breadbasket, from *pānis,* bread.] **—pan·ni·ered** *adj.*

pan·ni·kin (pánnikin) *n. British.* A small saucepan or metal cup. [Diminutive of PAN.]

Pan·no·ni·a (pa-nṓni-ə, pə-). An ancient Roman province in central Europe occupying parts of modern Hungary and Yugoslavia.

pa·no·cha (pə-nṓ-chə) *n.* Also **pa·no·che** (-chee). A coarse grade of Mexican sugar. [Mexican Spanish, diminutive of Spanish *pan,* bread, from Latin *pānis.*]

pan·o·ply (pánnəpli) *n., pl.* **-plies.** **1.** The complete arms and armour of a warrior. **2.** Any imposing array that covers or protects. [Greek *panoplia,* full suit of armour : PAN- + *hoplon*†, weapon.]

pan·op·tic (pan-óptik) *adj.* Also **pan·op·ti·cal** (-'l) Showing or seeing every part or aspect in one view. [From Greek *panoptēs,* all-seeing : PAN- + *optos,* visible.]

pan·o·ram·a (pánnə-raámə || -rámmə) *n.* **1.** An unlimited view of all visible objects over a wide area. **2.** A comprehensive picture of a chain of events or a specific subject: *a panorama of ancient history.* **3.** A picture or series of pictures exhibited a part at a time by being unrolled and passed before the spectator, thus representing a continuous scene. [PAN- + Greek *horāma,* sight, from *horān,* to see.] **—pan·o·ram·ic** (-rámmik) *adj.* **—pan·o·ram·i·cal·ly** *adv.*

panoramic sight *n.* An artillery sight that gives a view over a wide area.

pan·pipes (pán-pīps) *pl.n. Sometimes capital* **P.** *Sometimes singular.* A primitive wind instrument consisting of a series of pipes or reeds of graduated length bound together, and played by blowing across the top open ends. Also called "mouth organ", "Pandean pipes" "Pan's pipes", "syrinx". [PAN + PIPE.]

pan·sy (pánzi) *n., pl.* **-sies.** **1.** Any plant of the genus Viola, especially *V. wittrockiana,* the garden pansy, having rounded, velvety petals of various colours. See **wild pansy.** **2.** Deep to strong violet. **3.** *Slang.* A homosexual or very effeminate male. Used derogatorily. [Fanciful formation from French *pensée,* "thought", from the feminine past participle of *penser,* to think.]

pant (pant) *v.* **panted, panting, pants.** —*intr.* **1.** To breathe rapidly in short gasps, as after exertion. **2.** To give off or emit smoke, steam, or the like in loud puffs. **3.** To pulsate rapidly; throb. **4.** To yearn frantically: *"my spirit began to burn and pant"* (R.D. Blackmore). —*tr.* To utter hurriedly or breathlessly.
~*n.* **1.** The act of panting. **2.** A short, laboured breath; a gasp. **3.** A short, loud puff, as of steam from an engine. **4.** A throb; a pulsation. [Middle English *panten,* from Anglo-French *panter,* from Old French *pantaisier,* from Vulgar Latin *phantasiāre* (unattested), to fantasise, have nightmares, gasp with horror, from Latin *phantasia,* an apparition, fantasy, from Greek, from *phantazein,* to make visible, from *phainein,* to show.] **—pant·ing·ly** *adv.*

Pan·ta·gru·el·i·an (pántə-groo-élli-ən) *n.* Characteristic of or appropriate to Rabelais' character Pantagruel, noted for his ebullient, often coarse, humour and huge appetite. **—Pan·ta·gru·el·ism** (-grṓo-ə-liz'm) *n.*

pan·ta·lets, pan·ta·lettes (pántə-léts) *pl.n.* **1.** Long underdrawers, trimmed with ruffles extending below the skirt, worn by women in the mid-19th century. **2.** A pair of frills to be attached to the legs of such underdrawers. [Diminutive of PANTALOON.]

pan·ta·loon (pántə-lṓon || -lṓon) *n.* **1.** *Plural.* **a.** Formerly, men's tight trousers extending from waist to ankle. **b.** *Archaic.* Trousers of any kind. **2.** *Capital* **P.** A character in the commedia dell'arte, portrayed as a foolish old man with slippers and tight trousers. [French *pantalon,* from Italian *pantalone,* originally a nickname for Venetian characters in Italian comedies, from *Pantaleone,* a saint once popular in Venice.]

pan·tech·ni·con (pan-tékni-kən || -kon) *n. British.* **1.** A large van or lorry, especially one used for furniture removals. **2.** *Archaic.* A furniture warehouse. [Originally the name of a 19th-century bazaar in London where artistic things were sold : PAN- + Greek *tekhnikon,* neuter of *tekhnikos,* artistic, from *tekhnē,* art skill.]

pan·the·ism (pán-thee-iz'm, -thi-) *n.* **1.** The doctrine that God is, or is in, everything and that the various forces and workings of nature are modes or manifestations of his existence. **2.** Belief in and worship of all gods. Compare **deism, theism.** **—pan·the·ist** *n.* **—pan·the·is·tic** (-ísstik), **pan·the·is·ti·cal** *adj.*

pan·the·on (pánthi-ən, pan-theé-ən || -on) *n.* **1.** *Capital* **P.** A circular temple in Rome, completed in 25 B.C., and dedicated to all the gods. **2.** Any temple dedicated to all gods. **3.** All the gods of a people. **4.** A public building commemorating and dedicated to the great or revered figures of a nation. **5.** The most eminent figures in the history of a particular field: *the philosophers' pantheon.* [Middle English *Panteon,* the Pantheon, from Latin *Panthēon,* from Greek *pantheion* : PAN- + *theos,* god.]

pan·ther (pánthər) *n.* **1.** The leopard, *Panthera pardus,* especially in its black, unspotted form. **2.** *U.S.* Any of several similar or related animals, such as the puma or jaguar. [Middle English *panter,* from Old French *pantere,* from Latin *panthēra,* from Greek *panthēr*†.]

pant·ies (pántiz) *pl.n. Singular* **pan·tie, pan·ty.** *Informal.* A pair of women's or children's underpants. [From PANTS.]

pan·ti·hose, pan·ty·hose (pánti-hōz) *pl.n. Chiefly U.S. & South African.* A pair of woman's tights. [PANTIES + HOSE.]

pan·tile (pán-tīl) *n.* An S-curved roofing tile, laid so the down curve of one tile overlaps the up curve of the next one. [PAN + TILE (i.e., "dish-tile", from the concave shape).]

pan·ti·soc·ra·cy (pánt-i-sóckrə-si, -ī-) *n.* A utopian society in which everyone is equal and everyone rules. [PANTO- + ISOCRACY.]

pan·to (pántō) *n., pl.* **-tos.** *British Informal.* A pantomime.

panto–, pant– *comb. form.* Indicates all; for example, **pantisocracy, pantomorphic.** [From Greek *pas* (stem *pant-*), all.]

pan·tof·fle, pan·to·fle (pan-tóff'l) *n.* Also **pantoufle** (-tṓof'l). *Archaic.* A slipper. [Middle English *pantufle,* from Old French *pantoufle,* from Old Italian *pantofola,* perhaps from Medieval Greek *pantophellos,* "all cork" (of which medieval slippers were made) : *pas* (stem *pant-*), PAN- + *phellos*†, cork, cork oak.]

pan·to·graph (pánt-ə-graf, -graaf, -ō-) *n.* **1.** An instrument for copy-

PRONUNCIATION KEY

a, trap; aa, father; ai, fair;
ar, star; aw, lawn; ay, play;
b, bb, stab; rubber;
ch, church; ck, ticket;
d, dd, dead; ladder; e, dress;
ee, bee; er, defer; ew, few;
ewr, pure; ə, about;
ər, letter; f, ff, fife; differ;
g, gg, giggle; h, hat; i, kit;
ī, price; īr, fire; j, judge;
k, kick; l, ll, let; 'l, needle;
m, mm, man; n, nn, no;
'n, sudden; ng, thing; o, lot;
ō, no; ŏŏ, foot; ōō, shoe;
oor, poor; ow, cow;
owr, hour; oy, boy;
p, pp, pepper; r, rr, red;
s, ss, sauce; sh, ship;
t, tt, totter; th, thick; th, this;
smooth; u, cut; ur, turn;
v, vv, valve; w, wet; y, yes;
z, zz, zebra; zh, vision;
pleasure

IN FOREIGN WORDS:

aN, oN, Saint-Saëns;
hl, Llanelli; Hluhluwe;
kh, loch; lough; Khaled

STRESS MARK:

ín-sīt, insight; in-sít, incite

pantheon

A PLACE TO HONOUR GODS AND HEROES

Style of a Roman temple and a French memorial

In Imperial Rome, many individual gods had temples dedicated exclusively to them. However, there were a number of pantheons – from the Greek words *pan* for "all" and *theos* for "god" – which were temples for the worship of all the Roman gods. The most famous of these temples, known today simply as the Pantheon, was begun in Rome about 27 B.C. by the statesman and general Marcus Vipsanius Agrippa. He intended it to be a temple in the classical style, but after a fire in the 2nd century A.D. the Emperor Hadrian had it completely rebuilt as the present imposing circular building of elaborate brickwork.

It is noted for its massive dome, the largest Roman dome to survive intact. Until modern times, the Pantheon's dome was the largest in the world, with a diameter of some 43 metres (142 feet). The dome was mostly made of concrete containing pozzolana, a volcanic earth that, when mixed with lime, became waterproof and extremely durable.

The Pantheon was consecrated as a Christian church in A.D. 609. It is now dedicated to Saint Maria Rotunda. With the rise in the belief of one God, the meaning of a pantheon changed. In France, the world's other remaining pantheon – the domed, cruciform Panthéon – was originally designed in 1759 as the church of Sainte-Geneviève in Paris. But it was secularised in the 19th century and is now a civil temple of honour for the nation's heroes and famous men.

THE EYE OF THE PANTHEON *The central "eye", or oculus, in the dome of the Pantheon in Rome is 8 metres (27 feet) in diameter, and allows a shaft of light to stream in.*

ing a picture or diagram to any desired scale, consisting of styluses for tracing and copying, mounted on four jointed rods in the form of a parallelogram with extended sides. **2.** Any similarly linked framework, used as an extensible support or contact, as on the framework that collects current from overhead cables in an electric locomotive. [French *pantographe* : PANTO- + -GRAPH.]

pan·to·mime (pánta-mīm) *n.* **1.** *British.* A kind of musical play performed at Christmas time, usually based on fairy stories, and characterised by topical jokes, extravagant sets, and having specific conventions, especially farcical, deriving from the commedia dell' arte. **2. a.** A genre of theatrical performance invented in Rome in

the reign of Augustus, in which one actor played all the parts in mime, with music and singing in the background. **b.** The actor in this genre. **c.** Any of various revivals or derivatives of this genre. **3.** Acting that consists mostly of gesture. **4.** *Archaic & U.S.* **Mime** *(see).* **5.** *Informal.* A ridiculous or confused situation. ~*v.* **pantomimed, -miming, -mimes.** *Rare.* —*tr.* To represent by mime. —*intr.* To express oneself in mime. [Latin *pantomīmus,* "the complete mime" : PANTO- + *mimos,* MIME.] —**pan·to·mim·ic** (-mímmik), **pan·to·mim·i·cal** *adj.* —**pan·to·mim·ist** (-mīmist) *n.*

pan·to·then·ic acid (pánta-thénnik) *n.* A component of the vitamin B complex, $C_9H_{17}NO_5$, common in liver but found in all living tissue. [Greek *pantothen,* from all sides, from *pan,* all. See **pan-.**]

pan·toum (pan-tōom) *n.* A verse form consisting of quatrains in which the second and fourth lines are repeated as the first and third lines of the following quatrain, and in which the final line of the poem repeats the opening line. [French, from Malay *pantun.*]

pan·try (pántri) *n., pl.* **-tries.** A small room or cupboard, usually off a kitchen, where food, china, and the like are stored. [Middle English *pantrie,* from Old French *paneterie,* bread closet, from *panetier,* servant in charge of the bread, from *pan,* bread, from Latin *pānis.*]

pants (pants) *pl.n.* **1.** A pair of underpants. **2.** *Chiefly U.S.* Trousers. —**the pants off.** *Informal.* Thoroughly. Used in phrases such as *scare the pants off someone.* —**with (one's) pants down.** Unprepared or in an awkward situation. [Short for *pantaloons,* plural of PANTALOON.]

pant·suit (pánt-sewt, -sōot) *n.* Also **pants suit.** *Chiefly U.S.* A trouser suit.

panty. Variant of **pantie.**

pantyhose. Variant of **pantihose.**

Pan·zer (pán-zər; *German* -tsər) *adj.* Of, pertaining to, or designating the fast armoured mechanical units of the German army, especially during World War II: *a Panzer division.* ~*n.* **1.** An armoured tank in a Panzer unit. **2.** *Plural.* Panzer troops. [German *Panzer,* armour, from Middle High German *Panzier,* from Old French *pancier,* body-armour, from *panse,* body, from Vulgar Latin *pantica* (unattested), variant of Latin *pantex,* paunch.]

pap[1] (pap) *n.* **1.** *Archaic & Regional.* A teat or nipple. **2.** Something resembling a nipple. [Middle English *pappe,* from Scandinavian (imitative of sucking).]

pap[2] *n.* **1.** Soft or semiliquid food, as for infants. **2.** Something lacking real value or substance; drivel. [Middle English *pape,* probably from Latin *pappa,* baby talk for food.]

pa·pa (pa-paa ‖ *chiefly U.S.* paapa) *n.* Father. Used, especially formally, by children. [French, from Old French, from Late Latin, from Greek *pap(p)as.*]

pa·pa·cy (páypa-si) *n., pl.* **-cies.** **1.** The office and jurisdiction of a pope. **2.** The period of time during which a pope is in office. **3.** The system of church government headed by the pope. [Middle English *papacie,* from Medieval Latin *pāpātia,* from Late Latin *pāpa,* POPE.]

Pa·pa·do·pou·los (páppa-dóppoo-loss), **Georgios** (1919–). Greek colonel and political leader. He seized power in a military coup (1967), abolished the monarchy (1973), and proclaimed himself president, but was overthrown in a second military coup.

pa·pa·in (pa-páy-in, -pī-) *n.* An enzyme capable of digesting protein, obtained from the unripe fruit of the papaya and used as a meat tenderiser, and in medicine as a protein digestant. [From PAPAYA.]

pa·pal (páyp'l) *adj.* **1.** Of, pertaining to, or issued by the pope: *a papal bull.* **2.** Of or pertaining to the papacy: *papal succession.* **3.** Of or pertaining to the Roman Catholic Church. [Middle English, from Old French, from Medieval Latin *pāpālis,* from Late Latin *pāpa,* POPE.] —**pa·pal·ly** *adv.*

Papal States. Former states of central Italy, under papal sovereignty (756–1870). They were originally given by Pepin the Short to Pope Stephen II and confirmed in this by Charlemagne (774). Varying in size over time owing to political struggles, the papal possessions were reduced after the Austro-Italian war (1859) and in 1870 Italian troops occupied Rome. The papacy did not recognise this loss of power until the **Lateran Treaty** (1929), when the Vatican City was created a separate state.

Pa·pa·ni·co·la·ou's test (páppa-nícka-laa-ōoz) *n.* A **Pap test** *(see).*

pa·pa·raz·zo (páppa-rát-sō) *n., pl.* **-raz·zi** (-see). A reporter or photographer, especially a freelance one, who doggedly searches for sensational stories about, or takes candid pictures of, celebrities for magazines and newspapers. [Italian, probably from French *paperassier,* scribbler, from *paperasse,* scrap paper, from *papier,* paper, from Old French, PAPER.]

pa·pav·er·ine (pa-páyva-rin, -reen ‖ -pávva-) *n.* Also **pa·pav·er·in** (-rin). A nonaddictive opium derivative, $C_{20}H_{21}NO_4$, used medicinally as an antispasmodic to treat such conditions as colic and asthma. [From New Latin *Papaver* (genus name), from Latin *pāpāver,* POPPY.]

pa·paw, paw·paw (páw-paw, pa-páw) *n.* **1.** A papaya. **2.** A tree, *Asimina triloba,* of central North America, having small, fleshy, edible fruit. **3.** The fruit of this tree. Also called "custard apple". [Probably from Spanish *papaya,* PAPAYA.]

pa·pa·ya (pa-pí-a) *n.* **1.** An evergreen tropical American tree, *Carica papaya,* bearing large, yellow, edible fruit. **2.** The fruit of this tree. Also called "papaw". [Spanish, from Cariban.]

Pa·pe·e·te (paa-pi-áyti, pa-páyti, -péeti). Port on the island of Tahiti and capital of French Polynesia. It is now a tourist centre.

Pa·pen (paapən), **Franz von** (1879–1969). German politician. He

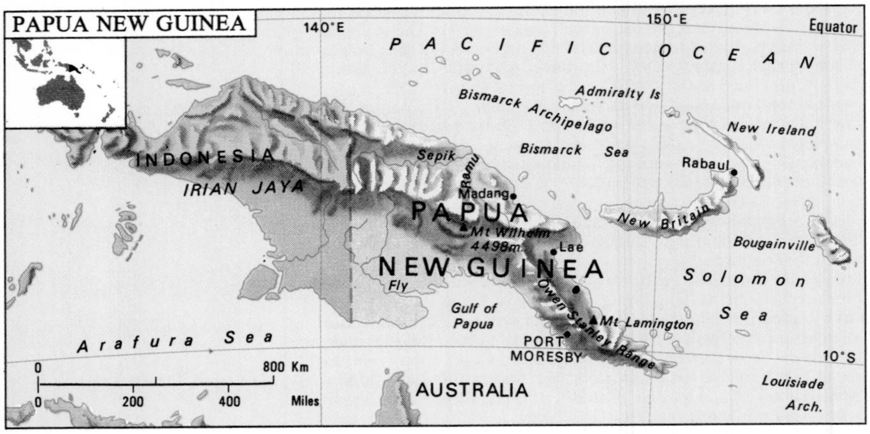

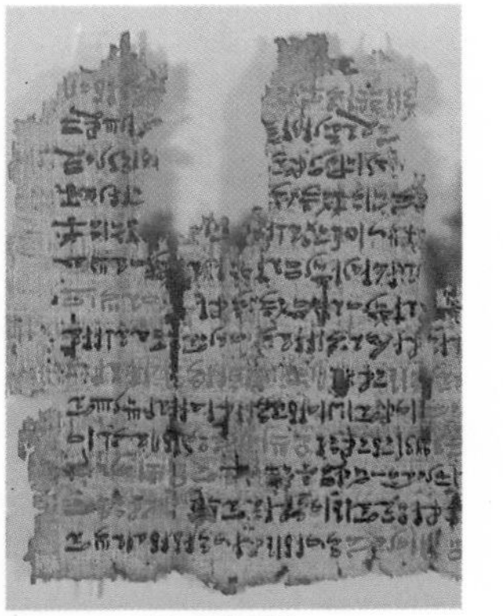

papyrus *About 5,500 years ago, the Egyptians discovered how to make a kind of paper from the papyrus plant, by laying two thin sheets of its pith at right-angles to each other and beating them into a sheet. The starch in the plant's juice formed a natural adhesive. This document on medicine, from the Egyptian Middle Kingdom, was written on papyrus in about 1700* B.C.

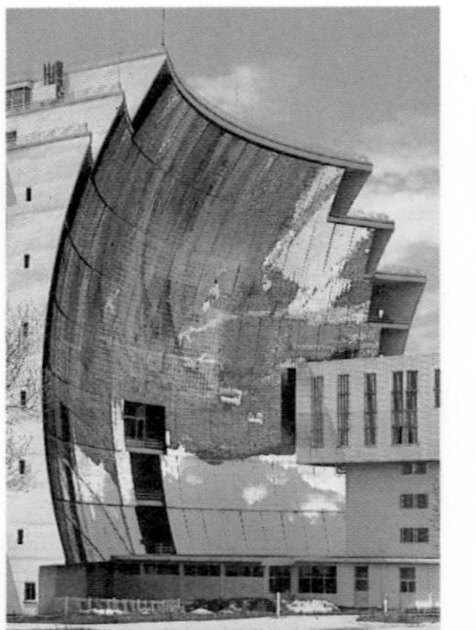

parabola *The reflecting surface of this French solar furnace at Odeillo in the Pyrenees forms a parabola, with the furnace room at its focus. On a hillside opposite, thousands of mirrors can be moved to direct the sun's rays on to the parabola; the pollution-free furnace can reach 3,500°C (6,332°F).*

served Hitler as vice-chancellor (1933–34) and as a diplomat. Although acquitted at the Nuremberg Trials, he was imprisoned for three years to undergo denazification.

pa·per (páypər) *n.* **1.** A thin sheet material made of cellulose pulp, derived mainly from wood, rags, and certain grasses, processed into flexible leaves or rolls by deposit from an aqueous suspension, and used chiefly for writing, printing, drawing, wrapping, and covering walls. **2.** A single sheet or leaf of this material. **3.** One or more sheets of this material, bearing writing or printing, such as: **a.** An official document. **b.** An essay, treatise, or scholarly dissertation. **c.** An examination, report, essay, or similar exercise by a student. **d.** A newspaper. **3.** *Sometimes capital* **P.** In Britain, either of two documents issued by the government discussing potential legislation, a **Green Paper** or **White Paper** *(both of which see).* **4.** *Plural.* A collection of letters, diaries, and other writings, especially those produced by one person. **5.** *Plural.* Documents establishing the identity of the bearer. **6.** *Plural.* **Ship's papers** *(see).* **7.** A negotiable document, such as a cheque or letter of credit. **8.** *Slang.* A free ticket to a theatre. **9.** *Plural.* Cigarette papers. **—on paper. 1.** In writing or print. **2.** In theory, as distinguished from actual performance or fact: *good on paper, but poor in reality.*
~tr.v. **papered, -pering, -pers. 1.** To wrap or cover in paper. **2.** To supply with paper. **3.** To cover with wallpaper. **4.** *Slang.* To fill (a theatre, for example) by issuing free passes: *paper the house.*
~adj. **1.** Made of or in the form of paper: *paper money.* **2.** Resembling paper in thinness or flimsiness. **3.** Existing only in printed or written form; notional; theoretical: *paper profits.* [Middle English *papir,* from Old French *papier,* from Latin *papȳrus,* paper, from Greek *papuros,* PAPYRUS.] **—pa·per·er** *n.* **—pa·per·y** *adj.*

pa·per·back (páypər-bak) *n.* A book or edition having a flexible paper binding and selling relatively cheaply.
~tr.v. **paperbacked, -backing, -backs.** To publish in paperback form. **—pa·per·back** *adj.* **—pa·per·back·er** *n.*

pa·per·board (páypər-bawrd || -bōrd) *n.* Pasteboard.

pa·per·bound (páypər-bownd) *adj.* Bound in paper; paperback.

pa·per·bark tree (páypər-baark) *n.* Any of various Australian trees of the genus *Melaleuca,* having papery bark shed in thin layers.

pa·per·boy (páypər-boy) *n.* A boy who delivers newspapers.

paper chase *n.* A cross-country run in which a trail of paper is left by one or more runners for the rest of the field to follow.

pa·per·clip (páypər-klip) *n.* A clip, usually a piece of bent wire, for holding sheets of paper together.

pa·per·girl (páypər-gurl) *n.* A girl who delivers newspapers.

pa·per·hang·er (páypər-hang-ər) *n.* One whose occupation is decorating walls with wallpaper. **—pa·per·hang·ing** *n.*

pa·per·knife (páypər-nīf) *n., pl.* **-knives** (-nīvz). A thin, blunt knife used for opening sealed envelopes, slitting uncut pages of books, and creasing paper.

pa·per·less (páypər-ləss, -liss) *adj.* Using information technology, as in the form of computers and word processors, to the extent that documentation on paper is not necessary: *a paperless office.*

paper mulberry *n.* A tree, *Broussonetia papyrifera,* native to Asia, having bark that can be processed into a paper-like fabric. See **tapa.**

paper nautilus *n.* A marine cephalopod mollusc of the genus *Argonauta,* having a paper-thin spiral shell. Also called "argonaut".

paper tape *n.* Paper in a long narrow strip with rows of holes punched across it, different combinations of holes representing different characters. It is used in telex machines, computers, and similar devices in which information is represented digitally.

paper tiger *n.* A person, nation, or thing that appears strong, invincible, and threatening but is in fact weak and often ineffectual.

pa·per·weight (páypər-wayt) *n.* A small heavy object, often decorative, placed on top of loose papers to keep them in place.

pa·per·work (páypər-wurk) *n.* Work, such as clerical work, involving the handling of reports, letters, forms, and the like.

pap·e·terie (páppətri || *French* pap-trée) *n.* A box used to hold paper and other writing materials. [French, stationery box, from *papier,* paper, from Old French, PAPER.]

Pa·pia·men·to (páp-yə-méntō) *n.* The Spanish-based creole language of the Netherlands Antilles. [Spanish, from *papia,* talk.]

pa·pi·er-mâ·ché (páppi-ay-máshay, -maáshay || *U.S. also* páypər-, -mə-sháy) *n.* A material made from paper pulp or shreds of paper mixed with glue or paste, that can be moulded into various shapes when wet and that becomes hard and suitable for varnishing when dry. [French, "chewed paper".] **—pa·pier-mâ·ché** *adj.*

pa·pil·la (pə-píllə) *n., pl.* **-pillae** (-píllee). Any small, nipple-like projection, such as a protuberance on the top of the tongue, at the root of a hair, or at the base of a developing tooth. [New Latin, from Latin, nipple, diminutive of *papula,* pimple.] **—pa·pil·lar·y** (pə-píllәri || *U.S.* páppi-lerri) *adj.* **—pa·pil·late** (pə-píl-ayt, páppil-, -ət, -it), **pa·pil·lose** (pə-píl-ōss, páppil-, -ōz) *adj.*

pap·il·lo·ma (páppi-lō-mə) *n., pl.* **-mata** (-mətə) or **-mas.** A small, benign epithelial tumour, usually occurring on the surface of a mucous membrane or the skin, such as a wart or corn. [PAPILL(A) + -OMA.] **—pap·il·lo·ma·tous** *adj.*

pap·il·lon (páppi-lon) *n.* A dog of a small breed with large, forward-facing ears and a long, fine coat that is white with coloured patches. [French, "butterfly" (referring to the appearance of the ears), ultimately from Latin *pāpiliō* (stem *pāpiliōn-*).]

pap·il·lote (páppi-lōt) *n.* **1.** A paper frill used to decorate the bone end of a cooked chop or cutlet. **2.** Greaseproof paper or foil in which some foods are cooked. [French, from *papillon,* butterfly.]

pa·pist (páypist) *n.* A Roman Catholic. Usually used derogatorily. [French *papiste,* from *pape,* POPE.] **—pa·pis·ti·cal** (pay-pístik'l, pə-) *adj.* **—pa·pi·stry** (páypistri) *n.*

pa·poose, pap·poose (pə-pōōss, pa-) *n.* Also **pap·poose.** A North American Indian infant or young child. [Algonquian *papoos.*]

pap·pus (páppəss) *n., pl.* **pappi** (páppī). A tuft of bristles, found on seeds of certain plants, such as dandelions and thistles, that aid dispersal. [Latin, from Greek *pappos,* grandfather, hence pappus.] **—pap·pose** (páppōss), **pap·pous** (páppəss) *adj.*

pap·py[1] (páppi) *adj.* **-pier, -piest.** Of or like pap; mushy; pulpy.

pappy[2] *n., pl.* **-pies.** *U.S. Informal.* Father. [Diminutive of PAPA.]

pa·pri·ka (pápprikə, pə-préekə, pa-) *n.* A mild, powdered seasoning made from sweet red peppers. [Hungarian, from Serbian, from *papar,* pepper, from Greek *peperi,* PEPPER.] **—pap·ri·ka** *adj.*

Pap test (pap) *n.* A test in which a smear of a bodily secretion, especially from the cervix or vagina, is fixed and examined for the presence of abnormal cells to detect cancer in an early stage. Also called "Pap smear", "Papanicolaou's test", "smear test". [Invented by George *Papanicolaou* (1883–1962), U.S. scientist.]

Pap·u·an (páp-oo-ən, paáp-, -yoo-) *n.* **1.** A native or inhabitant of Papua New Guinea. **2.** A member of a subgroup of an Oceanic Negroid people of Melanesia. **3.** Any of numerous languages of Papua New Guinea. **—Pap·u·an** *adj.*

Pa·pu·a New Guinea, State of (páp-oo-ə-, paáp-, -yoo-). Country in the southwest Pacific Ocean. A member of the Commonwealth, it consists of the eastern part of New Guinea, the Bismarck Archipelago, Bougainville, and other islands. Formerly an Australian territory, it gained independence in 1975 and exports copper, coffee, cocoa, timber, and copra. Area, 461 691 square kilometres (178,259 square miles). Population, 3,300,000. Capital, Port Moresby.

pap·ule (páppewl) *n.* Also **pap·u·la** (páppew-lə) *pl.* **-lae** (-lee). A small, inflammatory, congested spot on the skin; a pimple. [Latin *papula,* pimple.] **—pap·u·lar, pap·u·lif·er·ous** (-líffərəss) *adj.*

pap·y·rol·o·gy (páppi-rólləji) *n.* The study of ancient papyri. [From Greek *papuros,* PAPYRUS + -LOGY.] **—pap·y·ro·log·i·cal** (-rə-lójik'l) *adj.* **—pap·y·rol·o·gist** (-rólləjist) *n.*

pa·py·rus (pə-pīr-əss) *n., pl.* **-ri** (-pīr-ī) or **-ruses. 1.** A tall aquatic reedlike plant, *Cyperus papyrus,* of southern Europe and northern Africa. **2.** A kind of paper made from the pith stems of this plant, used by the ancient Egyptians, Greeks, and Romans as a writing material. **3.** A document written on this paper. [Middle English *papirus,* paper, from Latin *papȳrus,* from Greek *papuros*†.]

par (par) *n.* **1.** An accepted average; a normal standard: *up to par.* **2.** An equality of status, level, or value; an equal footing: *on a par.* **3.** *Finance.* **a.** The established face value of a monetary unit expressed in terms of a monetary unit of another country using the same metal standard. **b.** A condition of equality between the face value of a stock, bond, or other negotiable instrument and its current market value: *sell at par.* **4.** In golf, the number of strokes considered necessary to complete a hole or course in expert play.
~adj. **1.** Equal to the standard; normal. Used chiefly in the phrase *par for the course.* **2.** *Finance.* Of or pertaining to face value. [Latin *par,* equal.]

par. **1.** paragraph. **2.** parallel. **3.** parenthesis. **4.** parish.

pa·ra[1] (párrə) *n. Informal.* **1.** A paratrooper. **2.** A paragraph.

pa·ra[2] (paárə) *n.* A monetary unit equal to $^1/_{100}$ of the dinar of Yugoslavia. [Serbo-Croatian, from Turkish, from Persian *parāh,* "piece".]

par·a[3] (párrə) *adj. Chemistry & Physics.* **1.** Of, pertaining to, or designating positions in a benzene ring separated by two carbon atoms. Used in combination: *para-dichlorobenzene.* Also written italic *p-*: *p-dichlorobenzene.* **2.** Of, pertaining, to, or designating a polymer of a chemical compound. Used in combination: *paraformaldehyde.* **3.** Of, pertaining to, or designating a form of a diatomic molecule in which the nuclear spins are antiparallel. Used in combination: *parahydrogen.* Compare **ortho, meta.** [Independent use of PARA- (chemical prefix).]

para–[1], par– *comb. form.* Indicates: **1.** Alongside; for example, **paragenesis. 2.** Near or beside; for example, **parathyroid gland. 3.** Beyond; over and above; for example, **paralinguistics, paranormal. 4.** Incorrect; abnormal; for example, **paraesthesia. 5.** Resembling or similar to; for example, **paramilitary, paratyphoid fever.** **6.** Subsidiary or auxiliary to; for example **paramedical.** **7.** Isomeric to or polymeric to; for example, **paraldehyde.** [In borrowed Greek compounds, *para-* indicates: 1. Beside, to the side of, alongside, as in **paradigm, Paraclete.** 2. Beyond, as in **paradox.** 3. Wrongly, harmfully, unfavourably, as in **paralysis.** 4. Among, as in **parallax.** *Para-* is the preverbal form of the preposition *para,* beside, for.]

para–² *comb. form.* Indicates something that protects or stops; for example, **parachute, parasol.** [French, from Italian, from *parare,* to defend, from Latin *parāre,* to make ready.]

para·a·min·o·ben·zo·ic acid (pârrə-ə-mīnōben-zṓ-ik, -mēenō-) *n.* A naturally occurring compound, $NH_2C_6H_4CO_2H$, used in the preparations of lotions and creams for preventing sunburn.

para·a·min·o·sal·i·cyl·ic acid (pârrə-ə-mīnō-sál-i-síllik, -mēenō-) *n.* *Abbr.* **PAS, PASA** A drug, chemically similar to aspirin, used in the treatment of tuberculosis, usually in combination with isoniazid or streptomycin.

pa·rab·a·sis (pə-rábbə-siss) *n., pl.* **-ses** (-seez). In ancient Greek comedies, an address by the chorus to the audience. [Greek, a stepping forward (to address the audience), from *parabainein,* go forward : PARA- + *bainein,* to go.]

par·a·bi·o·sis (párrə-bī-ṓ-siss) *n. Biology.* The natural or artificial fusion of two organisms, as in the development of Siamese twins or the experimental joining of animals for research.

par·a·blast (párrə-blast) *n.* The food yolk of a meroblastic egg. [PARA- (resembling) + -BLAST.] **—par·a·blas·tic** (-blásstik) *adj.*

par·a·ble (párrəb'l) *n.* A simple story illustrating a moral or religious lesson, especially one told by Jesus in the Gospels. [Middle English, from Old French *parabole,* from Late Latin *parabola,* from Greek *parabolē,* juxtaposition, comparison, parable, from *paraballein,* to set beside : PARA- *para,* beside + *ballein,* to throw.]

pa·rab·o·la (pə-rábbələ) *n. Geometry.* A plane curve formed by the locus of points equidistant from a fixed line and a fixed point not on the line. It is a conic section with an eccentricity of 1, formed by a plane intersecting a conical surface parallel to the axis of the cone. [New Latin, from Greek *parabolē,* juxtaposition, parallelism (see **parable**); referring to the parallelism of the plane section containing the parabola and an element in the conical surface.]

par·a·bol·ic (párrə-bóllik) *adj.* Also **par·a·bol·i·cal** (-'l). **1.** Of or like a parable. **2.** Of or having the form of a parabola. **3.** Of or having the form of a paraboloid; generated by a parabola: *a parabolic antenna.* **—par·a·bol·i·cal·ly** *adv.*

pa·rab·o·loid (pə-rábbə-loyd) *n. Geometry.* A surface having sections that are parabolas; especially, one in which the sections parallel to two coordinate axes are parabolas, the sections parallel to the other axis being either an ellipse or circle (an *elliptic paraboloid*), or a hyperbola (a *hyperbolic paraboloid*). [PARABOL(A) + -OID.] **—pa·rab·o·loi·dal** (-lóyd'l) *adj.*

paraboloid of revolution *n. Geometry.* An elliptic paraboloid formed by revolving a parabola about its own axis.

Par·a·cel·sus (párrə-sél-səss), **Phipippus Aureolus,** born Theophrastus Bombastus von Hohenheim (*c.* 1493–1541). Swiss physician. He improved pharmacy, encouraged scientific experiments, and generally revolutionised European medicine.

pa·ra·ce·ta·mol (párrə-séetə-mol, -séttə-) *n.* A drug that relieves pain and reduces fever, commonly used as an alternative to aspirin. [From *para-acetylaminophenol.*]

pa·rach·ro·nism (pə-ráckrə-niz'm) *n.* An error made in a chronology, especially by giving too late a date. Compare **prochronism.** [PARA- (incorrect) + Greek *khronos,* time + -ISM, perhaps by analogy with *anachronism.*]

par·a·chute (párrə-shōōt) *n.* **1.** An apparatus used to retard free fall from an aircraft, consisting of a canopy attached by cords to a harness and worn or stored folded until deployed in descent. **2.** Any of various similar unpowered devices for retarding free-speeding or free-falling motion, as for example on some jets. **3.** A membranous, winglike extension between the limbs of flying squirrels and certain lizards; a patagium.
~*v.* **parachuted, -chuting, -chutes.** —*tr.* To drop (supplies, for example) by means of a parachute. —*intr.* To descend by means of a parachute. [French PARA- (protecting) + *chute,* fall, CHUTE.]
—par·a·chut·ist *n.*

Par·a·clete (párrə-kleet) *n.* **1.** The Holy Ghost as an advocate or counsellor. **2.** *Small* **p.** An advocate. [Middle English *Paraclit,* from Old French *Paraclet,* from Late Latin *Paraclētus,* from Greek *Paraklētos,* "the Comforter", advocate, "one called to help", from *parakalein,* to call to help : PARA- (alongside) + *kalein,* to call.]

pa·rade (pə-ráyd) *n.* **1. a.** A public procession on some festive or ceremonial occasion. **b.** The occasion or action of making such a procession. **c.** The event itself, or the persons involved: *the Easter parade.* **2. a.** A ceremonial inspection of troops. **b.** The troops taking part in such an inspection. **c.** The place of assembly for an inspection of troops. Also called "parade ground". **3.** A continuous succession, as of persons or things on display or being reviewed: *a parade of fashions.* **4.** In fencing, a parry. **5.** An ostentatious show; a pompous display: *make a parade of humanitarian zeal.* **6.** A public square or a promenade. **—on parade. 1.** Being displayed or reviewed. **2.** Behaving ostentatiously.
~*v.* **paraded, -rading, -rades.** —*tr.* **1.** *Military.* **a.** To assemble (troops) for a formal display or inspection. **b.** To cause (troops, for example) to go on a ceremonial march. **2.** To march or walk through or around. **3.** To exhibit ostentatiously; flaunt. —*intr.* **1.** *Military.* To assemble for a formal inspection. **2.** To take part in a parade. **3.** To promenade in a public place. Used with *through* or *along.* —See Synonyms at **show.** [French, from Italian *parata,* from Vulgar Latin *parāta* (unattested), "a making ready", from Latin *parāre,* to prepare.] **—pa·rad·er** *n.*

par·a·digm (párrə-dīm || -dim) *n.* **1.** A list of all the inflectional forms of a word taken as an illustrative example of the conjugation or declension to which it belongs. **2.** Any example or model used as a standard. **3.** In the philosophy of science, the prevailing scientific framework of theories and concepts within which a scientist works. [Late Latin *paradīgma,* from Greek *paradeigma,* model, from *paradeiknunai,* to compare, exhibit : PARA-, (alongside) + *deiknunai,* to show.] **—par·a·dig·mat·ic** (-dig-máttik, -dīg-) *adj.*

par·a·dise (párrə-dīss || *U.S. also* -dīz) *n.* **1.** *Often capital* **P.** The Garden of Eden. **2.** *Theology.* **a.** Heaven, the abode of righteous souls after death. **b.** An intermediate resting place for righteous souls awaiting the Resurrection. **3.** The Muslim heaven, regarded as a garden of sensual delights and pleasures. **4.** Any place of ideal beauty or loveliness. **5.** A state of delight. [Middle English *paradis,* from Old French, from Late Latin *paradīsus,* from Greek *paradeisos,* garden, park, paradise, from Avestan *pairi-daēza,* circumvallation, walled-in park : *pairi,* around + *daēza,* wall.] **—par·a·di·si·a·cal** (párrədi-sī-ik'l, -zī-), **par·a·di·sa·i·cal** (-sáy-ik'l, -záy-) *adj.* **—par·a·di·si·a·cal·ly, par·a·di·sa·i·cal·ly** *adv.*

par·a·dos (párrə-doss) *n.* A bank of earth, especially one backing a trench, that gives protection from the rear. [French : PARA- (protect) + *dos,* back, from Latin *dorsum.*]

par·a·dox (párrə-doks) *n., pl.* **-doxes. 1. a.** A seemingly absurd, contradictory statement that may nonetheless be true. **b.** A self-contradictory statement such as *I'm telling you the truth when I say I'm a liar.* **2.** A person, situation, or action exhibiting inexplicable or contradictory aspects. **3.** An assertion that is essentially self-contradictory, although perhaps based on a valid deduction from acceptable premises. **4.** A statement contrary to received opinion. [Latin *paradoxum,* from Greek *paradoxon,* from *paradoxos,* incredible, conflicting with expectation : PARA- (beyond) + *doxa,* opinion, from *dokein,* to think.] **—par·a·dox·i·cal** (-dóksik'l) *adj.* **—par·a·dox·i·cal·ly** *adv.* **—par·a·dox·i·cal·ness** *n.*

paradoxical sleep *n.* A stage of sleep characterised by **rapid eye movement** *(see)* and increased electrical activity of the brain. Compare **orthodox sleep.**

par·a·drop (párrə-drop) *n. Military.* The delivery of supplies or personnel to a place by parachute.
~*tr.v.* **paradropped, -dropping, -drops.** To deliver (something) by parachute. [PARA(CHUTE) + DROP.]

par·aes·the·sia (párress-théezi-ə) *n.* An abnormal sensation of prickling, tingling, or itching of the skin. [Latin, from Greek : PARA- (incorrect) + *aisthēsia,* from *aisthēsis,* sensation.] **—par·aes·thet·ic** (-théttik) *adj.*

par·af·fin (párrə-fin, -fèen, -fín, -féen) *n.* **1.** A liquid mixture of hydrocarbons obtained from petroleum and boiling in the range 150–300°C, used as a heating fuel and as a fuel for aircraft. Also called "paraffin oil", "kerosene". **2.** See **paraffin wax. 3.** See **liquid paraffin. 4.** A type of hydrocarbon, an **alkane** *(see).* Not in current technical usage.
~*tr.v.* **paraffined, -fining, -fins.** To saturate, impregnate, or coat with paraffin. [19th century : German, from Latin *parum,* (too) little + *affinis,* related, referring to its chemical inertia and lack of affinity to other substances.] **—par·af·fin·ic** (-fínnik) *adj.*
Usage: The term *kerosene* is used in the United States. In Britain, *paraffin* is used for the domestic fuel for portable heaters; *kerosene* is used in certain industrial contexts, and in particular for the fuel for jet aircraft.

paraffin wax *n.* A white or colourless waxy solid mixture of hydrocarbons obtained from petroleum and used to make candles, wax paper, lubricants, and sealing materials.

par·a·form·al·de·hyde (párrəfawr-mál-di-hīd) *n.* A white solid polymer of formaldehyde, $(HCHO)_n$, where *n* is at least 6, used as a disinfectant, a fumigant, and a fungicide. Also called "paraform".

par·a·gen·e·sis (párrə-jénni-siss) *n.* Also **par·a·ge·ne·sia** (-ji-néezi-ə). *Geology.* The successive order in which a formation of associated minerals is generated. [PARA- (alongside) + -GENESIS.] **—par·a·ge·netic** (-ji-néttik) *adj.*

par·a·go·ge (párrə-gṓji) *n.* Also **par·a·gogue** (-gog). The addition of a sound or syllable to the end of a word; for example, the addition of *-st* to *again* to make *against.* [Late Latin, from Greek *paragōgē,* alteration, derivation, from *paragein,* lead past, change : PARA- (beyond) + *agein,* to lead.] **—par·a·gog·ic** (-gójik) *adj.*

par·a·gon (párrə-gən || -gon) *n.* **1.** A model or pattern of excellence or perfection of a kind; a peerless example: *paragon of virtue.* **2. a.** An unflawed diamond weighing at least 100 carats. **b.** A very large spherical pearl. **3.** *Printing.* A type size of 20 points.
~*tr.v.* **paragoned, -goning, -gons.** *Archaic.* **1.** To compare. **2.** To match; equal. [Obsolete French, from Italian *paragone,* comparison, touchstone, from Medieval Greek *parakonē,* whetstone, from Greek *parakonan,* to sharpen against, to compare : *para,* alongside + *akonan,* to sharpen, from *akonē,* whetstone, from *akē,* point.]

par·a·graph (párrə-graaf, -graf) *n. Abbr.* **par., para. 1.** A distinct division of a written work or composition that expresses some thought or point relevant to the whole but is complete in itself and usually marked by beginning on a separate, indented line. **2.** A mark (¶) used to indicate where a new paragraph should begin or to serve as a reference mark. **3.** A brief article, notice, or announcement, as in a newspaper.

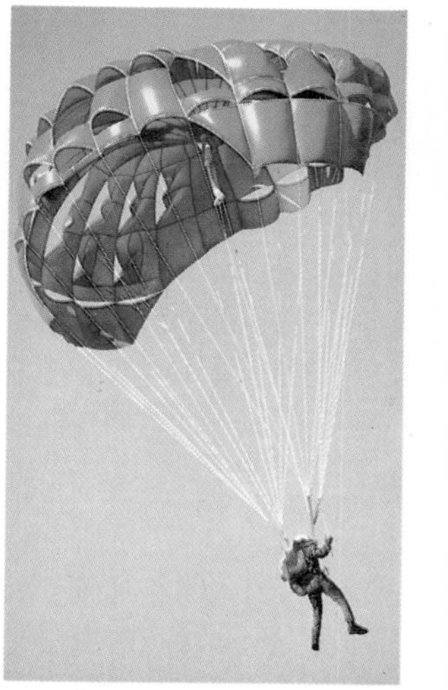

parachute *The earliest parachute – a large canvas umbrella stiffened with ribs – was used by a Frenchman, Louis Lenormand, in 1783. Modern parachutes are generally of synthetic material, and sporting versions, such as the one shown here, have vents which allow them to be steered.*

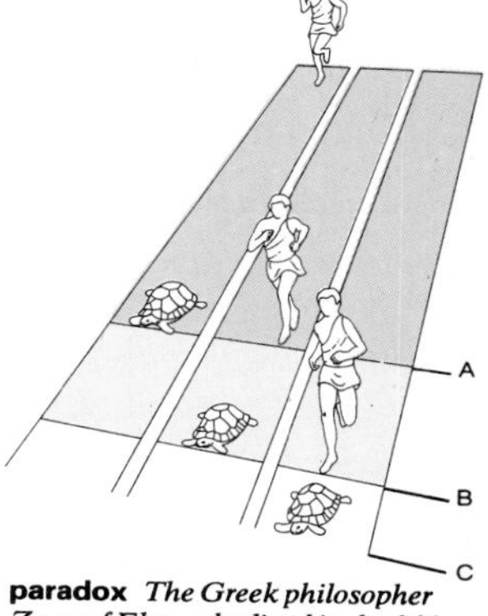

paradox *The Greek philosopher Zeno of Elea, who lived in the fifth century* B.C.*, devised a number of mathematical paradoxes, of which the most celebrated is that of Achilles and the tortoise. If Achilles runs ten times as fast as the tortoise and the tortoise has a 100-metre start, the tortoise will have moved 10 metres by the time Achilles reaches its original position (A). But by the time Achilles reaches B, the tortoise will have moved another metre to C, and by the time he reaches C it will have moved another tenth of a metre, and so on. To catch the tortoise, the number of metres Achilles must travel is 100 + 10 + 1 +* $\frac{1}{10}$ *+* $\frac{1}{100}$ *+ . . . Since this series is open-ended, the paradox comes to the absurd conclusion that Achilles will never overtake the tortoise; always, during the time it takes him to reach its last position, the tortoise has edged a little forward. Only in the 19th century, after calculus was developed, were mathematicians able to resolve the paradox and prove that Achilles did catch up.*

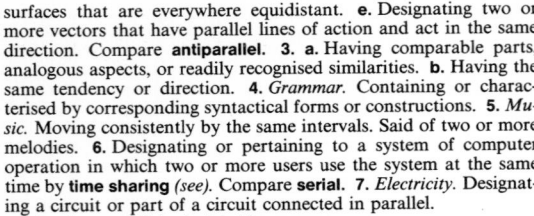

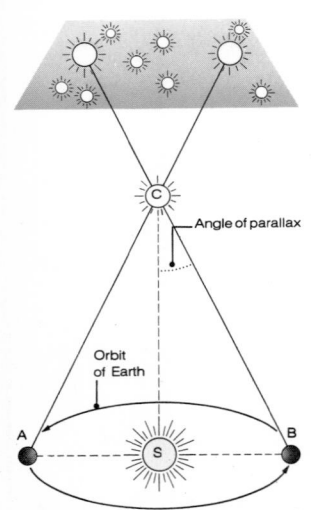

parallax *Up to a distance of about 100 light years, the visual phenomenon of parallax can be used to calculate the distance from Earth of stars. From opposite points A and B on the Earth's orbit around the Sun, the relative position of star C is measured against the background of more distant stars. The greater the shift in background, the greater the angle of parallax, and the closer the star is to the Earth.*

~*tr.v.* **paragraphed, -graphing, -graphs.** *Abbr.* **par. 1.** To divide or arrange in paragraphs. **2.** To express or put in a paragraph. [Medieval Latin *paragraphus,* sign marking a new section of writing, from Greek *paragraphos,* line to mark exchange in dialogue, from *paragraphein,* to write beside : PARA- (beside) + *graphein,* to write.] —**par·a·graph·ic** (-gráffik), **par·a·graph·i·cal** *adj.*

par·a·graph·i·a (párrə-graf-i-ə, -graaf-) *n. Psychiatry.* The writing of words or letters other than those intended or an inability to express ideas in writing, often resulting from certain disorders of the brain. [New Latin : PARA- (abnormal) + *-graphia,* "writing"; see -**graph.**]

Par·a·guay, Republic of (párrə-gwī, -gwī ‖ *chiefly U.S.* -gway). *Spanish.* **República del Paraguay.** Landlocked South American country. It is divided by the river Paraguay, with fertile lowlands and hills to the east, and the infertile Gran Chaco region to the west. The eastern more populous area produces cattle, oilseeds, sugar cane, and cotton. Area, 406 752 square kilometres (157,048 square miles). Population, 3,300,000. Capital, Asunción. —**Par·a·guay·an** (-gwī-ən ‖ -gwáy-) *adj. & n.*

Paraguay, River. South American river, 2 550 kilometres (1,585 miles) long. Rising in the Mato Grosso of Brazil, it flows south through Paraguay, joining the Paraná at the Argentine border.

Paraguay tea *n.* A tree, **maté** *(see),* or the beverage made from its leaves.

par·a·hy·dro·gen (párrə-hídrəjən) *n.* A form of hydrogen in which the two nuclei in each molecule have antiparallel spins; one of two possible forms of hydrogen, constituting 25 per cent of the gas at room temperature. Compare **orthohydrogen.**

par·a·keet, par·ra·keet (párrə-keet, -keet) *n.* Also **par·a·quet** (-ket). Any of various small parrots, usually having long, tapering tails and a predominantly green plumage. [Old French *paroquet,* perhaps a pet form of *Pierre,* from Latin *Petrus,* (the name, Peter).]

par·al·de·hyde (pə-rál-di-hīd, pa-) *n.* A colourless aromatic liquid polymer, $C_6H_{12}O_3$, of acetaldehyde, used as a solvent and as a sedative. [PAR(A) + (ACET)ALDEHYDE.]

par·a·lin·guis·tic (párrə-ling-gwístik) *adj.* Of or pertaining to nonlinguistic features of verbal communication such as gestures or intonation.

par·a·lin·guis·tics (párrə-ling-gwístiks) *n. Used with a singular verb.* The study of the paralinguistic features of verbal communication.

par·a·li·pom·e·na (párrə-lī-pómminə, -li-) *pl.n.* The books of Chronicles in the Douay Bible. [Middle English, from Late Latin, from Greek, "things omitted" (that is, not covered in Kings), from *paraleipein,* to omit: PARA- (to one side) + *leipein,* to leave.]

par·a·lip·sis, par·a·leip·sis (párrə-líp-siss) *n., pl.* **-ses.** A rhetorical device used to emphasise a statement by first saying that one will not speak of the subject in question and then speaking of it, for example, *to say nothing of her former accomplishments, which include winning the championship and 3 medals.* [Late Latin, from Greek, "a leaving aside", from *paraleipein.* See **paralipomena.**]

par·al·lax (párrə-laks) *n.* **1.** An apparent change in the position of an object when the observer changes position. **2.** *Astronomy.* **a.** Change in the observed position of a star or other celestial body resulting from motion of the earth. **b.** A measure of this effect; the angle subtended at the body by a line joining two extreme positions of observation. **c.** The distance of a celestial body as determined in this way. See **diurnal parallax, annual parallax, secular parallax.** [French *parallaxe,* from New Latin *parallaxis,* from Greek, change, from *parallassein,* to change, alternate : PARA- + *allassein,* to change, exchange, from *allos,* other.] —**par·al·lac·tic** (-láktik) *adj.*

par·al·lel (párrə-lel) *adj. Abbr.* **par. 1.** Being an equal distance apart at every point. **2.** *Geometry.* **a.** Designating two or more equidistant coplanar lines that do not intersect. Compare **skew. b.** Designating two or more planes that do not intersect. **c.** Designating a line and a plane that do not intersect. **d.** Designating curves or surfaces that are everywhere equidistant. **e.** Designating two or more vectors that have parallel lines of action and act in the same direction. Compare **antiparallel. 3. a.** Having comparable parts, analogous aspects, or readily recognised similarities. **b.** Having the same tendency or direction. **4.** *Grammar.* Containing or characterised by corresponding syntactical forms or constructions. **5.** *Music.* Moving consistently by the same intervals. Said of two or more melodies. **6.** Designating or pertaining to a system of computer operation in which two or more users use the system at the same time by **time sharing** *(see).* Compare **serial. 7.** *Electricity.* Designating a circuit or part of a circuit connected in parallel.

~*adv.* In a parallel relationship or manner.

~*n. Abbr.* **par. 1.** A surface or line that is equidistant from another. **2.** *Geometry.* One of a set of parallel geometric figures, usually lines. **3. a.** Anything that closely resembles or is analogous to something else. **b.** A comparison indicating likeness or analogy. **4.** The condition of being parallel; near similarity or exact agreement in particulars. **5.** *Geography.* Any of the imaginary lines joining places of equal latitude, encircling the earth parallel to the equator. **6.** *Printing.* A sign (‖), usually indicating material referred to in a note or reference. **7.** *Electricity.* A configuration of two or more two-terminal components connected between two points in a circuit with one terminal of each connected to each of the two points. Used chiefly in the phrase *in parallel.* See **series circuit.**

~*tr.v.* **parallelled** or *U.S.* **-leled, -lelling** or *U.S.* **-leling, -lels. 1.** To make or place parallel to. **2.** To be or extend parallel to. **3.** To be similar or analogous to. **4.** To be or provide an equal or match for. **5.** To show to be analogous; compare or liken. [Latin *parallēlus,* from Greek *parallēlos : para,* beside + *allēlōn,* of one another, from *allos,* other.]

parallel bars *pl.n.* A gymnastic apparatus, consisting of two horizontal bars supported on posts, often at different heights.

par·al·lel·e·pi·ped, par·al·lel·o·pi·ped (párrə-léllə-pī-ped, -le-léppi-, -pid) *n. Geometry.* A solid with six faces, each a parallelogram, having opposite pairs of faces congruent. [Greek *parallēlepipedon : parallēlos,* PARALLEL + *epipedon,* plane surface, from *epipedos,* level : *epi,* on + *pedon,* ground.]

par·al·lel·ism (párrə-lel-iz'm) *n.* **1.** The state or position of being parallel; a parallel relationship. **2.** Likeness, correspondence, or similarity in aspect, course, or tendency. **3. a.** The use of corresponding syntactical forms or literary devices. **b.** An instance of this. **4.** *Philosophy.* The doctrine that to every mental change there corresponds a concomitant, but causally unconnected, physical alteration.

par·al·lel·o·gram (párrə-léllə-gram) *n.* A four-sided plane figure with both pairs of opposite sides parallel. [Late Latin *parallēlogrammum,* from Greek *parallēlogrammon,* from *parallēlogrammos,* bounded by parallel lines : *parallēlos,* PARALLEL + *grammē,* line.]

parallelogram rule *n. Mathematics & Physics.* A rule for adding two vectors or vector quantities, such as forces or velocities, by forming a parallelogram in which two adjacent sides represent the vectors; their resultant is then indicated by the diagonal of the parallelogram through the point of intersection of the vectors.

parallel turn *n.* In skiing, a turn executed by shifting and dropping one's weight, keeping both skis parallel.

pa·ral·o·gism (pə-rál-ə-jiz'm) *n. Logic.* Fallacious or illogical reasoning; especially, a faulty argument of whose fallacy the reasoner is not aware. [French *paralogisme,* from Late Latin *paralogismus,* from Greek *paralogismos,* from *paralogos,* unexpected, beyond calculation : PARA- + *logos,* word.] —**pa·ral·o·gist** *n.* —**pa·ral·o·gis·tic** (-jistik) *adj.*

par·a·lyse, *U.S.* **par·a·lyze** (párrə-līz) *tr.v.* **-lysed, -lysing, -lyses. 1.** To affect with paralysis; cause to be paralytic. **2.** To make helpless or unable to move, as through emotion or fear. **3.** To impair the progress or functioning of; make inoperative or powerless. [From French *paralyser,* from *paralysie,* paralysis.] —**par·a·ly·sa·tion** (-záysh'n) *n.* —**par·a·lys·er** *n.*

pa·ral·y·sis (pə-rál-ə-siss) *n., pl.* **-ses** (-seez). **1.** Loss or impairment of the ability to move or have sensation in a bodily part as a result of injury to or disease of its muscles or nerve supply. **2.** Partial or complete inability to move or function; stoppage or impairment of activity. [Latin, from Greek *paralusis,* from *paraluein,* to loosen, disable : *para,* "unfavourably" + *luein,* to release.]

paralysis ag·i·tans (ájitanz) *n.* **Parkinson's disease** *(see).* [New Latin, "shaking palsy".]

par·a·lyt·ic (párrə-littik) *adj.* **1.** Affected with paralysis; paralysed. **2.** Of or pertaining to paralysis. **3.** *British Slang.* Very drunk.

~*n.* A person suffering from paralysis. [Middle English, from Old French *paralytique,* from Latin *paralyticus,* from Greek *paralutikos,* from *paralusis,* PARALYSIS.] —**par·a·lyt·i·cal·ly** *adv.*

par·a·mag·net (párrə-magnit) *n.* A paramagnetic substance.

par·a·mag·net·ism (párrə-mág-nit-iz'm, -nət) *n. Physics.* A type of magnetism occurring in substances with a positive magnetic susceptibility. It is caused by unpaired electron orbitals in the atoms which result in each atom having a dipole moment. An applied magnetic field tends to align these dipoles in such a way that for small fields and high temperatures the induced field is proportional to the applied field. Below the Curie point certain paramagnetic materials exhibit ferromagnetism. —**par·a·mag·net·ic** (-mag-néttik) *adj.* —**par·a·mag·net·ical·ly** *adv.*

Par·a·mar·i·bo (párrə-márri-bō). Capital and port of Surinam. It was founded by the French (1540), settled by the British (1630) and later taken over by the Dutch. Exports include bauxite and coffee.

paramatta. Variant of **parramatta.**

par·a·me·ci·um (párrə-meési-əm || -shi-) *n., pl.* **-cia** (-si-ə) or **-ums.** Any of various ciliate protozoans of the genus *Paramecium,* usually oval and having an oral groove for feeding. [New Latin, from Greek *paramēkēs,* oblong : PARA, (alongside) + *mēkos,* length.]

par·a·med·i·cal (párrə-méddik'l) *adj.* Of or designating auxiliary medical personnel, such as radiographers, laboratory technicians, and physiotherapists, or their work.

par·a·ment (párrəmənt) *n., pl.* **-ments** or **paramenta** (párrə-méntə). An ecclesiastical vestment or hanging. [Middle English, from Medieval Latin *parāmentum,* from *parāre,* to decorate, prepare.]

pa·ram·e·ter (pə-rámmitər) *n.* **1.** A variable or an arbitrary constant appearing in a mathematical expression, each value of which restricts or determines the specific form of the expression. **2.** *Usually plural. Informal.* Loosely: **a.** A fixed constraint or boundary: *keep within the parameters of our budget.* **b.** A characteristic and defining feature; a touchstone: *one of the parameters of democracy.* [New Latin : PARA- (alongside) + -METER.] **—par·a·met·ric** (párrə-méttrik) *adj.* **—par·a·met·ri·cal·ly** *adv.*

Usage: Using *parameter* in its fairly recent nonmathematical sense ("any defining or limiting factor") has attracted criticism on the grounds that it sounds pretentious. In general it is better to use one of the older, simpler words, such as *limit* or *constraint.*

par·a·mil·i·tar·y (párrə-mílli-təri, -tri || *U.S.* -terri) *adj.* **1.** Designating a group of people organised on a military pattern, especially as an auxiliary military force. **2.** Of or pertaining to such forces.

par·am·ne·si·a (párram-neézi-ə) *n. Psychology.* A distortion of memory in which fantasy and experience are confused. [PAR(A)- (resembling) + AMNESIA.]

pa·ra·mo (párrə-mō) *n., pl.* **-mos.** A high, treeless plain of tropical South America. [American Spanish, from Spanish *paramo*†, a wasteland.]

par·a·morph (párrə-mawrf) *n.* A mineral crystal formed or affected by paramorphism. [PARA- (subsidiary to) + -MORPH.]

par·a·mor·phism (párrə-mórf-iz'm) *n.* Structural alteration of a mineral without change of chemical composition. Also called "metastasis". **—par·a·mor·phic, par·a·mor·phous** *adj.*

par·a·mount (párrə-mownt) *adj.* **1.** Of chief concern or significance; primary; foremost: *of paramount importance.* **2.** Supreme in rank, power, or authority. —See Synonyms at **dominant.**

~*n. Rare.* A person of the highest power or authority; a supreme ruler. [Anglo-French *paramont,* "superior" (used of feudal overlordship) : Old French *par,* by, from Latin *per* + *amont,* above : *a,* to, from Latin *ad* + *mont,* mountain, from Latin *mōns* (stem *mont-*).] **—par·a·mount·cy** (-si) *n.* **—par·a·mount·ly** *adv.*

par·a·mour (párrə-moor) *n.* **1.** A lover, of either sex; especially, the lover of someone who is married. **2.** *Archaic.* A sweetheart. [Middle English, originally an adverb, "by way of love", from Old French *par amour* : *par,* by, from Latin *per* + *amour,* love, from Latin *amor,* from *amāre,* to love.]

Pa·ra·ná (párra-naá). Second-largest river in South America. Formed by the confluence of the rivers Grande and Paranaíba in southeast Brazil, it flows southwest for 2 900 kilometres (1,800 miles) through Paraguay, to join the river Uruguay at the Plata Estuary. It is important for navigation.

pa·rang (paá-rang) *n.* A short, heavy, straight-edged knife used in Malaysia and Indonesia as a tool and weapon. [Malay.]

par·a·noi·a (párrə-nóy-ə) *n.* **1.** A nondegenerative, limited, usually chronic psychosis characterised by delusions of persecution or of grandeur, defended by the afflicted with apparent logic and reason. **2.** Loosely, unwarranted fear or distrust of people or situations. [New Latin, from Greek, madness, from *paranoos,* demented : PARA- (beyond) + *nous,* mind.] **—par·a·noi·ac** (-ak) *adj. & n.*

par·a·noid (párrə-noyd) *adj.* **1.** Pertaining to, characteristic of, or suffering from paranoia: *a paranoid delusion.* **2.** Suggestive of paranoia; showing unreasonable distrust, suspicion, or an exaggerated sense of one's own importance.

~*n.* One afflicted with paranoia.

paranoid schizophrenia *n.* A type of schizophrenia resembling paranoia and characterised chiefly by delusions and hallucinations.

par·a·nor·mal (párrə-nórm'l) *adj.* Not within the range of normal experience or scientifically explainable phenomena. **—par·a·nor·mal·ly** *adv.*

par·an·thro·pus (pa-ránthrəpəss) *n., pl.* **-puses.** An extinct anthropoid ape of the genus *Paranthropus* (later renamed as a species of *Australopithecus),* known from remains found in South Africa. [New Latin : PAR(A)- (resembling) + Greek *anthrōpos,* man.]

par·a·pet (párrə-pit, -pet) *n.* **1.** A low, protective wall or railing along the edge of a roof, balcony, or similar structure. **2.** An earth or stone embankment protecting soldiers from enemy fire. —See Synonyms at **bulwark.** [French, from Italian *parapetto,* chest-high wall : PARA- (protecting) + *petto,* chest, from Latin *pectus.*] **—par·a·pet·ed** (párrə-pettid) *adj.*

par·aph (párrəf, pə-ráf) *n.* A flourish made after or below a signature, originally to prevent forgery. [French *parafe, paraphe,* from Old French *paraffe,* from Medieval Latin *paraphus,* from *paragraphus,* PARAGRAPH.]

par·a·pher·na·lia (párrəfər-náyli-ə) *n. Sometimes used with a plural verb.* **1.** Personal belongings. **2.** The articles used in some activity; equipment; gear: *drug paraphenalia.* **3.** Formerly, a married woman's personal property exclusive of her dowry. **4.** The accompanying problems or procedures involved in any project: *all the paraphernalia of moving.* [Medieval Latin *paraphernālia* (in sense 3), from Greek *parapherna* : PARA- (beyond) + *phernē,* dowry.]

par·a·phrase (párrə-frayz) *n.* **1.** A restatement of a text or passage in another form or other words, often to clarify meaning. **2.** The making of paraphrases, often used as a teaching device.

~*v.* **paraphrased, -phrasing, -phrases.** *—tr.* To express in a paraphrase. *—intr.* To compose a paraphrase. [French, from Latin *paraphrasis,* from Greek, from *paraphrazein,* to paraphrase : PARA- (alongside) + *phrazein,* to show.] **—par·a·phras·tic** (-frástik) *adj.*

pa·raph·y·sis (pə-ráffə-siss) *n., pl.* **-ses** (-seez). Any of the sterile filaments found among the sexual organs of certain fungi, algae, and mosses. [PARA- (subsidiary to) + Greek *phusis,* nature.]

par·a·ple·gia (párrə-pleéjə, -pleéji-ə) *n.* Complete paralysis of the lower body, including both legs, caused by injury to or disease of the spinal cord. [New Latin, from Greek *paraplēgia,* a stroke on one side, from *paraplēssein,* to strike on one side : PARA- (alongside) + *plēssein,* to strike.] **—par·a·ple·gic** (-pleéjik) *adj. & n.*

par·a·po·di·um (párrə-pōdi-əm) *n.,* **-dia** (-ə). Any of the lateral appendages of polychaete worms, which occur in pairs and are used in locomotion and respiration. [New Latin : PARA- + *-podium* (footlike part). See **podium.**]

par·a·psy·chol·o·gy (párrə-sī-kólləji) *n.* The study of phenomena such as telepathy, clairvoyance, and psychokinesis that are not explainable by known natural laws. **—par·a·psy·cho·log·i·cal** (-kə-lójik'l) *adj.* **—par·a·psy·chol·o·gist** (-kólləjist) *n.*

Par·a·quat (párrə-kwot, -kwat) *n.* A trademark for a poisonous, yellow, water-soluble solid used in solution as a weedkiller.

paraquet. Variant of **parakeet.**

Pa·rá rubber (pə-raá, paárə) *n.* Rubber obtained from various tropical South American trees of the genus *Hevea,* especially *H. brasiliensis.*

par·a·sang (párrə-sang) *n.* An ancient Persian unit of distance, usually estimated at about 5½ kilometres (3½ miles). [Latin *parasanga,* from Greek *parasangēs,* from Iranian, akin to Persian *farsang*†.]

par·a·se·le·ne (párrəsi-leé-ni) *n., pl.* **-nae** (-nee). A luminous spot on a lunar halo. Also called "mock moon", "moon dog". [New Latin : PARA- (resembling) + Greek *selēnē,* moon.] **—par·a·se·le·nic** (-lénnik) *adj.*

pa·ra·shah (párrə-shaa, paárə-) *n., pl.* **-shoth** (-shōt) or **-shioth** (-shi-ōt). Any of the portions of the Torah read on the Sabbath and on festivals in the synagogue. [Hebrew, "explanation".]

Par·a·shu·ra·ma (párrə-shoō-raámə) *n. Hinduism.* See **Rama.**

par·a·site (párrə-sīt) *n.* **1.** *Biology.* Any organism that grows, feeds, and is sheltered on or in a different organism while contributing nothing to the survival of its host. **2.** A person who habitually takes advantage of the generosity of others without making any useful return. **3.** In ancient Greece, one who was given free meals in return for his witty or cheeky conversation. [Old French, from Latin *parasītus,* from Greek *parasitos,* originally "fellow guest", later "parasite" : PARA- (beside) + *sitos,* grain, food.]

par·a·sit·ic (párrə-síttik) *adj.* Also **par·a·sit·i·cal** (-'l). **1.** Of, pertaining to, or characteristic of a parasite. **2.** Caused by a parasite, as certain diseases are. **—par·a·sit·i·cal·ly** *adv.*

par·a·sit·i·cide (párrə-sítti-sīd) *n.* Something used to destroy parasites. [From PARASIT(E) + -CIDE.] **—par·a·sit·i·cide, par·a·sit·i·ci·dal** (-sīd'l), **par·a·sit·i·cid·ic** (-síddik) *adj.* **—par·a·sit·i·ci·dal·ly** *adv.*

par·a·sit·ise, par·a·sit·ize (párrə-si-tīz, -sī-) *tr.v.* **ised, -ising, -ises.** To live on (a host) as a parasite.

par·a·sit·ism (párrə-sī-tiz'm) *n.* **1.** The characteristic behaviour or mode of existence of a parasite. **2.** A diseased condition resulting from parasitic infestation.

par·a·si·tol·o·gy (párrə-sī-tólləji) *n.* The scientific study of parasites. [From PARASIT(E) + -LOGY.] **—par·a·si·to·log·i·cal** (-sītə-lójik'l) *adj.* **—par·a·si·tol·o·gist** (-tólləjist) *n.*

par·a·sol (párrə-sol, -sól) *n.* A light, usually small umbrella carried, especially by women, for protection from the sun. [French, from Italian *parasole* : PARA- (protecting) + *sole,* sun, from Latin *sōl.*]

par·a·su·i·cide (párrə-soō-i-sīd, -séw-) *n.* **1. a.** An attempt to kill oneself that is not motivated by a genuine wish to die. **b.** The making of such attempts. **2.** A person who makes such an attempt.

par·a·sym·pa·thet·ic nervous system (párrə-símpə-théttik) *n. Anatomy.* The part of the autonomic nervous system originating in the central and back parts of the brain and in the lower part of the spinal cord that inhibits or opposes the physiological effects of the sympathetic nervous system, as in tending to stimulate digestive secretions, slowing the heart, and dilating blood vessels. Also called "craniosacral system".

par·a·syn·the·sis (párrə-sínthi-siss) *n. Grammar.* The formation of words by a combination of compounding and adding an affix, as in the formation of the word *freemasonry* from *free* plus *mason* plus *-ry,* rather than from *free* plus *masonry.* **—par·a·syn·thet·ic** (-sin-théttik) *adj.*

par·a·tax·is (párrə-táksiss) *n.* The coordination of grammatical elements such as phrases or clauses, without the use of coordinating elements such as conjunctions, as in *It was cold; the snows came.* Compare **asyndeton, hypotaxis.** [Greek, from *parataxis,* to arrange side by side : PARA- (beside) + *tassein,* to arrange.] **—par·a·tac·tic** (-táktik), **par·a·tac·ti·cal** *adj.* **—par·a·tac·ti·cal·ly** *adv.*

par·a·thi·on (párrə-thī-on) *n.* A highly poisonous liquid insecticide, $(C_2H_5O)_2P(S)OC_6H_4NO_2$. [PARA- + *thio(phosphate)* + -ON.]

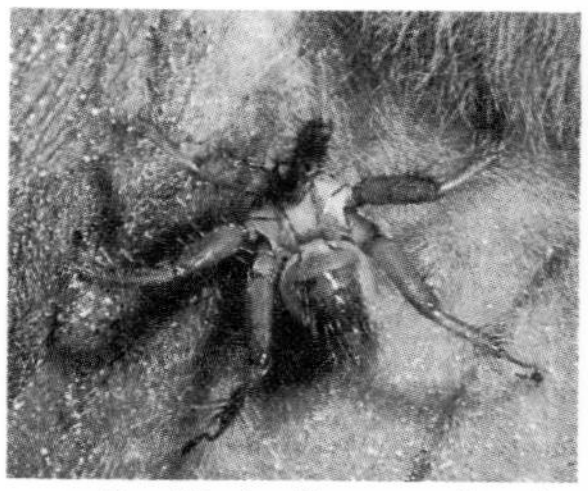

parasite *The bat fly, a member of the insect family* Nycteribiidae, *is a wingless parasite. It lives on the skin of bats.*

PRONUNCIATION KEY

a, trap; aa, father; ai, fair; ar, star; aw, lawn; ay, play; b, bb, stab; rubber; ch, church; ck, ticket; d, dd, dead; ladder; e, dress; ee, bee; er, defer; ew, few; ewr, pure; ə, about; ər, letter; f, ff, fife; differ; g, gg, giggle; h, hat; i, kit; ī, price; īr, fire; j, judge; k, kick; l, ll, let; 'l, needle; m, mm, man; n, nn, no; 'n, sudden; ng, thing; o, lot; ō, no; oō, foot; ōō, shoe; oor, poor; ow, cow; owr, hour; oy, boy; p, pp, pepper; r, rr, red; s, ss, sauce; sh, ship; t, tt, totter; th, thick; th, this; smooth; u, cut; ur, turn; v, vv, valve; w, wet; y, yes; z, zz, zebra; zh, vision; pleasure

IN FOREIGN WORDS:

aN, oN, Saint-Saëns; hl, Llanelli; Hluhluwe; kh, loch; lough; Khaled

STRESS MARK:

ín-sīt, insight; in-sīt, incite

par·a·thy·roid (párrə-thī́r-oyd) *adj.* **1.** Situated close to the thyroid gland. **2.** Of or pertaining to the parathyroid gland.
~*n.* The parathyroid gland.

parathyroid gland *n.* Any of four small kidney-shaped glands that lie in pairs near or within the lateral lobes of the thyroid gland and secrete parathyroid hormone.

parathyroid hormone *n.* A hormone, synthesised and secreted by the parathyroid glands, that raises the level of calcium in the blood. Deficiency results in tetany. Also called "parathormone".

par·a·troop·er (párrə-trōōpər) *n.* A member of the paratroops.

par·a·troops (párrə-trōōpss) *pl.n.* Infantry, trained and equipped to carry out parachute missions. [PARA(CHUTE) + TROOPS.] —**pa·ra·troop** *adj.*

par·a·ty·phoid (párrə-tī́foyd) *adj.* **1.** Resembling typhoid fever. **2.** Of or pertaining to paratyphoid fever.
~*n.* Paratyphoid fever.

paratyphoid fever *n.* An acute intestinal disease, similar to typhoid fever but less severe and caused by any of three bacteria of the genus *Salmonella.* Also called "paratyphoid".

par·a·vane (párrə-vayn) *n. Nautical.* A device equipped with sharp teeth and towed alongside a ship to cut the mooring cables of submerged mines. [PARA- (alongside) + VANE.]

par a·vion (par a-vyóɴ) *adv. French.* By aeroplane. Used as a label or notation on letters or articles sent by air mail.

par·boil (pár-boyl) *tr.v.* **-boiled, -boiling, -boils. 1.** To cook partially by boiling for a brief period. **2.** To subject to intense, often uncomfortable heat. [Middle English *parboilen,* "to boil thoroughly", later (by influence of PART) to parboil, from Old French *parbo(u)illir,* from Late Latin *perbullīre* : Latin *per,* thoroughly + *bullīre,* to boil.]

par·buck·le (pár-buck'l) *n.* **1.** A rope sling for rolling cylindrical objects up or down an inclined plane. **2.** A sling for raising or lowering a heavy object vertically.
~*tr.v.* **parbuckled, -ling, -les.** To raise or lower with a parbuckle. [Alteration (influenced by BUCKLE) of earlier *parbunkle*†.]

Par·cae (pár-see, -kī) *pl.n.* The three **Fates** *(see).* [Latin.]

par·cel (parss'l) *n.* **1.** Something wrapped up or packaged; a package. **2.** A portion or plot of land, usually a division of a larger area. **3.** A quantity of merchandise offered for sale. **4.** A group or company; a bunch. **5.** A distinct, often essential part of something. Used chiefly in the phrase *part and parcel.*
~*tr.v.* **parcelled,** or *U.S.* **-celed, -celling** or *U.S.* **-celing, -cels. 1.** To divide into portions or allotments and distribute. Usually followed by *out.* **2.** To make into a parcel or parcels; wrap; package. Sometimes followed by *up.* **3.** *Nautical.* To wind protective strips of canvas round (rope). [Middle English *parcelle,* from Old French, from Vulgar Latin *particella* (unattested), from Latin *particula,* portion, particle, diminutive of *pars* (stem *part-*), part.]

par·ce·nar·y (pár-si-nəri || *U.S.* -nerri) *n., pl.* **-ies.** *Law.* **Coparcenary** *(see).* [Anglo-French *parcenarie,* from Old French *parçonerie,* from *parçonier,* partner, PARCENER.]

par·ce·ner (pár-sənər) *n. Law.* A **coparcener** *(see).* [Anglo-French, from Old French *parçonier,* partner, from Vulgar Latin *partiōnārius* (unattested), from Latin *partītiō,* partition, from *partīre,* to divide, from *pars* (stem *part-*), part.]

parch (parch) *v.* **parched, parching, parches.** —*tr.* **1.** To make very dry, especially by the action of heat. **2.** To make thirsty. Usually used in the passive: *I'm parched.* **3.** To dry or roast (corn, peas, or the like) by exposing to heat. —*intr.* **1.** To become very dry: *The fields will soon parch in this heat.* **2.** To become thirsty. —See Synonyms at **burn.** [Middle English *parchen*†.]

Par·chee·si (paar-chée-si, -zi) *n.* A trademark for a board game based on the ancient game of **pachisi** *(see).*

parch·ment (párchmənt) *n.* **1.** The skin of a sheep or goat, prepared for writing or painting upon. **2.** A written text or drawing on a sheet of this material. **3.** Stiff, durable paper made in imitation of this material. [Middle English *perchement, parchemin,* from Old French *parchemin, parcamin,* from Vulgar Latin *particamīnum* (unattested), blend of Latin *Parthica (pellis),* "Parthian (leather)", and *pergamīna,* parchment, from Greek *pergamēnē,* from *Pergamēnos,* of Pergamun, from *Pergamon,* Pergamum in western Turkey (where it was first used as a substitute for papyrus).]

par·close (pár-klōz) *n.* A railing dividing a chapel or altar from the main body of a church. [Middle English, from Old French *parclos(e),* from past participle of *parclore,* to close off. See **per-, close.**]

pard (pard) *n. Archaic.* A leopard or other large cat. [Middle English *parde,* from Old French, from Latin *pardus,* from Greek *pardos,* from an Oriental source. See also **leopard.**]

par·da·lote (párdə-lōt) *n.* The **diamond bird** *(see).* [New Latin *pardalotus,* from Greek *pardalōtos,* having a leopard's spots, from *pardos* (stem *pardal-*), leopard.]

pard·ner (párdnər) *n. U.S. Regional.* A friend or partner. [Variant of PARTNER.]

par·don (párd'n) *tr.v.* **-doned, -doning, -dons. 1.** To release (a person) from punishment; forgive. **2.** To pass over (an offence) without punishment. **3.** To make courteous allowance for; to excuse: *Pardon me, but I must go.* —See Synonyms at **forgive.**
~*n.* **1. a.** The act of forgiving. **b.** Forgiveness; courteous overlooking or allowance. **2.** *Law.* **a.** The exemption of a convicted person from the penalties of an offence or crime by the power of the executor of the laws. **b.** The official document or warrant declaring such an exemption. **3.** Formerly, a papal indulgence.
~*interj.* Used as a polite or conventional apology for causing inconvenience, or as a request for spoken words to be repeated. [Middle English *pardonen,* from Old French *pardoner,* to give, pardon, from Late Latin *perdōnāre,* to give wholeheartedly : *per,* thoroughly + *dōnāre,* to give, from *dōnum,* gift.] —**par·don·a·ble** *adj.* —**par·don·a·bly** *adv.*

par·don·er (párd'n-ər) *n.* **1.** One who pardons. **2.** A medieval ecclesiastic authorised to raise money for religious works by granting papal indulgences to contributors.

pare (pair) *tr.v.* **pared, paring, pares. 1.** To remove the outer covering or skin of (a fruit or vegetable) by peeling with a knife or similar instrument. **2.** To remove the edges of (toenails, for example). **3.** To remove by or as if by cutting, clipping, or shaving. Used with *off* or *away: paring off lemon rind.* **4.** To lessen or diminish bit by bit; whittle away. Used with *off* or *down: paring expenditure down to a minimum.* [Middle English *paren,* from Old French *parer,* to prepare, from Latin *parāre.*]

Pa·ré (pa-ráy), **Ambroise** (*c.* 1510–90). French surgeon and pioneer of modern surgery. As an army surgeon he abandoned the cauterisation of amputated limbs with red-hot irons and boiling oil in favour of ligatures to tie off arteries.

par·e·gor·ic (párrə-górrik || -gáwrik) *n.* Camphorated tincture of opium, formerly taken internally for the relief of diarrhoea and intestinal pain. [Late Latin *parēgoricus,* from Greek *parēgorikos,* from *parēgoros,* encouraging, soothing, addressing : PARA- (beside), alongside + *agora,* assembly.]

pa·rei·ra (pə-ráirə) *n.* A drug prepared from the root of a South American plant, *Chondrodendron tomentosum,* used as a diuretic and tonic. [From Portuguese *parreira brava,* "wild vine".]

pa·ren·chy·ma (pə-réngkimə) *n.* **1.** *Anatomy.* The tissue characteristic of an organ, as distinguished from connective tissue. **2.** *Botany.* Tissue composed of soft, unspecialised, thin-walled cells. **3.** *Zoology.* A loose connective tissue occurring in flatworms and related invertebrates. [New Latin, from Greek *parenkhuma,* visceral flesh, from *parenkhein,* to pour in beside (from the belief that the tissues of the organs were poured in by their blood vessels) : PARA- (beside) + *en,* in + *khein,* to pour.] —**pa·ren·chy·mal, par·en·chym·a·tous** (párren-kímmətəss) *adj.* —**par·en·chym·a·tous·ly** *adv.*

par·ent (páir-ənt) *n.* **1.** A father or mother. **2.** A forefather; an ancestor; a progenitor. **3.** Any organism that produces or generates another. **4.** A guardian; a protector. **5.** The source or cause of something; the origin. **6.** *Physics & Chemistry.* A nucleus, atom, ion, or molecule that breaks up or changes to give a different nucleus, atom, or the like (the daughter). Also used adjectivally: *a parent ion.* [Middle English, from Old French, from Latin *parēns* stem *parent-*), from the present participle of *parere,* to give birth.] —**pa·ren·tal** (pə-rént'l) *adj.* —**pa·ren·tal·ly** *adv.* —**par·ent·hood** *n.*

par·ent·age (páir-əntij) *n.* **1.** Descent or derivation from parents or ancestors; lineage; ancestry. **2.** Derivation from a source; origin or cause. **3.** The state or relationship of being a parent.

parental generation *n.* A generation from which a genetic experiment begins. Compare **filial generation.**

par·en·ter·al (pə-réntərəl, pa-) *adj.* **1.** Located outside the alimentary canal. **2.** Taken into the body or administered in a manner other than through the digestive tract, as by intravenous or intramuscular injection. [PAR(A)- + ENTER(O)- + -AL.]

pa·ren·the·sis (pə-rén-thə-siss, -thi-) *n., pl.* **-ses** (-seez). *Abbr.* **par., paren. 1.** Either or both of the upright curved lines, (or), used to mark off explanatory or qualifying remarks in writing or printing. Also called "bracket", "round bracket". **2.** *Mathematics.* Such a mark used as one of a pair to enclose a sum, product, or other expression considered or treated as a collective entity in a mathematical operation. **3.** A qualifying or amplifying phrase occurring within a sentence in such a way as to form an interpolation independent of the surrounding syntactical structure; for example, in the sentence: *It was the best film —and I go to a lot —I have seen in a long time,* the words *and I go to a lot* constitute a parenthesis. **4.** An interruption of continuity; an interval; an interlude. [Late Latin, from Greek, "a putting in beside", from *parentithenai,* to insert : PARA- + *en,* in + *tithenai,* to put.]

pa·ren·the·sise, pa·ren·the·size (pə-rén-thə-sīz, -thi-) *tr.v.* **-sised, -sising, -sises. 1.** To insert as a parenthesis. **2.** To place between parenthetical marks. **3.** To insert a parenthesis or parentheses into.

par·en·thet·i·cal (párrən-théttik'l) *adj.* Also **par·en·thet·ic** (-théttik). **1.** Contained, or as if contained, in parentheses; qualifying or explanatory: *a parenthetical remark.* **2.** Using or containing parentheses. —**par·en·thet·i·cal·ly** *adv.*

par·ent·ing (páir-ənt-ing) *n.* The bringing up of children by or as by a parent.

pa·rer·gon (pa-rérg-ən, pə-, -ráirg-, -on) *n., pl.* **-ga.** *Formal.* Work done apart from one's main, primary, or professional work. [Latin, from Greek : PARA- + *ergon,* work.]

pa·re·sis (pə-rée-siss, pa-, párrə-siss) *n. Pathology.* **1.** Slight or partial paralysis. **2.** General paralysis. See **general paralysis of the insane.** [New Latin, from Greek, act of letting go, from *parienai,* to loose, let fall : PARA- (beside) + *hienai,* to throw.] —**pa·ret·ic** (-réttik) *n. & adj.* —**pa·ret·i·cal·ly** *adv.*

pa·re·u (paa-ráy-ōō) *n.* A rectangular piece of cloth worn in Polynesia as a wraparound skirt or loincloth. [Tahitian.]

pa·re·ve (paárəvə) *adj.* Also **par·ve** (párvə). *Judaism.* Designating or pertaining to foods that are prepared without meat, milk, or their derivatives, and that therefore may be eaten with meat or dairy dishes. [Yiddish *parev*†.]

par ex·cel·lence (paar éksə-loɴss, -lóɴss) *adv.* To the highest de-

PRONUNCIATION KEY

a, trap; aa, father; ai, fair;
ar, star; aw, lawn; ay, play;
b, bb, stab; rubber;
ch, church; ck, ticket;
d, dd, dead; ladder; e, dress;
ee, bee; er, defer; ew, few;
ewr, pure; ə, about;
ər, letter; f, ff, fife; differ;
g, gg, giggle; h, hat; i, kit;
ī, price; īr, fire; j, judge;
k, kick; l, ll, let; 'l, needle;
m, mm, man; n, nn, no;
'n, sudden; ng, thing; o, lot;
ō, no; ŏŏ, foot; ōō, shoe;
oor, poor; ow, cow;
owr, hour; oy, boy;
p, pp, pepper; r, rr, red;
s, ss, sauce; sh, ship;
t, tt, totter; th, thick; th, this;
smooth; u, cut; ur, turn;
v, vv, valve; w, wet; y, yes;
z, zz, zebra; zh, vision;
pleasure

IN FOREIGN WORDS:

aɴ, oɴ, Saint-Saëns;
hl, Llanelli; Hluhluwe;
kh, loch; lough; Khaled

STRESS MARK:

in-sī́t, insight; in-sī́t, incite

gree or epitome of something; pre-eminently. [French "by (way of) pre-eminence".]

par·fait (paar-fáy) *n.* **1.** A dessert made of cream, eggs, sugar, and flavouring frozen together. **2.** A dessert made of several layers of different flavours of ice cream garnished and served in a tall glass. [French, from *parfait,* perfect, from Latin *perfectus,* PERFECT.]

par·get (párjit) *n.* **1.** Plaster, roughcast, or any similar mixture used to coat walls or line chimneys. **2.** Ornamental plasterwork. **3.** A cement mixture used to waterproof outer walls.
~*tr.v.* **pargetted** or *U.S.* **-geted, -getting,** or *U.S.* **-geting, -gets.** To cover or adorn with parget. [Middle English *pargetten,* from Old French *parjeter,* to throw onto a surface : *par,* onto, from Latin *per* + *jeter,* to throw. See **jet** (stream).] **—par·get·ing** *n.*

par·he·lic circle (paar-héelik) *n.* A type of halo consisting of a large circle of white light lying parallel to the horizon and passing through the Sun. It is formed by reflection of sunlight by ice crystals in the atmosphere. Also called "parhelic ring". See **anthelion.**

par·he·li·on (paar-héeli-ən, -on) *n., pl.* **-helia** (-héeli-ə). *Meteorology.* A bright spot sometimes appearing to either side of the sun, often on a luminous ring or halo. Also called "mock sun", "sundog". [Latin *parēlion,* from Greek : PARA- (beside, beyond) + *hēlios,* sun.] **—par·he·lic** (-héelik, -héllik), **par·he·li·a·cal** (párhi-lī-ək'l) *adj.*

pa·ri·ah (pə-rī-ə, párri-ə) *n.* **1.** A social outcast. **2.** Formerly, a member of a low caste of agricultural and domestic workers in southern India and Burma. [Tamil *paraiyan,* drummer, from *parai,* drum (the pariahs having been originally a caste of drummers).]

pariah dog *n.* A **pye dog** *(see).*

Par·i·an (páir-i-ən) *adv.* **1.** Of or pertaining to the island of Paros or its inhabitants. **2.** Designating a type of white marble highly valued in ancient times for making statues. **3.** Designating a fine white porcelain.
~*n.* **1.** A native or inhabitant of Paros. **2.** Parian marble. **3.** Parian porcelain.

pa·ri·es (páir-i-eez) *n., pl.* **parietes** (pə-rī-i-teez). *Biology.* The wall of an organ. [New Latin, from Latin *pariēs*†, wall of a room.]

pa·ri·e·tal (pə-rī-it'l) *adj.* **1.** *Biology.* Pertaining to or forming the wall of a hollow structure. **2.** *Anatomy.* Of or pertaining to either of the parietal bones. **3.** *Botany.* Attached to the ovary wall. Said of the ovules or placenta in certain plants. [French *pariétal,* from Late Latin *parietālis,* from Latin *pariēs* (stem *pariet-*), PARIES.]

parietal bone *n. Anatomy.* Either of two large, irregularly quadrilateral bones, between the frontal and occipital bones, that together form the sides and top of the skull.

parietal lobe *n. Anatomy.* The division of each hemisphere of the brain that lies beneath each parietal bone.

par·i·mu·tu·el (párri-méwchoo-əl) *n., pl.* **pari-mutuels.** *Chiefly U.S.* A system of betting on races, or a machine that records bets under that system, a **totalisator** *(see).* [French *pari mutuel,* mutual stake.]

par·ing (páir-ing) *n. Often plural.* That which has been pared off or removed.

pa·ri pas·su (párri pássōō, paári paássōō) *adv. Latin.* With equal pace, speed, or progress; side by side: *proceed pari passu.*

Par·is¹ (párriss). *Greek Mythology.* The prince of Troy whose abduction of Helen provoked the Trojan War.

Par·is² (párriss || *French* pa-rée). Capital of France and of the Paris département. It is situated on the river Seine in the north of the country and is the administrative, cultural, and commercial centre of France. Capital of France since A.D. 987, it has witnessed many revolutions, including the French Revolution of 1789, and was occupied by the Germans during World War II. Its architecture includes the churches Nôtre Dame and Sacré Cœur, the Eiffel Tower, and the art galleries of the Louvre, the Jeu de Paume, and the Centre Pompidou. **—Pa·ris·i·an** (pə-rízzi-ən, -rízh'n) *adj. & n.*

Paris, Treaty of *n.* **1.** A treaty (1763) between Great Britain, France, and Spain that ended their participation in the Seven Year's War. **2.** A treaty (1783) between Great Britain and the United States that ended the War of American Independence. In this sense, also called "Treaty of Versailles".

Paris Commune *n.* **1.** The revolutionary committee that governed Paris from 1789 to 1795. **2.** The revolutionary government of Paris from March 18 to May 28, 1871. Also called the "Commune".

Paris green *n.* A poisonous emerald-green powder, $(CuO)_3As_2O_3 \cdot Cu(C_2H_3O_2)_2$ used as a pigment, insecticide, and wood preservative. [After PARIS, where it was once made.]

par·ish (párrish) *n. Abbr.* **par. 1.** In the Anglican, Roman Catholic, and some other churches, an administrative part of a diocese that has its own church. **2.** In England, a political division of a county for local civil government, usually corresponding to the ecclesiastical parish. **3.** Members of an ecclesiastical parish collectively; the community of parishioners. **—on the parish.** Formerly, receiving money or other welfare assistance, paid for and administered by the parish. [Middle English *paroche, parisshe,* from Old French *paroisse,* from Late Latin *parochia,* from Late Greek *paroikia,* from *paroikos,* Christian, from Greek, "neighbour", "sojourner", "stranger" : *para,* near, beside + *oikos,* house.]

parish clerk *n.* In the Church of England, a layperson appointed to lead the congregation in their part in church services and to help the parson with the administration of church business. The position may be amalgamated with that of **sexton** *(see).*

parish council *n.* In Britain, a civil body that administers the affairs of a parish.

pa·rish·ion·er (pə-ríshʼn-ər) *n.* A member of a parish. [Middle English *parisshoner,* perhaps from Old French *paroissien,* from *paroisse,* PARISH.]

par·ish-pump (párrish-púmp) *adj.* Of or designating an idea or outlook that is blinkered or parochial.

parish register *n.* The record of births, deaths, and marriages occurring in a parish.

par·i·son (párri-sən) *n.* A mass of glass, roughly rounded after removal from the furnace and prior to being blown or shaped. [From French *paraison,* from *parer,* to prepare.]

par·i·ty¹ (párrəti) *n., pl.* **-ties. 1.** Equality, as in amount, status, or value. **2.** Equivalence, correspondence, or resemblance. **3.** *Finance.* **a.** The equivalent in value of a sum of money expressed in terms of a different currency, at a fixed, official rate of exchange. **b.** The equivalence in value between coins of a different metal established at a fixed ratio. **c.** Equality of prices of goods or securities in two different markets. **4.** *Mathematics & Computing.* The comparative odd-even relationship between two integers. If both are odd, or both even, they are said to have the same parity; if one is odd and one even, they have different parity. Also used adjectivally: *a parity error.* **5.** *Symbol* **P** *Physics.* **a.** An intrinsic symmetry property of elementary particles that is characterised by the behaviour of the wave function of such particles under reflection through the origin of spatial coordinates. **b.** A quantum number, either +1 (even) or -1 (odd), that mathematically describes this property. [Latin *paritās* (stem *paritāt-*), from *pār,* equal.]

parity² *n.* **1.** The condition of having borne offspring. **2.** The number of children borne by one woman. [From -PAR(OUS) + -ITY.]

park (park) *n. Abbr.* **pk. 1.** A tract of land set aside for public use, such as: **a.** An expanse of enclosed grounds, sometimes landscaped, for recreational use within or adjoining a town or city. **b.** An enclosed area of land in which wild animals are kept: *a deer park* **c.** An extensive tract of land kept in its natural state: *a national park.* **2. a.** *U.S.* A stadium or enclosed playing field: *a ball park.* **b.** *British Slang.* A soccer pitch. **3.** A country estate, especially when including extensive gardens, woods, or the like. **4.** *Military.* **a.** An area where vehicles and artillery are stored and serviced. **b.** The materiel kept in such an area.
~*v.* **parked, parking, parks.** *—tr.* **1.** To put or leave (a car or other vehicle) for a time in a certain location, such as a garage or at the side of the road. **2.** To place (a spacecraft) in a temporary orbit, a *parking orbit.* **3.** *Informal.* To place, put, set, or leave somewhere: *Park your coats on this chair.* **4.** *Military.* To assemble (artillery or other equipment) in order. *—intr.* To park a vehicle. [Middle English, from Old French *parc,* enclosure, from Medieval Latin *parricus*†. See **paddock.**]

Park (park), **Chung Hee** (1917–79). President of South Korea (1963–79). Having fought as a general in the South Korean army, he came to power in a military coup (1961), became president, and later established martial law and assumed dictatorial powers (1972), ostensibly to resist invasion by North Korea. He was assassinated.

par·ka (párkə) *n.* **1.** A hooded fur jacket worn as an outer garment by Eskimos. **2.** A similar garment of warm cloth, worn for sports or outdoor work. [Aleutian, skin, from Russian, pelt of a reindeer, from Samoyed.]

Par·ker (párkər), **Charlie** (1920–55). U.S. black jazz musician. His brilliant technique as an alto saxophonist made him a legend in his own time, and influened the next generation of musicians.

Par·ker, Dorothy (Rothschild) (1893–1967). U.S. comic writer, poet, and critic. She was drama critic for Vanity Fair (1916-17) and book critic for the New Yorker (1927–33). She was noted for her satirical humour as in the short stories, *Here Lies* (1939).

parkin (párkin) *n.* A spicy, ginger-flavoured cake, popular especially in Northern England.

park·ing lot (párking) *n. U.S.* A **car park** *(see).*

parking meter *n.* A coin-operated meter monitoring the length of time that a car has been parked adjacent to it.

parking ticket *n.* A legal summons issued for a violation of parking regulations. Also called "ticket".

Par·kin·son's disease (párkin-sənz) *n.* A progressive neurological disease of the later years, characterised by muscular tremor, slowing of movement, partial facial paralysis, peculiarity of gait and posture, and weakness. Also called "parkinsonism", "paralysis agitans", "shaking palsy". [After James *Parkinson* (1755–1824), English surgeon.]

Par·kin·son's Law *n.* A satirical observation propounded as an economic law: "Work expands to fill the time available for its completion." [After C. Northcote *Parkinson* (1909), British writer.]

park·land (párk-land) *n.* **1.** A stretch of land set aside for public use, or enclosed as a park. **2.** Such stretches of land collectively.

park·way (párk-way) *n. Chiefly U.S.* A wide road, often having a middle strip planted with flower or shrubs.

park·y (párki) *adj.* **-ier, -iest.** *British Informal.* Chilly; cold. Said of weather. [19th century : perhaps from PERKY.]

parl. parliamentary.

Parl. Parliament.

par·lance (párlənss) *n.* **1.** A particular manner of speaking; a specified or personal language, style, or idiom: *legal parlance.* **2.** *Archaic.* Conversation, especially a parley or debate. [Old French, from *parler,* to speak, from Medieval Latin *parabolāre,* to PARLEY.]

par·lan·do (paar-lán-dō || *U.S.* -laán) Also **par·lan·te** (-tay). *adv. Music.* To be sung in a style suggestive of speech. Used as a direction. [Italian, from *parlare,* to speak, from Medieval Latin *parabolāre,* to PARLEY.] **—par·lan·do** *adj.*

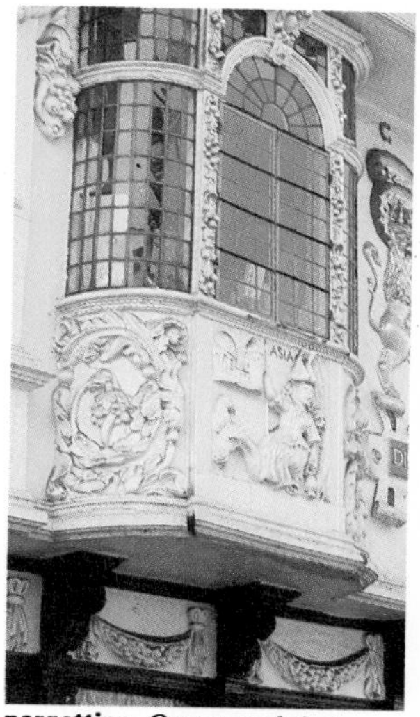

pargetting *Ornamental plaster work, seen here in Ipswich, Suffolk, England. The house was built in 1567.*

par·lay (pár-li, -lay) *tr.v.* **-layed, -laying, -lays.** *U.S.* **1.** To bet (an original wager and its winnings) on a subsequent event, as in a race or contest. **2.** To manoeuvre (an asset) to great advantage: *She parlayed her physical attributes into a film career.*
~*n. U.S.* A bet comprising the sum of an original wager plus its winnings, or a series of bets made in such a manner. [French *paroli*, a bet of this kind in faro, from Italian (Neapolitan), from *paro*, like, from Latin *pār*, equal.]

par·ley (párli) *n., pl.* **-leys.** A discussion or conference, especially between enemies over terms of truce or other matters.
~*v.* **parleyed, -leying, -leys.** —*intr.v.* To discuss, confer, or debate, as with an enemy or over a disagreement. —*tr.* To speak or converse in (a foreign language). Often used humorously. [French *parlée*, from the past participle of *parler*, to talk, from Old French, from Medieval Latin *parabolāre*, from Late Latin *parabola*, discourse, PARABLE.]

par·lia·ment (párlə-mənt, párli-, párli-ə-) *n.* **1.** A national representative body having supreme legislative powers within the state. **2.** *Capital* **P. a.** *Abbr.* **Parl.** In Britain, the highest legislative body, made up of the sovereign, the **House of Lords** and the **House of Commons**, (both of which see). **b.** The people composing such a body at any one time. **c.** Any of various equivalent bodies in other countries, as in most Commonwealth countries. **d.** The lower house or chamber of such a body. [Middle English, from Old French *parlement*, from *parler*, to talk. See **parley**.]

par·lia·men·tar·i·an (párlə-men-taír-i-ən, párli-, párli-ə-, -mən-) *n.* **1.** One who is expert in parliamentary procedures, rules, or debate. **2.** *Capital* **P.** A supporter of Parliament, as opposed to the king, during the English Civil War; a Roundhead. **3.** Broadly, a member of a parliament.
~*adj.* Of or pertaining to the Long Parliament or to the Roundheads. —**par·lia·men·tar·i·an·ism** *n.*

par·lia·men·ta·ry (párlə-mén-təri, párli-, párli-ə-, -tri) *adj. Abbr.* **parl.** Often *capital* **P. 1.** Of, pertaining to, or resembling Parliament or a parliament. **2.** Proceeding from, passed, or decreed by Parliament or a parliament. **3.** In accordance with the rules and customs of Parliament or a parliament: *Parliamentary procedure.* **4.** Having a parliament. **5.** Of or supporting Parliament during the English Civil War.

Parliamentary Commissioner for Administration *n.* In Britain, the **ombudsman** (see).

Parliamentary Undersecretary *n.* See **undersecretary**.

par·lour, *U.S.* **par·lor** (párlər) *n.* **1.** A room in a private home formerly reserved for the entertainment of visitors. **2.** A small room affording intimacy, such as: **a.** In a hotel, club, or the like, a room reserved for guests who desire a greater degree of privacy. **b.** In a monastery or convent, a room for receiving visitors and where conversation is permitted. **3.** *Chiefly U.S.* A room equipped and furnished for some special function or business: *a beauty parlour.*
~*adj.* Designating one who puts foward ideas, often extreme or radical, from a position of safety, and who never takes any action to promote them: *a parlour socialist.* [Middle English *parlour*, from Old French *parleur*, room used for conversation, from *parler*, to talk. See **parley**.]

parlour car *n. U.S.* A railway coach for day travel fitted with individual reserved seats.

parlour game *n.* A game, especially one that involves words, played indoors.

parlour maid *n.* A female servant employed to wait at table during meals.

par·lous (párləss) *adj. Archaic.* **1.** Perilous; dangerous. **2.** Shrewd; cunning.
~*adv.* Extremely; very. [Middle English, variant of *perilous*, from *peril*, PERIL.] —**par·lous·ly** *adv.*

Par·ma (pármə) City of Emilia Romagna, capital of Parma province, north Italy. Situated on the river Parma and near the Apennine Mountains, it was a cultural centre in the Middle Ages.

Parma violet *n.* A violet, *Viola odorata sempervirens*, cultivated for its fragrant lavender flowers.

Par·men·i·des (paar-ménni-deez). (c. 515– c. 450 B.C.). Greek philosopher. The greatest of the Eleatic school, he believed that reality is unchanging, permanent, and part of the world of being, of which all that can be said is that it is. He greatly influenced Plato.

Par·me·san (pármi-zan, -zon, -zán) *n.* A hard, dry Italian cheese made from skim milk and usually served grated as a garnish.
~*adj.* Of or from Parma. [French, from Italian *parmigiano*, of Parma.]

Par·mi·gia·ni·no (pármi-ja-néenō) (1503–40). Italian painter and etcher. His work is characterised by elongation of form and includes the *Madonna of the Long Neck* and his *Vision of St. Jerome.*

par·mi·gia·na (pármi-jáana) *adj.* Prepared with parmesan cheese: *veal parmigiana.* [Italian, feminine of *parmigiano*, Parmesan.]

Par·nas·si·an[1] (paar-nássi-ən) *adj.* Of, pertaining to, or symbolically associated with Mount Parnassus or with the world of poetry.

Parnassian[2] *n.* A member of a school of late 19th-century French poets whose work is characterised by detachment and emphasis on metrical form. [*Le Parnasse contemporain*, (1866), was the name of the group's first collection of poems.] —**Par·nas·si·an** *adj.*

Par·nas·sus, Mount (paar-nássəss). *Greek* **Par·na·ssós** (párna-sóss). Greek mountain, 2 457 metres (8,061 feet). Situated to the north of the Gulf of Corinth, it was held sacred in ancient times to Dionysus and Apollo. The oracle of Delphi was, and the modern town is, on its south side.

Par·nell (paar-nél), **Charles Stewart.** (1846–91). Irish politician and nationalist. He was president of the Irish National Land League (1879) and was imprisoned for his obstructive behaviour in the House of Commons (1881). He fought for Irish Home Rule in Parliament and supported the unsuccessful Home Rule Bill of Gladstone.

pa·ro·chi·al (pə-rṓki-əl) *adj.* **1.** Of, supported by, or located in a parish. **2.** Restricted to narrow scope; provincial: *parochial views.* [Middle English *parochiel*, from Old French *parochial*, from Late Latin *parochiālis*, from *parochia*, PARISH.] —**pa·ro·chi·al·ism** *n.* —**pa·ro·chi·al·i·ty** (-ál-əti) *n.* —**pa·ro·chi·al·ly** *adv.*

par·o·dy (párrədi) *n., pl.* **-dies. 1.** A literary, musical, or artistic work that broadly mimics characteristics of another work or a style and holds it up to ridicule. **2.** The genre or the compositon of such works; satirical mimicry. **3.** That which so unconvincingly attempts to be or imitate someone or something that it becomes an unintentional mockery; a travesty: *The trial was a parody of justice.* —See Synonyms at **caricature**.
~*tr.v.* **parodied, -dying, -dies.** To make a parody of. See Synonyms at **imitate**. [Latin *parōdia*, from Greek *parōidia*, "mock-song", burlesque poem : PARA- (beside, "quasi-") + *ōidē*, song.] —**pa·rod·ic** (pə-róddik), **pa·rod·i·cal** *adj.* —**par·o·dist** (párrədist) *n.*

pa·rol (pə-rṓl) *n. Law.* An oral utterance; word of mouth. Now used only in the phrase *by parol.*
~*adj. Law.* Given by word of mouth; not written: *give parol evidence. Compare* **documentary.** [French *parole*, "word", from Old French, from Vulgar Latin *paraula* (unattested), variant of Late Latin *parabola*, discourse, PARABLE.]

pa·role (pə-rṓl) *n.* **1.** *Law.* **a.** The release of a prisoner before his term has expired, on condition of continued good behaviour. **b.** The duration of such conditional release. Used in the phrase *on parole.* **2.** A password used by a military officer of the day or an officer on guard. **3.** Word of honour; especially, a promise given by a prisoner to observe the conditions of his parole. **4.** *Linguistics.* Language as actually used, or as realised in the actual speech and writing of a speech community, as opposed to its **langue** (see). Compare **performance.** —**on parole. 1.** Free from prison, subject to certain conditions, as a result of parole. **2.** *Informal.* Permitted a second chance, under close inspection, following an initial failure.
~*tr.v.* **paroled, -roling, -roles.** To release (a prisoner) on parole. [French, word of honour, "word", PAROL.] —**pa·ro·lee** (pə-rṓ-lée, párrō-) *n.*

par·o·no·ma·sia (párrə-nō-máy-zi-ə ‖ -zhə) *n.* A play on words; especially, a **pun** (see). [Latin, from Greek, from *paronomazein*, to call by a different name, to name besides : PARA- + *onomazein*, to name, from *onoma*, name.] —**par·o·no·mas·tic** (-mástik) *adj.* —**par·o·no·mas·ti·cal·ly** *adv.*

par·o·nym (párrənim) *n.* A paronymous word. [Greek *parōnumon*, from *parōnumos*, PARONYMOUS.] —**par·o·nym·ic** (-nímmik) *adj.*

pa·ron·y·mous (pə-rónnimoss) *adj.* Allied by derivation from the same root; having the same stem; cognate; for example, *beautiful* and *beauteous.* [Greek *parōnumos*, derivative : PARA- (beside) + *onuma*, *onoma*, name.] —**pa·ron·y·mous·ly** *adv.*

Pá·ros (páir-oss, párross). Greek island in the Aegean Sea. Situated in the Cyclades group to the south of the Greek mainland, it is famous for its white translucent marble, used in sculpture.

pa·rot·id gland (pə-róttid) *n.* Either of the largest of the paired salivary glands, located below and in front of each ear. Also called "parotid". [From Greek *parōtis* (stem *parotid*-) "(tumour) near the ear" : PARA- (beside) + *ōt*-, stem of *ous*, ear.]

par·o·ti·tis (párrə-títiss) *n.* Also **pa·rot·i·di·tis** (pə-rótti-dítiss). Inflammation of the parotid glands, as in mumps. [PAROT(ID) + -ITIS.] —**par·o·tit·ic** (-títtik) *adj.*

-parous *adj. comb. form.* Indicates giving birth to or bearing; for example, **multiparous.** [Latin *-parus*, from *parere*, to give birth to.]

pa·rou·si·a (pə-rṓō-si-ə, -rōw-, -zi-) *n.* The **Second Coming** (see). [Greek, "presence" : PARA- + *ousia*, being, from *einai*, to be.]

par·ox·ysm (párrək-siz'm) *n.* **1.** A sudden outburst of emotion or action: *a paroxysm of laughter.* **2.** *Pathology.* **a.** A crisis in or recurrent intensification of a disease. **b.** A spasm or fit; a convulsion. [French *paroxysme*, from Greek *paroxusmos*, irritation, exasperation, paroxysm, from *paroxunein*, to stimulate, irritate : PARA- (intensifier) + *oxunein*, to sharpen, goad, from *oxus*, sharp.] —**par·ox·ys·mal** (-sizm'l) *adj.* —**par·ox·ys·mal·ly** *adv.*

par·ox·y·tone (pə-rók-si-tōn, pa-) *adj.* In ancient Greek grammar, of or designating a word that has an acute accent on the penultimate syllable.
~*n.* A paroxytone word. [Greek *paroxutonos* : PARA- (beside) + *oxutonos*, OXYTONE.]

par·quet (pár-kay, -ki) *n.* **1. a.** Parquetry. **b.** A floor of parquetry. **2.** *U.S.* The stalls of a theatre, the **orchestra** (see).
~*tr.v.* **parqueted** (-kayd), **-queting** (-kay-ing), **-quets** (-kayz). **1.** To furnish (a room) with a floor of parquetry. **2.** To cover (a floor) with parquetry.
~*adj.* Made of parquetry: *a parquet floor.* [French, Old French, small enclosure, diminutive of *parc*, enclosure, PARK.]

par·quet·ry (párkitri) *n., pl.* **-ries.** Wood, often of contrasting colours, worked into an inlaid mosaic, used especially for floors. [French *parqueterie*, from *parquet*, theatre floor, PARQUET.]

parr (par) *n., pl.* **parrs** or collectively **parr.** A young salmon during the first two years of its life when it lives in fresh water. [18th century : origin obscure.]

Parr (par), **Catherine** (1512–48). Sixth wife of Henry VIII. The daughter of Sir Thomas Parr of Kendal, her marriage with Henry (1543) was her third.

parrakeet. Variant of **parakeet.**

par·ra·mat·ta, par·a·mat·ta (párrə-máttə) *n.* A light dress fabric made of a mixture of wool and cotton or silk. [After PARRAMATTA, where it was made.]

Par·ra·mat·ta (párrə-máttə). City of New South Wales, Australia. Situated on the Paramatta river, it is now a suburb of Sydney. It is the second oldest European settlement in Australia (founded 1790).

par·rel, par·ral (párrəl) *n. Nautical.* A sliding loop of rope or chain to which a running yard or gaff is fastened, permitting movement of the yard up and down the mast. [Middle English *perell,* from *parail,* equipment, aphetic variant of APPAREL.]

par·ri·cide (párri-sīd) *n.* **1.** One who murders his father or mother or other near relative. **2.** The act of committing such a murder. [Latin *parricīda* (the perpetrator) and *parricīdium* (the crime) : *parri-*†, "kin" + -CIDE.] **—par·ri·cid·al** (-sī́d'l) *adj.*

par·rot (párrət) *n.* **1.** Any of numerous tropical and semitropical birds of the order Psittaciformes, characterised by short, hooked bills, brightly coloured plumage, and, in some species, the ability to mimic human speech or other sounds. **2.** One who mindlessly imitates the words or actions of another.
~*tr.v.* **parroted, -roting, -rots.** To repeat or imitate without meaning or understanding. [Dialectal French *perrot,* from Old French *perroquet,* variant of *paroquet,* PARAKEET.] **—par·rot·ry** *n.*

parrot-fashion (párrət-fash'n) *adv.* Mechanically and without true understanding: *She learnt her notes parrot-fashion.*

parrot fever *n.* A virus disease, **psittacosis** *(see).*

par·rot·fish (párrət-fish) *n., pl.* **-fishes** or collectively **parrotfish.** Any of various brightly coloured tropical marine fishes of the family Scaridae, having jaws resembling a parrot's beak.

par·ry (párri) *v.* **-ried, -rying, -ries.** *—tr.* **1.** To deflect or ward off (a fencing thrust or sword, for example). **2.** To avoid, counter, or turn aside: *parried her questions.* *—intr.* To deflect or ward off a blow.
~*n., pl.* **parries. 1.** An act of deflecting or warding off a blow, especially in fencing. **2.** An evasive answer or action; an evasion. [French *Parez,* "Parry"! (in fencing), imperative of *parer,* to defend, parry, from Italian *parāre,* from Latin *parāre,* to prepare.]

Par·ry (párri), **Sir (Charles) (Hubert) Hastings** (1848–1918). British composer. He was the director of the Royal College of Music; his works include the oratorios *Judith, Job* (1892), and *King Sa* (1894), and the choral song *Jerusalem* (1916).

parse (parz || parss) *v.* **parsed, parsing, parses.** *—tr. Grammar.* **1.** To break (a sentence) down into component parts of speech with an explanation of the form, function, and syntactical relationship of each part. **2.** To describe (a word) by stating part of speech, form, and syntactical relationships in a sentence. *—intr.* To admit to being parsed: *His sentences do not parse easily.* [From Latin *pars,* part (in phrase *pars ōrātiōnis,* part of speech).] **—pars·er** *n.*

par·sec (pár-sek) *n. Symbol* **pc** A unit of length, used in astronomy, based on the distance from earth at which stellar parallax is one second of arc. It is equal to 3.2616 light-years or 3.0857×10^{13} kilometres. [PAR(ALLAX) + SEC(OND).]

Par·see, Par·si (pár-see, -sée) *n.* A member of a Zoroastrian religious sect, originally from Persia and now based mainly in western India. [Persian *Pārsī,* a Persian, from *Pārs,* Persia, from Old Persian *Pārsa,* PERSIA.] **—Par·see** *adj.* **—Par·see·ism** *n.*

Parsi·fal. See **Percival.**

par·si·mo·ni·ous (pár-si-mṓni-əss) *adj.* Marked by parsimony. See Synonyms at **stingy. —par·si·mo·ni·ous·ly** *adv.*

par·si·mo·ny (pár-si-məni || *U.S.* -mōni) *n.* **1.** Unusual or excessive frugality, especially with regard to money; extreme economy. **2.** Meanness; stinginess. [Middle English *parcimony,* from Latin *parsimōnia,* from *parcere* (past participle *parsus*), to spare.]

pars·ley (párssli) *n.* **1.** A widely cultivated herb, *Petroselinum crispum,* native to the Mediterranean region, having much-divided, curled leaves that are used as a garnish and for seasoning. **2.** Any of various superficially similar plants, such as **cow parsley** *(see).* [Middle English *persely, peresil,* from Old English *petersilie* and Old French *persil, perresil,* both from Late Latin *petrosīlium,* from Latin *petroselīnum,* from Greek *petroselinon,* rock parsley : *petra,* rock + *selinon,* parsley, CELERY.]

pars·nip (pársnip) *n.* **1.** A strong-scented plant, *Pastinaca sativa,* cultivated for its long, white, edible root. **2.** The root of this plant. [Middle English *pasnepe* (influenced by *nepe,* turnip), from Old French *pasnaie,* from Latin *pastināca,* parsnip, carrot, from *pastinum*†, a kind of two-pronged dibble.]

par·son (párss'n) *n.* **1.** In the Church of England, a clergyman with full legal control of a parish under ecclesiastical law. **2.** Loosely, any clergyman. [Middle English *persone,* parish priest, from Old French, person, parson, from Medieval Latin *persōna (ecclēsiae),* "PERSON (of the church)".]

par·son·age (párss'n-ij) *n.* The official residence of a parson.

parson bird *n.* The **tui** *(see).* [Referring to the white tuft at the throat, which resembles a clerical collar.]

parson's nose *n.* The fatty end part of the rump of a cooked fowl. Also called "pope's nose".

part (part) *n. Abbr.* **p., pt. 1. a.** A portion, division, or segment of a whole; a piece: *a book in three parts.* **b.** An essential constituent; a vital element of the whole. **2.** Any of several equal portions or fractions into which a whole may be divided: *a drink of two parts gin and one part vermouth.* **3.** *Mathematics.* An aliquot part. **4. a.** An organ, member, or other division of an animal or plant. **b.** *Plural.* See **private parts. 5.** A component that can be separated from a system: *a machine part.* **6. a.** A role given to an actor to play. **b.** The words of the role as spoken. **c.** These words written down. **7.** One's proper or expected share in responsibility or obligation; a duty: *It was not my part to give advice.* **8.** *Usually plural.* Ability; talent: *a man of many parts.* **9.** *Usually plural.* A region, land, or territory: *foreign parts.* **10.** *U.S.* A hair **parting** *(see).* **11.** *Music.* **a.** Any of the melodic lines in concerted music or in harmony. **b.** The individual score for it. **—for (one's) part.** So far as one is concerned. **—for the most part.** To the greater extent; generally; mostly. **—in good part.** With good grace: *to take a joke in good part.* **—in part.** To some extent; partly. **—on the part of.** By, felt by, or done by. **—play a part. 1.** To act in a dissembling or deceitful manner. **2.** To be significant or of use. Used with *in: played a part in the revival of folk music.* **—take part.** To join in; participate. Usually used with *in: He took part in the celebration.* **—take (someone's) part.** To side with someone in a disagreement; support: *He took her part in the argument.*
~*v.* **parted, parting, parts.** *—tr.* **1.** To divide or break into separate pieces, portions, sections, or the like: *parted the bread.* **2.** To separate by or as if by coming between; put or keep apart: *parted the boxers.* **3.** To comb (the hair) away from a dividing line on the scalp. **4.** *Informal.* To cause to abandon or leave: *He won't be parted from the television.* *—intr.* **1.** To divide or break; come apart: *The curtain parted in the middle.* **2.** To go away from one another; separate: *parted as friends.* **3.** To separate into ways going in different directions: *The road parts in the forest.* **4.** To leave; depart. Usually used with *from.* **5.** To die. Used euphemistically. —See Synonyms at **separate. —part with.** To give up; relinquish.
~*adv.* Partially; in part: *part yellow, part green.*
~*adj. Abbr.* **p., pt.** Not full or complete; partial: *a part owner.* [Middle English, from Old French, from Latin *pars* (stem *part-*).]

part. 1. participle. **2.** particular.

par·take (paar-táyk) *v.* **-took** (-to͝ok || -to͝ok), **-taken, -taking, -takes.** *—intr.* **1.** To take part or have a share; participate. Used with *in: partake in the festivities.* **2.** To take or be given part or portion. Usually used with *of: He partook of his mother's cake.* **3.** To have some quality or characteristic; show evidence. Used with *of: a nature that partook of the ferocity of the lion.* *—tr. Archaic.* To take or have part of; share. —See Synonyms at **share.** [Back-formation from *partaker,* from *part taker.*] **—par·tak·er** *n.*

par·tan (párt'n) *n. Scottish.* A crab. [Middle English of Celtic origin.]

part and parcel *n.* A basic part or essential function.

part·ed (pártid) *adj.* **1.** Separated or divided into parts; cleft. **2.** Kept apart; separated: *parted fingers.* **3.** *Botany.* Cleft almost to the base, so as to have distinct divisions or lobes; partite. **4.** *Archaic.* Deceased.

par·terre (paar-táir) *n.* A flower garden having the beds and paths arranged to form a pattern. [French, from Old French, from *par terre,* on the ground : *par,* on, from Latin *per* + *terre,* ground, from Latin *terra.*]

part exchange *n.* The system or an instance of paying for an object partly in money and partly by another object, often a second-hand object of the same type.

par·the·no·car·py (párthinō-kaarpi, paar-théenō-) *n. Botany.* The production of fruit without fertilisation or seed production. [Greek *parthenos*†, virgin + *-carpy,* from CARPOUS.]

par·the·no·gen·e·sis (párthinō-jénni-siss) *n.* **1.** *Biology.* Reproduction of organisms in which an unfertilised egg cell develops into an individual genetically identical to its parents. **2.** Human reproduction without apparent participation of the male; virgin birth. [New Latin : Greek *parthenos*†, virgin + -GENESIS.] **—par·the·no·ge·net·ic** (-jə-néttik) *adj.* **—par·the·no·ge·net·i·cal·ly** *adv.*

Par·the·non (pártha-non, -nan) *n.* A temple dedicated to Athena on the Acropolis at Athens, built (447–32 B.C.). The Elgin marbles formed an outside frieze. See feature, next page.

Par·thi·a (párthi-ə). Ancient region south of the Caspian Sea. Approximating to Khorasan in modern northeast Iran, it was part of the Persian Empire, but from 250 B.C. established and expanded its own empire to control the area between the rivers Euphrates and Indus. It was eventually overthrown by the Sassanian Persians (A.D. 226). **—Par·thi·an** *n. & adj.*

Parthian shot *n.* A remark, comment, or the like, directed in or as if in retreat, in simulation of the Parthian archers who shot at the enemy while feigning flight. Also called "parting shot".

par·tial (pársh'l) *adj.* **1.** Of, pertaining to, or affecting only part; not total; incomplete: *a partial truth.* **2.** Favouring one person or side over another or others; biased; prejudiced. **3.** Having a particular liking for someone or something; especially fond. Usually used with *to: very partial to fat Turkish cigarettes and strawberries.* **4.** *Mathematics.* Of, designating, or pertaining to operations or sequences of operations, such as differentiation and integration, when applied to only one of several variables in a function at a time.
~*n.* **1.** In music and acoustics, a **harmonic** *(see).* **2.** *Mathematics.* A partial derivative. [Middle English *parcial,* from Old French *partial,* from Late Latin *partiālis,* from Latin *pars* (stem *part-*), PART.] **—par·tial·ness** *n.*

partial derivative *n. Mathematics.* The derivative with respect to a single variable of a function of two or more variables, regarding other variables as constants. Also called "partial".

partial eclipse *n.* An eclipse in which a celestial body is only partly obscured.

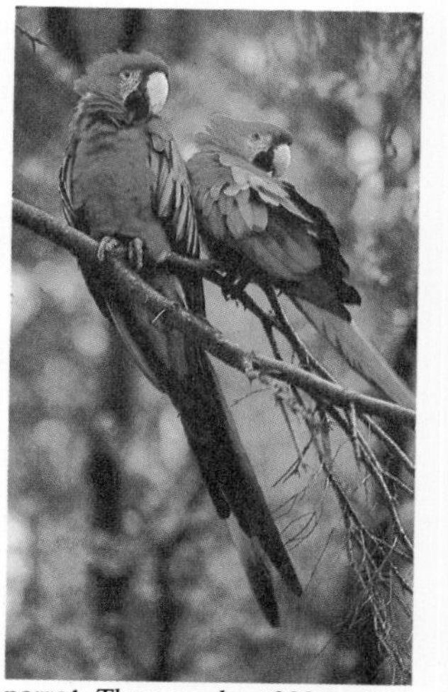

parrot *There are about 300 species of parrot – a family which includes macaws, cockatoos, and budgerigars – found worldwide in warm regions. They are brightly coloured and normally live in trees where they feed on fruit, nuts, and seeds. These are scarlet macaws, from Central and South America.*

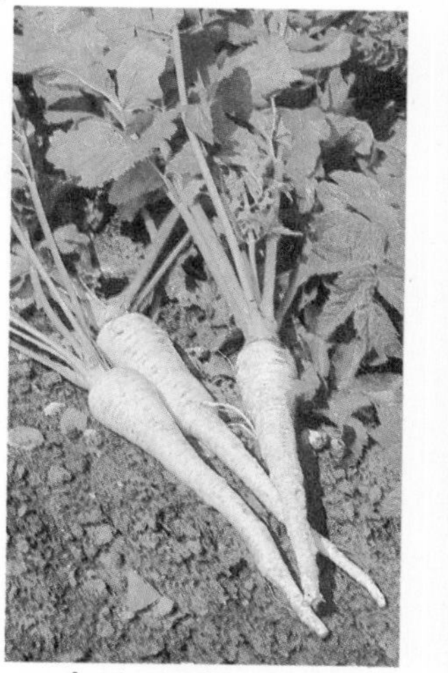

parsnip *A sweet-flavoured root vegetable related to the carrot.*

Parthenon

ARCHITECTURAL MASTERPIECE OF ANCIENT GREECE
The Parthenon, the most perfect Doric temple

The Parthenon is the architectural triumph of ancient Greece, and even the time-ravaged remains that stand above Athens today express the power and grace so brilliantly combined by its builders. The temples on the Acropolis were built after the Persian wars at the inspiration of Pericles to glorify Athens. None does so more than the Parthenon. It was built between 447 and 432 B.C. by Ictinus, to the oldest Greek order of building, the Doric. The entablature above the chunky, fluted columns includes sculptured blocks (metopes) showing battles between centaurs and Lapiths – semilegendary people of ancient Thessaly.

partial fraction *n.* Any of a set of fractions having an algebraic sum equal to a specified fraction, usually a ratio of polynomials.

par·ti·al·i·ty (pàrshi-ál-əti) *n., pl.* **-ties. 1.** The state or condition of being partial. **2.** Favourable prejudice or bias. **3.** A special fondness; a predilection: *a partiality for antiques.*

par·tial·ly (pársh'l-i) *adv.* **1.** In part; to a certain degree; partly. See Usage note at **partly. 2.** *Archaic.* **a.** In a prejudiced or biased manner. **b.** With special favour or fondness towards something or someone; with partiality.

partial pressure *n.* The individual pressure of one gas in a mixture of gases, equal to the pressure that the gas would exert if no other components were present. See **Dalton's Law.**

partial product *n. Mathematics.* A number formed in long multiplication by multiplying one number by a digit of the multiplier.

partial tone *n.* In music and acoustics, a **harmonic** *(see).*

par·ti·ble (pártəb'l) *adj.* Capable of being parted, divided, or separated; divisible. Said of estates or property. [Late Latin *partibilis,* from Latin *partīrī,* to divide, from *pars* (stem *part-*), PART.]

par·tic·i·pant (paar-tíssipənt ‖ pər-) *n.* One who participates or takes part in something.
~*adj.* Participating; taking part.

par·tic·i·pate (paar-tíssi-payt ‖ pər-) *intr.v.* **-pated, -pating, -pates.** To take part; join or share with others. Usually used with *in.* See Synonyms at **share.** [Latin *participāre,* from *particeps,* a partaker : *pars* (stem *part-*), PART + *-ceps,* "-taking".] —**par·tic·i·pance** (-pənss) *n.* —**par·tic·i·pa·tor** (-paytər) *n.*

par·tic·i·pa·tion (paar-tíssi-páysh'n ‖ pər-) *n.* **1.** The act of participating: *participation in a game.* **2.** A taking part or sharing, such as sharing in a company's profits or influencing its decision-making: *worker participation.*

par·ti·ci·ple (párti-sipp'l, pártsip'l ‖ paar-tíssip'l) *n. Abbr.* **p., part.** *Grammar.* A nonfinite form of a verb that is used with an auxiliary verb to indicate certain tenses, and that can also function independently as an adjective; for example, in the expressions *a glowing coal* and *a beaten dog, glowing* and *beaten* are participles. See **misrelated participle, past participle, present participle.** [Middle Eng-

lish, from Old French *participle, participe,* from Latin *participium,* from *particeps,* partaker (translation of Greek *metokhē*). See **participate.**] —**par·ti·cip·i·al** (-síppi-əl) *adj.* —**par·ti·cip·i·al·ly** *adv.*

par·ti·cle (pártik'l) *n.* **1.** A very small piece or part; a speck: *a particle of dust.* **2.** A very small amount, trace, or degree: *not a particle of doubt.* **3.** *Physics.* **a.** A body whose spatial extent and internal motion and structure, if any, are negligible. **b.** Any very small constituent of matter. **c.** An **elementary particle** *(see).* **4.** *Grammar.* **a.** In various languages, such as ancient Greek, any of a class of forms, such as prepositions or conjunctions, consisting of a single word that has no inflection. **b.** A suffix or prefix, such as *-ness* or *in-.* **5.** *Archaic.* A small division or section of something written, such as a clause of a document. **6. a.** A small piece of a consecrated Host. **b.** Any of the smaller, individual Hosts. [Middle English, from Latin *particula,* diminutive of *pars* (stem *part-*), PART.]

particle accelerator *n. Physics.* An **accelerator** *(see).*

par·ti·col·oured (párti-kullərd) *adj.* Having different parts or sections coloured differently; pied. [Middle English *party,* particoloured, from Old French *parti,* striped, from the past participle of *partir,* to divide, from Latin *partīre,* from *pars* (stem *part-*), PART.]

par·tic·u·lar (pər-tíckew-lər, -tík-yə-) *adj. Abbr.* **part. 1.** Of, belonging to, or associated with a single person, group, thing, or category; not general or universal: *his particular beliefs.* **2.** Separate and distinct from others; specific: *I wanted a particular hat.* **3.** Worthy of note; exceptional; special: *of particular interest.* **4. a.** Especially or excessively attentive to or concerned with details or niceties; fussy: *particular about his dress.* **b.** Detailed; full: *a particular account of the events.* **5.** *Logic.* Encompassing some, but not all, of a class or group; restricted. Said of a proposition. *Some snakes are venomous* is a particular proposition. Compare **universal. 6.** *Mathematics.* Designating a solution of a differential equation that is distinguished from the general representation of the set of all solutions by virtue of not involving arbitrary constants.
~*n.* **1.** An individual item, fact, or detail: *correct in every particular.* **2.** *Plural.* Items or details of information or news: *Tell us the particulars of your trip to China.* **3.** *Logic.* A particular proposition. —**in particular.** Particularly; especially. [Middle English *particuler,* concerned with details, from Old French, from Late Latin *particulāris,* from Latin *particula,* detail, PARTICLE.]

par·tic·u·lar·ise, par·tic·u·lar·ize (pər-tíckew-lə-rīz, -tík-yə-) *v.* **-ised, -ising, -ises.** —*tr.* **1.** To state or enumerate in detail; itemise. **2.** To mention or treat individually; specify; single out. —*intr.* To give particulars. —**par·tic·u·lar·i·sa·tion** (-rī-záysh'n ‖ *U.S.* -ri-) *n.* —**par·tic·u·lar·is·er** *n.*

par·tic·u·lar·ism (pər-tíckew-lə-riz'm, -tík-yə-) *n.* **1.** Exclusive adherence to or interest in one's own group, party, sect, or nation. **2.** A policy of allowing each state in a nation or federation to act independently. **3.** *Theology.* The belief that divine grace is reserved for a select group of people rather than for everyone. —**par·tic·u·lar·ist** *n.* —**par·tic·u·lar·is·tic** (-rístik) *adj.*

par·tic·u·lar·i·ty (pər-tíckew-lárrəti, -tík-yə-) *n., pl.* **-ties. 1.** The quality, or state, of being particular rather than general. **2.** Exactitude of detail, especially in description: *characters delineated with great particularity.* **3.** Attention to or concern with details; fastidiousness: *showed some particularity regarding his choice of friends.* **4.** A specific point or detail; a particular. **5.** *Rare.* An individual characteristic; a peculiarity.

par·tic·u·lar·ly (pər-tíckew-lər-li, -tík-yə-) *adv.* **1.** To a great degree; especially: *I particularly wanted to go for a walk.* **2.** With particular reference or emphasis; specifically: *Any colour will do, but I was thinking of blue particularly.* **3.** In a particular manner; severally; individually. **4.** With regard to particulars; in detail.

par·tic·u·late (paar-tíckew-lət, -lit, -layt) *adj.* **1.** Of, pertaining to, or formed of separate particles. **2.** *Genetics.* Designating the type of inheritance proposed by Gregor Mendel, in which characteristics are determined by discrete particles (genes). See **Mendel's laws.**

part·ing (párting) *n.* **1.** The act or process of separating or dividing. **2.** A division or separation: *the parting of the ways.* **3.** A departure or leave-taking. **4.** *British.* The line on the head where the hair is parted. Also *U.S.* "part". **5.** The act or time of a person's dying. Used euphemistically.
~*adj.* **1.** Given, received, or done at a departure or leave-taking: *a parting kiss.* **2.** *Literary.* Going away; leaving; departing. **3.** Dividing; separating.

parting shot *n.* A **parthian shot** *(see).*

par·ti pris (párti prée) *n., pl.* **partis pris** *(pronounced as singular).* *French.* An opinion or decision already arrived at; a prejudice. ["Side taken".]

par·ti·san¹, par·ti·zan (párti-zán, -zan ‖ -z'n, -s'n) *n.* **1.** A militant supporter of a party, cause, faction, person, or idea: *vociferous battle betwen partisans of the rival theories.* **2.** A member of a detached, often unofficially organised body of fighters who attack or harass an enemy within occupied territory; a guerrilla.
~*adj.* **1.** Of, pertaining to, or characteristic of a partisan or partisans. **2.** Favouring or supporting a single party or cause: *partisan politics.* [French, from Tuscan Italian *partigiano,* from *parte,* part, from Latin *pars* (stem *part-*), PART.] —**par·ti·san·ship** *n.*

par·ti·san², par·ti·zan (pártiz'n) *n.* A weapon, resembling a pike, having a long shaft surmounted by a blade with broad, projecting cutting edges, used chiefly in the 16th and 17th centuries. [Obsolete French *partizane,* from obsolete Italian *partesana,* "weapon used by a supporter", variant of (Tuscan) *partigiano,* PARTISAN (supporter).]

par·ti·ta (paar-téetə) *n. Music.* A set of related instrumental pieces, such as a series of variations or a suite. [Italian, from the feminine past participle of *partire.* See **partite.**]

par·tite (pár-tīt) *adj.* **1.** Divided into parts; parted. Often used in combination: *tripartite.* **2.** *Botany.* Parted. [Latin *partītus,* past participle of *partīre,* to divide, from *pars* (stem *part-*), PART.]

par·ti·tion (paar-tísh'n || pər-) *n.* **1. a.** The act or process of dividing something into parts. **b.** The state of being so divided. **2.** Something that separates, such as a thin wall dividing a larger area. **3.** A part or section into which something has been divided. **4.** *Mathematics.* **a.** An expression of a positive integer as a sum of positive integers. **b.** The decomposition of a set into a family of mutually exclusive sets. **5.** *Logic.* The analysis of a class into its component parts. **6.** *Chemistry.* The distribution of a substance between two different phases, as between two solvents. **7.** *Law.* A division of real property among joint owners or tenants.
~*tr.v.* **partitioned, -tioning, -tions. 1. a.** To divide into parts, pieces, or sections: *The island was partitioned.* **b.** *Law.* To divide (property) among several owners. **2.** To divide or separate by means of a partition. Often used with *off: partition an alcove off.* [Middle English *particioun,* from Old French *partition,* from Latin *partītiō* (stem *partītiōn,* from *partīre,* to divide. See **partite.**] **—par·ti·tion·er** *n.* **—par·ti·tion·ist** *n.* **—par·ti·tion·ment** *n.*

par·ti·tive (pártitiv) *adj.* **1.** Serving to divide something into parts. **2.** *Grammar.* Indicating a part as distinct from a whole. The phrase *some of the coffee* is a partitive construction. In certain inflected languages, such constructions are put into the genitive case.
~*n. Grammar.* **1.** A partitive word, such as *many* or *less.* **2.** A partitive construction or case. [Medieval Latin *partītīvus,* from Latin, from *partīre,* to divide. See **partite.**] **—par·ti·tive·ly** *adv.*

part·let (párt-lit, -lət) *n.* A woman's garment worn especially in the 16th century, consisting of a covering for the neck and shoulders, and having a band or ruffle at the neck. [Middle English *patelet,* from Old French *patelete,* band of cloth, diminutive of *patte,* paw, band. See **patten.**]

part·ly (pártli) *adv.* In part; in some degree; not completely.
Usage: *Partly* and *partially* are not usually interchangeable. *Partly* has the wider application, being used primarily when the emphasis is on the part as opposed to the whole of some physical thing *(a partly finished jigsaw),* or when the meaning is "to some extent" *(He is partly to blame). Partially* indirectly emphasises the whole of a condition or state, and generally means "to a limited degree" *(The move was partially successful).*

part·ner (pártnər) *n.* **1.** A person associated with another or others in some activity of common interest, especially: **a.** A member of a business partnership. **b.** A spouse. **c.** Either of two persons dancing together. **d.** Either of a pair or a team in a game or sport, such as bridge or tennis. **2.** *Usually plural. Nautical.* A wooden framework used to strengthen a ship's deck at the point where a mast or other structure passes through it.
~*tr.v.* **partnered, -nering, -ners. 1.** To make a partner of. **2.** To bring together as partners. **3.** To be the partner of. [Middle English *partener,* variant of *parcener,* from Anglo-French, PARCENER.]
Synonyms: *partner, colleague, ally, confederate, accomplice, associate.*

part·ner·ship (pártnər-ship) *n.* **1.** The state of being a partner; an association of partners. **2. a.** A contract entered into by two or more persons in which each agrees to share the labour and expenses in a joint business enterprise. **b.** The people involved in such a partnership. **c.** The relationship between these people.

part of speech *n. Grammar.* Any of a group of traditional classifications of words according to their functions in context. The chief ones are **noun, pronoun, verb, adjective, adverb, preposition, conjunction,** and **interjection** *(all of which see).* In addition, an **article** *(see),* is sometimes considered as belonging to this classification.

par·ton (pár-ton) *n.* A hypothetical elementary particle, such as a quark, suggested as a constituent of nucleons. [PART + -ON.]

par·took. Past tense of **partake.**

par·tridge (pártrij) *n., pl.* **-tridges** or collectively **partridge. 1.** Any of several plump-bodied Old World game birds, especially of the genera *Perdix* and *Alectoris.* **2.** *U.S.* Any of several similar or related birds. [Middle English *partrich,* from Old French *perdriz,* from Latin *perdix,* from Greek.]

par·tridge·ber·ry (pártrij-berri) *n., pl.* **-ries. 1.** A creeping, woody, evergreen plant, *Mitchella repens,* of eastern North America, having small white flowers and scarlet berries. Also called "twinberry". **2.** The fruit of this plant.

partridge wood *n.* The hard, durable, reddish-brown wood of a tropical American tree, *Andira inermis,* used for construction work and furniture. [Referring to its colour and striping.]

part song *n.* A song for three or more voice parts; especially, a short, unaccompanied piece for a choir.

part-time (párt-tīm) *adj.* For or during less than the customary time: *a part-time job.* **—part-time** *adv.* **—part-tim·er** *n.*

par·tu·ri·ent (paar-téwr-i-ənt || -tóor-) *adj.* **1.** About to bring forth young; being in labour. **2.** Of or pertaining to giving birth. **3.** About to produce or come forth with something, such as an idea or discovery. [Latin *parturiēns* (stem *parturient-*), present participle of *parturīre,* to be in labour, from *parere* (future participle *parturus*), to bear.] **—par·tu·ri·en·cy** *n.*

par·tu·ri·tion (pártewr-ísh'n) *n.* The act of giving birth; childbirth. [Late Latin *parturītiō* (stem *parturitiōn-*), from Latin *parturīre,* to be in labour. See **parturient.**]

part·work (párt-wurk) *n. British.* A series of magazines on a particular subject, issued in regular instalments, that builds up into a whole unit or book.

par·ty (párti) *n., pl.* **-ties. 1. a.** A social gathering for pleasure, amusement, or the like: *a cocktail party.* **b.** A group of persons gathered together to participate in some activity: *a sailing party.* **2.** *Sometimes capital* **P.** A permanent political group organised to promote and support its principles and candidates for public office: *the Labour Party.* **3.** *Law.* **a.** A person or group that has entered into a contract. **b.** A person or group involved in legal proceedings. **4.** A participant or accessory: *I won't be party to this corruption.* **5.** *Informal.* A person. Used humorously: *collapse of stout party!*
~*adj.* **1.** Of or appropriate to a social gathering or party: *a party dress; the party spirit.* **2.** Of, pertaining to, or supporting a political party. **3.** *Heraldry.* Divided into two parts. Said of a shield. [Middle English *partie,* part, party, from Old French, from the past participle of *partir,* to divide, from Latin *partīre.* See **partite.**]

party line *n.* **1.** A telephone line shared by two or more subscribers. **2.** The official policies, attitudes to particular issues, and principles of a political party to which loyal members are expected to adhere; especially, such policies, attitudes, and principles regarded as dogmatic. **—par·ty-line** (párti-līn) *adj.*

party politics *n.* Politics conducted merely for the sake of one's political party rather than for a greater cause, such as the good of the country.

par·ty-poop·er (párti-pōōpər) *n. Chiefly U.S. Slang.* One who declines to participate enthusiastically at a social gathering.

party wall *n. Law.* A wall built on the boundary line of adjoining properties and shared by two owners or tenants.

pa·rure (pə-róor, -réwr) *n.* A set of matched jewellery or other ornaments. [French, adornment, from Old French, from *parer,* to prepare, adorn, from Latin *parāre,* to prepare.]

par value *n.* The value imprinted on a share certificate or bond which provides the basis for interest, dividend, or share of capital; face value.

Par·va·ti (paar-vaátee). *Hinduism.* The wife of Siva.

parve. Variant of **pareve.**

par·ve·nu (párvə-new || -nōō) *n.* A person who has risen above his socioeconomic class without the background or qualifications for his new status, and is thought to be an upstart. [French, from the past participle of *parvenir,* to arrive, from Latin *parvenīre,* to come through : *per,* through + *venīre,* to come.] **—par·ve·nu** *adj.*

par·vis, par·vice (párviss) *n.* **1.** An enclosed courtyard or space in front of a palace or church. **2.** A portico or colonnade in front of a church. [Middle English *parvys,* from Old French *parvis,* from Late Latin *paradīsus,* enclosed garden, PARADISE.]

Parzival. See **Percival.**

pas (paa) *n., pl.* **pas** (paaz, *or as singular*). **1.** A dance step or series of steps. **2.** A dance. **3.** The right to go before; precedence. [French, from Latin *passus,* step, from the past participle of *pandere,* to stretch out.]

PAS, PASA para-aminosalicyclic acid.

Pas·a·de·na (pássə-déenə). City of southern California, United States. Situated northeast of Los Angeles, it is a holiday resort and has a specialised electronics industry.

pas·cal (pass-kál, -kaál, pássk'l) *n. Symbol* **Pa** An SI unit of pressure equal to a pressure of one newton per square metre. [After Blaise PASCAL.]

Pas·cal (pass-kál, -kaál, pásk'l) *n.* A high-level computing language used for dealing with alphabetic data, and widely used as a teaching language. [After Blaise PASCAL.]

Pas·cal (pass-kál), **Blaise** (1623–62). French mathematician, philosopher, and scientist. He invented a calculating machine, discovered that the pressure in a fluid is everywhere equal (leading to the invention of the hydraulic press and the barometer), and investigated the mathematical theory of probability and the differential calculus. After religious revelations (1654) he became a Jansenist; his posthumously published *Pensées* (1670) is a study of Christian beliefs, human nature, and the inadequacy of reason.

Pascal's triangle *n.* A triangular array of numbers in which each number is the sum of the two neighbouring numbers in the row above. [After Blaise PASCAL who devised it.]

pas·chal (paásk'l, pásk'l) *adj.* Of or pertaining to the Passover or to Easter. [Middle English *paskal,* from Old French *pascal,* from Late Latin *paschālis,* from *pascha,* Passover, Easter, from Late Greek *paska,* from Hebrew *pesaḥ,* PESACH.]

paschal lamb *n.* **1.** A lamb eaten at the feast of the Passover. **2.** *Capital* **P,** *capital* **L.** Jesus Christ.

pas de deux (də dő) *pl.* **pas de deux.** A ballet figure or dance for two persons. [French, "step for two".]

pa·se (paá-say) *n.* In bullfighting, a presentation and movement of the cape by the matador to attract, receive, and direct the charge of the bull. Also called "pass". [Spanish, "a passing", "pass", from *pasar,* to pass, from Vulgar Latin *passāre.* See **pass.**]

pasela. Variant of **bonsella.**

pash (pash) *n. Informal.* An infatuation. [Shortened from *passion.*]

pa·sha, pa·cha (paá-shə, pá-, pə-sha̋a) *n.* **1.** Formerly, a high official, especially a provincial governor, in the Ottoman Empire and various Islamic kingdoms. **2.** *Capital* **P.** A mode of address for or title of such an official or a person considered worthy of equal respect. When used as a title, it is placed after the surname: *Glubb Pasha.* [Turkish, probably from *baş,* chief.]

pa·sha·lik, pa·sha·lic (paáshə-lik) *n.* The jurisdiction of or territory presided over by a pasha. [Turkish.]

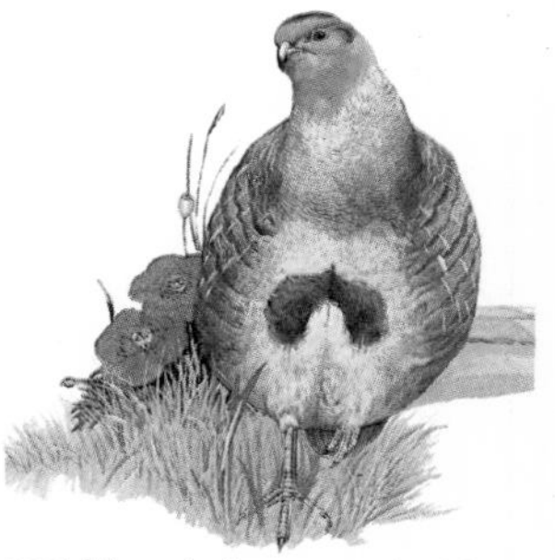

partridge *A plump game bird that lives mostly on the ground. It feeds largely on insects and plants, and nests in a grass-lined scrape in the earth. Partridges are common on farmland in Europe and parts of western Asia, and have been introduced to North America. This is the common partridge,* Perdix perdix.

PRONUNCIATION KEY

a, trap; aa, father; ai, fair; ar, star; aw, lawn; ay, play; b, bb, stab; rubber; ch, church; ck, ticket; d, dd, dead; ladder; e, dress; ee, bee; er, defer; ew, few; ewr, pure; ə, about; ər, letter; f, ff, fife; differ; g, gg, giggle; h, hat; i, kit; ī, price; īr, fire; j, judge; k, kick; l, ll, let; 'l, needle; m, mm, man; n, nn, no; 'n, sudden; ng, thing; o, lot; ō, no; ŏŏ, foot; ōō, shoe; oor, poor; ow, cow; owr, hour; oy, boy; p, pp, pepper; r, rr, red; s, ss, sauce; sh, ship; t, tt, totter; th, thick; th, this; smooth; u, cut; ur, turn; v, vv, valve; w, wet; y, yes; z, zz, zebra; zh, vision; pleasure

IN FOREIGN WORDS:

aN, ON, Saint-Saëns; hl, Llanelli; Hluhluwe; kh, loch; lough; Khaled

STRESS MARK:

ín-sīt, insight; in-sít, incite

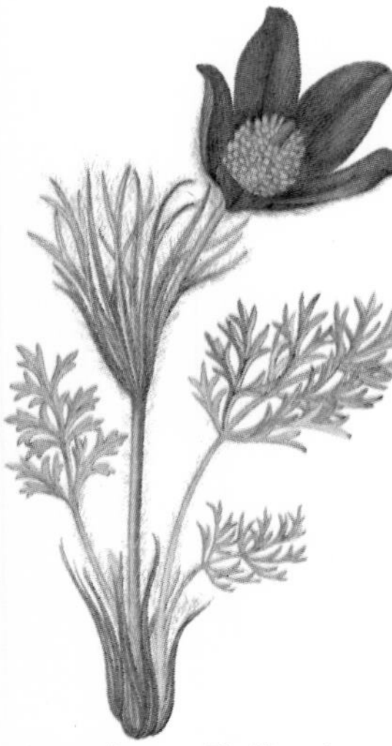

pasqueflower *The Eurasian pasqueflower,* Anemone pulsatilla – *also known as* Pulsatilla vulgaris – *is found among grasses on dry, chalky slopes. Some forms have reddish or whitish flowers instead of the violet one shown here.*

PRONUNCIATION KEY

a, trap; aa, father; ai, fair; ar, star; aw, lawn; ay, play; b, bb, stab; rubber; ch, church; ck, ticket; d, dd, dead; ladder; e, dress; ee, bee; er, defer; ew, few; ewr, pure; ə, about; ər, letter; f, ff, fife; differ; g, gg, giggle; h, hat; i, kit; ī, price; īr, fire; j, judge; k, kick; l, ll, let; 'l, needle; m, mm, man; n, nn, no; 'n, sudden; ng, thing; o, lot; ō, no; ŏŏ, foot; ōō, shoe; oor, poor; ow, cow; owr, hour; oy, boy; p, pp, pepper; r, rr, red; s, ss, sauce; sh, ship; t, tt, totter; th, thick; th, this; smooth; u, cut; ur, turn; v, vv, valve; w, wet; y, yes; z, zz, zebra; zh, vision; pleasure

IN FOREIGN WORDS:

aN, oN, Saint-Saëns; hl, Llanelli; Hluhluwe; kh, loch; lough; Khaled

STRESS MARK:

ín-sīt, insight; in-sī́t, incite

Pash·to (púsh-tō, pásh-) *n.* **1.** An Iranian language, one of the two official languages of Afghanistan. **2.** A speaker of this language. Also called "Pushtu," "Afghan". [Persian *pashtu,* from Afghan *pashtó,* from Old Persian *parshtā-,* "one who asks".] **—Pash·to** *adj.*

Pa·siph·a·ë (pa-síffi-ee,pə-). *Greek Mythology.* The wife of Minos and mother, by a white bull, of the Minotaur.

Pas·more (páss-mawr, paáss-), **(Edwin John) Victor** (1908–). British artist, founder of the London "Euston Road School" (1937). His early work shows the influence of cubism and fauvism, but after 1947 he produced colourful abstracts.

pa·so do·ble (paássō dṓblay, pássō) *n., pl.* **paso dobles. 1.** A Latin-American ballroom dance in duple time. **2.** A piece of music to which a paso doble is danced. [Spanish, "double step".] **—pa·so do·ble** *intr.v.*

Pa·so·li·ni (pássō-léeni; *Italian* paázō-), **Pier Paolo** (1922–75). Italian film director and writer. His films, frequently concerned with religion and Marxism, include *The Gospel According to St Matthew* (1964), *Theorem* (1968), and the sordid *Salo or the 120 days of Sodom* (1975). His murder was never solved.

pasque·flow·er (pásk-flowr, -paásk) *n.* Any of several plants of the genus *Anemone;* especially, the Eurasian species *A. pulsatilla,* having large purple white flowers and plumed fruit. [Earlier *passeflower* (influenced by Old French *pasque,* Easter), from Old French *passefleur* : *passer,* to PASS (surpass) + *fleur, flor,* FLOWER.]

pas·qui·nade (páskwi-náyd) *n.* A lampoon; especially, one posted in a public place.
~tr.v. **pasquinaded, -ading, -ades.** To ridicule with a pasquinade. [French, from Italian *pasquinata,* from *Pasquino,* nickname of an ancient statue in Rome on which lampoons were posted in the 16th century.] **—pas·qui·nad·er** *n.*

pass (paass || pass) *v.* **passed, passing, passes.** *—intr.* **1.** To move on or ahead; proceed: *The path was too narrow for us to pass.* **2.** To run; extend: *The river passes through our land.* **3.** To carry on despite obstacles: *pass through difficult years.* **4.** To catch up with and move past; overtake: *The sports car passed on the right.* **5.** To move past in time; elapse: *The days passed quickly.* **6.** To be transferred from one to another; circulate: *The wine passed round the table.* **7.** To be communicated or exchanged: *Abusive language passed between the two candidates.* **8.** To be transferred or conveyed to another by a will, deed, or the like: *The title passed to the eldest son.* **9.** To undergo transition from one condition, form, quality, or characteristic to another: *Daylight passed into darkness; joy passed into anger.* **10.** To come to an end; be terminated; subside: *His anger passed suddenly.* **11.** To cease to exist; die. Used euphemistically. **12.** To happen; take place: *What passed during the morning?* **13.** To be allowed to happen without notice or challenge: *Let their rude remarks pass.* **14.** To gain success in a test or examination by reaching the required standard: *Every pupil passed.* **15.** To be accepted as something different. Often used with *as* or *for: "would have his Noise and Laughter pass for Wit"* (William Wycherly). **16.** To be approved or adopted: *The motion to adjourn passed.* **17.** *Law.* **a.** To pronounce an opinion, judgment, or sentence. Used with *on* or *upon.* **b.** *Chiefly U.S.* To sit in judicial or legal investigation. Used with *on* or *upon: A jury passed on that issue.* **b.** To pronounce an opinion, judgment, or sentence. Used with *on* or *upon.* **18.** *Sports.* To hit, throw, or kick a ball, for example, to a teammate. **19.** In fencing, to thrust or lunge. **20. a.** In card games, to forgo one's turn to play or bid. **b.** In quizzes, board games, and similar contests, to miss a question or round of play by declining to attempt an answer or by opting to forgo one's turn. **21.** *Informal.* To decline an offer: *"Who's for another beer?" "I'll pass".* *—tr.* **1.** To go by without stopping; leave behind: *passed him on the final bend.* **2. a.** *Rare.* To go by without paying attention to; let go unmentioned. **b.** *Chiefly U.S.* To fail to pay (a dividend). **3.** To go beyond; exceed: *The returns passed all expectations.* **4.** To go across; go through: *pass enemy lines.* **5. a.** To gain success in (a test or examination) by reaching the required standard: *He passed every test.* **b.** To officially allow to pass a test, examination, or the like: *The instructor passed all the candidates.* **6. a.** To cause to move: *passed his hand over the fabric.* **b.** To cause to move into a specified position: *pass a cable round a cylinder.* **c.** To cause to move as part of a process: *pass liquid through a filter.* **7.** To cause to go by: *pass soldiers in review.* **8.** To allow to go by or elapse; spend: *passed the winter in Venice.* **9. a.** To cause to be transferred from one to another; circulate: *pass the news quickly.* **b.** To hand over to someone else: *pass the bread.* **c.** To circulate (money) fraudulently: *pass counterfeit banknotes.* **d.** *Law.* To transfer title or ownership of. **10.** *Sports.* To throw, hit, or kick (a ball, for example) to a teammate. **11.** To cross over; issue from: *No secrets pass her lips.* **12.** To discharge; void (bodily waste). **13. a.** To approve; adopt: *Parliament passed the bill.* **b.** To be sanctioned, ratified, or approved by: *The bill passed the House of Commons.* **14.** To pronounce; utter: *pass judgment.* **15.** To go past without noticing. Used with *by: passed them by.* **—bring to pass.** *Archaic.* To cause to happen. **—come to pass.** *Archaic.* To happen. **—pass away. 1.** To go away in time; end; terminate. **2.** To die. Used euphemistically. **3.** To spend or while away (time). **—pass off. 1.** To offer, sell, or put into circulation (an imitation of something) as genuine. **2.** To stop gradually: *The pain eventually passed off.* **3.** To take place or occur in a specified way: *passed off very well.* **4.** To consider superficially: *passed off the remark.* **—pass on. 1.** To transmit or convey. **2.** To move on. **3.** To die. Used euphemistically. **—pass out. 1.** To distribute. **2.** *Informal.* To faint. **3.** *British.* To finish a military course. **—pass over. 1.** To leave out; overlook; disregard. **2.** To die. Used euphemistically. **—pass up.** *Informal.* To reject; let go by: *pass up an opportunity.*
~n. **1.** The act of passing; passage. **2.** A way through or on which one can move or travel; especially, one in the form of a narrow gap between mountain peaks. **3. a.** A permit, ticket, or authorisation to come and go at will, as at restricted premises. **b.** A free ticket entitling one to use certain forms of public transport for a stated period of time. **c.** A ticket or card entitling one to admission to a usually specified place: *A backstage pass.* **d.** Written leave of absence from military duty. **e.** In South Africa, a **reference book** *(see).* **4.** A sweep or run by an aircraft over an area or target. **5.** A condition or situation, often critical in nature; a predicament: *This has come to a sorry pass.* **6.** A sexual invitation or overture: *He made passes at pretty girls.* **7.** A motion of the hand or the waving of a wand in conjuring. **8.** *Sports.* A transfer of a ball, for example, by hitting, kicking, or throwing between teammates. **b.** In fencing, a lunge or thrust. **10. a.** In card games, a refusal to bid, draw, bet, or play. **b.** In quizzes, board games, and similar contests, a refusal to attempt an answer or play. **11.** In bullfighting, a positioning or flourishing of the cape; a pase. —See Synonyms at **way.**
~interj. Used in card games, quizzes, and the like to indicate a refusal to bid, answer, attempt a play, or the like. [Middle English *passen,* to proceed, from Old French *passer,* from Vulgar Latin *passāre* (unattested), from Latin *passus,* step, pace, stride, from the past participle of *pandere,* to stretch out.]

Usage: *Passed* is the spelling used for the forms of the verb *pass* (past tense and past participle): *He passed/has passed the examination.* For all other uses (adjective, adverb, preposition), the spelling is *past.* The forms can have different meanings: *Passed examinations are better than failed ones, Past examinations can be forgotten.*

pass. 1. passenger. **2.** passive.

pass·a·ble (paáss-əb'l || páss-) *adj.* **1. a.** Capable of being passed: *a passable law.* **b.** Capable of being traversed, or crossed, as a road or stream may be. **2.** Acceptable for general circulation: *passable currency.* **3.** Satisfactory but not outstanding. **—pass·a·ble·ness** *n.* **—pass·a·bly** *adv.*

pas·sa·ca·glia (pássə-kaál-yə, -kál-) *n.* **1.** A 17th- and 18th-century musical form consisting of continuous variations on a ground bass in slow triple time. **2.** A dance to this music. Compare **chaconne.** [Italian, from Spanish *passacalle* : *pasar,* to pass, from (unattested) Vulgar Latin *passāre* (see **pass**) + *calle,* street, from Latin *callis*†, path.]

pas·sage[1] (pássij) *n.* **1.** The act or process of passing: **a.** A movement from one place to another; a going by, through, over, or across; a transit: *the passage of trains.* **b.** The process of elapsing: *the passage of time.* **c.** The process of passing from one state, condition, or stage to another; transition. **d.** The enactment into law of a legislative measure. **2.** A journey, especially one by air or water. **3. a.** The right to travel on something, especially a ship: *book a passage.* **b.** The price paid for this: *worked his passage.* **4.** The right, permission, or power to come and go freely. **5. a.** A channel or duct through, over, or along which something may pass: *the nasal passages.* **b.** A path, corridor or the like. **6 a.** An exchange of words, arguments, or vows between two persons. **b.** An exchange of blows. Used in the phrase *passage at arms.* **7.** A segment of a literary work: *a passage from Gibbon.* **8.** *Music.* **a.** A segment of a composition. **b.** A section of a composition lacking melodic or developmental value but allowing the performer an opportunity to attempt some virtuoso playing; especially, rapid scales and arpeggios. **9.** *Medicine.* An emptying of the bowels. —See Synonyms at **way.** [Middle English, from Old French, from *passer,* to PASS.]

passage[2] *v.* **-saged, -saging, -sages.** *—intr.* **1.** To move sideways in response to pressure applied by the rider to the other side. Used of a horse. **2.** To cause a horse to move in this way. Used of a rider. *—tr.* To cause (a horse) to passage. **—pas·sage** *n.*

passage hawk *n.* A young falcon or hawk that is captured while it is migrating.

pas·sage·way (pássij-way) *n.* A corridor.

pas·sant (páss'nt) *adj. Heraldry.* Designating a beast facing and walking towards the viewer's right with one front leg raised: *a lion passant.* [Middle English, from Old French, from the present participle of *passer,* to PASS.]

pass·book (paáss-bŏŏk || páss-, -bŏŏk) *n.* **1.** A small book held by a depositor, as with a building society, in which deposits and withdrawals are recorded. **2.** A book in which a merchant records credit sales. **3.** In South Africa, a **reference book** *(see).*

Pass·chen·daele (pásh'n-dayl). Village in Flanders, west Belgium. It was the site of the third Battle of Ypres (1917) in World War I, a British offensive resulting in the loss of 245,000 British troops.

pass degree *n.* A degree given by a college or university, indicating that a candidate has reached a standard entitling him to a degree but not an honours degree.

pas·sé (pássay, paássay, pa-sáy) *adj.* **1.** Out-of-date; no longer current or in fashion. **2.** Past the prime; faded; aged. [French, past participle of *passer,* to pass, from Old French, to PASS.]

passe·men·terie (pass-méntri, *French* -MON-trée) *n.* Ornamental trimming for a garment, such as braid, lace, or metallic beads. [French, from *passement,* from *passer,* from Old French, to PASS.]

pas·sen·ger (pássinjər) *n. Abbr.* **pass. 1.** A person who travels in a train, aeroplane, ship, bus, or other conveyance, without participating in its operation. **2.** *British Informal.* A member, as of a team,

who fails to contribute sufficient effort towards the work or enterprise undertaken. **3.** *Archaic.* A wayfarer or traveller.
~*adj.* Of or for passengers rather than goods: *a passenger train.* [Middle English *passyngere, passager,* from Old French *passager,* (adjective), passing, from *passage,* PASSAGE.]

passenger pigeon *n.* An extinct migratory bird, *Ectopistes migratorius,* abundant in North America until the late 19th century.

passe-par·tout (páss paar-tŏŏ, paáss-, -pər, -tŏŏ). **1.** Something enabling one to pass or go everywhere; especially, a master key. **2. a.** A mounting for a picture in which coloured tape forms the frame. **b.** The tape so used. **3.** A mat used in mounting a picture. [French, "pass everywhere".]

passe·pied (paáss-pyáy, páss-) *n.* **1.** A dance, originating in France, that resembles the minuet and became popular in England towards the end of the 17th century. **2.** A piece of music for this dance. [French, "pass-foot".]

pas·ser-by (paáss-ər-bí || páss-) *n., pl.* **passers-by** (-ərz-bí). A person who passes by, often by chance and on foot.

pas·ser·ine (pássə-rīn, -reen) *n.* A bird of the order Passeriformes, which includes perching birds and songbirds such as the jays, blackbirds, finches, warblers, and sparrows. More than half of all known birds belong to this order. [Latin *passerīnus,* from *passer*†, sparrow.] **—pas·ser·ine** *adj.*

pas seul (sōl) *n.* A dance or ballet figure performed by one person. [French, "step by oneself".]

pas·si·ble (pássib'l) *adj.* Capable of suffering; sensitive. [Middle English, from Old French, from Medieval Latin *passībilis,* from Latin *patī* (past participle *passus*), to suffer.] **—pas·si·bil·i·ty** (-bílləti) *n.*

pas·sim (pássim) *adv.* Throughout; frequently. Used in textual annotation to indicate that the word or passage occurs frequently in the work cited. [Latin *passim,* here and there, everywhere, scattered about, adverbial formation from *pandere,* to spread out, scatter.]

pass·ing (paáss-ing || páss-) *adj.* **1.** Of brief duration; transitory: *a passing fancy.* **2.** Cursory; superficial; casual: *a passing glance.* **3.** *Archaic.* Very; great: *" 'Tis a passing shame."* (Shakespeare).
~*adv. Archaic.* Very; surpassingly: *passing rich.*
~*n.* **1.** The act of one that passes or the state of having passed. **2.** A place where or a means by which one can pass. **3.** Death. Used euphemistically. **—in passing.** Casually or briefly, in the course of speaking about or doing something else: *mentioned in passing.*

passing bell *n.* A **death knell** *(see).*

passing note *n. Music.* A note that is not part of a particular melodic sequence but is placed between two notes or chords to provide a smooth transition from one to the other.

passing shot *n.* In tennis, a shot that is hit beyond the reach of an opponent at the net.

pas·sion (pásh'n) *n.* **1.** Any powerful emotion or appetite, such as love, joy, hatred, anger, or greed. **2. a.** Ardent adoring love. **b.** Strong sexual desire; lust. **c.** The object of such love or desire. **3. a.** Boundless enthusiasm: *a passion for travelling.* **b.** The object of such enthusiasm. **4.** An abandoned display of emotion, especially of anger: *a passion of remorse.* **5.** *Archaic.* Passivity, as opposed to action. **6.** *Archaic.* Martyrdom. **7.** *Capital* **P. a.** The sufferings of Christ in the period following the Last Supper and including the Crucifixion. **b.** A narrative of this (as in any of the Gospels), or a musical setting or serial pictorial representation of it. —See Synonyms below and at **feeling.** [Middle English, from Old French, from Late Latin *passiō* (stem *passiōn-*), (translation of Greek *pathos*), suffering, from Latin *patī* (past participle *passus*), to suffer.] **—pas·sion·less** *adj.* **—pas·sion·less·ly** *adv.*

Synonyms: *passion, fervour, enthusiasm, zeal, ardour.*

pas·sion·al (pásh'n'l) *adj.* Of or pertaining to passion.
~*n.* A book relating the sufferings of saints and martyrs.

pas·sion·ate (pásh'n-ət, -it) *adj.* **1.** Capable of or having intense feelings. **2.** Easily angered; bad-tempered. **3.** Amorous; lustful. **4.** Showing or expressing strong emotion; ardent: *a passionate speech against injustice.* **5.** Arising from or marked by passion: *a passionate rage.* **—pas·sion·ate·ly** *adv.*

pas·sion·flow·er (pásh'n-flowr) *n.* Any of various chiefly tropical American vines of the genus *Passiflora,* usually having large, showy flowers. Some species bear edible fruit. See **granadilla.** [From the imagined resemblance of its parts to aspects of Christ's Passion such as the crown of thorns, the nails, and the cross.]

passion fruit *n.* The edible fruit of the passionflower. Also called "granadilla".

Passion play *n.* A play representing the Passion of Christ.

Passion Sunday *n.* The last Sunday but one before Easter.

Pas·sion·tide (pásh'n-tīd) *n.* The fortnight between Passion Sunday and Easter.

Passion Week *n.* **1.** The week between Passion Sunday and Palm Sunday. **2.** See **Holy Week.**

pas·sive (pássiv) *adj.* **1.** Receiving or subjected to an action without responding or initiating an action in return. **2.** Accepting without objection or resistance; submissive; compliant: *passive obedience.* **3.** Not participating, acting, or operating; inert. **4.** *Finance.* Designating certain bonds or shares that do not bear interest. **5.** *Abbr.* **pass.** *Grammar.* Designating a verb form or voice used to indicate that the grammatical subject is the object of the action or the effect of the verb; for example, in the sentence *They were impressed by his manner,* the verb *were impressed* is in the passive voice. **6.** *Chemistry.* Rendered inactive. Said of metals that form a protective coating that prevents further reaction. **7.** *Electronics.* **a.** Having no source of power. **b.** Not amplifying or controlling a signal. **8.** Designating or relating to an aerial, satellite, or other device that receives or reflects radio waves, without emitting them. Compare **active.** —See Synonyms at **inactive.**
~*n. Abbr.* **pass.** *Grammar.* **1.** The passive voice. **2.** A verb or construction in this voice. [Middle English, from Latin *passīvus,* capable of suffering, from *patī* (past participle *passus*), to suffer.] **—pas·sive·ly** *adv.* **—pas·sive·ness, pas·siv·i·ty** (pa-sívvəti, pə-) *n.*

passive euthanasia *n.* Euthanasia effected by the withholding of treatment that would prolong the patient's life.

passive resistance *n.* Resistance to authority or law by nonviolent methods, such as refusal to comply or peaceful demonstrations.

passive smoking *n.* The inhaling of the smoke from the cigarettes, cigars, or pipes of others, regarded as a health hazard.

pas·siv·ism (pássiviz'm) *n.* **1.** Passive character or behaviour. **2.** The theory and practice of passive resistance. **—pas·siv·ist** *n.*

pass·key (paáss-kee || páss-) *n.* Any of various kinds of keys, such as a **master key** or **skeleton key** *(both of which see).*

pass laws *pl.n.* In South Africa, the laws and by-laws regulating black people's rights of movement and domicile. See **reference book.**

Pass·o·ver (paáss-ōvər || páss-) *n. Judaism.* A festival beginning on the evening of the 14th of Nisan and traditionally celebrated for eight days. It commemorates the escape of the Jews from Egypt. Exodus 12. Also called "Pesach", "Pesah". See **Seder.** [From the phrase *pass over,* translation of Hebrew *pesaḥ,* PESACH.]

pass·port (paáss-pawrt || páss-, -pōrt) *n.* **1.** An official document issued by a government that certifies the identity and citizenship of an individual and grants him permission to travel abroad. **2.** A permit issued by a foreign country allowing one to transport goods or to travel through that country. **3.** An official document issued to a ship, especially a neutral merchant ship in time of war, authorising it to leave port, or to enter certain waters freely. **4.** Anything that enables one to be admitted or accepted: *His wit was his passport into high society.* [French *passeport,* safe-conduct, permission to pass through a port : *passer,* to PASS + PORT.]

pas·sus (pássəss) *n., pl.* **passus** or **-suses.** A section or division of a story, poem, or the like, especially in medieval literature. [Latin, a stretch, section, from past participle of *pandere,* to stretch.]

pass·word (paáss-wurd || páss-) *n.* A secret word or phrase that certifies the speaker's identity, membership, or right to be admitted.

past (paast || past) *adj.* **1.** No longer current; gone by; finished. **2.** Having existed or occurred in, or belonging to, an earlier time; bygone: *past events.* **3.** Just gone by or elapsed: *in the past month.* **4.** Having served formerly in some official capacity: *a past president.* **5.** *Grammar.* Of, pertaining to, or designating a verb tense or form used to express an action, event, or condition completed or begun prior to the time it is expressed.
~*n.* **1. a.** The time before the present. Preceded by *the*: *in the past.* **b.** That which has occurred in the past: *came to terms with the past.* **2. a.** Former background, career, experiences, and activities: *a distinguished past.* **b.** A former period of someone's life kept secret, especially so that his or her reputation may be maintained: *a man with a past.* **3.** *Grammar.* **a.** The past tense. **b.** A verb form in the past tense.
~*adv.* **1.** Earlier than the present time; ago: *forty years past.* **2.** So as to pass by or go beyond: *He waved as he walked past.*
~*prep.* **1.** Beyond in time; later than; after: *It is past midnight.* **2. a.** Beyond in position: *the lake past the meadow.* **b.** Moving beyond: *drove past the wreckage.* **3.** Beyond the power, scope, extent, or influence of: *The problem is past understanding.* **4.** Beyond the number or amount of: *The child couldn't count past 20.* **—past it.** Unable to do those things which one could do in the past; no longer capable. **—would not put it past (someone).** To regard someone as having such competence, or of being of such a nature, as to be capable of a particular action or achievement. [Middle English *passed, past,* from the past participle of *passen,* to PASS.]

pas·ta (pástə || *chiefly U.S.* paástə) *n.* **1.** Paste or dough made of flour and water, used dried, as in macaroni, or fresh, as in ravioli. **2.** A prepared dish of pasta. [Italian, from Late Latin, PASTE.]

paste[1] (payst) *n.* **1.** A smooth viscous adhesive, such as flour and water or starch and water, used to join light materials, such as paper and cloth. **2.** Any similar soft, smooth, thick mixture. Often used in combination: *toothpaste.* **3.** A smooth dough of water, flour, and butter or other shortening, used in making pastry. **4.** A food that has been pounded until it is reduced to a smooth, creamy mass: *anchovy paste.* **5.** A sweet, doughy confection: *almond paste.* **6.** Moistened clay used in making porcelain or pottery. **7. a.** A hard, brilliant glass used in making artificial gems. **b.** A gem made of this glass. In this sense, also called "strass".
~*tr.v.* **pasted, pasting, pastes. 1.** To cause to adhere by applying paste. **2.** To cover with something to which paste has been applied: *He pasted the wall with posters.* [Middle English, from Old French, from Late Latin *pasta,* dough, paste, from Greek *pastē,* barley porridge, from *pastos,* sprinkled, from *passein,* to sprinkle.]

paste[2] *tr.v.* **pasted, pasting, pastes.** *Slang.* To punch, beat, or hit. [Alteration of BASTE (to beat).]

paste·board (páyst-bawrd || -bōrd) *n.* **1.** A thin, firm board made of sheets of paper pasted together or of pressed paper pulp, used especially to make book covers. **2.** *Slang.* **a.** A ticket. **b.** A playing card. **c.** A visiting card.
~*adj.* **1.** Made of pasteboard. **2.** Weak and pliable; flimsy. **3.** Fake; counterfeit.

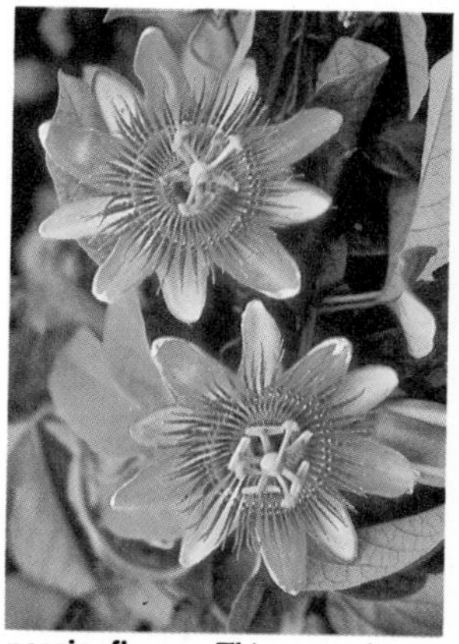

passionflower *This genus of flowering plants gets its name from its association with the Passion of Christ. The bloom's spiny centre is said to symbolise the crown of thorns, and the petals are said to represent ten of the 12 apostles. The two left out are Judas Iscariot – because he betrayed Christ – and Peter – because he denied Christ. This species is* Passiflora caerulea.

pas·tel (pást'l, pa-stél) n. 1. a. A dried paste made of ground and mixed pigment, chalk, water, and gum, used to make crayons. b. A crayon of this material. 2. A picture or sketch drawn with such a crayon. 3. The art or process of drawing with such crayons. 4. A soft, delicate hue; a light tint. 5. A sketchy or brief prose work. [French, from Italian *pastello*, from Late Latin *pastellus*, woad dye, crayon, diminutive of *pasta*, PASTE (referring to the paste of decocted woad twigs).] —**pas·tel** —adj. —**pas·tel·ist, pas·tel·list** n.

pas·tern (páss-tern, -tərn) n. 1. The part of a horse's foot between the fetlock and hoof. 2. The bone comprising this part. In this sense, also called "pastern bone". 3. A comparable part of the leg of a dog or other quadruped. [Middle English *pastron*, a horse's hobble, hence the part of the leg to which it is attached, from Old French *pasturon*, variant of *pasture*, a hobble, from Late Latin *pāstōria*, a sheep's hobble, from *pāstor*, PASTOR.]

Pas·ter·nak (pástər-nak; *Russian* pəsteer-nák), **Boris (Leonidovich).** (1890–1960). Russian author and translator. His *Dr. Zhivago* (1957), a novel of disillusionment with the Russian Revolution was banned by the Soviet authorities. Expelled by the Soviet Writers' Union (1958), he was forced to refuse the Nobel prize.

paste-up (páyst-up) n. 1. Any composition of light, flat objects pasted on a sheet of paper or other backing; a collage. 2. *Printing.* A layout consisting of type proofs, artwork, or both, exactly positioned and prepared for making a printing plate. In this sense, also *U.S.* "mechanical".

Pas·teur (pa-stór), **Louis.** (1822–95). French microbiologist and chemist. The founder of modern microbiology, he became professor at the Sorbonne (1867) and discovered that microorganisms in the air were responsible for fermentation in beer and milk. In investigating ways of excluding these organisms, he developed the process of pasteurisation. He also developed vaccines for anthrax, rabies, and chicken cholera.

pas·teur·i·sa·tion (páass-tər-ī-záysh'n, páss-, -chər, -tewr- ‖ *U.S.* -i-) n. The process of destroying most disease-producing microorganisms and limiting fermentation in milk, beer, and other liquids by application of heat. [Invented by Louis PASTEUR.]

pas·teur·ise, pas·teur·ize (páass-tər-īz, páss-, -chər-, -tewr-) tr.v. -ised, -ising, -ises. To subject (a liquid, especially milk) to pasteurisation. —**pas·teur·is·er** n.

Pasteur treatment n. A rabies treatment in which the growth of antibodies is stimulated during the incubation of the disease by increasingly strong inoculations of the attenuated rabies virus. Also called "pasteurism". [After Louis PASTEUR.]

pas·tic·cio (pa-stích-ō, -steéch-) n., pl. -ci (-ee). A work, especially of music, produced by borrowing fragments or motifs from various sources; a potpourri. [Italian, "pasty", "hotchpotch", from Medieval Latin *pastīcius*, pasty, from Late Latin *pasta*, PASTE.]

pas·tiche (pa-steésh, páss-teesh) n. 1. A dramatic, literary, or musical piece openly imitating the previous work of another artist, often with satirical intent. 2. A hotchpotch; a pasticcio. [French, from Italian *pasticcio*, PASTICCIO.]

pas·tille (páss-til, -teel, -t'l, pa-stéel) n. Also **pas·til** (-til, -t'l). 1. A small medicated or flavoured tablet; a lozenge. 2. A tablet containing aromatic substances, burned to fumigate or deodorise the air. 3. A paste or pastel for making crayons. 4. A pastel crayon. [French, from Latin *pāstillus*, roll, diminutive of *pānis*, bread.]

pas·time (páass-tīm ‖ páss-) n. An activity that occupies one's time pleasantly; something that interests, amuses, or diverts.

pas·ti·na (pa-steéna) n. Tiny pieces of macaroni, usually cooked in soups or used as baby food. [Italian, diminutive of *pasta*, pasta, from Late Latin, PASTE.]

pas·tis (pa-steéss) n. An alcoholic drink flavoured with anise. [French *pastis†*.]

past master n. Abbr. **P.M.** 1. One who has formerly held the position of master in an organisation such as a lodge or club. 2. A person thoroughly experienced and skilled in a particular craft.

pas·tor (páass-tər ‖ páss-) n. 1. A Christian minister in the capacity of having spiritual charge over a congregation or other group. 2. *Rare.* A shepherd. 3. A starling, *Sturnus roseus*, of south Europe and Asia, having a pink and black plumage. In this sense, also called "rosy pastor". [Middle English *pastour*, from Old French, from Latin *pāstor*, shepherd, from *pāscere* (past participle *pāstus*), to graze, feed. Sense 1 arises from a recurrent Biblical metaphor, seen in Psalms 23:1, John 10:11 and 21:15.]

pas·tor·al (páass-tərəl, páss-) adj. 1. Of or pertaining to shepherds, herdsmen, and others directly involved in animal husbandry. 2. Used for pasture. Said of land. 3. a. Of or pertaining to the country or country life; rural. b. Having the qualities of idealised country life, such as charming simplicity and a leisurely, carefree pace. 4. Of or designating an artistic work that portrays country life in this way. 5. Designating a branch of theology dealing with the relations between religious truth and spiritual needs or clerical duties. 6. Of or pertaining to a pastor or his duties. —See Synonyms at **rural**.
~n. 1. A literary or other artistic work that portrays rural life, usually in an idealised manner. 2. A letter from a pastor such as a bishop, to those in his care. 3. *Music.* A pastorale. [Middle English, from Latin *pāstōrālis*, from *pāstor*, shepherd, PASTOR.] —**pas·tor·al·ism** n. —**pas·tor·al·ist** n. —**pas·tor·al·ly** adv.

pas·to·rale (pásta-ráal, -ráali ‖ -rál) n., pl. -rali (-ráalee) or -rales. *Music.* 1. An opera or other vocal composition based on a rural theme or subject. 2. An instrumental composition with a tender melody in a moderately slow rhythm, suggestive of idyllic rural life.

Also called "pastoral". [Italian, from *pastorale*, pastoral, from Latin *pāstōrālis*, PASTORAL.]

pas·tor·al·ist (páass-tərə-list, trə- ‖ páss-) n. 1. *Australian.* A sheep farmer or cattle farmer. 2. *Rare.* One who writes pastorals.

pastoral staff n. A **crosier** (see).

pas·tor·ate (páass-tərə-rət, -rit ‖ pástə-) n. 1. The office, rank, or jurisdiction of a pastor. 2. A pastor's term of office with one congregation. 3. A body of pastors; pastors collectively.

past participle n. Abbr. **pp., p.p.** A verb form indicating past or completed action or time. It is used as a verbal adjective in phrases such as *finished work, baked beans,* and with auxiliaries to form the passive voice or perfect and pluperfect tenses in constructions such as *The work was finished.* Also called "perfect participle".

past perfect adj. Designating a verb tense, the **pluperfect** (see). ~n. 1. The pluperfect tense. 2. A verb in this tense.

pas·tra·mi (pə-stráami) n. A highly seasoned smoked beef, usually cut from the breast or shoulder. [Yiddish, from Romanian *pastramă*, from *păstra†*, to preserve.]

pas·try (páystri) n., pl. -tries. 1. A baked paste, of any of various kinds, made from flour, water, and shortening, sometimes with egg yolk, used for the crusts of pies, tarts, and the like. 2. Baked foods collectively, such as pies or tarts, made with this paste. 3. An individual cake or turnover made of flaky pastry, usually topped with icing, and having a sweet filling. [From PASTE.]

past tense n. A verb tense used to express an action, event, or condition that occurred or began in the past. For example, in *While she was sewing, he read aloud,* the verbs *was sewing* and *read* are in the past tense.

pas·tur·age (páass-chər-ij, -tewr- ‖ páss-) n. 1. The grass or other vegetation eaten by grazing animals. 2. a. Land covered with such grass or vegetation. b. A particular piece of such land. c. The right to graze cattle on such land. 3. The business of grazing cattle.

pas·ture (páass-chər, -tewr ‖ páss-) n. 1. The grass or other vegetation eaten as food by grazing animals. 2. a. Land on which such vegetation grows. b. A particular piece of such land.
~v. pastured, -turing, -tures. —tr. 1. To herd (animals) into a pasture to graze. 2. To provide (animals) with pasturage. Used of land. 3. To feed on (vegetation). Used of animals. 4. To use (land) for animals to graze on. —intr. To graze in a pasture. [Middle English, from Old French, from Late Latin *pāstūra*, from Latin *pāscere* (past participle *pāstus*), to pasture, feed.] —**pas·tur·a·ble** adj. —**pas·tur·er** n.

past·y[1] (páysti) adj. -ier, -iest. 1. Resembling paste in colour or consistency. 2. Pale and lifeless-looking. Said of the face or complexion. —**past·i·ness** (páysti-nəss, -niss) n.

pas·ty[2] (pásti, páasti) n., pl. -ties. *Chiefly British.* A pie consisting of an envelope of pastry with a filling of seasoned meat and sometimes vegetables, or of jam or fruit. [Middle English *pastee*, from Old French *paste*, from noun, dough, PASTE.]

past·y[3] (páysti) n., pl. -ies. Either of the patches used by a strip-tease performer to conceal her nipples. [From PASTE (to stick).]

PA system n. A **public-address system** (see).

pat[1] (pat) v. **patted, patting, pats.** —tr. 1. a. To tap gently with the open hand or with something flat. b. To tap or stroke lightly as a gesture of affection. 2. To mould by tapping gently with the hands or a flat implement. —intr. 1. To run or walk with a tapping sound. 2. To hit something or against something gently or lightly. ~n. 1. A light stroke or tap. 2. The sound made by such a stroke or tap, or by light footsteps. 3. A small mass of something, shaped by or as if by patting: *a pat of butter.* —**pat on the back.** *Informal.* A compliment, especially when intended as an encouragement. [Middle English *patte* (probably imitative).]

pat[2] adj. 1. Timely; opportune; fitting: *a pat answer.* 2. Needing no change; exactly right. 3. Glib; somewhat insincere: *Her reply was too pat to be convincing.*
~adv. *Informal.* 1. Without changing position; steadfastly. 2. Perfectly; precisely; aptly. —**have off pat.** *Informal.* To know or have memorised completely. —**stand pat.** *Chiefly U.S. Informal.* 1. To refuse to change one's position or opinion. 2. To decline to draw more cards to a poker hand. [Probably "with a hitting stroke", from PAT (to tap).] —**pat·ly** adv. —**pat·ness** n.

pat[3] n. —**on (one's) pat.** *Australian Slang.* One one's own; alone. [Rhyming slang, short for *Pat Malone*.]

Pat n. *Informal.* An Irishman. [Short for *Patrick,* a very common Christian name in Ireland.]

pat. patent; patented.

pa·ta·gi·um (pə-táy-ji-əm) n., pl. -gia (-ji-ə). *Zoology.* 1. A thin membrane extending between the fore and hind limb to form a wing or winglike extension, as in bats and flying squirrels. 2. An expandable, membranous fold of skin between the wing and body of a bird. [New Latin, from Latin, gold edging on a woman's tunic, from Greek *patageion* (unattested), "clattering gold braid", from *patagos*, a clatter (imitative).]

Pat·a·go·ni·a (pátta-góni-ə). Region of South America in Argentina and Chile. Extending southwards from the Río Colorado to the Straits of Magellan, it is a cool, semiarid plateau at the foot of the Andes. The chief occupation is the raising of sheep, and its mineral wealth includes oil, iron ore, and coal. —**Pat·a·go·ni·an** adj. & n.

pat·ball (pát-bawl) n. *Informal.* A game, especially tennis, when played at an unexpectedly low level of competence.

patch (pach) n. 1. A small piece of material affixed to another, larger piece to conceal or reinforce a weakened or worn area. 2. a. Any small piece of cloth used for patchwork. b. *Military.* A small cloth badge affixed to a sleeve or lapel to indicate the unit to which one belongs. **3.** A dressing or bandage applied to protect a wound or sore. **4.** A small pad or shield of cloth worn over an injured eye or to conceal a missing eye. **5.** A **beauty spot** *(see).* **6. a.** A small piece of land. **b.** *U.S.* The produce grown on such a piece of land: *a patch of beans.* **7.** *Informal.* A district for which a policeman, or a group of policeman, is responsible. **8.** A small part or section of a surface that differs from or contrasts with the whole: *The flowers made white patches against the grass.* **9.** A discoloured area on the skin or mucous membrane. **10.** A small piece or part of anything: *"that little patch of blue which prisoners call the sky"* (Oscar Wilde). **11.** A period of experience of a specified type: *went through a bad patch after the divorce.* **—not a patch on.** *Informal.* Not comparable to; not nearly as good as.

~tr.v. **patched, patching, patches. 1. a.** To put a patch or patches on, especially when mending clothes. **b.** To be a patch for or on. Used of material. **2. a.** To make by sewing scraps of material together: *patch a quilt.* **b.** To make by piecing various elements together, especially hastily: *They patched a plan together.* **3.** To mend, repair, or put together, especially hastily, clumsily, or poorly: *patching old costumes for the tour.* **4.** *Electronics & Computing.* To join up (circuits) temporarily by a connected board into which plugs may be fitted. **—patch up.** To settle; make up: *They patched up their quarrel.* [Middle English *pacche,* perhaps variant of *peche,* from Old French *pece, pieche,* PIECE.] **—patch·a·ble** *adj.* **—patch·er** *n.*

patch board *n. Electronics.* A **plugboard** *(see).*

patch·ou·li, pach·oo·li (páchōōli, pə-chōōli) *n., pl.* **-lis.** Also **patch·ou·ly** *pl.* **-lies. 1.** Any of several Asiatic trees of the genus *Pogostemon,* especially *P. patchouly* and *P. cablin,* having leaves that yield a fragrant oil used in the manufacture of perfumes. **2.** A perfume made from this oil. [Tamil *paccilai* : *paccu,* green + *ilai,* leaf.]

patch pocket *n.* A pocket consisting of a patch of material sewn onto the outside of a garment, as on a shirt or a pair of jeans, rather than inset through a slit in the fabric.

patch test *n.* A test for allergic sensitivity made by applying a suspected allergen to the skin in a small surgical pad.

patch·work (pách-wurk) *n.* **1.** Needlework consisting of various coloured patches of material sewn together, as in a quilt. **2.** A collection of miscellaneous or incongruous parts; a jumble: *a patchwork of outmoded theories.*

patch·y (páchi) *adj.* **-ier, -iest. 1.** Made up of or marked by patches: *a patchy pair of trousers.* **2.** Uneven in quality or performance: *patchy work.* **—patch·i·ly** *adv.* **—patch·i·ness** *n.*

patd. patented.

pate (payt) *n.* **1.** The head; especially, the top of the head: *a bald pate.* **2.** The brains; the intellect. [Middle English *pate*†.]

pâte (paat) *n.* Paste used in making porcelain and pottery. [French, patty, paste, from Old French *paste,* PASTE.]

pâ·té (páttay, pátti, *French* paa-táy) *n.* **1.** A firm meat paste often made with liver. **2.** A firm paste made of other ingredients, such as fish or vegetables. **3.** A small pastry filled with meat or fish. [French *paté(e),* from Old French *pasté(e),* from *paste,* PASTE.]

pâté de foie gras (də fwaá graá) *n.* A rich paste made from livers of specially fattened geese, usually flavoured with truffles. Also called "foie gras". [French, "pâté of fat liver".]

pa·tel·la (pə-téllə) *n., pl.* **-tellae** (-téllee). **1. a.** A flat, triangular bone located at the front of the knee joint. Also called "kneecap". **b.** *Biology.* Any dish-shaped formation. **2.** An ancient Roman pan or dish. [Latin, diminutive of *patina,* plate. See **paten.**] **—pa·tel·lar, pa·tel·late** (-tél-ət, -it, -ayt) *adj.*

pa·tel·li·form (pə-télli-fawrm) *adj.* Shaped like a pan, dish, or cup: *the patelliform shell of the limpet.* [New Latin *patelliformis* : PATELL(A) + -FORM.]

pat·en, pat·in (pátt'n) *n.* **1.** A plate, especially one used to hold the Eucharistic bread. **2.** A thin disc of metal. [Middle English *paten, pat(e)yn,* from Old French *patene,* from Latin *patina,* dish, pan, from Greek *patanē.*]

pa·ten·cy (páyt'n-si) *n.* **1.** The state or quality of being obvious. **2.** The state of being open.

pa·tent (páyt'nt, pátt'nt. *Note. Although the pronunciation* (páyt'nt) *is the general one in Britain,* (pátt'nt) *is preferred for the technical senses 1–3.) n. Abbr.* **pat. 1. a.** A grant made by a government to an inventor, assuring him the sole right to make, use, and sell his invention for a certain period of time. **b.** The official document certifying such a grant, **letters patent** *(see).* **2.** Something that is protected by such a grant. **3. a.** In the United States, a grant made by a government to an individual, conveying to him fee-simple title to public lands. **b.** The official document of such a grant. **c.** The land so granted. **4.** A sign or piece of evidence that one is entitled to possess something or has a certain quality, for example: *a patent of respectability.*

~adj. (for senses 2, 3, 6, 7, 8 usually páyt'nt) **1.** Open to general inspection; unsealed. Used chiefly in the phrase *letters patent.* **2.** Obvious; plain: *His insincerity was patent.* **3.** *Informal.* Ingenious; well-thought-out; well-constructed. **4.** *Abbr.* **pat.** Protected by a patent. **5.** *Abbr.* **pat.** Of, pertaining to, or dealing in patents: *patent law.* **6.** *Biology.* Spreading open; expanded. **7.** *Anatomy.* Open; unobstructed. Said of vessels, ducts, and other hollow parts. **8.** Ground and polished on both sides of the glass.

~tr.v. **patented, -enting, -ents.** *Abbr.* **pat. 1.** To obtain a patent on. **2.** To grant a patent to. [As noun, Middle English *(letters) patente,* letters patent, from Old French *(lettres) patentes,* from Medieval Latin *(litterae) patentes,* "open letter or document", from *patentes,* plural of *patens,* open, from the present participle of *patēre,* to be open.] **—pa·tent·a·bil·i·ty** (-ə-billəti) *n.* **—pa·tent·a·ble** *adj.*

pa·tent·ee (páyt'n-tée, pátt'n-) *n.* A person who has been granted a patent.

patent leather (páyt'nt) *n.* **1.** Black leather finished to a hard, glossy surface. **2.** Any of several synthetic materials having a similar appearance. [Made by a once-patented process.]

patent log *(usually* páyt'nt) *n. Nautical.* A torpedo-shaped instrument with rotary fins that is dragged from the stern of a vessel to measure the speed or distance travelled. Also called "screw log", "taffrail log".

pa·tent·ly (páyt'nt-li, *rarely* pátt'nt-) *adv.* Obviously; clearly; plainly.

patent medicine *n. (usually* páyt'nt) A drug or other medical preparation that is protected by a patent and can be bought without a prescription. Not in technical usage.

Patent Office *(usually* pátt'nt) *n.* A government department in which claims for patents are studied and patents are issued and recorded.

pat·en·tor (páyt'n-tər, pátt'n-, -tór) *n.* One that grants a patent.

patent right (pátt'nt, páyt'nt) *n.* The right granted by a patent; especially, the right to have exclusive manufacture and sale of an invention.

pa·ter (páytər) *n. British.* Father. Usually used humorously. [Latin.]

Pa·ter, Walter (Horatio). (1839–94). British critic and essayist. A humanist and believer in "art for art's sake", his works include *Imaginary Portraits* (1887) and *Plato and Platonism* (1893).

pa·ter·fa·mil·i·as (páytər-fə-mílli-ass, páttər-) *n., pl.* **patresfamilias** (páytreez-, páttreez-). The father of a family considered as head of the household. [Latin : *pater,* father + *familiās,* archaic genitive of *familia,* FAMILY.]

pa·ter·nal (pə-térn'l) *adj.* **1.** Of, pertaining to, or characteristic of a father; fatherly. **2.** Received or inherited from one's father. **3.** Related through one's father. [Medieval Latin *paternālis,* from Latin *paternus,* fatherly, from *pater,* father.] **—pa·ter·nal·ly** *adv.*

pa·ter·nal·ism (pə-térn'l-iz'm) *n.* A policy or practice of managing or governing people in a fatherly manner, especially by providing for their needs without giving them responsibility. **—pa·ter·nal·is·tic** (-ístik) *adj.* **—pa·ter·nal·is·ti·cal·ly** *adv.*

pa·ter·ni·ty (pə-térnəti) *n.* **1.** The fact or condition of being a father; fatherhood. **2.** Descent on a father's side; paternal descent. **3.** Authorship; origin. Also used adjectivally: *paternity leave; paternity suit.* [Old French *paternite,* from Late Latin *paternitās* (stem *paternitāt-*), from Latin *paternus,* fatherly, PATERNAL.]

pa·ter·nos·ter (páttər-nóstər) *n.* **1.** *Often capital* **P.** The **Lord's Prayer** *(see),* especially when recited in Latin. **2.** Any of the large beads on a rosary, on which the Lord's Prayer is said. **3.** A sequence of words spoken as a prayer or as a magic formula. **4.** A type of lift in which open compartments move continuously in a looped chain, passing each floor slowly enough for users to enter or alight. **5.** A weighted fishing line having several jointed attachments for hooks connected by beadlike swivels. [Latin *pater noster,* "our father".]

path (paath || path) *n., pl.* **paths** (paathz || pathz, paaths, paths). **1.** A trodden track or way. **2.** Any surface track or way. **3.** A way that allows forward movement: *clear a path through the forest.* **4.** The route or course along which something moves: *the path of a hurricane.* **5.** A course of action or conduct: *the path of righteousness.* —See Synonyms at **way.** [Middle English *path,* Old English *pæth.*] **—path·less** (-ləss, -liss) *adj.*

path. pathological; pathology.

-path *n. suffix.* Indicates: **1.** One who practises a specified type of alternative medicine; for example **naturopath. 2.** One who suffers from a specified disease; for example **psychopath.** [Sense 1, back-formation from -PATHY. Sense 2, from Greek *-pathēs,* -sufferer, from *pathos,* suffering, PATHOS.] **—-path·ic** *adj. suffix.*

Pa·than (pə-taán) *n.* A member of a Pashto-speaking tribal people of Indo-Iranian stock and Muslim religion, living chiefly in northwest Pakistan and Afghanistan. [Hindi *Paṭhan,* from Afghan *Pĕṣtana,* plural of *Pĕṣtūn,* an Afghan, from *pashtó,* the Afghan language. See **Pashto.**]

pa·thet·ic (pə-théttik) *adj.* **1.** Of, pertaining to, expressing, or arousing pity, sympathy, or tenderness; full of pathos: *the ragged children made a pathetic sight.* **2.** *Informal.* Inadequate: *a pathetic attempt.* **3.** *Informal.* Of little interest or worth; feeble; useless. —See Synonyms at **moving.** [French *pathétique,* from Late Latin *pathēticus,* from Greek *pathētikos,* from *pathētos,* liable to suffer, from *pathos,* passion, suffering.] **—pa·thet·i·cal·ly** *adv.*

Synonyms: *pathetic, pitiful, regrettable, lamentable.*

pathetic fallacy *n.* The attribution of human emotions or characteristics to inanimate things, as in romantic literature.

path·find·er (paáth-fīndər || páth-) *n.* **1.** One who discovers a way through or into unexplored regions. **2.** An aircraft of pilot who finds a target area and marks it by flares or other signalling devices. **2.** A radar system or radio beacon used for navigation or homing.

patho- *comb. form.* Indicates disease or suffering; for example, **pathogen.** [New Latin, from Greek *pathos,* emotion, suffering.]

path·o·gen (páthə-jen, -jən) *n.* Also **path·o·gene** (-jeen). Any agent that causes disease, especially a microorganism such as a bacterium or fungus. [PATHO- + -GEN.]

path·o·gen·e·sis (páthə-jenni-siss) *n.* Also **pa·thog·e·ny** (pə-thójəni). The origin and development of a diseased or morbid condition. [New Latin : PATHO- + -GENESIS.]

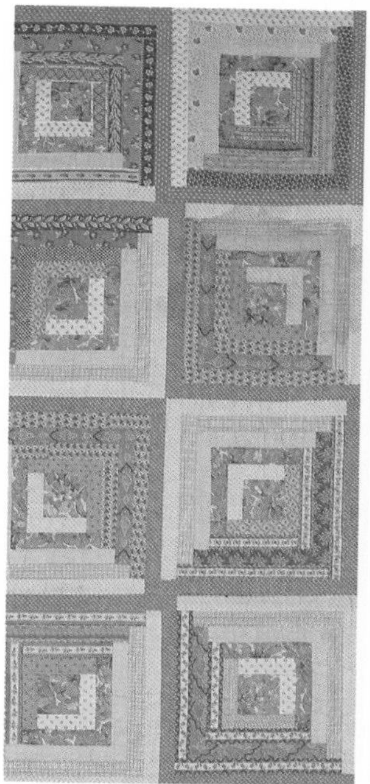

patchwork *An American patchwork quilt made around 1860 and now in the American Museum in Bath, England. Patchwork was developed as a way of using up scraps of fabric.*

path·o·gen·ic (páthə-jénnik) *adj.* Also **path·o·ge·net·ic** (páthō-jə-néttik, -je-). Capable of causing disease: *pathogenic bacteria.* —**path·o·gen·i·ci·ty** (-je-níssəti) *n.*

path·og·no·mon·ic (páthəg-nə-mónnik, pə-thóg-) *adj.* Distinctive or characteristic of a particular disease. Said of signs and symptoms. [From Greek *pathognōmonikos,* "indicating a disease" : PATH- + *gnōmonikos,* from *gnōmōn,* indicator, judge.]

pathol. pathological; pathology.

path·o·log·i·cal (páthə-lójik'l) *adj.* Also **path·o·log·ic** (-lójik). *Abbr.* **path., pathol.** 1. Of or pertaining to pathology. 2. Pertaining to or caused by disease. 3. Unhealthy or compulsive in behaviour: *a pathological liar.* —**path·o·log·i·cal·ly** *adv.*

pa·thol·o·gy (pə-thólləji) *n., pl.* **-gies.** *Abbr.* **path., pathol.** 1. The scientific study of the nature of disease, its causes, processes, development, and consequences. 2. The anatomical or functional manifestations of disease, or of a particular disease, for example changes in organs and tissues. [New Latin *pathologia* and Old French *pathologie,* from Greek *pathologia,* study of passions : PATHO- + -LOGY.] —**pa·thol·o·gist** *n.*

pa·thos (páythoss) *n.* 1. A quality in something or someone, or the evocation of such a quality in art or literature, that arouses feelings of pity, sympathy, tenderness, or sorrow in another: *the pathos of their parting.* 2. A feeling of sympathy or pity. [Greek, passion, suffering.]

Usage: Pathos (and *pathetic*) are general terms to do with the sense of "feeling pity or sympathy". *Bathos* (and *bathetic*) are quite different in meaning and more restricted in application, referring to the sudden intrusion of something banal or ordinary in an elevated or high-flown context, producing a sense of anticlimax.

path·way (páath-way ‖ páth-) *n.* 1. A path. 2. *Chemistry.* A particular chain of reactions leading to a given product.

-pathy *n. comb. form.* Indicates: 1. Feeling; perception; for example, **telepathy.** 2. **a.** Disease; a diseased condition; for example, **neuropathy. b.** A system of treating disease; for example, **homeopathy.** [Latin *-pathia,* from Greek *-patheia,* from *pathos,* PATHOS.]

pa·tience (páysh'nss) *n.* 1. The capacity of calm, uncomplaining endurance, or perseverance: *"This is the story of what a woman's patience can endure."* (Wilkie Collins). 2. Tolerant understanding: *had no patience with fools.* 3. The capacity to put up with delay and wait for the right moment. 4. *Chiefly British.* Any of various card games played by one person in which the cards have to be matched up in certain combinations. Also *U.S.* "solitaire".

Synonyms: patience, resignation, forbearance.

pa·tient (páysh'nt) *adj.* 1. Sharing or marked by patience. 2. Capable of bearing affliction with calmness.

~*n.* 1. A person or animal receiving medical treatment. 2. One who is the recipient of an action. [Middle English *pacient,* from Old French *patient,* from Latin *patiēns* (stem *patient-*), from the present participle of *patī,* to suffer.] —**pa·tient·ly** *adv.*

patin. Variant of **paten.**

pat·i·na (páttinə) *n.* 1. A thin layer of corrosion, usually brown or green, that appears on copper or copper alloys, such as bronze, as a result of natural or artificial oxidation. Compare **verdigris.** 2. The sheen produced by age and use on a surface. 3. Any surface appearance. [Italian, originally, "a mixture prepared in a bowl and used to coat calfskins", from Latin *patina,* shallow dish, plate. See **paten.**]

pa·tine (pa-téen) *tr.v.* **-tined, -tining, -tines.** *Rare.* To coat with a patina. [French, *patine,* from Old French *patene,* from Latin PATINA.]

pat·i·o (pátti-ō ‖ páati-) *n., pl.* **-os.** 1. An inner, roofless courtyard. 2. A usually paved area for dining or relaxation adjacent to a house or flat. [Spanish, courtyard.]

pa·tis·se·rie (pə-téessəri, pa-) *n.* 1. A bakery specialising in rich, fancy cakes and pastries. 2. Such cakes and pastries. [French *pâtisserie,* from Old French, "pastry", from *pâtissier,* pastry cook, from *pastitz* (unattested), pasty, from Vulgar Latin *pastīcium* (unattested), from Late Latin *pasta,* dough, PASTE.]

Pat·more (pát-mawr), **Coventry (Kersey Dighton)** (1823–96). British poet and critic. His works include *The Angel in the House* (1854–63). Associated with the pre-Raphaelite Brotherhood, he later underwent conversion to Roman Catholicism (1864).

Pat·mos, Pát·mos (pát-moss). Greek island of the Dodecanese group, in the southeastern Aegean Sea. It is where Saint John the Divine is reputed to have written the Book of Revelation.

Pat·na (pát-nə; *Hindi* pút-). Capital city of Bihar State, India. Situated on the Ganges, it is on the former site of Pataliputra, capital of the Maghda Kingdom (5th century B.C.) and the Maurya and Gupta Empire. It is now the centre of a rice-growing area.

Patna rice *n.* A type of rice having long grains, used chiefly in savoury dishes. [After PATNA.]

pat·ois (pátwaa; *French* pa-twá) *n., pl.* **patois** (-z, *or as singular*). 1. Any regional French or Swiss dialect. 2. A West Indian French Creole, such as that spoken in St. Lucia. 3. Any English Creole, especially Jamaican Creole. 4. Any regional dialect. 5. Illiterate or substandard speech. 6. The special jargon of a group; cant. [French, perhaps from Old French *patoier,* to handle roughly, from *patte,* paw.]

Pa·ton (páyt'n), **Alan** (1903–). South African novelist. He rose to international fame with *Cry, the Beloved Country* (1948), an indictment of South Africa's racial policies. His other books include *Debbie Go Home* (1961) and *The Long View* (1968). He was national president of the Liberal Party until 1968.

Pat·ras (páttrəss, pə-tráss). Port of western Greece. Situated on the east side of the Gulf of Patras in the north Peloponnese. It was a starting place for the Greek War of Independence (1821).

pat·res·fa·mil·i·as. Plural of **paterfamilias.**

patri– *prefix.* Indicates father; for example, **patriclinous.** [Latin *pater,* father, and Greek *patēr,* father.]

pa·tri·al (páytri-əl) *n. British.* A citizen of the United Kingdom who has the right to British nationality by virtue of birth, adoption, naturalisation, or registration in the United Kingdom; through being the child or grandchild of a patrial; or through being resident, with a certain status, in the United Kingdom for at least five years. —**pa·tri·a·li·ty** (-əl-iti) *n.*

pa·tri·arch (páytri-aark ‖ páttri-) *n.* 1. The paternal leader of a family or tribe. Compare **matriarch.** 2. In the Old Testament: **a.** Any of the progenitors of the human race before the Flood, from Adam to Noah. **b.** Abraham, Isaac, Jacob, or any of Jacob's 12 sons, the eponymous progenitors of the 12 tribes of Israel: *"and Jacob begat the twelve patriarchs"* (Acts 7:8). 3. In the early Christian church, any of the bishops of Rome, Constantinople, Jerusalem, Antioch, and Alexandria. 4. *Roman Catholic Church.* **a.** A bishop who holds the highest episcopal rank after the pope. **b.** The pope himself. 5. In the Eastern Orthodox Church: **a.** The bishop of Alexandria, Antioch, Constantinople, Jerusalem, Moscow, Serbia, or Romania. **b.** The bishop of Constantinople, as leader of the Greek Orthodox Church. Also called "ecumenical patriarch". 6. A high dignitary of the Mormon priesthood, empowered to invoke blessings. Also called "evangelist". 7. A man regarded as the founder or original head of an enterprise, organisation, or tradition. 9. A very old and venerable man; an elder. 10. The most venerable specimen in a group: *patriarch of the herd.* 11. Loosely, any man holding a powerful or authoritative position in a conventional hierarchy who insists on being heard, respected, and obeyed. Often used derogatorily. [Middle English *patriarke,* from Old French *patriarche,* from Late Latin *patriarcha,* from Greek *patriarkhēs* : *patria,* lineage, family, from *patēr,* father + -ARCH.]

pa·tri·ar·chal (páytri-árk'l ‖ páttri-) *adj.* Also **pa·tri·ar·chic** (-árkik). 1. Pertaining to or characteristic of a patriarch; venerable; dignified. 2. Of or pertaining to a patriarchy: *a patriarchal social system.* 3. Ruled by a patriarch: *a patriarchal see.* —**pa·tri·ar·chal·ly** *adv.* —**pa·tri·ar·chal·ism** *n.*

patriarchal cross *n.* A Latin cross having two horizontal bars, of which the upper is the shorter.

pa·tri·ar·chate (páytri-aark-ət, -ayt, -it ‖ páttri-) *n.* 1. The territory, residence, rule, or rank of a patriarch. 2. A patriarchy.

pa·tri·ar·chy (páytri-aarki ‖ páttri-) *n., pl.* **-chies.** 1. A system of social organisation in which descent and succession are traced through the male line. 2. The rule of a people or family by men. 3. A society or social system founded by men and serving their interests alone, so that they retain and inherit power, wealth, privileges, and opportunities that most women do not.

pa·tri·cian (pə-trísh'n) *n.* 1. A member of one of the noble families of the Roman Republic, which before the third century B.C. had exclusive rights to the Senate and the magistracies. Compare **plebeian.** 2. A dignity or title conferred by the Byzantine emperors. 3. A member of the hereditary ruling class in the medieval free cities of Italy and Germany. 4. A member of an aristocracy. 5. A person of notably superior upbringing, manners, and tastes. [Middle English *patricion,* from Old French *patricien,* from Latin *patricius,* (nobleman) of senatorial rank, from *patres,* "fathers", senators, from *pater,* father.] —**pa·tri·cian** *adj.* —**pa·tri·cian·ly** *adv.*

pa·tri·ci·ate (pə-tríshi-ət, -ayt, -it) *n.* 1. The rank of patrician. 2. Patricians as a class; nobility; aristocracy. [Latin *patriciātus,* from *patricius,* PATRICIAN.]

pat·ri·cide (páttri-sīd) *n.* 1. The act of murdering one's father. 2. One who murders his father. [Late Latin *patricīdium* (crime) and Latin *patricīda* (killer) : PATRI- + -CIDE.] —**pat·ri·cid·al** (-síd'l) *adj.*

Pat·rick, Saint (páttrik), (*c.* 385–460). Patron saint of Ireland. Probably born in south Wales, he was kidnapped by pirates and taken to Ireland, escaping after six years to France where he was ordained as a bishop (*c.* 430). Returning to Ireland as a Christian missionary (*c.* 432), he established a see at Armagh and helped to spread Christianity.

pat·ri·cli·nous (páttri-klínəss) *adj.* Also **pat·ro·cli·nous** (páttrō-, páttrə-), **pat·ro·cli·nal** (-klín'l). Mainly derived from the male line. Said of plants and animals. Compare **matriclinous.** [PATRI- + *-clinous,* from Greek *-klinēs,* leaning, from *klinein,* to lean.]

pat·ri·lin·e·al (páttri-línni-əl) *adj.* Relating to, based on, or tracing descent through the male line. Compare **matrilineal.**

pat·ri·lo·cal (páttri-lók'l) *adj. Anthropology.* Pertaining to the custom in some primitive societies of living in the home territory of a husband's family or tribe.

pat·ri·mo·ny (páttri-məni ‖ *U.S.* -mōni) *n., pl.* **-nies.** 1. An inheritance from a father or other ancestor. 2. A legacy; a heritage. 3. An endowment or estate belonging to a church. [Middle English *patrimoine,* from Old French, from Latin *patrimōnium,* from *pater,* father.] —**pat·ri·mo·ni·al** (-mōni-əl) *adj.* —**pat·ri·mo·ni·al·ly** *adv.*

pa·tri·ot (páytri-ət, páttri-) *n.* A person who loves, supports, and defends his country. [Old French *patriote,* compatriot, from Late Latin *patriōta,* from Greek *patriōtēs,* from *patris,* fatherland, from *patēr,* father.] —**pa·tri·ot·ic** (-óttik) *adj.* —**pa·tri·ot·i·cal·ly** *adv.* —**pa·tri·ot·ism** *n.*

pa·tris·tic (pə-trístik, pa-) *adj.* Also **pa·tris·ti·cal** (-'l). 1. Of or pertaining to patristics. 2. *Biology.* Designating similarity between different types of plants or animals due to common ancestry. [PATR(I)- + -IST + -IC.] —**pa·tris·ti·cal·ly** *adv.*

pa·tris·tics *n. Used with a singular verb.* The study of the teachings and lives of the fathers of the early Christian church. Also called "patrology".

pa·trol (pə-trṓl) *n.* **1.** The action of moving about an area for purposes of observation or security. **2.** A person or group of persons who carry out such an action. **3. a.** A military unit sent out on a reconnaissance mission. **b.** One or more vehicles, boats, ships, or aircraft assigned to guard or reconnoitre a given area. **4.** A small group, usually six, of Scouts or Guides, a division of a troop or company. —*v.* **patrolled, -trolling, -trols.** —*tr.* To engage in a patrol of. —*intr.* To engage in a patrol. [French *patrouiller*, from Old French *patouiller*, to paw or paddle around in mud: *patte*, paw (see **patten**) + *-ouiller*, imitative verb suffix.] —**pa·trol·ler** *n.*

patrol car *n.* A police car that patrols an area and is usually in radio contact with headquarters.

pa·trol·man (pə-trṓl-man, -mən) *n., pl.* **-men** (-men, -mən). **1.** *British.* A person employed by a motoring organisation to patrol a given area and go to the assistance of motorists who are in trouble. **2.** *Chiefly U.S.* A policeman or guard who patrols an assigned area.

pa·trol·o·gy (pə-trŏlləji) *n.* **1.** Patristics. **2.** A collection of the writings of the fathers of the early Christian church. [17th century : from Greek *patēr* (stem *patr-*), father + -LOGY.] —**pat·ro·log·i·cal** (páttrə-lójik'l) *adj.* —**pa·trol·o·gist** *n.*

patrol torpedo boat *n.* A PT boat (see).

patrol wagon *n. U.S.* A police van used to convey prisoners.

pa·tron (páytrən; *rarely* páttrən) *n.* **1.** Anyone who supports, protects, or champions; a benefactor: *a patron of the arts.* **2.** A regular customer. **3.** One who has the right to present a clergyman to an ecclesiastical benefice. **4.** In ancient Rome: **a.** The former owner of a freed slave who retained certain rights over him. **b.** The protector of a client. **5.** A patron saint. [Middle English *patroun*, from Old French *patron*, from Medieval Latin *patrōnus*, patron, patron saint, from Latin, defender, advocate, from *pater*, father.] —**pa·tron·al** (pə-trṓn'l, pa- ‖ *chiefly U.S.* páytron'l) *adj.*

pat·ron·age (páttrənij; *rarely* páytrənij) *n.* **1.** Support, encouragement, or championship from a patron. **2.** A patronising manner. **3.** The trade given to a commercial establishment by its customers. **4.** Customers or patrons collectively; clientele. **5.** The power or action of distributing governmental or political positions. **6.** The positions so distributed. **7.** The right to present a clergyman to an ecclesiastical benefice.

pa·tron·ess (páytrə-niss, páttrə-, -ness) *n.* A female patron.

pat·ron·ise, pat·ron·ize (páttrə-nīz ‖ *chiefly U.S.* páytrə-) *tr.v.* **-ised, -ising, -ises.** **1.** To act as a patron to; support. **2.** To go to regularly as a customer. **3.** To treat in an offensively condescending manner. —**pat·ron·is·er** *n.* —**pat·ron·is·ing·ly** *adv.*

patron saint *n.* The guardian saint of any nation, place, craft, activity, class, or person. Also called "patron".

pat·ro·nym·ic (páttrə-nímmik) *n.* A name derived from the first name of one's father or a paternal ancestor; especially, one formed by a suffix or prefix, as in *Johnson*, the son of John. In the Russian formula *Vladimir Ilyich Lenin*, *Ilyich* (son of Ilya) is a patronymic while *Lenin* is a true surname. Compare **metronymic.** [Late Latin *patronymicum*, from *patrōnymicus*, "derived from the name of a father", from Greek *patrōnumia*, patronymic : PATR(I)- + *onuma*, name.] —**pat·ro·nym·i·cal·ly** *adv.*

pa·troon (pə-trṓon) *n. U.S.* Formerly, a member of the Dutch West India Company who was granted proprietary and manorial rights in New York and New Jersey. [Dutch, from French *patron*, patron, from Old French, PATRON.]

pat·sy (pátsi) *n., pl.* **-sies.** *Chiefly U.S. Slang.* A person who is cheated, victimised, or made the butt of a joke. [20th century : origin obscure.]

pat·tée (páttay, pátti) *adj.* Having triangular arms that become wider towards the ends. Said of a cross. Often used after the noun: *a cross pattée.* [French *patte*, paw.]

pat·ten (pátt'n) *n.* A wooden sandal, shoe, or clog; especially, a wooden overshoe raised on a wooden or metal support. [Middle English *patin*, from Old French *patin*, from *patte*, a paw, hoof, from Vulgar Latin *patta*† (unattested).]

pat·ter[1] (páttər) *v.* **-tered, -tering, -ters.** —*intr.* **1.** To make a quick succession of light, soft taps: *Rain pattered on the roof.* **2.** To move with quick, light, soft steps. —*tr.* To cause to patter. —*n.* A succession of quick, light, tapping sounds. [Frequentative of PAT (tap lightly).]

pat·ter[2] *v.* **-tered, -tering, -ters.** —*intr.* **1.** To chatter glibly and rapidly. **2.** To mumble prayers in a mechanical manner. —*tr.* To utter in a glib, rapid, or mechanical manner. —*n.* **1.** Glib, rehearsed, rapid speech, as of an auctioneer, salesman, or comedian. **2.** The jargon of a particular group; cant. **3.** Meaningless talk; chatter. **4.** Rapid speech inserted into a song. [Middle English *patren*, *patern*, from Latin *pater(noster)*, PATER(NOSTER), from the mechanical recitation of the prayer.] —**pat·ter·er** *n.*

pat·tern (páttərn) *n.* **1.** A plan, diagram, or model to be followed in making things: *a dress pattern.* **2.** A representative sample; a specimen. **3. a.** An archetype. **b.** An ideal worthy of imitation: *a pattern of womanly virtues.* **4.** Any artistic or decorative design: *a paisley pattern.* **b.** A design of natural or accidental origin: *the pattern of ice crystals on a windowpane.* **5.** A recurrent set of features or characteristics: *behavioural patterns.* **6.** Form and style in an artistic

work or body of artistic works. **7. a.** The arrangement of identically aimed rifle shots upon a target. **b.** The distribution and spread of shot from a shotgun. **8.** A shape, usually wooden, embedded in sand to make a mould for metal casting. —*tr.v.* **patterned, -terning, -terns.** **1.** To make, mould, or design by following a pattern. Usually used with *on*, *upon*, or *after.* **2.** To cover or ornament with a design or pattern. [Alteration of Middle English *patron*, from Old French, from Medieval Latin *patrōnus*, patron, (hence) "something to be imitated", pattern. See **patron.**]

Pat·ti (pátti), **Adelina** (1843–1919). Spanish-born Italian soprano. She had a voice remarkable for its range, timbre, and flexibility.

Pat·ton (pátt'n), **George Smith Jr.** (1885–1945). U.S. general. A graduate from West Point (1909), during World War II he commanded the Seventh Army during the Sicilian campaign (1943) and led the Third Army in Europe, breaking through the German defences in Normandy and crossing France (1944) to reach eventually the Czech border (1945).

pat·ty (pátti) *n., pl.* **-ties.** **1.** A small pie. **2.** *Chiefly U.S.* A small, oval, flattened cake of chopped or minced food. [French *pâté*, small pie, from Old French *paste*, from *paste*, PASTE.]

pat·u·lous (páttew-ləss) *adj.* Also **pat·u·lent** (-lənt). *Botany.* Spreading or expanded: *patulous branches.* [Latin *patulus*, from *patēre*, to be open.] —**pat·u·lous·ly** *adv.* —**pat·u·lous·ness** *n.*

Pau (pō). Town in southwest France. Capital of the Pyrénées-Atlantiques département, it is a popular resort and produces textiles and leather. It was the seat of the kings of Navarre.

P.A.U. Pan American Union.

pau·a (pów-ə) *n.* A New Zealand abalone, *Haliotis iris,* having edible flesh and an ornamental shell used for decoration. [Maori.]

pau·ci·ty (páwssəti) *n.* **1.** Smallness of number; fewness. **2.** Smallness of quantity; a scarcity. [Middle English *paucite*, from Old French, from Latin *paucitās* (stem *paucitāt-*), from *paucus*, few.]

Paul VI (pawl), born Giovanni Battista Montini (1897–1978). Italian pope (1963–78). He reconvened the second Vatican Council, worked for reform within the Vatican, and reiterated the teachings of his church on contraception in the encyclical *Humanae Vitae* (On Human Life) (1968).

Paul, Saint (c. A.D. 5–67), also known as Saul of Tarsus, The Apostle to the Gentiles. Originally an anti-Christian, he had a vision on the road to Damascus that led to his conversion; his life and doctrines are set forth in the Acts of the Apostles and his epistles.

paul·dron (páwldrən) *n.* Either of two metal plates in a suit of armour designed to protect the shoulder. [French *espauleron*, from Old French *espaule* (*épaule*), shoulder. See **epaulette.**]

Pau·li (pówli), **Wolfgang** (1900–58). U.S. physicist. Born in Vienna, he was educated at Munich and Copenhagen and in 1925 formulated his **exclusion principle** of quantum theory. He was awarded the Nobel prize for physics (1945).

Pauli exclusion principle *n. Physics.* The **exclusion principle** (see). [After Wolfgang PAULI.]

Paul·ine (páwlīn) *adj.* Of or pertaining to St. Paul, his writings, or his teachings and the theological doctrines derived from them. —**Paul·in·ism** *n.* —**Paul·in·ist** *n.*

Pau·ling (páwling), **Linus Carl** (1901–). U.S. biochemist. For his work on the nature of chemical bonding received the Nobel prize for chemistry (1954). For his views against nuclear weapons, detailed in *No More War* (1958), he received the Nobel peace prize (1962). He was also awarded the 1971 International Lenin peace prize.

Paul Jones *n.* A dance in which partners are changed at a given signal. [After John Paul JONES.]

pau·low·ni·a (paw-lṓni-ə) *n.* Any of several trees of the genus *Paulownia,* native to the Orient, having large, heart-shaped leaves and clusters of purplish or white flowers. [New Latin, after Anna *Paulovna* (died 1865), Russian princess.]

paunch (pawnch) *n.* The belly; especially, a pot-belly: *"His hands clasped themselves over his capacious paunch."* (Virginia Woolf). —*tr.v.* **paunched, paunching, paunches.** To disembowel (an animal). [Middle English *paunche*, from Anglo-French, from Old French *pance*, from Latin *pantex*† (stem *pantic-*). —**paunch·i·ness** *n.* —**paunch·y** *adj.*

pau·per (páwpər) *n.* **1.** One who is extremely poor. **2.** Formerly, one who lived on public charity. —**pau·per·ism** *n.* —*tr.v.* **paupered, -pering, -pers.** To pauperise. [Latin, poor.]

pau·per·ise, pau·per·ize (páwpə-rīz) *tr.v.* **-ised, -ising, -ises.** To make a pauper of; impoverish. —**pau·per·i·sa·tion** (-rī-záysh'n ‖ U.S. -ri-) *n.*

pau·piette (pō-pyèt, paw-) *n.* A thin slice of meat wrapped round a savoury filling. [French, from Old French *poupe*, fleshy part, from Latin *pulpa*, PULP.]

pause (pawz) *intr.v.* **paused, pausing, pauses.** **1.** To cease or suspend activity for a time: *She paused to listen.* **2.** To linger; tarry: *pausing for a while at the café.* **3.** To hesitate: *He paused before accepting the task.* —*n.* **1.** A hiatus in action or activity; a temporary respite. **2.** A delay or suspended reaction, as from uncertainty; a hesitation: *After a pause, the audience burst into cheers.* **3.** A break, stop, or rest in speaking or reading for a calculated purpose or effect: *a pause to let the words sink in.* **4. a.** *Music.* A sign indicating a fermata. **b.** *Prosody.* A measured break or rest; a caesura. **5.** A reason for hesitation. Usually used in the phrase *give someone pause.* [Middle English, a pause, from Old French, from Latin *pausa*, from Greek *pausis*, a stopping, from *pauein*, to stop.]

pav *n. Australian Informal.* A dessert, *pavlova (see).*

pa·vane, pa·van (pə-váan, -ván, pávv'n) *n.* Also **pav·in** (pávvin). 1. A slow, stately court dance introduced into England in the 16th century. 2. A piece of music for this dance. [Old French *pavane,* from Old Spanish *pavana,* from Old Italian *(danza) pavanna,* "(dance) of Padua", dialectal variant of *padovana,* feminine of *padovano,* of Padua, from *Padova,* PADUA.]

Pa·va·rot·ti (pávvə-rótti), **Luciano** (1935-). Italian tenor. He sang in a local choir before winning a singing competition in Emilia-Romagna when aged 25. He made his debut at La Scala (1965), and now specialises in Verdi and Puccini.

pave (payv) *tr.v.* **paved, paving, paves.** 1. To cover with any hard, smooth surface that will bear traffic. 2. To cover uniformly, as if with a pavement. 3. To be or compose the pavement of. [Middle English *paven,* from Old French *paver,* from Latin *pavīre,* to strike, stamp.] —**pav·er** *n.*

pa·vé (pávvay) *n.* 1. A setting of precious stones placed together so closely that no metal shows: *a brooch in pavé.* 2. A paved surface. [French, from the past participle of *paver,* to PAVE.]

pave·ment (páyvmənt) *n.* 1. *Chiefly British.* A paved footway along the side of a road. Also *U.S.* "sidewalk". 2. A natural rock pavement resulting from weathering, glacial action, or wind erosion. 3. *U.S.* A hard, paved surface; especially, a roadway. 4. The material of which a pavement is made.

pavement artist *n.* 1. One who draws in chalks or crayons on the pavement in order to obtain money from passers-by. 2. One who executes and sells paintings and drawings, especially portraits of passers-by, in the street.

Pa·via (páavi-ə). Capital city of Pavia province, Lombardy, north Italy. Situated on the river Ticino, it was a centre of romanesque art in the 12th and 13th centuries, and is where St. Augustine is buried. It is now an agricultural centre.

pav·id (pávvid) *adj. Literary.* Fearful; frightened; timid. [Latin *pavidus,* from *pavēre,* to fear.]

pa·vil·ion (pə-víl'yən) *n.* 1. *British.* A building at the edge of a cricket pitch or other sports ground where players may change and rest. 2. An ornate tent, especially of the kind used by knights in medieval Europe. 3. **a.** A temporary, often open structure, used at parks or fairs for amusement or shelter. **b.** A display stand at an exhibition. 4. A building or other structure connected to a larger building; an annexe. 5. Any of a group of related buildings forming a complex, as of a hospital. 6. A part of a building that is higher than the rest and usually ornate. 7. The surface of a brilliant-cut gem that slants outwards from girdle to culet. ~*tr.v.* **pavilioned, -ioning, -ions.** 1. To shelter in or as if in a pavilion. 2. To provide with a pavilion or pavilions. [Middle English *pavilon,* from Old French *paveillon,* from Latin *pāpiliō†* (stem *pāpiliōn-*), butterfly, tent (from its resemblance to a butterfly's wings).]

pav·ing (páyving) *n.* 1. A pavement. 2. Material used to pave surfaces. Also used adjectivally: *a paving stone.*

pav·iour, *U.S.* **pav·ior** (páyv-yər) *n.* 1. A person who puts down paving. 2. Material or tools used for paving. [Middle English *pavier,* from *paven,* PAVE.]

pav·is, pav·ise (pávviss) *n.* A medieval shield large enough to protect the whole body. [Middle English, from Old French *pavais,* from Old Italian *pavese,* "of Pavia", from PAVIA, where pavises were first made.]

Pav·lov (páv-lov; *Russian* -ləf), **Ivan Petrovich** (1849–1936). Russian physiologist and experimental psychologist. For his research on the nature of digestion he received the Nobel prize for physiology and medicine (1904). He is best known for his work on conditioned reflexes in animals.

pav·lo·va (pav-lóvə) *n.* A meringue cake topped with fruit and whipped cream, popular especially in Australia and New Zealand. [After Anna PAVLOVA.]

Pav·lo·va (pav-lóvə; *Russian* pávləvə), **Anna** (1881–1931). Russian ballerina. Making her debut in 1899, she worked with Diaghilev in 1909 and from 1914 toured the world with her own company. Her most famous roles were in *Swan Lake* and *Les Sylphides.*

Pav·lo·vi·an (pav-lóvi-ən) *adj.* 1. Of or pertaining to Pavlov or his theories. 2. Loosely; automatic; mechanical: *a Pavlovian response.*

Pa·vo (páavō) *n.* A constellation in the Southern Hemisphere near Apus and Indus. [Latin *pāvō,* peacock (probably imitative), obscurely related to Greek *taōs,* a peacock. See also **peacock.**]

pav·o·nine (pávvə-nīn) *adj.* 1. Of or like a peacock. 2. Resembling a peacock's tail in colour, design, or iridescence. [Latin *pāvōnīnus,* from *pāvō,* peacock. See **peacock.**]

paw (paw) *n.* 1. The nailed or clawed foot of an animal. 2. *Informal.* A human hand, especially one that is large, clumsy, or dirty. ~*v.* **pawed, pawing, paws.** —*tr.* 1. To strike with the paw or paws. 2. To strike with a repeated scraping motion: "*His black charger pawed the straw*" (W.M. Thackeray). 3. To handle clumsily, rudely, or with amorous intent; caress awkwardly. —*intr.* 1. To scrape the ground with the forefeet: *The horse pawed restlessly.* 2. To make clumsy, grasping motions with the hands. [Middle English *pawe, powe,* from Old French *poue,* from Germanic *pauta* (unattested).] —**paw·er** *n.*

paw·ky (páwki) *adj.* **-ier, -iest.** *British Regional.* 1. Dryly humorous. 2. Shrewd; astute. [Northern English and Scottish dialect *pawk†,* a trick.] —**paw·ki·ly** *adv.* —**paw·ki·ness** *n.*

pawl (pawl) *n.* A hinged or pivoted device adapted to fit into a notch of a ratchet wheel to impart forward or prevent backward motion. Also called "detent". [Dutch *pal,* possibly from Latin *pālus,* stake.]

pawn¹ (pawn) *n.* 1. Something given as security for a loan; a pledge. 2. The condition of being held as a pledge against the payment of a loan: *jewels in pawn.* 3. A person serving as security; a hostage. 4. The act of pawning. ~*tr.v.* **pawned, pawning, pawns.** 1. To give or deposit as security for the payment of money borrowed. 2. To risk; hazard; stake: *pawn one's honour.* [Middle English *paun,* from Old French *pan, pand,* security, from West Germanic *panda* (unattested).] —**pawn·a·ble** *adj.* —**pawn·age** *n.* —**pawn·er, pawn·or** (-ər) *n.*

pawn² *n.* 1. *Abbr.* **P** A chessman of the lowest value, allowed to move one square at a time (or two squares for the first move) and capture on a one-space diagonal forward move. 2. A person or thing used to further the purposes of another. [Middle English *poun, pawne,* from Old French *poon, peon,* from Medieval Latin *pedō* (stem *pedōn-*), a foot soldier, from Latin *pēs* (stem *ped-*), foot.]

pawn·bro·ker (páwn-brōkər) *n.* One who lends money at interest in exchange for personal property left with him as security. —**pawn·bro·king** *n.*

Paw·nee (paw-née) *n., pl.* **-nees** or collectively **Pawnee.** 1. A member of a confederation of four North American Plains Indian peoples. 2. The language of this confederation.

pawn·shop (páwn-shop) *n.* The shop of a pawnbroker.

pawpaw. Variant of **papaw.**

pax (paks) *interj. British Slang.* Used to express a request for a truce, especially among schoolchildren. [Latin, peace.]

PAX, P.A.X. private automatic (telephone) exchange.

Pax·ton (pákstən), **Sir Joseph** (1801–65). British architect and landscape gardener. While working as chief gardener to the Duke of Devonshire he submitted the winning design for the Crystal Palace to house the Great Exhibition of 1851. He used a greenhouse he had designed as his model, producing one of the earliest examples of prefabricated construction, built of iron and glass.

pay¹ (pay) *v.* **paid** or **payed** (for sense 10), **paying, pays.** —*tr.* 1. To remunerate or recompense for goods or services rendered. 2. To give (money) in exchange for goods or services. Often used with *out.* 3. To give the indicated amount of (money owed); discharge (a debt or obligation): *pay taxes.* 4. To yield as recompense or return: *This job pays little.* 5. To undergo; subject oneself to: *pay the penalty.* 6. To bear the cost of: *He paid my way through university.* 7. To afford an advantage to; profit: *It paid him to be generous.* 8. To give or bestow: *pay compliments; pay attention.* 9. To make (a visit or call). 10. *Nautical.* To let out (a rope or cable) gradually. Used with *out.* —*intr.* 1. To make payment. 2. To discharge a debt or obligation. 3. To be profitable or worthwhile. —**pay back.** 1. To return borrowed money to. 2. To avenge oneself on; retaliate against: *paid him back for the unjust treatment he had received.* 3. To extend hospitality, for example, in like manner to: *paid her back for her kindness.* —**pay (one's) way.** To contribute one's own share; pay for oneself. —**pay up.** To pay the full amount demanded. ~*adj.* 1. Requiring payment to operate: *a pay telephone.* 2. Yielding valuable metal in mining: *pay stratum.* ~*n.* 1. The act of paying or state of being paid. 2. Money given in return for work done; a salary; wages. 3. Paid employment; hire: *the men in our pay.* 4. **a.** Recompense or reward: *His thanks were pay enough.* **b.** Retribution or punishment. 5. *Rare.* A person considered with regard to his credit or willingness to pay. [Middle English *payen,* from Old French *paier,* from Medieval Latin *pācāre,* to satisfy, pay, from Latin, to pacify, from *pāx* (stem *pāc-*), peace.]

pay² *tr.v.* **payed** or **paid, paying, pays.** *Nautical.* To coat or cover (seams of a ship, for example) with waterproof materials such as tar or asphalt. [Old French *peier,* from Latin *picāre,* to pitch, to tar, from *pix* (stem *pic-*), pitch.]

pay·a·ble (páy-əb'l) *adj.* 1. Requiring payment on a certain date; due. 2. That can or may be paid. 3. Capable of producing profit: *a payable business venture.* —**pay·a·bly** *adv.*

pay bed *n.* A bed in a British National Health Service hospital paid for by the user, who is treated as a private patient.

pay claim *n.* A demand for an increase in wages or salary.

pay·day (páy-day) *n.* The day on which wages are paid.

pay dirt *n. U.S.* 1. Earth, ore, or gravel with enough metal content to make mining profitable. 2. Something useful or profitable.

P.A.Y.E. *n.* Pay as you earn: a system of tax collection in Britain in which an employee's income tax is deducted from his pay by his employer and paid directly to the government.

payed. *Nautical.* Alternative past tense and past participle of **pay.**

pay·ee (pay-ée) *n.* A person to whom money is paid.

pay·er (páy-ər) *n.* 1. A person who pays. 2. A person named as responsible for paying a bill or note.

pay·ing guest (pay-ing) *n. Abbr.* **P.G.** A lodger or boarder.

pay·load (páy-lōd) *n.* 1. The revenue-producing part of a cargo. 2. *Aerospace.* **a.** The passengers, mail, bombs, or cargo in an aircraft. **b.** The warhead of a missile. **c.** In rockets and satellites, the data-collecting and transmitting equipment. **d.** In manned spacecraft, the personnel, life-support systems, and equipment necessary to accomplish missions.

pay·mas·ter (páy-maastər ‖ -mastər) *n. Abbr.* **pm.** An official or employee in charge of paying wages and salaries.

pay·ment (páymənt) *n. Abbr.* **payt., pt.** 1. The act of paying or state of being paid. 2. That which is paid; compensation; recompense. 3. One's due, reward, or punishment; a requital.

pay·nim (páynim) *n. Archaic.* Any non-Christian, especially a Muslim. [Middle English *painim,* from Old French *paienime,* from Late Latin *pāgānismus,* heathendom, from *pāgānus,* PAGAN.]

pay off *tr.v.* **1. a.** To pay the full amount owed on (a debt). **b.** To get revenge on. **2.** To pay the wages due to and discharge (an employee). **3.** *Informal.* To bribe. *—intr.v.* **1.** To give full return; be profitable: *The effort pays off in the long run.* **2.** *Nautical.* To turn to leeward. Used of a vessel.

pay·off (páy-off, -awff) *n.* **1. a.** Full payment of a salary or wages. **b.** The time of payment. **2.** *Informal.* A final settlement or reckoning; the climax of a narrative, especially of a joke, or of a sequence of events. **3.** Final retribution or revenge. **4.** *Informal.* A bribe.

pay·o·la (pay-ṓlə) *n. U.S. Slang.* **1.** Bribery; especially, the bribing of disc jockeys to promote records. **2.** Such a bribe. [PAY + (VICTR)OLA, originally of record payoffs.]

pay packet *n. British.* An envelope containing an employee's wages or salary, in the form of cash or a cheque. Also *U.S.* "pay envelope".

pay·phone (páy-fōn) *n.* A coin-operated telephone. Also called "call box", *U.S.* "pay station".

pay·roll (páy-rōl) *n.* **1.** A list of employees receiving wages, with the amounts due to each. **2.** The total sum of money to be paid out to employees at a given time.

pay·sage (pay-záazh) *n.* A representation of a rural scene in art; a landscape. [French, landscape, from *pays,* country, Old French *païs,* from Vulgar Latin *pagensis* (unattested), from Latin *pāgus,* rural district.] **—pay·sa·gist** *n.*

payt. payment.

Pb The symbol for the element lead [Latin *plumbum.*].

P.B. **1.** British Pharmacopoeia. **2.** prayer book.

PBX, P.B.X. private branch (telephone) exchange.

pc parsec.

pc. **1.** piece. **2.** price.

p.c. **1.** after meals [Latin *post cibum.*]. **2.** per cent. **3.** petty cash. **4.** postcard.

P.C. **1.** Parish Council; Parish Councillor. **2.** Past Commander. **3.** Police Constable. **4.** Post Commander. **5.** Privy Council; Privy Councillor.

p/c, P/C **1.** petty cash. **2.** prices current.

pct. *U.S.* per cent.

Pd The symbol for the element palladium.

pd. paid.

p.d. **1.** per diem. **2.** potential difference.

P.D. **1.** per diem. **2.** *U.S.* Police Department.

P.D.S.A. People's Dispensary for Sick Animals (in Britain).

pe (pay) *n.* The 17th letter of the Hebrew alphabet. [Hebrew *peh,* "mouth".]

PE **1.** physical education. **2.** potential energy. **3.** printers' error. **4.** probable error.

pea (pee) *n.* **1.** A climbing annual legume, *Pisum sativum,* grown in all temperate zones, and having compound leaves, small white flowers, and edible seeds in a green, elongated pod. **2.** Any of the rounded green seeds of the pea, cooked and eaten as a vegetable. **3.** *Plural.* The unopened pods of the pea plant. **4.** Any of several plants of the genus *Lathyrus,* such as the **sweet pea** *(see).* See **chick-pea, cowpea. 5.** *Australian Informal.* One that seems likely to succeed or win. Preceded by *the.* [Taken as singular of earlier *pease,* Middle English *pese,* Old English *pise,* from Late Latin *pīsa,* from Latin, plural of *pīsum,* pea, from Greek *pison*†, a pea.]

peace (peess) *n.* **1.** The absence of war or other hostilities. **2.** An agreement or treaty to end hostilities: *the Peace of Westphalia.* **3.** Freedom from quarrels and disagreement; harmonious relations: *They made peace with each other.* **4.** Public security; law and order: *disturbing the peace.* **5.** Calm; serenity: *peace of mind.* **—at peace.** **1.** In a state of tranquillity; serene. **2.** Free from strife. **—hold** or **keep (one's) peace.** To be silent. **—keep the peace.** To maintain or observe law and order. **—make (one's) peace with.** To be reconciled with; renew friendly relations with. [Middle English *pes, pais,* from Old French, from Latin *pāx* (stem *pāc-*).]

Peace (peess). River in British Columbia, Canada, flowing 1 520 kilometres (945 miles) from the Rocky Mountains through wheat-growing areas into the Slave river at Lake Athabaska.

peace·a·ble (péesəb'l) *adj.* **1.** Inclined or disposed to peace; promoting calm: *They met in a peaceable spirit.* **2.** Peaceful; undisturbed. **—peace·a·ble·ness** *n.* **—peace·a·bly** *adv.*

Peace Corps *n.* An organisation set up by the U.S. government in 1961 that trains and sends volunteers abroad to work with people of developing countries on projects for technological, agricultural, and educational improvement.

peace·ful (péessf'l) *adj.* **1.** Undisturbed by strife, turmoil, or disagreement; tranquil. **2.** Opposed to strife; peaceable. **3.** Of or characteristic of a condition of peace. —See Synonyms at **calm.** **—peace·ful·ly** *adv.* **—peace·ful·ness** *n.*

peace·mak·er (péess-maykər) *n.* One who makes peace, especially by settling the disputes of others. **—peace·mak·ing** *n.* & *adj.*

peace offering *n.* **1.** Any offering made to an adversary in the interests of peace or reconciliation. **2.** An offering made to God in thanksgiving; especially, a sacrificial offering as prescribed by Levitical law. Leviticus 3:2–6.

peace pipe *n.* A **calumet** *(see).*

peace·time (péess-tīm) *n.* A time of absence of war. **—peace·time** *adj.*

peach¹ (peech) *n.* **1.** A small tree, *Prunus persica,* native to China but widely cultivated throughout the temperate zones, having pink flowers and edible fruit. **2.** The soft, juicy, single-seeded fruit of this tree, having white or yellow flesh and downy, red-tinted, yellow skin. **3.** Yellowish pink to light orange. **4.** *Informal.* **a.** Any especially admirable or pleasing person or thing. **b.** A pretty girl. *~adj.* Of the colour peach. [Middle English *peche,* from Old French, from Late Latin *persica,* from Latin, plural of *persicum (mālum),* "Persian (apple)", from *Persicus,* PERSIAN.]

peach² *v.* **peached, peaching, peaches.** *—intr. Informal.* To inform on someone. *—tr. Obsolete.* To inform against. [Middle English *pechen,* aphetic variant of *impechen,* IMPEACH.]

peach·blow (péech-blō) *n.* A purplish-pink monochrome glaze used on Chinese porcelain. Also called "peachbloom".

peach Melba *n.* Also *French* **pêche Melba** (pesh). A dessert consisting of peach halves, ice cream, and raspberry sauce. [After Dame Nellie MELBA.]

peach·y (péechi) *adj.* **-ier, -iest.** **1.** Like a peach, especially in colour or texture. **2.** *U.S. Informal.* Splendid; fine. **—peach·i·ness** *n.*

pea·cock (pée-kok) *n.* **1. a.** A male peafowl of the genus *Pavo,* distinguished by its crested head, brilliant blue or green feathers, and long tail feathers that are marked with eyelike, iridescent spots and can be spread in a fanlike form. **b.** Loosely, a female peafowl of the genus *Pavo.* **2.** A glossy, greenish-black peafowl, *Afropavo congensis,* from the forests of central Africa, having white plumes on the head. Also called "Congo peacock". **3.** A common butterfly, *Inachis* (or *Nymphalis*) *io,* with red, brown, and black wings each bearing a bright, bluish-purple eyespot. **4.** A vain person given to self-display; a dandy.
~intr.v. **peacocked, -cocking, -cocks.** To strut about like a peacock; exhibit oneself in a vain way. [Middle English *pecok, pocok* : Old English *pēa,* peafowl, from Latin *pāvō,* peacock, obscurely related to Greek *taōs*†, peacock + *cok,* COCK.] **—pea·cock·ish, pea·cock·y** *adj.*

Peacock, Thomas Love (1785–1866). British novelist and poet. In the service of the East India Company (1819–56), he wrote seven novels, most of them satirical, attacking intellectual fashions and caricaturing the poets of the Romantic school, including his friend Shelley. His works include *Headlong Hall* (1816), *Crotchet Castle* (1831), and *Gryll Grange* (1860).

peacock blue *n.* Light to moderate greenish blue. **—pea·cock-blue** (péekok-blōō ‖ -bléw) *adj.*

pea crab *n.* Any of various small, globular crabs of the genus *Pinnotheres,* the females of which live as commensals within the shells of oysters and similar molluscs.

pea·fowl (pée-fowl) *n., pl.* **-fowls** or collectively **peafowl.** Any of three large pheasants, *Pavo cristatus,* of India and Ceylon, *P. muticus,* of southeastern Asia, or *Afropavo congensis,* of central Africa. [*Peacock* + *fowl.*]

peag, peage (peeg) *n.* North American Indian money, **wampum** *(see).* [Narraganset *wampompeag,* WAMPUM.]

pea green *n.* Moderate yellowish green. **—pea-green** (pée-gréen) *adj.*

pea·hen (pée-hen) *n.* The female peafowl.

pea jacket *n.* A short, double-breasted coat of heavy navy-blue wool, worn by sailors. Also called "pea coat". [Probably from Dutch *pijjakker* : *pij,* a kind of coarse cloth, from Middle Dutch *pīe*† + *jekker,* a jacket.]

peak¹ (peek) *n. Abbr.* **pk.** **1.** A tapering, projecting point; a pointed extremity: *peak of a cap; peak of a roof.* **2. a.** The pointed summit of a mountain. **b.** The mountain itself: *High Peak.* **3. a.** The point of a beard. **b.** A **widow's peak** *(see).* **4.** The point of greatest development, value, or intensity; height; maximum: *at the peak of her fame.* **5.** *Physics.* The highest value attained by a varying quantity: *a current peak.* **6.** *Nautical.* **a.** The narrow portion of a ship's hull at the bow or stern. **b.** The upper after corner of a fore-and-aft sail. **c.** The outermost end of a gaff. —See Synonyms at **summit.**
~v. **peaked, peaking, peaks.** *—tr.* **1.** *Nautical.* To raise (a gaff) above the horizontal. **2.** To raise (the blade of an oar) to a vertical position. **3.** To bring to a peak, head, or maximum. *—intr.* **1.** To be formed into a peak or peaks: *Beat the egg whites until they peak.* **2.** To achieve a maximum of development, value, or intensity.
~adj. Approaching or constituting the maximum: *peak efficiency.* [Perhaps back-formation from *peaked,* variant of dialect *picked,* pointed, from PICK (tool.]

peak² *intr.v.* **peaked, peaking, peaks.** *Rare.* To become sickly, emaciated, or pale. [16th century : origin obscure.]

Peak District. Plateau region mainly in Derbyshire, central England. A national park, it encompasses the southern Pennines and is crossed by rivers such as the Wye and Dove,which have cut gorges and caves in the limestone rock and produced potholes. Its maximum height is at Kinder Scout, 636 metres (2,088 feet).

Peake (peek), **Mervyn (Laurence)** (1911–68). British author and illustrator, born and partly educated in China. He is best known for his trilogy of Gothic fantasies *Titus Groan* (1946), *Gormenghast* (1950), and *Titus Alone* (1959). He also illustrated editions of *The Rime of the Ancient Mariner* (1943) and *Alice in Wonderland* (1946).

peaked (peekt) *adj.* Ending in a peak; pointed.

peak·y (péeki) *adj.* Having a sickly, pale or pinched appearance.

peal (peel) *n.* **1.** A ringing of a set of bells; especially, a change or set of changes, rung on bells. **2.** A set of bells tuned to each other; a chime; a carillon. **3.** A loud burst of noise or series of noises, as of laughter or thunder.
~v. **pealed, pealing, peals.** *—intr.* To sound in a peal; ring: *The bells pealed out.* *—tr.* To utter loudly and sonorously. [Middle

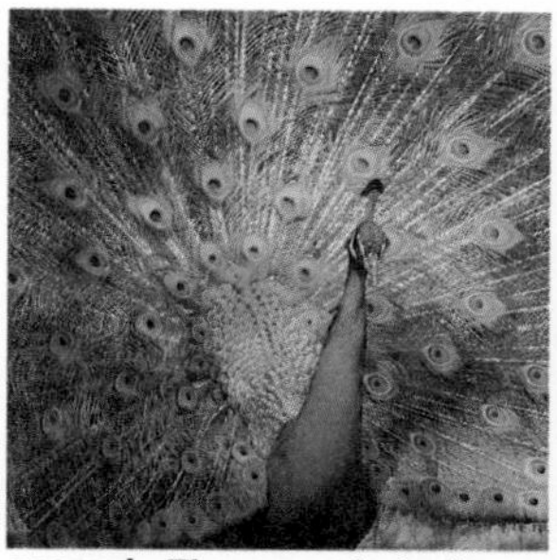

peacock *The eye-marked tail feathers of* Pavo cristatus, *the blue or Indian peacock (above), can grow up to 1.5 metres (5 feet) long. The train, which is lifted into a fan during courtship, is possessed only by the male. Each male may have a harem of up to five hens.*

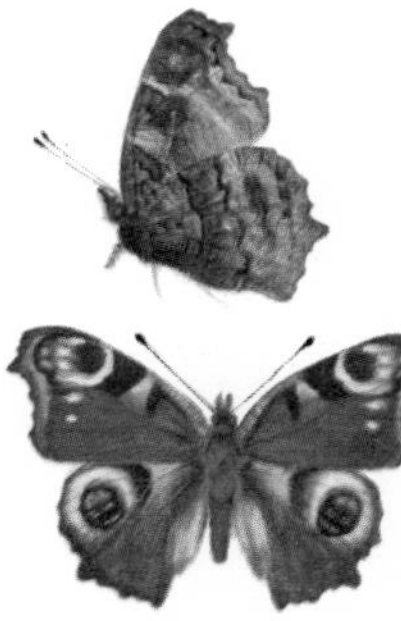

peacock butterfly Inachis io, *the peacock butterfly, is related to the tortoiseshell and red admiral. Adults hibernate in hollow trees or buildings, and the undersides of their wings are dull, looking like dead leaves when they are folded.*

pear

A SYMBOL OF LONGEVITY THAT BEARS FRUIT
The world's second most important fruit crop

The pear tree is a member of the rose family. As a fruit tree it is taller, straighter, and broader than most, and it lives longer – in China it is a symbol of longevity. Its wood is a warm, dark colour and, because it is relatively free from warping, it has been popular for use in veneering and for making musical instruments and mathematical drawing instruments.

The wild pear tree is thorny, with bitter, gritty fruit, and is used as a rootstock on to which cultivated varieties are grafted. In continental Europe, the quince is widely used as a rootstock for many varieties of pear, producing a smaller tree that fruits at an earlier age.

World-wide, pears are the second most important fruit crop after apples, but in the United States they rank third after apples and peaches. Thousands of varieties have been produced since pre-Christian times in Europe alone, but they can be divided into three categories: sweet or dessert pears, cooking pears, and hard, bitter varieties for making perry, a cider-like drink.

Although pears are cultivated in all countries that have temperate climates, the use of the crop varies. In North America and Australia, for example, half the production is preserved by canning, whereas in Europe most of the pear crop is eaten raw or freshly cooked.

Louise Bonne A dessert pear usually cultivated as a dwarf

William's Bon Chrétien Called a Bartlett when canned

Conference Sweet and juicy, and stores well

Doyenné du Comice Juicy and slightly cinnamon flavoured

Fertility A dessert variety, and a heavy cropper

Winter Nelis A small-to-medium-sized dessert variety

Packham's Triumph Sweet and juicy, an important Australian export crop

Common pear The wild fruit, itself probably a hybrid originally

Joséphine de Malines Juicy, with a rich, aromatic flavour

English *pele,* summons to church by bell, short for *appel,* an appeal, from *appelen,* to APPEAL.]

pean. Variant of **paean.**

pea·nut (pée-nut) *n.* **1.** A vine, *Arachis hypogaea,* native to tropical America and widely cultivated in semitropical regions. It has yellow flowers on stalks that bend over and grow into the soil so that the seed pods ripen underground. **2.** The edible, nutlike, oily seed of this vine, used for food and as a source of oil. Also called "goober", "groundnut", "monkey nut". **3.** *Plural. Slang.* A very small amount of money; a trifling sum: *Clothes were being sold for peanuts at the jumble sale.* **4.** *U.S. Slang.* A small or insignificant person.

peanut butter *n.* A paste made from roasted ground peanuts.

peanut oil *n.* The oil pressed from peanuts, used for cooking, in soaps, and as a pharmaceutical vehicle.

pear (pair) *n.* **1.** A widely cultivated tree, *Pyrus communis,* having glossy leaves, white flowers, and edible fruit. **2.** The gritty-textured fruit of this tree, spherical at the apex and tapering towards the base. [Middle English *pere,* Old English *peru, pere,* from Latin *pirus,* pear tree, *pirum,* pear; akin to Greek *apios,* pear tree.]

pearl[1] (perl) *n.* **1.** A smooth, lustrous, variously coloured deposit, chiefly calcium carbonate, formed around a grain of sand or other foreign matter in the shells of certain molluscs and valued as a gem. **2.** Mother-of-pearl; nacre. **3.** A person or object likened to a pearl in beauty or value. **4.** *Printing.* A type size, 5 points. **5.** *Plural.* A string of pearls. **6.** A bluish or greyish white.
~*v.* **pearled, pearling, pearls.** —*tr.* **1.** To decorate or cover with or as with pearls. **2.** To make into the shape or colour of pearls. —*intr.* **1.** To dive or fish for pearls or pearl-bearing molluscs. **2.** To form beads resembling pearls.
~*adj.* **1.** Made of or containing pearl. **2.** Having the shape or colour of pearls or mother of pearl. [Middle English *perle,* from Old French, from Vulgar Latin *per(nu)la* (unattested), diminutive of Latin *perna,* leg; ham, sea-mussel (from its ham-shaped peduncle).]

pearl[2]. Variant of **purl** (embroidery).

Pearl. See **Zhu Jiang** (river).

pearl ash *n. Chemistry.* **Potassium carbonate** *(see).*

pearl barley *n.* Barley rubbed into small, rounded grains, used in stews and soups.

pearl diver *n.* A person who dives in search of molluscs containing pearls. Also called "pearler".

pearl·er (pérlər) *n.* **1.** A pearl diver. **2.** A boat engaged in searching for pearls. **3.** Variant of **purler.**

pearl fish *n.* Any of various fishes of the family Carapidae, especially of the genus *Fierasfer,* that shelter inside sea cucumbers or occasionally pearl shells.

pearl grey *n.* Light bluish grey. —**pearl-grey** (pérl-gráy) *adj.*

Pearl Harbor. Inlet of the Pacific Ocean on Oahu Island, Hawaii, United States. Site of a U.S. naval base, it was the object of a surprise attack by the Japanese Air Force on December 7, 1941, which precipitated the United States into World War II.

pearl·ised, pearl·ized (pérlīzd) *adj.* Having a pearly finish: *pearlised nail varnish.*

pearl·ite (pérlīt) *n.* **1.** A mixture of ferrite and cementite forming distinct layers or bands in slowly cooled carbon steels. **2.** Variant of **perlite.** [French *perlite,* from *perle,* a soft gelatinous capsule, from Old French, PEARL + -ITE.]

pearl millet *n.* A tropical grass, *Pennisetum typhoideum,* having long, bulrush-like flowering spikes and whitish seeds that are used as food in the Old World.

pearl oyster *n.* Any of several bivalve marine molluscs of the genus *Pinctada* and related genera, of tropical waters. *P. margaritifera* is a major commercial source of pearls.

pearlwort (pérl-wurt ‖ -wawrt) *n.* Any of various short, tufted plants of the genus *Sagina* bearing tiny white or green flowers.

pearl·y (pérli) *adj.* **-ier, -iest. 1.** Resembling pearls: *pearly teeth.* **2.** Covered or decorated with pearls or mother-of-pearl.
~*n.* A pearly king or queen. **2. a.** *Plural.* The traditional costume worn by a pearly king or queen. **b.** A pearl button.

pearly everlasting *n.* A plant, *Anaphalis margaritacea,* having woolly, grey-green foliage and whitish, long-lasting flowers.

Pearly Gates *pl.n.* **1.** *Informal.* The gateway to heaven. **2.** *Small p, small g. British Slang.* The teeth.

pearly king *n.* A London costermonger wearing a ceremonial costume elaborately decorated with pearl buttons.

pearly nautilus *n.* The **chambered nautilus** *(see).*

pearly queen *n.* The wife of a pearly king, who wears a costume decorated in similar fashion.

pear·main (pair-mayn, pér-) *n.* Any of several varieties of red-skinned apple. [Middle English *parmayn,* a kind of pear, from Old French *parmain,* from Vulgar Latin *parmānus* (unattested), of PARMA.]

pear oil *n.* A solvent, **amyl acetate** *(see).*

Pears (peerz), **Sir Peter** (1910–). British tenor. He joined Sadlers Wells (1943) and performed the title role in *Peter Grimes,* written by his friend and associate Benjamin Britten. A founder with Britten of the Aldeburgh Festival (1948), he has had several roles created for him, including Aschenbach in *Death in Venice* (1974).

Pearse (peerss), **Patrick (Henry)** (1879–1916). Irish nationalist, poet, and teacher. A leader of the Gaelic revival, particularly in schools, and of the Irish Republican Brotherhood, he commanded the rebels in the Easter Rising (1916), becoming president of the provisional government in an independent Irish republic. After the defeat of the insurgents, he was court-martialled and shot.

Pear·son (péerss'n), **Lester (Bowles)** (1897–1972). Canadian Liberal prime minster (1963–68). He represented Canada at the United Nations, became chairman of NATO (1951), and received the Nobel peace prize (1957) for his key role in the negotiation of a solution to the Suez crisis (1956).
Pear·y (péer-i), **Robert (Edwin)** (1856–1920). U.S. rear-admiral and explorer. Making a total of eight Arctic voyages, on his last expedition he became the first man to reach the North Pole (1909).
Peary Land. Peninsula of northern Greenland. At its northernmost point, Cape Morris Jessup, it is 710 kilometres (440 miles) from the North Pole and is the world's most northerly point of land. A mountainous region, it was first explored by Robert Peary (1892).
peas·ant (pézz'nt) *n.* **1.** A member of the class comprising small farmers and tenants and labourers on the land where these constitute the main labour force in agriculture. **2.** A countryman; a rustic. **3.** *Informal.* An uncouth, crude, or ill-bred person; a boor. [Middle English *paissaunt,* from Old French *païsant,* from *païs,* country, from Medieval Latin *pāgēnsis,* "inhabitant of a district", rustic, peasant, from Latin *pāgus,* a district, canton, rural area.]
peas·ant·ry (pézz'ntri) *n.* **1.** The social class constituted by peasants. **2. a.** The condition or rank of a peasant. **b.** Conduct or manners thought to be characteristic of peasants.
pease (peez) *n., pl.* **pease** or **peasen** (-'n). *Obsolete.* A pea.
pease·cod, peas·cod (péez-kod) *n. Archaic.* The pod of the pea. [Middle English *pesecod* : *pese,* PEA + COD (pod).]
pease pudding *n. Chiefly British.* A purée made from boiled dried peas. [*Pease,* Old English *pise* (plural *pisan*), PEA.]
pea·shoot·er (pée-shootər) *n.* A toy consisting of a small tube through which dried peas or other pellets are blown at a target.
pea soup *n.* A purée or soup made of dried or fresh peas.
pea-soup·er (pée-sóopər, -sóopər) *n. Chiefly British Informal.* A dense yellow fog.
peat (peet) *n.* Partially decomposed, compacted vegetable matter, usually mosses or sedges, found in bogs and fens, and used as fertiliser and fuel. [Middle English *pete,* from Medieval Latin *peta,* probably from Celtic, akin to Medieval Latin *pecia, petia,* PIECE.] **—peat·y** *adj.*
peat bog *n.* A **bog** *(see).*
peat moss *n.* **1.** Any moss, especially of the genus *Sphagnum,* growing in fens. **2.** The partly decomposed remains of such mosses, used as a mulch and plant food. Also called "bog moss".
peau de soie (pō də swáa) *n.* A smooth, satiny fabric of silk or rayon. [French, "skin of silk".]
pea·vey (péevi) *n., pl.* **-veys.** Also **pea·vy** *pl.* **-vies.** *U.S.* A wooden lever with a metal point and a hinged hook near the end, used by lumberjacks to handle logs. [After Joseph *Peavey,* U.S. blacksmith, to whom its invention (about 1870) has been attributed.]
peb·ble (pébb'l) *n.* **1. a.** A small stone eroded smooth. **b.** *Geology.* A rock fragment larger than a gravel and smaller than a cobble, having a diameter of 4 to 64 millimetre (0.16 to 2.5 inches). **2. a.** Clear, colourless quartz; rock crystal. **b.** A lens made of such quartz. **3.** A crinkled surface, as on leather or paper. **4.** *Australian Informal.* An obstinate or intractable person or animal.
~*adj.* Designating a spectacle lens that is thick and has high powers of magnification.
~*tr.v.* **pebbled, -bling, -bles.** **1.** To pave or pelt with pebbles. **2.** To impart an irregularly rough, grainy surface to (leather or paper). [Middle English *pibbil, puble,* Old English *papol(stān)* : *papol-,* pebble (probably imitative) + *stān,* STONE.] **—peb·bly** *adj.*
pebble·dash (pébb'l-dash) *n. British.* Mortar in which small pebbles are embedded, used as a finish for outside walls.
~**pebbledashed, -dashing, -dashes.** *—tr.v. British.* To cover with pebbledash.
pe·can (pi-kán, -káan, pée-kan) *n.* **1.** A tree, *Carya illinoensis,* of the southern United States, having deeply furrowed bark and edible nuts. **2.** The smooth, thin-shelled, oval nut of the pecan. [Earlier *paccan,* from Algonquian, akin to Ojibwa *pagân,* hard-shell nut, Abnaki *pagann,* Cree *pakan.*]
pec·ca·ble (pécka-b'l) *adj.* Liable to sin. [Old French, from Latin *peccāre,* to sin. See **peccant.**] **—pec·ca·bil·i·ty** (-bílləti) *n.*
pec·ca·dil·lo (péckə-díllō) *n., pl.* **-loes** or **-los.** A small sin or fault. [Spanish *pecadillo,* diminutive of *pecado,* sin, from Latin *peccātum,* from *peccāre,* to sin. See **peccant.**]
pec·cant (péckənt) *adj.* **1.** Sinful; guilty. **2.** Violating a rule or accepted practice; erring; faulty. [Latin *peccāns* (stem *peccant-*), present participle of *peccāre,* to sin, stumble.] **—pec·can·cy** *n.* **—pec·cant·ly** *adv.*
pec·ca·ry (péckəri) *n., pl.* **-ries.** Either of two piglike, hoofed mammals, *Tayassu angulatus* or *T. pecari,* of southern North America, Central America, and South America, having dense, long, dark bristles. [Spanish *pecari,* from Carib *pakira.*]
pec·ca·vi (pe-káavee, -káyvī) *n., pl.* **-vis.** A confession of sin. [Latin, "I have sinned".]
pêche Melba *n. French.* A dessert, **peach Melba** *(see).*
Pe·chen·ga (pə-chéngə). *Finnish* **Pet·sa·mo** (pét-səmō). Port on the Barents Sea, northwest U.S.S.R. Ice-free, it has a large fishing fleet, and is the centre of a strategic mining region. The area was part of Finland from 1920 to 1944.
Pe·cho·ra (pə-chórə). River of European U.S.S.R. It rises in the Ural Mountains, and flows northwards for 1 790 kilometres (1,112 miles) to the Barents Sea, passing through the important Pechora coal basin.
peck¹ (pek) *v.* **pecked, pecking, pecks.** *—tr.* **1.** To strike with a beak or some sharp-pointed instrument. **2.** To make (a hole, for example) by striking repeatedly with the beak or a pointed instrument. **3.** To grasp and pick up with the beak: *The bird pecked insects from the log.* **4.** *Informal.* To kiss briefly and casually: *He pecked her on the cheek.* *—intr.* **1.** To make strokes with the beak or something pointed like a beak: *the noise of birds pecking outside.* **2.** To eat in small, sparing bits; nibble. Used with *at*: *pecking at her food.* **3.** To criticise repeatedly; nag; carp. Used with *at.*
~*n.* **1.** A stroke or light blow with the beak. **2.** A mark or hole made by such a stroke. **3.** *Informal.* A light, quick kiss. [Middle English *pecken,* probably from Middle Low German *pekken*†.]
peck² *n. Abbr.* **pk., pk** **1. a.** A unit of volume or capacity in the British Imperial System, used in dry measure, equal to 9.092 litres (554.84 cubic inches). **b.** A unit of volume or capacity in the U.S. system, used in dry measure, equal to 7.571 litres (537.605 cubic inches). **2.** A container holding or measuring this amount. **3.** *Informal.* A great deal: *a peck of troubles.* [Middle English, from Anglo-French *pek*†.]
peck·er (péckər) *n.* **1.** One who or that which pecks. **2.** *British Slang.* Courage; mettle; pluck. Used chiefly in the phrase *keep one's pecker up.* **3.** *U.S. Vulgar Slang.* The penis.
pecking order *n.* **1.** A hierarchy within certain flocks of birds, especially poultry, according to which each member submits to pecking and domination by the stronger or more aggressive members, and has the privilege of pecking and dominating the weaker members. Also called "peck order". **2.** Any supposedly similar hierarchy, for example, in a human group. [Translation of German *Hackordnung.*]
Peck·in·pah (péckin-paa), **(David) Sam(uel)** (1925–). U.S. film director. He began by working for television on such serials as *Gunsmoke.* His often violent films, several of which are westerns, include *The Wild Bunch* (1969), *Straw Dogs* (1971), *The Getaway* (1972), *Cross of Iron* (1977) and *Convoy* (1978).
peck·ish (péckish) *adj. Informal.* **1.** *Chiefly British.* Somewhat hungry. **2.** *U.S.* Peevish; irritable.
Peck·sniff·i·an (pek-sniffi-ən) *adj.* Addicted to fatuous and hypocritical talk of benevolence and other virtues. [After Seth *Pecksniff,* a character in Dickens' novel *Martin Chuzzlewit* (1844).]
pec·o·ri·no (péckə-réenō) *n.* A hard, pale yellow Italian cheese made from ewe's milk. [Italian (adjective), of ewes, from *pecora,* sheep, from Latin, cattle, plural of *pecu* (stem *pecor-*) herd, cattle.]
Pe·cos (páykəss). River of southern United States. It flows 1 180 kilometres (735 miles) across New Mexico and Texas, to join the Rio Grande.
Pécs (paakh). *German* **Fünf·kir·chen** (fünf-keerkhən). Industrial city of southwest Hungary, lying at the centre of the country's main coalmining region.
pec·tase (pék-tayz, -tayss) *n.* An enzyme found in certain fruits that catalyses the conversion of pectins to pectic acids.
pec·tate (pék-tayt) *n.* A salt or ester of pectic acid.
pec·ten (péktin) *n., pl.* **-tens** or **-tines** (-eez). *Zoology.* **1.** Any body structure or organ resembling a comb, such as the ridged part of the eye of reptiles and birds. **2.** A scallop of the genus *Pecten.* [New Latin, from Latin, comb.]
pec·tic acid (péktik) *n. Chemistry.* Any of several colloidal substances, essentially complex organic acids, derived from the sugar galactose. [French *pectique.* See **pectin.**]
pec·tin (péktin) *n.* Any of a group of complex colloidal substances of high molecular weight found in ripe fruits, such as apples, and used to form a gel when heated with sugar, as in jam-making. [French *pectine,* from *pectique,* from Greek *pēktikos,* coagulating, from *pēktos,* coagulated, from *pēgnunai,* to coagulate.] **—pec·tic, pec·tin·ous** *adj.*
pec·tin·ase (pékti-nayz, -nayss) *n.* A plant enzyme that catalyses the hydrolysis of pectin.
pec·ti·nate (pékti-nayt) *adj.* Also **pec·ti·nat·ed** (-naytid). Shaped like a comb; comblike. [Latin *pecten* (stem *pectin-*), comb, PECTEN + -ATE.] **—pec·ti·na·tion** (-náysh'n) *n.*
pec·to·ral (péktərəl) *adj.* **1.** *Anatomy.* Pertaining to the breast or chest: *a pectoral muscle.* **2.** Worn on the chest or breast: *a pectoral cross.*
~*n.* **1.** A chest muscle or organ. **2.** A pectoral fin. **3.** A medicine for chest diseases. **4.** An ornament or decoration worn on the chest. [Middle English, from Old French, of or worn on the chest, from Latin *pectorālis,* from *pectus* (stem *pector-*), breast.]
pectoral fin *n.* Either of the anterior pair of fins attached to the pectoral girdle of fishes. Also called "pectoral".
pectoral girdle *n. Zoology.* A skeletal structure in vertebrates, attached to and supporting the forelimbs or fins. Also called "pectoral arch", and, chiefly in humans, "shoulder girdle".
pec·u·late (péckew-layt) *v.* **-lated, -lating, -lates.** *—tr.* To embezzle or take for one's own use. *—intr.* To steal money or goods entrusted to one. [Latin *pecūlārī,* to embezzle, from *pecūlium,* "wealth in cattle", private property, from *pecu,* cattle.] **—pec·u·la·tion** (-láysh'n) *n.* **—pec·u·la·tor** *n.*
pe·cu·li·ar (pi-kéwli-ər, pə-) *adj.* **1.** Unusual or eccentric; strange; queer. **2.** Calling for special consideration or attention; distinct and particular. **3. a.** Exclusive; unique: *the peculiar attributes of beauty.* **b.** Belonging distinctively or especially to one person, group, or kind: *he spoke with an accent peculiar to his native county.* —See Synonyms at **characteristic, strange.**
~*n.* **1.** *British.* A church or parish under the jurisdiction of a diocese different from that in which it lies. **2.** *Rare.* Some privilege or

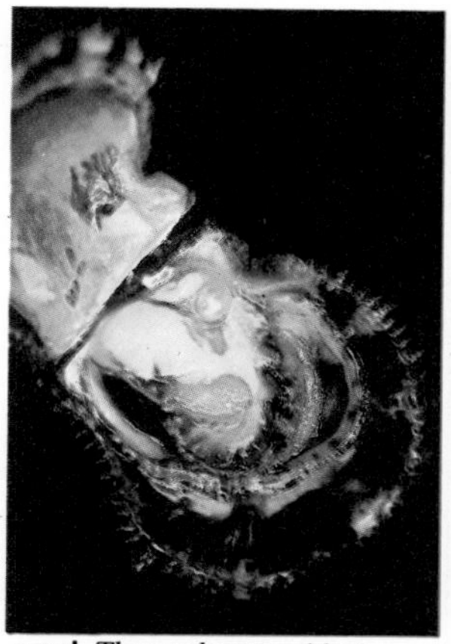

pearl *The pearl oyster – which belongs to the genus* Margaritifer *– has a shell lined with a smooth, iridescent substance known as nacre, or mother-of-pearl. If an irritant, such as a grain of sand, becomes trapped within its shell, the oyster gradually covers it with layers of nacre to reduce the friction, and this process forms the pearl. Cultured pearls, which take about four years to produce, are created by inserting an irritant artificially.*

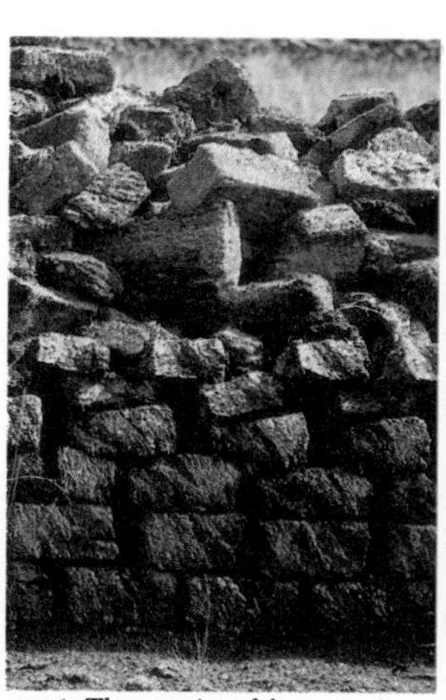

peat *The remains of decomposing vegetable matter, peat is found in boggy regions with temperate climates. It is the first stage in nature's production of coal, and is cut from the ground in blocks, dried and used as a fuel.*

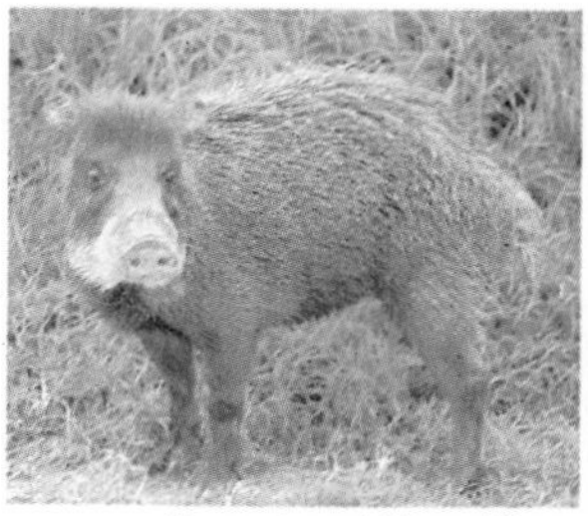

peccary *Peccaries, which are New World relatives of the pig, live in packs of about a dozen animals. A full-grown peccary can weigh up to about 30 kilograms (65 pounds).*

property that belongs exclusively to one. **3.** *Printing.* A **special sort** *(see).* [Middle English *peculier,* from Latin *pecūliāris,* individual, peculiar, of private property, from *pecūlium,* "wealth in cattle", private property, from *pecu,* cattle, wealth.] —**pe·cu·liar·ly** *adv.*

pe·cu·li·ar·i·ty (pi-kêwli-árrəti) *n., pl.* **-ties. 1.** The quality or state of being peculiar. **2. a.** A notable or distinctive feature or characteristic. **b.** An eccentricity; an idiosyncrasy; a quirk.

Peculiar People *pl.n. Sometimes small* **p,** *small* **p.** An evangelical Protestant denomination founded in 1838, the members of which believe in divine healing.

pe·cu·ni·ar·y (pi-kêwni-əri ‖ -erri) *adj.* **1.** Consisting of or pertaining to money: *a pecuniary loss; pecuniary motives.* **2.** Requiring the payment of money: *a pecuniary offence.* n. —See Synonyms at **financial.** [Latin *pecūniārius,* from *pecūnia,* "wealth in cattle", property, money, from *pecu,* cattle.]

ped-. 1. Variant of **paed-. 2.** Variant of **pedo-** (soil).

-ped, -pede *n. comb. form.* Indicates foot or feet; for example, **biped, centipede.** [Latin *pēs* (stem *ped-*), foot.]

ped·a·gog·ic (péddə-gójik, -gŏjik, -góggik) Also **ped·a·gog·i·cal** (-'l) *adj.* **1.** Of, pertaining to, or characteristic of teaching. **2.** Characterised by pedantic formality. —**ped·a·gog·i·cal·ly** *adv.*

ped·a·gog·ics (péddə-gójikss, -gŏjiks, -góggiks) *n. Used with a singular verb.* The art of teaching; education; pedagogy.

ped·a·gogue (pédda-gog) *n.* **1.** A schoolteacher; an educator. **2.** One who instructs in a pedantic or dogmatic manner. [Middle English *pedagoge,* from Old French *pedagogue,* from Latin *paedagō-gus,* from Greek *paidagōgos,* teacher, trainer (of boys) : *paid-,* PEDO- + *agōgos,* leader, from *agein,* to lead.] —**ped·a·gogu·ish** *adj.*

ped·a·go·gy (pédda-goji, -gŏji, -goggi) *n.* **1.** The art or profession of teaching. **2.** Preparatory training or instruction.

ped·al (pédd'l) *n.* **1. a.** A lever operated by the foot on various musical instruments, such as the piano, organ, or harp. **b.** Any of various electronic devices used to modify the signal from an electronic instrument, especially a guitar. **2.** A pedal point. **3.** A lever worked by the foot in a machine, such as a motor vehicle, bicycle, or sewing machine.
~*adj.* (in sense 1 also pèed'l) **1.** Pertaining to a foot or footlike part: *the pedal extremities.* **2.** *Music.* Pertaining to a pedal.
~*v.* **pedalled** or *U.S.* **pedaled, pedalling** or *U.S.* **-aling, -als.** —*intr.* **1.** To use or operate a pedal or pedals. **2.** To ride a bicycle. —*tr.* To operate the pedals of. [French *pédale,* from Italian *pedale,* (organ) pedal, from Latin *pedālis,* of the foot, from *pēs,* foot.]

pedal bin *n.* A small bin, typically for kitchen refuse, the lid of which is raised and lowered by a foot pedal.

ped·al·board (pedd'l-bawrd) *n.* A bank of foot-operated keys, as on an organ.

pe·dal·fer (pi-dál-fər) *n. Geology.* Soil rich in aluminium and iron and deficient in carbonates, characteristic of humid, high-temperature regions with forest cover. Compare **pedocal.** [PED(O)-(soil) + AL(UM) + Latin *ferrum,* iron.]

ped·a·lo (pédd'l-ō) *n., pl.* **-los** or **-loes.** A small pleasure boat propelled by paddle wheels operated by pedals. [From PEDAL.]

pedal point *n. Music.* A note, usually in the bass and on the tonic or the dominant, sustained through harmonic changes in the other parts. Also called "pedal".

pedal pushers *pl.n.* Calf-length women's and girls' slacks, originally worn for cycling.

ped·ant (pédd'nt) *n.* **1.** One who pays undue attention to book learning and formal rules or details without having a true insight or understanding. **2.** One who exhibits his learning or scholarship ostentatiously. **3.** *Archaic.* A schoolmaster; a pedagogue. [French, from Italian *pedante,* apparently from *peda-* as in PEDAGOGUE + -ANT.] —**pe·dan·tic** (pi-dántik, pe-), **pe·dan·ti·cal** *adj.* —**pe·dan·ti·cal·ly** *adv.*

ped·ant·ry (pédd'ntri) *n., pl.* **-ries. 1.** Excessive attention to detail or rules in learning or teaching. **2. a.** The habit of mind or manner characteristic of a pedant. **b.** An instance of pedantic behaviour.

ped·ate (péddayt) *adj.* **1.** *Zoology.* Having feet. **2.** Resembling or functioning as a foot or feet: *pedate appendages.* **3.** *Botany.* Having radiating lobes or divisions, with the lateral lobes cleft or divided: *a pedate leaf.* [Latin *pedātus,* from *pēs* (stem *ped-*), foot.]

ped·dle (pédd'l) *v.* **-dled, -dling, -dles.** —*tr.* **1.** To travel about selling (wares): *peddling goods from door to door.* **2.** To sell (narcotic drugs, for example), especially in small quantities. **3.** To try to spread or circulate (ideas or opinions). —*intr.* To travel about selling wares. [Back-formation from PEDLAR.]

ped·dler (péddlər) *n.* **1.** One who peddles, especially narcotic drugs. **2.** *U.S.* Variant of **pedlar.**

ped·er·ast, paed·er·ast (péddə-rast) *n.* One who practises pederasty. [Back-formation from PEDERASTY.]

ped·er·ast·y (péddə-rasti) *n.* Homosexual relations, especially between a male adult and a boy or young man. [New Latin *paederastia,* from Greek *paiderastia : pais* (stem *paid-*), boy + *erastēs,* lover (from *eros,* sexual love, EROS).]

pe·des. Plural of **pes.**

ped·es·tal (péddist'l) *n.* **1.** An architectural support or base, as for a column or statue. **2.** Either of the supports for a kneehole desk, usually consisting of a set of drawers. **3.** Any support or foundation. —**put on a pedestal.** To treat with exaggerated regard, ignoring imperfections.
~*tr.v.* **pedestalled** or *U.S.* **pedestaled, -talling** or *U.S.* **-taling, -tals.** To place on or provide with a pedestal. [Old French *piedestal,* from

Old Italian *piedestallo,* from *pie di stallo,* "foot of a stall" : *pie,* foot, from Latin *pēs + di,* of, + *stallo,* stall.]

pe·des·tri·an (pi-déstri-ən) *n.* A person travelling on foot; a walker, especially in town and cities.
~*adj.* **1.** Of, suitable for, pertaining to, or designed for pedestrians: *pedestrian traffic.* **2.** Going or performed on foot: *a pedestrian journey.* **3.** Commonplace; undistinguished; ordinary. [Latin *pedester,* going on foot, hence prosaic, from *pedes,* one who goes on foot, from *pēs* (stem *ped-*), a foot.] —**pe·des·tri·an·ism** *n.*

pedestrian crossing *n. British.* A place where pedestrians have priority over traffic when crossing the road. Also *U.S.* "crosswalk". See **pelican crossing, zebra crossing.**

pedestrian precinct *n.* An area in a town reserved for pedestrians and closed to vehicular traffic.

pedi- *comb. form.* Indicates foot; for example, **pediform.** [Latin, from *pēs* (stem *ped-*), foot.]

pediatrician. *U.S.* Variant of **paediatrician.**

ped·i·cel (péddi-sel, -səl) *n.* **1.** *Biology.* A small stalk, part, or organ, especially one serving as a support. **2.** *Botany.* **a.** Any of several small stalks bearing a single flower in an inflorescence. **b.** A support for a fern sporangium or moss capsule. **3.** The second segment of an insect's antenna. [New Latin *pedicellus,* diminutive of Latin *pedīculus,* little foot, pedicel, from *pēs,* a foot.]

ped·i·cel·late (péddi-séll-ət, -it, -ayt) *adj.* Also **ped·i·cel·lar** (-ər). Having or supported by a pedicel.

ped·i·cle (péddik'l) *n.* A pedicel.

pe·dic·u·lar (pi-díckewlər, pe-) *adj.* Of or caused by lice. [Latin *pedīculāris,* from *pedīculus,* louse, diminutive of *pedis,* louse.]

pe·dic·u·late (pi-díckew-lət, pe-, -lit, -layt) *adj.* Of or pertaining to marine fish of the order Pediculati (or Lophiiformes), which includes the anglerfish.
~*n.* A fish of this order. [New Latin *Pediculati,* "little-footed ones" (from the shape of their pectoral fins), from Latin *pedīculus,* little foot. See **pedicel.**]

pe·dic·u·lo·sis (pi-díckew-lŏ-siss, pe-) *n.* Infestation with lice. [New Latin : Latin *pedīculus,* louse (see **pedicular**) + -OSIS.] —**pe·dic·u·lous** (-ləss) *adj.*

ped·i·cure (péddi-kewr) *n.* **1. a.** Cosmetic care of the feet and toenails. **b.** A single cosmetic treatment of the feet and toenails. **2.** A chiropodist.
~*tr.v.* **pedicured, -curing, -cures.** To give a pedicure to. [French *pédicure :* PEDI- + Latin *cūrāre,* to take care of, from *cūra,* care.] —**ped·i·cur·ist** *n.*

ped·i·form (péddi-fawrm) *adj.* Shaped like a foot. [French *pédi-forme :* PEDI- + -FORM.]

ped·i·gree (péddi-gree) *n.* **1.** Recorded ancestry; lineage: *The young man's pedigree was impeccable.* **2.** A list of ancestors; a family tree. **3.** The recorded descent of a purebred animal. Also used adjectivally: *a pedigree cow.* **4.** A source or derivation. [Middle English *pedegru,* from Old French *pie de grue,* "crane's foot", from the three-line, claw-shaped mark formerly used to show the succession in a pedigree : *pie,* foot, from Latin *pēs + de,* of + *grue,* crane, from Latin *grūs.*] —**ped·i·greed** *adj.*

ped·i·ment (péddi-mənt) *n.* **1.** A wide, low-pitched gable surmounting the facade of a building in the Grecian style. **2.** A similar or derivative element used widely in architecture and decoration. **3.** A sloping rock surface, usually covered with alluvium, found in desert areas at the base of mountains. [Variant of earlier *perement,* probably variant (influenced by PEDI-) of PYRAMID.] —**ped·i·men·tal** (-mént'l) *adj.* —**ped·i·ment·ed** (-mentid, -məntid) *adj.*

ped·i·palp (péddi-palp) *n.* Either of the second pair of appendages in arachnids that are attached to the head and may be adapted as sensory organs, as in spiders, or as claws, as in scorpions. Also called "palp". [New Latin *pedipalpus.* See **pedi-, palp.**]

ped·lar (péddlər) *n.* Also *chiefly U.S.* **ped·dler, ped·ler.** One who peddles for a living; a hawker. [Middle English *pedlere,* earlier *pedder,* from *ped†,* wicker basket, pannier.]

pedo-¹, ped- *comb. form.* Indicates soil; for example, **pedalfer, pedocal.** [Greek *pedon,* earth, soil.]

pedo-². *Chiefly U.S.* Variant of **paedo-.**

ped·o·cal (péd-ō-kal, -ə-) *n. Geology.* A lime-rich soil of cool, semi-arid, and arid regions. Compare **pedalfer.** [PEDO- (soil) + Latin *calx,* lime, limestone, from Greek *khalix,* pebble, small stone.] —**ped·o·cal·ic** (-kálik) *adj.*

pe·dol·o·gy (pi-dólləji, pe-) *n.* The scientific study of soils, their origins, characteristics, and uses. Compare **agrology.** [PEDO- (soil) + -LOGY.] —**ped·o·log·ic** (péddə-lójik), **ped·o·log·i·cal** *adj.* —**ped·o·log·i·cal·ly** *adv.* —**pe·dol·o·gist** (-dólləjist) *n.*

pe·dom·e·ter (pi-dómmitər) *n.* An instrument that gauges the approximate distance travelled on foot by registering the number of steps taken. [French *pédomètre : pedo-,* variant of PEDI- + -METER.]

pe·dun·cle (pi-dúngk'l ‖ *U.S. also* pée-dungk'l) *n.* **1.** *Botany.* The main stalk of an inflorescence, or a stalk or stem bearing a solitary flower. **2.** *Zoology.* A stalklike structure in various invertebrate animals. **3.** *Anatomy.* A stalklike bundle of fibres, especially of nerve fibres, connecting different parts of the central nervous system. [New Latin *pedunculus,* diminutive of Latin *pēs* (stem *ped-*), a foot.] —**pe·dun·cu·lar** *adj.*

pe·dun·cu·late (pi-dúngkew-lət, pe-, -lit, -layt) *adj.* Also **pe·dun·cu·lat·ed** (-laytid). Having or supported by a peduncle.

pedunculate oak *n.* The common or English oak, *Quercus robur,* having acorns borne on long peduncles. See **oak.**

pee (pee) *intr.v.* **peed, peeing, pees.** *Slang.* To urinate.

~*n. Slang.* **1.** Urine. **2.** A act of urinating. [Euphemistic abbreviation, from *p* in PISS.]

Pee·bles (peeb'lz). Former county town of Peeblesshire, Scotland. Situated on the river Tweed, it is an agricultural centre and important for the manufacture of woollen goods.

Pee·bles·shire (peéb'lz-shər, -sheer, -shīr). Also **Tweed·dale.** Former county of southeast Scotland, now part of the Borders Region.

peek (peek) *intr.v.* **peeked, peeking, peeks.** **1.** To glance quickly. **2.** To look or peer furtively, as from a place of concealment.
~*n.* A furtive or brief look. [Middle English *piken*†.]

peek·a·boo (peék-ə-boo, -boo) *n. Chiefly U.S.* A child's game, **peep-bo** *(see).*
~*adj.* Having a pattern of small holes. Said of a garment or fabric. [PEEK + BOO; akin to Dutch *kiekeboe.*]

peel¹ (peel) *n.* The skin or rind of certain fruits, such as the orange or apple.
~*v.* **peeled, peeling, peels.** —*tr.* **1.** To strip or cut away the skin, rind, or bark from; pare. **2.** To strip away; pull off (an outer covering). **3.** To put (another player's ball) through a hoop in croquet. —*intr.* **1.** To lose or shed skin, bark, or other covering. **2.** To come off in thin strips or pieces, as bark, skin, or paint may. **3.** *Slang.* To remove one's clothes; undress. Often used with *off.* **—peel off.** To leave flight formation in order to land or make a dive. Used of an aircraft. [Middle English *pelen,* from Old French *peler,* to peel, remove hair from, from Latin *pilāre,* to plunder, "pile up (booty)", from *pīa,* "pile", PILLAR.]

peel² *n.* **1.** A long-handled, shovel-like tool used by bakers to move bread or pastries into and out of an oven. **2.** Formerly, a T-shaped pole, used by printers for hanging freshly printed sheets of paper to dry. [Middle English *pele,* from Old French, shovel, from Latin *pāla,* spade.]

peel³ *n.* Any of several fortified houses or towers constructed in the border area between Scotland and England in the 16th century. [Middle English *pel(e),* castle, small tower, (originally) palisade, from Anglo-French, from Latin *pālus,* stake.]

Peel (peel). Seaport of the Isle of Man, western Europe. Situated on the west coast, its chief industries are tourism and fishing.

Peel, Sir Robert (1788–1850). British Conservative prime minister (1834–35, 1841–46). Entering Parliament as a Tory (1809), he served as secretary for Ireland (1812–18) and was Home Secretary (1822–27, 1828–30), during which time he reorganised and consolidated the London police as the Metropolitan Police (1829) and helped to pass the Catholic Emancipation Act (1829). After the passing of the parliamentary Reform Bill (1832), he outlined the reforming programme of the emergent Conservative Party with the Tamworth Manifesto (1834). Following the split between the traditional protectionist Tories and the new Conservatives over free trade and the repeal of the Corn Laws (1846) his government fell, after which he gave his support to the Whigs.

peel·er¹ (peélər) *n.* **1.** A person or device that peels; especially, a kitchen implement for peeling the rind or skin from a fruit or vegetable. **2.** *U.S. Slang.* A striptease artist.

peeler² *n. British Slang.* A policeman. Not in current usuage. [After Sir Robert PEEL.]

pee·lie-wal·ly (peéli-wál-i) *adj. Scottish.* Pale and insipid-looking. [Perhaps reduplication of obsolete *wally,* faded, from *wallow,* to fade, Old English *walwian.*]

peel·ing (peéling) *n.* A piece or strip that has been peeled off, as of skin, bark, or rind.

peen (peen) *n.* The end of a hammerhead opposite the flat striking surface, often wedge-shaped or ball-shaped and used for chipping, indenting, and metalworking.
~*tr.v.* **peened, peening, peens.** To hammer, bend, or shape with a peen. [*Peen, pane,* perhaps from French *panne,* from Dutch *pen,* from Latin *pinna,* point.]

Pee·ne·münde (páynə-mündə). Fishing village in East Germany. Situated on the Isle of Usedom on the Baltic coast, it was a centre for the development of guided missiles prior to and during World War II (1937–45), producing the V1 flying bomb and the V2 rocket.

peep¹ (peep) *n.* **1.** A weak, shrill sound or utterance, like that of a young bird. **2.** Any slight sound or utterance: *I don't want to hear a peep out of you.* **3.** Any of various small North American sandpipers.
~*intr.v.* **peeped, peeping, peeps.** **1.** To utter short, soft, high-pitched sounds, like those of a baby bird. **2.** To speak in a thin, high-pitched voice. [Middle English *pepen* (imitative).]

peep² *v.* **peeped, peeping, peeps.** —*intr.* **1.** To look furtively; steal a quick glance. **2.** To peer through a small opening or from behind something: *"She stretched herself up on tiptoe, and peeped over the edge of the mushroom."* (Lewis Carroll). **3.** To become visible gradually, as though emerging from a hiding place: *At dawn the sun peeped over the horizon.* —*tr.* To cause to emerge or become partly visible.
~*n.* **1.** A quick or furtive look; a glance. **2.** A first glimpse or first appearance: *the peep of dawn.* [Middle English *pepen,* alteration of *piken,* PEEK.]

peep-bo (peép-bō) *n.* A child's game in which a person repeatedly covers and exposes his face to the cry of "peep-bo". Also called "bo-peep", *chiefly U.S.* "peekaboo".

peep·er¹ (peépər) *n.* A creature that peeps.

peeper² *n.* **1.** Someone who looks furtively. **2.** *Slang.* An eye.

peep·hole (peép-hōl) *n.* A small hole or crevice through which one may peep.

peeping Tom *n.* A man who derives sexual gratification from pruriently and secretly spying on the intimate behaviour of others; a voyeur. [From the story of *Peeping Tom* of Coventry, a tailor who was the sole person to peep at the naked Lady Godiva (and was struck blind).]

peep·show (peép-shō) *n.* An exhibition of pictures or objects, especially of an erotic nature, viewed through a small hole or magnifying glass. Also called "raree show".

peep sight *n.* A rear sight of a firearm consisting of an adjustable eyepiece with a small opening through which the front sight and the target are aligned.

peep·toe (peép-tō) *adj.* Also **peep·toed** (-tōd). Cut away to reveal the big toe or part of the toes. Said of a shoe.

pee·pul, pi·pal (peép'l) *n.* A fig tree, *Ficus religiosa,* of India, regarded as sacred by Buddhists. According to Buddhist tradition, this is the tree under which the Buddha attained enlightenment. Also called "bo tree". [Hindi *pīpal,* from Sanskrit *pippala.*]

peer¹ (peer) *intr.v.* **peered, peering, peers.** **1.** To look intently, searchingly, or with difficulty: *We peered through the mist.* **2.** To be partially visible; show: *The moon peered from behind a cloud.* —See Synonyms at **gaze.** [Perhaps contraction of APPEAR.]

peer² *n.* **1. a.** A nobleman. **b.** A member of the British peerage; a duke, marquis, earl, viscount, or baron. **2.** A person who has equal standing with another, as in rank, class, or age. **3.** *Archaic.* A companion; a fellow. [Middle English *peer(e),* from Old French *per,* equal, one's equal, (hence) nobleman, from Latin *pār,* equal.]

peer·age (peér-ij) *n.* **1.** The rank or title of a peer. **2.** The body of peers. **3.** A book listing peers and their families.

peer·ess (peér-iss, -ess) *n.* **1.** A woman who holds a life peerage. **2.** The wife or widow of a peer.

peer group *n.* Those of the same age and status as an individual.

peer·less (peér-ləss, -liss) *adj.* Without peer; unmatched; unequalled. **—peer·less·ly** *adv.* **—peer·less·ness** *n.*

peer of the realm *n., pl.* **peers of the realm.** *British.* A hereditary peer who has the right to sit in the House of Lords on his majority.

peeve (peev) *tr.v.* **peeved, peeving, peeves.** *Informal.* To annoy or make resentful; vex.
~*n. Informal.* **1.** A vexation; a grievance: *a pet peeve.* **2.** A resentful mood: *be in a peeve.* [Back-formation from PEEVISH.]

pee·ver (peévər) *n. Scottish Regional.* **1.** A tile, stone, or the like used in the game of hopscotch. **2.** *Plural.* The game of hopscotch itself. [Origin obscure.]

pee·vish (peévish) *adj.* **1.** Querulous; discontented; fretful. **2.** Ill-tempered. **3.** Contrary; fractious. [Middle English *pevish*†.] **—pee·vish·ly** *adv.* **—pee·vish·ness** *n.*

pee·wee (peé-wee) *n. U.S.* **1.** *Informal.* Any relatively or unusually small person or thing. **2.** Variant of **pewee.** [Whimsical formation based on WEE.] **—pee·wee** *adj.*

pee·wit, pe·wit (peé-wit) *n.* A bird, the **lapwing** *(see).* [Imitative of its call.]

peg (peg) *n.* **1.** A small cylindrical or tapered pin, as of wood, used to fasten things, such as floorboards, to mark a point, such as a boundary, or to plug a hole, such as the vent of a barrel. **2.** A similar pin forming a projection that may be used as a support, as for hanging clothes on. **3.** Any of the pins of a stringed musical instrument that are turned to tighten or slacken the strings so as to regulate their pitch. **4.** An implement fitted with a pointed prong or claw for tearing or catching. **5.** A degree or notch, especially in estimation. **6.** *Chiefly British.* A small alcoholic drink, especially brandy or whisky and soda. **7.** A pretext or occasion for: *a peg to hang one's grievances upon.* **8.** A **clothes peg** *(see).* **9.** *Informal.* A wooden leg. **10.** In croquet, a coloured post that players must hit in order to proceed. **—take (someone) down a peg.** To reduce the pride of; humble. **—off the peg.** *Chiefly British.* Bought ready to wear. Said of a garment. **—a square peg in a round hole.** A misfit.
~*v.* **pegged, pegging, pegs.** —*tr.* **1. a.** To put or insert a peg into. **b.** To provide (a barrel) with a vent and peg. **c.** To pierce or strike with or as with a peg. **2.** To designate or mark by means of pegs: *pegging the score in a cribbage game.* **3.** *Finance.* **a.** To stabilise or fix the prices of (securities, stocks, or the like) so as to minimise fluctuation. **b.** To fix levels of (prices, wages or the like), as by government legislation. **4.** To aim and throw (a missile, such as a stone or a ball) at or to a person or target. —*intr.* To proceed doggedly and steadily; hammer away; persist. Often followed by *away*: *pegging steadily away until the work's done.* **—peg out.** *Informal.* **1.** To become exhausted; collapse. **2.** *Informal.* To die. **3.** In croquet: **a.** To win a game by hitting the peg. **b.** To cause (an opponent's ball) to strike the peg. **4.** To score the winning point in cribbage. [Middle English *pegge,* probably from Middle Dutch.]

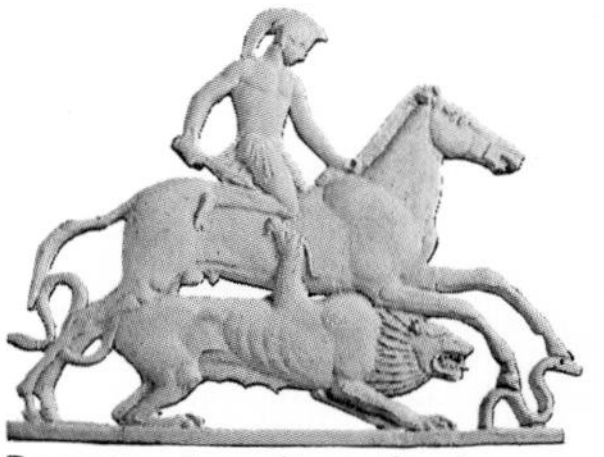

Pegasus *According to Greek legend, when the Gorgon Medusa was slain by the hero Perseus, the flying horse arose from her blood. Later Bellerophon rode the horse in his fight with the Chimera (above). Pegasus became a constellation in the sky when Bellerophon fell off while attempting to ride him to heaven.*

Peg·a·sus¹ (péggə-səss). *Greek Mythology.* The winged steed that caused Hippocrene, the fountain of the Muses on Helicon, to well forth with a stroke of his hoof; the mount of Bellerophon. [Latin, from Greek *Pegasos,* from *pēgē,* spring.]

Pegasus² *n.* A constellation in the Northern Hemisphere near Aquarius and Andromeda.

peg·board (pég-bawrd || -bōrd) *n.* **1.** A board for playing games such as cribbage, having holes into which pegs are inserted, either as part of a game or to keep score. **2.** Hardboard having rows of small holes into which hooks or pegs may be inserted.

peg leg *n. Informal.* An artificial leg, especially one made of wood.

peg·ma·tite (pég-mə-tīt) *n. Geology.* A very coarse-grained igneous rock, sometimes rich in rare elements such as uranium, tungsten, and tantalum. Most pegmatites are granite. [French : Greek *pēgma*

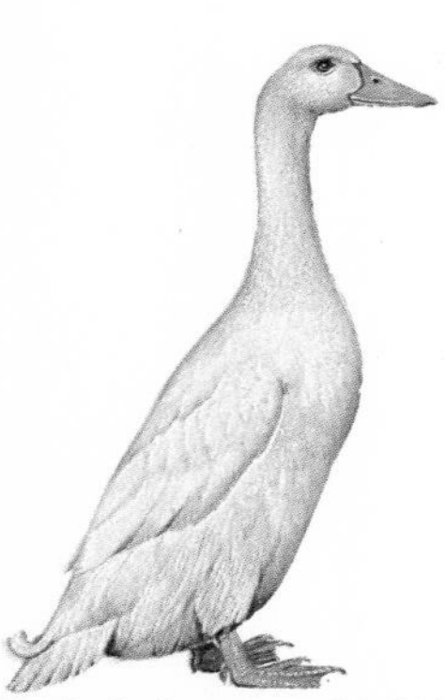

Pekin duck *A creamy-white bird with a bright yellow bill. It is similar to the Aylesbury duck, and is found in farmyards throughout the world.*

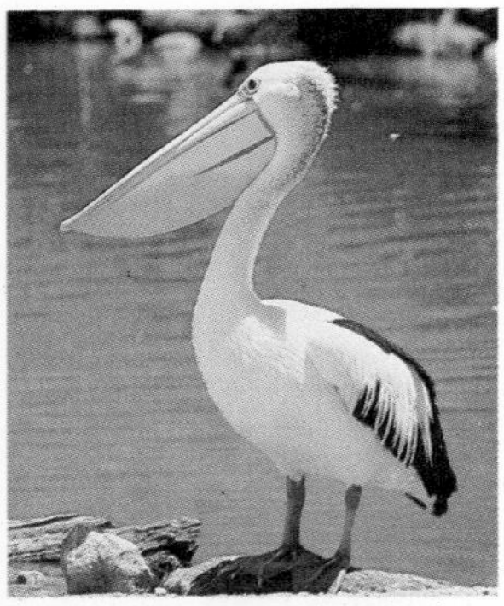

pelican *The pelican's huge beak pouch is used as a fishing net. Clumsy on land, pelicans are impressive fliers. This is the Australian pelican,* Pelecanus conspicillatus.

(stem *pēgmat-*), framework, from *pēgnunai,* to fasten + -ITE.] **—peg·ma·tit·ic** (-títtik) *adj.*

peg top *n.* A wooden spinning top, tapering to a usually metal point on which it rotates.

Pé·guy (pay-gée), **Charles (Pierre)** (1873–1914). French poet, nationalist, and publisher. He founded the journal *Cahiers de la quinzaine* (1900–14) in which he published his own work and that of other writers. Combining this with socialist and Catholic views, he also wrote *Notre Jeunesse* (1910), *Le Mystère de la charité de Jeanne d'Arc* (1910), and *Eve* (1913).

Pehlevi. Variant of **Pahlavi.**

P.E.I. Prince Edward Island.

pei·gnoir (páyn-waar, payn-wáar, pen-) *n.* A woman's loose-fitting dressing gown; a negligee. [French, "garment worn while combing the hair", from Old French *peigner,* to comb the hair, from Latin *pectināre,* from *pecten* (stem *pectin-*), comb.]

Pei·ping. See **Beijing.**

Peirce (perss), **Charles (Sanders)** (1839–1914). U.S. philosopher and logician. He founded pragmatism as a reaction against "useless" metaphysical speculation and theorising. He was also a pioneer in the development of modern formal logic, inspired by the algebraic laws and methods of De Morgan and Boole.

pej·o·rate (péjə-rayt) *tr.v.* **-ated, -ating, -ates.** To diminish in quality, status, or worth. [Back-formation from PEJORATIVE.]

pej·o·ra·tion (péjə-ráysh'n) *n.* **1.** The process or condition of worsening or degenerating. **2.** *Linguistics.* The process by which the semantic status of a word changes for the worse, over a period of time. For example, *egregious,* which formerly meant "distinguished", " has come to mean "conspicuously bad". Compare **amelioration.** [Medieval Latin *pējōrātiō* (stem *pējōrātiōn-*), from Late Latin *pējōrāre,* to become or make worse, from Latin *pējor,* worse.]

pe·jor·a·tive (pi-jórrətiv, pə-, péejə-rətiv || -raytiv, *U.S. also* péjə-) *adj.* **1.** Tending to make or become worse. **2.** Expressing disapproval.
~*n.* A pejorative word. **—pe·jor·a·tive·ly** *adv.*

pek·an (péckən) *n.* A mammal, the **fisher** *(see).* [Canadian French *pékan,* of Algonquian origin, akin to Abnaki *pékané.*]

peke (peek) *n. Informal.* A Pekingese dog.

Pe·kin (pee-kín, péekin) *n.* A large white duck of an Oriental breed, widely reared in the United States for food. [French *pékin,* from *Pékin,* Peking (Beijing).]

Peking. See **Beijing.**

Pe·king·ese (péeking-éez || -éess *for senses 1, 2.) n., pl.* **Pekingese.** Also **Pe·kin·ese** (péekin-). **1.** A resident or native of Peking (Beijing), China. **2.** The Chinese dialect of Peking (Beijing). **3.** A toy dog of a breed developed in China, having a flat nose, long hair, and short, bowed forelegs. **—Pe·king·ese** *adj.*

Peking man *n.* An early form of man whose fossil remains were found at Zhoukoudian (Choukoutien) near Beijing (Peking). The remains are classified as *Homo erectus,* but were formerly classified as *Sinanthropus pekinensis* or *Pithecanthropus pekinensis.*

pe·koe (péekō) *n.* A high-quality variety of black tea made from the leaves around the buds. [Chinese (Amoy) *peh ho* : *peh,* white + *ho,* down (referring to the downy appearance of the young leaves).]

pel·age (péllij) *n.* The coat of a mammal, consisting of hair, fur, wool, or other soft covering, as distinct from bare skin. [French, from Old French *pel, poil,* hair, from Latin *pilus.*]

Pe·la·gi·an·ism (pe-láyji-ə-niz'm, pi-) *n.* The theological doctrine propounded by Pelagius, and condemned as heresy by the Roman Catholic Church in A.D. 417. Included in its tenets were denial of original sin and affirmation of man's ability to be righteous by the exercise of free will. **—Pe·la·gi·an** *adj.* & *n.*

pe·lag·ic (pe-lájik, pi) *adj.* Of, pertaining to, or living in open oceans or seas rather than waters adjacent to land or inland waters. See **plankton, nekton.** [Latin *pelagicus,* from Greek *pelagikos,* from *pelagos,* sea.]

Pe·la·gi·us (pe-láyji-əss, pi-). (*c.* A.D. 360– *c.* 420). British heretical theologian. Settling in Rome (*c.* 380), he rejected St. Augustine's teachings on predestination and original sin, and in the heretical doctrine of Pelagianism proclaimed the free will of man to do good or evil. He was condemned by Pope Innocent I (417) and by the Council of Ephesus (431).

pel·ar·gon·ic acid (péllaar-gónnik, -gṓnik) *n.* A colourless or yellow oil, $CH_3(CH_2)_7COOH$, used as a petrol additive and in the manufacture of lacquers, plastics, and pharmaceuticals. Also called "nonanoic acid". [Obtained from the leaves of PELARGONIUM.]

pel·ar·go·ni·um (péllaar-gṓni-əm) *n.* Any of various plants and shrubs of the genus *Pelargonium,* which includes the geraniums. [New Latin, from Greek *pelargos,* a stork (from the long, beak-shaped capsules of the plants).]

Pe·las·gi·an (pe-láz-gi-ən, pi-, -ji-) *n.* A member of a people living in the region of the Aegean Sea before the coming of the Greeks. [Greek *Pelasgoi,* native name of unknown origin probably altered by folk etymology as if to mean "sea people", from *pelagos,* sea.] **—Pe·las·gi·an, Pe·las·gic** *adj.*

Pe·lé (péllay), born Edson Arantes do Nascimento (1940–). Brazilian footballer. One of the world's greatest inside forwards, he helped to win the World Cup for Brazil in 1958, 1962, and 1970. Playing for Santos (1955–74) and the New York Cosmos (1975–77), he scored more than 1,200 goals.

Pe·lée, Mount (pə-lay). Volcano on the West Indian island of Martinique. Its eruption (1902), with clouds of incandescent gas, destroyed the town of St. Pierre. **—Pe·lé·an** *adj.*

pel·er·ine (pélla-reen || *U.S. also* -rin, -réen) *n.* A woman's cape, usually short, with points descending in front. [French *pèlerine,* from the feminine of *pèlerin,* a pilgrim, from Late Latin *pelegrīnus,* PILGRIM.]

pelf (pelf) *n.* Wealth or riches, especially when dishonestly acquired. [Middle English, booty, from Old French *pelfre.* See **pilfer.**]

pel·ham (pélləm) *n.* A horse's bit, combining a curb and a snaffle. [Probably from the surname *Pelham.*]

pel·i·can (péllikən) *n.* Any of various large, web-footed birds of the genus *Pelecanus,* of tropical and warm regions, having under the lower bill a large pouch used for catching and holding fish. [Middle English *pelican,* Old English *pellican,* from Late Latin *pelicānus,* from Greek *pelekan, pelekinos,* from *pelekus,* an axe (probably from the shape of its bill), akin to Sanskrit *parasu,* an axe, probably of Mesopotamian origin.]

pelican crossing *n.* A pedestrian crossing where traffic lights are operated by the person wishing to cross the road. [Irregularly from *pe*destrian *li*ght *c*ontrolled *c*rossing.]

pe·lisse (pe-léess, pi-, pə-) *n.* **1.** A long cloak or outer robe, usually of fur or with a fur lining. **2.** A woman's loose, light cloak, often with openings for the arms. [French, from Medieval Latin *pellicia,* leather garment, cloak, from Latin *pellicius,* made of skin, from *pellis,* skin.]

pe·lite (péelīt) *n.* Any rock composed of fine fragments, of such components as clay, quartz particles, or rock flour. [Greek *pēlos*†, clay + -ITE.] **—pe·lit·ic** (pi-líttik) *adj.*

Pel·la (péllə). Ancient city of Greece. Capital of Macedonia, under Philip II (382–336 B.C.), it was the birthplace of his son Alexander the Great (356 B.C.).

pel·lag·ra (pe-láygrə, pi-, pə-, -lággrə || *U.S. also* -láagrə) *n.* A chronic disease caused by niacin deficiency, and characterised by skin eruptions, digestive and nervous disturbances, and eventual mental deterioration. [Italian : *pelle,* skin, from Latin *pellis* + Greek *agra,* seizure.] **—pel·lag·rous** *adj.*

pel·lag·rin (pe-láygrin, pi-, pə-, -lággrin || -láagrin) *n.* A person afflicted with pellagra. [From PELLAGRA.]

pel·let (péllit) *n.* **1.** A small, solid or densely packed ball or mass, as of bread, wax, or medicine. **2.** A bullet or piece of small shot. **3.** A stone ball, used as a catapult missile or as a primitive cannonball. **4.** A hard mass of undigestible food that is regurgitated by certain birds, especially birds of prey.
~*tr.v.* **pelleted, -leting, -lets. 1.** To make or form into pellets. **2.** To strike with pellets. [Middle English *pelet,* from Old French *pelote,* from Vulgar Latin *pilotta* (unattested), diminutive of Latin *pila,* ball, PILL.]

pel·li·cle (péllik'l) *n.* **1.** A thin skin or film, such as an organic membrane or a liquid film. **2.** A rigid outer layer of cytoplasm in certain single-celled organisms such as the euglenas. **3.** The thin outer covering of a mushroom cap. [Old French *pellicule,* from Medieval Latin *pellicula,* from Latin, diminutive of *pellis,* skin.] **—pel·lic·u·lar** (pe-líckewlər, pi-, pə-) *adj.*

pel·li·to·ry (pélli-təri, -tri) *n., pl.* **-ries. 1.** Any of various plants of the genus *Parietaria,* that grow on walls, rocks, and the like, and have clusters of small flowers arising at the leaf bases. **2.** A small plant, *Anacyclus pyrethrum,* of the Mediterranean region, containing a volatile oil once used for the relief of toothache and facial neuralgia. [Sense 1, altered from Middle English *peritorie, paritorie,* from Old French *paritaire,* from Late Latin *parietāria (herba),* "herb of the wall", from *parietārius,* belonging to walls, from Latin *pariēs* (stem *pariet-*), wall. See **paries.** Sense 2, altered from earlier *peletyr,* Middle English *peletre, peretre,* from Latin *pyrethrum,* PYRETHRUM.]

pell-mell (pél-mél) *adv.* **1.** In a jumbled, confused manner; helter-skelter. **2.** In frantic, disorderly haste; headlong. [French *pêle-mêle,* Old French *pesle mesle, mesle mesle,* reduplications of *mesle,* imperative of *mesler,* to mix, from Vulgar Latin *misculāre* (unattested), from Latin *miscēre.*] **—pell-mell** *adj.* & *n.*

pel·lu·cid (pe-léw-sid, pi-, -lṓō-) *adj.* **1.** Admitting the passage of light; transparent; translucent. **2.** Transparently clear in style or meaning: *pellucid prose.* [Latin *pellūcidus,* from *pellūcēre, perlūcēre,* to shine through : *per,* through + *lūcēre,* to shine.] **—pel·lu·cid·i·ty** (péllew-síddəti), **pel·lu·cid·ness** *n.* **—pel·lu·cid·ly** *adv.*

Pel·man·ism (pélmәniz'm) *n.* **1.** A system of training the memory. **2.** *Often small* **p.** A game in which playing cards are placed face down and the players try to turn up matching pairs. [Proprietary term, after the *Pelman* Institute, London.]

pel·met (pélmit) *n.* A piece of board or draped material fixed above a window or door to hide a curtain rail. [Probably from French *palmette,* PALMETTE (referring to ornamental palm-leaf design on cornice moulding).]

Pel·o·pon·nese (pélləpə-neess, -néess || -neez). Also **Pel·o·pon·ne·sus** (-néessəss). Peninsula of southern Greece, known as Morea in the Middle Ages. Joined to the mainland by the Isthmus of Corinth, it is largely mountainous with fertile coastal lowlands in the west and north. Ruled by Sparta until the fourth century B.C., it has many ruins, and produces currants, wine, and olives. **—Pel·o·pon·ne·sian** (-néesh'n, -néezh'n) *adj.*

Peloponnesian War *n.* A war between Athens and Sparta with their allies (431–404 B.C.) that was won by Sparta.

pe·lo·ri·a (pe-láw-ri-ə, pi-, pə- || -lṓ-) *n. Botany.* Unusual regularity in the form of a flower or other structure that is normally irregular. [New Latin, from Greek *pelōros,* monstrous, from *pelōr,* monster, prodigy.] **—pe·lor·ic** (-láwrik, -lórrik) *adj.*

pe·lo·rus (pi-láwrəss || -lṓrəss) *n., pl.* **-ruses.** A fixed compass card on which bearings relative to the ship's heading are taken. [Perhaps after *Pelorus*, pilot of Hannibal.]

pe·lo·ta (pə-lóttə, pe-, -lőtə) *n.* **1.** A fast game popular in the Basque country and Spanish America in which players hit a ball with a scoop-shaped wicker racket against any of three walls of a court. **2.** The ball used in this game. [Spanish, ball, augmentative of *pella*, from Latin *pila*, ball.]

pelt[1] (pelt) *n.* **1. a.** The skin of an animal with the fur or hair still on it. **b.** A stripped animal skin ready for tanning. **2.** An animal hide, especially one used as a garment. [Middle English, perhaps back-formation from PELTRY.]

pelt[2] *v.* **pelted, pelting, pelts.** —*tr.* **1.** To strike or assail repeatedly with or as with blows or missiles; throw things at; bombard. **2.** To cast, hurl, or throw (missiles). —*intr.* **1.** To beat or strike heavily and repeatedly. **2.** To move at a fast speed. **3.** To pour with rain. Often used with *down*.
—*n.* **1.** A sharp blow; a whack. **2.** A rapid pace; speed. Used chiefly in the phrase *at full pelt*. [Middle English *pelten*, perhaps from Latin *pultāre*, basin.] —**pelt·er** *n.*

pel·tast (péltast) *n.* In ancient Greece, a foot soldier who carried a spear and small leather shield. [Latin *peltasta*, from Greek *peltastēs*, from *peltē*, small shield.]

pel·tate (péltayt) *adj. Botany.* Having the leaf stalk attached near the centre of the surface, rather than at or near the margin. [New Latin *peltatus*, "having a shield", from Latin *pelta*, small light shield, from Greek *peltē*.] —**pel·tate·ly** *adv.*

Pel·ti·er effect (pélti-ay) *n.* The generation of heat at either of the two junctions of a thermocouple when it is passing current. Compare **Seebeck effect**. [After Jean *Peltier* (1785–1845), French physicist.]

Peltier element *n.* An electronic device consisting of metal strips that alternate with strips of n-type and p-type semiconductor so that when a current is passed heat is absorbed from one set of metallic strips and emitted from the other set, as a result of the Peltier effect. [After Jean *Peltier*.]

pel·try (péltri) *n.* Undressed pelts collectively. [Middle English, from Old French *peleterie*, from *peletier*, furrier, from *pel*, skin, from Latin *pellis*.]

pel·vic (pélvik) *adj.* Of, in, near, or pertaining to the pelvis.

pelvic fin *n.* Either of a pair of lateral hind fins of fishes, attached to the pelvic girdle. Also called "ventral fin".

pelvic girdle *n.* The skeletal structure of bone or cartilage by which the hind limbs or analogous parts are supported and joined to the vertebral column. Also called "pelvic arch", and in humans "hip girdle".

pel·vis (pél-viss) *n., pl.* **-vises** or **-ves** (-veez). *Anatomy.* **1.** A basin-shaped skeletal structure, composed of the innominate bones on the sides, the pubis in front, and the sacrum and coccyx behind. **2.** The renal pelvis (see). [New Latin, from Latin *pēlvis*, basin.]

pem·broke[1] (pémbrŏŏk ‖ -brŏk) *n.* A Welsh corgi of a breed characterised by a short tail and pointed ears. [After PEMBROKE.]

Pem·broke[2] (pém-brŏŏk, -brək ‖ -brŏk). Seaport in Dyfed, southwest Wales. Situated on Milford Haven, it has a medieval castle where Henry VII was born.

Pem·broke·shire (pém-brŏŏk-shər, -brək-, -sheer ‖ -brŏk-). Former county of southwest Wales, now part of Dyfed. Its coast is a national park, and tourism and dairy farming are important. Its county town was Haverfordwest.

pem·mi·can, pem·i·can (pémmikən) *n.* **1.** A food originally prepared by North American Indians from lean, dried strips of meat pounded into paste, mixed with fat and berries, and pressed into small cakes. **2.** A similar food made chiefly from beef, dried fruit, and suet, used as emergency rations. [Cree *pimikân*, from *pimii*, grease, fat.]

pem·phi·gus (pémfigəss, pem-fígəss) *n.* Any of several acute or chronic skin diseases characterised by itching blisters. The variety *pemphigus vulgaris* is a serious disease that spreads from the mucous membranes to large areas of skin. [New Latin, from Greek *pemphix* (stem *pemphig*-), drop, pustule, of imitative origin.]

pen[1] (pen) *n.* **1.** An instrument for writing or drawing with ink: **a.** Formerly, one made from a large quill with the nib split and sharpened. **b.** A tapering metal device with a split point, fitted to a metal, plastic, or wooden holder. It may be dipped in ink or supplied by a reservoir within the holder. **c.** A penholder and its pen together. See **ball-point pen, fountain pen. 2.** A writing instrument viewed as the writer's weapon or means of expression of ideas or opinions. **3.** A writer or author: *a hired pen.* **4.** A style of writing: *a witty pen.* **5.** The chitinous internal shell of a squid.
—*tr.v.* **penned, penning, pens.** To write or compose with a pen. [Middle English *penne*, from Old French, feather, pen, from Latin *penna*, feather (in Late Latin, also "pen").] —**pen·ner** *n.*

pen[2] *n.* **1.** A fenced enclosure for animals. **2.** The animals kept in such an enclosure. **3.** Any of various other enclosures, such as a bullpen or a playpen. **4.** A repair dock for submarines. **5.** In Jamaica: **a.** A farm where livestock is bred. **b.** A country estate.
—*tr.v.* **penned, penning, pens.** To confine in or as if in a pen. [Middle English *pen*, Old English *penn*.]

pen[3] *n.* A female swan. Compare **cob**. [Origin obscure.]

pen[4] *n. U.S. Slang.* A penitentiary. [Short for PENITENTIARY.]

pen., Pen. peninsula.

P.E.N. (pen) *n.* International Association of Poets, Playwrights, Editors, Essayists, and Novelists.

pe·nal (péen'l) *adj.* **1.** Of or pertaining to punishment, especially for

---

breaking the law. **2.** Subject to punishment; legally punishable: *a penal offence.* **3.** Prescribing or enumerating punishments or penalties for offences: *penal laws.* **4.** Serving as or constituting a means or place of punishment: *penal servitude.* [Middle English, from Old French, from Latin *poenālis*, from *poena*, penalty.] —**pe·nal·ly** *adv.*

penal code *n.* The body of laws relating to crimes and offences and the penalties for their commission.

pe·nal·ise, pe·nal·ize (péen'l-īz ‖ U.S. also pénn'l-) *tr.v.* **-ised, -ising, -ises. 1.** To subject to a penalty, especially for infringement of a law or official regulation. **2.** To impose a handicap on; place at a disadvantage. **3.** To make punishable by a penalty. —See Synonyms at **punish.** —**pe·nal·i·sa·tion** (-ī-záysh'n ‖ U.S. -i-) *n.*

pen·al·ty (pénn'lti) *n., pl.* **-ties. 1.** A punishment established by law or authority for a crime or offence. **2.** Something, especially a sum of money, required as a forfeit for an offence or to fulfil a contract or obligation. **3.** The disadvantage or painful consequences resulting from an action or condition. **4.** *Sports.* A handicap or loss of advantage imposed on a team or competitor for infraction of a rule. **5.** *Often plural.* In contract bridge, points scored by the opponents when the declarer fails to make his bid. [Anglo-French *penalte* (unattested), from Medieval Latin *poenālitās* (stem *poenālitāt*-), from Latin *poenālis*, PENAL.]

penalty area *n.* In soccer, the area in front of the goal where the goalkeeper may handle the ball and where a penalty kick may be awarded. Also called "penalty box".

penalty box *n.* **1.** In soccer, the penalty area. **2.** In ice hockey, the enclosure where penalised players sit.

penalty kick *n.* **1.** In soccer, a direct free kick at the goal awarded following a foul committed in the penalty area of the defending team and taken from the penalty spot, with only the goalkeeper in defence. **2.** In Rugby football, a kick awarded against a team for an infringement, such as a player's being offside.

penalty rate *n. Australian.* A special rate paid to people working outside the normal hours; overtime rate.

penalty spot *n.* In soccer, a mark 11 metres (12 yards) from the goalmouth from which a penalty kick is taken.

pen·ance (pénnənss) *n.* **1.** An act of self-mortification or devotion performed by way of demonstrating contrition for sin. **2.** *Ecclesiastical.* **a.** A sacrament that includes contrition, confession to a priest, acceptance of punishment, and absolution. **b.** A punishment imposed as a condition of absolution. **3.** A feeling of sorrow for one's wrongdoing or sin. —**do penance.** To show repentance by undergoing imposed or voluntary punishment. [Middle English *penaunce*, from Old French *penance*, from Latin *paenitentia*, penitence, from *paenitēns*, PENITENT.]

Pe·nang or **Pi·nang**[1] (pə-náng, pe-). State of Peninsular Malaysia. It is made up of Penang Island at the north end of the Strait of Malacca, and Province Wellesley on the mainland, and produces coconuts, rice, and rubber. George Town, the capital, is also called Penang.

Penang or **Pinang**[2]. See **George Town.**

pe·na·tes (pe-náatayz, pi-, pə-, -náyteez) *pl.n.* The Roman gods of the household, tutelary deities of the home and of the state, whose cult was closely connected and often identified with that of the **lares** (see). [Latin *Penātēs*, household gods, akin to *penus*†, the interior of a house (compare **penetrate**).]

pence (penss). *British.* Alternative plural of **penny.** Often used in combination: *twopence.* See Usage note at **penny.**

pen·cel or **pen·sil** (pén-s'l, -sil) *n.* A narrow flag, streamer, or pennon, especially one carried at the top of a lance or spear. [Middle English, from Anglo-French, contracted from Old French *penoncel*, diminutive of *penon*, PENNON.]

pen·chant (pón-shon, pénchənt) *n.* A strong inclination; a definite and continued liking. [French, from the present participle of *pencher*, to incline, from Vulgar Latin *pendicāre* (unattested), from Latin *pendēre*, to hang.]

pen·cil (pén-s'l, -sil) *n.* **1.** A narrow, generally cylindrical implement for writing, drawing, or marking, consisting of a thin rod of graphite, crayon, or similar substance encased in wood or held in a plastic or metal mechanical device. **2.** Something shaped or used like a pencil; especially, a narrow medicated or cosmetic stick: *a styptic pencil; an eyebrow pencil.* **3. a.** *Archaic.* An artist's brush, especially a fine one. **b.** An artist's style or technique in drawing or delineating. **c.** Descriptive skill. **4.** A narrow cone or cylinder of rays, especially light rays, forming a beam of small diameter. **5.** *Mathematics.* A family of geometrical figures that share a common property, such as all straight lines in a plane that pass through a fixed point.
—*tr.v.* **pencilled** or *U.S.* **penciled, -cilling** or *U.S.* **-ciling, -cils. 1.** To write or produce by using a pencil: *pencil a note.* **2.** To mark, shade, or colour with or as if with a pencil. —**pencil in.** To enter on note down provisionally in a diary, timetable, or the like. [Middle English *pensel, pencel,* from Old French *pincel,* from Vulgar Latin *pēnicellus* (unattested), from Latin *pēnicillus,* a brush, pencil, "small tail", diminutive of *pēnis,* tail.] —**pen·cil·ler** *n.*

pencil sharpener *n.* A device consisting of a blade within a cone used for giving a sharp point to a pencil.

pend (pend) *intr.v.* **pended, pending, pends. 1.** To wait for a decision or judgment. **2.** *Regional.* To hang; depend. [Latin *pendere,* to suspend, hang.]

pen·dant, pen·dent (péndənt) *n.* **1.** Something suspended from something else; especially, an ornament or piece of jewellery attached to a necklace or bracelet. **2.** A hanging lamp or chandelier. **3.** A sculptured ornament suspended from a vaulted Gothic roof or

---

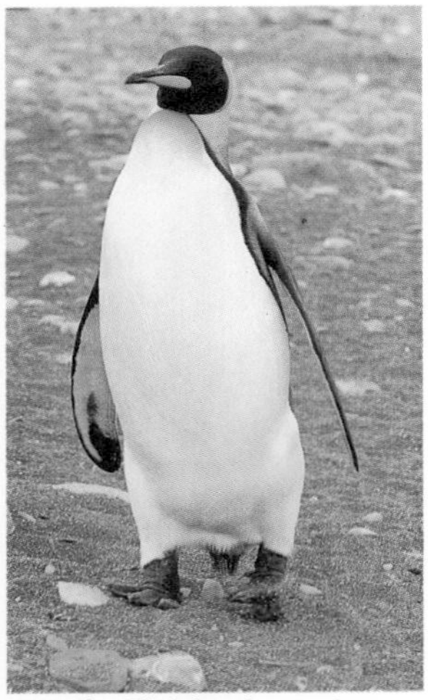

penguin *Flightless, but good swimmers, all 18 species of penguin live in the Southern Hemisphere, feeding on fish, squid, and crustaceans. This is the king penguin,* Aptenodytes patagonicus.

ceiling. **4. a.** Either of a matched pair; a parallel or companion piece. **b.** An additional thing or part that supplements or complements another; a complement. **5.** A short rope hanging from a mast or spar with an eye at its lower end to which fittings may be attached. **6.** *Nautical.* A **pennant** *(see).*
~adj. Variant of **pendent.** [Middle English *pendaunt,* from Old French *pendant,* from the present participle of *pendre,* to hang, from Vulgar Latin *pendere* (unattested), to hang, variant of Latin *pendēre,* to hang.]

pen·dent, pen·dant (péndənt) *adj.* **1.** Hanging down; dangling; suspended. **2.** Projecting; jutting; overhanging. **3.** Awaiting settlement; undecided; pending.
~n. Variant of **pendant.** [Middle English *penda(u)nt,* from Old French *pendant,* hanging. See **pendant.**] **—pen·dent·ly** *adv.*

pen·den·te li·te (pen-dénti lī́ti) *adj. Law.* While a lawsuit is pending; during litigation. [Latin, "with litigation pending".]

pen·den·tive (pen-déntiv) *n. Architecture.* An overhanging, triangular section of vaulting between the rim of a dome and each adjacent pair of the arches that support it. [French *pendentif,* "overhanging feature", from Latin *pendēns* (stem *pendent-*), present participle of *pendēre,* to hang.]

Pen·de·rec·ki (péndə-rétski), **Krzystof** (1933–). Polish experimental composer. Receiving wide acclaim for his *Passion and Death of our Lord Jesus Christ according to St. Luke* (1966), he developed his own musical notation, abandoning normal tempos and employing unconventional sounds. Other works include *Threnody to the Victims of Hiroshima* (1961), and two operas, *The Devils of Loudun* (1969), and *Paradise Lost* (1977–78).

pend·ing (pénding) *adj.* **1.** Not yet dealt with, decided, or settled; awaiting conclusion or confirmation. **2.** Impending; imminent.
~prep. **1.** While in process of; during. **2.** While awaiting; until. [Anglicised form of French *pendant,* from Old French, "hanging" (after Latin *pendēns* (stem *pendent-*), hanging, pending).]

pen·drag·on (pen-drággən) *n.* The supreme war leader of the post-Roman Celts of England and Wales. [Middle English, from Welsh : *pen,* chief, head, from Common Celtic *gwenno-* (unattested) + *dragon,* standard, from Latin *dracō,* cohort's standard, DRAGON.] **—pen·drag·on·ship** *n.*

pen·du·lar (péndewlər) *adj.* Of or resembling the motion of a pendulum; swinging back and forth.

pen·du·lous (péndewləss) *adj.* **1.** Hanging loosely. **2.** *Rare.* Wavering; undecided. [Latin *pendulus,* from *pendēre,* to hang.] **—pen·du·lous·ly** *adv.* **—pen·du·lous·ness** *n.*

pen·du·lum (péndewləm) *n.* **1. a.** A mass suspended from a fixed low-friction support at the end of a relatively light thread so that it is free to swing in a vertical plane under the influence of gravitational force only. Also called "simple pendulum". **b.** Any of several related, freely swinging configurations differing in mass distribution, suspension, and possible modes of motion. Also called "compound pendulum". **2.** Any such object used to regulate the movement of various devices, especially clocks. **3.** Something that swings back and forth from one course, opinion, or condition to another: *the pendulum of public opinion.* [New Latin, from Latin, neuter of *pendulus,* PENDULOUS.]

Pe·nel·o·pe (pi-néllәpi, pə-). In the *Odyssey,* the wife of Odysseus and mother of Telemachus, celebrated for her constancy.

pe·ne·plain, pe·ne·plane (péeni-playn, -pláyn) *n. Geology.* A nearly flat land surface representing an advanced stage of erosion. [Latin *paene, pēne,* almost + PLAIN.] **—pe·ne·pla·na·tion** (-plə-náysh'n) *n.*

pe·nes. Alternative plural of **penis.**

pen·e·tra·li·a (pénni-tráyli-ə) *pl.n.* **1.** The innermost parts of a building; especially, the sanctuary of a temple. **2.** Innermost or hidden parts; recesses: *the penetralia of the soul.* [Latin *penetrālia,* plural of *penetrāle,* innermost part, from *penetrālis,* inner, interior, from *penetrāre,* to PENETRATE.]

pen·e·trance (pénnitrənss) *n. Genetics.* **Expression** *(see).* [From PENETRANT.]

pen·e·trant (pénnitrənt) *adj.* Penetrating; piercing.
~n. Something that penetrates or is capable of penetrating. [Latin *penetrāns* (stem *penetrant-*), present participle of *penetrāre,* to PENETRATE.]

pen·e·trate (pénni-trayt) *v.* **-trated, -trating, -trates.** *—tr.* **1. a.** To enter or force a way into; pierce: *penetrated the enemy's territory.* **b.** To insert the penis into the vagina or anus of. **2. a.** To enter into and permeate: *The smell penetrated the entire building.* **b.** To cause to be permeated or diffused; steep. **3.** To grasp the inner significance of; understand: *penetrate a mystery.* **4.** To see through. **5.** To affect deeply, as by piercing the consciousness or emotions. **6.** To infiltrate: *The spy penetrated the enemy's intelligence service.* *—intr.* **1.** To pierce or enter into something; make a way in or through something. **2.** To gain admittance or access. **3.** To gain insight into something. [Latin *penetrāre,* from *penitus,* deeply, from *penus*†, the interior of a house.] **—pen·e·tra·bil·i·ty** (-trə-bílləti) *n.* **—pen·e·tra·ble** (-trəbj'l) *adj.* **—pen·e·tra·bly** *adv.* **—pen·e·tra·tor** (-traytər) *n.* **—pen·e·tra·tive** *adj.*

pen·e·trat·ing (pénni-trayting) *adj.* **1.** Able or seeming to penetrate: *a penetrating wind.* **2.** Keenly perceptive or understanding: *penetrating insight.* **—pen·e·trat·ing·ly** *adv.*

pen·e·tra·tion (pénni-tráysh'n) *n.* **1.** The act or process of piercing or penetrating something. **2.** The power or ability to penetrate. **3.** The extent to which a person or thing penetrates, especially: **a.** The extent to which an incursion or infiltration by a hostile force is successful. **b.** The depth reached by a projectile after hitting its target. **c.** In ball games, the depth to which the ball is sent into an opponent's playing area. **4.** Understanding; insight.

pen·e·trom·e·ter (pénni-trómmitər) *n.* **1.** A device for measuring the penetrating power of X-rays. **2.** A device for measuring the penetrability of semisolids. [PENETR(ATION) + -METER.]

pen friend *n.* A person with whom one corresponds regularly and forms a friendship, usually without meeting. Also called "pen pal".

pen·guin (péng-gwin) *n.* **1.** Any of various flightless marine birds of the family Spheniscidae, of cool regions of the Southern Hemisphere. They have scalelike, barbless feathers, flipper-like wings, and webbed feet. See **Adélie penguin, emperor penguin.** **2.** *Obsolete.* The great auk. [16th century : origin obscure.]

-penia *n. comb. form.* Indicates lack or deficiency; for example, **leukopenia.** [New Latin, from Greek *penia,* poverty, lack.]

pen·i·cil·la·mine (pénni-síllə-meen) *n.* A drug that is a chelating agent and is used to treat poisoning by various metals and also severe rheumatoid arthritis.

pen·i·cil·late (pénni-síl-ət, -it, -ayt) *adj.* Having or resembling a tuft or brush of fine hairs, such as those on caterpillars and certain grasses. [Latin *pēnicillus,* brush, PENCIL + -ATE.] **—pen·i·cil·late·ly** *adv.* **—pen·i·cil·la·tion** (-si-láysh'n) *n.*

pen·i·cil·lin (pénni-síllin) *n.* Any of several isomeric antibiotic compounds obtained from penicillium moulds, especially *Penicillium notatum* and *P. chrysogenum,* or produced biosynthetically, and used to treat a wide variety of bacterial infections. [New Latin *penicillium,* PENICILLIUM.]

pen·i·cil·li·um (pénni-sílli-əm) *n., pl.* **-liums** or **-lia** (-sílli-ə). Any of various moulds of the genus *Penicillium,* having a characteristic blue-green colour, and producing tufts of fine filaments. They grow on decaying fruits and ripening cheese, and are used in the production of penicillin and in making cheese. [New Latin, from Latin *pēnicillus,* brush, PENCIL.]

penile (péenīl) *adj.* Of or relating to the penis. [New Latin *penilis.*]

pen·ill (pénnihl) *n., pl.* **penillion** (pi-nílli-ən; *Welsh* (pe-níhl-yon). **1.** A form of improvised Welsh poetry sung in accompaniment to a tune played on a harp, especially at eisteddfods. **2.** A stanza of such poetry. [Welsh, verse, stanza.]

pen·in·su·la (pi-nín-sewlə, pə-, pe-, -shŏŏlə) *n. Abbr.* **pen., Pen.** A long projection of land into water. Compare **cape.** [Latin *pēninsula* : *paene,* almost + *īnsula,* an island.]

pen·in·su·lar (pi-nín-sew-lər, pə-, -shŏŏ-) *adj.* Of, pertaining to, or resembling a peninsula.
~n. An inhabitant of a peninsula.

Pen·in·su·lar War (pi-nín-sew-lər, pə-, -shŏŏ-). The part of the Napoleonic Wars fought against France in the Peninsula (Spain and Portugal) from 1808-14 by Britain, Portugal, and Spain.

pe·nis (pée-niss) *n., pl.* **-nises** or **-nes** (-neez). **1.** *Anatomy.* The male organ of copulation in higher vertebrates, and of urinary excretion in mammals. **2.** Any of various copulatory organs in males of lower animals. [Latin *pēnis,* tail, penis.]

penis envy *n.* **1.** In Freudian psychology, an emotional and sexual drive in women supposedly originating when a girl perceives her genitalia as a lack or castration. **2.** Loosely, a supposed envy in women of men's power, status, and dominance in society.

pen·i·tent (pénnitənt) *adj.* Feeling or expressing remorse for one's misdeeds or sins.
~n. **1.** One who is penitent. **2.** A person performing penance under the direction of a confessor. [Middle English, from Old French, from Latin *paenitēns* (stem *paenitent-*), present participle of *paenitēre,* to repent.] **—pen·i·tence** *n.* **—pen·i·tent·ly** *adv.*

pen·i·ten·tial (pénni-ténsh'l) *adj.* **1.** Of, pertaining to, or expressing penitence. **2.** Pertaining to or of the nature of penance.
~n. **1.** A book or set of church rules concerning the sacrament of penance. **2.** A penitent. **—pen·i·ten·tial·ly** *adv.*

pen·i·ten·tia·ry (pénni-tén-shəri, -shi-əri || *U.S.* -erri) *n., pl.* **-ries.** **1.** *Roman Catholic Church.* A tribunal of the Roman Curia, presided over by a cardinal designated in this office as the Grand Penitentiary, having jurisdiction in matters relating to penance, dispensations, and papal absolutions. **2.** *U.S.* A prison, especially one for those convicted of serious crimes.
~adj. **1.** Of or for the purpose of penance; penitential. **2.** Pertaining to or used for punishment or reform of wrongdoers. **3.** *U.S.* Resulting in or punishable by imprisonment in a penitentiary: *a penitentiary offence.* [Middle English *penitenciary,* penance officer, from Medieval Latin *penitentiārius,* from Latin *paenitentia,* repentance, from *paenitēns,* (stem *paenitent-*) PENITENT.]

pen·knife (pén-nīf) *n., pl.* **-knives** (-nīvz). A small pocketknife, usually with one or more blades that fold into the handle, originally used to make or sharpen quill pens.

pen·man (pén-mən) *n., pl.* **-men** (-mən). **1.** An author; a writer. **2.** An expert in penmanship. **3.** A copyist; a scribe.

pen·man·ship (pén-mən-ship) *n.* The art, skill, style, or manner of handwriting; calligraphy.

Penn (pen), **William** (1644–1718). English Quaker. Converted to Quakerism (1667), he was imprisoned in the Tower of London for his views (1668). In 1681 he was given a charter in Pennsylvania by the Crown in lieu of a debt to his late father, and proceeded to establish a colony practising religious toleration (1682).

pen·na (pénnə) *n., pl.* **pennae** (pénnee). Any of the larger feathers forming the visible plumage of a bird, as distinguished from the down feathers. [Latin, feather.] **—pen·na·ceous** (pe-náyshəss) *adj.*

pen name *n.* A literary pseudonym.

pen·nant (pénnənt) n. 1. *Nautical.* A long, narrow, relatively small flag, often triangular, used for signalling or for identification. Also called "pendant". 2. Any similar flag; a pennon. 3. *U.S. & Australian.* A flag used as an emblem or one awarded to the winner of a contest. [Blend of PENDANT and PENNON.]

pen·nate (pénnayt) adj. Also **pen·nat·ed** (-aytid). Feathered or winged. [Latin *pennātus*, winged, from *penna*, feather, wing.]

pen·ni (pénni) n., pl. **-nis** or **pennia** (-ə). A coin equal to ¹/₁₀₀ of the markka of Finland. [Finnish, perhaps from Middle Low German *pennige*, from West Germanic *panninga* (unattested).]

pen·ni·less (pénni-ləss, -liss, -less) adj. Entirely without money; very poor. —**pen·ni·less·ly** adv. —**pen·ni·less·ness** n.

Pen·nines (pénnīnz). Also **Pennine Chain.** Range of hills in north England. Extending from the Cheviot Hills in the north to the Vale of Trent in the south, its maximum height is at Cross Fell, 893 metres (2,930 feet). Its Pennine Way is used by walkers, and tourism and sheepfarming are important.

pen·ni·nite (pénni-nīt) n. A bluish-green form of **chlorite** *(see).* [German *Pennin*, Pennine Alps along the Swiss-Italian border (where it was discovered) + -ITE.]

pen·non (pénnən) n. 1. A long, narrow banner or streamer, often forked or triangular in shape, borne upon a lance. 2. A pointed or tapering banner or flag flown by a boat. 3. Any banner, flag, or pennant. 4. *Poetic.* A pinion; a wing. [Middle English, from Old French *penon*, augmentative of *penne*, feather, wing, from Latin *penna*.] —**pen·noned** adj.

pen·non·cel, pen·on·cel, pen·non·celle (pénnən-sel) n. A small pennon, flag, or streamer borne upon a lance. [Middle English *penoncelle*, from Old French *penoncel*, diminutive of *penon*, PENNON.]

penn'orth. Variant of **pennyworth.**

Penn·syl·va·ni·a (pén-sil-váyni-ə). State of northeast United States. It was established as a colony (1681) by the Quaker William Penn, who aimed to promote religious toleration. Its many industrial towns include the capital Harrisburg, Pittsburgh, and Philadelphia, and agriculture and dairy farming are important.

Pennsylvania Dutch n. 1. *Used with a plural verb.* The descendants of German and Swiss immigrants who settled in Pennsylvania in the 17th and 18th centuries. 2. German as spoken by this group. Also called "Pennsylvania German".

Penn·syl·va·ni·an (pén-sil-váyni-ən) adj. 1. Of or pertaining to the state of Pennsylvania. 2. *Geology. U.S.* Of, belonging to, or designating the Upper Carboniferous period.
~n. 1. A native or inhabitant of Pennsylvania. 2. *Geology. U.S.* The Upper Carboniferous period. Preceded by *the.*

pen·ny (pénni) n., pl. **-nies** or **pence** (penss) (for senses 1,3). 1. **a.** *Abbr.* **p.** A coin of the United Kingdom equal to ¹/₁₀₀ of a pound. Also called "new penny". **b.** *Abbr.* **d.** Formerly, a coin of the United Kingdom equal to ¹/₂₄₀ of a pound, or ¹/₁₂ of a shilling. **c.** A coin of the Republic of Ireland and of various dependent territories of the United Kingdom. 2. *Abbr.* **p.** *U.S. & Canadian.* A **cent** *(see).* 3. Any of various coins of small denomination. 4. A sum of money: *that must have cost a pretty penny.* —**pennies from heaven.** Unexpected good fortune. —**spend a penny.** *British.* To urinate. Used euphemistically. —**the penny drops.** Comprehension or realisation occurs, usually suddenly. —**turn an honest penny.** To earn money by honest work. —**two** or **ten a penny.** Very common and hence without much value. [Middle English *penny*, Old English *penig, penning*, from West Germanic *panninga* (unattested); probably akin to PAWN (security).]

Usage: The change to decimal currency in 1971 had several linguistic consequences for British English, to which the community is still reacting. Chief among these is the question of how to pronounce the conventional abbreviation *p*, as in *10p.* Immediately following decimalisation, the pronunciation "tenpence" was ambiguous, as it was unclear whether this would have meant ten "old" as opposed to "new" pence. (For a while, the forms *old pence* and *new pence* were used, but these have now largely died out as people have become familiar with the new system). The abbreviation *p*, pronounced (pee), came to be used as an alternative, and it quickly became the dominant form. However, many people find the abbreviated form unpleasant, and prefer the form *pence*, even in cases where the old singular form, *penny*, would have been used. There is now a trend for *pence* to be used in more formal styles, and *p* to be used informally. When used in isolation *pence* is pronounced (penss). In combination, it used to be pronounced (-pənss), for example *tenpence* (ténpənss). Since decimalisation this pronunciation has been giving way to (-pénss) even in combination: thus *tenpence* is pronounced (tén-pénss).

-penny adj. comb. form. Indicates costing or worth the specified number of pennies; for example, **tenpenny.**

pen·ny-a-lin·er (pénni-ə-līnər) n. A hack writer, especially a journalist.

penny black n. *Often capital P, capital B.* Any of a set of postage stamps, costing one penny and bearing the head of Queen Victoria on a black background, that were the first adhesive stamps issued.

pen·ny·cress (pénni-kress) n. Any of several plants of the genus *Thlaspi*, native to Europe, and characteristically having small, winged seed pods; especially, *T. arvense*, which grows as a weed on waste ground. [Perhaps variant of *penny grass*, from its round, flat pods.]

pen·ny·dread·ful (pénni-drédf'l) n. *Informal.* A piece of cheap, sensational popular fiction, such as a book or magazine.

pen·ny-far·thing (pénni-fárthing) n. An early bicycle with a very large front wheel driven directly by pedals, and a small back wheel. [Alluding to the relative size of the wheels.]

penny-pinch·ing (pénni-pinching) adj. *Informal.* Very mean or stingy with money. —**pen·ny-pinch·ing** n.

pen·ny-roy·al (pénni-róy-əl) n. A Eurasian plant, *Mentha pulegium*, having hairy leaves and small lilac-blue flowers. It yields a useful aromatic oil. [Variant of Middle English *puliol real*, from Anglo-French : Old French *poliol*, pennyroyal, from Latin *pūlegium*†, fleabane + *real, roial*, ROYAL.]

pen·ny·weight (pénni-wayt) n. *Abbr.* **dwt., pwt.** A unit of troy weight equal to 24 grains, ¹/₂₀ of a troy ounce or approximately 1.555 grams.

penny whistle n. A type of metal flageolet having six fingerholes. Also called "tin whistle".

pen·ny-wise (pénni-wīz) adj. Careful, often overcareful, in dealing with small sums of money or small matters. —**penny-wise, pound-foolish.** Careful with small sums but wasteful with large sums of money.

pen·ny·wort (pénni-wurt ‖ -wawrt) n. Any of several plants having rounded leaves suggestive of pennies, such as: 1. A Eurasian plant, *Umbilicus rupestris* (or *Cotyledon umbilicus*), having thick, rounded leaves and yellowish-green, bell-shaped flowers. This species is also called "navelwort". 2. A small, prostrate plant, *Hydrocotyle vulgaris*, having tiny pink flowers.

pen·ny·worth (pénni-wurth, -wərth, pénnərth) n. Also **penn'orth** (pénnərth). 1. As much as a penny will buy. 2. A small amount; a modicum. 3. A bargain.

pe·nol·o·gy, poe·nol·o·gy (pee-nólləji) n. The theory and practice of prison management and criminal treatment and rehabilitation. Compare **criminology.** [Latin *poena*, penalty, from Greek *poinē* + -LOGY.] —**pe·no·log·i·cal** (péenə-lójik'l) adj. —**pe·no·log·i·cal·ly** adv. —**pe·nol·o·gist** (-nólləjist) n.

penoncel. Variant of **pennoncel.**

pen pal n. A pen friend *(see).*

pen-push·er (pén-pōōshər) n. *Informal.* 1. Someone who deals with a large amount of paperwork, especially a clerk or other office worker. 2. A writer. —**pen-push·ing** n. & adj.

pensil. Variant of **pencel.**

pen·sile (pén-sīl) adj. 1. Hanging down loosely; suspended: *a pensile nest.* 2. Building a hanging nest. Said of birds. [Latin *pēnsilis*, from *pendēre* (past participle *pēnsus*), to hang.] —**pen·sile·ness** n. **pen·sil·i·ty** (pen-sílti) n.

pen·sion[1] (pénsh'n) n. A sum of money paid regularly by a government, company, patron, or the like as, for example, a retirement or injury benefit, in return for a service or by way of patronage.
~tr.v. **pensioned, -sioning, -sions.** 1. To grant a pension to. 2. To retire or dismiss with a pension. Usually used with *off.* [Middle English *pensioun*, from Old French *pension*, from Medieval Latin *pēnsiō* (stem *pēnsiōn-*), from Latin, payment, from *pendere* (past participle *pēnsus*), to weigh, pay.]

pen·sion[2] (pónss-yon, ponss-yón) n. A boarding house or small hotel in some continental countries, especially France. —**en pension** (-ON). *Chiefly British.* 1. Designating the system of hotel charges at a fixed rate per day or a longer period, inclusive of meals: *en pension terms.* 2. At such a rate or under such a system: *living en pension.* [French, boarding house, boarding school, originally "payment for the board and education of a child", extended use of Old French *pension*, payment, PENSION (grant).]

pen·sion·a·ble (pénsh'n-əb'l) adj. 1. Entitling one to receive a pension: *pensionable age.* 2. Conferring the right to a pension: *a pensionable job.*

pen·sion·ar·y (pénsh'n-əri, -ri ‖ -erri) adj. 1. Constituting a pension. 2. Receiving a pension. 3. Mercenary; venal.
~n., pl. **pensionaries.** 1. A pensioner. 2. A hireling.

pen·sion·er (pénsh'n-ər) n. 1. One who receives a pension; especially, one who receives a government retirement pension. 2. One who is dependent on the bounty of another.

pension fund n. A fund contributed to by employers and usually also employees to provide retirement and widows' pensions for employees.

pen·sive (pén-siv) adj. 1. Deeply or seriously thoughtful. 2. Suggesting or expressing deep, often melancholy thoughtfulness. [Middle English *pensif*, from Old French, from *penser*, to think, from Latin *pēnsāre*, frequentative of *pendere* (past participle *pēnsus*), to weigh.] —**pen·sive·ly** adv. —**pen·sive·ness** n.
Synonyms: pensive, contemplative, reflective, meditative.

penstemon. *Chiefly U.S.* Variant of **pentstemon.**

pen·stock (pén-stok) n. 1. A sluice or gate used to control a flow of water. 2. A pipe or conduit used to carry water to a waterwheel or turbine. [PEN (enclosure) + STOCK.]

pent (pent). Alternative past tense and past participle of **pen.**
~adj. *Poetic.* Pent-up.

penta-, pent- comb. form. Indicates five; for example, **pentameter, pentangular.** [Greek, from *pente*, five.]

pen·ta·chlo·ro·phe·nol (péntə-kláwrə-féenol, klórrə- ‖ -klōrə-, -nōl) n. A compound, C_6Cl_5OH, used in solution as a fungicide and wood preservative.

pen·ta·chord (péntə-kawrd) n. *Music.* 1. An instrument with five strings. 2. A series of five notes in a diatonic scale.

pen·ta·cle (péntək'l) n. A five-pointed star, often thought to have magical or mystical significance, formed by five straight lines connecting the vertices of a pentagon and enclosing another pentagon in the completed figure. Also called "pentagram", "pentangle". [Medieval Latin *pentaculum* (unattested) : Greek *penta-*, PENTA- + *-culum*, diminutive suffix.]

pen·tad (péntad) *n.* **1.** A group or series of five members. **2.** A five-year period. [Greek *pentas* (stem *pentad-*), from *pente*, five.]

pen·ta·dac·tyl (pèntə-dáktil) *adj.* Also **pen·ta·dac·ty·late** (-ayt, -ət, -it). Having five fingers or toes on each hand or foot. [Latin *pentadactylus*, from Greek *pentadaktulos* : PENTA- + *daktulos*, finger, DACTYL.]

pen·ta·gon (péntə-gən ‖ *U.S.* -gon) *n.* A polygon having five sides and five angles. **—the Pentagon.** The U.S. Department of Defence; the U.S. military comand. [Latin *pentagōnum*, from Greek *pentagōnon* : PENTA- + -GON.]

pen·tag·o·nal (pen-tággən'l) *adj.* **1.** Having five sides and five angles. **2.** Of or formed in pentagons. **—pen·tag·o·nal·ly** *adv.*

pen·ta·he·dron (pèntə-hée-drən) *n., pl.* **-drons** or **-dra** (-drə). A polyhedron having five plane surfaces. [New Latin : PENTA- + -HEDRON.] **—pen·ta·he·dral** *adj.*

pen·tam·er·ous (pen-támmərəss) *adj.* **1.** Having or divided into five similar parts. **2.** *Botany.* Having flower parts, such as petals, sepals, and stamens, in sets of five. [New Latin *pentamerus* : PENTA- + -MEROUS.] **—pen·tam·er·ism** *n.*

pen·tam·e·ter (pen-támmitər) *n.* **1.** A line of verse composed of five metrical feet; especially, a line of classical verse having a set metrical pattern consisting of four dactyls and two stressed feet. **2.** English verse composed in iambic pentameter. [Latin, from Greek *pentametros* : PENTA- + -METER.] **—pen·tam·e·ter** *adj.*

pen·tane (péntayn) *n.* Any of three isomeric alkanes, C_5H_{12}: **1.** *Normal pentane.* A colourless flammable liquid used as an anaesthetic, solvent, and in the manufacture of artificial ice. **2.** *Isopentane.* A colourless flammable liquid used as a solvent and in the manufacture of polystyrene foam. **3.** *Neopentane.* A colourless gas used in the manufacture of synthetic rubber. [PENT(A)- + -ANE.]

pen·tan·gu·lar (pen-táng-gewlər) *adj.* Having five angles.

pen·ta·no·ic acid (pèntə-nō-ik) *n.* A colourless liquid, $CH_3(CH_2)_3COOH$, used in making perfumes, flavourings, and pharmaceuticals. Also called "valeric acid". [PENTAN(E) + -OIC.]

pen·ta·prism (péntə-priz'm) *n.* A prism with a pentagonal cross-section, used especially in single-lens reflex cameras to deflect an image through the lens to the viewfinder.

pen·ta·quine (péntə-kween, -kwin) *n.* A drug used in the treatment of malaria. [PENTA- + QUIN(OLINE).]

pen·tar·chy (péntaarki) *n., pl.* **-chies.** **1.** Government by five rulers. **2.** A body of five rulers governing jointly. **3.** A country governed by five joint rulers. **4.** An association or federation of five governments, each ruled by a different leader. [Greek *pentarkhia* : PENTA- + -ARCHY.] **—pen·tar·chi·cal** (pen-tárkik'l) *adj.*

pen·ta·stich (péntə-stik) *n.* A poem, strophe, or stanza containing five lines. [Late Greek *pentastikhos*, of five verses : PENTA- + -stikhos, -STICH.]

Pen·ta·teuch (péntə-tewk ‖ -tōōk) *n.* The first five books of the Old Testament: Genesis, Exodus, Leviticus, Numbers, and Deuteronomy. [Late Latin *Pentateuchus*, from ecclesiastical Greek *Pentateukhos* : PENTA- + *teukhos*, a tool, case for papyrus rolls, scroll.] **—Pen·ta·teuch·al** (-téwk'l ‖ -tōōk'l) *adj.*

pen·tath·lon (pen-táth-lən, -lon) *n.* An athletic contest consisting of five events for each participant. Originating in the ancient Olympics, it was revived in the modern Olympics as the *modern pentathlon*, and consists of running, riding, swimming, fencing, and pistol shooting. [Greek : PENT(A)- + *athlon*, contest (see **athlete**).] **—pen·tath·lete** *n.*

pen·ta·tom·ic (pèntə-tómmik) *adj. Chemistry.* Designating a molecule that contains five atoms.

pen·ta·ton·ic scale (pèntə-tónnik) *n.* Any of various five-note musical scales, especially one composed of the first, second, third, fifth, and sixth notes of a diatonic scale.

pen·ta·va·lent (pèntə-váylənt) *adj. Chemistry.* Having a valency of 5; quinquevalent.

Pen·te·cost (pénti-kost ‖ -kawst) *n.* **1.** A festival of the Christian Church occurring on the seventh Sunday after Easter, to celebrate the descent of the Holy Ghost upon the disciples. Also called "Whit", "Whit Sunday". **2.** A Jewish festival, **Shavuot** (*see*). [Middle English *Pentecost*, Old English *Pentecosten*, from Late Latin *Pentēcostē*, from Greek *pentēkostē (hēmera)*, the fiftieth day (after the Resurrection), Pentecost, from *pentēkostos*, fiftieth, from *pentēkonta*, fifty : *pente*, five + *-konta*, "ten times".]

Pen·te·cos·tal (pénti-kóst'l ‖ -káwst'l) *adj.* **1.** Of, pertaining to, or occurring at Pentecost. **2.** Of, pertaining to, or designating any of various Christian religious congregations that seek to be filled with the Holy Ghost, in emulation of the disciples at Pentecost. **—Pen·te·cos·tal** *n.* **—Pen·te·cos·tal·ism** *n.*

pen·tene (pénteen) *n.* A colourless flammable alkene, C_5H_{10}, occurring in several isomeric forms. Formerly called "amylene". [PENT(A)- + -ENE.]

pent·house (pént-howss) *n.* **1. a.** A maisonette or flat situated on the roof of a building. **b.** A residence, often with a terrace, comprising the top floor of a block of flats. **c.** A structure housing machinery on the roof of a building. **2.** A shed or sloping roof attached to the side of a building or wall. [Alteration (assimilated to HOUSE) of Middle English *pentis*, from Old French *appentis*, from Medieval Latin *appenticium*, appendage, from Latin *appendix*, from *appendēre*, to append : *ad*, on + *pendēre*, to suspend, hang.]

pen·ti·men·to (pènti-méntō) *n.* **1.** The emergence in a painting of an underlying image, for example, an earlier painting, part of a painting, or original draft, that shows through the final picture, usually when the top layer of paint has become transparent with age. **2.** Such an underlying image. [Italian, "repentance", correction.]

Pent·land Firth (péntlənd). Strait, 32 kilometres (20 miles) long, separating north Scotland from the Orkney Islands. Despite its strong currents, it is a major shipping route.

pent·land·ite (péntlən-dīt) *n.* The principal ore of nickel, a light-brown nickel iron sulphide. [French; discovered by Joseph B. *Pentland* (died 1873), Irish scientist.]

pen·to·bar·bi·tone sodium (pènt-ō-bárbi-tōn, -ə-) *n.* A white crystalline or powdery barbiturate, $C_{11}H_{17}N_2NaO_3$, used as a sedative. Also called "sodium pentobarbital".

pen·tode (péntōd) *n.* An electronic valve with five electrodes. In addition to a cathode and an anode it has a control grid, a screen grid, and a suppressor grid situated between the screen and the anode. [PENTA- + Greek *hodos*, way.]

pen·to·san (pént-ə-san, -ō-) *n.* Any of a group of complex carbohydrates (hemicelluloses) such as xylan and araban, with the general formula $(C_5H_8O_4)n$, found with cellulose in many woody plants and yielding pentoses on hydrolysis. [PENTOS(E) + -AN.]

pen·tose (pén-tōss, -tōz) *n.* A sugar having five carbon atoms per molecule. [PENT(A)- + -OSE.]

pent·ox·ide (pent-ók-sīd) *n.* An oxide having five atoms of oxygen in the molecule. [PENT(A)- + OXIDE.]

pent·ste·mon (pent-stéemən, -stémmən, péntstimən) *n.* Also *chiefly U.S.* **pen·ste·mon** (pen-). Any of numerous plants of the North American genus *Penstemon*, having four fertile stamens and one bearded sterile stamen. [New Latin, irregularly from PENTA- + Greek *stēmōn*, warp (here representing "stamen").]

pent-up (pént-úp) *adj.* Not given expression; repressed: *pent-up anger.*

pen·tyl (pén-tīl, -til) *n. Chemistry.* The univalent organic radical C_5H_{11}, occurring in several isomeric forms in many organic compounds. Formerly called "amyl". [PENT(A)- + -YL.]

pentyl acetate *n.* A colourless combustible liquid, $CH_3COOC_5H_{11}$, used as a paint solvent and in flavourings, photographic films, and the extraction of penicillin.

pen·tyl·ene·tet·ra·zol (pèntileen-téttrə-zol ‖ -zōl) *n.* A drug, $C_6H_{10}N_4$, used as a stimulant of the central nervous system.

penuchle. Variant of **pinochle.**

pe·nult (pe-núlt, pi-, pə-, pénult ‖ pée-) *n.* The next to the last syllable in a word. Also called "penultima". [Latin *paenultimus*, last but one : *paene, pēne†*, almost + *ultimus*, farthest away, last, from *uls*, beyond.]

pe·nul·ti·mate (pe-núlti-mət, pi-, pə, -mit) *adj.* **1.** Next to last. **2.** Of or pertaining to the penult of a word: *penultimate stress.* ~*n.* **1.** The next to the last. **2.** The penult. [Latin *paenultimus*, PENULT.]

pe·num·bra (pi-núm-brə, pe-, pə-) *n., pl.* **-brae** (-bree) or **-bras.** **1.** A partial shadow between regions of complete shadow (umbra) and complete illumination occurring, for example, on parts of the earth from which a partial eclipse may be observed. **2.** *Astronomy.* The partly darkened fringe around a sunspot. [New Latin : Latin *paene, pēne†*, almost + UMBRA.] **—pe·num·bral, pe·num·brous** *adj.*

pe·nu·ri·ous (pi-néwr-i-əss, pe-, pə- ‖ -noór-) *adj.* **1.** Miserly; stingy. **2.** Poverty-stricken; needy. **3.** Yielding little; barren: *a penurious land.* [Medieval Latin *pēnūriōsus*, from *pēnūria*, PENURY.] **—pe·nu·ri·ous·ly** *adv.* **—pe·nu·ri·ous·ness** *n.*

pen·u·ry (pénnewr-i) *n.* **1.** Extreme want or poverty; destitution. **2.** Extreme dearth; barrenness; insufficiency. [Middle English, from Latin *paenūria, pēnūria†*, want, scarcity.]

Pe·nu·ti·an (pi-néw-ti-ən, -sh'n ‖ -nōō-) *n.* A family or phylum of North American Indian languages of Pacific coastal areas from California to British Columbia.

Pen·zance (pen-zánss, pən-; *locally* -zánss). Seaside resort in Cornwall, southwest England. A port for early crops from the Scilly Isles, its other industries include tourism and fishing.

pe·on (pée-ən, -on; *Spanish* pay-ón; *also for sense 2* pewn) *n., pl.* **peons** or **peones** (pay-ōneez). **1. a.** An unskilled labourer or farm worker of Latin America or the southwestern United States. **b.** Formerly, such a worker bound in servitude to a creditor. **2.** A native Indian or Ceylonese messenger, servant, or foot soldier. **3.** Any menial worker; a drudge. [Spanish *peon*, Portuguese *peão* and French *pion*, all from Medieval Latin *pedo* (stem *pedōn-*), a foot soldier, from Latin *pēs* (stem *ped-*), a foot.]

pe·on·age (pée-ənij) *n.* Also **pe·on·ism** (-əniz'm). **1.** The condition of being a peon. **2.** A system by which debtors are bound in servitude to their creditors until the debts are paid.

pe·o·ny, pae·o·ny (péerni, pée-əni) *n., pl.* **-nies.** Any of various garden plants of the genus *Paeonia*, having large yellow, pink, red, white, or creamy globular flowers. [Middle English *pione*, Old English *peonie*, from Latin *peōnia*, from Greek *paiōniā*, supposedly discovered by *Paiōn*, physician (of the gods). See **paean**.]

peo·ple (péep'l) *n., pl.* **people** or **peoples** (for senses 1, 2). **1.** A body of persons living in the same country under one national government; a nationality. **2.** A body of persons sharing a common religion, culture, language, or inherited condition of life. **3.** *Plural.* Persons in general; men, women, and children; human individuals collectively. **4.** *Plural.* The mass of ordinary persons; the populace. Usually preceded by *the*. **5.** *Usually plural.* **a.** The citizens of a nation, state, or other political unit. **b.** In certain forms of Marxist ideology, the proletariat: *a people's court.* **6.** *Plural.* Persons subordinate to or loyal to a ruler, superior, or employer. **7.** *Plural.* **a.** Family, relatives, or ancestors. **b.** Visitors; guests: *We're having people for dinner tonight.* **8.** *Plural.* Persons with regard to some characteristic, or considered as a group: *working people; young people.* **9.** *Plural.* Human beings considered as distinct from lower animals or inanimate things. **10.** *Plural.* A race or kind of beings distinct from human beings: *the little people.* —See Usage note at **nation.**

~*tr.v.* **peopled, -pling, -ples.** To furnish with a population; populate. [Middle English *peple, poeple,* from Old French *pueple, pople,* from Latin *populus.*] —**peo·pler** (pée·plər) *n.*

Usage: People is the usual word for a group of human beings, considered collectively and without differentiation: *Several people were in the room. Persons* is more restricted in use: it tends to be found in more formal and impersonal contexts, and is therefore typical of written rather than spoken English, particularly administrative and official English. In its singular form, *person* takes a singular pronoun (*If a person has an interest in politics, he will . . .*), though a plural form (*they*) is sometimes used in informal speech.
people's front *n.* A political coalition, a **popular front** *(see).*
People's Republic of China. See **China.**
Pe·o·ri·a (pee-áwri-ə ‖ -óri-). City in Illinois, United States. Situated where the Illinois river becomes Lake Peoria, it is a port and agricultural centre for the corn belt, and manufactures machinery.
pep (pep) *n. Informal.* Energy; high spirits; vim.

~*tr.v.* **pepped, pepping, peps.** *Informal.* To bring energy or liveliness to; invigorate. Usually followed by *up.* [Short for PEPPER.] —**pep·py** (péppi) *adj.* —**pep·pi·ness** *n.*
Pep·in the Short (péppin), also known as Pepin III (*c.* 715–768). King of the Franks (751–768). The father of Charlemagne, he came to the defence of Pope Stephen II against the king of the Lombards, Aistulf (754), and established the core territory of the Papal States.
pep·los (pépp-ləss, -loss) *n., pl.* **-loses.** Also **pep·lus** (-ləss). A loose outer robe worn by women in ancient Greece. Also called "peplum". [Greek *peplos†.*]
pep·lum (péppləm) *n., pl.* **-lums. 1.** A short overskirt or ruffle attached at the waistline. **2.** A peplos. [Latin, from *peplus,* PEPLOS.]
pe·po (péepō) *n., pl.* **-pos.** The fruit of any of various related plants, such as the cucumber and melon, having a hard rind, fleshy pulp, and numerous seeds. [Latin, melon, from Greek *pepōn.*]
pep·per (péppər) *n.* **1.** A woody vine, *Piper nigrum,* of the East Indies, having small, berry-like fruit. **2.** The dried, blackish fruit of this plant, used as a pungent condiment. When ground whole, it is called *black pepper,* and with the shell removed, *white pepper.* **3.** Any of several other plants of the genus *Piper,* such as cubeb, betel, and kava. **4.** Any of several varieties of a tropical plant, *Capsicum annuum* (or *C. frutescens*). **5.** The podlike fruit of any of these plants, varying in size, shape, colour, and degree of pungency. The milder types include the **sweet pepper** and **pimiento** *(both of which see),* and the more pungent types include the **chilli** *(see).* **6.** Any of various condiments made from the more pungent varieties of *C. annuum* (or *C. frutescens*), such as **cayenne pepper, chilli pepper,** and **paprika** *(all of which see).* In this sense, also called "hot pepper".

~*tr.v.* **peppered, -pering, pers. 1.** To season or sprinkle with pepper. **2.** To sprinkle liberally; dot. **3.** To pelt or shower with small missiles. **4.** To punish. **5.** To make (a speech or article, for example) lively and vivid as with wit or invective. [Middle English *peper,* Old English *pipor,* from Latin *piper,* from Greek *peperi,* from Sanskrit *pippalī,* berry.]
pep·per-and-salt (péppər-ənd-sáwlt ‖ -sólt) *adj.* Having a close mixture of black and white or brown and white. Said of hair or fabrics.
pep·per·corn (péppər-kawrn) *n.* **1.** A dried berry of the pepper vine *Piper nigrum.* **2.** Any small or insignificant thing.
peppercorn rent *n.* A nominal rent. [Referring to a peppercorn as representing a trifling sum.]
pep·pered moth (péppərd) *n.* A European moth, *Biston betularia,* that exists in two distinct forms, a black and white speckled form predominating in rural regions, and a black or melanic form that flourishes in industrial areas. See **pigmentation.**
pepper mill *n.* A small utensil for grinding peppercorns.
pep·per·mint (péppər-mint) *n.* **1.** A plant, *Mentha piperita,* having small purple or white flowers and downy leaves that yield a pungent oil. **2.** The oil from this plant, or a preparation made from it, used as flavouring. **3.** A sweet with this flavouring.
pep·pe·ro·ni (peppə-rōni) *n.* A variety of highly seasoned Italian salami. [Italian, *peperone,* chilli, from *pepere,* pepper.]
pepper pot *n.* **1.** A container with small holes in the top for sprinkling ground pepper. Also called "pepperbox". **2.** A thick West Indian stew of meat or fish, vegetables, and condiments.
pepper tree *n.* Any of several trees of the genus *Schinus;* especially, *S. molle,* native to South America, having yellowish-white flowers and red ornamental fruits with seeds that are used as a condiment.
pep·per·wort (péppər-wurt ‖ -wawrt) *n.* Any of several plants of the genus *Lepidium,* having small white flowers and winged, pungent fruits. Also *U.S.* "peppergrass".
pep·per·y (péppəri) *adj.* **1.** Of, like, or containing pepper; sharp or pungent in flavour. **2.** Vigorously sharp-tempered in disposition and manner: *a peppery general.* **3.** Sharp and stinging in style or content: *a peppery speech.* —**pep·per·i·ness** *n.*
pep pill *n. Informal.* Any tablet or capsule containing an ingredient

that stimulates the central nervous system; especially, any of the amphetamines.
pep·sin, pep·sine (pépsin) *n.* **1.** A digestive enzyme found in gastric juice that catalyses the breakdown of protein to peptides. **2.** A substance containing this enzyme, obtained from the stomachs of pigs and used as a digestive aid. [German *Pepsin,* from Greek *pepsis,* digestion, from *peptein,* to digest, cook.]
pep·sin·o·gen (pep-sínnəjən) *n.* An inert substance found in the cells of the gastric mucosa that is converted to pepsin during digestion by the action of hydrochloric acid. [PEPSIN + -GEN.]
pep talk *n.* A speech of exhortation delivered by a leader, as to team members or staff.
pep·tic (péptik) *adj.* **1. a.** Of or assisting digestion: *peptic secretion.* **b.** Induced by or associated with the action of digestive secretions. **2.** Of or involving pepsin. **3.** Capable of digesting.

~*n.* A digestive agent. [Latin *pepticus,* from Greek *peptikos,* from *peptein,* to digest.]
peptic ulcer *n.* An ulcer of the mucous membrane, especially of the stomach or oesophagus, caused by the action of digestive secretions.
pep·ti·dase (pépti-dayz, -dayss) *n.* An enzyme that hydrolyses peptides, releasing amino acids. [PEPTID(E) + -ASE.]
pep·tide (pép-tīd) *n.* Also **pep·tid** (-tid). Any of various natural or synthetic compounds containing two or more amino acids linked by the carboxyl group of one amino acid and the amino group of another. [PEPT(ONE) + -IDE.]
peptide bond *n.* The chemical bond, $-CO \cdot NH = CHCONHCH =$, between the organic acid groups and amino groups of neighbouring amino acids, constituting the primary linkage of all protein structures.
pep·tise, pep·tize (pép-tīz) *tr.v.* **-tised, -tising, -tises. 1.** To increase the dispersion of (a colloidal solution), by the addition of an electrolyte. **2.** To liquefy (a colloidal gel) to form a sol, by the addition of an electrolyte. [Greek *peptein,* to digest + -ISE.] —**pep·ti·sa·tion** (-tī-záysh'n ‖ *U.S.* -ti-) *n.*
pep·tone (péptōn) *n.* Any of various protein compounds obtained by acid or enzyme hydrolysis of natural protein and used as nutrients and culture media. [German *Pepton,* from Greek *pepton,* from *peptein,* to digest.] —**pep·ton·ic** (pep-tónnik) *adj.*
pep·to·nise, pep·to·nize (péptə-nīz) *tr.v.* **-nised, -nising, -nises. 1.** To convert (protein) into a peptone. **2.** To dissolve (food) by means of a proteolytic enzyme. **3.** To combine with peptone. —**pep·to·ni·sa·tion** (-nī-záysh'n ‖ *U.S.* -ni-) *n.*
Pepys (peeps), **Samuel** (1633–1703). English diarist. His diary, a detailed account of everyday life, includes descriptions of the Great Fire of London and the Great Plague.
Pe·quot (pée-kwot) *n., pl.* **-quots** or collectively **Pequot. 1.** A member of an Algonquian-speaking North American Indian people formerly living in southern New England. **2.** The language of this tribe. —**Pe·quot** *adj.*
per (per, *weak form* pər) *prep. Abbr.* **p. 1.** Through; by means of: *per bearer.* Used in business. **2.** To, for, or by each; for every: *40 miles per gallon.* **3.** According to; by the. Often used with *as: as per instructions.* —**as per usual.** As usual. Used humorously. [Latin.]
PER Professional and Executive Register (in Britain).
per- *prefix. Chemistry.* Indicates: **1.** A compound that includes an element in its highest oxidation state; for example, **perchloric acid. 2.** A compound that includes the peroxy group in its structure; for example, **hydrogen peroxide. 3.** A complete substitution or addition in an organic compound; for example, **perchloroethylene.** [Latin, from preposition *per,* through, by, away. In borrowed Latin compounds, *per-* indicates: 1. Through, as in **percolate.** 2. Throughout, to the end, as in **perennial, perorate.** 3. Thoroughly, completely, as in **perfect, perceive.** 4. Away, as in **perdition, peregrine.** 5. Destruction, as in **perfidy, perjure.** 6. Intensified action, as in **perfervid, perform.**]
per. 1. period. **2.** person.
per·ac·id (per-ássid) *n.* **1.** Any acid containing the peroxy group. **2.** An inorganic acid, such as perchloric acid, containing the largest proportion of oxygen in a series of related acids.
per·ad·ven·ture (pərəd-vénchər, pér-əd-, pérrəd-) *adv. Archaic.* Perhaps; perchance; it may be.

~*n. Archaic.* Uncertainty; doubt: *beyond peradventure.* [Middle English *per aventure :* Old French *per,* by + *aventure,* ADVENTURE.]
Pe·rak (paír-ə, péer-) State in the west of peninsular Malaysia. It has rich tin deposits and produces sugar, rubber, rice, and coconuts. Ipoh is the capital.
per·am·bu·late (pə-rámbew-layt) *v.* **-lated, -lating, -lates.** *Formal.* —*tr.* To traverse, especially in order to inspect. —*intr.* To walk about; roam; stroll. [Latin *perambulāre : per-,* through + *ambulāre,* to walk, AMBULATE.] —**per·am·bu·la·to·ry** (pə-rámb-yōolə-təri, -tri) *adj.* —**per·am·bu·la·tion** (-láysh'n) *n.*
per·am·bu·la·tor (pə-rámbew-laytər) *n. Chiefly British Formal.* A **pram** *(see).*
per an·num (ánnəm) *adv. Abbr.* **p.a., per an., per ann.** By the year; annually.
per·bo·rate (pər-báwr-ayt, pér- ‖ -bór-) *n.* A salt containing the radical BO_3, formed from a borate and hydrogen peroxide.
per·cale (pər-káyl, -káal) *n.* An opaque cotton fabric used to make sheets and clothing. [French, from Persian *pargālah†.*]
per·ca·line (pérkə-leen, -lin) *n.* A glazed fine cotton fabric used for linings. [French, from PERCALE.]
per cap·i·ta (káppitə) *adv.* Per person: *income per capita.* [Latin, "by heads".] —**per capita** *adj.*

percussion instruments

THE BEAT BEHIND AN ORCHESTRA
Musical instruments that are struck with a stick, beater, or hand

Music for a symphony orchestra, a band, or a pop group underlines its rhythms with percussion instruments – the collective name for the instruments that are played by being struck. In most cases they are struck directly by hand or with a stick or padded beater; but sometimes a pedal-operated beater is used, as with the bass drum.

The ancient Greeks used a small drum called a *tympanum* – a forerunner of the kettledrum – and large kettledrums appeared in European orchestras in the 17th century. Today's kettledrums, or timpani, are tuned to a definite pitch which can be altered mechanically by means of a pedal or by screws round the drumhead.

Other tuned percussion instruments include the glockenspiel, chimes, xylophone, and marimba. Those not tuned, and which always produce the same note when struck, include the bass drum, snare drum, tambourine, triangle, maracas, and cymbals.

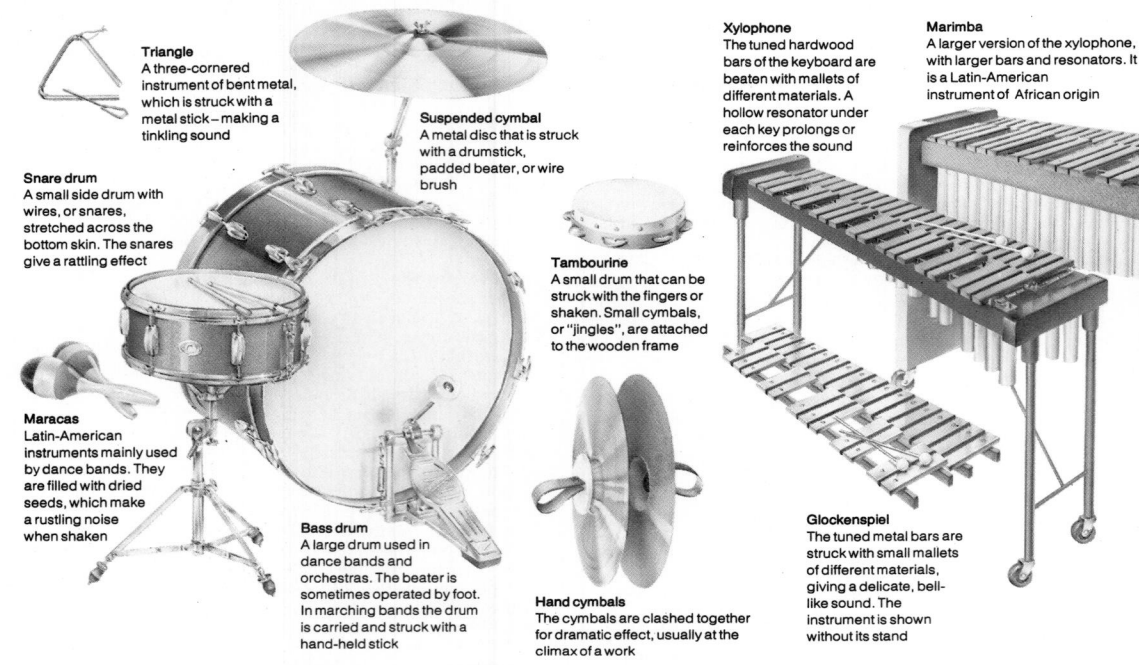

Triangle
A three-cornered instrument of bent metal, which is struck with a metal stick – making a tinkling sound

Snare drum
A small side drum with wires, or snares, stretched across the bottom skin. The snares give a rattling effect

Suspended cymbal
A metal disc that is struck with a drumstick, padded beater, or wire brush

Maracas
Latin-American instruments mainly used by dance bands. They are filled with dried seeds, which make a rustling noise when shaken

Bass drum
A large drum used in dance bands and orchestras. The beater is sometimes operated by foot. In marching bands the drum is carried and struck with a hand-held stick

Tambourine
A small drum that can be struck with the fingers or shaken. Small cymbals, or "jingles", are attached to the wooden frame

Hand cymbals
The cymbals are clashed together for dramatic effect, usually at the climax of a work

Xylophone
The tuned hardwood bars of the keyboard are beaten with mallets of different materials. A hollow resonator under each key prolongs or reinforces the sound

Marimba
A larger version of the xylophone, with larger bars and resonators. It is a Latin-American instrument of African origin

Glockenspiel
The tuned metal bars are struck with small mallets of different materials, giving a delicate, bell-like sound. The instrument is shown without its stand

---

per·ceive (pər-séev) *tr.v.* **-ceived, -ceiving, -ceives. 1.** To become aware of directly through any of the senses; especially, to see or hear. **2.** To take notice of; observe; detect. **3.** To become aware of in one's mind; achieve understanding of; apprehend. —See Synonyms at **see.** [Middle English *perceiven,* from Old French *perceivre,* from Latin *percipere,* "to seize wholly", "see all the way through" : *per-,* thoroughly + *capere,* to seize.] —**per·ceiv·a·ble** *adj.* —**per·ceiv·a·biy** *adv.*

per·ceived noise decibel (pər-séevd) *n. Abbr.* **PNdB.** A unit used to measure perceived noise levels by comparing them with the level of sound pressure of a reference sound that is judged to be of equal level by a normal listener.

per cent, per·cent (pər-sént) *adv. Abbr.* **p.c., pct.** *Symbol* **%** Per hundred; for or out of each hundred. Used to indicate that the preceding number is a percentage: *A quarter of ten is 25 per cent.* ~*n.* **1.** A hundredth part; a percentage part. **2.** *Plural.* Securities yielding a specified rate of interest: *the six per cents.* [Short for Latin *per centum,* by the hundred : *per,* by + *centum,* hundred.]

Usage: Per cent and *percentage* are both used to express quantity with relation to a whole. *Per cent* is always used in a specific sense, with a number: *60 per cent of the population agreed. Percentage* is never preceded by a number, and is generally qualified by a term indicating size (*A large percentage agreed*). It is also often used loosely in the sense of "a certain proportion" (*A percentage of the population objected*), but this has attracted criticism. The construction of the verb following is governed by the number of the noun used with *per cent/percentage: A large percentage of the patients are . . ., A large percentage of the population is . . .*

per·cent·age (pər-séntij) *n.* **1.** A fraction or ratio with 100 fixed and understood as the denominator. It is formed by multiplying a decimal equivalent of a fraction by 100. For example, 0.98 equals a percentage of 98. **2. a.** A specified proportion or share in relation to the whole: *in a high percentage of cases.* **b.** *Informal.* A certain proportion: *A percentage of the electorate never votes.* **3.** An allowance, commission, or the like that varies in proportion to a larger sum, such as total sales: *work for a percentage.* **4.** *Informal.* Advantage; gain.

per·cen·tile (pər-sént-īl) *n. Statistics.* A number scale of 100 equal divisions of a range of a set of statistical data, that indicates the value below which that percentage of the data lies. For example, a score higher than 97 per cent in an examination is in the 97th percentile. [From PER CENT.]

per·cept (pér-sept) *n.* **1.** The object of perception. **2.** An impression in the mind of something perceived by the senses, viewed as the basic component in the formation of concepts. [Back-formation from PERCEPTION.]

per·cep·ti·ble (pər-sép-tə-b'l, -ti-) *adj.* Capable of being perceived; discernible by the senses or mind. —**per·cep·ti·bil·i·ty** (-bílləti) *n.* —**per·cep·ti·bly** *adv.*

Synonyms: *perceptible, palpable, appreciable, noticeable, discernible.*

per·cep·tion (pər-sépsh'n) *n.* **1.** The process, act, or faculty of perceiving. **2.** The effect or product of perceiving. **3.** The awareness of the external world, or some aspect of it, through physical sensations and the interpretation of these by the mind. **4.** Any insight, intuition, or knowledge gained by perceiving. **5.** The ability or capacity to gain insight by perceiving. [Latin *perceptiō* (stem *perceptiōn-*), from *percipere* (past participle *perceptus*), to PERCEIVE.] —**per·cep·tion·al** *adj.*

per·cep·tive (pər-séptiv) *adj.* **1.** Of or pertaining to perception. **2. a.** Having the ability to perceive; keen in discernment. **b.** Marked by discernment and understanding; sensitive. —**per·cep·tive·ly** *adv.* —**per·cep·tiv·i·ty** (pér-sep-tívvəti) *n.*

per·cep·tu·al (pər-séptew-əl) *adj.* Of, based on, or involving perception. —**per·cep·tu·al·ly** *adv.*

Perceval. See **Percival.**

Per·ce·val (pérsiv'l), **Spencer** (1762–1812). British prime minister (1809–12). He was assassinated in the lobby of the House of Commons.

perch¹ (perch) *n.* **1.** A rod or branch serving as a roost for a bird. **2. a.** A place for resting or sitting, especially one that is high. **b.** A secure position. **3.** A pole used in acrobatics. **4. a.** A unit of length, the **rod** (*see*). **b.** One square rod of land. **5.** A unit of cubic measure used in stonework, usually 16.5 feet by 1 foot by 1.5 feet, or 24.75 cubic feet. **6.** A frame on which cloth is laid for examination of quality. **7.** A pole connecting the front and back axles in a wagon, carriage, or the like.

~*v.* **perched, perching, perches.** —*intr.* **1.** To alight or rest on a perch; roost. **2.** To stand, sit, rest, or be situated on some elevated place or position: *The child perched on the window sill.* —*tr.* **1.** To place on or as on a perch. **2.** To lay (cloth) on a perch in order to examine it. [Middle English *perche,* from Old French, from Latin *pertica,* stick, from Italic root *pert-* (unattested), pole.]

perch² *n., pl.* **-es** or collectively **perch. 1.** Any of various freshwater

perch *The European perch,* Perca fluviatilis *(above), can live for ten years, growing to more than 3 kilograms (6¼ pounds). Adult perch feed on smaller fish.*

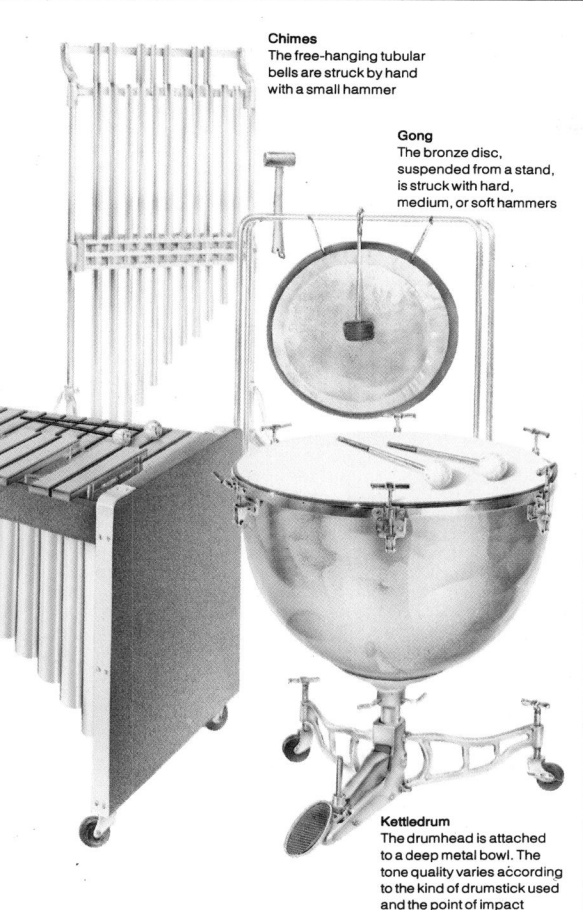

Chimes
The free-hanging tubular bells are struck by hand with a small hammer

Gong
The bronze disc, suspended from a stand, is struck with hard, medium, or soft hammers

Kettledrum
The drumhead is attached to a deep metal bowl. The tone quality varies according to the kind of drumstick used and the point of impact

fishes of the genus *Perca*, especially either of two edible species, *P. fluviatilis*, of Europe and *P. flavescens*, of North America. **2.** Any of various related or similar fishes, such as the **pike perch** *(see)*. [Middle English *perche*, from Old French, from Latin *perca*, from Greek *perkē*.]

per·chance (pər-cháanss, pér- ‖ -chánss) *adv. Archaic.* Perhaps; possibly. [Middle English *perchaunce*, from Old French *per chance, par chance : per, par*, by, + CHANCE.]

Per·che·ron (pérshə-ron ‖ pérchə-) *n.* A large draught horse of a breed developed in France. [French, from *Percheron*, a native of *le Perche*, district south of Normandy.]

perch·ing (pérching) *adj.* Having feet especially adapted for grasping a perch. Said of certain birds.

per·chlo·rate (pər-kláwr-ayt, pér- ‖ -klór-) *n.* An ester or a salt of perchloric acid.

per·chlo·ric acid (pər-klórrik, pér-, -kláwr-ik ‖ -klór-) *n.* A clear, colourless, hygroscopic liquid, $HClO_4$, explosively unstable under some conditions. It is a powerful oxidant and is used as a catalyst and in explosives.

per·chlor·o·eth·yl·ene (pər-kláwr-ō-éthi-leen, pér- ‖ -klór-) *n.* A colourless, nonflammable organic solvent, $Cl_2C:CCl_2$, used in dry-cleaning solutions and to dissolve a variety of waxes, tars, rubbers, and gums. Also called "tetrachloroethylene".

per·cip·i·ent (pər-síppi-ənt) *adj.* Having the power of perceiving; especially, perceiving keenly and readily.
~*n.* One that perceives. [Latin *percipiēns* (stem *pecipient-*), present participle of *percipere*, PERCEIVE.] —**per·cip·i·ence** *n.*

Per·ci·val, Per·ce·val (pérssiv'l). Also **Par·si·fal, Par·zi·val** (pár-sif'l). In Arthurian legend, a naive and virtuous young knight who is eventually granted a sight of the Holy Grail.

per·coid (pér-koyd) *n.* Also **per·coi·de·an** (per-kóydi-ən). Any member of the Percoidea, a large suborder of fishes that includes the perches, sunfishes, and groupers. [New Latin *Percoidea* : Latin *perca*, PERCH (fish) + -OID.] —**per·coid, per·coi·de·an** *adj.*

per·co·late (pérkə-layt) *v.* **-lated, -lating, -lates.** —*tr.* **1.** To cause (liquid, powder, or small particles) to pass through a porous substance or small holes; filter; sift. **2.** To pass or ooze through: *Water percolated the sand.* **3.** To make (coffee, for example) in a percolator. —*intr.* **1.** To drain or seep through a porous substance or filter. **2.** *Informal.* To become lively or active. **3.** *Informal.* To pass along gradually: *The news percolated down to me.*
~*n.* (-lət, -lit, -layt). A liquid that has been percolated. [Latin

percōlāre : per-, through + *cōlāre*, to filter, strain, from *cōlum*, sieve.] —**per·co·la·tion** (-láysh'n) *n.*

per·co·la·tor (pérkə-laytər. *Note: the pronunciation* pérkew-laytər *is not standard.) n.* A type of coffeepot in which hot water passes through ground coffee beans; especially, one in which boiling water is forced repeatedly up through a centre tube to filter through a small perforated container of ground coffee.

per con·tra (kóntrə) *adv. Latin.* On the contrary.

per·cuss (pər-kúss) *tr.v.* **-cussed, -cussing, -cusses.** To strike or tap firmly, as in medical percussion: *percuss a patient's chest.* [Latin *percutere* (past participle *percussus*), to strike hard : *per-* (intensive) + *quatere*, to strike.]

per·cus·sion (pər-kúsh'n) *n.* **1.** The striking together of two bodies, especially when noise is produced. **2.** The sound, vibration, or shock caused by such a striking together. **3.** The act of detonating a percussion cap in a firearm. **4.** A method of medical diagnosis in which various areas of the body, especially the chest, back, and abdomen, are tapped to determine by resonance the condition of internal organs. **5. a.** Musical percussion instruments collectively. **b.** The section of an orchestra consisting of these instruments. [Latin *percussiō* (stem *percussiōn-*), from *percutere*, to PERCUSS.]

percussion cap *n.* A thin metal cap containing gunpowder or some other detonator that explodes on being struck.

percussion instrument *n.* A musical instrument in which sound is produced by striking, such as a drum, xylophone, or cymbal.

per·cus·sion·ist (pər-kúsh'n-ist) *n.* One who plays percussion instruments.

per·cus·sive (pər-kússiv) *adj.* Of, pertaining to, or characterised by percussion. —**per·cus·sive·ly** *adv.* —**per·cus·sive·ness** *n.*

per·cu·ta·ne·ous (pér-kew-táyni-əss) *adj.* Passed, done, or effected through or by means of the skin. —**per·cu·ta·ne·ous·ly** *adv.*

Per·cy (pér-si), **Sir Henry,** also called Hotspur (1364–1403). English soldier. He plotted with his father, the Earl of Northumberland, to overthrow Henry IV. He was killed in battle at Shrewsbury.

Percy, Bishop Thomas (1729–1811). English antiquary and poet. The Bishop of Dromore from 1782, his chief work is *The Reliques of Ancient English Poetry* (1765), a selection of medieval ballads and songs, which stimulated the Romantic revival.

per di·em (dî-em, dée-) *adv. Abbr.* **p.d., P.D.** Per day.
~*n. Abbr.* **p.d., P.D.** An allowance for daily expenses.
~*adj. Abbr.* **p.d., P.D.** Reckoned on a daily basis: *per diem costs.* [Latin, "by the day".]

per·di·tion (pər-dish'n) *n.* **1. a.** The loss of the soul; eternal damnation. **b.** Hell. **2.** *Archaic.* Utter loss or ruin. [Middle English *perdicioun*, from Late Latin *perditiō* (stem *perditiōn-*), from Latin *perdere* (past participle *perditus*), to throw away, destroy, lose : *per-*, away + *dare*, to give.]

per·du, per·due (pér-dew, per-déw ‖ -dōō, -dóō) *adj.* Concealed; hidden. Used chiefly in the phrase *lie perdu.*
~*n. Obsolete.* A soldier sent on a dangerous mission. [French, "lost", from the past participle of *perdre*, to lose, from Latin *perdere*. See **perdition**.]

per·du·ra·ble (pər-déwr-əb'l ‖ -dóor-) *adj.* Extremely durable; permanent. [Middle English, from Old French, from Late Latin *perdūrābilis*, from *perdūrāre*, "to last throughout", endure : *per-*, throughout + *dūrāre*, to last.] —**per·du·ra·bil·i·ty** (-ə-bílləti) *n.* —**per·du·ra·bly** *adv.*

père (pair) *n. French.* Father. Used after a proper name to distinguish a father from a son who has the same name: *Dumas père.* Compare **fils**.

Père David's deer *n.* A large reddish-grey Chinese deer, *Elaphurus davidianus*, that survives only in captivity. [After Père Armand David (1826–1900), French missionary.]

per·e·gri·nate (pérrigri-nayt) *v.* **-nated, -nating, -nates.** —*intr.* To journey or travel from place to place usually for a long time and over great distances. —*tr.* To travel through or over. In both senses, often used humorously. [Latin *peregrīnārī*, to travel in foreign lands, from *peregrīnus*, foreigner. See **peregrine**.] —**per·e·gri·na·tion** (-náysh'n) *n.* —**per·e·gri·na·tor** *n.*

per·e·grine (pérri-grin, -green ‖ -grīn) *adj. Archaic.* **1.** Foreign; alien. **2.** Roving or wandering; migratory.
~*n.* The peregrine falcon. [Medieval Latin *peregrīnus*, from Latin, a foreigner, stranger, from *pereger*, being abroad : *per-*, away, + *ager*, land, field.]

peregrine falcon *n.* A widely distributed bird of prey, *Falco peregrinus*, having grey and white plumage, formerly much used in falconry. Also called "peregrine". [Middle English, translation of Medieval Latin *falco peregrinus*, "pilgrim falcon"; so named because young peregrines were caught in passage ("pilgrimage") from their breeding place, rather than taken from the nest.]

Per·el·man (pérrəlmən), **S(idney) J(oseph)** (1904–79). U.S. humorist. Beginning as a cartoonist, he became a scriptwriter on Marx Brothers films.

per·emp·to·ry (pə-rémp-təri, pérrəmp-, -tri) *adj.* **1.** Overbearing; imperious: *a peremptory manner.* **2.** Having the nature of or expressing command; urgent: *"a bell began to toll with a peremptory clang."* (Thomas Hardy). **3.** Not admitting denial or refusal; imperative: *a peremptory command.* **4.** *Law.* Precluding further debate or action: *a peremptory decree.* [Late Latin *peremptōrius*, "precluding debate", decisive, from *perimere* (past participle *peremptus*), to take away completely : *per-*, completely + *emere*, to obtain.] —**per·emp·to·ri·ly** *adv.* —**per·emp·to·ri·ness** *n.*

peregrine *This falcon can dive on its prey – often a grouse or pigeon – at speeds of up to 130 kilometres per hour (80 miles per hour). It kills the victim in midair with a single blow of its talons, then circles back to retrieve the body from the ground. Peregrines mate for life, often returning to the same eyrie year after year; they are found in all the world's continents except Antarctica.*

per·emp·tory challenge n. Law. The right of a defendant in a criminal trial to object to a certain number of proposed jurors.

pe·ren·nate (pérri-nayt, pə-rénnayt) intr.v. **-nated, -nating, -nates.** Rare. To survive from one growing season to the next, often with a period of reduced or arrested growth between seasons. Used of plants. [Latin perennātus, past participle of perennāre, to survive, continue : PER- (through) + -ennāre, from annus, year.]

per·en·ni·al (pə-rénni-əl) adj. **1.** Lasting or active through the year or through many years: the perennial snowcaps of the Alps. **2. a.** Lasting an indefinitely long time; everlasting; perpetual: perennial happiness. **b.** Appearing again and again; continually recurring. **3.** Botany. Having a life span of more than two years. Compare **annual, biennial.** —See Synonyms at **continual.** ~n. Botany. A perennial plant. [Latin perennis : per-, throughout + annus, year.] —**per·en·ni·al·ly** adv.

perf. perfect.

per·fect (pér-fikt ‖ -fékt) adj. Abbr. **perf. 1.** Lacking nothing essential to the whole; complete of its nature or kind. **2.** In a state of undiminished or highest excellence; without defect; flawless. **3.** Highly skilled or talented in a certain field or area. **4. a.** Faithfully reproducing an original; accurate; exact: a perfect reproduction of a painting. **b.** Corresponding in every respect to an ideal or conventionally recognised standard: the perfect host. **c.** Precise; correct: perfect pitch; perfect timing. **5.** Complete; thorough; utter: a perfect fool. **6.** Pure; undiluted; unmixed: perfect red. **7.** Excellent and delightful in all respects: a perfect day. **8.** Botany. Having both stamens and pistils in the same flower; monoclinous. **9.** Grammar. Of, pertaining to, or designating a verb form expressing action completed prior to a fixed point of reference in time. English verbs have three perfect tenses: the present (or simple) perfect, the pluperfect (or past perfect), and the future perfect. **10.** Of, pertaining to, or designating a number or quantity equal to an integral power of another number or quantity: 4, 9, and 16 are perfect squares. **11.** Music. **a.** Designating the three basic intervals of the octave, fourth, and fifth. **b.** Designating a cadence in which the final chord has its root in both bass and soprano. **12.** Designating a gas that obeys the ideal gas laws. ~n. Abbr. **perf.** Grammar. **1.** The perfect tense. **2.** A verb or verb form in this tense. ~tr.v. (usually pər-fékt) **perfected, -fecting, -fects. 1.** To bring to perfection or completion. **2.** To improve. **3.** To complete the printing of (a sheet) by printing the reverse side. [Middle English perfit, parfit, from Old French parfit, from Latin perfectus, finished, complete, excellent, from past participle of perficere, to complete : per-, completely + facere, to do.] —**per·fect·er** n. —**per·fect·ness** n.

Usage: In its absolute senses, it is not possible to use comparative and superlative forms with perfect in standard English. However, in the more general sense of "excellent", these forms are often used loosely: That's one of the most perfect specimens I've ever seen.

perfect binding n. A common method of binding sheets of paper without sewing, as in making paperback books, in which each cut sheet (page) is glued by one edge onto a stiff backing. —**per·fect-bound** (pérfikt-bównd) adj.

per·fect·i·ble (pər-féktəb'l) adj. Capable of becoming or being made perfect. —**per·fect·i·bil·i·ty** (-billəti) n.

per·fec·tion (pər-féksh'n) n. **1.** The state or quality of being perfect. **2.** The process or act of perfecting: Perfection of the plan took years. **3.** A person or thing that perfectly embodies something: Her pastry is culinary perfection. **4.** An instance or quality of excellence. —**to perfection** Perfectly: cooked to perfection.

per·fec·tion·ism (pər-féksh'n-iz'm) n. **1.** A belief that moral or spiritual perfection can be achieved by man in this life. **2.** A propensity for setting extremely high standards and being displeased with anything less. —**per·fec·tion·ist** n. & adj.

per·fec·tive (pər-féktiv) adj. **1.** Tending towards perfection. **2.** Grammar. Of or designating a verb in the perfective aspect. ~n. Grammar. **1.** The perfective aspect. **2.** A verb in the perfective aspect. —**per·fec·tive·ly** adv. —**per·fec·tive·ness, per·fec·tiv·i·ty** (pérfek-tívviti) n.

perfective aspect n. An aspect of verbs that expresses a completed action as distinct from a continuing or not necessarily completed action. Compare **imperfective aspect.** See **aspect.**

per·fect·ly (pér-fikt-li ‖ -fékt-) adv. **1.** In a perfect manner or to a perfect degree. **2.** Completely; fully; wholly: perfectly ridiculous.

perfect number n. A number that is equal to the sum of its integral factors, for example 28, whose divisors are 1,2,4,7, and 14. The first four perfect numbers are 6, 28, 496, and 8,128.

per·fec·to (pər-féktō) n., pl. **-tos.** A cigar of standard length, thick in the centre and tapering at each end. [Spanish, perfect, from Latin perfectus, PERFECT.]

perfect participle n. The **past participle** (see).

perfect pitch n. **Absolute pitch** (see).

perfect rhyme n. The commonest English rhyme, having identity in sound for the last accented vowel and any final consonants or syllables but with variation in the preceding consonant, for example, great, late; rider, spider; dutiful, unbeautiful. Also called "full rhyme", "true rhyme".

perfect square n. An integer that is the square of an integer.

perfect year n. In the Hebrew calendar, a year having 355 days or a leap year having 385 days.

per·fer·vid (per-férvid) adj. Literary. Impassioned; zealous; extravagantly eager. [New Latin perfervidus : per- (intensifier) + Latin fervidus, FERVID.] —**per·fer·vid·ly** adv. —**per·fer·vid·ness** n.

per·fi·dy (pérfidi) n., pl. **-dies.** Deliberate breach of faith; calculated violation of trust; treachery. [Latin perfidia, from perfidus, treacherous : per- (destruction) + fidēs, faith.] —**per·fid·i·ous** (pər-fiddi-əss) adj. —**per·fid·i·ous·ly** adv.

per·fo·li·ate (pər-fóli-ət, per-, -it, -ayt) adj. Designating a leaf that completely clasps the stem and is apparently pierced by it. [New Latin perfoliatus, "pierced through the leaf" : Latin per-, through + foliātus, "leaved", FOLIATE.] —**per·fo·li·a·tion** (-áysh'n) n.

per·fo·rate (pérfə-rayt) tr.v. **-rated, -rating, -rates. 1.** To pierce, punch, or bore a hole or holes in. **2.** To pierce or stamp (a sheet of paper, for example) with rows of holes, such as those between postage stamps, to allow easy separation. ~adj. (-rit, -rət, -rayt). Having a perforation or perforations. [Latin perforāre : per-, through + forāre, to bore.] —**per·fo·ra·ble** (-rəb'l) adj. —**per·fo·ra·tive** (-rətiv, -raytiv), **per·fo·ra·to·ry** (-rə-tri, -təri) adj. —**per·fo·ra·tor** (-raytər) n.

per·fo·ra·tion (pérfə-ráysh'n) n. **1.** The act of perforating, or state of being perforated. **2.** A hole or series or set of holes punched or bored through something. **3.** In stamp-collecting: **a.** Any of the small holes, or the set of such holes, punched between or around individual stamps on a sheet or roll for the purpose of easy separation. **b.** The method of dividing sheets or rolls of stamps in this way. Compare **roulette. 4.** The series of ridges and indentations along the edge of an object, especially a postage stamp, that has been detached, by tearing, along a perforated line.

per·force (pər-fórss, per- ‖ -fórss) adv. By necessity; willy-nilly. [Middle English par force, from Old French : par, by, + FORCE.]

per·form (pər-fórm) v. **-formed, -forming, -forms.** —tr. **1.** To begin and carry through to completion; do: perform an operation. **2.** To take action in accordance with the requirements of; fulfil (a promise or duty, for example.) **3. a.** To enact (a feat or role) before an audience. **b.** To give a public presentation of (a piece of music, for example). —intr. **1.** To carry out a particular activity; function, especially in a specified way: My car performs badly on wet roads. **2.** To fulfil an obligation or requirement; accomplish something as promised or expected. **3.** To portray a role or demonstrate some skill before an audience. **4.** To present a dramatic or musical work or other entertainment before an audience. [Middle English performen, from Anglo-French parformer, variant of Old French parfornir. (assimilated to forme, FORM) : par- (intensifier), from Latin per- + fornir, to FURNISH.] —**per·form·a·ble** adj. —**per·form·er** n.

Synonyms: perform, execute, accomplish, achieve, effect, fulfil, discharge.

per·form·ance (pər-fórmənss) n. **1.** The act of performing, or the state of being performed. **2.** The act or style of performing a work or role before an audience. **3. a.** The way in which someone or something functions. **b.** Excellence in functioning. Also used adjectivally: a high-performance car. **4.** A presentation, especially a theatrical one, before an audience. **5.** Something performed; an accomplishment; a deed. **6.** Informal. An instance of bad behaviour, such as a display of temper, usually in public. **7.** Informal. Something involving effort or difficulty: Moving house was quite a performance. **8.** Linguistics. The spoken and written utterances collectively of an individual user of language, as opposed to his linguistic **competence** (see). Compare **parole.**

performance test n. A psychological test that requires only nonverbal responses, used, for example, to test the intellectual ability of children with speech problems.

per·form·a·tive (pər-fórmətiv) adj. Philosophy & Linguistics. **1.** Designating an utterance that is itself an instance of the action it describes; for example utterances such as I promise that . . . or I command that . . . are instances of promising or commanding. **2.** Designating a verb used in such an utterance. ~n. A performative verb or utterance.

per·form·ing arts (pər-fórming) pl.n. Those arts, such as drama and music, which are realised in performance rather than directly by the creative artist.

per·fume (pérfewm ‖ U.S. also pər-féwm) n. **1.** A volatile liquid, distilled from flowers or prepared synthetically, that emits and diffuses a fragrant odour. **2.** Any agreeable scent or odour. —See Synonyms at **smell.** ~tr.v. (pər-féwm, per-, pérfewm) **perfumed, -fuming, -fumes.** To impregnate with fragrance; impart a pleasant odour to. [French parfum, probably from obsolete Italian parfumare, to smoke through : par-, through, from Latin per- + fumare, to smoke, from Latin fūmāre, from fūmus, smoke.]

per·fum·er (pər-féwmər, per-) n. A maker or seller of perfumes.

per·fum·er·y (pər-féwməri, per-) n., pl. **-ies. 1.** Perfumes in general. **2.** An establishment that specialises in making or selling perfume. **3.** The art of making perfume.

per·func·to·ry (pər-fúngk-təri, -tri) adj. Done or acting routinely and with little interest or care. See Synonyms at **superficial.** [Late Latin perfunctōrius, from Latin perfungi (past participle perfunctus), "to get through with" : per-, completely + fungī, to perform.] —**per·func·to·ri·ly** adv. —**per·func·to·ri·ness** n.

per·fuse (pər-féwz) tr.v. **-fused, -fusing, -fuses. 1.** To coat, suffuse, or permeate with liquid, colour, or light. **2.** To pour or diffuse (a liquid) over or through something. [Latin perfundere (past participle perfusus), to pour over or through : per-, through + fundere, to pour.] —**per·fu·sive** (-féw-siv, -ziv) adj.

per·go·la (pérgələ ‖ pər-gólə) n. An arbour or passageway with a roof of trelliswork on which climbing plants grow. [Italian, from Latin pergula, projecting roof, from pergere, to proceed.]

per·haps (pər-háps, praps) *adv.* Possibly; maybe; it may be that. [PER (by) + plural of HAP (chance).]

pe·ri (péer-i) *n.* **1.** In Persian mythology, a beautiful fairy. **2.** A beautiful or fairy-like being. [Persian *pārī;* akin to Avestan *pairika,* witch.]

peri– *prefix.* Indicates: **1.** About, around, encircling, or enclosing; for example, **periotic, periscope.** **2.** Close at hand, adjacent, or near; for example, **perihelion.** [Latin, from Greek, from *peri,* about, near, around.]

per·i·anth (pérri-anth) *n. Botany.* The outer organs of a flower, consisting of the calyx and corolla (the sepals and petals), or of either of these if the other is absent. [French *périanthe,* from New Latin *perianthium* : PERI- + ANTH(O)- + -IUM.]

per·i·apt (pérri-apt) *n.* An amulet or charm worn as protection against harm and disease. [Old French *periapte,* from Greek *periapton,* from *periaptos,* appended, from *periaptein,* to hang or fasten around : *peri-,* PERI- + *haptein,* to fasten (see **synapse**).]

per·i·blem (pérri-blem) *n. Botany.* A zone of tissue in the apical meristem of a root that develops into the cortex. [German, from Greek *periblēma,* protection, from *periballein,* to throw around : *peri-,* PERI- + *ballein,* to throw.]

per·i·car·di·tis (pérrikaar-dītiss) *n.* Inflammation of the pericardium. [New Latin : PERICARD(IUM) + -ITIS.]

per·i·car·di·um (pérri-kár-di-əm) *n., pl.* **-dia** (-di-ə). The membranous sac enclosing the heart. [New Latin, from Greek *perikardion,* from *perikardios,* around the heart : PERI- + *kardia,* heart.] **—per·i·car·di·ac** (-ak), **per·i·car·di·al** *adj.*

per·i·carp (pérri-kaarp) *n. Botany.* The casing of the seed or seeds within a fruit, developed from the ovary wall. [New Latin *pericarpium,* from Greek *perikarpion,* pod, shell : *peri-,* PERI- + -CARP.] **—per·i·car·pi·al** (-kárpi-əl) *adj.*

per·i·chon·dri·um (pérri-kón-dri-əm) *n., pl.* **-dria** (-dri-ə). *Anatomy.* The fibrous membrane covering the surface of cartilage except at joint endings. [New Latin : PERI- + CHONDR(O)- + -IUM.] **—per·i·chon·dri·al** *adj.*

per·i·clase (pérri-klayss, -klayz) *n.* A mineral form of magnesium oxide, MgO, usually occurring in isomeric crystals or grains. [German *Periklas,* from New Latin *periclasia,* "perfect cleavage (of the crystals)" : PERI- (around, hence above others, exceedingly) + -CLASE.]

Per·i·cles (pérri-kleez) (*c.* 495–429 B.C.). Athenian statesman and general. A great democrat and skilled orator, he controlled Athenian affairs during the city's most glorious era. He fostered cultural life, encouraging Sophocles and Phidias among others, and also ordered the building of the Parthenon. **—Per·i·cle·an** (perri-klée-ən) *adj.*

per·i·cli·nal (pérri-klīn'l) *adj.* **1.** Of or pertaining to a pericline. **2.** *Botany.* **a.** Designating a line of cell division parallel to the surface of the organ, as found in a meristem. **b.** Having tissue of one origin completely enclosed by tissue of a different origin. Said of certain chimaeras.

per·i·cline (pérri-klīn) *n.* **1.** A variety of albite occurring as elongated white crystals. **2.** A formation of stratified rock shaped like a dome or basin in which the slopes follow the direction of folding. Also called "dome". [Greek *periklinēs,* sloping on all sides : *peri-,* PERI- + *klinein,* to slope, lean.]

per·i·cra·ni·um (pérri-kráy-ni-əm) *n., pl.* **-nia** (-ni-ə). *Anatomy.* The external **periosteum** *(see)* that covers the outer surface of the skull. [New Latin, from Greek *perikranion,* from *perikranios,* around the skull : PERI- + *kranion,* CRANIUM.] **—per·i·cra·ni·al** *adj.*

per·i·cy·cle (pérri-sīk'l) *n. Botany.* The outermost layer of the stele of a plant, usually though not always consisting of a layer of cells. [French *péricycle,* from Greek *perikuklos,* spherical : *peri-,* PERI- + *kuklos,* CYCLE.] **—per·i·cy·clic** (-sīklik, -sícklik) *adj.*

per·i·cyn·thi·on (pérri-sínthi-ən) *n.* The point at which a spacecraft launched from the Earth into orbit round the Moon is nearest to the Moon. Compare **apocynthion, perilune.** [PERI- + *-cynthion,* from CYNTHIA (the Moon).]

per·i·derm (pérri-derm) *n. Botany.* An outer layer of tissue of plant roots and stems, consisting of the bark and the layer of growing tissue beneath the bark. [New Latin *peridermis* : PERI- + -DERM.] **—per·i·der·mal** (-dérm'l), **per·i·der·mic** (-dérmik) *adj.*

pe·rid·i·um (pə-ríd-i-əm) *n., pl.* **-ridia** (-i-ə). The covering of the spore-bearing organ in many fungi. [New Latin, from Greek *pēridion,* diminutive of *pēra*†, leather bag.] **—pe·rid·i·al** *adj.*

per·i·dot (pérri-dot || -dōt) *n.* A transparent, pale green variety of **olivine** *(see).* [French *péridot,* from Old French *peritot*†.] **—per·i·dot·ic** (-dóttik || -dōtik) *adj.*

per·i·do·tite (pérri-dōtit || *U.S. also* pə-ríddə-tīt) *n.* Any of a group of igneous rocks composed mainly of olivine and various pyroxenes and amphiboles. [French *péridotite,* from *péridot,* PERIDOT.]

per·i·gee (pérri-jee) *n.* The point nearest the Earth in the orbit of the Moon or a satellite. Compare **apogee.** [French *périgée,* from New Latin *perigeum,* from Greek *perigeion,* from *perigeios,* near the Earth : *peri-,* PERI- + *gē,* the Earth.] **—per·i·ge·an** *adj.*

per·i·gla·cial (pérri-gláy-sh'l, -si-əl) *adj.* Designating a region around a glacier.

per·i·gon (pérri-gən || -gon) *n.* An angle of 360°; a round angle. [PERI- + -GON.]

Pér·i·gueux (*French* perri-gö). Town in southwest France. Situated on the river Isle, it is capital of the Dordogne département.

pe·rig·y·nous (pə-ríjinəss) *adj. Botany.* **1.** Having sepals, petals, and stamens around the edge of a flat or cuplike receptacle containing the ovary. **2.** Designating flower parts arranged in this way: *perigynous stamens.* [New Latin *perigynus* : PERI- + -GYNOUS.] **—pe·rig·y·ny** (pə-ríjini) *n.*

per·i·he·li·on (pérri-héeli-ən) *n., pl.* **-helia** (-héeli-ə). The point nearest the Sun in the orbit of a planet or other body. Compare **aphelion.** [New Latin : PERI- + Greek *hēlios,* sun.]

per·il (pérrəl, pérril) *n.* **1.** A condition of imminent danger; exposure to the risk of harm or loss. **2.** Something that endangers; a serious risk. **—at (one's) peril.** At the risk of danger or punishment. —See Synonyms at **danger.**

~*tr.v.* **perilled** or *U.S.* **periled, -illing** or *U.S.* **-iling, -ils.** *Rare.* To expose to danger or the chance of injury; imperil. [Middle English, from Old French, from Latin *perīculum,* trial, danger.] **—per·il·ous** *adj.* **—per·il·ous·ly** *adv.*

per·i·lune (pérri-lōōn || -lewn) *n.* The point at which a spacecraft launched from the Moon into lunar orbit is nearest to the Moon. Compare **apolune, pericynthion.** [PERI- + Latin *lūna,* Moon, by analogy with *perigee.*]

per·i·lymph (pérri-limf) *n.* The fluid surrounding the structures of the internal ear in vertebrates.

pe·rim·e·ter (pə-rímmitər, pi-, pe-) *n.* **1.** *Mathematics.* **a.** A closed curve bounding a plane area. **b.** The length of such a boundary. **2.** Any outer boundary, such as the edge of a playing field or a fortified strip protecting a military position. **3.** A diagnostic instrument used to measure the extent of a person's field of vision. [French *périmètre,* from Latin *perimetros,* from Greek : *peri-,* PERI- + -METER.] **—per·i·met·ric** (pérri-méttrik), **per·i·met·ri·cal** *adj.* **—per·i·met·ri·cal·ly** *adv.*

per·i·morph (pérri-mawrf) *n.* A mineral that encloses a different mineral. Compare **endomorph.** [PERI- + -MORPH.] **—per·i·mor·phic** (-mórfik), **per·i·mor·phous** *adj.* **—per·i·mor·phism** *n.*

per·i·my·si·um (pérri-mízzi-əm) *n., pl.* **-mysia** (-mízzi-ə). A sheath of connective tissue enveloping bundles of muscle fibres. [New Latin : PERI- + Greek *mus,* muscle.]

per·i·na·tal (pérri-náyt'l) *adj.* Of, pertaining to, or occurring in the period from approximately three months before to one month after birth: *perinatal mortality.*

per·i·neph·ri·um (pérri-néf-ri-əm) *n., pl.* **-ria** (-ri-ə). The connective and fatty tissue surrounding the kidney. [New Latin, from Greek *perinephros,* fat around the kidney : *peri-,* PERI- + *nephros,* kidney.] **—per·i·neph·ral, per·i·neph·ri·al, per·i·neph·ric** *adj.*

per·i·ne·um (pérri-née-əm) *n., pl.* **-nea** (-née-ə). **1.** The portion of the body in the pelvis occupied by the urogenital passages and the rectum. **2.** The region between the scrotum and the anus in males, and between the posterior vulva junction and the anus in females. [New Latin, from Late Latin *perinaion,* from Greek : *peri-,* PERI- + *inan*†, to excrete.] **—per·i·ne·al** *adj.*

per·i·neu·ri·um (pérri-néwr-i-əm || -nóor-) *n., pl.* **-neuria** (-i-ə). A sheath of connective tissue enclosing a bundle of nerve fibres. [New Latin : PERI- + NEUR(O)- + -IUM.] **—per·i·neu·ri·al** *adj.*

pe·ri·od (péer-i-əd) *n. Abbr.* **per. 1.** An interval of time characterised by the occurrence of certain conditions or events: *slack periods.* **2.** An interval of time characterised by the prevalence of a specified culture, ideology, or technology: *artefacts of the pre-Columbian period.* **3.** A unit of geological time, longer than an epoch and shorter than an era. **4.** An interval regarded as a distinct evolutionary or developmental phase; a stage: *Picasso's blue period.* **5.** Any of various arbitrary temporal units, especially: **a.** A division of time allotted for teaching a class. **b.** A division of the playing time of a game. **6.** *Physics.* The time interval between two successive occurrences of any recurrent event or cycle; the reciprocal of frequency. **7.** An instance or occurrence of menstruation. **8.** A point or portion of time at which something is ended; a completion; a conclusion. **9.** The full pause at the end of a spoken sentence. **10.** *Chiefly U.S.* A **full stop** *(see).* **11. a.** In formal literary composition, a sentence of several carefully balanced clauses. **b.** *Plural.* Rhetorical language. **12.** A metrical unit of Greek verse consisting of two or more cola. **13.** *Music.* A group of two or more phrases within a composition, made up of eight or sixteen measures and terminating with a cadence. **14.** *Mathematics.* **a.** The smallest interval in the range of the independent variable required for a periodic function to begin another cycle. **b.** A group of digits separated by commas in a written number. **c.** The number of digits that repeat in a repeating decimal. For example, $^1/_7 = 0.142857142857\ldots$ has a six-digit period. **15.** *Astronomy.* **a.** The time taken for a heavenly body to complete one orbit or one rotation on its axis. **b.** The interval between two maximum emissions from a variable star. **16.** *Chemistry.* Any of the horizontal rows of elements in the periodic table. Compare **group.**

~*adv. Chiefly U.S.* Used to add finality and emphasis to a preceding statement: *I'm going, period!*

~*adj.* Of, belonging to, or representing a particular historical age or time: *a period piece; period furniture.* [Middle English *paryode,* from Old French *periode,* from Late Latin *periodus,* period of time, from Latin, sentence, from Greek *periodos,* circuit : *peri-* PERI- + *hodos,* way.]

per·i·o·date (perī-ə-dayt, pər-) *n.* A salt or ester of a periodic acid.

pe·ri·od·ic (péer-i-óddik) *adj.* Also **pe·ri·od·i·cal** (-'l). **1.** Having periods or repeated cycles. **2.** Happening or appearing at regular intervals. **3.** Taking place now and then; intermittent. [French *périodique,* from Latin *periodicus,* from Greek *periodikos,* from *periodos,* PERIOD.] **—pe·ri·od·i·cal·ly** *adv.*

Synonyms: *periodic, sporadic, intermittent, occasional, fitful.*

Pericles *A Greek bust of the Athenian orator and statesman who was responsible for the building of the Parthenon in Athens. The bust, now in the British Museum in London, bears Pericles' name in Greek characters across its base.*

per·i·od·ic acid (pér-ī-óddik) *n.* Any of several acids that contain more oxygen than iodic acid, especially HIO_4 and H_5IO_6.

pe·ri·od·i·cal (peer-i-óddik'l) *n.* A publication issued at regular intervals, usually of a week or longer. *~adj.* **1.** Of, pertaining to, or designating such a publication. **2.** Variant of **periodic.**

periodic function *n.* A mathematical function, such as sin *x* or cos *x*, whose value is repeated at regular invervals.

pe·ri·o·dic·i·ty (peer-i-ə-díssəti) *n.* The quality of being periodic; recurrence at regular intervals.

periodic law *n. Chemistry.* The principle that the properties of the elements recur periodically with increasing atomic number.

periodic system *n.* The classification of the chemical elements on the basis of the periodic law.

periodic table *n. Chemistry.* A tabular arrangement of the elements according to their atomic number.

per·i·o·don·tal (perri-ə-dónt'l, -ō-) *adj.* Of or designating tissue and structures surrounding and supporting the teeth. [PERI- + ODONT(O)- + -AL.]

per·i·o·don·tics (perri-ə-dóntiks, -ō-) *n. Used with a singular verb.* Also **per·i·o·don·tia** (-dónshə). The branch of dentistry dealing with periodontal disease. [New Latin *periodontium*, periodontal tissue : PERI- + ODONT(O)- + -IUM.] —**per·i·o·don·tic** *adj.* —**per·i·o·don·tist** *n.*

per·i·os·te·um (perri-óss-i-əm) *n., pl.* **-tea** (-ti-ə). A fibrous membrane covering all bones, except at points of articulation. [New Latin, from Late Latin *periosteon*, from Greek, from *periosteos*,

---

HOW NATURE'S ELEMENTS ARE RELATED

Discovering the pattern that puts atoms into families

Ninety-two chemical elements are found in nature. Each has a different number of protons in the nucleus of its atoms. Hydrogen has one proton, helium two, lithium three, and so on to uranium with 92. This number is known as the atomic number.

If the elements are set out in horizontal rows in order of their atomic number, they can be arranged in a pattern, or table, that brings out the similarities in their chemical properties. The pattern is known as the periodic table because elements with similar properties appear at regular, predictable intervals in the numerical order and fall into columns in the table. In

this way elements can be grouped into "families".

The periodic relationship between the elements was discovered by a Russian-born physicist, Dmitri Mendeleyev (1834–1907). He did not know of the existence of protons, but he did know that the atom of each element – and not all 92 were known at that time – had a different weight and that the weights increased at a regular, progressive rate.

In 1869, Mendeleyev wrote the names of the known elements on cards and placed the cards in rows and columns as in some fantastic game of patience. He shuffled his cards about for two years – and the results

were astonishing. When placed in a certain pattern in order of their atomic weight, with blank cards for obvious gaps in the progression, the elements in the vertical columns all had similarities in their chemical properties.

Using his table of elements, Mendeleyev was able to predict the existence, weight, and chemical properties of elements then unknown to man. Only in the 1930s, with the discovery of the internal structure of the atom, was the accuracy of Mendeleyev's table finally proved. By then, the elements he had predicted had been identified.

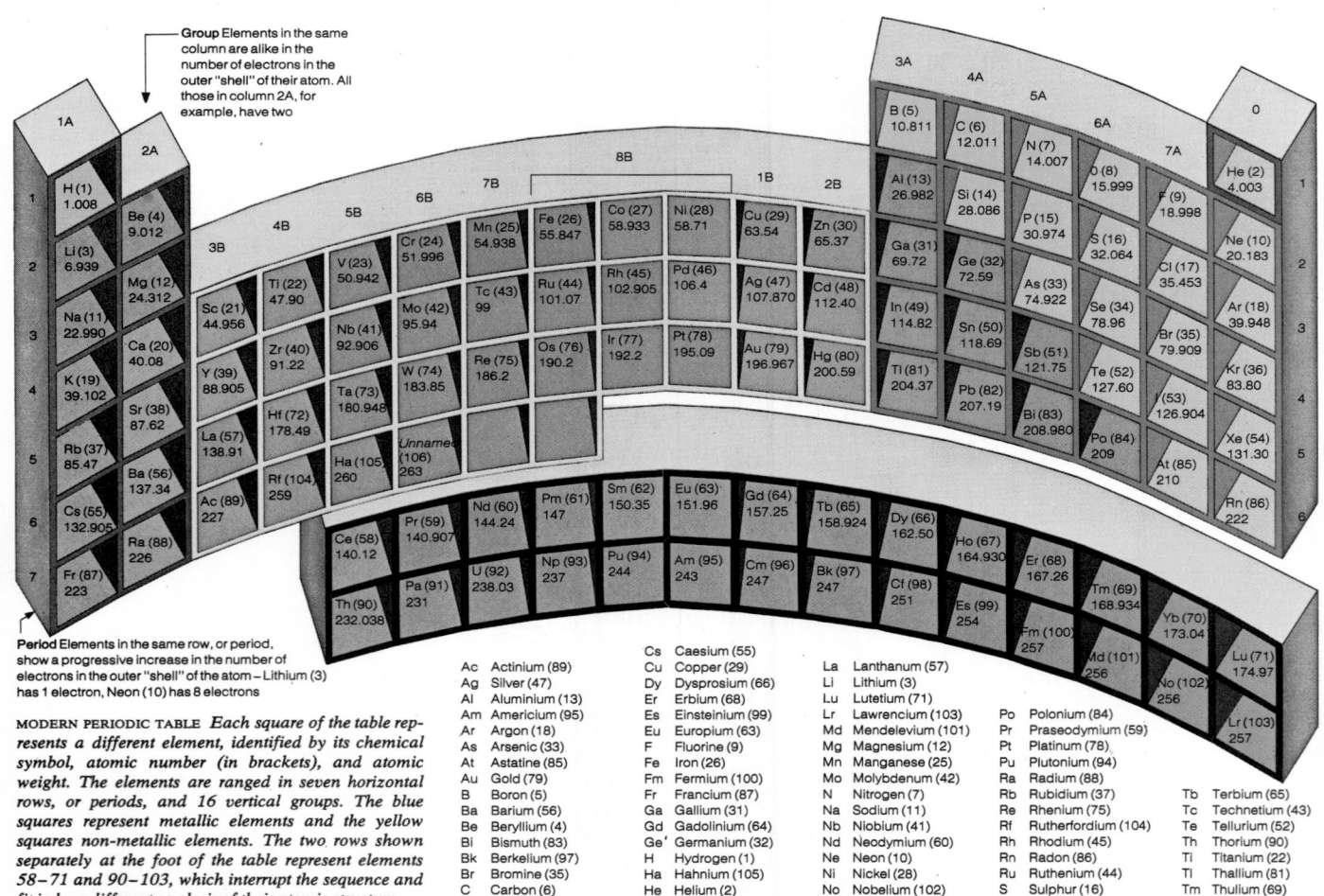

Group Elements in the same column are alike in the number of electrons in the outer "shell" of their atom. All those in column 2A, for example, have two

Period Elements in the same row, or period, show a progressive increase in the number of electrons in the outer "shell" of the atom – Lithium (3) has 1 electron, Neon (10) has 8 electrons

MODERN PERIODIC TABLE *Each square of the table represents a different element, identified by its chemical symbol, atomic number (in brackets), and atomic weight. The elements are ranged in seven horizontal rows, or periods, and 16 vertical groups. The blue squares represent metallic elements and the yellow squares non-metallic elements. The two rows shown separately at the foot of the table represent elements 58–71 and 90–103, which interrupt the sequence and fit in by a different analysis of their atomic structure.*

Since 1934, scientists have created elements beyond uranium – transuranium elements – by bombarding an element with neutrons. This transforms part of it into the element with the next highest atomic number. The method had been used to create 14 transuranium elements by 1982, giving a table of 106 elements.

Ac	Actinium (89)	Cs	Caesium (55)
Ag	Silver (47)	Cu	Copper (29)
Al	Aluminium (13)	Dy	Dysprosium (66)
Am	Americium (95)	Er	Erbium (68)
Ar	Argon (18)	Es	Einsteinium (99)
As	Arsenic (33)	Eu	Europium (63)
At	Astatine (85)	F	Fluorine (9)
Au	Gold (79)	Fe	Iron (26)
B	Boron (5)	Fm	Fermium (100)
Ba	Barium (56)	Fr	Francium (87)
Be	Beryllium (4)	Ga	Gallium (31)
Bi	Bismuth (83)	Gd	Gadolinium (64)
Bk	Berkelium (97)	Ge	Germanium (32)
Br	Bromine (35)	H	Hydrogen (1)
C	Carbon (6)	He	Helium (2)
Ca	Calcium (20)	Hf	Hafnium (72)
Cd	Cadmium (48)	Hg	Mercury (80)
Ce	Cerium (58)	Ho	Holmium (67)
Cf	Californium (98)	I	Iodine (53)
Cl	Chlorine (17)	In	Indium (49)
Cm	Curium (96)	Ir	Iridium (77)
Co	Cobalt (27)	K	Potassium (19)
Cr	Chromium (24)	Kr	Krypton (36)

La	Lanthanum (57)	Po	Polonium (84)
Li	Lithium (3)	Pr	Praseodymium (59)
Lu	Lutetium (71)	Pt	Platinum (78)
Lr	Lawrencium (103)	Pu	Plutonium (94)
Md	Mendelevium (101)	Ra	Radium (88)
Mg	Magnesium (12)	Rb	Rubidium (37)
Mn	Manganese (25)	Re	Rhenium (75)
Mo	Molybdenum (42)	Rf	Rutherfordium (104)
N	Nitrogen (7)	Rh	Rhodium (45)
Na	Sodium (11)	Rn	Radon (86)
Nb	Niobium (41)	Ru	Ruthenium (44)
Nd	Neodymium (60)	S	Sulphur (16)
Ne	Neon (10)	Sb	Antimony (51)
Ni	Nickel (28)	Sc	Scandium (21)
No	Nobelium (102)	Se	Selenium (34)
Np	Neptunium (93)	Si	Silicon (14)
O	Oxygen (8)	Sm	Samarium (62)
Os	Osmium (76)	Sn	Tin (50)
P	Phosphorus (15)	Sr	Strontium (38)
Pa	Proctactinium (91)	Ta	Tantalum (73)
Pb	Lead (82)		
Pd	Palladium (46)		
Pm	Promethium (61)		

Tb	Terbium (65)
Tc	Technetium (43)
Te	Tellurium (52)
Th	Thorium (90)
Ti	Titanium (22)
Tl	Thallium (81)
Tm	Thulium (69)
U	Uranium (92)
V	Vanadium (23)
W	Tungsten (74)
Xe	Xenon (54)
Y	Yttrium (39)
Yb	Ytterbium (70)
Zn	Zinc (30)
Zr	Zirconium (40)

around the bones : peri-, PERI- + osteon, bone.] —**per·i·os·te·al,
per·i·os·te·ous** adj.

per·i·os·ti·tis (pérri-oss-títiss) n. Inflammation of the periosteum.
—**per·i·os·tit·ic** (-títtik) adj.

per·i·ot·ic (pérri-ṓtik, -óttik) adj. 1. Situated around the ear. 2. Of or designating the bones immediately around the inner ear. [PERI- + OTIC.]

per·i·pa·tet·ic (pérripə-téttik) adj. 1. Walking about from place to place in the pursuit of one's business; itinerant. 2. Carried on while walking or moving from place to place: a peripatetic conversation. 3. British. Employed in a number of places and travelling between them; especially, working in more than one school: a peripatetic music teacher. [From PERIPATETIC.]

Per·i·pa·tet·ic (pérripə-téttik) adj. Of or pertaining to the philosophy or methods of teaching of Aristotle, who conducted discussions while walking about in the Lyceum of ancient Athens.
~n. 1. A member of Aristotle's school. 2. A follower of the philosophy of Aristotle; an Aristotelian. [Middle English, from Old French peripatetique, from Latin peripatēticus, from Greek peripatētikos, from peripatein, to walk about while teaching : peri-, PERI- + patein, to tread, walk.]

per·i·pe·te·ia (pérripə-tī́-ə, -tée-ə) n. Also **pe·rip·e·ty** (pə-ríppəti). An abrupt or unexpected change in a course of events or situation, especially in a drama or literary work. [Greek, from peripiptein, to change suddenly, "fall around" : peri-, PERI- + piptein, to fall.]

pe·riph·er·al (pə-ríffərəl, -ríffrəl) adj. Also **per·i·pher·ic** (pérri-férrik). 1. Pertaining to, located on, or constituting the periphery. 2. Not of central importance; minor or incidental.
~n. Computing. A peripheral device. —**pe·riph·er·al·ly** adv.

peripheral device n. A device used to feed information into or extract information from a computer, such as a keyboard, printer, or magnetic tape unit, or a device outside the main store in which information is stored. Also called "peripheral", "peripheral unit".

peripheral nervous system n. The part of the nervous system comprising the cranial nerves, the spinal nerves, and the autonomic nervous system.

peripheral vision n. Antatomy. Vision in which images fall upon parts of the retina outside the macula lutea.

pe·riph·er·y (pə-riff-əri, pe-) n., pl. **-ies.** 1. a. The outermost part or region within a precise boundary. b. The region or area immediately beyond a precise boundary. c. Broadly, an area forming an imprecise boundary; the fringe or edge of something, especially of a social group. 2. Mathematics. a. A perimeter (see). b. The surface of a solid. 3. Anatomy. A region in which nerves end. [Middle English peripherie, from Late Latin peripherīa, from Greek periphereia, from peripherēs, carrying around, from peripherein, to carry around : peri-, PERI- + pherein, to carry.]

pe·riph·ra·sis (pə-ríffrə-siss, pe-) n., pl. **-ses** (-seez). 1. The use of indirect or roundabout methods of expression. 2. An indirect expression; a circumlocution. [Latin, from Greek, from periphrazein, to express in a roundabout way : peri-, PERI- + phrazein, to say.]

per·i·phras·tic (pérri-frástik) adj. 1. Of or characterised by periphrasis. 2. Grammar. Constructed by using an auxiliary word rather than an inflected form; for example, the phrases the word of his father and his father did say are periphrastic, while his father's word and his father said are inflected. —**per·i·phras·ti·cal·ly** adv.

pe·rip·ter·al (pə-ríptərəl, pe-) adj. Architecture. Built with a row of columns on all sides. [Latin peripteros, from Greek, "flying around" : peri-, PERI- + pteron, wing.]

pe·rique (pə-réek) n. A strongly flavoured, black tobacco grown in Louisiana and used in various blends. [Louisiana French, said to be after Périque, nickname of Pierre Chenet, planter who introduced tobacco-growing in Louisiana.]

per·i·sarc (pérri-saark) n. Zoology. A horny external covering that encloses the colonies of certain hydrozoans. [PERI- + Greek sarx (stem sark-), flesh.] —**per·i·sar·cal** (-sárk'l), **per·i·sar·cous** adj.

per·i·scope (pérri-skōp) n. Any of various optical instruments that contain reflecting elements, such as mirrors and prisms, to permit observation from a position displaced from a direct line of sight, as from a submerged submarine or a trench below ground level. [PERI- + -SCOPE.] —**per·i·scop·ic** (-skóppik) adj.

per·ish (pérrish) v. **-ished, -ishing, -ishes.** —intr. 1. To die, especially in a violent or untimely manner. 2. To pass from existence; die out or away. 3. To decay; rot away. —tr. To destroy or rot away; cause to perish. [Middle English perisshen, from Old French perir (present stem periss-), from Latin perīre, to pass away : per-, away + īre, to go.]

per·ish·a·ble (pérrishə-b'l) adj. Liable to perish, decay, or spoil.
~n. Plural. Perishable foodstuffs. —**per·ish·a·bil·i·ty** (-bílləti), **per·ish·a·ble·ness** n. —**per·ish·a·bly** adv.

per·ished (pérrisht) adj. Informal. 1. Debilitated or extremely distressed because of cold. 2. Feeling extremely cold; frozen.

per·ish·er (pérrishər) n. British Informal. An annoying young person or child; a rascal.

per·ish·ing (pérrishing) adj. Informal. 1. Unpleasantly or distressingly cold; freezing: It's perishing outside. 2. Damned; confounded: Stop that perishing dog barking.
~adv. Informal. Very. Used as an intensive. —**per·ish·ing·ly** adv.

per·i·sperm (pérri-sperm) n. Botany. The nutritive tissue in the seeds of many plants that is derived from the nucellus and deposited outside the embryo sac.

pe·ris·so·dac·tyl (pə-ríssō-dák-til, -t'l) adj. Zoology. 1. Having an odd number of toes. 2. Of or designating certain hoofed mammals,

---

periscope

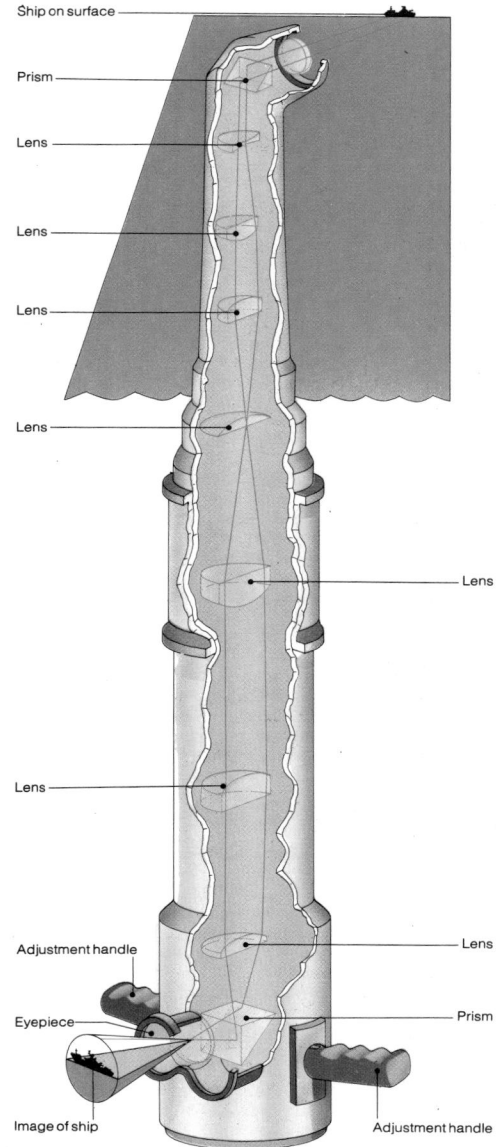

BENDING THE LINE OF SIGHT
How prisms and mirrors can move an image

The simplest form of periscope consists of two mirrors angled at 45° and placed with one higher than the other so that an image is reflected from the top of the instrument down to the observer at its base. This simple device was much used for observation in the trenches during World War I, when sniper fire made it dangerous for a man to poke his head out. It is often used by people in crowds to see a procession, for example, over the heads of those in front.

More sophisticated periscopes, such as those used in submarines, work on the same basic principle but use prisms instead of mirrors. When set at a certain angle, a right-angled prism reflects a beam of light through 90° and allows only about 4 per cent of the light to be lost, so the intensity of the image is retained even when the periscope is very long. Submarine periscopes incorporate several lenses to increase magnification and alter the field of view.

Not all periscopes are designed to give a simple vertical shift to the image. For example, those used in armoured cars may also shift the image horizontally. Different prisms can be used to move the image through any angle.

Ship on surface

Prism

Lens

Lens

Lens

Lens

Lens

Lens

Lens

Lens

Adjustment handle

Eyepiece

Prism

Image of ship

Adjustment handle

ADJUSTABLE LENSES Handles at the base of a submarine periscope enable the observer to adjust the lenses in order to obtain a magnified image and a wider field of vision.

---

such as horses and rhinoceroses, of the order Perissodactyla, that have an odd number of toes.

~n. *Zoology*. A hoofed mammal of this order. [Greek *perissodaktulos* : *perissos*, excessive, uneven, from *peri-*, PERI- (around, hence beyond) + *daktulos*, DACTYL.] —**pe·ris·so·dac·ty·lous** *adj.*

per·i·stal·sis (pérri-stál-siss ‖ -stáwl-) *n., pl.* **-ses** (-seez). Involuntary wavelike muscular contractions that propel contained matter along tubular organs, as in the alimentary canal. [New Latin, from *peristalticus*, of peristalsis, from Greek *peristaltikos*, compressing around, from *peristulon*, *peristulos*, surrounded by columns : *peri-*, PERI- + *stellein*, to place, set.] —**per·i·stal·tic** *adj.*

per·i·stome (pérri-stóm) *n.* **1.** *Botany*. A circular row of toothlike appendages surrounding the mouth of a moss capsule. **2.** *Zoology*. The area around the mouth in certain invertebrates. [New Latin *peristoma* : PERI- + -STOME.] —**per·i·sto·mal** (-stóm'l), **per·i·sto·mi·al** (-stómi-əl) *adj.*

per·i·style (pérri-stīl) *n. Architecture.* **1.** A series of columns surrounding a temple or other structure, or enclosing a court. **2.** A court enclosed by such columns. [French *péristyle*, from Latin *peristylum*, from Greek *peristulon*, from *peristulos*, surrounded by columns : *peri-*, PERI- + *stulos*, pillar.] —**per·i·sty·lar** (-stílər) *adj.*

per·i·the·ci·um (pérri-thée-si-əm, -shi-) *n., pl.* **-cia** (-si-ə). A flask-shaped fruiting body in certain fungi, containing ascospores. [New Latin : PERI- + Greek *thēkion*, diminutive of *thēkē*, a case, chest.]

per·i·to·ne·um (pérri-tə-née-əm, -tō-) *n., pl.* **-nea** (-née-ə). The membrane lining the walls of the abdominal cavity and covering the viscera. [Late Latin *peritonēum*, from Greek *peritonaion*, neuter of *peritonaios*, stretched across, from *peritonos*, stretched around or over : *peri-*, PERI- + *tenein*, to stretch.] —**per·i·to·ne·al** *adj.*

per·i·to·ni·tis (pérri-tə-nítiss, -tō-) *n.* Inflammation of the peritoneum. [New Latin : PERITON(EUM) + -ITIS.]

pe·rit·ri·cha (pə-ríttrikə) *pl.n. Singular* **per·i·trich** (pérri-trik). **1.** Bell-shaped or tubular microorganisms of the order Peritrichida, characterised by a wide oral opening surrounded by cilia. **2.** Bacteria entirely covered with cilia. [New Latin : PERI- + Greek *thrix* (stem *trikh-*), hair.] —**pe·rit·ri·chous** *adj.*

per·i·wig (pérri-wig) *n.* A wig or peruke. [Earlier *perwyke*, from Old French *perruque*, PERUKE.]

per·i·win·kle[1] (pérri-wingk'l) *n.* A winkle (see). [16th century : origin obscure.]

periwinkle[2] *n.* **1.** Any of several trailing, evergreen plants of the genus *Vinca*; especially, *V. minor*, having blue flowers. Also *U.S.* "myrtle". **2.** Light purplish-blue. Also called "periwinkle blue". [Variant (influenced by PERIWINKLE, snail) of Middle English *pervenke*, from Old French *pervenche*, from Latin *pervinca*, shortening of *vincapervinca*†.] —**per·i·win·kle** *adj.*

per·jure (pérjər) *tr.v.* **-jured, -juring, -jures.** To render (oneself) guilty of perjury by deliberately giving false evidence or testifying falsely under oath. [Middle English *perjuren*, from Old French *perjurer*, from Latin *perjūrāre* : *per-* (destruction) + *jūrāre*, to swear.] —**per·jur·er** *n.*

per·ju·ry (pérjəri) *n., pl.* **-ries. 1.** *Law.* The deliberate, wilful giving of false, misleading, or incomplete evidence or testimony by a witness under oath in a judicial proceeding, whether given in a court or by affidavit. **2.** Any violation of an oath or promise. [Middle English *perjurie*, from Anglo-French *parjurie*, from Latin *perjūrium*, from *perjūrus*, perjured, from *perjūrāre*, to PERJURE.] —**per·ju·ri·ous** (pər-jóor-i-əss, per-) *adj.* —**per·ju·ri·ous·ly** *adv.*

perk[1] (perk) *v.* **perked, perking, perks.** —*intr.* **1.** To stick up or jut out jauntily, as a dog's ears might. Often used with *up*. **2.** To regain one's animation or good spirits. Used with *up*. —*tr.* **1.** To raise smartly and quickly. Often used with *up*. **2.** To make vigorous and lively again; cheer. Often used with *up*. **3.** To make more attractive, trim, or smart in appearance. Often used with *up*. [Middle English *perken*, perhaps from Anglo-French *perquer*, to perch, from *perque*, rod, from Latin *pertica*. See **perch** (roost).]

perk[2] *n.* **1.** A payment or profit received in addition to a regular wage or salary, especially one received regularly or expected as one's due. **2.** Any extra benefit received through one's employment. Also formally called "perquisite". —See Synonyms at **right**. [Shortened from PERQUISITE.]

perk[3] *v.* **perked, perking, perks.** —*intr.* To percolate. Used of coffee. —*tr.* To cause (coffee) to percolate. [Shortened from PERCOLATE.]

Per·kin's mauve (pérkinz) *n.* A dye, **mauveine** (see). [After Sir William *Perkin* (1838–1907), British chemist who developed it.]

perk·y (pérki) *adj.* **-ier, -iest. 1.** Cheerful and brisk; jaunty. **2.** Assertive and confident. —**perk·i·ly** *adv.* —**perk·i·ness** *n.*

per·lite, pearlite (pérlīt) *n.* A natural volcanic glass similar to obsidian but having distinctive concentric cracks and a relatively high water content. In a fluffy heat-expanded form it is used as a lightweight aggregate in plaster and concrete and in thermal and acoustic insulation. [French. See **pearl**, **-ite**.] —**per·lit·ic** (pər-líttik) *adj.*

perm[1] (perm) *n.* **1.** A treatment producing long-lasting artificial waves in the hair through any of various processes, especially by applying chemicals to the hair while wet, winding it on rollers, and drying with heat. **2.** The hairstyle produced by such treatment. See **cold wave**. Also called "permanent wave", *U.S.* "permanent".

~*tr.v.* **permed, perming, perms.** To give a perm to. [Shortened from PERMANENT WAVE.]

perm[2] *tr.v.* **permed, perming, perms.** To make a selection and com-

bination of (matches and their results) on a football-pools' coupon; make a permutation of.

~*n.* A **permutation** (see), on a football-pools' coupon. [Shortened from PERMUTATION.]

Perm (perm ‖ *Russian* pyairm). City and region of the R.S.F.S.R., U.S.S.R., situated on the river Kama.

perm. permanent.

per·ma·frost (pérmə-frost ‖ -frawst) *n.* Permanently frozen, rock, soil, and subsoil continuous in polar regions and occurring locally in perennially frigid areas. [PERMA(NENT) + FROST.]

Perm·al·loy (perm-ál-oy ‖ pérmə-loy) *n.* A trademark for any of several alloys of nickel and iron, often with small amounts of other elements, having exceptionally high magnetic permeability.

per·ma·nence (pérmənənss) *n.* The condition or quality of being permanent.

per·ma·nen·cy (pérmənən-si) *n., pl.* **-cies. 1.** Permanence. **2.** Someone or something permanent.

per·ma·nent (pérmənənt) *adj. Abbr.* **perm. 1.** Fixed and changeless; lasting or meant to last indefinitely. **2. a.** Not expected to change for a long or indefinite period: *my permanent address.* **b.** *Often capital* **P.** Designating a high-ranking member of a government department whose position is not affected by changes in the government: *Permanent Secretary to the Treasury.*

~*n. U.S.* A perm for the hair. [Middle English, from Old French, from Latin *permanēns* (stem *permanent-*), present participle of *permanēre*, to remain throughout : *per-*, throughout + *manēre*, to remain.] —**per·ma·nent·ly** *adv.*

permanent magnet *n.* A material that retains induced magnetic properties after it is removed from a magnetic field; a ferromagnet.

Permanent Under Secretary *n.* An Under Secretary (see).

permanent wave *n.* A hairstyle or hair treatment, a **perm** (see).

permanent way *n. British.* The rails, sleepers, and roadbed of a railway track.

per·man·ga·nate (pər-máng-gə-nayt, -nit, -nət) *n.* Any of the salts of permanganic acid, all of which are strong oxidising agents. [PERMANGAN(IC ACID) + -ATE.]

permanganate of potash *n.* Potassium permanganate (see).

per·man·gan·ic acid (pérmang-gánnik) *n.* An unstable inorganic acid, $HMnO_4$, existing as a strongly oxidising, aqueous solution.

per·me·a·bil·i·ty (pérmi-ə-bílləti) *n.* **1.** The property or condition of being permeable. **2.** *Physics.* **Magnetic permeability** (see). **3.** The rate of diffusion of a pressurised gas through a porous material.

per·me·a·ble (pérmi-əb'l) *adj.* Capable of being permeated. [Late Latin *permeābilis*, from Latin *permeāre*, to PERMEATE.] —**per·me·a·bly** *adv.*

per·me·ance (pérmi-ənss) *n.* **1.** The act of permeating. **2.** A measure of the ability of a magnetic circuit to conduct magnetic flux; the reciprocal of **reluctance** (see). [Latin *permeāns*, present participle of *permeāre*, to PERMEATE.]

per·me·ate (pérmi-ayt) *v.* **-ated, -ating, -ates.** —*tr.* **1.** To spread or flow throughout; pervade. **2.** To pass through the openings or interstices of: *liquid permeating a membrane.* —*intr.* To spread; penetrate; diffuse. [Latin *permeāre* : *per-*, through + *meāre*, to go, pass.] —**per·me·ant** (-ənt), **per·me·a·tive** (-ətiv, -aytiv) *adj.* —**per·me·a·tion** (-áysh'n) *n.*

per men·sem (mén-sem) *adv. Latin.* By the month or for each month.

Per·mi·an (pérmi-ən) *adj.* Of, belonging to, or designating the geological time, system of rocks, and sedimentary deposits of the sixth and last period of the Palaeozoic era.

~*n. Geology.* The Permian period. Preceded by *the*. [After *Perm*, former Russian province (see PERM), where the rock strata were first identified.]

per mill, per mil (mil) *adv.* By the thousand; per thousand. [*mill, mil*, from Latin *mille*, a thousand.]

per·mis·si·ble (pər-míssə-b'l) *adj.* That can be permitted, tolerated, or accepted; allowable: *maximum permissible dosage.* —**per·mis·si·bil·i·ty** (-bílləti), **per·mis·si·ble·ness** *n.* —**per·mis·si·bly** *adv.*

per·mis·sion (pər-mísh'n) *n.* **1.** The act of permitting. **2.** Consent, especially formal consent; leave; authorisation. [Middle English, from Old French, from Latin *permissiō* (stem *permissiōn-*), from *permittere* (past participle *permissus*), to PERMIT.]

per·mis·sive (pər-míssiv) *adj.* **1.** Granting permission; allowing. **2.** Permitting discretion, as distinct from prescriptive. **3.** Lenient, tolerant, or liberal, especially when based on or reflecting a belief that there should be as few restraints as possible in matters of sexual morality. **4.** *Archaic.* Not forbidden; permitted. —**per·mis·sive·ly** *adv.* —**per·mis·sive·ness** *n.*

per·mit (pər-mít) *v.* **-mitted, -mitting, -mits.** —*tr.* **1.** To allow (something); consent to; tolerate. **2.** To give permission to; authorise. **3. a.** To afford opportunity for; make possible. **b.** To allow as possible; admit of. —*intr.* To afford opportunity; allow. —**permit of.** To allow as a possibility; permit.

~*n.* (pérmit ‖ *U.S. also* pər-mít). **1.** Permission; leave. **2.** A document or certificate giving permission to do something; a licence; a warrant. [Latin *permittere* : *per-*, through + *mittere*, to let go, send.] —**per·mit·ter** *n.*

Usage: *Permit* may be followed by *of* when it means "admit; be open to the possibility": *The wording permits (of) only one interpretation.* The use of this construction in the general sense of "allow" is considered nonstandard: the sentence *The law does not permit of their doing that* would in standard English be *The law does not permit their doing that* or *The law does not permit them to do that.*

per·mit·tiv·i·ty (pérmi-tívvəti) *n., pl.* **-ties.** *Physics.* **1.** A measure of the ability of a medium to transmit an electric field, expressed as the ratio of its electric displacement to the intensity of the field at some point. Also called "absolute permittivity". See **electric constant. 2.** The ratio of electric flux density produced by an electric field in a medium to that produced in a vacuum by the same field. Also called "relative permittivity", "dielectric constant". [From PERMIT.]

per·mu·ta·tion (pérmew-táysh'n) *n.* **1.** A complete change; a transformation. **2.** The act of changing the arrangement or order of a given set of objects in a group. **3.** *Mathematics.* An ordered arrangement of all or some of the elements of a set. **4.** Broadly, any of the variations possible in a given situation: *permutations of our original plan.* **5.** A particular selection and combination of matches and their results, made on a football-pools' coupon. In this sense, also called "perm". **—per·mu·ta·tion·al** *adj.*

per·mute (pər-méwt) *tr.v.* **-muted, -muting, -mutes. 1.** To change the order of. **2.** *Mathematics.* To subject to permutation. [Middle English *permuten,* from Old French *permuter,* from Latin *permūtāre* : *per-,* completely + *mūtāre,* to change.] **—per·mut·a·ble** *adj.*

per·ni·cious (pər-níshəss) *adj.* **1. a.** Tending to cause death or serious injury; deadly. **b.** Causing great harm; destructive; ruinous. **2.** Causing moral injury; evil: *a pernicious philosophy.* [Latin *perniciōsus,* from *perniciēs,* destruction : *per-,* completely + *nex* (stem *nec-*), death.] **—per·ni·cious·ly** *adv.* **—per·ni·cious·ness** *n.*

pernicious anaemia *n.* A severe anaemia associated with failure to absorb vitamin B_{12}.

per·nick·e·ty (pər-níckəti) *adj.* Also *U.S.* **per·snick·e·ty** (-sníckəti) *Informal.* **1.** Fussy; very strict in matters of detail. **2.** Involving or showing minute attention to detail. [19th century (Scottish) : origin obscure.]

Pe·rón (pe-rón), **Juan (Domingo)** (1895–1974). Argentinian soldier and politician, president (1946–55, 1973–74). As vice-president (1944) in a right-wing military government he developed a personal following among urban workers. Imprisoned by democrats in 1945, he was released following street demonstrations in his favour, and was elected president in 1946. While restricting civil liberties he carried out social reforms. His second wife, (María) Eva (Duarte de) Perón (1919–52), known as Evita, won popularity for her charitable works. Perón was overthrown by the army in 1955, but returned from exile to become president again in 1973. He was succeeded in office by his third wife, María Estela (Martínez de) Perón (1931–), known as Isabelita, who was ousted by the army in 1976.

per·o·ne·al (pérrə-née-əl) *adj. Anatomy.* Of or pertaining to the fibula or to the outer portion of the leg. [New Latin *peroneus,* of the fibula, from *perone,* fibula, from Greek *peronē,* "pin, buckle".]

per·o·rate (pérrə-rayt) *intr.v.* **-rated, -rating, -rates. 1.** To make a peroration. **2.** To speak at great length, often in an inflated, pompous manner; declaim. [Latin *perōrāre,* to harangue at length : *per-,* thoroughly, to the end + *ōrāre,* to speak.]

per·o·ra·tion (pérrə-ráysh'n) *n.* The concluding part of a speech or written discourse, usually consisting of a formal recapitulation.

per·ox·i·dase (pə-róksi-dayss, -dayz) *n.* An enzyme found in most plant cells and some animal cells that catalyses peroxide oxidation reactions. [PEROXID(E) + -ASE.]

per·ox·ide (pə-rók-sīd) *n. Chemistry.* **1. Hydrogen peroxide** (see). **2.** Any compound containing oxygen that yields hydrogen peroxide with an acid, such as sodium peroxide, Na_2O_2.
~ *tr.v.* **peroxided, -iding, -ides. 1.** To treat with peroxide. **2.** To bleach (hair) with hydrogen peroxide.

peroxide blonde *n.* A person, usually a woman, having hair dyed or bleached with or as if with hydrogen peroxide.

peroxy-, peroxo- *comb. form.* Indicates the presence of the peroxide group in a chemical compound; for example, **peroxysulphuric acid.**

per·oxy·sul·phu·ric acid (pə-róksi-sul-féwr-ik) *n.* A white unstable crystalline acid, H_2SO_5, used as an oxidising agent. Also called "Caro's acid", "persulphuric acid".

per·pend (pər-pénd) *v.* **-pended, -pending, -pends.** *Archaic.* —*tr.* To wonder about; ponder. —*intr.* To wonder; reflect. [Latin *perpendere,* to consider carefully : *per-,* thoroughly + *pendere,* to consider, weigh.]

per·pen·dic·u·lar (pér-pən-díckew-lər ‖ -pen-) *adj.* **1.** *Mathematics.* Intersecting at or forming right angles. **2.** At right angles to the horizontal; vertical. **3.** Vertical or very steep; precipitous, as a cliff face or mountainside might be. **4.** *Often capital* **P.** Designating a style of English Gothic architecture of the 14th–16th centuries, characterised by emphasis of the vertical element and especially by vertical lines in window tracery. —See Synonyms at **vertical.**
~ *n.* **1.** A line or plane perpendicular to a given line or plane. **2.** A perpendicular position. **3.** A device, such as a plumb line, used in marking the vertical from a given point. **4.** A vertical or nearly vertical line or plane. [Middle English *perpendiculer,* from Old French, from Latin *perpendiculārius,* from *perpendiculum,* plumb line : *per-,* thoroughly + *pendēre,* to hang + *-culum,* instrumental suffix.] **—per·pen·dic·u·lar·i·ty** (-lárrəti) *n.*

per·pe·trate (pér-pi-trayt, -pə-) *tr.v.* **-trated, -trating, -trates. 1.** To be guilty of; commit: *perpetrate a crime.* **2.** To carry out; perform (an act, especially one considered outrageous or bad): *perpetrate a practical joke.* [Latin *perpetrāre,* to accomplish : *per-,* completely + *patrāre,* to do, "perform in the capacity of a father", from *pater,* father.] **—per·pe·tra·tion** (-tráysh'n) *n.* **—per·pe·tra·tor** (-ər) *n.*

---

perpendicular

SOARING TO THE HEAVENS
Tall towers that marked the climax of English Gothic architecture

Most medieval churches in Britain – those built between the late 12th century and early 16th – were designed in one of three distinct styles known collectively as Gothic. Perpendicular, the last of these styles to be developed, began in about 1380 and dominated English architecture for more than 200 years.

During this period, builders turned away from the narrow arches of earlier Gothic designs. With the broader arches were larger windows with rectilinear tracery, slender columns, and tall, majestic towers. The effect was to make churches seem to be reaching towards heaven, and it is this vertical emphasis that gives the Perpendicular style its name. Several outstanding examples of the style, also noted for its fan vaulting, still survive. Among them are King's College Chapel in Cambridge (1446–1515) and the Henry VII Chapel in Westminster Abbey (1503–12).

POINTING THE WAY *Strong vertical lines in the stonework and a huge stained-glass window – both typical of Perpendicular architecture – dominate the 14th-century east front of York Minster.*

WHEELS WITHIN WHEELS *Decorative ribs radiate from supporting columns to form a complex cluster of fan vaults with pendants in the Henry VII Chapel in Westminster Abbey.*

per·pet·u·al (pər-péchoo-əl, -péttew-) *adj.* **1.** Lasting for eternity. **2.** Lasting for an indefinitely long time. **3.** Having effect or having tenure for an unlimited duration or for a complete lifetime: *a treaty of perpetual friendship.* **4.** Ceaselessly repeated or continuing without interruption: *perpetual nagging.* **5.** Flowering throughout the growing season. —See Synonyms at **continual.**
∼*n.* A plant that flowers throughout the growing season. [Middle English *perpetuel,* from Old French, from Latin *perpetuālis,* from *perpetuus,* continuous, permanent, from *perpes* (stem *perpet-*), throughout, uninterrupted : *per-,* thoroughly + *petere,* to go towards.] **—per·pet·u·al·ly** *adv.* **—per·pet·u·al·ness** *n.*

perpetual calendar *n.* A chart or mechanical device that indicates the day of the week corresponding to any given date over a period of many years.

perpetual motion *n.* The hypothetical continuous and perpetual operation of an isolated mechanical device or other closed system, without loss of energy and without an external energy source.

per·pet·u·ate (pər-péchoo-ayt, -péttew-) *tr.v.* **-ated, -ating, -ates.** **1.** To make perpetual. **2.** To prolong the existence or memory of: *a myth perpetuated by repetition.* [Latin *perpetuāre,* from *perpetuus,* PERPETUAL.] **—per·pet·u·a·tion** (-áysh'n), **per·pet·u·ance** (-ənss) *n.* **—per·pet·u·a·tor** (-aytər) *n.*

per·pe·tu·i·ty (pér-pə-téw-əti || -tóo-) *n., pl.* **-ties.** **1.** The quality, state, or condition of being perpetual: *"The perpetuity of the Church was an article of faith."* (Morris West). **2.** Time without end; eternity. **3.** *Law.* **a.** The condition of an estate that is limited so as to be inalienable either perpetually or longer than the period determined by law. **b.** An estate so limited. **4.** *Finance.* An annuity payable indefinitely. **—in perpetuity.** For ever.

Per·pi·gnan (pàir-peen-yoN, pér-, -yóN). Town in southern France, capital of Pyrénées-Orientales département. Situated on the river Têt, it is a tourist and agricultural centre.

per·plex (pər-pléks) *tr.v.* **-plexed, -plexing, -plexes.** **1.** To fill with uncertainty or bewilderment; confuse or puzzle. **2.** To make confusedly intricate; complicate: *Her explanation only perplexed the matter even more.* —See Synonyms at **puzzle.** [From obsolete adjective *perplex,* involved, perplexed, from Latin *perplexus,* intricate : *per-,* thoroughly + *plectere* (past participle *plexus*), to weave, entwine.] **—per·plex·ed·ly** (-pléksid-li, -plékst-) *adv.*

per·plex·i·ty (pər-pléksəti) *n., pl.* **-ties.** **1.** The state or condition of being perplexed or puzzled; bewilderment. **2.** The state or condition of being intricate or complicated: *the perplexity of life in the 20th century.* **3.** Something that perplexes.

per pro·cu·ra·ti·o·nem (prōkewr-áyshi-ōnem, próckewr-, -àati-) *prep. Abbr.* **per pro, per proc., p.p.** *Latin.* On behalf of.

per·qui·site (pérkwizit) *n.* **1.** *Formal.* A **perk** *(see).* **2.** A tip; a gratuity. **3.** Something claimed as an exclusive right: *the perquisite of the upper classes.* —See Synonyms at **right.** [Middle English, from Medieval Latin *perquīsītum,* acquisition, perquisite, from the past participle of Latin *perquīrere,* to search for : *per-,* thoroughly + *quaerere,* to seek.]

Per·rault (pérrō, pe-rṓ), **Charles** (1628–1703). French writer. His *Tales of Mother Goose* (*c.* 1697) includes Tom Thumb, Puss in Boots, and Sleeping Beauty.

per·ron (pérrən) *n.* **1.** A platform at the entrance of a large building or a church. **2.** A flight of steps leading to such a platform. [Middle English, from Old French, from Vulgar Latin *petro* (stem *petron-*) (unattested), augmentative of *petra,* stone.]

per·ry (pérri) *n., pl.* **-ries.** A fermented alcoholic beverage made from pears. [Middle English *pereye,* from Old French *pere,* from Vulgar Latin *pirātum* (unattested), from Latin *pirum,* PEAR.]

Per·ry (pérri), **Fred(erick John)** (1909–). British tennis player. He won the Wimbledon men's singles title in three consecutive years (1934–36), a record only surpassed by Björn **Borg.**

Pers. Persia; Persian.

per·salt (pér-sawlt || -solt) *n.* A salt of a peracid.

per se (sáy, sée) *adv.* In or by itself; as such; intrinsically. [Latin *per sē* : *per,* by, PER + *sē* (accusative), self.]

per·se·cute (pér-si-kewt) *tr.v.* **-cuted, -cuting, -cutes.** **1.** To oppress or harass with ill-treatment; especially, to subject to severe penalties because of political or religious dissent. **2.** To annoy persistently; bother. [Middle English, from Old French *persecuter,* back-formation from *persecuteur,* pursuer, from Late Latin *persecutor,* from Latin *persequī* (past participle *persecūtus*), to pursue : *per-,* throughout, to the end + *sequī,* to follow.] **—per·se·cu·tive, per·se·cu·to·ry** (-kewtəri, -kéwtəri || *U.S. also* -kew-tawri, -tōri) *adj.* **—per·se·cu·tor** (-kewtər) *n.*

per·se·cu·tion (pér-si-kéwsh'n) *n.* **1.** The act or practice of persecuting. **2.** The state or condition of being persecuted. **3.** A period during which people are persecuted. **—per·se·cu·tion·al** *adj.*

persecution complex *n.* A psychological delusion that other people feel hostility towards one or are attempting to victimise one.

Per·se·id (pér-si-id) *n., pl.* **-ids** or **Per·se·i·des** (pər-sée-i-deez, per-). *Astronomy.* Any of a shower of meteors that appears to originate in the vicinity of the constellation Perseus during August. [New Latin *Perseïdes,* plural of *Perseis,* daughter of PERSEUS.]

Per·seph·o·ne (per-séffəni, pər-). *Greek Mythology.* The wife of Hades and queen of the underworld; identified with Proserpina.

Per·se·us[1] (pér-sewss || -si-əss, -sooss). *Greek Mythology.* The son of Zeus and Danae who slew Medusa and rescued Andromeda.

Perseus[2] *n.* A constellation in the Northern Hemisphere near Andromeda and Auriga.

per·se·ver·ance (pér-si-véer-ənss) *n.* **1.** The holding to a course of action, belief, or purpose without giving way; steadfastness. **2.** The Calvinistic doctrine that those who have been chosen by God will continue in a state of grace to the end and will finally be saved.
Synonyms: *perseverance, persistence, tenacity, steadfastness.*

per·sev·er·a·tion (pər-sévvə-ráysh'n) *n. Psychology.* **1.** Continued or repetitive activity or actions; specifically: **a.** The uncontrollable repetition of a word, phrase, or gesture. **b.** The spontaneous recurrence of a thought, image, phrase, or tune in the mind. **2.** The retention in new and inappropriate circumstances of a form of behaviour or a working pattern from other circumstances; broadly, unadaptability.

per·se·vere (pér-si-véer) *intr.v.* **-vered, -vering, -veres.** To persist in or remain constant to a purpose, idea, or task in the face of obstacles or discouragement. [Middle English *perseveren,* from Old French *perseverer,* from Latin *persevērāre,* from *persevērus,* very serious : *per-* (intensifier) + *sevērus,* serious, severe.] **—per·se·ver·ing·ly** *adv.*

Per·shing (pér-shing, -zhing), **John J(oseph)** (1860–1948). U.S. general. He commanded the U.S. Expeditionary Force sent to Europe in 1917, and later became U.S. chief of staff (1921–24).

Persia. *Abbr.* **Pers.** See **Iran.**

Per·sian (pér-sh'n || -zh'n) *adj. Abbr.* **Pers.** Of or pertaining to Persia or Iran, its people, languages, or culture.
∼*n.* **1.** A native or inhabitant of ancient or modern Persia or modern Iran. **2.** The Iranian language of the Persians, of the West Iranian group of Indo-European languages, in any of its several historical forms, Old Persian, Avestan, Pahlavi, Middle Persian, and modern Iranian.

Persian cat *n.* A domestic cat of a breed having long, silky fur.

Persian Gulf. See The **Gulf.**

Persian lamb *n.* **1.** The lamb of the karakul sheep of Asia. **2.** The glossy, tightly curled fur obtained from such a lamb, usually when it is three or four days old. In this sense, also called "caracul".

per·si·car·i·a (pér-si-kàir-i-ə) *n.* Any of various plants of the genus *Polygonum* having spikes of pink or white flowers. Common persicaria, *P. persicaria,* is also called "redshank". [New Latin, from Latin *persicum,* peach.]

per·si·flage (pér-si-flaazh, pàir-, -flaazh) *n.* **1.** A light, bantering style in writing or speaking. **2.** Idle, good-natured banter. [French, from *persifler,* to banter : *per-* (intensive), from Latin + *siffler,* to whistle, hiss, boo, from Vulgar Latin *sīfilāre* (unattested), from Latin *sībilāre.*]

per·sim·mon (per-símmən, pər-) *n.* **1.** Any of various chiefly tropical trees of the genus *Diospyros,* such as the Chinese persimmon *D. Kaki,* having orange-red fruit that is edible only when completely ripe. **2.** The fruit of any of these trees. [Of Algonquian origin; akin to Cree *pasiminan,* dried fruit, Delaware *pasīmēnan.*]

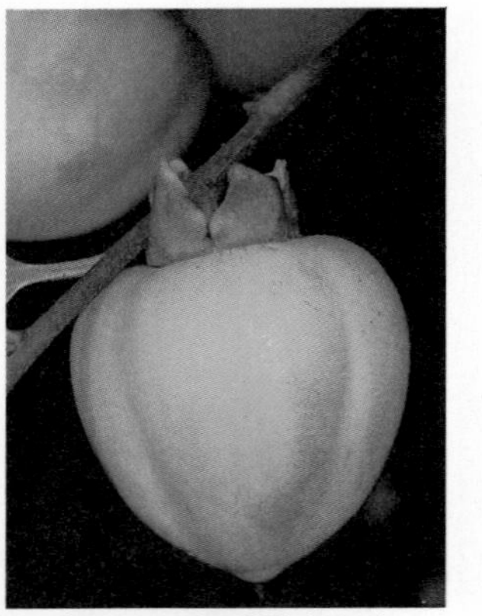

persimmon *The edible fruit of some trees of the genus* Diospyros. *Approximately the size of an orange, the fruit is grown extensively in China and Japan, and remains on the trees in autumn long after the leaves have fallen. It is extremely bitter until ripe.*

per·sist (pər-síst || -zíst) *intr.v.* **-sisted, -sisting, -sists.** **1.** To hold firmly and steadfastly to some purpose, state, belief, or course of action, despite obstacles, warnings, or setbacks. **2.** To continue in existence; last: *The pain persisted for several months.* [Latin *persistere* : *per-* (intensive) + *sistere,* to stand firm.]

per·sist·ence (pər-síss-tənss || -zíss-) *n.* Also **per·sis·ten·cy** (-tən-si). **1.** The act of persisting. **2.** The quality of being persistent; perseverance; tenacity. **3.** The continuance of an effect after the cause is removed: *persistence of vision.* —See Synonyms at **perseverance.**

per·sist·ent (pər-síss-tənt || -zíss-) *adj.* **1.** Refusing to give up or let go; persevering obstinately. **2.** Insistently repetitive or continuous. **3.** Continuing to exist, often in spite of action designed to prevent this; enduring: *a persistent rumour; a persistent superconducting current.* **4.** *Botany.* Lasting past maturity without falling off. Said of certain leaves or flowers. **5.** *Zoology.* **a.** Retained permanently, rather than disappearing in an early stage of development: *the persistent gills of axolotls.* **b.** Continuing to grow after the normal period of growth. [Back-formation from *persistence,* or PERSIST + -ENT.] **—per·sist·ent·ly** *adv.*

persnickety. *U.S.* Variant of **pernickety.**

per·son (pérss'n) *n. Abbr.* **per.** **1.** A living human being, especially as distinguished from an animal or thing. **2.** A human being considered without reference to his or her sex. See **-person.** **3.** The composite of characteristics that make up an individual personality. **4. a.** The living body of a human being. **b.** The body together with its clothing: *a pistol concealed about his person.* **c.** The penis. Used in the phrase *expose one's person.* **5.** *Archaic.* Guise; character. **6.** Physique and general appearance. **7.** *Law.* A human being or organisation with legal rights and duties. **8.** *Theology.* The separate individualities of the Father, Son, and Holy Spirit, as distinguished from the essence of the Godhead that unites them. **9.** *Grammar.* **a.** Any of three groups of pronoun forms with corresponding verb inflections that distinguish between the speaker (first person), the individual addressed (second person), and the individual or thing spoken of (third person). **b.** Any of the different forms or inflections expressing these distinctions. **—in person.** Physically present. —See Usage note at **people.** [Middle English *persone, person,* from Old French *persone,* from Latin *persōna,* mask (especially one worn by an actor), hence the character played by an actor, probably from Etruscan *phersu,* mask.]

-person *n. suffix.* Indicates are holding a specified position or doing a specified job, for example, **salesperson, chairperson.**
Usage: In recent years titles or job descriptions in which a person's sex is explicitly represented (such as *chairman, barman*) have attracted the criticism of those concerned with the status of women's rights in society. It is argued that such suffixes as *-man*

Persia

THE FIRST OF THE FABULOUS EMPIRES

Cyrus II founded Persia's lasting civilisation

Almost 3,000 years ago, Aryan tribes settled at the crossroads of Europe and Asia and formed one of the world's most durable civilisations. They called it Iran, land of the Aryans, but it is better known as Persia after the Parsua, the warrior tribe that turned it into the first of the great empires.

About 546 B.C., Cyrus II, King of Parsa, overthrew the other dominant tribe of Iran, the Medes, and conquered all the neighbouring lands from Assyria in the west to India in the east. He named this the Achaemenid empire after an ancestor, Achaemenes. The empire reached its peak under Darius I (521–486 B.C.) and his son, Xerxes (486–465 B.C.); during this time the Persians administered 20 provinces and narrowly failed to conquer Greece, when Xerxes was defeated at the sea battle of Salamis (480).

Since then, waves of invaders have poured across Persia's temperate plateau, only to have their culture absorbed into the Persian way of life. Alexander the Great conquered the empire (334 B.C.) and stayed there, seduced by its attractions. For 500 years (223 B.C. to A.D. 226), Parthians, fearsome horsemen from central Asia, ruled Persia, keeping the Romans at bay and preserving the country's personality.

The Sassanids (A.D. 246–642) restored Persian sovereignty, and built a network of roads and a capital at Ctesiphon. This brilliant dynasty fell to the most cataclysmic of all Persia's invaders, Bedouin Arabs who swarmed into the country, lured by its wealth. Although poorly armed, they were inspired by a new faith, Islam. They swept aside the Sassanids and grafted their religion, Shi'ism, onto the Persian culture. Under their dynamism, mathematics and science flowered and the Persian language, enriched by Arabic, became the literary idiom of Islam.

Alongside this renaissance, Persia retained its old customs and crafts. Goldsmiths and brass-beaters worked in the open bazaars; architecture and the decorative art of tile glazing reached new heights; carpet weaving flourished. There were later invasions. The Seljuks, a Turkish tribe (1037–1220); the Mongols (1220–1380); Tamerlane's Timurids (1380–1500); the Qajars, another Turkish tribe (1787–1925). None had the impact of the Islamic incursion. Modern Persia became known as Iran in 1935.

EMPIRE BUILDER *This ancient marble head of an Achaemenid king is most likely a bust of the Persian empire's first great ruler, Cyrus II. In 546 B.C., this warlord moulded the lands of Media and Parsa into a single kingdom, then swept out to bring most of Middle Eastern Asia under his heel.*

symbolise the biases of a male-dominated society and should be avoided where possible. Consequently the neutral *-person* form has come to be increasingly used, especially in American English.

per·so·na (pər-sŏ́-nə, per- ‖ -naa) *n., pl.* **-nae** (-nee, -nī) (for sense 1) or **-nas** (for senses 2, 3). **1.** A character in a dramatic or literary work. **2.** *Psychology.* The role that a person assumes in order to display his conscious intentions to himself and to others. Compare **anima. 3.** A person's public image. [Latin *persōna,* mask, PERSON.]

per·son·a·ble (pérss'n-əb'l) *adj.* Pleasing in appearance or personality; attractive. **—per·son·a·ble·ness** *n.*

per·son·age (pérss'n-ij) *n.* **1. a.** A person. **b.** A person of distinction. **2.** A historical or fictional character. [Middle English, from Old French, from *persone,* PERSON.]

per·so·na gra·ta (per-sŏ́-nə grá́a-tə, pər- ‖ *U.S. also* gráttə) *n., pl.* **personae gratae** (-nee -tee, -nī -tī). A person who is acceptable; especially, a diplomat who is fully acceptable to a foreign government. [Latin, "an acceptable person".] **—per·so·na gra·ta** *adj.*

per·son·al (pérss'n'l, -n'l) *adj.* **1.** Of or pertaining to a particular person; private; one's own: *personal affairs.* **2.** Characterised by or involving action on the part of a particular person, rather than of a representative: *a personal appearance; took a personal interest in the case.* **3.** Done to or for or directed towards a particular person: *a personal favour.* **4. a.** Concerning or referring to a person's individual character and his intimate affairs or interests, especially in a critical or hostile manner: *an uncalled-for, highly personal remark.* **b.** Making or tending to make personal remarks: *He always becomes personal in an argument.* **5.** Of or pertaining to the body or physical being: *personal cleanliness.* **6.** Pertaining to or having the nature of a person or self-conscious being: *a personal God.* **7.** *Law.* Pertaining to a person's movable property: *personal effects.* Compare **real. 8.** *Grammar.* Of or pertaining to grammatical person.

personal assistant *n. Abbr.* **P.A.** A person who assists an executive, usually in a secretarial capacity.

personal column *n.* The section of a newspaper or magazine containing brief classified advertisements, announcements, and especially private messages.

personal equation *n.* **1.** The tendency of a person, based on his individual characteristics, to subjectivity or error. **2.** The resulting variation in observation, judgment, and reasoning. **3.** The allowance or correction made for such variation.

per·son·al·ise, per·son·al·ize (pérss-nəl-īz, -'n'l-) *tr.v.* **-ised, -ising, -ises. 1.** To endow with personal or human qualities; personify. **2.** To have printed or marked with one's initials or name: *personalised stationery.* **3.** *U.S.* To take (remarks, for example) as applying to oneself, and usually as an insult.

per·son·al·ism (pérss-nəl-iz'm, -'n'l-) *n.* **1.** The quality of being characterised by purely personal modes of expression or behaviour; idiosyncrasy. **2.** *Philosophy.* Any of various trends of subjective idealism emphasising the importance of individuals, and regarding personality as the key to the interpretation of reality. **—per·son·al·ist** *n. & adj.* **—per·son·al·is·tic** (-istik) *adj.*

per·son·al·i·ty (pér-sə-nál-əti) *n., pl.* **-ties. 1.** The state or quality of being a person. **2. a.** The dynamic character, self, or psyche that constitutes and animates the individual person and makes his experience of life unique. **b.** A person as the embodiment of distinctive traits of mind and behaviour. **3.** The pattern of collective behavioural, temperamental, emotional, and mental traits of an individual. **4.** The distinctive qualities of an individual; especially, those distinguishing personal characteristics that make one socially appealing. **5. a.** A person of prominence or notoriety; a celebrity: *personalities in the news.* **b.** A person with an amusing or striking turn of mind; a character. **6.** *Plural.* Remarks of a personal nature, especially when offensive. **7.** The characteristics of a place or situation that give it a distinctive quality. **—See Synonyms at disposition.** [Middle English *personalite,* from Old French, from Late Latin *persōnālitās* (stem *persōnālitāt-*), from Latin *persōnālis,* personal, from *persōna,* PERSON.]

per·son·al·ly (pérss-nəli, -'n'l-i) *adv.* **1.** In person; without the intervention of another. **2.** As far as oneself is concerned: *Personally, I don't care how much it costs.* **3.** As a person: *I admire his skill but dislike him personally.* **4.** As applying to oneself, and usually as a criticism: *Don't take his remarks personally.*

personal pronoun *n.* A pronoun indicating speaker, person spoken to, or person or thing spoken about. The personal pronouns in the subject form in current English are: *I, we, you, he, she, it, they.*

personal property *n. Law.* Temporary or movable property as distinguished from real property.

per·son·al·ty (pérss-'n'l-ti, -nəl-) *n., pl.* **-ties.** *Law.* Personal property. [Anglo-French *personalté,* from Late Latin *persōnālitās,* PERSONALITY.]

persona non grata (*see* **persona grata;** non, nŏn) *n., pl.* **personae non gratae.** *Abbr.* **p.n.g.** A person who is not acceptable or welcome; especially, a diplomat not acceptable to a foreign government. [Latin, "unacceptable person".] **—persona non grata** *adj.*

per·son·ate¹ (pér-sə-nayt) *tr.v.* **-ated, -ating, -ates. 1.** To impersonate (a character); play the role or portray the part of. **2.** To endow with personal qualities; personify. **3.** *Law.* To assume the identity of (a person) with intent to deceive. [From PERSON.] **—per·son·a·tion** (-náysh'n) *n.* **—per·son·a·tive** (-nətiv, -naytiv) *adj.* **—per·son·a·tor** (-naytər) *n.*

per·son·ate² (pér-sə-nayt, -nət, -nit) *adj. Botany.* Designating a corolla having the upper lip arched and the lower lip protruding so that the throat is nearly closed. [Latin *persōnātus,* masked, from *persōna,* mask, PERSON.]

per·son·i·fi·ca·tion (pər-sónnifi-káysh'n, per-) *n.* **1.** The personifying of something abstract or inanimate, as: **a.** A rhetorical figure of speech in which objects or abstractions are endowed with human qualities or are represented as possessing human form, as in *Hunger sat shivering on the road* or *Flowers danced about the lawn.* **b.** The artistic representation of an abstract quality or idea as a person. **2.** A person or thing exemplifying to a remarkable degree a specified quality or idea; an embodiment: *a personification of bigotry.*

per·son·i·fy (pər-sónni-fī, per-) *tr.v.* **-fied, -fying, -fies. 1.** To think of or represent (an object or abstraction) as having personality or the qualities, thoughts, or movements of a living human being. **2.** To represent (an object or abstraction) by a human figure. **3.** To represent (an abstract quality or idea): *He personifies evil.* **4.** To be the embodiment or perfect example of: *She personified liberalism.* [French *personnifier,* from *personne,* person, from Old French *persone,* PERSON.] **—per·son·i·fi·er** *n.*

per·son·nel (pér-sə-nél) *n.* **1.** The body of persons employed by or active in an organisation, business, or service: *military personnel.* **2.** The administrative division of an organisation concerned with the recruitment and well-being of its personnel. [French, from Old French *personal,* personal, from Late Latin *personālis,* from Latin *persōna,* mask, PERSON.]

per·spec·tive (pər-spéktiv) *n.* **1.** Any of various techniques for representing three-dimensional objects and depth relationships on a two-dimensional surface. *Linear perspective* renders depth by using actual or suggested lines that intersect in the background to delimit relative size from background to foreground. *Aerial* or *atmospheric perspective* renders depth by changes of form, size, tone, and colour with recession of objects from the picture plane. **2.** Any picture representing objects in this way. **3.** A view or vista. **4.** The appearance of objects in depth as perceived by normal binocular vision. **5. a.** The relationship of aspects of a subject to one another and to a whole: *a perspective of history.* **b.** Any of such aspects. **6.** Subjective evaluation of the relative significance of facts or things; one's personal point of view. **7.** An objective and well-balanced evaluation or point of view: *get things in perspective.* [Middle English, from Medieval Latin *perspectīva (ars),* optics, from Late Latin *perspectīvus,* of a view, from Latin *perspicere* (past participle *perspectus*), to see through or into, inspect : *per-* (intensive) + *specere,* to look.] **—per·spec·tive** *adj.* **—per·spec·tive·ly** *adv.*

per·spec·tiv·ism (pər-spéktiv-iz'm) *n. Sometimes capital* **P.** *Philosophy.* The doctrine that reality can be accurately understood only from several different points of view.

Per·spex (pér-speks) *n.* A trademark for a clear acrylic plastic used as a substitute for glass.

per·spi·ca·cious (pér-spi-káyshəss) *adj.* Acutely discerning, perceptive, or understanding. [Latin *perspicāx,* clear-sighted, from *perspicere,* to see through. See **perspective.**] **—per·spi·ca·cious·ly** *adv.* **—per·spi·cac·i·ty** (pér-spi-kássəti), **per·spi·ca·cious·ness** *n.*

per·spi·cu·i·ty (pér-spi-kéw-əti) *n.* **1.** The quality of being perspicuous; clarity of expression or exposition. **2.** Perspicacity.

per·spic·u·ous (pər-spíckew-əss, per-) *adj.* Clearly expressed or

presented; easy to understand; lucid. [Latin *perspicuus,* from *per-spicere,* to see through. See **perspective.**] **—per·spic·u·ous·ly** *adv.* **—per·spic·u·ous·ness** *n.*

per·spi·ra·tion (pér-spə-ráysh'n, -spi-) *n.* **1.** The salty moisture excreted through the pores of the skin by the sweat glands; sweat. **2.** The act or process of perspiring. **—per·spir·a·to·ry** (-spír-ə-tri, -təri) *adj.*

per·spire (pər-spír) *v.* **-spired, -spiring, -spires.** *—intr.* To excrete perspiration through the pores of the skin. *—tr.* To expel through external pores; exude. [French *perspirer,* from Old French, from Latin *perspīrāre,* breathe through : *per-,* through + *spīrāre,* to blow, breathe.]

per·suade (pər-swáyd) *tr.v.* **-suaded, -suading, -suades. 1.** To induce (someone) to follow a course of action, as by argument, reasoning, or entreaty: *persuaded him to part with his money.* Sometimes used with *into: She would not be persuaded into leaving.* **2.** To make (someone or oneself) believe something; convince: *persuaded me that she was right.* [Latin *persuādēre* : *per-* (intensive) + *suādēre,* to persuade, urge.] **—per·suad·a·ble** *adj.* **—per·suad·er** *n.*

    Synonyms: *persuade, induce, prevail on, convince.*

per·sua·si·ble (pər-swáy-zəb'l, -səb'l) *adj.* That can be persuaded; persuadable. **—per·sua·si·bil·i·ty** (-zə-bílləti) *n.*

per·sua·sion (pər-swáyzh'n) *n.* **1. a.** The act of persuading or attempting to persuade. **b.** The state of being persuaded. **2.** The ability or power to persuade. **3.** A strong conviction or belief. **4. a.** A body of religious beliefs; a religion: *worshippers of various persuasions.* **b.** Those who adhere to such beliefs; a sect. **5.** Any grouping or faction. **—See Synonyms at opinion.** [Latin *persuāsiō* (stem *per-suāsiōn-*), from *persuādēre,* to PERSUADE.]

per·sua·sive (pər-swáy-siv, -ziv) *adj.* Tending or having the power to persuade: *a persuasive argument.* **—per·sua·sive·ly** *adv.* **—per·sua·sive·ness** *n.*

per·sul·phu·ric acid (pér-sul-féwr-ik) *n.* **Peroxysulphuric acid** *(see).*

pert (pert) *adj.* **perter, pertest. 1.** Impudently bold; saucy: *a pert little girl.* **2.** High-spirited; vivacious: *a pert old lady.* **3.** Jaunty: *a pert little hat.* [Middle English, short for Old French *apert,* straightforward, open, from Latin *aperīre* (past participle *apertus*), to open, and from Old French *aspert,* from Latin *expertus,* EXPERT.] **—pert·ly** *adv.* **—pert·ness** *n.*

pert. pertaining.

per·tain (pər-táyn, per-) *intr.v.* **-tained, -taining, -tains. 1.** To have reference; relate: *evidence pertaining to the accident.* **2.** To belong as an adjunct or accessory: *the farm and all the lands which pertain to it.* **3.** To be fitting or suitable. [Middle English *partenen,* from Old French *partenir,* from Latin *pertinēre,* to relate to, reach to : *per-,* to, thoroughly + *tenēre,* to hold.]

Perth¹ (perth). City in Tayside Region, east Scotland, situated on the river Tay. A former capital of Scotland, it is where James I was murdered (1437) and where John Knox preached against idolatry (1559).

Perth². Capital of Western Australia. Situated on the Swan river, it was founded in 1829, and expanded with the discovery of gold at

---

perspective

SPACE AND MOVEMENT IN PAINTING

Perspective creates the illusion of a three-dimensional space on a flat surface

It was not until the 15th century that artists learnt how to introduce the effect of space and movement into their work. The ancient Egyptians, for example, were more interested in telling a story or showing objects separately than in giving an appearance of depth and solidity. The study of perspective by Renaissance artists and mathematicians resulted in the discovery of a means of projecting the illusion of a three-dimensional space onto a two-dimensional surface.

    Pioneered by the Florentine architect Filippo Brunelleschi (1377–1446), the new discovery was quickly taken up by Italian painters like Masaccio (1401–28), Paolo Uccello (1397–1475), and Piero della Francesca (c. 1410–92), and by the German Albrecht Dürer (1471–1528). For 400 years linear perspective dominated European painting, and it was only in the late 19th century that artists turned to colour and shading to give the impression of depth.

    Linear perspective makes use of the observation that objects appear to get smaller, and parallel lines to converge, the closer they are to the horizon. The architect Leone Battista Alberti (1404–72) formulated mathematical rules to show how this effect could be created in art. On a flat surface like a painting, roofs, pavements and other horizontal lines converge. If continued, they would meet at a "vanishing point" on the horizon. Vertical shapes like trees and pillars diminish in size as they recede.

PERSPECTIVE IN ART *In this picture,* The Tribute Money, *painted by the Italian artist Masaccio about 1427, perspective is used to indicate relative distances between objects. The horizontal lines of the building on the right are drawn so that they would converge at a vanishing point on the horizon roughly at the centre of the picture. The figures and trees in the painting get gradually smaller in size the nearer they are to the horizon, giving the effect of distance.*

Kalgoorlie in the 1890s. It is now a commercial and cultural centre, and a market centre for agricultural products.

Perth·shire (pérth-shər, -sheer, -shĭr) *n.* Former county of Scotland, now in the Central and Tayside Regions. It is largely mountainous.

per·ti·na·cious (pérti-náyshəss) *adj.* **1.** Holding firmly or tenaciously to some purpose, belief, or opinion. **2.** Stubbornly or perversely persistent. —See Synonyms at **obstinate.** [Latin *pertināx* : *per-*, thoroughly, completely + *tenāx*, tenacious, from *tenēre*, to hold.] —**per·ti·na·cious·ly** *adv.* —**per·ti·na·cious·ness** *n.*

per·ti·nac·i·ty (pérti-nássəti) *n.* The quality or state of being pertinacious.

per·ti·nent (pérti-nənt) *adj.* Having a clear connection with a specific matter; apposite. See Synonyms at **relevant.** [Middle English, from Old French, from Latin *pertinēns* (stem *pertinent-*), present participle of *pertinēre*, to reach, concern, PERTAIN.] —**per·ti·nence** (-nənss), **per·ti·nen·cy** *n.* —**per·ti·nent·ly** *adv.*

per·turb (pər-túrb, per-) *tr.v.* **-turbed, -turbing, -turbs. 1.** To disturb greatly; make uneasy or anxious. **2.** To throw into great disorder. **3.** *Physics.* To cause perturbation to (an electron or celestial body). [Middle English *perturben,* from Old French *perturber,* from Latin *perturbāre* : *per-*, thoroughly + *turbāre*, to throw into disorder, from *turba*, confusion, probably from Greek *turbē*, disorder.]

per·tur·ba·tion (pér-tər-báysh'n, -tur-) *n.* **1. a.** The act of perturbing. **b.** The state or condition of being perturbed; agitation. **2.** Something that perturbs. **3.** *Physics.* Variation in a designated orbit, as of an electron or planet, resulting from the influence of one or more external bodies.

per·tus·sis (pər-tússiss) *n.* A disease, **whooping cough** *(see).* [New Latin : Latin *per-* (intensive) + *tussis,* a cough, TUSSIS.] —**per·tus·sal** *adj.*

Pe·ru (pə-róo). Republic of western South America. It rises from the Pacific Ocean to the Andes, 6 768 metres (22,205 feet) at Mt. Huascaran, descending again to the forested Amazon Basin. Conquered by the Spanish (1533), who destroyed its Inca civilisation, it regained its independence in 1824 and lost its southern territories to Chile in the War of the Pacific (1879–83). It has considerable mineral resources, including copper, iron, silver, zinc, and oil, while its agricultural products include maize, cotton, sugar, and coffee. Fishing and livestock are also important, and industrial production is expanding rapidly. Area, 1 285 216 square kilometres (496,225 square miles). Population, 18,600,000. Capital, Lima.

Pe·ru·gia (pə-róo-jə, pe-, -ji-ə). Capital of mountainous Perugia province, Umbria, central Italy. It is an agricultural trade centre and its products include furniture, glassware, and chocolates.

Pe·ru·gi·no (pérroo-jéenō), born Pietro di Cristoforo Vannucci (*c.* 1445–1523). Italian painter, born near Perugia (from which his name derives). His outstanding works include a fresco in the Sistine Chapel, *Christ giving the Keys to St. Peter.*

pe·ruke (pə-róok, pe-) *n.* A wig, especially one of a type worn by men in the 17th and 18th centuries; a periwig. [French *perruque,* from Italian *parrucca, perrucca†,* head of hair, wig.]

pe·rus·al (pə-róo'l, pe-) *n.* The act or an instance of perusing.

pe·ruse (pə-róoz, pe-) *tr.v.* **-rused, -rusing, -ruses. 1.** To read or examine, especially with great care. **2.** To read, especially in a casual or leisurely fashion. [Middle English *perusen,* to use up, perhaps from Anglo-Latin *perusāre* (unattested) : *per-* (intensive) + Vulgar Latin *usāre* (unattested), to USE.] —**pe·rus·er** *n.*

Pe·rutz (pə-róots), **Max Ferdinand** (1914–). British chemist, of Austrian birth. He used the technique of X-ray diffraction to discover the structure of haemoglobin. In 1962 he shared the Nobel prize for this work, with John Kendrew (born 1917).

Pe·ru·vi·an (pə-róovi-ən, pe-) *adj.* Of or pertaining to Peru, its inhabitants, or their culture.
~*n.* A native or inhabitant of Peru. [New Latin *Peruvia,* Peru + -AN.]

Peruvian bark *n.* A medicinal bark, **cinchona** *(see).*

perv (perv) *n.* **1.** *Slang.* A pervert. **2.** *Australian Slang.* A glance that is sexually inviting or suggestive.
~*intr.v.* **perved, perving, pervs.** *Australian Slang.* To glance or stare in a sexually suggestive manner. [Shortened from PERVERT.]

per·vade (pər-váyd, per-) *tr.v.* **-vaded, -vading, -vades.** To spread right through; be present throughout; permeate: *"A marvellous stillness pervaded the world."* (Joseph Conrad). [Latin *pervādere* : *per-*, through + *vādere,* to go.] —**per·va·sion** (-váyzh'n) *n.*

per·va·sive (pər-váy-siv, per- ‖ -ziv) *adj.* Having the quality of pervading or tendency to pervade. [Latin *pervāsus,* past participle of *pervādere,* to PERVADE.] —**per·va·sive·ly** *adv.* —**per·va·sive·ness** *n.*

per·verse (pər-vérss, per-) *adj.* **1. a.** Having a disposition to oppose and contradict. **b.** Characterised by or arising from such a disposition. **2.** Directed away from what is right or good; perverted. **3.** Obstinately persisting in an error or fault; wrongly self-willed or stubborn. **4.** Irritable; peevish. —See Synonyms at **contrary.** [Middle English *pervers,* from Old French, from Latin *pervertere* (past participle *perversus*), to PERVERT.] —**per·verse·ly** *adv.* —**per·verse·ness** *n.*

per·ver·sion (pər-vérsh'n, per- ‖ -vérzh'n) *n.* **1.** The act of perverting or the state of being perverted. **2.** A sexual practice or act considered abnormal. **3.** An incorrect interpretation or perverted form. —**per·ver·sive** (-vér-siv ‖ -ziv) *adj.*

per·ver·si·ty (pər-vérss-əti, per-) *n., pl.* **-ties. 1.** The quality or state of being perverse. **2.** An instance of being perverse.

per·vert (pər-vért, per-) *tr.v.* **-verted, -verting, -verts. 1. a.** To cause to turn from what is considered morally right; corrupt. **b.** To cause to deviate from what is natural or normal. **2.** To employ for a wrong or improper purpose; misuse. **3.** To interpret incorrectly; distort; misconstrue. **4.** To bring to a worse condition; debase.
~*n.* (pér-vert). One who practises sexual perversion. [Middle English *perverten,* from Old French *pervertir,* from Latin *pervertere,* to turn the wrong way, turn around : *per-*, completely + *vertere,* to turn.] —**per·vert·er** *n.* —**per·vert·i·ble** *adj.*

per·vert·ed (pər-vértid, per-) *adj.* **1.** Deviating greatly from what is considered proper and correct: *a perverted idea of justice.* **2.** Of, pertaining to, or practising sexual perversion. —**per·vert·ed·ly** *adv.*

per·vi·ous (pérvi-əss) *adj.* **1.** Allowing passage or entrance; permeable: *material pervious to water.* **2.** Open to arguments, ideas, or change. [Latin *pervius* : *per-*, through + *via,* way, road.] —**per·vi·ous·ly** *adv.* —**per·vi·ous·ness** *n.*

pes (payz, peez ‖ payss) *n., pl.* **pedes** (péd-eez, -ayz). *Biology.* A foot or footlike part, especially: **1.** The human foot. **2.** The corresponding part in other higher vertebrates. [New Latin, from Latin *pēs,* foot.]

Pe·sach, Pe·sah (páy-saakh) *n.* Passover *(see).* [Hebrew *pesaḥ,* a passing over, from *pāsaḥ,* to pass over.]

Pe·sca·ra (pess-káara) *n.* Seaport of Italy, capital of Pescara province. Situated on the Adriatic coast it is a resort.

pe·se·ta (pə-sáytə, pe-) *n. Abbr.* **p., pta. 1.** The basic monetary unit of Spain, equal to 100 centimos. **2.** A coin worth one peseta. [Spanish, diminutive of PESO.]

pe·se·wa (péssə-wə, -waa) *n., pl.* **pesewa** or **pesewas.** A monetary unit equal to $1/100$ of the cedi of Ghana.

Pe·sha·war (pə-sháa-wər, pe-, -sháw-). Strategic city in north Pakistan. Situated 18 kilometres (11 miles) from the eastern end of the Khyber Pass, it has for centuries been a major trading centre for central Asia.

pes·ky (péski) *adj.* **-kier, -kiest.** *Chiefly U.S. Informal.* Troublesome; annoying: *a pesky mosquito.* [Probably irregularly from PEST.] —**pes·ki·ly** *adv.* —**pes·ki·ness** *n.*

pe·so (páy-sō ‖ péssō) *n., pl.* **-sos.** *Abbr.* **p. 1. a.** The basic monetary unit of Argentina, Bolivia, Chile, Colombia, Cuba, the Dominican Republic, Mexico, and the Philippines, equal to 100 centavos. **b.** The basic monetary unit of Uruguay, equal to 100 centesimos. **2.** A coin or note worth one peso. [Spanish, "weight", from Latin *pēnsum,* from *pendere* (past participle *pēnsus*), to weigh.]

pes·sa·ry (péssəri) *n., pl.* **-ries.** *Medicine.* **1.** Any of various contraceptive or supportive devices placed and worn in the vagina. **2.** A medicated vaginal suppository. [Middle English *pessarie,* from Medieval Latin *pessārium,* from Late Latin *pessum, pessus,* from Greek *pessos,* oval stone for games.]

pes·si·mism (péssi-miz'm ‖ pézzi-) *n.* **1.** A tendency to take the gloomiest and least hopeful possible view of a situation. **2.** The doctrine or belief that this is the worst of all possible worlds and that all things ultimately tend towards evil. **3.** The doctrine or be-

PERU

COLOMBIA

Equator

ECUADOR

Putumayo

Chira

Piura

Marañon

Iquitos

Amazon

Chiclayo

BRAZIL

Cordillera

Trujillo

Chan Chan

Huascaran
▲ 6768m.

Chimbote

10°S

Oriental

Callao

Rimac

LIMA

Huancayo

Machu Picchu

Cuzco

BOLIVIA

PACIFIC
OCEAN

Arequipa

Lake
Titicaca

20°S

CHILE

| 0 | 400 | 800 Km |

| 0 | 200 | 400 | Miles |

80°W   70°W

lief that the evil in the world outweighs the good. [French *pessimisme,* from Latin *pessimus,* worst.] —**pes·si·mist** *n.* —**pes·si·mis·tic** (-místik) *adj.* —**pes·si·mis·ti·cal·ly** *adv.*

pest (pest) *n.* 1. An annoying person or thing; a nuisance. 2. An injurious plant or animal, especially one harmful to man, crops, or livestock. 3. *Archaic.* A pestilence. [French *peste,* from Latin *pestis†,* plague.]

Pes·ta·loz·zi (péstə-lótsi), **Johann Heinrich** (1746–1827). Swiss educationalist. He opened homes and schools for poor children, and in works such as *How Gertrude Teaches Her Children* (1801) described his theory that a child should be taught to think, rather than to learn by rote.

pes·ter (péstər) *tr.v.* **-tered, -tering, -ters.** To harass with petty annoyances or repeated demands; bother. See Synonyms at **harass.** [Probably from Old French *empestrer,* to tie up (an animal), impede, from Vulgar Latin *impastōriāre* (unattested) : *in,* on, in + *pastōria* (unattested), the tying up of an animal, from Late Latin *pāstūra,* PASTURE; influenced by PEST.] —**pes·ter·er** *n.*

pest·house (pést-howss) *n.* Formerly, a hospital for patients suffering from plague or some other infectious disease; a lazaretto.

pes·ti·cide (pésti-sīd) *n.* Any chemical that is used to kill pests, especially insects and rodents. [From PEST + -CIDE.] —**pes·ti·cid·al** (-sīd'l) *adj.*

pes·tif·er·ous (pess-tíffərəss) *adj.* 1. Producing or breeding infectious disease. 2. Infected with or contaminated by an epidemic disease. 3. Morally evil or corrupting; pernicious. 4. *Informal.* Irritating; annoying. [Middle English, from Latin *pestiferus* : *pestis,* PEST + -FEROUS.] —**pes·tif·er·ous·ly** *adv.*

pes·ti·lence (péstilənss) *n.* 1. Any usually fatal epidemic disease, especially bubonic plague. 2. An epidemic of such a disease. 3. A pernicious, evil influence or agent.

pes·ti·lent (péstilənt) *adj.* 1. Tending to cause death; deadly; fatal. 2. Infected or contaminated with a contagious disease. 3. Morally, socially, or politically harmful; pernicious. 4. Extremely irritating or annoying. [Middle English, from Latin *pestilēns* (stem *pestilent-*), from *pestis,* plague, PEST.]

pes·ti·len·tial (pésti-lénsh'l) *adj.* 1. Of or pertaining to pestilence. 2. Tending to cause epidemic disease; pestiferous. 3. Pernicious or troublesome; pestilent.

pes·tle (péss'l; *also* pést'l) *n.* 1. A club-shaped hand tool for grinding or mashing substances in a mortar. 2. A large bar moved vertically to stamp or pound, as in a press or mill. ~*v.* **pestled, -tling, -tles.** —*tr.* To pound, grind, or mash with a pestle. —*intr.* To use a pestle. [Middle English *pestel,* from Old French, from Latin *pistillum.*]

pet¹ (pet) *n.* 1. A tame animal kept for amusement or companionship. 2. Any object of the affections. 3. A person especially loved or indulged; a favourite: *teacher's pet.* ~*adj.* 1. Kept as a pet: *a pet cat.* 2. Of or pertaining to pets: *pet food.* 3. Especially cherished or indulged; favourite: *a pet daughter.* ~*v.* **petted, petting, pets.** —*tr.* 1. To treat or regard as a pet; indulge or pamper. 2. To stroke or caress gently. 3. To fondle or caress in an erotic way. —*intr.* To fondle and caress in an erotic way. [16th century (Scottish and northern English dialect) : origin obscure.] —**pet·ter** *n.*

pet² *n.* A fit of bad temper or pique. ~*intr.v.* **petted, petting, pets.** To be sulky and peevish. [16th century: origin obscure.]

pet. petroleum.

Pé·tain (pe-tán), **Henri Philippe** (1856–1951). French military leader. As a general in World War I, he became a national hero for successfully defending Verdun (1916). Appointed head of state in 1940, he accepted the terms of surrender to Germany, and headed the pro-German government of unoccupied Vichy France until 1942. After the Liberation he was condemned to death, a sentence later commuted to life imprisonment.

pet·al (pétt'l) *n. Botany.* A separate, often brightly coloured segment of a corolla. Compare **sepal.** [New Latin *petalum,* from Greek *petalon,* leaf.] —**pet·alled** *adj.*

-petal *adj. comb. form.* Indicates a moving towards or seeking; for example, **centripetal.** [New Latin *-petus,* from Latin *petere,* to seek.]

pet·al·if·er·ous (pétt'l-íffərəss) *adj.* Bearing petals. [From PETAL + -FEROUS.]

pet·al·o·dy (pétt'l-ōdi) *n.* A condition in some plants where the stamens or other floral parts take on the appearance and function of petals. [Greek *petalōdēs,* leaflike, from *petalon,* leaf, PETAL.] —**pet·al·o·dic** (-óddik) *adj.*

pet·al·oid (pétt'l-oyd) *adj.* Resembling a petal; petal-like.

pet·al·ous (pétt'l-əss) *adj.* Having petals; petalled.

pé·tanque (pay-tónk) *n.* A type of **boules** (*see*), played especially in southern France. [Provençal, from *ped tanco,* (with the) foot fixed (to the ground or spot).]

pe·tard (pe-tárd, pi-) *n.* 1. Formerly, a small bell-shaped bomb used to breach a gate or wall. 2. A firework that explodes with a loud noise. —**hoist with (one's) own petard.** Suffering harm as a result of one's own cleverness or scheming. [French *pétard,* from *péter,* to break wind, from *pet,* a fart, from Latin *pēditum,* from *pēdere,* to break wind.]

pet·cock (pét-kok) *n.* A small valve or tap used to drain or reduce pressure from pipes, radiators, and boilers. [Perhaps PET(TY) + COCK.]

pe·te·chi·a (pi-téeki-ə, pe- ‖ *U.S. also* -técki-ə) *n., pl.* **-chiae** (-ee). A small spot on a body surface, such as the skin or mucous membrane, caused by a minute haemorrhage. [New Latin, from Italian *petecchia†,* skin spot.] —**pe·te·chi·al** *adj.* —**pe·te·chi·ate** (-ət, -it, -ayt) *adj.*

pe·ter¹ (péetər) *intr.v.* **-tered, -tering, -ters.** 1. To diminish gradually. Usually used with *out.* 2. *Chiefly U.S.* To become exhausted. Used with *out: all petered out.* [U.S. mining slang, *peter†.*]

peter² *n. Slang.* 1. A prison cell. 2. A safe or strongbox. [Perhaps from the name *Peter.*]

peter³ *n.* In bridge and other card games, a conventional sequence of play designed to indicate to one's partner the strength of one's hand in a particular suit. It usually involves playing a high card and then a low card in that suit. ~*intr.v.* **petered, -tering, -ters.** To play a peter. [From PETER (verb), to give out, diminish gradually.]

Pe·ter (péetər) *n.* Either of the two books of the New Testament attributed to St. Peter.

Peter I, known as Peter the Great (1672–1725). Tsar of Russia (1682–1725) who turned his country into a major European power. From 1682 he ruled jointly with his half-brother Ivan V, under the regency of Ivan's elder sister, Sophia. Effectively sole ruler from 1689, Peter campaigned against the Turks and Persians, and led Russia, Poland, and Denmark to victory over Sweden in the Battle of Poltava (1709). Extending Russian territory around the Baltic and Caspian shores, he also founded the Russian navy and reformed the administration of the state.

Peter, Saint, called "Simon Peter" (died *c.* A.D. 67). The chief of the Apostles; traditionally regarded as first Bishop of Rome. [Greek *petros,* stone, rock, translation of Aramaic *Kēphā,* surname conferred upon the Apostle by Jesus: "*thou art Peter, and upon this rock I will build my church*" (Matthew 16:1).]

Pe·ter·bor·ough (péetər-brə, -bərə, -burrə). City in Cambridgeshire, eastern England, situated on the river Nene. Catherine of Aragon is buried in its 12th-century cathedral. It was made a new town (1967), is an agricultural centre, and produces bricks and diesel engines.

Pe·ter·head (péetər-héd). Port in Grampian Region, northeast Scotland. The Old Pretender landed there in 1715. It is a service centre for the North Sea oil industry. Its industries include fishing, engineering, and the quarrying of granite.

Pe·ter·loo massacre (péetər-loo) *n.* The violent dispersing by cavalry of a meeting of English radicals in Manchester on August 16, 1819. The incident became a symbol of repression. [After St. Peter's Fields (in Manchester) + WATERLOO.]

pe·ter·man (péetər-mən) *n., pl.* **-men** (-mən, -men). *British Slang.* A criminal who specialises in opening safes.

Peter Pan *n.* 1. A man who clings to his childhood and remains emotionally or psychologically a boy; a chronically immature man. 2. A man who looks much younger than he is. [After the central character in J.M. Barrie's play, *Peter Pan* (1904).]

Peter principle *n.* The principle that in a hierarchy, a person competent for certain tasks will be promoted to others he is less able to fulfil, and will thus find his own level of incompetence. [From *The Peter Principle* (1969), book by L. Peter and R. Hull.]

pe·ter·sham (péetər-shəm) *n.* 1. A thick woollen fabric. 2. An overcoat made of such a fabric. 3. A stiff, ribbed silk braid. [After Viscount *Petersham* (died 1851), British army officer.]

Pe·ter·son (péetər-s'n), **Oscar (Emmanuel)** (1925–). Canadian jazz pianist. His style is noted for its technical accomplishment.

Peter's pence *n.* Also **Peter pence.** 1. A tax, originally of one penny per household, paid in medieval England to the Papal See. 2. An annual voluntary contribution made by Roman Catholics towards the expenses of the Holy See. [From St. PETER, as symbolising the papacy.]

pet·i·o·lar (pétti-ōlər) *adj. Biology.* Of, pertaining to, or growing on a petiole.

pet·i·o·late (pétti-ə-layt ‖ *U.S. also* -ō-lət) *adj.* Also **pet·i·o·lat·ed** (-laytid). *Biology.* Having a petiole.

pet·i·ole (pétti-ōl) *n.* 1. *Botany.* The stalk by which a leaf is attached to a stem; a leafstalk. 2. *Zoology.* The slender, stalklike connection between the thorax and abdomen in certain insects. [New Latin *petiolus,* from Late Latin *petiolus, peciolus,* small foot, fruit stalk, irregularly from Latin *pediculus,* diminutive of *pēs* (stem *ped-*), foot.]

pet·i·o·lule (pétti-ō-lewl, péeti-, -ō-, -lōol) *n. Botany.* The stalk of a leaflet in a compound leaf. [New Latin *petiolulus,* diminutive of *petiolus,* PETIOLE.]

pet·it, pet·ty (pétti) *adj. Law.* Lesser; minor. [Middle English, from Old French *petit,* "small", perhaps from Gallo-Roman (unattested) *pittitto-* (perhaps imitative of children's speech).]

Pe·tit (pə-tée), **Roland** (1924–). French dancer and choreographer. An innovator in contemporary ballet, he has introduced both realism and fantasy in works that include *The Strolling Players* (1945) and *Carmen* (1949).

pe·tit bour·geois (pétti bóor-zhwáa, pə-tée) *n., pl.* **petits bourgeois.** Also **petty bourgeois.** A member of the petite bourgeoisie, often considered as narrow-minded, conservative, and self-righteous. —**pe·tit-bour·geois** *adj.*

pe·tite (pə-téet) *adj.* Small, slender, and trim. Said of a girl or woman. [French, feminine of PETIT.]

petite bourgeoisie *n.* Also **petty bourgeoisie.** The class that includes small businessmen, skilled manual workers, and low-ranking white-collar staff; the lower middle classes.

pet·it four (pétti fóor, pə-tée fór ‖ fór) *n., pl.* **petits fours** or **petit fours** (-z, *or pronounced as singular*). A small, rich biscuit or cake, often decorated and eaten at tea or after a meal. [French, small cake, from *four,* oven.]

pe·ti·tion (pi-tísh'n, pə-) *n.* **1.** A written document bearing many signatures, requesting action on a particular issue from those in authority. **2.** A solemn supplication or request to a superior authority; an entreaty. **3.** *Law.* **a.** A formal written application asking a court for a specific judicial action: *a petition for appeal.* **b.** The act of making such a request. **c.** That which is asked for in any such request.
~*v.* **petitioned, -tioning, -tions.** —*tr.* **1.** To address a petition to. **2.** To ask for by petition; request formally. —*intr.* To make a request or entreaty. Often followed by *for*: *petition for retrial.* [Middle English *peticioun,* from Old French *petition,* from Latin *petītiō* (stem *petītiōn-*), attack, solicitation, from *petere* (past participle *petītus*), to seek, demand.] —**pe·ti·tion·ar·y** (-əri || -erri) *adj.* —**pe·ti·tion·er** *n.*

pe·ti·ti·o prin·ci·pi·i (pi-tíshiō prin-síppi-ī, -kíppi-) *n. Logic.* The fallacy of assuming in the premise of an argument that which one wishes to prove in the conclusion; begging the question. [Medieval Latin, "postulation of the beginning".]

pet·it juror (pétti) *n.* A member of a petit jury.

pet·it jury (pétti) *n.* A jury of 12 persons that sits at civil and criminal trials. Also called "trial jury". Compare **grand jury.**

pet·it larceny (pétti) *n.* In the United States and formerly in Britain, theft of objects whose value is below a certain designated figure. Compare **grand larceny.**

pe·tit maître (pə-tée méttr) *n.* A dandy. [French, "small master".]

pet·it mal (pétti mál || *U.S. also* maál) *n. Pathology.* A mild form of epilepsy characterised by frequent but transient lapses of consciousness and only rare spasms or falling. Compare **grand mal.** [French, "small illness".]

pet·it point (pétti póynt; *French* pə-tée pwáN) *n.* **1.** A small stitch used in needlepoint. **2.** Needlepoint done with such a stitch. Compare **gros point.** [French, "small point".]

pe·tit pois (pə-tée pwaá, pétti) *pl.n.* Small tender green peas. [French, small peas.]

Pet·ra (péttrə, péetrə). Ancient ruined city of southwest Jordan. It was capital of the Nabataeans, prospering as an important East-West trading post from the fourth century B.C. until its capture by the Romans (A.D. 106). It was rediscovered in 1812.

Pet·rarch (péttraark; *also* péetraark), born Francesco Petrarca (1304–74). Italian poet and scholar who, with Dante and Boccaccio, instituted the literary Renaissance in Italy. A Florentine by birth, his works unite classical scholarship with Christian belief in the spirit of humanism. He is especially remembered for his love sonnets dedicated to Laura. —**Pet·rarch·an** (pe-trárkən, pi-) *adj.*

Petrarchan sonnet *n.* A sonnet in a form of Italian origin comprising an octave with the rhyme pattern *abbaabba,* and a sestet of various rhyme patterns such as *cdccdc* or *cdecde.*

pet·rel (péttrəl) *n.* Any of various sea birds of the order Procellariiformes, especially the **storm petrel** *(see).* [Variant of earlier *pitteral*†.]

Pe·tri dish (péetri) *n.* A shallow dish with a loose-fitting cover, used especially to culture microorganisms for research. [After Julius R. *Petri* (died 1921), German bacteriologist.]

Pe·trie (péetri), **Sir (William Matthew) Flinders** (1853–1942). British archaeologist. He is especially known for his excavations in Egypt which began with work on the pyramids at Giza in 1880. His published works include *Methods and Aims of Archaeology* (1904).

pet·ri·fac·tion (péttri-fáksh'n) *n.* Also **pet·ri·fi·ca·tion** (-fi-káysh'n). **1. a.** The process of petrifying; the conversion of organic matter into stone or a stony substance. **b.** Something resulting from this process. **2.** The state of being petrified, as by fear. [From PETRIFY (by analogy with, for example, STUPEFACTION).]

pet·ri·fy (péttri-fī) *v.* **-fied, -fying, -fies.** —*tr.* **1.** To convert (wood or other organic matter) into stone or a stony substance by structural impregnation with dissolved minerals. **2.** To cause to become stiff or stonelike; deaden. **3.** To stun or paralyse with terror. —*intr.* To become stony, especially by mineral replacement of organic matter. [French *petrifier* : Latin *petra,* stone, from Greek + *facere,* to make.]

Pe·trine (péetrīn) *adj.* **1.** Of or pertaining to St. Peter. **2.** Of or pertaining to the pope considered as a successor of St. Peter.

petro– *comb. form.* Indicates: **1.** Rock or stone; for example, **petrology.** **2.** Petroleum; for example, **petrochemistry.** [Greek *petros,* stone and *petra,* rock.]

pet·ro·chem·i·cal (péttrō-kémmik'l) *n.* Any chemical derived from petroleum or natural gas. —**pet·ro·chem·i·cal** *adj.*

pet·ro·chem·is·try (péttrō-kémmistri) *n.* The chemistry of petroleum and its derivatives.

pet·ro·dol·lar (péttrō-dollər) *n.* A dollar earned by an oil-producing country from its exports, especially as part of a reserve to be invested abroad.

pet·ro·glyph (péttrə-glif, péttrō-) *n.* A usually prehistoric carving or line drawing on rock. —**pet·ro·glyph·ic** (-gliffik) *adj.*

pe·trog·ra·phy (pe-tróggrə-fi, pi-) *n.* The description and classification of rocks. [PETRO- + -GRAPHY.] —**pe·trog·ra·pher** (-fər) *n.* —**pet·ro·graph·ic** (péttrə-gráffik), **pet·ro·graph·i·cal** *adj.* —**pet·ro·graph·i·cal·ly** *adv.*

pet·rol (péttrəl) *n. Chiefly British.* A volatile mixture of flammable liquid hydrocarbons derived from crude petroleum and used principally as a fuel for internal-combustion engines and as an illuminant, thinner, and solvent. As a fuel it usually contains antiknock compounds and corrosion inhibitors. Also *U.S.* "gasoline". [French *pétrole* (in the phrase *essence de pétrole*), from Old French *petrole,* from Medieval Latin *petroleum,* PETROLEUM.]

pet·ro·la·tum (péttrə-láytəm, péttrō-, -laátəm) *n.* A colourless to amber gelatinous semisolid, obtained from petroleum, consisting of various alkanes and alkenes, and used in lubricants and medicinal ointments. Also called "petroleum jelly". [New Latin, from Medieval Latin *petroleum,* PETROLEUM.]

petrol bomb *n.* A bottle containing petrol, stoppered by a wick, and thrown as a weapon when the wick is lit.

pe·tro·le·um (pi-trṓli-əm, pə-) *n. Abbr.* **pet.** A natural, yellow-to-black, thick, flammable liquid hydrocarbon mixture found principally beneath the earth's surface and processed for fractions including natural gas, petrol, naphtha, kerosene, fuel and lubricating oils, paraffin wax, asphalt, and a wide variety of derivative products. Also called "crude oil", "rock oil". [Medieval Latin : PETRO- + *oleum,* oil.]

petroleum ether *n.* A volatile mixture of the higher alkane liquids obtained as a fraction of petroleum distillation and used as a solvent.

petroleum jelly *n.* Petrolatum.

pe·trol·ic (pi-tróllik, pə-) *adj.* Derived from petroleum.

pe·trol·o·gy (pi-tróllәji, pə-, pe-) *n.* The study of the origin, composition, structure, and alteration of rocks. [PETRO- + -LOGY.] —**pet·ro·log·ic** (péttrə-lójik), **pet·ro·log·i·cal** *adj.* —**pet·ro·log·i·cal·ly** *adv.* —**pe·trol·o·gist** (-tróllәjist) *n.*

petrol station *n. British.* A **filling station** *(see).*

pet·ro·nel (péttrə-nel) *n.* A firearm or large pistol used by cavalry soldiers in the 16th and 17th centuries. [French *petrinal,* variant of *poitrinal* (noun), from adjective, "of the chest" (the butt end was designed to rest on the chest while firing), from *poitrine,* chest, from Vulgar Latin *pectorina* (unattested), from Latin *pectus* (stem *pectōr-*), chest.]

pe·tro·sal (pe-trṓss'l, pə-) *adj.* Also **pet·rous** (péttrəss). *Anatomy.* Pertaining to or located near the portion of the temporal bone that surrounds the inner ear. [Latin *petrōsus,* PETROUS.]

pet·rous (péttrəss) *adj.* **1.** Of, pertaining to, or resembling rock; stony; hard. **2.** *Anatomy.* Variant of **petrosal.** [Latin *petrōsus,* rocky, from *petra,* rock, from Greek.]

pet·ti·coat (pétti-kōt) *n.* **1.** An item of woman's underwear, made of a light fabric and having the form either of a skirt or of a dress or slip. **2.** *Slang.* A woman or girl.
~*adj.* **1.** Female; feminine. **2.** Of or by women: *petticoat government.* [Middle English *petycote* : PETTY + COAT.]

pet·ti·fog (pétti-fog || -fawg) *intr.v.* **-fogged, -fogging, -fogs.** To act like a pettifogger. [Back-formation from PETTIFOGGER.]

pet·ti·fog·ger (pétti-foggər || -fawgər) *n.* **1.** An unscrupulous lawyer. **2.** A person who pays excessive attention to small details; an extremely fussy person; a quibbler. [PETTY + *fogger,* unscrupulous dealer, perhaps after *Fugger,* 15th-16th century family of merchants in Augsburg, Germany.]

pet·tish (péttish) *adj.* Ill-tempered; peevish; petulant. [Probably from PET (ill temper).] —**pet·tish·ly** *adv.* —**pet·tish·ness** *n.*

pet·ti·toes (pétti-tōz) *pl.n.* Pig's trotters considered as food. [16th century (originally, offal), from Old French *petite oie,* "little goose", giblets of a goose; assimilated to *petty toes.*]

pet·ty (pétti) *adj.* **-tier, -tiest.** **1.** Small, trivial, or insignificant in quantity or quality: *petty grievances.* **2.** Having or showing a contemptibly narrow-minded and ungenerous nature: *a petty outlook.* **3.** Of subordinate or inferior rank. **4.** *Law.* Variant of **petit.** —See Synonyms at **trivial.** [Middle English *pety,* small, variant of *petit,* PETIT.] —**pet·ti·ly** *adv.* —**pet·ti·ness** *n.*

petty bourgeois. Variant of **petit bourgeois.**

petty bourgeoisie. Variant of **petite bourgeoisie.**

petty cash *n. Abbr.* **p.c., p/c, P/C** A small fund of money for incidental expenses, as in an office. Also *U.S.* "float".

petty officer *n. Abbr.* **P.O., p.o.** A naval noncommissioned officer ranking between a chief petty officer and a leading seaman, and equivalent in rank to a sergeant in the army.

petty sessions *n. Used with a singular verb.* **1.** A magistrate's court. **2.** A sitting of a magistrate's court.

pet·u·lant (péttew-lənt || péchoo-) *adj.* Unreasonably irritable or ill-tempered; peevish. [French *pétulant,* saucy, from Latin *petulāns* (stem *petulant-*), present participle of *petulāre* (unattested), to jab at, frequentative of *petere,* to attack.] —**pet·u·lance, pet·u·lan·cy** *n.* —**pet·u·lant·ly** *adv.*

pe·tu·ni·a (pi-téwn-iə, pə- || -tṓōn-) *n.* Any of various widely cultivated plants of the genus *Petunia,* native to tropical America, having funnel-shaped flowers in various shades. [New Latin, from obsolete French *petun,* tobacco, from Tupi *petyn, petyma.*]

pe·tun·tse, pe·tun·tze (pi-túnt-si, pə-, -tṓōnt-, -say) *n.* A variety of feldspar sometimes mixed with kaolin in Chinese porcelain. [Chinese *bái dùn zi,* "white heap".]

Pev·en·sey (pévv'nzi). Village in East Sussex, southeast England. Now situated inland as a result of the retreating sea, it is where William the Conqueror landed in 1066. It is one of the Cinque Ports and has the remains of a Norman castle and Roman fort.

Pevs·ner (pévz-nər), **Antoine** (1886–1962). Russian sculptor and painter, a pioneer of constructivism. He initiated the movement with *The Realist Manifesto* (1920), written jointly with his brother Naum Gabo. Pevsner moved to Paris in 1923 after the movement's abstract tendencies fell out of favour with the Bolshevik authorities.

Pevsner, Sir Nikolaus (Bernhard Leon) (1902–). British writer on architecture, born in Germany. He held professorial chairs in

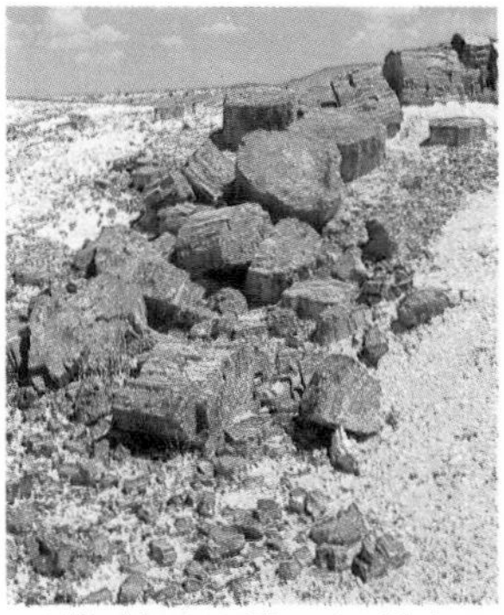

petrified forest *These jumbled rocks were trees about 170 million years ago. Long after the trees fell and were buried by layers of mud, sand and volcanic ash, they became petrified – turned to stone – as mineral-rich water seeped into the trunks, eventually replacing each cell in the wood with a matching crystal of quartz. Later, erosion brought the stone trees back to the surface, where they now form part of the Petrified Forest National Park in the U.S. state of Arizona.*

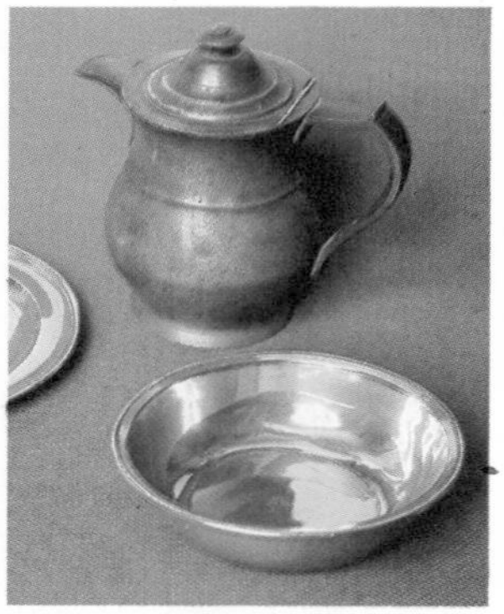

pewter *In the Middle Ages, this tin-based alloy replaced wood as a material for tableware. It remained unrivalled until the end of the 18th century, when manufacturers first produced relatively cheap porcelain and earthenware in large quantities. This pewter tableware was made in America in the mid-19th century.*

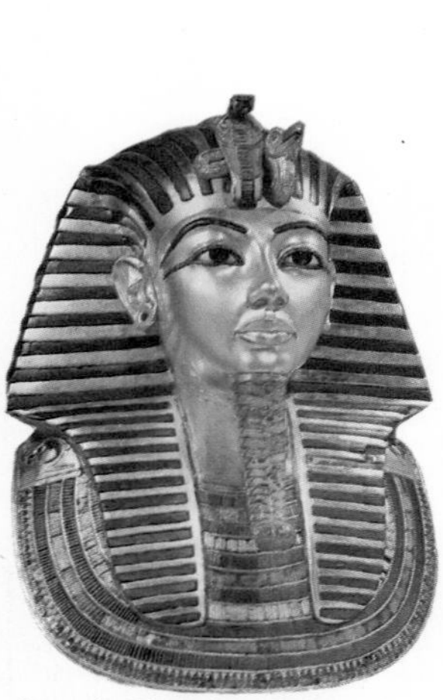

pharaoh *This solid gold funeral mask of the Egyptian pharaoh Tutankhamun was placed over the head and shoulders of his linen-wrapped mummy more than 3,000 years ago. It was found when his tomb was rediscovered in 1922 by the British archaeologist Howard Carter.*

fine art at Cambridge, Oxford, and London and is known for his standard survey *The Buildings of England* (1951–74).

pew (pew) *n.* **1.** A bench for the congregation in a church. **2.** A small enclosure or box of seats in a church, especially one formerly reserved for a particular family or group of regular churchgoers. **3.** *British Informal.* A seat. Used chiefly in the phrase *take a pew.* [Middle English *pewe, puwe,* from Old French *puie,* raised seat, balcony, from Latin *podia,* plural of *podium,* podium, balcony, from Greek *podion,* small foot, base, diminutive of *pous* (stem *pod-*), foot.]

pewit. Variant of **peewit.**

pew·ter (péwtər) *n.* **1.** Any of numerous silver-grey alloys of tin with various amounts of antimony, copper, and lead, formerly used widely for fine kitchen utensils and tableware. **2.** Pewter articles collectively. [Middle English *pewtre,* from Old French *peutre, peautre,* variant of *peltre,* tin, from (unattested) Vulgar Latin *peltrum*†.] **—pew·ter** *adj.*

pe·yo·te (pay-ṓti) *n.* Also **pe·yo·tl** (-ṓt'l). **1.** A cactus, **mescal** *(see).* **2.** A hallucinatory drug derived from the tubercles of this cactus. [Mexican Spanish, from Nahuatl.]

pf. 1. pfennig. **2.** preferred.

pfen·nig (fénnig; *German* pfénnikh) *n., pl.* **-nigs** or **pfennige** (-ə). *Abbr.* **pf., pfg.** A coin equal to $^1/_{100}$ of the Deutsche mark of West Germany and the mark of East Germany. [German *Pfennig,* from Old High German *pfenning,* from West Germanic *panninga* (unattested). See also **penny, penni.**]

pfg. pfennig.

PG *adj.* In Britain, designating a rating for films, equivalent to the former "A" rating, containing some scenes that may be unsuitable for young children. [*p*arental *g*uidance.]

Pg. Portugal; Portuguese.

P.G. 1. paying guest. **2.** postgraduate.

PGA Professional Golfers' Association.

pH *n. Chemistry.* A measure of the acidity or alkalinity of a solution calculated as the common logarithm of the reciprocal of the hydrogen ion concentration in moles per cubic decimetre of solution and numerically equal to 7 for neutral solutions. pH increases with increasing alkalinity and decreases with increasing acidity. [*p*otential of *H*ydrogen.]

ph. phase.

Phae·drus (féedrəss) (first century A.D.). A Thracian-born freedman of the emperor Augustus, author of a collection of fables based on those attributed to Aesop.

phae·ton (fáyt'n, fáy-ət'n) *n.* A light, open, four-wheeled carriage, usually drawn by a pair of horses. [French *phaéton,* after *Phaéton,* French form of *Phaethon,* son of Helios who attempted to drive the chariot of the sun.]

phage (fayj) *n.* A **bacteriophage** *(see).*

-phage *n. comb. form.* Indicates something that eats or destroys; for example, **bacteriophage.** [Greek *-phagos,* from *phagein,* to eat.]

phag·e·dae·na, phag·e·de·na (fáji-déenə) *n.* An ulcer of the skin and subcutaneous tissues that spreads rapidly and causes sloughing off of the skin. [Latin, from Greek *phagedaina,* from *phagein,* to consume, eat.]

phago- *comb. form.* Indicates eating or destroying; for example, **phagocyte.** [Greek, from *phagein,* to eat.]

phag·o·cyte (fág-ə-sīt, -ō-) *n. Physiology.* A cell such as a leucocyte that engulfs and digests cells, microorganisms, or other foreign bodies in the bloodstream and tissues. [PHAGO- + -CYTE.] **—phag·o·cyt·ic** (-síttik) *adj.*

phag·o·cy·to·sis (fág-ə-sī-tṓ-siss, -ō-) *n. Physiology.* The envelopment and digestion of bacteria or other foreign bodies by phagocytes. [New Latin : PHAGOCYT(E) + -OSIS.]

-phagous *adj. comb. form.* Indicates eating or tending to eat; for example, **phyllophagous.** [Latin *-phagus,* from Greek *-phagos,* eating, from *phagein,* to eat.]

-phagy, -phagia *n. comb. form.* Indicates an eating or consumption; for example, **cytophagy, dysphagia.** [Greek *-phagia,* from *phagein,* to eat.]

pha·lan·ge·al (fa-lán-ji-əl, fə-, fál-ən-jée-əl || fáyl-) *adj. Anatomy.* Of or pertaining to a phalanx or phalanges.

pha·lan·ger (fə-lánjər) *n.* Any of various small, arboreal marsupials of the family Phalangeridae, of Australia and adjacent islands, having a long tail and dense, woolly fur. [New Latin, from PHALANX, "toe bone" (with reference to the peculiar structure of the second and third toes of its hind feet).]

pha·lan·ges (fa-lánjeez, fə- || *U.S. also* fay-) *pl.n. Singular* **phalanx** or **pha·lange** (fál-anj || *U.S.* fáyl-, fə-lánj). *Anatomy.* The bones of the fingers or toes.

phal·an·ster·y (fál-ən-stri, -stəri || -sterri) *n., pl.* **-ies. 1.** A community of the followers of Charles **Fourier** *(see).* Also called "phalanx". **2.** The buildings of such a community. [French *Phalanstère* : *phalange,* phalanx, from New Latin *phalanx,* PHALANX + *monastère,* monastery, from Late Latin *monastērium,* MONASTERY.] **—phal·an·ste·ri·an** (-stéer-i-ən) *n.* & *adj.* **—phal·an·ste·ri·an·ism** *n.*

pha·lanx (fál-angks || *chiefly U.S.* fáyl-) *n., pl.* **-lanxes** or **phalanges** (fa-lánjeez, fə- || fay-). **1.** An ancient Greek formation of infantry carrying overlapping shields and long spears, perfected by Philip II of Macedon and used by Alexander the Great. **2.** Any close-knit or compact body of people. **3.** A phalanstery. **4.** *Anatomy.* Singular of **phalanges.** [Latin, from Greek, wooden beam, finger bone, line of battle.]

phal·a·rope (fál-ə-rōp) *n.* Any of several wading birds of the family Phalaropodidae, having lobed toes that enable them to swim. [French, from New Latin *phalaropus* : Greek *phalaris,* coot (which has a white patch on the head), from *phalaros,* having a white spot + *-pus,* from Greek *pous,* foot.]

phal·lic (fál-ik) *adj.* **1.** Of, pertaining to, or resembling a phallus. **2.** Of or pertaining to the cult of the phallus as an embodiment of generative power. [Greek *phallikos,* from *phallos,* PHALLUS.]

phal·lo·cen·tric (fál-ō-séntrik, -ə-) *adj.* Dominated by men or male preoccupations and interests.

phal·lo·crat (fál-ə-krat, -ō-) *n.* One who believes in male superiority; a male chauvinist. **—phal·lo·crat·ic** (-kráttik) *adj.*

phal·lus (fál-əss) *n., pl.* **phalli** (-ī) or **-luses. 1.** A representation of the penis and testes as an embodiment of generative power. **2. a.** The penis. **b.** The sexually undifferentiated tissue in the embryo that becomes the penis or clitoris. [Late Latin *phallus,* penis, from Greek *phallos.*]

-phane *n. comb. form.* Indicates resemblance or similarity to a specified material; for example, **cellophane.** [Greek *-phanēs,* appearing, shining, from *phainesthai,* to appear.]

phan·er·o·crys·tal·line (fánnərō-krístə-līn, -lin) *adj.* Designating igneous or metamorphic rocks having a crystalline structure in which the crystals are visible to the naked eye. [Greek *phaneros,* visible + CRYSTALLINE.]

phan·er·o·gam (fánnər-ə-gam, -ō-) *n. Botany.* A plant that produces flowers and true seeds; a spermatophyte. No longer in technical usage. Compare **cryptogam.** [New Latin *phanerogamus,* "one having visible reproductive parts" : Greek *phaneros,* visible, from *phainein,* to show + -GAMOUS.] **—phan·er·o·gam·ic** (-gámmik), **phan·er·og·a·mous** (fánnə-róggəməss) *adj.*

phan·er·o·phyte (fánnərō-fīt, fə-nérrə-) *n.* A perennial plant that bears its dormant buds well above soil level. [Greek *phaneros,* visible + -PHYTE.]

phan·tasm (fán-taz'm) *n.* **1.** Something apparently seen but having no physical reality; a phantom. **2.** An illusory mental image. **3.** In Platonic philosophy, objective reality as perceived and distorted by the five senses. [Middle English *fantasme,* from Old French, from Latin *phantasma,* apparition, spectre, from Greek, from *phantazein,* to make visible, from *phainein,* to show.] **—phan·tas·mal** (fan-tázm'l), **phan·tas·mic** (-tázmik) *adj.*

phan·tas·ma·go·ri·a (fán-tazmə-górri-ə, fan-tázmə-, -gáwri- || -gṓri-) *n.* **1.** A fantastic sequence of haphazardly associative imagery, as seen in dreams or fever. **2.** Any scene of constant and bewildering change. [Originally, the name of an early 19th-century magic-lantern show producing optical illusions, from PHANTASM + an obscure second element.] **—phan·tas·ma·gor·ic** (-górrik || -gáwrik), **phan·tas·ma·gor·i·cal** *adj.*

phantasy. Variant of **fantasy.**

phan·tom (fántəm) *n.* **1.** Something apparently seen, heard, or sensed, but having no physical reality; a ghost; a spectre. **2.** An image that appears only in the mind.
~*adj.* **1.** Unreal; ghostlike. **2.** *Pathology.* Designating an organ, structure, or condition that does not exist but appears to from various signs and symptoms. [Middle English *fantosme, fantome,* from Old French, from Latin *phantasma,* PHANTASM.]

phantom limb *n.* The sensation that a limb or part of a limb still exists after it has been amputated, usually because pain appears to come from the amputated part.

phantom pregnancy *n.* A condition in which symptoms of pregnancy, such as an enlarged abdomen, occur in a nonpregnant woman. Caused by the secretion of pituitary hormones, it is usually the result of an emotional disorder. Also called "pseudocyesis".

-phany *n. comb. form.* Indicates a manifestation or sudden appearance; for example, **epiphany.** [Greek *-phania,* from *phainein,* to show.]

Phar·aoh (fáir-ō) *n. Often small* **p. 1.** A king of ancient Egypt. **2.** A tyrant. [Late Latin *Pharaō,* from Greek *Pharaō,* transcription of Hebrew *Par'ōh,* from an Egyptian word meaning "great house".] **—Phar·a·on·ic** (-ay-ónnik) *adj.*

pharaoh ant *n.* A small reddish ant, *Monomorium pharaonis,* originally of tropical countries but now a pest of heated buildings in temperate regions.

Phar·i·sa·ic (fárri-sáy-ik || -záy-) *adj.* **1.** Of or pertaining to the Pharisees. **2.** *Small* **p.** Variant of **pharisaical.**

phar·i·sa·ical (fárri-sáy-ik'l || -záy-) *adj.* Also **pharisaic.** Hypocritically self-righteous and censorious. **—phar·i·sa·i·cal·ly** *adv.* **—phar·i·sa·i·cal·ness** *n.*

phar·i·sa·ism (fárri-say-iz'm) *n.* Also **phar·i·see·ism** (-see-). **1.** Hypocritical observance of the letter of religious or moral law without regard for the spirit; sanctimoniousness. **2.** *Capital* **P.** The doctrines and practices of the Pharisees.

phar·i·see (fárri-see) *n.* **1.** *Capital* **P.** A member of an ancient Jewish sect that emphasised strict interpretation and observance of the Mosaic law in both its oral and written form. Compare **Sadducee. 2.** A hypocritically self-righteous person. [Middle English *pharise,* Old English *farise,* from Late Latin *pharisaeus,* from Greek *pharisaios,* from Aramaic *perīshayyā,* plural of *perīsh,* "separated".]

phar·ma·ceu·ti·cal (fármə-séwtik'l, -sóotik'l,) *adj.* Also **phar·ma·ceu·tic** (farmə-séwtik, -sóotik). Of or pertaining to pharmacy or pharmacists.
~*n.* A pharmaceutical product or preparation. [Late Latin *pharmaceuticus,* from Greek *pharmakeutikos,* from *pharmakeutēs,* pharmacist, from *pharmakeuein,* to give drugs, from *pharmakon,* drug. See **pharmaco-.**] **—phar·ma·ceu·ti·cal·ly** *adv.*

phar·ma·ceu·tics (fármə-séwtiks, -sóotiks) *n.* **1.** *Used with a singu-*

lar verb. Pharmacy. **2.** *Used with a plural verb.* Pharmaceutical remedies.

phar·ma·cist (fármə-sist) *n.* A person trained in pharmacy.

pharmaco- *comb. form.* Indicates drugs; for example, **pharmacology.** [Greek *pharmakon†*, drug, poison, potion.]

phar·ma·cog·no·sy (fármə-kóg-nə-si) *n.* The branch of pharmacology dealing with crude natural drugs. [PHARMACO- + Greek -*gnōsia*, knowledge, from -GNOSIS.] —**phar·ma·cog·no·sist** *n.* —**phar·ma·cog·nos·tic** (-kog-nóstik) *adj.*

phar·ma·col·o·gy (fármə-kóllə ji) *n.* The science of drugs, including their composition, uses, and effects. [PHARMACO- + -LOGY.] —**phar·ma·co·log·i·cal** (-kə-lójik'l), *adj.,* —**phar·ma·co·log·i·cal·ly** *adv.* —**phar·ma·col·o·gist** (-kóllojist) *n.*

phar·ma·co·poe·ia, phar·ma·co·pe·ia (fármə-kə-pée-ə, -kō-) *n.* **1.** A book containing an official list of medicinal drugs together with articles on their preparation and use. **2.** The range of drugs used in medicine. [New Latin, from Greek *pharmakopoiia*, preparation of drugs, from *pharmakopoios*, preparing drugs : PHARMACO- + -*poios*, "making", from *poiein*, to make.] —**phar·ma·co·poe·ial** (-əl) *adj.* —**phar·ma·co·poe·ist** (-ist) *n.*

phar·ma·cy (fármə-si) *n., pl.* **cies. 1.** The science of preparing and dispensing drugs. **2.** A place where drugs are prepared; a dispensary. [Middle English *farmacie*, from Old French, from Late Latin *pharmacia*, from Greek *pharmakeia*, from *pharmakon*, drug.]

pha·ros (fáir-oss) *n. Literary.* A lighthouse. [From *Pharos*, formerly an island in the bay of Alexandria, celebrated in antiquity for its lighthouse.]

pha·ryn·ge·al (fárrin-jée-əl, fə-rínji-əl, fa-) *adj.* Also **pha·ryn·gal** (fə-ríng-g'l, fa-). Of, pertaining to, located in, going to, or coming from the pharynx: *pharyngeal air-stream mechanism.* ~*n.* Also **pha·ryn·gal.** A speech sound produced in the pharynx. [New Latin *pharyngeus*, from *pharynx*, PHARYNX.]

phar·yn·gi·tis (fárrin-jí-tiss) *n.* Inflammation of the pharynx. [New Latin : PHARYNG(O)- + -ITIS.]

pharyngo-, pharyng- *comb. form.* Indicates pharynx; for example, **pharyngoscope, pharyngitis.** [New Latin, from Greek *pharungo-*, from *pharunx*, PHARYNX.]

phar·yn·gol·o·gy (fárring-góllə-ji, fárrin-) *n.* The medical study of the pharynx and its diseases. [PHARYNGO- + -LOGY.] —**phar·yn·go·log·i·cal** (-gə-lójik'l) *adj.* —**phar·yn·gol·o·gist** (-jist) *n.*

pha·ryn·go·scope (fə-ríng-gə-skōp, fa-, -gō-) *n.* An instrument used in examining the pharynx. [PHARYNGO- + -SCOPE.] —**phar·yn·gos·co·py** (fárring-góskəpi, fárrin-) *n.*

phar·yn·got·o·my (fárring-góttəmi, fárrin-) *n., pl.* **-mies.** A surgical incision of the pharynx. [PHARYNGO- + -TOMY.]

phar·ynx (fárringks) *n., pl.* **pharynges** (fə-rínjeez, fa-) or **pharynxes.** The section of the digestive tract that extends from the nasal cavities and mouth to the oesophagus. [New Latin, from Greek *pharunx*, throat, pharynx.]

phase (fayz) *n. Abbr.* **ph. 1.** Any one of a sequence of distinct apparent forms. **2.** A distinct stage of development: *The war fell into three clear phases.* **3.** A temporary manner, attitude, or pattern of behaviour: *a passing phase.* **4.** *Astronomy.* Any of the cyclically recurring apparent forms of the Moon or a planet. **5.** *Physics.* **a.** A particular stage in a periodic process or phenomenon. **b.** The fraction of a complete cycle elapsed as measured from a given reference point and often expressed as an angle. **6.** *Chemistry.* A discrete homogeneous part of a material system that is mechanically separable from the rest, as is ice from water. **7.** *Biology.* A characteristic form or appearance that occurs in a cycle or that distinguishes some individuals of a group. **8.** *Biology.* A stage in cell division. —**in** (or **out of**) **phase.** *Physics.* Reaching (or not reaching) corresponding phases at the same time, as two waves might. ~*tr.v.* **phased, phasing, phases. 1.** To plan or carry out systematically by phases: *a phased withdrawal of troops.* **2.** To bring into harmony or efficient joint functioning. Often used with *with*: *phase one process with another.* —**phase in.** To introduce slowly by one stage at a time. —**phase out.** To eliminate or withdraw slowly by one stage at a time. [Back-formation from *phases* (plural), from New Latin *phasis*, from Greek, appearance, phase of the Moon, from *phainein*, to show.] —**pha·sic** (fáyzik) *adj.*

phase-contrast microscope (fáyz-kón-traast ‖ -trast) *n.* A microscope that renders differences in the phase of light transmitted or reflected by a specimen as variations in contrast. Also called "phase microscope".

phase modulation *n.* In telecommunications, the variation of the phase of a carrier wave by an amount proportional to the amplitude of a modulating signal.

phase rule *n.* A rule stating that the number of degrees of freedom in a material system at equilibrium is equal to the number of components minus the number of phases plus the constant 2. For example, the system of water vapour, water, and ice has zero degrees of freedom, since three phases of one component coexist.

-phasia *n. comb. form.* Indicates a specified type of speech disorder; for example, **dysphasia.** [New Latin, from Greek, speech, from *phasis*, utterance, from *phanai*, to say, speak.]

phat·ic (fáttik) *adj.* Designating utterances that assert a friendly social relationship rather than conveying specific thoughts or ideas. Much conversation about the weather, for example, is merely phatic. [From the term *phatic communion*, coined by B. Malinowski : Greek *phatos*, spoken, from *phanai*, to speak.]

Ph.D. Doctor of Philosophy [Latin *Philosophiae Doctor*].

pheas·ant (fézz'nt) *n., pl.* **-ants** or collectively **pheasant.** Any of

various game birds of the family Phasianidae, native to the Old World, characteristically having long tails and, in the males of many species, brilliantly coloured plumage. [Middle English *fesaunt, fesant,* from Old French *fesan, faisan,* from Latin *phasiānus,* from Greek *phasianos,* "the Phasian (bird)", of the river Phasis in the Caucasus, from *Phāsis,* the river Phasis.]

pheasant's eye *n.* **1.** Any of various plants of the genus *Adonis;* especially *A. annua,* which has small scarlet flowers and finely divided leaves. **2.** A narcissus, *Narcissus poeticus,* having white petals and a shallow, red-rimmed, yellow corona. In this sense, also called "narcissus".

phel·lem (fél-əm, -em) *n. Botany.* **Cork cambium** (see). [Greek *phellos,* cork + -*em,* as in PHLOEM.]

phel·lo·derm (fél-ō-derm, -ə-) *n.* The soft cortex tissue that forms on the inner side of the phellogen of some trees. [Greek *phellos,* cork + -DERM.] —**phel·lo·der·mal** (-dérm'l) *adj.*

phel·lo·gen (fél-ō-jen, -ə-jən) *n.* A tissue in woody plants, from which cork and phelloderm develop. [Greek *phellos,* cork + -GEN.] —**phel·lo·ge·net·ic** (-jə-néttik, -je-), **phel·lo·gen·ic** (-jénnik) *adj.*

phe·nac·e·tin (fi-nássə-tin, fe-) *n.* An analgesic drug, **acetophenetidin** (see). [PHEN(O)- + ACET(O)- + -IN.]

phen·a·cite (fénnə-sīt) *n.* A rare natural beryllium silicate, coloured yellow, brown, or pale rose, occurring as vitreous crystals sometimes used as gems. [Greek *phenax†* (stem *phenak-*), an impostor (from its resemblance to quartz).]

phe·nan·threne (fi-nán-threen, fe-) *n.* A colourless crystalline compound, $C_{14}H_{10}$, obtained by fractional distillation of coal-tar oils and used in dyes, drugs, and explosives. [PHEN(O)- + ANTHR(ACENE.]

phen·ar·sa·zine chloride (fin-ár-sə-zeen, fen-) *n.* A highly poisonous yellow crystalline compound, $C_{12}H_9AsClN$, used as a poison gas and sometimes with tear gas.

phen·a·zine (fénnə-zeen) *n.* A yellow crystalline compound, $C_6H_4N_2C_6H_4$, used in the manufacture of dyes.

phe·net·ic (fi-néttik) *adj. Biology.* Of, pertaining to, or designating a system of classification based on observed similarities and differences between organisms rather than on their supposed evolutionary relationships. [*Phenotype* + gen*etic.*]

phen·e·tole (fénni-tōl) *n.* A colourless, oily, phenyl ether, $C_6H_5OC_2H_5.$

phenix. *U.S.* Variant of **phoenix.**

pheno-, phen- *comb. form. Chemistry.* Indicates: **1.** Showing or displaying; for example, **phenocryst. 2.** A compound derived from, containing, or related to benzene; for example, **phenol, phenothiazine.** [Greek *phainein,* to show. Sense 2 is from French *(acide) phénique,* an early name for phenol, from Greek *phainein* (so named because it was originally extracted from illuminating gas).]

phe·no·bar·bi·tone (féen-ō-bárbi-tōn, -ə-) *n.* Also **phe·no·bar·bi·tal** (-t'l). A white, shiny, crystalline compound, $C_{12}H_{12}N_2O_3$, used in medicine as a sedative, for treating insomnia, and as a hypnotic.

phe·no·cop·y (féen-ō-koppi, -ə-) *n., pl.* **-ies.** *Genetics.* **1.** An environmentally induced phenotypic variation that closely resembles a genetically determined character. **2.** A characteristic or organism existing as such a variation. [PHENO(TYPE) + COPY.]

phe·no·cryst (féen-ō-krist, fén-, -ə-) *n.* A conspicuous crystal embedded in a finer-grained groundmass giving a porphyritic texture. [PHENO- + CRYST(AL).] —**phe·no·crys·tic** (-krístik) *adj.*

phe·nol (féen-ol ‖ -ōl) *n. Chemistry.* **1.** A caustic, poisonous, white, crystalline compound, C_6H_5OH, derived from benzene and used in various resins, plastics, disinfectants, and pharmaceuticals. Also called "carbolic acid". **2.** Any of a class of aromatic organic compounds having at least one hydroxyl group attached directly to the benzene ring. [PHEN(O)- + -OL.] —**phe·no·lic** (fi-nóllik, fee ‖ nōlik) *adj.*

phenolic resin *n.* Any of various synthetic thermosetting resins, obtained by the reaction of phenols with simple aldehydes and used to make moulded products and as coatings and adhesives.

phe·nol·o·gy (fi-nóllə-ji) *n.* The study of periodic biological phenomena, such as flowering, breeding, and migration, especially as related to climate. [PHENO(MENON) + -LOGY.] —**phe·no·log·i·cal** (féenə-lójik'l) *adj.* —**phe·nol·o·gist** (-jist) *n.*

phe·nol·phthal·ein (féen-ol-tháyl-een, -thál-, -thál-, -i-in ‖ -ōl-) *n.* A pale yellow crystalline powder, $(C_6H_4OH)_2C_2O_2C_6H_4$, used as an acid-base indicator, in making dyes, and as a cathartic.

phe·nom·e·nal (fi-nómmin'l) *adj.* **1.** Of or pertaining to a phenomenon or phenomena. **2.** Extraordinary; outstanding; remarkable. **3.** *Philosophy.* Known or derived through the senses, rather than through the mind. —**phe·nom·e·nal·ly** *adv.*

phe·nom·e·nal·ism (fi-nómmin'l-iz'm) *n. Philosophy.* The doctrine that the sole objects of knowledge are perceptual experiences. —**phe·nom·e·nal·ist** *n.* —**phe·nom·e·nal·is·tic** (-ístik) *adj.* —**phe·nom·e·nal·is·ti·cal·ly** *adv.*

phe·nom·e·nol·o·gy (fi-nómmi-nóllə-ji) *n.* **1.** The study of all possible appearances in human experience, during which considerations of objective reality and of purely subjective response are temporarily left out of account. **2.** A philosophical movement based on such study, originated by Edmund Husserl about 1905. [German *Phänomenologie* : PHENOMENO(N) + -LOGY.] —**phe·nom·e·no·log·i·cal** (-nə-lójik'l) *adj.* —**phe·nom·e·no·log·i·cal·ly** *adv.* —**phe·nom·e·nol·o·gist** (-nóllə-jist) *n.*

phe·nom·e·non (fi-nómmi-nən ‖ *U.S.* -non) *n., pl.* **-na** (-nə) or **-nons** (for sense 2). **1.** Any occurrence or fact that is directly perceptible by the senses. **2. a.** An unusual, significant, or unaccountable fact or occurrence; a marvel. **b.** A person outstanding for some extreme quality or achievement: *"I thought Mr. Barkis a phenomenon of respectability."* (Charles Dickens). **3.** *Philosophy.* That which appears real to the senses, regardless of whether its underlying existence is proved or its nature understood. Compare **noumenon. 4.** *Physics.* An observable event. [Late Latin *phaenomenon,* from Greek *phainomenon,* from *phainomenos,* present participle of *phainesthai,* to appear, from *phainein,* to show.]

phe·no·thi·a·zine (fēenō-thī-ə-zeen) *n.* A greenish organic compound, $C_{12}H_9NS$, used in insecticides, anthelmintics, and dyes.

phe·no·type (fēen-ō-tīp, -ə-) *n. Genetics.* **1.** The environmentally and genetically determined observable appearance of an organism. Compare **genotype. 2.** An individual or group of organisms exhibiting a particular phenotype. [German *Phänotypus:* PHENO- + TYPE.] —**phe·no·typ·ic** (-típpik), **phe·no·typ·i·cal** *adj.* —**phe·no·typ·i·cal·ly** *adv.*

phen·ox·ide (fi-nók-sīd, fe-) *n.* Any of various salts of phenol containing the ion $C_6H_5O^-$.

phen·yl (fēen-īl, fén-, -'l) *adj. Chemistry.* Designating, containing, or combined with the group C_6H_5, derived from benzene. Usually used in combination: *phenylalanine.* [PHEN(O)- + -YL.] —**phe·nyl·ic** (fi-nillik, fe-) *adj.*

phen·yl·al·a·nine (fēenīl-ál-ə-neen, fénn'l-) *n.* A natural amino acid, $C_6H_5CH_2CH(NH_2)COOH$, that occurs as a constituent of many proteins and is extracted for use as a dietary supplement. It is normally converted to tyrosine in the body; a failure in this reaction causes phenylketonuria.

phen·yl·ene (fénn'l-een) *n.* An organic radical, C_6H_4, derived from benzene by removal of two hydrogen atoms.

phenylene blue *n.* **Indamine** (*see*).

phe·nyl·ke·to·nu·ri·a (fēenīl-kée-tō-néwr-i-ə, fénn'l-, -tə- ‖ -nóor-) *n.* A congenital defect of protein metabolism that causes excessive accumulation of phenylalanine in the blood and leads to mental retardation unless detected and remedied. [New Latin : PHENYL + KETONE + -URIA.] —**phe·nyl·ke·to·nu·ric** *adj. & n.*

phe·nyl·thi·o·car·bam·ide (fēenīl-thī-ō-kárbə-mīd, fénn'l-) *n. Abbr.* **PTC** A crystalline compound, $C_7H_8N_2S$, the taste of which is determined by a pair of genes. If one or both genes are dominant the compound is bitter to the taster, if neither is dominant it is tasteless. Also called "phenylthiourea".

pher·o·mone (férrə-mōn) *n.* A substance that is externally secreted by certain animals and induces a behavioural or physiological response in other animals of the same species. [Greek *pherein,* to bear + *hormone.*] —**pher·o·mo·nal** (-mōn'l) *adj.*

phew (few) *interj.* Used to express relief, fatigue, surprise, or disgust.

phi (fī) *n.* The 21st letter in the Greek alphabet, written Φ, φ. Transliterated in English as *ph,* or *f* in modern Greek words. [Greek.]

phi·al (fī-əl) *n.* A small bottle, a **vial** (*see*). [Middle English *fiole,* from Old French, from Old Provençal *fiola,* from Latin *phiala,* vessel, saucer, from Greek *phialē†,* broad vessel.]

Phi Beta Kappa *n.* **1.** A fraternity of American university students and graduates whose members are chosen on the basis of high academic standing. It is the oldest fraternity in the United States (founded 1776). **2.** A member of this fraternity. [From the initials of the Greek phrase *philosophia biou kubernētēs,* "philosophy the guide of life" (motto of the society).]

Phi·di·as (fī-di-ass, fíddi-) (*c.* 500 – *c.* 430 B.C.). Athenian sculptor, considered by his contemporaries the greatest in Greece. He supervised work on the Parthenon, and his statue of Zeus at Olympia was listed as one of the Seven Wonders of the World.

phil. philosopher; philosophical; philosophy.

Phil. 1. Philippians (New Testament). **2.** Philippines.

phil–. Variant of **philo–.**

Phil·a·del·phi·a (fillə-délfi-ə) City in Pennsylvania, United States, situated on the Delaware river. It was founded in 1681 by William Penn. Its industries include textiles and oil refining, and its port exports grain and timber. The signing of the Declaration of Independence (1776) and the drafting of the U.S. Constitution (1787) both took place here.

Philadelphia lawyer *n. U.S.* A lawyer of great ingenuity in the discovery and manipulation of subtle legalisms.

phil·a·del·phus (fillə-délfəss) *n. Botany.* The **mock orange** (*see*).

Phi·lae (fī-lee). Submerged island in the river Nile, southeast Egypt. It is the former site of ancient ruins, most of which were removed to the island of Agilkia before the completion of the Aswan High Dam.

phi·lan·der (fi-lándər) *intr.v.* **-dered, -dering, -ders.** To engage in love affairs frivolously or casually; flirt. Used of a man. [From *Philander,* a traditional literary name for a lover, mistakenly adopted from Greek *philandros,* "loving men", "loving one's husband" : PHIL(O)- + *anēr* (stem *andr-*), man.] —**phi·lan·der·er** *n.*

phil·an·throp·ic (fil-ən-thróppik, -an-) *adj.* Also **phil·an·throp·i·cal.** Showing, engaged in, or practising philanthropy: *a philanthropic gesture; a philanthropic donation.* —**phil·an·throp·i·cal·ly** *adv.*

phi·lan·thro·py (fi-lánthrə-pi) *n., pl.* **-pies. 1.** The effort or wish to increase the well-being of humanity, as by charitable works. **2.** Love of humanity in general. **3.** An action or institution designed to promote human welfare. [Late Latin *philanthrōpia,* from Greek *philanthrōpia,* benevolence, from *philanthrōpos,* "lover of mankind" : PHIL(O)- + *anthrōpos,* man.] —**phi·lan·thro·pist** (-pist) *n.*

phi·lat·e·ly (fi-láttə-li) *n.* The collection and study of postage stamps, postmarks, and related materials; stamp-collecting.

[French *philatélie :* PHILO- + Greek *atelēs,* tax-free (here used as a rendering of the old postmark *franc de port,* "carriage-free"; see **frank**):* A- (without) + *telos,* charge.] —**phil·a·tel·ic** (fillə-téllik) *adj.* —**phil·a·tel·i·cal·ly** *adv.* —**phi·lat·e·list** (-list) *n.*

–phile, –phil *n. comb. form.* Indicates one having a strong affinity or fondness for; for example, **Anglophile.** [French *-phile* or New Latin *-philus,* from Greek *philos,* beloved, dear, loving.]

Philem. Philemon (New Testament).

Phi·le·mon¹ (fī-lée-mən, fi-, -mon). A friend and convert of St. Paul.

Philemon² *n. Abbr.* **Philem.** A book of the New Testament, a short epistle to Philemon by St. Paul.

phil·har·mon·ic (fil-aar-mónnik, -ər-, -haar-) *adj. Often capital* **P.** Devoted to or appreciative of music. Used chiefly in the names of symphony orchestras, choirs, or musical societies.
~*n. Often capital* **P.** A symphony orchestra or choir, or the group that supports it. [French *philharmonique,* from Italian *filarmonico : fil-,* PHILO- + *armonico,* harmonic.]

phil·hel·lene (fil-hélleen) *n.* Also **phil·hel·len·ist** (-héllənist). **1.** One who admires Greece or the Greeks. **2.** Formerly, one who advocated the national independence of Greece. [Greek *philellēn :* PHIL(O)- + HELLENE.] —**phil·hel·len·ic** (he-léenik) *adj.* —**phil·hel·len·ism** (-hélləniz'm) *n.*

–philia *n. comb. form.* Indicates: **1.** Tendency towards; for example, **haemophilia. 2.** Abnormal attraction to; for example, **necrophilia.** [New Latin, from Greek *philia,* friendship, from *philos,* loving.] —**philiac** *n. & adj. comb. form.*

–philic. Variant of **-philous.**

Phil·ip II¹ (fillip) (*c.* 382–336 B.C.). King of Macedon (359–336) and father of Alexander the Great. He created a powerful army which finally defeated a Greek coalition at Chaeronea (338), and achieved a peace settlement in which all the states except Sparta took part.

Philip II² (1527–98). King of Spain (1556–98). A devout Catholic, he married Mary I of England (1554) to seal an alliance in defence of the Netherlands. From his father, Charles V, he acquired the kingdom of Naples and Sicily (1554) and the duchy of Milan (1540), the Low Countries (1555), and territories in the Americas (1556). When Charles abdicated in 1556, Philip was left a huge empire which he tried to maintain through a series of costly wars. In 1588, he launched the ill-fated Armada against England.

Philip, Prince, Duke of Edinburgh (1921–). Husband of Queen Elizabeth II. He was born in Corfu but educated mainly in Britain. He served in the Royal Navy in World War II and took up British citizenship in 1947. He was created Duke of Edinburgh on the eve of his wedding to Elizabeth later that year. In 1956 he introduced the Duke of Edinburgh's Award Scheme to encourage the leisure activities of young people between 14 and 25 years of age.

Philip, Saint¹. One of the Apostles; said to have spread the Gospel in Asia Minor. Matthew 10:3; Acts 1:13.

Philip, Saint². Called "the Evangelist". Christian leader of the first century A.D.

Phi·lip·pi (filli-pī, fi-líppī). Ancient town in Macedonia, Greece; the scene of the defeat of Brutus and Cassius by Mark Antony and Octavian (42 B.C.). —**Phi·lip·pi·an** (fi-líppi-ən) *n. & adj.*

Phi·lip·pi·ans (fi-líppi-ənz) *n. Used with a singular verb. Abbr.* **Phil.** A book of the New Testament, the epistle of Saint Paul to the Christians of Philippi.

Phi·lip·pic (fi-líppik) *n.* **1.** Any of the orations of Demosthenes against Philip of Macedon in the fourth century B.C. **2.** Any of the orations of Cicero against Mark Antony in 44 B.C. **3.** *Small* **p.** Any verbal denunciation characterised by invective.

Philippine mahogany *n.* Any of various Philippine hardwood trees of the genus *Shorea* and related genera.

Phil·ip·pines, Republic of the (filli-peenz, *rarely* -pīnz ‖ -péenz). Country in southeast Asia. It consists of over 7,000 islands, most of which are uninhabited. The largest islands are Luzon and Mindanao. The country is mountainous and heavily forested, and relies on agriculture, but manufacturing is expanding. Coconut products, copper, sugar, and forest products are the chief exports. The islands were colonised by the Spaniards, transferred to the United States (1898) following the Spanish-American war, and, after Japanese occupation in World War II, were granted independence (1946). Ferdinand Marcos, elected president in 1965, became virtual president for life with dictatorial powers in 1976. Area, 300 000 square kilometres (115,831 square miles). Population, 51,600,000. Capital, Manila. —**Phil·ip·pine** (filli-peen, *rarely* -pīn) *adj.*

Philippine Sea. Region of the west Pacific Ocean. Situated immediately to the east of the Philippines, it reaches its maximum depth in the Philippines Trench (10 540 metres; 34,578 feet).

Phi·lis·tine (filliss-tīn ‖ *U.S.* -steen, *also* fi-liss-) *n.* **1.** A member of the warlike people of ancient Philistia in southwestern Palestine. **2.** *Usually small* **p.** A boorish and uncultured person, especially one who is proud of his ignorance and actively antagonistic to intellectual or artistic matters.
~*adj.* **1.** Of or pertaining to the ancient Philistines. **2.** *Sometimes small* **p.** Lacking in or hostile to culture: *philistine cuts in arts spending.* [Middle English, from Late Latin *Philistīnus,* from Late Greek *Philistinos,* from Hebrew *Pelishtī,* Philistia, from *pelesheth,* "land of the Philistines".] —**Phi·lis·tin·ism** (-tin-iz'm) *n.*

Phillips Screw *n.* A trademark for a screw with a cross-shaped groove in its head, used with a matching screwdriver.

phil·lu·me·ny (fi-léwmə-ni, -lōōmə-) *n.* The collection and study of

matchbox labels. [PHILO- + Latin *lumen*, light + -Y.] **—phil·lu·men·ist** *n.*

Phi·lo (fī́-lō) **, Judaeus** (died A.D. *c.* 50). Jewish philosopher and historian. The author of many treatises, he is especially known for trying to interpret the Scriptures in terms of Greek philosophy.

philo-, phil-. Indicates love; for example, **philology, philanthropy.** [New Latin, from Greek, from *philos,* loving.]

phil·o·den·dron (fílla-dén-dran) *n., pl.* **-drons** or **-dra** (-dra). Any of various climbing tropical American plants of the genus *Philodendron,* many of which are cultivated as house plants for their heart-shaped, glossy green leaves. [New Latin, from Greek, from *philodendros,* "tree-loving" : PHILO- + *dendron,* tree.]

phi·lol·o·gy (fi-lólla-ji) *n. Abbr.* **philol.** 1. The study of language; especially, **historical linguistics** (*see*). 2. *Archaic.* Literary study or classical scholarship. [French *philologie,* from Old French, from Latin *philologia,* love of learning, from Greek : PHILO- + -LOGY.] **—phil·o·log·i·cal** (fílla-lójik'l) *adj.* **—phil·o·log·i·cal·ly** *adv.* **—phi·lol·o·gist** (-jist), **phi·lol·o·ger** (-jar) *n.*

Phil·o·mel (fíl-a-mel, -ō-) *n.* Also **Phil·o·me·la** (-méela ‖ -máyla). *Poetic.* The nightingale personified. [From PHILOMELA.]

Phil·o·me·la (fílla-méela ‖ -máyla). *Greek Mythology.* A princess of Athens who, after being raped and having her tongue cut out by Tereus, king of Thrace, was turned into either a swallow or a nightingale.

phil·o·pro·gen·i·tive (fíllō-prō-jénnativ) *adj.* 1. Producing many offspring; prolific. 2. Loving one's own offspring or children in general. 3. Of or pertaining to love of children. **—phil·o·pro·gen·i·tive·ly** *adv.* **—phil·o·pro·gen·i·tive·ness** *n.*

philos. philosopher; philosophical; philosophy.

phi·los·o·pher (fi-lóssafar) *n.* 1. *Abbr.* **phil., philos.** A student of or specialist in philosophy. 2. A person who lives and thinks according to a particular philosophy. 3. A writer or thinker whose intellectual or ideological theories are used as the basis of a policy, cult, or school of thought: *the philosopher of monetarism.* 4. A person who remains calm and rational even under the most trying of circumstances. 5. *Archaic.* An alchemist. [Middle English *philosophre,* from Old French *philosophe,* from Latin *philosophus,* from Greek *philosophos* "loving wisdom" : PHILO- + *sophos,* wise.]

philosophers' stone, philosopher's stone *n.* 1. In alchemy: **a.** The substance held to have the power of transmuting baser metals into gold. **b.** The **elixir** (*see*). 2. Anything, such as a principle or idea, thought capable of effecting spiritual or other regeneration.

phil·o·soph·i·cal (fílla-sóffik'l) *adj.* Also **phil·o·soph·ic** (-sóffik). *Abbr.* **phil., philos.** 1. Of, pertaining to, or based on a system of philosophy. 2. Characteristic of or befitting a philosopher; enlightened; wise. 3. Serene and stoical in the face of difficulties. **—phil·o·soph·i·cal·ly** *adv.*

phi·los·o·phise, phi·los·o·phize (fi-lóssa-fīz) *v.* **-phised, -phising,**

-phises. *—intr.* 1. To talk or speculate in a philosophical manner. 2. To indulge in moralistic and often superficial reasoning. *—tr.* 1. To make (a theory or view) philosophical. 2. To explain (an event, decision, or the like) in a philosophical way. **—phi·los·o·phis·er** *n.*

phi·los·o·phy (fi-lóssafi) *n., pl.* **-phies.** *Abbr.* **phil., philos.** 1. **a.** Love and pursuit of wisdom by intellectual means. **b.** The investigation of causes and laws underlying reality. **c.** A particular system of philosophical inquiry or demonstration. 2. Inquiry into the nature of things based on logical reasoning rather than empirical methods. 3. The critique and analysis of fundamental beliefs as they come to be conceptualised and formulated. 4. Formerly, the investigation of natural phenomena and its systematisation in theory and experiment, as in alchemy, astrology, or astronomy: *natural philosophy.* 5. All the disciplines presented in university curricula of science and the liberal arts, except medicine, law, and theology: *Doctor of Philosophy.* 6. The science comprising logic, ethics, aesthetics, metaphysics, and epistemology. 7. The general principles underlying a particular branch of study, field of activity, or approach to practical problems: *the philosophy of history; monetarist philosophy.* 8. The system of values by which one lives. 9. The calmness and detachment thought to befit a philosopher. [Middle English *philosophie,* from Old French, from Latin *philosophia,* from Greek, from *philosophos,* "loving wisdom". See **philosopher.**]

–philous, –philic *adj. comb. form.* Indicates a love of or attraction to something; for example, **photophilous, lyophilic.** [Greek *philos,* beloved, dear, loving.]

phil·tre, *U.S.* **phil·ter** (fíltar) *n.* 1. A love potion. 2. Any magic potion or charm. [French *philtre,* from Latin *philtrum,* from Greek *philtron,* "love charm", from *philein,* to love, from *philos,* beloved.]

phi·mo·sis (fī-mṓ-siss) *n.* Abnormal narrowing of the opening of the foreskin, which prevents its being drawn back over the tip of the penis. [New Latin, from Greek, a muzzling, from *phimos,* muzzle.]

phiz (fiz) *n.* Also **phiz·og** (fizzog) *Slang.* A face or facial expression. Not in current usage. [Alteration and shortening of PHYSIOGNOMY.]

Phiz. See Hablot Knight **Browne.**

phle·bi·tis (fli-bī́tiss, flee-, fle-) *n. Pathology.* Inflammation of a vein. [PHLEB(O)- + -ITIS.] **—phle·bit·ic** (-bíttik) *adj.*

phleb-, phleb- *comb. form.* Indicates a vein; for example, **phlebotomy, phlebitis.** [Greek, from *phleps†* (stem *phleb-*), vein.]

phle·bot·o·mise, phle·bot·o·mize (fli-bóttamīz, flee-, fle-) *tr.v.* **-mised, -mising, -mises.** *Medicine.* To perform a phlebotomy on.

phle·bot·o·my (fli-bótta-mi, flee-, fle-) *n., pl.* **-mies.** *Medicine.* The therapeutic practice of opening a vein to draw blood. Also called "venesection". [Middle English *flebotomye,* from Old French *flebotomie,* from Late Latin *phlebotomia,* from Greek, "blood-letting" : PHLEBO- + -TOMY.] **—phleb·o·tom·ic** (flébba-tómmik, fléeba-), **phleb·o·tom·i·cal** *adj.* **—phle·bot·o·mist** (-mist) *n.*

Phleg·e·thon (flégga-thən, -thon). *Greek Mythology.* A river of fire, one of the six rivers of Hades. [Greek, from *phlegethein,* to blaze, from *phlegein,* to burn.]

phlegm (flem) *n.* 1. *Physiology.* Thick mucus secreted by the respiratory mucosa. 2. One of the four humours of ancient physiology. 3. Sluggishness of temperament. 4. Calm self-possession; equanimity. [Middle English *fleume,* from Old French, from Late Latin *phlegma,* body moisture, from Greek, flame, inflammation, phlegm, from *phlegein,* to burn.] **—phlegm·y** (flémmi) *adj.*

phleg·mat·ic (fleg-máttik) *adj.* Having or suggesting a calm, unexcitable temperament; unemotional. [Middle English from Old French from Late Latin *phlegmaticus,* from Greek *phlegmatikos,* having phlegm, from *phlegma* (stem *phlegmat-*), PHLEGM.]

phlo·em (flṓ-em) *n. Botany.* The nutrient-conducting tissue of vascular plants, consisting of sieve tubes and other cellular material. Also called "bast". Compare **xylem.** [German *Phloem,* from Greek *phloios, phloos,* bark.]

phlo·gis·tic (flo-jístik, fla- ‖ flṓ-) *adj.* 1. Of or pertaining to phlogiston. 2. *Medicine.* Of or pertaining to inflammation or fever.

phlo·gis·ton (flo-jíss-tan, fla-, -ton ‖ flṓ-) *n.* A hypothetical substance formerly thought to be a volatile constituent of all combustible substances released as flame in combustion. [New Latin, from Greek, from *phlogistos,* "inflammable", from *phlogizein,* to set on fire, from *phlox* (stem *phlog-*), flame, from *phlegein,* to burn.]

phlog·o·pite (flógga-pīt) *n.* A yellow to dark-brown mica, $KMg_3AlSi_3O_{10}(OH)_2$, used in insulation. [German *Phlogopit,* from Greek *phlogōpos,* "fiery-looking" : *phlox* (stem *phlog-*), flame (see **phlogiston**) + *ōps,* eye.]

phlox (floks) *n., pl.* **phlox** or **phloxes.** Any plant of the genus *Phlox,* chiefly native to North America but widely cultivated, having lance-shaped leaves and clusters of white, red, or purple flowers. [New Latin, from Latin, a flower, from Greek, wallflower, flame, from *phlegein,* to burn.]

phlyc·te·na, phlyc·tae·na (flik-tée-na) *n., pl.* **-nae** (-nee). *Medicine.* A small blister; a vesicle. [New Latin, from Greek *phluktaina,* blister, from *phluein, phluzein,* to boil over.]

Phnom Penh (pnóm pén, nóm, pə-nóm). Capital of Kampuchea (Cambodia). Situated at the head of the Mekong Delta, it was a loyalist stronghold during the civil war (1970–75) but suffered greatly, with most of its population being dispersed after its fall to the Khmer Rouge (1976). It was a thriving port and a cultural and commercial centre, producing textiles, shipping, and dried fish.

–phobe *n. comb. form.* Indicates one that fears, often irrationally, or is averse to or lacks an affinity for something specified; for example, **xenophobe.** [Greek *-phobos,* fearing, from *phobos,* fear, flight.]

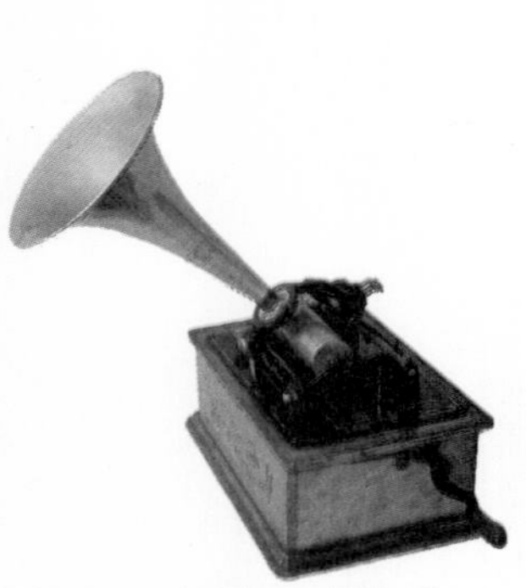

phonograph *Thomas Edison's standard phonograph in the Science Museum, London. These early clockwork phonographs, which used a needle running in the grooves of a cylinder, were the forerunners of modern record players.*

pho·bi·a (fṓb-i-ə) *n.* **1.** A persistent, abnormal, or irrational fear of something specified. **2.** Any strong fear, dislike, or aversion. [New Latin, independent use of *-phobia,* -PHOBIA.] **—pho·bic** (-ik) *adj.*

-phobia *n. comb. form.* Indicates persistent, irrational, abnormal, or intense fear; for example, **hypnophobia.** [New Latin, from Late Latin, from Greek, from *phobos,* fear, flight.]

-phobic *adj. comb. form.* Indicates: **1.** Having an abnormal fear or dread of; for example, **arachnophobic. 2.** Lacking an affinity for; for example, **lyophobic.** [-PHOBIA + -IC.]

Pho·bos (fṓb-oss, fób-) *n. Astronomy.* The larger and inner of the two satellites of the planet Mars.

phoe·be (féebi) *n.* Any of several small dull-coloured North American birds of the genus *Sayornis.* [Imitative of its call.]

Phoe·be[1] (féebi). *Greek Mythology.* The goddess Artemis. [Greek *Phoibē,* from *phoibos,* shining.]

Phoe·be[2] (féebi) *n.* **1.** *Poetic.* The moon. **2.** *Astronomy.* The ninth, smallest, and outermost of the major satellites of Saturn. [From PHOEBE.]

Phoe·bus (féebəss). *Greek Mythology.* Apollo, the god of the sun. [Greek *phoibos,* radiant.]

Phoe·ni·cia (fi-néesh-ə, -nísh-, -i-ə). Ancient name for the coastal areas of modern Syria and Lebanon. It was settled by a Semitic people descended from the Canaanites who established a trading empire (*c.* 1200 B.C.) along the Mediterranean. Its chief colony was at Carthage, North Africa, with others in Spain, Cyprus, and Sicily, and its chief towns were Sidon and Tyre.

Phoe·ni·cian (fi-néesh-'n, -nísh-, -i-ən) *n.* **1.** A native, inhabitant, or subject of ancient Phoenicia. **2.** The Northwest Semitic language of ancient Phoenicia. [Middle English *Phenicien,* from Old French, from Latin *Phoenīcius,* from Greek *phoinix,* PHOENIX, also a Phoenician (the association is unexplained).] **—Phoe·ni·cian** *adj.*

phoe·nix (féeniks) *n.* **1.** A mythological bird that consumed itself by fire after 500 years, and rose renewed from its ashes. **2.** A person or thing that has been restored to a new existence from destruction, downfall, or ruin. **3.** A person or thing of unsurpassed excellence or beauty; a paragon. [Middle English *fenix,* from Old French, from Latin *phoenix,* from Greek *phoinix,* phoenix, purple, Phoenician.]

Phoenix[1]. Town in Arizona, United States. Situated on the river Salt, it is in a dairy and citrus fruit region, is a health resort, and produces textiles, aircraft, steel, and aluminium.

Phoenix[2] *n. Astronomy.* A constellation in the Southern Hemisphere near Tucana and Sculptor.

Phoenix Islands. See **Kiribati.**

phon (fon) *n.* A unit of loudness equal to the number of decibels a sound is above a reference tone having a frequency of 1000 hertz and a given root-mean-square sound pressure. [Greek *phōnē,* sound.]

phon. phonetic; phonetics; phonology.

pho·nate (fō-náyt || *U.S.* fṓ-nayt) *v.* **-nated, -nating, -nates.** *—intr.* To utter vocal sounds; vocalise. *—tr.* To utter (a sound). [PHON(O)- + -ATE.] **—pho·na·tion** (-náysh'n) *n.* **—pho·nat·o·ry** (fṓnə-təri, -tri, fō-náy- || *U.S.* -tawri, -tōri) *adj.*

phone[1] (fōn) *n. Linguistics.* Any individual sound as realised in speech. [Greek *phōnē,* sound, voice.]

phone[2] *n.* A telephone.
~*v.* **phoned, phoning, phones.** *—intr.* To telephone. *—tr.* **1.** To telephone (someone). **2.** To impart (information or news, for example) by telephone. [Short for TELEPHONE.]
Usage: This form of *telephone* is a word in its own right, is not usually preceded by an apostrophe ('phone) in written English.

-phone *n. comb. form.* Indicates: **1.** A sound or sound-emitting device; for example, **radiophone. 2.** A speaker of a specified language; for example, **Anglophone.**
~*adj. comb. form.* Indicates speaking a specified language; for example, **Francophone.** [Greek *phōnē,* sound, voice.]

phone-in (fṓn-in) *n.* A live radio or television programme in which listeners telephone the studio to answer quiz questions, respond to charity appeals, or put questions and views to the presenter or a panel of guests for discussion.

pho·neme (fṓn-eem) *n. Linguistics.* Any of the classes of speech sounds in a given language or accent that have the potential to distinguish words one from another. The initial consonant sounds in *leaf* and *reef* belong to different phonemes (l) and (r) respectively, since these words are distinct in meaning. [French *phonème,* from Greek *phōnēma,* an utterance, from *phōnein*; See **phonetic.**]

pho·ne·mic (fə-néemik, fō-) *adj.* Also **pho·ne·mat·ic** (fṓni-máttik, fónni-) **1.** Of, pertaining to, or having the characteristics of a phoneme. **2.** Of or pertaining to phonemics. **3.** Serving to differentiate the meaning of otherwise identical utterances. **4.** Pertaining to or designating speech sounds that belong to different phonemes. **—pho·ne·mi·cal·ly** *adv.*

pho·ne·mi·cise, pho·ne·mi·cize (fə-néemi-sīz, fō-) *tr.v.* **-cised, -cising, -cises.** To analyse (speech sounds) into phonemes. **—pho·ne·mi·ci·sa·tion** *n.*

pho·ne·mics (fə-néemiks, fō-) *n. Used with a singular verb. Linguistics.* The study and establishment of the phonemes of a language. **—pho·ne·mi·cist** (-néemi-sist) *n.*

phonet. phonetic; phonetics.

pho·net·ic (fə-néttik, fō-) *adj. Abbr.* **phon., phonet. 1.** Of or pertaining to phonetics. **2.** Representing the sounds of speech with a set of distinct symbols, each denoting a single sound: *phonetic spelling.* **3.** Altering the conventional spelling of a word so as to better represent its pronunciation; for example, the spelling *kwik* for *quick.* **4.** Employing more than the minimum number of symbols necessary to differentiate the meaning of utterances. **5.** Designating the distinction between any speech sounds, whether or not these are phonemes. [New Latin *phoneticus,* from Greek *phōnētikos,* from *phōnein,* to sound, from *phōnē,* sound, voice.] **—pho·net·i·cal·ly** *adv.*

phonetic alphabet *n.* **1.** A standardised set of symbols used in phonetic transcription. See **International Phonetic Alphabet. 2.** In telecommunications, any of various systems of code words for identifying letters in voice communication, such as *Charlie* standing for *C, Foxtrot* for *F,* and the like.

pho·ne·ti·cian (fṓni-tísh'n, fónni-) *n.* An expert in phonetics.

pho·net·ics (fə-néttiks, fō-) *n. Used with a singular verb. Abbr.* **phon., phonet. 1.** The science or study of the sounds of speech, their production, reception, combination, description, classification, and representation by written symbols. **2.** The system of sounds of a particular language.

pho·ney (fṓni) *adj.* **-nier, niest.** Also *chiefly U.S.* **pho·ny.** *Informal.* **1.** Not genuine or real; spurious; fake: *a phoney painting.* **2.** Having a false manner or image; insincere.
~*n., pl.* **phoneys** or **-nies.** *Informal.* **1.** Something not genuine; a fake. **2.** A person who projects false feelings or a false image. [20th century : origin obscure.] **—pho·ni·ly** *adv.* **—pho·ni·ness** *n.*

phon·ic (fónnik, fṓnik) *adj.* **1.** Of, pertaining to, or having the nature of sound, especially speech sound. **2.** Of or pertaining to phonics. [PHON(O)- + -IC.] **—phon·i·cal·ly** *adv.*

phon·ics (fónniks) *n. Used with a singular verb.* **1.** The study or science of sound; acoustics. Not in current technical usage. **2.** A method of teaching reading and pronunciation by training learners to recognise the phonetic value of letters and syllables.

phono–, phon– *comb. form.* Indicates sound or a voice; for example, **phonology.** [Greek *phōnē,* sound, voice.]

pho·no·gram (fṓnə-gram) *n.* A character, symbol, or sequence of symbols, as in a phonetic alphabet, representing a word or phoneme in speech. [PHONO- + -GRAM.] **—pho·no·gram·ic, pho·no·gram·mic** (-grámmik) *adj.* **—pho·no·gram·i·cal·ly, pho·no·gram·mi·cal·ly** *adv.*

pho·no·graph (fṓnə-graaf, -graf) *n.* **1.** An early machine for recording and reproducing sounds using a wax cylinder. **2.** *U.S.* A **gramophone** *(see).* [PHONO- + -GRAPH.] **—pho·no·graph·ic** (-gráffik) *adj.* **—pho·no·graph·i·cal·ly** *adv.*

pho·nog·ra·phy (fə-nóggrə-fi, fō-) *n.* **1.** The science or practice of transcribing speech by means of symbols representing elements of sound; phonetic transcription. **2.** Any system of writing or shorthand based on phonetic transcription. [PHONO- + -GRAPHY.] **—pho·nog·ra·pher** (-fər), **pho·nog·ra·phist** (-fist) *n.*

pho·no·lite (fṓn-ə-līt, -ō-) *n.* A volcanic rock composed principally of orthoclase and nepheline. Also called "clinkstone". [French, from German *Phonolith* : PHONO- + -LITH (it clinks when struck).] **—pho·no·lit·ic** (-líttik) *adj.*

pho·nol·o·gy (fə-nólləji, fō-) *n. Abbr.* **phon., phonol. 1.** The study of the sound system of a language or of two or more related languages. **2.** The sound system of a given language. [PHONO- + -LOGY.] **—pho·no·log·i·cal** (fṓnə-lójik'l, fónnə-) *adj.* **—pho·no·log·i·cal·ly** *adv.* **—pho·nol·o·gist** (-jist) *n.*

pho·nom·e·ter (fə-nómmitər, fo-, fō-) *n.* A device that measures the intensity of sound, usually calibrated in phons. [PHONO- + -METER.] **—pho·no·met·ric** (fṓnə-méttrik, fónnə-), **pho·no·met·ri·cal** *adj.*

pho·non (fṓn-on) *n. Physics.* The quantum of thermal energy in a crystal lattice, used especially in mathematical models to calculate vibrational properties of solids. There are two types of phonon: *acoustic,* corresponding to longitudinal motion of the lattice points, and *optic,* corresponding to transverse motion. [PHON(O)- + -ON.]

pho·no·re·cep·tion (fṓnō-ri-sép-sh'n) *n.* Perception of or response to sound waves. **—pho·no·re·cep·tor** (-tər) *n.*

pho·no·scope (fṓn-ə-skōp, -ō-) *n.* A device that produces a visible display of the mechanical properties of a sounding body, especially of musical instruments. [PHONO- + -SCOPE.]

pho·no·type (fṓn-ə-tīp, -ō-) *n.* **1.** A phonetic symbol used in printing. **2.** Text printed in phonetic symbols. **—pho·no·typ·ic** (-típpik), **pho·no·typ·i·cal** *adj.* **—pho·no·typ·i·cal·ly** *adv.*

pho·no·typ·y (fṓn-ə-tīpi, -ō-) *n.* The practice of transcribing speech sounds by means of phonetic symbols. **—pho·no·typ·ist** *n.*

phony. *Chiefly U.S.* Variant of **phoney.**

-phony *n. comb. form.* Indicates sound of a specified kind; for example, **telephony.** [Greek *-phōnia,* from *phōnē,* sound.]

phoo·ey (fōō-i) *interj.* Used as an exclamation of disgust, disbelief, disappointment, or contempt. [Imitative.]

-phore *n. comb. form.* Indicates a bearer or producer of; for example, **semaphore.** [Greek *-phoros,* bearing, from *pherein,* to bear.]

-phoresis *n. comb. form.* Indicates transmission; for example, **electrophoresis.** [Greek *phorēsis,* a bearing, from *phorein,* frequentative of *pherein,* to bear.]

phor·mi·um (fáwr-mi-əm) *n.* A genus of perennial plants, grown chiefly for their long, stiff, bladelike leaves; especially, *P. tenax* (New Zealand flax), often used as a border plant.

-phorous *adj. comb. form.* Indicates bearing or producing; for example, **gonophorous.** [Greek *-phoros,* from *pherein,* to bear.]

phos- *comb. form.* Indicates the presence of light; for example, **phosgene.** [Greek *phōs,* light.]

phos·gene (fóss-jeen, fóz-) *n.* A colourless volatile liquid or gas, $COCl_2$, used as a poison gas and in making glass, dyes, resins, and plastics. Also called "carbonyl chloride". [PHOS- (from the former method of obtaining the compound by exposure to sunlight) + -gene, variant of -GEN.]

phos·ge·nite (fózji-nīt) n. A rare fluorescent secondary mineral, Pb₂(Cl₂CO₃), occurring as white, yellow, or grey tetragonal crystals. [German *Phosgenit* : PHOSGENE + -ITE.]

phosph-. Variant of **phospho-.**

phos·pha·gen (fósfə-jen) n. Phosphocreatine. [PHOSPHA(TE) + -gen.]

phos·pha·tase (fósfə-tayz, -tayss) n. Any of numerous enzymes that catalyse the hydrolysis of phosphoric acid esters to phosphate ions. [PHOSPHAT(E) + -ASE.]

phos·phate (fóss-fayt, *rarely* -fət, -fit) n. **1.** *Chemistry.* Any salt or ester of phosphoric acid containing mainly pentavalent phosphorus and oxygen. **2.** A fertiliser containing phosphorus compounds. [French *phosphat*, from *phosphore*, phosphorous, from New Latin *phosphorus*, PHOSPHORUS.] —**phos·phat·ic** (foss-fáttik, fóss-) adj.

phosphate rock n. Any of various sedimentary rocks composed largely of apatite, or guano deposits, both of which are used as fertiliser and as a source of phosphorous compounds.

phos·pha·tide (fósfə-tīd) n. A phospholipid.

phos·pha·tise, phos·pha·tize (fósfə-tīz) v. **-tised, -tising, -tises.** —*tr.* **1.** To change into a phosphate or phosphorus. **2.** To treat with phosphate or phosphoric acid. —*intr.* To change into or become a phosphate. —**phos·pha·ti·sa·tion** (-tī-záysh'n ‖ U.S. -ti-) n.

phos·pha·tu·ri·a (fósfə-téwr-i-ə ‖ -tóor-) n. A condition in which excessive phosphates are discharged in the urine. [New Latin : PHOSPHAT(E) + -URIA.] —**phos·pha·tu·ric** (-ik) adj.

phos·phene (fóss-feen) n. A luminous visual sensation experienced when the eyeball is pressed. [PHOS- + Greek *phainein*, to show.]

phos·phide (fóss-fīd) n. A compound of phosphorus and a more electropositive element. [PHOSPH(O)- + -IDE.]

phos·phine (fóss-feen) n. **1.** A colourless, spontaneously flammable poisonous gas, PH₃, having a garlic-like smell and is used as a doping agent for solid-state components. **2.** A synthetic yellow dye. [PHOSPH(O)- + -INE.]

phos·phite (fóss-fīt) n. Any salt of phosphorous acid.

phospho-, phosph- *comb. form.* Indicates the presence of phosphorus; for example, **phosphocreatine.** [French, from *phosphore*, phosphorus, from New Latin *phosphorus*, PHOSPHORUS.]

phos·pho·cre·a·tine (fóss-fō-krée-ə-teen, -fə-) n. Also **phos·pho·cre·a·tin** (-tin). An organic compound, C₄H₁₀N₃O₅P, found in vertebrate tissues, capable of providing physiological energy as in muscular contraction. Also called "phosphagen".

phos·pho·lip·id (fóss-fə-líppid, -fō-) n. Any of a group of compound lipids consisting of phosphoric acid, fatty acids, and a nitrogenous base, forming an important part of cell membranes. Also called "phosphatide".

phos·pho·ni·um (foss-fóni-əm, fóss-) n. A univalent radical, PH₄, derived from phosphine. [PHOSPH(O)- + (AMM)ONIUM.]

phos·pho·pro·tein (fóss-fō-prṓ-teen, -fə-, -tee-in) n. Any of a group of proteins, containing chemically bound phosphoric acid.

phos·phor (fóss-fər ‖ -fawr) n. **1.** Any substance that can be stimulated to emit light by incident radiation. **2.** Something exhibiting phosphorescence. [French *phosphore*, from New Latin *phosphorus*, PHOSPHORUS.]

phosphor bronze n. A hard, strong, corrosion-resistant bronze containing up to 0.5 per cent phosphorus and used in electric switches, springs, and chains.

phos·pho·resce (fósfə-réss) intr.v. **-resced, -rescing, -resces.** To exhibit phosphorescence. [Back-formation from *phosphorescent* : PHOSPHOR + -ESCENT.]

phos·pho·res·cence (fósfə-réss'nss) n. Persistent emission of light following exposure to and removal of incident radiation. Compare **fluorescence, bioluminescence.** [From PHOSPHOR.] —**phos·pho·res·cent** adj. —**phos·pho·res·cent·ly** adv.

phos·phor·ic (foss-fórrik, fóss- ‖ -fáwrik; U.S. *also* fósfərik) adj. Of, pertaining to, or containing phosphorus, especially in a valency state higher than that of a comparable phosphorous compound.

phosphoric acid n. A clear colourless liquid, H₃PO₄, used in fertilisers, soaps and detergents, food flavouring, and pharmaceuticals.

phos·pho·rism (fósfər-iz'm) n. Chronic phosphorus poisoning from ingestion or inhalation. [PHOSPHOR(US) + -ISM.]

phos·pho·rite (fósfər-īt) n. **1.** A fibrous variety of **apatite** (*see*). **2.** A concretionary mass of rock consisting predominantly of calcium phosphate. [PHOSPHOR(US) + -ITE.]

phos·pho·rous (fósfərəss ‖ U.S. *also* foss-fáwrəss, -fṓrəss) adj. Of, pertaining to, or containing phosphorus, especially in the trivalent state.

phosphorous acid n. *Chemistry.* A white or yellowish hygroscopic crystalline solid, H₃PO₃, used as a reducing agent and to produce phosphite salts.

phos·pho·rus (fósfərəss) n. **1.** *Symbol* **P** A highly reactive, poisonous, nonmetallic element occurring naturally in phosphates, especially apatite, and existing in three allotropic forms, white (sometimes yellow), red, and black. It is an essential constituent of living cells and, depending on the allotropic form, is used in safety matches, pyrotechnics, incendiary shells, fertilisers, glass, and steel. Atomic number 15, atomic weight 30.9738, melting point (white) 44.1°C, boiling point 280°C, relative density (white) 1.83, valencies 3, 5. **2.** Any phosphorescent substance. [New Latin, from Greek *phōsphoros*, "light-bearing" (so named from the fact that white phosphorus is phosphorescent in air) : PHOS- + -PHOROUS.]

phosphorus pentoxide n. A white solid, P₂O₅, produced by burning phosphorus. It has an affinity for water, with which it forms phosphoric acid.

phos·pho·ryl·ase (foss-fórri-layz, fósfəri-, -layss) n. *Biochemistry.* Any of a group of enzymes that catalyse the production of glucose-1-phosphate from glycogen. [PHOSPHOR(US) + -YL + -ASE.]

phos·pho·ryl·ate (foss-fórri-layt, fósfəri-) tr.v. **-ated, -ating, -ates.** To change (an organic substance) into an organic phosphate. [PHOSPHOR(US) + -YL + -ATE.] —**phos·pho·ryl·a·tion** (-láysh'n) n.

phos·sy jaw (fóssi) n. *Informal.* Degeneration of the bone of the lower jaw caused by prolonged exposure to phosphorus fumes. [*phossy*, shortened from PHOSPHORUS.]

phot (fōt, fot) n. *Physics.* A unit of illumination equal to one **lumen** (*see*) per square centimetre. [Greek *phōs* (stem *phōt-*), light.]

pho·tic (fṓtik) adj. **1.** Of or pertaining to light. **2.** *Biology.* Pertaining to the production of light by organisms. **3.** Pertaining to or designating the upper zone or region of a body of water, into which sunlight penetrates. [PHOT(O)- + -IC.]

pho·to (fṓtō) n., pl. **-tos.** *Informal.* A photograph.

photo-, phot- *comb. form.* Indicates: **1.** Light; for example, **photosynthesis, photic. 2.** Photographic; for example, **photomontage.** [Greek *phōs* (stem *phōt-*), light.]

pho·to·ac·tin·ic (fṓtō-ak-tínnik) adj. Able to emit actinic radiation.

pho·to·ac·tive (fṓtō-áktiv) adj. **1.** Capable of responding to photoelectric stimulation. **2.** Capable of responding to light by chemical reaction. —**pho·to·ac·tiv·i·ty** (-ak-tívvəti) n.

pho·to·au·to·troph·ic (fṓtō-áwt-ə-trṓffik, -ō-, -trṓfik) adj. *Biology.* Capable of using light as a source of energy in the synthesis of food from inorganic materials.

pho·to·bi·ot·ic (fṓtō-bī-óttik) adj. *Biology.* Depending on light for the continuance of life and growth.

pho·to·call (fṓtō-kawl) n. A gathering of people on some special occasion to enable the press to take photographs of them.

pho·to·cath·ode (fṓtō-káthōd) n. A cathode that emits electrons when it is illuminated.

pho·to·cell (fṓtō-sel) n. *Electronics.* A **photoelectric cell** (*see*).

pho·to·chem·is·try (fṓtō-kémmistri) n. The chemistry of the interactions of radiant energy and chemical systems. —**pho·to·chem·i·cal** (-kémmik'l) adj.

pho·to·chro·mic (fṓtō-krṓmic) adj. **1.** Of or designating a substance exhibiting photochromism. **2.** Of or pertaining to transparent materials containing compounds exhibiting photochromism.

pho·to·chro·mism (fṓtō-krṓmiz'm) n. The ability of certain compound materials, especially treated plastics, to darken or change colour when exposed to visible or near ultraviolet light and to revert to their original transparency or colour when the light source is removed.

pho·to·chron·o·graph (fṓtō-krónnə-graaf, -graf) n. A device for measuring small intervals of time by the length of a trace made by a light beam on a moving photographic film. —**pho·to·chron·og·ra·phy** n.

pho·to·com·pose (fṓtō-kəm-pṓz ‖ -kom-) tr.v. **-posed, -posing, -poses.** To prepare (written or graphic matter) for printing by photocomposition; filmset; photoset. —**pho·to·com·pos·er** n.

pho·to·com·po·si·tion (fṓtō-kómpə-zísh'n) n. The projection of the image of type characters, by photomechanical or electronic means, onto photographic film, which is used to prepare printing plates. Also called "filmsetting", "phototypesetting".

pho·to·con·duc·tiv·i·ty (fṓtō-kón-duk-tívvəti) n. *Physics.* The increase in electrical conductivity of certain semiconductors when exposed to light. —**pho·to·con·duc·tive** (-kən-dúktiv ‖ -kon-) adj. —**pho·to·con·duc·tion** n.

pho·to·cop·i·er (fṓtō-koppi-ər, -kóppi-) n. A device for photographically reproducing written, printed, or graphic material.

pho·to·cop·y (fṓtō-koppi; *as verb also* -kóppi) tr.v. **-copied, -copying, -copies.** To make a photographic reproduction of (printed, written, or graphic material). ~n., pl. **photocopies.** A photographic reproduction.

pho·to·cur·rent (fṓtō-kurrənt) n. *Physics.* An electric current produced by illumination of a photoelectric material.

pho·to·dis·in·te·gra·tion (fṓtō-diss-ínti-gráysh'n) n. *Physics.* Nuclear disintegration or transformation caused by absorption of gamma rays, or other high-energy radiation.

pho·to·dy·nam·ic (fṓtō-dī-námmik) adj. *Biology.* Of or pertaining to the effect of light on organisms. —**pho·to·dy·nam·ics** n.

pho·to·e·las·tic·i·ty (fṓtō-dee-lass-tíssəti, -i-) n. *Physics.* The effect of distortion of a solid on its optical properties; especially, the production of double refraction in crystals by applied stress. —**pho·to·e·las·tic** adj.

pho·to·e·lec·tric (fṓtō-i-léktrik) adj. Also **pho·to·e·lec·tri·cal** (-'l). Of or pertaining to electric effects, such as increased electrical conduction, caused by illumination. —**pho·to·e·lec·tri·cal·ly** adv. —**pho·to·e·lec·tric·i·ty** (-lek-tríssəti, -éllek-, -éelek-) n.

photoelectric cell n. An electronic device having an electrical output that varies in response to incident radiation, especially to visible light. Also called "electric eye", "magic eye", "photocell".

photoelectric effect n. *Physics.* The ejection of electrons from a substance by incident electromagnetic radiation, especially by visible and ultraviolet light.

pho·to·e·lec·tron (fṓtō-i-lék-tron) n. *Physics.* An electron released or ejected from a substance by the photoelectric effect.

pho·to·e·mis·sion (fṓtō-i-mísh'n) n. *Physics.* The emission of photoelectrons, especially from metallic surfaces.

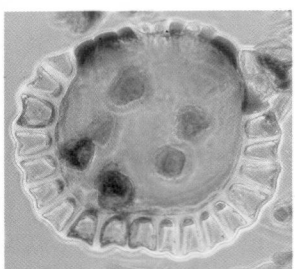

photomicrograph *A photograph taken through a microscope. This example is of the spore-bearing structure in a fern.*

pho·to·en·grave (fṓtō-in-gráyv, -en-) *tr.v.* **-graved, -graving, -graves.** To reproduce by photoengraving. —**pho·to·en·grav·er** *n.*

pho·to·en·grav·ing (fṓtō-in-gráyving, -en-) *n.* **1.** The process of reproducing graphic or printed material by transferring the image photomechanically to a plate or other surface in etched relief for printing. **2.** A plate prepared by this method. **3.** A reproduction made by this method.

photo finish *n.* **1.** The end of a race in which the leading contestants cross the finishing line so close together that the winner must be determined by a photograph taken at the moment of crossing. **2.** *Informal.* Any extremely close finish or result.

Pho·to·fit (fṓtō-fit) *n.* A trademark for a system of, or the equipment for, creating a picture of the face of a criminal suspect, missing person, or the like. The process involves combining photographs of individual facial features into a composite portrait, on the basis of a description. Compare **Identikit**.

pho·to·flash (fṓtō-flash) *n.* In photography, a **flashbulb** *(see).*

pho·to·flood (fṓtō-flud) *n.* A reusable electric lamp that produces a bright continuous light for photographic illumination.

pho·to·fluor·og·ra·phy (fṓtō-flōo-ə-róggrəfi, -floor-) *n. Medicine.* The process of taking photographs *(photofluorograms)* of fluoroscopic images. [PHOTO- + FLUORO- + -GRAPHY.] —**pho·to·fluor·o·graph·ic** (-rə-gráffik) *adj.*

photog. photograph; photographer; photography.

pho·to·gel·a·tine process (fṓtō-jélla-tin) *n.* In photography, **collotype** *(see).*

pho·to·gene (fṓt-ō-jeen, -ə-) *n. Physiology.* A retinal **afterimage** *(see).* [PHOTO- + -gene, variant of -GEN.]

pho·to·gen·ic (fṓt-ə-jénnik, -ō-, *rarely* -jéenik) *adj.* **1.** Having a physical appearance, especially facial characteristics, that photographs well. **2.** *Biology.* Producing or emitting light; phosphorescent. **3.** *Rare.* Caused or produced by light. [PHOTO- + -GENIC.] —**pho·to·gen·i·cal·ly** *adv.*

pho·to·ge·ol·o·gy (fṓtō-jee-ólləji, -ji-) *n.* The study of geology and geological phenomena by means of aerial and satellite photography.

pho·to·gram (fṓtə-gram) *n.* **1.** A shadowy image produced without a camera by placing an object in contact with film or photosensitive paper and exposing to light. **2.** *Archaic.* A photograph. [PHOTO- + -GRAM.]

pho·to·gram·me·try (fṓt-ō-grámmətri, -ə-) *n.* **1.** The process of making maps or scale drawings by aerial or other photography. **2.** The process of making precise measurements by the use of photography. [PHOTOGRAM + -METRY.] —**pho·to·gram·met·ric** (-grə-méttrik) *adj.* —**pho·to·gram·me·trist** (-grámmətrist) *n.*

pho·to·graph (fṓtə-graaf, -graf) *n. Abbr.* **photog.** An image, especially a positive print, recorded by a camera and reproduced on a photosensitive surface.
~*v.* **photographed, -graphing, -graphs.** —*tr.* To take a photograph of. —*intr.* **1.** To practise photography. **2.** To appear in photographs in a specified way: *She photographs well.* [PHOTO- + -GRAPH.]

pho·tog·ra·pher (fə-tóggrəfər) *Abbr.* **photog.** A person who takes photographs, especially as a profession.

pho·to·graph·ic (fṓtə-gráffik) *adj.* Also **pho·to·graph·i·cal** ('l). **1.** Of, pertaining to, or produced by photography. **2.** Used in photography: *a photographic lens.* **3.** Resembling a photograph; especially, representing or simulating something with great accuracy and fidelity of detail. **4.** Capable of retaining facts or forming accurate and lasting impressions, often after reading or seeing something for only a short time: *had a photographic memory.* —**pho·to·graph·i·cal·ly** *adv.*

photographic magnitude *n.* The magnitude of a star as measured from a photographic plate, taking into account the difference in colour sensitivity between the emulsion and the eye.

pho·tog·ra·phy (fə-tóggrəfi) *n. Abbr.* **photog.** **1.** The process of creating optical images on photosensitive surfaces. **2.** The art, practice, or occupation of taking and printing photographs, slides, or films. [PHOTO- + -GRAPHY.]

pho·to·gra·vure (fṓt-ə-grə-véwr, -ō-) *n.* **1.** The process of printing from an intaglio plate on which an image has been engraved by means of photography. **2.** A picture or reproduction, or graphic material generally, produced by this process.

pho·to·he·li·o·graph (fṓtō-héeli-ə-graaf, -graf) *n.* A refracting telescope equipped to photograph the sun.

pho·to·i·on·i·sa·tion (fṓtō-ī-ən-ī-záysh'n || *U.S.* -i-) *n.* The ionisation of an atom or molecule as a result of exposure to radiation. See **ionising radiation**.

pho·to·jour·nal·ism (fṓtō-júrn'l-iz'm) *n.* Journalism making extensive use of photographs rather than written material as a means of reporting news. —**pho·to·jour·nal·ist** *n.*

pho·to·ki·ne·sis (fṓtō-kī-née-siss, -ki-) *n. Biology.* Movement as a response to light. —**pho·to·ki·net·ic** (-néttik) *adj.*

pho·to·lith·o·graph (fṓt-ō-líth-ə-graaf, -ə-, -líth-, -ō-, -graf) *tr.v.* **-graphed, -graphing, -graphs.** To reproduce by means of photolithography.
~*n.* A picture made by photolithography. —**pho·to·li·thog·ra·pher** (-li-thóggrəfər) *n.*

pho·to·li·thog·ra·phy (fṓtō-li-thóggrəfi, -lī-) *n.* **1.** A planographic printing process using plates prepared by photographic means. Also "photolith". **2.** *Electronics.* A technique for making printed circuits, integrated circuits, and the like by photographically reproducing a pattern for electroplating, etching, or diffusion. —**pho·to·lith·o·graph·ic** (-líthə-gráffik) *adj.*

pho·to·lu·mi·nes·cence (fṓtō-lōomi-néss'nss, -léwmi-) *n.* **Luminescence** *(see)* produced by infrared radiation, visible light, or ultraviolet radiation. —**pho·to·lu·mi·nes·cent** *adj.*

pho·tol·y·sis (fō-tóllə-siss) *n.* Chemical decomposition induced by light or other radiant energy. [New Latin : PHOTO- + -LYSIS.] —**pho·to·lyt·ic** (fṓt-ə-líttik, -ō-) *adj.*

photom. photometry.

pho·to·map (fṓt-ō-map, -ə-) *n.* A map made by superimposing orientating data on an aerial photograph.

pho·to·me·chan·i·cal (fṓtō-mi-kánnik'l) *adj.* Of, pertaining to, or designating any of various methods by which plates are prepared for printing by means of photography.
~*n.* A piece of artwork or paste-up of typeset material that is ready to be processed into a printing plate by photographic means. —**pho·to·me·chan·i·cal·ly** *adv.*

pho·tom·e·ter (fō-tómmitər) *n.* An instrument for measuring a property of light, especially luminous intensity or flux. [PHOTO- + -METER.]

pho·tom·e·try (fō-tómmətri) *n. Abbr.* **photom.** *Physics.* The measurement of the properties of light, especially of luminous intensity. [PHOTO- + -METRY.] —**pho·to·met·ric** (fṓt-ə-méttrik, -ō-), **pho·to·met·ri·cal** *adj.* —**pho·tom·e·trist** (-tómmətrist) *n.*

pho·to·mi·cro·graph (fṓtō-míkrə-graaf, -míkrō-, -graf) *n.* A photograph made through a microscope. Compare **microphotograph**.
~*tr.v.* **photomicrographed, -graphing, -graphs.** To photograph through a microscope. —**pho·to·mi·crog·ra·pher** (-mī-króggrəfər) *n.* —**pho·to·mi·cro·graph·ic** (-gráffik) *adj.* —**pho·to·mi·crog·ra·phy** (-mī-króggrəfi) *n.*

pho·to·mon·tage (fṓtō-món-taázh) *n.* **1.** A technique of making a composite picture by assembling several photographs or pieces of photographs, often in combination with other types of graphic material. **2.** A composite picture produced by this technique.

pho·to·mul·ti·pli·er (fṓtō-múlti-plī-ər) *n.* A device for detecting and measuring electromagnetic radiation, consisting of a photocathode to detect the radiation and an electron multiplier to amplify it and produce a detectable electric signal.

pho·to·mur·al (fṓtō-méwr-əl) *n.* A mural made from a very much enlarged photograph or a montage of photographs.

pho·ton (fṓ-ton) *n. Physics.* The quantum of electromagnetic energy, generally regarded as a discrete, stable **elementary particle** *(see)* having zero mass, no electric charge, and carrying angular and linear momentum. [PHOT(O)- + -ON.] —**pho·ton·ic** (-tónnik) *adj.*

pho·to·nas·ty (fṓtō-nasti) *n. Botany* A nastic movement in which the stimulus is light. [PHOTO- + -NASTY.] —**pho·to·nas·tic** *adj.*

pho·to·neu·tron (fṓtō-néw-tron || -nōo-) *n.* A neutron produced by an atomic nucleus as a result of a photodisintegration.

pho·to·nu·cle·ar (fṓtō-néwkli-ər || -nōokli-) *adj. Physics.* Of, pertaining to, or designating a nuclear reaction induced by photons.

pho·to·off·set (fṓtō-óff-set, -áwf-) *n.* **Offset printing** *(see).*

pho·to·pe·ri·od (fṓtō-péer-i-əd) *n. Biology.* The relative exposure of an organism to daylight as a proportion of the total day, considered especially with regard to the effect on growth and functioning. —**pho·to·pe·ri·od·ic** (-óddik), **pho·to·pe·ri·od·i·cal** *adj.* —**pho·to·pe·ri·od·ism** (-əd-iz'm) *n.*

pho·toph·i·lous (fō-tóffiləss) *adj.* Also **pho·to·phil·ic** (fṓt-ə-fillik, -ō-) *Biology.* Growing or functioning best in strong light. [PHOTO- + -PHILOUS.] —**pho·toph·i·ly** (-tóffili) *n.*

pho·to·pho·bi·a (fṓt-ō-fóbi-ə, -ə-) *n.* **1.** Abnormal sensitivity, especially of the eyes, to light. **2.** *Psychology.* An abnormal dread of or aversion to sunlight or well-lit places. [PHOTO- + -PHOBIA.] —**pho·to·pho·bic** (-fóbik) *adj.*

pho·to·pi·a (fō-tópi-ə) *n.* Daylight vision with eyes adapted to normal bright light. [New Latin : PHOT(O)- + -OPIA.] —**pho·to·pic** (-tóppik, -tōpik) *adj.*

pho·to·pol·y·mer (fṓtō-póllimər) *n.* Any polymeric material that is sensitive to light.

pho·to·re·al·ism (fṓtō-réer-liz'm, -rée-ə-) *n.* A style of painting that attempts to imitate the effects of still photography, especially by painting in very fine detail and using commonplace subject matter. —**pho·to·re·al·ist** *n.*

pho·to·re·cep·tion (fṓtō-ri-sép-sh'n, -rə-) *n. Biology.* The detection or perception of visible light; vision; sight. —**pho·to·re·cep·tive** (-tiv) *adj.*

pho·to·re·cep·tor (fṓtō-ri-séptər, -rə-) *n.* A photoreceptive nerve and the cell or organ that it serves.

pho·to·re·con·nais·sance (fṓtō-ri-kónni-s'nss, -rə- || -z'nss) *n. Military.* Photographic aerial reconnaissance.

pho·to·sen·si·tise, *or U.S.* **pho·to·sen·si·tize** (fṓtō-sén-sə-tīz) *tr.v.* **-tised, -tising, -tises.** To make (an organism or substance) sensitive to light. —**pho·to·sen·si·ti·sa·tion** (-tī-záysh'n || *U.S.* -ti-) *n.*

pho·to·sen·si·tive (fṓtō-sén-sətiv) *adj.* Sensitive to light. —**pho·to·sen·si·tiv·i·ty** (-sə-tívvəti) *n.*

pho·to·set (fṓtō-set) *tr.v.* **-set, -setting, -sets.** *Printing.* To photocompose.

pho·to·sphere (fṓt-ə-sfeer, -ō-) *n.* The surface of a star, especially of the Sun. —**pho·to·spher·ic** (-sférrik || -sféer-ik) *adj.*

Pho·to·stat (fṓt-ō-stat, -ə-) *n.* **1.** A trademark for a device used to make quick, direct-reading negative or positive photographic copies of written, printed, or graphic material. **2.** *Sometimes small* **p.** A copy made by Photostat.
~*tr.v.* **Photostatted** *or U.S.* **-stated, -statting** *or U.S.* **-stating, -stats.** *Often small* **p.** To make a copy of by Photostat. [PHOTO- + -STAT.] —**Pho·to·stat·ter** *n.* —**Pho·to·stat·ic** (-státtik) *adj.*

pho·to·syn·the·sis (fōtō-sínthə-siss) *n.* **1.** The process by which chlorophyll-containing cells in green plants convert incident light to chemical energy and synthesise organic compounds from inorganic compounds, especially carbohydrates from carbon dioxide and water, with the simultaneous release of oxygen. **2.** A similar process occurring in certain bacteria. —**pho·to·syn·thet·ic** (-sin-théttik) *adj.* —**pho·to·syn·thet·i·cal·ly** *adv.*

pho·to·syn·the·sise, pho·to·syn·the·size (fōtō-sínthə-sīz) *v.* **-sised, -sising, -sises.** —*tr.* To synthesise by the process of photosynthesis. —*intr.* To perform the process of photosynthesis.

pho·to·tax·is (fōtō-táksiss) *n.* Also **pho·to·tax·y** (-taksi). *Biology.* The movement of an organism in response to a source of light. [PHOTO- + -TAXIS.] —**pho·to·tac·tic** (-táktik) *adj.*

pho·to·tel·e·graph (fōtō-télli-graaf, -graf) *tr.v.* **-graphed, -graphing, -graphs.** To transmit (printed or other graphic material) by **facsimile** (*see*). —**pho·to·te·leg·ra·phy** (-ti-léggrəfi) *n.* —**pho·to·tel·e·graph·ic** (-gráffik), **pho·to·tel·e·graph·i·cal** *adj.* —**pho·to·tel·e·graph·i·cal·ly** *adv.*

pho·to·ther·a·py (fōtō-thérrəpi) *n.* The treatment of disease, especially certain skin conditions, with light, including infrared and ultraviolet radiation. Also called "phototherapeutics".

pho·tot·o·nus (fō-tóttənəss) *n. Biology.* Sensitivity of an organism caused by exposure to light. [PHOTO- + TONUS.] —**pho·to·ton·ic** (fōt-ō-tónnik, -ə-) *adj.*

pho·to·tran·sis·tor (fōtō-tran-síss-tər, -traan-, -zíss-) *n. Electronics.* A transistor having highly photosensitive electrical characteristics.

pho·tot·ro·pism (fōtō-trōp-iz'm, fō-tóttrəp-) *n.* Also **pho·tot·ro·py** (-i). *Botany.* Growth or movement of a plant part in response to a source of light. [PHOTO- + -TROPISM.] —**pho·to·trop·ic** (-tróppik, -trōpik) *adj.* —**pho·to·trop·i·cal·ly** *adv.*

pho·to·tube (fōtō-tewb ‖ -tōōb) *n. Electronics.* An electron tube with a photocathode.

pho·to·type·set·ter (fōtō-típ-settər) *n.* Any of various machines used in photocomposition.

pho·to·type·set·ting (fōtō-típ-setting) *n. Printing.* **Photocomposition** (*see*).

pho·to·vol·ta·ic (fōtō-vol-táy-ik ‖ -vōl-) *adj. Electronics.* Capable of producing a voltage when exposed to radiant energy, especially visible light.

photovoltaic effect *n.* The difference in potential produced when electromagnetic radiation falls on a thin film of one solid deposited on the surface of another solid, especially when those solids are semiconductors.

pho·to·zin·co·graph (fōtō-zíngkə-graaf, -graf) *tr.v.* **-graphed, -graphing, -graphs.** To make (a print) by photozincography. ~*n.* A print produced by photozincography.

pho·to·zin·cog·ra·phy (fōtō-zing-kóggrəfi) *n.* A photoengraving process in which sensitised zinc plates are used.

phr. phrase.

phras·al (fráyz'l) *adj.* Of, pertaining to, or consisting of a phrase or phrases. —**phras·al·ly** *adv.*

phrasal verb *n. Grammar.* A verb combined with an adverb or preposition or both, that functions as a unit and usually means more than the sum of its parts; for example, *give in,* meaning to yield, or *hang back,* meaning to hesitate, are phrasal verbs.

phrase (frayz) *n. Abbr.* **phr.** **1.** Any sequence of words intended to have meaning. **2.** A brief, apt, and cogent expression, such as *at a stroke.* **3.** A particular or characteristic style of verbal expression. **4.** *Grammar.* A group of two or more words in sequence that form a syntactic unit or group of syntactic units, but, especially in English, not containing a finite verb. **5.** A series of dance movements forming a unit in a choreographic pattern. **6.** *Music.* A segment of a composition constituting a more or less distinctive melody, usually consisting of about four bars and ending in a cadence. ~*tr.v.* **phrased, phrasing, phrases.** **1.** To express in words: *a tactfully phrased reply.* **2.** To pace or mark off (something read aloud or spoken) by pauses. **3.** *Music.* To divide (a passage) into phrases. [Latin *phrasis,* from Greek, speech, style of speech, from *phrazein,* to show, explain.]

phrase book *n.* A book, often pocket-sized, that gives common and useful expressions in a foreign language with their translations.

phrase marker *n. Linguistics.* The representation of a sentence's grammatical structure, usually by a tree diagram.

phra·se·o·gram (fráyzi-ə-gram, -ō-) *n.* A symbol, such as one used in shorthand, that denotes a particular phrase.

phra·se·o·graph (fráyzi-ə-graaf, -ō-, -graf) *n.* A phrase having a phraseogram. —**phra·se·o·graph·ic** (-gráffik) *adj.*

phra·se·ol·o·gist (fráyzi-óllǝjist) *n.* A person who uses epigrammatic phrases or a particular phraseology.

phra·se·ol·o·gy (fráyzi-óllǝji) *n., pl.* **-gies.** **1.** The way in which words and phrases are used in speech or writing; style. **2.** The characteristic mode of expression used by a particular person or group; parlance: *nautical phraseology.* [New Latin *phraseologia* : PHRASE + -LOGY.] —**phra·se·o·log·i·cal** (-ǝ-lójik'l) *adj.*

phras·ing (fráyzing) *n.* **1.** The manner in which an expression is phrased; wording. **2.** *Music.* **a.** The division of a passage into phrases. **b.** The manner in which phrases are rendered or interpreted as in a performance.

phra·try (fráytri) *n., pl.* **-tries.** **1.** In ancient Greece, a subdivision of a tribe or phyle, being originally a kinship group and surviving in classical Athens as a division in the political and military organisation of the state. **2.** *Anthropology.* An exogamous subdivision of the

---

photosynthesis

HOW PLANTS USE THE SUN'S ENERGY

Green cells trigger all the world's food chains

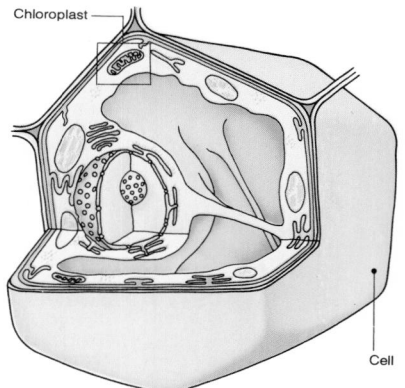

Chloroplast — Cell

The power of the Sun is trapped by the leaves of plants on Earth and used to produce food by a process called photosynthesis. When sunlight strikes the plant leaves, chlorophyll molecules – which give the leaves their green colour – are agitated into generating tiny electric currents. These electric currents split the water that has been sucked into the plant by its roots into separate particles involving oxygen gas and hydrogen atoms.

The oxygen is given off into the atmosphere to form a vital part of the air we breathe. The hydrogen is combined with carbon dioxide absorbed from the surrounding air by pores in the leaves to form a sugar. Such sugars are the basic building blocks of plants. Photosynthesis not only provides the oxygen that keeps most animals alive, but it is the basis of all the world's food chains. Animals such as sheep and cattle eat plants and convert them into protein, which is consumed by meat-eaters such as man. In water, bacteria and blue-green and other algae carry out a similar photosynthesis, creating a water-borne food chain similar to that on land.

KEY TO LIFE *Inside the plant cell, chloroplasts trigger the photosynthesis by converting sunlight to electricity. This creates the food for plant growth that is the starting point for all the food chains of the living world.*

HOW SUNLIGHT, WATER, AND CARBON DIOXIDE CREATE SUGARS IN A CHLOROPLAST

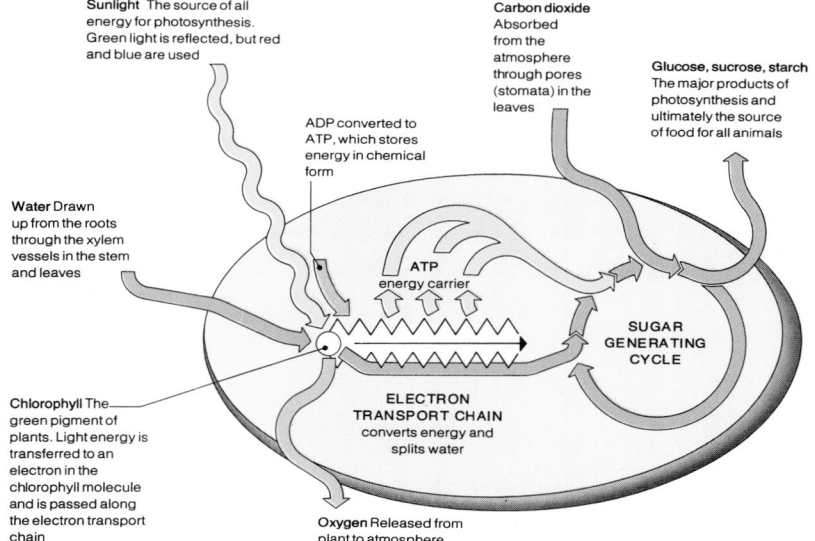

Sunlight The source of all energy for photosynthesis. Green light is reflected, but red and blue are used

Carbon dioxide Absorbed from the atmosphere through pores (stomata) in the leaves

Glucose, sucrose, starch The major products of photosynthesis and ultimately the source of food for all animals

ADP converted to **ATP**, which stores energy in chemical form

Water Drawn up from the roots through the xylem vessels in the stem and leaves

ATP energy carrier

SUGAR GENERATING CYCLE

Chlorophyll The green pigment of plants. Light energy is transferred to an electron in the chlorophyll molecule and is passed along the electron transport chain

ELECTRON TRANSPORT CHAIN converts energy and splits water

Oxygen Released from plant to atmosphere

The electric charge that is created in photosynthesis is used to form adenosine triphosphate (ATP) from adenosine diphosphate (ADP) by the addition of a phosphate molecule. ATP holds in chemical form energy that is later needed to convert carbon dioxide to sugar.

---

tribe, comprising two or more related clans. [Greek *phratria,* from *phratēr,* fellow clan member.] —**phra·tric** (fráytrik) *adj.*

Phraya. See **Chao Praya.**

phre·at·ic (free-áttik) *adj. Geology.* Of, pertaining to, or designating **ground water** (*see*). [Greek *phrear* (stem *phreat-*), a well.]

-phrenia *n. comb. form.* Indicates mental disorder; for example, **schizophrenia.** [Greek *phrēn,* mind.]

phren·ic (frénnik ‖ frénik) *adj.* **1.** *Archaic.* Of or pertaining to the mind. **2.** *Anatomy.* Of or pertaining to the diaphragm: *the phrenic nerve.* [New Latin *phrenicus* : PHREN(O)- + -IC.]

phre·ni·tis (fri-nítiss, fre-) *n. Pathology.* **1.** **Encephalitis** (*see*). **2.** Inflammation of the diaphragm. **3.** Frenzy; delirium. [Late Latin *phrenītis,* from Greek *phrenitis* : *phrēn,* diaphragm, mind + -ITIS.] —**phre·nit·ic** (-níttik) *adj.*

phreno-, phren– *comb. form.* Indicates: **1.** The mind; for example, **phrenology.** **2.** The diaphragm; for example, **phrenic.** [Greek *phrēn,* diaphragm, mind.]

phre·nol·o·gy (fri-nóllə-ji, fre-) *n. Abbr.* **phrenol.** The now discredited practice of studying character and mental capacity from the shape and irregularities of the skull. [PHRENO- + -LOGY.] —**phren·o·log·ic** (frénnə-lójik ‖ frēenə-), **phren·o·log·i·cal** *adj.* —**phre·nol·o·gist** (-nóllə-jist) *n.*

Phryg·i·a (fríji-ə). Former kingdom of western and central Asia Minor. It reached the peak of its prosperity in the eighth century B.C.

Phryg·i·an (fríji-ən) adj. **1.** Of or pertaining to Phrygia or its people, language, and culture. **2.** Music. **a.** Of or designating a mode of the ancient Greeks. **b.** Of or designating an authentic church mode with tonic E and dominant C.
~n. **1.** A native or inhabitant of Phrygia. **2.** The Indo-European language of the Phrygians.

Phrygian cap n. A soft cap with a forward-curving peak, represented in ancient Greek art as part of the attire worn by Phrygians. Compare **liberty cap**.

PHS Public Health Service (in the United States).

phthal·ein (tháy-leen, fthál-, thál-, -i-in) n. Any of a group of chemical compounds formed by a combination of phthalic anhydride with a phenol, from which certain synthetic dyes are derived. [PHTHAL(IC) + -EIN.]

phthal·ic (thál-ik, fthál-, tháyl-) adj. Chemistry. **1.** Of, pertaining to, or derived from naphthalene. **2.** Pertaining to phthalic acid. [Short for naphthalic : (NA)PHTH(A) + AL(COHOL) + -IC.]

phthalic acid n. A colourless, crystalline organic acid, $C_6H_4(COOH)_2$, prepared from naphthalene and used in the synthesis of dyes, perfumes, and other organic compounds.

phthalic anhydride n. A white, crystalline compound, $C_6H_4(CO)_2O$, used in the manufacture of phthaleins and other dyes, resins, plasticisers, and insecticides.

phthal·in (thál-in, fthál-, tháyl-) n. Any of various colourless compounds derived from the reduction of phthaleins.

phthal·o·cy·a·nine (thál-ō-sí-ə-neen, fthál-, tháyl-) n. Any of several stable, light-fast, blue or green organic pigments derived from the basic compound $(C_6H_4C_2N)_4N_4$, and used in enamels, printing inks, linoleum, and plastics. [PHTHAL(IC) + CYANINE.]

phthi·ri·a·sis (thi-rí-ə-siss ‖ U.S. also thī-) n. Pathology. Infestation with lice; pediculosis. [Latin phthiriasis, from Greek phtheiriasis : phtheir, louse + -IASIS.]

phthis·ic (tízzik, thí-sik, fthí-) n. Archaic. **1.** Phthisis. **2.** Asthma (see). [Sense 2, from Middle English ptisike, from Old French tisique, from Latin phthisicus, from Greek phthisikos, consumptive, from phthisis, PHTHISIS.] —**phthis·ic, phthis·i·cal** adj.

phthi·sis (thí-siss, fthí-, tí-) n. Also archaic **phthis·ic** (-sik, tízzik). Pathology. **1.** Tuberculosis (see) of the lungs. **2.** Wasting away or emaciation and atrophy of the body or part of the body. [Latin, from Greek, from Greek phthinein, phthien, to decay, waste away.]

phut (fut) n. A heavy, dull sound, as of impact with an inflatable object. —**go phut.** Informal. To collapse or fail. [Hindi phatnā, burst, collapse (imitative).]

phyco– comb. form. Indicates algae; for example, **phycology**. [Greek phukos†, seaweed.]

phy·col·o·gy (fī-kóllə-ji) n. The branch of botany concerned with the study of algae. [PHYCO- + -LOGY.] —**phy·co·log·i·cal** (fīkə-lójik'l) adj. —**phy·col·o·gist** (-kóllə-jist) n.

phy·co·my·cete (fīkō-mí-seet, -mī-séet) n. Botany. Any of various filamentous aquatic fungi, including certain moulds and mildews. [New Latin phycomycetes : PHYCO- + -MYCETE.] —**phy·co·my·ce·tous** (-séetəss) adj.

phy·la. Plural of **phylum**.

phy·lac·ter·y (fi-láktəri) n., pl. -ies. **1.** Judaism. Either of two small leather boxes, each containing strips of parchment inscribed with quotations from the Hebrew Scriptures. One is strapped to the forehead and the other to the left arm by religiously observant Jewish men during morning worship, except on Sabbath and holidays. **2.** Literary. **a.** An amulet **b.** A reminder. [Middle English filakterie, from Late Latin phylactērium, from Greek phulaktērion, safeguard, from phulaktēr, guard, from phulax (stem phulak-), guard.]

phy·lax·is (fi-lák-siss) n. Inhibiting of infection by the body. [Greek phulaxis, "a guarding", from phulassein, to guard.] —**phy·lac·tic** (-tik) adj.

phy·le (fí-li) n., pl. -lae (-lee). A large grouping of citizens, based on kinship, constituting the largest political subdivision of an ancient Greek city-state. [Greek phulē, tribe.] —**phy·lic** adj.

phy·let·ic (fī-léttik) adj. Biology. Of, pertaining to, or reflecting the phylogeny or evolutionary development of an organism. [New Latin phylesis, a genus development, from Greek phulon, tribe, class, race.] —**phy·let·i·cal·ly** adv.

–phyll n. comb. form. Indicates leaf; for example, **chlorophyll**. [Greek phullon, leaf.]

phyl·lite (fil-īt) n. A metamorphic rock, similar to slate but often having a wavy, silky lustre, and a distinctive cleavage. [PHYLL(O)- + -ITE.]

phyllo–, phyll– comb. form. Indicates leaf; for example, **phylloclade**. [New Latin, from Greek phullon, leaf.]

phyl·lo·clade (fil-ō-klayd, -ə-) n. Also **phyl·lo·clad** (-klad). Botany. A cladophyll (see). [New Latin phyllocladium : PHYLLO- + Greek klados, a branch.]

phyl·lode (fil-ōd) n. Botany. Also **phyl·lo·di·um** (fi-lṓdi-əm) pl. -dia (-ə). A flattened leafstalk that performs the functions of a leaf. [New Latin phyllodium, from Greek phullōdēs, like a leaf : PHYLL(O)- + -ODE (like).] —**phyl·lo·di·al** adj.

phyl·loid (fil-oyd) adj. Botany. Resembling a leaf; leaflike. [New Latin phylloides : PHYLL(O)- + -OID.]

phyl·lome (fil-ōm) n. Botany. A leaf, or a plant structure that functions as a leaf. [PHYLL(O)- + -OME.] —**phyl·lom·ic** (fī-lómik, -lómmik) adj.

phyl·loph·a·gous (fi-lóffəgəss) adj. Zoology. Feeding on leaves. [PHYLLO- + -PHAGOUS.]

phyl·lo·pod (fillə-pod) n. Any of various crustaceans of the order Phyllopoda, having swimming and respiratory appendages that resemble leaves.
~adj. Also **phyl·lop·o·dous** (fi-lóppədəss). **1.** Possessing leaflike feet. **2.** Of or pertaining to the phyllopods. [New Latin phyllopoda, "leaf-footed" : PHYLLO- + -POD.] —**phyl·lop·o·dan** (fi-lóppədən) adj. & n.

phyl·lo·qui·none (fillō-kwi-nṓn) n. A form of **vitamin K** (see), occurring in plants.

phyl·lo·tax·y (fillə-taksi) n. Also **phyl·lo·tax·is** (-táksiss). Botany. **1.** The arrangement of leaves on a stem. **2.** The principles governing leaf arrangement. [New Latin : PHYLLO- + -TAXIS.] —**phyl·lo·tac·tic** (-táktik), **phyl·lo·tac·ti·cal** adj.

–phyllous adj. comb. form. Indicates a specified kind or number of leaves; for example, **heterophyllous**. [New Latin -phyllus, from Greek phullon, leaf.]

phyl·lox·e·ra (fillok-séer-ə, fi-lóksər-ə) n., pl. -rae (-ee) or -ras. Any of several small insects of the genus Phylloxera; especially, P. vitifoliae, a species very destructive of grape crops. [New Latin : PHYLLO- + Greek xēros, dry.] —**phyl·lox·e·ran** adj. & n.

phy·log·e·ny (fī-lójəni) n., pl. -nies. Also **phy·lo·gen·e·sis** (fīlō-jénnə-siss) pl. -ses (-seez). Biology. The evolutionary development of a species, genus, or other taxonomic rank. Compare **ontogeny**. [Greek phulē, tribe, clan, and phulon, tribe, race + -GENY.] —**phy·lo·ge·net·ic** (-jə-néttik), **phy·lo·gen·ic** (-jénnik) adj. —**phy·lo·ge·net·i·cal·ly** adv.

phy·lum (fí-ləm) n., pl. -la (-lə). **1.** Biology. A taxonomic division of the animal kingdom or, less commonly, the plant kingdom, directly above a class in size. **2.** Linguistics. A large division of related families of languages or linguistic stocks, especially of the New World. [New Latin, from Greek phulon, tribe, class, race.]

phys. **1.** physical. **2.** physician. **3.** physicist; physics. **4.** physiological; physiology.

phys·i·at·rics (fizzi-áttriks) n. Used with a singular verb. U.S. **Physiotherapy** (see). [PHYS(IO)- + -IATRICS.] —**phys·i·at·ric, phys·i·at·ri·cal** adj. —**phys·i·at·rist** (-áttrist) n.

phys·ic (fízzik) n. Archaic. **1.** Any medicine or drug. **2.** A cathartic. **3.** The art of healing or profession of medicine. **4.** Physics.
~tr.v. **physicked, -icking, -ics.** Archaic. **1.** To treat with or as if with medicine. **2.** To act upon as a cathartic; purge. [Middle English fisike, from Old French fisique, from Latin physica, natural medicine or science, physics, from Greek phusikē, from phusikos, natural, from phusis, nature, from phuein, to bring forth, make grow.]

phys·i·cal (fízzik'l) adj. Abbr. **phys. 1.** Of or pertaining to the body, as distinguished from the mind or spirit; bodily; corporeal : physical strength. **2.** Of or pertaining to material things: physical environment. **3.** Of or pertaining to matter and energy or the sciences dealing with them, especially physics. **4. a.** Highly conscious of or communicating through one's body. **b.** Involving a great deal of physical contact: a physical game, with a lot of hard tackles.
~n. U.S. A physical examination. [Middle English phisycal, from Medieval Latin physicālis, medicinal, from Latin physica, natural medicine. See physic.] —**phys·i·cal·ly** adv.

physical anthropology n. The science of human evolutionary biology, genetic development, racial variation, and classification. Also called "somatology". Compare **cultural anthropology**.

physical chemistry n. The scientific analysis of the properties and behaviour of chemical systems primarily by physical theory and technique as, for example, the thermodynamic analysis of macroscopic chemical phenomena.

physical education n. Abbr. **PE.** Education, training, and practice in physical exercise, team games, gymnastics, and the like, especially as part of a school curriculum.

physical examination n. A medical examination to detect illness or dysfunction and, especially, to determine physical fitness for a particular activity or service. Also British "medical", U.S. "physical".

physical geography n. The study of the natural features of the Earth's surface, including land forms, oceans, seas, soils, the atmosphere, and the distribution of fauna and flora. Also called "physiography".

phys·i·cal·ism (fízzik'l-iz'm) n. Philosophy. The doctrine that all phenomena can be described in terms of time and space, and consequently that any meaningful statement other than an analytic and tautological one, can in principle be reduced to an empirically verifiable physical statement. —**phys·i·cal·ist** n. —**phys·i·cal·is·tic** (-istik) adj.

physical jerks pl.n. British Informal. Physical exercises.

physical medicine n. The branch of medicine that treats physical disabilities, such as those resulting from rheumatism or polio.

physical quantity n. Physics. A **quantity** (see).

physical science n. Any of the sciences, such as physics, chemistry, astronomy, and geology, that analyses the nature and properties of energy and nonliving matter. Compare **life science**.

physical therapy n. U.S. Physiotherapy (see).

phy·si·cian (fi-zísh'n) n. Abbr. **phys. 1.** A person qualified to practise medicine, especially in areas other than surgery; a medical doctor. **2.** Archaic. Any person who heals or exerts a healing influence. [Middle English fisicien, from Old French, from fisique, PHYSIC.]

phys·i·cist (fízzi-sist) n. Abbr. **phys.** A scientist who specialises in physics.

Phrygian cap A detail from a Coptic textile of the fourth or fifth century A.D., now in the British Museum, London. The cap was the typical headgear of the Phrygians, a people who settled in central Turkey in the eighth century B.C.

phys·i·co·chem·i·cal (fízziko̅-kémmik'l) adj. Of or pertaining to physical chemistry or the physical and chemical aspects of a phenomenon. [*Physico-*, "physics and", + CHEMICAL.]

phys·ics (fízziks) n. *Used with a singular verb.* Abbr. **phys.** 1. The science of matter and energy and of interactions between the two. It is based on mathematics and grouped in traditional fields such as acoustics, optics, mechanics, thermodynamics, and electromagnetism. In modern physics, relativity and quantum theory are used and other areas of study include atomic and nuclear physics, cryogenics, solid-state physics, particle physics, and astrophysics. 2. Physical properties, interactions, processes, or laws: *the physics of supersonic flight.* 3. *Archaic.* The study of the natural or material world and phenomena; natural science or natural philosophy. [Plural of PHYSIC (translation of Latin plural *physica*, natural science).]

physio-, phys- comb. form. Indicates: 1. Natural or nature; for example, **physiography.** 2. Physical; for example, **physiotherapy.** [Greek *phusio-*, from *phusis*, nature, from *phuein*, to make grow.]

phys·i·og·no·my (fízzi-ónnə-mi ‖ -óg-nə-) n., pl. **-mies.** 1. The art or practice of judging human character from facial features. 2. Facial features, especially when regarded as revealing character. 3. The aspect and character of an inanimate or abstract entity: *the physiognomy of the Midlands.* [Learned respelling of Middle English *fysnamye, phisnomye*, from Old French *phizonomie*, from Medieval Latin *phisionomia*, from Late Greek *phusiognōmia*, short for Greek *phusiognōmonia* : PHYSIO- + *gnōmōn*, "judge", "interpreter".] **—phys·i·og·nom·ic** (-ə-nómmik ‖ -əg-), **phys·i·og·nom·i·cal** adj. **—phys·i·og·nom·i·cal·ly** adv. **—phys·i·og·no·mist** (-mist) n.

phys·i·og·ra·phy (fízzi-óggrə-fi) n. Physical geography (see). [PHYSIO- + -GRAPHY.] **—phys·i·og·ra·pher** (-fər) n. **—phys·i·o·graph·ic** (-ə-gráffik), **phys·i·o·graph·i·cal** adj. **—phys·i·o·graph·i·cal·ly** adv.

physiol. physiological; physiology.

phys·i·o·log·i·cal (fízzi-ə-lójik'l) adj. 1. Of or pertaining to physiology. 2. In accordance with or characteristic of the normal functioning of a living organism. **—phys·i·o·log·i·cal·ly** adv.

physiological saline n. A salt solution, saline (see).

phys·i·ol·o·gy (fízzi-óllə-ji) n. Abbr. **phys., physiol.** 1. The biological science of essential and characteristic life processes, activities, and functions. 2. All the vital processes of an organism, organ, or tissue. [Latin *physiologia*, from Greek *phusiologia*, study of nature : PHYSIO- + -LOGY.] **—phys·i·ol·o·gist** n.

phys·i·o·ther·a·py (fízzi-ō-thérrə-pi) n. Medicine. The study or practice of the therapeutic use of physical methods or agents, such as remedial exercises, massage, or infrared and ultraviolet rays. Also *U.S.* "physical therapy", "physiatrics". **—phys·i·o·ther·a·peu·tic** (-péwtik) adj. **—phys·i·o·ther·a·pist** n.

phy·sique (fi-zéek) n. The body, considered with reference to its proportions, muscular development, and appearance: *a muscular physique.* [French, from adjective, "physical", from Latin *physicus*, natural, from Greek *phusikos*; see physic.]

phy·so·clis·tous (fí-sō-klístəss) adj. Having an air bladder that is not joined to the alimentary canal, as in certain fishes. [Greek *phusa*, bladder + *-clistous*, from Greek *kleistos*, closed.]

phy·so·stig·mine (fí-sō-stíg-meen) n. A colourless or pink alkaloid, $C_{15}H_{21}N_3O_2$, extracted from the Calabar bean, and used especially in eyedrops to restrict the size of the pupil and to relieve pressure in the eyeball. Also called "eserine". [New Latin *Physostigma* (genus of the Calabar bean) : Greek *phusa*, bellows, bladder + STIGMA.]

phy·sos·to·mous (fí-sóstəməss) adj. Having a connecting tube between the air bladder and a part of the alimentary canal, as in certain fishes. [Greek *phusa*, bellows, bladder + -STOME + -OUS.]

-phyte n. comb. form. Botany. Indicates a plant with a specified character or habitat; for example, **xerophyte.** [Greek *phuton*, plant, from *phuein*, to make grow.]

phyto-, phyt- comb. form. Indicates plant or plant life; for example, **phytogenesis.** [New Latin, from Greek *phuto-*, from *phuton*, plant, from *phuein*, to make grow.]

phy·to·gen·e·sis (fíto̅-jénnə-siss) n. Also **phy·tog·e·ny** (fí-tójəni). The origin and evolutionary development of plants. [PHYTO- + -GENESIS.] **—phy·to·ge·net·ic** (-jə-néttik) adj. **—phy·to·ge·net·i·cal·ly** adv.

phy·to·gen·ic (fíto̅-jénnik) adj. Also **phy·tog·e·nous** (fí-tójənəss). Having a plant origin, as coal has. [PHYTO- + -GENIC.]

phy·to·ge·og·ra·phy (fíto̅-ji-óggrə-fi) n. The study of the distribution of plants. **—phy·to·ge·og·ra·pher** (-fər) n. **—phy·to·ge·o·graph·i·cal** (-jée-ə-gráffik'l), **phy·to·ge·o·graph·ic** adj.

phy·tog·ra·phy (fí-tóggrəfi) n. The science of plant description; descriptive botany. [PHYTO- + -GRAPHY.]

phy·to·hor·mone (fíto̅-hór-mōn) n. A growth substance (see).

phy·to·lite (fíto̅-līt, -ə-) n. Also **phy·to·lith** (-lith). A fossil plant. [PHYTO- + -LITE.]

phy·tol·o·gy (fí-tólləji) n. The study of plants; botany. [New Latin *phytologia* : PHYTO- + -LOGY.] **—phy·to·log·ic** (fíta-lójik), **phy·to·log·i·cal** adj.

phy·ton (fí-ton) n. A segment of a plant sufficiently large to be able to grow independently if given appropriate conditions. [New Latin, from Greek *phuton*, plant, from *phuein*, to make grow.] **—phy·ton·ic** (fí-tónnik) adj.

phy·to·pa·thol·o·gy (fíto̅-pə-thóllə-ji) n. The study of the origin, nature, and prevention of plant diseases. **—phy·to·path·o·log·i·cal** adj. **—phy·to·pa·thol·o·gist** (-jist) n.

phy·toph·a·gous (fí-tóffə-gəss) adj. Feeding on plants, including shrubs and trees. Said especially of certain insects. [PHYTO- + -PHAGOUS.] **—phy·toph·a·gy** (-ji) n.

phy·to·plank·ton (fít-ō-plángk-tən, -ə-) n. Minute, floating aquatic plants. **—phy·to·plank·ton·ic** (-tónnik) adj.

phy·to·so·ci·ol·o·gy (fíto̅-sō-si-óllə-ji ‖ -shi-) n. The branch of ecology that deals with the characteristics, relationships, and distribution of associated plants. **—phy·to·so·ci·o·log·i·cal** (-ə-lójik'l) adj. **—phy·to·so·ci·o·log·i·cal·ly** adv. **—phy·to·so·ci·ol·o·gist** n.

phy·to·tox·ic (fíto̅-tóksik) adj. Poisonous to plants. **—phy·to·tox·ic·i·ty** (-tok-síssəti) n.

phy·to·tox·in n. Any poison, such as curare or strychnine, that is derived from a plant.

phy·to·tron (fíto̅-tron) n. A building, often divided into many compartments, in which plants can be grown under controlled conditions. [PHYTO- + -TRON.]

pi¹ (pī) n., pl. **pis.** 1. The 16th letter in the Greek alphabet, written Π, π. Transliterated in English as *P, p.* 2. Symbol π Mathematics. A transcendental number, approximately 3.14159, representing the ratio of the circumference to the diameter of a circle and appearing as a constant in a wide range of mathematical problems. [Greek. The mathematical sense is from the first letter of Greek *periphireia*, PERIPHERY, and *perimetros*, PERIMETER.]

pi². Chiefly U.S. Variant of **pie** (printing).

pi³ adj. British Informal. Pious; sanctimonious. [Shortening.]

pi·a (pí-ə, pée-ə) n. Anatomy. The pia mater. **—pi·al** adj.

pi·ac·u·lar (pī-áckewlər) adj. In the Christian Church: 1. Making expiation or atonement for a sacrilege: *piacular sacrifice.* 2. Requiring expiation; wicked; blameworthy. [Latin *piācularis*, from *piāculum*, sin offering, propitiatory sacrifice, from *piāre*, to appease, atone for, from *pius*, pious.]

Piaf (pée-af, p-yaff), **Edith**, born Edith Giovanna Gassion (1915–63). French cabaret singer. Her songs include *Milord, La vie en rose*, and *Non, je ne regrette rien*, which became a personal anthem.

pi·affe (pi-áf) intr.v. **piaffed, piaffing, piaffes.** In dressage, to perform the piaffer. [French *piaffer*, to strut.]

pi·af·fer (pi-áffər) n. A dressage movement in which a horse trots very slowly or on the spot with high action of the legs. [French, from *piaffer*, to strut.]

Pia·get (pee-á-zhay, -áa-), **Jean** (1896–1980). Swiss child psychologist. He studied the development of intellectual awareness through the successive stages of childhood, systematically observing changes in such conceptions as justice and guilt.

pi·a ma·ter (pí-ə máytər, pée-ə máatər) n. Anatomy. The fine vascular membrane that envelops the brain and spinal cord under the arachnoid membrane and the dura mater. Also called "pia". [Medieval Latin (translation of Arabic *al'umm ragīgah*, "tender mother").]

pi·an·ism (péer-niz'm, pée-ə-, pi-ánniz'm) n. Technique, artistry, or execution in piano playing.

pi·a·nis·si·mo (pée-ə-níssi-mō, peer-, pée-aa-) adv. Abbr. **pp, pp.** Music. Very softly or quietly. Used as a direction. ~n., pl. **pianissimos.** Music. A part of a composition that is to be played pianissimo. [Italian, superlative of PIANO (softly).] **—pi·a·nis·si·mo** adj.

pi·an·ist (péer-nist, pée-ə-, pi-ánnist) n. One who plays the piano.

pi·a·nis·tic (péer-nístik, pée-ə-) adj. 1. Of or pertaining to the piano. 2. Well-adapted to the piano. **—pi·a·nis·ti·cal·ly** adv.

pi·an·o¹ (p-yánnō, -yaánō, pi-ánnō, -aánō) n., pl. **-os.** A musical instrument with a manual keyboard actuating hammers that strike wire strings set vertically in an upright frame or horizontally in a roughly triangular frame, producing sounds that may be softened or sustained by means of pedals. [Italian, short for PIANOFORTE.]

pi·a·no² (p-yaánō, pi-aánō) adv. Abbr. **p, p.** Music. Softly; quietly. Used as a direction. ~n., pl. **pianos.** Music. A passage to be played softly. [Italian, from Late Latin *plānus*, smooth, from Latin, even.] **—pi·a·no** adj.

piano accordion n. An accordion that has a piano-like keyboard played by the right hand.

pi·an·o·for·te (p-yánnō-fórt-i, -yaánō-, pi-aánō-, -fawrti ‖ U.S. also -fawrt, -fōrt) n. A piano. [Italian, from *piano e forte*, soft and loud.]

Pi·a·no·la (peer-nōlə, pée-ə-, p-ya-) n. A trademark for a mechanical piano that plays music automatically according to the perforations on a paper roll by means of pedal-operated bellows.

piano player n. 1. A pianist. 2. Any of various automatic devices for playing a piano.

piano trio n. 1. An instrumental ensemble for playing chamber music, consisting of a piano, violin, and cello. 2. A piece of music written for such an ensemble.

pi·as·sa·va (pée-ə-sáavə) n. Also **pi·as·sa·ba** (-sáabə). 1. Either of two Brazilian palm trees, *Attalea funifera* or *Leopoldinia piassaba*, from which a strong, coarse fibre is obtained. 2. The fibre of either of these trees, used for making ropes, brushes, and brooms. [Portuguese *piassaba*, from Tupi *piaçába*.]

pi·as·tre, pi·as·ter (pi-ástər, -áastər) n. 1. A coin equal to ¹/₁₀₀ of the pound of Egypt, Lebanon, Sudan, and Syria. 2. The basic monetary unit of the former South Vietnam, equal to 100 cents. 3. Formerly, a Spanish dollar; a piece of eight. [French *piastre*, from Italian *piastra (d'argento)*, plate (of silver), from Latin *emplastra, emplastrum*, PLASTER.]

pi·az·za (pi-átsə, -ádzə, -áatsə ‖ U.S. -ázzə, -áazə) n., pl. **-zas** (for all senses) or **piazze** (-átsay, -áatsay) (for sense 1). 1. A public square in an Italian town. 2. British. A roofed and arcaded passageway; a colonnade. 3. U.S. A verandah; a porch. [Italian, from Latin *pla-*

Picasso

THE PRODIGIOUS MASTER OF 20TH-CENTURY ART
Picasso's restless mind sought the shapes behind the shapes

Pablo Picasso (1881–1973) is the dominant figure of 20th-century art. He was born in Màlaga, Spain, the son of an art teacher. He showed precocious talent while a pupil at Barcelona (1895–1903), and from 1900 spent much of his time in Paris, settling there in 1904. Paris was the inspiration of his blue period, during which he painted – with blue predominant – the city's prostitutes and destitutes.

His rose period (1905–7), all circuses and harlequins, was more cheerful. Picasso became influenced by Gauguin's primitive art and Cézanne's search for colour and form. Cézanne told him: "Look for the spheres, cones, and cylinders in life". Picasso took him at his word. With Georges Braque, he launched cubism (1908–14), looking in analytical ways at the outlines of familiar subjects, as in *Portrait of Clovis Sagot* (1909), *Violin and Grapes* (1912), *Girl and Mandolin* (1910). Picasso broke up his pictures into solid fragments, looking for shapes and the space behind.

In the 1920s and 1930s, Picasso's restless imagination switched to etching, sculpture, surrealism, and stage designing. *Guernica* (1937), his most famous painting, was inspired by the bombing of the Basque town of Guernica by German aeroplanes. Picasso became a Communist. He twice accepted the Lenin Peace Prize, but angered the French by rejecting their Legion of Honour (1967). He died leaving a hoard of his work. Much of it was given to the French government in lieu of death duties and is to be permanently housed in Paris.

A MASTER'S MASTERPIECE *Picasso's huge protest at war and fascism was finished within a few weeks of Guernica's destruction by German bombs. A tangle of people and horses shriek in protest at the carnage, apparently overseen by a rampant bull. A naked* *electric light bulb offers the bare promise of hope. The work was given to the Spanish Republican Government and kept in New York at Picasso's request "Until democracy returned to Spain". It was taken to a permanent place at the Prado, Madrid, in 1981.*

tea, broad street, courtyard, from Greek *plateia,* from *platus,* broad, flat.]

pi·broch (pée-brok, -brokh) *n.* A series of variations on a traditional dirge or martial theme for the highland bagpipes. [Scottish Gaelic *piobaireachd,* pipe music, from *piobair,* piper, from *píob,* pipe.]

pi·ca¹ (píkə) *n.* **1.** A printer's unit of type size, equal to 12 points or about 0.42 centimetres (¹/₆ inch). **2.** An equivalent unit of composition measurement used in determining the dimensions of lines, illustrations, or printed pages. **3.** A size of letters in typewriting, having 10 characters to the inch, the equivalent of 12-point printing type. [Probably from Anglo-Latin *píca,* PIE (church almanac).]

pica² *n.* A craving for unnatural food such as mud or cloth, as occurs occasionally in hysteria and pregnancy. [New Latin, from Latin *píca,* magpie (from its omnivorous nature).]

pic·a·dor (píckə-dawr; *Spanish* peéka-thór) *n., pl.* **-dors** or **-dores** (-tháwrayss). A horseman in a bullfight who lances the bull's neck muscles so that it will tend to keep its head low for the subsequent stages. [Spanish, from *picar,* to prick, pierce. See *picaro.*]

Pic·ar·dy (píckərdi). *French* **Picardie.** Region and former province of northern France, now mainly in the Somme *département.* Stretching from the English Channel along the rivers Somme and Oise, its main industries are agriculture and the production of textiles. It was the scene of heavy fighting during both World Wars.

pic·a·resque (píckə-résk || *U.S. also* peéka-) *adj.* **1.** Of or involving clever rogues or adventurers. **2.** Of, pertaining to, or characteristic of the *picaresque novel,* in which the rogue-hero and his escapades are depicted episodically with broad realism and satire. [French, from Spanish *picaresco,* from *picaro,* rogue, PICARO.]

pic·a·ro (píckə-rō, peéka-) *n., pl.* **-ros** (-rōz; *Spanish* -ròss). An adventurer; a rogue. [Spanish, "rogue", from *picar,* to wound lightly, "to prick", from Vulgar Latin *piccáre* (unattested), to pick, from *piccus* (unattested), woodpecker, from Latin *pícus.*]

pic·a·roon (píckə-roón) *n.* **1. a.** A pirate. **b.** A rogue or thief. **2.** A pirate ship.

~*intr.v.* **picarooned, -rooning, -roons.** To act as a pirate. [Spanish *picarón,* augmentative of *picaro,* PICARO.]

Pi·cas·so (pi-kássō || *U.S. also* -káa-sō), **Pablo (Ruiz y)**, (1881–1973). Spanish painter, perhaps the most prolific and versatile artist of this century. Among his many works are *Les Demoiselles d'Avignon* (1907) and *Guernica* (1937).

pic·a·yune (píckə-yoón || *U.S.* pícki-) *adj. U.S.* **1.** Of little value or importance; paltry. **2.** *Informal.* Petty; mean.

~*n.* **1.** A Spanish-American coin, a half real, formerly used in parts of the southern United States. **2.** In the United States, a five-cent piece. **3.** *Chiefly U.S. Informal.* Something of very small value; a trifle: *not worth a picayune.* [French *picaillon,* small copper coin, from Provençal *picaioun†.*]

pic·ca·lil·li (píckə-lílli) *n., pl.* **-lis.** A pickled relish made of various chopped vegetables, mustard, and hot spices. [Perhaps blend of PICKLE and CHILLI.]

pic·ca·nin (píckə-nin) *n. Chiefly South African Informal.* A black African child. [Shortened from PICCANINNY.]

pic·ca·nin·ny (píckə-nínni) *n., pl.* **-nies.** Also *chiefly U.S.* **pick·a·nin·ny.** A small black or Aboriginal child. Often considered offensive.

~*adj.* Very small; tiny. [Originally West Indian, from Spanish *pequeño,* small, or Portuguese *pequenino,* little one, from *pequeno,* small.]

pic·co·lo¹ (píckə-lō) *n., pl.* **-los.** A small flute pitched an octave above a regular flute. [Shortened from *piccolo flute,* from PICCOLO (adjective).]

piccolo² *adj.* Designating a musical instrument considerably smaller than the usual size: *a piccolo trumpet; a piccolo concertina.* [Italian *piccolo†,* small.]

pice (píss) *n., pl.* **pice.** An Indian coin of low value, a **paisa** *(see).*

pi·ce·ous (pí-si-əss) *adj.* **1.** Of, pertaining to, or resembling pitch. **2.** Glossy black in colour. [Latin *piceus,* from *pix* (stem *pic-*), pitch.]

pich·i·ci·e·go (píchi-see-áygō) *n.* Also **pich·i·ci·a·go** (-áygō, -áagō) *pl.* **-gos.** **1.** An extremely small armadillo, *Chlamyphorus truncatus,* of Argentina, having pale-pink armour and white hair. **2.** A similar South American armadillo, *Burmeisteria retusa,* having yellow-brown armour and whitish hair. [Spanish, perhaps from Guarani *pichey,* armadillo + Spanish *ciego,* blind, from Latin *caecus.*]

pick¹ (pik) *v.* **picked, picking, picks.** —*tr.* **1.** To select from or as if from a group: *picked the best.* **2. a.** To pull or pluck off: *pick an apple.* **b.** To gather in by picking: *pick cotton.* **c.** To gather the harvest from: *picked a field.* **3. a.** To remove the outer covering of; pluck: *pick a chicken clean of feathers.* **b.** To tear off bit by bit: *pick meat from the bones.* **4. a.** To probe (the teeth or nose, for example) to remove extraneous matter. **b.** To scratch or try to remove (a spot, for example) with the fingernails. **5.** To untangle and isolate (threads) as in weaving. **6.** To break up, pierce, or dig by means of a sharp, pointed instrument, such as a pick. **7.** To make (a hole) with a sharp instrument. **8.** To seek and discover (a flaw): *He picked holes in their argument.* **9.** To take up (food) with the beak; peck: *The parrot picked its seed.* **10. a.** To steal the contents of (a person's pocket). **b.** To steal (money, for example) from a person's pocket. **11.** To open (a lock) without the use of the key. **12.** To make (one's way) carefully: *picked her way through the mud.* **13.** To provoke: *pick a fight.* **14.** To pluck the strings of (a musical instrument). *—intr.* **1.** To decide with care or forethought: *pick and choose.* **2.** To work with a pick. **3.** To harvest or gather fruit, crops, or the like. **4.** To eat food sparingly and without apparent appetite: *just picked at his meal.* **—**See Synonyms at **choose. —pick at.** *Informal.* To find fault with or make petty criticisms about; nag: *She picks at him day and night.* **—pick off.** To shoot after singling out: *I picked the ducks off one by one.* **—pick on. 1.** To tease or bully. **2.** To select, especially for something unpleasant. **—pick out. 1. a.** To discern from the surroundings; distinguish: *At last we managed to pick out his face in the crowd.* **b.** To cause to stand out by the use of a different colour; distinguish from a background: *pick out the design in green.* **c.** To distinguish or select from a mass of detail. **2.** To play (music) slowly by or as if by ear: *He managed to pick out the tune.* **—pick over.** To sort out or examine item by item, especially in order to select the best.

~n. **1.** The act of picking, especially with a pointed instrument. **2.** The act of selecting or choosing; choice: *Take your pick.* **3.** That which is selected or regarded as the most desirable; the best or choicest one: *the pick of the crop.* **4.** The amount or quantity of a crop that is picked by hand. **5.** *Printing.* **a.** A particle of dirt or paper caught in type or a printing plate, and causing a mark or smudge on the printed sheet. **b.** The mark so produced. [Middle English *piken,* to pierce, probably from Old French *piquer,* to prick, pick, from Vulgar Latin *piccāre* (unattested), to prick, pierce.]

pick[2] *n.* **1.** A tool for breaking hard surfaces, consisting of a curved bar sharpened at one or both ends and fitted to a long handle. **2.** Anything used for picking, such as an ice pick or a toothpick. **3.** *Music.* A **plectrum** *(see).* [Middle English *pik,* probably a variant of PIKE (pole).]

pick[3] *n.* **1.** A weft thread in weaving. **2.** A passage or throw of the shuttle in a loom.

~tr.v. **picked, picking, picks. 1.** To throw (a shuttle) across the loom. **2.** *Archaic.* To cast; pitch: *"as high as I could pick my lance"* (Shakespeare). [Middle English *pykken,* to throw (a shuttle), to cast, variant of *picchen,* to PITCH.]

pickaback. Variant of **piggyback.**

pickaninny. *Chiefly U.S.* Variant of **piccaninny.**

pick·axe (pík-aks) *n.* A pick, usually with a point at one end of the head and chisel edge at the other.

~v. **pickaxed, -axing, -axes.** *—intr.* To use a pickaxe. *—tr.* To use a pickaxe on. [Alteration (influenced by AXE) of Middle English *pikois, pikeis,* pickaxe, from Old French *picois,* from *pic,* pickaxe, perhaps from *piquer,* to prick. See **picket.**]

picked (pikt) *adj.* Chosen by careful selection.

pick·er[1] (píckər) *n.* **1.** One that picks; especially, a machine or person that harvests crops or gathers fruit. **2.** A machine that separates and cleans the fibres of wool, cotton, or the like.

picker[2] *n.* In weaving, the part of a loom that throws the shuttle across it.

pick·er·el (píckrəl, píckərəl) *n., pl.* **-els** or collectively **pickerel.** A young pike. [Middle English *pikerel,* diminutive of *pik, pike,* PIKE (fish).]

pick·et (píckit) *n.* **1. a.** A person or persons stationed outside a place of employment, usually during a strike, to express grievance or protest and discourage entry by nonstriking employees or customers. **b.** A person or persons present outside any building to protest. **2.** A pointed stake driven into the ground to support a fence, secure a tent, tether animals, mark points in surveying or, when pointed at the top, serve as part of a defensive barrier. **3.** *Military.* A detachment of one or more soldiers positioned in front of their lines to give advance warning of enemy approach.

~v. **picketed, -eting, -ets.** *—tr.* **1.** To enclose, secure, tether, mark out, or fortify with pickets. **2.** *Military.* **a.** To post as a picket. **b.** To guard with a picket. **3.** To post a picket or act as a picket at (a place of work, for example) during a strike or demonstration. *—intr.* To act or serve as a picket. [French *piquet,* from *piquer,* to prick, from *pic,* PICK (tool).] **—pick·et·er** *n.*

picket fence *n.* A fence of pointed, upright pickets.

picket line *n.* A line or procession of people picketing a place of business or otherwise staging a public protest.

Pick·ford (pík-fərd), **Mary,** born Gladys Mary Smith (1893–1979). U.S. star of the silent screen, born in Canada. Known as "America's Sweetheart", her films included *Pollyanna* (1919).

pick·in (píckin) *n. West African.* A small child. Also *West Indian* "pickney" [Variant of PICCANINNY, or from Portuguese *pequeno,* small.]

pick·ings (píckingz) *pl.n.* Something that is or may be picked, as: **a.** Leftovers. **b.** Profits, spoils, or a share of spoils.

pick·le (píck'l) *n.* **1. a.** *Often plural.* Any edible product, especially vegetables or fruit, that has been preserved and flavoured in a solution of brine or vinegar. **b.** A relish containing such vegetables or fruit. **c.** *Chiefly U.S.* A cucumber thus preserved and flavoured. **2.** A solution of brine or vinegar; often spiced, for preserving and flavouring food. **3.** An acid or other chemical solution used as a bath to remove scale and oxides from the surface of metals before plating or finishing. **4.** *Informal.* A troublesome, embarrassing, or difficult situation. **5.** *British Informal.* A naughty child.

~tr.v. **pickled, -ling, -les. 1.** To preserve or flavour in a solution of brine or vinegar. **2.** To treat (metal) in a chemical bath. [Middle English *pekille,* from Middle Dutch and Middle Low German *pekel*†.]

pick·led (píck'ld) *adj.* **1.** Preserved in or treated with pickle. **2.** *Informal.* Drunk.

pick·lock (pík-lok) *n.* **1.** A person who picks locks; especially, a thief. **2.** An instrument for picking a lock.

pick-me-up (pík-mee-up, -mi-) *n. Informal.* A drink, often alcoholic, taken as a stimulant or restorative.

pick·pock·et (pík-pockit) *n.* One who steals from pockets or handbags.

pick up *tr.v.* **1.** To take up or gather up by hand: *pick up your toys.* **2.** To take on (passengers, freight, survivors, hitchhikers, or the like). **3.** *Informal.* **a.** To go and fetch; collect: *pick the kids up from school.* **b.** To get or acquire without deliberate planning: *pick up a bargain.* **c.** To acquire (skill, knowledge, or understanding) over a period of time. **4.** To bring by chance or intent within sight or hearing: *picked up a foreign station.* **5.** To gain or recover (speed). **6.** *Informal.* To take into custody; arrest: *The coastguard picked up five smugglers.* **7.** To accept the responsibility of paying: *pick up the bill.* **8.** *Slang.* To make casual acquaintance with, usually in anticipation of sexual relations. *—intr.v. Informal.* To improve in condition or activity: *Sales will pick up next autumn.*

pick-up, pick·up (pík-up) *n.* **1. a.** The action or process of picking up: *the pick-up and delivery of farm produce.* **b.** Capacity for acceleration: *a sports car with good pick-up.* **c.** *Informal.* An improvement in condition or activity: *a pick-up in sales.* **2.** *Informal.* **a.** A place where passengers, freight, or the like are picked up. Also used adjectivally: *a pick-up point.* **b.** Passengers, freight, or the like to be picked up. **3.** *Slang.* A stranger with whom casual acquaintance is made, usually in anticipation of sexual relations. Often used derogatorily. **4.** A light truck with an open body and low sides used for making light deliveries. Also called "pick-up truck". **5. a.** *Electronics.* A device that converts the oscillations of a gramophone needle into electrical impulses for subsequent conversion into sound. **b.** A device on an electric guitar that converts the vibrations of the strings into electric signals for subsequent amplification and conversion into sound. See **crystal pickup, magnetic pickup. 6.** In radio and television: **a.** The reception of waves for conversion to electrical impulses. **b.** The apparatus used for such reception.

~adj. Designating a musical group formed at short notice for a specific performance, as opposed an established one.

Pick·wick·i·an (pik-wícki-ən) *adj.* **1.** Characterised by simplicity and benevolence. **2.** Understood or meant in a sense other than the obvious or literal one. Said of words or their sense. [After Mr. Pickwick in Dickens' *The Pickwick Papers* (1837).]

pick·y (píckí) *adj.* **-ier, -iest.** *Informal.* Excessively meticulous; fussy.

pic·nic (pík-nik) *n.* **1. a.** A meal taken to be eaten in the open air on an excursion to the seaside or the country, for example. **b.** An excursion or outing in which food is taken to be eaten in the open air. **c.** Any informal or makeshift meal eaten in the open air. **2.** *Slang.* An easy task or pleasant experience: *Teaching's no picnic.*

~intr.v. **picnicked, -nicking, -nics.** To go on or participate in a picnic. [French *piquenique,* perhaps a reduplication (influenced by obsolete French *nique,* a trifle) of *piquer,* to pick, peck, from Old French. See **picket.**] **—pic·nick·er** *n.*

pico– *comb. form. Symbol* **p** Indicates one million millionth, 10^{-12}; for example, *picosecond.* [Spanish *pico,* small quantity, peak, from *picar,* to prick. See **picaro.**]

Pi·co del·la Mi·ran·do·la (péekō déllə mi-rándələ), **Giovanni, Conte** (1463–94). Italian humanist and philosopher. He tried to reconcile Christianity, Platonism, and Hebrew philosophy, but attracted papal censure.

pic·o·line (píckə-leen, pīkə-, -lin) *n.* Any of three isomeric liquid methylpyridine bases, C_6H_7N, derived from coal tar, horse urine, and bone oil and used as an industrial solvent. [Latin *pix* (stem *pic-*), pitch + -OL + -INE.]

pi·cot (pée-kō, pee-kṓ, pi-) *n.* A small embroidered loop forming an ornamental edging, as on ribbons, handkerchiefs, or hems.

~tr.v. **picoted** (-kōd, -kṓd), **-coting** (-kō-ing, -kṓ-), **-cots** (-kōz, -kṓz). To trim with edging. [French, "small point", diminutive of *pic,* peak, point, prick, from *piquer,* to prick. See **picket.**]

pic·o·tee (píckə-tée) *n.* A carnation of a type having pale petals bordered by a darker colour. [French *picoté,* furnished with points, from *picoter,* to mark with points or pricks, from PICOT.]

pic·rate (píckrayt) *n.* A salt or ester of picric acid. [PICR(O)- + -ATE.]

pic·ric acid (píckrik) *n.* A poisonous, explosive yellow crystalline solid, $C_6H_2(NO_2)_3OH$, used in explosives, dyes, and antiseptics. Also called "trinitrophenol". [PICR(O)- + -IC.]

PRONUNCIATION KEY

a, trap; aa, father; ai, fair; ar, star; aw, lawn; ay, play; b, bb, stab; rubber; ch, church; ck, ticket; d, dd, dead; ladder; e, dress; ee, bee; er, defer; ew, few; ewr, pure; ə, about; ər, letter; f, ff, fife; differ; g, gg, giggle; h, hat; i, kit; ī, price; īr, fire; j, judge; k, kick; l, ll, let; 'l, needle; m, mm, man; n, nn, no; 'n, sudden; ng, thing; o, lot; ō, no; ŏŏ, foot; ōō, shoe; oor, poor; ow, cow; owr, hour; oy, boy; p, pp, pepper; r, rr, red; s, ss, sauce; sh, ship; t, tt, totter; th, thick; th, this; smooth; u, cut; ur, turn; v, vv, valve; w, wet; y, yes; z, zz, zebra; zh, vision; pleasure

IN FOREIGN WORDS:

aN, oN, Saint-Saëns; hl, Llanelli; Hluhluwe; kh, loch; lough; Khaled

STRESS MARK:

ín-sīt, insight; in-sī́t, incite

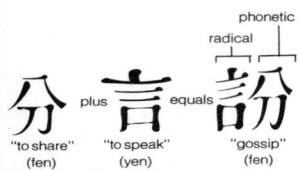

分 plus 言 equals 訬
"to share"   "to speak"   "gossip"
(fen)   (yen)   (fen)

pictograph *Chinese characters are pictographic in origin, but the relationship between image and meaning is no longer immediately apparent, because the original pictures used have been reduced to symbols. Modern Chinese characters – as in the word for "gossip" (above) – are made up of two pictographic elements: a radical, which indicates the general meaning; and a phonetic component, which indicates the pronunciation.*

pic·rite (píckrīt) *n.* A coarse-grained igneous rock consisting of olivine and augite with small quantities of plagioclase feldspar. [PICRO- (containing magnesium) + -ITE.]

picro– *comb. form.* Indicates something bitter; for example, **picrotoxin**. [Greek *pikro-*, from *pikros*, bitter.]

pic·ro·tox·in (píckrə-tóksin, píckrō-) *n.* A bitter powder, $C_{30}H_{34}O_{13}$, used as a stimulant and antidote for barbiturate poisoning.

Pict (pikt) *n.* A member of an ancient northern British people. They came into conflict with the Britons, and later made raids on Roman garrisons. By about A.D. 900, they had effectively disappeared, having been assimilated with the Scots. [Middle English, from Late Latin *Pictī* (plural), probably alteration of the indigenous name by folk etymology, as if to mean "the painted (i.e. tattooed) people", from *pictus*, past participle of *pingere*, to paint.]

Pict·ish *adj.* Of or pertaining to the Picts or their language. —*n.* The language of the Picts, extinct by the tenth century, and known chiefly from place names.

pic·to·graph (pík-tə-graaf, -tō-, -graf) *n.* Also **pic·to·gram** (-gram). **1.** A picture representing a word or idea; a hieroglyph. **2.** A record in hieroglyphic symbols. **3.** A pictorial representation of numerical data or relationships as by charts, symbols, or the like. [Latin *pictus*, past participle of *pingere*, to paint + -GRAPH.] —**pic·to·graph·ic** (-gráffik) *adj.* —**pic·to·graph·i·cal·ly** *adv.* —**pic·tog·ra·phy** (pik-tóggrəfi) *n.*

Pic·tor (píktər) *n.* A constellation in the Southern Hemisphere near Columba and Dorado. [Latin, painter, from *pingere* (past participle *pictus*), to paint.]

pic·to·ri·al (pik-táwri-əl ‖ -tóri-) *adj.* **1.** Pertaining to, characterised by, or composed of pictures. **2.** Of or pertaining to painting, drawing, or etching. **3.** Represented in a picture. **4.** Having vivid imagery; graphic: *pictorial prose.* **5.** Illustrated by pictures. —*n.* An illustrated periodical. [Late Latin *pictōrius*, from Latin *pictor*, painter. See **Pictor.**] —**pic·to·ri·al·ly** *adv.*

pic·ture (pík-chər) *n.* **1. a.** A visual representation or image painted, drawn, photographed, or otherwise rendered on a surface. Also used adjectivally: *a picture postcard.* **b.** An image in the mind: *a vivid picture of the attack.* **2.** Any visible image, especially one on a flat surface: *the picture reflected in the lake.* **3.** A vivid or realistic verbal description: *a Shakespearean picture of guilt.* **4.** A person or object that bears a striking resemblance to another: *the picture of her mother.* **5.** A person, object, or scene that typifies or embodies an emotion, state of mind, or mood: *a picture of embarrassment.* **6.** The circumstances of an event or time considered as a scene; a situation: *Their defeat changed the picture.* **7.** A cinematic film. **8.** *Plural. British.* **a.** A cinema. **b.** A showing of a film at a cinema. **9.** Someone or something that is very beautiful: *She looked a picture in her new dress.* —**in the picture.** Apprised of the relevant facts; informed. —**out of the picture. 1.** Irrelevant. **2.** No longer in contention; too far behind to be capable of victory.
—*tr.v.* **pictured, -turing, -tures. 1.** To make a visible representation or picture of. **2.** To form a mental image of; visualise: *I can't picture her as a nurse.* **3.** To describe vividly in words; make a verbal picture of: *pictured her heroism glowingly.* [Middle English, from Latin *pictūra*, from *pingere* (past participle *pictus*), to paint.]

picture card *n.* A **court card** (see).

picture hat *n.* A wide-brimmed hat, often highly decorated, originally worn by women in the 18th century.

picture palace *n. British.* A cinema. Not in current usage.

pic·tur·esque (pík-chə-résk) *adj.* **1.** Constituting or suggesting a striking or attractive picture; suitable for a picture: *the picturesque emerald hills of Ireland.* **2.** Striking or interesting in an unusual way; irregularly or quaintly attractive. **3.** Strikingly expressive or vivid: *picturesque language.* [Alteration (influenced by PICTURE) of French *pittoresque*, from Italian *pittoresco*, from *pittore*, painter, from Latin *pictor*, from *pingere* (past participle *pictus*), to paint.] —**pic·tur·esque·ly** *adv.* —**pic·tur·esque·ness** *n.*

picture tube *n.* A television tube (see).

picture window *n.* A large window, usually of a single sheet of glass, giving out on to an attractive view.

picture writing *n.* **1.** The recording of events using pictures or symbols, such as in early hieroglyphs. **2.** A writing system that uses pictographs.

pic·ul (pík'l) *n.* Any of various units of weight used in the Far East; especially, a Chinese unit equal to about 60 kilograms (133 pounds). [Malay *pīkul*, a man's load.]

pid·dle (pídd'l) *intr.v.* **-dled, -dling, -dles. 1.** To spend time aimlessly; diddle. **2.** *Informal.* To urinate. [Perhaps from PEDDLE. In sense 2, perhaps blend of PISS + PUDDLE.]

pid·dling (pídd'l-ing, píddling) *adj. Informal.* Beneath consideration; trifling; trivial.

pid·dock (píddək) *n.* Any of various marine bivalve molluscs of the family Pholadidae, capable of boring into wood, rock, and other materials. [18th century: origin obscure.]

pidg·in (píjin) *n.* A simplified form of speech, usually a mixture of two or more languages, that has a rudimentary grammar and vocabulary and is used for communication between groups speaking different languages. Compare **creolised language.** [From PIDGIN ENGLISH.] —**pidg·in** *adj.*

pidgin English *n. Sometimes capital* **P.** A pidgin based on English and used originally as a trade language in Far Eastern ports. [A pidgin rendering of *business English.*]

pie¹ (pī) *n.* A baked food consisting of a shell of pastry and a filling of fruit, meat, cheese, or other ingredients, usually covered with a pastry crust. [Middle English *pie*, perhaps "magpie" (comparing the mixture in a pie to the various items a magpie might collect).]

pie² *n. Archaic.* A bird, the **magpie** (see). [Middle English, from Old French, from Latin *pīca*.]

pie³ *n.* A former monetary unit of India and Pakistan. [Hindi *pā'ī*, from Sanskrit *pādikā*, quarter, from *pāda*, foot, leg, quarter.]

pie⁴ *n.* An almanac of services used in the English church before the Reformation. [Medieval Latin *pīca*, almanac, PICA.]

pie⁵ *n.* Also *chiefly U.S.* **pi'** *pl.* **pis. 1.** *Printing.* Type that has been jumbled or thrown together at random. **2.** Any jumble or disorder: *An army without ranks fell to pie.*
—*v.* **pied, pieing, pies.** Also **pi, pied, piing, pies.** *Printing.* —*tr.* To jumble or mix up (type). —*intr.* To become jumbled.

pie·bald (pī-bawld) *adj.* Spotted or patched, especially in black and white: *a piebald horse.*
—*n.* A piebald animal, especially a horse. Compare **skewbald.** [PIE (magpie) + BALD.]

piece (peess) *n.* **1.** A thing considered as a unit or element of a larger quantity or class; a portion: *a piece of string.* **2.** A portion or part that has been separated from a whole: *a piece of cake.* **3. a.** An object that is one member of a group or class: *a piece of furniture.* **b.** Such an object considered as particularly fine, valuable, or rare: *a collector's piece.* **4.** An artistic, musical, or literary work or composition. **5.** An instance; a specimen: *a piece of folly.* **6.** *Informal.* One's fully expressed opinion; one's mind: *speak one's piece.* **7.** A coin or counter: *a ten-pence piece.* **8.** In various board games, any of the counters or men used in playing. **9.** In chess, any of the figures other than a pawn. **10.** A firearm, especially a rifle. **11.** A person, especially a woman, considered in terms of sexual attractiveness. Usually considered offensive. **12.** *Scottish.* A sandwich or slice of buttered bread. **13.** *U.S. Regional.* A short or manageable distance. —**a piece of (one's) mind.** *Informal.* Frank or aggressive criticism or censure. —**go to pieces. 1.** To break into small pieces; fall apart. **2.** *Informal.* To lose mental and emotional self-control; break down. —**a nasty piece of work.** *British Informal.* A cruel or unpleasant person. —**of a piece. 1.** Belonging to the same kind or class. **2.** Internally consistent and predictable; forming a coherent whole.
—*tr.v.* **pieced, piecing, pieces. 1.** To mend or put together by joining or uniting the pieces of: *He pieced together the vase.* **b.** To combine the parts or pieces of in such a way as to be able to understand or draw conclusions from: *tried to piece the story together.* **2.** To join (broken threads) when spinning. —**piece out. 1.** To eke out; cause to last. **2.** To increase by adding a piece to. [Middle English, from Anglo-French, Old French *pece*, from Medieval Latin *pecia, petia,* from Gaulish *pettia†* (unattested).]

pièce de ré·sis·tance (p-yéss də ráyzi-stónss, rézzi-) *n.* **1.** The principal dish of a meal. **2.** The most outstanding item or event in a group or series, especially in a series of artistic works. [French.]

piece goods *pl.n.* Fabrics made and sold in standard lengths.

piece·meal (péess-meel) *adv.* **1.** Piece by piece; gradually: *articles acquired piecemeal.* **2.** In pieces; apart.
—*adj.* Accomplished or made piece by piece or in separate stages; fragmentary. [Middle English *pecemele: pece,* PIECE + *-mele,* by a certain measure, Old English *mælum,* dative plural of *mæl,* a point of time. See **meal.**]

piece of cake *n. Informal.* Something that is very easy to perform, obtain, operate, or the like.

piece of eight *n., pl.* **pieces of eight.** An obsolete Spanish silver coin.

piece rate *n.* A fixed rate of payment per number of products turned out.

piece·work (péess-wurk) *n.* Work paid for according to the number of items produced. —**piece·work·er** *n.*

pie chart *n.* A circular chart having radii dividing the circle into sectors proportional to the relative size of the quantities represented. Also called "pie graph". [From PIE (pastry).]

Pieck (peek), **Wilhelm** (1876–1960). German communist statesman, president of the German Democratic Republic (1949–60).

pie·crust (pī-krust) *n.* The baked pastry of a pie.
—*adj.* Designating a piece of furniture with an ornamental moulding like the edge of a piecrust.

pied (pīd) *adj.* Patchy in colour; splotched; piebald. [Middle English, from PIE (magpie), from its piebald colouring.]

pied-à-terre (p-yéd-aa-taír, p-yáyd-, p-yáyt-) *n., pl.* **pieds-à-terre** *(pronounced as singular). French.* A secondary or temporary lodging: *a small pied-à-terre in the city.* [French, "foot to the ground".]

pied·mont (péed-mont) *adj. Geology.* Formed or lying at the foot of a mountain or mountain range: *a piedmont plain.*
—*n. Geology.* A piedmont area or region. [French, from Italian *piémonte,* PIEDMONT.]

Pied·mont (péed-mont, p-yéd-, -mənt). *Italian.* **Pie·mon·te** (p-ye-móntay). Autonomous region of northwest Italy. It includes part of the Alps and Po valley, and Asti, Novara, and Torino are among its provinces. It formed the heartland of modern Itlay during the Risorgimento (from 1814), and its capital, Turin, was Italy's first national capital. —**Pied·mon·tese** (eez) *n. & adj.*

Pied Piper *n.* **1.** In German legend, a piper who rid the town of Hamelin of its rats by leading them away with his music. When he was refused due payment he led away the children of the town as well. Also called "Pied Piper of Hamelin". **2.** *Often small* **p.** A person who lures away others to follow him.

pied wagtail *n.* A British subspecies of the white wagtail (*Motacilla*

alba), *Motacilla alba yarrellii,* having black and white plumage and a long black tail. Also called "water wagtail".
pie-eyed (pī-īd) *adj. British Slang.* Drunk.
pie graph *n.* A **pie chart** *(see).*
pie in the sky *n. Informal.* False expectation; unwarranted hope. **—pie-in-the-sky** *adj.*
pie•man (pī-mən) *n., pl.*- **men** (-mən, -men). *British Archaic.* A person who sells pies.
pier (peer) *n.* **1. a.** A platform extending from a shore over water and supported by piles or pillars, used to secure, protect, and provide access to ships or boats. **b.** Such a structure supporting various buildings used predominantly for entertainment. **2.** A supporting structure at the junction of connecting spans of a bridge. **3.** *Architecture.* Any of various vertical supporting structures, especially: **a.** A pillar, rectangular in cross-section, supporting an arch or roof. **b.** The portion of a wall between windows or openings. **c.** A reinforcing structure that projects from a wall; a buttress. [Middle English *per, pere,* from Anglo-Latin *pera*†.]
pierce (peerss) *tr.v.* **pierced, piercing, pierces. 1.** To cut or pass through or into, with or as if with a sharp instrument; stab; penetrate. **2.** To make a hole or opening in; perforate. **3.** To make a way through: *The path pierced the wilderness.* **4. a.** To sound sharply through: *His shout pierced the din.* **b.** To shine through: *His torch pierced the darkness.* **5.** To succeed in discerning or understanding: *He pierced the heart of the mystery.* **6.** To affect penetratingly; move deeply; transfix: *pierced by anguish.*
~intr. To penetrate into or through something: *The rocket pierced through space.* [Middle English *percen,* from Old French *percer, percier,* from Vulgar Latin *pertūsiāre* (unattested), from Latin *pertundere* (past participle *pertūsus*), to pierce through : *per,* through + *tundere,* to thrust.] **—pierc•er** *n.* **—pierc•ing•ly** *adv.*
pierced (peerst) *adj.* Designating an ear having a tiny hole made in the lobe to hold an earring.
pier glass *n.* A long mirror formerly hung on the portion of wall (pier) between windows.
Pi•e•ri•an (pī-éer-i-ən, -érri-) *adj.* Of or pertaining to the Muses or to artistic inspiration. [After the PIERIAN SPRING.]
Pierian Spring. 1. *Greek Mythology.* A fountain in Pieria in ancient Macedonia, sacred to the Muses. **2.** A source of inspiration, especially to artists and poets.
Pie•ro del•la Fran•ces•ca (p-yáir-ō déllə fran-chéskə) (*c.* 1420–92). Italian painter of the Renaissance. His mature works include a fresco cycle, *The Story of the True Cross* (1452–66), Arezzo.
Pier•rot (péer-ō; *French* p-ye-rō) *n.* **1.** A stock male character in traditional French pantomime having a whitened face and floppy white clothing. **2.** *Small* **p.** A clown, doll, or the like similarly dressed and made up. [French, diminutive of *Pierre,* from Latin *Petrūs,* (the name Peter).]
pier table *n.* A table designed to stand between windows, under a pier glass.
pi•e•tà (pée-ay-taá) *n. Often capital* **P.** A painting, drawing, or sculpture of the Virgin Mary holding and mourning over the dead body of Jesus. [Italian, "pity", from Latin *pietās,* PIETY.]
Pie•ter•mar•itz•burg (péetər-márrits-burg). Capital of Natal province, Republic of South Africa. Founded (1838) by the Boers, it lies in an agricultural region.
pi•e•tism (pī-ə-tiz'm) *n.* **1.** Piety. **2.** Affected or exaggerated piety. **3.** *Capital* **P.** A reforming movement in the German Lutheran Church during the 17th and 18th centuries, which strove to renew the devotional ideal in the Protestant religion. [German *Pietismus,* from Latin *pietās,* PIETY.] **—pi•e•tist** *n.* **—pi•e•tis•tic** (-tístik), **pi•e•tis•ti•cal** *adj.* **—pi•e•tis•ti•cal•ly** *adv.*
pi•e•ty (pī-əti) *n., pl.* **-ties. 1.** Religious devotion and reverence to God. **2.** Devotion and reverence to parents and family. **3.** A pious act or thought. **4.** The state or quality of being pious. [French *piété,* from Latin *pietās* (stem *pietāt-*), from *pius,* PIOUS.]
piezo– *comb. form.* Indicates pressure; for example, **piezometer.** [Greek *piezein,* to squeeze, press.]
pi•e•zo•e•lec•tric crystal (pī-éezō-i-léktrik, péezō-, pee-étsō-) *n.* Any of certain crystals lacking a centre of symmetry, such as quartz, that when subjected to stress produces a **potential difference** *(see)* between its two stressed surfaces.
pi•e•zo•e•lec•tric•i•ty (pī-éezō-éllek-trissəti, péezō-, pee-étsō-, -i-lek- || -trízzəti) *n.* The generation of electricity or of electric polarity in dielectric crystals subjected to mechanical stress, and, conversely, the generation of stress in such crystals subjected to an applied voltage. Also called "piezoelectric effect". **—pi•e•zo•e•lec•tric** (-i-léktrik), **pi•e•zo•e•lec•tri•cal** *adj.* **—pi•e•zo•e•lec•tri•cal•ly** *adv.*
pi•e•zom•e•ter (pī-eez-ómmitər, péez-, pée-ets-) *n.* Any instrument for measuring pressure, especially high pressure. [PIEZO- + -METER.] **—pi•e•zo•met•ric** (-ə-méttrik, -ō-), **pi•e•zo•met•ri•cal** *adj.* **—pi•e•zom•e•try** (-ómmətri) *n.*
pif•fle (píff'l) *intr.v.* **-fled, -fling, -fles.** *Informal.* To talk or act in a feeble or futile way.
~n. Informal. Foolish or futile talk or ideas; nonsense. [Imitative.]
pif•fling (píffling) *adj.* Futile and trivial; silly.
pig (pig) *n.* **1.** Any of several mammals of the family Suidae, having short legs, cloven hoofs, bristly hair, and a cartilaginous snout used for digging; especially, the domesticated pig, *Sus scrofa.* **2.** The edible parts of a pig; pork. **3.** *Informal.* A person regarded as being unpleasantly dirty, piglike, greedy, or gross. **4.** See **guinea pig. 5. a.** An oblong block of metal, chiefly iron or lead, poured from a smelting furnace. **b.** A mould in which such metal is cast. **c. Pig iron** *(see).* **6.** *Slang.* A policeman. Used derogatorily. **7.** *British Informal.* A tedious or difficult thing. **8.** *Regional.* A segment of an orange, apple, or other fruit. **—a pig in a poke.** Something that is obtained without first being inspected, or whose value is unknown. **—make a pig of (oneself).** To be greedy or self-indulgent.
~v. **pigged, pigging, pigs.** *—intr.* **1.** To give birth to pigs; farrow. **2.** To act in a greedy, dirty or piggish way. *—tr. Informal.* To eat (food) greedily; gobble. **—pig it.** To live in a piglike way. [Middle English *pigge,* probably from Old English *picga*† (unattested).]
pig bed *n.* A bed of sand in which pigs of iron are cast.
pi•geon (píj-ən, -in) *n.* **1.** Any of various birds of the widely distributed family Columbidae, characteristically having deepchested bodies, small heads, and short legs; especially, *Columba livia* or any of its domesticated varieties. This species is also called "rock dove". **2.** *Slang.* One who is easily swindled; a dupe. **3.** *British Informal.* Responsibility; affair: *It's not my pigeon.* [Middle English *pijon,* from Old French, young bird, pigeon, from Late Latin *pīpiō* (stem *pīpiōn-*), squab, young chirping bird, from *pīpīre,* to chirp.]
pigeon chest *n.* A chest deformity marked by a projecting sternum, such as may occur as the result of rickets. Also called "chicken breast". **—pi•geon-chest•ed** *adj.*
pi•geon-heart•ed (píj-ən-hártid, -in-) *adj.* Lacking courage; cowardly.
pi•geon•hole (píj-ən-hōl, -in-) *n.* **1.** The small hole or holes for nesting, in a pigeon loft. **2.** A small compartment or recess for holding papers; a cubbyhole. **3.** *Informal.* A category or classification.
~tr.v. **pigeonholed, -holing, -holes. 1.** To place or file in a pigeonhole. **2.** To classify mentally; categorise. **3.** To put aside and ignore; shelve.
pigeon pea *n.* **Dhal** *(see).*
pi•geon-toed (píj-ən-tōd, -in-) *adj.* Having the toes turned inwards.
pi•geon•wing (píj-ən-wing, -in-) *n.* A dance step performed by jumping and clapping the feet together. [Probably a translation of French *ailes de pigeon,* a ballet term for a leap in which the dancer's legs imitate the motion of a bird's wings.]
pig•ger•y (píggəri) *n., pl.* **-ies. 1.** A place where pigs are kept. **2.** Greediness or slovenliness; piggishness. [PIG + -ERY.]
pig•gin (píggin) *n.* A small wooden bucket with one stave projecting above the rim for use as a handle. Also called "pipkin". [16th century : origin obscure.]
pig•gish (píggish) *adj.* **1.** Like a pig; greedy; dirty. **2.** *British Informal.* Stubborn; pig-headed. **—pig•gish•ly** *adv.* **—pig•gish•ness** *n.*
Pig•gott (píggət), **Lester (Keith)** (1935–). British jockey. He has won the Derby a record eight times, the Ascot Gold Cup 11 times, and has had more than 3,000 winners.
pig•gy (piggi) *n., pl.* **-gies.** A little pig. Used especially by children. *~adj.* **piggier, -giest.** Piggish.
pig•gy•back (píggi-bak) *n.* Also **pick•a•back** (pícka-). **1.** A ride on the shoulders or back of another person. **2.** A method of transporting vehicles by loading them onto another vehicle such as a train or a specially designed lorry.
~tr.v. **piggybacked, -backing, -backs.** Also **pick•a•back.** To carry or transport by piggyback.
~adj. Of, pertaining to, or designating a piggyback. **2.** *Informal.* Of or pertaining to a method of transplant surgery in which the new organ is initially supported by the existing organ, which is left in the body until the transplant has established itself: *a piggyback heart.* **—pig•gy•back** *adv.*
piggy bank *n.* A child's receptacle for holding money, often shaped like a pig, and having a slot into which coins are inserted.
pig-head•ed (píg-héddid) *adj.* Stubborn, especially in a stupid or belligerent way. See Synonyms at **obstinate. —pig-head•ed•ly** *adv.* **—pig-head•ed•ness** *n.*
pig iron *n.* Crude iron cast in blocks or pigs. Also called "pig".
pig•jump (píg-jump) *intr.v.* **-jumped, -jumping, -jumps.** *Australian & N.Z.* To kick out with the hind legs, keeping the front legs rigid and on the ground. Used of a horse.
pig Latin *n.* A coded jargon in which the initial consonant of each word is transposed to the end of that word with *-ay* (ay) added to form a new syllable, as *igpay atinlay* for *pig Latin.*
pig•let (píg-lət, -lit) *n.* A young pig.
pig•ment (píg-mənt) *n.* **1.** Any substance or matter used as colouring. **2.** Dry colouring matter, usually an insoluble powder to be mixed with a vehicle to produce paint and similar products. **3.** *Biology.* A substance, such as chlorophyll or haemoglobin, that produces a characteristic colour in plant or animal tissue.
~tr.v. (*also* pig-mént) **pigmented, -menting, -ments.** To colour with pigment. [Latin *pigmentum,* from *pingere,* to paint.] **—pig•men•tar•y** (-əri || -erri) *adj.*
pig•men•ta•tion (píg-mən-táysh'n, -men-) *n. Biology.* **1.** Coloration of tissues by pigment. **2.** Deposition of pigment by cells.
pigment cell *n.* A **chromatophore** *(see).*
pigmy. Variant of **pygmy.**
Pigmy. Variant of **Pygmy.**
pig•nut (píg-nut) *n.* **1.** Either of two trees, *Carya glabra* or *C. ovalis,* of the eastern United States, bearing nuts with slightly bitter kernels. **2.** The nut of either of these trees. **3.** A plant, the **earthnut** *(see),* or its tuberous root.
pig•root (píg-rōōt) *intr.v.* **-rooted, -rooting, -roots.** *Australian & N.Z.* To pigjump.
pig's ear *n.* **1.** A large, sweet, flaky biscuit, shaped like a cloverleaf. **2.** *Informal.* A messy or clumsy performance of a task: *You've made a right pig's ear of these accounts.*

pig *One of the most useful of farm animals: its flesh is used for food, its bristles for brushes and its skin for hides. The Large White pig (above) is primarily reared for bacon.*

pigeon *Grain and plants are the pigeon's chief diet. The young are fed on a milky substance secreted in the adults' crop which provides them with protein. Pigeons are the only birds to produce a milk similar to that of mammals. The European wood pigeon, shown here, is regarded as a major agricultural pest, because of the immense damage it does to crops.*

pigmentation *Many animals, such as chameleons and some fish, can change their colouring, or pigmentation, to match their surroundings. These two peppered moths are both of the same species, but have adapted to different environments. The original type is speckled, and is therefore unobtrusive on lichen-covered trees. The upper one is more common near sooty, polluted cities.*

pig's fry n. The offal, such as the heart and liver, of a pig, fried together and eaten.

pig·skin (píg-skin) n. 1. The skin of a pig. 2. Leather made from this. —**pig·skin** adj.

pig·stick (píg-stik) intr.v. **-sticked, -sticking, -sticks.** To hunt wild boar on horseback with a spear. —**pig·stick·er** n. —**pig·stick·ing** n.

pig·sty (píg-stī) n., pl. **-sties.** 1. A shelter or pen where pigs are kept. 2. Chiefly British. A filthy or very untidy place. Also U.S. "pigpen".

pig·swill (píg-swil) n. 1. Leftover food or other edible matter used to feed pigs. Also called "pig's wash". 2. Informal. Extremely poor-quality food.

pig·tail (píg-tayl) n. 1. A plait of hair that hangs down behind the head. 2. Either of a pair of similar plaits at the sides of the head. 3. A twisted roll of tobacco. —**pig·tailed** adj.

pig·weed (píg-weed) n. 1. A coarse weed, Amaranthus retroflexus, having hairy leaves and spikes of green flowers. Also called "red-root". 2. U.S. A plant, **fat hen** (see).

pi·ka (pī́ka, péékə) n. Any of several small, tailless, harelike mammals of the genus Ochotona, of the mountains of North America and Eurasia. Also called "cony". [Tungus (East Siberia) piika.]

pike[1] (pīk) n. 1. A weapon consisting of a long wooden shaft with a pointed steel or iron head, formerly used by infantry. 2. Any spike or sharp point, such as the tip of a spear.
~tr.v. **piked, piking, pikes.** To pierce or kill with a pike. [Middle English, Old English pīc†, prick, point.]

pike[2] n., pl. **pikes** or collectively **pike.** 1. A freshwater game and food fish, Esox lucius, of the Northern Hemisphere, having a long snout and sometimes attaining a length of over 1½ metres (four feet). 2. Any of various similar or related fishes. [Middle English, perhaps from PIKE (spike), referring to the shape of its jaw.]

pike[3] n. A turnpike (see). [Short for TURNPIKE.]

pike[4] n. Chiefly British Regional. A mountain or hill peak. [Middle English, akin to Norwegian dialectal pīk†.]

pike·let (pī́k-lət, -lit) n. 1. British Regional. A small, flat crumpet. 2. Australian & N.Z. A small, flat drop scone. [West Midlands dialect, shortened from Welsh bara pyglyd, pitchy bread.]

pike·man (pī́k-mən) n., pl. **-men** (-mən). 1. The keeper of a turnpike. 2. Formerly, a soldier armed with a pike.

pike·perch (pī́k-perch) n., pl. **-perches** or collectively **pikeperch.** Any of various fishes related to the perches and resembling the pike, such as the **walleye** (see).

pik·er (pī́kər) n. Informal. A timid, cautious person, often mean and petty, who tends to back out of situations or shirk work. [Middle English, perhaps special use from PIKE (weapon).]

pike-staff (pī́k-staaf ‖ -staf) n., pl. **-staffs** or **-staves** (-stayvz). 1. The shaft of a pike. 2. A walking stick tipped with a metal spike. [PIKE (point) + STAFF.]

pi·lar (pī́lər) adj. Of or covered with hair. [New Latin pilaris, from Latin pilus, a hair.]

pi·las·ter (pi-lástər) n. Architecture. A rectangular column with a capital and base, set into a wall to ornament it. [Old French pilastre, from Italian pilastro, from Medieval Latin pilastrum, from Latin pīla, PILLAR.]

Pi·late (pī́lət), **Pontius** (First century A.D.). Roman governor of Judaea (A.D. 26–36). He ordered Christ's crucifixion (allegedly with some reluctance). He is referred to by the Jewish authors Josephus and Philo, who both allude to his political insensitivity.

pi·lau, pi·law (pi-lów, -law) n. Also **pi·laf, pi·laff** (pil-af, pi-láf, pee- ‖ Chiefly U.S. -laaf). A dish consisting of rice cooked in a spicy seasoned stock, often with meat, shellfish, or vegetables. Also used adjectivally: pilau rice. [Turkish pilāw, from Persian pilāw from Osmanli pilau†, "rice porridge".]

pil·chard (pílchərd) n. Any of various small marine fishes related to the herrings; especially, a commercially important edible species, Sardina pilchardus, of European waters. [16th century: pilcher†.]

pile[1] (pīl) n. 1. A quantity of objects stacked, thrown, or having fallen together in a heap; a mound. 2. Often plural. Informal. A large accumulation or quantity: piles of trouble. 3. Informal. A large sum of money; a fortune. 4. A funeral pyre. 5. Informal. A very large building or complex of buildings. 6. Physics. A **nuclear reactor** (see). 7. Electricity. A **voltaic pile** (see).
~v. **piled, piling, piles.** —tr. 1. To set or stack in a pile or heap. Sometimes used with up. 2. To load with a pile: He piled the table with books. —intr. 1. To become or form a heap or pile. Often used with up. 2. Informal. To move in a disorderly mass or group. Used with in, on, off, or out: pile out of a car. —**pile it on.** Informal. To exaggerate. [Middle English, from Old French, heap, heap of stone, from Latin pīla, PILLAR.]

pile[2] n. 1. A heavy beam of timber, concrete, or steel, driven into the earth as a foundation or support for a structure. 2. Heraldry. A wedge-shaped charge, usually pointing downwards.
~tr.v. **piled, piling, piles.** 1. To drive piles into. 2. To support or provide with piles. [Middle English pile, pointed shaft, stake, Old English pīl, from West Germanic pīla (unattested), from Latin pīlum, heavy javelin, pestle.]

pile[3] n. 1. a. Cut or uncut loops of yarn forming the surface of certain fabrics, such as velvet, plush, and carpeting. Compare **nap.** b. Any such filament or loop of yarn. 2. The surface so formed. 3. Soft, fine hair, fur, or wool. [Middle English, probably from Anglo-French pyle, from Latin pilus, hair.] —**piled** adj.

pi·le·at·ed (pī́li-aytid, pílli-) adj. Also **pi·le·ate** (-ət, -it, -ayt). 1. Botany. Having a pileus. 2. Zoology. Having a crest, as certain birds do. [Latin pīleātus, from PILEUS.]

pile-driv·er (pī́l-drīvər) n. 1. A machine that drives piles (beams) into the earth by means of a steam hammer or by raising a weight between guideposts and dropping it on the head of the pile. 2. Informal. A powerful punch or kick.

pi·le·ous (pī́li-əss, pílli-) adj. Biology. Hairy. [Latin pilus, hair.]

piles (pīlz) pl.n. Haemorrhoids (see). Not in technical usage. [Plural of pile, from Latin pila, ball. See **pill.**]

pi·le·um (pī́li-əm, pílli-) n., pl. **pilea** (-ə). Zoology. The top of a bird's head, extending from the base of the bill to the nape. [New Latin, from Latin pīleus, felt cap, PILEUS.]

pile up intr.v. Informal. To crash; collide. Used especially of motor vehicles. —tr. To cause to crash or collide.

pile-up (pī́l-up) n. Informal. A collision involving several motor vehicles.

pi·le·us (pī́li-əss, pílli-) n., pl. **pilei** (-ī). 1. Botany. The umbrella-like cap of the reproductive body of certain fungi, such as mushrooms. 2. A round, brimless skullcap worn in ancient Rome. [New Latin, from Latin pīleus, pilleus, felt cap.]

pile·wort (pī́l-wurt ‖ -wawrt) n. The **lesser celandine** (see).

pil·fer (pílfər) v. **-fered, -fering, -fers.** —tr. To steal (a small amount or inexpensive item); filch. —intr. To steal or filch. —See Synonyms at **rob.** [Middle English, from Anglo-French, Old French pelfrer, to rob, despoil, from pelfre†, booty.] —**pil·fer·age** (-ij) n. —**pil·fer·er** n.

pil·grim (pil-grim) n. 1. A religious devotee who journeys to a shrine or sacred place. 2. One who embarks on a quest for some end conceived as sacred. 3. Any traveller. 4. Capital P. A Pilgrim Father. [Middle English pelegrim, from Old French peligrin, from Late Latin pelegrīnus, alteration of Latin peregrīnus, PEREGRINE.]

pil·grim·age (pilgrim-ij) n. 1. A journey to a sacred place or shrine. 2. Any long journey or search, especially one of exalted purpose or moral significance.
~intr.v. **pilgrimaged, -aging, -ages.** To go on a pilgrimage.

Pilgrim Father n. pl. **Pilgrim Fathers.** A member of the group of English Puritans that founded the colony of Plymouth in New England in 1620. Also called "Pilgrim", "Founding Father".

pi·lif·er·ous (pī-liffərəss, pi-) adj. 1. Botany. Designating the outermost layer of cells, in the region behind a root apex, that are elongated to form root hairs. 2. Bearing or terminating in a hair or hairs. [Latin pilus, hair + -FEROUS.]

pil·i·form (pī́li-fawrm, pílli-) adj. Botany. Resembling a hair. [Latin pilus, hair + -FORM.]

pil·ing (pī́l-ing) n. 1. The act of driving building piles into the earth. 2. Building piles collectively. 3. A structure composed of piles.

Pil·i·pi·no (pílli-péenō) n. The national language of the Philippines, based primarily on Tagalog, and having many Spanish and local dialectal elements. [Tagalog, from pilipino, Filipino, from Philippine Spanish, FILIPINO.]

pill[1] (pil) n. 1. A small pellet or tablet of medicine, sometimes coated, taken by swallowing whole or chewing. 2. Sometimes capital P. Informal. An oral contraceptive. Usually preceded by the. 3. Slang. Something considered to resemble a pill, such as a tennis ball. 4. Anything distasteful or unpleasant, but necessary: a bitter pill to swallow. 5. Slang. An insipid or ill-natured person.
~v. **pilled, pilling, pills.** —tr. 1. To dose with pills. 2. To make into pills. —intr. To form small balls resembling pills: a jumper that pills. [Middle Dutch pile, probably from Latin pilula, diminutive of pila†, ball.]

pill[2] v. **pilled, pilling, pills.** —tr. 1. Archaic. To pillage (people or a place). 2. Archaic & Regional. To peel. —intr. Archaic. To pillage. [Middle English pillen, perhaps from Old English pylan, from Latin pilāre, from pilus, hair; influenced by Old French piller, to plunder.]

pil·lage (pílij) v. **-laged, -laging, -lages.** —tr. 1. To rob (people or a place) of goods by violent seizure; plunder. 2. To take as spoils. —intr. To take spoils by robbery and violence.
~n. 1. The act of pillaging. 2. Something pillaged; spoils. [Middle English, from Old French, from piller, to tear up, maltreat, plunder, from pille, dialectal variant of peille, rag, cloth, probably from Latin pilleus, felt cap.] —**pil·lag·er** n.

pil·lar (pílər) n. 1. Architecture. A slender, freestanding, vertical support; a column. 2. Any similar structure used for decoration. 3. Someone or something similar in function or shape: a pillar of strength; a pillar of flame. 4. One who occupies a central or responsible position: a pillar of the state. —**from pillar to post.** From one place or situation to another; hither and thither.
~tr.v. **pillared, -laring, -lars.** To support or decorate with a pillar or pillars. [Middle English piler, from Old French pilier, from Vulgar Latin pīlāre (unattested), extension of Latin pīla†, pillar.]

pillar box n. British. A bright red, pillar-shaped public post box.

pil·lar-box red (pílər-boks) n. Bright red; scarlet. —**pillar-box red** adj.

Pillars of Hercu·les Two peaks, Gibraltar and Jebel Musa, one on each side of the Strait of Gibraltar, at the entrance to the Mediterranean sea.

pill·box (píl-boks) n. 1. A small box for pills usually having a shallow, cylindrical shape. 2. A woman's small, round hat. 3. A roofed concrete emplacement for a machine gun or other weapon.

pill bug n. A **woodlouse** (see).

pil·lion (píl-yən) n. A pad or cushion for a passenger behind the saddle on a motorcycle, scooter, or horse. Also used adjectivally: a pillion passenger.
~adv. On a pillion: ride pillion. [Scottish Gaelic pillean, diminutive of peall, covering, cushion, from Latin pellis, skin, hide.]

pilaster A pavilion framed by the rectangular columns known as pilasters, at Stoke Bruerne, Northamptonshire, England. It was designed by the architect Inigo Jones (1573–1652).

pil·li·winks (pílli-wingks) n. A medieval instrument of torture for squeezing the fingers and thumbs. [Middle English *pyrewinkes*†.]

pil·lo·ry (pílləri) n., pl. **-ries.** 1. A wooden framework with holes for the head and hands, in which offenders were formerly locked to be exposed to public scorn as punishment. 2. Public humiliation or exposure to scorn.
~tr.v. **pilloried, -rying, -ries.** 1. To put in a pillory as punishment. 2. To expose to public ridicule and abuse. [Middle English, from Anglo-Latin *pillorium*, from Old French *pilori*, probably from Provençal *espilori*†.]

pil·low (píllō) n. 1. A cushion for the head, used especially during sleep, consisting of a cloth case stuffed with something soft, such as down, feathers, or foam rubber. 2. Something similar in function or shape: *a pillow of moss.* 3. The pad on which bobbin lace is made.
~tr.v. **pillowed, -lowing, -lows.** 1. To rest (one's head) on or as if on a pillow. 2. To act as a pillow for. [Middle English *pilwe*, Old English *pyle, pylu*, from Latin *pulvīnus*†, pillow.] —**pil·low·y** adj.

pillow block n. *Engineering.* A block that encloses and supports a journal or shaft; a bearing.

pil·low·case (píllō-kayss) n. A removable covering for a pillow, usually of cotton or linen. Also called "pillowslip".

pill·wort (píl-wurt ‖ -wawrt) n. An aquatic Eurasian fern, *Pilularia globulifera*, with pill-like spore-producing bodies.

pillow lace n. **Bobbin lace** (see).

pi·lo·car·pine (pílō-kár-peen) n. Also **pi·lo·car·pin** (-pin). A poisonous alkaloid, $C_{11}H_{16}N_2O_2$, obtained from the leaves of the jaborandi tree and used to increase the secretion of various glands, and, as eye drops, to constrict the pupil. [From New Latin *Pilocarpus*, genus of the jaborandi : Greek *pilos*, felt + -CARPOUS.]

pi·lose (pí-lōz, -ōss) adj. Covered with fine, soft hair. [Latin *pilōsus*, from *pilus*, a hair.]

pi·lot (pílət) n. 1. One who operates or is licensed to operate an aircraft or spacecraft in flight. 2. **a.** One who is licensed to take charge of and steer a ship into and out of port or through dangerous waters, though not himself belonging to the ship's crew. **b.** The helmsman of a ship. 3. One who guides or directs a course of action for others. 4. The part of a tool, machine or machine that leads or guides the whole. 5. A pilot light (see). 6. Something that serves as a test, trial, or model, such as a television programme produced as a prototype of a series being considered for transmission.
~tr.v. **piloted, -loting, -lots.** 1. To serve as the pilot of. 2. To steer, or control the course of.
~adj. 1. Serving as a tentative model for future experiment or development: *a pilot film; a pilot study.* 2. Serving or leading as a guide: *a pilot beacon.* [French *pilote*, from Italian *pilota*, alteration of obsolete *pedota*, from Medieval Greek *pēdōtēs* (unattested), from Greek *pēda*, plural of *pēdon*, rudder, steering oar.]

pi·lot·age (pílətij) n. 1. *Nautical.* **a.** The technique or act of piloting. **b.** The fee paid to a pilot. 2. Navigation of an aircraft by visual identification of landmarks.

pilot balloon n. A small balloon used to determine wind velocity.

pilot cell n. A storage battery cell tested to determine the condition of the entire battery.

pilot cloth n. A thick, dark, blue cloth used for seamen's coats and similar garments.

pilot engine n. A locomotive engine sent ahead of a train to check the track for safety.

pilot fish n. A marine fish, *Naucrates ductor*, that often swims in company with larger fishes, especially sharks.

pi·lot·house (pílət-howss) n. A **wheelhouse** (see).

pi·lot·ing (píləting) n. 1. The occupation or service of a pilot. 2. *Nautical.* Coastal navigation by reference to landmarks, buoys, soundings, and the like. See **celestial navigation**.

pilot lamp n. A small electric lamp wired to light in response to specified conditions in an electric circuit. Also called "pilot light".

pilot light n. 1. A small gas flame that is kept burning constantly in order to ignite a gas burner, as in a cooker, or the main burner, as in a boiler. Also called "pilot". 2. A pilot lamp.

pilot officer n. The lowest-ranking commissioned officer in the Royal Air Force and various other air forces, ranking below a flying officer and equivalent in rank to a second lieutenant in the Army or a midshipman in the Navy.

pilot plant n. A small version of an industrial plant built to provide experience and design data for the full-scale plant.

pilot whale n. Any of several small, dark-coloured whales of the genus *Globicephala*. Also called "blackfish".

pils·ner, pil·sen·er (pílz-nər, pílss-) n. A strong, pale lager. [After *Pilsen* (PLZEŇ), Czechoslovakia, where it was originally brewed.]

Pilt·down man (pílt-down) n. A species of early man, *Eoanthropus dawsoni*, postulated from bones found in an early Pleistocene gravel bed in 1912, and proved in 1953 to have been a forgery based on the artificial modification and juxtaposition of the cranium of a modern man and the mandible of an orang-utan. [After the site near *Piltdown* Common, Sussex, identified by Charles Dawson (died 1916), English lawyer and amateur palaeontologist.]

pil·ule (píl-yōōl) n. A pill, especially a little pill. [French, from Latin *pilula*, diminutive of *pila*, ball. See **pill**.] —**pil·u·lar** (píl-lew-lər) adj.

Pi·ma (péema) n., pl. **-mas** or collectively **Pima.** 1. A member of a North American Indian people living in southern Arizona and northern Mexico. 2. The Uto-Aztecan language of this people. —**Pi·man** adj.

pi·men·to (pi-méntō) n., pl. **-tos.** 1. A tree, the **allspice** (see), or its

berries. 2. The **pimiento** (see). [Spanish *pimiento*, pepper, from Late Latin *pigmenta*, plural of *pigmentum*, plant juice, PIGMENT.]

pi meson n. *Physics.* A subatomic particle, the **pion** (see).

pi·mien·to (pi-méntō, -mi-éntō) n., pl. **-tos.** Also **pi·men·to.** 1. A sweet pepper (see). 2. The mild, ripe, red fruit of certain sweet peppers, used in salads, cookery, and as stuffing for green olives. Also called "red pepper". [Spanish, pepper, allspice, PIMENTO.]

pimp (pimp) n. 1. A man who solicits clients for a prostitute or brothel. 2. A man who procures prostitutes for a client or patron; a pander. 3. *Australian & N.Z. Slang.* A person who betrays secrets; an informer or telltale.
~intr.v. **pimped, pimping, pimps.** 1. To serve as a pimp. 2. *Australian & N.Z. Slang.* To betray secrets or be a telltale. Often used with *on.* [19th century : origin obscure.]

pim·per·nel (pímpər-nel, -n'l) n. 1. Any plant of the genus *Anagallis*, especially the scarlet pimpernel, *A. arvensis*, whose small, red, starlike flowers close in bad weather. Also called "poor man's weatherglass", "shepherd's weatherglass". 2. Any of various similar or related plants, such as the yellow pimpernel, *Lysimachia nemorum.* [Middle English *pympernele*, from Old French *pimpernelle*, from Vulgar Latin *piperīnella* (unattested), from Latin *piper*, PEPPER.]

pim·ple (pímp'l) n. A small swelling of the skin, sometimes containing pus; a papule or pustule. [Middle English *pinple*, nasalised form from Old English *piplian*†, to break out in pimples.] —**pim·pled, pim·ply** adj.

pin (pin) n. 1. A short, straight, stiff piece of wire with a blunt head and a sharp point, used especially for fastening. 2. Anything resembling a pin in shape or use, such as a hairpin or safety pin. 3. An ornament, brooch, or badge, especially a thin one, fastened to the clothing by means of a pin. 4. Something of little or no value: *"I would not care a pin."* (Shakespeare). 5. A slender, cylindrical piece of wood or metal for holding or fastening parts together, or serving as a support for suspending one thing from another, such as: **a.** A thin rod for securing the ends of fractured bones. **b.** A peg for fixing the crown to the root of a tooth. **c.** See **cotter pin**. 6. *Nautical.* **a.** See **belaying pin**. **b.** See **thole pin**. 7. *Music.* Any of the pegs securing the strings, and regulating their tension, on a stringed instrument. 8. The part of a key stem entering a lock. 9. The safety clasp in a hand grenade, whose removal releases the spring that activates the detonation process. 10. See **rolling pin**. 11. Any of the wooden clubs at which the ball is aimed in various bowling games. 12. In golf, the pole bearing a pennant to mark a hole. 13. In chess: **a.** The act of pinning an opponent's piece. **b.** The position of a piece when pinned. 14. In wrestling, a hold that prevents one's opponent from moving, especially one pressing both his shoulders to the ground. 15. A small beer cask holding 20.5 litres (4.5 gallons). 16. *Plural. Informal.* The legs: *steady on his pins.*
~tr.v. **pinned, pinning, pins.** 1. To fasten or secure with or as if with a pin or pins. 2. **a.** To transfix. **b.** To place in a position of trusting dependence. Used with *on* or *to: He pinned his faith on an absurdity.* 3. **a.** In wrestling, to secure (one's opponent) in an immobilising hold, especially when pressing both his shoulders to the ground. **b.** To hold fast; immobilise: *He was pinned under the wreckage.* 4. *Informal.* To attribute (a wrongdoing or crime). Used with *on: The murder was pinned on the wrong man.* 5. In chess, to prevent the moving of (a piece) without exposing a more valuable piece to capture. —**pin down.** 1. To oblige (someone) to make a definite response or commitment. 2. To specify clearly; locate precisely: *I had a feeling of sadness but couldn't pin down its cause.*
~adj. Having a grain suggestive of the heads of pins: *pin leather.* [Middle English *pin*, peg, Old English *pinn*, probably from Latin *pinna*, quill.]

pi·ña cloth (péen-yə) n. A soft, sheer fabric made from the fibres of pineapple leaves. [Spanish *piña*, pineapple, pinecone, from Latin *pīnea*, from *pīnus*, PINE.]

pi·ña co·la·da (péen-yə kə-lá-adə, ko-, kō-) n. A cocktail consisting of dark rum, pineapple juice, and coconut milk or syrup. [Spanish, "strained pineapple".]

pin·a·fore (pínnə-fawr ‖ -fōr) n. A sleeveless garment like an apron, usually with a bib, worn over clothing in order to protect it. [PIN (verb) + AFORE (originally pinned on dress).]

pinafore dress n. A sleeveless, collarless dress designed to be worn over a jumper or blouse.

Pinang. See **Penang**.

pi·nas·ter (pí-nástər) n. A pine tree, *Pinus pinaster*, native to the Mediterranean region, having large cones and a characteristic pyramidal form. Also called "maritime pine", "cluster pine". [Latin *pīnaster*, a wild pine : *pīnus*, PIN(E) + -ASTER.]

pin·ball (pín-bawl) n. A game played on a board or machine in which the player operates a plunger to shoot a ball down a slanted surface having obstacles and targets; especially, a slot-machine game in which a player propels a number of small steel balls, one at a time, into a slanted area containing electronic devices that, when touched by the ball, register points for the contestant. Also used adjectively: *a pinball machine.*

pince-nez (pánss-náy, pínss-, -nay) n., pl. **pince-nez** (*pronounced as singular*). Glasses, without arms or side pieces, that are held in position by being clipped to the bridge of the nose. [French, "pinch-nose" : *pincer*, to PINCH + *nez*, nose, from Latin *nāsus*.]

pin·cer (pín-sər) n. Anything resembling either of the grasping parts of pincers.

pincer movement n. Also **pincers movement**. A military manoeu-

pine *Any evergreen conifer with needles arranged in groups of two, three or five qualifies as a pine. This is a Scots pine, which survives in a few natural forests in the Scottish Highlands, but is usually grown as a timber tree in commercial plantations.*

pineapple *The pineapple plant is a native of South and Central America, and resembles a small yucca tree. The edible aromatic fruit weighs up to 2 kilograms (4½ pounds).*

vre in which the enemy is attacked from two flanks with the aim of encirclement.

pin·cers (pín-sərz) *pl.n.* **1.** A grasping tool having a pair of jaws and handles pivoted together to work in opposition. **2.** The articulated, prehensile claws of certain arthropods, such as the lobster. [Middle English *pynsour,* a pincer, from Old French *pinceour* (unattested), from *pincier,* to PINCH.]

pinch (pinch) *v.* **pinched, pinching, pinches.** *—tr.* **1.** To squeeze between the thumb and a finger, the jaws of a tool, or other edges. **2.** To squeeze or bind (a part of the body) in such a way as to cause discomfort or pain: *The shoes pinch my toes.* **3.** To nip, wither, or shrivel: *buds pinched by the frost.* **4.** To cause to become thin or tired-looking, as from lack of food, emotional stress, or the like: *Her face was pinched with grief.* **5.** To give an inadequate supply to; stint: *The children were pinched of food.* **6.** *Informal.* To steal. **7.** *Slang.* To arrest. **8.** To move by means of a pinch bar. **9.** *Nautical.* To head (a boat) too close into the wind. **10.** To cause to have very little money. Usually used in the passive: *very pinched for cash at the moment.* **11.** To cut off the tips of (buds or shoots). Usually used with *back* or *down.* *—intr.* **1.** To press, squeeze, or bind painfully: *This collar pinches.* **2.** To be miserly or excessively frugal. **3.** *Nautical.* To sail too close to the wind. **4.** To become narrow and then give out altogether. Used of a vein of ore.
~n. **1.** The act or an instance of pinching. **2. a.** An amount of something that can be held between thumb and forefinger: *a pinch of rosemary.* **b.** A very small amount. **3.** A painful, difficult, or straitened circumstance: *to feel the pinch.* **4.** *Slang.* A theft or robbery. **5.** *Slang.* An arrest or police raid. **—at a pinch.** In extreme circumstances; if unavoidable. [Middle English *pinchen,* to pinch, prick, from Old North French *pinchier* (unattested), variant of Old French *pincier,* from Gallo-Roman *pinctiare, punctiare* (unattested), from Latin *pungere* (past participle *punctus*), to prick.]

pinch bar *n.* A crowbar with a pointed projection at one end.

pinch·beck (pínch-bek) *n.* **1.** An alloy of zinc and copper used as imitation gold. **2.** A cheap imitation.
~adj. **1.** Made of pinchbeck. **2.** Imitation; spurious. [Invented by Christopher *Pinchbeck* (1670?–1732), English watchmaker.]

pinch·cock (pínch-kok) *n.* A clamp used to regulate or close a flexible tube, especially in laboratory apparatus.

pinch effect *n. Physics.* The radial constriction of a **plasma** *(see),* caused by the interaction of its internal electric currents and its self-generated magnetic field.

pinch-pen·ny (pínch-penni) *n., pl.* **-nies.** A mean or niggardly person; a miser.
~adj. Miserly; mean.

pin curl *n.* A coiled strand of hair, usually damp, secured with a hairclip and combed into a wave or curl when dry.

pin·cush·ion (pín-kōōsh'n) *n.* A small, firm cushion in which pins are stuck when not in use.

Pin·dar (pín-dər, -daar) (*c.* 518–438 B.C.). Greek poet. He is remembered especially for his *Odes.*

Pin·dar·ic (pin-dárrik) *adj.* **1.** Pertaining to or characteristic of the poetic style of Pindar. **2.** Of or characteristic of a Pindaric ode.
~n. Often plural. A Pindaric ode.

Pindaric ode *n.* **1.** An ode in the form developed by Pindar, consisting of a series of triads formed by the strophe, antistrophe, and epode. **2.** An ode based on an adaptation of this form, with irregular stanzas and rhyme schemes, especially as practised by English poets of the 17th and 18th centuries.

pine[1] (pīn) *n.* **1.** Any of various evergreen trees of the genus *Pinus,* having needle-shaped leaves in clusters and bearing cones. Many are valued for shade and ornament and for their wood and resinous sap, which yields turpentine and pine tar. **2.** Loosely, any coniferous tree, especially of the family Pinaceae, such as the cedar, spruce, or fir. **3.** The wood of any of these trees. **4.** Any of various similar but unrelated plants, such as the screw pine or ground pine. [Middle English *pine,* from Old English *pīn* and Old French *pin,* from Latin *pīnus.*]

pine[2] *v.* **pined, pining, pines.** *—intr.* **1.** To suffer intense longing or yearning. Usually used with *for*: *pining for home.* **2.** To wither or waste away from longing or grief. Usually used with *away.* *—tr. Archaic.* To grieve or mourn for. **—See Synonyms at yearn.**
~n. Archaic. Intense longing or grief. [Middle English *pinen,* Old English *pīnian,* from *pīne* (unattested), torture, from Latin *poena,* penalty, from Greek *poinē,* punishment.] **—pin·y, pin·ey** *adj.*

pin·e·al (pínni-əl, pī-née-əl) *adj.* Pertaining to the pineal body. [French *pinéal,* from Latin *pīnea,* pine cone, from *pīneus,* of the pine, from *pīnus,* PINE.]

pineal body *n.* A small glandlike structure in the brain of vertebrates. In animals it secretes melatonin but its functions in humans are uncertain. Also called "pineal gland", "epiphysis".

pineal eye *n.* An extension of the pineal body that forms an eyelike protuberance on the head in certain reptiles and primitive cartilaginous fish.

pine·ap·ple (pīn-app'l) *n.* **1.** A tropical American plant, *Ananas comosus,* having large, swordlike leaves and a large, fleshy, edible fruit consisting of the flowers fused into a compound whole with a terminal tuft of leaves. **2.** The fruit of this plant. **3.** *Slang.* A small hand grenade. [Originally "pine cone" (from the resemblance of the fruit to a pine cone), Middle English *pinappel* : PINE + APPLE.]

pineapple weed *n.* A low-growing annual plant, *Matricaria matricarioides,* having greenish-yellow, rayless flower heads and a smell of pineapple when crushed.

pine cone *n.* The woody conical reproductive structure of a pine tree.

pine marten *n.* An arboreal musteline mammal, *Martes martes,* found in woods, especially pine woods, of northern Europe.

pi·nene (pī-neen) *n.* Either of two isomeric terpene liquids, $C_{10}H_{16}$, that are the main constituents of oil or spirits of turpentine. [PIN(E) + -ENE.]

pine needle *n.* The needle-shaped leaf of a pine tree.

pine nut *n.* The edible seed of certain pines.

Pi·ne·ro (pi-néer-ō), **Sir Arthur Wing** (1855–1934). British playwright. Abandoning a career in law, he won fame as a writer of immensely popular farces, such as *Dandy Dick* (1887). His later plays include *The Second Mrs Tanqueray* (1893).

pin·er·y (pīnəri) *n., pl.* **-ies.** **1.** A hothouse or plantation for the cultivation of pineapples. **2.** A forest of pine trees.

pine tar *n.* A viscous or semisolid brown to black substance produced by the destructive distillation of pine wood and used in roofing preparations, paints and varnishes, and as an antiseptic.

pi·ne·tum (pī-née-təm) *n., pl.* **-ta** (-tə). An area planted with pine trees or related conifers, especially for botanical study. [Latin *pīnētum,* pine-wood, from *pīnus,* PINE.]

piney. Variant of **piny.**

pin·feath·er (pín-fethər) *n.* In birds, a growing feather still enclosed in its horny sheath; especially, one just emerging through the skin.

pin·fold (pín-fōld) *n.* A pound for stray animals, such as sheep.
~tr.v. **pinfolded, -folding, -folds.** To confine in or as if in a pinfold. [Middle English *pyn(de)fold,* Old English *pundfald* : *pund-,* POUND (enclosure) + *fald,* FOLD.]

ping (ping) *n.* A brief, high-pitched sound, such as that made by a bullet striking metal.
~intr.v. **pinged, pinging, pings.** To produce a ping. [Imitative.]

pin·go (píng-gō) *n.* A mound of gravel or earth occurring in arctic regions as a result of pressure from water trapped between newly frozen ice and the permafrost beneath it. [Eskimo.]

Ping-Pong (píng-pong) *n.* **1.** A trademark for table-tennis equipment. **2.** *Small* **p**, *small* **p.** The game of table tennis.

pin·guid (píng-gwid) *adj.* **1.** Oily, greasy, or fatty. **2.** Designating soil that is rich and fertile. [Latin *pinguis,* fat + -ID.] **—pin·guid·i·ty** (-gwíddəti) *n.*

pin·head (pín-hed) *n.* **1.** The head of a pin. **2.** Anything small, trifling, or insignificant. **3.** *Slang.* A stupid person. **—pin·head·ed** (-héddid) *adj.*

pin·hole (pín-hōl) *n.* A tiny puncture made by or as if by a pin.

pinhole camera *n.* An elementary camera having a pinhole instead of a lens.

pin·ion[1] (pín-yən) *n.* **1.** A bird's wing. **2.** The outer rear edge of a bird's wing, containing the primary feathers. **3.** A primary feather of a bird.
~tr.v. **pinioned, -ioning, -ions.** **1. a.** To remove or bind the wing feathers of (a bird) to prevent flight. **b.** To cut or bind (the wings of a bird). **2.** To restrain or immobilise (a person) by binding the arms. **3.** To fix in one place; make fast: *He jabbed with his fork and pinioned a piece of meat.* [Middle English *pynyon,* from Old French *pignon,* from Vulgar Latin *pinniō,* stem *pinniōn-* (unattested), augmentative of Latin *pinna, penna,* a feather, wing.]

pinion[2] *n.* A small cogwheel that engages or is engaged by a larger cogwheel or a rack. [French *pignon,* alteration of obsolete *pignol,* from Vulgar Latin *pīneolus,* from Latin *pīnea,* pine cone, from *pīnus,* PINE.]

pin·ite (pín-īt, pīn-) *n.* A hydrous, usually amorphous mineral silicate of aluminium and potassium. [German *Pinit*; found at *Pini,* mine in Saxony.]

pink[1] (pingk) *n.* **1.** Any of various plants of the genus *Dianthus,* often cultivated for their fragrant flowers. **2.** Any of various similar plants of other genera. **3.** A flower of any of these plants. **4.** The highest degree of excellence or perfection: *He is in the pink of condition.* **5.** Any of a group of colours pale reddish in hue, of medium to high lightness, and low to moderate saturation. **6. a.** Any object of this colour. **b.** Pink clothing. **7.** *British.* **a.** The scarlet coat of a huntsman. **b.** A huntsman wearing a scarlet coat. **8.** *Slang.* A person regarded as being half-heartedly Communist or left-wing. Used derogatorily.
~adj. **pinker, pinkest.** **1.** Of the colour pink. **2.** *British.* Designating the scarlet coat worn by a huntsman. **3.** *Slang.* Half-heartedly or mildly left-wing or Communist. Used derogatorily. [Perhaps short for obsolete *pink eye,* "small eye" (from the shape of the flower), from obsolete Dutch *pinck oog(en),* "small eye(s)", (also) conjunctivitis : *pin(c)k*†, small, the little finger + *oog,* eye.] **—pink·ish** *adj.* **—pink·ness** *n.* **—pink·y** *adj.*

pink[2] *tr.v.* **pinked, pinking, pinks.** **1.** To stab lightly with a pointed weapon; prick. **2.** To decorate with a perforated pattern. **3.** To cut with pinking shears. [Middle English *pynken,* probably of Low German origin; akin to Low German *pinken*†, to peck.]

pink[3] *n.* Also **pink·ie** (píngki), **pink·y,** *pl.* **-ies.** *Nautical.* A sailing vessel with a narrow stern. [Middle English *pynk,* from Middle Dutch *pin(c)ke*†.]

pink[4] *intr.v.* **pinked, pinking, pinks.** To knock because of faulty combustion. Used of a car engine. [Imitative.]

pink elephants *pl.n.* Hallucinations resulting from excessive consumption of alcohol. Used humorously.

Pink·er·ton (píngkərtən) **Allan.** (1819–84). U.S. detective, born in Scotland. In 1850 he founded Pinkerton's National Detective Agency, later the most famous in the United States.

pink·eye (pĭngk-ī) n. Acute contagious conjunctivitis, characterised by inflamed eyelids and eyeballs. Not in technical usage. [See **pink** (colour).]

pink gin n. A drink made from gin, water, and angostura bitters.

pink·ie (pĭngki) n. Also **pink·y**, pl. **-ies.** Chiefly Scottish & U.S. Informal. **1.** The little finger. **2.** Variant of **pink** (sailing vessel). [Dutch pinkje, diminutive of pink, little finger, from obsolete pin(c)k†.]

pinking shears pl.n. Sewing scissors with notched or serrated blades. They are used to finish edges of cloth with a scalloped or zigzag pattern, for decoration or to prevent fraying.

pink·o (pĭngkō) n., pl. **-os** or **-oes.** Chiefly U.S. A person regarded as mildly left-wing or Communist. Used derogatorily. —**pink·o** adj.

Pink·ster, Pinx·ster (pĭngkstər) n. U.S. Regional. Whit Sunday or Whitsuntide. [Dutch, PENTECOST.]

pin money n. Money for incidental expenses, for example money given by a man to his wife or his daughter for her personal expenses. **2.** Extra money, earned for example from part-time work, that does not contribute to the family budget or household expenses, or is spent on non-essential items. [Originally, a small sum for buying hat-pins or hairpins.]

pin·na (pĭnnə) n., pl. **pinnae** (pĭnnee) or **-nas. 1.** Botany. Any of the leaflets of a pinnate leaf. **2.** Zoology. A feather, wing, fin, or similar appendage. **3.** Anatomy. The external part of the ear; the auricle. [Latin pinna, penna, wing, feather.] —**pin·nal** adj.

pin·nace (pĭn-əss, -iss) n. Nautical. **1.** A small sailing boat formerly used as a tender for merchant and war vessels. **2.** Any small ship or ship's boat. [French pinace, from Old Spanish pinaza or Italian pinaccia, from (unattested) Vulgar Latin pīnācea (nāvis), "(ship) of pine-wood", from Latin pīnus, pine tree.]

pin·na·cle (pĭnnək'l) n. **1.** Architecture. A small turret or spire on a roof or buttress. **2.** Any tall, pointed formation, such as a mountain peak. **3.** The highest point; the summit; the acme: the pinnacle of achievement. —See Synonyms at **summit.**
~tr.v. **pinnacled, -cling, -cles. 1.** To furnish with a pinnacle. **2.** To place on or as if on a pinnacle. [Middle English pin(n)acle, from Old French, from Late Latin pinnāculum, "little wing," from Latin pinna, feather, wing.]

pin·nate (pĭn-ayt, -ət, -it) adj. Also **pin·nat·ed** (pi-náytid, pĭnnayt-id). **1.** Resembling a feather; pennate. **2.** Botany. Having leaflets, lobes, or divisions in a feather-like arrangement on each side of a common axis, as many compound leaves do. [Latin pinnātus, feathered, from pinna, feather.] —**pin·nate·ly** adv.

pin·nat·i·fid (pi-nátti-fid, -náyti-) adj. Botany. Having pinnately cleft lobes or divisions reaching about halfway to the midrib. Said of certain leaves. [Latin pinnātus, PINNATE + -FID.] —**pin·nat·i·fid·ly** adv.

pin·nat·i·sect (pi-nátti-sekt, -náyti-) adj. Botany. Divided nearly to the midrib. Said of certain leaves. [PINNATI- + -SECT.]

pin·ni·ped (pĭnni-ped) adj. Also **pin·ni·pe·di·an** (-péedi-ən). Zoology. Of or belonging to the Pinnipedia, an order of aquatic mammals that includes the seals, walruses, and similar animals having finlike flippers for locomotion.
~n. A mammal belonging to this order. [Latin pinna, feather, wing, PINNA + -PED.]

pin·nule (pĭnnewl) n. Also **pin·nu·la** (pĭnnew-lə) pl. **-lae** (-lee). **1.** Botany. Any of the lobes of a leaflet of a pinnately compound leaf. **2.** Zoology. A feather-like or plumelike organ or part, such as a small fin, or any of the appendages of a crinoid. [New Latin pinnula, from Latin, diminutive of pinna, penna, feather, wing, fin.] —**pin·nu·lar** (-lər) adj.

pin·ny (pĭnni) n., pl. **-nies.** Informal. A pinafore or apron.

Pi·no·chet (U·gar·te) (peenō-shay; Spanish -chét), **Augusto** (1915–). Chilean general. He led the group of officers who, in 1973, overthrew the elected government of Salvador Allende. Appointed president in 1974, he directed a notoriously brutal junta.

pi·noch·le, pi·noc·le, pe·nuch·le (pee-nuck'l, -nock'l) n. **1.** A game of cards, played chiefly in the United States, for two to four persons, played with a special pack of 48 cards, with points being scored by taking tricks and forming certain combinations. **2.** The combination of the queen of spades and jack of diamonds in this game. [19th century : origin obscure.]

pi·not noir (peenō nwar) n. A variety of black grape used for making Champagne and red Burgundy wine. [French, "black pinot" : pinot, variant of pineau, diminutive of pin, pine (tree); comparing the shape of its grape clusters to pine cones.]

pin·point (pĭn-poynt) n. **1.** An extremely small thing; a particle; a bit: a pinpoint of light. **2.** A tiny or insignificant spot: the pinpoint of ground upon which we stand. **3.** Military. **a.** A point on a map indicating a strictly defined target. **b.** A precisely identified and limited target. **4.** The sharp tip of a pin.
~tr.v. **pinpointed, -pointing, -points. 1. a.** To locate and identify precisely: Our radar pinpointed the planes. **b.** To define or delimit precisely. **2.** Military. To take precise aim at: pinpoint a target.
~adj. **1.** Characterised by meticulous precision: He spots flaws with pinpoint accuracy. **2.** Minuscule; tiny: pinpoint creatures.

pin·prick (pĭn-prik) n. **1.** A slight puncture made by or as if by a pin. **2.** An insignificant wound. **3.** A minor annoyance.
~v. **pinpricked, -pricking, -pricks.** —tr. To puncture with or as if with a pin. —intr. To make a slight puncture with a pin.

pins and needles n. Used with a singular or plural verb. A tingling felt in a part of the body numbed from lack of circulation.

pin·scher (pĭnshər) n. See **Doberman pinscher.**

pin·stripe (pĭn-strīp) n. **1.** A thin stripe on a fabric. **2.** A kind of fabric with thin stripes, often used for men's suits. Also used adjectively: a pinstripe suit.

pint (pīnt) n. Abbr. **p., pt., o. 1. a.** A unit of volume or capacity, used in liquid measure, equal to one eighth of a gallon, in Britain 0.568 litre (20 fluid ounces), and in the United States 0.473 litre (16 fluid ounces). **b.** A unit of volume or capacity used in dry measure in the United States, equal to one half of a quart or 0.5506 litre. **2.** A container such as a milk bottle having such a capacity, or the amount of a substance that can be contained in it. **3.** British Informal. **a.** A pint of beer. **b.** A drink of beer in a pub. [Middle English pinte, from Old French, probably from Medieval Latin pincta, "painted mark (on a measuring container)", from Vulgar Latin pinctus (unattested), painted. See **pinto.**]

pint·a¹ (pīntə) n. Informal. A pint of milk. [From pronunciation of pint of, as in the slogan, "Drinka pinta milka day".]

pin·ta² (pĭn-tə, -taa; Spanish peén-) n. A contagious skin disease prevalent in tropical America, caused by spirochaete microorganisms, and characterised by extreme thickening and localised discoloration of the skin. [American Spanish, from Spanish, painted mark, from the feminine of Vulgar Latin pinctus (unattested), painted. See **pinto.**]

pin·ta·de·ra (pĭntə-daír-ə) n. A decorative seal or stamp, of the Neolithic period and early American cultures, usually made of terracotta and thought to have been used for applying pigment to the skin. [Spanish, instrument for painting, from pintar, to PAINT.]

pin·tail (pĭn-tayl) n., pl. **-tails** or collectively **pintail.** A duck, Anas acuta, of the Northern Hemisphere, having grey, brown, and white plumage and a sharply pointed tail in the male.

Pin·ter (pĭntər), **Harold** (1930–). British playwright, actor, and director. His plays, which include The Caretaker (1959) and The Homecoming (1965), are known for their elusive dialogue and atmosphere of menace. —**Pin·ter·esque** (-ésk) adj.

pin·tle (pĭnt'l) n. An upright pin or bolt used as a pivot; specifically: **1.** Nautical. The pin on which a rudder turns. **2.** The pin on a gun carriage. **3.** A pin or bolt on the back of a towing vehicle to which a towed vehicle is attached. [Middle English pintel, "penis", Old English pintel†.]

pin·to (pĭntō) n., pl. **-tos** or **-toes.** U.S. Any horse with irregular spots or markings.
~adj. U.S. Irregularly marked; piebald. [American Spanish, from obsolete Spanish, "painted", "spotted", from Vulgar Latin pinctus (unattested), variant of Latin pictus, past participle of Latin pingere, to paint.]

pint-size (pīnt-sīz) adj. Also **pint·sized** (-sīzd). Informal. Of small dimensions; diminutive.

pin-up (pĭn-up) n. **1.** A picture to be pinned up on a wall; especially, a photograph of a sexually attractive person or a nude or partially dressed person. **2.** A person considered as a suitable model for such a picture. **3.** A photograph of a celebrity.
~adj. U.S. Designed to be attached to a wall: a pin-up lamp.

pin·wheel (pĭn-weel, -hweel) n. **1.** A firework, a small **catherine wheel** (see). **2.** A cogwheel with a circle of pins at right angles to its face, used as a tripping device. **3.** U.S. A toy, a **windmill** (see).

pin·work (pĭn-wurk) n. The fine stitches raised in needlepoint lace from the surface of a motif.

pin·worm (pĭn-wurm) n. A small nematode worm, Enterobius vermicularis, that infects the human intestines and rectum, especially in children. Also called "threadworm".

pin wrench n. A wrench having a projection designed to fit a hole in the object to be turned.

pinx·it (pĭngksit) n. Abbr. **pinx.** Latin. He or she painted (this). Formerly used as part of the painter's signature on a painting.

Pinxter. Variant of **Pinkster.**

pin·yin (pĭn-yin) n. A system of transliteration of Chinese characters into Roman characters, introduced in China in 1957. [Chinese, "spell sound".]

pi·o·let (pée-ə-lay, -láy) n. A kind of ice axe. [French, diminutive of French dialectal piola, small axe, ultimately from Old Provençal apcha, apia, axe, from Germanic; akin to Old High German hāppa, sickle.]

pi·on (pī-on) n. Symbol π Physics. Any of three elementary particles in the meson family, pi zero, pi minus, and pi plus, having zero spin, negative parity, and 0, + 1, and − 1 times the charge of the electron respectively. The pi zero has a lifetime of 9×10^{-16} second and decays into photons, while the two pions have lifetimes of about 2.5×10^{-8} and decay into leptons. They are exchanged between particles in the strong remaining interaction. Also called "pi meson". [Shortened from PI MESON.]

pi·o·neer (pī-ə-néer) n. **1.** One who ventures into unknown or unclaimed territory to settle. Also used adjectively: a pioneer spirit. **2.** An innovator in a particular field: a pioneer in aviation. Also used adjectively: pioneer research. **3.** A military engineer employed in the construction and fortification of roads, bridges, or the like, and the maintenance of communication lines. **4.** Ecology. A plant species that is one of the first to establish itself in a previously barren environment.
~v. **pioneered, -neering, -neers.** —tr. **1.** To initiate or participate in the development of: men who pioneered the submarine. **2. a.** To explore or open up (a region). **b.** To be a pioneer to (travellers, for example); conduct. —intr. To act as a pioneer. [French pionnier, from Old French peon(n)ier, originally "a foot soldier sent out to clear the way", from pion, peon, foot soldier. See **peon.**]

pi·ous (pī-əss) adj. **1.** Having or showing reverence and earnest

pinnacle The slender outlines of the pinnacled clock tower at Trinity College, Cambridge, England.

compliance in the observance of religion; devout. **2. a.** Marked by conspicuous devoutness. **b.** Marked by false devoutness; solemnly hypocritical. **3.** Not secular; devotional: *pious readings.* **4.** Professing or exhibiting a strict, traditional sense of virtue and morality; high-minded: *the pious instructions of his parents.* **5.** Well-intentioned but having little likelihood of being realised. Used chiefly in the phrase *a pious hope.* **6.** *Archaic.* Having filial reverence; dutiful. [Latin *pius.*] **—pi·ous·ly** *adv.* **—pi·ous·ness** *n.*

pip¹ (pip) *n.* **1.** The seed of a fleshy fruit, such as an apple or orange. **2.** A rootstock of certain flowering plants, especially lily of the valley. **3.** *U.S. Informal.* Something remarkable of its kind: *a pip of a plan.* [Shortened from PIPPIN.]

pip² *tr.v.* **pipped, pipping, pips.** *British Slang.* **1.** To strike with a gunshot; hit. **2.** To defeat, especially at the last moment: *He was pipped at the post.* **3.** To blackball. [Perhaps from PIP (dot on dice, hence, "small ball").]

pip³ *n.* **1.** A dot indicating a unit of numerical value on playing cards, dice, or dominoes. **2.** *British Informal.* A shoulder insignia indicating the rank of certain officers in the British Army. **3.** A radar signal. **4.** Any of the segments found on the surface of a pineapple. [16th century : *peepe*†.]

pip⁴ *v.* **pipped, pipping, pips.** *—tr.* To break through (an eggshell) in hatching. *—intr.* To peep or chirp, as a young bird does.
∼n. A short, high-pitched signal, especially one of a series constituting a time signal in a radio transmission. [Variant of PEEP (peek) and PEEP (cheep).]

pip⁵ *n.* **1. a.** A disease of birds, characterised by a thick mucous discharge that forms a crust in the mouth and throat. **b.** The crust symptomatic of this disease. **2.** *British Slang.* A bad mood or depression. Preceded by *the*: *She gives me the pip.* [Middle English *pippe,* from Middle Dutch, phlegm, mucus, from West Germanic *pipit* (unattested), probably from Vulgar Latin *pīppīta,* (earlier) *pītīta* (both unattested), alterations of Latin *pītuīta,* phlegm.]

pi·pa (pe͞epə) *n.* A South American toad, *Pipa pipa,* the female of which carries her fertilised eggs on her back, where they develop in pits in the skin. Also called "Surinam toad". [Surinam dialect *pipá* (feminine), *pipál* (masculine), of African origin.]

pip·age (pīpij) *n.* **1.** The transmission of liquids through pipes. **2.** The charge for such transmission. **3.** Pipes; piping.

pipal. Variant of **peepul.**

pipe (pīp) *n.* **1. a.** Any hollow cylinder or tubular conveyance for a fluid or gas. **b.** A section or piece of such a tube. **2. a.** An instrument for smoking, consisting of a tube of wood or clay with a mouthpiece at one end and a small bowl at the other. **b.** The amount of tobacco or other substance to fill the bowl of a smoking pipe; a pipeful. **3. a.** *Biology.* A tubular part or organ. **b.** *Plural. Informal.* The human respiratory system or vocal cords. **4.** *Abbr.* **p. a.** A wine cask having a capacity of 105 gallons (457 litres). **b.** This volume as a unit of liquid measure. **5.** *Abbr.* **p.** *Music.* **a.** A tubular wind instrument, such as a flute. **b.** Any of the tubes in an organ. **c.** *Plural.* A small wind instrument, consisting of tubes of different lengths bound together: *pipes of Pan.* **d.** *Plural.* A set of bagpipes. **e.** A primitive type of flute that was played with one hand while the other beat a drum or tabor. **6.** *Archaic.* The sound of the voice, especially as used in singing or acting. **7.** A birdcall. **8. a.** *Nautical.* A kind of whistle used for signalling crew members: *a boatswain's pipe.* **b.** The sound this pipe makes. **9.** *Mining.* **a.** A vertical, cylindrical vein of ore. **b.** Any of the vertical veins of eruptive origin in which diamonds are found in South Africa. **10.** *Geology.* An eruptive passageway opening into the crater of a volcano. **11.** A cone-shaped cavity in a steel ingot, formed during cooling by unequal contraction. **—put that in your pipe and smoke it.** That is the situation whether you like it or not.
∼v. **piped, piping, pipes.** *—tr.* **1. a.** To convey (liquid or gas) by means of pipes. **b.** To supply or convey as if by means of a pipe. **2.** To provide or connect with pipes. **3. a.** To play (a tune) on a pipe or pipes: *"Piper, pipe that song again."* (William Blake). **b.** To lead by playing on pipes. **4.** *Nautical.* To call (crew members, for example) by sounding the boatswain's pipe. **5.** To utter in a shrill, reedy tone. **6.** To furnish (a garment or fabric) with piping. **7. a.** To force (icing, for example) through a tube or forcing bag fitted with a nozzle to make a decorative pattern. **b.** To make (a decorative pattern) in this way. *—intr.* **1.** To play on a pipe. **2.** To speak shrilly; make a shrill sound. **3.** To chirp or whistle, as a bird does. **4.** *Nautical.* To call on a boatswain's pipe. **5.** In metallurgy, to develop conical cavities. **—pipe down.** *Informal.* To stop talking; be quiet. **—pipe up.** To speak up, especially in a small, shrill voice. [Middle English *pipe,* Old English *pīpe,* from Common Germanic *pīpa* (unattested), from Common Romance *pīpa* (unattested), from Latin *pīpāre,* to chirp.] **—pip·y** *adj.*

pipe·clay (pīp-klay) *n.* A fine white clay used in making tobacco pipes and pottery, in calico printing, and in whitening leather.

pipe cleaner *n.* A pliant, tufted piece of wire used for cleaning the stem of a tobacco pipe.

piped music *n.* Prerecorded background music as played continuously in supermarkets, airports, or the like.

pipe dream *n.* A wishful, fantastic notion or hope. [From the fantasies induced by opium.]

pipe·fish (pīp-fish) *n., pl.* **-fishes** or collectively **pipefish.** Any of various slim, elongated marine or freshwater fishes of the family Syngnathidae, characterised by a tubelike snout and an external covering of bony plates. Also called "needlefish".

pipe·fit·ting (pīp-fitting) *n.* **1. a.** The act or work of joining pipes together. **b.** A branch of the plumbing trade that deals specifically with the installation and repair of piping systems. **2.** A section of pipe used to join two or more pipes together.

pipe·ful (pīp-fo͝ol) *n., pl.* **-fuls.** The amount required to fill a pipe.

pipe·line (pīp-līn) *n.* **1.** A long pipe, often buried underground, for the conveyance of water, gas, or petroleum products. **2.** A channel by which information of a generally secret or confidential nature is transmitted. **3.** A line of communication or route of supply: *a new pipeline for medical supplies.* **—in the pipeline.** On the way to being accomplished or realised: *a promotion in the pipeline.*
∼tr.v. **pipelined, -lining, -lines.** **1.** To convey by means of a pipeline. **2.** To lay a pipeline through.

pipe organ *n.* A musical instrument, an **organ** *(see).*

pip·er (pīpər) *n.* One who plays a pipe or the bagpipes.

Pip·er (pīpər), **John (Egerton Christmas)** (1903–). British painter and writer. He has also designed stage sets, as well as stained-glass windows for Coventry Cathedral.

pi·per·a·zine (pi-pérrə-zeen, pī-, -zin) *n.* A colourless crystalline compound, $C_4H_{10}N_2$, used to inhibit corrosion, in insecticides, and as an anthelmintic. [PIPER(INE) + AZ(O)- + -INE.]

pi·per·i·dine (pi-pérri-deen, pī-, -din) *n.* A colourless liquid, $C_5H_{10}NH$, a strong base used in the manufacture of rubber and as a curing agent in epoxy resins. [PIPER(INE) + -IDE + -INE.]

pip·er·ine (píppər-een, -īn, -in) *n.* A crystalline alkaloid, $C_{17}H_{19}NO_3$, extracted from black pepper, and used as flavouring and as an insecticide. [Latin *piper,* PEPPER + -INE.]

pi·per·o·nal (pi-pérrə-n'l, pī-, píppərō-, -nal) *n.* A white powder, $C_8H_6O_3$, having a floral odour, used as flavouring and in perfume. Also called "heliotropin". [PIPER(INE) + -ON(E) + -AL.]

pipe·stone (pīp-stōn) *n.* A heat-hardened compacted red clay used by American Indians for making tobacco pipes.

pi·pette, pi·pet (pi-pét ‖ *chiefly U.S.* pī-) *n. Chemistry.* Any of variously shaped glass tubes, open at both ends, usually calibrated, and used especially to transfer small volumes of liquid from one container to another. [French, diminutive of *pipe,* PIPE.]

pipe·wort (pīp-wurt ‖ -wawrt) *n.* An aquatic plant, *Ericocaulon septangulare,* having submerged, narrow, translucent leaves and small greyish flowers in a flat, button-like cluster.

pipe wrench *n.* A wrench with two serrated jaws, one adjustable, used for gripping and turning pipes. Compare **Stillson wrench.**

pip·ing (pīping) *n.* **1.** A system of pipes, such as one used in plumbing. **2.** *Music.* **a.** The act of playing on a pipe. **b.** The music produced by a pipe. **3.** A shrill, high-pitched sound. **4.** A rounded strip of cloth, sometimes covering a cord, used for trimming the seams and edges of garments or furniture covers. **5.** Rounded strands produced by forcing a substance such as icing through a tube or forcing bag with a nozzle, used to decorate food.
∼adj. **1.** Playing on a pipe. **2.** Making a high-pitched sound with little resonance, as does a pipe.
∼adv. Used as an intensive: *piping hot.*

pip·i·strelle (píppi-strél) *n.* Any small bat of the genus *Pipistrellus,* especially *P. pipistrellus.* [French, from Italian *pipistrello, vipistrello,* ultimately from Latin *vespertilio,* bat, from *vesper,* evening.]

pip·it (píppit) *n.* Any of various widely distributed songbirds of the genus *Anthus,* characteristically having brownish upper plumage and a light, streaked breast. The meadow pipit, *A. pratensis,* was formerly also called "titlark". [Imitative of its note.]

pip·kin (píp-kin) *n.* **1.** A small earthenware or metal cooking pot. **2.** A **piggin** *(see).* [16th century : origin obscure.]

pip·pin (píppin) *n.* **1.** Any of several varieties of eating apple. **2.** *Informal.* An admired person or thing. Not in current usage. [Middle English *pepin, pipin,* seed, seedling apple, from Old French *pepin,* from Common Romance stem *pipp-* (suggestive of the small size of the seed).]

pipsqueak (píp-skweek) *n.* A small or insignificant person. Used derogatorily. [Originally a name given to a small artillery shell used by the Germans in World War I : PIP (dot) + SQUEAK.]

pi·quant (pe͞ek-ənt, -ON, -aant ‖ *U.S. also* píkwənt) *adj.* **1.** Pleasantly pungent in taste or odour; spicy. **2.** Interesting yet having a disconcerting or troubling effect: *a piquant reversal of roles.* **3.** *Archaic.* Causing hurt pride or feelings; stinging: *a piquant answer.* [Old French, present participle of *piquer,* to pierce, prick, PIQUE.] **—pi·quan·cy** (-ən-si) *n.* **—pi·quant·ly** *adv.*

pique (peek) *n.* A feeling of resentment or vexation arising from wounded pride or vanity: *an old man's fit of pique.*
∼tr.v. **piqued, piquing, piques.** **1.** To cause to feel resentment or vexation; injure the pride of: *piqued by her snub.* **2.** To provoke; arouse: *The portrait piqued my curiosity.* **3.** To pride (oneself). Used with *on* or *upon*: *piqued themselves on their style.* [Old French, "a pricking", from *piquer,* to prick, from Vulgar Latin *piccāre* (unattested), perhaps from Latin *pīcus,* magpie, woodpecker.]

pi·qué (pe͞e-kay ‖ *U.S. also* pi-káy) *n.* A tightly woven fabric with various raised patterns, produced especially by a double warp. [French, "quilting", from *piquer,* to backstitch (as in quilting), to prick, PIQUE.]

pi·quet (pi-két, -káy) *n.* A card game for two people, played with a pack from which all cards below the seven (aces being high) are removed. [French, of obscure origin.]

pi·ra·cy (pīr-ə-si) *n., pl.* **-cies.** **1.** Robbery committed at sea. **2.** Any illegal act, such as kidnapping, committed at sea or in the air. **3.** The unauthorised use or reproduction of copyright material.

Pi·rae·us (pīr-ée-əss). *Greek* **Pi·re·evs** or **Pi·rai·évs** (pee-re-éffs).

PRONUNCIATION KEY

a, trap; aa, father; ai, **fair**; ar, **star**; aw, **lawn**; ay, **play**; b, bb, stab; **rubber**; ch, **church**; ck, ticket; d, dd, **dead**; **ladder**; e, **dress**; ee, **bee**; er, **defer**; ew, **few**; ewr, **pure**; ə, about; ər, letter; f, ff, **fife**; **differ**; g, gg, **giggle**; h, **hat**; i, **kit**; ī, **price**; īr, **fire**; j, **judge**; k, **kick**; l, ll, let; 'l, needle; m, mm, **man**; n, nn, **no**; 'n, sudden; ng, **thing**; o, **lot**; ō, **no**; o͝o, **foot**; o͞o, **shoe**; oor, **poor**; ow, **cow**; owr, **hour**; oy, **boy**; p, pp, **pepper**; r, rr, red; s, ss, **sauce**; sh, **ship**; t, tt, **totter**; th, **thick**; th, **this**; **smooth**; u, cut; ur, **turn**; v, vv, **valve**; w, **wet**; y, **yes**; z, zz, **zebra**; zh, vision; pleasure

IN FOREIGN WORDS:

aN, ON, **Saint-Saëns**; hl, **Llanelli**; **Hluhluwe**; kh, loch; **lough**; **Khaled**

STRESS MARK:

in-sīt, insight; in-sīt, incite

Port of Athens, Greece, situated on the Saronic Gulf. It is the main industrial part of the city.

pi·ra·gua (pi-ráag-wə, -rág-) *n.* **1.** A canoe made by hollowing out a tree trunk; a dugout. **2.** A flat-bottomed sailing boat with two masts. [Spanish, from Carib *piraguas.*]

Pi·ran·del·lo (pírrən-déllō, péer-ən-), **Luigi** (1867–1936). Italian playwright, novelist, and short-story writer. His work examines the relativity of truth and the elusiveness of identity, as in *Six Characters in Search of an Author* (1922) and *Henry IV* (1922). Pirandello won the Nobel prize for literature in 1934.

Pi·ra·ne·si (péer-ə-náy-zi, -si), **Giovanni Battista** (1720–78). Italian artist, known for his architectural etchings. His studies of Rome and its ruins contributed to the emergence of neoclassicism.

pi·ra·nha (pi-ráan-ə, -yə) *n.* Any of several tropical American freshwater fishes of the genus *Serrasalmus.* They are voraciously carnivorous and often attack and destroy living animals. [Portuguese, from Tupi, variant of *piraya,* scissors.]

pi·ra·ru·cu (pi-ráarə-kōō) *n.* A fish, the **arapaima** *(see).* [Portuguese *pirarucú,* from Tupi *pirá-rucú,* "red fish" : *pirá,* fish + *(u)rucú,* red.]

pi·rate (pír-ət, -it) *n.* **1.** One who robs at sea or plunders the land near the sea without commission from a sovereign nation. **2.** A ship used for this purpose. **3.** One who operates without proper authorisation, especially: **a.** One who makes use of or reproduces the work, especially copyright material, of another, without permission or illicitly: *a video pirate.* **b.** One who broadcasts on an unauthorised radio wavelength. Also used adjectivally: *a pirate radio station.*
~*v.* **pirated, -rating, -rates.** —*tr.* **1.** To attack and rob (a ship at sea). **2.** To seize (goods) by piracy. **3.** To make use of or reproduce (another's work) illicitly. —*intr.* To act as a pirate. [Middle English, from Latin *pīrāta,* from Greek *peiratēs,* "attacker", from *peiran,* to attempt, attack, from *peira,* an attempt.] **—pi·rat·ic** (pīr-áttik), **pi·rat·i·cal** *adj.* **—pi·rat·i·cal·ly** *adv.*

pi·rog (pi-rōg) *n., pl.* **-rogen** (-ən), **-roghi** (-ee) or **-rogi.** A large Russian pastry made of dough with various stuffings of meat, fish, rice, eggs, and vegetables. [Russian, probably from *pir,* feast, party.]

pi·rogue (pi-rōg) *n.* A canoe made from a hollowed tree trunk; a piragua. [French, from Spanish *piragua,* PIRAGUA.]

pir·ou·ette (pírroo-ét) *n.* In ballet, a full turn of the body on the tip of the toe or on the ball of the foot.
~*intr.v.* **pirouetted, -etting, -ettes.** To execute a pirouette. [French, from Old French *pirouet†,* a spinning top.]

pi·rozh·ki, pi·rosh·ki (pi-rózh-ki, -rósh-) *pl.n. Singular* **pi·rozh·ok** (pírrə-zhók). Small Russian pastries made with various fillings. [Russian, small pocket of pastry, diminutive of PIROG.]

Pi·sa (pée-zə; *Italian* -sa). Capital of Pisa province, Tuscany, Italy. Situated on the river Arno near the Ligurian Sea, it was a commercial and artistic centre (12th and 13th centuries), its many historical monuments include its leaning Romanesque bell tower.

pis al·ler (péez-állay || *U.S.* -a-láy) *n. French.* A course of action adopted for want of a better alternative. [French, "worst to go".]

Pi·sa·nel·lo (pée-zə-néllō; *Italian* -sa-), born Antonio Pisano; also called Vittore Pisano (*c.*1395–*c.*1455). Italian artist and medallist. In his own day he was celebrated for his medallions; he is especially admired today for his sketches of the natural world.

Pi·sa·no (pee-záa-nō, -sáa-), **Andrea,** born Andrea da Pontedera (*c.* 1290–*c.*1348). Italian sculptor and architect. He worked mainly in Florence where he executed the bronze door of the Baptistery.

pis·ca·ry (pískəri) *n., pl.* **-ries. 1.** *Law.* The right to fish. Used chiefly in the phrase *common of piscary,* meaning the right to fish in waters belonging to another. **2.** A place in which to fish. [Middle English *piscairie,* from Medieval Latin *piscāria,* right to fish, from Latin, neuter plural of *piscārius,* of fish or fishing, from *piscis,* fish.]

pis·ca·to·ri·al (pískə-táwri-əl || -tōri-) *adj.* Also **pis·ca·to·ry** (-tri, -təri) **1.** Of or pertaining to fish, fishermen, or fishing. **2.** Involved in or devoted to fishing. [Latin *piscātōrius,* of fish or fishing, from *piscātor,* fisherman, from *piscārī,* to fish, from *piscis,* fish.] **—pis·ca·to·ri·al·ly** *adv.*

Pi·sces (pí-seez, písk-eez, píss-) *n.* **1.** A constellation in the equatorial region of the Northern Hemisphere near Aries and Pegasus. **2. a.** The 12th sign of the **zodiac** *(see).* Also called the "Fish", the "Fishes". **b.** One born under this sign. **3.** A taxonomic group that includes the cartilaginous and bony fishes. [Middle English, from Medieval Latin, "the Fishes", from plural of Latin *piscis,* fish.] **—Pi·sce·an** *n. & adj.*

pisci– *comb. form.* Indicates fish; for example, **pisciform.** [From Latin *piscis,* fish.]

pi·sci·cul·ture (píssi-kulchər || píski-, pí-si-) *n.* The breeding, hatching, and rearing of fish under controlled conditions. **—pi·sci·cul·tur·al** (-kúlchərəl) *adj.* **—pi·sci·cul·tur·ist** (-kúlchərist) *n.*

pi·sci·form (píssi-fawrm || píski-, pí-si-) *adj.* Having the shape of a fish. [PISCI- + -FORM.]

pi·sci·na (pi-sée-nə, -sí-, -shée-) *n., pl.* **-nae** (-nee) or **-nas.** *Ecclesiastical.* A stone basin with a drain for carrying away the water used in ceremonial ablutions. Also called "sacrarium". [Medieval Latin, from Latin, fish tank, from *piscis,* fish.] **—pis·ci·nal** *adj.*

pi·scine (píss-īn || pisk-, píss-, -in, -een) *adj.* Of, pertaining to, or typical of a fish or fishes. [Medieval Latin *piscīnus,* from *piscis,* fish.]

Pi·scis Aus·tri·nus (pí-siss oss-trīnəss, píssiss, awss-) *n.* A constellation in the Southern Hemisphere near Aquarius and Grus. [New Latin, "(the) Southern Fish".]

pi·sciv·o·rous (pi-sívvə-rəss || pí-, -skívvə-) *adj.* Feeding on fish; fish-eating. [PISCI- + -VOROUS.]

pish (pish) *interj.* Used to express disdain.

pi·shogue (pi-shōg) *n. Irish.* **1.** Black magic; sorcery; witchcraft. **2.** An evil spell; an incantation. [Irish *píseog,* witchcraft.]

pi·si·form (píssi-fawrm, pí-si-) *adj.* Suggestive of a pea in size or shape; pealike.
~*n. Anatomy.* A small bone at the junction of the ulna and the wrist. [Latin *pīsum,* PEA + -FORM.]

pis·mire (píss-mīr, píz-) *n.* An ant. [Middle English *pissemyre,* from *pisse,* PISS (from the urinous smell of an anthill) + obsolete *mire,* ant, probably from Scandinavian; akin to Danish *myre,* ant.]

pi·so·lite (pí-sō-līt, -sə-) *n. Geology.* A concretionary limestone composed of globules more than 2 millimetres in diameter. [New Latin *pisolithus,* "pea stone" : Greek *pisos, pison,* PEA + -LITE.] **—pi·so·lit·ic** (-líttik) *adj.*

piss (piss) *v.* **pissed, pissing, pisses.** —*intr.* **1.** *Vulgar.* To urinate. **2.** *Vulgar Slang.* To rain. Often used with *down.* —*tr. Vulgar.* **1.** To discharge (blood, for example) with the urine. **2.** To wet or soak with urine. **—piss about** or **around.** *Vulgar Slang.* To behave in a silly or time-wasting fashion. **—piss off.** *Vulgar Slang.* **1.** To annoy, irritate, or anger. **2.** To go, depart, or leave. **—piss on** or **over.** *Vulgar Slang.* To defeat or vanquish utterly.
~*n. Vulgar.* **1.** Urine. **2.** An act of urinating. **—take the piss out of.** *Vulgar Slang.* To make fun of.
~*interj. Vulgar Slang.* Used to express anger, frustration, or disappointment. [Middle English, from Old French *pisser,* from Vulgar Latin *pisare* (unattested), of imitative origin.]

Pis·sar·ro (pi-sáarō), **Camille** (1830–1903). French impressionist painter. He took part in all eight impressionist exhibitions (1874–86), chiefly producing rural scenes.

piss artist *n. British Vulgar Slang.* **1.** A person who is known to drink alcohol and who often behaves in a high-spirited or buffoonish way. **2.** A very incompetent or unreliable person.

pissed (pist) *adj.* **1.** *British Vulgar Slang.* Drunk; intoxicated. **2.** *U.S. Slang.* Annoyed; irritated.

pis·soir (píss-waar, pee-swáar) *n. French.* A public urinal.

piss-up (píss-up) *n. British Vulgar Slang.* A drinking bout, especially one involving a group of people.

pis·ta·chi·o (piss-táshi-ō, -táashi-, -táchi-) *n., pl.* **-os.** Also **pis·tache** (-tásh). **1.** A tree, *Pistacia vera,* of the Mediterranean region and western Asia, bearing small hard-shelled nuts. **2.** The nut of this tree, having an edible, oily, green kernel. Also called "pistachio nut". **3.** Moderate to light yellowish green. [Italian *pistaccio,* from Latin *pistācium,* from Greek *pistakion,* pistachio nut, from *pistakē,* pistachio tree, from Persian *pistah†.*]

pis·ta·reen (pistə-réen) *n.* A small silver coin used in America and the West Indies during the 18th century. [Probably altered from Spanish *peseta,* PESETA.]

piste (peest) *n.* **1.** A ski slope or run of densely packed snow. **2.** The area in which a fencing bout takes place. [French, racetrack.]

pis·til (pístil) *n. Botany.* The female reproductive organ of a flower, including the stigma, style, and ovary. [French *pistil,* from Latin *pistillum,* PESTLE.]

pis·til·late (pístil-ayt, -ət, -it) *adj. Botany.* **1.** Having a pistil or pistils. **2.** Bearing pistils but no stamens: *pistillate flowers.*

pis·tol (píst'l) *n.* A firearm designed to be held and fired with one hand. **—hold a pistol to (someone's) head.** To bring overwhelming pressure to bear on (someone) to comply with one's wishes.
~*tr.v.* **pistolled** or *U.S.* **-oled, -tolling,** or *U.S.* **-toling, -tols.** To shoot with a pistol. [French *pistole,* from German *Pistole,* from Czech *pišťala,* "pipe", akin to Russian *pischal,* shepherd's pipe.]

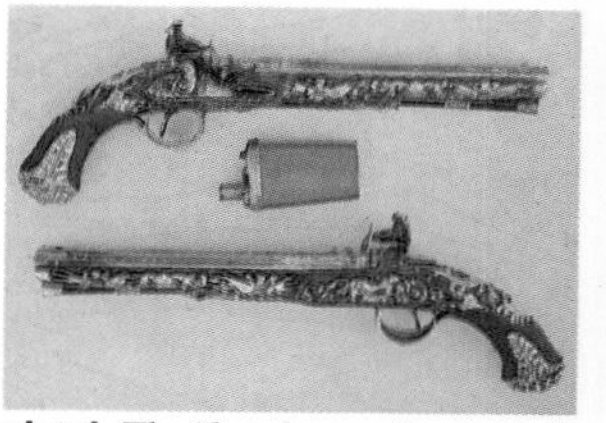

pistol *The "hand gonne" appeared in the first half of the 16th century. This pair of flintlock pistols was made in London for the Prince Regent, in 1815.*

pis·tole (pi-stōl, pístōl) *n.* An obsolete gold coin, used in various European countries until the late 19th century. [French, variant of *pistolet,* perhaps "small pistol" (originally a name given in jest to Spanish coins which were smaller than French coins, as a pistol is smaller than a harquebus), from *pistole,* PISTOL.]

pis·to·leer (pístə-léer) *n.* Formerly, a soldier armed with a pistol.

pistol grip *n.* **1.** The grip of a pistol, shaped to fit the hand. **2.** A similar grip sometimes used on a rifle or other firearm. **3.** A grip used on certain tools, such as a saw, shaped to fit the hand.

pis·tol-whip (píst'l-wip, -hwip) *tr.v.* **-whipped, -whipping, -whips.** *Chiefly U.S.* To beat with a pistol barrel.

pis·ton (pístən) *n.* **1.** A solid cylinder or disc that fits into a larger cylinder and moves back and forth under fluid pressure, as in a reciprocating engine, or displaces or compresses fluids, as in pumps and compressors. **2.** *Music.* A valve mechanism in brass instruments for altering pitch. [French, from Old French, from Old Italian *pistone, pestone,* augmentative of *pestello,* PESTLE.]

piston ring *n.* An adjustable split metal ring that fits round a piston and closes the gap between the piston and cylinder wall.

piston rod *n.* A **connecting rod** *(see)* that is attached to a piston.

pit¹ (pit) *n.* **1.** A relatively deep hole in the ground. **2. a.** An area excavated for minerals. Often used in combination: *a chalkpit.* **b.** A coal mine. **c.** The shaft of a coal mine. **3.** A trap consisting of a concealed hole in the ground; a pitfall. **4.** Hell. Preceded by *the.* **5.** An enclosed space, often one dug in the ground, in which animals, such as dogs or gamecocks, are placed for fighting. Often used in combination: *a cockpit.* **6. a.** The lowest surface of a body, organ, or part: *the pit of the stomach.* **b.** A small indentation in the skin left by disease or injury; a pockmark. **7. a.** An **orchestra pit** *(see).* **b.** *Chiefly British.* The ground floor of a theatre. **c.** Those who sit in this area. **8.** *U.S.* The section of an exchange where

pitcher plant *A type of carnivorous plant which attracts insects by means of nectar secreted inside its lip. Once inside the vaselike pitcher, the insects slide down into a pool of enzymes, where they drown and are digested. This is a North American species,* Sarracenia flava.

trading in a specific commodity is carried on. **9.** *Botany.* A thin-walled area in the wall of lignified plant cells. **10.** A box sunk into a sports ground and filled with sand or other material to cushion the fall of athletes taking part, for example, in the long jump or the triple jump. **11. a.** A sunken area in a garage floor from which mechanics may inspect or work on the underside of vehicles. **b.** *Often plural.* A place beside a motor-racing track where cars or motorcycles may be serviced during a race. **12.** *Plural. Slang.* The most wretched or disagreeable place or condition. Preceded by *the.* —See Synonyms at **hole.**
~*v.* **pitted, pitting, pits.** —*tr.* **1.** To make cavities, depressions, or scars in: *"the mountain was pitted with deep craters"* (Muriel Spark). **2.** To place in contest against another; set in direct opposition: *"a man pitted in conflict against the sea"* (D.H. Lawrence). **3.** To put, bury, or store in a pit. —*intr.* **1.** To become marked with small pits. **2.** To retain an impression after being indented, as by a fingernail. Used of skin. [Middle English *pitt,* Old English *pytt,* from West Germanic *putti* (unattested), from Latin *puteus,* a pit, well.]

pit² *n. Chiefly U.S.* The single, central kernel of certain fruits, such as a peach or cherry; a stone.
~*tr.v. Chiefly U.S.* **pitted, pitting, pits.** To extract pits from (fruit). [Perhaps from Dutch, from Middle Dutch *pit(te),* from West Germanic *pithan* (unattested), PITH.]

pi·ta¹ (péetə) *n.* Any of several plants of the genus *Agave,* that yield a strong fibre. Also called "istle", "ixtle". [Spanish, from Quechua.]

pita². Variant of **pitta.**

pit·a·pat (píttə-pát, -pat) *intr.v.* **-patted, -patting, -pats. 1.** To move with a series of quick, tapping steps. **2.** To make a repeated tapping sound.
~*n.* A series of quick steps, taps, or beats.
~*adv.* With a rapid tapping sound. [Imitative.]

Pit·cairn Islands (pít-kairn). Small group of volcanic islands in the south Pacific Ocean. The largest, Pitcairn Island, was settled by nine fleeing mutineers of the Bounty (1790) together with some Tahitians. It is a British dependency. See map at **Pacific Ocean.**

pitch¹ (pich) *n.* **1.** Any of various thick, dark, sticky substances obtained from the distillation residue of coal tar, wood tar, or petroleum, and used for waterproofing, roofing, caulking, and paving. **2.** Any of various natural bitumens, such as mineral pitch or asphalt, having similar uses. **3.** A resin derived from the sap of various coniferous trees, such as the pines.
~*tr.v.* **pitched, pitching, pitches.** To smear or cover with or as if with pitch. [Middle English *pich,* Old English *pic,* from Latin *pix* (stem *pic-*).] —**pitch·i·ness** *n.* —**pitch·y** *adj.*

pitch² *v.* **pitched, pitching, pitches.** —*tr.* **1.** To throw, usually forcefully, in a specified direction. **2.** In cricket, to bowl (a ball) so that it lands in a specific place. **3.** To put up or in position; establish: *pitch a tent.* **4.** To set firmly; implant; embed: *pitched the cricket stumps in the ground.* **5. a.** To fix the level of: *pitch one's expectations high.* **b.** To set the character and course of: *He pitched his speech to the party line.* **6.** To set at a specified pitch of music or sound. **7.** In card games, to lead (a card), thus establishing the trump suit. **8.** In golf, to strike (a ball) with great elevation and backspin so as to minimise movement on landing. **9.** To tell. Used chiefly in the phrase *pitch someone a yarn.* —*intr.* **1.** To land on the ground at a specified place: *The ball pitched near the wicket.* **2.** In baseball, to play in the position of pitcher. **3.** To plunge; fall, especially forwards: *He pitched over the railing.* **4.** To stumble around; lurch. **5.** To dip bow and stern alternately. Used of a ship or an aircraft. Compare **roll. 6.** To slope downwards: *The hill pitched steeply.* **7.** To set up living quarters; encamp; settle. —**pitch for.** *Informal.* To try to obtain something, especially through persuasion: *pitching for more business.* —**pitch in.** *Informal.* **1.** To set to work vigorously. **2.** To join forces with others; help; cooperate. —**pitch into.** *Informal.* To attack verbally or physically; assault. —**pitch on.** *Informal.* To choose.
~*n.* **1.** An act or instance of pitching. **2. a.** In cricket, the spot where a bowled ball lands. **b.** In baseball, a throw of the ball by the pitcher for action by the batter. **3. a.** The playing area in certain ball games such as football or hockey. **b.** In cricket, the rectangular area between the wickets, 22 yards by 10 feet. In this sense, also called "wicket". **4.** *Nautical.* The alternate dip and rise of a craft's bow and stern. **5. a.** Any steep downward slant. **b.** The degree of such a slant. **6.** *Architecture.* **a.** The angle of a roof. **b.** The highest point of a structure: *the pitch of an arch.* **7.** A point or stage of development or intensity, especially an extreme point: *reached a pitch of excitement.* **8.** The subjective quality of a complex sound, dependent on frequency, loudness, and intensity, and often measured as the frequency of a pure note of a given intensity judged equivalent to the complex sound by a normal ear. **9.** *Music.* **a.** The relative position of a note in a scale, as determined by its frequency. **b.** Any of various standards that establish a frequency for each musical note, used in the tuning of instruments: *high pitch, low pitch.* See **concert pitch. 10. a.** The distance travelled by a screw in a single revolution. **b.** The distance between two corresponding points on adjacent screw threads or gear teeth. **c.** The distance between two corresponding points on a helix. **11.** The distance a propeller would travel in an ideal medium during one complete revolution, measured parallel to the shaft of the propeller. **12. a.** *Slang.* A set talk designed to persuade: *sales pitch.* **b.** The place or stand of a vendor, hawker, or the like. **13.** A card game, **all fours** *(see).* **14.** In golf, a shot that is pitched. In this sense, also called "pitch shot". —**queer (someone's) pitch.** *Informal.* To spoil the chances or plans of. [Middle English *picchen,* to pierce, fix, set, throw, Old English *picc(e)an* (unattested), to prick, thrust, peculiar causative of *pician* (unattested), PICK (prick).]

pitch accent *n. Linguistics.* **Tonic accent** *(see).*

pitch-and-toss (pích-ən-tóss || -táwss) *n.* A game in which the player who comes closest to hitting a mark with a coin is entitled to toss all the other coins, and keep those that land heads up.

pitch-black (pích-blák) *adj.* Extremely dark or black.

pitch·blende (pích-blend) *n.* The principal ore of uranium, a brownish-black mineral of uranium dioxide with small amounts of uranium decay products. It is the chief source of radium. Also called "uraninite". [German *Pechblende* : *Pech,* pitch (from its black colour), from Latin *pix* + BLENDE.]

pitch circle *n.* An imaginary circle passing through the teeth of a gearwheel, having a radius that would enable it to touch but not overlap a similar circle on a mating gear.

pitch-dark (pích-dárk) *adj.* Extremely dark.

pitched battle *n.* **1.** A battle fought in close contact by troops whose formation and tactics have been carefully planned. **2.** Any fierce combat or dispute. [From the past participle of PITCH (to put in position, array for battle).]

pitch·er¹ (píchər) *n.* **1.** One that pitches. **2.** In baseball, the player who throws the ball from the mound to the batter. **3.** In golf, an iron club with a sharply inclined head.

pitcher² *n.* **1. a.** A large vessel for liquids made of clay, earthenware, or the like, and usually having two handles and a spout for pouring. **b.** Any large jug. **2.** *Botany.* A juglike part, such as the leaf of a pitcher plant. [Middle English *picher,* from Old French *pichier, bichier,* from Frankish *bikari* (unattested), BEAKER.]

pitcher plant *n.* Any of various insectivorous plants of the genera *Sarracenia, Heliamphora, Darlingtonia, Nepenthes,* and *Cephalotus,* having leaves modified to form juglike organs that trap insects.

pitch·fork (pích-fawrk) *n.* A large fork with sharp, widely spaced prongs for lifting and pitching hay.
~*tr.v.* **pitchforked, -forking, -forks. 1.** To lift or toss with a pitchfork. **2.** To force or thrust into a place or position very suddenly. [Middle English *pychforke,* alteration of *pikforke* (through wrong association with *picchen,* to toss, PITCH) : probably PICK + FORK.]

pitch·man (pích-mən) *n., pl.* **-men** (-mən). *U.S. Informal.* A pedlar or vendor of small wares, especially one with a colourful sales talk.

pitch pine *n.* **1.** Any of various American pine trees yielding pitch or turpentine, such as *Pinus rigida* of eastern North America. **2.** The wood of any of these trees.

pitch pipe *n. Music.* A small pipe that, when sounded, gives the standard pitch for a piece of music or for tuning an instrument.

pitch·stone (pích-stōn) *n.* Any of various glassy volcanic rocks distinguished by their dark lustre and relatively high water content. [Translation of German *Pechstein.*]

pit·e·ous (pítti-əss) *adj.* **1.** Arousing pity; pathetic. **2.** *Archaic.* Pitying; compassionate. —See Usage note at **pitiable.** [Middle English *piteus, pitous,* from Old French *piteus,* from *pite,* PITY.] —**pit·e·ous·ly** *adv.* —**pit·e·ous·ness** *n.*

pit·fall (pít-fawl) *n.* **1.** A trap made by digging a hole in the ground and concealing its opening. **2.** Any danger or difficulty that is not easily anticipated or avoided.

pith (pith) *n.* **1.** *Botany.* The soft, spongelike substance in the centre of stems and branches of most vascular plants. Also called "medulla". **2.** The white fibrous tissue between the rind and the pulp in such fruits as oranges and grapefruits. **3.** The essential or central part of anything; the essence; the gist. **4.** Force; strength; vigour.
~*tr.v.* **pithed, pithing, piths. 1.** To remove the pith from (a plant stem). **2.** To sever or destroy the spinal cord of (a laboratory animal), usually by means of a needle inserted into the vertebral canal. **3.** To kill (animals) by cutting the spinal cord. [Middle English *pithe,* Old English *pitha,* from West Germanic *pithon†* (unattested). See also **pit** (stone of fruit).]

pit·head (pít-hed) *n.* The top of a mine shaft, especially of a coal mine, including the hoisting gear and ancillary buildings.

pith·e·can·thro·pus (píthi-kan-thrṓ-pəss, -kánthrə-) *n., pl.* **-pi** (-pī). A member of the former genus *Pithecanthropus,* thought to indicate the existence of a primate between man and ape. It is now reclassified as *Homo erectus.* See **Java man, Peking man.** [New Latin : Greek *pithēkos†,* ape + -ANTHROPUS.] —**pith·e·can·thro·poid** *adj.*

pith helmet *n.* A light sun hat made from dried pith; a topi.

pith·os (píth-os) *n., pl.* **-thoi** (-oy). *Archaeology.* A large jar used for storing goods such as oil or grain. [Greek.]

pith·y (píthi) *adj.* **-ier, -iest. 1.** Consisting of or resembling pith. **2.** Precisely meaningful; cogent and terse. —See Synonyms at **concise.** —**pith·i·ly** *adv.* —**pith·i·ness** *n.*

pit·i·a·ble (pítti-əb'l) *adj.* **1.** Arousing or deserving of pity or compassion. **2.** Arousing disdainful pity; paltry; despicable. —**pit·i·a·ble·ness** *n.* —**pit·i·a·bly** *adv.*

Usage: *Pitiable, pitiful,* and *piteous* are often interchangeable. However, *pitiable* tends to be used in contexts where the wretchedness of a condition is being emphasised *(the pitiable circumstances those people live in)*; *pitiful* often introduces a sense of "contemptible" *(they earn a pitiful wage)*; *piteous* stresses the arousal of compassionate feelings *(a piteous sight).*

pit·i·ful (píttif'l) *adj.* **1.** Arousing pity; pathetic. **2.** So inferior or insignificant as to be contemptible; mean; paltry. **3.** *Archaic.* Filled with pity or compassion. —See Synonyms at **pathetic.** —See Usage note at **pitiable.** —**pit·i·ful·ly** *adv.* —**pit·i·ful·ness** *n.*

pit·i·less (pítti-ləss, -liss) *adj.* Having no pity; without mercy. See Synonyms at **cruel.** —**pit·i·less·ly** *adv.* —**pit·i·less·ness** *n.*

Pit·man (pít-mən), **Sir Isaac** (1813–97). British inventor of the Pitman shorthand system (1837). It was based on the sound rather than the written appearance of words.

pi·ton (pee-ton; *French* pee-tón) *n.* A metal spike fitted at one end with an eye or ring through which to pass a rope, used in mountain climbing. [French, from Old French, "nail", from Romance root *pitt-*, pointed thing.]

Pi·tot-stat·ic tube (péetō-státtik ‖ pee-tṓ-) *n.* A device consisting of a Pitot tube and a static tube combined to measure simultaneously total and static pressure in a fluid stream. It can be used in aircraft to determine relative wind speed.

Pi·tot tube (péetō ‖ *U.S.* pée-tō) *n.* A device used to measure the total pressure of a fluid stream. It is essentially a tube attached to a manometer at one end with its other end pointing upstream. [After Henri *Pitot* (1695–1771), French physicist.]

pit pony *n.* A small horse or pony, formerly used in coal mines for haulage.

pit·saw (pít-saw) *n.* A large saw for cutting logs, hand-operated by two men, one of whom stands on the log and the other in a pit underneath.

Pitt (pit), **William, 1st Earl of Chatham,** also known as Pitt the Elder (1708–78). British statesman and orator. He became an M.P. in 1735, and was associated with the Whig faction, opposing Robert Walpole. He was Paymaster General (1746–55) and Secretary of State (1756–57, 1757–61) for much of the Seven Years' War. In 1766–68 he formed an all-party ministry that failed to cope with the crisis in the American colonies, and he resigned through ill health.

Pitt, William, also known as Pitt the Younger (1759–1806). British statesman and prime minister (1783–1801, 1804–06). The son of William Pitt the Elder, he became an M.P. in 1781 and as Chancellor of the Exchequer (1782–83) began a lifelong rivalry with Charles James Fox. He became at 24 the youngest prime minister in British history. His India Act (1784) and Canada Act (1791) laid the basis of future colonial administration. In response to Irish unrest, he accomplished the Act of Union between Ireland and Britain (1800). The Napoleonic wars dominated Pitt's second ministry. He negotiated an alliance with Russia and Austria which collapsed after Napoleon's victory at Austerlitz (1805).

pit·ta, pi·ta (pítta, péeta) *n.* A flat, oval, slightly leavened kind of bread, which can be slit open to take a filling, originally from Greece and the Middle East. [Modern Greek.]

pit·tance (pítt'nss) *n.* **1.** A meagre allowance of money: *She lives on a pittance.* **2.** A very small salary or remuneration. **3.** A small amount or portion of anything. [Middle English *pitaunce,* from Old French *pitance,* from Medieval Latin *pittantia,* from Vulgar Latin *pietantia* (unattested), pious donation, portion (of food) given to monastics, from *pietārī,* to be charitable, from Latin *pietās,* piety, from *pius,* pious.]

pit·ter-pat·ter (pítta-pattar, -páttar) *n.* A rapid series of light, tapping sounds.
~*intr.v.* **-tered, -tering, -ters.** To move with or make a pitter-patter: *rain pitter-pattered on the road.*
~*adv.* With a series of light, tapping sounds. [Imitative.]

Pitts·burgh (pits-burg). City in southwest Pennsylvania. Situated at the confluence of the Allegheny, Monongahela, and Ohio rivers, it is the country's largest inland river port. It produces coal and steel.

pi·tu·i·tar·y (pi-téw-i-tri, -təri ‖ -tṓ-, -terri) *n., pl.* **-ies. 1.** *Anatomy.* The pituitary gland. **2.** *Medicine.* An extract from the anterior or posterior lobes of the pituitary gland, prepared for therapeutic use.
~*adj.* **1.** Of or pertaining to the pituitary gland. **2.** *Archaic.* Of or secreting phlegm or mucus; mucous. [Latin *pītuītārius,* from *pītuīta,* phlegm.]

pituitary gland *n. Anatomy.* A small, oval endocrine gland attached to the base of the vertebrate brain, the secretions of which control the other endocrine glands and influence growth, metabolism, and maturation. Also called "hypophysis", "pituitary body".

pit·u·ri (píchəri) *n.* An Australian shrub, *Duboisia hopwoodii,* the leaves of which yield a narcotic. [From a native Australian name.]

pit viper *n.* Any of various venomous snakes of the family Crotalidae, such as the copperhead or rattlesnake, characterised by a small pit on each side of the head.

pit·y (pítti) *n., pl.* **-ies. 1. a.** Sorrow or grief aroused by the misfortune of another; compassion for another's suffering. **b.** Concern or regret for one considered inferior or less favoured; condescending sympathy. **2.** A regrettable or disagreeable fact or necessity. —**for pity's sake.** Used to express angry frustration or an embittered plea: *Go away, for pity's sake!* —**more's the pity.** Regrettably; so much the worse: *I didn't see it, more's the pity.* —**take pity on.** To attempt to alleviate the misfortune of another.
~*v.* **pitied, pitying, pities.** —*tr.* To feel pity for. —*intr. Archaic.* To feel pity. [Middle English *pite,* from Old French *pit(i)e,* from Late Latin *pietās* (stem *pietāt-*), compassion, extended sense of Latin *pietās,* piety, from *pius,* pious.] —**pit·y·ing·ly** *adv.*

Synonyms: pity, compassion, commiseration, sympathy, condolence.

pit·y·ri·a·sis (pítti-rí-ə-siss) *n.* Any of various skin diseases of humans and animals, characterised by epidermal shedding of flaky scales. [Greek *pituriasis,* from *pituron†,* grain husk, dandruff.]

più (pew) *adv. Music.* More. Used in directions to performers, as in *più forte,* more loudly. [Italian, from Latin *plūs,* more.]

Pius V, Saint, born Michele Ghislieri (1504–72). Pope (1566–72).

He supported the Inquisition and encouraged the suppression of Protestantism in France and the Netherlands. In 1570 he excommunicated Elizabeth I of England. He was cononised in 1712.

Pius XII, born Eugenio Pacelli (1876–1958). Italian pope (1939–58). As Papal Secretary of State he negotiated the concordat with Nazi Germany (1933). During World War II he believed the best way to achieve peace was to maintain formal relations with all the belligerents but he was much criticised for not speaking out against the persecution of the Jews.

Piute. Variant of **Paiute.**

piv·ot (pívvət) *n.* **1.** A short rod or pointed shaft on which a related part rotates or swings; a fulcrum. **2.** A person or thing that chiefly determines the course or effect of something; the essential component. **3.** A person who helps to keep the order and direction of wheeling troops. **4.** The act of turning on or as if on a pivot.
~*v.* **pivoted, -oting, -ots.** —*tr.* To mount on, attach by, or furnish with a pivot or pivots. —*intr.* To turn on or as if on a pivot: *It all pivots on her decision.* [French, of obscure origin.]

pi·vo·tal *adj.* **1.** Of, pertaining to, or being a pivot. **2.** Of vital importance; crucial. —**pi·vot·al·ly** *adv.*

pix¹ (piks) *pl.n. Informal.* Photographs or films. [Abbreviation of *pictures.*]

pix². Variant of **pyx.**

pix·el (píks-el) *n.* An element of a computer graphics display on a VDU. [From PIX + *el*ement.]

pix·ie, pix·y (píksi) *n., pl.* **-ies.** A fairy-like or elfin creature. [17th century : origin obscure.]

pix·i·lat·ed, pix·il·lat·ed (píksi-laytid) *adj.* **1.** Behaving as if led by pixies; bemused; whimsical; eccentric. **2.** *Slang.* Drunk. [From *pixy-led,* altered after past participles such as TITILLATED.]

Pi·zar·ro (pi-záa-rō; *Spanish* pee-thá-), **Francisco** (1475–1541). Spanish conquistador. In 1530 with some 180 men he crossed the Andes and in 1532 reached the heart of the Inca empire. He captured and killed its emperor, Atahualpa, at Cajamarca, and entered Cuzco in 1533. Within two years he subdued the whole empire and founded Lima as his capital (1535).

pizz. *Music.* pizzicato.

piz·za (péet-sə) *n.* A baked dish of Italian origin consisting of a shallow breadlike crust typically covered with a spiced mixture of tomatoes and cheese, and sometimes other ingredients, such as anchovies, meat, or olives. [Italian.]

piz·zazz, pe·zazz (pi-záz, pə-) *n. Slang.* Flamboyant; zest or flair. [Imitative.]

piz·ze·ri·a (péetsə-rée-ə) *n.* A place where pizzas are made, sold, and eaten. [Italian, from PIZZA.]

piz·zi·ca·to (pítsi-káatō) *adv. Abbr.* **pizz.** *Music.* Played by plucking rather than bowing the strings of an instrument, such as a violin.
~*n., pl.* **pizzicatos** or **-ti.** A passage or note played in this manner. [Italian, past participle of *pizzicare,* to pluck, pinch, from *pizza,* to prick, pinch, from Old Italian *pizza,* a point, edge, from Gallo-Roman *pīnts-, pīts-* (unattested). See also **pinch.**] —**piz·zi·ca·to** *adj.*

piz·zle (pízz'l) *n.* The penis of an animal, especially that of a bull. [Earlier *peezel,* from Low German *pēsel,* diminutive of Middle Low German *pēse,* sinew, penis, perhaps an early borrowing of Latin *pēniculus,* diminutive of *pēnis,* PENIS.]

PK psychokinesis.

pk. 1. pack. **2.** park. **3.** peak. **4.** peck.

pkg. package.

pkt. packet.

pl. 1. place. **2.** plate. **3.** plural.

Pl. Place (used in street names).

P.L.A. Port of London Authority.

PL/1 *n.* A high-level symbolic language designed for programming computers. [*Program Language Number 1.*]

plac·a·ble (plack-əb'l, *rarely* pláyk-) *adj. Rare.* Easily calmed or pacified; tolerant. [Middle English, agreeable, from Old French, placable, from Latin *plācābilis,* from *plācāre,* to calm, appease.] —**plac·a·bil·i·ty** (-ə-billəti) *n.* —**plac·a·bly** *adv.*

plac·ard (plák-aard, -ərd) *n.* **1.** A printed or written announcement for display in a public place; a poster: *demonstrators carrying placards with slogans.* **2.** A nameplate, as on the door of a house.
~*tr.v.* **placarded, -arding, -ards. 1.** To announce or advertise (a message or product) on a placard. **2.** To post placards on or in. **3.** To display as a placard. [Middle English *placquart,* plate, breastplate, from Old French *plaquart,* from *plaquier,* to plaster, from Middle Dutch *placken†,* to patch, paste. See also **plaque.**] —**placard·er** *n.*

pla·cate (plə-káyt, *rarely* play- ‖ *U.S.* pláy-kayt, plá-) *tr.v.* **-cated, -cating, -cates.** To allay the anger of, especially by making concessions; appease. See Synonyms at **pacify.** [Latin *plācāre,* to calm, appease.] —**pla·cat·er** *n.* —**pla·ca·tion** (-káysh'n) *n.* —**pla·ca·to·ry** (-əri) *n.*, **pla·ca·tive** (plə-káytiv, pláckətiv) *adj.*

place (playss) *n.* **1.** A portion of space; an area with definite or indefinite boundaries. **2.** Such an area, for example a building, set aside for a specified activity: *a place of worship.* **3.** A definite location, especially: **a.** A house, flat, or other residence: *My place or yours?* **b.** A business establishment or office. **c.** A particular town or city. **4.** *Usually* *Abbr.* **P.** *Abbr.* **Pl.** A public square or street with houses in a town. **5. a.** A space for one person to sit or stand, for example as a passenger or spectator. **b.** A setting for one person at a table. **6.** A position regarded as belonging to someone or something else; stead: *I was chosen in his place.* **7.** A particular point that one has reached; especially, a point up to which one has read in a book: *I lost my place.* **8.** A position figuratively occupied by a thing, group, or activity in a larger complex; an existing function; a role: *the place of trade unions in society.* **9.** Proper or customary location or order: *Everything is in place.* **10. a.** A social status entailing a certain mode of behaviour: *the days when servants knew their place.* **b.** An appropriate right or duty: *It's not my place to criticise.* **c.** A location or situation requiring a particular mode of behaviour: *This is not the place for flippancy.* **11. a.** A position of eminence: *a place in history.* **b.** A position as a member of a selective body, for example as an employee of a firm or member of a team: *She's got a place at Oxford.* **12. a.** A relative position in a series, especially in a series classified according to achievement: *went up to third place in the hit parade.* **b.** *British.* A position as one of the first three (or, sometimes, four) horses to finish a race, and especially as either the second or third horse. **c.** A specified stage in a list of points to be made, as in an argument: *In the first place, they have no right to protest.* **13.** *Abbr.* **pl.** The position of a number in relation to other numbers in a series. See **decimal place.** **—all over the place.** In confusion or disarray. **—give place to. 1.** To make space or room for. **2.** To be superseded by. **—go places.** *Informal.* To enjoy increasing success. **—in place of.** Instead of. **—know (one's) place.** To be aware of one's position of inferiority and act accordingly. **—out of place. 1.** Inappropriate. **2.** In the wrong place. **—put (someone) in his place.** To cause (someone who is arrogant or conceited) to be humbled. **—take (one's) place.** To take up a usual or specified position: *took his place at the front.* **—take place.** To occur; happen.

~*v.* **placed, placing, places.** *—tr.* **1.** To put in a specified position; set. **2.** To put in a specified relation or order: *Place the words in alphabetical order.* **3.** To arrange for (a person or thing) to receive appropriate treatment, especially: **a.** To find accommodation or employment for. **b.** To invest (money). **c.** To lay (an order or bet, for example). **d.** To find a publisher for (a book). **e.** To have (an advertisement, for example) displayed or published. **4.** To appoint to a post: *placed in a key position.* **5.** To rank in an order or sequence: *I'd place him second best.* **6.** To put, lay, or fix: *placed emphasis on her appearance.* **7.** To recollect clearly the circumstances or context of: *I can't place him now.* **8.** To adjust (one's speaking or singing voice) for the best possible effects. **9.** To declare the position of (a horse, runner, or other contestant), especially amongst the first three finishes of a race. *—intr. U.S.* To arrive among the first three finishers in a race; especially, to finish in second place. [Middle English, space, locality, from Old French, from Latin *platea,* "broad street", space, from Greek *plateia (hodos),* "broad(way)", from feminine of *platus,* broad.]

Place (playss), **Francis** (1771–1854). British radical. A prosperous London tailor, he fought for trade union rights. He helped to draft the People's Charter (1838) from which Chartism was born.

pla·ce·bo (plə-sée-bō, pla-; *in sense 1 also* -cháy-) *n., pl.* **-bos** or **-boes. 1.** *Roman Catholic Church.* The service or office of vespers for the dead. **2. a.** *Medicine.* A substance containing no active drug given to a patient who thinks he is ill who believes it to be an active drug, to humour him or to effect a cure *(the placebo effect)* by changing his psychological attitude by this deception. **b.** An inactive substance used as a control in an experiment. **3.** Anything lacking intrinsic remedial value, done or given to humour another. [Medieval Latin, from the first word of the first antiphon of the service, *Placēbo (Dominō in rēgiōne vivōrum),* "I shall please (the Lord in the land of the living)", from *placēre,* to please.]

place card *n.* A card that bears a name indicating where a person must sit at a dinner table.

place kick *n.* In Rugby football, a kick made when the ball is propped up in a fixed position on the ground. **—place-kick** (pláyss-kik) *v.* **—place-kick·er** *n.*

place·man (pláyss-mən) *n., pl.* **-men** (-mən). *Chiefly British.* A person appointed to an office as a reward for loyalty rather than merit, especially one who will serve the interests of the appointer.

place mat *n.* A protective table mat, often decorative, on which dishes and plates are placed at mealtimes.

place·ment (pláyss-mənt) *n.* **1. a.** The act of placing or arranging. **b.** The state of being placed or arranged. **2.** The act or business of finding jobs, lodgings, or other positions for applicants. **3.** In racket games such as tennis or squash, the act or practice of accurately placing the ball in parts of the court.

pla·cen·ta (plə-sén-tə) *n., pl.* **-tas** or **-tae** (-tee). **1.** *Anatomy.* A vascular, membranous organ that develops in female mammals during pregnancy and provides the foetus with nutrients and removes waste products via the umbilical cord. Following birth, the placenta is expelled as part of the afterbirth. **2.** *Botany.* **a.** The part of the ovary to which the ovules are attached. **b.** In nonflowering plants, the tissue that bears the spore cases. [Latin, flat cake, from Greek *plakoenta,* accusative of *plakoeis, plakous,* flat, flat cake, from *plax* (stem *plak-*), flat surface.]

pla·cen·tal (plə-sént'l, pla-) *adj.* Also **pla·cen·tate** (-séntayt). Having a placenta. Said especially of animals.

plac·en·ta·tion (pláss-en-táysh'n, -'n-) *n.* **1.** *Zoology.* **a.** The formation of a placenta. **b.** The type or structure of a placenta. **2.** *Botany.* The way in which the placenta is arranged in or attached to the ovary.

plac·er (plássər) *n.* **1.** A glacial or alluvial deposit of sand or gravel containing deposits of heavy minerals such as gold, platinum, and diamonds. **2.** A place where such a deposit is washed to extract its mineral content. [American Spanish, "shoal", from *plaza,* place, from Latin *platea,* "broad road", PLACE.]

placer mining *n.* The obtaining of minerals from placers by washing or dredging. **—placer miner** *n.*

plac·id (plássid) *adj.* Having a calm appearance or temperament; not easily excited or upset. See Synonyms at **calm.** [French, from Latin *placidus,* pleasing, gentle, from *placēre,* to please.] **—pla·cid·i·ty** (pla-síddəti, plə-), **plac·id·ness** *n.* **—plac·id·ly** *adv.*

plack·et (pláckit) *n.* A slit in a dress, blouse, or skirt to make the garment easy to put on or take off or to give access to a pocket. [Earlier *plackerd,* dress, petticoat, originally, "breastplate", variant of PLACARD.]

plac·oid (pláckoyd) *adj. Zoology.* Platelike, as the hard, toothlike scales of sharks, skates, and rays are. [Greek *plax* (stem *plak-*), flat surface, plate + -OID.]

pla·fond (plə-fón, pla-, -FÓN) *n.* A ceiling, especially one that is decorated, as with paintings. [French, from *plat,* flat + *fond,* bottom.]

pla·gal (pláyg'l) *adj. Music.* **1.** Designating a medieval mode having a range from the fourth below to the fifth above its final note. **2.** Designating a cadence with the subdominant chord immediately preceding the tonic chord. Compare **authentic.** [Medieval Latin *plagālis,* from *plaga,* plagal mode, from *plagius,* plagal, from Medieval Greek *plagios (ēkhos),* plagal (mode), from Greek *plagios,* placed sideways, oblique, from *plagos,* side.]

plage (plaazh) *n. Astronomy.* A **flocculus** *(see).*

pla·gia·rise, pla·gia·rize (pláyj-ə-rīz, -i-ə-) *v.* **-rised, -rising, -rises.** *—tr.* **1.** To steal and use (the ideas or writings of another) as one's own. **2.** To appropriate passages or ideas from (another) to use as one's own. *—intr.* To take and use as one's own the writings or ideas of another. [From PLAGIARY.] **—pla·gia·ris·er** *n.*

pla·gia·rism (pláyj-ə-riz'm, -i-ə-) *n.* **1.** The act of plagiarising. **2.** That which is plagiarised. [From PLAGIARY.] **—pla·gia·rist** *n.* **—pla·gia·ris·tic** (-rístik) *adj.*

pla·gia·ry (pláyj-əri, -i-əri || -i-erri) *n., pl.* **-ries.** *Archaic.* **1.** Plagiarism. **2.** A plagiarist. [Originally "kidnapper", from Latin *plagiārius,* from *plagium,* kidnapping, from *plaga,* net.]

plagio- *comb. form.* Indicates a slanting or inclining; for example, **plagiotropism.** [Greek *plagios,* placed sideways, oblique, from *plagos,* side.]

pla·gi·o·clase (pláyji-ō-klayz, pláji-, -ə-, -klayss) *n.* Any of a common rock-forming series of triclinic feldspars consisting of mixtures of sodium and calcium aluminium silicates. Also called "plagioclase feldspar". [German *Plagioklas* : PLAGIO- + -CLASE.] **—pla·gi·o·clas·tic** (-klástik) *adj.*

pla·gi·o·cli·max (pláyji-ō-klī-maks, pláji-, -ə-) *n. Ecology.* A stable plant community that, because of environmental factors such as grazing pressure, cannot develop into a natural climax.

pla·gi·ot·ro·pism (pláyji-ō-trōp-iz'm, pláji-, -ə-, -óttrəp-) *n. Biology.* A tendency, especially in lateral roots, to grow at an oblique angle to the direction of the stimulus. [PLAGIO- + -TROPISM.] **—pla·gi·o·trop·ic** (-tróppik, -trōpik) *adj.* **—pla·gi·o·trop·i·cal·ly** *adv.*

plague (playg) *n.* **1.** A highly infectious, usually fatal, epidemic disease, especially bubonic plague. **2.** A sudden influx, as of destructive or harmful insects: *a plague of locusts.* **3.** *Informal.* Any cause for annoyance; a nuisance: *the plague of their chatter.* **4.** A disaster or affliction, or calamity, especially one seen as a punishment. **—a plague on.** *Archaic.* Used as a curse: *A plague on your good deeds!*

~*tr.v.* **plagued, plaguing, plagues. 1.** To harass, pester, or annoy: *plagued their parents with silly questions.* **2.** To afflict with or as if with plague or any other evil. —See Synonyms at **harass.** [Middle English, a blow, calamity, malignant disease, from Old French, from Late Latin *plāga,* from Latin, a stroke, wound, probably from Greek *plaga, plēgē,* stroke.] **—plagu·er** *n.*

pla·guy, pla·guey (pláygi) *adj.* Irritating; bothersome. **—pla·gui·ly** (-li) *adv.*

plaice (playss) *n., pl.* **plaices** or collectively **plaice. 1.** An edible marine flatfish, *Pleuronectes platessa,* of western European waters. **2.** *U.S.* Any related flatfish, such as *Hippoglossoides platessoides* of North American Atlantic waters. [Middle English, from Old French *plaïs, plaïz,* from Late Latin *platessa,* "flatfish".]

plaice *An edible flatfish which feeds on flat-bottomed, sandy seabeds in the North Atlantic. Newly hatched fish have an eye on each side of the head. As they grow, the left eye moves up and over the head, and the fish's right side becomes its back. This is the European species,* Pleuronectes platessa.

plaid (plad || playd) *n.* **1.** A long, rectangular piece of woollen cloth of a tartan or checked pattern worn over one shoulder as part of Scottish Highland costume. **2.** Cloth with a tartan or checked pattern.

~*adj.* **1.** Made of plaid. **2.** Having a tartan or checked pattern. [Scottish Gaelic *plaide†.*]

Plaid Cymru (plīd kŏomri) *n.* The Welsh Nationalist party. It is dedicated to the cause of autonomy for Wales and the promotion of the Welsh language. [Welsh, party of Wales.]

plain (playn) *adj.* **plainer, plainest. 1.** Free from obstructions; open to view; clear: *plain sight.* **2.** *Rare.* Having no visible elevation or depression; flat; level. **3.** Easily understood; clearly evident; obvious to the mind: *make one's intention plain.* **4.** Uncomplicated; easily done; simple: *plain needlework.* **5.** Straightforward; frank; candid: *plain speaking.* **6. a.** Not mixed with other substances; pure: *plain water.* **b.** Containing no raising agents: *plain flour.* **7. a.** Common in rank or station; ordinary: *a plain man.* **b.** Without affectation or pretension. **8.** Not ruled; without lines. Said of paper. **9.** Not rich or elaborate: *plain food.* **10.** With little ornamentation or decoration: *a plain dress.* **11.** Not dyed, twilled, or patterned: *a plain fabric.* **12.** Not beautiful or handsome; unattractive: *a plain face.* **13.** Sheer; utter; unqualified: *plain stupidity.*

14. Not in code: *a plain message.* **15.** Designating the basic, simple knitting stitch. —See Synonyms at **evident.**
~*n.* **1.** An extensive, level, treeless land region, such as a valley floor or a plateau summit. **2.** In knitting, plain stitch.
~*adv.* In a clear or obvious manner: *plain stupid.* [Middle English, from Old French, from Latin *plānus,* flat, clear.] —**plain·ly** *adv.* —**plain·ness** *n.*
plain·chant (pláyn-chaant ‖ -chant) *n.* Plainsong. [French, from Medieval Latin *cantus plānus,* PLAINSONG.]
plain chocolate *n.* A dark, bitter chocolate made without milk. Compare **milk chocolate.**
plain clothes *pl.n.* Ordinary, civilian clothes as opposed to uniform, especially police uniform. —**plain-clothes** (pláyn-klōthz, -klōz) *adj.*
plain-laid (pláyn-layd) *adj.* Designating a rope made of three strands laid together with a right-hand twist.
plain sailing *n.* **1.** Easy sailing over a direct course. **2.** Easy, unimpeded progress. [Alteration of *plane sailing* (navigation using PLANE angles).]
Plains Indian *n.* A member of any of the North American Indian peoples that once inhabited the Great Plains of North America.
plains·man (pláynz-mən) *n., pl.* **-men** (-mən, -men). An inhabitant or settler of a plains region, especially the prairie regions of the United States.
plain·song (pláyn-song ‖ -sawng) *n. Music.* **1. Gregorian chant** *(see).* **2.** Any medieval liturgical music without strict meter and traditionally sung without accompaniment. Also called "plainchant". [Translation of Medieval Latin *cantus plānus.*]
plain-spo·ken (pláyn-spōkən, -spókən) *adj.* Blunt; frank.
plain stitch *n.* In knitting, the basic, simple stitch, producing either a flat surface, as in stocking stitch, or a ribbed surface, as in garter stitch. Compare **purl stitch.**
plaint (playnt) *n.* **1.** *Archaic & Poetic.* **a.** A complaint. **b.** An utterance of grief or sorrow; a lamentation. **2.** *Law.* A statement of grievance submitted to a court as a request for redress. [Middle English *pleinte, plaint,* from Old French *plainte,* from Latin *planctus,* past participle of *plangere,* to strike (one's breast), lament.]
plain·tiff (pláyntif) *n. Law.* The party that institutes a suit in a court. Compare **defendant.** [Middle English *plaintif,* from Old French, from adjective *plaintif,* PLAINTIVE.]
plain·tive (pláyntiv) *adj.* Expressing restrained sorrow; mournful; melancholy: *the plaintive sound of wind in the trees.* [Middle English *pleintif,* from Old French *plaintif,* from *plainte,* lamentation, PLAINT.] —**plain·tive·ly** *adv.* —**plain·tive·ness** *n.*
plain weave *n.* A weave in which the filling threads and the warp threads interlace alternately, forming a checked pattern. Also called "taffeta weave".
plait (plat ‖ playt) *n.* **1.** A length of interwoven strands, especially of hair. **2.** A pleat.
~*tr.v.* **plaited, plaiting, plaits. 1.** To interweave (hair, grass, thread, or the like) into a plait. **2.** To make by plaiting. [Middle English, fold, crease, from Old French *pleit,* from Vulgar Latin *plic(i)tus* (unattested), from Latin *plicitus,* variant past participle of *plicāre,* to fold.] —**plait·er** *n.*
plan (plan) *n.* **1.** Any detailed scheme, programme, or method worked out beforehand for the accomplishment of an object: *a plan of attack.* **2.** A proposed or tentative project or course of action: *Do you have any plans for the evening?* **3.** A systematic arrangement of details; an outline or sketch: *the plan of a story.* **4.** A drawing or diagram made to scale showing the structure or arrangement of something: *a town plan; the plan of a building.* **5.** In rendering perspective, one of several imaginary planes perpendicular to the line of vision between the viewer and the object being depicted.
~*v.* **planned, planning, plans.** —*tr.* **1.** To formulate a scheme or programme for the accomplishment or attainment of: *plan a campaign.* **2.** To have as a specified aim or purpose; intend: *They plan to go to the beach.* **3.** To draw or make a graphic representation of. —*intr.* To make a plan. Often used with *on* or *for.* [French, as "level ground", "plane", from Latin *plānum,* from *plānus,* flat; as "ground plan", "map", altered from *plant* (in sense influenced by Italian *pianta,* ground plan or design), from *planter,* to plant, from Latin *plantāre. See* **plant.**]
pla·nar (pláyn-ər ‖ -aar) *adj.* **1.** Of, pertaining to, or situated in a plane. **2.** Flat: *a planar surface.* [Late Latin *plānāris,* from Latin *plānum,* level surface, from *plānus,* flat, PLAIN.] —**pla·nar·i·ty** (play-nárrəti, plə-) *n.*
pla·nar·i·an (plə-naír-i-ən) *n.* Any of various flatworms of the order Tricladida, having broad, ciliated bodies and a three-branched digestive cavity. [New Latin *Planaria* (genus), from Latin *plānus,* flat.]
planar process *n.* A method of manufacturing semiconductor devices in which impurities are diffused through holes etched into an oxide layer formed on a silicon substrate, producing a diffused junction.
pla·na·tion (play-náysh'n, plə-) *n.* Lateral erosion, as of a valley, by a running stream. [From PLANE (level surface).]
planch·et (plánchit) *n.* A flat disc of metal ready for stamping as a coin; a coin blank. [Diminutive of *planch,* board, Middle English *plaunche,* from Old French *planche,* from Latin *planca. See* **plank.**]
plan·chette (plaan-shét, plon-) *n.* A small triangular board with a pointer supported by two casters and a vertical pencil which is said to spell out messages from the spirit world when the operator's

fingers are placed lightly upon it. [French, diminutive of Old French *planche,* board. See **planchet.**]
Planck (plangk), **Max (Karl Ernst Ludwig)** (1858–1947). German physicist. While professor at the university of Berlin (1889–1928) he originated the quantum theory (1900); he was awarded the Nobel prize (1918), and his theory was applied by Einstein, Bohr, and others to transform 20th-century physics.
Planck's constant *n. Symbol* **h** *Physics.* The constant of proportionality relating the quantum of energy that can be possessed by radiation to the frequency of that radiation. Its value is approximately 6.6262×10^{-34} joule seconds. [After Max PLANCK.]
Planck's formula *n.* The formula, put forward by Planck, by which the distribution of energy in **black-body radiation** *(see)* over a narrow frequency range is expressed as a function of frequency and temperature.
plane[1] (playn) *n.* **1.** *Geometry.* A surface containing all the straight lines connecting any two points on it. **2.** Any flat or level surface. **3.** A level of development, existence, or achievement. **4.** An aeroplane or hydroplane. **5.** *Aeronautics.* A supporting surface of an aircraft; an aerofoil or wing.
~*adj.* **1.** *Geometry.* Designating a figure lying in a plane: *a plane curve.* **2.** Flat. —See Synonyms at **level.** [Latin *plānum,* a flat surface, from *plānus,* flat.] —**plane·ness** *n.*
plane[2] *n.* **1.** A carpenter's tool with an adjustable blade for smoothing and levelling wood. **2.** A flat, trowel-shaped tool for smoothing the surface of clay, sand, or plaster in a mould.
~*v.* **planed, planing, planes.** —*tr.* **1.** To smooth or finish with or as if with a plane. **2.** To remove with a plane. Used with *off* or *away.* —*intr.* **1.** To work with a plane. **2.** To act as a plane. [Middle English, from French *plane, plaine,* from Late Latin *plāna,* from *plānāre,* to plane, from *plānus,* level.]
plane[3] *intr.v.* **planed, planing, planes. 1.** To rise partly out of the water, as a hydroplane does at high speeds. **2.** To soar or glide. [French *planer,* to soar (with wings stretched on a level), from *plan,* a level surface, from Latin *plānum,* from *plānus,* flat.]
plane[4] *n.* The **plane tree** *(see).*
plane angle *n.* An angle formed by two straight lines in a plane.
plane geometry *n.* The geometry of planar figures.
plane polarisation *n.* A form of polarisation of electromagnetic radiation in which the waves are restricted to vibration in one plane.
plan·er (pláynər) *n.* **1.** One that planes. **2.** A machine tool for smoothing and planing the surfaces of wood or metal. **3.** *Printing.* A smooth block of wood used to level a forme of type.
plane sailing *n.* **1.** The calculation of the position of a ship on the basis that it is sailing on a plane and not the curved surface of the earth. **2.** See **plain sailing.**
plan·et (plánnit) *n.* **1.** A nonluminous celestial body illuminated by light from a star, such as the Sun, around which it revolves. In the **Solar System** *(see)* there are nine known major planets: Mercury, Venus, Earth, Mars, Jupiter, Saturn, Uranus, Neptune, and Pluto. **2.** In ancient astronomy, any of the seven celestial bodies (Mercury, Venus, the Moon, the Sun, Mars, Jupiter, and Saturn) visible to the naked eye and thought to revolve about a fixed Earth. **3.** *Astrology.* Any of the seven revolving celestial bodies that in conjunction with the stars are supposed to influence human affairs and personalities. [Middle English *planete,* from Old French, from Late Latin *planēta,* from Greek *planēs, planētēs,* plural of *planētos,* wandering planet, from *planasthai,* to wander.] See feature, next page.
plane table *n.* A portable surveying instrument consisting essentially of a drawing board and a ruler mounted on a tripod and used to sight and map topographical details.
plan·e·tar·i·um (plánni-taír-i-əm) *n., pl.* **-iums** or **-ia** (-i-ə). **1.** An apparatus or model representing the Solar System. **2.** A device for projecting images of celestial bodies in their courses, on the inner surface of a hemispherical dome. **3.** A building or room containing such a device, with seats for an audience. [PLANET + -ARIUM.]
plan·e·tar·y (plánni-tri, -təri ‖ -terri) *adj.* **1.** Of, pertaining to, or resembling the physical or orbital characteristics of a planet or the planets. **2.** Terrestrial; mundane; earthly. **3.** Wandering; erratic: *planetary life.* **4.** Designating or pertaining to a **gear train** *(see),* consisting of a central gear with an internal ring gear and one or more pinions.
planetary nebula *n.* Any of several objects in the Galaxy, each consisting of a hot, blue-white, central star surrounded by an envelope of expanding gas. See **Ring Nebula.**
plan·e·tes·i·mal (plánni-téssim'l ‖ -tézzim'l) *n. Astronomy.* **1.** Any of the innumerable small bodies consisting of interstellar dust, thought to have been present in the presolar medium. **2.** In the planetesimal hypothesis, any of the innumerable small bodies thought to have been formed from gaseous solar material. [PLANET + (INFINIT)ESIMAL.] —**plan·e·tes·i·mal** *adj.*
planetesimal hypothesis *n.* The hypothesis put forward by T.C. Chamberlain and F.R. Moulton in 1906 to account for the formation of the planets in the Solar System. It states that gas drawn off from the young Sun and another star as they passed close to each other condensed into planetesimals, which then by gravitational aggregation and accretion formed the planets. Compare **nebular hypothesis, presolar nebular hypothesis.**
plan·e·toid (plánnitoyd) *n. Astronomy.* An **asteroid** *(see).* —**plan·e·toi·dal** *adj.*
plane tree *n.* Any of several trees of the genus *Platanus,* having ball-shaped fruit clusters, large leaves with pointed lobes, and, usu-

planet

THE ROTATING SATELLITES OF OUR OWN SOLAR SYSTEM

Nine major bodies constantly circle the Sun

A planet is a nonluminous body of matter in space, revolving around a luminous star from which it gets its light. There are nine known major planets circling the Sun in our Solar System and they are listed below. It is not known precisely how the planets were created, but one widely accepted theory is that they were formed about 4,600 million years ago from a cloud of swirling gas and dust. Matter collided and contracted under its own gravitational force and coalesced into the planets with, at their centre, the largest body of all, the Sun, which contains 99.9 per cent of all the matter in the Solar System.

PLANET	Distance from Sun Kilometres (miles)	Diameter Kilometres (miles)	Length of day	Length of year	Mass relative to Earth	Escape velocity Kilometres/sec (miles/sec)	Mean surface temperature	Number of known satellites (moons)
MERCURY	57 900 000 (36,000,000)	4880 (3,032)	58 days 15 hr 36 min	87.97 days	0.055	4.25 (2.64)	+350°C	0
VENUS	108 200 000 (67,200,000)	12 104 (7,521)	243 days	224.7 days	0.815	10.36 (6.43)	+475°C	0
EARTH	149 600 000 (92,960,000)	12 756 (7,926)	23 hr 56 min 4 sec	365.26 days	1.0	11.18 (6.95)	+22°C	1
MARS	227 900 000 (141,600,000)	6787 (4,217)	24 hr 37 min 23 sec	686.98 days	0.108	5.02 (3.12)	−23°C	2
JUPITER	778 300 000 (483,600,000)	142 800 (88,700)	9 hr 50 min 30 sec	4,332.59 days	317.943	59.64 (37.06)	−123°C	16
SATURN	1 427 000 000 (886,700,000)	120 000 (74,500)	10 hr 14 mins	10,759.22 days	95.195	35.41 (22.0)	−180°C	21+
URANUS	2 869 600 000 (1,783,100,000)	51 800 (32,200)	16 hr (?)	30,685.4 days	14.605	21.41 (13.3)	−218°C	5
NEPTUNE	4 496 600 000 (2,794,100,000)	49 500 (30,800)	18 hr (?)	60,195 days	17.232	23.52 (14.61)	−228°C	2
PLUTO	5 900 000 000 (3,666,000,000)	2320 (1,440)	6 days 9 hr 18 min	90,475 days	0.002	1.0 (0.6)	−230°C (?)	1

DETAILS OF THE PLANETS *The distance from the Sun is an average, as the planets' orbits are elliptical. The day is the length of axial rotation, and the year is the time each planet takes to complete a revolution around the Sun. Both are measured in units of Earth time. The mass, or the amount of matter that each planet consists of, is given as a multiple of Earth's mass. Escape velocity is the minimum speed a body must reach in order to escape the planet's gravity.*

ally, outer bark that flakes off in patches. Also called "plane", "platan". See **London plane.** [*Plane,* from Middle English, from Old French, from Latin *platanus,* from Greek *platanos,* from *platus,* broad (from its broad leaves).]

planet wheel *n.* Any of the small gear wheels in an **epicyclic train** *(see).*

plan·gent (plánjənt) *adj.* **1.** Striking with a reverberating sound, as waves do against the shore. **2. a.** Loud and resounding, as is the sound of bells. **b.** Expressing sadness; plaintive: *plangent strains.* [Latin *plangens* (stem *plangent-*), present participle of *plangere,* to strike (one's breast).] —**plan·gen·cy** *n.* —**plan·gent·ly** *adv.*

plani–. Variant of **plano-.**

pla·nim·e·ter (pla-nímmitər, plə- ‖ play-) *n.* An instrument that measures the area of a plane figure as a mechanically coupled pointer traverses the figure's perimeter. [French *planimètre* : PLANI- + -METER.] —**plan·i·met·ric** (plánni-méttrik ‖ pláyni-), **pla·ni·met·ri·cal** *adj.* —**pla·ni·met·ri·cal·ly** *adv.* —**pla·nim·e·try** (-nímmətri) *n.*

plan·ish (plánnish) *tr.v.* **-ished, -ishing, -ishes.** To flatten, smooth, toughen, or polish (metal) by rolling or hammering. [French *planir* (present stem *planiss-*), to make level, from *plan,* level, from Latin *plānus.*] —**plan·ish·er** *n.*

pla·ni·sphere (plánni-sfeer, pláyni-) *n.* **1.** A representation of a sphere or part of a sphere on a plane surface. **2.** *Astronomy.* A polar projection of the celestial sphere on a chart equipped with an adjustable overlay to show the stars visible at a particular time and place. [Middle English *planispherie,* from Medieval Latin *plānisphaerium* : PLANI- + -SPHERE.] —**pla·ni·spher·ic** (-sférrik) *adj.*

plank (plangk) *n.* **1.** A long piece of timber cut thicker than a board. **2. a.** *Chiefly U.S.* Any of the policies of a political platform. **b.** Loosely, anything that supports a position: *the chief plank in their argument.* —**walk the plank.** To be forced, as by pirates, to walk down a plank extended over the side of a ship so as to drown. ∼*tr.v.* **planked, planking, planks.** **1.** To furnish, lay, or cover with planks. **2.** To put or set down emphatically or with force. **3.** *U.S.* To bake or grill and serve (fish or meat) on a plank. **4.** *Informal.* To pay at once. Usually used with *down* or *out.* [Middle English *plank(e),* from Old North French *planke,* from Latin *planca.*]

plank·ing (plángking) *n.* Planks considered collectively.

plank-sheer (plángk-sheer) *n.* A horizontal timber forming the outer edge of the upper deck of a wooden ship. Also called "covering board". [Altered (by association with PLANK and SHEER) from earlier *planshire,* Middle English *plancher,* from Old French *planchier,* from *planche,* plank, from Latin *planca.*]

plank·ton (plángk-tən, -ton) *n. Biology.* Plant and animal organisms, generally microscopic, that float or drift in great numbers in fresh or salt water. Compare **nekton.** [German, from Greek, "wanderer", neuter of *planktos,* wandering, from *plazesthai,* to wander, drift.] —**plank·ton·ic** (-tónnik) *adj.*

plan·ner (plánnər) *n.* One who plans; especially, an official responsible for planning architectural development and the use of land.

plan·ning (plánning) *n.* The making of plans, especially for future building and land use. Also used adjectively: *planning department.*

planning permission *n.* Permission from a local or government authority to build on a site, or to alter a building or its use.

plano–, plani– *comb. form.* Indicates flatness; for example, **planometer, planimeter.** [Latin *plānus,* flat.]

pla·no·con·cave (pláynō-kón-kayv, -kən-káyv) *adj.* Flat or plane on one side and concave on the other. Said of a lens.

pla·no·con·vex (pláynō-kón-veks, -kən-véks) *adj.* Flat or plane on one side and convex on the other. Said of a lens.

pla·nog·ra·phy (plə-nóggrəfi, pla-, play-) *n.* A process for printing from a smooth surface, such as lithography or offset. [PLANO- + -GRAPHY.] —**pla·no·graph** (pláyn-ə-graaf, -ō-, -graf) *tr.v.* —**pla·no·graph·ic** (pláyn-ə-gráffik, -ō-) *adj.* —**pla·no·graph·i·cal·ly** *adv.*

pla·nom·e·ter (pla-nómmitər, plə- ‖ play-) *n.* A flat metal plate for gauging the accuracy of a plane surface in precision metalworking; a surface plate. [PLANO- + -METER.] —**plan·o·met·ric** (plán-ō-méttrik, pláyn-, -ə-) *adj.* —**pla·nom·e·try** (-nómmətri) *n.*

plant (plaant ‖ plant) *n.* **1.** Any organism that characteristically has cellulose cell walls, grows by synthesising inorganic substances, lacks the power of locomotion, and lacks specialised sensory organs and nervous tissue. **2.** A plant having no permanent woody stem; a herb, as distinguished from a tree or shrub. *Note:* In this dictionary, *plant* is used in this sense rather than the word *herb,* to avoid confusion with the medicinal and cookery senses of the latter term. **3. a.** Equipment, including machinery, tools, instruments, and fixtures, and the buildings containing them, necessary for any industrial or manufacturing operation. **b.** A factory or other place where industrial processes are carried out. **4.** *U.S.* The buildings, equipment, and fixtures of any institution. **5.** *Informal.* A person secretly placed amongst others in order to observe, spy on, or mislead them. **6.** *Informal.* **a.** A misleading piece of evidence placed so as to be discovered. **b.** Something, especially stolen goods, fraudulently placed so as to incriminate a person. **7.** *Slang.* A scheming trick; a swindle. **8.** In snooker, a situation in which a red ball can be potted by being hit by another red ball that has been hit by the cue ball. ~*tr.v.* **planted, planting, plants. 1.** To place or set (seeds, roots, cuttings, or young plants) in the ground to grow. **2. a.** To furnish or supply (a plot of land) with plants or seeds. **b.** To stock (water) with fish or spawn. **c.** To introduce (an animal) into an area. **3.** To fix or set firmly in position: *He planted both feet on the ground.* **4.** To establish or set up; found: *plant a colony.* **5.** To implant (an idea, sentiment, or the like) in the mind; introduce and establish firmly. **6.** *Informal.* **a.** To place or station (a person) for the purposes of observation, spying, misleading, or the like: *Detectives were planted all over the store.* **b.** To place (something) for the purpose of deception: *plant false evidence.* **7.** *U.S. Informal.* To hide by burying. **8.** *Slang.* To deliver (a blow or punch). [Middle English *plante,* from Old French and Old English, from Latin *planta,* shoot, from *plantāre,* to plant, "drive in with the sole of the foot", from *planta,* sole of the foot.] **—plant·a·ble** *adj.*

Plan·tag·e·net (plan-tájə-nət, -táj-, -nit) *n.* A family and, especially, a line of English kings from Henry II to Richard III (1154–1485) who succeeded the Norman monarchs and descended from Queen Matilda's marriage to Geoffrey, Count of Anjou. The line includes the Angevin, Lancastrian, and Yorkist kings, and ended with the accession of the Tudors. [Middle English, from Old French, sprig of broom (an insignia in the crest of the Counts of Anjou) : Latin *planta,* sprig + *genista,* broom.] **—Plan·tag·e·net** *adj.*

plan·tain¹ (plántin, pláantin) *n.* Any of various plants of the genus *Plantago*; especially, *P. major,* a weed with a rosette of broad leaves and a spike of small, greenish flowers. See **ribgrass.** [Middle English, from Old French, from Latin *plantāgō* (stem *plantagin-*), from *planta,* sole of the foot (from its broad leaves).]

plan·tain² *n.* **1.** A large tropical plant, *Musa paradisiaca,* resembling the banana and bearing similar fruit. **2.** The green-skinned, starchy fruit of this plant, used as a staple food in tropical regions. [Spanish *plántano,* plane tree, from Medieval Latin *plantanus,* variant of Latin *platanus,* PLANE TREE.]

plantain lily *n.* Any of several plants of the genus *Hosta,* native to Asia, widely cultivated for their broad leaves and white, blue, or lilac flowers. Also called "hosta", "day lily".

plan·tar (plánt-ər || -aar) *adj.* Of, pertaining to, or located on the sole of the foot. [Latin *plantāris,* from *planta,* sole of the foot.]

plan·ta·tion (plan-táysh'n, plaan-) *n.* **1.** An area under cultivation. **2.** A group of cultivated trees or plants. **3.** A large estate or farm on which crops such as cotton, tobacco, or sugar are grown and harvested, often by resident workers. **4.** Formerly, a newly established colony or settlement.

plant community *n.* A distinct group of plants that grow in the same habitat and are to some extent dependent on each other.

plant·er (pláant-ər || plánt-) *n.* **1. a.** One who plants. **b.** A machine or tool for planting or sowing seeds. **2.** The owner or manager of a plantation. **3.** An early settler or colonist. **4.** A decorative container for house plants.

plan·ti·grade (plánti-grayd) *adj. Zoology.* Walking with the entire lower surface of the foot on the ground, as humans and bears do. ~*n.* A plantigrade animal. Compare **digitigrade.** [French, from New Latin *plantigradus* : Latin *planta,* sole of the foot + -GRADE.]

plant kingdom *n.* One of the main divisions of the living world, comprising the algae, bryophytes, pteridophytes, and seed plants, and usually the fungi. Compare **animal kingdom, mineral kingdom.**

plant louse *n.* An **aphid** *(see).*

plan·u·la (plánnew-lə) *n., pl.* **-lae** (-lee). The free-swimming, ciliated larva of a coelenterate. [New Latin, from Latin, little plane (from the flatness of the larva), from *plānus,* flat, level.] **—plan·u·lar** *adj.*

plaque (plak, plaak) *n.* **1.** A flat plate, slab, or disc that is ornamented or engraved for mounting, as on a wall for decoration or on a monument for information. **2.** A small pin or brooch worn as an ornament or a badge of membership. **3.** *Pathology.* A small, disc-shaped formation or growth; a patch. **4. Dental plaque** *(see).* **5.** In bacteriology, a clear area in a colony of bacterial cells caused by the localised destruction of bacteria by a bacteriophage. [French, from Old French, metal plate, coin, from Middle Dutch *placke,* from *placken*†, to patch, paste. See also **placard.**]

plash¹ (plash) *n.* **1.** A light splash. **2.** The sound of such a splash. ~*v.* **plashed, plashing, plashes.** —*tr.* To spatter (liquid) about; splash. —*intr.* To splash lightly. [Perhaps from Dutch *plassen,* from Middle Dutch *plasschen* (imitative).]

plash² *tr.v.* **plashed, plashing, plashes.** To interweave (branches, for example); pleach. [Middle English, from Old French *plassier,* from Vulgar Latin *plectiare* (unattested), from Latin *plectere,* to plait.]

plash·y (pláshi) *adj.* **-ier, -iest. 1.** Marshy; wet. **2.** Plashing or splashing.

-plasia, -plasy *n. comb. form.* Indicates growth or change; for example, **hypoplasia, heteroplasy.** [New Latin, from Greek *plasis,* moulding, from *plassein,* to mould.]

plasm (plázz'm) *n.* **1.** See **germ plasm. 2.** Plasma.

-plasm *n. comb. form. Biology.* Indicates the material characteristically forming cells; for example, **protoplasm.** [From PLASMA.]

plas·ma (plázmə) *n.* Also **plasm** (plázz'm). **1. a.** *Physiology.* The clear, yellowish fluid portion of blood, lymph, or intramuscular fluid in which cells are suspended. **b.** *Medicine.* Cell-free, sterilised **blood plasma** *(see),* used in transfusions. **2.** Protoplasm or cytoplasm. **3. Whey** *(see).* **4.** *Physics.* An electrically neutral, highly ionised gas composed of ions, electrons, and neutral particles. [New Latin, extended use of Late Latin *plasma,* a form, mould, from Greek, from *plassein,* to mould.] **—plas·mat·ic** (plaz-máttik), **plas·mic** (plázmik) *adj.*

plasma engine *n.* A hypothetical engine for use in space that generates thrust by emitting a jet of plasma.

plas·ma·gel (plázmə-jel) *n. Biology.* A jelly-like state of cytoplasm, characteristically occurring in the periphery of the cell.

plas·ma·gene (plázmə-jeen) *n. Genetics.* A self-reproducing hereditary structure in cell cytoplasm that functions in a manner analogous to, but independent of, chromosomal genes. **—plas·ma·gen·ic** (-jénnik, -jéenik) *adj.*

plasma membrane *n. Biology.* The semipermeable membrane that encloses the cytoplasm of a cell.

plas·ma·pher·e·sis (plázmə-férrə-siss) *n.* The method of obtaining quantities of plasma, rather than whole blood, from donors for the purpose of transfusion. [New Latin, from PLASMA + Greek *aphesis,* a removal, from *aphairein,* to take away: *apo,* off, away + *hairein,* to take.]

plas·ma·sol (plázmə-sol || -sōl, *U.S. also* -sawl) *n. Biology.* A state of cytoplasm that is more liquid than plasmagel and is found in the interior of the cell. [PLASMA + SOL (colloid).]

plas·min (plázmin) *n. Biochemistry.* A proteolytic enzyme in plasma that dissolves fibrin in blood clots. Also called "fibrinolysin". [PLASM(O)- + -IN.]

plasmo-, plasm- *comb. form.* Indicates plasma or resemblance to plasma; for example, **plasmolysis, plasmin.** [New Latin PLASMA.]

plas·mo·des·ma (pláz-mə-déz-mə, -mō-) *n., pl.* **-mata** (-mətə). Also **plas·mo·desm** (-dezz'm). *Biology.* A strand of living cytoplasm connecting two plant cells that are otherwise functionally separate. [New Latin : PLASMO- + Greek *desma,* a bond, from *dein,* to bind.]

plas·mo·di·um (plaz-mṓdi-əm) *n., pl.* **-dia** (-ə). **1.** Any protozoan of the genus *Plasmodium,* which includes the parasites that cause malaria. **2.** A naked, multinucleate mass of protoplasm such as that characteristic of the vegetative phase of the slime moulds. [New Latin : PLASMO- + -ODE + -IUM.]

plas·mo·lyse, *U.S.* **plas·mo·lyze** (plázmə-līz) *v.* **-lysed, -lysing, -lyses.** —*tr.* To subject to plasmolysis. —*intr.* To undergo plasmolysis. [Back-formation from PLASMOLYSIS.]

plas·mol·y·sis (plaz-móllə-siss) *n. Biology.* Shrinkage or contraction of the protoplasm in a plant or bacterial cell, caused by loss of water through osmosis. [PLASMO- + -LYSIS.] **—plas·mo·lyt·ic** (plázmə-líttik) *adj.* **—plas·mo·lyt·i·cal·ly** *adv.*

plas·mo·some (plázmə-sōm) *n. Biology.* A **nucleolus** *(see).*

-plast *n. comb. form.* Indicates an organised unit of living matter; for example, **protoplast.** [Greek *plastos,* moulded. See **plastic.**]

plas·ter (pláastər || plástər) *n.* **1.** A mixture of lime, sand, and water, sometimes with hair or other fibre added, that hardens to a smooth solid and is used for coating walls and ceilings. **2.** A **sticking plaster** *(see).* **3.** Plaster of Paris. **4.** A pastelike mixture applied to a part of the body for healing or cosmetic purposes. **5.** A **mustard plaster** *(see).*
~*tr.v.* **plastered, -tering, -ters. 1.** To cover, coat, or repair with plaster or similar material. **2.** To cover by or as if by pasting; especially, to cover conspicuously or to excess. **3.** To apply a plaster to. **4.** To cause to adhere to another surface: *"His hair was plastered to his forehead."* (William Golding). **5.** To make smooth by applying a sticky substance. Used with *down*: *plastered down with hair oil.* **6.** *Slang.* To inflict injury, damage, or defeat on: *plastered by the bombers.* [Middle English *plaster,* Old English *plaster,* from Medieval Latin *plastrum,* short for Latin *emplastrum,* from Greek *emplastron, emplaston,* salve, from *emplastos,* past participle of *emplassein,* to daub on, plaster : *em-, en,* in + *plassein,* to mould, plaster.] **—plas·ter·er** *n.*

plas·ter·board (pláastər-bawrd || plástər-, -bōrd) *n.* A thin, rigid board or sheet of layers of fibreboard or paper, with a plaster core, used to cover walls and ceilings.

plaster cast *n.* **1.** A mould or cast of a piece of sculpture or other object made with plaster of Paris. **2.** *Medicine.* A **cast** *(see).*

plas·tered (pláastərd || plástərd) *adj. Slang.* Drunk.

plas·ter·ing (pláast-ər-ing, -ring || plást-) *n.* **1.** A layer or coating of plaster. **2.** *Informal.* A heavy defeat.

plaster of Paris *n.* Any of a group of gypsum cements, essentially hemihydrated calcium sulphate, $2CaSO_4{\cdot}H_2O$, a white powder that forms a paste when mixed with water and hardens into a solid. It is used in making small moulded articles and in surgical casts. Also called "plaster". [Middle English; originally made in *Paris.*]

plaster saint *n. Informal.* A deceptively pious and upright person.

plas·tic (plástik, pláastik) *adj.* **1.** Capable of being shaped or formed; pliable: *Clay is a plastic substance.* **2.** Pertaining to or dealing with shaping or modelling: *the plastic arts.* **3.** Giving form or shape to a substance. **4.** Easily influenced; impressionable. **5.** Made of a plastic or plastics: *a plastic garden hose.* **6.** *Informal.* Synthetic or artificial in taste or appearance: *plastic food.* **7.** *Physics.* Capable of undergoing continuous deformation without breaking or returning to the original size. Said of solids. **8.** *Biology.* Capable of changing or developing tissue; formative. Said of cells and tissues. —See Synonyms at **flexible.**

PRONUNCIATION KEY

a, trap; aa, father; ai, fair; ar, star; aw, lawn; ay, play; b, bb, stab; rubber; ch, church; ck, ticket; d, dd, dead; ladder; e, dress; ee, bee; er, defer; ew, few; ewr, pure; ə, about; ər, letter; f, ff, fife; differ; g, gg, giggle; h, hat; i, kit; ī, price; īr, fire; j, judge; k, kick; l, ll, let; 'l, needle; m, mm, man; n, nn, no; 'n, sudden; ng, thing; o, lot; ō, no; o͞o, foot; o͞o, shoe; oor, poor; ow, cow; owr, hour; oy, boy; p, pp, pepper; r, rr, red; s, ss, sauce; sh, ship; t, tt, totter; th, thick; th, this; smooth; u, cut; ur, turn; v, vv, valve; w, wet; y, yes; z, zz, zebra; zh, vision; pleasure

IN FOREIGN WORDS:

aN, oN, Saint-Saëns; hl, Llanelli; Hluhluwe; kh, loch; lough; Khaled

STRESS MARK:

ín-sīt, insight; in-sít, incite

~n. Any of various materials based on polymerised organic compounds, often with additives such as pigments, fillers, or plasticisers. They can be moulded, extruded, or cast into various shapes and coatings, or drawn into filaments used as textile fibres. [French *plastique,* from Latin *plasticus,* from Greek *plastikos,* fit for moulding, from *plastos,* moulded, from *plassein,* to mould.] —**plas·ti·cal·ly** *adv.* —**plas·tic·i·ty** (plass-tíssəti, plaass-) *n.*

-plastic *adj. comb. form.* Indicates a forming or growing; for example, **cytoplastic.** [Greek *plastikos,* fit for moulding, PLASTIC.]

plastic bullet *n.* A cylindrical piece of plastic, about 10 centimetres (4 inches) long, intended to be fired low among members of a disorderly crowd to disperse it.

plastic explosive *n.* A type of high explosive in the form of a mouldable jelly, used with a detonator.

Plas·ti·cine (pláss-tə-seen, plaáss-, -ti-) *n.* A trademark for a putty-like modelling material used especially by children.

plas·ti·cise, plas·ti·cize (plásti-sīz, plaásti-) *v.* -**cised, -cising, -cises.** —*tr.* To make plastic. —*intr.* To become plastic.

plas·ti·cis·er (plásti-sīzər, plaásti-) *n.* Any of various substances added to plastics or other materials to keep them soft or pliable.

plastic money *n.* Credit cards. Used humorously.

plastic surgery *n.* Cosmetic or remedial surgery to remodel, repair, or restore injured or defective tissue or body parts. —**plastic surgeon** *n.*

plas·tid (plástid, plaástid) *n. Biology.* Any of several specialised cytoplasmic structures occurring in plant cells and in some plantlike organisms, and having various physiological functions. [German *Plastid, Plastiden* (plural), from Greek *plastides,* feminine plural of *plastēs,* moulder, sculptor, from *plastos,* moulded, from *plassein,* to mould.] —**plas·tid·i·al** (plass-tíddi-əl, plaass-) *adj.*

plas·tron (pláss-trən, -tron) *n.* 1. A breastplate worn under a coat of mail. 2. A protective breastplate worn by fencers. 3. A trimming on the front of a bodice. 4. The front of a man's dress shirt. 5. *Zoology.* The ventral surface of the shell of a turtle or tortoise. 6. *Anatomy.* The breastbone together with the cartilages associated with it. [Old French, from Old Italian *piastrone,* augmentative of *piastra,* "metal plate", from Latin *emplastra, emplastrum,* PLASTER.] —**plas·tral** (-trəl) *adj.*

-plasty *n. comb. form.* Indicates plastic surgery; for example, **dermatoplasty.** [Greek *-plastia,* from *plastos,* moulded. See **plastic.**]

-plasy. Variant of **-plasia.**

plat¹ (plat) *tr.v.* **platted, platting, plats.** *Regional.* To plait or braid. ~*n. Regional.* A plait. [Middle English *platen,* variant of *plaiten,* to PLAIT.]

plat² 1. *Archaic.* A small area of ground; a patch. 2. *U.S.* A chart, plan, or the like, especially one showing the proposed design of a town or group of buildings. [Variant of PLOT.]

plat. 1. platform. 2. platoon.

Pla·ta, Rí·o de la (plaáta, rée-ō dellə). *English* **River Plate** (playt). Estuary in South America, formed by the confluence of the rivers Paraná and Uruguay. It proceeds into the Atlantic Ocean.

plat·an (plátt'n) *n.* A plane tree *(see).* [Middle English, from Latin *platanus,* PLANE TREE.]

plat·an·na (plát-ánnə) *n. South African.* See **xenopus.**

plate (playt) *n.* 1. **a.** A shallow dish in which food is served or from which it is eaten. **b.** The contents of such a dish. **c.** The amount a plate will hold; a plateful. **d.** *U.S.* A whole course served on such a dish. 2. *U.S.* Food and service for one person at a meal: *dinner at a set price per plate.* 3. **a.** Household utensils covered with a thin layer of precious metal, such as gold or silver. **b.** Articles, in a church for example, made of gold and silver. **c.** A dish passed among a congregation for the collection of offerings. 5. **a.** A smooth, flat, relatively thin, rigid body of uniform thickness. 6. **a.** A sheet of hammered, rolled, or cast metal. **b.** A very thin plated coat or layer of metal. **c.** Metal or metal objects coated with such a layer. 7. **a.** A flat piece of metal forming part of a machine: *a boiler plate.* **b.** A flat piece of metal on which something is engraved. **c.** A number plate on a motor vehicle. 8. **a.** A thin piece of metal used for armour. **b.** Armour made of this. 9. *Abbr.* **pl.** *Printing.* **a.** A sheet of metal, plastic, rubber, paperboard, or other material converted into a printing surface, such as an electrotype or stereotype. **b.** A print of a woodcut, lithograph, or other engraved material, especially when reproduced in a book. **c.** A full-page book illustration, often in colour and printed on paper different from that used on the text pages. 10. *Abbr.* **pl.** *Photography.* A light-sensitive sheet of glass or metal upon which an image can be recorded. 11. A **dental plate** *(see).* 12. *Architecture.* In wood-frame construction, a horizontal member, capping the exterior wall studs, upon which the roof rafters rest. 13. In baseball, a flat piece of heavy rubber set in the ground that is used to define the place over which the ball must be thrown by a pitcher for a strike. Also called "home plate". 14. *Sports.* **a.** A dish, cup, or other trophy offered as a prize. **b.** A contest, especially a horse race, offering such a prize. 15. *Anatomy & Zoology.* **a.** A thin, flat layer or scale. **b.** A platelike part or organ. 16. *Electronics.* **a.** An electrode, as in a storage battery or capacitor. **b.** *U.S.* The anode in a thermionic valve. 17. Any of the regions of the earth's crust. See **plate tectonics.** —**on a plate.** So as to be easily available or taken without effort. —**on (one's) plate.** *Informal.* Requiring one's attention: *I've a lot on my plate just now.* ~*tr.v.* **plated, plating, plates.** 1. To coat or cover with a thin layer of metal. 2. To armour. 3. *Printing.* To make a stereotype or electrotype from. 4. To give a glossy finish to (paper) by pressing between metal sheets or rollers. [Middle English, from Old French,

from feminine of *plat,* flat, from Vulgar Latin *plattus* (unattested), from Greek *platus,* broad, flat.]

pla·teau (pla-tṓ, plə-, plátto) *n., pl.* **-teaus** or **-teaux** (-z). 1. An elevated and comparatively level expanse of land; tableland. 2. A relatively stable or quiescent period or state; a levelling off: *a plateau of business activity.* 3. A flat region on a graph. [French, from Old French *platel,* a flat piece, from *plat,* flat, from Vulgar Latin *plattus* (unattested), from Greek *platus,* broad, flat.]

plat·ed (pláytid) *adj.* 1. Coated with a thin layer of metal. Often used in combination: *gold-plated.* 2. Covered or furnished with plates or sheets of metal. Often used in combination: *armour-plated.* 3. Knitted with two kinds of wool, one on the face and one on the back.

plate·ful (pláyt-fŏŏl) *n., pl.* **-fuls.** 1. The amount of food or other substance that a plate will hold. 2. A generous portion of food.

plate glass *n.* Rolled and polished flat glass containing few impurities, used for mirrors and windows.

plate·lay·er (pláyt-lay-ər) *n. British.* A person who lays and maintains railway track.

plate·let (pláyt-lət, -lit) *n.* An irregular-shaped disc, smaller than a red blood cell, that is found in the blood of vertebrates and promotes coagulation. Also called "blood platelet", "thrombocyte". [Diminutive of PLATE.]

plate·mark (pláyt-maark) *n.* A mark on metal, a **hallmark** *(see).*

plat·en (plátt'n) *n.* 1. A flat plate in a printing press that serves to position the paper and hold it against the inked type. 2. The roller on a typewriter against which the keys strike. [Earlier *plattin,* from Old French *platine,* from *plate,* PLATE.]

plat·er (pláytər) *n.* 1. One that plates. 2. *Slang.* An inferior racehorse.

plate tectonics *n.* 1. The theory that the earth's crust is composed of a series of rigid plates and that movement of these plates in relation to each other is responsible for all the features of the earth's surface. 2. The study of the earth's crust based on this theory.

plat·form (plát-fawrm) *n. Abbr.* **plat.** 1. A floor or horizontal surface raised above the level of the adjacent area, especially: **a.** A stage for public speaking. **b.** A raised area alongside the tracks in a railway station where passengers may alight from or board trains. 2. An area in certain buses reserved for the conductor, next to the seating area. 3. A thick raised sole or heel on certain types of shoes and boots. Also used adjectively: *platform soles.* 4. The declared policies with which a political figure or group makes an appeal to an electorate. [French, "ground plan", from Old French, "flat form" : feminine of *plat,* flat (see **plateau**) + *forme,* FORM.]

platform balance *n.* An equal-arm balance having two flat platforms above the beam and frequently using a sliding rider instead of weights.

platform scale *n.* A weighing instrument consisting of a platform coupled to an automatic system of levers and adjustable weights, designed to move a pointer over a scale.

Plath (plath), **Sylvia** (1932–63). U.S. poet. She established her reputation with her collection *The Colossus* (1960). In 1963 she committed suicide, and her posthumous collection *Ariel* (1968) contains poems of intense anguish.

plat·ing (pláyting) *n.* 1. A thin layer or coating of metal, such as gold or silver. 2. A covering or layer of metal sheets or plates.

pla·tin·ic (plə-tínnik) *adj. Chemistry.* Of, pertaining to, or containing platinum. Said especially of compounds containing platinum with a valency of 4. [PLATIN- + -IC.]

plat·i·nise, plat·i·nize (plátti-nīz) *tr.v.* **-nised, -nising, -nises.** To coat with platinum, as by electroplating or vacuum evaporation. [PLATIN(I)- + -IZE.]

plat·i·nised (plátti-nīzd) *adj.* Coated or treated with platinum; especially, coated with finely divided platinum: *platinised asbestos.*

platino-, platin-, platini- *comb. form.* Indicates the presence or characteristics of platinum: for example, **platinotype, platinoid.**

plat·i·noid (plát-noyd) *adj.* Like platinum. ~*n.* 1. An alloy of copper, nickel, tungsten, and zinc, formerly used in electric coils. 2. Any metal resembling platinum chemically, especially osmium, iridium, or palladium. [PLATIN(O)- + -OID.]

plat·i·no·type (pláttinō-tīp) *n.* 1. A process formerly used for making photographic prints, using a finely precipitated platinum salt and an iron salt in the sensitising solution to produce photographic prints in platinum black. 2. A photographic print produced by this process. [PLATINO- + -TYPE.]

plat·i·nous (pláttinəss) *adj. Chemistry.* Of, pertaining to, or containing platinum. Said especially of compounds containing platinum with a valency of 2.

plat·i·num (pláttinəm) *n.* 1. *Symbol* Pt A silver-white metallic element occurring worldwide, usually mixed with other metals such as iridium, osmium, or gold. It is ductile and malleable, does not oxidise in air, and is used in electrical components, jewellery, dentistry, electroplating, and as a catalyst. Atomic number 78, atomic weight 195.09, melting point 1773.5°C, boiling point 3827°C, relative density 21.45, valencies 2, 4. 2. Medium to light bluish grey. [New Latin, from Spanish *platina,* PLATINA.]

platinum black *n.* A fine black powder of metallic platinum, used as a catalyst and as a gas absorbent.

platinum blonde *n.* 1. A very light silver-blond hair colour. 2. A person having hair of this colour. See Usage note at **blond.** —**platinum blonde** *adj.*

platinum metals *pl.n.* The group of chemically related elements ruthenium, osmium, rhodium, iridium, palladium, and platinum.

---

plate tectonics

THE WORLD'S CONTINENTS ARE ON THE MOVE
Mountains rise up and earthquakes shake the Earth

Some 200 million years ago, all the continents of the world were grouped together in a single supercontinent which geologists call Pangaea (from the Greek word that means "all earth"). Beneath the Earth's outer shell, or lithosphere, there is a molten layer, called the asthenosphere, through which slow convection currents exercised their force on Pangaea. Gradually the single landmass broke up and separate pieces of it began moving to their present positions.

The lithosphere is composed of a number of rigid plates colliding or growing apart or sliding past each other. This movement is continuous and measurable – the Atlantic Ocean expands by a few centimetres a year as Europe and America draw apart. The Indian Ocean is also expanding but the Pacific and the Mediterranean are becoming smaller.

Where continental plates collide they cause the Earth's crust to buckle and throw up mountains – the

Himalayas have been pushed up by the constant pressure of the Indian plate on the Asian plate.

Ocean ridges occur where molten rock rises through a rift fault in the ocean floor to form new lithosphere. The oceanic plate becomes larger and is forced against a continental plate, forming a subduction zone. Here the less dense ocean floor sinks back into the Earth's molten interior, perhaps under the pressure of gravity or convection currents.

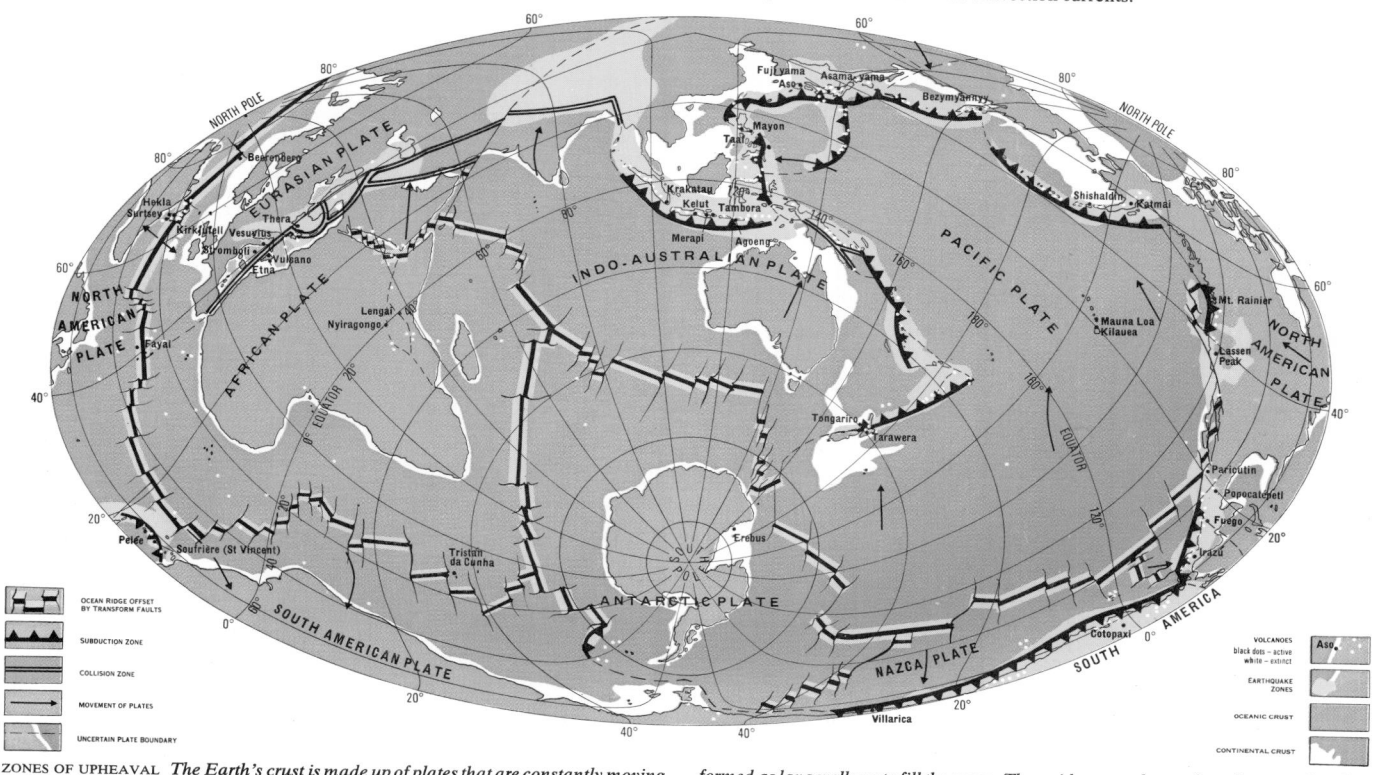

ZONES OF UPHEAVAL *The Earth's crust is made up of plates that are constantly moving. The areas where two plates push together – subduction or collision zones – make up the world's volcano and earthquake belts. Where plates move apart, mid-ocean ridges are formed as lava wells up to fill the space. These ridges are also earthquake areas. In other parts of the world, including California, two plates travelling in the same direction at slightly different speeds grind jerkily past each other.*

---

plat·i·tude (plátti-tewd ‖ -tōōd) *n.* **1.** A trite, unoriginal, sententious remark or statement. **2.** Lack of originality; triteness. [French, "flatness", from *plat*, flat, from Old French, from Vulgar Latin *plattus* (unattested), from Greek *platus*, broad, flat.] —**plat·i·tud·i·nise** (-téwd-i-nīz ‖ -tōōd-) *intr.v.* —**plat·i·tu·di·nous** (-téwd-inəss ‖ -tōōd-) *adj.*

Pla·to (pláytō) (c. 428–347 B.C.). Greek philosopher, a major influence on Western thought. An Athenian aristocrat, he became a devoted admirer of Socrates. In about 386 he founded the Academy, where he taught and wrote for much of the rest of his life. Plato presented his philosophy in the form of dramatic *Dialogues* in which Socrates conducts the discussions, as in *The Republic*, where he proposes a system for educating rulers as "philosopher kings".

Pla·ton·ic (plə-tónnik ‖ *U.S. also* play-) *adj.* Also **Pla·ton·i·cal** (-'l). **1.** Of, pertaining to, or characteristic of Plato or his philosophy. **2. a.** *Often small* p. Transcending physical desire and tending towards the purely spiritual or ideal: *platonic love.* **b.** *Small* p. Intimate, but not indulging in sexual intimacy: *a platonic relationship.* [Latin *Platonicus*, from Greek *Platōn*, Plato.] —**Pla·ton·i·cal·ly** *adv.*

Pla·to·nise, Pla·to·nize (pláytə-nīz) *v.* **-nised, -nising, -nises.** —*intr.* To adopt or adhere to the philosophy of Plato. —*tr.* To explain in accordance with Platonic philosophy.

Pla·to·nism (pláyt'n-iz'm) *n.* The philosophy of Plato, especially the view that asserts that the phenomena of the world are an imperfect and transitory copy of a transcendent world of archetypal forms. —**Pla·to·nist** *n.*

pla·toon (plə-tōōn) *n. Abbr.* **plat. 1.** A subdivision of a military company divided into squads or sections. **2.** A body of persons working together. [French *peloton*, "little ball", group of soldiers, from Old French *pelote*, from Vulgar Latin *pilotta* (unattested), diminutive of Latin *pila*, ball. See **pill**.]

Platt·deutsch (plát-doych) *n.* The Low German vernacular of northern Germany. [German, from Dutch *platduits* : *plat*, flat, low, clear, from Middle Dutch, from Old French, flat (see **platitude**) + *Duitsch*, German, from Middle Dutch *duutsch*.]

plat·te·land (pláttə-lant) *n. South African.* Rural districts; country areas. [Afrikaans, "flat land".] —**plat·te·land·er** (-landər) *n.*

plat·ter (pláttər) *n.* **1. a.** A large, shallow, often wooden dish or plate, used especially for serving food. **b.** A meal served on such a dish. **2.** *Chiefly U.S. Slang.* A gramophone record. [Middle English *plater*, from Anglo-French, from Old French *plate*, **PLATE**.]

plat·y¹ (pláyti) *adj.* **-ier, -iest.** Designating soil or minerals occurring in flaky layers.

platy² (plátti) *n., pl.* **platy, platys,** or **platies.** Any of several small freshwater fishes of the genus *Xiphophorus*, of southern North America; especially, *X. maculatus*, a colourful aquarium fish. Also called "platyfish". [New Latin *Platypoecilus*, "flat and colourful" (Greek *poikilos*, variegated), from Greek *platus*, broad, flat.]

platy– *comb. form.* Indicates flatness; for example, **platyhelminth.** [Greek *platus*, broad, flat.]

plat·y·hel·minth (plátti-hélminth) *n. Zoology.* Any of various parasitic and nonparasitic worms of the phylum Platyhelminthes, such as a tapeworm or a planarian, characteristically having a flattened body. Also called "flatworm". [**PLATY-** + Greek *helmis* (stem *helminth-*), parasitic worm.] —**plat·y·hel·min·thic** (-hel-mínthik) *adj.*

plat·y·pus (plátti-pəss ‖ -pōōss) *n., pl.* **-puses.** The duck-billed **platypus** (*see*). [New Latin, from Greek *platupous*, "flat-footed" : **PLATY-** + *pous*, foot.]

plat·yr·rhine (plátti-rīn) *adj.* Also **plat·yr·rhin·i·an** (plátti-rínni-ən). **1.** *Anthropology.* Having a broad, flat nose. **2.** *Zoology.* Of or designating the New World monkeys, many of which are characterised by widely separated nostrils.

~n. Also **plat·yr·rhin·i·an**. A platyrrhine person or monkey. [New Latin *Platyrrhina*, "flat-nosed ones", from *platyrrhinus*, flat-nosed, from Greek *platurrhis, platurrhinos* : PLATY- + Greek *rhis* (stem *rhin-*), nose (see **rhino-**).]

plau·dit (pláwdit) n. Usually plural. Enthusiastic approbation or praise; especially, critical approval. [Originally "an appeal for applause", from Latin *plaudite*, imperative of *plaudere*, to applaud.]

plau·si·ble (pláwz-ə-b'l, -i-) adj. 1. Seemingly or apparently valid, likely, or acceptable: *a plausible excuse*. 2. Giving a deceptive impression of truth, acceptability, or reliability; specious. [Originally "deserving applause", acceptable, from Latin *plausibilis*, from *plaudere* (past participle *plausus*), to applaud, acclaim.] —**plau·si·bil·i·ty** (-billəti), **plau·si·ble·ness** n. —**plau·si·bly** adv.

plau·sive (pláw-siv, -ziv) adj. 1. Showing or expressing praise or approbation; applauding. 2. Obsolete. Plausible. [Latin *plaudere*, to applaud.]

Plau·tus (pláwtəss), **Titus Maccius** (c. 254–184 B.C.). Roman comic dramatist. Twenty-one of his comedies survive, all adapted from Greek sources to which he added his own earthy Roman humour. His imitators included Shakespeare and Molière.

play (play) v. **played, playing, plays.** —intr. 1. To occupy oneself in amusing or diverting activities; especially, to engage in childish games. 2. a. To take part in a game. b. To participate in a betting game; gamble. 3. To act in jest or sport. 4. To deal or behave carelessly or indifferently; toy; trifle. Usually used with *with*. 5. To allow a specified type of play. Used of a sports ground: *the court is playing slow*. 6. a. To act or behave in a specified way: *play fair*. b. Informal. To cooperate: *I asked them but they won't play*. 7. To act or perform, especially in a dramatic production. 8. To perform on a musical instrument. 9. To emit sound or be sounded in performance: *The band is playing*. 10. To be performed or shown, as in a theatre or cinema: *Othello is playing next week*. 11. To move or seem to move quickly, lightly, or irregularly: *The breeze played on the water*. 12. To function or operate uninterruptedly; especially, to discharge a steady stream: *The fountains played in the courtyard*. 13. To move or operate freely within a bounded space, as machine parts do. —tr. 1. a. To perform or act (a role or part) in a dramatic performance. b. To assume the role of; act as: *play Iago*. 2. To put on or perform (a drama or other theatrical work) on or as if on the stage. 3. To put on or produce a theatrical, musical, or other performance in (a specified place): *played Bristol last week*. 4. To pretend to be; mimic the activities of: *The boys played cowboys and Indians*. 5. To participate in (a game or sport). 6. To compete against in a game or sport. 7. a. To occupy or work at (a position) in a game: *He plays goalkeeper*. b. To employ the position of in a game: *play Russell at centre forward*. c. To use or move (a card, piece, or the like) in a game: *play the ace*. d. To make (a shot or stroke), as in tennis: *played a forehand*. 8. To perform or put into effect, especially as a trick or deception: *play a joke on someone*. 9. To use or manipulate (two or more competitors, for example) for one's own interests: *play them against each other*. 10. a. To bet on; wager. b. To make a wager on. 11. à. To perform on (a musical instrument): *play the guitar*. b. To perform (music) on an instrument or instruments. 12. To cause (a record or record player, for example) to emit recorded sounds. 13. To discharge, set off, or cause to operate in or as if in a continuous stream: *play a hose on a fire*. 14. To cause to move rapidly, lightly, or irregularly: *play lights over the dance floor*. 15. In angling, to exhaust (a hooked fish) by allowing it to pull on the line. —**play about** or **around**. 1. To act in a silly or frivolous way, often so as to annoy: *Stop playing about and tell me!* —**play along**. To deceive or give a false impression to. —**play along with**. To cooperate with a plan or person, for example, especially out of self-interest. —**play at**. To participate in or engage in half-heartedly or frivolously. —**play down**. To minimise the importance of; make little of: *play down one's failings*. —**play down to**. To act or behave in a condescending manner towards. —**play on**. Also **play upon** (for sense 1). 1. To take advantage of (another's attitudes or feelings) for one's own interests. 2. In cricket, to allow the ball to hit the wicket after hitting it. Used of a batsman. —**play (oneself) in**. To introduce or accustom (oneself) gradually to a new situation. —**play out**. 1. To do or play until completed; finish. 2. To accompany the departure of with music. —**play up**. Informal. 1. To emphasise or publicise: *play up one's conquests*. 2. To act or behave in a way so as to cause irritation or discomfort. 3. To engage in an activity wholeheartedly. —**play up to**. Informal. 1. To support (another actor) in a performance. 2. To try to ingratiate oneself with.

~n. 1. a. A dramatic work written for performance on the stage; a drama. b. The performance of such a work. 2. Activity engaged in for enjoyment or recreation, especially as a childish pastime. 3. Fun or jesting: *done in play*. 4. a. The act of carrying on or engaging in a game or sport. b. The manner or way of playing a game or sport. 5. A manner or method of dealing with people generally. Used especially in the phrases *foul play* and *fair play*. 6. A turn, move or action in a game: *It's your play*. 7. Participation in betting; gambling. 8. Sports. The condition of a ball, puck, or similar object in active or legitimate use or motion during a game. Used in the phrases *in play* and *out of play*. 9. Action, motion, or use: *the play of the imagination*. 10. Quick, often irregular movement or action, especially of light or colour: *the play of the light*. 11. Movement or space or scope for movement: *give the rope more play*. —**bring** or **call into play**. To cause to operate; activate. —**make a play for**. Informal. To attempt to attract or obtain by using art, wiles, or

skill. —**make great play with**. To exploit enthusiastically. [As verb, Middle English *playen*, from Old English *plegan*; as noun, Middle English *pley, play*, Old English *plega*.] —**play·a·ble** (pláy-əb'l) adj.

pla·ya (plī-ə) n. U.S. 1. An inland drainage basin, surrounded by sheets of saline or alkaline crust and containing a shallow lake. 2. The lake in such a basin. [Spanish, "shore", from Medieval Latin *plagia*, from Greek, sides, neuter plural of *plagios*. See **plagio-**.]

play-act (pláy-akt) intr.v. **-acted, -acting, -acts.** 1. To play a pretended role; make believe. 2. To behave in an overdramatic or artificial manner. —**play-acting** n. —**play-actor** n.

play back tr.v. To replay (a recording). —intr. 1. In cricket, to step back in order to hit the ball. 2. To replay a recording.

play·back (pláy-bak) n. 1. The act or process of replaying a newly made record or tape. 2. A method of or apparatus for reproducing sound recordings.

play·bill (pláy-bil) n. 1. A poster announcing a theatrical performance. 2. U.S. A programme for a theatrical performance.

play·boy (pláy-boy) n. A wealthy, often suave, carefree man, especially one who regularly indulges in the pleasures of nightclubs, sports, and female company.

play·er (pláy-ər) n. 1. One who participates in a game or sport, especially professionally. 2. One who performs in theatrical roles; an actor. 3. One who plays a musical instrument. 4. The mechanism actuating a player piano. 5. An apparatus for reproducing recorded sound: *a cassette player*. 6. A gambler. 7. A trifler.

Player, Gary (Jim) (1935–). South African professional golfer, winner of numerous international tournaments.

player piano n. A mechanically operated piano that uses a perforated paper roll to actuate the keys.

play·ful (pláyf'l) adj. 1. Full of fun and good spirits; frolicsome; sportive: *a playful kitten*. 2. Humorous; jesting: *a playful comment*. —**play·ful·ly** adv. —**play·ful·ness** n.

Synonyms: playful, mischievous, impish, waggish, frivolous.

play-go·er (pláy-gō-ər) n. One who regularly attends the theatre.

play·ground (pláy-grownd) n. 1. An outdoor area set aside for recreation and play, as in a school; especially, one containing seesaws, swings, and the like. 2. Broadly, any area in which one may enjoy oneself: *The Riviera is a millionaire's playground*.

play·group (pláy-grōōp) n. A supervised gathering of children of preschool age where they can engage in games and other activities.

play·house (pláy-howss) n. 1. A theatre. 2. A small house for children to play in. 3. U.S. A child's toy house; a doll's house.

playing card n. Any of a pack of cards with a design designating its value in the colour of one of the four **suits** (see), and used in various card games.

playing field n. A field for games such as cricket and soccer.

play·mate (pláy-mayt) n. A companion in play or recreation.

play off intr.v. 1. To use or manipulate (two or more competitors) especially for one's own interests: *She played her two suitors off against each other*. 2. Sports. To establish the winner of (a tie) by playing an additional game or series of games. —intr.v. Sports. To participate or meet in a play-off.

play-off (pláy-off, -awff) n. Sports. 1. A final game or series of games played to break a tie. 2. U.S. A series of games played to determine a championship.

play·pen (pláy-pen) n. A portable enclosure in which a baby or young child can be left to play.

play·room (pláy-rōōm, -rŏŏm) n. A room designed or set aside for recreation or playing.

play·school (pláy-skōōl) n. Educational activities based on play for preschool children.

play·suit (pláy-sewt, -sōōt) n. A garment designed for a young child to play in.

play·thing (pláy-thing) n. 1. Something to play with; a toy. 2. One treated as a toy: *a plaything of fate*.

play·time (pláy-tīm) n. Time devoted to recreation, especially as a break from school lessons.

play·wright (pláy-rīt) n. One who writes plays; a dramatist.

pla·za (pláázə, plázzə) n. A public square or similar open area, especially in towns or cities of Spanish-speaking countries. [Spanish, from Vulgar Latin *plattea* (unattested), variant of Latin *platea*, broad street. See **place**.]

plc, PLC, p.l.c., P.L.C. public limited company.

plea (plee) n. 1. An appeal or entreaty: *a plea for leniency*. 2. An excuse; a pretext: *"Necessity, the tyrant's plea"* (Milton). 3. Law. a. In civil cases, a defendant's answer to the declaration made by the plaintiff. b. In criminal law, the answer of the accused to a charge or indictment. c. Formerly, an action or suit. [Middle English *plai(d), plee*, a lawsuit, pleading, from Anglo-French *plai, ple*, Old French *plaid*, legal action, agreement, decree, from Medieval Latin *placitum*, from Latin, "something agreeable", opinion, decision, from the neuter of *placitus*, pleasing, agreeable, from the past participle of *placēre*, to please.]

plea bargaining n. The practice, especially between defending and prosecuting counsel, of reaching agreement over the charge on which the defendant should stand trial, normally resulting in the defendant pleading guilty to a less serious offence than that with which he could otherwise be charged (and would be so charged, were he to plead not guilty).

pleach (pleech ‖ playch) tr.v. **pleached, pleaching, pleaches.** To plait or interlace (branches or twigs, for example), especially in making a hedge or an arbour. [Middle English *plechen*, from Old

North French *plechier*, from Latin *plectere* (past participle *plexus*), to weave, plait.]

plead (pleed) *v.* **pleaded** or *Chiefly U.S. & Scottish* **pled** (pled), **pleading**, **pleads.** —*intr.* **1.** To appeal earnestly; implore; beg: *pleaded with her to stay.* **2.** To argue or offer persuasive reasons for or against something. **3.** To furnish or provide an argument or appeal: *His misfortunes plead for him.* **4.** *Law.* **a.** To put forward a plea of a specified nature in a court of law: *plead guilty.* **b.** To enter an answer or pleading on behalf of a defendant or as part of the prosecution in a law action. **c.** To address a court as a lawyer or advocate. —*tr.* **1.** To assert or put forward as defence, vindication, or excuse; submit as a plea: *plead illness.* **2.** To present as an answer to a charge, indictment, or declaration made against one. **3. a.** *Law.* To argue or present (a case) in a court of law. **b.** To present the arguments for (a cause). [Middle English *pleden*, from Anglo-French, from Old French *plaidier.* See **plea.**] —**plead·a·ble** *adj.* —**plead·er** *n.*

plead·ing (plée·ding) *n.* **1. a.** The act of entreating or making a plea. **b.** A plea or entreaty thus made. **2.** *Law.* **a.** The art or procedure of one who acts as an advocate in a law court. **b.** The act or technique of drawing up or presenting pleas in legal cases. **c.** A formal statement, generally written, propounding the cause of action or the defence of a legal case. **d.** *Plural.* The consecutive statements, allegations, and counterallegations made in turn by plaintiff and defendant, or prosecutor and accused, until a single issue is reached upon which the trial may be held. —**plead·ing·ly** *adv.*

pleas·ance (plézz'nss) *n. Archaic.* **1.** A secluded, landscaped area, such as the garden of a mansion. **2.** Pleasure or a source of pleasure. [Old French *(maison de) plaisance,* "(house of) pleasure", from *plaisant,* PLEASANT.]

pleas·ant (plézz'nt) *adj.* **1.** Giving or affording pleasure or enjoy-

---

playing cards

THE MYSTERIOUS ORIGINS OF PLAYING CARDS

Were they first known in China, Arabia, or Europe?

Playing cards may have originated in China, where they were developed from paper money, or they may have been invented independently in Europe, where they were first heard of in Italy in 1300. Or they may have been introduced to Europe by the Arabs, after they conquered Sicily and Spain.

The modern deck was developed from the 78-card Tarot deck, used for both fortune-telling and games, which has four suits – swords, cups, coins, and batons.

Today's familiar 52-card deck emerged in France in the early 15th century. Italian and Spanish cards still have the Tarot suits. The German suits are hearts, bells, acorns, and leaves. The French and English suits are spades, hearts, diamonds, and clubs, although the "club" of English-speaking countries is really a trefoil, and the "spade" is the head of a pike.

1500 *German card suits are bells, leaves, hearts, and acorns. This bell of 1500 is probably a knave.*

1678 *An English card illustrating the Popish Plot of 1678, a supposed plan to murder Charles II.*

ORIENTAL CARDS

In India and Iran, cards are all handmade on slivers of wood, cardboard, fabric, or leather. The cards are handpainted and coated with lacquer, making them much thicker than factory-produced European cards.

IRAN *This Shah (or King) is one of 25 cards in the Iranian pack of five suits.*

1840 *Some English cards of the 19th century made the suit signs into scenes – in this case a sword fight.*

MODERN *Double-headed cards were introduced in the 18th century, but did not become standard until after 1870.*

INDIA *A Mir (or King) of the Moon suit in one type of pack. Most Indian cards are circular.*

ment; agreeable. **2.** Pleasing in manner, appearance, or other personal qualities. **3.** Fair and comfortable. **4.** *Obsolete.* Merry; lively. —See Synonyms at **amiable.** [Middle English *plesaunt,* from Old French *plaisant,* from the present participle of *plaisir,* to PLEASE.] **—pleas·ant·ly** *adv.* **—pleas·ant·ness** *n.*

pleas·ant·ry (plézz'ntri) *n., pl.* **-ries. 1.** A jesting, entertaining, or humorous remark or action: *exchanged pleasantries.* **2.** Pleasingly humorous style or manner in conversation or at social occasions. [French *plaisanterie,* from *plaisant,* PLEASANT.]

please (pleez) *v.* **pleased, pleasing, pleases.** *—tr.* **1.** To give enjoyment, pleasure, or satisfaction to; make glad or contented. **2.** *Formal.* To be the will or desire of. Used impersonally with *it: May it please you to accept our gifts.* *—intr.* **1.** To give satisfaction or pleasure; be agreeable. **2.** To have the will or desire; wish: *Do whatever you please.* **—be pleased to.** *Formal.* To be willing to; agree to: *He was pleased to grant me an audience.* **—please (oneself).** To do or act as one likes. **—if you please. 1.** If it is your will, desire, or pleasure. **2.** If you can believe or imagine it. Used as an ironical expression of indignation or surprise.

~interj. Used: **1.** To indicate a polite request. **2.** To express an earnest wish or protest. [Middle English *plaisen, plesen,* from Old French *plaisir,* from Latin *placēre.*]

Usage: The usual intensive accompanying *pleased* in British English is *very;* In American English, *very much* is also used, and often preferred. The usual prepositions following *pleased* are *with (He was pleased with my work), about (He was pleased about my new job),* and *at (He was pleased at seeing me win). Over* is sometimes used informally instead of *about* and *at,* but is open to criticism.

pleas·ing (pleézing) *adj.* Giving pleasure or enjoyment; agreeable; gratifying. **—pleas·ing·ly** *adv.* **—pleas·ing·ness** *n.*

pleas·ur·a·ble (plézh-ərəb'l, -rəb'l) *adj.* Agreeable; gratifying. **—pleas·ur·a·ble·ness** *n.* **—pleas·ur·a·bly** *adv.*

pleas·ure (plézhər) *n.* **1. a.** An enjoyable sensation or emotion; *got pleasure from swimming.* **b.** Satisfaction; delight: *I'll do it with pleasure.* **2.** A source of enjoyment, gratification, or delight. **3.** Amusement, diversion, or worldly enjoyment: *"Pleasure . . . is a safer guide than either right or duty."* (Samuel Butler). Also used adjectivally: *a pleasure cruise.* **4.** Sensual gratification or indulgence. **5.** One's preference, wish, or choice: *What is your pleasure?*

~v. **pleasured, -uring, -ures.** *—tr.* **1.** *Archaic.* To give pleasure or enjoyment to; please; gratify. **2.** To gratify sexually. Used euphemistically. *—intr. Archaic.* To take pleasure; delight. Often used with *in.* [Middle English *plesure,* (earlier) *plesir,* from Old French *plaisir,* noun use of *plaisir,* to PLEASE.]

Synonyms: *pleasure, enjoyment, delight, joy.*

pleasure principle *n.* In psychoanalysis, the drive to seek immediate gratification of instinctual needs and to reduce pain. [Translation of German *Lustprinzip.*]

pleat (pleet) *n.* A fold in cloth or other material, made by doubling the material upon itself and then pressing or stitching into place.

~tr.v. **pleated, pleating, pleats.** To press or arrange in pleats. [Middle English, variant of PLAIT.]

pleb (pleb) *n.* *Informal.* A person of the lower classes; a plebeian. Used derogatorily. [Short for PLEBEIAN.] **—pleb·by** (plébbi) *adj.*

plebe (pleeb) *n.* A freshman at the U.S. Military or Naval Academy. [Short for PLEBEIAN.]

ple·be·ian (pli-beé-ən) *adj.* **1.** Of or pertaining to the Roman plebs. In this sense, compare **patrician. 2.** Of, belonging to, or characteristic of common people. **3.** Crude; vulgar; low: *plebeian tastes.*

~n. **1.** A member of the Roman plebs. **2.** A member of the lower classes. **3.** Someone who is vulgar or coarse. [Latin *plēbēius,* from *plēbs,* common people.] **—ple·be·ian·ism** *n.*

pleb·i·scite (plébbi-sīt, -sit) *n.* **1.** A direct vote in which the entire electorate of a country, region, or other political unit is invited to accept or refuse the measure, programme, or government of the person or party initiating the consultation. **2.** Such a vote whereby a population exercises the right of national self-determination. Compare **referendum.** [French *plébiscite,* from Latin *plēbiscītum,* people's decree : *plēbi,* genitive of *plēbs,* common people + *scītum,* decree, from *sciscere* (past participle *scītus*), to approve, decree, "to seek to know", from *scīre,* to know.]

plebs (plebz) *n.* **1.** The common people of ancient Rome. **2.** The common people; the populace. [Latin *plēbs.*]

plec·tog·nath (plék-tog-nath, -təg-) *n.* Any of various tropical marine fishes of the order Tetraodontiformes (or Plectognathi), which includes the triggerfishes, puffers, trunkfishes, and others. [New Latin *Plectognathi,* "ones having twisted jaws" (from their ankylosed jaws) : Greek *plektos,* past participle of *plekein,* to weave, twist + *-gnathi,* plural of *-gnathus,* -GNATHOUS.] **—plec·tog·nath** *adj.*

plec·trum (plék-trəm) *n., pl.* **-trums** or **-tra** (-trə). Also **plec·tron** (-trən || -tron). A small, thin, flexible piece of metal, plastic, bone, or other material, used to pluck the strings of certain musical instruments, such as the guitar or lute. Also called "pick". [Latin, from Greek *plēktron,* from *plēssein* (stem *plek-*), to strike + *-tron,* instrumental suffix.]

pled. Alternative past tense and past participle of **plead.**

pledge (plej) *n.* **1.** A formal promise to do something, such as the performance of an obligation or duty, or to refrain from doing something. **2. a.** Something given or held as security to guarantee payment of a debt or fulfilment of an obligation. **b.** The condition of something thus given or held: *put an article in pledge.* **3.** Something, such as an item of personal property, put in pawn. **4.** Something given as a token or sign. **5.** The act of drinking to someone; a toast. **—take the pledge.** To make a solemn vow to abstain from drinking alcoholic drinks.

~tr.v. **pledged, pledging, pledges. 1.** To offer or guarantee by a solemn promise. **2.** To bind or secure by or as if by a pledge. **3.** To deposit as security; pawn. **4.** To drink a toast to. —See Synonyms at **devote.** [Middle English *pleg(g)e,* from Old French *plege,* from Late Latin *plebium,* from *plebire,* to pledge, probably from Frankish *plegan* (unattested), to guarantee (influenced by Latin *praebēre,* to offer).]

pledg·ee (pléj-eé) *n.* **1.** A person to whom something is pledged. **2.** A person with whom something is deposited as a pledge.

pledg·er (pléjər) *n.* One who makes or gives a pledge.

pledg·or, pledge·or (pléj-ór) *n.* A person who deposits property as a pledge.

-plegia *n. comb. form. Medicine.* Indicates a form of paralysis; for example, **paraplegia.** [New Latin, from Greek *plēgē,* a stroke, blow, from *plēssein* (stem *plēg-*), to strike.]

Plei·ad[1] (plī́-əd, pleé-) *n., pl.* **Pleiades** (-eez). *Sometimes small* **p.** A group of seven illustrious persons. [French *Pléiade,* the name adopted by Ronsard (*c.* 1553) to designate himself and his six most eminent companions among the poets of the "brigade", in allusion to a group of Alexandrian poets named after the PLEIADES.]

Pleiad[2], **Pleiade** *n. Greek Mythology.* Any of the Pleiades.

Pleiad[3], **Pleiade** *n. Astronomy.* Any of the stars in the Pleiades.

Plei·a·des[1] (plī́-ədeez, pleé-) *pl.n. Greek Mythology.* The seven daughters of Atlas (Maia, Electra, Celaeno, Taygeta, Merope, Alcyone, and Sterope), who were changed into stars.

Pleiades[2] *pl.n. Astronomy.* An open star cluster in the constellation Taurus, consisting of several hundred stars, of which six or seven are visible to the naked eye. Also called the "Seven Sisters".

pleio-. Variant of **pleo-.**

Pleiocene. Variant of **Pliocene.**

plei·ot·ro·pism (plī-óttrə-piz'm) *n.* Also **plei·ot·ro·py** (-óttrəpi). *Genetics.* The control or determination of more than one characteristic or function by a single gene. [Greek *ple(i)ōn,* more + -TROPISM.] **—plei·o·trop·ic** (plī-ə-tróppik) *adj.* **—plei·o·trop·i·cal·ly** *adv.*

Pleis·to·cene (plī́-stə-seen, -stō-) *adj. Geology.* Of, belonging to, or designating the geological time, rock series, and sedimentary deposits of the earlier of the two epochs of the Quaternary period, characterised by the alternate appearance and recession of northern glaciation and the appearance of the progenitors of man.

~n. Geology. The Pleistocene epoch or system of deposits. Preceded by *the.* [Greek *pleistos,* most + -CENE.]

ple·na·ry (pleén-əri, plén-) *adj.* **1.** Complete in all aspects or essentials; full; absolute: *plenary powers.* **2.** Fully attended by all qualified members: *a plenary session.*

~n. A plenary session or meeting of an organisation; a plenum. [Late Latin *plēnārius,* from Latin *plēnus,* full.] **—ple·na·ri·ly** *adv.* **—ple·na·ri·ness** *n.*

plenary indulgence *n. Roman Catholic Church.* An indulgence that remits the full temporal punishment incurred by a sinner.

plen·i·po·ten·ti·ar·y (plénnipə-tén-shəri, -shi-əri || *U.S. also* -shi-erri) *adj.* **1.** Invested with or conferring full powers. **2.** Absolute; full: *plenipotentiary power.*

~n., pl. **plenipotentiaries.** A person, especially an ambassador or diplomat, fully authorised to represent a government. [Medieval Latin *plēnipotentiārius,* from Late Latin *plēnipotens* : Latin *plēnus,* full + *potens,* POTENT.]

plen·i·tude (plénni-tewd || -tōōd) *n.* **1.** Abundance; copiousness. **2.** The condition of being full, ample, or complete. [Middle English, fullness, from Old French, from Latin *plēnitūdō,* from *plēnus,* full.]

plen·te·ous (plénti-əss) *adj.* **1.** Abundant; copious. **2.** Producing or yielding in abundance. [Middle English *plenti(v)ous,* from Old French *plentiveus,* from *plentif,* abundant, from *plente(t),* PLENTY.] **—plen·te·ous·ly** *adv.* **—plen·te·ous·ness** *n.*

plen·ti·ful (plénti̇f'l) *adj.* **1.** Existing in great quantity or ample supply. **2.** Providing or producing an abundance: *a plentiful harvest.* **—plen·ti·ful·ly** *adv.* **—plen·ti·ful·ness** *n.*

plen·ty (plénti) *n.* **1.** A full or wholly adequate amount or supply; as much as one could want: *plenty of time.* **2.** A large quantity or amount; abundance: *goods in plenty.* **3.** A condition of general abundance or prosperity: *peace and plenty.*

~adj. Plentiful; abundant. Always used after the noun or pronoun: *That's plenty.*

~adv. Chiefly U.S. Informal. Sufficiently; quite: *It's plenty hot.* [Middle English *plent(i)e, plentet,* from Old French *plente(t),* from Latin *plēnitās* (stem *plēnitat*), from *plēnus,* full.]

ple·num (pleén-əm || plén-) *n., pl.* **-nums** or **plena** (-ə). **1. a.** A condition in which air or other gas, in an enclosure, is at a pressure greater than that outside the enclosure. **b.** An enclosure in which such a condition exists. **2.** In the philosophy of the Stoics, the whole of space regarded as being filled with matter. **3.** An assembly or meeting with all members present. **4.** Fullness. [Latin, neuter of *plēnus,* full.] **—ple·num** *adj.*

pleo-, pleio-, plio- *comb. form.* Indicates more; for example, **pleomorphism, pleiotropism, Pliocene.** [Greek *pleiōn, pleōn,* more.]

ple·och·ro·ism (pli-óckrō-iz'm) *n.* The property possessed by some crystals of exhibiting different colours when viewed along different axes. Compare **dichroism.** [PLEO- + -CHRO(OUS) + -ISM.] **—ple·o·chro·ic** (pleé-ə-krṓ-ik) *adj.*

ple·o·mor·phism, plei·o·mor·phism (pleé-ə-mórf-iz'm, -ō-) *n.* **1.** *Chemistry.* **Polymorphism** *(see).* **2.** *Biology.* The occurrence of two or more structural forms during a life cycle, especially of cer-

PRONUNCIATION KEY

a, trap; aa, father; ai, fair;
ar, star; aw, lawn; ay, play;
b, bb, stab; rubber;
ch, church; ck, ticket;
d, dd, dead; ladder; e, dress;
ee, bee; er, defer; ew, few;
ewr, pure; ə, about;
ər, letter; f, ff, fife; differ;
g, gg, giggle; h, hat; i, kit;
ī, price; īr, fire; j, judge;
k, kick; l, ll, let; 'l, needle;
m, mm, man; n, nn, no;
'n, sudden; ng, thing; o, lot;
ō, no; ŏŏ, foot; ōō, shoe;
oor, poor; ow, cow;
owr, hour; oy, boy;
p, pp, pepper; r, rr, red;
s, ss, sauce; sh, ship;
t, tt, totter; th, thick; th, this;
smooth; u, cut; ur, turn;
v, vv, valve; w, wet; y, yes;
z, zz, zebra; zh, vision;
pleasure

IN FOREIGN WORDS:

aN, ON, Saint-Saëns;
hl, Llanelli; Hluhluwe;
kh, loch; lough; Khaled

STRESS MARK:

ín-sīt, insight; in-sīt, incite

tain plants. [PLEO- + -MORPH + -ISM.] —**ple·o·mor·phic** (-mórfik) *adj.*

ple·o·nasm (plée-ə-naz'm) *n.* **1.** The use of more words than are required to express an idea; redundancy. **2.** An instance of this. **3.** A superfluous word or phrase. [Late Latin *pleonasmus*, from Greek *pleonasmos*, "superabundance", from *pleonazein*, to be more than enough, from *ple(i)ōn*, more.] —**ple·o·nas·tic** (-nástik) *adj.* —**ple·o·nas·ti·cal·ly** *adv.*

ple·o·pod (plée-ə-pod) *n. Zoology.* An appendage of crustaceans, a swimmeret (*see*). [PLEO- + -POD.]

ple·si·o·sau·rus (plée-si-ə-sáwrəss, -ō- || -zi-) *n., pl.* **-sauri** (-sáwrī). Also **ple·si·o·saur** (-sawr). A large, long-necked marine reptile of the extinct suborder Plesiosauria, common in Europe and North America during the Mesozoic era. [New Latin, from Greek *plēsios*, near + -SAURUS.]

plessor. *Medicine.* Variant of **plexor.**

pleth·o·ra (pléthərə) *n.* **1.** A superabundance; an excess. **2.** An excess of blood in the circulatory system or in one organ or area. [Late Latin *plēthōra*, from Greek *plēthōra*, *plēthōrē*, fullness, from *plēthein*, to be full.]

ple·thor·ic (ple-thórrik, pli- || -tháwrik, pléthərik) *adj.* **1. a.** Excessive in quantity; superabundant: *plethoric wealth.* **b.** Inflated in style; turgid: *plethoric prose.* **2.** Characterised by an overabundance of blood. —**ple·thor·i·cal·ly** *adv.*

ple·thys·mo·graph (plə-thíz-mə-graf, ple-, -thiss-, -graaf) *n.* An instrument used to measure changes in the volume of fluid in a part of the body, such as a limb, caused by fluctuations in blood pressure. [Greek *plēthusmos*, enlargement + -GRAPH.] —**ple·thys·mog·ra·phy** (pléthiz-móggrəfi, pléthiss-) *n.*

pleu·ra¹ (plóor-ə || pléwr-ə) *n., pl.* **pleurae** (-ee). *Anatomy.* Either of two membranous sacs, each of which lines one side of the thoracic cavity and envelops the contiguous lung, reducing the friction of respiratory movements to a minimum. [Medieval Latin, from Greek *pleura†*, side, rib.] —**pleu·ral** *adj.*

pleu·ra². Plural of **pleuron.**

pleu·ri·sy (plóor-ə-si, -i- || pléwr-) *n. Pathology.* Inflammation of the pleura, characterised by pain in the chest or side that becomes worse on deep breathing or coughing. [Middle English *pleresye, pluresy,* from Old French *pleurisie,* from Late Latin *pleurisis,* for Latin *pleurītis,* from Greek *pleurītis,* from *pleura†*, side, rib.] —**pleu·rit·ic** (plóor-rittik || pléwr-) *adj.*

pleuro-, pleur- *comb. form.* Indicates: **1.** The side; for example, **pleurodont. 2.** The pleura; for example, **pleuropneumonia.** [New Latin, from Greek *pleura†*, side, rib.]

pleu·ro·dont (plóor-ə-dont || pléwr-) *adj. Zoology.* **1.** Having the teeth attached by their sides to the inner side of the jaw, as in some lizards. **2.** Attached in this way: *pleurodont teeth.* ~*n.* An animal with pleurodont teeth. [PLEUR(O)- + -ODONT.]

pleu·ron (plóor-on || pléwr-) *n., pl.* **pleura** (-ə) *Zoology.* Either of the two lateral parts of the cuticle covering each of the body segments of arthropods. [New Latin, from Greek *pleuron, pleura†*, rib, side.]

pleu·ro·pneu·mo·nia (plóor-ō-new-móni-ə || pléwr-, -nōō-) *n. Pathology.* Pneumonia aggravated by pleurisy.

pleu·ro·pneu·mo·ni·a-like organism (plóor-ō-new-móni-ə-līk || pléwr-, -nōō-) *n. Abbr.* **PPLO** Any of a group of tiny, nonmotile, bacteria-like organisms formerly thought to cause a disease resembling pneumonia but now known to be harmless.

pleu·rot·o·my (ploor-róttəmi || plew-) *n., pl.* **-mies.** Surgical incision into the pleura. [PLEURO- + -TOMY.]

pleus·ton (plóo-stən, -ston || pléw-) *n.* Plants, such as algae, that float upon the surface of bodies of fresh water. [Greek *pleusis,* sailing, from *plein,* to sail + (PLANK)TON.] —**pleus·ton·ic** (plōo-stónnik || pléw-) *adj.*

plex·i·form (plék-si-fawrm) *adj.* Similar to or having the form of a plexus; complicated in structure. [PLEX(US) + -FORM.]

Plex·i·glas (plék-si-glaass || -glass) *n. U.S.* A trademark for a light, permanently transparent, weather-resistant thermoplastic form of polymethyl methacrylate.

plex·im·e·ter (plek-símmitər) *n. Medicine.* A small, thin plate held against the body and struck with a plexor in the technique of percussion (*see*). [PLEX(OR) + -METER.] —**plex·i·met·ric** (pléksi-méttrik) *adj.* —**plex·im·e·try** (plek-simmətri) *n.*

plex·or (pléksər) *n.* Also **ples·sor** (pléssər). *Medicine.* A small, rubber-headed hammer used with a pleximeter, in diagnosis by percussion (*see*) and also in testing nervous reflexes. [Greek *plēxis,* stroke, from *plēssein,* to strike.]

plex·us (pléksəss) *n., pl.* **plexus** or **-uses. 1.** *Anatomy.* A structure in the form of a network, especially of nerves, blood vessels, or lymphatics: *the solar plexus.* **2.** Any interlacing of parts; a network. [New Latin, from Latin, network, from *plexus,* past participle of *plectere,* to plait.]

pli·a·ble (plí-əb'l) *adj.* **1.** Easily bent or shaped; flexible. **2. a.** Receptive to change; adaptable. **b.** Easily influenced, persuaded, or swayed; tractable. —See Synonyms at **flexible.** —**pli·a·bil·i·ty** (-ə-billəti), **pli·a·ble·ness** *n.* —**pli·a·bly** *adv.*

pli·an·cy (plí-ən-si) *n.* The quality or condition of being pliant.

pli·ant (plí-ənt) *adj.* **1.** Easily bent or flexed; supple; limber. **2.** Easily altered or modified to fit conditions; adaptable. **3.** Yielding readily to influence or command; docile; compliant. —See Synonyms at **flexible.** [Middle English, from Old French, present participle of *plier,* to bend, fold, from Latin *plicāre,* to fold.] —**pli·ant·ly** *adv.* —**pli·ant·ness** *n.*

pli·ca (plíkə) *n., pl.* **plicae** (plí-see). **1.** *Zoology & Anatomy.* A fold or

ridge as of skin, membrane, or shell. **2.** A matted and encrusted state of the hair, resulting from dirt and vermin. [Medieval Latin, a fold, plait, from Latin *plicāre,* to fold.] —**pli·cal** (plík'l) *adj.*

pli·cate (plí-kayt) *adj.* Also **pli·cat·ed** (-id). Arranged in folds like those of a fan; pleated: *plicate leaves.* [Latin *plicātus,* past participle of *plicāre,* to fold.] —**pli·cate·ly** *adv.* —**pli·cate·ness** *n.*

pli·ca·tion (plí-káysh'n) *n.* Also **plic·a·ture** (plickə-chər, -tewr). **1. a.** The act or process of folding. **b.** The state of being folded. **2.** A fold. **3.** A surgical technique in which folds are sutured in the walls of a hollow organ to reduce its size.

pli·é (plée-ay) *n.* A movement in ballet in which the knees are bent while the back remains straight and the feet remain flat on the floor. [French, from past participle of *plier,* to bend.]

pli·er (plí-ər) *n.* One who plies (a trade).

pli·ers (plí-ərz) *pl.n.* Any of variously shaped tools having a pair of pivoted jaws, used for holding, bending, or cutting.

plight¹ (plīt) *n.* A condition or situation of difficulty or adversity. See Synonyms at **predicament.** [Middle English *plit,* from Anglo-French, Old French *pleit, ploit,* "a fold", from Vulgar Latin *plicitum* (unattested), from Latin *plicitus,* past participle of *plicāre,* to fold.]

plight² *tr.v.* **plighted, plighting, plights.** *Archaic.* **1.** To promise or bind by a solemn pledge; especially, to betroth. **2.** To give or pledge (one's word or oath, for example): *plight one's troth.* ~*n. Archaic.* **1.** A solemn pledge, as of faith. **2.** An engagement. [Middle English, Old English *pliht* (noun), peril.] —**plight·er** *n.*

plim·soll, plim·sole (plím-səl || -sōl) *n. British.* A light rubber-soled cloth shoe, worn especially as a sports shoe. Also called "gymshoe", and, in southwest England and in Wales, "dap". [Probably because the rubber rim resembles a PLIMSOLL LINE.]

Plimsoll line *n.* Any of a set of lines on the hull of a merchant ship to indicate the depth to which it may be legally loaded under specific conditions. Also called "load line", "Plimsoll mark". [After Samuel *Plimsoll* (1824–98), Member of Parliament who supported the British Merchant Shipping Act (1876).]

plink (plingk) *n.* A light tinkling sound. ~*v.* **plinked, plinking, plinks.** —*intr.* To produce a plink. —*tr.* To cause to plink.

plinth (plinth) *n.* **1.** A block or slab upon which a pedestal, column, or statue is placed. **2.** The base block at the intersection of the skirting board and the vertical frame round a doorway. **3.** A continuous course of stones supporting a wall. Also called "plinth course". **4.** A square base, as on a vase. [French *plinthe,* from Latin *plinthus,* from Greek *plinthos†,* brick, square stone block.]

Plin·y¹ (plínni), Latin name Gaius Plinius Secundus; also known as Pliny the Elder (A.D. 23–79). Roman writer and administrator. He is remembered chiefly for his encyclopedic *Natural History.*

Pliny². Latin name Gaius Plinius Caecilius Secundus; also known as Pliny the Younger (c. A.D. 61–113). Roman politician and writer, the nephew of Pliny the Elder. His correspondence provides much valuable information about Roman life, and includes a letter from Bithynia which gives one of the first accounts of the early Christians.

plio-. Variant of **pleo-.**

Pli·o·cene (plí-ə-seen, -ō-) *adj. Geology.* Of, belonging to, or designating the geological time, rock series, and sedimentary deposits of the last of the five epochs of the Tertiary period, characterised by the appearance of distinctly modern plants and animals. ~*n. Geology.* The Pliocene epoch or system of deposits. Preceded by *the.* [Greek *pleiōn,* more + -CENE.] —**Pli·o·cen·ic** (-sénnik, -séenik) *adj.*

plis·sé (plée-say || U.S. pli-sáy) *n.* **1.** A puckered texture of cloth created by treating fabric with a caustic soda. **2.** Fabric having such a texture. [French, past participle of *plisser,* to fold, pleat.]

PLO Palestine Liberation Organisation.

plod (plod) *v.* **plodded, plodding, plods.** —*intr.* **1.** To move or walk heavily or laboriously; trudge. **2.** To work or act perseveringly or monotonously; drudge. Used with *at, on,* or *upon.* —*tr.* To make (one's way) or trudge heavily and slowly along or over. ~*n.* **1.** The act of moving or walking heavily and slowly. **2. a.** A laborious journey. **b.** A laborious piece of work. **3.** The sound made by a heavy step. [16th century: imitative.] —**plod·ding·ly** *adv.*

plod·der (plóddər) *n.* One who moves or, especially, works steadily but laboriously and unimaginatively.

plodge (ploj) *intr.v.* **plodged, plodging, plodges.** *Northeastern English.* To wade or paddle, especially in the sea. ~*n. Northeastern English.* An act of wading or paddling. [Akin to PLOD, perhaps influenced by PLUNGE; imitative.]

-ploid *adj. & n. comb. form. Biology.* Indicates a specified multiple of a set of chromosomes; for example, **polyploid.** [Greek *-ploos,* -fold + -OID.] —**-ploidy** *n. comb. form.*

plonk¹ (plongk) *v.* **plonked, plonking, plonks.** *Informal* —*tr.* **1.** To fling down or drop heavily or abruptly. Often used with *down: He plonked the goods down on the counter.* **2.** To play (the piano, for example) badly. —*intr.* **1.** To fall or be dropped heavily or abruptly. **2.** To play a piano or other instrument badly. ~*n.* **1.** An abrupt or heavy fall or drop. **2.** The sound made by this. [Variant of PLUNK.] —**plonk** *adv.*

plonk² *n. Informal.* Wine of indifferent quality. [Originally Australian slang, probably from French *(vin) blanc,* white (wine).]

plonk·o (plóngk-ō) *n., pl.* **-os.** Also **plonk·ie** (-i). *Australian Informal.* An alcoholic, especially one addicted to cheap wine; a wino. [PLONK (wine) + -O.]

plop (plop) *v.* **plopped, plopping, plops.** —*intr.* To fall or move

plover Pluvialis squatarola, *the grey plover (above), is a shore bird, foraging for small shellfish, worms, and insects along beaches and mudflats. It breeds only in the high Arctic tundras of Canada and Russia, but outside the northern summer some birds migrate as far south as the coasts of South America and Australia.*

plum *Some species of this Northern Hemisphere fruit tree grow up to 10 metres (33 feet) high; others are merely shrubs. The fruits become prunes when dried.*

with a sound like that of an object falling into water without splashing. —*tr.* To drop or move so as to make such a sound.
~*n.* A plopping sound or movement. [19th century : imitative.] **—plop** *adv.*

plo·sion (plṓzh'n) *n. Phonetics.* The sudden release of breath in the articulation of a plosive. Also called "explosion". Compare **implosion.** [From EXPLOSION.]

plo·sive (plṓ-siv, -ziv) *adj. Phonetics.* Designating a speech sound whose articulation requires, at some stage, the complete closure of both the nasal and the oral passage, as in the sound of (p) in *top.*
~*n. Phonetics.* A plosive speech sound. Also called "explosive". [French, from *explosif,* EXPLOSIVE.]

plot (plot) *n.* **1.** A small piece of ground, generally used for a specific purpose. **2. a.** A graphic representation, as on a chart. **b.** Something located on a graph. **c.** *U.S.* A ground plan, as for a building; a chart; a diagram. **3.** A plan of the main series of events or an outline of the action of a story, drama, or the like. **4.** A secret plan, usually to accomplish a hostile or illegal purpose; a scheme. —See Synonyms at **conspiracy. —the plot thickens.** Matters are becoming more complex, often with intriguing or sinister overtones.
~*v.* **plotted, plotting, plots.** —*tr.* **1. a.** To represent graphically, as on a chart: *plot a ship's course.* **b.** To make a plan or map of. **2.** To prearrange secretly or deviously: *plot an assassination.* **3.** To conceive and arrange the action and incidents of: *plot a novel.* **4. a.** To locate (points or other figures) on a graph mathematically by means of coordinates. **b.** To draw (a curve) connecting points on a graph. —*intr.* To devise secretly; conspire. [In the sense "a piece of ground" (and hence the extended senses "plan", "diagram"), Middle English *plot(te),* Old English *plot*†. In the sense "secret plan", from *complot,* from Old French *complote*†.] **—plot·ter** *n.*

Plo·ti·nus (plō-tī́nəss, plo-) (*c.* A.D. 205–270). Greek philosopher. He initiated neoplatonism, developing Plato's teaching along mystic lines which suggest some knowledge of Oriental philosophy.

plough (plow) *n.* Also *chiefly U.S.* **plow. 1.** A farm implement consisting of a heavy blade or blades at the end of a beam, usually pulled by a draught animal or tractor and used for breaking up and turning over soil in preparation for sowing. **2.** Any implement with a similar function, such as a snowplough. **3.** Ploughed land. **4.** *British Slang.* Failure in an examination. **—put** or **set (one's) hand to the plough.** To start a piece of work. **—the Plough.** *Astronomy.* A group of seven bright stars forming part of the constellation Ursa Major. Also called "Charles' Wain", *U.S.* "Big Dipper".
~*v.* **ploughed, ploughing, ploughs.** Also *Chiefly U.S.* **plow, plowed, plowing, plows.** —*tr.* **1. a.** To break and turn over (earth) with a plough. **b.** To dig in (stubble, for example) with a plough. **2. a.** To form (a furrow, for example) with a plough. **b.** To make or form with driving force: *ploughed his way through the crowd.* **3.** To make furrows or indentations in. **4.** To cut through (water): *plough the high seas.* **5.** *British Slang.* To fail (a candidate) in an examination. —*intr.* **1.** To break and turn up earth with a plough. **2.** To admit of being ploughed: *Rocky earth ploughs poorly.* **3.** To move or progress in the manner of a plough. Usually used with *through.* **4.** To proceed laboriously; plod. **5.** *British Slang.* To fail an examination. **—plough back.** To reinvest (earnings or profits) in one's business. **—plough into.** *Informal.* **1.** To strike with force. **2.** To undertake (a task, for example) with eagerness and vigour. [Middle English *plou, plogh,* Old English *plōg, plōh,* from late Germanic *plōgaz* (unattested), of Italic origin.] **—plough·er** *n.*

plough·boy (plów-boy) *n.* **1.** A boy who leads or guides a team of animals in ploughing. **2.** A country boy.

plough·land (plów-land) *n.* **1.** In medieval England, a unit of land area roughly equivalent to the area capable of being ploughed by a team of eight oxen in a single year. **2.** Land under cultivation or suitable for cultivation.

plough·man (plów-mən) *n., pl.* **-men** (-mən, -men). **1.** A person who ploughs. **2.** A farmer or rustic.

ploughman's spikenard *n.* A European plant, *Inula conyza,* having clusters of yellowish flower heads. Also called "fleawort".

plough·share (plów-shair) *n.* The cutting blade of a plough; a share.

plov·er (plúvvər ‖ *U.S. also* plṓvər) *n., pl.* **-ers** or collectively **plover. 1.** Any of various widely distributed wading birds of the family Charadriidae, including the lapwing, having rounded bodies, short tails, and short bills. **2.** Any of various similar or related birds. [Middle English, from Old French *plovier,* from Vulgar Latin *pluviārius, ploviārius* (unattested), "rain-bird" (reason for naming obscure), from Latin *pluvia,* rain, from *pluere,* to rain.]

Plow·right (plów-rīt), **Joan (Anne),** The Lady Olivier (1929–). British actress. She is admired for her work in the modern theatre, especially in the socially aware plays of the 1950s, including Osborne's *The Entertainer* (1958, filmed 1960).

ploy (ploy) *n.* **1.** A tactic or stratagem, as in a conversation or game, to obtain an advantage. **2.** An activity; an occupation or amusement. [18th century (Scottish) : origin obscure.]

P.L.P. Parliamentary Labour Party (in Britain).

P.L.R. Public Lending Right.

plu. plural.

pluck (pluk) *v.* **plucked, plucking, plucks.** —*tr.* **1.** To detach by grasping and pulling abruptly with the fingers; pick: *pluck a flower.* **2.** To pull out the hair or feathers of: *pluck a chicken.* **3.** To give an abrupt pull to; tug at: *pluck a sleeve.* **4.** *Music.* To sound (the strings of an instrument) by pulling and releasing them with the fingers or a plectrum. **5.** *Slang.* To rob or swindle. —*intr.* To give an abrupt pull; tug. Used with *at.* **—pluck up.** To gather, raise, or summon up (one's courage, for example).
~*n.* **1.** The act of plucking; a tug; a snatch. **2.** Resourceful courage and daring in the face of difficulties; spirit. **3.** The heart, liver, windpipe, and lungs of a slaughtered animal. [Middle English *plukken,* Old English *pluccian,* from West Germanic *plukkōn* (unattested), from Vulgar Latin *piluccāre* (unattested), to remove the hair, pluck, irregularly from *pilus,* hair.] **—pluck·er** *n.*

pluck·y (plúcki) *adj.* **-ier, -iest.** Having or showing courage or spirited resourcefulness in trying circumstances. See Synonyms at **brave. —pluck·i·ly** *adv.* **—pluck·i·ness** *n.*

plug (plug) *n.* **1.** An object, such as a cork, rubber disc, or wad of cloth, used to stop a hole or gap. **2. a.** A fitting, with metal prongs for insertion in a fixed socket, used to connect an appliance to a power supply. **3.** A **spark plug** *(see).* **4. a.** A flat cake of pressed or twisted tobacco. **b.** A portion of chewing tobacco. **5.** *Geology.* A mass of igneous rock filling the opening, or vent, of a volcano. **6.** *Informal.* A favourable public mention, as of a commercial product, especially television or radio. **7.** *U.S. Slang.* Something inferior, useless, or defective; especially, an old, worn-out horse.
~*v.* **plugged, plugging, plugs.** —*tr.* **1.** To fill (a hole) tightly with or as with a plug or stopper; stop up. **2.** To use as a plug: *plugged a cork in a bottle.* **3.** To connect (an electrical appliance) to a socket. Used with *in.* **4.** *Slang.* **a.** To hit with a bullet; shoot. **b.** To hit with the fist; punch. **5.** *Informal.* **a.** To make favourable public mention of (a product, for example). **b.** To advertise or publicise (a song, for example) by constant repetition. —*intr.* **1.** To function by being connected to an electrical outlet. Used with *in.* **2.** *Informal.* To work doggedly and persistently at some activity. Often used with *away* or *along*: *plug away at homework.* **3.** *Slang.* To fire bullets. [Middle Dutch *plugge*†.] **—plug·ger** *n.*

plug·board (plúg-bawrd ‖ -bōrd) *n. Electronics.* A board containing a number of sockets used for patching circuits. Also called "patch board".

plug hat *n. U.S. Slang.* A man's stiff silk hat. [Probably because the head fits into it like a plug.]

plug·hole (plúg-hōl) *n.* The main drainage hole in a bath, basin, or other fixture into which a plug fits.

plug in *intr.v.* **1.** To connect an applicance to an electrical power source by inserting its plug into a socket. **2.** *Chiefly U.S. Slang.* To become aware of or in touch with something: *It's time to face facts and plug in to the real world.* —*tr.v.* To cause to be plugged in.

plug-in (plúg-in) *adj.* Designating an appliance that works by being plugged in to an electrical power source.
~*n.* A plug-in appliance or piece of equipment.

plug-ug·ly (plúg-úggli) *n., pl.* **-lies.** *U.S. Slang.* A gangster or ruffian.
~*adj.* Very ugly. [After the *plug-ugly* gangs in 19th-century New York, whose members wore PLUG HAT(S).]

plum[1] (plum) *n.* **1.** Any of several shrubs or small trees of the genus *Prunus*; especially, *P. domestica,* bearing smooth-skinned, fleshy, edible fruit with a single hard-shelled seed. **2.** The fruit of any of these trees. **3. a.** Any of several trees bearing plumlike fruit. **b.** The fruit of such a tree. **4.** A raisin, when added to a pudding or cake. **5.** Dark purple to deep reddish purple. **6.** *Informal.* Something that is the best of its kind or that is especially desirable, such as a good position. Also used adjectivally: *a plum job.* [Middle English *plum(me), plowme,* Old English *plūme,* from West Germanic, from Latin *prūnum.* See **prune.**]

plum[2]**.** *Informal.* Variant of **plumb.**

plum·age (plṓō-mij ‖ pléw-) *n.* **1.** The feathers of a bird. **2.** Feathers used ornamentally. **3.** Elaborate dress; finery. [Middle English, from Old French, from *plume,* PLUME.]

plu·mate (plṓō-mayt, -mət, -mit) *adj. Biology.* Resembling or possessing a plume or feather. [Latin *plūmātus,* feathered, from *plūma,* a feather.]

plumb (plum) *n.* **1.** A weight suspended from the end of a line, used to determine water depth or to establish a true vertical. **2.** The truly vertical position of a freely suspended plumb line. **—out of** or **off plumb.** Not vertical.
~*adj.* Also **plum** (for sense 2). **1.** Exactly vertical. **2.** *Chiefly U.S. Informal.* Utter; sheer: *a plumb fool.* —See Synonyms at **vertical.**
~*adv.* Also **plum** (for sense 2). **1.** In a vertical or perpendicular line. **2.** *Chiefly U.S. Informal.* Utterly; completely: *plumb tired.*
~*v.* **plumbed, plumbing, plumbs.** —*tr.* **1.** To test the alignment or angle of with a plumb line. **2.** To straighten or make perpendicular. Usually used with *up.* **3.** To determine the depth of; sound. **4.** To reach or experience (the lowest point or worst extreme of something). **5.** To examine closely; probe into. **6.** To connect to a water supply or drain; fit as part of the plumbing system. Often used with *in*: *She plumbed in the washing machine.* —*intr.* **1.** To be connected to a water supply or drain. Usually used with *in*: *That washing machine will plumb in easily.* **2.** To work as a plumber. [Middle English *plumbe, plombe,* from Old French *plombe,* from Latin *plumbum,* lead.] **—plumb·a·ble** *adj.*

plum·ba·go (plum-báygō) *n., pl.* **-gos. 1.** Graphite. **2.** Any plant of the genus *Plumbago,* the **leadwort** *(see).* [Latin *plumbāgō,* lead ore, leadwort, from *plumbum,* lead.]

plumb bob *n.* A usually conical piece of metal attached to the end of a plumb line. Also called "plummet".

plumb·er (plúmmər) *n.* A workman who installs and repairs pipes and plumbing fixtures for water and drainage. [Middle English *plummer*, from Old French *plommier*, from Late Latin *plumbārius*, lead worker, from Latin *plumbum*, lead.]

plumber's helper *n.* A device having a large suction cup at the end of a handle, used to clear drains; a plunger.

plumber's snake *n.* A plumber's tool, a **snake** *(see)*.

plumb·er·y (plúmmәri) *n.*, *pl.* **-ies.** *Rare.* **1.** A plumber's workshop or place of business. **2.** A plumber's work; plumbing.

plum·bic (plúmbik) *adj. Chemistry.* Of, pertaining to, or containing lead. Said especially of compounds that contain lead with a valency of 4. [From Latin *plumbum*, lead.]

plum·bi·con (plúmbi-kon) *n. Electronics.* A type of television camera tube in which the optical image is detected by a semiconducting lead oxide layer. [From Latin *plumbum*, lead + ICON.]

plumb·ing (plúmming) *n.* **1.** The pipes, fixtures, and other apparatus of a water or sewage system. **2.** The work or trade of a plumber. **3.** The act of using a plumb line.

plum·bism (plúmbiz'm) *n.* **Lead poisoning** *(see)*.

plumb line *n.* **1.** A line from which a weight is suspended to determine verticality or depth. **2.** A line regarded as directed exactly towards the earth's centre of gravity.

plum·bous (plúmbәss) *adj.* Of, pertaining to, or containing lead. Said especially of compounds that contain lead with a valency of 2. [Late Latin *plumbōsus*, full of lead, from *plumbum*, lead.]

plumb rule *n.* A narrow strip of wood with a plumb line and bob attached, used to test for a true vertical.

plum cake *n.* A kind of rich cake containing raisins, currants, and often other dried fruit.

plum duff *n.* A boiled suet pudding made with raisins or currants.

plume (ploōm || plewm) *n.* **1.** A feather, especially one that is large and ornamental. **2.** A large feather or cluster of feathers worn as an ornament or symbol of rank, as on a helmet. **3.** A token of honour or achievement. **4.** A feather-like structure, form, or object: *a plume of smoke.* **5.** *Biology.* A feathery structure, such as the cluster of fine hairs on certain fruits and seeds.
~*tr.v.* **plumed, pluming, plumes.** **1.** To decorate, cover, or supply with or as if with plumes. **2.** To smooth (itself or its feathers); preen. Used of a bird. **3.** To pride or congratulate (oneself). Used with *on* or *upon*. [Middle English, from Old French, from Latin *plūma*.] **—plum·y** *adj.*

plume·let (ploōm-lәt, -lit || pléwm-) *n.* A small plume.

plum·met (plúmmit) *n.* **1.** A **plumb bob** *(see)*. **2.** Anything that weighs down or oppresses.
~*intr.v.* **plummeted, -meting, -mets.** To drop straight down; plunge. [Middle English *plomet*, from Old French *plombet*, ball of lead, diminutive of *plomb*, lead, from Latin *plumbum*.]

plum·my (plúmmi) *adj.* **-mier, -miest.** **1.** Made of, resembling, or full of plums. **2.** Having or designating a deep, rich voice and exaggerated articulation, often considered upper-class or over-refined. **3.** *Informal.* Desirable; good: *a plummy job.*

plu·mose (ploō-mōss, -mōz || pléw-) *adj.* **1.** Having plumes or feathers; feathered. **2.** Resembling a feather or plume; feathery. [Latin *plūmōsus*, from *plūma*, a feather.] **—plu·mose·ly** *adv.* **—plu·mos·i·ty** (ploō-mόssәti || plew-) *n.*

plump¹ (plump) *adj.* **plumper, plumpest.** **1. a.** Overweight in an attractive way. **b.** Well-rounded and full in form: *plump cheeks.* **2.** Abundant; ample: *a plump reward.* —See Synonyms at **fat.**
~*v.* **plumped, plumping, plumps.** —*tr.* To make full or well-rounded. Often used with *up*: *plump up a pillow.* —*intr.* To become rounded or full. Often used with *up.* [Middle English, from Middle Dutch, from Middle Low German *plomp, plump*, thick, blunt, dull, probably akin to *plumpen*, to PLUMP.] **—plump·ish** *adj.* **—plump·ly** *adv.* **—plump·ness** *n.*

plump² *v.* **plumped, plumping, plumps.** —*intr.* **1.** To drop abruptly or heavily: *plump into a chair.* **2. a.** To make one choice out of several possibilities. **b.** To vote for or choose only one, in a situation in which more than one could have been chosen. In both senses, used with *for.* **3.** To give all one's support or praise. Used with *for.* —*tr.* **1.** To drop or throw down heavily or abruptly: *plump an ice cube into a glass.* **2.** To utter or say abruptly. Used with *out* or *in.*
~*n.* **1.** A heavy or abrupt fall or collision. **2.** The sound of this.
~*adj.* Blunt; direct.
~*adv.* **1.** With a heavy or abrupt impact. **2.** Straight down. **3.** Without qualification; bluntly. [Middle English, from Middle Low German *plumpen*, to plunge into water (probably imitative).]

plum pudding *n.* **Christmas pudding** *(see)*.

plum tomato *n.* A variety of tomato that produces long, oval fruits, which are often tinned.

plu·mule (ploō-mewl || pléw-) *n.* **1.** A down feather. **2.** *Botany.* The rudimentary bud of a plant embryo, which becomes the shoot of the seedling. [Latin *plūmula*, diminutive of *plūma*, feather.] **—plu·mu·lose** (-ōss, -ōz) *adj.*

plun·der (plúndәr) *v.* **-dered, -dering, -ders.** —*tr.* **1.** To rob (a person or place) of goods by force, especially in time of war; pillage; loot. **2.** To seize wrongfully or by force; steal. —*intr.* To take booty; rob; pillage. —See Synonyms at **rob.**
~*n.* **1.** Property stolen by fraud or force; booty. **2.** The act or practice of plundering. [Middle Dutch *plunderen* or Frisian *plunderje*, "to rob (of household goods)", akin to Middle Dutch *plunde, plunne*†, household goods, clothes.] **—plun·der·a·ble** *adj.* **—plun·der·er** *n.* **—plun·der·ous** *adj.*

plun·der·age (plúndәrij) *n.* **1.** The act of plundering; pillage. **2.** *Maritime Law.* **a.** The embezzling of goods on board a ship. **b.** The goods so acquired.

plunge (plunj) *v.* **plunged, plunging, plunges.** —*tr.* **1.** To thrust or throw forcefully into a substance or place: *Plunge the lobsters into boiling salted water.* **2.** To cast suddenly or violently into a specified state or situation: *The room was plunged into darkness.* —*intr.* **1.** To throw oneself into a substance or place. **2.** To throw oneself earnestly or wholeheartedly into a specified state or activity. **3.** To enter violently or speedily. **4.** To descend steeply; fall precipitously, as a road or cliff might. **5.** To move forwards and downwards violently. **6.** *Informal.* To speculate or gamble extravagantly.
~*n.* **1.** An act or instance of plunging. **2. a.** A place or area for diving or plunging, as a swimming pool. **b.** A swim; a dip. **—take the plunge.** **1.** To take a decisive, difficult step. **2.** *Informal.* To get married. [Middle English *plungen, plongen*, from Old French *plonger, plungier*, from Vulgar Latin *plumbicāre* (unattested), to sound with a plumb, from Latin *plumbum*, lead.]

plunge bath *n.* A bath deep enough to jump or plunge into.

plung·er (plúnjәr) *n.* **1.** One that plunges. **2.** A part that operates with a repeated thrusting or plunging movement, such as a piston. **3.** A device consisting of a rubber suction cup attached to the end of a stick, used to clean out clogged drains and pipes.

plunging fire *n.* Gunfire that reaches its target at an almost perpendicular angle, as from guns situated at a higher level than the target.

plunging neckline *n.* A neckline of a garment cut very low and having a very steep U- or V-shape.

plunk (plungk) *v.* **plunked, plunking, plunks.** *Informal.* —*tr.* **1.** To strum or pluck (the strings of a musical instrument or the instrument itself). **2.** To throw or place heavily or abruptly. Used with *down*: *plunk one's money down.* —*intr.* **1.** To emit a hollow, twanging sound. **2.** To drop or fall abruptly or heavily; plump.
~*n. Informal.* **1.** A short, hollow, twanging sound. **2.** *Chiefly U.S.* A heavy blow or stroke.
~*adv. Informal.* **1.** With a short, hollow thud. **2.** Exactly; precisely: *plunk in the centre.* [Imitative.] **—plunk·er** *n.*

plu·per·fect (ploō-pér-fikt || pléw-, -fekt) *adj. Abbr.* **plup., plupf.** *Grammar.* Of or designating a verb tense used to express action completed prior to a stated or implied past time.
~*n.* **1.** The pluperfect tense, formed in English with the past participle of a verb and one or more auxiliaries; for example, in the sentence *He had gone by the time we arrived, had gone* is in the pluperfect. **2.** A verb or form in this tense. Also called "past perfect". [New Latin *plūsperfectum*, contracted from Latin *(tempus praeteritum) plūs quam perfectum*, "(past tense) more than perfect" (translation of Greek *khronos hupersuntelikos*) : Latin *plūs*, more + *quam*, than + *perfectus*, PERFECT (tense).]

plu·ral (plόor-әl || pléwr-) *adj. Abbr.* **pl., plu., plur.** **1.** Of or composed of more than one member, set, or kind. **2.** Of or relating to a grammatical form that designates more than one of the things or persons stated. Compare **dual, singular.**
~*n. Grammar.* **1.** The plural number or form. **2.** A word or word element in this form. [Middle English *plurel, plural*, from Old French *plurel*, from Latin *plūrālis*, from *plūs* (stem *plūr-*), more.] **—plu·ral·ly** *adv.*

plu·ral·ise, plu·ral·ize (plόor-ә-līz || pléwr-) *v.* **-ised, -ising, -ises.** —*tr.* **1.** To make plural. **2.** To express in the plural. —*intr.* **1.** To become plural. **2.** To hold more than one position or ecclesiastical benefice at one time. **—plu·ral·i·sa·tion** (-lī-záysh'n || *U.S.* -li-) *n.*

plu·ral·ism (plόor-ә-liz'm || pléwr-) *n.* **1.** The condition of being plural. **2.** A condition of society in which numerous ethnic, religious, or cultural groups remain distinct but coexist within one nation. **3.** The belief that political power should not be wielded by central government alone, but shared by regional councils and organisations. **4.** The holding by one person of more than one position or office, especially two or more ecclesiastical benefices, at one time. **5.** *Philosophy.* **a.** The doctrine that reality is composed of many ultimate substances. **b.** The belief that no single explanatory system or view of reality can account for all the phenomena of life. Compare **monism, dualism.**

plu·ral·ist (plόor-ә-list || pléwr-) *n.* **1.** A person who holds more than one office, especially two or more ecclesiastical benefices, at one time. **2.** One who adheres to philosophical pluralism. **3.** One who advocates cultural pluralism. **—plu·ral·is·tic** (-lísstik) *adj.*

plu·ral·i·ty (ploor-rál-әti || plew-) *n.*, *pl.* **-ties.** *Abbr.* **plur.** **1.** The state or fact of being plural. **2.** A large number or amount; a multitude. **3.** *Ecclesiastical.* **a.** Pluralism. **b.** The offices or benefices held by a pluralist. **4.** *U.S.* A **relative majority** *(see)*. **5.** The larger or greater part of anything.

plural marriage *n.* Marriage to more than one partner at the same time or during one period; polygamy.

pluri- *comb. form.* Indicates more than one or many; for example, **pluricellular.** [Latin *plūs* (stem *plūr-*), more, *plures* (plural); several.]

plus (pluss) *prep.* **1.** Added to. **2.** Increased by; along with: *earnings plus dividends.*
~*adj.* **1. a.** Involving or pertaining to addition. **b.** Positive, as on a scale; more than zero. **2.** Added or extra: *a plus benefit.* **3.** *Informal.* Increased to a further degree: *personality plus.* **4.** Slightly more than: *a mark of C plus.* **5.** *Electricity.* Positive.
~*conj.* What is more; in addition.
~*n.* **1.** The plus sign (+). **2.** A positive quantity. **3.** A favourable factor: *Clear weather was a plus for the trip.* [Latin *plūs*, more.]
Usage: Within a sentence, *plus* can be a preposition (like *together with*) rather than a conjunction, and therefore a following

PRONUNCIATION KEY

a, **trap**; aa, **father**; ai, **fair**; ar, **star**; aw, **lawn**; ay, **play**; b, bb, **stab**; **rubber**; ch, **church**; ck, **ticket**; d, dd, **dead**; **ladder**; e, **dress**; ee, **bee**; er, **defer**; ew, **few**; ewr, **pure**; ә, **about**; әr, **letter**; f, ff, **fife**; **differ**; g, gg, **giggle**; h, **hat**; i, **kit**; ī, **price**; īr, **fire**; j, **judge**; k, **kick**; l, ll, **let**; 'l, **needle**; m, mm, **man**; n, nn, **no**; 'n, **sudden**; ng, **thing**; o, **lot**; ō, **no**; ōō, **foot**; ōō, **shoe**; oor, **poor**; ow, **cow**; owr, **hour**; oy, **boy**; p, pp, **pepper**; r, rr, **red**; s, ss, **sauce**; sh, **ship**; t, tt, **totter**; th, **thick**; th, **this**; **smooth**; u, **cut**; ur, **turn**; v, vv, **valve**; w, **wet**; y, **yes**; z, zz, **zebra**; zh, **vision**; **pleasure**

IN FOREIGN WORDS:

aN, oN, **Saint-Saëns**; hl, **Llanelli**; **Hluhluwe**; kh, **loch**; **lough**; **Khaled**

STRESS MARK:

ín-sīt, insight; in-sít, incite

verb may be singular or plural depending on the number of the subject: *Their strength plus their spirit makes them very strong. Their resources plus their determination make them very strong.*

plus fours *pl.n.* Loose knickerbockers bagging below the knees, traditionally worn by men for golf. [From the phrase *plus four inches,* the length added to ordinary knickerbockers to make them overhang the knees.]

plush (plush) *n.* A fabric of silk, rayon, cotton, or other material, having a thick, deep pile.
~*adj.* **1.** Made of or covered with plush. **2.** *Informal.* Ostentatiously luxurious, as in furnishings. [From obsolete French *pluche,* from Old French *p(e)luche,* from *peluch(i)er,* to pluck, from Vulgar Latin *pilūccāre* (unattested), "to remove the hair," irregularly from *pilus,* hair.] —**plush·ly** *adv.*

plush·y (plúshi) *adj.* **-ier, -iest. 1.** Resembling plush in texture. **2.** *Informal.* Plush; luxurious: *a plushy office.* —**plush·i·ly** *adv.* —**plush·i·ness** *n.*

plus-mi·nus (plúss-mīnəss, -mīnəss) *adv. Chiefly South African.* Approximately, more or less: *at plus-minus 6.30 a.m.* [Probably from the arithmetical sign (±).]

plus sign *n.* The symbol (+), as in *2 + 2 = 4,* used to indicate addition or a positive quantity. Also called "plus". Compare **minus sign.**

plus twos *pl.n.* Trousers similar to, but less wide than, plus fours.

Plu·tarch (plōō-taark ‖ pléw-), (*c.*46–120 A.D.). Greek academic. He wrote the *Parallel Lives,* a collection of biographies which Shakespeare used in his Roman plays.

Plu·to¹ (plōōtō ‖ pléwtō). *Roman Mythology.* The god of the dead and ruler of the underworld, identified with the Greek Hades. [Latin, from Greek *Ploutōn,* "rich one", from *ploutos,* wealth.]

Pluto² *n.* The ninth and farthest planet from the Sun, having a sidereal period of revolution about the Sun of 248.4 years, 4.5 thousand million kilometres (2.8 thousand million miles) distant from the Earth at perihelion and 7.4 thousand million kilometres (4.6 thousand million miles) at aphelion, and a diameter approximately one fifth that of the Earth. [After PLUTO (god).]

plu·toc·ra·cy (plōō-tóckrə-si ‖ plew-) *n., pl.* **-cies. 1.** Government by the wealthy. **2.** A wealthy class that controls a government. **3.** A government or state in which the wealthy rule. [Greek *ploutokratia* : *ploutos,* wealth + -CRACY.] —**plu·to·crat** (plōō-tə-krat, -tō-) *n.* —**plu·to·crat·ic** (-króttik) *adj.* —**plu·to·crat·i·cal·ly** *adv.*

plu·ton (plōō-ton ‖ pléw-) *n.* Igneous rock formed beneath the surface of the earth by consolidation of magma. [Probably back-formation from PLUTONIC.]

Plu·to·ni·an (plōō-tōni-ən ‖ plew-) *adj.* Also **Plu·ton·ic** (-tónnik). **1.** Of or pertaining to Pluto or the underworld. **2.** Of or pertaining to the planet Pluto.

plu·ton·ic (plōō-tónnik ‖ plew-) *adj. Geology.* Of deep igneous or magmatic origin: *plutonic water.* [From PLUTO (referring to the infernal regions).]

plu·to·ni·um (plōō-tóni-əm ‖ plew-) *n. Symbol* **Pu** A naturally radioactive, silvery, metallic transuranic element, occurring in uranium ores and produced artificially by neutron bombardment of uranium, having fifteen isotopes with masses ranging from 232 to 246 and half-lives from 20 minutes to 76 million years. It is a radiological poison, specifically absorbed by bone marrow, and is used, especially the highly fissionable isotope Plutonium-239, as a reactor fuel and in nuclear weapons. Atomic number 94, melting point 639.5°C, boiling point 3,226.8°C, relative density 19.8, valencies 3, 4, 5, 6. [Discovered shortly after NEPTUNIUM, and named by analogy after the planet PLUTO (beyond the planet Neptune).]

plu·vi·al (plōō-vi-əl ‖ pléw-) *adj.* **1.** Of or pertaining to rain; rainy. **2.** *Geology.* Caused by rain.
~*n.* A period of prolonged rain causing geological change. [Latin *pluviālis,* from *pluvia,* rain. See **pluvious.**]

Pluto

A REMOTE AND FRIGID WORLD

The planet that proved to be much smaller than predicted

Pluto, the ninth planet, was discovered in 1930 by the American astronomer Clyde Tombaugh. Its position had been predicted by another American, Percival Lowell, who died in 1916. The prediction had been made on the basis of irregularities in the movements of the giant planets Uranus and Neptune, which indicated that they were being influenced by an invisible body. When Pluto's size was measured however, it was surprisingly small – no more than 2320 kilometres (1,440 miles) in diameter, or one-fifth of the diameter of the Earth. It is probably made up of a mixture of ice and rock, with a surface temperature of −230°C (−382°F). It is not massive enough to cause any measurable effects upon other planets, and so the planet Lowell sought may remain to be discovered.

Pluto has a much more eccentric orbit than those of the other planets. It takes 248 years to go once round the Sun, and at its closest it moves further in towards the Sun than the orbit of Neptune, so between 1979 and 1999 Neptune, not Pluto, is "the outermost planet". In 1977 it was found that Pluto has a moon, which is one-third the diameter of Pluto, and moves round it every 6.3 days. Both Pluto and its moon, Charon, may have layers of frozen methane on their surfaces.

Even in the world's largest telescopes Pluto looks like nothing more than a dim star, and very sensitive techniques are needed to show Pluto and Charon separately.

HOW A PLANET WAS FOUND *Clyde Tombaugh found Pluto when checking two photographs of the same area of sky taken on January 23 and 29, 1930, at the Lowell Observatory, Arizona, as part of an intensive search for the planet. He noticed that one point* *had moved position. It was indeed a planet, but it was not exactly what he was looking for. Scientists had predicted a gaseous giant, not a tiny lump of ice and rock. But Pluto's discovery was a triumph: it was the first planet to be discovered with photography.*

Planet location guide

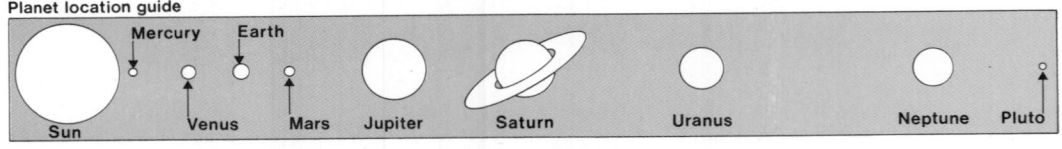

pluvio– *comb. form.* Indicates rain; for example, **pluviometer.** [Latin *pluvia,* rain. See **pluvious.**]

plu·vi·om·e·ter (plōō-vi-ómmitər || pléw-) *n.* A device for measuring rainfall, a **rain gauge** *(see).* [French *pluviomètre* : PLUVIO- + -METER.] **—plu·vi·o·met·ric** (-ō-méttrik, -ə-), **plu·vi·o·met·ri·cal** *adj.* **—plu·vi·o·met·ri·cal·ly** *adv.* **—plu·vi·om·e·try** (-ómmətri) *n.*

plu·vi·ous (plōō-vi-əss || pléw-) *adj.* Also **plu·vi·ose** (-ōss, -ōz). Characterised by heavy rainfall; rainy. [Middle English *pluvyous,* from Latin *pluviōsus,* from *pluvia,* rain, from *pluvius,* rainy, from *pluvere,* to rain.] **—plu·vi·os·i·ty** (-vi-óssiti) *n.*

ply¹ (plī) *tr.v.* **plied, plying, plies.** *Rare.* **1.** To join together, as by moulding or twisting. **2.** To double over (cloth, for example).
~*n., pl.* **plies. 1.** A layer, as of doubled-over cloth or of paper. **2.** Any of the sheets of wood glued together to form plywood. **3.** Any of the strands twisted together to make yarn, rope, or thread. Used in combination to indicate a specified number of strands, twists, or folds: *three-ply.* **4.** *Rare.* A bias; an inclination. [Middle English *plien,* from Old French *plier,* from Latin *plicāre,* to fold.]

ply² *v.* **plied, plying, plies.** *—tr.* **1.** To use diligently as a tool or weapon; wield: *plies an axe.* **2.** To engage in (a trade, for example); practise diligently. **3.** To traverse or sail over regularly: *plied the coastal routes.* **4.** To continue supplying or offering to: *plying her guests with food.* **5.** To assail vigorously. *—intr.* **1.** To traverse a route or course regularly: *A boat plies between the islands.* **2.** To perform or work diligently or regularly: *plied at the weaver's trade.* **3.** *Nautical.* To work against the wind by a zigzag course; tack. [Middle English *(ap)plien,* to employ, APPLY.]

Plym·outh¹ (plímməth). Port of Devon, southwest England. On Plymouth Sound between the Plym and Tamar estuaries, it has long been important as a naval station. Sir Francis Drake sailed from here to fight the Spanish Armada and it was the last port of call for the *Mayflower* before she sailed to America (1620). Since 1914 Plymouth has comprised the three towns of Plymouth, Stonehouse, and Devonport.

Plymouth². Town in Massachusetts, United States, southeast of Boston on Plymouth Bay. It was the landing point for the Pilgrim Fathers of the *Mayflower* (1620). Tourism, fishing, and electronics are important.

Plymouth Brethren *n.* A strict puritanical Protestant sect founded in 1830 in Plymouth, England.

ply·wood (plī-wōōd) *n.* A structural material made of thin layers of wood glued tightly together, usually with the grains of adjoining layers at right angles to each other. [PLY (layer) + WOOD.]

Pl·zeň *(Czech* p'lzeň). *German* **Pil·sen** (pílz'n). Capital of West Bohemia, Czechoslovakia. Situated on the river Berounka, it is most famous for its Pilsner beer, brewed since the Middle Ages.

Pm The symbol for the element promethium.

pm. 1. paymaster. **2.** premium.

p.m. 1. post meridiem. **2.** post-mortem. **3.** post-mortem examination.

P.M. 1. past master. **2.** postmaster; postmistress. **3.** post meridiem. **4.** post-mortem examination. **5.** prime minister. **6.** provost marshal.

PMBX private manual branch (telephone) exchange.

P.M.G. 1. Paymaster general. **2.** postmaster general.

PMT *n.* **1.** Premenstrual tension. **2.** A photomechanical transfer.

p.n., P/N promissory note.

PNdB. Perceived noise decibel.

pneum. pneumatic.

pneu·ma (néwmə || nōōmə) *n.* The soul or vital spirit. [Greek *pneuma,* blast of wind, breath, divine inspiration, spirit.]

pneu·mat·ic (new-máttik || nōō-) *adj. Abbr.* **pneum. 1.** Of or pertaining to air or other gases. **2.** Of or pertaining to pneumatics. **3.** Run by or using compressed air. **4.** Filled with air, especially compressed air: *a pneumatic tyre.* **5.** Having air cavities, as do the bones of many birds. **6.** Having or pertaining to shapely, full breasts: *"Uncorseted, her friendly bust/Gives promise of pneumatic bliss."* (T.S. Eliot). **7.** Of or pertaining to the pneuma; spiritual.
~*n.* A pneumatic tyre. [French *pneumatique,* from Latin *pneumaticus,* from Greek *pneumatikos,* from *pneuma* (stem *pneumat-*), wind, spirit.] **—pneu·mat·i·cal·ly** *adv.* **—pneu·ma·tic·i·ty** (néw-mə-tíssəti || nōō-) *n.*

pneu·mat·ics (new-máttiks || nōō-) *n. Used with a singular verb.* The study of the mechanical properties of air and other gases.

pneumatic trough *n. Chemistry.* A flat dish filled with water or other liquid, used in laboratory experiments for collecting gases by displacement of liquid from an inverted container.

pneumato– *comb. form.* Indicates: **1.** Air; for example, **pneumatophore. 2.** Breath or breathing; for example, **pneumatometer. 3.** Spirit or spirits; for example, **pneumatology.** [Greek *pneuma* (stem *pneumat-*), blast of wind, breath, spirit.]

pneu·ma·tol·o·gy (néw-mə-tólləji || nōō-) *n.* **1.** The doctrine or study of spiritual beings and phenomena; especially, the belief in spirits intervening between man and God. **2.** The Christian doctrine of the Holy Ghost. **3.** *Archaic.* Psychology. [New Latin *pneumatologia* : PNEUMATO- + -LOGY.] **—pneu·ma·to·log·ic** (-tə-lójik), **pneu·ma·to·log·i·cal** *adj.* **—pneu·ma·tol·o·gist** (-tólləjist) *n.*

pneu·ma·tom·e·ter (néw-mə-tómmitər || nōō-) *n.* A device for measuring the pressure of inspiration or expiration in the lungs. [PNEUMATO- + -METER.] **—pneu·ma·tom·e·try** (-tómmətri) *n.*

pneu·mat·o·phore (new-máttə-fawr || nōō-, -fōr) *n.* **1.** *Zoology.* A gas-filled sac serving as a float in certain colonial organisms, such as the Portuguese man-of-war. **2.** *Botany.* A specialised root in certain aquatic plants, such as the mangrove, that grows upwards and through which exchange of respiratory gases occurs.

pneumo–, pneum– *comb. form.* Indicates: **1.** The lung or respiratory organs; for example, **pneumograph. 2.** Air or gas; for example, **pneumothorax.** [Greek *pneuma,* wind, breath, spirit.]

pneu·mo·ba·cil·lus (néw-mō-bə-sílləss || nōō-) *n., pl.* **-cilli** (-síllī). A rod-shaped bacterium, *Klebsiella pneumoniae,* associated with respiratory infections, especially pneumonia.

pneu·mo·coc·cus (néw-mə-kóckəss, -ō- || nōō-) *n., pl.* **-cocci** (-kók-sī). A spherical bacterium, *Streptococcus pneumoniae,* that causes pneumonia. **—pneu·mo·coc·cal** *adj.*

pneu·mo·co·ni·o·sis (néw-mō-kōni-ṓ-siss || nōō-) *n.* Also **pneu·mo·no·co·ni·o·sis** (-mōnō-). Any lung disease caused by prolonged inhalation of mineral or metallic dusts, characterised by breathlessness and coughing. [New Latin : PNEUMO- + Greek *konia, konis,* dust + -OSIS.]

pneu·mo·gas·tric (néw-mō-gástrik || nōō-) *adj.* **1.** Of or involving the lungs and the stomach. **2.** Relating to the vagus nerve. In this sense, not in current technical usage.

pneumogastric nerve *n. Anatomy.* The **vagus** *(see).* Not in current technical usage.

pneu·mo·graph (néw-mō-graf, -mə-, -graaf || nōō-) *n.* A device for recording chest movements during respiration. [PNEUMO- + -GRAPH.] **—pneu·mo·graph·ic** (-gráffik) *adj.*

pneu·mo·nec·to·my (néw-mə-néktəmi || nōō-) *n., pl.* **-mies.** Also **pneu·mec·to·my** Surgical removal of a lung or of lung tissue. [Greek *pneumōn,* lung (see **pneumonic**) + -ECTOMY.]

pneu·mo·nia (new-mṓni-ə || nōō-) *n.* A disease marked by inflammation of one lung (*single pneumonia*) or both (*double pneumonia*), which become nonfunctional owing to the presence of pus in the air sacs, and caused by viruses, bacteria, and physical and chemical agents. [New Latin, from Greek, from *pneumōn,* lung, from *pneuma,* breath.]

pneu·mon·ic (new-mónnik || nōō-) *adj.* **1.** Pertaining to, affected by, or similar to pneumonia. **2.** Of, affecting, or pertaining to the lungs; pulmonary. [New Latin *pneumonicus,* from Greek *pneumonikos,* of the lungs, from *pneumōn,* lung.]

pneu·mon·it·is (néw-mə-nītiss) *n.* Inflammation of the lungs that is restricted to the walls of the air sacs. [PNEUMON- + -ITIS.]

pneu·mo·tho·rax (néw-mō-tháwr-aks, -mə- || nōō-, -thṓr-) *n.* Accumulation of air or gas in the pleural cavity, occurring as a result of disease or injury, or formerly induced to collapse the lung in the treatment of tuberculosis and other lung diseases.

p.n.g. persona non grata.

p-n junction (pée-én) *n. Electronics.* A junction between a p-type and an n-type semiconducting region, used in rectifiers and in transistors. [*P-n,* abbreviation of *P*ositive-*n*egative.]

Po¹ The symbol for the element polonium.

Po² (pō). Italy's longest river, 652 kilometres (405 miles). Rising in the western Alps, it flows eastwards to a delta on the Adriatic Sea.

p.o. 1. petty officer. **2.** post office.

P.O. 1. Personnel Officer. **2.** petty officer. **3.** postal order. **4.** post office.

poach¹ (pōch) *tr.v.* **poached, poaching, poaches.** To cook gently in a boiling or simmering liquid: *fish poached in wine.* [Middle English *pochen,* from Old French *poch(i)er* (originally of shelled eggs, to cook so that the whites form pockets), from *poche,* pocket, from Frankish *pokka* (unattested).]

poach² *v.* **poached, poaching, poaches.** *—intr.* **1.** To trespass on another's property in order to take fish or game. **2.** To take fish or game in a forbidden area. **3.** To take, acquire, or appropriate something or someone by devious or unfair means. **4.** To become muddy or broken up from being trampled. Used of land. *—tr.* **1.** To trespass on (another's property) for fishing or hunting. **2.** To take (fish or game) illegally. **3.** To take, acquire, or appropriate (something or someone) by devious or unfair means: *was accused of poaching staff from a rival company.* **4.** In tennis and similar games, to play (a shot that should have been taken by one's partner). **5.** To make (land) muddy or broken up by trampling. [Earlier *poche,* perhaps from French *pocher,* to pocket. See **poach** (cookery).]

poach·er¹ (pōchər) *n.* A vessel or dish designed for the poaching of food, such as eggs or fish.

poacher² *n.* A person who poaches on the property of another.

po·chard (pṓchərd) *n.* Any of various diving ducks of the genera *Aythya* and *Netta;* especially, *A. ferina,* of Europe, the male of which has grey and black plumage and a reddish head.

pock (pok) *n.* **1.** A pustule caused by smallpox or a similar eruptive disease. **2.** A mark or scar left in the skin by such a pustule; a pockmark. [Middle English *pokke,* Old English *pocc,* from Germanic.] **—pock·y** *adj.*

pock·et (póckit) *n.* **1. a.** A small, flat pouch or pouchlike piece of material sewn into a garment and used to carry small articles. **b.** A piece of material sewn onto the outside of a garment with the top edge open. **2. a.** A small sack or bag. **b.** *Chiefly South African.* A sack, used as a rough measure, in which commodities such as potatoes or sugar are sold in bulk. **3.** Any receptacle, cavity, or opening similar in shape or purpose to a garment pocket, such as a compartment on the inside of a car door, or a receptacle on the back of an aeroplane seat or inside a suitcase. **4.** Supply of money; financial means. **5.** *Mining.* **a.** A small cavity in the earth containing ore. **b.** A small body or accumulation of ore. **6.** Any of the pouchlike receptacles at the corners and sides of a billiard table. **7.** In Austra-

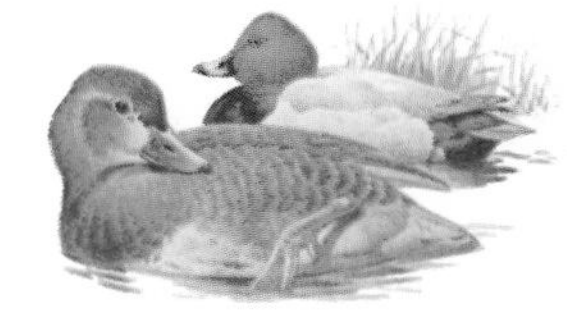

pochard *A freshwater duck of European lakes and rivers which can dive to 3 metres (about 10 feet) to feed on roots, buds, and seeds. The adult female (above, foreground) has brown plumage; the male has a red head, black breast, and a pale grey body.*

PRONUNCIATION KEY

a, trap; aa, father; ai, fair; ar, star; aw, lawn; ay, play; b, bb, stab; rubber; ch, church; ck, ticket; d, dd, dead; ladder; e, dress; ee, bee; er, defer; ew, few; ewr, pure; ə, about; ər, letter; f, ff, fife; differ; g, gg, giggle; h, hat; i, kit; ī, price; īr, fire; j, judge; k, kick; l, ll, let; 'l, needle; m, mm, man; n, nn, no; 'n, sudden; ng, thing; o, lot; ō, no; ōō, foot; ōō, shoe; oor, poor; ow, cow; owr, hour; oy, boy; p, pp, pepper; r, rr, red; s, ss, sauce; sh, ship; t, tt, totter; th, thick; th, this; smooth; u, cut; ur, turn; v, vv, valve; w, wet; y, yes; z, zz, zebra; zh, vision; pleasure

IN FOREIGN WORDS:

aN, oN, Saint-Saëns; hl, Llanelli; Hluhluwe; kh, loch; lough; Khaled

STRESS MARK:

ín-sīt, insight; in-sī́t, incite

lian Rules football, a side position at either end of the field. **8.** A small, isolated or protected area or group. **9.** An **air pocket** (see). —See Synonyms at **hole.** —**in** (or **out**) **of pocket.** Having gained (or lost) money. —**in** (one's) **pocket.** Under one's influence or control. —**line** (one's) **pockets.** To profit dishonestly by one's position. —**put** (one's) **hand in** (one's) **pocket.** To pay for something or donate money.

~*adj.* **1.** Suitable for or capable of being carried in one's pocket: *a pocket edition.* **2.** Small; miniature.

~*tr.v.* **pocketed, -eting, -ets. 1.** To place in or as if in one's pocket. **2.** To take possession of for oneself, especially dishonestly. **3.** To accept or tolerate (an insult, for example). **4.** To suppress or conceal: *He pocketed his pride.* **5.** *U.S.* To prevent (a bill) from becoming law by delaying its signing until the adjournment of the legislative body. Used of the U.S. president. See **pocket veto. 6.** In billiards, snooker, and similar games, to hit (a ball) directly or indirectly into a pocket. [Middle English *poket,* from Anglo-French *poket(e),* diminutive of *poke, poque,* bag, POKE.] —**pock·et·a·ble** *adj.* —**pock·et·er** *n.*

pocket battleship *n.* A small battleship built to conform with limitations on size and armament established by treaty.

pocket billiards *n.* The game of **pool** (see).

pock·et·book (póckit-boŏk ‖ -boōk) *n.* **1. a.** A small notebook. **b.** A pocket-sized folder or case used to hold money and papers. **2.** *U.S.* A handbag. **3.** *U.S.* A pocket-sized, usually paperbound book.

pocket borough *n.* A borough in England, prior to the Reform Act of 1832, whose representation was controlled by a single person or family. Compare **rotten borough.**

pock·et·ful (póckit-foŏl) *n., pl.* **-fuls** or **pocketsful.** As much as a pocket will hold.

pocket gopher *n.* A gopher (see).

pocket handkerchief. 1. A small handkerchief kept in a garment pocket. **2.** Something small and square or rectangular, such as a tiny garden or lawn.

pock·et·knife (póckit-nīf) *n., pl.* **-knives** (-nīvz). A small knife with a blade or blades folding into the handle.

pocket money *n.* **1.** Money given at regular intervals to a child, usually by the parents. **2.** Money for incidental or minor expenses.

pocket mouse *n.* Any of various small, North American burrowing rodents of the genus *Perognathus,* having external cheek pouches.

pocket veto *n.* In the United States: **1.** The president's indirect veto of a bill presented to him within ten days of Congressional adjournment, by his retaining the bill unsigned until Congress adjourns. **2.** A similar action exercised by a state governor or other chief executive.

pock·mark (pók-maark) *n.* **1.** A pitlike scar left on the skin by smallpox or another eruptive disease. **2.** A pit or scar on a surface. —*tr.v.* **pockmarked, -marking, -marks.** To disfigure with pockmarks. —**pock·marked** *adj.*

po·co (pṓkō) *adv. Music.* Somewhat; a little. Used as a direction: *poco adagio.* [Italian, little, from Latin *paucus,* little, few.]

po·co a po·co (pṓkō-a-pṓkō, -aa-) *adv. Music.* Gradually; little by little. Used as a direction: *poco a poco diminuendo.* [Italian.]

po·co·cu·ran·te (pṓkō-kewr-ránti, -koō-) *adj.* Indifferent; unconcerned; apathetic.

~*n.* One who does not care; an unconcerned person. [Italian, "little caring".] —**po·co·cu·ran·tism** *n.*

pod[1] (pod) *n.* **1.** *Botany.* **a.** The long, two-valved fruit of a leguminous plant, such as the pea, which contains several seeds and usually dries and splits open when ripe. **b.** The seed case of such a fruit. **c.** Any of several similar fruits. **2.** A podlike protective covering. **3.** *Aeronautics.* A streamlined housing that encloses engines, machine guns, or fuel, carried externally on aircraft.

~*v.* **podded, podding, pods.** —*intr.* **1.** To bear or produce pods. **2.** To expand or swell like a pod. —*tr.* To remove (seeds, peas, beans, or the like) from a pod. [17th century : back formation from dialect *podware†,* crops, bagged vegetables.]

pod[2] *n.* **1.** A school of seals or whales. **2.** A small flock of birds. [19th century (U.S.) : origin obscure.]

pod[3] *n.* **1.** The lengthways groove in certain boring tools, such as augers. **2.** The socket for holding the bit in a boring tool. [16th century : perhaps variant of PAD (cushion).]

-pod, -pode *n. comb. form.* Indicates a specified kind or number of feet; for example, **cephalopod, tripod.** [New Latin *-podius, -poda,* from Greek *pous* (stem *pod-*), foot.] —**-podous** *adj. comb. form.*

po·dag·ra (pə-dággrə, pṓ-, po-, póddəgrə) *n. Pathology.* Gout, especially of the big toe. [Middle English, from Latin, from Greek, "trap for the feet", foot disease, gout : *pous* (stem *pod-*), foot + *agra, agrē,* seizure.] —**po·dag·ral, po·dag·ric** *adj.*

pod·dy (póddi) *n. pl.* **-dies.** *Australian.* A calf requiring to be handfed.

~*adj.* Requiring to be handfed. Said especially of a lamb or calf. [From adjective, fat, from dialect *pod,* fat protruding belly, special use of POD (seed vessel).]

po·des·ta (po-désta, pṓ- ‖ *Italian* pódess-táʹa) *n.* **1.** A governor appointed by Frederick Barbarossa to rule over one or more of the Lombard cities. **2.** The chief magistrate or officer in any of the republics of medieval Italy. **3.** Under the Fascist regime in Italy, the chief magistrate or mayor in any of the Italian communes except Rome and Naples. **4.** A subordinate magistrate or judge in some modern Italian towns. [Italian *podestà, potestà,* from Latin *potestās* (stem *potestāt-*), power, magistrate, from *potis,* able.]

Pod·gor·ny (pod-górni, *Russian* pud-), **Nikolai Viktorovich** (1903–83). Soviet politician. He became president of the U.S.S.R. (1965) but resigned (1977) when displaced by Brezhnev.

podg·y (póji) *adj.* **-ier, -iest.** Also *chiefly U.S.* **pudg·y** (púji). Short and plump; chubby. See Synonyms at **fat.** —**podg·i·ly** *adv.* —**podg·i·ness** *n.*

po·di·a·try (pə-dī-ətri, pō-) *n. U.S.* **Chiropody** (see). [Greek *pous* (stem *pod-*), foot + -IATRY.] —**po·di·a·trist** *n.*

po·di·um (pṓ-di-əm) *n., pl.* **-dia** (-di-ə) or **-ums. 1.** An elevated platform, as for an orchestral conductor or lecturer; a dais. **2.** *Architecture.* A low wall serving as foundation. **3.** A wall circling the arena of an ancient amphitheatre. **4.** *Zoology.* Any structure resembling or functioning as a foot. [Latin, raised platform, balcony, from Greek *podion,* "small foot", base, from *pous* (stem *pod-*), foot.]

-podium *n. comb. form.* Indicates a part that resembles a foot; for example, **monopodium.** [New Latin, from Greek *podion,* "small foot", from *pous,* foot.]

pod·o·phyl·lin (póddō-fíllin) *n.* A bitter-tasting resin obtained from the dried root of the **May apple** (see), and used as a laxative. [New Latin *podophyllum,* "(plant with) footlike leaves" : Greek *pous* (stem *pod-*), foot + *phullon,* a leaf + -IN.]

pod·zol (pód-zol) *n.* Also **pod·sol** (-sol). A leached soil formed mainly in cool, humid climates. [Russian, "ash ground" : *pod,* bottom, ground + *zola,* ashes.] —**pod·zol·ic** (pod-zóllik) *adj.*

pod·zo·lise, pod·zo·lize (pód-zo-līz) *v.* **-lised, lising, lises.** Also **pod·so·lise** (-so-) *v.* —*tr.* To make (soil) acidic by leaching out bases; form into a podzol. —*intr.* To become acidic by leaching; become a podzol. Used of soil. —**pod·zol·i·sa·tion** (-lī-záysh'n ‖ *U.S.* -li-) *n.*

Poe (pō), **Edgar Allan** (1809–49). U.S. author. His macabre stories and poems, such as *The Fall of the House of Usher* (1839) and *Ligeia* (1840), had widespread influence, especially on Baudelaire and Mallarmé in France.

P.O.E. 1. port of embarkation. **2.** port of entry.

po·em (pṓ-im, -əm, -em) *n.* **1.** A composition designed to convey a vivid and imaginative sense of experience, characterised by the use of condensed language, chosen for its sound and suggestive power as well as its meaning, and by the use of such literary techniques as structured metre, natural cadences, rhyme, and imagery. **2.** Any composition in verse rather than in prose. **3.** Any literary composition written with an intensity of language or conscious use of stylistic devices more characteristic of poetry than of prose: *a prose poem.* **4.** Any creation, object, or experience thought to embody the lyrical beauty or structural perfection characteristic of poetry. [French *poème* or Latin *poēma,* from Greek *poiēma, poēma,* "created thing", work, poem, from *poiein,* to make, create.]

poenology. Variant of **penology.**

po·e·sy (pṓ-i-zi, -e- ‖ -si) *n., pl.* **-sies.** *Archaic.* **1.** Poetry. **2. a.** The art or practice of composing poems. **b.** The inspiration involved in composing poetry. **3.** Poems collectively. [Middle English *poesie,* from Old French, from Common Romance *poēsia* (unattested), variant of Latin *poēsis,* from Greek *po(i)ēsis,* "a making", "creation", poetry, from *poiein,* to make, create.]

po·et (pṓ-it, -et) *n.* **1.** A writer of poems. **2.** One who is especially gifted in the perception and expression of the beautiful or lyrical. [Middle English *poete,* from Old French, from Latin *poēta,* from Greek *poiētēs,* "maker", poet, from *poiein,* to make, create.]

Synonyms: poet, bard, versifier, rhymer, rhymester, poetaster.

po·et·as·ter (pṓ-i-táss-tər, -ə- ‖ -táyss-) *n.* An inferior poet. See Synonyms at **poet.** [New Latin : Latin *poēt(a),* POET + -ASTER.]

po·et·ess (pṓ-i-tiss, -ə-, -tess) *n.* A female poet. Sometimes considered offensive. See Usage note at **-ess.**

po·et·ic (pō-éttik) *adj.* Also **po·et·i·cal** (-'l). **1.** Of or pertaining to poetry. **2.** Having a quality or style characteristic of poetry: *poetic diction.* **3.** Suitable as a subject for poetry: *a poetic love affair.* **4.** Of, pertaining to, or befitting a poet: *poetic insight.* **5.** Having or showing the sensitivity or insight of a poet. **6.** Characterised by romantic imagery: *a poetic account.* [From French *poétique,* from Latin *poēticus,* from Greek *poiētikos,* inventive, ingenious, from *poiētēs,* "maker", POET.]

po·et·i·cal (pō-éttik'l) *adj.* **1.** Variant of **poetic. 2.** Fancifully depicted or embellished; idealised. —**po·et·i·cal·ly** *adv.*

po·et·i·cise, po·et·i·cize (pō-étti-sīz) *tr.v.* **-ised, -ising, -ises.** To give a poetic quality to.

po·et·i·cism (pō-étti-siz'm) *n.* A poetic term or expression that has become no longer vivid or evocative.

poetic justice *n.* An outcome whereby a person receives his just deserts in a manner peculiarly or ironically appropriate.

poetic licence *n.* The liberty taken, especially by an artist or writer, in deviating from conventional form or fact to achieve a desired effect.

po·et·ics (pō-éttiks) *n. Used with a singular verb.* **1.** Literary criticism that deals with the nature, forms, and laws of poetry. **2.** A treatise on or study of poetry or aesthetics. **3.** Poetic utterances or feelings.

po·et·ise, po·et·ize (pṓ-i-tīz, -ə-) *v.* **-ised, -ising, -ises.** —*intr.* To write or express oneself in poetry. —*tr.* To give poetic expression to. —**po·et·is·er** *n.*

poet laureate *n., pl.* **poets laureate** or **poet laureates.** A poet appointed by the British sovereign to compose poems for State occasions, who is a member of the Royal Household.

po·et·ry (pṓ-i-tri, -ə- ‖ póytri) *n.* **1.** The art or work of a poet. **2. a.** Poems regarded as forming a division of literature. **b.** The poetic works of a given author, group, nation, or genre. **3.** Any piece of literature written in metre; verse. **4.** Prose that resembles a poem, as in form, sound, or other qualities. **5.** The essence of or characteristic quality possessed by a poem or poems. **6.** A quality that suggests poetry, as in grace, beauty, or harmony: *the poetry of dance movements.* [Middle English, from Medieval Latin *poētria,* from Latin *poēta,* POET.]

po-faced (pō-fáyst) *adj.* Having a neutral or stern expession. [*Po,* variant (after French pronunciation) of POT.]

pogge (pog) *n.* A marine European fish, *Agonus cataphractus,* with a body covering of bony plates, a large broad head, and a long tapering tail. [17th century : origin obscure.]

po·go·ni·a (pə-gṓni-ə) *n.* Any of various small terrestrial orchids of the genus *Pogonia,* of the North Temperate Zone, having pink or whitish flowers. [New Latin, "bearded plant" (from the yellow hair covering the lip of its flower), from Greek *pōgōn*†, beard.]

po·go stick (pṓgō) *n.* A strong stick with footrests and a heavy spring set into the bottom end, propelled along the ground by hopping. [20th century : origin obscure.]

po·grom (póg-rəm, -rom, pə-grom) *n.* An organised and often officially encouraged massacre or persecution of a minority group, especially a Jewish community. [Russian, "like thunder", devastation : *po-,* like, from *po,* at, by, next to + *grom,* thunder.]

po·hu·tu·ka·wa (pō-hóotə-kaa-wə) *n.* A New Zealand tree, *Metrosideros excelas,* with red flowers and hard, heavy red wood used for marine timber work. [Maori.]

poi (poy, pṓ-i) *n.* A Hawaiian food made from taro root cooked, pounded to a paste, and fermented. [Hawaiian.]

-poiesis *n. comb. form.* Indicates making, creating, or producing; for example, **haematopoiesis.** [From Greek *poiēsis,* a making, creation, from *poiein,* to make.] **—-poietic** *adj. comb. form.*

poign·ant (póyn-yənt, -ənt, *also* póyg-nənt) *adj.* **1.** Appealing to the emotions; affecting; touching: *poignant sentiment.* **2.** Piercing; incisive: *poignant criticism.* **3.** Keenly distressing to the mind: *poignant anxiety.* **4.** Relevant; to the point: *"Her illustrations were apposite and poignant."* (Charles Lamb). **5.** Agreeably intense or stimulating: *poignant delight.* **6. a.** *Archaic.* Sharp or sour to the taste; piquant. **b.** Sharp or pungent to the smell: *a poignant perfume.* —See Synonyms at **moving.** [Middle English *poynaunt, pugnaunt,* pointed, sharp, from Old French *puignant,* present participle of *poindre,* from Latin *pungere,* to prick, pierce.] **—poign·an·cy, poign·ance** *n.* **—poign·ant·ly** *adv.*

poi·ki·lo·therm (póykil-ə-therm, -ō-) *n. Zoology.* A poikilothermic organism, such as a fish or reptile. [Greek *poikilos,* various, variant + -THERM.]

poi·ki·lo·ther·mic (póykil-ə-thérmik, -ō-) *adj.* Also **poi·ki·lo·ther·mal** (-thérm'l). *Zoology.* Having a body temperature that varies with the external environment; cold-blooded. Compare **homoiothermic.** **—poi·ki·lo·ther·mism, poi·ki·lo·ther·my** *n.*

poi·lu (pwaa-lóo, *French* -lü) *n., pl.* **-lus** (*pronounced as singular, or -z*). *World War I Slang.* A French front-line soldier. [French, "hirsute", hence (slang) pugnacious, from *poil,* hair, from Latin *pilus.*]

Poin·ca·ré (pwaNka-ráy), **Jules Henri** (1854–1912). French mathematician. He made a distinguished contribution to experimental physics and theoretical astronomy, as well as pure and applied mathematics, anticipating Einstein's work on relativity.

Poincaré, Raymond (1860–1934). French politician. A cousin of Jules Henri Poincaré, he held office as ninth president of the Republic (1913–20) and served for three terms as prime minister (1912–13, 1922–24, and 1926–29).

poin·ci·an·a (póyn-si-áanə || *U.S.* -ánnə) *n.* **1.** Any of various tropical trees of the genus *Poinciana,* having large orange or red flowers. **2.** A related tree, the **royal poinciana** *(see).* [New Latin, after M. de *Poinci,* 17th-century governor of French Antilles.]

poin·set·ti·a (poyn-sétti-ə) *n.* A tropical American shrub, *Euphorbia pulcherrima,* having petal-like, usually scarlet, bracts beneath yellow flowers, widely grown as a house plant. [New Latin; discovered by J.R. *Poinsett* (1799–1851), U.S. minister to Mexico.]

point (poynt) *n. Abbr.* **pt. 1.** The sharp or tapered end of something: *the point of a knife.* **2.** Something that has a sharp or tapered end, such as a knife or needle. **3.** A tapering extension of land projecting into water; a promontory; a cape. **4.** A mark formed by or as if by the sharp end of something. **5.** A mark or dot used in printing or writing. **6.** A mark used in punctuation; especially, a full stop. **7.** See **decimal point. 8.** *Phonetics.* A diacritical mark used to differentiate or modify vowels and consonants, such as a **vowel point** *(see).* **9.** Any of the protruding marks used in certain methods, such as Braille, of writing and printing for the blind. **10.** *Geometry.* A dimensionless geometric object having no property but position. **11.** A position, place, or situation; a spot: *a good point to begin.* **12.** A specified degree, condition, or limit in a scale, course, or the like: *a melting point.* **13. a.** One of the 32 equal divisions marked at the circumference of a mariner's compass card that indicate direction. **b.** The distance or interval of 11 degrees, 15 minutes between any two adjacent markings. **14.** Any distinct condition or degree: *the point of no return.* **15.** A specific moment in time: *At this point she left.* **16.** A crucial situation in a course of events. **17.** An important, essential, or primary factor: *missed the whole point.* **18.** A purpose, goal, advantage, or reason: *can't see any point in continuing.* **19.** The major idea or essential part of a concept or narrative: *get to the point of the story.* **20.** A significant, outstanding, or effective idea, argument, or suggestion: *made some excellent points.* **21.** A separate or individual item or element; a detail: *several points worth noting.* **22. a.** A striking or distinctive characteristic or quality: *his good points.* **b.** A quality or characteristic that is important or distinctive; especially, a standard characteristic used to judge an animal. **c.** *Plural.* The extremities of a horse, dog, or the like: *a bay pony with white points.* **23.** A single unit, as in counting, rating, or measuring. **24.** *U.S.* A unit of credit used in marking academic achievement. **25.** A unit of scoring or counting in a game or sport: *won the match on points.* **26.** The stiff and attentive stance taken by a hunting dog. **27.** *Electricity.* **a.** An electrical contact, especially one in the distributor of a car engine or crystal set. **b.** *Chiefly British.* A **power point** *(see).* **28.** *Finance.* A unit of value used to quote or state the current prices of stocks, commodities, or the like. **29.** A unit equal to .0001 used in calculating a rate of exchange in U.S. dollars: *The pound gained three points against the dollar.* **30.** *Printing.* A unit of type size equal to 0.01384 inch, or approximately $^1/_{72}$ of an inch. **31.** A jeweller's unit of mass equal to 2 milligrammes or 0.01 carat. **32. a.** Needlepoint. **b.** Bobbin lace. **33.** *Often plural.* **a.** A device consisting of two sections of railway track and the accompanying apparatus, used to transfer trains from one track to another. **b.** The junction of railway tracks at such a device. **34.** A ribbon or cord with a metal tag at the end, used to fasten clothing in the 16th and 17th centuries. **35.** In cricket: **a.** The position of a fielder on the off side straight out from the batsman, as if at the point of his bat. **b.** A fielder in this position. **36.** In boxing, the top of the chin, as a spot for delivering a blow. **37.** In backgammon, any of the tapered divisions of the board. **38.** A small body of troops that goes ahead of or behind the main force to reconnoitre. **39.** An aggressive stance or stroke made holding a bayonet. **40.** The act of pointing. **—beside the point.** Having nothing to do with the subject; irrelevant. **—in point.** By way of example. Used chiefly in the phrase *a case in point.* **—in point of fact.** As a matter of fact. **—make a point of.** To take special care or pains to. **—make (one's) point.** To prove oneself successfully to be right. **—not to put too fine a point on it.** To speak frankly or bluntly. **—on the point of.** At the moment immediately prior to; about to: *on the point of surrendering.* **—off the point.** Away from the subject in question. **—score points off.** To make points at the expense of (someone). **—stretch a point. 1.** To make an exception. **2.** To exaggerate. **—to the point.** Relevant; apposite. **—up to a point.** To some extent but not entirely: *You are right up to a point.*
~*v.* **pointed, pointing, points.** *—tr.* **1.** To direct or aim: *point a weapon.* **2.** To cause to head: *pointed us in the right direction.* **3.** To indicate the position or direction of: *point the way.* **4.** To sharpen (a pencil, for example); provide with a point. **5.** To separate with a decimal point. Used with *off.* **6.** To mark with a point or full stop; punctuate. **7.** To mark (a consonant) with a vowel point. **8.** To give emphasis to (a remark, for example); stress. Often used with *up.* **9.** To indicate the presence and position of (game) by standing immobile and directing the muzzle towards it. **10.** To fill and finish the joints of (brickwork, for example) with cement or mortar. *—intr.* **1.** To direct attention or indicate position with or as if with the finger. Usually used with *at* or *to.* **2.** To turn the mind or thought in a particular direction: *The facts all point to one conclusion.* **3.** To be turned or faced in a given direction; aim. **4.** To perform the action of a hunting dog scenting game and gazing towards it fixedly. **5.** *Nautical.* To sail close to the wind. **—point out.** To call attention to; indicate. [Middle English *poynt,* from Old French *point,* a prick, dot, small particle, and *pointe,* pointed end or tip, respectively from Latin *punctum* and *puncta* from the neuter and feminine of *punctus,* past participle of *pungere,* to pierce, prick.]

point-blank (póynt-blángk) *adj.* **1.** Aimed straight at the mark or target; especially, aimed straight without allowing for the drop in a projectile's course: *a point-blank shot.* **2. a.** So close to a target that a weapon may be aimed directly at it. **b.** Close enough so that missing the target is unlikely or impossible: *point-blank range.* **3.** Straightforward; blunt: *a point-blank accusation.*
~*adv.* **1.** With a straight aim; directly; straight: *The policeman fired point-blank.* **2.** Without hesitation, deliberation, or equivocation: *answer point-blank.* [Probably POINT (verb) + BLANK (white centre spot of a target).]

point d'ap·pui (pwaN da-pwée) *n., pl.* **points d'appui** (*pronounced as singular*). **1.** *Military.* Formerly, a secure position or base serving as a support for operations in the field. **2.** A base or support. [French, point of support.]

point defect *n. Crystallography.* A defect in a crystal lattice occurring at a single lattice point; a vacancy or an interstitial.

point-de·vice (póynt-di-víss) *adj. Archaic.* Scrupulously correct or neat; precise. [Middle English *at point devis,* probably from Anglo-French *à point devis* (unattested), "arranged to (the) point" : *à point,* to perfection + *devis,* "divided", arranged, from Latin *divisus,* past participle of *dīvidere,* to divide.] **—point-de·vice** *adv.*

point duty *n.* In Britain, the duty of a traffic warden or constable stationed at a junction, roundabout, or the like, to regulate traffic.

pointe (poynt) *n.* In ballet, the tip of the toes. [French.]

point·ed (póyntid) *adj.* **1.** Having an end coming to a point. **2.** Sharp; cutting: *a pointed question.* **3.** Obviously directed at or making reference to a particular target: *pointed wit.* **4.** Clearly evident or conspicuous; emphasised; marked: *a pointed lack of interest.* **5.** Characterised by the use of a pointed crown, as in Gothic architecture: *a pointed arch.* **—point·ed·ly** *adv.* **—point·ed·ness** *n.*

point·er (póyntər) *n.* **1.** One that sharpens, directs, indicates, or points. **2.** A scale indicator on a watch, balance, or other measuring instrument. **3.** A long, tapered stick for indicating objects on a chart, blackboard, or the like. **4.** A hunting dog of a breed having a short-haired coat that is usually white with black or brownish spots. **5.** *Informal.* A suggestion; a hint; a piece of advice. **—the Pointers.** In the constellation of the Plough, the two stars which align with the Pole Star and can be used to indicate north.

poin·til·lism (pwántee-iz'm, póyn-, -til-) *n.* A method of painting exemplified by Seurat and his followers in late 19th-century France consisting of the juxtaposition of dots of primary colours which blend in the viewer's eye from a distance, giving brighter secondary colours. Compare **divisionism.** [French *pointillisme,* from *pointiller,* to paint small dots, from *pointille,* small point or dot, from Italian *puntiglio,* diminutive of *punto,* point, dot, from Latin *punctum,* from the neuter past participle of *pungere,* to pierce, prick.] **—poin·til·list** *n. & adj.* **—poin·til·lis·tic** (-istik) *adj.*

point·ing (póynting) *n.* **1.** Cement or mortar used to fill up cracks or spaces in joints, as in brickwork. **2.** A method of marking psalms to indicate how irregular lines are to be chanted.

point lace *n.* A type of handmade lace, **needlepoint** *(see).*

point·less (póynt-ləss, -liss) *adj.* **1.** Meaningless; irrelevant: *a pointless remark.* **2.** Ineffectual; futile: *It would be pointless to complain.* **—point·less·ly** *adv.* **—point·less·ness** *n.*

point of honour *n., pl.* **points of honour.** A matter that affects one's honour or reputation.

point of inflection *n. Mathematics.* A stationary point on a curve at which the tangent to the curve changes from rotating in one direction to rotating in the other, as the curve passes through the point.

point of no return *n.* A stage or point reached in a course of action after which turning back or stopping is no longer possible.

point of order *n.* A question as to whether that which is being discussed is in order or allowed by the rules.

point of reference *n.* A reference *(see).*

point-of-sale (póynt-əv-sáyl) *adj.* Of, provided for, or situated at the place where purchases are made: *point-of-sale advertising.*

point of view *n.* **1.** The position from which something is observed or considered; a standpoint. **2.** A manner of viewing things; an attitude.

points·man (póynts-mən) *n., pl.* **-men** (-mən, -men). A person who operates the points on a railway line. Also *U.S.* "switchman".

point source *n. Optics.* A source of light or other radiation that can be regarded as having negligible size.

point system *n.* **1.** *Printing.* A system of measurement by the **point** *(see).* **2.** Any system of printing or writing for the blind that uses an alphabet of raised symbols or dots that correspond to letters, such as Braille. **3.** A system of evaluating and averaging achievement, as in education, by awarding numerical units or points.

point-to-point (póynt-tə-póynt) *n.* A cross-crountry or steeplechase race over a course marked by flags, often organised by a recognised hunt club or other body.

poise¹ (poyz) *v.* **poised, poising, poises.** *—tr.* **1.** To carry or hold in equilibrium; balance. **2.** To hold steady or raised, as in readiness: *with hands poised.* *—intr.* To be balanced or held in suspension; hover: *poise on the brink.*
~n. **1.** The state or condition of being balanced or held in equilibrium; stability; balance. **2.** Freedom from awkwardness or embarrassment; assurance; composure. **3.** The bearing or deportment of the head or body; mien. **4.** A state or condition of hovering or being suspended. [Middle English *poisen, peisen,* to weigh, from Old French *poiser, peser,* from Vulgar Latin *pēsāre* (unattested), variant of Latin *pensāre,* frequentative of *pendere,* to weigh.]

poise² (pwaaz) *n.* A centimetre-gram-second unit of dynamic viscosity equal to one dyne-second per square centimetre. [French, after Jean Louis Marie *Poiseuille* (1799–1869), French physician.]

poised (poyzd) *adj.* **1.** Assured; composed. **2.** Held balanced or steady in readiness: *stood poised for the jump.*

poi·son (póyz'n) *n.* **1.** Any substance that causes injury, illness, or death, especially by chemical means. **2.** Anything that is destructive, corruptive, or fatal: *the poison of her criticism.* **3.** A substance that inhibits or retards a chemical reaction or deactivates a catalyst. **4.** A substance in a nuclear reactor that absorbs neutrons without undergoing fission, thereby slowing down the chain reaction.
~tr.v. **poisoned, -soning, -sons. 1.** To give poison to; kill or harm with poison. **2.** To put poison on or into: *poison a cup.* **3. a.** To pollute: *Fumes poisoned the air.* **b.** To have a harmful influence on; corrupt, ruin, taint, or embitter: *Jealousy poisoned their friendship.* **4.** To inhibit or retard (a chemical or nuclear reaction).
~adj. Poisonous. [Middle English *poysoun,* potion, poisonous drink, from Old French *poison,* from Latin *pōtiō* (stem *pōtiōn-*), from *pōtāre,* to drink.] **—poi·son·er** *n.*

poison gas *n.* Any lethal or crippling vapour such as phosgene or chlorine, used in warfare.

poison hemlock *n. U.S.* A poisonous plant, **hemlock** *(see).*

poison ivy *n.* A North American shrub or vine, *Rhus radicans,* having leaflets in groups of three, small green flowers, and whitish berries, causing a rash on contact.

poi·son·ous (póyz'n-əss) *adj.* **1. a.** Capable of harming or killing by or as if by poison. **b.** Broadly, toxic or venomous. **2.** Containing a poison. **3.** Marked by apparent ill will; malicious: *a poisonous glance.* **4.** *Informal.* Objectionable; unpleasant. **—poi·son·ous·ly** *adv.* **—poi·son·ous·ness** *n.*

poison-pen letter (póyz'n-pén) *n.* A letter or note, usually anonymous, containing abusive or malicious information about the recipient or a third party.

Pois·son distribution (pwássoN, pwaa-sóN) *n. Statistics.* A probability distribution used to describe the occurrence of events in a large number of independent repeated trials. [After S.D. *Poisson* (1781–1840), French mathematician.]

Poi·tiers (pwáat-yay, pwaat-yáy). Capital of Vienne département, west France. It was the capital of the former province of Poitou and the site of many battles, including the defeat of the French (under John II) by the English (under Edward the Black Prince) in 1356. An agricultural centre, it also produces chemicals and electrical equipment.

poke¹ (pōk) *v.* **poked, poking, pokes.** *—tr.* **1.** To push or jab, as with a finger or arm; prod. **2.** To make (a hole or pathway, for example) by or as if by prodding, thrusting, or poking. **3.** To cause to project; stick: *A seal poked its head out of the water.* **4.** To stir (a fire) by prodding the wood or coal with a poker or stick. **5.** To strike; punch. **6.** *Slang.* To have sexual intercourse with. *—intr.* **1.** To make thrusts or jabs with a stick, poker, or the like. Used with *at.* **2.** To pry or meddle; intrude: *poking into another's business.* **3.** To search or look in a curious manner: *poking around in the drawer.* **4.** To thrust forward; appear; protrude: *His head poked from under the blankets.* **5.** *Chiefly U.S.* To live or proceed in a slow or lazy manner; dawdle; potter. Often used with *along.*
~n. **1.** A push, thrust, or jab. **2.** A punch or blow with the fist. **3.** *U.S.* A person who moves slowly or aimlessly; a dawdler. [Middle English *poken,* from Middle Dutch and Middle Low German *poken,* to strike, thrust (probably imitative).]

poke² *n.* **1.** A large bonnet having a projecting brim at the front, worn especially in the 18th and 19th centuries. Also called "poke bonnet". **2.** The brim of such a bonnet. [From POKE (to thrust).]

poke³ *n. Chiefly Regional.* A sack or bag. [Middle English, from Old North French *poque,* variant of Old French *poche,* pocket, from Frankish *pokka* (unattested), bag.]

pok·er¹ (pōkər) *n.* One that pokes; specifically, a metal rod used to stir a fire.

poker² *n.* Any of various card games played by two or more players who bet on the value of their hands. [19th century : origin obscure.]

poker face *n.* A face lacking any interpretable expression. [From the impassive face of an expert poker player.] **—pok·er-faced** (pōkər-fáyst, -fayst) *adj.*

poker machine *n. Australian.* A fruit machine. Also informally called "pokie".

po·key (pōki) *n., pl.* **-keys.** Also **pok·y** *pl.* **-kies.** *Chiefly U.S. Slang.* Jail; prison.
~adj. Variant of **poky.** [From POKY.]

pok·y, poke·y (pōki) *adj.* **-ier, -iest.** *Informal.* **1.** Small and cramped: *a poky flat.* **2.** *U.S.* Dawdling; dull; slow.
~n. Chiefly U.S. Slang. Variant of **pokey.** [From POKE, to thrust, (hence, slang) to confine.]

Pol. Poland; Polish.

Po·lack (pō-lak ‖ *U.S.* -laak) *n.* **1.** *Chiefly U.S. Slang.* A person of Polish descent or birth. Used derogatorily. **2.** *Obsolete.* A native of Poland; a Pole. [Polish *Polak.*] **—Po·lack** *adj.*

Po·land, People's Republic of (pōland). Polish **Pol·ska** (pól-ska). Country in eastern Europe. It is largely an undulating plain rising to the Carpathian Mountains in the south, and is crossed by the rivers Vistula and Warta. Becoming a united state in the 10th century, it was a great power during the 15th and 16th centuries but was partitioned in 1772, 1793, and 1795, after which it disappeared until reformed in 1918. Occupied by the Germans (1939–45), it has had Communist rule since 1948. Poland is largely an agricultural country, although industry has grown considerably since World War II. Economic troubles led to riots over the price of food in 1970, 1976, and 1980–81, culminating in strikes, the declaration of martial law, and the suppression of the free trade union, Solidarity, coupled with the threat of Soviet invasion (1981–82). Area, 312 677 square kilometres (120,725 square miles). Population, 36,000,000. Capital, Warsaw.

POLAND

Po·lan·ski (pə-lánski), **Roman** (1933–). Polish film director. His films, such as *Rosemary's Baby* (1968), *Chinatown* (1974), and *Tess* (1980), are notable for their brooding menace and black humour.
po·lar (pṓlər) *adj.* **1. a.** Of, pertaining to, or designating a pole. **b.** Measured from or referred to a pole or poles: *polar diameter.* **2.** Pertaining to, connected with, or located near the North Pole or South Pole. **3.** Occupying or characterised by opposite extremes. **4.** Serving as a guide, as a polestar or a pole of the earth might. **5.** Central or pivotal. [New Latin *polāris,* from Latin *polus,* POLE.]
polar angle *n.* The angle formed by the polar axis and the radius vector in a polar coordinate system.
polar axis *n.* The fixed reference axis from which the polar angle is measured in a polar coordinate system.
polar bear *n.* A large, white-furred bear, *Thalarctos maritimus,* of Arctic regions.
polar body *n. Genetics.* A minute cell produced and ultimately discarded in the development of an ovum, containing little or no cytoplasm but having one of the nuclei derived from the first or second meiotic division of the oocyte.
polar cap *n.* **1. a.** A high-altitude icecap. **b.** The polar regions of ice. **2.** *Astronomy.* Any differentiated polar region of a planet.
polar circle *n.* The **Arctic Circle** or **Antarctic Circle** *(both of which see).*
polar coordinate *n.* Either of two coordinates, the radius vector or the polar angle, that together can be used to specify the position of any point in a plane.
polar distance *n. Astronomy.* The angular distance between the celestial pole and the point to be measured on the celestial sphere.
po·lar·im·e·ter (pṓlə-rímmitər) *n.* An instrument used to measure the rotation of the plane of polarisation of polarised light, or the degree of polarisation of light passing through an optically active compound or sample. **—po·lar·i·met·ric** (-ri-méttrik) *adj.* **—po·lar·im·e·try** (-rímmətri) *n.*
Po·lar·is (pō-láariss, pə-, -lárriss) *n.* **1.** A star of the second magnitude in the constellation Ursa Minor, almost at the north celestial pole. Also called "North Star", "Pole Star". **2.** A U.S. Navy intermediate range surface-to-surface ballistic missile. [New Latin *(Stella) Polāris,* polar (star).]
po·lar·i·sa·tion (pṓlə-rī-záysh'n || *U.S.* -ri-) *n.* **1.** The uniform and nonrandom elliptical, circular, or linear variation of a wave characteristic, especially of vibrational orientation, in light or other radiation. **2.** The partial or complete polar separation of positive and negative electric charge in a nuclear, atomic, molecular, or chemical system. **3.** A concentration, as of groups, forces, or interests, about two conflicting or contrasting positions.
po·lar·i·scope (pō-lárri-skōp, pə-) *n.* An instrument for ascertaining, measuring, or exhibiting the properties of polarised light, or for studying the interactions of polarised light with optically transparent media.
po·lar·ise, po·lar·ize (pṓlə-rīz) *v.* **-ised, -ising, -ises.** *—tr.* **1.** To induce polarisation in; impart polarity to. **2.** To cause to concentrate about two conflicting or contrasting positions. *—intr.* To become polarised. **—po·lar·is·a·ble** *adj.* **—po·lar·is·er** *n.*
po·lar·i·ty (pō-lárrəti, pə-) *n., pl.* **-ties. 1.** Intrinsic separation into contrasting or opposile poles; intrinsic polar alignment or orientation, especially with respect to a physical property: *magnetic polarity.* **2.** The possession or manifestation of two opposing attributes, tendencies, or principles: *political polarity.* **3.** A specified polar extreme: *an electric terminal with positive polarity.*
po·lar·og·ra·phy (pṓlə-róggrəfi) *n.* An electrochemical method of quantitative or qualitative analysis based on the relationship between an increasing current passing through the solution being analysed and the increasing voltage used to produce the current. [From POLAR(ISATION) + -GRAPHY.] **—po·lar·o·graph·ic** (pō-lárrə-gráffik, pə-) *adj.* **—po·lar·o·graph·i·cal·ly** *adv.*
Po·lar·oid (pṓlə-royd) *n.* **1.** A trademark for a specially treated, transparent plastic capable of polarising light passing through it, used in sunglasses and other glare-reducing optical devices. **2. a.** A trademark for a type of camera that develops the film and produces prints within a few seconds of taking the photograph. **b.** A photograph taken with such a camera.
Polar Regions *pl.n.* The land and water areas surrounding the North and South poles.
pol·der (pṓl-dər, pól-) *n.* An area of low-lying land, especially in the Netherlands, that has been reclaimed from a body of water and is protected by dykes. [Middle Dutch *polre, polder*†.]
pole[1] (pōl) *n. Abbr.* **p. 1.** Either axial extremity of any axis through a sphere. **2.** Either of the regions contiguous to the extremities of the earth's rotational axis, the **North Pole** or the **South Pole** *(both of which see).* **3.** *Physics.* See **magnetic pole. 4.** *Electricity.* Either of two oppositely charged terminals, as in an electric cell or battery. **5.** *Astronomy.* See **celestial pole. 6.** *Biology.* **a.** A structurally or physiologically distinct region at either axial extremity of a nucleus, cell, or organism. **b.** Either end of the spindle formed in a cell during mitosis or meiosis. **7.** Either of two antithetical ideas, propensities, forces, or positions. **8.** Any fixed point of reference. **9.** *Geometry.* The origin in a polar coordinate system; the polar angle vertex. **—poles apart.** Having very different opinions, views, tastes, or the like. [Middle English, from Latin *polus,* from Greek *polos,* axis of the sphere, firmament.]
pole[2] *n.* **1.** A long, relatively slender, and generally rounded piece of wood or other material. **2.** The long, tapering, wooden shaft extending up from the front axle of a vehicle to the collars of the animals drawing it; a tongue. **3. a.** A unit of length, a **rod** *(see).* **b.** A unit of area equal to a square rod (30¼ square yards). **4.** *Nautical.* A small or light spar. **5.** In horseracing, the starting position nearest the inner rail on the inside lane. **—under bare poles.** *Nautical.* Having no sails up. Said of a sailing vessel. **—up the pole.** *Informal.* **a.** Crazy; mad. **b.** Misguided or mistaken.
~v. **poled, poling, poles.** *—tr.* **1.** To propel with a pole. **2.** To support (plants) with a pole. **3.** To strike, poke, or stir with a pole. **4.** To stir (molten metal) with a green pole that introduces carbon and deoxidises the substance by reacting with the oxygen. *—intr.* **1.** To propel a boat, raft, or the like with a pole. **2.** To use ski poles to gain speed or turn. [Middle English *po(o)le,* Old English *pāl,* from Common Germanic, from Latin *pālus,* stake.]
Pole (pōl) *n.* A native or inhabitant of Poland.
pole·axe (pṓl-aks) *n.* **1.** A battle-axe used in the Middle Ages, consisting of an axe, or an axe, hammer, and pick combination, with a long shaft. **2.** An axe having a hammer face opposite the blade, used to slaughter cattle.
~tr.v. **poleaxed, -axing, -axes.** To strike or fell with or as if with a poleaxe. [Middle English *pollax* : POLL (head) + AXE.]
pole·cat (pṓl-kat) *n.* **1.** A carnivorous mammal, *Mustela putorius,* of Europe, Asia, and northern Africa, having dark brown or black fur. It emits a foul-smelling fluid when alarmed. **2.** Any of several similar or related animals, especially the ferret in Britain or the skunk in the United States. [Middle English *polcat* : *pol-*† (meaning unknown) + CAT.]
pole horse *n.* A horse harnessed to the pole, or tongue, of a vehicle. Also called "poler".
po·lem·ic (pə-lémmik, po-, pō-) *n.* **1. a.** A controversy or argument, especially one that is a refutation of or an attack upon a particular opinion, doctrine, or the like. **b.** Loosely, any virulent criticism. **2.** A person engaged in or inclined to controversy, argument, or refutation.
~adj. Also **po·lem·i·cal** (-'l). Of, pertaining to, or given to controversy, argument, or refutation. [Medieval Latin *polemicus,* controversialist, from Greek *polemikos,* of war, hostile, opposed, from *polemos*†, war.] **—po·lem·i·cal·ly** *adv.*
po·lem·i·cist (pə-lémmi-sist, po-, pō-) *n.* Also **pol·e·mist** (-lémmist, póllimist). A person who writes or is skilled in polemics.
po·lem·ics (pə-lémmiks, po-, pō-) *n.* *Used with a singular verb.* The art or practice of argument or controversy, especially in support of or against a doctrine or belief.
pol·e·mol·o·gy (pól-i-mólləji, -e-, -ə-) *n.* The study of wars and conflicts between nations. [Greek *polemos,* war + -LOGY.] **—pol·e·mo·log·i·cal** (-mə-lójik'l) *adj.* **—pol·e·mol·o·gist** *n.*
po·len·ta (pō-léntə, pə-) *n.* A thick porridge made from maize and eaten especially in Italy. [Italian, from Latin, pearl barley.]
pol·er (pṓlər) *n.* **1.** One that propels, supports, conveys, or strikes with a pole. **2.** A pole horse.
Pole Star (pṓl-staar) *n.* **1.** A star, **Polaris** *(see).* **2.** *Small* **p,** *small* **s.** A guiding principle.
pole vault *n. Sports.* A field event in which the contestant jumps or vaults over a high crossbar with the aid of a long flexible pole.
pole-vault (pṓl-vawlt || -volt) *intr.v.* **-vaulted, -vaulting, -vaults.** *Sports.* To perform or compete in the pole vault. **—pole-vault·er** *n.*
poleyn (pṓlayn) *n.* A piece of armour protecting the knee.
po·lice (pə-léess || pō-, pṓleess) *n., pl.* **police. 1. a.** The government department established to maintain order, enforce the law, and prevent and detect crime. **b.** An official civil force, or body of persons, established and maintained for this purpose; a police force. **c.** *Used with a plural verb.* The members of such a force collectively. **2. a.** Any group of persons resembling the police force of a community in organisation or function: *military police.* **b.** *Used with a plural verb.* The members of such a group. **3.** *Archaic.* The regulation and control of the affairs of a community, especially with respect to the maintenance of order, law, health, morals, safety, and other matters affecting general welfare.
~tr.v. **policed, -licing, -lices. 1.** To regulate, control, or keep in order with or as if with police. **2.** *U.S.* To make (a military area) neat in appearance. [Originally "policy", "government organisation", from French, from Late Latin *polītia,* administration of the commonwealth, from Latin *polītīa,* the state, from Greek *politeia,* polity, citizenship, from *politēs,* citizen, from *polis,* city.]
police court *Law.* **1.** Formerly, a magistrate's court. **2.** Formerly in Scotland, a district court.
police dog *n.* A dog, especially a German shepherd, trained to aid the police.
police force *n.* A body of persons trained in methods of law enforcement and crime prevention and detection, and given authority to maintain the peace, safety, and order of the community.
po·lice·man (pə-léess-mən, pléess-) *n., pl.* **-men** (-mən). A male member of a police force.
police officer *n.* A policeman or policewoman; especially, a constable.
police state *n.* A country or other political unit in which the government exercises rigid and repressive controls over social, economic, and political life, especially by means of a secret police force.
police station *n.* The headquarters of a unit of a police force where those under arrest are first charged.
po·lice·wom·an (pə-léess-wŏŏmən, pléess-) *n., pl.* **-women** (-wimmin). *Abbr.* **P.W.** A female member of a police force.
pol·i·cy[1] (pól-ə-si, -i-) *n., pl.* **-cies. 1.** Any overall plan or course of

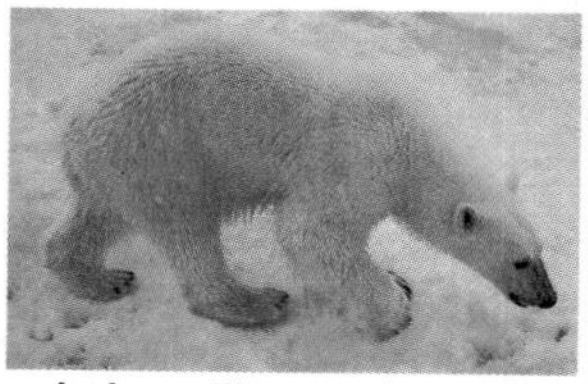

polar bear *These wandering Arctic hunters feed mainly on seals. When fully grown, they can be 2.5 metres long (more than 8 feet), and can weigh up to 720 kilograms (nearly 1,600 pounds).*

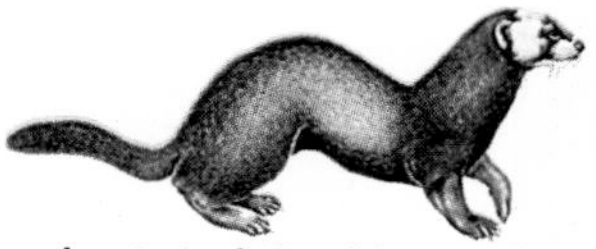

polecat *A relative of the weasel, the common Eurasian polecat usually lives in a woodland burrow. It is a good swimmer but a poor climber. Polecats are meat-eaters, hunting small animals such as rabbits, birds, and snakes. They are also known to have made stores of frogs for winter food – sometimes hoarding as many as 120 in larders in their burrows. The polecat bites the frogs at the base of the skull, paralysing but not killing them, so that they stay fresh for long periods.*

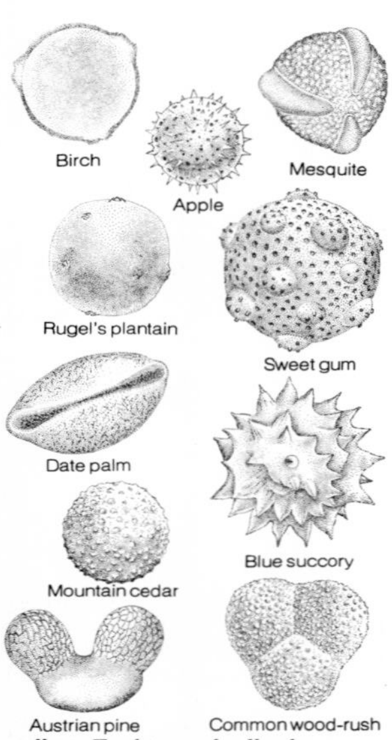
Birch
Apple
Mesquite
Rugel's plantain
Sweet gum
Date palm
Blue succory
Mountain cedar
Austrian pine
Common wood-rush
pollen *Each type of pollen has a distinctive shape. The material of the protective spore coat is so durable that botanists have been able to use pollen grains found in ancient rocks to identify plant species that grew millions of years ago.*

action adopted, as by a government, political party, or business organisation, designed to influence and determine immediate and long-term decisions or actions: *foreign policy; company personnel policy.* **2. a.** A course of action, guiding principle, or procedure considered to be expedient, prudent, or advantageous: *Honesty is the best policy.* **b.** Prudence, shrewdness, or sagacity in practical matters. **3.** *Scottish.* The park surrounding a country seat or large house. [Middle English *policye,* polity, commonwealth, policy, from Old French *policie,* from Latin *polītīa,* state, from Greek *politeia,* citizenship, from *politēs,* citizen, from *polis,* city.]

policy² *n., pl.* **-cies.** A written contract or certificate of insurance. [French *police,* from Provençal *poliss(i)a* or Italian *polizza,* probably from Medieval Latin *apodixa,* from Latin *apodīxis,* from Greek *apodeixis,* "a showing or making known", proof, from *apodeiknunai,* to show off, make known : *apo,* off, from + *deiknunai,* to show.]

pol·i·cy·hol·der (pól-ə-si-hōldər, -i-) *n.* A person or organisation that holds an insurance policy.

po·li·o (pṓli-ō) *n.* Poliomyelitis.

po·li·o·my·e·li·tis (pō-li-ō-mī́-ə-lī́tiss) *n.* An infectious viral disease occurring mainly in children and in its severest form attacking the central nervous system and producing paralysis, muscular atrophy, and often deformity. Also called "infantile paralysis", "polio". [Greek *polios,* grey + MYELITIS.]

po·lis (pól-iss) *n., pl.* **-leis** (-īss || -ayss) A city-state of ancient Greece. [Greek *polis,* city.]

pol·ish (póllish) *v.* **-ished, -ishing, -ishes.** *—tr.* **1.** To make smooth and shiny by abrasion or chemical action. **2.** To free from coarseness; make elegant; refine: *polish one's manners.* **3.** To remove flaws from; perfect or complete: *polish one's piano technique.* *—intr.* **1.** To become smooth or shiny by or as if by rubbing. **2.** To become perfect or refined. **—polish off.** *Informal.* **1.** To complete or finish quickly: *polish off a meal.* **2.** To eliminate or dispose of: *He polished off his enemies.* **—polish up.** To improve by study or practice. Often used with *on*: *polish up your singing.*
~n. **1.** Smoothness or shininess of surface or finish. **2.** A substance applied to smooth, colour, or shine a surface: *shoe polish.* **3.** The act or process of polishing. **4.** Elegance of style or manners; refinement. [Middle English *polisshen,* from Old French *polir* (present stem *poliss-*), from Latin *polīre.*] **—pol·ish·er** *n.*

Po·lish (pṓlish) *adj. Abbr.* **Pol.** Of or pertaining to Poland, its inhabitants, or their language or culture.
~n. Abbr. **Pol. 1.** The West Slavonic language that is the major language of Poland. **2.** *Used with a plural verb.* The people of Poland. [From POLE.]

pol·ished (póllisht) *adj.* **1.** Refined; elegant; cultured. **2.** Impeccable; accomplished; flawless. **3.** Having the husk removed. Said of grains of rice. **3.** Having no imperfections or errors; flawless.

Pol·it·bu·ro (póllit-bewr-ō, pə-lít-) *n., pl.* **-ros.** The chief political and executive committee of a Communist party, as in the U.S.S.R. [Russian *Polit(icheskoe) Buro,* political bureau.]

po·lite (pə-lī́t || pō-) *adj.* **-litre, -litest. 1.** Marked by consideration for others, correct manners, or tact; courteous. **2.** Refined; elegant; cultivated: *polite society.* [Middle English *polyt,* polished, smoothed, from Latin *polītus,* past participle of Latin *polīre,* to POLISH.] **—po·lite·ly** *adv.* **—po·lite·ness** *n.*
Synonyms: *polite, civil, courteous, genteel.*

pol·i·tesse (pólli-téss) *n.* Courteous formality; politeness. [French, from Italian *politezza, pulitezza,* cleanliness, from *pulīto,* "polished", clean, from Latin *polītus,* past participle of *polīre,* to POLISH.]

pol·i·tic (pól-ətik, -itik) *adj.* **1.** Artful; ingenious; shrewd: *a politic diplomat.* **2.** Using, displaying, or proceeding from policy; prudent; judicious: *a politic decision.* **3.** Crafty; unscrupulous; cunning. **4.** Political. Now archaic except in the phrase *the body politic.* [Middle English *polytyk,* "political", pursuing a policy, prudent, from Old French *politique,* from Latin *polīticus,* from Greek *politikos,* of a citizen, from *politēs,* citizen, from *polis,* city.] **—pol·i·tic·ly** *adv.*

po·lit·i·cal (pə-líttik'l || pō-) *adj.* **1.** Of or pertaining to the study, structure, or affairs of government or the state, especially in regard to civil policy-making rather than military, legal, or administrative matters. **2.** Having a definite or organised policy or structure of government. **3.** Of or pertaining to policies or parties within a state: *strong political views.* **4.** Of or pertaining to the citizens of a state: *political rights.* **5.** Of or pertaining to the security of the government or state: *a political offence.* **6.** Very interested or active in politics: *I'm not a political person, I'm afraid.* **7.** Having or influenced by partisan interests; not neutral, objective, or unbiased: *The English legal system must never become a political institution.* **8.** Arising from or influenced by partisan or selfish factors, rather than the merits of the case: *a purely political decision; His promotion must have been political.* **—po·lit·i·cal·ly** *adv.*

political animal *n.* **1.** A person who is skilled or experienced in the art of political subterfuge and who uses it to advance his personal interests or career. **2.** A person who is extremely interested or involved in politics. **3.** Any person, or human beings in general, considered as being unavoidably influenced by politics.

political asylum *n.* The protection offered by a state to a foreigner who has left or wishes to leave his own country for political reasons.

political economy *n.* The science of economics. Not in current usage.

political lesbian *n.* A feminist who chooses for ideological reasons to abstain from sexual relations with men, whether or not she then engages in lesbianism. **—political lesbianism** *n.*

political prisoner *n.* A person imprisoned for any act a state considers hostile, especially the expression of views in conflict with its ideology, or for any offence it may consider to endanger its security. Compare **prisoner of conscience.**

political science *n.* The study of the history, processes, principles, and structure of government and of political institutions. **—political scientist** *n.*

pol·i·ti·cian (pólli-tísh'n) *n.* **1. a.** One who is actively involved in politics, especially party politics. **b.** One who holds or seeks a political office. **2.** One skilled or experienced in the science or administration of government. **3.** One skilled at or given to scheming and manoeuvring.

po·lit·i·cise, po·lit·i·cize (pə-lítti-sīz || pō-) *v.* **-cised, -cising, -cises.** *—intr.* To engage in or discuss politics. *—tr.* To make political in character or awareness. **—po·lit·i·ci·sa·tion** (-sī-záysh'n) *n.*

pol·i·tick·ing (pólli-ticking) *n.* **1.** Involvement in politics, especially for one's personal advantage. **2.** Canvassing for votes.

po·lit·i·co (pə-líttikō) *n., pl.* **-cos.** *Informal.* A politician or political agitator. Often used derogatorily. [Italian and Spanish, "political", from Latin *polīticus,* POLITIC.]

pol·i·tics (pól-ə-tiks, -i-) *n.* *Usually used with a singular verb.* **1.** The art or science of power and government. **2.** The policies, goals, or affairs of a government or state or of the groups or parties within it. **3. a.** The conducting of or engaging in political affairs, often professionally. **b.** The business, activities, or profession of a person so involved. **4.** The methods or tactics involved in managing a state or government. **5. a.** The scheming and manoeuvring for power and personal advantage that occurs within a given group: *office politics.* **b.** A political aspect inherent in a given situation or sphere: *sexual politics.* **6.** *Used with a plural verb.* Opinions or principles dealing with political subjects: *Her politics are conservative.*

pol·i·ty (pólləti) *n., pl.* **-ties. 1.** The form of government of a nation, state, church, or organisation. **2.** Any organised society, such as a nation, having one specific form of government. **3.** The supervision of public affairs; political administration. **4.** The condition of having a government or being politically organised. [From Latin *polītīa,* POLICY.]

pol·ka (pólkə, pṓlkə) *n.* **1.** A lively dance consisting of three steps and a skip, originating in Bohemia, performed by couples in duple time. **2.** A piece of music for this dance. [French and German, from Czech *pulka,* half-step, from *pul,* half.] **—pol·ka** *intr.v.*

pol·ka dot (pólkə, pṓlkə, pṓkə) *n.* **1.** Any of a number of dots or round spots forming a pattern on cloth. **2.** A pattern or fabric marked with such dots. [Perhaps a respelling of *poke a dot.*]

poll (pōl) *n.* **1.** The casting and registering of votes in an election. **2.** The number of votes cast or recorded. **3.** A tax required for voting, a **poll tax** *(see).* **4.** A list or record of persons, especially for taxing or voting purposes. **5. a.** Any sampling of opinion on an issue in a given group: *took a poll of the class.* **b.** An **opinion poll** *(see).* **6.** The head, especially the top of the head where hair grows. **7.** The blunt or broad end of a hammer, axe, or other similar tool. **—go to the polls.** To vote. Used of a country or electorate.
~v. **polled, polling, polls.** *—tr.* **1.** To receive (a specified number of votes). **2.** To register (a person), especially for voting purposes. **3.** To receive or record the votes of. **4.** To cast (a vote or ballot). **5.** To canvass (a person, area, or sample group of persons) to survey general opinion. **6.** To cut off or trim (hair, horns, or wool, for example). **7.** To trim or cut off the hair, wool, branches, or horns of: *poll sheep.* *—intr.* To vote in an election. [Middle English *pol, polle,* head (whence the Modern English senses of "counting by heads", "registering of votes"), of Low German origin perhaps akin to Middle Low German *polle*†.] **—poll·er** *n.*

pol·lack, pol·lock (póllək) *n., pl.* **-lacks** or collectively **pollack.** A marine food and game fish, *Pollachius pollachius,* related to the cod, occurring chiefly in northern Atlantic waters. [17th century : from Scottish *podlock*†.]

pol·lard (pól-ərd || -aard) *n.* **1.** A tree whose top branches have been cut back to the trunk so that it may produce a dense growth of new shoots. **2.** An animal, such as an ox, goat, or sheep, that no longer has its horns.
~tr.v. **pollarded, -larding, -lards.** To change into a pollard. [From POLL.]

polled (pōld) *adj.* Having no horns; hornless.

pol·len (póllən) *n. Botany.* The fine, powder-like material produced by the anthers of flowering plants and by the male cones of conifers, which contains the male gametes and functions as the male element in fertilisation. [New Latin, from Latin, flour, dust.]

pollen analysis *n.* **Palynology** *(see).*

pollen count *n.* The average number of pollen grains in a cubic yard or other standard volume of air over a 24-hour period at a particular time and place, used to estimate the possible severity of hay-fever attacks.

pollen tube *n. Botany.* The slender tube that grows from a grain of pollen down the style of a pollinated plant to the ovule, and conveys male gametes which fertilise the egg cell.

pol·lex (pólleks) *n., pl.* **pollices** (pólli-seez). The innermost forelimb digit; the thumb. [Latin, thumb.] **—pol·li·cal** *adj.*

pollin–, pollini– *comb. form..* Indicates pollen; for example, **pollinosis, polliniferous.** [New Latin *pollen* (stem *pollin-*), POLLEN.]

pol·li·nate, pol·len·ate (pólli-nayt) *tr.v.* **-nated, -nating, -nates.** *Botany.* To convey or transfer pollen from an anther or male cone to a stigma or female cone of (a plant or flower) in the process of fertilisation. [New Latin *pollen* (stem *pollin-*), POLLEN.] **—pol·li·na·tion** (-náysh'n) *n.* **—pol·li·na·tor** *n.*

pol·lin·ic (po-línnik, pə-) *adj. Botany.* Of or pertaining to pollen.

pol·li·nif·er·ous, pol·len·if·er·ous (pólli-níffərəss) *adj.* **1.** Producing or yielding pollen. **2.** Adapted for carrying pollen, as a bee's legs are. [POLLINI- + -FEROUS.]

pol·lin·i·um (po-lín-i-əm, pə-) *n., pl.* **-ia** (-i-ə). *Botany.* A mass of agglutinated pollen grains, found in the flowers of most orchids and milkweeds. [New Latin : POLLIN- + -IUM.]

pol·li·no·sis, pol·len·o·sis (pólli-nṓ-siss) *n. Pathology.* Allergic reaction to pollen, as in disorders such as hay fever or asthma. [New Latin : POLLIN- + -OSIS.]

pol·li·wog, pol·ly·wog (pólli-wog) *n. U.S.* An immature frog or toad; a tadpole. [Middle English *polwygle : pol, polle,* POLL (head) + *wiglen, wigelen,* to WIGGLE.]

pollock. Variant of **pollack.**

Pol·lock (póllək), **Jackson** (1912–56). U.S. artist. After early surrealist work, he turned to the technique of action painting, throwing or dripping paint onto a very large canvas.

poll·ster (pṓlstər) *n.* A person who conducts opinion polls.

poll tax *n.* A former tax levied, especially in the United States, on persons rather than on property, often as a requirement for voting. Also called "poll".

pol·lut·ant (pə-lṓo-t'nt, -léw-) *n.* Anything that pollutes; especially, any gaseous, chemical, or organic waste that contaminates air, soil, or water.

pol·lute (pə-lṓot, -léwt) *tr.v.* **-luted, -luting, -lutes.** **1.** To contaminate (the environment) with harmful or poisonous substances. **2.** To render morally impure; corrupt. **3.** To make ceremonially impure; profane; desecrate. [Middle English *polluten,* from Latin *polluere* (past participial stem *pollut-*).] —**pol·lut·er** *n.* —**pol·lu·tive** *adj.*

pol·lu·tion (pə-lṓo-sh'n, -léw-) *n.* **1.** The act or process of polluting or the state of being polluted. **2.** The contamination of soil, water, or the atmosphere by the discharge of noxious substances. **3.** Broadly, any public nuisance attributable to a particular cause: *noise pollution.*

Pol·lux[1] (pólləks) *Greek Mythology.* One of the twin sons of Zeus and Leda. See **Castor and Pollux.**

Pollux[2] *n. Astronomy.* A first-magnitude star in the constellation Gemini. [After the mythical twin POLLUX.]

Pol·ly (pólli) *n.* A name for a parrot.

Pol·ly·an·na (pólli-ánnə) *n.* A foolishly or blindly optimistic person. [After the title character in *Pollyanna* (1913), novel by Eleanor Porter (1868–1920).]

po·lo (pṓlō) *n.* **1.** A game of Oriental origin played by two teams of three or four players on horseback, equipped with long-handled mallets for driving a small wooden ball through the opponents' goal. **2.** Any similar game, such as water polo. [Balti *polo,* "ball," akin to Tibetan *bo-lo.*] —**po·lo·ist** *n.*

Po·lo (pṓlō), **Marco** (*c.* 1254–1324). Venetian traveller. His father Niccolo and uncle Maffeo had already made one successful trading expedition to the court of the Mongol Emperor Kublai Khan in China before they took Marco with them in 1271. He entered Kublai's diplomatic service and undertook missions to all parts of the Mongol Empire before returning to Venice in 1295. His memoirs were for hundreds of years the West's chief source of knowledge of the Orient.

pol·o·naise (póllə-nayz || pṓlə-) *n.* **1.** A stately, marchlike dance in triple time, consisting mainly of a promenade of couples. **2.** A piece of music for this dance. **3.** A woman's dress of the 18th century, having a fitted bodice and draped cutaway skirt, worn over an elaborate underskirt. [French, from the feminine of *polonais,* Polish, from Medieval Latin *Polōnia,* Poland.]

polo neck *n.* **1.** A soft, high, turning collar worn turned down so as to fit closely about the neck. **2.** A sweater having such a collar. —**polo-neck** *adj.*

po·lo·ni·um (pə-lṓni-əm) *n. Symbol* **Po** A naturally radioactive metallic element, occurring in minute quantities as a product of radium disintegration and produced by bombarding bismuth with neutrons. It has many isotopes ranging in mass number from 193 to 218, of which polonium-210, with a half-life of 134.8 days, is the most readily available. Atomic number 84, melting point 254°C, boiling point 962°C, relative density 9.32, valencies 2, 4, 6. [Latin *Polōnia,* Poland, native country of its discoverers, the Curies.]

po·lo·ny (pə-lṓni) *n., pl.* **-nies.** *British.* A large, lightly seasoned sausage made chiefly from pork, usually eaten cold and sliced in salads or sandwiches. Also called "Bologna sausage". [Probably from *Bologna (sausage).*]

Polska. See **Poland.**

pol·ter·geist (póltər-gīst, pṓltər-) *n.* A noisy, mischievous spirit that manifests itself by slamming doors, moving objects, and the like. [German *Poltergeist : poltern,* to make noises, rattle, knock, from Middle High German *boldern, buldern* + German *Geist,* ghost, from Old High German *geist.*]

pol·troon (pol-trṓon) *n.* A base coward. Not in current usage. [French *poltron,* from Italian *poltrone,* perhaps augmentative of *poltro,* lazy person.] —**pol·troon·er·y** *n.*

pol·y (pólli) *n., pl.* **polys.** *Informal.* A polytechnic.

poly– *comb. form.* Indicates: **1.** More than one, many, or much; for example, **polygamy.** **2.** More than usual; abnormal or excessive; for example, **polydipsia.** **3.** A polymer; for example, **polythene, polyester.** [Greek *polus,* much, many.]

pol·y·a·del·phous (pólli-ə-délfəss) *adj. Botany.* Having or designating stamens arranged in three or more groups by means of their united stalks or filaments. Said of flowers. [POLY- + Greek *adelphos,* brother + -OUS.]

pol·y·am·ide (pólli-ám-īd, -id) *n. Chemistry.* A polymer containing repeated amide linkages, as in various kinds of nylon.

pol·y·a·mine (pólli-áymeen) *n.* Any of a group of organic compounds that contain two or more amino groups.

pol·y·an·dry (pólli-andri) *n.* **1.** The state or practice of having more than one husband at a single time. **2.** *Botany.* The condition in flowers of having an indefinite number of stamens. **3.** The practice of a female animal's mating with more than one male during a single breeding season. [Greek *poluandria,* from *poluandros :* POLY- + -ANDROUS.] —**pol·y·an·drous** (-ándrəss) *adj.*

pol·y·an·thus (pólli-ánthəss) *n., pl.* **-thuses.** Any of a group of hybrid garden primroses, especially *Primula polyantha,* having clusters of variously coloured flowers. [New Latin, from Greek *poluanthos,* "having many flowers" : POLY- + -ANTHOUS.]

polyanthus narcissus *n.* A bulbous plant, *Narcissus tazetta,* native to Eurasia, having clusters of fragrant white or yellow flowers.

pol·y·a·tom·ic (pólli-ə-tómmik) *adj. Chemistry.* Having three or more atoms as constituents. Said especially of molecules.

pol·y·ba·sic (pólli-báy-sik) *adj. Chemistry.* Polyprotic.

pol·y·ba·site (pólli-báy-sīt, pə-líbbə-) *n.* A black mineral with a metallic lustre, containing silver, copper, antimony, arsenic, and sulphur, essentially $(Ag,Cu)_{16}(Sb,As)_2S_{11}$, often found in veins of silver. [German *Polybasit :* POLY- + BAS(IS) + -ITE.]

Po·ly·bi·us (po-líbbi-əs(s), pə-) (*c.*201–120 B.C.). Greek historian. His 40-volume history of Rome in the second and third centuries B.C. has mostly been lost.

pol·y·car·bon·ate (pólli-kárbə-nayt, -nit, -nət) *n.* Any of a class of clear, strong polyester resins, made from phosgene and dihydric phenols, and used in moulded articles.

pol·y·car·pel·lar·y (pólli-kaar-pélləri || U.S. -kárpə-lerri) *adj.* Having or consisting of many carpels. [POLY- + CARPEL + -ARY.]

pol·y·car·pic (pólli-kárpik) *adj. Botany.* Also **pol·y·car·pous** (-pəss) (for sense 1). **1.** Having fruit with two or more carpels. **2.** Producing flowers and fruit several times in one season. [POLY- + -CARPOUS.] —**pol·y·car·py** *n.*

pol·y·cen·trism (pólli-séntriz'm) *n.* The principle or advocacy, especially in Communism, of more than one possible dogma or political centre. —**pol·y·cen·trist** *n. & adj.*

pol·y·chaete (pólli-keet) *n.* Any of various marine worms of the class Polychaeta, including the lugworms, bristleworms, and ragworms, having paired, flattened, bristle-tipped organs of locomotion. [New Latin *Polychaeta,* from Greek *polukhaitēs,* with much hair : POLY + *khaitē,* long hair, CHAETA.] —**pol·y·chaete, pol·y·chae·tous** (-kéetəss) *adj.*

pol·y·chro·mat·ic (pólli-krō-máttik, -krə-) *adj.* Also **pol·y·chro·mic** (-krṓmik), **pol·y·chro·mous** (-krṓməss). **1.** Having many colours or manifesting changes of colour. **2.** *Physics.* Having a mixture of wavelengths. Said of light and other electromagnetic radiation. **3.** *Physics.* Having a mixture of energies. Said of streams of particles. —**pol·y·chro·ma·tism** (-krṓmə-tiz'm) *n.*

pol·y·chro·mat·o·phil·i·a (pólli-krō-máttə-fílli-ə, -krṓmətə-) *n.* Also **pol·y·chro·mo·phil·i·a** (-krṓmə-). Susceptibility to staining with more than one type of dye, as seen in diseased red blood cells. [POLY- + CHROMATO- + -PHILIA.] —**pol·y·chro·mat·o·phil·ic** *adj.*

pol·y·chrome (pólli-krōm) *adj.* **1.** Having many or various changing colours; polychromatic. **2.** Made or decorated in many or various colours.

~*n.* An object having or decorated in many colours. [Greek *polukhrōmos :* POLY- + -CHROME.]

pol·y·chro·my (pólli-krōmi) *n.* The art of employing many colours in decoration, especially as used in ancient architecture or pottery.

pol·y·con·ic projection (pólli-kónnik) *n. Geography.* A conic map projection having distances between meridians along every parallel of latitude equal to those distances on a globe. The central geographical meridian is a straight line and the others are curved, while the parallels are arcs of circles.

pol·y·cot·ton (pólli-kótt'n) *n.* A textile composed of a mixture of cotton and polyester fibres.

pol·y·cot·y·le·don (pólli-kótti-léed'n) *n. Botany.* A plant having several cotyledons. —**pol·y·cot·y·le·don·ous** *adj.*

pol·y·cy·clic (pólli-sīklik, -sicklik) *adj. Chemistry.* Of or designating a compound with molecules that contain three or more rings of atoms.

pol·y·cy·thae·mi·a (pólli-sī-théemi-ə) *n. Pathology.* A condition marked by an abnormally large number of red cells in the blood. [POLY- + CYT(O)- + -HAEMIA.]

pol·y·dac·tyl (pólli-dáktil) *adj.* Also **pol·y·dac·ty·lous** (-əss). Having more than the normal number of fingers or toes.

~*n.* A polydactyl person or animal. [Greek *poludaktulos :* POLY- + DACTYL.] —**pol·y·dac·tyl·ism, pol·y·dac·ty·ly** *n.*

pol·y·dem·ic (pólli-démmik) *adj. Ecology.* Occurring in or inhabiting two or more regions. [POLY- + (EN)DEMIC.]

pol·y·dip·si·a (pólli-dípsi-ə) *n.* Excessive or abnormal thirst. [New Latin : POLY- + Greek *dipsa,* thirst.] —**pol·y·dip·sic** *adj.*

pol·y·em·bry·o·ny (pólli-émbri-əni, -em-brī-əni) *n. Biology.* The development of more than one embryo from a single egg or ovule, as occurs in the development of identical twins. [POLY- + Late Latin *embryō* (stem *embryōn-*) + -Y.] —**pol·y·em·bry·on·ic** (-émbri-ónnik) *adj.*

pol·y·es·ter (pólli-éstər) *n. Chemistry.* Any of numerous synthetic resins, produced chiefly by reaction of dibasic acids with dihydric

polo *Polo is thought to have been first played by the Persians, possibly as long ago as 500 B.C. It spread, in the 19th century, to Europe and the United States from India where it had become popular with the British stationed there.*

alcohols. Reinforced polyester resins are light, strong, and weather-resistant, and are used in boat hulls, swimming pools, waterproof fibres, adhesives, and moulded parts. [POLY(MER) + ESTER.] —**pol·y·es·ter·i·fi·ca·tion** (-ifi-káysh'n) *n.*

pol·y·eth·ene (pólli-étheen) *n.* A synthetic material, **polythene** *(see).* Also called "polyethylene".

pol·y·ether (pólli-éethər) *n.* Any of a large number of synthetic polymeric materials containing C-O-C linkages, as in the epoxy resins.

po·lyg·a·la (pə-líggələ) *n.* A plant, the **milkwort** *(see).* [New Latin *Polygala,* from Latin, from Greek *polugalon* : POLY- + *gala,* milk.]

po·lyg·a·mist (pə-líggəmist) *n.* One who practises polygamy.

po·lyg·a·my (pə-líggəmi) *n.* **1.** The state or practice of having more than one spouse at any one time, especially more than one wife, or in the case of animals, more than one female mate. **2. a.** The condition of having both hermaphrodite and unisexual flowers on the same plant. **b.** The condition of having hermaphrodite and unisexual flowers on different plants of the same species. [Old French *polygamie,* from Late Latin *polygamia,* from Greek *polugamia* : POLY- + -GAMY.] —**po·lyg·a·mous** *adj.* —**po·lyg·a·mous·ly** *adv.*

pol·y·gene (pólli-jeen) *n.* Any of a set of cooperating genes, each producing a small quantitative effect on a single characteristic.

pol·y·gen·e·sis (pólli-jénni-siss) *n.* The derivation of a species or type from more than one ancestor. Compare **monogenesis.** —**pol·y·ge·net·ic** (-jə-néttik), **pol·y·gen·ic** (-jénnik) *adj.*

pol·y·glot (pólli-glot) *adj.* Speaking, writing, written in, or composed of several languages.

~*n.* **1.** A person with a reading, writing, or speaking knowledge of several languages. **2.** A book, especially the Bible, containing versions of the same text in different languages. **3.** A mixture or confusion of languages. [French *polyglotte,* from Greek *poluglōttos* : POLY- + *glōtta, glōssa,* tongue.] —**pol·y·glot·ism, pol·y·glot·tism** *n.*

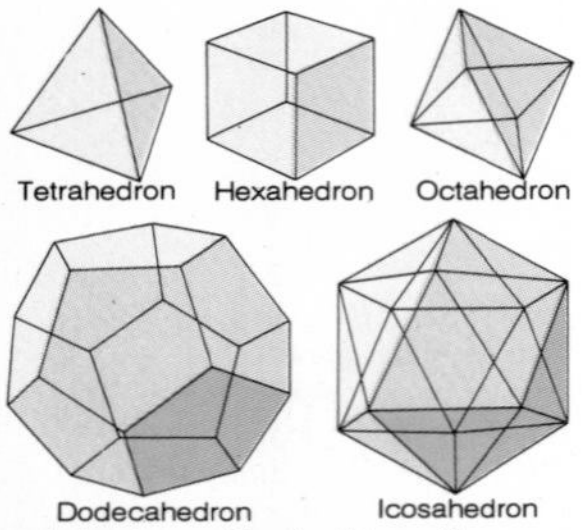
Tetrahedron
Hexahedron
Octahedron
Dodecahedron
Icosahedron

polyhedron *Each of these five regular polyhedra has identical regular faces and identical angles. There are no other shapes with these properties.*

pol·y·gon (pólli-gən || -gon) *n.* A closed plane figure bounded by three or more line segments. [Late Latin *polygōnum,* from Greek *polugōnon,* from *polugōnos,* "having many angles" : POLY- + -GON.] —**po·lyg·o·nal** (pə-líggən'l) *adj.* —**po·lyg·o·nal·ly** *adv.*

po·lyg·o·num (pə-líggənəm) *n.* Any of numerous plants of the widely distributed genus *Polygonum,* including knotgrass and bistort, characterised by stems with knotlike joints and heads of small pink or white flowers. [New Latin, from Greek *polugonon,* knotgrass : POLY- + *gonu,* knee.]

pol·y·graph (pólli-graaf, -graf) *n.* **1.** An instrument that simultaneously records changes in such physiological processes as heartbeat, blood pressure, and respiration, and is sometimes used in lie detection. **2.** A device that produces simultaneous copies of matter written, printed, or drawn. **3.** An author who is prolific or who writes many varying works. [Greek *polugraphos,* "writing a lot" : POLY- + -GRAPH.] —**po·lyg·ra·pher** (pə-líggrəfər) *n.* —**pol·y·graph·ic** (-gráffik) *adj.*

po·lyg·y·ny (pə-lijəni) *n.* **1.** The condition or practice of having more than one wife or female mate at a single time. **2.** The condition in flowers of having many styles. [POLY- + Greek *gunē,* woman.] —**po·lyg·y·nous** *adj.*

pol·y·he·dral angle (pólli-héedrəl). *Geometry.* A configuration formed by three or more planes having intersections that form a common vertex. Compare **solid angle.**

pol·y·he·dron (pólli-héedrən, -hé-) *n., pl.* **-drons** or **-dra** (-drə). *Geometry.* A solid bounded by polygons. [New Latin, from Greek *poluedron,* neuter of *poluedros,* having many sides or seats : POLY- + -HEDRON.] —**pol·y·he·dral** *adj.*

pol·y·his·tor (pólli-hístər) *n.* A polymath. [Greek *poluistōr* : POLY- + *histōr,* learned.] —**pol·y·his·tor·ic** (-hiss-tórrik || -táwrik) *adj.*

pol·y·hy·dric (póli-hídrik) *adj.* Also **pol·y·hy·drox·y** (póli-hī-dróksi). *Chemistry.* Containing at least two hydroxyl groups.

Pol·y·hym·ni·a (pólli-hím-ni-ə). *Greek Mythology.* The Muse of sacred song, poetry, and mime. [Latin, from Greek *Polumnia,* from *polumnos,* abounding in songs : POLY- + *humnos,* HYMN.]

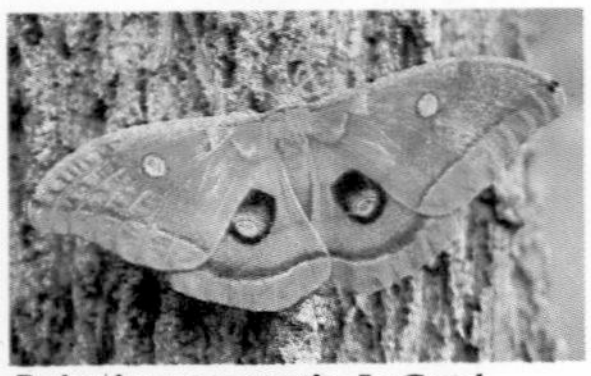

Polyphemus moth *In Greek mythology, Polyphemus was a one-eyed giant, and this silkworm moth is so named because of the single eyelike marking on each of its hind wings.*

pol·y·mas·ti·gote (pólli-másti-gōt) *adj. Zoology.* Having a tuftlike arrangement of flagella. [POLY- + Greek *mastix*† (stem *mastig-*), whip + -ATE.]

pol·y·math (pólli-math) *n.* A person of great or varied learning. [Greek *polumathēs* : POLY- + *math-,* stem of *manthanein,* to learn.] —**pol·y·math, pol·y·math·ic** (-máthik) *adj.*

pol·y·mer (póllimər) *n. Chemistry.* A substance formed by linkage of numerous natural and synthetic compounds of usually high molecular weight of two or more repeated units. [From POLYMERIC.]

pol·y·mer·ic (pólli-mérrik) *adj. Chemistry.* Of, pertaining to, or consisting of a polymer. [Greek *polumerēs,* having many parts : POLY- + -MEROUS.] —**pol·y·mer·i·cal·ly** *adv.* —**po·lym·er·ism** (pə-límmə-riz'm, póllimə-) *n.*

pol·y·mer·ise, pol·y·mer·ize (póllimə-rīz, pə-límmə-) *v.* **-ised, -ising, -ises.** *Chemistry.* —*tr.* To cause (a chemical compound) to form a polymer. —*intr.* To react to form a polymer. Used of compounds. —**pol·y·mer·i·sa·tion** (-rī-záysh'n || *U.S.* -ri-) *n.*

po·lym·er·ous (pə-límmərəss) *adj. Biology.* Consisting of numerous parts. [POLY- + -MEROUS.]

pol·y·me·thyl methacrylate (pólli-méethīl, -méthil) *n.* A clear synthetic material used extensively as a substitute for plate glass.

pol·y·morph (pólli-mawrf) *n.* **1.** *Biology.* An organism characterised by polymorphism. **2.** *Chemistry.* A specific crystalline form of a compound or mineral that can crystallise in different forms. **3.** Any of a group of white blood cells that have a lobed nucleus and granular cytoplasm. Also called "polymorphonuclear leucocyte". [From *polymorphous,* having many forms, from Greek *polumorphos* : POLY- + -MORPHOUS.]

pol·y·mor·phism (pólli-mórfiz'm) *n.* **1.** *Biology.* The occurrence of different forms, stages, or colour types in organisms of the same species. **2.** *Chemistry.* Crystallisation of a compound or mineral in at least two distinct forms. —**pol·y·mor·phic** (-mórfik), **pol·y·mor·phous** *adj.*

pol·y·myx·in (pólli-míksin) *n. Medicine.* Any of various mainly toxic antibiotics derived from strains of the soil bacterium *Bacillus polymixa* and used to treat a variety of infections. [New Latin *(Bacillus) polymixa* : POLY- + MYX(O)- + -IN.]

Pol·y·ne·sia (pólli-néezh-ə, -i-ə, -néezi-ə, -néeshə). A division of the Pacific islands, including New Zealand and the many smaller islands in the southern and central Pacific. The smaller islands are mostly coral islands and the larger ones volcanic. See also **Melanesia, Micronesia.** See map at **Pacific Ocean.**

Pol·y·ne·sian (pólli-née-zh'n, -zhi-ən, -zi-ən, -sh'n) *adj.* Of or pertaining to Polynesia, its inhabitants, culture, or languages.

~*n.* **1.** A member of the native peoples of Polynesia, including the Hawaiians, Maoris, Samoans, and Tahitians. **2.** A subfamily of Austronesian languages spoken in Polynesia.

pol·y·neu·ri·tis (pólli-newr-rítiss, -new- || -noor-, -nōō-) *n.* Any disorder involving inflammation of all the peripheral nerves.

pol·y·no·mi·al (pólli-nṓmi-əl) *adj.* Of, pertaining to, or consisting of more than two names or terms.

~*n.* **1.** *Biology.* A taxonomic name consisting of more than two terms. **2.** *Mathematics.* **a.** An algebraic function of two or more summed terms, each term consisting of a constant multiplier and one or more variables raised, in general, to integral powers. For example, the general form of a polynomial of degree *n* in a single real variable *x* is $a_0x^n + a_1x^{n-1} + \ldots + a_{n-1}x + a_n$ where $a_0, a_1, \ldots, a_n$ are real numbers with $a_0 \neq 0$ and *n* is a positive integer. **b.** Any mathematical expression of two or more terms. Also called "multinomial". [POLY- + (BI)NOMIAL.]

pol·y·nu·cle·o·tide (pólli-néw-kli-ə-tīd || -nōō-) *n.* A compound consisting of a chain of linked nucleotides, such as the nucleic acids DNA and RNA.

po·lyn·ya (póllin-yaa, -yaá) *n.* A large area of open water surrounded by sea ice. [Russian *polyn'ya,* from *polyĭ,* open.]

pol·y·on·y·mous (pólli-ónniməss) *adj.* Having or called by several different names. [POLY- + -ONYM + -OUS.]

pol·yp (póllip) *n.* **1.** *Zoology.* A coelenterate having a cylindrical body and an oral opening usually surrounded by tentacles, such as a hydra or coral. Compare **medusa. 2.** *Pathology.* A growth protruding from the mucous lining of an organ, such as the nose. In this sense, also called "polypus". [French *polype,* octopus, from Latin *polypus,* from Greek *polupous,* "many-footed" : POLY- + *pous,* foot.] —**pol·yp·oid** *adj.*

pol·y·par·y (pólli-pəri || *U.S.* -perri) *n., pl.* **-ies.** Also **pol·y·par·i·um** (-páir-i-əm) *pl.* **-ia** *Zoology.* The common framework and base of a polyp colony, especially of coral. [From POLYP.]

pol·y·pep·tide (pólli-péptīd) *n. Biochemistry.* A **peptide** *(see)* containing between 10 and 100 amino acids.

pol·y·pet·al·ous (pólli-pétt'l-əss) *adj. Botany.* Having distinctly separate petals: *a polypetalous corolla.*

pol·y·pha·gi·a (pólli-fáy-jə, -ji-ə) *n.* An excessive or pathological desire to eat. [New Latin, from Greek *poluphagia,* from *poluphagos,* eating much, POLYPHAGOUS.] —**pol·y·pha·gi·an** *adj.*

po·lyph·a·gous (pə-líffəgəss) *adj. Zoology.* Feeding on or utilising a variety of foods. [Greek *poluphagos,* eating much : POLY- + -PHAGOUS.]

pol·y·phase (pólli-fayz) *adj. Electricity.* Having, using, or pertaining to two or more alternating electrical signals with the same amplitudes but different phases; multiphase.

Pol·y·phe·mus (pólli-féeməss). *Greek Mythology.* The Cyclops who confined Odysseus and his companions in a cave until Odysseus blinded him and escaped.

pol·y·phone (pólli-fōn) *n. Phonetics.* A written character or combination of characters having two or more phonetic values, such as the letter *c* in *cake* and *certain.* [POLY- + -PHONE.]

pol·y·phon·ic (pólli-fónnik) *adj.* **1.** *Music.* **a.** Of or pertaining to polyphony. **b.** Of or designating an instrument that can sound more than one note at a time. **2.** Having many voices. **3.** *Phonetics.* Of or pertaining to a polyphone. —**pol·y·phon·i·cal·ly** *adv.*

polyphonic prose *n.* Prose that has a distinct rhythmic pattern and uses poetic devices so as to give the effect of verse, especially when read aloud.

po·lyph·o·ny (pə-líffəni, po-) *n., pl.* **-nies. 1.** The simultaneous combination of two or more independent melodic parts, especially when in close harmonic relationship; counterpoint. Compare **homophony, monophony. 2.** A style of composition, or a piece of music, incorporating polyphony. **3.** The representation of two or more sounds by one written character, such as the *c* in *cake* and *certain.* [Greek *poluphōnia,* variety of tones, from *poluphōnos,* having many tones : POLY- + *phōnē,* sound, PHONE.] —**po·lyph·o·nous** *adj.* —**po·lyph·o·nous·ly** *adv.*

pol·y·phy·let·ic (pólli-fī-léttik) *adj. Biology.* Pertaining to or characterised by development from more than one ancestral type. —**pol·y·phy·let·i·cal·ly** *adv.*

pol·y·phy·o·dont (pólli-fī-ə-dont) *adj.* Having many sets of teeth that develop and are shed in succession. [New Latin, "producing many teeth", from Greek *poluphuēs* (POLY- + *-phuēs,* from *phuein,* to bring forth) + -ODONT.]

pol·y·ploid (pólli-ployd) *adj. Genetics.* Having more than twice the normal haploid chromosome number.
~*n. Genetics.* An organism with more than two sets of chromosomes. [POLY- + -PLOID.] —**pol·y·ploi·dic** (-plóydik) *adj.* —**pol·y·ploi·dy** (-ploydi) *n.*

pol·yp·noe·a (po-lípni-ə, pə-, póllip-née-ə) *n.* Very rapid breathing; panting. [New Latin : POLY- + Greek *pnoia*, breathing, from *pnein*, to breathe.] —**pol·yp·ne·ic** *adj.*

pol·y·pod (pólli-pod) *adj.* Also **po·lyp·o·dous** (pə-líppədəss). Having numerous legs. Said of insect larvae and similar organisms.
~*n.* A polypod animal or organism. [Greek *polypous* (stem *polypod-*), "many-footed" : POLY- + *pous*, foot.]

pol·y·po·dy (pólli-pədi, -pŏdi) *n., pl.* **-dies.** Any of various ferns of the widely distributed genus *Polypodium*, having simple or compound fronds and creeping rootstocks. Also called "wall fern". [Middle English *polypodie*, from Latin *polypodium*, from Greek *polupodion*, diminutive of *polupous*, POLYPOD.]

pol·y·pore (pólli-pawr ‖ -pŏr) *n.* A **pore fungus** (see).

pol·y·pro·pyl·ene (pólli-prṓpi-leen) *n.* A synthetic, strong, polymeric material made from propene and used extensively in making moulded articles, such as kitchenware, toys, and chairs. Also called "polypropene".

pol·y·pro·tic (pólli-prṓtik) *adj. Chemistry.* Designating an acid with two or more replaceable hydrogen atoms in each molecule; polybasic. [POLY- + PROT(ON) + -IC.]

pol·yp·tych (pólliptik) *n.* A decorated altarpiece or panel having four or more hinged sections which can be folded together. [Greek *poluptukhos*, having many folds : POLY- + *ptukhē*, a fold, from *ptussein*†, to fold.]

pol·y·pus (pólli-pəss) *n., pl.* **-pi** (-pī) or **-puses.** *Pathology.* A polyp (see). [Latin, POLYP.]

pol·y·rhyth·mic (pólli-ríthmik) *adj. Music.* Designating a composition or performer that has or uses several different rhythms, as for different parts, simultaneously. —**pol·y·rhythm** (-rith'm) *n.*

pol·y·sac·cha·ride (pólli-sáckə-rīd) *n.* Also **pol·y·sac·cha·rose** (-rōz, -rōss). A carbohydrate consisting of a group of nine or more monosaccharides joined by glycosidic bonds, such as starch and cellulose.

pol·y·se·my (pólli-seemi, pə-líssəmi) *n.* The quality or condition of an individual word having several different meanings at a given time. —**pol·y·se·mous** (pólli-séeməss, pə-líssəməss) *adj.*

pol·y·sep·al·ous (pólli-sépp'l-əss) *adj. Botany.* Having distinctly separated sepals.

pol·y·some (pólli-sŏm) *n.* A structure in the cytoplasm of cells that consists of a group of ribosomes associated with messenger RNA. Also called "polyribosome". [POLY- + -SOME.]

pol·y·so·mic (pólli-sŏmik) *adj. Genetics.* Having an excess number of one or more chromosomes, but not all. [POLY- + (CHROMO)SOM(E) + -IC.] —**pol·y·so·my** (pólli-sŏmi) *n.*

pol·y·sper·my (pólli-spermi) *n.* The entry of several sperms into an ovum during fertilisation. —**pol·y·sper·mic** (-spérmik) *adj.*

po·lys·ti·chous (pə-lístikəss, po-) *adj.* Arranged in two or more series or rows. Said especially of leaves on a stem.

pol·y·sty·rene (pólli-stír-een) *n.* A polymeric form of styrene used either as a hard, rigid plastic for moulded articles, or as a white, light, expanded foam for packing and thermal insulation.

pol·y·sul·phide (pólli-súlfīd) *n. Chemistry.* A sulphur compound containing at least two sulphur atoms linked together per molecule.

pol·y·syl·lab·ic (pólli-si-lábbik) *adj.* 1. Having more than three syllables. 2. Characterised by words having more than three syllables. —**pol·y·syl·lab·i·cal·ly** *adv.*

pol·y·syl·la·ble (pólli-sílləb'l) *n.* A polysyllabic word. [Medieval Latin *polysyllaba*, feminine of *polysyllabus*, polysyllabic, from Greek *polusullabos* : POLY- + *sullabē*, SYLLABLE.] —**pol·y·syl·lab·i·cism** (-si-lábbi-siz'm), **pol·y·syl·la·bism** (-silləbiz'm) *n.*

pol·y·syn·de·ton (pólli-síndi-tən ‖ -ton) *n.* The repetition of connectives or conjunctions in close succession for rhetorical effect, as in the phrase *here and there and everywhere.* [Late Greek *polusundeton*, from *polusundetos*, using many connectives : Greek, POLY- + *sundetos*, bound together (see **syndetic**).]

pol·y·syn·thet·ic (pólli-sin-théttik) *adj. Linguistics.* Designating a language, such as Eskimo, in which many of the elements of a sentence or phrase are combined into one word and do not exist separately; holophrastic. Compare **synthetic**.

pol·y·tech·nic (pólli-ték-nik) *adj.* 1. Pertaining to technical training. 2. Pertaining to or dealing with many arts or sciences.
~*n.* In Britain, a college of higher education specialising in the teaching of technical and vocational subjects and applied sciences up to degree level. [French *polytechnique*, from Greek *polutekhnos*, skilled in many arts : POLY- + *tekhnē*, art.]

pol·y·tene (pólli-teen) *adj. Genetics.* Designating a chromosome in which the chromatids have remained unseparated after duplicating, resulting in a very large chromosome with conspicuous transverse bands.

pol·y·tet·ra·fluor·o·eth·y·lene (pólli-téttrə-flóor-ō-éthi-leen) *n. Abbr.* **PTFE** A waxy, opaque-white, thermoplastic resin (-C₂F₄)*n*, thermally stable, resistant to acids, alkalis, and oxidising agents, and having an extremely low coefficient of friction. It is used as a low-friction coating, especially for nonstick pans and for chemical-resistant gaskets, seals, and hoses. A trademark is "Teflon".

pol·y·the·ism (pólli-thee-iz'm, -thée-) *n.* The worship of or belief in more than one god. [French *polythéisme*, from Greek *polutheos*,

believing in many gods : POLY- + *theos*, god.] —**pol·y·the·ist** *n.* —**pol·y·the·is·tic** (-thee-ístik) *adj.*

pol·y·thene (pólli-theen) *n.* Any of various synthetic polymeric materials made from ethene and used in moulded articles, pipes, coatings, and textiles. There are two main forms: *low-density polythene*, which is soft and flexible, and *high-density polythene*, which is harder and rigid. Also called "polyethylene", "polyethene". [Shortened from *polyethylene*.]

po·lyt·o·cous (pə-líttəkəss, po-) *adj. Biology.* Producing many offspring or ova at a single time. [Greek *polutokos*, bearing numerous offspring : POLY- + *tokos*, offspring, from *tiktein*, to beget.]

pol·y·to·nal·i·ty (pólli-tō-nál-əti) *n. Music.* The use or occurrence of two or more keys simultaneously in a composition. —**pol·y·ton·al** (-tŏn'l) *adj.* —**pol·y·ton·al·ly** *adv.*

pol·y·troph·ic (pólli-tróffik ‖ -trófik) *adj.* 1. *Biology.* Obtaining nourishment from various types of organic material. 2. *Pathology.* Characterised by or pertaining to excessive nutrition. [Greek *polytrophos*, well-fed : POLY- + *trephein*, to feed.]

pol·y·typ·ic (pólli-típpik) *adj.* Also **pol·y·typ·i·cal** (-'l). Existing in, having, or involving many different forms or types.

pol·y·un·sat·u·rat·ed (pólli-un-sáchə-raytid, -sáchoor-, -sáttewr-) *adj.* Of, pertaining to, or containing long chains of carbon atoms with numbers of double carbon-carbon linkages. Said especially of natural fats and oils used in margarines and cooking oils.

pol·y·ure·thane (pólli-yóor-ə-thayn; *also, wrongly,* -theen) *n.* Also **pol·y·ure·than** (-than). Any of various thermoplastic or thermosetting resins, of varying flexibility, used in paints, varnishes, adhesives, foams, and electrical insulation. Also called "urethane".

pol·y·u·ri·a (pólli-yóor-i-ə) *n. Pathology.* Excessive passage of urine, as in diabetes. [POLY- + -URIA.] —**pol·y·u·ric** *adj.*

pol·y·va·lent (pólli-váylənt) *adj.* 1. *Microbiology.* Containing, sensitive to, or interacting with more than one kind of antigen, antibody, toxin, or microorganism. 2. *Chemistry.* **a.** Having more than one valency. **b.** Having a valency of 3 or higher; multivalent. [POLY- + *valent*, from VALENCE.] —**pol·y·va·lence**, **pol·y·va·len·cy** *n.*

pol·y·vi·nyl (pólli-vín'l, -vínil) *adj.* Designating any of a group of polymerised thermoplastic vinyl compounds, such as PVC.

polyvinyl acetate *n. Abbr.* **PVA.** A common, clear, thermoplastic resin used in paints and adhesives.

polyvinyl chloride *n.* See **PVC.**

pol·y·zo·an (pólli-zṓ-ən) *n.* Any aquatic invertebrate animal of the phylum Polyzoa (or Bryozoa), consisting of a colony of polyp-like individuals. Also called "bryozoan". [New Latin *Polyzoa* : POLY- + -ZOA.] —**pol·y·zo·an** *adj.*

pol·y·zo·ar·i·um (pólli-zō-áir-i-əm) *n., pl.* **-aria** (-i-ə). Also **pol·y·zo·a·ry** (-zṓ-əri) *pl.* **-ries.** *Zoology.* A polyzoan colony or its supporting skeletal structure. [POLY- + -ZO(A) + -ARIUM.] —**pol·y·zo·ar·i·al** (-zō-áir-i-əl) *adj.*

pol·y·zo·ic (pólli-zṓ-ik) *adj. Biology.* 1. Forming or consisting of a colony of zooids. 2. Having many sporozoites. [POLY- + -ZOIC.]

pom (pom) *n. Australian & N.Z. Slang.* A British person; a pommy.

pom·ace (púmmiss) *n.* 1. The pulpy refuse remaining after the juice has been pressed from apples or other fruit. 2. Any similar pulpy material, such as that remaining after the extraction of oil from nuts, seeds, or fish. [Middle English, from Medieval Latin *pōmācium*, cider, from Latin *pōmum*, apple.]

po·ma·ceous (po-máyshəss, pō-) *adj.* 1. Of, pertaining to, or characteristic of apples. 2. Of, pertaining to, or bearing pomes. [New Latin *pomaceus* : Latin *pōmum*, apple (see **pomace**) + -ACEOUS.]

po·made (po-máad, pə-, -máyd ‖ pō-) *n.* A perfumed ointment applied to the hair. Also called "pomatum".
~*tr.v.* **pomaded, -mading, -mades.** To apply pomade to. [French *pommade*, from Italian *pomata*, hair ointment (originally apple-scented), from *pomo*, apple, from Latin *pōmum*.]

po·man·der (pō-mándər, pə- ‖ pō-mandər) *n.* 1. A mixture of aromatic substances carried in an apple-shaped container, formerly regarded as a protection against infection and now used to perfume rooms, wardrobes, or the like. 2. A case or box for holding this mixture. [Middle English, variant of Old French *pome d'embre*, from Medieval Latin *pōmum de ambra*, "apple" or "ball of amber" : *pōmum*, apple, POME + *de*, of + *ambra*, AMBER.]

Pom·bal (pom-bál), **Sebastião José de Carvalho e Melo, Marquês de** (1699-1782). Portuguese statesman. As chief minister during most of the reign of King Joseph (1750-77), he was both a ruthless despot and a social and economic reformer.

pom·be (pómbay) *n. East African.* An alcoholic drink made from grain, especially from millet. [Swahili.]

pome (pōm) *n. Botany.* A fleshy fruit in which the ovary and seeds are enclosed in an enlarged receptacle, such as the apple, pear, or quince. [Middle English, from Old French *pomme, pome*, apple, from Vulgar Latin *pōma* (unattested), from Latin *pōmum*.]

pome·gran·ate (pómmi-grannit, pómmə-, póm- ‖ *U.S. also* púm-) *n.* 1. A semitropical shrub or small tree, *Punica granatum*, native to Asia, and widely cultivated for its edible fruit. 2. The fruit of this tree, having a tough, reddish rind, and containing many seeds enclosed in a juicy red pulp with a mildly acid flavour. [Middle English *poumgarnei, pomegranard*, from Old French *pome grenate* : *pome*, apple, POME + *grenate*, having many seeds, from Latin *grānātus*, from *grānum*, grain.]

pom·e·lo (pómmi-lō, púmmi-) *n., pl.* **-los.** The **grapefruit** or **shaddock** (*both of which see*). [19th century : origin obscure.]

Pom·e·ran·i·a (pómmə-ráyni-ə). Former region of central Europe,

pomegranate *Originally the pomegranate grew only in Asia. But it is now grown in most parts of the world for its edible fruit (above) and as an ornamental tree for its scarlet flowers.*

now absorbed into East Germany and Poland (1945). It extends from the Baltic Sea to the river Vistula in a low-lying plain.

Pom·er·a·ni·an (pómmə-ráyni-ən) *adj.* Of or relating to Pomerania or its people.
~*n.* **1.** A native or inhabitant of Pomerania. **2.** A toy dog of a breed having long, silky hair and a small body.

pom·fret cake (púm-frit, póm-) *n.* A soft, round, flat, liquorice sweet. Also called "pomfret", "Pontefract cake". [From *Pomfret*, earlier form of PONTEFRACT, where it was originally made.]

pom·i·cul·ture (pómmi-kulchər ‖ *U.S.* pŏmi-) *n.* The cultivation of fruit. [Latin *pōmum*, fruit, POME + CULTURE.]

po·mif·er·ous (po-míffərəss, pō-) *adj. Botany.* Bearing pomes. [Latin *pōmifer*, fruit-bearing : *pōmum*, fruit, POME + -FER.]

pom·mel (púmm'l, póm'l) *n.* **1.** A knob on the hilt of a sword or other weapon. **2.** The raised front part of a saddle; a saddlebow.
~*tr.v.* **pommelled** or *U.S.* **pommeled**, **-melling** or *U.S.* **-meling**, **-mels.** To beat; pummel. [Middle English *pomel*, from Old French, from Vulgar Latin *pōmellum* (unattested), rounded knob, diminutive of Latin *pōmum*, fruit, apple, POME.]

pom·my, pom·mie (pómmi) *n., pl.* **-mies.** *n. Sometimes capital* P. *Australian & N.Z. Slang.* A British person. Often used derogatorily. [20th century : origin obscure.]

po·mol·o·gy (po-móllǝji) *n.* The scientific study and cultivation of fruit. [New Latin *pomologia* : Latin *pōmum*, fruit, POME + -LOGY.] —**po·mo·log·i·cal** (pómmǝ-lójik'l ‖ *U.S.* pŏmǝ-) *adj.* —**po·mo·log·i·cal·ly** *adv.* —**po·mol·o·gist** (-móllǝjist) *n.*

Pomona. See **Mainland.**

pomp (pomp) *n.* **1.** Dignified or magnificent display; splendour. **2.** Vain or ostentatious display. [Middle English, from Old French *pompe*, from Latin *pompa*, from Greek *pompē*, "a sending", solemn procession, from *pempein*†, to send.]

pom·pa·dour (póm-pǝ-door, pón-, -dawr ‖ -dōr) *n.* **1.** A woman's hairstyle, popular in the 18th century, formed by sweeping the hair straight up from the forehead, into a high, turned-back roll. **2.** A man's hair style with the hair brushed up from the forehead. [Invented by the Marquise de POMPADOUR.]

Pom·pa·dour (póm-pǝ-door, pón-, -dawr ‖ -dōr), **Marquise de**, also known as Madame de Pompadour; born Jeanne Antoinette Poisson (1721–64). Mistress of King Louis XV of France. She was popularly blamed for engineering France's alliance with Austria, which led to the disastrous Seven Years' War (1756–63).

pom·pa·no (póm-pǝ-nō, púm-) *n., pl.* **-nos** or collectively **pompano**. Any of several marine food fishes of the genus *Trachinotus*; especially, *T. glancus*, of tropical and temperate Atlantic waters. [Spanish *pámpano*†.]

Pom·pei·i (pom-páy-ee). Ancient city of Campania, southern Italy. Situated on the Gulf of Naples, it was buried by the eruption of Mt. Vesuvius (A.D. 79). Since its rediscovery (1748), excavations have provided an invaluable insight into ancient Roman life.

Pom·pey (pómpi), also called Pompey the Great; Latin name Cneius Pompeius Magnus (106–48 B.C.). Roman general and statesman. He suppressed the slave revolt led by Spartacus and campaigned on the Empire's eastern frontiers. He joined Julius Caesar and Crassus to form a ruling triumvirate in 60 B.C. He broke with Caesar in 50 B.C. but was defeated by him at Pharsala in 48 B.C. and fled to Egypt, where he was murdered.

Pom·pi·dou (pompi-dōō; *French* poN-pee-dōō), **Georges (Jean Raymond)** (1911–74). French statesman and president. He served as adviser (1944–46) and personal assistant (1958–59) to de Gaulle, helping to draft the constitution of the Fifth Republic. He was prime minister four times and helped to negotiate a settlement between France and the Algerians (1961) and to defuse the student revolt (1968). He succeeded de Gaulle as president (1969–74).

pom-pom[1] (póm-pom) *n.* **1.** In World War I, a variety of large machine gun using one-pound shells. **2.** In World War II, an automatic, rapid-fire, antiaircraft cannon. [Imitative.]

pompom[2] *n.* Also **pom·pon** (póm-pon). **1.** A tuft or ball of wool, feathers, or other material worn as a decoration, especially on a hat. **2.** A small, button-like flower of certain chrysanthemums and dahlias. [French *pompon*†.]

pom·pous (pómpǝss) *adj.* **1.** Characterised by an exaggerated show of dignity or self-importance; pretentious. **2.** Pretentious in speech or manner. **3.** *Archaic.* Characterised by pomp or stately display; ceremonious. [Middle English, from Old French *pompeux*, from Late Latin *pompōsus*, from Latin *pompa*, POMP.] —**pom·pos·i·ty** (-póssǝti) *n.* —**pom·pous·ly** *adv.* —**pom·pous·ness** *n.*

'pon (pon). *Archaic.* Contraction of *upon*.

ponce (ponss) *n. Chiefly British.* **1.** A man who lives off the earnings of a prostitute; a pimp. **2.** *Slang.* A flashy, showy, and often effeminate man. Used derogatorily.
~*intr.v.* **ponced, poncing, ponces.** **1.** To be a ponce. **2.** *Slang.* **a.** To act in a flashy, showy, and often effeminate manner. Usually used with *about* or *around*. **b.** To do something in an ostentatious, inefficient, or frivolous manner. Usually used with *about* or *around*. [Perhaps from POUNCE.]

Ponce de Le·ón (pónss dǝ lée-ǝn; *Spanish* pón-thay the-lay-ón), **Juan** (1460–1521). Spanish explorer. He sailed with Columbus on his second voyage (1493–94) and started the settlement of Puerto Rico in 1508, becoming its governor (1509–12). He discovered Florida in 1513 but when starting a settlement there in 1521 he was killed in a skirmish with the local Indians.

pon·cey, pon·cy (pón-si) *adj. Slang.* Characteristic of a ponce; especially, flashy or showy. Used derogatorily.

pon·cho (pónchō) *n., pl.* **-chos.** **1.** A blanket-like cloak having a hole in the centre for the head, worn originally in South America. **2.** A similar garment worn instead of a jacket or coat, or as a shawl. [American Spanish, from Araucanian *pontho*, woollen fabric.]

pond (pond) *n.* A still body of water, smaller than a lake, often of artificial construction.
~*v.* **ponded, -ponding, ponds.** —*intr.* To form a pond. —*tr.* To confine in, or as if in, a pond; dam up. [Middle English *ponde*, *pounde*, enclosure, Old English *pund*-.]

pon·der (póndǝr) *v.* **-dered, -dering, -ders.** —*tr.* To weigh mentally; consider carefully. —*intr.* To meditate; deliberate; reflect. Often used with *on* or *upon*. [Middle English *ponderen*, from Old French *ponderer*, from Latin *ponderāre*, to weigh, ponder, from *pondus* (stem *ponder-*), weight.] —**pon·der·er** *n.*

pon·der·a·ble (póndǝrǝ-b'l) *adj.* Capable of being weighed or assessed; appreciable.
~*n.* A factor or consideration that can be assessed. —**pon·der·a·bil·i·ty** (-bíllǝti) *n.*

pon·der·ous (póndǝr-ǝss) *adj.* **1.** Having great weight; massive; huge. **2.** Graceless or unwieldy from weight. **3.** Lacking fluency; laboured; dull: *a ponderous speech.* —See Synonyms at **heavy.** [Middle English, from Old French *pondereux*, from Latin *ponderōsus*, from *pondus* (stem *ponder-*), weight.] —**pon·der·ous·ly** *adv.* —**pon·der·ous·ness, pon·der·os·i·ty** *n.*

Pon·di·cher·ry (póndi-chérri, -shérri). Union Territory of southeast India. On the Coromandel coast, it was a former French territory (founded 1674), reverting to Indian control in 1954.

pond lily *n.* The **water lily** *(see).*

Pon·do (póndō) *n., pl.* **-dos** or collectively **Pondo.** A member of a Xhosa-speaking black people of southern Africa, living chiefly in Pondoland in Transkei. —**Pon·do** *adj.*

pon·dok (pón-dok) *n.* Also **pon·dok·kie** (pon-dócki). *South African.* **1.** A crude or roughly built hut or shelter; a shack. **2.** A very small or dilapidated house. [Afrikaans, perhaps from Malay, hut, or from Hottentot, hut.]

pond scum *n.* Any of various freshwater algae that form a usually greenish scum on the surface of stagnant water.

pond skater *n.* Any water insect of the family Gerridae, having a slender body and long legs used to skim across the water's surface. Also called "skater", "water strider".

pond·weed (pónd-weed) *n.* **1.** Any of various submerged or floating aquatic plants of the genus *Potamogeton.* **2.** Any of various similar plants, such as **Canadian pondweed** *(see).*

pone (pōn, pŏni) *n.* In card games, the player on the dealer's right or, in two-handed games, the dealer's opponent. [Latin, "play!", from second-person singular imperative of *ponere*, to put, place.]

pong (pong) *n. British Informal.* An unpleasant smell; a stink.
~*intr.v.* **ponged, ponging, pongs.** *British Informal.* To give off an unpleasant smell; stink. [20th century : origin obscure.] —**pong·y** (póng-gi) *adj.*

pon·gee (pónjee, pon-jée) *n.* **1.** A soft, thin undyed cloth of Chinese or Indian silk with a knotty weave. **2.** A synthetic fabric resembling this. [Mandarin Chinese *běn zhī*, "homemade" : *běn*, own, self + *zhī*, weave.]

pon·gid (póng-gid, pónjid) *n.* Any primate of the family Pongidae; an **anthropoid ape** *(see).*
~*adj.* Of or pertaining to the family Pongidae. [New Latin *Pongidae*, from *Pongo* (genus), from Congolese *mpongo*, ape.]

pon·go (póng-gō) *n., pl.* **-gos.** *British Military Slang.* A serviceman, especially one in the army. [From PONG.]

pon·iard (pón-yǝrd, -yaard) *n.* A dagger.
~*tr.v.* **poniarded, -iarding, -iards.** To stab with a poniard. [French *poignard*, from *poing*, fist, from Old French, from Latin *pugnus.*]

pons (ponz) *n., pl.* **pontes** (pónteez). *Anatomy.* **1.** Any slender tissue joining two parts of an organ. **2.** The **pons varolii.** [Latin *pōns*, bridge.]

pons as·i·no·rum (ássi-náwrǝm ‖ -nórǝm) *n.* **1.** A proposition in the first book of Euclid, stating that the angles opposite the equal sides of an isosceles triangle are equal. **2.** A problem difficult for beginners. [Latin, "asses' bridge" (the fifth proposition of Euclid mentioned in sense 1, supposedly very difficult to "cross" : *pōns*, PONS + *asinōrum*, genitive plural of *asinus*, ASS.]

pons va·ro·li·i (vǝ-rŏli-ī) *n.* A band of nerve fibres in the brain connecting the medulla oblongata and the mesencephalon below the cerebellum. Also called "pons". [New Latin, "bridge of Varoli", after Constanzo *Varoli* (1542–75), Italian surgeon and anatomist.]

pont (pont) *n. South African.* A flat-bottomed ferryboat, moved by a cable, rope, or chain attached at both sides of a river bank. [Afrikaans, from Dutch, ferryboat, PUNT.]

Pon·ta Del·ga·da (póntǝ del-gaádǝ). Largest city of the Azores, situated on São Miguel Island. It is a tourist centre and fuelling point for shipping.

Pon·te·fract (pónti-frakt; *formerly* púm-frit). Town in West Yorkshire, northern England. Britain's first parliamentary election by secret ballot was held here in 1872. Coalmining and the production of liquorice sweets, pomfret cakes, are important.

Pontefract cake *n.* A **pomfret cake** *(see).*

Pon·tic (póntik) *adj.* Of or pertaining to the Black Sea region. [Latin *Ponticus*, from Greek *Pontikos*, from *Pontos*, PONTUS.]

pon·ti·fex (pónti-feks) *n., pl.* **pontifices** (pon-tíffi-seez). **1.** In ancient Rome, a member of the Pontifical College, the highest college of priests, headed by the *Pontifex Maximus.* **2.** A pontiff. [Latin,

Pompeii *The temple of Apollo at Pompeii, with Vesuvius in the background. The building was preserved, like others in the town, by the ash which buried it when Vesuvius erupted in* A.D. *79.*

probably from Etruscan, reshaped by folk etymology as if to mean "bridge-maker".]

pon·tiff (póntif) *n.* **1. a.** The pope. **b.** *Archaic.* A bishop. **2.** A pontifex. [French *pontif,* from Latin *pontifex,* PONTIFEX.]

pon·tif·i·cal (pon-tíffik'l) *adj.* **1.** Pertaining to, characteristic of, or suitable for a pope or bishop. **2.** Having the dignity, pomp, or authority of a pontiff. **3.** Pompously authoritative. ~*n.* **1.** *Plural.* The vestments and insignia of a pontiff. **2.** A book of ceremonies and rites for a bishop. [Latin *pontificālis,* from *pontifex,* PONTIFEX.] —**pon·tif·i·cal·ly** *adv.*

pon·tif·i·cate (pon-tíffi-kət, -kit, -kayt) *n.* The office or term of office of a pontiff. ~*intr.v.* (-kayt) **pontificated, -cating, -cates. 1.** To serve as a pontiff. **2.** To speak or behave with pompous authority. [Latin *pontificātus,* from *pontifex,* PONTIFEX.]

pon·ti·fy (pónti-fī) *intr.v.* **-fied, -fying, -fies.** To speak or behave with pompous authority; pontificate.

pon·til (póntil) *n.* A glassmaker's tool, a *punty (see).* [French, perhaps from Italian *puntello,* d minutive of *punto,* point, from Latin *punctum,* from the neuter past participle of *pungere,* to prick.]

pon·tine (póntīn) *adj.* **1.** Of or pertaining to bridges. **2.** Pertaining to the **pons varolii** *(see).* [Latin *pōns* (stem *pont-*), bridge.]

Pontine Marshes. Reclaimed area in south Latium, central Italy. Drainage was completed in the 1930s, destroying malarial breeding grounds and providing rich agricultural land.

Pontius Pilate. See **Pilate.**

Pont l'É·vê·que (pón lay-vék) *n.* A soft-centred square French cheese made of whole cows' milk. [After *Pont L'Évêque,* town in northern France.]

pon·to·nier (pónta-néer) *n. Military.* A person in charge of pontoons or engaged in the construction of pontoon bridges. [French *pontonnier,* from *ponton,* PONTOON.]

pon·toon¹ (pon-tóon, pón-) *n.* **1. a.** A flat-bottomed boat or other structure used to support a floating bridge. **b.** A floating structure serving as a dock. **2.** A float on a seaplane. [French *ponton,* floating bridge, from Old French, from Latin *pontō* (stem *pontōn-*), boat bridge, from *pōns,* bridge.]

pontoon² *n.* **1.** A card game in which the aim is to hold cards that have a score higher than those of the banker, but no higher than 21. **2.** A winning hand in this game, consisting of an ace and a court card or ten, that adds up to exactly 21. Also called "vingt-et-un", "twenty-one". [Probably from French *vingt-et-un,* twenty-one.]

pontoon bridge *n.* A temporary floating bridge using pontoons for support. Also called "bateau bridge".

Pon·tus (póntəss). Ancient kingdom in northeast Asia Minor. Situated on the south shore of the Black Sea, it reached its peak under Mithridates VI but declined after his defeat by Pompey (c.65 B.C.).

Pon·ty·pool (pónt-i-pool, *welsh* -ə-). Town in Gwent, southeast Wales. Situated on the South Wales coalfield, it began smelting iron ore in 1577 and was an early centre for the manufacture of tinplate.

Pon·ty·pridd (pónt-i-préeth, *Welsh* -ə-). Town in Mid Glamorgan, South Wales. Coalmining and light engineering are important.

po·ny (póni) *n., pl.* **-nies. 1.** A horse of any of several small breeds, not over 14.2 hands high. **2.** *Informal.* A racehorse. **3.** *U.S.* A translation or summary used as an aid in studying or examinations; a **crib** *(see).* **4.** Anything small for its kind, such as a liqueur glass. **5.** *British Slang.* The sum of 25 pounds. ~*intr.v.* **ponied, -nying, -nies.** *U.S. Slang.* To pay money owed or due. Used with *up.* [Earlier *powny,* probably from obsolete French *poulenet,* diminutive of *poulain,* from Late Latin *pullāmen,* from Latin *pullus,* foal.]

pony express *n.* In the United States, a postal system using relays of ponies; specifically, the system in operation from St. Joseph, Missouri, to Sacramento, California (1860-61).

po·ny·tail (póni-tayl) *n.* A hairstyle, as for girls or women, in which the hair is clasped at the back so as to hang down like a tail.

pony trekking *n.* The practice or pastime of riding cross-country on ponies.

poo (poo) *n. Informal.* Faeces. Used by or to young children. ~*intr.v.* **pooed, pooing, poos.** *Informal.* To defecate. Used by or to young children. [Imitative.]

pooch (pooch) *n. Chiefly U.S. Informal.* A dog. [20th century : origin obscure.]

pood (pood) *n.* A former Russian weight equivalent to about 16.4 kilograms (36 pounds). [Russian *pud,* from Old Norse *pund,* POUND.]

poo·dle (pood'l) *n.* A dog of any of various breeds originally developed in Europe as hunting dogs, having thick, curly hair, and ranging in size from the fairly large standard poodle to the very small toy poodle. [German *Pudel(hund),* "poodle (dog)", probably from Low German *pudeln,* to splash, "splashing dog" (because the poodle was originally trained as a water dog); akin to Old English *pudd,* ditch. See **puddle.**]

poof, pouffe, pouf (poof, poof) *n.* Also **poove** (poov), **puff.** *British Slang.* **1.** A male homosexual. Used derogatorily. **2.** An effeminate or weak man. —**poof·y, poov·ey** *adj.* [19th century : perhaps akin to PUFF (noun), in the sense "braggart".]

poof·ter (poof-tər, póof-) *n. British Slang.* A poof. Also called "woofter".

pooh (poo) *interj.* Used to express disdain or disgust. [Imitative.]

Pooh-Bah (poo-baa) *n.* A pompous, ostentatious official; especially, one who, holding many offices, fulfils none of them. [After the Lord-High-Everything-Else in W.S. Gilbert's *Mikado* (1885).]

pooh-pooh (poo-poo) *tr.v.* **-poohed, -poohing, -poohs.** *Informal.* To express contempt or disdain for; dismiss or make light of. [Reduplication of POOH.]

pool¹ (pool) *n.* **1.** A small body of still water; a small pond. **2.** A puddle of any liquid. **3.** A deep place in a river or stream. **4.** A **swimming pool** *(see).* **5.** An underground reservoir, as of oil or gas. [Middle English, Old English *pōl,* from West Germanic *pōla-, pōl-* (unattested).]

pool² *n.* **1.** In certain gambling games, the total amount staked by all players. **2. a.** A supply of people with certain skills, material resources, or the like that can be drawn on: *a typing pool.* **b.** Any grouping of resources for the common advantage of the participants: *a car pool.* **3.** *Finance. Chiefly U.S.* **a.** A mutual fund established by a group of shareholders for speculating in or manipulating prices of securities. **b.** The persons or parties participating in such a combination. **4. a.** An agreement between competing business concerns to establish controls over production, market, and prices for common profit. **b.** The group of concerns participating in such an agreement. **5.** In fencing, a match in which each member of a team fences successively with each member of an opposing team. **6.** Any of several games played on a six-pocket billiard table, usually with 15 object balls and a cue ball. Also called "pocket billiards". Compare **billiards.** ~*v.* **pooled, pooling, pools.** —*tr.* To combine (money, funds, or interests) into a common stock for mutual benefit. —*intr.* To join or form a pool. [French *poule,* stakes, target (as in *jeu de la poule,* "game of the hen"), hen, from Late Latin *pullus,* hen, from Latin, young of an animal.]

Poole (pool). Coastal resort of Dorset, southwest England. It was once an important port, but today relies on such industries as pottery, chemicals, boatbuilding, and tourism.

pool·room (pool-room, -room) *n. U.S.* A commercial establishment or room for the playing of pool or billiards.

pools (poolz) *pl.n. Informal.* The **football pools** *(see).*

pool table *n.* A six-pocket billiard table on which pool is played.

poon (poon) *n.* **1.** Any of several trees of the genus *Calophyllum,* of southern and eastern Asia, having light, hard wood used for masts and spars. **2.** The wood or medicinal oil obtained from any of these trees. [Singhalese *pūna,* probably from Tamil *punnai.*]

Poo·na (poona). City of central western India. Situated in the western Ghats, Maharashtra state, it was captured by the British in 1817. Mild in climate, it became and remains a resort town and military centre. It also has cotton and paper mills.

poop¹ (poop) *n. Nautical.* **1.** The superstructure at the stern of a ship. **2.** The poop deck. ~*tr.v.* **pooped, pooping, poops.** *Nautical.* **1.** To break over the stern of (a ship). Used of waves. **2.** To be subjected to the breaking of (waves). Used of a ship or ship's stern. [Middle English, from Old French *poupe,* from Latin *puppis†.*]

poop² *tr.v.* **pooped, pooping, poops.** *U.S. Slang.* To cause to become fatigued or exhausted; tire. Usually used in the passive. —**poop out.** *U.S.* To give up because of exhaustion: *poop out of the race.* [20th century : origin obscure.]

poop³ *n. U.S. Slang.* Inside information. [20th century : origin obscure.]

poop deck *n. Nautical.* The deck at the stern of a ship built above the main deck. Also called "poop".

poor (poor, por ‖ pôr) *adj.* **poorer, poorest. 1. a.** Having little or no wealth and few or no possessions; poverty-stricken. **b.** *Law.* Dependent on charity or public funds; destitute. **c.** Wanting or lacking in financial or other resources: *an area poor in timber and coal.* **2. a.** Lacking in mental or moral quality; ignoble: *a poor loser; a poor spirit.* **b.** Inferior; inadequate; inefficient: *a poor memory.* **3. a.** Lacking desirable elements or constituents: *Poor soil leads to poor milk.* **b.** Bad or ill; weak: *poor health.* **4. a.** Lacking in value or quality; trivial: *a poor exchange.* **b.** Lacking in quantity: *poor attendance.* **5. a.** Humble: *in my poor opinion.* **b.** Needing or deserving pity; pitiable: *poor old Sarah, in trouble again.* [Middle English *povere, poure,* from Old French *povre,* from Latin *pauper.*] —**poor·ness** *n.*

poor box *n.* A box, especially in a church, for collecting charitable donations.

poor·house (poor-howss, pór- ‖ pôr-) *n.* Formerly, an establishment maintained at public expense as a place for the accommodation and sometimes employment of paupers; a workhouse.

poori. Variant of **puri.**

poor law *n.* Formerly, a law or system of laws providing for public relief and support of the poor.

poor·ly (poor-li, pór- ‖ pôr-) *adv.* In a poor manner. ~*adj.* In poor health; ailing; ill: *Emily's feeling poorly.* See Synonyms at **sick.**

poor man's weatherglass *n.* A plant, the scarlet pimpernel. See **pimpernel.** [So called because its blossoms open only in fair weather.]

poor relation *n.* Something thought of as inferior when compared with a similar thing or class of things; something overshadowed by or receiving less attention than another.

poor white *n.* A member of a socially deprived, exploited, and poverty-stricken class of white farmers and labourers, especially in the American South and South Africa. Often used derogatorily.

poove. Variant of **poof.**

pop¹ (pop) *v.* **popped, popping, pops.** —*intr.* **1.** To make a short, light, explosive sound. **2.** To burst open with such a sound. **3.** To

THE COMIC-STRIP WORLD OF POP ART

A dynamic glorification of 20th-century mass-produced objects and images

Pop art originated in England and America in the late 1950s and early 1960s. It aimed to portray all aspects of popular culture, and in order to do this the movement focused on contemporary personalities and celebrities as well as on commercial and mundane objects that were in daily use; for the first time products such as soup tins, Coca-Cola bottles, advertisements, and comic strips were invested with aesthetic interest. Roy Lichtenstein, Andy Warhol, and Robert Rauschenberg were among the foremost American pop artists. In England the leading artists were Richard Hamilton, Peter Blake, and David Hockney.

WHAAM *Oil on two canvas panels by Roy Lichtenstein (1963). Born in 1923, Lichtenstein pioneered the pop art movement in America. He concentrated on comic-strip cartoons, reproducing them so exactly that he even incorporated the colour dots used in commercial printing. Later he made use of the comic strip to portray subjects other than cartoons.*

CAMPBELL SOUP CAN *This painting by Andy Warhol (1965) is in the Museum of Modern Art, New York.*

move quickly or unexpectedly; appear abruptly: *pop round to the shops; she popped up from nowhere.* **4.** To open wide suddenly so as to protrude: *His eyes popped with interest.* **5.** In baseball, to hit a short high fly ball that can be caught by an infielder. **6.** To shoot a pistol or other firearm. —*tr.* **1.** To cause to make a sharp bursting sound: *beer bottles being popped open.* **2.** To cause to burst open or explode with such a sound. **3.** To put or thrust quickly or suddenly: *She popped the crisp into her mouth.* **4.** To fire (a pistol or other firearm). **5.** To fire at; shoot. **6.** *British Informal.* To pawn: *He popped all the silver.* **7.** *Slang.* To take or swallow (drugs in pill form), usually habitually. —**pop off.** *Informal.* **1.** To leave abruptly or hurriedly. **2.** To die. **3.** *U.S.* To speak in a burst of vehement anger.
~*n.* **1.** A sudden, light, explosive sound. **2.** A shot with a firearm. **3.** *Informal.* A non-alcoholic, flavoured, carbonated drink, such as lemonade. —**in pop.** *British Informal.* In pawn; pawned.
~*adv.* **1.** With a popping sound. **2.** Abruptly or unexpectedly. [Middle English *poppen* (imitative).]

pop² *n.* **1.** A father. **2.** An old man. In both senses, used as a familiar term of address. [Short for *poppa,* variant of PAPA.]

pop³ *n.* Pop music (see).
~*adj.* **1.** Of, pertaining to, or specialising in pop. **2.** Of, pertaining to, or suggestive of pop art. [Short for POPULAR.]

Pop *n.* A club and debating society at Eton College.

pop. **1.** popular. **2.** population.

pop art *n.* A form of art that depicts objects of everyday life and adapts techniques of commercial art, such as comic strips.

pop·corn (póp-kawrn) *n.* **1.** A variety of maize, *Zea mays everta,* having hard kernels that burst when heated to form white, irregularly shaped puffs. **2.** The edible, popped kernels of popcorn. [Contraction of *popped corn.*]

pope¹ (pōp) *n.* **1.** Often capital **P.** The bishop of Rome and head of the Roman Catholic Church on earth, and considered by Catholics to be, by apostolic succession from St. Peter, the vicar of Christ on earth. **2.** *Eastern Orthodox Church.* **a.** A priest. **b.** The patriarch of Alexandria. **3.** The head of the Coptic Church in Egypt. **4.** Any figure considered to have unquestioned authority: *the pope of surrealism.* [Middle English, Old English *pāpa,* from Late Latin, from Greek *pappas,* title of bishops, PAPA.]

pope² *n.* A fish, the ruffe (see). [From POPE (prelate).]

Pope, Alexander (1688–1744). English poet. He is best known for the famous satirical, mock-epic poems *The Rape of the Lock* (1712; 1714) and *The Dunciad* (1728; 1743). He also wrote philosophical poems such as *An Essay on Man* (1733–34), and edited Shakespeare and translated Homer.

pope·dom (pōpdəm) *n.* The office, jurisdiction, or tenure of a pope; the papacy.

pop·er·y (pōpəri) *n.* The doctrines, practices, and rituals of the Roman Catholic Church. Used derogatorily.

pope's nose *n.* The **parson's nose** (see).

pop-eyed (póp-īd) *adj.* **1.** Having bulging eyes. **2.** Amazed; astonished: *popeyed at the spectacle.*

pop-gun (póp-gun) *n.* A toy gun that operates by compressed air, firing corks or pellets with a popping noise.

pop·in·jay (póppin-jay) *n.* **1.** A vain, supercilious person; a fop. **2.** *Archaic.* A parrot. [Middle English *papejay, papengay,* parrot, from Old French *papegai,* from Spanish *papagayo,* from Arabic *ba-baghā.*]

pop·ish (pópish) *adj.* Of or pertaining to the popes or the Roman Catholic Church. Used derogatorily. —**pop·ish·ly** *adv.* —**pop·ish·ness** *n.*

Popish Plot *n.* See Titus **Oates.**

pop·lar (pópplər) *n.* **1.** Any of several fast-growing deciduous trees of the genus *Populus,* having triangular leaves and soft, light wood. See **aspen, cottonwood, Lombardy poplar. 2.** The wood of any of these trees. **3.** Loosely, the **tulip tree** (see). [Middle English *poplere,* from Anglo-French, Old French *poplier,* earlier *pople,* from Latin *pōpulus.*]

pop·lin (pópplin) *n.* A light, ribbed fabric of silk, rayon, wool, or cotton, used in making clothing and upholstery. [Obsolete French *papeline,* from Italian *papalina,* feminine of *papalino,* papal, from Medieval Latin *papalis,* from Late Latin *papa,* POPE (the fabric was first made at the papal town of Avignon).]

pop·lit·e·al (pop-lítti-əl, póppli-tée-əl) *adj.* Of or pertaining to the part of the leg behind the knee joint. [New Latin *popliteus,* from Latin *poples†* (stem *poplit-*), the hollow of the knee.]

pop music *n.* Modern music, often electrically amplified, typically using simple melodies and strong rhythms and having a broad, popular appeal, especially to young people. Also called "pop".

Po·po·ca·te·petl, Mount (póppə-kátta-pétt'l; *Spanish* -ka-táy-pett'l). Dormant volcano in central Mexico. It is 5 452 metres (17,887 feet) high.

pop·o·ver (póp-ōvər) *n.* A very light, puffy, hollow muffin of American origin, made with eggs, milk, and flour. [So called because it pops up over the rim of the baking tin.]

pop·pa·dom, pop·pa·dum (póppədəm) *n.* A thin, round, savoury Indian biscuit, usually fried in oil and served with curry.

pop·per (póppər) *n.* **1.** One that pops. **2.** A **press-stud** (see). **3.** *Slang.* A drug, **amyl nitrite** (see), inhaled for sensual gratification. **4.** *Chiefly U.S.* A basket or pan in which popcorn is popped.

Pop·per (póppər), **Sir Karl (Raimund),** (1902–). British philosopher, born in Austria. He proposed that any theory, to qualify as a scientific theory, must in principle be falsifiable. His best-known works are *The Logic of Scientific Discovery* (1934), *The Open Society and its Enemies* (1945), and *The Poverty of Historicism* (1957). —**Pop·per·i·an** (po-péer-i-ən) *adj.*

pop·pet (póppit) *n.* **1.** A poppet valve. **2.** *Nautical.* **a.** A small wooden strip on the gunwale of a boat that forms or supports the oarlocks. **b.** Any of the beams of a launching cradle supporting a ship's hull. **3.** *Chiefly British.* A sweet, endearing person, animal, or child; a darling. [Middle English *popet,* child, doll, PUPPET.]

poppet valve *n.* An intake or exhaust valve, operated by springs and cams, that opens by axial motion. Also called "poppet".

pop·ping crease (pópping) *n.* In cricket, a line four feet in front of

poppy *The field poppy,* Papaver rhoeas, *sheds its petals after only one day, but a vigorous plant may produce up to 400 flowers in succession during the summer. Often the first wild flower to colonise waste land, the poppy became a symbol of Remembrance Day because it thrived on the battlefields of Flanders after World War I.*

the wicket and parallel with the bowling crease at which the batsman stands when receiving a ball and behind which he must keep his bat or foot to avoid being stumped. Also called "batting crease".

pop·ple (pópp'l) *intr.v.* **-pled, -pling, -ples.** To move in a tossing, bubbling, or rippling manner, as choppy water does.
~*n.* **1.** Choppy or bubbling water. **2.** The sound made by boiling liquid. [Middle English *poplen,* from Middle Dutch *popelen†,* quiver (imitative).]

pop·py (póppi) *n., pl.* **-pies. 1.** Any of numerous plants of the genus *Papaver,* of temperate regions, having conspicuous red, orange, or white flowers, and a milky white juice. See **opium poppy. 2.** Any of several similar or related plants, such as the **California poppy** and the **horned poppy** *(both of which see).* **3.** The narcotic extracted from the opium poppy. **4.** Vivid red to reddish orange. **5.** An artificial poppy worn on Remembrance Sunday and days leading up to it. [Middle English *popi,* Old English *popig, popaeg,* altered from Vulgar Latin *papāvum* (unattested), variant of Latin *papāver†.*]

pop·py·cock (póppi-kok) *n.* Senseless talk; nonsense. [Dutch dialect *pappekak,* "soft dung" : *pap,* soft food, pap, from Middle Dutch *pappe,* probably from Latin *pappa,* father, food + *kak,* dung, from *kakken,* to defecate, from Latin *cacāre.*]

Poppy Day *n.* **Remembrance Sunday** *(see).* [From the custom of wearing artificial poppies, after the *Flanders poppy,* flower chosen to commemorate the casualties of the World Wars.]

pop·py·head (póppi-hed) *n.* **1.** The seed capsule of a poppy. **2.** An ornamental carving on the top end of a church bench or pew.

pop-shop (póp-shop) *n. British Informal.* A pawnshop.

Pop·si·cle (pópsik'l) *n. U.S.* A trademark for an ice lolly.

pop·sy, pop·sie (pópsi) *n., pl.* **-sies.** *British Informal.* **1.** A young, pretty woman. **2.** A girlfriend. [Irregularly from POPPET + -Y.]

pop·u·lace (póppew-ləss, -liss) *n.* **1.** The common people; the masses. **2.** A population. [French, from Italian *popolaccio,* rabble, from *popolo,* the people, from Latin *populus.*]

pop·u·lar (póppewlər) *adj. Abbr.* **pop. 1.** Widely liked or appreciated by the public. **2. a.** Liked by friends, associates, or acquaintances; sought after for company. **b.** Liked or appreciated by an individual or group: *Cats are not popular with me.* **3.** Of, representing, or carried on by the common people or the people at large: *a popular uprising.* **4.** Fit for or reflecting the taste and intelligence of the broad mass of people: *a popular newspaper.* **5.** Accepted by, originating with, or prevalent among the people in general: *a popular misunderstanding.* **6.** Suited or appealing to ordinary people, as by being within their financial means: *popular prices.* [Latin *populāris,* of the people, from *populus,* people.] **—pop·u·lar·ly** *adv.*

popular front *n.* Any of various political coalitions formed in European countries during the 1930s, as an alliance of democratic, leftwing, and revolutionary parties having common interests in the struggle against reaction and fascism.

pop·u·lar·ise, pop·u·lar·ize (póppewlə-rīz) *tr.v.* **-ised, -ising, -ises.** To make popular; especially, to cause to become readily intelligible to the layman: *a programme popularising science.* **—pop·u·lar·i·sa·tion** (-rī-zaysh'n || *U.S.* -ri-) *n.* **—pop·u·lar·is·er** *n.*

pop·u·lar·i·ty (póppew-lárrəti) *n.* The quality or state of being popular, especially of being widely admired or sought after.

popular music *n.* Light music, typically being melodic and emotionally evocative, and having a broad, popular appeal.

pop·u·late (póppew-layt) *tr.v.* **-lated, -lating, -lates. 1.** To supply with inhabitants, as by colonisation; fill with people. **2.** To inhabit or become inhabitants of. **3.** *Physics & Chemistry.* To cause (quantum states or energy levels) to be occupied. [Medieval Latin *populāre,* to people, from Latin *populus,* people.]

pop·u·la·tion (póppew-láysh'n) *n. Abbr.* **p., pop. 1. a.** All the people inhabiting a specified area. **b.** The total number of such people. **2.** The total number of inhabitants of a particular race, class, or group in a specified area. **3.** The act or process of furnishing with inhabitants. **4.** *Ecology.* All the organisms that constitute a specific interbreeding group, especially a species, inhabiting a specified habitat. **5.** *Statistics.* The entire set of individuals, items, or scores from which a sample is drawn. Also called "universe". **6.** *Astronomy.* Either of two classes to which stars can be assigned according to their age, distribution, and content of metal: *population I,* which contains young, luminous, metal-rich stars found in the spiral arms of galaxies; and *population II,* which contains older, metal-deficient stars found in the Galactic halo.

population density *n.* The number of people, plants, or animals in a given unit area.

population explosion *n.* A sudden sharp increase in population caused by a rise in the birth rate or a decline in the death rate, or both. [Late Latin *populātiō,* from Latin *populus,* people.]

population inversion *n. Physics.* A condition in which the usual or unexcited energy level of atoms in laser material is less heavily populated than a higher level, making stimulated emission and laser action possible.

pop·u·lism (póppew-liz'm) *n.* **1.** A political philosophy directed to the needs of the common people and advocating a more equitable distribution of wealth and power. **2.** A style of political or personal conduct displaying identification with the interests, attitudes, or activities of the common people.

pop·u·list (póppewlist) *n.* **1.** An advocate of populism. **2.** *Capital* **P.** A member of a U.S. political party, *the Populist Party* or *People's Party,* formed in 1892 to represent agrarian interests and disappearing in the early years of the 20th century.
~*adj.* Pertaining to or characteristic of populism or its advocates.

pop·u·lous (póppewləss) *adj.* Containing many people or inhabitants; thickly settled or populated. [Middle English *populus,* from Latin *populōsus,* from *populus,* people.] **—pop·u·lous·ly** *adv.* **—pop·u·lous·ness** *n.*

pop-up (póp-up) *adj.* **1.** Having a mechanism that springs upwards or makes an object spring upwards: *a pop-up toaster.* **2.** Designating a book having paper or pages cut and folded in such a way that, when opened, pictures of figures and objects spring up.

por·bea·gle (pór-beeg'l) *n.* A shark, *Lamna nasus,* of temperate Atlantic waters. Also called "mackerel shark". [Cornish *porghbugel†.*]

por·ce·lain (pórss-lin, pór-sə-, -layn || pōrss-, pōr-sə-) *n.* **1.** A hard, white, translucent ceramic made by firing a pure clay and glazing with variously coloured fusible materials; china. Also used adjectivally: *a porcelain vase.* **2.** An object or objects collectively made of this material. [French *porcelaine,* from Old French *pourcelaine,* from Italian *porcellana,* "of a sow", hence cowry shell, hence porcelain (from the resemblance of the shell to a sow's vulva), from *porcella,* diminutive of *porca,* sow, from Latin, feminine of *porcus,* swine.] **—por·ce·la·ne·ous** (-sə-láyni-əss) *adj.* See feature, next page.

porcelain clay *n.* **Kaolin** *(see).*

porcelain enamel *n.* A silicate glass fired on metal. Also called "vitreous enamel".

porch (porch || pōrch) *n.* **1.** A covered platform, usually having a separate roof, at an entrance to a house. **2.** *U.S.* An open or enclosed gallery or room attached to the outside of a building; a verandah. **3.** *Archaic.* A portico or covered walk. **—the Porch.** Zeno's Stoic school of philosophy, so named from the portico in Athens where he instructed his pupils. [Middle English *porche,* from Old French, from Latin *porticus,* PORTICO.]

por·cine (pór-sīn) *adj.* Of, pertaining to, or resembling a pig. [Latin *porcīnus,* from *porcus,* pig.]

por·cu·pine (pórkew-pīn) *n.* Any of various rodents, especially of the genera *Hystrix* and *Erethizon,* characteristically covered with long, sharp quills or spines. [Middle English *porkepin,* from Old French *porc espin,* "spiny pig", from Vulgar Latin *porcospīnus* (unattested) : Latin *porcus,* pig + *spīna,* thorn.]

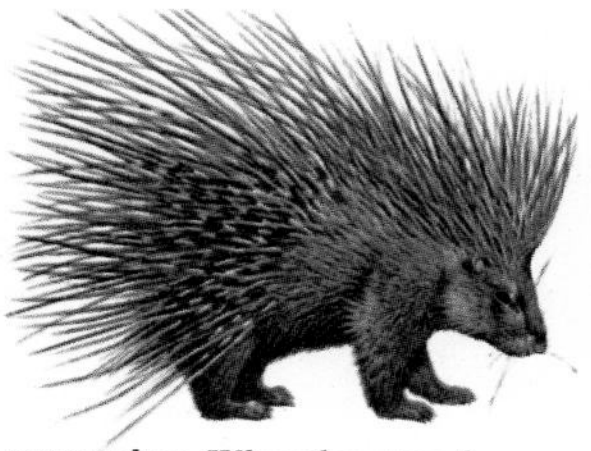

porcupine *When threatened, a porcupine erects its sharp, sometimes barbed, quills and shakes them in warning. If actually attacked, it turns its back to drive the quills into the attacker's face. The quills are easily detached and may remain embedded in the attacker, but the porcupine cannot shoot its quills. Porcupines are found in Europe, Asia, Africa, and America.*

porcupine fish *n.* Any of various spiny tropical marine fishes of the family Diodontidae; especially, *Diodon holocanthus,* capable of inflating itself when attacked.

porcupine grass *n.* Any of various Australian grasses of the genus *Triodia.* See **spinifex.**

pore¹ (por || pōr) *intr.v.* **pored, poring, pores. 1.** To read or study carefully and attentively. Usually used with *over*: *pore over a book.* **2.** To meditate deeply; ponder. Usually used with *over.* **3.** *Rare.* To gaze steadily or earnestly. [Middle English *pouren†.*]

pore² *n.* **1.** A minute orifice, such as one in the skin of an animal, serving as an outlet for perspiration, or in a plant leaf or stem, serving as a means of absorption and transpiration. **2.** Any minute surface opening or passageway, as in a rock. [Middle English, from Old French, from Latin *porus,* from Greek *poros,* passage.]

pore fungus *n.* Any fungus having a crustlike fruiting body with a pitted or porous surface. Also called "polypore".

por·gy (pórgi) *n., pl.* **-gies** or collectively **porgy. 1.** Any of various North American marine fishes of the family Sparidae. **2.** Any of several similar or related fishes. [18th century : **origin obscure.**]

po·rif·er·an (pə-ríffərən, paw-) *n.* Any animal of the phylum Porifera, which includes the sponges. [New Latin *Porifera,* neuter plural of *porifer,* bearing pores : Latin *porus,* PORE + -FER.] **—po·rif·er·al, po·rif·er·an** *adj.*

po·rif·er·ous (pə-ríffərəss, paw-) *adj.* **1.** Having pores. **2.** *Zoology.* Of or pertaining to the phylum Porifera, which includes the sponges. [From PORE + -FEROUS.]

pork (pork || pōrk) *n.* The flesh of a pig used as food. [Middle English, from Old French *porc,* pig, from Latin *porcus.*]

pork barrel *n. U.S. Slang.* A government project or appropriation benefiting a specific area and constituents.

pork·er (pórkər || pōrkər) *n.* **1.** A fattened young pig. **2.** *Informal.* One who resembles a pig, as in being fat and greedy.

pork·ling (pórk-ling || pōrk-) *n.* A young or small pig.

pork pie *n.* A thick-crusted pie filled with minced pork and usually served cold.

pork·pie hat (pórk-pī || pōrk-) *n.* A man's hat having a low, flat crown and a brim that can be turned up or down. [From a fancied reemblance.]

pork·y (pórki || pōrki) *adj.* **1.** Pertaining to or resembling pork: *a porky flavour.* **2.** *Informal.* Fat or fleshy. **—pork·i·ness** *n.*

porn (pórn) *n. Slang.* Pornography.
~*adj. Slang.* Also **por·no** (pórnō). Pornographic.

por·nog·ra·phy (pawr-nóggrəfi) *n.* **1.** Written, graphic, or other material intended solely to excite feelings of sexual lust, and usually considered obscene. **2.** The trade in or production of such material. **3.** Any activity, or representations of it, considered obscene or offensive: *the pornography of violence.* [Greek *pornographos,* writing about prostitutes : *pornē,* harlot, prostitute + -GRAPH.] **—por·nog·ra·pher** *n.* **—por·no·graph·ic** (pórnə-gráffik) *adj.*

por·o·mer·ic (páw-rə-mérrik || pō-) *adj.* Permeable to water vapour. Said of synthetic materials used in making shoes, for example.
~ *n.* A poromeric material. [PORE + -MER + -IC.]

po·ros·i·ty (paw-róssəti, pə- || pō-) *n., pl.* **-ties. 1.** The state or property of being porous. **2.** *Geology.* A measure of this property, equal to the volume of air in a rock divided by the total volume. **3.** A

PRONUNCIATION KEY

a, trap; aa, father; ai, fair;
ar, star; aw, lawn; ay, play;
b, bb, stab; rubber;
ch, church; ck, ticket;
d, dd, dead; ladder; e, dress;
ee, bee; er, defer; ew, few;
ewr, pure; ə, about;
ər, letter; f, ff, fife; differ;
g, gg, giggle; h, hat; i, kit;
ī, price; īr, fire; j, judge;
k, kick; l, ll, let; 'l, needle;
m, mm, man; n, nn, no;
'n, sudden; ng, thing; o, lot;
ō, no; o͝o, foot; o͞o, shoe;
oor, poor; ow, cow;
owr, hour; oy, boy;
p, pp, pepper; r, rr, red;
s, ss, sauce; sh, ship;
t, tt, totter; th, thick; th, this;
smooth; u, cut; ur, turn;
v, vv, valve; w, wet; y, yes;
z, zz, zebra; zh, vision;
pleasure

IN FOREIGN WORDS:

aɴ, oɴ, Saint-Saëns;
hl, Llanelli; Hluhluwe;
kh, loch; lough; Khaled

STRESS MARK:

ín-sīt, insight; in-sī́t, incite

porcelain

THE SEARCH TO MAKE TRUE PORCELAIN
Chinese porcelain exported to Europe starts a craze for "Chinaware"

The type of ceramic called porcelain was being produced in China in the 8th century. It was composed of kaolin (china clay) and petuntse (a mineral similar to English Cornish stone). When fired to about 1,300°C (2,370°F) it becomes a tough, vitreous material, cool white in colour and translucent when thin.

Ming porcelain exported to Europe in the 15th century started a craze for blue-and-white chinaware, and European potters began to imitate it. About 1580, potters in Italy created a glassy material, called Medici porcelain, that looked something like porcelain. It was a mixture of white clay and powdered glass, fired to less than 1,050°C (1,922°F). French potters of the 17th century made "soft-paste" porcelain in a similar way. Because this glassy material was more fragile than true, "hard-paste" porcelain, the search for true porcelain continued.

Johann Böttger, a ceramist in Saxony, discovered how to make porcelain early in the 18th century and the Royal Saxon Porcelain factory at Meissen had a virtual monopoly for 40 years. But by 1750 there were hard-paste porcelain factories all over Europe. Soft-paste porcelain was made until about 1800 at many centres, including Sevres, Chelsea, Bow, and Derby.

By 1800 a hybrid porcelain paste that included bone ash had been developed in England. Called bone china, it is tough, white, and translucent when thin, and cheaper to make than hard-paste porcelain, which it largely replaced in Britain.

CHINESE PORCELAIN *The owner of this vase, which was made during the Yuan dynasty in the 14th century, buried it for safety. It was excavated in China in 1964.*

ITALIAN PORCELAIN *This soft-paste vase, with its enamelled Chinese figures, was made in the Capodimonte factory in Italy in the 1740s.*

GERMAN PORCELAIN *Johann Böttger, the first European to make hard-paste porcelain, produced this coffee-pot in Meissen, about 1719.*

ENGLISH BONE CHINA *This modern cup and saucer is made from a hybrid paste containing bone ash, probably first used about 1750.*

structure or part that is porous. [Middle English, from Medieval Latin *porōsitās* (stem *porōsitāt-*), from *porōsus*, POROUS.]

po·rous (páwr-əss ‖ pŏr-) *adj.* **1.** Having or full of pores. **2.** Admitting the passage of gas or liquid through pores or interstices. [Middle English, from Medieval Latin *porōsus*, from Latin *porus*, PORE.] —**po·rous·ly** *adv.* —**po·rous·ness** *n.*

porous pot *n. Chemistry.* A plate or container of porous fireclay, used to separate electrolytes in a cell or to support a semipermeable membrane.

por·phy·ri·a (pawr-fírri-ə) *n.* A hereditary disease involving disturbance in the metabolism of porphyrins and producing symptoms of mental confusion, neuritis, and abdominal pain. [New Latin, from PORPHYRIN, which colours the faeces of porphyria patients.]

por·phy·rin (pórfi-rin) *n. Biochemistry.* Any of various nitrogen-containing, heterocyclic organic compounds occurring widely in plant and animal tissues and providing the foundation structure for haemoglobin, chlorophyll, and certain enzymes. [Greek *porphura*, PURPLE (from its colour).]

por·phy·ry (pórf-iri, -əri) *n., pl.* **-ries.** *Geology.* Igneous rock containing relatively large conspicuous crystals, especially feldspar, in a fine-grained matrix. [Middle English *porfurie*, red or purple stone, from Medieval Latin *porphyrium*, from Latin *porphyrītēs*, purple-coloured stone, from Greek *porphurītēs*, from *porphura*, PURPLE.] —**por·phy·rit·ic** (-i-ríttik), **por·phy·rit·i·cal** *adj.*

por·poise (pórpəss) *n., pl.* **-poises** or collectively **porpoise. 1.** Any of several gregarious aquatic mammals of the genus *Phocaena* and related genera, of oceanic waters, characteristically having a blunt snout and a triangular dorsal fin. **2.** Broadly, any of several related mammals, such as the **dolphin** *(see).* [Middle English *porpoys*, from Old French *porpois*, from Vulgar Latin *porcopiscis* (unattested) : Latin *porcus*, a pig + *piscis*, fish.]

por·ridge (pórrij) *n.* **1.** Oatmeal or similar ground grain, cooked in milk or water and often eaten at breakfast. **2.** *British Slang.* A prison sentence; time in prison. —**do porridge.** *British Slang.* To serve a sentence in prison. [Variant (influenced by Middle English *porray*, a pottage) of POTTAGE.]

por·rin·ger (pórrinjər) *n.* A shallow cup or bowl with a handle. [Alteration of *pottinger*, Middle English *potinger, poteger*, from Old French *potager*, from *potage*, POTTAGE.]

port¹ (port ‖ pôrt) *n. Abbr.* **pt. 1. a.** A town having a harbour for ships taking on or discharging cargoes. **b.** A place on a waterway that provides a harbour for a nearby town. **2.** A place of shelter; a haven. **3.** A **port of entry** *(see).* [Middle English, from Old English and Old French, both from Latin *portus*, house door, port.]

port² *n.* The left-hand side of a ship or aircraft when facing forwards. Compare **starboard.** ~*adj.* On the left-hand side. ~*tr.v.* **ported, porting, ports.** To turn or shift (the helm of a vessel) to the left. [17th century : probably referring to the side of a ship usually facing the port.]

port³ *n.* **1.** *Nautical.* **a.** An opening in the side of a ship used for access. **b.** A porthole. **2.** An opening for a gun to be fired through, as in a tank or wall. **3.** An opening, as in a cylinder or valve face, for the passage of steam or fluid. **4.** *Scottish.* A gateway or portal, as to a town. **5.** A point at which data can be input or output for a computer. [Middle English, opening, from Old French *porte*, gate, door, from Latin *porta.*]

port⁴ *n.* **1.** A rich, sweet fortified wine of Portugal. **2.** Any of various similar wines produced in other countries. [Short for *Oporto*, port in northwest Portugal (Portuguese *o porto*, "the port"), from which it was shipped.]

port⁵ *tr.v.* **ported, porting, ports.** *Military.* To carry (a rifle, sword, or other weapon) diagonally across the body, with the muzzle or blade near the left shoulder. ~*n.* **1.** *Military.* The position of a rifle or other weapon when ported. **2.** The manner in which a person carries himself; bearing. [Middle English, "a bearing", from Old French, from *porter*, to bear, from Latin *portāre.*]

Port. Portugal; Portuguese.

port·a·ble (pór-təb'l ‖ pôr-) *adj.* **1.** Capable of being carried. **2.** Easily carried or moved. **3.** *Archaic.* Endurable; bearable. ~*n.* Something that is portable, such as a light typewriter. [Middle English, from Old French, from Late Latin *portābilis*, from Latin *portāre*, to carry.] —**port·a·bil·i·ty** (-tə-bílləti), **port·a·ble·ness** *n.* —**port·a·bly** *adv.*

Port Adelaide. Chief port of South Australia, serving Adelaide.

port·age (pórt-ij ‖ pôrt-, pawr-taázh) *n.* **1. a.** The act or process of carrying; transport. **b.** The cost of such transporting. **2. a.** The carrying of boats and supplies overland between two waterways. **b.** A place, track, or route used in such transporting. ~*v.* **portaged, -aging, -ages.** —*tr.* To transport by portage. —*intr.* To carry boats and supplies overland. [Middle English, from Old French, from Medieval Latin *portāgium*, from Latin *portāre*, to carry.]

por·tal (pórt'l ‖ pôrt'l) *n.* **1.** A doorway, entrance, or gate; especially, one that is large and imposing. **2.** *Often plural.* Any entrance or means of entrance: *portals of knowledge.* ~*adj.* Of or pertaining to the portal vein. [Middle English, from Old French, from Medieval Latin *portāle*, a city gate, porch, from *portālis*, of a gate, from Latin *porta*, a gate.]

portal system *n.* A vein or group of veins that terminates at both ends in a capillary bed, such as the *hepatic portal system.*

por·tal-to-por·tal (pórt'l-tə-pórt'l ‖ pôrt'l-tə-pôrt'l) *adj.* Chiefly U.S.

Of or based on the time spent on an employer's property, from the moment of arrival to that of departure: *portal-to-portal pay.*

portal vein *n. Anatomy.* A vein that conducts blood from one organ to another organ other than the heart.

por·ta·men·to (pór-tə-mén-tō || pōr-) *n., pl.* **-ti** (-tee). *Music.* A smooth, uninterrupted glide in passing from one tone to another, especially with the voice or a bowed string instrument. [Italian, "a carrying", from *portare,* to carry, from Latin *portāre.*]

Port Arthur. See **Lüda.**

por·ta·tive (pór-tətiv || pōr-) *adj.* **1.** Portable. **2.** Of or pertaining to carrying. [Middle English *portatif,* from Old French, from Latin *portāre,* to carry.]

Port-au-Prince (pórt-ō-prínss; *French* -práNss). Capital of Haiti, West Indies. It is the country's chief port and commercial centre.

Port Blair (blair). Administrative centre and main port of the Andaman and Nicobar Islands, lying on South Andaman Island.

port·cul·lis (pórt-kúlliss || pōrt-) *n.* A sliding grille of iron or wood suspended in the gateway of a fortified place in such a way that it can be quickly lowered in case of attack. [Middle English *porculis, port colice,* from Old French *porte coleïce* : *porte,* gate, from Latin *porta* + *coleïce,* feminine of *couleïs,* sliding, from *couler,* to slide, from Latin *colāre,* to strain, from *cōlum,* sieve.]

Porte (port || pōrt) *n.* The government or court of the Ottoman Empire. [French *(la Sublime) Porte,* "(the High) Gate" (translation of Turkish *Bab-i Ali*), from Old French *porte,* gate, PORT.]

porte-co·chère, porte-co·chere (pórt-ko-sháir || pōrt-, -kō-) *n.* **1.** A supported roof projecting from an entrance to a building, such as a hotel, providing shelter for those getting in and out of vehicles. **2.** Formerly, a carriage entrance leading into a courtyard. [French *porte cochère,* "coach-door" : Old French *porte,* gate, PORT + *cochère,* for coaches, from *coche,* COACH.]

Port Elizabeth. Seaport and industrial centre in southeast Cape Province, Republic of South Africa It was settled by the British in 1799. Its industries include vehicle assembly and fruit canning.

por·tend (pawr-ténd || pōr-) *tr.v.* **-tended, -tending, -tends.** To serve as an omen or warning of; presage. See Synonyms at **foretell.** [Middle English *portenden,* from Latin *portendere: por-,* variant of PRO- + *tendere,* to stretch.]

por·tent (pór-tent || pōr-) *n.* **1.** An indication of something momentous or calamitous about to occur; an omen. **2.** Prophetic or threatening significance: *a vision of dire portent.* **3.** Something amazing or miraculous; a marvel. [Latin *portentum,* from *portendere* (past participle *portentus*), to PORTEND.]

por·ten·tous (pawr-téntəss || pōr-) *adj.* **1.** Marked by pompousness; pretentiously weighty. **2.** Full of unspecifiable significance; exciting wonder and awe; prodigious: *a portentous monster.* **3.** Of the nature of or constituting a portent; foreboding; ominous. **—por·ten·tous·ly** *adv.* **—por·ten·tous·ness** *n.*

por·ter¹ (pórt-ər || pōrt-) *n.* **1. a.** A person employed to carry luggage, as at a hotel or railway station. **b.** A person who accompanies an expedition of explorers or mountaineers and carries equipment and supplies; a bearer. **2.** *U.S.* A railway employee who waits on passengers. [Middle English *portour,* from Old French *porteur,* from Late Latin *portātor,* from Latin *portāre,* to carry.]

porter² *n. Chiefly British.* **1.** A gatekeeper; a doorman, especially in a large building. **2.** A person in charge of the entrance and entrance hall of a building such as a college, who deals with enquiries and often has caretaking responsibilities. **3.** *Roman Catholic Church.* Formerly, an ordinand in the lowest of the minor orders. [Middle English, from Old French *portier,* from Late Latin *portārius,* from Latin *porta,* a gate.]

porter³ *n.* A dark beer resembling light stout, made from malt browned by drying at a high temperature. [Shortened from *porter's beer* or *ale* (originally brewed especially for porters).]

Por·ter (pórt-ər || pōrt-), **Cole** (1893–1964). U.S. composer. He wrote the music and lyrics for musical comedies such as *High Society* and *Kiss Me Kate.* Among his popular songs is *Night and Day.*

Porter, Katherine Anne (1890–1980). U.S. writer. Her volumes of shorts stories include *Flowering Judas* (1930) and *Pale Horse, Pale Rider* (1939). Her only novel is *Ship of Fools* (1962).

por·ter·age (pór-tərij || pōr-) *n.* **1.** The carrying of parcels or goods as done by porters. **2.** The charge for this.

por·ter·house (pór-tər-howss || pōr-) *n.* **1.** In 19th-century America, an alehouse or chophouse. **2.** A cut of beef taken from the chump end of the sirloin, having a T-bone and a piece of fillet. In this sense also called "porterhouse steak". [PORTER (beer) + HOUSE.]

port·fo·li·o (pórt-fóli-ō || pōrt-) *n., pl.* **-os.** **1. a.** A portable case used for holding loose sheets of paper, drawings, maps, and the like. **b.** Such a case used for holding official documents such as those of a government ministry. **2.** The office, post, or responsibility of a cabinet member or minister of state. **3. a.** An itemised list of the investments, securities, and other financial assets owned by a bank, investment organisation, or other investor. **b.** The investments and assets so listed. [Italian *portafoglio* : *portare,* to carry, from Latin *portāre* + *foglio,* leaf, sheet, from Latin *folium.*]

Port Glasgow. Town in Strathclyde Region, west central Scotland. It is situated on the river Clyde estuary to the west of Glasgow. Its industries include shipbuilding and engineering.

Port Har·court (hár-kərt, -kawrt). Deepwater port in southeast Nigeria. It is the centre of the country's oil industry.

port·hole (pórt-hōl || pōrt-) *n.* **1.** A small, usually circular window in a ship's side. **2.** An opening in a fortified wall; an embrasure.

por·ti·co (pór-tikō || pōr-) *n., pl.* **-coes** or **-cos.** A porch or walkway with a roof supported by columns, often leading to the entrance of a building. [Italian, from Latin *porticus,* porch, from *porta,* a gate.] **—por·ti·coed** *adj.*

por·ti·ère, por·ti·ere (pór-ti-áir || pōr-) *n.* A heavy curtain hung across a doorway. [French *portière,* from *porte,* door, from Old French, gate, PORT.]

por·tion (pór-sh'n || pōr-) *n.* **1.** A section or quantity within a larger thing; a part of a whole. **2.** A part separated from a whole. **3.** A part that is allotted to a person or group, such as: **a.** The amount of food or of a specific dish, served to one person at a meal; a helping. **b.** The part of an estate received by an heir. **4.** *Archaic.* A woman's dowry. **5.** *Archaic.* One's allotment of human destiny; one's lot or fate: *Liars will have their portion in Hell.*
~*tr.v.* **portioned, -tioning, -tions.** **1.** To divide into parts or shares for distribution; parcel out. Usually used with *out.* **2.** *Archaic.* To provide with a share, inheritance, or dowry. [Middle English, from Old French, from Latin *portiō* (stem *portiōn-*).] **—por·tion·a·ble** *adj.* **—por·tion·er** *n.* **—por·tion·less** *adj.*

Port Jackson. Also **Sydney Harbour.** Inlet of the Pacific Ocean in New South Wales, Australia. The fine harbour is spanned by Sydney Harbour Bridge (opened 1932), the world's second longest steel arch bridge, with a span of 503 metres (1,652 feet).

Port·land (pórt-lənd, pōrt-). Deepwater port and largest city in Oregon, United States. It is a major exporter of wood, grain, and fruit.

Portland, Isle of. Peninsula in Dorset, south England, connected to the mainland by Chesil Bank. Its limestone quarries have provided the stone for such buildings as St. Paul's Cathedral, London.

Portland, William Henry Cavendish Bentinck, 3rd Duke of (1738–1809). British statesman. He was twice prime minister, first as a Whig (1783) and later as a Tory (1807–09).

Portland cement *n.* A hydraulic cement made by heating a mixture of limestone and clay in a kiln and pulverising the resultant clinker. [It resembles *Portland stone,* quarried at the Isle of PORTLAND.]

Port Laoi·se or **Port Laoighi·se** (léeshə). County town of Laois, Leinster province, Republic of Ireland. It is a market town, and its industries include malting and flour milling.

Port Lou·is (lōō-iss, lōō-i). Capital and seaport of Mauritius. Founded in 1735 by the French, it exports sugar and rum.

port·ly (pórtli || pōrtli) *adj.* **-lier, -liest.** **1.** Being stout and corpulent and having a dignified bearing. Said especially of an adult man. **2.** *Archaic.* Stately; majestic; imposing. —See Synonyms at **fat.** [From PORT (bearing).] **—port·li·ness** *n.*

port·man·teau (pórt-mán-tō || pōrt-) *n., pl.* **-teaus** or **-teaux** (-tōz). *Chiefly British.* A large suitcase that opens into two hinged compartments. [French *portemanteau,* from Old French, "coat-carrier" : *porter,* to carry, from Latin *portāre* + MANTEAU.]

portmanteau word *n.* A word formed by merging the sounds and meanings of two different words; a blend; for example, *chortle,* from *chuckle* and *snort.* ["You see, it's like a *portmanteau* . . . there are two meanings packed up in one word". (Lewis Carroll).]

Port·mei·ri·on (pórt-mîr-i-ən, -máir-; *Welsh* -yon). Coastal resort in north Wales, near Porthmadog in Gwynedd. Begun in 1926 by Sir Clough William-Ellis, it resembles the Italian village of Portofino.

Port Mo·res·by (mórz-bi || mōrz-). Capital of Papua New Guinea. It is a major commercial centre and port.

port of call *n.* **1.** A port where ships dock in the course of voyages to load or unload cargo, obtain supplies, or undergo repairs. **2.** A stopping-place on a journey; a place visited.

port of entry *n. Abbr.* **P.O.E.** A place where travellers or goods may officially enter or leave a country. Also called "port".

Port of Spain. Capital and chief port of Trinidad and Tobago, West Indies. It is situated on Trinidad, on the Gulf of Paria.

Por·to No·vo (pórtō nóvō). Capital and chief port of Benin, West Africa. It was an important centre of the slave trade and the capital of a native kingdom during the 19th century.

por·trait (pór-trit, -trət, -trayt || pōr-) *n.* **1.** A painting, photograph, or other visual likeness, usually of a person; especially, one showing the face. **2.** A verbal picture or description, especially of a person. **3.** Any close likeness of one thing to another. [French, from Old French, from the past participle of *portraire,* PORTRAY.]

por·trait·ist (pór-trətist || pōr-) *n.* A person who makes portraits, especially a painter or photographer.

por·trai·ture (pór-tri-chər, -trə-, -tewr || pōr-) *n.* **1.** The practice or art of making portraits. **2.** A portrait. **3.** Portraits collectively.

por·tray (pawr-tráy || pōr-) *tr.v.* **-trayed, -traying, -trays.** **1.** To depict or represent pictorially; make a picture of. **2.** To depict or describe in words. **3.** To represent dramatically, as on the stage. [Middle English *portraien,* from Old French *portraire,* from Latin *prōtrahere,* to draw forth, reveal (in Medieval Latin, also "to portray") : *prō,* forth + *trahere,* to draw.] **—por·tray·a·ble** *adj.* **—por·tray·er** *n.*

por·tray·al (pawr-tráy-əl || pōr-) *n.* **1.** The act or process of depicting or portraying. **2.** A representation or description.

por·tress (pór-triss, -trəss, -tress || pōr-) *n.* A female doorkeeper or porter, especially in a convent.

Port Sa·id (saá-eed, sīd). City in northeast Egypt, on the Mediterranean coast. It was founded in 1859 at the entrance to the new Suez Canal. Its main industry is the fuelling and servicing of ships.

Port Sa·lut (pór-sə-lōō, -sa-; *French* -sa-lü) *n.* A mild, semihard fermented French cheese, made originally by Trappist monks.

Ports·mouth (pórts-məth || pōrts-). City in Hampshire, southern England. It is situated on Portsea Island at the entrance to Portsmouth Harbour and is Britain's main naval base.

Port Stanley. Also **Stanley.** Capital of the Falkland Islands, lying

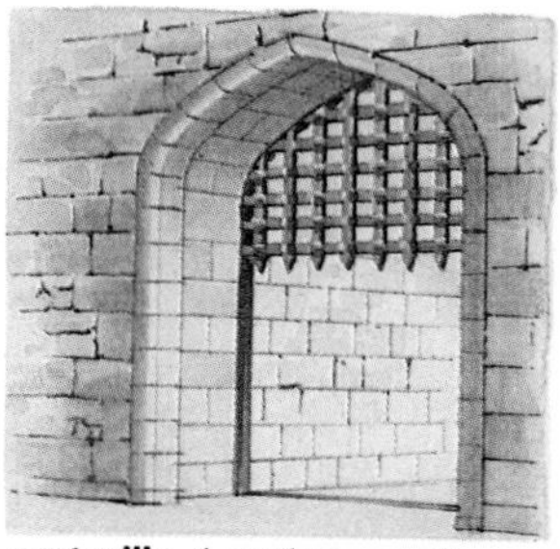

portcullis *A grating – usually made of metal or iron-plated oak – used to block the entrances to medieval castles. It was raised and lowered by rope and pulley.*

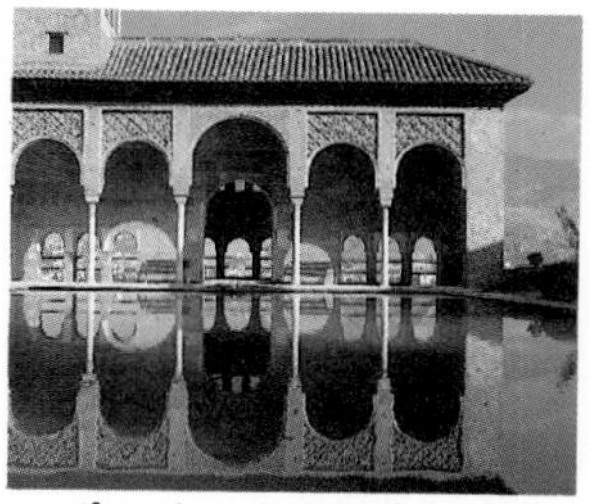

portico *A portico, or colonnaded porch, at the Alhambra, seat of the Moorish kings of Spain at Granada.*

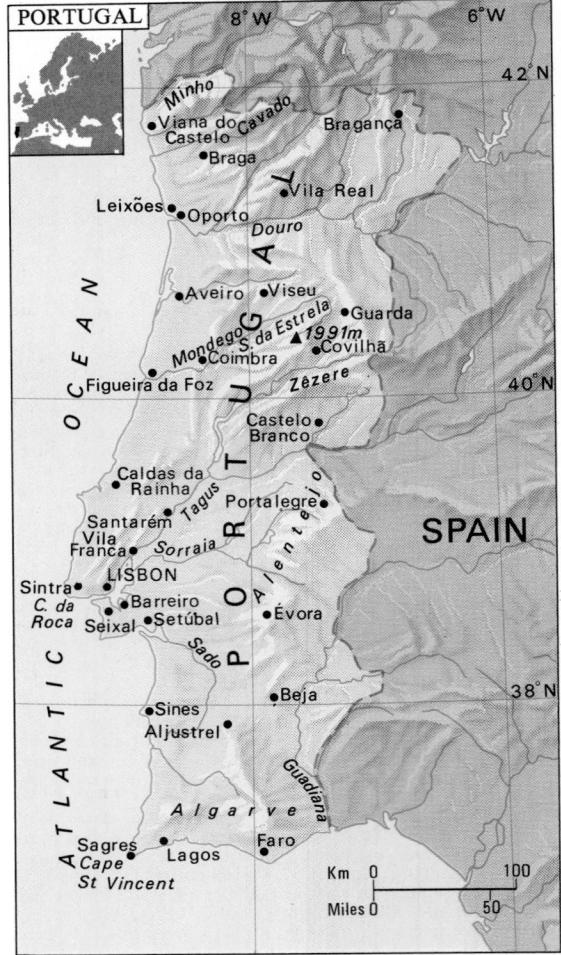

PORTUGAL

Minho
Viana do Castelo
Cávado
Bragança
Braga
Vila Real
Leixões • Oporto
Douro
Aveiro • Viseu
S. da Estrela
Mondego ▲1991m Guarda
Coimbra Covilhã
Figueira da Foz Zêzere
Castelo Branco
Caldas da Rainha
Tagus
Santarém Portalegre
Vila Franca Sorraia
Sintra LISBON
C. da Roca
Barreiro • Évora
Seixal • Setúbal
Sado
Beja
Sines
Aljustrel
Algarve
Guadiana
Sagres
Cape Lagos Faro
St Vincent

OCEAN
ATLANTIC
PORTUGAL
Alentejo
SPAIN

8°W   6°W
42°N
40°N
38°N

Km 0   100
Miles 0   50

on East Falkland Islands. It is the islands' only town and chief port.

Port Sudan. Chief port of Sudan, on the Red Sea. It was founded in 1907 as the terminus of the railway to the Nile valley.

Port Tal·bot (táwl-bət ‖ tól-, tál-). Town in West Glamorgan, South Wales, situated at the mouth of the river Avon on Swansea Bay. Its many steelworks were affected by cutbacks in the late 1970s.

Por·tu·gal (pór-tew-g'l, -choo- ‖ pór-). *Abbr.* **Port.** Republic of southwest Europe, situated on the Iberian peninsula. Its coastal plain rises to mountains in the north and east. It is one of western Europe's poorer countries, but manufacturing is expanding, and in 1979 provided nearly as many jobs as farming. Textiles and clothing, chemicals, cork, wine, wood, fish, and fruit are the main exports. There are rich mineral resources, including tungsten, copper, and uranium. Tourism is important in the economy, as is the money sent home by overseas workers. Portugal became a kingdom in the 12th century, and during the 15th century established an empire as a result of exploring Africa, discovering Brazil, and finding the sea route to India. It was ruled by Spain (1580–1640), invaded by France (1807), and in 1910 became a republic later ruled by the fascist dictator Salazar. A peaceful military coup (1974) overthrew Salazar's successor, Marcello Caetano, and 1975 saw the return to democratic civilian rule. Madeira and the Azores are integral parts of Portugal, but its African territories achieved independence in the 1970s. Area, 92 082 square kilometres (35,553 square miles). Population, 9,900,000. Capital, Lisbon.

Por·tu·guese (pór-tew-géez, -choo- ‖ pór-, -géess) *adj. Abbr.* **Pg.**, **Port.** Of or pertaining to Portugal, its people, culture, or language. ~*n., pl.* **Portuguese.** *Abbr.* **Pg.**, **Port.** 1. A native or inhabitant of Portugal. 2. The Romance language of Portugal, Brazil, and various former Portuguese territories.

Portuguese East Africa. See **Mozambique.**

Portuguese Guinea. See **Guinea-Bissau, Republic of.**

Portuguese man-of-war *n.* A complex, colonial hydrozoan organism of the genus *Physalia*, of warm seas, having a bluish, bladder-like float from which are suspended numerous long, stinging tentacles capable of inflicting severe injury.

Portuguese West Africa. See **Angola.**

por·tu·lac·a (pór-tew-láckə, -choo-, -láykə ‖ pór-) *n.* Any plant of the genus *Portulaca*, having fleshy stems and leaves; especially, *P. grandiflora*, cultivated for its showy flowers that open only in sunlight. This species is also called "rose moss". See **purslane.** [New

Latin, from Latin *portulāca*, purslane, from *portula*, diminutive of *porta*, gate, from the gatelike covering on its capsule.]

pos. 1. position. 2. positive.

pose¹ (pōz) *v.* **posed, posing, poses.** *—intr.* 1. To assume or hold a particular position or posture, as in sitting for a portrait. 2. To affect a particular mental attitude or play a part, usually in order to impress. 3. To represent oneself in a given character or as other than what one is: *He posed as a vicar in order to enter people's houses. —tr.* 1. To place (a model, for example) in a specific position. 2. To propound or assert; put forward: *pose a problem.* ~*n.* 1. A bodily attitude or position, especially one assumed for an artist or photographer. 2. An affected attitude of mind or body. [Middle English *posen,* from Old French *poser,* from Late Latin *pausāre,* to cease, from Latin *pausa,* a pause, from Greek *pausis,* from *pauein,* to pause; confused in some senses with Latin *pōnere* (past participle *positus*), to place.]

pose² *tr.v.* **posed, posing, poses.** *Rare.* To puzzle or confuse with a difficult question or problem. [Short for *appose,* Middle English *apposen, opposen,* to confront with objections, from Old French *opposer,* to OPPOSE.]

Po·sei·don (pə-síd'n, po-). *Greek Mythology.* The god of the sea, earthquakes, and horses; brother of Zeus; identified with the Roman god Neptune. [Latin, from Greek *Poseidōn†.*]

Posen. See **Poznán.**

pos·er¹ (pózər) *n.* A person who poses.

poser² *n.* A baffling question or problem.

po·seur (pō-zér, -zőr) *n.* A person who affects a particular attitude, character, or manner to impress others. [French, from Old French *poser,* POSE.]

posh (posh) *adj. Informal.* 1. Smart, rich, or fashionable; exclusive: *a posh car.* 2. Refined; upper-class: *a posh accent.* ~*adv. Informal.* In a refined or upper-class manner. Used chiefly in the phrase *to talk posh.* [19th century : origin obscure. One unsubstantiated explanation cites the acronym for "port (side) out, starboard home", referring to accommodation on the shady and hence expensive side of ships sailing between England and India.]

pos·it (pózzit) *tr.v.* **-ited, -iting, -its.** 1. To place in position. 2. To put forward as a fact or truth or for the sake of argument; postulate. —See Synonyms at **presume.** [Latin *pōnere* (past participle *positus*), to place. See **position.**]

po·si·tion (pə-zísh'n ‖ pō-) *n. Abbr.* **pos.** 1. A place or location. 2. **a.** The right or appropriate place: *The guns were in position.* **b.** An advantageous place: *manoeuvre for position.* **c.** *Military.* An area occupied by troops for a strategic purpose. 3. **a.** The way in which something is placed. **b.** The arrangement of bodily parts; posture: *a standing position.* **c.** The arrangement of the pieces at any one time in a game of chess, draughts, or the like. 4. A mental posture; a point of view: *the government's position on foreign aid.* 5. A situation or state relative to certain circumstances: *in a difficult position.* 6. Social standing or status; rank. 7. A post of employment; a job. 8. *Sports.* In team games, the part of the playing-area for which a particular player is responsible. 9. The act or process of positing. **b.** The principle or proposition posited. 10. *Music.* The arrangement of the notes in a chord, either *close position,* in which the notes are relatively near to one another, or *open position,* in which they are relatively widely spaced. 11. *Music.* **a.** Any of the points on the fingerboard of a string instrument, at which the string may be stopped to produce a true note. **b.** Any of seven lengths to which a trombone tube is extended in normal playing. 12. In Greek and Latin verse, the condition in which a syllable is metrically long as a result of the placing of a short vowel before at least two successive consonants. 13. *Finance.* The holding of securities or commodities by a dealer, either above *(long position)* or below *(short position)* the quantity he has undertaken to deliver. —**in a position to.** Able or entitled to. ~*tr.v.* **positioned, -tioning, -tions.** To place in position. [Old French, from Latin *positiō* (stem *position-*), from *pōnere* (past participle *positus*), to place.] —**po·si·tion·al** *adj.* —**po·si·tion·er** *n.*

positional notation *n.* The common method of representing numbers by a set of digits, with the position of a digit in a string giving the power of the base of the system. For example, in decimal notation the number 12 indicates $(1 \times 10) + 2$; the number 212 indicates $(2 \times 10^2) + (1 \times 10) + 2$. In binary notation the base is 2, so the decimal 12 is indicated by 1100; that is, $(1 \times 2^3) + (1 \times 2^2) + (0 \times 2) + 0$. The same number in octal notation would be 14; that is, $(1 \times 8) + 4$.

pos·i·tive (póz-ə-tiv, -i-) *adj. Abbr.* **pos.** 1. Characterised by or displaying certainty, acceptance, or affirmation: *a positive answer.* 2. Measured or moving in a direction of increase, progress, improvement, or forward motion. 3. Explicitly or openly expressed or laid down: *a positive demand.* 4. Admitting of no doubt; irrefutable. 5. Determined or settled in opinion or assertion; confident; sure: *a positive manner.* 6. Overconfident; dogmatic. 7. Constructive rather than censorious or destructive; helpful or beneficial: *positive criticism.* 8. Concerned with matters of fact rather than value; descriptive and empirical: *positive economics.* 9. Composed of or characterised by the presence, rather than the absence, of particular qualities or attributes; real: *a positive benefit.* 10. Without relation to or comparison with anything else; absolute. 11. *Informal.* Used as an intensive: *She is a positive angel.* 12. *Mathematics.* Pertaining to or designating: **a.** A quantity greater than zero. **b.** The sign $(+)$. **c.** A quantity, number, angle, or direction opposite to another designated as negative. 13. *Physics.*

Pertaining to or designating electric charge of a sign opposite to that of an electron. **14.** *Medicine.* **a.** Indicating the presence of a particular disease, condition, or organism: *a positive Wassermann test.* **b.** Indicating the presence of the **Rh factor** *(see).* **15.** *Biology.* Indicating or characterised by response or motion towards the source of a stimulus: *positive tropism.* Compare **negative.** **16.** In photography, having the areas of light and dark in their original and normal relationship, or having natural colours, as in a print made from a negative. **17.** *Grammar.* Expressing or involving the simple, uncompared degree of comparison of adjectives or adverbs. Compare **comparative, superlative.** **18.** Driven by or generating power directly through intermediate parts having little or no play: *positive drive.* **19.** Designating a lens or mirror capable of converging a beam of radiation.

~n. **1.** That which is positive. **2.** *Philosophy.* That which is given or perceptible to the senses. **3.** *Mathematics.* A quantity greater than zero. **4.** *Physics.* A positive electric charge. **5.** In photography, an image in which the lights and darks or colours appear as they do in nature. **6.** *Grammar.* **a.** The positive degree of an adjective or adverb. **b.** An adjective or adverb expressing the positive degree; for example, the simple form *bright* as opposed to the forms *brighter* or *brightest.* [Middle English, from Old French *positif,* from Latin *positīvus,* arbitrarily laid down, dogmatic, from *pōnere* (past participle *positus*), to place.] **—pos·i·tive·ness** *n.*

positive discrimination *n.* Discrimination designed to remedy previous injustices or to make up for an existing discriminatory state of affairs; especially, the treating of a person or social group more favourably because of some disadvantage possessed, such as being physically handicapped or being a member of a racial minority.

positive feedback *n.* A type of **feedback** *(see)* in which an increase in output causes an increase in input.

pos·i·tive·ly (póz-ə-tiv-li, -i-) *adv.* **1.** In a positive manner. **2.** *Informal.* Used as an intensive: *Silly?—She's positively certifiable.*

positive prescription *n. Law.* **Prescription** *(see).*

positive vetting *n.* A form of thorough security checking, performed by the Ministry of Defence, on any civil servants likely to be handling confidential or politically sensitive information.

pos·i·tiv·ism (póz-ə-tiv-iz'm, -i-) *n.* **1. a.** A philosophical doctrine contending that sense perceptions are the only admissible basis of human knowledge and precise thought. **b.** A philosophical system based upon this doctrine; especially, the system of Auguste **Comte** *(see),* designed to supersede theology and metaphysics, and depending on a hierarchy of the sciences, beginning with mathematics and culminating in sociology. **2.** The application of positivism in logic, epistemology, and ethics. See **logical positivism.** **3.** Dogmatic certainty, as in speculation and argument. **—pos·i·tiv·ist** *n.* **—pos·i·tiv·is·tic** (-vísstik) *adj.*

pos·i·tron (pózzi-tron) *n. Symbol* e⁺ The **antiparticle** *(see)* of the electron. Also called "antielectron". [POSI(TIVE) + (ELEC)TRON.]

pos·i·tron·i·um (pózzi-trṓni-əm) *n. Physics.* A short-lived entity formed when electron and a positron are bound together in a configuration resembling the hydrogen atom. [From POSITRON.]

po·sol·o·gy (pə-sólləji, po-) *n.* The branch of medicine concerned with the science of the dosage of drugs and other agents. [French *posologie,* from Greek *posos,* how much.]

poss. 1. possession. **2.** possessive. **3.** possible; possibly.

pos·se (póssi) *n.* **1.** *U.S.* A posse comitatus. **2.** *U.S.* Any body of armed men with legal authority. **3.** *Informal.* Any large body of people, usually with a shared purpose. **—in posse.** *Law.* Possible; potential. [Short for POSSE COMITATUS.]

posse com·i·ta·tus (kómmi-taáatəss, -táytəss) *n. U.S.* A body of men that a sheriff or other peace officer is empowered to summon to aid in maintaining peace or capturing a criminal, for example. Also called "posse". [Medieval Latin *posse comitātūs,* "force of the county" : *posse,* power, from Latin, to be able, have power (see **potent**) + *comitātūs,* genitive of *comitātus,* COUNTY.]

pos·sess (pə-zéss || pō-) *tr.v.* **-sessed, -sessing, -sesses.** **1.** To have as property; own. **2.** To have as a quality, characteristic, or other attribute. **3.** To acquire mastery of or have knowledge of: *possess valuable data.* **4.** To gain or exert influence or control over; dominate: *Fury possessed him.* **5.** *Rare.* To control or maintain (one's nature) in a particular state or condition: *Possess your heart in patience.* **6.** To have sexual intercourse with. Used of a man. **7.** *Archaic.* To gain or seize. [Middle English *possessen,* from Old French *possesser,* from Latin *possīdere* (past participle *possessus*), "to sit as master", take possession of : *posse,* to be able + *sīdere,* to sit down and from Latin *possidēre* (past participle *possessus*), to own, possess : *posse,* to be able + *sedēre,* to sit.] **—pos·ses·sor** *n.*

pos·sessed (pə-zést || pō-) *adj.* **1.** Owning, having, or mastering something such as property or knowledge. Used with *of*: *possessed of vital secrets; possessed of a sharp tongue.* **2.** Influenced or controlled by a strong emotion or idea, by or as if by an evil spirit or other force. Often used with *by* or *with: possessed with an urge to kill; a man possessed.* **3.** *Rare.* Self-possessed; calm or collected.

pos·ses·sion (pə-zésh'n || pō-) *n.* **1.** The act or fact of possessing. **2.** The state of being possessed. **3.** *Abbr.* **poss.** That which is owned or possessed. **4.** *Plural.* Wealth or property. **5.** *Abbr.* **poss.** *Law.* Actual control, holding, or occupancy with, or without, rightful ownership. **6.** Any territory subject to foreign control. **7.** Self-control. **8.** The state of being dominated by, or as if by, evil spirits or by a strong emotion or idea. **9.** *Sports.* Control of the ball, puck, or the like. —See Synonyms at **assets.**

pos·ses·sive (pə-zéssiv || pō-) *adj. Abbr.* **poss.** **1.** Of or pertaining to ownership or possession. **2.** Having or manifesting a desire to control or dominate: *a possessive husband.* **3.** *Grammar.* Of, pertaining to, or designating a noun or pronoun case that expresses belonging or a similar relation.

~n. Abbr. **poss.** *Grammar.* **1.** The possessive case. **2.** A possessive form or construction. **—pos·ses·sive·ly** *adv.* **—pos·ses·sive·ness** *n.*

possessive adjective *n. Grammar.* A pronominal adjective expressing possession. In the sentences *This is my duty* and *It is their fate,* the possessive adjectives are *my* and *their.*

possessive pronoun *n. Grammar.* Any of several pronouns expressing possession and capable of replacing noun phrases. In current English, they are: *mine, his, hers, its, ours, yours, theirs, whose.*

pos·ses·so·ry (pə-zéssəri) *adj.* **1.** Of, pertaining to, or having possession. **2.** *Law.* Depending on or arising from possession.

pos·set (póssit) *n.* A spiced drink of hot sweetened milk curdled with wine or ale. [Middle English *poshet, poshot*†.]

pos·si·bil·i·ty (póssə-bílləti, póssi-) *n., pl.* **-ties.** **1.** The fact or state of being possible. **2.** Something possible. **3.** A contestant or candidate capable of winning or being chosen. **4.** *Plural.* Capacity for favourable development; potential: *The possibilities of microtechnology are unlimited.*

pos·si·ble (póss-əb'l, -ib'l) *adj. Abbr.* **poss.** **1.** Capable of happening, existing, or being true without contradicting proven facts, laws, or circumstances. **2.** Capable of occurring or being done without offence to character, nature, or custom; suitable or acceptable: *the only possible answer.* **3.** Capable of favourable development; potential. **4.** That may or may not occur; of uncertain likelihood.

~n. A possibility; especially, a candidate or contestant who has a strong chance of being selected or achieving success. [Middle English, from Old French, from Latin *possibilis,* from *posse,* to be able.]

Synonyms: *possible, practical, workable, practicable, feasible, viable.*

pos·si·bly (póss-əbli, -ibli) *adv.* **1.** Perhaps; maybe. **2.** In any way at all; under any circumstances: *She can't possibly have said that.*

pos·sum (póss'm) *n., pl.* **-sums** or (for sense 1) collectively **possum.** **1.** A marsupial, the **opossum** *(see).* **2.** *Australian & N.Z.* A **phalanger** *(see).* **—play possum.** To pretend to be dead, asleep, or unaware in order to deceive an opponent.

Pos·sum (póssem) *n.* A trademark for a device that enables paralysed patients to operate such instruments as typewriters by means of blowing or extremely light touch.

post¹ (pōst) *n.* **1.** A long piece of wood, metal, or other material set upright in the ground to serve as a marker or support. **2.** Anything resembling this. **3.** The starting or finishing point at a racecourse, usually marked by a pole. **4.** *Informal.* A goal post.

~tr.v. **posted, posting, posts.** **1. a.** To place (an announcement), as by sticking or pinning in public view. Sometimes used with *up.* **b.** To cover (a wall, for example) with posters; placard. Often used with *over.* **2.** To announce by or as if by posters: *post banns.* **3.** To denounce publicly. **4.** To publish (a name, especially of a missing ship) on a list. [Middle English *post,* Old English *post,* from West Germanic *posta* (unattested), from Latin *postis.*]

post² *n.* **1.** A military base where troops are stationed. **2.** The grounds and buildings of a military base. **3.** *Military. British.* Either of two bugle calls, *first post* or *last post,* sounded in the evening as a signal to retire to quarters. **4.** An assigned position or station, as of a guard or sentry. **5.** A position of employment; especially, an appointed public office. **6.** A place to which anyone is assigned for duty or work. **7.** A **trading post** *(see).*

~tr.v. **posted, posting, posts.** **1.** To assign to a position or station: *post a sentry.* **2.** To appoint to a naval or military command. **3.** To appoint or assign (someone) to a position or job in a distant location: *was posted to Libya as consul.* [French *poste,* from Old Italian *posto,* from Vulgar Latin *postum* (unattested), contraction of Latin *positum,* neuter past participle of *pōnere,* to place.]

post³ *n.* **1. a.** Letters, packages, and other material collected, handled, and delivered by the Post Office or some other delivery system; mail. **b.** The system of delivering such items; the postal system. **2. a.** A particular delivery or collection of postal material: *missed the second post.* **b.** Postal material from or for a specific person or organisation: *He opened her post.* **3. a.** A postbox; a letter box. **b.** A post office. **4.** *Capital* **P.** Used as part of the title of certain newspapers: *The Sunday Post.* **5. a.** Formerly, any of a series of relay stations along a fixed route, furnishing fresh riders and horses for the delivery of mail on horseback. **b.** A rider on such a mail route; a courier. **—by return of post.** By the next post in the opposite direction.

~v. **posted, posting, posts.** *—intr.* **1.** To travel in stages or relays. **2.** *Archaic.* To travel quickly; speed or hasten. **3.** To bob up and down in the saddle in rhythm with a horse's trotting gait. *—tr.* **1.** To send (a letter, package, or the like) by post. **2.** To inform of the latest news. Usually used in the passive: *keep me posted.* **3.** To send by mail in a system of relays on horseback. **4.** In bookkeeping: **a.** To transfer (an item or items) to a ledger. **b.** To make the necessary entries in (a ledger).

~adv. **1.** By post. **2.** By post horse. **3.** With great speed; rapidly. [French *poste,* from Italian *posta,* from Vulgar Latin *posta* (unattested), contraction of Latin *posita,* feminine past participle of *pōnere,* to place.]

post– *prefix.* Indicates: **1.** After in time; later; subsequent to; for example, **postdate, postgraduate.** **2.** After in position; behind; posterior to; for example, **postfix, postaxial.** ***Note:*** Many compounds other than those entered here may be formed with *post-.* In

PRONUNCIATION KEY

a, trap; aa, father; ai, fair; ar, star; aw, lawn; ay, play; b, bb, stab; rubber; ch, church; ck, ticket; d, dd, dead; ladder; e, dress; ee, bee; er, defer; ew, few; ewr, pure; ə, about; ər, letter; f, ff, fife; differ; g, gg, giggle; h, hat; i, kit; ī, price; īr, fire; j, judge; k, kick; l, ll, let; 'l, needle; m, mm, man; n, nn, no; 'n, sudden; ng, thing; o, lot; ō, no; ŏŏ, foot; ōō, shoe; oor, poor; ow, cow; owr, hour; oy, boy; p, pp, pepper; r, rr, red; s, ss, sauce; sh, ship; t, tt, totter; th, thick; th, this; smooth; u, cut; ur, turn; v, vv, valve; w, wet; y, yes; z, zz, zebra; zh, vision; pleasure

IN FOREIGN WORDS:

aN, oN, Saint-Saëns; hl, Llanelli; Hluhluwe; kh, loch; lough; Khaled

STRESS MARK:

ín-sīt, insight; in-sít, incite

forming compounds, *post-* is now usually joined with the following element without space or hyphen: *postwar.* However, if the second element begins with a *t* or a capital letter, it is separated with a hyphen: *post-traumatic, post-Victorian.* Compounds made up of the Latin word *post* and another Latin form are hyphenated. Those entered here are **post-bellum, post-mortem,** and **post-obit.** [Latin, from *post,* behind, after.]

post·age (pṓstij) *n.* The charge for delivering an item of post.

postage stamp *n.* A small printed, usually adhesive, label issued by a government and sold in various denominations to be affixed to items of mail as evidence of the payment of postage.

post·al (pṓst'l) *adj.* **1.** Of or pertaining to post or the Post Office. **2.** Sent or delivered by post: *a postal ballot.* —**post·al·ly** *adv.*

postal order *n.* A money order *(see),* bought from and only payable at a post office.

post·ax·i·al (pṓst-áksi-əl) *adj. Anatomy.* Located behind an axis of the body, especially behind to the fibula or the ulna.

post·bag (pṓst-bag) *n.* **1.** The usually large amount of post from the public received by a public figure, a radio or television programme, or other institution or person. **2.** A mailbag *(see).*

post·bel·lum (pṓst-bélləm) *adj.* Of, during, or designating the period after a war, especially the American Civil War. [Latin *post,* after + *bellum,* war.]

post·box (pṓst-boks) *n.* A box, usually metal and set into a wall, or a **pillar box** *(see),* into which outgoing post is put for collection by a postal service. Also called "letter box".

post·boy (pṓst-boy) *n.* **1.** *Rare.* A boy or man who carries or delivers post. **2.** A postilion.

post·card (pṓst-kaard) *n. Abbr.* **p.c.** A card, often bearing a picture on one side, with space for an address, postage stamp, and short message. Also called "card".

post·ca·va (pṓst-ká·avə, -káyvə) *n. Anatomy.* The inferior **vena cava** *(see).* —**post·ca·val** *adj.*

post chaise *n.* A closed, four-wheeled, horse-drawn carriage, formerly used to transport post and passengers. Also called "chaise". [POST (mail) + CHAISE.]

post·code (pṓst-kōd) *n.* In the United Kingdom, a combination of letters and figures, that specifies the location of a postal address, and is used in the automatic sorting of post by the Post Office. Also called "postal code", *U.S.* "zip code".

post·con·cil·i·ar (pṓst-kən-síl-li-ər ‖ -kon-) *adj.* Designating, pertaining to, or characteristic of the Roman Catholic Church since the Second Vatican Council (1962–65).

post·date (pṓst-dáyt) *tr.v.* **-dated, -dating, -dates. 1.** To put a date on (a cheque, letter, or document) that is later than the actual date. **2.** To occur later than; follow in time.

post·di·lu·vi·an (pṓst-di-lṓovi-ən ‖ -lἐwvi-) *adj.* Also **post·di·lu·vi·al** (-əl). Existing or occurring after the biblical Flood.
—*n.* A person or thing living after the biblical Flood.

post·doc·tor·al (pṓst-dóktərəl) *adj.* Of, pertaining to, designating, or engaged in academic study beyond a doctoral degree.

post·er (pṓstər) *n.* **1. a.** A large printed placard, bill, or announcement, often illustrated, posted to advertise or publicise something. **b.** An illustration, picture, reproduction of a painting, or the like, on a large sheet of paper, often used to decorate the wall of a room. **2.** One who posts bills or notices.

poster art *n.* An art form characteristically used in advertising or decorative posters.

poste res·tante (pṓst réstoNt, ri-stóNt) *n.* **1.** Used on an item such as a letter to indicate that it should be held at a particular post office until claimed by the addressee. **2.** The department of a post office dealing with such post. Also *U.S.* "general delivery". [French, "remaining mail" : *poste,* POST (mail) + *restante,* from *rester,* to REST.]

pos·te·ri·or (po-stéer-i-ər ‖ pō-) *adj.* **1.** Located behind a part or towards the rear of a structure. **2.** *Zoology & Anatomy.* Pertaining to the caudal (hind) end of the body in an animal or the dorsal (back) side in man. **3.** *Botany.* Next to or nearest the main stem or axis. Said of flowers and buds. **4.** Coming after in order; following. **5.** Following in time; later; subsequent. Compare **anterior.**
—*n.* The buttocks. Used humorously or euphemistically. [Latin, comparative of *posterus,* coming after, next, from *post,* after.]
—**pos·te·ri·or·ly** *adv.*

pos·te·ri·or·i·ty (po-stéer-i-órrəti ‖ pō-) *n.* The condition of being posterior in location or time.

pos·ter·i·ty (po-stérrəti ‖ pō-) *n.* **1.** Future generations. **2.** All of a person's descendants. [Middle English *posterite,* from Old French *posterite,* from Latin *posteritās* (stem *posteritāt-*), from *posterus,* next. See **posterior.**]

pos·tern (póss-tərn, pṓss-, -tern) *n.* A small, usually private, rear gate, especially one in a fort or castle.
—*adj.* Situated at the back or side. [Middle English *posterne,* from Old French *posterne,* variant of *posterle,* from Late Latin *posterula,* diminutive of *postera,* back door, from the feminine of *posterus,* coming after. See **posterior.**]

poster paint *n.* Opaque watercolour paint in bright colours. Also called "poster colour".

post exchange *n. Often capital P,* capital E. *Abbr.* **PX** *U.S.* A shop or set of shops on a military base for the sale of tax-free merchandise and services to military personnel and their families.

post·ex·il·i·an (pṓst-ig-zíll-i-ən ‖ -eg-, -ek-síll-) *adj.* Also **post·ex·il·ic** (-ik). Of, pertaining to, or designating the period of Jewish history following the Babylonian captivity (after 586 B.C.).

post·fix (pṓst-fíks) *tr.v.* **-fixed, -fixing, -fixes.** To add at the end of something; suffix.
—*n.* (pṓst-fiks). A suffix. —**post·fix·al** (-fíks'l), **post·fix·i·al** *adj.*

post-free (pṓst-frée) *adj.* Free of postal charges or with postage prepaid. —**post-free** *adv.*

post·gla·ci·al (pṓst-glάy-si-əl, -sh'l) *adj. Geology.* Pertaining to or occurring during the time following a glacial period.

post·grad·u·ate (pṓst-gráddew-ət, -it) *adj. Abbr.* **P.G.** Of, pertaining to, designating, or pursuing advanced study beyond the level of a bachelor's or equivalent degree.
—*n.* A person engaged in such study.

post·haste (pṓst-hάyst) *adv.* With great speed; hastily; rapidly.
—*n. Archaic.* Great speed; rapidity. [Originally *post, haste,* a direction on letters : POST (courier) + HASTE (imperative).]

post hoc er·go prop·ter hoc (pṓst hók ἐrgō próptər hók) *n. Latin.* The fallacy of assuming or arguing that because one event or situation comes after another, it must in some way be the result of it. ["After this, therefore on account of this".]

post horn *n.* A simple horn formerly blown to announce the arrival of a coach, especially a mail coach.

post horse *n.* Formerly, a horse kept at inns and post houses to be used by post riders or hired by travellers.

post house *n.* A public house or inn where post horses were kept in former times.

post·hu·mous (pṓstewməss) *adj.* **1.** Occurring or continuing after one's death: *a posthumous award; posthumous fame.* **2.** Published after the author's death: *a posthumous book.* **3.** Born after the death of the father: *a posthumous child.* [Latin *posthumus,* "last", alteration (influenced by *humus,* earth, and taken as "after burial") of *postumus,* superlative of *posterus,* coming after, next. See **posterior.**]
—**post·hu·mous·ly** *adv.* —**post·hu·mous·ness** *n.*

post·hyp·not·ic suggestion *n.* A suggestion made to a hypnotised person specifying an action to be performed in a subsequent waking state.

pos·tiche (po-stéesh, pósteesh ‖ *U.S.* also paw-) *adj.* **1.** Added superfluously or inappropriately. Said especially of architectural ornamentation. **2.** Artificial; false.
—*n.* **1.** Something false; a sham. **2.** A small hairpiece. [French, from Italian *posticcio,* fake, counterfeit, from *posto,* added, placed, from Latin *positus,* past participle of *pōnere,* to place.]

pos·til·i·on, pos·til·li·on (po-stílli-ən, -stíl-yən ‖ pō-) *n.* A person who rides the near (left-hand) horse of the leading pair to guide a team of horses drawing a coach. [French *postillon,* from Italian *postiglione,* from *posta,* POST (mail).]

post·im·pres·sion·ism, post·im·pres·sion·ism (pṓst-im-présh'n-iz'm) *n. Often capital* P. A school of painting in France in the late 19th century, exemplified by artists such as Cézanne, Gauguin, and van Gogh, who rejected the objective naturalism of impressionism and used form and colour in freer and more individually subjective ways. —**post·im·pres·sion·ist** *n. & adj.* —**post·im·pres·sion·is·tic** (-ístik) *adj.*

post·ing (pṓsting) *n.* An appointment to a job or post, especially to a military or public position, or to one overseas.

post·lude (pṓst-lṓod, -lewd) *n.* **1. a.** An organ voluntary played at the end of a church service. **b.** A concluding piece of music. **2.** A final chapter or phase. [POST- + (PRE)LUDE.]

post·man (pṓst-mən) *n., pl.* **-men** (-mən). A man employed by the Post Office to collect and deliver post. Also *chiefly U.S.* "mailman".

post·mark (pṓst-maark) *n.* An official mark printed over the stamp on an item of post; especially, one that cancels the stamp and records the date and place of posting.
—*tr.v.* **postmarked, -marking, -marks.** To stamp with a postmark.

post·mas·ter (pṓst-maastər ‖ -mastər) *n. Abbr.* **P.M.** An official in charge of a local post office. —**post·mas·ter·ship** *n.*

postmaster general *n., pl.* **postmasters general.** *Abbr.* **P.M.G.** The executive head of certain national postal services.

post·me·rid·i·an (pṓst-mə-ríddi-ən) *adj.* Of, pertaining to, or taking place in the afternoon.

post me·rid·i·em (pṓst mə-ríddi-əm, -em) *adv. Abbr.* **p.m.** After noon. Used chiefly in the abbreviated form to specify the hour: *10.30 p.m.* [Latin *post merīdiem,* after midday : *post,* after + *merīdiem,* accusative of *merīdiēs,* midday, noon (see **meridian**).]

post·mil·le·nar·i·an (pṓst-mílli-naír-i-ən) *adj.* Of or pertaining to postmillennialism.
—*n.* A person who believes in postmillennialism. Compare **premillenarian.** —**post·mil·le·nar·i·an·ism** *n.*

post·mil·len·ni·al (pṓst-mi-lénni-əl) *adj.* Happening or existing after the millennium.

post·mil·len·ni·al·ism (pṓst-mi-lénni-əl-iz'm) *n.* The doctrine that Christ's second coming will follow the millennium. Also called "postmillenarianism". Compare **premillennialism.** —**post·mil·len·ni·al·ist** *n.*

post·mis·tress (pṓst-miss-triss, -trəss) *n. Abbr.* **P.M.** A woman in charge of a local post office.

post·mod·ern·ism, post·mod·ern·ism (pṓst-móddərniz'm) *n.* Either of two trends in art, literature, and architecture, which largely reject the theories and practices of modernism. One of the trends reverts to more traditional, formal, even classical approaches; the other seeks to go beyond art, form, and meaning altogether, and favours works which are anarchic, outrageous, or transitory.

post·mor·tem (pṓst-mór-tem, -təm) *adj. Abbr.* **p.m. 1.** Occurring or done after death. **2.** Of or pertaining to a post-mortem examination.

~*n.* **1.** A post-mortem examination, especially an **autopsy** *(see).* **2.** *Informal.* An analysis or review of some completed event, especially of a failure or defeat. [Latin, after death.]

post·na·sal (pōst-náyz'l) *adj.* At the rear part of the nasal cavity.

postnasal drip *n.* The chronic secretion of mucus from the posterior nasal cavities, resulting in congestion and coughing.

post·na·tal (pōst-náyt'l) *adj.* Of or occurring during the period immediately after birth. —**post·na·tal·ly** *adv.*

postnatal depression *n.* A period of depression and anxiety experienced by a mother after having given birth, sometimes manifested by aggression towards the baby.

post·nup·tial (pōst-núp-sh'l, -ch'l) *adj.* Happening after marriage. —**post·nup·tial·ly** *adv.*

post·o·bit (pōst-óbit, -óbbit) *adj.* Also **post·o·bit·u·ar·y** (pōst-ə-bíttew-əri ‖ -erri). Coming into effect after a person's death.

~*n.* A bond given by a borrower promising to repay a debt after the death of a person from whose estate he expects to inherit. Also called "post-obit bond". [Latin *post obitum,* after death : *post,* after + *obitum,* accusative of *obitus,* death (see **obituary**).]

post office *n. Abbr.* **P.O., p.o.** **1.** *Capital* P, *capital* O. The public department responsible for all postal services, and, in many countries, for telecommunications as well. **2.** Any local office where post is received, sorted, and delivered, stamps and other postal matter are sold, and certain financial business is conducted.

post office box *n. Abbr.* **P.O.B., P.O. box.** A private rented box,

---

postimpressionism

THE POSTIMPRESSIONIST SCHOOL

A group of 19th-century painters who influenced 20th-century art

The term postimpressionism was never used by the postimpressionist painters; it was coined retrospectively in 1910 by the English art critic Roger Fry when he mounted an exhibition in London of the work of the French painters Paul Cézanne (1839–1906) and Paul Gauguin (1848–1903), and the Dutch painter Vincent van Gogh (1853–90).

Postimpressionism describes a school of painting that flourished in France in the last two decades of the 19th century. Most postimpressionist artists began as impressionists and continued to base their style on the colour innovations of the impressionist movement. However, they moved away from the objectivity of the impressionists, who tried to represent what the eye actually sees. The postimpressionists painted pictures that were entirely subjective and which captured the artist's own highly personalised ideas, emotions, and imagination.

This individualistic and intellectual approach to art led to an increased interest in ways of showing emotion in its most dramatic and compelling form and in the structural qualities of a subject. And it heralded the surrealist, futurist, cubist, expressionist, and fauvist movements of 20th-century art.

VAN GOGH *Poppy Field was painted in 1890 by van Gogh at Saint-Rémy, near Arles in France. The artist moved to France in 1886, and there, inspired by the landscape, created his most outstanding work. His rich, energetic brush strokes and dynamic use of brilliant colour portray his innermost perceptions.*

GAUGUIN *Paul Gauguin painted* Contes Barbares *(above) in 1902 in the Marquesas Islands. He died there a year later. His style, one of the most distinctive, uses large areas of strong unbroken colour to create a direct emotional effect. His paintings are full of symbolic and psychological depth; one of his main themes is the contrast between the savage and civilised world.*

CÉZANNE *Mont Sainte-Victoire (left) typifies Cézanne's striving to give a feeling of monumental permanence to his subject matter instead of portraying a fleeting moment, as impressionist art did. He juxtaposed subtle colours to create the illusion of depth and volume in his work. He painted many landscapes and still-lifes, but also figure groups and some portraits.*

pigeonhole, or the like in a post office, to which post can be addressed and delivered, and where it is kept until collected.

post·op·er·a·tive (pôst-ópp-ərətiv, -rətiv ‖ -əraytiv) *adj.* Of, administered, or occurring in the period shortly after surgery. —**post·op·er·a·tive·ly** *adv.*

post·or·bi·tal (pôst-órbit'l) *adj. Anatomy.* Located behind the eye or eye socket: *a postorbital bone.*

post·paid (pôst-páyd) *adj. Abbr.* **p.p., ppd.** With the postage paid in advance.

post·par·tum (pôst-pártəm) *adj.* Of or occurring in the period shortly after childbirth. [Latin *post partum,* after birth : *post,* after + *partum,* accusative of *partus,* a bringing forth, from the past participle of *parere,* to bear.]

post·pone (pə-spôn, pôst-pôn) *tr.v.* **-poned, -poning, -pones. 1.** To delay until a future time; put off. **2.** *Rare.* To place after in importance; subordinate. [Latin *postpônere,* to place after : *post,* after + *pônere,* to put, place.] —**post·pon·a·ble** *adj.* —**post·pone·ment** *n.* —**post·pon·er** *n.*

post·po·si·tion (pôst-pə-zísh'n) *n. Grammar.* **1.** The placing of a word or particle after the word which it modifies or to which it is grammatically related. **2.** A word or particle so placed. In *what for?* and *homewards, for* and *-wards* are postpositions. [French, from Old French *postposer,* to place after, from Latin *postPONE.*] —**post·po·si·tion·al** *adj.* —**post·po·si·tion·al·ly** *adv.*

post·pos·i·tive (pôst-póz-ə-tiv, -i-) *adj. Grammar.* Of, pertaining to, or designating a word or particle characterised by postposition: *a postpositive adjective.* Compare **prepositive.**
~*n.* A postpositive word or particle. [Late Latin *postpositīvus,* from Latin *postpônere* (past participle *postpositus*), to place after, POSTPONE.] —**post·pos·i·tive·ly** *adv.*

post·pran·di·al (pôst-prándi-əl) *adj.* Following or after any meal, especially dinner. Often used humorously.

post·script (pôst-skript) *n. Abbr.* **p.s., P.S. 1.** A message appended at the end of a letter after the writer's signature. **2.** Additional information appended to a book, article, or the like. [Latin *postscriptum,* from *postscrībere* (past participle *postscriptus*), to write after : *post,* after + *scrībere,* to write.]

post·trau·mat·ic (pôst-traw-máttik, -trow-) *adj.* Following injury or resulting from it: *post-traumatic amnesia.*

pos·tu·lant (póstewlənt) *n.* **1.** A person submitting a request or application; a petitioner. **2.** A candidate for admission into a religious order. Compare **novice.** [French, from Latin *postulāns* (stem *postulānt-*), present participle of *postulāre,* to demand, POSTULATE.] —**pos·tu·lan·cy, pos·tu·lant·ship** *n.*

pos·tu·late (póstew-layt) *tr.v.* **-lated, -lating, -lates. 1.** To make claim for; demand. **2.** To put forward for consideration as true or real with no proof: *He postulated the presence of ghosts to explain the strange noises.* **3.** To assume as a premise or axiom; take for granted, especially in a mathematical or logical proof or theorem. **4.** To appoint or promote (a person) provisionally, subject to higher authorisation. —See Synonyms at **presume.**
~*n.* (-lit, -lət, -layt). **1.** Something assumed as being self-evident or generally accepted, as used as a basis for an argument. **2.** A fundamental element; a basic principle. **3.** *Logic & Mathematics.* An axiom. **4.** A requirement; a prerequisite. [Latin *postulāre,* to request, demand.] —**pos·tu·la·tion** (-láysh'n) *n.*

pos·tu·la·tor (póstew-laytər) *n.* **1.** One who postulates. **2.** *Roman Catholic Church.* A church official who presents a plea for canonisation or beatification. [Medieval Latin. See **postulate.**]

pos·ture (póss-chər, -tewr) *n.* **1.** A position or attitude of the body or of bodily parts: *a sitting posture.* **2.** A characteristic way of bearing one's body, especially the trunk and head; carriage: *learning good posture.* **3.** A pose; a particular bodily position, such as one assumed by an artist's model. **4.** The arrangement of the parts of any object. **5.** The present condition or tendency of something: *the military posture of a nation.* **6.** A frame of mind affecting one's behaviour; an overall attitude: *a posture of tolerance.* **7.** An exaggerated or unnatural attitude or mode of behaviour; a pose.
~*v.* **postured, -turing, -tures.** —*intr.* To assume an exaggerated or unnatural pose or mental attitude; pose for effect. —*tr.* To put in a posture; position. [French, from Italian *postura,* from Latin *positūra,* position, from *pônere* (past participle *positus*), to place.] —**pos·tur·al** *adj.* —**pos·tur·er, pos·tur·ist** *n.*

post·vo·cal·ic (pôst-vô-kál-ik) *adj.* Designating a consonant or consonantal sound directly following a vowel.

post·war (pôst-wáwr) *adj.* Occurring after a particular war.

post·wom·an (pôst-wŏomən) *n., pl.* **-women** (-wimmin). A female postman.

po·sy (pôzi) *n., pl.* **-sies. 1.** A flower or small bunch of flowers. **2.** *Archaic.* A brief verse or sentimental phrase, especially when inscribed on a trinket. [Variant of POESY.]

pot¹ (pot) *n.* **1. a.** Any of various usually domestic containers made of metal, glass, or pottery, such as a short, cylindrical vessel for holding jam, a rounded juglike vessel for liquid tea or coffee, or a round, fairly deep cooking vessel with a handle. **b.** Such a vessel and its contents: *a pot of soup; a pot of tea.* **c.** The amount that such a vessel will hold. **2. a.** A large drinking cup; a tankard. **b.** A drink, usually of beer, contained in such a cup. **3.** An artistic or decorative ceramic vessel of any size or shape. **4. a.** A flowerpot. **b.** Something resembling a domestic pot in appearance or function, such as a chimney pot or chamber pot. **5.** A vessel, usually gold, silver, or silverplate, awarded as a sports prize. **6.** A trap for fish, crustaceans, or eels, consisting of a wicker or wire basket: *a lobster pot.*

7. In gambling card games, the total amount staked by all the players in one hand. **8.** *U.S. Informal.* A common fund to which the members of a group contribute and upon which they draw for certain stated purposes. **9.** *Informal.* **a.** *Plural.* A great deal; a large amount: *pots of money.* **b.** A large amount of money: *made a pot.* **10.** *Informal.* A pot-belly *(see).* **11.** In billiards, snooker, and similar games, a shot intended to send a ball into a pocket. **12.** *Informal.* A pot shot *(see).* —**go to pot.** *Informal.* To deteriorate.
~*v.* **potted, potting, pots.** —*tr.* **1.** To place or plant in a pot: *pot a plant.* **2.** To preserve (food) in a pot. **3.** To cook in a pot. **4.** To shoot (game) for food rather than for sport. **5.** *Informal.* To shoot with a pot shot. **6.** *Informal.* To win or capture; bag. **7.** In billiards, snooker, and similar games, to hit (a ball) directly or indirectly into a pocket. **8.** *Informal.* To make (a child) sit on a potty. —*intr. Informal.* To take a pot shot. [Middle English, Old English *pott,* from Vulgar Latin *pottus* (attested only in Late Latin).]

pot² *n. Chiefly Northern British.* A pothole.

pot³ *n. Informal.* Cannabis *(see).* [Perhaps shortened from Mexican Spanish *potiguaya†.*]

pot. potential.

po·ta·ble (pôtə-b'l) *n. Often plural.* Drinkable liquid.
~*adj.* Fit to drink. [French, from Late Latin *pōtābilis,* from Latin *pōtāre,* to drink.] —**po·ta·bil·i·ty** (-bílləti), **po·ta·ble·ness** *n.*

po·tage (po-tăazh) *n. French.* A thick soup. [Old French, contents of a pot, from *pot,* POT.]

po·tam·ic (pə-támmik, po-) *adj.* Of or pertaining to rivers. [Greek *potamos,* river.]

pot·a·mol·o·gy (póttə-móllɔji) *n.* The scientific study of rivers. [Greek *potamos,* river + -LOGY.]

pot·ash (póttash) *n.* **1.** Potassium carbonate. **2.** Potassium hydroxide. **3.** Any of several compounds containing potassium, especially soluble compounds, such as potassium oxide, potassium chloride, and various potassium sulphates, used chiefly in fertilisers. [Singular of earlier *pot ashes* (translation of obsolete Dutch *potasschen*) : POT + plural of ASH (so called because first obtained by evaporating the lye of wood ashes in iron pots).]

potash feldspar *n.* Potassium feldspar *(see).*

potash muriate *n. Chemistry.* Potassium chloride *(see).*

po·tas·si·um (pə-tássi-əm) *n. Symbol* **K** A soft, silver-white, light, highly or explosively reactive metallic element obtained by electrolysis of its common hydroxide and found in, or converted to, a wide variety of salts used in fertilisers and soaps. Atomic number 19, atomic weight 39.102, melting point 63.2°C, boiling point 765.5°C, relative density 0.856, valency 1. [New Latin, from *potassa,* potassium monoxide, from English POTASH.] —**po·tas·sic** *adj.*

potassium-argon dating *n.* A method of dating rocks and minerals by measuring the isotope argon–40 in the sample, present as a result of the radioactive decay of the naturally occurring isotope potassium-40. The technique can be used for ages up to 10^{10} years.

potassium bitartrate *n.* A white crystalline solid or powder, $KHC_4H_4O_6$, used in baking powder, in the tinning of metals, and as a component of laxatives. Also called "cream of tartar".

potassium bromide *n.* A white crystalline solid or powder, KBr, used as a sedative, in photographic emulsion, and in spectroscopy. Also called "bromide".

potassium carbonate *n.* A transparent, white, deliquescent, granular powder, K_2CO_3, used in making glass, pigments, ceramics, and soaps. Also called "pearl ash", "potash".

potassium chlorate *n.* A moderately poisonous crystalline compound, $KClO_3$, used as an oxidising agent, bleach, and disinfectant, and in making explosives, matches, and fireworks.

potassium chloride *n.* A colourless crystalline solid or powder, KCl, used in fertilisers and in the preparation of potassium compounds. Also called "potassium muriate", "potash muriate".

potassium cyanide *n.* A poisonous white compound, KCN, used in extracting gold and silver from ores, electroplating, photography, and as a fumigant and insecticide. Also called "cyanide".

potassium dichromate *n.* A bright yellowish-red crystalline compound, $K_2Cr_2O_7$, used as an oxidising agent, and in pyrotechnics, explosives, and safety matches.

potassium feldspar *n.* Any member of the feldspar group of minerals that comprises silicates of aluminium and potassium. Orthoclase and microcline are the most common members of the group. Also called "potash feldspar".

potassium hydroxide *n.* A caustic deliquescent solid, KOH, used as a bleach and in detergents and soaps, matches, and many potassium compounds. Also called "caustic potash", "lye".

potassium nitrate *n.* A transparent or white crystalline compound, KNO_3, used to pickle meat and in explosives, matches, rocket propellants, and fertilisers. Also called "nitre", "saltpetre".

potassium permanganate *n.* A dark purple crystalline compound, $KMnO_4$, used as an oxidising agent, disinfectant, and in deodorisers and dyes. Also called "permanganate of potash", "purple salt".

potassium sulphate *n.* A colourless or white crystalline compound, K_2SO_4, used in medicine, glassmaking, fertilisers, and as a reagent in analytical chemistry.

po·ta·tion (pō-táysh'n, pə-) *n. Formal.* **1.** The act of drinking. **2.** A drink, especially an alcoholic drink. [Middle English *potacioun,* from Old French *potation,* from Latin *pōtātiō* (stem *pōtātiōn-*), drinking, from *pōtāre,* to drink.]

po·ta·to (pə-táytō) *n., pl.* **-toes. 1.** A plant, *Solanum tuberosum,* native to South America and widely cultivated for its starchy, edible tubers. **2.** A tuber of this plant, which is cooked and eaten as a vegetable. Also called "Irish potato", "white potato". **3.** Any of several similar plants; especially, the **sweet potato** *(see).* [Spanish *patata,* from Taino *batata.*]

potato beetle *n.* The **Colorado beetle** *(see).*

potato chip *n.* **1.** *Australian, N.Z., & U.S.* A crisp. **2.** *British.* A chip.

po·ta·to·ry (pṓtə-təri, -tri) *adj. Formal.* Of, pertaining to, or given to drinking. [Latin *pōtātōrius,* from *pōtāre,* to drink.]

pot-au-feu (pót-ō-fér; *French* -fö) *n.* A thick French soup in which meat and vegetables are simmered, sometimes with rice or pasta. [French, "pot on the fire".]

pot-bel·ly (pót-belli, -bélli) *n., pl.* **-lies.** **1.** A protruding abdominal region; a fat, rounded stomach. Also informally called "pot". **2.** A person having a pot-belly. **—pot-bel·lied** *adj.*

pot-belly stove *n. Chiefly U.S.* A short rounded stove in which wood or coal is burned. Also called "pot-bellied stove".

pot·boil·er (pót-boylər) *n.* A literary or artistic work of poor quality, produced as quickly as possible for profit. [So called because the income enables one to keep a cooking pot on the boil, that is, sustains the necessities of life.]

pot-bound (pót-bownd) *adj.* Designating a pot plant whose roots no longer have enough space in the flowerpot to grow, and whose growth above the surface is consequently poor or retarded.

pot·boy (pót-boy) *n. Chiefly British.* Formerly, a boy or man working in an inn or a public house serving customers and doing chores.

po·teen (po-téen, -chéen) *n.* Also **po·theen** (po-théen). Irish whiskey that is distilled unlawfully. [Irish Gaelic *poitín,* small pot, whiskey made in a private still, diminutive of *pota,* POT.]

Po·tem·kin (pə-témkin; *Russian* pət-yómkin), **Grigory Alexandrovich, Prince** (1739–91). Russian soldier and statesman. He became Catherine II's lover and lifelong favourite. He built up the Black Sea Fleet, annexed the Crimea, and campaigned against the Turks (1787–91).

po·ten·cy (pṓt'n-si) *n., pl.* **-cies.** Also **po·tence** (pṓt'nss) **1.** The quality or state of being potent. **2.** Inherent capacity for growth and development; potentiality. —See Synonyms at **strength.**

po·tent (pṓt'nt) *adj.* **1.** Possessing inner or physical strength; powerful. **2.** Capable of commanding attention; able to convince: *potent arguments.* **3.** Having great control or authority. **4.** Capable of causing strong physiological or chemical effects, as medicines or alcoholic drinks might. **5.** Able to achieve sexual penetration of the female and to father children. Said of a male. [Middle English (Scottish), from Latin *potēns* (stem *potent-*), present participle of Old Latin *potēre* (unattested) (superseded by *posse*), to be able, have power.] **—po·tent·ly** *adv.* **—po·tent·ness** *n.*

po·ten·tate (pṓt'n-tayt) *n.* **1.** One who has the power and position to rule over others; a monarch. **2.** One who dominates or leads any group or endeavour: *an industrial potentate.* [Middle English *potentat,* from Old French, from Late Latin *potentātus,* from Latin, power, rule, from *potēns,* POTENT.]

po·ten·tial (pə-ténsh'l, pō-) *adj. Abbr.* **pot.** **1.** Possible but not yet realised; capable of being but not yet in existence; latent: *"Every admirer is a potential enemy."* (Cyril Connolly). See Synonyms at **latent.** **2.** *Grammar.* Expressing possibility, capability, or power. Said of a verb or verb form: *the potential subjunctive.*
~*n. Abbr.* **pot.** **1.** The inherent ability or capacity for growth, development, or coming into being: *Women have a potential for political influence that has never been realised.* **2.** The ability to succeed; unrealised talent: *She has great potential.* **3.** *Grammar.* A potential verb form. **4.** *Physics.* The work required to bring a unit electric charge, magnetic pole, or mass from an infinitely distant position to a designated point in a static electric, magnetic, or gravitational field, respectively. **5.** *Electricity.* The potential energy of a unit charge at any point in an electric circuit measured with respect to a specified reference point in the circuit or to earth; voltage. [Middle English *potencial,* from Old French, from Late Latin *potentiālis,* powerful, from *potentia,* latent power, from Latin, potency, from *potēns,* POTENT.] **—po·ten·tial·ly** *adv.*

potential difference *n. Symbol* **V** The difference in electrical potential between two points in a circuit or other system; the work done in moving unit electric charge from one point to the other.

potential energy *n.* The energy of a particle or system of particles derived from position, rather than motion, with respect to a specified reference state taken as zero energy. Compare **kinetic energy.**

po·ten·ti·al·i·ty (pə-ténshi-ál-əti, pō-) *n., pl.* **-ties.** **1.** Inherent capacity for growth, development, or coming into existence. **2.** Something possessing this capacity.

po·ten·ti·ate (pə-ténshi-ayt, pō-) *tr.v.* **-ated, -ating, -ates.** **1.** To make possible or effective. **2.** To increase (the effectiveness) of two drugs, hormones, or the like by administering them in combination. [POTENCY + -ATE, by analogy with *substantiate.*] **—po·ten·ti·a·tion** (-áysh'n) *n.*

po·ten·til·la (pṓt'n-tíllə) *n.* Any of numerous plants or shrubs of the genus *Potentilla,* of the North Temperate Zone. See **cinquefoil.** [New Latin, from Medieval Latin, garden valerian, from Latin *potēns,* POTENT.]

po·ten·ti·om·e·ter (pə-ténshi-ómmitər, pō-) *n. Electricity.* **1.** An instrument for measuring an unknown voltage or potential difference by comparison with a standard voltage. **2.** Any three-terminal resistor with an adjustable centre connection, widely used for volume control in radio and television receivers.

pot·head (pót-hed) *n. Slang.* A person who habitually smokes cannabis.

poth·er (pó*th*ər) *n.* **1.** A commotion; a disturbance. **2.** A state of nervous activity; fuss. **3.** A choking cloud of smoke or dust.
~*v.* **pothered, -ering, -ers.** *—tr.* To make confused; trouble; worry. *—intr.* To be overly concerned with trifles; fuss. [16th century : origin obscure.]

pot·herb (pót-herb || *U.S. also* -erb) *n.* Any plant whose leaves, stems, or flowers are cooked and eaten or used as seasoning.

pot·hole (pót-hōl) *n.* **1.** A hole in the rocky bed of a stream, formed by the grinding effect of pebbles whirled round by eddies. **2.** A deep hole or pit, especially in a road surface. **3.** Loosely, a vertical cave system, especially in the Pennines of northern England.
~*intr.v.* **potholed, -holing, holes.** To explore underground caves, especially vertical cave systems, as a hobby or sport. **—pot·hol·er** *n.* **—pot·hol·ing** *n.*

pot·hook (pót-hŏŏk || -hōōk) *n.* **1.** A bent or hooked piece of iron for hanging a pot or kettle over an open fire. **2.** A curved iron rod with a hooked end used for lifting hot pots, irons, or stove lids. **3.** A curved, S-shaped mark made by children learning to write.

pot·house (pót-howss) *n. British Archaic.* A small, rough public house or tavern. Used derogatorily.

pot·hunt·er (pót-huntər) *n.* **1.** One who hunts game for food, ignoring the rules of sport. **2.** One who participates in contests simply to win prizes. **—pot·hunt·ing** *adj. & n.*

po·tiche (po-téesh) *n.* A vase or jar with a round or polygonal body tapering at the neck and having a removable cover. [French, from *pot,* POT.]

po·tion (pṓsh'n) *n.* A liquid drink or dose, especially of medicinal, magic, or poisonous content. [Middle English *pocioun,* from Old French *potion,* from Latin *pōtiō* (stem *pōtiōn-*), from *pōtāre* (alternative past participle *pōtus*), to drink.]

Pot·i·phar (pótti-fər, -faar). Pharaoh's chief officer, who purchased Joseph as a slave. Genesis 39:1–20.

pot·latch (pót-lach) *n.* A ceremonial feast among North American Indians living on the Pacific coast of Washington, British Columbia, and Alaska, at the end of which the host distributes valuable gifts or destroys property to show that he can afford to do so. [Chinook, from Nootka *patlatsh,* giving, gift.]

pot luck *n.* Whatever food happens to be available. **—take pot luck.** **1.** To take whatever food is offered. **2.** To choose at random.

pot marigold *n.* A plant, *Calendula officinalis,* native to southern Europe, often grown for its showy yellow or orange flowers, the dried florets of which were formerly used for seasoning.

pot marjoram *n.* **Marjoram** *(see).*

Po·to·mac (pə-tṓmak). River in the eastern United States. Rising in the Allegheny Mountains of West Virginia, it flows 462 kilometres (287 miles) to the Atlantic Ocean at Chesapeake Bay. Washington D.C. stands at its highest navigable point.

po·to·roo (pṓtə-rōō) *n., pl.* **-roos.** *Australian.* A **kangaroo rat** *(see).* [From a native Australian name.]

pot·pie (pót-pī) *n.* A mixture of meat or poultry and vegetables covered with a pastry crust and baked in a deep dish.

pot plant *n.* **1.** A cultivated plant grown in a flowerpot; especially, one used as a house plant. **2.** *Informal.* A cannabis plant.

pot·pour·ri (pō-pŏŏrri || *U.S.* -pōō-rée) *n., pl.* **-ris.** **1.** A combination of various incongruous elements. **2.** A miscellaneous anthology or collection. **3.** A mixture of dried flower petals and spices, kept in a jar and used to scent the air. [French *pot pourri* (translation of Spanish OLLA PODRIDA) : POT + *pourri,* rotten, from the past participle of *pourrir,* to rot, from Vulgar Latin *putrīre* (unattested), variant of Latin *putrēre, putrēscere,* from *puter,* rotten.]

pot-roast, pot roast (pót-rōst) *n.* A piece of meat, usually beef, that is browned and then cooked until tender, often with vegetables, in a covered pot.
~*tr.v.* **pot-roasted, -roasting, -roasts.** To cook (meat) in this way.

Pots·dam (póts-dam). City in East Germany, on the river Havel. It was the administrative capital of the Prussian province of Brandenburg, and the location of the Potsdam Conference (1945).

pot·sherd (pót-sherd) *n.* Also **pot·shard** (-shard). A fragment of broken pottery, as found in an archaeological excavation. Also called "shard", "sherd". [Middle English : POT + SHARD.]

pot shot *n.* **1.** A shot aimed to kill, without regard for sporting rules. **2. a.** A random shot. **b.** A shot fired at an animal or person within easy range. [Referring to shots fired by a hunter who kills game only for his pot.]

pot still *n.* A still used in whisky-making, in which the mash is heated directly.

pot·stone (pót-stōn) *n.* An impure variety of soapstone once used to make cooking vessels.

pot·ta·ble (póttə-b'l) *adj.* Designating a ball in billiards, snooker, or similar games that can be potted relatively easily.

pot·tage (póttij) *n.* **1.** A thick soup or stew of vegetables and sometimes meat. **2.** *Archaic.* Porridge. [Middle English *potage,* from Old French, *potage,* POTAGE.]

pot·ted (póttid) *adj.* **1. a.** Placed in a pot. **b.** Grown in a pot, as a plant. **2.** Preserved in a pot or jar. **3.** *Chiefly British Informal.* Shortened or summarised often in a crude or superficial way: *a potted history of the Church.* **4.** *Chiefly U.S. Slang.* Intoxicated.

pot·ter¹ (póttər) *n.* A person who makes earthenware pots, dishes, or other vessels. [Middle English, Old English *pottere,* from POT.]

potter² *v.* **-tered, -tering, -ters.** Also *chiefly U.S.* **put·ter** (púttər). *—intr.* **1.** To occupy oneself aimlessly; tinker about. Usually used

potato *This native South American plant, which is related to the tomato, has flourished in Europe since the 16th century. The flower is inconspicuous, but the underground tubers from which the plant is propagated are a staple food in many countries.*

with *about.* **2.** To move about or do things slowly or feebly. Often used with *about.* —*tr.* To waste (especially time) in idling. Used with *away.* [Frequentative of dialect *pote*, to poke, from Old English *potian*, to thrust.] —**pot·ter·er** *n.*

Pot·ter (póttər), **Beatrix** (1866–1943). British writer and illustrator of children's books. *The Tale of Peter Rabbit* (1902) was the first in a series of perennially popular works.

Potter, Stephen (1900–70). British writer. He is remembered chiefly for his humorous books offering advice on outwitting and outshining other people. These include *Gamesmanship* (1947), *Lifemanship* (1950), and *One-Upmanship* (1952).

Pot·ter·ies, The (póttəriz). Trent Valley region of Staffordshire, north-central England. Situated around Stoke-on-Trent, it includes the towns of Burslem, Hanley, Longton, Fenton, and Tunstall. Josiah Wedgwood founded his pottery here (1769). It became the centre of the English pottery industry in the 19th century.

pot·ter's clay (póttərz) *n.* A clay suitable for making pottery or for modelling, low in iron content. Also called "potter's earth".

---

pottery

THE FINE ART OF BAKING AND GLAZING CLAY

Ancient techniques adapted by artists through the ages

The main types of pottery – earthenware, stoneware, and porcelain – differ in their clays and in the degree of heat needed to harden them. Throughout history, clay has been used to make vessels – simply pressed into shape, built up in rolls, or formed on a wheel. About 25,000 years ago man found that clay models hardened when baked in a fire, but pottery was first made about 7000 B.C. in western Asia. By about 3500 B.C. the potter's wheel was in use in Mesopotamia.

Early earthenware pots were fired at a relatively low temperature, about 500°C (932°F), and were porous. By 1500 B.C. potters were using a glassy paste to decorate pots, but it was 300 B.C. before a waterproof glaze for earthenware was developed. Stoneware was first made by the Chinese about 1400 B.C. They discovered a clay that would become non-porous if fired at about 1,150°C (2,102°F), and so needed no glaze. The Chinese were also the first to make porcelain, during the T'ang dynasty (A.D. 618–907). It was made from kaolin and petuntse and needed firing at about 1,300°C (2,372°F). It is the hardest type of pottery and can be made very thin.

Fine pottery was made in ancient Greece, 7th–17th century China, America before Columbus, and Islamic Persia, Turkey, and Spain. Meissen in Germany, Sèvres in France, and Chelsea and Worcester in England were famed for porcelain in the 18th and 19th centuries.

PERSIAN POTTERY *This earthenware ewer was made in the 12th century in Kashan, a province of Persia noted for its lustreware. The ewer was press-moulded and decorated with metallic lustre, a carved pattern, and blue and turquoise glaze.*

CHELSEA PORCELAIN *This figure group, made about 1750, shows how fine, hard clay will hold minute detail with great sharpness.*

MODERN VASE *The ancient techniques were used to produce this simply shaped stoneware vase made by the British artist Hans Coper in 1968.*

---

potter's wheel *n.* A revolving, horizontal disc, operated electrically or by treadle, upon which clay is shaped manually.

potter wasp *n.* Any of various wasps of the genus *Eumenes*, characteristically building pot-shaped nests of clay.

pot·ter·y (póttəri) *n., pl.* **-ies. 1.** Ware, such as vases, pots, bowls, or plates, made of stoneware, earthenware or porcelain. **2.** The craft or occupation of a potter. **3.** The establishment in which this craft is pursued. [Middle English, from Old French *poterie*, from *potier*, POTTER.]

potting shed *n.* A garden shed in which plants can be grown and protected from harsh weather before being planted outside.

pot·tle (pótt'l) *n.* **1.** A pot or drinking vessel with a two-quart capacity. **2.** The liquid contained in such a vessel. **3.** An old liquid measure equal to about two quarts. **4.** A small basket of strawberries. [Middle English *potel*, from Old French, diminutive of POT.]

pot·to (póttō) *n., pl.* **-tos. 1.** Any of several small African primates of the genera *Perodicticus* and *Arctocebus*; especially *P. potto*, having woolly fur. **2.** The **kinkajou** (see). [Probably from Guinea dialect; akin to Wolof *pata*, a tailless monkey.]

Pott's disease (pots) *n.* Tuberculosis of the spine often resulting in deformity. [After Percivall *Pott* (1714–88), British surgeon.]

pot·ty¹ (pótti) *adj.* **-tier, -tiest.** *Chiefly British Informal.* **1.** Somewhat silly or crazy; foolish. **2.** Of little importance; trivial. [Perhaps from the phrase *to go to pot*, to deteriorate, and from POT (liquor).]

potty² *n., pl.* **-ties.** A child's chamber pot.

pot·ty-trained (pótti-traynd) *adj. Informal.* Designating a child who has learnt to use a potty or lavatory; toilet-trained.

pot-wal·lop·er (pót-wolləpər, -wólləpər) *n.* Also **pot-wal·ler** (-wollər, -wáwlər). In some English boroughs before 1832, a man entitled to vote as a result of having his own fireplace. [Literally, "pot-boiler", from POT + dialect *wallop, wall*, to boil, from Old English *weallan*, to boil.]

pouch (powch) *n.* **1.** A small flexible receptacle; a bag. **2.** A small bag of leather or other relatively nonporous material for carrying loose pipe tobacco. **3.** *Archaic.* A purse for small coins. **4.** A leather bag for carrying powder or small-arms ammunition. **5.** A bag for mail, especially one for diplomatic dispatches. **6.** Anything resembling a bag in shape: *He had pouches under his eyes.* **7.** *Zoology.* A saclike structure, such as the cheek pockets of the hamster, or the external abdominal pocket in which marsupials carry their young. **8.** *Anatomy.* A small saclike structure occurring as an outgrowth of a larger structure. **9.** *Scottish.* A pocket.
~*v.* **pouched, pouching, pouches.** —*tr.* **1.** To place in or as if in a pouch; pocket: *He pouched all the money.* **2.** To cause to resemble a pouch in shape. **3.** To swallow. Used of certain birds and fishes. —*intr.* To assume the form of a pouch or pouchlike cavity. [Middle English *pouche*, from Old French *po(u)che*, from Frankish *pokka* (unattested).] —**pouch·y** *adj.*

pouffe, pouf (poof) *n.* **1. a.** A large, firm cushion used as a seat. **b.** A small, soft, backless couch. **2.** A woman's hairstyle popular in the 18th century, characterised by high rolled puffs. **3.** Any part of a dress or other garment gathered into a puff. **4.** A rounded soft pad used to stiffen or give body to puffs in the hair, or puffs in a garment. **5.** Variant of **poof.** [French (imitative).]

pou·lard, pou·large (poo-laard ‖ *U.S.* poo-lárd) *n.* A young hen that has been spayed for fattening. Compare **capon.** [French *poularde*, from Old French *pollarde*, from *polle, poule*, hen, from Vulgar Latin *pulla* (unattested), from Latin *pullus*, young of an animal.]

Pou·lenc (poo-langk; *French* poo-láNk), **Francis** (1899–1963). French composer, member of Les Six. His works range from song cycles like *Le Bestiaire* (1919) to the operas *Les Mamelles de Tirésias* (1947) and *Dialogue des Carmélites* (1957).

poult (pōlt ‖ polt) *n.* A young domestic fowl or related bird. [Middle English *pult*, short for *polet, poulet*, pullet, from Old French *poulet*, diminutive of *poule*, hen, chicken. See **poulard.**]

poul·ter·er (pōl-tərər ‖ pól-) *n.* A poultry dealer. [Middle English *poulter*, poulterer, from Old French *pouletier*, from *poulet*, POULT.]

poul·tice (pōl-tiss ‖ pól-) *n.* A moist, soft mass of bread, meal, kaolin, or other adhesive substance, usually heated, spread on cloth, and applied to warm, moisten, or stimulate an aching or inflamed part of the body. Also called "cataplasm". [Earlier *pultes* (taken as singular), from Medieval Latin *pultēs*, pulp, thick paste, from Latin, plural of *puls* (stem *pult-*), pap, possibly from Greek *poltos*, porridge.] —**poul·tice** *tr.v.*

poul·try (pōl-tri ‖ pól-) *n.* Domestic fowls, such as chickens, turkeys, ducks, or geese. [Middle English *pultrie*, from Old French *pouleterie*, from *pouletier*, POULTERER.]

pounce¹ (pownss; *West Indian also* pungss) *v.* **pounced, pouncing, pounces.** —*intr.* **1.** To spring or swoop with intent to seize someone or something. Used with *on, upon*, or *at.* **2.** To attack suddenly and unexpectedly. —*tr. Rare.* To seize with or as if with talons. ~*n.* **1.** The act of pouncing. **2.** The talon or claw of a bird of prey. [Middle English, talon, claw (hence verb, to seize), probably variant of *punson*, PUNCHEON.] —**pounc·er** *n.*

pounce² *n.* **1.** A fine powder formerly used to seal the porous surfaces of paper and parchment and prepare them for writing on. **2.** A fine powder, such as pulverised charcoal, dusted over a stencil to transfer a design to an underlying surface. ~*tr.v.* **pounced, pouncing, pounces. 1.** To sprinkle, smooth, or treat with pounce. **2.** To transfer (a stencilled design) with pounce. [French *ponce*, from Vulgar Latin *pōmex* (unattested), variant of Latin *pūmex*, PUMICE.] —**pounc·er** *n.*

pounce³ *tr.v.* **pounced, pouncing, pounces.** To ornament (metal, for example) by perforating from the back with a pointed implement. [Middle English *pounsen,* variant of *pounsonen,* from Old French *poinçonner,* to prick, stamp, from *poinçon,* pointed tool. See **punch, puncheon.**]

pounce box *n.* A small box with a perforated top, formerly used to sprinkle sand or pounce on writing paper to dry the ink.

poun·cet box (pówn-sit, -sət) *n.* A small perfume box with a perforated top. [Perhaps from *pounced box* (perforated box).]

pound[1] (pound; *West Indies also* pungd) *n., pl.* **pound** or **pounds.** **1.** *Abbr.* **lb a.** A unit of mass in the avoirdupois system equal to 7,600 grains and divided into 16 ounces. It is equivalent to 0.453592 kilogram. Also called "pound avoirdupois". **b.** A unit of weight in the troy system equal to 5,760 grains and divided into 12 ounces. It is equal to 0.373242 kilogram. Also called "pound troy". **c.** A unit of weight in the apothecaries' system equal to 5,760 grains or one pound troy. **2.** A unit of weight differing in various countries and times, especially one equal to half a kilogram. **3.** A British unit of force equal to the weight of a standard one-pound mass where the local acceleration of gravity is 32.174 feet per second per second. Also called "pound force". **4.** *Symbol* £ **a.** The basic monetary unit of the United Kingdom, equal to 100 new pence; before 1971 it was equal to 20 shillings or 240 old pence. Also called "pound sterling". **b.** The basic monetary unit of various dependent territories of the United Kingdom, equal to 100 pence. **c.** The Irish **punt** *(see).* **5. a.** The basic monetary unit of Lebanon, Sudan, Syria, and Egypt, equal to 100 piastres. **b.** The basic monetary unit of Cyprus and Malta, equal to 1,000 mils. **c.** Formerly, the basic monetary unit of Israel, equal to 100 agorot. It is now worth 1/10 of the shekel. **6.** A former monetary unit of Scotland before the Union, usually worth a small fraction of the pound sterling. Also called "pound Scots". **7.** A coin or note worth one pound. [Middle English *po(u)nd,* Old English *pund,* from Latin *pondō* (a weight of 12 ounces).]

pound[2] *v.* **pounded, pounding, pounds.** *—tr.* **1.** To strike or hammer with a heavy blow or blows. **2.** To drive (something) in or out with repeated blows; hammer. **3.** To beat to a powder or pulp; pulverise or crush. **4.** To instil by persistent and emphatic repetition: *pound knowledge into their heads.* **5.** To assault with heavy gunfire. *—intr.* **1.** To strike vigorous, repeated blows. Often used with *on* or *at*: *He pounded on the table.* **2.** To move along heavily and noisily. **3.** To pulsate rapidly and heavily: *Her heart pounded.* **4.** To work or move laboriously: *a ship pounding through heavy seas.* **5.** To assault an enemy position with heavy gunfire. Often used with *away at.* **6.** To do something in a vigorous attacking way: *pounded away at the typewriters.* **—pound out.** To produce something by or as if by pounding: *pounding out his new novel.*
~n. **1.** A heavy blow. **2.** The sound of a heavy blow; a thump. **3.** The act of pounding. [Alteration (with unhistorical *d*) of earlier *p(o)unne,* Middle English *pounen,* Old English *pūnian*†, probably from Germanic.]

pound[3] *n.* **1.** A public enclosure for the confinement of stray livestock or dogs. **2.** A place in which impounded property is held until redeemed. **3.** An enclosure in which animals or fish are trapped or kept. **4.** A place of confinement for lawbreakers.
~tr.v. **pounded, pounding, pounds.** To impound. [Middle English *pound,* Old English *pund-,* as in *pundfald;* compare PINFOLD.]

Pound, Ezra (Loomis) (1885–1972). U.S. poet. He was instrumental in establishing the modernist movement in poetry. As a result of his pro-Fascist stance during World War II, he was confined to a mental hospital in the United States until 1958, when he returned to Italy. His best-known work is the unfinished sequence of poems, the *Cantos* (1925–60).

pound·age (pówndij) *n.* **1.** A tax or commission based on value per pound (sterling). **2.** A rate or charge based on weight in pounds. **3.** Weight measured in pounds.

pound·al (pównd'l) *n. Abbr.* **pdl.** A unit of force in the foot-pound-second system of measurement, equal to the force required to accelerate a standard one-pound mass one foot per second per second. [*pound* quint*al.*]

pound cake *n.* A rich cake containing eggs and originally made with a pound each of flour, butter, and sugar.

pound·er (pówndər) *n.* **1. a.** Something weighing a pound. **b.** Something weighing a specified number of pounds. Used in combination: *a quarter-pounder.* **2.** A gun firing shells that weigh a specified number of pounds. Used in combination: *an eighteen-pounder.* **3. a.** Something costing a pound. **b.** Something worth a specified number of pounds. Used in combination: *a five-pounder.*

pound-fool·ish (pównd-fōōlish) *adj.* Unwise in dealing with large sums of money or important matters. See **penny-wise.**

pound of flesh *n.* Something owed and harshly insisted upon. [From Antonio's debt in Shakespeare's *Merchant of Venice.*]

pour (por ‖ pōr) *v.* **poured, pouring, pours.** *—tr.* **1.** To make (a fluid or granular solid) stream or flow. **2.** To send forth, produce, express, or utter copiously, as if in a stream or flood. **—pour out.** To give unrestrained expression to: *poured out his tale of woe.* *—intr.* **1.** To stream or flow continuously or profusely. **2.** To rain hard or heavily. **3.** To go forth or stream in large numbers or quantities. **4.** To fill cups with tea, coffee, or the like: *Will you pour?*
~n. A pouring or flowing forth; especially, a downpour of rain. [Middle English *pouren*†.] **—pour·er** *n.*

pour·boire (pōōr-bwaar, pōōr-bwár) *n.* Money given as a gratuity; a tip. [French, "for drinking".]

pour·par·ler (pōōr-párlay ‖ -paar-láy) *n.* Conversation or discussion preliminary to negotiation. [French, "for speaking".]

pour point *n.* The lowest temperature at which an oil or other liquid will pour when cooled under given conditions.

pousse-ca·fé (pōōss-ka-fáy) *n.* **1.** A brandy or liqueur served after dinner with coffee. **2.** *Chiefly U.S.* A drink consisting of several layers of liqueurs. [French, "coffee pusher".]

pous·sette (pōō-sét) *n.* A country-dance figure in which a couple or couples join hands and dance round one another. [French, from *pousse,* a push, from *pousser,* to push, from Old French, from Latin *pulsāre,* frequentative of *pellere,* to push, beat.] **—pous·sette** *intr.v.*

pous·sin (pōō-sáɴ) *n.* A young chicken, five to six weeks old and weighing about one and a half pounds, reared for eating. [French.]

Poussin, Nicolas (1594–1665). French painter. His landscapes and historical and religious subjects are considered some of the finest examples of the classical style.

pout[1] (powt) *v.* **pouted, pouting, pouts.** *—intr.* **1.** To protrude the lips in an expression of displeasure or sulkiness. **2.** To show displeasure or disappointment; sulk. **3.** To project or protrude: *His lips pouted in expectation of a kiss.* *—tr.* **1.** To push out or protrude (the lips). **2.** To utter or express with a pout.
~n. **1.** A protrusion of the lips, especially as an expression of sullen or childish discontent. **2.** *Sometimes plural.* A fit of petulant sulkiness. [Middle English *pouten,* perhaps from Old English *pūtian* (unattested), to swell, be inflated, from Germanic.]

pout[2] *n., pl.* **pout** or **pouts.** **1.** Any of various European food fishes related to the cod; especially, the **bib** or the **Norway pout** *(both of which see).* **2.** Any of various other fishes, such as the **eelpout** *(see).* [Middle English *poute* (unattested), Old English *-pūte* (as in *aelepūte,* eelpout), from Germanic; akin to POUT (expression).]

pout·er (pówtər) *n.* **1.** Any of a breed of pigeons capable of distending the crop until the breast becomes puffed out. **2.** One who pouts.

pov·er·ty (póvvərti) *n.* **1. a.** The state or condition of being poor; lack of the means of providing material needs or comforts. **b.** The renunciation by religious persons of the right to personal property. **2.** Lack of something necessary or desirable; insufficiency; paucity: *a poverty of talent.* **3.** Deficiency in amount; scantiness: *the poverty of his vocabulary.* **4.** Unproductiveness; infertility: *the poverty of the soil.* [Middle English *poverte,* from Old French, from Latin *paupertās* (stem *paupertāt-*), from *pauper,* poor.]

poverty line *n.* A level of income that is considered a minimum for a decent standard of living.

poverty trap *n.* A situation in which a person's net income will fall through taxation or loss of benefits if his gross income increases.

pow (pow) *n.* The sound of a blow, collision, or explosion.
~interj. Used to imitate the sound of a blow, collision, or explosion. [Imitative.]

POW, P.O.W. prisoner of war.

pow·an (pów-ən) *n.* Any of various related freshwater fishes; especially, the whitefish *Coregonus clupeoides,* found in Scottish lakes. Also called "lake herring". [Scottish variant of POLLAN.]

pow·der (pówdər) *n.* **1.** A substance consisting of ground, pulverised, or otherwise finely dispersed solid particles. **2.** Any of various preparations in this form, such as certain medicines, and detergents; especially, a flesh-coloured cosmetic powder used on the face to give a matt complexion. **3. a.** An explosive mixture, **gunpowder** *(see).* **b.** Any of various similar explosive substances. **4.** Powder snow. **—keep (one's) powder dry.** To wait for a suitable opportunity to deal with an opponent.
~v. **powdered, -dering, -ders.** *—tr.* **1.** To reduce to powder; pulverise. **2.** To dust or cover with or as if with powder; apply powder or small specks or particles to. *—intr.* **1.** To become pulverised; turn to powder. **2.** To use powder as a cosmetic. [Middle English *poudre,* from Old French, from Latin *pulvis* (stem *pulver-*).] **—pow·der·er** *n.*

powder blue *n.* Moderate to pale blue. [The colour of powdered smalt.] **—pow·der-blue** (pówdər-blōō) *adj.*

pow·dered (pówdərd) *adj.* Produced in the form of a powder.

powder flask *n.* A small flask or similar receptacle formerly used for carrying gunpowder.

powder horn *n.* A container consisting of an animal's horn capped at the open end, formerly used to carry gunpowder.

powder keg *n.* **1.** A barrel for holding gunpowder or other explosives. **2.** A potentially explosive thing or situation.

powder magazine *n.* A storage place for gunpowder.

powder metallurgy *n.* The technology of powdered metals, especially the production and use of metallic powders for making objects by pressure and heating.

powder puff *n.* A soft pad for applying cosmetic or talcum powder.

powder room *n.* A public lavatory for women.

powder snow *n.* Loose, dry snow on the ground, making an ideal skiing surface. Also called "powder".

pow·der·y (pówdəri) *adj.* **1.** Composed of or similar to powder. **2.** Dusted or covered with or as if with powder. **3.** Easily made into powder; friable.

powdery mildew *n.* **1.** Any of various plant diseases caused by fungi of the family Erysiphaceae and resulting in a white, powdery growth appearing mostly on the upper surface of leaves. **2.** Any of the fungi causing such a disease.

Pow·ell (pów-əl, pō-, -il), **Anthony** (1905–). British novelist. His 12-volume novel cycle *A Dance to the Music of Time* is a social satire portraying Nicholas Jenkins and his upper-class friends.

Powell, (John) Enoch (1912–). British politician. He became a Conservative M.P. in 1950. His controversial views on immigration and his opposition to membership of the European Community

potter's wheel *The invention of the potter's wheel in Mesopotamia in about 3500 B.C. revolutionised the making of ceramics shortly before the invention of the wheel itself revolutionised transport.*

powder horn *Gunpowder for flintlock firearms was kept in an animal's horn. A hole in the base of the horn acted as a funnel for loading the powder into the weapon.*

cost him his place in the Shadow Cabinet and, eventually, he felt unable to remain in the Conservative Party. He was elected as Ulster Unionist Council M.P. for South Down in October 1974. —**Pow·el·ism** n. —**Pow·el·lite** n. & adj.

pow·er (pów-ər, powr) n. **1.** The ability or capacity to act or perform effectively. **2.** Often plural. **a.** A specific capacity, faculty, or aptitude: his powers of concentration. **b.** Natural abilities or capacities: at the height of her powers. **3.** Strength or force exerted or capable of being exerted; might. **4. a.** The ability or official capacity to exercise control; authority. **b.** A right; a prerogative. **5.** A person, group, or nation having great influence or control over others. **6.** The might of a nation, political organisation, or similar group. **7.** Forcefulness; effectiveness. **8.** Informal. A large number or amount: a power of good. **9.** Physics. The rate at which work is done, mathematically expressed as the first derivative of work with respect to time and commonly measured in units such as the watt and horsepower. **10. a.** The ability to do work; energy. **b.** The capacity to make machines and other physical systems operate, or to generate light and heat: wave power. **c.** Electrical or mechanical energy as opposed to unaided human energy. Also used adjectivally: power tools; a power saw; a power loom. **11.** Mathematics. **a.** An **exponent** (see). **b.** The number of elements in a finite set. **12.** Optics. A measure of the **magnification** (see) of an optical instrument, such as a microscope or telescope. **13.** Plural. **a.** Deities; supernatural spirits. **b.** In medieval angelology, the sixth group of angels in the hierarchical order of nine. See **angel**. **14.** Archaic. An armed force. —See Synonyms at **strength**. —**the powers that be.** The authorities; those in power.
~tr.v. **powered, -ering, -ers.** To supply with power, especially mechanical power.
~adj. Designating or pertaining to a mechanical device in which the force or torque applied by an operator is amplified by an engine: power brakes; power steering. [Middle English pouer, from Old French poeir, povoir, from poeir, to be able, from Old Latin potēre (unattested) (superseded by posse).]

power base n. A position that allows a person or group to build up and consolidate power, usually through the support of a committed following: used the young turks of the party as his power base.

pow·er·boat (pów-ər-bōt, powr-) n. A **motorboat** (see).

power broker n. One who exerts influence over those in power, especially by promising or withdrawing the support of his followers. —**pow·er·brok·ing** n.

power cut n. An interruption in the supply of electricity to a particular area.

power dive n. A downward plunge of an aircraft accelerated by both gravity and engine power. —**pow·er-dive** (pów-ər-dīv, powr-) v.

power drill n. **1.** A portable electric drill. **2.** A large drilling machine having a vertical, motorised drill set in a table stand.

pow·er·ful (pów-ər-f'l, powr-) adj. **1.** Having or capable of exerting power. **2.** Strong in effect. **3.** Chiefly U.S. Regional. Great: It did a powerful lot of good. —**pow·er·ful·ly** adv. —**pow·er·ful·ness** n.

pow·er·house (pów-ər-howss, powr-) n. **1.** A power station. **2.** A person or group having great strength or contributing greatly to the activity of a body: the nation's intellectual powerhouse.

pow·er·less (pów-ər-lass, pówr-, -liss) adj. **1.** Lacking strength or power; helpless; ineffectual. **2.** Lacking legal or other authority. —**pow·er·less·ly** adv. —**pow·er·less·ness** n.

power of appointment n. Law. A power, granted by deed or will, giving a person the authority to assign an estate, or an interest in it, to any person (general power) or to a person from a particular group (special power).

power of attorney n. Abbr. P/A, P.A. Law. A legal instrument authorising one to act as another's attorney, legal representative, or agent; legal authority to act on behalf of another. Also called "procuration".

power pack n. Electronics. A compact, often portable, device that converts supply current to direct or alternating current as required by specific equipment.

power plant n. **1.** All the equipment, including structural members, that constitutes a unit power source: the power plant of a lorry. **2.** A complex of structures, machinery, and associated equipment for generating power, especially electric power.

power point n. A device into which an electric plug can be inserted in order to connect it with a circuit. Also called "point".

power politics n. Used with a singular verb. International diplomacy in which each nation uses or threatens to use military or economic power to further its own interests. [Translation of German Machtpolitik.]

power series n. Mathematics. A sum of successively higher integral powers of a variable or combination of variables, each multiplied by a constant coefficient.

power-shar·ing (pów-ər-shair-ing, powr-) n. A system whereby minority parties or interests exercise some measure of political power in cooperation with the majority. —**power-shar·ing** adj.

power shovel n. A large, usually mobile machine having a boom, a dipper stick, and a bucket for excavating.

power station n. A building housing equipment for generating electricity.

pow-wow (pów-wow) n. **1. a.** A conference or meeting with or of North American Indians. **b.** Informal. Any conference or gathering for discussion. **2.** Among some North American Indians, a medicine man. **3.** A North American Indian ceremony in which incantations and dancing are used to invoke divine aid in hunting, in battle, or against disease.
~intr.v. **powwowed, -wowing, -wows.** To hold a powwow. [Algonquian; akin to Narraganset powwaw, magician.]

Pow·ys (pów-iss, pō-). Inland mountainous county of central Wales, created in 1974 from Radnorshire, Breconshire, and Montgomeryshire.

Powys, John Cowper (1872–1963). British author. His brothers Theodore Francis (1875–1953) and Llewelyn (1884–1939) were also writers. John Cowper wrote poetry and long, mystical novels set in the West Country, such as A Glastonbury Romance (1932).

pox (poks) n. **1.** Any disease characterised by purulent skin eruptions, such as chicken pox or smallpox. **2.** Syphilis. —**a pox on (someone or something).** Archaic. Used to wish misfortune and calamity on someone or something. [Alteration of pocks, plural of POCK (mark).]

Poz·nań (póz-nan; Polish -nañ). German **Pos·en** (pōz'n). Capital of Poznań Province in west Poland, situated on the river Warta. It was the residence of the Polish kings until 1296. During World War II, it was occupied by Germany and badly damaged. In 1956, it was the scene of severe rioting over economic and political problems.

poz·zuo·la·na (pót-swə-láanə) n. Also **poz·zo·la·na** (pót-sə-). **1.** A siliceous volcanic ash used to produce hydraulic cement. **2.** Any of various artificially produced substances resembling this ash. [Italian pozzolana, "of Pozzuoli", town near Vesuvius.] —**poz·zuo·la·nic** adj.

pp Music. pianissimo.

pp. 1. pages. **2.** past participle. **3.** Music. pianissimo.

p.p. 1. parcel post. **2.** parish priest. **3.** past participle. **4.** per procurationem. **5.** postpaid.

P.P. 1. parish priest. **2.** postpaid.

ppd. 1. postpaid. **2.** prepaid.

pph. pamphlet.

P.P.S. 1. Parliamentary Private Secretary. **2.** additional postscript. [Latin post postscriptum].

p.q. previous question.

P.Q. Province of Quebec.

Pr The symbol for the element praseodymium.

PR public relations.

pr. 1. pair. **2.** present. **3.** price. **4.** printing. **5.** pronoun.

Pr. 1. priest. **2.** prince. **3.** Provençal.

P.R. 1. proportional representation. **2.** public relations. **3.** Puerto Rico.

praam, pram (praam, pram) n. **1.** A flat-bottomed boat used especially in the Baltic as a barge. **2.** Chiefly British. A small dinghy having a flat, snub-nosed bow. [Dutch, from Middle Dutch praem, from Old Slavonic pramŭ.]

prac·ti·ca·ble (práktika-b'l) adj. **1.** Capable of being effected, done, or executed; feasible. **2.** Capable of being used for a specified purpose: a practicable way of entry. —See Synonyms at **possible**. —See Usage note at **practical**. [French practicable, from pratiquer, to PRACTISE.] —**prac·ti·ca·bil·i·ty** (-bílləti) n. —**prac·ti·ca·bly** adv.

prac·ti·cal (práktik'l) adj. **1.** Of, pertaining to, governed by, or acquired through practice or action, rather than theory, speculation, or ideals. **2.** Manifested in or involving practice. **3.** Actually engaged in some work or occupation. **4.** Capable of being used or put into effect. **5. a.** Functioning well in actual use; suitable for its purpose: Season tickets are very practical. **b.** Designed to serve a purpose without elaboration: practical low-heeled shoes. **6.** Concerned with the production or operation of something useful: Woodworking is a practical art. **7.** Level-headed, efficient, and down-to-earth. **8.** Being actually so in almost every respect; virtual: a practical disaster. —See Synonyms at **possible**.
~n. An examination testing a student's practical ability in a subject: a chemistry practical. [Late Latin practicus, practical, from Greek praktikos, from praktos, to be done, from prattein, prassein, to practise.] —**prac·ti·cal·i·ty** (prákti-kál-əti), **prac·ti·cal·ness** n.

Usage: Practical and practicable are sometimes confused. A practical solution to a problem is one of proven effectiveness; a practicable solution is one that is capable of being put into effect, though it may not necessarily solve the problem. There may be several practicable suggestions for dealing with a situation, but not all of these may be practical ones. Practicable is not used of people, and thus lacks the sense of down-to-earth efficiency which is apparent in such contexts as John is a very practical person. In contemporary usage, practical seems to be taking over some of the senses of practicable, but the trend is open to criticism.

practical joke n. A mischievous trick played on a person especially to cause him or her to feel embarrassment or indignity.

prac·ti·cal·ly (práktikli) adj. **1.** In a way that is practical. **2.** In every important respect; virtually. **3.** Almost.

Usage: Practically is now widely used in such senses as "in effect": The species is practically extinct; and "nearly": He had practically finished eating when I arrived. These uses are often criticised on the grounds that, as the events in question have not taken place "in practice", the word practically is inappropriate.

practical nurse n. U.S. A professional nurse who is trained but not registered. Compare **registered nurse**.

prac·tice (práktiss) n. **1.** A habitual or customary action or way of doing something: make a practice of being punctual. **2. a.** Repeated performance of an activity in order to learn or perfect a skill. **b.** Archaic. The skill so learned or perfected. **c.** The condition of being skilled through repeated performance: He is out of practice at *golf.* **3.** The act or process of doing something; a performance. **4.** The exercise of an occupation or profession, such as medicine or law: *set up in practice as a solicitor.* **5.** The business of a professional person, such as a solicitor or doctor: *How large is the practice?* **6.** *Plural.* Habitual actions or acts, especially when they are objectionable, questionable, or unacceptable. **7.** The methods of procedure used in a court of law. **8.** *Archaic.* **a.** The act of tricking. **b.** A stratagem; a trick. —See Synonyms at **habit.** [Middle English *practisen,* from Old French *practiser, pratiquer,* from Medieval Latin *practicāre,* from Late Latin *practicus,* PRACTICAL.]

Usage: Both the noun and the verb are usually spelt with a *c* in American English. In British English, only the noun has a *c*; the verb has an *s.* Confusion sometimes arises when the noun and past participle are used adjectivally: *a practice match* but *a practised tennis-player.*

prac·tise, *U.S.* **prac·tice** (práktiss) *v.* **-tised, -tising, -tises.** —*tr.* **1.** To do or perform habitually or customarily; make a habit of. **2.** To exercise or perform repeatedly in order to acquire or polish a skill: *practise a dance step.* **3.** *Chiefly U.S.* To give lessons or repeated instructions to; drill: *to practise students in handwriting.* **4.** To work at, especially as a profession: *practise law.* **5.** To carry out in action; act in accordance with: *practise one's religion.* **6.** To take advantage of; impose upon. Used with *on* or *upon.* —*intr.* **1.** To do or perform something habitually or repeatedly. **2.** To do something repeatedly in order to acquire or polish a skill. **3.** To work at a profession.

prac·tised (práktist) *adj.* **1.** Proficient; skilled; expert. **2.** Acquired or brought to perfection by practice.

prac·tis·ing (prákti-sing) *adj.* **1.** Actively professing and adhering to the beliefs, way of life, or principles of: *a practising Christian.* **2.** Actively employed as or engaged in the profession of: *She is both a novelist and a practising barrister.*

prac·ti·tion·er (prak-tísh'n-ər) *n.* One who practises an occupation, profession, or technique: *a medical practitioner.* [From earlier *practician,* from obsolete French *practicien,* from *pra(c)tique,* practice, from Late Latin *practicus,* PRACTICAL.]

prae-. Variant of **pre-.**

prae·di·al, pre·dial (préedi-əl) *adj.* **1.** Pertaining to land or its products. **2.** Attached to or arising from land or landed property: *praedial serfs.* [Medieval Latin *praediālis,* of an estate, from Latin *praedium,* estate, from *praes,* surety.]

praefect. Variant of **prefect.**

prae·mu·ni·re (préemew-nír-i) *n. Law.* **1.** Formerly in Britain, the offence of appealing to or obeying a foreign court or authority, such as that of the Pope, thus challenging the supremacy of the Crown. **2.** The writ charging this offence. **3.** The penalty for this offence. [Middle English, from Medieval Latin *praemūnīre (facias),* "that you warn (someone to appear)" (words in the writ), from Latin *praemūnīre,* to fortify (meaning influenced by *praemonēre,* to forewarn) : *prae,* before + *mūnīre,* to fortify.]

prae·no·men (pree-nōmən) *n., pl.* **-nomina** (-nómminə ‖ -nōminə) or **-nomens.** In ancient Rome, any first or personal name. Compare **cognomen, nomen.** [Latin *praenōmen* : *prae,* before + *nōmen,* name.] **—prae·nom·i·nal** (-nómmin'l) *adj.*

prae·tor (prée-tər, -tawr) *n.* A high elected magistrate of the Roman Republic, ranking below the consuls. [Latin *praetor,* "leader", "chief", from *praeīre,* to go before : *prae-,* in front of + *īre,* to go.] **—prae·tor·ship** *n.*

prae·to·ri·an (pree-táwri-ən, pri- ‖ -tōri-) *adj.* **1.** Of or pertaining to a praetor or the praetorship. **2.** *Capital* **P.** Of, pertaining to, or characteristic of the Praetorian Guard.
~*n.* **1.** An ex-praetor. **2.** *Capital* **P.** A member of the Praetorian Guard or of a group having comparable position and power.

Prae·to·ri·an Guard (pree-táwri-ən, pri-) *n.* **1.** The elite guard of the Roman emperors, usually numbering about 5,000 men, whose notoriously bribable allegiance on many occasions determined the imperial succession. **2.** A member of this guard. [Originally the bodyguard of a praetor under the Roman Republic.]

Prae·to·ri·us (pri-táwri-əss; *German* pre-tōri-ōoss), **Michael,** born Michael Schultheiss; also known as Michael Schulz (1571–1621). German composer. He wrote a number of hymns, dances, and madrigals. His *Syntagma Musicum* (1615–19) is an account of the musical theory and instruments employed in his time.

prag·mat·ic (prag-máttik) *adj.* Also **prag·mat·i·cal** (-'l) **1. a.** Dealing with facts or actual occurrences; based on or dealing with immediate circumstances rather than theoretical considerations; practical. **b.** Active rather than contemplative. **2.** Pertaining to the study of events and historical phenomena with emphasis on their practical outcome. **3.** Of or pertaining to pragmatism. **4.** Of or pertaining to the affairs of a state. **5.** *Rare.* Interfering; bossy.
~*n.* **1.** A pragmatic sanction. **2.** *Rare.* A meddler; a busybody. [Latin *pragmaticus,* skilled in affairs, from Greek *pragmatikos,* from *pragma* (stem *pragmat-*), deed, affair, from *prattein,* to do.] **—prag·mat·i·cal·ly** *adv.*

prag·mat·ics (prag-máttiks) *n. Usually used with a singular verb.* The branch of semiotics concerned with the relations between signs or expressions and their users.

pragmatic sanction *n.* An edict issued by a sovereign that becomes part of the fundamental law of the land.

prag·ma·tism (prágmə-tiz'm) *n.* **1.** *Philosophy.* The theory, developed by Charles S. Peirce and William James, that the meaning of a proposition or course of action lies in its observable consequences, and that the sum of these consequences constitutes its meaning. **2.** A method or tendency in the conduct of political affairs characterised by the rejection of theory and precedent, and by the use of practical means and expedients. **3.** A pragmatic outlook or way of behaving. **—prag·ma·tist** *n.* **—prag·ma·tis·tic** (-tístik) *adj.*

prag·ma·tise, prag·ma·tize (prágmə-tīz) *tr.v.* **-tised, -tising, -tises.** To consider or represent as real or actual.

Prague (praag). *Czechoslovakian* **Pra·ha** (praaha) Capital of Czechoslavakia, lying on the river Vltava in central Bohemia. It became the capital of newly independent Czechoslovakia in 1918. In 1968 Soviet forces entered the city following the "Prague Spring", a period in which the city had become the focus of the movement for greater economic and political freedom led by Alexander Dubček. Prague is the leading Czech industrial centre.

prai·rie (prair-i) *n.* An extensive area of flat or rolling temperate grassland, especially in central North America. [French, from Old French *praerie,* from Vulgar Latin *prātāria* (unattested), from Latin *prātum*†, meadow.]

prairie chicken *n.* Either of two grouse, *Tympanuchus cupido* or *T. pallidicinctus,* of western North America, having deep-chested bodies and mottled brownish plumage. Also called "prairie hen".

prairie dog *n.* Any of several burrowing rodents of the genus *Cynomys,* of west-central North America. They have yellowish fur, a barklike call, and live in large communities.

prairie oyster *n.* **1.** A raw egg immersed in a liquid, usually Worcester sauce or vinegar, and swallowed whole, especially as a remedy for a hangover. **2.** *U.S. Regional & Canadian.* A testicle of a calf, cooked and served as food.

Prairie Provinces. Region of west central Canada: the provinces of Manitoba, Alberta, and Saskatchewan.

prairie schooner *n.* A canvas-covered wagon, similar to but lighter than the **Conestoga wagon** *(see),* used by pioneers crossing the North American prairies.

prairie wolf *n.* The **coyote** *(see).*

praise (prayz) *n.* **1.** An expression of warm approval or admiration; strong commendation. **2.** The glorification and extolling of a deity, ruler, or hero. **3.** *Archaic.* A reason for praise; merit. **—praise be.** Used to express gratitude or relief. **—sing the praises of.** To praise highly and publicly.
~*tr.v.* **praised, praising, praises. 1.** To express warm approval of or admiration for; commend; applaud. **2.** To extol or exalt; worship. [Middle English *preisen,* from Old French *presier,* to prize, praise, from Late Latin *pretiāre,* from Latin *pretium,* price.] **—prais·er** *n.*

Synonyms: *praise, acclaim, commend, extol, laud.*

praise·wor·thy (práyz-wurthi) *adj.* Meriting praise; highly commendable. **—praise·wor·thi·ly** *adv.* **—praise·wor·thi·ness** *n.*

Pra·krit (praa-krit) *n.* **1.** Any of the vernacular languages of India, as opposed to the literary language, **Sanskrit** *(see).* **2.** Any of the various ancient Indic languages on which the modern vernaculars are based. [Sanskrit *prākrta,* vulgar, vernacular : *pra-,* before + *krta,* made, from *kr,* to make.] **—Pra·krit·ic** (-kríttik) *adj.*

pra·line (praa-leen ‖ práy-, *U.S. also* práw-) *n.* A crisp confection or sweet made of nut kernels stirred in boiling sugar syrup until brown. It is often crushed and used as a flavouring. [French, invented by the cook of César de Choiseul, Count du Plessis-*Praslin,* French field-marshal (1598–1675).]

prall·tril·ler (praal-trillər) *n. Music.* A melodic detail or embellishment, consisting of a mordent (a rapid alteration of two notes), using the auxiliary note above the principal note. Also called "inverted mordent". [German *Pralltriller,* "elastic trill" : *prallen,* to rebound (akin to Middle High German *prellen*†) + *triller,* trill, from Italian *trillo,* TRILL.]

pram[1] (pram) *n.* A small carriage for babies and children consisting of a cot and a supporting structure on four, or sometimes three, wheels, which can be pushed. Also called "perambulator", *U.S.* "baby carriage". [Shortened from PERAMBULATOR.]

pram[2]**.** Variant of **praam.**

prance (praanss ‖ pranss) *intr.v.* **pranced, prancing, prances. 1. a.** To spring forward on the hind legs. Used of a horse. **b.** To move with a succession of such springs or bounds. **2.** To ride a horse that moves in this way. **3.** To walk or move about in a lively manner; spring; strut.
~*n.* An act of prancing. [Middle English *prauncen*†.] **—pranc·er** *n.* **—pranc·ing·ly** *adv.*

pran·di·al (prándi-əl) *adj.* Of or relating to a meal, especially dinner. [Latin *prandium,* late breakfast.] **—pran·di·al·ly** *adv.*

prang (prang) *n. Informal.* **1.** A crash, accident, or collision, especially in an aircraft or car. **2.** The destruction of a target by bombing.
~*v.* **pranged, pranging, prangs.** *Informal.* —*tr.* **1.** To crash or damage in a collision. **2.** To bomb. —*intr.* To crash an aircraft or other vehicle. [Imitative.]

prank[1] (prangk) *n.* A mischievous trick; a practical joke. [16th century : origin obscure.]

prank[2] *v.* **pranked, pranking, pranks.** —*tr.* To decorate or dress ostentatiously or gaudily. —*intr.* To make an ostentatious display. [Akin to Dutch *pronk*†, finery and *pronken*†, to strut.]

prank·ster (prángkstər) *n.* One who plays tricks or pranks.

pra·se·o·dym·i·um (práy-zi-o-dímmi-əm, -si-) *n. Symbol* **Pr** A soft, yellow, malleable, ductile rare-earth element that develops a characteristic green tarnish in air. It occurs naturally with other rare earths in monazite and is used to colour glass yellow, as a core material for carbon arcs, and in metallic alloys. Atomic number 59,

prairie dog *This squirrel of the North American plains lives underground in communal burrows containing up to 1,000 animals. It gets its name from its doglike warning bark.*

atomic weight 140.907, melting point 935°C, boiling point 3,127°C, relative density 6.64, valencies 3, 4. [New Latin, contraction of *praseodidymium* : Greek *prasios*, leek-green, from *prason*, leek + DIDYMIUM.]

prat (prat) *n.* **1.** *British Informal.* A stupidly pretentious or incompetent person. **2.** *Archaic & Vulgar.* The buttocks. [Perhaps imitative of the sound of spanking.]

prate (prayt) *v.* **prated, prating, prates.** —*intr.* To talk idly and at great length; chatter. —*tr.* To utter idly or to little purpose. ～*n.* Empty, foolish, or trivial talk. [Middle English *praten*, akin to Middle Dutch and Middle Low German *prāten* (perhaps imitative).] —**prat·er** *n.* —**prat·ing·ly** *adv.*

prat·fall (prát-fawl) *n. Chiefly U.S.* **1.** An embarrassing mistake or failure. **2.** A fall on the buttocks. [PRAT + FALL.]

prat·in·cole (prátting-kōl, práyting-) *n.* Any of several swallow-like Old World birds of the genus *Glareola* and related genera, having brown and black plumage. [New Latin *pratincola*, "meadow-dweller" : Latin *prātum*, meadow (see **prairie**) + *incola*, inhabitant.]

pra·tique (prátteek, pra-téek) *n. Nautical.* Clearance granted to a ship to proceed into port after compliance with quarantine or health regulations. [French, PRACTICE.]

prat·tle (pratt'l) *v.* **-tled, -tling, -tles.** —*intr.* To talk idly or meaninglessly; babble. —*tr.* To utter in a childish or silly way. ～*n.* Childish or meaningless sounds; babble. [Frequentative of PRATE (akin to Low German *prateln*).] —**prat·tler** *n.*

prawn (prawn) *n.* Any of various edible marine crustaceans of the genus *Palaemon* and related genera, closely related to and resembling the shrimps. ～*intr.v.* **prawned, prawning, prawns.** To fish for prawns. [Middle English *prayne*†.] —**prawn·er** *n.*

prax·i·ol·o·gy, prax·e·ol·o·gy (práksi-óllǝji) *n.* The study of human conduct. [From PRAXIS + -LOGY.]

prax·is (práks-iss) *n., pl.* **-es** (-eez). **1.** Practical application or exercise of a branch of learning. **2.** Habitual or established practice; custom. [Medieval Latin, from Greek, doing, action, from *prattein*, *prassein*, to do.]

Prax·it·e·les (prak-sítti-leez) (mid-fourth century B.C.). Athenian sculptor. His few surviving works include *Hermes carrying Dionysus*, discovered at Olympia (1877).

pray (pray) *v.* **prayed, praying, prays.** —*intr.* **1.** To utter or address prayer to a god or some other object of worship. **2.** To make a fervent request; plead; beg. —*tr.* **1.** To say a prayer or prayers to. **2.** To ask (someone) imploringly; beseech. Often used to introduce an entreaty or question: *Pray, be careful.* **3.** To make a devout or earnest request for: *I pray your indulgence.* **4.** To move or bring by prayer or entreaty. [Middle English *preyen*, from Old French *preier*, from Latin *precārī*, to entreat, from *prex* (stem *prec-*), prayer.]

pray·er[1] (práy-ǝr) *n.* One who prays.

prayer[2] (praír) *n.* **1. a.** The practice of addressing God in words or through meditation, as in praise, gratitude, sorrow, or intercession. **b.** An instance of this. **c.** A specially worded form used in addressing God. **d.** A petition or act of devotion to any object of worship. **2.** *Sometimes capital* P. A religious service in which praying predominates: *morning prayer.* **3. a.** Any fervent request. **b.** The thing so requested: *His safe arrival was their prayer.* **4.** *Slang.* The slightest chance of achieving something: *you haven't a prayer!* [Middle English *preyere*, from Old French *preiere*, from Medieval Latin *precāria*, written petition, prayer, from Latin, feminine of *precārius*, obtained by entreaty, from *precārī*, to entreat, PRAY.]

prayer beads *pl.n.* A string of beads for keeping count of the prayers one is saying; a rosary.

prayer book *n.* **1.** A book containing prayers and other forms of worship. **2.** *Usually capital* P, capital B. *Abbr.* **P.B.** The Book of Common Prayer.

prayer·ful (praír-f'l) *adj.* **1.** Inclined to pray frequently; devout. **2.** Characterised by or conducive to prayer. —**prayer·ful·ly** *adv.* —**prayer·ful·ness** *n.*

prayer mat *n.* A small mat or carpet knelt on by Muslims when praying. Also called "prayer rug".

prayer meeting *n.* An evangelical service, especially one held on a weekday evening, in which the laity participate by singing, praying, or testifying.

prayer shawl *n.* A large, lightweight shawl worn, especially by Jews, during prayer. See **tallith.**

prayer wheel *n.* A cylinder inscribed with or containing written prayers and revolved on an axis, used especially by the Buddhists of Tibet.

praying mantis *n.* A green or brownish predatory insect, *Mantis religiosa*, that, while at rest, folds its front legs as if in prayer.

P.R.B. Pre-Raphaelite Brotherhood.

pre– *prefix.* Indicates: **1.** An earlier or prior time; for example, **prearrange, pre-Columbian. 2.** Preliminary or preparatory work or activity; for example, **preschool. 3.** A location in front or anterior; for example, **preaxial.** *Note:* Many compounds other than those entered here may be formed with *pre-*. In this dictionary, *pre-* is normally joined with the following element without space or hyphen: *prearrange.* However, many users prefer the hyphenated form, especially if the second element begins with a capital letter: *pre-Christian,* or the letter *e: pre-eminent.* [Middle English, from Old French, from Latin *prae-*, from *prae*, before, in front. In Latin compounds, *prae-* indicates: 1. Before in time, as in **prescient. 2.** Before in position, in front, as in **premorse. 3.** Before in degree or

importance, superior, exceeding, as in **preponderate. 4.** Intensifying action, as in **prepotent.**

preach (preech) *v.* **preached, preaching, preaches.** —*tr.* **1.** To expound upon in writing or speech; especially, to urge acceptance of or compliance with (specified religious or moral principles). **2.** To deliver (a sermon, lengthy advice, or the like). —*intr.* **1.** To deliver a sermon. **2.** To give religious or moral instruction, especially in a drawn-out, tiresome manner. [Middle English *prechen*, from Old French *prechier*, from Late Latin *praedīcāre*, from Latin, to proclaim : *prae*, before + *dīcāre*, to say.]

preach·er (préechǝr) *n.* **1.** A Protestant clergyman; a minister. **2.** One who preaches.

preach·i·fy (préechi-fī) *intr.v.* **-fied, -fying, -fies.** *Informal.* To preach tediously and didactically. —**preach·i·fi·ca·tion** (-fi-káysh'n) *n.*

preach·ment (préechmǝnt) *n.* **1.** The act of preaching. **2.** A tiresome or unwelcome moral lecture; tedious sermonising.

preach·y (préechi) *adj.* **-ier, -iest.** *Chiefly U.S. Informal.* Inclined to preach.

pre·ad·am·ite (prée-áddǝmīt) *n.* **1.** One supposed to have been in existence before Adam (traditionally thought to have been the first man, created by God). **2.** One who holds that there were people in existence before Adam. [PRE- + ADAM + -ITE.] —**pre·ad·am·ite** *adj.*

pre·ad·ap·ta·tion (prée-áddap-táysh'n, -áddǝp-) *n.* The condition of an organism or group of organisms of having one or more characteristics that would be advantageous, and therefore enhance its chances of survival, in a changed environment.

pre·ad·o·les·cence (prée-áddǝ-léss'nss) *n.* The period between childhood and adolescence, often designated as between the ages of ten and twelve. —**pre·ad·o·les·cent** *n. & adj.*

pre·am·ble (prée-ámb'l, prée-amb'l) *n.* **1.** A preliminary statement; especially, the introduction to a formal document, explaining its purpose. **2.** An introductory occurrence or fact; a preliminary. [Middle English, from Old French *preambule*, from Medieval Latin *praeambulum*, from Late Latin *praeambulus*, walking in front : *prae*, in front + *ambulāre*, to walk.] —**pre·am·bu·lar·y** (prée-ámbew-lǝri ‖ *U.S.* -lerri) *adj.*

pre·am·pli·fi·er (prée-ámplifī-ǝr) *n.* An electronic circuit or device that detects and sufficiently amplifies weak signals, especially from a radio receiver, for subsequent amplification stages. Also informally called "preamp".

pre·ar·range (prée-ǝ-ráynj) *tr.v.* **-ranged, -ranging, -ranges.** To arrange in advance. —**pre·ar·range·ment** *n.*

pre·a·tom·ic (prée-ǝ-tómmik) *adj.* Of or pertaining to the period preceding the use of atomic energy.

pre·au·di·ence (prée-áwdi-ǝnss) *n.* In Britain, the right of certain lawyers belonging to various ranks to be heard before others, when there is no particular order in which business is to be heard in court. The Attorney-General and the Solicitor-General take precedence in most matters, followed by Queen's Counsel and then junior barristers (in the order in which they were called to the bar).

pre·ax·i·al (prée-áksi-ǝl) *adj.* Anatomically positioned in front of a body axis. —**pre·ax·i·al·ly** *adv.*

preb·end (prébbǝnd) *n.* **1.** A clergyman's stipend, drawn from a special endowment belonging to his cathedral or church. **2.** The property or tithe providing the endowment for such a stipend. **3.** The clergyman who receives such a stipend; a prebendary. [Middle English *prebende*, from Old French, from Medieval Latin *praebenda*, from Late Latin, from Latin, "things to be given", from *praebēre*, to grant : *prae*, forth + *habēre*, to hold, offer.] —**preb·en·dal** (pri-bénd'l) *adj.*

preb·en·dar·y (prébbǝn-dǝri, -dri ‖ -derri) *n., pl.* **-ies. 1.** A clergyman who receives a prebend. **2.** In the Anglican Church, a clergyman holding the honorary title of prebend without a stipend.

prec. preceding.

Pre·cam·bri·an, Pre-cam·bri·an (prée-kámbri-ǝn) *adj.* Of, belonging to, or designating the oldest and largest division of geological time, preceding the Cambrian, often subdivided into the Archaeozoic and Proterozoic eras, and characterised by the appearance of primitive forms of life. ～*n.* The Precambrian era. Preceded by *the.*

pre·can·cel (prée-kánss'l) *tr.v.* **-celled** or *U.S.* **-celed, -celling** or *U.S.* **-celing, -cels.** To cancel a postage stamp before posting. ～*n.* A precancelled stamp or envelope.

pre·can·cer·ous (prée-kán-sǝrǝss) *adj.* Designating a growth that is not malignant but will become so if left untreated.

pre·car·i·ous (pri-kaír-i-ǝss, prǝ-) *adj.* **1.** Dangerously lacking in security or stability. **2.** Subject to chance or unknown conditions. **3.** Based upon uncertain or unproved premises: *a precarious argument.* **4.** *Archaic.* Dependent on the will or favour of another. [Latin *precārius*, dependent on prayer, from *precārī*, to entreat, from *prex* (stem *prec-*), entreaty, prayer.] —**pre·car·i·ous·ly** *adv.*

pre·cast (prée-kaást ‖ -kást) *tr.v.* **-cast, -casting, -casts.** To form (concrete or other building materials) into structurally useful shapes, typically blocks, before use. —**pre·cast** *adj.*

prec·a·to·ry (préckǝ-tǝri, -tri ‖ pri-káy-, prǝ-) *adj.* Also **prec·a·tive** (-tiv). Relating to or expressing entreaty or supplication. [Late Latin *precātōrius*, from *precārī*, to entreat. See **precarious.**]

pre·cau·tion (pri-káwsh'n, prǝ-) *n.* **1.** An action taken in advance to protect against possible failure or danger; a safeguard. **2.** Caution practised in advance; forethought; circumspection. [French *précaution*, from Late Latin *praecautiō*, from Latin *praecavēre*, to guard against before : *prae*, before + *cavēre*, to guard against.]

pre·cau·tion·ar·y (pri-káwsh'n-əri, prə-, -ri || -erri) *adj.* Also **pre·cau·tion·al** (-'l). **1.** Of or constituting a precaution. **2.** Advising or exercising precaution.

pre·cau·tious (pri-káwshəss, prə-) *adj.* Exercising precaution. **—pre·cau·tious·ly** *adv.* **—pre·cau·tious·ness** *n.*

pre·cede (pri-seéd, preé-) *v.* **-ceded, -ceding, -cedes.** *—tr.* **1.** To come before in time; exist or occur prior to. **2.** To come before in order or rank; surpass; outrank. **3.** To be or go in a position in front of or in advance of. **4.** To preface; introduce: *precede a speech with an anecdote.* *—intr.* To exist or go before. [Middle English *preceden,* from Old French *preceder,* from Latin *praecēdere* : *prae,* before + *cēdere,* to go.]

pre·ced·ence (préssi-d'nss, preéssi-, preé-seé-, pri-) *n.* Also **pre·ced·en·cy** (-i). **1.** The act or state of preceding. **2.** Priority in importance, position, rank, or the like. **3.** A ceremonial order of rank, observed especially on formal occasions.

Usage: The preposition that follows the phrases *take/have precedence* is *over* (less often *of,* which tends to be more formal). One also gives precedence *to.* The noun *precedent* may be followed by *of (the precedent of staying for a year)* or *for (there is no precedent for doing that).* The adjective , when used after a verb, is followed by *to (His statement was precedent to mine).*

prec·e·dent (préssi-dənt, preéssi-) *n.* **1.** An act or instance that may be used as an example in dealing with or justifying subsequent similar cases. **2.** *Law.* A judicial decision that may be used as a standard in subsequent similar cases.
~adj. (pri-seéd'nt; *rarely* préssidənt). Preceding; prior. —See Usage note at **precedence.** [Middle English, from Old French, from Latin *praecēdēns,* present participle of *praecēdere,* PRECEDE.] **—prec·e·dent·ed** (-dentid) *adj.* **—pre·ced·ent·ly** (pri-seéd'ntli) *adv.*

prec·e·den·tial (préssi-dénsh'l, preéssi-) *adj.* **1.** Of, pertaining to, or serving as a precedent. **2.** Having precedence.

pre·ced·ing (pri-seéding, preé-) *adj. Abbr.* **prec.** Existing or coming before in time, place, rank, or sequence; previous.

pre·cen·tor (pri-séntər, preé-) *n.* **1.** One who directs the singing of the congregation or choir in a church. **2.** In some cathedrals, a member of the clergy who is in charge of music. [Late Latin, from Latin *praecinere,* to sing before : *prae,* before + *canere,* to sing.] **—pre·cen·to·ri·al** (preé-sen-táwri-əl || -tṓri-) *adj.* **—pre·cen·tor·ship** *n.*

pre·cept (preé-sept) *n.* **1.** A rule or principle imposing a particular standard of action or conduct. **2.** *Law.* An order or direction from one official to another as: **a.** A writ or warrant. **b.** *British.* A written order from a sheriff with instructions for holding an election. **3.** *British.* An order from a county council to a rating authority for the levying of rates. [Middle English, from Latin *praeceptum,* from *praecipere* (past participle *praeceptus*), to take beforehand, warn, teach : *prae,* before + *capere,* to take.]

pre·cep·tive (pri-séptiv) *adj.* **1.** Of or expressing a precept. **2.** Giving precepts; didactic. **—pre·cep·tive·ly** *adv.*

pre·cep·tor (pri-séptər || preé-septər) *n.* A teacher; an instructor. [Middle English *preceptur,* from Latin *praeceptor,* teacher, from *praecipere,* to teach. See **precept.**] **—pre·cep·to·ri·al** (preé-sep-táwri-əl || -tṓri-) *adj.* **—pre·cep·to·ri·al·ly** *adv.* **—pre·cep·tor·ship** *n.*

pre·cep·to·ry (pri-séptəri) *n., pl.* **-ries.** In the Order of the Knights Templars: **1.** A subordinate community. **2.** The buildings of such a community.

pre·cep·tress (pri-sép-trəss, -triss) *n.* A female preceptor.

pre·cess (pri-séss, preé-) *intr.v.* **-cessed, -cessing, -cesses.** *Physics & Astronomy.* To move in or be subjected to precession. [Back-formation from PRECESSION.]

pre·ces·sion (pri-sésh'n, preé-) *n.* **1.** The act or state of preceding; precedence. **2.** *Physics.* A complex motion executed by a rotating body in which the axis of rotation changes orientation when the body is subject to an applied torque. A torque of constant magnitude will cause the axis to describe a conical locus at a constant angular velocity. **3.** *Astronomy.* Precession of the equinoxes. [New Latin *praecessio,* from Medieval Latin *praecessiō* (stem *praecessiōn-*), a going forward, from Latin *praecēdere* (past participle *praecessus*), PRECEDE.] **—pre·ces·sion·al** *adj.*

precession of the equinoxes *n. Astronomy.* A slow westward shift of the equinoctial points along the plane of the ecliptic at a rate of 50.27 seconds of arc per year, resulting from precession of the Earth's axis of rotation.

pre·cinct (preé-singkt) *n.* **1.** *Usually plural.* **a.** A place or enclosure marked off by definite limits, especially one that surrounds a church, cathedral, or the like. **b.** A boundary. **2.** *Plural.* Neighbourhood; environs. **3.** A part of a town designed for a specified purpose: *a shopping precinct.* **4.** *U.S.* In a town or city: **a.** A district to be patrolled by the police. **b.** An electoral district. [Middle English *precincte,* from Medieval Latin *praecinctum,* "enclosure", from Latin *praecingere* (past participle *praecinctus*), to gird about : *prae,* before, around + *cingere,* to gird.]

pre·ci·os·i·ty (préshi-óssəti, préssi-) *n., pl.* **-ties.** Extreme meticulousness or overrefinement, as in language. [Middle English *preciousite,* from Old French *precieusite,* (stem *preciōsitāt-*) from Latin *pretiōsitās,* from *pretiōsus* PRECIOUS.]

pre·cious (préshəss) *adj.* **1.** Of high cost or worth; valuable: *precious metal.* **2.** Highly esteemed; cherished. **3.** Dear; beloved. **4.** Affectedly dainty or overrefined. **5.** *Informal.* **a.** Arrant; thoroughgoing. **b.** Used as an intensive to express anger or irritation: *Take your precious books, for all I care!* —See Synonyms at **costly.**
~n. One who is precious; a darling.
~adv. Used as an intensive: *precious little to eat!* [Middle English, from Old French *precieus, precios,* from Latin *pretiōsus,* from *pretium,* price.] **—pre·cious·ly** *adv.* **—pre·cious·ness** *n.*

precious stone *n.* Any of various minerals, such as diamond, ruby, or sapphire, valued for their rarity or appearance.

prec·i·pice (préss-i-piss, -ə-) *n.* **1.** An extremely steep, high face of a cliff or mass of rock. **2.** The brink of a dangerous situation. [Old French, from Latin *praecipitium,* from *praecipitāre,* to throw headlong. See **precipitate.**]

pre·cip·i·ta·ble (pri-síppitəb'l) *adj.* Capable of being precipitated. [From PRECIPITATE.]

pre·cip·i·tant (pri-síppitənt) *adj.* **1.** Rushing or falling headlong. **2.** Impulsive in thought or action; rash. **3.** Abrupt or unexpected; sudden. —See Usage note at **precipitate.**
~n. Any substance that causes precipitation. [French *précipitant,* from Latin *praecipitāns,* present participle of *praecipitāre,* to throw headlong, PRECIPITATE.] **—pre·cip·i·tance, pre·cip·i·tan·cy** *n.* **—pre·cip·i·tant·ly** *adv.*

pre·cip·i·tate (pri-síppi-tayt, prə-) *v.* **-tated, -tating, -tates.** *—tr.* **1.** To throw from or as from a great height; hurl downwards. **2.** To cause to happen before anticipated or required. **3.** *Meteorology.* To cause (water vapour) to condense as rain, snow, dew, frost, sleet, or hail. **4.** *Chemistry.* To cause (a solid substance) to be separated from a solution. *—intr.* **1.** *Meteorology.* To condense and fall. **2.** *Chemistry.* To be separated from a solution as a precipitate. **3.** To fall headlong. —See Synonyms at **speed.**
~adj. (-tət, -tit || -tayt). **1.** Speeding headlong; moving rapidly and heedlessly. **2.** Acting with excessive haste or impulse; lacking due deliberation. **3.** Occurring suddenly or unexpectedly. —See Synonyms at **reckless.**
~n. (-tayt, -tət, -tit). *Chemistry.* A solid or solid phase separated from a solution, usually as a suspension of particles, which may subsequently settle. [Latin *praecipitāre,* to throw headlong, from *praeceps,* headlong : *prae,* in front + *caput,* head.] **—pre·cip·i·tate·ly** *adv.* **—pre·cip·i·tate·ness** *n.* **—pre·cip·i·ta·tive** (-tətiv, -taytiv) *adj.* **—pre·cip·i·ta·tor** (-taytər) *n.*

Usage: *Precipitate, precipitant,* and *precipitous,* and their corresponding adverbs, are sometimes confused. *Precipitate* and *precipitant* apply primarily to rash, overhasty human actions: *That was a very precipitate remark; He acted precipitantly when he resigned. Precipitous* is used primarily of physical steepness: *The precipitous west face of the mountain.*

pre·cip·i·ta·tion (pri-síppi-táysh'n, prə-) *n.* **1. a.** The act of precipitating. **b.** The state of being precipitated. **2.** Abrupt or impulsive haste. **3.** *Meteorology.* **a.** Deposition of water droplets or ice particles condensed from atmospheric water vapour as rain, snow, dew, frost, sleet, or hail. **b.** The quantity of such substances falling in a specific area within a specific period. **4.** *Chemistry.* The production of a precipitate.

pre·cip·i·tin (pri-síppitin, prə-) *n. Biochemistry.* An antibody that reacts with an antigen to form a precipitate. [PRECIPIT(ATE) + -IN.]

pre·cip·i·tous (pri-síppitəss, prə-) *adj.* **1.** Like a precipice; extremely steep. **2.** Having several precipices. **3.** *Nonstandard.* Precipitate. —See Usage note at **precipitate.** [French *précipiteux,* from Old French, from Latin *praecipitium,* PRECIPICE.] **—pre·cip·i·tous·ly** *adv.* **—pre·cip·i·tous·ness** *n.*

pré·cis (práy-see; *rarely* préssee || *U.S. also* pray-seé) *n., pl.* **précis** (-z). A concise summary of the essential facts or statements of a book, article, or other text; an abstract.
~tr.v. **précised** (-seed), **-cising** (-see-ing), **-cises** (-seez). To make a précis of. [French *précis,* "precise", from Old French *precis,* PRECISE.]

pre·cise (pri-sī́ss, prə-) *adj.* **1.** Clearly expressed or delineated; distinct; definite: *precise ideas.* **2.** Of or producing great exactness or accuracy: *a precise measurement; precise instruments.* **3.** Exactly corresponding to what is indicated; correct: *the precise amount of seasoning.* **4.** Strictly distinguished from others; very: *at that precise moment.* **5.** Strictly correct in manners, behaviour, or the like: *precise in his dress.* [Old French *precis,* from Latin *praecīsus,* shortened, from *praecīdere,* to cut off in front, shorten : *prae,* in front + *caedere,* to cut.] **—pre·cise·ly** *adv.* **—pre·cise·ness** *n.*

pre·ci·sian (pri-sízh'n, prə-) *n.* A person who is strict and precise in adherence to established rules, forms, or standards; especially, one who is strict in matters of religion or morality. [From PRECISE.] **—pre·ci·sian·ism** *n.*

pre·ci·sion (pri-sízh'n, prə-) *n.* The state or quality of being precise.
~adj. Precise in nature, action, or performance: *a precision tool; precision handling.* [French *précision,* from Latin *praecīsiō* (stem *praecīsiōn-*), act of cutting, from *praecīdere,* to cut off in front, abridge. See **precise.**] **—pre·ci·sion·ist** *n.*

pre·clin·i·cal (preé-klínnik'l) *adj.* **1.** Occurring in the early stages of a disease, before diagnosis is possible. **2.** Preparing for, or pertaining to the studies that prepare for, the study of medicine.

pre·clude (pri-klṓod || -kléwd) *tr.v.* **-cluded, -cluding, -cludes.** **1.** To make impossible or impracticable by previous action; prevent. **2.** To bar or prevent (a person) from something; debar. —See Synonyms at **prevent.** [Latin *praeclūdere* : *prae,* in front + *claudere,* to close.] **—pre·clu·sion** (-klṓozh'n || -kléwzh'n) *n.* **—pre·clu·sive** (-klṓo-siv || -kléw-, -ziv) *adj.* **—pre·clu·sive·ly** *adv.*

pre·co·cial (pri-kṓsh'l, prə-) *adj.* Covered with down and capable of moving about when first hatched. Said of birds. Compare **altricial.**

PRONUNCIATION KEY

a, trap; aa, father; ai, fair;
ar, star; aw, lawn; ay, play;
b, bb, stab; rubber;
ch, church; ck, ticket;
d, dd, dead; ladder; e, dress;
ee, bee; er, defer; ew, few;
ewr, pure; ə, about;
ər, letter; f, ff, fife; differ;
g, gg, giggle; h, hat; i, kit;
ī, price; īr, fire; j, judge;
k, kick; l, ll, let; 'l, needle;
m, mm, man; n, nn, no;
'n, sudden; ng, thing; o, lot;
ō, no; ŏŏ, foot; ōō, shoe;
oor, poor; ow, cow;
owr, hour; oy, boy;
p, pp, pepper; r, rr, red;
s, ss, sauce; sh, ship;
t, tt, totter; th, thick; th, this;
smooth; u, cut; ur, turn;
v, vv, valve; w, wet; y, yes;
z, zz, zebra; zh, vision;
pleasure

IN FOREIGN WORDS:

aN, oN, Saint-Saëns;
hl, Llanelli; Hluhluwe;
kh, loch; lough; Khaled

STRESS MARK:

ín-sīt, insight; in-sī́t, incite

pre-Columbian pottery *A Mochica pot, in the form of a man in a deerskin with a rope around his neck, possibly posing in a sacrificial role. The Mochica civilisation – in the Moche valley, on the north coast of Peru – flourished from about 200* B.C. *It ended in about* A.D. *600, nearly 900 years before the arrival of Columbus.*

[New Latin *praecoces,* precocial birds, from Latin *praecox,* PRECOCIOUS.]

pre·co·cious (pri-kṓshəss, prə-) *adj.* **1. a.** Characterised by unusually early development or maturity, especially in mental aptitude. **b.** Aping the manners and speech of adults: *a precocious brat.* **2.** Manifesting or characterised by premature or unusually early development. **3.** *Botany.* Blossoming before the leaves sprout. [Latin *praecox,* "ripening before its time", from *praecoquere,* to cook or ripen before : *prae,* before + *coquere,* to cook, ripen.] **—pre·co·cious·ly** *adv.* **—pre·co·cious·ness, pre·coc·i·ty** (-kóssəti) *n.*

pre·cog·ni·tion (prée-kog-nísh'n) *n.* **1.** Knowledge of something in advance of its occurrence. **2.** In Scots law, an unsworn statement given by a witness in advance of a trial. [Late Latin *praecognitiō,* from Latin *praecognōscere* (past participle *praecognitus*), to know before : *prae,* before + *cognōscere,* to know (see **cognition**).] **—pre·cog·ni·tive** (prée-kóg-nitiv) *adj.*

pre-Co·lum·bi·an (prée-kə-lúmbi-ən) *adj.* Of, relating to, or originating in the Americas before the voyages of Columbus.

pre·con·ceive (prée-kən-séev || -kon-) *tr.v.* **-ceived, -ceiving, -ceives.** To form an opinion or conception of (a matter) beforehand, without knowledge or experience: *preconceived ideas.*

pre·con·cep·tion (prée-kən-sépsh'n || -kon-) *n.* **1.** An opinion or conception formed in advance of actual knowledge. **2.** A prejudice.

pre·con·di·tion (prée-kən-dísh'n || -kon-) *n.* A condition that must exist or be established before something can occur or be considered; a prerequisite.
~*tr.v.* **preconditioned, -tioning, -tions.** To condition, train, or accustom in advance.

pre·co·nise, pre·co·nize (prée-kən-īz) *tr.v.* **-nised, -nising, -nises.** **1.** To command or announce in public. **2.** To call or summon in public. **3.** *Roman Catholic Church.* To publicly approve the nomination of (a new bishop). Used of the pope. [Middle English, from Medieval Latin *praeconizare,* from *praeco* (stem *praecon-*), herald.] **—pre·co·ni·sa·tion** (-ī-záysh'n || *U.S.* -i-) *n.*

pre·con·scious (prée-kónshəss) *adj.* **1. a.** *Psychology.* Of or designating mental contents capable of being recalled although not present in the conscious mind. **b.** Designating the part of the mind held to be the region of such contents. **2.** Before the development of consciousness. —See Usage note at **conscious.** **—pre·con·scious·ly** *adv.*

pre·con·tract (prée-kón-trakt) *n.* An agreement or contract, as of marriage, entered into beforehand.
~*v.* (-kən-trákt || -kon-) **precontracted, -tracting, -tracts.** —*tr.* **1.** To engage (a person) in a contract of marriage by previous agreement. **2.** To establish previously by contract. —*intr.* To enter into a contract beforehand.

pre·cook (prée-kóók || -kóók) *tr.v.* **-cooked, -cooking, -cooks.** To cook in advance, or cook partially before final cooking.

pre·crit·i·cal (prée-kríttik'l) *adj.* Prior to the occurrence of a critical condition.

pre·cur·sor (pri-kúrssər, prée-) *n.* **1.** One that precedes and indicates or announces someone or something to come; a forerunner; a harbinger. **2.** One that precedes another; a predecessor. **3.** A substance that is converted into another substance during a chemical or biochemical reaction. [Latin *praecursor,* from *praecurrere,* to run before : *prae,* before + *currere,* to run.]

pre·cur·so·ry (pri-kúrss-əri, prée-) *adj.* Also **pre·cur·sive** (-iv). **1.** Preceding in the manner of a precursor; preliminary; introductory. **2.** Suggesting or indicating something to follow; premonitory.

pred. predicate.

pre·da·cious, pre·da·ceous (pri-dáyshəss, pre-) *adj.* Living by seizing or taking prey; predatory. Said of such animals as lions and hawks. [Latin *praedārī,* to plunder. See **predatory.**] **—pre·da·cious·ness, pre·dac·i·ty** (-dássəti) *n.*

pre·date (prée-dáyt) *tr.v.* **-dated, -dating, -dates.** **1.** To mark or designate with an earlier date than the actual one. **2.** To precede in time; antedate.

pre·da·tion (pri-dáysh'n, pre-) *n.* **1.** The act or practice of plundering or marauding. **2.** A feeding relationship in an ecological community in which one species of animal (the predator) captures, kills, and eats another (the prey). [Latin *praedātiō* (stem *praedātiōn-*), from *praedārī,* to plunder. See **predatory.**]

pred·a·tor (préddə-tər || -tawr) *n.* One that is predatory; especially, an animal that lives by preying upon others. [Latin *praedātor,* from *praedārī,* to plunder. See **predatory.**]

pred·a·to·ry (préddə-tri, -təri) *adj.* **1.** Of, pertaining to, or characterised by plundering, pillaging, or marauding: *a predatory war.* **2.** Preying on other animals; predacious. **3.** *Informal.* Addicted to or characterised by a tendency to exploit or destroy others for one's own gain. [Latin *praedātōrius* from *praedārī,* to plunder, from *praeda,* booty.] **—pred·a·to·ri·ly** *adv.* **—pred·a·to·ri·ness** *n.*

pre·de·cease (prée-di-séess, -də-) *tr.v.* **-ceased, -ceasing, -ceases.** To die before (some other person). **—pre·de·cease** *n.*

pred·e·ces·sor (prée-di-sessər, -séssər || *chiefly U.S.* préddə-) *n.* **1.** One who precedes another in time, especially in an office or position. **2.** Something that has been succeeded by another. **3.** An ancestor or forefather. [Middle English *predecessour,* from Old French *predecesseur,* from Late Latin *praedecessor* : Latin *prae,* before + *dēcessor,* one who leaves, from *dēcessus,* past participle of *dēcēdere,* to die, go away : *dē,* away + *cēdere,* to go.]

pre·del·la (pri-déllə) *n., pl.* **delle** (-déllay). **1. a.** An altar platform. **b.** Ornamentation on the front side of this platform. **2. a.** A raised shelf at the back of the altar. **b.** Ornamentation on the front side of this shelf. [Italian, stool, step, perhaps from Old High German *bret,* board.]

pre·des·ti·nar·i·an (prée-desti-náir-i-ən, pree-désti-, pri-) *adj.* **1.** Of or pertaining to predestination. **2.** Believing in or based on the doctrine of predestination.
~*n.* One who believes in the doctrine of predestination. **—pre·des·ti·nar·i·an·ism** *n.*

pre·des·ti·nate (prée-désti-nayt, pri-) *tr.v.* **-nated, -nating, -nates.** **1.** To destine or determine in advance; foreordain. **2.** *Theology.* To predestine.
~*adj.* (-nət, -nit, -nayt). Foreordained; predestined. [Middle English *predestinaten,* from Latin *praedestināre,* PREDESTINE.]

pre·des·ti·na·tion (prée-desti-náysh'n, pree-désti-, pri-) *n.* **1.** The act of predestining, or the condition of being predestined. **2.** *Theology.* **a.** The act whereby God is believed to have foreordained all things. **b.** The doctrine that God has foreordained all things, especially the salvation, or damnation, of individual souls. **3.** Destiny.

pre·des·tine (prée-déstin, pri-) *tr.v.* **-tined, -tining, -tines.** **1.** To fix upon, decide, or decree in advance; foreordain. **2.** *Theology.* To foreordain by divine will or decree; predestinate. [Middle English *predestinen,* from Old French *predestiner,* from Latin *praedestināre* : *prae,* before + *dēstināre,* to determine, DESTINE.]

pre·de·ter·mi·nate (prée-di-térmi-nət, -nit, -nayt) *adj.* Determined or established beforehand.

pre·de·ter·mine (prée-di-términ) *tr.v.* **-mined, -mining, -mines.** **1.** To determine, decide, or establish in advance. **2.** To influence or sway towards an action or opinion; give a tendency to beforehand; predispose. [Late Latin *praedēterminãre* : *prae,* before + *dētermināre,* DETERMINE.] **—pre·de·ter·mi·na·tion** (-áysh'n) *n.* **—pre·de·ter·mi·na·tive** (-ətiv || -aytiv) *adj.* **—pre·de·ter·min·er** *n.*

predial. Variant of **praedial.**

pred·i·ca·ble (préddi-kəb'l) *adj.* Capable of being stated or predicated.
~*n.* **1.** Something that can be predicated; a quality or attribute. **2.** *Logic.* Any of five general attributes of the Aristotelian class, *genus, species, property, difference,* and *accident,* designating the peculiar relation that a predicate bears to its subject, regardless of the quantity or quality of a proposition. [Medieval Latin *praedicābilis,* from Late Latin *praedicāre,* to proclaim, PREDICATE.] **—pred·i·ca·bil·i·ty** (-kə-bílləti), **pred·i·ca·ble·ness** *n.*

pre·dic·a·ment (pri-dícka-mənt, prə- *for senses 1, 2;* préddikə- *for sense 3*) *n.* **1.** A troublesome, embarrassing, or ludicrous situation. **2.** *Archaic.* A specified state or condition. **3.** *Logic.* A state or classification of existence. [Middle English, from Late Latin *praedicāmentum* (translation of Greek *katēgoria,* category), something predicated, condition (especially an unpleasant one), from *praedicāre,* to proclaim, PREDICATE.] **—pre·dic·a·men·tal** (-ménť'l) *adj.* **—pre·dic·a·men·tal·ly** *adv.*
Synonyms: *predicament, plight, dilemma, quandary.*

pred·i·cant (préddikənt) *adj.* Concerned with preaching.
~*n.* A member of a religious order dedicated to preaching. [Latin *praedicāns* (stem *praedicānt-*), present participle of *praedicāre,* to speak in public. See **predicate.**]

pred·i·cate (préddi-kayt) *v.* **-cated, -cating, -cates.** —*tr.* **1.** To base or establish (a concept, statement, or action). Used with *on* or *upon*: *He predicates his argument on these facts.* **2.** *Logic.* **a.** To state or affirm as an attribute or quality of: *predicate aggressiveness of mankind.* **b.** To make (a term or expression) the predicate of a proposition. **3.** To carry the connotation of; imply. **4.** To proclaim; assert; declare. —*intr.* To make a statement or assertion.
~*n.* (-kət, -kit, -kayt; *also* préedi-). *Abbr.* **pred.** **1.** *Grammar.* The part of a sentence or clause that expresses something about the subject. It regularly consists of a verb and may include objects, modifiers, or complements of the verb; for example in the simple sentences: *The house is white* and *The man hit the dog;* the words *is white* and *hit the dog* are predicates. **2.** *Logic.* Whatever is stated about the subject of a proposition.
~*adj.* (-kət, -kit, -kayt). **1.** *Grammar.* Of or belonging to the predicate of a sentence or clause. **2.** Predicated; stated. [Late Latin *praedicāre,* to proclaim, from Latin : *prae,* in front of, in public + *dicāre,* to say.] **—pred·i·ca·tion** (-káysh'n) *n.*

predicate calculus *n.* The branch of symbolic logic dealing not only with relations between propositions as a whole, but also with their internal structure, especially the relation between subject and predicate. Symbols are used to represent the subject and predicate of the proposition and the existential or universal quantifier is used to denote whether the proposition is universal or particular in its application. Compare **propositional calculus.**

pre·dic·a·tive (pri-díckətiv, prə- || préddi-kaytiv) *adj. Grammar.* Pertaining to or designating an adjective, noun, or construction that follows certain verbs, typically copula verbs, and applies directly to the subject of the verb. For example, in the sentence *The young girl is ill, ill* is a predicative adjective. Compare **attributive.**
~*n. Grammar.* A predicative word or construction, especially an adjective. **—pre·dic·a·tive·ly** *adv.* **—pre·dic·a·tive·ness** *n.*

pred·i·ca·to·ry (préddi-kaytəri, -káytəri || *U.S.* -kə-tawri, -tōri) *adj.* Of, pertaining to, or characteristic of preaching or a preacher. [Late Latin *praedicātōrius,* from *praedicāre,* to proclaim, PREDICATE.]

pre·dict (pri-díkt, prə-) *v.* **-dicted, -dicting, -dicts.** —*tr.* To state, tell about, or make known in advance, especially on the basis of special knowledge; foretell: *predict the weather.* —*intr.* To foretell what will happen; prophesy. —See Synonyms at **foretell.** [Latin *praedīcere* (past participle *praedictus*), to foretell : *prae,* before + *dīcere,* to tell, say.]

pre·dict·a·ble (pri-díkt-əb'l, prə-) *n.* **1.** That may be predicted or anticipated. **2.** Having no element of originality: *predictable opinions.* **—pre·dict·a·bil·i·ty** (-ə-bílləti) *n.* **—pre·dict·a·bly** *adv.*

pre·dic·tion (pri-díksh'n, prə-) *n.* **1.** The act of foretelling or predicting. **2.** Something foretold or predicted; a prophecy. **—pre·dic·tive** (-díktiv) *adj.* **—pre·dic·tive·ly** *adv.* **—pre·dic·tive·ness** *n.*

pre·dic·tor (pri-díktər, prə-) *n.* **1.** One that predicts. **2.** An instrument that enables an anti-aircraft gun to track enemy aircraft.

pre·di·gest (prée-dī-jést, -di-) *tr.v.* **-gested, -gesting, -gests.** To subject (food) to a partial artificial process to assist with digestion. **—pre·di·ges·tion** (-jéss-chən, -jésh-) *n.*

pred·i·kant (préddi-kant, práydi-) *n.* In South Africa, a minister of the Dutch Reformed Church. [Dutch, from Latin *praedicāns* (stem *praedicant-*). See **predicant.**]

pre·di·lec·tion (prée-di-léksh'n || *chiefly U.S.* préddə-) *n.* A preference or partiality; a predisposition. [French *prédilection,* from Medieval Latin *praedīligere,* to prefer : Latin *prae,* before + *dīligere,* to love, choose (see **diligent**).]

pre·dis·pose (prée-diss-pṓz) *tr.v.* **-posed, -posing, -poses. 1.** To make (someone) inclined to something in advance; put into a certain frame of mind for something: *His good manners predispose people to like him.* **2.** To make susceptible or liable. **3.** *Archaic.* To settle or dispose of in advance. **—pre·dis·pos·al** *n.*

pre·dis·po·si·tion (prée-díspə-zísh'n) *n.* **1.** The state of being predisposed; a tendency or inclination. **2.** Susceptibility to a particular type of disease.

pred·ni·sone (préd-ni-sōn) *n.* A synthetic corticosteroid drug, similar to cortisone, used to treat rheumatic, inflammatory, and allergic conditions. [Apparently *pregnant* + *diene* + *cortisone.*]

pre·dom·i·nant (pri-dómminənt, prə-) *adj.* **1.** Having greatest ascendancy, importance, influence, authority, or force. **2.** Most common or conspicuous; prevailing: *the predominant colour was red.* —See Synonyms at **dominant.** [Old French, from Medieval Latin *praedomināns* (stem *praedominant-*), present participle of *praedominārī,* PREDOMINATE.] **—pre·dom·i·nance, pre·dom·i·nan·cy** *n.* **—pre·dom·i·nant·ly** *adv.*

pre·dom·i·nate (pri-dómmi-nayt, prə-) *v.* **-nated, -nating, -nates.** —*intr.* **1.** To be of greater power, importance, or quantity; be most important or outstanding. **2.** To have authority, power, or controlling influence; prevail. Often used with *over.* —*tr. Rare.* To dominate or prevail over. [Latin *praedominārī,* to subdue beforehand : *prae,* before + *dominārī,* to DOMINATE.] **—pre·dom·i·nate·ly** (-nət-li, -nit-) *adv.* **—pre·dom·i·nat·ing·ly** *adv.* **—pre·dom·i·na·tion** (-náysh'n) *n.* **—pre·dom·i·na·tor** (-naytər) *n.*

pre·ec·lamp·si·a (prée-ik-lámpsi-ə, -ek-) *n.* A condition affecting pregnant women, marked by high blood pressure, swelling of the ankles, and the presence of protein in the urine.

pre·em·i·nent (prée-émmi-nənt, pri- || -nent) *adj.* Superior to all others; outstanding. See Synonyms at **dominant.** [Late Latin *praeēminēns* (stem *praeēminent-*), from Latin, present participle of *praeēminēre,* to excel : *prae,* in front of + *ēminēre,* to stand out (see **eminent**).] **—pre·em·i·nence** *n.* **—pre·em·i·nent·ly** *adv.*

pre·empt (prée-émpt, pri-) *v.* **-empted, -empting, -empts.** —*tr.* **1. a.** To stop (a person) doing something by taking advance action. **b.** To take advance action to counteract (a plan, for example). **2.** To exercise one's right to buy (property, for example) before others. **3.** To seize; take over. **4.** *Chiefly U.S.* To settle on (public land) so as to obtain the right to buy before others. —*intr.* In bridge, to make a pre-emptive bid. [Back-formation from PRE-EMPTION.] **—pre·emp·tor** (-ər, -awr) *n.* **—pre·emp·to·ry** (-əri) *adj.*

pre·emp·tion (prée-émpsh'n, pri-) *n.* **1.** An act or instance of pre-empting. **2. a.** The right to purchase something before others. **b.** A purchase made using such a right. [Medieval Latin *praeemptiō* (stem *praeemptiōn-*), from *praeemere,* to buy beforehand : *prae,* before + *emere,* to buy.]

pre·emp·tive (prée-émptiv, pri-) *adj.* **1.** Of, pertaining to, or characteristic of pre-emption. **2.** Designed to anticipate and frustrate opposition: *a pre-emptive strike against the enemy.* **3.** Designating or characteristic of a high bid in bridge that is intended to prevent the opposing players from bidding. **—pre·emp·tive·ly** *adv.*

preen (preen) *v.* **preened, preening, preens.** —*tr.* **1.** To smooth or clean (feathers) with the bill. Used of a bird. **2.** To adorn or trim (oneself) carefully; primp. **3.** To take pride or satisfaction in (oneself). Used with *on*: *preening themselves on having won another victory.* —*intr.* **1.** To dress up; primp. **2.** To smooth or clean feathers with the bill. Used of a bird. [Middle English *preinen, proinen, prunen,* perhaps a variant of PRUNE, influenced by dialect *preen*†, to pierce.] **—preen·er** *n.*

pre·ex·il·i·an (prée-ig-zílli-ən, -eg-, -ek-, -sílli-) *adj.* Also **pre·ex·il·ic** (-zillik, -síllik). Pertaining to the history of the Jewish people prior to their exile in Babylonia at the end of the sixth century B.C.

pre·ex·ist (prée-ig-zíst, -eg- || -ik-) *v.* **-isted, -isting, -ists.** —*intr.* To exist before. —*tr.* To exist before (something): *dinosaurs that preexisted mammals.* **—pre·ex·ist·ence** *n.* **—pre·ex·ist·ent** *adj.*

pref. 1. preface; prefatory. **2.** preference; preferred. **3.** prefix.

pre·fab (prée-fab || -fáb) *n.* A prefabricated part or building.

pre·fab·ri·cate (prée-fábbri-kayt) *tr.v.* **-cated, -cating, -cates. 1.** To construct or manufacture in advance. **2.** To produce standard sections of (a house, for example) that can be easily assembled. **—pre·fab·ri·ca·tion** (-káysh'n) *n.* **—pre·fab·ri·ca·tor** (-kaytər) *n.*

pref·ace (préf-əss, -iss) *n. Abbr.* **pref. 1. a.** A statement or essay, usually by the author, introducing a book and explaining its scope, intention, or background. **b.** The introductory section of a speech. **2.** Anything introductory or preliminary. **3.** *Usually capital* **P.** A thanksgiving prayer ending with the Sanctus and introducing the Eucharistic prayer of the Roman Catholic Mass.
∼*tr.v.* **prefaced, -acing, -aces. 1.** To introduce by or provide with a preliminary statement or essay. **2.** To serve as an introduction to. [Middle English, from Old French, from Medieval Latin *prefātia,* alteration of Latin *praefātiō,* a saying beforehand, from *praefārī,* to say beforehand : *prae,* before + *fārī,* to speak.] **—pref·ac·er** *n.*

pref·a·to·ry (préffə-təri, -tri) *adj.* Also **pref·a·to·ri·al** (-táwri-əl || -tōri-) *Abbr.* **pref.** Of the nature of, or serving as, an introductory statement or essay; preliminary. [Latin *prefātiō,* PREFACE.] **—pref·a·to·ri·ly** *adv.*

pre·fect (prée-fekt) *n.* Also **prae·fect** (for senses 1, 3). **1.** Any of several high military or civil officials, such as magistrates or administrators, of ancient Rome. **2. a.** In some countries, such as France or Italy, a high-ranking administrative official in the provinces. **b.** The chief of police in Paris. **3.** *Roman Catholic Church.* A cardinal presiding over a congregation of the Curia. **4.** In some schools, a senior pupil authorised with a limited disciplinary power over other pupils. [Middle English, from Old French, from Latin *praefectus,* overseer, chief, from the past participle of *praeficere,* to place at the head of : *prae,* before + *facere,* to do.]

prefect apostolic *n., pl.* **prefects apostolic.** A Roman Catholic priest with broad jurisdiction in an area where no bishop has been appointed.

pre·fec·ture (prée-fek-tewr, -choor, -chər) *n.* **1. a.** The office or authority of a prefect. **b.** The district under the control of a prefect. **2.** The residence or offices of a prefect. **—pre·fec·tur·al** *adj.*

pre·fer (pri-fér, prə- || *West Indies also* préffər) *tr.v.* **-ferred, -ferring, -fers. 1.** To choose rather than another or others as better or more to one's taste; value more highly; like better: *prefer to walk; prefers cider to beer.* **2.** *Law.* To give priority or precedence to (a creditor). **3.** *Law.* To enter, prosecute, or offer for consideration or resolution before a legal body: *He preferred charges against her for theft.* **4.** To promote. [Middle English *preferren,* from Old French *preferer,* from Latin *praeferre,* to hold or set before : *prae,* before + *ferre,* to bear.] **—pre·fer·rer** *n.*

Usage: When the object of *prefer* is an infinitive the construction following is introduced by *rather than*: *I prefer to ride rather than to walk.* It is possible to omit the second *to* (. . . *to ride rather than walk*), but it is not acceptable in standard English to omit *rather.* In all other constructions, *prefer* is followed by *to*: *I prefer riding to walking; I prefer whisky to gin. Than* can never be used in such constructions, though *rather than* is sometimes heard in informal speech (*I prefer whisky rather than gin).* In such cases, stricter usage prefers the *to* construction, or an alternative containing *have (I would rather have whisky than gin)* or *instead of (I would rather have whisky instead of gin).*

pref·er·a·ble (préf-rəb'l, préffə- || pri-fér-əb'l, prə-) *adj.* More desirable or worthy; preferred. **—pref·er·a·bil·i·ty** (-rə-bílləti || -ə-), **pref·er·a·ble·ness** *n.* **—pref·er·a·bly** *adv.*

pref·er·ence (préf-rənss, préffə-) *n. Abbr.* **pref. 1. a.** The selecting of someone or something over another or others. **b.** Someone or something so chosen. **2.** The state of being better liked or more highly valued. **3.** *Law.* **a.** The paying of one or more creditors by an insolvent debtor before, or to the exclusion of, other creditors. **b.** The right to be so paid. **4.** The granting of precedence or advantage to one over all others, as to one country or group of countries in levying duties. —See Synonyms at **choice.** [French *préférence,* from Medieval Latin *praeferentia,* from Latin *praeferēns,* present participle of *praeferre,* PREFER.]

preference shares *pl.n. British.* Shares with a fixed rate of dividend, that entitle their holders to priority of payment, over those who hold ordinary shares. Also *U.S.* "preferred stock". Compare **ordinary shares.**

pref·er·en·tial (préffə-rénsh'l) *adj.* **1.** Of, having, providing, or obtaining advantage or preference: *The old patients receive preferential treatment.* **2.** Manifesting or originating from partiality or preference, as in international trade: *preferential tariff rates.* **—pref·er·en·tial·ism** *n.* **—pref·er·en·tial·ist** *n.* **—pref·er·en·tial·ly** *adv.*

preferential voting *n.* A system of voting in which the voter indicates his choices in order of preference.

pre·fer·ment (pri-férmənt, prə-) *n.* **1.** The act of advancing to a higher position or office; promotion. **2.** A position, appointment, or rank giving advancement. [Middle English *preferrement,* from *preferren,* PREFER.]

pre·fig·u·ra·tion (prée-fíggə-ráysh'n || *chiefly U.S.* -fíggew-) *n.* **1.** The act of representing, suggesting, or imagining in advance. **2.** Something that prefigures. **—pre·fig·ur·a·tive** (-rətiv) *adj.* **—pre·fig·ur·a·tive·ly** *adv.* **—pre·fig·ur·a·tive·ness** *n.*

pre·fig·ure (prée-fíggər, pri- || *chiefly U.S.* -fíggewr) *tr.v.* **-ured, -uring, -ures. 1.** To suggest, indicate, or represent by an antecedent form or model; presage; foreshadow: *The art and theories of Cézanne prefigured the cubist school of art.* **2.** To imagine or picture to oneself in advance. [Middle English *prefiguren,* from Late Latin *praefigūrāre,* to shape beforehand : *prae,* before + *figūrāre,* to shape, from *figūra,* FIGURE.] **—pre·fig·ure·ment** *n.*

pre·fix (prée-fiks, -fiks) *tr.v.* **-fixed, -fixing, -fixes. 1.** To put or fix something before. **2.** To add as a prefix.
∼*n.* (prée-fiks; *rarely* préffiks). **1.** *Abbr.* **pref.** *Grammar.* An affix put before a word that changes or modifies the meaning; for exam-

PRONUNCIATION KEY

a, **trap**; aa, **father**; ai, **fair**;
ar, **star**; aw, **lawn**; ay, **play**;
b, bb, **stab**; **rubber**;
ch, **church**; ck, **ticket**;
d, dd, **dead**; **ladder**; e, **dress**;
ee, **bee**; er, **defer**; ew, **few**;
ewr, **pure**; ə, **about**;
ər, **letter**; f, ff, **fife**; **differ**;
g, gg, **giggle**; h, **hat**; i, **kit**;
ī, **price**; īr, **fire**; j, **judge**;
k, **kick**; l, ll, **let**; 'l, **needle**;
m, mm, **man**; n, nn, **no**;
'n, **sudden**; ng, **thing**; o, **lot**;
ō, **no**; ŏŏ, **foot**; ōō, **shoe**;
oor, **poor**; ow, **cow**;
owr, **hour**; oy, **boy**;
p, pp, **pepper**; r, rr, **red**;
s, ss, **sauce**; sh, **ship**;
t, tt, **totter**; th, **thick**; th, **this**;
smooth; u, **cut**; ur, **turn**;
v, vv, **valve**; w, **wet**; y, **yes**;
z, zz, **zebra**; zh, **vision**;
pleasure

IN FOREIGN WORDS:

aN, oN, **Saint-Saëns**;
hl, **Llanelli**; **Hluhluwe**;
kh, **loch**; **lough**; **Khaled**

STRESS MARK:

ín-sīt, insight; in-sít, incite

ple, in the word *disbelieve, dis-* is a prefix. See **combining form. 2.** A title placed before a person's name. [New Latin *praefixum*, a prefix, from Latin *praefīgere* (past participle *praefīxus*), to fix before : *prae*, before + *fīgere*, to fix.] —**pre·fix·al** *adj.* —**pre·fix·al·ly** *adv.*

pre·for·ma·tion (prée-fawr-máysh'n) *n.* **1.** The act of shaping or forming in advance; prior formation. **2.** *Biology.* A now invalidated biological theory that all parts of a future organism exist completely formed in the germ cell and develop only by increasing in size. —**pre·for·ma·tion·ism** *n.*

pre·fron·tal lobe (prée-frúnt'l) *n.* The part of each cerebral hemisphere of the brain situated in front of the frontal lobe.

prefrontal lobotomy *n.* A surgical operation, a **leucotomy** *(see).*

preg·gers (préggərz) *adj. Chiefly British Informal.* Pregnant.

preg·na·ble (prég-nəb'l) *adj.* Vulnerable to seizure or capture, as a fort. [Earlier *preignable*, Middle English *prenable*, from Old French, from *prendre*, to take, capture, from Latin *prehendere*.] —**preg·na·bil·i·ty** (-nə-billəti) *n.*

preg·nan·cy (prég-nən-si) *n., pl.* **-cies. 1.** The condition of being pregnant. **2.** The period during which a developing foetus is carried within the uterus.

preg·nant (prég-nənt) *adj.* **1.** Carrying a developing foetus within the uterus. **2.** Creative; inventive. **3.** Fraught with implications: *a pregnant silence.* **4. a.** Abounding; profuse. **b.** Filled; charged; fraught: *pregnant with meaning.* **5.** Producing results; fruitful; momentous: *a pregnant decision.* [Middle English, from Latin *praegnāns* (stem *praegnānt-*), variant of *praegnās*, probably *prae*, before + *gnascī*, be born.] —**preg·nant·ly** *adv.*

pre·heat (prée-héet) *tr.v.* **-heated, -heating, -heats.** To heat beforehand: *preheat the oven for 30 minutes.*

pre·hen·sile (pri-hén-sīl, prée- ‖ *U.S.* -s'l) *adj.* Adapted for seizing or holding, especially by wrapping around an object: *a prehensile tail.* [French *préhensile*, from Latin *prehendere* (past participle *prehensus*), to seize.] —**pre·hen·sil·i·ty** (prée-hen-sílləti) *n.*

pre·hen·sion (pri-hénsh'n) *n. Formal.* **1.** The act of grasping or seizing. **2. a.** Apprehension by the senses. **b.** Understanding. [Latin *prehensiō* (stem *prehensiōn-*), from *prehendere* (past participle *prehensus*), to seize.]

pre·his·tor·ic (prée-hiss-tórrik, -iss- ‖ -táwrik) *adj.* Also **pre·his·tor·i·cal** (-'l) **1.** Of, pertaining to, or belonging to the era before recorded history. **2.** Very old-fashioned or out-of-date. Used humorously. —**pre·his·tor·i·cal·ly** *adv.*

pre·his·to·ry (prée-hístri, -hístəri) *n.* **1.** The history of mankind in the period before written or recorded history, investigated by archaeology. **2.** The study of this. **3.** The history of the earlier stages of an event or incident. —**pre·his·to·ri·an** (prée-hiss-táwri-ən, -iss- ‖ -tóri-) *n.*

pre·ig·ni·tion (prée-ig-nísh'n) *n.* The ignition of fuel in an internal-combustion engine before the spark passes through the fuel.

pre·judge (prée-júj) *tr.v.* **-judged, -judging, -judges.** To judge beforehand without adequate evidence. [French *préjuger*, from Latin *praejūdicāre* : *prae*, before + *jūdicāre*, to judge, from *jūdex*, JUDGE.] —**pre·judg·er** *n.* —**pre·judg·ment, pre·judge·ment** *n.*

prej·u·dice (préj-ŏŏ-diss, -ə-) *n.* **1. a.** An adverse judgment or opinion formed beforehand or without knowledge or examination of the facts. **b.** A preconceived preference or idea; a bias. **2.** The act or state of holding unreasonable preconceived judgments or convictions. **3.** Irrational suspicion or hatred of a particular group, race, or religion. **4.** Detriment or injury caused to a person by the preconceived and unfavourable conviction of another or others. Now rare except in the phrases in *or to the prejudice of.* —**without prejudice to.** *Law.* Without affecting any right or claim.
~*tr.v.* **prejudiced, -dicing, -dices. 1.** To cause (a person) to judge prematurely and irrationally; bias. **2.** To affect injuriously or detrimentally by some judgment or act. [Middle English, from Old French, from Latin *praejūdicium* : *prae*, before + *jūdicium*, judgment, from *jūdex*, JUDGE.]

prej·u·di·cial (préj-ŏŏ-dísh'l, -ə-) *adj.* Causing or of the nature of prejudice; detrimental. —**prej·u·di·cial·ly** *adv.*

prel·a·cy (prélla-si) *n., pl.* **-cies. 1. a.** The office or station of a prelate. **b.** Prelates collectively. Also called "prelature". **2.** Church government administered by prelates. Often used derogatorily. In this sense, also called "prelatism".

prel·ate (prél-ət, -it) *n.* A bishop or an abbot, or one having a similar status in the church. [Middle English *prelat*, from Old French, from Medieval Latin *praelātus*, from Latin (past participle of *praeferre*, to bear before, prefer) : *prae*, before + *-lātus*, "carried".] —**pre·lat·ic** (pri-láttik) *adj.*

prelate nul·li·us (núl-i-əss, nŏŏl-, nŏŏl-) *n.* A Roman Catholic prelate, usually a titular bishop, who has jurisdiction over a territory not in a diocese but subject directly to the Holy See. [PRELATE + Latin *nūllīus*, of nobody, from *nūllus*, NULL.]

pre·lect (pri-lékt) *intr.v.* **-lected, -lecting, -lects.** To lecture or discourse in public. [Latin *praelegere* (past participle *praelēctus*) : *prae*, in front of, in public + *legere*, to read.] —**pre·lec·tion** *n.* —**pre·lec·tor** *n.*

pre·li·ba·tion (prée-lī-báysh'n) *n. Rare.* A foretaste. [Latin *praelībātiō* (stem *praelībātiōn-*), from *praelībāre*, to taste beforehand : *prae*, before + *lībāre*, to taste.]

pre·lim·i·nar·y (pri-límmin-ri, prə-, -əri, -lím'nəri ‖ -erri) *adj.* Prior to or preparing for the main matter, action, or business; introductory; prefatory.
~*n., pl.* **preliminaries. 1.** Something, such as a statement or action, that is antecedent or preparatory. **2. a.** An academic test or exami-

nation that is preparatory to one that is longer, more complex, or more important. **b.** *Sports.* An early qualifying stage of a competition: *got through the preliminaries but was knocked out in the first round.* **3.** *Plural. Printing.* Material that precedes the actual text of a book, such as the title pages, preface, or dedication. Also informally called "prelims". [French *préliminaire*, from Medieval Latin *praelīmināris* : *prae*, before + *līmināris*, of a threshold, from *līmen*, threshold, lintel (see **limen**).] —**pre·lim·i·nar·i·ly** *adv.*

pre·lims (pri-límz, prée-limz) *pl.n. Informal.* **1.** Preliminary examinations. **2.** Material that precedes the actual text of a book; preliminaries.

pre·lit·er·ate (prée-líttər-ət, -it) *adj.* Of or pertaining to any culture not having a written language.

prel·ude (préllewd ‖ *U.S. also* práy-lŏŏd, prée-) *n.* **1.** That which precedes or introduces a performance, event, or action. **2.** *Music.* A piece or movement serving as an introduction to a musical composition, as: **a.** An independent piece of moderate length that precedes a fugue. **b.** The opening section of a **suite** *(see).* **c.** The overture to an opera or oratorio, or a similar piece played before one of the acts of an opera. **d.** A piece played before a church service; an introductory voluntary. **3.** *Music.* A short composition in a free style, usually for piano or orchestra.
~*v.* **preluded, -luding, -ludes.** —*tr.* **1.** To serve as a prelude to. **2.** To introduce with or as if with a prelude. —*intr.* To serve as a prelude or introduction. [Old French, from Medieval Latin *praelūdium*, from Latin *praelūdere*, to play beforehand : *prae*, before + *lūdere*, to play, from *lūdus*, game.] —**pre·lud·er** *n.* —**pre·lu·di·al** (pri-lŏŏdi-əl, pre-, -léwdi-) *adj.*

prem. premium.

pre·mar·i·tal (prée-márrit'l, pri-) *adj.* Occurring before marriage: *premarital sex.*

pre·ma·ture (prémmə-tewr, préema-, -tèwr, -choor, -chóor, -chər ‖ -toor, -tóor) *adj.* **1.** Occurring, growing, or existing prior to the customary, correct, or assigned time; uncommonly or unexpectedly early: *a premature end.* **2.** Too hurried or impulsive. **3.** Born or occurring after a gestation period of less than the normal time: *a premature baby.* [Latin *praemātūrus* : *prae*, before + *mātūrus*, ripe, MATURE.] —**pre·ma·ture·ly** *adv.* —**pre·ma·ture·ness, pre·ma·tu·ri·ty** (-téwr-əti, -chóor- ‖ -tóor-) *n.*

pre·max·il·la (prée-mak-síllə) *n., pl.* **-maxillae** (-síllee). Either of two bones located in front of and between the maxillary bones in the upper jaw of vertebrates. —**pre·max·il·lar·y** (-sílləri ‖ *U.S.* -máksi-lerri) *adj.*

pre·med (prée-méd) *n. Informal.* Premedication.

pre·med·i·ca·tion (prée-méddi-káysh'n) *n.* Drugs, including a sedative, administered before a general anaesthetic to prepare a patient for surgery.

pre·med·i·tate (prée-méddi-tayt, pri-) *v.* **-tated, -tating, -tates.** —*tr.* To plan, arrange, or plot (a deed or events) in advance. —*intr.* To meditate or deliberate beforehand. [Latin *praemeditārī* : *prae*, before + *meditārī*, MEDITATE.] —**pre·med·i·ta·tive** (-tətiv, -taytiv) *adj.* —**pre·med·i·ta·tor** (-taytər) *n.*

pre·med·i·tat·ed (prée-méddi-taytid, pri-) *adj.* Characterised by deliberate purpose, previous consideration, and some degree of planning. —**pre·med·i·tat·ed·ly** *adv.*

pre·med·i·ta·tion (prée-méddi-táysh'n, pri-, prée-) *n.* **1.** The act of speculating, arranging, or plotting in advance. **2.** *Law.* The contemplation and plotting of a crime in advance, showing intent to commit the crime.

pre·men·stru·al tension (prée-ménstrew-əl) *n.* *Abbr.* **P.M.T.** A group of symptoms including emotional disturbance, fatigue, irritability, and sometimes depression that affects some women for up to about a week before menstruation. It is associated with retention of water and salts in the tissues.

pre·mier (prém-yər, -i-ər ‖ *U.S.* pri-méer, préemi-ər) *adj.* **1.** First in status or importance; chief. **2.** First to occur or exist; earliest.
~*n.* **1.** The head of government in some countries, as, for example a **prime minister** *(see).* **2.** The chief executive of a Canadian province or an Australian state. [Middle English *primier*, from Old French *premier*, first, chief, from Latin *prīmārius*, of the first rank, from *prīmus*, first.] —**pre·mier·ship** *n.*

prem·i·ere (prémmi-air, -ər ‖ *U.S.* pri-méer, prim-yáir) *n.* **1.** The first public presentation of a film, play, or other performance. **2.** The leading lady of a theatre company.
~*v.* **premiered, -miering, -mieres.** —*tr.* To present the first public performance of. —*intr.* To have its first public presentation. [French, feminine of *premier*, first, chief, PREMIER.]

pre·mil·le·nar·i·an (prée-mílli-naír-i-ən) *adj.* Of or pertaining to premillennialism.
~*n.* A person who believes in premillennialism. Compare **postmillenarian.**

pre·mil·len·ni·al (prée-mi-lénni-əl) *adj.* Of or happening before the millennium.

pre·mil·len·ni·al·ism (prée-mi-lénni-əl-iz'm) *n.* The belief that Christ's second coming will immediately precede the millennium. Compare **postmillennialism.** —**pre·mil·len·ni·al·ist** *n.*

Prem·in·ger (prémminjər), **Otto (Ludwig)** (1906–). Austrian-born U.S. film director. Among his most successful films are *Laura* (1944) and *Anatomy of a Murder* (1959).

prem·ise (prémmiss) *n.* Also **prem·iss** (for sense 1). **1. a.** A proposition upon which an argument is based or from which a conclusion is drawn. **b.** *Logic.* One of the first two propositions (major or minor) of a syllogism, from which the conclusion is drawn. **2.** *Plu-*

ral. Law. **a.** In a document, matter previously referred to; the aforesaid. **b.** The preliminary or explanatory statements or facts of a document, as in a conveyance or deed. **3.** *Plural.* **a.** Land and the buildings upon it. **b.** A building or part of a building. **—on** (or **off**) **the premises.** Inside (or outside) a building, shop, restaurant or the like together with its adjoining grounds.

~*v.* (prémmiss, pri-míz). **premised, -ising, -ises.** —*tr.* **1.** To state in advance as introduction or explanation. **2.** To state or assume in an argument. —*intr.* To make a premise. [Middle English *premisse*, from Old French, from Medieval Latin *praemissa (prōpositiō),* "(proposition) put before", from Latin *praemissus,* past participle of *praemittere,* to send ahead : *prae,* before + *mittere,* to send.]

pre·mi·um (préemi-əm) *n., pl.* **-ums.** *Abbr.* **pm., prem. 1.** A prize awarded for a particular act. **2.** Something offered free or at a reduced price, as an inducement to buy. **3.** A sum of money or bonus paid in addition to a regular price, salary, or other amount. **4.** *U.S.* The amount paid, often in addition to the interest, to obtain a loan. **5.** The amount paid or payable, often in installments, for an insurance policy. **6.** The amount at which something is valued above its par or nominal value, as money or securities. **7.** Payment for training in a trade or profession. **8.** An unusual or high value: *put a premium on honesty and hard work.* —See Synonyms at **bonus.** **—at a premium. 1.** Above par or an average. **2.** In great demand; more valuable than usual.

~*adj.* Of high quality. [Latin *praemium,* profit derived from booty, "that which is obtained before others" : *prae,* before + *emere,* to take.]

Premium Bond *n.* In Britain, a bond that can be bought from the government, that, while earning no interest, entitles the holder to the chance of a monthly cash prize. Also officially called "Premium Savings Bond".

pre·mo·lar (prée-mólər) *n.* Any of eight bicuspid teeth located in pairs on each side of the upper and lower jaws, behind the canines and in front of the molars. **—pre·mo·lar** *adj.*

pre·mo·ni·tion (prémmə-nísh'n, préemə-) *n.* **1.** A warning in advance; a forewarning. **2.** A presentiment of the future; a foreboding. [Old French, from Late Latin *praemonitiō* (stem *praemonitiōn-*), from Latin *praemonēre,* to warn beforehand : *prae,* before + *monēre,* to warn.] **—pre·mon·i·to·ri·ly** (pri-mónni-trəli, -tərili) *adv.* **—pre·mon·i·to·ry** *adj.*

pre·morse (pri-mórss) *adj.* *Biology.* Abruptly truncated, as though bitten or broken off: *premorse leaves.* [Latin *praemorsus,* past participle of *praemordēre,* to bite off in front : *prae,* in front + *mordēre,* to bite.]

pre·mu·ni·tion (prée-mew-nísh'n) *n.* Relative immunity to severe infection as a result of inducing an active low-grade infection. [Latin *praemūnitiō* (stem *praemūnitiōn-*), fortification beforehand, from *praemūnīre,* to fortify beforehand : *prae,* before + *mūnīre,* to fortify.] **—pre·mune** (-méwn) *adj.*

pre·na·tal (prée-náyt'l) *adj.* Existing or taking place prior to birth; preceding birth. **—pre·na·tal·ly** *adv.*

prenatal diagnosis *n.* Examination of a pregnant woman in order to discover genetic, developmental, or other abnormalities in the foetus. Techniques used include **amniocentesis** and **foetoscopy** (both of which see).

pren·tice (préntiss) *n. Archaic.* An apprentice.

~*adj. Archaic.* **1.** Of or pertaining to an apprentice. **2.** Inexperienced; unskilled.

prentice piece *n.* Formerly, a piece of work done by an apprentice at the end of his indenture to show that he had mastered his craft.

pre·oc·cu·pan·cy (prée-óckewpən-si, pri-) *n.* **1.** The act or right of taking possession before others; preoccupation. **2.** The state of being preoccupied or engrossed.

pre·oc·cu·pa·tion (pree-óckew-páysh'n, pri-, prée-) *n.* **1.** The state of being preoccupied; absorption of the attention or intellect. **2.** Something that preoccupies or engrosses the mind. **3.** Possession or occupation in advance; preoccupancy.

pre·oc·cu·pied (pree-óckew-pīd, pri-, prée-) *adj.* **1. a.** Absorbed in thought; engrossed. **b.** Excessively concerned with something; distracted. **2.** Formerly or already occupied. **3.** Already used and therefore unavailable for further use. Said of taxonomic names.

pre·oc·cu·py (pree-óckew-pī, pri-, prée-) *tr.v.* **-pied, -pying, -pies. 1.** To occupy completely the mind or attention of; engross. **2.** To occupy or take possession of in advance or before another. [Latin *praeoccupāre* : *prae,* before + *occupāre,* to OCCUPY.]

pre·or·dain (prée-awr-dáyn) *tr.v.* **-dained, -daining, -dains.** To appoint, decree, or ordain in advance; foreordain. **—pre·or·dain·ment, pre·or·di·na·tion** (-di-náysh'n) *n.*

prep (prep) *adj. Informal.* Preparatory: *a prep school.*

~*n. Informal.* **1.** The preparing of lessons; homework. **2.** Time set aside for this.

prep. 1. preparation; preparatory. **2.** preposition.

pre·pack (prée-pák) *tr.v.* **-packed, -packing, -packs.** To wrap or pack (products) before marketing them.

prep·a·ra·tion (préppə-ráysh'n) *n. Abbr.* **prep. 1.** The act or process of preparing. **2.** The state of being made ready beforehand; readiness. **3.** *Usually plural.* Preliminary measures that serve to make ready for something: *preparations for the wedding reception.* **4.** A substance, such as a medicine, prepared for a particular purpose. **5.** *Music.* **a.** The anticipation of a dissonant note by means of its introduction as a consonant note in the preceding chord. **b.** The

note so used. **6. a.** Homework, especially at a boarding school. **b.** Time set aside for this.

pre·par·a·tive (pri-párrətiv, prə-) *adj.* Serving or tending to prepare or make ready; preparatory.

~*n.* That which prepares for something following. **—pre·par·a·tive·ly** *adv.*

pre·par·a·to·ry (pri-párra-tri, prə-, -təri) *adj. Abbr.* **prep. 1.** Serving to make ready or prepare. **2.** Preliminary; introductory. **3.** Occupied in or pertaining to preparation. **—preparatory to.** In preparing for. **—pre·par·a·to·ri·ly** *adv.*

preparatory school *n.* **1.** In Britain, a school, usually private, for pupils up to the age of 13, attended in preparation for public schools. Also informally called "prep school". **2.** In the United States, a school, usually private, preparing pupils for college.

pre·pare (pri-paír, prə-) *v.* **-pared, -paring, -pares.** —*tr.* **1.** To make ready for a specified purpose or for some act, event, or experience: *prepared the fish for cooking; wasn't prepared for the shock.* **2. a.** To put together or make by combining various elements or ingredients; manufacture; compound. **b.** To subject to a treatment or process: *prepare fruit by boiling with sugar.* **c.** To compose (a speech, for example) for subsequent use. **3.** To fit out; equip: *The troops were prepared for service in the Arctic.* **4.** *Music.* To lead up to and soften (a dissonance or its impact) by means of preparation. —*intr.* To put things or oneself in readiness; get ready. [Middle English *preparen,* from Old French *preparer,* from Latin *praeparāre,* to prepare in advance : *prae,* before + *parāre,* to prepare.] **—pre·par·ed·ly** (-paírd-li, -paír-id-) *adv.* **—pre·par·er** *n.*

pre·pared (pri-paírd, prə-) *adj.* **1.** Made ready. **2.** Willing: *Both sides were prepared to meet.*

pre·par·ed·ness (pri-paír-id-nəss, prə-, -paírd-, -niss) *n.* The state of being prepared; especially, military readiness for war.

pre·pay (prée-páy) *tr.v.* **-paid, -paying, -pays.** To pay or pay for beforehand. **—pre·pay·ment** *n.*

pre·pense (pri-pénss) *adj. Law.* Contemplated in advance; premeditated. Used chiefly in the phrase *malice prepense.* [Variant of obsolete *prepensed, purpensed,* from Middle English *purpensen,* think of in advance, from Old French *pourpenser,* to premeditate : *pour,* forth, before, from Latin *prō-* + *penser,* think, from Latin *pensāre,* frequentative of *pendere,* to weigh.] **—pre·pense·ly** *adv.*

pre·pon·der·ance (pri-póndər-ənss, prə-) *n.* Also **pre·pon·der·an·cy** (-ən-si). Superiority, as in weight, quantity, power, or importance.

pre·pon·der·ant (pri-póndərənt, prə-) *adj.* Being superior, as in power, force, or importance; predominant. See Synonyms at **dominant.** **—pre·pon·der·ant·ly** *adv.*

pre·pon·der·ate (pri-póndə-rayt, prə-) *intr.v.* **-ated, -ating, -ates. 1.** To exceed something else in weight. **2.** To be greater, as in power, force, quantity, or importance; predominate. **3.** *Archaic.* To be weighed down, as one end of a balance. [Latin *praeponderāre* : *prae,* in front of, exceeding + *ponderāre,* to weigh, from *pondus* (stem *ponder-*), weight.] **—pre·pon·der·at·ing·ly** *adv.* **—pre·pon·der·a·tion** (-ráysh'n) *n.*

prep·o·si·tion (préppə-zísh'n) *n. Abbr.* **prep.** *Grammar.* **1.** In some languages, a word that indicates the relation of a substantive to a verb, an adjective, or another substantive. Some English prepositions are *at, by, in, to, from,* and *with.* **2.** Any word or construction of similar function, such as *with regard to* or *concerning.* [Middle English *preposicioun,* from Latin *praepositiō* (translation of Greek *prothesis*), from *praepōnere* (past participle *praepositus*), to place in front : *prae,* in front + *pōnere,* to place.]

prep·o·si·tion·al (préppə-zísh'n'l) *adj.* **1.** Pertaining to, composed of, or used as a preposition. **2.** Designating, pertaining to, or inflected in the prepositional.

~*n.* **1.** The grammatical case in certain Indo-European languages, such as Russian, that is used only as the object of prepositions. **2.** A form or construction in this case. **—prep·o·si·tion·al·ly** *adv.*

prepositional phrase *n. Grammar.* A phrase consisting of a preposition and the noun it governs and having adjectival or adverbial value; for example, in the phrases *a dress of wool* and *written in haste,* the prepositional phrases are *of wool* (adjectival value) and *in haste* (adverbial value).

pre·pos·i·tive (pri-pózzətiv, prée-) *adj. Grammar.* Put before; prefixed: *a prepositive adjective.* Compare **postpositive.**

~*n. Grammar.* A word or particle put before another word. [Late Latin *praepositīvus,* from *praepōnere* (past participle *praepositus*), to place in front. See **preposition.**] **—pre·pos·i·tive·ly** *adv.*

pre·pos·sess (préepə-zéss) *tr.v.* **-sessed, -sessing, -sesses. 1.** To preoccupy the mind of to the exclusion of other thoughts or feelings. **2.** To influence beforehand for or against someone or something; prejudice; bias. **3.** To impress favourably in advance.

pre·pos·sess·ing (préepə-zéssing) *adj.* Impressing favourably; pleasing. **—pre·pos·sess·ing·ly** *adv.* **—pre·pos·sess·ing·ness** *n.*

pre·pos·ses·sion (préepə-zésh'n) *n.* **1.** A preconception or prejudice. **2.** The state of being preoccupied with thoughts, opinions, or feelings, especially ones that are favourable.

pre·pos·ter·ous (pri-póstrəss, prə-, -póstərəss) *adj.* Contrary to nature, reason, or common sense; absurd. See Synonyms at **foolish.** [Latin *praeposterus,* "inverted", perverted, absurd : *prae-,* before + *posterus,* coming after, following, next, from *post,* after.] **—pre·pos·ter·ous·ly** *adv.* **—pre·pos·ter·ous·ness** *n.*

pre·po·ten·cy (prée-pōt'n-si, pri-) *n.* **1.** The state or condition of being prepotent; predominance. **2.** *Genetics.* The capacity of one parent to transmit more characteristics to the offspring than the

Pre-Raphaelite painting *"The Order of Release" by John Everett Millais (1829–96), one of the founders of the Pre-Raphaelite movement. The Pre-Raphaelites reacted to the thrusting materialism of the 19th century by seeking a return to what they saw as the innocence and sincerity of early Renaissance painting.*

other parent. **3.** *Botany.* The capacity of some pollen to cause fertilisation more readily than pollen from another source.

pre·po·tent (prée-pōt'nt, pri-) *adj.* Also **pre·po·ten·tial** (-pə-ténsh'l, -pō-). **1.** Greater in power, influence, or force; predominant. **2.** *Genetics.* Showing prepotency. [Middle English, from Latin *praepotēns* (stem *praepotent-*), present participle of *praeposse,* to be very powerful : *prae-* (intensifier) + *posse,* to be able or powerful.] **—pre·po·tent·ly** *adv.*

prep·py, prep·pie (préppi) *n., pl.* **-pies.** *U.S. Informal.* A student or graduate of the U.S. preparatory school system.
~*adj. U.S. Informal.* Of, pertaining to, or being a preppy; especially, having the conservative tastes and values or dressing in the neat, casual style, characteristic of a preppy.

pre·print *n.* A printing or copy of a book, report, document, or the like, issued in advance of general publication or distrubution.
~*tr.v.* **preprinted, -printing, -prints.** To print and issue in advance of general publication.

prep school *n. Informal.* A **preparatory school** *(see).*

pre·puce (prée-pewss) *n.* **1.** The **foreskin** *(see).* **2.** A structure corresponding to the foreskin covering the glans of the clitoris. [Middle English, from Old French, from Latin *praepūtium.*] **—pre·pu·tial** (-péwsh'l, pri-) *adj.*

pre·quel (preekwəl) *n.* A film, book, or the like that is made or written after another which is about the same subject, but that relates events that occurred prior to those related in the previous film, book, or the like. [PRE- or PRE(VIOUS) + (SE)QUEL.]

Pre-Raph·a·el·ite (prée-ráf-ə-līt, -ráffi-, -ráffay- || *U.S. also* -ráyffi-, -ráafi-) *n.* A painter or writer belonging to or influenced by the Pre-Raphaelite Brotherhood, a society founded in 1848 by Rossetti and others to advance the style and spirit of Italian painting before Raphael. **—Pre-Raph·a·el·it·ism** *n.* **—Pre-Raph·a·el·ite** *adj.*

pre·re·cord (prée-ri-kórd, -rə-) *tr.v.* **-corded, -cording, -cords.** To record beforehand; especially, to record (a broadcast) in advance of transmission.

pre·re·cord·ed (prée-ri-kórdid, -rə-) *adj.* **1.** Recorded beforehand: *prerecorded laughter.* **2.** Bearing a commercial recording; not blank: *prerecorded tapes.*

pre·req·ui·site (prée-rékwizit, pri-) *adj.* Required as a prior condition to something. See Synonyms at **necessary.**
~*n.* That which is prerequisite.
Usage: As a noun, *prerequisite* is followed by *of* or *for,* and occasionally by *to*: *Hard work is a prerequisite for success.* As an adjective, it is followed by *to*: *Hard work is prerequisite to success.*

pre·rog·a·tive (pri-róggətiv, prə-) *n.* **1. a.** An exclusive right or privilege held by a person or group, especially a hereditary or official right. **b.** See **Royal Prerogative. 2.** Any characteristically exclusive right or privilege. **3.** A natural advantage making one superior: *Thinking is one of man's prerogatives.* —See Synonyms at **right.**
~*adj.* Of, arising from, or exercising a prerogative. [Middle English, from Old French, from Latin *praerogātīva (centuria),* "(century) chosen to vote first", from *praerogātīvus,* asked to vote first, from *praerogāre,* to ask before others : *prae-,* before + *rogāre,* to ask.]

pres. 1. present (time). **2.** president.

Pres. President.

pres·age (préssij) *n.* **1.** An indication or warning of a future occurrence; an omen; a portent. **2.** A feeling or intuition of what is going to occur; a presentiment; a foreboding. **3.** *Rare.* A prediction.
~*v.* **pre·sage** (préssij, pri-sáyj) **presaged, -saging, -sages.** *—tr.* **1.** To indicate or warn of in advance; portend. **2.** To have a presentiment of. **3.** To foretell or predict. *—intr.* To make or utter a prediction. —See Synonyms at **foretell.** [Middle English, from Latin *praesāgium,* foreboding, from *praesāgīre,* to perceive beforehand : *prae-,* before + *sāgīre,* to perceive.] **—pre·sage·ful** (pri-sáyj-f'l) *adj.*

pres·by·o·pi·a (préz-bi-ṓpi-ə || préss-) *n.* The inability of the eye to focus sharply on nearby objects, resulting from hardening of the lens with advancing age; longsightedness. [New Latin : Greek *presbus,* old man + -OPIA.] **—pres·by·op·ic** (-óppik) *adj.*

pres·by·ter (préz-bi-tər || préss-) *n.* **1.** In the early Christian church, an elder of the congregation. **2.** In various hierarchical churches, a priest. **3.** In the Presbyterian Church: **a.** A teaching elder. **b.** A ruling elder. [Late Latin, an elder, from Greek *presbuteros,* a priest, "older", comparative of *presbus,* old man.]

pres·byt·er·ate (prez-bíttər-ət, -it, -ayt || press-) *n.* **1.** The office of a presbyter. **2.** The body or order of presbyters.

pres·by·te·ri·al (préz-bi-téer-i-əl || préss-) *adj.* Of or pertaining to a presbyter or the presbytery. **—pres·by·te·ri·al·ly** *adv.*

pres·by·te·ri·an (préz-bi-téer-i-ən || préss-) *adj.* **1.** Of or pertaining to ecclesiastical government by presbyters. **2.** *Capital* **P.** Of or pertaining to a Presbyterian Church.
~*n. Capital* **P.** A member or adherent of a Presbyterian Church. **—pres·by·te·ri·an·ism** *n.*

Presbyterian Church *n.* Any of various Protestant churches governed by presbyters and traditionally Calvinist in doctrine. In England, the Presbyterian Church became part of the **United Reformed Church** *(see),* in 1972.

pres·by·ter·y (préz-bi-tri, -təri || préss-, *U.S.* -terri) *n., pl.* **-ies. 1.** In the Presbyterian Church: **a.** A court composed of the ministers and representative elders of a particular locality. **b.** The district represented by this court. **2.** Presbyters collectively. **3.** Government of a church by presbyters. **4.** The section of the church east of the choir where the main altar is situated; a sanctuary. **5.** *Roman Catholic Church.* The residence of a priest. [Middle English *presbytory,* from Late Latin *presbyterium,* a council of presbyters, from Greek *presbuterion,* from *presbuteros,* priest, PRESBYTER.]

pre·school (prée-skōōl) *adj.* Of or pertaining to children below the age at which they begin full-time education.

pre·sci·ence (préssi-ənss, préshi- || prée-si-) *n.* Knowledge of actions or events before they occur; foreknowledge; foresight. **—pre·sci·ent** (-ənt) *adj.* **—pre·sci·ent·ly** *adv.*

pre·scind (pri-sínd, prée-) *v.* **-scinded, -scinding, -scinds.** *—tr.* To separate or divide, especially so as to consider individually. Used with *from.* *—intr.* To withdraw one's attention. Used with *from.* [Latin *praescindere,* to cut off in front : *prae-,* in front + *scindere,* to cut off.]

pre·scribe (pri-skrī́b, prə-) *v.* **-scribed, -scribing, -scribes.** *—tr.* **1.** To set down as a rule or guide; ordain; enjoin. **2.** *Medicine.* To order or recommend the use of (a drug, treatment, or the like). *—intr.* **1.** To establish rules, laws, or directions. **2.** *Medicine.* To order or recommend a remedy or treatment. **3.** *Law.* To assert a right or title to something on the grounds of prescription. [Middle English *prescriben,* to hold by right of prescription, from Medieval Latin *prescrībere,* to claim by such right, from Latin *praescrībere,* to write at the beginning, prescribe : *prae-,* before, in front + *scrībere,* to write.] **—pre·scrib·er** *n.*

pre·script (prée-skript) *n.* Something prescribed, especially a rule or regulation of conduct.
~*adj.* (prée-skript, pri-skrípt). Established as a rule; set down; prescribed. [Latin *praescriptum,* from *praescrībere* (past participle *praescriptus*), PRESCRIBE.]

pre·scrip·ti·ble (pri-skrípt-əb'l) *adj.* Capable of, subject to, or derived from prescription. **—pre·scrip·ti·bil·i·ty** (-ə-bíllәti) *n.*

pre·scrip·tion (pri-skrípsh'n, prə-) *n.* **1. a.** The act of prescribing. **b.** That which is prescribed. **2.** *Medicine.* **a.** A written instruction by a doctor for the preparation and administration of a medicine. **b.** A prescribed medicine. **c.** An ophthalmologist's or optometrist's written instruction for the grinding of corrective lenses. **3.** A formula directing the preparation or correction of anything. **4.** *Law.* **a.** The process of acquiring title to property by reason of uninterrupted possession of specified duration. Also called "positive prescription". **b.** The limitation of time beyond which an action, debt, or crime is no longer valid or enforceable. Also called "negative prescription". [Middle English *prescripcion,* from Old French *prescription,* from Latin *praescriptiō* (stem *praescriptiōn-*), a writing in front, from *praescrībere,* PRESCRIBE.]

prescription charge *n.* In Britain, a tax levied as a charge for each medicine or appliance supplied under the National Health Service.

pre·scrip·tive (pri-skríptiv, prə-) *adj.* **1.** Sanctioned or authorised by long-standing custom or usage. **2.** Making or giving injunctions, directions, laws, or rules. **3.** *Law.* Acquired by or based upon uninterrupted possession. **4.** *Linguistics.* Of or designating a grammar that seeks to lay down rules for the usage of language, as opposed to just describing it. Compare **descriptive. —pre·scrip·tive·ly** *adv.*

pre·scrip·tiv·ism (pri-skríptiv-iz'm, prə-) *n.* **1.** *Philosophy.* The doctrine that ethical propositions prescribe a course of action or a code of morality and are not true or false. Compare **emotivism, descriptivism. 2.** *Linguistics.* The doctrine that a grammar should be prescriptive.

pres·ence (prézz'nss) *n.* **1.** The state or fact of being present. **2.** Immediate proximity in time or space. **3. a.** The area immediately surrounding a great personage, especially a sovereign granting an audience. **b.** A great or imposing person. **4.** A person's manner of carrying himself; bearing. **5.** A person or thing, especially a supernatural being, that is felt to be present. **6.** A person or body of persons present in a given place; especially, military personnel protecting a national interest. **7.** Charismatic bearing or authority, as in an actor. —See Synonyms at **bearing.**

presence of mind *n.* Ability to think and act efficiently, especially when under pressure.

pre·sen·ile dementia (prée-séen-īl || -sén-) *n.* Any of several conditions, especially **Alzheimer's disease** *(see),* characterised by deterioration of mental abilities in young or middle-aged people.

pre·se·nil·i·ty (prée-si-nílləti, -sə-) *n.* Reduction of mental or physical abilities, normally associated with age, occuring in young or middle-aged people. **—pre·se·nile** *adj.*

pres·ent¹ (prézz'nt) *n.* **1.** A moment or period in time designated as being intermediate between past and future; now. **2.** *Abbr.* **pr., pres.** *Grammar.* **a.** The present tense. **b.** A verb form in the present tense. **3.** *Plural. Law.* The document or instrument in question: *be it known by these presents.*
~*adj.* **1.** Being, pertaining to, existing, or occurring at a moment or period in time considered as the present: *present events.* **2.** At hand; nearby; in the vicinity. **3.** Existing or occurring within; contained in. **4.** *Abbr.* **pr., pres.** *Grammar.* Designating a verb tense or form that expresses current time. **5.** *Obsolete.* Readily available; immediate. [Middle English, from Old French, from Latin *praesēns* (stem *praesent-*), present participle of *praeesse,* to be before one, be present : *prae-,* in front of + *esse,* to be.]

pre·sent² (pri-zént, prə-) *v.* **-sented, -senting, -sents.** *—tr.* **1.** To introduce, especially with formal ceremony: *She was presented to the king.* **2. a.** To bring before the public: *present a play.* **b.** *British.* To act as a presenter on (a radio or television programme). **3. a.** To hand over or give, especially as a gift or award: *presented a huge bill; presented the cheque to the winner.* **b.** To hand over or give to, especially formally: *presented him with a gold watch.* **4.** To offer to

the view or mind; show: *presented a sharp contrast.* **5. a.** To constitute or entail: *This presents a challenge to us all.* **b.** To face; confront: *presented me with a dilemma.* **6.** To offer for consideration: *An idea presented itself.* **7. a.** To point or aim (a weapon). **b.** To salute with (a weapon)). Used chiefly in the phrase *present arms.* **8.** To recommend (a clergyman) for a benefice. **9.** *Law.* **a.** To offer to a legislature or court for consideration. **b.** To bring a charge or accusation against. **10.** To represent or depict in a particular manner: *He presented himself to us as a benefactor.* —*intr.* To be directed towards the neck of the womb and vagina during labour. Used of part of an unborn child. —See Synonyms at **offer.** —**present (oneself).** To arrive or appear.
~*n.* **pres•ent** (prézz'nt). A gift. [Middle English *presenten,* from Old French *presenter,* from Latin *praesentāre,* from *praesēns,* PRESENT (adjective).]

pre•sent•a•ble (pri-zént-əb'l, prə-) *adj.* **1.** Fit to be given, displayed, or offered. **2.** Of decent enough appearance to be fit for introduction to others. —**pre•sent•a•bil•i•ty** (-ə-bílləti), **pre•sent•a•ble•ness** *n.* —**pre•sent•a•bly** *adv.*

pres•en•ta•tion (prézz'n-táysh'n || *chiefly U.S.* prée-zen-, -z'n-) *n.* **1. a.** The act of presenting or offering someone or something, as for acceptance or approval. **b.** The state of being presented. **c.** The manner or style in which someone or something is presented; especially, the way in which a commercial product is promoted through design, packaging, and advertising. **2.** A performance, as of a play. **3. a.** A formal ceremony at which something, such as an award or prize, is presented. **b.** Something that is presented. Also used adjectivally: *a presentation copy of a book.* **4.** A formal introduction, such as at court. **5.** The act or right of nominating a clergyman to a benefice. **6.** The process of offering for consideration. **7.** *Medicine.* The position of the foetus in the uterus at birth, with respect to the neck of the uterus. —**pres•en•ta•tion•al** *adj.*

pre•sent•a•tive (pri-zéntətiv, prə-) *adj.* **1.** Having the capacity or function of bringing an idea or image to mind. **2.** *Philosophy.* **a.** Perceived or capable of being perceived directly rather than through association. **b.** Having the ability to so perceive. **3.** Capable of nominating or of being nominated to an ecclesiastical benefice. —**pre•sent•a•tive•ness** *n.*

pres•ent-day (prézz'nt-dáy) *adj.* Current.

pres•en•tee (prézz'n-tée) *n. U.S.* **1.** A person who is presented. **2.** A person to whom something is given.

pre•sent•er (pri-zéntər, prə-) *n.* **1.** One who presents. **2.** *British.* One who introduces a radio or television programme.

pre•sen•tient (pri-sén-shi-ənt, -sh'nt || -zén-) *adj.* Having a presentiment or presentiments. [Latin *praesentiēns* (stem *praesentient-*), present participle of *praesentīre,* to have a presentiment. See **presentiment.**]

pre•sen•ti•ment (pri-zénti-mənt, -sénti-) *n.* A sense of something about to occur; a premonition. See Synonyms at **apprehension.** [Obsolete French, from Old French *presentir,* to have a presentiment, from Latin *praesentīre,* to perceive beforehand : *prae-,* before + *sentīre,* to perceive.]

pres•ent•ly (prézz'ntli) *adv.* **1.** In a short time; soon; directly: *She will arrive presently.* **2.** *U.S.* At this time or period; now: *He is presently staying with us.* **3.** *Archaic.* Immediately.

Usage: In American English, *presently* is being increasingly used to mean "at this time, now", a trend which has attracted much criticism. This usage has so far had little influence on British English, where the meaning of "in a short time, soon", is standard.

pre•sent•ment (pri-zént-mənt, prə-) *n.* **1.** The act of presenting; presentation. **2.** Something presented, such as a picture or exhibition. **3.** *Law.* **a.** The act of submitting or presenting a formal statement of a legal matter to a court or authorised person. **b.** A report written by a jury or a similar body. **4.** *Finance.* The presenting of a bill or note for payment.

present participle *n. Grammar.* A participle expressing present action, in English formed by the infinitive plus *-ing* and used: **1.** To express present action in relation to the time indicated by the finite verb in its clause. **2.** To form certain compound tenses of the verb. **3.** To function as a verbal adjective.

present perfect *n. Grammar.* **1.** The verb tense expressing action completed at the present time. This tense is formed in English by combining the present tense of *have* with a past participle; for example in the sentence: *He has spoken,* the words *has spoken* constitute the present perfect. **2.** A verb in this tense.

present tense *n. Grammar.* The verb tense expressing action in the present time or habitual action in the past and future; for example, in the sentence *She drinks her coffee quickly,* the verb *drinks* is in the present tense.

pre•serv•a•tive (pri-zérvətiv, prə-) *n.* Something used to preserve; especially, a chemical used in foods to inhibit decay. —**pre•serv•a•tive** *adj.*

pre•serve (pri-zérv, prə-) *v.* **-served, -serving, -serves.** —*tr.* **1.** To protect from injury, peril, or other adversity; maintain in safety. **2. a.** To keep in a good, healthy condition: *moisturising cream preserves the skin.* **b.** To keep or maintain in an unchanged form: *Her name will be preserved.* **3.** To keep or maintain intact. **4. a.** To prepare (food) so as to prevent decomposition, as by bottling or salting. **b.** To prepare (fruit, for example) by boiling with sugar, so as to prevent decomposition or make jam. **5.** To prevent (organic bodies) from decaying or spoiling. **6.** To keep or protect (game or fish) for one's private hunting or fishing. —*intr.* **1.** To prepare fruit or other foods for storage. **2.** To maintain a private area stocked with game or fish. —See Synonyms at **defend.**
~*n.* **1.** Something that acts to preserve; a preservative. **2.** *Often plural.* Fruit that has been preserved by boiling with sugar, especially for use as jam. **3.** An area maintained: **a.** For the protection of wildlife. **b.** *U.S.* For natural resources. **4.** Something considered to be the special domain or sphere of certain persons: *Ancient Greek is the preserve of scholars.* [Middle English *preserven,* from Old French *preserver,* from Medieval Latin *praeservāre,* "to guard beforehand" : Latin *prae-,* before + *servāre,* to keep, guard.] —**pre•serv•a•bil•i•ty** (-ə-bílləti) *n.* —**pre•serv•a•ble** *adj.* —**pres•er•va•tion** (prézzər-váysh'n) *n.* —**pre•serv•er** *n.*

pre•set (prée-sét) *tr.v.* **-set, -setting, -sets.** To set (controls, for example) in advance.

pre•shrunk (prée-shrúngk) *adj.* Shrunk during manufacture to minimise subsequent shrinkage.

pre•side (pri-zíd, prə-) *intr.v.* **-sided, -siding, -sides. 1.** To occupy a place of authority, as, for example, a chairman or president. **2.** To possess or exercise authority or control. **3.** *Music.* To be the featured instrumental performer: *presided at the piano.* [French *presider,* from Latin *praesidēre,* "to sit in front of", superintend : *prae-,* before + *sedēre,* to sit.] —**pre•sid•er** *n.*

pres•i•den•cy (prézzi-dən-si || -den-) *n., pl.* **-cies.** The office, function, or term of a president.

pres•i•dent (prézzi-dənt || -dent) *n. Abbr.* **p., P., pres., Pres. 1.** One appointed or elected to preside over an organised body of people, such as an assembly or meeting. **2.** *Often capital* **P.** The chief executive of a republic. **3.** *Sometimes capital* **P. a.** *U.S.* The chief officer of a branch of government. **b.** *U.S.* The chief executive officer of a business corporation. **c.** The chief officer of a society, club, university college, or any similar body. [Middle English, from Old French, from Latin *praesidēns* (stem *praesident-*), present participle of *praesidēre,* PRESIDE.] —**pres•i•den•tial** (-dénsh'l) *adj.* —**pres•i•den•tial•ly** *adv.* —**pres•i•dent•ship** *n.*

pres•i•dent-e•lect (prézzi-dənt-i-lékt || -dent-, -ə-) *n.* A person who has been elected president but has not yet begun his term of office.

pre•sid•i•o (pri-séedi-ō, -síddi-, -zíddi-) *n., pl.* **-os.** A garrison; a military post, especially in a country under Spanish control. [Spanish, from Latin *praesidium,* garrison, fortification, from *praesidēre,* "to sit in front of", guard, PRESIDE.]

pre•sid•i•um (pri-síddi-əm, -zíddi-) *n.* **1.** Any of various permanent executive committees in Communist countries having power to act for a larger governing body. **2.** *Capital* **P.** A committee of the Supreme Soviet, headed by the premier, and constituting the highest policy-making body of the U.S.S.R. [Russian *prezidium,* from Latin *praesidium.* See **presidio.**]

pre•sig•ni•fy (prée-síg-ni-fī) *tr.v.* **-fied, -fying, -fies.** To betoken or signify beforehand; prefigure; foreshadow.

Pres•ley (prézli), **Elvis (Aaron)** (1935–77). U.S. rock and roll singer. Following his first popular record success, *Heartbreak Hotel* (1956), he embarked on a career that was to encompass over thirty films and the sale of over 150 million copies of his records.

presolar nebular hypothesis *n.* A theory put forward to account for the origin of the Sun and the Solar System in which gas and dust from the interstellar medium contracted under the influence of gravity to form a nebula. The dust particles in the nebula became centres of accretion for matter, forming planetismals which in turn coalesced and accreted matter to form the bodies in the Solar System. Compare **planetismal, primitive solar-nebula hypothesis.**

press¹ (press) *v.* **pressed, pressing, presses.** —*tr.* **1. a.** To exert steady weight or force against; bear down on: *The wrestler pressed his opponent down.* **b.** To apply pressure to or push, as with a finger: *pressed the button.* **2. a.** To squeeze the juice or other contents from. **b.** To extract (juice, for example) by squeezing or compressing. **3. a.** To apply steady force to, so as to make compact, reshape, or flatten: *pressed flowers.* **b.** To smooth, flatten, or shape (clothing) using steam or steady pressure from an iron. **4.** To clasp or embrace closely. **5.** To seek to influence as by insistent arguments; entreat insistently. **6.** To attempt to force to action; urge on; spur. **7.** To place in trying or constraining circumstances; distress; harass: *pressed by lack of money; pressed for time.* **8.** To lay stress upon; emphasise: *pressed her point.* **9.** To advance or carry on vigorously: *pressed his attack.* **10.** To put forward importunately or insistently: *They pressed their claim.* **11.** To manufacture (a record) from a mould or matrix. **12.** To lift (a weight) first to the shoulders and then above the head. Used of a weightlifter. —*intr.* **1.** To exert force or pressure. **2.** To weigh heavily, as on the mind. **3.** To advance eagerly; push forward: *let's press on with the next course.* **4.** To require haste; be urgent. **5.** To press clothes or other material. **6.** To assemble closely and in large numbers; crowd. **7.** To employ urgent persuasion or entreaty; ask earnestly or persistently. —See Synonyms at **urge.**
~*n.* **1.** Any of various machines or devices that apply pressure. Often used in combination: *a winepress.* **2.** Any of various machines used for printing; a **printing press** *(see).* **3. a.** A place or establishment where matter is printed. **b.** *Often capital* **P.** A printing or publishing firm: *The Nonesuch Press.* **4.** The method, art, or business of printing. **5. a.** The news media as a whole; especially, the newspapers. Preceded by *the.* Also used adjectivally: *a press release.* **b.** The people involved in the news media; especially, reporters and photographers. Preceded by *the.* **c.** The material dealt with in the news media; especially, reviews or editorial comment: *The new play received a bad press.* **6.** The act of gathering in large

PRONUNCIATION KEY

a, trap; aa, father; ai, fair; ar, star; aw, lawn; ay, play; b, bb, stab; rubber; ch, church; ck, ticket; d, dd, dead; ladder; e, dress; ee, bee; er, defer; ew, few; ewr, pure; ə, about; ər, letter; f, ff, fife; differ; g, gg, giggle; h, hat; i, kit; ī, price; īr, fire; j, judge; k, kick; l, ll, let; 'l, needle; m, mm, man; n, nn, no; 'n, sudden; ng, thing; o, lot; ō, no; ŏŏ, foot; ōō, shoe; oor, poor; ow, cow; owr, hour; oy, boy; p, pp, pepper; r, rr, red; s, ss, sauce; sh, ship; t, tt, totter; th, thick; th, this; smooth; u, cut; ur, turn; v, vv, valve; w, wet; y, yes; z, zz, zebra; zh, vision; pleasure

IN FOREIGN WORDS:

aN, oN, Saint-Saëns; hl, Llanelli; Hluhluwe; kh, loch; lough; Khaled

STRESS MARK:

ín-sīt, insight; in-sít, incite

numbers or of pushing forward. **7.** A large gathering; a throng. **8. a.** The act of applying pressure. **b.** The state of being pressed. **9.** The haste or urgency of business or affairs. **10.** The set of proper creases in a garment or fabric, formed by ironing. **11.** An upright cupboard or case used for storing clothing, books, or other articles. **12.** In weightlifting, the act of pressing a weight. —**at** or **in press.** Being printed. —**go to press.** To start printing or being printed. [Middle English *pressen,* from Old French *presser,* from Latin *pressāre,* frequentative of *premere* (past participle *pressus*), to press.]

press² *tr.v.* **pressed, pressing, presses. 1.** To force into military service; impress. **2.** To use in a manner different from the usual or intended. Used chiefly in the phrase *press into service.*
~*n.* Conscription or impressment into service, especially into the navy. [Alteration (by association with PRESS, to apply pressure, compel) of earlier *prest,* to give money to (recruits), from Middle English *prest,* money given to recruits, from Old French, "loan", from *prester,* to lend, from Latin *praestāre,* to place something at someone's disposal, furnish : *prae-,* PRE- + *stāre,* to stand.]

press agent *n. Abbr.* **P.A.** A person employed to arrange advertising and favourable publicity for an actor, theatre, or the like.

press agency *n.* A **news agency** (see).

press box *n.* A section reserved for reporters, as in a sports stadium.

press conference *n.* An interview held for news reporters and photographers by a politician or other public figure.

press·er (préssər) *n.* **1.** A person who presses clothes. **2.** Any of various devices that apply pressure to a product in manufacturing.

press gallery *n.* An area above the ground floor reserved for the press, as in a parliament.

press gang *n.* A company under an officer with the task of pressing men into military, especially naval, service.

press-gang (préss-gang) *tr.v.* **-ganged, -ganging, -gangs. 1.** To press into military service. **2.** To force (a person) to do something unwillingly.

press·ing (préssing) *adj.* **1.** Demanding immediate attention; urgent: *a pressing need.* **2.** Importunate; insistent: *a pressing invitation.* —See Synonyms at **urgent.**
~ *n.* **1.** A series of gramophone records produced at one time. **2.** Any of these records. —**press·ing·ly** *adv.*

press·man (préss-mən, -man) *n., pl.* **-men** (-mən, -men). **1.** A printing press operator. **2.** *British.* A journalist.

press·mark (préss-maark) *n.* A mark in or on a book indicating where it should be placed in a library.

press officer *n.* A person employed by an organisation to liaise with and answer enquiries from the press.

press of sail *n. Nautical.* The greatest amount of sail that a ship can carry safely. Also called "press of canvas".

pres·sor (préss-ər, -awr) *n.* An agent that increases blood pressure. [Latin *premere* (stem *press-*), to PRESS.] —**pres·sor** *adj.*

press release *n.* An announcement or official account of an event, performance, or other news or publicity item issued to the press.

press·room (préss-rōōm, -rŏŏm) *n.* The room in a printing or newspaper publishing establishment that contains the presses.

press secretary *n.* A person who manages the public affairs and press conferences of a public figure.

press·stud (préss-stud) *n.* A small metal or plastic fastener for clothes, that works by having its two parts pushed together. Also chiefly *U.S.* "snap fastener".

press-up (préss-up) *n.* A physical exercise performed by lying with the face and palms to the floor and by pushing the body up and down with the arms. Also *U.S.* "push-up".

pres·sure (préshər) *n.* **1. a.** The act of pressing. **b.** The condition of being pressed. **2.** The application of continuous force by one body upon another that it is touching; compression. **3. a.** *Abbr.* **p** *Physics.* Force applied over a surface, measured as force per unit of area. It is measured in pascals, pounds per square inch, or the like. **b.** *Meteorology.* See **atmospheric pressure. 4.** A constraining influence upon the mind or will, as, for example, a moral force: *brought pressure to bear upon the government.* **5.** Urgent claim or demand; harassment: *working under pressure.* **6.** A burdensome, distressing, or weighty condition; oppression, as of grief. **7.** *Obsolete.* A mark made by application of force or weight; an impression.
~*tr.v.* **pressured, -suring, -sures.** To bring pressure upon (a person), as by influence or persuasion. [Middle English, from Latin *pressūra,* from *premere,* to PRESS.]

pressure cabin *n.* A pressurised section of an aircraft.

pressure cooker *n.* An airtight metal pot that uses steam under pressure at high temperature to cook food quickly.

pressure gauge *n.* **1.** A device for measuring fluid pressure. **2.** A device for measuring the pressure of explosions.

pressure group *n.* Any group that exerts pressure on legislators and public opinion to advance or protect its interests.

pressure point *n.* Any of several places on the skin where an artery lies over a bone, and where pressure may be applied to stop bleeding from a wound beyond that point.

pressure ridge *n.* A ridge of floating ice formed as two ice floes push against each other.

pressure sore *n.* A **bed sore** (see).

pressure suit *n.* A garment that is worn in high-altitude aircraft or in spacecraft to compensate for low-pressure conditions. Compare **G-suit.**

pressure system *n.* Any system of high or low atmospheric pressure, such as a depression or anticyclone.

pres·sur·ise, pres·sur·ize (préshər-īz) *tr.v.* **-ised, -ising, -ises. 1.** To coerce (a person) with pressure, especially into a course of action. **2.** To maintain normal air pressure in (an enclosure, such as an aircraft or submarine). **3.** To put (gas or liquid) under a greater than normal pressure. —**pres·sur·i·sa·tion** (-ī-záysh'n ‖ *U.S.* -i-) *n.*

press·work (préss-wurk) *n.* **1.** The directing or running of a printing press. **2.** The matter printed by a printing press.

Pres·tel (préss-tel) *n.* A trademark for a system operated by British Telecom for transmitting a wide variety of computer-stored information over the telephone system in viewdata form, and allowing viewers to return information to the computer.

pres·ti·dig·i·ta·tion (présti-díji-táysh'n) *n.* Manual skill and dexterity in the execution of tricks; sleight of hand. [French, from *prestidigitateur,* juggler, from *preste,* nimble, from Latin *praestus* (see *presto*) + Latin *digitus,* finger.] —**pres·ti·dig·i·ta·tor** (-taytər) *n.*

pres·tige (press-téezh, préss- ‖ -téej) *n.* **1.** Prominence or influential status achieved through success, renown, or wealth. **2.** The power to command admiration in a group.
~*adj.* Possessing or conferring prestige. [French, originally "illusion brought on by magic", phantasmagoria, from Latin *praestigiae,* "juggler's tricks", illusions, alteration of *praestrigiae* (unattested), from *praestringere,* to bind up, dazzle, blind : *prae-,* before + *stringere,* to bind, tighten.] —**pres·tig·ious** (-tíjəss, -tíji- ‖ -téeji-) *adj.* —**pres·tig·ious·ly** *adv.* —**pres·tig·ious·ness** *n.*

pres·tis·si·mo (press-tíssimō) *adv. Music.* At as fast a tempo as possible. Used as a direction.
~*n., pl.* **prestissimos.** *Music.* A section or passage to be played in this manner. [Italian, superlative of PRESTO.] —**pres·tis·si·mo** *adj.*

pres·to (préstō) *adv.* **1.** *Music.* In rapid tempo. Used as a direction. **2.** Suddenly; at once. Used chiefly in the phrase *hey presto.*
~*n., pl.* **prestos.** *Music.* A section or passage to be played presto. [Italian, from Latin *praestus,* ready, from *praestō†,* at hand.] —**pres·to** *adj.*

Pres·ton (préstən). County town of Lancashire, northwest England. Situated on the river Ribble, it is a port and has textile and engineering industries. Cromwell defeated the Royalists here in 1648.

Pres·ton·pans (préstən-pánz). Town in Lothian Region, east central Scotland. It was the site of the defeat of the English by the Jacobites under Charles Edward Stuart (Bonnie Prince Charlie) (1745).

pre·stress (prée-stréss) *tr.v.* **-stressed, -stressing, -stresses.** To subject (material) to stress before applying a load, so as to counterbalance applied stresses under loaded conditions.

prestressed concrete *n.* Reinforced concrete in which the reinforcing wires or bars have been subjected to stress before forming the concrete, so as to strengthen the material under load.

Prest·wick (prést-wik). Town in Strathclyde Region, Scotland. Situated on the Firth of Clyde, it is famous for its golf course. Scotland's international airport is located here.

pre·sum·a·ble (pri-zéwm-əb'l, prə-, -zōōm- ‖ -zhōōm-) *adj.* Capable of being presumed or taken for granted; reasonable as a supposition; probable. —**pre·sum·a·bly** *adv.*

pre·sume (pri-zéwm, prə-, -zōōm ‖ -zhōōm) *v.* **-sumed, -suming, -sumes.** —*tr.* **1.** To take for granted; assume. **2.** *Law.* To take as being proved in the absence of contrary evidence. **3.** To engage oneself in, without authority or permission; venture; dare. Often used with an infinitive. —*intr.* **1.** To act overconfidently; take liberties. **2.** To take unwarranted advantage of something. Used with *on* or *upon: presumed upon her kindness.* —See Synonyms at **conjecture.** [Middle English *presumen,* from Old French *presumer,* from Late Latin *praesūmere,* to venture, from Latin, "to take in advance", presuppose, foresee, assume : *prae-,* before + *sūmere,* to take.] —**pre·sum·ed·ly** (-idli) *adv.* —**pre·sum·er** *n.*

Synonyms: presume, suppose, postulate, assume, posit.

pre·sump·tion (pri-zúmpsh'n, prə-) *n.* **1.** Behaviour or language that is boldly arrogant or offensive; effrontery. **2.** The act of presuming or accepting as true. **3.** Acceptance or belief based on reasonable evidence; an assumption or supposition. **4.** A condition or basis for accepting or presuming. **5.** *Law.* An inference as to the truth of an allegation or proposition, based on probable reasoning, in the absence of, or prior to, actual proof or disproof. [Middle English *presumpcion,* from Old French, from Latin *praesumptiō* (stem *praesumptiōn-*), from *praesūmere,* PRESUME.]

pre·sump·tive (pri-zúmptiv, prə-) *adj.* **1.** Providing a reasonable basis for belief or acceptance. **2.** Founded on probability or presumption: *an heir presumptive.* **3.** *Zoology.* Designating a cell or cells of an embryo that differentiate into a particular structure or organ. —**pre·sump·tive·ly** *adv.*

pre·sump·tu·ous (pri-zúmp-tew-əss, prə-, -choo-, -chəss, -shəss) *adj.* **1.** Excessively forward or bold, especially because of excessive self-confidence; arrogant. **2.** *Obsolete.* Presumptive. [Middle English, from Old French *presumptueux,* from Late Latin *praesumptuōsus,* audacious, from *praesumptiō,* audacity, PRESUMPTION.] —**pre·sump·tu·ous·ly** *adv.* —**pre·sump·tu·ous·ness** *n.*

pre·sup·pose (prée-sə-póz) *tr.v.* **-posed, -posing, -poses. 1.** To assume or suppose in advance; take for granted. **2.** To require or involve necessarily as an antecedent condition: *Intelligent speaking presupposes intelligent thinking.* [Middle English *presupposen,* from Old French *presupposer,* from Medieval Latin *praesuppōnere* : *prae-,* before + *suppōnere,* to SUPPOSE.] —**pre·sup·po·si·tion** (-suppə-zísh'n) *n.*

pret. preterite.

pre·tax (prée-táks) *adj.* Before taxation.

pre·tence, *U.S.* **pre·tense** (pri-ténss, prə- || *U.S. also* préé-tenss) *n.* **1.** The act of pretending; a false appearance or action intended to deceive. **2.** A false or studied show of something; an affectation. **3.** A false reason or excuse; a pretext. **4.** Something imagined or pretended; a piece of make-believe. **5.** A mere show without reality; an outward appearance. Used with *at*: *There was some pretence at negotiating.* **6.** A right asserted with or without foundation; a claim. **7.** Ostentation; pretentiousness. [Middle English, from Anglo-French *pretense,* from Medieval Latin *praetensa* (unattested), from Latin *pretendere,* to PRETEND.]

Usage: *Pretence* has the general meaning, derived from the verb *pretend,* of "act of pretending": *He made a pretence of doing his homework. Pretension* is a more specific term meaning "unsupported claim": *He has pretensions to being a writer.* Occasionally, *pretence* is used in place of the latter, but careful writers prefer to distinguish the two.

pre·tend (pri-ténd, prə-) *v.* **-tended, -tending, -tends.** *—tr.* **1.** To affect; feign. **2.** To claim or allege insincerely or falsely; profess: *She pretended to be simple.* **3.** To represent fictitiously in play; make believe: *You pretend to be Romeo.* **4.** *Informal.* To take upon oneself; venture: *I won't pretend to tell you, a novelist, how to write.* *—intr.* **1.** To feign an action, character, or the like, as in play. **2.** To put forward a claim. Used with *to*: *pretended to the throne.*

~adj. Informal. Imaginary; taken as such, especially for the purposes of a game: *pretend money.* [Middle English *pretenden,* from Latin *praetendere,* "to stretch forth", hold out as a pretext, assert : *prae-,* before + *tendere,* to stretch.]

Synonyms: *pretend, feign, dissemble, fake, simulate.*

pre·tend·ed (pri-téndid, prə-) *adj.* **1.** Falsely asserted or alleged: *pretended loyalty.* **2.** False; untrue; feigned. **—pre·tend·ed·ly** *adv.*

pre·tend·er (pri-téndər, prə-) *n.* **1.** One who simulates, pretends, or alleges falsely; a hypocrite or dissembler. **2. a.** One who sets forth a claim. **b.** A claimant to a throne. **3.** *Capital* **P.** In British history: **a.** James Edward **Stuart** *(see),* the Old Pretender. **b.** Charles Edward **Stuart** *(see),* the Young Pretender.

pre·ten·sion (pri-ténsh'n, prə-) *n.* **1.** A specious allegation; a pretext. **2.** An asserted, but usually unproved, claim to something, such as a privilege, right, or other position of distinction or importance. **3.** An asserted but unsupported claim, as to some merit or skill: *no pretensions to being a chess player.* See Usage note at **pretence. 4.** Pretentiousness; ostentation; display.

pre·ten·tious (pri-ténshəss, prə-) *adj.* **1. a.** Claiming or demanding a position of distinction or merit, especially when unjustified: *a pretentious play.* **b.** Affecting or adopting any mannerism, habit, style of dress, or the like, simply for the sake of appearance. **2.** Making an extravagant outer show; ostentatious. **—pre·ten·tious·ly** *adv.* **—pre·ten·tious·ness** *n.*

pret·er·ite, pret·er·it (préttrit, préttərit) *adj. Abbr.* **pret., pt.** *Grammar.* Designating the verb tense that expresses or describes a past or completed action or condition; for example, in the sentence *Mary bought cakes, bought* is in the preterite tense.

~n. Abbr. **pret., pt.** *Grammar.* **1.** The verb form expressing or describing a past or completed action or condition; the past tense. **2.** A verb in this form. [Middle English, past, past tense, from Old French, from Latin *praeteritus,* gone by, past, past participle of *praeterīre,* to go by, pass : *praeter,* beyond, comparative of *prae-,* before + *īre,* to go.]

pret·er·i·tion (préttə-rísh'n) *n.* **1.** The act of passing by, disregarding, or omitting. **2.** In Roman Law, the neglect of a testator to mention a legal heir or heirs in his will. **3.** *Theology.* The passing over of the non-elect by God. [Late Latin *praeteritiō* (stem *praeteritiōn-*), from Latin *praeterīre,* to go by, pass over. See **preterite.**]

pre·ter·i·tive (pri-térrətiv, prə-) *adj. Grammar.* Designating a verb limited to a past tense or past tenses.

pre·ter·mit (préétər-mít) *tr.v.* **-mitted, -mitting, -mits.** *Formal.* **1.** To disregard intentionally, or allow to pass unnoticed or unmentioned. **2.** To fail to do or include; omit; neglect. **3.** To desist from temporarily. [Latin *praetermittere,* to let go by : *praeter,* beyond (see **preterite**) + *mittere,* to let go.] **—pre·ter·mis·sion** (-mísh'n) *n.* **—pre·ter·mit·ter** *n.*

pre·ter·nat·u·ral (préétər-nách-rəl, -náchoo-, -náchə-) *adj.* **1.** Out of or beyond the normal course of nature; differing from the natural; abnormal **2.** Transcending the natural or material order, often connoting divinity; supernatural. [Medieval Latin *praeternātūrālis,* from Latin *praeter nātūram,* beyond nature : *praeter,* beyond + accusative of *nātūra,* NATURE.] **—pre·ter·nat·u·ral·ism** *n.* **—pre·ter·nat·u·ral·ly** *adv.* **—pre·ter·nat·u·ral·ness** *n.*

pre·text (préé-tekst) *n.* An ostensible or professed purpose.

~tr.v. **pretexted, -texting, -texts.** To allege as an excuse: *"I shall pretext a catastrophe."* (Aldous Huxley). [Latin *praetextus,* outward show, pretence, from past participle of *praetexere,* to weave in front, cloak, disguise, pretend : *prae-,* before + *texere,* to weave.]

Pre·to·ri·a (pri-táwri-ə, prə- || -tőri-). Administrative capital of Transvaal province and the Republic of South Africa. Founded in 1855, its industries include steel making and food processing.

Pre·to·ri·us (pri-táwri-əss, prə- || -tőri-; *Afrikaans* -üss), **Andries Wilhelmus Jacobus** (1799–1853). Afrikaner politician and soldier. Leading the Great Trek to the Natal, he defeated the Zulus (1838), then, seeking independence from the British, trekked on to the Transvaal. Following the Boer victory (1848), he secured independence for the area as a republic, and for the Orange Free State. His son, Marthinus Wessel Pretorius (1819–1901), was president of both states, and was leader of the Boers in the first Boer War (1880–81).

pret·ti·fy (prítti-fī) *tr.v.* **-fied, -fying, -fies.** To make pretty, especially in a superficial or insubstantial way. Often used derogatorily. **—pret·ti·fi·ca·tion** (-fi-káysh'n) *n.* **—pret·ti·fi·er** *n.*

pret·ty (prítti) *adj.* **-tier, -tiest. 1.** Pleasing or attractive to the eye or ear, especially in a graceful or delicate way: *a pretty girl; a pretty tune.* **2.** Excellent; fine; good. Often used ironically: *That's a pretty mess you've got us into!* **3.** *Archaic.* Gallant; fine. **4.** Effeminate; foppish: *a pretty boy.* **5.** *Informal.* Considerable in size or extent: *a pretty fortune.* —See Synonyms at **beautiful.**

~adv. Informal. **1.** To a fair degree; somewhat; moderately: *He is a pretty good student.* **2.** Very; extremely: *a pretty good judge of character.* **—sitting pretty.** *Informal.* In favourable circumstances; in a good position.

~n., pl. **pretties.** *Informal.* One that is pleasing or pretty.

~tr.v. **prettied, -tying, -ties.** *Informal.* To make pretty. Used with *up*: *pretty up the house.* [Middle English *prety, praty,* clever, skilfully made, fine, Old English *prættig,* cunning, tricky, from *prætt,* trick, wile, craft, from West Germanic *pratt-*† (unattested).] **—pret·ti·ly** *adv.* **—pret·ti·ness** *n.*

pretty-pretty (prítti-pritti) *adj.* Pretty in a contrived way.

pre·tu·ber·cu·lous (préé-tew-bérkew-ləss || -tōō-) *adj.* Pertaining to the stage at which tuberculosis is established, occurring before the actual development of symptoms.

pret·zel (préts'l) *n.* A glazed, salted biscuit, usually baked in the form of a loose knot or stick. [German *Pretzel, Brezel,* from Old High German *brezitella,* from Medieval Latin *brachiatellum* (unattested), diminutive of *brachītum* (unattested), "armlet", hence a ring-shaped cake, from Latin *bracchium,* arm, from Greek *brakhiōn.*]

pre·vail (pri-váyl, prə-) *intr.v.* **-vailed, -vailing, -vails. 1.** To be greater in strength or influence; triumph or win a victory. Often used with *over* or *against*: *let common sense prevail.* **2.** To be most common or frequent; be predominant. **3.** To be in force, use, or effect; be current. **4.** To use persuasion or inducement successfully. Used with *on, upon,* or *with.* —See Synonyms at **persuade.** [Middle English *prevayllen,* from Latin *praevalēre,* to be more powerful : *prae-,* before, beyond + *valēre,* to be strong.] **—pre·vail·er** *n.*

pre·vail·ing (pri-váyling, prə-) *adj.* **1.** Most frequent or common; predominant. **2.** Generally current; widespread; prevalent. **3.** To be met with at a given time: *the prevailing circumstances.* **—pre·vail·ing·ly** *adv.* **—pre·vailing·ness** *n.*

Synonyms: *prevailing, prevalent, current, rife.*

prev·a·lent (prévvələnt) *adj.* **1.** Widely or commonly occurring. **2.** Generally accepted or practised. See Synonyms at **common, prevailing.** [Latin *praevalēns* (stem *praevalent-*), present participle of *praevalēre,* to PREVAIL.] **—prev·a·lence** *n.* **—prev·a·lent·ly** *adv.*

pre·var·i·cate (pri-várri-kayt, prə-) *intr.v.* **-cated, -cating, -cates. 1.** To stray from or evade the truth; equivocate. **2.** To speak or act evasively; quibble. [Latin *praevāricārī,* to walk crookedly, deviate from one's course, collude : *prae-,* before, beyond + *vāricāre,* to straddle, from *vāricus,* straddling, from *vārus,* stretched, bent, knock-kneed (see **varus**).] **—pre·var·i·ca·tion** (-káysh'n) *n.* **—pre·var·i·ca·tor** (-kaytər) *n.*

pre·ven·i·ent (pri-véeni-ənt, préé-, prə-) *adj.* **1.** Antecedent; previous; preceding. **2.** Expectant; anticipatory. **3.** Seeking or tending to prevent. [Latin *praeveniēns* (stem *praevenient-*), present participle of *praevenīre,* to come before, precede, anticipate : *prae-,* before + *venīre,* to come.] **—pre·ven·i·ent·ly** *adv.*

pre·vent (pri-vént, prə-; *for sense 4,* préé-) *v.* **-vented, -venting, -vents.** *—tr.* **1.** To keep from happening, as by some prior action; avert; thwart. **2.** To keep (someone) from doing something; hinder; impede. Often used with *from.* **3.** *Archaic.* To anticipate or counter in advance. **4.** *Archaic.* To come before; precede. *—intr.* To be an obstacle: *There will be a picnic, if nothing prevents.* [Middle English *preventen,* to anticipate, from Latin *praevenīre,* to come before, anticipate : *prae-,* before + *venīre,* to come.] **—pre·vent·a·bil·i·ty** (-ə-bílləti), **pre·vent·i·bil·i·ty** *n.* **—pre·vent·a·ble, pre·vent·i·ble** *adj.* **—pre·vent·er** *n.*

Synonyms: *prevent, preclude, obviate, forestall.*

Usage: When *prevent* is followed by the *-ing* form of a verb, formal English requires that any preceding noun be in the possessive case: *He prevented Jean's leaving.* Less formally, the noun may be used without any possessive marker and followed by *from*: *He prevented Jean from leaving.* A construction lacking both *from* and the possessive ending is sometimes used, especially in British English, but attracts criticism: *He prevented Jean leaving.*

pre·ven·tion (pri-vénsh'n, prə-) *n.* **1.** The act of preventing. **2.** A hindrance; an obstacle.

pre·ven·tive (pri-vént-iv, prə-) *adj.* Also **pre·ven·ta·tive** (-ətiv). **1.** Designed or used to prevent or hinder; acting as an obstacle; precautionary. **2.** *Medicine.* Thwarting or warding off illness or disease; prophylactic. **3.** In Britain, designating the branch of Customs that is concerned with intercepting smuggling.

~n. Also **pre·ven·ta·tive. 1.** Something that prevents; an obstacle. **2.** *Medicine.* Something used to ward off illness. **—pre·ven·tive·ly** *adv.* **—pre·ven·tive·ness** *n.*

Pré·vert (pray-váir), **Jacques** (1900–77). French poet and screenplay writer. His poetry, which is surrealist, exuberant, and humorous, deals in the main with Parisian low life. His scripts include *Les Enfants du Paradis* (1945).

pre·view (préé-vew, -véw) *n.* Also *U.S.* **pre·vue** (for sense 1). **1.** An

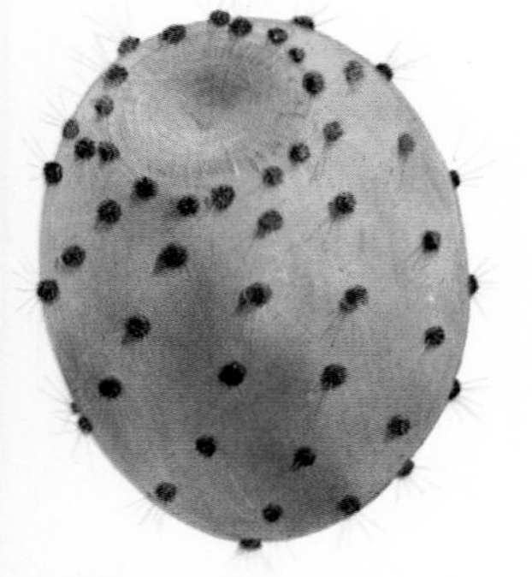

prickly pear *The edible fruit of some species of* Opuntia *cacti.* Opuntia ficus-india, *shown here, is a native of Mexico.*

advance showing of a film, an art exhibition, or some other event to an invited audience, prior to public presentation. **2.** Broadly, any advance viewing or exhibition.

~*v.* **previewed, -viewing, -views.** Also *U.S.* **pre·vue, -vued, -vuing, -vues.** —*tr.* To view or exhibit in advance. —*intr.* To be shown or exhibited in advance.

Prev·in (prévvin), **André (George)** , born Andreas Ludwig Priwin (1929–). German-born U.S. conductor, arranger, and composer. Winner of four Academy Awards for his film scores, he later gained recognition in the world of classical music.

pre·vi·ous (prée̋v-yəss, -i-əss) *adj.* **1.** Existing or occurring prior to something else in time or order; antecedent. **2.** *Informal.* Premature; hasty. **—previous to.** Prior to; before. [Latin *praevius,* going before, leading the way : *prae-,* before + *via,* way.] **—pre·vi·ous·ly** *adv.* **—pre·vi·ous·ness** *n.*

previous question *n. Abbr.* **p.q.** In parliamentary procedure, a motion to not take a vote on the issue being debated, which, if carried, ends the debate, but if defeated, means that an immediate vote on the issue must be taken. Compare **closure.**

pre·vise (pri-víz, prée̋-) *tr.v.* **-vised, -vising, -vises.** *Rare.* **1.** To foresee. **2.** To notify in advance. [Latin *praevidēre* (stem *praevīs-*) : *prae-,* before + *vidēre,* to see.] **—pre·vi·sion** (-vízh'n) *n.* **—pre·vi·sion·al** *adj.*

pre·vo·cal·ic (prée̋-vō-kál-ik, -və-) *adj. Phonetics.* Preceding a vowel.

pre·war (prée̋-wáwr) *adj.* Existing or occurring before a particular war.

prex·y (préksi) *n., pl.* **-ies.** *U.S. Slang.* A president, especially of a college or university. [Shortened variant of PRESIDENT.]

prey (pray) *n.* **1.** Any creature hunted or caught for food; a quarry. **2.** One that can be damaged or hurt; a victim: *The district fell prey to the developers.* **3.** *Archaic.* Something taken by violence; booty.

~*intr.v.* **preyed, preying, preys. 1.** To hunt, catch, or eat as prey. **2.** To victimise someone or make a profit at someone's expense. **3.** To plunder or pillage. **4.** To exert a grave or harmful effect: *Remorse preyed upon his mind.* [Middle English *preye,* from Old French *preie,* from Latin *praeda,* booty, prey.] **—prey·er** *n.*

Pri·am (prí-əm, -am). *Greek Mythology.* King of Troy, the father of Paris and Hector, killed when his city fell to the Greeks.

pri·ap·ic (prī-áppik, -áypik) *adj.* Also **pri·a·pe·an** (prí-ə-pée̋-ən). Phallic. [From PRIAPUS.]

pri·a·pism (prí-əp-iz'm) *n.* Persistent, usually painful, erection of the penis, especially as a consequence of disease. [French *priapisme,* from Late Latin *priāpismus,* from Greek *priapismos,* from *priapizein,* "to act like Priapus", be lewd, from *Priapos,* PRIAPUS.]

pri·a·pus (prī-áypəss) *n.* **1.** *Capital* **P.** The Graeco-Roman god of procreation, guardian of gardens and vineyards, and personification of the erect phallus. **2.** An image of the god Priapus, such as a statuette with a large, erect penis. [Latin, from Greek *Priapos*†.]

Prib·i·lof Islands (prí-bi-loff). Also **Fur Seal Islands.** Group of volcanic islands lying in the central Bering Sea, the breeding ground of the Alaska fur seal and an internationally recognised seal reserve.

price (prīss) *n. Abbr.* **pr. 1.** The sum of money or goods asked or given for something. **2.** The cost at which something is obtained: *Victory must be achieved at any price.* **3.** The cost of bribing someone. **4.** A reward offered for the capture or killing of a person. **5.** *Archaic.* Value or worth. **6.** Betting odds. **—at a price.** At considerable cost. **—what price.** *Chiefly British.* Used in questions to indicate: **1.** The unlikelihood of something specified taking place: *What price inflation coming down?* **2.** A disparaging attitude to something specified: *What price United's performance?*

~*tr.v.* **priced, pricing, prices. 1.** To fix or establish a price for: *shoes priced at nineteen pounds.* **2.** To find out the price of: *spent the day pricing dresses.* [Middle English *pris,* price, value, praise, from Old French, from Latin *pretium,* price, value, reward.]

Synonyms: *price, charge, fee, cost, expense, expenditure, outlay.*

price control *n.* The imposition of a maximum level upon the prices of certain goods by a government, especially in a time of economic crisis.

price index *n.* A number relating prices of a group of commodities to their prices during a particular base period.

price·less (príss-ləss, -liss) *adj.* **1.** Of inestimable worth; invaluable. **2.** Highly amusing, absurd, or odd. —See Synonyms at **costly.**

price support *n. Economics.* A system of maintaining a minimum price for certain goods, especially agricultural products of the European Economic Community, whereby the Community or a government undertakes to buy them if the market price falls below an agreed level.

price tag *n.* **1.** A label attached to a piece of merchandise indicating its price. **2.** The cost of something: *Success carried a high price tag.*

price war *n.* A situation in which suppliers in the same market cut their prices in a competitive battle to increase their sales.

pri·cey (prí-si) *adj.* **-ier, -iest.** *Informal.* Expensive.

prick (prik) *n.* **1. a.** The act of piercing or pricking. **b.** The sensation of being pierced or pricked. **2.** Any painful or stinging feeling or reflection: *the pricks of remorse.* **3.** A small mark or puncture made by a pointed object. **4.** A pointed object, such as a goad, thorn, or the like. **5. a.** *Vulgar.* A penis. **b.** *Vulgar Slang.* A foolish or disagreeable person. **—kick against the pricks.** To hurt or torment oneself by futile resistance.

~*v.* **pricked, pricking, pricks.** —*tr.* **1. a.** To puncture lightly. **b.** To puncture so as to cause injury. **2.** To sting with a mental or emotional pang. **3.** *Archaic.* To incite; impel: *"My duty pricks me on"* (Shakespeare). **4.** To mark or delineate on a surface by means of small punctures: *prick a pattern.* **5.** *Nautical.* To measure with dividers on a chart. **6.** To cause to rise sharply or stiffly. Used chiefly with *up*: *The dog pricked up his ears.* **7.** To transplant (seedlings) prior to a final planting. Used chiefly with *out* or *off.* —*intr.* **1.** To pierce or puncture something. **2.** To feel a stinging or pricking sensation. **3.** *Archaic.* To ride at a gallop. [Middle English *prik(ke),* Old English *prica,* pricked mark, puncture, from West Germanic *prikk-* (unattested).]

prick·er (príckər) *n.* **1.** Anything, such as a tool, that pricks. **2.** *U.S.* A prickle or thorn.

prick·et (príckit) *n.* **1. a.** A small spike for holding a candle upright. **b.** A candlestick having such a spike. **2.** A male deer before his antlers branch. [Middle English *priket,* from *prik,* PRICK.]

prick·le (prick'l) *n.* **1.** A small, sharp point arising from the epidermis of a branch, leaf, or other plant structure, and containing no woody or vascular tissue. **2.** A spine, as on a hedgehog. **3.** A pricking or tingling sensation.

~*v.* **prickled, -ling, -les.** —*tr.* **1.** To prick, as with a thorn. **2.** To cause a tingling sensation in. —*intr.* **1.** To feel or cause a tingling or pricking. **2.** To rise or stand up like prickles. [Middle English *prikle, prikel,* from Old English *pricel(s),* from West Germanic *prikkil-* (unattested), diminutive of *prikk-,* PRICK.]

prick·ly (príckli, prick'l-i) *adj.* **-lier, -liest. 1.** Having prickles or sharp spines. **2.** Tingling; smarting; stinging. **3. a.** Touchy; irritable. **b.** Causing irritation: *a prickly problem.* **—prick·li·ness** *n.*

prickly heat *n.* A noncontagious skin complaint, **miliaria** *(see).*

prickly pear *n.* **1.** Any of various cacti of the genus *Opuntia,* having bristly flattened or cylindrical joints, showy, usually yellow flowers, and ovoid, sometimes edible fruit. See **cholla, nopal. 2.** The fruit of any of these plants.

prickly poppy *n.* Any of various plants of the genus *Argemone,* chiefly of tropical America, having large yellow or white flowers and prickly leaves, stems and pods.

pride (prīd) *n.* **1.** A sense of one's own proper dignity or value; self-respect. **2.** Pleasure or satisfaction taken in one's work, achievements, or possessions: *took pride in her garden.* **3. a.** A cause or source of pride: *These men were their country's pride.* **b.** The best representative or member of a group, class, or the like: *She was the pride of the three sisters.* **c.** The most successful or thriving condition; the prime: *the flush and pride of youth.* **4. a.** An excessively high opinion of oneself; conceit; arrogance. **b.** In traditional Christianity, the consideration or personification of this condition as the first of the seven deadly sins. **5. a.** Mettle or spirit in horses. **b.** *Archaic.* The state of sexual desire or heat, especially in female animals; rut. **6.** A company of lions. —See Synonyms at **flock. —pride of place.** The best or most important position.

~*v.* **prided, priding, prides.** —*tr.* To esteem (oneself) for. Used with *on* or *upon*: *I pride myself on this garden.* —*intr. Rare.* To indulge in self-esteem; glory. [Middle English *pride, prude, prute,* Old English *prȳte, prȳde,* from *prūt, prūd,* PROUD.] **—pride·ful** *adj.* **—pride·ful·ly** *adv.* **—pride·ful·ness** *n.*

Pride, Thomas (died 1658). English colonel in the Parliamentary army. In 1648 he led his regiment to Parliament and expelled about 150 Presbyterian and Royalist members who were opposed to the condemnation of Charles I ("Pride's Purge"); he was one of the signatories of Charles' death warrant.

prie-dieu (prée̋d-yér, -yṓ) *n., pl.* **-dieus** or **-dieux** (-z). A low desk with space for a book above and with a footpiece below for kneeling in prayer. [French *prie-Dieu,* "pray God".]

pri·er, pry·er (prí-ər) *n.* One who pries.

priest (preest) *n.* **1.** *Abbr.* **P., Pr.** In the Roman Catholic, Eastern Orthodox, Anglican, Armenian, and separated Catholic hierarchies, an ordained minister ranking below a bishop but above a deacon and having authority to pronounce absolution and administer sacraments. **2.** A minister in a non-Christian religion.

~*tr.v.* **priested, priesting, priests.** *Archaic.* To ordain or admit to the priesthood. [Middle English *pre(e)st, preost,* from Old English *prēost,* from Vulgar Latin *prester* (unattested), contracted from Late Latin *presbyter,* from Greek *presbuteros,* "elder", comparative of *presbus,* old man.]

priest·craft (prée̋st-kraaft || -kraft) *n.* The art and practice of being a priest; especially, priests' influence on or involvement in secular affairs and issues. Used derogatorily.

priest·ess (prée̋ss-tiss, -tess, -téss) *n.* A female priest in a non-Christian religion.

priest·hood (prée̋st-hŏŏd) *n.* **1.** The character, office, or vocation of a priest. **2.** The clergy.

Priest·ley (prée̋stli), **J(ohn) B(oynton)** (1894–). British author. His robust and perceptive novels, including *The Good Companions* (1929), have enjoyed great popularity, as have his plays. These include *Laburnum Grove* (1933), a social comedy, and *Dangerous Corner* (1932), an examination of the nature of time and perception.

Priestley, Joseph (1733-1804). English scientist. He is best known for his work on the isolation of gases, and for the discovery of oxygen (1774). As a Presbyterian minister, he influenced the Unitarian movement.

priest·ly (prée̋st-li) *adj.* **-lier, -liest.** Of, pertaining to, or befitting a priest or priests. **—priest·li·ness** *n.*

priest-rid·den (prée̋st-ridd'n) *adj.* Dominated or heavily influenced by priests. Used derogatorily.

priest's hole (prée̋sts-hōl) *n.* Also **priest-hole** (prée̋st-). Formerly in

Britain, a hiding-place used to conceal and protect Roman Catholic priests.

prig (prig) *n.* **1.** A person regarded as overprecise, affectedly arrogant, smug, or narrow-minded. **2.** *Archaic.* A coxcomb. **3.** *British Slang.* A petty thief or pickpocket. Not in current usage. ~*tr.v.* **prigged, prigging, prigs.** *British Slang.* To steal or pilfer. Not in current usage. [16th century (cant, "tinker") : origin obscure.] —**prig·ger·y** (príggəri) *n.* —**prig·gish** *adj.* —**prig·gish·ly** *adv.*

prim (prim) *adj.* **primmer, primmest. 1.** Precise, neat, or trim. **2.** Excessively formal or strict in matters of convention or morality. ~*v.* **primmed, primming, prims.** —*tr.* To fix (the face or mouth) in a prim expression. —*intr.* To assume a prim expression. [Old French *prin, prime*, very fine, excellent, from Latin *prīmus*, first, PRIME.] —**prim·ly** *adv.* —**prim·ness** *n.*

prim. 1. primary. **2.** primitive.

pri·ma ballerina (préemə) *n., pl.* **prima ballerinas.** The leading female dancer in a ballet company. Compare **ballerina.** [Italian, "first ballerina".]

pri·ma·cy (prímə-si) *n., pl.* **-cies. 1.** The state or condition of being first or foremost. **2.** The office or province of an ecclesiastical primate. [Middle English, from Medieval Latin *prīmātia*, from *prīmās*, PRIMATE.]

pri·ma don·na (préemə dónnə ‖ *U.S. also* prímmə) *n., pl.* **prima donnas. 1.** The leading female soloist in an opera company. **2.** A temperamental and conceited person. [Italian, "first lady".]

primaeval. Variant of **primeval.**

pri·ma fa·cie (prímə fáy-shee, -shi-ee, -see, -si-ee ‖ *chiefly U.S.* -shə) *adv.* At first sight; before closer inspection. [Latin.] —**pri·ma-fa·cie** *adj.*

prima-facie evidence *n. Law.* Evidence that would if uncontested, establish a fact or raise a presumption of a fact.

pri·mal (prím'l) *adj.* **1.** Being first in time; original; archetypal. **2.** Primitive in character. **3.** Of first importance; primary. ~*n.* A reliving of a painful experience, often dating from an earlier period of one's life, which may be evoked for therapeutic purposes, as in primal therapy. ~*v.* **primalled, -malling, -mals.** —*intr.* To experience a primal. —*tr.* To cause or help to primal. [Medieval Latin *prīmālis,* from Latin *prīmus*, first.]

primal scream *n.* A scream that may be emitted during or as if during a primal.

primal therapy *n.* A form of psychotherapy in which attempts are made to make patients relive painful earlier experiences, as of infancy and sometimes birth, the reliving of which with full intensity is held to produce permanent positive physical and psychological changes. —**primal therapist** *n.*

pri·ma·ri·ly (prím-rəli, -ərəli ‖ prī-mérrəli, prí-, *U.S. also* prí-merrəli) *adv.* **1.** At first; originally. **2.** Chiefly; principally.

pri·ma·ry (prím-əri ‖ -erri) *adj. Abbr.* **prim. 1.** Occurring first in time, development, or sequence; earliest; original: *primary source.* **2.** Of or designating education for children up to the age of 11. **3.** Of standing first in a list, series, or sequence: *primary negotiations.* **4.** First or best in degree, quality, or importance: *a primary consideration.* **5.** *Geology.* **a.** Of, pertaining to, or designating the earliest periods of geological development up to and including the Palaeozoic era; Precambrian. Not in current technical usage. **b.** Designating features of a rock that developed at the time of formation. **6. a.** Of or designating a fundamental or basic part of an organised whole: *Word play is a primary element in Shakespeare's language.* **b.** Of or designating certain basic, natural industries, such as fishing or forestry, or their products. **7.** Immediate; direct: *a primary effect.* **8.** Of or pertaining to the basic colours from which all other colours may be derived. See **primary colour. 9.** *Linguistics.* **a.** Having a word root or other linguistic element as a basis that cannot be further analysed or broken down. Said of the derivation of a word or word element. **b.** Referring to present or future time. Said of the various present and future tenses in Latin, Greek, and Sanskrit. **10.** *Electricity.* Of, pertaining to, or designating an inducting current, circuit, or coil. **11.** Of, pertaining to, or designating the main flight feathers projecting along the outer edge of a bird's wing. **12.** *Chemistry.* **a.** Pertaining to the replacement of one of several atoms or radicals in a compound by another atom or radical. **b.** Having a carbon atom attached solely to one other carbon atom in a molecule. **13.** Of, pertaining to, or designating plant growth derived solely from apical meristems present in the embryo. ~*n., pl.* **primaries.** *Abbr.* **prim. 1. a.** One that is first in time, order, or sequence. **b.** One that is first or best in degree, quality, or importance. **c.** One that is fundamental or basic. **2.** A primary colour. **3.** Any of the main flight feathers projecting along the outer edge of a bird's wing. **4.** An inducting electric current, circuit, or coil. **5.** *Astronomy.* A celestial body, especially a star, to which the orbit of a satellite, or secondary, is referred. **6.** A **cosmic ray** (see). **7.** In the United States: **a.** A meeting of the registered voters of a political party for the purpose of nominating candidates and for choosing delegates to their party convention. **b.** A preliminary election in which the registered voters of a political party nominate candidates for office. [Middle English, from Latin *prīmārius,* of the first rank, chief, basic, from *prīmus*, first.]

primary accent *n.* The strongest stress or accent in a word; for example, in the word *typical*, the first syllable carries the primary accent. Also called "primary stress". Compare **secondary accent, tertiary accent.**

primary cell *n.* A cell in which an irreversible chemical reaction generates electricity. Also called "galvanic cell", "voltaic cell". Compare **secondary cell.**

primary coil *n.* An electrically conducting coil, as in a transformer, that carries an inducting current. Also called "primary winding".

primary colour *n.* A colour belonging to any of three groups, each of which is regarded as generating all colours. These groups are: **1.** *Additive, physiological,* or *light* primaries—red, green, and blue. Lights of red, green, and blue wavelengths may be mixed to produce all colours. **2.** *Subtractive* or *colorant* primaries—magenta, yellow, and cyan. Substances that reflect light of one of these wavelengths and absorb (subtract) other wavelengths may be mixed to produce all colours. **3.** *Psychological* primaries—red, yellow, green, and blue, plus the achromatic pair black and white. All colours may be subjectively conceived as mixtures of these.

primary group *n.* In sociology, a group of people in regular personal and social contact, such as a family or team of workers. Compare **secondary group.**

primary radiation *n.* Cosmic radiation as it enters the Earth's atmosphere.

primary school *n.* A school for children between the ages of 5 or 6 and 11.

pri·mate (prí-mət, -mit, -mayt *for sense 1*; -mayt *for sense 2*) *n.* **1.** A bishop of highest rank in a province or country, such as the Archbishop of Canterbury who is the *Primate of all England.* **2.** Any member of the order Primates, which includes the monkeys, apes, and humans, typically having dexterous hands and feet, binocular vision, and a well-developed brain. ~*adj.* Of, pertaining to, or belonging to the order Primates. [Middle English *primat*, from Old French, from Medieval Latin *prīmās* (stem *prīmāt-*), archbishop, from Latin "of the first rank", chief, leader, from *prīmus*, first.] —**pri·ma·tial** (prī-máysh'l) *adj.*

prime (prīm) *adj.* **1.** First in excellence, quality, or value: *prime beef.* **2.** First in degree or rank; chief: *Money was his prime motive.* **3.** First or early in time, order, or sequence. **4.** *Mathematics.* Designating a prime number. —See Synonyms at **chief.** ~*n.* **1.** The earliest or first part, such as the break of day or the season of spring. **2.** *Mathematics.* A prime number. **3.** The age of maximum physical health and intellectual vigour: *the prime of life.* **4.** The period or phase of ideal or peak condition. **5.** In fencing, the first of eight positions of thrust and parry. **6.** A mark (′) written above and to the right of a letter in order to distinguish it from the same letter already in use or to designate a related quantity or thing, such as feet, minutes of angle, or minutes of time. **7.** In religious observance: **a.** The second of the seven *canonical hours (see).* **b.** *Rare.* The time of day set aside for this prayer, usually about 6:00 a.m. **8.** *Music.* **a.** The tonic or keynote of a scale. **b.** A zero interval between notes. ~*v.* **primed, priming, primes.** —*tr.* **1.** To make ready; prepare. **2.** To prepare (a gun, mine, or grenade) for firing by inserting a charge of gunpowder or a primer or by releasing the safety pin. **3.** To prepare for operation, as by pouring water into a pump or petrol into a carburettor. **4.** To prepare (a surface) for painting by covering with size, primer, or an undercoat. **5.** To prepare with information. **6.** To fortify: *primed him with brandy.* —*intr.* To prepare someone or something for future action or operation. [Middle English, from Old French, feminine of *prin*, from Latin *prīmus*, first; the canonical hour derives from Old English *prīm*, from Latin *prīma (hōra)*, first (hour), from the feminine of *prīmus*.] —**prime·ly** *adv.* —**prime·ness** *n.*

prime meridian *n.* The zero meridian, (0°), from which longitude east and west is measured and which passes through Greenwich.

prime minister *n. Abbr.* **P.M. 1.** A chief minister appointed by a ruler. **2.** *Often capital* P, *capital* M. In some countries, such as Britain, the chief minister who leads the government. —**prime ministership, prime ministry** *n.*

prime mover *n.* **1.** The initial force, such as electricity, wind, or gravity, that engages or moves a machine. **2.** That which is regarded as the initial source of energy directed towards a goal. **3.** Any machine or mechanism that converts natural energy into work. **4.** In Aristotelian philosophy, the self-moved being that causes all motion.

prime number *n.* A number that has itself and one as its only factors.

prim·er¹ (prímər ‖ *chiefly U.S.* prímmər) *n.* **1.** A school textbook. **2.** A book that covers the basic elements of any subject: *a primer of Freudian psychology.* [Middle English, from Anglo-French, from Medieval Latin *prīmārium (manuāle)*, "basic handbook", from Latin *prīmārius,* basic, PRIMARY.]

prim·er² (prímər) *n.* **1.** A cap or tube containing a small amount of explosive used to detonate the main explosive charge of a firearm or mine. **2.** Someone or something that primes or causes to be primed. **3.** An undercoat of paint or size applied to prepare a surface, as for painting. [From PRIME (verb).]

prime rate *n.* The lowest rate of interest on bank loans at any given time and place, offered to preferred borrowers.

pri·me·ro (pri-maír-ō) *n.* A gambling card game, popular in Elizabethan England. [Alteration of Spanish *primera*, feminine of *primero*, "first", from Latin *prīmarius*, principal, from *prīmus*, first.]

prime time *n.* The hours, usually during the evening, when television attracts its largest audience, so that companies can charge high rates for advertising. Also used adjectivally: *a prime-time slot.*

pri·me·val, pri·mae·val (prī-méev'l) *adj.* Belonging to the first or earliest age: *the primeval swamp.* [Latin *prīmaevus,* in the first period of life : *prīmus,* first + *aevum,* age.] **—pri·me·val·ly** *adv.*

prime vertical *n. Astronomy.* The great circle that passes through an observer's zenith at right angles to the celestial meridian and intersects the horizon at the east and west points.

prim·i·grav·i·da (prīmi-grávvi-də) *n., pl.* **-das** or **-dae** (-dee). *Medicine.* A woman who is pregnant for the first time. [New Latin, from Latin (feminines) *prima,* first + *gravida,* GRAVID.]

prim·ing (prīming) *n.* **1.** The explosive used to ignite a charge. **2.** A preliminary coat of paint or size applied to a surface.

pri·mip·a·ra (prī-míppə-rə) *n., pl.* **-aras** or **-arae** (-ree). *Medicine.* A woman who has borne only one child. [Latin : *prīmus,* first + *-para,* feminine of *-parus,* -PAROUS.] **—pri·mi·par·i·ty** (prīmi-párrəti) *n.* **—pri·mip·a·rous** (-rəss) *adj.*

primrose *There are over 500 species in the primrose genus; this is* Primula vulgaris. *They grow wild throughout the Northern Hemisphere in cool or mountainous areas and are common garden plants.*

prim·i·tive (prímmə-tiv, prímmi-) *adj. Abbr.* **prim. 1.** Of or pertaining to an earliest or original stage or state: *the primitive Church.* **2.** Characterised by simplicity or crudity; unsophisticated: *primitive weapons.* **3.** Of or pertaining to early stages in the evolution of human culture: *primitive societies.* **4.** *Linguistics.* Serving as the basis for derived or inflected forms: *"Pick" is the primitive word from which "picket" is derived.* **5.** *Mathematics.* Any form in geometry or algebra from which another form is derived. **6. a.** Of or pertaining to late medieval or pre-Renaissance European painters. **b.** Loosely, of or pertaining to any unsophisticated painting. **c.** Of or designating one who paints in a primitive style. **7.** *Geology.* Of or pertaining to rocks formed by the first solidification of the earth's crust. **8.** *Biology.* Occurring in or characteristic of an early stage of development or evolution.
~*n.* **1.** A person belonging to a primitive society. **2.** Someone or something at a low or early stage of development. **3. a.** One belonging to an early stage in the development of a culture or artistic trend; especially, a painter of the pre-Renaissance period. **b.** An artist having a primitive style. **c.** A work by a primitive painter. **4.** *Linguistics.* A word or word element from which another word or inflected form of the word is derived. Compare **derivative.** [Middle English *primitif,* from Old French, from Latin *prīmitīvus,* first of its kind, from *prīmitus,* at first, in the first place, from *prīmus,* first.] **—prim·i·tive·ly** *adv.* **—prim·i·tive·ness, prim·i·tiv·i·ty** (-tivvəti) *n.*

primitive solar-nebula hypothesis *n.* A theory of the origin of the Solar System that combines elements of the **nebular hypothesis** and the **planetismal hypothesis** (*both of which see*). It states that dust and gas condensed from galactic matter, forming a *presolar medium* which contracted under its own gravity and eventually led to the formation of the Sun and planetismals, which in turn accreted further matter to form the planets, their satellites, and the rest of the bodies in the Solar System.

prim·i·tiv·ism (prímmə-tiv-iz'm, prímmi-) *n.* **1.** The state or quality of being primitive. **2.** A belief that modern civilisation would benefit by a return to or consideration of primitive culture, customs, or ideas. **3.** The style of primitive painters. **—prim·i·tiv·ist** *adj. & n.* **—prim·i·tiv·is·tic** (-ístik) *adj.*

Primitive Methodism *n.* A form of Methodism characterised by evangelical fervour, that broke away from the official church early in the 19th century and was readmitted in 1932. **—Primitive Methodist** *adj. & n.*

pri·mo (prée-mō) *n., pl.* **-mos** or **-mi** (-mee). *Music.* The principal part in a duet or ensemble composition. [Italian, "first", from Latin *prīmus.*] **—pri·mo** *adj.*

Pri·mo de Ri·ve·ra (préemō day ri-váir-ə), **Miguel** (1870–1930). Spanish general and politician. He seized power (1923) and established a military directorate to run the country. Political dissent and ill-health forced his resignation (1930). His son José Antonio (1903–36) founded the Falangist movement, and was executed by the Loyalists in the Civil War.

pri·mo·gen·i·tor (prī-mō-jénnitər, -mə-) *n.* The earliest ancestor or forefather. [Medieval Latin : Latin *prīmus,* first + GENITOR.]

pri·mo·gen·i·ture (prī-mō-jénni-chər, -mə-, -choor, -tewr) *n.* **1.** The state or condition of being the first-born or eldest child. **2.** *Law.* The right of the eldest child, especially the eldest son, to inherit the entire estate of one or both parents. Compare **ultimogeniture.** [Medieval Latin *prīmōgenitūra* : Latin *prīmus,* first + *genitūra,* birth, from *gignere* (stem *genit-*), to beget.] **—pri·mo·gen·i·tar·y** (-tri, -təri || -terri), **pri·mo·gen·i·tal** *adj.*

pri·mor·di·al (prī-mórdi-əl, prī-) *adj.* **1.** Happening at, belonging to, or characteristic of the beginning of time or history. **2.** Fundamental; seeming to have always existed: *primordial images in myths.* **3.** *Biology.* Belonging to or characteristic of the earliest stage of development of an organism or part.
~*n.* A basic principle. [Middle English, from Late Latin *prīmōrdiālis,* from Latin *prīmōrdium,* origin, from *prīmōrdius,* original : *prīmus,* first + *ordīrī,* to begin.] **—pri·mor·di·al·ly** *adv.*

primordial soup *n.* The suspension of organic molecules thought to have been the origin of life. Compare **spontaneous generation, abiogenesis.**

pri·mor·di·um (prī-mórdi-əm, prī-) *n., pl.* **-dia** (-ə). An organ or part in its earliest stage of development. [Latin, "origin". See **primordial.**]

primp (primp) *v.* **primped, primping, primps.** —*tr.* To neaten (one's hair, for example) with considerable attention to detail. —*intr.* To primp oneself. [Dialectal variant of PRIM.]

prim·rose (prím-rōz) *n.* **1.** Any of various plants of the genus *Primula*; especially, *P. vulgaris,* which has single, pale yellow flowers on long, hairy stalks. See **bird's eye primrose. 2.** See **evening primrose. 3.** Pale yellow. [Middle English *primerose,* from Old French, from Medieval Latin *prīma rosa,* "first (or earliest) rose" : Latin *prīma,* feminine of *prīmus,* first + *rosa,* ROSE.] **—prim·rose** *adj.*

primrose path *n.* A life of ease or pleasure, especially at the risk of eventual ruin.

prim·u·la (prímmewlə) *n.* Any plant of the genus *Primula,* which includes the primrose, cowslip, oxlip, and polyanthus. [Medieval Latin, feminine noun from *prīmulus,* diminutive of *prīmus,* first.]

pri·mum mo·bi·le (prī-məm mṓbi-li, prée-, -lay) *n.* **1.** In medieval astronomy, the tenth and outermost concentric sphere of the universe, thought to revolve around the Earth from east to west in 24 hours and believed to cause the other nine spheres to revolve with it. **2.** A prime mover. [Medieval Latin, "first moving (thing)", a translation of Arabic *al-muḥarrik al-awwal.*]

pri·mus (prīməss) *n., pl.* **-muses.** The first in rank of the bishops of the Scottish Episcopal Church. [Medieval Latin *prīmus,* from Latin, first.]

Pri·mus (prīməss) *n.* A trademark for a small, portable, oil-burning cooking stove.

pri·mus in·ter pa·res (prī-məss íntər párreez) *n. Latin.* The first among equals.

prin. 1. principal. **2.** principle.

prince (prinss) *n.* **1.** *Archaic.* A hereditary ruler; a king. **2.** *Abbr.* **P., Pr.** The ruler of a principality or a small state. **3.** *Abbr.* **P., Pr.** A male member of a royal family; especially, in Britain, the son or grandson of a monarch. **4.** *Abbr.* **P., Pr.** A nobleman of varying status in different countries. **5.** An outstanding man in any group: *John Wesley was the prince of preachers.* [Middle English, from Old French, from Latin *princeps* (stem *princip-*), first in rank, sovereign, ruler : *prīmus,* first + *cipere,* variant of *capere,* to take.]

Prince Albert *n. U.S.* A man's long, double-breasted frock coat. [Popularised by Prince *Albert* Edward, later EDWARD VII.]

prince consort *n.* The husband of a sovereign queen.

prince·dom (prínss-dəm) *n.* **1.** The territory ruled by a prince; a principality. **2.** The rank or status of a prince.

Prince Edward Island. Island province of southeast Canada, situated in the Gulf of St. Lawrence and separated from the mainland by the Northumberland Strait.

prince·ling (prínss-ling) *n.* Also **prince·let** (-lət, -lit). A prince of minor status or importance.

prince·ly (prínss-li) *adj.* **-lier, -liest. 1.** Of or befitting a prince. **2.** Sumptuous; lavish. **—prince·li·ness** *n.* **—prince·ly** *adv.*

Prince of Darkness. A name for **Satan.**

Prince of Peace. A name for **Christ.**

Prince of the Church *n.* A cardinal in the Roman Catholic Church.

Prince of Wales *n.* **1.** A title given to the eldest son of a British sovereign. **2.** A male holding this title.

prince regent *n.* A prince who rules the country, as during the absence or incapacity of a sovereign.

prince royal *n.* The eldest son of a sovereign.

prince's-feath·er (prínssiz-fé*th*ər) *n.* An annual plant, *Amaranthus hypochondriacus,* having dense, feathery, red flower clusters.

prin·cess (prin-séss, prín-; *before a name,* prín-sess, -səss, -siss) *n.* **1.** *Archaic.* A hereditary female ruler; a queen. **2.** The female ruler of a principality. **3.** A female member of a royal family other than the monarch; especially, in Britain, the daughter or grand-daughter of a monarch. **4.** A noblewoman of varying rank in different countries. **5.** The wife of a prince. **6.** Any woman thought of as having the status or qualities of a princess.
~*adj.* Designed to hang in smooth, close-fitting, unbroken lines from shoulder to flared hem: *a princess dress.* [Middle English *princesse,* from Old French, feminine of PRINCE.]

princess royal *n.* The eldest daughter of a sovereign.

Prince·ton (prínss-tən). Town in west central New Jersey, United States. It is the site of the defeat of the British under James Grant and Lord Cornwallis by George Washington's forces (1777). Today it is noted chiefly for its university.

prin·ci·pal (prín-sip'l) *adj. Abbr.* **prin.** First, highest, or foremost in importance, rank, worth, or degree; chief. See Synonyms at **chief.**
~*n. Abbr.* **prin. 1.** One who holds a position of presiding rank; especially, the head of a college, school, or the like. **2.** A main participant in a given situation. **3.** A person having a leading or starring role in a dramatic work. **4.** *Finance.* **a.** The capital or main body of an estate or financial holding, as distinguished from the interest or revenue from it. **b.** A sum of money owed as a debt, upon which interest is calculated. **5.** *Law.* **a.** A person who empowers another to act as his representative. **b.** The person having prime responsibility for an obligation, as distinguished from one who acts as surety or as an endorser. **c.** One who commits or is an accomplice to a crime. **6.** The main truss or rafter that supports and gives form to a roof. **7.** Either of the participants in a duel. **8.** *Capital* **P.** An administrative officer of the British government service in the grade between Assistant Secretary and Senior Executive Officer. **9.** *Music.* **a.** A player leading any of the instrumental groupings in an orchestra. **b.** An organ stop, the four-foot diapason. [Middle English, from Old French, from Latin *principālis,* first, original, hence overseer, ruler, from *princeps,* first one in rank, chief, PRINCE.] **—prin·ci·pal·ly** (-sipli, -sip'l-i) *adv.*

Usage: *Principal* and *principle* are often confused in spelling, but they have no senses in common. *Principal* is both an adjective and a noun, with senses to do with "leading, chief": *the principal violinist; the principal of the college. Principle* is only a noun, pertaining to basic truths, laws, or rules: *the principle of self-government.*

PRONUNCIATION KEY

a, trap; aa, father; ai, fair; ar, star; aw, lawn; ay, play; b, bb, stab; rubber; ch, church; ck, ticket; d, dd, dead; ladder; e, dress; ee, bee; er, defer; ew, few; ewr, pure; ə, about; ər, letter; f, ff, fife; differ; g, gg, giggle; h, hat; i, kit; ī, price; īr, fire; j, judge; k, kick; l, ll, let; 'l, needle; m, mm, man; n, nn, no; 'n, sudden; ng, thing; o, lot; ō, no; ŏŏ, foot; ōō, shoe; oor, poor; ow, cow; owr, hour; oy, boy; p, pp, pepper; r, rr, red; s, ss, sauce; sh, ship; t, tt, totter; th, thick; th, this; smooth; u, cut; ur, turn; v, vv, valve; w, wet; y, yes; z, zz, zebra; zh, vision; pleasure

IN FOREIGN WORDS:

aN, oN, Saint-Saëns; hl, Llanelli; Hluhluwe; kh, loch; lough; Khaled

STRESS MARK:

ín-sīt, insight; in-sīt, incite

principal axis *n.* **1.** An imaginary line that passes through the centres of curvature of a system of lenses or mirrors. **2.** Any of the three mutually perpendicular axes about which the moment of inertia of a body is a maximum.

principal boy *n.* The leading young male character in a pantomime, played by a woman. Compare **dame.**

principal focus *n.* A focal point *(see).*

prin·ci·pal·i·ty (prín-si-pál-əti) *n., pl.* **-ties. 1.** A territory ruled by a prince or from which a prince derives his title. **2.** The position, authority, or jurisdiction of a prince; sovereignty. **3.** *Plural.* In medieval angelology, one of the nine orders of angels. See **angel.**

principal parts *pl.n.* In traditional grammars of inflected languages, the primary forms of a verb from which all other forms may be derived. In English, the principal parts are generally considered to be the present infinitive *(play, eat),* the past tense *(played, ate),* the past participle *(played, eaten),* and the present participle *(playing, eating).* **Note:** In this dictionary, all inflected forms of verbs are given. For regular verbs, this includes, in addition to the principal parts, the third-person singular form *(plays, eats),* which is listed following the present participle.

prin·cip·i·um (prin-síppi-əm) *n., pl.* **-ia** (-ə). A principle, especially one that is basic. [Latin, basis, origin, PRINCIPLE.]

prin·ci·ple (prín-sip'l) *n. Abbr.* **prin. 1.** A basic truth, law, or assumption: *the principles of democracy.* **2. a.** A rule or standard, especially of good behaviour. **b.** Moral or ethical standards or judgments collectively. **3.** A fixed or predetermined policy or mode of action: *acting on the principle of every man for himself.* **4.** A basic, essential, quality or element determining intrinsic nature or characteristic behaviour. **5.** A scientific rule or law concerning, for example: **a.** Natural phenomena: *the principle of relativity.* **b.** Mechanical processes: *the principle of jet propulsion.* **6.** A basic source; an origin. **7.** A constituent imparting a distinctive character. **—in principle.** With regard to the idea or proposal in itself, rather than the practicalities: *In principle I'd love to come, but I'm afraid I'm too ill.* —See Usage note at **principal.** [Middle English, origin, commencement, hence fundamental quality or truth, modification of Old French *principe,* from Latin *principium,* from *princeps,* first. See **prince.**]

prin·ci·pled (prín-sip'ld) *adj.* Motivated by or based on moral or ethical principles.

prink (pringk) *v.* **prinked, prinking, prinks.** *—tr.* To adorn (oneself) in a showy manner. *—intr.* To primp. [Probably alteration of PRANK (adorn).] **—prink·er** *n.*

print (print) *n.* **1.** A mark or impression made in or upon a surface by pressure: *the print of footsteps in the sand.* **2. a.** A device or implement, such as a stamp, die, or seal, used to press markings on or into a surface. **b.** Something formed or marked by such a device: *a print of butter.* **3. a.** Lettering or other impressions produced in ink from type by a printing press or other means. **b.** Matter, such as newspaper publications, produced by such a process. **c.** The state or form of matter so produced. **d.** A newspaper or periodical. **4.** A design or picture transferred from an engraved plate, wood block, lithographic stone, or other medium. **5.** A photographic image transferred to paper or a similar surface, usually from a negative. **6.** A fabric or garment with a dyed pattern that has been pressed onto it, usually by engraved rollers. **7.** A fingerprint. **—in print. 1.** In printed or published form. **2.** Still offered for sale by the publisher: *books in print.* **—out of print.** No longer offered for sale by the publisher.

~*v.* **printed, printing, prints.** *—tr.* **1.** To press (a mark or design, for example) onto or into a surface. **2.** To make an impression on or in (a surface) with a stamp, seal, die, or similar device. **3.** To press (a stamp or similar device) onto or into a surface to leave a marking. **4.** To produce by means of pressed type on a paper surface, with or as if with a printing press. **5.** To offer in printed form; publish. **6.** To write in unjoined characters similar to those commonly used in print. **7.** To impress firmly in the mind or memory. **8.** To produce (a positive photograph) by passing light through a negative onto sensitised paper. *—intr.* **1.** To work as a printer. **2.** To write in unjoined characters similar to those commonly used in print. **3.** To produce or receive an impression, marking, or image. **4.** To produce a book, newspaper, or the like, by printing. [Middle English *pri(e)nte, pre(i)nte,* from Old French *preinte,* from the past participle of *preindre,* to press, from Latin *premere.*]

print. printing.

print·a·ble (príntəb'l) *adj.* **1.** Capable of being printed or of producing a print. **2.** Regarded as fit for publication.

printed circuit *n.* An electronic circuit in which the conducting connections are formed by depositing a metal, such as copper, in predetermined patterns on an insulating substrate. Other materials, especially semiconductors, may also be deposited to form various electronic components.

print·er (príntər) *n.* **1.** A person who operates a printing press. **2.** A typesetter. **3.** Loosely, a person involved in the business of printing. **4.** One that prints. **5.** The part of a word processor or computer that produces printed matter.

printer's devil *n.* An apprentice in a printing establishment.

print·er·y (príntəri) *n., pl.* **-ies.** *U.S.* **1.** A place where typographic printing is done. **2.** A factory where fabrics are printed.

print·ing (príntïng) *n. Abbr.* **pr., print., ptg. 1.** The process, art, or business of producing printed material by means of inked type and a printing press or by similar means. **2. a.** The act of one that prints. **b.** Matter that is printed. **3.** All the copies of a book or

---

SPREADING THE WORD QUICKLY AND ACCURATELY
How letterpress printing opened up mass communication

Printing, the repeated reproduction on paper of words in ink, gave man the means of mass communication. Suddenly, thousands of leaflets, pamphlets, or books could be reproduced in a fraction of the time it took a whole team of men to copy by hand a single publication.

Ancient Babylonians had put their information in seals of baked clay. The Egyptians wrote on papyrus; the Romans on parchment, an untanned leather. Medieval monks copied prayers and bibles on paper, once the secret of paper-making had been learned from the Chinese. But, until printing was invented, the main forms of communication were speech and drama.

In the 1040s in China, books were first printed from individual clay characters held in an iron frame. Metal type was used in Korea around 1400. The process – letterpress printing – was invented independently in Europe about 1440 by Johann Gutenberg of Mainz, west Germany. Using single moulds, he was able to cast, in a mixture of tin and lead, all the letters he wanted. Composed together into words and sentences and locked into frames and inked, they could be printed over and over again. Gutenberg's technique, printing from a raised surface, has scarcely changed, and has been used to produce most of the millions upon millions of books and newspapers printed since. The development of lithography in Germany (1798) made it simpler to reproduce colour pictures, and in 1895, the engraving of copper plates was adapted to reproduce photographs, by etching light and shade onto the plate in a series of dots.

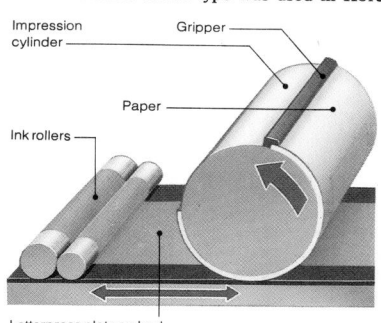

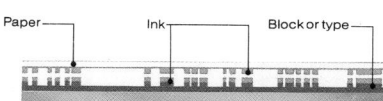

LETTERPRESS *In the oldest form of printing, letterpress, the letters and images to be reproduced are raised above the areas to be left blank. The type and plates are locked into a frame, placed on a flat bed, inked by rollers, and the paper to be printed is gently rolled across it. For high-speed printing of newspapers and magazines, the raised images are impressed on a curved, metal stereotype cast from a papier mâché mould, then fixed to a cylinder on a rotary press.*

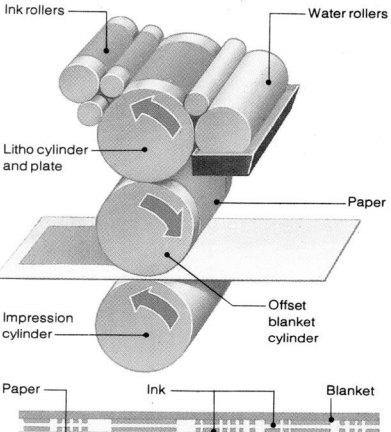

LITHOGRAPHY *Images are photographically exposed onto a flexible metal plate, which is developed chemically so that image areas accept greasy ink and non-image areas only water (grease and water repel each other). The plate is wetted and inked and the image printed onto paper. In offset lithography, the image is transferred to a rubber blanket and then onto the paper.*

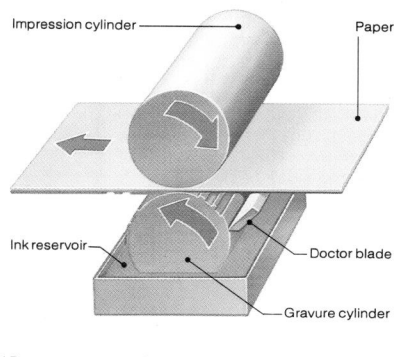

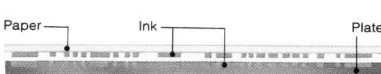

PHOTOGRAVURE *Printing images are exposed photographically onto a plate or copper cylinder, which is then etched into cells or recesses. The cylinder runs in an ink reservoir, which fills the recesses with ink. A "doctor" blade wipes off surface ink, then the image is printed on paper carried by an impression cylinder. The deeper, ink-filled, cells create the darker areas.*

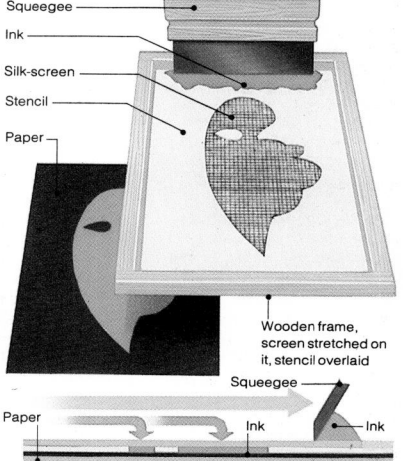

SILK-SCREEN *A process used for advertising and display work. A stencil to blank out the non-image areas is hand-cut or photographically reproduced. A screen of silk, nylon, or metal mesh is stretched over a frame, and the stencil laid on it. Ink is forced with a rubber squeegee through the screen and onto the paper. The process is repeated for each different colour used.*

other publication that are printed at one time. Compare **edition.** **4.** Written unjoined characters resembling those appearing in print.

printing office *n.* An establishment where printed material is produced, especially one that is officially authorised.

printing press *n.* A machine that transfers lettering or images by the contact of various forms of inked surface with paper or similar material fed into it. Also called "press". See **flat-bed press, rotary press, web press.**

print out *intr.v.* To print as a computer function; produce print-out. —*tr.v.* To produce (information) as print-out.

print-out (prínt-owt) *n.* The printed output of a computer.

print run *n.* The number of copies printed during a continuous operation of a printing press.

print shop *n.* A printers' workplace.

pri·or[1] (prī́-ər) *adj.* **1.** Preceding in time or order: *a prior commitment.* **2.** Preceding in importance or value: *a prior consideration.* —**prior to.** Before; earlier than. [Latin. See **prior** (cleric).]

prior[2] *n.* **1.** A monk in charge of a priory, or ranking next under the abbot of an abbey. **2.** One of the ruling magistrates of the medieval Italian republic of Florence. [Middle English *pri(o)ur,* from Old English and Old French *prior,* both from Medieval Latin *prior,* from Late Latin, superior officer, administrator, from Latin, former, superior.] —**pri·or·ate** (-ət, -it) *n.* —**pri·or·ship** *n.*

pri·or·ess (prī́-ər-iss, -ess) *n.* A nun at the head of a priory or ranking next below an abbess in an abbey. [Middle English *prioresse,* from Old French, feminine of PRIOR.]

pri·or·i·ty (prī-órrəti || *U.S. also* -áwrəti) *n., pl.* **-ties. 1.** Precedence, especially as established by order of importance or urgency. Also used adjectivally: *priority booking.* **2. a.** An established right to precedence. **b.** Anything which has or claims precedence: *Accuracy was not one of her priorities.* **c.** The right of a vehicle to proceed rather than give way to other traffic. **3.** A preceding or coming earlier in time. [Middle English *priorite,* from Old French, from Medieval Latin *priōritās* (stem *priōritāt-*), from Latin *prior,* PRIOR.]

pri·or·y (prī́-əri) *n., pl.* **-ies.** A monastery or convent governed by a prior or prioress. [Middle English *priorie,* from Anglo-French, from Medieval Latin *priōria,* from PRIOR.]

Pri·pet (préepit). *Russian* **Pri·pyat** (pri-pyát). River in the western U.S.S.R. Rising near the Polish border in northwest Ukraine, it flows 800 kilometres (500 miles) generally eastwards through the Pripet Marshes to join the river Dnepr near Kiev.

prise, prize (prīz) *tr.v.* **prised, prising, prises.** To move, open, or force with or as if with a lever.
~*n.* Leverage. [Middle English *prisen* (verb, from noun), from Old French *prise,* lever, instrument for forcing, from past participle of *prendre,* from Latin *prehendere,* to seize.]

prism (prízz'm) *n.* **1.** *Mathematics.* A polyhedron having parallel, congruent polygons as bases and parallelograms as sides. **2.** A homogeneous transparent solid, usually with triangular bases and rectangular sides, used to produce or analyse a continuous spectrum. **3.** A crystalline solid having three or more similar faces parallel to a single axis. [Late Latin *prisma,* from Greek, "a thing sawn", prism, from *priein*†, to saw.]

pris·mat·ic (priz-máttik) *adj.* Also **pris·mat·i·cal** (-'l). **1.** Of, pertaining to, or resembling a prism. **2.** Refracting light as a prism does. **3.** Multicoloured; iridescent. —**pris·mat·i·cal·ly** *adv.*

pris·ma·toid (prízmə-toyd) *n. Mathematics.* A polyhedron having all vertices lying in one of two parallel planes. [New Latin *prismatoides* : Greek *prisma* (stem *prismat-*), PRISM + -OID.] —**pris·ma·toi·dal** (-tóyd'l) *adj.*

pris·moid (príz-moyd) *n.* A prismatoid whose bases and sides are equal in number and whose faces are parallelograms or trapezoids. [French *prismoïde* : *prisme,* prism, from Late Latin *prisma,* PRISM + -OID.] —**pris·moi·dal** *adj.*

pris·on (prízz'n) *n.* **1.** A place where persons convicted or accused of crimes are confined; a jail. **2.** Any place or condition of forced confinement or constraint. **3.** Imprisonment.
~*tr.v.* **prisoned, -oning, -ons.** *Rare.* To imprison. [Middle English *priso(u)n, prisun,* from Old French *prison,* "seizure, imprisonment", from Latin *pre(n)siō,* contraction from *prehensiō* (stem *prehensiōn-*), from *prehendere,* to seize.]

pris·on·er (príz-nər, prízz'n-ər) *n.* **1.** A person held in custody, captivity, or a condition of forcible restraint, especially while awaiting trial or serving a prison sentence. **2.** One deprived of freedom of action or expression: *a prisoner of fate.*

prisoner of conscience *n.* A person imprisoned for political or religious views. Compare **political prisoner.**

prisoner of war *n. Abbr.* **POW, P.O.W.** A person, especially a member of the armed services, taken captive by or surrendering to enemy forces during wartime.

pris·sy (príssi) *adj.* **-sier, -siest.** Finicky, fussy, and prudish. [Blend of PRIM and SISSY.] —**pris·si·ly** *adv.* —**pris·si·ness** *n.*

pris·tine (príss-teen, -tīn || *U.S. also* pri-stéen) *adj.* **1.** Of, pertaining to, or typical of the earliest time or condition; primitive or original. **2. a.** Remaining in a pure state; uncorrupted. **b.** Loosely, not soiled; fresh; clean. [Latin *prīstinus,* original.]

prith·ee (prí-thi, -thee || *chiefly U.S.* -thee) *interj. Archaic.* Please; I pray thee. [Earlier *preythe,* from (I) *pray thee.*]

priv. private.

pri·va·cy (prívvə-si, prī́və-) *n., pl.* **-cies. 1.** The condition of being secluded or isolated from the view of, or from contact with, others. **2.** Concealment; secrecy.

pri·vate (prī́-vət, -vit) *adj. Abbr.* **priv., pvt. 1.** Secluded from the sight, presence, or intrusion of others: *a private bathroom.* **2. a.** Of or confined to one person; personal: *private opinions.* **b.** Exclusive to a small group, usually a pair: *a private joke.* **3.** Not available for public use, control, or participation: *a private club.* **4.** Belonging to a particular person or persons, as opposed to the public or the government: *private property.* **5.** Not holding an official or public position. **6.** Not public; intimate; secret: *private tragedy.*
~*n.* **1.** *Abbr.* **Pvt.** A serviceman of the lowest rank in many armies, marine corps, and civilian organisations, ranking below lance-corporal in the British army. **2.** *Plural. Informal.* The genitals. —**in private.** Secretly; confidentially. [Middle English *privat,* from Latin *prīvātus,* not belonging to the state, not in public life, deprived of office, from the past participle of *prīvāre,* to deprive, release, from *prīvus,* single, individual, deprived of.] —**pri·vate·ly** *adv.* —**pri·vate·ness** *n.*

private bill *n.* A bill put before a legislative body, dealing with the affairs of an individual or organisation, such as a local authority, rather than with national matters.

private carrier *n.* A carrier by land, water, or air, such as an airline company, which reserves the right to decide whether it will carry particular passengers or goods. Compare **common carrier.**

private detective *n.* A privately employed detective as distinguished from one belonging to a public police force. Also informally called "private eye".

private enterprise *n.* **1.** Business activities unregulated by state ownership or control; privately owned business in general. **2.** A privately owned business enterprise, especially one in a system of free enterprise or laissez-faire capitalism. **3.** Loosely, capitalism.

pri·va·teer (prīvə-téer) *n.* **1.** A ship privately owned and manned but authorised by a government during wartime to attack enemy vessels. **2.** The commander or any crew member of such a ship.
~*intr.v.* **privateered, -teering, -teers.** To sail or serve as a privateer. [From PRIVATE (adjective) by analogy with *volunteer.*]

private income *n.* An income derived from trusts, investments, or the like, rather than from employment.

private law *n.* The branch of law which deals with or affects the rights of, and the relations between, private individuals. Compare **public law.**

private limited company *n. Finance.* A limited, liability company whose shares are distributed privately rather than by public subscription and can be transferred only under special conditions. Compare **public limited company.**

private member *n.* A member of the British Parliament who does not hold office in the government or in his party.

private member's bill *n.* In Britain, a bill presented to Parliament sponsored by a private member rather than the government.

private parts *pl.n.* The genitals. Used euphemistically.

private patient *n. Chiefly British.* A patient who meets the costs of medical treatment either by direct payment or through private insurance rather than through the National Health Service.

private practice *n. Chiefly British.* Medical practice, or a business based upon it, in which treatment is given and paid for by private arrangement rather than through the National Health Service.

private school *n.* A school run and supported by private individuals or by a charity or other body rather than by a government or public agency, and usually charging fees. See **public school.**

private sector *n.* The section of a state's economy that is under the control of privately owned enterprises, rather than of government departments or public corporations. Compare **public sector.**

pri·va·tion (prī-váysh'n) *n.* **1. a.** Lack of the basic necessities or comforts of life. **b.** The condition resulting from such lack. **2.** An act, condition, or result of deprivation or loss. [Middle English *privacion,* from Old French *privation,* from Latin *prīvātiō* (stem *prīvātiōn-*), from *prīvāre,* to deprive. See **private.**]

pri·vat·ise, pri·vat·ize (prī́-vət-īz, -vit-) *v.* **-ised, -ising, -ises.** —*tr.* To transfer or sell (public assets, such as national industries) to private ownership. —*intr.* To transfer public assets to private ownership. —**pri·vat·i·sa·tion** (-ī-záysh'n || *U.S.* -i-) *n.*

priv·a·tive (prívvətiv, prī-váytiv) *adj.* **1.** Causing deprivation, lack, or loss. **2.** *Grammar.* Altering the meaning of a term from positive to negative.
~*n. Grammar.* A privative prefix or suffix, such as *a-, non-, un-,* or *-less.* [Latin *prīvātīvus,* from *prīvāre,* to deprive. See **private.**] —**priv·a·tive·ly** *adv.*

priv·et (prívvit) *n.* Any of several trees or shrubs of the genus *Ligustrum,* having pointed leaves, clusters of white tubular flowers, and black to purple berries; especially *L. ovalifolium* which is widely planted as hedging. [16th century : origin obscure.]

privet hawk *n.* A large hawk moth, *Sphinx ligustri,* the larvae of which feed mostly on privet and lilac.

priv·i·lege (prívvilij) *n.* **1. a.** A special advantage, immunity, permission, right, or benefit granted to or enjoyed by an individual, race, sex, class, or caste. **b.** Such a right or advantage held as a result of status or rank, and exercised to the exclusion or detriment of others. **2.** The principle of granting and maintaining privileges: *a society based on privilege.* **3.** Any of the basic rights to which a nation's citizen is entitled by the constitution. **4.** The rights and immunities of members of Parliament enjoyed by virtue of their position, such as immunity from libel charges based on allegations made within the legislative chambers. **5.** The right extended to or claimed by priests, lawyers, and certain public officials to withhold confidential information from the police or tribunals. **6.** The right of the press to publish defamatory material when reporting court or parliamen-

PRONUNCIATION KEY

a, trap; aa, father; ai, fair; ar, star; aw, lawn; ay, play; b, bb, stab; rubber; ch, church; ck, ticket; d, dd, dead; ladder; e, dress; ee, bee; er, defer; ew, few; ewr, pure; ə, about; ər, letter; f, ff, fife; differ; g, gg, giggle; h, hat; i, kit; ī, price; īr, fire; j, judge; k, kick; l, ll, let; 'l, needle; m, mm, man; n, nn, no; 'n, sudden; ng, thing; o, lot; ō, no; ŏŏ, foot; ōō, shoe; oor, poor; ow, cow; owr, hour; oy, boy; p, pp, pepper; r, rr, red; s, ss, sauce; sh, ship; t, tt, totter; th, thick; th, this; smooth; u, cut; ur, turn; v, vv, valve; w, wet; y, yes; z, zz, zebra; zh, vision; pleasure

IN FOREIGN WORDS:

aN, oN, Saint-Saëns; hl, Llanelli; Hluhluwe; kh, loch; lough; Khaled

STRESS MARK:

ín-sīt, insight; in-sī́t, incite

tary proceedings in which such material is presented. **7.** *U.S. Finance.* Any option to buy or sell a stock, including **put, call, spread,** and **straddle** *(all of which see).* —See Synonyms at **right**.

~*tr.v.* **privileged, -leging, -leges. 1.** To grant a privilege to. **2.** To free or exempt. Used with *from.* [Middle English, from Old French, from Latin *prīvilēgium,* law affecting an individual, prerogative : *prīvus,* single, individual + *lēx* (stem *lēg-*), law.]

priv·i·leged (prĭvvilĭjd) *adj.* **1.** Enjoying a privilege or having privileges: *a privileged childhood.* **2.** Protected against any action for defamation: *a privileged remark.* **3.** Protected against demands for publication or access: *privileged information.*

priv·i·ty (prĭvvəti) *n., pl.* **-ties. 1.** Knowledge of something private or secret shared between individuals, especially with the implication of approval or consent. **2.** *Law.* **a.** A relationship between parties that is held to be sufficiently close and direct to support a legal claim on behalf of or against another person with whom this relationship exists. **b.** A successive or mutual interest in or relationship to the same property. [Middle English *privete, privite,* a secret, privacy, from Old French, from Medieval Latin *prīvitās* (stem *prīvitāt-*), from Latin *prīvus,* single, private.]

priv·y (prĭvvi) *adj.* **-ier, -iest. 1.** Sharing in or having knowledge of something private or secret. Used with *to: privy to another's thoughts and desires.* **2.** *Rare.* Belonging or proper to a person (such as the British sovereign) in his private rather than his official capacity: *Privy Council.* **3.** *Archaic.* Concealed; secret.

~*n., pl.* **privies. 1. a.** *Archaic & U.S.* A lavatory. **b.** An outhouse. **2.** *Law.* Any of the parties having an interest in the same matter. [Middle English *prive,* secret, private, acquainted with, from Old French *prive,* from Latin *prīvātus,* PRIVATE.] —**priv·i·ly** *adv.*

Privy Council *n. Abbr.* **P.C. 1.** A council of the British sovereign that now consists of all current and former cabinet ministers and certain senior legal and ecclesiastical officials in private capacity and others appointed as a high honour, membership being for life. In certain cases its Judicial Committee acts as a supreme appellate court in the Commonwealth. **2.** A similar council in various other countries which serves as an advisory body to the head of state. —**Privy Councillor** *n.*

Privy Purse *n. Sometimes small* **p,** *small* **p. 1.** The sum of money assigned to the British sovereign, or any of various other sovereigns, for the private expenses of the royal household. **2.** The official in charge of the private expenses of the British royal household. Also officially called "Keeper of the Privy Purse".

Privy Seal *n.* In Britain, a royal seal attached to certain documents as proof that they are issued by royal authority.

prix fixe (prēe fĭks, fēeks) *n., pl.* **prix fixes** *(pronounced as singular).* **1.** A **table d'hôte** *(see).* **2.** The price at which a table d'hôte meal is offered. Compare **à la carte**. [French, "fixed price".]

prize¹ (prīz) *n.* **1.** Something offered or won as an award for achieving superiority or excellence in competition with others. **2.** Something offered for winning in a raffle, lottery, or other game of chance. **3.** Anything worth striving for or aspiring to.

~*adj.* **1.** Offered or given as a prize: *a prize cup.* **2.** Given a prize, or likely to win a prize: *a prize cow.* **3.** Worthy of a prize; first-class. Often used ironically: *a prize idiot.*

~*tr.v.* **prized, prizing, prizes. 1.** To value highly; esteem, cherish, or treasure. **2.** *Rare.* To estimate the worth of; appraise; evaluate. —See Synonyms at **appreciate**. [Middle English *pris* (noun), variant of PRICE; verb, Middle English, from Old French *preisier* (stem *pris-*), to PRAISE.]

prize² *n.* **1.** Something seized by force or taken as booty; especially, an enemy ship and cargo captured at sea during wartime. **2.** Something valuable taken from another. **3.** The act of seizing; capture. [Middle English *pris(e),* from Old French *prise,* from Vulgar Latin *pre(n)sa* (unattested), "something seized", from the past participle of Latin *pre(he)ndere,* to seize.]

prize.³ Variant of **prise**.

prize court *n. Law.* A court authorised to determine and allocate claimants' shares to goods seized at sea during wartime.

prize fight *n.* A match fought between professional boxers for money. —**prize fighter** *n.* —**prize fighting** *n.*

prize money *n.* **1.** Money constituting a prize or prizes. **2.** Money representing a part of the value of ships or property captured at sea, formerly allocated for division between those taking part in the capture. In this sense, also called "prize bounty".

prize ring *n.* **1.** The platform enclosed by ropes in which contending boxers meet. **2.** Professional boxing. Preceded by *the.*

p.r.n. *Medicine.* as the situation demands [Latin *pro re nata.*]

pro¹ (prō) *n., pl.* **pros.** *Abbr.* **p. 1.** An argument in favour of something; an affirmative consideration. Used chiefly in the phrase *pros and cons.* **2.** One who supports a proposal or takes the affirmative side in debate.

~*prep.* In favour of.

~*adv.* In favour of something; affirmatively.

~*adj.* Favouring; supporting. [Middle English, from Latin *prō,* for.]

pro² *n., pl.* **pros.** *Informal.* **1.** A professional, especially in sports. **2.** An expert in any field of endeavour. **3.** A prostitute.

~*adj. Informal.* Professional: *pro football.* [Short for PROFESSIONAL.]

pro–¹ *prefix.* Indicates: **1.** Favour or support; for example, **prorevolutionary. 2.** Acting as; for example, **proconsul, properdin.** *Note:* Many compounds other than those entered here may be formed with *pro-.* In this dictionary, when forming compounds, *pro-* is nor-

mally joined with the following element without space or hyphen: *profascist.* However, many users prefer the hyphenated form, especially when the second element begins with a capital letter: *pro-American.* It is also preferable to use the hyphen when the second element begins with *o* or when forming the compound brings together three or more vowels that would be confusing to read: *pro-aesthetic.* [In borrowed Latin compounds, *prō-* indicates: **1.** Forwards, forth, in public, as in **project, proclaim. 2.** Forwards and downwards, as in **profligate. 3.** Away, as in **prodigal. 4.** In front of, before, as in **prohibit. 5.** Anterior, before, in anticipation of, as in **provide. 6.** Onwards, forwards, as in **progress. 7.** Extending out, as in **prolong. 8.** Substituting for, acting as, as in **pronominal. 9.** On behalf of, for, as in **prosit. 10.** Intensified action, as in **promiscuous.** Latin *prō-,* from *prō,* before, in front of, according to, for.]

pro–² *prefix.* Indicates before in time or position, or forwards; for example, **prophage, procarp, procephalic.** [Greek *pro,* before, in front of, forward.]

pro., Pro. professional.

P.R.O. 1. Public Records Office. **2.** public relations officer.

pro·a (prō-ə) *n.* A swift Malayan sailing boat with a triangular sail and a single outrigger. [Earlier *parao, prau,* from Malay *pĕrāhŭ,* probably from Marathi *pąḍāv.*]

pro-am (prō-ám) *adj. Chiefly U.S.* Of, pertaining to, or designating a sports competition in which both professional and amateur players take part. [*professional* + *amateur.*]

pro and con *adj.* Also **pro and contra.** For and against.

~*prep.* For and against. See **pro.** [Latin *pro,* for + *contra,* against.]

prob. 1. probable; probably. **2.** problem.

prob·a·bi·lism (prόbbəb'l-iz'm) *n.* **1.** *Philosophy.* The doctrine that probability is a sufficient basis for belief and action, since certainty in knowledge is unattainable. **2.** *Roman Catholic Church.* A principle that when there is doubt as to the moral rectitude of an action, that opinion which favours liberty may be followed, provided that it is theologically probable, even though the contrary may be equally, or even more, probable. —**prob·a·bi·list** *n.* —**prob·a·bi·lis·tic** (-ĭstĭk) *adj.*

prob·a·bil·i·ty (prόbbə-bĭllə́ti) *n., pl.* **-ties. 1.** The quality or condition of being probable; likelihood. **2.** A probable situation, condition, or event. **3.** *Statistics.* A number expressing the likelihood of occurrence of a specific event, such as the ratio of the number of experimental results that would produce the event to the total number of results considered possible. If the probability is 1 the event is certain to happen, if it is 0 it is certain not to happen. —**in all probability.** Most probably; very likely.

probability density function *n. Statistics.* A function that enables the probability for any value or interval within a range to be determined and formulas for parameters to be established. Also called "density", "density function".

probability theory *n.* A branch of mathematics dealing with the statistical evaluation of the probability of random occurrences.

prob·a·ble (prόbbəb'l) *adj. Abbr.* **prob. 1.** Likely to happen or to be

---

probability

HEADS OR TAILS?

The mathematics behind the toss of a coin

Blaise Pascal, a 17th-century French mathematician, was one of the first scholars to study the laws of chance and so open the way for the science of statistics. The number triangle below – which gives the chances of each outcome possible when one or more coins are tossed together – was devised by him and is known as Pascal's triangle. In each row each number is the sum of the two above. The "6 coins" row shows the probabilities if six coins are tossed. The sum of the numbers in the row, 64, is the total number of possible results. One possible result is six heads and no tails; the chance of this happening is 1 in 64. Another possible result is five heads and one tail; the Pascal triangle shows that its probability is 6 in 64.

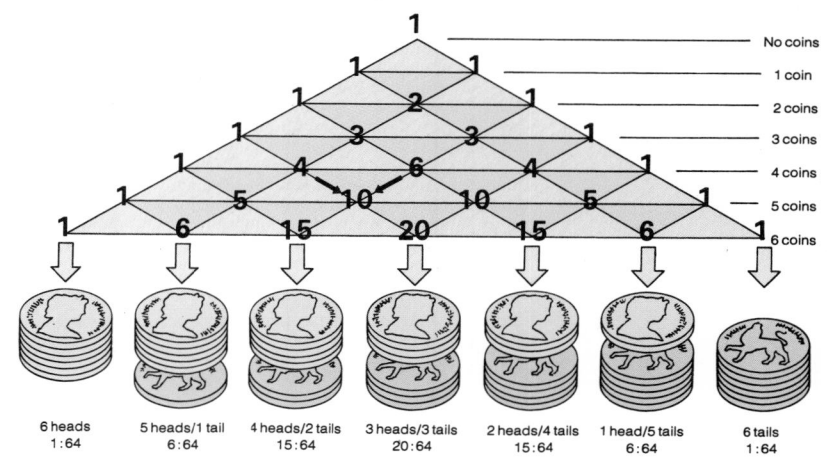

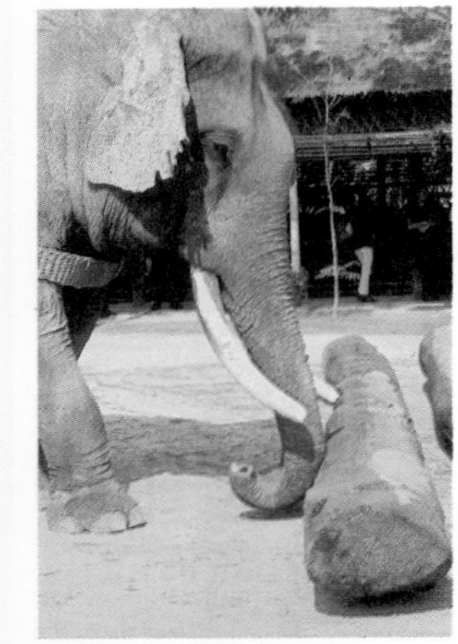

proboscis *The only surviving member of the scientific order* Proboscidea – *the trunked animals – is the elephant. It uses its muscular proboscis to lift food and water to its mouth, and is used in Asia as a ceremonial means of transport and in the timber industry.*

true. 2. Relatively or most likely but not certain; plausible. 3. *Theology.* Of or pertaining to moral opinions and actions for the lawfulness of which intrinsic reasons or extrinsic authority may be adduced; possible; provable.
~*n. Informal.* A candidate or competitor who is likely to be selected or successful. [Middle English, from Old French, from Latin *probābilis,* provable, laudable, from *probāre,* to approve, PROVE.]

probable cause *n. Law.* Reasonable grounds for belief that an accused person is guilty as charged and accordingly that further legal action is justified.

prob·a·bly (próbbəbli; *informally also* prób-bli, próbbli, próbbəli) *adv. Abbr.* **prob.** Most likely; very likely; presumably.

pro·band (prṓ-band) *n.* In genealogical or medical surveys, the ancestor or member of a family who is adopted as the starting point for the purposes of a study. [Latin *probandus,* gerundive of *probāre,* to test.]

pro·bang (prṓ-bang) *n.* A flexible rod used in surgery to displace foreign bodies stuck in the oesophagus. [Alteration (influenced by PROBE) of earlier *provang* (so named by the inventor).]

pro·bate (prṓ-bayt, -bət, -bit) *adj. U.S.* Of or pertaining to a probate court or its action.
~*n.* 1. Legal establishment of the validity of a will. 2. A document certifying such validity. 3. *Chiefly U.S.* The right to validate wills.
~*tr.v.* **probated, -bating, -bates.** *U.S.* To establish the validity of (a will). [Middle English *probat,* from Latin *probātum,* something proved, from *probāre,* to examine, demonstrate as good, PROVE.]

probate court *n. U.S.* A court limited to the jurisdiction of probating wills and administering estates.

pro·ba·tion (prə-báysh'n, prō-) *n.* 1. A trial period in which a person's fitness for membership in a working or social group is tested. 2. *Law.* The action of suspending the sentence of one convicted of an offence and granting provisional freedom, under the supervision of a probation officer, on the promise of good behaviour. 3. *Chiefly U.S.* A trial period in which a student is permitted to redeem poor results or bad conduct. 4. The status of a person on probation. 5. The act or process of testing or being tested. [Middle English *probacioun,* from Old French *probation,* from Latin *probātiō* (stem *probātiōn-*), from *probāre,* to try, PROVE.] —**pro·ba·tion·al, pro·ba·tion·ar·y** (-ri, -əri || -erri) *adj.* —**pro·ba·tion·al·ly** *adv.*

pro·ba·tion·er (prə-báysh'n-ər, prō-) *n.* A person on probation prior to membership of a body.

probation officer *n.* A social worker who under the direction of a court supervises, and gives support to an offender on probation.

pro·ba·tive (prṓbə-tiv) *adj.* Also **pro·ba·to·ry** (-tri, -təri, prə-báytəri, prō-). 1. Serving to test, try, or prove. 2. Furnishing evidence or proof. [Middle English *probatiffe,* from Latin *probātīvus,* of proof, from *probāre,* to try, PROVE.]

probe (prōb) *n.* 1. Any object or device used to investigate an unknown configuration or condition. 2. A slender, flexible instrument used to explore a wound or body cavity. 3. The act of exploring or searching with the aid of such an instrument. 4. An investigation into the nature of something; especially, an investigation conducted by a legislative committee into corrupt practices. Used especially in journalism. 5. *Electronics.* An electrical lead attached to a measuring or detecting instrument, used for testing circuits. 6. Loosely, any act of examining or testing. 7. A **space probe** *(see).*
~*v.* **probed, probing, probes.** —*tr.* 1. To explore with a probe. 2. To test or examine: *probed their defences; probing her motives.* 3. To investigate (a matter, especially a public scandal) throroughly; delve into. —*intr.* To conduct an exploratory investigation; search. [Medieval Latin *proba,* examination, from Late Latin, proof, test, from Latin *probāre,* to test, PROVE.] —**prob·er** *n.*

pro·bi·ty (prṓbəti) *n.* Complete and confirmed integrity; uprightness. See Synonyms at **honesty.** [Old French *probité,* from Latin *probitās* (stem *probitāt-*), goodness, honesty, from *probus,* good, honest, virtuous.]

prob·lem (prób-ləm, -lem, -lim) *n. Abbr.* **prob.** 1. A question or situation that presents uncertainty, perplexity, or difficulty. 2. A person who is difficult to deal with. 3. A question put forward for consideration, discussion, or solution.
~*adj.* 1. Difficult to deal with or handle: *a problem child.* 2. Dealing with a social or moral problem: *a problem play.* [Middle English *probleme,* from Old French, from Latin *problēma,* from Greek *problēma,* "thing thrown forward", projection, obstacle, problem, from *proballein,* to throw forward : *pro-,* forward + *ballein,* to throw.]

prob·lem·at·i·cal (prób-lə-máttik'l, -li-, -le-) *adj.* Also **prob·lem·at·ic** (-máttik). 1. Posing a problem; difficult to solve. 2. Open to doubt; debatable. —**prob·lem·at·i·cal·ly** *adv.*

pro·bos·cid·i·an (prṓ-boss-íddi-ən) *n.* Also **pro·bos·ci·de·an** (-íddi-ən, -i-dée-ən). An animal belonging to the Proboscidea, an order of mammals that is characterised by a trunk or proboscis and includes the elephant. —**pro·bos·cid·i·an** *adj.*

pro·bos·cis (prō-bóssiss, prə-) *n., pl.* **-cises** or **-boscides** (-bóssi-deez). 1. A long, flexible snout or trunk, such as that of an elephant. 2. A slender, tubular feeding and sucking structure of some insects. 3. A human nose, especially a prominent one. Used humorously. [Latin, from Greek *proboskis* : *pro-,* in front + *boskein,* to feed.]

proboscis monkey *n.* A monkey, *Nasalis larvatus,* native to the forests of Borneo, the male of which has a large, long nose.

proboscis worm *n.* A marine work; the **nemertean** *(see).*

proc. 1. proceedings. 2. process.

pro·caine hydrochloride (prṓ-kayn) *n.* A white crystalline powder, $C_{13}H_{20}O_2N_2 \cdot HCl$, used as a local anaesthetic in medicine and dentistry. A trademark is "Novocain". [PRO- (in place of) + (CO)-CAINE.]

pro·cam·bi·um (prō-kámbi-əm) *n. Botany.* A layer of meristematic tissue from which the vascular tissue is formed. [PRO- (before) + CAMBIUM.] —**pro·cam·bi·al** *adj.*

pro·carp (prṓ-kaarp) *n. Botany.* A specialised female reproductive organ in certain algae. [New Latin *procarpium* : PRO- (before) + -CARP.]

procaryote. Variant of **prokaryote.**

pro·ca·the·dral (prṓ-kə-thée̋drəl) *n.* A church functioning as the cathedral church of a diocese.

pro·ce·dur·al (prə-séejər-əl, prō-, -séed-yər-) *adj.* Of or pertaining to procedure, especially of a court of law or parliamentary body.

pro·ce·dure (prə-séejər, prō-, -séed-yər) *n.* 1. A manner of proceeding; a way of performing or effecting something. 2. An act composed of steps; a course of action. 3. A set of established forms or methods for conducting the affairs of a business, legislative body, or court of law. [French *procédure,* from Old French, from *proceder,* PROCEED.]

pro·ceed (prō-séed, prə-) *intr.v.* **-ceeded, -ceeding, -ceeds.** 1. a. To go forwards or onwards, especially after an interruption; continue. b. To resume speaking. 2. To undertake and carry on some action or process. 3. To move on in an orderly manner. 4. a. To come into being; arise. b. To issue forth; originate. Used of the Holy Spirit. c. To come out; emerge: *cries proceeding from next door.* 5. To institute and conduct a legal action. Used with *against.* [Middle English *proceden,* from Old French *proceder,* from Latin *prōcēdere* : *prō-,* forward + *cēdere,* to go.] —**pro·ceed·er** *n.*

pro·ceed·ing (prō-séeding, prə-) *n.* 1. A course of action; a procedure. 2. A continuing of an action. 3. *Plural.* A sequence of events occurring at a particular place or time. 4. *Plural. Abbr.* **proc.** A record of business carried on by a society or other organisation; minutes. 5. *Law.* a. *Plural.* Litigation. b. The instituting or conducting of litigation.

pro·ceeds (prṓ-seedz) *pl.n.* The amount of money derived from a commercial or fund-raising venture; profits; yield.

pro·ce·phal·ic (prṓ-se-fál-ik, -ke-, -sə-) *adj. Anatomy.* Pertaining or belonging to the front of the head. [PRO- (in front) + -CEPHALIC.]

proc·ess[1] (prṓ-sess, -siss || *chiefly U.S.* próss-ess, -əss) *n. Abbr.* **proc.** 1. A system of operations in the production of something. 2. A series of actions, changes, or functions that bring about an end or result: *the peacemaking process.* 3. The course or passage of time. 4. Ongoing movement; progression. 5. *Law.* a. A summons or writ ordering a defendant to appear in court. b. The total set or number of summonses or writs issued in a particular proceeding. c. The entire course of a judicial proceeding. 6. *Biology.* A part extending or projecting from an organ or organism; an appendage. 7. Any of various photomechanical or photoengraving methods.
~*tr.v.* **processed, -essing, -esses.** 1. To put through the steps of a prescribed procedure. 2. To prepare, treat, or convert by subjecting to some special process: *processed cheese; to process film.* 3. *Law.* To serve with a summons or writ. 4. To institute legal proceedings against; prosecute. 5. *Computing.* To subject (numbers, text, or other data) to modification by program.
~*adj. Abbr.* **proc.** 1. *Chiefly U.S.* Prepared or converted by a special treatment. 2. Made by or used in photomechanical or photoengraving methods: *a process print.* [Middle English *proces(se),* from Old French *proces,* from Latin *prōcessus,* from the past participle of *prōcēdere,* to PROCEED.]

pro·cess[2] (prə-séss, prō-) *intr.v.* **-cessed, -cessing, -cesses.** *Rare.* To move along or go in or as if in a procession. [Back-formation from PROCESSION.]

pro·ces·sion (prə-sésh'n) *n.* 1. The act of proceeding, moving along, or issuing forth. 2. a. A group of persons, vehicles, or objects moving along in an orderly and formal manner, usually in a long line. b. The movement of such a group. 3. Any continuous and orderly course: *the procession of the seasons.*
~*intr.v.* **processioned, -sioning, -sions.** *Rare.* To form or go in a procession. [Middle English, from Old French, from Late Latin *prōcessiō* (stem *prōcessiōn-*), religious procession, from Latin, a marching forward, from *prōcēdere,* to PROCEED.]

pro·ces·sion·al (prə-sésh'n 'l) *adj.* Of, pertaining to, or suitable for a procession.
~*n.* 1. A book containing the ritual observed during a religious procession. 2. A hymn sung when the clergy enter a church at the beginning of the service. 3. Any music intended to be played or sung during a procession. —**pro·ces·sion·al·ly** *adv.*

pro·ces·sor (prṓ-sess-ər, -siss- || *chiefly U.S.* pró-) *n.* 1. One who processes. 2. The **central processing unit** *(see)* of a computer.

process printing *n.* Printing from multiple, usually four, halftone images, each inked with a different colour such that the composite impression will reproduce the colours of the original.

pro·cess-serv·er (prṓ-sess-sérvər, -siss- || pró-) *n.* A sheriff's officer who delivers summonses or writs.

pro·cès-ver·bal (prō-sáy-vair-bál, -báal) *n., pl.* **-baux** (-bṓ). 1. An official record of diplomatic negotiations. 2. In France, a detailed official record of a legal charge or other proceedings. [French, "verbal proceedings", originally referring to evidence delivered orally by illiterate subaltern police officers.]

pro·chron·ism (prṓkrən-iz'm, prókrən-) *n.* An anachronism consisting in assigning something too early a date. Compare **parachronism.** [PRO- + Greek *khronos,* time + -ISM.]

pro•claim (prə-kláym, prō-) *tr.v.* **-claimed, -claiming, -claims. 1.** To announce officially and publicly; declare. **2.** To indicate unmistakably; make plain. **3.** To praise; extol. [Middle English *procla(y)men,* from Old French *proclamer,* from Latin *prōclāmāre* : *prō-,* forward, forth + *clāmāre,* to cry out.] **—pro•claim•er** *n.*

proc•la•ma•tion (prócklə-máysh'n) *n.* **1.** The act of proclaiming. **2.** Something proclaimed; especially, an official public announcement.

pro•clit•ic (prō-klíttik, prṓ-) *adj. Linguistics.* Forming an accentual unit with the following word and thus having no independent accent. Compare **enclitic.**
~*n.* A proclitic word. [New Latin *procliticus,* formed by analogy with Late Latin *encliticus,* ENCLITIC : Greek *pro-,* forward + *klinein,* to lean.]

pro•cliv•i•ty (prō-klívvəti, prə-) *n., pl.* **-ties.** A natural propensity or inclination; a predisposition. [Latin *prōclīvitās,* from *prōclīvus,* sloping forward : *prō-,* forward + *clīvus,* slope, hill.]

pro•con•sul (prṓ-kón-s'l) *n.* **1.** A provincial governor of consular rank in ancient Rome. **2.** A high administrator in any of various territories of the European colonial empires. [Middle English, from Latin, combined from *prō consule,* (one acting) for a consul : *prō-,* for + CONSUL.] **—pro•con•su•lar** (-sew-lər || -sə-) *adj.* **—pro•con•su•late** (-sew-lət, -lit || -sə-) *n.*

pro•cras•ti•nate (prō-krásti-nayt, prə-) *v.* **-nated, -nating, -nates.** *—intr.* To put off doing something until a future time. *—tr. Rare.* To postpone or delay needlessly. [Latin *prōcrāstināre,* "to put forward to tomorrow" : *prō-,* forward + *crāstinus,* of tomorrow, from *crās*†, tomorrow.] **—pro•cras•ti•na•tion** (-náysh'n) *n.* **—pro•cras•ti•na•tor** (-naytər) *n.*

pro•cre•ate (prṓ-kri-ayt, -áyt) *v.* **-ated, -ating, -ates.** *—tr.* **1.** To beget (offspring). **2.** To produce or create; originate. *—intr.* To beget offspring; reproduce. [Latin *prōcreāre* : *prō-,* forward, forth + *creāre,* to CREATE.] **—pro•cre•ant** (-ənt) *adj.* **—pro•cre•a•tion** (-áysh'n) *n.* **—pro•cre•a•tor** (-ər) *n.*

pro•cre•a•tive (prṓ-kri-aytiv, -áytiv) *adj.* **1.** Capable of reproducing; generative. **2.** Of or directed towards procreation: *procreative instinct.*

pro•crus•te•an (prō-krústi-ən, prə)- *adj.* Producing or designed to produce conformity by ruthless or arbitrary means. [After *Procrustes,* from Greek *Prokroustēs,* "stretcher", name of legendary robber who stretched or shortened captives to fit an iron bed.]

procrustean bed *n. Often capital* **P.** An arbitrary standard to which exact conformity is forced.

pro•cryp•tic (prō-kríptik) *adj. Zoology.* Having a pattern or coloration adapted for natural camouflage. [Probably PRO(TECT) + CRYPTIC.]

procto–, proct– *comb. form.* Indicates rectum or anus; for example, **proctology.** [Greek *prōktos,* anus.]

proc•tol•o•gy (prok-tólləji) *n.* The physiology and pathology of the rectum and anus. [PROCTO- + -LOGY.] **—proc•to•log•ic** (próktə-lójik), **proc•to•log•i•cal** *adj.* **—proc•to•log•i•cal•ly** *adv.* **—proc•tol•o•gist** (-tólləjist) *n.*

proc•tor (próktər) *n.* **1.** In certain universities and schools, an official responsible for discipline and for invigilating at examinations. **2.** An agent or representative, especially one hired to collect tithes or to conduct a court case on another's behalf. **3.** In the Church of England, an elected clerical member of a synod.
~*v.* **proctored, -toring, -tors.** *—tr. U.S.* To serve as proctor at (an examination). *—intr.* To serve as a proctor. [Middle English *proc(u)tour,* agent, deputy, contraction of *procuratour,* PROCURATOR.] **—proc•to•ri•al** (prok-táwri-əl || -tōri-) *adj.*

proc•to•scope (próktə-skōp) *n.* An instrument for examining the rectum. [PROCTO- + -SCOPE.] **—proc•to•scop•ic** (-skóppik) *adj.* **—proc•tos•co•py** (prok-tóskəpi) *n.*

pro•cum•bent (prō-kúmbənt) *adj.* **1.** *Botany.* Trailing along the ground; prostrate: *a procumbent vine.* **2.** Lying face down; prone. [Latin *prōcumbens* (stem *prōcumbent-*), present participle of *prōcumbere,* to fall forward, bend down : *prō-,* forward, down + *-cumbere,* to lie down.]

proc•u•ra•tion (próckewr-áysh'n) *n* **1.** The act or process of procuring or being procured. **2.** *Law.* The criminal act of procuring women for purposes of prostitution. **3.** *Law.* **a.** The appointment or duties of an agent or legal representative. **b.** The document certifying such appointment or duties. **c. Power of attorney** *(see).*

proc•u•ra•tor (prók-yŏŏ-raytər, próckewr-aytər) *n.* **1.** An agent having power of attorney. **2.** A Roman official acting as a financial agent of the emperor or as the administrator of a minor province. [Middle English *procuratour,* from Old French, from Latin *prōcūrātor,* from *prōcūrāre,* to take care of, PROCURE.] **—proc•u•ra•to•ri•al** (-ə-táwri-əl || -tōri-), **proc•u•ra•to•ry** (-ətri, -ətəri, -áytəri) *adj.*

procurator fiscal *n.* In Scotland, an official who serves as coroner and public prosecutor. Also called "fiscal".

pro•cure (prə-kéwr, prō-) *v.* **-cured, -curing, -cures.** *—tr.* **1.** To obtain; acquire. **2.** To bring about; effect: *procure a solution.* **3.** To obtain (a child or woman) to serve as a prostitute. *—intr.* To obtain girls or women to serve as prostitutes. [Middle English *procuren,* to take care of, gain, obtain, from Old French *procurer,* from Late Latin *prōcūrāre,* to obtain, from Latin, to take care of, manage for someone else : *prō-,* for, on behalf of + *cūrāre,* to take care of.] **—pro•cure•ment** *n.*

pro•cur•er (prə-kéwr-ər, prō-) *n.* **1.** One who procures. **2.** A pander.

pro•cur•ess (prə-kéwr-iss, prō-, próckewr-, -ess) *n.* A female procurer.

Pro•cy•on (prṓ-si-ən || -on) *n.* A double star in the constellation Canis Minor. [Latin, from Greek *Prokuōn,* "before the dog star" : *pro-,* before + *kuōn,* dog.]

prod (prod) *tr.v.* **prodded, prodding, prods. 1.** To jab or poke, as with a pointed instrument. **2.** To rouse to action; urge; goad.
~*n.* **1.** The act or an instance of prodding. **2.** Anything pointed used to prod; a goad. **3.** An incitement or reminder; a stimulus. [16th century : perhaps imitative.] **—prod•der** *n.*

Prod *n. Informal.* Also **Prod•dy, Prod•die** (próddi) *pl.* **-dies.** A Protestant. Used derogatorily. **—Prod, Prod•dy** *adj.*

prod. 1. produce; produced. **2.** product.

prod•i•gal (próddig'l) *adj.* **1.** Recklessly wasteful; extravagant. **2.** Extremely generous. **3.** Profuse; lavish: *prodigal praise.*
~*n.* A person given to luxury or extravagance; a spendthrift or profligate. [Latin *prōdigus,* from *prōdigere,* to drive away, squander : *prōd-,* variant of *prō-,* forth, away + *agere,* to drive.] **—prod•i•gal•ly** *adv.*

prod•i•gal•i•ty (próddi-gál-əti) *n., pl.* **-ties. 1.** Extravagant wastefulness. **2.** Profuse generosity. **3.** Extreme abundance; lavishness.

pro•di•gious (prə-díjəss) *adj.* **1.** Impressively great in size, force, or extent; enormous. **2.** Extraordinary; marvellous. **3.** *Obsolete.* Portentous; ominous. [Latin *prōdigiōsus,* from *prōdigium,* omen, portent, PRODIGY.] **—pro•di•gious•ly** *adv.* **—pro•di•gious•ness** *n.*

prod•i•gy (próddiji) *n., pl.* **-gies. 1.** A person with exceptional talents or powers: *a child prodigy.* **2.** An act, object, or event so extraordinary or rare as to inspire wonder; a marvel. **3.** *Archaic.* An omen or portent. [Latin *prōdigium,* prophetic sign, marvel.]

pro•drome (prṓ-drōm) *n.* An early symptom of a disease, often different in nature from the later symptoms. [French, from Greek *prodromos,* precursor : *pro-,* forward + *dromos,* running.] **—pro•dro•mal** (prō-drṓm'l), **pro•drom•ic** (prō-drómmik) *adj.*

pro•duce (prə-déwss || prō-, -dŏŏss) *v.* **-duced, -ducing, -duces.** *—tr.* **1.** To bring forth; yield. **2.** To create by mental or physical effort. **3.** To manufacture. **4. a.** To cause to occur or exist; give rise to. **b.** To give birth to. **5.** To bring forward; exhibit. **6.** *British.* To interpret and supervise the acting and artistic design of (a play, for example). **7.** To sponsor and present to the public: *produce a film.* **8.** In geometry, to extend (an area or volume) or lengthen (a line). *—intr.* To make or yield the customary product or products.
~*n.* (pród-yōōss || -ōōss, *chiefly U.S.* prṓd-) *Abbr.* **prod.** Something produced; a product; especially, agricultural products collectively. [Latin *prōdūcere,* to lead or bring forth : *prō-,* forward + *dūcere,* to lead.] **—pro•duc•i•ble** *adj.*

pro•duc•er (prə-déw-sər || prō-, -dṓō-) *n.* **1.** One that produces. **2.** *Economics.* A person or organisation that grows or manufactures goods or provides services for sale. **3. a.** A person who arranges the finance, hiring of actors, and other practical business in the making of a cinematic film or the staging of a play. Compare **director. b.** *British.* The person who supervises and instructs the actors or participants in a radio or television production, and is responsible for the overall artistic interpretation. **4.** A furnace that manufactures producer gas. **5.** *Ecology.* Any organism that is the first stage in a food chain, such as bacteria or green plants, building up foods from and feeding on inorganic matter. Compare **consumer.**

producer gas *n.* A gas used as fuel, generated by passing air with steam over burning coke or coal, to yield a combustible mixture of nitrogen, carbon monoxide, and hydrogen. Also called "air gas".

producer goods *pl.n. Economics.* **Capital goods** *(see).*

prod•uct (pród-ukt, -əkt) *n. Abbr.* **prod. 1. a.** Anything produced by human or mechanical effort or by a natural process. **b.** An article considered as merchandise: *redesign the product.* **c.** Marketable goods collectively: *What the company needs is product.* **d.** A person who has undergone a specified type of training or education: *a grammar school product.* **2.** A direct result; a consequence. **3.** *Chemistry.* A substance produced by a chemical change. **4.** *Mathematics.* **a.** The result obtained by performing multiplication. **b.** A **scalar product** *(see).* **c.** A **vector product** *(see).* [Latin *prōductum,* from the past participle of *prōdūcere,* to PRODUCE.]

pro•duc•tion (prə-dúksh'n || prō-) *n.* **1.** The act or process of producing. **2.** *Economics.* The creation of value or wealth by producing goods and services. **3.** Something produced; a product. **4. a.** The total number of products; output. **b.** The rate at which products are produced. **5. a.** *British.* The artistic supervision and interpretation of a stage play or other live public entertainment. **b.** A public performance or showing of such an entertainment. **c.** A version of a play or similar work with a particular interpretation and staging: *a new production of Fidelio.* **6.** Mass production. Also used adjectivally: *a production model.* **7.** *Informal.* **a.** A great effort. **b.** An unnecessarily complicated procedure; a fuss. **—pro•duc•tion•al** *adj.*

production line *n.* **1.** An **assembly line** *(see).* **2.** A method of mass-producing goods using a continuous flow of components, which are assembled on a moving conveyor. **3.** Any system or institution whose products or graduates emerge regularly and systematically and have standardised characteristics. **—pro•duc•tion-line** (prə-dúksh'n-līn || prō-) *adj.*

pro•duc•tive (prə-dúktiv || prō-) *adj.* **1.** Producing or capable of producing. **2.** Producing abundantly; fertile; prolific. **3.** Yielding favourable or useful results; constructive. **4.** *Economics.* Of or involved in the creation of goods and services to produce wealth or value. **5.** Resulting in. Used with *of: difficulties productive of dispute.* **—pro•duc•tive•ly** *adv.* **—pro•duc•tiv•i•ty** (pród-uk-tívvəti, prṓd-, -ək-), **pro•duc•tive•ness** *n.*

product liability *n.* Legal responsibility on the part of a manufac-

PRONUNCIATION KEY

a, trap; aa, father; ai, fair; ar, star; aw, lawn; ay, play; b, bb, stab; rubber; ch, church; ck, ticket; d, dd, dead; ladder; e, dress; ee, bee; er, defer; ew, few; ewr, pure; ə, about; ər, letter; f, ff, fife; differ; g, gg, giggle; h, hat; i, kit; ī, price; īr, fire; j, judge; k, kick; l, ll, let; 'l, needle; m, mm, man; n, nn, no; 'n, sudden; ng, thing; o, lot; ō, no; ŏŏ, foot; ōō, shoe; oor, poor; ow, cow; owr, hour; oy, boy; p, pp, pepper; r, rr, red; s, ss, sauce; sh, ship; t, tt, totter; th, thick; th, this; smooth; u, cut; ur, turn; v, vv, valve; w, wet; y, yes; z, zz, zebra; zh, vision; pleasure

IN FOREIGN WORDS:

aN, oN, Saint-Saëns; hl, Llanelli; Hlhuhluwe; kh, loch; lough; Khaled

STRESS MARK:

ín-sīt, insight; in-sī́t, incite

turer, as opposed to a retailer, to ensure that a product is safe or good quality, and fit for its purpose.

pro·em (prṓ-em) n. A short introduction; a preface. [Middle English *proheme*, from Old French *pro(h)eme*, from Latin *prooemium*, from Greek *prooimion*, prelude : *pro-*, before + *oimē*, song, from *oimos*, way, path.] —**pro·e·mi·al** (prō-ēemi-əl ‖ U.S. also -émmi-) adj.

prof., Prof. professor.

prof·a·na·tion (próffə-náysh'n) n. The act or an instance of profaning; desecration.

pro·fane (prə-fáyn, prō-) adj. 1. Showing contempt or irreverence towards God or sacred things; blasphemous. 2. Nonreligious in subject matter, form, or use; secular: *sacred and profane music*. 3. Not initiated into the mysteries of ritual. 4. Vulgar; coarse. ~tr.v. profane, -faning, -fanes. 1. To treat with irreverence. 2. To put to an improper, unworthy, or degrading use; abuse. [Middle English *prophane*, from Old French, from Medieval Latin *prophānus*, variant of Latin *profānus*, "before (i.e., outside) the temple", hence not sacred, secular, impious : *pro-*, before + *fānum*, temple.] —**pro·fan·a·to·ry** (-fánnə-tri, -təri) adj. —**pro·fane·ly** adv. —**pro·fane·ness** n. —**pro·fan·er** n.
    Synonyms: profane, blasphemous, sacrilegious.

pro·fan·i·ty (prə-fánnəti, prō-) n., pl. -ties. 1. The condition or quality of being profane. 2. a. Abusive, vulgar, or irreverent language. b. The use or an instance of such language.

pro·fess (prə-féss, prō-) v. -fessed, -fessing, -fesses. —tr. 1. To affirm openly; declare or claim. 3. To claim skill in or knowledge of. 4. To affirm belief in: *profess Catholicism*. 5. To receive into a religious order. —intr. 1. To make an open affirmation. 2. To take the vows of a religious order. [Latin *profitērī* (past participle *professus*), to declare publicly : *pro-*, forth, in public + *fatērī*, to acknowledge, confess.]

pro·fessed (prə-fést, prō-) adj. 1. According to one's own admission; self-confessed: *a professed hedonist*. 2. Self-proclaimed but pretended. 3. Belonging to a profession. 4. Having taken the vows of a religious order. —**pro·fess·ed·ly** (-féssid-li) adv.

pro·fes·sion (prə-fésh'n ‖ prō-) n. 1. An occupation or vocation requiring training, as in law, theology, or the sciences. 2. The body of qualified persons of any specific occupation or field. 3. The act or an instance of professing; a declaration; a claim. 4. An avowal of faith in a religion, especially on first being accepted into it. 5. The taking of vows by a person joining a religious order. [Middle English, vow made on entering a religious order, from Old French, from Latin *professiō* (stem *professiōn-*), declaration, confession, from *profitērī*, PROFESS.]

pro·fes·sion·al (prə-fésh'n'l ‖ prō-) adj. 1. Of, pertaining to, engaged in, or suitable for a profession. 2. Engaged in a specific activity as a source of livelihood. 3. Performed by persons receiving pay. 4. Having great skill or experience in a particular field or activity. ~n. Abbr. pro., Pro. 1. A person following a profession. 2. One who earns his livelihood as a sportsman, either playing or coaching. 3. One who has an assured competence in a particular field or occupation. —**pro·fes·sion·al·ly** adv.

professional foul n. Sports. In team games, a deliberate foul, usually committed when the opposing team seems certain of scoring.

pro·fes·sion·al·ism (prə-fésh'n'l-iz'm ‖ prō-) n. 1. Professional status, methods, character, or standards. 2. The use of professional players in organised sports.

pro·fes·sor (prə-féssər ‖ prō-) n. 1. Abbr. prof., Prof. a. A tutor of the highest rank in a university or comparable institution. b. U.S. A teacher or instructor. 2. One who professes. [Middle English *professour*, from Latin *professor*, from *profitērī*, PROFESS.] —**pro·fes·so·ri·al** (próf-ə-sáwri-əl, -i-, -e- ‖ -sōri-) adj. —**pro·fes·so·ri·al·ly** adv. —**pro·fes·sor·ship** (-ship) n.

prof·fer (próffər) tr.v. -fered, -fering, -fers. To offer; tender. See Synonyms at **offer**. ~n. The act of proffering; an offer. [Middle English *profren*, from Old French *p(o)roffrir* : *por-*, from Latin *prō-*, forth + *offrir*, to offer, from Latin *offerre*, "to carry towards" : *ob-*, to, towards + *ferre*, to carry.] —**prof·fer·er** n.

pro·fi·cien·cy (prə-físh'n-si ‖ prō-) n., pl. -cies. The state or quality of being proficient; skill; competence.

pro·fi·cient (prə-fish'nt ‖ prō-) adj. Performing in a given art, skill, or branch of learning with expert correctness and facility; adept. ~n. Rare. An adept; an expert. [Latin *proficiens* (stem *proficient-*), present participle of *proficere*, to make progress. See **profit**.] —**pro·fi·cient·ly** adv.
    Synonyms: proficient, adept, skilled, skilful.

pro·file (prṓ-fīl; old-fashioned -feel) n. 1. a. A side view of an object or structure, especially of a human head. b. A representation of an object or structure seen from the side. 2. An outline of any object. 3. A biographical essay presenting the subject's most noteworthy characteristics and achievements. 4. a. A graph or table representing numerically the extent to which a person or thing shows various tested characteristics: *an organisational profile*. b. The characteristics represented. 5. a. A vertical section of the soil at any point of the earth's surface down to the parent rock, showing the different horizons. b. A graphical representation of this section. Also called "soil profile". 6. a. A vertical section of the earth's crust at any point showing the different layers of rock. b. A graphical representation of this section. —See Synonyms at **form**. ~tr.v. profiled, -filing, -files. 1. To draw or shape a profile of.

2. To write a profile of. [Italian *profilo*, from *profilare*, to draw in outline : *pro-*, forward + *filare*, to spin, draw a line, from Late Latin *fīlāre*, to spin, from Latin *fīlum*, thread, string.]

prof·it (próffit) n. 1. An advantageous gain or return; a benefit. 2. The return received on a business undertaking after all operating expenses have been met. 3. Economics. The prospect of such return considered as the chief motivation in all activity in a capitalist economy. 4. Often plural. a. The return received on an investment after all charges have been paid. b. The rate of increase in the net worth of a business enterprise in a given accounting period. c. Income received from investments or property. d. The amount received for a commodity or service in excess of the original cost. ~v. profited, -iting, -its. —intr. 1. To make a gain or profit. 2. To be advantageous; benefit. —tr. To be beneficial to. [Middle English, from Old French, from Latin *prōfectus*, advance, progress, success, profit, from the past participle of *prōficere*, to go forward, accomplish, be advantageous : *prō-*, for + *facere*, to do, make.]

prof·it·a·ble (próffit-əb'l) adj. 1. Beneficial; advantageous. 2. Yielding a financial profit. —**prof·it·a·bil·i·ty** (-ə-bílləti), **prof·it·a·ble·ness** n. —**prof·it·a·bly** adv.

profit and loss n. An account showing net and gross profit or loss over a given period. —**prof·it·and-loss** (próffit-ənd-lóss) adj.

prof·i·teer (próffi-téer) n. One who makes excessive profits on commodities in short supply. ~intr.v. profiteered, -teering, -teers. To act as a profiteer.

prof·i·te·role (próffitə-rōl, prə-fíttə-, -rōl) n. A small, round case of choux pastry usually filled with cream and served with a chocolate sauce. [Fench, diminutive of *profit*, PROFIT.]

prof·it-shar·ing (próffit-shair-ing) n. A system by which employees receive a share of the profits of a business enterprise. —**prof·it-shar·ing** adj.

prof·li·gate (próffli-gət, -git ‖ -gayt) adj. 1. Given over to dissipation; dissolute. 2. Recklessly wasteful; wildly extravagant. ~n. A profligate person; a wastrel. [Latin *prōflīgātus*, from the past participle of *prōflīgāre*, to strike down, destroy, ruin : *prō-*, forward, down + *flīgere*, to strike.] —**prof·li·ga·cy** (-gə-si) n.

pro for·ma (prō fórmə) adv. Latin. As a matter of, or according to, form. —**pro for·ma** adj.

pro·found (prə-fównd ‖ prō-; West Indian also -fúngd) adj. -er, -est. 1. Situated at, extending to, or coming from a great depth; deep. 2. Coming as if from the depths of one's being: *profound contempt*. 3. Thoroughgoing; far-reaching. 4. Penetrating beyond what is superficial or obvious: *a profound thinker*. 5. Unqualified; absolute; complete. [Middle English *profounde*, from Old French *profond*, *profund*, from Latin *profundus* : *pro-*, before + *fundus*, bottom.] —**pro·found·ly** adv. —**pro·found·ness** n.

pro·fun·di·ty (prə-fúndəti ‖ prō-) n., pl. -ties. 1. Great depth. 2. Depth of intellect, feeling, or meaning. 3. Something profound or abstruse. [Middle English *profundite*, from Old French, from Late Latin *profunditās* (stem *profunditāt-*), from *profundus*, deep, PROFOUND.]

pro·fuse (prə-féwss ‖ prō-) adj. 1. Plentiful; overflowing. 2. Giving or given freely and abundantly; extravagant. Usually used with *in* or *with*: *profuse in his compliments*. [Middle English, from Latin *prōfūsus*, from the past participle of *prōfundere*, to pour forth : *prō-*, forth + *fundere*, to pour.] —**pro·fuse·ly** adv. —**pro·fuse·ness** n.

pro·fu·sion (prə-féwzh'n ‖ prō-) n. 1. The state of being profuse; abundance. 2. Lavish or unrestrained expense; extravagance. 3. A profuse outpouring or display.

prog[1] (prog) n. British Informal. A proctor. —tr.v. progged, progging, progs. British Informal. To subject to a proctor's authority. [Shortening.]

prog[2] n. British Informal. A programme. [Shortening.]

prog. 1. programme. 2. progress; progressive.

pro·gen·i·tive (prō-jénnətiv) adj. Capable of producing offspring; fertile. [Middle English. See **progenitor**.]

pro·gen·i·tor (prō-jénnitər, prə-) n. 1. A direct ancestor. 2. An originator of a line of descent. 3. Any founder or precursor of a trend or tradition. [Middle English *progenitour*, from Old French *progeniteur*, from Latin *prōgenitor*, from *prōgenitus*, past participle of *prōgignere*, to beget : *prō-*, forth + *gignere*, to beget.]

prog·e·ny (prójəni) n., pl. -nies. 1. Children or descendants; offspring. 2. A result of creative effort; a product. [Middle English *progenie*, from Old French, from Latin *prōgeniēs*, descent, descendants, from *prōgignere*, to beget. See **progenitor**.]

pro·ges·ta·tion·al (prō-jess-táysh'n'l) adj. 1. Preceding gestation. 2. Preceding ovulation.

pro·ges·ter·one (prō-jéstə-rōn, prə-) n. A female hormone, $C_{21}H_{30}O_2$, secreted by the corpus luteum of the ovary prior to ovulation, which prepares the uterus for implantation of a fertilised ovum. [PRO- (acting for) + GES(TATION) + STER(OL) + -ONE.]

pro·ges·to·gen (prō-jéstə-jən, -jen) n. Any substance having an action like progesterone. [PROGEST(ERONE) + -GEN.]

pro·glot·tid (prō-glót-id) n., pl. -tids. Also **pro·glot·tis** (-iss) pl. -tides (-i-deez). Any of the segments of a tapeworm. [New Latin *proglottis* (stem *proglottid-*), from Greek *proglōssis*, tip of the tongue (from its shape) : *pro-*, before + *glōssa*, *glōtta*, tongue.] —**pro·glot·tic**, **pro·glot·ti·de·an** (-i-dée-ən, prō-glot-; also prō-glo-tíddi-ən) adj.

prog·na·thous (prog-náy-thəss, próg-nə-) adj. Also **prog·nath·ic** (-náthik). Having one or both jaws projecting forward to a considerable degree. [PRO- (in front, projecting) + -GNATHOUS.] —**prog·na·thism** (próg-nə-thiz'm) n.

prog·no·sis (prog-nṓ-siss) n., pl. -ses (-seez). 1. a. A prediction of the probable course and outcome of a disease. **b.** The likelihood of recovery from a disease. **2.** Any forecast or prediction. [Late Latin, from Greek *prognōsis,* from *progignōskein,* to foreknow, predict : *pro-,* before + *gignōskein,* to know.]

prog·nos·tic (prog-nóstik, prəg-) *adj.* **1.** Of, pertaining to, or acting as a prognosis. **2.** Predicting; foretelling.
~*n.* **1.** A sign or omen of some future happening. **2.** A symptom indicating the future course of a disease. [Medieval Latin *prognōsticus,* from Greek *prognōstikos,* from *progignōskein,* to predict. See **prognosis.**]

prog·nos·ti·cate (prog-nósti-kayt, prəg-) *tr.v.* **-cated, -cating, -cates. 1.** To predict, using present indications as a guide. **2.** To foreshadow; portend. [Medieval Latin *prognōsticāre,* from *prognōsticus,* PROGNOSTIC.] **—prog·nos·ti·ca·tor** (-kaytər) *n.* **—prog·nos·ti·ca·tion** (-káysh'n) *n.*

pro·gram (prṓ-gram || -grəm) *n.* **1.** A set of instructions, written in a suitable programming language, that are fed into a computer to enable it to perform logical or arithmetical operations on data. **2.** *U.S.* Variant of **programme.**
~*v.* **programmed** or *U.S.* **programed, -gramming** or *U.S.* **-graming, -grams.** *—tr.* **1.** To supply (a computer) with a program or programs. **2.** To organise or convert (data) into a program. **3.** *U.S.* Variant of **programme.** *—intr.* To write a computer program. **—pro·gram·ma·ble** (-əb'l, prō-grám-) *adj.*

pro·gramme, *U.S.* **pro·gram** (prṓ-gram || -grəm) *n.* **1. a.** A listing of the order of events and other pertinent information for some public presentation. **b.** A booklet containing such information sold at concerts, plays, and similar events. **2.** The presentation itself. **3.** A radio or television show. **4.** Any organised list or schedule of procedures or activities. **5.** A schedule of projects to be carried out: *a building programme.* **6.** A syllabus.
~*tr.v.* **programmed** or *U.S.* **programed, -gramming** or *U.S.* **-graming, -grammes** or *U.S.* **-grams. 1.** To include or schedule in a programme. **2.** To design (a plan, for example) as a definite programme. **3.** To cause (a machine, animal, or person) to follow a set procedure; control or direct the behaviour of. [French *programme,* from Late Latin *programma,* public notice, from Greek, from *prographein,* to set forth as a public notice : *pro-,* before + *graphein,* to write.] **—pro·gram·mat·ic** (-grə-máttik) *adj.*

pro·grammed learning (prṓ-gramd || -grəmd) *n.* A system of instruction, relying largely on textbooks or machines and requiring minimal supervision by teachers.

programme music *n.* Music intended to convey ideas or suggest the episodes of a story. Compare **absolute music.**

pro·gram·mer, pro·gram·er (prṓ-grammər || -grəmmər) *n.* **1.** One who prepares a computer program. **2.** A person who schedules radio or television programmes.

pro·gram·ming language (prṓ-gram-ing || -grəm-) *n.* Any of various coded systems of words and symbols used to write instructions to a computer in familiar notation rather than directly in a machine code. See **high-level language, low-level language.**

pro·gress (prṓ-gress || *chiefly U.S.* pró-, -grəss) *n.* **1.** Movement towards a goal. **2.** Development; unfolding. **3.** Steady improvement, as of a society or civilisation: *a believer in progress.* **4.** *Chiefly British.* A state journey made by a sovereign through the realm. **—in progress.** Under way; currently being done or made.
~*intr.v.* (prə-gréss, prō-) **-gressed, -gressing, -gresses. 1.** To advance; proceed. **2.** To advance towards a more desirable form or condition. [Middle English *progresse,* from Latin *prōgressus,* from past participle of *prōgredī,* to go forward : *prō-,* forward + *gradī,* to step, go.]

progress chaser *n.* A person whose task is to encourage or exhort those working on a project and to monitor their output, to ensure that progress is maintained.

pro·gres·sion (prə-grésh'n, prō-) *n.* **1.** The act of or an instance of progressing. **2. a.** A sequence, as of events. **b.** The movement from one item in such a sequence to the next. **3.** *Mathematics.* A series of numbers or quantities, each derived from the one preceding by some consistent operation. See **arithmetic progression, geometric progression. 4.** *Music.* A succession of notes or chords or the modulation from one to the next. —See Synonyms at **series. —pro·gres·sion·al** *adj.*

pro·gres·sion·ism (prə-grésh'n-iz'm, prō-) *n.* The doctrine that society or nature has progressed, is progressing, or ought to progress towards a higher and more desirable state. **—pro·gres·sion·ist** *n.*

pro·gres·sive (prə-gréssiv, prō-) *adj.* **1.** Moving forward; ongoing; advancing. **2.** Proceeding in steps; continuing steadily by increments. **3. a.** Believing in or striving for constant improvement or new advances. **b.** Characterised by an advance over the established forms; very modern: *progressive rock music.* **c.** Promoting or favouring political and social reform. **4.** *Capital* **P.** Of or belonging to a Progressive Party. **5.** Of, designating, pertaining to, or influenced by a theory of education characterised by emphasis on the individual needs and capacities of each child and informality of curriculum. **6.** Of or denoting a tax system in which the rate of taxation increases as the taxable amount increases. **7.** *Pathology.* Continuously spreading or increasing in severity. **8.** *Grammar.* Designating a verb form or aspect that expresses an action or condition in progress; continuous. In English, it is formed by adding the suffix *-ing* to the root verb form.
~*n.* **1.** A person who favours or strives for advances or reform in politics, education, or other fields. **2.** *Capital* **P.** One who belongs to a Progressive Party. **3. a.** The progressive form of a verb. **b.** A verb in this form. **—pro·gres·sive·ly** *adv.* **—pro·gres·sive·ness** *n.*

Progressive Party *n.* **1.** A South African political party existing between 1959 and 1975, having broadly liberal policies. **2.** Any of three U.S. political parties, formed in 1912 (under the leadership of Theodore Roosevelt), 1924, and 1948 respectively.

Progressive Reform Party *n.* A South African political party formed in 1975 by the merging of the Progressive Party with the *Reform Party,* a group of former members of the **United Party** *(see).* It is now the official opposition.

pro·gres·siv·ism (prə-gréssiv-iz'm, prō-) *n.* The doctrines and practice of political or educational progressives.

pro·hib·it (prə-híbbit, prō-) *tr.v.* **-ited, -iting, -its. 1.** To forbid by authority. **2.** To prevent or debar. [Middle English *prohibiten,* from Latin *prōhibēre,* to hold in front, hinder, hold back : *prō-,* in front + *habēre,* to hold.]

Usage: The usual preposition following this verb is *from (The law prohibits you from doing that),* but the following constructions are also used: *The law prohibits doing that; The law prohibits your doing that.* The construction *The law prohibits you doing that* is also found but is not acceptable.

pro·hi·bi·tion (prṓ-i-bísh'n, -hi-) *n.* **1.** The act of prohibiting or state of being prohibited. **2.** A law, order, or decree that forbids something. **3.** *Law.* An order from the High Court forbidding a lower court or tribunal from deciding a particular case. In this sense, also officially called "Order of Prohibition". **4. a.** The forbidding by law of the manufacture, transportation, sale, and possession of alcoholic drinks. **b.** *Capital* **P.** The period (1920–33) during which such a law was in force in the United States.

pro·hi·bi·tion·ist (prṓ-i-bísh'n-ist, -hi-) *n.* **1.** One in favour of banning the manufacture and sale of alcoholic drinks. **2.** A member of a party in the United States that advocated the Prohibition.

pro·hib·i·tive (prə-híbbitiv, prō-) *adj.* Also **pro·hib·i·to·ry** (-híbbi-tri, -təri). **1.** Prohibiting or likely to prohibit. **2.** Preventing or discouraging something, such as purchase or use: *prohibitive costs.* **—pro·hib·i·tive·ly** *adv.*

proj·ect (prój-ekt, -ikt || prṓj-) *n.* **1.** A plan or proposal. **2.** An undertaking requiring concerted effort. **3.** A research undertaking.
~*v.* **pro·ject** (prə-jékt, prō-), **-jected, -jecting, -jects.** *—tr.* **1.** To thrust outwards or forwards. Compare **retroject. 2.** To throw forwards; hurl; impel. **3.** To transport in one's imagination. **4.** *Psychology.* To externalise and attribute (an emotion, for example) to someone or something else. Used with *onto.* **5.** To direct (one's voice) so as to be heard clearly at a distance. **6.** To form a plan or intention for; intend. Used especially in the past participle: *my projected tour of Wales.* **7. a.** To cause (an image) to appear upon a surface. **b.** To cast (light or shadow). **8.** To produce a projection of. **9. a.** To use as a basis for estimates or predictions: *If you project these figures to next year, you will see that prices should rise.* **b.** To estimate; predict: *projected a ten per cent rise.* **10.** To convey or represent vividly to an audience: *projects himself poorly.* *—intr.* **1.** To extend forwards or out; protrude. **2.** To direct one's voice so as to be heard clearly at a distance. [Middle English *proiecte,* from Latin *prōjectum,* a projecting, projection, from the past participle of *prō(j)icere,* to throw forth : *prō-,* forth + *jacere,* to throw.]

pro·jec·tile (prə-jék-tīl, prō-, prój-ik-, -ek- || *chiefly U.S.* -t'l) *n.* **1.** A fired, thrown, or otherwise projected object, such as a bullet, having no capacity for self-propulsion. **2.** A self-propelling missile, such as a rocket.
~*adj.* (*always* -jék-). **1.** Capable of being impelled or hurled forwards. **2.** Driving forwards; impelling. **3.** *Zoology.* Capable of being thrust outwards; protrusile. [New Latin *prōjectilis,* from Latin *prō(j)icere,* to throw forth, PROJECT.]

pro·jec·tion (prə-jéksh'n, prō-) *n.* **1.** The act of projecting or state of being projected. **2.** Something that thrusts outwards; a protuberance. **3.** A plan for an anticipated course of action. **4.** A prediction made after all available information has been examined. **5. a.** The process of projecting a filmed image onto a screen or other viewing surface. **b.** The image so projected. **6.** The image of a geometric figure produced by a coordinate mapping. **7.** A system of intersecting lines, such as the grid of a map, on which part or all of the globe or the celestial sphere may be represented as a plane surface. See **map projection. 8.** *Psychology.* The naive or unconscious attribution of one's own feelings, attitudes, or desires to others. **—pro·jec·tion·al** *adj.*

pro·jec·tion·ist (prə-jéksh'n-ist, prō-) *n.* **1.** One who operates a film projector. **2.** A map-maker.

pro·jec·tive (prə-jéktiv, prō-) *adj. Mathematics.* **1.** Pertaining to or made by projection. **2.** Extending outwards; projecting. **3.** Designating a property of a geometric figure that does not vary when the figure undergoes projection. **—pro·jec·tive·ly** *adv.*

projective geometry *n.* The study of geometric properties that are invariant under projection.

projective test *n.* A psychological test in which a subject's responses to relatively unstructured standard stimuli, such as a series of abstract patterns or incomplete sentences, are analysed to obtain information about the personality or sometimes intelligence.

pro·jec·tor (prə-jéktər, prō-) *n.* **1.** A machine for projecting an image onto a screen. **2.** A device for projecting a beam of light. **3.** One who devises plans or projects.

pro·kar·y·ote, pro·car·y·ote (prō-kárri-ōt) *n.* Any organism in which the genetic material is not bounded by a nuclear membrane but exists free in the cytoplasm. Prokaryotes consist mainly of the bacteria and blue-green algae. Compare **eukaryote.** [PRO- + KARYO- + *-ote,* as in *zygote.*] **—pro·kar·y·o·tic** (-óttik) *adj.*

Pro·kof·i·ev (prə-kóffi-ef), **Sergei Sergeyevich** (1891–1953). Russian composer. He wrote seven symphonies, several operas, ballets, and concertos. His glittering, inventive compositions include the opera *The Love of Three Oranges.* In 1948 his works were denounced as undemocratic by the Soviet government.

pro·lac·tin (prō-láktin) *n.* A pituitary hormone that, in mammals, stimulates and controls the secretion of milk, and stimulates the production of progesterone by the corpus luteum in the ovary. Also called "luteotrophic hormone". [PRO- (forth) + LACT(O)- + -IN.]

pro·la·mine (prō-ləm-in, prō-lám-, -een) *n.* Also **pro·la·min** (-in). Any of a class of simple proteins found in wheat, rye, and other grains. [PROL(INE) + AM(MONIA) + -INE.]

pro·lapse (prō-laps, prō-láps) *intr.v.* **-lapsed, -lapsing, -lapses.** *Medicine.* To fall or slip out of place.
~*n.* Also **pro·lap·sus** (prō-lápsəss). *Medicine.* The falling down or slipping out of place of an organ or part, such as the uterus. [Late Latin *prōlapsus,* a falling, from Latin, past participle of *prōlābī,* to fall or slip down : *prō-,* forward, down + *lābī,* to fall, slip.]

pro·late (prṓ-layt, prō-láyt) *adj.* Designating the shape of a solid, especially of a spheroid, having its polar axis longer than its equatorial diameter; cigar-shaped. Compare **oblate.** [Latin *prōlātus,* stretched out (used as past participle of *prōferre,* to bring forward, stretch out) : *prō-,* forth + *-lātus,* "carried".] **—pro·late·ly** *adv.* **—pro·late·ness** *n.*

pro·la·tive (prō-láy-tiv, prṓlə-) *adj. Grammar.* Serving to extend or complete predication, as an infinitive verb does when joined without *to* to an auxiliary verb. For example, the word *hope* in *we must hope* is a prolative verb or infinitive. [PROLAT(E) + -IVE.]

prole (prōl) *n. Informal.* A member of the working class; a proletarian. Used derogatorily. [Shortened from PROLETARIAN; popularised by George Orwell's novel *1984.*]

pro·leg (prṓ-leg) *n.* Any of the stubby limbs on the abdominal segments of insect larvae. [PRO- (for, serving as) + LEG.]

pro·le·gom·e·non (prō-le-gómmi-nən, -li-, -non) *n., pl.* **-na** (-nə). A critical introduction, usually to a scholarly text. [Greek, from the present passive participle of *prolegein,* to say beforehand : *pro-,* before + *legein,* to say.] **—pro·le·gom·e·nous** *adj.*

pro·lep·sis (prō-léep-siss, -lép-) *n., pl.* **-ses** (-seez). **1.** The rhetorical device of anticipating and answering an objection or argument before one's opponent has put it forward. **2.** The use of a descriptive word in anticipation of the act or circumstances that would make it applicable. In the sentence *That gambler is a dead man: Sam Sneak has sworn to get him,* the use of the adjective *dead* indicates a prolepsis. [Late Latin, rhetorical anticipation, from Greek *prolēpsis,* from *prolambanein,* to take beforehand, anticipate : *prō-,* before + *lambanein,* to take.] **—pro·lep·tic** (-tik), **pro·lep·ti·cal** *adj.*

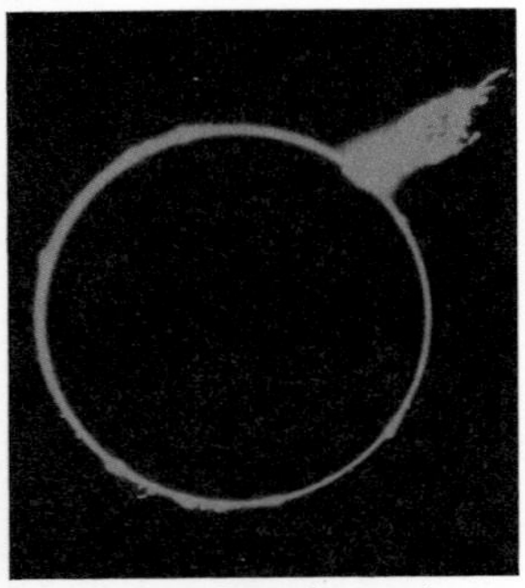
prominence *In a solar prominence, hot gases can lash out nearly 1 000 000 kilometres (600,000 miles) from the surface of the Sun.*

pro·le·tar·i·an (prṓ-li-táir-i-ən, -le-, -lə-) *adj.* Of, pertaining to, or characteristic of the proletariat.
~*n.* A member of the proletariat. [Latin *prōlētārius,* Roman citizen of the lowest class (who serves the state only by producing offspring), from *prōlēs,* offspring.] **—pro·le·tar·i·an·ism** *n.*

pro·le·tar·i·at (prō-li-táir-i-ət, -le-, -lə-, -at) *n.* **1. a.** The class of industrial wage earners who, possessing neither capital nor means of production, must earn their living by manual labour. **b.** The poorest class of working people. **2.** In ancient Rome, the people who possessed no property, constituting the lowest class of citizens. [French *prolétariat,* from Latin *prōlētārius,* PROLETARIAN.]

pro·lif·er·ate (prō-líffə-rayt, prə-) *v.* **-ated, -ating, -ates.** *—intr.* **1.** To reproduce or produce new growth or parts rapidly and repeatedly: *cells proliferating.* **2.** To increase or spread at a rapid rate. *—tr.* To cause to grow or increase rapidly. [French *prolifère,* from Medieval Latin *prōlifer,* producing offspring, PROLIFEROUS.] **—pro·lif·er·a·tion** (-ráysh'n) *n.* **—pro·lif·er·a·tive** (-rətiv, -raytiv) *adj.*

pro·lif·er·ous (prō-líffərəss, prə-) *adj.* **1.** *Biology.* Reproducing freely by means of buds and side branches. **2.** *Botany.* Freely producing buds or offshoots, sometimes from abnormal places. [Medieval Latin *prōlifer,* producing offspring : Latin *prōlēs,* offspring + -FEROUS.]

pro·lif·ic (prō-líffik, prə-) *adj.* **1.** Producing offspring or fruit in great abundance; fertile. **2.** Producing abundant works or results. [Medieval Latin *prōlificus* : Latin *prōlēs,* offspring + *-ficus,* from *facere,* to make.] **—pro·lif·i·cal·ly** *adv.*

pro·line (prṓ-leen, -lin) *n.* An amino acid, $C_5H_9O_2N$, found in proteins. [German *Prolin* : P(YR)ROL(E) + -INE.]

pro·lix (prṓ-liks, prō-líks) *adj.* **1.** Wordy and tedious. **2.** Tending to speak or write at great length; long-winded. [Middle English, from Old French *prolixe,* from Latin *prōlixus,* "poured forth", extended, abundant : *prō,* forth + *-lixus,* from *liquēre,* to be liquid.] **—pro·lix·i·ty** (prō-líksəti, prə-) *n.* **—pro·lix·ly** *adv.*

pro·loc·u·tor (prō-lóckewtər) *n.* A presiding officer or chairman, especially of the lower house of a convocation in the Anglican Church. [Middle English, from Latin *prōlocūtor,* "one who speaks out", advocate, from *prōloquī,* to speak out, plead : *prō-,* forth + *loquī,* to speak.]

pro·logue, *U.S.* **pro·log** (prṓ-log, *rarely* -lōg || *U.S. also* -lawg) *n.* **1.** The lines introducing a discourse or play. **2.** The character or actor who delivers these lines. **3.** An introductory act or event.
~*tr.v.* **prologued** or *U.S.* **prologed, -loguing** or *U.S.* **-loging, -logues** or *U.S.* **-logs.** To add a prologue to. [Middle English *prolog,* from Old French *prolog(u)e,* from Latin *prologus,* from Greek *prologos,* (speaker of) a prologue, : *pro-,* before + *legein,* to speak.]

pro·logu·ise, pro·logu·ize (prṓ-lo-gīz; *rarely* pró-, -lō- || *U.S. also* -law-) *intr.v.* **-ised, -ising, -ises.** Also *U.S.* **pro·log·ize** (*sometimes* -jīz). To write or deliver a prologue. **—pro·logu·is·er** *n.*

pro·long (prō-lóng, prə- || *U.S. also* -láwng) *tr.v.* **-longed, -longing, -longs.** Also **pro·lon·gate** (prṓ-long-gayt, pró- || *chiefly U.S.* prə-lóng-gayt, prō-, -láwng-), **-gated, -gating, -gates. 1.** To lengthen in duration; protract. **2.** To lengthen in extent. [Middle English *prolongen,* from Old French *prolonguer,* from Late Latin *prōlongāre* : Latin *prō-,* out, extending + *longus,* LONG.] **—pro·lon·ga·tion** (prō-long-gáysh'n, pró- || -lawng-) *n.*
Synonyms: *prolong, protract, extend.*

pro·lu·sion (prō-lóō-zh'n, prə-, -léw-) *n.* **1.** A preliminary exercise in writing. **2.** An essay written as a preface to a more detailed work. [Latin *prōlūsiō* (stem *prōlūsiōn-*), from *prōlūdere* (past participle *prōlūsus*), to play or practise beforehand : *prō-,* before + *lūdere,* to play.] **—pro·lu·so·ry** (-sə-ri, -zə-) *adj.*

prom (prom) *n.* **1.** *British Informal.* **a.** A promenade. **b.** A promenade concert. **2.** *U.S.* A ball or formal dance held for a high-school or college class. [Short for PROMENADE.]

prom. promontory.

prom·e·nade (prómmə-naád, -naad; -náyd *for noun sense 4 and intransitive verb sense 2*) *n.* **1.** A leisurely walk, especially one taken in a public place as a social activity. **2.** A public place for such walking, especially along the seafront. In this sense, also informally called "prom". **3. a.** A formal ball. **b.** A formal march by the guests at the opening of a ball. **4.** A march executed between the figures of a square dance or country dance.
~*v.* **promenaded, -nading, -nades.** *—intr.* **1.** To go on a leisurely walk. **2.** To execute a promenade in square or country dancing. *—tr.* **1.** To take a promenade along or through. **2.** To take or display on or as if on a promenade. [French, from *se promener,* to take a walk, from Late Latin *prōmināre,* to drive forward : *prō-,* forward + *mināre,* to drive, from Latin *minārī,* to threaten, from *minae,* threats.]

promenade concert *n. Chiefly British.* A concert in which part of the audience stands rather than sits. Also informally called "prom".

promenade deck *n.* The upper deck or a section of the upper deck on a passenger ship where the passengers can promenade.

prom·e·nad·er (prómmə-naádər; *for sense 1 also* -náydər) *n.* **1.** One who promenades. **2.** One attending a promenade concert.

Pro·me·the·an (prə-méethi-ən, prō-) *adj.* **1.** Pertaining to or suggestive of Prometheus. **2.** Boldly creative; life-bringing.
~*n.* One who is Promethean in manner or actions.

Pro·me·theus (prə-mée-thewss, prō, -thi-əss || -thōōss). *Greek Mythology.* A Titan who stole fire from the gods to give to humankind and was punished by being chained to a rock where a vulture gnawed at his liver.

pro·me·thi·um (prə-méethi-əm, prō-) *n. Symbol* **Pm** A radioactive rare-earth element prepared by fission of uranium or by neutron bombardment of neodymium, having 14 isotopes with mass numbers ranging from 140 to 154, and used as a source of beta rays. Atomic number 61, melting point 1,080°C, boiling point 2,460°C, valency 3. [New Latin, after PROMETHEUS (referring to the fire of a nuclear furnace).]

prom·i·nence (prómmi-nənss) *n.* Also **prom·i·nen·cy** (-nən-si). **1.** The condition or quality of being prominent. **2.** Something that is prominent; a projection. **3.** Emphasis or importance. **4.** *Astronomy.* A tonguelike cloud of luminous gas rising from the sun's surface, visible as part of the corona during a total solar eclipse.

prom·i·nent (prómminənt) *adj.* **1.** Projecting outwards; protuberant. **2.** Immediately noticeable; conspicuous. **3.** Widely known; eminent. [Latin *prōminēns* (stem *prōminent-*), present participle of *prōminēre,* to jut out, project : *prō-,* forth + *-minēre,* to jut.] **—prom·i·nent·ly** *adv.*

prom·is·cu·i·ty (prómmiss-kéw-əti || prṓ-miss-) *n., pl.* **-ties. 1.** The state or character of being promiscuous. **2.** Promiscuous sexual intercourse. **3.** An indiscriminate mixture; a hotchpotch.

pro·mis·cu·ous (prə-mískew-əss || prō-) *adj.* **1.** Characterised by casual association with many sexual partners. **2.** Consisting of diverse and unrelated parts or individuals; confused. **3.** Lacking standards of selection; indiscriminate. **4.** Casual; random. [Latin *prōmiscuus,* mixed : *prō-* (intensifier), thoroughly + *miscēre,* to mix.] **—pro·mis·cu·ous·ly** *adv.* **—pro·mis·cu·ous·ness** *n.*

prom·ise (prómmiss) *n.* **1.** A declaration giving assurance that one will or will not do something; a vow. **2.** Something which one has undertaken to give or perform. **3.** Indication of future excellence or success: *a child with great promise.*
~*v.* **promised, -ising, -ises.** *—tr.* **1.** To pledge or offer assurance. Followed by an infinitive or clause. **2.** To make a promise of; pledge oneself to give. **3.** To afford a basis for expecting: *That clear sky promises a hot afternoon.* *—intr.* **1.** To make a promise. **2.** To afford a basis for expectation. Often used with *well* or *fair.* [Middle English *promys(se),* from Latin *prōmissum,* from the neuter past participle of *prōmittere,* "to send forth", promise : *prō-,* forth + *mittere,* to let go, send.] **—prom·is·er** *n.*

Promised Land *n.* **1.** The land of Canaan, promised to Abraham and his descendants. Genesis 12:7. **2.** *Small* **p.**, *small* **l.** Any place or time of anticipated happiness.

prom·is·ee (prómmiss-ée) *n. Law.* An individual to whom a promise is made.

prom·is·ing (prómmiss-ing) *adj.* Likely to develop in a desirable or successful way. **—prom·is·ing·ly** *adv.*

prom·i·sor (prómmiss-ór) *n. Law.* An individual who makes a promise.

prom·is·so·ry (prómmiss-əri, prə-míss-) *adj.* **1.** Containing, involving, or having the nature of a promise. **2.** *Insurance.* Of or designating the preliminary undertakings or guarantees indicating how the provisions of an insurance contract will be carried out after it is signed. [Medieval Latin *prōmissōrius,* from Latin *prōmissor,* one who promises, from *prōmittere,* to PROMISE.]

promissory note *n. Abbr.* **p.n., P/N** A written promise to pay or repay a specified sum of money at a stated time or on demand. Also called "note", "note of hand".

prom·mer (prómmər) *n. British Informal.* One attending a promenade concert. [From PROM.]

pro·mo (prṓmō) *n. Informal.* An advertising or publicity campaign. Also used adjectivally: *promo material.* [Shortened from PROMOTION or PROMOTIONAL.]

prom·on·to·ry (prómmən-tri, -təri) *n., pl.* **-ries.** *Abbr.* **prom. 1.** A high ridge of land or rock jutting out into a sea or other expanse of water. **2.** *Anatomy.* A projecting bodily part. [Medieval Latin *prōmontōrium,* alteration of Latin *prōmunturium* : probably from *prō-,* forward + *mōns* (stem *mont-*), mountain.]

pro·mote (prə-mṓt || prō-) *tr.v.* **-moted, -moting, -motes. 1. a.** To raise to a more important or responsible job or rank. **b.** *Chiefly U.S.* To advance (a student) to the next, higher course or class. **2.** To contribute to the progress or growth of; further. **3.** To urge the adoption of; advocate. **4.** To attempt to sell or popularise by advertising or by securing financial support. —See Synonyms at **advance.** [Middle English *promoten,* from Latin *prōmovēre* (past participle *prōmōtus*), to move forward, advance : *prō-,* forward, onwards + *movēre,* to move.]

pro·mot·er (prə-mṓtər || prō-) *n.* **1.** An active supporter; an advocate. **2.** A finance and publicity organiser, as of a boxing match. **3.** *Chemistry.* A substance added to a catalyst in small amounts to increase its activity.

Promoter of the Faith *n. Roman Catholic Church.* The official name for a **devil's advocate** *(see).*

pro·mo·tion (prə-mṓsh'n || prō-) *n.* **1.** The act of promoting. **2.** An advancement in rank or responsibility. **3.** Encouragement; furtherance. **4. a.** Advertising or other publicity. **b.** An advertising or publicity campaign. **—pro·mo·tion·al** *adj.* **—pro·mo·tion·al·ly** *adv.*

pro·mo·tive (prə-mṓtiv || prō-) *adj.* Tending to promote.

prompt (prompt) *adj.* **1.** On time; punctual. **2.** Done without delay. **3.** Ready for action; quick to respond.
~*adv.* Exactly on time: *Come at two o'clock prompt.*
~*tr.v.* **prompted, prompting, prompts. 1.** To press into action; incite. **2.** To give rise to; inspire. **3.** To assist with a reminder; remind. **4.** In theatrical productions, to give a cue to (a performer who has forgotten his lines).
~*n.* **1. a.** The act of prompting or giving a cue. **b.** The information suggested; a reminder or cue. **2.** A theatrical prompter. **3.** *Finance.* **a.** A prompt note. **b.** The time limit stipulated in a prompt note. [Middle English, from Old French, from Latin *promptus,* "brought to light", "visible", hence, at hand, ready, prompt, from the past participle of *prōmere,* to bring forth, make manifest : *prō-,* forth + *emere,* to take.] **—promp·ti·tude, prompt·ness** *n.* **—prompt·ly** *adv.*

prompt·book (prómpt-bŏŏk- || -bŏŏk) *n.* An annotated script used by a theatre prompter.

prompt·er (prómptər) *n.* **1.** One who prompts. **2.** One who gives cues to actors.

prompt neutron *n.* A neutron instantaneously emitted (within 10^{-8} second) in nuclear fission. Compare **delayed neutron.**

prompt note *n.* A notice sent to the purchaser of goods reminding him of the amount due to the seller and the date on which it is due. Also called "prompt".

prompt side *n. Abbr.* **P.S.** The side of the stage on which the prompter sits: in Britain, to the left of an actor facing the audience, in the United States, to the right.

prom·ul·gate (próm-'l-gayt, -mul- || prṓ-, *U.S. also* prō-múl-) *tr.v.* **-gated, -gating, -gates. 1.** To make known (a decree, law, or doctrine) by public declaration; announce officially. **2.** To put (a law) into effect by formal public announcement. [Latin *prōmulgāre* : *prō-,* forth + *mulgēre,* to milk, cause to emerge.] **—prom·ul·ga·tion** (-gáysh'n) *n.* **—prom·ul·ga·tor** (-gaytər) *n.*

pro·my·ce·li·um (prṓ-mī-séeli-əm) *n., pl.* **-lia** (-ə). *Botany.* A germ tube produced by certain fungal spores.

pron. 1. pronominal; pronoun. **2.** pronounced; pronunciation.

pro·nate (prō-náyt, prṓnayt) *tr.v.* **-nated, -nating, -nates.** To turn (the palm of the hand or inner surface of a forelimb) downwards or backwards. [Late Latin *prōnāre,* to bend forward, bow, from Latin *prōnus,* PRONE.] **—pro·na·tion** (-náysh'n) *n.*

pro·na·tor (prō-náytər || *U.S.* prṓ-naytər) *n.* A forearm or forelimb muscle that effects pronation.

prone (prōn) *adj.* **1.** Lying with the front or face downwards; prostrate. **2.** Tending or liable: *prone to mischief.* Often used in combination: *accident-prone.* [Middle English, from Latin *prōnus,* "bending" or "leaning forward".] **—prone·ly** *adv.* **—prone·ness** *n.*
Usage: *prone, supine, prostrate. Prone* always means lying face downwards. *Supine* also means lying down, but always on one's back. *Prostrate* can mean lying down in either position, and suggests placing oneself, being thrown, or collapsing into this position..

pro·neph·ros (prō-néf-ross, prṓ-, -rəss) *n., pl.* **-roi** (-roy) or **-ra** (-rə). A primitive kidney that disappears early in the embryonic development of higher vertebrates. [New Latin : Greek *pro-,* before + *nephros,* kidney.] **—pro·neph·ric** (-rik) *adj.*

prong (prong || *U.S. also* prawng) *n.* **1.** A sharply pointed part of a tool or instrument, such as a tine of a fork. **2.** Any sharply pointed projection. **3.** Anything that can be used in combination with something else to attack an enemy or tackle a problem, such as a unit of troops or a policy: *the three prongs of our attack on inflation.*
~*tr.v.* **pronged, pronging, prongs.** To pierce with a prong. [Middle English *pronge, prange,* forked instrument; perhaps akin to Middle Low German *prange,* pinching instrument, from Germanic *prang-* (unattested), pinch.]

pronged (prongd || prawngd) *adj.* **1.** Having a specified number of prongs. **2.** Coming from a specified number of directions at once.

prong·horn (próng-hawrn || práwng-) *n., pl.* **-horns** or collectively **pronghorn.** A small deer, *Antilocapra americana,* resembling an antelope and having small forked horns, found on North American plains. Also called "prongbuck", "pronghorn antelope".

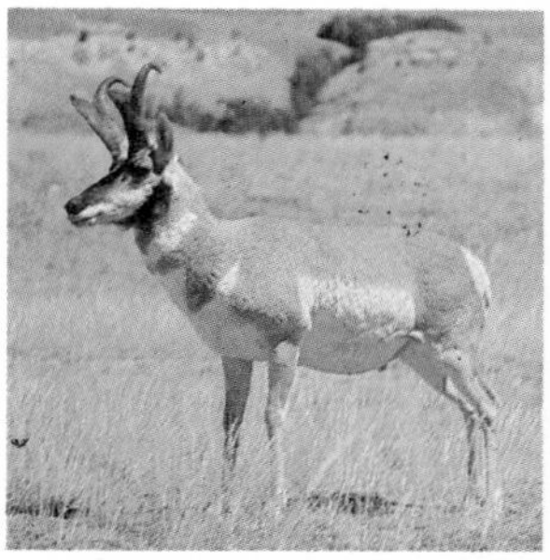
pronghorn *The only surviving member of the family* Antilocapridae, *the pronghorn resembles the antelope and was once found from Mexico to Canada. Now, however, it is confined to the plains of North America.*

pro·nom·i·nal (prō-nómmin'l, prə-) *adj. Abbr.* **pron., pronom. 1.** Of, pertaining to, or functioning as a pronoun. **2.** Resembling a pronoun, as by specifying a person, place, or thing, while functioning primarily as another part of speech. *His* in *his choice* is a pronominal adjective. [Late Latin *prōnōminālis,* from Latin *prōnōmen,* PRONOUN.] **—pro·nom·i·nal·ly** *adv.*

pro·nom·i·nal·ise, pro·nom·i·nal·ize (prō-nómmin'l-z, prə-) *tr.v.* **-ised, -ising, -ises.** To treat as or make into a pronoun. **—pro·nom·i·nal·i·sa·tion** (-ī-záysh'n || *U.S.* -i-) *n.*

pro·noun (prṓ-nown || *West Indies also* -nung) *n. Abbr.* **pron., pr.** Any of a class of words that function as substitutes for nouns or noun phrases and denote persons or things asked for, previously specified, or understood from the context. [Middle English *pronom,* from Latin *prōnōmen* : *prō-,* in place of + *nōmen,* name.]

pro·nounce (prə-nównss || prō-; *West Indies also* -núngss) *v.* **-nounced, -nouncing, -nounces.** —*tr.* **1. a.** To articulate (a word or speech sound). **b.** To articulate in the approved manner. **2.** To transcribe (a word) in phonetic symbols. **3.** To state officially and formally; declare. **4.** To declare to be in a specified condition: *The doctor pronounced the victim dead.* **5.** To deliver (a verdict or opinion, for example). —*intr.* **1.** To declare one's opinion or make a pronouncement. Used with *on.* **2.** To articulate words. [Middle English *pronuncen, pronouncen,* from Old French *prononcier,* from Latin *prōnuntiāre,* to speak in public, declare : *prō-,* forth, in public + *nuntiāre,* to declare, from *nuntius,* message, messenger.] **—pro·nounce·a·ble** *adj.* **—pro·nounc·er** *n.*

pro·nounced (prə-nównst || prō-; *West Indies also* -núngst) *adj. Abbr.* **pron. 1.** Spoken; voiced. **2.** Distinct; strongly marked. **—pro·nounced·ly** (-nównst-li, -nówn-sid-) *adv.* **—pro·nounced·ness** *n.*

pro·nounce·ment (prə-nównss-mənt || prō-; *West Indies also* -núngss-) *n.* **1.** A formal declaration. **2.** An authoritative statement.

pron·to (próntō) *adv. Informal.* Without delay; quickly. [Spanish, from Latin *promptus,* PROMPT.]

pro·nu·cle·us (prṓ-néw-kli-əss, prō- || -nŏŏ-) *n., pl.* **-clei.** (-ī). The haploid nucleus of a sperm or egg prior to fusion of the nuclei in fertilisation. **—pro·nu·cle·ar** *adj.*

pro·nun·ci·a·mien·to (prə-nún-si-ə-méntō || prō-, -nŏŏn-, -thi-) *n., pl.* **-tos. 1.** An edict or proclamation, especially when announcing a coup d'état. **2.** Any authoritarian pronouncement. [Spanish.]

pro·nun·ci·a·tion (prə-nún-si-áysh'n || prō-, -nówn-) *n. Abbr.* **pron. 1.** The act or manner or an instance of articulating speech. **2.** The approved manner of pronouncing a particular word or sound. **3.** A phonetic transcription of a word. **—pro·nun·ci·a·tion·al** *adj.*

pro·oes·trus (prō-éess-trəss, prō- || *U.S.* -éss-) *n.* The period of the oestrous cycle immediately before oestrus.

proof (prŏŏf || prŏŏf) *n.* **1.** The evidence establishing the validity of a given assertion. **2.** Conclusive demonstration of something. **3.** The testing or validation of something by experiment or trial. **4.** *Archaic.* Proven impenetrability. **5.** *Law.* The evidence used to determine the verdict or judgment in a case. **6.** In Scots law, trial before a judge rather than a jury. **7.** The validation of a proposition by application of specified rules, as of induction or deduction, to assumptions, axioms, and sequentially derived conclusions. **8.** The strength of an alcoholic drink with reference to **proof spirit** *(see).* **9.** *Printing.* A trial sheet of printed material that is checked against the original version and on which corrections are made. Also called "proof sheet". **10.** In engraving, a trial impression of a plate, stone, or block. **11.** In photography, a trial print.
~*adj.* **1.** Fully or successfully resistant; impervious. Used with *against* or in combination: *proof against fire; waterproof.* **2.** Of standard alcoholic strength. **3.** Used in proving or making corrections.
~*v.* **proofed, proofing, proofs.** —*tr.* **1.** To make or run off (a printed or engraved proof). **2.** To proofread (copy). **3.** To make resistant or impervious. —*intr.* To proofread. [Middle English *pre(o)ve, prof, prove,* from Old French *pre(o)ve,* from Late Latin *proba,* from Latin *probāre,* to test, PROVE.]

proof·read (prŏŏf-reed || prŏŏf-) *v.* **-read** (-red), **-reading, -reads.** —*tr.* To read (copy or a printer's proof) against the original typescript, printed version, or manuscript in order to check that they are correct. —*intr.* To correct a printer's proof while reading against the original version. **—proof·read·er** *n.*

proof spirit *n.* An alcohol-water mixture or an alcoholic drink containing 49.28 per cent ethanol by weight or 57.1 per cent by volume and having a relative density of 0.92 at 15.56°C (60°F). In the

PRONUNCIATION KEY

a, trap; aa, father; ai, fair; ar, star; aw, lawn; ay, play; b, bb, stab; rubber; ch, church; ck, ticket; d, dd, dead; ladder; e, dress; ee, bee; er, defer; ew, few; ewr, pure; ə, about; ər, letter; f, ff, fife; differ; g, gg, giggle; h, hat; i, kit; ī, price; īr, fire; j, judge; k, kick; l, ll, let; 'l, needle; m, mm, man; n, nn, no; 'n, sudden; ng, thing; o, lot; ō, no; ŏŏ, foot; ōō, shoe; oor, poor; ow, cow; owr, hour; oy, boy; p, pp, pepper; r, rr, red; s, ss, sauce; sh, ship; t, tt, totter; th, thick; th, this; smooth; u, cut; ur, turn; v, vv, valve; w, wet; y, yes; z, zz, zebra; zh, vision; pleasure

IN FOREIGN WORDS:

aN, oN, Saint-Saëns; hl, Llanelli; Hluhluwe; kh, loch; lough; Khaled

STRESS MARK:

ín-sīt, insight; in-sīt, incite

United States, proof spirit contains 50 per cent ethanol by volume at 15.56°C (60°F).

prop¹ (prop) *n.* **1.** Anything used to support or shore something up. **2.** A person or thing serving as a support or stay. **3. a.** In Rugby football, either of the two forwards who play on the left or right of the front row of the scrum. **b.** The position of such a player. In both senses, also called "prop forward".
~*tr.v.* **propped, propping, props. 1.** To keep from falling; support, especially by means of a rigid object. Often used with *up.* **2.** To lean or rest for support. Usually used with *against.* [Middle English *proppe,* probably from Middle Dutch *proppe†,* vine-prop, stopper.]

prop² *n.* A stage **property** *(see).*

prop³ *n. Informal.* A propeller.

prop– *comb. form. Chemistry.* Indicates derivation from propionic acid; for example, propane. [From PROPIONIC (ACID).]

prop. 1. proper; properly. **2.** property. **3.** proposition. **4.** proprietary; proprietor.

pro·pae·deu·tic (prō-pee-dew-tik ‖ -pi-, -doo-) *adj.* Providing introductory instruction.
~*n. Often plural.* Preparatory instruction. [Greek *propaideuein,* to teach beforehand : *pro-,* before + *paideuein,* to rear or educate, from *pais* (stem *paid-*), child.]

prop·a·ga·ble (próppəgəb'l) *adj.* Capable of being propagated.

prop·a·gan·da (próppə-gándə) *n.* **1.** The systematic propagation or discrediting of a given doctrine or cause by circulating polemical material, such as posters or leaflets. **2.** Material disseminated by the champions or opponents of a doctrine or cause. [From PROPAGANDA FIDE.] —**prop·a·gan·dism** *n.* —**prop·a·gan·dist** *n.* —**prop·a·gan·dis·tic** (-gan-dístik) *adj.* —**prop·a·gan·dis·ti·cal·ly** *adv.*

Prop·a·gan·da Fi·de (próppə-gándə fēeday) *n. Roman Catholic Church.* The Congregation of the Roman Curia that has authority in the matters of preaching the gospel and of administering Church missions. Also called "Propaganda". [Italian, short for the New Latin title *Sacra Congregatio de Propaganda Fide,* Sacred Congregation for Propagating the Faith, from Latin *prōpāgāndus,* gerundive of *prōpāgāre,* to PROPAGATE.]

prop·a·gan·dise, prop·a·gan·dize (próppə-gánd-īz) *v.* **-dised, -dising, -dises.** —*tr.* **1.** To spread (a doctrine or opinion) by means of propaganda. **2.** To subject (a person or group of persons) to propaganda. —*intr.* To spread propaganda.

prop·a·gate (próppə-gayt) *v.* **-gated, -gating, -gates.** —*tr.* **1.** To cause (animals) to breed. **2.** To breed (offspring). **3.** To multiply (plants) by cuttings, graftings, or the like. **4.** To transmit (characteristics) from one generation to another. **5.** To make known; promote or spread. **6.** *Physics.* To cause (a wave, for example) to move through a medium; transmit. —*intr.* **1.** *Physics.* To move through a medium. **2.** To breed or multiply. [Latin *prōpāgāre,* to propagate (plants) by means of slips, from *prōpāgo, prōpāgēs,* slip, shoot, offspring : *prō,* forth + *pāgo,* from *pangere,* to layer.] —**prop·a·ga·tive** (-gətiv, -gaytiv) *adj.*

prop·a·ga·tion (próppə-gáysh'n) *n.* **1.** Increase or spread, as by natural reproduction. **2.** Dissemination, as of a belief: *propagation of the Gospel.* —**prop·a·ga·tion·al** *adj.*

prop·a·ga·tor (próppə-gaytər) *n.* One that propagates; especially, a tray with a clear glass or plastic cover containing soil in which seeds or cuttings are raised.

prop·a·gule (próppə-gewl) *n.* A plant structure, such as a bud, bulb, or tuber, that becomes detached from the parent plant and develops into a new individual. [From PROPAGATE + -ULE.]

pro·pane (prō-payn) *n.* A colourless alkane gas, C_3H_8, found in natural gas and petroleum, and used as fuel. [PROP- + -ANE.]

pro·pane-di·ol (prō-payn-dī-ol ‖ -ōl) *n. Chemistry.* Propylene glycol *(see).*

pro·pa·no·ic ac·id (prōpə-nó-ik) *n. Chemistry.* Propionic acid *(see).* [PROPANE + -IC.]

pro·pa·nol (prōpə-nol ‖ -nōl) *n.* A colourless, liquid alcohol that occurs in two isomeric forms, 1-propanol, $CH_3CH_2CH_2OH$, and 2-propanol, $CH_3CHOHCH_3$. Both forms are used as solvents. Also called "propyl alcohol". [PROPAN(E) + -OL.]

pro·pa·none (prōpə-nōn) *n. Chemistry.* An organic ketone, acetone *(see).*

pro·par·ox·y·tone (prō-pə-róksi-tōn, -pa-, -tən) *adj.* Having an acute accent on the antepenult in Classical Greek.
~*n.* A proparoxytone word. [Greek *proparoxutonos : pro-,* before + PAROXYTONE.] —**pro·par·ox·y·ton·ic** (-tónnik) *adj.*

pro pa·tri·a (prō páttri-ə, páatri-, -aa). *Latin.* For one's country.

pro·pel (prə-pél) *tr.v.* **-pelled, -pelling, -pels.** To cause to move or sustain in motion. [Middle English *propellen,* from Latin *prōpellere : prō,* forward + *pellere,* to drive.]

pro·pel·lant, pro·pel·lent (prə-péllənt ‖ prō-) *n.* **1.** Something that propels or provides thrust, such as an explosive charge or a rocket fuel. **2.** The gas used in a domestic aerosol spray.
~*adj.* Serving to propel; propelling.

pro·pel·ler (prə-péllər) *n.* Any of various related simple machines for propelling aircraft or boats, especially one having radiating blades mounted on a revolving power-driven shaft. Also called "screw", "screw propeller".

propeller shaft *n.* **1.** The shaft that drives a propeller. **2.** The shaft in a motor vehicle that transmits power from the gearbox to the differential. Also called "prop shaft".

pro·pel·ling pencil (prə-pélling ‖ prō-) *n.* A pencil in which the lead can be retracted, extended, or replaced.

pro·pe·nal (prōpi-nal) *n. Chemistry.* An organic aldehyde, acrolein *(see).*

pro·pend (prō-pénd, prə-) *intr.v.* **-pended, -pending, -pends.** *Archaic.* To have a propensity towards. [Latin *prōpendēre,* to hang forward or downwards, be inclined or favourable : *prō-,* forward, down + *pendēre,* to hang.]

pro·pene (prō-peen) *n.* A colourless, flammable alkene gas, C_3H_6, obtained by cracking petroleum and used in organic synthesis. Also called "propylene".

pro·pe·no·ic acid (prō-pee-nō-ik, -pi-) *n. Chemistry.* An organic acid, acrylic acid *(see).*

pro·pen·si·ty (prə-pén-səti, prō-) *n., pl.* **-ties.** An innate inclination; a tendency; a bent. [From archaic *propense,* inclined, from Latin *prōpensus,* past participle of *prōpendēre,* to be inclined or favourable, PROPEND.]

prop·er (próppər) *adj. Abbr.* **prop. 1.** Suitable; fitting; appropriate: *the proper moment.* **2.** Out-and-out; thorough: *a proper rascal.* **3.** Worthy of the name: *take one's medicine like a proper man.* **4.** Meeting a requisite standard of competence or validity. **5. a.** Within the strict limitation of the term. Used after the noun: *France proper.* **b.** Rigorously correct; exact. **6.** Characteristically belonging to the being or thing in question. Used after the noun and with *to: an optical effect proper to fluids.* **7. a.** Seemly; decorous in behaviour. **b.** Displaying exaggerated propriety or gentility. **8.** *Mathematics.* Designating a subset of a given set when the latter has at least one element not in the subset. **9.** *Ecclesiastical.* Belonging to the proper of the day. —See Synonyms at **fit.**
~*adv.* Thoroughly: *He got told off good and proper.*
~*n. Sometimes capital* P. *Ecclesiastical.* **1.** The parts of the Mass or Divine Office that vary according to the particular day or feast. **2.** An office to be said on an appointed day or feast. Compare **ordinary.** [Middle English *propre,* one's own, distinctive, correct, proper, from Old French, from Latin *proprius,* one's own, personal, particular.] —**prop·er·ly** (*informally also* próppli) *adv.* —**prop·er·ness** *n.*

proper adjective *n.* An adjective formed from a proper noun.

pro·per·din (prō-pérdin) *n.* A natural protein in human blood serum that helps provide immunity to Gram-negative bacteria and viruses. Not in technical usage. [Perhaps PRO- (acting as) + Latin *perdere,* "to give away", squander, hence, to destroy : *per-,* away, to destruction + *dare,* to give + -IN.]

proper fraction *n.* **1.** A numerical fraction in which the numerator is less than the denominator; a common fraction that is less than one. **2.** A polynomial fraction in which the numerator is of lower degree than the denominator. Compare **improper fraction.**

proper motion *n. Astronomy.* The component of a star's motion in space, relative to the sun, that is perpendicular to the line of sight.

proper noun *n.* A noun designating by name a being or thing without a limiting modifier. Also called "proper name". Compare **common noun.**

prop·er·tied (próppər-tid ‖ -teed) *adj.* Owning land or securities as a principal source of revenue.

prop·er·ty (próppərti) *n., pl.* **-ties.** *Abbr.* **prop. 1.** The right of possession, use, and disposal of something; ownership. **2.** A possession, or possessions collectively. **3.** Something tangible or intangible to which its owner has legal title. **4.** A piece of land, such as that on which a house stands or that used for farming. **5.** Any article, except costumes and scenery, used on the set or stage of a film, play, or musical. Also called "prop". **6. a.** A characteristic trait or peculiarity. **b.** A special capability or power; a virtue. **c.** A quality serving to define or describe an object or substance. **d.** A characteristic attribute possessed by all members of a class. **e.** *Logic.* A predicable that is common and peculiar to the whole of a species and is necessarily predicated of its essence without being part of that essence. —See Synonyms at **asset, quality.** [Middle English *proprete,* from Old French *propr(i)ete,* from Latin *proprietās* (stem *proprietāt-*), ownership, peculiarity, from *proprius,* own, particular, PROPER.]

prop forward *n.* A player in Rugby football, a **prop** *(see).*

pro·phage (prō-fayj) *n.* A noninfectious association between a bacterial virus and a bacterium, in which the viral chromosomes link with the bacterial chromosomes but do not cause disruption of the bacterial cell or promote replication of the virus itself. [PRO- (before) + -PHAGE.]

pro·phase (prō-fayz) *n. Biology.* The first stage in cell division in meiosis and mitosis, during which chromosomes become visible and the nuclear membrane begins to disintegrate. See **diakinesis, diplotene, leptotene, pachytene, zygotene.**

proph·e·cy (próffə-si, próffi-) *n., pl.* **-cies. 1.** A prediction. **2. a.** The inspired utterance of a prophet, viewed as a declaration of divine will. **b.** Such a revelation transmitted orally or in writing. **c.** The quality or activity of receiving and transmitting such relevations. [Middle English *propheci(e), prophesye,* from Old French *profecie, prophecie,* from Latin *prophētīa,* from Greek *prophēteia,* from *prophētēs,* PROPHET.]
Usage: Prophecy and prophesy are sometimes confused in spelling. *Prophecy* is the noun; *prophesy* the verb. Their pronunciations are also different.

proph·e·sy (próffi-sī, próffə-) *v.* **-sied, -sying, -sies.** —*tr.* **1.** To reveal by divine inspiration. **2.** To predict. **3.** To prefigure; foreshow. —*intr.* **1.** To reveal the will of God. **2.** To predict the future. **3.** To speak as a prophet. —See Synonyms at **foretell.** —See Usage note at **prophecy.** [Middle English *prophecien,* from Old French *prophecier,* from *prophecie,* PROPHECY.] **—proph·e·si·er** *n.*

proph·et (próffit) *n.* **1.** A person who speaks by divine inspiration or as the interpreter through whom divine will is expressed. **2.** One who predicts the future. **3.** The chief spokesman of a cause. **—the Prophet. 1.** *Islam.* Muhammad. **2.** In the Mormon Church, Joseph Smith. **—the Prophets.** The prophetic writings of the Hebrew Scriptures; the second main division of the Old Testament. [Middle English *prophet(e), profete,* from Old French, from Latin *prophēta,* from Greek *prophētēs,* "one who speaks beforehand" : *pro-,* before + *-phētēs,* "speaker", from *phanai,* to say.]

proph·et·ess (próffit-iss, -ess) *n.* A female prophet.

pro·phet·ic (prə-féttik, prō-) *adj.* Also **pro·phet·i·cal** (-'l). **1.** Of or belonging to a prophet or prophecy. **2.** Of the nature of prophecy. **—pro·phet·i·cal·ly** *adv.* **—pro·phet·i·cal·ness** *n.*

pro·phy·lac·tic (próffi-láktik || *chiefly U.S.* prṓfi-) *adj.* Acting to defend against or prevent something, especially disease; protective. *~n.* **1.** A prophylactic medicine, device, or measure. **2.** Something intended as a precaution. **3.** *Chiefly U.S.* Any contraceptive device, especially a condom. [Greek *prophulaktikos,* from *prophulassein,* to stand on guard before (a place), take precautions against : *pro-,* before + *phulassein,* to guard, protect, from *phulax,* a guard.] **—pro·phy·lac·ti·cal·ly** *adv.*

pro·phy·lax·is (próffi-lák-siss || *chiefly U.S.* prṓfi-) *n., pl.* **-laxes** (-seez). The prevention of or protective treatment for disease. [New Latin, from Greek *prophulaktikos,* PROPHYLACTIC.]

pro·pin·qui·ty (prə-píngkwəti, prō-, pro-) *n.* **1.** Nearness in place or time; proximity. **2.** Kinship. **3.** Similarity in nature. [Middle English *propinquite,* from Latin *propinquitās* (stem *propinquitāt-*), from *propinquus,* near.]

pro·pi·o·nate (prṓpi-ə-nayt) *n.* A salt or ester of propionic acid. [PROPION(IC ACID) + -ATE.]

pro·pi·on·ic acid (prṓpi-ónnik) *n.* A fatty acid, $CH_3CH_2CO_2H$, prepared synthetically and used in a salt form as a mould inhibitor in bread. Also called "propanoic acid". [French *propionique* : Greek *pro-,* before, first (because this acid is first in order among the fatty acids) + *piōn,* fat + -IC.]

pro·pi·ti·ate (prə-píshi-ayt, prō-) *tr.v.* **-ated, -ating, -ates.** To conciliate (an offended power); appease. [Latin *propitiāre,* from *propitius,* PROPITIOUS.] **—pro·pi·ti·a·ble** *adj.* **—pro·pi·ti·at·ing·ly** *adv.* **—pro·pi·ti·a·tive** (-ətiv, -aytiv) *adj.* **—pro·pi·ti·a·tor** (-aytər) *n.*

pro·pi·ti·a·tion (prə-píshi-áysh'n, prō-) *n.* **1.** The act of propitiating. **2.** Something that propitiates; especially, an offering to a god.

pro·pi·ti·a·to·ry (prə-píshi-ətri, prō-, -písh-, -ətəri) *adj.* Of or offered in propitiation; conciliatory.
~n., pl. **propitiatories.** In ancient Jewish ceremony, the **mercy seat** *(see).* **—pro·pi·ti·a·to·ri·ly** *adv.*

pro·pi·tious (prə-píshəss || prō-) *adj.* **1.** Presenting favourable circumstances; auspicious. **2.** Kindly; gracious. —See Synonyms at **favourable.** [Middle English *propycyous,* from Old French *propicius,* from Latin *propitius,* favourable, kind.] **—pro·pi·tious·ly** *adv.* **—pro·pi·tious·ness** *n.*

prop-jet (próp-jet) *n.* A **turboprop** *(see).*

prop·o·lis (próppəliss) *n.* A resinous substance used by bees in making their hives. [Latin, from Greek, suburb, hence (unexplained sense development) bee glue : *pro-,* before, beyond + *polis,* city.]

pro·po·nent (prə-pṓnənt || prō-) *n.* **1.** One who argues in support of something; an advocate. **2.** *Law.* A person who applies for probate of a will. [Latin *prōpōnēns* (stem *prōpōnent-*), present participle of *prōpōnere,* to PROPOSE.]

pro·por·tion (prə-pór-sh'n || prō-, -pṓr-) *n.* **1.** A part considered in relation to the whole. **2.** A relationship between things or parts of things with respect to comparative magnitude, quantity, or degree. **3.** A relationship between quantities, such that if one varies, another varies in a manner dependent on the first; a ratio. **4.** Harmonious relationship; symmetry. **5.** *Usually plural.* Dimensions; size: *He has the proportions of a giant.* **6.** *Mathematics.* A relationship of equality between two ratios. Four quantities, *a, b, c, d,* are said to be in proportion if $a/b = c/d$.
~tr.v. **proportioned, -tioning, -tions. 1.** To adjust so that proper relations between parts are attained. **2.** To adjust in degree, quantity, or other measure, in relation to something else. [Middle English *proporcioun,* from Old French *proportion,* from Latin *prōportiō* (stem *prōportiōn-*) (translation of Greek *analogia,* analogy), from the phrase *prō portiōne,* "for the share of", proportionally : *prō,* for + *portiō,* share, portion.] **—pro·por·tion·a·ble** *adj.* **—pro·por·tion·a·bly** *adv.* **—pro·por·tion·er** *n.* **—pro·por·tion·ment** *n.*
Synonyms: *proportion, harmony, symmetry, balance.*

pro·por·tion·al (prə-pór-sh'n'l || prō-, -pṓr-) *adj.* **1.** Forming a relationship with other parts or quantities; being in proportion. **2.** Properly related in size or other measurable characteristics. **3.** *Mathematics.* Having a constant ratio.
~n. Any of the quantities in a mathematical proportion. **—pro·por·tion·al·i·ty** (-sh'n-áləti) *n.* **—pro·por·tion·al·ly** *adv.*

proportional representation *n. Abbr.* **P.R.** Representation of all parties in an elective body in proportion to their share of the total vote cast in an election. Compare **first-past-the-post.**

pro·por·tion·ate (prə-pór-sh'n-ət, -it || prō-, -pṓr-, -ayt) *adj.* Being in due proportion; proportional.
~tr.v. (-ayt) **proportionated, -ating, -ates.** To make proportionate. **—pro·por·tion·ate·ly** (-ət-li, -it- || -ayt-) *adv.* **—pro·por·tion·ate·ness** *n.*

pro·pos·al (prə-pṓz'l || prō-) *n.* **1.** The act of proposing. **2.** A plan or scheme that is proposed; a suggestion. **3.** An offer of marriage.

pro·pose (prə-pṓz || prō-) *v.* **-posed, -posing, -poses.** *—tr.* **1.** To put forward for consideration, discussion, or adoption: *propose new methods.* **2.** To present or nominate (a person) for a position, office, or membership. **3.** To offer (a toast). **4.** To purpose; intend. *—intr.* To form or make a proposal, especially of marriage. [Middle English *proposen,* from Old French *proposer,* from Latin *prōpōnere* (past participle *prōpositus*), to put or set forth, declare, propound : *prō,* forward + *pōnere,* to place.] **—pro·pos·er** *n.*

prop·o·si·tion (próppə-zísh'n) *n. Abbr.* **prop. 1.** A plan or scheme suggested for consideration or acceptance. **2.** *Informal.* A matter or person requiring special handling. **3.** A suggested business offer, arrangement, or the like. **4.** A subject for discussion or analysis, as in a debate. **5.** *Logic.* **a.** A statement in which the subject is affirmed or denied by the predicate and can or is shown to be true or false. **b.** A statement containing only logical constants and having a fixed truth-value. **6.** *Informal.* An offer of sexual intercourse.
~tr.v. **propositioned, -tioning, -tions.** *Informal.* To propose a private bargain to; especially, to make an offer of sexual intercourse to. [Middle English *proposicioun,* from Old French *proposition,* from Latin *prōpositiō* (stem *prōpositiōn-*), from *prōpōnere,* PROPOSE.] **—prop·o·si·tion·al** (-'l) *adj.* **—prop·o·si·tion·al·ly** *adv.*

propositional calculus *n.* The branch of symbolic logic dealing with the relationships formed between propositions by such connectives as *and, or,* and *if* as opposed to their internal structure. Compare **predicate calculus.**

propositional function *n. Logic.* An expression having the form of a proposition, but containing undefined symbols for the substantive elements. It becomes a proposition when appropriate values are assigned to the symbols.

pro·pos·i·tus (prə-pózzi-təss, prō-) *n., pl.* **-ti** (-tī). *Law.* One from whom a line of descent is traced. [New Latin, specialised use of the past participle of Latin *prōpōnere,* to place before, PROPOSE.]

pro·pound (prə-pównd, prō- || *West Indies also* -pungd) *tr.v.* **-pounded, -pounding, -pounds. 1.** To put forward for consideration; set forth. **2.** *Law.* To present (a will) before the proper authority to obtain probate. [Alteration of earlier *propoune,* Middle English (Scottish) *proponen,* from Latin *prōpōnere,* to PROPOSE.] **—pro·pound·er** *n.*

propr. proprietor.

pro·prae·tor (prṓ-préetər, prō-) *n.* A Roman official appointed, usually immediately after holding the praetorship, to be the chief administrator of a province. [Latin, from *prō praetōre,* (one acting) for a praetor : *prō,* for + PRAETOR.] **—pro·prae·to·ri·al** (-táwri-əl || -tṓri-), **pro·prae·to·ri·an** *adj.*

pro·pri·e·tar·y (prə-prī́-ə-tri, -təri || prō-, -terri) *adj. Abbr.* **prop., pty. 1.** Of or pertaining to a proprietor or to proprietors collectively. **2.** Exclusively owned; private. **3.** Befitting an owner: *a proprietary air.* **4.** Owned by a private individual or corporation under a trademark or patent. **5.** *Medicine.* Of or designating a medical preparation or agent made and distributed under a trade name.
~n., pl. **proprietaries.** *Abbr.* **prop., pty. 1.** A proprietor. **2.** A group of proprietors. **3.** Ownership; proprietorship. **4.** Formerly, the governor of a proprietary American colony. **5.** A proprietary medicine or agent. [Late Latin *proprietārius,* from Latin *proprietās,* property, PROPRIETY.] **—pro·pri·e·tar·i·ly** *adv.*

proprietary colony *n.* Any of certain early North American colonies, such as Carolina and Pennsylvania, that were granted by the Crown in the 17th century to one or more Lords Proprietary, who had full governing rights.

pro·pri·e·tor (prə-prī́-ə-tər || prō-) *n. Abbr.* **prop., propr. 1.** A person who has legal title to something; an owner. **2.** The owner or owner-manager of a business or other institution. [Alteration of PROPRIETARY (noun).] **—pro·pri·e·to·ri·al** (-táwri-əl || -tṓri-) *adj.* **—pro·pri·e·to·ri·al·ly** *adv.* **—pro·pri·e·tor·ship** *n.*

pro·pri·e·tress (prə-prī́-ə-triss, -tress || prō-) *n.* A female proprietor.

pro·pri·e·ty (prə-prī́-əti || prō-) *n., pl.* **-ties. 1.** The quality of being fitting or proper; appropriateness. **2. a.** Conformity to prevailing customs and usages. **b.** *Plural.* The usages and customs considered to be correct in polite society. Preceded by *the.* —See Synonyms at **etiquette.** [Middle English *propriete,* ownership, one's own nature, idiosyncrasy, from Old French, from Latin *proprietās* (stem *proprietāt-*), from *proprius,* PROPER.]

pro·pri·o·cep·tor (próppri-ō-séptər, -ə-) *n.* A sensory receptor, chiefly in muscles, tendons, and joints, that responds to stimuli arising within the organism. [Latin *proprius,* one's own + (RE)CEPTOR.] **—pro·pri·o·cep·tive** *adj.*

prop root *n.* A root growing from above ground into the soil and helping to support the plant stem, as in maize.

prop shaft *n.* A **propeller shaft** *(see).*

prop·to·sis (prop-tṓ-siss) *n., pl.* **-ses** (-seez). Forward displacement of an organ, such as the eyeball. [Late Latin, from Greek *proptōsis,* a falling forward, from *propiptein,* to fall forward : *pro-,* forward + *piptein,* to fall.]

pro·pul·sion (prə-púl-sh'n || prō-) *n.* **1.** The process of driving or propelling. **2.** A driving or propelling force. [Medieval Latin *prōpulsiō* (stem *prōpulsiōn-*), from Latin *prōpellere* (past participle *prōpulsus*), to drive forward, PROPEL.] **—pro·pul·sive, pro·pul·so·ry** (-səri) *adj.*

pro·pyl (prṓ-pil, -pīl) *n. Chemistry.* A univalent organic radical with composition C_3H_7, derived from propane. [PROP- + -YL.]

prop·y·lae·um (próppi-lée-əm, prṓ-pī-) *n., pl.* **-laea** (-lée-ə). *Architecture.* An entrance or vestibule to a temple or group of buildings.

Also called "propylon". [Latin, from Greek *propulaion* : *pro-*, before + *pulē*, gate.]
propyl alcohol *n. Chemistry.* **Propanol** *(see).*
pro·pyl·ene (prṓpi-leen) *n. Chemistry.* **Propene** *(see).* [PROPYL + -ENE.]
propylene glycol *n.* A colourless viscous hygroscopic liquid, $CH_3CH(OH)CH_2OH$, used in antifreeze solutions, in hydraulic fluids, and as a solvent. Also called "propanediol".
pro ra·ta (prṓ raatə; *old-fashioned* ráytə || *U.S. also* ráttə) *adj.* In proportion. [Latin *pro rata (parte),* according to the calculated (share).] **—pro ra·ta** *adv.*
pro·rate (prō-ráyt, -rayt) *v.* **-rated, -rating, -rates.** *U.S.* *—tr.* To divide, distribute, or assess proportionately. *—intr.* To settle affairs on the basis of proportional distribution. [From PRO RATA.] **—pro·rat·a·ble** (-ráytəb'l) *adj.* **—pro·ra·tion** (-ráysh'n) *n.*
pro·rogue (prə-rṓg, prō-) *tr.v.* **-rogued, -roguing, -rogues.** To discontinue the sessions of (a parliament or similar body) for a period of time. [Middle English *prorogen,* from Old French *prorog(u)er,* from Latin *prōrogāre,* "to ask publicly (for an extension of one's term of office)", prolong, defer : *prō-,* forward, in public + *rogāre,* to ask.] **—pro·ro·ga·tion** (prṓ-rə-gáysh'n, prórrə-) *n.*
pros- *prefix.* Indicates: **1.** Near, to, or towards; for example, **prosenchyma. 2.** In front; for example, **prosencephalon.** [Greek, from *pros,* near, at, towards, to.]
pro·sa·ic (prō-záy-ik, prə-) *adj.* **1.** Of or like prose; not poetic. **2. a.** Matter-of-fact; straightforward. **b.** Lacking in imagination and spirit; dull; ordinary. [Late Latin *prōsaicus,* from Latin *prōsa,* PROSE.] **—pro·sa·i·cal·ly** *adv.* **—pro·sa·ic·ness** *n.*
pro·sa·ism (prṓ-zay-iz'm) *n.* **1.** A quality or style that is prosaic. **2.** A prosaic expression, phrase, or word.
pro·sce·ni·um (prə-séeni-əm, prō-) *n., pl.* **-nia** (-ə). **1.** In a modern theatre, the area located between the curtain and the orchestra. **2.** In an ancient theatre, the stage, located between the background and the orchestra. [Latin, from Greek *proskēnion* : *pro-,* before + *skēnē,* "tent", stage-building used as background (see **scene**).]
proscenium arch *n.* In a traditional theatre, the arch over the front of and framing the stage.
pro·sciut·to (prō-shóo-tō, pro-) *n., pl.* **-ti** (-ti). A type of spiced Italian ham. [Italian, from *pro-,* beforehand, PRE- + *asciutto,* dried.]
pro·scribe (prō-skrī́b, prə-) *tr.v.* **-scribed, -scribing, -scribes. 1.** To denounce or condemn; specifically, to outlaw or banish. **2.** To prohibit; forbid. **3.** In ancient Rome, to publish the name of (a person) as outlawed and confiscate his property. [Latin *prōscrībere,* to publish in writing, proscribe : *prō-,* in front, publicly + *scrībere,* to write.] **—pro·scrib·er** *n.*
pro·scrip·tion (prō-skríp-sh'n, prə-) *n.* **1.** The act of proscribing; prohibition. **2.** The condition of being proscribed. **—pro·scrip·tive** *adj.* **—pro·scrip·tive·ly** *adv.*
prose (prōz) *n.* **1.** Ordinary speech or writing, as distinguished from verse. **2.** Commonplace expression or quality. **3.** A piece of English prose to be translated into another language as an exercise. **4.** *Roman Catholic Church.* Formerly, a hymn of irregular metre sung after the gradual at Mass.
~adj. Written in prose.
~v. **prosed, prosing, proses.** *—tr.* To make into prose. *—intr.* **1.** To write prose. **2.** To speak or write in a dull, tiresome style. [Middle English, from Old French, from Latin *prōsa (ōrātiō),* "straightforward discourse", from *prōsus, prorsus,* straightforward, direct, from *prōversus,* past participle of *prōvertere,* to turn forward : *prō-,* forward + *vertere,* to turn.]
pros·e·cute (próssi-kewt) *v.* **-cuted, -cuting, -cutes.** *—tr.* **1.** To pursue or persist in so as to complete. **2.** To carry on (a trade, for example); practise. **3. a.** To initiate legal or criminal court action against. **b.** To seek to obtain or enforce by legal action. *—intr.* **1.** To initiate and conduct legal proceedings. **2.** To act as prosecutor. [Middle English *prosecuten,* to follow, from Latin *prōsequī* (past participle *prōsecūtus*), to follow up or forward : *prō-,* forward + *sequī,* to follow.]
prosecuting attorney *n. U.S.* An attorney empowered to prosecute cases on behalf of a government and the people.
pros·e·cu·tion (próssi-kéwsh'n) *n.* **1. a.** The act of prosecuting. **b.** The state of being prosecuted. **2.** The institution and carrying out of a legal proceeding. **3.** The lawyers who act on behalf of the Crown or State in criminal proceedings. **4.** The act or process of carrying out or continuing something.
pros·e·cu·tor (próssi-kewtər) *n.* **1.** One who prosecutes. **2.** One who initiates and carries out a legal action, especially criminal proceedings. **3.** *Law.* The barrister or advocate conducting the prosecution in criminal proceedings. Also called "public prosecutor".
pros·e·lyte (próssi-līt, próssə-) *n.* A convert to a religion or doctrine, especially a recent convert.
~v. Variant of **proselytise.** [Middle English *proselite,* from Late Latin *prosēlytus,* from Greek *prosēlutos,* "one who comes to a place", stranger, religious convert.] **—pros·e·lyt·er** *n.*
pros·e·lyt·ise, pros·e·lyt·ize (próssi-lit-īz, próssə-) *v.* **-ised, -ising, -ises.** Also **proselyte, -lyted, -lyting, -lytes.** *—intr.* **1.** To make proselytes. **2.** Loosely, to promote or speak enthusiastically on behalf of a cause. **3.** *Archaic.* To become a proselyte; convert. *—tr.* **1.** To convert from one belief or faith to another. **2.** Loosely, to try to win (a person) to a cause one espouses. **—pros·e·lyt·i·sa·tion** (-ī-záysh'n || *U.S.* -i-) *n.* **—pros·e·lyt·is·er** *n.*
pros·e·lyt·ism (próssi-lit-iz'm, próssə- || -līt-) *n.* **1.** The practice of proselytising. **2.** The state of being a proselyte; conversion. **—pros·e·lyt·i·cal** (-líttik'l) *adj.* **—pros·e·lyt·ist** (-lit-ist || -līt-) *n.*
pros·en·ceph·a·lon (próss-en-séff'l-on, -kéff'l-, -ən) *n. Anatomy.* The **forebrain** *(see).* [New Latin : PROS- (before, in front) + ENCEPHALON.] **—pros·en·ce·phal·ic** (-si-fál-ik, -ki-) *adj.*
pros·en·chy·ma (pross-éngkimə) *n. Botany.* Tissue consisting of elongated cells with tapering ends, occurring in supporting and conducting tissue. [New Latin : PROS- (near, towards) + (PAR)ENCHYMA.] **—pros·en·chym·a·tous** (-eng-kímmətəss) *adj.*
prose poem *n.* A short work, often a single paragraph, written as prose but employing poetic techniques and imagery.
Pro·ser·pi·na (prə-sérpinə, pro- || prō-, -zérpinə). Also **Pros·er·pine** (próssər-pīn). *Roman Mythology.* The wife of Pluto and daughter of Jupiter and Ceres; the goddess of the underworld, corresponding to the Greek Persephone.
pro·sim·i·an (prō-símmi-ən) *adj.* Of or belonging to the Prosimii, a primitive suborder of primates that includes the lemurs, lorises, and tarsiers. [New Latin *Prosimii* : *pro-,* before + Latin *simia,* ape, from *simus,* snub-nosed, from Greek *simos* (see **simian**).] **—pro·sim·i·an** *n.*
pro·sit (prṓ-zit, -sit, prōst) *interj.* Your health! Used as a drinking toast. [German, from Latin, "may it be advantageous".]
pros·o·dist (próss-ədist || próz, prṓz-) *n.* A specialist in prosody.
pros·o·dy (próssədi || próz-ədi, prṓz-) *n. pl.* **-dies.** *Abbr.* **pros. 1.** The science of versification, covering such aspects as metrical, rhythmical, and stanzaic forms. **2.** A particular system of versification. [Middle English *prosodye,* from Latin *prosōdia,* tone or accent of a syllable, from Greek *prosōidia,* accompanied song, modulation of voice, pronunciation, diacritical mark : *pros-,* to, in addition to + *ōidē,* song, lay, ode.] **—pro·sod·ic** (prə-sóddik, prō- || -zóddik) *adj.* **—pro·sod·i·cal·ly** *adv.*
pro·so·po·poe·ia, pro·so·po·pe·ia (próss-ə-pə-pée-ə, -ō- || *U.S. also* prə-sṓ-, prō-) *n.* In rhetoric: **1.** The impersonation of an absent or imaginary speaker. **2.** Personification, as of abstractions or inanimate objects. [Latin *prosopopoiia,* from Greek *prosōpopoiia,* dramatisation : *prosōpon,* face, mask, dramatic character : *pros,* towards + stem *op-,* to see + *poiein,* to make.] **—pro·so·po·poe·ial** *adj.*
pros·pect (próspekt) *n.* **1. a.** Something expected; a possibility. **b.** Expectation: *no prospect of a job.* **2.** *Plural.* Chances for success, especially with regard to wealth or social position. **3. a.** A potential customer. **b.** A candidate deemed likely to succeed. **4.** The direction in which an object, such as a building, faces. **5.** An extensive or distant view or scene presented to the eye: *a pleasant prospect.* **6.** The act of surveying or examining. **7.** In mining: **a.** The location or probable location of a mineral deposit. **b.** An actual or probable deposit. **c.** The mineral yield obtained by working an ore.
~v. (prə-spékt, próspekt) **prospected, -pecting, -pects.** *—tr.* To explore (a region) for gold or other mineral deposits. *—intr.* To explore for mineral deposits. Often used with *for.* [Middle English *prospecte,* from Latin *prōspectus,* distant view, vista, from the past participle of *prōspicere,* to look forward, foresee : *prō-,* forward + *specere,* to look.]
Synonyms: *prospect, outlook, expectation.*
pro·spec·tive (prə-spéktiv, pro- || prō-) *adj.* **1.** Looking forward in time; characterised by foresight. **2.** Being in prospect; likely to become: *the prospective bridegroom.* **—pro·spec·tive·ly** *adv.*
pros·pec·tor (prə-spéktər, pro- || próspektər) *n.* One who explores an area for natural deposits, such as gold or oil.
pro·spec·tus (prə-spéktəss || prō-) *n.* **1.** A formal summary of a proposed commercial, literary, or other venture. **2.** A brochure published by an institution, such as a school or university, giving such details as facilities and charges. [Latin, PROSPECT.]
pros·per (próspər) *v.* **-pered, -pering, -pers.** *—intr.* To be fortunate or successful; thrive. *—tr. Archaic.* To cause to be successful. [Middle English *prosperen,* from Old French *prosperer,* from Latin *prosperāre,* to make fortunate, from *prosperus,* fortunate.]
pros·per·i·ty (pross-pérrəti, prəss-) *n., pl.* **-ties.** The condition of being prosperous and having good fortune or financial success.
pros·per·ous (próspræss, próspərəss) *adj.* **1.** Having success; flourishing. **2.** Affluent; well-to-do. **3.** Propitious; favourable. **—pros·per·ous·ly** *adv.* **—pros·per·ous·ness** *n.*
pros·ta·glan·din (próstə-glándin) *n.* Any of various substances composed of fatty acids and having hormone-like activity, found especially in mammals. [From *prostate gland* + -IN.]
pros·tate (próss-tayt; *rarely* -tit) *n.* A gland in male mammals that secretes a liquid that forms a part of the semen. Also called "prostate gland". [New Latin *prostata,* from Greek *prostatēs,* "stander before (the bladder)", from *proïstanai,* to cause to stand in front : *pro-,* in front + *histanai,* to cause to stand.] **—pros·tate, pros·tat·ic** (pross-táttik) *adj.*
pros·ta·tec·to·my (próstə-téktəmi) *n., pl.* **-mies.** The surgical removal of all or part of the prostate. [PROSTAT(E) + -ECTOMY.]
pros·ta·ti·tis (próstə-tī́tiss) *n.* Inflammation of the prostate.
pros·the·sis (pross-thée-siss, próss-thə-) *n., pl.* **-ses** (-seez). **1.** The artificial replacement of a limb, tooth, or other body part. **2.** An artificial device used in such replacement. **3.** *Linguistics.* Variant of **prothesis.** [Late Latin, addition of a letter or syllable, from Greek, attachment, addition, from *prostithenai,* to put to, add : *pros-,* in addition + *tithenai,* to place, put.] **—pros·thet·ic** (-théttik) *adj.* **—pros·thet·i·cal·ly** *adv.*
prosthetic group *n. Biochemistry.* The nonpeptide part of a conjugated protein, such as the haem group in haemoglobin.

PRONUNCIATION KEY

a, trap; aa, father; ai, fair; ar, star; aw, lawn; ay, play; b, bb, stab; rubber; ch, church; ck, ticket; d, dd, dead; ladder; e, dress; ee, bee; er, defer; ew, few; ewr, pure; ə, about; ər, letter; f, ff, fife; differ; g, gg, giggle; h, hat; i, kit; ī, price; īr, fire; j, judge; k, kick; l, ll, let; 'l, needle; m, mm, man; n, nn, no; 'n, sudden; ng, thing; o, lot; ō, no; ŏŏ, foot; ōō, shoe; oor, poor; ow, cow; owr, hour; oy, boy; p, pp, pepper; r, rr, red; s, ss, sauce; sh, ship; t, tt, totter; th, thick; th, this; smooth; u, cut; ur, turn; v, vv, valve; w, wet; y, yes; z, zz, zebra; zh, vision; pleasure

IN FOREIGN WORDS:

aN, oN, Saint-Saëns; hl, Llanelli; Hluhluwe; kh, loch; lough; Khaled

STRESS MARK:

ín-sīt, insight; in-sī́t, incite

pros·thet·ics (pross-théttiks) *n. Used with a singular verb.* Prosthetic surgery. **—pros·the·tist** (-thée-tist, próss-thə-) *n.*

pros·tho·don·tics (próss-thə-dóntiks, -thō-) *n. Used with a singular verb.* Also **pros·tho·don·ti·a** (-dón-shə, -shi-ə). Prosthetic dentistry. [From PROSTH(ESIS) + -ODONT + -ICS.] **—pros·tho·don·tist** *n.*

pros·ti·tute (prósti-tewt || -tōōt) *n.* **1.** One who solicits and accepts payment for sexual services, especially a woman or girl who accepts payment from men, or a man or boy who engages in homosexual practices for payment. **2.** One who sells or degrades his abilities or name for money or an unworthy cause.
~*tr.v.* **prostituted, -tuting, -tutes. 1.** To offer (oneself or another) for sexual hire. **2.** To degrade (oneself or one's talents) for money or an unworthy cause. [Latin *prōstitūta,* from the past participle of *prōstituere,* to expose publicly, prostitute : *prō-,* forth, in public + *statuere,* to set, place, from *stare* (past participle *status*), to stand.] **—pros·ti·tu·tor** (-ər) *n.*

pros·ti·tu·tion (prósti-téwsh'n || -tóosh'n) *n.* **1.** The act or practice of prostituting. **2.** The act of offering or devoting one's talents to an unworthy use or cause.

pro·sto·mi·um (prō-stṓmi-əm) *n.* The part of the head end of an earthworm or other annelid that bears tentacles, a sucker, or feeding appendages.

pros·trate (pro-stráyt, prə- || *chiefly U.S.* próstrayt) *tr.v.* **-trated, -trating, -trates. 1.** To make (oneself) bow or kneel down in humility or adoration. **2.** To throw down flat. **3. a.** To make very weak or exhausted; overcome. **b.** To cause to be submissive; overthrow.
~*adj.* (próss-trayt; *rarely* -trət, -trit). **1.** Lying face down, as in submission. **2.** Lying down full-length. **3. a.** Physically or emotionally exhausted; incapacitated. **b.** Overthrown or defeated. **4.** *Botany.* Growing along the ground. —See Usage Note at **prone.** [Middle English *prostrat* (adjective), from Latin *prōstrātus,* past participle of *prōsternere,* to throw down, prostrate : *prō-,* down before + *sternere,* to stretch out, cast down.] **—pros·tra·tor** (-ər) *n.*

pros·tra·tion (pro-stráysh'n, prə-) *n.* **1. a.** The act of prostrating oneself. **b.** The state of being prostrate. **2.** Total exhaustion.

pro·style (prṓ-stīl) *adj. Architecture.* Having a row of columns across the front only, as in some Greek temples.
~*n.* A prostyle building or portico. [Latin *prostylos,* from Greek *prostulos,* having pillars in front : *pro-,* in front + *stulos,* pillar.]

pros·y (prṓzi) *adj.* **-ier, -iest. 1.** Matter-of-fact; dry; prosaic. **2.** Dull; commonplace. **—pros·i·ly** *adv.* **—pros·i·ness** *n.*

prot-. Variant of **proto-.**

Prot. 1. Protectorate. **2.** Protestant.

pro·tac·tin·i·um (prṓtak-tínni-əm) *n. Symbol* **Pa** A rare radioactive element chemically similar to uranium, having 12 known isotopes, the most common of which is protactinium 231 with a half-life of 32,480 years. Atomic number 91, melting point about 1,600°C, relative density 15.37, valency 4 or 5. [New Latin : PROT(O)- + ACTINIUM (because it disintegrates into actinium).]

pro·tag·o·nist (prō-tággənist, prə-) *n.* **1. a.** The leading character in Greek drama. **b.** The leading character in any play, novel, or other literary work. **2.** Any leading or principal figure; especially, one who initiates a political policy. [Greek *prōtagōnistēs* : PROT(O)- + *agōnistēs,* actor, from *agōnizesthai,* to contend, from *agōnia,* a contest, from *agōn,* gathering, contest, from *agein,* to lead.]
Usage: Traditionally, *protagonist* has the sense of "leader" or (in literary works) "leading character". It is therefore considered improper to use a phrase such as *chief protagonist* (for it contains a redundant word) or to use the word in the plural, when only one literary work is being referred to. However, the word is extending its meaning, and is now often used in the sense of "leader in a matter of importance", as well as in the sense of "partisan" or "champion": *She was a staunch protagonist of the liberation movement.* See also **antagonist.**

Pro·tag·o·ras of Abdera (prō-tággə-rass, prə-, -rəss) (*c.* 490–*c.* 421 B.C.). Greek philosopher. He is said to have coined the maxim, "Man is the measure of all things."

pro·ta·mine (prṓtə-meen, -min) *n.* Also **pro·ta·min** (-min). Any of the group of the simplest proteins that are highly basic, soluble in water, not coagulated by heat, and yield only amino acids, chiefly arginine, upon hydrolysis. [PROT(O)- + -AMINE.]

pro·tan·drous (prō-tándrəss) *adj.* Also **pro·tan·dric** (-tándrik). Having male gametes that mature before the female gametes. Said of certain plants and hermaphrodite animals. Compare **protogynous.** [PROTO- + -ANDROUS.] **—pro·tan·dry** (-tándri) *n.*

pro·ta·no·pi·a (prṓtə-nṓpi-ə) *n.* A form of partial colourblindness in which perception of red is defective, and reds, yellows, and greens are confused. [New Latin : PROT(O)- + AN- (without) + -OPIA.] **—pro·ta·nope** (-nōp) *n.* **—pro·ta·nop·ic** (-nóppik) *adj.*

prot·a·sis (próttə-siss) *n.* **1.** *Grammar.* A subordinate clause expressing the condition in a conditional sentence. Compare **apodosis. 2.** The introductory part of a classical drama. [Late Latin, proposition, from Greek, "a stretching forward", proposition, premise, from *proteinein,* to stretch forward, offer, propose : *prō-,* before + *teinein,* to stretch.]

pro·te·a (prṓti-ə) *n.* Any shrub of the southern African genus *Protea,* having showy, conelike flower heads. [New Latin, from PROTEUS (referring to the many different forms of the shrub.]

pro·te·an (prō-tée-ən, prṓti-) *adj.* Readily taking on different characters or forms; changeable. [From PROTEUS.]

pro·te·ase (prṓti-ayz, -ayss) *n.* An enzyme that catalyses the hydrolytic breakdown of proteins. Also called "proteolytic enzyme". [PROTE(IN) + -ASE.]

pro·tect (prə-tékt, prō-) *tr.v.* **-tected, -tecting, -tects. 1.** To keep from harm, attack, or injury; guard. **2.** *Economics.* To help (domestic industry) by imposing tariffs on imported goods. **3.** *Commerce.* To assure payment of (drafts or notes, for example) by setting aside funds in advance. —See Synonyms at **defend.** [Latin *prōtegere* (past participle *prōtectus*), to cover in front, protect : *prō-,* in front + *tegere,* to cover.] **—pro·tect·ing·ly** *adv.*

pro·tec·tion (prə-téksh'n, prō-) *n.* **1.** The act of protecting. **2.** The condition of being protected. **3.** One that protects. **4.** A document, such as a passport, guaranteeing safe conduct to travellers. **5.** *Economics.* A tariff system protecting domestic industries from foreign competition. **6.** *Informal.* **a.** Money extorted by racketeers in exchange for a promise of freedom from molestation. Also called "protection money". **b.** Freedom from molestation obtained in this way. **—pro·tec·tion·al** *adj.*

pro·tec·tion·ism (prə-téksh'n-iz'm, prō-) *n. Economics.* The theory, policy, or system of protecting domestic industries from foreign competition. **—pro·tec·tion·ist** *n.* & *adj.*

pro·tec·tive (prə-téktiv, prō-) *adj.* **1.** Adapted or intended to afford protection. **2.** Of, pertaining to, or designed to protect domestic industries from foreign competition: *a protective tariff.* **3.** Showing or expressing often undue concern over the safety or welfare of others: *too protective towards him.* **—pro·tec·tive** *n.* **—pro·tec·tive·ly** *adv.* **—pro·tec·tive·ness** *n.*

protective colouring *n. Zoology.* **1.** Colour and markings of an animal that help it to appear inconspicuous in its surroundings so that it is less likely to be seen by predators; camouflage. **2. Batesian mimicry** *(see).*

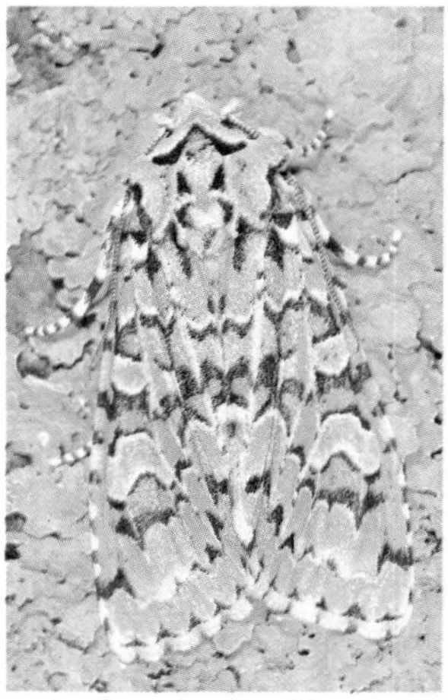

protective colouring *Many insect species have evolved elaborately patterned markings to enable them to hide from predators. This European moth – the Merveille du Jour,* Griposia aprilina *– has wings which match the lichen-covered trees on which it rests.*

pro·tec·tor (prə-téktər, prō-) *n.* **1.** A person who protects; a guardian. **2.** *Usually capital* **P.** Formerly, a title given to one who ruled during the absence, minority, or illness of the monarch. **—pro·tec·tor·al** *adj.* **—pro·tec·tor·ship** *n.*

pro·tec·tor·ate (prə-téktər-ət, prō-, téktr-, -it) *n. Abbr.* **Prot. 1.** A relationship of protection and partial control assumed by a superior power over a dependent country or region. **2.** The protected country or region. **3.** *Capital* **P. a.** The government, office, or term of a protector. **b.** The government of England under Oliver Cromwell (1653–58) and his son Richard (1658–59).

pro·tec·to·ry (prə-téktəri, prō-) *n., pl.* **-ries.** Formerly, an institution run by the Roman Catholic Church providing for the welfare of destitute children.

pro·té·gé (prót-ə-zhay, prṓt-, -e-, -ay- || *U.S. also* -zháy) *n. Feminine* **pro·té·gée.** One whose welfare, training, or career is promoted by an influential person. [French, from the past participle of *protéger,* to PROTECT.]

pro·te·id (prṓ-tee-id, -teed) *n.* A protein. Not in technical usage.

pro·tein (prṓ-teen, -tee-in) *n.* **1.** Any of a group of complex nitrogenous organic compounds of high molecular weight that contain amino acids as their basic structural units and that occur in all living matter and are essential for the growth and repair of animal tissue. Foods containing a high proportion of protein include meat, eggs, and cheese. **2.** The nutritional value provided by food containing any or a combination of these compounds: *You need more protein.* [French *protéine,* "primary substance (to the body)", from Late Greek *proteios,* primary, from Greek *prōtos,* first.] **—pro·tein·a·ceous** (-áyshəss; *also* -tin-), **pro·tein·ic** (-téenik), **pro·tei·nous** *adj.*

pro·tein·ase (prṓ-teen-ayz, -tee-in-, -ayss) *n.* A protease that hydrolyses proteins into polypeptides.

pro·tein·ate (prṓ-teen-ayt, -tee-in-) *n.* A protein compound.

pro·tein·u·ri·a (prṓ-teen-yóor-i-ə, -tee-in-) *n. Pathology.* **Albuminuria** *(see).*

pro tem (prṓ tém) *adv.* Pro tempore. **—pro tem** *adj.*

pro tem·po·re (prō témpəri) *adv. Abbr.* **p.t.** For the time being; temporarily. [Latin.] **—pro tem·po·re** *adj.*

proteo– *comb. form.* Indicates protein; for example, **proteolysis.**

pro·te·o·clas·tic (prṓti-ō-kástik) *adj.* Of, pertaining to, or causing proteolysis; proteolytic. [PROTEO- + -CLASTIC.]

pro·te·ol·y·sis (prṓti-óllə-siss) *n.* The breaking down of proteins into simpler, soluble substances, as in digestion. [PROTEO- + -LYSIS.] **—pro·te·o·lyt·ic** (-ə-líttik) *adj.*

proteolytic enzyme *n.* **Protease** *(see).*

pro·te·ose (prṓti-ōz, -ōss) *n.* Any of several water-soluble substances created as a product of partial digestion of protein. Also *U.S.* "albumose". [PROTE(O)- + -OSE.]

Prot·er·o·zo·ic (próttər-ō-zṓ-ik, prṓtər-, -ə-) *adj. Geology.* Of, belonging to, or designating the geological time and deposits of the Precambrian era between the Archaeozoic era and the Cambrian period of the Palaeozoic era.
~*n. Geology.* The Proterozoic period. Preceded by *the.* [Greek *proteros,* earlier, anterior + -ZOIC.]

pro·test (prə-tést, prō- || prṓ-test) *v.* **-tested, -testing, -tests.** —*tr.* **1.** To promise or affirm with earnest solemnity: *The accused protested innocence.* **2.** *Law.* To declare (a bill of exchange or promissory note) dishonoured or refused. **3.** *Literary.* To proclaim or make known. **4.** *U.S.* To object to, especially in a formal statement. —*intr.* **1. a.** To express strong objection, disagreement, or annoyance. Used with *about, against,* or *at.* **b.** To hold a rally or meeting to voice disapproval or objection. **2.** To make an earnest avowal or affirmation. —See Synonyms at **object.**
~*n.* (prṓ-test). **1.** A formal declaration of disapproval or objection issued by a concerned party. **2.** Any individual or collective gesture or display of objection or disapproval. Also used adjectivally: *a protest song.* **3.** *Law.* **a.** A formal statement drawn up by a notary

for a creditor, declaring that the debtor has refused to accept or honour a bill of exchange or promissory note. **b.** A formal declaration made by a taxpayer, stating that the tax demanded is illegal or excessive and reserving the right to contest it. **4.** A formal written statement by the master of a ship giving the circumstances and details of a disaster, injury, or the like, that occurred at sea. **5.** *Sports.* A formal objection lodged against a player or other competitor. **—under protest.** Against one's will; expressing disagreement or objections. [Middle English *protesten,* from Old French *protester,* from Latin *prōtestārī,* to declare in public, testify, protest : *prō-,* forth, in public + *testārī,* to be a witness, make a will, from *testis,* a witness, will.] **—pro·test·er** *n.* **—pro·test·ing·ly** *adv.*

prot·es·tant (próttistənt; *also* prə-téstənt, prō-) *n. Rare.* One who makes a declaration or protest. **—prot·es·tant** *adj.*

Prot·es·tant (próttistənt) *n. Abbr.* **Prot. 1.** A member of any of the Christian churches, such as the Anglican, Baptist, Methodist, or Presbyterian, descending from those that seceded from the Church of Rome at the time of the Reformation, denying the universal authority of the Pope and emphasising the principle of justification by faith. **2.** Any of those who adhered to the doctrine of Luther and, in 1529, protested against the decree of the Diet of Spires commanding submission to the authority of Rome.
~adj. Of or pertaining to Protestants or Protestantism. [Latin *prōtestāns* (stem *prōtestānt-*), present participle of *prōtestārī,* to PROTEST.]

Protestant Episcopal Church *n.* The autonomous branch of the Anglican Communion in the United States. Also called "Episcopal Church".

Prot·es·tant·ism (próttistənt-iz'm) *n.* **1.** Adherence to a Protestant church. **2.** The religion fostered by the Protestant movement. **3.** Protestants or the Protestant churches collectively.

pro·tes·ta·tion (prōt-ess-táysh'n, prótt-, -iss-) *n.* **1.** An emphatic declaration. **2.** A strong or formal expression of dissent.

Pro·teus (prō-tewss,-ti-əss || -tōōss). *Greek Mythology.* A sea god who could change his shape at will.

pro·tha·la·mi·on (prōthə-láymi-ən || -on) *n., pl.* **-mia** (-ə). Also **pro·tha·la·mi·um** (-əm) *pl.* **-mia** (-ə). A song in celebration of a wedding; an epithalamium. [Coined by Edmund Spenser : PRO- (before) + Greek *epithalamion,* EPITHALAMIUM.]

pro·thal·lus (prō-thál-əss, prō-) *n., pl.* **-li** (-ī). Also **pro·thal·li·um** (-i-əm) *pl.* **-lia** (-i-ə). *Botany.* A small, flat mass of tissue, produced by a germinating spore of certain pteridophytes and gymnosperms, that bears sexual organs. [New Latin : Greek *pro-,* in front of, before + *thallos,* a shoot.] **—pro·thal·li·al** *adj.*

proth·e·sis (próthə-siss) *n., pl.* **-ses** (-seez). Also **pros·the·sis** (for sense 1). **1.** *Linguistics.* The addition of a phoneme at the beginning of a word to ease pronunciation or to form a new word. **2.** In the Eastern Orthodox Church, the preparation of the Eucharistic elements for consecration. [Greek, from *protithenai,* to put before : *pro-,* before + *tithenai,* to put, place.] **—pro·thet·ic** (prə-théttik, prō-) *adj.* **—pro·thet·i·cal·ly** *adv.*

proth·o·no·tar·y (prōth-ə-nōtəri, -ō-, prō-thónnə-tri, -təri || -terri) *n., pl.* **-ies.** Also **pro·to·no·tar·y** (prōt-, -tónnə-). **1.** Formerly, the principal clerk in certain courts of law. **2.** *Roman Catholic Church.* One of a college of twelve ecclesiastics charged with the registry of important pontifical proceedings. **3.** *Archaic.* A chief scribe. [Middle English *prothonotarie,* from Late Latin *prōtonotārius* : PROTO- + *notārius,* "of shorthand", secretary, from *nota,* mark, shorthand character.] **—pro·tho·no·tar·i·al** (-táir-i-əl) *adj.*

pro·tho·rax (prō-tháw-raks, prō- || -thō-) *n., pl.* **-axes** or **-thoraces** (-rə-seez). The anterior division of the thorax of an insect, bearing the first pair of legs. **—pro·tho·rac·ic** (prō-thaw-rássik || -thə-) *adj.*

pro·throm·bin (prō-thrómbin, prō-) *n.* A plasma protein that is converted into thrombin during blood coagulation.

pro·tist (prōtist) *n. Biology.* Any of the single-celled organisms of the kingdom Protista, which includes protozoans, bacteria, fungi, some algae, and other forms not readily classified as either plants or animals. [New Latin *Protista,* "simplest organisms", from Greek *prōtista,* neuter plural of *prōtistos,* the very first, primal, from *prōtos,* first.] **—pro·tist·an** *adj. & n.* **—pro·tis·tol·o·gy** (prōtiss-tólləji) *n.*

pro·ti·um (prō-ti-əm || *U.S. also* -shi-) *n.* The most abundant isotope of hydrogen, H^1, with atomic mass 1. [New Latin : PROT(O)- + -IUM.]

proto-, prot- *comb. form.* Indicates: **1.** The earliest form or the first in rank or time; for example, **protium, protoplast, prototype. 2.** *Capital* **P.** The earliest form of a language as reconstructed by comparative linguistics; for example, **Proto-Germanic. 3.** *Chemistry.* The member of a series that has the least amount of a specified element or radical; for example, **protoporphyrin.** [Greek *prōtos,* first.]

pro·to·col (prō-tə-kol, -tō- || -kōl) *n.* **1. a.** The forms of ceremony, precedence, and etiquette observed by diplomats and heads of state. **b.** Any rules or code of behaviour or etiquette. **2.** The first copy of a treaty or other document prior to its ratification. **3.** Any official record of a transaction or negotiations, especially one that is used as a preliminary draft for a document, such as a treaty. **4.** The official formulae annexed to a charter, papal bull, or the like. —See Synonyms at **etiquette.**
~v. **protocolled** or *U.S.* **-coled, -colling** or *U.S.* **-coling, -cols.** *—intr.* To form or issue protocols. *—tr.* To record or embody in a protocol. [Earlier Scottish *prothocoll,* from Old French *prothocole,* from Medieval Latin *protocollum,* from Late Greek *prōtokollon,* first sheet glued to binding of a book, bearing a table of contents : PROTO- + *kolla,* glue.] **—pro·to·col·ar** (-kóllər), **pro·to·col·a·ry** (-kólləri), **pro·to·col·ic** (-kóllik) *adj.*

Pro·to-Ger·man·ic (prōtō-jer-mánnik) *n.* The hypothetical prehistoric language that was the ancestor of the Germanic languages.

pro·tog·y·nous (prō-tójinəss) *adj.* Having female gametes that mature before the male gametes. Said of certain plants and hermaphrodite animals. Compare **protandrous.** [PROTO- + -GYNOUS.] **—pro·tog·y·ny** *n.*

pro·to·his·to·ry (prōtō-hístri, -hístəri) *n.* The study of human culture, or a particular instance of it, just prior to its earliest recorded history. **—pro·to·his·tor·ic** (-hiss-tórrik || -táwrik) *adj.*

pro·to·hu·man (prōtō-héwmən) *n.* A member of any of several species of prehistoric primates resembling modern man but more primitive in development. **—pro·to·hu·man** *adj.*

Pro·to-In·do-Eur·o·pe·an (prōtō-índō-yoor-ə-pée-ən) *n.* The hypothetical, reconstructed ancestor of the Indo-European languages.

pro·to·lan·guage (prōtō-lang-gwij) *n. Linguistics.* A language that is reconstructed by comparative linguistics as the hypothetical ancestor of another existing language or group of languages. Compare **Ursprache.**

pro·to·lith·ic (prō-tō-líthik, -tə-) *adj.* Of, pertaining to, or characteristic of the very beginning of the Stone Age; eolithic. [PROTO- + -LITHIC.]

pro·to·mar·tyr (prōtō-maartər) *n.* **1.** The first Christian martyr, Saint Stephen. **2.** The first martyr in a cause.

pro·to·mor·phic (prō-tō-mórfik, -tə-) *adj.* Primitive in structure or form. [PROTO- + -MORPHIC.]

pro·ton (prō-ton) *n. Symbol* **p** *Physics.* A stable, positively charged elementary particle in the baryon family having a mass 1,836 times that of the electron. It is a constituent of all atomic nuclei. See **neutron, particle.** [Greek *prōton,* neuter of *prōtos,* first.] **—pro·ton·ic** (prō-tónnik) *adj.*

pro·to·ne·ma (prōtə-néemə) *n., pl.* **-nemata** (-néemətə, -némmətə). *Botany.* A green, threadlike structure that arises on germination of a moss spore, and that eventually develops into a mature plant. [PROTO- + Greek *nēma,* thread.] **—pro·to·ne·mal** (-néem'l), **pro·to·ne·ma·tal** (-néemət'l, -némmət'l) *adj.*

proton number *n.* **Atomic number** *(see).*

protonotary. Variant of **prothonotary.**

proton synchrotron *n. Physics.* A ring-shaped **synchrotron** *(see)* that uses a frequency modulated accelerating voltage to accelerate protons to energies of the order 10^9 electronvolts. Also called "proton accelerator".

pro·to·path·ic (prōtə-páthik) *adj.* Of, pertaining to, or designating the cutaneous sensory reception of gross pressure, pain, heat, or cold. Compare **epicritic.** [Medieval Greek *prōtopathēs,* affected first, from Greek *prōtopathein,* to feel or be affected first : PROTO- + *paskhein,* to feel, experience.] **—pro·top·a·thy** (prō-tóppəthi) *n.*

pro·to·plasm (prō-tə-plaz'm, -tō-) *n.* A complex, jelly-like colloidal substance constituting the living matter of plant and animal cells, and performing the basic life functions. See **cytoplasm, nucleoplasm.** [German *Protoplasma* : PROTO- + -PLASM.] **—pro·to·plas·mic** (-plázmik), **pro·to·plas·mal** (-plázm'l), **pro·to·plas·mat·ic** (-plaz-máttik) *adj.*

pro·to·plast (prō-tə-plast, -tō-) *n.* **1.** *Biology.* The protoplasm and plasma membrane of a plant or bacterial cell after the cell wall has been removed. **2.** *Rare.* A prototype. [Old French *protoplaste,* from Late Latin *prōtoplastus,* "first formed", from Greek *prōtoplastos* : PROTO- + -PLAST.] **—pro·to·plas·tic** (-plástik) *adj.*

pro·to·por·phy·rin (prōtō-pórfərin) *n.* A metal-free porphyrin, $C_{34}H_{34}N_4O_4$, which, with iron, forms haem.

Pro·to-Sem·i·tic (prōtō-si-míttik, -se-, -sə-) *n.* The hypothetical common ancestor of the Asiatic (Eastern) branch of Hamito-Semitic, from which Arabic, Canaanite, Aramaic, Ethiopic, and Ugaritic are descended.

pro·to·star (prōtō-staar) *n.* A mass of gas and dust in interstellar space that is thought to contract to form a star.

pro·to·stele (prō-tō-steel, -tə-, -steelee) *n. Botany.* A type of stele commonly found in roots that lacks pith and has a solid core of xylem. **—pro·to·ste·lic** (-steelik) *adj.*

pro·to·troph·ic (prōtə-tróffik, -trōfik) *adj.* Obtaining nourishment by the assimilation of inorganic materials. Said of plants and bacteria. [PROTO- + -TROPH(Y) + -IC.] **—pro·tot·roph·y** (prō-tóttrəfi) **pro·to·troph** (prōtə-trof) *n.*

pro·to·type (prō-tə-tīp, -tō-) *n.* **1.** An original type, form, or instance that serves as a model on which later stages are based or judged. **2.** An early and typical example. **3.** *Biology.* A primitive or ancestral form or species. [French, from Greek *prōtotupon,* original form, archetype, from neuter of *prōtotupos,* "in the first form", original : PROTO- + -TYPE.] **—pro·to·typ·al** (-tīp'l), **pro·to·typ·ic** (-tippik), **pro·to·typ·i·cal** *adj.*

pro·to·xy·lem (prō-tə-zī-lem, -tō-, -ləm) *n. Botany.* The first type of xylem that is formed from the procambium. Compare **metaxylem.**

pro·to·zo·an (prō-tə-zō-ən, -tō-) *n., pl.* **-zoans** or **-zoa** (-zō-ə). Also **pro·to·zo·on** (-on). Any of the single-celled, usually microscopic organisms of the phylum or subkingdom Protozoa, which includes the most primitive forms of animal life. [New Latin *Protozoa* : PROTO- + -ZOAN.] **—pro·to·zo·an, pro·to·zo·ic** (-zō-ik) *adj.*

pro·to·zo·ol·o·gy (prō-tə-zō-ólləji, -tō-, -zoo-) *n.* The biological study of protozoans. **—pro·to·zo·o·log·i·cal** (-zō-ə-lójik'l, -zōō-) *adj.* **—pro·to·zo·ol·o·gist** (-ólləjist) *n.*

pro·tract (prə-trákt, prō-) *tr.v.* **-tracted, -tracting, -tracts. 1.** To draw out or lengthen in time; prolong, especially unnecessarily. **2.** In

PRONUNCIATION KEY

a, trap; aa, father; ai, fair;
ar, star; aw, lawn; ay, play;
b, bb, stab; rubber;
ch, church; ck, ticket;
d, dd, dead; ladder; e, dress;
ee, bee; er, defer; ew, few;
ewr, pure; ə, about;
ər, letter; f, ff, fife; differ;
g, gg, giggle; h, hat; i, kit;
ī, price; īr, fire; j, judge;
k, kick; l, ll, let; 'l, needle;
m, mm, man; n, nn, no;
'n, sudden; ng, thing; o, lot;
ō, no; ōō, foot; ōō, shoe;
oor, poor; ow, cow;
owr, hour; oy, boy;
p, pp, pepper; r, rr, red;
s, ss, sauce; sh, ship;
t, tt, totter; th, thick; th, this;
smooth; u, cut; ur, turn;
v, vv, valve; w, wet; y, yes;
z, zz, zebra; zh, vision;
pleasure

IN FOREIGN WORDS:

aN, oN, Saint-Saëns;
hl, Llanelli; Hluhluwe;
kh, loch; lough; Khaled

STRESS MARK:

ín-sīt, insight; in-sít, incite

surveying, to draw to scale by means of a scale and protractor; plot. **3.** *Anatomy.* To extend or protrude. —See Synonyms at **prolong.** [Latin *prōtrahere* (past participle *prōtractus*), to drag out, lengthen : *prō-*, out, extending + *trahere,* to drag, pull.] —**pro·tract·ed·ly** *adv.* —**pro·tract·ed·ness** *n.* —**pro·trac·tive** *adj.*

pro·trac·tile (prə-trák-tīl, prō- || *U.S.* -til, -t'l) *adj.* Also **pro·tract·i·ble** (-təb'l). *Zoology.* Capable of being protracted; extensible. —**pro·trac·til·i·ty** (prō-trak-tílləti) *n.*

pro·trac·tion (prə-tráksh'n, prō-) *n.* **1. a.** The act of protracting. **b.** The state of being protracted. **2.** A drawing made to scale. **3.** The irregular lengthening of a normally short syllable.

pro·trac·tor (prə-tráktər, prō-) *n.* **1.** A semicircular instrument for measuring and constructing angles. **2.** An adjustable pattern used by tailors. **3.** A surgical instrument for removing foreign objects, especially bullets, from the body.

pro·trude (prə-trōōd, prō- || -tréwd) *v.* **-truded, -truding, -trudes.** —*tr.* To push or thrust outwards. —*intr.* To jut out; project. [Latin *prōtrūdere* : *prō-*, forth + *trūdere,* to thrust.] —**pro·trud·ent** (-'nt) *adj.*

pro·tru·sile (prə-trōō-sīl, prō- || -tréw-, *U.S.* -sil, -s'l) *adj.* Also **pro·tru·si·ble** (-sib'l). Capable of being thrust outwards, as the tongue is. [PROTRUS(ION) + -ILE.] —**pro·tru·sil·i·ty** (prō-trōō-sílləti || -trew-) *n.*

pro·tru·sion (prə-trōō-zh'n, prō- || -tréw-) *n.* **1. a.** The act of protruding. **b.** The state of being protruded. **2.** Something that protrudes.

pro·tru·sive (prə-trōō-siv, prō- || -tréw-, -ziv) *adj.* **1.** Tending to protrude; protruding. **2.** Unduly or disagreeably conspicuous; obtrusive. —**pro·tru·sive·ly** *adv.* —**pro·tru·sive·ness** *n.*

pro·tu·ber·ance (prə-téw-bərənss, prō- || -tōō-) *n.* Also **pro·tu·ber·an·cy** (-i) *pl.* **-cies.** **1.** That which protrudes; a bulge or knob. **2.** The condition of being protuberant.

pro·tu·ber·ant (prə-téw-bərənt, prō- || -tōō-. *The popular pronunciation* prə-trōōbərənt *reflects a nonstandard blending of this word with* **protrudent**) *adj.* Swelling outwards; bulging. [Late Latin *prōtūberāns* (stem *prōtūberānt-*), present participle of *prōtūberāre,* to PROTUBERATE.] —**pro·tu·ber·ant·ly** *adv.*

pro·tu·ber·ate (prə-téw-bə-rayt, prō- || -tōō-) *intr.v.* **-ated, -ating, -ates.** *Rare.* To swell or bulge out. [Late Latin *prōtūberāre* : *prō-*, forth, outwards + *tūber,* swelling, bump.] —**pro·tu·ber·a·tion** (ráysh'n) *n.*

proud (prowd) *adj.* **prouder, proudest.** **1.** Feeling pleasurable satisfaction over an attribute or act by which one's stature is measured. **2.** Occasioning pride; gratifying: *a proud moment.* **3.** Marked by exacting or constraining self-respect: *too proud to accept charity.* **4.** Having excessive self-esteem; haughty; arrogant. **5.** Of great dignity; honoured: *a proud name.* **6.** Majestic; magnificent. **7.** Occasioned by pride, expressing pride: *a proud smile.* **8.** Spirited or excited. Said of animals: *a proud mare.* **9.** Projecting slightly from a surrounding surface; not flush: *the sockets are proud of the wall.* ~*adv.* So as to project slightly from a surface. —**do (someone) proud.** To be very generous towards; especially, to entertain on a lavish scale. [Middle English *proud,* late Old English *prūt, prūd,* from Old French *prod, prud,* good, gallant, brave, from Late Latin *prōde,* advantageous, from Latin *prōdesse,* to be beneficial : *prōd-*, variant of *prō-*, for + *esse,* to be. Sense 9 and adverb : 16th century, "overgrown, swollen".] —**proud·ly** *adv.* —**proud·ness** *n.*

Synonyms: *proud, arrogant, haughty, disdainful, supercilious.*

proud flesh *n. Pathology.* The swollen flesh around a healing wound. [Middle English, from PROUD (swollen).]

Prou·dhon (prōōdoN, prōō-dóN), **Pierre Joseph** (1809–65). French political theorist and economist. Best-known for his theory that "all property is theft" in his *Qu'est-ce que la propriété* (1840).

Proust (prōōst), **Joseph-Louis** (1754–1826). French chemist. He discovered that compounds contain fixed proportions of elements by weight: the law of definite proportions.

Proust, Marcel (1871–1922). French novelist. His masterpiece was the 12-volume *A la recherche du temps perdu* (published 1913–27), strongly autobiographical in theme, and an exploration of memory and perception. —**Prous·ti·an** (prōōsti-ən) *adj. & n.*

proust·ite (prōōstīt) *n.* A red silver ore, Ag_3AsS_3, occurring in hexagonal crystals often in association with other silver-bearing minerals. [After Joseph-Louis PROUST.]

Prout (prowt), **William** (1785–1850). British chemist and physician. *Prout's Hypothesis* showed that all atomic weights are multiples of that of hydrogen and he also discovered that gastric juices in the stomach contain hydrochloric acid.

prov. **1.** province; provincial. **2.** provisional.

Prov. **1.** Provençal. **2.** Proverbs (Old Testament). **3.** Provost.

prove (prōōv) *v.* **proved, proved** or **proven** (prōōv'n. *There is also a spelling-pronunciation* prōv'n), **proving, proves.** —*tr.* **1.** To establish the truth or validity of by presentation of argument or evidence. **2.** *Law.* To establish the authenticity of (a will). **3.** To determine the quality of by testing or scientific experiment. **4.** *Mathematics.* **a.** To validate (a hypothesis or proposition) by a proof. **b.** To verify (the result of a calculation). **5.** *Printing.* To make a sample impression of (type). **6.** *Archaic.* To experience: *"And we will all the pleasures prove"* (Christopher Marlowe). —*intr.* **1.** To turn out: *"a very agreeable companion may . . . prove a very improper . . . friend"* (Lord Chesterfield). **2.** To rise to the desired degree before baking. Used of dough. —See Synonyms at **confirm.** [Middle English *proven,* to put to test, prove, from Old French *prover,* from Latin *probāre,* to test, demonstrate as good, from *probus,* good, virtuous.] —**prov·a·bil·i·ty** (prōōvə-bílləti), **prov·a·ble·ness** *n.* —**prov·a·ble** *adj.* —**prov·a·bly** *adv.* —**prov·er** *n.*

Usage: *Proved* is the preferred past participle form of this verb in British English: *He has proved his point. Proven* is less often used, and tends to be found in formal (especially legal) contexts. But it is the preferred form in American English, and is normal in both American and British English when used adjectivally before a noun.

prov·en (prōōv'n; prōv'n) *adj.* Having been put to the test and shown to be valid: *proven ability.* See **not proven.** —**prov·en·ly** *adv.*

prov·e·nance (próvvə-nənss || *U.S. also* -naanss) *n.* The place of origin; derivation. [French, from *provenant,* present participle of *provenir,* to come forth, originate, from Latin *prōvenīre* : *prō-*, forth + *venīre,* to come.]

Pro·ven·çal (próv-oN-saal, -'n- || *U.S. also* prōv-, prə-vénss'l) *n. Abbr.* **Prov., Pr.** **1.** A native or inhabitant of Provence, France. **2.** The Romance language of Provence, especially the literary language of the troubadours. —**Pro·ven·çal** *adj.*

Pro·vence (pro-vóNss, prō-, -vaanss). Region and former province of southeast France. It extends from the Alps westwards to the Rhône valley and from the Mediterranean northwards to the former province of Dauphiné, and is a distinct cultural region with its own language, Provençal, in which the medieval troubadours composed their love lyrics. Tourism is important, especially along the Riviera, and wine and fruit are the chief products.

prov·en·der (próvvindər) *n.* **1.** Dry food, such as hay, used as fodder for livestock. **2.** *Informal.* Food or provisions. [Middle English *provendre,* from Old French *provend(r)e,* from Medieval Latin *prōbenda,* fodder, alteration of Late Latin *praebenda,* support, subsistence, pension, "things to be supplied", from *praebendus,* gerundive of *prae(hi)bēre,* to hold forth, supply : *prae-*, before + *habēre,* to hold.]

pro·ve·ni·ence (prə-veen-i-ənss, prō-, -yənss) *n.* A source or origin of something. [Latin *prōveniēns* (stem *prōvenient-*), present participle of *prōvenīre,* to come forth. See **provenance.**]

pro·ven·tric·u·lus (prō-ven-tríckew-ləss) *n., pl.* **-li** (-lī). *Zoology.* **1.** The glandular part of the stomach anterior to the gizzard in birds. **2.** The thick-walled, muscular stomach of insects and crustaceans. Also called "gizzard". [New Latin : PRO- (in front of) + Latin *ventriculus,* stomach, gizzard, VENTRICLE.] —**pro·ven·tric·u·lar** (-lər) *adj.*

prov·erb (próvverb) *n.* **1.** A short, pithy saying in frequent and widespread use, expressing a well-known truth or fact. **2.** A person or thing recognised as a typical example; one that is proverbial. —See Synonyms at **saying.**

~*tr.v.* **proverbed, -erbing, -erbs.** **1.** To give the character of a proverb to. **2.** To make into a proverb. [Middle English *proverbe,* from Old French, from Latin *prōverbium,* "set of words put forth" : *prō-*, forth + *verbum,* word.]

pro·ver·bi·al (prə-vérbi-əl, pro- || prō-) *adj.* **1.** Of the nature of a proverb. **2.** Expressed in a proverb or proverbs. **3.** Widely referred to, as if the subject of a proverb; well known. —**pro·ver·bi·al·ly** *adv.*

Prov·erbs (próvverbz) *n. Used with a singular verb. Abbr.* **Prov.** A book of the Old Testament.

pro·vide (prə-vīd || prō-) *v.* **-vided, -viding, -vides.** —*tr.* **1.** To furnish; supply: *You can provide the drinks.* **2.** To give; afford: *the delay provided an opportunity to reflect.* **3.** To set down as a stipulation: *The contract provides that in case of injury you will be excused.* **4.** *Ecclesiastical.* Formerly, to appoint to a an ecclesiastical benefice, especially when the benefice has not yet become vacant. **5.** *Rare.* To make ready; prepare. —*intr.* **1.** To take measures in preparation. Used with *for* or *against.* **2.** To supply means of subsistence. Used with *for.* **3.** To make a stipulation or condition: *The will doesn't provide for such a contingency.* [Middle English *providen,* to foresee, make provision, from Latin *prōvidēre* : *prō-*, beforehand, in anticipation of + *vidēre,* to see.] —**pro·vid·er** *n.*

pro·vid·ed (prə-vīdid || prō-) *conj.* On the condition; if and only if. Often followed by *that*: *She will go, provided that I stay behind.*

Usage: When a requirement is explicitly set forth, the standard construction is *provided that* (or simply *provided*): *You may leave, provided that you have finished the job.* The use of *providing* is common in informal speech, but attracts criticism in written English.

prov·i·dence (próvvi-dənss || -denss) *n.* **1.** Care or preparation in advance; foresight. **2.** Prudent management; economy. **3.** The care, guardianship, and control exercised by a deity. **4.** *Capital* **P.** God, especially when viewed as a guardian and protector.

Providence. Seaport and capital of Rhode Island in the United States, situated where the Providence river joins Narragansett Bay. Its industries include jewellery, printing, and textiles.

prov·i·dent (próvvi-dənt || -dent) *adj.* **1.** Providing for future needs or events; showing foresight. **2.** Frugal; economical. [Middle English, from Latin *prōvidēns* (stem *prōvident-*), present participle of *prōvidēre,* to foresee, PROVIDE.] —**prov·i·dent·ly** *adv.*

prov·i·den·tial (próvvi-dénsh'l) *adj.* **1.** Of or resulting from divine providence. **2.** Happening as if through divine intervention; fortunate; opportune. —**prov·i·den·tial·ly** *adv.*

provident society *n.* A **friendly society** *(see).*

pro·vid·ing (prə-vīding || prō-) *conj.* On the condition; provided. Sometimes followed by *that.* See Usage note at **provided.**

prov·ince (próvvinss) *n. Abbr.* **prov.** **1.** A territory governed as an administrative or political unit of a country or empire, such as Saskatchewan in Canada. **2.** Any of various lands outside Italy conquered by the Romans and administered by them as self-contained units. **3.** An ecclesiastical division of territory under the jurisdiction of an archbishop. **4.** *Plural.* Areas of a country situated away from the capital or national cultural centre. Preceded by *the.* **5.** A comprehensive area of knowledge, activity, or interest. **6.** The range of one's proper duties and functions; scope; jurisdiction. **7.** *Ecology.* A subdivision of a **region** *(see).* [Middle English *provynce,* from Old French *province,* from Latin *prōvincia*†.]

pro·vin·cial (prə-vínsh'l || prō-) *adj.* **1.** *Abbr.* **prov.** Of or pertaining to a province. **2.** Of or supposedly characteristic of people from the provinces; not fashionable or sophisticated. **3.** Limited in perspective; narrow and self-centred.
~*n.* **1.** A native or inhabitant of the provinces. **2.** A person who has supposedly provincial ideas or habits. **—pro·vin·cial·ism, pro·vin·ci·al·i·ty** (-vínshi-ál-əti) *n.* **—pro·vin·cial·ly** *adv.*

proving ground *n.* A place for testing new devices or theories.

pro·vi·rus (prṓ-vīr-əss) *n.* A virus that does not cause lysis and has become part of the host cell, and is transmitted from one cell generation to the next in the chromosome.

pro·vi·sion (prə-vízh'n || prō-) *n.* **1.** The act of supplying or fitting out. **2.** That which is provided. **3.** A preparatory measure: *make provision for our distinguished guest.* **4.** *Plural.* A stock of necessary supplies, especially food. **5.** A stipulation or qualification; especially, a clause in a document or agreement. **6.** The appointment of an ecclesiastical clergyman to a benefice before it is vacant.
~*tr.v.* **provisioned, -sioning, -sions.** To supply with provisions. [Middle English, foresight, precaution, from Old French, from Latin *prōvīsiō* (stem *prōvīsiōn-*), from *prōvīsus,* past participle of *prōvidēre,* to PROVIDE.] **—pro·vi·sion·er** *n.*

pro·vi·sion·al (prə-vízh'n-'l || prō-) *adj.* Also **pro·vi·sion·ar·y** (-əri || -erri) (for sense 1). **1.** *Abbr.* **prov.** Provided for the time being, pending permanent arrangements: *a provisional plan.* See Synonyms at **transient. 2.** *Capital* **P.** Of, pertaining to, or designating the wing of both the Irish Republican Army and Sinn Fein formed by the split in those organisations, that emphasises the use of terrorist methods to achieve the unification of Ireland. Compare **Official.**
~*n.* **1.** A stamp that is issued temporarily by a post office until the normal issue is available. **2.** *Capital* **P.** A member of the Provisional Irish Republican Army or Sinn Fein. **—pro·vi·sion·al·ly** *adv.*

provisional licence *n.* A licence issued for a fixed period to a person who is learning to drive a motor vehicle, that carries certain restrictions, for example not allowing the holder to drive a car alone.

pro·vi·so (prə-vízō, prō-) *n., pl.* **-sos** or **-soes. 1.** A clause in a document making a qualification, condition, or restriction. **2.** Any condition or stipulation. [Middle English, from Medieval Latin *prōvīsō (quod),* provided (that), from *prōvīsus,* past participle of *prōvidēre,* to PROVIDE.]

pro·vi·so·ry (prə-vízəri || prō-) *adj.* Depending on a proviso; conditional. **—pro·vi·so·ri·ly** *adv.*

pro·vi·ta·min (prṓ-víttə-min, prō-, -vítə-) *n.* A substance, such as carotene (provitamin A), that is converted into a vitamin in animal bodies.

Pro·vo (prṓvō) *n., pl.* **-vos.** Also *locally* **Pro·vie** (prṓvee). A member of the Provisional IRA or Sinn Fein. [Shortened from PROVISIONAL (*IRA* or *Sinn Fein*).] **—Pro·vo** *adj.*

prov·o·ca·tion (próvvə-káysh'n) *n.* **1.** The act of provoking or inciting. **2.** Something that provokes; a cause of irritation. **3.** *Law.* Action by one person that causes another person to lose self-control and kill the doer, not amounting to a defence but reducing the gravity of the crime from murder to manslaughter.

pro·voc·a·tive (prə-vóckətiv || prō-) *adj.* Tending to arouse or excite a response, especially anger, curiosity, or sexual interest. **—pro·voc·a·tive·ly** *adv.* **—pro·voc·a·tive·ness** *n.*

pro·voke (prə-vṓk || prō-) *tr.v.* **-voked, -voking, -vokes. 1.** To incite to anger or resentment. **2.** To stir or incite to action; arouse. **3.** To bring on by inciting. —See Synonyms at **annoy.** [Middle English *provoken,* from Old French *provoquer,* from Latin *prōvocāre,* to call forth, challenge : *prō-,* forth + *vocāre,* to call.] **—pro·vok·ing·ly** *adv.*
Synonyms: *provoke, incite, excite, stimulate, arouse, rouse, stir.*

pro·vo·lo·ne (provo-lṓnay) *n.* A hard Italian curd cheese.

prov·ost (próvvəst || *U.S. also* prṓ-vost, -vəst) *n. Abbr.* **prov. 1.** The chief officer of a Scottish burgh. **2. a.** In the Anglican Church, the highest official in certain cathedrals, especially one of the modern foundation. **b.** In the Roman Catholic Church, the head of a cathedral chapter. **3.** The head of certain colleges at Cambridge and Oxford. [Middle English *provost,* from Old English *profost* and Old French *provost,* both from Medieval Latin *prōpositus, praepositus,* from Latin *praepositus,* "(one) placed before (others)", president, superintendent, from the past participle of *praepōnere,* to place before or over : *prae-,* before + *pōnere,* to place.] **—prov·ost·ship** *n.*

pro·vost court (prə-vṓ || *U.S.* prṓvō) *n.* A military court for the trial of minor offences committed in occupied hostile territories.

pro·vost guard (prə-vṓ || *U.S.* prṓvō) *n. Chiefly U.S.* A detail of soldiers on police duty under a provost marshal.

pro·vost marshal (prə-vṓ || *U.S.* prṓvō) *n. Abbr.* **P.M.** The head of military police.

prow (prow) *n.* **1.** The painted front part of a ship's hull; the bow. **2.** A similar projecting part of anything. [French *pro(u)e,* probably from Italian dialect *prua,* from Latin *prōra,* from Greek *prōira.*]

prow·ess (prów-iss, -ess) *n.* **1.** Outstanding skill or ability. **2.** Outstanding strength, courage, or daring, especially in battle. [Middle English *prowesse,* from Old French *proesse,* from *prou,* variant of *prod, prud,* gallant, brave, PROUD.]

prowl (prowl) *v.* **prowled, prowling, prowls.** —*tr.* To roam through stealthily, as if in search of prey or plunder. —*intr.* To move around furtively or with predatory intent.
~*n.* An act of prowling: *on the prowl.* [Middle English *prollen*†.]

prowl car *n. U.S.* A police patrol car.

prowl·er (prówl-ər) *n.* One who prowls; especially, a man who prowls at night, intent on theft, voyeurism, or sexual molestation.

prox. proximo.

prox·i·mal (próksim'l) *adj.* **1.** Nearest; proximate. **2.** *Biology.* Near the central part of the body or a point of attachment or origin: *the proximal end of a bone.* Compare **distal.** [Latin *proximus,* nearest, next, PROXIMATE.] **—prox·i·mal·ly** *adv.*

prox·i·mate (próksi-mət, -mit) *adj.* **1.** Closely related in space, time, or order; nearest; next. **2.** Approximate. [Latin *proximātus,* past participle of *proximāre,* to come near, from *proximus,* nearest.] **—prox·i·mate·ly** *adv.*

prox·i·me ac·ces·sit (próksi-mi ak-séssit, -may, ək-) *n.* **1.** One who has second place after the winner of an academic prize or distinction. **2.** A second prize. [Latin, "(he) came very near".]

prox·im·i·ty (prok-símməti) *n.* The state, quality, or fact of being near or next in space or time; closeness. [Old French *proximite,* from Latin *proximitās,* from *proximus,* nearest. See **proximate.**]

proximity fuse *n.* An electronic device for detonating a projectile as it approaches a target, as in antiaircraft shells. Also "VT fuse".

prox·i·mo (próksi-mō) *adv. Abbr.* **prox.** *Archaic.* Of or in the following month: *on the 15th proximo.* Compare **ultimo, instant.** [Latin *proximō (mense),* in the next (month), ablative of *proximus,* nearest, next. See **proximate.**]

prox·y (próksi) *n., pl.* **-ies. 1.** A person authorised to act for another; an agent or substitute. **2.** The authority to act for another. **3.** The written authorisation for such action. **—by proxy.** By means of an intemediary. [Middle English *procusie, proxcy,* contractions of *procuracie,* from Anglo-French, from Medieval Latin *prōcūrātia,* from Latin *prōcūrātiō,* a caring for, from *prōcūrātus,* past participle of *prōcūrāre,* to take care of, PROCURE.]

prude (prōōd || prewd) *n.* A person who is over-concerned with being or seeming to be proper or modest, especially with regard to sex. [French, short for Old French *pr(e)udefemme,* virtuous woman, "fine thing of a woman" : *preu,* virtuous, variant of *prod, prud* (see **proud**) + *de,* of + *femme,* woman.] **—prud·er·y** (-əri) *n.*

pru·dence (prṓōd'nss || préwd'nss) *n.* **1.** The state, quality, or fact of being prudent or sensible. **2.** Careful management; economy.

pru·dent (prṓōd'nt || préwd'nt) *adj.* **1.** Wise in handling practical matters; exercising good judgment or common sense. **2.** Careful with regard to one's own interests; provident. **3.** Careful about one's conduct; circumspect; discreet. [Middle English, from Old French, from Latin *prūdēns* (stem *prūdent-*), foreseeing, wise, contraction of *prōvidēns,* PROVIDENT.] **—pru·dent·ly** *adv.*

pru·den·tial (prōō-dénsh'l || prew-) *adj.* **1.** Arising from or characterised by prudence. **2.** Exercising prudence, good judgment, or common sense. **—pru·den·tial·ly** *adv.*

Prud·hoe Bay (prúddō, prṓōdō). Inlet of the Arctic Ocean, north Alaska, United States. Oil was discovered here (1968), and it is connected to Valdez on the south coast by the trans-Alaska pipeline.

prud·ish (prṓōd-ish || préwd-) *adj.* Having an excessive regard for propriety, modesty, or morality, especially that of others; prim. **—prud·ish·ly** *adv.* **—prud·ish·ness** *n.*

pru·i·nose (prṓō-i-nōz, -nōss || préw-) *adj. Botany.* Having a white, powdery covering or bloom. [Latin *pruīnōsus,* covered with frost, from *pruīna,* hoarfrost.]

prune¹ (prōōn || prewn) *n.* **1.** The partially dried fruit of any of several varieties of the common plum, *Prunus domestica.* **2.** *Chiefly British Informal.* A foolish or ineffectual person. [Middle English *prun(n)e,* from Old French *prune,* from Vulgar Latin *prūna* (unattested), from Latin, plural of *prūnum,* plum; akin to Greek *proumnon,* from an unknown source in Asia Minor.]

prune² *v.* **pruned, pruning, prunes.** —*tr.* **1.** To cut off or remove dead or living parts or branches of (a plant, shrub, or tree) to improve shape or growth. **2.** To remove or cut out as superfluous. **3.** To remove superfluous material from; cut down: *prune the budget.* —*intr.* To remove branches or parts from a plant. [Middle English *prouynen,* from Old French *pro(o)ignier, from* Vulgar Latin *prōrotundiāre* (unattested), to cut roundedly in front : Latin *prō-,* in front + *rotundus,* round, circular.] **—prun·er** *n.*

pru·nel·la (prōō-néllə || prew-) *n.* Also **pru·nel·lo** (-néllō). A strong, heavy fabric of worsted twill, used chiefly for shoe uppers, clerical robes, and academic gowns. [French *prunelle,* "sloe", here perhaps "sloe-coloured stuff". See **prunelle.**]

pru·nelle (prōō-nél || prew-) *n.* A green, sloe-flavoured French liqueur. [French, "sloe", diminutive of *prune,* plum.]

pru·ri·ent (prṓor-i-ənt || préwr-) *adj.* **1.** Obsessively interested in improper matters, especially those of a sexual nature. **2.** Characterised by or arousing such interest: *prurient thoughts.* [Latin *prūriēns* (stem *prūrient-*), present participle of *prūrīre,* to itch, be lascivious.] **—pru·ri·ence, pru·ri·en·cy** *n.* **—pru·ri·ent·ly** *adv.*

pru·ri·go (proor-rígō, prōō- || prew-) *n.* A chronic, inflammatory skin disease characterised by eruption and severe itching. [Latin, an itching, from *prūrīre,* to itch.] **—pru·rig·i·nous** (-ríjinəss) *adj.*

pru·ri·tus (proor-rítəss, prōō- || prew-) *n. Pathology.* **1.** Severe itching, usually of undamaged skin. **2.** Any condition characterised by this. [Latin, from *prūrīre,* to itch.] **—pru·rit·ic** (-ríttik) *adj.*

Prus·sia (prúshə). Former north German state, now in West Germany, East Germany, and Poland. Bordering the Baltic sea, it was

PRONUNCIATION KEY

a, trap; aa, father; ai, fair; ar, star; aw, lawn; ay, play; b, bb, stab; rubber; ch, church; ck, ticket; d, dd, dead; ladder; e, dress; ee, bee; er, defer; ew, few; ewr, pure; ə, about; ər, letter; f, ff, fife; differ; g, gg, giggle; h, hat; i, kit; ī, price; īr, fire; j, judge; k, kick; l, ll, let; 'l, needle; m, mm, man; n, nn, no; 'n, sudden; ng, thing; o, lot; ō, no; ŏŏ, foot; ōō, shoe; oor, poor; ow, cow; owr, hour; oy, boy; p, pp, pepper; r, rr, red; s, ss, sauce; sh, ship; t, tt, totter; th, thick; th, this; smooth; u, cut; ur, turn; v, vv, valve; w, wet; y, yes; z, zz, zebra; zh, vision; pleasure

IN FOREIGN WORDS:

aN, oN, Saint-Saëns; hl, Llanelli; Hluhluwe; kh, loch; lough; Khaled

STRESS MARK:

ín-sīt, insight; in-sít, incite

established in the 13th century by the victory of the Teutonic knights over the heathen Prussians. It became a hereditary duchy in 1525, and united with the Mark of Brandenburg in 1618. It became the Kingdom of Prussia in 1701 and under Frederick the Great took Silesia and parts of Poland. Prussia gained further territories at the Congress of Vienna (1815) and expanded under Bismarck to form the North German Confederation (1867) and the German Empire (1871). After World War I it became a republic much reduced in size (1918) and was dissolved completely after World War II (1946–47) by the Allies. Berlin was the capital.

Prus·sian (prúsh'n) *adj.* **1.** *Abbr.* **Prus., Pruss.** Of or pertaining to Prussia, its people, or their language and culture. **2.** Similar to or suggestive of the Junkers and the military class of Prussia, especially in being sternly disciplined.
~*n.* **1.** Any of the western Balts inhabiting the region between the Vistula and the Neman in ancient times. **2.** A Baltic inhabitant of Prussia. **3.** A German inhabitant of Prussia. **4.** See **Old Prussian.**

Prussian blue *n.* **1.** An insoluble dark blue pigment and dye, ferric ferrocyanide or one of its modifications. **2.** **Iron blue** *(see).* **3.** Moderate to deep greenish blue. [Discovered in Berlin (1704) by H. de Diesbach, a maker of artist's colours.] **—Prus·sian blue** *adj.*

Prus·sian·ise, Prus·sian·ize (prúsh'n-īz) *tr.v.* **-ised, -ising, -ises.** To make Prussian in character or organisation, as by imposing rigid discipline. **—Prus·sian·i·sa·tion** (-ī-záysh'n || *U.S.* -i-) *n.*

prus·si·ate (prúshi-ət, prússi-, -it, -ayt) *n. Chemistry.* **1.** A ferrocyanide or ferricyanide. **2.** A salt of hydrocyanic acid; a cyanide. [French : from *(acide) prussique,* PRUSSIC (ACID) + -ATE.]

prus·sic acid (prússik) *n. Chemistry.* **Hydrocyanic acid** *(see).* [French *acide prussique,* because obtained from Prussian blue.]

pry[1] (prī) *intr.v.* **pried, prying, pries.** To look or enquire closely, curiously, or inquisitively, especially in a furtive manner. Often used with *into.*
~*n., pl.* **pries.** **1.** An act of prying. **2.** An excessively inquisitive person. [Middle English *prien,* perhaps related to PEER.] **—pry·ing·ly** *adv.*

pry[2] *tr.v.* **pried, prying, pries.** *U.S.* To prise, as with a lever. [From PRISE, mistaken for third person singular, as if *pries.*]

pryer. Variant of **prier.**

Prynne (prin), **William** (1600–69). English political agitator. A Puritan, he was imprisoned (1633) and had his ears cut off for his pamphlet, *Historiomastix,* an attack on the theatre which insulted the Queen. He was later branded on both cheeks for pamphleteering, and again imprisoned (1650) for writings attacking the Commonwealth.

Prze·wal·ski's horse (pshi-vál-skiz, pshe-, shə- || -skeez) *n.* A Mongolian wild horse with an erect mane, *Equus przewalskii* (or *E. caballus przewalskii*), now an endangered species. [After N.M. *Przewalski* (1839–88), Russian explorer who discovered it.]

Ps. Psalm; Psalms (Old Testament).

p.s. **1.** passenger steamer. **2.** postscript.

P.S. **1.** permanent secretary. **2.** Police Sergeant. **3.** postscript. **4.** private secretary. **5.** prompt side.

Psa. Psalm; Psalms (Old Testament).

psalm (saam || solm, saalm) *n.* **1.** A sacred song; a hymn. **2.** *Usually capital* **P.** *Abbr.* **Ps., Psa.** Any of the sacred songs or hymns collected in the Old Testament Book of Psalms.
~*tr.v.* **psalmed, psalming, psalms.** To sing of or celebrate in psalms. [Middle English *(p)salm,* Old English *(p)sealm,* from Late Latin *psalmus,* from Greek *psalmos,* song sung to the harp, psalm (translation of Hebrew *mizmōr,* song, psalm), from *psallein,* to pluck, play the harp.]

psalm·ist (saám-ist || sólm-, saálm-) *n.* A writer or composer of psalms. **—the Psalmist.** King David, to whom many of the scriptural psalms are traditionally attributed.

psalm·o·dy (saá-mədi, sál- || sól-, saál-) *n., pl.* **-dies.** **1.** The singing of psalms in divine worship. **2.** The composition or arranging of psalms for singing. **3.** A collection of psalms. [Middle English *psalmodie,* from Late Latin *psalmōdia,* from Late Greek, from Greek, singing to the harp : *psalmos,* PSALM + *ōidē,* song, ode.] **—psalm·o·dist** *n.*

Psalms (saamz || solmz, saalmz). *Abbr.* **Ps., Psa.** A book of the Old Testament, the Book of Psalms, containing 150 songs.

Psal·ter (sáwl-tər || sól-) *n. Often small* **p.** **1.** A book containing the Book of Psalms or a particular version of it in liturgical use. **2.** A musical setting for the Psalms. **3.** The Psalms. [Middle English *(p)salter, sauter,* from Old English *(p)saltere* and Old French *(p)sautier,* both from Late Latin *psaltērium,* early Christian transference of Greek *psaltērion,* psalm, song, PSALTERY.]

psal·te·ri·um (sawl-téer-i-əm || sol-) *n., pl.* **-teria** (-téer-i-ə). The third division of the stomach of ruminants, the **omasum** *(see).* [New Latin, from Late Latin, PSALTER (when slit open its folds fall apart like the leaves of a book).] **—psal·te·ri·al** *adj.*

psal·ter·y (sáwl-təri || sól-) *n., pl.* **-ies.** An ancient, stringed musical instrument played by plucking the strings with the fingers or a plectrum. [Middle English *(p)salterie, sautre,* from Old French *(p)salterie, sauter(i)e,* from Latin *psaltērium,* from Greek *psaltērion,* from *psallein,* to pluck, play upon a stringed instrument.]

psam·mite (sámmīt) *n.* Metamorphosed arenaceous rock. [French : Greek *psammos,* sand + -ITE.] **—psam·mit·ic** (sam-íttik) *adj.*

pse·phite (sée-fīt) *n.* A rock consisting of relatively large fragments embedded in a finer matrix. [French, from Greek *psēphos,* pebble.] **—pse·phit·ic** (see-fíttik) *adj.*

pse·phol·o·gy (si-fóllə-ji, se-) *n.* The study of electoral systems and voting trends and behaviour. [Greek *psēphos,* pebble, vote (from the use of pebbles to cast votes in ancient Greece) + -LOGY.] **—pseph·o·log·i·cal** (séefə-lójik'l, séffə-) *adj.* **—pse·phol·o·gist** *n.*

pseud (sewd, sōōd) *n. Chiefly British Informal.* A pretentious, superficial, or affected person. [Shortened from PSEUDO.] **—pseud** *adj.*

pseud. pseudonym.

pseud·ax·is (sew-dáksiss, sōō-) *n. Botany.* A **sympodium** *(see).* [PSEUD(O)- + AXIS.] **—pseud·ax·i·al** *adj.*

pseud·e·pig·ra·pha (séw-di-píggrə-fə, sōō-) *pl. n. Sometimes capital* **P.** **1.** Spurious writings; specifically, writings falsely attributed to Biblical characters or times. **2.** A body of Jewish religious texts written between 200 B.C. and A.D. 200 and spuriously ascribed to various prophets and kings of Hebrew Scriptures. [Greek, neuter plural of *pseudepigraphos,* falsely ascribed : PSEUDO- + *epigraphein,* to ascribe : *epi,* on, upon + *graphein,* to write.] **—pseud·e·pig·ra·phal** (-f'l), **pseud·ep·i·graph·ic** (-deppi-gráffik), **pseud·ep·i·graph·i·cal, pseud·e·pig·ra·phous** (-píggrə-fəss) *adj.*

pseu·do (séw-dō, sōō-) *adj.* False or counterfeit; fake. [Middle English, from PSEUDO-.]

pseudo–, pseud– *comb. form.* Indicates: **1.** Inauthenticity; sham; for example, **pseudoscience. 2.** Deceptive similarity; for example, **pseudopodium.** ***Note:*** Many compounds other than those entered here may be formed with *pseudo-.* In this dictionary in forming compounds, *pseudo-* is normally joined with the following element without a space or hyphen: *pseudoscience.* However, many users prefer the hyphenated form, and it is used here if the second element begins with a capital letter: *pseudo-Americanism.* It is also preferable to use the hyphen if the second element begins with *o* or if forming the compound brings together three or more vowels that would be confusing to read. [Middle English, from Late Latin, from Greek *pseudēs,* false, from *pseudein†,* to lie.]

pseu·do·carp (séw-dō-kaarp, sōō-, -də-) *n. Botany.* A fruit, such as the pear, apple, or strawberry, that contains fleshy tissue developed from floral parts as well as the ovary. Also called "accessory fruit". [PSEUDO- + -CARP.] **—pseu·do·car·pous** (-kárpəss) *adj.*

pseu·do·cy·e·sis (séw-dō-sī-ée-siss, sōō-, -də-) *n.* **Phantom pregnancy** *(see).*

pseu·do·her·maph·ro·dit·ism (séw-dō-her-máffrə-dī-tiz'm, sōō-, -də-) *n.* An abnormal condition, present at birth, in which the external genital organs resemble those of the opposite sex.

pseu·do·morph (séw-dō-mawrf, sōō-, -də-) *n.* **1.** A false, deceptive, or irregular form. **2.** *Mineralogy.* A mineral having the crystalline form of another mineral rather than that normally characteristic of its composition. [PSEUDO- + -MORPH.] **—pseu·do·mor·phic** (-mórfik), **pseu·do·mor·phous** (-mórfəss) *adj.* **—pseu·do·mor·phism** (-mórf-iz'm) *n.*

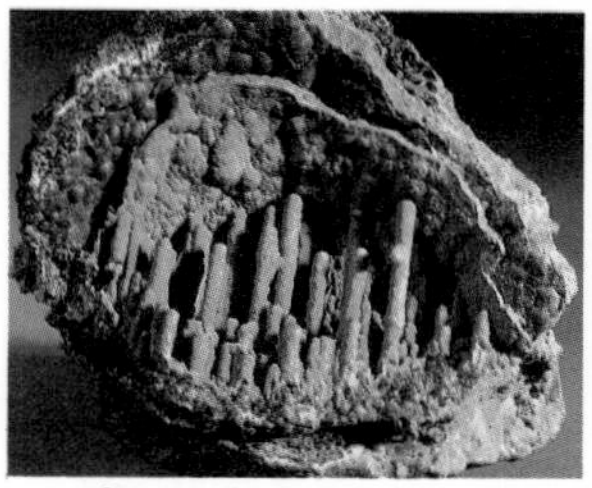

pseudomorph *A pseudomorph is a mineral appearing in the crystal form of another. This is pseudomorphous malachite found in the Ural mountains of Russia.*

pseu·do·nym (séw-də-nim, sōō- || -dō-) *n. Abbr.* **pseud.** A fictitious name, especially one assumed by an author. [French *pseudonyme,* from Greek *pseudōnumon,* neuter of *pseudōnumos* : PSEUD(O)- + -ONYM.] **—pseu·don·y·mous** (sew-dónniməss, sōō-) *adj.*

pseu·do·po·di·um (séw-də-pōdi-əm, sōō-, -dō-) *n., pl.* **-dia** (-ə). Also **pseu·do·pod** (-pod). A temporary protrusion of the cytoplasm of a cell, serving, in organisms such as the amoeba, as a means of locomotion and of surrounding and ingesting food. [PSEUDO- + -PODIUM.]

pseu·do·sci·ence (séw-dō-sī-ənss, sōō-) *n.* An unscientific or trivially scientific theory, methodology, or activity that appears to be or is presented as scientific. **—pseu·do·sci·en·tif·ic** (-ən-tíffik) *adj.* **—pseu·do·sci·en·tist** *n.*

pseud·y (séw-di, sōō-) *adj.* **-ier, -iest.** *Informal.* Pretentious or insincere. [From PSEUD.] **—pseud·i·ness** *n.*

psf, p.s.f. pounds per square foot.

pshaw (pshə, pshaw, shaw) *interj.* Used to indicate impatience, irritation, disapproval, or disbelief.

psi (psī || sī) *n.* The 23rd letter in the Greek alphabet, written Ψ, ψ. Transliterated in English as *ps.* [Late Greek, from Greek *psei,* originally (in the alphabet used at Athens) written ΦΣ.]

psi, p.s.i. pounds per square inch.

psi·lo·cy·bin (sī-lə-sībin, sí-, -lō-) *n.* A phosphate, $C_{12}H_{17}N_2O_4P$, that is the hallucinogen in the fungus *Psilocybe mexicana.* [New Latin *Psilocybe,* from Greek *psīlos,* bald + *kubē,* head (referring to its appearance) + -IN.]

psi·lom·e·lane (sī-lómmilayn) *n.* A black, hydrated oxide ore of manganese. [Greek *psilos,* mere, bare + *melas* (stem *melan-*), black.]

psi·lo·phyte (sī-lō-fīt, -lə-) *n.* Any of a group of simple vascular plants, the Psilophyta, that appeared early in the Palaeozoic era and were the first of the land plants.

psi particle *n.* An elementary particle in the meson family, believed to consist of a charmed quark and its antiquark, the discovery of which led to the concept of charm in physics. Also called "J particle", "J psi particle". [Greek *psi* (arbitrary designation).]

psit·ta·cine (síttə-sīn, -sin) *adj.* Of, pertaining to, or characteristic of parrots. [Latin *psittacīnus,* from *psittacus,* parrot, from Greek *psittakos†.*]

psit·ta·co·sis (síttə-kō-siss) *n.* A virus disease of parrots and related birds, communicable to human beings, in whom it produces high fever, nosebleeds, and complications similar to pneumonia. Also called "parrot fever". [New Latin : Latin *psittacus,* parrot (see **psittacine**) + -OSIS.] **—psit·ta·cot·ic** (-kóttik, -kōtik) *adj.*

pso·as (sō-ass, -əss) *n. Anatomy.* Either of two hip muscles, *psoas major,* which flexes the hip joint, and *psoas minor,* a slender muscle that is often absent. [Greek, accusative plural of *psoa*, interpreted as singular.]

pso·ri·a·sis (so-rī́-ə-siss, saw-, sə-) *n.* A chronic, noncontagious skin disease characterised by inflammation and red, scaly patches. [New Latin, from Greek *psōriasis*, from *psōrian*, to have the itch, from *psōra*, itch, from *psēn*, to rub, scratch.] **—pso·ri·at·ic** (sáw-ri-áttik, só- || sṓ-) *adj.*

pst, psst (pst) *interj.* Used as a whisper to attract somebody's attention, especially without others noticing.

PST, P.S.T. Pacific Standard Time.

P.S.V. public service vehicle (in Britain).

psych, psyche (sīk) *tr.v.* **psyched, psyching, psychs.** *Informal.* **1.** To put (a person, especially onself) into the right psychological frame of mind, as for a performance or competition. Usually used with *up.* **2.** To undermine the confidence of by using psychological tactics. Often used with *out*: *She psyched out her opponent by insults.*

psych. psychological; psychologist; psychology.

psy·che (sī́-ki, -kee) *n.* **1.** The soul or spirit, as distinguished from the body. **2.** *Psychiatry.* The mind functioning as the centre of thought, feeling, and behaviour, and consciously or unconsciously adjusting and relating the body to its social and physical environment. [Latin, from Greek *psukhē*, breath, life, soul.]

Psy·che (sī́-ki, -kee). *Classical Mythology.* A maiden loved by Eros and united with him after Aphrodite's jealousy was overcome. She became the personification of the soul.

psy·che·del·i·a (sī́ki-déeliə, -délli-) *pl.n.* **1.** The world of psychedelic drugs, those who take them, and the effects produced by them. **2.** The music, art, books, or other artefacts that deal with or are supposed to suggest or evoke psychedelic experiences. [PSYCHEDELIC + -IA.]

psy·che·del·ic (sī́ki-déllik) *adj.* **1.** Of, pertaining to, or generating hallucinations, distortions of perception, and, occasionally, states resembling psychosis: *psychedelic drugs.* **2.** Producing an effect similar to the effects of psychedelic drugs: *psychedelic art.*
~*n.* A psychedelic drug. [From PSYCHE (mind) + Greek *dēlos*, clear, visible.]

psy·chi·a·trist (sī-kī́-ə-trist, si-, sə-) *n.* A doctor specially trained to practise psychiatry.

psy·chi·a·try (sī-kī́-ə-tri, si-, sə-) *n.* The medical study, diagnosis, treatment, and prevention of mental or emotional disorders. [PSYCH(O)- + -IATRY.] **—psy·chi·at·ric** (sī́-ki-áttrik), **psy·chi·at·ri·cal** *adj.* **—psy·chi·at·ri·cal·ly** *adv.*

psy·chic (sī́kik) *adj.* Also **psy·chi·cal** (-'l). **1.** Of or pertaining to the human mind or psyche. **2. a.** Of or pertaining to extraordinary, especially extrasensory and nonphysical, mental processes or forces, such as extrasensory perception and telepathy. **b.** Proceeding from or produced by such processes or forces. **c.** Designating a person who is especially responsive to such processes or forces.
~*n.* **1.** A psychic person. **2.** A medium. [Greek *psukhikos*, from *psukhē*, soul, life, PSYCHE.] **—psy·chi·cal·ly** *adv.*

psy·chics (sī́kiks) *n.* *Used with a singular verb.* The analysis, examination, and study of psychic phenomena.

psy·cho (sī́kō) *n., pl.* **-chos.** *Slang.* A psychopath. **—psy·cho** *adj.*

psycho–, psych– *comb. form.* Indicates the mind or mental processes; as, **psychology.** [Greek *psukhē*, breath, life, PSYCHE.]

psy·cho·a·cous·tics (sī́kō-ə-kóostiks) *n.* *Used with a singular verb.* The study of sound in relation to its reception, both physiological and psychological.

psy·cho·ac·tive (sī́kō-áktiv) *adj.* Having an effect on the mind.

psy·cho·an·a·lyse, psy·cho·an·a·lyze (sī́kō-ánnə-līz) *tr.v.* **-lysed, -lysing, -lyses.** To analyse and treat by psychoanalysis. [Back-formation from PSYCHOANALYSIS.]

psy·cho·a·nal·y·sis (sī́kō-ə-nál-ə-siss) *n.* **1.** A method of psychotherapy originated by Sigmund Freud, based on the exploration of unconscious mental processes as manifested in dreams and disturbed relationships with others. Its aim is to reveal repressed anxieties and overcome the effects of bad experiences in early childhood, typically using the technique of free association. **2.** A technique of research into human behaviour and mental processes using the methods and theories of psychoanalysis. **3.** A theory of human psychology, based on the findings of psychoanalysis, concerning the structure of the mind and the effect of unconscious mental processes on behaviour. **—psy·cho·an·a·lyst** (-ánnə-list) *n.* **—psy·cho·an·a·lyt·ic** (-ánnə-líttik), **psy·cho·an·a·lyt·i·cal** *adj.* **—psy·cho·an·a·lyt·i·cal·ly** *adv.*

psy·cho·bab·ble (sī́kō-babb'l) *n.* Psychoanalytic jargon. [Coined in 1975 by R.D. Rosen, author of *Psychobabble.*]

psy·cho·bi·ol·o·gy (sī́kō-bī-óllәji) *n.* The study of the interactions between mental and biological processes as they affect personality.

psy·cho·chem·i·cal (sī́kō-kémmik'l) *adj.* Causing psychological changes or mental disorders.
~*n.* A psychochemical substance, such as a drug or gas.

psy·cho·dra·ma (sī́kō-draamə, -dráamə || *U.S. also* -drámmə) *n.* **1.** A psychotherapeutic and analytic technique in which individuals spontaneously play out roles based on their personal histories. **2.** A psychological drama. **—psy·cho·dra·mat·ic** (-drə-máttik) *adj.*

psy·cho·dy·nam·ics (sī́kō-dī-námmiks) *n.* *Used with a singular verb.* **1.** The interaction of various mental or emotional processes, especially when they are considered as constituents of a system of interrelated forces. **2.** Behavioural analysis in terms of motives or drives. **—psy·cho·dy·nam·ic** *adj.*

psy·cho·gen·e·sis (sī́kō-jénnə-siss) *n.* **1. a.** The origin and development of psychological processes, personality, or behaviour. **b.** The origin of the soul. **2.** The psychological or mental, as opposed to the physiological or physical, origin of something. **—psy·cho·ge·net·ic** (-jə-néttik) *adj.* **—psy·cho·ge·net·i·cal·ly** *adv.*

psy·cho·gen·ic (sī́kō-jénnik) *adj.* Having a psychological rather than physiological origin. Said of certain disorders. [PSYCHO- + -GENIC.] **—phy·cho·gen·ic·al·ly** *adv.*

psy·cho·geri·at·rics (sī́kō-jérri-áttriks) *n.* The psychiatry of the mental disorders of old people. **—psycho·ger·i·at·ric** *adj.*

psy·chog·no·sis (sī-kog-nṓ-siss) *n. Rare.* The study of the psyche. [PSYCHO- + -GNOSIS.] **—psy·chog·nos·tic** (-nóstik) *adj.*

psy·cho·his·to·ry (sī́ko-históri) *n.* The study of individual and collective psychology as it influences and is affected by the historical process: *the psychohistory of the Nazi holocaust.* **—psy·cho·his·tor·i·cal** (-his-tórrik'l) *adj.* **—psy·cho·his·tor·i·cal·ly** *adv.*

psy·cho·ki·ne·sis (sī́kō-kī-née-siss, -ki-) *n.* **1.** *Abbr.* **PK** In parapsychology, the production of motion, especially in inanimate and remote objects, by the exercise of psychic powers. **2.** *Psychiatry.* Uninhibited, maniacal motor response. [PSYCHO- + -KINESIS.] **—psy·cho·ki·net·ic** (-kī-néttik, -ki-) *adj.*

psychol. psychological; psychologist; psychology.

psy·cho·lin·guis·tics (sī́kō-ling-gwístiks) *n.* *Used with a singular verb.* A branch of linguistics concerned with the mental and psychological aspects of language and speech, such as, for example, the childhood acquisition of language. **—psy·cho·lin·guist** (-líng-gwist) *n.* **—psy·cho·lin·guis·tic** *adj.*

psy·cho·log·i·cal (sī́kə-lójik'l) *adj.* Also *rare* **psy·cho·log·ic.** *Abbr.* **psych., psychol. 1.** Of or pertaining to psychology. **2.** Of, pertaining to, or derived from the mind or emotions: *Your fear of water is purely psychological—you're a perfectly good swimmer.* **3.** Capable of influencing the mind or emotions. **—psy·cho·log·i·cal·ly** *adv.*

psychological moment *n.* The time when the mental state of a person is most likely to produce the desired response.

psychological warfare *n.* The use of tactics in warfare designed to undermine the courage, loyalty, or morale of the enemy.

psy·chol·o·gise, psy·chol·o·gize (sī-kóllə-jīz) *v.* **-gised, -gising, -gises.** *—tr.* To explain (behaviour) in terms of psychology. *—intr.* To investigate behaviour using psychological concepts.

psy·chol·o·gism (sī-kóllə-jiz'm) *n.* The application or use, often spurious, of psychological theories to interpret or explain phenomena in other sciences or in the arts, as in history or literature.

psy·chol·o·gist (sī-kólləjist) *n.* *Abbr.* **psych., psychol.** A person trained to perform psychological research or therapy.

psy·chol·o·gy (sī-kólləji) *n., pl.* **-gies.** *Abbr.* **psych., psychol. 1.** The science concerned with understanding and explaining mental processes and behaviour. **2.** The emotional and behavioural characteristics of an individual, group, or activity: *the psychology of war.* **3.** Subtle tactical action or argument: *She used poor psychology on her employer.* [New Latin *psychologia* : PSYCHO- + -LOGY.]

psy·cho·met·rics (sī́k-ə-méttriks, -ō-) *n.* *Used with a singular verb.* **1.** The measurement of psychological variables, such as intelligence, aptitude, or emotional disturbance. **2.** The mathematical, especially statistical, design of psychological tests and measures. **—psy·cho·met·ric, psy·cho·met·ri·cal** *adj.* **—psy·cho·met·ri·cal·ly** *adv.* **—psy·cho·me·tri·cian** (-me-trísh'n, -mə- || sī-kómmə-), **psy·chom·e·trist** (sī-kómmə-trist) *n.*

psy·chom·e·try (sī-kómmətri) *n.* **1.** Psychometrics. **2.** In parapsychology, the supposed ability to divine facts about events, objects, or people, through proximity to them or through touching them. [PSYCHO- + -METRY.]

psy·cho·mo·tor (sī́kō-mṓtər) *adj.* Of or pertaining to muscular activity associated with mental processes.

psy·cho·neu·ro·sis (sī́kō-newr-rṓ-siss || -noor-, -new-, -nóo-) *n., pl.* **-ses** (-seez). *Psychology.* **Neurosis** *(see).* **—psy·cho·neu·rot·ic** (-róttik) *adj. & n.*

psy·cho·path (sī́k-ə-path, -ō-) *n.* A person with a personality disorder, especially one manifested in aggressively antisocial behaviour, amoral attitudes, and continually fluctuating moods. [From PSYCHOPATHY.] **—psy·cho·path·ic** (-páthik) *adj.*

psy·cho·pa·thol·o·gy (sī́kō-pə-thóllə-ji) *n.* The study of pathological mental disorders. **—psy·cho·path·o·log·ic** (-páthə-lójik), **psy·cho·path·o·log·i·cal** *adj.* **—psy·cho·pa·thol·o·gist** (-thóllə-jist) *n.*

psy·chop·a·thy (sī-kóppəthi) *n.* A mental disorder or disease. [PSYCHO- + -PATHY.]

psy·cho·phar·ma·col·o·gy (sī́kō-fármə-kóllə-ji) *n.* A branch of pharmacology concerned with the study and use of drugs that affect the mind. **—psy·cho·phar·ma·co·log·i·cal** (-kə-lójik'l) *adj.* **—psy·cho·phar·ma·col·o·gist** (-kóllə-jist) *n.*

psy·cho·phys·ics (sī́kō-fízziks) *n.* *Used with a singular verb.* The psychological study of relationships between physical stimuli and sensory responses. **—psy·cho·phys·i·cal** *adj.* **—psy·cho·phys·i·cal·ly** *adv.* **—psy·cho·phys·i·cist** (-fízzi-sist) *n.*

psy·cho·phys·i·ol·o·gy (sī́kō-fízzi-ólləji) *n.* The study of correlations between mental processes and physiology. **—psy·cho·phys·i·o·log·i·cal** (-ə-lójik'l) *adj.* **—psy·cho·phys·i·o·log·i·cal·ly** *adv.*

psy·cho·pro·phy·lax·is (sī́kō-próffi-láksiss || *chiefly U.S.* -prṓfi-) *n.* The use of psychological conditioning to prepare a woman for natural childbirth. **—psy·cho·pro·phy·lac·tic** (-láktik) *adj.*

psy·cho·sex·u·al (sī́kō-sék-sew-əl, -shoo-, -shwəl) *adj.* Of or pertaining to the psychological aspects of sex or the mental processes relating to it. **—psy·cho·sex·u·al·i·ty** (-ál-əti) *n.*

psy·cho·sis (sī-kṓ-siss) *n., pl.* **-ses** (-seez). Any severe mental disorder, with or without organic damage, characterised by deterioration of normal intellectual and social functioning and by partial or com-

PRONUNCIATION KEY

a, trap; aa, father; ai, fair; ar, star; aw, lawn; ay, play; b, bb, stab; rubber; ch, church; ck, ticket; d, dd, dead; ladder; e, dress; ee, bee; er, defer; ew, few; ewr, pure; ə, about; ər, letter; f, ff, fife; differ; g, gg, giggle; h, hat; i, kit; ī, price; īr, fire; j, judge; k, kick; l, ll, let; 'l, needle; m, mm, man; n, nn, no; 'n, sudden; ng, thing; o, lot; ō, no; ŏŏ, foot; ōō, shoe; oor, poor; ow, cow; owr, hour; oy, boy; p, pp, pepper; r, rr, red; s, ss, sauce; sh, ship; t, tt, totter; th, thick; th, this; smooth; u, cut; ur, turn; v, vv, valve; w, wet; y, yes; z, zz, zebra; zh, vision; pleasure

IN FOREIGN WORDS:

aN, oN, Saint-Saëns; hl, Llanelli; Hluhluwe; kh, loch; lough; Khaled

STRESS MARK:

in-sīt, insight; in-sī́t, incite

plete withdrawal from reality. Compare **neurosis**. [New Latin : PSYCH(O)- + -OSIS.]

psy·cho·so·mat·ic (sīkō-sə-máttik, -sō-) *adj.* Of or pertaining to phenomena that exhibit an interaction of the physiological and the psychological, especially disorders, such as high blood pressure, that may be initiated or aggravated by mental stress.

psy·cho·sur·ger·y (sīkō-súrj-əri) *n.* Brain surgery when used to treat mental disorders. —**psy·cho·sur·gi·cal** (-ik'l) *adj.*

psy·cho·tech·nics (sīkō-ték-niks) *n. Used with a singular verb. Chiefly U.S.* The practical or technological use of psychology, as in analysis of social or industrial problems. —**psy·cho·tech·ni·cal** *adj.* —**psy·cho·tech·ni·cian** (-tek-nísh'n) *n.*

psy·cho·ther·a·py (sīk-ō-thérrə-pi, -ə-) *n.* 1. Treatment of emotional and psychosomatic disorders based on the application of psychological knowledge, rather than exclusively on the use of drugs, surgery, or other physical treatment. 2. Psychotherapy using depth psychology, by contrast with behaviour therapy. —**psy·cho·ther·a·peu·tic** (-péwtik) *adj.* —**psy·cho·ther·a·pist** (-pist) *n.*

psy·chot·ic (sī-kóttik) *n.* One suffering from a psychosis. [From PSYCHOSIS.] —**psy·chot·ic** *adj.* —**psy·chot·i·cal·ly** *adv.*

psy·chot·o·mi·met·ic (sī-kóttō-mi-méttik, -mī-) *adj.* Designating a drug, such as LSD, that is capable of causing psychosis or psychotic symptoms.
~*n.* A psychotomimetic drug. [PSYCHOT(IC) + MIMETIC.]

psy·cho·trop·ic (sīkō-tróppik, -trōpik) *adj.* Affecting the moods or mental processes. Said of a drug. [PSYCHO- + -TROPIC.] —**psy·cho·trop·ic** *n.* —**psy·cho·trop·i·cal·ly** *adv.*

psychro– *comb. form.* Indicates cold; for example, **psychrometer**. [Greek *psukhros†*, cold.]

psy·chrom·e·ter (sī-krómmitər) *n.* A hygrometer that uses the difference in readings between two thermometers, one having a wet bulb ventilated to cause evaporation and the other having a dry bulb, as a measure of atmospheric moisture. Also called "wet-and-dry-bulb thermometer". [PSYCHRO- + -METER.]

psy·chro·phil·ic (sīk-rō-fíllik, -rə-) *adj. Biology.* Thriving at relatively low temperatures, usually between 0 and 25°C. Said of certain bacteria. Compare **mesophilic, thermophilic**. [PSYCHRO- + -PHIL(E) + -IC.]

psyl·la (síllə) *n.* Also **psyl·lid** (síllid). Any of various plant lice of the family Chermidae (or Psyllidae), especially *Psylla mali*, a pest that infests apple trees. [Greek *psulla*, flea.]

Pt The symbol for the element platinum.

pt. 1. part. 2. payment. 3. pint. 4. point. 5. port. 6. preterite.

p.t. 1. past tense. 2. pro tempore.

P.T. 1. Pacific Time. 2. physical therapy. 3. physical training. 4. postal telegraph. 5. purchase tax (formerly, in Britain).

pta. peseta.

P.T.A. 1. Parent-Teacher Association. 2. passenger transport authority (in Britain).

Ptah (ptaa, taa) *n.* In ancient Egypt, the creator god and the god of Memphis, represented in the form of a mummy.

ptar·mi·gan (tármigən) *n., pl.* **-gans** or collectively **ptarmigan.** A game bird, *Lagopus mutus*, of the grouse family, inhabiting arctic and subarctic regions of the Northern Hemisphere. It has feathered feet and plumage that is brownish-grey in summer, grey in autumn, and white in winter. [Alteration (by pseudo-learned association with Greek *pteron*, wing) of Scottish Gaelic *tarmachan*, diminutive of *tarmach†*.]

Pte. private (in the British and various other armies).

–pter *n. comb. form.* Indicates wings or winglike parts; for example, **ornithopter.** [New Latin *-ptera*, from Greek *-pteros*, -PTEROUS.]

pter·i·dol·o·gy (térri-dóllə-ji) *n.* The study of ferns. [Greek *pteris* (stem *pterid-*), fern, from *pteron*, feather + -LOGY.] —**pter·i·do·log·i·cal** (-də-lójik'l) *adj.* —**pter·i·dol·o·gist** (-dóllə-jist) *n.*

pter·i·do·phyte (térri-dō-fīt, -də-; *also* te-ríddə-, tə-) *n. Botany.* Any plant of the division Pteridophyta, including the ferns, and horsetails, that reproduces by spores and has vascular tissue. [New Latin *Pteridophyta* : Greek *pteris*, fern (see **pteridology**) + -PHYTE.] —**pter·i·do·phyt·ic** (-fíttik), **pter·i·doph·y·tous** (-dóffitəss) *adj.*

pter·i·do·sperm (térri-dō-sperm, -də-; *also* te-ríddə-, tə-) *n.* The **seed fern** (see).

ptero– *comb. form.* Indicates feather, wing, or winglike part; for example, **pterodactyl.** [Greek *pteron*, feather, wing.]

pter·o·dac·tyl (térrə-dáktil, térrō-) *n.* Any of various extinct flying reptiles of the family Pterodactylidae. See **pterosaur.** [New Latin *Pterodactylus*, "wing-finger" : PTERO- + DACTYL.]

pter·o·pod (térrə-pod, térrō-) *n.* Any of various small marine gastropod molluscs of the order Pteropoda, that swim with winglike expanded lobes of the foot. Also called "sea butterfly". [New Latin *Pteropoda*, "wing-footed ones", from Greek *pteropous*, wing-footed : PTERO- + *-pous*, -POD.] —**pter·o·pod** *adj.*

pter·o·saur (térrə-sawr, térrō-) *n.* Any of various extinct flying reptiles of the order Pterosauria, including the pterodactyls, of the Jurassic and Cretaceous periods, characterised by wings consisting of a flap of skin supported by the very long fourth digit on each front limb. [New Latin *Pterosauria*, "winged lizards" : PTERO- + -*sauria*, plural of -SAURUS.]

–pterous, –pteran *adj. comb. form.* Indicates a specified number or kind of wings; for example, **dipterous.** [Greek *-pteros*, -winged, from *pteron*, feather, wing.]

pter·y·goid (térrig-oyd) *adj. Anatomy.* Of or designating either of two processes in the skull attached to the body of the sphenoid bone.

~*n. Anatomy.* Either of these processes. Also called "pterygoid process". [Greek *pterugoeidēs* : *pterux*, wing, from *pteron*, feather, wing + -OID.]

PTFE polytetrafluoroethylene.

ptg. printing.

ptis·an (tízz'n, ti-zán) *n.* A **tisane** (see). [Middle English *tisan*, peeled barley, barley water, from Old French, from Medieval Latin *tisana*, variant of Latin *ptisana*, from Greek *ptisanē*, from *ptissein*, to peel, crush.]

P.T.O, **p.t.o.** please turn over.

Ptol·e·ma·ic (tóllə-máy-ik) *adj.* 1. Of or pertaining to the astronomer Ptolemy. 2. Of or pertaining to the Ptolemies or to Egypt during their rule, 323 B.C. to 30 B.C.

Ptolemaic system *n.* The astronomical system of Ptolemy, having the Earth at the centre of the universe, with the Moon, planets, and the stars revolving about it.

Ptol·e·ma·ist (tóllə-máy-ist) *n.* An adherent of or believer in the astronomical system of Ptolemy.

Ptol·e·my (tólləmi), born, Claudius Ptolemaeus (*c.* A.D. 90–*c.* 168). Graeco-Egyptian mathematician and geographer. His work, preserved at the Great Library in Alexandria, was translated into Arabic, spread across the Islamic world, and was reintroduced to Europe, where it had a great influence on medieval and Renaissance scholars. His *Geographike hyphegesis* inspired Columbus.

Ptolemy I Soter (*c.* 367– *c.* 284 B.C.). Macedonian soldier, king, and historian. One of Alexander the Great's generals, he became governor of Egypt after his death, and eventually (305) proclaimed himself king, founding the Ptolemaic dynasty. He founded the Library at Alexandria, and recorded Alexander's campaigns.

Ptolemy XIII Theos Philopator (63–47 B.C.). King of Egypt. Following his succession to the throne (51 B.C.) with his sister and wife, Cleopatra, he exiled her (48 B.C.) to Syria. Julius Caesar, however, supported the reinstatement of Cleopatra, and Ptolemy was killed in the subsequent civil war.

pto·maine, pto·main (tō-mayn, tō-máyn, tə-) *n.* Any of various basic nitrogenous materials, some poisonous, produced by the putrefaction and decomposition of protein. [French *ptomaïne*, from Italian *ptomaina*, from Greek *ptōma*, "fall, fallen body", corpse, from *piptein*, to fall.]

ptomaine poisoning *n.* Food poisoning. Ptomaines were formerly erroneously considered a cause of all food poisoning.

pto·sis (tō-siss) *n.* Abnormal and permanent lowering of an organ; especially, drooping of the upper eyelid caused by muscle failure. [New Latin, from Greek *ptōsis*, fall, from *piptein*, to fall.] —**pto·tic** (tōtik, tóttik) *adj.*

pts. 1. parts. 2. payments. 3. pints. 4. points. 5. ports.

pty. proprietary.

pty·a·lin (tī-ə-lin) *n.* A salivary enzyme in humans and some other animals that hydrolyses starch into dextrins and ultimately maltose. [Greek *ptualon*, saliva, from *ptuein*, to spit + -IN.]

pty·a·lism (tī-ə-liz'm) *n.* Excessive flow of saliva. [Greek *ptualon*, saliva. See **ptyalin**.]

p-type (pée-tīp) *adj. Electronics.* Of or designating a semiconductor or its type of conductivity, in which the majority of carriers are holes rather than electrons. Compare **n-type.** [*Positive type.*]

Pu The symbol for the element plutonium.

pub (pub) *n. Chiefly British.* A place where alcoholic drinks are sold under licence to be consumed on or off the premises, which often also provides light meals. Also used adjectivally: *a pub lunch.*
~*intr.v.* **pubbed, pubbing, pubs.** To have a drink in a pub. Used chiefly in the phrase *go pubbing.* [Short for PUBLIC HOUSE.]

pub. 1. public. 2. publication. 3. published; publisher; publishing.

pub crawl —*n. Slang.* A round of drinking in several pubs in succession. —**pub-crawl** (púb-krawl) *intr.v.* —**pub-crawl·er** *n.*

pube (pewb) *n. Informal.* A pubic hair. [Short for *pubic hair.*]

pu·ber·ty (péwbər-ti) *n.* The stage of maturation in early adolescence in which the individual becomes physiologically capable of sexual reproduction and the secondary sexual characteristics appear. [Middle English *puberte*, from Latin *pūbertās* (stem *pūbertāt-*), from *pūber*, adult.] —**pu·ber·al, pu·ber·tal** (-t'l) *adj.*

pu·ber·u·lent (pew-bérrew-lənt ‖ -bérrə-) *adj.* Also **pu·ber·u·lous** (-ləss). *Biology.* Covered with minute hairs or very fine down; finely pubescent. [Latin *pūber*, grown up, adult, (of plants) downy.]

pu·bes (péw-beez). Plural of **pubis.**
~*n., pl.* **pubes.** *Anatomy.* The pubic region. [Latin *pūbēs.*]

pu·bes·cence (pew-béss'nss) *n.* 1. The attainment or onset of puberty. 2. a. A covering of soft down or short hairs, as on certain plants and insects. b. The state of being pubescent.

pu·bes·cent (pew-béss'nt) *adj.* 1. Reaching or having reached puberty. 2. Covered with short hairs or soft down. [French, from Latin *pūbēscens* (stem *pūbēscent-*), present participle of *pūbēscere*, to reach puberty, from *pūber*, adult.]

pu·bic (péwbik) *adj.* Of, pertaining to, or in the region of the lower part of the abdomen, the pubis, or the pubes. [From PUBES.]

pu·bis (péw-biss) *n., pl.* **-bes** (-beez). The forward portion of either of the hipbones, at the juncture forming the front arch of the pelvis. [New Latin (*os*) *pubis*, bone of the groin, from Latin *pūbis*, genitive of *pūbēs*, PUBES.]

publ. 1. publication. 2. published; publisher.

pub·lic (púbblik) *adj. Abbr.* **pub.** 1. Of, concerning, or affecting the community or the people as a whole: *public affairs.* 2. Maintained for or open to be used by the whole community. 3. Participated in or able to be attended by the whole community: *public worship.*

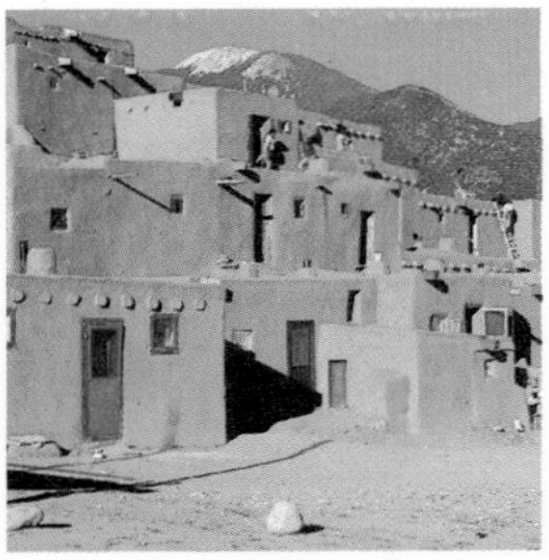

pueblo *These multistorey buildings gave their Spanish name to the Indians whose traditional homes they are: the Pueblo peoples of New Mexico and the southwestern United States. Jutting beams support the roof of each house and take the weight of the rooms above.*

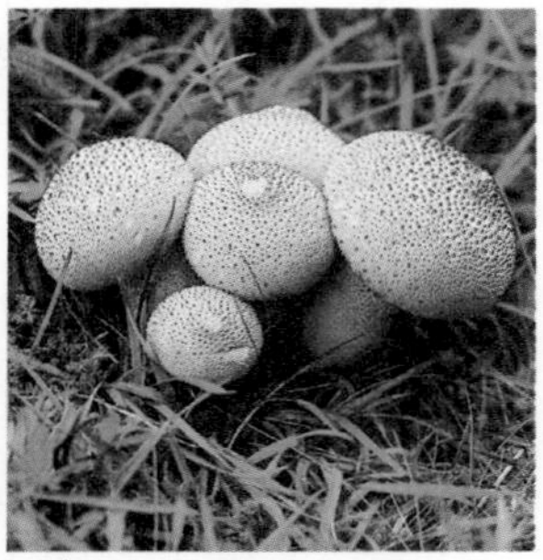

puffball *Many of these common fungi are edible until maturity. Then they become powdery inside and puff out spores if disturbed. Some species grow up to 120 centimetres (4 feet) across. The British species,* Lycoperdon perlatum gemnatum *(above), grows mostly in woodlands.*

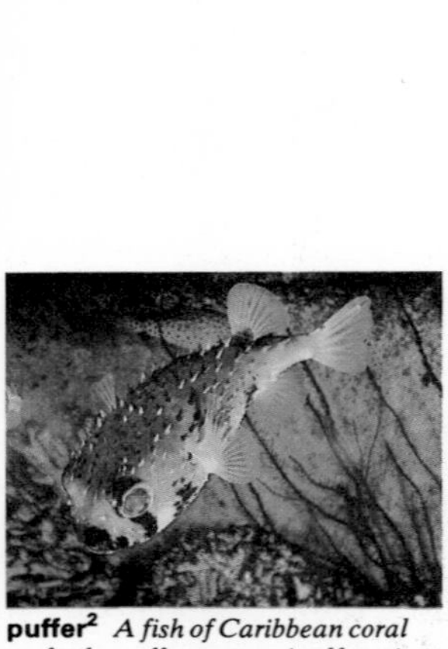

puffer[2] *A fish of Caribbean coral reefs, the puffer protects itself against predators by inflating its spiky body.*

4. Connected with or acting on behalf of the people, community, or government, rather than concerned with private matters or interests: *public office.* **5. a.** Open to the knowledge or judgment of all: *a public scandal.* **b.** Known or recognised by many people: *a public figure.* **—go public. 1.** To offer shares for sale to the public, especially for the first time. Used of a private company. **2.** To appeal directly to the public, as by means of the media, instead of going through the usual internal channels or complaints procedures. **—make public.** To cause to be known by several or many people or the people at large.
~*n. Abbr.* **pub. 1.** The community or the people as a whole. **2.** A group of people sharing a common specified interest: *the reading public.* **3.** Admirers or followers, especially of a famous person. [Middle English *publique, publyk,* from Old French *public, publique,* from Latin *pūblicus,* alteration of *poplicus,* from *populus,* people.] **—pub·lic·ness** *n.*

pub·lic-ad·dress system (púbblik-ə-dréss) *n. Abbr.* **PA** An electronic amplification apparatus installed and used for broadcasting in public areas. Also called "PA system".

pub·li·can (púbbli-kən) *n.* **1.** *Chiefly British.* The keeper of a public house; a tavernkeeper. **2.** A collector of public taxes or tolls in the ancient Roman Empire. [Middle English, from Old French *publicain,* from Latin *pūblicānus,* contractor for public revenues, from *pūblicum,* public revenue, from *pūblicus,* PUBLIC.]

pub·li·ca·tion (púbbli-káysh'n) *n. Abbr.* **pub., publ. 1.** The act or process of publishing printed matter. **2.** Any printed material offered for sale or distribution, such as a book or periodical. **3.** The communication of information to the public. **4.** *Law.* The act of making defamatory information public. [Middle English *publicatioun,* from Old French, from Late Latin *pūblicātiō* (stem *pūblicātiōn-*), from *pūblicāre,* to make public, from Latin *pūblicus,* PUBLIC.]

public company *n.* A **public limited company** *(see).*

public convenience *n. Chiefly British.* A lavatory that is available for use by the general public. Also called "convenience".

public corporation *n.* In Britain, a state-owned organisation responsible for the management of a nationalised industry.

public defender *n.* In the United States, a lawyer or staff of lawyers, usually publicly appointed, having responsibility for the legal defence of those unable to afford or obtain legal assistance.

public domain *n.* **1.** The status of publications, products, and processes that are not protected under patent or copyright. **2.** *U.S.* Land owned and controlled by the state or federal government.

public enemy *n.* A person, usually a criminal, who is considered to be especially dangerous to the community.

public gallery *n.* A gallery in a parliament or council chamber where the public may sit and listen to proceedings.

public house *n. Chiefly British.* A pub.

pub·li·cise, pub·li·cize (púbbli-sīz) *tr.v.* **-cised, -cising, -cises.** To give publicity to; bring to public attention; advertise.

pub·li·cist (púbbli-sist) *n.* A person who publicises something or someone; especially, a press or publicity agent.

pub·lic·i·ty (pub-líssəti, pəb-) *n.* **1.** Information that concerns a person, group, event, or product and is disseminated through various forms of the media to attract public notice. **2.** Public interest, notice, or notoriety achieved by the spreading of such information. **3.** The act, process, or occupation of disseminating information to gain public interest. **4.** The condition of being public. [French *publicité,* from *public,* PUBLIC.]

public law *n.* **1.** The branch of law dealing with the state or government and the way it relates to individuals or other governments. Compare **private law. 2.** A law affecting the public.

public lending right *n. Abbr.* **P.L.R.** The right of an author to receive royalties when his books are lent by a public library.

public library *n.* A noncommercial library for the use of the general public, usually supported by public funds.

public limited company *n. Finance. Abbr.* **PLC, p.l.c., P.L.C.** A limited liability company whose shares are made available for subscription by the public rather than distributed privately, and can be transferred freely on the open market. Also called "public company". Compare **private limited company.**

pub·lic·ly (púbblikli) *adv.* **1.** In a public manner; not privately; openly. **2.** By or with consent of the public.

public nuisance *n.* **1.** *Law.* An illegal act that causes harm to the community at large rather than to a particular individual. **2.** *Informal.* A person who is considered to be obnoxious by many people.

public opinion *n.* The views of the public, especially on a matter of public concern or interest.

public prosecutor *n.* **1.** A government official who prosecutes criminal actions on behalf of the state or community. **2.** A **prosecutor** *(see).*

public relations *n. Usually used with a singular verb. Abbr.* **PR, P.R. 1.** The methods and activities employed by an individual, organisation, or government to promote a favourable relationship and good image with the public. **2.** The degree of success achieved in such a relationship. **3.** The staff employed to promote such a relationship. **4.** The art or science of establishing such a relationship.

public school *n.* **1.** In Britain, a private, independent, secondary, fee-paying school at which the pupils usually board. Compare **comprehensive, grammar school, secondary modern school. 2.** Loosely, any school maintained by the state.

public sector *n.* The section of the economy that is under the control of government departments or public corporations, including nationalised industries, national and local government, welfare, and education. Compare **private sector. —public-sector** *adj.*

public servant *n.* A person who holds a government position by election or by appointment.

public service *n.* **1.** Employment within a governmental system, especially within the civil service. **2.** A service performed for the benefit of the public. Also used adjectivally.

public speaking *n.* The art or process of making speeches before an audience. **—public speaker** *n.*

pub·lic-spir·i·ted (púbblik-spírritid) *adj.* Motivated by or showing active devotion to the good of the community; concerned for the public welfare. **—pub·lic-spir·it·ed·ness** *n.*

public utility *n.* **1.** An industrial organisation that provides an essential service or commodity, such as water, electricity, transport, or communication, to the public, and is usually under state ownership or control. Also called "public utility company". **2.** *Usually plural. Finance.* Shares issued by such a company.

public works *pl.n.* Construction projects, such as motorways or dams, financed by public funds and constructed by a government for the benefit or use of the general public.

pub·lish (púbblish) *v.* **-lished, -lishing, -lishes.** *—tr.* **1.** To prepare and issue (printed material) for public distribution or sale. **2.** To bring to the public attention; announce. *—intr.* **1.** To issue a publication. **2.** To be the author of a published work. [Middle English *publishen,* from Old French *publier* (stem *publiss-*), from Latin *pūblicāre,* to make public, from *pūblicus,* PUBLIC.] **—pub·lish·a·ble** *adj.*

pub·lish·er (púbblishər) *n. Abbr.* **pub., publ.** A person or company engaged in publishing printed material.

pub·lish·ing (púbblishing) *n.* The business, people, or work involved in the publication of books, periodicals, and the like.

Puc·ci·ni (po͞o-chéeni, po͞o-), **Giacomo** (1858–1924). Italian composer. A major composer of the verismo movement, he wrote in a style that is especially noted for its lyrical qualities. His works, which continue to enjoy enormous popularity, include *La Bohème* (1896), *Tosca* (1900), and *Madame Butterfly* (1904).

puce (pewss) *n.* Deep red to dark greyish purple. [French *(couleur) puce,* "flea (colour)", from Latin *pūlex,* flea.] **—puce** *adj.*

puck (puk) *n.* A hard rubber disc used in ice hockey as the playing and scoring medium. [19th century : origin obscure.]

Puck *n.* In English folklore, a mischievous sprite. Also called "Robin Goodfellow". [Middle English *p(o)uke,* Old English *pūca*†.]

pucka. Variant of **pukka.**

puck·er (púckər) *v.* **-ered, -ering, -ers.** *—tr.* To gather into small wrinkles or folds. *—intr.* To become contracted and wrinkled.
~*n.* A wrinkle or wrinkled part, as in tightly stitched cloth. [Originally "to form a pocket", perhaps from POCKET.]

puck·ish (púckish) *adj.* Mischievous; impish: *a puckish grin.* [From PUCK.] **—puck·ish·ly** *adv.* **—puck·ish·ness** *n.*

pud·ding (po͝odding) *n.* **1. a.** A sweet dessert, usually containing flour or a cereal product, that has been boiled, steamed, or baked. **b.** A savoury dish baked in suet pastry, with a pudding-like consistency. **c.** Any mixture with a soft, pudding- or porridge-like consistency. **2.** A sausage-like preparation made with minced meat or various other ingredients stuffed into a bag or skin and boiled. **3.** The sweet course of a meal. **—in the pudding club.** *Informal.* Pregnant. [Middle English, from Old French *boudin,* from Vulgar Latin *botellīnus* (unattested), diminutive of Latin *botellus,* sausage.]

pudding stone *n.* A rock, a **conglomerate** *(see).*

pud·dle (púdd'l) *n.* **1.** A small pool of water, especially one formed by rain. **2.** A small pool of any liquid. **3.** A tempered paste of wet clay and sand used as waterproofing.
~*v.* **puddled, -dling, -dles.** *—tr.* **1.** To make muddy. **2.** To work (clay or sand) into a thick, watertight paste. **3.** *Metallurgy.* To process (impure metal) by puddling. *—intr.* **1.** To splash or dabble in or as if in a puddle. Used with *about.* **2.** To dabble or fuss in a disorganised fashion: *always puddling about with his papers but never gets his desk cleared.* [Middle English *podel, pothel,* diminutive of Old English *pudd*†, ditch.] **—pud·dly** (púdd'l-i, púddli) *adj.*

pud·dler (púdd'l-ər, púddlər) *n.* **1.** One who puddles iron or clay. **2.** One who puddles about.

pud·dling (púdd'l-ing, púddling) *n.* **1.** *Metallurgy.* The purification of impure metal, especially pig iron, by agitation of a molten bath of the metal in an oxidising atmosphere. **2.** Compaction of wet clay or a similar material to make a watertight paste.

pu·den·cy (péwd'n-si) *n.* Modesty; shame; prudishness. [Late Latin *pudentia,* shame, from Latin *pudēns* (stem *pudent-*), present participle of *pudēre,* to feel shame.]

pu·den·dum (pew-dén-dəm) *n., pl.* **-da** (-də). *Often plural.* The human external genital organs, especially a woman's. [New Latin, from Late Latin *pudenda,* from Latin *pudendus,* gerundive of *pudēre,* to be ashamed.] **—pu·den·dal** *adj.*

pudgy. Variant of **podgy.**

pueb·lo (pwéb-lō, po͞o-éb-) *n., pl.* **-los. 1.** A community dwelling, up to five storeys high, built of stone or adobe by Indian tribes of the southwestern United States. **2.** *Capital* **P.** A member of a tribe, such as the Hopi or Zuñi, inhabiting such dwellings. **3.** An Indian village of the southwestern United States. [Spanish, "people", "population", from Latin *populus,* people.]

puer·ile (péwr-īl ‖ péw-ər-, *chiefly U.S.* -il) *adj.* **1.** Immature; childish. **2.** Pertaining to childhood. [French *puéril,* from Latin *puerīlis,* from *puer,* child, boy.] **—puer·ile·ly** *adv.* **—puer·ile·ness** *n.*

puer·il·ism (péwr-il-iz'm ‖ péw-ər-) *n. Psychiatry.* Infantile or child-

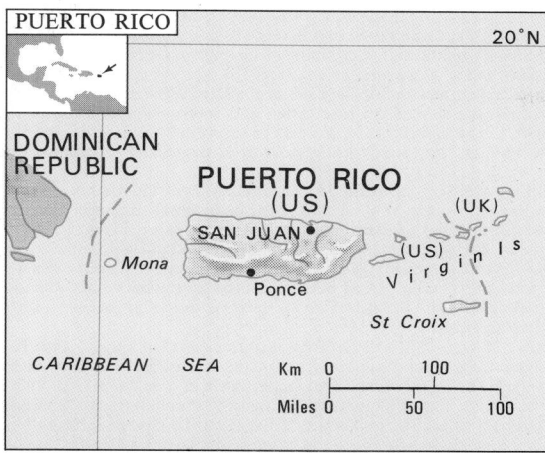

ish behaviour exhibited by an adult suffering from a mental illness. [PUERILE + -ISM.]

puer·il·i·ty (pewr-rílləti, péwr- ‖ péw-ə-) *n., pl.* **-ties. 1.** The condition of being puerile. **2.** A childish action, idea, or utterance.

pu·er·per·al (pew-érpərəl) *adj. Medicine.* Connected with, resulting from, or following childbirth. [Latin *puerperus,* bearing young : *puer,* child + -PAROUS.]

puerperal fever *n.* Infection of the womb and of the bloodstream following childbirth. Also called "childbed fever".

pu·er·pe·ri·um (péwr-péer-i-əm, péw-ər-) *n.* The approximate six-week period after childbirth to return of normal uterine size. [Latin, childbirth, from *puerperus,* PUERPERAL.]

Puer·to Ri·co, Commonwealth of (pwér-tō réekō, pwár-, -tə). Island in the West Indies. Self-governing but associated with the United States, it is largely mountainous and densely populated. Its chief industries include textiles, chemicals, the breeding of cattle, and sugar production. Large-scale emigration to the United States (1940s and 1950s) has declined and there is a small independence movement. Area, 8 897 square kilometres (3,434 square miles). Population, 3,300,000. Capital, San Juan. —**Puer·to Ric·an** *adj. & n.*

puff (puf) *n.* **1. a.** A short, forceful exhalation of breath. **b.** A short, sudden gust of wind. **c.** A brief, sudden emission of air, vapour, or smoke. **d.** A short, sibilant sound produced by a puff. **2.** An amount of vapour, smoke, or similar material released in a puff. **3.** An act of drawing in and expelling the breath, as in smoking tobacco. **4.** *Rare.* A swelling or rounded protuberance. **5.** A light, flaky pastry. **6.** See **powder puff. 7.** A soft roll of hair forming part of a hairstyle. **8.** A portion of fabric that is gathered at the edges and full in shape. **9.** An extravagantly flattering recommendation of a book, play, or the like, especially in a newspaper. **10.** Variant of **pouffe. 11.** *U.S.* An eiderdown. **12.** *Genetics.* A swelling seen in certain areas of giant chromosomes.
~*v.* **puffed, puffing, puffs.** —*intr.* **1.** To blow in puffs. **2.** To come forth in a puff or puffs. **3.** To breathe forcefully and rapidly; pant. **4.** To emit or move while emitting puffs of smoke, vapour, or the like: *The train puffed.* **5.** To take puffs on a cigarette, pipe, or cigar. **6.** To swell or seem to swell, as with air or pride. Often used with *up* or *out.* —*tr.* **1.** To emit or give forth in a puff or puffs. **2.** To impel with puffs. **3.** To smoke (a cigar, for example). **4.** To inflate or distend. **5.** To fill with pride or conceit. Used with *out* or *up: all puffed up by her recent success.* **6.** To publicise with exaggerated praise. **7.** To cause to be out of breath. Usually used in the passive with *out.* [Middle English *puffen,* Old English *puffan* (unattested), imitative.] —**puff·i·ly** *adv.* —**puff·i·ness** *n.*

puf·fy (púffi) *adj.* **puffier, puffiest. 1.** Swollen or bloated: *puffy eyes after a night spent crying.* **2.** Breathless.

puffed sleeve (puft) *n.* A short sleeve, gathered at both ends so that it stands out from the shoulder. Also called "puff sleeve".

puff·ad·der (púff-addər) *n.* A venomous African viper, *Bitis arietans,* having crescent-shaped yellowish markings. [South African Dutch and Afrikaans *pofadder : pof,* puff + ADDER; so called because it inflates its body when aroused.]

puff·ball (púff-bawl) *n.* Any of various fungi of the genus *Lycoperdon* and related genera, having a ball-shaped fruiting body that, when broken open, releases the enclosed spores in puffs of dust.

puff·er (púffər) *n.* **1.** One that puffs. **2.** Any of various marine fishes of the family Tetraodontidae, that are capable of swelling up. Also called "blowfish", "swellfish".

puff·e·ry (púffəri) *n.* Exaggerated praise or recommendation.

puf·fin (púffin) *n.* Any of several sea birds of the genera *Fratercula* and *Lunda,* of northern regions, characteristically having black and white plumage and a vertically flattened, brightly coloured bill. Also called "sea parrot". [Middle English *poffo(u)n, pophyn†.]*

puff pastry *n.* Dough that is rolled and folded in layers, and that expands in baking to form a rich, light, flaky pastry.

pug¹ (pug) *n.* A small dog of a breed originating in China, having a snub nose, wrinkled face, square body, short smooth hair, and a curled tail. [16th century : perhaps of Dutch origin.]

pug² *n.* **1.** Clay ground and kneaded with water into a plastic consistency for forming bricks or pottery. **2.** A machine for grinding and mixing clay.
~*tr.v.* **pugged, pugging, pugs. 1.** To knead (clay) with water. **2.** To fill in with clay or mortar. **3.** To cover or pack with clay, mortar, sawdust, or felt in order to soundproof. [16th century : origin obscure.]

pug³ *n.* A footprint, track, or trail, especially of an animal.
~*tr.v.* **pugged, pugging, pugs.** To track by pugs. [Hindi *pag,* probably from Sanskrit *padakah,* foot, from *pada.*]

pug⁴ *n. Slang.* A boxer. [Shortened from PUGILIST.]

pug·gree, pug·ree (púggri) *n.* Also **pug·ga·ree, pug·a·ree,** (púg-gəri). A band or scarf wrapped around the crown of a hat. [Hindi *pagrī,* from Sanskrit *parikara;* akin to Arabic *pairikara,* turban.]

pu·gi·lism (péwjil-iz'm) *n.* The skill or practice of fighting with the fists; boxing. [Latin *pugil,* fighter, from *pugnus,* fist.]

pu·gi·list (péwjil-ist) *n.* One who fights with the fists; especially, a professional boxer. —**pu·gi·lis·tic** (-ístik) *adj.*

Pu·gin (péwjin), **Augustus Welby Northmore** (1812–52). British architect. A convert to Roman Catholicism and a leader of the neo-Gothic movement, which he advocated in his book *Contrasts* (1836), he designed many Catholic churches and cathedrals. He also collaborated with **Barry** on the interior of Westminster Palace.

pug·na·cious (pug-náyshəss) *adj.* Eager to fight; having a quarrelsome disposition. See Synonyms at **belligerent.** [Latin *pugnāx* (stem *pugnāc-),* fond of fighting, from *pugnāre,* to fight, from *pugnus,* fist.] —**pug·na·cious·ly** *adv.* —**pug·na·cious·ness, pug·nac·i·ty** (-nássəti) *n.*

puffin *The puffin's large, brightly coloured bill has given it the alternative name of sea parrot. The colours remain only during the breeding season; the outer layers of the bill are shed in the autumn.*

Pugin

ARCHITECT OF VICTORIAN ENGLAND'S GOTHIC REVIVAL
Pugin sought to express the spirit of Christianity

Augustus Welby Northmore Pugin was 21 years old when, in 1833, he was converted to the Roman Catholic faith, and resolved to build churches that would be "the perfect expression of all we should hold sacred".

Pugin hated what he called the "pagan" churches built in the classical style of the Renaissance. He felt that the architecture of a society reflected its moral quality, and that the Gothic architecture of the Middle Ages was a faithful expression of the Christian spirit. His book *True Principles of Pointed or Christian Architecture* appeared in 1841.

Born in London in 1812, Pugin was the son of an architectural draughtsman and editor of books on Gothic details. In 1835 – the year after the Houses of Parliament were burned down – it was Pugin who masterminded the detailed Gothic design and interior that won the architect Charles Barry the contract to rebuild them.

Four years later he began to design St. Chad's Cathedral, Birmingham, the first Gothic cathedral to be built in England·for some 400 years. Among his other outstanding monuments are St. Giles's Church, Cheadle, Staffs (1841–46), and St. Augustine's Church in Ramsgate, Kent (1846–51), where he lived.

For much of his life Pugin suffered from ill health and the effects of overwork. In 1851 he was committed to the London lunatic asylum, known as Bedlam, and died after his release the following year. "I have done the work of a hundred years in only forty" he declared shortly before the end. "It has worn me out."

FURNISHINGS OF THE HOUSE OF LORDS *During the last eight years of his life, Pugin made 2,000 designs for the interior of the House of Lords. Despite increasing ill health, he coped with orders for every kind of furnishing – from the royal throne down to fireguards, candlesticks, and inkstands.*

pug nose *n.* A short nose that is flattened and turned up at the end. [Probably from PUG (dog).] **—pug-nosed** (púg-nōzd) *adj.*

puis·ne (péwni) *adj. Law.* Lower in rank; junior.
~*n. Law.* One of lesser rank; especially, an associate judge. [Old French, "born afterwards". See **puny.**]

puis·sance (pwée-SONSS, -SÓNSS, *for sense 1; for sense 2, also* péw-i-s'nss, pwíss'nss) *n.* **1.** An equestrian competition testing a horse's ability to jump heights. **2.** *Archaic & Poetic.* Power; potency; might.

puis·sant (pwée-SONT, -SÓNT, péw-i-s'nt, pwíss'nt) *adj. Archaic & Poetic.* Mighty; powerful; potent. [Middle English *puissaunt,* from Old French, from Gallo-Roman *possiantem* (unattested), from Latin *posse,* to be powerful.] **—puis·sant·ly** *adv.*

puke (pewk) *v.* **puked, puking, pukes.** *Slang. —intr.* To vomit. Sometimes used with *up. —tr.* To vomit (something) up.
~*n. Slang.* **1.** Vomit. **2.** The act of vomiting. [16th century.]

puk·ka, puck·a (púckə) *adj.* **1.** Genuine; authentic. **2.** Superior; first-class. **3.** Correct; right and proper. [Hindi *pakkā,* cooked, ripe, firm, from Sanskrit *pakva.*]

pul (pōōl) *n., pl.* **puls** or **puli** (-i, -ee). A coin of Afghanistan, equal to 1/100 of the afghani. [Persian, from Turkish, possibly from Late Greek *phollis,* bellows, money bag, from Latin *follis.*]

pu·la (pōō-laa, -lə) *n., pl.* **-la** or **-las.** The standard monetary unit of Botswana, introduced in 1976. [Tswana, "rain".]

Pu·la (pōō-lə, -laa). *Italian* **Po·la** (pō-la). Town in Croatia, northwest Yugoslavia. Situated on the Istrian peninsula on the Adriatic coast, it was an Austrian naval base (1815–1918) before passing to Italy (1919) and finally Yugoslavia (1947). It has many historical remains, notably the massive Roman stadium.

pul·chri·tude (púlkri-tewd || -tōōd) *n. Literary.* Physical beauty. [Middle English *pulcritude,* from Latin *pulchritūdō,* from *pulcher*†, beautiful.] **—pul·chri·tu·di·nous** (-téwdi-nəss || -tōōdi-) *adj.*

pule (pewl) *intr.v.* **puled, puling, pules.** To whine; fret. [Earlier *pewle, peule,* probably from French *piauler* (imitative).] **—pul·er** *n.*

pu·li[1] (pōōl-i, péwl-, -ee) *n., pl.* **-lis** or **pulik** (-ik). A long-haired sheepdog of a Hungarian breed. Also called "Hungarian puli". [Hungarian.]

pu·li[2]. Alternative plural of **pul.**

Pu·lit·zer prize (pōōl-itsər, *also* péwl-) *n.* Any of several awards established by the U.S. publisher Joseph Pulitzer (1847–1911) and conferred annually in the United States for accomplishments in U.S. journalism, literature, and music.

pull (pōōl) *v.* **pulled, pulling, pulls.** *—tr.* **1.** To apply force to so as to cause or tend to cause motion towards the source of the force. **2.** To remove from a fixed position; extract: *pull teeth.* Usually used with *away, off,* or *out.* **3.** To tug at; jerk or tweak. **4.** To rip or tear; rend. **5.** To stretch (toffee, for example) repeatedly. **6.** To strain (a muscle, for example) injuriously. **7.** *Informal.* To attract; draw. **8.** *Informal.* To perform or bring about successfully. Often used with *off: You'll never pull off a bank robbery.* **9.** *Slang.* To draw out (a knife or gun) in readiness for use. **10.** In cricket, to strike (a ball) aggressively from the off to the leg side by forcing it across the line of the body. **11.** In golf or baseball, to hit (a ball) in the direction one is facing when the swing is carried through, as to the left of a right-handed player. **12. a.** To operate (an oar) in rowing. **b.** To transport or propel by rowing. **c.** To be rowed by: *That boat pulls six oars.* **13.** To rein in (a horse) to keep it from winning a race. **14.** *Printing.* To produce (a print or impression) from type. **15.** To remove the feathers from (a bird); pluck. *—intr.* **1. a.** To exert force in pulling something. **b.** To tug or jerk. Used with *at.* **2. a.** To move: *The bus pulled away from the kerb.* **b.** To move in a vehicle: *She pulled away from the kerb.* **3.** To drink or inhale deeply. Often used with *at* or *on.* **4.** To row a boat. **5.** To strain repeatedly at the bit. Used of a horse. **—pull about.** To subject to rough physical treatment. **—pull a fast one.** *Informal.* To use a sly or underhand trick to gain advantage. **—pull ahead.** To move in front by going faster. **—pull apart** or **to pieces. 1.** To separate the parts of forcefully. **2.** To criticise severely or unfairly. **—pull down.** To dismantle or demolish (a building or structure). **—pull for.** To hope or cheer for the success of. **—pull (oneself) together.** To regain one's composure. **—pull together.** To make a joint effort; cooperate.
~*n.* **1.** The action or process of pulling or being pulled. **2.** Force exerted in pulling, or required to overcome resistance in pulling. **3.** Any sustained effort: *a long pull across the mountains.* **4.** Something used for pulling, such as a knob on a drawer. **5.** A deep inhalation or swallow, as on a cigar or of a drink. **6.** *Informal.* A means of gaining special advantage; influence: *She has pull with the boss.* **7.** *Informal.* Ability to draw or attract; popular appeal. **8.** A stroke or hit that pulls the ball in cricket, golf, or baseball. **9.** A spell or period of rowing. **10.** The act of reining in a horse, especially when racing. **11.** *Printing.* A print or impression. **12.** The force required to draw back the trigger of a firearm or a bow. [Middle English *pullen,* to pull, pluck, Old English *pullian*†.] **—pull·er** *n.*

pull·back (pōōl-bak) *n.* **1.** The act or process of pulling or moving something back; especially, an orderly withdrawal of troops. **2.** Any device for holding or drawing something back.

pul·let (pōōllit) *n.* A young hen, especially of the common domestic fowl, usually less than one year old. [Middle English *polet, pulet,* from Old French *poulet, pollet,* diminutive of *poul,* cock, *poule,* hen, from Latin *pullus,* young of an animal, chick.]

pul·ley (pōōlli) *n., pl.* **-leys. 1.** A simple machine used to change the direction and point of application of a pulling force, especially for lifting weights, consisting essentially of a wheel with a grooved rim in which a pulled rope or chain is run. **2.** A wheel turned by or driving a belt. [Middle English *po(u)ley,* from Old French *po(u)lie,* from Vulgar Latin *polidium* (unattested), probably from Late Greek *polidion* (unattested), diminutive of Greek *polos,* pole, pivot.]

pull in *intr.v.* **1.** To stop at a station. Used of a train. **2. a.** To stop in a lay-by, at a motorway café, or the like. **b.** To move over to or stop at the side of the road. Used of a motor vehicle or a driver. *—tr.v.* **1.** *Chiefly British.* To catch or arrest (a criminal or suspect). **2.** To make or earn (a profit or sum of money). **3.** To attract (a crowd).

pull-in (pōōl-in) *n. British.* A café at the side of the road.

Pull·man (pōōlmən) *n.* A well furnished railway carriage, usually with individual sleeping compartments. Also called "Pullman car". [After George M. *Pullman* (1831–97), U.S. industrialist.]

pul·lo·rum disease (pōō-láwr-əm || pə-, -lṓr-) *n.* A severe contagious diarrhoea of young poultry, caused by the bacterium *Salmonella pullorum.* [Latin *pullorum,* genitive plural of *pullus,* young animal, PULLET.]

pull out *intr.v.* **1.** To depart from a station. Used of a train. **2. a.** To move from a stationary position at the side of a road. Used of a vehicle. **b.** To move out of a lane of traffic in order to pass another vehicle. **3.** To withdraw from a situation or commitment. **4.** *Military.* To withdraw from a site of battle. **5.** To change from a dive into level flight. *—tr.v.* To withdraw (troops) from a battle.

pull·out (pōōl-owt) *n.* **1.** A withdrawal, especially of troops. **2.** *Aeronautics.* The change from a dive into level flight. **3.** Something designed to be pulled out, such as a leaflet in a book or magazine. **—pull·out** *adj.*

pull over *intr.v.* **1.** To bring a vehicle to a stop at the side of a road. **2.** To move to the side of the road in order to stop or to allow faster vehicles to pass.

pull·o·ver (pōōl-ōvər) *n.* A garment, such as a sweater, that is put on by being drawn over the head. **—pull·o·ver** *adj.*

pull-tab (pōōl-tab) *n.* A **tab** (*see*) on a can of drink.

pull through *intr.v.* Also **pull round.** To recover from an illness or setback. *—tr.v.* To cause to recover from an illness or setback.

pull·through (pōōl-thrōō) *n.* Something designed to be pulled through; specifically, a long soft brush or piece of material for cleaning the inside of a wind instrument such as a saxophone.

pul·lu·late (púllew-layt) *intr.v.* **-lated, -lating, -lates. 1.** To put forth sprouts or buds; germinate. **2.** To breed rapidly or abundantly. **3.** To teem; swarm. [Latin *pullulāre,* to grow, sprout, from *pullulus,* diminutive of *pullus,* young animal, PULLET.] **—pul·lu·la·tion** (-láysh'n) *n.* **—pul·lu·la·tive** (-lətiv, -laytiv) *adj.*

pull up *intr.v.* **1.** To come to a halt. Used of a vehicle. **2.** To move to a place or position that is level or ahead, as in a race. Used with *with. —tr.v.* **1.** To bring (a vehicle, horse, or the like) to a halt. **2.** To reprimand or scold. **3.** To stop (a person who is doing something wrong, making mistakes, or the like).

pull-up (pōōl-up) *n.* An exercise for strengthening the arms, performed by hanging by the hands from an overhead bar and pulling the body upwards until the chin is even with or above the bar.

pul·mo·nar·y (púl-mənri, pōōl-, -mənəri || -mə-nerri) *adj.* **1.** Of or pertaining to the lungs. **2.** Having lungs or lunglike organs. [Latin *pulmōnārius,* from *pulmō,* (stem *pulmōn-*), lung.]

pulmonary artery *n.* An artery in which deoxygenated blood travels directly from the right ventricle of the heart to the lungs.

pulmonary vein *n.* A vein in which oxygenated blood travels directly from the lungs to the left atrium of the heart.

pul·mo·nate (púl-mə-nət, pōōl-, -nit, -nayt) *adj.* **1.** Having lungs or lunglike organs. **2.** Pertaining to the Pulmonata, an order of gastropods including snails and slugs, in which the mantle cavity is modified to function as a lung.
~*n.* A pulmonate mollusc. [Latin *pulmōnātus,* from *pulmō,* lung. See **pulmonary.**]

pul·mon·ic (pul-mónnik, pōōl-) *adj.* Pulmonary.

pulp (pulp) *n.* **1.** A soft, moist, shapeless mass of matter. **2.** The soft, juicy part of fruit. **3.** A mass of pressed vegetable matter; *apple pulp.* **4.** A mixture of cellulose material, such as wood, paper, and rags, ground up and moistened to make paper. **5.** The soft inner structure of a tooth, consisting of nerve and blood vessels. **6.** In mining, a mixture of powdered ore and water. **7.** Magazines and books collectively, that contain sensational or pornographic subject matter and are characteristically printed on rough, unfinished paper. Also used adjectivally: *pulp fiction.* **—reduce (someone) to pulp.** To cause (someone) to be incapable of thought or action, as through fear, shock, or the like.
~*v.* **pulped, pulping, pulps.** *—tr.* **1.** To reduce to pulp. **2.** To remove the pulp from (fruit). *—intr.* To be reduced to a pulp. [Latin *pulpa*†, solid flesh, pulp.] **—pulp·ous, pulp·y** *adj.*

pul·pit (pōōl-pit || púl-) *n.* **1.** An elevated platform, lectern, or stand used in preaching or conducting a religious service. **2.** Any similar raised platform, such as one used by harpooners in a whaling boat. **3. a.** Clergymen collectively. Preceded by *the.* **b.** The profession of preaching the Christian message. **4.** Any medium of communication through which a person expresses a opinion, especially regularly. [Middle English, from Latin *pulpitum*†, scaffold, platform.]

pulp·wood (púlp-wōōd) *n.* Soft wood, such as spruce or pine, used in making paper.

pul·que (pōōl-ki, pōōl-, -kay) *n.* An alcoholic milky drink made in Mexico from various species of agave. [Mexican Spanish; perhaps akin to Nahuatl *poliuhqui, puliuhqui,* decomposed, spoilt.]

pul·sar (púl-saar) *n. Astronomy.* Any of numerous small, dense stars

PRONUNCIATION KEY

a, trap; aa, father; ai, fair; ar, star; aw, lawn; ay, play; b, bb, stab; rubber; ch, church; ck, ticket; d, dd, dead; ladder; e, dress; ee, bee; er, defer; ew, few; ewr, pure; ə, about; ər, letter; f, ff, fife; differ; g, gg, giggle; h, hat; i, kit; ī, price; īr, fire; j, judge; k, kick; l, ll, let; 'l, needle; m, mm, man; n, nn, no; 'n, sudden; ng, thing; o, lot; ō, no; ōō, foot; ōō, shoe; oor, poor; ow, cow; owr, hour; oy, boy; p, pp, pepper; r, rr, red; s, ss, sauce; sh, ship; t, tt, totter; th, thick; th, this; smooth; u, cut; ur, turn; v, vv, valve; w, wet; y, yes; z, zz, zebra; zh, vision; pleasure

IN FOREIGN WORDS:

aN, oN, Saint-Saëns; hl, Llanelli; Hluhluwe; kh, loch; lough; Khaled

STRESS MARK:

ín-sīt, insight; in-sít, incite

that emit regular pulses of radiation, usually radio waves, as a result of their rapid rotation. [From *puls*ating *star.*]

pul·sate (pul-sáyt || *chiefly U.S.* púl-sayt) *intr.v.* **-sated, -sating, -sates. 1.** To expand and contract rhythmically; throb. **2.** To quiver. [Latin *pulsāre,* frequentative of *pellere* (past participle *pulsus*), to push, beat, strike.] **—pul·sa·tive** (púl-sətiv, pul-sáytiv) *adj.*
Synonyms: *pulsate, beat, palpitate, throb.*

pul·sa·tile (púl-sə-tīl || *U.S.* -til) *adj.* Pulsating; vibrating. [Medieval Latin *pulsātilis,* from Latin *pulsāre,* to PULSATE.]

pul·sa·ting star (pul-sáyting || *chiefly U.S.* púl-sayting) *n.* A star that periodically becomes brighter as its outer layers expand and contract.

pul·sa·tion (pul-sáysh'n) *n.* **1.** The act of pulsating. **2.** A single beat, throb, or vibration.

pul·sa·tor (pul-sáytər) *n.* A pulsating device or machine, such as a pump.

pul·sa·to·ry (púl-sə-tri, -təri, pul-sáytəri) *adj.* Having rhythmical vibration or movement; pulsating.

pulse¹ (pulss) *n.* **1.** *Physiology.* The rhythmical throbbing of arteries produced by the regular contractions of the heart. **2.** Any regular beating rhythm. **3.** A single throb or beat. **4.** *Physics & Electronics.* A transient amplification or intensification of a characteristic of a system, especially of a wave characteristic, followed by return to equilibrium or steady state: *a signal pulse; a beam pulse.* **5.** The perceptible emotions or sentiments of a group: *the pulse of the electorate.* **6.** *Informal.* Energy; vitality: *the pulse of the party.*
~intr.v. **pulsed, pulsing, pulses.** To throb or vibrate; pulsate. [Middle English *pous, puls,* from Old French *pous, pols,* from Latin *pulsus,* beating, striking, from the past participle of *pellere,* to push, beat, strike.] **—pulse·less** *adj.*

pulse² *n.* **1.** The edible seeds of certain pod-bearing plants, such as lentils. **2.** A plant yielding such seeds. [Middle English *pols, puls,* from Old French *po(u)ls,* porridge, from Latin *puls,* pottage made of meal and pulse, possibly from Greek *poltos,* porridge.]

pulse-height analyser (púlss-hīt) *n.* An electronic device that sorts signal pulses into predetermined ranges of amplitude.

pulse·jet (púlss-jet) *n.* A type of ramjet in which air intake and combustion occur intermittently, producing rapid periodic bursts of thrust.

pulse modulation *n. Electronics.* Modulation by coded variation of the amplitude or other characteristic of wave pulses.

pul·sim·e·ter (pul-símmitər) *n.* Also **pul·som·e·ter** (-sómmitər). *Medicine.* An instrument that measures the frequency or strength of the pulse. [PULSE + -METER.]

pul·som·e·ter (pul-sómmitər) *n.* **1.** A pump for raising water by the pulsed condensation of steam. Also called "vacuum pump". **2.** Variant of **pulsimeter.** [PULSE + -METER.]

pul·ver·a·ble (púl-vrəb'l, -vərəb'l) *adj.* Capable of being pulverised.

pul·ver·ise, pul·ver·ize (púlvə-rīz) *v.* **-ised, -ising, -ises.** *—tr.* **1.** To pound, crush, or grind to a powder or dust. **2.** To demolish, defeat, or destroy. *—intr.* To be ground or reduced to powder or dust. [Old French *pulveriser,* from Late Latin *pulverizāre,* from Latin *pulvis* (stem *pulver-*), dust.] **—pul·ver·is·a·ble** *adj.* **—pul·ver·i·sa·tion** (-rī-záysh'n || *U.S.* -ri-) *n.* **—pul·ver·is·er** *n.*

pul·ver·u·lent (pul-vérrewlənt) *adj.* **1.** Made of, covered with, or crumbling to fine powder or dust. **2.** Powdery; dusty; crumbly. [Latin *pulverulentus,* dusty, from *pulvis,* dust. See **pulverise.**]

pul·vil·lus (pul-víl-əss) *n., pl.* **-li** (-ī). Any of the soft, cushion-like pads between the claws of an insect's foot. [Latin, diminutive of *pulvīnus*†, cushion.]

pul·vi·nate (púlvi-nayt) *adj.* Also **pul·vi·nat·ed** (-naytid). **1.** Having a convex face. Said of a frieze. **2.** *Botany.* Having a swelling at the base. Said of a leafstalk. [Latin *pulvīnātus,* from PULVINUS.]

pul·vi·nus (pul-vī́-nəss) *n., pl.* **-ni** (nī). *Botany.* A swelling at the base of a leafstalk, which, through changes in turgor, can alter the position of the leaf. [Latin *pulvīnus*†, cushion.]

pu·ma (péwmə) *n.* A large American wild cat, *Panthera concolor* (or *Felis concolor*), resembling a short-legged lioness. Also called "cougar", "mountain lion". [Spanish, from Quechua.]

pum·ice (púmmiss) *n.* A porous, lightweight volcanic rock with the same composition as rhyolite, often used as an abrasive. Also called "pumice stone".
~tr.v. **pumiced, -icing, -ices.** To clean, polish, or smooth with pumice. [Middle English *pomys,* from Old French *pomis,* from Latin *pūmex.*] **—pu·mi·ceous** (pew-míshəss) *adj.* **—pum·ic·er** *n.*

pum·mel (púmm'l) *tr.v.* **-melled** or *U.S.* **-meled, -melling** or *U.S.* **-meling, -mels.** To beat or hit with or as if with the fists. [From POMMEL (originally, to beat with the pommel of a sword).]

pump¹ (pump) *n.* A machine or device for transferring a liquid or gas from a source or container through tubes or pipes to another container or receiver.
~v. **pumped, pumping, pumps.** *—tr.* **1.** To raise or cause to flow by means of a pump. **2.** To inflate with gas by means of a pump. Often used with *up.* **3.** To remove the water from. Often used with *out.* **4.** To cause to operate with the up-and-down motion of a pump handle. **5.** To propel, eject, or insert with a pump. **6.** *Physics.* To supply (a laser) with sufficient energy to achieve population inversion. **7.** *Informal.* **a.** To question closely or persistently for information. **b.** To gain or force (information) from a person by persistent questioning: *They pumped the truth from him.* **8. a.** To fill with a steady stream of something, such as bullets or information. **b.** To supply or fill somebody or something with (a steady flow of something): *pumped money into the project.* *—intr.* **1.** To operate a pump. **2.** To raise or move gas or liquid with a pump. **3.** To gush or flow, especially in regular spurts. **4.** To move up and down in the manner of a pump handle. [Middle English *pumpe, pompe* (nautical use), from Middle Low German *pumpe* or Middle Dutch *pompe,* probably imitative.] **—pump·er** *n.*

pump² *n.* **1.** A low-heeled woman's shoe with no fastenings. **2.** A light shoe used for dancing and certain sports. [16th century.]

pum·per·nick·el (púmpə-nick'l, pŏŏmpər-) *n.* A dark, sourish bread made from whole, coarsely ground rye. [German *Pumpernickel* : early New High German *Pumpern,* a fart (imitative) + *Nickel,* "devil", general pejorative (see **nickel**); so named from being hard to digest.]

pump gun *n.* A gun or rifle that may be reloaded by means of a sliding magazine under the barrel.

pump·kin (púmp-kin, púm- || púng-) *n.* **1.** A coarse, trailing vine, *Cucurbita pepo,* cultivated for its fruit. **2.** The large, round fruit of this vine, with thick, orange-yellow rind, orange, pulpy flesh, and many seeds. **3.** Either of two similar vines, *C. maxima* or *C. moschata,* bearing large, pumpkin-like squashes. [Variant (influenced by -KIN) of earlier *pumpion, pompon,* from Old French *popon, pompon,* from Latin *pepō,* from Greek *pepōn,* a large melon (edible only when ripe), from *pepōn,* ripe, from *peptein,* to cook, ripen.]

pun¹ (pun) *n.* A play on words, sometimes on different senses of the same word and sometimes on the similar sense or sound of different words; for example, words of the dying Mercutio in *Romeo and Juliet:* "ask for me tomorrow, and you shall find me a grave man".
~intr.v. **punned, punning, puns.** To make a pun or puns. [Probably short for obsolete *pundigrion,* perhaps a fanciful alteration of Italian *puntiglio,* "fine point", diminutive of *punto,* POINT.] **—pun·ning·ly** *adv.*

pun² *tr.v.* **punned, punning, puns.** *British Regional.* To pack down (rubble or earth) by ramming and pounding it. [Dialect variant of POUND (verb).]

pu·na (pŏŏnə) *n.* **1.** A high, dry, bleak plateau within the Andes of Bolivia or Peru, sparsely covered with coarse grasses and stunted shrubs. **2.** The vegetation of a puna. [Quechua.]

punch¹ (punch) *n.* **1.** A tool for making holes in a material: *a leather punch.* **2.** A tool for forcing a pin, bolt, or rivet in or out of a hole. **3.** A tool for stamping a design on a surface. **4.** A **countersink** *(see).* **5.** A device for punching cards *(card punch)* or paper tape *(tape punch)* for use in a computer.
~v. **punched, punching, punches.** *—tr.* To use a punch on. *—intr.* To use a punch. [Short for PUNCHEON (punching tool).]

punch² *tr.v.* **punched, punching, punches. 1.** To hit with a sharp blow of the fist. **2.** To poke or prod with a stick. **3.** *Western U.S.* To herd (cattle), especially as a profession.
~n. **1.** A blow with the fist. **2.** *Informal.* Vigour or forcefulness: *His writing lacks punch.* **—pull (one's) punches.** *Informal.* **1.** To hold back deliberately from giving full force to one's blows. **2.** To lessen deliberately the full impact of one's words; especially, to not be outspoken in one's criticism. [Middle English *punchen,* variant of *pounsen,* POUNCE (to perforate).] **—punch·er** *n.*

punch³ *n.* A mixed drink consisting of fruit juices, water, sugar, spices, or the like, usually with a wine or spirit base, and often hot. [Perhaps from Hindi *pānch,* from Sanskrit *pañca,* five (originally prepared with five ingredients).]

Punch *n.* The quarrelsome hook-nosed husband of Judy in the comic puppet show, *Punch and Judy.* **—pleased as Punch.** Highly pleased; gratified. [Short for PUNCHINELLO.]

punch·bag (púnch-bag) *n.* Also *U.S.* **punching bag.** A large, heavy, stuffed bag, usually of canvas, suspended from above and designed to be punched with the fists for exercise or boxing training.

punch·ball (púnch-bawl) *n.* **1.** A small inflated bag or ball, usually of leather, either suspended from above or supported on a springy pole and designed to be punched with the fists for exercise or boxing training. **2.** A punchbag.

punch·bowl (púnch-bōl) *n.* A large bowl from which punch or other drinks may be served by means of a ladle.

punch-drunk (púnch-drúngk, -drungk) *adj.* **1.** Suffering from the effects of repeated blows on the head. **2.** Acting in a dazed manner.

punched card (puncht) *n.* Also **punch card.** A card punched with holes or notches to represent letters and numbers or with a pattern of holes to represent related data, for use in a computer.

punched tape *n.* Also **punch tape.** Paper tape in which holes are punched to represent data to be processed by a computer.

pun·cheon¹ (púnchən) *n.* **1.** A short, wooden upright used in structural framing. **2.** A piece of broad, heavy timber, roughly dressed, with one face finished flat. **3.** A punching, perforating, or stamping tool, especially one used by a goldsmith. [Middle English *ponchon, pons(y)on,* a sharp tool, from Old French *po(i)nchon, poinçon,* from Vulgar Latin *punctiō* (unattested), from *punctiāre* (unattested), to pierce, prick, from Latin *pungere* (past participle *punctus*), to prick.]

puncheon² *n.* **1.** A cask with a capacity of between 320 and 550 litres (70 and 120 gallons). **2.** This specific volume of liquid used as a measure. [Old French *po(i)nçon, po(i)nchon*†.]

Pun·chi·nel·lo (púnchi-néllō) *n., pl.* **-los** or **-loes. 1.** The short, fat, comic-looking character in an Italian puppet show and probable prototype of the English Punch. **2.** A person thought to resemble this puppet. [Variant of earlier *policinello,* from Italian dialect (Neapolitan) *polecenella,* perhaps diminutive of *polecena,* young turkey cock (from the puppet's beaklike nose), from *pulcino,* chicken, from Late Latin *pullicenus,* diminutive of Latin *pullus,* PULLET.]

puma *The second largest American wild cat after the jaguar, a full-grown puma can weigh more than 100 kilograms (220 pounds). Once ranging from British Columbia to Patagonia, it is now restricted to wilderness areas.*

punch line *n.* The line or part of a joke or humorous story that gives the point of the whole and causes amusement.
punch press *n.* A power press fitted with punches and dies for cutting, forming, or imprinting metal, plastic, or the like.
punch-up (púnch-up) *n. Chiefly British Slang.* A fist fight.
punch·y (púnchi) *adj.* **-ier, -iest.** *Informal.* **1.** Having force, vigour, or zest: *a punchy advert.* **2.** Punch-drunk. **—punch·i·ly** *adv.*
punc·tate (púngk-tayt) *adj.* Also **punc·tat·ed** (-táytid || -taytid). Having tiny spots, points, or depressions. [New Latin *punctatus,* from Latin *punctum,* pricked mark, POINT.] **—punc·ta·tion** (-táysh'n) *n.*
punc·til·i·o (pungk-tílli-ō) *n., pl.* **-tilios. 1.** A fine or petty point of etiquette. **2.** Precise observance of formalities or etiquette. [Italian *puntiglio,* "fine point", diminutive of *punto,* POINT.]
punc·til·i·ous (pungk-tílli-əss) *adj.* **1.** Attentive to the finer points of etiquette and formal conduct. **2.** Showing attention to detail; precise; scrupulous. —See Synonyms at **meticulous.** [French *pointilleux,* from *pointille,* "fine point", from Italian. See **punctilio.**] **—punc·til·i·ous·ly** *adv.* **—punc·til·i·ous·ness** *n.*

pupa *A caterpillar building the cocoon in which it will pupate, or undergo the transformation to adult. The pupa is the third stage – egg, larva, pupa, adult – in the metamorphic life cycle of insects such as bees, moths, and butterflies.*

punc·tu·al (púngk-tew-əl, -choo-, -chŏŏl) *adj.* **1. a.** Acting or arriving exactly at the time appointed; prompt. **b.** Always observant of or keeping to appointed times. **2.** Paid or accomplished at or by the appointed time. **3.** *Archaic.* Precise; exact. **4.** Confined to or being a point in space. [Middle English, from Medieval Latin *punctuālis,* "to the point", from Latin *punctum,* pricked mark, POINT.] **—punc·tu·al·i·ty** (-ál-əti), **punc·tu·al·ness** *n.* **—punc·tu·al·ly** *adv.*
punc·tu·ate (púngk-tew-ayt, -choo-) *v.* **-ated, -ating, -ates.** *—tr.* **1.** To provide (a text) with punctuation marks. **2.** To interrupt periodically. **3.** To stress; emphasise. *—intr.* To use punctuation. [Medieval Latin *punctuāre,* to mark with a point, punctuate, from Latin *punctum,* pricked mark, point, from the past participle of *pungere,* to prick, pierce.] **—punc·tu·a·tive** (-aytiv) *adj.* **—punc·tu·a·tor** (-aytər) *n.*
punc·tu·a·tion (púngk-tew-áysh'n, -choo-) *n.* **1.** The use of standard marks and signs in writing and printing to separate words into sentences, clauses, and phrases, as in order to clarify meaning, give intonation, or provide emphasis. **2.** The marks so used. **3.** An act or instance of punctuating.
punctuation mark *n.* Any of a set of marks or signs used to punctuate texts; for example, the comma (,) or the full stop (.).
punc·ture (púngk-chər) *v.* **-tured, -turing, -tures.** *—tr.* **1.** To pierce with a pointed object. **2.** To make (a hole) by piercing. **3.** To cause to collapse by piercing. **4.** To depreciate; deflate: *She punctured his ego.* *—intr.* To be pierced or punctured.
~n. **1.** An act or instance of puncturing. **2.** A hole or depression made by a sharp object; especially, a hole in a pneumatic tyre. [Middle English, from Latin *punctūra,* a pricking, puncture, from *pungere* (past participle *punctus*), to prick.] **—punc·tur·a·ble** *adj.*
pun·dit (púndit) *n.* Also **pan·dit** (for sense 1). **1.** A Brahmanic scholar, learned in Sanskrit and in Hindu philosophy, religion, and law. **2.** A learned person or a person who claims to be an expert. [Hindi *paṇḍit,* from Sanskrit *paṇḍita,* a learned man, from Dravidian (akin to Telegu *paṇḍa,* wisdom).] **—pun·dit·ry** (-ri) *n.*

puppet *Richly painted two-dimensional puppets are operated by rods in a Javanese shadow play. This type of puppet theatre was developed in Java about 1,000 years ago, and the puppets enact scenes from Indian and Javanese mythology.*

pung (pung) *n. U.S.* A low box sleigh drawn by one horse. [Shortened from *tom-pong, tow-pong,* of Algonquian origin, akin to TOBOGGAN.]
pun·gent (púnjənt) *adj.* **1.** Having a sharp, acid taste or smell. **2.** Penetrating; biting; caustic: *pungent satire.* **3.** *Biology.* Pointed: *a pungent leaf.* [Latin *pungēns* (stem *pungent-*), present participle of *pungere,* to prick, sting.] **—pun·gen·cy** *n.* **—pun·gent·ly** *adv.*
Pu·nic (péwnik) *adj.* **1.** Of or pertaining to ancient Carthage or its people. **2.** Having the characteristic of treachery attributed to the Carthaginians by the Romans.
~n. The West Semitic language of ancient Carthage, a dialect of Phoenician. [Latin *Pūnicus,* earlier *Poenicus,* from *Poenus,* a Carthaginian, from Greek *Phoinix,* Phoenician.]
Punic Wars *pl.n.* Three wars waged by Rome against Carthage (264–241 B.C., 218–201 B.C., and 149–146 B.C.) in which Rome finally defeated Carthage and annexed its territory.
pun·ish (púnnish) *v.* **-ished, -ishing, -ishes.** *—tr.* **1.** To subject (a person) to a penalty, such as imprisonment, a fine, or a beating, for a crime, fault, offence, or misbehaviour. **2.** To inflict a penalty on a criminal or wrongdoer for (a crime or offence, for example). **3.** To handle roughly; injure; hurt. **4.** *Informal.* To deplete (a stock or supply) heavily. *—intr.* To give punishment. [Middle English *punissen, punyschen,* from Old French *punir* (stem *puniss-*), from Latin *pūnīre, poenīre,* from *poena,* penalty, punishment, from Greek *poinē.*] **—pun·ish·er** *n.* **—pun·ish·ing·ly** *adv.*
Synonyms: *punish, chastise, discipline, castigate, penalise.*
pun·ish·a·ble (púnnish-əb'l) *adj.* Liable to or deserving punishment.
pun·ish·ment (púnnish-mənt) *n.* **1. a.** An act of punishing. **b.** The condition of being punished. **2.** A penalty imposed for wrongdoing, as for a crime or offence. **3.** *Informal.* Rough handling.
pu·ni·tive (péwnətiv) *adj.* Inflicting or aiming to inflict punishment; punishing. [French *punitif,* from Medieval Latin *pūnītīvus,* from Latin *pūnīre* (past participle *pūnītus*), PUNISH.] **—pu·ni·tive·ly** *adv.* **—pu·ni·tive·ness** *n.*
Pun·jab or **Pan·jab** (pún-jaáb, -jaab; *also* pŏŏn- || *U.S. also* -jáb). Region of the northwest Indian subcontinent. It was ruled by the Sikhs until annexation by the British (1849) and was divided along religious lines in 1947. West Punjab passed to Pakistan, and is now the province of Punjab, East Punjab remaining Indian. East Punjab was further divided (1966) into linguistic areas to form the present Indian states of Punjab and Haryana.
Pun·ja·bi (pún-jaábi, pun-, *also* pŏŏn-, pōōn- || *U.S. also* -jábbi) *n.* Also **Pan·ja·bi** (for sense 2). **1.** A native or inhabitant of the Punjab. **2.** The Indic language spoken in the Punjab, belonging to the Indo-European family. **—Pun·jab·i** *adj.*
punk¹ (pungk) *n.* **1.** A youth culture that developed in Britain in the late 1970s among fans of punk rock, characterised by a rejection of middle-class values and standard pop culture, and the adoption of a deliberately aggressive and outrageous personal appearance, often involving startling make-up and hairstyles, and leather clothing. **2.** A young person belonging to this culture. **3.** Punk rock. [Shortened from *punk rock(er).*]
punk² (pungk) *n.* **1.** Dry, decayed wood, used as tinder. **2.** Any of various substances that smoulder when ignited, used to light fireworks. **3. a.** An object of little value or poor quality. **b.** Such objects collectively; rubbish. **4.** *Slang.* Any disreputable or worthless person. **5.** *Chiefly U.S. Slang.* **a.** A young ruffian or petty criminal. **b.** An inexperienced or callow youth.
~adj. Slang. Of poor quality; worthless. [18th century.]
punk³ *n.* **1.** *Archaic.* A passive homosexual; a catamite. **2.** A prostitute. [16th century : origin obscure.]
pun·ka, pun·kah (púngkə) *n.* A fan used especially in India, made of a palm frond or strip of cloth hung from the ceiling and moved manually or by machine. [Hindi *pankhā,* from Sanskrit *pakṣaka,* fan, from *pakṣa,* shoulder, wing.]
punk rock *n.* A type of rock music that developed in the late 1970s, characterised by a spirit of aggression and defiance embodied typically in loud, raucous singing, offensive lyrics, and driving rhythms. [PUNK (worthless, rotten) + ROCK (music).] **—punk rocker** *n.*
pun·net (púnnit) *n. British.* A small, square basket used for holding soft fruit. [Perhaps diminutive of dialect *pun,* POUND (weight).]
pun·ster (pún-stər) *n.* A maker of puns.
punt¹ (punt) *n.* An open, flat-bottomed boat with squared ends, propelled by a long pole and used in shallow waters.
~v. **punted, punting, punts.** *—tr.* **1.** To propel (a boat) with a pole. **2.** To carry in a punt. *—intr.* **1.** To propel a punt. **2.** To travel in a punt as a leisure activity. [Middle Low German *punte, punto,* ferryboat, from Latin *pontō,* a Gaulish vessel, apparently from *pōns* (stem *pont-*), bridge.] **—punt·er** *n.*
punt² (punt) *n.* In soccer, Rugby football, or similar games, a kick in which the ball is dropped from the hands and kicked before it touches the ground.
~v. **punted, punting, punts.** *—tr.* To propel (a ball) by means of a punt. *—intr.* To execute a punt. [Probably from dialectal *bunt, punt†,* to push, kick.]
punt³ (punt) *intr.v.* **punted, punting, punts. 1.** In gambling games such as roulette or faro, to lay a bet against the bank. **2. a.** To gamble; bet. **b.** To bet on a horse race. [French *ponter,* from *ponte,* bet against the banker, from Spanish *punto,* "point", "ace", from Latin *punctum,* POINT.] **—punt·er** *n.*
punt⁴ (pŏŏnt) *n.* **1.** The basic monetary unit of the Republic of Ireland, equal to 100 pence. **2.** A note worth one punt. Also called "pound".
Pun·ta A·re·nas (pŏŏntə aráy-nass). The world's southernmost city, lying on the Strait of Magellan in Chile. It is an oil port, with military and naval installations, and a tourist centre.
pun·ty (púnti) *n., pl.* **-ties.** In glassmaking, an iron rod on which molten glass is handled. Also called "pontil". [Variant of PONTIL.]
pu·ny (péwni) *adj.* **-nier, -niest. 1.** Of inferior size, strength, or significance; weak. **2.** Feeble; ineffectual: *a puny attempt.* [Phonetic spelling of PUISNE, from Old French "born afterwards" : *puis,* afterwards, from Vulgar Latin *postius* (unattested), comparative of Latin *post,* after + *ne,* born, from Latin *nātus,* past participle of *nāscī,* to be born.] **—pu·ni·ly** *adv.* **—pu·ni·ness** *n.*
pup (pup) *n.* **1.** A young dog; a puppy. **2.** The young of certain other animals, such as the seal. **3.** *British Informal.* An insolent person. **4.** *Informal.* An object or item that turns out to be worthless or inferior. Used chiefly in such phrases as *buy a pup* or *be sold a pup.* **—in pup.** Pregnant. Said of a bitch.
~intr.v. **pupped, pupping, pups.** To give birth to pups. [Back-formation from PUPPY.]
pu·pa (péw-pə) *n., pl.* **-pae** (-pee) or **-pas.** The nonmobile stage in the metamorphosis of many insects, following the larval stage and preceding the adult form, during which many internal changes occur. Compare **nymph.** [New Latin *pupa,* from Latin *pūpa,* girl, doll, feminine of *pūpus,* boy.] **—pu·pal** *adj.*
pu·pate (pew-páyt || *U.S.* péw-payt) *intr.v.* **-pated, -pating, -pates.** To become a pupa. **—pu·pa·tion** (pew-páysh'n) *n.*
pu·pil¹ (péw-p'l, -pil) *n.* **1.** A student under the direct supervision of a teacher. **2.** *Law.* A minor under the supervision of a guardian. [Middle English *pupille,* orphan, ward, (hence) pupil, from Old French, from Latin *pūpillus,* diminutive of *pūpus,* boy.]
pupil² *n.* The apparently black circular aperture in the centre of the iris of the eye through which light passes to the retina. [Middle English *pupilla* and Old French *pupille,* both from Latin *pūpilla,* "little orphan girl", pupil (by analogy with Greek *korē,* little girl, doll, pupil of the eye, originally referring to the miniature reflections that can be seen by looking closely at another's eye), feminine of *pūpillus,* PUPIL.]
pu·pil·lage, *U.S.* **pu·pil·age** (péwpilij) *n.* **1.** The state or period of being a pupil. **2. a.** The practical training received by an inexperi-

enced barrister in the chambers of an experienced barrister. **b.** The period of time spent in such training.

pu·pil·lar·y¹, pu·pi·lar·y (péwpi-lәri || -lerri) *adj.* Of or pertaining to a ward or a student.

pupillary², pupilary *adj.* Of or affecting the pupil of the eye.

pu·pip·a·rous (pew-pippәrәss) *adj.* Producing well-developed young that are ready to pupate. [PUPA + -PAROUS.]

pup·pet (púppit) *n.* **1.** A small figure of a person or animal, having jointed parts animated from above by strings or wires; a marionette. **2.** A similar figure having a cloth body and hollow head, designed to be fitted over and manipulated by the hand or finger. **3.** A toy representing a human figure; a doll. **4.** A person or group whose behaviour is determined by the will of others.
~*adj.* **1.** Of or pertaining to puppets. **2.** Sponsored and controlled by another or others while professing autonomy: *a puppet state.* [Middle English *popet, popette,* small child, doll, from Old French *poupette,* diminutive of *poupe* (unattested), doll, from Vulgar Latin *puppa* (unattested), doll, from Latin *pūpa. See* **pupa.**]

pup·pet·eer (púppi-téer) *n.* A person who operates and entertains with puppets or marionettes.

pup·pet·ry (púppitri) *n., pl.* **-ries. 1.** The art of making puppets and presenting puppet shows. **2.** The actions of puppets. **3.** Stilted or artificial dramatic performance.

Pup·pis (púppiss) *n.* A constellation in the Southern Hemisphere near Canis Major and Pyxis. [Latin, "the ship", from *puppis,* POOP (stern).]

pup·py (púppi) *n., pl.* **-pies. 1.** A young dog; a pup. **2.** A conceited or inexperienced youth. [Middle English *popi,* from Old French *po(u)pee,* doll, toy, plaything, from Vulgar Latin *puppa* (unattested). See **puppet.**] **—pup·py·ish** *adj.*

puppy fat *n.* The fatty tissue or fat appearance of a child or adolescent. It usually becomes less noticeable with age.

puppy love *n.* Adolescent love or infatuation.

pup tent *n.* A **shelter tent** *(see).*

Pur·beck marble (púr-bek) *n.* A nonmarine marble, used in architecture and sculpture on account of its high gloss. [After Isle of *Purbeck,* Dorset, the peninsula where it is quarried.]

pur·blind (púr-blīnd) *adj.* **1.** Having poor vision; nearly or partly blind. **2.** Slow in understanding or discernment; dull. [Middle English *pur(e)blind,* originally "totally blind" : PURE (completely) + BLIND.] **—pur·blind·ly** *adv.* **—pur·blind·ness** *n.*

Pur·cell (púr-s'l, -sel; *also* -sél), **Henry** (1659–95). English composer. As organist at Westminster Abbey and Composer in Ordinary to the Chapel Royal, he was the leading musical figure of Restoration England.

pur·chas·a·ble (púr-chәss-әb'l, -chiss-) *adj.* **1.** Capable of being bought. **2.** Capable of being bribed; venal. **—pur·chas·a·bil·i·ty** (-ә-bíllәti) *n.*

pur·chase (púr-chәss, -chiss) *tr.v.* **-chased, -chasing, -chases. 1.** To obtain in exchange for money or its equivalent; buy. **2.** To acquire by effort; earn. **3.** *Law.* To acquire (property) legally by means other than inheritance. **4.** To raise, haul, or hold with a mechanical device such as a lever or wrench.
~*n.* **1.** That which is bought. **2. a.** The act of buying. **b.** Acquisition through the payment of money or its equivalent. **3.** *Law.* **a.** The acquisition of property other than by inheritance. **b.** Annual rent or income, especially from land. **4.** A grip applied manually or mechanically to move something or prevent it from slipping. **5.** A tackle, lever, or other device used to obtain mechanical advantage. **6.** A position, as of a lever or one's feet, affording means to move or secure a weight. **7.** Any means of increasing power, influence, or advantage. [Middle English *po(u)rchasen,* from Old French *po(u)rchacier, purchacier,* to pursue, seek to obtain : *po(u)r-,* for, from Latin *prō* + *chacier,* to CHASE.] **—pur·chas·er** *n.*

purchase tax *n.* Formerly, a tax in Britain on certain consumer goods, especially non-essential, luxury items. It was replaced in 1973 by value-added tax.

purchasing agent *n. Abbr.* **P.A.** A person acting as another's agent in making purchases.

purchasing power *n.* **1.** The ability of a person or group to purchase, generally measured by income. **2.** The value of a particular monetary unit in terms of the goods or services it will buy.

pur·dah (púr-daa, -dә) *n.* **1.** A curtain used to screen Hindu or Muslim women from men or strangers, especially in India. **2.** In India, the system of secluding women, especially of high rank, from public view. **3.** Seclusion, or ostracism resulting from embarrassment or disgrace. Used humorously: *After his blunder, he was in purdah for weeks.* [Hindi *pardā,* screen, veil, from Persian *pardah*†.]

pure (pewr) *adj.* **purer, purest. 1.** Having a homogeneous or uniform composition; not mixed: *pure oxygen.* **2.** Free from adulterants or impurities; full-strength: *pure chocolate.* **3.** Free from dirt, defilement, or pollution; clean. **4.** Free from foreign elements: *keeping the language pure.* **5.** Containing nothing inappropriate or extraneous: *a pure production of Hamlet.* **6. a.** Complete: *by pure chance.* **b.** Thorough; utter: *pure folly.* **7.** Free or relatively free from taint, sin, or faults. **8.** Chaste; virgin. **9.** Of unmixed blood or ancestry. **10.** *Genetics.* Breeding true to parental type; homozygous: *a pure line.* **11.** *Music.* Free from discordant qualities. **12.** *Phonetics.* Articulated with a single unchanging speech sound; monophthongal: *a pure vowel.* **13.** Theoretical rather than applied: *pure science.* **14.** *Philosophy.* Free from empirical elements: *pure reason.* [Middle English *pur, pure,* from Old French *pur* (feminine *pure*), from Latin *pūrus,* clean.] **—pure·ness** *n.*

pure·bred (péwr-bréd) *adj.* Of a strain established through breeding many generations of unmixed stock. **—pure·bred** (-bred) *n.*

pu·rée (péwr-ay; *rarely* póor- || *U.S.* pew-ráy, -rée) *tr.v.* **-réed, -réeing, -rées.** To convert (vegetables or fruit, for example) to a semisolid state, as by cooking and pressing through a strainer.
~*n.* Food so prepared. [French, from Old French *purer,* to purify, strain, from Latin *pūrāre,* to purify, from *pūrus,* PURE.]

Pure Land Buddhism *n.* A form of Buddhism widely followed in Japan, which teaches salvation through faith in, and the calling on the name of, the Buddha Amida. Also called "Jodo".

pure·ly (péwrli) *adv.* **1.** In a pure manner. **2.** Innocently; chastely. **3.** Totally; entirely: *purely by chance.*

pur·fle (púrf'l) *tr.v.* **-fled, -fling, -fles.** To finish or decorate the border or edge of (a table or violin, for example).
~*n.* Also **pur·fling** (púrfling). An ornamental border or edging. [Middle English *purfilen,* from Old French *porfiler,* to weave, from Vulgar Latin *prōfīlāre* (unattested), to draw in outline : Latin *prō,* forth, out + *fīlum,* thread.]

pur·ga·tion (pur-gáysh'n) *n.* The act of purging or purifying.

pur·ga·tive (púrgәtiv) *adj.* Tending to cleanse or purge.
~*n. Medicine.* A purgative agent, a **laxative** *(see).*

pur·ga·to·ri·al (púrgә-táwri-әl || -tőri-) *adj.* **1.** Serving to purify of sin; expiatory. **2.** Of, pertaining to, or resembling purgatory.

pur·ga·to·ry (púrgә-tri, -tәri) *n., pl.* **-ries. 1.** *Roman Catholic Church.* A state in which the souls of those who have died in grace must expiate venial sins. **2.** Any place or condition of expiation, suffering, or remorse.
~*adj.* Tending to cleanse or purge. [Middle English *purgatorie,* from Medieval Latin *purgātōrium,* from Late Latin *purgātōrius,* from Latin *purgāre,* to PURGE.]

purge (purj) *v.* **purged, purging, purges.** —*tr.* **1. a.** To free from impurities; purify. **b.** To remove (impurities and other elements) by or as if by cleansing. **2.** To rid of sin, guilt, or defilement. **3.** *Law.* **a.** To clear (a person) of a charge or imputation. **b.** To atone for (an offence) by being punished. **4.** To rid (a nation, political party, or other group) of persons considered to be undesirable. **5.** *Medicine.* **a.** To cause evacuation of (the bowels). **b.** To induce evacuation of the bowels in (a patient). —*intr.* **1.** To become pure or clean. **2.** To undergo or cause an emptying of the bowels.
~*n.* **1.** The act or process of purging. **2.** That which purges; especially, a medicinal purgative. **3.** The ridding of dissidents and others considered undesirable from a government, political party, or the like. [Middle English *purgen,* from Old French *purger,* from Latin *purgāre, pūrigāre* (unattested), to cleanse : *pūrus,* PURE + *agere,* to lead.] **—purg·er** *n.*

pu·ri (póor-i) *n.* A light, flat wheat cake of Pakistani or northern Indian origin, usually deep-fried in fat. [Hindi, from Sanskrit *purah,* cake.]

Pu·ri (pőō-ree). Also **Jagannath** or **Juggernaut.** Seaport in Orissa, east central India. It is a major centre of pilgrimage for Hindus.

pu·ri·fi·ca·tor (péwr-i-fi-kaytәr) *n.* A cloth used to clean the chalice and paten and the lips and fingers of the celebrant at the Eucharist.

pu·ri·fy (péwr-i-fī) *v.* **-fied, -fying, -fies.** —*tr.* **1.** To rid of impurities; cleanse. **2.** To rid of foreign or objectionable elements. **3.** To free from sin, guilt, or other defilement. —*intr.* To become clean or pure. [Middle English *purifien,* from Old French *purifier,* from Latin *pūrificāre,* to make pure : *pūrus,* PURE + *facere,* to make.] **—pu·ri·fi·ca·tion** (-fi-káysh'n) *n.* **—pu·rif·i·ca·to·ry** (-fi-kaytәri, -káytәri, -fickәtri) *adj.* **—pu·ri·fi·er** *n.*

Pu·rim (péwr-im, póor-; *Hebrew* pōō-réem) *n. Judaism.* A holiday in the month of Adar, celebrating the deliverance of the Jews from the threatened massacre by Haman. Esther 9:20–22. [Hebrew *pūrīm,* plural of *pūr,* lot (from the lots cast by Haman to determine the day of destruction of the Jews), from Akkadian *pūru,* stone.]

pu·rine (péwr-een, -in) *n.* **1.** A colourless crystalline compound, $C_5H_4N_4$, used in organic synthesis and metabolism studies. **2.** Any of a group of naturally occurring organic compounds derived from or having molecular structures related to purine, including uric acid, adenine, guanine, and caffeine. [German *Purin* : blend of Latin *pūrus,* PURE + New Latin *uricus,* URIC (ACID) (in which it is found) + -INE.]

pur·ism (péwr-iz'm) *n.* Strict observance of or insistence upon traditional correctness, especially of language. [French *purisme,* from *pur,* PURE.]

pur·ist (péwr-ist) *n.* One who practises or urges strict correctness, especially in the use of words. **—pu·ris·ti·cal** (pewr-rístik'l) *adj.* **—pu·ris·ti·cal·ly** *adv.*

pu·ris·tic *adj.* **1.** Characterised by purism. **2.** *Capital* **P.** Of or pertaining to Katharevousa.
~*n. Capital* **P.** A variety of Modern Greek **Katharevousa** *(see).*

Pu·ri·tan (péwr-i-tәn) *n.* **1.** A member of a group of English Protestants who, in the 16th and 17th centuries, after the Reformation, sought further simplification of the ceremonies and creeds of the Church of England and strict religious discipline. **2.** *Small* **p.** One who lives in accordance with the precepts of the Puritans; especially, one who regards luxury or pleasure as sinful.
~*adj.* **1.** Of or pertaining to the Puritans or Puritanism. **2.** *Small* **p.** Characteristic of a puritan; puritanical. [Late Latin *pūritās,* purity, from *pūrus,* PURE, by analogy with *Catharan,* CATHAR.]

pu·ri·tan·i·cal (péwr-i-tánnik'l) *adj.* Also **pu·ri·tan·ic** (-tánnik). **1.** Rigorous in religious observance; marked by stern morality. **2.** *Capital* **P.** Of, pertaining to, or characteristic of the Puritans. Used derogatorily. **—pu·ri·tan·i·cal·ly** *adv.* **—pu·ri·tan·i·cal·ness** *n.*

PRONUNCIATION KEY

a, trap; aa, father; ai, fair; ar, star; aw, lawn; ay, play; b, bb, stab; rubber; ch, church; ck, ticket; d, dd, dead; ladder; e, dress; ee, bee; er, defer; ew, few; ewr, pure; ә, about; әr, letter; f, ff, fife; differ; g, gg, giggle; h, hat; i, kit; ī, price; īr, fire; j, judge; k, kick; l, ll, let; 'l, needle; m, mm, man; n, nn, no; 'n, sudden; ng, thing; o, lot; ō, no; ŏŏ, foot; ōō, shoe; oor, poor; ow, cow; owr, hour; oy, boy; p, pp, pepper; r, rr, red; s, ss, sauce; sh, ship; t, tt, totter; th, thick; th, this; smooth; u, cut; ur, turn; v, vv, valve; w, wet; y, yes; z, zz, zebra; zh, vision; pleasure

IN FOREIGN WORDS:

aN, oN, Saint-Saëns; hl, Llanelli; Hluhluwe; kh, loch; lough; Khaled

STRESS MARK:

ín-sīt, insight; in-sít, incite

purple emperor *This beautiful woodland butterfly,* Apatura iris, *whose wings are quite differently coloured on top (lower illustration) and underneath (upper illustration), is attracted to carrion, manure, and foul mud – possibly because of the presence of salts.*

Pu·ri·tan·ism (péwr-i-tən-iz'm) *n.* **1.** The practices and doctrines of the Puritans. **2.** *Small* **p.** Scrupulous moral rigour; especially, hostility to social pleasures and indulgences.
pu·ri·ty (péwr-əti) *n.* **1.** The quality or condition of being pure. **2.** *Physics.* The proportion of a single-frequency spectral component in a mixture of achromatic and spectral colours. [Middle English, from Old French *pureté*; assimilated to Late Latin *pūritās* (stem *pūritāt-*), from Latin *pūrus,* PURE.]
purl[1] (purl) *intr.v.* **purled, purling, purls.** To flow or ripple with a murmuring sound. Used chiefly of water.
~*n.* The motion or sound made by rippling water. [16th century : probably imitative; akin to Norwegian *purla*†.]
purl[2] *v.* **purled, purling, purls.** Also **pearl** (for transitive sense 2 and intransitive sense 2). —*tr.* **1.** To knit with a purl stitch. **2.** To edge or finish with lace or embroidery. —*intr.* **1.** To do knitting with a purl stitch. **2.** To edge or finish with lace or embroidery.
~*n.* Also **pearl** (for senses 2 and 3). *Abbr.* **p. 1.** The inversion of a knit stitch; a purl stitch. **2.** A decorative edging of lace or embroidery. **3.** Gold or silver wire used in embroidery. [Earlier *pirl*†; perhaps akin to PURL (ripple).]
pur·ler (púrlər) *n.* Also **pear·ler** (for sense 2). *Informal.* **1.** *British.* **a.** A blow throwing one forwards. **b.** A headlong fall. Used chiefly in the phrases *come a purler* or *take a purler.* **2.** *Australian.* One that is outstanding or excellent.
pur·lieu (púr-lew || -lōō) *n.* **1.** Any outlying or neighbouring area; specifically, in former times, land beyond the perimeter of a forest but still partly subject to hunting laws. **2.** *Plural.* Outskirts; environs. **3.** A place that one frequents. [Middle English *purlewe,* perhaps alteration of Anglo-French *puralée,* perambulation, from the past participle of Old French *poraler, puraler,* to traverse : *por,* through, from Latin *prō,* forth + *aler,* to go, probably from Vulgar Latin *amlāre* (unattested), from Latin *ambulāre,* to walk.]
pur·lin, pur·line (púrlin) *n.* Any of several horizontal timbers supporting the rafters of a roof. [Middle English *purly(o)n*†.]
pur·loin (púr-loyn, pur-lóyn || pər-) *v.* **-loined, -loining, -loins.** —*tr.* To steal; filch. —*intr.* To commit theft. [Middle English *purloynen,* to remove, from Anglo-French *purloigner,* "to put far away" : Old French *pur-,* away, from Latin *prō-,* away + *loign,* far, from Latin *longē,* far, from *longus,* long.] —**pur·loin·er** *n.*
purl stitch *n.* An inverted knitting stitch. Also called "purl".
pur·ple (púrp'l) *n.* **1.** Any of a group of colours with a hue between that of violet and red. **2.** Cloth of this colour, formerly worn as a symbol of royalty or high office. **3.** A pigment or dyeing agent used to produce such cloth. **4.** Imperial, royal, or other high rank. **5.** The cloth worn by or the rank or office of a cardinal or bishop.
~*adj.* **1.** Of the colour purple. **2.** Royal or imperial; regal. **3.** Elaborate and ornate: *purple prose.*
~*v.* **purpled, -pling, -ples.** —*tr.* To make purple. —*intr.* To become purple. [Middle English *purpel, purpyl,* Old English *purple,* altered by dissimilation from *purpuran,* of purple, from *purpura,* purple cloth, from Latin, purple. See **purpura.**]
purple emperor *n.* A Eurasian butterfly, *Apatura iris,* having a purple sheen on the upper side of the wing in the male.
purple gallinule *n.* **1.** A dark, bluish-purple waterfowl, *Porphyrio porphyrio,* resembling a large moorhen. **2.** A similar American bird, *Porphyrula martinica,* with a blue-purple breast and green back.
purple heart *n.* Also **pur·ple·heart** (púrp'l-haart) (for senses 1, 2). **1.** Any of several tropical American trees of the genus *Peltogyne,* valued for their decorative wood. **2.** The purplish heartwood of any of these trees. **3.** *Chiefly British Informal.* A purple, heart-shaped amphetamine tablet containing the drug Drinamyl.
Purple Heart *n.* The U.S. Armed Forces medal of the Order of the Purple Heart, awarded to servicemen wounded in action.
purple loosestrife *n.* A marsh plant, *Lythrum salicaria,* having long spikes of purple flowers.
purple patch *n.* **1.** An extravagant, florid, or ornate passage of literary writing. **2.** Broadly, any brief performance that is unusually stylish or effective. Also called "purple passage".
purple salt *n. Chemistry.* **Potassium permanganate** *(see).*
purple sprouting broccoli *n.* See **broccoli.**
pur·plish (púrplish, púrp'l-ish) *adj.* Having a somewhat purple tint.
pur·port (pər-pórt, pur-, púr-pərt, -pawrt || -pōrt; -pōrt) *tr.v.* **-ported, -porting, -ports. 1.** To contain the claim or profession (to be or do something). **2.** To have or give the appearance, often falsely, of being, professing, or intending. —See Synonyms at **mean.**
~*n.* (púr-pawrt, -pərt || -pōrt). **1.** The apparent meaning; the import or significance. **2.** The purpose or intention. —See Synonyms at **meaning.** [Middle English *purporten,* to imply, from Old French *porporter,* to embody, contain, from Medieval Latin *prōportāre,* to carry forth : Latin *prō,* forth + *portāre,* to carry.] —**pur·port·ed·ly** (pər-pórt-id-li, pur- || -pōrt-) *adv.*
pur·pose (púrpəss) *n.* **1.** The object towards which one strives or for which something exists; a goal; an aim. **2.** A result or effect that is intended or desired. **3.** Determination; resolution. **4.** The matter at hand; the point at issue: *Let's return to the purpose.* —See Synonyms at **intention.** —**on purpose.** Deliberately.
~*tr.v.* **purposed, -posing, -poses.** To intend or resolve to perform or accomplish. [Middle English *porpos, purpos,* from Old French, from *porposer, purposer,* to design, intend, from Latin *prōpōnere* (past participle *prōpositus*), to put forward, PROPOSE.]
pur·pose-built (púrpəss-bílt) *adj.* Built specifically for the purpose being served: *a purpose-built ski-resort.*
pur·pose·ful (púrpəss-f'l) *adj.* **1.** Having a purpose; intentional. **2.** Having or manifesting purpose; determined. —See Usage note at **purposely.** —**pur·pose·ful·ly** *adv.* —**pur·pose·ful·ness** *n.*
pur·pose·less (púrpəss-ləss, -liss) *adj.* Without any purpose; aimless; pointless. —**pur·pose·less·ly** *adv.* —**pur·pose·less·ness** *n.*
pur·pose·ly (púrpəss-li) *adv.* **1.** With a particular purpose in mind. **2.** On purpose; intentionally.
Usage: *Purposely, purposefully,* and *purposively* are sometimes confused. Of the three, *purposely* is the most general term, meaning "deliberately, on purpose". *Purposefully* adds the nuance of "acting in a determined way", and *purposively* adds the nuance of "acting so as to achieve a particular end". Some contexts allow all three words, but usually a distinction is maintained: *He purposely left the room, so I could sleep* and *He purposefully left the room, to fetch the papers. Purposively* tends to be restricted to psychological or behavioural description: *This organism acts purposively.*
pur·pos·ive (púrpəss-iv) *adj.* **1.** Having or serving a purpose. **2.** Purposeful as opposed to aimless or random. —See Usage note at **purposely.** —**pur·pos·ive·ly** *adv.* —**pur·pos·ive·ness** *n.*
pur·pu·ra (púrpewr-ə) *n.* A skin rash made up of small purple spots caused by subcutaneous bleeding. [Latin, from Greek *porphura,* purple (dye), shellfish from which it was obtained, from Semitic.]
pur·pure (púrpewr) *n. Heraldry.* The colour purple. [Old English and Old French *purpre,* from Latin *purpura.* See **purpura.**] —**pur·pure** *adj.*
pur·pur·in (púrpewr-in) *n.* A red crystalline derivative of anthraquinone, $C_{14}H_5O_2(OH)_3$, used as a stain in biology. [Latin *purpura,* purple (see **purpura**) + -IN.]
purr (pur) *n.* **1.** The characteristic softly vibrant sound of a cat, understood to express pleasure or contentment. **2.** Any similar sound, such as the idling of a well-tuned motor car.
~*v.* **purred, purring, purrs.** —*intr.* To emit a purr. —*tr.* To utter or express by means of a purr: *purred their approval.* [Imitative.]
purse (purss) *n.* **1.** A small bag or pouch for carrying money, especially coins. **2.** *U.S.* A woman's handbag. **3.** Anything that resembles a bag or pouch. **4.** Available wealth or resources; money. **5.** A sum of money collected as a present or offered as a prize.
~*tr.v.* **pursed, pursing, purses.** To gather or contract (the lips or brow) into wrinkles or folds; pucker. [Middle English *purs,* Old English *purs,* from Late Latin *bursa,* bag, oxhide, from Greek *bursa,* leather, hide.]
purs·er (púrssər) *n.* The officer in charge of money matters and welfare of passengers on a ship. [Middle English, from *purs,* PURSE.]
purse seine (sayn) *n.* A fishing seine that is pursed or drawn into the shape of a bag to enclose the catch.
purse strings *pl.n.* **1.** The strings that tighten and close the opening of an old-fashioned purse. **2.** Control of finance or money supply.
purs·lane (púrss-lin, -layn) *n.* **1.** A trailing weed, *Lythrum portula* (or *Peplis portula*), having small yellow flowers, reddish stems, and fleshy leaves that are sometimes used in salads. Also called "water purslane". **2.** Any of various similar but unrelated plants, such as sea purslane. [Middle English *purcelan, purslane,* from Old French *porcelaine,* cowrie shell, from Late Latin *porcillāgo,* from Latin *porcil(l)āca, portulāca.*]
pur·su·ance (pər-séw-ənss, -sōō- || -shōō-) *n.* The carrying out or putting into effect of a plan, idea, or the like.
pur·su·ant (pər-séw-ənt, -sōō- || -shōō-) *adj.* Proceeding from and conformable to; in accordance with. Used with *to.*
~*adv.* Also **pur·su·ant·ly.** Accordingly; consequently. [Middle English *poursuiant,* from Old French, present participle of *poursuivre,* PURSUE.]
pur·sue (pər-séw, -sōō || -shōō) *v.* **-sued, -suing, -sues.** —*tr.* **1.** To follow in an effort to overtake or capture; chase. **2.** To strive to gain or accomplish. **3.** To proceed along the course of; follow: *pursue the original plan.* **4.** To carry further; advance: *pursued the argument.* **5.** To be engaged in (a vocation or hobby, for example). **6.** To follow closely; harass. —*intr.* **1.** To chase; follow. **2.** To continue; carry on. [Middle English *pursuen,* from Anglo-French *pursuer,* from Old French *po(u)rsuivre, po(u)rsuir,* from Vulgar Latin *prōsequere* (unattested), from Latin *prōsequī* : *prō-,* forth, onward + *sequī,* to follow.] —**pur·su·a·ble** *adj.* —**pur·su·er** *n.*
pur·suit (pər-séwt, -sōōt || -shōōt) *n.* **1.** The act or an instance of chasing or pursuing. **2.** The act of striving: *pursuit of success.* **3.** An activity engaged in: *academic pursuits.* **4.** A cycling race, usually on a circular track, in which two riders or teams, beginning some distance apart, attempt to overtake each other. [Middle English *pursu(i)te,* from Old French *poursuite,* from *poursuivre,* PURSUE.]
pur·sui·vant (púr-si-vənt, -swi-) *n.* **1.** In the British Colleges of Heralds, an officer ranking below a herald. **2.** *Archaic.* A follower, messenger, or attendant. [Middle English *pursevant,* from Old French *pours(u)ivant,* follower, from the present participle of *poursuivre,* PURSUE.]
pur·sy (púrssi || pússi) *adj.* **-sier, -siest. 1.** Short of wind. **2.** Fat; corpulent. [Middle English *pursy, pursive,* from Anglo-French *porsif,* Old French *polsif,* from *polser,* to wheeze, be short of breath, from Latin *pulsāre,* to pulse. See **pulsate.**] —**purs·i·ness** *n.*
pur·te·nance (púrtinənss) *n. Archaic.* An animal's viscera or inner organs, especially the heart, liver, and lungs. [Middle English *purtenaunce,* "appurtenance", "accessory", alteration of Old French *partenance,* pertinence, from PERTINENT.]
pu·ru·lence (péwr-ōō-lənss, -rew-) *n.* **1.** The condition of discharging or containing pus. **2.** Pus.
pu·ru·lent (péwr-ōō-lənt, -rew-) *adj.* Containing or discharging pus.

[Latin *pūrulentus* : *pūs* (stem *pūr-*), pus + -ULENT.] **—pu·ru·lent·ly** *adv.*

pur·vey (pər-váy, pur- ‖ *U.S. also* púr-vay) *tr.v.* **-veyed, -veying, -veys.** To supply (food or information, for example); furnish. [Middle English *purveien, porveien,* from Old French *porveeir, porveioir,* from Latin *prōvidēre,* to foresee, PROVIDE.]

pur·vey·ance (pər-váy-ənss, pur-) *n.* The act of procuring supplies.

pur·vey·or (pər-váy-ər, pur-) *n.* **1.** A person who furnishes provisions, especially food. **2.** A distributor; a dispenser.

pur·view (púr-vew) *n.* **1.** The extent or range of function, power, or competence; scope. **2.** Range of vision, comprehension, or experience; outlook. **3.** *Law.* The body, scope, or limit of a statute. [Middle English *purveu, purvewe,* proviso, provisional clause, from Anglo-French *purveu,* "(it is) provided" (word used to introduce a proviso), from Old French *porveu,* past participle of *porveeir,* to provide, PURVEY.]

pus (puss) *n.* A viscous, yellowish-white fluid formed in infected tissue, consisting chiefly of leucocytes, cellular debris, and liquefied tissue elements. [Latin *pūs.*]

Pu·san (pōō-sán). Seaport in southeast Korea. Capital of South Kyongsang province, it is the nearest point on the Asiatic mainland to Japan and was a United Nations supply base during the Korean War. It is a commercial and industrial centre.

Pu·sey (péwzi), **Edward Bouverie** (1800–82). British theologian. A member of the Oxford Movement, he advocated a revival of ceremony and Catholicism in the Anglican church. **—Pu·sey·ism** (-iz'm) *n.* **—Pu·sey·ite** (-īt) *n.*

push (pŏŏsh) *v.* **pushed, pushing, pushes.** *—tr.* **1.** To exert force against (an object) to move it away. **2.** To move by exerting force in this manner; thrust; shove. **3.** To force (an enemy or opposing team) to move back or retreat: *pushed the tank battalion back.* **4.** To force (one's way): *He pushed his way through the crowd.* **5.** To urge on or encourage, especially in a forceful way: *They push us hard at school.* **6.** *Informal.* To bear hard upon; press: *pushed for time.* **7.** To extend or enlarge: *push civilisation past the frontier.* **8.** *Informal.* **a.** To promote or market (a product). **b.** To sell (a narcotic) illegally. **c.** To advocate or seek support for: *push the idea.* **9.** *Sports.* To hit (a ball) with a slow, precise stroke, rather than with a sharp rap or swinging stroke. *—intr.* **1.** To exert outward force against something. **2.** To advance despite difficulty or opposition; press forward. **3.** To expend great or vigorous effort, especially to bring about or obtain something. Oten used with *for*: *pushing for an enquiry.* **—push along.** *Informal.* To depart; set out. **—push off. 1.** *Informal.* **a.** To depart; set out. **b.** To go away or withdraw hastily. Often used in the imperative. **2.** To cause (a boat, for example) to begin to move. **—push on.** To continue. **—push (someone) about** or **around.** *Informal.* To bully someone or order him about. **—push through.** To force the acceptance or adoption of (a bill or amendment, for example).
~*n.* **1.** The act of pushing; a thrust. **2.** A vigorous or insistent effort towards an end. **3.** A provocation to action; a stimulus. **4.** *Informal.* Persevering energy; enterprise. **5.** A struggle; a strain: *It'll be a push but we can do it.* **6.** *Australian Informal.* A group of people; a clique. **—at a push.** With some difficulty. **—give (someone) the push.** *Informal.* **1.** To dismiss (someone) from a job. **2.** To end an emotional relationship with (someone). [Middle English *posshen, pusshen,* from Old French *polser, poulser,* to push, beat, from Latin *pulsāre,* frequentative of *pellere* (past participle *pulsus*), to push, beat.]

push·ball (pŏŏsh-bawl) *n.* **1.** A game, played chiefly in the United States, in which two opposing teams attempt to push a heavy ball, 1.83 metres (six feet) in diameter, across a goal. **2.** The ball so used.

push-bike (pŏŏsh-bīk) *n. Informal.* A bicycle operated solely by pedalling, as distinct from a motorised bicycle.

push button *n.* A small button that activates an electric circuit.

push-but·ton (pŏŏsh-butt'n) *adj.* Operated by or as if by push buttons: *push-button warfare.*

push·cart (pŏŏsh-kaart) *n.* A light cart pushed by hand; a barrow.

push·chair (pŏŏsh-chair) *n.* A light, folding, four-wheeled chair for wheeling small children about.

push·er (pŏŏshər) *n.* **1.** One that pushes. **2.** An energetically ambitious person. **3.** *Informal.* A person who sells drugs illegally. **4.** A utensil, used by a child, for pushing food onto a spoon or fork.

push·ing (pŏŏshing) *adj.* **1.** Energetic; enterprising. **2.** Aggressive; forward; presumptuous.
~*adv. Informal.* Almost; nearly: *pushing 40.* **—push·ing·ly** *adv.*

Push·kin (pŏŏsh-kin), **Alexandr Sergeyevich** (1799–1837). Russian poet. He wrote the verse novel *Eugene Onegin* (1825–31), the play *Boris Godunov* (1831), and many narrative and lyrical poems and short stories, all considered classics of their genre. He is regarded as the founder of the Russian literary language.

push·o·ver (pŏŏsh-ōvər) *n. Informal.* **1.** Anything easily accomplished. **2.** A person or group easily defeated or taken advantage of.

push-pull (pŏŏsh-pŏŏl) *adj.* Designating an arrangement of two identical electronic devices that act 180° out of phase with each other in order to minimise distortion.

push·rod (pŏŏsh-rod) *n.* Also **push rod.** A rod moved by a cam to operate the valves in an internal-combustion engine.

push-start (pŏŏsh-staart) *n.* A method of starting a motor vehicle by pushing it, then putting it into gear, so that the engine turns.
~*tr.v.* (*also* -stárt) **push-started, -starting, -starts.** To start (a motor vehicle) in this way.

Push·tu (púsh-tōō, -tōō; *also* pŏŏsh-) *n.* An Iranian language, **Pashto** *(see).*

push-up (pŏŏsh-up) *n. U.S.* A **press-up** *(see).*

push·y (pŏŏshi) *adj.* **-ier, -iest.** *Informal.* Disagreeably forward or aggressive. **—push·i·ly** *adv.* **—push·i·ness** *n.*

pu·sil·lan·i·mous (péw-si-lánniməss, -zi-) *adj.* Lacking courage; cowardly. [Late Latin *pūsillanimis* : Latin *pūsillus,* very small, weak, from *pūsus,* boy + *animus,* mind, soul.] **—pu·sil·la·nim·i·ty** (-lə-nímməti) *n.* **—pu·sil·lan·i·mous·ly** *adv.*

puss[1] (pŏŏss) *n. Informal.* **1.** A cat. **2.** A girl or young woman. Used affectionately. **3.** *Archaic.* A hare. [Probably from Middle Low German *pūs*†.]

puss[2] *n. Slang.* **1.** The mouth. **2.** The face. [Irish *bus,* lip, mouth, from Old Irish, lip.]

puss moth *n.* A Eurasian moth, *Cerura vinula,* the caterpillar of which has a forked tail and prominent eyespots at the anterior end to alarm predators. [From PUSS (cat), referring to its furry body.]

puss·y[1] (pŏŏssi) *n., pl.* **-ies. 1.** *Informal.* A cat. **2.** *Vulgar Slang.* **a.** The female genitals. **b.** Women collectively, considered as sexual objects. [See **puss** (cat).]

pus·sy[2] (pússi) *adj.* **-sier, -siest.** Resembling or containing pus.

puss·y·foot (pŏŏssi-fŏŏt) *intr.v.* **-footed, -footing, -foots. 1.** To move stealthily or cautiously. **2.** *Informal.* To act or proceed cautiously or timidly to avoid committing oneself.

pussy willow *n.* **1.** A North American shrub or small tree, *Salix discolor,* having silky, pale grey catkins. **2.** Any of several similar willows.

pus·tu·lant (pústewlənt) *adj.* Causing pustules to form.
~*n.* An agent that produces pustules.

pus·tu·late (pústew-layt) *v.* **-lated, -lating, -lates.** *—tr.* To cause (tissue) to form pustules. *—intr.* To form pustules.
~*adj.* (-lət, -lit, -layt). Covered with pustules.

pus·tu·la·tion (pústew-láysh'n) *n.* **1.** The formation or appearance of pustules. **2.** A pustule.

pus·tule (pústewl) *n.* **1.** A slight, inflamed raised area of the skin filled with pus. **2.** Any small swelling similar to a blister or pimple. [Middle English, from Old French, from Latin *pustula,* a blister.] **—pus·tu·lar** (-ər) *adj.*

pusz·ta (pŏŏsh-tə) *n.* Temperate grassland on the plains of Hungary. [Hungarian.]

put (pŏŏt) *v.* **put, putting, puts.** *—tr.* **1.** To place in a specified location; set: *put the cat out; put words into her mouth.* **2.** To cause to be in a specified condition: *put one's room in order; She put his mind at rest.* **3.** To cause to undergo something; subject: *was put to death.* **4.** To assign; attribute: *put a false interpretation on events; put the blame on his wife.* **5.** To estimate. Used with *at*: *He put the time at five o'clock.* **6.** To impose: *put a tax on cigarettes; put an end to his agony.* **7.** To bet; wager (a stake). **8.** To hurl with an overhand pushing motion: *put the shot.* **9.** To bring up for consideration or judgment: *The committee put the question.* **10.** To express; state: *putting it bluntly.* **11.** To render in a specified language or literary form: *put prose into verse.* **12.** To adapt: *lyrics put to music.* **13.** To urge or force to some action: *put an outlaw to flight.* **14.** To apply: *We must put our minds to it.* **15.** To impart; invest: *put some effort into it.* **16.** To cause to penetrate. Used with *through*: *put her hand through the window.* *—intr.* To proceed: *The ship put into the harbour.* **—put about. 1.** *Nautical.* **a.** To change direction; go from one tack to another. **b.** To cause (a ship) to put about. **2.** To spread (a rumour or news, for example). **—put across. 1.** To state so as to be understood or accepted. **2.** To convey (an impression): *She puts across an image of haughtiness.* **3.** To project or give a specified impression of (oneself): *He put himself across rather feebly at the interview.* **—put aside** or **by. 1.** To save for later use; reserve. **2.** To abandon; discard. **—put away. 1.** To save or keep in reserve. **2.** *Informal.* To confine in an institution, such as a mental hospital. **3.** To consume (food or drink), especially in large quantities. **—put back. 1.** To postpone for or until a specified time: *The meeting is being put back for 24 hours.* **2.** To cause delay or disruption to. **—put forth. 1.** To grow: *The plant put forth leaves.* **2.** To offer for consideration. **—put forward. 1.** To propose (an idea, for example). **2.** To nominate, as for a position of authority. **—put in. 1.** *Nautical.* To enter a port or harbour. **2.** To insert; interject. **3.** To submit (a form, for example). **4.** To apply or enter: *put in for the job.* **5.** To devote or contribute (work, time, or money, for example). **6. a.** To cause (a political party, for example) to be elected. **b.** In cricket, to make (the opposing team) bat. **—put it about. 1.** To spread information or rumour. **2.** *Slang.* To be sexually promiscuous. **—put one across** or **over on.** *Informal.* To trick or deceive (someone), especially into believing a claim or excuse. **—put out. 1.** To extinguish: *put out a fire.* **2.** *Nautical.* To leave, as from a port: *The ship put out to sea.* **3.** To blind (eyes), as by poking. **4.** To publish. **5.** To inconvenience: *I was put out by her late arrival.* **6.** To confuse; disconcert. **7.** To dislocate: *put his back out.* **—put over. 1.** To communicate or put across. **2.** *U.S.* To achieve. **—put through. 1. a.** To connect (a caller) by telephone. **b.** To make (a telephone call). **2.** To carry to a successful termination. **—put upon.** To impose on; take advantage of. Used in the passive: *He was put upon by his friends.*
~*n.* **1.** An act of putting the shot. **2.** *Finance.* An option to sell a stipulated amount of stock or securities within a stated time and at a fixed price. Compare **call, straddle.**
~*adj. Informal.* Fixed; stationary: *Stay put.* [Middle English *put(t)en* (unattested), Old English *pūtian*†, to push, thrust.]

PRONUNCIATION KEY

a, trap; aa, father; ai, **fair**; ar, **star**; aw, **lawn**; ay, **play**; b, bb, stab; **rubber**; ch, **church**; ck, **ticket**; d, dd, **dead**; **ladder**; e, **dress**; ee, **bee**; er, **defer**; ew, **few**; ewr, **pure**; ə, about; ər, letter; f, ff, **fife**; **differ**; g, gg, **giggle**; h, **hat**; i, **kit**; ī, **price**; īr, **fire**; j, **judge**; k, **kick**; l, ll, **let**; 'l, **needle**; m, mm, **man**; n, nn, **no**; 'n, **sudden**; ng, **thing**; o, **lot**; ō, **no**; ŏŏ, **foot**; ōō, **shoe**; oor, **poor**; ow, **cow**; owr, **hour**; oy, **boy**; p, pp, **pepper**; r, rr, **red**; s, ss, **sauce**; sh, **ship**; t, tt, **totter**; th, **thick**; th, **this**; **smooth**; u, **cut**; ur, **turn**; v, vv, **valve**; w, **wet**; y, **yes**; z, zz, **zebra**; zh, **vision**; **pleasure**

IN FOREIGN WORDS:

aN, oN, **Saint-Saëns**; hl, **Llanelli**; **Hluhluwe**; kh, **loch**; **lough**; **Khaled**

STRESS MARK:

ín-sīt, insight; in-sít, incite

pu·ta·men (pew-táy-men, -mən) *n., pl.* **-tamina** (-támminə). *Botany.* A hard, shell-like covering, such as that enclosing the kernel of a peach. [New Latin, from Latin *putāmen,* clippings, prunings, shells, from *putāre,* to prune, cut.] **—pu·tam·i·nous** (pew-támminəss) *adj.*

pu·ta·tive (péw-tətiv, pew-táytiv) *adj.* Generally regarded as such; supposed; reputed: *his putative mother.* [Middle English, from Old French *putatif,* from Late Latin *putātīvus,* from Latin *putāre,* to compute, consider.] **—pu·ta·tive·ly** *adv.*

put down *tr.v.* **1. a.** To write down; record. **b.** To record a promise or arrangement made by (someone): *Put her down for Tuesday.* **c.** To record or have recorded on a list. **d.** To list or table on an agenda: *put down a motion on overseas aid.* **2.** To repress; defeat. **3.** *Informal.* To express rejection or criticism of. **4.** To kill (an animal) mercifully. **5.** To attribute or ascribe: *Put it down to inexperience.* **6.** To regard or estimate: *I'd put her down for a liar.* **7.** To land (an aircraft). **8.** To stop reading (a book, for example). *—intr.v.* To land. Used of an aircraft.

put-down (pŏŏt-down) *n. Slang.* A dismissal or rejection, especially in the form of a critical or slighting remark.

put·log (pút-log, pŏŏt- || *U.S. also* -lawg) *n.* Also **put·lock** (-lok). Any of the short pieces of timber that support a scaffolding floor. [17th century : origin obscure.]

put off *tr.v.* **1.** To delay or postpone (a meeting, for example). **2.** To avoid meeting (a person) by giving an excuse. **3.** To annoy by distracting. **4.** To cause (someone) to feel dislike for (someone or something). **5.** To disconcert; make apprehensive.

put·off (pŏŏt-off, -awf) *n. Chiefly U.S.* A pretext for inaction.

put on *tr.v.* **1.** To clothe oneself with; don. **2.** To apply or activate: *put on the brake.* **3.** To present; perform: *put on a play.* **4.** To assume affectedly: *put on a funny accent.* **5.** To switch on (an electrical appliance). **6. a.** To increase in: *put on weight.* **b.** To add: *put on ten runs after tea.* **7.** To cause to be connected, as on the telephone. **8.** *U.S.* To tease or mislead (someone).

put-on (pŏŏt-on || -awn) *adj.* Pretended; feigned.
~n. U.S. Informal. **1.** The act of teasing or misleading someone, especially for amusement. **2.** Something intended as a hoax or joke.

put-put (pút-put) *n. Slang.* **1.** A small engine. **2.** The noise made by such an engine. **3.** A boat or vehicle operated by such an engine. Also used adjectivally: *a put-put engine.*
~intr.v. **put-putted, -putting, -puts. 1.** To make the sound of a put-put engine. **2.** To travel in or on, or as if in or on, a put-put boat or vehicle. [Imitative.]

pu·tre·fac·tion (péwtri-fáksh'n) *n.* **1.** The partial decomposition of organic matter by microorganisms, producing foul-smelling matter. **2.** Putrefied matter. **3.** The condition of being putrefied. [Middle English *putrefaccioun,* from Late Latin *putrefactiō* (stem *putrefactiōn-*), from Latin *putrefacere,* PUTREFY.] **—pu·tre·fac·tive** (péwtri-fáktiv), **pu·tre·fa·cient** (-fáysh'nt) *adj.*

pu·tre·fy (péwtri-fī) *v.* **-fied, -fying, -fies.** *—tr.* **1.** To decompose (something); cause to decay. **2.** To make gangrenous. *—intr.* **1.** To decompose. **2.** To become gangrenous. **—**See Synonyms at **decay.** [Middle English *putrefien,* from Old French *putrefier,* from Latin *putrefacere* : *puter,* rotten + *facere,* to make.]

pu·tres·cence (pew-tréss'nss) *n.* **1.** A putrescent character or condition. **2.** Putrid matter.

pu·tres·cent (pew-tréss'nt) *adj.* **1.** Becoming putrid; putrefying. **2.** Of or pertaining to putrefaction. [Latin *putrēscens,* present participle of *putrēscere* (stem *putrēscent-*), to grow rotten, inceptive of *putrēre,* to be rotten, from *puter,* rotten.]

pu·tres·ci·ble (pew-tréssə-b'l) *adj.* Subject to putrefaction. [French, from Late Latin *putrēscibilis,* from Latin *putrēscere,* to grow rotten. See **putrescent.**] **—pu·tres·ci·bil·i·ty** (-bílləti) *n.*

pu·tres·cine (pew-tréss-een, -in) *n.* A colourless amine, $NH_2(CH_2)_4NH_2$, occurring in putrefying animal substances; 1,4-diaminobutane. [Latin *putrēscere,* become rotten (see **putrescent**) + -INE.]

pu·trid (péwtrid) *adj.* **1.** In a decomposed, foul-smelling state; rotten. **2.** Proceeding from or displaying putrefaction. **3.** Corrupt; morally rotten. **4.** *Slang.* Extremely objectionable or worthless; vile. [Latin *putridus,* from *putrēre,* to be rotten. See **putrescent.**] **—pu·trid·i·ty** (pew-tríddəti), **pu·trid·ness** *n.* **—pu·trid·ly** *adv.*

putsch (pŏŏch) *n. Sometimes capital* **P.** A sudden attempt by a group to overthrow a government. [German, from Swiss German, a thrust (imitative).]

putt (put) *n.* In golf, a light stroke made on the putting green in an effort to place the ball into the hole.
~v. **putted, putting, putts.** *—tr.* To hit (the ball) with such a stroke on the green. *—intr.* To putt the ball. [Variant of PUT.]

put·tee (pútti || pu-tée) *n.* Also **put·ty** *pl.* **-ties. 1.** A strip of cloth wound spirally around the leg from ankle to knee, for covering and protection. **2.** A rectangular canvas legging with small straps and buckles, covering the lower leg between mid-calf and ankle. [Hindi *paṭṭī,* from Sanskrit *paṭṭikā,* from *paṭṭa†,* cloth band.]

put·ter¹ (púttər) *n.* **1.** In golf, a short, stiff-shafted club used for putting. **2.** A golfer who is putting.

put·ter² (pŏŏtər) *n.* **1.** One that puts. **2.** An athlete who puts the shot.

putter³. *U.S.* Variant of **potter.**

putting green *n.* **1.** In golf, the area at the end of a fairway in which the hole is placed, having turf more closely mown than the rest of the course. **2.** An area for practising putting.

put·to (pŏŏt-ō) *n., pl.* **-ti** (-ee, -i). A figure of a small boy or cherub in painting, sculpture, and ornamentation.

put·ty (pútti) *n., pl.* **-ties. 1.** A doughlike cement made by mixing whiting and linseed oil, used to fill holes in woodwork and secure panes of glass. **2.** Any substance with a similar consistency or function. **3.** A fine lime cement used as a finishing coat on plaster. **4.** Yellowish or light greyish brown. **5.** A person or group that is very compliant, impressionable, or easily influenced: *His accomplices were putty in his hands.*
~tr.v. **puttied, -tying, -ties.** To fill, cover, or secure with putty. [French *potée,* from Old French, contents of a pot, a potful, from *pot,* a pot, from Middle Low German, from Vulgar Latin *pottus* (attested only in Late Latin).]

put up *tr.v.* **1.** To erect; build. **2.** To preserve, as in glass jars: *put up jam.* **3.** To nominate. **4.** To provide (funds) in advance. **5.** To provide lodgings for: *put someone up for the night.* **6.** To incite to some action: *put someone up to a prank.* **7.** To raise and arrange (long hair) in a style. **8.** To offer (property) for sale. **9.** To offer or show (resistance, for example), especially when hard-pressed: *put up a fight.* **10.** To raise or increase: *put up the price.* **11.** *Archaic.* To sheath (a sword). *—intr.v.* **1.** To stay in lodgings. **2.** To stand as a candidate. **—put up with.** To endure patiently; tolerate.

put-up (pŏŏt-up, -úp) *adj. Informal.* Planned or prearranged secretly. Used chiefly in the phrase *a put-up job.*

puy (pwee) *n.* A small extinct volcanic cone. [French.]

puz·zle (puzz'l) *v.* **-zled, -zling, -zles.** *—tr.* **1.** To cause uncertainty and indecision in; perplex. **2.** To clarify or solve (something confusing) by reasoning or study. Used with *out*: *He puzzled out the significance of her statement.* *—intr.* To ponder a problem in an effort to solve or understand it. Often used with *over* or *about.*
~n. **1.** One that puzzles. **2.** A toy, game, testing device, or the like, that tests ingenuity. See **jigsaw puzzle. 3.** The condition of being perplexed; bewilderment. [16th century : origin obscure.] **—puz·zle·ment** (-mənt) *n.* **—puz·zler** (púzzlər, púzz'l-ər) *n.*

Synonyms: *puzzle, perplex, mystify, bewilder, confound, baffle.*

PVC *n.* Polyvinyl chloride: a common thermoplastic resin used in a wide variety of manufactured products, including raincoats, garden hoses, gramophone records, and floor tiles.

pvt., Pvt. private.

P.W. policewoman (in Britain).

P.W.D. Public Works Department.

pwt. pennyweight.

PX *U.S.* post exchange; Post Exchange.

py–. Variant of **pyo–.**

py·a (pyaa, pi-áa) *n.* A coin equal to 1/100 of the kyat of Burma. [Burmese.]

py·ae·mi·a (pī-éemi-ə) *n.* Blood poisoning due to the presence of pus-forming bacteria. [New Latin : PY(O)- + -AEMIA.] **—py·ae·mic** *adj.*

pyc·nid·i·um (pik-níddi-əm) *n., pl.* **-nidia** (-ə). *Botany.* A rounded or flask-shaped asexual fruiting body containing spores. It occurs in certain fungi. [New Latin : Greek *puknos,* thick + *-idium,* Latin diminutive suffix, from Greek *-idion.*] **—pyc·nid·i·al** *adj.*

pyc·nom·e·ter (pik-nómmitər) *n.* A standard vessel used in measuring the relative density of materials. [Greek *puknos,* thick, dense + METER.]

pye dog (pī) *n.* A stray, untamed domestic dog in Asia. Also called "pariah dog". [Hindi *pāhī,* pariah, outsider.]

py·e·li·tis (pī-ə-lī-tiss) *n.* Inflammation of the pelvis of the kidney, usually caused by bacterial infection. [New Latin *pyelo-,* pelvis, from Greek *puelos,* basin + -ITIS.] **—py·e·lit·ic** (-líttik) *adj.*

py·e·log·ra·phy (pī-ə-lóggrəfi) *n.* Examination of the kidneys by means of X-ray pictures (*pyelograms*). [New Latin *pyelo-,* pelvis (see **pyelitis**) + -GRAPHY.] **—py·e·lo·graph·ic** (-lə-gráffik) *adj.*

py·e·lo·ne·phri·tis (pī-ə-lō-ni-frítiss, -ne-) *n.* Inflammation of both the kidney and the pelvis of the ureter. [New Latin *pyelo-,* pelvis (see **pyelitis**) + NEPHRITIS.]

py·gid·i·um (pī-jíddi-əm) *n., pl.* **-gydia** (-ə). The posterior body region of certain invertebrates. [New Latin, from Greek *pugidion,* diminutive of *pugē†,* rump.] **—py·gid·i·al** *adj.*

Pyg·ma·li·on (pig-máyli-ən, -mályən). *Greek Mythology.* A king of Cyprus who carved and then fell in love with a statue of a woman, which Aphrodite brought to life as Galatea.

pyg·my, pig·my (píg-mi) *n., pl.* **-mies.** An individual of unusually small size or significance.
~adj. **1.** Unusually or atypically small. **2.** Of little importance or stature. [Middle English *pigmie,* from Latin *pygmaeus,* dwarfish, from Greek *pugmaios,* from *pugmē,* fist, the length from the elbow to the knuckles.] **—pyg·mae·an, pyg·me·an** (pig-mée-ən) *adj.*

Pyg·my, Pig·my (píg-mi) *n., pl.* **-mies. 1.** A member of any of several African and Asian peoples with a hereditary stature of from four to five feet. **2.** In Greek legend, a member of a race of dwarfs.
~adj. Of or pertaining to the Pygmies.

py·ja·mas, *U.S.* **pa·ja·mas** (pi-jáaməz, pə- || *U.S. also* -jámməz) *pl.n.* **1.** A loose-fitting garment consisting of trousers and a jacket, worn especially for sleeping. **2.** Loose-fitting trousers worn in the Orient. [Hindi *pāejāma* : Persian *pāī,* leg, foot, from Middle Persian + *jāmah†,* garment.] **—py·ja·ma** (-jáamə || -jámmə) *adj.*

pyk·nic (pík-nik) *adj. Anthropology.* Characterised by short, stocky, and powerful stature; endomorphic. [Greek *puknos,* thick, dense.] **—pyk·nic** *n.*

py·lon (pī-lən || -lon) *n.* **1.** A steel tower supporting high-tension electric cables forming part of the grid system. **2.** *Aeronautics.* A tall tower used to guide pilots, especially as a marker for the turning point in a race. **3.** A large structure marking an entrance or ap-

PRONUNCIATION KEY

a, trap; aa, father; ai, fair; ar, star; aw, lawn; ay, play; b, bb, stab; rubber; ch, church; ck, ticket; d, dd, dead; ladder; e, dress; ee, bee; er, defer; ew, few; ewr, pure; ə, about; ər, letter; f, ff, fife; differ; g, gg, giggle; h, hat; i, kit; ī, price; īr, fire; j, judge; k, kick; l, ll, let; 'l, needle; m, mm, man; n, nn, no; 'n, sudden; ng, thing; o, lot; ō, no; ŏŏ, foot; ōō, shoe; oor, poor; ow, cow; owr, hour; oy, boy; p, pp, pepper; r, rr, red; s, ss, sauce; sh, ship; t, tt, totter; th, thick; th, this; smooth; u, cut; ur, turn; v, vv, valve; w, wet; y, yes; z, zz, zebra; zh, vision; pleasure

IN FOREIGN WORDS:

aN, oN, Saint-Saëns; hl, Llanelli; Hluhluwe; kh, loch; lough; Khaled

STRESS MARK:

ín-sīt, insight; in-sít, incite

proach; specifically, a monumental gateway in the form of a pair of truncated pyramids serving as the entrance to an ancient Egyptian temple. **4.** A streamlined casing for attaching an external engine pod or fuel tank to the body of an aircraft. [Greek *pulōn,* gateway, from *pulē,* a gate.]

py·lo·rus (pī-láw-rəss || pi-, -lṓ-) *n., pl.* **-ri** (-rī). The passage connecting the stomach and the duodenum. [Late Latin *pylōrus,* from Greek *pulōros,* "a gatekeeper" : *pulē,* a gate + *ouros,* watcher, from *horan,* to see.] **—py·lor·ic** (-lórrik, -láwrik || -lṓrik) *adj.*

Pym (pim), **John** (1584–1643). English politician. A Somerset squire, he became a leading Parliamentary opponent of Charles I, moving the bills of impeachment against his advisers. Charles' attempts to arrest him (1642) in the House of Commons precipitated the Civil War, in which his coordination of military activity earned him the title "King" Pym.

pyo–, py– *comb. form.* Indicates pus; for example, **pyorrhoea, pyaemia.** [Greek *puon,* pus.]

py·o·der·ma (pī́-ō-dérmə) *n.* Any skin disease in which pus is produced. [New Latin : PYO- + -DERMA.] **—py·o·der·mic** *adj.*

py·o·gen·e·sis (pī́-ō-jénnə-siss) *n. Pathology.* Pyosis. [PYO- + -GENESIS.] **—py·o·gen·ic** (-jénnik) *adj.*

Pyong·yang (pyóng-yáng). *Japanese* **Heijo.** Capital of North Korea. Situated on the river Taedong, it was rebuilt after its destruction by U.S. bombing during the Korean War (1950–53). In a coal and iron region, its industries include heavy engineering and textiles.

py·or·rhoe·a (pī́-ə-reér, -rée-ə) *n.* **1.** A discharge of pus. **2.** Inflammation of the gum and tooth sockets leading to loosening of the teeth. [New Latin : PYO- + -RRHEA.] **—py·or·rhoe·al** *adj.*

py·o·sis (pī-ṓ-siss) *n.* The formation of pus. Also called "pyogenesis". [New Latin, from Greek *puōsis* : PY(O)- + -OSIS.]

pyr–. Variant of **pyro–.**

py·ra·can·tha (pī́r-ə-kánthə) *n.* A shrub of the genus *Pyracantha,* the **fire thorn** *(see).* [New Latin, from Greek *purakantha,* name of a shrub : PYR(O)- + Greek *akantha,* thorn.]

pyr·a·lid (pírrə-lid) *n.* Also **py·ral·i·did** (pi-rál-i-did). Any of various small or medium-sized moths of the large, widely distributed family Pyralididae. [New Latin *pyralididae,* from *pyralis* (genus), from Greek *puralis,* fabulous insect supposed to live in fire, from *pur,* fire.] **—pyr·a·lid** *adj.*

pyr·a·mid (pírrə-mid) *n.* **1.** In geometry, a polyhedron with a polygonal base and triangular faces meeting in a common vertex. **2.** Anything having such a shape or structure. **3.** A massive monument found especially in Egypt, having a rectangular base and four triangular faces culminating in a single apex, and serving as a tomb or temple. **4.** *Plural.* A game similar to billiards played with 15 coloured balls and a cue ball. **5.** *Anatomy.* Any of various approximately pyramidal structures, as in the medulla of the kidney.
~*v.* **pyramided, -miding, -mids.** *—tr.* **1.** To place or build in the shape of a pyramid. **2.** To build (an argument or thesis, for example) progressively from a basic general premise. **3.** *Finance. U.S.* To speculate in (securities or property) by making a series of buying and selling transactions in which paper profits are used as margin for making further purchases. *—intr.* **1.** To assume the shape of a pyramid. **2.** To increase rapidly and on a widening base. **3.** *Finance. U.S.* To pyramid securities or property. [Latin *pyramis* (stem *pyramid-*), from Greek *puramis*†.] **—py·ram·i·dal** (pi-rámmid'l), **pyr·a·mid·ic** (pírrə-míddik), **pyr·a·mid·i·cal** *adj.* **—py·ram·i·dal·ly** (pi-rámmid'l-i) *adv.*

pyr·a·mid·ing (pírrə-midding) *n. Finance.* A system of business organisation in which a holding company controls subsidiary companies which are themselves holding companies, thereby achieving a concentration of power by means of limited capital ownership.

pyramid selling *n.* A system of selling in which one person with the right to sell certain goods sells part of this right or part of a consignment to others, who repeat this procedure, with only those at the bottom end of this pyramidal structure actually selling the goods.

py·ran (pī́r-an, -án) *n.* An unsaturated ring compound, C_5H_5O, having two double bonds and, depending on the position of these, two isomers. [PYR(O)- + -AN.]

py·ra·nom·e·ter (pī́r-ə-nómmitər) *n.* A **solarimeter** *(see).* [Greek *pur,* fire + *ano,* up + -METER.]

py·rar·gy·rite (pīr-árji-rīt, pī-) *n.* A deep red to black silver ore with the composition Ag_3SbS_3. Also called "ruby silver". [German *Pyrargyrit* : PYR(O)- + Greek *arguros,* silver + -ITE.]

py·ra·zole (pī́r-ə-zōl) *n.* A crystalline ring compound, $C_3H_4N_2$, consisting of a five-membered ring having two double bonds. [PYR(O)- + AZOLE.]

pyre (pīr) *n.* A heap of combustible material, especially one for burning a corpse as a funeral rite. [Latin *pyra,* from Greek *pura,* from *pur,* fire.]

py·rene[1] (pī́r-een, -reén) *n.* The one-seeded stone of certain single fruits. [New Latin *pyrena,* from Greek *purēn.*]

py·rene[2] (pī́r-een) *n.* A tetracyclic hydrocarbon, $C_{16}H_{10}$, obtained from coal tar. [PYR(O)- + -ENE.]

Pyrenean mountain dog *n.* A dog of an ancient breed originating in central Europe, typically having a large, powerful body with a coat of thick, fine, white hair.

Pyr·e·nees (pírrə-neéz). *French* **Pyrénées;** *Spanish* **Pirineos.** Mountain range in southwest Europe, separating France from the Iberian Peninsula. It rises to 3 404 metres (11,168 feet) at Pico de Aneto, and includes the Principality of Andorra. **—Pyr·e·ne·an** (pírrə-neé-ən) *adj.*

py·re·noid (pīr-reé-noyd, pī́r-ə-) *n.* Any of the protein granules of certain algae and some other lower plants in which starch is formed. [PYREN(E) (fruit stone; from the shape of its nucleus) + -OID.]

py·re·thrin (pīr-reéth-rin, pī- || *U.S. also* -réth-) *n.* Either of two viscous liquid esters, $C_{21}H_{28}O_3$ or $C_{22}H_{28}O_5$, that are extracted from pyrethrum flowers and are used as insecticides. See **cinerin.** [French *pyréthrine* : PYRETHR(UM) + -IN.]

py·re·thrum (pīr-reéth-rəm, pī- || *U.S. also* -réth-) *n.* **1.** Any of various Old World plants of the genus *Chrysanthemum* (or *Tanacetum*) having showy, daisy-like flowers; especially, *C. cinerariaefolium,* widely cultivated as a source of insecticide. **2.** An insecticide prepared from the dried flowers of pyrethrum plants. **3.** A medicinal preparation made from the root of a related plant, *Anacyclus pyrethrum,* used to stimulate the flow of saliva. In this sense, also called "pyrethrum root". [Latin, from Greek *purethron,* feverfew, from *puretos,* fever, from *pur,* fire.]

py·ret·ic (pīr-réttik, pī-, pi-) *adj.* Characterised or affected by fever; feverish. [New Latin *pyreticus,* from Greek *puretikos,* from *puretos,* fever, from *pur,* fire.]

Py·rex (pī́r-eks) *n.* A trademark for any of various types of heat- and chemical-resistant glass used for ovenware and tableware.

py·rex·i·a (pīr-réksi-ə, pī-, pi-) *n.* Fever. [New Latin, from Greek *purexis,* from *puressein,* to have a fever, from *puretos,* fever. See **pyretic.**] **—py·rex·i·al, py·rex·ic** *adj.*

pyr·he·li·om·e·ter (pīr-heéli-ómmitər, pər-) *n.* Any of various devices that measure all or restricted components of solar radiation. [PYR(O)- + HELIO- + -METER.]

pyr·i·dine (pírri-deen) *n.* A flammable, colourless or yellowish liquid base, C_5H_5N, used to synthesise vitamins and drugs, as a solvent, and as a denaturant for alcohol. [PYR(O)- + -ID + -INE.] **—py·rid·ic** (pīr-ríddik, pī-, pi-) *adj.*

pyr·i·dox·ine (pírri-dók-seen, -sin) *n.* Also **pyr·i·dox·in** (-sin). A pyridine derivative, $C_8H_{11}O_3N$, occurring in plant and animal tissues and active in various metabolic processes. Also called "vitamin B_6". [PYRID(INE) + OX- + -INE.]

pyr·i·form (pírri-fawrm) *adj.* Pear-shaped: *a pyriform organ.* [New Latin *pyriformis* : Medieval Latin *pyrum,* variant of Latin *pirum,* PEAR + -FORM.]

py·rim·i·dine (pīr-rímmi-deen, pī-, pi-) *n.* **1.** A liquid and crystalline organic base, $C_4H_4N_2$. **2.** Any of several basic compounds, such as uracil, cytosine, or thymine, having a molecular structure similar to pyrimidine and found in living matter as a nucleotide component. [German *Pyrimidin,* variant of PYRIDINE.]

py·rite (pī́r-īt) *n.* A yellow to brown, widely occurring mineral sulphide, FeS_2, used as an iron ore and to produce sulphur dioxide for sulphuric acid. Also called "fool's gold", "iron pyrites". [Latin *pyrītēs,* PYRITES.] **—py·rit·ic** (pīr-ríttik, pī-), **py·rit·i·cal** *adj.*

py·ri·tes (pīr-rīteez, pī-, pi-, pə-) *n., pl.* **pyrites.** Any of various natural metallic sulphides. [Latin *pyrītēs,* flint, pyrite, from Greek *puritēs (lithos),* "fire (stone)", from *puritēs,* of fire, from *pur,* fire.]

py·ro (pī́r-ō) *adj. Chemistry.* Of, pertaining to, or designating an acid derived from an anhydride and having a water content intermediate between those of the ortho and meta acids. Used in combination: **pyrosulphuric acid.** Compare **meta, ortho.**

pyro–, pyr– *comb. form.* Indicates: **1.** Fire or heat; for example, **pyrotechnic. 2.** Resulting from or by the action of fire or heat; for example, **pyrography. 3.** A mineral that changes its properties when heat is applied; for example **pyromorphite. 4.** *Chemistry.* A new substance obtained by heating another substance; for example **pyrophosphoric acid.** [Greek *pur,* fire.]

py·ro·cat·e·chol (pī́r-ō-kátti-chol, -ə-, -kol || -chōl, -kōl) *n.* A colourless, crystalline organic compound, $C_6H_4(OH)_2$, used as an antiseptic and photographic developer. [PYRO- + CATECH(U) + -OL.]

py·ro·cel·lu·lose (pī́r-ō-séllew-lōz, -ə-, -lōss) *n.* A cellulose nitrate used as a component of smokeless powder.

py·ro·chem·i·cal (pī́r-ō-kémmik'l, -ə-) *adj.* Of or designating high-temperature chemical activity. **—py·ro·chem·i·cal·ly** *adv.*

py·ro·clas·tic (pī́r-ō-klástik, -ə-) *adj.* Made up of fragments ejected from a volcano. Said of a rock. [PYRO- + -CLAST + -IC.]

py·ro·e·lec·tric (pī́r-ō-i-léktrik, -ə-) *adj.* Exhibiting or pertaining to pyroelectricity.
~*n.* A pyroelectric material.

py·ro·e·lec·tric·i·ty (pī́r-ō-éllek-tríssəti, -i-lék-, -ée-lek- || -trízzəti) *n.* The polarisation of electric charge in a crystal by change of temperature.

py·ro·gal·lol (pī́r-ō-gál-ol, -ə- || -ōl) *n.* A white, lustrous crystalline compound, $C_6H_3(OH)_3$, used as a photographic developer and to treat skin diseases; 1,2,3-trihydroxybenzene. Also called "pyrogallic acid". [PYRO- + GALL(IC) + -OL (hydroxyl group).] **—py·ro·gal·lic** *adj.*

py·ro·gen (pī́r-ə-jen, -ō-, -jən) *n.* A substance that produces fever. [PYRO- + -GEN.]

py·ro·gen·ic (pī́r-ə-jénnik, -ō-) *adj.* Also **py·rog·e·nous** (pīr-rójənəss, pī-). **1.** Producing or produced by fever. **2.** Caused by or generating heat. **3.** *Geology.* Igneous.

py·rog·ra·phy (pīr-róggrəfi, pī-) *n.* **1.** The art or process of producing designs on wood, leather, or other material by using heated tools or a fine flame. **2.** A design made by this process. [PYRO- + -GRAPHY.] **—py·ro·graph** (pī́r-ə-graaf, -ō-, -graf) *n.* **—py·rog·ra·pher** (-róggrəfər) *n.* **—py·ro·graph·ic** (-gráffik) *adj.*

py·ro·lig·ne·ous (pī́r-ō-líg-ni-əss, -ə-) *adj.* Made by the destructive distillation of wood.

pyroligneous acid *n.* A mixture of methanol, acetic acid, acetone,

pyramid *Of the seven wonders of the ancient world, only the pyramids still stand. The pyramid on the left was built for the pharaoh Mycerinus and the one in the centre for Chephren. But the oldest and largest of the three is the Great Pyramid of Khufu (Cheops) which was built about 2575 B.C., and is about 140 metres high (450 feet).*

pyrite *The name of this mineral comes from the Greek word for fire. Pyrite will make sparks if struck with a harder material.*

various tars, and related products from wood distillation, used in meat smoking. Also called "wood vinegar".

py·ro·lu·site (pĭr-ō-lṓo-sīt, -ə-, -lḗw-) *n.* A soft, black to dark grey ore of manganese, consisting essentially of manganese dioxide. [German *Pyrolusit* : PYRO- + Greek *lousis*, a washing, from *louein*, to wash + -ITE (it is used in purifying glass).]

py·ro·lyse, py·ro·lyze (pĭr-ə-līz, -ō-) *tr.v.* **-lysed, -lysing, -lyses.** To subject (something) to pyrolysis. [PYRO- + -LYSE.]

py·rol·y·sis (pīr-rólla-siss, pī-) *n.* Chemical change caused by heat. [PYRO- + -LYSIS.] **—py·ro·lyt·ic** (pĭr-ə-líttik, -ō-) *adj.*

py·ro·man·cy (pĭr-ə-man-si, -ō-) *n.* Divination by fire or flames. [Middle English *piromance*, from Old French *pyromancie*, from Late Latin *pyromantia*, from Greek *puromanteia* : PYRO- + -MANCY.] **—py·ro·man·tic** (-mántik) *adj.*

py·ro·ma·ni·a (pĭr-ə-máyn-i-ə, -ō-, -máyn-yə) *n.* The uncontrollable impulse to start fires. [PYRO- + -MANIA.] **—py·ro·ma·ni·ac** (-i-ak) *adj. & n.* **—py·ro·ma·ni·a·cal** (-mə-nī-ək'l) *adj.*

py·ro·met·al·lur·gy (pĭr-ō-mi-tál-ər-ji, -ə-, -me-, -métt'l-urji) *n.* Metallurgy that depends on the action of heat, involving such processes as smelting.

py·rom·e·ter (pīr-rómmitər, pī-) *n.* An electrical thermometer used for measuring high temperatures. [PYRO- + -METER.] **—py·ro·met·ric** (pĭr-ə-méttrik, -ō-), **py·ro·met·ri·cal** *adj.* **—py·rom·e·try** (-rómmətri) *n.*

py·ro·mor·phite (pĭr-ə-mórfīt, -ō-) *n.* A lead ore $(PbCl)Pb_4(PO_4)_3$, occurring in green, brown, or yellow crystals. [German *Pyromorphit* : PYRO- + MORPH(O)- + -ITE.]

py·rone (pĭr-ōn) *n. Chemistry.* A type of organic compound having a six-membered ring formed by five carbon atoms and one oxygen atom. [PYR(O)- + -ONE.]

py·rope (pĭr-ōp) *n.* A deep-red garnet, $Mg_3Al_2Si_3O_{12}$, used as a gem. [Middle English *pirope*, from Old French, from Latin *pyrōpus*, gold bronze, fiery garnet, from Greek *purōpos*, "fiery-eyed" : PYR(O)- + Greek *ōps*, eye.]

py·ro·phor·ic (pĭr-ə-fórrik, -ō- ‖ -fáwrik) *adj.* **1.** Spontaneously igniting in air. **2.** Producing sparks by friction. [Greek *purophoros*, "fire-bearing" : PYRO- + -PHOROUS.]

py·ro·phos·phate (pĭr-ō-fóss-fayt, -ə-) *n.* A salt of pyrophosphoric acid.

py·ro·phos·phor·ic acid (pĭr-ō-foss-fórrik, -ə- ‖ -fáwrik; *U.S. also* -fósfərik) *n.* A syrupy viscous liquid, $H_4P_2O_7$, used as a catalyst and in organic chemical manufacture. [PYRO- + PHOSPHORIC (it is made by heating a phosphoric acid).]

py·ro·phyl·lite (pĭr-ō-fil-īt, -ə-, -róffi-līt) *n.* A silvery white or pale-green mineral, hydrous aluminium silicate, $Al_2Si_4O_{10}(OH)_2$, occurring naturally in soft, compact masses. [German *Pyrophyllit* : PYRO- + PHYLL(O)- + -ITE (its foliations spread when heated).]

py·ro·sis (pīr-rṓ-siss, pī-) *n. Chiefly U.S.* Heartburn. [Greek *purōsis*, a burning, from *pouroun*, to burn, from *pur*, fire.]

py·ro·stat (pĭr-ə-stat, -ō-) *n.* **1.** An automatic sensing device that activates an alarm or extinguisher in the event of fire. **2.** A high-temperature thermostat. [PYRO- + -STAT.]

py·ro·sul·phate (pĭr-ō-súl-fayt, -ə-) *n.* A salt of pyrosulphuric acid. [PYROSULPH(URIC ACID) + -ATE (salt).]

py·ro·sul·phu·ric acid (pĭr-ō-sul-féwr-ik, -ə-) *n.* A heavy, oily, colourless to dark-brown liquid, $H_2S_2O_7$, produced by adding sulphur trioxide to concentrated sulphuric acid and used in petroleum refining and explosives.

py·ro·tech·nic (pĭr-ə-ték-nik, -ō-) *adj.* Also **py·ro·tech·ni·cal** (-'l). **1.** Of or pertaining to fireworks. **2.** Resembling fireworks; brilliant: *a pyrotechnic wit.* [PYRO- + Greek *tekhnikos*, of art or skill. See **technical**.] **—py·ro·tech·ni·cal·ly** *adv.*

py·ro·tech·nics (pĭr-ə-ték-niks, -ō-) *n.* Also **py·ro·tech·ny** (-tek-ni) (for sense 1). **1.** *Used with a singular verb.* The art of manufacturing or setting off fireworks. **2.** *Used with a singular or plural verb.* A fireworks display. **3.** *Used with a singular or plural verb.* A brilliant display, as of rhetoric or wit, or of virtuosity in the performing arts. **—py·ro·tech·nist** *n.*

py·rox·ene (pĭr-rókseen, pī-) *n.* Any of a group of crystalline mineral silicates common in igneous and metamorphic rocks and containing two metallic oxides, usually magnesium, iron, calcium, or sodium. [French *pyroxène*, "stranger to fire" (i.e., foreign substance in igneous rocks) : PYRO- + Greek *xenos*, stranger.] **—py·rox·en·ic** (pĭr-ok-sénnik) *adj.*

py·rox·e·nite (pīr-róksi-nīt, pī-) *n.* An igneous rock consisting chiefly of pyroxenes.

py·rox·y·lin (pīr-róksi-lin, pī-) *n.* Also **py·rox·y·line** (-leen, -lin). A highly flammable nitrocellulose used in the manufacture of collodion, plastics, and lacquers. [PYRO- + XYL(O)- + -IN.]

pyr·rhic¹ (pírrik) *n.* A Greek metrical foot composed of two short syllables. [Latin, from Greek *(pous) purrhikhios*, pyrrhic (foot), from *purrhikhē*, PYRRHIC (dance).] **—pyr·rhic** *adj.*

pyrrhic² *n.* An ancient Greek war dance imitative of actual fighting. [Latin, from Greek *purrhikhē*, traditionally supposed to be from *Purrhikhos*, the name of its inventor.] **—pyr·rhic** *adj.*

Pyrrhic victory A victory involving great losses on the victor's part. [After *Pyrrhus*, (c. 318–272 B.C.), King of Epirus, whose tactical victories against the Romans failed to avert his defeat.]

Pyr·rhon·ism (pírrən-iz'm) *n.* **1.** The sceptical philosophy of Pyrrho of Elis (c. 360–270 B.C.); especially, the doctrine that nothing can be known as absolutely certain. **2.** Loosely, scepticism or philosophic doubt. **—Pyr·rhon·ist** *n.*

pyr·rho·tite (pírrə-tīt, pírrō-) *n.* Also **pyr·rho·tine** (-tīn). A brownish-bronze weakly magnetic mineral iron sulphide. When it contains nickel, it is a nickel ore, and is used for making sulphuric acid. Also called "magnetic pyrites". [German *Pyrrhotin*, from Greek *purrhotēs*, redness, from *purrhos*, fiery, red, from *pur*, fire.]

pyr·role (pírrōl, *also* pi-rṓl) *n.* A yellowish or brown oil, C_4H_5N, with an odour similar to chloroform and used to manufacture a wide variety of drugs. Also called "azole". [Greek *purrhos*, red, tawny, from *pur*, fire + -OLE.] **—pyr·rol·ic** (pi-róllik, -rṓlik) *adj.*

pyr·rol·i·dine (pi-rólli-deen, -rṓli-, -din) *n.* A colourless heterocyclic base, $C_4H_9N_1$, made synthetically by the hydrogenation of pyrrole and occurring in tobacco leaves. [PYRROLE + -IDE + -INE.]

py·ru·vic acid (pīr-rṓo-vik, pī- ‖ -réw-) *n.* A colourless liquid, $CH_3COCOOH$, formed as a fundamental intermediate in protein and carbohydrate metabolism. [PYR(O)- + Latin *uva*, grape.]

Py·thag·o·ras (pī-thággə-rass, -rəss ‖ *U.S.* pi-) (c. 580–c. 500 B.C.). Greek philosopher, theologian, and mathematician. The school he founded in southern Italy taught spiritual growth through asceticism and the study of musical harmony and geometry. Though his famous theorem was known previously, he was the first to prove its universal validity. His insight into the relationship between numbers and the perceived universe gives him claim to be the first true mathematician.

Pythagoras' theorem *n.* The theorem that in a right-angled triangle the square of the length of the hypotenuse is equal to the sum of the squares of the lengths of the other two sides.

Py·thag·o·re·an·ism (pī-thággə-réer-niz'm, -rée-ə- ‖ *U.S.* pi-) *n.* The philosophy of Pythagoras, chiefly distinguished by its description of reality in terms of arithmetical relationships and the doctrine of the transmigration of souls. **—Py·thag·o·re·an** (pī-thággə-réern, -rée-ən ‖ *U.S.* pi-) *n. & adj.*

Pyth·e·as (píthi-ass, -əss) (fourth century B.C.). Greek navigator. Based in Marseilles, he passed through the Straits of Gibraltar and explored the Atlantic coasts of Europe, Britain, and possibly Iceland. His voyages are described by Strabo (c. 60 B.C.–A.D. 21).

Pyth·i·a (píthi-ə) *n.* The oracular priestess of Apollo at Delphi.

Pyth·i·an (píthi-ən) *adj.* **1.** Of or pertaining to Delphi, the temple of Apollo at Delphi, or its oracle. **2.** Of or pertaining to the Pythian games. [Latin *Pythius*, from Greek *Puthios*, from *Puthō*, *Puthōn*, ancient name of Delphi, after the serpent PYTHON.] **—Pyth·ic** *adj.*

Pythian games *pl.n.* In ancient Greece, a pan-Hellenic athletics festival held every four years at Delphi in honour of Apollo.

py·thon (píth'n ‖ *U.S. also* pī-thon) *n.* Any of various large, nonvenomous Old World snakes of the family Pythonidae, that coil around and crush their prey. [After PYTHON.]

Py·thon (píth'n ‖ *U.S. also* pī-thon) *n. Greek Mythology.* A dragon or serpent that was the tutelary demon of the oracular cult at Delphi until killed and expropriated by Apollo.

Py·thon·esque *adj.* Designating, displaying, or pertaining to a style of humour characterised by bizarre and far-fetched imaginative associations, brutal or outrageous visual jokes, and zany behaviour. [After the B.B.C. television series, *Monty Python's Flying Circus*.]

py·tho·ness (píthə-ness,-niss) *n.* **1.** Pythia. **2.** A prophetess. [Middle English *phitonesse*, from Old French *phitonise*, *pithonise*, from Late Latin *pȳthōnissa*, from Greek *Puthōn*, PYTHON.]

py·thon·ic (pī-thónnik) *adj.* **1.** Of, pertaining to, or resembling a python. **2.** Of or like an oracle; prophetic.

py·u·ri·a (pī-yoór-i-ə) *n.* The abnormal condition of pus in the urine. [New Latin : PY(O)- + -URIA.]

pyx, pix (piks) *n.* **1.** *Roman Catholic Church.* **a.** A container in which the Eucharist is carried. **b.** A container in which supplies of wafers for the Eucharist are kept. **2.** A chest in the British mint in which specimen coins are placed to await assay. [Middle English *pyxe*, from Latin *pyxis*, box, from Greek *puxis*, box.]

pyx·id·i·um (pik-síddi-əm) *n., pl.* **-idia** (-ə). *Botany.* A seed capsule having a circular lid that falls off to release the seeds. Also called "pyxis". [New Latin, from Greek *puxidion*, diminutive of *puxis*, PYXIS.]

pyx·is (pík-siss) *n., pl.* **pyxides** (-si-deez). *Botany.* A pyxidium.

Pyxis *n.* A constellation in the Southern Hemisphere, near Antlia and Puppis. [New Latin *Pyxis (nautica)*, "the Mariner's Compass", from Greek *puxis*, box, PYXIS.]

pyrotechnics *Pyrotechnics in the form of a fireworks display on the Rhine at Düsseldorf, West Germany. The term comes from Greek words meaning "skill with fire".*

q, Q (kew) *n., pl.* **q's** or *rare* **qs, Qs,** or **Q's. 1.** The 17th letter of the modern English alphabet. **2.** Any of the speech sounds represented by this letter.

q, Q, q., Q. *Note:* As an abbreviation or symbol, *q* may be a small or a capital letter, with or without a full stop. Established forms or those generally preferred precede the definition. When no form is given, all four forms are in general use in that sense. **1. q.** quart. **2. q.** quarter. **3. q.** quarterly. **4. q., Q.** quarto. **5. Q** *Chess.* queen. **6. Q.** Queen. **7. q.** query. **8. q.** question. **9. Q** quetzal. **10. q.** quintal. **11. q.** quire. **12.** *Physics.* heat. **13.** The 17th in a series; 16th when *J* is omitted.

Qaddafi, Moammar al-. See Moammar al-**Gaddafi.**

Qah·re·man·shahr (kȧ́ari-man-shár). Formerly **Ker·mān·shāh** or **Kir·mān·shāh** (kér-, kúr-). Capital of Qahremanshahr province, western Iran, founded by the Sassanids in the fourth century A.D. It is a market centre for a rich agricultural region.

Qandahar. See **Kandahar.**

Qa·tar, State of (ka-taár). Independent country, bordering the Gulf. It consists of the peninsula of Qatar which is mainly desert. Its economy is primarily based on large resources of onshore and offshore oil and gas. Qatar was a British protectorate from 1916 until 1971. Area, 11 000 square kilometres (4,247 square miles). Population, 300,000. Capital, Doha. See map at **Gulf States.**

QB *Chess.* queen's bishop.

Q.B. Queen's Bench.

QBP *Chess.* queen's bishop's pawn.

Q.C. Queen's Counsel.

Q.E.D. which was to be demonstrated or proved. Used to indicate that an incontrovertible conclusion has been reached. [Latin *quod erat demonstrandum.*]

Q.E.F. which was to be done. [Latin *quod erat faciendum.*]

Q factor *n.* **1.** A measure of the efficiency of a resonant circuit given by $(I/R)(L/C)^{1/2}$, where R is the resistance, L the inductance, and C the capitance of the circuit. Also called "quality factor". **2.** The heat released in a nuclear reaction, usually expressed in electronvolts. Also called "Q value". [Sense 2, *Q* (heat) + FACTOR.]

Q fever *n.* A disease of livestock caused by the rickettsia, *Coxiella burnettii,* that can be transmitted to humans and causes severe headaches and pneumonia. [From *Q*ueensland, Australia, where it was first identified.]

qilin. Variant of **kylin.**

Qin. See **Ch'in.**

Qing. See **Ch'ing.**

Qing·hai or **Ch'ing-hai** or **Tsing·hai** (chíng-hí). Province in northwestern China, named after one of the largest salt lakes in China, Qinghai Hu, which is also known by its Mongol name, Koko Nor, meaning "Blue Sea".

QKt *Chess.* queen's knight.

QKtP *Chess.* queen's knight's pawn.

ql. quintal.

Q.M. quartermaster.

Q.M.G. Quartermaster General.

qn. question.

Qom (kom, kawm, khawm). Also **Qum** or **Kum.** City in central Iran, on the main route connecting the capital Tehran with southern Iran. It is an important holy city for Shiite Muslims and pilgrims flock to visit the tomb of Fatima, sister of Imam Riza.

qoph (koff, kōof, kawf, kōf) *n.* The 19th letter of the Hebrew alphabet. [Hebrew *qōph,* from a Northwest Semitic word meaning "eye of a needle".]

QP *Chess.* queen's pawn.

q. pl. as much as you please. [Latin *quantum placet.*]

qq. questions.

Qq. quartos.

qq.v. which (things) see. [New Latin *quae vide.*]

QR *Chess.* queen's rook.

qr. 1. quarter. **2.** quarterly. **3.** quire.

QRP *Chess.* queen's rook's pawn.

q.s. as much as suffices. [Latin *quantum sufficit.*]

Q-ship (kéw-ship) *n.* A merchant ship carrying concealed guns as a trap for unsuspecting enemy ships. [From *Q,* perhaps representing *query.*]

QSO *Astronomy.* quasi-stellar object.

QSRS *Astronomy.* quasi-stellar radio source.

qt. 1. quantity. **2.** quart.

q.t. *n. Informal.* Quiet. Used in the phrase *on the q.t.*

qto. quarto.

qty. quantity.

qu. 1. queen. **2.** query. **3.** question.

qua (kway, kwaa) *adv.* By virtue of being; as; in the capacity of. [Latin *quā,* ablative singular feminine of *quī,* who.]

quack¹ (kwak) *n.* The characteristic harsh, rasping call of a duck. ∼*intr.v.* **quacked, quacking, quacks.** To emit a quack. [Imitative; compare Dutch *kwakken* and German *quacken.*]

quack² *n.* **1.** An untrained person who pretends to have medical knowledge. **2.** *Informal.* A doctor or surgeon. **3.** A charlatan; a mountebank. Also used adjectively: *quack remedies.* ∼*v.* **quacked, quacking, quaks.** —*intr.* To act as a quack. —*tr.* To offer or advertise (a cure, for example) in extravagant terms. [Shortened from QUACKSALVER.] —**quack·er·y** *n.*

quack·sal·ver (kwák-sal-vər) *n. Archaic.* A quack; a charlatan. [Dutch *quacksalver* : probably from obsolete *quacken,* to chatter + *salf,* SALVE.]

quad¹ (kwod) *n. Informal.* A quadrangle.

quad² *n. Printing.* A piece of type metal lower than the raised typeface, used for filling spaces and blank lines. Formerly called "quadrat".

quad³ *n. Informal.* A quadruplet (*see*).

quad. 1. quadrangle. **2.** quadrant. **3.** quadrilateral.

quadr–. Variant of **quadri-.**

quad·ran·gle (kwód-rang-g'l) *n. Abbr.* **quad. 1.** In geometry, a plane figure consisting of four points, no three of which are collinear, connected by straight lines. **2. a.** A rectangular area surrounded on all four sides by buildings: *an Oxford college quadrangle.* **b.** The buildings bordering this area. [Middle English, from Old French, from Late Latin *quadr(i)angulum,* from Latin, neuter of *quadr(i)angulus,* having four angles : QUADR(I)- + *angulus,* ANGLE.] —**quad·rang·u·lar** (kwod-ráng-gew-lər) *adj.*

quad·rant (kwódrənt) *n. Abbr.* **quad. 1.** In geometry: **a.** A circular arc subtending a central angle of 90°; a quarter of the circumference of a circle. **b.** The plane area bounded by two perpendicular radii and the arc they subtend. **c.** Any of the four areas into which a plane is divided by the reference axes in a coordinate system, designated *first, second, third,* and *fourth,* counting clockwise from the area in which both coordinates are positive. **2.** Anything, such as a machine part, that is shaped like a quarter circle. **3.** An early instrument for measuring altitudes, consisting of a graduated arc with a movable radius for measuring angles. [Middle English, quarter of a day, from Latin *quadrāns* (stem *quadrant-*), fourth part, quarter; akin to *quattuor,* four.]

quad·ra·phon·ic (kwódrə-fónnik) *adj.* Of, pertaining to, or reproduced by a high-fidelity sound system with equipment for the reproduction of sound from four separate channels. Compare **stereophonic.** [Irregularly from QUADR(I)- + PHONIC.] —**quad·ra·phon·ics, quad·raph·o·ny** (kwod-ráffəni, kwód-) *n.*

quad·rat (kwódrət) *n.* **1.** *Printing.* A quad (type metal). Not in current technical usage. **2. a.** A square or rectangular area of vegetation, usually one square metre, selected at random for study of its plants, which are regarded as typical of the surrounding area. **b.** A rectangular frame used to mark out such an area. [Middle English, variant of QUADRATE.]

quad·rate (kwód-rət, -rit, -rayt) *adj.* **1.** *Zoology.* Of, pertaining to, or designating a bone or cartilaginous structure of the skull, joining the upper and lower jaws in birds, fish, reptiles, and amphibians. **2.** *Archaic.* Square or rectangular. ∼*n.* **1.** A quadrate bone. **2.** An approximately square or cubic area, space, or object. ∼*intr.v.* (kwo-dráyt, kwə- ‖ *U.S.* kwód-rayt) **quadrated, -rating,**

-rates. To correspond; agree; square. Often used with *with*. [Middle English, square, from Latin *quadrātus*, past participle of *quadrāre*, to make square, from *quadrus*, a square.]

quad·rat·ic (kwo-dráttik, kwə-, kwó-) *adj.* Of, pertaining to, or containing equations whose terms are of the second degree or less. [From QUADRATE.] —**quad·rat·ic** *n.*

quadratic equation *n.* An equation of the second degree, having the general form $ax^2 + bx + c = 0$, where *a*, *b*, and *c* are constants.

quadratic formula *n.* The formula $x = [-b \pm \sqrt{(b^2 - 4ac)}]/2a$, used to calculate the roots of a quadratic equation.

quad·rat·ics (kwo-dráttiks, kwə-, kwó-) *n. Used with a singular verb.* The algebra of quadratic equations.

quad·ra·ture (kwódrə-chər, -tewr) *n.* **1.** The process of making something square. **2.** *Mathematics.* The process of constructing a square equal in area to a given surface. **3.** *Astronomy.* Any configuration in which the angular separation of two celestial bodies, as measured from a third, is 90°. **4.** *Electronics.* The state in which two alternating signals of the same frequency differ in phase by 90°.

quad·ren·ni·al (kwo-drénni-əl, kwó-) *adj.* **1.** Happening once in four years. **2.** Lasting for four years.
~*n.* An event occurring every four years. —**quad·ren·ni·al·ly** *adv.*

quad·ren·ni·um (kwo-drénni-əm, kwó-) *n., pl.* **-ums** or **-nia** (-ə). A period of four years. [Latin *quadr(i)ennium* : QUADR(I)- + *annus*, year.]

quadri-, quadr– *comb. form.* Indicates four; for example, **quadriceps, quadric.** [Latin; akin to *quattuor*, four.]

quad·ric (kwódrik) *adj.* Of, pertaining to, or designating geometric surfaces that are defined by quadratic equations. [QUADR(I)- + -IC.]

quad·ri·cen·ten·ni·al (kwódri-sen-ténni-əl) *n. Chiefly U.S.* A 400th anniversary. —**quad·ri·cen·ten·ni·al** *adj.*

quad·ri·ceps (kwódri-seps) *n., pl.* **quadriceps** or **-cepses** (-sepsiz). The large four-part extensor muscle at the front of the thigh. [New Latin : QUADRI- + (BI)CEPS.] —**quad·ri·cip·i·tal** (-síppit'l) *adj.*

quad·ri·ga (kwo-dréegə, kwə-, -drígə) *n.* In classical times, a chariot drawn by four horses.

quad·ri·lat·er·al (kwódri-láttrəl, -láttərəl) *n. Abbr.* **quad.** In geometry, a four-sided polygon.
~*adj. Abbr.* **quad.** Having four sides.

qua·drille¹ (kwə-dríl, kwo-, *rarely* kə-) *n.* **1.** A dance of French origin composed of five figures and performed by four or more couples. **2.** A piece of music for this dance in 6/8 and 2/4 time. [French, originally "one of the four divisions of an army, group of knights at a tournament", from Spanish *cuadrilla*, diminutive of *cuadra*, "square", from Latin *quadra*.]

quadrille² *n.* A card game popular during the 18th century, played by four people with a pack of 40 cards. [French, perhaps from Spanish *cuartillo*, from *cuarto*, fourth, from Latin *quārtus*; assimilated to QUADRILLE (dance).]

quad·ril·li·on (kwó-dríl-iən, kwo-, kwə-) *n.* **1.** *British.* The cardinal number represented by 1 followed by 24 zeros, usually written 10^{24}. **2.** *U.S.* The cardinal number represented by 1 followed by 15 zeros, usually written 10^{15}. [French : QUADR(I)- + (M)ILLION.] —**quad·ril·li·on** *adj.* —**quad·ril·li·onth** *n. & adj.*

quad·ri·no·mi·al (kwódri-nómi-əl) *n.* A polynomial with four terms. [QUADRI- + -nomial (as in binomial).]

quad·ri·par·tite (kwódri-pártīt) *adj.* **1.** Consisting of or divided into four parts. **2.** Involving four participants.

quad·ri·ple·gi·a (kwódri-plée-jə, -ji-ə) *n. Medicine.* Paralysis of all four limbs. Also called "tetraplegia". [QUADRI- + -PLEGIA.] —**quad·ri·ple·gic** (-pléejik) *adj. & n.*

quad·ri·va·lent (kwódri-váylənt) *adj. Chemistry.* **1.** Having four valencies. **2.** *Rare.* Having a valency of four; tetravalent. —**quad·ri·va·lence, quad·ri·va·len·cy** *n.*

quad·riv·i·um (kwo-drívvi-əm) *n., pl.* **-ia** (-ə). The higher division of the seven liberal arts in the Middle Ages, composed of geometry, astronomy, arithmetic, and music. Compare *trivium.* [Late Latin, from Latin, "place where four ways meet" : QUADRI- + *via*, way.]

quad·roon (kwo-dróon, kwə-) *n.* A person having one Negro grandparent. [Spanish *cuarterón*, from *cuarto*, quarter, from Latin *quārtus.*]

quad·ru·ma·nous (kwo-dróomə-nəss) *adj.* Also **quad·ru·ma·nal** (-n'l). Having four feet with opposable first digits, as do primates other than humans. [New Latin *quadrumana* (noun), neuter plural of *quadrumanus* : *quadru-*, variant of QUADRI- + *manus*, hand.]

quad·ru·ped (kwódroo-ped, *rarely* -pid) *n.* A four-footed animal.
~*adj.* Four-footed. [Latin *quadrupēs* : *quadru-*, variant of QUADRI- + -PED.] —**quad·ru·pe·dal** (-pédd'l, kwo-dróopid'l) *adj.*

quad·ru·ple (kwóddroop'l, kwo-dróop'l, kwə- ‖ -dréwp'l, *also* -drúpp'l) *adj.* **1.** Consisting of or having four parts, members, or copies. **2.** Multiplied by four; four times as much, as many, or as large. **3.** *Music.* Having four beats to the measure: *quadruple time.*
~*n.* A fourfold amount.
~*v.* **quadrupled, -pling, -ples.** —*tr.* To multiply or increase by four; quadruplicate. —*intr.* To be multiplied fourfold. [French, from Latin *quadruplus* : *quadru-*, variant of QUADRI- + *plus*, -fold.]

quad·ru·plet (kwóddroo-plit, -plet, -plət, kwo-dróo- ‖ -dréw-, *also* -drú-) *n.* **1.** A group or combination of four associated by common properties or behaviour. **2.** Any of four offspring born in a single birth. In this sense, also informally called "quad".

quad·ru·pli·cate (kwo-dróopli-kət, -kit, -kayt) *adj.* **1.** Multiplied by four; quadruple. **2.** Fourth in a group or set of four.
~*n.* **1.** Any of a set of four. **2.** A set of four copies.

~*v.* (-kayt) **quadruplicated, -cating, -cates.** —*tr.* To multiply by four. —*intr.* To become quadruplicated. [Latin *quadruplicātus*, past participle of *quadruplicāre*, to multiply by four, from *quadruplex*, fourfold : *quadru-*, variant of QUADRI- + -plex, -fold.] —**quad·ru·pli·cate·ly** *adv.* —**quad·ru·pli·ca·tion** (-káysh'n) *n.*

quad·ru·plic·i·ty (kwóddroo-plíssəti) *n.* The state of being quadruple or of being multiplied by four. [Latin *quadruplex*, fourfold. See **quadruplicate.**]

quaes·tor (kwéest-ər, -awr ‖ *U.S. also* kwést-) *n.* Any of various public officials in ancient Rome responsible for finance or administration in various areas of government. [Middle English *questor*, from Latin *quaestor*, from *quaerere* (past participial stem *quaesīt-*), to seek, ask.] —**quaes·to·ri·al** (kwee-stáwri-əl ‖ kwe-, -stóri-) *adj.* —**quaes·tor·ship** *n.*

quaff (kwoff, kwaaf ‖ kwaf) *v.* **quaffed, quaffing, quaffs.** —*tr.* To drink deeply. —*intr.* To take a long, deep draught.
~*n.* A long, deep draught. [Perhaps imitative.] —**quaff·er** *n.*

quag·ga (kwággə ‖ kwáagə; *South African* kwákhə) *n.* A zebra-like mammal, *Equus quagga*, of southern Africa, that has been extinct since the late 19th century. [Xhosa *iqwara.*]

quag·gy (kwóggi, kwággi) *adj.* **-gier, -giest. 1.** Like a marsh; soggy. **2.** Soft; flabby. [From *quag*, marshy place; akin to dialect *quag*, to tremble, shake (imitative).]

quag·mire (kwóg-mīr, kwág-) *n.* **1.** A bog or swamp. Also called "quag". **2.** A difficult or precarious situation from which extrication is almost impossible. [From *quag* (see QUAGGY) + MIRE.]

qua·hog (kwáw-hog, kwáa-, káw- ‖ *U.S. also* kố-, -hawg) *n.* An edible clam, *Venus mercenaria*, having a hard, rounded shell. [Narraganset *poquaûhock.*]

quaich, quaigh (kwaykh) *n.* A two-handled Scottish drinking cup of varying size. [Scottish Gaelic *cuach*, from Old Irish *cúach*, from Latin *caucus*, drinking cup, from Greek *kauka, kaukion.*]

Quai d'Or·say (káy dór-say, dawr-sáy). Quay on the left bank of the river Seine in Paris, which has given its name to the French Ministry of Foreign Affairs located there.

quail¹ (kwayl) *n., pl.* **quails** or *collectively* **quail. 1.** Any of various small partridge-like Old World birds of the family Phasianidae; especially, *Coturnix coturnix*, having mottled brown plumage and a distinctive cry. **2.** Any of various similar or related New World birds, such as the **bobwhite** *(see).* [Middle English *quaille*, from Old French, from Medieval Latin *coacula* (imitative of its cry).]

quail² *intr.v.* **quailed, quailing, quails.** To lose courage; recoil in fear; cower. See Synonyms at **recoil.** [Middle English *quailent*, to decline, fail, give way.]

quaint (kwaynt) *adj.* **quainter, quaintest. 1.** Agreeably curious, especially in an old-fashioned way: *a quaint little old cottage.* **2.** Unfamiliar or unusual in character; odd; strange: *what quaint manners you have.* **3.** Inappropriate; illogical: *They fought the war out of a quaint sense of honour.* —See Synonyms at **strange.** [Middle English *queinte, cointe*, clever, skilfully made, from Old French *cointe*, expert, elegant, from Latin *cognitus*, past participle of *cognōscere*, to be acquainted with : *com-*, with + *gnōscere*, to know.] —**quaint·ly** *adv.* —**quaint·ness** *n.*

quake (kwayk) *intr.v.* **quaked, quaking, quakes. 1.** To shake or tremble with instability or shock: *The ground quaked.* **2.** To shiver or tremble, as with cold or strong emotion: *quaking with rage.* —See Synonyms at **shake.**
~*n.* **1.** An instance of quaking; a shake. **2.** *Informal.* An earthquake. [Middle English *quaken*, Old English *cwacian*, from Germanic *kwei-* (unattested), to shake.] —**quak·i·ly** *adv.* —**quak·y** *adj.*

Quak·er (kwáykər) *n.* A member of the Religious Society of Friends *(see).* Not used officially by the Friends. [From QUAKE, probably in allusion to the admonition of George Fox, founder of the Society, to "tremble at the word of the Lord".] —**Quak·er** *adj.* —**Quak·er·ism** *n.* —**Quak·er·ly** *adj. & adv.*

quak·ing aspen (kwáyking) *n.* A tree, the aspen *(see).*

quaking grass *n.* Any of several grass species of the genus *Briza*, having delicate, spreading panicles with ovoid spikelets. [Referring to its motion in wind.]

qual·i·fi·ca·tion (kwóllifi-káysh'n) *n.* **1.** Any quality, accomplishment, or ability that makes a person suitable for a particular position or task. **2.** A degree, diploma, or other evidence of successful completion of a course of study or training: *left school without any qualifications.* **3.** A condition or circumstance that must be met or complied with. **4.** A restriction or modification: *an offer with a number of qualifications.*

qual·i·fied (kwólli-fīd) *adj.* **1.** Having the appropriate qualifications for an office, position, or task. **2.** Limited, restricted, or modified: *gave qualified approval.* —**qual·i·fied·ly** (-fīd-li ‖ -fī-idli) *adv.*

qual·i·fi·er (kwólli-fī-ər) *n.* **1.** One that qualifies or has qualified: *Five qualifiers proceeded to the final.* **2.** A preliminary round or heat in a contest of selection process. **3.** *Grammar.* A **modifier** *(see).*

qual·i·fy (kwólli-fī) *v.* **-fied, -fying, -fies.** —*tr.* **1.** To describe by enumerating the characteristics or qualities of; characterise. **2.** To make competent or suitable for an office, position, or task. **3.** To authorise to work or act legally. **4.** To modify, limit, or restrict, as by giving exceptions. **5.** To make less harsh or severe; moderate. **6.** *Grammar.* To modify the meaning of (a word or phrase). —*intr.* **1.** To be or to become qualified. **2.** To reach the later or final stages of a contest or selection process by competing successfully in earlier rounds. [French *qualifier*, from Medieval Latin *quālificāre*, to attribute a quality to : Latin *quālis*, of what kind (see **quality**) + *facere*, to make.]

qual·i·ta·tive (kwólli-tətiv, -taytiv) *adj.* Of, pertaining to, or concerning quality or qualities: *A purely qualitative assessment, taking no account of number or size.* [Late Latin *quālitātivus,* from Latin *quālitās,* QUALITY.] **—qual·i·ta·tive·ly** *adv.*

qualitative analysis *n.* Chemical determination of the constituents of a substance without regard to quantity. Compare **quantitative analysis.**

Qua·li·täts·wein (kwólli-táyts-vīn; *German* kvál-ee-) *n.* **1.** A designation awarded to a wine produced in Germany, officially testifying to its quality and its origin in any of several specified regions. **2.** A wine thus endorsed. [German, "quality wine".]

qual·i·ty (kwólləti) *n., pl.* **-ties.** *Abbr.* **qlty. 1.** A characteristic or attribute of something; a property; a feature: *Her worst quality is her impatience.* **2.** The natural or essential character of something: *the hard quality of mahogany.* **3.** Degree or grade of excellence: *goods of low quality.* **4.** Excellence; superiority. **5.** *Archaic.* **a.** High social position. **b.** People of high social position. Preceded by *the.* **6.** *Music.* Timbre, as determined by overtones. **7.** *Phonetics.* The character of a vowel sound determined by the size and shape of the oral cavity and the amount of resonance with which the sound is produced. **8.** *Logic.* The positive or negative character of a proposition. **9.** *Informal.* A newspaper or magazine of a relatively high intellectual standard, and usually having a relatively low circulation.
~*adj.* Having high quality; excellent: *quality goods; quality entertainment.* [Middle English *qualite,* from Old French, from Latin *quālitās* (stem *quālitāt-*), from *quālis,* of what kind.]
Synonyms: *quality, property, attribute, character, trait.*

quality factor *n.* The **Q factor** *(see).*

quality of life *n.* The degree of emotional, intellectual, or cultural satisfaction in one's everyday life, as distinct from the degree of material comfort. Compare **standard of living.**

qualm (kwaam, kwawm || kwaalm) *n.* **1.** *Often plural.* A feeling of misgiving, uneasiness, or doubt, especially over a matter of conscience. **2.** A sudden feeling of sickness, faintness, or nausea. [16th century : origin obscure.] **—qualm·ish** *adj.* **—qualm·ish·ly** *adv.*
Synonyms: *qualm, scruple, compunction, misgiving, reservation.*

quamash. Variant of **camass.**

quan·da·ry (kwóndəri || kwóndri) *n., pl.* **-ries.** A state of uncertainty or perplexity; a dilemma. See Synonyms at **predicament.** [16th century : origin obscure.]

quan·dong, quan·dang (kwón-dong) *n.* **1.** A shrubby Australian tree, *Santalum acuminatus* which, yields an edible fruit containing an edible seed. Also called "native peach". **2.** An Australian tree the brush quandong, *Elaeocarpus grandis,* producing straw-coloured, easily worked timber. [From a native Australian language.]

quan·go (kwáng-gō) *n., pl.* **-gos.** A *quasi-a*utonomous *n*ational *g*overnment (or *n*ongovernmental) *o*rganisation: any of numerous government-sponsored agencies or authorities with independent powers.

quant (kwont) *n.* A long pole used manually to propel a flat-bottomed boat, such as a punt, over shallow waterways. [Perhaps from Latin *contus,* from Greek *kontos,* pole for propelling a boat.] **—quant** *v.*

Quant (kwont), **Mary** (1934–). British fashion designer. She opened her first boutique in 1957 with her husband, Alexander Plunket Greene, and by the 1960s had become one of the world's most influential designers. She was awarded the O.B.E. in 1966.

quan·ta. Plural of **quantum.**

quan·tal (kwónt'l) *adj. Physics.* **1.** Of or pertaining to a quantum or a quantised system. **2.** Existing in only one of two possible states.

quan·ta·some (kwóntə-sōm) *n. Botany.* Any of the small particles occurring on the surface of the membranes of chloroplasts on which are thought to be the functional units of photosynthesis. [Probably from Latin *quanta,* "how many", plural of QUANTUM + -SOME.]

quan·tic (kwóntik) *n. Mathematics.* A homogeneous polynomial having two or more variables, as in $x^3 + x^2y + y^2x + y^3$. See **quadric, cubic, quartic.** [Latin *quantus,* how much + -IC.]

quan·ti·fi·er (kwónti-fī-ər) *n.* **1.** One that quantifies. **2.** *Grammar.* A modifier indicating range, quantity, or application, such as *many* or *four.* **3.** *Logic.* An operator, or its symbol, indicating range, quantity, or application; especially, a *universal quantifier,* which indicates that every object of the kind specified is being referred to, and an *existential quantifier,* which indicates that at least one such object does actually exist.

quan·ti·fy (kwónti-fī) *tr.v.* **-fied, -fying, -fies. 1.** To determine or express the quantity of: *One cannot quantify the value of a human life.* **2.** *Logic.* To limit the quantity of (a term or proposition) by prefixing a quantifier such as *all, some,* or *none.* [Medieval Latin *quantificāre* : *quantus,* how great + *facere,* to make.] **—quan·ti·fi·a·ble** (-fī-əb'l || -fī-əb'l) *adj.* **—quan·ti·fi·ca·tion** (-fi-káysh'n) *n.*

quan·tise, quan·tize (kwónt-īz) *tr.v.* **-tised, -tising, -tises.** *Physics.* **1.** To limit the possible values of (a magnitude or quantity) to a set of discrete values by quantum mechanical rules. **2.** To replace the dynamic variables of (a system) by the corresponding quantum mechanical operators in order to calculate the behaviour of the system. [QUANT(UM) + -ISE.] **—quan·ti·sa·tion** (-ī-záysh'n || *U.S.* -i-) *n.*

quan·ti·ta·tive (kwónti-tətiv, -taytiv) *adj.* **1. a.** Expressed or capable of expression as a quantity. **b.** Of, pertaining to, or susceptible of measurement. **c.** Pertaining to or based upon duration of sound rather than stress. Said especially of classical verse. [Medieval Latin *quantitātivus,* from Latin *quantitās,* QUANTITY.] **—quan·ti·ta·tive·ly** *adv.*

quantitative analysis *n.* Chemical determination of the amounts or proportions of constituents in a substance. Compare **qualitative analysis.**

quan·ti·ty (kwóntəti) *n., pl.* **-ties.** *Abbr.* **qt., qty. 1. a.** A number or amount of anything, either specified or indefinite. **b.** A considerable amount or number. **2.** The measurable, countable, or comparable property or aspect of a thing. **3.** Anything serving as the object of a mathematical operation. **4.** *Phonetics.* The length of a vowel or consonant sound expressed in terms of the time needed to produce it. **5.** *Logic.* The exact character of a proposition in respect of its universality, singularity, or particularity. **6.** *Physics.* An attribute that can be measured and assigned a value of a certain number of units. In this sense, also called "physical quantity". [Middle English *quantite,* from Old French, from Latin *quantitās* (stem *quantitāt-*), from *quantus,* how great.]

quantity surveyor *n.* A person who estimates, usually as a profession, the amounts and overall cost of the materials and labour needed in the construction of a building.

quan·tum (kwón-təm) *n., pl.* **-ta** (-tə). **1.** The quantity or amount of something. **2.** A specific portion of something. **3.** Something that may be counted or measured. **4.** *Physics.* A discrete, indivisible amount of some quantity, especially energy or angular momentum, by which a given system may change in any process. [Latin, neuter of *quantus,* how great.]

quantum chromodynamics *n. Physics.* **Chromodynamics** *(see).*

quantum electrodynamics *n. Physics.* The quantum-mechanical theory of the properties and interactions of charged elementary particles with each other and with electromagnetic radiation.

quantum gravitation *n. Physics.* A theory of gravitation in which interactions are caused by the exchange of particles (gravitons).

quantum jump *n.* **1.** *Physics.* The transition of an atomic or molecular system from one discrete energy level to another. It usually occurs with absorption or emission of radiation having energy equal to the difference between the two levels. **2.** Any abrupt change or step from one level or category to a quite different one, especially in knowledge or information. Also called "quantum leap".

quantum mechanics *n. Mathematics & Physics.* A formulation of the early ideas arising from quantum theory. It is used to interpret atomic and nuclear phenomena. See **wave mechanics, matrix mechanics, black-body radiation.**

quantum number *n. Physics.* Any of a set of real numbers that individually characterise the properties and collectively specify the state of a particle or of a system which is quantised.

quantum state *n. Physics.* Any one of the possible states of a system described by quantum theory.

quantum statistics *n. Physics.* The use of statistics to determine the properties of large numbers of particles by calculating the distribution of the particles over possible quantum states. See **Fermi-Dirac statistics, Bose-Einstein statistics.**

quantum theory *n.* A mathematical theory of physical systems that was developed to account for several physical phenomena that could not be explained by classical mechanics. It postulates that a system can gain or lose energy only in descrete amounts (quanta). Further developments led to the theory of **wave-particle duality** *(see)* and were formalised in quantum mechanics.

quar. 1. quarter. **2.** quarterly.

quar·an·tine (kwórrən-teen, *rarely* -tīn || *U.S. also* kwáwrən-) *n.* **1. a.** A period of time, originally lasting 40 days, during which a vehicle, a person, an animal, or goods suspected of carrying a contagious disease are detained at their port of entry under enforced isolation to prevent disease from entering a country. **b.** A place for such detention. **2.** Enforced isolation or restriction of free movement imposed to prevent a contagious disease from spreading. **3.** Any enforced isolation.
~*tr.v.* **quarantined, -tining, -tines. 1.** To place in quarantine. **2.** To isolate politically or economically. [Italian *quarantina,* period of forty days, from *quaranta,* forty, from Latin *quadrāgintā.*]

quark[1] (kwaark, kwawrk) *n. Physics.* Any of a hypothetical set of fermions having electric charges of magnitude one third or two thirds that of the electron, proposed (together with their antiparticles) as the fundamental units of baryons and mesons. [From a line in James Joyce's *Finnegans Wake,* "three quarks for Muster Mark".]

quark[2] (kwaark, kfaark) *n.* A low-fat, soft cheese made of skimmed milk and often served mixed with fruit.

quar·rel[1] (kwórrəl || kwáwrəl) *n.* **1.** An angry dispute; a disagreement; an argument. **2.** A cause for dispute or argument: *We have no quarrel with the findings.*
~*intr.v.* **quarrelled** or *U.S.* **quarreled, -relling** or *U.S.* **-reling, -rels. 1.** To engage in a quarrel; argue angrily. **2.** To disagree; differ. **3.** To find fault with something; complain. —See Synonyms at **argue.** [Middle English, (cause for) complaint, from Old French, from Latin *querēla,* from *querī,* to complain.] **—quar·rel·ler** *n.*

quarrel[2] *n.* **1.** A bolt for a crossbow. **2.** A small diamond-shaped or square pane of glass in a latticed window. [Middle English *quarel,* from Old French, from Vulgar Latin *quadrellus* (unattested), diminutive of Late Latin *quadrus,* square.]

quar·rel·some (kwórrəl-səm || kwáwrəl-) *adj.* Characterised by quarrelling or tending to quarrel. See Synonyms at **belligerent.**

quar·ri·on (kwórri-ən) *n.* A parrot, the **cockatiel** *(see).* [Probably from an Australian native name.]

quar·ry[1] (kwórri || kwáwri) *n., pl.* **-ries. 1.** A bird or other animal that is hunted, or such animals collectively; prey; game. **2.** Any object of pursuit. [Middle English *querre,* entrails of a beast given

quarry² *A quarry at Carrara in Italy, whose fine white marble has been prized by sculptors from Roman times to the present day. The Renaissance artist Michelangelo carved his statue of David from a single block of unflawed Carrara marble.*

to the hounds, from Anglo-French, Old French *cuiree,* variant of *co(u)ree,* from Vulgar Latin *corāta,* viscera, from Latin *cor,* heart.]

quarry² *n., pl.* **-ries. 1.** An open excavation or pit from which stone is obtained by digging, cutting, or blasting. **2.** A source from which material, such as information, can be extracted.
~*v.* **quarried, -rying, -ries.** —*tr.* **1.** To cut, dig, blast, or otherwise obtain (stone) from a quarry. **2.** To obtain (information) by long, careful searching. **3.** To use (land) as a quarry. —*intr.* To obtain material from or as if from a quarry. [Middle English *quarey, quarere,* from Old French *quarriere,* from *quarre* (unattested), "square stone", from Latin *quadrus,* square.] **—quar·ri·er** *n.*

quarry³ *n., pl.* **-ries. 1.** A square or diamond shape. **2.** A pane of glass of this shape. [Variant of QUARREL (bolt).]

quart¹ (kwawrt || kawrt) *n. Abbr.* **q., qt.** A unit of liquid measure equal to two pints or a quarter of a gallon, and equivalent: **1.** In the British imperial system, to 1.136 litres. **2.** In the U.S. customary system, to 0.946 litres. [Middle English, from Old French *quarte, quārta,* feminine of Latin *quārtus,* fourth.]

quart² (kart) *n.* In card games like piquet, a sequence of four cards in one suit. [French *quarte,* fourth, QUARTE.]

quar·tan (kwáwrt'n) *adj.* Occurring every fourth day, counting inclusively, or every 72 hours. Said of a fever.
~*n.* A recurrent malarial fever, occurring every 72 hours. Also called "quartan malaria". [Middle English *quarteyne,* from Old French *quartaine,* from Latin *quārtāna (fēbris),* "quartan fever", from *quārtānus,* of the fourth, from *quārtus,* fourth.]

quarte, quart (kart) *n.* The fourth regular position in fencing. [French, "fourth", "quart", from Old French. See **quart.**]

quar·ter (kwáwtər || kwáwrtər, káwtər) *n. Abbr.* **q., qr., quar. 1.** Any of four equal parts of something. **2. a.** A period of fifteen minutes. **b.** The point on a clock's face marking either 15 minutes after or 15 minutes before an hour. Also called "quarter-hour". **3.** A coin equal to one fourth of the dollar of the United States and Canada. **4. a.** One fourth of a year; three months. **b.** *U.S.* An academic term lasting for approximately three months. **5.** *Astronomy.* **a.** One-fourth of the period of the Moon's revolution around the Earth. **b.** Either of two of the visible phases of the Moon: the *first quarter,* from new moon until it approaches fullness; and the *third quarter,* from after fullness until it has disappeared in the sunrise. **6.** *Sports. Chiefly U.S.* Any of four equal periods of playing time into which some games are divided. **7.** A fourth of any of various units of weight or measure, as of a yard, a mile, a pound, or a hundredweight. **8.** *British.* A measure of grain equal to approximately eight bushels. **9. a.** Any of the four major divisions of the compass: north, south, east, or west. **b.** A fourth of the distance between any two of the 32 divisions of the compass. **10. a.** The general direction on either side of a ship located 45 degrees off the stern. **b.** Any of the four major divisions of the horizon as determined by the four points of the compass. **c.** Any region or area of the earth thought of as falling in such a specified division. **11. a.** The upper portion of the aft side of a ship, usually between the aftermost mast and the stern. **b.** The part of a yard between the slings and the yardarm. **12.** *Heraldry.* Any of four divisions of a shield. **13.** Any of the four limbs of a carcass of an animal, usually including the adjoining parts. **14.** Either side of a horse's hoof. **15.** The part of the side of a shoe between the heel and the vamp. **16.** *Plural.* A place of residence; specifically, the buildings or barracks housing military personnel. **17.** *Usually plural.* A proper or assigned station or place, as for officers and crew on a warship. **18.** A district or section, as of a city, especially characterised by a specified group of people or activity: *the Latin quarter.* **19.** *Often plural.* An unnamed person or group of persons considered as a source of something, such as help or information: *got help from the highest quarters; no news from that quarter.* **20.** Mercy or clemency, especially when shown to an enemy: *gave no quarter.*
~*v.* **quartered, -tering, -ters.** —*tr.* **1. a.** To cut or otherwise divide into four equal or equivalent parts. **b.** To quartersaw (a log). **2.** To divide or separate into a number of parts. **3.** Formerly, to cut or dismember (a human body) into four parts: *hung, drawn, and quartered.* **4.** *Heraldry.* **a.** To divide (a shield) into four equal areas with vertical and horizontal lines. **b.** To place (a charge) in a quarter or quarters. **5. a.** To mark or place (holes, for example) a fourth of a circle apart. **b.** To fix (one machine part) at right angles to its connecting part. **6.** To provide (soldiers, for example) with lodgings. **7.** To traverse (an area of ground) laterally back and forth while slowly moving forward. Used especially of hunting dogs. —*intr.* **1.** To take up or be assigned lodgings. **2.** To traverse an area of ground by ranging over it from side to side.
~*adj.* **1.** Being one of four equal or equivalent parts. **2.** Being a fourth of a standard or usual value. [Middle English, from Old French *quartier,* from Latin *quārtārius,* from *quārtus,* fourth.]

quar·ter·age (kwáwtərij) *n.* A monetary allowance, wage, or payment made or received quarterly.

quar·ter·bound (kwáwtər-bównd) *adj.* Bound in leather or similar material only along the spine and adjoining part of the boards, as is this dictionary.

quarter day *n.* Any of the four days of the year regarded as the beginning of a new season or quarter, when most quarterly payments are due. In England, Wales, and Ireland, these days are Lady Day, Midsummer Day, Michaelmas, and Christmas; in Scotland they are Candlemas, Whit Sunday, Martinmas, and Lammas.

quar·ter·deck (kwáwtər-dek) *n.* The after part of the upper deck of a sailing ship, usually reserved for officers.

quar·ter·fi·nal (kwáwtər-fín'l) *n.* In a competition or tournament, any of four matches constituting a round or stage whose winners go on to play in the semifinal round. **—quar·ter·fi·nal** *adj.*

quarter horse *n.* A strong saddle horse of a breed developed in the western United States. [Formerly trained for races of up to a quarter of a mile.]

quar·ter·ing (kwáwtəring) *n. Heraldry.* **1.** The combining of different coats of arms on one shield, thereby showing the uniting of different families. **2.** *Plural.* The coats of arms so displayed.

quar·ter·light (kwáwtər-līt) *n. British.* A small triangular window in the front of a car, next to the main side window.

quar·ter·ly (kwáwtərli) *adj. Abbr.* **q., qr., quar. 1.** Occurring or appearing at regular intervals of three months: *a quarterly magazine; a quarterly payment.* **2.** Having four sections. Said of a heraldic shield.
~*n., pl.* **quarterlies.** *Abbr.* **q., qr., quar.** A publication issued regularly every three months. **—quar·ter·ly** *adv.*

quar·ter·mas·ter (kwáwtər-maastər || -mastər) *n. Abbr.* **Q.M. 1.** A military officer responsible for the food, clothing, and equipment of troops. **2.** A naval petty officer responsible for the steering of a ship, and other navigational duties. [From QUARTER (residence).]

Quartermaster General *n. Abbr.* **Q.M.G.** A military officer in charge of the branch of the army that deals with food, clothing, equipment, and other supplies.

quar·tern (kwáwt'n || kwáwtərn) *n.* **1.** A fourth of something. **2.** *British.* A loaf weighing about four pounds. [Middle English *quarteron,* from Old French, from *quartier,* QUARTER.]

quarter note *n. Music. Chiefly U.S.* A note, the **crotchet** *(see).*

quar·ter-phase (kwáwtər-fayz) *adj. Electronics.* Two-phase.

quar·ter·saw (kwáwtər-saw) *tr.v.* **-sawed, -sawed** or **-sawn, -sawing, -saws.** To saw (a log) into quarters lengthways along its axis.

quarter sessions *n. Law.* Formerly in Britain, a court held at least four times a year to try offences and hear appeals. In 1972 it was abolished and its jurisdiction transferred to the crown courts.

quar·ter·staff (kwáwtər-staaf || -staf) *n., pl.* **-staves** (-stayvz). A long wooden staff, formerly used as a weapon.

quarter tone *n. Music.* Half a **semitone** *(see).*

quar·tet, quar·tette (kwáwr-tét, káwr-) *n.* **1.** A musical composition for: **a.** Four singers. **b.** Four instruments, especially stringed instruments. **2.** A group of four performing musicians. **3.** Any set of four persons or things. [French *quartette,* Italian *quartetto,* diminutive of *quarto,* fourth, from Latin *quārto.* See **quarto.**]

quar·tic (kwáwrtik || káwrtik) *adj. Mathematics.* Of or pertaining to the fourth degree; biquadratic.
~*n. Mathematics.* An algebraic equation of the fourth degree. Also called "biquadratic". [From Latin *quārtus,* fourth.]

quar·tile (kwáwr-tīl || káwr-, *U.S.* -t'l) *n. Statistics.* The value of the boundary at the 25th, 50th, or 75th percentiles of a frequency distribution divided into four parts, each containing a quarter of the population. [Medieval Latin *quārtīlis,* of a quartile, from Latin *quārtus,* fourth. See **quarto.**] **—quar·tile** *adj.*

quar·to (kwáwrtō) *n., pl.* **-tos.** *Abbr.* **q., Q., qto. 1.** The page size obtained by folding a whole sheet into four leaves. **2.** A book composed of pages of this size or folded in this way. Also written *4to, 4°.* **3.** A size of paper, 8 by 10 inches (203 by 256 millimetres). [Latin *(in) quārto,* in quarter, from *quārtus,* fourth.] **—quar·to** *adj.*

quartz (kwáwrts || káwrts) *n.* **1.** A hard, crystalline, vitreous mineral form of silicon dioxide, SiO_2, found worldwide in such varieties as agate, chalcedony, chert, flint, opal, and rock crystal. It may be clear and transparent (as in rock crystal) or any of various colours, such as purple (as in amethyst) or yellow (as in citrine). **2.** Quartz glass.
~*adj.* **1.** Made of quartz. **2.** Designating a timepiece that is regulated by electronic circuitry using a small quartz crystal to operate its mechanism and produce a high degree of accuracy. [From German *Quarz,* from Middle High German *quarz,* from old West Slavonic *kwardy,* hard.]

quartz crystal *n.* A small crystal of quartz accurately cut along certain axes so that it can be vibrated at a particular frequency, used for its piezoelectric properties to produce an electrical signal of constant known frequency.

quartz glass *n.* A pure silica glass, highly transparent to ultraviolet radiations.

quartz·if·er·ous (kwáwrts-íffərəss) *adj.* Containing quartz.

quartz-i·o·dine lamp (kwáwrts-ī-ə-deen || *U.S. also* -əd'n, -ə-dīn) *n.* A type of lamp, used especially for car headlights, having a quartz envelope containing inert gas with a small amount of iodine vapour and a tungsten filament. The iodine vapour improves the brightness of the lamp. Also called "quartz-iodide lamp".

quartz·ite (kwáwrts-īt) *n.* A metamorphic rock resulting from the recrystallisation of sandstone.

qua·sar (kwáy-zaar, -saar) *n. Astronomy.* A member of any of several classes of starlike objects having exceptionally large red shifts that are often emitters of radio frequency as well as visible radiation and have apparently immense speeds, energies, and distances from Earth. Also called "quasi-stellar object". [*Quas*i stell*ar.*]

quash (kwosh) *tr.v.* **quashed, quashing, quashes. 1.** *Law.* To set aside or annul. **2.** To put down or suppress forcibly and completely. [Middle English *quassen,* from Old French *quasser, casser,* from Late Latin *cassāre,* from Latin *cassus,* empty, void.]

qua·si (kwáy-zī, kwaá-, kwá-, -sī, -zi) *adv.* To some degree; almost or somewhat. Usually used in combination: *quasi-scientific literature.*

~*adj.* Resembling but not being something specified. Used in combination: *a quasi-victory.* [Latin *quasi,* as if : *quam,* than, how, as + *sī,* if.]

Qua·si·mo·do (kwáazi-mṓdō; *Italian* kwa-zéemodo), **Salvatore** (1901–68). Italian poet. Though his earlier work drew on an idyllic childhood in Sicily, his postwar writing, such as *Il falso e vero verde* (1956), reflects concern over social issues. He was awarded the Nobel prize in 1959.

qua·si·stel·lar object (kwáyzī-stéllər, kwáazī-) *n. Abbr.* **QSO** A quasar.

quasi-stellar radio source *n. Abbr.* **QSRS** *Astronomy.* A quasi-stellar object which is only detected by its radio emission. Not in technical usage.

quas·sia (kwóshə) *n.* **1. a.** A tree, *Quassia amara,* of tropical America, having bright scarlet flowers. **b.** The wood or bark of this tree. **2.** A bitter substance obtained from the wood and bark of this tree and related trees, used in medicine and as an insecticide. [New Latin, after Graman *Quassi,* 18th-century native of Surinam, who discovered its medicinal properties.]

qua·ter·nar·y (kwə-térnəri, kwo- || *U.S. also* kwóttər-nerri) *adj.* **1.** Consisting of four; in fours. **2.** *Chemistry.* **a.** Designating a compound having four groups connected to a nitrogen or phosphorus atom. **b.** Designating a compound consisting of four different atoms or radicals.

~*n., pl.* **quaternaries. 1.** The number four. **2.** A set of four objects. [Middle English, set of four, from Latin *quaternārius,* consisting of four each, from *quaternī,* four each, from *quater,* four times.]

Qua·ter·nar·y (kwə-térnəri, kwo- || *U.S. also* kwóttər-nerri) *adj. Geology.* Of, belonging to, or designating the geological time and system of rocks, and sedimentary deposits of the second period of the Cenozoic era, from the end of the Tertiary (two million years ago) to the present, characterised by the appearance and development of human beings, and including the Pleistocene and Holocene epochs.

~*n. Geology.* The Quaternary period or system of deposits. Preceded by *the.* [From QUATERNARY (fourth).]

quaternary ammonium compound *n. Chemistry.* Any of a class of compounds containing an ion NR_4^+, where R is an organic group or a hydrogen atom.

qua·ter·ni·on (kwə-térni-ən, kwo-) *n.* **1.** A set of four persons or items. **2.** *Mathematics.* An element of a system of four dimensional vectors obeying laws similar to those of complex numbers. [Middle English, from Late Latin *quaterniō* (stem *quaterniōn-*), from Latin *quaternī,* four each. See **quaternary.**]

quat·rain (kwóttrayn || kwo-tráyn) *n.* A stanza of verse having four lines that often rhyme alternately. [French, from Old French, from *quatre,* four, from Latin *quattuor.*]

quat·re·foil (káttrə-foyl, káttər-) *n.* **1.** A figure of a flower with four petals or a leaf with four leaflets, especially in heraldry. **2.** *Architecture.* An ornament or tracery with four foils or lobes. **3.** *Geometry.* A curve that has four lobes. [Middle English *quaterfoile,* set of four leaves : *quater-,* four, from Old French *quatre* + FOIL (leaf).]

quat·tro·cen·to (kwóttrō-chéntō, kwáttrō-) *n.* The 15th-century period of Italian art and literature. [Italian, short for *(mil)quattro cento,* "(one thousand) four hundred".]

qua·ver (kwáyvər) *v.* **-vered, -vering, -vers.** —*intr.* **1.** To quiver, as from weakness or emotion; tremble. Used especially of the voice. **2.** To speak in a quivering voice. **3.** To produce a trill on a musical instrument or in singing. —*tr.* To utter or sing in a trilling or trembling voice.

~*n.* **1.** *Music.* A note having an eighth of the time value of a whole note. Also *U.S.* "eighth note". **2.** A quivering sound. **3.** A trill. [Middle English *quaveren,* frequentative of obsolete *quaven* (imitative), to tremble, from Germanic; akin to Low German *quabbeln,* to tremble.] —**qua·ver·ing·ly** *adv.* —**qua·ver·y** *adj.*

quay (kee) *n.* A wharf or reinforced bank, such as one that juts out from a harbour, where ships are loaded or unloaded. [Earlier *key,* Middle English *key, kay,* from Old French *chai, cay,* from Gaulish *caio,* rampart, retaining wall.]

quay·age (kée-ij) *n.* **1.** A charge for the use of a quay. **2.** The space available for or on quays. **3.** Quays collectively.

quay·side (kée-sīd) *n.* The area alongside or forming a quay. —**quay·side** *adj.*

quean (kween) *n.* **1.** *Scottish.* A young woman, especially one who is not married. **2.** *Archaic.* An impudent or disreputable woman; especially, a prostitute. [Middle English *quen(e),* Old English *cwene,* woman, wife, from Germanic.]

quea·sy (kwéezi) *adj.* **-sier, -siest. 1.** Nauseated or easily nauseated. **2.** Causing nausea or sickness: *queasy food.* **3. a.** Causing uneasiness. **b.** Uneasy; troubled. **4.** Easily troubled: *a queasy conscience.* [Middle English *coysy, qwesye,* perhaps originally "wounded", from Anglo-French, Old French *coisi* (unattested), akin to *coisier,* to injure.] —**quea·si·ly** *adv.* —**quea·si·ness** *n.*

Que·bec[1] (kwi-bék). *French* **Qué·bec** (kay-bék). Capital of Quebec province, Canada, situated at the confluence of the St. Lawrence and St. Charles rivers in the southeast of the country. A picturesque city, it is the hub of French Canadian culture. It is chiefly a distribution and manufacturing centre with a wide range of industries including timber, printing, textiles, shipbuilding, and iron and steel production. Tourism is also important.

Quebec[2]. Largest province in Canada, in the east of the country. Most of it is part of the Laurentian (or Canadian) Shield, a plateau of hard rock which was scoured by ice sheets and glaciers and is now rich in minerals and timber. Between this block and the Appalachian Mountains in the south lies the valley of the St. Lawrence river. Montreal is at the centre of this rich agricultural strip, which provides cereals and dairy products. Originally a French colony known as New France or Canada (1534–1763), the province still retains French language and customs, and there is a strong separatist movement. Capital, Quebec.

que·bra·cho (ki-bráachō, kay-) *n., pl.* **-chos. 1.** Any of several South American trees having very hard wood; especially, *Aspidosperma quebracho,* the bark of which is used in medicine, and trees of the species *Schinopsis,* whose barks yield tannin. **2.** The bark or wood of any of these trees. [American Spanish, variant of *quiebrahacha,* "axe-breaker" : *quiebra,* from *quebrar,* to break + *hacha,* axe.]

Quech·ua (kéch-wə, -waa || kéchoo-ə, ke-chóo-) *n., pl.* **-uas** or collectively **Quechua.** Also **Quich·ua** (kích-), **Kech·ua. 1.** A member of a South American Indian people originally constituting the ruling class of the Incan Empire. **2.** The language of this people, still spoken by other Indian peoples of Peru, Ecuador, Bolivia, Chile, and Argentina. [Spanish, from Quechua *kkechúwa,* "plunderer", "robber".] —**Quech·uan** *n. & adj.*

queen (kween) *n. Abbr.* **qu. 1.** A female monarch or ruler. **2.** The wife or widow of a king. **3.** A woman, or a thing personified as a woman, who is eminent or supreme in a specified field or area: *a beauty queen; the queen of my heart.* **4.** *Abbr.* **Q** The most powerful piece in chess, able to move in any direction in a straight or diagonal line. **5.** A playing card bearing the figure of a queen, next above the jack and below the king in each suit. **6.** The fertile, fully developed female in a colony of social bees, ants, or termites. **7.** *Slang.* **a.** One who is showily effeminate: *a drag queen.* **b.** A male homosexual. Used derogatorily.

~*v.* **queened, queening, queens.** —*tr.* **1.** To make (a woman) a queen. **2.** *Chess.* To convert (a pawn) into a queen, when it has reached the far end of the board. —*intr.* To reign as queen. —**queen it.** *Slang.* To act or behave in a showy, effeminate manner. [Middle English *qu(e)ene,* Old English *cwēn,* woman, wife, queen, from Germanic.] —**queenship** *n.*

Queen Anne *n.* The style of English architecture (characterised by classical decoration and red brickwork) and furniture (characterised especially by fine upholstery and wood inlays) typical of the reign of Queen Anne (1702–14). Often used adjectivally.

Queen Anne's lace *n.* A widely distributed plant, *Daucus carota,* native to Eurasia, having finely divided leaves and flat clusters of small white flowers. Also called "wild carrot".

Queen Anne's War *n.* See **War of the Spanish Succession.**

queen cake *n.* A small sponge cake often iced or containing currants and sometimes baked in the shape of a heart.

Queen Charlotte Islands. Group of islands off the coast of British Columbia, western Canada. Logging and fishing are the main occupations and the native Indians are renowned for their canoe building. Masset in the north of Graham Island is the chief town.

queen consort *n.* The wife of a reigning king.

queen dowager *n.* The widow of a king.

Queen Elizabeth Islands. Also (until 1954) **Par·ry Islands** (párri). The northern part of the Arctic Archipelago, which forms part of the Northwest Territories of Canada. The islands possess rich oil deposits, exploited since the early 1960s.

queen·ly (kwéenli) *adj.* **-lier, -liest. 1.** Of or resembling a queen. **2.** Pertaining to or befitting a queen. —**queen·li·ness** *n.*

queen mother *n.* A dowager queen who is the mother of the reigning monarch.

queen of puddings *n.* A sweet pudding consisting of a moist jam and breadcrumb mixture topped with meringue.

Queen of the May *n.* A **May Queen** *(see).*

queen post *n.* Either of two upright supporting posts set vertically between the rafters and the tie beam at equal distances from the apex of a roof. Compare **king post.**

Queens (kweenz). Borough of New York City, in the United States at the western end of Long Island, and coextensive with Queen's County.

Queen's Bench *n. Abbr.* **Q.B.** One of the divisions of the English High Court of Justice. Also called "King's Bench" during the reign of a king.

Queens·ber·ry Rules (kwéenz-bri, -bəri || -berri) *pl. n.* **1.** A boxing code of fair play developed in 1867 by the eighth Marquis of Queensberry. **2.** Broadly, any set of rules that prescribe fair play.

Queen's Counsel *n. Abbr.* **Q.C.** A member of a group of pre-eminent barristers nominally appointed to serve as counsel to the British Crown. Also called "King's Counsel" during the reign of a king.

Queen's County. See **Leix.**

Queen's English *n.* British English as traditionally spoken by the middle and upper-middle classes, especially in the south of England, considered to be a standard of correctness. Also called "King's English" during the reign of a king.

queen's evidence *n.* Evidence given for the crown by an accused person against an accomplice in a British legal proceeding. Also called "king's evidence" during the reign of a king.

Queen's highway *n.* In Britain, any public road. Also called "King's highway" during the reign of a king.

Queens·land (kwéenz-lənd, -land. *Note: in Australia usually* -land.) Second largest state in Australia, in the northeast of the country. It includes the adjacent islands in the Pacific Ocean and the Gulf of Carpentaria. The Great Barrier Reef runs along its eastern coastline, and the coastal plains give way to the high peaks of the Great

PRONUNCIATION KEY

a, trap; aa, father; ai, fair; ar, star; aw, lawn; ay, play; b, bb, stab; rubber; ch, church; ck, ticket; d, dd, dead; ladder; e, dress; ee, bee; er, defer; ew, few; ewr, pure; ə, about; ər, letter; f, ff, fife; differ; g, gg, giggle; h, hat; i, kit; ī, price; īr, fire; j, judge; k, kick; l, ll, let; 'l, needle; m, mm, man; n, nn, no; 'n, sudden; ng, thing; o, lot; ō, no; ŏŏ, foot; ōō, shoe; oor, poor; ow, cow; owr, hour; oy, boy; p, pp, pepper; r, rr, red; s, ss, sauce; sh, ship; t, tt, totter; th, thick; th, this; smooth; u, cut; ur, turn; v, vv, valve; w, wet; y, yes; z, zz, zebra; zh, vision; pleasure

IN FOREIGN WORDS:

aN, oN, Saint-Saëns; hl, Llanelli; Hluhluwe; kh, loch; lough; Khaled

STRESS MARK:

ín-sīt, insight; in-sī́t, incite

Dividing Range. There are grasslands on the western hills and vast plains further west. Agriculture and manufacturing are both economically important, and there is also considerable mineral wealth, including copper, coal, gold, bauxite, uranium, oil, and gas. The first settlement, in 1824, was a penal colony. Brisbane is the capital city.

queen's metal *n.* A form of britannia metal containing a small amount of zinc.

Queen's Regulations *n.* The military laws governing discipline, punishment, and the code of conduct of members of the armed forces. Also called "King's Regulations" during the reign of a king.

Queen's shilling *n.* See **King's shilling.**

Queen's speech *n.* In Britain, the **Speech from the Throne** *(see).*

queen truss *n.* A building truss having queen posts.

queer (kweer) *adj.* **queerer, queerest. 1.** Deviating from the expected or normal; strange: *a queer situation.* **2.** Odd or unconventional in behaviour; eccentric. **3.** Arousing suspicion. **4.** *Slang.* Fake; counterfeit. **5.** Unwell; queasy. **6.** *Informal.* Homosexual. Often used derogatorily. —See Synonyms at **strange.**
~*n. Informal.* A homosexual, especially a male one. Used derogatorily. **2.** Counterfeit money.
~*tr.v.* **queered, queering, queers.** *Informal.* **1.** To ruin or spoil. **2.** To put into a bad position. [Perhaps from German *quer,* perverse, cross, from Middle High German *twerch, querch,* from Old High German *twerh, dwerah.* See **thwart.**] **—queer·ly** *adv.* **—queer·ness** *n.*

quern *Querns have been used for grinding grain into flour since before 5000 B.C. Early querns consisted simply of two stones rubbed together by hand. Rotary querns like this one date from Greek and Roman times. Grain poured into the central hollow of the revolving upper stone is channelled to the grinding surfaces and emerges as fine meal through holes in the fixed lower stone.*

Queer Street *n. Chiefly British.* Difficulties, especially financial ones.

que·le·a (kwéeli-ə) *n.* A small African finch, *Quelea quelea,* with brown plumage and a red bill, that is a serious pest of grain crops. [New Latin, perhaps from Medieval Latin *qualea,* QUAIL.]

quell (kwel) *tr.v.* **quelled, quelling, quells. 1.** To put down forcibly; suppress: *quelled the riot.* **2.** To pacify; calm: *quelled her fears.* [Middle English *quellen,* to kill, destroy, Old English *cwellan,* from Germanic.]

Quemoy. See **Jinmen.**

quench (kwench) *tr.v.* **quenched, quenching, quenches. 1.** To put out; extinguish. **2.** To suppress; stifle; put down. **3.** To slake; satisfy. **4.** To cool (hot metal) by thrusting into water or other liquid. **5.** To reduce (sparking or oscillation) in an electronic circuit. **6.** To suppress (luminescence, fluorescence, or electrical discharge, for example) by adding a deactivating agent. [Middle English *quenchen,* Old English *ācwencan.*] **—quench·a·ble** *adj.* **—quench·er** *n.*

Que·neau (kə-nṓ), **Raymond** (1903–79). French novelist and poet. His bizarre, erudite humour, full of puns and surrealism, cloaked a profound pessimism. Notable among his works are *Le Chien-dent* (1933) and *Zazie dans le Métro* (1959).

Quetzalcoatl *The Aztec god of civilisation is thought to have had a historical counterpart in an early king of the Toltec people, who dominated Mexico before the Aztecs. The Aztecs believed that Quetzalcoatl would one day return from the east to rule again – and when the Spanish conquistadores landed in 1519, their leader, Hérnan Cortés, was welcomed as the god.*

que·nelle (kə-nél, ki-) *n.* A dumpling, especially of pounded fish, bound with eggs and poached in stock or water. [French.]

quer·ce·tin (kwérssi-tin) *n.* A yellow, powdered crystalline compound, $C_{15}H_{10}O_7$, synthesised or occurring as a glycoside in the rind and bark of numerous plants, and used medicinally to treat abnormal capillary fragility. [Latin *quercētum,* oak forest, from *quercus,* oak.]

que·rist (kwéer-ist) *n. Rare.* A questioner; an enquirer. [Latin *quaerere,* to seek, ask.]

quern (kwern) *n.* **1.** A hand-turned grain mill consisting of two stone wheels, one resting upon the other. **2.** A small hand mill for grinding spices. [Middle English *querne,* Old English *cweorn,* from Germanic.]

quer·u·lous (kwérrōō-ləss, kwérrew-) *adj.* **1.** Given to complaining or fretting; peevish. **2.** Expressing a complaint or grievance; grumbling; fretful. [Latin *querulus,* from *querī,* to complain.] **—quer·u·lous·ly** *adv.* **—quer·u·lous·ness** *n.*

que·ry (kwéer-i) *n., pl.* **-ries. 1.** A question; an inquiry. **2.** A doubt in the mind. **3.** *Abbr.* **q., qu.** A notation, usually (?), calling attention to an item to question its validity or accuracy.
~*tr.v.* **queried, -rying, -ries. 1.** To express doubt or uncertainty about; question. **2.** *Chiefly U.S.* To put a question to (a person). **3.** To mark with a query, as to question validity or accuracy. —See Synonyms at **ask.** [Variant (influenced by ENQUIRY) of earlier *quaere,* from Latin, imperative of *quaerere,* to seek, ask.]

quest (kwest) *n.* **1.** The act or an instance of seeking or pursuing something; a search. **2.** In medieval romance, an expedition undertaken by a knight in order to perform some prescribed feat: *the quest for the Holy Grail.* **—in quest of.** In pursuit of; seeking.
~*v.* **quested, questing, quests.** —*intr.* **1.** To make a search; go on a quest. **2.** To search for game. Used of a hunting dog. —*tr. Archaic.* To seek; search for. [Middle English *queste,* from Old French, from Vulgar Latin *quaesita* (unattested), from Latin, feminine past participle of *quaerere,* to seek.] **—quest·er** *n.*

ques·tion (kwéss-chən, kwésh-, *also* kwést-yən) *n. Abbr.* **q., qn., qu. 1.** An expression of enquiry that invites or calls for a reply; an interrogative sentence, phrase, or gesture. **2.** A subject or point open to controversy; an unsettled issue. **3.** A matter or problem, especially one conditioned by or considered in terms of a specified factor: *a question of ethics.* **4.** A point or subject under discussion or being considered. **5.** A proposition brought up for consideration by an assembly. **6.** Uncertainty; doubt. **7.** Possibility; chance: *no question of my giving in.* **—beg the question. 1.** To presuppose the conclusion in one's argument. **2.** To equivocate. **—call into question.** To cast doubt upon. **—out of the question.** Not worth considering; impossible. **—pop the question.** *Informal.* To propose marriage.
~*v.* **questioned, -tioning, -tions.** —*tr.* **1.** To put a question to. **2.** To interrogate (a witness or suspect, for example). **3.** To express doubt about; dispute. —*intr.* To ask questions. —See Synonyms at **ask.** [Middle English, from Old French, from Latin *quaestiō* (stem *quaestiōn-*), from *quaerere* (past participle *quaestus*), to seek, ask.] **—ques·tion·er** *n.* **—ques·tion·ing·ly** *adv.*

ques·tion·a·ble (kwéss-chən-əb'l, kwésh-) *adj.* **1.** Open to doubt; uncertain; problematic. **2.** Of dubious morality or respectability. —See Synonyms at **doubtful. —ques·tion·a·bil·i·ty** (-əbílliti), **ques·tion·a·ble·ness** *n.* **—ques·tion·a·bly** *adv.*

question mark *n.* **1.** A punctuation symbol (?) written, in English, at the end of a sentence or phrase to indicate a direct question. Also called "interrogation mark", "interrogation point", "interrogative". **2. a.** This symbol used to indicate uncertainty, as in dating a museum specimen, for example: (*?10th century*). **b.** *Informal.* An unknown factor; a situation of doubt or insecurity.

ques·tion·mas·ter (kwéss-chən-maass-tər, kwésh- || -mass-) *n. British.* One who chairs a quiz game, as on the radio or television.

ques·tion·naire (kwéss-chə-náir, kwésh-, késs-; kwést-yən-, kést-) *n.* A printed form containing a set of questions, especially one used for gathering information from people, as in a survey. [French, from *questionner,* to question, from *question,* QUESTION.]

question time *n.* In Britain, a period during a parliamentary session when questions may be put to certain ministers concerning matters for which they are responsible.

Quet·ta (kwéttə). Capital city of Baluchistan province in Pakistan, situated on the main route north to Afghanistan via the Bolan Pass. It is an important trade centre.

quet·zal (kwét-s'l, két- || ket-saál, -sál) *n., pl.* **-zals** or **-zales** (-saál-ayss, -ayz). **1.** A Central American bird, *Pharomacrus mocino,* having brilliant bronze-green and red plumage and, in the male, long flowing tail feathers. **2.** *Abbr.* **Q a.** The basic monetary unit of Guatemala, equal to 100 centavos. **b.** A coin worth one quetzal. [American Spanish, from Nahuatl *quetzalli,* tail feather.]

Quet·zal·co·a·tl (kéts'l-kō-átt'l, -aát'l). A god of the Toltecs and Aztecs, represented as a plumed serpent.

queue (kew) *n.* **1.** A line or file of people or vehicles waiting to do something, such as board a bus, or to receive attention in turn, as at a shop counter. **2.** A long plait of real or artificial hair worn hanging down the back of the neck; a pigtail. **—jump the queue.** To do something or receive attention before one's turn has come.
~*intr.v.* **queued, queuing, queues.** To wait in a queue. Often used with *up.* [French, tail, line, from Old French *coe, cue,* from Latin *cauda,* tail.]

queue-jump·ing (kéw-jumping) *n.* The practice or an act of making sure one does something or receives attention before one's turn has come. **—queue-jump·er** *n.* **—queue-jump·ing** *adj.*

Que·zon City (káy-son, -zon || *U.S.* -sawn). City adjoining Manila on the island of Luzon, in the Philippines. It was the country's capital from 1948 to1976.

quib·ble (kwíbb'l) *intr.v.* **-bled, -bling, -bles. 1.** To make exaggerated distinctions or raise objections to unimportant details: *quibbling over trivialities.* **2.** *Archaic.* To make a pun.
~*n.* **1.** A petty distinction or minor objection. **2.** *Archaic.* A pun. [From obsolete *quib,* pun, perhaps from Latin *quibus,* dative and ablative plural of *quī,* who, which (used in legal documents and hence associated with quips and quibbles).]

quiche (keesh) *n.* A usually savoury tart consisting of beaten eggs with cheese, bacon, or other ingredients baked in an unsweetened pastry shell. [French, probably from German (dialectal) *Küche,* diminutive of *Kuchen,* cake, from Old High German *kuocho.*]

quick (kwik) *adj.* **quicker, quickest. 1.** Moving or functioning rapidly and energetically; speedy: *a quick worker.* **2.** Occupying a brief space of time: *a quick chat over lunch.* **3.** Understanding, thinking, or learning with speed and dexterity; intellectually sharp. **4.** Perceiving with speed and sensitivity; alert; keen. **5.** Done or occurring in a relatively short time; prompt; immediate. **6.** Hasty or sharp in reacting: *quick to attack her opponents.* **7.** *Archaic.* Pregnant. Used especially in the phrase *quick with child.* **8.** *Archaic.* Alive. —See Synonyms at **fast, nimble.**
~*n.* **1.** Sensitive or raw exposed flesh, as under the fingernails. **2.** The most personal and sensitive area of the emotions: *cut to the quick.* **3.** The vital core of a thing; the essence. Used chiefly in the phrase *the quick of the matter.* **4.** *British.* Quickset.
~*adv.* Quickly; promptly.
~*interj.* Used to urge quick action or response. [Middle English *qui(c)ke,* swift, lively, alive, Old English *cwic(u),* living, alive, from Germanic.] **—quick·ness** *n.* **—quick·ly** *adv.*

Usage: *Quick* is occasionally used as an adverb in informal speech (especially in the imperative: *Come quick!*), but *quickly* is the preferred form in formal speech and writing. See also **slow.**

quick assets *pl. n.* Liquid assets, including cash on hand and assets readily convertible to cash.

quick-change (kwík-cháynj) *adj.* Of or designating an actor, entertainer, or other performer, who must quickly change costume on a number of occasions during the performance.

quick·en (kwíckən) *v.* **-ened, -ening, -ens.** —*tr.* **1.** To make more rapid; speed up; accelerate. **2.** To make alive; vitalise. **3.** To excite and stimulate; stir. —*intr.* **1.** To become more rapid. **2.** To show life; come or return to life: *"and the weak spirit quickens"* (T.S. Eliot). **3. a.** To reach the stage of pregnancy when the foetus can be

felt to move. Used of the mother. **b.** To make these first movements, thus showing signs of life. Used of a foetus. —See Synonyms at **speed.** —**quick·en·er** n.

quick-fire (kwĭk-fīr) adj. Suggesting rapid gunfire: quick-fire questions.

quick-freeze (kwĭk-frēez) tr.v. **-froze** (-frōz), **-frozen** (-frōz′n), **-freezing, -freezes.** To freeze (food) by a process sufficiently rapid to retain natural flavour, nutritional value, or other properties.

quick·ie (kwĭcki) n. Informal. Something made, done, or consumed rapidly or hastily.

quick·lime (kwĭk-līm) n. Chemistry. **Calcium oxide** (see). [So called because it is the first substance produced by heating limestone.]

quick march n. A march done in quick time, especially by soldiers. —interj. Used as a command for such a march.

quick·sand (kwĭk-sand) n. A bed of loose sand and mud mixed with water forming a soft, shifting mass that yields easily to pressure and may suck down any denser object resting on its surface.

quick·set (kwĭk-set) n. Chiefly British. **1. a.** Cuttings or slips of a plant suitable for hedges. **b.** A single slip or cutting of such a plant. **2.** A hedge consisting of such plants. —**quick·set** adj.

quick·sil·ver (kwĭk-sĭlvər) n. The element **mercury** (see). —adj. Unpredictable; mercurial. [Middle English quicksilver, Old English cwicseolfor (translation of Latin argentum vivum) : QUICK, "living" + SILVER.]

quick·step (kwĭk-step) n. A fast ballroom dance. —**quick·step** intr.v.

quick-tem·pered (kwĭk-tĕmpərd) adj. Easily aroused to anger.

quick time n. A military marching pace of 120 steps per minute.

quick-wit·ted (kwĭk-wĭttid) adj. Showing mental alertness or agility: a quick-witted reply. See Synonyms at **shrewd, intelligent.** —**quick-wit·ted·ly** adv. —**quick-wit·ted·ness** n.

quid¹ (kwĭd) n., pl. **quid** or rare **quids.** British Informal. A pound sterling. —**quids in.** Informal. In a good or advantageous position, especially for making money. [Probably from Latin quid, something, perhaps alluding to QUID PRO QUO; compare French quibus, "wherewithal".]

quid² n. A cut of something to be chewed, such as tobacco. [Dialect variant of CUD.]

quid·di·ty (kwĭddəti) n., pl. **-ties. 1.** The real nature of a thing; the essence. **2.** A hairsplitting distinction; a quibble. [Medieval Latin quidditās, from Latin quid, what, something, anything.]

quid·nunc (kwĭd-nungk) n. Archaic. A busybody; a gossip. [Latin quid nunc?, "What now?".]

quid pro quo (kwĭd prō kwō) n., pl. **quid pro quos.** An equal exchange or substitution. [Latin, "something for something".]

qui·es·cent (kwi-ĕss′nt) adj. **1.** Inactive or still; dormant. **2.** Medicine. Designating a disease that is in an inactive or undetectable phase. —See Synonyms at **latent.** [Latin quiēscēns (stem quiēscent-), present participle of quiēscere, to be QUIET.] —**qui·es·cence** n. —**qui·es·cent·ly** adv.

qui·et (kwī-ət) adj. **-eter, -etest. 1.** Making no noise; silent. **2.** Free of noise; hushed. **3.** Calm and unmoving; still. **4.** Free from disturbance and agitation; untroubled. **5.** Restful; soothing. **6.** Characterised by tranquillity; serene; peaceful. **7.** Not showy or brash; restrained; unobtrusive. **8.** Private; unnoticed: a quiet word; quiet anger. —**keep quiet about.** To let no one know about; say nothing about. —See Synonyms at **calm, still.** —n. The quality or condition of being quiet; silence; tranquillity; repose. —**on the quiet.** Secretly; surreptitiously. —v. **quieted, -eting, -ets.** —intr. To quieten. [Middle English, from Old French, from Latin quiētus, from the past participle of quiēscere, to be quiet, be at rest, from quiēs, quiet.] —**qui·et·ness** n.

qui·et·en (kwī-ət′n) v. **-ened, -ening, -ens.** —tr. **1.** To cause to become silent or at rest; soothe or silence. **2.** To calm or allay (fears, for example). —intr. To become quiet. Usually used with down: The child had been crying but soon quietened down. —See Synonyms at **pacify.** [QUIET + -EN.] —**qui·et·en·er** n.

qui·et·ism (kwī-ət-iz′m) n. **1.** A form of Christian mysticism requiring passive contemplation and the joyful surrender of the will. **2.** A state of quietness and passivity. —**qui·et·ist** adj. & n. —**qui·et·is·tic** (-ĭstik) adj. —**qui·et·is·tic·al·ly** adv.

quiet sun n. Astronomy. The Sun at a time when there is very little sunspot activity.

qui·e·tude (kwī-i-tewd, -ə- ‖ -tōod) n. A condition of tranquillity. [Medieval Latin quiētūdō, from Latin quiētus, QUIET.]

qui·e·tus (kwī-ay-təss, -ée-) n. **1.** Something that serves to suppress, check, or eliminate. **2.** Release from life; death. **3.** Anything that kills or eliminates; a deathblow. **4.** A final discharge, as of a duty or debt. [Medieval Latin quiētus (est), "(he is) discharged", from Latin quiētus, at rest, released, QUIET.]

quiff (kwĭf) n. British. **1.** A tuft of hair brushed up to a peak over the forehead and sometimes lacquered. **2.** A strand or curl of hair that falls over the forehead. [20th century; akin to **coif.**]

quill (kwĭl) n. **1.** The hollow, stemlike main shaft of a feather. Also called "calamus". **2.** Any of the larger wing or tail feathers of a bird. Also called "quill feather". **3.** A writing pen made from such a feather. Also called "quill pen". **4.** A plectrum for a stringed musical instrument of the clavichord type. **5.** A toothpick made from the stem of a feather. **6.** Any of the sharp hollow spines of a porcupine or hedgehog. **7.** A musical pipe having a hollow stem. **8.** A spindle or bobbin, originally a length of reed or cane, around which yarn is wound in weaving. **9.** A small roll of dried bark,

especially cinnamon. **10.** In machinery, a hollow shaft that rotates on a solid shaft when gears are engaged. —v. **quilled, quilling, quills.** —intr. To wind thread or yarn onto a quill. —tr. To make or press small ridges in (fabric). [Middle English quil(le); akin to Middle Low German quiele†.]

Quil·ler-Couch (kwĭllər-kōoch), **Sir Arthur (Thomas)** (1863–1944). British critic and writer. He is best known as the editor of the Oxford Book of English Verse (1900) (under the pen-name "Q").

quil·let (kwĭllit) n. Archaic. A verbal nicety or subtlety; a quibble. [Perhaps short for obsolete quillity, variant of QUIDDITY.]

quilt (kwĭlt) n. **1.** A bed coverlet or blanket made of two layers of fabric with a layer of cotton, wool, feathers, or down in between, all stitched firmly together, usually in a crisscross design. **2.** A duvet. **3.** Any thick cover of protective material. —v. **quilted, quilting, quilts.** —tr. **1.** To make into a quilt by stitching together (layers of fabric). **2.** To make like a quilt: quilt a skirt. **3.** To pad and stitch ornamentally. **4.** To sew up between layers of fabric. —intr. **1.** To make a quilt. **2.** To do quilted needlework. [Middle English quilte, from Old French cuilte, from Latin culcita, sack filled with feathers, mattress.]

quilt·ing (kwĭlting) n. **1.** Material used to make quilts. **2.** Quilted material.

quim (kwĭm) n. British Vulgar Slang. A woman's genitals. [16th century : origin obscure.]

Quim·per (kan-páir, kám-). Administrative centre of the Finistère département in Brittany, northwestern France. It is famous for its pottery and fine Gothic cathedral.

quin (kwĭn) n. British. A **quintuplet** (see).

quin– comb. form. Indicates cinchona or cinchona bark; for example, quinidine. [Spanish quina, cinchona bark, short for quinaquina, perhaps from Quechua.]

qui·na·ry (kwīnəri) adj. **1.** Of, pertaining to, or based on the number five. **2.** Consisting of five things or parts. [Latin quinārius, from quinī, five each, distributive of quinque, five.]

qui·nate (kwīnayt) adj. Arranged in groups of five: quinate leaflets. [Latin quinī, five each.]

quince (kwĭnss) n. **1.** A tree, Cydonia oblonga, native to Asia, having white flowers and apple-like fruit. **2.** The aromatic, many-seeded fruit of this tree, edible only when cooked. [Middle English quynce, plural of quyn, quince, from Old French c(o)oin, from Latin cotōneum, cydōneum (mālum), "Cydonian (apple)", from Greek kudōnion, from Kudōnia, CYDONIA.]

quin·cen·te·nar·y (kwĭn-sen-tēen-əri, -tén-) n., pl. **-naries.** Also chiefly U.S. **quin·cen·ten·ni·al** (-tĕnni-əl). **1.** A five-hundredth anniversary. **2.** A celebration of this. [Irregularly from Latin quinque, five + CENTENARY.] —**quin·cen·te·nar·y, quin·cen·ten·ni·al** adj.

quin·cunx (kwĭn-kungks) n. An arrangement of five objects, with one at each corner of a rectangle and one at the centre, as in the five on a dice. [Latin quincunx (stem quincunc-), five twelfths of a Roman coin (as denoted by five dots or dashes so arranged) : quinque, five + uncia, a twelfth part.] —**quin·cun·cial** (kwĭn-kúnsh′l) adj. —**quin·cun·cial·ly** adv.

quin·dec·a·gon (kwĭn-déckə-gən, kwĭn- ‖ -gon) n. Geometry. A polygon having 15 sides and 15 angles. [Irregularly from Latin quindecim, fifteen + -GON.] —**quin·dec·a·gon·al** (-di-kággən′l) adj. —**quin·dec·a·gon·al·ly** adv.

quin·de·cen·ni·al (kwĭn-di-sénni-əl, -de-) adj. **1.** Occurring once every 15 years. **2.** Lasting 15 years. [Latin quindecim, fifteen + annus, year.] —**quin·de·cen·ni·al·ly** adv.

quin·i·dine (kwĭnni-deen) n. A colourless crystalline alkaloid, $C_{20}H_{24}N_2O_2$, resembling quinine and used in treating certain heart disorders and malaria. [QUIN- + -ID(E) + -INE.]

qui·nine (kwi-néen, kwĭnneen ‖ U.S. kwĭ-nīn, kwĭ-). n. **1.** A bitter, colourless, amorphous powder or crystalline alkaloid, $C_{20}H_{24}N_2O_2$·$3H_2O$, derived from certain cinchona barks and used to treat malaria, though now largely replaced by less toxic drugs. **2.** Any of various compounds or salts of this alkaloid. [QUIN- + -INE.]

quin·oid (kwĭn-oyd) n. Chemistry. A substance resembling quinone in structure or physical properties. [QUIN(ONE) + -OID.]

qui·noi·dine (kwi-nóy-deen, -din) n. A brownish-black mixture of alkaloids remaining after extraction of crystalline alkaloids from cinchona bark, used as a quinine substitute. [QUIN- + -OID + -INE.]

quin·o·line (kwĭnnə-leen, -lin) n. An aromatic organic base, C_9H_7N, having a pungent tarlike odour, synthesised or obtained from coal tar, and used as a preservative and in making antiseptics and dyes. [QUIN- + -OL + -INE.]

quin·one (kwi-nōn, kwĭn-ōn) n. Chemistry. Any of a class of aromatic compounds found widely in plants; especially, the yellow crystalline form $C_6H_4O_2$, used in making dyes, in tanning hides, and in photography. [QUIN- + -ONE.]

quin·o·noid (kwĭnnə-noyd, kwi-nōn-oyd) adj. Chemistry. Of, containing, or resembling quinone, in structure or properties.

quin·qua·ge·nar·i·an (kwĭng-kwə-ji-nair-i-ən) n. A person fifty years old, or between fifty and sixty years of age. —adj. Of or characteristic of a fifty-year-old. [Latin quinquāgēnārius, consisting of fifty, from quinquāgēnī, fifty each, from quinquāginta, fifty.]

Quin·qua·ges·i·ma (kwĭng-kwə-jéssimə) n. The Sunday before the beginning of Lent; the first day of Shrovetide. Also called "Quinquagesima Sunday". [Medieval Latin quinquāgēsima, from Latin, fiftieth, from quinquāginta, fifty.]

quince A bushy, fast-growing fruit tree of the genus Cydonia, which is thought to have originated in Central Asia. The fruit has a delicious smell, but is bitter and hard unless cooked. It was held sacred by the ancient Greeks and, according to one legend, was the forbidden fruit in the Garden of Eden.

quinque– *comb. form.* Indicates five; for example, **quinquefoliate**. [Latin *quinque*, five.]

quin·que·fo·li·ate (kwing-kwi-fṓli-ət, -it, -ayt) *adj. Botany.* Having five leaves, leaflets, or leaflike parts. [QUINQUE- + Latin *folium*, leaf, FOIL.]

quin·quen·ni·al (kwing-kwénni-əl, kwin-) *adj.* 1. Happening once every five years. 2. Lasting for five years. ~*n.* 1. A fifth anniversary. 2. A period of five years. —**quin·quen·ni·al·ly** *adv.*

quin·quen·ni·um (kwing-kwénni-əm, kwin-) *n., pl.* -**ums** or -**quennia.** A period of five years. [Latin : QUINQUE- + *annus*, year.]

quin·que·va·lent (kwing-kwi-váylənt) *adj. Chemistry.* Pentavalent. —**quin·que·va·lence** *n.*

quin·sy (kwinzi) *n.* Acute inflammation of the tonsils and surrounding tissue, leading to the formation of an abscess. [Middle English *quinesye*, from Old French *quinencie*, from Medieval Latin *quinancia*, from Greek *kunanchē*, dog quinsy, sore throat : *kuōn*, hound + *ankhein*, to strangle.]

quint (kint, kwint) *n.* In piquet and similar games, a sequence of five cards of the same suit in one hand. [French, from Latin *quinta*, feminine of *quintus*, fifth.]

quin·tain (kwintin) *n.* 1. A post, or a target mounted on a post, to be tilted at especially by horsemen. 2. The exercise of tilting. [Middle English *quintaine*, from Old French, from Latin *quintāna via*, the fifth street in a Roman camp, supposedly used for military exercises, from *quintānus*, fifth in rank, from *quintus*, fifth.]

quin·tal (kwint'l) *n. Abbr.* **q., ql.** 1. A unit of mass in the metric system equal to 100 kilograms (220 pounds). 2. A short hundredweight, 100 pounds (45.36 kilograms). [Middle English, from Old French, from Medieval Latin *quintāle*, from Arabic *qintār*, KANTAR.]

quin·tar (keen-tár) *n.* A monetary unit, equal to $1/100$ of the lek of Albania. [Albanian *qintar*.]

quinte (kaNt) *n.* In fencing, the fifth in a series of eight parrying positions. [Old French, fifth.]

quin·tes·sence (kwin-téss'nss) *n.* 1. The pure, highly concentrated essence of something. 2. The purest or most typical example; the embodiment: *Her manners were the quintessence of courtesy.* 3. In ancient and medieval philosophy, the fifth and highest essence (after the four elements of earth, air, fire, and water), thought to be the substance of the heavenly bodies and latent in all things. [Middle English, from Old French *quinte essence*, from Medieval Latin *quinta essentia* (translation of Greek *pemptē ousia*, fifth essence) : Latin *quinta*, feminine of *quintus*, fifth + *essentia*, ESSENCE.]

quin·tes·sen·tial (kwinti-sénsh'l) *adj.* 1. Being most typical; expressing the essence of the thing or person specified. 2. Having the nature of a quintessence; pure and concentrated in nature. —**quin·tes·sen·tial·ly** *adv.*

quin·tet, quin·tette (kwin-tét, kwin-) *n.* 1. A group of five persons or things; especially, a group of five musicians. 2. A musical composition for five voices or instruments. [French *quintette*, from Italian *quintetto*, from *quinto*, fifth, from Latin *quintus*, fifth.]

quin·tile (kwin-tīl) *n.* 1. *Astrology.* The aspect of planets distant from each other by 72° or a fifth of the zodiac. 2. *Statistics.* The portion of a frequency distribution containing a fifth of the total sample. [Latin *quintus*, fifth.]

quin·til·li·on (kwin-tíl-yən, kwin-) *n.* 1. *British.* The cardinal number represented by 1 followed by 30 zeros, usually written 10^{30}. 2. *U.S.* The cardinal number represented by 1 followed by 18 zeros, usually written 10^{18}, equivalent to the British trillion. [Latin *quintus*, fifth + (M)ILLION.] —**quin·til·li·on** *adj.* —**quin·til·li·onth** *n. & adj.*

quin·tu·ple (kwin-tew-p'l, kwin-téw- ‖ -tōō-, -tṓo-, *also* -tupp'l) *adj.* 1. Consisting of or having five parts, members, or copies. 2. Multiplied by five; five times as much, as many, or as large. ~*n.* A fivefold amount or number. ~*v.* **quintupled, -pling, -ples.** —*tr.* To multiply or increase by five. —*intr.* To be multiplied fivefold. [French, from Late Latin *quintuplex* : Latin *quintus*, fifth + -*plex*, -fold.]

quin·tu·plet (kwin-tew-plit, -plet, -plət; kwin-téw- ‖ -túpplət) *n.* 1. A group or combination of five associated by common properties or behaviour. 2. Any of five offspring born in a single birth. In this sense, also called "quin". [From QUINTUPLE.]

quin·tu·pli·cate (kwin-téw-pli-kət, -kit, -kayt ‖ -tṓo-) *adj.* 1. Multiplied by five; fivefold. 2. Being the fifth of a set of copies. ~*n.* 1. Any of a set of five. 2. A set of five copies. ~*tr.v.* (-kayt) **quintuplicated, -cating, -cates.** 1. To make five copies of. 2. To multiply by five. [Late Latin *quintuplicātus*, from *quintuplicāre*, to make fivefold, from *quintuplex*, QUINTUPLE.]

quip (kwip) *n.* 1. A brief, witty remark delivered offhand. 2. A cleverly sarcastic remark; a verbal thrust; a gibe. 3. A quibble. —See Synonyms at **joke.** ~*intr.v.* **quipped, quipping, quips.** To make a quip or quips. [Earlier *quippy*, perhaps from Latin *quippe*, indeed, certainly (often used ironically), from *quid*, what.]

qui·pu, quip·pu (kée-pōō) *n.* A device consisting of variously coloured and knotted cords attached to a base rope, used by the Incas of Peru for calculating and recording. [Spanish *quipo*, from Quechua *quipu*.]

quire¹ (kwīr) *n. Abbr.* **q., qr.** 1. A set of 24 or sometimes 25 sheets of paper of the same size and stock; $1/20$ ream. 2. 4 sheets of paper folded to form 8 leaves, or 16 pages. 3. A set of all leaves required for a book before binding. ~*tr.v.* **quired, quiring, quires.** To fold or arrange in quires. [Middle English, from Old French *quaer*, set of four sheets, from Vulgar Latin *quaternum* (unattested), from Latin *quaternī*, set of four, from *quater*, four.]

quire² *n. Archaic.* A choir (see).

Quir·i·nal (kwirrin'l) *n.* One of the seven hills of Rome, the site of the Quirinal Palace, the residence of the head of state of Italy since 1870.

quirk (kwurk) *n.* 1. A peculiarity of behaviour; an oddity; a whim. 2. An unpredictable or unaccountable act or event: *a quirk of fate*. 3. **a.** A sudden sharp turn or twist. **b.** A flourish in handwriting, drawing, or music. 4. An equivocation; a quibble; a subterfuge. 5. A quip. 6. *Architecture.* A lengthways groove on a moulding. —See Synonyms at **eccentricity.** [16th century : origin obscure.] —**quirk·i·ly** *adv.* —**quirk·i·ness** *n.* —**quirk·y** *adj.*

quis·ling (kwízling) *n.* A traitor who serves as the puppet of the enemy occupying his country. [After Vidkun QUISLING.]

Quis·ling (kwíz-ling; *Norwegian* kvíss-), **Vidkun,** born Abraham Lauritz Jonsson (1887–1945). Norwegian politician. Forming the fascist National Union Party (1933), he went on to become minister president (1942) under the Nazi occupation. Following the Axis surrender (1945), he was tried and executed for treason.

quit (kwit) *v.* **quitted** *or chiefly U.S.* **quit, quitting, quits.** —*tr.* 1. To end one's involvement with; leave abruptly: *"You and I are on the point of quitting the theatre of our exploits"* (Lord Nelson). 2. To give up; relinquish; put aside. 3. To leave; depart from 4. *Chiefly U.S.* To discontinue; cease; stop. 5. *Archaic.* To rid oneself of by paying: *quit a debt.* 6. *Archaic.* To conduct or acquit (oneself). —*intr.* 1. To cease to perform. 2. To give up as in defeat; stop. 3. To leave rented premises: *notice to quit.* 4. To leave a job. ~*adj.* Absolved of a duty or obligation; free; released. Often used with *of.* [Middle English *quiten*, to set free, release, from Old French *quiter*, from Medieval Latin *quiētāre*, to set free, quit, discharge, from Latin *quiētus*, freed, QUIET.]

Usage: **Quitted** and **quit** are both used as past tense and past participle forms of this verb. **Quit** is standard in American English (*She quit her job*). In British usage, *quitted* is often used, but is slowly being replaced by *quit*, which is nowadays the more common variant. Many British speakers dislike the use of *quit* in the general sense of "stop" (*She has quit smoking*) because of its American overtones and would never allow it in formal contexts.

quit·claim (kwít-klaym) *n. Law.* The transfer of a title, right, or claim to another. ~*tr.v.* **quitclaimed, -claiming, -claims.** To renounce all claim to (a possession or right). [Middle English *quiteclaimen* (verb), from Old French *quiteclamer*, "to declare free" : *quite*, free, QUIT + *clamer*, to CLAIM.]

quite (kwīt) *adv.* 1. To the greatest extent; entirely; completely: *quite alone; not quite finished.* 2. Actually; truly; really: *quite different.* 3. **a.** Somewhat; fairly: *quite easy.* **b.** To only a limited degree: *I quite liked it, but felt it could have been better.* —**quite a** *or* **an.** 1. Considerable. Used to qualify an indefinite noun: *quite a few; quite a gap.* 2. *Informal.* Exceptional; extraordinary; impressive: *quite an establishment.* —**quite something.** *Informal.* Something extraordinary or impressive. ~*interj.* Also **quite so.** Used to indicate agreement. [Middle English, from adjective, "free", rid of, from Old French, from Latin *quiētus*, freed, QUIET.]

Usage: Many people have objected to the "weaker" senses of *quite*, where the word means "rather, somewhat" (*It's quite warm today*), preferring to restrict it to the more positive senses of "entirely" (*quite certain*) and "actually" (*quite ill*). However, the weaker sense is very widely used, especially in informal speech. Nowadays, it is felt to be somewhat pedantic to criticise a phrase such as *quite all right* as containing a redundancy, or a phrase such as *quite similar* as containing a contradiciton, and this kind of use will often be heard even in formal speech. *Quite a(n)*, indicating indefinite quantity, is generally acceptable (*Quite a large number stayed away*); but when indicating extraordinary quality (*quite a show*), it is informal.

Qui·to (kéetō). Capital city of Ecuador and capital of Pichincha province. It is an educational, cultural, manufacturing, and political centre and was the northern capital of the Inca empire.

quit·rent (kwít-rent) *n.* Formerly, a rent paid by a freeman in lieu of services required of him by feudal custom.

quits (kwits) *adj.* Even with someone by payment or requital. —**call it quits.** To agree that something, such as a dispute or debt, is settled on both sides. [Middle English, "discharged", "paid up", from Medieval Latin *quittus*, QUIT.]

quit·tance (kwítt'nss) *n.* 1. Release from a debt, obligation, or penalty. 2. A document or receipt certifying such a release. 3. Something given as requital or recompense; repayment. [Middle English *quitance*, from Old French, from *quiter*, to free, discharge a debt, QUIT.]

quit·ter (kwíttər) *n. Informal.* One who gives up easily.

quit·tor (kwíttər) *n.* An inflammation of the hoof cartilage of horses and other solid-hoofed animals, characterised by degeneration of hoof tissue, formation of a slough, and fistulous sores. [Middle English *quiture*, perhaps from Old French, decoction, from Latin *coctūra*, from *coquere* (past participle *coctus*), to cook.]

quiv·er¹ (kwívvər) *v.* **quivered, -ering, -ers.** —*intr.* To shake with a slight rapid motion; tremble; vibrate. —*tr.* To cause to quiver. —See Synonyms at **shake.** ~*n.* The act or motion of quivering. [Middle English *quiveren*, from QUIVER (nimble).]

quiver² *n.* **1.** A portable case for arrows. **2.** A case full of arrows. [Middle English, from Anglo-French *quiver* (unattested), Old French *cuivre*, from West Germanic.]

quiver³ *adj. Obsolete.* Nimble; brisk. [Middle English *quiver*, Old English *cwifer-*.]

quiv·er·ful (kwívvər-foŏl) *n., pl.* **-fuls. 1.** The amount held by a quiver. **2.** A large number; a sizeable quantity. Often used in the phrase *a quiverful of children.*

qui vive (kée véev) *n.* Alert watchfulness or vigilance. Used chiefly in the phrase *on the qui vive.* [French, "(Long) live who?" (a sentinel's challenge demanding to know the allegiance of the person approaching).]

quix·ot·ic (kwik-sóttik) *adj.* Also **quix·ot·i·cal** (-'l). Caught up in the romance of noble deeds or unreachable ideals; romantic, absent-minded, and unpractical. [After DON QUIXOTE.] **—quix·ot·i·cal·ly** *adv.* **—quix·o·tism** (kwiksət-iz'm) *n.*

quiz (kwiz) *tr.v.* **quizzed, quizzing, quizzes. 1.** To question closely or repeatedly; interrogate. **2.** To test the knowledge of by posing questions. **3.** *Archaic.* To poke fun at; mock. **4.** *Archaic.* To look at questioningly or mockingly, especially through a quizzing glass. *~n., pl.* **quizzes. 1.** A short oral or written test of knowledge. **2.** A competition in which the knowledge of the contestants is tested by questioning, especially as an entertainment, as on a radio or television programme. Also used adjectively: *a quiz show.* **3.** A questioning or inquiry. **4.** *Archaic.* **a.** A practical joke. **b.** An eccentric person. [18th century : origin obscure.] **—quiz·zer** *n.*

quiz·zi·cal (kwízzik'l) *adj.* **1.** Suggesting humorous or ironical puzzlement; questioning. **2.** Teasing; mocking: *"his face wore a somewhat quizzical, almost impertinent air"* (Lawrence Durrell). **—quiz·zi·cal·i·ty** (kwízzi-kál-əti) *n.* **—quiz·zi·cal·ly** *adv.*

quiz·zing glass (kwízzing) *n.* A small monocle.

Qum. See **Qom.**

Qum·rān (koŏm-ráan, -rán). Village on the northwest coast of the Dead Sea in the part of Jordan occupied by Israel in 1967, thought to be the city of Salt mentioned in Joshua 15:62. It includes Khirbat Qumrān, ruins left by a community of Essenes, a Jewish sect, which flourished there from the mid-second century B.C. until A.D. 68, when it was finally destroyed by Vespasian's army. Remains of the sect's library, the Dead Sea Scrolls, were first found by local shepherds in 1947 in caves at Qumrān.

quod (kwod) *n. British Slang.* Prison. [17th century : origin obscure.]

quod·li·bet (kwódli-bet) *n.* **1.** A theological or philosophical argument, especially done as an exercise. **2.** A musical medley. [Middle English, scholastic debate, disputation, from Medieval Latin *quodlibetum*, from Latin *quodlibet*, what you please : *quod*, what + *libet*, it pleases, from *libēre*, to please.]

quoin, coign (koyn, kwoyn) *n.* **1. a.** An exterior angle of a wall or other masonry. **b.** A stone serving to form such an angle; a cornerstone. **2.** A keystone. **3.** *Printing.* A wedge-shaped block used to lock type in a chase. **4.** A wedge used to raise the level of a gun. *~tr.v.* **quoined, quoining, quoins.** To provide, secure, or raise with a quoin or quoins. [Variant of COIN (corner).]

quoit (koyt, kwoyt) *n.* A flat ring of iron or rope used in the game of quoits. *~tr.v.* **quoited, quoiting, quoits.** To throw in the manner of a quoit. [Middle English *coite*†.]

quoits (koyts, kwoyts) *n. Used with a singular verb.* A game in which quoits are thrown at a stake, with points awarded for encircling it.

quok·ka (kwóckə) *n.* A small rare wallaby, *Setonix brachyurus*, occurring mainly on the islands off the coast of Western Australia. [From a native Australian language.]

quon·dam (kwón-dam, -dəm) *adj.* That once was; former: *a quondam friend.* [Latin, formerly, from *quom*, when.]

quo·rate (kwáw-rayt, -rət, -rit ‖ kwŏ-) *adj.* Constituting or having a quorum. [QUOR(UM) + -ATE.]

quo·rum (kwáw-rəm ‖ kwŏ-) *n.* The minimum number of officers or members of a committee, organisation, or assembly, usually a majority, who must be present for the valid transaction of business. [Middle English, a quorum of justices of the peace, from Latin texts of commissions reading, for example, *quorum vos . . . duos esse volumus*, "of whom we wish that you be . . . two", genitive plural of *quī*, who.]

quot. quotation.

quo·ta (kwŏtə) *n.* **1.** A share, as of goods to be distributed or work to be done, assigned to a group or to each member of a group; an allotment. **2.** A stipulated number, proportion, or amount, as of persons who may be admitted or of goods that may be imported: *import quotas.* [Medieval Latin, from Latin, feminine of *quotus*, of what number. See **quote.**]

quot·a·ble (kwŏt-əb'l) *adj.* Suitable for or worth quoting. **—quot·a·bil·i·ty** (-ə-bílləti) *n.* **—quot·a·bly** *adv.*

quo·ta·tion (kwŏ-táysh'n, kwə-) *n. Abbr.* **quot. 1.** The act of quoting. **2.** A passage that is quoted. **3.** An estimate of costs or prices: *She gave me a quotation for painting the house.* **4.** *Commerce.* **a.** The quoting of current prices and bids for shares and goods. **b.** The prices or bids cited. **5.** Registration given by the Stock Exchange to a company, allowing the company's shares and stock to be dealt in on the Stock Exchange. **—quo·ta·tion·al** *adj.* **—quo·ta·tion·al·ly** *adv.*

quotation mark *n.* Either of a pair of punctuation marks used to mark the beginning and end of a passage attributed to another and repeated word for word. They appear in the form (" ") (double quotation marks) or (' ') (single quotation marks). Also called "inverted comma", informally "quote".

quote (kwŏt) *v.* **quoted, quoting, quotes.** *—tr.* **1.** To repeat or copy the words of (another), usually with acknowledgement of the source. **2.** To cite or refer to for illustration or proof. **3.** To state (a price) for securities, goods, or services. *—intr.* **1.** To give a quotation, as from a book. **2.** To be registered on the Stock Exchange, as a company whose shares and stocks may be dealt in. *~n. Informal.* **1.** A quotation. **2.** A quotation mark. [Middle English, to mark (chapters, references, or the like) with numbers, from Medieval Latin *quotāre*, from Latin *quotus*, of what number, from *quot*, how many.] **—quot·er** *n.*

quoth (kwŏth) *tr.v. Archaic.* Uttered; said. Used only in the first and third persons, with the subject following: *"Quoth the raven 'Nevermore!'."* (Edgar Allen Poe). [Middle English *quoth*, Old English *cwæth*, he said, from *cwethan*, to say.]

quo·tha (kwŏthə) *interj. Archaic.* Used to express surprise or sarcasm, after quoting the word or phrase of another. [Contraction of *quoth he.*]

quo·tid·i·an (kwŏ-tíddi-ən, kwo-) *adj.* **1.** Recurring daily. Said particularly of attacks of malaria. **2.** Everyday; commonplace. [Middle English *cotidien*, from Old French, from Latin *quotīdiānus*, from *quotīdiē*, each day : *quot*, how many, as many as + *diēs*, day.]

quo·tient (kwŏsh'nt) *n.* **1.** The quantity resulting from division of one quantity by another; the number of times one quantity must be multiplied to make up another. **2.** *Informal.* The rate or proportion of some specified quality: *a high anxiety quotient amongst those with dangerous occupations.* [Middle English *quocient*, from Latin *quotiēns*, how many times, from *quot*, how many.]

Qur'an. Variant of **Koran.**

q.v. Which see. Used to indicate a cross-reference. [Latin, *quod vide.*]

Q value *n. Physics.* The **Q factor** *(see).*

Qwa·qwa In South Africa, the tribal homeland for the South Sotho people.

R

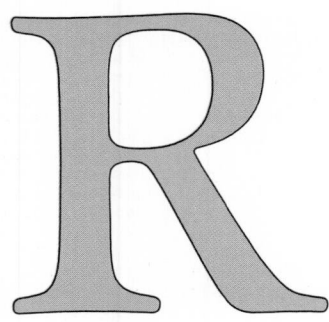

Ra *This bronze falcon head represents Ra, the ancient Egyptian sun god whose boat was believed to sail across the sky each day. It was thought to be towed back through the underworld each night. Since Ra was the supreme Egyptian deity, the pharaohs used "son of Ra" as one of their titles.*

rabbit *The rabbit probably originated in Spain, but is now found in most parts of the world. Farmers consider it a serious pest, and myxomatosis – a disease affecting only rabbits and a few hares – was introduced in the 1950s to control the rabbit population. The disease was spread deliberately through Australia from 1950, but it reached England from mainland Europe in 1953 only by accident.*

r, R (ar) *n., pl.* **r's** or *rare* **rs, Rs** or **R's. 1.** The 18th letter of the modern English alphabet. **2.** Any of the speech sounds represented by this letter.

r, R, r., R. *Note:* As an abbreviation or symbol, *r* may be a small or a capital letter, with or without a full stop. Established forms or those generally preferred precede the definition. When no form is given, all four forms are in general use in that sense. **1. R** *Chemistry.* gas constant. **2. R.** rabbi. **3. R** *Chemistry.* radical. **4. r, R** radius. **5. r., R.** railway. **6. R** rand. **7. r.** range. **8. r.** rare. **9. R, R.** Réaumur (scale). **10. R.** rector. **11. R.** regiment. **12. R.** Regina. **13. R., r.** registered (trademark). **14. R.** regius. **15. R.** Republican (party) (in the United States). **16. r, R** resistance (electricity). **17. R** *Ecclesiastical.* response. **18. r.** retired. **19. R.** Rex. **20. r., R.** right. **21. r., R.** river. **22. r., R.** road. **23. r.** rod (unit of length). **24. R** röntgen (unit of radiation). **25. R** rook (in chess). **26. r., R.** rouble. **27. R.** royal. **28. r.** rubber (in card games). **29. r, r.** *Sports.* run. **30. r., R.** rupee. **31.** Rydberg constant. **32.** The 18th in a series; 17th when *J* is omitted.

Ra (ra). Also **Re** (ray). The sun god, the supreme deity of the ancient Egyptians, represented as a man usually with the head of a hawk crowned with a solar disc and uraeus. [Egyptian *ra'.*]

Ra The symbol for the element radium.

R.A. 1. rear admiral. **2.** *Astronomy.* right ascension. **3.** Royal Academy; Royal Academician. **4.** Royal Artillery.

R.A.A.F. Royal Australian Air Force.

Ra·bat (rə-baát). Capital of Morocco, situated on the Atlantic Ocean at the mouth of the Bou Regreg river. There have been settlements here since ancient times, and it became a Muslim fortress (*c.* A.D. 700).

rabato. Variant of **rebato.**

Ra·baul (raa-bówl, rə-). Port in the northeast of the island of New Britain, Papua New Guinea. The town is surrounded by active volcanoes and was severely damaged by eruptions in 1937.

Rabbah Ammon, Rabbath Ammon. See **Amman.**

rab·bet (rábbit) *n.* Also **re·bate** (rée-bayt, rábbit). **1.** A cut or groove along or near the edge of a piece of wood that allows another piece to fit into it to form a joint. **2.** A joint made in this manner. ~*v.* **rabbeted, -beting, -bets.** —*tr.* **1.** To cut a rabbet in. **2.** To join by a rabbet. —*intr.* To be joined by a rabbet. [Middle English *rabet,* from Old French *rabat,* a beating down, from *rabattre,* to beat down, reduce : *re-,* back + *abattre,* to beat down : *a-,* from Latin *ad-,* to + *battre,* to beat, from Latin *battuere.*]

rab·bi (ráb-ī) *n., pl.* **-bis.** Also **rab·bin** (rábbin). **1.** *Abbr.* **R.** The ordained spiritual leader of a Jewish congregation. **2.** Formerly, a person authorised to interpret Jewish law. [Hebrew *rabbī,* my master : *rabh,* great one + *-ī,* my.]

rab·bin·ate (rábbin-ayt) *n.* The office or function of a rabbi.

Rab·bin·ic (ra-bínnik, rə-) *n.* The Hebrew language as used in the learned writings of the rabbis of the medieval period.

rab·bin·i·cal (ra-bínnik'l, rə-) *adj.* Also **rab·bin·ic** (-bínnik). Of, pertaining to, or characteristic of rabbis, or their views, learning, writings, or language. —**rab·bin·i·cal·ly** *adv.*

rab·bin·ism (rábbin-iz'm) *n.* Rabbinical teachings and traditions.

rab·bin·ist (rábbin-ist) *n.* A strict observer of the Talmud and of rabbinical traditions. —**rab·bin·is·tic** (-ístik).

rab·bit (rábbit) *n., pl.* **-bits** or collectively **rabbit. 1.** Any of various long-eared, short-tailed, burrowing mammals of the family Leporidae, such as the commonly domesticated Old World species *Oryctolagus cuniculus.* **2.** *U.S.* Loosely, a hare. **3.** The fur of a rabbit or hare. **4.** *Informal.* One who plays a particular game or sport badly. ~*intr.v.* **rabbited, -biting, -bits. 1.** To hunt rabbits. **2.** *Slang.* To talk at length, usually trivially and often rapidly. Often used with *on.* [Middle English *rabet,* probably from Old French; akin to Walloon *robete,* diminutive of Flemish *robbe†.*] —**rab·bit·er** *n.*

rabbit fever *n.* A disease, tularaemia (*see*).

rab·bit·fish (rábbit-fish) *n., pl.* **-fishes** or collectivly **rabbitfish. 1.** A fish, the **chimaera** (*see*); especially, the species *Chimaera monstrosa,* of European seas. Also called "ratfish". **2.** Any fish of the family Siganidae, of tropical Indo-Pacific waters, having a rounded, rabbit-like snout and spiny fins.

rabbit punch *n.* A chopping blow to the back of the neck.

rab·ble¹ (rább'l) *n.* **1.** A tumultuous mob. **2.** A group of persons regarded with contempt: *a rabble of penniless aristocrats.* **3.** The lower classes. Used derogatorily, preceded by *the.* [Middle English *rabble†.*]

rabble² *n.* Also **rab·bler** (rábblər). *Metallurgy.* **1.** An iron bar with one end bent like a rake, used to stir and skim molten iron in puddling. **2.** Any of various similar tools or mechanically operated devices used in roasting or refining furnaces. ~*tr.v.* **rabbled, -bling, -bles.** *Metallurgy.* To stir or skim (molten iron) with a rabble. [French *râble,* fire shovel, from Old French *roable,* from Medieval Latin *rotabulum,* from Latin *rutābulum,* from *ruere†* (past participle *rutus*), to rake up.]

rab·ble-rous·er (rább'l-rowzər) *n.* One who incites a crowd to action or violence; a demagogue.

Ra·be·lais (rábbə-lay, ráb- ‖ -láy), **François** (*c.* 1494–1553). French humanist and satirist. A Franciscan, then a Benedictine monk, he studied medicine at Montpellier. His satirical tales attacked medieval scholasticism and superstition: the most popular are *Pantagruel* (1532) and *Gargantua* (1534). Despite his religious sincerity, his works are full of high-spirited vulgarity.

Rab·e·lai·si·an (rábbə-láyzi-ən ‖ *U.S. also* -láyzh'n) *adj.* Pertaining to or characteristic of the works of Rabelais; broadly and lustily humorous.

ra·bi (rúbbi) *n.* **1.** In India and Pakistan, a crop that is harvested at the beginning of spring. Compare **kharif. 2.** In north India, the cool dry or winter season. [Urdu, spring crop, from Arabic *rabī',* spring.]

Ra·bi (rúbbi, raábi) *n.* Also **Ra·bi·a** (rə-bée-ə). Either the third or the fourth month of the Muslim calendar. [Arabic *rabī',* spring.]

Ra·bi (raábi), **Isidor Isaac** (1898–). Austrian-born U.S. physicist. He is particularly noted for his work on magnetic forces within the atom. He was awarded the Nobel prize (1944).

rab·id (rábbid, *also* ráybid) *adj.* **1.** Of or afflicted with rabies. **2.** Fanatical; extreme. **3.** Raging; uncontrollable: *rabid thirst.* [Latin *rabidus,* raving, from *rabere,* to rave.] —**rab·id·i·ty** (rə-bíddəti, ra-, ray-), **rab·id·ness** *n.* —**rab·id·ly** *adv.*

ra·bies (ráy-beez, -biz, -bi-eez) *n.* An acute, infectious, often fatal viral disease of most warm-blooded animals, especially wolves, cats, and dogs, that is transmitted to humans by the bite of infected animals. It affects the central nervous system and is characterised by convulsions and aversion to water. Also called "hydrophobia". [New Latin, from Latin *rabiēs,* rage, from *rabere,* to rave.] —**ra·bi·et·ic** (ráybi-éttik) *adj.*

R.A.C. 1. Royal Armoured Corps. **2.** Royal Automobile Club.

rac·coon, ra·coon (ra-koŏn, rə-) *n., pl.* **-coons** or collectively **raccoon. 1.** A carnivorous North American mammal, *Procyon lotor,* having greyish-brown fur, black, masklike facial markings, and a bushy, black-ringed tail. Also *U.S.* "coon". **2.** The fur of this animal. **3.** Any of various similar or related animals. [Algonquian (Virginia) *aroughcoune, arathkone.*]

raccoon dog *n.* A wild dog, *Nyctereutes procyonoides,* of east Asia, having golden-brown hair and black eye patches like those of a raccoon.

race¹ (rayss) *n.* **1. a.** A local geographic or global human population distinguished as a more or less distinct group by genetically transmitted physical characteristics. **b.** The division of mankind according to such characteristics: *discrimination on the grounds of race.* **2.** Loosely, any species, especially mankind as a whole: *the human race.* **3.** Any group of people united or classified together on the basis of common history, nationality, or geographical distribution. **4.** A genealogical line; a lineage; a family. **5.** Any group of people having a particular characteristic, profession, or the like in common: *the race of statesmen.* **6.** *Biology.* **a.** A plant or animal population that differs from others of the same species in one or more hereditary traits; a subspecies. **b.** A breed or strain, as of domestic animals. —See Usage Note at **nation.** [French, group of people, generation, from Italian *razza†.*]

race[2] *n.* **1. a.** A competition of speed, such as in running or riding. **b.** *Plural.* A series of such competitions, especially in horse riding, held at a specific time on a regular course: *winning money at the races.* **2.** Any contest or pursuit of supremacy: *the race for top position.* **3. a.** Steady or rapid onward movement. **b.** *Archaic.* A steady onward movement, course, or span: *the sun's race.* **c.** *Archaic.* A human lifetime. **4. a.** A strong or swift current of water. **b.** The channel of such a current. **c.** An artificial channel built to transport water and utilise its energy. **5.** A groovelike part of a machine in which a moving part slides or rolls; especially, any of the rings holding the balls or rollers in a bearing. Also called "raceway". **6.** *Australian.* A fenced track for sheep or other livestock, especially one leading to a dip. **7.** *Aeronautics.* A **slipstream** *(see).*
~*v.* **raced, racing, races.** —*intr.* **1.** To compete in a contest of speed. **2.** To move rapidly or at top speed. **3.** To run too rapidly because of decreased resistance or a lighter load. Used of engines. —*tr.* **1.** To compete against in a contest of speed. **2.** To cause (an animal or vehicle) to compete in such a contest, especially habitually or professionally. **3.** To cause to move rapidly or at top speed. **4.** To cause (an engine with the gears disengaged, for example) to run too fast. [Middle English *ra(a)s,* from Old Norse *rās.*]

race[3] *n.* A root, especially of ginger. [Old French *rais, raiz,* root, from Latin *rādix* (stem *rādīc-*).]

race·card, race card (ráyss-kaard) *n.* A printed list or programme of the races, their times, and their runners, at a race meeting. Also called "card".

race·course (ráyss-kawrss || -kōrss) *n.* A course or track laid out for horseracing.

race·horse (ráyss-hawrss) *n.* A horse bred and trained to race.

ra·ceme (rə-seém, ra-, ray-) *n.* *Botany.* An inflorescence in which stalked flowers are arranged singly along a common main axis with the youngest at the top, as in the lily of the valley. [Latin *racēmus*†, stalk of a cluster of grapes, bunch of berries.]

race meeting *n.* A series of races, usually horse races, held at a particular time or place.

ra·ce·mic (rə-seémik, ra-, ray-, -sémmik) *adj.* Of or designating a chemical mixture containing equal quantities of dextrorotatory and laevorotatory isomers so that it does not have a net optical activity. [French *racémique,* from Latin *racēmus,* RACEME.]

racemic acid *n.* An optically inactive form of tartaric acid, $C_4H_6O_6 \cdot H_2O$, that can be separated into dextrorotatory and laevorotatory components and is sometimes found in grape juice during winemaking.

ra·ce·mi·form (rə-seémi-fawrm, ra-, ray-) *adj.* *Botany.* Resembling a raceme in form. [RACEME + -FORM.]

ra·ce·mise, ra·ce·mize (rássi-mīz) *v.* **-mised, -mising, -mises.** —*tr.* To convert (an optically active compound) into an optically inactive racemic mixture. —*intr.* To become racemic; change into a racemic mixture. —**rac·e·mi·sa·tion** (-mī-záysh'n || *U.S.* -mi-) *n.*

rac·e·mism (rə-seém-iz'm, rássim-) *n.* *Chemistry.* The condition or state of being racemic.

rac·e·mose (rássim-ōz, -ōss) *adj.* **1.** *Botany.* Designating any inflorescence in which the main axis continues to grow at the tip so that the oldest flowers are at the bottom and the youngest towards the tip. **2.** *Anatomy.* Having a structure of clustered parts. Said of glands. [Latin *racēmōsus,* full of clusters, from *racēmus,* RACEME.] —**rac·e·mose·ly** *adv.*

rac·er (ráyssər) *n.* **1.** One that takes part in races or is capable of great speed. **2.** Any of various fast-moving North American snakes of the genus *Coluber.*

race relations *pl.n.* Interaction and relationships between people of different races, especially with reference to their quality in a given social environment.

race riot *n.* A riot inspired by racial hatred or resentment, especially one resulting in a violent confrontation between groups of people of different races.

race suicide *n.* The gradual extinction of a people or race caused by the birth rate falling below the death rate as a result of an intentional limitation on the number of children.

race·track (ráyss-trak) *n.* **1.** A track, circuit, or course laid out for motor racing, greyhound racing, or the like. **2.** *U.S.* A racecourse.

race·way (ráyss-way) *n.* **1.** An artificial channel for transporting water. **2.** A racetrack. **3.** A machine **race** *(see).*

Ra·chel (ráychəl). The second wife of Jacob and mother of his sons Joseph and Benjamin. Genesis 29–35. [Hebrew *rāḥēl,* "ewe".]

ra·chis (ráy-kiss) *n., pl.* **-chises** or **-chides** (-ki-deez). *Biology.* A main axis or shaft, such as the main stem of an inflorescence, the shaft of a contour feather, or the spinal column. [New Latin, from Greek *rhakhis,* spine, backbone.] —**ra·chi·al** *adj.*

ra·chi·tis (ra-kītiss, rə-) *n.* A childhood and infant disease, **rickets** *(see).* [New Latin, from Greek *rhakhitis,* disease of the spine : RACHIS + -ITIS.] —**ra·chit·ic** (-kíttik) *adj.*

Rach·man·i·nov (rak-mánni-nof || rakh-, *U.S.* raak-maáni-; *Russian* -nəf), **Sergei (Vasilyevich)** (1873–1943). Russian composer. A virtuoso pianist, he excelled at the interpretation of the late Romantic composers; his own work is essentially a continuation of the genre. He left Russia (1917) to live in Switzerland and latterly in the United States.

Rach·man·ism (rák-mən-iz'm) *n.* The severe exploitation and intimidation, often violent, of slum tenants by a landlord or landlords. [After Perec *Rachman* (1920–1962), Polish-born British landlord who practised such intimidation.]

ra·cial (ráysh'l) *adj.* **1.** Pertaining to or typical of a race or races, or an ethnic group or groups. **2.** Arising from or based upon differences between races, especially physically distinguished human races, or ethnic groups. —**ra·cial·ly** *adv.*

Ra·cine (ra-seén), **Jean** (1639–99). French playwright. The greatest tragedian of the French classical period, he wrote plays based on classical Greek and Roman themes, which include *Andromaque* (1667), *Britannicus* (1669), and *Phèdre* (1677). —**Ra·cin·i·an** *adj.*

ra·cism (ráyssiz'm) *n.* Also **ra·cial·ism** (ráysh'l-izm). **1.** The belief that certain races, especially one's own, are inherently superior to others. **2.** Discriminatory behaviour or practices based on this view. —**rac·ist, ra·cial·ist** *n. & adj.*

rack[1] (rak) *n.* **1.** A framework or stand for holding or displaying various articles, especially: **a.** A small frame or ridged structure on which washed crockery or cutlery is placed to drain: *a plate rack.* **b.** A receptacle for livestock feed: *a hay rack.* **c.** A secure ledge for luggage. **d.** A series of hooks in a frame: *a hat rack.* **e.** A frame for holding bombs in an aeroplane. **f.** *Printing.* An upright framework for holding cases of type or galley proof. **g.** *U.S.* In billiards, snooker, and the like, a **frame** *(see).* **2.** A toothed bar that meshes with another toothed structure, such as a pinion or gearwheel. **3.** An instrument of torture, consisting of a frame on which the victim's body is stretched. Often preceded by *the.* —**on the rack.** Under great strain or in anguish.
~*tr.v.* **racked, racking, racks. 1.** To place in or upon a rack. **2.** To torture by means of the rack. **3.** To torment; make suffer: *racked with pain.* **4.** To subject to stress or violent shaking. **5.** To strain with great effort; make heavy or taxing demands on. **6.** To rack-rent. **7.** To move (a machine part) by use of a toothed rack. —**rack up.** *U.S. Slang.* To accumulate: *rack up points.* [Middle English *rekke, rakke,* probably from Middle Dutch *rec,* framework, *recken,* to stretch, from Germanic.] —**rack·er** *n.*

rack[2] *n.* A rapid, showy gait of a horse, in which each foot strikes the ground separately. Also called "single-foot".
~*intr.v.* **racked, racking, racks.** To go or move with this gait. [Perhaps of Arabic origin and akin to *rikwa,* easy-paced.]

rack[3], wrack (rak) *n.* A thin mass of wind-driven clouds.
~*intr.v.* **racked** or **wracked, racking** or **wracking, racks** or **wracks.** To be driven by the wind. Used of clouds. [Middle English *rak,* probably from Scandinavian, akin to Swedish *rak.*]

rack[4], wrack *n.* Destruction; decay. Now used only in the phrase *rack and ruin.* [Variant of WRACK (ruin).]

rack[5] *tr.v.* **racked, racking, racks.** To drain or draw off (wine or cider) from the dregs. [Middle English *rakken,* from Provençal *arracar,* from *raca*†, dregs, stems and husks of grapes.]

rack[6] *n.* **1.** A rib cut of lamb between the shoulder and the loin. **2.** A crown roast of lamb. [Perhaps from RACK (framework).]

rack-and-pin·ion (rák-ən-pín-yən) *n.* A device for the conversion of rotary to linear motion, consisting of a pinion and a mated rack.

rack·et[1], rac·quet (rákit) *n.* **1.** A light bat with a long handle attached to a head consisting of a nearly elliptical hoop strung with a network of catgut, nylon, or silk, used in various ball games. **2.** A snowshoe resembling the head of a racket. [French *rachette, raquette,* from Italian *racchetta,* from dialectal Arabic *râḥet,* palm of the hand.]

racket[2] *n.* *Informal.* **1.** A clamour; an uproar; a din. **2. a.** A business that obtains money through fraud or extortion. **b.** An illegal or dishonest practice. **3.** *Informal.* Any business or job. **4.** A lively and often dissipated social life. —See Synonyms at **noise.**
~*intr.v.* **racketed, -eting, -ets.** To lead a lively and often dissipated social life. Often used with *about.* [16th century (clamour) : probably imitative.]

rack·et·eer (ráki-teér) *n.* One engaged in an illegal business.
~*intr.v.* **racketeered, -eering, -eers.** To engage in a dishonest racket.

rack·et-press (rákit-press) *n.* A frame usually consisting of two rigid pieces kept pressed together by a spring or screws and nuts, used to keep the head of a racket in shape.

rack·ets, rac·quets (rákits) *n.* *Used with a singular verb.* A game resembling squash, played on a four-walled court.

rack·et-tail (rákit-tayl) *n.* Any of various birds having a racket-shaped tail, especially certain hummingbirds and kingfishers.

rack·et·y (rákiti) *adj.* Noisy; raucous; rowdy.

Rack·ham (rákəm), **Arthur** (1867–1939). British book illustrator. His graceful, ethereal style was best suited to fairy stories, such as *Peter Pan* (1906); among his other works is an edition of *A Christmas Carol* (1915).

rack railway *n.* A **cog railway** *(see).*

rack-rent (rák-rent) *n.* An exorbitant rent.
~*tr.v.* **rack-rented, -renting, -rents.** To exact exorbitant rent for or from. [From RACK (to torture).] —**rack-rent·er** *n.*

ra·con (ráy-kon) *n.* A radar beacon. [*Ra*dar beacon.]

rac·on·teur (rák-on-túr, -ON-) *n.* One who recounts stories and anecdotes with skill and wit. [French, from Old French, from *raconter,* to tell : *re-,* again + *aconter,* tell, count : *a-,* from Latin *ad-,* to + *co(u)nter,* to COUNT.]

racoon. Variant of **raccoon.**

racquet. Variant of **racket.**

rac·y (ráyssi) *adj.* **-ier, -iest. 1.** Full-flavoured; piquant or pungent: *a racy wine.* **2.** Vigorous; lively: *a racy manner.* **3.** Humorous and slightly sexually improper; risqué. [From RACE (lineage, in the sense of a distinctive kind).] —**rac·i·ly** *adv.* —**rac·i·ness** *n.*

rad (rad) *n.* *Physics.* A unit of energy absorbed from ionising radi-

raccoon Procyon lotor, *the raccoon or coon (above), is a meat-eating mammal native to North America. It often hunts beside lakes and streams, searching with its hands underwater for clams and frogs – a habit which has given rise to a mistaken belief that it washes its food before eating it.*

PRONUNCIATION KEY

a, trap; aa, father; ai, fair;
ar, star; aw, lawn; ay, play;
b, bb, stab; rubber;
ch, church; ck, ticket;
d, dd, dead; ladder; e, dress;
ee, bee; er, defer; ew, few;
ewr, pure; ə, about;
ər, letter; f, ff, fife; differ;
g, gg, giggle; h, hat; i, kit;
ī, price; īr, fire; j, judge;
k, kick; l, ll, let; 'l, needle;
m, mm, man; n, nn, no;
'n, sudden; ng, thing; o, lot;
ō, no; ŏŏ, foot; ōō, shoe;
oor, poor; ow, cow;
owr, hour; oy, boy;
p, pp, pepper; r, rr, red;
s, ss, sauce; sh, ship;
t, tt, totter; th, thick; th, this;
smooth; u, cut; ur, turn;
v, vv, valve; w, wet; y, yes;
z, zz, zebra; zh, vision;
pleasure

IN FOREIGN WORDS:

aN, oN, Saint-Saëns;
hl, Llanelli; Hluhluwe;
kh, loch; lough; Khaled

STRESS MARK:

in-sīt, insight; in-sít, incite

ation, equal to 0.01 joule per kilogram of irradiated material. [Short for RADIATION.]

rad 1. radian. **2.** radiator.

rad. 1. radical. **2.** radio. **3.** radius. **4.** radix.

RADA, R.A.D.A. (ráadə). In Britain, the Royal Academy of Dramatic Art.

ra·dar (ráydaar) *n.* **1.** A method of detecting distant objects and determining their position, velocity, or other characteristics by analysis of very high frequency radio waves reflected from their surfaces. **2.** The equipment used in such detection. [*Radio detection and ranging.*]

radar astronomy *n.* The technique of investigating celestial objects in the solar system by reflecting radio waves off them and detecting and analysing the reflected waves.

radar beacon *n.* A fixed device that sends or receives, amplifies, alters, and returns a radar signal, permitting a distant receiver to determine its bearing and sometimes its range. Also called "racon".

radar picket *n.* A ship or aircraft posted, usually during hostilities, to keep a radar watch for approaching aircraft.

ra·dar·scope (ráydaar-skōp) *n. Electronics.* The oscilloscope viewing screen of a radar receiver. [RADAR + (OSCILLO)SCOPE.]

Rad·cliffe (rád-klif), **Ann,** born Ann Ward (1764–1823). British novelist. She pioneered the "Gothic" novel. Although her books, including *The Mysteries of Udolpho* (1794), were popular thrillers, they also had a notable influence on the Romantic movement.

Rad·cliffe-Brown (rád-klif-brówn), **Alfred Reginald** (1881–1955). British anthropologist. His work on kinship, based on field work among the Andaman islanders and Australian Aborigines, laid the foundations of British anthropology.

rad·dle[1] (rádd'l) *tr.v.* **-dled, -dling, -dles.** To twist together or interweave. [Old French *rudelle, redelle,* rod twisted between upright stakes, perhaps from Middle High German *reidel.*]

radial symmetry *A rose window in the basilica of St. Francis, in Assisi, Italy. Bisect the composition anywhere and each half will be a mirror image of the other.*

radar

"SEEING" THINGS OUT OF SIGHT

How objects are detected by bouncing radio waves

Radar enables objects like ships and aircraft to be detected and precisely located at long distances or in poor visibility. Radio waves are bounced off the object, and the returning echo monitored.

The distance to the object is measured by the time taken for the radio waves to be reflected back to the radar aerial, and the location is indicated by the direction in which the aerial is pointing when the signal is received. This information is shown by light spots displayed on the scaled screen of a cathode-ray tube – the tube used in a television set.

Radar was developed in Britain in the 1930s from the ideas of the Italian radio pioneer Guglielmo Marconi. By the outbreak of World War II, a chain of radar stations along Britain's south and east coasts was capable of detecting aircraft more than 160 kilometres (100 miles) away. Now it can detect missiles up to 3200 kilometres (2,000 miles) distant, and be used to locate typhoons and thunderstorms as well as help the police to catch speeding motorists.

AIR-TRAFFIC CONTROL *Approaching aircraft are shown by flight numbers on a radar screen, and their positions located on a superimposed map.*

raddle[2]. Variant of **ruddle.**

rad·dled (rádd'ld) *adj.* Worn-out, as by debauchery or general deterioration. Usually said of a person. [Probably alluding to the heavily rouged face of an old or debauched person. See **ruddle.**]

ra·di·al (ráydi-əl) *adj.* **1. a.** Of, pertaining to, or arranged like rays or the radii of a circle. **b.** Radiating from or converging to a common centre. **2.** Having or characterised by parts so arranged or so radiating. **3.** Moving or directed along a radius. **4.** *Anatomy.* Of, pertaining to, or near the radius or forearm: *the radial nerve.* **5.** Developing symmetrically about a central point. **6.** Radial-ply. ~*n.* **1.** A radial part, such as a ray, spoke, or radius. **2.** Any basal fin ray in a bony fish. **3.** A radial-ply tyre. [Medieval Latin *radiālis,* from Latin *radius,* rod, ray. See **radius.**] —**ra·di·al·ly** *adv.*

radial engine *n.* An internal-combustion engine, as formerly used in propeller-driven aircraft, with radially arrayed cylinders.

ra·di·al-ply (ráydi-əl-plī) *adj.* Designating a vehicle tyre in which the cords in the fabric casing run radially, giving flexibility to the walls of the tyre. Compare **cross-ply.**

radial symmetry *n.* **1.** Symmetrical arrangement of constituents, especially of radiating parts, about a central point. **2.** *Biology.* The arrangement of the parts of an organism around a central axis such that a vertical cut through the axis in any plane produces two halves that are mirror images of each other. Compare **bilateral symmetry.**

ra·di·an (ráydi-ən) *n. Abbr.* rad *Mathematics.* A unit of angular measure equal to the angle subtended at the centre of a circle by an arc of length equal to the radius of the circle. It is equal to $360/2\pi^\circ$, or approximately $57°17'44.6''$. [RADI(US) + -AN.]

ra·di·ance (ráydi-ənss) *n.* Also **ra·di·an·cy** (-ən-si). **1.** The quality or state of being radiant. **2.** *Physics.* The radiant energy emitted per unit time in a given direction by a projected unit area of an emitting surface. Compare **irradiance.**

ra·di·ant (ráydi-ənt) *adj.* **1.** Emitting heat or light. **2.** Consisting of or emitted as radiation: *radiant heat.* **3. a.** Filled with light; bright. **b.** Glowing or beaming, as with health or happiness. **4.** *Physics.* Designating photometric quantities that depend on energy measurements rather than on measurements of visible light: *radiant exitance.* In this sense, compare **luminous.** —See Synonyms at **bright.** ~*n.* **1.** An object or point from which light or heat rays are emitted. **2.** *Astronomy.* The apparent celestial origin of a meteoric shower. **3.** The part of a gas fire or other heater that gives out heat. [Latin *radiāns* (stem *radiant-*), present participle of *radiāre,* to RADIATE.] —**ra·di·ant·ly** *adv.*

radiant efficiency *n. Symbol* η_e *Physics.* A measure of the efficiency of a source of radiation, equal to the power it emits divided by the power consumed by the source.

radiant energy *n. Physics.* Energy transferred by radiation, especially by an electromagnetic wave.

radiant exitance *n. Symbol* M_e *Physics.* The radiant flux emitted from a surface per unit area at a given point.

radiant flux *n. Symbol* ϕ_e *Physics.* The rate of flow of energy as electromagnetic radiation.

radiant heat *n.* Heat transferred as radiation, especially as infrared radiation.

radiant intensity *n. Symbol* I_e *Physics.* The radiant flux per unit solid angle emitted from a given point.

ra·di·ate (ráydi-ayt) *v.* **ated, -ating, -ates.** —*intr.* **1.** To emit radiation. **2.** To issue or emerge in rays. **3.** To spread out or converge radially, in the manner of the spokes of a wheel. —*tr.* **1.** To emit (heat or light, for example). **2.** To diffuse or cause to go out from or as if from a centre. **3.** To manifest in a glowing manner: *He radiated confidence.* **4.** To illuminate; light up. ~*adj.* (also **-ət, -it**). **1.** *Botany.* Having rays, raylike parts, or ray flowers: *a radiate inflorescence.* **2.** *Biology.* Characterised by **radial symmetry** (*see*). **3.** Surrounded with rays. Said of a representation of a head, especially on a coin. [Latin *radiāre,* to emit beams, furnish with spokes, from *radius,* ray. See **radius.**]

ra·di·a·tion (ráydi-áysh'n) *n.* **1.** The act or process of radiating. **2.** *Physics.* **a.** The emission and propagation of waves or particles. **b.** The propagating waves or particles, such as light, sound, radiant heat, or particles emitted by radioactivity. **3.** *Anatomy.* Radial arrangement of parts, as of a group of nerve fibres connecting different areas of the brain. **4.** *Biology.* A form of evolution, **adaptive radiation** (*see*).

radiation pattern *n. Electronics.* A diagram representing the strength of emission of electromagnetic radiation and its direction around a transmitting aerial.

radiation sickness *n.* Illness induced by ionising radiation, ranging in severity from nausea, vomiting, headache, and diarrhoea to loss of hair and teeth, reduction in red and white blood cell count, extensive haemorrhaging, sterility, and death.

ra·di·a·tive (ráydi-ətiv, -aytiv) *adj. Physics.* Of or involving the emission of radiation, especially electromagnetic radiation.

ra·di·a·tor (ráydi-aytər) *n.* **1. a.** A heating device consisting of a series of connected pipes or a flat structure containing ducts, through which hot water or steam can be circulated in a central-heating system. **b.** A similar portable device containing oil, which is heated electrically. **2. a.** A cooling device, as in automotive engines, through which water or other fluids circulate as a coolant. **b.** The grille at the front of such a device on a motor vehicle. **3.** *Physics.* A body that emits radiation. **4.** A transmitting aerial.

rad·i·cal (ráddik'l) *adj.* **1.** Arising from or going to a root or source. **2. a.** Affecting the basis of something; fundamental in its effect: *a radical revision of the procedure.* **b.** Broadly, having a profound or far-reaching effect: *radical reductions in staff levels.* **3.** Advocating or intended to effect fundamental or throroughgoing changes, especially of economic and political structures. **4.** *Linguistics.* Of or designating a word root. **5.** *Botany.* Of, pertaining to, or growing from the root. **6.** *Medicine.* Designating treatment directed to the complete cure of a disease rather than simply to the relief of symptoms. ~*n.* **1.** One who advocates profound political, social, or other change. **2.** *Mathematics. Abbr.* **rad.** The root of a quantity as indicated by the radical sign. **3.** *Chemistry. Abbr.* **R** An atom or group of atoms with at least one unpaired electron. **4.** *Linguistics. Abbr.* **rad.** A word element, a **root** (see). [Middle English, of the root, fundamental, from Late Latin *rādīcālis*, having roots, from Latin *rādix* (stem *rādic-*), root.] —**rad·i·cal·ly** *adv.* —**rad·i·cal·ness** *n.*

radical chic *n.* **1.** The adoption or affectation by people in fashionable society of radical left-wing policies and opinions and the styles and tastes associated with these views. **2.** Such people collectively. [Coined by Tom WOLFE.]

radical expression *n.* A mathematical expression or form in which radical signs appear.

rad·i·cal·ise, rad·i·cal·ize (ráddik'l-īz) *tr.v.* **-ised, -ising, -ises.** To make radical or more radical, especially in political affairs. —**rad·i·cal·i·sa·tion** (-ī-záysh'n || *U.S.* -i-) *n.*

rad·i·cal·ism (ráddik'l-iz'm) *n.* **1.** The doctrines or practices of political or other radicals. **2.** The state or quality of being radical.

radical sign *n.* **1.** The sign √ placed before a quantity, indicating extraction of the root designated by a raised integral index. When extracting a square root, the index is customarily omitted. **2.** This sign together with a horizontal bar extending from its top to the end of the expression from which a root is to be extracted.

rad·i·cand (ráddi-kand, -kánd) *n.* The quantity under a radical sign: *3 is the radicand of* √ *3.* [Latin *rādīcandum*, neuter gerundive of *rādīcāre*, to take root, from *rādix*, root. See **radical.**]

rad·i·ces. Alternative plural of **radix.**

rad·i·cle (ráddik'l) *n.* **1.** *Botany.* The part of the plant embryo that develops into the primary root. **2.** *Anatomy.* A small structure resembling a root, such as a fibril of a nerve. [Latin *rādīcula,* diminutive of *rādix* (stem *rādīc-*), root.]

ra·di·i. Alternative plural of **radius.**

ra·di·o (ráydi-ō) *n., pl.* **-os.** *Abbr.* **rad. 1.** The use of electromagnetic waves in the approximate frequency range from 10 kilohertz to 300 000 megahertz to transmit or receive electric signals without wires connecting the points of transmission and reception. **2.** Communication of audible signals, such as music, encoded in electromagnetic waves so transmitted and received. **3. a.** Transmission of programmes for the public by this means; radio broadcasting as an industry or medium. **b.** Programmes transmitted by radio: *The radio was interesting last night.* **c.** Used in the title of certain broadcasting stations: *Radio 3.* **4. a.** The equipment used to transmit radio signals; a transmitter. **b.** The equipment used to receive radio signals; a receiver. **c.** A complex of equipment capable of both transmitting and receiving radio signals. **5.** A message sent by radio. ~*adj.* **1.** Of, pertaining to, or sent by radio. **2.** Of, pertaining to, or designating oscillations of **radio frequency** (see). ~*v.* **radioed, -oing, -os.** —*tr.* **1.** To transmit a message to, or communicate with, by radio. **2.** To broadcast by radio. —*intr.* To transmit a message by radio. [Short for RADIOTELEGRAPHY.]

radio– *comb. form.* Indicates emission and propagation of radiation; for example, **radioactive.** [From RADIATION.]

ra·di·o·ac·tive (ráydi-ō-áktiv) *adj. Physics.* Of or exhibiting radioactivity. —**ra·di·o·ac·tive·ly** *adv.*

radioactive dating *n.* Any method of determining the age of organic material, such as wood or fossils, using the decay rates of naturally occurring radioactive isotopes. See **radiocarbon dating.**

radioactive decay *n.* A progressive decrease in the number of radioactive atoms in a substance by spontaneous nuclear disintegration or transformation. Also called "decay".

radioactive series *n.* A group of nuclides related by a sequence of radioactive decay processes in which the heavier members of the group are transformed into successively lighter ones, the lightest being stable. Also called "decay chain".

ra·di·o·ac·tiv·i·ty (ráydi-ō-ak-tívvəti) *n.* **1.** The spontaneous emission of radiation, either directly from unstable atomic nuclei or as a consequence of a nuclear reaction. The radiation so emitted, including alpha particles, nucleons, electrons, and gamma rays.

radio astronomy *n.* The study of celestial objects and phenomena by observation and analysis of emitted or reflected radio waves.

ra·di·o·au·tog·ra·phy (ráydi-ō-aw-tóggrəfi) *n.* **Autoradiography** (see).

radio beacon *n.* A fixed radio transmitter that broadcasts distinctive signals as a navigational aid.

radio beam *n.* A focused beam of radio signals transmitted by a radio beacon to guide aircraft or ships. Also called "beam".

ra·di·o·bi·ol·o·gy (ráydi-ō-bī-óllə-ji) *n.* **1.** The study of the effects of radiation on living organisms. **2.** The use of radioactive tracers to study biological processes. —**ra·di·o·bi·o·log·i·cal** (-bī-ə-lójik'l) *adj.* —**ra·di·o·bi·o·log·i·cal·ly** *adv.* —**ra·di·o·bi·ol·o·gist** (-ollə-jist) *n.*

radio cab *n.* A licensed taxi operating from a central unit to which customers can telephone to hire cabs. Also called "radio taxi".

radio car *n.* A car equipped with a mobile radio transmitter, used for example in outside-broadcast radio programmes.

ra·di·o·car·bon (ráydi-ō-kárbən) *n.* Radioactive carbon, especially **carbon 14** (see).

radiocarbon dating *n.* A technique of radioactive dating in which the age of a specimen can be calculated by measuring its content of carbon-14, absorbed from the atmosphere during its lifetime, which decays at a known rate. Also called "carbon dating".

ra·di·o·chem·is·try (ráydi-ō-kémmistri) *n.* The chemistry of radioactive materials. —**ra·di·o·chem·i·cal** *adj.*

radio compass *n.* A navigational aid consisting of an automatic radio receiver that determines the transmission direction of incoming radio waves.

ra·di·o·el·e·ment (ráydi-ō-éllimənt) *n.* Any naturally occurring or artificially produced radioactive element.

radio frequency *n. Abbr.* **RF 1.** The frequency of the waves transmitted by a specific radio station. **2.** Any frequency in the range within which radio waves may be transmitted, from about 10 kilohertz to about 300 000 megahertz. Radio frequency groups are: *very low frequency* (vlf), 10 to 30 kilohertz; *low frequency* (lf), 30 to 300 kilohertz; *medium frequency* (mf), 300 to 3 000 kilohertz; *high frequency* (hf), 3 000 to 30 000 kilohertz; *very high frequency* (vhf), 30 to 300 megahertz; *ultrahigh frequency* (uhf), 300 to 3 000 megahertz; *superhigh frequency* (shf), 3 000 to 30 000 megahertz; *extremely high frequency* (ehf), 30 000 to 300 000 megahertz.

ra·di·o·ge·nic (ráydi-ō-jénnik) *adj.* Caused by radioactivity. [RADIO- + -GENIC.]

ra·di·o·gram (ráydi-ō-gram) *n.* **1.** *British.* A unit resembling a small cabinet and containing a radio and record-player. **2.** A message transmitted by wireless telegraphy. **3.** A radiograph.

ra·di·o·graph (ráydi-ō-graaf, -graf) *n.* An image produced on a radiosensitive surface, such as a photographic film, by radiation other than visible light, especially X-rays passed through an object, or by photographing a fluoroscopic image. Also called "radiogram". ~*tr.v.* **radiographed, -graphing, -graphs.** To make a radiograph of. [RADIO- + -GRAPH.]

ra·di·og·ra·phy (ráydi-óggrəfi) *n.* Examination of the internal structure of a solid object by passing X-rays or gamma rays through it to produce a radiograph. The technique is used in industry and medicine. See **radiology.** —**ra·di·og·ra·pher** (-óggrəfər) *n.* —**ra·di·o·graph·ic** (-ə-gráffik, -ō-) *adj.* —**ra·di·o·graph·i·cal·ly** *adv.*

radio ham *n.* A licensed amateur radio operator who broadcasts and receives radio messages on his own equipment, as a hobby. Also informally called "ham".

ra·di·o·im·mu·no·as·say (ráydi-ō-i-méwnō-ə-sáy, -ássay) *n.* The technique of using radioactively labelled substances, particularly hormones, to measure the amounts of particular antibodies or hormones in the blood. [RADIO- + IMMUNNE + ASSAY.]

radio interferometer *n.* A form of radio telescope in which two or more separate receiving antennae are connected to a single detector, information being obtained by analysis of the interference patterns produced by detected radio waves.

ra·di·o·i·so·tope (ráydi-ō-Ī-sə-tōp) *n.* A naturally or artificially produced radioactive isotope of an element.

ra·di·o·lar·i·an (ráydi-ō-laír-i-ən) *n.* Any of various marine protozoans of the order Radiolaria, having rigid siliceous skeletons and radiating spicules. [New Latin *Radiolaria,* from Late Latin *radiolus,* small sunbeam, diminutive of Latin *radius,* ray. See **radius.**]

ra·di·o·lo·ca·tion (ráydi-ō-lə-káysh'n, -lō-) *n.* The detection of distant objects by radar.

ra·di·ol·o·gy (ráydi-óllə-ji) *n.* **1.** The use of ionising radiation for radiotherapy and medical diagnosis; especially, the use of X-rays in medical radiography or fluoroscopy. **2.** Radioscopy. [RADIO- + -LOGY.] —**ra·di·o·log·i·cal** (-ə-lójik'l) *adj.* —**ra·di·ol·o·gist** (-óllə-jist) *n.*

ra·di·o·lu·cent (ráydi-ō-lṓoss'nt, -léwss'nt) *adj.* Allowing the passage of radiation, especially X-rays. [RADIO- + (TRANS)LUCENT.]

ra·di·om·e·ter (ráydi-ómmitər) *n.* Any of various devices for detecting or measuring radiation. See **Crookes radiometer.** [RADIO- + -METER.] —**ra·di·o·met·ric** (-ə-méttrik, -ō-) *adj.* —**ra·di·om·e·try** (-ómmətri) *n.*

ra·di·o·nu·clide (ráydi-ō-néw-klīd || -nṓo-) *n.* A radioactive nuclide.

ra·di·o·paque (ráydi-ō-páyk) *adj.* Also **ra·di·o·o·paque** (-ō-ō-). Absorbing, and therefore being opaque to, radiation, especially X-rays. Radiopaque substances are used, for example, in medical radiography as contrast media. [RADIO- + OPAQUE.]

ra·di·o·phone (ráydi-ō-fōn) *n.* A radiotelephone. —**ra·di·o·phon·ic** (-fónnik) *adj.*

ra·di·o·pho·to·graph (ráydi-ō-fṓtə-graaf, -graf) *n.* Also **ra·di·o·pho·to** (-fṓtō). A photograph transmitted by radio waves, each image point being reproduced by a received electric impulse. —**ra·di·o·pho·tog·ra·phy** (-fə-tóggrəfi) *n.*

ra·di·o·scope (ráydi-ō-skōp) *n.* A **fluoroscope** (see). [RADIO- + -SCOPE.]

ra·di·os·co·py (ráydi-óskəpi) *n.* The examination of the inner structure of opaque objects by X-rays or other penetrating radiation. Also called "radiology". [RADIO- + -SCOPY.] —**ra·di·o·scop·ic** (-ə-skóppik, -ō-) *adj.* —**ra·di·o·scop·i·cal** *adj.*

ra·di·o·sen·si·tive (ráydi-ō-sén-si-tiv) *adj.* Sensitive to radiation. Said especially of certain forms of cancer.

ra·di·o·sonde (ráydi-ō-sond) *n.* An instrument carried aloft, chiefly by balloon, to gather and transmit meteorological data.

radio source *n.* A celestial source of radio waves, such as a quasar or supernova remnant.

radio spectrum *n.* The entire range of electromagnetic communications frequencies, including those used for radio, radar, and television; the radio-frequency spectrum.

radio telescope *Radio telescopes – like this one in West Germany – are used by astronomers to "listen" to the stars. Radio signals from space are reflected from a giant dish on to a central antenna and then analysed to produce a radio map of the universe. Pulsars and quasars – celestial bodies which are powerful natural radio transmitters – were both first identified by radio astronomy.*

ragged robin *The wild flower* Lychnis flos-cuculi *or ragged robin (above) is also called bachelor's buttons in parts of Britain. Country girls used to put several of them under an apron, naming them after local boys; the one that opened first told the girl who she might marry.*

ragwort *A late-flowering relative of the daisy that gets its name from its ragged leaves. It is mildly poisonous.*

radio taxi *n.* A **radio cab** *(see).*

ra·di·o·tel·e·graph (ráydi-ō-télli-graaf, -graf) *n.* **1.** The sending of messages by radiotelegraphy. **2.** A message sent by this means. **—ra·di·o·tel·e·graph** *v.* **—ra·di·o·tel·e·graph·ic** (-graffik) *adj.*

ra·di·o·te·leg·ra·phy (ráydi-ō-ti-léggrəfi, -te-, -tə-) *n.* **Wireless telegraphy** *(see).*

ra·di·o·tel·e·phone (ráydi-ō-télli-fōn) *n.* A telephone in which audible communication is established by radio. Also called "radiophone", "wireless telephone". **—ra·di·o·tel·e·phon·ic** (-fónnik) *adj.* **—ra·di·o·te·leph·o·ny** (-ti-léffəni, -te-, -tə-) *n.*

radio telescope *n.* A sensitive, directional radio-antenna system used to detect and analyse radio waves from space.

ra·di·o·ther·a·py (ráydi-ō-thérrəpi) *n.* The treatment of disease, particularly cancer, with radiation, especially by selective irradiation with X-rays or other ionising radiation and by ingestion of radioisotopes.

radio wave *n.* A radio-frequency electromagnetic wave. Formerly called "Hertzian wave".

radio window *n.* A region in the radio spectrum (10 000 to 40 000 megahertz) in which radio waves are not absorbed by the atmosphere or reflected by the ionosphere and can pass between Earth and space.

rad·ish (ráddish || réddish) *n.* **1.** Any of various plants of the genus *Raphanus;* especially, *R. sativus,* having a thickened, edible root. **2.** The pungent root of this plant, eaten raw as an appetiser and in salads. [Middle English *radiche,* Old English *rædic,* from Latin *rādix* (stem *rādīc-*), root.]

ra·di·um (ráydi-əm) *n. Symbol* **Ra** A rare brilliant-white, luminescent, highly radioactive metallic element having 16 isotopes of which radium 226 with a half-life of 1,622 years is the most common. It is used in cancer radiotherapy, as a neutron source for some research purposes, and as a constituent of luminescent paints. Atomic number 88, melting point 700°C, boiling point 1,737°C, valency 2. [New Latin, from Latin *radius,* ray (radium emits rays that penetrate opaque matter). See **radius.**]

radium therapy *n.* The use of radium in radiotherapy, especially in treating cancer.

ra·di·us (ráydi-əss) *n., pl.* **-dii** (-ī) or **-uses. 1.** *Abbr.* **R, r, rad. a.** A line segment that joins the centre of a circle with any point on its circumference. **b.** A line segment that joins the centre of a sphere with any point on its surface. **c.** A line segment that joins the centre of a closed figure, such as a polygon or ellipse, to a point on the circumference. **2.** The length of any such line segment. **3.** A measure of circular area or extent: *every family within a radius of 25 miles.* **4.** A measure of range of activity or influence. **5.** A radial part or structure, such as a mechanically pivoted arm or the spoke of a wheel. **6.** *Anatomy.* **a.** A long, prismatic, slightly curved bone, the shorter and thicker of the two forearm bones, located on the outer side of the ulna. **b.** A similar bone in many vertebrates. [Latin *radius*†, spoke of a wheel, ray.]

radius of curvature *n.* In geometry, the reciprocal of the curvature of a given curve at a given point.

radius vector *n. Mathematics.* **1.** A line segment that joins any variable point to the origin of polar or spherical coordinates. **2.** The length of such a line segment.

ra·dix (ráydiks) *n., pl.* **-dices** (ráydi-seez, ráddi-) or **-dixes. 1.** *Biology.* A root or point of origin. **2.** *Abbr.* **rad.** *Mathematics.* The base of a system of numbers, as 2 is of the binary system and 10 is of the decimal system. [Latin *rādix,* root.]

radix point *n.* A **decimal point** *(see).*

Rad·nor·shire (rád-nər-shər, -sheer, *also* -nawr- || -shīr). *Welsh.* **Sir Fae·sy·fed** (shéer vī-súvved). Former county of east central Wales. A mountainous region, known for its sheep rearing, it became part of the new county of Powys (1974).

ra·dome (ráy-dōm) *n.* A domelike protective housing for a radar antenna used especially in certain aircraft. [*ra*dar + *dome.*]

ra·don (ráy-don) *n. Symbol* **Rn** A colourless, radioactive, inert gaseous element formed by disintegration of radium. It is used as a radiation source in radiotherapy and to produce neutrons for research. Atomic number 86, atomic weight 222, melting point −71°C, boiling point −61.8°C, relative density (solid) 4, valency 0, half-life 3.823 days. [New Latin : RAD(IUM) + *-on,* suffix indicating inert gases.]

rad·u·la (ráddew-lə) *n., pl.* **-lae** (-lee). *Zoology.* In molluscs, a ribbon-like strip on the tongue, bearing rows of horny teeth used for scraping food. [New Latin, from Latin *rādula,* scraper, from *rādere,* to scrape.] **—rad·u·lar** *adj.*

RAF, R.A.F. (*often* raf) *n.* In Britain, the Royal Air Force.

raf·fi·a, raph·i·a (ráffi-ə) *n.* **1.** An African palm tree, *Raphia ruffia,* having large leaves that yield a useful fibre. Also called "raffia palm". **2.** The fibre of these leaves, used for mats, baskets, and other products. [Malagasy.]

raf·fi·nose (ráffin-ōz, -ōss) *n.* A white crystalline sugar, $C_{18}H_{32}O_{16}$, obtained from cottonseed meal and sugar beets. [French, from *raffiner,* to refine : *re-,* again + *affiner,* to refine : *a-,* to, from Latin *ad-* + *fin,* refined, from Old French, FINE.]

raff·ish (ráffish) *adj.* **1.** Vulgar; showy. **2.** Slightly disreputable; rakish. [Probably from dialectal *raff,* trash, from Middle English *raf.* See **raft** (amount).] **—raff·ish·ly** *adv.* **—raff·ish·ness** *n.*

raf·fle[1] (ráff'l) *n.* **1.** The disposing of an item as a prize in a competition by a lottery, in which the winning ticket is chosen at random. **2.** The competition itself.
~*v.* **raffled, -fling, -fles.** —*tr.* To dispose of in a raffle. Often used with *off.* —*intr.* To conduct or take part in a raffle. [Middle English *rafle,* a type of dice game, from Old French *raffle*†, act of snatching.] **—raf·fler** *n.*

raffle[2] *n.* Rubbish; debris. [Middle English, perhaps from Old Fench *ne rafle,* nothing at all.]

Raf·fles (ráff'lz), **Sir (Thomas) Stamford (Bingley)** (1781–1826). British colonial administrator. He is best known for his acquisition (1819) of Singapore for the East India Company, and his founding of the city there. He was also a founder and first president of London Zoo.

raf·fle·si·a (ra-fléez-i-ə || -fléezh-ə) *n.* Any of various parasitic leafless plants of the tropical Asian genus *Rafflesia;* especially, *R. arnoldi,* having large flowers smelling of rotten meat and pollinated by carrion flies. [New Latin, after Sir Stamford RAFFLES.]

raft[1] (raaft || raft) *n.* **1.** A flat structure, typically made of planks, logs, or barrels, that floats on water and is used for transport or as a platform for swimmers. **2.** A **life raft** *(see).* **3.** A collection of floating ice, logs, or debris. **4.** In building, a layer of reinforced concrete used as a foundation to distribute the weight of a building, especially on subsiding ground.
~*v.* **rafted, rafting, rafts.** —*tr.* **1.** To convey on a raft. **2.** To make a raft from. —*intr.* To travel by raft. [Middle English *rafte,* from Old Norse *raptr,* beam, rafter.]

raft[2] *n. U.S. Informal.* A great number, amount, or collection; a lot. [Variant of Scottish *raff,* trash, from Middle English *raf,* perhaps from Scandinavian, akin to Old Norse *hreppa,* to catch, from Germanic *hrap-* (unattested).]

raft·er (raáf-tər || ráf-) *n.* Any of the sloping beams that support a pitched roof. [Middle English *rafter,* Old English *ræfter,* from Germanic.]

rag[1] (rag) *n.* **1.** A scrap of cloth. **2.** Such scraps collectively, used, for example, as stuffing material or for pulp in papermaking. Also used adjectivally: *the rag content of a sheet of paper.* **3.** A scrap or fragment. **4.** *Slang.* A newspaper, especially one regarded as sensational or contemptible. **5.** *Plural.* **a.** Threadbare or tattered clothing. **b.** *Informal.* Clothes. **6.** *British Informal.* A flag. **7.** A jagged piece; a rough projection. **—chew the rag.** *Informal.* To complain. [Middle English *ragge,* probably back-formation from RAGGED.]

rag[2] *tr.v.* **ragged, ragging, rags.** *Slang.* **1.** To tease; taunt. **2.** To scold. **3.** *British.* To play a practical joke upon.
~*n. British.* **1.** A practical joke; a prank. **2.** A period during a college term when students hold comic parades and other activities to raise money for charity. Also used adjectivally: *rag week.* [18th century : origin obscure.]

rag[3] *n.* **1.** A roofing slate with one rough surface. **2.** Any coarsely textured rock. [Middle English *ragghe*†, later associated with RAG (cloth).]

rag[4] *tr.v.* **ragged, ragging, rags.** To compose or play (a piece of music) in ragtime.
~*n.* A piece of music written in ragtime. [Short for RAGTIME.]

ra·ga (raágə, raag) *n.* A traditional form in Hindu music, consisting of a theme that expresses some aspect of religious feeling and sets forth a tonal system on which variations are improvised within a prescribed framework of typical progressions, melodic formulas, and rhythmic patterns. [Sanskrit *rāga,* colour, musical colour.]

rag·a·muf·fin (rággə-muffin) *n.* A dirty or unkempt child. [After *Ragamoffyn,* demon in *Piers Plowman* (*c.* 1393), probably based on RAG (cloth).]

rag-and-bone man (rág-ən-bṓn) *n.* A person who buys or gathers old clothes, furniture, and other junk, and sells it. Also *U.S.* "junk man".

rag·bag (rág-bag) *n.* A jumbled collection; a mixture.

rag bolt *n.* A bolt having a jagged projection on the shank keeping it in place when driven in.

rag doll *n.* A doll made from or stuffed with scraps of cloth.

rage (rayj) *n.* **1. a.** Extreme, vehement anger; fury. **b.** A fit of anger. **2.** Furious intensity, as of a storm or disease. **3.** Burning desire or passion. **4.** *Informal.* A fad; a craze. —See Synonyms at **anger. —all the rage.** *Informal.* Very fashionable.
~*intr.v.* **raged, raging, rages. 1.** To speak or act furiously. **2.** To move with great violence or intensity. **3.** To spread, prevail, or continue unchecked. [Middle English, from Old French, from Vulgar Latin *rabia* (unattested), from Latin *rabiēs,* madness, from *rabere,* to rave.]

rag·ged (rággid) *adj.* **1.** Tattered. **2.** Dressed in tattered or threadbare clothes. **3.** Unkempt or shaggy. **4.** Having a rough surface or edges; jagged. **5.** Uneven; sloppy; lacking smoothness or polish: *a ragged performance.* **6.** Harsh; rasping: *a ragged cry.* [Middle English, from Old Norse *roggvathr,* tufted, from *rogg*†, tuft of fur.] **—rag·ged·ly** *adv.* **—rag·ged·ness** *n.*

ragged robin *n.* A plant, *Lychnis flos-cuculi,* native to Eurasia, having reddish or white flowers with deeply lobed petals. Also called "cuckooflower". [From the ragged appearance of the petals.]

ragged school *n.* Formerly, a free school for poor children.

ra·gi (raági, rággi) *n.* A grass, *Eleusine coracana,* of Africa and Asia, where it is cultivated for its edible grain. [Hindi *rāgī,* from Sanskrit, from Dravidian *rāki* (unattested).]

rag·lan (rágglən) *n.* A loose coat, jacket, or sweater with slanted shoulder seams and with the sleeves extending in one piece to the neckline.
~*adj.* Having the shoulder seams extending diagonally from armhole to neckline: *a raglan sleeve.* [After Lord RAGLAN.]

Rag·lan (rágglən), **Fitzroy James Henry Somerset, 1st Baron**

radio wave

SILENT SIGNALS IN THE EMPTY AIR
How radio waves send sounds around the world

A radio wave is an electromagnetic signal that travels at the speed of light, and can be picked up by a receiving aerial similar to the one from which it was transmitted. Decoded, it reproduces the same sound waves that were converted by electricity into the electromagnetic signals at the transmitter. The idea that such signals could exist was put forward in 1864 by the Scots physicist, James Clerk Maxwell (1831–79). His theory of electromagnetism was proved correct in

1888, when a German physicist, Heinrich Hertz (1857–94) put an electric charge on two metal spheres, separated by a small gap. A few feet away he held another two spheres, also separated by a small gap. When a spark flashed between the two charged spheres, a similar spark flashed across the second gap. This was because the electric field produced a displacement current in empty space. This is the basis of all radio communication. An electric charge moved

rapidly up and down an aerial sets up a changing electric field. This sets up a changing magnetic field at right angles. The magnetic field sets up another changing electric field at right angles to itself, and so on. These changing waves travel at the speed of light. An aerial placed in their path has a current created in it matching that from the transmitter. Convert the current to sound waves, and you can hear sounds originated hundreds of kilometres away.

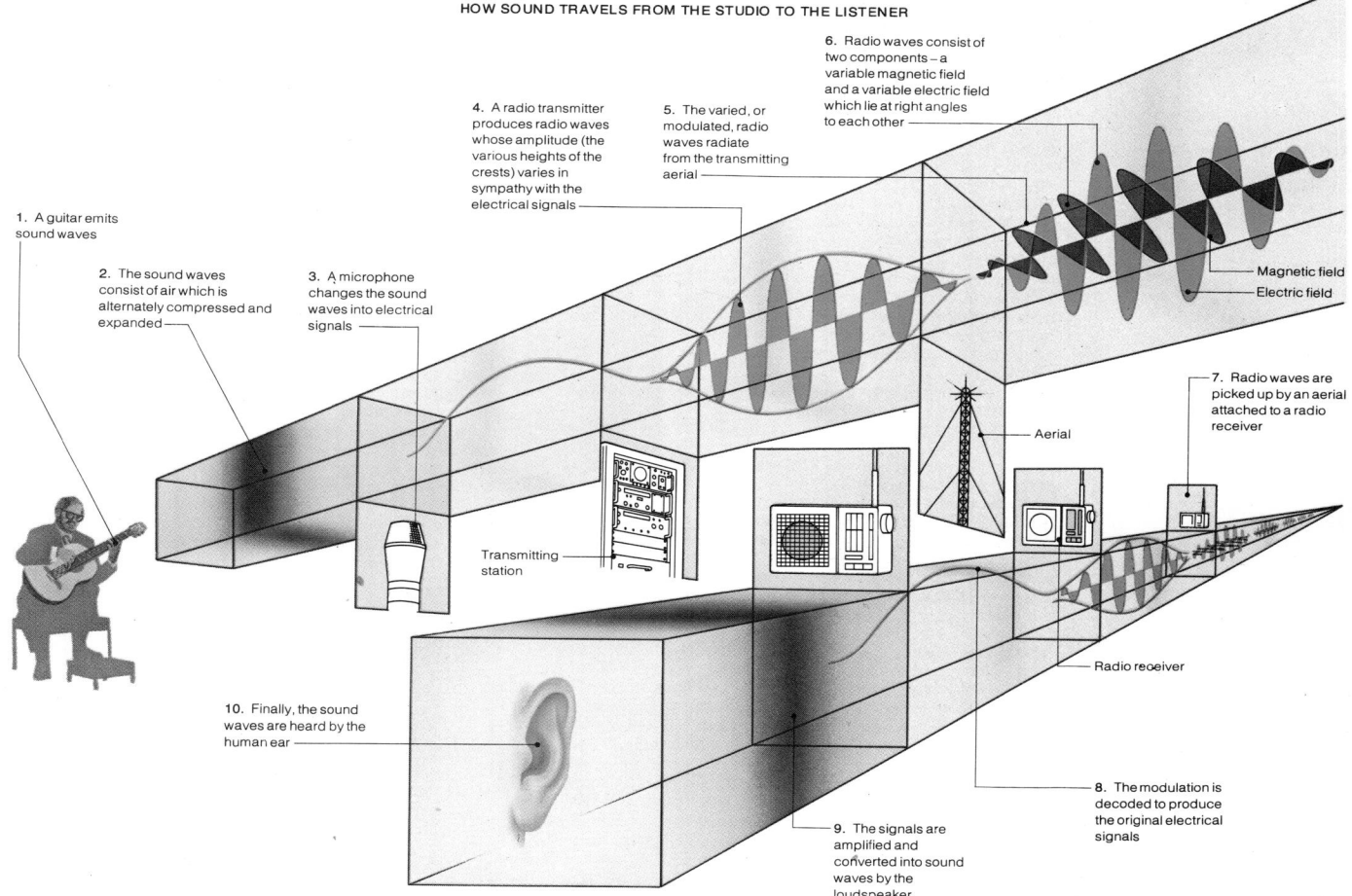

HOW SOUND TRAVELS FROM THE STUDIO TO THE LISTENER

1. A guitar emits sound waves

2. The sound waves consist of air which is alternately compressed and expanded

3. A microphone changes the sound waves into electrical signals

4. A radio transmitter produces radio waves whose amplitude (the various heights of the crests) varies in sympathy with the electrical signals

5. The varied, or modulated, radio waves radiate from the transmitting aerial

6. Radio waves consist of two components – a variable magnetic field and a variable electric field which lie at right angles to each other

Magnetic field

Electric field

7. Radio waves are picked up by an aerial attached to a radio receiver

Aerial

Transmitting station

Radio receiver

8. The modulation is decoded to produce the original electrical signals

9. The signals are amplified and converted into sound waves by the loudspeaker

10. Finally, the sound waves are heard by the human ear

Radio waves are transmitted at the speed of light – about 299 800 kilometres (186,000 miles) a second. The lengths of the waves – that is, the distance from one crest to another – vary. Long-wave radio is transmitted at wavelengths of 1000–2000 metres, medium-wave at 187–577 metres, and short-wave at 10–100 metres. The frequency of the waves, measured in hertz after the

physicist who discovered them, is the number of waves that pass a stationary point in one second. The shorter the radio wave, the higher the frequency. Very high frequency bands (VHF) have wavelengths of 1–10 metres, and these are used for local TV and radio broadcasting. The term for thousands of cycles a second is kilohertz, and the term for millions of cycles is

megahertz. Radio waves can be sent round the world because they bounce back from a layer of the ionosphere, about 90 kilometres (55 miles) above the Earth. Because of the Earth's curvature, they bounce back to a point hundreds of kilometres from where they were transmitted. The Earth's surface bounces them back to the ionosphere, and so on round the world.

(1788–1855). British field marshal. He lost an arm at Waterloo and rose to become military secretary to Wellington (1827–52) and commander of the British forces in the Crimean War.

ra·gout (rággōō, ra-gōō) *n.* A rich stew of meat and vegetables. [French *ragoût,* from *ragoûter,* to renew the taste : *re-,* again + *a-,* from Latin *ad,* to + *goût,* taste, from Latin *gustus.*]

rag·tag (rág-tag) *n.* Rabble; riffraff. Also called "ragtag and bobtail".

~*adj.* Also **rag·gle·tag·gle** (rágg'l-tagg'l). Low, coarse, and unkempt; ragged. [RAG (scrap) + TAG.]

rag·time (rág-tīm) *n.* A style of jazz characterised by elaborately syncopated rhythm in the melody and a steadily accented accompaniment. [Perhaps from *ragged time,* referring to the syncopation.]

rag trade *n. Informal.* The clothing trade. Preceded by *the.*

Ragusa. See Dubrovnik.

rag·weed (rág-weed) *n.* **1.** Any American plant of the genus *Ambrosia;* especially, *A. artemisiifolia* or *A. trifida,* whose profuse pollen is

a chief cause of hay fever. Also called "bitterweed". **2.** The ragwort. [From the raggedness of the leaves.]

rag·worm (rág-wurm) *n.* Any of various marine polychaete worms of the genus *Nereis;* especially, *N. cultrifera,* swimming by means of paired, paddle-like appendages. Also *U.S.* "clamworm". [Referring to the raglike appearance of its appendages.]

rag·wort (rág-wurt ‖ -wawrt) *n.* Any of several plants of the genus *Senecio,* having yellow daisy-like flowers; especially, *S. jacobaea,* of Europe. Also called "ragweed". [From the raggedness of the leaves.]

raid (rayd) *n.* **1. a.** A sudden attack, such as one made by thieves for seizing something. **b.** A swift incursion, especially into hostile territory, in order to accomplish a specific task, such as the destruction of enemy installations. **c.** A sudden and forcible invasion by the police. **2.** An act of depleting resources, as if by carrying them off in an attack. Often used humorously: *made a raid on our savings.* **3.** An attempt by speculators to drive stock prices down by selling.

rail² *There are more than 100 species of rail around the world. The water rail (above), which is native to Europe and Asia, is a marshland bird that seldom emerges from its cover among the reeds. It can often be detected by its hollow, squealing cry.*

rainbow *The giant arc of a rainbow is created through refraction of the sun's rays by particles of water in the atmosphere, each droplet acting as a tiny prism.*

rainbow trout *Introduced to Europe from North America, the rainbow trout is a prized game fish. It grows fast, feeding at the surface largely on hovering insects, and a three-year-old specimen can be up to 500 millimetres (20 inches) long.*

~v. **raided, raiding, raids.** *—tr.* To make a raid on. *—intr.* To conduct or participate in a raid. [Middle English, Scottish dialect form of Old English *rād,* ROAD.] **—raid·er** *n.*

rail¹ (rayl) *n.* **1.** A bar or series of bars placed, usually horizontally, some distance above the ground and supported by vertical posts or a solid structure, as in a railing, balustrade, fence, or the like. **2. a.** A bar or rod attached to a wall and used to hang objects from: *a picture rail.* **b.** A bar or rod on the side of a staircase used to hold on to for support or balance: *a hand rail.* **3.** A steel bar used, usually in pairs, as a track for a railway, tramway, or the like. **4.** The railway as a means of transport: *We went by rail.* **5.** A horizontal piece of wood in a door or in panelling. **—off the rails.** *Chiefly British.* **1.** Haywire; out of control. **2.** Behaving oddly or erratically.
~tr.v. **railed, railing, rails. 1.** To supply with a rail or rails. **2.** To enclose or separate with a rail or rails. Usually used with *off* or *in.* [Middle English *raile,* from Old French *reille,* bar, from Latin *rēgula,* rod, straight piece of wood.]

rail² *n., pl.* **rails** or collectively **rail.** Any of various marsh birds of the family Rallidae, characteristically having brownish plumage and short wings adapted for only short flights. [Middle English *ra(i)le,* from Old French *raale,* from Old Northern French *raille,* Vulgar Latin *rasc(u)la* (unattested), perhaps imitative.]

rail³ *intr.v.* **railed, railing, rails.** To use bitter, harsh, or abusive language. Used with *at* or *against.* [Middle English *railen,* from Old French *railler,* to mock, from Old Provençal *ralhar,* to scold, from Vulgar Latin *ragulāre* (unattested), to bray, from Late Latin *ragere*†, to neigh, roar.] **—rail·er** *n.*

rail·head (ráyl-hed) *n.* **1.** The farthest point on a railway to which rails have been laid. **2.** *Military.* The section of a railway where supplies are unloaded.

rail·ing (ráyling) *n.* **1. a.** *Often plural.* A banister, balustrade, or fence made of rails. **b.** The upper, longitudinal part of a balustrade. **2.** Rails collectively. **3.** Material for making rails.

rail·ler·y (ráyləri) *n., pl.* **-ies. 1.** Good-natured teasing or ridicule; banter. **2.** An instance of this. [French *raillerie,* from Old French *railler,* to RAIL (to use harsh language).]

rail·road (ráyl-rōd) *n. U.S.* A railway.
~tr.v. **railroaded, -roading, -roads.** *Informal.* **1.** To pressure or coerce. Often used with *into*: *railroaded us into signing the contract.* **2.** To push or force hurriedly by exerting unfair pressure. Usually used with *through*: *They railroaded the bill through Parliament.*

rail·way (ráyl-way) *n. Abbr.* **r., R., Rwy., Ry. 1.** A road composed of parallel steel rails providing a track for locomotive-drawn trains and other rolling stock. **2.** The entire system of such track, together with the land, stations, rolling stock, and other property used in rail transport. **3.** Any similar transport system using a fixed track: *a cable railway.* **4.** Any track on which something can move.

rai·ment (ráymənt) *n. Archaic.* Clothing; garments. [Middle English *rayment,* short for obsolete *arrayment,* from Old French *araiement, araie,* an array, from *arayer,* to ARRAY.]

rain (rayn) *n.* **1. a.** Water condensed from atmospheric vapour, falling to earth in drops. **b.** The descent of such water. **c.** A fall of such water; a rainstorm or shower. **d.** Rainy weather. **2.** The rapid falling of anything in large numbers or quantities. **3.** *Plural.* The rainy season or seasonal rainfalls, as in certain tropical areas. **—as right as rain.** *British.* Quite all right; fine; healthy. **—rain or shine. 1.** Regardless of the weather. **2.** Under all circumstances.
~v. **rained, raining, rains.** *—intr.* **1.** To fall in drops of water from the clouds: *It rained every day.* **2.** To fall like rain. **3.** To release rain. *—tr.* **1.** To send or pour down. **2.** To offer, give, or deal out abundantly or forcefully: *His opponent rained blows on him.* **—rain off.** *British.* To cause the postponement or cancellation of (a picnic or sports event, for example) because of rain. Often used in the passive. [Middle English *reyn, rain,* Old English *regn, rēn, regnian,* from Germanic.]

rain·bird (ráyn-burd) *n.* Any of various birds, such as the green woodpecker, whose cry is supposed to indicate the approach of rain.

rain·bow (ráyn-bō) *n.* **1. a.** An arc of colours appearing in the sky opposite the sun as a result of the refractive dispersion of sunlight in drops of rain or mist. **b.** Any similar arc, as in a waterfall mist or graded display of colours. **2.** An illusory objective or hope: *chasing the rainbow of a quick fortune.* [Middle English *reinbowe,* Old English *rēnboga* : RAIN + BOW.]

rainbow bird *n.* A brightly coloured Australian bee-eater, *Merops ornatus.*

rainbow trout *n.* A North American food fish, *Salmo gairdneri,* having a reddish longitudinal band and black spots.

rain check *n. U.S.* A ticket stub for an outdoor sports event entitling the holder to admission at a future date if the original event is rained off. **—take a rain check.** To postpone acceptance of an offer on the understanding that the offer may be taken up later.

rain·coat (ráyn-kōt) *n.* A waterproof or water-resistant coat.

rain·drop (ráyn-drop) *n.* A drop of rain.

Raine (rayn), **Kathleen (Jessie)** (1908–). British poet and critic. Her poetic work, as in the collection *Stone and Flower* (1943), is both visionary and lyrical.

rain·fall (ráyn-fawl) *n.* **1.** A shower or fall of rain. **2.** *Meteorology.* The total quantity of water, as measured by a rain gauge, condensed or precipitated as rain, snow, hail, dew, hoar frost, rime, or sleet in a given area and time interval.

rain forest *n.* A dense evergreen forest occupying a tropical region with a large annual rainfall (over 250 centimetres or 100 inches).

rain gauge *n.* A device for measuring rainfall. Also called "pluviometer", "udometer".

Rai·ni·er III (ráyni-ay), **Prince de Monaco** (1923–). Ruling Prince of Monaco (1949–). He succeeded his grandfather Louis II, and relinquished many of his absolutist powers in 1962. He married the U.S. film star Grace Kelly in 1956.

Rai·ni·er, Mount (ráyni-ər, ray-néer). Mountain in Mount Rainier National Park, Washington State, United States. At 4 392 metres (14,408 feet), it is the highest peak in the Cascade Range.

rain·mak·er (ráyn-maykər) *n.* A person supposedly capable of producing rain by artificial or supernatural means, especially among American Indians.

rain·mak·ing (ráyn-mayking) *n.* **1.** The ceremony and rituals observed by a rainmaker. **2.** *Informal.* **Cloud seeding** *(see).*

rain·out (ráyn-owt) *n.* Radioactive fallout carried down by rain.

rain·proof (ráyn-proof || -proof) *adj.* Impenetrable by rain. Said of coverings such as clothes or roofs. **—rain·proof** *tr.v.*

rain shadow *n.* A region with a relatively low rainfall, sheltered by adjacent high ground from prevailing, rain-bearing winds.

rain·spout (ráyn-spowt) *n.* A spout draining a roof gutter.

rain·storm (ráyn-stawrm) *n.* A storm accompanied by rain.

rain tree *n.* A Central American tree, *Samarea saman,* widely planted as an ornamental in the tropics, having red-and-yellow flowers and leaflets that close when it starts to rain.

rain·wash (ráyn-wosh) *n. Geology.* Decomposed rock and similar matter washed away by rain.

rain·wat·er (ráyn-wawtər || *U.S. also* -wottər) *n.* Water precipitated as rain, as opposed to well water or tapwater, with little dissolved mineral matter.

rain·wear (ráyn-wair) *n.* Waterproof clothing.

rain·y (ráyni) *adj.* **-ier, -iest.** Characterised by, full of, or bringing rain. **—rain·i·ly** *adv.* **—rain·i·ness** *n.*

rainy day *n.* A time of need or trouble.

Rais or **Retz** (ray), **Gilles de** (1404–40). French marshal. A commander in the victorious campaigns of 1428–31 against the English, he later resorted to alchemy and witchcraft to finance his excessive lifestyle. He was tried and executed for murdering about 140 children, and entered folklore as Bluebeard.

raise (rayz) *v.* **raised, raising, raises.** *—tr.* **1.** To move or cause to move upwards or to a higher position; elevate; lift. **2. a.** To place or set upright; make erect. **b.** To cause to project or stand up or out. **c.** To cause (a blister, for example) to form. **3.** To erect or build. **4. a.** To cause to arise, appear, or exist. **b.** To awaken from or as if from death. **5.** To increase in size, quantity, or worth: *raise prices.* **6.** To increase in intensity, degree, strength, or pitch: *raise one's expectations.* **7.** To elevate in rank or dignity; promote. **8. a.** To grow or breed. **b.** To bring up; rear. **9.** To put forward for consideration. **10.** *Law.* To begin or set (a lawsuit) in operation. **11.** To express or utter (a cry or shout, for example). **12.** To bring about; cause; provoke: *raise a cheer.* **13.** To arouse or stir up: *raise a revolt.* **14.** To gather together; collect: *raise money.* **15.** To cause (dough) to puff up. **16.** To end or abandon (a siege, blockade, or the like). **17.** To remove or withdraw (an order). **18. a.** To increase (a poker bet). **b.** To bet more than (a preceding bettor in poker). **c.** To increase the bid of (one's bridge partner). **19.** *Nautical.* To bring (a shoreline or another ship, for example) into sight by approaching nearer. **20.** To establish radio contact with. **21.** To bring up the nap on the surface of (fabric). **22.** *Scottish.* To make angry; enrage. **23.** *Mathematics.* To multiply (a number) by a certain power or by itself a certain number of times: *4 raised to the power 3* (4^3) *equals 64.* *—intr.* To increase the stakes in poker or gambling. —See Synonyms at **lift.**
~n. **1.** An act of raising or increasing. **2.** *Chiefly U.S.* An increase in salary; a rise. [Middle English *reisen, raisen,* from Old Norse *reisa.*] **—rais·er** *n.*

raised (rayzd) *adj.* **1.** Represented in relief, as a design might be; embossed. **2.** *U.S.* Leavened by yeast.

raised pie *n.* A tall, straight-sided, usually savoury, pie made from hot-water crust pastry that has been moulded over a base, such as a large jam jar, or set in a pie mould.

rai·sin (ráyz'n) *n.* A sweet grape of several varieties, dried either in the sun or artificially. [Middle English *raisin,* from Old French, grape, from Latin *racēmus,* RACEME.]

rai·son d'ê·tre (ráy-zoN-déttr, -dáytrə) *n., pl.* **raisons d'être** *(pronounced as singular).* Reason for being; point or justification for existing. [French.]

raj (raaj; *also* raazh) *n.* In India, dominion or sovereignty. **—the (British) Raj.** British rule in India. [Hindi *rāj,* reign, from Sanskrit *rājā,* from *rājati,* he rules.]

Raj·ab (rújəb, rə-jáb) *n.* The seventh month of the Muslim calendar. [Arabic.]

ra·jah, ra·ja (ráajə) *n.* A prince, chief, or ruler in India and certain other eastern countries such as Malaysia. [Hindi *rājā,* from Sanskrit *rājan,* king.]

Ra·ja·sthan (ráajə-staan). State in northwest India formed (1848) from a number of former principalities of Rajputana. It is divided into the Thar desert in the west and the more fertile Deccan plateau in the east. The two regions are separated by the Aravalli Mountains, which yield salt, sandstone, marble, coal, mica, and gypsum. The state capital is Jaipur.

Raj·put, Raj·poot (ráaj-poot || -poot) *n.* A member of a Hindu people claiming descent from the warlike and powerful rulers of north India from the 8th to the 13th century.

rake[1] (rayk) *n.* **1.** A long-handled implement with a row of projecting teeth at its head, used to gather leaves or mown grass, or to loosen or smooth earth. **2.** Any similarly shaped implement, as for removing ashes from an oven or drawing betting chips across a table. **3.** Any of various toothed and often wheeled mechanical implements used for gathering hay, straw, or the like.
~*v.* **raked, raking, rakes.** —*tr.* **1.** To gather or move with or as if with a rake. **2.** To smooth, scrape, or loosen with a rake or similar implement. **3.** To search or examine thoroughly. **4.** To scrape; scratch; graze. **5.** To aim heavy gunfire along the length of. **6.** To direct one's gaze along the length of: *rake the horizon.* —*intr.* **1.** To use a rake. **2.** To conduct a search. **—rake in.** To gain (money) in abundance. **—rake up.** To revive or bring to light: *rake up a scandal.* [Middle English *rake,* Old English *raca, racu.*] **—rak•er** *n.*

rake[2] *n.* A profligate, sexually promiscuous man. [Short for RAKEHELL.]

rake[3] *v.* **raked, raking, rakes.** —*intr.* To slant or incline from the vertical, as a ship's funnel does. —*tr.* To cause to lean or slant.
~*n.* **1.** Inclination from the vertical or from the horizontal. **2.** A slope or slant; especially the slope from the back of a theatre stage down to the front. **3.** The angle between the cutting edge of a tool and a plane perpendicular to the working surface to which the tool is applied. **4.** *Aeronautics.* The angle of inclination of an aircraft's wings. [17th century : probably akin to German *ragen*†, to project.]

rake•hell (ráyk-hel) *n. Archaic.* A rake; a roué.
~*adj. Archaic.* Dissolute; profligate. [Probably from the phrase, *to rake hell.*]

rake-off (ráyk-off, -awf) *n. Slang.* A percentage or share of the profits of an enterprise, especially one given or accepted as a bribe. [From the rake used by a croupier in a gambling house.]

rake's progress *n.* A continuous and dissolute decline; a descent into vice. [From William Hogarth's series of engravings, *A Rake's Progress* (1735).]

rak•i, rak•ee (raáki, raa-keé || rácki) *n.* A brandy of Turkey and the Balkan Peninsula, distilled from grapes or plums and flavoured with anise. [Turkish *rāqī.*]

rak•ish[1] (ráykish) *adj.* **1.** *Nautical.* Having a trim, streamlined appearance: *"We were schooner-rigged and rakish, with a long and lissom hull"* (John Masefield).. **2.** Dashing; jaunty; smart. [From RAKE (to incline), from the raked masts on some fast pirate ships.] **—rak•ish•ly** *adv.* **—rak•ish•ness** *n.*

rakish[2] *adj.* Characteristic of a roué or rake; debauched; dissolute. **—rak•ish•ly** *adv.* **—rak•ish•ness** *n.*

rale, râle (raal) *n.* An abnormal crackling sound heard through a stethoscope over the lungs. [French *râle,* from *râler,* to make a rattling sound in the throat, from Old French, probably from Vulgar Latin *rasclāre* (unattested), to scrape.]

Ra•leigh (ráw-li, raá-). Capital of North Carolina, United States, in the eastern part the state.

Ra•leigh (ráwli, raáli, rál-i), **Sir Walter** (*c.* 1554–1618). British explorer, admiral, and writer. A favourite of Elizabeth I, he campaigned in Ireland and Cadiz, explored Guiana, colonised Virginia, and introduced tobacco and the potato to Europe. Found guilty of treason by James I, he was released for yet another expedition to Guiana, and was executed on its failure. His literary output includes memoirs, poetry, and a history of the world.

ral•len•tan•do (rál-ən-tán-dō, -en- || *U.S.* raál-, -taán-) *adv. Abbr.* **rall.** *Music.* So as to slacken gradually in tempo; ritardando. Used as a direction.
~*n., pl.* **rallentandos.** *Music.* A passage or movement performed with a gradual reduction in tempo. [Italian, slowing down, from *rallentare,* to relax : *re-* (intensifier) + *allentare,* to slow down, from Late Latin *allentāre* : Latin *ad-,* to + *lentus,* slow.] **—ral•len•tan•do** *adj.*

ral•line (rál-īn || -in) *adj.* Of, pertaining to, or belonging to the Rallidae, a family of birds containing the rails, crakes, and coots.

ral•ly[1] (rál-i) *v.* **-lied, -lying, -lies.** —*tr.* **1.** To call together for a common purpose; assemble. **2.** To reassemble and restore to order. **3.** To rouse or revive (one's strength, for example) from inactivity or decline. —*intr.* **1.** To meet for a common purpose. **2.** To join in a common effort or for a common purpose: *The workers rallied round to help.* **3.** To reassemble for a renewed effort, especially after being dispersed: *The brigade rallied for a final attack.* **4.** To recover abruptly from a setback or disadvantage. **5.** To show sudden improvement in health or spirits. **6.** *Finance.* To improve or rise after a fall. Said of stock market prices. **7.** In tennis and similar games, to exchange several strokes. —See Synonyms at **gather.**
~*n., pl.* **rallies. 1.** An assembly, especially one intended to inspire enthusiasm for a cause. **2. a.** A reassembling, as of dispersed troops. **b.** The signal ordering this. **3.** A sharp improvement in health, vigour, or spirits. **4.** *Finance.* A notable rise in market prices and active trading after a decline. **5.** In tennis and similar games, an exchange of several strokes. **6.** A race in which cars are driven over a fixed course with specific rules. [French *rallier,* from Old French *ralier* : *re-,* again + *alier,* to unite, ALLY.] **—ral•li•er** *n.*

rally[2] *tr.v.* **-lied, -lying, -lies.** To tease good-humouredly; banter. [French *railler,* from Old French, to RAIL (abuse).] **—ral•li•er** *n.*

ram (ram) *n.* **1.** A male sheep. **2.** *Capital* **R.** A constellation and sign of the zodiac, **Aries** *(see).* **3.** Any of several devices used to drive, batter, or crush by forceful impact: **a.** A weapon, the **battering-ram** *(see).* **b.** The weight that drops in a pile driver or steam hammer. **c.** The plunger or piston of a force pump or hydraulic press. **4. a.** A projection on the prow of a warship, used to batter or cut into an enemy vessel. **b.** A ship having such a projection. **5.** A pump, a **hydraulic ram** *(see).*
~*v.* **rammed, ramming, rams.** —*tr.* **1.** To strike or drive against with a heavy impact; butt. **2.** To force, press, or drive down or into place. **3.** To cram; stuff. —*intr.* To crash; collide. [Middle English *ram,* Old English *ramm,* from Germanic *ramma-* (unattested).] **—ram•mer** *n.*

ram *Male sheep are known as rams. Above is a male bighorn, a wild sheep native to western North America. In ancient Egypt, the ram was believed to be the embodiment of the soul, and several ancient Egyptian gods are depicted with a ram's head. Below is the ram god of Mendes, a holy town in the Nile delta.*

RAM (ram) *n.* Random-access memory.

R.A.M. Royal Academy of Music (in Britain).

Ra•ma (raámə, raam) *n. Hinduism.* Any of three of the incarnations of Vishnu, regarded as heroes: Balarama, Parashurama, and especially Ramachandra. [Sanskrit *Rāma*†, dark-coloured, black.]

Ra•ma•chan•dra (raámə-chúndrə) *n. Hinduism.* The seventh of Vishnu's incarnations and hero of the Hindu epic poem *Ramayana.* Also called "Rama".

Ram•a•dan, Ram•a•dhan (rámmə-daán, raámə-, -dán) *n.* Also **Ram•a•zan** (-zaán, -zán). **1.** The ninth month of the Muslim year, spent in fasting from sunrise to sunset. **2.** The fasting itself. [Arabic *Ramaḍān,* the hot month, from *ramaḍ,* dryness.]

Ra•man (raámən), **Sir Chandrasekhara (Venkata)** (1888–1970). Indian physicist. A specialist in spectroscopy, he discovered the Raman effect, for which he was awarded the Nobel prize (1930).

Raman effect *n. Physics.* The alteration in frequency and random alteration in phase of light scattered in a material medium, used for investigating the structure of molecules. [After Sir C.V. RAMAN.]

Raman spectroscopy *n. Physics.* A form of spectroscopy for investigating the structure of molecules by analysing the spectrum *(Raman spectrum)* of light scattered from a sample. [After Sir C.V. RAMAN.]

Ra•ma•nu•ja (raámə-nóojə) (11th century A.D.). Indian theologian. Rejecting the impersonal tradition of Hindu deities, he founded the *bhakti* movement, advocating devotion to the personalised deity Vishnu and a greater involvement with the temporal world.

ra•mate (ráymayt) *adj.* Having branches. [Latin *rāmus,* branch.]

Ra•ma•ya•na (raa-mī́-ənə, -maá-yənə) *n.* A Sanskrit epic poem of ancient India, regarded as sacred by Hindus. It relates the adventures of Ramachandra. Compare **Mahabharata.** [Sanskrit *Rāmāyana* : *Rāma,* RAMA + *-ayana,* suffix meaning "pertaining to".]

Ram•bert (róm-bair), **Dame Marie,** born Cyvia Rabbam; also known as Miriam Rambach (1888–1982). Polish-born British ballet dancer and producer. She joined Diaghilev in 1913, became a British citizen in 1918, and, with her husband, founded the Carmargo Society (later the Ballet Rambert) in 1920. A teacher of many outstanding dancers, she greatly influenced ballet in Britain.

ram•ble (rámb'l) *intr.v.* **-bled, -bling, -bles. 1.** To walk or wander aimlessly and for pleasure; stroll or roam. **2.** To follow an irregularly winding course of motion or growth. **3.** To speak or write with many digressions. —See Synonyms at **wander.**
~*n.* A leisurely stroll. [Probably from Middle Dutch *rammelen,* (of animals) to wander about in sexual heat, from *rammen,* to copulate with; akin to RAM.]

ram•bler (rámblər) *n.* **1.** One who rambles. **2.** A person who takes long country walks, especially as a regular leisure pursuit. **3.** A variety of cultivated rose having weak stems that trail over the ground, other vegetation, and the like. In this sense, also called "rambler rose".

ram•bling (rámbling) *adj.* **1.** Extended over an irregular area; sprawling: *a large, rambling Elizabethan house.* **2.** Lengthy and desultory; long-winded. **—ram•bling•ly** *adv.*

Ram•bouil•let[1] (róN-boō-yáy). Town in the département of Yvelines, north France, set in the forest of Rambouillet. Its famous chateau is the official summer residence of French presidents.

Ram•bouil•let[2] (róm-boō-yay, rám-, -lay) *n.* Any of a breed of merino sheep of French origin, raised for wool and meat. [After RAMBOUILLET.]

ram•bunc•tious (ram-búngkshəss) *adj. U.S. Informal.* Boisterous; disorderly. [Probably variant of RUMBUSTIOUS.]

ram•bu•tan (ram-bóot'n) *n.* **1.** A tree, *Nephelium lappaceum,* of Southeast Asia, bearing edible, oval red fruit with soft spines. **2.** The fruit of this tree. [Malay *rambutan,* from *rambut,* hair, from the hairy covering of the fruit.]

R.A.M.C. Royal Army Medical Corps (in Britain).

Ra•meau (raámō, raa-mṓ, ra-), **Jean Philippe** (1683–1764). French composer and critic. Although he was an organist, it is his orchestral works which display the greatest innovations. His opera-ballets include *Les Indes galantes* (1735).

ram•e•kin, ram•e•quin (rámmi-kin, rám-) *n.* **1.** A cheese preparation made with eggs, breadcrumbs, or pastry, baked and served in individual dishes. **2.** A small individual dish used for both baking and serving this. [French *ramequin,* from Middle Dutch *rameken,* diminutive of *ram,* cream, from Middle Low German *rōm(e).*]

ra•men•tum (rə-mén-təm) *n., pl.* **-ta** (-tə). Any of the brown scaly structures on the stems of fern fronds. [New Latin, from Latin *rādere,* to scrape + *-mentum,* -MENT.]

ra•mi. Plural of **ramus.**

ram•ie (rámmi, raámi) *n.* **1.** A woody Asian plant, *Boehmeria nivea,* having broad leaves. **2.** The flaxlike fibre from the stem of this plant, used in making fabrics and cordage. [Malay *rami.*]

ram•i•fi•ca•tion (rámmifi-káysh'n) *n.* **1.** The act or process of branching out or dividing into branches. **2.** A branch or other subordinate part extending from a main body. **3.** An arrangement of

PRONUNCIATION KEY

a, trap; aa, father; ai, fair;
ar, star; aw, lawn; ay, play;
b, bb, stab; rubber;
ch, church; ck, ticket;
d, dd, dead; ladder; e, dress;
ee, bee; er, defer; ew, few;
ewr, pure; ə, about;
ər, letter; f, ff, fife; differ;
g, gg, giggle; h, hat; i, kit;
ī, price; īr, fire; j, judge;
k, kick; l, ll, let; 'l, needle;
m, mm, man; n, nn, no;
'n, sudden; ng, thing; o, lot;
ō, no; ŏŏ, foot; ōō, shoe;
oor, poor; ow, cow;
owr, hour; oy, boy;
p, pp, pepper; r, rr, red;
s, ss, sauce; sh, ship;
t, tt, totter; th, thick; th, this;
smooth; u, cut; ur, turn;
v, vv, valve; w, wet; y, yes;
z, zz, zebra; zh, vision;
pleasure

IN FOREIGN WORDS:

aN, oN, Saint-Saëns;
hl, Llanelli; Hluhluwe;
kh, loch; lough; Khaled

STRESS MARK:

ín-sīt, insight; in-sī́t, incite

branches or branching parts. **4.** A development or consequence growing out of and often complicating a problem, plan, or statement.

ram·i·form (rámmi-fawrm) *adj.* Branchlike or branching. [RAMUS + -FORM.]

ram·i·fy (rámmi-fī) *v.* **-fied, -fying, -fies.** —*tr.* To divide into, or cause to extend in, branches or branchlike parts. —*intr.* To branch out or become divided into branches. [French *ramifier,* from Medieval Latin *rāmificāre,* from Latin *rāmus,* branch.]

ra·min (ra-mín) *n.* **1.** Any of various trees of the genus *Gonystylus,* native to Southeast Asia; especially *G. bancanus,* valued for its pale hardwood. **2.** The wood of any such tree. [Malay.]

ram·jet (rám-jet) *n.* **1.** A jet engine that compresses and heats its air intake for the fuel mixture by means of a specially shaped intake duct. It has no revolving parts and operates only at speed, requiring take-off assistance. **2.** An aircraft propelled by such an engine. Also called "athodyd".

ra·mose (ráy-mōz, -mōss, ra-mōss) *adj.* Having many branches. [Latin *rāmōsus,* from *rāmus,* branch.]

ra·mous (ráyməss) *adj.* **1.** Of or resembling branches. **2.** Branching; ramose. [Latin *rāmōsus,* RAMOSE.]

ramp[1] (ramp) *n.* **1.** A sloping passage or roadway connecting different levels, as of a building or road. **2.** *Architecture.* A concave bend of a handrail where a sharp change in level or direction occurs, such as at a stair landing. **3.** A mobile staircase for entering and leaving an aeroplane. **4.** A sudden bump or change in level in a road surface, sometimes introduced deliberately to keep traffic to a low speed. **5.** A small platform straddling a cable, hosepipe, or the like and enabling vehicles to pass over it without touching it. **6.** A short upward projection from which a person or vehicle may be launched, as on a ski-jump or aircraft-carrier. [French *rampe,* from *ramper,* to slope, creep, from Old French to RAMP.]

ramp[2] *intr.v.* **ramped, ramping, ramps. 1.** To act threateningly or violently; rage. **2.** To assume a threatening stance. **3.** To stand in the rampant position.
~*n.* The act of ramping. [Middle English *rampen,* from Old French *ramper,* to climb, rear up, from Frankish *rampōn* (unattested).]

ramp[3] *n. British.* A fraudulent act; a swindle. [19th century : origin obscure.]

ram·page (rámpayj, ram-páyj) *n.* A course of violent, frenzied, and destructive action or behaviour. —**on the rampage.** Behaving violently and destructively.
~*intr.v.* (ram-páyj). **rampaged, -paging, -pages.** To rush about wildly or violently; rage. [18th century (Scottish) : perhaps from RAMP (to rear up).] —**ram·pag·er** (-páyjər) *n.*

ram·pa·geous (ram-páyjəss) *adj.* Raging; frenzied: *"The hot rampageous horses of my will"* (W.H. Auden). —**ram·pa·geous·ly** *adv.* —**ram·pa·geous·ness** *n.*

ram·pant (rámpənt) *adj.* **1.** Extending unchecked; unrestrained; widespread. **2.** Characterised by ungoverned vehemence and extravagance. **3.** Rearing or ramping on the hind legs. **4.** *Heraldry.* Rearing on the left hind leg with the forelegs raised, the right above the left, and usually with the head in profile. **5.** *Architecture.* Springing from a support or abutment higher at one side than at the other. Said of an arch or vault. [Middle English *rampaunt,* from Old French *rampant,* present participle of *ramper,* to climb, RAMP.] —**ram·pan·cy** *n.* —**ram·pant·ly** *adv.*

ram·part (rám-paart, -pərt) *n.* **1.** A fortification consisting of an elevation or embankment, often provided with a parapet. **2.** Anything that serves to protect or defend: *The cliff was a rampart against the ocean.* —See Synonyms at **bulwark.**
~*tr.v.* **ramparted, -parting, -parts.** To protect or defend with or as if with a rampart. [French *rempart,* from *remparer,* to fortify : *re-* (intensifier) + *emparer,* to defend, fortify, from Provençal *antparar, amparar,* from Vulgar Latin *anteparāre* (unattested), to prepare for defence : Latin *ante-,* before + *parāre,* to prepare.]

ram·pi·on (rámp-yən, -i-ən) *n.* **1.** A Eurasian plant, *Campanula rapunculus,* having clusters of bluish flowers and an edible root used in salads. **2.** Any of various similar plants of the genus *Phyteuma.* [Probably from Old French *raiponce,* from Medieval Latin *rapontium,* probably from Latin *rāpa, rāpum,* turnip, RAPE.]

ram·rod (rám-rod) *n.* **1.** A metal rod used to force the charge into a muzzleloading firearm. **2.** A rod used to clean the barrel of a firearm. **3.** A person who resembles a ramrod in inflexibility.

Ram·say (rámzi), **Allan** (1713–84). Scottish portrait painter. He was court painter to George III. His portraits include George's wife, Queen Charlotte (National Portrait Gallery, London), and Jean-Jacques Rousseau (National Gallery, Edinburgh).

Ramsay, Sir William (1852–1916). Scottish chemist. Investigating his colleague Rayleigh's discovery that atmospheric nitrogen seemed heavier than laboratory-prepared nitrogen, he discovered the inert gases argon (1894), helium (1895), neon, xenon, and krypton (1898). He was awarded the Nobel prize (1904).

Ram·ses (II) (rám-seez, rámmi-), also known as Ramses the Great. (*c.*1300–1224 B.C.). Egyptian king. He is best known for his prodigious building activities: most famous archaeological sites in Egypt bear some evidence of his patronage. Known to the Greeks as Sesostris, he was probably the king connected with the Jewish exodus from Egypt.

Ram·sey (rámzi), **Sir Alf(red Ernest)** (1922–). English football manager and player. He was appointed England manager in 1963

Ramses The most important of the Egyptian kings called Ramses was Ramses II The Great. This statue of him was carved in about 1250 B.C.

and masterminded England's victory in the 1966 World Cup, but resigned in 1974.

Rams·gate (rámz-git, -gayt). Port and resort in Kent, southeast England. It is a major yachting centre and has a busy commercial harbour as well. It became a popular resort in the 19th century. There is a hovercraft service to Calais, France.

ram·shack·le (rám-shack'l) *adj.* Likely to fall apart because of shoddy construction or lack of maintenance; rickety. [Back-formation from *ramshackled, ransackled,* from *ransackle,* frequentative of Middle English *ransaken,* to RANSACK.]

ram's horn *n. Judaism.* A **shofar** (*see*).

Ram Singh (rám síng, ráam) (1816–85). Indian religious leader. As chief of the Kuka sect of Sikhs, he organised an early civil disobedience campaign against the British, but was imprisoned when his more fanatical followers attacked Muslims. He later died in exile.

ram·son (rám-z'n, -s'n) *n. Usually plural.* **1.** A broad-leaved Eurasian garlic, *Allium ursinum,* having a bulbous root used in salads and relishes. **2.** The root of this plant. [Middle English *ramsyn,* Old English *hramsan* (plural of *hramsa*), mistaken as singular.]

ram·til (rám-til) *n.* An African plant, *Guizotia abyssinica,* grown for its oil-rich seeds. The seed is called "Niger seed". [Hindi *rāmtil* : Sanskrit *rāma,* dark (see **Rama**) + *tila†,* sesame.]

ram·u·lose (rámmew-lōz, -lōss) *adj.* Also **ram·u·lous** (-ləss). *Biology.* Having numerous small branches. [Latin *rāmulōsus,* from *rāmulus,* diminutive of *rāmus,* branch, RAMUS.]

ra·mus (ráy-məss) *n., pl.* **-mi** (-mī). *Biology & Anatomy.* A branchlike part of a structure, such as a branch of a nerve fibre or a thin process projecting from a bone. [New Latin, from Latin, branch.]

ran. Past tense of **run.**

Ran (ran). *Norse Mythology.* The goddess of the sea who caught drowning persons in her net.

R.A.N. Royal Australian Navy.

Rance (raanss, RONSS). River in northwest France. 100 kilometres (62 miles) long, it flows from Landes du Mene northeastwards across Brittany to enter the English Channel through the Golfe de St. Malo. The world's first marine power station using the energy of the tides was opened on its estuary in 1966.

ranch (raanch ‖ ranch) *n.* **1.** An extensive farm, especially one in North America, on which large herds of cattle, sheep, or horses are raised. **2.** Any large farm on which a particular crop or kind of animal is raised. **3.** A fish farm in the open sea for breeding migratory fish such as salmon.
~*intr.v.* **ranched, ranching, ranches.** To work on or manage a ranch. [Mexican Spanish *rancho,* from Spanish, mess room, from Old Spanish *rancher, ranchar,* be billeted, from Old French *ranger,* to put in a line, from *renc,* line, row, from Frankish *hring* (unattested), ring.]

ranch·er (raán-chər ‖ rán-) *n.* One who owns, manages, or works on a ranch.

ran·che·ro (raan-chaír-ō ‖ ran-) *n., pl.* **-ros.** *Southwestern U.S.* A rancher. [Mexican Spanish, from *rancho,* RANCH.]

ranch house *n.* **1.** The building on a ranch occupied by its owner or manager. **2.** A rectangular, one-storey house with a low-pitched roof, a style common on Western U.S. ranches.

ranch·man (raánch-mən ‖ ránch-) *n., pl.* **-men** (-mən). *U.S.* A rancher.

ranch mink *n.* An American mink bred in captivity from Alaskan and Labrador strains for special pelt colours and qualities.

ran·cho (raán-chō ‖ rán-) *n., pl.* **-chos.** *Southwestern U.S.* **1.** A hut or group of huts in which ranch workers live. **2.** A ranch. [Mexican Spanish, RANCH.]

ran·cid (rán-sid) *adj.* **1.** Stale or decomposed. Said of fats or oils. **2.** Having the disagreeable odour or taste of decomposed oils or fats; sour; rank. **3.** Disagreeable; mean-spirited; nasty: *a scowling, rancid old man.* [Latin *rancidus,* from *rancēre†* (unattested), to stink.] —**ran·cid·i·ty** (ran-síddəti), **ran·cid·ness** *n.*

ran·cour, *U.S.* **ran·cor** (rángkər) *n.* Bitter resentment; deep-seated ill will. [Middle English *rancour,* from Old French, from Late Latin *rancour* (stem *rancōr-*), rancidity, from *rancēre,* to stink. See **rancid.**] —**ran·cor·ous** *adj.* —**ran·cor·ous·ly** *adv.* —**ran·cor·ous·ness** *n.*

rand[1] (rand, raant, ront) *n., pl.* **rand** or **rands. 1.** The basic monetary unit of the Republic of South Africa, equal to 100 cents. **2.** A note or coin worth one rand. [After *the Rand,* WITWATERSRAND.]

rand[2] (rand, raant, ront) *n., pl.* **rands** or **rande** (-ə). *South African.* A ridge of hills or an extended area of high ground. [Afrikaans, from Dutch, strip, ridge, from Germanic *randa* (unattested), rim, edge.]

rand[3] (rand) *n.* **1.** A strip of leather inserted between the heel and sole of a shoe or boot. **2.** *British Regional.* A border or space around something, such as the unploughed area around a field. [Middle English, Old English, rim, margin, border, from Germanic.]

Rand, the. See **Witwatersrand.**

ran·dan (rán-dan) *n.* **1.** A type of boat designed to be rowed by three persons. **2.** The way of rowing this boat, in which the persons fore and aft use one oar each, and the person in the middle uses two. [19th century : origin obscure.]

R & B rhythm and blues.

R & D research and development.

ran·dom (rándəm) *adj.* **1.** Having no specific pattern or objective; lacking causal relationships; haphazard. **2.** *Statistics.* **a.** Of or designating a phenomenon that does not produce the same outcome or consequences every time it occurs under identical circumstances. **b.** Of or designating an event having a relative frequency of occurrence that approaches a stable limit as the number of observations of the event increases to infinity. **c.** Of or designating a sample drawn from a population so that each member of the population has an equal chance to be drawn. **d.** Of or pertaining to a member of such a sample: *a random number.* —See Synonyms at **chance.** **—at random.** Without definite method or purpose; unsystematically: *chose one man at random from the volunteers.* [Middle English *randoun,* from Old French *randon,* haphazard, from *randir,* to run, from Frankish *rant*† (unattested), a running.] **—ran·dom·ly** *adv.*

ran·dom-ac·cess (rándəm-ák-sess) *adj. Computing.* Giving access directly to any required part of a computer store: *a random-access memory.* Also called "direct access". Compare **sequential access.** See **read-write.**

ran·dom·ise, ran·dom·ize (rándəm-īz) *tr.v.* **-ised, -ising, -ises.** To make random, especially for scientific experimentation. **—ran·dom·i·sa·tion** (-ī-záysh'n || *U.S.* -i-) *n.*

random variable *n. Statistics.* A variable having numerical values determined by the results of a chance experiment. Also called "stochastic variable".

ran·dy (rándi) *adj.* **-dier, -diest. 1.** *Chiefly British Slang.* Sexually aroused; lustful. **2.** Coarse and shrewish. Said of a woman. ~*n., pl.* **randies.** *Chiefly Scottish.* A shrewish woman. [Scottish, from *rand,* variant of RANT.] **—rand·i·ly** *adv.* **—rand·i·ness** *n.*

ranee. Variant of **rani.**

rang. Past tense of **ring.**

ran·ga·ti·ra (rúng-gə-téer-ə, ráng-) *n. N.Z.* A Maori chief or noble person. [Maori.]

range (raynj) *n. Abbr.* **r. 1. a.** The extent of perception, knowledge, experience, or ability of someone or something. **b.** The area or sphere covered by or included in something; the scope: *Personal relations lie outside the range of sociology.* **c.** The limits within which something is valid or applicable; effective scope: *a long-range weather forecast; within the range of possibilities.* **2. a.** An amount or extent of variation: *a wide price range.* **b.** *Music.* The extent of pitch variation within the capacity of a voice or instrument. **c.** The limits between which a meter or other measuring instrument can be operated. **3. a.** The maximum or effective distance that can be traversed, as by bullets or by radiation. **b.** The distance to a target. **4.** The maximum distance that a ship or other vehicle can travel before exhausting its fuel supply. **5.** A place for shooting at targets. **6.** A testing area in which rockets and missiles are fired and flown. **7.** *U.S.* An extensive area of open land on which livestock wander and graze. **8.** The geographical region in which a particular kind of plant or animal normally lives or grows. **9.** The act of or opportunity for wandering or roaming over a large area: *gave free range to her imagination.* **10.** *Mathematics.* **a.** The totality of points in a set established by a **mapping** *(see).* Also called "codomain". Compare **domain. b.** The order of the highest nonzero determinant contained in a given matrix. **11.** *Statistics.* A measure of dispersion equal to the difference or interval between the smallest and largest of a set of quantities. **12.** A class, rank, or order. **13.** An extended group or series, especially of mountains. **14.** Any of a series of double-faced bookcases in a library stack room. **15.** A set of products or services of the same general type; a line: *a new range of sportswear.* **16.** A large cooking stove of a type usually heated by solid fuel and having one or more ovens, on which several foods may be cooked at the same time. **17.** The action or an act of ranging. **18.** *Geology.* A mineral belt.
~*v.* **ranged, ranging, ranges.** —*tr.* **1.** To arrange or dispose in a particular order, especially in rows or lines. **2.** To assign to a particular category; classify. **3.** To align (a gun or telescope, for example) with a target; train; sight. Usually used with *on.* **4.** To determine the distance of (a target). **5.** To move or travel over or through (a region), as in exploration. **6.** *Printing.* To set (lines of type) so that they are flush with the margin. **7.** *Nautical.* To uncoil (an anchor cable) on deck so that the anchor may descend easily. **8.** *U.S.* To turn (livestock) out onto a range to graze. —*intr.* **1.** To vary within specified limits: *Her humour ranged from subtle irony to practical jokes.* **2.** To extend in a particular direction: *a river ranging to the east.* **3.** To extend in the same direction. **4.** To move over or through a given area as in exploration: *"his eye . . . ranged with delight over the treasures"* (Washington Irving). **5.** To roam or wander; rove. Used with *over.* **6.** To live or grow within a particular region. Used with *over.* **7.** To be capable of reaching a specified distance: *Our missiles range farther than theirs.* **8.** *Printing.* To lie flush at the margin. Said of lines of type. —See Synonyms at **wander.** [Middle English, series, line, from Old French *range, renge,* range, rank, from *renc, reng,* line, row, from Frankish *hring* (unattested), circle, ring.]

range finder *n.* Any of various optical, electronic, or acoustical instruments used to determine the distance of an object.

range light *n. Nautical.* **1.** Any of two or more lights used to guide a ship through a narrow channel at night. **2.** *Plural.* Two or more lights in a pattern on a powered vessel, used at night to indicate its course or size.

rang·er (ráynjər) *n.* **1.** *British.* The keeper of a royal forest or park. **2.** A person employed to patrol and guard a forest. **3.** *Usually capital* **R.** A senior member of the Girl Guides. **4.** *Capital* **R.** A member of a group of U.S. soldiers specially trained for making raids. Compare **commando. 5.** A wanderer or rover.

rang·ing rod (ráynjing) *n.* A patterned pole used as a marker in surveying. Also called "ranging pole".

Ran·goon (ráng-gōōn, rang-). Capital city and chief port of Burma. Lying on the river Rangoon near its entrance into the Gulf of Martaban, it is the natural focus of Burma's transport network, and its commercial and industrial centre. The major exports are rice, cotton, timber, rubber, and petroleum products. Rangoon is dominated by the golden-spired Shwe Dagon Pagoda. It was severely damaged by an earthquake and tidal wave in 1930.

rang·y (ráynji) *adj.* **-ier, -iest. 1.** Having slender, long limbs. **2.** *Chiefly U.S.* Providing ample range; roomy.

ra·ni (raá-nee, raa-neé) *n., pl.* **-nis.** Also **ra·nee. 1.** The wife of a rajah. **2.** A reigning Hindu princess or queen. [Hindi *rānī,* from Sanskrit *rājñī,* feminine of *rājan,* king.]

Ran·jit Singh (rún-jit síng), **Maharaja** (1780–1839). Sikh prince of the Punjab. After capturing Lahore (1799), he proclaimed himself maharajah, and wrested control of the Punjab from the Afghans and Pathans, thus earning himself the title "Lion of the Punjab".

Ran·jit·singh·ji Vi·bha·ji (rúnjit-síng-jee vee-baá-jee), **Kumar Shri, Maharajah Jam Sahib of Nawanagar** (1872–1933). Indian prince, cricketer and politician. He was an enlightened prince and chancellor of the Chamber of Princes (1932). As a cricketer, he was a spectacular batsman who played for Sussex and England, and the first player to score 3,000 runs in a single season (1899).

rank¹ (rangk) *n.* **1. a.** A relative position in society. **b.** An official position or grade: *the rank of sergeant.* **c.** A relative position or degree of value in any graded scale: *"The critical power is of lower rank than the creative."* (Matthew Arnold). **d.** High or eminent station or position: *persons of rank.* **2.** A row, line, series, or range of people or things. **3.** *Military.* **a.** A line of soldiers, vehicles, or other military equipment standing side by side in close order. Compare **file. b.** *Plural.* The armed forces. **c.** *Plural.* Members of the armed forces excluding officers. Preceded by *the* or *other.* **4.** Any of the horizontal lines of squares on a chessboard. **5.** *Mathematics.* The number of rows of the greatest order determinant extracted from a given matrix. **6.** *Music.* A row or set of pipes in an organ that are controlled by the same stop. **7.** A place where taxis park while waiting to be hired. **—break ranks. 1.** *Military.* To fail to remain in line, especially during battle. **2.** To fail to support one's colleagues in a joint enterprise. **—close ranks.** To consolidate strength, as when under threat or attack. **—pull rank.** To use one's superior position to get one's way or gain an advantage.
~*v.* **ranked, ranking, ranks.** —*tr.* **1.** To place in a row or rows. **2.** To give a particular order or position to; classify. **3.** *U.S.* To outrank or take precedence over. —*intr.* **1.** To hold a particular rank or place: *rank first.* **2.** *Chiefly U.S.* To hold a senior position or have authority or precedence. [Old French *ranc, renc,* rank, RANGE.]

rank² *adj.* **ranker, rankest. 1.** Growing profusely or with excessive vigour: *rank weeds.* **2.** Yielding a profuse, often excessive, crop; highly fertile: *rank earth.* **3.** Strong and offensive in odour or taste. **4.** Indecent; disgusting. **5.** Absolute; complete: *a rank amateur.* —See Synonyms at **flagrant.** [Middle English *rank,* Old English *ranc,* haughty, full-grown, overbearing, from Germanic.] **—rank·ly** *adv.* **—rank·ness** *n.*

Rank (rangk), **J(oseph) Arthur, 1st Baron** (1888–1972). British film producer and entrepreneur. A Methodist evangelist, he saw in films a means of spreading Christianity. He soon became aware of the commercial possibilities, and made his first secular film in 1935. In 1946 he founded the Rank Organisation and virtually controlled the British film industry, with a wide network of concerns covering every aspect of production and distribution.

Rank, Otto (1884–1939). Austrian psychologist. A protégé of Freud, though later disowned by him, he studied the psychiatric aspects of myth and creativity, and also suggested that emotional disorders could be caused at the time of birth.

rank and file *pl. n.* **1.** The common soldiers of an army excluding officers. **2.** Those who form the major portion of any group or organisation, excluding the leaders and officers.

Ran·ke (rángkə), **Leopold von** (1795–1886). German historian. He is best known for pioneering the modern methods of exhaustively analysing source documents; his *History of the Latin and Teutonic Nations 1494–1535* (1824) and subsequent works on Prussian, French, English, Spanish, Italian, and Serbian history are regarded as the first examples of modern historical criticism.

rank·er (rángkər) *n. British.* **1.** A soldier in the ranks. **2.** A commissioned officer who has risen from the ranks.

Ran·kine scale (ráng-kin) *n.* A scale of absolute temperature using Fahrenheit degrees, in which the freezing point of water is 491.69° and the boiling point of water is 671.69°. [After William J.M. Rankine (1820–72), Scottish physicist.]

rank·ing (rángking) *adj. Chiefly U.S.* High-ranking; preeminent.
~*n.* A place or position on a usually specified scale: *has a high ranking on the squash ladder.*

ran·kle (rángk'l) *intr.v.* **-kled, -kling, -kles. 1.** To cause persistent irritation or resentment. **2.** *Archaic.* To become sore or inflamed; fester. [Middle English *ranclen,* from Old French *rancler, draoncler,* from *rancle, draoncle,* ulcer, festering sore, from Late Latin *dracunculus,* something twisted like a serpent, from Latin, diminutive of *dracō* (stem *dracōn-*), serpent.]

ran·sack (rán-sak) *tr.v.* **-sacked, -sacking, -sacks. 1.** To search or examine (a room or box, for example) thoroughly, usually disordering the contents in the process. **2.** To search (a house or town, for example) for plunder; pillage. —See Synonyms at **rob.** [Middle English *ransaken,* from Old Norse *rannsaka,* search a house : *rann,*

PRONUNCIATION KEY

a, trap; aa, father; ai, fair; ar, star; aw, lawn; ay, play; b, bb, stab; rubber; ch, church; ck, ticket; d, dd, dead; ladder; e, dress; ee, bee; er, defer; ew, few; ewr, pure; ə, about; ər, letter; f, ff, fife; differ; g, gg, giggle; h, hat; i, kit; ī, price; īr, fire; j, judge; k, kick; l, ll, let; 'l, needle; m, mm, man; n, nn, no; 'n, sudden; ng, thing; o, lot; ō, no; ŏŏ, foot; ōō, shoe; oor, poor; ow, cow; owr, hour; oy, boy; p, pp, pepper; r, rr, red; s, ss, sauce; sh, ship; t, tt, totter; th, thick; th, this; smooth; u, cut; ur, turn; v, vv, valve; w, wet; y, yes; z, zz, zebra; zh, vision; pleasure

IN FOREIGN WORDS:

aN, oN, Saint-Saëns; hl, Llanelli; Hluhluwe; kh, loch; lough; Khaled

STRESS MARK:

ín-sīt, insight; in-sít, incite

house, from Common Germanic *razn-* (unattested) + *-saka,* search.] **—ran·sack·er** *n.*

ran·som (rán-səm) *n.* **1.** The release of a person or property in return for payment of a stipulated price. **2.** The price or payment demanded or paid. **3.** *Theology.* A redemption from sin and its consequences. **—hold to ransom. 1.** To confine or retain possession of (a person or property) until a stipulated price is paid. **2.** To try to force concessions from: *The unions are holding the country to ransom.*
~*tr.v.* **ransomed, -soming, -soms. 1.** To obtain the release of (a person or property) by paying a certain price. **2. a.** To hold captive or keep possession of while demanding such a payment. **b.** To release after receiving a ransom. **3.** *Theology.* To deliver from sin and its consequences. [Middle English *ransoun,* from Old French *ran·çon,* from Latin *redemptiō,* REDEMPTION.] **—ran·som·er** *n.*

Ran·som (rán-səm), **John Crowe** (1888–1974). U.S. poet and critic. Best known for his critical work *The New Criticism* (1941). His collections of poetry include *Chills and Fever* (1924).

Ran·some (rán-səm), **Arthur (Mitchell)** (1884–1967). British writer. He was a prominent journalist, recording travels through such places as the U.S.S.R. and the Far East, but is best known as the author of several children's books, including *Swallows and Amazons* (1931).

rant (rant) *v.* **ranted, ranting, rants.** —*intr.* To speak or declaim in a violent, loud, or vehement manner. Often used in the phrase *rant and rave.* —*tr.* To exclaim with violence or extravagance.
~*n.* **1.** Violent, loud, or extravagant speech. **2.** *Chiefly Scottish.* Wild or uproarious merriment. [Probably from Dutch *ranten*†.] **—rant·er** *n.* **—rant·ing·ly** *adv.*

ran·u·la (ránnew-lə) *n., pl.* **-lae** (-lee). A cyst on the underside of the tongue caused by obstruction of a duct or a salivary gland. [New Latin, from Latin, swelling in tongues of cattle, diminutive of *rāna*†, frog.]

ra·nun·cu·lus (rə-núngkew-ləss) *n., pl.* **-luses** or **-li** (-lī). Any plant of the genus *Ranunculus,* including the buttercups, typically having yellow flowers. [New Latin, from Latin *rānunculus,* diminutive of *rāna*†, frog.]

R.A.O.C. Royal Army Ordnance Corps (in Britain).

rap¹ (rap) *v.* **rapped, rapping, raps.** —*tr.* **1.** To hit sharply and swiftly; strike. **2.** To utter sharply and abruptly. Used with *out.* —*intr.* **1.** To strike a quick, light blow or blows; knock. **2.** *Chiefly U.S. Informal.* To talk freely; chat. **3.** *Chiefly U.S.* To improvise words and vocal sounds to an instrumental accompaniment.
~*n.* **1.** A quick, light blow or knock. **2.** A knocking or tapping sound. **3.** *Chiefly U.S.* A talk, conversation, or discussion. **4.** *Informal.* **a.** A reprimand or censure. **b.** Unpleasant consequences of wrongdoing, especially when one is not personally to blame. Used in the phrase *take the rap.* **5.** *Slang.* A prison sentence. **—beat the rap.** *U.S. Slang.* To escape punishment or be acquitted of a charge. [Middle English *rappen,* akin to Norwegian *rappe,* Swedish *rappa,* (imitative).] **—rap·per** *n.*

rap² *n.* **1.** A counterfeit halfpenny passed in Ireland during the 18th century. **2.** *Informal.* The least bit: *I don't care a rap.* [Short for Irish Gaelic *ropaire*†, counterfeit halfpenny.]

ra·pa·cious (rə-páyshəss) *adj.* **1.** Taking by force; plundering. **2.** Greedy; avaricious. **3.** Subsisting on live prey. Said especially of birds. [Latin *rapax* (stem *rapāc-*), from *rapere,* to seize.] **—ra·pa·cious·ly** *adv.* **—ra·pa·cious·ness, ra·pac·i·ty** (-pássəti) *n.*

rape¹ (rayp) *n.* **1. a.** The crime of forcing a female to submit to sexual intercourse without her consent. **b.** Such a crime committed against a male. **2.** The fact of having been raped. **3.** *Archaic.* The act of seizing and carrying off by force; abduction. **4.** Abusive or improper treatment; violation; profanation: *a rape of justice.* **5.** The act of plundering or despoiling a country or city, especially in war.
~*v.* **raped, raping, rapes.** —*tr.* **1.** To force (especially a female) to submit to sexual intercourse. **2.** *Archaic.* To seize and carry off by force. **3.** To plunder or pillage. —*intr.* To commit rape. [Middle English, from Old French *raper,* from Latin *rapere,* to seize.] **—rap·ist** *n.*

rape² *n.* A Eurasian plant, *Brassica napus,* cultivated for its seed, which yields a useful oil, and as fodder. Also called "colza". See **cole.** [Middle English, from Latin *rāpa, rāpum,* turnip.]

rape³ *n. Often plural.* The refuse of grapes left after the extraction of the juice in wine making. [French *râpe,* grape stalk, from Old French *rasper,* to scrape off, RASP.]

rape oil *n.* The edible oil extracted from rapeseed, also used as a lubricant and in the manufacture of various products.

rape·seed (ráyp-seed) *n.* The seed of the rape plant.

Raph·a·el¹ (ráf-ay-əl, -ayl, -i-əl), born Raffaello Sanzio or Santi (1483–1520). Italian painter, one of the towering figures of the High Renaissance. He came to early prominence in Florence, but his most famous paintings were done in Rome, especially the great frescoes for the Stanza della Segnatura in the Vatican. Completed in 1511, they include *The School of Athens* and the *Triumph of Religion,* also called *Disputà.* In Rome, too, he painted what is considered his greatest altarpiece, the *Sistine Madonna* (1512), and many portraits. **—Raph·a·el·esque** (-ésk) *adj.*

Raph·a·el² (ráf-ay-əl, ráyf-, -i-, -ī-, -el, ráffayl ‖ ráyf-). One of the archangels. [Hebrew *Rophā'ēl,* "God has healed".]

ra·phe, rha·phe (ráy-fi) *n., pl.* **-phae** (-fee). *Biology.* A seamlike line or ridge between two similar parts, as in the scrotum, the coat of certain seeds, or the valves of a diatom. [New Latin, from Greek *rhaphē,* seam, from *rhaptein,* to sew.]

raphia. Variant of **raffia.**

ra·phide (ráy-fīd, rá-) *n., pl.* **-phides** (-z, ráffi-deez). Also **ra·phis** (-fiss) *pl.* **-phides.** *Botany.* Any of a bundle of needle-shaped crystals, composed chiefly of calcium oxalate, occurring in many plant cells. [Back-formation from *raphides,* plural, from New Latin, from Greek *rhaphis* (stem *rhaphid-*), needle, from *rhaptein,* to sew.]

rap·id (ráppid) *adj.* **1.** Moving, acting, or occurring with great speed; swift. **2.** Happening in a very short time: *a rapid change.* —See Synonyms at **fast.**
~*n. Usually plural.* A fast-flowing section of a river usually caused by a sudden steepening of the riverbed. [Latin *rapidus,* hurrying, seizing, from *rapere,* to seize.] **—rap·id·ly** *adv.* **—ra·pid·i·ty** (rə-píd-dəti, ra-), **rap·id·ness** *n.*

rapid eye movement *n. Abbr.* **REM** Constant movement of the eyeballs behind the closed eyelids during **paradoxical sleep** (see), occurring when dreaming takes place.

rap·id-fire (ráppid-fīr) *adj.* **1.** Designed to fire shots in rapid succession. **2.** Marked by continual, rapid occurrence: *rapid-fire questions.*

rapid transit *n. Chiefly U.S.* An urban passenger-transport system using elevated or underground trains or a combination of both.

ra·pi·er (ráyp-yər, -i-ər) *n.* **1.** A long, slender, two-edged sword with a cuplike hilt, used in the 16th and 17th centuries. **2.** An 18th-

rape² *Brassica napus, or rape, has been cultivated since ancient times. The seed is pressed to yield edible oil and the plant is used as cattle food. It is closely related to the garden swede, and to the mustard plant.*

Raphael

ARTIST OF THE HIGH RENAISSANCE

Master of inventiveness in gesture and grouping

Raphael (1483–1520) was a master of composition, and the grace and harmony of his paintings exemplify the ideals of the High Renaissance. He was the most assimilative genius of his age, absorbing and applying the techniques of both Leonardo da Vinci and Michelangelo without being an imitator of either.

The son of an Umbrian painter, Raphael trained with the painter Perugino, possibly in Perugia. At the age of 21 he moved to Florence. His *Madonna and Child* groups of this period reflect Leonardo's influence, particularly in their treatment of light and shade. Raphael went to Rome in 1508, commissioned by Pope Julius II to decorate a set of Vatican apartments; his frescoes in the Stanza della Segnatura include the outstanding *Disputà* and *School of Athens.* In 1514 he succeeded Bramante as architect of St. Peter's.

When Raphael died at the age of 37, his last painting, *The Transfiguration,* was unfinished, and was completed by Giulio Romano, an assistant in his large and flourishing studio. Despite his short life, Raphael's influence on the work of succeeding ages is unparalleled in the history of art.

MADONNA DEL GRANDUCA *Raphael's Madonna paintings are noted for their serenity and tenderness of expression. This one in the Palazzo Pitti, Florence, dates from about 1505.*

century, lighter, sharp-pointed sword lacking a cutting edge and used only for thrusting. [French *rapière*, originally *(espée) rapière†*, rapier (sword).]

rap·ine (ráp-īn, -in) *n. Law.* Forcible seizure of another's property; plunder. [Middle English *rapyne*, from Old French *rapine*, from Latin *rapīna*, from *rapere*, to RAPE (seize).]

rap·pa·ree (ráppə-rée) *n.* 1. A freebooting soldier of 17th-century Ireland. 2. *Archaic.* A bandit or robber. [Irish Gaelic *rapaire*, short pike, either from English RAPIER or French *rapière*, RAPIER.]

rap·pee (ra-pée) *n.* A strong snuff made from a dark, coarse tobacco. [French *râpé*, "grated" (as tobacco), from *râper*, to grate, from Old French *rasper*, to RASP.]

rap·pel (ra-pél) *n.* The act or method of descending from a mountainside or cliff by means of a double rope passed under one thigh and over the opposite shoulder, or through karabiners attached to a harness.
~*intr.v.* **rappelled, -pelling, -pels.** To descend from a steep height by rappel. [French, "recall", from Old French *rapel*, from *rapeler*, to summon, recall : *re-*, again + *apeler*, to summon, APPEAL.]

rap·port (ra-pór, rə- ‖ -pôr) *n.* A relationship; especially, one of mutual trust or emotional affinity. [French, from *rapporter*, to bring back, yield, from Old French *raporter* : *re-*, back, again + *aporter*, to bring, from Latin *apportāre* : *ad-*, to + *portāre*, to carry.]

rap·por·teur (ráp-awr-tér ‖ -ôr-) *n.* A person appointed by a committee who prepares reports for it or records its proceedings. [French. See **rapport**.]

rap·proche·ment (ra-prósh-mon ‖ *U.S.* -prôsh-) *n.* A re-establishing of cordial relations, as between two countries. [French, from *rapprocher*, to bring together : *re-*, again + *approcher*, to approach, from Late Latin *appropriāre* : Latin *ad-*, to + *prope*, near.]

rap·scal·li·on (rap-skál-i-ən) *n.* A rascal; a scamp. [Variant of obsolete *rascallion*, perhaps from RASCAL.]

rapt (rapt). *adj.* 1. Transported with powerful emotion; enraptured. 2. Deeply absorbed; engrossed. 3. Expressing rapture: *a rapt expression on her face.* [Middle English, from Latin *raptus*, "seized", from the past participle of *rapere*, to seize.]

rap·tor (ráp-tər, -tawr) *n.* A bird of prey. [Latin, "one who seizes", from *raptus*, RAPT.]

rap·to·ri·al (rap-táwri-əl ‖ -tôri-) *adj.* 1. Subsisting by seizing prey; predatory. 2. Adapted for the seizing of prey. Said of the feet of birds of prey. 3. Of, pertaining to, or characteristic of birds of prey.

rap·ture (rápchər) *n.* 1. The state of being transported by a powerful emotion; great joy; ecstasy. 2. *Often plural.* An expression or utterance of great delight. 3. *Archaic.* The transporting of a person from one place to another, especially to heaven. —See Synonyms at **ecstasy.**
~*tr.v.* **raptured, -turing, -tures.** *Archaic.* To enrapture. [Medieval Latin *raptūra*, "ecstasy", from Latin *raptus*, RAPT.]

rap·tur·ous (rápchərəss) *adj.* Expressing great joy or delight; ecstatic. —**rap·tur·ous·ly** *adv.* —**rap·tur·ous·ness** *n.*

ra·ra a·vis (rárə ávviss, ráir-ə áyviss) *n., pl.* **rara avises** or **rarae aves** (ráarī ávvayz, ráir-ee áyveez). A rare or unique person or thing. [Latin, "rare bird".]

rare[1] (rair) *adj.* **rarer, rarest.** 1. *Abbr.* **r.** Infrequently occurring; uncommon; unusual. 2. Highly valued owing to unusualness; special. 3. Thin in density; rarefied. Said of gases. 4. Of unusual excellence; exceptional: *a rare novel.* [Middle English, from Latin *rārus*, loose, thin, scarce, remarkable.] —**rare·ness** *n.*

rare[2] *adj.* **rarer, rarest.** Underdone so as to retain redness. Said of meat. [Variant of obsolete *rear*, half-cooked (originally of eggs) Middle English *rere*, Old English *hrēr*.] —**rare·ness** *n.*

rare·bit (ráirbit) *n.* A cheese dish, **Welsh rabbit** *(see).* [Folk-etymological variant of (WELSH) RABBIT.]

rare earth *n.* 1. Any of various oxides of the rare-earth elements. 2. Loosely, a rare-earth element.

rare-earth element (ráir-érth) *n.* Any of a group of metallic elements with atomic numbers from 57 to 71. Also called "rare earth", "lanthanide", "lanthanon". [Originally contrasted with the so-called "common-earth elements" (calcium, magnesium, and aluminium).]

rar·ee show (rár-ee) *n.* 1. A peepshow *(see).* 2. A street show. [From RARE (excellent).]

rar·e·fac·tion (ráir-i-fáksh'n) *n.* Also **rar·e·fi·ca·tion** (-fi-káysh'n). 1. The act or process of rarefying. 2. The state of being rarefied. —**rar·e·fac·tive** *adj.*

rar·e·fied (ráir-i-fīd) *adj.* 1. Belonging or restricted to a small and select group; esoteric. 2. Marked by a lofty or exalted style or quality: *a rarefied academic atmosphere.*

rar·e·fy (ráir-i-fī) *v.* **-fied, -fying, -fies.** —*tr.* 1. To make thin, less compact, or less dense. 2. To purify or refine. —*intr.* To become thin, less dense, or purer. [Middle English *rarefien*, from Old French *rarefier*, from Latin *rārēfacere* : *rārus*, RARE + *facere*, to make.] —**rar·e·fi·a·ble** (-fī-əb'l ‖ -fī-) *adj.*

rare gas *n. Chemistry.* An inert gas *(see).*

rare·ly (ráirli) *adv.* 1. Not often; seldom; infrequently: *"The truth is rarely pure and never simple."* (Oscar Wilde). 2. In an unusual degree; exceptionally. 3. *Regional.* With uncommon excellence.
Usage: The use of *ever* following *rarely* is commonly used for emphasis in informal speech (*I rarely ever go there*), but in formal contexts it is criticised as redundant. Generally acceptable are such combinations as *rarely if ever* and *rarely or never.*

rare·ripe (ráir-rīp) *adj. U.S.* Ripening early.

~*n. U.S.* A fruit or vegetable that ripens early. [*Rare-*, variant (perhaps influenced by RARE, underdone) of RATHE.]

rar·ing (ráir-ing) *adj. Informal.* Full of eagerness; enthusiastic. Followed by an infinitive: *We're raring to go.* [From dialectal *rare*, variant of REAR (to arouse, raise up).]

rar·i·ty (ráir-əti) *n., pl.* **-ties.** 1. Something that is especially valued because it is rare. 2. The quality or state of being rare; infrequency of occurrence.

Ra·ro·ton·ga (ráir-ə-tóng-gə). A volcanic island in the South Pacific Ocean, site of Avarua, capital of the Cook Islands.

R.A.S. 1. Royal Agricultural Society 2. Royal Astronomical Society.

ras·bo·ra (raz-báw-rə ‖ -bô-) *n.* Any of various tropical fishes of the genus *Rasbora*, of which several brightly coloured species are kept in home aquariums. [From a native East Indian name.]

ras·cal (rásk'l ‖ rásk'l) *n.* 1. An unscrupulous or dishonest person; a scoundrel. 2. One who is playfully mischievous; a scamp. Often used affectionately or humorously, especially of children. 3. *Archaic.* One belonging to the rabble.
~*adj. Archaic.* Of or suited to the rabble; base. [Middle English, from Old French *rascaille*, rabble, perhaps from Old Northern French *rasque* (unattested), dregs, mud, filth, from Vulgar Latin *rasica* (unattested), from Latin *rādere*, to scrape. Compare **rash** (eruption).] —**ras·cal·ly** *adj.*

ras·cal·i·ty (raa-skál-əti ‖ -ra) *n., pl.* **-ties.** 1. The behaviour or character of a rascal. 2. A base or mischievous act.

rase. Variant of **raze.**

rash[1] (rash) *adj.* **rasher, rashest.** 1. Acting without forethought or due caution; impetuous. 2. Characterised by or resulting from ill-considered haste or boldness: *a rash decision.* —See Synonyms at **reckless.** [Middle English *rasch*, nimble, quick, eager, perhaps from Middle Dutch *rasch*; probably cognate with RATHE.] —**rash·ly** *adv.* —**rash·ness** *n.*

rash[2] *n.* 1. Any eruption of the skin in spots or blotches. 2. An outbreak of many instances within a brief period: *a rash of defections to the other party.* [Possibly from obsolete French *rache*, from Old French *rasche*, scurf, from *raschier*, to scratch, from Vulgar Latin *rasciāre* (unattested), to scrape, from Latin *rādere* (past participle *rāsus*).]

rash·er (ráshər) *n.* A thin slice of bacon or ham to be fried or grilled. [16th century : origin obscure.]

Ras·mus·sen (ráss-mə-sən ‖ *U.S.* raáss-), **Knud Johan Victor** (1879–1933). Danish explorer and ethnologist. Of Eskimo descent, he spent much of his time in Arctic America studying the inhabitants, and argued that the Eskimo and the Red Indian were descended from common ancestor.

ra·so·ri·al (rə-sáw-ri-əl, -záw- ‖ -sô-, -zô-) *adj.* Characteristically scratching the ground for food. Said of poultry. [Late Latin *rāsor*, "scraper", from Latin *rādere* (past participle *rāsus*), to scrape.]

rasp (raasp ‖ rasp) *v.* **rasped, rasping, rasps.** —*tr.* 1. To file or scrape with a rasp. 2. To utter in a rough, grating tone. 3. To irritate; grate upon (nerves or feelings). —*intr.* 1. To grate; scrape harshly. 2. To make a harsh, grating sound.
~*n.* 1. A coarse file having abrasive, pointed projections. 2. The act of filing with a rasp. 3. A harsh, grating sound. [Middle English *raspen*, from Old French *rasper*, from Old High German *raspōn*, from Germanic *hrap-* (unattested), to snatch. See **raffle**.] —**rasp·er** *n.* —**rasp·ing·ly** *adv.* —**rasp·y** *adj.*

ras·pa·to·ry (ráaspə-tri, -təri ‖ ráspə-) *n., pl.* **-ies.** A surgical instrument used for scraping the surface of a bone. [Medieval Latin *raspatorium* (unattested), or French *raspatoire*, from Old French *rasper*, *raspe*, RASP.]

rasp·ber·ry (ráaz-bri, ráass-, -bəri ‖ ráz-, ráss-, -berri) *n., pl.* **-ries.** 1. Any of various shrubby, usually prickly plants of the genus *Rubus*, bearing edible berries, such as *R. idaeus*, of Europe. 2. The fruit of any of these plants, consisting of a mass of small, fleshy, usually red drupelets. 3. Moderate to dark or purplish red. 4. *Slang.* A derisive or contemptuous sound made by vibrating the extended tongue and the lips while exhaling. [From obsolete *raspis†* + BERRY.] —**rasp·ber·ry** *adj.*

Ras·pu·tin (rass-péw-tin, -póo-), **(Grigory Yefimovich)**, born G. Y. Novykh (1872–1916). Russian monk and faith healer. A Siberian peasant, he preached and lived a peculiar religious life of "sinning in order to be forgiven" (Rasputin can mean debauchee). His relative success in treating the Tsarevich's haemophilia and his magnetic personality gained him great influence at the Imperial court. He was murdered by nobles anxious to uphold the monarchy.

Ras·ta (rástə, *also* rústə) *n., pl.* **-tas.** *Informal.* A Rastafarian. Also called "Rastaman".

Ras·ta·fa·ri·an, Ras Ta·fa·ri·an (rástə-fáir-i-ən) *n.* A member of a cult of black nationalists, originating in Jamaica, who regard Ras Tafari, the title and surname of the former Ethiopian emperor **Haile Selassie** *(see),* as God. They typically have dreadlocks and wear beret-like hats called toms. —**Ras·ta·fa·ri·an·ism** *n.* —**Ras·ta·fa·ri·an** *adj.*

ras·ter (rástər) *n. Electronics.* A pattern of lines produced by scanning an electron beam, as on a television screen. [German *Raster*, screen, from Latin *rastrum*, rake, from *rādere* (past participial stem *rās-*), to scrape.]

rat (rat) *n.* 1. Any of various long-tailed rodents resembling, but larger than, mice; especially, any of the genus *Rattus*, such as the common black rat, *R. rattus.* See **brown rat.** 2. Any of various similar animals. 3. *Slang.* A despicable, sneaky person, especially one

rattle *This rattle was used by a shaman or medicine man of a North American Indian tribe as a charm to heal the sick. Made of wood in the shape of a bird, it is decorated with a human figure and a frog.*

who abandons his associates in time of trouble. **4.** *Slang.* A blackleg; a scab. **5.** *Chiefly U.S. Slang.* One who informs on or betrays his associates. **—smell a rat.** *Slang.* To suspect that something underhand or treacherous is going on.
~*intr.v.* **ratted, ratting, rats. 1.** To hunt for or catch rats, especially with the aid of dogs. **2.** *Slang.* To desert or betray one's associates or friends. Used with *on.* [Middle English *rat,* Old English *ræt,* from Germanic *ratt-* (unattested).]

ra·ta *n.* Either of two New Zealand trees of the genus *Metrosideros, M. robusta* or *M. lucida,* having crimson flowers and hard wood.

rat·a·ble, rate·a·ble (ráyt-əb'l) *adj.* **1.** Capable of being rated, estimated, or appraised. **2.** *British.* Liable to assessment or rates. **—rat·a·bil·i·ty** (-ə-bílləti), **rat·a·ble·ness** *n.* **—rat·a·bly** *adv.*

ratable value *n. British.* The value at which property is assessed by a local authority for the payment of rates. Also called "ratal".

rat·a·fi·a (ráttə-féer, -fée-ə) *n.* Also **rat·a·fee** (-fee). **1.** A liqueur flavoured with fruit kernels or almonds. **2.** A small macaroon flavoured with almonds. [French, from West Indian French Creole.]

rat·al (ráyt'l) *n. British.* Ratable value.
~*adj. British.* Of or pertaining to rates or their payment or assessment. [RAT(E) + -AL.]

ratan. Variant of **rattan.**

rat·a·plan (ráttə-plan) *n.* A tattoo, as of a drum, the hooves of a galloping horse, or machine-gun fire. [French (imitative).]

rat-a-tat-tat (ráttə-tát-tát) *n.* A series of short, sharp sounds, such as those made by knocking on a door. [Imitative.]

ra·ta·touille (ráttə-tóo-i, -twée) *n.* A vegetable stew made from tomatoes, peppers, courgettes, and aubergines. [French (dialect), from *touiller,* to stir.]

rat·bag (rát-bag) *n.* **1.** *Chiefly Australian & N.Z. Slang.* A scoundrel or rascal. Sometimes used affectionately or humorously. **2.** *British Informal.* An obnoxious person. **—rat·bag·ger·y** (-əri) *n.*

rat-bite fever (rát-bīt) *n.* Either of two infectious diseases contractible from the bite of a rat: **1.** That arising from *Streptobacillus moniliformis* and characterised by skin inflammation, back and joint pains, headache, and vomiting. **2.** That arising from *Spirillum minus,* with ulceration at the site of the bite, a purplish rash, and recurrent fever. Also called "rat-bite disease".

rat-catch·er (rát-kachər) *n.* A person who rids houses of rats or other vermin.

ratch·et (ráchit) *n.* **1.** A mechanism consisting of a pawl, or hinged catch, that engages the sloping teeth of a bar, permitting motion in one direction only. **2.** The pawl, wheel, or bar of such a mechanism. **3.** The toothed wheel in such a mechanism. Also called "ratchet wheel". [French *rochet,* from Old French *rocquet,* head of a lance, from Frankish *rokko* (unattested), a distaff.]

rate[1] (rayt) *n.* **1. a.** A measured quantity, as of speed, cost, or value, calculated by its relation to some other quantity: *at the rate of 60 miles per hour; the birth rate.* **b.** A ratio that is fixed as a standard between two sums, quantities, or the like: *the rate of exchange.* **2.** The speed at which something moves, changes, or progresses: *driving at a very dangerous rate.* **3.** The cost per unit of a commodity or service. **4.** A charge or payment calculated in relation to any particular sum or quantity. **5.** A specified level of relative quality. Used in combination: *first-rate; tenth-rate.* **6.** *Plural.* In Britain, a tax on property assessed and levied by a local authority to pay for local services. **—at any rate.** Whatever the case may be; anyway.
~*v.* **rated, rating, rates.** *—tr.* **1.** To calculate the value of; appraise. **2.** To place in a particular rank or grade. **3.** To regard or account: *The play was rated a great success.* **4.** To value for purposes of taxation. **5.** To specify the performance limits of (a machine or firearm, for example). **6.** *Informal.* To think highly of: *I don't really rate this job.* **7.** *Informal.* To merit or deserve: *rate special treatment.* *—intr.* **1.** To be ranked in a particular class or grade. **2.** *Chiefly U.S. Informal.* To have status, importance, or influence. —See Synonyms at **estimate.** [Middle English, from Old French, from Medieval Latin *rata,* calculated, fixed, from the feminine past participle of Latin *rērī,* to calculate.] **—rat·er** *n.*

rate[2] *tr.v.* **rated, rating, rates.** To berate angrily. [Middle English *raten,* perhaps from Old Norse *hrata.*]

ra·tel (ráy-t'l, -tel || *South African* ráat'l) *n.* An animal, the **honey badger** *(see).* [Afrikaans *ratel*†.]

rate of exchange *n.* The ratio at which the unit of currency of one country may be, or is, exchanged for the unit of currency of another country. Also called "exchange rate".

rate·pay·er (ráyt-payər) *n. British.* One who is liable to pay rates.

rat·fink (rát-fingk) *n. U.S. Slang.* A contemptible, obnoxious, or otherwise undesirable person. [RAT (to betray) + FINK.]

rat·fish (rát-fish) *n., pl.* **-fishes** or collectively **ratfish. 1.** A fish, *Hydrolagus affinis,* of Pacific waters, having a long, narrow tail. **2.** The **rabbitfish** *(see).*

Rat·haus (rát-howss; *German* ráat-) *n. German.* In Germany, a government or municipal building; a town hall.

rathe (rayth, raath || rath) *adj. Archaic & Poetic.* **1.** Appearing or ripening early in the year. **2.** Prompt; eager. [Middle English *rathe,* early, rapid, Old English *hræd, hræth,* from Germanic.]

Ra·the·nau (ráatə-now), **Walter** (1867–1922). German industrialist and politician, one of the leading figures in the period of German reconstruction after World War I. As foreign minister (1922), he negotiated the Treaty of Rapallo with the U.S.S.R. He was assassinated by anti-Semites shortly afterwards.

rath·er (ráa-thər || rá-; -thér *for sense 7*) *adv.* **1.** More readily; preferably: *I'd rather stay at home.* **2.** With more reason, logic, wisdom, or other justification. **3.** With more accuracy: *He's my friend, or rather he was my friend.* **4.** To a certain extent; somewhat: *rather nice.* **5.** On the contrary: *Locks are not for opening doors; rather, they are for keeping them firmly shut.* **6.** *West & South African.* Instead or in preference: *I don't feel like swimming—let's go for a walk rather.* **7.** *Chiefly British.* Most certainly. Used as an emphatic affirmative reply. **8.** *Obsolete.* More quickly; earlier. [Middle English *rather,* Old English *hrathor,* comparative of *hrathe, hræth,* early, RATHE.]

Usage: In constructions expressing preference, *rather* is generally preceded by *would,* either in full or abbreviated form *('d),* when followed by a bare infinitive: *I would rather leave now than stay until midnight. Should* is also possible in this construction. When followed by a clause, *rather* may also be preceded by *had: I had rather you left now,* and this is especially common in American English, where there is also a preference for *had* in statements using the infinitive construction. Of course, in informal speech, the distinction between *would* and *had* in statements disappears, as both are reduced to *'d.* Nor is there a usage issue in relation to question forms, where *would* is the only possible construction: *Would you rather stay? Would you rather I stayed?*

When pronouns follow *rather than,* they may occur either in subject or object form, depending on their role in relation to the rest of the sentence. For example, in the sentence *I asked you rather than him, him* is the object because it is governed by the verb *ask,* whereas in *You, rather than he, caused the trouble,* the pronoun *he* is used because it is part of the subject of the verb *cause.* In informal speech, however, there is a tendency for object forms to be used universally.

rat·i·fi·ca·tion (ráttifi-káysh'n) *n.* The action of officially and formally confirming something, such as a treaty or constitution.

rat·i·fy (rátti-fī) *tr.v.* **-fied, -fying, -fies.** To give formal sanction to; approve and so make valid. See Synonyms at **approve, confirm.** [Middle English *ratifien,* from Old French *ratifier,* from Medieval Latin *ratificāre* : Latin *ratus,* "fixed" (see **rate**) + *facere,* to make.] **—rat·i·fi·er** *n.*

rat·i·ne (ra-téen) *n.* Also **rat·i·né** (rátti-nay || *U.S.* -náy). A loosely woven fabric with a coarse, knotted texture. [French, past participle of *ratiner*†, to adorn.]

rat·ing[1] (ráyting) *n.* **1.** A place assigned on a scale; a standing. **2.** In the Royal Navy and certain other navies, an ordinary seaman. **3.** An evaluation of the financial status of a business or an individual: *has a very good credit rating.* **4.** A specified performance limit, as of capacity, range, or operational capability: *power rating.* **5.** *Plural.* An estimate of the number of listeners or viewers of a particular radio or television programme, used as an index of its popularity. **6.** Any of the classes into which racing yachts are divided according to tonnage, dimensions, or the like.

rating[2] *n.* A scolding.

ra·ti·o (ráy-shi-ō || *U.S. also* -shō) *n., pl.* **-tios. 1.** The relation in number between two similar magnitudes, determined by the number of times an object exists in one quantity as compared with the other: *the ratio of managerial staff to all employees.* **2.** *Mathematics.* The relative size of two quantities expressed as the quotient of one divided by the other: *The ratio of 7 to 4 is written 7:4 or 7/4.* [Latin *ratiō,* computation, from *rērī* (past participle *ratus*), to consider.]

ra·ti·oc·i·nate (rátti-óssi-nayt || *U.S. also* ráshi-, -ṓ-si-) *intr.v.* **-nated, -nating, -nates.** To reason methodically and logically. [Latin *ratiōcināre,* from *ratiō,* RATIO.] **—ra·ti·oc·i·na·tion** (-náysh'n) *n.* **—ra·ti·oc·i·na·tive** (-nətiv, -naytiv) *adj.* **—ra·ti·oc·i·na·tor** (-náytər) *n.*

ra·tion (rásh'n || *U.S. also* ráysh'n) *n.* **1.** *Often plural.* A fixed portion; especially, an amount of food, clothing, fuel, or the like, allotted to persons in military service or to civilians in times of scarcity. Also used adjectivally: *a ration book.* **2.** *Plural.* Provisions. **3.** An allotted, deserved, or sufficient amount: *He's used up his ration of goodwill.*
~*tr.v.* **rationed, -tioning, -tions. 1.** To supply with rations. **2. a.** To distribute in restricted allocations, as during wartime. **b.** To give sparingly, as if in rations. Often used with *out*: *The stern father rationed even his love out to his sons.* —See Synonyms at **distribute.** [French, from Latin *ratiō* (stem *ratiōn-*), RATIO.]

ra·tion·al (rásh'n'l) *adj.* **1.** Having or exercising the ability to reason. **2.** Of sound mind; sane. **3.** Manifesting or based upon reason; logical. **4.** *Mathematics.* Designating an algebraic expression or equation in which no variable appears in an irreducible radical or with a fractional exponent. [Latin *ratiōnālis,* from *ratiō,* reason, RATIO.] **—ra·tion·al·ly** *adv.* **—ra·tion·al·ness** *n.*

ra·tion·ale (ráshə-náal, *rarely* -i) *n.* **1.** The fundamental reasons for something; a logical basis. **2.** An exposition of principles or reasons. [Latin *ratiōnāle,* neuter of *ratiōnālis,* RATIONAL.]

ra·tion·al·ise, ra·tion·al·ize (rásh'n'l-īz) *v.* **-ised, -ising, -ises.** *—tr.* **1.** To make conformable to reason; make rational. **2.** To interpret from a rational standpoint. **3.** *Psychology.* To devise self-satisfying but inadequate reasons for (one's behaviour), especially while being unaware of unconscious motivation. **4.** *Mathematics.* To remove radicals without changing the value of (an expression) or roots of (an equation). **5.** *Chiefly British.* To bring modern, efficient methods to (an industry, for example). *—intr.* **1.** To think in a rational or logical way. **2.** *Psychology.* To rationalise one's behaviour. **—ra·tion·al·i·sa·tion** (-ī-záysh'n || *U.S.* -i-) *n.* **—ra·tion·al·is·er** *n.*

ra·tion·al·ism (rásh'n'l-iz'm) *n.* **1.** *Theology.* **a.** The theory that the exercise of reason, rather than the acceptance of authority or spiritual revelation, provides the only valid basis for belief, and that

PRONUNCIATION KEY

a, trap; aa, father; ai, fair;
ar, star; aw, lawn; ay, play;
b, bb, stab; rubber;
ch, church; ck, ticket;
d, dd, dead; ladder; e, dress;
ee, bee; er, defer; ew, few;
ewr, pure; ə, about;
ər, letter; f, ff, fife; differ;
g, gg, giggle; h, hat; i, kit;
ī, price; īr, fire; j, judge;
k, kick; l, ll, let; 'l, needle;
m, mm, man; n, nn, no;
'n, sudden; ng, thing; o, lot;
ō, no; ŏŏ, foot; ōō, shoe;
oor, poor; ow, cow;
owr, hour; oy, boy;
p, pp, pepper; r, rr, red;
s, ss, sauce; sh, ship;
t, tt, totter; th, thick; th, this;
smooth; u, cut; ur, turn;
v, vv, valve; w, wet; y, yes;
z, zz, zebra; zh, vision;
pleasure

IN FOREIGN WORDS:

aN, oN, Saint-Saëns;
hl, Llanelli; Hluhluwe;
kh, loch; lough; Khaled

STRESS MARK:

ín-sīt, insight; in-sít, incite

reason is the prime source of spiritual truth. **b.** The rejection of religion on the grounds that it can have no logical or rational basis. **2.** In ethics, the theory that the exercise of reason provides the only valid basis for moral beliefs and rules of conduct. **3.** *Philosophy.* The theory, as exemplified in the philosophy of Descartes and Spinoza, that the exercise of reason, rather than empiricism, provides the only valid basis for and source of knowledge. Compare **empiricism.** **—ra·tion·al·ist** *n. & adj.* **—ra·tion·al·is·tic** (-ístik) *adj.* **—ra·tion·al·is·ti·cal·ly** *adv.*

ra·tion·al·i·ty (ráshə-nál-əti) *n., pl.* **-ties.** **1.** The quality or condition of being rational. **2.** A rational belief or practice.

rational number *n.* Any number capable of being expressed as an integer or quotient of integers.

rat·ite (rát-īt) *adj.* Designating any of a group of flightless birds having a flat breastbone without the keel characteristic of most flying birds and feathers lacking barbs.
~n. A ratite bird, such as the ostrich, emu, or kiwi. [New Latin *Ratitae* (group), from Latin *ratis,* raft (so named in allusion to the "keelless" sternum).]

rat kangaroo *n.* Any of various Australian marsupials of the subfamily Potoroinae, similar to kangaroos but having a long, ratlike face.

rat·line, rat·lin (rát-lin) *n. Nautical.* **1.** Any of the small ropes fastened horizontally to the shrouds of a ship and forming a ladder for going aloft. **2.** The rope used for this purpose.

RATO rocket assisted takeoff.

ra·toon, rat·toon (ra-tōōn) *n.* A basal shoot sprouting from a plant such as the banana, pineapple, or sugar cane.
~v. **ratooned** or **rattooned, -tooning, -toons.** *—intr.* To produce or grow as a ratoon or ratoons. *—tr.* To propagate (a crop) from ratoons. [Spanish *retoño,* sprout, from *retoñar,* to sprout : *re-,* again + *otoñar,* to grow in the autumn, from *otoño,* autumn, from Latin *autumnus,* AUTUMN.]

rat race *n. Informal.* Ceaseless, hectic, and fiercely competitive activity, especially when involving a struggle for power or promotion: *As a merchant banker you can't avoid the rat race.*

rats (rats) *interj. Informal.* Used to express contemptuous disbelief or irritation.

rats·bane (ráts-bayn) *n.* **1.** *Literary.* Rat poison. **2.** Arsenic trioxide.

rat snake *n.* Any of several nonvenomous, rodent-eating snakes such as those of the genera *Elaphe* and *Ptyas.*

rat-tail (rát-tayl) *adj.* Also **rat-tailed** (-tayld). **1.** Shaped like a rat's tail: *a rat-tail file.* **2.** Designating a spoon whose handle is prolonged like a tail along the back of the bowl.
~n. **1.** A fish, the **grenadier** *(see).* **2. a.** A horse's tail that is hairless. **b.** A horse with such a tail. **3.** A round file shaped like a rat's tail, used especially to widen holes in metal. In this sense also called "rat's tail".

rat·tan, ra·tan (rə-tán, ra-) *n.* **1.** Any of various climbing palms of the genera *Calamus, Daemonorops,* or *Plectomia,* of tropical Asia, having long, tough, slender stems. **2.** The stems of any of these palms, used to make wickerwork. **3.** A switch, stick, or cane made from such a stem. [Malay *rotan,* probably from *raut,* trim.]

rat·ter (ráttər) *n.* **1.** A cat, dog, or person who catches and kills rats. **2.** *Slang.* A deserter, betrayer, or traitor.

Rat·ti·gan (ráttigən), **Sir Terence (Mervyn)** (1911–77). British playwright. He first made his name with two farces, *French Without Tears* (1936) and *While the Sun Shines* (1943). Perhaps his best-known play is *The Winslow Boy* (1946), which won a New York Critics' Award. He was knighted in 1971.

rat·tle[1] (rátt'l) *v.* **-tled, -tling, -tles.** *—intr.* **1.** To make or emit a quick succession of short, sharp sounds, as of pebbles being shaken in a container. **2.** To move with such sounds: *a train rattling along the track.* **3.** To talk rapidly and at length, usually without much serious content. Used with *on.* *—tr.* **1.** To cause to rattle. **2.** To utter or perform rapidly or effortlessly: *rattle off a list of names.* **3.** *Informal.* To disconcert; unnerve; fluster.
~n. **1.** A rapid succession of short, percussive sounds. **2.** A device for producing these sounds, such as a baby's toy. **3.** A rattling sound in the throat caused by obstructed breathing. **4.** The series of horny structures at the end of a rattlesnake's tail. **5.** Loud or rapid talk; babble. **6.** Idle or trivial chatter. **7.** An incessant talker. **8.** Any of several related European plants having a seed capsule that rattles, such as the red rattle, *Pedicularis palustris,* or the yellow rattle, *Rhinanthus minor.* [Middle English *ratelen,* from Middle Low German *rattelen,* akin to Middle High German *razzeln*†.]

rattle[2] *tr.v.* **-tled, -tling, -tles.** *Nautical.* To secure ratlines to (a rigging). Used with *down.* [Back-formation from *rattling,* variant of RATLINE.]

rat·tle·box (rátt'l-boks) *n.* Any of various plants or shrubs of the genus *Crotalaria,* having inflated pods in which the seeds rattle.

rat·tle·brain (rátt'l-brayn) *n. Informal.* A talkative, foolish person. Also called "rattlehead", "rattlepate". **—rat·tle·brained** (-braynd) *adj.*

rat·tler (ráttlər) *n.* **1.** One who or that which rattles. **2.** *Informal.* An outstanding example of something. **3.** *Chiefly U.S.* A rattlesnake. **4.** *U.S. Informal.* A goods train.

rat·tle·snake (rátt'l-snayk) *n.* Any of various venomous New World snakes of the genera *Crotalus* and *Sistrurus,* having at the end of the tail a series of loosely attached, horny segments that can be vibrated to produce a rattling or buzzing sound.

rattlesnake plantain *n.* Any of various small orchids of the genus *Goodyera,* having mottled or striped leaves and spikes of whitish flowers. [From its leaves, which resemble a rattlesnake's skin.]

rat·tle·trap (rátt'l-trap) *n. Informal.* A rickety, worn-out vehicle.

rat·tling (rátt'l-ing, ráttling) *adj. Informal.* **1.** Animated; brisk: *rattling conversation.* **2.** Very good.
~adv. Informal. Very; especially: *a rattling good yarn.*

rat·tly (rátt'l-i, ráttli) *adj.* Rattling or apt to rattle; clattering.

rattoon. Variant of **ratoon.**

rat·trap, rat-trap (rát-trap) *n.* **1.** Any of various traps used for catching rats. **2.** A bicycle pedal of a type having metal teeth, and often a toe clip, to provide a firm grip for the foot.

rat·ty (rátti) *adj.* **-tier, -tiest.** **1.** Of or characteristic of rats. **2.** Infested by rats. **3.** *Chiefly British Slang.* Peevish; irritable. **4.** *Slang.* Unkempt and dirty. Said of hair. **5.** *U.S. Slang.* Dilapidated and shabby. **—rat·ti·ly** *adv.* **—rat·ti·ness** *n.*

rau·cous (ráwkəss) *adj.* Rough-sounding and harsh. [Latin *raucus,* hoarse, harsh.] **—rau·cous·ly** *adv.* **—rau·cous·ness** *n.*

raun·chy (ráwnchi) *adj.* **-chier, -chiest.** **1.** *Chiefly U.S. Slang.* **a.** Earthy; coarse; vulgar. **b.** Smutty; indecent. **2.** *Informal.* Marked by loud, driving rhythms. Said especially of rock music. [20th century : origin obscure.] **—raunch·i·ly** *adv.* **—raunch·i·ness** *n.*

Rausch·en·berg (rówsh'n-berg), **Robert** (1925–). U.S. painter and sculptor. He developed an individual, somewhat pop-art style out of the collage and *objet trouvé* methods. One of his most notable works is *The Bed* (1955), which consists of his own bed, daubed with paint and hung vertically.

rau·wol·fi·a (raw-wŏŏlfi-ə, row-) *n.* Any of various tropical trees and shrubs of the genus *Rauwolfia;* especially, *R. serpentina,* of southeast Asia. The root of this species is the source of alkaloid drugs such as reserpine, formerly used as tranquillisers but now used chiefly to treat high blood pressure. [New Latin, after Leonhard *Rauwolf* (died 1596), German botanist.]

rav·age (rávvij) *v.* **-aged, -aging, -ages.** *—tr.* To destroy or despoil; devastate: *Invaders ravaged the countryside; a face ravaged by grief.* *—intr.* To wreak destruction.
~n. **1.** The act or practice of ravaging. **2.** *Usually plural.* Damage; destructive effects: *the ravages of disease.* [French, from Old French, from *ravir,* to RAVISH.] **—rav·ag·er** *n.*

rave[1] (rayv) *v.* **raved, raving, raves.** *—intr.* **1.** To speak wildly, irrationally, or incoherently: *raving like a madman.* **2.** To roar; rage. **3.** *Informal.* To speak with wild enthusiasm: *He raved about her looks.* **4.** To speak in an angry and vehement manner. **5.** *British Slang.* To engage in wild, festive activities. Often used in the phrase *rave it up.* *—tr.* To utter in a wild and unrestrained manner.
~n. **1.** The state or act of raving. **2.** *British Slang.* A wild party. **3.** *British Slang.* A current fashion or trend.
~adj. Informal. Wildly enthusiastic: *rave reviews.* [Middle English *raven,* to be delirious, wander, from Old Northern French *ravert*†.]

rave[2] *n.* A framework or rail attached to the side of a cart. [Variant of dialect *rathe*†.]

rav·el (rávv'l) *v.* **-elled** or *U.S.* **-eled, -elling** or *U.S.* **-eling, -els.** *—tr.* **1.** To separate the fibres or threads of (cloth, for example); unravel. Often used with *out.* **2.** To clarify by separating the aspects of. Often used with *out: "Must I ravel out my weaved-up folly"* (Shakespeare). **3.** To entangle or knot. **4.** To complicate or confuse. *—intr.* **1.** To become separated into component threads; unravel; fray. Used of cloth. **2.** To become entangled, knotted, or confused.
~n. **1.** A broken or frayed thread. **2.** A tangle or knot. [Dutch *rafelen,* to unravel, from obsolete Dutch *ravelen*†, to entangle.] **—rav·el·ler** *n.*

Ra·vel (ra-vél), **Maurice** (1875–1937). French composer, with Debussy the leading figure of the so-called Impressionist school. He is perhaps best known for his piano compositions, especially *Pavane pour une infante défunte* (1899) and *Le Tombeau de Couperin* (1917). He wrote two piano concertos, one for the left hand only (1931). His other major orchestral scores include the song cycle, *Schéhérazade* (1903), and the ballet, *Daphnis et Chlóe* (1912).

rave·lin (ráv-lin, rávvə-) *n.* A triangular, embanked salient outside the main ditch of a fortress. [French, from obsolete Italian *ravellino, rivellino,* perhaps from diminutive of *riva,* bank, from Latin *rīpa.*]

rav·ell·ing (rávv'l-ing) *n.* A thread or fibre that has become separated from a woven material.

rav·el·ment (rávv'l-mənt) *n. Archaic.* Confusion or entanglement.

ra·ven[1] (ráyv'n) *n.* **1.** A large bird, *Corvus corax,* related to the crow, having black plumage and a croaking cry. **2.** Shiny black. [Middle English *raven,* Old English *hræfn,* from Germanic.] **—ra·ven** *adj.*

rav·en[2] (rávv'n) *v.* **-ened, -ening, -ens.** *—tr.* **1.** To consume greedily; devour. **2.** To seek or seize (prey or plunder). *—intr.* **1.** To seek or seize prey or plunder. **2.** To eat ravenously; be voracious.
~n. Variant of **ravin.** [Old French *raviner,* ravage, seize by force, from Vulgar Latin *rapīnāre* (unattested), from Latin *rapīna,* rapine, from *rapere,* to seize.] **—rav·en·er** *n.*

rav·en·ing (rávv'n-ing) *adj.* **1.** Predatory; voracious. **2.** *Archaic.* Rabid. **—rav·en·ing·ly** *adv.*

Ra·ven·na (rə-vénnə). Capital of Ravenna province in Emilia-Romagna, north central Italy. It is an agricultural market and industrial centre, connected to the Adriatic coast by canal. Ravenna rose to importance under the Romans and is famous for its colourful mosaics and for its Roman and Byzantine buildings.

rav·en·ous (rávv'n-əss, rávvin-) *adj.* **1.** Extremely hungry; famished. **2.** Greedy; rapacious; voracious: *ravenous for power.* [Middle Eng-

rattlesnake *There are about 30 species of rattlesnake, ranging in size from 300 millimetres (1 foot) to 2.5 metres (8 feet). All are pit vipers, so called because they are able to seek their prey in the dark by means of heat-sensitive pits near their nostrils.*

raven *The sinister appearance of these large coal-black crows gathering to feed on a carcass has given them an unsavoury reputation. A small flock of ravens is kept at the Tower of London; legend has it that the Tower will fall if the birds leave.*

lish, rapacious, from Old French *ravineux,* from *raviner,* to RAVEN.] **—rav•en•ous•ly** *adv.* **—rav•en•ous•ness** *n.*

rav•er (ráyvər) *n. British Slang.* A person who appears to lead a very exciting and uninhibited social life.

rave-up (ráyv-up) *n. British Slang.* A wild party; a rave.

ra•vi•gote (rávvi-gōt, -gŏt) *n.* A vinegar sauce spiced with minced onion, capers, and herbs, served with boiled meats or fish. [French, from *ravigoter,* to add new vigour : *re-,* again + *a-,* to, from Latin *ad-* + *vigueur,* vigour, from Latin *vigor,* VIGOUR.]

rav•in, rav•en (rávvin) *n. Poetic.* **1.** Plundering or pillage. **2.** Something taken as prey. **3.** The act or practice of preying. [Middle English *ravine,* from Old French, rapine, from Latin *rapīna,* from *rapere,* to seize.]

ra•vine (rə-véen) *n.* A deep, narrow cleft or gorge in the earth's surface, especially one worn by the flow of water. [French, mountain torrent, from Old French, rapine. See **ravin.**]

rav•ing (ráyving) *adj.* **1.** Talking or behaving irrationally; wild: *a raving maniac.* **2.** *Informal.* Exciting admiration or notice: *a raving beauty.*
~*adv.* Used as an intensive: *raving mad.*
~*n. Often plural.* Delirious, irrational speech. **—rav•ing•ly** *adv.*

ra•vi•o•li (rávvi-ṓli || *U.S. also* raávi-) *pl.n.* **1.** Small casings of pasta filled with chopped meat, cheese, or other ingredients and usually served with a sauce. **2.** *Used with a singular verb.* A dish consisting of ravioli. [Italian, plural of dialectal *raviolo,* diminutive of *rava,* turnip, from Latin *rāpa,* turnip.]

rav•ish (rávvish) *tr.v.* **-ished, -ishing, -ishes. 1.** *Literary.* To seize and carry away by force. **2.** *Literary.* To rape; deflower; violate. **3.** To enrapture. Usually used in the passive: *ravished by his charm.* [Middle English *ravisshen,* from Old French *ravir* (present stem *raviss-*), from Vulgar Latin *rapīre* (unattested), from Latin *rapere,* seize.] **—rav•ish•er** *n.* **—rav•ish•ment** *n.*

rav•ish•ing (rávvishing) *adj.* **1.** Entrancing; delightful. **2.** *Informal.* Extremely beautiful; gorgeous. **—rav•ish•ing•ly** *adv.*

raw (raw) *adj.* **1.** Uncooked: *raw meat.* **2.** Being in a natural condition; not subjected to manufacturing, refining, or finishing processes: *raw wool.* **3.** Untrained and inexperienced: *a raw recruit.* **4.** *Chiefly U.S.* Recently finished; fresh: *raw plaster.* **5.** Having subcutaneous tissue exposed: *a raw wound.* **6.** Penetratingly damp and cold. **7.** *Informal.* Cruel and unfair. **8.** Outspoken; crude. **9.** Undiluted; neat. Said of spirits. **10.** Not analysed or modified. Said of statistics. **11.** Unhemmed or unfinished. Said of the edge of cloth. **—in the raw. 1.** In a crude or unrefined state. **2.** *Informal.* Nude; naked. **—on the raw.** On a sensitive area or topic: *Her comment about small men touched him on the raw.* [Middle English *raw,* Old English *hrēaw.*] **—raw•ly** *adv.* **—raw•ness** *n.*

Ra•wal•pin•di (ráwl-píndi, raá-wəl-). City in the Punjab, north Pakistan, lying in the foothills of the Himalayas. It is an important industrial and commercial centre, its industries including oil refining, railway engineering, chemicals, furniture, and textiles. After the British occupied the Punjab (1849), it became a major British military outpost. It was the temporary capital of Pakistan (1959–70), during the building of the new capital, Islamabad.

raw•boned (ráw-bōnd) *adj.* Having a lean, gaunt frame with prominent bones.

raw•hide (ráw-hīd) *n.* **1.** The untanned hide of cattle or other animals. **2.** A whip or rope made of such hide.

ra•win•sonde (ráy-win-sond) *n.* A meteorological balloon carrying instruments and a radar target, used for measuring wind speed in the upper atmosphere. [*Ra*dar + *win*d + radio *sonde.*]

Rawl•plug (ráwl-plug) *n.* A trademark for a small hollow plug of plastic or wool fibre, inserted into holes to secure nails and screws.

raw material *n.* **1.** *Often plural.* The natural products or basic materials on which manufacturing processes are carried out to give finished products. **2.** Somebody or something regarded as having the basic attributes or potential for a particular purpose.

raw sienna *n.* **1.** A brownish-yellow pigment made from untreated sienna. **2.** Brownish orange to light brown. Also called "sienna".

raw silk *n.* **1.** Untreated silk as reeled from the cocoon. **2.** Fabric woven from such silk.

Raws•thorne (ráwss-thawrn), **Alan** (1905–71). British composer. His works include *Theme and Variations* for two violins (1938) and the *Symphonic Studies* (1939), as well as three symphonies, various concertos, and vocal and chamber music.

ray[1] (ray) *n.* **1.** A thin line or narrow beam of radiation, especially of light. **2.** Any graphic or other representation of such a line. **3.** A slight trace or hint; a gleam. **4.** In geometry, a straight line extending indefinitely from a point. **5.** Any structure having the form of lines extending from a point. **6.** *Botany.* A ray flower. **7.** *Zoology.* **a.** Any of the bony spines supporting the membrane of a fish's fin. **b.** Any of the arms of a starfish or related animal.
~*v.* **rayed, raying, rays.** *—tr.* **1.** To send out as rays; emit. **2.** To decorate with rays or radiating lines. **3.** To cast rays upon; irradiate. *—intr.* To extend or issue forth in rays. Used of lines or light, for example. [Middle English, from Old French *rai,* from Latin *radius.* See **radius.**]

ray[2] *n.* Any of various marine cartilaginous fishes of the order Rajiformes (or Batoidei), having large, winglike, pectoral fins horizontally flattened bodies, and narrow tails. See **electric ray.** [Middle English *raye,* from Old French *raie,* from Latin *raia*†.]

ray[3], **re** (ray) *n. Music.* In tonic sol-fa, a syllable representing the second note of a diatonic scale. [Middle English, from Medieval Latin. See **gamut.**]

Rayleigh scattering *The changing colours of the sky at midday and dusk were first explained by the English mathematician Lord Rayleigh (1842–1919). He discovered that light waves – like other types of electromagnetic radiation – are broken up, or scattered, as they pass through the air, and that some wavelengths are scattered more than others. Which wavelengths dominate depends both on the size and on the number of molecules and particles through which the light passes. The size of the air molecules and dust particles in the Earth's atmosphere has the effect of scattering wavelengths at the blue end of the Sun's spectrum about five times more strongly than wavelengths at the red end – which is why the sky normally appears blue. At sunset and sunrise, however, when sunlight has to pass through a thicker layer of atmosphere, the greater number of molecules and particles in its path has the effect of absorbing the blue wavelengths – and allowing the redder colours in the spectrum to shine through.*

Ray[1] (ray), **Man** (1890–1976). U.S. artist. A founder of the Dadaist movement, he moved to Paris (1921) and experimented with surrealism. He later became a fashion photographer and film-maker.

Ray[2] (rī, ray), **Satyajit** (1921–). Indian film director, the most acclaimed of his generation. His films, such as *Pather Panchali* (1955) and *Distant Thunder* (1974), are notable for their realistic portrayal of everyday life, and artistic composition of their camera-work.

ray flower *n.* Any of the flat, strap-shaped marginal flowers in the flower head of certain composite plants, such as the daisy. Also called "ray floret". Compare **disc flower.**

ray gun *n.* In science fiction, a weapon that emits rays that can paralyse, stun, kill, or vaporise.

Ray•leigh (ráyli), **John William Strutt, 3rd Baron** (1842–1919). British physicist. He was awarded the 1904 Nobel prize for his discovery, with Sir William Ramsay, of the inert gas argon. His son, Robert John Strutt, the 4th Baron, (1875–1947), developed the radiocarbon method of determining the age of rocks.

Rayleigh scattering *n.* The scattering of light waves by particles with dimensions much smaller than their wavelengths, resulting in angular separation of colours, and responsible for the reddish colour of sunset and the blue of the sky. [Explained by Lord RAYLEIGH in 1871.]

ray•less (ráy-ləss, -liss) *adj.* **1.** Lacking rays: *a rayless flower.* **2.** Lacking light; gloomy: *a rayless dungeon.*

ray•on (ráy-on, *rarely* -ən) *n.* **1.** Any of several similar synthetic textile fibres produced by forcing a cellulose solution through fine spinnerets and solidifying the resulting filaments. **2.** Any fabric made from such fibres. [From RAY (light).] **—ray•on** *adj.*

raze, rase (rayz) *tr.v.* **razed** or **rased, razing** or **rasing, razes** or **rases. 1.** To tear down or demolish; level to the ground. **2.** To erase. **3.** *Archaic.* To scrape; graze. —See Synonyms at **ruin.** [Middle English *rasen,* from Old French *raser,* from Vulgar Latin *rasāre* (unattested), from Latin *rādere* (past participle *rāsus*), to scrape.]

ra•zee (ray-zée, *also* rázzee) *n., pl.* **-ees.** Formerly, a sailing ship made smaller by the removal of its upper deck or decks.
~*tr.v.* **razeed, -eeing, -ees.** To remove the upper deck or decks from (a sailing ship). [French *rasée,* from *raser,* to shave close.]

ra•zor (ráyzər) *n.* **1.** A sharp-edged cutting instrument, used especially for shaving the face. **2.** An instrument with electrically driven blades, used for shaving.
~*tr.v.* **razored, -oring, -ors.** To use a razor on; shave or cut with a razor. [Middle English *raso(u)r,* from Old French *rasor,* from *raser,* to scrape, RAZE.]

ra•zor•back (ráyzər-bak) *n.* **1.** A whale, the **rorqual** *(see).* **2.** A semi-wild pig of the southeastern United States, having a narrow body with a ridged back. **3.** *U.S.* A sharp, ridged hill.

ra•zor•bill (ráyzər-bil) *n.* A sea bird, *Alca torda,* of the northern Atlantic, having black-and-white plumage and a flattened, white-ringed bill. Also called "razorbilled auk".

razor cut *n.* A hairstyle produced by trimming the hair fairly short with a razor in layers so that it tapers towards the nape of the neck.

ra•zor-edge (ráyzər-ej, -éj) *n.* **1.** A keen, sharp edge, as of a knife or mountain ridge. **2.** A thin dividing line: *the razor-edge of legality.* **3.** A critical or dangerous state of affairs. Used especially in the phrase *on a razor-edge.* Also called "razor's edge".

razor shell *n.* Any of various long, narrow burrowing bivalve molluscs of the family Solenidae. Also *U.S.* "razor clam".

razz (raz) *n. U.S. Slang.* A derisive sound, a **raspberry** *(see).*
~*tr.v.* **razzed, razzing, razzes.** *Chiefly U.S. Slang.* To deride, heckle, or tease. [Short for *razzberry,* variant of RASPBERRY.]

raz•zi•a (rázzi-ə) *n., pl.* **-zias.** A raid carried out for plunder or slaves, especially as formerly practised by Muslims in North Africa. [French, from Arabic (Algerian) *gazīa,* from Arabic *gazwa.*]

raz•zle (rázz'l) *n. Slang.* **1.** A wild spree, especially a drinking spree. Used chiefly in the phrase *on the razzle.* **2.** A razzle-dazzle. [Shortened from RAZZLE-DAZZLE.]

razzle-dazzle (rázz'l-dazz'l, -dázz'l) *n.* **1.** An exciting, glittering display, especially one intended to dazzle or impress, as in advertising. **2.** Ebullient energy; vigour. **3.** A razzle. [Reduplication of DAZZLE.]

razz•ma•tazz (ráz-mə-táz, -taz) *n.* Also **razz•a•ma•tazz** (rázzə-). Noisy excitement and show, especially when designed to impress or attract. [Variant of RAZZLE-DAZZLE.]

Rb The symbol for the element rubidium.

RBC red blood cell.

RBE *Physics.* relative biological effectiveness.

R.C. 1. Red Cross. **2.** reinforced concrete. **3.** Reserve Corps. **4.** Roman Catholic.

R.C.A. 1. Royal College of Art. **2.** Royal Canadian Academy. **3.** Radio Corporation of America.

R.C.A.F. Royal Canadian Air Force.

R.C.M. Royal College of Music.

R.C.M.P. Royal Canadian Mounted Police.

R.C.N. 1. Royal Canadian Navy. **2.** Royal College of Nursing.

R.C.O. Royal College of Organists.

R.C.P. Royal College of Physicians.

rcpt. receipt.

R.C.S. 1. Royal College of Science. **2.** Royal College of Surgeons. **3.** Royal Corps of Signals.

rct. recruit.

R.C.T. Royal Corps of Transport.

R.C.V.S. Royal College of Veterinary Surgeons.

rd rod (unit of length).

rd. 1. road. **2.** round.

Rd. road.

R.D. *Finance.* refer to drawer.

re[1]. *Music.* Variant of **ray.**

re[2] (ree, ray) *prep.* Concerning; in reference to; in the case of. Used in commercial or legal contexts. [Latin *rē,* from *rēs,* thing.]

Re The symbol for the element rhenium.

Re. Variant of **Ra.**

re– *prefix.* Indicates: **1.** Restoration to a previous or improved condition or position; for example, **repay, rehouse, redecorate. 2.** Repetition of a previous action; for example, **reactivate.** ***Note:*** Many compounds other than those entered here may be formed with *re-*. In forming compounds *re-* is normally, in this dictionary, joined with the following element without space or hyphen: *reopen.* If the second element begins with *e,* it is preferable to separate it with a hyphen: *re-entry.* However, such compounds may often be found written solid and are indicated here as fully acceptable variants. If a compound that resembles a familiar word is intended in a special sense, the hyphen is necessary to make the distinction: *re-creation,* meaning "creation anew". The hyphen may also be necessary to clarify an unusual nonce formation: *re-realignment,* or a compound that produces a series of three or more vowels: *re-aerify.* [Middle English *re-,* from Old French, from Latin *re-, red-,* in the following senses: 1. Back, as in **rebuke.** 2. Back to an earlier state or condition, as in **repair.** 3. Back in place, as in **remain.** 4. Backward, away, as in **refract.** 5. Again, repeatedly, in return for, as in **respond.** 6. Behind, as in **relinquish.** 7. Contrary, in the sense of negating, as in **repeal.** 8. Against, as in **reluctant.** 9. In response to, as in **requiem.** 10. As an intensive, as in **revere.**]

Re. rupee.

R.E. 1. Religious Education. **2.** Right Excellent. **3.** Royal Engineers. **4.** Royal Exchange.

're (ər). Contraction of *are.*

reach (reech) *v.* **reached, reaching, reaches.** —*tr.* **1.** To stretch out or put forth (a bodily part); extend. Often used with *out: reached her hand out to touch the ceiling.* **2.** To touch or take hold of by extending some bodily part, especially the hand or something held therein: *Can you reach the table?* **3.** To get to, go as far as, or arrive at: *reach maturity; reach the end of a journey.* **4.** To communicate with; contact: *You can reach me at the office.* **5. a.** To extend as far as: *His property reached the edge of the forest.* **b.** To carry as far as: *His cry reached our ears.* **6.** To aggregate or amount to. **7.** *Informal.* To give or hand over to someone: *Reach me the sugar.* **8.** To hit or strike, especially in fencing or boxing. **9.** To make an impression on; affect: *reached the hearts of thousands.* —*intr.* **1.** To extend or thrust out something. **2.** To try to grasp, touch, or attain something: *reach for a gun; reach for the stars.* **3. a.** To extend in time or space: *His land reaches to the bottom of the hill.* **b.** To extend in influence or effect: *The effects of their policies reach throughout the land.* **4.** *Nautical.* To sail with the wind abeam.
~*n.* **1.** The act or an instance of reaching out. **2.** Power of or capicity for reaching, as: **a.** The extent or distance something can reach. **b.** The range or scope of influence or effect: *beyong the reach of the law.* **c.** The extent of one's ability to attain or achieve: *The larger model is beyond our reach.* **3.** An unbroken expanse of water, especially on a river or canal. **4.** *Plural.* A level, position, or grouping: *the upper reaches of the civil service.* **5.** A pole connecting the rear axle of a vehicle, such as a wagon, with the front. **6.** *Nautical.* The tack of a sailing vessel with the wind abeam. [Middle English *rechen,* Old English *rǣcan,* from West Germanic *raikjan* (unattested). —**reach·er** *n.*

Synonyms: *reach, achieve, attain, gain, compass, accomplish.*

reach-me-down (reéch-mi-down) *n.* Something of inferior quality through being secondhand or imitative. Also used adjectivally: *churned out plodding, reach-me-down verse.*

re·act (ri-ákt, ree-) *v.* **-acted, -acting, -acts.** —*intr.* **1.** To act in response or opposition to some former act or state. Used with *against, on,* or *upon.* **2. a.** To be affected or influenced by circumstances or events. **b.** *Medicine.* To be affected, especially adversely by a drug, allergen, or the like. **3.** *Chemistry.* To undergo chemical change. —*tr. Chemistry.* To cause (substances) to undergo chemical change. [RE- + ACT, influenced by Medieval Latin *reagere* (past participle *reactus*), to react.]

re·ac·tance (ri-áktənss, ree-) *n. Symbol* **X** Opposition to the flow of alternating electric current caused by the inductance and capacitance in a circuit. See **impedance.**

re·ac·tant (ri-áktənt, ree-) *n.* A substance participating in a chemical reaction; especially, a directly reacting substance present at the initiation of the reaction.

re·ac·tion (ri-áksh'n, ree-) *n.* **1. a.** A response to a stimulus or former action; especially, a response indicating a person's feelings or views about something. **b.** Reciprocal action between two things. **2.** A reverse or opposing action. **3. a.** A tendency to revert to a former state. **b.** A tendency, as in art and especially politics, towards conservatism and opposition to progressive trends. **4.** A chemical change or transformation in which a substance decomposes, combines with other substances, or interchanges constituents with other substances. **5.** A **nuclear reaction** *(see).* **6.** A force produced in a system by an applied force, equal in magnitude to the applied force and acting in the opposite direction. **7. a.** The effect of a drug; especially, an adverse effect. **b.** The effect of a substance upon a person who is allergic to that substance. **c.** An adverse response by a person to such drugs or allergens. **8.** A period of depression, exhaustion, mental disorder, or the like, as occurs following shock or excessive exertion.

re·ac·tion·ar·y (ri-áksh'n-əri, ree-, -ri || -erri) *adj.* Also **re·ac·tion·ist** (-ist). Characterised by reaction; especially, opposing progressive trends or wishing to return to a former, outmoded state.
~*n., pl.* **reactionaries.** A person who is reactionary.

reaction engine *n.* An engine that develops thrust by the expulsion of matter, especially ignited fuel gases. Also "reaction motor".

reaction time *n. Biology.* The time interval between the application of a stimulus and the detection of a response.

reaction turbine *n.* A type of turbine in which part of the torque is produced by pressure from fluid moving out of the rotating part.

re·ac·ti·vate (ri-ákti-vayt, ree-) *tr.v.* **-vated, -vating, -vates. 1.** To make active again. **2.** To restore the effectiveness or ability to function of. —**re·ac·ti·va·tion** (-váysh'n) *n.*

re·ac·tive (ri-áktiv, ree-) *adj.* **1.** Tending to be responsive or to react to a stimulus. **2.** Characterised by reaction. **3.** *Chemistry & Physics.* Tending to participate in reactions. **4.** *Electricity.* Having electrical reactance.

reactive depression *n.* Mental depression that arises in response to unfavourable external circumstances without necessarily reflecting deep-seated personality or physiological problems.

re·ac·tor (ri-áktər, ree-) *n.* **1.** A person or thing that reacts. **2.** *Electricity.* A circuit element, such as a coil, used to introduce reactance into a circuit. **3.** *Physics.* A **nuclear reactor** *(see).*

read (reed) *v.* **read** (red), **reading, reads.** —*tr.* **1.** To comprehend, take in the meaning of, or be able to convert into the intended sound (something written or printed) by looking at or, in the case of blind people, touching the characters or words and interpreting them. **2.** To utter or render aloud (something written or printed). **3.** To have the knowledge of (a language) necessary to understand printed or written material: *I can read Russian but I can't speak it.* **4. a.** To seek to interpret the true nature or meaning of (someone or something) through close scrutiny: *read the sky for signs of snow.* **b.** To ascertain the true thoughts, intent, or mood of: *He read her mind.* **5.** To interpret the signs or arrangement of: *read a map.* **6.** To ascribe a special meaning or interpretation, often mistakenly, to (something read, heard, experienced, or observed): *He read her tears as sadness, not joy: Don't read too much into what he says.* **7. a.** To foretell or predict (the future). **b.** To foretell the future by interpreting the arrangement of (lines on a hand or tea leaves, for example). **8.** To perceive, receive, or comprehend (a signal, message, or its sender): *I read you loud and clear.* **9.** To be engaged in the study of: *read law at university.* **10.** To learn or get knowledge from (something written or printed): *He read that crime was rife.* **11.** To have or adopt as a reading in a particular passage: *For "color" read "colour".* **12.** To indicate, register, or show: *The dial reads 0°.* **13.** To be interpreted as; mean: *The law reads that he is guilty.* **14.** To obtain or detect and transfer (information) from a computer storage device. **15.** To cause to be in a specified state by reading: *read me to sleep.* **16.** To interpret or be able to interpret (musical notation) and reproduce the appropriate notes. **17.** In various sports to anticipate correctly (the moves or tactics of one's teammates or opponents). —*intr.* **1.** To read printed or written characters, as of words or music. **2.** To utter or render aloud the words that one is reading. **3.** To learn by reading. Used with *about* or *of: I read about it in the paper.* **4.** To have a particular wording: *The line reads thus.* **5.** To have a specified character or quality for the reader: *His poems read well.* **6.** To study: *reading for the bar.* —**read (oneself) in.** In the Anglican Church, to enter into a benefice by a public reading of the Thirty-nine Articles. —**read up.** To acquire information or improve one's skill by reading or studying. Often used with *on.*
~*n.* **1.** The act or an instance of reading. **2.** Material suitable for reading or something to be read: *a good read.*
~*adj.* (red). Informed by reading; learned. Used in combination: *well-read.* [Read (infinitive), read (past tense and past participle); Middle English *reden, redde, red,* Old English *rǣdan,* to advise, explain, read, *rǣdde, rǣden,* from Germanic *rǣdhan* (unattested).]

Read (reed), **Sir Herbert (Edward)** (1893–1968). British poet and literary and art critic. His first volume of poetry, *Naked Warriors,* appeared in 1919, the *Collected Poems* in 1966. He is more famous as a critic, for books such as *Art and Industry* (1934), *Art and society* (1937), *Art and Alienation* (1967), *Form in Modern Poetry* (1932), and *Phases of English Poetry* (1950).

read·a·ble (reéd-əb'l) *adj.* **1.** Capable of being read easily; legible. **2.** Pleasurable or interesting to read. —**read·a·bil·i·ty** (-ə-billəti), **read·a·ble·ness** *n.* —**read·a·bly** *adv.*

Reade (reed), **Charles** (1814–84). British novelist. His best-known work was *The Cloister and the Hearth* (1861).

read·er (reédər) *n.* **1.** One who reads, especially, a person who enjoys reading very much. **2.** A professional reciter of literary works. **3. a.** In the Roman Catholic Church, a **lector. b.** In the Anglican Church, a **lay reader** *(see).* **4.** A person employed by a publisher to read and evaluate manuscripts. **5.** A corrector of printers' proofs; a proofreader. **6.** *Chiefly British.* A senior university lecturer. **7.** *U.S.* A teaching assistant who reads and grades examination papers. **8.** A textbook of reading exercises designed as part of a course for people learning to read, especially for children. **9.** A computer device for converting data from one form into another.

read·er·ship (reédər-ship) *n.* **1.** The readers collectively or the total number of readers of a publication or publications. **2.** *Chiefly British.* The office or rank of a reader in a university.

PRONUNCIATION KEY

a, trap; aa, father; ai, fair; ar, star; aw, lawn; ay, play; b, bb, stab; rubber; ch, church; ck, ticket; d, dd, dead; ladder; e, dress; ee, bee; er, defer; ew, few; ewr, pure; ə, about; ər, letter; f, ff, fife; differ; g, gg, giggle; h, hat; i, kit; ī, price; īr, fire; j, judge; k, kick; l, ll, let; 'l, needle; m, mm, man; n, nn, no; 'n, sudden; ng, thing; o, lot; ō, no; ŏŏ, foot; ōō, shoe; oor, poor; ow, cow; owr, hour; oy, boy; p, pp, pepper; r, rr, red; s, ss, sauce; sh, ship; t, tt, totter; th, thick; th, this; smooth; u, cut; ur, turn; v, vv, valve; w, wet; y, yes; z, zz, zebra; zh, vision; pleasure

IN FOREIGN WORDS:

aN, oN, Saint-Saëns; hl, Llanelli; Hluhluwe; kh, loch; lough; Khaled

STRESS MARK:

ín-sīt, insight; in-sít, incite

read·i·ly (réddili, rédd'l-i) *adv.* **1.** Promptly; quickly. **2.** Willingly. **3.** Easily; without difficulty or hindrance.

read·i·ness (réddi-nəss, -niss) *n.* The quality or state of being ready or willing.

read·ing (réeding) *n.* **1.** The skill of being able to read. Also used adjectivally: *reading age.* **2.** Written or printed material. **3.** The act of rendering aloud written or printed matter. **4.** An official or public recitation of written material: *the reading of a will.* **5. a.** A personal interpretation or perception: *What's your reading of the situation?* **b.** A personal interpretation or appraisal of a text or passage. **6.** The precise form of a particular passage in a text. **7.** The information indicated by a gauge or graduated instrument. **8.** In parliamentary procedure, the formal presentation of a bill to a legislative body at any of the stages of its passage; the *first reading* is for the introduction of the bill; the *second reading* is for approving the general principles of the bill; the *third reading* is for the accepting of details of the bill as debated in committee.
~*adj.* Designed or used for reading: *a reading lamp.*

Read·ing (rédding). Administrative centre of Berkshire, southern England, situated at the confluence of the rivers Thames and Kennet. It is an important railway junction, and its industries include electronics, printing, brewing, and engineering.

Reading, Rufus Daniel Isaacs, 1st Marquess of. (1860–1935). British politician and lawyer. Of Jewish extraction, he became the first commoner to achieve a marquessate in over a century. He was in turn a Liberal M.P. (1904–13), Attorney-General (1910–13), Lord Chief Justice (1913–18, 1919–21), ambassador to the United States (1918–19), Viceroy of India (1921-26), and Foreign Secretary (1931).

re·ad·just (rée-ə-júst) *v.* **-justed, -justing, -justs.** —*tr.* To adjust or arrange again —*intr.* To adjust or adapt oneself, as to a new environment or changed circumstances. **—re·ad·just·er** *n.* **—re·ad·just·ment** *n.*

read-on·ly (réed-ōnli) *adj. Computing.* Designating or pertaining to devices in which the information held cannot be changed: *a read-only memory.* Compare **random-access.**

read out *tr.v.* **1.** To read (a text, passage, or the like) aloud. **2.** *U.S.* To expel by proclamation from a social, political or other group.

read-out (réed-owt) *n.* Presentation of computer data, usually in digital form, from calculations or storage, often displayed on a V.D.U. Compare **print-out.**

read-write (réed-rīt) *adj. Computing.* **1.** Of, pertaining to, or designating hardware or software enabling the transfer of information to and from magnetic tape or disk: *a read-write head.* **2.** Designating a memory in which the information held may be altered or read at will. See **random-access.**

read·y (réddi) *adj.* **-ier, -iest. 1.** Prepared or available for service or action. **2.** Mentally disposed; willing: *He was ready to believe them.* **3.** Liable or about to do something. Used with an infinitive: *ready to leave.* **4.** Prompt in understanding or reacting: *a ready intelligence; a ready response.* **5.** Available: *ready money.* **—at the ready. 1.** In position for aiming and firing. Said of a rifle. **2.** In a position for immediate use or action.
~*tr.v.* **readied, readying, readies.** To cause to be ready. [Middle English *redy,* Old English *rǣde,* from Germanic *raidh-* (unattested), prepare.]

read·y-made (réddi-máyd) *adj.* **1.** Made to a set pattern rather than to individual specifications. Compare **made-to-order. 2.** Already existing and available for use: *a ready-made answer.* **3.** Unoriginal and commonplace: *ready-made prose.*
~*n.* **1.** Something that is ready-made. **2.** In art, especially in Dada, an ordinary object, or group of objects, such as a rubbish bin or pile of bricks, that is removed from its original surroundings and viewed as a work of art.

read·y-mix (réddi-miks) *n.* Liquid concrete mixed before delivery to the site at which it is used.

read·y reckoner *n.* A table of conversions, percentages, discounts, or the like, used as an aid in calculation.

read·y-to-wear (réddi-tə-wáir, -tōō-) *adj.* Made to a set pattern; off-the-peg; ready-made. Said of clothes.

re·af·firm (rée-ə-fúrm) *tr.v.* **-firmed, -firming, -firms.** To affirm or assert again. **—re·af·fir·ma·tion** (rée-affər-máysh'n) *n.*

re·af·for·est (rée-ə-fórrist) *tr.v.* **-ested, -esting, -ests.** Also **re·for·est** (rée-fórrist). To replace or plant trees in (an area that was formerly a forest). **—re·af·for·est·a·tion** (-áysh'n), **re·for·est·a·tion** *n.*

Rea·gan (ráygən), **Ronald** (1911–). U.S. actor and politician. After a moderately successful career in Hollywood, mainly as an actor in B movies, he was elected governor of California (1966), a post he held for the Republicans for eight years. In 1980, he was elected president of the United States.

re·a·gent (ree-áyjənt, ri-) *n.* Any substance used in a chemical reaction to detect, measure, examine, or produce other substances. [RE- + AGENT, after REACT.]

re·a·gin (ri-áyjin, ree-) *n.* An antibody present in the blood of individuals allergic to a particular substance (allergen). Subsequent contact with the allergen provokes a reaction with the antibody that is responsible for the allergic response. [*Reagent* + -IN.]

re·al[1] (reerl, rée-əl, reel) *adj.* **1.** Being or occurring in fact or actuality; having verifiable existence: *a real fortune.* **2.** True and actual; not illusory or fictitious: *the real explanation.* **3.** Emphatically having all the attributes normally associated with the specified person or thing: *a real man.* **4.** Genuine and authentic; not artificial or spurious. **5.** *Philosophy.* Existing actually and objectively; not contingent. **6.** *Physics & Chemistry.* Designating a gas in which deviations from ideal gas behaviour occur because of interactions between the constituent gas molecules. **7.** Of, pertaining to, or designating an image formed by light rays that converge in space. **8.** *Mathematics.* Of, pertaining to, or designating the non-imaginary part of a complex quantity. **9.** *Law.* Consisting of or pertaining to stationary or fixed property, such as buildings or land. Compare **personal. 10.** *Economics.* Valued according to current purchasing power rather than the nominal amount: *real incomes.* **11.** *Informal.* Used as an intensive: *a real idiot.* **—for real.** *Slang.* Not illusory or experimental; genuine and serious. **—the real.** The totality of actual, existing things, as opposed to imaginary things.
~*adv. Chiefly U.S. Informal.* Very: *real sorry.* [Middle English, of real property or things, from Anglo-French, from Late Latin *reālis,* actual, real, from Latin *rēs,* thing.] **—real·ness** *n.*

Synonyms: *real, actual, true, authentic, concrete, existent, genuine, tangible, veritable.*

re·al[2] (ray-aál) *n., pl.* **reals** or **-ales** (-ayz, *Spanish* -ess). A former Spanish silver monetary unit. [Spanish, from *real,* "royal", from Latin *rēgālis,* regal, from *rēx* (stem *rēg-*), king.]

re·al[3] (ray-aál) *n., pl.* **reals** or **reis** (rayss, *Portuguese* raysh). Either of two former monetary units of Portugal and Brazil. [Portuguese, from *real,* "royal". See **real** (Spanish coin).]

real ale *n.* Beer that is put in cask while the yeast is still alive and thus matures in the cask. It is usually rich and strong. Compare **keg beer.**

real estate *n. Chiefly U.S. Law.* **Real property** *(see).*

real image *n. Optics.* An optical image that is formed by converging rays.

re·al·gar (ri-álgər, ree-, -gaar) *n.* A soft orange or red arsenic ore, As_2S_2, used in fireworks, tanning, and as a pigment. [Middle English, from Medieval Latin, from Arabic *rajh al-ghār,* powder (of) the mine or cave.]

re·al·i·sa·tion (réer-lī-záysh'n, rée-ə- || *U.S.* -li-) *n.* **1.** The act or fact of realising, or the condition of being realised. **2.** The result of realising.

re·al·ise, re·al·ize (réer-līz, rée-ə- || rée-līz) *v.* **-ised, -ising, -ises.** —*tr.* **1. a.** To comprehend completely or correctly. **b.** To become aware of; notice. **2.** To make real or actualise (a plan or ambition, for example): *realise a dream.* **3.** To make or cause to appear realistic. **4.** To obtain or achieve, as gain or profit: *realise a return on an investment.* **5.** To bring in (a sum) as profit by sale. **6.** To convert (property) into money. **7.** *Music.* To complete or reconstruct in full (a part or harmonies, especially for a piece of baroque music) from the figured base. **8.** *Phonetics.* To produce the sound of (a phoneme) in speech; articulate. —*intr.* To become conscious or aware of something. [French *réaliser,* from Old French *realiser,* from *real,* real, from Late Latin *reālis,* REAL.] **—re·al·is·a·ble** *adj.* **—re·al·is·er** *n.*

re·al·ism (réer-liz'm, rée-ə-) *n.* **1.** Inclination towards literal truth rather than towards the abstract, romantic, or ideal. **2.** Inclination towards a pragmatic, practical, and material way of life rather than an idealistic or morally absolute one. **3.** *Often capital* **R.** In art and literature, a style favouring the representation of life or objects as they actually exist rather than romanticising or idealising them or presenting them in an abstract form. **4.** *Philosophy.* **a.** The doctrine that universal or general ideas and principles have an objective existence. Compare **nominalism. b.** The doctrine that the objects of perception exist independently of the perceiver. Compare **idealism. c.** Broadly, the view that theories, especially scientific or other explanatory theories, are objectively true or false.

re·al·ist (réer-list, rée-ə-) *n.* **1.** One inclined to literal truth and pragmatism. **2.** A person who practises or believes in artistic or philosophical realism. Also used adjectivally: *a realist doctrine.*

re·al·is·tic (réer-lístik, reer-, rée-ə- || rée-lístik) *adj.* **1.** Inclined towards the literal truth, as opposed to the abstract, romantic, or ideal. **2. a.** Closely resembling the object, scene, or person being represented; lifelike: *a realistic landscape.* **b.** Concerned with or seeking to represent what is objectively real, as in art or literature. **3.** Of or pertaining to philosophical realism. **4.** Practical-minded as opposed to idealistic; pragmatic: *Let's be realistic now and agree to at least a few of their demands.*

re·al·i·ty (ri-álləti, ree-) *n., pl.* **-ties. 1.** The quality or state of being actual or true. **2.** A person, entity, or event that is actual. **3.** The totality of all things possessing actuality, existence, or essence. **4.** That which exists objectively and in fact. **5.** *Philosophy.* The sum of all that is real, absolute, and unchangeable. **—in reality.** In actual fact.

re·al·ly (réerli, rée-ə-li || réeli) *adv.* **1.** In reality or fact. **2.** Truly; thoroughly. **3.** Used as an intensive: *You really shouldn't have done it.*
~*interj.* Used to express mild surprise, incredulity, or boredom.

realm (relm) *n.* **1.** A kingdom. **2.** Any field, sphere, or province: *the realm of science.* [Middle English *realme, reaume,* from Old French, from Latin *regimen,* system of government, from *regere,* to rule.]

real number *n.* Any rational or irrational number. See **number.**

re·al·po·li·tik (ray-ál-polli-teek) *n. Often capital* **R.** A harshly realistic national policy having as its sole principle the advancement of the national interest. [German, "realistic politics".]

real presence *n. Theology.* The doctrine that Christ's actual body and blood are present in the Eucharist.

real property *n. Law.* Fixed property, such as buildings and land. Also *chiefly U.S.* "real estate", "realty".

real tennis (reel, *rearely* rayl) *n.* An early form of tennis, from which lawn tennis developed. It is played in a large indoor court having a specially marked-out floor, high cement walls on three sides, and a buttress on the fourth side, off which the ball may be played. Also called "royal tennis", *U.S.* "court tennis".

real time *n. Computing.* A computer response which occurs almost at the same rate as the data that has been input. **—real-time** *adj.*

re·al·tor (réerl-tər, rée-əl-, réel-, -tawr, *also* ri-ál-, ree-) *n. Often Capital* **R.** *U.S.* An estate agent. [From REALTY.]

re·al·ty (réerl-ti, rée-əl-, réel-) *n., pl.* **-ties.** *Law. Chiefly U.S.* Real property. [REAL + -TY.]

ream¹ (reem) *n.* **1.** *Abbr.* **rm.** A quantity of paper, formerly 480 sheets, now 500 sheets or, in a printer's ream, 516 sheets. **2.** *Usually plural.* An extensive amount, as of paper or written or printed material: *wrote reams of verse.* [Middle English *rem(e),* from Old French *remme,* from Arabic *rizmah,* bundle.]

ream² *tr.v.* **reamed, reaming, reams. 1.** To form, shape, taper, or enlarge (a hole) with or as if with a reamer. **2.** To remove (material) by reaming. **3.** *U.S.* To squeeze the juice out of (fruit) with a squeezer. [19th century : perhaps from Middle English *remen,* to make room, Old English *rȳman,* to widen.]

ream·er (réemər) *n.* **1.** Any of various tools used to shape or enlarge holes. **2.** *U.S.* A lemon or orange squeezer. **3.** One that reams.

reap (reep) *v.* **reaped, reaping, reaps.** *—tr.* **1.** To cut (a crop) for harvest with a scythe, sickle, or reaper. **2.** To harvest (a crop so cut). **3.** To harvest a crop from. **4.** To obtain as a result of effort. *—intr.* **1.** To cut or harvest a crop. **2.** To obtain a return or reward. [Middle English *repen,* Old English *rīpan*†.]

reap·er (réepər) *n.* **1.** One who reaps. **2.** A machine for harvesting grain or pulse crops.

re·ap·por·tion (rée-ə-pórsh'n || -pṓrsh'n) *tr.v.* **-tioned, -tioning, -tions.** To distribute anew. **—re·ap·por·tion·ment** *n.*

re·ap·prais·al (rée-ə-práyz'l) *n.* A new or fresh appraisal or evaluation. **—re·ap·praise** *v.*

rear¹ (reer) *n.* **1.** The hind part of something. **2.** The point or area farthest from the front of something. **3.** The part of a military deployment usually farthest from the fighting front. **4.** *Informal.* The buttocks. **—bring up the rear.** To be last, as in in a line or race. *~adj.* Of, at, or located in the rear. [Short for ARREAR.]

rear² *v.* **reared, rearing, rears.** *—tr.* **1.** To care for (a child or children) during the early stages of life; bring up. **2.** To lift upright; raise. **3.** To build; erect. **4.** To tend (growing plants or animals). *—intr.* **1.** To rise on the hind legs, as a horse does. Often used with *up.* **2.** To rise high in the air; tower. Often used with *up* or *over.* [Middle English *reren,* to lift up, raise, Old English *rǣran;* akin to RAISE.] **—rear·er** *n.*

rear-ad·mi·ral (réer-ádmərəl) *n. Abbr.* **Rear Adm., R.A.** An officer of the Royal Navy and various other navies ranking between a vice admiral and a commodore, equivalent in rank to a major general in the Army and an air vice marshal in the Air Force.

rear·guard (réer-gaard) *n.* A detachment of troops that protects the rear of a military force.
~adj. Designating policies or actions designed to ward off attack while retreating or to resist almost inevitable change or certain defeat. [Middle English *reregarde,* from Old French : *rere,* backward, behind, from Latin *retrō* + *garde,* AGUARD.]

rear light *n.* Either of a pair of red lights on the back of a motor vehicle. Also called "rear lamp", *chiefly U.S.* "taillight".

re·arm (rée-árm, ree-) *v.* **-armed, -arming, -arms.** *—tr.* **1.** To arm again. **2.** To equip with better weapons. *—intr.* To arm oneself again. **—re·ar·ma·ment** (-əmənt) *n.*

rear·most (réer-mōst) *adj.* Farthest in the rear; last.

re·ar·range (rée-ə-ráynj, réer-) *tr.v.* **-ranged, -ranging, -ranges.** To change or restore the arrangement of. **—re·ar·range·ment** *n.*

rear·view mirror (réer-véw) *n.* **1.** A small adjustable mirror centrally attached at the top or bottom the windscreen in a motor vehicle to allow the driver a view of what is directly behind. **2.** A similar mirror attached to the handlebar of a motorcycle or bicycle.

rear·ward¹ (réer-wərd) *adj.* Directed towards or situated at the rear. *~adv. Chiefly U.S.* Rearwards.

rear·ward² (réer-wawrd) *n.* A posistion at rear; especially the rearguard of an armed force. [Middle English *rerewarde,* from Anglo-French : *rere,* behind, from Latin *retrō* + *warde,* guard, from Germanic.]

rear·wards (réer-wərdz) *adv.* Also *chiefly U.S.* **rearward.** Towards, to, or at the rear.

rea·son (réez'n) *n.* **1.** The basis or motive for an action, decision, or conviction. **2.** A declaration or argument advanced to explain or justify an action, decision, or conviction. **3.** An underlying fact or cause that provides a logical justification for a premise or occurrence. **4. a.** The power to think, judge, and draw logical conclusions. **b.** The intellect as opposed to emotions, feelings, instincts, or intuitions. **5.** Good judgment; sound sense; intelligence. **6.** A sound mental state; sanity. **7.** *Logic.* A premise, usually the minor premise, of an argument. —See Synonyms below and at **mind.** —See Usage note at **because, cause. —by reason of.** Because of. **—in** or **within reason.** Within the bounds of good sense or practicality. **—listen to reason.** To allow oneself to be persuaded by logical or sensible arguments. **—reasons of State.** A political justification for an action or measure. **—stand to reason.** To be logical or likely. Usually used impersonally: *It stands to reason that he will win.* **—with reason.** With good cause; justifiably.
~v. **reasoned, -soning, -sons.** *—intr.* **1.** To use the faculty of reason; think logically. **2.** To talk or argue logically and persuasively. **3.** To seek to persuade someone with reasons. Used with *with.* **4.** *Archaic.* To engage in conversation or discussion: *"Come . . . let us reason together"* (Isaiah 1:18). *—tr.* **1.** To determine, solve, or conclude by logical thinking. Often used with *out.* **2.** To seek to persuade (someone) with reasons. Used with *out of* or *into.* **3.** To discuss; debate. [Middle English *reisun,* from Old French, from Vulgar Latin *ratiōne* (unattested), from Latin *ratiō* (stem *ratiōn-*), calculation, judgment, reasoning, from *ratus,* past participle of *rērī,* to think, reason.] **—rea·son·er** *n.*
Synonyms: *reason, intuition, understanding, discernment, judgment.*

rea·son·a·ble (réez'n-əb'l) *adj.* **1.** Capable of reasoning; rational. **2.** Governed by or in accordance with reason or sound thinking. **3.** Within the bounds of common sense or normal expectations. **4.** Not excessive or extreme; fair; moderate. **—rea·son·a·bil·i·ty** (-ə-bílləti), **rea·son·a·ble·ness** *n.* **—rea·son·a·bly** *adv.*

rea·soned (réez'nd) *adj.* Having been well thought out; reasonable: *a reasoned argument.*

rea·son·ing (réez'n-ing) *n.* **1.** The mental processes of one who reasons; especially, the drawing of conclusions or inferences from observation, facts, or hypotheses. **2.** The particular evidence or arguments used in this procedure.

re·as·sure (rée-ə-shóor, réer-, -shór || -shéwr) *tr.v.* **-sured, -suring, -sures. 1.** To restore confidence to. **2.** To assure again. **3.** To reinsure. **—re·as·sur·ance** *n.* **—re·as·sur·ing·ly** *adv.*

reast. Variant of **reest.**

reata. Variant of **riata.**

Ré·au·mur, Re·au·mur (ráy-ə-mewr, -ō-, -mər) *adj. Abbr.* **R, R., Réaum.** Designating or indicated on a temperature scale that registers the freezing point of water as 0° and the boiling point as 80°. [Introduced by René de RÉAUMUR.]

Ré·au·mur (ráy-ə-mewr, -ō-, -mər, *French* -múr), **René Antoine Ferchault de** (1683–1757). French physicist and natural scientist, one of the leading figures of 18th-century science. He is best known for his invention of the alcohol thermometer (c. 1730) and the temperature scale named after him, but he also developed opaque glass and wrote a six-volume study of insects (1734–42).

reave¹ (reev) *v.* **reft** (reft) or **reaved, reaving, reaves.** *Archaic. —tr.* **1.** To seize and carry off forcibly. **2.** To deprive of; bereave. Used with *of. —intr.* To rob, plunder, or pillage. [Middle English *reven,* to plunder, Old English *rēafian.*]

reave² *tr.v.* **reft** (reft) or **reaved, reaving, reaves.** *Archaic.* To break or tear apart. [Middle English *reven,* variant (influenced by *riven,* RIVE) of REAVE (seize).]

Reb¹ (reb) *n. Sometimes small* **r.** *U.S. Informal.* A Confederate soldier in the American Civil War. [Short for REBEL.]

Reb² *n.* A Jewish title of respect, approximately equivalent to "Mr." or "Sir", but used with the first name rather than the surname. [Yiddish, from Hebrew *rabbī,* my teacher, RABBI.]

re·bar·ba·tive (ri-bárbətiv, rə-) *adj.* Extremely unattractive; repellent. [French *rébarbatif,* from Old French *rebarber,* "to face beard to beard", face an enemy, hence, to be repellent : *re-,* back, against + *barbe,* beard, from Latin *barba.*]

re·bate¹ (rée-bayt, ri-báyt, rə-) *n.* A deduction from an amount to be paid or a return of part of an amount already paid.
~tr.v. **rebated, -bating, -bates. 1.** To deduct or return (an amount) from a payment or bill. **2.** *Archaic.* To dull or blunt (a weapon, for example). **3.** *Archaic.* To lessen; diminish. [Middle English *rebaten,* to deduct, subtract, from Old French *rabattre,* to beat down again, reduce : *re-,* again + *abattre,* to beat down : *a-,* to, from Latin *ad-* + *battre,* to beat, from Latin *battuere.*] **—re·bat·er** *n.*

rebate². Variant of **rabbet.**

re·ba·to (ri-baátō) *n., pl.* **-tos.** Also **ra·ba·to** (rə-). A stiff, flaring collar of lace or other fabric, worn by both men and women in the early part of the 17th century. [Old French *rabat,* turndown collar, from *rabattre,* to turn down again, REBATE.]

re·bec, re·beck (réebek, rébbek) *n.* A pear-shaped, two- or three-stringed musical instrument of medieval times, played with a bow. [Old French *rebec,* variant (influenced by *bec,* beak, because of the shape of the instrument) of *rebebe,* from Old Provençal *rebab,* from Arabic (dialectal) *rebāb.*]

Re·bec·ca, Re·bek·ah (ri-béckə, rə-). The wife of Isaac and the mother of Jacob and Esau. Genesis 24:1–67.

re·bel (ri-bél, rə-) *intr.v.* **-belled, -belling, -bels. 1.** To refuse allegiance to and oppose by force an established government or ruling authority. Often used with *against.* **2.** To resist or defy any authority or generally accepted convention. **3.** To feel or express strong unwillingness or distaste: *rebelled at the unwelcome suggestion.*
~n. **reb·el** (rébb'l). **1.** A person who rebels or is in rebellion. **2.** A person who refuses to comply with accepted conventions.
~adj. **reb·el** (rebb'l). **1.** Of, pertaining to, or consisting of rebels. **2.** Rebellious; defiant. [Middle English *rebellen,* from Old French *rebeller,* from Latin *rebellāre,* to make war again : *re-,* again + *bellāre,* to make war, from *bellum,* war.]

re·bel·li·on (ri-bél-i-ən, rə-) *n.* **1.** An uprising or organised opposition intended to change or overthrow an existing government or ruling authority. **2.** An act or show of defiance towards any authority or established convention. [Middle English, from Old French, from Latin *rebelliō* (stem *rebelliōn-*), from *rebellāre,* to REBEL.]
Synonyms: *rebellion, revolt, insurrection, uprising, coup d'état, revolution, mutiny.*

re·bel·li·ous (ri-bél-i-əss, rə-) *adj.* **1.** Participating in or inclined to-

PRONUNCIATION KEY

a, **trap**; aa, **father**; ai, **fair**;
ar, **star**; aw, **lawn**; ay, **play**;
b, bb, **stab**; **rubber**;
ch, **church**; ck, **ticket**;
d, dd, **dead**; **ladder**; e, **dress**;
ee, **bee**; er, **defer**; ew, **few**;
ewr, **pure**; ə, **about**;
ər, **letter**; f, ff, **fife**; **differ**;
g, gg, **giggle**; h, **hat**; i, **kit**;
ī, **price**; īr, **fire**; j, **judge**;
k, **kick**; l, ll, **let**; 'l, **needle**;
m, mm, **man**; n, nn, **no**;
'n, **sudden**; ng, **thing**; o, **lot**;
ō, **no**; o͝o, **foot**; o͞o, **shoe**;
oor, **poor**; ow, **cow**;
owr, **hour**; oy, **boy**;
p, pp, **pepper**; r, rr, **red**;
s, ss, **sauce**; sh, **ship**;
t, tt, **totter**; th, **thick**; th, **this**;
smooth; u, **cut**; ur, **turn**;
v, vv, **valve**; w, **wet**; y, **yes**;
z, zz, **zebra**; zh, **vision**;
pleasure

IN FOREIGN WORDS:

aɴ, oɴ, **Saint-Saëns**;
hl, **Llanelli**; **Hluhluwe**;
kh, **loch**; **lough**; **Khaled**

STRESS MARK:

ín-sīt, insight; in-sī́t, incite

rebus *A picture taken from an early 20th-century children's book. The story attached to the puzzle explains that the rebus was designed by an ingenious beggar and set beside him in the street. Curious passers-by then had to pay to discover its meaning. The solution: 'For a period, I ate next to nothing.'*

wards rebellion. **2.** Of or characteristic of a rebel. **3.** Resisting management or control; unruly. —See Synonyms at **insubordinate.** **—re·bel·li·ous·ly** *adv.* **—re·bel·li·ous·ness** *n.*

Re·ber (ráybər), **Grote** (1911–). U.S. astronomer. He built the world's first radio telescope in 1937, and has continued to play an active part in the development of subsequent telescopes.

re·bind (rée-bīnd) *tr.v.* **-bound** (-bownd || *West Indies also* -búngd), **-binding, -binds.** To bind again; especially, to put a new binding on (a book).

re·birth (rée-búrth, ree- || -burth) *n.* **1.** A second or new birth; a reincarnation. **2.** A spiritual regeneration. **3.** A renaissance or revival.

re·bore (rée-bawr || -bōr) *n.* The process of drilling out the cylinder of an engine and fitting a slightly larger piston.
~*tr.v.* (-bór || -bṓr) **rebored, -boring, -bores.** To give (an engine) a rebore.

re·born (rée-bórn, ree-) *adj.* Born again; emotionally or spiritually revived or regenerated.

re·bound (ri-bównd, rée- || *West Indies also* -búngd) *v.* **-bounded, -bounding, -bounds.** *—intr.* **1.** To spring or bounce back after hitting or colliding with something. **2.** To harm the person responsible for an act, especially an act of malice: *Their efforts to discredit me rebounded on them.* **3.** To re-echo; resound. *—tr.* To cause to rebound.
~*n.* (rée-bownd, -bównd, ri- || *West Indies also* -búngd). **1.** A springing or bounding back; a recoil. **2.** In soccer, hockey, and other ball games, a ball that has rebounded, as off a goal post. **3.** *Informal.* One whose affections are sought by someone on the rebound: *Does she really love him or is he just a rebound?* **—on the rebound. 1.** In the act of springing or bounding back. **2.** In reaction to disappointment, rejection, or depression: *marriage on the rebound.* [Middle English *rebounden,* from Old French *rebondir* : *re-,* again, back + *bondir,* to resound, BOUND (leap).]

re·bo·zo (ri-bṓ-zō, -sō; *Spanish* -thō, -sō) *n., pl.* **-zos.** A long scarf worn over the head and shoulders, especially by Mexican women. [Spanish *rebozo*†.]

re·broad·cast (rée-bráwd-kaast || -kast) *tr.v.* **-cast** or **-casted, -casting, -casts. 1.** To repeat the broadcast of (a programme). **2.** To receive and send out (a broadcast) again. **—re·broad·cast** *n.*

re·buff (ri-búf) *n.* **1.** A blunt or abrupt repulsing or refusal, as to an offer of help or sympathy or to a person making unwelcome advances; a snub. **2.** Any check or abrupt setback to progress or action.
~*tr.v.* **rebuffed, -buffing, -buffs. 1.** To refuse or reject bluntly or contemptuously; snub. **2.** To repel or drive back. —See Synonyms at **refuse.** [Old French *rebuffer,* from Italian *ribuffare,* to scold, rebuff, from *ribuffo,* reprimand : *re-,* back, again, from Latin + *buffo,* puff, gust (imitative).]

re·build (rée-bíld, ree-) *tr.v.* **-built** (-bílt), **-building, -builds. 1.** To build again. **2.** To make extensive structural repairs to. **3.** To restore, as from a condition of ruin: *plans to rebuild the economy.*

re·buke (ri-béwk, rə-) *tr.v.* **-buked, -buking, -bukes.** To criticise or reprove sharply; reprimand. —See Synonyms at **admonish.**
~*n.* A sharp reproof. [Middle English *rebuken,* from Old Northern French *rebuke;* akin to Old French *buchier,* to beat, chop down wood, from *busche,* log.]

re·bus (réebəss) *n., pl.* **-buses.** A riddle whose answer, composed of words or syllables, is depicted by symbols or pictures that suggest the sounds or give clues to the meanings of the words or syllables they represent. [Latin *rēbus,* by things, from *rēs,* thing.]

re·but (ri-bút) *v.* **-butted, -butting, -buts.** *—tr.* **1.** To refute, especially by offering opposing evidence or arguments, as in a legal case. **2.** *Archaic.* To repel. *—intr.* To present opposing evidence or arguments. [Middle English *rebuten,* from Old French *rebuter* : *re-,* again, back + *buter,* to BUTT.]

re·but·tal (ri-bútt'l) *n.* The act of rebutting.

re·but·ter (ri-búttər) *n.* **1.** One that refutes or rebuts. **2.** *Law.* The defendant's answer to the plaintiff's surrejoinder.

rec (rek) *n. Informal.* A recreation ground.

rec. 1. receipt. **2.** recipe. **3.** record; recorder; recording. **4.** recreation.

re·cal·ci·trant (ri-kál-si-trənt, rə-) *adj.* Stubbornly resistant to authority, domination, or guidance. See Synonyms at **unruly.**
~*n.* A recalcitrant person. [Latin *recalcitrāns* (stem *recalcitrant-*), present participle of *recalcitrāre,* to kick back : *re-,* back, again + *calcitrāre,* to kick, from *calx* (stem *calc-*), heel.] **—re·cal·ci·trance, re·cal·ci·tran·cy** *n.*

re·cal·esce (rée-kə-léss) *intr.v.* **-esced, -escing, -esces.** To undergo recalescence. Used of a cooling metal.

re·ca·les·cence (rée-kə-léss'nss) *n. Metallurgy.* A sudden increase of heat in a cooling metal caused by an exothermic structural change. [Latin *recalescens* (stem *recalescent-*), present participle of *recalescere,* to grow warm again : *re-,* back, again + *calescere,* become warm, from *calēre,* to be warm.] **—re·ca·les·cent** *adj.*

re·call (ri-káwl, rə-) *tr.v.* **-called, -calling, -calls. 1.** To call back; ask or order to return. **2.** To summon back, as from a daydream or digression, to awareness of or concern with the subject or situation at hand. **3. a.** To remember or recollect. **b.** To cause to remember. **4.** To cancel, take back, or revoke. **5.** To request purchasers to return (defective goods, for example). **6.** To bring back; restore.
~*n.* (*also* rée-kawl). **1.** The act of recalling or summoning back; especially, an official order to return. **2.** A signal, such as a bugle call, used to summon servicemen back to their posts. **3.** The ability to remember information or experiences. **4.** The act of revoking or cancelling. **5.** *Computing.* A measure of the efficiency of an information retrieval system. **—re·call·a·ble** *adj.*

Ré·ca·mier (ray-kámmi-ay), **Jeanne Françoise Julie Adélaide,** born Julie Bernard (1777–1849). French society hostess. Through her beauty and wit she attracted many influential figures to her *salon,* and she was painted by David and Gérard.

re·cant (ri-kánt) *v.* **-canted, -canting, -cants.** *—tr.* To make a formal retraction or disavowal of (a statement or belief to which one has previously committed oneself). *—intr.* To make a formal retraction or disavowal of a previous statement or previously held belief. [Latin *recantāre* : *re-,* back + *cantāre,* sing, chant, frequentative of *canere,* sing.] **—re·can·ta·tion** (rée-kan-táysh'n) *n.* **—re·cant·er** *n.*

re·cap[1] (rée-káp, ree-) *tr.v.* **-capped, -capping, -caps. 1.** To replace a cap or caplike covering on. **2.** *U.S.* To bond new rubber onto the tread and lateral surface of (a worn car tyre).
~*n.* (rée-kap). *U.S.* A tyre thus reconditioned.

re·cap[2] (rée-kap, -káp) *tr.v.* **-capped, -capping, -caps.** *Informal.* To recapitulate.
~*n. Informal.* A recapitulation. [Short for RECAPITULATE.]

re·ca·pit·u·late (rée-kə-píttew-layt) *v.* **-lated, -lating, -lates.** *—tr.* **1.** To repeat in concise form the main points of (a speech, discussion, or the like); sum up. **2.** *Biology.* To appear to repeat (the evolutionary stages of the species) during the embryonic development of the individual organism. *—intr.* To summarise the main points. [Late Latin *recapitulāre* : *re-,* back, again + *capitulāre,* to put under headings, from Latin *capitulum,* heading, small head, diminutive of *caput,* head.] **—re·ca·pit·u·la·tive** (-lətiv, -laytiv), **re·ca·pit·u·la·to·ry** (-lə-tri, -təri, -laytəri || -láytəri) *adj.*

re·ca·pit·u·la·tion (rée-kə-píttew-láysh'n) *n.* **1.** The act or process of recapitulating. **2.** A summary or concise review. **3.** *Biology.* The apparent repetition of some evolutionary stages of the species during embryonic development. Also called "palingenesis". **4.** *Music.* The restatement of the exposition of a theme after its development, forming the final section of a movement in sonata form.

re·cap·tion (ri-kápsh'n, rée-) *n. Law.* The act of claiming and retaking that which has been wrongfully taken or detained, such as goods or a child. It is legal so long as there is no breach of the peace. [RE- + CAPTION ("seizure").]

re·cap·ture (rée-kápchər) *tr.v.* **-tured, -turing, -tures. 1.** To capture again; retake or recover. **2.** To recall or revive the feeling or quality of: *an attempt to recapture that wonderful moment.* **3.** *U.S.* To acquire by the government procedure of recapture.
~*n.* **1. a.** The act of recapturing. **b.** The condition of being recaptured. **2.** Anything recaptured. **3.** *U.S.* The lawful taking by a government of a fixed amount of the profits of a public utility company in excess of a stipulated rate of return.

re·cast (rée-kaást || -kást) *tr.v.* **-cast, -casting, -casts. 1.** To mould again: *recast a bell.* **2.** To set down or present (ideas, for example) in a new or different arrangement. **3.** To change the cast of (a theatrical production, film, or the like).
~*n.* (rée-kaast || -kast). **1.** The act or process of recasting. **2.** Something produced by recasting.

rec·ce (récki) *v.* **-ced** or **-ceed, -ceing, -ces.** *Slang.* To reconnoitre.
~*n. Slang.* A reconnaissance. [Shortening.]

recd., rec'd. received.

re·cede (rée-séed) *tr.v.* **-ceded, -ceding, -cedes.** To cede back; yield or grant to one formerly in possession.

re·cede (ri-séed, rée-) *intr.v.* **-ceded, -ceding, -cedes. 1.** To move back or away from a limit, point, or mark. **2.** To slope backwards. **3.** To become or seem to become more distant. **4.** To become less; diminish. **5.** To withdraw or retreat from an agreement, stated position, or the like. **6. a.** To gradually cease to grow above the forehead or on the temples. Used of a man's hair. **b.** To move backwards from the forehead. Used of a man's hairline. [Latin *recēdere,* to go back : *re-,* back, again + *cēdere,* to go.]

re·ceipt (ri-séet, rə-) *n. Abbr.* **rec., rcpt., rept., rec't, rect. 1.** A written acknowledgement that a stipulated article, sum of money, or delivery of merchandise has been received. **2. a.** The act of receiving something. **b.** The fact of being received. **3.** *Usually plural.* The quantity or amount of something received: *cash receipts.* **4.** *Archaic & Regional.* A recipe.
~*tr.v.* **receipted, -ceipting, -ceipts. 1.** To mark (a bill) as having been paid. **2.** *Chiefly U.S.* To give or write a receipt for (money paid or goods delivered). [Middle English *receite,* from Old Northern French, from Medieval Latin *recepta,* from Latin *recipere* (past participle *receptus*), to take, RECEIVE.]

re·ceiv·a·ble (ri-séevəb'l, rə-) *adj.* **1.** Suitable for being received or accepted, especially as payment. **2.** Awaiting or requiring payment; due or collectable: *accounts receivable.*
~*n. Plural.* Business assets represented by the total amount of accounts due for payment.

re·ceive (ri-séev, rə-) *v.* **-ceived, -ceiving, -ceives.** *—tr.* **1. a.** To take or acquire (something given or offered). **b.** To take or accept (something delivered or transmitted, such as a letter or telephone call). **2.** To acquire knowledge of or information about: *receive bad news.* **3.** To have (a blessing or title, for example) bestowed on one. **4.** To meet with; experience: *receive sympathetic treatment.* **5.** To have inflicted or imposed on oneself: *receive a penalty.* **6.** To bear the weight or force of; support. **7.** To take or intercept the impact of (a blow, for example). **8.** To take in, hold, or contain. **9.** To admit as to a state or society: *receive new members.* **10.** To greet or welcome, especially in a formal manner. **11.** To perceive or acquire mentally: *receive a bad impression.* **12.** To accept as valid or regard with approval: *theories that are widely received.* **13.** To respond or react to in the specified way: *His suggestion was received with howls of derision.* **14.** To listen to and formally and authoritatively acknowledge: *receive an oath of allegiance.* **15.** To take (the sacraments). **16.** *Chiefly British.* To accept and pay for (goods known to be stolen), especially in order to resell them. **17.** To face (the service), as in tennis. *—intr.* **1.** To acquire or get something; be a recipient. **2.** To admit or welcome guests or visitors. **3.** To partake of the Eucharist. **4.** *Electronics.* To convert incoming electrical or electromagnetic waves into visible or audible signals. **5.** *Chiefly British.* To accept and pay for goods known to be stolen, especially in order to resell them. **6.** To be required to face and return the service, as in tennis. [Middle English *receiven,* from Old Northern French *receivre,* from Latin *recipere,* to take back, regain : *re-*, back, again + *capere,* to take.]

re•ceived (ri-séevd, rə-) *adj.* **1.** Generally accepted or believed. **2.** Conventional; clichéd: *received wisdom.* Often used derogatorily.

Received Pronunciation *n. Abbr.* **R.P.** The form of English pronunciation based typically on that of the upper and upper-middle classes in England, having no characteristics peculiar to any region within England and being generally accepted within England as a de facto standard accent.

re•ceiv•er (ri-séevər, rə-) *n.* **1.** One who receives something; a recipient. **2.** An official appointed to receive and account for money due. **3.** *Law.* A person appointed by a court administrator to take into custody property or funds of others that are pending litigation, such as the property or funds of a person declared bankrupt or of unsound mind. **4.** One who knowingly buys or receives stolen goods. **5.** A receptacle intended for a specific purpose, as for collecting the products of distillation. **6.** *Electronics.* A device, such as a part of a radio, television set, or telephone, that receives incoming electrical or electromagnetic signals and converts them to perceptible forms.

re•ceiv•er•ship (ri-séevər-ship, rə-) *n. Law.* **1.** The office or functions of a receiver. **2.** The state of being held in the custody of a receiver.

re•ceiv•ing end (ri-séeving, rə-) *n. Informal.* A position in which one is subjected directly to an unpleasant experience, especially criticism or abuse. Used chiefly in the phrase *on the receiving end.*

receiving order *n. Law.* A court order appointing a receiver to take custody of the property or funds of a debtor when an act of bankruptcy has been established.

re•cen•sion (ri-sénsh'n, rə-) *n.* **1.** A critical revision of a text incorporating the most plausible elements found in varying sources. **2.** A text so revised. [Latin *recēnsiō* (stem *recēnsiōn-*), a reviewing, an enumeration, from *recēnsēre,* to survey again, review : *re-*, again, back + *cēnsēre,* to estimate, assess.]

re•cent (réess'nt) *adj.* **1.** Of, belonging to, or occurring at a time immediately prior to the present. **2.** Modern; new. **3.** *Capital* **R.** *Geology.* Of, belonging to, or designating the Holocene epoch.
~n. Capital **R.** *Geology.* The **Holocene epoch** *(see).* Preceded by *the.* [Latin *recēns* (stem *recent-*), fresh, new.] **—re•cen•cy, re•cent•ness** *n.* **—re•cent•ly** *adv.*

re•cept (rée-sept) *n.* A mental image formed from what is common to successive perceptions. [RE- + (CON)CEPT.]

re•cep•ta•cle (ri-séptək'l, rə-) *n.* **1.** Something that holds or contains; a container. **2.** *Botany.* **a.** The tip of a flower stalk, that bears and supports the floral organs. **b.** In certain seaweeds, the part of the blade that bears the reproductive structures. [Latin *receptāculum,* from *receptāre,* to take again, frequentative of *recipere* (past participle *receptus*), to RECEIVE.]

re•cep•tion (ri-sépsh'n, rə-) *n.* **1.** The act or process of receiving or accepting or of being received or accepted. **2. a.** A welcome, greeting, or acceptance: *a friendly reception.* **b.** A response or reaction: *Her speech got a very hostile reception.* **3.** A formal social function held to meet guests, as after a wedding, or entertain visitors, such as foreign dignitaries. **4.** *Electronics.* **a.** The action of receiving electrical or electromagnetic signals. **b.** The condition or quality of received signals. **6. a.** The place, as in an office or hospital, where clients or visitors are received and appointments made. **b.** The place in a hotel where guests register or make reservations. [Latin *receptiō* (stem *receptiōn-*), from *recipere* (past participle *receptus*), to RECEIVE.]

re•cep•tion•ist (ri-sépsh'n-ist, rə-) *n.* A person employed, as in an office, hotel, or hospital, to receive callers or clients, answer the telephone, and deal with enquiries.

re•cep•tive (ri-séptiv, rə-) *adj.* **1.** Capable of or qualified for receiving. **2.** Ready or willing to receive favourably. **3.** Quick to apprehend new ideas, impressions, or the like. **—re•cep•tive•ly** *adv.* **—re•cep•tiv•i•ty** (rée-sep-tívvəti, ré-), **re•cep•tive•ness** *n.*

re•cep•tor (ri-séptər) *n. Anatomy.* A cell or group of cells specialised to sense or to receive stimuli.

re•cess (ri-séss, rə-, rée-sess) *n.* **1.** A temporary cessation of customary activities or proceedings, such as at the end of a Parliamentary session: *the Easter recess.* **2.** The period of such cessation. **3.** *Usually plural.* A remote, secret, or secluded place. **4.** *Anatomy.* An indentation or small hollow in an organ. **5.** An alcove.
~v. **recessed, -cessing, -cesses.** *—tr.* **1.** To place in a recess. **2.** To create or fashion a recess in. **3.** *U.S.* To suspend for a recess. *—intr. U.S.* To take a recess. [Latin *recessus,* from the past participle of *recēdere,* to RECEDE.]

re•ces•sion (rée-sésh'n) *n.* The act of restoring possession to a former owner.

re•ces•sion (ri-sésh'n, rə-) *n.* **1.** A decline in economic activity that occurs during a period of otherwise increasing prosperity, but is not as severe as a depression. **2.** The act of withdrawing or receding back. **3.** The filing out of clergy and choir members after a church service. [Latin *recessiō* (stem *recessiōn-*), from *recessus,* RECESS.]

re•ces•sion•al (ri-sésh'n'l, rə-) *adj.* Of or pertaining to recession.
~n. A hymn that accompanies the exit of the clergy and choir after a service.

re•ces•sive (ri-séssiv, rə-) *adj.* **1.** Tending to go backwards or recede. **2.** *Genetics.* Of, pertaining to, or designating an allele that does not produce a phenotypic effect when paired with a dominant allele. Compare **dominant. 3.** *Phonetics.* Designating a stress that falls near the beginning of a polysyllabic word.
~n. Genetics. **1.** A recessive allele or trait. **2.** An organism having a recessive trait. **—re•ces•sive•ly** *adv.*

ré•chauf•fé (ray-shṓ-fay || *U.S.* ráy-shō-fáy) *n.* **1.** Leftover food that is warmed up. **2.** Old material reworked or rehashed. [French, "warmed up", from *réchauffer,* to heat again, from Old French : *re-*, again, back + *chauffer,* to warm (see **chafe**).]

re•cher•ché (rə-sháir-shay || *U.S.* -sháy) *adj.* **1.** Highly sought after; rare. **2.** Exquisite; refined. **3.** Familiar or known only to experts or connoisseurs. **4.** Overrefined; affected and forced. [French, past participle of *rechercher,* to search for, RESEARCH.]

re•chris•ten (rée-kríss'n) *tr.v.* **-ened, ening, ens. 1.** To christen again. **2.** To rename.

re•cid•i•vism (ri-síddi-viz'm) *n.* A tendency to relapse into a former pattern of behaviour; especially, a tendency to return to criminal habits. [From *recidivist,* from French *récidiviste,* relapser, from *récidiver,* to relapse, from Medieval Latin *recidīvāre,* from Latin *recidīvus,* a falling back, from *recidere,* fall back : *re-*, back, again + *cadere,* fall.] **—re•cid•i•vist** *n.* **—re•cid•i•vis•tic** (-vístik), **re•cid•i•vous** *adj.*

Re•ci•fe (re-séefi) Formerly **Pernambuco.** Capital of the state of Pernambuco in eastern Brazil. It is a busy port and industrial centre.

recip. reciprocal; reciprocity.

rec•i•pe (réssi-pi, réssə-, -pee) *n.* **1.** *Abbr.* **rec.** A formula for preparing a mixture or compound, especially in cooking or pharmacology, with a list of measured ingredients and often a set of directions for their use or application. **2.** *Symbol* ℞ A medical prescription. Not in current technical usage. **3.** A procedure or set of circumstances likely to lead to a specified end: *a recipe for disaster.* [Latin, "take", imperative of *recipere,* to take, RECEIVE.]

re•cip•i•ence (ri-síppi-ənss, rə-) *n.* Also **re•cip•i•en•cy** (-ən-si). The capacity to receive; receptivity.

re•cip•i•ent (ri-síppi-ənt, rə-) *adj.* Functioning as a receiver.
~n. **1.** One that receives or is receptive. **2.** *Medicine.* A person who receives blood or transplanted tissue from a donor. [Latin *recipiēns* (stem *recipient-*), present participle of *recipere,* to RECEIVE.]

re•cip•ro•cal (ri-sípprə-k'l, rə-) *adj.* **1.** Performed or given in return: *a reciprocal present.* **2.** Interchanged, given, or owed by each of two parties to the other: *reciprocal funds.* **3.** Performed, experienced, or felt by both sides: *reciprocal hatred.* **4.** Equivalent or corresponding. **5.** *Grammar.* Expressing mutual action or relationship. Said of some verbs and compound pronouns. **6.** *Mathematics.* Of or pertaining to a quantity divided into 1.
~n. **1.** Anything that is reciprocal to something else; a converse or complement. **2.** *Mathematics.* The quotient of a specific quantity divided into 1. For example, the reciprocal of 7 is $^1/_7$; the reciprocal of $^2/_3$ is $^3/_2$. [Latin *reciprocus,* alternating, returning.] **—re•cip•ro•cal•i•ty** (-kál-əti), **re•cip•ro•cal•ness** *n.* **—re•cip•ro•cal•ly** *adv.*

reciprocal ohm *n. Physics.* A **siemens** *(see).*

reciprocal pronoun *n. Grammar.* A pronoun or pronominal phrase expressing mutual action or relationship, such as *each other.*

re•cip•ro•cate (ri-sípprə-kayt, rə-) *v.* **-cated, -cating, -cates.** *—tr.* **1.** To give or take mutually; interchange. **2.** To show or feel in response or return. **3.** To cause to move back and forth alternately. *—intr.* **1.** To move back and forth alternately. **2.** To give and take something mutually. **3.** To make a return for something given or done. **4.** To be complementary or equivalent. [Latin *reciprocāre,* to move back and forth, from *reciprocus,* RECIPROCAL.] **—re•cip•ro•ca•tive** (-kətiv, -kaytiv) *adj.* **—re•cip•ro•ca•tor** (-kaytər) *n.*

re•cip•ro•cat•ing engine (ri-sípprə-kávting, rə-) *n.* An engine having a crankshaft turned by linearly reciprocating pistons.

re•cip•ro•ca•tion (ri-sípprə-káysh'n, rə-) *n.* **1.** An alternating back-and-forth movement. **2.** The act or fact of reciprocating; a mutual giving or receiving; an interchange.

rec•i•proc•i•ty (réssi-próssəti) *n., pl.* **-ties.** *Abbr.* **recip. 1.** A reciprocal condition or relationship. **2.** A mutual or cooperative interchange of favours or privileges; especially, one constituting a commercial policy or trade agreement between two or more parties.

re•ci•sion (ri-sízh'n, rə-) *n.* The act or an instance of rescinding; an annulment or cancellation. [Latin *recīsiō* (stem *recīsiōn-*), a cutting off, from *recīsus,* past participle of *recīdere,* to cut down : *re-*, back, back down, again + *caedere,* to cut.]

recit. *Music.* recitative.

re•cit•al (ri-sīt'l, rə-) *n.* **1.** A public reciting of poetry or prose. **2.** A retelling in detail; a narration. **3.** Something thus told. **4.** A performance of music or dance, especially by a soloist or small ensemble. **5.** *Law.* A preliminary part of a document setting out relevant facts. **—re•cit•al•ist** *n.*

PRONUNCIATION KEY

a, trap; aa, father; ai, fair;
ar, star; aw, lawn; ay, play;
b, bb, stab; rubber;
ch, church; ck, ticket;
d, dd, dead; ladder; e, dress;
ee, bee; er, defer; ew, few;
ewr, pure; ə, about;
ər, letter; f, ff, fife; differ;
g, gg, giggle; h, hat; i, kit;
ī, price; īr, fire; j, judge;
k, kick; l, ll, let; 'l, needle;
m, mm, man; n, nn, no;
'n, sudden; ng, thing; o, lot;
ō, no; o͝o, foot; o͞o, shoe;
oor, poor; ow, cow;
owr, hour; oy, boy;
p, pp, pepper; r, rr, red;
s, ss, sauce; sh, ship;
t, tt, totter; th, thick; th, this;
smooth; u, cut; ur, turn;
v, vv, valve; w, wet; y, yes;
z, zz, zebra; zh, vision;
pleasure

IN FOREIGN WORDS:

aN, oN, Saint-Saëns;
hl, Llanelli; Hluhluwe;
kh, loch; lough; Khaled

STRESS MARK:

ín-sīt, insight; in-sī́t, incite

rec·i·ta·tion (réssi-táysh'n) *n.* **1.** The act of reciting poetry or prose from memory, especially in a public performance. **2.** The material so recited.

rec·i·ta·tive[1] (ri-sítətiv, réssi-taytiv) *adj.* Pertaining to or having the character of a recital or recitative.

rec·i·ta·tive[2] (réssitə-téev) *n.* Also **re·ci·ta·ti·vo** (-téevō; *Italian* ré-chee-ta-) *pl.* **-vi** (-vee) or **-vos** (-vōz). *Abbr.* **recit.** **1.** A musical style used in opera and oratorio, in which the text is declaimed in the rhythm of natural speech with slight melodic variation. **2.** A passage rendered in this form. [Italian *recitativo,* from *recitare,* to recite, from Latin *recitāre,* to RECITE.]

re·cite (ri-sít, rə-) *v.* **-cited, -citing, -cites.** *—tr.* **1.** To repeat aloud or declaim (a poem or passage) that has been rehearsed or memorised, especially before an audience or teacher. **2.** To relate in detail. **3.** To list or enumerate. *—intr.* To deliver a recitation. [Middle English *reciten,* from Old French *reciter,* from Latin *recitāre,* to read out, cite again : *re-,* back, again + *citāre,* to CITE.] **—re·cit·er** *n.*

reck (rek) *v.* **recked, recking, recks.** *Archaic & Regional. —tr.* To take heed of; be concerned about: *He does not reck death. —intr.* To take heed; have caution. [Middle English *recken, recchen,* to be careful, to take care, Old English *reccan†, recan* (unattested).]

reck·less (rék-ləss, -liss) *adj.* **1. a.** Heedless or careless. **b.** Headstrong; rash: *a reckless lover.* **2.** Having no regard for consequences; uncontrolled; wild: *a reckless driver.* [Middle English *recheles, reckeles,* Old English *rēcelēas.*] **—reck·less·ly** *adv.* **—reck·less·ness** *n.*

Synonyms: *reckless, adventurous, rash, precipitate, foolhardy, audacious, daring.*

reck·on (réckən) *v.* **-oned, -oning, -ons.** *—tr.* **1.** To count or compute. **2.** To consider as being; regard as. **3.** *Informal.* To think or assume. **4.** *Slang.* To think well of; regard highly: *I don't reckon him as captain. —intr.* **1.** To make a calculation; figure. Often used with *up.* **2.** To make assumptions about something; place reliance. Used with *on* or *upon*: *reckon on financial aid.* **3.** To make allowance for a possibility; anticipate something. Used with *on* or *upon*: *I didn't reckon on your being here.* —See Synonyms at **calculate, consider.** **—reckon with.** **1.** To come to terms or settle accounts with. **2.** To recognise as significant: *a force to be reckoned with.* **—reckon without.** To fail to take into account. [Middle English *reknen,* Old English *gerecenian,* to enumerate, from Germanic.]

reck·on·er (réckənər) *n.* **1.** One that reckons. **2.** A handbook of mathematical tables to facilitate computation; a ready reckoner.

reck·on·ing (réckəning) *n.* **1.** Computation. **2.** An itemised bill or statement of a sum due. **3.** The settlement of a bill or account. **4.** Calculation of the position of a ship, aircraft, or the like. **5.** Judgment of or retribution for past misdeeds. Used chiefly in the phrase *day of reckoning.*

re·claim (ri-kláym, rée-) *tr.v.* **-claimed, -claiming, -claims.** **1.** To make (marshland or desert, for example) suitable for cultivation or habitation, as by stabilising, irrigating, or fertilising. **2.** To procure (usable substances) from refuse or waste products. **3.** To turn (a person) from error, evil, or barbarism; reform. **4.** To demand or effect the return of. **5.** *Archaic.* To tame (a falcon, for example). **6.** To produce (land) by filling in an area previously submerged by the sea. —See Synonyms at **recover, save.**

~n. The act of reclaiming or condition of being reclaimed. [Middle English *reclamen,* to call back, from Old French *reclamer,* from Latin *reclāmāre,* to exclaim against : *re-,* back, against + *clāmāre,* to call out.] **—re·claim·a·ble** *adj.* **—re·claim·ant, re·claim·er** *n.*

rec·la·ma·tion (récklə-máysh'n) *n.* **1.** The act or process of reclaiming or condition of being reclaimed. **2.** A restoration, as to usefulness, or morality. [Old French, a protest, from Latin *reclāmātiō* (stem *reclamātiōn-*), cry of opposition, from *reclāmāre,* to RECLAIM.]

ré·clame (ray-klaam, re-) *n.* **1.** Public acclaim. **2.** A taste or flair for publicity. [French, publicity, from *réclamer,* to reclaim, from Old French *reclamer,* to RECLAIM.]

rec·li·nate (récklin-ayt) *adj. Botany.* Bent or turned downwards towards the base. Said especially of leaves and stems. [Latin *reclīnātus,* past participle of *reclīnāre,* to RECLINE.]

re·cline (ri-klín, rə-) *v.* **-clined, -clining, -clines.** *—tr.* To cause to assume a leaning or supine position. *—intr.* To lie back or down. [Middle English *reclinen,* from Old French *recliner,* from Latin *reclīnāre* : *re-,* back, again + *-clīnāre,* to bend.] **—rec·li·na·tion** (récli-náysh'n) *n.* **—re·clin·er** *n.*

re·cluse (ri-kloóss ‖ -kléwss, *U.S. also* rék-loōss, -loōz) *n.* One who withdraws to live in solitude and seclusion; a hermit.

~adj. Withdrawn from the world; solitary. [Middle English *reclus(e),* from Old French, past participle of *reclure,* to shut up, from Latin *reclūdere,* to close off, unclose, open : *re-* (intensifive), again + *claudere,* to close. **—re·clu·sion** (-kloózh'n ‖ -kléwzh'n) *n.*]

re·clu·sive (ri-kloó-siv ‖ -kléw-, -ziv) *adj.* **1.** Seeking or preferring seclusion or isolation. **2.** Providing seclusion: *a reclusive hut.*

re·cog·ni·sance, re·cog·ni·zance (ri-kóg-ni-z'nss, rə-, -kónni-) *n.* **1.** *Law.* **a.** An obligation of record entered into before a court or magistrate by which a person binds himself to perform a particular act, such as to appear in court or pay a sum of money. **b.** A sum of money pledged to assure the performance of such an act. **2.** *Archaic.* A recognition. [Middle English *recognizance, reconissaunce,* recognition, from Old French *reconoissance,* from *reconoistre,* to RECOGNISE.] **—re·cog·ni·sant** *adj.*

rec·og·nise, rec·og·nize (réckəg-nīz, *also* réckə-. *Note: the pronunciation* réckə-nīz, *although used by many educated speakers, is widely condemned). tr.v.* **-nised, -nising, -nises.** **1.** To know or be aware that (something perceived) has been perceived by oneself before: *recognise a face.* **2.** To know or identify from past experience or knowledge: *recognise a red-winged blackbird.* **3. a.** To realise; comprehend and appreciate fully: *recognised the value of the discovery.* **b.** To perceive or acknowledge the validity or reality of: *recognise a demand.* **4.** To acknowledge the presence of; greet: *refused to recognise me in the street.* **5.** To give permission to (a person) to speak in a debate. Used especially of a chairman. **6.** To acknowledge or accept the national status of (a new government). **7.** To show approval or appreciation of: *recognise services rendered.* [Old French *reconoistre* (stem *reco(g)noiss-*), from Latin *recognōscere,* to know again : *re-,* again + *cognōscere,* to know : *co-,* with + *gnōscere,* become acquainted.] **—rec·og·nis·a·ble** (-nīzəb'l, *also* -nīzəb'l) *adj.* **—rec·og·nis·a·bly** *adv.* **—rec·og·nis·er** *n.*

rec·og·nised (réckəg-nīzd, *also* réckə-. *See note at* **recognise**). *adj.* Generally approved or acknowledged as meeting appropriate requirements: *a recognised brand or paint.*

rec·og·ni·tion (réckəg-nísh'n, *also* réckə- *See note at* **recognise.**) *n.* **1.** The act of recognising or state of being recognised, especially: **a.** An awareness that something perceived has previously been perceived by oneself. **b.** An acknowledgment, as of a claim or fact. **2.** Attention or favourable notice: *Her achievements won her general recognition.* **3.** An acknowledgment of the national status of a new government by another nation. [Latin *recognitiō* (stem *recognitiōn-*), from *recognōscere* (past participle *recognitus*), to RECOGNISE.] **—re·cog·ni·to·ry** (ri-kóg-ni-tri, -təri), **re·cog·ni·tive** *adj.*

re·coil (ri-kóyl, rə-) *intr.v.* **-coiled, -coiling, -coils.** **1.** To spring back, as a shotgun does when fired. **2.** To shrink back, as in fear or repugnance. **3.** To harm the person responsible for an act, especially an act of malice. Used with *on* or *upon: Vice recoils upon the guilty men.*

~n. (rée-koyl, ri-kóyl). **1.** The amount of space used by a firearm as it recoils upon firing. **2.** The act or state of recoiling. [Middle English *recoilen, reculen,* from Old French *reculer* : *re-,* back, again + *cul,* backside, from Latin *cūlus.*] **—re·coil·er** *n.*

Synonyms: *recoil, blench, cower, quail, cringe, flinch, shrink.*

re-col·lect (rée-kə-lékt) *tr.v.* **-lected, -lecting, -lects.** **1.** To collect again. **2.** To calm or control (oneself).

rec·ol·lect (réckə-lékt) *v.* **-lected, -lecting, -lects.** *—tr.* To recall to mind; remember. *—intr.* To have a recollection; remember. [Medieval Latin *recolligere* (past participle *recollectus*), to recall, from Latin, to gather again : *re-,* again + *colligere,* to gather, COLLECT.] **—rec·ol·lec·tive** *adj.* **—rec·ol·lec·tive·ly** *adv.*

rec·ol·lec·tion (réckə-léksh'n) *n.* **1.** The act or power of recollecting. **2.** Something recollected. —See Synonyms at **memory.**

re·com·bi·nant (rée-kómbinənt, ree-) *n.* An individual in which genetic recombination has occurred.

~adj. Of, pertaining to, or characterised by genetic recombination. [RECOMBIN(E) + -ANT.]

recombinant DNA *n.* DNA prepared by laboratory manipulation in which genes from one species are combined with those of another species.

re·com·bi·na·tion (rée-kómbi-náysh'n) *n.* The formation in an offspring of gene combinations not present in either of its parents.

re·com·mence (rée-kə-ménss) *v.* **-menced, -mencing, -mences.** To begin or commence again.

rec·om·mend (réckə-ménd) *tr.v.* **-mended, -mending, -mends.** **1.** To commend to the attention of another as reputable, worthy, or desirable. **2.** To make attractive or acceptable: *He has little to recommend him.* **3.** To counsel or advise (a particular course of action). **4.** *Archaic.* To commit to the charge of another: *recommended his soul to God.* [Middle English *recommenden,* from Medieval Latin *recommendāre* : Latin *re-,* again + *commendāre,* to COMMEND.] **—rec·om·mend·a·ble** *adj.* **—rec·om·mend·er** *n.*

rec·om·men·da·tion (réckə-men-dáysh'n, -mən-) *n.* **1.** The act of recommending. **2.** Something that recommends; specifically, a favourable statement concerning a person's character or qualifications. **3.** Someone or something that is recommended. **—rec·om·men·da·to·ry** (-mén-də-tri, -təri, -dáytəri) *adj.*

re·com·mit (rée-kə-mít) *tr.v.* **-mitted, -mitting, -mits.** **1.** To commit again. **2.** To refer (a bill) to a committee again, for further consideration. **—re·com·mit·ment, re·com·mit·tal** *n.*

rec·om·pense (réckəm-penss) *tr.v.* **-pensed, -pensing, -penses.** **1.** To reward or pay for services. **2. a.** To award compensation for (loss or damage, for example); make a return for. **b.** To award compensation to.

~n. **1.** Amends made for something, such as damage or loss. **2.** Payment in return for something given or done, such as services. [Middle English *recompensen,* from Old French *recompenser,* from Late Latin *recompensāre* : Latin *re-,* back, again + *compensāre,* to COMPENSATE.]

re·com·pose (rée-kəm-pṓz ‖ -kom-) *tr.v.* **-posed, -posing, -poses.** **1.** To compose again. **2.** To restore to composure; calm. **—re·com·po·si·tion** (rée-kompə-zísh'n) *n.*

re·con (rée-kon) *n.* The smallest genetic unit that is capable of recombination. [*Recombination* + -ON.]

rec·on·cil·a·ble (réckən-síl-əb'l, -síl-) *adj.* Capable of reconciliation or able to be reconciled. **—rec·on·cil·a·bil·i·ty** (-ə-bílləti), **rec·on·cil·a·ble·ness** *n.* **—rec·on·cil·a·bly** *adv.*

rec·on·cile (réckən-sīl) *tr.v.* **-ciled, -ciling, -ciles.** **1.** To re-establish friendship between. **2.** To settle or resolve (a dispute, for example). **3.** To bring to acceptance or acquiescence: *reconcile oneself to de-*

feat. **4.** To make compatible or consistent. Often used with *to* or *with*: *reconcile my way of thinking with yours.* **5.** To purify (a consecrated place) in a special ceremony, after an act of desecration. [Middle English *reconcilen,* from Old French *reconcilier,* from Latin *reconciliāre* : *re-,* again + *conciliāre,* to CONCILIATE.] **—rec·on·cile·ment, rec·on·cil·i·a·tion** (-sílli-áysh'n) *n.* **—rec·on·cil·er** *n.* **—rec·on·cil·i·a·to·ry** (-sílli-ətri, -ətəri) *adj.*

rec·on·dite (réckən-dīt, ri-kóndīt, rə-) *adj.* **1.** Not easily understood; abstruse: *the recondite origin of life.* **2.** Concerned with abstruse or obscure subjects: *recondite scholarship.* [Latin *reconditus,* past participle of *recondere,* to hide, put up again : *re-,* again + *condere,* bring together.] **—rec·on·dite·ly** *adv.* **—rec·on·dite·ness** *n.*

re·con·di·tion (rée-kən-dísh'n || -kon-) *tr.v.* **-tioned, -tioning, -tions.** **1.** To restore by repairing, renovating, or rebuilding. **2.** To overhaul and restore to good working order.

re·con·nais·sance (ri-kónni-s'nss, rə-, -kónnə- || -z'nss) *n.* **1.** The process or activity of investigating or surveying. **2. a.** A preliminary survey made of a region to examine its terrain or to determine the disposition of enemy forces. **b.** A party making such a survey. [French, from Old French *reconoissance,* RECOGNISANCE.]

re·con·noi·tre, *U.S.* **re·con·noi·ter** (réckə-nóytər || réekə-) *v.* **-tred** or *U.S.* **-tered, -tring** or *U.S.* **-tering, -tres** or *U.S.* **-ters.** *—tr.* To make a preliminary inspection of (an area or enemy positions, for example). *—intr.* To make a reconnaissance.

~*n.* An act of reconnoitring. [Obsolete French *reconnoître,* from Old French *reconoistre,* RECOGNISE.] **—re·con·noi·tr·er** *n.*

re·con·sid·er (rée-kən-síddər || -kon-) *v.* **-ered, -ering, -ers.** *—tr.* To consider (a decision, for example) again, with a view to possible revision. *—intr.* To consider a matter again and, especially, to come to a different decision. **—re·con·sid·er·a·tion** (-áysh'n) *n.*

re·con·sti·tute (rée-kón-sti-tewt || -tōōt) *tr.v.* **-tuted, -tuting, -tutes.** **1.** To restore the constitution of (a concentrate or dried food, for example), as by the addition of water. **2.** To restore to existence or to an original condition; reconstruct. **—re·con·sti·tu·tion** (-téwsh'n || -tōōsh'n) *n.*

re·con·struct (rée-kən-strúkt || -kon-) *tr.v.* **-structed, -structing, -structs.** **1.** To construct again; rebuild. **2. a.** To remake (something that is incomplete or damaged) guided by the available evidence: *reconstruct the orchestral score from the piano version.* **b.** To represent (an occurrence, such as a crime or historical event) in dramatic form on the basis of available evidence.

re·con·struc·tion (rée-kən-strúksh'n || -kon-) *n.* **1.** The act or result of reconstructing. **2.** *Capital* **R.** The period (1865–77) in the United States after the Civil War during which the states of the Southern Confederacy were reorganised prior to their full readmission to the Union. **3.** *Finance.* **Reorganisation** *(see).* **—re·con·struc·tive** *adj.*

re·con·vey (rée-kən-váy || -kon-) *tr.v.* **-veyed, -veying, -veys.** To convey back to a former owner or place. **—re·con·vey·ance** *n.*

rec·ord (réckawrd || *chiefly U.S.* réckərd) *n. Abbr.* **rec.** **1. a.** An account made in an enduring form, especially in writing, that preserves the knowledge or memory of events or facts. **b.** The fact or condition of serving as such an account for future reference: *a newspaper of record.* **2.** Something on which such an account is made. **3.** *Often plural.* Information or data on a particular subject collected and preserved: *look up parish records.* **4.** The known history of performance or achievement: *a fine war record.* **5.** The best performance known officially, as in a sport: *broke the world record.* **6.** *Law.* **a.** An account officially written and preserved as evidence or testimony. **b.** An account of judicial or legislative proceedings written and preserved as evidence. **c.** The documents or volumes containing such evidence. **7.** A disc structurally coded to reproduce sound when played on a record player; a gramophone record. Also used adjectivally: *a record company.* **8.** Anything that provides a source of information about the past or preserves facts for reference: *Pop music is a record of contemporary youth culture.* **9.** An official report kept by the police of an individual's previous convictions. **10.** *Computing.* A small amount of data that is stored, processed, and retrieved as a single convenient unit. **—for the record.** For the sake of accuracy; as an official fact. **—off the record.** Confidentially or unofficially; not for publication. **—on record. 1.** Noted in official recordings of past facts or events: *the warmest summer on record.* **2.** Officially recorded or noted for public disclosure: *He is on record as having stated his acceptance of the new regime.*

~*v.* **re·cord** (ri-kórd, rə-) **-corded, -cording, -cords.** *—tr.* **1.** To set down for preservation in writing or other permanent form. **2.** To serve as a source of information about or as evidence of: *Her novel records a past way of life.* **3.** To register or indicate: *A thermometer records temperatures.* **4. a.** To register (a voice or piece of music, for example) in permanent form by mechanical or electrical means for reproduction. **b.** To perform (a piece of music, for example) that is to be registered in this way. *—intr.* To record something.

~*adj.* **rec·ord** (réckawrd || *chiefly U.S.* réckərd). *Abbr.* **rec.** Establishing a record: *a record crowd.* [Middle English *recorde,* from Old French *record,* from *recorder,* to record, from Latin *recordārī,* to remember, think over : *re-,* again + *cor* (stem *cord-*), mind, heart.]

rec·ord-break·ing (réckawrd-brayking || réckərd-) *adj.* That establishes a new record: *a record-breaking time.*

re·cord·ed delivery (ri-kórdid, rə-) *n.* **1.** A service provided by the Post Office that makes an official record of the posting and delivery of mail. **2.** A delivery of post provided by this service.

~*adv.* By or using this service.

re·cord·er (ri-kórdər, rə-) *n.* **1.** One that records, such as: **a.** An instrument for recording measurements. **b.** An official who records proceedings. **c.** A **tape recorder** *(see).* **2.** A fipple flute with eight fingerholes existing in various ranges. **3.** *Law.* In England and Wales, a barrister or solicitor of at least ten years' standing who acts as a part-time judge in the crown court and can also sit as a judge for a county court. **4.** *Capital* **R.** Used as part of the title of certain newspapers: *The Halifax Recorder.*

re·cord·ing (ri-kórding, rə-) *n. Abbr.* **rec.** **1.** A gramophone record or magnetic tape or wire upon which sound has been recorded. **2.** The sounds so recorded. **3.** The process of registering sound in a permanent form on a record or tape. **4.** A radio or television programme that has been prerecorded.

Recording Angel *n.* An angel who supposedly registers the good and evil acts of every person.

recording studio *n.* See **studio.**

record player *n.* A device for playing gramophone records, consisting of a single unit having a turntable, a pickup for converting vibrations of the needle into electrical signals, an amplifier, and one or more loudspeakers.

re·count (rée-kównt || *West Indies also* -kúngt) *tr.v.* **-counted, -counting, -counts.** To count again.

~*n.* (rée-kownt, *rarely* -kównt). An additional count; especially, a second count of votes cast in an election.

re·count (ri-kównt || *West Indies also* -kúngt) *tr.v.* **-counted, -counting, -counts.** **1.** To narrate the facts or details of. **2.** To enumerate. [Middle English *recounten,* from Old French *reconter* : *re-,* again, back + *conter, compter,* to relate, COUNT.] **—re·count·al** *n.*

re·coup (ri-kōōp) *v.* **-couped, -couping, -coups.** *—tr.* **1.** To receive or get back an equivalent for; make up for: *recoup the loss.* **2.** To return as an equivalent for; reimburse. **3.** *Law.* To deduct or withhold (part of something due) for a legally recognised reason. *—intr.* To regain a former favourable position. **—**See Synonyms at **recover.** [Middle English *recoupen,* from Old French *recouper,* to cut back, retrench : *re-,* back + *couper,* to cut, strike, from *coup,* blow, COUP.] **—re·coup·a·ble** *adj.* **—re·coup·ment** *n.*

re·course (ri-kórss, rə- || -kōrss, *also* rée-kawrss, -kōrss) *n.* **1.** A turning or applying to a person or thing for aid or security: *have recourse to the courts.* **2.** One that is turned or applied to for aid or security: *His only recourse was the police.* See Usage note at **resort.** **3.** *Law.* The right to demand payment from the endorser of a bill of exchange or other commercial paper when the first party liable fails to pay. **—without recourse.** Disclaiming liability for nonpayment. Used as a formula by an endorser of a bill of exchange to avoid liability. [Middle English *recours,* from Old French, from Latin *recursus,* a running back, from *recurrere,* to run back : *re-,* again, back + *currere,* to run.]

re-cov·er (rée-kúvvər) *tr.v.* **-ered, -ering, -ers.** To cover again.

re·cov·er (ri-kúvvər, rə-) *v.* **-ered, -ering, -ers.** *—tr.* **1. a.** To get back or regain possession or control of (property). **b.** To retrieve; make up for: *recovered the time lost in the strike.* **2.** To restore (oneself) to a normal state, as after an illness or setback. **3.** To regain the use or enjoyment of: *recovered his health; land recovered from the sea.* **4.** *Law.* To gain as compensation by means of a favourable judgment in a civil lawsuit: *recover damages.* **5.** To derive (useful substances) from waste material. *—intr.* **1.** To regain a normal or usual condition or state, as of health or economic development. Often used with *from.* **2.** To receive a favourable judgment in a civil lawsuit. **3.** In swimming or rowing, to stretch the arm or oar forwards ready to take another stroke. [Middle English *recoveren,* from Old French *recoverer,* from Latin *recuperāre,* to RECUPERATE.] **—re·cov·er·a·ble** *adj.* **—re·cov·er·er n.**

Synonyms: *recover, reclaim, regain, recoup, retrieve.*

re·cov·er·y (ri-kúvvəri, rə-) *n., pl.* **-ies.** **1.** An act, instance, process, or duration of recovering; recuperation. **2.** A return to a normal condition. **3.** Something gained or restored in recovering. **4.** The obtaining of usable substances from unusable sources, such as waste material. **5.** *Law.* The process of recovering compensation, damages, or the like by a lawsuit. **6.** In fencing, the returning to an on guard position. **7.** In swimming or rowing, the action of recovering. **8.** In golf, a stroke to bring a ball out of a bunker or away from the rough.

recovery room *n.* A hospital room used for the care and observation of patients immediately after surgery.

rec·re·ant (réckri-ənt) *adj. Literary.* **1.** Unfaithful or disloyal to a belief, promise, or cause. **2.** Craven or cowardly.

~*n. Literary.* **1.** A faithless or disloyal person; an apostate. **2.** A coward. [Middle English *recreant,* from Old French, present participle of *recroire,* to yield, surrender, from Medieval Latin *recrēdere* : Latin *re-,* back, contrarily + *crēdere,* entrust, believe.] **—rec·re·ance, rec·re·an·cy** *n.* **—rec·re·ant·ly** *adv.*

re-cre·ate (rée-kri-áyt, -kree-) *tr.v.* **-ated, -ating, -ates.** To reproduce (something that formerly existed); create anew. **—re-cre·a·tion** *n.*

rec·re·ate (réckri-ayt) *v.* **-ated, -ating, -ates.** *—tr.* To impart fresh life to; refresh mentally or physically. *—intr.* To take recreation; amuse oneself. [Latin *recreāre,* to create anew : *re-,* back, again + *creāre,* to CREATE.] **—rec·re·a·tive** (-ətiv, -aytiv) *adj.*

rec·re·a·tion (réckri-áysh'n) *n. Abbr.* **rec.** **1.** Refreshment of one's mind or body through diverting activity. **2.** A form of relaxation or pleasurable exercise that fosters this. **—rec·re·a·tion·al** *adj.*

recreation ground *n.* A piece of public land used for recreational activities, often equipped with swings, slides, and the like.

rec·re·ment (réckri-mənt) *n.* Waste matter; refuse; dross. [Latin

PRONUNCIATION KEY

a, **trap**; aa, **father**; ai, **fair**; ar, **star**; aw, **lawn**; ay, **play**; b, bb, **stab**; **rubber**; ch, **church**; ck, **ticket**; d, dd, **dead**; **ladder**; e, **dress**; ee, **bee**; er, **defer**; ew, **few**; ewr, **pure**; ə, **about**; ər, **letter**; f, ff, **fife**; **differ**; g, gg, **giggle**; h, **hat**; i, **kit**; ī, **price**; īr, **fire**; j, **judge**; k, **kick**; l, ll, **let**; 'l, **needle**; m, mm, **man**; n, nn, **no**; 'n, **sudden**; ng, **thing**; o, **lot**; ō, **no**; ŏŏ, **foot**; ōō, **shoe**; oor, **poor**; ow, **cow**; owr, **hour**; oy, **boy**; p, pp, **pepper**; r, rr, **red**; s, ss, **sauce**; sh, **ship**; t, tt, **totter**; th, **thick**; th, **this**; **smooth**; u, **cut**; ur, **turn**; v, vv, **valve**; w, **wet**; y, **yes**; z, zz, **zebra**; zh, **vision**; **pleasure**

IN FOREIGN WORDS:

aN, oN, **Saint-Saëns**; hl, **Llanelli**; **Hluhluwe**; kh, **loch**; **lough**; **Khaled**

STRESS MARK:

ín-sīt, insight; in-sít, incite

redcurrant *This fruit-bearing shrub was first cultivated in northwest Europe, but the name comes partly from Greece. Redcurrants, like other currants, are so called because of the berries' similarity to the raisins of Corinth.*

PRONUNCIATION KEY

a, trap; aa, father; ai, fair; ar, star; aw, lawn; ay, play; b, bb, stab; rubber; ch, church; ck, ticket; d, dd, dead; ladder; e, dress; ee, bee; er, defer; ew, few; ewr, pure; ə, about; ər, letter; f, ff, fife; differ; g, gg, giggle; h, hat; i, kit; ī, price; īr, fire; j, judge; k, kick; l, ll, let; 'l, needle; m, mm, man; n, nn, no; 'n, sudden; ng, thing; o, lot; ō, no; o͝o, foot; o͞o, shoe; oor, poor; ow, cow; owr, hour; oy, boy; p, pp, pepper; r, rr, red; s, ss, sauce; sh, ship; t, tt, totter; th, thick; th, this; smooth; u, cut; ur, turn; v, vv, valve; w, wet; y, yes; z, zz, zebra; zh, vision; pleasure

IN FOREIGN WORDS:

aN, ON, Saint-Saëns; hl, Llanelli; Hluhluwe; kh, loch; lough; Khaled

STRESS MARK:

ín-sīt, insight; in-sít, incite

recrēmentum : *re-*, back, again + *cernere*, to separate, sift.] **—rec·re·men·tal** (-mént'l) *adj.*

re·crim·i·nate (ri-krímmi-nayt, rə-) *v.* **-nated, -nating, -nates.** *—tr.* To accuse in return. *—intr.* To counter one accusation with another. [Medieval Latin *recrīmināre* : Latin *re-*, again, back + *crīmināre*, to accuse, from *crīmen*, accusation.] **—re·crim·i·na·tive** (-nətiv, -naytiv), **re·crim·i·na·to·ry** (-nətri, -nətəri, -náytəri) *adj.* **—re·crim·i·na·tor** (-naytər) *n.*

re·crim·i·na·tion (ri-krimmi-náysh'n, rə-) *n.* **1.** The act of recriminating, especialy in a bitter way; mutual accusation. **2.** A countercharge.

re·cru·desce (rée-kro͞o-déss, réckro͞o-) *intr.v.* **-desced, -descing, -desces.** To break out anew after a dormant or inactive period. Used especially of something undesirable, such as a disease or state of discontent. [Latin *recrūdēscere* : *re-*, again + *crūdēscere*, to get worse, from *crūdus*, harsh, raw.] **—re·cru·des·cence** *n.* **—re·cru·des·cent** *adj.*

re·cruit (ri-kro͞ot, rə- || -kréwt) *v.* **-cruited, -cruiting, -cruits.** *—tr.* **1.** To enlist for military service. **2.** To strengthen or raise (an armed force) by enlistment. **3. a.** To obtain (new members or employees, for example). **b.** To supply with new members or employees. **4.** To enrol (another) in support of oneself or one's ideas. **5.** To replenish. **6.** To renew or restore (health or vitality). *—intr.* **1.** To seek or enlist new members or recruits. **2.** To regain lost health or strength; recover.

∼n. **1.** *Abbr.* **rct.** A newly enlisted member of a military force; especially, one of the lowest rank or grade. **2.** A new member of any organisation or body. [Obsolete French dialect *recrute*, new growth, from *recrue*, past participle of *recroître*, to grow again, from Latin *recrēscere* : *re-*, again + *crēscere*, to grow.] **—re·cruit·er** *n.* **—re·cruit·ment** *n.*

re·crys·tal·lise, re·crys·tal·lize (rée-kríst'l-īz) *v.* **-lised, -lising, -lises.** *—tr.* To dissolve (a substance) and then crystallise, especially so as to purify. *—intr.* **1.** To be recrystallised. **2.** To form new crystals or crystal structure. Used of a deformed metal. **—re·crys·tal·li·sa·tion** (-ī-záysh'n || *U.S.* -i-) *n.*

rec't receipt.

rect. **1.** receipt. **2.** rectangle; rectangular. **3.** rectified. **4.** rector; rectory.

rec·tal (rékt'l) *adj.* Pertaining to, near, or administered via the rectum. **—rec·tal·ly** *adv.*

rec·tan·gle (rék-tang-g'l) *n. Abbr.* **rect.** *Geometry.* A parallelogram with a right angle. [Medieval Latin *rēctangulum* : Latin *rēctus*, right + *angulus*, ANGLE.]

rec·tan·gu·lar (rek-táng-gew-lər) *adj. Abbr.* **rect.** **1.** Having the shape of a rectangle. **2.** Having right angles. Said of a geometric figure, such as a spherical triangle. **3.** Having or pertaining to lines or planes that are mutually perpendicular: *a rectangular coordinate system.* **4.** Having a base that is a rectangle. Said of geometric solids. **—rec·tan·gu·lar·i·ty** (-lárrəti) *n.* **—rec·tan·gu·lar·ly** *adv.*

rectangular coordinate *n. Geometry.* A coordinate in a **Cartesian coordinate system** *(see)* that has the coordinate axes at right angles.

rectangular hyperbola *n. Geometry.* A hyperbola for which the two asymptotes are at right angles. It has an equation of the form $xy = e$ in Cartesian coordinates.

rec·ti·fi·er (rékti-fī-ər) *n.* **1.** A person or thing that rectifies. **2.** *Electricity.* A device, such as a diode, that converts alternating current to direct current. **3.** A worker who blends or dilutes whisky or other alcoholic beverages. **4.** *Chemistry.* A condenser used to separate or purify.

rec·ti·fy (rékti-fī) *tr.v.* **-fied, -fying, -fies.** **1.** To set right; correct. **2.** To correct by calculation or adjustment. **3.** *Chemistry.* To refine or purify, especially by distillation. **4.** *Electricity.* To convert (alternating current) into direct current. **5.** To adjust (the proof of alcoholic spirit) by adding water or other liquids. —See Synonyms at **correct.** [Middle English *rectifien*, from Old French *rectifier*, from Medieval Latin *rēctificāre* : Latin *rēctus*, straight + *facere*, to make.] **—rec·ti·fi·a·ble** *adj.* **—rec·ti·fi·ca·tion** (-fi-káysh'n) *n.*

rec·ti·lin·e·ar (rékti-línni-ər) *adj.* Moving in, consisting of, bounded by, or characterised by a straight line or lines. [Late Latin *rēctilīneus* : *rēctus*, straight + *līnea*, LINE.] **—rec·ti·lin·e·ar·ly** *adv.*

rec·ti·tude (rékti-tewd || -to͞od) *n.* **1.** Moral uprightness. **2.** Rightness, as of intellectual judgment. **3.** Straightness. [Middle English, from Old French, from Late Latin *rēctitūdō*, from Latin *rēctus*, straight.]

rec·to (réktō) *n., pl.* **-tos.** The right-hand page of a book or front side of a leaf, as opposed to the **verso** *(see).* [Latin *rēctō (foliō)*, on the right side of (a page), ablative of *rēctus*, right, straight.]

rec·tor (réktər) *n. Abbr.* **R., rect.** **1. a.** In the Church of England, a clergyman who has charge of a parish and formerly owned the tithes from it. **b.** In other Episcopalian churches, a clergyman in charge of a parish. **2.** *Roman Catholic Church.* A priest appointed to be the administrative as well as spiritual head of a church or other institution such as a seminary or university. **3. a.** The principal of certain schools, colleges, and universities. **b.** In Scottish universities, a representative, often a prominent public figure, elected by the students to the governing body. [Latin *rēctor*, governor, from *rēctus*, past participle of *regere*, to rule.] **—rec·tor·ate** (-ət, -it) *n.* **—rec·to·ri·al** (rek-táwri-əl || -tōri-) *adj.*

rec·to·ry (rέktri, réktəri) *n., pl.* **-ries.** *Abbr.* **rect.** **1.** The house in which a rector lives. **2.** A rector's office.

rec·trix (rék-triks) *n., pl.* **rectrices** (-tri-seez, *also* -trī-seez). Any of the stiff main feathers of a bird's tail. [Latin, feminine of *rēctor*, governor (the feathers help regulate flight). See **rector.**]

rec·tum (rék-təm) *n., pl.* **-tums** or **-ta** (-tə). The portion of the large intestine extending from the sigmoid flexure of the colon to the anal canal. Also called "back passage". [New Latin *rectum (intestinum)*, straight (intestine), from Latin *rēctus*, straight.]

rec·tus (rék-təss) *n., pl.* **-ti** (-tī). Any of various straight muscles, as of the abdomen, eye, neck, and thigh. [New Latin, from Latin *rēctus*, straight.]

re·cum·bent (ri-kúmbənt, rə-) *adj.* **1.** Lying down; reclining. **2.** Resting; idle. **3.** *Biology.* Resting upon the surface from which it arises: *a recumbent organ.* **4.** *Geology.* Designating or pertaining to a fold in a rock formation in which the strata in the fold lie almost parallel to those in the rest of the formation. [Latin *recumbēns* (stem *recumbent-*), present participle of *recumbere*, to lie down : *re-*, back, again + *-cumbere*, to lie.] **—re·cum·bence, re·cum·ben·cy** *n.* **—re·cum·bent·ly** *adv.*

re·cu·per·ate (ri-kéwpə-rayt, rə-, -ko͞opə-) *v.* **-ated, -ating, -ates.** *—intr.* **1.** To return to health or strength; recover. **2.** To recover from financial loss. *—tr.* **1.** To restore to health or strength. **2.** To regain. [Latin *recuperāre* : RE- + *cup-*, from *capere*, to take.] **—re·cu·per·a·tion** (-ráysh'n) *n.* **—re·cu·per·a·tive** (-rətiv, -raytiv), **re·cu·per·a·to·ry** (-rətri, -rətəri, -ráytəri) *adj.*

re·cu·per·a·tor (ri-kéwpə-raytər, -rə-) *n.* A heat exchanger using the waste heat from the flue gases of a furnace to heat the incoming air.

re·cur (ri-kúr, rə-) *intr.v.* **-curred, -curring** (-kúr-ing, *rarely* -kúrring), **-curs.** **1.** To happen or come up again or repeatedly. **2.** To return to one's thoughts or attention: *a recurring nightmare.* **3.** To to back, as in thought, memory, or discourse. Used with *to.* **4.** *Mathematics.* To occur or be repeated an infinite number of times. Used of digits or groups or digits in a repeating decimal faction. —See Synonyms at **return.** [Latin *recurrere*, to run back : *re-*, back + *currere*, to run.] **—re·cur·rence** (-kúrrənss) *n.*

re·cur·rent (ri-kúrrənt, rə-) *adj.* **1.** Occurring or appearing again or repeatedly; returning regularly. **2.** *Anatomy.* Running in a reverse direction. Said of arteries and nerves that turn back on themselves. **—re·cur·rent·ly** *adv.*

recurring decimal *n. Mathematics.* A **repeating decimal** *(see).*

recurrent fever *n.* **Relapsing fever** *(see).*

re·cur·sion (ri-kúrsh'n, rə- || -kúrzh'n) *adj. Mathematics & Logic.* **1.** A repeated process or formula for generating or defining a series of terms, such as successive terms in a polynomial expression. Used adjectivally. **2.** An expression generated in this way. [Late Latin *recursiō* (stem *recursiōn-*), a return, from Latin *recurrere* (past participle *recursus*), to RECUR.] **—re·cur·sive** (-kúr-siv) *adj.*

re·cur·vate (ri-kúrv-ət, -it, -ayt) *adj.* Bent or curved backwards. [Latin *recurvātus*, past participle of *recurvāre*, to RECURVE.]

re·curve (rée-kúrv) *v.* **-curved, -curving, -curves.** *—tr.* To bend or curve backwards or downwards. *—intr.* To become recurved. [Latin *recurvāre* : *re-*, back, backward + *curvāre*, to curve, from *curvus*, CURVE.] **—re·cur·va·tion** (rée-kur-váysh'n) *n.*

rec·u·sant (réckewz'nt, ri-kéwz'nt, rə-) *n.* **1.** A Roman Catholic who refused to attend the services of the Church of England between the reigns of Henry VIII and George II. **2.** A dissenter; a nonconformist. [Latin *recusāns* (stem *recusant-*), present participle of *recusāre*, to refuse : *re-*, contrary to, back + *causa*, CAUSE.] **—rec·u·san·cy** (réckewz'nssi, ri-kéwz'nssi, rə-) *n.* **—rec·u·sant** *adj.*

re·cuse (ri-kéwz, rə-) *tr.v.* **-cused, -cusing, -cuses.** To challenge or object to (a judge or juror) on such grounds as his prejudice or disqualification. [Latin *recusāre*, to refuse. See **recusant.**]

re·cy·cle (rée-sīk'l) *tr.v.* **-cled, -cling, -cles.** **1.** To put or pass through a cycle again, as for further treatment. **2.** To start a different cycle in. **3. a.** To make new use of or to process for re-use (used and discarded objects and material). **b.** To extract useful materials from (rubbish, waste, or the like). **c.** To extract and reuse (useful substances found in waste). **—re·cy·cla·ble** *adj.*

red¹ (red) *n.* **1.** Any of a group of colours that may vary in lightness and saturation, whose hue resembles that of fresh blood; the hue of the long-wavelength end of the spectrum; one of the additive or light primaries; one of the psychological primary hues, evoked in the normal observer by the long-wavelength end of the spectrum. See **primary colour.** **2.** A pigment or dye having or giving this hue. **3.** Something that has this hue such as: **a.** Clothing or material: *She wore red.* **b.** A red ball used in some games, such as billiards, snooker, or croquet. **c.** One of the two colours on which bets may be placed in roulette and rouge-et-noir. **d.** A **red light** *(see).* **4.** *Often capital* **R.** *Informal.* **a.** A Communist or radical revolutionary activist. **b.** A supporter or member of a Communist or left-wing socialist party. **c.** *Slang.* A citizen of a Communist country. *Often used derogatorily.* **—in the red.** Having a debit rather than a credit balance; in debt. **—see red.** To become suddenly furious.

∼adj. **redder, reddest.** **1.** Having a colour resembling that of blood. **2.** Reddish in colour, or having parts that are reddish in colour. Used in animal and plant names: *red fox; red oak.* **3. a.** Designating hair or an animal's coat having a colour ranging from orange and copper-coloured, to reddish brown. **b.** Having a coppery skin tone. **4.** Having a ruddy or flushed complexion, as from exertion or embarrassment. **5.** Bloodshot or red-rimmed. Said of eyes. **6.** Coloured by the skins of the black grapes from which it is made. Said of wine. **7.** Involving or concerned with bloodshed or violence. **8.** *Often capital* **R.** **a.** Radical or revolutionary in nature: *red political theories.* **b.** Of, pertaining to, or caused by revolution or revolutionaries: *a red scare.* **c.** Communist or having a Communist government: *Red China.* **9.** Designating one of the three quark colours. The other two are blue and green. [Middle English *red, read*, Old English *rēad.*] **—red·ly** *adv.* **—red·ness** *n.*

red². Variant of **redd**.
red. reduced; reduction.
re•dact (ri-dákt) *tr.v.* **-dacted, -dacting, -dacts. 1.** To draw up or draft (a proclamation or edict, for example). **2.** To make ready for publication; edit or revise. [Latin *redigere* (past participle *redactus*), to collect, drive back : *re-*, back + *agere*, to drive, do.] **—re•dac•tor** (ri-dák-tər || -tawr) *n.* **—re•dac•tion** (ri-dáksh'n) *n.*
red admiral *n.* A Eurasian butterfly, *Vanessa atalanta*, the wings of which are black with red and white markings.
red alert *n.* A state of readiness for an imminent danger, such as a natural disaster or enemy attack.
red algae *pl.n.* Algae of the division Rhodophyta, characteristically red or reddish in colour and including dulse and similar seaweeds.
re•dan (ri-dán) *n.* A fortification consisting of two walls that form a salient angle. [French, from earlier *redent*, a notching : RE- + *dent*, tooth.]
red•back spider (réd-bak) *n.* A poisonous long-legged Australian spider, *Latrodectus hasseltii*, the female of which has a round black abdomen with a red marking on the back.
red bark *n.* A form of cinchona that is reddish in colour and has a high alkaloid content.
red beds *pl.n. Geology.* Sequences of red sedimentary rocks, especially sandstones or shales, formed in a highly oxidising environment, the iron present being oxidised to red ferric oxide.
red biddy *n. Slang.* Cheap red wine with added methylated spirits.
red blood cell *n. Abbr.* **RBC.** An **erythrocyte** *(see).* Also called "red blood corpuscle".
red-blood•ed (réd-blúddid) *adj. Informal.* Strong, brave, or virile.
red•breast (réd-brest) *n.* Any of various birds with a red breast; especially the **robin** *(see).*
red•brick (réd-brik, -brik) *adj.* Of or designating a British university dating from the late 19th century, especially as distinguished from Oxford or Cambridge, and from those founded since World War II.
Red•bridge (réd-brij). Borough in northeastern London, England. It was created (1965) by the merger of the boroughs of Ilford, Wanstead, and Woodford, and parts of Dagenham and Chigwell.
Red Brigade *n.* A terrorist group formed in Italy in 1969 and committed to the abolition of capitalist society.
red•bud (réd-bud) *n.* Any of several American shrubs or small trees of the genus *Cercis.* See **Judas tree.**
red•cap (réd-kap) *n.* **1.** *British Informal.* A member of the military police. **2.** A European bird, the **goldfinch** *(see).*
red carpet *n.* **1.** A carpet laid down for important visitors, as outside the door of a public building. **2.** Deferential or ceremoniously hospitable treatment. Used chiefly in the phrase *roll out the red carpet.* Also used adjectivally: *red-carpet treatment.*
red cedar *n.* **1.** A tall evergreen coniferous tree, *Thuya plicata*, of western North America. Also called "savin". **2.** The reddish, aromatic, durable wood of this or of similar trees.
red cell *n.* An **erythrocyte** *(see).* Also called "red corpuscle".
Red China. An informal name for the People's Republic of **China.**
red clover *n.* A Eurasian plant, *Trifolium pratense*, widely naturalised and planted as a forage or cover crop. It has leaflets in groups of three and globular heads of fragrant, rose-purple flowers.
red•coat (réd-kōt) *n.* Formerly, a British soldier.
red coral *n.* Any of various corals of the genus *Corallium*, having pinkish-red skeletons used to make jewellery and ornaments.
Red Crescent *n.* **1.** A branch of the Red Cross Society in a Muslim country. **2.** The emblem of such a branch.
Red Cross *n.* **1.** *Abbr.* **R.C.** An international organisation, formed according to the terms of the Geneva Convention of 1864, for the care of the wounded, sick, and homeless in wartime and now also during and following natural disasters. Also officially called "Red Cross Society". **2.** Any national branch of this organisation. **3.** The emblem of the organisation, a Geneva cross or red Greek cross on a white background.
red•cur•rant (réd-kúrrənt) *n.* **1.** Any of several shrubs of the genus *Ribes* that are cultivated for their small, acid-tasting, red fruits. **2.** The fruit of such a shrub, used to make jams and other preserves. Also used adjectivally: *redcurrant jelly.*
redd, red (red) *tr.v.* **redd** or **redded, redding, redds.** *Chiefly Scottish.* To put in order; arrange. Used with *up.* [Middle English *redden*, probably variant of *ridden*, to RID.]
red deer *n.* A common Eurasian deer, *Cervus elaphus*, having a reddish-brown coat and many-branched antlers.
red•den (rédd'n) *v.* **-dened, -dening, -dens.** *—tr.* To make red or redder. *—intr.* To become red; to become flushed or to blush.
red•dish (réddish) *adj.* Mixed or tinged with red; somewhat red. **—red•dish•ness** *n.*
reddle. Variant of **ruddle.**
red duster *n. British Informal.* The **Red Ensign** *(see).*
red dwarf *n. Astronomy.* Any of a small class of mostly main-sequence stars that are generally cool and small.
rede (reed) *tr.v.* **reded, reding, redes.** *Archaic.* **1.** To give advice to; counsel. **2.** To interpret; explain or tell.
~n. Archaic. **1.** Advice or counsel. **2.** An interpretation or narration. [Middle English *reden*, to guide, direct, Old English *rǣdan.*]
re•dec•o•rate (rée-déckə-rayt) *v.* **-rated, -rating, -rates.** *—tr.* To change the décor of, as by painting and renewing furnishings. *—intr.* To change the décor of a room, building, or the like. **—re•dec•o•ra•tion** (-ráysh'n) *n.*
re•deem (ri-deém, rə-) *tr.v.* **-deemed, -deeming, -deems. 1. a.** To recover ownership of by paying a stipulated sum. **b.** To recover (pawned goods or mortaged land, for example) by payment. **2.** To pay off (a promissory note or loan, for example). **3.** To turn in (coupons or trading stamps, for example) and receive something in exchange. **4.** To fulfil (an oath, pledge, or promise). **5. a.** To convert (tokens or shares, for example) into cash. **b.** To convert (banknotes) into specie. Used of a bank. **6.** To rescue or set free by paying a ransom. **7.** *Theology.* To save from a state of sinfulness and its consequences. **8.** To make up for; make amends for. **9.** To put (oneself) back in favour. —See Synonyms at **save.** [Middle English *redemen*, from Latin *redimere*, to buy back : *red-*, *re-*, back, again + *emere*, to take, buy.]
re•deem•a•ble (ri-deéməb'l, rə-) *adj.* **1.** Capable of being converted into cash. Said, for example, of tokens or shares. **2.** Able to be repaid and thereby cancelled either at a fixed date or subject to notice. Said, for example, of bonds or debentures. **3.** Capable of being saved or redeemed.
re•deem•er (ri-deémər, rə-) *n.* **1.** One who redeems; a saviour. **2.** *Capital* **R.** Jesus Christ, who, in Christian belief, redeemed mankind from sinfulness by his death on the cross.
re•deem•ing (ri-deéming, rə-) *adj.* Making up for or compensating for other faults or inadequacies: *He has one redeeming feature.*
re•de•fine (reé-di-fín, -də-) *tr.v.* **-fined, -fining, -fines.** To define again, especially in a different way.
re•demp•tion (ri-démp-sh'n, rə-, -dém-) *n.* **1.** The act or an instance of redeeming or the condition of being redeemed. **2.** A recovery of something pawned or mortgaged; a repurchase. **3. a.** The payment of an obligation, such as a government's payment of the value of its bonds. **b.** The conversion of banknotes into specie by a bank. **4.** *Theology.* Salvation from sin through Christ's death on the Cross. **5.** Release from a danger or evil. **—beyond** or **past redemption.** No longer able to be saved, made good, or restored. [Middle English *redempcioun*, from Old French *redemption*, from Latin *redemptiō* (stem *redemptiōn-*), from *redimere* (past participle *redemptus*), to REDEEM.] **—re•demp•tion•al, re•demp•tive, re•demp•to•ry** (-tri, -təri) *adj.*
re•demp•tion•er (ri-démpsh'n-ər, rə-) *n.* In Colonial America, an emigrant from Europe who paid for his voyage by serving as a bondservant for a stipulated period.
Re•demp•tor•ist (ri-démptərist) *n.* A member of a Roman Catholic order, the Congregation of the Most Holy Redeemer, founded by St. Alphonsus de Liguori in 1732 to do missionary work. [Latin *redemptor*, redeemer.]
Red Ensign *n.* A red flag with the Union Jack in the inner top corner; the ensign of the British Merchant Navy.
re•de•ploy (reé-di-plóy, -də-) *tr.v.* **-ployed, -ploying, -ploys. 1.** To move (military forces) from one combat zone to another. **2.** To assign new tasks to (workers). **—re•de•ploy•ment** *n.*
re•de•sign (reé-di-zín, -də-) *tr.v.* **-signed, -signing, -signs.** To produce a new design for. **—re•de•sign** *n.*
re•de•vel•op (reé-di-véllәp, -də-) *v.* **-oped, -oping, -opes.** *—tr.* **1.** To develop (something) again. **2.** *Photography.* To tone or intensify (a developed negative) by a second developing process. **3.** To rebuild (an area, for example) according to new plans. *—intr.* To develop again. **—re•de•vel•op•er** *n.* **—re•de•vel•op•ment** *n.*
redevelopment area *n.* An urban area that is replanned and almost completely rebuilt.
red•eye (réd-ī) *n.* **1.** *U.S. Slang.* Whiskey of an inferior grade. **2.** Any of several red-eyed fishes; especially, the **rudd** *(see).*
red-faced (réd-fáyst) *adj.* Having a flushed face owing to embarrassment, anger, intoxication, or the like. **—red-faced•ly** *adv.*
red•fin (réd-fin) *n.* Any of several small, freshwater fishes of the genus *Notropis*, such as *N. cornutus*, that have reddish fins and are often kept in aquariums.
red fir *n.* **1.** An evergreen coniferous tree, *Abies magnifica*, of California and Oregon, having reddish wood valued as timber. **2.** The wood of this tree, or of similar trees, such as the **Douglas fir** *(see).*
red fire *n.* Any of various combustible compounds, especially containing salts of lithium or strontium, that burn with a bright red flame and are used in flares and fireworks.
red•fish (réd-fish) *n., pl.* **-fishes** or collectively **redfish. 1.** A male salmon that has just spawned. Compare **blackfish. 2.** Any of several fishes that are reddish in colour; especially, a bright-red, European food fish, *Sebastes marinus* of North Atlantic waters.
red fox *n.* Any of several foxes of the genus *Vulpes*, having reddish fur; especially, *V. vulpes*, of the Northern Hemisphere.
Red•ford (réd-fərd), **Robert** (1937–). U.S. actor and film director. His reputation as one of the biggest box-office stars was established in films such as *Butch Cassidy and the Sundance Kid* (1969), *The Candidate* (1972), *The Way We Were* (1973), *The Sting* (1973), and *All the President's Men* (1976). For the first film he directed, *Ordinary People*, he won an Academy Award as best director (1981).
red giant *n. Astronomy.* Any of a class of stars that are usually cool, very large, and are believed to be formed in the final stages of the evolution of certain stars.
Red•grave (réd-grayv), **Sir Michael (Scudamore)** (1908–). British actor. Beginning his stage career with the Liverpool Repertory Theatre in 1934, he went on to become one of the leading actors of his generation, especially in the plays of Shakespeare. His films include *The Lady Vanishes* (1938), the *Dam Busters* (1954), and *Goodbye Mr. Chips* (1969). His daughters Lynn Redgrave (1943–) and Vanessa Redgrave (1937–), and his son Corin Redgrave (1939–), are all experienced stage and screen actors.
Redgrave, Vanessa (1937–). British actress, daughter of Sir Michael. She won the *Evening Standard* award as best actress (1961) for her performances in *The Taming of the Shrew* and *As You Like*

red deer *Native to the woodlands of Europe, Asia, and northwest Africa, the red deer has long been hunted for both sport and food. The stags and hinds live separately except during the autumn breeding season.*

red fox *The red fox is the common fox of Europe and Asia. Adaptable in habits and diet, it manages to thrive even in towns and cities.*

redpoll *Redpolls are seed-eaters and make their nests in pine, birch, and alder trees. The male redpoll (above) is distinguished by its red forehead and pink breast.*

redshank *For most of the year, redshanks are sociable birds, often gathering in large flocks on muddy open shores. But from mid-April to June, mating pairs retire to build their nests away from the flock in damp grassy areas or marshland. The birds breed in Europe and Asia, but most migrate during the northern winter, sometimes as far as India and South Africa.*

red squirrel *Of the 200 species of squirrel, the red and grey squirrels are the most common. The red squirrel (above) is a Eurasian species that lives particularly in pine woods. In many parts of Britain, though, it has been supplanted by the imported North American grey.*

It with the Royal Shakespeare company. Her films include *Morgan, a Suitable Case for Treatment* (1966), *Isadora* (1969), and *Julia* (1977), for which she won an Academy Award as best supporting actress.

red grouse *n.* A reddish-brown grouse, *Lagopus lagopus* occurring on the moorlands of Great Britain and Ireland. Formerly called "moorcock".

Red Guard *n.* A member of a militant Chinese youth organisation that denounced opposition to the **Cultural Revolution** *(see).*

red gum[1] *n.* **1.** Any of several Australian trees of the genus *Eucalyptus,* especially, *E. camaldulensis.* **2.** The hard, reddish wood of any of these trees.

red gum[2] *n.* A disease, **strophulus** *(see).*

red-hand·ed (réd-hándid) *adj.* In the act of committing, or having just committed, a crime; in flagrante delicto: *caught red-handed.* —**red-hand·ed** *adv.* —**red-hand·ed·ly** *adv.*

red hat *n.* **1.** A large, red, tasselled hat presented to a newly created cardinal. It is never worn. **2.** This hat as a symbol of a cardinal's office.

red·head (réd-hed) *n.* **1.** A person with red hair. **2.** A North American duck, *Aythya americana,* of which the male has black and grey plumage and a reddish head.

red heat *n.* **1.** The temperature of a red-hot substance. **2.** The physical condition of a red-hot substance.

red herring *n.* **1.** Something that draws attention away from the matter or issue at hand. **2.** A smoked herring having a reddish colour. [From the use of red herring to give the scent in exercising hunting dogs.]

red-hot (réd-hót) *adj.* **1.** Heated so as to emit red light (a temperature of about 500°C). **2.** Very hot. **3.** Heated, as with excitement, anger, or enthusiasm. **4.** New; very recent: *red-hot information.*

red-hot poker *n.* Any of several plants of the African genus *Kniphofia,* cultivated as garden plants for their cylindrical heads of red or yellow flowers.

re·di·a (réedi-ə) *n., pl.* **-diae** (-ee). A larva of parasitic flukes that gives rise to other rediae or to cercaria larvae. [New Latin, after Francesco *Redi* (1629–97), Italian naturalist.]

Re·dif·fu·sion (ree-di-féwzh'n) *n.* A trademark for a system of **cable television** *(see).*

Red Indian *n.* A North American Indian.

red·in·gote (rédding-gōt) *n.* **1.** A man's long double-breasted overcoat with a full skirt. **2.** A woman's full-length unlined coat or dress open down the front to show a dress or underskirt. [French, from English *riding coat.*]

red·in·te·grate (red-ínti-grayt, rid-) *v.* **-grated, -grating, -grates.** —*tr.* To restore to a complete, whole, or harmonious state. —*intr. Psychology.* To undergo redintegration. [Middle English, from Latin *redintegrāre* : *red-,* RE- + *integrāre,* to INTEGRATE.]

red·in·te·gra·tion (red-ínti-gráysh'n, rid-) *n.* **1.** *Psychology.* The revival of a complete previous mental state due to recurrence of part of the complex of stimuli that gave rise to that previous mental state. **2.** The act or process or redintegrating.

re·dis·tri·bute (ree-diss-tríbbewt ‖ -distri-bewt) *tr.v.* **-uted, -uting, -utes.** To distribute again in a different way; reallocate. —**re·dis·tri·bu·tion** (ree-distri-béwsh'n) *n.* —**re·dis·trib·u·tive** (ree-diss-tríb-bewtiv ‖ -distri-bewtiv) *adj.*

red lead *n.* A bright-red powder, Pb_3O_4, used in paints, glass, pottery, and pipe-joint packing. Also called "minium".

red-let·ter (réd-léttər) *adj.* Memorable: *a red-letter day.* [From the rubrication of feasts in church calendars.]

red light *n.* **1.** A red traffic light or other signal to stop. Also called "red". **2.** A danger signal.

red-light district (réd-lît) *n.* A district containing many brothels.

red man *n. Informal.* A North American Indian. Often considered offensive.

red meat *n.* Dark-coloured meat, such as beef or lamb. Compare **white meat.**

Red·mond (réd-mənd), **John Edward** (1856–1918). Irish politician. Succeeding Parnell as the leader of the Parliamentary Home Rule movement, he achieved many of the movement's objectives. His support for Britain during World War I and the rise of Sinn Fein undermined his influence.

red mullet *n. British.* Any marine fish of the family Mullidae, several species of which are used as food. Also *U.S.* "goatfish".

red·neck (réd-nek) *n. Informal.* **1.** Any of the white rural labouring class in the southern United States. **2.** *Chiefly U.S.* A manual worker having bigoted views. Used derogatorily. [Referring to the sunburnt necks of labourers.]

re·do (ree-dŏo) *tr.v.* **-did** (-díd), **-done** (-dún), **-doing, -does** (-dúz). **1.** To do again. **2.** To redecorate thoroughly; refurbish.

red ochre *n.* **1.** A natural red mixture of clay and iron oxide; an **ochre** *(see).* **2.** A refined form of this mixture used as pigment.

red·o·lent (réddələnt) *adj.* **1.** Having or emitting fragrance; pleasantly odorous. **2.** Smelling. Used with *of: boatyards redolent of tar.* **3.** Evocative or reminiscent. Used with *of* or *with: music redolent of Mozart.* [Middle English, from Old French, from Latin *redolēns* (stem *redolent-*), present participle of *redolēre,* to emit an odour : *red-, re-,* in response, back + *olēre,* to smell.] —**red·o·lence, red·o·len·cy** *n.* —**red·o·lent·ly** *adv.*

Re·don (rə-dón), **Odilon** (1840–1916). French painter, lithographer, and etcher, regarded by the surrealists as one of their forerunners. He first gained notice by his eerie, dreamlike lithographs, and was especially famous for his paintings of flowers.

re·dou·ble (ree-dúbb'l, ri-) *v.* **-bled, -bling, -bles.** —*tr.* **1.** To increase or intensify greatly: *redouble one's efforts.* **2.** To double. **3.** *Archaic.* To echo or re-echo. **4.** To double (a double) in bridge. —*intr.* **1.** To increase or intensify greatly: *Our efforts redoubled.* **2.** To be doubled; become twice as much or as great. **3.** *Archaic.* To echo; reverberate. **4.** To double a double in bridge.

re·doubt (ri-dówt, rə-) *n.* **1.** A small, often temporary defensive fortification, usually standing alone. **2.** Any defensive stronghold. **3.** Any place of refuge. [French *redoute,* from obsolete Italian *ridotta,* from Medieval Latin *reductus,* concealed place, from Latin, withdrawn, from the past participle of *redūcere,* withdraw : *re-,* back + *dūcere,* to lead.]

re·doubt·a·ble (ri-dówtəb'l, rə-) *adj.* **1. a.** Awesome; fearsome. **b.** Formidable. **2.** Worthy of respect or honour. [Middle English, from Old French *redoutable,* from *redouter,* to dread : *re-* (intensive) + *douter,* to fear, DOUBT.] —**re·doubt·a·bly** *adv.*

re·dound (ri-dównd, rə-) ‖ *West Indies also* -dúngd) *intr.v.* **-dounded, -dounding, -dounds.** **1.** To have an effect or consequence. **2.** To return, rebound, or recoil. Used with *on* on *upon.* **3.** *Archaic.* To contribute; accrue. [Middle English *redounden,* to abound, from Old French *redonder,* from Latin *redundāre,* to overflow : *red-, re-* (intensive) + *undāre,* to overflow, surge, from *unda,* wave.]

re·dox (ree-doks) *n. Chemistry.* **Oxidation-reduction** *(see).* Also used adjectively; *a redox reaction.* [*Red*uction of *ox*idation.]

red pepper *n.* **1.** A **pimiento** *(see).* **2. Cayenne pepper** *(see).*

red pine *n.* A New Zealand coniferous tree, *Dacrydium cupressinum.* Also called "rimu".

Red Planet *n. Informal.* The planet **Mars** *(see).* Preceded by *the.*

red·poll (réd-pōl, -pol) *n.* Any of several finches of the genus *Acanthis;* especially *A. flammea,* having brownish plumage and a red crown.

Red Poll *n.* Also **Red Polled.** Any of a breed of reddish, hornless cattle developed in England and raised for dairy and meat products.

---

red shift

MOVEMENT ALTERS WAVELENGTH

Why colour is a clue to the movement of stars

Light from the stars changes colour for the same reason that the whistle of a passing train changes pitch – because of a phenomenon known as the Doppler effect. Christian Doppler, the 19th-century Austrian physicist who first explained the phenomenon, showed that the wavelength of light or sound waves changes according to the movement of the wave source. Waves from a source moving towards an observer bunch up and become shorter; waves from a receding source are strung out, making them longer than normal. So the pitch of a train whistle rises as the train approaches, because higher sounds have shorter wavelengths, then drops as the train moves away.

Similarly, light from a star approaching the Earth appears bluer than it should because lines in the spectrum of starlight have shifted towards the blue end of the spectrum. Conversely, light from a receding star appears redder than it should. Lines in the spectrum are shifted towards the red end, a phenomenon known as the red shift. Light from all the distant galaxies so far observed is "red-shifted" to a considerable degree, indicating that the galaxies are moving away from the Earth at very high speeds, and thus that the universe as a whole is expanding.

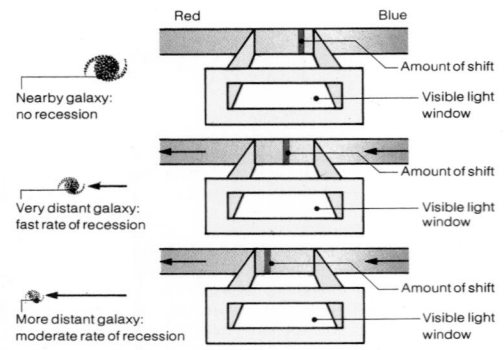

RECEIVING GALAXIES *As distant galaxies recede from the Earth, their light shifts towards the red end of the part of the spectrum visible to the human eye (represented as the "visible light window" above). The amount of shift shows how fast different galaxies are receding and what their present distance is from the Earth.*

re·draft (rée-dra̋aft || -dráft) *tr.v.* **-drafted, -drafting, -drafts.** To make a new or revised version of (a written document, for example). ~*n.* **1.** A second draft; a revision. **2.** A second bill of exchange on a drawee for the amount of a dishonoured bill plus costs.

re·dress (ri-dréss, rə-) *tr.v.* **-dressed, -dressing, -dresses. 1.** To set right; remedy or rectify. **2.** To make amends for. **3.** To adjust (a balance, for example) so as to produce a condition of equality. —See Synonyms at **correct.**
~*n.* (ri-dréss, rə- || rée-dress). **1.** Satisfaction or amends for wrong done; compensation. **2. a.** Correction or setting right. **b.** A means of rectification: *We had no redress.* —See Synonyms at **reparation.** [Middle English *redressen,* from Old French *redresser* : *re-,* back + *dresser,* to make straight, DRESS.] —**re·dress·able, re·dress·i·ble** *adj.* —**re·dress·al** *n.* —**re·dress·er, re·dres·sor** *n.*

red salmon *n.* The **sockeye salmon** *(see).*

Red Sea. Sea running northwest from the Gulf of Aden to the Sinai Peninsula in Egypt, where it branches into the Gulf of Aqaba to the east and the Gulf of Suez to the west. It has been joined to the Mediterranean Sea by the Suez Canal since 1869 and is one of the world's major shipping routes, connecting Europe with the Far East and Australia. It is coloured red at certain times of the year owing to the reddish algae that appear in it.

red setter *n.* An **Irish setter** *(see).*

red·shank (réd-shangk) *n.* **1.** An Old World wading bird, *Tringa totanus,* having long red legs. **2.** A plant, **persicaria** *(see).*

red shift, red·shift (réd-shift, -shift) *n.* **1.** An increase apparent in the wavelength of radiation emitted by a receding celestial body as a consequence of the **Doppler effect** *(see)* as seen by a stationary observer. Compare **blue shift. 2.** A similar increase in wavelength resulting from the presence of a high gravitational field. In this sense, also called "Einstein shift", "gravitational red shift".

red·shift (réd-shift) *v.* **-shifted, -shifting, -shifts.** —*tr.* To cause (radiation or spectral lines) to change to a longer wavelength. —*intr.* To move or change to a longer wavelength.

red-short (réd-shórt) *adj.* Brittle when red-hot. Said of iron or steel. —**red-short·ness** *n.*

red·skin (réd-skin) *n. Informal.* A North American Indian. Usually considered offensive.

red snapper *n.* Any of several tropical and semitropical marine food fishes of the genus *Lutjanus,* having red or reddish bodies.

red spider *n.* Also **red spider mite.** See **spider mite.**

Red Spot *n. Astronomy.* A very large, reddish, variable oval patch (about 1 400 kilometres by up to 48 000 kilometres) occurring south of the equator in the atmosphere of the planet Jupiter. Also called "Great Red Spot".

red squirrel *n.* **1.** A Eurasian squirrel, *Sciurus vulgaris* having reddish or tawny fur. **2.** Any of several reddish North American squirrels. See **chickadee.**

red·start (réd-staart) *n.* **1.** Any bird of the Eurasian genus *Phoenicurus;* especially, *P. phoenicurus,* of Europe, which has a greyish plumage with a black throat and a red tail. **2.** A North American bird, *Setophaga ruticilla,* the male of which is black with orange markings on wings and tail. [RED + obsolete *start,* tail, from Middle English *stert,* Old English *steort.*]

red tape *n.* Official requirements and procedures, such as the filling in of forms, considered as an obstructive bureaucratic device. [From the tape used to tie English governmental documents.]

red tide *n.* Ocean waters coloured by the proliferation of red, one-celled, plantlike animals occurring in sufficient numbers to kill fish.

re·duce (ri-déwss, rə- || -dóoss) *v.* **-duced, -ducing, -duces.** —*tr.* **1. a.** To lessen in extent, amount, number, degree, price, or other quality; diminish. **b.** To degrade or lower in rank, position, social circumstances, or the like. **2.** To gain control of, especially by conquest. **3.** To put in order or arrange systematically. **4.** To separate into components by analysis. **5.** To bring to a specified state or condition, as by simplification or transformation: *reduced him to tears.* **6.** To powder or pulverise. **7.** To cause (meat juices, for example) to thicken by evaporating excess water. **8.** *Chemistry.* **a.** To remove oxygen from (a compound), as in the smelting of metal ores. **b.** To add hydrogen to (a compound), as in hydrogenation reactions. **c.** To add electrons to (a compound, ion, or group), as in the change of ferric ions (Fe^{3+}) to ferrous ions (Fe^{2+}). **9.** *Mathematics.* To simplify the form of (an expression) without changing the value. **10.** To remove some of the silver from (an emulsion) forming a photographic image. **11.** To restore (a fracture or dislocation, or a fractured or displaced body part) to normal. —*intr.* **1. a.** To become diminished. **b.** To lose weight, as by dieting. **2.** To amount to or be viewable as something specified. Used with *to*: *the problem reduces to a question of time and money.* **3.** To thicken, especially by evaporation. Used of sauces and other liquids. **4.** *Chemistry.* To undergo reduction; lose oxygen or gain hydrogen or electrons. Used of chemical compounds. —See Synonyms at **decrease.** [Middle English *reducen,* to bring back, from Latin *redūcere* : *re-,* back, again + *dūcere,* to lead.] —**re·duc·i·bil·i·ty** (-ə-billəti) *n.* —**re·duc·i·ble** *adj.* —**re·duc·i·bly** *adv.*

re·duced (ri-déwst, rə- || -dóost) *adj.* **1.** Less in extent, amount, number, degree, price, or other quality: *at a reduced rate.* **2.** Less prosperous than formerly: *in reduced circumstances.*

re·duc·er (ri-déwssər, rə- || -dóossər) *n.* **1.** One that reduces. **2.** A chemical solution for reducing the density of photographic negatives or prints. **3.** A threaded cylinder for connecting pipes of different diameter.

re·duc·ing agent (ri-déwssing || -dóossing) *n.* A substance that chemically reduces other substances.

re·duc·tase (ri-dúkt-ayz, rə-, -ayss) *n.* Any enzyme that catalyses biochemical reduction reactions. [REDUCT(ION) + -ASE.]

re·duc·ti·o ad ab·sur·dum (ri-dúk-ti-ō ad əb-súrdəm, -shi-, ab-) *n.* **1.** Disproof of a proposition by showing the absurdity of its inevitable conclusion. **2.** Proof of a proposition by disproving its negation by means of reductio ad absurdum. **3.** The following through of a principle or idea to absurdity. [Latin, "reduction to absurdity"].

re·duc·tion (ri-dúksh'n, rə-) *n. Abbr.* **red. 1. a.** The act or process of reducing. **b.** The process or state of being reduced. **2. a.** The result of reducing. **b.** A reprographic copy of a picture, text, or the like, that is smaller than the original. **3.** The amount by which anything is lessened or diminished. **4.** The process of reducing or a chemical reaction in which something is reduced. Compare **oxidation. 5. a.** The cancelling of common factors in the numerator and denominator of a fraction. **b.** The converting of a fraction to its decimal equivalent. [Middle English *reduccion,* from Old French *reduction,* from Late Latin *reductiō* (stem *reductiōn-*), from Latin, from *redūcere,* to REDUCE.] —**re·duc·tion·al, re·duc·tive** *adj.*

reduction division *n. Biology.* **1.** The first meiotic division, in which the chromosome number is halved. **2. Meiosis** *(see).*

re·duc·tion·ism (ri-dúksh'n-iz'm, rə-) *n.* **1.** The systematic reduction of complicated information or objects to simple components. **2.** The theory or belief that a complex system can be understood completely on the basis of its simple constituents. —**re·duc·tion·ist** *n. & adj.*

re·dun·dan·cy (ri-dún-dən-si) *n., pl.* **-cies.** Also **re·dun·dance** (-dənss). **1.** The state, condition, or quality of being redundant, especially: **a.** Superfluity or excess. **b.** Unnecessary repetition. **c.** *Chiefly British.* The losing of a job that has been eliminated; dismissal from a position that then ceases to exist: *the threat of redundancy.* **2.** *Chiefly British.* **a.** An instance of the loss of a job which has been eliminated: *They made 13 redundancies.* **b.** Loosely, compensation for being made redundant; redundancy payment. **3.** Duplication or repetition of elements in electronic or mechanical equipment to provide alternative functional channels in case of failure. **4.** Repetition of parts or all of a message to circumvent transmission errors.

re·dun·dant (ri-dúndənt) *adj.* **1.** Exceeding what is necessary or natural; superfluous. **2.** Needlessly repetitive; verbose. **3.** Copious or profuse. **4.** *Chiefly British.* Unemployed or about to be unemployed because of the elimination of one's job. [Latin *redundāns* (stem *redundant-*), present participle of *redundāre,* to overflow, run back : *red-, re-,* back + *undāre,* to overflow, from *unda,* wave.] —**re·dun·dant·ly** *adv.*

re·du·pli·cate (ri-déwpli-kayt, rə- || -dóopli-) *v.* **-cated, -cating, -cates.** —*tr.* **1.** To repeat or redouble. **2.** *Linguistics.* **a.** To double (the initial syllable or all of a root word) to produce an inflectional or derivational form. **b.** To form (a new word) by doubling all or part of a word. —*intr.* To be doubled.
~*adj.* (-ət, -it). **1.** Doubled. **2.** *Botany.* Having outward-curved margins: *reduplicate petals.* [Late Latin *reduplicāre* : Latin *re-,* again + *duplicāre,* to DUPLICATE.]

re·du·pli·ca·tion (ri-déwpli-káysh'n, rə- || -dóopli-) *n.* **1.** Reduplicating or the state of being reduplicated. **2.** A product or result of reduplicating. **3.** A word formed by or containing a reduplicated element. **4.** The added element in a word form that is reduplicated. —**re·du·pli·ca·tive** (-kətiv, -kaytiv) *adj.* —**re·du·pli·ca·tive·ly** *adv.*

re·du·vi·id (ri-déwvi-id, rə- || -dóovi-) *n.* Any bloodsucking insect of the family Reduviidae. [New Latin *Reduviidae,* from Latin *reduvia, redivia,* hangnail, exuviae : *red-,* RE- + *-uvia,* from *-uere,* to put on.] —**re·du·vi·id** *adj.*

red·wa·ter (réd-wawtər || *U.S. also* -wottər) *n.* A disease of cattle caused by infestation with the protozoan *Babesia bovis* and characterised by the passage of red urine due to the destruction of red blood cells.

red whortleberry *n.* A shrub, the **cowberry** *(see).*

red·wing (réd-wing) *n.* A European thrush, *Turdus iliacus,* having reddish feathers under the wings and a white eyestripe.

red·wood (réd-wood) *n.* **1.** A very tall evergreen coniferous tree, *Sequoia sempervirens,* of coastal and northern California. Compare **giant sequoia. 2.** The soft, reddish wood of this tree. **3.** Any of various woods of reddish colour or yielding red dye.

reebok. Variant of **rhebok.**

re·ech·o, re·echo (ree-éckō, ri-) *v.* **-oed, -oing, -oes.** —*intr.* **1.** To be repeated again and again by or as if by an echo. **2.** To resound or reverberate with or as if with repeated echoes. —*tr.* To echo back repeatedly.

reed (reed) *n.* **1. a.** Any of various tall aquatic grasses having jointed, hollow stalks; especially, any of the genus *Phragmites,* such as *P. communis.* **b.** The stalk of any of these plants. **c.** A mass of reeds. **d.** Reeds collectively, especially for use as thatching material. **2.** A primitive wind instrument made of such a hollow stalk. **3.** *Music.* **a.** A flexible strip of cane or metal set into the mouthpiece of certain musical instruments to produce tone by vibrating in response to a stream of air. **b.** An instrument, such as an oboe or clarinet, fitted with a reed. **4.** A narrow, movable frame on a loom, fitted with reed or metal strips that separate the warp threads. **5.** *Architecture.* A reeding. **6.** An ancient Hebrew unit of length, equivalent to six cubits.
~*tr.v.* **reeded, reeding, reeds. 1.** To thatch with reed. **2.** *Architec-*

redstart *The European redstart,* Phoenicurus phoenicurus *(above), gets its name from its reddish tail;* steort *is an Old English word for tail. The birds nest in tree holes or in hollows on the ground in Europe and western Asia, and migrate for the northern winter to tropical Africa. They feed mainly on insects.*

redwing *The European redwing,* Turdus iliacus *(above), is one of the smaller members of the thrush family; fully grown, it is about 21 centimetres (8¼ inches) long. It breeds in northern Europe and Asia, building nests of grass in trees, bushes, or on the ground, and migrates as far as North Africa in winter.*

reed *Tall grasses have been used since prehistoric times to make clothing and domestic goods such as mats. The reed boat shown here is used by the Uru people of Lake Titicaca in South America.*

ture. To decorate with reeding. [Middle English *rede, reod,* Old English *hrēod.*]

Reed (reed), **Sir Carol** (1906–76). British film director, one of the most acclaimed of the post-World War II era. His most notable films since the war were *The Third Man* (1949), *Our Man in Havana* (1959), *The Agony and the Ecstasy* (1965), and *Oliver!* (1968), the last of which won him an Academy Award.

Reed, John (1887–1920). U.S. journalist and Communist leader. As a reporter in World War I he was in Petrograd during the October Revolution (1917), and recorded the experience in his famous book, *Ten Days That Shook the World* (1919), the best eye-witness account of the Bolshevik seizure of power. Expelled from the U.S. Socialist Convention in 1919, he organised the left-wing splinter group of the movement into the Communist Labour party. In 1919 he returned to the U.S.S.R., where he worked in the department of propaganda. He died of typhus and was buried in the Kremlin.

reed·buck (reéd-buk) *n.* Any of several African antelopes of the genus *Redunca,* having incurved horns. Also called "nagor". [Translation of Afrikaans *rietbok.*]

reed bunting *n.* A common European bunting, *Emberiza schoeniclus,* that frequents reed beds and has a brownish plumage. The head of the male is black in summer. Also called "reed sparrow".

reed grass *n.* A perennial Eurasian grass, *Glyceria maxima,* having tall erect stems and growing in rivers and ponds.

reed·ing (reéding) *n.* **1.** *Architecture.* A convex decorative moulding having parallel strips resembling thin reeds. **2.** The indentations on the edge of a coin; milling.

reed·ling (reédling) *n.* A bird, the **bearded reedling** *(see).*

reed mace *n.* Any of various reedlike marsh plants of the genus *Typha;* especially, *T. latifolia,* having dense, cylindrical heads of small brown flowers. Also called "bulrush", "cat's tail".

reed organ *n.* Any of various keyboard instruments in which vibrating reeds produce notes when acted upon by currents of air.

reed pipe *n.* An organ pipe with a reed that vibrates and produces a note when air is forced through it. Compare **flue pipe.**

reed stop *n.* A stop on an organ made up of reed pipes. Compare **flue stop.**

re·ed·u·cate (reé-éddew-kayt, ree-) *tr.v.* **-cated, -cating, -cates. 1.** To educate again or anew; especially, to indoctrinate (criminals and political dissidents, for example) for purposes of rehabilitation. **2.** To retrain to function effectively, especially in a new working capacity. **—re·ed·u·ca·tion** (-káysh'n) *n.*

reed warbler *n.* An Old World warbler of the genus *Acrocephalus;* especially, *A. scirpaceus,* which frequents reed beds and has reddish-brown plumage.

reed·y (reédi) *adj.* **-ier, -iest. 1.** Full of reeds. **2.** Made of reeds. **3.** Resembling a reed especially in being slender or fragile. **4.** Having or designating a tone like that of a reed instrument; shrill or high-pitched. **—reed·i·ness** *n.*

reef[1] (reef) *n.* **1.** *Geology.* A strip or ridge of rocks, sand, or soil that rises to or near the surface of a body of water. **2.** A **coral reef** *(see).* **3.** In mining, a vein of ore. **4.** In Africa, the Precambrian gold-bearing conglomerates. —See Usage note at **shoal.** [Earlier *riff,* from Middle Dutch *rif,* ridge, perhaps from Old Norse, rib, ridge.] **—reef·y** *adj.*

reef[2] *n. Nautical.* A portion of a sail rolled and tied down to lessen the area exposed to the wind.
~*v.* **reefed, reefing, reefs.** —*tr.* **1.** To reduce the size of (a sail) by tucking in a part and tying it to or rolling it around a yard. **2.** To shorten (a topmast or bowsprit) by taking part in. —*intr.* To reduce the size of a sail by taking in reefs. [Middle English *riff,* from Old Norse *rif,* ridge, rib.]

Reef, the. See **Witwatersrand.**

reef·er[1] (reéfər) *n.* **1.** One who reefs, such as a midshipman. **2.** A short, heavy, close-fitting, double-breasted jacket. In this sense also called "reefing jacket".

reefer[2] *n. Slang.* A marijuana cigarette. Not in current usage. [Perhaps from REEF (to roll up and shorten a sail).]

reef knot *Reef knots are used to make a long rope from two shorter ones. The Greeks and Romans were familiar with this knot; it is one of the few to be accurately depicted in ancient works of art.*

reef knot *n.* A common knot composed of two overhand knots with ends lying parallel. Also called "flat knot", *U.S.* "square knot".

reek (reek) *v.* **reeked, reeking, reeks.** —*intr.* **1. a.** To give off or become permeated with a strong and unpleasant odour. **b.** *Regional.* To give off smoke, steam, or fumes. **2.** To be pervaded by something, especially of an unpleasant nature: *The whole business reeks of corruption.* —*tr.* **1.** To emit or exude (smoke or odours, for example). **2.** To process or treat by exposing to the action of smoke.
~*n.* **1.** A strong and offensive odour; a stench. **2.** *Regional.* Vapour; smoke; steam. [Middle English *reken,* Old English *rēocan,* from Germanic.] **—reek·er** *n.* **—reek·y** *adj.*

reel[1] (reel) *n.* **1.** A cylinder, spool, or frame that turns on an axis and is used for winding rope, tape, or other flexible materials. **2.** Such a device attached to a fishing rod to let out or wind up the line. **3.** *British.* A small spool with wide ends round which sewing thread is wound. **4. a.** The wire, film, or other material wound on a reel. **b.** The quantity of such material wound on one reel.
~*tr.v.* **reeled, reeling, reels. 1.** To wind upon a reel. **2.** To wind or draw on a reel. Used with *in, out,* or *up*: *reel in a fish.* **3.** To recite rapidly and effortlessly. Used with *off.* [Middle English *reel,* Old English *hrēol*†.] **—reel·a·ble** *adj.*

reel[2] *v.* **reeled, reeling, reels.** —*intr.* **1.** To be thrown off balance or fall back: *He reeled under the blow.* **2.** To stagger, lurch, or sway, as from drunkenness. **3.** To go round and round in a whirling motion. **4.** To feel dizzy. —*tr.* To cause to reel.
~*n.* A staggering, swaying, or whirling movement. [Middle English *relen,* probably from REEL (spool).] **—reel·er** *n.*

reel[3] *n.* **1.** Any of various fast dances in 4/4 time, of Scottish origin. **2.** The music for a reel. [From REEL (whirl).]

reel-to-reel (reél-tə-reél, -tōō-) *adj.* Of, using, or designating magnetic tape that is wound onto one typically exposed reel from another: *reel-to-reel tape recorder.* Compare **cassette.**

re-en·act, re·enact (reé-i-nákt, -e-) *tr.v.* **-acted, -acting, -acts. 1.** To act out again (an earlier incident, for example). **2.** To enact (a law, for example) again or anew. **—re-en·act·ment** *n.*

re-en·trant, re·en·trant (ree-éntrənt, ri-) *adj.* Pointing inwards.
~*n.* **1.** A re-entrant angle or part. **2.** A marked indentation into a landform.

re-entrant angle *n.* An interior angle of a polygon greater than 180°.

re-en·try, re·en·try (ree-éntri) *n., pl.* **-tries. 1.** The act of entering again or anew; a second or subsequent entry. **2.** *Law.* The recovery of possession of premises by the lessor under a right reserved in the lease or contract. **3.** In bridge and whist: **a.** The act of regaining the lead by taking a trick. **b.** The card that will take a trick and thus regain the lead. **4.** *Aerospace.* The return of a missile or spacecraft into the earth's atmosphere.

reest (reest) *intr.v.* **reested, reesting, reests.** *Chiefly Scottish.* To stop suddenly and refuse to budge; baulk. Used of a horse. [Probably variant of Scottish *arreest,* to ARREST.] **—reest·y** *adj.*

reeve[1] (reev) *n.* **1.** A high officer of local administration appointed by the Anglo-Saxon kings. **2.** In the later medieval period, a bailiff or steward of a manor. **3.** Any of various minor local officers. **4.** The elected president of a local council in some parts of Canada. [Middle English *reve, reeve,* Old English *(ge)rēfa,* from *rōf* (unattested), assembly.]

reeve[2] *tr.v.* **rove** (rōv) or **reeved, reeving, reeves.** *Nautical.* **1.** To pass (a rope or rod) through a hole, ring, pulley, or block. **2.** To fasten (a block, for example) by such a procedure. [Probably from Dutch *rēven,* to REEF (sail).]

reeve[3] *n.* A bird, the female **ruff** *(see).* [17th century.]

Reeves (reevz), **William Pember** (1857–1932). New Zealand politician. He entered the New Zealand parliament as a Liberal in 1887 and as Minister of Labour (1891–96) was chiefly responsible for introducing the most progressive welfare and labour legislation then known in the world. He resigned his seat in 1896 to write a history of New Zealand, *The Long White Cloud* (1898), and other books. From 1905 to 1908 he was high commissioner to London and from 1908 to 1919 director of the London School of Economics.

re-ex·am·ine, re·ex·am·ine (reé-ig-zámmin, -eg-, -ik-) *tr.v.* **-ined, -ining, -ines. 1.** To examine again or anew; review. **2.** *Law.* To question (one's own witness) again after cross-examination. Used of a lawyer. **—re-ex·am·i·na·tion** (-áysh'n) *n.*

re-ex·port, re·ex·port (reé-ek-spórt, -ik-, *also* -ékspawrt || -spṓrt) *tr.v.* **-ported, -porting, -ports.** To export (imported goods), often after processing.
~*n.* (reé-ék-spawrt || -spōrt). **1.** The act of re-exporting. **2.** Something re-exported. **—re-ex·por·ta·tion** (-spawr-táysh'n || -spōr-) *n.*

ref (ref) *n. Informal.* A referee at a sports event.

ref. 1. referee. **2.** reference; referred. **3.** refining. **4.** reformation; reformed. **5.** refunding.

re·face (reé-fáyss) *tr.v.* **-faced, -facing, -faces. 1.** To renew or repair the surface of (a building, for example). **2.** To give a new facing to (a garment, for example).

re·fect (ri-fékt, rə-) *tr.v.* **-fected, -fecting, -fects.** *Archaic.* To supply with food and drink. [Latin *reficere* (past participle *refectus*), to refresh : *re-,* again + *facere,* to make.]

re·fec·tion (ri-féksh'n, rə-) *n. Archaic.* **1.** Refreshment with food and drink. **2.** A light meal or repast. [Middle English *refeccioun,* from Old French *refection,* from Latin *refectiō* (stem *refectiōn-*), a restoring, from *reficere,* to refresh. See **refect.**]

re·fec·to·ry (ri-féktəri, rə-; *also, chiefly in monasteries,* réffik-tri, réffi-, -təri) *n., pl.* **-ries.** A room where meals are served, as in an institution such as a monastery or college. [Late Latin *refectōrium,* from Latin *reficere,* to REFECT.]

re·fer (ri-fér, rə-) *v.* **-ferred, -ferring, -fers.** —*tr.* **1.** To direct to a source for help or information: *refer a patient to a specialist.* **2.** *Formal.* To assign or attribute (an effect, for example) to some cause; ascribe responsibility for: *referred the cure to prayer.* **3.** To assign to or regard as belonging to a specified category, place, or time: *referred sharks to the fishes; referred dinosaurs to prehistoric times.* **4.** To submit (a matter in dispute) to an authority for arbitration, decision, or examination. **5.** To direct a person's attention to: *referred the article to me.* **6.** *British.* To fail (a student, for example) in an examination. **7.** To return (a text, for example) to its originator for improvement. **8.** To cause or experience: *referred pain.* Used with *to,* or sometimes *back to,* in most senses. —*intr.* **1.** To pertain; concern; apply: *a provision referring only to officers.* **2.** To allude or direct notice or attention; make reference. **3.** To have recourse, as for information or authority. Used with *to* in all senses. [Middle English *refer(r)en,* from Old French *referer,* from Latin *referre,* refer to, carry back : *re-,* back, again + *ferre,* to carry.] **—ref·er·a·ble** (réffrəb'l), **re·fer·ra·ble** (ri-fér-əb'l, rə-) *adj.* **—re·fer·ral** (ri-fér-əl) *n.* **—re·fer·rer** *n.*

Usage: In the general sense of "directing to a source", formal usage avoids the use of *refer back,* unless the implication is that a second act of reference is involved *(I referred him back to the passage he had mentioned earlier). Let me refer you to a good book on the subject* is the standard form, *back* being unnecessary.

ref·e·ree (réffə-rée) *n. Abbr.* **ref. 1.** One to whom something is referred, as for settlement or decision; an arbitrator. **2.** *Sports.* An official supervising and judging play, as in boxing and football. **3. a.** One willing to testify to the ability or character of an applicant, especially for employment. **b.** One who carefully reads a new scientific or scholarly work to decide whether it should be published. **4.** *Law.* A judicial official to whom certain cases are referred for adjudication, especially in civil cases in which both parties agree to this procedure or in which complex documents must be analysed. See **Official Referee.** —See Synonyms at **judge.**
~*v.* **refereed, -reeing, -rees.** —*tr.* To judge or supervise as referee. —*intr.* To act as referee.

ref·er·ence (réffrənss, réffərənss) *n. Abbr.* **ref. 1.** The act of referring or the state of being referred. **2.** That to which something refers. **3.** Relation, connection, or correspondence: *with reference to your complaint.* **4. a.** A direction or attention: *many references to learned journals.* **b.** An allusion, as to a person, event, or situation. **5. a.** A note in a publication referring the reader to another passage or source. **b.** The passage or source so referred to. **c.** A mark directing the reader to a footnote or other information. Also called "reference mark". **6.** *Law.* The submission of a case to a referee. **7. a.** A statement by one person attesting to another's ability, experience, character, or creditworthiness. **b.** Someone willing to provide such a testimonial. **8. a.** A source of information and facts: *works of reference.* Also used adjectivally: *a reference library.* **b.** The act of searching for information: *for quick reference.* **9.** An object or activity taken as a norm; a standard: *using the dollar as a reference.* Also called "point of reference". —*tr.v.* **referenced, -encing, -ences. 1.** To furnish (a text or publication, for example) with references. **2.** To refer to or quote as a reference. **—ref·er·enc·er** *n.* **—ref·er·en·tial** (réffə-rénsh'l) *adj.*

reference book *n.* **1.** A book, such as a dictionary or an encyclopedia, that is consulted for specific points of information, rather than read continuously. **2.** In South Africa, an identity document, recording domicile and employment record and other personal information, that all black adults are required to carry in white areas. In this sense, also called "pass", "passbook".

reference group *n. Sociology.* A group of people whose standards and behaviour affect and are admired by a person not necessarily in the group. Compare **membership group, peer group.**

ref·er·en·dum (réffə-rén-dəm) *n., pl.* **-dums** or **-da** (-də). **1. a.** The submission of a proposed public measure or actual statute to a direct popular vote. **b.** Such a vote. Compare **plebiscite. 2.** The submission of any matter concerning a group to the direct vote of its members. **3.** A note from a diplomat to his government requesting instructions. [Latin, neuter gerundive of *referre,* to REFER.]

ref·er·ent (réffrənt, réffərənt) *n.* **1.** One that is referred to; specifically, the object, event, or idea that a word, phrase, or sign represents. **2.** One that refers. **3.** *Logic.* The first term in a proposition, from which the relation proceeds; for example, in the sentence *Dogs like bones, dogs* is the referent. [Latin *referēns* (stem *referent-*), present participle of *referre,* REFER.] **—ref·er·ent** *adj.*

re·ferred pain (ri-férd, rə-) *n.* Pain felt in a part of the body other than the site of the disease or injury.

ref·fo, re·fo (réffō) *n., pl.* **-fos.** *Australian Slang.* A refugee, usually from Europe.

re·fill (rée-fíl) *v.* **-filled, -filling, -fills.** —*tr.* To fill again. —*intr.* To become full again.
~*n.* (rée-fil, *rarely* -fíl). **1.** A product, such as an ink cartridge, intended to replace the used contents of a container. **2. a.** A second or subsequent filling. **b.** *British Informal.* A further measure of a drink, especially an alcoholic drink, poured into a person's glass or cup when it is empty.

re·fine (ri-fín, rə-) *v.* **-fined, -fining, -fines.** —*tr.* **1.** To remove unwanted substances from; purify. **2.** To separate (crude oil, for example) into distinct substances. **3.** To remove by purifying. Used with *out* or *away.* **4.** To free from coarse characteristics; make more elegant, polished, or subtle. **5.** To improve, as by making more precise: *refine a theory.* —*intr.* **1.** To become free of impurities. **2.** To acquire polish or elegance. **3.** To use subtlety and precise distinctions in thought or speech. **4.** To make improvements, as by making something clearer or more precise. Used with *on* or *upon.* [RE- + FINE (verb).] **—re·fin·a·ble** *adj.* **—re·fin·er** *n.*

re·fined (ri-fínd, rə-) *adj.* **1.** Free from coarseness or vulgarity; polite; genteel. **2.** Free of impurities; purified. **3.** Precise to a fine degree; subtle; exact.

re·fine·ment (ri-fín-mənt, rə-) *n.* **1. a.** An act or process of refining. **b.** The state or quality of being refined. **2.** The result of refining; an improvement or elaboration. **3.** Fineness of thought, manners, or expression; polish; cultivation. **4.** A precise phrasing; a subtlety or subtle distinction. —See Synonyms at **culture.**

re·fin·er·y (ri-fínəri, rə-) *n., pl.* **-ies.** An industrial plant for purifying a crude substance, such as petroleum, sugar, fat, or ore.

re·fit (rée-fít) *v.* **-fitted, -fitting, -fits.** —*tr.* To prepare and equip for further or additional use; especially, to modernise and re-equip (a ship, for example). —*intr.* To be made ready for further use.
~*n.* (rée-fit, -fít). **1.** An act or process of refitting, especially of a ship. **2.** A secondary or subsequent preparation of supplies and equipment. **—re·fit·ment** *n.*

refl. 1. reflection; reflective. **2.** reflex; reflexive.

re·flate (rée-fláyt) *v.* **-flated, -flating, -flates.** —*tr. Economics.* To cause reflation in (a country's economy, for example). —*intr. Economics.* To cause reflation. Used of a government authority. Compare **deflate.**

re·fla·tion (rée-fláysh'n) *n. Economics.* An increase of the money in circulation, effected by a government in order to increase consumer demand and thereby to stimulate the economy. **—re·fla·tion·a·ry** (-ri, -əri || -erri) *adj.*

re·flect (ri-flékt, rə-) *v.* **-flected, -flecting, -flects.** —*tr.* **1.** To throw or bend back (heat, light, or sound, for example) from a surface. **2.** To form an image of; mirror. **3.** To manifest or express: *His work reflects intelligence.* **4.** *Mathematics.* To transform by reversing the sign of one coordinate. **5.** To consider, think, or realise: *He reflected that all was well.* **6.** To throw or bring (credit or discredit, for example) onto someone or something. **7.** *Archaic.* To bend back. —*intr.* **1.** To be thrown or bent back. Used especially of heat, light, or sound. **2. a.** To give back a likeness: *This surface reflects.* **b.** To become mirrored: *The statue reflected in the water.* **3.** To think, meditate, or consider seriously. Often used with *on* or *upon.* **4. a.** To bring blame or reproach. Used with *on* or *upon.* **b.** To cause the character of a person or thing to appear in a specified light. Used with *on* or *upon*: *The argument reflects badly on you.* [Middle English *reflecten,* from Old French *reflecter,* from Latin *reflectere,* to bend back : *re-,* back + *flectere,* to FLEX.]

re·flec·tance (ri-fléktənss, rə-) *n.* The ratio of the total radiant flux (as of light) reflected by a surface to the total falling on the surface. Compare **absorptance, transmittance.**

reflecting telescope *n.* An optical telescope in which the principal image-forming element is a parabolic or spherical mirror. Also called "reflector". Compare **refracting telescope.**

re·flec·tion (ri-fléksh'n, rə-) *n.* Also *chiefly British* **re·flex·ion.** *Abbr.* **refl. 1.** The act of reflecting or state of being reflected. **2.** Something reflected, such as light, radiant heat, sound, or an image. **3. a.** Concentration of the mind; careful consideration. **b.** A result of such consideration, communicated or not; a thought. **4. a.** An imputation of censure or discredit; reproach. Used chiefly in the phrase *cast reflections on* or *upon.* **b.** An expression, often discreditable, of the character of a person or thing. Used with *on* or *upon*: *a reflection on your honesty.* **5. a.** The act or an instance of bending back. **b.** *Anatomy.* A structure or part bent back upon itself. **6.** *Mathematics.* **a.** A transformation in which the sign of one coordinate is reversed. **b.** A symmetry relationship involving such a transformation. **—re·flec·tion·al** *adj.* **—re·flec·tion·less** *adj.*

reflection nebula *n.* See **nebula.**

re·flec·tive (ri-fléktiv, rə-) *adj. Abbr.* **refl. 1. a.** Of, pertaining to, produced by, or resulting from reflection. **b.** Capable of or producing reflection. **2.** Meditative; pensive. —See Synonyms at **pensive. —re·flec·tive·ly** *adv.* **—re·flec·tive·ness** *n.*

re·flec·tiv·i·ty (rée-flek-tívvəti) *n., pl.* **-ties. 1.** The quality of being reflective. **2.** The ability to reflect. **3.** *Physics.* The ratio of the intensity of the total radiation, as of light, reflected from a surface to the total falling on the surface.

re·flec·tor (ri-fléktər, rə-) *n.* **1.** That which reflects. **2.** A surface that reflects radiation. **3.** A small red reflective disc or strip, usually attached to the rear of a vehicle to increase its visibility. **4.** A reflecting telescope. **5.** *Physics.* A layer of material placed around the core of a nuclear reactor to reflect neutrons back into the core.

re·flet (rə-fláy) *n.* A lustrous or iridescent effect, as on pottery. [French, from Italian *riflesso,* reflection.]

re·flex (rée-fleks) *adj. Abbr.* **refl. 1.** *Physiology.* Of or designating an action or response performed without conscious control, such as a sneeze, blink, or hiccup. **2.** Broadly, of or designating any action or response performed unintentionally, automatically, or without deliberation: *a reflex response to danger.* **3.** Reflected or directed back upon the source: *reflex thoughts; reflex effort.* **4.** Designating light that is reflected. **5.** Turned, thrown, or bent backwards.
~*n. Abbr.* **refl. 1.** *Physiology.* A response to a stimulus performed without conscious control. **2.** *Psychology.* An automatic, instinctive, or mechanical response to a situation or other stimulus. **3.** *Plural.* The ability to respond to outside influences, usually considered in terms of speed: *For karate you need fast reflexes.* **4.** Reflection or an image produced by reflection. **5.** See **reflex camera. 6.** A linguistic form when viewed as descended from a usually specified earlier form; for example, *mother* and *fire* are reflexes of the Indo-European *māter* and *pūr* respectively.
~*tr.v.* (ri-fléks, rə-) **reflexed, -flexing, -flexes. 1.** To bend, turn back, or reflect. **2.** To cause to undergo a reflex process. [Latin *reflexus,* past participle of *reflectere,* to REFLECT.]

reflex angle *n.* An angle greater than 180° and less than 360°.

reflex arc *n.* The neural path of a physiological reflex, the simplest form of which consists of a sensory neurone and a motor neurone linked in the brain or spinal cord by a synapse.

reflex camera *n.* A camera fitted with a mirror to reflect the exact focused image onto a coupled viewing screen.

re·flex·ive (ri-fléksiv, rə-) *adj.* **1.** *Abbr.* **refl.** *Grammar.* Pertaining to, involved in, or expressing an action or relationship affecting the agent, subject, or source of the action; for example, in *She dressed herself,* the verb *dressed* and the pronoun *herself* are reflexive. **2.** *Logic.* Designating such a relationship. **3.** Designating or pertaining to a relation that is independent of the order of the terms. For example, equality is reflexive, for if $a = b$ then $b = a$. **4.** Of or pertaining to a reflex.

PRONUNCIATION KEY

a, trap; aa, father; ai, fair; ar, star; aw, lawn; ay, play; b, bb, stab; rubber; ch, church; ck, ticket; d, dd, dead; ladder; e, dress; ee, bee; er, defer; ew, few; ewr, pure; ə, about; ər, letter; f, ff, fife; differ; g, gg, giggle; h, hat; i, kit; ī, price; īr, fire; j, judge; k, kick; l, ll, let; 'l, needle; m, mm, man; n, nn, no; 'n, sudden; ng, thing; o, lot; ō, no; ŏŏ, foot; ōō, shoe; oor, poor; ow, cow; owr, hour; oy, boy; p, pp, pepper; r, rr, red; s, ss, sauce; sh, ship; t, tt, totter; th, thick; th, this; smooth; u, cut; ur, turn; v, vv, valve; w, wet; y, yes; z, zz, zebra; zh, vision; pleasure

IN FOREIGN WORDS:

aɴ, ᴏɴ, Saint-Saëns; hl, Llanelli; Hluhluwe; kh, loch; lough; Khaled

STRESS MARK:

ín-sīt, insight; in-sī́t, incite

~*n.* A reflexive verb or pronoun. **—re•flex•ive•ly** *adv.* **—re•flex•ive•ness, re•flex•iv•i•ty** (rée-flek-sívvəti) *n.*

re•flex•ol•o•gy (rée-flek-sólləji) *n.* **1.** The study of reflexes. **2.** The practice of foot massage to treat ailments in all parts of the body.

ref•lu•ent (réffloo-ənt) *adj. Rare.* Flowing back; ebbing. [Latin *refluēns* (stem *refluent-*), present participle of *refluere,* flow back : *re-,* back + *fluere,* flow.] **—ref•lu•ence** *n.*

re•flux (rée-fluks) *n.* **1.** The process or an act of flowing back; ebb. **2.** The pathological flow of liquid against its normal direction of movement, such as the flow of stomach contents into the oesophagus. **3.** *Chemistry.* The process of refluxing. Also used adjectivally: *reflux extraction.*
~*tr.v.* **refluxed, -fluxing, -fluxes.** *Chemistry.* To boil (a liquid) in a vessel attached to a condenser so that the liquid continuously condenses and runs back into the vessel. This process is used for extracting substances or carrying out reactions. [Middle English : RE- + FLUX.]

refo. Variant of **reffo.**

reforest. Variant of **reaforrest.**

re•form (rée-fórm) *v.* **-formed, -forming, -forms.** *—tr.* To form again. *—intr.* To become formed again.

re•form (ri-fórm, rə-) *v.* **-formed, -forming, -forms.** *—tr.* **1.** To improve, as by alteration, correction of error, or abolition of abuses and malpractices. **2.** To abolish (abuses or malpractices). **3.** To cause (a person) to abandon irresponsible or immoral practices. **4.** *Chemistry.* To change the structure of (hydrocarbons in petroleum) by heat and pressure, usually using catalysts, so as to produce hydrocarbons suitable for petrol. *—intr.* To abandon irresponsible or immoral practices. **—**See Synonyms at **correct.**
~*n.* **1.** The correction of abuses or evils. **2.** A change for the better; an improvement.
~*adj.* Pertaining to or favouring reform. [Middle English *reformen,* from Old French *reformer,* from Latin *refōrmāre* : *re-,* again, back + *fōrmāre,* to form, from *fōrma,* FORM.] **—re•form•a•ble** *adj.* **—re•form•a•bil•i•ty** (-ə-bílləti) *n.* **—re•form•a•tive** *adj.* **—re•form•er** *n.*

ref•or•ma•tion (réffər-máysh'n, *rarely* réffawr-) *n. Abbr.* **ref. 1.** The act of reforming or the state of being reformed. **2.** *Capital* **R.** The 16th-century movement that aimed at reforming Western Christianity, resulting in the separation of the Protestant churches from the Roman Catholic Church. **—ref•or•ma•tion•al** *adj.*

re•for•ma•to•ry (ri-fórmə-tri, -tər-i) *adj.* Serving or tending to reform.
~*n., pl.* **reformatories.** In many countries but no longer in Britain, a penal institution for the discipline, reformation, and training of juvenile and first offenders. Also called "reform school". [REFORMAT(ION) + -ORY.]

re•formed (ri-fórmd, rə-) *adj. Abbr.* **ref. 1.** Improved in conduct or character. **2.** *Capital* **R.** Of, pertaining to, or denoting the Protestant churches that follow the teachings of Calvin and Zwingli. **3.** *Capital* **R.** Of, pertaining to, or designating Reform Judaism.

re•form•ism (ri-fórm-iz'm, rə-) *n.* The advocacy of social or economic reform, especially in contrast to revolution. **—re•form•ist** *n.*

Reform Judaism *n.* A branch of Judaism introduced in the 19th century that endeavours to reconcile historical Judaism with modern life without requiring strict observance of traditional law. Compare **Conservative Judaism, Orthodox Judaism.**

re•fract (ri-frákt, rə-) *tr.v.* **-fracted, -fracting, -fracts. 1.** To deflect (light, for example) by refraction. **2.** To measure the refractive power of (a lens, for example). [Latin *refringere* (past participle *refractus*), to break off : *re-,* away, backwards + *frangere,* to break.]

refract•ing telescope (ri-frákting) *n.* A telescope in which the final image is produced entirely by lenses. Also called "refractor". Compare **reflecting telescope.**

re•frac•tion (ri-fráksh'n, rə-) *n. Abbr.* **refr. 1.** *Physics.* The deflection of a propagating wave, as of light or sound, at the boundary between two mediums, or in a passage through a medium of non-uniform density, occurring when the speed of the wave is different in the different mediums or regions. **2.** *Astronomy.* The apparent positional elevation of celestial objects caused by deflection of light entering the Earth's atmosphere. **3. a.** The capacity of the eye to refract light. **b.** The measurement of the angle through which an eye refracts light. **—re•frac•tion•al** *adj.*

re•frac•tive (ri-fráktiv, rə-) *adj.* **1.** Of or pertaining to refraction. **2.** Causing refraction. Said especially of such materials as diamond, with a high refractive index. **—re•frac•tive•ly** *adj.* **—re•frac•tive•ness, re•frac•tiv•i•ty** (rée-frak-tívvəti) *n.*

refractive index *n. Physics.* The ratio of the speed of light in a vacuum to the speed of light in the medium under consideration. Also called "index of refract".

re•frac•tom•e•ter (rée-frak-tómmitər) *n.* Any of several optical instruments that measure indices of refraction. **—re•frac•to•met•ric** (ri-fráktə-méttrik, rə-) *adj.* **—re•frac•tom•e•try** (-tómmətri) *n.*

re•frac•tor (ri-fráktər, rə-) *n.* **1.** One that refracts. **2.** A refracting telescope.

re•frac•to•ry (ri-fráktəri, rə-) *adj.* **1.** Obstinate; unmanageable. **2.** Difficult to melt or work; resistant to heat. **3.** Not responsive to treatment. **4.** *Physiology.* Designating the period following transmission of a nerve impulse during which a neurone will not respond to further stimulation. **—**See Synonyms at **unruly.**
~*n., pl.* **refractories. 1.** Any of various materials such as alumina, silica, and magnesite that do not significantly deform or change chemically at high temperatures. **2.** *Plural.* Bricks of such materials and of various shapes used to line furnaces. [Earlier *refractary,* from Latin *refractārius,* from *refringere* (past participle *refractus*), to break off, REFRACT.] **—re•frac•to•ri•ly** *adv.* **—re•frac•to•ri•ness** *n.*

re•frain[1] (ri-fráyn, rə-) *v.* **-frained, -fraining, -frains.** *—intr.* To hold oneself back; abstain. Used with *from. —tr. Archaic.* To restrain or hold back; curb. [Middle English *refreynen,* from Old French *refrener,* from Latin *refrēnāre,* hold back, bridle : *re-,* back + *frēnum,* bridle.] **—re•frain•er** *n.* **—re•frain•ment** *n.*

refrain[2] *n.* **1. a.** A phrase or verse repeated at intervals throughout a song or poem, especially at the end of each stanza. **b.** Music for the refrain of a poem. **2.** Loosely, a tune. **3.** A repetitious utterance or theme. [Middle English *refreyn,* from Old French *refrain,* from *refraindre,* to echo, break off (a refrain "breaks off" to recur at intervals), from Vulgar Latin *refrangere* (unattested), from Latin *refringere,* to break off, REFRACT.]

re•fran•gi•ble (ri-fránj-ib'l, rə-) *adj.* Capable of being refracted. [New Latin *refrangibilis,* from *refrangere,* variant of Latin *refringere,* to REFRACT.] **—re•fran•gi•bil•i•ty** (-ibílləti), **re•fran•gi•ble•ness** *n.*

re•fresh (ri-frésh, rə-) *v.* **-freshed, -freshing, -freshes.** *—tr.* **1.** To revive (a person) with or as if with rest, food, or drink. **2.** To make cool, clean, or damp; freshen. **3.** To restore by some treatment: *refresh the paintwork.* **4.** To renew by stimulation: *refresh one's memory. —intr.* **1.** To take refreshment. **2.** To become revived; reinvigorate. [Middle English *refresshen,* from Old French *refreschir, refreschier* : *re-,* again + *freis, fresche,* FRESH.]

re•fresh•er (ri-fréshər, rə-) *n.* **1.** One that refreshes. **2.** *British.* An extra payment made to a barrister during a prolonged legal case.
~*adj.* Serving to reacquaint one with material previously studied: *a refresher course.*

re•fresh•ing (ri-fréshing, rə-) *adj.* **1.** Serving to refresh. **2.** Pleasantly new and different; unusual. **—re•fresh•ing•ly** *adv.*

re•fresh•ment (ri-fréshmənt, rə-) *n.* **1.** The act of refreshing or state of being refreshed; reinvigoration; revival. **2.** Something that refreshes, such as food or drink. **3.** *Plural.* A light meal or snack and drinks.

re•frig•er•ant (ri-fríjərənt, rə-) *adj.* **1.** Cooling or freezing; refrigerating. **2.** *Medicine.* Reducing fever.
~*n.* **1.** A substance, such as air, ammonia, water, or carbon dioxide, used to produce refrigeration, either as the working substance of a refrigerator or by direct absorption of heat. **2.** *Medicine.* Any agent used to produce cooling or reduce fever.

re•frig•er•ate (ri-fríjə-rayt, rə-) *tr.v.* **-ated, -ating, -ates. 1.** To cool or chill (a substance). **2.** To preserve (food) by chilling. [Latin *refrigerāre* : *re-,* repeatedly, again + *frigerāre,* to make cool, from *frigus* (stem *frigor-*), cool.] **—re•frig•er•a•tion** (-ráysh'n) *n.* **—re•frig•er•a•tive** (-rətiv || -raytiv) *adj.* & *n.* **—re•frig•er•a•to•ry** (-rə-təri, -tri, -raytəri) *adj.*

re•frig•er•a•tor (ri-fríjə-raytər, rə-) *n.* An apparatus for reducing and maintaining the temperature of a chamber below the temperature of the external environment; for example, a household appliance for keeping food and drink. Also informally called "fridge".

re•frin•gent (ri-frínjənt, rə-) *adj.* Of, pertaining to, or producing refraction; refractive. [Latin *refringēns* (stem *refringent-*), present participle of *refringere,* to REFRACT.]

reft. Alternative past tense and past participle of **reave.**

re•fu•el (rée-féw-əl, -féwl) *v.* **-elled** or *U.S.* **-eled, -elling** or *U.S.* **-eling, -els.** *—tr.* To supply again with fuel. *—intr.* To take on a fresh supply of fuel.

ref•uge (réffewj) *n.* **1.** Protection or shelter, as from danger or hardship. **2.** A place providing protection or shelter; a haven or sanctuary; specifically, a place providing shelter for victims of domestic violence. **3.** Anything to which one may turn for help, relief, or escape: *Silence was his only refuge.* **4.** *British.* A **traffic island** *(see).* **—**See Synonyms at **shelter.**
~*v.* **refuged, -uging, -uges.** *Archaic. —tr.* To give refuge to. *—intr.* To take refuge. [Middle English, from Old French, from Latin *refugium,* from *refugere,* flee back : *re-,* away, back + *fugere,* to flee.]

ref•u•gee (réffew-jée) *n.* A person who flees to find refuge; especially, one who escapes from invasion, oppression, or persecution, often to another country. [French *réfugié,* from the past participle of *réfugier,* to put in a refuge, from *refuge,* REFUGE.]

re•ful•gent (ri-fúljənt, rə-) *adj.* Shining radiantly; brilliant; resplendent. [Latin *refulgēns* (stem *refulgent-*), present participle of *refulgēre,* to flash back : *re-,* back + *fulgēre,* to flash.] **—re•ful•gence, re•ful•gen•cy** *n.* **—re•ful•gent•ly** *adv.*

re•fund[1] (ri-fúnd, rə-, rée-) *v.* **-funded, -funding, -funds.** *—tr.* **1.** To return or repay; give back. **2.** To repay (a person); reimburse. *—intr.* To make repayment.
~*n.* (rée-fund). **1.** A repayment of funds. **2.** The amount repaid. [Middle English *refunden,* to pour back, from Old French *refunder,* from Latin *refundere* : *re-,* back + *fundere,* to pour.] **—re•fund•er** (-fúndər) *n.* **—re•fund•ment** *n.*

re•fund[2] (rée-fúnd) *tr.v.* **-funded, -funding, -funds. 1.** To fund anew. **2.** *Finance.* To pay back (a debt) with new borrowing; especially, to replace (a bond issue) with a new bond issue.

re•fur•bish (rée-fúrbish, ri-, rə-) *tr.v.* **-bished, -bishing, -bishes.** To make clean or fresh again; renovate. **—re•fur•bish•ment** *n.*

re•fus•al (ri-féwz'l, rə-) *n.* **1.** The act of refusing. **2.** The opportunity to accept or reject; option: *He gave me first refusal.*

re•fuse[1] (ri-féwz, rə-) *v.* **-fused, -fusing, -fuses.** *—tr.* **1.** To make known or declare that one is unwilling to, or will not, do, accept,

PRONUNCIATION KEY

a, trap; aa, father; ai, fair;
ar, star; aw, lawn; ay, play;
b, bb, stab; rubber;
ch, church; ck, ticket;
d, dd, dead; ladder; e, dress;
ee, bee; er, defer; ew, few;
ewr, pure; ə, about;
ər, letter; f, ff, fife; differ;
g, gg, giggle; h, hat; i, kit;
ī, price; īr, fire; j, judge;
k, kick; l, ll, let; 'l, needle;
m, mm, man; n, nn, no;
'n, sudden; ng, thing; o, lot;
ō, no; ŏŏ, foot; ōō, shoe;
oor, poor; ow, cow;
owr, hour; oy, boy;
p, pp, pepper; r, rr, red;
s, ss, sauce; sh, ship;
t, tt, totter; th, thick; th, this;
smooth; u, cut; ur, turn;
v, vv, valve; w, wet; y, yes;
z, zz, zebra; zh, vision;
pleasure

IN FOREIGN WORDS:

aN, oN, Saint-Saëns;
hl, Llanelli; Hluhluwe;
kh, loch; lough; Khaled

STRESS MARK:

ín-sīt, insight; in-sī́t, incite

give, or allow. **2.** To be unwilling and fail to jump (an obstacle). Used of a horse. *—intr.* To decline to do, accept, allow, or give something. [Middle English *refusen,* from Old French *refuser,* from Vulgar Latin *refūsāre* (unattested), from Latin *refundere* (past participle *refūsus*), to pour back. See **refund.**] **—re·fus·er** *n.*

Synonyms: *refuse, decline, reject, spurn, rebuff, ignore.*

ref·use[2] (réffewss) *n.* Anything discarded or rejected as useless or worthless; rubbish; waste matter.

~adj. Discarded or rejected as useless or worthless. [Middle English, something rejected, from Old French *refus,* refusal, from *refuser,* to REFUSE.]

re·fuse·nik (ri-féwznik, rə-) *n.* A Soviet citizen whose application for a visa to emigrate has been refused. [REFUSE + -NIK.]

ref·u·ta·tion (réffew-táysh'n) *n.* Also **re·fu·tal** (ri-féwt'l, rə-). **1.** The act of refuting. **2.** Something that refutes.

re·fute (ri-féwt, rə-) *tr.v.* **-futed, -futing, -futes. 1.** To prove (a statement or argument) to be false or erroneous; disprove. **2.** To prove (a person) to be wrong. [Latin *refutāre,* rebut, drive back.] **—ref·ut·a·bil·i·ty** (réff-ewtə-bílləti, ri-féwtə-) *n.* **—ref·ut·a·ble** *adj.* **—ref·ut·a·bly** *adv.* **—re·fut·er** *n.*

Usage: There is a widespread use of *refute* with the meaning "to deny", but it attracts criticism as it lacks the strong sense of "proof" that is inherent in the word.

reg (reg) *n.* A flat, stony desert, especially in the Sahara, where sheets of gravel and pebbles cover the surface. [Arabic.]

reg. 1. regent. **2.** regiment. **3.** region. **4.** register; registered. **5.** registrar. **6.** registry. **7.** regular; regularly. **8.** regulation. **9.** regulator.

Reg. 1. Regent. **2.** Regina.

re·gain (ri-gáyn, rée-) *tr.v.* **-gained, -gaining, -gains. 1.** To recover possession of; get back again. **2.** To manage to reach again. **—**See Synonyms at **recover. —re·gain·er** *n.*

re·gal[1] (rée'g'l) *adj.* **1.** Pertaining to a king or queen; royal. **2.** Belonging to or befitting a king or queen: *regal attire.* **3.** Dignified; stately. [Middle English, from Old French, from Latin *rēgālis,* royal, from *rēx* (stem *rēg-*), king.] **—re·gal·ly** *adv.*

regal[2] *n.* A small, portable reed organ often used in dramatic works in the 16th and 17th centuries. [French *régale,* perhaps feminine of *régal,* REGAL.]

re·gale (ri-gáyl, rə-) *v.* **-galed, -galing, -gales.** *—tr.* **1.** To delight or entertain; give pleasure to: *regaled us with folk songs.* **2.** To entertain sumptuously with food and drink; provide a feast for. *—intr.* To feast. **—**See Synonyms at **amuse.**

~n. Obsolete. **1.** A great feast; a sumptuous repast. **2.** A choice food or drink; a delicacy. **3.** Refreshment. [French *régaler,* from Old French *regaler,* from *regal,* REGAL.] **—re·gale·ment** *n.*

re·ga·li·a (ri-gáyli-ə, rə-) *pl.n. Often used with a singular verb.* **1.** The emblems and symbols of royalty, such as the crown and sceptre. **2.** The distinguishing symbols of any rank, office, order, or society. **3.** Magnificent attire; finery. [Medieval Latin *rēgālia,* plural of *rēgāle,* royal prerogative, from Latin, neuter of *rēgālis,* REGAL.]

re·gal·i·ty (ri-gál-əti, ree-) *n., pl.* **-ties. 1.** Royalty or sovereignty; kingship or queenship. **2.** A country or area under a monarch; a kingdom. **3.** The rights or privileges of a king or queen.

re·gard (ri-gárd, rə-) *v.* **-garded, -garding, -gards.** *—tr.* **1.** To look upon or consider in a specified way: *I regard him as a fool.* **2.** To look at attentively; observe closely. **3.** To have great affection or admiration for: *She regards her father highly.* **4.** To relate to, concern, or refer to: *This item regards your question.* **5.** To consider or take account of. **6.** *Obsolete.* To take care of. *—intr.* **1.** To look; gaze. **2.** To give heed; pay attention. **—as regards.** Relating to; concerning. **—**See Synonyms at **consider.**

~n. **1.** Careful thought or attention; concern; heed: *He gives little regard to his appearance.* **2.** Respect, affection, or esteem: *He has won the regard of all.* **3.** A look or gaze. **4.** *Plural.* Sentiments of respect or affection; good wishes: *send one's regards.* **5.** Reference or relation: *with regard to this case.* **6.** A particular point or respect: *I agree in this regard.* **7.** *Obsolete.* Appearance or aspect. [Middle English *regarden,* from Old French *regarder, reguarder,* to look at, regard : *re-,* back, back at + *guarder, garder,* to GUARD.]

Synonyms: *regard, esteem, admiration, approbation.*

Usage: *Regard* occurs in a range of constructions, some of which require an additional *-s* in standard English. Thus one has: *to have regard to* ("to take into account"), *to have regard for* ("to show consideration for"), *with regard to* ("concerning"), and *without regard to* ("without taking into account"), alongside *as regards* ("concerning"), *give one's regards to* ("greet"), and *kind regards* (as a letter ending). In informal English, there is a tendency to use the *-s* form more widely, as in *with regards to,* but this attracts criticism. The use of *regarding* and *respecting* as prepositions *(Regarding your visit . . .)* is also sometimes criticised. When the sense of "a particular" is required, formal usage prefers *respects* to *regards*: *In some respects, she is a good choice.* As a verb with the sense of "consider", *regard* is normally used with *as (I regard it as a good thing).*

re·gar·dant (ri-gárd'nt, rə-) *adj. Heraldry.* With the face turned backwards in profile: *a lion regardant.* [Middle English, from Old French, from *regarder,* to REGARD.]

re·gard·ful (ri-gárdf'l, rə-) *adj.* **1.** Showing regard; observant; heedful. Often used with *of.* **2.** Showing deference; respectful; considerate. **—re·gard·ful·ly** *adv.* **—re·gard·ful·ness** *n.*

re·gard·ing (ri-gárding, rə-) *prep.* In reference to; with respect to; concerning. See Usage note at **regard.**

re·gard·less (ri-gárd-ləss, rə-, -liss) *adj.* Heedless; unmindful. Often used with *of.*

~adv. In spite of everything; anyway. **—re·gard·less·ly** *adv.* **—re·gard·less·ness** *n.*

re·gat·ta (ri-gáttə, rə- || -gaátə) *n.* A boat race or series of boat races. [Italian (Venetian dialect) *regatta, regata*†, gondola race.]

regd. registered.

re·ge·late (réeji-layt) *intr.v.* **-lated, -lating, -lates.** To undergo regelation. [RE- + Latin *gelāre,* to freeze.]

re·ge·la·tion (réeji-láysh'n) *n.* **1.** Successive melting and freezing of ice when pressure is applied and relaxed at the interface of two blocks of ice. **2.** The fusion of two blocks of ice by regelation.

re·gen·cy (réejən-si) *n., pl.* **-cies. 1.** The office, area of jurisdiction, or government of a regent or regents. **2.** A person or group selected to govern in place of a king or other ruler in the case of minority, absence, incompetence, or sickness. **3.** The period during which a regent governs, especially: **a.** *Capital* **R.** In British history, the period 1811–20 during which George, Prince of Wales (later George IV) was regent for his father George III. **b.** *Capital* **R.** In French history, the period 1715–23 during which Philippe, Duke of Orléans, was regent for the young Louis XV.

~adj. Usually capital **R.** Of, pertaining to, or characteristic of the style, especially in furniture, prevalent during the Regency periods in Britain and France.

re·gen·er·a·cy (ri-jénnərə-si, rə-, rée-) *n.* The state of being regenerated.

re·gen·er·ate (ri-jénnə-rayt, rə-, -rée) *v.* **-ated, -ating, -ates.** *—tr.* **1.** To reform or revitalise spiritually or morally. **2.** To form, construct, or create anew. **3.** *Biology.* To replace (a lost or damaged organ or part) by formation of new tissue. **4.** *Electronics.* To amplify (a signal in a radio receiver, for example) by positive feedback. *—intr.* **1.** To become formed or constructed again. **2.** To undergo spiritual conversion or rebirth. **3.** To effect regeneration.

~adj. (ri-jénnə-rət, -rit, rə-). **1.** Spiritually or morally revitalised. **2.** Restored; refreshed; renewed. [Latin *regenerāre,* to reproduce : *re-,* again + *generāre,* to beget, GENERATE.] **—re·gen·er·a·ble** *adj.* **—re·gen·er·a·tive** (-rətiv || -raytiv) *adj.* **—re·gen·er·a·tive·ly** *adv.*

re·gen·er·a·tion (ri-jénnə-ráysh'n, rə-, rée-) *n.* **1.** The act or process of regenerating or the state of being regenerated. **2.** Spiritual or moral revival or rebirth. **3.** *Biology.* The regrowth of lost or destroyed parts or organs.

re·gen·er·a·tor (ri-jénnə-raytər, rə-, rée-) *n.* One that regenerates.

Re·gens·burg (*German* ráygənss-boork). Formerly **Rat·is·bon** (ráttiz-bon). Town in the state of Bavaria, West Germany. It is a commercial, industrial, and transport centre. Dating from Roman times, it was the permanent seat of the Imperial Diet (1663–1806), and passed to Bavaria in 1810.

re·gent (réejənt) *n. Abbr.* **reg., regt., Regt. 1.** One who rules during the minority, absence, or disability of a sovereign. **2.** *Archaic.* One acting as a ruler or governor. **3.** In the United States, a person serving on a board that governs a university or other educational institution or system. [Middle English, from Old French, ruling, from Medieval Latin *regēns* (stem *regent-*), from Latin, present participle of *regere,* to rule.] **—re·gent** *adj.*

regent bird *n.* An Australian bowerbird, *Sericulus chrysocephalus.*

reg·gae (réggay, réggi) *n.* A type of popular music originating in the West Indies with an insistent rhythm heavily accentuating the third beat of the bar. [20th century : of West Indian origin.]

Reg·gio di Calabria (réj-ō). Also **Reggio** or **Reggio Calabrio.** Seaport and industrial centre in Calabria, southwest Italy. Originally a Greek colony, it was taken by the Romans in 270 B.C.

Reggio nell'E·mi·lia (nel e-méel-yə). Also **Reggio** or **Reggio Emilia.** Capital city of the province of Reggio nell'Emilia in north Italy on the river Crostolo. It lies on the ancient Via Emilia and is a commercial centre for the surrounding rich agricultural area.

reg·i·cide (réji-sīd) *n.* **1.** The killing of a king. **2.** One who kills or helps to kill a king. [Latin *rēx* (stem *rēg-*), king + -CIDE.] **—reg·i·ci·dal** (-sīd'l) *adj.*

re·gime, ré·gime (ray-zhéem, re-, ri-) *n.* **1. a.** A system of management or government. **b.** A government holding power, especially a totalitarian one. **2.** A social system or pattern. **3.** A regimen. **4.** The pattern of seasonal fluctuation in a climate or in the volume of a river. **5.** *Informal.* The accepted way of doing or running things: *the new office regime.* [French *régime,* from Latin *regimen,* from *regere,* to rule.]

reg·i·men (réji-mən, -men) *n.* **1.** A system of therapy: *a dietetic regimen.* **2.** A set of rules or prescribed procedure for regulating life or achieving some end. [Middle English, from Latin, REGIME.]

reg·i·ment (réjimənt) *n.* **1.** *Abbr.* **reg., regt., Regt.** A permanent military unit consisting of at least two battalions and sometimes other units and usually commanded by a colonel. **2.** A large, organised group. **3.** *Archaic.* Rule: *"the monstrous regiment of women"* (John Knox).

~tr.v. (réji-mént) **regimented, -menting, -ments. 1.** To organise or form into a regiment or regiments. **2.** To appoint to a regiment. **3.** To put into order; systematise. **4.** To force uniformity and discipline upon. [Middle English, from Old French, from Late Latin *regimentum,* from Latin *regere,* to rule.] **—reg·i·men·tal** *adj.* **—reg·i·men·tal·ly** *adv.* **—reg·i·men·ta·tion** (-men-táysh'n) *n.*

reg·i·men·tals (réji-mént'lz) *pl.n.* **1.** The uniform and insignia characteristic of a particular regiment. **2.** Military dress.

Re·gi·na[1] (ri-jīnə, rə-) *n. Abbr.* **R., Reg. 1.** The reigning queen. Used as a title and signature on documents. **2.** *Law.* The Crown. Used in lawsuits when the monarch is a queen: *Regina v. Jones.* [Latin.]

Regina[2]. Capital of Saskatchewan province, Canada, built on the

Regency *The Royal Pavilion at Brighton, England was built between 1815 and 1823 by the Regency architect John Nash. Regency architecture combined oriental and French influences with classical Greek styles, and was characterised by the use of delicate iron balconies, stucco plasterwork, and tall windows.*

Indian settlement of Wascana. It is a major agricultural centre.

re·gion (réejən) *n. Abbr.* **reg.** **1.** Any large, usually continuous segment of a surface or space; an area. **2.** A large and indefinite portion of the Earth's surface. **3.** A specific district or territory. **4.** A field of interest or activity; a sphere. **5.** A part of the Earth characterised by distinctive animal or plant life. **6.** An area of the body having natural or arbitrarily assigned boundaries: *the abdominal region.* **7.** *Usually plural.* The different areas of a country excluding the capital: *Politics in the regions differs from politics in Westminster.* **8.** Range; vicinity: *a price in the region of £5,000.* **9.** *Mathematics.* A **domain** *(see).* —See Synonyms at **area.** [Middle English *regioun,* kingdom, from Old French *region,* from Latin *regiō* (stem *regiōn-),* direction, boundary, from *regere,* to direct.]

re·gion·al (réejən'l) *adj.* **1.** Of, pertaining to, or characteristic of a large geographical region. **2.** Of, pertaining to, or characteristic of a particular region or district; localised. **3.** Of, belonging to, or characteristic of a form of a language that is distributed in identifiable geographical areas and has identifiable phonetic, structural, and other differences from the standard form of the language; dialectal. **—re·gion·al·ly** *adv.*

regional ileitis *n. Medicine.* Inflammation, thickening, and ulceration of any part of the digestive tract, particularly the ileum. Also called "Crohn's disease".

re·gion·al·ise, re·gion·al·ize (réejən'l-īz) *tr.v.* **-ised, -ising, -ises.** To divide into regions for administrative purposes; especially, to divide into partially autonomous administrative units. **—re·gion·al·i·sa·tion** (-ī-záysh'n || *U.S* -i-) *n.*

re·gion·al·ism (réejən'l-iz'm) *n.* **1.** The political division of territory into partially autonomous regions. **2.** The theory or advocacy of such a political system. **3.** Attachment to one's native region. **4.** A feature, as of language, associated with a particular region.

ré·gis·seur (réji-súr; *French* rayzhee-sőr) *n., pl.* **-seurs** (-súrz, -sőr). *French.* The director of a ballet.

reg·is·ter (réjistər) *n. Abbr.* **reg.** **1.** A formal or official recording of items, names, or actions. **2.** A book for such entries. **3.** An entry in a register. **4.** A device that automatically indicates a quantity or number. **5.** An adjustable, grille-like device through which heated or cooled air is released into a room. **6.** *Music.* **a.** The range of an instrument or voice. **b.** A part of such a range that has similar quality. **c.** A group of matched organ pipes; a stop. **7.** The style or form of language typically used in particular social situations: *scientific register; colloquial register.* **8.** *Printing.* **a.** The exact alignment of printed lines for columns on both sides of a page. **b.** The exact alignment of different colour plates in the printing of a picture. **9.** *Computing.* A specific location in a storage device, especially one assigned to a particular operation.

~*v.* **registered, -tering, -ters.** —*tr.* **1.** To enter in a register; record officially; enrol. **2.** To indicate, as on an instrument or scale. **3.** To show (emotion). **4.** To cause (post) to be officially recorded by payment of a fee. **5.** To cause to align or correspond. —*intr.* **1.** To place or cause placement of one's name in a register or on an official list: *We registered to vote.* **2.** To be indicated, as on an instrument or scale. **3.** To be shown. **4.** To create an impression on someone's mind. **5.** To be aligned; correspond. [Middle English *registre,* from Old French, from Medieval Latin *registrum, regest(r)um,* from Late Latin *regesta,* list, neuter plural past participle of Latin *regerere,* to bring back : *re-,* back + *gerere,* to bring, carry.] **—reg·is·ter·er** *n.* **—reg·is·tra·ble** (réjistrəb'l) *adj.*

registered post *n.* **1.** Mail that is recorded by the post office when sent and is insured by payment of a fee against loss or damage. **2.** The Post Office service by which such mail is sent.

registered nurse *n. Abbr.* **R.N.** *U.S.* A trained nurse who has passed a state registration examination.

reg·is·trant (réjistrənt) *n.* One who registers or is registered.

reg·is·trar (réji-strár, -straar) *n. Abbr.* **reg., regr.** **1.** One who is in charge of registers or official records. **2.** *British.* An official in charge of a registry office, who is licensed to perform marriages. **3.** An officer in a college or university who keeps records of the enrolment and academic standing of students. **4.** *British.* A specialist physician or surgeon in a hospital, subordinate to a consultant, but senior to a house physician or house surgeon.

reg·is·tra·tion (réji-stráysh'n) *n.* **1.** A registering, as of voters or students. **2.** The number of persons registered; an enrolment. **3.** An entry in a register. **4. a.** A selected combination of organ stops. **b.** The technique of selecting and adjusting organ stops.

registration number *n.* The official set of numerals and letters on the number plates of a motor vehicle indicating when and where it was registered.

registration plate *n.* A **number plate** *(see).*

reg·is·try (réjistri) *n., pl.* **-tries.** *Abbr.* **reg.** **1.** Registration. **2.** A ship's registered nationality. **3.** A place where registers are kept.

registry office *n. British.* **1.** An office where official records of births, marriages, and deaths are kept and where civil marriages are performed by a registrar. **2.** Formerly, an employment agency for the hire of domestic servants.

Re·gi·us professor (réeji-əss, réej-) *n.* One holding a professorship established by royal bounty at any of certain older British universities. [Latin *rēgius,* royal, from *rēx* (stem *rēg-*), king + PROFESSOR.]

reg·let (rég-lit, -lət) *n.* **1.** *Architecture.* A narrow, flat moulding. **2.** *Printing.* A flat piece of wood used to separate lines of type. [French *réglet,* from Old French *reglet,* from *regle,* rule, straight edge, from Latin *rēgula,* rule.]

reg·nal (régnəl) *adj.* Designating a specified year of a sovereign's reign calculated from the date of accession: *in her thirtieth regnal year.* [Medieval Latin *regnālis,* from Latin *rēgnum,* REIGN.]

reg·nant (régnənt) *adj.* **1. a.** Reigning; ruling. **b.** Ruling in one's own right and not merely as a consort: *Queen regnant.* **2.** Predominant. **3.** Widespread; prevalent. [Latin *regnāns* (stem *regnant-*), present participle of *regnāre,* to reign, from *rēgnum,* REIGN.]

reg·o·lith (réggə-lith) *n.* Loose material, including soils, broken rock, volcanic ash, and glacial material, overlying the bedrock. Also called "mantle rock". [Greek *rhēgos,* blanket + -LITH.]

re·gorge (ri-górj) *v.* **-gorged, -gorging, -gorges.** —*tr.* To disgorge. —*intr.* To flow back again. [French *regorger,* from Old French : *re-,* back + *gorger,* to gorge, from *gorge,* throat, GORGE.]

reg·o·sol (rég-ə-sol, -ō- || -sōl) *n.* An unconsolidated azonal soil formed from alluvium or sands. [Greek *rhēgos,* blanket + Latin *solum,* soil.]

regr. registrar.

re·grate (ri-gráyt) *tr.v.* **-grated, -grating, -grates.** **1.** Formerly, to purchase (goods, especially foodstuffs) in order to resell at a profit at or near the same marketplace. **2.** To retail or sell again (goods so purchased). [Middle English *regraten,* from Old French *regrater,* from *regratier* : perhaps *re-,* against + *grater,* to scratch, from Germanic.]

re·gress (ri-gréss, rə-) *intr.v.* **-gressed, -gressing, -gresses.** To go back; return to a previous condition, state, or behaviour pattern.
~*n.* (rée-gress). **1.** Return or withdrawal. **2.** The act of reasoning from an effect to a cause. [Latin *regressus,* past participle of *regredī,* to go back : *re-,* back + *gradī,* to step, go.]

re·gres·sion (ri-grésh'n, rə-) *n.* **1.** Reversion; retrogression. **2.** Relapse to a less perfect or developed state. **3.** *Psychology.* Reversion to a more primitive or less mature behaviour pattern. **4.** *Statistics.* The tendency for the expected value of a random variable to approach more closely the mean value of its set than does the independent variable by means of which it was predicted.

re·gres·sive (ri-gréssiv, rə-) *adj.* **1.** Tending to return or revert. **2.** Characterised by regression or a tendency to regress. **3.** Designating taxation in which the rate lessens as the amount taxed increases. **—re·gres·sive·ly** *adv.* **—re·gres·sive·ness** *n.*

re·gret (ri-grét, rə-) *tr.v.* **-gretted, -gretting, -grets.** **1.** To feel disappointed, distressed, or repentant about. **2.** To feel sorrow or grief over; mourn.
~*n.* **1.** Distress, repentance, sorrow, or disappointment over a desire unfulfilled or an action performed or not performed. **2.** A sense of loss and longing for someone or something gone. **3.** *Often plural.* An expression of grief or disappointment; especially, a courteous declining to accept an invitation. [Middle English *regretten,* from Old French *regreter,* to lament : perhaps *re-* (intensifive), again + Old Norse *grata,* to moan, sob.]
Synonyms: *regret, sorrow, grief, anguish, woe, heartache.*

re·gret·ful (ri-grét-f'l, rə-) *adj.* Full of regret or sorrow. **—re·gret·ful·ly** *adv.* **—re·gret·ful·ness** *n.*

re·gret·ta·ble (ri-gréttəb'l, rə-) *adj.* Eliciting or deserving regret. See Synonyms at **pathetic.**

regret·ta·bly (ri-gréttəbli, rə-) *adv.* **1.** In a regrettable manner. **2.** It is regrettable that: *Regrettably, the book won't be finished on time.*

re·group (rée-gróop), *v.* **-grouped, -grouping, -groups.** —*intr.* To become an ordered group or formation again after dispersal or disordering: *We regrouped after the attack.* —*tr.* To cause to regroup.

regt., Regt. **1.** regent. **2.** regiment.

reg·u·lar (réggewlər) *adj. Abbr.* **reg.** **1.** Customary, usual, or normal. **2.** Orderly, even, or symmetrical. **3.** Conforming to set procedure, principle, or discipline. **4.** Methodical; well-ordered. **5.** Occurring at fixed intervals; periodic. **6.** Constant; not varying. **7.** Formally correct; proper. **8.** Having the required qualifications for an occupation. **9.** Perfect; complete; thorough: *a regular villain.* **10.** *U.S. Informal.* Good; nice: *a regular guy.* **11.** *Botany.* Having similar and symmetrically arranged parts. **12.** *Grammar.* Belonging to a standard mode of inflection or conjugation. **13.** Belonging to a religious order and bound by its rules: *the regular clergy.* Compare **secular.** **14.** In geometry: **a.** Having equal sides and equal angles. Said of polygons. **b.** Having faces that are congruent regular polygons with congruent polyhedral angles. Said of polyhedra. **15.** Belonging to or constituting the permanent army of a nation. **16.** Menstruating or defecating at normal intervals. **17.** In crystallography, having radial symmetry. —See Synonyms at **normal.**
~*n. Abbr.* **reg.** **1.** A soldier belonging to a regular army. **2.** *Informal.* A habitual customer or patron. **3.** A clergyman or other member of a religious order. [Middle English *reguler,* under religious rule, from Old French, from Latin *rēgulāris,* containing rules, from *rēgula,* rule, ruler.] **—reg·u·lar·i·ty** (-lárriti) *n.* **—reg·u·lar·ly** *adv.*

reg·u·lar·ise, reg·u·lar·ize (réggewlə-rīz) *tr.v.* **-ised, -ising, -ises.** To make regular; cause to conform. **—reg·u·lar·i·sa·tion** (-rī-záysh'n || *U.S.* -ri-) *n.*

reg·u·late (réggewlayt) *tr.v.* **-lated, -lating, -lates.** **1.** To control or direct according to a rule or procedure. **2.** To adjust in conformity to a specification or requirement. **3.** To adjust (a mechanism) for accurate and proper functioning. [Late Latin *rēgulāre,* from Latin *rēgula,* a rule.] **—reg·u·la·tive** (-lətiv, -laytiv), **reg·u·la·to·ry** (-laytəri, -láy-, -lə-, -tri) *adj.*

reg·u·la·tion (réggewláysh'n) *n. Abbr.* **reg.** **1.** The act of regulating. **2.** A principle, rule, or law designed to control or govern behaviour. **3.** A governmental order having the force of law. **4.** The ability of an embryo to continue normal development following injury to or alteration of a structure.

PRONUNCIATION KEY

a, trap; aa, father; ai, fair; ar, star; aw, lawn; ay, play; b, bb, stab; rubber; ch, church; ck, ticket; d, dd, dead; ladder; e, dress; ee, bee; er, defer; ew, few; ewr, pure; ə, about; ər, letter; f, ff, fife; differ; g, gg, giggle; h, hat; i, kit; ī, price; īr, fire; j, judge; k, kick; l, ll, let; 'l, needle; m, mm, man; n, nn, no; 'n, sudden; ng, thing; o, lot; ō, no; ŏŏ, foot; ōō, shoe; oor, poor; ow, cow; owr, hour; oy, boy; p, pp, pepper; r, rr, red; s, ss, sauce; sh, ship; t, tt, totter; th, thick; th, this; smooth; u, cut; ur, turn; v, vv, valve; w, wet; y, yes; z, zz, zebra; zh, vision; pleasure

IN FOREIGN WORDS:

aN, ON, Saint-Saëns; hl, Llanelli; Hluhluwe; kh, loch; lough; Khaled

STRESS MARK:

ín-sīt, insight; in-sít, incite

~*adj. Abbr.* **reg.** Prescribed in accordance with a rule or standard procedure: *a regulation uniform.*
reg·u·la·tor (réggewlaytər) *n. Abbr.* **reg. 1.** One that regulates. **2. a.** The mechanism in a watch by which its speed is governed. **b.** An accurate clock used as a standard for timing other clocks. **3. a.** A device to maintain uniform speed in a machine; a governor. **b.** A device to control the flow of gases, liquids, or electric current.
regulator gene *n.* A gene that controls the expression of an **operon** *(see).*
reg·u·lus (réggew-ləss) *n., pl.* **-li** (-lī) or **-luses.** *Metallurgy.* **1.** The metallic part of a charge that sinks under the slag to the bottom of a furnace or crucible. **2.** A relatively impure product of various ores in smelting, **matte** *(see).* [Medieval Latin *rēgulus,* from Latin, a petty king (this metallic antimony combines readily with gold, the king of metals), diminutive of *rēx,* king.] **—reg·u·line** (-līn, -lin) *adj.*
Regulus *n.* A bright triple star in the constellation Leo. Also called "Alpha Leonis".
Regulus, Marcus Atilius (died *c.* 250 B.C.). Roman general, hero of the First Punic War. Appointed consul in 267 B.C. and again in 256 B.C., he was captured by the Carthaginians in 255, and sent to sue for peace with the Roman senate; instead Regulus pleaded with the senate to reject the enemy's proposals. He returned to Carthage rather than break his parole, and died there.
re·gur (rég-ər, ráyg-) *n.* A dark coloured tropical soil, notably in the cotton-growing area of the northwest Deccan, India. Also called "tropical black earth". [Hindi *regar.*]
re·gur·gi·tate (ri-gúrji-tayt, rée-) *v.* **-tated, -tating, -tates.** *—intr.* **1.** To rush or surge back. **2.** To bring partially digested food back into the mouth to feed the young. Used especially of certain birds. *—tr.* **1.** To cause to pour back; especially, to vomit up (partially digested food). **2.** To bring (partially digested food) back into the mouth. Used especially of certain birds. **3.** To reproduce (facts, for example) in an unthinking fashion. [Medieval Latin *regurgitāre* : *re-,* back + Late Latin *gurgitāre,* to engulf, flood, from Latin *gurges,* a whirlpool.] **—re·gur·gi·ta·tion** (-táysh'n) *n.*
re·ha·bil·i·tate (rée-ə-billi-tayt, -hə-) *tr.v.* **-tated, -tating, -tates. 1.** To restore (a handicapped or delinquent person, for example) to useful life through education and therapy. **2.** To reinstate the good name of. **3.** To restore the former rank, privileges, or rights of. [Medieval Latin *rehabilitāre* : Late Latin *re-,* again + *habilitāre,* HABILITATE.] **—re·ha·bil·i·ta·tion** (-táysh'n) *n.* **—re·ha·bil·i·ta·tive** (-tətiv -taytiv) *adj.*
re·hash (rée-hásh) *tr.v.* **-hashed, -hashing, -hashes.** To repeat, rework, or rewrite (old material) without significant alteration.
~*n.* (rée-hash). A repeated or unoriginal account; a rehashing. [RE- + HASH (to chop over).]
re·hear (rée-héer) *tr.v.* **-heard** (-hérd), **-hearing, -hears. 1.** To hear again. **2.** *Law.* To give a second consideration to (a case).
re·hears·al (ri-hérss'l, rə-) *n.* **1.** The act or an instance of practising for a performance, especially for a public performance. **2.** A verbal repetition; a detailed enumeration: *a rehearsal of his woes.*
re·hearse (ri-hérss, rə-) *v.* **-hearsed, -hearsing, -hearses.** *—tr.* **1. a.** To practise (all or part of a play, concert, entertainment, or the like) in preparation for a public performance. **b.** To make rehearse; direct in rehearsal. **2.** To perfect or cause to perfect (an action) by repetition. **3.** To retell or recite. **4.** To list or enumerate. *—intr.* To rehearse a concert, entertainment, play, or the like. [Middle English *rehercen,* from Old French *rehercer,* to repeat, originally "to harrow again" : *re-,* again + *hercer,* to harrow, from *herce,* a harrow, from Latin *hirpex* (see **hearse**).] **—re·hears·er** *n.*
re·heat (rée-héet) *tr.v.* **-heated, -heating, -heats. 1.** To add fuel to (exhaust gas in a jet engine) in order to give further combustion and improve the power. **2.** To heat again.
~*n.* The process of reheating exhaust gases in a jet engine.
Re·ho·bo·am (rée-ə-bṓ-əm, -hə-) *n. Often small* **r.** A large wine bottle often used for champagne, holding the equivalent of six standard bottles. [After *Rehoboam,* son of King Solomon (by analogy with JEROBOAM).]
re·house (rée-hówz) *tr.v.* **-housed, -housing, -houses.** To put or re-establish in a new, usually improved, dwelling or shelter.
Reich (rīk; *German* rīkh) *n.* The territory or government of a German empire or republic; specifically: the *First Reich,* the Holy Roman Empire (ninth century to 1806); the *Second Reich,* the German Empire (1871–1919); the Weimar Republic (1919–33); and the *Third Reich* (1933–45). [German, from Old High German *rīhhi,* realm.]
Reich, Wilhelm (1897–1957). Austrian psychologist. He was Freud's assistant in Vienna (1922–28), but rejected his ideas. In 1939 he settled in the United States, where he claimed to discover a new kind of energy called *orgone,* discharged through sexual release. In 1954 the Food and Drug Administration ordered the destruction of all *orgone accumulators,* boxes in which Reich advised patients to sit to restore this energy. For defying a ban and continuing to publish, Reich was convicted of contempt of court in 1956, and died in prison.
Reichs·mark (rīks-maark; *German* rīkhs-) *n., pl.* **reichsmark** or **-marks.** *Abbr.* **RM.** A former monetary unit of Germany, until 1948, having a value of 100 Reichspfennigs. See **Deutsche mark.** [German : *Reichs,* genitive of REICH + MARK (money).]
Reichs·pfen·nig (rīks-fennig; *German* rīkhs-pfennikh) *n.* A former bronze German coin, worth 1/100 of a Reichsmark. See **pfennig.** [German : *Reichs,* genitive of REICH + PFENNIG.]
Reichs·tag (rīks-taag; *German* rīkhs-taak) *n.* **1.** The representative and legislative assembly of the German Empire (1871–1919) and of the Weimar Republic (1919–33). **2.** The building in Berlin in which the assembly met. [German : *Reichs,* genitive of REICH + *Tag,* council, diet, from *tagen,* to deliberate.]
Reid (reed), **Sir George Houston** (1845–1918). Australian politician, born in Scotland. He was premier of New South Wales (1894–99) and prime minister of Australia (1904–05). He was knighted in 1909, served as high commissioner to London (1910–15), and sat in the British parliament (1916–18).
re·i·fy (rée-i-fī, ráy-) *tr.v.* **-fied, -fying, -fies.** To regard or treat (an abstraction or ideal) as if concretely or materially existing. [Latin *rēs,* a thing + -FY.] **—re·i·fi·ca·tion** (-fi-káysh'n) *n.* **—re·i·fi·er** *n.*
reign (rayn) *n.* **1.** The exercise of sovereign power, as by a monarch. **2.** A period during which sovereignty is held. **3.** Dominance or widespread influence: *the reign of reason.*
~*intr.v.* **reigned, reigning, reigns. 1.** To exercise sovereign power. **2.** To hold the title of sovereign, but with limited authority. **3.** To be predominant or prevalent. [Middle English *rei(n)gne,* from Old French *reigne,* from Latin *rēgnum,* from *rēx* (stem *rēg-*), a king.]
reign·ing (ráyning) *adj.* Designating the current holder of a championship or other competitive title: *the reigning Miss World.*
Reign of Terror *n.* **1.** The period (1793–94) of the French Revolution during which thousands of persons were executed. **2.** *Small* **r,** *small* **t.** Any period of widespread violence or intimidation.
Reik (rīk), **Theodor** (1888–1969). U.S. psychologist, born in Vienna. He was one of Freud's students and worked with him (1910–38), after which he settled in the United States. His numerous books included *The Secret Self* (1952), and *Myth and Guilt* (1957).
re·im·burse (rée-im-búrss) *tr.v.* **-bursed, -bursing, -burses. 1.** To repay: *He reimbursed his creditors.* **2.** To pay back or compensate (a person) for money spent, or losses or damages incurred. [RE- + obsolete *imburse,* to pay, to pocket money, from Old French *embourser* : EN- + *borser,* to obtain money, from *borse,* a purse, from Late Latin *bursa,* "oxhide", from Greek, hide, skin.] **—re·im·burs·a·ble** *adj.* **—re·im·burse·ment** *n.*
re·im·port (rée-im-pórt ‖ -pṓrt) *tr.v.* **-ported, -porting, -ports.** To bring back into a country (goods made from raw materials originally exported from that country).
~*n.* (-ím-pawrt ‖ -pōrt) **1.** The act of reimporting. **2.** Goods reimported. **—re·im·por·ta·tion** (-táysh'n) *n.*
re·im·pres·sion (rée-im-présh'n) *n.* **1.** A second or subsequent impression. **2.** A reprinting of a book.
Reims (raNss). *English* **Rheims** (reemz). City in the département of Marne in northeast France on the river Vesle. It is a major marketing centre for champagne wines. The site of the coronation of most French kings after Louis VII (1137), it has a fine Gothic cathedral. The German surrender was signed at Allied headquarters in Reims at the end of World War II (May 1945).
rein (rayn) *n.* **1. a.** *Plural.* A pair of long, narrow leather straps attached to the bit of a bridle and used by a rider or driver to control a horse or other animal. **b.** Any strap forming part of a harness, such as a bearing rein. **2.** *Plural.* A harness used to control a young child. **3.** *Often plural.* Any means of restraint, check, or guidance. **4.** *Often plural.* Any means of control: *the reins of government.* **—draw rein. 1.** To exert pressure on the reins. **2.** To slow or stop. **—give (free) rein to.** To release from restraints. **—keep a tight rein on.** To exercise close control over.
~*v.* **reined, reining, reins.** *—tr.* **1.** To check or hold back (a horse or other animal). Often used with *in, back,* or *up.* **2.** To guide or control. **3.** *Archaic.* To equip with reins. *—intr.* To control a horse or other animal with reins. Often used with *in, back,* or *up.* [Middle English *re(i)ne,* from Old French *re(s)ne,* from Vulgar Latin *retina* (unattested), from Latin *retinēre,* to RETAIN.]
re·in·car·nate (ree-íng-kaar-nayt, rée-in-kár-) *tr.v.* **-nated, -nating, -nates.** To furnish with another body; incarnate again. Usually used in the passive: *believed he'd be reincarnated as a snake.*
~*adj.* (rée-in-kár-nət, -nit, -nayt). Reborn in another body; reincarnated. **—re·in·car·na·tion** (rée-in-kaar-náysh'n) *n.*
rein·deer (ráyn-deer) *n., pl.* **-deers** or collectively **reindeer.** A large deer, *Rangifer tarandus,* of arctic regions of the Old World and Greenland, having branched antlers in both sexes. It is identical to the caribou, but can be domesticated. [Middle English *reyndere,* from Old Norse *hreindyri* : *hreinn,* reindeer + *dyr,* deer.]
reindeer moss *n.* An erect, greyish, branching lichen, *Cladonia rangiferina,* of arctic regions, used as food for reindeer.
re·in·fec·tion (rée-in-féksh'n) *n.* A second infection that follows recovery from a previous infection by the same causative agent.
re·in·force (rée-in-fórss ‖ -fṓrss) *tr.v.* **-forced, -forcing, -forces. 1.** To give more force or effectiveness to; strengthen; support. **2.** *Military.* To strengthen with additional manpower or equipment. **3.** To strengthen, as by adding extra support or padding. **4.** To increase in number. **5.** *Psychology.* To encourage by means of reinforcement. [RE- + *inforce,* variant of ENFORCE.]
reinforced concrete *n. Abbr.* **R.C.** Poured concrete containing steel bars or metal netting to increase its tensile strength. Also called "ferroconcrete".
re·in·force·ment (rée-in-fórss-mənt ‖ -fṓrss-) *n.* **1.** The act or process of reinforcing, or the condition of being reinforced. **2.** Something that reinforces. **3.** *Often plural.* Additional troops, vessels, or equipment sent to support a military action. **4.** *Psychology.* **a.** The occurrence or experimental introduction of an unconditioned stimulus along with a conditioned stimulus. **b.** The strengthening

reindeer *Reindeer, or caribou, are domesticated in Lappland and used as draught animals as well as for their meat, milk, and hides.*

of a conditioned response by such means. **c.** The strengthening of an instrumental or operant conditioned response leading to satisfaction; reward. **d.** Loosely, any condition strengthening learning.

Rein·hardt (rín-haart), **Django** (1910–53). Belgian Gypsy jazz guitarist. He began his professional career in 1922. His left hand was mutilated in a fire in 1928, but he devised a fingering technique to overcome the disability. In 1934, with Stephane Grappelli and others, he founded the Quintette du Hot Club de France.

Reinhardt, Max (1873–1943). Austrian stage actor, producer, and director. He managed his own theatre in Berlin (1902–05); in 1919 he founded the *Grosse Schauspielhaus,* and in 1920 the Salzburg Festival. In 1933 he fled Germany and settled in the United States. He was famous for his ambitious stage-setting and crowd scenes.

reins (raynz) *pl.n. Archaic.* **1.** The kidneys, loins, or lower back region. **2.** The seat of the affections and passions, which were formerly regarded as having their source in the kidneys and loins. [Middle English, from Old French, from Latin *rēnēs.* See **renal.**]

re·in·state (rée-in-stáyt) *tr.v.* **-stated, -stating, -states.** To restore to a previous condition or position. **—re·in·state·ment** *n.*

re·in·sure (rée-in-shóor, -shór || -shéwr) *tr.v.* **-sured, -suring, -sures. 1.** To insure again. **2.** To insure by transferring in whole or in part a risk or contingent liability already covered under an existing contract. **—re·in·sur·ance** *n.* **—re·in·sur·er** *n.*

re·in·vest (rée-in-vést) *tr.v.* **-vested, -vesting, -vests.** To invest (capital or earnings) again. Used especially of receipts derived from a securities portfolio. **—re·in·vest·ment** *n.*

reis. Alternative plural of **real** (Portuguese monetary unit).

re·is·sue (rée-íshoo, -íssew) *tr.v.* **-sued, -suing, -sues.** To issue again; make available again.
~*n.* **1.** A second or subsequent issue, as of a book altered in format or price. **2.** A reprinting of postage stamps from unchanged plates.

re·it·er·ate (ree-íttə-rayt) *tr.v.* **-ated, -ating, -ates.** To say or do over again; repeat. [Latin *reiterāre* : *re-,* again + *iterāre,* ITERATE.] **—re·it·er·a·tion** (-ráysh'n) *n.* **—re·it·er·a·tive** (-rətiv, -raytiv) *adj.* **—re·it·er·a·tive·ly** *adv.*

Reith of Stonehaven (reeth), **John (Charles Walsham), 1st Baron** (1889–1971). British radio, television, and airline manager. As director-general (1927–38) of the BBC, he helped to establish its framework and ensure its independence of government control. In 1938 he became chairman of Imperial Airways, which he merged with British Airways to form the new British Overseas Airways Corporation in 1939. He was director of Combined Operations Material at the Admiralty (1943–45) and chairman of the Commonwealth Telecommunications Board (1946–50).

reive (reev) *intr.v.* **reived, reiving, reives.** *Northern British.* To raid, rob, or plunder. [Variant of REAVE.] **—reiv·er** *n.*

re·ject (ri-jékt, rə-) *tr.v.* **-jected, -jecting, -jects. 1.** To refuse to accept, recognise, or make use of; repudiate. **2.** To refuse to consider or grant; deny. **3.** To refuse affection or recognition to (a person). **4.** To discard as defective or useless; throw away. **5.** To spit out or vomit. **6.** To fail to accept (transplanted tissues or organs) owing to immunological incompatibility. —See Synonyms at **refuse.**
~*n.* (rée-jekt). Something or someone that has been rejected as unsatisfactory or below standard. [Middle English *rejecten,* from Latin *rejicere* (past participle *rejectus*), to throw back : *re-,* back, away + *jacere,* to throw.] **—re·ject·er** (ri-jéktər, rə-) *n.*

re·jec·tion (ri-jéksh'n, rə-) *n.* **1.** The act or process of rejecting. **2.** The condition of being rejected. **3.** Something rejected.

re·jec·tor (ri-jéktər, rə-) *n.* One that rejects; specifically, an electronic circuit that cuts out signals of a designated frequency range. Compare **acceptor.**

re·jig (rée-jíg) *tr.v.* **-jigged, -jigging, -jigs. 1.** To re-equip (a factory, workshop, or the like) with different machines or equipment. **2.** *Informal.* To revise, rework, or rearrange. **—re·jig·ger** *n.*

re·joice (ri-jóyss, rə-) *v.* **-joiced, -joicing, -joices.** —*intr.* **1.** To feel or be joyful. **2.** To possess or be lucky in possessing something. Used with *in*: *He rejoiced in the name of Herbert Sidebottom.* —*tr.* To fill with joy; gladden. [Middle English *rejoicen,* from Old French *rejoir* (stem *rejoiss-*) : *re-* (intensive) + *joir,* to be joyful, from Latin *gaudēre.*] **—re·joic·er** *n.*

re·joic·ing (ri-jóyssing, rə-) *n.* The feeling or expressing of joy or an instance of this; joyful celebration.

re·join[1] (rée-jóyn, ri-) *v.* **-joined, -joining, -joins.** —*tr.* **1.** To come again into the company of: *rejoined his regiment.* **2.** To join or put together again; reunite. —*intr.* To be or become joined again.

re·join[2] (ri-jóyn, rə-) *v.* **-joined, -joining, -joins.** —*tr.* To say as a reply. —*intr.* **1.** To respond; answer. **2.** *Law.* To answer a plaintiff's replication. [Middle English *rejoinen,* from Old French *rejoindre* : *re-,* back, again + *joindre,* to JOIN.]

re·join·der (ri-jóyndər, rə-) *n.* **1.** An answer, especially in response to a reply. **2.** *Law.* A second pleading by a defendant, in answer to a plaintiff's replication. [Middle English *rejoyner,* from Old French *rejoindre* (substantive infinitive), to REJOIN (answer).]

re·ju·ve·nate (ri-jóov-ə-nayt, rə-, -i-) *tr.v.* **-nated, -nating, -nates. 1.** To restore the youthful vigour or appearance of. **2.** To stimulate (a stream) to renewed erosive activity, as by a local uplift of land or an increase in precipitation. [RE- + Latin *juvenis,* a youth.] **—re·ju·ve·na·tion** (-náysh'n) *n.* **—re·ju·ve·na·tor** (-náytər) *n.*

re·ju·ve·nes·cence (ri-jóov-ə-néss'nss, rée-, -i-) *n.* The act of making youthful again; rejuvenation. **—re·ju·ve·nes·cent** *adj.*

re·kin·dle (rée-kínd'l) *v.* **-kindled, kindling, -kindles.** —*tr.* **1.** To relight. **2.** To revive or renew: *rekindle one's interest in books.* —*intr.* To be relit or revived.

rel. **1.** relating. **2.** relative; relatively. **3.** released. **4.** religion; religious.

re·lapse (ri-láps, rə-) *intr.v.* **-lapsed, -lapsing, -lapses. 1.** To fall back into or revert to a former habit or state. **2.** To regress after partial recovery from illness. **3.** To slip back into bad ways; backslide.
~*n.* (*also* rée-laps). The act or an instance of relapsing. [Latin *relapsus,* past participle of *relābī,* to slide back : *re-,* back + *lābī,* to slide.] **—re·laps·er** *n.*

relapsing fever *n.* Any of several infectious diseases characterised by chills and fever, and caused by spirochaetes of the genus *Borrelia* transmitted by lice and ticks. Also called "recurrent fever".

re·late (ri-láyt, rə-) *v.* **-lated, -lating, -lates.** —*tr.* **1.** To narrate or tell. **2.** To bring into logical or natural association. —*intr.* **1.** To have connection, relation, or reference. Used with *to.* **2.** To form mutually responsive relationships; interact with others in an effective manner. Sometimes used with *to.* —See Synonyms at **join.** [Latin *relātus* (past participle of *referre,* to carry back, REFER) : *re-,* back + *-lātus,* "carried".] **—re·lat·er** *n.*

re·lat·ed (ri-láytid, rə-) *adj.* **1.** Connected; associated. **2.** Connected by kinship, marriage, or common origin. **3.** *Music.* Having a specified harmonic connection. **—re·lat·ed·ness** *n.*

re·la·tion (ri-láysh'n, rə-) *n.* **1.** A logical or natural association between two or more things; relevance of one to another; a connection. **2.** The connection of people by blood or marriage; kinship. **3.** A person related to another by blood or marriage; a relative. **4.** The mode or way in which a person or thing is connected with another. **5.** *Plural.* The connections or associations drawing together persons, groups, or nations in personal, business, or diplomatic affairs: *public relations.* **6.** Reference; regard: *in relation to your query.* **7. a.** The act of telling or narrating. **b.** A narrative; an account. **8.** *Plural.* Sexual intercourse.

re·la·tion·al (ri-láysh'n'l, rə-) *adj.* **1.** Of or arising from kinship. **2.** Indicating or constituting relations. **3.** *Grammar.* Expressing a syntactic relation.

re·la·tion·ship (ri-láysh'n-ship, rə-) *n.* **1.** The condition or fact of being related. **2.** Connection by blood or marriage; kinship. **3. a.** A particular kind of connection existing between people having dealings with one another: *I have a good working relationship with my boss.* **b.** A close emotional connection between two people.

rel·a·tive (réllətiv) *adj. Abbr.* **rel. 1.** Having pertinence or relevance; connected; related. **2.** Considered in comparison with something else. **3.** Dependent upon or interconnected with something else for intelligibility or significance; not absolute. **4.** Referring to or qualifying an antecedent. **5.** *Grammar.* Designating a pronoun that introduces a relative clause and has reference to an antecedent. In the sentence *He who hesitates is lost,* the relative pronoun is *who.* Compare **demonstrative, interrogative. 6.** *Music.* Having the same key signature. Said of major and minor scales and keys. **7.** *Physics & Chemistry.* Pertaining to or designating a physical quantity that is expressed as a ratio of the measured value to the value for some standard system: *relative density; relative humidity.*
~*n.* **1. a.** One related by kinship; a relation. **b.** One related by a common origin. **2.** One that is relative. **3.** *Grammar.* A relative term. [Middle English *relatif,* from Old French, from Late Latin *relātīvus,* from Latin *relātus.* See **relate.**] **—rel·a·tive·ly** *adv.* **—rel·a·tive·ness** *n.*

relative atomic mass *n. Symbol* **A_r** *Chemistry.* **Atomic weight** *(see).*

relative biological effectiveness *n. Abbr.* **RBE** *Physics.* A measure of the capacity of a specific ionising radiation to produce a specific biological effect, usually expressed as the dose of a standard type of radiation relative to the dose of the ionisation in question required to produce the effect.

relative clause *n. Grammar.* A dependent clause introduced by a relative pronoun. In the sentence *He who hesitates is lost,* the relative clause is *who hesitates.*

relative density *n. Symbol* **d** The density of a substance relative to the density of some standard substance; specifically: **1.** The ratio of the density of a liquid or solid substance to the density of water. Unless otherwise specified, it is assumed that the substance is at room temperature (20° C) and the water is at its temperature of maximum density (4° C). Also called "specific gravity". **2.** The ratio of the density of a gas to the density of hydrogen, usually under conditions of standard temperature and pressure.

relative humidity *n. Abbr.* **r.h.** The ratio of the amount of water vapour in the air at a specific temperature to the maximum capacity of the air at that temperature. Compare **absolute humidity.**

relative majority *n.* The number of votes cast for the winning candidate that exceed those cast for the runner-up, when no one candidate receives more than 50 per cent of all votes cast. Also *U.S.* "plurality". Compare **absolute majority.**

relative molecular mass *n. Symbol* **M_r** *Chemistry.* **Molecular weight** *(see).*

relative permeability *n. Symbol* μ_r *Physics.* The ratio of the magnetic permeability of a given medium to that of free space (that is, to the magnetic constant).

relative permittivity *n. Symbol* ϵ_r *Physics.* The ratio of the electric permittivity of a given medium to that of free space (that is, to the electric constant). Also called "dielectric constant".

relative pitch *n.* **1.** The pitch of a note as determined by its position in a scale. **2.** The ability to recognise or produce a note by mentally establishing a relationship between its pitch and that of a recently heard note. Compare **absolute pitch.**

PRONUNCIATION KEY

a, trap; aa, father; ai, fair; ar, star; aw, lawn; ay, play; b, bb, stab; rubber; ch, church; ck, ticket; d, dd, dead; ladder; e, dress; ee, bee; er, defer; ew, few; ewr, pure; ə, about; ər, letter; f, ff, fife; differ; g, gg, giggle; h, hat; i, kit; ī, price; īr, fire; j, judge; k, kick; l, ll, let; 'l, needle; m, mm, man; n, nn, no; 'n, sudden; ng, thing; o, lot; ō, no; oo, foot; ōō, shoe; oor, poor; ow, cow; owr, hour; oy, boy; p, pp, pepper; r, rr, red; s, ss, sauce; sh, ship; t, tt, totter; th, thick; th, this; smooth; u, cut; ur, turn; v, vv, valve; w, wet; y, yes; z, zz, zebra; zh, vision; pleasure

IN FOREIGN WORDS:

aN, oN, Saint-Saëns; hl, Llanelli; Hluhluwe; kh, loch; lough; Khaled

STRESS MARK:

ín-sīt, insight; in-sít, incite

rel·a·tiv·ism (réllətiv-iz'm) *n.* Any of various philosophical attitudes holding that moral value, knowledge, or truth is not absolute but relative, for example to an individual, historical circumstances, or a theoretical framework.

rel·a·tiv·ist (réllətivist) *n.* **1.** A proponent of relativism. **2.** A physicist specialising in the theories of relativity.

rel·a·tiv·is·tic (rélləti-vistik) *adj.* **1.** Of or pertaining to relativism. **2.** *Physics.* **a.** Of, pertaining to, or resulting from speeds that are approaching the speed of light: *relativistic increase in mass.* **b.** Of or pertaining to phenomena explicable by Special or General relativity: *relativistic mechanics.*

rel·a·tiv·i·ty (réllə-tívvəti) *n.* **1.** The quality or state of being relative. **2.** A state of dependence in which the existence, quality, or significance of one entity is determined by that of another. **3.** A theory of relative motion, space, and time developed by Albert Einstein in two parts. **Special relativity** (1905) deals with uniform motion at constant relative velocity, and is based on the principles that the speed of light is a constant, irrespective of the the motion of the observer, and that physical laws are the same for all observers. **General relativity** (published 1916) extends this to non-uniform (accelerated) motion and is applied particularly to gravitation.

re·la·tor (ri-láytər, rə-) *n.* One who relates or narrates.

re·lax (ri-láks, rə-) *v.* **-laxed, -laxing, -laxes.** *—tr.* **1.** To make lax or loose: *relax one's grip.* **2.** To make less severe, formal, or strict. **3.** To reduce in intensity; slacken. **4.** To relieve from effort or strain. *—intr.* **1.** To take one's ease; rest. **2.** To become lax or loose. **3.** To become less severe. **4.** To become less formal or tense. [Middle English *relaxen,* from Latin *relaxāre : re-,* back + *laxāre,* to loosen, from *laxus,* lax, loose.] **—re·lax·a·ble** *adj.* **—re·lax·er** *n.*

re·lax·ant (ri-láksənt, rə-) *n.* A drug or therapeutic treatment that relaxes or relieves muscular or nervous tension. *~adj.* Tending to relax or to relieve tension.

re·lax·a·tion (réelak-sáysh'n, réllək-) *n.* **1. a.** The act of relaxing. **b.** The state of being relaxed. **2.** Refreshment of body or mind; recreation: *play golf for relaxation.* **3.** A loosening or slackening. **4.** A reduction in strictness or severity. **5.** *Physiology.* The return to normal length of inactive muscle or muscle fibres following contraction. **6.** *Physics.* The return or adjustment of a system to equilibrium following a small displacement or abrupt change. **7.** *Mathematics.* A numerical method in which the errors, or residuals, resulting from an initial approximation are reduced by succeeding approximations until all errors are within specific limits. *—See Synonyms at* **rest.** **—re·lax·a·tive** (ri-láksətiv, rə-) *adj. & n.*

relaxation time *n.* *Physics.* The time required for an exponential variable to decrease to 1/*e* (0.368) of its initial value.

re·laxed (ri-lákst, rə-) *adj.* **1.** Free from strain or tension. **2.** Informal or easy-going in manner. **—re·laxed·ly** (re-láksidli) *adv.* **—re·laxed·ness** *n.*

re·lax·in (rī-láksin, rə-) *n.* A female hormone secreted by the corpus luteum in the final stages of pregnancy that causes the cervix to dilate and relaxes the pelvic ligaments in childbirth. [RELAX + -IN.]

re·lay (rée-láy) *tr.v.* **-laid** (-láyd), **-laying, -lays.** To lay again.

re·lay (rée-lay, ri-láy) *n.* **1.** A crew of labourers who relieve another crew at work; a shift. **2.** A fresh team, as of horses or dogs, to relieve weary animals in a hunt, task, or journey. **3.** An act of passing something along from one person, group, or station to another. **4.** A relay race, or any one of its lengths or laps. **5.** An automatic electromagnetic or electromechanical device that responds to a small current or voltage change by activating switches or other devices in an electric circuit. *~tr.v.* (ri-láy, rə-, rée-lay), **relayed, -laying, -lays.** **1.** To pass or send along by or as if by relay: *relay a message.* **2.** To supply with fresh relays. **3.** *Electronics.* To control or retransmit by means of a relay. **4.** *British.* To broadcast from a theatre, concert hall, or the like via a transmitter. [Middle English *relai,* from Old French, from *relaier,* to relay, leave behind : *re-,* back + *laier,* to leave, variant of *laissier,* from Latin *laxāre,* to loosen, from *laxus,* lax, loose.]

relay race *n.* A race between two or more teams, in which each team member runs only a set part of the race, and then is relieved by another member of his team.

relay station *n.* An installation for receiving telecommunications signals and amplifying and retransmitting them.

re·lease (rée-léess) *tr.v.* **-leased, -leasing, -leases.** To lease again.

re·lease (ri-léess, rə-) *tr.v.* **-leased, -leasing, -leases.** **1.** To set free from confinement, restraint, or bondage; liberate. **2.** To free, unfasten, or let go of. **3.** To relieve from debt or obligation. **4. a.** To allow performance, sale, publication, distribution, or circulation of. **b.** To make known or available. **5.** To relinquish (a right or claim, for example). **6.** *Chemistry.* To free from chemical combination. *~n.* **1.** A deliverance; liberation. **2.** An authoritative discharge from an obligation or from prison. **3.** An unfastening or letting go of something caught or held fast. **4.** A device or catch for locking or releasing a mechanism. **5. a.** A freeing or issuing of something for general publication, use, or circulation: *a film on general release.* **b.** Something thus issued or released: *a press release; a record release.* **6.** *Law.* **a.** The relinquishment of a right, title, or claim to another. **b.** The document authorising such a relinquishment. [Middle English *relesen,* from Old French *relessier, relaissier,* from Latin *relaxāre,* to RELAX.]

re·leas·er (ri-léessər, rə-) *n.* **1.** One that releases. **2.** *Zoology.* Any stimulus or combination of stimuli that elicits an instinctive behavioural pattern.

rel·e·gate (rél-i-gayt, -ə-) *tr.v.* **-gated, -gating, -gates.** **1.** To send or

---

relativity

HOW THINGS MOVE IN RELATION TO EACH OTHER
The theory that cast new light on the workings of the universe

The theory of relativity was proposed by Albert Einstein, the German-born mathematical physicist, early this century. It is based on the assumption that all motion is relative and that absolute rest is meaningless. That is, rest and motion do not exist by themselves – they depend on comparing one object with another.

For example, if a vehicle is travelling at 145 kilometres (90 miles) an hour towards another vehicle approaching it head on at 115 kilometres (70 miles) an hour, the velocity of the vehicles relative to each other is 260 kilometres (160 miles) an hour.

This relative velocity, however, applies to the two vehicles only in connection with each other. The velocity of the first vehicle relative to the Earth is 145 kilometres (90 miles) an hour. Relative to the sun it is about 29 000 kilometres (18,000 miles) an hour. Einstein also put forward the ideas that mass and energy were equivalent, and that time and space were inseparable – not independent concepts as had been previously supposed.

Einstein expounded his theory in two parts – the special theory of relativity (1905), which applies to observers or systems in uniform relative motion, and the general theory of relativity (1915), which deals also with observers in accelerated motion.

The special theory is developed from two principles: first, that the laws of natural phenomena are the same for all observers, and second, that the velocity of light is constant for all observers regardless of their own velocity. From these basic principles Einstein deduced that mass and energy are interchangeable, and are related by the simple-sounding formula $E = mc^2$, where E is energy, m is mass, and c is the speed of light.

The formula shows that a small mass can be converted into a huge amount of energy. This idea led to, amongst other things, the invention of the atom bomb, and unlocked the secret of how the sun shines. Both processes are nuclear reactions in which a tiny amount of nuclear mass is liberated as light and heat.

Other findings of the special theory are that if a body moves at a high velocity relative to an observer, the observer sees that the length of the body has apparently contracted and that time for the body has slowed down.

These changes are significant only for speeds close to the speed of light. For example, if the body is a metre rule with a clock strapped to it, the observer will measure the length of the rule to be less than a metre and the clock will appear to be running slowly compared with the observer's clock. The observer will also see that the mass of the body increased with its velocity. For this reason it is impossible to travel faster than the speed of light, for at that speed mass becomes infinite.

In the general theory, Einstein showed that the presence of massive bodies in space – or more specifically the presence of their gravitational fields – distorts space itself, so that the shortest distance between two points becomes a curve rather than a straight line. Light also is bent by the gravitational field of a massive body.

Many verifications of Einstein's theory have arisen in modern physics, especially in the fields of astrophysics and nuclear physics.

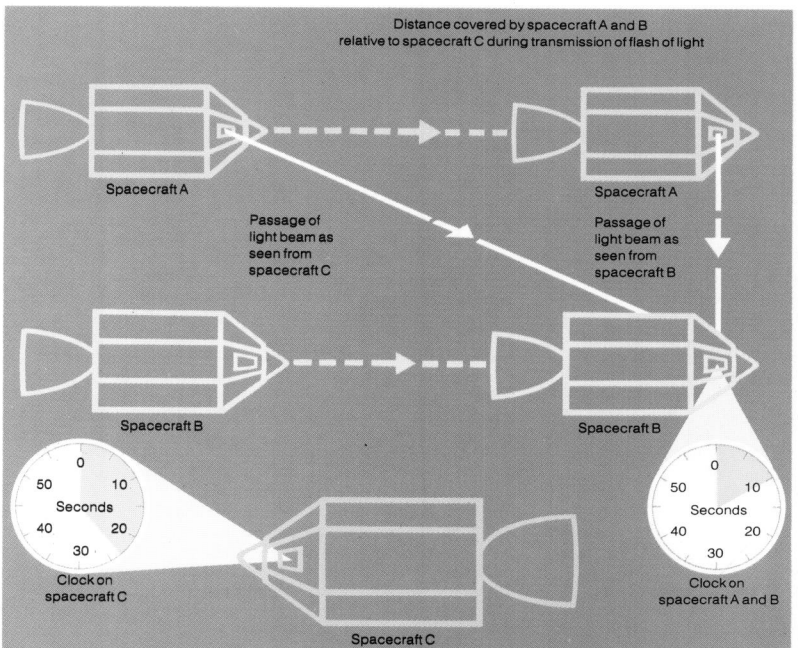

Distance covered by spacecraft A and B relative to spacecraft C during transmission of flash of light

Spacecraft A

Spacecraft A

Passage of light beam as seen from spacecraft C

Passage of light beam as seen from spacecraft B

Spacecraft B

Spacecraft B

0 10 20 30 40 50 Seconds
Clock on spacecraft C

0 10 20 30 40 50 Seconds
Clock on spacecraft A and B

Spacecraft C

WHEN TIME SLOWS DOWN *Because the speed of all motion is relative to something else, time does not pass at the same rate for all observers. Consider, for instance, what happens when spacecraft A and B, flying side by side, pass spacecraft C going in the opposite direction.*

If a flash of light is sent from A to B it is seen by both craft as following a straight line, because neither craft is moving relative to the other. But seen from C the flash follows a diagonal line, *from the position of A when the flash was emitted to the position of B when it was received.*

This diagonal line is longer than the distance between spacecraft A and B, and since the speed of light is constant, the time interval between emission and arrival must seem longer when viewed from C than from A or B. If A and B pass C at 90 per cent of the speed of light, and the flash takes 10 seconds from A to B, to observers in C it will seem to take 23 seconds.

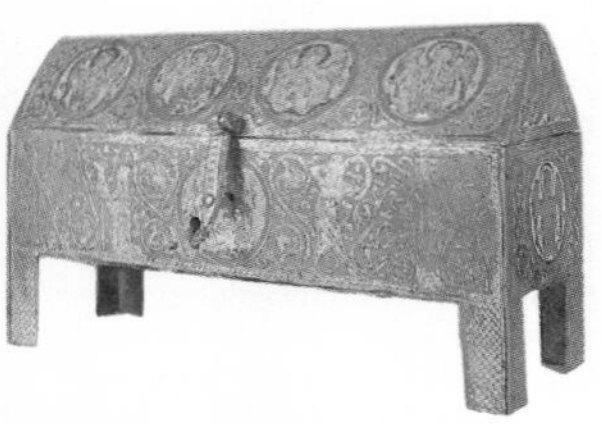

reliquary *A 13th-century French reliquary, decorated in enamel with angels in medallions. Reliquaries are used to store holy relics such as bones of saints.*

PRONUNCIATION KEY

a, trap; aa, father; ai, **fair**; ar, **star**; aw, **lawn**; ay, **play**; b, bb, **stab**; **rubber**; ch, **church**; ck, **ticket**; d, dd, **dead**; **ladder**; e, **dress**; ee, **bee**; er, **defer**; ew, **few**; ewr, **pure**; ə, **about**; ər, **letter**; f, ff, **fife**; **differ**; g, gg, **giggle**; h, **hat**; i, **kit**; ī, **price**; īr, **fire**; j, **judge**; k, **kick**; l, ll, **let**; 'l, **needle**; m, mm, **man**; n, nn, **no**; 'n, **sudden**; ng, **thing**; o, **lot**; ō, **no**; ŏŏ, **foot**; ōō, **shoe**; oor, **poor**; ow, **cow**; owr, **hour**; oy, **boy**; p, pp, **pepper**; r, rr, **red**; s, ss, **sauce**; sh, **ship**; t, tt, **totter**; th, **thick**; th, **this**; **smooth**; u, **cut**; ur, **turn**; v, vv, **valve**; w, **wet**; y, **yes**; z, zz, **zebra**; zh, **vision**; **pleasure**

IN FOREIGN WORDS:

aN, oN, **Saint-Saëns**; hl, **Llanelli**; **Hluhluwe**; kh, **loch**; **lough**; **Khaled**

STRESS MARK:

ín-sīt, insight; in-sī́t, incite

consign, especially to an obscure or inferior place, position, or condition. **2.** To move to a lower division. Used of a sports team, especially one in a Football League. **3.** To refer or assign (a matter or task, for example) for decision or execution. **4.** To cast out; banish; exile. [Latin *relēgāre,* to send away : *re-,* back, away + *lēgare,* to send.] **—rel·e·ga·tion** (-gáysh'n) *n.*

re·lent (ri-lént, rə-) *intr.v.* **-lented, -lenting, -lents.** To become softened or gentler in attitude, temper, or determination; go back on a harsh decision. —See Synonyms at **yield.** [Middle English *relenten,* from Medieval Latin *relentāre* (unattested) : *re-* (intensive), again + *lentāre,* soften, from Latin, bend, from *lentus,* pliable.]

re·lent·less (ri-lént-ləss, rə-, -liss) *adj.* **1.** Unyielding; pitiless: *relentless persecution.* **2.** Steady and persistent; unremitting: *the relentless advance of the tide.* **—re·lent·less·ly** *adv.* **—re·lent·less·ness** *n.*

rel·e·vant (rél-i-vənt, -ə-) *adj.* **1.** Related to the matter at hand; to the point; pertinent. **2.** *Linguistics.* Serving to distinguish one phoneme from others; distinctive. [Medieval Latin *relevāns* (stem *relevant-*), from Latin, present participle of *relevāre,* to lift up, RELIEVE.] **—rel·e·vance, rel·e·van·cy** *n.* **—rel·e·vant·ly** *adv.*

Synonyms: *relevant, pertinent, germane, material, apt, apposite, apropos.*

re·li·a·ble (ri-lī́-əb'l, rə-) *adj.* Capable of being relied upon; trustworthy; dependable. **—re·li·a·bil·i·ty** (-ə-bílləti), **re·li·a·ble·ness** *n.* **—re·li·a·bly** *adv.*

re·li·ance (ri-lī́-ənss, rə-) *n.* **1.** The act of relying. **2.** Confidence; dependence; trust. **3.** Something or someone depended on; a mainstay. —See Synonyms at **trust.**

re·li·ant (ri-lī́-ənt, rə-) *adj.* Dependent; relying or trusting. Used with *on.* **—re·li·ant·ly** *adv.*

rel·ic (réllik) *n.* Also *archaic* **rel·ique** (réllik, ri-léek). **1.** Something that has survived the passage of time; especially, an object or custom whose original cultural environment has disappeared. **2.** *Biology.* A relict. **3.** Something cherished for its age or associations with a person, place, or event; a keepsake. **4.** An object of religious veneration; especially, an article reputed to be associated with a saint or martyr. **5.** Anything old, leftover, or remaining; a remnant. **6.** *Plural.* A corpse; the remains of a dead person. [Middle English *relik(e),* from Old French *relique,* from Late Latin *reliquiae,* remains (especially of a martyr), from Latin, from *relinquere,* to leave behind, RELINQUISH.]

rel·ict (réllikt) *n.* **1.** *Biology.* An organism or species of an earlier time surviving in an environment that has undergone considerable change. **2.** *Rare.* A widow.
~adj. Geology. Pertaining to something that has survived, such as structures or minerals after destructive processes. [Latin *relictus,* past participle of *relinquere,* to leave behind, RELINQUISH.]

re·lief (ri-léef, rə-) *n.* **1. a.** Ease from or lessening of pain or discomfort. **b.** Ease or lessening of a burden or something imposed, such as a levy: *tax relief.* **2. a.** Anything that lessens pain, discomfort, fear, anxiety, or the like. **b.** The feeling of buoyancy or well-being that immediately follows the removal or lessening of anxiety, pain, discomfort, or the like. **3.** Assistance, in the form of money or food, given to the needy, aged, or to the inhabitants of any disaster-stricken region. **4. a.** A release from a job, post, or duty, as of a sentinel. **b.** The person or group of persons taking over the duties of another. **5. a.** The projection of figures or forms from a flat background, or such a projection that is apparent only, as in painting. **b.** Any work of art featuring such projection. Also called "relievo." **6.** *Geography.* The variations in elevation of any area of the earth's surface. **7.** Distinction or prominence resulting from contrast: *Her dark hat brought her pallor into relief.* **8.** A diversion; a pleasant or amusing change: *light relief.* **9.** A bus, aircraft, ferry, or train that supplements or replaces an existing service. **10.** The act of raising a siege or blockade. **11.** *Law.* The obtaining of reparation or redress. **12.** In feudal law, a payment made by the heir of a deceased tenant to a lord for the privilege of succeeding to the tenant's estate. **—on relief.** *U.S.* Receiving government funds because of need or poverty. [Middle English, from Old French, from *relever,* to RELIEVE.]

relief map *n.* A map that depicts land configuration, as with contour lines, shading, or colours.

relief model *n.* A three-dimensional model of land configuration.

relief road *n.* A road, such as a bypass, that takes traffic away from another overcongested road or roads or a town.

re·lieve (ri-léev, rə-) *tr.v.* **-lieved, -lieving, -lieves. 1.** To lessen or alleviate (something painful, oppressive, or distressing); ease: *hypnotic suggestion may relieve pain.* **2.** To free from pain, anxiety, fear, or the like. **3. a.** To furnish assistance or aid to. **b.** To raise a siege or blockade of. **4.** To release (a person) from obligation or oppression, as by law or legislation. **5.** To free from a particular duty by providing or acting as a substitute. **6.** To make less oppressive, monotonous, or uniform: *a laugh relieved the tension.* **7.** To make distinct or effective through contrast; set off: *A black sash relieves a white gown.* **8.** *Informal.* To rob; take from: *I was relieved of my handbag.* **—relieve (oneself).** To empty one's bowels or bladder. [Middle English *releven,* from Old French *relever,* relieve, raise again, from Latin *relevāre* : *re-,* again + *levāre,* to raise.] **—re·liev·a·ble** *adj.* **—re·liev·er** *n.*

Synonyms: *relieve, allay, alleviate, assuage, comfort, lighten, soothe, mitigate.*

re·liev·ing arch *n.* An arch built for reinforcement, or to distribute weight more evenly.

re·lie·vo (ri-léevō, rə-) *n., pl.* **-vos.** Relief in art and architecture. [Italian *rilievo,* from *rilievare,* to emphasise, raise, from Latin *relevāre,* to RELIEVE.]

re·lig·ion (ri-líjən, rə-) *n. Abbr.* **rel., relig. 1.** The expression of man's belief in and reverence for a superhuman power or powers regarded as creating or governing the universe. **2.** Any personal or institutionalised system of beliefs or practices embodying this belief or reverence: *the Hindu religion.* **3.** The spiritual or emotional attitude of one who recognises the existence of a superhuman power or powers. **4.** Any objective pursued with zeal or conscientious devotion: *A collector might make a religion of his hobby.* **5.** The monastic way of life. **6.** *Archaic.* Sacred rites or practices. [Middle English *religioun,* from Old French *religion,* from Latin *religiō* (stem *religiōn-*), bond between man and the gods, perhaps from *religāre,* to bind back : *re-,* back + *ligāre,* to bind, fasten.]

re·lig·ion·ism (ri-líjə-niz'm, rə-) *n.* Excessive or affected religious zeal. **—re·lig·ion·ist** *n.*

re·li·gi·ose (ri-líji-ōss, rə-, -ōz) *adj.* Excessively religious, particularly in an affected or sentimental manner. [From RELIGIOUS.]

re·lig·i·os·i·ty (ri-líji-óssəti, rə-) *n., pl.* **-ties. 1.** The state of being religious. **2.** Excessive or affected piety.

re·lig·ious (ri-líjəss, rə-) *adj. Abbr.* **rel. 1.** Of, pertaining to, or teaching religion. **2.** Adhering to or manifesting religion; pious; godly. **3.** Extremely scrupulous or conscientious. **4.** Pertaining to or belonging to an order taking vows of poverty, chastity, and obedience.
~n., pl. **religious.** *Abbr.* **rel** A person belonging to a religious order, especially a monk or nun. [Middle English, from Old French, from Latin *religiōsus,* from *religiō,* RELIGION.] **—re·li·gious·ly** *adv.* **—re·li·gious·ness** *n.*

Religious Society of Friends *n.* A Christian sect founded in about 1650 in England by George Fox; it has no ritual, formal creed, or priesthood, and rejects violence. Preceded by *the.* Also known as the "Society of Friends", "Quakers".

re·line (rée-lī́n) *tr.v.* **-lined, -lining, -lines. 1.** To make new lines on. **2.** To put a new lining in (a garment, for example).

re·lin·quish (ri-língkwish, rə-) *tr.v.* **-quished, -quishing, -quishes. 1.** To retire from; give up; abandon. **2.** To put aside or desist from (something practised, professed, or intended). **3.** To surrender; renounce. **4.** To let go or release (a grasp, for example). [Middle English *relinquysshen,* from Old French *relinquir* (stem *relinquiss-*), from Latin *relinquere,* to leave behind : *re-,* behind + *linquere,* to leave.] **—re·lin·quish·er** *n.* **—re·lin·quish·ment** *n.*

Synonyms: *relinquish, yield, resign, abdicate, abandon, surrender, cede, waive, forgo, renounce.*

rel·i·quar·y (rélli-kwəri || *U.S.* -kwerri) *n., pl.* **-ies.** A receptacle, such as a coffer or shrine, for keeping or displaying religious relics. [French *relinquaire,* from Medieval Latin *reliquiārium,* from *reliquia,* singular of Late Latin *reliquiae,* remains. See **relic.**]

re·liq·ui·ae (ri-líkwi-ee, rə-) *pl.n.* Remains, especially of fossil organisms. [Latin.]

rel·ish (réllish) *n.* **1.** An appetite for something; an appreciation or liking: *a relish for luxury.* **2. a.** Pleasure; zest. **b.** Anything that lends pleasure or zest. **3.** A spicy or savoury condiment, such as pickles or chutney. **4.** The flavour of a food, especially when appetising. **5.** A trace or suggestion of some pleasurable quality.
~v. **relished, -ishing, -ishes.** *—tr.* **1.** To enjoy; take pleasure in. **2.** To look forward to with eagerness: *I don't relish the prospect of working this weekend.* **3.** To like the flavour of. **4.** To give flavour to; spice. *—intr.* To have a pleasing or distinctive taste. —See Synonyms at **like.** [Alteration (through influence of -ISH) of obsolete *reles,* a taste, from Old French *reles,* variant of *relais,* something remaining, from *relaissier,* to leave behind, release, from Latin *relaxāre,* to loosen, RELAX.] **—rel·ish·a·ble** *adj.*

re·live (rée-lív) *v.* **-lived, -living, -lives.** *—tr.* To undergo again (an experience, for example), especially in the imagination.

re·lo·cate (rée-lō-káyt) || *U.S. also* -lṓ-kayt) *v.* **-cated, -cating, -cates.** *—tr.* To establish (one's home, a factory, or the like) in a new place. *—intr.* To become established in a new home, area, or place of business: *The company relocated in the suburbs.* **—re·lo·ca·tion** *n.*

re·lu·cent (ri-lṓō-sənt, -léw-) *adj. Literary.* Reflecting light; shining. [Latin *relūcēns* (stem *relūcent-*), present participle of *relūcēre,* to shine back : *re-,* back + *lūcēre,* to shine.]

re·luct (ri-lúkt, rə-) *intr.v.* **-lucted, -lucting, -lucts.** *Archaic.* To show reluctance. [Latin *reluctārī,* to struggle against : *re-,* against + *luctārī,* to struggle.]

re·luc·tance (ri-lúktənss, rə-) *n.* Also *rare* **re·luc·tan·cy** (-tən-si). **1.** The state of being reluctant; unwillingness. **2.** *Physics.* A magnetic quantity analogous to electric resistance and equal in a closed magnetic circuit to the ratio of magnetomotive force (analogous to voltage) to magnetic flux (analogous to current).

re·luc·tant (ri-lúktənt, rə-) *adj.* **1.** Unwilling; averse: *reluctant to help.* **2.** Marked by unwillingness. **3.** *Archaic.* Offering resistance; opposing. [Latin *reluctāns* (stem *reluctant-),* present participle of *reluctārī,* to struggle against, RELUCT.] **—re·luc·tant·ly** *adv.*

rel·uc·tiv·i·ty (rélluk-tívvəti, rée-luk-, ri-lúk-) *n., pl.* **-ties.** *Physics.* A measure of the resistance of a material to the establishment of a magnetic field within it, equal to the reciprocal of **magnetic permeability** *(see).* [*Reluctance* + *conductivity.*]

re·lume (ri-lṓōm, -léwm) *tr.v.* **-lumed, -luming, -lumes.** *Poetic.* To make bright or clear again; illuminate again. [RE- + (IL)LUME.]

re·ly (ri-lī́, rə-) *intr.v.* **-lied, -lying, -lies. 1.** To use unquestioningly for support, assistance, or the like; to have as one's main recourse; depend. Used with *on* or *upon.* **2.** To trust; have confidence. Used

with *on* or *upon*: *rely on the children to behave.* [Middle English *relien*, to gather, rally, from Old French *relier*, from Latin *religāre*, to bind back : *re-*, back + *ligāre*, to fasten, to tie.]
  Synonyms: *rely, trust, depend, bank, count.*
REM¹ *n.* See **rapid eye movement.**
REM², rem *n.* See **roentgen equivalent man.**
rem. remittance.
re·main (ri-máyn, rə-) *intr.v.* **-mained, -maining, -mains. 1.** To continue in a specified condition, quality, or place. **2.** To stay or be left over after the removal, departure, loss, or destruction of others. **3.** To be left as still to be dealt with: *A cure remains to be found.* **4.** To endure or persist: *Despite therapy his fears remained.* —See Synonyms at **stay.** [Middle English *remaynen*, from Old French *remanoir, remaindre*, from Latin *remanēre*, to stay behind : *re-*, back in place + *manēre*, to stay.]
re·main·der (ri-máyndər, rə-) *n.* **1.** Something that is left over after other parts have been taken away; the rest. **2.** *Mathematics.* **a.** In division, the dividend minus the product of the divisor and quotient. **b.** In subtraction, the **difference** *(see).* **3.** *Law.* An estate effective and enjoyable only after the termination of another estate created at the same time. **4.** A copy of a book remaining with a publisher after sales have fallen off, usually sold at a reduced price. *~adj.* Remaining; leftover.
  ~tr.v. **remaindered, -dering, -ders.** To sell (books) as remainders. [Middle English *remaynder*, from Old French *remainder*, from *remaindre*, to REMAIN.]
  Synonyms: *remainder, rest, residue, residuum, residuals, balance, remnant, leavings, remains, relic.*
re·mains (ri-máynz, rə-) *pl.n.* **1.** All that is left after other parts have been taken away, used up, or destroyed. **2.** A corpse. **3.** The unpublished writings of a deceased author. **4.** Ancient ruins or fossils. —See Synonyms at **remainder.**
re·make (rée-máyk) *tr.v.* **-made** (-máyd), **-making, -makes.** To make anew; reconstruct.
  ~n. (rée-mayk). **1.** An instance of making anew. **2.** Something made again; a new version of something: *a remake of an old film.*
re·mand (ri-máand, rə- ‖ -mánd) *tr.v.* **-manded, -manding, -mands. 1.** To send or order back. **2.** *Law.* To hold on bail or send back (a defendant in criminal proceedings) to prison, to another court, or to another agency for further proceedings. **—on remand.** Remanded on bail or in custody.
  ~n. **1.** The state of being remanded. **2.** The act of remanding. **3.** A person remanded. [Middle English *remaunden*, from Old French *remander*, from Late Latin *remandāre*, to send back word : Latin *re-*, back + *mandāre*, to send word.] **—re·mand·ment** *n.*
remand home *n.* Formerly, an institution for juvenile offenders due to appear before a court. Also called "remand centre".
rem·a·nence (rémmənənss) *n.* **1.** *Rare.* The state of remaining or enduring. **2.** *Physics.* The magnetic induction that remains in a material after removal of the magnetising field. [Middle English *remanent*, remaining, from Latin *remanēns* (stem *remanent-*), present participle of *remanēre*, to REMAIN.] **—rem·a·nent** *adj.*
re·mark (ri-márk, rə-) *v.* **-marked, -marking, -marks.** *—tr.* **1.** To say or write briefly and casually as a comment. **2.** To take notice of; observe. *—intr.* To make a comment or observation. Used with *on* or *upon.* —See Synonyms at **see.**
  ~n. **1.** The act of noticing or observing; observation; mention: *a place worthy of remark.* **2.** A casual or brief expression of opinion; a comment. **3.** Variant of **remarque.** [French *remarquer* : RE- (intensive) + MARK.] **—re·mark·er** *n.*
re·mark·a·ble (ri-márkəb'l, rə-) *adj.* **1.** Worthy of notice. **2.** Extraordinary; striking; uncommon. **—re·mark·a·ble·ness** *n.* **—re·mark·a·bly** *adv.*
re·marque, re·mark (ri-márk, rə-) *n.* **1.** A mark made in the margin of a plate in engraving to indicate its stage of development prior to completion. **2.** A print or proof from a plate carrying such a mark. [French, from *remarquer*, to REMARK.]
Re·marque (rə-márk), **Erich Maria** (1898–1970). German-born U.S. novelist. From his experience in the trenches in World War I he drew the material for his first, and most famous, novel, *All Quiet on the Western Front* (1929).
re·match (rée-mach) *n.* *Sports.* A contest between opponents who have previously met each other in competition.
Rem·brandt (rém-brant, -brənt), born Rembrandt Harmenszoon van Rijn (1606–69). Dutch painter, generally regarded as the greatest master of the Dutch school. He worked in his native town of Leiden until *c.* 1632, thereafter chiefly in Amsterdam. Most of his early paintings were on religious and allegorical themes and display, in their mastery of light and shade, the influence of Caravaggio. In Amsterdam, he established himself as the city's leading portrait painter. Among his most famous paintings are the group portraits, *The Shooting Company of Captain Frans Banning Cocq* (1642; known also as *The Night Watch*) and *The Syndics of the Cloth Guild* (1662). His series of self-portraits (1629–69) records the progress of his life with great perception. **—Rem·brandt·esque** *adj.*
R.E.M.E., RE·ME (*often* rèemi) *n.* Royal Electrical and Mechanical Engineers.
re·me·di·a·ble (ri-méedi-əb'l, rə-) *adj.* Capable of being remedied. **—re·me·di·a·ble·ness** *n.* **—re·me·di·a·bly** *adv.*
re·me·di·al (ri-méedi-əl, rə-) *adj.* **1.** Supplying a remedy. **2.** Intended to correct something, such as a physical defect. **3.** Designating or pertaining to teaching methods intended to cater for backward or slow pupils: *remedial classes.* **—re·me·di·al·ly** *adv.*

Rembrandt

THE PASSING YEARS ARE CAPTURED IN HIS SELF-PORTRAITS
An artist who was fascinated by growing old

One of the greatest artists of all time, the Dutch painter Rembrandt van Rijn (1606–69) is noted for the vigour and realism of his work, particularly his portraits. His powers of observation and deep psychological insight are evident not only in his portraits, but also in his striking religious paintings and landscapes.

All his life Rembrandt was fascinated with light and shade, and in many of his works a concentrated light falls on a central figure set in a shadowy background. Ageing also fascinated him, and his many self-portraits record the gradual alteration of his features with a searching understanding and sincerity.

His success as a portrait painter began in 1632 with *The Anatomy Lesson of Dr Tulp,* and reached its peak in 1642 with his celebrated *Night Watch.* During this successful period, when he had many commissions and pupils, he married (1634) Saskia van Uylenborch, who brought him a good dowry and who features in many of his works; she died in 1642.

Despite his wealth, extravagant living and waning popularity led him into financial difficulties and eventually bankruptcy (1656). But Rembrandt's powers remained undiminished; he continued teaching, and in these difficult years produced works of insight, compassion, and technical mastery – such as *The Jewish Merchant* (1650) and *Old Jew in an Armchair* (1652). The self-portraits he had begun as a young man continued with ever greater depth of feeling, and rank among the most tender expressions ever executed in paint.

MASTER OF THE PORTRAIT *Rembrandt's fascination with age drove him to paint a series of self-portraits which capture his development from a lively youth to a disillusioned old man. Here he is about 60.*

rem·e·dy (rémmidi, rémmədi) *n., pl.* **-dies. 1.** Something, such as medicine or therapy, that relieves pain, cures disease, or corrects a disorder. **2.** Something that corrects any evil, fault, or error. **3.** *Law.* A legal means of preventing or correcting a wrong or enforcing a right. **4.** The allowance by a mint for deviation from the standard weight or quality of coins.
  ~tr.v. **remedied, -dying, -dies. 1.** To relieve or cure (a disease or disorder). **2.** To counteract or rectify (an error, wrong, or defect); set right. —See Synonyms at **correct.** [Middle English *remedie*, from Anglo-French *remedie*, from Latin *remedium*, medicine : *re-*, again + *medērī*, to heal.] **—rem·e·di·less** *adj.*
re·mem·ber (ri-mémbər, rə-) *v.* **-bered, -bering, -bers.** *—tr.* **1. a.** To

bring back to the mind through an act of memory. **b.** To become aware of or think of again. **2.** To recall to the mind with effort or determination. **3.** To retain in the mind; keep carefully in memory: *remember a poem.* **4.** To keep (someone) in mind as worthy of affection, reward, or recognition: *he remembered her in his will.* **5.** To reward with a gift or tip. **6.** To mention (someone, usually oneself) to another as sending greetings: *Remember me to your mother.* **7.** *Archaic.* To remind. *—intr.* To have or use the faculty of memory. [Middle English *remembren,* from Old French *remembrer,* from Late Latin *rememorārī,* to remember again : *re-,* again + *memorārī,* to remind, from Latin *memor,* mindful.] **—re•mem•ber•a•ble** *adj.* **—re•mem•ber•er** *n.*

re•mem•brance (ri-mémbrənss, rə-) *n.* **1.** The act of remembering. **2.** The state of being remembered. **3.** Something serving to celebrate or honour the memory of a person or event; a memorial. **4.** The length of time over which one's memory extends. **5.** Something remembered; a reminiscence. **6.** A memento or souvenir. **7.** *Plural.* Greetings. —See Synonyms at **memory.** [Middle English, from Old French, from *remember,* to REMEMBER.]

re•mem•branc•er (ri-mémbrən-sər, rə-) *n.* **1.** One that causes another to remember; a reminder. **2.** *Capital* **R. a.** An officer of the British judiciary responsible for collecting debts due to the Crown. In this sense, also called "King's (or Queen's) Remembrancer". **b.** An official who represents the City of London on ceremonial occasions, before parliamentary committees, and the like.

Remembrance Sunday *n.* In Britain, the Sunday nearest November 11, when those who died in both World Wars are remembered and honoured. Also called "Poppy Day", "Remembrance Day".

re•mex (reé-meks) *n., pl.* **remiges** (rémmi-jeez). A quill or flight feather of a bird's wing. [New Latin, from Latin *rēmex* (stem *rēmig-*), oarsman : *rēmus,* oar + *agere,* to drive.] **—re•mig•i•al** (ri-míji-əl, rə-) *adj.*

re•mind (ri-mínd, rə-) *tr.v.* **-minded, -minding, -minds.** To cause (someone) to remember or think of. Used with *of,* an infinitive, or a clause: *The song reminded me of summer; Remind me to give you the address.* **—re•mind•er** *n.*

Rem•ing•ton (rémmingtən), **Eliphalet** (1793–1861). U.S. arms manufacturer. In 1816 he began making flintlock rifles and in 1847 he manufactured the U.S. navy's first breech-loading rifle, the Jenks carbine. His Remington Arms Company became a major arms supplier to the U.S. government, and, under his son Philo (1816–89), a major manufacturer of sewing machines and typewriters.

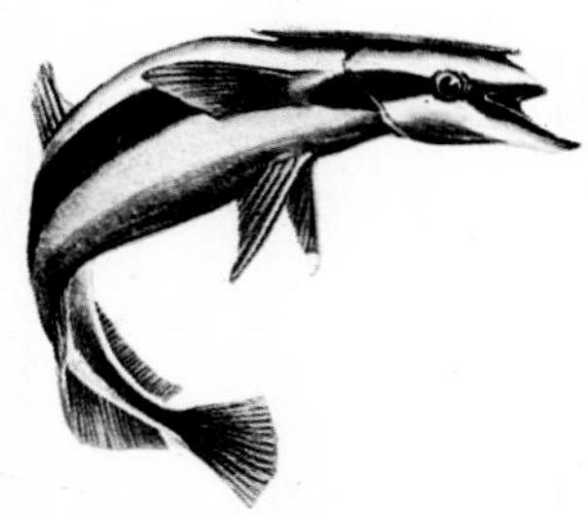

remora *A sea fish with a suction pad on its head by which it attaches itself to sharks, whales, and turtles. It feeds mainly on the skin parasites of its carrier. There are about ten species, growing from 30 to 90 centimetres (1 to 3 feet) long.*

rem•i•nisce (rémmi-níss) *intr.v.* **-nisced, -niscing, -nisces.** To recollect and tell of past experiences or events. [Back-formation from REMINISCENT.]

rem•i•nis•cence (rémmi-níss'nss) *n.* **1.** The act or process of recalling the past. **2.** A thing remembered; a memory. **3.** *Often plural.* A narration or account of past experiences. **4.** An event that brings to mind a similar, former event. —See Synonyms at **memory.** [Late Latin *reminiscentia.* See **reminiscent.**]

rem•i•nis•cent (rémmi-níss'nt) *adj.* **1.** Having the quality of or containing reminiscence or reminiscences. **2.** Tending to recall or suggest: *an evening reminiscent of happier times.* [Late Latin *reminiscens* (stem *reminiscent-*), present participle of *reminiscī,* to recollect : RE- + *min-,* from *mēns* (stem *ment-*), mind.] **—rem•i•nis•cent•ly** *adv.*

re•mise[1] (ri-míz, rə-) *tr.v.* **-mised, -mising, -mises.** *Law.* To relinquish a claim to; surrender by deed. [Middle English, from Old French, from the feminine past participle of *remettre,* to remit, from Latin *remittere,* to REMIT.]

re•mise[2] (rə-meéz, ri-) *n.* In fencing, a second thrust made after the first has failed.
~intr.v. **remised, -mising, -mises.** To make a remise. [French, from past participle of *remettre,* to put back. See **remit.**]

re•miss (ri-míss, rə-) *adj.* **1.** Lax in attending to duty; negligent. **2.** Inclined to idleness; slack. [Middle English, from Latin *remissus,* slack, past participle of *remittere,* to REMIT.] **—re•miss•ness** *n.*

re•mis•si•ble (ri-míssə-b'l, rə-) *adj.* Capable of being remitted or forgiven. **—re•mis•si•bil•i•ty** (-bílləti) *n.*

re•mis•sion (ri-mísh'n, rə-) *n.* **1. a.** The act of remitting. **b.** The condition of being remitted. **2. a.** Release, as from a debt, penalty, or obligation. **b.** Forgiveness; pardon. **3.** A lessening of intensity or degree; an abatement; especially, a temporary abatement of the symptoms of a disease.

re•mit (ri-mít, rə-) *v.* **-mitted, -mitting, -mits.** *—tr.* **1.** To send (money), as by post. **2. a.** To cancel (a penalty or punishment). **b.** To pardon; forgive. **3.** To restore to an original condition; put back. **4. a.** *Law.* To refer (a case) back to a lower court for further consideration. **b.** To refer (a matter) back for further consideration to a committee, authority, or the like. **5.** To relax; slacken. **6.** To defer; postpone. *—intr.* **1.** To send money. **2.** To diminish; abate.
~n. (reémit). **1.** A case remitted to a lower court. **2. a.** A matter for further consideration by a committee or authority. **b.** An area of study or enquiry for a committee or authority. [Middle English *remitten,* from Latin *remittere,* to send back, release : *re-,* back + *mittere,* to send.] **—re•mit•ta•ble** (ri-míttəb'l, rə-) *adj.*

re•mit•tal (ri-mítt'l, rə-) *n.* Remission.

re•mit•tance (ri-mítt'nss, rə-) *n. Abbr.* **rem. 1.** Money or credit sent to someone. **2.** The act of sending money or credit.

remittance man *n.* A person living abroad on funds sent from home, especially in former times.

re•mit•tent (ri-mítt'nt, rə-) *adj.* Characterised by temporary abatements in severity. Said especially of diseases.
~n. A remittent fever. **—re•mit•tence, re•mit•ten•cy** *n.* **—re•mit•tent•ly** *adv.*

re•mit•ter (ri-míttər, rə-) *n.* Also **re•mit•tor** (for sense 3). **1.** *Law.* The principle or act by which an individual holds property by a valid title dated prior to a defective title under which he at first held ownership. **2.** *Law.* The act of transferring a case for decision to another court, generally a lower one. **3.** One that remits.

rem•nant (rémnənt) *n.* **1.** Something left over; a remainder. **2.** A leftover piece of fabric remaining after the rest has been used or sold. **3.** A surviving trace or vestige, as of a former condition. **4.** *Often plural.* A small, remaining group of people. —See Synonyms at **remainder.**
~adj. Remaining; leftover. [Middle English *remenant,* from Old French, present participle of *remanoir, remaindre,* to REMAIN.]

re•mod•el (reé-módd'l) *tr.v.* **-elled** or *U.S.* **-eled, -elling** or *U.S.* **-eling, -els. 1.** To model again. **2.** To remake with a new structure or in a new style; reconstruct; renovate. **—re•mod•el•ler** *n.*

re•mon•e•tise, re•mon•e•tize (reé-múnni-tīz ‖ -mónni-) *tr.v.* **-tised, -tising, -tises.** To restore (silver, for example) to use as legal tender. **—re•mon•e•ti•sa•tion** (-tī-záysh'n ‖ *U.S.* -ti-) *n.*

re•mon•strance (ri-mónstrənss, rə-) *n.* **1.** The act of remonstrating. **2.** A speech or gesture of protest, opposition, or reproof; especially, a formal statement of public grievances.

re•mon•strant (ri-mónstrənt, rə-) *adj.* Characterised by remonstrance; expostulatory.
~n. **1.** One who remonstrates or signs a remonstrance. **2.** *Capital* **R. a.** Any of the Dutch Arminians who, in 1610, formally stated the grounds of their dissent from strict Calvinism. **b.** A member of the Protestant denomination founded by these dissenters.

re•mon•strate (rémmən-strayt, ri-món-, rə-) *v.* **-strated, -strating, -strates.** *—tr.* To say or plead in protest, objection, or reproof. *—intr.* To make objections; argue or plead against some action: *remonstrate with one's superiors.* —See Synonyms at **object.** [Medieval Latin *remōnstrāre,* to demonstrate : Latin *re-,* completely + *monstrāre,* to show, from *monstrum,* an omen, a portent, from *monēre,* to warn.] **—re•mon•stra•tion** (-stráysh'n) *n.* **—re•mon•stra•tive** (ri-mónstrətiv ‖ rémmən-straytiv) *adj.* **—re•mon•stra•tor** *n.*

re•mon•tant (ri-móntənt, rə-) *adj.* Blooming more than once during a season, as certain roses do.
~n. A remontant rose. [French, "rising again", from the present participle of *remonter,* to rise again, REMOUNT.]

rem•o•ra (rémmərə, ri-máw-rə ‖ -mṓ-) *n.* Any of several marine fishes of the family Echeneidae, having on the head a sucking disc with which they attach themselves to larger animals, ships, or other moving objects. Also called "suckerfish", "shark sucker". [Latin, "delay" (they were believed to be able to delay ships by sticking to them) : *re-,* back + *mora,* a delay.]

re•morse (ri-mórss, rə-) *n.* **1.** Moral anguish arising from repentance for past misdeeds; bitter regret. **2.** *Obsolete.* Compassion. [Middle English, from Old French *remors,* from Medieval Latin *remorsus,* from Latin, a biting back, from the past participle of *remordēre,* to bite again : *re-,* again + *mordēre,* to bite.] **—re•morse•ful** *adj.* **—re•morse•ful•ly** *adv.* **—re•morse•ful•ness** *n.*

re•morse•less (ri-mórss-ləss, rə-, -liss) *adj.* **1.** Having no pity or compassion; merciless. **2.** Relentless, very persistent. **—re•morse•less•ly** *adv.* **—re•morse•less•ness** *n.*

re•mote (ri-mṓt, rə-) *adj.* **-moter, -motest. 1. a.** Located far away; relatively distant in space: *Our hotel was remote from the city centre.* **b.** Outlying; isolated; out-of-the-way: *a remote hamlet.* **2.** Distant in time: *the remote past.* **3. a.** Very slight or faint: *hadn't the remotest interest in what I was saying.* **b.** Having only a vague connection: *a cause very remote from everyday concerns.* **4.** Being distantly related by blood or marriage: *a remote descendant.* **5.** Distant in manner; aloof. **6.** Of, pertaining to, or designating computing devices or systems situated at some distance from the central computer that communicate with it usually by means of cables. —See Synonyms at **distant.** [Latin *remōtus,* past participle of *removēre,* to move back or away : *re-,* back, away + *movēre,* to move.] **—re•mote•ly** *adv.* **—re•mote•ness** *n.*

remote control *n.* The direction of an activity, process, or machine from a distant point, as by radioed instructions or coded signals.

ré•mou•lade (rémmə-láyd, rémmōō-, -laád) *n.* A piquant cold sauce for cold poultry, meat, and shellfish, made of mayonnaise with chopped pickles, capers, anchovies, and herbs. [French *rémoulade,* variant of Picard dialect *ramolas,* horseradish, variant of Latin *armoracea,* of Italic origin.]

re•mould (reé-mṓld) *tr.v.* **-moulded, -moulding, -moulds.** To mould again; especially, to mould new rubber walls and tread on (a tyre).
~n. (reé-mōld). Anything remoulded; especially, a remoulded tyre.

re•mount (reé-mównt) *tr.v.* **-mounted, -mounting, -mounts. 1.** To mount again. **2.** To supply with fresh horses.
~n. (*also* reé-mownt). A fresh horse. [Middle English *remounten,* from Old French *remonter* : *re-,* again + *monter, munter,* to MOUNT.]

re•mov•a•ble (ri-mṓōvə-b'l, rə-) *adj.* Capable of being removed. **—re•mov•a•bil•i•ty** (-bílləti), **re•mov•a•ble•ness** *n.* **—re•mov•a•bly** *adv.*

re•mov•al (ri-mṓōv'l, rə-) *n.* **1. a.** The act of removing. **b.** The fact of being removed. **2.** Relocation, as of a home or business. Also used adjectivally: *a removal van.* **3.** Dismissal, as from office.

re•mov•a•list (rə-mṓōv'l-ist) *n. Australian.* A person or business engaged in moving household or office furniture to a new location.

re•move (ri-mṓōv, rə-) *v.* **-moved, -moving, -moves.** *—tr.* **1.** To move from a position occupied: *remove the dishes from the table.*

2. To convey from one place to another: *removed the family to safety.* 3. To take from one's person; doff: *remove one's hat.* 4. To do away with; eliminate: *remove stains; removed his anxieties.* 5. To dismiss from office. —*intr.* 1. To change one's place of residence or business; move. 2. *Poetic.* To depart; go away.
~*n.* 1. The act of removing; a removal. 2. The distance or degree of space, time, or status that separates persons or things: *at one remove from poverty.* 3. *British.* An intermediate class or form in certain schools, especially private schools. 4. A dish that succeeds another at a meal. [Middle English *removen,* from Old French *remouvoir,* from Latin *removēre,* to move back : *re-,* back + *movēre,* to move.] **—re•mov•er** *n.*

re•moved (ri-mo͞ovd, rə-) *adj.* 1. Distant in space, time, or nature; remote. 2. Separated in relationship by a specified degree of descent: *My first cousin's child is my first cousin once removed.* 3. *Archaic.* Succeeded by another dish at a meal: *fish removed by beef.* —See Synonyms at **distant.** **—re•mov•ed•ly** (-mo͞ovidli) *adj.* **—re•mov•ed•ness** *n.*

re•mu•ner•ate (ri-méwnə-rayt, rə-) *tr.v.* **-ated, -ating, -ates.** 1. To pay (a person) for goods provided, services rendered, or losses incurred. 2. To compensate for; make up for: *remunerate his efforts.* [Latin *remūnerāre* : *re-,* intensive + *mūnerāre,* to give, from *mūnus,* a gift.] **—re•mu•ner•a•bil•i•ty** (-rə-bílləti) *n.* **—re•mu•ner•a•ble** *adj.* **—re•mu•ner•a•tor** *n.*

re•mu•ner•a•tion (ri-méwnə-ráysh'n, rə-) *n.* 1. An act of remunerating. 2. That which remunerates; recompense; payment.

re•mu•ner•a•tive (ri-méwnə-rətiv, rə- || -raytiv) *adj.* 1. Likely to be well remunerated; profitable. 2. Serving to remunerate. **—re•mu•ner•a•tive•ly** *adv.* **—re•mu•ner•a•tive•ness** *n.*

Re•mus (réeməss). *Roman Mythology.* The twin brother of **Romulus** *(see).*

ren•ais•sance (ri-náyss'nss, rə-, rén-ay-sonss, -e-, -sónss || *U.S. also* -zónss) *n.* 1. A rebirth; a revival. 2. *Capital* **R.** a. The humanistic revival of classical art, literature, and learning that originated in Italy in the 14th century and later spread throughout Europe. b. The period of this revival (roughly 14th–16th century). 3. *Sometimes capital* **R.** Any similar period of revived intellectual or artistic achievement or enthusiasm: *the Celtic Renaissance.*
~*adj. Capital* **R.** 1. Of, pertaining to, or characteristic of the Renaissance or its artistic and intellectual works and styles. 2. Of or designating the style of architecture and decoration prevalent during the Renaissance. [French, a rebirth, from Old French, from *renaistre* (present stem *renais-*), to be born again, from Latin *renascī* : *re-,* again + *nascī,* to be born.] See feature, next page.

Renaissance man or **woman** *n.* A man or woman whose intellectual interests and achievements are wide-ranging; especially, one whose talents encompass both the arts and the sciences.

re•nal (réen'l) *adj.* Of, pertaining to, resembling, or in the region of the kidneys. [French *rénal,* from Late Latin *rēnālis,* from Latin *rēnēs*†, kidneys.]

renal pelvis *n.* A small funnel-shaped cavity in the kidney in which urine collects before being discharged into the ureter. Also called "pelvis".

re•nas•cence (ri-náss'nss, rə-, -náyss'nss) *n.* 1. A new birth or life; a rebirth. 2. A cultural revival; a renaissance.

re•nas•cent (ri-náss'nt, rə, -náyss'nt) *adj.* Coming into being again; showing renewed growth or vigour. [Latin *renascēns* (stem *renascent-*), present participle of *renascī,* to be born again. See **renaissance.**]

ren•coun•ter (ren-kówntər) *n. Archaic.* 1. An unplanned meeting. 2. A sudden encounter with an enemy.
~*v.* **rencountered, -tering, -ters.** *Archaic.* —*tr.* To meet unexpectedly. —*intr.* To have an unexpected meeting. [French *rencontre,* from *rencontrer,* to have a (hostile) meeting : *re-,* again, against + *encontrer,* to ENCOUNTER.]

rend (rend) *v.* **rent** (rent) **rending, rends.** —*tr.* 1. a. To tear or pull; wrench. b. To rip apart or into pieces; split. 2. To remove forcibly; wrest. 3. To penetrate and disturb as if by tearing: *Screams rent the silence.* 4. To cause pain or distress to (the heart, for example). —*intr.* To burst; come apart. —See Synonyms at **tear.** [Middle English *renden,* Old English *rendan.*] **—rend•er** *n.*

ren•der (réndər) *tr.v.* **-dered, -dering, -ders.** 1. To submit or present for consideration, payment, or approval: *render a bill.* 2. To give or make available: *render assistance.* 3. To give what is due or proper: *asked much and rendered little.* 4. To give in return or retribution: *render an apology for his rudeness.* 5. To surrender or relinquish; yield. 6. To represent in, as in painting, writing, or music; depict in artistic form: *This poem renders precisely the pains of love.* 7. To perform an interpretation of (a musical piece, for example). 8. To express in another language or form; translate. 9. To pronounce formally; hand down (a verdict, for example). 10. To cause to become; make: *"This study renders men acute, inquisitive"* (Edmund Burke). 11. To reduce, convert, or melt down (fat) by heating. 12. To coat (brick, for example) with plaster or cement.
~*n.* A payment in kind, services, or cash from a tenant to a feudal lord. [Middle English *rendren,* to give in return, relinquish, from Old French *rendre,* to give back, from Vulgar Latin *rendere* (unattested), variant of Latin *reddere* : *re-,* back + *dare,* to give.] **—ren•der•a•ble** *adj.* **—ren•der•er** *n.*

ren•der•ing (réndəring) *n.* A coat of plaster, cement, or the like covering a surface.

ren•dez•vous (rón-di-vo͞o, rón-, -day-) *n., pl.* **-vous** (-vo͞oz). 1. a. An arrangement or appointment to meet. b. A prearranged meeting place; especially, an assembly point for troops, ships, or spacecraft. 2. The meeting itself. 3. A popular gathering place.
~*v.* **rendezvoused** (-vo͞od), **-vousing** (-vo͞o-ing), **-vous** (-vo͞oz). —*tr.* To bring together (persons or military units) at a prearranged time and place. —*intr.* To meet together at a prearranged time and place. [Old French, from *rendez vous,* "present yourselves" : *rendez,* imperative of *rendre,* to RENDER + *vous,* you.]

ren•di•tion (ren-dísh'n) *n.* 1. The act of rendering. 2. An interpretation of a musical score or dramatic piece. 3. A performance of a musical or dramatic work. 4. A translation, often interpretive. [Obsolete French, from Old French *rendre,* to give back, RENDER.]

ren•dzi•na (ren-dzéenə, -jéenə) *n.* A dark soil which develops under grass on limestone and chalk. [Russian, from Polish *redzina.*]

ren•e•gade (rénni-gayd) *n.* 1. One who rejects a religion, cause, allegiance, or group for another; a deserter. 2. An outlaw; a rebel.
~*adj.* Of or like a renegade; treacherous. [Spanish *renegado,* from Medieval Latin *renegātus,* one who denies, renegade, from the past participle of *renegāre,* to deny : Latin *re-,* intensive + *negāre,* to deny.]

re•nege, re•negue (ri-néeg, rə-, -nayg, -neg) *v.* **-neged** or **-negued, -neging** or **-neguing, -neges** or **-negues.** —*intr.* 1. To fail to carry out a promise or commitment: *renege on a contract.* 2. In card games, to fail to follow suit when able and required by the rules to do so. —*tr. Obsolete.* To renounce; disown.
~*n.* The act of reneging in card games. [Medieval Latin *renegāre,* to deny. See **renegade.**] **—re•neg•er** *n.*

re•ne•go•ti•ate (réeni-gōshi-ayt) *tr.v.* **-ated, -ating, -ates.** To negotiate anew; especially, to revise the terms of (a contract) so as to limit or get back excess profits gained by the contractor. **—re•ne•go•ti•a•ble** *adj.* **—re•ne•go•ti•a•tion** (-áysh'n) *n.*

re•new (ri-néw, rə- || -no͞o) *v.* **-newed, -newing, -news.** —*tr.* 1. To make new or as if new again; restore. 2. To take up again; resume. 3. To repeat so as to reaffirm: *renewed her promise of support.* 4. To regain (spiritual or physical vigour); revive. 5. a. To arrange for the extension of: *renew a contract.* b. To extend the period of loan of: *renew a library book.* 6. To replenish. 7. To bring into being again; re-establish. —*intr.* 1. To become new again. 2. To start again. 3. To renew a contract, lease, or other agreement.

re•new•a•ble (ri-néw-ə-b'l, rə- || -no͞o-) *adj.* 1. Able to be renewed. 2. Designating an energy source, such as the sun or wave power, that may be considered for practical purposes as inexhaustible. **—re•new•a•bil•ity** (-bílləti) *n.*

re•new•al (ri-néw-əl, rə- || -no͞o-) *n.* 1. a. The act or an instance of renewing. b. The state of being renewed. 2. Something renewed.

re•new•ed•ly (ri-néw-idli, rə- || -no͞o-) *adv.* Over again; anew.

Ren•frew (rén-fro͞o). Royal burgh on the river Clyde in Strathclyde Region, western Scotland. It is mainly an industrial centre and it is the site of Glasgow Airport.

Ren•frew•shire (rén-fro͞o-shər, -sheer, -shīr). Former county of west central Scotland. In 1975 it became part of the Strathclyde Region.

Re•ni (rénni), **Guido** (1575–1642). Italian painter and engraver, forerunner of late 17th-century Roman classicism. He worked in Rome and his native Bologna. His best-known works are the *Crucifixion of St. Peter* (1605) and the *Aurora* fresco (1613–14).

reni–, reno– *comb. form.* Indicates kidney or kidneys; for example, **reniform** [Latin *rēnēs,* kidneys.]

ren•i•form (rénni-fawrm, réeni-) *adj.* Shaped like a kidney: *a reniform leaf.* [RENI- + -FORM.]

ren•in (réenin || rénnin) *n.* A protein-digesting enzyme, released by the kidneys in response to stress, which acts to raise blood pressure. [RENI- + -IN.]

re•ni•tent (ri-nīt'nt, rə-, rénni-) *adj. Rare.* 1. Resisting pressure; not pliant. 2. Reluctant to yield or be swayed; recalcitrant. [Latin *renītens* (stem *renītent-*), present participle of *renītī,* to struggle against, resist : *re-,* back, against + *nītī,* to press forward, push.] **—ren•i•tence, ren•i•ten•cy** *n.*

Ren•ner (rénnər), **Karl** (1870–1950). Austrian politician, president of the Austrian republic (1945–50). After the abdication of the Emperor Charles I, he became the first chancellor (1919–20) of the Austrian republic. In 1945 he became prime minister, foreign minister, and later president of the liberated republic.

Rennes (ren). Capital of the Ille-et-Vilaine département, northwest France. It is a railway junction and agricultural market centre.

ren•net (rénnit) *n.* 1. The inner lining of the fourth stomach of calves and other young mammals. 2. A dried extract of this lining especially from young calves, used to curdle milk. [Middle English *rennet,* Old English *rynet* (unattested).]

ren•nin (rénnin) *n.* A milk-coagulating enzyme produced by the stomach. It is an active constituent of rennet and is used in making cheeses and junkets. Also called "chymosin". [RENN(ET) + -IN.]

Re•no (réenō). City in western Nevada, United States, lying on the river Truckee. Tourism is the major industry and the city is noted for the ease with which a divorce may by obtained owing to the state's short-term residence requirements.

Re•noir (rə-nwár), **Jean** (1894–1978). French film director. The son of the painter Auguste Renoir, he won great acclaim for the artistry of films such as *La Grande illusion* (1937), *La Bête humaine* (1938), and *La Règle du jeu* (1939).

Renoir, Pierre Auguste (1841–1919). French impressionist painter. In the 1870s he began to exhibit at the Impressionist salons. He developed the so-called "rainbow palette", from which black was eliminated. Among his best-known paintings are *Le Moulin de la galette* (1876) and *Les Parapluies* (1883). In the mid-1880s he devel-

PRONUNCIATION KEY

a, trap; aa, father; ai, **fair;** ar, star; aw, lawn; ay, play; b, bb, stab; **rubber;** ch, **church;** ck, ticket; d, dd, **dead;** ladder; e, dress; ee, bee; er, defer; ew, **few;** ewr, **pure;** ə, about; ər, letter; f, ff, **fife;** differ; g, gg, **giggle;** h, hat; i, kit; ī, price; īr, fire; j, **judge;** k, **kick;** l, ll, let; 'l, needle; m, mm, man; n, nn, no; 'n, sudden; ng, **thing;** o, lot; ō, no; o͝o, **foot;** o͞o, shoe; oor, **poor;** ow, **cow;** owr, **hour;** oy, **boy;** p, pp, **pepper;** r, rr, red; s, ss, **sauce;** sh, **ship;** t, tt, totter; th, **thick;** th, **this;** smooth; u, cut; ur, **turn;** v, vv, valve; w, **wet;** y, yes; z, zz, zebra; zh, vision; pleasure

IN FOREIGN WORDS:

aN, oN, **Saint-Saëns;** hl, **Llanelli; Hluhluwe;** kh, loch; **lough; Khaled**

STRESS MARK:

ín-sīt, insight; in-sít, incite

THE FLOWERING OF EUROPEAN CULTURE

The civilisation of ancient Rome inspires a new artistic movement

Renaissance is a French word meaning rebirth, and is used to describe the developments in architecture, painting, and sculpture which began in Florence in the early 1400s and spread through Italy and across Europe by 1600. It was part of an intellectual movement that made man rethink his relationship with God and nature and stimulated scientific discoveries.

In the 14th century, the Italian poet and writer Petrarch put forward the idea that since the fall of the Roman Empire, Italy had been in the Dark Ages, a period of decline and ignorance. If man could return to the styles and ideas of the Roman Empire there would be a new age of glory. Modern studies show that the Roman Empire was not the peak of human achievement and that the Dark Ages were not a cultural gap, but this myth achieved a strong hold on the Italian imagination. It stimulated the study of Roman art and civilisation and led to the discovery of ancient Greek literature, philosophy, and science. This Graeco-Roman revival led to a new Humanist movement that acknowledged man's feelings and aspirations without displacing God's importance in art or philosophy.

The Renaissance saw the establishment of portraiture, frequently with landscape backgrounds, as an accepted art form. Portraiture developed through the patronage of the wealthy trading classes who were willing to pay for being immortalised in pictures. There was a new use of light and shade in painting to create the illusion of reality. The architect Brunelleschi calculated the mathematical rules governing perspective and these were eagerly adopted by painters.

The Italian Renaissance divides into three periods. The Early Renaissance (1420–90) was marked by men such as Brunelleschi, the sculptor Donatello, and the painters Masaccio, Piero della Francesca, Botticelli, Mantegna, and Bellini. Brunelleschi revived the style of classical Roman architecture but adapted it to create a new harmony and style. Donatello gave his figures a new feeling of energy with minute details learned from studies of the human body. In painting, the artists portrayed emotion, which added to the realism of their work.

In the High Renaissance (1490–1520), the architect Donato Bramante revised the designs for St. Peter's Basilica in classical style. Other artists of the time included Leonardo da Vinci and Raphael; they helped to perfect the realistic style of painting. The sculptor, painter, and architect Michelangelo worked from the end of the Early Renaissance into the Mannerist period (1520–1600). He could portray accurately the human body from any angle. Mannerism was an experimental period when artists began to assert their independence from classical ideas. It coincided with unease in the Roman Catholic Church as the rise of northern European protestantism confronted it – the period known as the Reformation.

In northern Europe, the Flemish painter Jan van Eyck was an early developer of oil paints and used vivid colours to paint reality in its smallest detail. Also in the Flemish school Hieronymous Bosch and Pieter Bruegel used realism to convey symbolic and sinister messages, and in Germany Albrecht Dürer portrayed the religious turmoil of the age.

BEGINNINGS OF RENAISSANCE PAINTING *The artist Masaccio (1401–28) is credited with the founding of Renaissance painting. His* Expulsion of Adam and Eve from Paradise *(left) is one of a series of frescoes in the Brancacci Chapel in Florence. It shows not only a more realistic sense of perspective but also portrays emotion in the characters. In contrast with the earlier International Gothic style, where figures were almost expressionless, his figures show the full horror of their fate. Masaccio employed the perspective rules of Brunelleschi. His frescoes served as examples to other painters throughout the next century.*

THE PERFECTION OF TECHNIQUE *Leonardo da Vinci (1452–1519) probably painted his* Ginevra de Benci *(above) as a wedding portrait in 1473–74. It conveys a melancholy mood, with the subject wearing an ambiguous expression and seeming to assess the viewer with critical eyes; perhaps the marriage was not of her choice. Apart from her face, all the light areas are small and irregular, and the spikiness of the leaves contrasts with the softness of her hair. The painting shows a considerable advance on the techniques of Masaccio 50 years earlier; technical progress in the 500 years since has been much slower.*

oped a more classical manner, as in *Le Jugement de Paris* (*c.* 1914).

re·nounce (ri-nównss, rə-) *v.* **-nounced, -nouncing, -nounces.** —*tr.* **1.** To give up (a title or activity, for example), especially by formal announcement. **2.** To reject; disown. —*intr.* **1.** In card games, to fail to follow suit because one does not hold a card of the required suit. **2.** *Law.* To give up a right. —See Synonyms at **relinquish.**
~*n.* In card games: **1.** An act of renouncing. **2.** An opportunity to renounce. [Middle English *renouncen,* from Old French *renoncer,* from Latin *renūntiāre,* to bring back word, protest against, report : *re-,* back, against + *nūntiāre,* inform, from *nūntium,* message.] **—re·nounce·ment** *n.* **—re·nounc·er** *n.*

ren·o·vate (rén-ə-vayt, -ō-) *tr.v.* **-vated, -vating, -vates.** **1.** To restore to an earlier, good condition; improve by repairing or remodelling. **2.** To impart new vigour to; revive. [Latin *renovāre* : *re-,* again + *novāre,* to make new, from *novus,* new.] **—ren·o·va·tion** (-váysh'n) *n.* **—ren·o·va·tor** (-vaytər) *n.*

re·nown (ri-nówn, rə-) *n.* **1.** The quality of being honoured and acclaimed; celebrity. **2.** *Archaic.* Report; rumour. —See Synonyms at **fame.** [Middle English *renoun(e),* from Old French *renon, renom,* from *renomer,* to name again, make famous : *re-,* again, from Latin + *nomer,* to name, from Latin *nōmināre,* from *nōmen,* a name.]

re·nowned (ri-nównd, rə-) *adj.* Having renown; famous.

rent¹ (rent) *n.* **1. a.** Payment, usually of an amount fixed by contract, made by one person or agency at stated regular intervals in return for the right to occupy or use the land or property of another. **b.** A similar payment made for the use of a facility or service provided by another, such as a telephone. **2.** *Economics.* **a.** The return derived from cultivated or improved land after deduction of all production costs. **b.** The revenue yielded by a piece of land in excess of that yielded by the poorest or least favourably located land, under equal market conditions.
~*v.* **rented, renting, rents.** —*tr.* **1.** To obtain occupancy or use of (another's property, or a facility or service provided by another) in return for regular payments. **2.** To grant temporary occupancy or use of (one's own property or a service) in return for regular payments. Often used with *out.* —*intr.* To be rented or be available for renting: *The cottage rents at £200 a week.* [Middle English *rente,* income from property, from Old French, from Vulgar Latin *rendita* (unattested), from the feminine past participle of *rendere* (unattested), to RENDER.] **—rent·a·ble** *adj.*

rent². Past tense and past participle of **rend.**
~*n.* **1.** An opening made by or as if by rending; a rip or gap. **2.** A breach of relations between people or groups; a rift.

rent-a- *comb. form.* Indicates: **1.** For hire; for example, **rent-a-car.** **2.** *Informal.* Hired, paid, or induced to act as the thing or persons specified; for example, **rent-a-crowd, rent-a-mob.** In this sense, used derogatorily or humorously.

rent·al (rént'l) *n.* **1.** An amount charged as rent. **2.** A list of tenants and rents. **3.** *Chiefly U.S.* Property available for renting. **4.** The act of renting.
~*adj.* Of, concerning, or available for rent.

rente (rONT) *n., pl.* **rentes** (*pronounced as singular*). *French.* **1.** Annual income, especially from government bonds; annuity. **2. a.** *Usually plural.* The government bonds of various European countries, especially of France. **b.** The interest paid on these bonds.

rent·er (réntər) *n.* **1.** One who receives payment in exchange for the use of his property by another. **2.** One who pays rent for the use of another's property; a tenant. **3.** *British.* One who distributes films, in return for payment, to commercial cinemas.

rent-free (rént-frée) *adj.* Not subject to rent.
~*adv.* Without having to pay, or without paying, rent.

ren·ti·er (rónti-ay, *French* rONt-yáy) *n. French.* One who derives an unearned income from rents or investments.

rent-roll (rént-rōl) *n.* **1.** A list of property owned by an individual, together with the rent due and received from it. **2.** The income accruing to an individual from such property.

rent strike *n.* A collective refusal, for example by all the tenants in one building or area, to pay rent, usually as a form of protest or in order to bring rents down.

re·num·ber (rée-númbər) *tr.v.* **-bered, -bering, -bers.** To number again or in a different order.

re·nun·ci·a·tion (ri-nún-si-áysh'n, rə-) *n.* **1.** The act or an instance of renouncing: *the renunciation of pleasures.* **2.** A declaration in which something is renounced. [Middle English, from Latin *renūntiātiō* (stem *renūntiātiōn-*) from *renūnitiāre,* to RENOUNCE.] **—re·nun·ci·a·tive** (-ətiv || -aytiv), **re·nun·ci·a·to·ry** (-ə-təri, -tri) *adj.*

re·o·pen (rée-ōpən, ri-) *v.* **-pened, -pening, -pens.** —*tr.* To open or take up again. —*intr.* To start again; resume.

re·or·der (rée-órdər, ri-) *v.* **-dered, -dering, -ders.** —*tr.* **1.** To order again. **2.** To straighten out or put in order again. **3.** To rearrange. —*intr.* To order the same goods again.
~*n.* A further order of goods previously supplied.

re·or·gan·i·sa·tion (rée-órgə-nī-záysh'n, ri- || *U.S.* -ni-) *n.* **1.** The act or process of organising again or differently. **2.** *Finance.* A thorough alteration of the structure of a business enterprise, especially after a bankruptcy. In this sense, also called "reconstruction".

re·or·gan·ise, re·or·gan·ize (rée-órgə-nīz, ri-) *v.* **-ised, -ising, -ises.** —*tr.* To organise again or anew. —*intr.* To undergo or effect changes in organisation. **—re·or·gan·is·er** *n.*

re·or·i·ent·ate (rée-áwri-en-tayt, -órri-, -ən- || -ōri-) *tr.v.* **-ated, -ating, -ates.** **1.** To change the direction of; give a new orientation to. **2.** To change the general views or way of thinking of. **—re·or·ien·ta·tion** (-táysh'n) *n.*

re·o·vi·rus (rée-ō-vīr-əss) *n.* Any of a group of spherical, RNA-containing viruses that are widely distributed in humans. They are found in the respiratory and digestive tracts but do not appear to cause disease. [*R*espiratory *e*nteric *o*rphan *virus.*]

rep¹, repp (rep) *n.* A ribbed or corded fabric of various materials, such as cotton, wool, or silk. [French *reps*†.]

rep² *n. Informal.* A representative; a travelling salesman.

rep³ *n. Physics.* A unit of absorbed radiation dose, equal to the absorbed dose in water that has been exposed to one roentgen. The rep has been largely replaced by the **rad** *(see).* [*R*oentgen + *e*quivalent + *p*hysical.]

rep⁴ *n. Informal.* **1.** A **repertory company** *(see).* **2. Repertory** *(see).*

rep. **1.** repair. **2.** report. **3.** reporter. **4.** representative. **5.** reprint. **6.** republic.

Rep. **1.** *U.S.* representative. **2.** republic. **3.** *U.S.* Republican (Party).

re·pack·age (rée-páckij) *tr.v.* **-aged, -aging, -ages.** To package again or anew; especially, to put in a new kind of package.

re·pair¹ (ri-páir, rə-) *tr.v.* **-paired, -pairing, -pairs.** **1.** To restore to sound condition after damage or injury; mend. **2.** To set right; remedy: *repair an oversight.* **3.** To renew or revitalise. **4.** To make up for or compensate for (a loss or wrong, for example).
~*n. Abbr.* **rep.** **1.** The work, act, or process of repairing: *beyond repair.* **2.** General condition after use or maintenance: *in good repair.* **3. a.** An instance of repairing. **b.** Something that has been repaired. [Middle English *repairen,* from Old French *reparer,* from Latin *reparāre* : *re-,* back (to an earlier state) + *parāre,* to put in order, prepare.] **—re·pair·a·ble** *adj.* **—re·pair·er** *n.*

repair² *intr.v.* **-paired, -pairing, -pairs.** *Formal.* **1.** To betake oneself; go: *We all repaired to the restaurant.* **2.** To resort; go for help.
~*n. Archaic.* **1.** An act of going or sojourning. **2.** A place to which one goes frequently or habitually; a haunt. [Middle English *repairen,* to return, from Old French *repairer,* from Late Latin *repatriāre,* to REPATRIATE.]

re·pair·man (ri-páir-mən, rə-) *n., pl.* **-men** (-mən, -men). A man whose occupation is making repairs: *a bicycle repairman.*

re·pand (ri-pánd, rə-) *adj. Botany.* Having a wavy margin: *a repand leaf.* [Latin *repandus,* bent back : *re-,* back, backwards + *pandus,* bent, turned, past participle of *pandere,* to spread.]

rep·a·ra·ble (répprə-b'l, réppərə-b'l) *adj.* Also **re·pair·a·ble** (re-páirəb'l, rə-). Able to be repaired or made good. **—rep·a·ra·bil·i·ty** (-bílləti) *n.* **—rep·a·ra·bly** *adv.*

rep·a·ra·tion (réppə-ráysh'n) *n.* **1. a.** The act or process of repairing. **b.** The condition of being repaired. **2.** The act or process of making amends; expiation. **3.** Something done or paid to make amends; compensation. **4.** *Plural.* Compensation or remuneration required of a defeated nation for damage or injury during a war. [Middle English *reparacioun,* from Old French *reparation,* from Late Latin *reparātiō* (stem *reparātiōn-*), from Latin *reparāre,* to REPAIR.]
Synonyms: *reparation, redress, amends, restitution, indemnity.*

re·par·a·tive (ri-párrətiv, rə-) *adj.* Also **re·par·a·to·ry** (ri-párrə-təri, rə-, -tri). **1.** Tending to repair. **2.** Of, pertaining to, or of the nature of reparations.

rep·ar·tee (rép-aar-tée || -ər-, *U.S. also* -táy) *n.* **1.** A swift, witty reply; a ready or spirited retort. **2.** Witty and spirited conversation characterised by such replies. **3.** Skill in making such replies or conversation. —See Synonyms at **wit.** [French *repartie,* from *repartir,* to reply readily, from Old French, to depart again : *re-,* again + *partir,* to part, from Latin *partīre,* from *pars,* a part.]

re·par·ti·tion (réepaar-tísh'n) *n.* **1.** Distribution; apportionment. **2.** A partitioning again or in a different way.
~*tr.v.* **repartitioned, -tioning, -tions.** To partition again; redivide.

re·past (ri-páast, rə- || -pást) *n.* **1.** *Formal.* A meal, or the food eaten or provided at a meal. **2.** *Obsolete.* Food; nourishment. [Middle English, from Old French, from *repaistre,* to feed, from Late Latin *repascere,* to feed again : Latin *re-,* again + *pascere,* to feed.]

re·pa·tri·ate (rée-páttri-ayt, ri- || *chiefly U.S.* -páytri-) *tr.v.* **-ated, -ating, -ates.** To return to the country of birth, citizenship, or ownership: *repatriate war refugees; repatriate the stolen statue.*
~*n.* (-ət, -it, -ayt). Someone who has been repatriated. [Late Latin *repatriāre* : Latin *re-,* back + *patria,* native country.] **—re·pa·tri·a·tion** (-áysh'n) *n.*

re·pay (ri-páy, rée-) *v.* **-paid** (-páyd), **-paying, -pays.** —*tr.* **1.** To pay back (money); refund. **2.** To pay (someone) back, either in return or in compensation. **3.** To make compensation for; make a return for. **4.** To make or do in return: *repay a call.* —*intr.* To make repayment or recompense. **—re·pay·a·ble** *adj.* **—re·pay·ment** *n.*

re·peal (ri-péel, rə-) *tr.v.* **-pealed, -pealing, -peals.** To revoke or rescind; withdraw or annul officially or formally: *Parliament repealed the law.* —See Synonyms at **nullify.**
~*n.* The act or process of repealing. [Middle English *repelen,* from Anglo-French *repeler,* from Old French *rapeler* : *re-,* back, contrary + *apeler,* to APPEAL.] **—re·peal·a·ble** *adj.* **—re·peal·er** *n.*

re·peat (ri-péet, rə-) *v.* **-peated, -peating, -peats.** —*tr.* **1.** To utter or state again. **2.** To utter in duplication of another's utterance. **3.** To recite from memory. **4.** To pass on (something told in confidence) to another. **5.** To do, experience, or produce again. **6.** To manifest or express (oneself) in the same way or words: *History repeats itself.* —*intr.* **1.** To do or say something again. **2.** To occur more than once; recur. **3.** To strike the hour, half-hour, or quarter-hour, when a spring is pressed. Used of a watch or clock. **4.** To fire, or be capable of firing, several shots without being reloaded. Used of a gun. **5.** *Informal.* To be tasted again, often as a result of belching,

PRONUNCIATION KEY

a, trap; aa, father; ai, fair; ar, star; aw, lawn; ay, play; b, bb, stab; rubber; ch, church; ck, ticket; d, dd, dead; ladder; e, dress; ee, bee; er, defer; ew, few; ewr, pure; ə, about; ər, letter; f, ff, fife; differ; g, gg, giggle; h, hat; i, kit; ī, price; īr, fire; j, judge; k, kick; l, ll, let; 'l, needle; m, mm, man; n, nn, no; 'n, sudden; ng, thing; o, lot; ō, no; ŏŏ, foot; ōō, shoe; oor, poor; ow, cow; owr, hour; oy, boy; p, pp, pepper; r, rr, red; s, ss, sauce; sh, ship; t, tt, totter; th, thick; th, this; smooth; u, cut; ur, turn; v, vv, valve; w, wet; y, yes; z, zz, zebra; zh, vision; pleasure

IN FOREIGN WORDS:

aN, oN, Saint-Saëns; hl, Llanelli; Hluhluwe; kh, loch; lough; Khaled

STRESS MARK:

ín-sīt, insight; in-sít, incite

after having been swallowed. Used of food: *Onions repeat on me.*
~*n.* **1.** The act of repeating. Also used adjectivally: *a repeat performance.* **2.** Something repeated; especially, a television or radio programme that has been broadcast before. **3.** *Music.* **a.** A passage or section that is repeated. **b.** A sign usually consisting of a vertical pair of dots, indicating a passage to be repeated. **4. a.** A repeated or duplicate order for goods. **b.** The goods so ordered. [Middle English *repeten,* from Old French *repeter,* from Latin *repetere,* to go back to, seek again : *re-,* again + *petere,* to go to, seek.]

re·peat·ed (ri-péetid, rə-) *adj.* Said, done, or occurring again and again. **—re·peat·ed·ly** *adv.*

re·peat·er (ri-péetər, rə-) *n.* **1.** Someone or something that repeats. **2.** A watch or clock with a pressure-activated mechanism that strikes the hour and, often the half-hour and quarter-hour. **3.** A repeating firearm. **4.** An electrical circuit in a transmission line for amplifying and retransmitting signals, to compensate for power losses.

repeating decimal *n.* A decimal in which, after a certain digit, a pattern of one or more digits is repeated indefinitely, as in 1.5461616161. . . . Also called "circulating decimal", "recurring decimal".

repeating firearm *n.* A firearm capable of firing several times without reloading. Also called "repeater".

re·pel (ri-pél, rə-) *v.* **-pelled, -pelling, -pels.** —*tr.* **1.** To drive back; ward off or keep away: *repel insects.* **2.** To offer successful resistance to; fight off: *repel an invasion.* **3.** To refuse to accept; reject: *repel an offer.* **4.** To turn away from; spurn. **5.** To cause aversion or distaste in: *His rudeness repels everyone.* **6.** To be resistant to; be incapable of absorbing or mixing with. **7.** To present an opposing force to; push back or away by a force: *Electric charges of the same sign repel each other.* —*intr.* **1.** To offer a resistant force to something. **2.** To cause aversion or distaste. [Middle English *repellen,* from Latin *repellere* : *re-,* back + *pellere,* to drive.] **—re·pel·er** *n.*

Usage: *Repel* and *repulse* both have the physical sense of driving back or off: an invasion, for example, may be repelled or repulsed. *Repulse* may also apply to rebuffing or rejecting someone in a hostile or impolite manner *(I repulsed every attempt he made to get to know me)*; but only *repel* is used in the sense of causing distaste or aversion to someone *(The picture repelled me).*

re·pel·lent (ri-péllənt, rə-) *adj.* Also *rare* **re·pel·lant.** **1.** Serving or tending to repel; capable of repelling something. **2.** Inspiring aversion or distaste; repulsive. **3.** Resistant or impervious to an often specified substance. Often used in combination: *a water-repellent fabric.* —See Synonyms at **hateful.**
~*n.* Also *rare* **re·pel·lant.** Something that repels; especially: **1.** A substance used to repel insects. **2.** A substance or treatment for making a fabric or surface impervious or resistant to something. **—re·pel·lence, re·pel·len·cy** *n.*

re·pent¹ (ri-pént, rə-) *v.* **-pented, -penting, -pents.** —*intr.* **1.** To feel remorse or self-reproach for what one has done or failed to do; be contrite. **2.** To feel such remorse or regret for past conduct as to change one's mind regarding it. Used with *of: He repented of his severity.* **3.** To feel remorse or contrition for one's sins and to renounce sinful ways. —*tr.* **1.** To feel regret or self-reproach for. **2.** To change one's mind regarding (past conduct). [Middle English *repenten,* from Old French *repentir* : *re-,* in response to + *pentir,* to be sorry, from Vulgar Latin *penitīre* (unattested), to cause to repent, from Latin *paenitēre* (see **penitent**).] **—re·pent·er** *n.*

re·pent² (réepənt) *adj. Botany.* Creeping along the ground; prostrate. [Latin *rēpēns* (stem *rēpent-*), present participle of *rēpere,* to creep.]

re·pen·tance (ri-péntənss, rə-) *n.* **1.** Remorse or contrition for past conduct or sin. **2.** The act or process of repenting.

re·pen·tant (ri-péntənt, rə-) *adj.* Characterised by or demonstrating repentance; penitent. **—re·pen·tant·ly** *adv.*

re·per·cus·sion (réepər-kúsh'n) *n.* **1.** An effect, influence, or result, often indirect, produced by an event or action. **2.** A recoil, rebounding, or reciprocal motion after impact. **3.** A reflection, especially of sound; an echo. [Latin *repercussiō* (stem *repercussiōn-*), from *repercussus,* past participle of *repercutere,* to cause to rebound : *re-,* back + *percutere,* to PERCUSS.] **—re·per·cus·sive** *adj.*

rep·er·toire (réppər-twaar) *n.* Also **rep·er·to·ry** (-təri, -tri). **1.** The stock of songs, plays, operas, or other pieces that a player or company is able to perform. **2.** The range or number of skills or special accomplishments of a particular person or group. [French *répertoire,* from Late Latin *repertōrium,* REPERTORY.]

rep·er·to·ry (réppər-təri, -tri) *n., pl.* **-ries.** **1.** A repertoire. **2. a.** The performance of plays by a theatrical company, from a specific repertoire, usually in alternation. Also informally called "rep". **b.** A repertory company. **3.** A storehouse or other place where a stock of things is kept. **4.** Something stored in or as if in such a place; a stock or collection: *a repertory of photographic techniques.* [Late Latin *repertōrium,* from Latin *repertus,* past participle of *reperīre,* to find out, find again : *re-,* again + *parīre,* to produce, invent.] **—rep·er·to·rial** (-táwri-əl || -tōri-əl) *adj.*

repertory company *n.* **1.** A theatrical company that presents and performs plays from a specific repertoire. **2.** A theatrical company presenting a number of plays for a limited period during a season. Also called "repertory", informally "rep".

rep·e·tend (réppi-tend, -ténd) *n.* **1.** A word, sound, or phrase that is repeated; a refrain. **2.** *Mathematics.* The digit or group of digits that repeats infinitely in a repeating decimal; for example, 61 in 1.54616161. . . . [Latin *repetendum,* neuter gerundive of *repetere,* to REPEAT.]

ré·pé·ti·teur (ray-pétti-tér, ri-, -tőr) *n.* A coach for opera singers, ballet dancers, or other artists. [French.]

rep·e·ti·tion (réppi-tísh'n, réppə-) *n.* **1.** The act or process of repeating; the saying, doing, or producing of something again. **2.** A recitation or recital, especially of prepared or memorised material. **3.** Something repeated; a copy or reproduction. [Latin *repetītiō* (stem *repetītiōn-*), from *repetere,* to REPEAT.]

rep·e·ti·tious (réppi-tíshəss, réppə-) *adj.* Characterised by or filled with repetition, especially needless or tedious repetition. **—rep·e·ti·tious·ly** *adv.* **—rep·e·ti·tious·ness** *n.*

re·pet·i·tive (ri-péttitiv, rə-, -péttətiv) *adj.* Characterised by repetition; tending to repeat. **—re·pet·i·tive·ly** *adv.* **—re·pet·i·tive·ness** *n.*

re·phrase (rée-fráyz, ri-) *tr.v.* **-phrased, -phrasing, -phrases.** To phrase again; especially, to state in a new, clearer, or different way.

re·pine (ri-pín, rə-) *intr.v.* **-pined, -pining, -pines.** To be discontented or low in spirits; complain or fret. [RE- + PINE (pain).]

repl. replacement.

re·place (ri-pláyss, rée-) *tr.v.* **-placed, -placing, -places.** **1. a.** To place again. **b.** To put back in place. **2.** To take or fill the place of; supplant or supersede. **3.** To be or provide a substitute for. **4.** To provide a new version of, especially by purchase: *replaced the broken lamp.* **—re·place·a·ble** *adj.* **—re·plac·er** *n.*

Synonyms: *replace, supplant, displace, supersede.*

re·place·ment (ri-pláyssmənt, rée-) *n. Abbr.* **repl.** **1.** The act or process of replacing or of being replaced. **2.** One that replaces, such as a player who takes the place of an injured colleague in a team. **3.** *Chemistry.* A type of reaction in which one atom or group in a compound is replaced by another. See **substitution.** **4.** *Geology.* A process in which one mineral is gradually replaced by another through deposition and removal.

re·plant (rée-pláant || -plánt) *tr.v.* **-planted, -planting, -plants.** **1.** To plant something again, or in a new place. **2.** To supply with new plants: *replant a window box.* **3.** *Chemistry.* A type of reaction in which one atom or group in a compound is replaced by another. See **substitution.**
~*n.* (rée-plaant || -plant). Something that has been replanted.

re·play (rée-pláy) *tr.v.* **-played, -playing, -plays.** To play over again: *replay a match; replay a tape.*
~*n.* (rée-play). **1.** The act or process of replaying something. **2.** Something replayed; especially: **a.** A football match between two teams whose previous meeting has ended in a draw. **b.** A part of a television broadcast showing a particular sequence or piece of action, sometimes in slow motion. See **action replay.**

re·plen·ish (ri-plénnish, rə-) *tr.v.* **-ished, -ishing, -ishes.** **1.** To fill or make complete again; add a new stock or supply to: *replenish the larder.* **2.** To renew a supply of. [Middle English *replenisshen,* from Old French *replenir* (present stem *repleniss-*) : *re-,* again + *plenir,* to fill, from *plein,* full.] **—re·plen·ish·er** *n.* **—re·plen·ish·ment** *n.*

re·plete (ri-pléet, rə-) *adj.* **1.** Plentifully supplied; abounding. Used with *with.* **2.** Filled to satiation; gorged. [Middle English *replet,* from Old French, from Latin *replētus,* past participle of *replēre,* to refill : *re-,* again + *plēre,* to fill.] **—re·plete·ness** *n.*

re·ple·tion (ri-pléesh'n, rə-) *n.* **1.** The condition of being fully supplied or completely filled. **2.** A state of excessive fullness.

re·plev·i·a·ble (ri-plévvi-əb'l, rə-) *adj.* Also **re·plev·is·a·ble** (-səb'l). *Law.* Capable of being recovered by replevin.

re·plev·in (ri-plévvin, rə-) *n.* Also **re·plev·y** (-plévvi). *Law.* **1.** An action to recover personal property unlawfully taken. **2.** The recovery of property by this action subject to the recoverer's willingness to have the matter settled finally in court. **3.** The writ or procedure by which the property is recovered.
~*tr.v.* **replevined, -ining, -ins.** *Law.* To replevy. [Middle English *replevyn,* from Anglo-French *replevine,* a pledge, from Old French *replevir,* to recover, "to pledge back" : *re-,* back + *plevir,* pledge, from Frankish *plegan* (unattested).]

re·plev·y (ri-plévvi, rə-) *tr.v.* **-ied, -ying, -ies.** *Law.* To regain possession of (goods) by a writ of replevin.
~*n. Law.* Replevin. [Anglo-French *replevir,* from Old French. See **replevin.**]

rep·li·ca (répplikə) *n.* **1.** A copy or reproduction of a work of art, especially one made by the original artist. **2.** Any copy or close reproduction, especially one on a smaller scale. [Italian, from *replicare,* to repeat, from Latin *replicāre,* to REPLICATE.]

rep·li·cate (réppli-kayt) *tr.v.* **-cated, -cating, -cates.** **1.** To duplicate, copy, reproduce, or repeat. **2.** To fold over; bend (something) back upon itself.
~*adj.* (-kət, -kit, -kayt). Also **rep·li·cat·ed** (-kaytid). Folded over or bent back upon itself: *a replicate leaf.* [Late Latin *replicāre,* to repeat, from Latin, to fold back : *re-,* back + *plicāre,* to fold.]

rep·li·ca·tion (réppli-káysh'n) *n.* **1.** A fold or a folding back. **2.** A reply; a response, especially to an answer. **3.** *Law.* The plaintiff's response to the defendant's answer or plea. **4.** An echo or reverberation. **5.** A copy or reproduction. **6.** The act or process of duplicating or reproducing something. **7.** The process by which exact copies of genetic material, such as DNA molecules, are produced.

re·ply (ri-plí, rə-) *v.* **-plied, -plying, -plies.** —*intr.* **1.** To give an answer in speech or writing. **2.** To respond by some action or gesture: *He replied by shrugging his shoulders.* **3.** To echo. **4.** *Law.* To answer a defendant's plea. —*tr.* To say or give as an answer: *He replied that he was ill.* —See Synonyms at **answer.**

~*n., pl.* **replies. 1.** An answer in speech or writing. **2.** A response by action or gesture. **3.** *Law.* A plaintiff's speech or argument in answer to that of a defendant. [Middle English *replien,* from Old French *replier,* to fold back, reply, from Latin *replicāre,* to REPLICATE.] —**re·pli·er** *n.*

reply-paid (ri-plī́-páyd, rə-) *adj.* **1.** With the reply prepaid by the sender. Said especially of a telegram. **2.** With the postage paid by the addressee. Said of a postcard, envelope, or the like.

re·point (rée-póynt) *tr.v.* **-pointed, -pointing, -points.** To reset (bricks) in new mortar or cement; point (brickwork) again.

ré·pon·dez s'il vous plaît (re-póɴday sée vŏŏ pláy, ray-). *Abbr.* **R.S.V.P.** *French.* Please reply. Used on formal invitations.

re·port (ri-pórt, rə- || -pōrt) *n. Abbr.* **rep., rept., rpt. 1.** An account, a result of an investigation, an announcement, or the like that is prepared, presented, or delivered, usually in formal or organised form. **2.** A formal, detailed account of the proceedings or transactions of a group. **3.** *Usually plural. Law.* A published collection of authoritative accounts of court cases or of judicial decisions. **4.** Rumour or gossip; common talk: *According to report, they eloped.* **5.** Reputation; repute: *a man of bad report.* **6.** An explosive noise: *the sharp report of a rifle.* **7.** *British.* An account and summary of a pupil's work, achievement, progress, and behaviour at school.

~*v.* **reported, -porting, -ports.** —*tr.* **1.** To make or present an account of (an inquiry, for example), often officially, formally, or regularly. **2.** To relate or tell about: *reported the discovery in a learned journal.* **3.** To write or provide an account or summary of for publication or broadcast. **4.** To submit or relate the results of considerations concerning: *The committee reported the bill.* **5.** To carry back and repeat to another. **6.** To complain about or denounce: *Report him to the police.* —*intr.* **1.** To make a report. **2.** To serve as a reporter for a newspaper, broadcasting company, or other news medium. **3.** To present oneself: *report for duty.* **4.** To be accountable: *He reports directly to the chairman.* [Middle English, from Old French, from *reporter,* to carry back, from Latin *reportāre,* "to carry back" : *re-,* back + *portāre,* to carry.] —**re·port·a·ble** *adj.*

re·port·age (ri-pórt-ij, réppawr-táazh || -pōrt-, réppōr-, réppər-) *n.* **1.** The reporting of news or information of general interest. **2.** The style of such reporting.

re·port·ed·ly (ri-pórt-idli, rə- || -pōrt-) *adv.* By report; supposedly.

reported speech *n.* **Indirect speech** *(see).*

re·port·er (ri-pórt-ər, rə- || -pōrt-) *n. Abbr.* **rep. 1.** A person who reports. **2.** A writer, investigator, or (especially on radio and television) presenter of news stories. **3.** A person authorised to write and issue official accounts of judicial or legislative proceedings. —**rep·or·to·ri·al** (réppawr-táwri-əl, réppər-, rée-pawr- || -pōr-, -tōri-) *adj.*

report stage *n.* The stage in the passage of a bill through the British Parliament when the committee examining it has completed its work and resubmits the bill to the House of Commons.

re·pose¹ (ri-pṓz, rə-) *n.* **1. a.** The act of resting; a rest. **b.** The state of being at rest; relaxation. **2.** Peace of mind; freedom from anxiety; composure. **3.** Calm; tranquillity. —See Synonyms at **rest.**

~*v.* **reposed, -posing, -poses.** —*tr.* **1.** To lay (oneself or part of one's body) down. **2.** To rest or relax (oneself). —*intr.* **1.** To lie at rest; relax. **2.** To lie or be supported by something. **3.** To lie dead: *repose in the grave.* [Middle English *reposen,* from Old French *reposer, repauser,* from Late Latin *repausāre* : *re-* (intensifier), again + *pausāre,* to rest, from Latin *pausa,* a stop, pause, from Greek *pausis,* from *pauein,* to stop.] —**re·pos·al** *n.* —**re·pos·er** *n.*

repose² *tr.v.* **-posed, -posing, -poses.** To place (faith or trust, for example) in. [Middle English *reposen* : RE- + POSE (formed by analogy with Latin *repōnere,* to put back).]

re·pose·ful (ri-pṓzf'l, rə-) *adj.* Expressing repose; calm. —**re·pose·ful·ly** *adv.* —**re·pose·ful·ness** *n.*

re·pos·it (ri-pózzit, rə-) *tr.v.* **-ited, -iting, -its.** To put away; store. [Latin *repōnere* (past participle *repositus*), to put back, replace : *re-,* back + *pōnere,* to place.] —**re·po·si·tion** (rée-pə-zísh'n, réppə-) *n.*

re·pos·i·to·ry (ri-pózzi-təri, rə-, -tri) *n., pl.* **-ries. 1.** A place where things may be put for safekeeping. **2.** A warehouse. **3.** A museum. **4.** A burial vault; a tomb. **5.** One that contains or is a store for something specified: *She was a repository of ancient herbal lore.* **6.** One who is entrusted with secrets or confidential information.

re·pos·sess (rée-pə-zéss || -pō-) *tr.v.* **-sessed, -sessing, -sesses. 1.** To take back possession of (property), as from someone who has not kept up hire-purchase repayments; regain possession of. **2.** To give back possession to. —**re·pos·ses·sion** *n.*

re·pous·sé (rə-pŏŏ-say, ri- || -pŏŏ-sáy) *adj.* **1.** Raised in relief. Said of a design worked in metal. **2.** Decorated with raised designs.

~*n.* **1.** A design hammered in relief. **2.** The technique of hammering such a design. [French, past participle of *repousser,* to push back, from Old French : *re-,* back + *pousser,* to PUSH.]

repp. Variant of **rep** (fabric).

repr. representing.

rep·re·hend (réppri-hénd, réppra-) *tr.v.* **-hended, -hending, -hends.** To reprove; censure. See Synonyms at **criticise.** [Middle English *reprehenden,* from Latin *reprehendere,* rebuke, hold back : *re-,* back + *prehendere,* to seize.]

rep·re·hen·si·ble (réppri-hén-si-b'l, réppra-, -sə-) *adj.* Deserving of rebuke or censure; blameworthy. [Late Latin *reprehēnsibilis,* from Latin *reprehendere* (past participle *reprehēnsus*), to REPREHEND.] —**rep·re·hen·si·bil·i·ty** (-bílləti), **rep·re·hen·si·ble·ness** *n.* —**rep·re·hen·si·bly** *adv.*

rep·re·hen·sion (réppri-hénsh'n, réppra-) *n.* Rebuke; censure.

rep·re·sent (réppri-zént, réppra-) *tr.v.* **-sented, -senting, -sents. 1. a.** To stand for; symbolise. **b.** To indicate or communicate by signs or signals. **2.** To depict; portray. **3.** To present clearly to the mind. **4.** To point out forcefully: *represented the need for caution.* **5.** To describe or put forward (a person or thing) as an embodiment of some specified quality. **6. a.** To serve as the official and authorised delegate or agent for; act as a spokesman for. **b.** To be present in the name of. **7.** To serve as an example of: *The class of mammals is represented by seven species in this museum.* **8.** To be the equivalent of. **9. a.** To stage (a play, for example); present; produce. **b.** To act the part or role of. —See Synonyms at **mean.** [Middle English *representen,* from Latin *repraesantāre,* show, bring back : *re-,* back, again + *praesentāre,* to PRESENT.] —**rep·re·sent·a·ble** *adj.* —**rep·re·sent·a·bil·i·ty** (-ə-bílləti) *n.*

rep·re·sen·ta·tion (réppri-zen-táysh'n, réppra-, -zən-) *n.* **1.** The act of representing or the state of being represented. **2.** That which represents. **3.** *Often plural.* **a.** An account or statement, as of facts, allegations, or arguments. **b.** An expostulation; a protest: *make representations to a higher authority.* **4.** A presentation or production, as of a play. **5.** The state or condition of serving as an official delegate, agent, or spokesman. **6.** The right or privilege of being represented by delegates having a voice in a legislative body. **7.** *Law.* A statement of fact made by one party in order to induce another party to enter into a contract.

rep·re·sen·ta·tion·al (réppri-zen-táysh'n'l, réppra-, -zən-) *adj.* Of or pertaining to representation, especially to realistic and naturalistic graphic representation in art, as opposed to abstraction.

rep·re·sen·ta·tion·al·ism (réppri-zen-táysh'n'l-iz'm, réppra-, -zən-) *n.* Also **rep·re·sen·ta·tion·ism** (-táysh'n-iz'm) (for sense 1). **1.** *Philosophy.* A theory of perception that holds that since external objects are perceived through the mediation of the human mind, they can never be perceived directly as they really are, but only as representations of the "real" object. **2.** The practice and active support of representational art.

rep·re·sen·ta·tive (réppri-zéntətiv, réppra-) *n. Abbr.* **rep., Rep. 1.** A person or thing serving as an example or type for others of the same classification; a typical instance. **2. a.** One qualified to serve as an authorised official delegate or agent. **b.** One present in the name of another person or body. **c.** One who travels around on behalf of a company, trying to obtain orders or custom. **3. a.** A member of a governmental body, usually legislative, chosen by popular vote. **b.** In the United States, a member of the House of Representatives, the lower house of Congress, or of a state legislature.

~*adj.* **1.** Representing, depicting, portraying, or able to do so. **2.** Authorised to act as an official delegate or agent. **3.** Of, pertaining to, or characteristic of government by representation. **4.** Exemplary of others in the same class; typical. —**rep·re·sen·ta·tive·ly** *adv.* —**rep·re·sen·ta·tive·ness** *n.*

re·press (ri-préss, rə-) *tr.v.* **-pressed, -pressing, -presses. 1.** To hold back; restrain: *repress a laugh.* **2.** To suppress; quell: *repress a rebellion.* **3.** To control forcibly and oppresively; subjugate: *His parents repressed him in childhood.* **4.** *Psychology.* To force (memories, ideas, or fears, for example) into the subconscious mind. [Middle English *repressen,* from Latin *reprimere* (past participle *repressus*) : *re-,* back + *premere,* to press.] —**re·press·i·ble** *adj.* —**re·pres·sive** *adj.* —**re·pres·sive·ly** *adv.* —**re·pres·sive·ness** *n.*

re·pres·sion (ri-présh'n, rə-) *n.* **1. a.** The action of repressing. **b.** The state of being repressed. **2.** The unconscious exclusion of painful impulses, desires, or fears from the conscious mind.

re·pres·sor, re·press·er (ri-préssər, rə-) *n.* **1.** One that represses. **2.** *Biology.* A protein that prevents the synthesis of other proteins by interfering with the action of DNA.

re·prieve (ri-préev, rə-) *tr.v.* **-prieved, -prieving, -prieves. 1.** To postpone or cancel the punishment of. **2.** To bring relief to.

~*n.* **1. a.** The postponement or cancellation of a punishment. **b.** A warrant for such a postponement or cancellation. **2.** Temporary relief, as from danger or pain. [Variant of earlier *reprive, repry,* from Middle English *repryen,* from Old French *reprendre* (past participle *repris*), to take back, from Latin *reprehendere,* to hold back, REPREHEND.] —**re·priev·a·ble** *adj.*

rep·ri·mand (réppri-maand, -maánd || -mánd, -mand) *tr.v.* **-manded, -manding, -mands.** To rebuke or censure severely. See Synonyms at **admonish.**

~*n.* (-maand || -mand). A severe or formal rebuke or censure. [French *reprimender,* from *reprimende,* a reprimand, ultimately from Latin *reprimenda,* neuter plural gerundive of *reprimere,* to REPRESS.]

re·print (rée-print) *n. Abbr.* **rep. 1.** Something that has been printed again; especially: **a.** A new or additional edition; a facsimile impression of an original. **b.** An offprint; a separately printed excerpt. **2.** A facsimile of a stamp printed after the original issue of the stamp has ceased.

~*tr.v.* (rée-prínt) **reprinted, -printing, -prints.** To print again; make a new copy or edition of. —**re·print·er** *n.*

re·pri·sal (ri-prī́z'l, rə-) *n.* **1.** *Often plural.* Retaliation for an injury with the intent of inflicting at least as much injury in return. **2.** The forcible seizure of an enemy's goods or subjects in retaliation for inflicted injuries. **3.** An act or instance of any kind of retaliation. [Middle English *reprisail,* from Anglo-French *reprisaille,* from Medieval Latin *repraesālia,* contraction of *repraehensālia,* from Latin *reprehensus,* past participle of *reprehendere,* to REPREHEND.]

re·prise (ri-préez, rə-) *n.* **1.** *Music.* A repetition of a phrase or verse; a return to an original theme. **2.** A repetition; a repeat.

~*tr.v.* **reprised, -prising, -prises.** —*tr.* To repeat; make a reprise

PRONUNCIATION KEY

a, trap; aa, father; ai, fair; ar, star; aw, lawn; ay, play; b, bb, stab; rubber; ch, church; ck, ticket; d, dd, dead; ladder; e, dress; ee, bee; er, defer; ew, few; ewr, pure; ə, about; ər, letter; f, ff, fife; differ; g, gg, giggle; h, hat; i, kit; ī, price; īr, fire; j, judge; k, kick; l, ll, let; 'l, needle; m, mm, man; n, nn, no; 'n, sudden; ng, thing; o, lot; ō, no; ŏŏ, foot; ōō, shoe; oor, poor; ow, cow; owr, hour; oy, boy; p, pp, pepper; r, rr, red; s, ss, sauce; sh, ship; t, tt, totter; th, thick; th, this; smooth; u, cut; ur, turn; v, vv, valve; w, wet; y, yes; z, zz, zebra; zh, vision; pleasure

IN FOREIGN WORDS:

aɴ, oɴ, Saint-Saëns; hl, Llanelli; Hluhluwe; kh, loch; lough; Khaled

STRESS MARK:

ín-sīt, insight; in-sī́t, incite

of. [Middle English, from Old French, "a taking back", from the feminine past participle of *reprendre*, to take back, from Latin *reprehendere*, to REPREHEND.]

re-pro (réeprō) *n. Informal.* Reproduction furniture. —*adj. Informal.* Made to resemble an antique: *a repro chair.*

re-proach (ri-prōch, rə-) *tr.v.* **-proached, -proaching, -proaches.** 1. To blame for something; rebuke; censure. 2. *Archaic.* To bring shame upon; disgrace. —See Synonyms at **admonish.** —*n.* 1. Censure; rebuke; blame. 2. That which causes rebuke or blame. 3. Disgrace; shame. —**beyond reproach.** So good as to preclude any possibility of criticism. [Middle English *reprochen*, from Old French *reprochier*, from Vulgar Latin *repropiāre* (unattested), bring back near : Latin *re-*, back + *prope*, near.] —**re-proach-a-ble** *adj.* —**re-proach-a-ble-ness** *n.* —**re-proach-a-bly** *adv.* —**re-proach-er** *n.*

re-proach-ful (ri-prōch-f'l, rə-) *adj.* Expressing reproach or blame. —**re-proach-ful-ly** *adv.* —**re-proach-ful-ness** *n.*

rep-ro-bate (rép-rə-bayt, -rō-, -bət, -bit) *n.* 1. A morally unprincipled person; a rogue; a scoundrel. Often used humorously or affectionately. 2. *Theology.* One who is predestined to damnation. —*adj.* 1. Morally unprincipled; shameless. 2. *Theology.* Rejected by God and without hope of salvation. —*tr.v.* (-bayt) **reprobated, -bating, -bates.** 1. To disapprove of; condemn. 2. *Theology.* To abandon to eternal damnation. [Late Latin *reprobātus*, past participle of *reprobāre*, to reprove : Latin *re-*, back, against + *probāre*, to test, PROVE.] —**rep-ro-ba-tion** (-báysh'n) *n.*

re-pro-duce (rée-prə-déwss || -prō-, -dōoss) *v.* **-duced, -ducing, -duces.** —*tr.* 1. To produce a counterpart, image, or copy of. 2. *Biology.* To generate (offspring) by sexual or asexual means. 3. To produce again or anew; re-create. 4. To bring to mind again (a memory, for example). —*intr.* 1. To generate offspring. 2. To undergo copying. —**re-pro-duc-er** *n.* —**re-pro-duc-i-ble** *adj.*

re-pro-duc-tion (rée-prə-dúksh'n || -prō-) *n.* 1. The act of reproducing or of being reproduced. 2. That which is reproduced, especially with reference to its faithfulness to an original: *disappointed by the poor quality of the sound reproduction.* 3. A copy of a work of art, antique, or the like. Also used adjectivally: *reproduction furniture.* 4. *Biology.* The sexual or asexual process by which organisms generate others of the same kind.

reproduction proof *n. Printing.* A proof of metal type made for reproduction through a photographic process such as photo-offset lithography.

re-pro-duc-tive (rée-prə-dúktiv || -prō-) *adj.* 1. Of or pertaining to reproduction. 2. Tending to reproduce. —**re-pro-duc-tive-ly** *adv.* —**re-pro-duc-tive-ness** *n.*

rep-ro-graph-ics (répprə-gráffiks, réeprō-) *n. Usually used with a singular verb.* 1. The technique of reprography. 2. The materials, equipment, and processes used in reprography.

re-prog-ra-phy (ri-próggrəfi, rée-) *n.* The process of reproducing, reprinting, or copying graphic material by mechanical, electronic means. [REPRO(DUCE) + -GRAPHY.] —**rep-ro-graph-ic** (répprə-gráffik, réeprə-) *adj.* —**rep-ro-graph-i-cal-ly** *adv.*

re-proof¹ (ri-prōōf, rə- || -prōof) *n.* An act or expression of reproving; a rebuke.

re-proof² (rée-prōōf || -prōof) *tr.v.* **-proofed, -proofing, -proofs.** 1. To make a new proof of (printed matter). 2. To make resistant again, as by making heatproof or waterproof.

re-prove (ri-prōōv, rə-) *tr.v.* **-proved, -proving, -proves.** To rebuke for a fault or misdeed; scold. See Synonyms at **admonish.** [Middle English *reproven*, from Old French *reprover*, from Late Latin *reprobāre*, REPROBATE.] —**re-prov-a-ble** *adj.* —**re-prov-er** *n.* —**re-prov-ing-ly** *adv.*

rept. 1. receipt. 2. report.

rep-tant (réptənt) *adj. Biology.* Creeping or crawling. [Latin *reptāns* (stem *reptant-*), present participle of *reptāre*, to crawl, frequentative of *repere*, to crawl.]

rep-tile (rép-tīl || *U.S. also* -t'l, -til) *n.* 1. Any of various coldblooded, usually egg-laying vertebrates of the class Reptilia, such as a snake, lizard, crocodile, turtle, or dinosaur, having an external covering of scales or horny plates, and breathing by means of lungs. 2. A despicable or repulsive person. —*adj.* 1. Of, pertaining to, or characteristic of reptiles. 2. Despicable; repulsive. 3. *Archaic.* Creeping. [Middle English *reptil*, from Old French *reptile*, from Late Latin *reptile*, neuter of *reptilis*, creeping, from Latin *repere*, to creep.]

rep-til-i-an (rep-tílli-ən) *adj.* 1. Of or pertaining to reptiles. 2. Resembling or characteristic of a reptile. 3. Repulsive, contemptible, or devious. —*n.* A reptile.

Rep-ton (réptən), **Humphry** (1752–1818). English landscape gardener. Like Capability Brown, he planned carefully informal gardens, though with more classical elements in them. His work is best seen at Cobham Hall, Kent, and at Sheringham Hall, Norfolk.

re-pub-lic (ri-púbblik, rə-) *n. Abbr.* **rep., Rep., Repub.** 1. Any political order that is not a monarchy. 2. **a.** A constitutional form of government, especially a democratic and representative one, in which the head of state is not a monarch, and supreme power is vested in the people or their elected representatives. **b.** A country having such a form of government. 3. A particular republican administration constituting a stage in a country's political history: *the third republic.* 4. Any group of people working freely and equally for the same cause: *the republic of letters.* 5. An autonomous or partially autonomous political and territorial unit belonging to a sovereign federation; specifically, such a unit in the U.S.S.R. or Yugoslavia. [French *république*, from Latin *rēspūblica* : *rēs*, a thing, matter, affair + *pūblica*, feminine of *pūblicus*, PUBLIC.]

re-pub-li-can (ri-púbblikən, rə-) *adj.* 1. Of, pertaining to, or characteristic of a republic. 2. In favour of a republican form of government. 3. *Capital* **R. a.** *Abbr.* **R., Rep., Repub.** Of, belonging to, or supporting the Republican Party of the United States. **b.** Of, belonging to, or supporting the nationalist cause in Ireland, opposed to the partition of Ireland and seeking reunification. **c.** Of, belonging to, or supporting the government side in the Spanish Civil War. —*n.* 1. A person who favours a republican form of government. 2. *Capital* **R. a.** A member of the Republican Party of the United States. **b.** A supporter of the republican cause in Ireland. **c.** A supporter of the Republican side in the Spanish Civil War. —**re-pub-li-can-ism** *n.*

Republican calendar *n.* The **Revolutionary calendar** (*see*).

re-pub-li-can-ise, re-pub-li-can-ize (ri-púbblikə-nīz, rə-) *tr.v.* **-ised, -ising, -ises.** To make republican. —**re-pub-li-can-i-sa-tion** (-nī-záysh'n || *U.S.* -ni-) *n.*

Republican Party *n.* 1. One of the two major political parties of the United States, organised in 1854 to oppose slavery. 2. The Democratic-Republican Party, a former political party of the United States, organised in 1792 by Thomas Jefferson. See **Democratic Party.**

re-pub-li-ca-tion (rée-púbbli-káysh'n) *n.* 1. The act of republishing. 2. That which is republished.

re-pub-lish (rée-púbblish) *tr.v.* **-lished, -lishing, -lishes.** 1. To publish anew or again. 2. *Law.* To revive (a cancelled will, for example). —**re-pub-lish-er** *n.*

re-pu-di-ate (ri-péwdi-ayt, rə-) *tr.v.* **-ated, -ating, -ates.** 1. To reject emphatically as unfounded or unjust. 2. **a.** To refuse to recognise the validity or authority of. **b.** To refuse to pay. 3. **a.** To disown (a son or a wife, for example). **b.** To refuse to have any dealings with. [Latin *repudiāre*, to reject, cast off, from *repudium*, a casting off.] —**re-pu-di-a-tive** (-ətiv ||, -aytiv) *adj.* —**re-pu-di-a-tor** *n.*

re-pu-di-a-tion (ri-péwdi-áysh'n) *n.* 1. The act of repudiating or the state of being repudiated. 2. The act of refusing to acknowledge a contract or debt.

re-pugn (ri-péwn, rə-) *v.* **-pugned, -pugning, -pugns.** *Archaic.* —*tr.* To oppose or resist. —*intr.* To be opposed; conflict. [Middle English *repugnen*, from Old French *repugner*, from Latin *repugnāre*, to fight against : *re-*, against + *pugnāre*, to fight.]

re-pug-nance (ri-púg-nənss, rə-) *n.* Also **re-pug-nan-cy** (-nən-si). 1. Extreme dislike or aversion. 2. Contradiction; inconsistency.

re-pug-nant (ri-púg-nənt, rə-) *adj.* 1. Offensive; distasteful; repulsive. 2. Contradictory; inconsistent. [Middle English, from Old French, from Latin *repugnāns* (stem *repugnant-*), present participle of *repugnāre*, REPUGN.] —**re-pug-nant-ly** *adv.*

re-pulse (ri-púlss, rə-) *tr.v.* **-pulsed, -pulsing, -pulses.** 1. To drive back; repel. 2. To spurn or reject with rudeness, coldness, or denial. —See Usage note at **repel.** —*n.* 1. The act of repulsing or the fact of being repulsed. 2. Rejection; refusal. [Latin *repulsus*, past participle of *repellere*, to REPEL.] —**re-puls-er** *n.*

re-pul-sion (ri-púlsh'n, rə-) *n.* 1. The act of repulsing, or the condition of being repulsed. 2. Extreme aversion or dislike. 3. *Physics.* A force that tends to increase the distance between two bodies having like magnetic poles or like electric charges.

re-pul-sive (ri-púl-siv, rə-) *adj.* 1. Causing repugnance, extreme dislike, or aversion; disgusting. 2. Tending to repel or drive off. 3. *Physics.* Opposing in direction: *a repulsive force.* —**re-pul-sive-ly** *adv.* —**re-pul-sive-ness** *n.*

rep-u-ta-ble (réppewtə-b'l) *adj.* Having a good reputation; honourable; trustworthy: *buy from a reputable dealer.* —**rep-u-ta-bil-i-ty** (-billəti) *n.* —**rep-u-ta-bly** *adv.*

rep-u-ta-tion (réppew-táysh'n) *n.* 1. The general estimation in which a person or thing is held by the public; what is known, said, or thought about a person. 2. The state or fact of being highly thought of or having a good reputation. 3. A specified character or trait ascribed to a person or thing: *a reputation for courtesy.* [Middle English *reputacion*, from Latin *reputātiō* (stem *reputātiōn-*), a reckoning, from *reputāre*, to consider, REPUTE.]

re-pute (ri-péwt, rə-) *tr.v.* **-puted, -puting, -putes.** To consider, suppose, or regard. Usually used in the passive. —*n.* 1. Reputation. 2. Good reputation. —See Synonyms at **fame.** [Middle English *reputen*, from Old French *reputer*, from Latin *reputāre*, to count over, consider : *re-*, over, again + *putāre*, to compute, consider.]

re-put-ed (ri-péwtid, rə-) *adj.* Generally considered or supposed.

re-put-ed-ly (ri-péwtidli, rə-) *adv.* According to what is generally believed or supposed.

req. 1. require; required. 2. requisition.

re-quest (ri-kwést, rə-) *tr.v.* **-quested, -questing, -quests.** 1. To ask for; express a desire for. 2. To ask (a person) to do something. —*n.* 1. An expressed desire; an act of asking. 2. That which is asked for. —**by request.** In response to an expressed desire. —**in request.** In great demand. —**on request.** When asked for. —*adj.* Having been desired or demanded: *a request performance.* [Middle English, from Old French *requester*, from *requeste*, a request, from Vulgar Latin *requaesita* (unattested), from Latin *requīrere*, to seek again, REQUIRE.]

Usage: As a noun, *request* is generally followed by *for*: *He made a request for an increase in salary.* For the verb, however, formal English prefers alternative constructions: *He requested an increase from his boss* is preferred to *He requested his boss for an increase* or *He requested his boss to give him an increase.*

request stop *n.* A stop on a bus or coach route at which one must signal to the vehicle's driver if one wishes to be picked up.

re·qui·em (réckwi-əm, -em ‖ *U.S. also* ráykwi-, réekwi-) *n.* **1.** *Capital* **R.** *Roman Catholic Church.* **a.** A mass for a deceased person or persons. **b.** A musical composition for such a mass. **2.** Any hymn, composition, or service for the dead. [Middle English, from Latin (first word of the introit of the mass for the dead), accusative of *requiēs,* rest : *re-,* again + *quiēs,* rest.]

req·ui·es·cat (réckwi-éss-kat ‖ -kaat) *n.* A prayer for the repose of the souls of the dead. [Latin, "may he (or she) rest", from *requiescere,* to rest : *re-,* again + *quiescere,* to be quiet, rest, from *quiēs,* quiet, rest.]

re·quire (ri-kwír, rə-) *tr.v.* **-quired, -quiring, -quires. 1.** To have use for as a necessity; need. **2.** To ask or demand formally or authoritatively: *His presence was required in court.* **3.** To compel or oblige. **4.** To call for; demand as necessary or appropriate: *matters requiring our attention.* [Middle English *requiren,* from Old French *requere,* from Vulgar Latin *requaerere* (unattested), from Latin *requīrere,* to seek again, search for, inquire : *re-,* again + *quaerere,* to seek, to ask.] **—re·quir·a·ble** *adj.* **—re·quir·er** *n.*

re·quired (ri-kwírd, rə-) *adj. Abbr.* **req.** Needed; essential: *required reading.* See Synonyms at **necessary.**

re·quire·ment (ri-kwír-mənt, rə-) *n.* **1.** That which is required; something needed or wanted. **2.** Something obligatory; a prerequisite.

req·ui·site (réckwizit) *adj.* Required; necessary; essential.

~*n.* A necessity; something needed, especially for a particular purpose: *toilet requisites.* See Synonyms at **need.** [Middle English, from Latin *requisītus,* past participle of *requīrere,* to REQUIRE.] **—req·ui·site·ly** *adv.* **—req·ui·site·ness** *n.*

req·ui·si·tion (réckwi-zísh'n) *n. Abbr.* **req. 1. a.** A formal written request for something that is needed. **b.** An order claiming something for official, especially military, use. **c.** The act of making any such request or claim. **2.** A necessity; a requirement. **3.** The state or condition of being needed or put into service. **4.** A formal request made by one government to another, demanding the return of a criminal.

~*tr.v.* requisitioned, -tioning, -tions. **1.** To demand, as for military needs or in a time of emergency. **2.** To make demands of.

re·quit·al (ri-kwít'l, rə-) *n.* **1.** The act of requiting. **2.** Return, as for an injury or for some friendly act.

re·quite (ri-kwít, rə-) *tr.v.* **-quited, -quiting, -quites. 1.** To make repayment or return for: *requite another's love.* **2.** To repay (a person): *requited the stranger for his help.* **3.** To avenge. [RE- + obsolete *quite,* variant of QUIT.] **—re·quit·a·ble** *adj.* **—re·quit·er** *n.*

re·read (rée-réed) *tr.v.* **-read** (-réd), **-reading, -reads.** To read again; especially, to read (a work) with a fresh critical approach.

rere·dos (réer-doss) *n.* **1.** A decorative screen or facing on the wall at the back of an altar. **2.** The back of an open hearth of a fireplace. [Middle English, from Old French *areredos : arere,* back, behind, from Vulgar Latin *ad retrō* (unattested) : Latin *ad,* to + *retrō,* backwards + *dos,* back, from Latin *dorsum.*]

re·run (rée-run) *n.* A repeat broadcast, production, or showing of a television series, play, or the like.

~*tr.v.* (-rún) **reran** (-rán), **-running, -runs.** To present a second production, broadcast, or showing of.

---

reptile

LIVING RELATIVES OF THE DINOSAURS

Reptiles were the first vertebrates to spend their lives on land

The Reptile class includes the various groups of dinosaur – the largest-known land animals – which have been extinct for some 65 million years. Four groups of reptile survive today – snakes and lizards, crocodiles, turtles, and the primitive tuatara. All life on this planet began in the water and, over the long process of evolution, reptiles were the first vertebrates to adapt to living their entire life-cycle on land. They evolved from primitive amphibians. Although some reptiles, crocodiles and turtles for example, have returned to live in the water, all reptiles breathe through lungs, not through gills. Newly born or freshly hatched reptiles do not pass through a period as aquatic larvae but are like miniature adults. They are cold-blooded creatures, whose behaviour, not body function, is adapted to maintain them at an ideal temperature; they shun great heat or cold and bask in the sun for warmth.

LIZARD *The lizard (below) belongs to the order* Squamata, *whose members have scales covering the body. Some lizards can shed part of the tail if it is caught by a predator. Each vertebra has a preformed point at which to break. The new tail that grows is stumpy and formed round cartilage, not new bone.*

TUATARA *Most of this order, the* Rhynchocephalia, *is extinct and the tuatara (left), found only on islands off New Zealand, is the sole survivor. It is a small, lizard-like creature but its teeth are fused to the edges of its jaws – not set in sockets. The female lays up to 15 eggs which take 15 months to hatch.*

TURTLE *The marine turtles and the land tortoises compose the order* Chelonia. *The turtle (right) has flippers where the tortoise has feet. Turtles lay their eggs on land, but newly hatched young go straight to the sea to escape predators.*

CROCODILE *The order* Crocodilia, *the crocodiles, are the largest living reptiles and they live mainly in tropical rivers. Alligators, caymans, and gavials, are of similar appearance to the crocodile but the difference by which each can be recognised is in the number of teeth on each side of the jaw: crocodiles have 14 or 15, alligators and caymans have between 17 and 22, and gavials have 27–29. The crocodile also differs in that one tooth on each side of its lower jaw sticks out when its mouth is closed. All are adapted to life in the water, having raised eyes and nostrils so that they can see and breathe almost submerged. Valves in their throats keep water out of the lungs as they dive.*

res. 1. research. 2. reserve. 3. residence; resident; resides. 4. resolution.

res adjudicata. Variant of **res judicata.**

re·sale (rée-sayl, -sáyl) n. The selling again of a purchase. Also used adjectivally: *resale value.*

resale price maintenance n. Abbr. **R.P.M.** An agreement among manufacturers or between wholesalers and retailers not to sell goods below a fixed price, usually imposed by the manufacturer. Such an agreement in Britain is only legal when shown to be in the public interest.

re·scind (ri-sínd, rǝ-) tr.v. **-scinded, -scinding, -scinds.** To void; repeal. See Synonyms at **nullify.** [Latin *rēscindere,* to cut off, abolish : *re-* (intensive) + *scindere,* to cut.] —**re·scind·a·ble** adj. —**re·scind·er** n. —**re·scind·ment** n.

re·scis·sion (ri-sízh'n, rǝ-) n. The act of rescinding. [Late Latin *rescissiō* (stem *rescissiōn-*), from Latin *rescissus,* past participle of *rēscindere,* RESCIND.]

re·scis·so·ry (ri-síss-ǝri, rǝ-, -síz-) adj. Pertaining to rescission or having the effect or power of rescinding. [Late Latin *rescissōrius,* from Latin *rescissus,* past participle of *rescindere,* RESCIND.]

re·script (rée-skript) n. 1. A formal decree or edict. 2. An act of rewriting or something that is rewritten. 3. In ancient Rome, a reply from the Roman emperor to a magistrate's query on a point of law. 4. *Roman Catholic Church.* A response from the Pope to a question regarding discipline or doctrine. [Latin *rescriptum,* from the neuter past participle of *rescribere,* to write back or in reply : *re-,* back + *scribere,* to write.]

res·cue (réskew) tr.v. **-cued, -cuing, -cues.** 1. To save, as from danger or imprisonment. 2. *Law.* To take from legal custody by force. —See Synonyms at **save.**
~n. 1. An act of freeing or saving. Also used adjectivally: *a rescue team.* 2. *Law.* Removal from legal custody by force. [Middle English *rescuen,* from Old French *rescourre,* from Vulgar Latin *reexcutere* (unattested), to drive away, shake off : Latin *re-* (intensive) + *excutere,* to shake out or off : *ex,* out + *quatere,* to shake.] —**res·cu·a·ble** adj. —**res·cu·er** n.

re·search (ri-sérch, rǝ-, -zérch, rée-serch) n. Abbr. **res.** 1. Investigation or inquiry in order to gather new information or to collate what is already known about a subject, especially as an academic pursuit. Also used adjectivally: *a research grant.* 2. Information gathered during such a course of investigation or inquiry.
~v. **researched, -searching, -searches.** —intr. To engage in or perform research. —tr. 1. To study or investigate thoroughly. 2. To carry out research for. [From obsolete French *recerche, recercher,* to seek out, to search again : *re-,* again + *cerch(i)er,* to SEARCH.] —**re·search·er** n.

re·seat (rée-séet) tr.v. **-seated, -seating, -seats.** 1. To fit (a valve, for example) in a new seating. 2. To provide with a different or new seat or seats.

ré·seau, re·seau (rézzō, ray-zó ‖ ree-, ri-) n., pl. **-seaus** (-z, or pronounced as singular) or **-seaux** (-z, or pronounced as singular). 1. A net or mesh foundation for lace. 2. *Astronomy.* A reference grid of fine lines forming uniform squares on a photographic plate or print, used in measuring stars, for example. 3. In colour photography, a mosaic screen of fine lines of three colours. [French, from Old French *reseuil,* diminutive of *raiz, roiz,* a net, from Latin *rētis, rēte.*]

re·sect (ri-sékt, ree-) tr.v. **-sected, -secting, -sects.** To perform a resection of or pare down. [Latin *resectus,* past participle of *resecāre,* to cut off : *re-,* back, off + *secāre,* to cut.]

re·sec·tion (ri-séksh'n, ree-) n. The surgical removal of part of an organ or structure.

re·se·da (réssidǝ, rézzidǝ, ri-séedǝ ‖ for sense 2, U.S. also ráyzi-daa) n. 1. Any plant of the genus *Reseda,* which includes the mignonette. 2. Greyish or dark green to yellow green or light olive. [New Latin, from Latin *resēdā†.*] —**re·se·da** adj.

re·sem·blance (ri-zémblǝnss, rǝ-) n. 1. The condition or quality of resembling something; similarity in nature, form, or appearance; likeness. 2. The extent to or manner in which something resembles something else. 3. A point in which one thing or person resembles another; a likeness. —See Synonyms at **likeness.**

re·sem·ble (ri-zémb'l, rǝ-) tr.v. **-bled, -bling, -bles.** To have a similarity to; be like. [Middle English *resemblen,* from Old French *resembler* : *re-* (intensifier) + *sembler,* to be like, from Latin *simulāre, similāre,* to imitate, from *similis,* like.] —**re·sem·bler** n.

re·sent (ri-zént) tr.v. **-sented, -senting, -sents.** To feel indignantly aggrieved at (an act, situation, or person). [From obsolete French *resentir,* to feel strongly : *re-* (intensive) + *sentir,* to feel, from Latin *sentīre.*]

re·sent·ful (ri-zent-f'l) adj. Full of, characterised by, or inclined to feel resentment. —**re·sent·ful·ly** adv. —**re·sent·ful·ness** n.

re·sent·ment (ri-zéntmǝnt) n. Indignation, bitterness, or ill will felt towards an act, situation, or person. See Synonyms at **anger.**

re·ser·pine (réssǝrpin, ri-sér-pin, -peen) n. A white to yellowish powder, $C_{33}H_{40}N_2O_9$, isolated from the roots of certain species of rauwolfia, especially *Rauwolfia serpentina,* and used as a sedative and tranquilliser. [German *Reserpin,* from New Latin *Rauwolfia serpentina,* a species of snakeroot.]

res·er·va·tion (rézzǝr-váysh'n) n. 1. The act of reserving; a keeping back or withholding. 2. Something that is kept back or withheld. 3. **a.** A limiting qualification, condition, or exception. **b.** A misgiving or doubt: *has reservations about his reliability.* See Synonyms at **qualm.** 4. A tract of land set apart, especially in the United States, for a special purpose, as one for the use of a North American In-

dian people. 5. **a.** An arrangement by which something, such as a ticket or hotel accommodation, is secured in advance. **b.** That which is so secured. **c.** The record or promise of such an arrangement. 6. *British.* A strip of land between two carriageways of a road. Also called "reserve". 7. *Law.* **a.** A clause in a conveyance retaining for the grantor a right or interest in the estate conveyed. **b.** The right or interest so retained. 8. In the Christian Church, the practice of keeping consecrated hosts in a church after the celebration of the Eucharist.

re·serve (ri-zérv, rǝ-) tr.v. **-served, -serving, -serves.** 1. To keep back or save for future use or treatment, or for a special purpose. 2. **a.** To set apart for a particular person or use. **b.** To secure (a ticket or hotel room, for example) in advance; book. 3. To keep or secure for oneself; retain: *I reserve the right to disagree.* 4. To refrain from giving or expressing (judgment) immediately, especially in order to obtain further evidence. —See Synonyms at **keep.**
~n. Abbr. **res.** 1. Something kept back or saved for future use or a special purpose. 2. The state of being kept back, set aside, or saved: *funds held in reserve.* 3. A reservation, condition, or qualification: *accepted her story without reserve.* 4. The keeping of one's feelings, thoughts, or affairs to oneself. 5. Self-restraint in action or expression; reticence. 6. Lack of enthusiasm; sceptical caution. 7. An amount of capital held back from investment by a bank or a portion of profits not distributed by a company in order to meet probable or possible demands. 8. An area of public land kept for a particular purpose: *a game reserve.* 9. A central reservation, especially on a motorway. 10. *Often plural.* **a.** A fighting force kept uncommitted until strategic need arises. **b.** The part of a country's armed forces not on active duty but subject to call in an emergency. 11. *Sports.* **a.** An extra member of a team kept in readiness in case any of the playing members should be injured or unable to play. **b.** *Plural.* The second or substitute team of a club. 12. A reserve price.
~adj. Held in or forming a reserve: *a reserve supply of food.* [Middle English *reserven,* from Old French *reserver,* from Latin *reservāre,* to keep back : *re-,* back + *servāre,* to save, keep.] —**re·serv·a·ble** adj. —**re·serv·er** n.

reserve bank n. Any of the 12 main banks of the U.S. Federal Reserve System.

reserve currency n. Foreign currency that is kept in reserve by a government for the paying of international debts.

re·served (ri-zérvd, rǝ-) adj. 1. Held in reserve; kept back or set aside. 2. Not outgoing in manner or speech; undemonstrative; reticent. —See Synonyms at **humble.** —**re·serv·ed·ly** (-zérvidli) adv. —**re·serv·ed·ness** (-zérvid-nǝss, -niss) n.

reserved occupation n. *British.* An occupation that exempts one from conscription into the armed forces.

reserve price n. The minimum fixed price at which property will be sold at an auction.

re·serv·ist (ri-zérvist, rǝ-) n. A member of a military reserve.

res·er·voir (rézzǝr-vwaar ‖ rézzǝ-) n. 1. A body of water collected and stored in a natural or artificial lake. 2. A receptacle or chamber for storing a fluid. 3. *Anatomy.* A **cisterna** (see). 4. A large supply of something; a reserve: *a reservoir of gratitude.* [French *réservoir,* from *réserver,* to RESERVE.]

re·set (rée-sét) tr.v. **-set, -setting, -sets.** 1. To set (a broken bone or printing type, for example) again. 2. To change the setting of (a dial, for example); especially, in computing, to set (a counting device) back to zero or some other given value.
~n. (rée-set). 1. An act of resetting. 2. Something that is reset. —**re·set·ter** n.

res ges·tae (ráyss géss-tī, ráyz, jéss-, -tee) pl.n. 1. Things done; deeds. 2. *Law.* The facts of a case that are admissible in evidence. [Latin.]

resh (resh, raysh) n. The 20th letter of the Hebrew alphabet, corresponding to the letter *r* in English. [Hebrew *rēsh,* from *rōsh,* "head".]

re·shuf·fle (rée-shúff'l) tr.v. **-fled, -fling, -fles.** 1. To shuffle again. 2. To reorganise the allocation of positions or jobs within (a cabinet or board of directors, for example).
~n. (rée-shuff'l). An act of reshuffling; especially, a reshuffling of positions or jobs.

re·side (ri-zíd, rǝ-) intr.v. **-sided, -siding, -sides.** 1. *Formal.* To live in a place for an extended or permanent period of time. 2. To be inherently present; exist. Used with *in.* 3. To be vested. Used with *in.* [Middle English *residen,* from Old French *resider,* from Latin *residēre,* "to sit back", "remain sitting" : *re-,* back, back in place + *sedēre,* to sit.] —**re·sid·er** n.

res·i·dence (rézzidǝnss) n. Abbr. **res.** 1. The place in which one lives; a dwelling; an abode. 2. The act or a period of residing somewhere. 3. **a.** A large house or mansion. **b.** A residency. —**in residence.** Living in or appointed to a particular place or institution in order to carry out a specified job or set of duties: *writer in residence.*

res·i·den·cy (rézzi-dǝn-si ‖ -den-) n., pl. **-cies.** 1. **a.** A protected state in which the powers of the protecting state are exercised by a resident representative; specifically, such a territory in India during the British Raj. **b.** The official residence of such a representative. 2. Residence. 3. A long-term engagement for a musical group to appear and play at a particular venue. 4. *U.S.* The period during which a doctor receives specialised clinical training.

res·i·dent (rézzi-d'nt ‖ -dent) n. Abbr. **res.** 1. One who resides in a particular place; a long-term or permanent inhabitant as opposed to a visitor. 2. **a.** Formerly, the British representative of a governor general at an Indian native court. **b.** Formerly, a representative of the British government in a protected state. **3.** A nonmigratory bird or other animal. **4.** *U.S.* A doctor serving his period of residency. ~*adj.* **1.** Dwelling in a particular place; residing. **2.** Living somewhere in connection with duty or work. **3.** Inherently present. **4.** Nonmigratory. Said of birds and other animals. **5.** *Informal.* Acting in a specified capacity as a member of a group: *our resident expert on football.*

res·i·den·tial (rézzi-dénsh'l) *adj.* **1.** Of, pertaining to, or involving residence: *a residential course.* **2.** Having residence; especially, residing in a place for occupational reasons: *a residential social worker.* **3.** Of, suitable for, or limited to private residences.

res·i·den·ti·ar·y (rézzi-dén-shəri || -shi-erri) *adj.* **1.** Having a residence, especially an official one. **2.** Involving or required to live in an official residence.

~*n., pl.* **residentiaries.** **1.** A resident. **2.** A clergyman required to live in an official residence.

re·sid·u·al (ri-zíddew-əl, rə-) *adj.* **1.** Pertaining to or characteristic of a residue. **2.** Remaining as a residue. **3.** Persisting: *residual resentment.*

~*n.* **1.** The quantity left over at the end of a process; a remainder. **2.** *Statistics.* **a.** The difference between a given single value and the mean value of a number of observations. **b.** The difference between an observed value and the theoretical value. **3.** *Usually plural. U.S.* Payment made to a performer on a recorded television programme for repeat showings. —See Synonyms at **remainder.**

re·sid·u·ar·y (ri-zíddew-əri, rə- || -erri) *adj.* **1.** Of, pertaining to, or constituting a residue. **2.** *Law.* Entitled to the residue of an estate.

res·i·due (rézzi-dew || -doō) *n.* **1.** The remainder of something after removal of a part. **2.** Matter remaining after completion of any abstractive chemical or physical process, such as evaporation, combustion, distillation, or filtration; a residuum. **3.** *Law.* The remainder of a testator's estate after all claims, debts, and bequests are satisfied. Also called "residuum". **4.** *Geology.* Rock, soil, or the like produced by weathering of other rocks with associated removal of material. —See Synonyms at **remainder.** [Middle English, from Old French *residu,* from Latin *residuum,* from *residuus,* remaining, from *residēre,* RESIDE.]

re·sid·u·um (ri-zíddew-əm, rə-) *n.* **1.** Something remaining after removal of a part; a residue. **2.** *Law.* Residue. —See Synonyms at **remainder.** [Latin, RESIDUE.]

re-sign (rée-sín) *tr.v.* **-signed, -signing, -signs.** To sign anew.

re·sign (ri-zín, rə-) *v.* **-signed, -signing, -signs.** —*tr.* **1.** To give over or submit (oneself); force (oneself) to acquiesce. **2.** To give up (a job or position). **3.** To relinquish (a privilege, right, or claim). —*intr.* To give up one's job or office, especially by giving formal notice: *resign from the army.* —See Synonyms at **relinquish.** [Middle English *resignen,* from Old French *resigner,* from Latin *resignāre,* to unseal, resign : *re-,* back + *signāre,* to seal, sign, from *signum,* a mark, sign.] —**re·sign·er** *n.*

res·ig·na·tion (rézzig-náysh'n) *n.* **1.** The act of resigning. **2.** An oral or written statement that one is resigning a position or office. **3.** Unresisting acceptance; passive submission. —See Synonyms at **patience.**

re·signed (ri-zínd, rə-) *adj.* Feeling or marked by resignation; acquiescent. —**re·sign·ed·ly** (-zínidli) *adv.*

re·sile (ri-zíl, rə-) *intr.v.* **-siled, -siling, -siles.** **1.** To draw back; recoil. **2.** To spring back; especially, to resume a prior position or form after being stretched or pressed. [Latin *resilīre,* to leap back, recoil : *re-,* back + *salīre,* to leap.]

re·sil·i·ence (ri-zílli-ənss, rə-) *n.* Also **re·sil·ien·cy** (-ən-si). **1.** The ability to recover quickly from illness, change, or misfortune; buoyancy. **2.** The property of a material that enables it to resume its original shape or position after being bent, stretched, or compressed; elasticity. —**re·sil·i·ent** *adj.* —**re·sil·i·ent·ly** *adv.*

res·in (rézzin) *n.* **1.** Any of numerous clear to translucent, yellow or brown, solid or semisolid substances of plant origin, such as copal, rosin, and amber, obtained as exudations and used principally in lacquers, varnishes, synthetic plastics, and pharmaceuticals. **2.** Any of numerous similar polymerised synthetic materials or chemically modified natural resins including thermoplastic materials, such as polyvinyl, polystyrene, and polyethylene, and thermosetting materials, such as polyesters, epoxies, and silicones, that are used with fillers, stabilisers, pigments, and other components to form plastics. ~*tr.v.* **resined, -ining, -ins.** To treat or rub with a resin; apply resin to. [Middle English *resyn,* from Old French *resine,* from Latin *rēsīna,* from Greek *rhētinē*†.] —**res·in·ous** *adj.*

res·in·ate (rézzi-nayt) *tr.v.* **-ated, -ating, -ates.** To impregnate, permeate, or flavour with a resin.

resin canal *n.* A long intercellular channel found in certain conifers, such as pine, which is lined with glandular cells that secrete resin into the cavity. Also called "resin duct".

res·in·if·er·ous (rézzi-níffərəss) *adj.* Yielding resin.

res·in·oid (rézzi-noyd) *adj.* Characteristic of, pertaining to, or containing resin.

~*n.* A resinoid synthetic, especially a thermosetting resin.

re·sist (ri-zíst, rə-) *v.* **-sisted, -sisting, -sists.** —*tr.* **1.** To strive or work against; fight off; oppose actively. **2.** To remain firm against the action or effect of; withstand: *resist rust.* **3.** To keep from giving in to or enjoying; abstain from: *could not resist a cake.* —*intr.* To offer resistance; act in opposition. —See Synonyms at **oppose.** ~*n.* A substance that can cover and protect a surface, as from corrosion. [Middle English *resisten,* from Latin *resistere,* to stand back, resist : *re-,* back, against + *sistere,* to place.] —**re·sist·er** *n.*

re·sis·tance (ri-zístənss, rə-) *n.* **1.** The act or an instance of resisting, or the capacity to resist. **2.** Any force that tends to oppose or retard motion. **3.** The natural ability of the body to ward off disease. **4.** *Symbol* **r, R** *Electricity.* **a.** The opposition to the flow of electric current characteristic of a medium, substance, or circuit element. Also used adjectivally: *resistance loss.* **b.** A resistor. **5.** *Physics.* Any of various physical quantities analogous to electrical resistance, measuring such properties as opposition to sound. **6.** In psychoanalysis, a process in which the ego opposes the conscious recall of unpleasant experiences. **7.** *Often capital* **R.** An underground organisation engaged in a struggle for the national liberation of a country under military occupation. Also used adjectivally: *a resistance movement.*

resistance thermometer *n. Physics.* An accurate type of thermometer in which temperature is measured by determining the electrical resistance of a coil of thin wire, usually platinum.

resistance welding *n.* A method of welding by forcing two pieces of metal together and passing a high electric current across the junction, so as to heat the metals by the contact resistance at the junction.

re·sis·tant (ri-zístənt, rə-) *adj.* **1.** Showing or marked by resistance. **2.** Able to withstand the effects of heat, corrosion, or the like. Often used in combination: *rust-resistant.*

re·sist·i·ble (ri-zístə-b'l, rə-) *adj.* Capable of being resisted. —**re·sist·i·bil·i·ty** (-bílləti) *n.* —**re·sist·i·bly** *adv.*

re·sis·tive (ri-zístiv, rə-) *adj.* Capable of or tending towards resistance; resisting. —**re·sis·tive·ly** *adv.*

re·sis·tiv·i·ty (réeziss-tívviti, ri-zíss-, rə-, rézziss-) *n.* **1.** The capacity for or tendency towards resistance. **2.** *Electricity.* The resistance per unit length of a substance with uniform unit cross-sectional area; the reciprocal of conductivity. Formerly called "specific resistance".

re·sist·less (ri-zíst-ləss, rə-, -liss) *adj. Archaic.* **1.** Incapable of being resisted. **2.** Powerless to resist. —**re·sist·less·ly** *adv.*

re·sis·tor (ri-zístər, rə-) *n.* An electric circuit element used to provide resistance. Also called "resistance".

re·sit (rée-sít) *tr.v.* **-sat, -sitting, -sits.** To take (an examination) again. —**re·sit** (rée-sit) *n.*

res ju·di·ca·ta (ráyss jōōdi-kaátə, ráyz, réez) *n.* Also **res ad·ju·di·ca·ta** (a-jōōdi-). An adjudicated precedent in law that cannot be altered. [Latin, "thing decided".]

Res·nais (re-náy), **Alain** (1922–). French film director. His two most famous films, *Hiroshima, Mon Amour* (1959) and *Last Year in Marienbad* (1961), classed him as a member of the New Wave. Recent films include *Providence* (1977) and *My American Uncle.*

re·sol·u·ble (ri-zóllew-b'l, rə-) *adj.* Capable of being resolved; resolvable. [Late Latin *resolūbilis,* from Latin *resolvere,* RESOLVE.] —**re·sol·u·bil·i·ty** (-bílləti), **re·sol·u·ble·ness** *n.*

res·o·lute (rézzə-lōōt, -lewt) *adj.* **1.** Characterised by firmness or determination. **2.** Pursuing a fixed purpose; unwavering. [Latin *resolūtus,* past participle of *resolvere,* to RESOLVE.] —**res·o·lute·ly** *adv.* —**res·o·lute·ness** *n.*

res·o·lu·tion (rézzə-lōō-sh'n, -léw-) *n. Abbr.* **res.** **1.** The state or quality of being resolute; firm determination. See Synonyms at **courage.** **2.** The act of resolving to do something. **3.** A course of action determined or decided upon. **4.** A formal statement of a decision or expression of opinion put before or adopted by an assembly. **5.** The action or process of separating or reducing something into its constituent parts: *the prismatic resolution of sunlight into its spectral colours.* **6.** *Medicine.* The subsiding or termination of an abnormal condition, as of a fever or inflammation. **7.** The act or process of finding a solution, as of a problem or puzzle. **8.** *Music.* **a.** The progression of a dissonant note or chord to a consonant note or chord. **b.** The note or chord to which such a progression is made. **9.** *Physics.* The efficiency with which an instrument or technique can separate or distinguish the component parts of something; resolving power.

re·sol·u·tive (ri-zóllewtiv, rə-, rézzə-lōōtiv, -lewtiv) *adj.* Having the power to disintegrate or dissolve something.

re·solv·a·ble (ri-zólv-əb'l, rə- || *Southern England also* -zṓlv-) *adj.* Capable of being resolved; solvable. —**re·solv·a·bil·i·ty** (-ə-bílləti), **re·solv·a·ble·ness** *n.*

re·solve (ri-zólv, rə- || *Southern England also* -zṓlv) *v.* **-solved, -solving, -solves.** —*tr.* **1. a.** To make a firm decision about (a matter of controversy, for example); settle: *resolve a question.* **b.** To decide upon (a course of action); determine: *resolved to tell the truth.* **2.** To cause (a person) to reach a decision. **3.** To decide or express by formal vote. **4.** To separate (something) into constituent parts. **5.** To change or convert. Usually used reflexively: *His resentment resolved itself into resignation.* **6.** To find a solution to; solve. **7.** To remove or dispel (doubts or misunderstandings); clear up. **8.** To bring to a conclusion: *resolve a conflict.* **9.** *Medicine.* To reduce (an inflammation). **10.** *Music.* To cause (a note or chord) to progress from dissonance to consonance. **11.** *Chemistry.* To separate (a racemic compound or mixture) into its optically active constituents. **12.** *Optics.* **a.** To render visible and distinguish parts of (an image). **b.** To separate or distinguish (different lines) in a spectrum. **13.** *Mathematics.* To separate (a vector, for example) into coordinate components. **14.** *Obsolete.* To melt or dissolve (something). —*intr.* **1.** To reach a decision. Used with *on* or *upon*: *resolve on a proposal.* **2.** To become separated or reduced to constituents. Used with *into.* **3.** *Music.* To undergo resolution. —See Synonyms at **decide.**

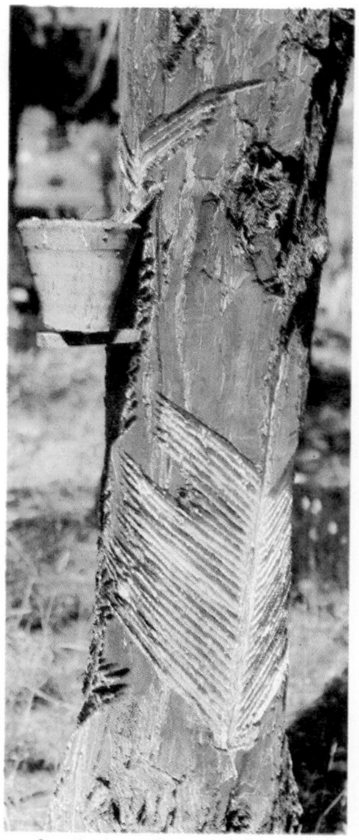

resin *A natural or synthetic substance used chiefly as a binding agent in the manufacture of paints and varnishes. Rosin – a dark, solid substance – is made from the resin of pine trees. The sap of the tree is milked into a container through cuts in the bark (above), then distilled to produce turpentine and rosin. Rosin is used on the bows of stringed musical instruments to increase the friction between the bow and the strings.*

~*n.* **1.** Firmness of purpose; determination. **2.** A decision; a fixed purpose. **3.** *U.S.* A formal resolution made by a deliberative body. [Middle English *resolven,* to analyse, untie, solve, from Latin *resolvere,* to release, unbind, annul, resolve : *re-* (intensive), again + *solvere,* untie, release.] **—re•solv•er** *n.*

re•solved (ri-zólvd, rə- || -zṓlvd) *adj.* Fixed in purpose; firmly determined; resolute. **—re•solv•ed•ly** (-idli) *adv.*

re•sol•vent (ri-zólv-ənt, rə- || -zṓlv-) *adj.* **1.** Causing or capable of causing separation into constituents; solvent. **2.** Causing reduction in inflammation or swelling.

~*n.* A resolvent substance, especially: **1.** A solvent. **2.** A medicine that reduces inflammation or swelling.

re•solv•ing power (ri-zólv-ing, rə- || -zṓlv-) *n. Physics.* A measure of the ability of an instrument to resolve optical images or spectra.

res•o•nance (rézzənənss) *n.* **1.** The quality or condition of being resonant. **2.** *Physics.* **a.** The enhancement of the response of an electrical or mechanical system to a periodic driving force when the driving frequency is equal to the natural undamped frequency of the system. **b.** The condition of a system of subatomic particles in which the probability of a particular reaction, as for example nuclear capture of a neutron, is a maximum; the occurrence of a cross-section maximum. **c.** The event corresponding to such a maximum, especially the particle state so formed, having only a few possible modes of decay and characterised by a lifetime considerably longer than neighbouring states. **3.** The intensification and prolongation of sound, especially of a musical note, produced by sympathetic vibration. **4.** *Medicine.* The sound produced by diagnostic percussion of the chest, abdomen, or other hollow organ. **5.** *Chemistry.* The phenomenon occurring in a chemical compound whereby its molecular structure can be represented by two or more conventional structures, the actual structure being regarded as a hybrid form of the representations. Used adjectivally: *a resonance hybrid.* **6.** *Phonetics.* The intensification of vocal tones during articulation, as by the air cavities of the mouth and nasal passages.

res•o•nant (rézzənənt) *adj.* **1.** Of, pertaining to, or exhibiting resonance. **2.** Having a prolonged, subtle, stimulating effect beyond the initial impact: *resonant Shakespearean verse.* **3.** Producing resonance: *resonant frequency excitation.* [Latin *resonāns* (stem *resonant-*), present participle of *resonāre,* to RESOUND.] **—res•o•nant•ly** *adv.*

resonant circuit *n.* An electrical circuit with inductance and capacitance chosen to produce a specific value of the natural frequency of the circuit. Also called "resonator".

res•o•nate (rézzə-nayt) *intr.v.* **-nated, -nating, -nates. 1.** To exhibit resonance or resonant effects. **2.** To resound. [Latin *resonāre,* to RESOUND.] **—res•o•na•tion** (-náysh'n) *n.*

res•o•na•tor (rézzə-naytər) *n.* **1.** A resonating system. **2.** A hollow chamber or cavity with dimensions chosen to permit internal resonant oscillation of electromagnetic or acoustical waves of specific frequencies. **3.** *Electronics.* **a.** Any of various microwave-generating tubes or devices containing such resonant chambers or cavities. **b.** A resonant circuit.

re•sorb (ree-sórb, ri-, -zórb) *v.* **-sorbed, -sorbing, -sorbs.** *—tr.* **1.** To absorb again. **2.** *Biology.* To dissolve and assimilate (bone tissue, for example). *—intr.* To be resorbed. [Latin *resorbēre* : *re-,* back + *sorbēre,* to suck.] **—re•sorp•tion** (-sórp-sh'n, -zórp-) *n.*

res•or•cin•ol (ri-zór-si-nol, rə- || -nōl) *n.* Also **res•or•cin** (-sin). A white crystalline compound, $C_6H_4(OH)_2$, used to treat certain skin diseases and in dyes, resin adhesives, and pharmaceuticals. [RES(IN) + ORC(HIL) + -IN + -OL.]

re-sort (rée-sórt) *tr.v.* **-sorted, -sorting, -sorts.** To sort again.

re•sort (ri-zórt, rə-) *intr.v.* **-sorted, -sorting, -sorts. 1.** To seek assistance, relief, or an expedient; have recourse. Used with *to*: *The government resorted to censorship of the press.* **2.** To go customarily or frequently; repair. Used with *to.*

~*n.* **1.** A place frequented by people for holidays or recreation: *a winter resort.* **2.** A customary or frequent going or gathering: *a popular place of resort.* **3.** A person or thing turned to for aid or relief: *a last resort.* **4.** The act of turning to a person or thing for aid or relief; recourse. [Middle English *resorten,* return, revert, from Old French *resortir,* to come out again, to resort : *re-,* again + *sortir,* to go out (see **sortie**).]

Usage: *Resort* and *recourse* are used in slightly different constructions in standard English: for example, *He resorted to force, He had recourse to force.* To *have resort to* is often heard, but the usage attracts criticism. Similarly, standard usage requires *as a last resort,* not *as a last recourse.*

re•sound (ri-zównd, rə-) *v.* **-sounded, -sounding, -sounds.** *—intr.* **1.** To be filled with sound; reverberate. **2.** To make a loud, long, or reverberating sound. **3.** To become famous, celebrated, or extolled. *—tr.* **1.** To send back (sound); re-echo. **2.** To extol; celebrate. [Middle English *resounen,* from Old French *resoner,* from Latin *resonāre,* to sound again, echo : *re-,* again + *sonāre,* to sound.]

re•sound•ing (ri-zównding, rə-) *adj.* **1.** Resonating or reverberating; loud: *resounding applause.* **2.** Emphatic; decisive: *a resounding victory.* **—re•sound•ing•ly** *adv.*

re•source (ri-zórss, -sórss, rə- || -zṓrss, -sṓrss, *or with initial stress* rée-sawrss) *n.* **1.** Something that can be used for support or help: *financial and human resources.* **2.** An available supply that can be drawn upon when needed. **3.** The ability to deal effectively with a difficult or troublesome situation; initiative; capability. **4.** Any means of coping with a difficult situation. **5. a.** *Plural.* The total means available to a country for its economic and political development, including such elements as mineral wealth, manpower, and armaments. **b.** *Plural.* The total means available to a company for increasing production or profit, including such elements as plant, labour, and raw materials. **c.** Any such element considered individually. [French *ressource,* from Old French *ressourse,* relief, recovery, from *resourdre,* to rise again, from Latin *resurgere* : *re-,* again + *surgere,* to rise, SURGE.]

re•source•ful (ri-zórss-f'l, rə-, -sórss-, || -sṓrss-, -zṓrss-) *adj.* Readily able to act effectively, especially in a difficult situation or emergency; capable. **—re•source•ful•ly** *adv.* **—re•source•ful•ness** *n.*

resp. 1. respective; respectively. **2.** respiration.

re•spect (ri-spékt, rə-) *tr.v.* **-spected, -specting, -spects. 1.** To feel or show esteem for; honour. **2.** To show consideration for; avoid violation of; treat with deference. **3.** *Archaic.* To relate or refer to.

~*n.* **1.** A feeling of deferential regard; honour; esteem. **2.** The state of being regarded with honour or esteem. **3.** Willingness to show consideration or regard: *Have some respect for her feelings.* **4.** *Plural.* Polite expressions of consideration or deference: *pay one's respects.* **5.** A particular aspect, feature, or detail: *is identical in many respects.* **6.** Relation; reference. Used chiefly in the phrases *in respect of* and *with respect to.* **—pay (one's) last respects.** To show signs of respect to a dead person before or at a funeral. **—with respect.** Used by a speaker to introduce a statement that disagrees with or rejects a remark just made by a previous speaker. [Latin *respectus,* past participle of *respicere,* to regard, look back : *re-,* back + *specere,* to look.] **—re•spect•ful** *adj.* **—re•spect•ful•ly** *adv.* **—re•spect•ful•ness** *n.*

re•spect•a•bil•i•ty (ri-spéktə-bílləti, rə-) *n., pl.* **-ties. 1.** The quality, state, or characteristic of being respectable. **2.** Respectable members of a community.

re•spect•a•ble (ri-spéktəb'l, rə-) *adj.* **1.** Meriting respect or esteem; worthy. **2.** Conforming or tending to conform to conventionally accepted moral standards and behaviour. **3.** Of moderately good quality: *a respectable day's work.* **4.** Considerable in amount, number, or size: *a respectable sum of money.* **5.** Of reasonable social standing; honest and decent. **6.** Having an acceptable appearance; presentable: *a respectable hat.* **—re•spect•a•ble•ness** *n.* **—re•spect•a•bly** *adv.*

re•spec•ter (ri-spéktər, rə-) *n.* One who respects. **—no respecter of persons.** One that does not treat the rich or powerful with undue favour.

re•spect•ing (ri-spékting, rə-) *prep.* In relation to; concerning.

re•spec•tive (ri-spéktiv, rə-) *adj. Abbr.* **resp.** Belonging or pertaining to two or more persons or things regarded individually; particular: *"The two women stood by their respective telephones"* (Doris Lessing). **—re•spec•tive•ness** *n.*

re•spec•tive•ly (ri-spéktivli, rə-) *adv. Abbr.* **resp.** Singly in the order designated or mentioned: *gave Paul and Anne a book and a record respectively.*

re•spell (rée-spél) *tr.v.* **-spelled** or **-spelt** (-spélt), **-spelling, -spells.** To spell again or in a new way, especially by using a phonetic alphabet.

Re•spi•ghi (re-spéegi), **Ottorino** (1879–1936). Italian composer. He wrote prolifically in almost every form, but little of his music is now performed, except for the symphonic poems *The Fountains of Rome* (1917) and *The Pines of Rome* (1924).

res•pi•ra•ble (réspir-əb'l, ri-spī́r-, rə-) *adj.* **1.** Suitable for breathing. **2.** Capable of or adapted for breathing. **—res•pi•ra•bil•i•ty** (-ə-bílləti) *n.*

res•pi•ra•tion (réspə-ráysh'n, réspi-) *n. Abbr.* **resp. 1.** The act or process of inhaling and exhaling; breathing. **2.** The metabolic process by which an organism assimilates oxygen, oxidises organic substances in the cells, with the release of energy, and releases carbon dioxide and other products of oxidation.

res•pi•ra•tor (réspə-raytər, réspi-) *n.* **1.** An apparatus used in administering artificial respiration, such as an **iron lung** *(see).* **2.** A screenlike device worn over the mouth or nose, or both, to protect the respiratory tract.

res•pi•ra•to•ry (ri-spī́r-ə-tri, re-, rə-, réspirə-, -təri, réspi-raytəri) *adj.* Of, pertaining to, affecting, or used in respiration.

respiratory distress syndrome *n.* A condition in newborn, especially premature, infants, in which the lungs are imperfectly expanded, leading to extreme difficulty in breathing. Also called "hyaline membrane disease".

re•spire (ri-spī́r, rə-) *v.* **-spired, -spiring, -spires.** *—intr.* **1.** To breathe in and out; inhale and exhale. **2.** To undergo the metabolic process of respiration. **3.** *Archaic.* To breathe easily again, as after a period of exertion or trouble. *—tr.* To inhale and exhale (air); breathe. [Middle English *respyren,* to breathe again, from Latin *respīrāre* : *re-,* again + *spīrāre,* to breathe.]

res•pite (réss-pit, -pīt || ri-spī́t, rə-) *n.* **1. a.** A temporary cessation or postponement, usually of something disagreeable. **b.** An interval of rest or relief. **2.** The temporary suspension of a death sentence; a reprieve.

~*tr.v.* **respited, -piting, -pites. 1.** To provide with a period of temporary rest or relief. **2. a.** To grant (someone) a reprieve. **b.** To grant a reprieve from (a punishment or sentence). [Middle English *respit,* from Old French, from Latin *respectus,* a looking back, a refuge, from the past participle of *respicere,* to look back : *re-,* back + *specere,* to look.]

re•splen•dent (ri-spléndənt, rə-) *adj.* Splendid or dazzling in appearance; brilliant. [Middle English, from Latin *resplendēns* (stem *resplendent-*), present participle of *resplendēre,* to shine brightly : *re-*

PRONUNCIATION KEY

a, trap; aa, father; ai, fair; ar, star; aw, lawn; ay, play; b, bb, stab; rubber; ch, church; ck, ticket; d, dd, dead; ladder; e, dress; ee, bee; er, defer; ew, few; ewr, pure; ə, about; ər, letter; f, ff, fife; differ; g, gg, giggle; h, hat; i, kit; ī, price; īr, fire; j, judge; k, kick; l, ll, let; 'l, needle; m, mm, man; n, nn, no; 'n, sudden; ng, thing; o, lot; ō, no; o͝o, foot; o͞o, shoe; oor, poor; ow, cow; owr, hour; oy, boy; p, pp, pepper; r, rr, red; s, ss, sauce; sh, ship; t, tt, totter; th, thick; th, this; smooth; u, cut; ur, turn; v, vv, valve; w, wet; y, yes; z, zz, zebra; zh, vision; pleasure

IN FOREIGN WORDS:

aN, oN, Saint-Saëns; hl, Llanelli; Hluhluwe; kh, loch; lough; Khaled

STRESS MARK:

ín-sīt, insight; in-sī́t, incite

(intensive) + *splendēre,* to shine.] **—re·splen·dence, re·splen·den·cy** *n.* **—re·splen·dent·ly** *adv.*

re·spond (ri-spónd, rə-) *v.* **-sponded, -sponding, -sponds.** *—intr.* **1.** To make a reply; answer. **2.** To act in return or in answer. **3.** To react; especially, to react positively or cooperatively: *The patient responded well to the treatment.* *—tr.* To say in reply; answer. —See Synonyms at **answer.**

~n. **1.** *Architecture.* A pilaster supporting an arch. **2.** A chanted or sung response in a liturgy. [Latin *respondēre,* "to promise in return" : *re-,* back, in return + *spondēre,* to promise.] **—re·spon·der** *n.*

re·spon·dent (ri-spóndənt, rə-) *adj.* **1.** Giving or given as a response. **2.** *Law.* Being a defendant.

~n. **1.** A person who responds. **2.** *Law.* A defendant, especially in a divorce suit. **—re·spon·dence, re·spon·den·cy** *n.*

re·sponse (ri-spónss, rə-) *n.* **1.** A reply or answer. **2.** Any act of responding; a reaction: *Public response has been overwhelming.* **3. a.** A reaction, such as that of an organism or mechanism, to a specific stimulus. **b.** A measure of this; for example, the ratio of the output signal of an electronic device to the input signal. **4.** *Abbr.* **R. a.** That which is spoken or sung by a congregation or choir in answer to the officiating minister or priest. **b.** A responsory. **5.** In the game of bridge, a bid made in reply to a partner's bid. [Middle English *respons,* from Old French, from Latin *responsum,* from past participle of *respondēre,* "to promise in return", RESPOND.]

re·spon·si·bil·i·ty (ri-spón-sə-bílləti, rə-) *n., pl.* **-ties. 1.** The state or fact of being responsible. **2.** A thing or person that one is answerable for; a duty, obligation, or burden. **3.** The power or ability to act without superior authority or guidance; the quality of being responsible.

re·spon·si·ble (ri-spón-səb'l, rə-) *adj.* **1. a.** Legally or ethically accountable for the care or welfare of another. **b.** Having control or authority over something; in charge: *She is responsible for sales.* **2.** Involving personal accountability or ability to act without guidance or superior authority. **3.** Being the source, explanation, or cause of something. Used with *for*: *He was responsible for the accident.* **4. a.** Capable of making moral, practical, or rational decisions on one's own, and therefore answerable for one's behaviour. **b.** Able to be trusted or depended upon; reliable. **5.** Based upon or characterised by good judgment or sound thinking. **6.** Having the means to pay debts or fulfil obligations. **7.** Required to render account; answerable. Used with *to*: *The cabinet is responsible to Parliament.* [From obsolete French, correspondent to, from Latin *respondēre,* to RESPOND.] **—re·spon·si·bly** *adv.*

Synonyms: *responsible, answerable, accountable, liable.*

re·spon·sive (ri-spón-siv, rə-) *adj.* **1.** Answering or replying; responding. **2.** Readily reacting, as to suggestions, influences, stimuli, or efforts. **3.** Containing or using responses: *responsive liturgy.* **—re·spon·sive·ly** *adv.* **—re·spon·sive·ness** *n.*

re·spon·so·ry (ri-spón-səri, rə-) *n., pl.* **-ries.** A chant or anthem recited or sung after a reading in a church service. Also called "response". [Middle English, from Late Latin *responsōria,* from Latin *respondēre* (past participle *responsus*), RESPOND.]

re·spon·sum (ri-spón-səm, rə-) *n., pl.* **-sa** (-sə). An answer by a rabbi to a question concerning Jewish law or its observance. [Latin, response.]

re·spray (rée-spráy) *tr.v.* **-sprayed, -spraying, -sprays.** To spray (a car, for example) again, as to renew or change the colour of the paintwork. **—re·spray** (rée-spray) *n.*

res pu·bli·ca (ráyss pŏŏblikə, ráyz) *n.* The state; the republic. [Latin. See **republic.**]

rest¹ (rest) *n.* **1. a.** The act or state of ceasing from work, activity, or motion; quiet. **b.** A period during which someone is not required to work or something is not used: *gave the engine a rest.* **2.** Peace, ease, or refreshment resulting from sleep or the cessation of an activity. **3.** Sleep or quiet relaxation. **4.** The repose of death: *laid to rest.* **5.** Relief or freedom from disquiet or disturbance. **6.** Mental or emotional tranquillity. **7.** Termination or absence of motion. **8.** *Music.* **a.** An interval of silence corresponding to any of the possible time values within the measure. **b.** A mark or symbol indicating such a pause and its length. **9.** In prosody, a short pause in a line of verse; a caesura. **10.** A device used as a support or prop. Often used in combination: *a footrest.* **11.** In billiards, snooker, and similar games, a **bridge** *(see).* **12.** A place for lodging or shelter, especially for sailors or travellers. Often used in the name of a hotel, inn, or the like. **—at rest. 1.** In a state of rest or repose, especially: **a.** Asleep. **b.** Dead. **c.** Motionless. **2.** Free from anxiety or distress.

~v. **rested, resting, rests.** *—intr.* **1.** To refresh oneself by ceasing work or activity or by lying down, sleeping, or relaxing in some other manner. **2.** To cease temporarily from work, motion, or activity. **3.** To sleep. **4. a.** To be at peace or ease; be tranquil. **b.** To have peace in death: *resting in Highgate cemetery.* **5.** To remain in a particular state; receive no further attention: *let the issue rest here.* **6.** To be supported; lie, lean, or sit. Used with *in, on, upon,* or *against.* **7.** To be imposed or vested as a responsibility or burden. Used with *on, upon,* or *with*: *The final decision rests with the chairman.* **8.** To depend or rely. Used with *on, upon,* or *with*: *His argument rests on a false assumption.* **9.** To be located or be in a specified place: *now rests in the British Museum.* **10.** To settle, fall, or be fixed: *his eyes rested on her.* **11.** To remain; linger. Used with *on* or *upon.* **12.** *Law.* To cease voluntarily the presentation of evidence in a case. *—tr.* **1. a.** To give rest or repose to; refresh by rest. **b.** To stop using, cultivating, or working. **2.** To place, lay, or lean for ease, support, or repose. **3.** To base or ground: *rested his conclusion on that fact.* **4.** To fix or direct (the eyes or gaze, for example). **5.** *Law.* To cease voluntarily the introduction of evidence in (a case). [Middle English *reste,* Old English *reste, ræst,* rest, resting place, from Common Germanic *rast-* (unattested).] **—rest·er** *n.*

Synonyms: *rest, relaxation, repose, leisure, ease, comfort.*

rest² *n.* **1.** That part which is left over after something has been removed; the remainder. **2.** *Used with a plural verb.* The ones remaining: *The rest are coming later.* —See Synonyms at **remainder.**

~intr.v. **rested, resting, rests. 1.** To be or continue to be; remain: *rest easy.* **2.** *Obsolete.* To remain or be left over. [Middle English, from Old French *reste,* from *rester,* to remain, from Latin *restāre,* to keep back, stand firm : *re-,* back + *stāre,* to stand.]

rest³ *n.* On medieval armour, a support for the butt of a lance on the side of the breastplate, used when charging. [Middle English *(a)rest,* an arresting, from Old French, from *arester,* to ARREST.]

re·state (rée-stáyt) *tr.v.* **-stated, -stating, -states.** To state again or in a new form. **—re·state·ment** *n.*

res·tau·rant (réstə-RON, rést-, -ront, -rənt) *n.* A place where meals are served, usually for payment, to the public. [French, "restorative", from *restaurer,* to restore, from Old French *restorer,* to RESTORE.]

restaurant car *n. British.* A **dining car** *(see).*

res·tau·ra·teur (réss-tərə-túr, -torrə-, -tawrə- || -tŏŏr) *n.* Also *nonstandard* **res·taur·ant·eur** (-tə-ron-, -tə-RON-). The manager or owner of a restaurant or restaurants. [French, from *restaurer,* to restore. See **restaurant.**]

rest cure *n.* A complete rest from one's usual activities taken as part of a course of treatment, especially treatment for nervous disorders.

rest energy *n. Physics.* The energy equivalent of the rest mass of a body, equal to the rest mass multiplied by the speed of light squared.

rest·ful (rést-f'l) *adj.* **1.** Giving tranquillity. **2.** At rest; quiet. —See Synonyms at **comfortable. —rest·ful·ly** *adv.* **—rest·ful·ness** *n.*

rest·har·row (rést-harrō) *n.* Any of several Old World plants of the genus *Ononis,* having tough, woody stems and roots, and pink, purplish, or yellow pealike flowers. [Middle English *(a)resten,* ARREST + HARROW (because its roots obstruct or "arrest" the harrow).]

rest home *n.* A place for the care of the elderly or frail.

rest·ing (résting) *adj.* **1. a.** In a state of inactivity or rest. **b.** Out of work. Said euphemistically of an actor. **2.** *Biology.* Dormant. Said especially of spores that germinate after a prolonged period.

resting cell *n. Biology.* A cell that is not actively in the process of dividing.

resting place *n.* The grave. Used euphemistically, chiefly in the phrase *last resting place.*

resting potential *n. Physiology.* The difference in charge that exists between the inside and outside of the cell membrane of a nonconducting nerve or muscle cell.

res·ti·tu·tion (résti-téw-sh'n || -tŏŏ-) *n.* **1.** The act of restoring to the rightful owner something that has been taken away, lost, or surrendered. **2.** The act of making good or compensating for loss, damage, or injury; indemnification; reparation. **3.** A return to or restoration of a previous state or position; for example, the return of a system to its original state after deformation. —See Synonyms at **reparation.**

res·tive (réstiv) *adj.* **1.** Impatient or nervous under restriction, delay, or pressure; uneasy; restless. **2.** Difficult to control; refractory; unruly. [Middle English *restyffe,* unwilling to move, stationary, from Old French *restif,* from Vulgar Latin *restīvus* (unattested), remaining stationary, from Latin *restāre,* to keep back : *re-,* back + *stāre,* to stand.] **—res·tive·ly** *adv.* **—res·tive·ness** *n.*

rest·less (rést-ləss, -liss) *adj.* **1.** Without quiet, repose, or rest: *a restless night.* **2.** Unable or unwilling to rest or relax: *a restless child.* **3.** Never still or motionless: *the restless sea.* **4.** Agitated or uneasy. **—rest·less·ly** *adv.* **—rest·less·ness** *n.*

rest mass *n.* The physical mass of a body that is at rest relative to the observer.

re·stock (rée-stók) *tr.v.* **-stocked, -stocking, -stocks.** To stock again; furnish new stock for.

res·to·ra·tion (réss-tə-ráysh'n, -taw-) *n.* **1.** The act of restoring or reinstating someone or something, or the state of being restored: *the restoration of the death penalty.* **2.** The repairing and refurbishing of furniture, buildings, or works of art to return them to something close to their original condition. **3.** That which has been restored, such as a renovated building. **—the Restoration. 1.** The return of Charles II to the British throne in 1660. **2. a.** The period between the return of Charles II and the Revolution of 1688. **b.** Loosely, the period from 1660 until the end of the 17th century. Also used adjectivally: *Restoration prose.*

Restoration comedy *n.* A genre of dramatic comedy characterised by social satire and wit that flourished especially during the period of the Restoration in England, from about 1660 until the end of the 17th century.

re·stor·a·tive (ri-stórrə-tiv, rə-, re-, -stáwrə- || -stṓrə-) *adj.* Tending to renew or restore something, such as health or strength.

~n. Something that restores or revives, such as a drug.

re·store (ri-stór, rə- || -stṓr) *tr.v.* **-stored, -storing, -stores. 1.** To bring back into existence or use; re-establish: *restore law and order.* **2.** To bring back to a previous, normal, or original condition, as by repair, cleaning, or reconstruction: *restore a work of art.* **3.** To put (a person) back in a prior position: *restore the emperor to the throne.* **4.** To give or bring back; make restitution of: *restore the stolen*

PRONUNCIATION KEY

a, trap; aa, father; ai, fair;
ar, star; aw, lawn; ay, play;
b, bb, stab; rubber;
ch, church; ck, ticket;
d, dd, dead; ladder; e, dress;
ee, bee; er, defer; ew, few;
ewr, pure; ə, about;
ər, letter; f, ff, fife; differ;
g, gg, giggle; h, hat; i, kit;
ī, price; īr, fire; j, judge;
k, kick; l, ll, let; 'l, needle;
m, mm, man; n, nn, no;
'n, sudden; ng, thing; o, lot;
ō, no; ŏŏ, foot; ōō, shoe;
oor, poor; ow, cow;
owr, hour; oy, boy;
p, pp, pepper; r, rr, red;
s, ss, sauce; sh, ship;
t, tt, totter; th, thick; th, this;
smooth; u, cut; ur, turn;
v, vv, valve; w, wet; y, yes;
z, zz, zebra; zh, vision;
pleasure

IN FOREIGN WORDS:

aN, oN, Saint-Saëns;
hl, Llanelli; Hluhluwe;
kh, loch; lough; Khaled

STRESS MARK:

ín-sīt, insight; in-sít, incite

funds. [Middle English *restoren,* from Old French *restorer,* from Latin *restaurāre* : *re-,* back + *instaurāre,* to renew.] **—re·stor·er** *n.*

re·strain (ri-stráyn, rə-) *tr.v.* **-strained, -straining, -strains. 1. a.** To control; check; repress. **b.** To hold (a person) back; prevent. Used with *from: restrained them from going.* **2.** To deprive of freedom or liberty. **3.** To limit or restrict. [Middle English *restreynen,* from Old French *restraindre* (present stem *restrain-*), from Latin *restringere,* to RESTRICT.] **—re·strain·a·ble** *adj.*

Synonyms: *restrain, restrict, curb, check, inhibit.*

re·strained (ri-stráynd, rə-) *adj.* Showing or exercising restraint or self-restraint. **—re·strain·ed·ly** (-stráynidli) *adv.*

re·strain·er (ri-stráynər, rə-) *n.* A substance, often potassium bromide, added to photographic developer to reduce the fog on the film.

re·straint (ri-stráynt, rə-) *n.* **1.** The act of holding back or restraining. **2.** Loss or abridgment of freedom. **3.** Any influence that inhibits or restrains; a limitation. **4.** An instrument or means of controlling or restraining. **5. a.** Control or repression of feelings. **b.** Avoidance of excess or outlandishness. [Middle English *restreinte,* from Old French *restrainte,* from the past participle of *restraindre,* RESTRAIN.]

restraint of trade *n.* Any action or condition that tends to prevent free competition in business, such as the creation of a monopoly or the limiting of a market.

re·strict (ri-stríkt, rə-) *tr.v.* **-stricted, -stricting, -stricts.** To hold down or keep within limits. See Synonyms at **limit, restrain.** [Latin *restringere* (past participle *restrictus*), to bind back tight : *re-,* back + *stringere,* to bind.]

re·strict·ed (ri-stríktid, rə-) *adj.* **1.** Subject to limits or restrictions. **2.** Not for general circulation. Said of documents. **3.** *British.* Designating a zone or area in which speed limits or parking restrictions for vehicles apply. **4.** *Chiefly U.S.* Excluding or unavailable to certain groups. **—re·strict·ed·ly** *adv.*

re·stric·tion (ri-strík sh'n, rə-) *n.* **1.** The act of limiting or restricting. **2.** The state of being limited or restricted. **3.** Something that restricts; a limiting or restraining factor, condition, or regulation.

re·stric·tive (ri-stríktiv, rə-) *adj.* **1.** Tending or serving to restrict. **2.** *Grammar.* Designating a subordinate clause, phrase, or term considered to limit the application or reference of the word or word group that it modifies, thus being essential to the meaning of the sentence and usually not marked off by commas. In the sentence *People who read a great deal have large vocabularies,* the restrictive clause is *who read a great deal.* Compare **nonrestrictive. —re·stric·tive·ly** *adv.*

restrictive practice *n. British.* **1.** An agreement between buyers and sellers that interferes with or prevents free competition and is viewed as being against the public interest, for example fixing the prices, quantities, or quality of goods traded. Also called "restrictive trade practice". **2.** An agreement or activity by a trade union or its members that affects another union, other employees, or employers, as in reserving certain jobs for particular unions.

rest room *n. Chiefly U.S.* A public lavatory.

re·sult (ri-zúlt, rə-) *intr.v.* **-sulted, -sulting, -sults. 1.** To occur or exist as a consequence. Often used with *from.* **2.** To end in a particular way. Used with *in.* **3.** *Law.* To revert to a former owner owing to having been partially or ineffectually disposed of. Used of property. —See Synonyms at **follow.**

~n. **1.** The consequence of a particular action, operation, or course; an outcome. **2.** A particular consequence. **3.** *Often plural.* A positive or useful effect: *He may be stern but he certainly gets results.* **4.** *Often plural.* An answer or finding arrived at through research or calculation: *published the results of the survey.* **5.** *Often plural.* The final score, mark, or outcome of any encounter or endeavour involving competition: *football results; the election result.* **6.** *British Informal.* A win, especially in a team sport: *England need a result to square the cricket series.* —See Synonyms at **effect.** [Middle English *resulten,* from Medieval Latin *resultāre,* from Latin, to leap back, rebound : *re-,* back + *saltāre,* to leap, frequentative of *salīre,* to leap.]

re·sul·tant (ri-zúltənt, rə-) *adj.* Issuing or following as a consequence or result.

~n. **1.** That which results; an outcome. **2.** *Mathematics & Physics.* A vector or vector quantity that results from the addition or two or more vectors, for example, a net force resulting from the simultaneous application of other component forces. Also used adjectivally: *resultant force; resultant velocity.*

re·sume (ri-zéwm, rə-, -zóōm || -zhóōm) *v.* **-sumed, -suming, -sumes.** *—tr.* **1.** To continue after interruption or adjournment. **2.** To occupy or take again: *resume your seats.* **3.** To take on or take back again: *resume a gift.* *—intr.* To continue after interruption or adjournment. [Middle English *resumen,* from Old French *resumer,* from Latin *resūmere,* to take up again : *re-,* again + *sūmere,* to take up.] **—re·sum·a·ble** *adj.* **—re·sum·er** *n.*

rés·u·mé (réz-yoo-may, ráyz-, -oo- || -ə-, -máy) *n.* **1.** A summing up; a summary. **2.** *U.S.* A curriculum vitae. [French, from the past participle of *résumer,* to RESUME.]

re·sump·tion (ri-zúmpsh'n, rə-) *n.* The act or an instance of resuming. [Middle English, from Old French, from Late Latin *resūmptiō* (stem *resūmptiōn-*), from Latin *resūmere,* RESUME.]

re·su·pi·nate (ri-séw-pi-nət, rə-, -sóō-, -nit, -nayt) *adj. Biology.* Inverted or seemingly turned upside-down. [Latin *resupīnatus,* bent back, past participle of *resupīnāre,* to bend back : *re-,* back + *supīnus,* SUPINE.] **—re·su·pi·na·tion** (-náysh'n) *n.*

re·su·pine (ri-séw-pīn, -sóō- || rée-sə-, réssə-, -pín) *adj.* Lying on the back; supine. [Latin *resupīnus,* from *resupīnāre.* See **resupinate.**]

re·surge (ri-súrj, rə-) *intr.v.* **-surged, -surging, -surges. 1.** To rise again; re-emerge to prominence or vitality. **2.** To sweep or surge back again. [Latin *resurgere* : *re-,* again + *surgere,* SURGE.]

re·sur·gent (ri-súrjənt, rə-) *adj.* Rising or tending to rise or emerge again; resurging. **—re·sur·gence** *n.*

res·ur·rect (rézzə-rékt) *v.* **-rected, -recting, -rects.** *—tr.* **1.** To bring back to life; raise from the dead. **2.** To bring back into practice, notice, or use. *—intr.* To rise from the dead; return to life. [Back-formation from RESURRECTION.]

res·ur·rec·tion (rézzə-réksh'n) *n.* **1.** A rising from the dead or returning to life. **2.** The state of those who have returned to life. **3.** A returning or bringing back to practice, notice, or use; a revival. **—the Resurrection. 1.** The rising again of Christ on the third day after the Crucifixion. **2.** The rising again of the dead at the Last Judgment. [Middle English *resurreccion,* from Old French *resurrection,* from Late Latin *resurrēctiō* (stem *resurrēctiōn-*), from Latin *resurgere* (past participle *resurrēctus*), to RESURGE.] **—res·ur·rec·tion·al** *adj.*

res·ur·rec·tion·ist (rézzə-réksh'n-ist) *n.* Formerly, one who stole bodies from the grave in order to sell them for dissection.

resurrection plant *n.* Any of several plants that appear dead during dry periods and expand and continue to grow under moist conditions; especially, the **rose of Jericho** *(see).*

re·sus·ci·tate (ri-sússi-tayt, rə-) *v.* **-tated, -tating, -tates.** *—tr.* To restore consciousness, vigour, or life to. *—intr.* To return to life or consciousness; revive. [Latin *resuscitāre,* to revive : *re-,* again + *suscitāre,* to raise, stir up : *sub-,* below, up from below + *citāre,* to set moving, from *citus,* quick, past participle of *ciēre, cīre,* to stir.] **—re·sus·ci·ta·ble** (-təb'l) *adj.* **—re·sus·ci·ta·tion** (-táysh'n) *n.* **—re·sus·ci·ta·tive** (-tətiv, -taytiv) *adj.* **—re·sus·ci·ta·tor** (-taytər) *n.*

ret (ret) *tr.v.* **retted, retting, rets.** To moisten or soak (flax or hemp, for example) to soften and separate the fibres by partial rotting. [Middle English *reten,* perhaps from Old Norse *reyta* (unattested), from Germanic *rutjan* (unattested), to ROT.]

ret. 1. retain. **2.** retired. **3.** return; returned.

re·ta·ble (ri-táyb'l || rée-tayb'l, réttəb'l) *n.* A structure forming the back of an altar, especially: **1.** An overhanging shelf for lights and ornaments. **2.** A frame enclosing carved or painted panels. [French, from Spanish *retablo,* from Medieval Latin *retabulum* (unattested), shortening of *retrōtabulum,* structure at the back of an altar : *retrō-,* back + *tabulum,* table, from Latin *tabula,* board, tablet (see **table**).]

re·tail (rée-tayl, *rarely* ree-táyl) *n.* The sale of commodities in small quantities direct to the consumer.

~adj. Of, pertaining to, or engaged in the sale of goods in this way.

~adv. At retail; from a retailer.

~v. (ree-táyl, ri-, rée-tayl) **retailed, -tailing, -tails.** *—tr.* **1.** To sell in small quantities. **2.** To tell and retell (a story, especially gossip or scandal) in detail. *—intr.* To be sold at retail: *retails at about five pounds.* [Middle English *retaile,* "division", from Old French *retaille,* from *retailler,* to cut up : *re-* (intensive) + *tailler,* to cut (see **tailor**).] **—re·tail·er** (*usually* rée-taylər) *n.*

retail price index *n.* In Britain, an official monthly price index showing the changes in the retail prices of those goods and services typically bought by the average consumer.

re·tain (ri-táyn, rə-) *tr.v.* **-tained, -taining, -tains. 1. a.** To keep or hold in one's possession. **b.** To continue to have: *he retained their support.* **2.** To continue to adopt (a practice or name, for example); maintain: *The American edition retains the British spelling.* **3.** To keep or hold in a particular place, condition, or position. **4.** To keep in mind; remember. **5.** To hire (a barrister) by the payment of a preliminary fee. **6.** To keep in one's service or pay. —See Synonyms at **keep.** [Middle English *reteinen,* from Old French *retenir,* from Latin *retinēre* : *re-,* back + *tenēre,* to hold.] **—re·tain·a·ble** *adj.* **—re·tain·ment** *n.*

re·tained object (ri-táynd, rə-) *n.* An object in a passive construction that is identical to the object in the corresponding active construction, such as *story* in *Susan was told the story by John.*

re·tain·er[1] (ri-táynər, rə-) *n.* **1.** A person or thing that keeps or retains. **2. a.** One who served in a noble household, as in the feudal period, but who ranked higher than a servant; an attendant. **b.** A domestic servant, especially one who has been with the same family for a long period of time. **3.** Any device, frame, or groove that restrains or guides something.

retainer[2] *n.* **1.** The act of retaining a barrister or other adviser, or the fact of being so retained. **2. a.** A preliminary fee paid to engage the services of a barrister, consultant, or other professional. **b.** A regular fee paid to an outside consultant so that one may call upon his services when required. **3.** A fee paid to reserve rented accommodation or retain it during one's absence.

re·take (rée-táyk, ree-) *tr.v.* **-took** (-tóōk || -tóōk), **-taken** (-táykən), **-taking, -takes. 1.** To take back or again. **2.** To photograph or film again.

~n. (rée-tayk). **1.** A taking again. **2.** A scene or shot that has been or is to be filmed or photographed again. **—re·tak·er** *n.*

re·tal·i·ate (ri-tál-i-ayt, rə-) *v.* **-ated, -ating, -ates.** *—intr.* **1.** To return like for like; especially, to return evil for evil. **2.** To respond to aggression with another attack. *—tr.* To pay back (an injury) in kind. [Latin *retaliāre,* repay in kind : *re-,* back + *tāliō,* punishment in kind.] **—re·tal·i·a·tion** (-áysh'n) *n.* **—re·tal·i·a·to·ry** (-ə-təri, -tri) *adj.*

re·tard (ri-tárd, rə-) v. **-tarded, -tarding, -tards.** —tr. To impede or delay; cause to proceed slowly. —intr. To become delayed. —See Synonyms at **delay, hinder.**

~n. Rare. Retardation. [Middle English retarden, from Old French retarder, from Latin retardāre : re-, back, back in place + tardāre, to delay, from tardus, slow (see **tardy**.)] —**re·tard·er** n.

re·tar·dant (ri-tárdənt, rə-) n. Something that retards; specifically, a substance that slows down chemical reaction.

~adj. Causing retardation.

re·tar·date (ri-tárd-ayt, rə-, -ət, -it) n. A mentally retarded person.

re·tar·da·tion (réetaar-dáysh'n) n. Also **re·tard·ment** (re-tárdmənt). 1. The act of retarding. 2. The condition of being retarded. 3. The extent to which, or amount by which, something is retarded. 4. Psychology. **Mental deficiency** (see).

re·tard·ed (ri-tárdid, rə-) adj. Relatively slow or backward in mental or emotional development or in academic achievement.

retch (rech, reech) intr.v. **retched, retching, retches.** To try to vomit or make the motion of vomiting.

~n. The act or sound of this, usually involuntary. [Ultimately from Old English hrǣcan, to cough up phlegm, from Germanic (imitative).]

retd retired.

re·te (réeti) n., pl. **retia** (rée-ti-ə, -shə). An anatomical mesh or network, as of veins or nerves. [New Latin, from Latin rēte, a net.]

re·tell (rée-tél) tr.v. **-told** (-tóld), **-telling, -tells.** To relate or tell again.

re·ten·tion (ri-ténsh'n, rə-) n. 1. The act of retaining. 2. The condition of being retained. 3. The capacity to remember; memory; remembrance. 4. The ability to retain. 5. Pathology. Involuntary withholding of normally eliminated bodily wastes or secretions. [Middle English retencion, from Old French, from Latin retentiō (stem retentiōn-), from retinēre, **RETAIN**.]

re·ten·tion·ist (ri-ténsh'n-ist, rə-) n. One who favours the retention of something; especially, one who favours the retention of capital punishment.

re·ten·tive (ri-téntiv, rə-) adj. Having the ability, tendency, or capacity to retain: a retentive memory. —**re·ten·tive·ness, re·ten·tiv·i·ty** (-tívvəti) n.

re·think (rée-thíngk) v. **-thought** (-tháwt), **-thinking, -thinks.** —tr. To consider or think through again, especially in order to resolve difficulties or with a view to changing one's opinion. —intr. To rethink something; think again.

~n. (rée-thingk). An act of rethinking.

re·ti·ar·y (rée-ti-əri, -shi- ‖ U.S. -erri) adj. Of, resembling, or forming a net or web. [From Latin rēte, net.]

ret·i·cent (rétti-sənt) adj. 1. Characteristically silent or taciturn in temperament; reserved in speech. 2. Unwilling to make disclosures or give information. 3. Restrained or reserved in style. [Latin reticēns (stem reticent-), present participle of reticēre, to keep silent : re- (intensive), again + tacēre, to be silent.] —**ret·i·cence** n. —**ret·i·cent·ly** adv.

ret·i·cle (réttik'l) n. A **graticule** (see). [Latin rēticulum, diminutive of rēte, net.]

re·tic·u·lar (ri-tíckewlər, re-, rə-) adj. 1. Netlike. 2. Intricate; entangled. [New Latin reticularis, from Latin rēticulum, **RETICLE**.]

re·tic·u·late (ri-tíckewlət, re-, rə-, -lit, -layt) adj. Resembling or forming a network: reticulate veins of a leaf.

~v. (-layt) **reticulated, -lating, -lates.** —tr. 1. To make a net or network of. 2. To mark with lines resembling a network. —intr. To form a net or network. [Latin rēticulātus, from rēticulum, **RETICLE**.]

re·tic·u·la·tion (ri-tíckewláysh'n, re-, rə-) n. A network.

ret·i·cule (rétti-kewl) n. 1. A woman's handbag of a former type, often in the form of a pouch with a drawstring and originally made of a netted fabric. 2. A **graticule** (see). [French réticule, from Latin rēticulum, **RETICLE**.]

re·tic·u·lo·cyte (ri-tíckew-lō-sīt, re-, rə-) n. An immature red blood cell containing a network of filaments. [**RETICUL(UM)** + **-CYTE**.]

re·tic·u·lo·en·do·the·li·al system (ri-tíckew-lō-èndō-théeli-əl, re-, rə-) n. The widely diffused bodily system comprising all phagocytic cells except the leucocytes. [From **RETICUL(UM)** + **ENDOTHELIAL**.]

re·tic·u·lum (ri-tíckew-ləm, re-, rə-) n., pl. **-la** (-lə). 1. A netlike formation or structure; a network. 2. Zoology. The second compartment of the stomach of ruminant mammals, lined with a membrane having honeycombed ridges. [Latin rēticulum, **RETICLE**.]

Re·tic·u·lum (ri-tíck-yōōləm, re-, ri-) n. A constellation in the Southern Hemisphere near Dorado and Horologium. [Latin rēticulum, **RETICLE**.]

Re·tief (rə-téef), **Piet(er)** (1780–1838). One of the leaders of the Great Trek, he was murdered by the Zulu chief Dingane.

re·ti·form (rée-ti-fawrm, rétti-) adj. Arranged like a net; reticulate. [Latin rēte, net + **-FORM**.]

ret·i·na (réttinə ‖ U.S. also rétnə) n., pl. **-nas** or **-nae** (rétti-nee ‖ U.S. also rétnee). A delicate, multilayer, light-sensitive membrane lining the inner eyeball and connected by the optic nerve to the brain. [Middle English rethina, from Medieval Latin retina, from Latin rēte, net.] —**ret·i·nal** adj.

ret·i·nal (réttin'l) n. A crystalline retinal pigment, $C_{19}H_{27}CHO$, a component of **rhodopsin** (see). Also called "retinene". [Greek rhētīnē, resin + **-AL**.]

ret·i·ni·tis (rétti-nītiss) n. Pathology. Inflammation of the retina. [**RETIN(O)-** + **-ITIS**.]

retino-, retin- comb. form. Indicates the retina; for example, **retinitis**.

re·ti·nol (rétti-nol ‖ -nōl) n. 1. **Rosin oil** (see). 2. A derivative of **vitamin A** (see). [Greek rhētīnē, resin + **-OL**.]

ret·i·no·scope (rétti-nə-skōp, -nō) n. An optical instrument for examining refraction of light in the eye. Also called "skiascope". [**RETINO-** + **-SCOPE**.]

ret·i·nos·co·py (rétti-nóskəpi) n. Medical examination and analysis of the refractive properties of the eye. Also called "skiascopy". [**RETINO-** + **-SCOPY**.] —**ret·i·no·scop·ic** (-nə-skóppik, -nō-) adj.

ret·i·nue (rétti-new ‖ -nōō) n. The attendants, aides, or retainers accompanying a person of importance or rank. [Middle English retenue, from Old French, from the feminine past participle of retenir, to **RETAIN**.]

re·ti·ral (ri-tír-əl, rə-) n. Chiefly Scottish. Retirement from work or office.

re·tire (ri-tír, rə-) v. **-tired, -tiring, -tires.** —intr. 1. To go away; depart, as for rest, seclusion, or shelter. 2. To go to bed. 3. To give up one's occupation, office, or the like, so as to live at leisure on one's income, savings, or pension. 4. To fall back; retreat. 5. To withdraw from a competition or contest, as through injury. 6. In cricket, to voluntarily suspend or terminate one's innings, as through injury. —tr. 1. To remove from office or active service. 2. To lead back or away (troops, for example) from action; withdraw. 3. To take out of circulation: retire bonds. 4. In baseball, to put out (a batter or side); dismiss. [French retirer : re-, back + tirer, to draw (see **tier**.)]

re·tired (ri-tírd, rə-) adj. Abbr. **ret., retd** 1. Withdrawn; secluded. 2. Having given up business or office, usually because of age.

re·tire·ment (ri-tír-mənt, rə-) n. 1. The act of retiring. 2. The condition of being retired, as from one's former occupation or office. 3. Seclusion or privacy. 4. A retreat; a place of seclusion. —See Synonyms at **solitude.**

retirement age n. The age at which workers generally retire; especially, the age at which a retirement pension is payable.

retirement pension n. British. The pension paid by the government to a retired man over 65 or a woman over 60. Formerly called "old age pension".

re·tir·ing (ri-tír-ing, rə-) adj. 1. Shy and modest; reticent. See Synonyms at **humble, shy.** 2. At which one retires: retiring age. —**re·tir·ing·ly** adv.

retiring collection n. A collection taken as people leave after a church service, performance, or other gathering.

re·tool (rée-tōōl) tr.v. **-tooled, -tooling, -tools.** To fit out anew with tools; especially, to re-equip (a factory or workshop).

re·tort¹ (ri-tórt, rə-) v. **-torted, -torting, -torts.** —tr. 1. To return in kind; pay back. 2. a. To reply; especially, to answer in a quick, sharp manner. b. To present a counterargument to. —intr. To make a retort. —See Synonyms at **answer.**

~n. 1. A quick, incisive reply; especially, one that turns the first speaker's words to his own disadvantage. 2. A counterargument. [Latin retorquēre (past participle retortus), to bend back : re-, back + torquēre, to bend, twist.] —**re·tort·er** n.

re·tort² (ri-tórt, rə- ‖ U.S. also rée-tawrt) n. A closed laboratory vessel with an outlet tube, used for distillation, sublimation, or decomposition by heat. [French retorte, from Medieval Latin retorta, feminine of Latin retortus, "bent back" (the neck of the vessel is bent over), from retorquēre, to bend back, **RETORT**.]

retort² Antoine Lavoisier, the 18th-century French chemist, used this retort in a famous experiment which demonstrated the presence of oxygen in the air. Any vessel used for the distillation or separation of substances is called a retort.

re·tor·tion, re·tor·sion (ri-tórsh'n, rə-) n. Retaliation in kind by a state upon the citizens of another state. [**RETORT** + **-ION**, perhaps by analogy with **CONTORTION**.]

re·touch (rée-túch) tr.v. **-touched, -touching, -touches.** 1. To add new details or touches to (make-up or a painting, for example), for correction or improvement. 2. Photography. To improve or change (a negative or print) by adding details or removing flaws.

~n. (rée-tuch). 1. A detail changed or improved in a painting, photograph, or the like. 2. A painting, photograph, or the like, that has been retouched. 3. The act or art of altering or retouching.

re·trace (rée-tráyss, ri-) tr.v. **-traced, -tracing, -traces.** 1. To trace back to the source or origin. 2. To go back over (a route): retrace one's steps. 3. To go back over in one's mind. —**re·trace·a·ble** adj.

re·tract (ri-trákt, rə-) v. **-tracted, -tracting, -tracts.** —tr. 1. To take back or disavow (a statement, accusation, offer, or verbal contract); recant. 2. To draw back or in: The turtle retracted its head. 3. To withdraw or pull back (machinery, especially the undercarriage of an aircraft). 4. Phonetics. a. To utter (a sound) with the tongue drawn back. b. To draw back (the tongue). —intr. 1. To take back or disavow a statement, accusation, or the like. 2. To be withdrawn or pulled back. 3. To shrink or draw back. [Middle English retracten, from Old French retracter, from Latin retractāre, to handle again, frequentative of retrahere (past participle retractus), to draw back : re-, back, again + trahere, to draw.] —**re·tract·a·bil·i·ty** (-ə-bílləti) n. —**re·tract·a·ble, re·tract·i·ble** adj. —**re·trac·ta·tion** (rée-trak-táysh'n) n. —**re·trac·tive** adj.

re·trac·tile (ri-trák-tīl, rə- ‖ U.S. also -t'l) adj. Capable of being drawn back or in: Cats have retractile claws. —**re·trac·til·i·ty** (rée-trak-tílləti) n.

re·trac·tion (ri-tráksh'n, rə-) n. 1. The act of recanting or disavowing a statement, accusation, or the like. 2. The act or power of drawing back or of being drawn back.

re·trac·tor (ri-tráktər, rə-) n. 1. One that retracts. 2. Anatomy. A muscle, such as a flexor, that retracts an organ or part. 3. Medicine.

An instrument that holds back the edges of a wound or surgical incision.

re·tral (reétrəl, réttrəl) *adj.* **1.** *Biology.* At, close to, or towards the back. **2.** Backward; reverse. [Latin *retrō,* backward, behind.] **—re·tral·ly** *adv.*

re-tread (reé-tréd) *tr.v.* **-trod** (-tród), **-trodden** (-tródd'n), **-treading, -treads.** To tread (one's steps or route, for example) again.

re·tread (reé-tréd) *tr.v.* **-treaded, -treading, -treads.** To fit (a rubber tyre) with a new tread.
~*n.* (reé-tred). A retreaded tyre.

re·treat (ri-treét, rə-) *n.* **1.** The act of retiring or withdrawing. **2.** A quiet, private, or secure place; a refuge. **3.** A period of seclusion, retirement, or solitude. **4. a.** The withdrawal of a military force from a dangerous position or from an enemy attack. **b.** The signal for such a withdrawal, made on a drum or trumpet. **5.** *Military.* A bugle call signalling the lowering of the flag at sunset. **6. a.** A period spent in spiritual renewal, as through prayer, contemplation, or spiritual reading. **b.** A place, such as a monastery, where such a period can be spent. **7.** An institution, often private, for the treatment of alcoholics, the mentally ill, or others in need of care. —See Synonyms at **shelter. —beat a retreat. 1.** *Military.* To give a signal for withdrawal of forces. **2.** To withdraw; flee.
~*v.* **retreated, -treating, -treats.** —*intr.* **1. a.** To withdraw or retire. **b.** To withdraw from a battle. Used of troops. **2.** To slope backwards; recede. —*tr.* In chess, to move (a piece) back. [Middle English *retret,* from Old French *retrait,* from the past participle of *retraire,* to draw back, from Latin *retrahere,* to RETRACT.]

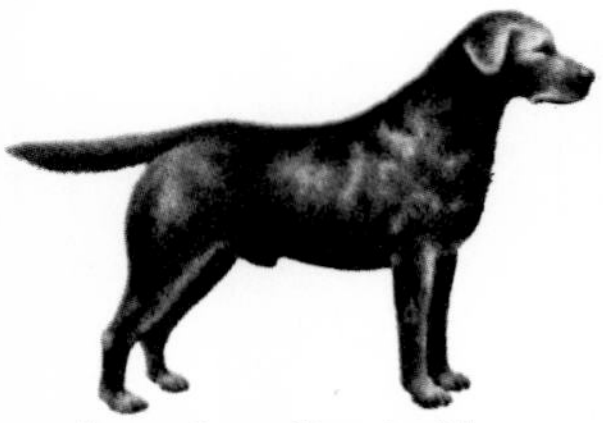

retriever *Several breeds of dogs have been trained as retrievers and used to pick up shot game. This is a black labrador, a North American breed which was introduced to Europe by fishermen in the early 19th century.*

re·trench (ri-trénch, rə-) *v.* **-trenched, -trenching, -trenches.** —*tr.* **1.** To cut down or curtail (expenditure or costs). **2. a.** To delete (parts of a literary work). **b.** To shorten or abridge (a literary work). **3.** To deduct or remove. **4.** *Military.* To provide with a retrenchment. —*intr.* To curtail expenses; economise. [From obsolete French *retrencher,* from Old French *retrenchier* : *re-* (intensive), again + *trenchier,* to cut off (see **trench**).]

re·trench·ment (ri-trénchmənt, rə-) *n.* **1.** The act or result of retrenching; especially, the cutting down of expenditure. **2.** *Military.* An inner line of defence, usually consisting of a trench and parapet.

re·tri·al (reé-trī-əl) *n.* A second trial, as of a legal case.

ret·ri·bu·tion (réttri-béwsh'n) *n.* **1.** Something given or demanded in repayment; especially, punishment or vengeance for a wrong or injury. **2.** *Theology.* Punishment or reward distributed in a future life according to performance in this one. [Middle English *retribucion,* from Old French *retribution,* from Late Latin *retribūtiō* (stem *retribūtiōn-*), from Latin *retribuere,* to pay back : *re-,* back + *tribuere,* to grant, pay (see **tribute**).]

re·trib·u·tive (ri-tríbbew-tiv, rə- || réttri-béw-) *adj.* Also **re·trib·u·to·ry** (-təri, -tri). Of, involving, or characterised by retribution.

re·trib·u·ti·vism (ri-tríbbewti-viz'm, rə-) *n.* The belief that criminals ought to be punished for the sake of vengeance rather than in order to prevent crime or rehabilitate the criminal. **—re·trib·u·ti·vist** *n.*

re·triev·al (ri-treév'l, rə-) *n.* **1.** An act or the process of retrieving. **2.** The possibility of repossession or restoration: *beyond retrieval.*

re·trieve (ri-treév, rə-) *v.* **-trieved, -trieving, -trieves.** —*tr.* **1.** To get back; regain. **2.** To revive; restore. **3. a.** To put right; rectify. **b.** To rescue, as from trouble or danger. **4.** To recall to mind; remember. **5.** To find and carry back; fetch. **6.** To manage to return (a difficult shot), as in tennis. **7.** *Computing.* To obtain (stored data) from a disk, tape, or other storage device. —*intr.* To find and bring back game. Used of a dog. —See Synonyms at **recover.**
~*n.* The act of retrieving. [Middle English *retreven,* to find again, from Old French *retrover* : *re-,* again + *trover,* to find, perhaps from Vulgar Latin *tropāre* (unattested), to write, compose, from Latin *tropus,* trope, a manner of singing, a song, from Greek *tropos,* "a turning".] **—re·triev·a·bil·i·ty** (-ə-bílləti) *n.* **—re·triev·a·ble** *adj.* **—re·triev·a·bly** *adv.*

re·triev·er (ri-treévər, rə-) *n.* **1.** One that retrieves. **2.** A dog of any of several breeds developed and trained to retrieve game; especially, a golden retriever.

ret·ro (réttrō) *n.* A **retrorocket** *(see).*

retro– *prefix.* Indicates: **1.** Backwards or back; for example, **retrorocket. 2.** Situated behind; for example, **retrolental.** [Latin *retrō,* backwards, behind.]

ret·ro·act (réttrō-ákt) *intr.v.* **-acted, -acting, -acts. 1.** To act in opposition or reciprocally. **2.** To be retroactive in application. Used of a law or pay rise, for example.

ret·ro·ac·tion (réttrō-áksh'n) *n.* **1.** A retroactive action. **2.** An opposing or reciprocal action; a reaction.

ret·ro·ac·tive (réttrō-áktiv) *adj.* **1.** Influencing or applying to a period prior to enactment. **2.** Effective from a date in the past: *a retroactive pay increase.* [French *rétroactif,* from Latin *retroactus,* past participle of *retroagere,* to drive back : RETRO- + *agere,* to drive.] **—ret·ro·ac·tive·ly** *adv.* **—ret·ro·ac·tiv·i·ty** (-ak-tívvəti) *n.*

ret·ro·cede (réttrō-seéd, réttra-, reétrə-) *v.* **-ceded, -ceding, -cedes.** —*intr.* To go back; recede. —*tr.* To cede or give back; return. [Latin *retrōcēdere,* to go back : RETRO- + *cēdere,* to go.] **—ret·ro·ces·sion** (-sésh'n) *n.*

ret·ro·choir (réttrō-kwīr, réttra-, reétrə-) *n.* The area behind the high altar in a cathedral or large church. [Medieval Latin *retrochorus* : RETRO- + CHOIR.]

ret·ro·flex (réttrō-fleks, réttra-, reétrə-) *adj.* Also **ret·ro·flexed** (-flekst). **1.** Bent, curved, or turned backwards. **2.** *Phonetics.* Pronounced with the tip of the tongue turned back against the roof of the mouth.
~*n.* A retroflex consonant. [New Latin *retroflexus,* from Late Latin *retrōflectere,* to bend back : RETRO- + Latin *flectere,* to bend, FLEX.] **—ret·ro·flex·ion, ret·ro·flec·tion** (-fléksh'n) *n.*

ret·ro·grade (réttrō-grayd, réttra-, reétrə-) *adj.* **1.** Moving or tending backwards; retiring; retreating. **2.** Inverted or reversed, especially in order. **3. a.** Reverting to an earlier or inferior condition; declining or degenerating. **b.** Reversing or obstructing progress: *a retrograde decision.* **4.** *Astronomy.* **a.** Having or pertaining to orbital motion in an opposite direction to that of the Earth about the Sun. **b.** Having or pertaining to motion about a given planet in an opposite sense to the planet's orbital motion around the Sun. **c.** Having an apparent clockwise rotation, resulting from the fact that the rotational period is greater than the orbital period. Said of a planet such as Venus. **d.** Having or designating an apparent backward motion on the celestial sphere, resulting from the fact that the orbital velocity about the Sun is lower that that of the Earth.
~*intr.v.* **retrograded, -grading, -grades. 1.** To move or seem to move backwards. **2.** To decline; degenerate; deteriorate. [Middle English, from Latin *retrōgradus* : RETRO- + *gradus,* a step, grade.] **—ret·ro·gra·da·tion** (-gray-dáysh'n, -grə-) *n.*

ret·ro·gress (réttrō-gréss, -gress, réttra-, reétrə-) *intr.v.* **-gressed, -gressing, -gresses. 1.** To return to an earlier, inferior, or less complex condition. **2.** To go or move backwards. [Latin *retrōgradī* (past participle *retrōgressus*), to go backwards : RETRO- + *gradī,* to step.] **—re·tro·gres·sive** *adj.* **—re·tro·gres·sive·ly** *adv.*

ret·ro·gres·sion (réttrō-grésh'n, réttra-, reétrə-) *n.* **1.** The act or process of deteriorating or declining. **2.** *Biology.* A return to a less complex or more primitive state or stage.

ret·ro·ject (réttrō-jékt, réttra-, reétrə-) *tr.v.* **-jected, -jecting, -jects.** To throw backwards. Compare **project.** [RETRO- + *-ject,* as in PROJECT (verb).]

ret·ro·len·tal (réttrō-lént'l, réttra-, reétrə-) *adj.* Behind a lens, especially the lens of the eye. [RETRO- + New Latin *lens* (stem *lent-*), LENS + -AL.]

ret·ro·rock·et (réttrō-rockit, réttra-, reétrə-) *n.* A rocket engine used to retard, arrest, or reverse the motion of an aircraft, missile, spacecraft, or other vehicle. Also called "braking rocket", "retro".

re·trorse (ri-trórss, rə-, reé-trawrss) *adj.* Directed or turned backwards or downwards. Said especially of plant parts. [Latin *retrōrsus,* contraction of *retrōversus* : RETRO- + *versus,* "turned", past participle of *vertere,* to turn.] **—re·trorse·ly** *adv.*

ret·ro·spect (réttrō-spekt, réttra-, reétrə-) *n.* A review, survey, or contemplation of things in the past. Used chiefly in the phrase *in retrospect.*
~*v.* (*also* -spékt) **retrospected, -specting, -spects.** *Archaic.* —*intr.* **1.** To contemplate the past. **2.** To refer back. Used with *to.* —*tr.* To look back on or contemplate (things past). [Latin *retrōspectus,* past participle of *retrōspicere,* to look back at : RETRO- + *specere,* to look at.] **—ret·ro·spec·tion** (-spéksh'n) *n.*

ret·ro·spec·tive (réttrō-spéktiv, réttra-, reétrə-) *adj.* **1.** Looking back on, contemplating, or directed towards the past. **2.** Looking or directed backwards. **3.** Applying to or influencing the past; retroactive. **4.** Of, pertaining to, or designating an exhibition showing the entire work of an artist or school over a period of years or a representative selection of an artist's entire work.
~*n.* A retrospective art exhibition. **—ret·ro·spec·tive·ly** *adv.*

re·trous·sé (rə-trōō-say, ri-) *adj.* Turned up at the end. Said of a nose. [French, past participle of *retrousser,* to turn back, from Old French : *re-,* back + *trousser,* to TRUSS.]

ret·ro·ver·sion (réttrō-vérsh'n, -vérzh'n, réttra-, reétrə-) *n.* **1.** A turning or tilting backwards. **2.** The state of being turned or tilted backwards. [Latin *retrōversus,* RETRORSE.]

re·try (reé-trī) *tr.v.* **-tried, -trying, -tries.** To try (a law case) again.

ret·si·na (ret-seénə, rétsinə) *n.* A resinated Greek wine. [Modern Greek, from Italian *resina,* resin, from Latin *rēsīna,* RESIN.]

re·turn (ri-túrn, rə-) *v.* **-turned, -turning, -turns.** —*intr.* **1.** To go or come back, as to an earlier condition or place. **2.** To revert in speech, thought, or practice. **3.** To recur; appear again: *Her cold has returned.* **4.** To answer; retort; respond. —*tr.* **1.** To send, put, give, or carry back: *return surplus supplies to the store.* **2.** To give or send back in reciprocation: *return a compliment.* **3.** To produce or yield (profit or interest) as a result of labour, investment, or expenditure. **4.** To reflect or send back (light or sound). **5. a.** To submit (a writ, report, or statement) to a judge or other person in authority. **b.** To render or deliver (a verdict). **c.** To declare to be as specified: *was returned not guilty.* **6.** To say in reply. **7.** To elect or re-elect, as to a legislative body. **8.** In card games, to respond to (a partner's lead) by leading the same suit. **9.** *Architecture.* To place (a wall moulding or the like) at an angle to or turned away from the previous line of direction. **10.** In racket games and certain other sports, to hit, throw, or play (a ball) back: *struggled to return his opponent's serve.*
~*n. Abbr.* **ret. 1.** The act or state of going, coming, bringing, or sending back. **2. a.** Something that is brought or sent back, such as a defective or unsold article. **b.** Something that goes or comes back. **3.** A recurrence, as of a periodic occasion or event. **4. a.** Something exchanged for that received; a repayment. **b.** The repaying or reciprocating of something received. **5.** A reply; a response; an answer. **6. a.** The profit made on an exchange of goods or other commercial transaction. **b.** *Often plural.* A profit or yield, as from labour or investments. **c.** The profit per unit, as in the manufacturing of a particular product. **7.** A statement, report, or compilation of data, typically one of a formal or official character that is submitted to an

appropriate authority, especially: **a.** A statement of a person's income for tax purposes, or the form on which such a statement is made. **b.** *Usually plural.* A report on the vote in an election. **8.** In card games, a lead that responds to the lead of one's partner. **9.** In racket games and certain other sports: **a.** The act of returning the ball to one's opponent. **b.** The ball so returned. **10.** *Architecture.* **a.** The extension of a moulding, projection, or other part at an angle (usually 90°) to the main part. **b.** A part of a building set at an angle to the façade. **11.** A channel, such as a pipe, carrying something back to its source. **12.** A return ticket. **13.** *Law.* **a.** A report by a sheriff or other officer of the court showing how he has discharged a duty laid upon him. **b.** The bringing or sending back of a writ, subpoena, or other document, with a short written report on it, by a sheriff or other officer, to the court from which it was issued. —**by return of post.** *British.* By the following post. —**many happy returns (of the day).** Used as an expression of greetings or congratulations to a person on his or her birthday.
~*adj.* **1.** Of or for coming back: *the return voyage.* **2.** Given, sent, or done in reciprocation or exchange: *a return visit.* **3.** Played or staged a second time, offering the original loser a chance to win: *a return boxing match.* **4. a.** Reversing or changing direction. **b.** Formed by a reversal or change in direction, 'as a bend in a road. **5.** *Chiefly British.* Of or designating a ticket entitling the holder to travel to a destination and back again, usually within a stated period. [Middle English *reto(u)rnen,* from Old French *retorner,* from Vulgar Latin *retornāre* (unattested), to turn back : Latin *re-,* back + *tornāre,* to turn in a lathe, from *tornus,* lathe, from Greek *tornos.*] —**re·turn·er** *n.*
re·turn·a·ble (ri-túrnəb'l, rə-) *adj.* **1. a.** Capable of being returned or brought back. **b.** Designating a bottle or other container that is returned when empty to the vendor, who refunds a deposit paid at the time of purchase. **2.** Legally required to be returned. ~*n.* A returnable bottle or container.
return crease *n.* In cricket, either of two lines at right angles to the bowling creases, from a line inside of which the bowler must bowl the ball.
re·turn·ing officer (ri-túrning, rə-) *n.* An official who is in charge of an election and announces the number of votes cast for each candidate.
re·tuse (ri-téwss, rə- ‖ -tōoss) *adj.* Having a rounded or blunt apex with a shallow notch. Said chiefly of leaves. [Latin *retūsus,* past participle of *retundere,* to beat back : *re-,* back + *tundere,* to strike, beat.]
Retz. See **Rais, Gilles de.**
Reu·ben¹ (rōo-bin, -bən ‖ réw-) Jacob's eldest son, the ancestor of one of the tribes of Israel. Genesis 29:32. [Hebrew *Re'ū-bēn,* "behold, a son" (from Genesis 29:32) *ra'u,* imperative plural of *ra'ah,* to behold, see + *ben,* son.]
Reuben² *n.* The tribe of Israel descended from Reuben.
re·u·ni·fy (ree-yōoni-fī, rée-) *tr.v.* **-fied, -fying, -fies.** To make whole again; restore (especially a divided country) to a united state. —**re·u·ni·fi·ca·tion** (rée-yōoni-fi-káysh'n, ree-yōoni-) *n.*
re·un·ion (rée-yōon-yən, ree-, ri-, -yōon-) *n.* **1.** The act of reuniting. **2.** The state of being reunited. **3.** A gathering of the members of a group, such as a family, who have been separated.
Ré·u·nion (ráy-ōon-yón; *French* -ün-). One of the Mascarene Islands, east of Madagascar in the Indian Ocean. It is an overseas département of France. It consists mainly of one active and several extinct volcanoes, with settlement and cultivation in the coastal lowlands. Sugar, molasses, and rum are the main exports. St. Denis is the capital and chief port. See map at **Indian Ocean.**
re·u·nite (rée-yōo-nīt, -yōo-) *v.* **-nited, -niting, -nites.** —*tr.* To bring together again. —*intr.* To come together again. [Medieval Latin *reūnīre* : *re-,* again + *ūnīre,* to UNITE.]
Reu·ter (róytər), **Paul Julius, Baron von,** born Israel Beer Josaphat (1816–99). German industrialist, the founder of Reuter's Telegraph Company. In 1849 he began his own small pigeon post service in Germany. Two years later he settled in London and opened a news office. By 1858 he had succeeded in having his foreign telegrams published by the English press. He eventually built up worldwide cable connections.
rev (rev) *n. Informal.* **1.** A revolution, as of an engine. **2.** A revolution per minute. ~*v.* **revved, revving, revs.** *Informal.* —*tr.* To increase the speed of (an engine). Often used with *up.* —*intr.* To operate at an increased speed. Often used with *up.*
rev. **1.** revenue. **2.** reverse; reversed. **3.** review; reviewed. **4.** revise; revision. **5.** revolution. **6.** revolving.
Rev. **1.** Revelation (New Testament). **2.** Reverend (title).
re·val·o·rise, re·val·o·rize (rée-vál-ə-rīz) *tr.v.* **-rised, -rising, -rises.** To establish a new value for (currency, assets, or the like). [Back-formation from *revalorisation,* from French : RE- + VALORISATION.] —**re·val·o·ri·sa·tion** (rée-vál-ə-rī-zaysh'n ‖ U.S. -ri-) *n.*
re·val·ue (rée-vál-yōo) *tr.v.* **-ued, -uing, -ues.** Also U.S. **re·val·u·ate, -ated, -ating, -ates.** To give a new value to (currency), especially an increased value. Compare **devalue.** —**re·val·u·ation** (rée-val-yoo-áysh'n) *n.*
re·vamp (rée-vámp) *tr.v.* **-vamped, -vamping, -vamps.** **1.** To patch up or restore; renovate. **2.** To revise or reconstruct (a manuscript, for example). **3.** To vamp (a shoe or boot) anew. ~*n.* The act, process, or result of revamping.
re·vanch·ism (ri-vánch-iz'm, rə-, -vónsh-) *n.* A foreign policy motivated by a desire to regain territory that was lost to an enemy

[French *revanche,* revenge, from *revancher,* to revenge, from Old French *revencher,* to REVENGE.] —**re·vanch·ist** *n. & adj.*
rev counter *n. Informal.* An instrument for counting the rate at which an engine is revolving; a tachometer.
Revd Reverend.
re·veal¹ (ri-véel, rə-) *tr.v.* **-vealed, -vealing, -veals.** **1.** To divulge or disclose; make known. **2.** To bring to view; expose; show. **3.** To make known by divine or supernatural means, as through revelation. Used of God. [Middle English *revelen,* from Old French *reveler,* from Latin *revēlāre,* to unveil, reveal : *re-,* back, back to a prior condition + *vēlāre,* to veil, from *vēlum,* a veil.] —**re·veal·a·ble** *adj.* —**re·veal·er** *n.* —**re·veal·ment** *n.*
Synonyms: reveal, expose, disclose, divulge, impart, betray.
reveal² *n. Architecture.* The internal, vertical side of a recess or opening, as of a doorway or window. [From obsolete *revale,* to lower, from Old French *revaler* : RE- + *avaler,* to lower (see **vail**).]
re·vealed religion (ri-véeld, rə-) *n.* Religion that is based on ideas or beliefs gained through revelation by God rather than through natural reasoning.
re·veal·ing (ri-véeling, rə-) *adj.* **1.** Significant; telling. **2.** Showing parts of the body considered to be sexually inviting: *a revealing dress.* —**re·veal·ing·ly** *adv.*
re·veil·le (ri-vál-i, rə-, -vélli) ‖ U.S. révvəli) *n.* **1.** The sounding of a bugle early in the morning to awaken and summon persons in a military camp or garrison. **2.** The first military formation of the day. [French *réveillez,* imperative of *réveiller,* to rouse, awaken, from Old French *reveiller* : *re-,* again + *veiller,* to rouse, from Latin *vigilāre,* to watch, from *vigil,* awake.]
rev·el (révv'l) *intr.v.* **-elled** or U.S. **-eled, -elling** or U.S. **-eling, -els.** **1.** To take great pleasure or delight. Used with *in: revels in scandal.* **2.** To engage in uproarious festivities; make merry. ~*n. Often plural.* A noisy, festive occasion. [Middle English *revelen,* from Old French *reveller,* to make noise, "to rebel", from Latin *rebellāre,* to REBEL.] —**rev·el·ler** *n.*
rev·e·la·tion (révvə-láysh'n) *n.* **1.** An act of revealing or something revealed; especially, a dramatic disclosure of something not previously known or realised. **2.** Something that reveals unexpected qualities or provides fresh understanding. **3.** *Theology.* A manifestation of divine will or truth. [Middle English, from Old French, from Late Latin *revēlātiō* (stem *revēlātiōn-*), from Latin *revēlāre,* REVEAL.] —**rev·e·la·tion·al** *adj.*
Rev·e·la·tion *n. Abbr.* **Rev.** Also **Revelations.** The last book in the New Testament, attributed to St. John. Also called the "Apocalypse", the "Revelation of St. John the Divine".
rev·e·la·tion·ist (révvə-láysh'n-ist) *n.* One who believes in divine revelation.
rev·el·ry (révv'l-ri) *n., pl.* **-ries.** Boisterous merrymaking. —**rev·el·rous** *adj.*
rev·e·nant (révvənənt) *n.* **1.** One that returns after an absence. **2.** One who returns after death; a ghost. [French, from the present participle of *revenir,* to return, from Latin *revenīre* : *re-,* again, back + *venīre,* to come.]
re·venge (ri-vénj, rə-) *tr.v.* **-venged, -venging, -venges.** **1.** To inflict punishment in return for (injury or insult); retaliate. **2.** To seek or take vengeance for (oneself or another person). —See Usage note at **avenge.** ~*n.* **1.** Vengeance; retaliation. **2.** The act of taking vengeance. **3.** A desire for revenge; vindictiveness. **4.** An opportunity for, or instance of, getting one's own back for an earlier reversal or defeat. [Middle English *revengen,* from Old French *revenger, revencher,* from Late Latin *revindicāre,* to avenge : Latin *re-* (intensive), again + *vindicāre,* to VINDICATE.]
re·venge·ful (ri-vénj-f'l, rə-) *adj.* Desiring revenge. See Synonyms at **vindictive.** —**re·venge·ful·ly** *adv.* —**re·venge·ful·ness** *n.*
rev·e·nue (révvə-new, révvi-; -venue sometimes ri-vénnew, rə- ‖ -nōo) *n. Abbr.* **rev.** **1.** The income of a government from all sources appropriated for the payment of public expenses. **2.** Yield from property or investment; income. **3.** A single source of income. **4.** A government department set up to collect public funds. Also used adjectivally: *a revenue officer.* [Middle English, return, return to place, from Old French, from the feminine past participle of *revenir,* to return, from Latin *revenīre* : *re-,* back, again + *venīre,* to come.]
revenue cutter *n.* A small, armed coastguard boat formerly used in patrols to catch smugglers.
revenue tariff *n.* A tariff imposed to raise public funds rather than to affect trade.
re·ver·ber·ate (ri-vérbə-rayt, rə-) *v.* **-ated, -ating, -ates.** —*intr.* **1.** To re-echo; resound. **2.** To be repeatedly reflected. **3.** To rebound or recoil; redound. —*tr.* **1.** To re-echo (a sound). **2.** To reflect (heat or light) repeatedly. [Latin *reverberāre,* to cause to rebound : *re-,* back + *verberāre,* to whip, lash, from *verbera,* whips, rods.] —**re·ver·ber·a·tion** (-ráysh'n) *n.* —**re·ver·ber·ant, re·ver·ber·a·tive** (-rətiv ‖ -raytiv) *adj.* —**re·verb·e·ra·tor** *n.*
reverberation pedal *n.* On a piano, the **sustaining pedal** (*see*).
reverberation time *n.* The time taken for a sound in a room to diminish in intensity by 60 decibels, used as a measure of the acoustic properties of the room.
re·ver·ber·a·to·ry (ri-vérbə-rə-tri, -təri, -ráytəri) *adj.* Of, pertaining to, or causing reverberation. ~*n.* A reverberatory furnace.
reverberatory furnace *n.* A furnace for smelting metals in which

the fuel and the ore are separated and the heat is reflected onto the ore by a curved roof. Also called "reverberatory".

re•vere (ri-véer, rə-) *tr.v.* **-vered, -vering, -veres.** To regard with awe, great respect, or devotion; venerate. [Latin *reverērī*: *re-* (intensive), again + *verērī*, to respect, feel awe of.] **—re•ver•er** *n.*

Synonyms: *revere, worship, venerate, adore, idolise.*

Re•vere (ri-véer, rə-), **Paul** (1735–1818). U.S. revolutionary hero. On April 18, 1775, he went on his famous ride to Concord, celebrated in a poem by Longfellow, to warn the people of Massachusetts that a British expedition was advancing towards Lexington.

rev•er•ence (révvərənss, révvrənss) *n.* **1.** A feeling of profound awe and respect and often of love; veneration. **2.** An act of showing respect; especially, an obeisance. **3.** The state of being revered. **4.** *Archaic & Irish. Capital* **R.** A title of respect for a clergyman. Preceded by *His* or *Your.* —See Synonyms at **honour.**
~*tr.v.* **reverenced, -encing, -ences.** To regard with reverence.

rev•er•end (révvərənd, révvrənd) *adj.* **1.** Deserving of reverence. **2.** Pertaining to or characteristic of the clergy; clerical. **3.** *Often capital* **R.** *Abbr.* **Rev., Revd** Designating a member of the clergy. ~*n. Informal.* A clergyman. [Middle English, from Old French, from Latin *reverendus*, gerundive of *reverērī*, REVERE.]

Reverend Mother *n.* A title of or form of address for the superior of a convent.

rev•er•ent (révvərənt, révvrənt) *adj.* Feeling or expressing reverence. [Middle English, from Latin *reverēns* (stem *reverent-*), present participle of *reverērī*, REVERE.] **—rev•er•ent•ly** *adv.*

rev•er•en•tial (révvə-rénsh'l) *adj.* Showing reverence: *a reverential tone of voice.* **—rev•er•en•tial•ly** *adv.*

rev•er•ie (révvəri) *n.* **1. a.** Absent-minded musing; daydreaming. **b.** A daydream: *a reverie of years long past.* **2.** *Music.* A piece of music evoking a dreamy state. **3.** *Archaic.* A fantastic or deluded notion. [Middle English, from Old French, from *rever*†, to dream.]

re•vers (ri-véer, rə-, -váir) *n., pl.* **revers** (-z). A part of a garment turned back to show the reverse side, such as a lapel. [French, from Old French, REVERSE.]

re•ver•sal (ri-vérss'l, rə-) *n.* **1.** An act or instance of reversing. **2.** The state of being reversed. **3.** An unfavourable change: *a reversal of fortune.* **4.** *Law.* A changing or setting aside, as of a lower court's decision by an appellate court.

re•verse (ri-vérss, rə-) *adj. Abbr.* **rev. 1. a.** Turned backwards in position, direction, or order; opposite; contrary. **b.** Upside-down, back to front, or inverted. **2.** Moving or acting in a manner contrary to the usual. **3.** Causing backward movement: *reverse gear.* **4.** *Printing.* Having the black and white areas reversed.
~*n. Abbr.* **rev. 1.** The opposite or contrary of something. **2. a.** The back or rear of something. **b.** The side of a coin not carrying the principal design. Compare **obverse. 3.** A change to an opposite position, condition, or direction. **4.** A change in fortune from better to worse; a setback. **5. a.** A mechanism for reversing movement, as a gear in a motor vehicle. **b.** The reverse position or operating condition of such a mechanism. **—in reverse.** In the contrary direction, order, or position. **—the reverse of.** Far from; not at all.
~*v.* **reversed, -versing, -verses.** —*tr.* **1. a.** To turn to the opposite direction or tendency. **b.** To cause to move in a direction opposite to the normal one: *reverse a car.* **2.** To turn inside out or upside down. **3.** To exchange the positions of; transpose. **4.** To cause to be completely different or opposite in character or effect: *reversed their policy on wage restraint.* **5.** *Law.* To revoke or annul (a decision or decree). **6.** To cause (the charge for a telephone call) to be paid by the recipient. —*intr.* **1. a.** To turn or move in the opposite direction. **b.** To move backwards. **2.** To reverse the action of an engine. [Middle English *revers*, from Old French, from Latin *reversus*, past participle of *revertere*, REVERT.] **—re•verse•ly** *adv.* **—re•vers•er** *n.*

reverse-charge call *n. Chiefly British.* A telephone call that is paid for by the recipient. Also called "transfer charge call", *U.S., Australian, & N.Z.* "collect call".

reversed fault *n. Geology.* A fault in which older beds on one side of the fault plane are thrust over younger beds on the other side as a result of compression. Also called "reverse fault".

reverse forecast *n.* A bet in which any of two, three,or more horses are backed to finish in any of the first two, three, or more places. Compare **forecast bet.**

reverse tran•scrip•tase (tran-skríp-tayz, traan-, -tayss) *n.* An enzyme that allows synthesis of DNA.

re•ver•si (ri-vér-si, rə-) *n.* A game played on a draughts board with counters that are coloured differently on each side. These are turned over when captured and become the captor's pieces. [French. See **reverse.**]

re•vers•i•ble (ri-vér-səb'l, rə-, -si-) *adj.* **1.** Capable of being reversed or revoked, or of returning to a former state. **2.** *Chemistry & Physics.* Capable of successively assuming or producing either of two states: *a reversible reaction.* **3.** In thermodynamics, pertaining to or occurring by processes that are at thermodynamic equilibrium: *a reversible electric cell.* **4.** Patterned, woven, or finished so that either side may be worn or used as the outer side: *a reversible coat.*
~*n.* A reversible item of clothing. **—re•vers•i•bil•i•ty** (-bílləti), **re•vers•i•ble•ness** *n.* **—re•vers•i•bly** *adv.*

re•vers•ing light (ri-vérssing, rə-) *n.* A light on the back of a motor vehicle that is automatically illuminated when reverse gear is engaged.

re•ver•sion (ri-vérsh'n, rə-, -vérzh'n) *n.* **1.** A return to a former condition, belief, or practice. **2.** A turning away or in the opposite direction. **3.** *Genetics.* Loosely, **atavism** *(see).* **4.** *Law.* **a.** The return of an estate or an interest in it to the grantor or his heirs after the grant has expired. **b.** The estate thus returned. **c.** The right to succeed to such an estate. **5.** The right or expectation of obtaining or succeeding to something at a future time. **6.** The sum payable by an insurance company on an insured person's death.

re•ver•sion•ar•y (ri-vérsh'n-əri, rə-, -vérzh'n- || *U.S.* -erri) *adj. Law.* Also **re•ver•sion•al** (-vérsh'n'l, -vérzh'n'l). Of or connected with the reversion of an estate.

re•ver•sion•er (ri-vér-sh'n-ər, -zhn-) *n. Law.* A person entitled to receive an estate in reversion.

re•vert (ri-vért, rə-) *intr.v.* **-verted, -verting, -verts. 1.** To return to a former, often less desirable, condition, practice, subject, or belief. **2.** *Law.* To return to the former owner or his heirs. Used of money or property. **3.** *Biology.* To return to a simpler or more primitive form or condition. Used of organisms, organs, and the like. [Middle English *reverten*, from Old French *revertir*, from Latin *revertere*, to turn back : *re-*, back + *vertere*, to turn.] **—re•vert•er** *n.* **—re•vert•i•ble** *adj.* **—re•ver•tive** *adj.*

re•vest (rée-vést) *tr.v.* **-vested, -vesting, -vests.** To vest (power or possession, for example) once again in a person or agency. [Middle English *revesten*, to dress (in ecclesiastical garments), from Old French *revestir*, from Late Latin *revestīre*, to clothe again : Latin *re-*, again + *vestīre*, to clothe, from *vestis*, clothes.]

re•vet (ri-vét, rə-) *v.* **-vetted, -vetting, -vets.** —*tr.* To face (a wall of earth) with a layer of stone or other suitable material. —*intr.* To construct a revetment. [French *revêtir*, from Old French *revestir*, to clothe again. See **revest.**]

re•vet•ment (ri-vétmənt, rə-) *n.* **1.** A facing, as of masonry, used to support an embankment, wall, or the like. **2.** A barricade against explosives.

re•view (ri-véw, rə-) *v.* **-viewed, -viewing, -views.** —*tr.* **1.** To look over, study, or examine again. **2.** To consider retrospectively; look back on. **3.** To examine with an eye to criticism or correction. **4.** To write or give a critical report on (a book or artistic production). **5.** *Law.* To examine (an action or verdict), especially in a higher court, in order to correct possible errors. **6.** To subject to a formal inspection, especially a military inspection. —*intr.* **1.** To go over or re-examine material. **2.** To act as a reviewer, especially for a newspaper or magazine. **3.** *U.S.* To revise, as for an examination.
~*n. Abbr.* **rev. 1.** A re-examination or reconsideration. **2.** A retrospective view or survey. **3.** An inspection or examination for the purpose of evaluating something. **4.** A published report or essay giving a critical estimate of an artistic work or performance, for example. **5.** A periodical publication devoted primarily to such reports. **6.** A formal military inspection. **7.** *Law.* An examination of an action or verdit, especially by a higher court, in order to correct possible errors. **8.** An entertainment, a **revue** *(see).* [From obsolete French *revoir* (past participle *reveu*), to see again, look over : *re-*, again, over + *voir*, to see, from Latin *vidēre*.] **—re•view•a•ble** *adj.*

re•view•al (ri-véw-əl, rə-) *n.* The act or an instance of reviewing.

re•view•er (ri-véw-ər, rə-) *n.* One who reviews; specifically, a critic writing for a newspaper or magazine.

re•vile (ri-vīl, rə-) *v.* **-viled, -viling, -viles.** —*tr.* To denounce with abusive language; rail against. —*intr.* To use abusive language. —See Synonyms at **malign, scold.** [Middle English *revilen*, from Old French *reviler* : *re-* (intensive), again + *vil*, VILE.] **—re•vile•ment** *n.* **—re•vil•er** *n.* **—re•vil•ing•ly** *adv.*

re•vis•al (ri-vīz'l, rə-) *n.* The act of revising; revision.

re•vise (ri-vīz, rə-) *v.* **-vised, -vising, -vises.** —*tr.* **1.** To change or modify: *revise an earlier opinion.* **2.** *British.* To restudy or go over (academic work), especially in preparation for an examination. —*intr.* To restudy work for an examination. **3.** To prepare a newly edited version of (a text). —See Synonyms at **correct.**
~*n. Abbr.* **rev.** (|| *U.S. also* rée-vīz) *Printing.* A proof made from an earlier proof on which corrections have been made. [Latin *revīsere*, to look back : *re-*, again, back + *vīsere*, to look at, from *vidēre* (past participle *vīsus*), to see.] **—re•vis•a•ble** *adj.* **—re•vis•er** *n.*

Re•vised Standard Version (ri-vīzd, rə-) *n. Abbr.* **R.S.V.** A modern American revision (1946–57) of the American Standard edition of the English Bible, in the King James tradition.

Revised Version *n. Abbr.* **R.V., Rev. Ver.** A revision of the King James Version of the Bible, prepared by a committee of scholars from Britain and the United States (1870–84).

re•vi•sion (ri-vízh'n, rə-) *n. Abbr.* **rev. 1.** The act or procedure of revising. **2.** The result of revising; a corrected or new version. **3.** *British.* The process or activity of revising for an examination. **—re•vi•sion•al, re•vi•sion•ar•y** (-əri || *U.S.* -erri) *adj.*

re•vi•sion•ism (ri-vízh'n-iz'm, rə-) *n.* **1.** A policy of modification or change, especially of a political or religious doctrine. **2.** *Often capital* **R.** A recurrent tendency within the Communist movement to revise Marxist theory in such a way as to provide justification for a retreat from the original doctrine. Often used derogatorily. **—re•vi•sion•ist** *n. & adj.*

re•vis•it (rée-vízzit) *tr.v.* **-ited, -iting, -its.** To visit again.
~*n.* A second or repeated visit. **—re•vis•i•ta•tion** (-áysh'n) *n.*

re•vi•so•ry (ri-vīzəri, rə-) *adj.* Of, pertaining to, effecting, or having the power of revision.

re•vi•tal•ise, re•vi•tal•ize (rée-vīt'l-īz) *tr.v.* **-ised, -ising, -ises.** To impart new life or vigour to; restore the vitality of. **—re•vi•tal•i•sa•tion** (-ī-záysh'n || *U.S.* -i-) *n.*

re•viv•al (ri-vīv'l, rə-) *n.* **1.** The act of reviving, or the condition of being revived. **2. a.** A restoration to use, acceptance, activity, or vigour after a period of obscurity or quiescence. **b.** A return to use or fashion, as of former styles, manners, or activities: *the Gothic Revival.* **3.** A new presentation of a play, film, or the like. **4.** A reawakening of faith or interest in religion. **5.** An evangelistic meeting or series of meetings for the purpose of reawakening religious faith, often characterised by impassioned preaching and public declarations of faith.

re·viv·al·ism (ri-vī́v'l-iz'm, rə-) *n.* The spirit or activities characteristic of religious revivals.

re·viv·al·ist (ri-vī́v'l-ist, rə-) *n.* **1.** A person who promotes or leads religious revivals. **2.** A person who revives practices or ideas of an earlier time. **—re·viv·al·ist, re·viv·al·is·tic** (-ístik) *adj.*

re·vive (ri-vī́v, rə-) *v.* **-vived, -viving, -vives.** *—tr.* **1.** To bring back to life or consciousness; resuscitate. **2.** To impart new health, vigour, or spirit to. **3.** To restore to use, currency, activity, or notice. **4.** To restore the validity or effectiveness of. **5.** To renew in the mind; recall. **6. a.** To put on a new production of (a stage work). **b.** To bring back (a former artistic style, for example) into popularity or fashion. *—intr.* **1.** To return to life or consciousness. **2.** To regain health, vigour, or good spirits. **3.** To return to use, currency, or notice; flourish again. **4.** To return to validity, effectiveness, or operative condition. [Middle English *reviven,* from Old French *revivre,* from Late Latin *revīvere* : Latin *re-,* again + *vīvere,* to live.] **—re·viv·er** *n.*

re·viv·i·fy (ree-vívvi-fī, ri-, ree-) *tr.v.* **-fied, -fying, -fies.** To impart new life to. [French *revivifier,* from Late Latin *revīvificāre* : *re-,* again + *vīvificāre,* to VIVIFY.] **—re·viv·i·fi·ca·tion** (-fi-káysh'n) *n.*

rev·i·vis·cence (révvi-víss'nss, rée-vī-, ri-vívviss'nss, rə-) *n.* A return to life or vigour; a revival. [Late Latin *reviviscentia,* from Latin *reviviscere,* "to start to live again", ultimately from *vivere,* to live.] **—rev·i·vis·cent** *adj.*

rev·o·ca·ble, re·vok·a·ble (révvəkə-b'l, ri-vṓkə-, rə-) *adj.* Capable of being revoked. **—rev·o·ca·bil·i·ty** (-bílləti), **rev·o·ca·ble·ness** *n.* **—rev·o·ca·bly** *adv.*

rev·o·ca·tion (révvə-káysh'n) *n.* The act of revoking, or the condition of being revoked; cancellation; repeal. **—rev·o·ca·to·ry** (révvəkə-tri, ri-vṓkə-, rə-, -təri) *adj.*

re·voke (ri-vṓk, rə-) *v.* **-voked, -voking, -vokes.** *—tr.* To void or annul by recalling, withdrawing, or reversing; cancel; rescind: *revoke a decree.* *—intr.* In card games, to fail to follow suit when one is required and able to do so. —See Synonyms at **nullify.**
~n. In card games, an act of revoking; a failure to follow suit. [Middle English *revoken,* from Old French *revoquer,* from Latin *revocāre,* to call back : *re-,* back + *vocāre,* to call.] **—re·vok·er** *n.*

re·volt (ri-vṓlt || -vólt) *v.* **-volted, -volting, -volts.** *—intr.* **1.** To institute or take part in a rebellion against authority, especially that of the state; rebel or mutiny. **2.** To be affected by or turn away in disgust or revulsion. Used with *against, at,* or *from.* *—tr.* To fill with disgust or abhorrence; repel.
~n. **1.** An uprising against state authority; a rebellion. **2.** Any act of protest or rejection. **3.** The state of a person or persons in rebellion: *be in revolt.* —See Synonyms at **rebellion.** [French *révolter,* from Italian *rivoltare,* from Vulgar Latin *revolvitāre* (unattested), from Latin *revolvere,* to roll back, REVOLVE.] **—re·volt·er** *n.*

re·volt·ing (ri-vṓlt-ing || -vólt-) *adj.* **1.** Causing disgust; repulsive; abhorrent. **2.** *Informal.* Nasty; disagreeable. **—re·volt·ing·ly** *adv.*

rev·o·lute (révvə-lo͞ot, -lewt) *adj. Botany.* Rolled back on the undersurface from the tip or margins, as some leaves are. [Latin *revolūtus,* past participle of *revolvere,* to roll back, REVOLVE.]

rev·o·lu·tion (révvə-lo͞osh'n, -léwsh'n) *n. Abbr.* **rev. 1.** A sudden political overthrow brought about from within a given system, especially: **a.** A forcible substitution of rulers or of ruling cliques: *a palace revolution.* **b.** Seizure of state power by the militant vanguard of a subject class or nation. —See Synonyms at **rebellion. 2.** A recognisably momentous change in any situation, field, or sphere or actvity: *the revolution in physics.* **3. a.** Orbital motion about a point, especially as distinguished from axial rotation: *the planetary revolution about the Sun.* **b.** A turning or rotational motion about an axis. **c.** A single complete cycle of such orbital or axial motion. [Middle English *revolucioun,* from Old French *revolution,* from Late Latin *revolūtiō* (stem *revolūtiōn-*), from Latin *revolvere* (past participle *revolūtus*), REVOLVE.]

rev·o·lu·tion·ar·y (révvə-lo͞osh'n-əri, -léwsh'n- || *U.S.* -erri) *adj.* **1.** Of, pertaining to, or bringing about a political or social revolution. **2.** Characterised by or resulting in radical change: *a revolutionary discovery.* **3.** Completely original or new: *a revolutionary approach to public relations.* **4.** Moving in circles; revolving. **5.** *Capital* **R. a.** Of or pertaining to any of various other revolutions, especially the French Revolution. **b.** Of or pertaining to the activities or period of the War of American Independence.
~n., pl. **revolutionaries.** Also *chiefly U.S.* **rev·o·lu·tion·ist.** One who advocates or fights in a revolution.

Revolutionary calendar *n.* The calendar introduced in France on October 24, 1793, by the National Convention and abolished under Napoleon on December 31, 1805, reckoning time from September 22, 1792, the date of the founding of the First Republic, and reckoning ten months to the year. Also called "Republican calendar".

rev·o·lu·tion·ise, rev·o·lu·tion·ize (révvə-lo͞osh'n-īz, -léwsh'n-) *tr.v.* **-ised, -ising, -ises. 1.** To bring about a radical change in; alter extensively or drastically. **2.** To cause (a country) to undergo a political, industrial, or social revolution. **3.** To imbue with revolutionary principles. **—rev·o·lu·tion·is·er** *n.*

re·volve (ri-vólv, rə- || *Southern England also* -vṓlv) *v.* **-volved, -volving, -volves.** *—intr.* **1.** To orbit a central point. **2.** To turn on an axis; rotate. **3.** To recur in cycles or at periodic intervals. *—tr.* **1.** To cause to revolve. **2.** *Literary.* To think over (a problem); ponder or reflect on. **3.** To have as a central theme or concern. Used with *about* or *around*: *The family seems to revolve around the dog.* —See Synonyms at **turn.** [Middle English *revolven,* from Latin *revolvere,* to roll back : *re-,* back + *volvere,* to roll.] **—re·volv·a·ble** *adj.*

re·volv·er (ri-vólv-ər, rə- || *Southern England also* -vṓlv-) *n.* **1.** A pistol having a revolving cylinder with several cartridge chambers. **2.** One that revolves.

re·volv·ing credit (ri-vólv-ing, rə- || -vṓlv-) *n.* **1.** *Finance.* A bank credit that can be drawn on for: **a.** A limited total amount that is renewable as soon as it is paid back. **b.** A limited amount at any one time, with no limit on the number of times. **2.** A form of credit made available to customers of a retail shop, whereby they are allowed a constant stipulated amount of credit in return for regular payment to the shop.

revolving door *n.* A door having several partitions attached to a central axis on which it turns, thus keeping out draughts.

revolving fund *n. Finance.* A fund of money from which loans or investments are made, which is kept at a constant level by repayment of the loans with interest or by the returns from the investments that it finances.

re·vue, re·view (ri-véw, rə-) *n.* An entertainment consisting of sketches, songs, and dances, often satirising current events, trends, and personalities. [French, from Old French, past participle of *revoir,* to REVIEW.]

re·vul·sion (ri-vúlsh'n, rə-) *n.* **1.** A sudden and strong change or reaction in feeling; especially, a feeling of violent disgust or loathing. **2.** A withdrawing or turning away from something. **3.** *Medicine.* Treatment of a diseased part or organ by diverting the blood to another part of the body, as by counterirritation. [Latin *revulsiō* (stem *revulsiōn-*), from *revellere* (past participle *revulsus*), to pull back or away : *re-,* back + *vellere,* to pull, tear.]

re·vul·sive (ri-vúl-siv, rə-) *n. Medicine.* A substance that produces revulsion. [REVULS(ION) + -IVE.] **—re·vul·sive** *adj.*

Rev. Ver. Revised Version (of the Bible).

re·ward (ri-wáwrd, rə-) *n.* **1. a.** Something given or received in recompense for worthy behaviour or a service rendered. **b.** Requital or retribution for harm done. **2.** Money offered for some special service, such as the return of a lost article or the capture of a criminal. **3.** A satisfying return or result; a profit. —See Synonyms at **bonus.**
~tr.v. **rewarded, -warding, -wards. 1.** To bestow a reward on. **2.** To give a reward because of or in return for: *They rewarded his bravery with a medal.* **3.** To satisfy or gratify: *Her patience was rewarded.* [Middle English *rewarden,* to heed, regard, reward, from Anglo-French *rewarder,* "to look at" : *re-* (intensive) + *warder,* to watch over, from Germanic.] **—re·ward·er** *n.*

re·ward·ing (ri-wáwrding, rə-) *adj.* Worthwhile or gratifying: *a rewarding experience.* **—re·ward·ing·ly** *adv.*

re·wa·re·wa (rée-wə-rée-wə, ráy-, ré-, -ráy-, -ré-) *n.* A New Zealand tree, *Knightia excelsa,* the red, figured timber of which is used in cabinetmaking. Also called "honeysuckle". [Maori.]

re·wind (rée-wī́nd) *tr.v.* **-wound** (-wównd), **-winding, -winds.** To wind again or anew.
~n. (rée-wīnd). The act or process of rewinding something, such as film or tape. **—re·wind·er** *n.*

re·wire (rée-wī́r) *tr.v.* **-wired, -wiring, -wires.** To provide with new wiring.

re·word (rée-wúrd) *tr.v.* **-worded, -wording, -words.** To state, express, or compose again using different words.

re·work (rée-wúrk) *tr.v.* **-worked, -working, -works. 1.** To work over again; revise or rewrite. **2.** To use (a theme or metaphor, for example) in a new or different context, often in an altered form. **3.** To subject to a repeated or new process.

re·write (rée-rī́t) *tr.v.* **-wrote** (-rṓt), **-written** (-rítt'n), **-writing, -writes.** To write again, especially in a different form.
~n. (rée-rīt). Something that has been rewritten. **—re·writ·er** *n.*

Rex² (reks) *n. Abbr.* **R. 1.** The reigning king. Used as a title and signature on documents. **2.** *Law.* The Crown. Used in lawsuits when the monarch is a king: *Rex v. Overton.* [Latin *rēx,* king.]

Rey·kja·vik or **Rey·kja·vík** (ráyk-yə-vik, -veek). Capital city and chief port of Iceland, lying on Faxaflói bay in the southwest of the country. The centre of the cod-fishing industry, it is the commercial and industrial hub of Iceland.

Rey·nard (rén-ərd, -aard, ráynaard). The fox, as personified in folklore and fable.

Rey·naud (re-nṓ), **Paul** (1878-1966). French politician. He held several cabinet posts in the 1930s before becoming prime minister in March, 1940. In October, he was arrested by the Vichy regime of Pétain, tried in 1942, and imprisoned in Germany (1942–45). After the war he served as finance minister (1948), and later helped to draw up the constitution for the Fifth Republic (1958).

Reyn·olds (rénn'ldz), **Sir Joshua** (1723–92). British painter, the first president of the Royal Academy. He was the leading painter of his day and one of the most important in the history of English painting. In the course of his lifetime he painted more than 2,000 historical subjects and portraits.

Reynolds number *n. Physics.* A dimensionless number characterising the type of flow in a fluid, used especially in the study of the effects of viscosity and velocity control in fluid systems. [After Osborne *Reynolds* (1842–1912), British physicist.]

PRONUNCIATION KEY

a, trap; aa, father; ai, fair; ar, star; aw, lawn; ay, play; b, bb, stab; rubber; ch, church; ck, ticket; d, dd, dead; ladder; e, dress; ee, bee; er, defer; ew, few; ewr, pure; ə, about; ər, letter; f, ff, fife; differ; g, gg, giggle; h, hat; i, kit; ī, price; īr, fire; j, judge; k, kick; l, ll, let; 'l, needle; m, mm, man; n, nn, no; 'n, sudden; ng, thing; o, lot; ō, no; o͝o, foot; o͞o, shoe; oor, poor; ow, cow; owr, hour; oy, boy; p, pp, pepper; r, rr, red; s, ss, sauce; sh, ship; t, tt, totter; th, thick; th, this; smooth; u, cut; ur, turn; v, vv, valve; w, wet; y, yes; z, zz, zebra; zh, vision; pleasure

IN FOREIGN WORDS:

aN, oN, Saint-Saëns; hl, Llanelli; Hluhluwe; kh, loch; lough; Khaled

STRESS MARK:

ín-sīt, insight; in-sī́t, incite

Re·za Shah Pah·la·vi (ráyzə, re-záa; páalə-vée), born Reza Khan (1877–1944). Iranian soldier, shah of Iran from 1925 to 1941. In 1935 he officially changed the name of Persia to its older name, Iran. He did much to modernise Iranian life, but in 1941 Soviet and British forces occupied Iran and forced him to abdicate in favour of his son, Muhammad Reza Shah.

RF radio frequency.

R factor *n* A genetic element in bacteria that gives them immunity or resistance to antibiotics and is transmitted from one bacterium to another by conjugation. [*Resistance factor.*]

R.F.C. Rugby Football Club.

R.G.S. Royal Geographical Society.

Rh 1. The symbol for the element rhodium. 2. rhesus. See **Rh factor**.

r.h. right hand.

R.H. Royal Highness.

R.H.A. Royal Horse Artillery.

rhab·do·man·cy (ráb-də-man-si, -dō-) *n.* Divination by means of a wand or a rod, especially in searching for underground water or ores. [Late Greek *rhabdomanteia* : *rhabdos,* rod + -MANCY.] —**rhab·do·man·cer** *n.*

rhab·do·my·o·ma (ráb-dō-mī-ṓ-mə, -də-) *n., pl.* -**mas** or -**mata** (-mətə). *Pathology.* A benign tumour in striated muscular fibres. [New Latin, from Greek *rhabdos,* rod + MYOMA.]

Rhad·a·man·thine (ráddə-mán-thīn, -thin) *adj.* Of or characteristic of Rhadamanthus; especially, rigorously and uncompromisingly adhering to the letter of the law.

Rhad·a·man·thus (ráddə-mánthəss). *Greek Mythology.* The judge of the dead in the underworld.

Rhae·ti·a (rée-shiə, -sh-ə). An ancient Alpine Roman province that included portions of modern Switzerland and Austria. —**Rhae·ti·an** *adj* & *n.*

Rhae·to-Ro·man·ic (réetō-rō-mánnik, -rə-) *adj.* Also **Rhae·to-Ro·mance** (-mánss). Of or belonging to a group of closely related Romance dialects spoken in southern Switzerland, northern Italy, and the Tyrol.

~*n.* Also **Rhae·to-Ro·mance.** These dialects considered as a distinct Romance language.

rhaphe. Variant of **raphe.**

rhap·sod·ic (rap-sóddik) *adj.* Also **rhap·sod·i·cal** (-'l). 1. Of, resembling, or characteristic of a rhapsody. 2. Impassioned or enthusiastic; ecstatic. —**rhap·sod·i·cal·ly** *adv.*

rhap·so·dise, rhap·so·dize (rápsə-dīz) *v.* -**dised,** -**dising,** -**dises.** —*intr.* To express oneself in an immoderately enthusiastic manner. —*tr.* To recite in the manner of a rhapsody.

rhap·so·dist (ráp-sədist) *n.* Also **rhap·sode** (-sōd). 1. In ancient Greece, a reciter of epic poetry, especially of the works of Homer. 2. A person who uses extravagantly enthusiastic or impassioned language.

rhap·so·dy (rápsədi) *n., pl.* -**dies.** 1. **a.** Exalted or excessively enthusiastic expression of feeling in speech or writing. **b.** *Often plural.* An extravagant expression of enthusiasm. 2. In ancient Greece, an epic poem, or a portion of one, suitable for uninterrupted recitation. 3. A literary work written in an impassioned or exalted style. 4. *Music.* A composition that is free or irregular in form, often improvisatory in character, and typically has a melodic content based on folk tunes. [Latin *rhapsōdia,* from Greek *rhapsōidia,* from *rhapsōidos,* "weaver of songs", rhapsodist : *rhaptein,* to sew together + *ōidē,* ode, song.]

rhat·a·ny (rátt'n-i) *n., pl.* -**nies.** 1. Either of two South American shrubs, *Krameria triandra* or *K. argentea,* having thick, fleshy roots. 2. The dried root of either of these plants, formerly used as an astringent. Also called "krameria". [Spanish *ratania,* from Quechua *ratánya.*]

rhbdr. rhombohedron.

rhe·a (reer, rée-ə) *n.* Any of several flightless South American birds of the genus *Rhea,* resembling the ostrich but somewhat smaller and having three toes instead of two. [New Latin *Rhea,* arbitrarily named after RHEA.]

Rhe·a (reer, rée-ə). *Greek Mythology.* One of the Titans, the wife of Cronos and mother of Zeus.

rhe·bok, ree·bok (rée-buk, -bok) *n.* An antelope, *Pelea capreolus,* that is found in southern Africa and has brownish-grey hair. [From Dutch *reebok,* ROEBUCK.]

Rhee (ree), **Syngman** (1875–1965). Korean politician, president of South Korea (1948–60). After World War II he was a key figure in the administration of American-occupied South Korea and in 1948 he became the first president of the Republic of Korea. He was re-elected in 1952, 1956, and 1960, but in May, 1960, he was forced from office by public demonstrations and went into exile in Hawaii.

Rheims. See **Reims.**

Rhein. See **Rhine.**

rhe·mat·ic (ri-máttik, ree-) *adj.* 1. Of or pertaining to word formation. 2. Derived from or pertaining to a verb. [Greek *rhēmatikos,* from *rhēma,* word, verb.]

Rhen·ish (rénnish, réenish) *adj.* Of or pertaining to the river Rhine or the lands bordering on it.

~*n. Archaic.* Rhine wine.

rhe·ni·um (réeni-əm) *n.* Symbol **Re** A rare dense silvery-white metallic element with a very high melting point. It is used for electrical contacts and with tungsten for high-temperature thermocouples. Atomic number 75, atomic weight 186.2, melting point 3,180°C, boiling point 5,627°C, relative density 21.02, valencies 1, 2, 3, 4, 5, 6, 7. [New Latin, from Latin *Rhēnus,* the RHINE.]

rheo– *comb. form.* Indicates a flow or current; for example, **rheol·ogy.** [Greek *rheos,* current, stream, from *rhein,* to flow.]

rhe·o·base (rée-ō-bayss) *n.* The weakest nerve impulse that is needed to produce a response in a tissue.

rhe·ol·o·gy (ree-óllə ji) *n.* The study of the deformation and flow of matter. [RHEO- + -LOGY.] —**rhe·o·log·i·cal** (rée-ə-lójik'l) *adj.* —**rhe·ol·o·gist** (-óllə jist) *n.*

rhe·om·e·ter (ree-ómmitər) *n.* An instrument for measuring the flow of viscous liquids, as of blood. [RHEO- + -METER.]

rhe·o·stat (rée-ə-stat, -ō-) *n.* A continuously variable electrical resistor used to regulate current, typically having a coil of wire with a sliding contact. [RHEO- + -STAT.] —**rhe·o·stat·ic** (-státtik) *adj.*

rhe·o·tax·is (rée-ə-táksiss, -ō-) *n.* The movement of an organism in response to a current, usually of water. [RHEO- + -TAXIS.] —**rhe·o·tac·tic** (-ták-tik) *adj.*

rhe·sus baby (rée-səss) *n.* A baby affected by **haemolytic disease** *(see).*

rhesus factor *n.* Rh factor *(see).*

rhesus monkey *n.* A brownish macaque monkey, *Macaca mulatta,* of India, used extensively in biological experimentation. [New Latin *rhesus,* arbitrarily from Latin *Rhēsus,* name of a mythological king of Thrace.]

rhe·tor (rée-tər ‖ -tawr) *n.* 1. A teacher of rhetoric in ancient Greece or Rome. 2. An orator. In this sense, often used disparagingly. [Middle English, from Medieval Latin *rēthor,* from Greek *rhētōr.*]

rhet·o·ric (réttərik) *n. Abbr.* **rhet.** 1. The study of the elements used in literature and public speaking, such as content, structure, cadence, and style. 2. The art of oratory, especially the persuasive use of language to influence the thoughts and actions of listeners. 3. **a.** Affectation, grandiloquence, or insincerity in speech or writing. **b.** Speech or writing that is impressive or persuasive, but often insincere or empty. [Middle English *rethorik,* from Old French *rethorique,* from Latin *rhētorica,* from Greek *rhētorikē (tekhnē),* "rhetorical (art)", from *rhētorikos,* rhetorical, from *rhētōr,* RHETOR.]

rhe·tor·i·cal (ri-tórrik'l, rə-) *adj.* 1. Concerned primarily with style or effect; showy, inflated, or insincere. 2. Of or pertaining to rhetoric; oratorical. —**rhe·tor·i·cal·ly** *adv.*

rhetorical question *n.* A question to which no answer is required or expected, or to which only one answer may be made.

rhet·o·ri·cian (réttə-rísh'n) *n.* 1. An expert in or teacher of rhetoric. 2. An eloquent speaker or writer. 3. One given to verbal extravagance.

rheum (rōom ‖ rewm) *n.* A watery or thin mucous discharge from the eyes or nose. [Middle English *reume,* from Old French, from Latin *rheuma,* from Greek, stream, humour of the body, rheum.] —**rheum·y** *adj.*

rheu·mat·ic (rōo-máttik, roo- ‖ rew-) *adj.* Of, pertaining to, or afflicted with rheumatism.

~*n.* 1. A person suffering from rheumatism. 2. *Plural. Informal.* Pains due to rheumatism. [Middle English *rewmatyk,* from Latin *rheumaticus,* troubled with rheum, from Greek *rheumatikos,* subject to rheum, from *rheuma,* stream, body humour, RHEUM.]

rheumatic fever *n.* A severe disease occurring chiefly in children as a complication of streptococcal infection of the throat, characterised by fever and painful inflammation of the joints, and frequently·resulting in permanent damage to the valves of the heart.

rheu·mat·ick·y (rōo-máttiki, rōo- ‖ rew-) *adj. Informal.* Suffering from stiffness or pain in the joints, such as that caused by rheumatism.

rheu·ma·tism (rōomə-tizz'm ‖ réwmə-) *n.* Any of several disorders, such as fibrositis and rheumatoid arthritis, that affect the muscles, tendons, joints, or bones, and are characterised by discomfort and disability. [Latin *rheumatismus,* rheum, catarrh, from Greek *rheumatismos,* from *rheumatizesthai,* to suffer from a flux, from *rheuma,* stream, flux, RHEUM.]

rheu·ma·toid (rōomə-toyd ‖ réwmə-) *adj.* Of, resembling, or afflicted with rheumatism. —**rheu·ma·toi·dal·ly** *adv.*

rheumatoid arthritis *n.* A chronic disease marked by stiffness and inflammation of the membranes of the joints, weakness, loss of mobility, and deformity.

rheumatoid factor *n.* An antibody present in the blood serum of many patients with rheumatoid arthritis that can be a means of diagnosing the disease.

rheu·ma·tol·o·gy (rōomə-tóllə ji ‖ réwmə-) *n.* The branch of medicine concerned with the diagnosis and treatment of rheumatic diseases. [RHEUMAT(ISM) + -LOGY.] —**rheu·ma·tol·o·gist** *n.*

Rh factor *n.* Any of several antigens on the surface of red blood cells of Rh positive blood that induce adverse reactions with blood cells that lack these antigens (Rh negative cells). Also called "rhesus factor". [First discovered in the blood of RHESUS MONKEYS.]

R.H.G. Royal Horse Guards.

rhi·nal (rīn'l) *adj.* Of or pertaining to the nose; nasal. [RHIN(O)- + -AL.]

Rhine (rīn). *German* Rhein; *French* Rhin (raN); *Dutch* Rijn. Longest river in western Europe, about 1 320 kilometres (820 miles) long. Its two principal headwaters, the Vorder Rhine and Hinter Rhine, rise in the Swiss Alps, and join near Chur to form the Rhine proper. The Rhine carries more traffic than any other waterway in the world. The chief commodities that are transported are iron ore, coal, petroleum, sand, gravel, and steel products. Canals link the river with the Maas, Rhône-Saône, Marne, and Danube valleys, thus forming a comprehensive waterway network.

rhea *The large flightless rhea resembles the ostrich and is native to South America. It is the male bird which builds the nest and incubates the eggs.*

rhesus monkey *An intelligent, reddish-brown species of macaque found in Southeast Asia and considered sacred in some parts of India. One of the most widely used research animals, the rhesus monkey helped in the discovery of the Rh, or rhesus, factor in human blood.*

Rhine·land (rín-land, -lənd). A historical region in modern West Germany, consisting of those areas adjoining the Rhine.

Rhine·land-Pa·lat·i·nate (rín-land-pə-látti-nət, -lənd-, -nit, -nayt). *German* **Rhein·land-Pfalz** (rín-lant-pfálts). State (land) in West Germany. It consists of forested uplands intersected by fertile river valleys, the chief rivers being the Rhine and Mosel. The cultivation of vines is widespread and some of Germany's best-known wines are produced there. The state is nevertheless heavily industrialised. Mainz is the capital.

rhi·nen·ceph·a·lon (rínen-séffə-lon, -kéffə-, -lən) *n., pl.* **-la** (-lə). The olfactory region of the brain, in the cerebrum. [RHIN(O)- + ENCEPHALON.] **—rhi·nen·ce·phal·ic** (-si-fál-ik) *adj.*

rhine·stone (rín-stōn) *n.* A colourless, artificial gem of paste or glass, often with facets that sparkle in imitation of diamond. [Translation of French *caillou du Rhin;* originally made at Strasbourg.]

Rhine wine *n.* **1.** Any of several typically white wines produced in the Rhine valley. **2.** Any similar light, dry wine produced elsewhere.

rhi·ni·tis (rī-nítiss) *n.* Inflammation of the nasal mucous membranes, as occurs in the common cold. [New Latin : RHIN(O)- + -ITIS.]

rhi·no[1] (rínō) *n., pl.* **-nos.** *Informal.* A rhinoceros.

rhino[2] *n. British Slang.* Money; cash. Not in current usage. [17th century : origin obscure.]

rhino-, rhin- *comb. form.* Indicates nose or nasal; for example, **rhinoscopy, rhinitis.** [Greek *rhis*† (stem *rhin-*), nose.]

rhi·noc·er·os (rī-nóssərəss) *n., pl.* **-oses** or collectively **rhinoceros.** Any of several large, thick-skinned, herbivorous mammals of the family Rhinocerotidae, of Africa and Asia, having one or two upright horns on the snout. An example is the one-horned Indian rhinoceros, *Rhinoceros unicornis.* [Middle English *rinoceros,* from Latin *rhīnocerōs,* from Greek *rhinokerōs,* "nose-horned" : RHINO- + *keras,* horn.] **—rhi·noc·e·rot·ic** (-nóss-ə-róttik, -i-) *adj.*

rhinoceros beetle *n.* Any of several scarabaeid beetles having one or more rhinoceros-like horns on the head, such as *Oryctes rhinoceros,* a pest of oriental coconut palms.

rhinoceros bird *n.* The **oxpecker** *(see).*

rhi·nol·o·gy (rī-nóllәji) *n.* The anatomy, physiology, and pathology of the nose. [RHINO- + -LOGY.] **—rhi·nol·o·gist** *n.*

rhi·no·plas·ty (rínō-plasti) *n.* Plastic surgery of the nose. [RHINO- + -PLASTY.] **—rhi·no·plas·tic** (-plástik) *adj.*

rhi·nos·co·py (rī-nóskəpi) *n.* Examination of the nasal passages. [RHINO- + -SCOPY.]

rhi·no·vi·rus (rínō-vīr-əss) *n* Any of a group of RNA-containing viruses that cause the common cold and other infections of the respiratory tract.

rhizo-, rhiz- *comb. form.* Indicates a root; for example, **rhizomorphous, rhizoid.** [Greek *rhiza,* root.]

rhi·zo·bi·um (rī-zṓ-bi-əm) *n., pl.* **-bia** (-bi-ə). Any of various nitrogen-fixing bacteria of the genus *Rhizobium* that form nodules on the roots of leguminous plants such as clover and beans. [New Latin *Rhizobium* : RHIZO- + Greek *bios,* life.]

rhi·zo·carp (rízō-kaarp) *n.* **1.** A plant having persistent roots but stems and leaves that die down at the end of each growing season. **2.** A plant that produces subterranean flowers and fruit. [RHIZO- + -CARP.] **—rhi·zo·car·pous** (-kárpəss) *adj.*

rhi·zo·ceph·a·lan (rízō-séff'l-ən) *n.* Any of various small aquatic crustaceans of the order Rhizocephala that are parasitic on other crustaceans. [New Latin *Rhizocephala,* "root-headed ones" (from the rootlike processes extending from the limbless body) : RHIZO- + *-cephala,* from *-cephalus,* -CEPHALOUS.] **—rhi·zo·ceph·a·lous** *adj.*

rhi·zo·gen·ic (rízō-jénnik) *adj.* Also **rhi·zo·ge·net·ic** (-jə-néttik), **rhi·zog·e·nous** (rī-zójənəss). *Botany.* Giving rise to roots: *rhizogenic tissue.* [RHIZO- + -GENIC.]

rhi·zoid (rí-zoyd) *adj.* Rootlike.

~*n.* **1.** A slender, rootlike filament by which mosses, liverworts, and ferns attach to the substratum and absorb nourishment. **2.** A rootlike extension of the thallus of a fungus. [RHIZ(O)- + -OID.] **—rhi·zoi·dal** (rī-zóyd'l) *adj.*

rhi·zome (rí-zōm) *n. Botany.* A rootlike, usually horizontal stem growing under or along the ground, and sending out roots from its lower surface, and leaves or shoots from its upper surface. Also called "rootstock", "rootstalk". [New Latin *rhizoma,* from Greek *rhizōma,* mass of roots of a tree, from *rhizousthai,* to take root, from *rhiza,* root.] **—rhi·zom·a·tous** (rī-zómmə-təss, -zṓmə-) *adj.*

rhi·zo·morph (rízō-mawrf) *n.* A rootlike part, such as the threadlike structure in certain fungi, consisting of strands of hyphae. [RHIZO- + -MORPH.]

rhi·zo·mor·phous (rízō-mórfəss) *adj. Botany.* Having the form of a root. [RHIZO- + -MORPHOUS.]

rhi·zoph·a·gous (rī-zóffəgəss) *adj.* Feeding on roots. [RHIZO- + -PHAGOUS.]

rhi·zo·pod (rízō-pod) *n.* Any protozoan of the class Rhizopoda, such as an amoeba, characteristically moving and taking in food by means of pseudopodia. [New Latin *Rhizopoda,* "root-footed" (from its rootlike pseudopodia) : RHIZO- + -POD.] **—rhi·zop·o·dan** (rī-zóppədən) *adj. & n.* **—rhi·zop·o·dous** *adj.*

rhi·zo·pus (ríz-ə-pəss, -ō-) *n.* Any of various often destructive fungi of the genus *Rhizopus,* such as *R. nigricans,* the common bread mould. [New Latin, "one having rootlike feet" (from its rhizoids) : RHIZO- + Greek *pous,* foot (see **-pod**).]

rhi·zo·sphere (rí-zō-sfeer, -zə-) *n.* The soil immediately surrounding the root system of a plant.

rhi·zot·o·my (rī-zóttəmi) *n., pl.* **-mies.** Surgical severance of spinal nerve roots to relieve severe pain or muscle spasm. [RHIZO- + -TOMY.]

Rh negative *adj.* Lacking an **Rh factor** *(see).*

rho (rō) *n.* The 17th letter in the Greek alphabet written P, ρ. Transliterated in English as *rh* or *r.* [Greek *rhō,* perhaps shortened from *rhōs,* head, of Semitic origin, akin to Hebrew *rēsh, rōsh,* "head", RESH.]

rho·da·mine (rṓdə-meen, -min) *n.* Any of several synthetic red to pink dyes. [RHOD(O)- + AMINE (the dyes are prepared from aminophenol).]

Rhode Island (rōd ílənd, īlənd ‖ *U.S.* rō-dílənd). State in New England, northeast United States. It is the smallest state in the Union but one of the most densely populated. Manufacturing is the chief employer, metalwares, textiles, and plastics being the main products. Fishing and tourism are important, and the state's resorts include Newport. Providence is the capital.

Rhode Island Red *n.* A domestic fowl of an American breed having dark reddish-brown feathers and producing brown eggs.

Rhodes (rōdz). *Greek* **Ró·dhos** (róthoss). Largest island in the Greek Dodecanese group, lying off the southwest coast of Turkey. The interior is mountainous but the island has fertile coastal strips and valleys where wheat, tobacco, cotton, olives, vines, oranges, and vegetables are grown. Tourism is also economically important. Rhodes, the capital, was founded in 408 B.C. and was the site of the Colossus of Rhodes, one of the Seven Wonders of the World, which was destroyed (*c.* 244 B.C.) by an earthquake.

Rhodes (rōdz), **Cecil (John)** (1853–1902). British industrialist and imperialist. In 1870 he went to South Africa and a year later staked a claim in the Kimberley diamond fields. In 1880 he founded the De Beers Mining Company, and he organised the British South Africa Company in 1889, thus gaining a virtual monopoly over mining in South Africa. In 1890 he became prime minister of the Cape Colony, but was forced to resign (1896) after being implicated in the Jameson Raid of 1895. He spent the rest of his life developing Rhodesia. He left a large fortune, most of which he willed to public causes such as the Rhodes scholarships.

Rhodes, Wilfred (1877–1973). English cricketer. He played for Yorkshire from 1898 to 1930 and in his career took 4187 first-class wickets (an all-time record) and made nearly 40,000 runs. On 16 occasions he did the double of 100 wickets and 1,000 runs in a season, and he had a long and distinguished test record as one of the greatest all-rounders in the history of the game.

Rhodesia. See **Zimbabwe.** **—Rho·de·sian** *adj. & n.*

Rho·de·sia and Ny·as·a·land, Federation of (rō-deé-shə, -zhə, -si-ə, -zi-ə; nī-ássə-land, ni-, *properly* nyássə-). From 1953 to 1963, a federation in central Africa consisting of the self-governing colony of Southern Rhodesia (now Zimbabwe) and the British protectorates of Northern Rhodesia (now Zambia) and Nyasaland (now Malawi).

Rhodesian man *n.* An extinct species of man, with a low forehead and massive brow ridges, whose fossil remains were found in central Zambia (formerly Northern Rhodesia), now classified as *Homo sapiens rhodesiensis.*

Rhodesian ridgeback *n.* A large dog of a breed developed in Africa, having short, yellowish-tan hair that forms a ridge along the back. Also called "ridgeback".

Rhodes Scholarship *n.* A scholarship available to students from the United States and certain other countries to study at Oxford University. **—Rhodes scholar** *n.*

rho·di·um (rṓdi-əm) *n. Symbol* **Rh** A hard, durable, silvery-white metallic element that is used to form high-temperature alloys with platinum and is plated on other metals to produce a durable corrosion-resistant coating. Atomic number 45, atomic weight 102.905, melting point 1,966°C, boiling point 3,727°C, relative density 12.41, valencies 2, 3, 4, 5, 6. [New Latin, "rose red" (from the colour of its compounds), from Greek *rhodon,* rose.]

rhodo-, rhod- *comb. form.* Indicates rose or rose-red; for example, **rhodolite.** [Greek *rhodon,* rose.]

rho·do·chro·site (rṓdo-krṓ-sīt) *n.* A naturally occurring impure form of manganese carbonate, $MnCO_3$, light-pink to rose-red in colour with a pearly or vitreous lustre, used as a manganese ore. [German *Rhodochrosit* : RHODO- + Greek *khrōsis,* colouring, from *khrōs, khroos,* colour, skin + -ITE.]

rho·do·den·dron (rṓ-də-déndrən, -di-) *n.* Any of various evergreen shrubs of the widely cultivated genus *Rhododendron,* of the North Temperate Zone, having clusters of variously coloured flowers. See **azalea.** [New Latin, from Latin, from Greek, "rose tree" : RHODO- + Greek *dendron,* tree.]

rho·do·lite (rṓdə-līt, róddə-) *n.* A rose-red or pink variety of garnet, used as a gem. [RHODO- + -LITE.]

rho·do·nite (rṓdə-nīt, róddə-) *n.* A pink to rose-red mineral, essentially $MnSiO_3$, used as an ornamental stone. Also called "manganese spar". [German *Rhodonit* : Greek *rhodon,* rose + -ITE.]

rho·dop·sin (rō-dóp-sin, rə-, ro-) *n.* The light-sensitive pigment in the retinal rods of the eyes, consisting of opsin and retinal. Also called "visual purple". [RHODO- + Greek *opsis,* sight + -IN.]

rhomb. Variant of **rhombus.**

rhom·ben·ceph·a·lon (rómben-séff'l-on, -kéff'l-, -ən) *n.* The portion of the embryonic brain from which the metencephalon, myelencephalon, and subsequently the cerebellum, pons, and medulla

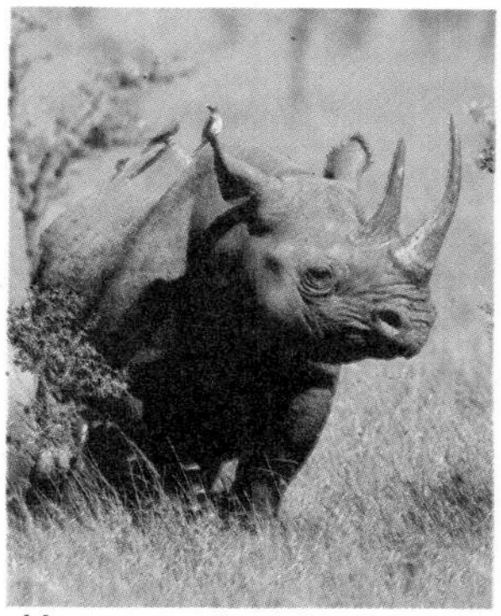

rhinoceros *A hoofed mammal found in Africa and Asia, the rhinoceros is chiefly solitary and lives on leaves and grass. Some of its five species have a single horn, but others – such as the African black (above) – have two.*

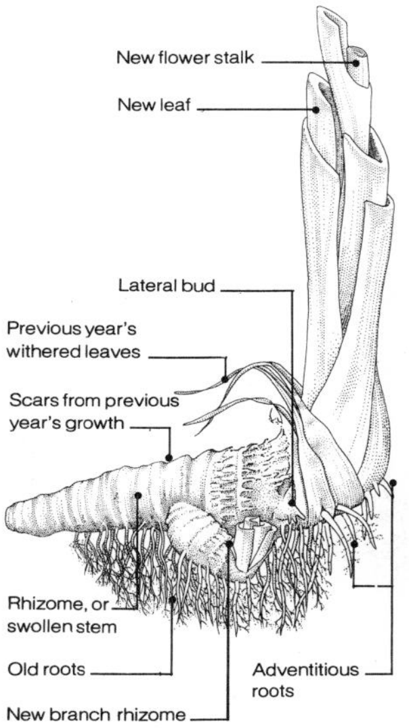
New flower stalk
New leaf
Lateral bud
Previous year's withered leaves
Scars from previous year's growth
Rhizome, or swollen stem
Old roots
Adventitious roots
New branch rhizome

rhizome *Plants which spread by means of underground stems, or rhizomes, include all the grasses and the iris shown here. Rhizomes burrow horizontally through the soil, storing food in winter and in spring throwing out new shoots above and roots below.*

oblongata develop. Also called "hindbrain". [New Latin : RHOMB(US) + ENCEPHALON.]

rhom·bic (rómbik) *adj.* **1.** Having the shape of a rhombus. **2.** *Crystallography.* **Orthorhombic** *(see).*

rhom·bo·he·dron (rómbō-hée-drən) *n., pl.* **-drons** or **-dra** (-drə). *Abbr.* **rhbdr.** A prism with six faces, each a rhombus. [New Latin : RHOMBUS + -HEDRON.] —**rhom·bo·he·dral** *adj.*

rhom·boid (róm-boyd) *n.* **1.** A parallelogram with unequal adjacent sides. **2.** Either of two muscles in the upper part of the back. ~*adj.* Having a shape like a rhomboid. [Greek *rhomboeidēs* : RHOMBUS + -OID.] —**rhom·boi·dal** (-bóyd'l) *adj.*

rhom·bus (róm-bəss) *n., pl.* **-buses** or **-bi** (-bī). Also **rhomb** (rom). An equilateral parallelogram. [Latin, from Greek *rhombos,* bullroarer, magic wheel, rhombus.]

rhon·chus (róng-kəss) *n., pl.* **-chi** (-kī). A coarse sound somewhat like snoring, usually caused by secretion in the bronchial tube. [Late Latin, snoring, from Greek *rhonkhos, rhonkos.*] —**rhon·chal, rhon·chi·al** (-ki-əl) *adj.*

Rhon·dda (rónthə). District in Mid Glamorgan, Wales, extending along the valleys of the rivers Rhondda Fawr and Rhondda Fach. The chief industry, coalmining, has declined in importance since the 1920s and 1930s and there has been a steady decrease in population in recent decades.

Rhône (rōn). Major European river, about 800 kilometres (500 miles) long. It issues from the Rhône Glacier in the Swiss Alps, and flows through Lake Geneva, then southwards through France to the Mediterranean. The river is important for hydroelectric power, and its valley south of Lyon is noteworthy for its excellent vineyards. The Rhône-Saône valley is a main north-south communications route. South of Lyon the river is navigable and an extensive canal system links it with other major rivers.

rho·tic (rótik) *adj. Phonetics.* **1.** Pertaining to, designating, or speaking a variety of English in which the consonant sound (r) has not been lost before a consonant sound or pause. Thus Scottish English is rhotic; Southern English is not. **2.** Designating a consonant sound which is a variety of (r). [From the Greek letter RHO.]

r.h.p. rated horsepower.

Rh positive *adj.* Containing an **Rh factor** *(see).*

rhu·barb (róo-baarb ‖ réw-) *n.* **1.** Any of several plants of the genus *Rheum,* characterised by large, long-stalked leaves; especially, *R. rhaponticum,* the common garden rhubarb, having long, green or reddish, acid leafstalks that are edible when cooked and sweetened. **2.** The dried, bitter-tasting rhizome and roots of *R. palmatum* or *R. officinale,* of central Asia, used as a laxative. **3.** *U.S. Slang.* A heated discussion, quarrel, or fight. ~*interj.* Used to convey an indistinct mumbling sound, as for background noise in a play. [Middle English *rubarbe,* from Old French *r(e)ubarbe,* probably from Medieval Latin *reubarb(ar)um,* probably alteration of *rha barbarum,* barbarian rhubarb : Late Latin *rha,* rhubarb, from Greek *rha, rhēon,* probably from *Rha,* former name of the Volga, on whose banks rhubarb was grown, + Latin *barbarus,* BARBAROUS.]

rhumb (rum ‖ rumb) *n.* **1.** A rhumb line. **2.** Any of the points of the mariner's compass. [Earlier *rumb,* from Old Spanish *rumbo* and Old French *rumb,* modifications (influenced by Latin *rhombus,* RHOMBUS) of Middle Dutch *ruum, rume,* room, space.]

rhumba. Variant of **rumba.**

rhum·ba·tron (rúmbə-tron) *n. Electronics.* A **cavity resonator** *(see).* [RHUMBA (rumba) + -TRON (alluding to the rhythmical variations of the waves).]

rhumb line *n.* **1.** An imaginary line that cuts all the Earth's meridians at a given constant angle. Also called "loxodrome", "loxodromic curve". **2.** The course of a ship following such a line; a course sailed using a constant compass bearing.

rhyme (rīm) *n.* Also *archaic* **rime. 1.** Correspondence of terminal sounds of words or of lines of verse. See **assonance, consonance, feminine rhyme, masculine rhyme. 2.** A poem or verse having a regular correspondence of sounds, especially at the ends of lines: *a nursery rhyme.* **3.** Poetry or verse of this kind. **4.** A word that corresponds with another in terminal sound, such as *night* and *fight,* and *baboon* and *harpoon.* ~*v.* **rhymed, rhyming, rhymes.** Also *archaic* **rime.** —*intr.* **1.** To form a rhyme; correspond in sound: *Death rhymes with breath.* **2.** To compose rhymes or verse. **3.** To make use of rhymes in composing verse. —*tr.* **1.** To put into rhyme or compose with rhymes. **2. a.** To use (a word or words) as a rhyme or rhymes. **b.** To pronounce as a rhyme. [Middle English *rime, ryme,* from from Medieval Latin *rithmus,* variant of Latin *rhythmus,* RHYTHM.]

rhym·er (rīmər) *n.* One who composes verse, especially of low quality. See Synonyms at **poet.**

rhyme royal *n.* A stanza form consisting of seven lines in iambic pentameter with the first line rhyming with the third, the second with the fourth and fifth, and the last two with each other.

rhyme·ster (rīm-stər) *n.* One who makes up light verse that rhymes. See Synonyms at **poet.**

rhym·ing slang (rīming) *n. British.* A type of humorous slang in which a word is replaced by a word or words that rhyme with it; for example, *brown bread* meaning *dead,* and *mince pies* meaning *eyes,* are instances of rhyming slang. Often only the first element is used, as *plates* (meaning *feet*) from *plates of meat.*

rhyn·cho·ce·phal·i·an (ringkō-si-fál-i-ən, -fáyl-) *adj.* Of or belonging to the Rhynchocephalia, an order of lizard-like reptiles of which only one species, the tuatara, is extant.

~*n.* A rhynchocephalian reptile. [New Latin *Rhynchocephalia* : Greek *rhunkhos,* snout, bill, beak + CEPHAL(O)- + -IA.]

rhy·o·lite (rī-ə-līt, -ō-) *n.* A fine-grained extrusive, acid igneous rock, the mineralogical equivalent of granite, consisting largely of quartz and feldspar, and often mica. [German *Rhyolit* : irregularly from Greek *rhuax,* stream (of lava), from *rhein,* to flow + -ITE.] —**rhy·o·lit·ic** (-littik) *adj.*

Rhys (reess), **Jean** (1894–1979). British novelist and short-story writer, born in Dominica. She went to Paris, where she published the collection of stories *The Left Bank* (1927). Her other works include *Voyage in the Dark* (1934), *Wide Sargasso Sea* (1966).

rhythm (ríth'm) *n.* **1. a.** Any kind of movement characterised by the regular recurrence of strong and weak elements: *the rhythm of the tides.* **b.** Action characterised by a smooth, regular, settled movement: *The crowd put the tennis player off his rhythm.* **2.** Nonrandom variation, especially uniform or regular variation, of any quantity or condition characterising a process, as in the body. **3.** *Music.* **a.** The part of music concerned with patterns of sound based on such elements as accent and tempo. **b.** A specified kind of this rhythm: *a waltz rhythm.* **4. a.** The metrical flow of sound with a regulated pattern of long and short, or accented and unaccented syllables, best exemplified in poetry or verse. **b.** A specified kind of such a metrical flow: *sprung rhythm.* **5.** In painting, sculpture, and other visual arts, a regular or harmonious pattern created by lines, forms, and colours. [French *rhythme,* from Latin *rhythmus,* from Greek *rhuthmos,* recurring motion, rhythm, akin to *rhein,* to flow.]

Synonyms: rhythm, metre, cadence, beat.

rhythm and blues *n. Abbr.* **R & B.** An urban form of blues using electrically amplified instruments, developed in the United States in the 1940s.

rhyth·mi·cal (ríthmik'l) *adj.* Also **rhyth·mic** (ríthmik). Pertaining to or characterised by rhythm; especially, recurring with measured regularity. —**rhyth·mi·cal·ly** *adv.*

rhyth·mics (ríthmiks) *n. Used with a singular verb.* The study of rhythm.

rhyth·mist (ríthmist) *n.* One who is expert in, or has a keen sense of, rhythm.

rhythm method *n.* A birth-control method dependent on avoidance of sexual intercourse during the ovulatory phase of the menstrual cycle.

rhythm section *n.* The members of a musical band or group, such as the drummer and bass guitarist, that supply the rhythm.

rhy·ton (rī-t'n, -ton) *n.* In ancient Greece, a drinking vessel or horn tapering to a hole in the bottom through which the wine could run. [Greek *rhuton,* from *rhutos,* flowing, from *rhein,* to flow.]

R.I. **1.** Rhode Island. **2.** Royal Institution. **3.** King and Emperor [Latin *Rex et Imperator*]. **4.** Queen and Empress [Latin *Regina et Imperatrix*].

ri·a (reer, rée-ə) *n.* A long narrow sea inlet, caused by flooding of a narrow valley , which unlike a fiord deepens towards the sea, and is typically found in southwest Ireland and northwest Spain. [Spanish, "river mouth".]

Riad. See **Riyadh.**

ri·al (rī-əl, ree-áal) *n.* **1. a.** The basic monetary unit of Iran, equal to 100 dinars. **b.** A coin worth one rial. **2.** The basic monetary unit of the Yemen Arabic Republic, equal to 100 fils. [Persian, from Arabic *riyāl,* from Spanish *real,* REAL (coin).]

ri·al·to (ri-ál-tō, ree-) *n., pl.* **-tos.** An exchange or trading centre. [After the *Rialto,* Venice, an island forming the centre of the city.]

ri·a·ta, re·a·ta (ree-áatə, -áttə) *n. U.S.* A lariat; a lasso. [Spanish *(la) reata,* (the) lasso, LARIAT.]

rib (rib) *n.* **1. a.** Any of the long, curved bones occurring, in humans, in 12 pairs and extending from the spine to or towards the breastbone and enclosing the heart and lungs. **b.** A similar bone in most other vertebrates. **2.** Any part or piece considered similar to a rib and serving to shape or support: *the rib of an umbrella.* **3.** A cut of meat enclosing one or more ribs. **4.** Any of the curved members attached to the keel of a boat and extending upwards and outwards to form the framework of the hull. **5.** Any of the formed transverse pieces along the length of an aeroplane wing used to establish shape. **6.** *Architecture.* **a.** An arch or a projecting arched member of a vault. **b.** Any of the curved pieces of an arch. **7. a.** A knitting stitch formed by working alternate plain and purl on one row, reversing this order on the next, and so on. **b.** The evenly ridged pattern formed by this. **c.** Material knitted in rib, usually found at the collar, waist, and neck of a woollen garment. **8.** *Botany.* Any of the main veins of a leaf or similar organ. **9.** A ridge of a mountain. **10.** *Mining.* A vein of ore. ~*tr.v.* **ribbed, ribbing, ribs. 1.** To shape, support, or provide with a rib or ribs. **2.** To work in rib: *Rib 30 rows, then cast off.* **3.** To make with ridges or raised markings. **4.** *Informal.* To tease or make fun of. [Middle English *rib(be),* Old English *rib(b),* from Germanic.]

R.I.B.A. Royal Institute of British Architects.

rib·ald (ríbb'ld ‖ ríbawld) *adj.* Characterised by or indulging in vulgar, lewd, coarse humour. See Synonyms at **coarse.** ~*n.* A ribald person. [Middle English *ribaud,* retainer of low rank, lewd person, rascal, blasphemer, from Old French *ribauld, ribaut,* from *riber,* to be wanton, from Old High German *rīban,* to be in heat, copulate, "to rub".]

rib·ald·ry (ríbb'ldri) *n., pl.* **-ries.** Ribald language or joking.

rib·and (ríbbənd) *n. Archaic.* A ribbon, especially one used as a decoration. [Middle English, from Old French *riban,* probably from a Germanic compound of BAND.]

rib·band (ríbbənd) n. A length of flexible wood or metal used to hold the ribs of a ship in place while the exterior planking or plating is being applied. [RIB + BAND (strip).]

Rib·ben·trop (ríbbən-trop), **Joachim von** (1893–1946). German politician. In 1938 Hitler made him foreign minister, and he played a major role in the negotiation of the German-Soviet non-aggression pact of 1939. He remained foreign minister until Hitler's death in 1945. He was convicted of war crimes at Nuremberg and hanged.

rib·bing (ríbbing) n. 1. Ribs collectively. 2. An arrangement of ribs, as in a boat. 3. Knitted rib. 4. *Informal.* An instance of teasing.

rib·bon (ríbbən) n. 1. A narrow strip or band of fine fabric, such as satin or velvet, finished at the edges and used for trimming or tying. 2. Anything resembling a ribbon, such as a measuring tape. 3. *Plural.* Tattered or ragged strips: *a dress torn to ribbons.* 4. An inked strip of cloth used for making the impression of typed characters, as in a typewriter. 5. A band of coloured cloth signifying an award, as of a military decoration or membership in an order. 6. *Plural. Informal.* Reins for driving horses.
~*tr.v.* **ribboned, -boning, -bons.** 1. To decorate or tie with ribbons. 2. To tear into ribbons or shreds. [Middle English *riban,* variant of RIBAND.]

ribbon development n. Land development marked by continuous building along a road leading away from a town and not having a natural social centre.

rib·bon·fish (ríbbən-fish) n., *pl.* **-fishes** or collectively **ribbonfish.** Any of several marine fishes, chiefly of the genus *Trachipterus,* having long, narrow, compressed bodies. See *oarfish.*

rib·bon·wood (ríbbən-wŏŏd) n. A New Zealand evergreen tree, *Hoheria populnea,* the timber of which is used in cabinetmaking and the bark for making cord.

ribbon worm n. A *nemertean (see).*

rib cage n. The enclosing structure formed by the ribs and the bones to which they are attached.

Ri·be·ra (ree-baír-ə), **José de,** also known as Lo Spagnoletto (1591–1652). Spanish painter. He studied in Rome (*c.* 1613–14) where he came under the influence of Caravaggio. In 1616 he settled in Naples. He painted chiefly religious subjects but also secular subjects such as *The Laughing Girl with Tambourine.*

ri·bo·fla·vin (ríbō-fláyvin) n. A crystalline orange-yellow pigment, $C_{17}H_{20}O_6N_4$, that is part of the vitamin B complex, being essential for carbohydrate metabolism. It is found in milk, leafy vegetables, fresh meat, and egg yolks, and produced synthetically. Also called "lactoflavin", "vitamin B₂", "vitamin G". [RIBO(SE) + FLAVIN.]

ri·bo·nu·cle·ase (ríbō-néw-kli-ayz, -ayss ‖ -nōō-) n. *Abbr.* **RNAase.** Any of various enzymes that promote the hydrolysis of RNA.

ri·bo·nu·cle·ic acid (ríbō-new-klée-ik, -kláy- ‖ -nōō-) n. See **RNA.** [RIBO(SE) + NUCLEIC ACID.]

ri·bose (rí-bōz, -bōss) n. A pentose sugar, $C_5H_{10}O_5$, occurring as a component of ribonucleic acid and certain coenzymes. [German *Ribon(säure),* a tetrahydroxyl acid from which ribose is obtained : *Ribon-,* arbitrary alteration of English *arabinose,* ribose : (GUM) ARAB(IC) + -IN + -OSE + *Säure,* acid.]

ribosomal RNA n. *Abbr.* **rRNA.** The RNA that forms a constituent of ribosomes.

ri·bo·some (ríbə-sōm) n. Any of numerous spherical cytoplasmic particles, consisting of RNA and protein, that are the sites of protein synthesis in the cell. [RIBO(SE) + -SOME (body).] —**ri·bo·so·mal** (-sōm'l) *adj.*

rib·wort (ríb-wurt ‖ *U.S. also* -wawrt) n. A weedy plant, *Plantago lanceolata,* having lancelike, ribbed leaves and a dense spike of small whitish flowers.

Ri·car·do (ri-kárdō), **David** (1772–1823). English political economist, one of the chief founders of the so-called classical school of economists. His most important work, *Principles of Political Economy and Taxation* (1817), supported the law of supply and demand in a free market. He also enunciated the "labour theory of value" which was taken up by Marx.

Ric·ci (réechi), **Matteo** (1552–1610). Italian Jesuit. He was sent as a missionary to China in 1582. His reports of life in China were the first knowledgeable accounts of Chinese life received by the West.

Riccio, David. See **Rizzio, David.**

rice (ríss) n. 1. A cereal grass, *Oryza sativa,* that is cultivated extensively in warm climates, and is a staple food throughout the world. 2. The starchy edible seed of this grass.
~*tr.v.* **riced, ricing, rices.** *U.S.* To sieve (food) to the consistency of rice. [Middle English *rys, ryce,* from Old French *ris,* from Italian *riso,* from Latin *orȳza,* from Greek *oruzon, oruza,* from East Iranian *vrīz-* (unattested), akin to Sanskrit *vrīhi†.*]

rice-bird (ríss-burd) n. Any of various birds that frequent rice fields, such as the Java sparrow.

rice bowl n. An area where rice is grown in abundance.

rice paper n. A thin, edible paper made chiefly from the pith of the rice-paper tree.

rice-pa·per tree (ríss-paypər) n. A shrub or small tree, *Tetrapanax papyriferum,* of eastern Asia, grown as a source of fibre for rice paper.

rice pudding n. A dessert made from rice baked in sweetened milk.

ri·cer·car (ree-chər-kár, -cher-, -chair-) n. *Music.* Also **ri·cer·ca·re** (-ay). A composition developing a basic theme, similar to a fugue.

rice weevil n. A small, destructive insect, *Sitophilus oryzae,* that infests stored grain and cereal products.

rich (rich) *adj.* **richer, richest.** 1. Possessing great wealth; owning much money, goods, or land. 2. Composed of rare or valuable materials; made with fine or elaborate craftsmanship; costly: *a rich brocade.* 3. Of great worth; valuable. 4. Elaborate or sumptuous: *a rich feast.* 5. Plentiful; abundant; ample. 6. Abundantly or copiously supplied. Used with *in* or *with: rich in tradition.* 7. Abounding in natural resources: *a rich land.* 8. Producing or yielding much; abundant: *a rich harvest.* 9. Of or designating food that contains a large or excessive proportion of tasty, fatty ingredients, such as eggs, butter, or cream: *a rich sauce.* 10. Pleasing and satisfying to the senses, owing to a quality such as fullness, mellowness, or intensity: *a rich tenor voice; a rich blue.* 11. Containing a large proportion of fuel to air. Said of a fuel mixture. 12. *Informal.* Full of amusement; satisfyingly funny: sometimes used ironically: *That's rich!* [Middle English *riche,* originally powerful, great, partly from Old French *riche,* from Frankish *ríki* (unattested), and partly from Old English *ríce.*] —**rich·ly** *adv.* —**rich·ness** n.

Rich·ard I (ríchərd), also known as Richard Coeur de Lion (Richard the Lionheart) (1157–99). King of England (1189–99), third son and successor of Henry II. He set out on the Third Crusade in 1190 and gained, by a treaty with Saladin, access for Christians to Jerusalem. He was captured by Leopold V of Austria in 1192, handed over to the Emperor Henry VI, and ransomed in 1194. He was in England in 1194, before returning to France where he was slain in a minor engagement.

Richard II (1367–1400). King of England (1377–99), son of the Black Prince and successor to his grandfather, Edward III. At the age of 14 he made a heroic appearance before the rebels taking part in the Peasants' Revolt (1381), placating them with promises of concessions which were immediately revoked. From 1386 until the end of his reign he was at odds with the baronial opposition in Parliament and his rule became increasingly authoritarian. In 1399 Richard took over the estates of his uncle John of Gaunt. John's heir, Henry Bolingbroke, was imprisoned in Pontefract Castle where he died.

Richard III (1452–85). King of England (1483–85), younger brother of Edward IV and last of the Yorkist kings. When Edward IV died in 1483, Richard seized his two sons, including the rightful heir, Edward V, and imprisoned them in the Tower of London. Richard was then crowned king. The two princes were murdered in the Tower, possibly on Richard's orders. In 1485 Richard was slain at the Battle of Bosworth Field.

Rich·ards (ríchərdz), **Sir Gordon** (1902–). British jockey. He won the jockey's championship every year from 1925 to 1953; except 1926, 1930, and 1941. He set the record of 269 victories in one season in 1947 and over his career rode 4,870 winners.

Richards, I(vor) A(rmstrong) (1893–1979). British literary critic and grammarian. In the 1920s he collaborated with Charles Ogden in the formulation of Basic English, publishing with him *The Foundations of Aesthetics* (1921) and *The Meaning of Meaning* (1923).

Rich·ard·son (ríchərd-sən), **Henry Handel,** pen name of Ethel Richardson Robertson (1870–1946). Australian novelist. She lived in England after 1903 and published her first novel, *Maurice Guest,* in 1908. Her best work is usually considered to be the trilogy of Australian life, *The Fortunes of Richard Mahony* (1930).

Richardson, Sir Ralph (David) (1902–). British stage and film actor. He made his great reputation chiefly as a character actor. He is noted for his strong characterisation in his performances of classic roles as well as in contemporary works, such as Pinter's *No Man's Land* (1975). He was knighted in 1947.

Richardson, Samuel (1689–1761). English novelist. He worked as a printer until the age of 50, when he began to write his first work, *Pamela* (1740). It was written in the form of a series of letters as were its successors, *Clarissa Harlowe* (1747–48) and *The History of Sir Charles Grandison* (1753–54).

Richardson, Tony (1928–). British film director. He established his reputation in the 1950s with a series of films in the then prevailing mood of social realism, *Look Back in Anger* (1958), *A Taste of Honey* (1961), and *The Loneliness of the Long Distance Runner* (1962). Other films which he directed include *Tom Jones* (1962).

Rich·bo·rough (rích-brə, -bərə ‖ -burrə). Site of the Roman port of Rutupiae, situated on the river Stour just north of Sandwich, Kent and now inland.

Riche·lieu (réesh-lyer, -lew; *French* -əl-yō), **Armand Jean du Plessis, Duc de** (1585–1642). French prelate and statesman, chief minister of Louis XIII, generally known as Cardinal Richelieu. He worked devotedly to strengthen the authority of the monarchy, suppressing numerous conspiracies by the nobles and directing France during the Thirty Years' War (1618–48). He founded the French Academy in 1635.

rich·en (ríchən) *tr.v.* **-ened, -ening, -ens.** *Rare.* To make rich.

rich·es (ríchiz) *pl.n.* 1. Abundant wealth. 2. Valuable or precious possessions. [Middle English *riches, richesse,* wealth (taken as a plural), from Old French, from *riche,* powerful, RICH.]

Rich·ler (ríchlər), **Mordecai** (1931–). Canadian writer. His comic novels are predominantly concerned with Jewish themes, and include *The Apprenticeship of Duddy Kravitz* (1959), *The Incomparable Atuk* (1963), and *Cocksure* (1968).

rich·ly (ríchli) *adv.* 1. In a rich way or manner. 2. In full measure; thoroughly: *richly rewarded.*

Rich·mond¹ (ríchmənd). Market town and tourist centre in North Yorkshire, England, situated on the river Swale.

Richmond². Capital of Virginia, eastern United States. Situated on the James river, it is a port exporting coal and tobacco, and it manufactures tobacco products and chemicals. Settled in 1637, it was capital of the Confederacy during the American Civil War.

Richmond-upon-Thames. Borough of southwest Greater London, England. Largely residential, it has within its boundaries Richmond Park, Kew Gardens, and Hampton Court Palace.

Rich·ter (ríkhtər), Hans (1843–1916). Hungarian conductor. He was especially famous for his performances of Wagner, and he helped Wagner to prepare the final scores of *Die Meistersinger* and the *Ring* cycle. He was conductor of the Hallé Orchestra in Manchester (1900–1911).

Richter, Svyatoslav Teofilovich (1915–). Soviet pianist, much admired for his interpretation of Schubert and Beethoven. He was not heard in the West until 1960, when he performed in Finland and the United States.

Richter scale (*also* ríktər) n. A logarithmic scale ranging from 1 to 10, used to express the magnitude of an earthquake. [After Charles F. *Richter* (born 1900), U.S. seismologist.]

Richt·ho·fen (ríkht-hōf'n), Manfred, Baron von, also known as the Red Baron (1892–1918). German pilot. During World War I he was credited with shooting down 80 enemy aircraft, making him the leading ace of the war. He was killed in action in 1918.

ri·cin (rī-sin, ríssin) n. A highly poisonous protein extracted from castor-oil beans and used as a biochemical reagent. [Latin *ricinus†*, castor-oil plant.]

ri·cin·o·le·ic acid (rissin-ō-lée-ik, rī-sin-, -óli-ik) n. An unsaturated fatty acid, $C_{18}H_{34}O_3$, prepared from castor oil and used in making soaps and in textile finishing. [Latin *ricinus*, castor-oil plant (see **ricin**) + OLEIC.]

rick¹ (rik) n. A stack of hay, straw, or similar material, especially when covered or thatched for protection from the weather.
~*tr.v.* **ricked, ricking, ricks.** To pile in ricks. [Middle English *reke*, Old English *hrēac*, akin to Old Norse *hraukr†*.]

rick² *tr.v.* **ricked, ricking, ricks.** *British.* To sprain, strain, or pull (one's back, for example).
~*n.* A sprain or similar injury. [Middle English *wricken*, from Middle Low German *wricken†*, to sprain.]

rick·ets (ríckits) n. *Used with a singular verb.* A deficiency disease resulting from a lack of vitamin D, characterised by defective bone growth, and occurring chiefly in children. Also called "rachitis". [Variant of RACHITIS.]

rick·ett·si·a (ri-két-si-ə) n., pl. **-siae** (-si-ee). Any of various microorganisms, mostly of the genus *Rickettsia*, carried as parasites by ticks, fleas, and lice. Transmitted to humans, they cause diseases such as typhus, Q fever, and trench fever. [After Howard T. *Ricketts* (1871–1910), U.S. pathologist.] —**rick·ett·si·al** *adj.*

rick·et·y (rick-əti, -i-ti) *adj.* **-ier, -iest. 1.** Likely to break or fall apart; shaky. **2.** Feeble with age; infirm: *a rickety old man.* **3.** Of, having, or resembling rickets. [From RICKETS.] —**rick·et·i·ness** n.

rick·ey (rícki) n., pl. **-eys.** A drink of soda water, lime juice, and usually gin. [20th century : origin obscure.]

rick·rack, ric·rac (rík-rak) n. A flat, narrow braid in zigzag form, used as a trimming. [Reduplication of RACK (to torture).]

rick·shaw (rík-shaw) n. A small two-wheeled oriental carriage drawn by one or two men. Also called "jinricksha". [Short for JINRICKSHA.]

ric·o·chet (ríckə-shay, -shet, -sháy, -shét) *intr.v.* **-cheted** (-shayd) or **-chetted** (-shettid), **-cheting** (-shay-ing) or **-chetting** (-shetting), **-chets.** To rebound at least once from a surface or surfaces. Used of a projectile, such as a bullet.
~*n.* An instance of such deflection. [French *ricochet†*.]

ri·cot·ta (ri-kóttə) n. An Italian cottage cheese made from the whey drained from other cheeses made with sheep's milk. [Italian, from Latin *recocta*, feminine past participle of *recoquere*, to cook again : *re-*, again + *coquere*, to cook.]

R.I.C.S. Royal Institution of Chartered Surveyors.

ric·tus (ríktəss) n. The expanse of an open mouth, a bird's beak, or similar structure. [Latin *rictus*, from the past participle of *ringī†*, to gape.] —**ric·tal** *adj.*

rid (rid) *tr.v.* **rid** or **ridded, ridding, rids.** To free from something objectionable or undesirable: *Let me rid your mind of fear.* —**get rid of.** To dispose of. [Middle English *rud(d)en, rid(d)en*, from Old Norse *rythja* (past participle *ruddr*), from Germanic *rudjan* (unattested).] —**rid·der** n.

rid·dance (rídd'nss) n. A welcome removal of or deliverance from something. —**good riddance.** Used to express relief at the removal or prospect of the removal of an unwanted person or thing. [RID + -ANCE.]

rid·den (rídd'n). Past participle of **ride.**
~*adj.* Dominated; oppressed. Usually used in combination: *disease-ridden; cliché-ridden.*

rid·dle¹ (rídd'l) *tr.v.* **-dled, -dling, -dles. 1.** To pierce with numerous holes; perforate. **2.** To put through a coarse sieve. **3.** To permeate and thereby weaken or damage: *riddled with errors.*
~*n.* A coarse sieve for separating and grading materials such as gravel: *a potato riddle.* [Middle English *rid(d)len*, to sift, from *riddil*, sieve, Old English *hriddel, hridder*.] —**rid·dler** n.

riddle² n. **1.** A question or statement requiring one to puzzle over it to answer or understand; a conundrum. **2.** Something perplexing; an enigma.
~*v.* **riddled, -dling, -dles.** —*tr.* To solve or explain (a riddle). —*intr.* **1.** To solve or propound riddles. **2.** To speak in riddles. [Middle English *redel(es), ridil*, Old English *rædelse*, from *rædan* (unattested), to READ.] —**rid·dler** n.

ride (rīd) *v.* **rode** (rōd), **ridden** (rídd'n), **riding, rides.** —*intr.* **1.** To

sit on, control, and be conveyed by an animal or a machine: *riding sidesaddle on the horse.* **2.** To be conveyed or transported, as in a vehicle, boat, or aircraft: *ride in a bus.* **3.** To travel over a surface: *This car rides well.* **4.** To lie at anchor. Used of a ship. **5.** *Literary.* To seem to be floating in space: *a star riding in the sky.* **6.** To progress effortlessly; be swept along as if by some relentless force: *rode to power on a surge of patriotism.* **7.** *Archaic.* To carry a rider or support something in a particular manner. **8.** To lie over something; overlap. Used especially of bones. **9.** To work or move from the proper place. Used with *up: Her tight skirt kept riding up.* **10.** To continue undisturbed by any action: *We let the problem ride.* —*tr.* **1.** To sit on, control, and be transported by: *ride a bike.* **2.** To be supported or carried upon. **3.** To travel over, along, or through: *ride the roads.* **4.** To rest upon by overlapping; overlie. **5.** To take part in or do by riding: *He rode his last race.* **6.** To control or dominate. **7.** To cause to ride, as by taking on one's shoulders: *riding his son on his back.* **8.** To keep (a vessel) at anchor. **9.** *U.S. Informal.* To tease or ridicule. **10.** To mount so as to copulate with. —**ride down. 1.** To catch up and overtake on horseback. **2.** To trample under horses' hooves. —**ride high.** To be elated, as from success. —**ride out.** To withstand or survive successfully. —**ride roughshod over.** To take a course of action without regard for the feelings, opinions, or welfare of.
~*n.* **1.** An excursion or journey by any means of conveyance, as on horseback, in a car, or on a boat. **2.** A path made for riding on horseback, especially through woodlands. **3.** At funfairs or similar places, any of various entertainments in which persons ride for pleasure or excitement. **4.** An experience of a specified type to which one is subjected: *The committee gave the minister a rough ride.* —**take for a ride.** *Informal.* To deceive or swindle. [Ride, rode, ridden; Middle English *riden, rad* (or *rod*), *riden*, Old English *rīdan, rād, riden* (unattested), from Germanic.]

rid·er (rídər) n. **1.** One who or that which rides; especially, one who rides horses. **2.** *Plural.* Material, such as iron plates, added to a ship's frame to strengthen it. **3.** A clause, usually having little relevance to the main issue, added to a document, such as a parliamentary bill. **4.** An amendment or addition, as to a document or statement: *The jury added a rider to the verdict.* **5.** A small weight that can slide along an arm of a chemical balance, used to make small changes to the balancing weight. **6.** *Mathematics.* A problem that can be posed arising from a theorem, especially in geometry. **7.** *Mining & Geology.* A thin seam lying over a thicker seam.

ridge (rij) n. **1.** The long, narrow upper section or crest of something: *ridge of a wave.* **2.** A long, narrow land elevation; a long hill or chain of mountains. **3.** A long, narrow, or crested part of the body: *the ridge of the nose.* **4.** The horizontal line formed by the juncture of two sloping planes; especially, the line formed by the surfaces of a roof. **5.** Any narrow raised strip, as in cloth or on ploughed land. **6.** *Meteorology.* An area of high pressure extending from the centre of an anticyclone and separating two low-pressure regions.
~*v.* **ridged, ridging, ridges.** —*tr.* To mark with, form into, or provide with ridges. —*intr.* To form into ridges. [Middle English *rigge*, back, ridge, Old English *hrycg*, from Germanic.] —**ridg·y** *adj.*

ridge·back (ríj-bak) n. A dog, a **Rhodesian ridgeback** (see).

ridge·ling, ridg·ling (ríjling) n. In veterinary medicine, a male animal, such as a horse, with one or two undescended testicles. Also called "rig". [Obsolete *ridgel*, probably "(animal) with testes near the back", from RIDGE.]

ridge·pole (ríj-pōl) n. **1.** A horizontal beam at the ridge of a roof, to which the rafters are attached. **2.** The horizontal pole at the top of a tent. Also called "ridge beam", "ridge piece".

ridge·way (ríj-way) n. *British.* A road, track, or other path along the top of a hill or range of hills.

rid·i·cule (ríddi-kewl) n. **1.** Words or actions intended to evoke contemptuous laughter at or feelings towards a person or thing. **2.** Subjection to such a contemptuous attitude.
~*tr.v.* **ridiculed, -culing, -cules.** To deride, mock, or make fun of. [French *ridicule*, from Latin *rīdiculum*, joke, jest, from *rīdiculus*, laughable, RIDICULOUS.] —**rid·i·cul·er** n.

Synonyms: ridicule, mock, taunt, twit, deride, gibe.

ri·dic·u·lous (ri-díckewlss, rə-) *adj.* Deserving or inspiring ridicule; absurd or preposterous; silly or laughable. See Synonyms at **foolish.** [Latin *rīdiculōsus, rīdiculus*, laughable, from *rīdēre†*, to laugh.] —**ri·dic·u·lous·ly** *adv.* —**ri·dic·u·lous·ness** n.

rid·ing¹ (rīding) n. The action or skill of one who rides on horseback.
~*adj.* Pertaining to, used in, or worn for riding: *a riding school; riding boots.*

riding² n. **1.** Formerly, one of the three administrative divisions of Yorkshire, England: North Riding, East Riding, and West Riding. **2.** Any similar administrative division; specifically, in Canada, a parliamentary constituency. [Middle English *riding, rithing* (with loss of the initial *th-* due to preceding *-t* in *east, west*), Old English *thrithing* (unattested), "thirding", from Old Norse *thrithjungr*, third part, from *thrithi*, third.]

riding habit n. The costume worn by a horsewomen, especially in former times.

riding lamp n. A lamp or light hung on a boat, ship, or other vessel, that is at anchor.

Rid·ley (rídli), Nicholas (c. 1500–55). English Protestant churchman and martyr. He was appointed Bishop of London in 1550 and helped to prepare the Edwardian prayer books. Under the Catholic

rickshaw *A traditional hand-pulled rickshaw in Calcutta, India. Modern rickshaws are often modified tricycles, which are pedalled instead of pulled.*

Mary I he was tried as a heretic and burnt at Oxford with Latimer.

Ri·dol·fi (ri-dólfi), **Roberto** (1531–1612). Florentine banker who settled in London (1555) and conspired against Elizabeth I. A Catholic and supporter of Mary Queen of Scots, he helped to plan a rebellion (1570–71) backed by Spain. The plot was discovered while Ridolfi was organising support abroad, but his fellow-conspirator, the Duke of Norfolk, was exposed and executed.

Rie·beeck (rée-bayk), **Jan van** (1619–77). Dutch administrator. Trained as a doctor, he joined the Dutch East India Company and in 1652 headed an expedition which founded Cape Town.

Rie·fen·stahl (rééf'n-shtaal), **Leni** (1902–). German film director and photographer. In her youth she made pro-Nazi films, including *Triumph of the Will* (1934) and *The Olympic Games* (1936), covering the Berlin Olympics. Her later works include photographic studies of Sudanese peoples, among them *Last of the Nuba* (1973).

ri·el (ree-él) *n.* The basic monetary unit of Kampuchea, divided into 100 sen.

Rie·mann (rée-man), **Georg Friedrich Bernhard** (1826–66). German mathematician, a pioneer of non-Euclidean geometry. From 1851 he developed an approach, now known as Riemannian geometry, by which a generalised space was studied without a prior framework for calculating distances between points. His work influenced Einstein's theory of relativity.

Rie·mann·i·an geometry (ree-mánni-ən) *n.* A non-Euclidean geometry based on the postulate that there are no parallel lines. Also called "elliptic geometry". [After G. F. B. RIEMANN.]

Ries·ling (reéss-ling, réez-) *n.* **1.** A sweet or dry white wine with a light, flowery bouquet produced especially in Germany and Alsace. **2.** The type of grape used in the making of this wine. [German, earlier *Rüssling*†.]

rif·amp·i·cin (rif-ámpi-sin) *n.* An antibiotic active against various infections, used chiefly to treat tuberculosis. [From *rifamycin*, earlier *rifomycin* (*r*eplication *i*nhibiting *f*ungus + -MYCIN), its source + *ampicillin* (to which it is comparable in efficacy).]

rife (rīf) *adj.* **rifer, rifest. 1.** Frequently or commonly happening or appearing; widespread; prevalent. **2.** Abundant; numerous. **3.** Abounding; full. Used with *with*: *That department is rife with incompetents.* —See Synonyms at **prevailing.** [Middle English *rif, ryfe,* Old English *rȳfe,* probably from Old Norse *rífr,* acceptable.]

riff (rif) *n.* In jazz and rock music, a short rhythmic phrase repeated so as to provide a rhythmic impulse. [20th century: origin obscure.]

Riff (rif) *n.* A member of a Berber people of the Rif country in northern Morocco, Africa.

rif·fle (ríff'l) *n.* **1.** The act of shuffling cards. **2.** *Mining.* **a.** The sectional stone or wood bottom lining of a sluice, arranged to trap mineral, especially gold, particles. **b.** A groove or block in such a lining. **3.** *U.S.* **a.** A rocky shoal or sandbar lying just below the surface of a waterway. **b.** A stretch of choppy water caused by such such a shoal or sandbar; a rapid.
~*v.* **riffled, -fling, -fles.** —*tr.* **1.** To shuffle (playing cards) by holding part of a pack in each hand and raising up the edges before releasing them to fall alternately in one stack. **2.** To thumb through (the pages of a book, for example). —*intr.* **1.** To shuffle cards. **2.** To thumb through pages. **3.** To become choppy. [Perhaps blend of RUFFLE (disturb) and RIPPLE.]

rif·fler (rífflər) *n.* A file with curved ends suitable for scraping. [Old French *rifloir,* from *rifler*†, to scratch, file.]

riff·raff (rif-raf) *n.* Worthless, uncultured, or disreputable persons. Used derogatorily. [Middle English *riffe raffe, rif and raf,* one and all, from Old French *rif et raf* : *rifler,* to file (see **riffler**) + *raffe,* a sweeping, from Middle High German *raffen,* to snatch (see **raffle**).]

ri·fle[1] (rīf'l) *n.* **1.** A firearm with a rifled bore designed to be fired from the shoulder. **2.** An artillery piece or naval gun that has been rifled. **3.** *Plural.* Troops armed with rifles.
~*tr.v.* **rifled, -fling, -fles.** To cut spiral grooves within (a gun barrel, for example) to improve the accuracy of the projectile's flight. [Originally "spiral groove", from *rifle,* to cut spiral grooves, from Old French *rifler,* to file. See **riffler.**]

rifle[2] *tr.v.* **-fled, -fling, -fles. 1. a.** To ransack with intent to steal. **b.** To plunder; pillage. **2.** To rob; strip bare: *rifle a safe.* [Middle English *riflen,* from Old French *rifler,* to scratch, file, plunder. See **riffler.**] —**ri·fler** *n.*

ri·fle·bird (rīf'l-burd) *n.* Any of several birds of paradise of the genus *Ptiloris,* of Australia and New Guinea. [From its cry.]

ri·fle·man (rīf'l-mən, -man) *n., pl.* **-men** (-mən, -men). **1.** One trained or expert in firing a rifle; especially a private in a rifle regiment of the British Army. **2.** A New Zealand wren, *Acanthisitta chloris.*

rifle range *n.* An area set aside for shooting practice at targets, using rifles.

ri·fle·ry (rīf'l-ri) *n.* **1.** The art and practice of marksmanship.

ri·fling (rīfling) *n.* Spiral grooves cut inside a gun barrel.

rift[1] (rift) *n.* **1.** A narrow fissure, cleft, or chink, as in rock. **2.** A break in friendly relations.
~*v.* **rifted, rifting, rifts.** —*intr.* To split open; burst; break. —*tr.* To cause to split open or break. [Middle English *rift, ryft,* from Scandinavian, akin to Danish *rift,* breach.]

rift[2] *n. U.S.* **1.** A shallow area in a waterway. **2.** The backwash of a wave that has broken upon a beach. [Probably variant of *riff,* dialectal variant of REEF.]

rift valley *n.* A long, narrow depression in the earth's surface formed when the land sinks between two fairly parallel faults.

rig[1] (rig) *tr.v.* **rigged, rigging, rigs. 1.** To fit out or provide (an aircraft, for example) with equipment. **2. a.** To equip (a ship) with sails, shrouds, and yards. **b.** To fit (sails, shrouds, and the like) to masts and yards. **3.** *Informal.* To dress, clothe, or adorn: *rigged out in her best dress.* **4.** To make, construct, or erect, often in haste or in a makeshift manner. Often used with *up.* **5.** To manipulate dishonestly for personal gain: *rig a competition.*
~*n.* **1.** The arrangement of masts, spars, and sails on a sailing vessel: *a square rig.* **2. a.** Any special equipment or gear for a particular purpose. **b.** A citizens' band receiver and transmitter. **3.** The installation and apparatus used for drilling oil and gas wells. **4.** *Slang.* A lorry. **5.** *U.S.* A vehicle with one or more horses harnessed to it. [Middle English *riggen,* probably from Scandinavian, akin to Norwegian *rigga.*]

rig[2] *n.* A **ridgeling** *(see).*

Ri·ga (réegə, *formerly also* rīgə). City and port in western U.S.S.R. Situated on the Baltic coast on the Gulf of Riga, it is capital of the Latvian S.S.R. A member of the Hanseatic League from 1282, it passed to Poland (1581), Sweden (1621), and Russia (1710), and was capital of the independent state of Latvia (1919–40).

rig·a·doon (ríggə-dóōn) *n.* **1.** A lively jumping quickstep for one couple. **2.** Music for this dance, usually in rapid duple time. [French *rigaudon, rigodon,* said to have been invented by a famous dancing master of Marseille named *Rigaud.*]

rigamarole. Variant of **rigmarole.**

rig·a·to·ni (rìggə-tōni) *n.* Large, ribbed, macaroni tubes, slightly curved and cut into short lengths. [Italian, plural of *rigato,* past participle of *rigare,* to draw a line, corrugate, from *riga,* line, from Germanic.]

Ri·gel (rī-jəl, -g'l) *n.* A bright double star in the constellation Orion. [Arabic *rijl,* (Orion's) foot.]

rig·ger[1] (ríggər) *n.* **1.** One who rigs, specifically: **a.** One who fits rigging to sailing ships. **b.** One who assembles or aligns aircraft parts or parachutes. **c.** One who works with hoisting tackle, cranes, pulleys, and scaffolds. **d.** One who works on an oil rig.

rigger[2] *n.* A metal bracket attached to the side of a racing or rowing boat that supports a rowlock. Also called "outrigger".

rig·ging (rígging) *n.* **1.** The system of ropes, chains, and tackle used to support and control the masts, sails, and yards of a sailing vessel. **2.** Any system of gear for a specific task.

right (rīt) *adj.* **righter, rightest.** *Abbr.* **R., r., rt. 1.** In accordance with or conformable to justice, law, morality, or similar principle: *right action.* **2.** In accordance with fact, reason, or truth; correct: *the right answer.* **3.** Fitting, proper, or appropriate: *the right one for the job.* **4.** Most favourable, desirable, or convenient: *the right time to act.* **5.** In a satisfactory state or condition; in good order: *I'll put it right in a moment.* **6.** Mentally sound or normal; sane: *in one's right mind.* **7.** Physically normal or healthy; well: *Are you feeling quite right?* **8.** Intended to be worn facing outwards or towards an observer: *the right side of cloth.* **9. a.** *Archaic.* Genuine; not spurious. **b.** *Informal.* Real; thorough: *I felt a right fool.* **10. a.** Designating, belonging to, or located on the side of the body to the east when the subject is facing north. **b.** Designating or located on the corresponding side of anything that can be considered to have a front: *the bird's right wing.* **c.** Designating or located on that side of anything which an observer directly facing it perceives to be on or towards his right side. **11.** *Often capital* **R.** Of or tending towards the political Right. **12.** In geometry: **a.** Formed by or in reference to a line or plane that is perpendicular to another line or plane. **b.** Having the axis perpendicular to the base. Said of solids: *right cone.* **13.** *Archaic.* Straight; uncurved; direct: *a right line.*
~*n.* **1.** That which is just, morally good, legal, proper, or fitting: *Two wrongs don't make a right.* **2. a.** The right side or direction: *My house is on the right.* **b.** That which is on or towards the right side or direction. **3.** *Often capital* **R. a.** The individuals and groups pursuing generally conservative or reactionary political policies, in opposition to broadly egalitarian or socialist policies. **b.** Support for such policies measured in terms of an imaginary political continuum: *moving further to the right.* **4.** In boxing, the right hand or a blow given by the right hand. **5.** That which is due to anyone by law, tradition, or nature: *She was given her rights.* **6.** A just or legal claim or title. **7.** *Finance.* **a.** A shareholder's privilege of buying additional shares in a company at a special price, usually at par or at a price below the current market value. **b.** *Often plural.* A privilege of subscribing for a particular stock or bond. —**by right** or **rights.** Justly; properly. —**in (one's) own right.** By virtue of one's own position, efforts, or achievements. —**to rights.** In a satisfactory or orderly condition: *set the place to rights.*
~*adv.* **1.** In a straight line; directly; straight. Often used with *to, into,* or *through*: *He went right to the heart of the matter.* **2.** Properly; suitably; conveniently; well: *The suit doesn't fit right.* **3.** Exactly; just: *It happened right over there.* **4.** Immediately: *She will be right down.* **5.** Completely; thoroughly; quite: *The wind blew right through him.* **6.** According to law, morality, or justice. **7.** Accurately; correctly. **8.** On or towards the right side or direction. **9. a.** *Archaic.* Extremely: *He answered right well.* **b.** *Regional.* Very; thoroughly: *had a right good time.* **10.** Very. Used in certain titles: *the Right Reverend; Right Honourable.* —**right, left, and centre.** From or on every side.
~*v.* **righted, righting, rights.** —*tr.* **1.** To put in or restore to an upright or proper position: *They righted their boat.* **2.** To put in order or set right; correct. **3.** To make reparation or amends for; redress: *right a wrong.* —*intr.* To regain an upright position.
~*interj.* Used to indicate assent, agreement, or comprehension.

PRONUNCIATION KEY

a, trap; aa, father; ai, fair;
ar, star; aw, lawn; ay, play;
b, bb, stab; rubber;
ch, church; ck, ticket;
d, dd, dead; ladder; e, dress;
ee, bee; er, defer; ew, few;
ewr, pure; ə, about;
ər, letter; f, ff, fife; differ;
g, gg, giggle; h, hat; i, kit;
ī, price; īr, fire; j, judge;
k, kick; l, ll, let; 'l, needle;
m, mm, man; n, nn, no;
'n, sudden; ng, thing; o, lot;
ō, no; ŏŏ, foot; ōō, shoe;
oor, poor; ow, cow;
owr, hour; oy, boy;
p, pp, pepper; r, rr, red;
s, ss, sauce; sh, ship;
t, tt, totter; th, thick; th, this;
smooth; u, cut; ur, turn;
v, vv, valve; w, wet; y, yes;
z, zz, zebra; zh, vision;
pleasure

IN FOREIGN WORDS:

aN, oN, Saint-Saëns;
hl, Llanelli; Hluhluwe;
kh, loch; lough; Khaled

STRESS MARK:

ín-sīt, insight; in-sít, incite

—**right on.** *Chiefly U.S. Slang.* Used to express enthusiastic approval or agreement. [Middle English *riht, right,* Old English *riht.*]
—**right-er** *n.* —**right-ness** *n.*

Synonyms: *right, privilege, prerogative, perk, franchise, birthright, title.*

right about turn *n.* See **about-turn.**

right angle *n.* An angle formed by the perpendicular intersection of two straight lines; an angle of 90 degrees. —**at right angles.** Forming such an angle.

right-an-gled (rīt-ang-gl'd, -áng-) *adj.* Forming or containing one or more right angles: *a right-angled triangle.*

right ascension *n. Abbr.* **R.A.** The angular distance of a celestial body or point on the celestial sphere, measured eastwards from the vernal equinox along the celestial equator to the hour circle of the body or point, and expressed in degrees or in hours.

right away *adv.* Without hesitation; immediately.

right-eous (rīt-yəss, rīchəss) *adj.* 1. Meeting accepted standards of what is right and just; morally right; virtuous. 2. Having justification or good reason: *righteous anger.* See Synonyms at **moral.** [Middle English *rightwise, ryghtuous,* Old English *rihtwīs : riht,* RIGHT + *wīs,* WISE (way).] —**right-eous-ly** *adv.* —**right-eous-ness** *n.*

right-ful (rīt-f'l) *adj.* 1. Right or proper; just. 2. Having a just or proper claim: *Return this dog to its rightful owner.* 3. Held or owned by just or proper claim: *This dog is my rightful property.* —**right-ful-ly** *adv.* —**right-ful-ness** *n.*

right-hand (rīt-hánd) *adj.* 1. Of or located on the right: *a right-hand drive car.* 2. Directed towards the right side: *a right-hand turn.* 3. Of, for, or done by the right hand. —**righthand-er** *n.*

right-hand-ed (rīt-hándid) *adj.* 1. Using the right hand more easily or skilfully than the left. 2. Done with the right hand. 3. Made to be used by the right hand. 4. Turning or spiralling from left to right; clockwise. —**right-hand-ed-ness** *n.*

right-hand man *n.* A subordinate who is a close associate of his superior.

right-ism (rītiz'm) *n. Sometimes capital* **R.** Reactionary or conservative political activities or ideas. —**right-ist** *adj. & n.*

right-ly (rītli) *adv.* 1. With correctness or certainty: *I can't rightly say when I'll come.* 2. **a.** Uprightly; with honesty. **b.** Justifiably: *She was rightly angered.* 3. Properly; suitably.

right-mind-ed (rīt-mīndid) *adj.* Having principles and views based on what is considered to be right. —**right-mind-ed-ness** *n.*

right-o (rī-tó) *interj. British Informal.* Used to express assent. [RIGHT + O.]

right of asylum *n.* The right of receiving **asylum** *(see).*

right of search *n. Law.* The right of a warring nation to stop any neutral vessel on the high seas and search it for contraband.

right of way *n.* 1. *Law.* **a.** The right to pass over property owned by another party. **b.** The path or thoroughfare on which such passage is made. 2. *U.S.* The strip of land over which facilities such as motorways, railways, or power lines are built. 3. The customary or legal right of a person, vessel, or vehicle to pass in front of another.

rights issue *n.* An offer of new shares by a company to its shareholders at a preferential price.

right whale *n.* Any of several whalebone whales of the Balaenidae family, characterised by a large head and absence of a dorsal fin.

right wing *n.* 1. The political right. 2. A division holding relatively conservative views within a larger political group. —**right-wing** (rīt-wíng) *adj.* —**right-wing-er** *n.*

rig-id (ríjid) *adj.* 1. Not bending; stiff; inflexible. 2. Not moving; fixed. 3. Rigorous; harsh; severe. 4. Scrupulously strict; undeviating: *a rigid point of view.* —See Synonyms at **stiff.** [French *rigide,* from Latin *rigidus,* from *rigēre,* to be stiff.] —**rig-id-ly** *adv.* —**rig-id-ness** *n.*

ri-gid-i-ty (ri-jíddəti) *n., pl.* -**ties.** 1. The state or quality of being rigid; stiffness; inflexibility. 2. An instance of being rigid.

rigidity modulus *n. Symbol* ζ *Physics & Engineering.* A modulus of elasticity measuring the response of a material to torsion or other shear, given by the ratio of the shear stress to the shear strain. Also called "shear modulus".

rig-ma-role (ríg-mə-rōl) *n.* Also **rig-a-ma-role** (ríggə-). 1. Confused, rambling, or incoherent speech or writing; nonsense. 2. A complicated and petty set of procedures. [Alteration of obsolete *ragman roll,* list, catalogue (in Middle English referring to a written roll used in a game of chance), of obscure origin.]

rig-or (ríggər, rī-gawr, -gər) *n.* 1. *Medicine.* An attack of shivering or trembling with a sensation of coldness, which marks the start of a fever. 2. *Physiology.* A state of rigidity in living tissues or organs, as caused by shock, that prevents response to stimuli. 3. *U.S.* Variant of **rigour.** [Middle English, from Latin *rigor,* stiffness, severity, from *rigēre,* to be stiff.]

rig-or-ism (rígga-riz'm) *n.* Severity or strictness in conduct, judgment, or practice; especially, in Roman Catholic theology, the stance that the rigorous or strict course is to be preferred in doubtful matters of conscience. —**rig-or-ist** *n.* —**rig-or-is-tic** (-rístik) *adj.*

rigor mor-tis (mórtiss) *n.* Muscular stiffening following death, due to chemical change in the tissues. [Latin, "the stiffness of death".]

rig-or-ous (ríggərəss) *adj.* 1. Characterised by or acting with rigour; rigid and severe. 2. Full of rigours; trying; harsh: *a rigorous climate.* 3. Demanding or characterised by strict accuracy or observance of standards: *rigorous tests.* —See Synonyms at **burdensome.** —**rig-or-ous-ly** *adv.* —**rig-or-ous-ness** *n.*

rig-our, *U.S.* **rig-or** (ríggər) *n.* 1. Strictness or severity, as in temperament, action, or judgment. 2. A harsh or trying circumstance;

a hardship: *the rigours of winter.* 3. Harshness or austerity in living, especially as part of religious observance. [Middle English, from Old French, from Latin *rigor,* from *rigēre,* to be stiff.]

Rig-Ve-da (ríg-váydə || -véedə) *n.* The most ancient collection of Hindu sacred verses. [Sanskrit *ṛigveda : ṛic* (stem *ṛig-),* "praise", hymn + *veda,* "knowledge", sacred writing, Veda.]

Ri-je-ka (ree-yécka). *Italian.* **Fiu-me** (féw-may). Yugoslavia's largest port, situated in the northwest of the country. An Italian force under Gabriele D'Annunzio seized it from the Hungarians in 1919, and it was formally awarded to Italy by a treaty of 1924. In 1947 it was transferred to Yugoslavia.

rijs-ta-fel (ríss-taaf'l) *n.* A Dutch-Indonesian meal of rice served with piquant side dishes of meat and vegetables.

Riks-mål (réeks-mawl) *n.* **Bokmål** *(see).*

rile (rīl) *tr.v.* **riled, riling, riles.** 1. To vex; anger; irritate. 2. *U.S.* To stir up (liquid). [Variant of ROIL.]

Ri-ley (rīli). *British.* —**lead** or **live the life of Riley.** *Informal.* To lead a life of pleasure and easy enjoyment. [20th century : the reason for the choice of the name is unknown.]

Riley, Bridget (Louise) (1931–). British painter, a leading exponent of op art. Working from predetermined mathematical grids, she produced undulating optical patterns of lines and squares, usually in black and white. Her most characteristic work was done in the early 1960s, and includes *Fall* (1963).

Ril-ke (rílkə), **Rainer Maria** (1875–1926). Austrian poet, born in Prague. His verse is marked by a strain of mystic lyricism, his collections including *The Book of Hours* (1905), *Sonnets to Orpheus,* (1923), and *The Duino Elegies* (1923).

rill (ril) *n.* Also **rille** (for sense 2). 1. A small brook; a rivulet. 2. Any of various long, narrow, straight depressions on the Moon's surface. [Dutch *ril* or Low German *rille.*]

rill-et (ríllit) *n.* A small rill.

rim (rim) *n.* 1. The border, edge, or margin of an object, especially one that is circular. 2. The circular outer part of a wheel farthest from the axle; specifically, the circular metal structure around which a tyre is fitted. —See Synonyms at **border.**
~*tr.v.* **rimmed, rimming, rims.** 1. To furnish with a rim; put a rim around; border. 2. *Sports.* To roll round the rim of (a hole, basket, or cup) without falling in. Used of a ball. [Middle English *rime, rym,* Old English *rima,* from Germanic *rimō* (unattested).]

Rim-baud (rámbō, *French* raN-bṓ), **(Jean) Arthur** (1854–91). French poet. His stormy relationship with Verlaine is alluded to in the prose poem *Une Saison en Enfer* (1873). Rimbaud gave up writing at 19 and lived an adventurous life in Europe, the Near East, and North Africa, dying in Marseille at the age of 37. A collection of his poems, *Les Illuminations* (1886), was published by Verlaine and strongly influenced the Symbolist movement.

rime¹ (rīm) *n.* Granular ice formed from supercooled fog droplets accumulating on the windward side of trees and other objects.
~*tr.v.* **rimed, riming, rimes.** To cover with or as if with rime. [Middle English *rim,* Old English *hrīma,* from Germanic *hrīmaz* (unattested), hoarfrost.] —**rim-y** *adj.*

rime² Variant of **rhyme.**

rime riche (réem réesh) *n., pl.* **rimes riches** (*pronounced as singular*). Rhyme using words or parts of words that are pronounced identically but have different meanings, for example, *write-right* or *portdeport.* [French, "rich rhyme".]

Ri-mi-ni (rímmini, réemini). Popular Adriatic resort in Emilia-Romagna, Italy. It has many Roman and medieval remains.

ri-mose (rī-mṓss, -mōz) *adj.* Full of chinks, cracks, or crevices. [Latin *rīmōsus,* from *rīma,* cleft, crevice, fissure.] —**ri-mose-ly** *adv.* —**ri-mos-i-ty** (rī-móssəti) *n.*

Rim-sky-Kor-sa-kov (rímski kór-sə-kof, *Russian* -sə-kəf), **Nikolai Andreyevich** (1844–1908). Russian composer. His music often incorporates Russian folk themes; his many operas include *The Snow Maiden* (1881), and he is especially remembered for his orchestral piece *Scheherezade* (1888).

ri-mu (réemōō) *n.* A tree, the **red pine** *(see).* [Maori.]

rind (rīnd) *n.* A tough outer covering, such as bark, the skin of some fruits, or the surface layer on cheese or bacon. [Middle English *rinde,* Old English *rind(e).*]

rin-der-pest (ríndər-pest) *n.* An acute, contagious virus disease, chiefly of cattle, characterised by ulceration of the intestinal tract. Also called "cattle plague". [German *Rinderpest : Rinder,* plural of *Rind,* ox, cow, from Old High German *(h)rind* + *Pest,* pestilence, plague, from Latin *pestis,* PEST.]

rin-for-zan-do (rín-fawrt-sán-dō, réen- || *U.S.* -sáan-) *adv. Music.* With a sudden increase of emphasis. Used as a direction. [Italian, present participle of *rinforzare,* to reinforce : *ri-,* from Latin *re-,* again + *inforzare,* from Old French *enforcier,* to ENFORCE.]

ring¹ (ring) *n.* 1. Any circular object, form, or arrangement with an empty circular centre: *blew smoke rings; a ring of bystanders.* 2. A small circular band, generally made of precious metal, often set with jewels, and worn on a finger: *a wedding ring.* 3. Any circular band used for carrying, holding, or containing something: *a napkin ring.* 4. An electric element, gas burner, or the like, used as a source of heat, especially for cooking. 5. A circular movement or course, as in dancing. 6. An enclosed, usually circular area in which exhibitions, sports, or contests take place: *a circus ring.* 7. **a.** A rectangular arena set off by stakes and ropes, in which boxing or wrestling contests are held. **b.** The sport of boxing. Preceded by *the.* 8. **a.** An enclosed area in which bets are placed at a racecourse. **b.** Bookmakers collectively. 9. **a.** An exclusive group of persons acting privately or illegally to advance their own interests, as in business or politics. **b.** A group of dealers illegally agreeing not to bid against each other at an auction, so as to achieve a lower sale price for a lot which is then reauctioned amongst themselves. **10. a.** A circular strip of bark removed from a tree trunk or branch to inhibit or stop growth. **b.** *Botany.* An **annual ring** *(see).* **11.** A field of contenders in a contest: *an unknown candidate entering the ring.* **12.** In geometry, the planar area between two concentric circles; an annulus. **13.** Any of the turns comprising a spiral or helix. **14.** *Chemistry.* A group of atoms chemically bound in a manner graphically representable as a circular form. Also called "closed chain". **—run rings round.** *Informal.* To show far greater skill than.

~*v.* **ringed, ringing, rings.** *—tr.* **1.** To surround with a ring; encircle. **2.** To form into a ring or rings, as by cutting. **3.** To ornament or supply with a ring or rings. **4.** To remove a circular strip of bark around the circumference of (a tree trunk or branch) in order to kill it or retard its growth; ring-bark. **5.** To put a ring in the nose of (a pig, bull, or other animal). **6.** To hem in (cattle or other animals) by riding in a circle around them. **7.** To toss a ring over (a peg) in a game. **8.** To put a ring round the leg of (a bird) for subsequent identification. *—intr.* **1.** To form a ring or rings. **2.** To move, run, or fly in a spiral or circular course. [Middle English *ring,* Old English *hring,* from Germanic.]

ring² *v.* **rang** (rang) or *nonstandard* **rung** (rung), **rung, ringing, rings.** *—intr.* **1.** To give forth a clear, resonant sound when caused to vibrate. **2.** To cause a bell or bells to sound. **3. a.** To sound a bell in order to summon someone. **b.** To make a telephone call: *I'll ring later.* **4.** To have a sound or character suggestive of a specified quality: *a perception that rings true.* **5.** To be filled with sound; resound. **6.** To persist vividly in the mind: *his plea still ringing in my ear.* **7.** To hear a persistent humming or buzzing: *ears ringing from the blast.* *—tr.* **1.** To cause (a bell, chimes, or the like) to ring. **2.** To produce (a sound) by or as if by ringing. **3. a.** To announce, proclaim, or signal by or as if by ringing. **b.** To summon or usher in in this way. Used with *in* or *out*: *ring in the new year.* **4.** To telephone (someone). Often used with *up.* **5.** To test (a coin, for example) for quality by the sound it produces when struck against something. **—ring back.** To return a telephone call or make another call later on. **—ring off.** To end a telephone call. **—ring up.** **1.** To make a telephone call. **2.** To record (a price) on a cash register.

~*n.* **1.** The sound created by a bell or other sonorous, vibrating object. **2.** Any loud sound, especially one that is repeated or continued. **3.** A telephone call. **4.** A suggestion of a particular quality: *Her offer has a suspicious ring.* **5.** A set of bells. **6.** An act or instance of sounding a bell. [Middle English *ringen,* Old English *hringan.* Rang, rung; Middle English *rang, rungen,* analogous formations to verbs such as SING.]

ring-bark (ríng-baark) *tr.v.* **-barked, -barking, -barks.** To ring (a tree trunk or branch).

ring binder *n.* A booklike file with two or more cicular clasps inside the spine that can be opened to allow loose leaves to be inserted.

ring·bolt (ríng-bōlt || -bolt) *n.* A bolt having a ring fitted through an eye at its head.

ring·bone (ríng-bōn) *n.* A bony growth on the fetlock, pastern, or coffin bone of a horse's foot, usually causing lameness. [It tends to spread around a horse's foot like a ring.]

ring·dove (ríng-duv) *n.* **1.** An Old World pigeon, *Streptopelia risoria,* having black markings forming a half circle on the neck. Also called "Barbary dove". **2.** The **wood pigeon** *(see).*

ringed (ríngd) *adj.* **1.** Wearing a ring or rings. **2.** Encircled or surrounded by bands or rings. **3.** Having ringlike markings.

rin·gent (rínjənt) *adj. Biology.* Having gaping liplike parts, as the corolla of some flowers or the shells of certain bivalves do. [Latin *ringēns* (stem *ringent-*), present participle of *ringī,* to open wide the mouth, gape. See **rictus.**]

ring·er¹ (ríng-ər) *n.* **1.** One that rings. **2.** A horseshoe or quoit thrown so that it encircles the peg.

ringer² *n.* **1.** One that sounds a bell or chime. **2.** *Informal.* A person who bears a striking resemblance to another. **3.** *U.S. Slang.* A contestant entered dishonestly into a competition.

Ring·er's solution (ríngərz) *n.* A solution of the chlorides of sodium, potassium, and calcium, used to maintain living tissues and organs *in vitro* and to treat dehydration. [After Sydney *Ringer* (died 1910), British physician.]

ring fence *n.* A fence that completely surrounds a property.

ring finger *n.* The fourth finger of the hand, especially the left hand, as counted from the thumb.

ring·git (ríng-git) *n.* The basic monetary unit of Malaysia, divided into 100 sen.

ring·hals (ríng-halss, ríngk-, -alss) *n., pl.* **ringhals.** Also **rink·hals** (ríngk-). An African snake, *Haemachates haemachatus,* that spits venom. Also called "spitting cobra", "spitting snake". [Afrikaans *ringhals, rinkals,* "ring-necked" : *ring,* ring, circle, from Middle Dutch *rinc* + *hals,* neck, from Middle Dutch.]

ring·lead·er (ríng-leedər) *n.* A person who leads others, especially in unlawful or improper activities.

ring·let (ríng-lət, -lit) *n.* **1.** A spirally curled lock of hair. **2.** A small circle or ring. **3.** Any of various butterflies of the family Satyridae having brownish wings marked with white rings. **—ring·let·ed** *adj.*

ring main *n.* A mains electrical circuit in a building, as in which the outlet sockets are connected in a single closed ring to the mains supply.

ring·mas·ter (ríng-maastər || -mastər) *n.* A person in charge of the performances in a circus ring.

Ring Nebula *n.* A planetary nebula in the constellation Lyra. [From its resemblance to a smoke ring.]

ring-necked pheasant (ríng-nekt) *n.* A widely distributed bird, *Phasianus colchicus,* native to the Old World, the male of which has brightly coloured plumage and a white ring around the neck.

ring ousel *n.* A European thrush, *Turdus torquatus,* of mountainous regions, the male of which is black with a white neck band.

ring-pull (ríng-pōōl) *n.* A **tab** *(see),* especially on a canned drink.

ring road *n.* A road that encircles a town or city, used as a bypass for motorists. Also called "orbital".

ring·side (ríng-sīd) *n.* **1.** The area or seats immediately outside an arena or ring, as at a boxing match. **2.** Any place providing a close view of a spectacle. Also used adjectivally: *ringside seats.*

ring·tail (ríng-tayl) *n.* **1.** An animal with ringlike markings on its tail; especially, the **cacomistle** *(see).* Also called "ring-tailed cat". **2.** Any of various Australian phalangers with prehensile tails.

ring-tailed (ríng-tayld) *adj.* **1.** Having a tail with ringlike markings. **2.** Having a tail that curls to form a ring.

ring·worm (ríng-wurm) *n.* Any of a number of contagious skin diseases caused by several related fungi, and characterised by ring-shaped, scaly, itching patches on the skin. Also called "tinea".

rink (ringk) *n.* **1.** An area surfaced with smooth ice for skating, hockey, or curling. **2.** A smooth floor suited for roller-skating. **3.** A building that houses a surface prepared for skating. **4.** A section of a bowling green large enough for play. **5.** A team of players in quoits, bowling, or curling. [Middle English (Scottish) *rinc,* jousting area, perhaps from Old French *renc, ranc,* row, range, RANK.]

rinkhals. Variant of **ringhals.**

rinse (rinss) *tr.v.* **rinsed, rinsing, rinses. 1.** To wash lightly with water. **2.** To remove (soap, dirt, or impurities) from clothing or hair, for example, by rinsing in clean water.

~*n.* **1.** The act or an instance of rinsing. **2.** The water or other solution used in this process. **3. a.** A cosmetic solution used in conditioning or tinting the hair. **b.** A hairstyle treated with such a solution. [Middle English *ryncen,* from Old French *rincer, raincier*†.] **—rins·er** *n.*

Ri·o de Ja·nei·ro (réē-ō də jə-néer-ō, day; *Portuguese* réē-ōō di zhə-náy-rōō). Also **Rio.** Chief seaport and former capital of Brazil, lying on Guanabara Bay in the southeast of the country. Brazil's second largest city, it is backed by towering mountains, the most spectacular of which are Sugar Loaf Mountain and Corvocado peak, which is surmounted by a colossal statue of Christ. A tourist centre, it has magnificent beaches, including the famous Copacabana. It is also a cultural, financial, commercial, manufacturing, and transport centre.

Ri·o Gran·de (réē-ō grándi, rī-ō gránd). Also **Río Bravo (del Norte).** River in the southern United States. Rising in the San Juan Mountains of southwestern Colorado, it flows 3 035 kilometres (1,885 miles) south, then southeast, to the Gulf of Mexico. For much of its length it forms the border between United States and Mexico.

ri·ot (rī-ət) *n.* **1.** A wild or turbulent disturbance created by a large number of people. **2.** *Law.* A violent disturbance of the public peace by three or more persons assembled for a common private purpose. Also used adjectivally: *riot police.* **3.** An unrestrained outbreak, as of laughter or passions. **4.** A wild profusion, as of colours. **5. a.** Unrestrained merrymaking; revelry. **b.** *Archaic.* Debauchery. **6.** *Slang.* An irresistibly funny person or thing. **7.** In hunting, the following by a hound of the scent of the wrong prey. **—run riot. 1.** To move or act with wild abandon. **2.** To grow luxuriantly or abundantly.

~*v.* **rioted, -oting, -ots.** *—intr.* **1.** To take part in a riot. **2.** To live wildly or engage in uncontrolled revelry. *—tr. Literary.* To waste (money or time) in wild or wanton living. Used with *away* or *out.* [Middle English *riot(e),* debauchery, revel, riot, from Old French *ri(h)ot(e),* from *r(u)ihoter*†, to quarrel.] **—ri·ot·er** *n.*

Riot Act *n.* **1.** A law, enacted in England in 1715, providing that if 12 or more persons unlawfully assemble and disturb the public peace, they must disperse upon proclamation or be considered guilty of felony. **2.** *Small* **r,** *small* **a.** Any severe or forceful warning or reproach. Used chiefly in the phrase *read the riot act.*

Rí·o·tin·to, Mi·ñas de (méen-yass day réē-ō tíntō). Also **Río Tinto.** Town in Huelva province, Andalucia, Spain. It is famous for its mineral deposits, first worked by the Phoenicians.

ri·ot·ous (rī-ətəss) *adj.* **1.** Of, pertaining to, or resembling a riot. **2.** Taking part in or inciting to riot or uproar. **3.** Uproarious; boisterous. **4.** Dissolute; profligate. **5.** Abundant or luxuriant: *a riotous growth.* **—ri·ot·ous·ly** *adv.* **—ri·ot·ous·ness** *n.*

rip¹ (rip) *v.* **ripped, ripping, rips.** *—tr.* **1.** To cut or tear apart roughly or energetically; slash: *ripped open the parcel.* **2.** To remove by cutting or tearing roughly: *ripped the plaster off her leg.* **3.** To split or saw (wood) along the grain. **4.** *Informal.* To produce, display, or exclaim suddenly. Used with *out*: *ripped out a gun; ripped out a vicious oath.* *—intr.* **1.** To become torn or split apart. **2.** *Informal.* To move quickly or violently. **3.** *Informal.* To make a vehement verbal attack. Used with *into*: *ripped into her opponent's record.* **—let rip.** To give full vent to one's feelings: *let rip and told him what she thought of him.* —See Synonyms at **tear.**

~*n.* **1.** A torn or split place, especially along a seam; a tear. **2.** The act of ripping. [Middle English *rippen*†.] **—rip·per** *n.*

rip² *n.* **1.** An area of turbulence in the sea caused by the meeting of tidal streams, or by a tidal stream suddenly entering shallow water.

2. An area of turbulence in the sea caused when water carried up a shore by strong waves returns down the shore. Also called "rip current", "rip tide". [Perhaps from RIP (the act of tearing).]

rip³ *n. Archaic.* **1.** A dissolute person. **2.** An old or worthless horse. [Perhaps shortened variant of REPROBATE.]

R.I.P. rest in peace. [Latin *requiescat in pace.*]

ri·par·i·an (rī-páiri-ən, ri-) *adj.* **1.** Of, on, or pertaining to the bank of a river. **2.** Designating a right due to an owner of riparian land, for example a right to fish.
~*n.* One who owns riparian land. [Latin *rīpārius,* from *rīpa,* bank, shore.]

rip·cord (ríp-kawrd) *n.* **1.** A cord pulled to release the pack of a parachute. **2.** A cord pulled to release gas from a balloon.

rip current *n.* A rip (in the sea).

ripe (rīp) *adj.* **1.** Fully developed or mature; especially, ready for harvesting or consumption: *ripe pears.* **2.** Resembling matured fruit, as in fullness: *a ripe figure.* **3.** Sufficiently advanced in preparation or ageing to be used: *ripe cheese.* **4.** Thoroughly matured, as by study or experience; seasoned: *ripe judgment.* **5.** Advanced in years: *the ripe old age of 85.* **6.** Fully developed; prepared to do or undergo something; ready: *ripe for picking.* **7.** Sufficiently advanced; opportune. Said of time. [Middle English *ripe,* Old English *rīpe.*] **—ripe·ly** *adv.* **—ripe·ness** *n.*

rip·en (rī́pən) *v.* **-ened, -ening, -ens.** —*tr.* To make ripe; cause to mature. —*intr.* To become ripe; mature. **—rip·en·er** *n.*

ri·pi·e·no (ríppi-áynō, rip-yénnō) *n. Music.* A passage in which the whole orchestra plays. [Italian, "full".]

rip off *tr.v. Slang.* **1.** To exploit, swindle, cheat, or defraud. **2.** To steal: *ripped off a case of whisky.* **3.** To steal from; rob: *Shoplifters ripped off the store.*

rip-off (ríp-off, -awff) *n. Slang.* **1. a.** An act of exploitation or overcharging. **b.** Something that is overpriced. **2.** A theft.

Rip·on (rīppən). Market town of North Yorkshire, England, famous for its cathedral (12th–16th century).

ri·poste, ri·post (ri-póst, -pṓst) *n.* **1.** A quick, retaliatory action or retort. **2.** In fencing, a quick thrust given after parrying an opponent's lunge.
~*intr.v.* **riposted, -posting, -postes.** To make a riposte. [French, from Italian *risposta,* answer, feminine past participle of *rispondere,* to answer, from Latin *respondēre,* to RESPOND.]

rip·ping (rípping) *adj. British Informal.* Wonderful; splendid. Not in current usage.

rip·ple¹ (rípp'l) *v.* **-pled, -pling, -ples.** —*intr.* **1.** To form or display little undulations or waves on the surface, as on disturbed water. **2. a.** To flow with such undulations or waves on the surface. **b.** To have a movement resembling rippling water: *rippling muscles.* **3.** To rise and fall gently in tone or volume: *Laughter rippled.* —*tr.* To cause to form small waves or undulations.
~*n.* **1.** A slight wave or undulation. **2.** Anything resembling such undulations in appearance: *ripples in the fabric.* **3.** A sound that gently rises and falls. **4.** *Electronics.* A small alternating, usually undesirable, signal superimposed on an otherwise constant signal. **5.** *U.S.* A small rapid. [17th century (verb) : origin obscure.] **—rip·pler** *n.* **—rip·pling·ly** *adv.* **—rip·ply** *adj.*

ripple² *n.* A comblike, toothed instrument for removing seeds from flax and other fibres.
~*tr.v.* **rippled, -pling, -ples.** To remove seeds from (flax or other fibres) with a ripple. [Middle English *rip(e)len,* to remove seeds, from Germanic, akin to Middle Low German *repelen.*]

rip·plet (ríplit) *n.* A little wave or ripple.

rip·rap (ríp-rap) *n. U.S.* **1.** A loose assemblage of broken stones erected in water or on soft ground as a foundation. **2.** The broken stones used for this.
~*tr.v.* **riprapped, -rapping, -raps.** *U.S.* **1.** To construct a riprap in or upon. **2.** To strengthen with a riprap. [Reduplication of RAP (to strike).]

rip-roar·ing (ríp-rawring || -rōring) *adj. Informal.* Noisy, lively, and exciting. [RIP + (UP)ROAR(IOUS).]

rip·saw (ríp-saw) *n.* A coarse-toothed handsaw for cutting wood along the grain.

rip·snort·er (ríp-snawrtər) *n. Slang.* A person or thing remarkable for strength, intensity, or excellence. **—rip·snort·ing** *adj.*

rip tide *n.* A rip (*see*) (in the sea).

Rip·u·ar·i·an (rippew-áir-i-ən) *adj.* Of or designating a group of Franks who lived along the Rhine, near Cologne, in the fourth century. **—Rip·u·ar·i·an** *n.* [Medieval Latin *Ripuārius*†.]

Rip Van Winkle (ríp van wíngk'l) *n.* One who is completely unaware of current trends and conditions. [After a character who slept for 20 years in a tale (1819) by Washington Irving.]

rise (rīz) *v.* **rose** (rōz), **risen** (rízz'n), **rising, rises.** —*intr.* **1.** To assume a standing position after lying, sitting, or kneeling. **2.** To get out of bed, especially after a night's rest. **3.** To move from a lower to a higher position; ascend. **4.** To increase in height or level: *The lake rose after the rain.* **5.** To appear above the horizon: *The Sun rises in the East.* **6.** To extend upwards; be prominent: *The tower rose above the hill; a cliff rising to 200 metres.* **7.** To slant or slope upwards: *Fields rose above the river.* **8.** To originate; come into existence: *a storm rising in the north.* **9.** To be built or erected. **10.** To appear at the surface of the water. Used of fish. **11.** To puff up or become larger during cooking or as a result of leavening: *Bread dough rises.* **12.** To become stiff and erect: *Hackles rose.* **13.** To increase in quantity, value, or price: *rising prices.* **14. a.** To increase in intensity, force, pitch, or prominence: *The temperature rises in summer.* **b.** To register an increase: *The index rose sharply.* **15.** To attain a higher status: *rose in her esteem.* **16. a.** To become apparent to the mind or senses: *Fears rose to haunt him.* **b.** To become elated: *Her spirits rose.* **17.** To uplift oneself to meet a demand: *rose to the challenge.* **18.** To return to life. **19.** To rebel. Often used with *up.* **20.** To close a session of an official assembly; adjourn. —*tr.* **1.** To cause to rise. **2.** *Nautical.* To cause (a distant object at sea) to become visible above the horizon by advancing closer.
~*n.* **1.** The act of rising; an ascent. **2.** The degree of elevation or ascent; an upward slope. **3.** The appearance of the Sun or other heavenly body above the horizon. **4.** An increase in height, as of the level of water. **5.** A gently sloping hill or elevation. **6.** An origin, beginning, or source: *the rise of a river.* **7.** *British.* An increase in salary or wages. **8.** The emergence of a fish seeking food or bait at the water's surface. **9.** An increase in price, worth, quantity, or degree. **10.** An increase in intensity, volume, or pitch. **11.** Elevation in social status, prosperity, or importance. **12.** The height of a flight of stairs or of a single step. **—get** or **take a rise out of.** *Slang.* To provoke or tease (someone) successfully. **—give rise to.** Give occasion or opportunity to: *give rise to doubt.* [Rise, rose, risen; Middle English *risen, ros, risen,* Old English *rīsan, rās, risen.* (*Rās* and *risen* are attested only in compounds.)]
Synonyms: *rise, ascend, climb, soar, mount.*

ris·er (rī́zər) *n.* **1.** A person who rises, especially from sleep: *a late riser.* **2.** The vertical part of a stair step.

ris·i·bil·i·ty (ríz-i-bílləti, rī́z-, -ə-) *n., pl.* **-ties.** **1.** The ability or tendency to laugh. **2.** Laughter; hilarity.

ris·i·ble (ríz-ib'l, rī́z-, -ə-) *adj.* **1.** Capable of laughing or inclined to laugh. **2.** Pertaining to or used in laughter. **3.** Apt to excite laughter; ludicrous; laughable. [Late Latin *rīsibilis,* from Latin *rīdēre* (past participle *rīsus*), to laugh. See **ridiculous.**] **—ris·i·bly** *adv.*

ris·ing (rī́zing) *adj.* **1.** Ascending, sloping upwards, or advancing: *rising ground.* **2.** Approaching maturity or prominence; emerging: *the rising generation; a rising young actress.*
~*n.* **1.** An uprising; a revolt. **2.** A prominence or projection. **3.** The leaven or yeast used to make dough rise in baking.
~*adv.* Almost or approaching a specified age.

rising damp *n.* Damp that enters a building through the foundations, rising up the walls by capillary action.

risk (risk) *n.* **1.** The possibility of suffering harm or loss; danger: *There is the risk we won't return.* **2.** A factor, element, or course involving uncertain danger; a hazard: *The stormy weather is a risk we shall have to take.* **3.** *Insurance.* **a.** The danger or probability of loss to the insurer. **b.** The amount that the insurance company stands to lose. **c.** A person or thing considered with respect to the possibility of loss to an insurer: *a poor risk.* —See Synonyms at **danger.**
~*tr.v.* **risked, risking, risks.** **1.** To expose to a chance of loss or damage; hazard. **2.** To incur the risk of: *risking death.* **3.** To take the risk arising from: *I'll risk staying another hour.* [French *risque(r),* from Italian *risco*†, danger, *riscare*†, to run into danger.] **—risk·er** *n.*

risk capital *n. British.* Money invested in an enterprise subject to risk, such as a new business venture.

risk·y (ríski) *adj.* **-ier, -iest.** **1.** Accompanied by or involving risk or danger; hazardous. **2.** Risqué. **—risk·i·ness** *n.*

Ri·sor·gi·men·to (ri-sórji-méntō, -zórji-) *n.* The period of or the movement for the liberation and political unification of Italy, beginning about 1750 and lasting until 1870. [Italian, "resurrection", from *risorgere,* to resurrect, from Latin *resurgere,* to rise again : *re-,* again + *surgere,* to rise. See **surge.**]

ri·sot·to (ri-zóttō, -sóttō) *n.* An Italian dish of rice cooked in stock with grated cheese or vegetables and seasonings, often served with chopped meat or seafood. [Italian, from *riso,* rice.]

ris·qué (ríss-kay, rée̋ss- || riss-káy) *adj.* Suggestive of or bordering on indelicacy or impropriety: *a risqué joke.* [French, from the past participle of *risquer,* to RISK.]

ris·sole (ríssōl) *n.* A small ball or cake made with a minced meat or fish mixture coated with breadcrumbs and egg, and usually fried. [French, from Old French *roissole,* from (unattested) Vulgar Latin *russeola (pasta),* "reddish (pastry)", from the feminine of Late Latin *russeolus,* diminutive of Latin *russeus,* reddish, from *russus,* red.]

ris·so·lé (ríssō-lay, rée-sō-, -láy) *adj.* Browned by frying. [French, past participle of *rissoler,* to brown by deep frying, from *rissole,* RISSOLE.]

ri·sus sar·do·ni·cus (rée-səss saar-dónnikəss, rī́-) *n.* A fixed, abnormal grin seen, for example, in cases of tetanus. [(New) Latin, sardonic laugh.]

ri·tar·dan·do (ríttaar-dán-dō || *U.S.* -daan-) *adv. Abbr.* **rit., ritard.** *Music.* Gradually slowing in tempo. Used as a direction. [Italian, from Latin *retardandum,* gerund of *retardāre,* to RETARD.]

rite (rīt) *n.* **1.** The prescribed or customary form for conducting a religious or other solemn ceremony: *the rite of baptism.* **2.** A ceremonial act or series of acts: *fertility rites.* **3.** *Often capital* **R.** The liturgy of a Christian church, especially one of the historical forms of the Eucharistic service: *the Anglican Rite.* **4.** *Often capital* **R.** A branch or division of the Christian church as determined by specific liturgy and law: *Catholics of the Latin Rite.* **5.** Any formal practice, custom, or procedure. [Middle English *ryte,* from Latin *rītus.*]

rite of passage *n.* A ceremony, as in a primitive society, that marks a person's change of status, for example at puberty or on marriage.

ri·tor·nel·lo (ríttər-néllō, ríttawr-) *n., pl.* **-nelli** (-néllee) or **-los.** *Mu-*

PRONUNCIATION KEY

a, trap; aa, father; ai, fair;
ar, star; aw, lawn; ay, play;
b, bb, stab; rubber;
ch, church; ck, ticket;
d, dd, dead; ladder; e, dress;
ee, bee; er, defer; ew, few;
ewr, pure; ə, about;
ər, letter; f, ff, fife; differ;
g, gg, giggle; h, hat; i, kit;
ī, price; īr, fire; j, judge;
k, kick; l, ll, let; 'l, needle;
m, mm, man; n, nn, no;
'n, sudden; ng, thing; o, lot;
ō, no; ŏŏ, foot; ōō, shoe;
oor, poor; ow, cow;
owr, hour; oy, boy;
p, pp, pepper; r, rr, red;
s, ss, sauce; sh, ship;
t, tt, totter; th, thick; th, this;
smooth; u, cut; ur, turn;
v, vv, valve; w, wet; y, yes;
z, zz, zebra; zh, vision;
pleasure

IN FOREIGN WORDS:

aN, oN, Saint-Saëns;
hl, Llanelli; Hluhluwe;
kh, loch; lough; Khaled

STRESS MARK:

ín-sīt, insight; in-sī́t, incite

sic. **1.** An instrumental interlude recurring between verses in a vocal work. **2.** A passage for full orchestra in a baroque concerto grosso. **3.** An instrumental interlude in early 17th-century opera. [Italian, a refrain, diminutive of *ritorno,* return, from *ritornare,* to return, from Vulgar Latin *retornāre* (unattested), to RETURN.]

rit·u·al (rítchōō-əl, ríttew-, ríchōōl) *n.* **1.** The prescribed form or order of conducting a religious or solemn ceremony. **2.** A body of ceremonies or rites. **3.** A book of rites or ceremonial forms. **4. a.** A ceremonial act or a series of such acts. **b.** The performance of such acts. **5.** Any habitual detailed method of procedure: *Her household chores have become a ritual with her.*
~*adj.* **1.** Of or characterised by a rite or rites. **2.** Performed as a rite or ritual: *a ritual fire dance.* [Latin *rītuālis,* from *rītus,* RITE.] **—rit·u·al·ly** *adv.*

rit·u·al·ise, rit·u·al·ize (rítchōō-ə-līz, ríttew-) *v.* **-ised, -ising, -ises.** *—intr.* To engage in or practise ritualism. *—tr.* To make into or convert to ritual. **—rit·u·al·i·sa·tion** (-ī-záysh'n ‖ *U.S.* -i-) *n.*

rit·u·al·ism (rítchōō-ə-liz'm, ríttew-) *n.* **1.** The study, practice, or observance of ritual. **2.** Insistence upon or adherence to ritual.

rit·u·al·ist (rítchōō-ə-list, ríttew-) *n.* **1.** An authority on or student of ritual. **2.** A person who practises or advocates the observance of ritual. **—rit·u·al·ist** *adj.*

rit·u·al·is·tic (rítchōō-ə-lístik, ríttew-) *adj.* Pertaining to, characterised by, or devoted to ritual or ritualism. **—rit·u·al·is·ti·cal·ly** *adv.*

ritz·y (rítsi) *adj.* **-ier, -iest.** *Informal.* Elegant; luxurious and fashionable. [From the *Ritz* hotels founded by César Ritz (1850–1918), Swiss hotelier.]

riv·age (rívvij) *n. Archaic.* A coast, shore, or bank. [Middle English, from Old French, from *rive,* bank, shore, from Latin *rīpa.*]

ri·val (rī′l) *n.* **1.** A person who attempts to equal or surpass another, or who pursues the same object as another; a competitor: *They were rivals for the same job.* **2.** One that equals or almost equals another in some respect. **—See Synonyms at opponent.**
~*adj.* Acting as or being a rival; competing.
~*v.* **rivalled** or *U.S.* **rivaled, -valling** or *U.S.* **-valing, -vals.** *—tr.* **1.** To attempt to equal or surpass. **2.** To be the equal of; be a match for: *"rivalled the beauties of the best Grecian architecture"* (Henry

Fielding). *—intr. Archaic.* To be a competitor or rival; compete. Used with *with.* [Latin *rīvālis,* "one using the same brook as another", rival, from *rīvālis,* of a brook, from *rīvus,* brook.]
Synonyms: compete, rival, vie, emulate.

ri·val·ry (rī′l'ri) *n., pl.* **-ries. 1.** The act or an instance of competing or emulating. **2.** The state or condition of being a rival.

rive (rīv) *v.* **rived, rived** or **riven** (rívv'n), **riving, rives.** *Archaic. —tr.* **1.** To rend or tear apart. **2.** To break into pieces, as by a blow; cleave or split asunder. **3.** To break or distress (the heart or spirit, for example). *—intr.* To be or become broken or split. [Middle English *riven,* from Old Norse *rifa.*]

riv·er (rívvər) *n.* **1.** *Abbr.* **R., r., riv.** A large natural stream of water flowing towards an ocean, lake, or other body of water. **2.** Any stream or abundant flow resembling this: *rivers of blood.* **—sell down the river.** To betray or deceive. **—up the river.** *U.S. Slang.* In or to prison. [Middle English, from Anglo-French *rivere,* river bank, river, from Vulgar Latin *rīpāria* (unattested), feminine of Latin *rīpārius,* on a bank, from *rīpa,* bank.]

Ri·ver·a (ri-vérrə), **Diego** (1886–1957). Mexican artist. His murals celebrate the struggle for independence and draw inspiration from his socialist beliefs, exalting the Indian peasantry at the expense of the ruling classes.

river basin *n.* A basin (sense 5) *(see).*

riv·er·bed (rívvər-bed) *n.* The area covered or once covered by water, between the banks of a river.

river horse *n. Informal.* The hippopotamus *(see).*

Riv·er·i·na (rívvə-réenə). Region of New South Wales, Australia. Situated between the rivers Murray, Lachlan, and Murrumbidgee, it consists mainly of a fertile plain, producing wheat, rice, and fruit.

riv·er·ine (rívvə-rīn ‖ -rin) *adj.* **1.** Pertaining to or resembling a river. **2.** Located on or inhabiting the banks of a river; riparian.

riv·er·side (rívvər-sīd) *n.* The bank of a river.
~*adj.* On or close to a bank of a river.

riv·et (rívvit, rívvət) *n.* A metal bolt or pin, having a head on one end, used to fasten metal plates or other objects together by inserting the shank through a hole in each piece and hammering down the plain end so as to form a new head.
~*tr.v.* **riveted, -eting, -ets. 1.** To fasten or secure with, or as if with,

---

river

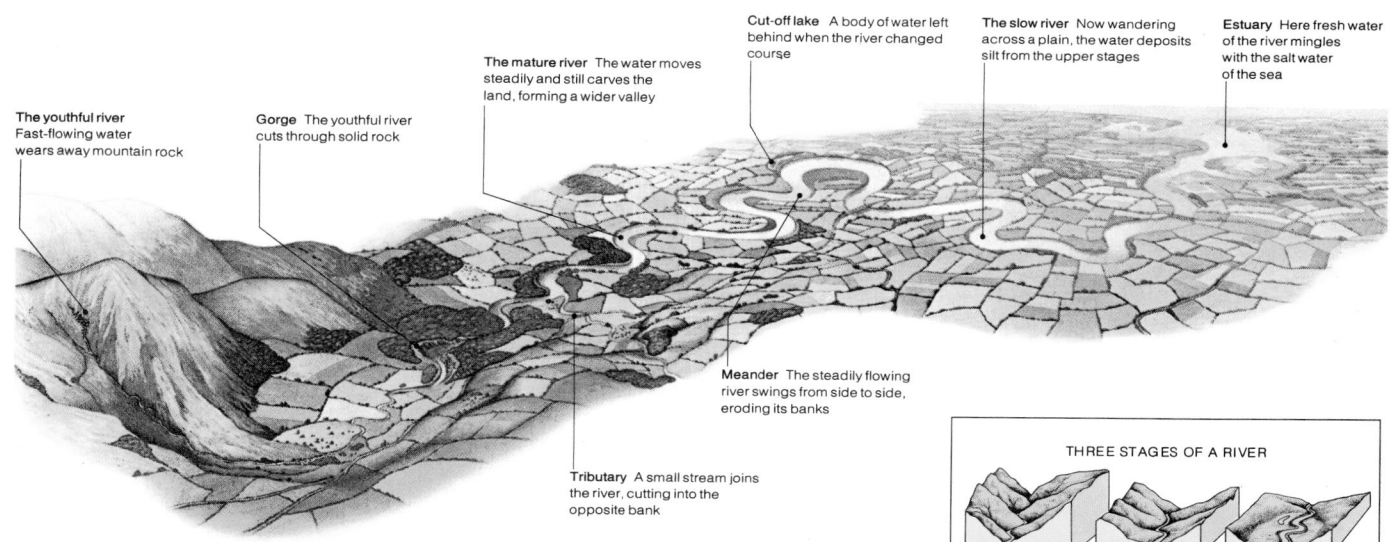

THE WINDING ROUTE TO THE SEA

How a river changes the face of the countryside

A river is a natural, flowing stream of water that cuts its own course through the land until it reaches the sea, a lake, or another river. On its way, it constantly changes the landscape. Most rivers have their sources in mountains or uplands and are fed by rain or melting snow. They begin as torrents, channelling a downward route through the rock or soil. Each particle a river removes, whether a grain of sand or a boulder, adds to its cutting power and helps to wear away its course.

In the mountains, the river course is known as the torrent stage. It cuts steep, V-shaped valleys, litters the bed with boulders, and plunges over waterfalls. These are formed where hard rock adjoins soft rock. The soft rock is worn away faster, leaving a sudden, vertical plunge, often many metres deep. As the river pours out of the high ground into its valley stage, the water moves more smoothly, and other streams join it as tributaries. Swollen by the extra flood, the river

widens and the sides of its valley become shallower.

As it reaches the flatlands of the coastal plain or lakeside, the river begins to loop, or meander, often changing course. Though flowing quietly, it still reshapes the country, depositing silt among the eddies of inner bends, to create gentle, often muddy, banks and eating away the outer banks. Large quantities of soil carried from the upper reaches, build up as mudflats and sandbanks at its estuary.

The youthful river Fast-flowing water wears away mountain rock

Gorge The youthful river cuts through solid rock

The mature river The water moves steadily and still carves the land, forming a wider valley

Cut-off lake A body of water left behind when the river changed course

The slow river Now wandering across a plain, the water deposits silt from the upper stages

Estuary Here fresh water of the river mingles with the salt water of the sea

Meander The steadily flowing river swings from side to side, eroding its banks

Tributary A small stream joins the river, cutting into the opposite bank

THREE STAGES OF A RIVER

The fast-flowing torrent reach of a river cuts a steep-sided, V-shaped valley. In the mid, or valley, stage, the V starts to open out, until in the final stage the river takes a constantly changing course across flat country to the sea.

ANATOMY OF A RIVER *In its upper stages, the torrent is often strong enough to move boulders and the river flow is broken and turbulent – rushing around and over obstacles. At the wider, valley stage, most rivers are deeper and navigable, and freshwater fish feed and breed among the eddies and the vegetation* *at the water's edge. On the flatlands near its mouth, the river deposits mud and silt, often creating new and rich stretches of farmland, called alluvial plains. Some rivers form a delta at their mouths – a tract of land built up from deposited sediment, through which the river diverges into a number of channels on its course to the sea.*

a rivet. **2.** To hammer the headless end of (a bolt, pin, or similar device) so as to form a head and fasten something. **3.** To fasten or secure firmly; fix. **4.** To engross; grip: *riveted by the scene.* [Middle English *ryvette*, from Old French *rivert*, to fix.] —**riv·et·er** *n.*

riv·et·ing (rívvit-ing, rívvət-) *adj.* Completely absorbing the attention; fascinating.

Riv·i·er·a (rivvi-aír-ə) *n.* **1.** The coastal region stretching along the Mediterranean Sea from Hyères in southeast France to La Spezia, Italy, that includes the fashionable resorts of Cannes, Monte Carlo, Nice, and St. Tropez. Preceded by *the.* **2.** *Small* **r.** **2.** Any resort area extending along a coastline. [Italian, "shore", from Vulgar Latin *rīpāria* (unattested). See **river.**]

ri·vi·ère (rívvi-aír) *n.* A necklace of diamonds or other precious stones, generally in one strand. [French, short for *rivière de diamants*, "stream of diamonds", from Old French *rivere*, RIVER.]

riv·u·let (rívvew-lət, -lit) *n.* A small brook or stream; a streamlet.

[Earlier *rivelet*, probably from Italian *rivoletto*, diminutive of *rivolo*, small stream, from Latin *rīvulus*, diminutive of *rīvus*, brook, stream.]

Ri·yadh or **Ri·ad** (rée-ad, ri-yáad). Capital of Saudi Arabia. Situated in an oasis in Nejd province, of which it is capital, it was once a walled town. The impact of the country's oil wealth has made it a commercial centre with much modern architecture.

ri·yal (ri-yáal, rée-al) *n.* Also **ri·al** (for sense 1). **1.** The basic monetary unit of Saudi Arabia, equal to 100 halalas. **2.** The basic monetary unit of the Yemen Arabic Republic, equal to 100 fils. [Arabic *riyāl*, from Spanish *real*, REAL (coin).]

R.L. Rugby league.

RM reichsmark.

rm. 1. ream. **2.** room.

R.M. 1. Royal Mail. **2.** Royal Marines.

R.M.A. Royal Military Academy.

rms root mean square.

R.M.S. 1. Royal Mail Service. **2.** Royal Mail Steamer.

Rₙ The symbol for the element radon.

R.N. Royal Navy.

RNA *n.* Ribonucleic acid: a nucleic acid occurring in all living cells, consisting of a single-stranded chain of alternating phosphate and ribose units with the bases adenine, guanine, cytosine, and uracil bonded to the ribose. RNA occurs in several forms, mostly in the cytoplasm, and has an essential role in protein syntheses. See **messenger RNA, ribosomal RNA, transfer RNA.**

RNAase *n.* Ribonuclease (*see*).

R.N.A.S. 1. Royal Navy Air Service. **2.** Royal Navy Air Station.

R.N.L.I. Royal National Lifeboat Institution.

R.N.R. Royal Naval Reserve.

R.N.V.R. Royal Naval Volunteer Reserve.

R.N.Z.A.F. Royal New Zealand Air Force.

R.N.Z.N. Royal New Zealand Navy.

ro. rood (measure).

roach¹ (rōch) *n., pl.* **roaches** or collectively **roach. 1.** A freshwater game fish, *Rutilus rutilus*, of northern Europe, having reddish fins. **2.** Any of various similar or related fishes. [Middle English *roche*, from Old French *rochet*.]

roach² *n.* 1. *U.S.* An insect, the **cockroach** (*see*). **2.** *Slang.* The butt or filter, usually homemade, of a marijuana cigarette.

roach³ *n. Nautical.* The upward curvature of the bottom edge of a square sail intended to prevent chafing. [18th century : origin obscure.]

Roach, Hal (1892–). U.S. film director. His film company produced comedies featuring Harold Lloyd, Laurel and Hardy, and others, and he directed films such as *Fraternally Yours* (1933) and *Of Mice and Men* (1940).

road (rōd) *n. Abbr.* **Rd., rd., R., r. 1. a.** An open way, generally public and usually having a hard tarmac or other surface, for the passage of vehicles, persons, and animals. **b.** *Capital* **R.** Used as part of certain street names: *Old Kent Road.* **2.** A course or path: *the road to success.* **3.** A passage or tunnel in a mine. **4.** *U.S.* A railway. **5.** *Usually plural. Nautical.* A **roadstead** (*see*). —**hit the road.** *Informal.* To begin a journey. —**on the road. 1.** On tour. Said especially of a theatrical company. **2.** Travelling or moving around, especially as a salesman or vagrant. —**one for the road.** A last drink before setting out. [Middle English *rood, rode*, riding, journey, Old English *rād*.]

road·bed (rōd-bed) *n.* **1. a.** The foundation upon which the sleepers, rails, and ballast of a railway are laid. **b.** A layer of ballast directly under the sleepers. **2.** The foundation and surface of a road.

road·block (rōd-blok) *n.* An obstruction across a road set up, as by the police or army, for purposes of detection, security, or defence.

road hog *n. Informal.* A driver who drives inconsiderately and selfishly, often keeping his vehicle near the middle of the road.

road·hold·ing (rōd-hōlding) *n.* The ability of a motor vehicle to retain its grip or hold on a surface without skidding.

road·house (rōd-howss) *n.* An inn, restaurant, or nightclub situated on a road, especially in the countryside.

road·ie (rōdi) *n., pl.* **-ies.** A person who is responsible for the travelling arrangements of a pop group on tour, and who supervises their instruments and equipment. Also called "road manager".

road metal *n.* Crushed or broken stone, cinders, or similar material used in the construction and repair of roads and roadbeds.

road·run·ner (rōd-runnər) *n.* A swift-running, crested bird, *Geococcyx californianus*, of southwestern North America, having streaked, brownish plumage and a long tail.

road sense *n.* The ability to use public roads and negotiate traffic safely.

road show *n.* A touring entertainment, especially one given by pop groups or similar artists.

road·side (rōd-sīd) *n.* The area bordering on a road.

road·stead (rōd-sted) *n. Nautical.* A sheltered, offshore anchorage area for ships. Also called "roads".

road·ster (rōd-stər) *n.* **1.** An open car having no back seats. **2.** A horse for riding on a road.

road test *n.* A test designed to assess the performance and roadworthiness of a vehicle by driving it on a road. —**road-test** *tr.v.*

road·way (rōd-way) *n.* A road, especially the part over which vehicles travel.

road·work (rōd-wurk) *n.* Outdoor long-distance running, especially as part of a sportsman's training.

road·works (rōd-wurks) *pl.n.* Construction or repair works on a road, often causing a delay for motorists.

---

road

4,000 YEARS OF ROAD-BUILDING
The ribbons of stone and asphalt that speeded up travel

Paved roads for wheeled vehicles were constructed as early as the third millennium B.C. in Egypt, Mesopotamia, and China, but Darius the Great, ruler of the Persian Empire (521–486 B.C.), built the first imperial road system. Roads connecting the provinces with the several capital cities ensured rapid communications with his army and messengers. The Romans later built a network of paved roads to link cities and forts across their empire.

As the ancient empires declined, their roads fell into disrepair and it was not until the 18th century in Europe that military requirements led to a revival of road-building by governments. A subsequent expansion of trade, accompanied by an increase in wheeled traffic, influenced governments to encourage interest in scientific road-building. Pierre Tresaguet (1716–96), inspired by the archaeology of classical civilisations, introduced into France construction methods similar to those of the Romans. Thomas Telford (1757–1834) introduced his methods into Britain, and both he and John McAdam (1756–1836) improved upon them.

When, during the 20th century, motor cars with pneumatic tyres raised intolerable levels of dust from crushed-stone road surfaces, a wearing course of tar was laid on the surface of a McAdam road and called a tarmacadam or tarmac road. Concrete was first used during the 1920s to pave Italian motorways.

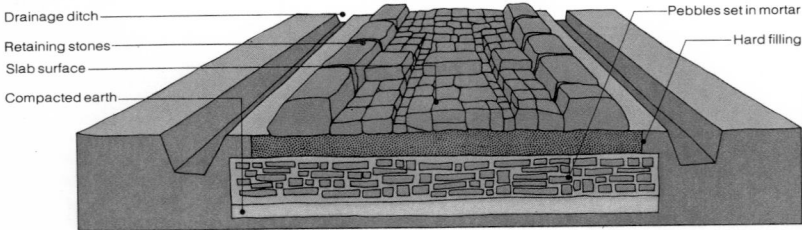

ROMAN *The road was founded on compacted earth covered with pebbles set in mortar. This was overlaid with a hard filling that was cambered (curved) and sometimes paved with stone slabs.*

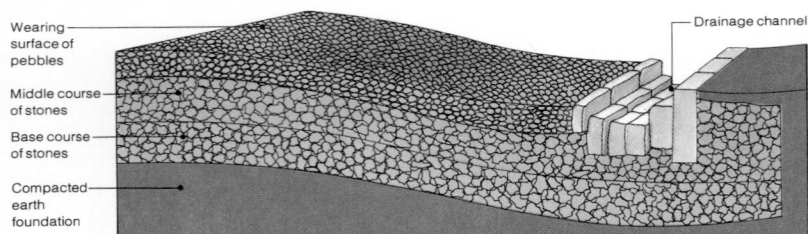

McADAM *A cambered foundation of compacted earth formed the base of the road. It was covered with two 100 millimetre (4 inch) courses of stones, and a wearing surface of pebbles which the steel wheels of horse-drawn wagons and coaches gradually crushed and smoothed to a fine dust.*

MODERN *Today's motorways have a thick sub-base of pebbly material, a base layer of concrete, a layer of tar or rolled asphalt, and a wearing course of rolled asphalt. The hard shoulder is asphalted.*

road·worth·y (rṓd-wurthi) *adj.* Fit to be driven on a public road. Said of a motor vehicle. **—road·worth·i·ness** *n.*

roam (rōm) *v.* **roamed, roaming, roams.** *—intr.* To move or travel without purpose or plan; rove; wander. *—tr.* To wander over or through. —See Synonyms at **wander.**

~n. The act of roaming. [Middle English *romen*†.] **—roam·er** *n.*

roan (rōn) *adj.* **1.** Having a chestnut *(strawberry roan),* bay *(red roan),* or black *(blue roan)* coat thickly sprinkled with white or grey hairs. Said chiefly of horses. **2.** Made or prepared from roan leather.

~n. **1.** The characteristic colouring of a roan horse. **2.** A roan horse or other animal. **3.** A soft, flexible sheepskin leather, often treated to resemble morocco, and used in bookbinding. In this sense, also called "roan leather". [Old French *roan*†.]

Ro·a·noke Island (rṓ-ə-nōk, rṓ-nōk). Island off the coast of North Carolina, United States, and the site of the first English colonies in North America. They were founded at the instigation of Sir Walter Raleigh (1585, 1587), but by 1591 all the colonists had disappeared, perhaps killed by Indians or by disease.

roar (ror || rōr) *v.* **roared, roaring, roars.** *—intr.* **1.** To utter a loud, deep, prolonged sound, especially in distress, rage, or excitement. **2.** To utter a loud, harsh, growling sound, like that characteristic of a lion. **3.** To laugh loudly or excitedly. **4.** To make or produce a harsh, loud noise or din: *the wind roaring in the trees.* **5.** To move or operate with a loud noise: *roared through the town on motorbikes.* **6.** To breathe with a rasping sound. Used of a horse. *—tr.* **1.** To utter or express with a deep, loud, and prolonged sound. **2.** To bring (oneself) into a specified state by roaring: *The crowd roared itself hoarse.*

~n. **1.** A loud, deep sound or cry, as of a person in distress or rage. **2.** The loud, deep cry characteristic of a lion. **3.** A loud, prolonged noise, such as that produced by waves, motorbikes, or gunfire. **4.** A loud burst of laughter. [Middle English *roren, raren,* Old English *rārian* (imitative).] **—roar·er** *n.*

roar·ing (ráwring || rṓring) *adj. Informal.* Very lively or successful; thriving: *a roaring trade.*

~adv. Informal. Extremely; very: *roaring drunk.*

Roaring Forties. The area of the southern oceans south of latitude 40°S, characterised by constant, strong northwest to west winds, gales, and damp, raw weather.

roast (rōst) *v.* **roasted, roasting, roasts.** *—tr.* **1.** To cook (meat, for example), as: **a.** With dry heat, especially with fat in an oven. **b.** By direct exposure to dry heat, as over an open fire or in hot ashes. **2.** To prepare (coffee beans, for example) for use by heating. **3.** To dry, brown, or parch by exposing to heat. **4.** To expose to great or excessive heat. **5.** *Metallurgy.* To heat (ores) in a furnace in order to dehydrate, purify, or oxidise. **6.** *Informal.* To criticise or ridicule harshly. *—intr.* **1.** To cook meat or other food in an oven. **2.** To undergo roasting. **3.** *Informal.* To feel extremely hot.

~n. **1.** Something roasted. **2.** A cut of meat suitable or prepared for roasting. **3.** The act or process of roasting.

~adj. Roasted: *roast chicken.* [Middle English *rosten,* from Old French *rostir,* probably from Old High German *rōsten,* from *rōst,* grate, gridiron, from Germanic *raust* (unattested).]

roast·er (rṓstər) *n.* **1.** One that roasts. **2.** A special dish or apparatus for roasting. **3.** Something fit for roasting, such as a chicken.

rob (rob) *v.* **robbed, robbing, robs.** *—tr.* **1.** To take property from (a place, person, or persons) illegally, by using or threatening to use violence or force; commit robbery against: *robbed by muggers; robbed a bank.* **2.** To deprive (a person) of something belonging, desired, or legally due by any unjust procedure: *rob a person of his reputation.* **3.** To deprive of something important, essential, or desirable: *robbed the joke of its point.* *—intr.* To commit or engage in robbery. [Middle English *robben,* from Old French *rober,* from Germanic.] **—rob·ber** *n.*

Synonyms: *rob, steal, burgle, filch, pilfer, thieve, plunder, loot, ransack.*

rob·a·lo (róbbə-lō, rṓbə-) *n., pl.* **-los** or collectively **robalo.** Any of various chiefly tropical marine food and aquarium fishes of the family Centropomidae, such as the **snook** *(see).* [Spanish *róbalo, robálo,* probably modification of *lobaro* (unattested), from *lobo,* wolf, "wolflike fish", from Latin *lupus.*]

Robbe-Gril·let (rob-gree-yáy), **Alain** (1922–). French novelist. He is an exponent of the French new novel, on which he has written in *Vers un nouveau roman* (1964). His novels include *Jealousy* (1957), in which the action is presented through the clinically detached prose of an observer who neither speaks nor appears in person. He has directed his own films, *L'Immortelle* (1963) and *Trans-Europe Express* (1967).

Rob·ben Island (rób-in, -ən). Small island in Table Bay, South Africa, 10 kilometres (6 miles) from Cape Town. A penal settlement, the island houses many South African political prisoners.

robber baron *n.* A feudal lord who robbed travellers passing through his domain.

robber crab *n.* A large Indo-Pacific crab, *Birgo latus,* that feeds on coconuts broken open with its pincers. Also called "coconut crab".

robber fly *n.* Any of various predatory flies of the family Asilidae, characteristically having long, bristly legs.

rob·ber·y (róbbəri) *n., pl.* **-ies.** **1.** The act of unlawfully taking the property of another by the use of force or intimidation. **2.** An instance of this.

Robbia, della. See **della Robbia.**

Rob·bins (róbbinz), **Jerome** (1918–). U.S. choreographer. Trained as a dancer, he staged his first ballet in 1944 and later won fame for creating the dance sequences in hit musicals such as *West Side Story* (1957) and *Fiddler on the Roof* (1964).

robe (rōb) *n.* **1.** A long, loose, flowing outer garment, especially: **a.** An official garment worn on formal occasions to show office or rank, as by a judge or high church official. **b.** *U.S.* A dressing gown or bathrobe. **2.** *Plural.* Clothes in general; dress. **3.** *U.S.* A blanket or covering made of fur, cloth, or other material: *a lap robe.*

~v. **robed, robing, robes.** *—tr.* To clothe or dress in or as if in a robe or robes. *—intr.* To put on a robe or robes. [Middle English, from Old French, from Vulgar Latin *rauba* (unattested), "clothes taken away as booty", robe, from Germanic; akin to ROB.]

Rob·ert I (róbbərt), known as Robert the Bruce (1274–1329). King of Scotland (1306–29). He seized the crown in 1306 and gradually extended his control over Scotland. In 1314 he won effective independence from England by his victory at Bannockburn, formally acknowledged by England at the treaty of Northampton (1328). He is buried in Dunfermline Abbey, Scotland.

Robert II[1] (1316–90). The first Stuart King of Scotland (1371–90). The son of Walter, the Steward of Scotland, by a daughter of Robert the Bruce, he several times acted as regent during the exile and captivity of David II. Known as the Steward, he succeeded David and initiated the Stuart dynasty.

Robert II[2], known as Robert Curthose (*c.* 1054–1134). Duke of Normandy (1087–1106), the eldest son of William the Conqueror. He acquired Normandy on the Conqueror's death, but the English crown went to Robert's younger brother, William Rufus. After his return from the first Crusade he planned to contest the English crown with the new king, his youngest brother, Henry I, but was defeated by Henry at Tinchebrai (1106) in Normandy. He was held captive in England for the rest of his life.

Rob·erts (róbbərts), **Frederick Sleigh, 1st Earl** (1832–1914). British soldier, commander in chief of the British army during the second Boer War (1899–1902). He won the Victoria Cross during the Indian Mutiny (1857–8) and in the Boer War he led the victorious advance on Pretoria.

Roberts, Tom, born Thomas William Roberts (1856–1931). Australian painter, born in England. He studied in Europe (1881–85) and later brought impressionism to Australia.

Robe·son (rṓb-sən), **Paul** (1898–1976). Black U.S. actor and singer. He won fame playing the title role in Eugene O'Neill's *Emperor Jones* (1925), further establishing his reputation in *Showboat* (1928) in which he sang *Ol' Man River,* a song with which he is especially associated. In 1943 he played the title role in a record-breaking New York run of *Othello.* A campaigner for civil rights, Robeson was attracted to Communism in the late 1940s.

Robes·pierre (rṓbz-pyair; *French* rōbz-pyáir), **Maximilien François Marie Isidore** (1758–94). French revolutionary leader. A radical lawyer, he became an early member of the Jacobin club. The chief architect of the Reign of Terror, Robespierre was famous for his austere and incorruptible character. He introduced laws permitting the confiscation of property and arrest of suspected traitors. A reaction to these measures led to his arrest and execution.

rob·in (róbbin) *n.* **1.** A small Eurasian songbird, *Erithacus rubecula,* having an orange breast and a brown back. **2.** A similar North American songbird, *Turdus migratorius.* Also called "American robin". **3.** Any of various birds resembling a robin. [Middle English, from Old French, from the name *Robin.*]

Robin Goodfellow. See **Puck.**

Rob·in Hood (róbbin hŏŏd). Legendary English outlaw. He is first mentioned in *Piers Plowman* (*c.* 1377), and ballads concerning his exploits became popular in the following centuries. Though he may have been an entirely mythical folk hero, various historical prototypes have been suggested, including a 12th-century Earl of Huntingdon and a disinherited follower of Simon de Montfort.

ro·bin·i·a (rə-bínni-ə, ro-, rō-) *n.* Any tree of the genus *Robinia;* especially, the **false acacia** *(see).* [New Latin, after Jean *Robin* (died 1629), French botanist.]

Rob·in·son (róbbin-sən), **Edward G,** born Emmanuel Goldenberg (1893–1973). U.S. film actor, born in Romania. He made his reputation in gangster films, such as *Little Caesar* (1930) and *Kid Galahad* (1937), and later played character parts, as in *Double Indemnity* (1944) and *The Cincinatti Kid* (1965).

Robinson, John (Arthur Thomas) (1919–). British churchman. As Bishop Suffragan of Woolwich (1959–69) he published *Honest to God* (1963), a controversial appraisal of New Testament teaching in the context of the modern world. He has lectured in theology at Trinity College, Cambridge, since 1969.

Robinson, Sugar Ray, born Walker Smith (1921–). U.S. boxer. He was six times world champion, once as a welterweight (1946–51) and five times as middleweight (1951–60).

Robinson, (William) Heath (1872–1944). British cartoonist and book illustrator. He is especially remembered for his humorous drawings of fantastic inventions collected in *Absurdities* (1934), among other volumes.

Robinson Cru·soe (krŏŏsō). The hero of Daniel Defoe's novel *Robinson Crusoe* (1719), a shipwrecked sailor who lived for years on a small tropical island.

ro·bo·rant (rṓbə-rənt, róbbə-) *adj.* Restoring vigour or strength.

~n. A roborant drug; a tonic. [Latin *rōborāns* (stem *rōborant-*), present participle of *rōborāre,* to strengthen, from *rōbur,* strength.]

ro·bot (rō-bot, -bət) *n.* **1.** An externally manlike mechanical device capable of performing human tasks or behaving in a human man-

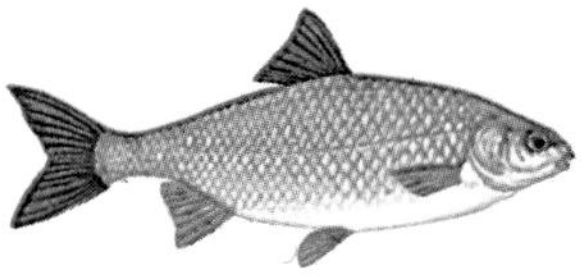

roach *A widespread and common freshwater fish growing to about 35 centimetres (14 inches). Roach are fished for food in eastern Europe, but are used mainly as game fish elsewhere.*

roadrunner *The poor flight of the roadrunner gives this bird its name since it is most often seen running along roads or across open land. A relative of the cuckoo, it is found in southwest North America, and feeds on lizards, snakes, and insects.*

robin *Many birds of the thrush family found throughout the world are called robins. The American robin is the largest, while the European robin,* Erithacus rubecula *(above) – which grows to about 14 centimetres (5½ inches) – frequently becomes very tame.*

rocking horse *A "safety" or "swing" rocking horse, a type first made in the 1870s and in common use from 1900 onwards.*

PRONUNCIATION KEY

a, trap; aa, father; ai, fair; ar, star; aw, lawn; ay, play; b, bb, stab; rubber; ch, church; ck, ticket; d, dd, dead; ladder; e, dress; ee, bee; er, defer; ew, few; ewr, pure; ə, about; ər, letter; f, ff, fife; differ; g, gg, giggle; h, hat; i, kit; ī, price; īr, fire; j, judge; k, kick; l, ll, let; 'l, needle; m, mm, man; n, nn, no; 'n, sudden; ng, thing; o, lot; ō, no; o͝o, foot; o͞o, shoe; oor, poor; ow, cow; owr, hour; oy, boy; p, pp, pepper; r, rr, red; s, ss, sauce; sh, ship; t, tt, totter; th, thick; th, this; smooth; u, cut; ur, turn; v, vv, valve; w, wet; y, yes; z, zz, zebra; zh, vision; pleasure

IN FOREIGN WORDS:

aN, oN, Saint-Saëns; hl, Llanelli; Hluhluwe; kh, loch; lough; Khaled

STRESS MARK:

ín-sīt, insight; in-sī́t, incite

ner. **2.** Any machine or device that works automatically or by remote control; especially, a machine in a factory that can be programmed to perform a variety of different tasks normally done by humans. Also called "automaton". **3.** A person who works mechanically without original thought. **4.** *South African.* A set of traffic lights. [Czech (in Karel Čapek's play *R.U.R. (Rossum's Universal Robots),* 1920), from *robota,* compulsory labour, drudgery.] **—ro·bot·ism** *n.* **—ro·bot·is·tic** (-ísstik) *adj.*

robot bomb *n.* A **flying bomb** *(see).*

ro·bot·ics (rō-bóttiks, rə-) *n.* The science of the designing, building, and application of robots. [ROBOT + -ICS.]

robot pilot *n.* An **automatic pilot** *(see).*

Rob Roy (rób róy), born Robert Macgregor (1671–1734). Scottish clan chief and cattle dealer. He was outlawed (1712) for failing to pay his debts and began a career of banditry which lasted until his arrest in 1722. He was pardoned in 1727. Sir Walter Scott's novel *Rob Roy* (1818) was based on his career.

Rob·son (rób-sən), **Dame Flora** (1902–). British actress. She made her stage debut in 1921 and won acclaim for her roles in classical drama; since 1931 she has also appeared in many films.

ro·bust (rō-búst, rə- || rō-bust) *adj.* **1.** Full of health and strength; vigorous; hardy. **2.** Powerfully built; hefty. **3.** Sturdy in construction. **4.** Requiring or suited to physical strength or endurance: *robust work.* **5.** Boisterous; rough. **6.** Marked by richness and fullness; full-bodied: *a robust wine.* **7.** Down-to-earth; straightforward: *a robust intellect.* —See Synonyms at **healthy.** [Latin *rōbustus,* oaken, from *rōbur, rōbus,* oak, strength.] **—ro·bust·ly** *adv.* **—ro·bust·ness** *n.*

roc (rok) *n.* A legendary bird of prey of enormous size and strength. [From Spanish *rocho,* from Arabic *rukhkh,* from Persian *rukh*†.]

ro·caille (ro-kī́, rō-) *n.* The light, shell-like, curving decoration used in rococo architecture. [French, "rockwork", from Old French *roche,* ROCK.]

roc·am·bole (róckəm-bōl) *n.* **1.** A European plant, *Allium scorodoprasum,* having a garlic-like bulb. **2.** The bulb of this plant, used as a seasoning. [French, from German *Rockenbolle,* "distaff bulb" : *Rocken,* distaff, from Old High German *rocko* + *Bolle,* bulb, from Old High German *bolla,* ball.]

Roch·dale (róch-dayl). Industrial town of Greater Manchester, northwest England. The birthplace of the cooperative movement (1844), its industries include textiles, engineering, and asbestos.

Roche (rosh), **Mazo de la** (1885–1961). Canadian novelist. She wrote 15 novels about the Whiteoak family of Jalna, the first of which was *Jalna* (1927).

Rochelle, La. See **La Rochelle.**

Ro·chelle powder (ro-shél) *n.* A cathartic, **Seidlitz powder** *(see).*

Rochelle salt *n.* A colourless efflorescent crystalline compound, $KNaC_4H_4O_6{\cdot}4H_2O$, used in making mirrors, in electronics, and as a laxative. [After LA ROCHELLE.]

roche mou·ton·née (rōsh mo͞o-tə-náy, rósh, -to-) *n., pl.* **roches moutonnées** (*pronounced as singular, or* -z). A glacially moulded mass of rock, worn smooth on the upstream side by abrasion, the downstream side being rough as a result of the plucking action of the ice. Also called "sheepback". [French, "fleecy rock".]

Roch·es·ter[1] (róchistər). Port of Kent, southeast England. Situted on the estuary of the river Medway just west of Chatham, it was held by the Romans, and has a Norman castle and a cathedral.

Rochester[2]. Port of New York State, United States, situated on the river Genesee on the south side of Lake Ontario.

Rochester, John Wilmot, 2nd Earl of (1647–80). British poet. A wit and libertine at the court of Charles II, he is especially remembered for his satirical writings, which include *A Satire Against Mankind* (1675), and for his amorous poems.

roch·et (róchit) *n.* A ceremonial vestment made of linen or lawn, worn by bishops and other church dignitaries. [Middle English, from Old French, from Frankish *rok* (unattested), coat.]

rock[1] (rok) *n.* **1.** Any relatively hard naturally formed mass of mineral or petrified matter; stone. **2. a.** A relatively large body of such material, as a cliff or peak. **b.** *Chiefly U.S.* A relatively small piece or fragment of such material; a stone. **3.** *Geology.* Any naturally formed mineral mass or aggregate that constitutes a significant part of the earth's crust. **4.** A person or thing suggestive of a mass of stone in stability, solidity, or strength: *St. Peter was the rock upon which the church was built.* **5.** *Usually plural. U.S. Slang.* Money. **6.** *Slang.* A large gem, especially a diamond. **7.** *Chiefly British.* A kind of hard sweet, usually peppermint-flavoured, and produced as a brightly coloured stick. **—on the rocks. 1.** *Informal.* In a state of destruction or ruin: *Their marriage is on the rocks.* **2.** Without money; bankrupt. **3.** Served over ice cubes without water or a mixer. **—The Rock.** *Informal.* The Rock of **Gibraltar** *(see).* [Middle English *rokke,* from Old Northern French *roque,* variant of Old French *roche,* from Medieval Latin *rocca*†.]

rock[2] *v.* **rocked, rocking, rocks.** *—intr.* **1.** To move back and forth or from side to side, especially gently or rhythmically: *The boat rocked on the waves.* **2.** To sway violently, as from a blow or shock; shake. **3.** To be washed and panned in a cradle or rocker. Used of ores. **4.** To dance to rock'n'roll music. *—tr.* **1.** To sway back and forth or from side to side; especially, to soothe or lull to sleep: *rocked the baby in his arms.* **2.** To cause to shake or sway violently. **3.** To disturb or distress deeply; shock: *The scandal rocked the town.* **4.** To wash or pan (ore) in a cradle or rocker. **5.** In mezzotint engraving, to roughen (a copper plate) with various rockers and roulettes. —See Synonyms at **swing.**

~n. **1.** The act of rocking. **2.** A rocking motion. **3. Rock 'n' roll** *(see).* **4. Rock music** *(see).* [Middle English *rokken,* Old English *roccian,* perhaps from Germanic *rukk-* (unattested).] **—rock·ing·ly** *adv.*

rock·a·bil·ly (róckə-billi) *n.* A form of rock music combining elements of country music and rhythm and blues. [*Rock* music + hill*billy.*]

Rock·all (rók-awl). Uninhabited British islet, situated in the Atlantic Ocean 350 kilometres (220 miles) off the Hebrides.

rock-and-roll. Variant of **rock 'n' roll.**

rock bass *n.* **1.** A freshwater food fish, *Ambloplites rupestris,* of eastern and central North America. **2.** Any of various similar or related fishes.

rock bottom *n.* The lowest level; the absolute bottom: *Prices have reached rock bottom.* **—rock-bot·tom** (rók-bóttəm) *adj.*

rock-bound (rók-bownd) *adj.* Hemmed in by or bordered with rocks: *a rock-bound lake.*

rock cake *n.* A small, sweet, relatively hard cake containing dried fruit and usually having a rough surface. Also called "rock bun".

rock crystal *n.* Transparent colourless quartz.

rock dove *n.* A bird, *Columba livia,* native to Europe but widely distributed elsewhere, having grey plumage with iridescent neck markings. It is the ancestor of the common domestic pigeon. Also called "rock pigeon".

Rock·e·fel·ler (róckə-fellər), **John D(avison)** (1839–1937). U.S. business magnate. He made his wealth through founding the Standard Oil Company (1870), the first major oil monopoly in the United States. From 1890 he established a number of institutions to promote medical research and education. His philanthropic concerns were developed by his son, John D(avison) Rockefeller Jr. (1874–1960).

Rockefeller, Nelson A(ldrich) (1908–79). U.S. Republican politician, the grandson of John D. Rockefeller. He was governor of New York (1958–73), and vice-president (1974–77).

rock·er (róckər) *n.* **1.** Any of various mechanical devices or parts that operate with a rocking motion. **2.** A rocking chair. **3.** A rocking horse. **4.** Either of the two curved pieces upon which a cradle, rocking chair, or similar device rocks. **5.** *Mining.* A cradle for washing or panning ores. **6.** A small steel plate with a curved, toothed edge, used to roughen a copper plate for a mezzotint. **7.** An ice skate with a curved blade. **8.** *Sometimes capital* **R.** In Britain, especially in the 1960s, a youth belonging to a gang of motorcyclists, typically having slicked-back hair and wearing a leather jacket, and often in conflict with **mods** *(see).* **—off (one's) rocker.** *Slang.* Out of (one's) mind; crazy.

rocker arm *n.* A pivoted lever, as in an internal-combustion engine, used to transfer cam or pushrod motion to a valve stem.

rock·er·y (róckəri) *n., pl.* **-ies.** A small-scale rock garden, usually forming part of a larger garden.

rock·et[1] (róckit) *n.* **1. a.** Any device propelled by ejection of matter, especially by the high-velocity ejection of the gaseous combustion products produced by internal ignition of solid or liquid fuels, used for launching a spacecraft or as a signal, for example. **b.** A rocket engine. **2. a.** A weapon carrying an explosive or other warhead, and using rocket power. **b.** An incendiary weapon with a rounded hollow warhead filled with explosives and formerly fired from a ship. **3.** A firework for aerial display that rises vertically then explodes and sprays a shower of coloured stars. Also called "skyrocket". **4.** *British Slang.* A strong reproof or reprimand.

~v. **rocketed, -eting, -ets.** *—intr.* **1.** To move or fly directly and swiftly, as a rocket does. **2.** To rise rapidly or unexpectedly: *prices rocketed.* *—tr.* **1.** To assault with rockets. **2.** To carry by means of a rocket. [French *roquette,* from Italian *rocchetto,* diminutive of *rocca,* ROCK (referring to cylindrical shape of firework).]

rocket[2] *n.* **1.** A plant, *Eruca sativa,* native to Eurasia, having yellowish-white flowers and leaves that are sometimes used in salads. **2.** Any of several related plants, especially one of the genera *Sisymbrium,* such as *S. irio* (London rocket), *Cakile* (sea rocket), or *Diplotaxis* (wall rocket). [French *roquette,* from Italian *ruchetta,* diminutive of *ruca,* from Latin *ērūca,* "caterpillar," plant with downy stems, perhaps from *er,* hedgehog.]

rock·et·eer (rócki-téer) *n.* A person who designs, launches, studies, or pilots rockets.

rocket engine *n.* An engine that propels, especially one that propels spacecraft or aircraft, by means of rockets.

rocket motor *n.* A rocket engine, especially one using solid propellants.

rock·et·ry (róckitri) *n.* The science and technology of rocket design, construction, and flight.

rock·et·sonde (róckit-sond) *n.* Recording equipment adapted for use on a rocket, and used for observation in the upper atmosphere.

rock·fish (rók-fish) *n., pl.* **-fishes** or collectively **rockfish. 1.** Any of various fishes living among rocks. **2.** Any of various fishes, chiefly of the genus *Sebastodes,* of Pacific waters.

rock flour *n.* Pulverised rock produced, for example, along the faces of a moving fault or during movement of a glacier.

rock garden *n.* A rocky area in which plants especially adapted to such terrain are cultivated.

rock hopper *n.* A New Zealand penguin, *Eudyptes crestatus,* with a yellow head crest.

Rock·ies (róckiz). The **Rocky Mountains** *(see).*

rock·ing chair (rócking) *n.* A chair mounted on rockers or springs, so that the sitter may rock on it.

rocking horse *n.* A toy horse large enough for a child to ride, mounted upon rockers or springs.

rock·ling (róckling) *n., pl.* **-lings** or collectively **rockling**. Any of various small marine fishes of the family Gadidae, of North Atlantic coastal waters, having barbels around the mouth. [ROCK (stone) + LING (fish).]

rock lobster *n.* The **spiny lobster** *(see)*.

rock music *n.* A form of western popular music that became established in the late 1950s, growing out of various types of U.S. folk music, such as blues and gospel, and is characterised by strong repetitive rhythms. Also called "rock".

rock'n'roll, rock-and-roll (rók-ən-ról) *n.* **1.** Popular music combining elements of rhythm and blues with country and western music, and having a heavily accented beat. Also called "rock". **2.** A form of jive which developed from jitterbug in response to rock music, originating in the 1950s among U.S. blacks. [In 1950s black American slang, *rock and roll* represents sexual intercourse.] —**rock'n'roll** *adj. & intr.v.* —**rock'n'rol·ler** *n.*

rock oil *n.* *Chiefly British.* **Petroleum** *(see)*.

rock·oon (ro-koon) *n.* A rocket carrying scientific instruments to study the upper atmosphere that is carried to a certain height by balloon, then fired. [*Rock*et + ball*oon*.]

rock pigeon *n.* The **rock dove** *(see)*.

rock plant *n.* Any plant adapted for growing among rocks or in rocky ground.

rock python *n.* The **amethystine python** *(see)*.

rock-ribbed (rók-ríbd) *adj.* **1.** Having rocks or rock outcroppings. **2.** Stern and unyielding.

rock·rose (rók-rōz) *n.* Any of various plants or shrubs of the genus *Helianthemum* and related genera, having roselike yellow, white, or reddish flowers, and often cultivated as garden ornamentals.

rock salmon *n.* *British.* Any of various coarse fish, such as the dogfish, that are used as food.

rock salt *n.* A mineral form of common salt (sodium chloride). Also called "halite".

rock samphire *n.* A plant, **samphire** *(see)*.

rock·shaft (rók-shaaft ‖ -shaft) *n.* A shaft that oscillates or rocks upon its bearings, but does not revolve.

rock·work (rók-wurk) *n.* Ornamental stonework, as in a rock garden or rockery.

rock·y[1] (rócki) *adj.* **-ier, -iest. 1.** Consisting of, containing, or abounding in rock or rocks. **2.** Resembling or suggesting rock; firm or hard; tough; unyielding. **3.** Marked by obstructions or difficulties: *the rocky road to success.* —**rock·i·ness** *n.*

rock·y[2] *adj.* **-ier, -iest. 1.** Unsteady; unstable; shaky. **2.** *Informal.* Weak, dizzy, or nauseous. —**rock·i·ness** *n.*

Rocky Mountains. Also **Rockies.** Mountain system of west North America, forming the Continental Divide. It extends 4 800 kilometres (3,000 miles) from the north Mexican border to the Yukon but is sometimes taken to include its continuation through the Yukon to Alaska. It rises to 4 399 metres (14,431 feet) at Mount Elbert and in its extended form to 6 050 metres (19,850 feet) at Mount Logan.

ro·co·co (rə-kókō, rō- ‖ *U.S. also* rókə-kō) *n.* **1.** A style of art, developed from the baroque, that originated in France (about 1720) and soon spread throughout Europe; especially, this style used in architecture and decoration, characterised by elaborate, profuse designs of scrolls and curves intended to produce a delicate effect. **2.** *Music.* The style immediately following the baroque in Europe (about 1726 to 1775). See feature, next page. ~*adj.* **1.** Of or in rococo style. **2.** Profuse or elaborate; overdone; florid: *rococo writing.* [French, fanciful alteration of ROCAILLE.]

rod (rod) *n.* **1.** A straight, thin piece or bar of metal, wood, or other material: *a curtain rod.* **2.** A shoot or stem cut from, or growing as part of, a woody plant. **3.** A stick, or a bundle of sticks, used for beating, as for punishment. **4.** A **fishing rod** *(see)*. **5.** A wand or staff symbolising power or authority. **6.** Power or dominion, especially of a tyrannical nature: *"under the rod of a cruel slavery."* (John Henry Newman). **7.** A metal bar in a machine: *a piston rod.* **8.** A measuring stick. **9.** See **levelling rod. 10.** A **lightning conductor** *(see)*. **11.** A **divining rod** *(see)*. **12.** *Abbr.* **rd, r. a.** A linear measure equal to 5.5 yards, 16.5 feet, or 5.03 metres. Also called "pole", "perch". **b.** A square rod, equal to 30.25 square yards. **13.** *Chiefly U.S. Vulgar.* A penis. **14.** *Anatomy.* Any of various rod-shaped cells in the retina that contain the pigment rhodopsin and are sensitive to dim light. Compare **cone. 15.** Any elongated microorganism; especially, a bacterium. **16.** *U.S. Slang.* A pistol or revolver. [Middle English *rodd*, Old English *rodd*.]

rode. Past tense of **ride.**

ro·dent (ród'nt) *n.* Any of various mammals of the order Rodentia, such as a mouse, rat, squirrel, or beaver, characterised by large, continuously growing incisors adapted for gnawing or nibbling. ~*adj.* **1.** Gnawing. **2.** Of or pertaining to rodents. [New Latin *Rodentia*, from Latin *rōdēns* (stem *rodent*-), present participle of *rōdere*, to gnaw.]

ro·dent·i·cide (rō-dénti-sīd) *n.* An agent used to kill rodent pests. [RODENT + -CIDE.]

rodent ulcer *n.* A malignant tumour of the face, especially the lips and nostrils, that destroys the underlying muscle and bone.

ro·de·o (rō-dáy-ō, rə-; *also* rōdi-ō) *n., pl.* **-os.** In North America: **1.** A cattle roundup. **2.** An enclosure for keeping cattle that have been rounded up. **3.** A public entertainment including riding broncos, lassoing, and similar displays. [Spanish, from *rodear*, to surround, from Latin *rotāre*, to ROTATE.]

Rodg·ers (rójərz), **Richard (Charles)** (1902–79). U.S. composer. He collaborated with the librettist Lorenz Hart (1895–1943) on *Pal Joey* (1940) and other musicals, but is especially remembered for those he produced with Oscar Hammerstein II, including *Oklahoma!* (1943), *South Pacific* (1949), *The King and I* (1951), and *The Sound of Music* (1959).

Ro·din (rō-daN, *French* rō-dáN), **(François) Auguste (René)** (1840–1917). French sculptor. He first exhibited at the Paris Salon in 1877, and later won an immense reputation for the originality of his compositions, which recall Michelangelo in their sense of tragic grandeur. His controversial public commissions included *The Burghers of Calais* (1894) and an effigy of Balzac in his dressing gown. His most ambitious work was the *Gates of Hell* on which he worked from the 1880s until his death. See feature, page 1457.

rod·o·mon·tade (róddə-mon-táyd, -moN-, -táad) *n.* **1.** Often plural. Pretentious boasting or bragging; bluster. **2.** A pretentious boast. See Synonyms at **bombast.** ~*adj.* Pretentiously boastful or bragging. ~*intr.v.* **rodomontaded, -tading, -tades.** To boast or brag; bluster; rant. [French, from obsolete Italian *rodomontada*, from *rodomonte*, braggart, after *Rodomonte*, a boastful Moorish king in the epics *Orlando Innamorato* (1487) and *Orlando Furioso* (1516).]

Rod·ri·go (rod-réegō), **Joaquin** (1902–). Spanish composer. Blind from the age of three, he has written many works, especially for guitar, including the *Concierto de Aranjuez* (1940), often blending the classsical tradition with picturesque folk elements.

roe[1] (rō) *n.* **1.** The egg-laden ovary of a fish. Also called "hard roe". **2.** The egg mass of certain crustaceans, such as the lobster. **3. Soft roe** *(see)*. [Middle English *roof, roughe, row,* from Middle Low German or Middle Dutch *roge*.]

roe[2] *n., pl.* **roes** or collectively **roe**. A **roe deer** *(see)*.

roe·buck (rō-buk) *n.* A male roe deer.

roe deer *n.* A small Eurasian deer, *Capreolus capreolus*, having a brownish coat and short, branched antlers in the male. Also called "roe." [*Roe*, Middle English *ro, ra(a)*, Old English *rā, rāha*, from Germanic.]

roent·gen, rönt·gen (rónt-gən, rúnt-, rúrnt-, rónt-, jən ‖ rént-) *n.* *Symbol* **R** A unit of radiation dosage, for X-rays or gamma rays, the dose that will produce ions of one sign having a total charge of 0.258×10^{-3} coulomb when totally absorbed in one kilogram of dry air under standard conditions. See **rad.** [After Wilhelm Konrad ROENTGEN.]

Roent·gen or **Rönt·gen** (*German* róntgən), **Wilhelm Konrad** (1845–1923). German physicist. He discovered X-rays and developed X-ray photography, revolutionising medical diagnosis, and was awarded the first Nobel prize for physics (1901).

roentgen equivalent man *n. Abbr.* **REM** A unit of radiation dose that would produce the same effect in a person as one roentgen of X-rays or gamma rays.

roent·gen·ise, roent·gen·ize (rónt-gə-nīz, rúnt-, rúrnt-, rónt-, -jə- ‖ rént-) *tr.v.* **-ised, -ising, -ises.** To subject to the action of X-rays. —**roent·gen·i·sa·tion** (-nī-záysh'n ‖ *U.S.* -ni-) *n.*

Roentgen ray *n.* An **X-ray** *(see)*.

ro·ga·tion (rō-gáysh'n, rə-) *n.* **1.** *Usually plural.* A solemn prayer or supplication, especially as chanted during the rites of the Rogation Days. **2.** A law proposed by a tribune or consul to the people of ancient Rome for acceptance or rejection. [Middle English *rogacioun*, from Latin *rogātiō* (stem *rogātiōn*-), from *rogāre*, to ask, supplicate.] —**ro·ga·tion·al** *adj.*

Rogation Days *pl.n. Ecclesiastical.* The three days preceding Ascension Day, designated as days of special prayer.

rog·a·to·ry (róggə-təri, -tri, rō-gáytəri, rə-) *adj. Law.* **1.** Requesting information, especially with proper authorisation: *rogatory letters.* **2.** Empowered to carry out investigations: *a rogatory commission.* [French *rogatoire*, from Medieval Latin *rogātōrius*, from Latin *rogāre*, to ask, supplicate.]

rog·er[1] (rójər) *interj. Often capital* **R. 1.** Used in telecommunications to indicate that a message has been received and understood. **2.** *Slang.* Used to express agreement or understanding. ~*n. Often capital* **R.** The **Jolly Roger** *(see)*. [From the name *Roger*, in signalling code representing *R* and (message) received.]

roger[2] *v.* **-ered, -ering, -ers.** *British Vulgar.* —*tr.* To have sexual intercourse with. —*intr.* To have sexual intercourse. [From obsolete *roger*, penis, humorous use of *Roger*, man's name.]

Rog·ers (rójərz), **Ginger**, born Virginia McMath (1911–). U.S. actress and entertainer. She is best remembered for her partnership with Fred Astaire in a number of 1930s film musicals, including *Top Hat* (1935), *Follow the Fleet* (1936), and *Shall We Dance* (1937).

Rog·et (rózhay, rō-zhay), **Peter Mark** (1779–1869). British philologist and polymath. A physician and secretary of the Royal Society, he was the author of the *Thesaurus of English Words and Phrases* (1852), which has appeared in many subsequent editions.

rogue (rōg) *n.* **1.** An unprincipled and dishonest person; a scoundrel. **2.** A person who is playfully mischievous; a rascal or scamp. Used humorously. **3.** *Archaic.* A wandering beggar; a vagrant or vagabond. **4.** A vicious and solitary animal; especially, an elephant separated from its herd. **5.** An organism, especially a cultivated plant, that shows an undesirable variation from a standard. ~*v.* **rogued, roguing, rogues.** —*tr.* **1.** To defraud. **2. a.** To remove (diseased or abnormal specimens) from a group, as of plants of the

roe deer *A small Eurasian deer which barks like a dog when alarmed. Both sexes are almost tailless and the male has only very short antlers.*

same variety. **b.** To remove such specimens from (a field, for example). —*intr.* To remove undesired plant specimens.

~*adj.* **1.** Vicious and solitary. Said of an animal. **2.** Taking an independent and often rebellious stance; maverick: *a rogue trade union.* **3.** Defective. Said especially of a new motor vehicle. [16th century (cant) : origin obscure.]

ro·guer·y (rōgəri) *n., pl.* **-ies. 1.** Behaviour characteristic of a rogue; trickery. **2.** An unprincipled or dishonest act. **3.** A mischievous act.

rogues' gallery *n.* **1.** A collection of photographs of criminals maintained in police files and used for making identifications. **2.** Broadly, any collection of people of some particular, usually disreputable, type, such as criminals.

ro·guish (rōgish) *adj.* **1.** Dishonest or unprincipled. **2.** Playfully mischievous. —**ro·guish·ly** *adv.* —**ro·guish·ness** *n.*

Röhm (röm), **Ernst** (1887–1934). German soldier and politician. He took part in the Munich putsch (1923) and in 1930 was appointed chief of staff of the Sturmabteilung, or Brownshirts, a uniformed branch of the Nazi party. Under Rohm the S.A. became a paramilitary force which threatened to rival the authority of the regular army. In 1934, Hitler had Röhm and other leaders executed.

roil (royl) *v.* **roiled, roiling, roils.** —*tr.* **1.** To make (a liquid) muddy or cloudy by stirring up sediment. **2.** To displease or disturb; irritate; vex. —*intr.* To be in a state of turbulence or agitation. [Perhaps from Old French *ruiler,* to mix mortar, from Late Latin *regulāre,* to REGULATE.]

roil·y (róyli) *adj.* **-ier, -iest.** *U.S.* **1.** Muddy; cloudy. **2.** Agitated.

roist·er (róystər) *intr.v.* **-ered, -ering, -ers. 1.** To engage in boisterous merrymaking; revel noisily. **2.** To behave in a blustering manner; swagger. [Probably from Old French *rustre,* churl, boor, alteration of *ruste,* rude, rough, churlish, from Latin *rūsticus,* RUSTIC.] —**roist·er·er** *n.* —**roist·er·ous** *adj.* —**roist·er·ous·ly** *adv.*

Ro·ki·tan·sky (rócki-tán-ski), **Karl, Freiherr von** (1804–78). Austrian pathologist, a pioneer of pathological anatomy. He helped to establish the study of disease autopsy as a medical science.

---

rococo

A FRENCH ART STYLE OF CHARM AND ELEGANCE

Avoiding pomposity with scrolls and frills

During the early 18th century, French patrons and artists reacted against the massiveness and pomposity of the Baroque style and adopted a lighter, smaller-scale style that came to be known as Rococo.

Rococo – originally a term of abuse applied to overelaborate works – was coined later in the century, probably by combining the French *rocaille* (rock) and *coquille* (shell), both of which were favourite Rococo motifs. It was primarily a decorative style, predominantly French, but also adopted in southern Germany, where the style was mainly used in churches. Art historians generally regard it as an aspect of, rather than a successor to, the Baroque style.

Rococo was characterised by a profusion of ornate scrolls and curves and was first used in metalwork and interior decoration. French architects, furniture makers, and artists adopted it and used it to transform the courts of northern Europe and Russia. French artists – chiefly Antoine Watteau, François Boucher, and Jean Fragonard – created a new genre of Rococo painting, charming, wistful, lightweight, and sometimes mildly erotic, in which courtiers dally in leafy gardens with pretty, gaily dressed young ladies.

Both Baroque and Rococo styles were superseded in the second half of the 18th century when discoveries in classical art inspired a passion for a new style, neoclassicism, which lasted well into the 19th century.

MEISSEN FIGURES *In this Meissen porcelain of 1770, a shepherd and sleeping shepherdess, breast exposed, form a scene reflecting the French taste for pastoral fantasy.*

THE SWING *Fragonard's painting of 1768 or 1769 is considered to express the essence of Rococo art, which was by then already in decline. The flirtatious young girl on the swing, her silk and lace dress billowing around her, kicks off her slipper above her lover's head, allowing him a delectable glimpse of leg and petticoat. Fragonard was a virtuoso who could turn his hand instantly to accord with different tastes – in this case the romanticised eroticism demanded by his client.*

HEAVEN'S GATES *The ornate ceiling of the Wieskirche at Steingaden, Bavaria, typifies the German religious use of the Rococo style, which in France was purely secular.*

Ro·land (rṓlənd, ro-lóN). A legendary hero, nephew of Charlemagne killed in battle at Roncesvalles (A.D. 778).

role, rôle (rōl) *n.* **1.** A character or part to be played by an actor in a dramatic production. **2.** The behaviour expected of or associated with an individual or group in society, as determined by social position, sex, or other factors. **3.** A function or position: *your role as a journalist.* [French *rôle,* from Old French *rol(l)e,.* roll (on which a part is written), from Medieval Latin *ro(tu)lus, ro(tu)la,* roll of parchment, from Latin *rotulus,* small wheel. See **roll.**]
Usage: The use of the circumflex accent is still common in formal English, but the unaccented form is more common nowadays, and is particularly widespread in American English.

role-play·ing (rṓl-play-ing) *n.* **1.** The usually subconscious adoption of behaviour or attitudes felt to be characteristic of a given position in society. **2.** The taking on of another's position and psychological perspective, usually in order to evaluate responses to likely situations or problems, especially as a training method for social workers and others or as a technique in psychotherapy. —**role-play** *n.*

role reversal *n.* The adoption of a social role opposite to that normally taken by the subject.

rolf¹ (rolf) *intr.v.* **rolfed, rolfing, rolfs.** *Chiefly U.S. Slang.* To vomit.

rolf² (rolf, rōf) *tr.v.* **rolfed, rolfing, rolfs.** To administer rolfing to. —**rolf·er** *n.*

Rolfe (rōf, *also* rolf), **Frederick William,** also known by his pen name of Baron Corvo (1860–1913). British novelist. A convert to Roman Catholicism he was an unsuccessful candidate for the priesthood and vented his frustration in his most famous work *Hadrian the Seventh* (1904), the story of a convert who becomes pope.

rolf·ing (rṓlf-ing, rōf-) *n.* Deep massage designed to relieve muscular and emotional tension and to reorientate the body to the force of gravity. [After Ida *Rolf* (1897–1979), U.S. physiotherapist.]

roll (rōl) *v.* **rolled, rolling, rolls.** —*intr.* **1.** To move forward along a surface by revolving on an axis or by repeatedly turning over. **2.** To travel or be moved on wheels or rollers. **3.** To travel or be carried in a vehicle: *rolled past the cornfields in the car.* **4. a.** To move or flow with an undulating rhythm: *The waves rolled towards the shore.* **b.** To be carried on a stream. **5. a.** To operate: *The presses began to roll.* **b.** *Informal.* To get underway; proceed: *The political campaign began to roll.* **6.** To go by; elapse. Used with *on, away,* or *by: The hours rolled on.* **7.** To recur periodically; progress as in cycles. Sometimes used with *round* or *around: Summer has rolled round again.* **8.** To move in a periodic revolution, as does a planet in its orbit. **9.** To turn and twist from side to side: *The puppy rolled in the mud.* **10.** To rotate: *His eyes rolled with fright.* **11.** To turn round or revolve on or as on an axis. **12.** To extend or appear to extend in gentle rises and falls: *rolling hills.* **13.** To move or rock from side to side. Used of a ship. Compare **pitch.** **14.** To walk with a swaying, unsteady motion. **15.** To form the shape of a ball or cylinder. Often used with *up: The caterpillar rolled up.* **16.** To become flattened by or as if by pressure applied by a roller. **17.** To make a deep, prolonged, surging sound. Said especially of thunder. **18.** To make a sustained, trilling sound, as do certain birds. **19.** *U.S.* To wander; travel round: *rolling from town to town.* —*tr.* **1.** To cause to move forward along a surface by revolving on an axis, or by repeatedly turning over. **2.** To move or push along on or as if on wheels or rollers: *roll the plane out of the hangar.* **3.** To impel or send onwards in a steady, undulating motion: *The sea rolls its waves onto the sand.* **4.** To impart a swaying, rocking motion to: *Heavy seas rolled the ship.* **5.** To cause to turn round or rotate: *roll one's eyes.* **6.** To pronounce or utter with a trill: *You must roll your "r's" when speaking Spanish.* **7.** To utter or emit in full, sonorous tones. **8.** To beat (a drum) with a continuous series of short blows. **9. a.** To wrap (something) round and round upon itself or around something else. Often used with *up: roll up a scroll.* **b.** To form (oneself) into a ball, as a hedgehog does. **10. a.** To envelop or enfold in a covering: *roll laundry in a sheet.* **b.** To shape into a ball or cylinder, as by rubbing between the hands or turning over and over: *rolled a cigarette; rolled snow into a ball.* **11.** To spread, compress, or flatten by applying pressure with a roller: *roll out dough.* **12.** *Printing.* To apply ink to (type) with a roller or rollers. **13.** To cause (a film camera, for example) to operate. **14.** *U.S.* To throw (dice) in craps or other games. **15.** *U.S. Slang.* To rob (a drunken, sleeping, or otherwise helpless person). —See Synonyms at **turn.** —**roll about.** *Informal.* To be overcome with laughter. —**roll in. 1.** To arrive in large numbers; pour in. **2.** *Informal.* To arrive at one's destination: *rolled in late again.* **3.** *Informal.* To abound in; be plentifully supplied with: *rolling in money.* —**roll (one's) own.** *Slang.* To make one's own cigarettes.
~*n.* **1.** The act or an instance of rolling. **2. a.** Anything rolled up in the form of a cylinder: *a roll of carpet.* **b.** A length of leather or other material that may be wound up, with pockets for storing toiletries, tools, or other useful objects. **3.** A quantity of something, such as cloth or wallpaper, rolled into a cylinder, often considered as a unit of measure. **4.** A piece of parchment or paper bearing an inscription that may be or is rolled up; a scroll. **5.** A register or catalogue. **6.** A list of names of persons belonging to a given group: *call the roll.* **7.** A mass of something in cylindrical or rounded form: *a roll of tobacco.* **8. a.** A small rounded portion of bread, that may be cut in half, buttered, and filled: *a cheese roll.* **b.** A cake or pudding made by rolling up dough on which a filling has been spread: *a jam roll.* **c.** Any food that is prepared by rolling up, especially by wrapping pastry round a filling: *a sausage roll.* **9.** A rolling, swaying, or rocking motion or gait. **10.** A gentle swell or undulation of a

surface: *the roll of the plains.* **11.** A deep reverberation or rumble. **12.** A rapid succession of short sounds: *the roll of a drum.* **13.** A trill: *the roll of her "r's."* **14.** A resonant, rhythmical flow of words. **15.** A roller; especially, a cylinder on which to roll something up or with which to flatten something. **16.** *Architecture.* A volute on a Corinthian or Ionic capital. **17.** A gymnastic movement in which the body performs a complete turn on itself, normally head over heels. **18.** A manoeuvre in which an aeroplane makes a single, complete rotation about its longitudinal axis without changing direction or losing altitude. **19.** *U.S. Slang.* Money; especially, a wad of paper money. —**strike off the rolls.** To deprive of membership, especially membership of a professional body after malpractice; expel. [Middle English *rol(l)en,* from Old French *rol(l)er,* from Vulgar

---

Rodin

THE SCULPTOR OF THE 19TH CENTURY
A new realism inspired by classical art

François Auguste Rodin (1840–1917) was the most influential sculptor of the 19th century. Taking his inspiration from Renaissance artists and classical Greek sculptors, he gave his figures a vivid sense of realism by placing them in convincing postures and giving them an appearance of movement.

Rodin, who was born in Paris, produced his first important work in bronze, called *Bronze Age,* in 1877. This male figure was so lifelike that some people thought it was cast from a living model. In 1880 he began his major life's work, called the *Gates of Hell,* which was inspired by Dante's poem *The Inferno.* It was never finished but it provided ideas for several of his most famous pieces including *The Kiss, The Thinker, Eve,* and *The Old Courtesan.*

Rodin often stimulated the imagination of his audience by leaving part of the stone unsculptured, so giving the impression that his figure had recently emerged. His work was a bridge between classical and modern styles and inspired Brancusi, Maillol, and the sculptures of Matisse.

MONUMENT TO BALZAC *Rodin's statue of Balzac was finished in 1898 but rejected by the committee that commissioned it. It was erected in the boulevard Raspail, Paris, in 1939.*

Latin *rotulāre* (unattested), from Latin *rotulus, rotula*, small wheel, from *rota*, wheel.]

Rol·land (ro-lóɴ), **Romain** (1866–1944). French novelist, biographer, dramatist, and man of letters. His varied works include *Jean Christophe* (1904–12), a ten-volume novel about a German musical genius. His essentially pacifist philosophy was much influenced by Tolstoy and Gandhi. He was awarded the Nobel prize for literature in 1915.

roll bar, roll-bar (rŏl-baar) *n.* A strong steel frame reinforcing the roof of a car for protection in case the car should roll over, found especially in cars used for race events.

roll call *n.* **1.** The reading aloud of a list of names of people, as in a classroom or barracks, to determine who is absent. **2.** The time fixed for such a reading.

roll-call vote (rŏl-kawl) *n. U.S.* **1.** A procedure of voting in a legislative assembly or other body, in which each member votes when his name is called from the roll. **2.** An instance of such a voting procedure.

rolled gold (rŏld) *n.* Metal with a thin decorative layer of gold, used especially in jewellery, pens, and the like. Also *U.S.* "filled gold".

rolled oats *n. Used with a singular or plural verb.* **1.** Flakes produced by simultaneously heating and flattening hulled oat grains between rollers. **2.** A breakfast cereal made by simmering such flakes in water or milk.

rolled-steel joist (rŏld-steel) *n.* An **RSJ** (see).

roll·er (rŏl-ər) *n.* **1.** One that rolls. **2.** Any of various cylindrical devices, specifically: **a.** A small, spokeless wheel, such as that of a roller skate or caster. **b.** An elongated cylinder upon which something is wound, such as a window blind or roll of foil. **c.** A heavy cylinder used to perform levelling or crushing operations. **d.** *Printing.* A cylinder, usually of hard rubber, used to ink the type before the paper is impressed. **e.** A cylinder of wire mesh, foam rubber, or other material around which a strand of hair is wound to produce a soft curl or wave. **f.** A device for spreading paint, consisting of a revolving cylinder of foam rubber or fibre fitted to a bracket and handle. **g.** A small steel cylinder in a roller bearing. **h.** Any of a set of revolving cylinders along which heavy objects may be rolled. **3.** A roller bandage. **4.** A heavy, swelling wave that breaks on the coast. **5.** Any of various birds of the family Coraciidae, mostly of warm regions of the Old World, having bright-blue wings, stocky bodies, and hooked bills, and noted for their aggressiveness. **6.** A tumbler pigeon of a breed that somersaults during flight. **7.** *Australian.* A wool-shed hand who trims and rolls fleeces after shearing. **8.** A steamroller (see).

roller bandage *n.* A long strip of bandage in the form of a roll.

roller bearing *n.* A bearing using rollers to reduce friction between machine parts.

roller coaster *n.* A steep, sharply banked, elevated railway with small open passenger cars, operated as a fairground attraction. Also called "big dipper", "switchback".

roller derby *n.* A relay race on roller skates; especially, a type of race run mainly in the United States on an oval track with two teams of skaters often involving aggressive tactics.

roller disco *n.* **1.** Dancing on roller skates to disco music. **2.** A discotheque designed for this type of dancing.

roller skate *n.* A skate having four small wheels instead of a runner, for skating on pavements and hard, smooth surfaces.

roll·er-skate (rŏl-ər-skayt) *intr.v.* **-skated, -skating, -skates.** To skate on roller skates. **—roller skater** *n.*

roller towel *n.* A long towel with its ends sewn together that is hung from a roller.

roll film *n.* Photographic film rolled on a spool.

rol·lick (rŏllik) *intr.v.* **-licked, -licking, -licks.** To behave or move in a carefree, frolicsome manner; romp.
~*n.* A carefree escapade; a lark. [Probably a blend of ROMP and ROLL and FROLIC.] **—rol·lick·some, rol·lick·y** *adj.*

rol·lick·ing (rŏlliking) *adj.* Carefree and high-spirited; boisterous. **—rol·lick·ing·ly** *adv.*

roll·ie (rŏl-i) *n. British Slang.* A **roll-up** (see).

roll·ing (rŏl-ing) *adj.* Progressive; developing or increasing with time: *rolling devolution.*

rolling hitch *n. Nautical.* A hitch for tying the end of one rope to a spar or the middle of another rope. The knot jams when tension is applied.

rolling mill *n.* **1.** A factory in which metal is rolled into sheets, bars, or other forms. **2.** A machine used for rolling metal.

rolling pin *n.* A smooth cylinder usually of wood and with a handle at each end, used for rolling out pastry or dough.

rolling stock *n.* The locomotives, carriages, wagons, and other wheeled vehicles used on a railway.

rolling stone *n.* A wanderer or other person of restless or unsettled habits.

Rolling Stones, The. British rock group, in the vanguard of the 1960s revolution in popular music. It consisted originally of Mick Jagger (1943–), Brian Jones (1942–69), Keith Richard (1943–), Charlie Watts (1941–), and Bill Wyman (1936–). Its many hit records include the singles *Satisfaction,* and *Honky Tonk Women.*

rolling strike *n.* An industrial strike in which groups within one work force strike in sequence, usually one group each day.

roll-mop (rŏl-mop) *n.* Also **roll·mops** *pl.* **rollmops.** A marinated fillet of herring sometimes wrapped around a gherkin or onion, and served as an hors d'oeuvre. [German *Rollmops : rollen,* to ROLL + *Mops,* pug dog.]

roll·neck (rŏl-nek) *n. Chiefly British.* **1.** A high neck on a garment, especially a sweater, that may be folded over. Also used adjectivally: *a rollneck sweater.* **2.** A sweater or other garment with such a neck.

roll on *tr.v.* To apply or put on by means of a rolling action.
~*interj. British Informal.* Used to express eager impatience for some specified event or time: *roll on Christmas!*

roll-on (rŏl-on) *n.* **1.** A liquid deodorant applied by a revolving ball in the mouth of a container. Also used adjectivally: *a roll-on deodorant.* **2.** A woman's corset made of light elastic material.

roll-on roll-off *adj.* **1.** Designating a ferry or other ship designed so that large or heavy vehicles can drive on and drive off. **2.** Of, pertaining to, or designating systems of transport operating in this way: *roll-on roll-off cargo.*

Rolls (rŏlz), **Charles Stewart** (1877–1910). British car manufacturer. In 1906 he merged his firm with that of car designer Henry Royce to form Rolls Royce Ltd., subsequently one of the world's most prestigious car manufacturers. Rolls was also an aviation pioneer. He died in an air crash.

roll-top desk (rŏl-top) *n.* A desk fitted with a flexible, sliding lid made of parallel slats. Also called "roll top".

roll up *intr.v.* **1.** *Informal.* To arrive, especially in a vehicle. **2.** *Informal.* To come along; gather round. **3.** To pile up or increase; become progressively larger. —*tr.v. Military.* To drive (the enemy's flank or line) round and back on itself.

roll-up (rŏl-up) *n.* **1.** *British Informal.* A cigarette put together by the smoker with a cigarette paper and tobacco. **2.** *Australian.* A gathering or assembly of people.

ro·ly-po·ly (rŏli-pŏli) *adj.* Short and plump; pudgy.
~*n., pl.* **roly-polies. 1.** A roly-poly person. **2.** *Chiefly British.* A pudding made by rolling up jam or fruit in pastry dough and cooking it. Also called "roly-poly pudding". [Perhaps from ROLL + POLL (head).]

ROM (rom) *n. Computing.* A read-only memory.

rom. roman (type).

Rom. 1. Roman. **2.** Romance (language). **3.** Romans (New Testament).

Roma. See Rome.

Ro·ma·ic (rō-máy-ik) *n. Rare.* Modern vernacular Greek. [Modern Greek *Rhōmaikos,* from Greek, Roman (especially, of the eastern Roman Empire at Byzantium), from *Rhōmē, Rhōma,* Rome, from Latin *Rōma,* ROME.] **—Ro·ma·ic** *adj.*

ro·maine (rō-máyn) *n. Chiefly U.S.* A lettuce, the **cos** (see). [French, from the feminine of *Romain,* Roman, from Old French, ROMAN.]

ro·ma·ji (rōmaa-jee) *n.* The Roman alphabet as used to transliterate Japanese. [Japanese, from *Roman.*]

ro·man (rōmən) *n. Sometimes capital R Abbr.* **rom.** The most common style of type, characterised by upright letters having serifs and vertical lines thicker than horizontal lines. This definition is printed in roman. Compare **italic.**
~*adj. Sometimes capital R Abbr.* **rom.** Of, set in, or printed in roman. [It represents the style used in ancient Roman inscriptions and manuscripts.]

Ro·man (rōmən) *adj. Abbr.* **Rom. 1.** Of, pertaining to, derived from, or characteristic of Rome and its people, especially ancient Rome. **2.** Of, in, pertaining to, or characteristic of the Latin language. **3.** Of or pertaining to the Roman Catholic Church. **4.** Of or designating an architectural style developed by the ancient Romans, characterised by great, round arches and barrel vaults, masonry construction, and classical orders as decorative features
~*n. Abbr.* **Rom. 1.** A native, resident, or citizen of Rome, especially ancient Rome. **2.** The Italian language as spoken in Rome. **3.** A member of the Roman Catholic Church. [Middle English *Roman* and *Romain,* respectively from Old English *Rōmān,* a Roman, and Old French *Romain,* Roman, a Roman, both from Latin *Rōmānus,* from *Rōma,* ROME.]

ro·man à clef (rō-món a kláy, -món aa) *n., pl.* **romans à clef** (-mónz, *or pronounced as singular). French.* A novel in which actual persons, events, or places are depicted in fictional guise. ["Novel with key".]

Roman alphabet *n.* **1.** The alphabet evolved by the ancient Romans from that of the Greeks by way of the Etruscan alphabet, consisting of 23 letters upon which are founded the modern western European alphabets. Also called "Latin alphabet". **2.** Any of the modern alphabets derived from this.

Roman calendar *n.* A lunar calendar used by the ancient Romans until it was superseded by the **Julian calendar** (see) in 46 B.C. It consisted of ten months and in each month designated the day of the new moon as the **calends** (see), the day of the full moon as the **ides** (see), and the ninth day before the ides as the **nones** (see). Dates were calculated backwards from these three points.

Roman candle *n.* A firework consisting of a tube from which streams of sparks are ejected. [Originated in Italy.]

Roman Catholic *adj. Abbr.* **R.C., Rom. Cath.** Of, designating, belonging to, or pertaining to the Roman Catholic Church.
~*n.* A member of the Roman Catholic Church.

Roman Catholic Church *n. Abbr.* **R.C.Ch.** The Christian church recognising the primacy of the see of Rome and the authority of the Pope characterised by a hierarchical structure of bishops and priests in which doctrinal and disciplinary authority are dependent upon apostolic succession. Also called "Catholic Church", "Church of Rome".

Roman Catholicism *n.* The doctrines, practices, and institutions of the Roman Catholic Church. Also called "Catholicism".

Romanesque

ART INSPIRED BY RELIGION

A rich combination of styles

Romanesque was the art style that began in France and northern Italy in the late 9th century and spread across Europe to reach its peak in the 11th and early 12th centuries; after this it began to develop into the Gothic style. It was expressed mainly through architecture, with the characteristics – derived from Roman architecture – of thick walls and semicircular arches supported by squat cylindrical columns. The development of cross-vaulting enabled builders to give churches stone ceilings rather than the traditional wooden roofs, which were subject to the risk of fire.

Throughout the political chaos of the Dark Ages in Europe, the Church had been the guardian of learning. With the return of a degree of stability in the 10th century, there was a rise in the number of monasteries and an increase in church building. The monastery of Cluny, north of Lyons in France, was particularly influential. Its third head, Abbot Hugh, was a builder who toured Europe and advised on the plans of over 1,000 buildings. The second abbey church of Cluny, built by his predecessor, inspired copies throughout Europe, including Durham cathedral. After 1066, Romanesque was spread through England by the Normans who also took it to Sicily and southern Italy.

Romanesque artists decorated the new churches with sculptures, frescoes, illuminated gospels, and missals (books containing the Mass). They drew on many styles, including Roman, Byzantine, Islamic, and barbarian sources.

PISA CATHEDRAL *This Romanesque building in Italy, begun in 1063, is faced with grey-green and white marble and mosaic inlays. The façade consists of tiers of arcades ascending into the gable. There is an elliptical dome at the crossing point of the nave and transepts.*

ro·mance (rə-mánss, rō- ‖ rô-manss) *n.* **1.** A long, medieval narrative in prose or verse, telling of the adventures of chivalric heroes. **2. a.** Any long, fictitious tale of heroes and extraordinary or mysterious events, usually set in a distant time and place. **b.** Any sequence of real events resembling such a tale in excitement, nobility, or idealised love. **3.** The class of literature of such tales. **4.** A quality suggestive of the adventure, mystery, and idealised exploits found in such tales. **5.** A novel, story, or film dealing with a love affair, especially in a sentimental fashion. **6.** The class or style of fictional works about idealised love. **7. a.** A love affair; especially, a short-lived but passionately idealistic attachment of two young people. **b.** Love or romantic involvement, especially when idealised. **c.** A strong, usually short-lived attachment or enthusiasm. **8.** Inclination towards love, adventure, or mystery; romantic spirit. **9.** A fictitiously embellished account or explanation. **10.** A short, lyrical song or instrumental piece.
~*v.* **romanced, -mancing, -mances.** —*intr.* **1.** To invent, write, or recount tales or adventure, nobility, or love. **2.** To tell extravagant and exaggerated lies. **3.** To think or behave in a romantic manner. —*tr. Informal.* To behave romantically towards; woo. [Middle English roma(u)ns, roma(u)nce, French, work written in French, from Old French romanz, romant, from Vulgar Latin *Rōmānicē* (unattested), in the vernacular (as opposed to *Latinē*, in Latin), from

Latin *Rōmānicus,* Roman, made in Rome, from *Rōmānus,* ROMAN.]
—**ro·manc·er** *n.*
Ro·mance (rə-mánss, rō-, rô-manss) *adj. Abbr.* **Rom.** Of, designating, or belonging to any of the languages that developed from Latin, the principal ones being French, Italian, Portuguese, Romanian, and Castilian Spanish and Catalan.
~*n.* The Romance languages. [From ROMANCE (French, "the Roman tongue").]
Roman Empire *n.* **1.** The lands governed by the ancient Romans. In A.D. 395 it was divided into the East Roman Empire or **Byzantine Empire** *(see)* and the **West Roman Empire** *(see).* **2.** The government of Rome and its lands from 27 B.C by Augustus and the later emperors. **3.** Any empire held to be the successor of the Roman Empire, such as the Byzantine Empire or Holy Roman Empire.
Rom·a·nes (rómma-niss, -ness) *n.* The Gypsy language; Romany. [Romany.]
Ro·man·esque (rōman-ésk) *adj.* **1.** Of, pertaining to, or designating a transitional style of European architecture prevalent from the 9th to the 12th century, and characterised by rounded arches, massive vaulting, and thick walls. See **Norman. 2.** Of, pertaining to, or designating the styles in art prevalent in this period.
~*n.* The Romanesque style. [From ROMAN.]
ro·man-fleuve (rō-món flérv, flòv) *n., pl.* **romans-fleuves** *(pronounced as singular). French.* A long novel, often in many volumes, chronicling the history of an individual, family, or community. Also called "saga novel". See **novel sequence.** [French, "river-novel" (because the development of its plot is now rapid, now slow, like the flow of a river), coined by Romain Rolland.]
Roman holiday *n.* **1.** A time of enjoyment derived from the suffering of others. **2.** Any savage and spectacular entertainment reminiscent of the staged public battles of Roman gladiators. [So called from the gladiatorial contests of the ancient Romans.]
Ro·ma·ni·a or **Ru·ma·ni·a** or **Rou·ma·ni·a, Socialist Republic of** (roō-máyni-ə, roō-, rō-). Republic of southeast Europe. It is dominated by the Carpathians, with the Transylvanian uplands to the northwest, and lower Danubian plains in the southeast. Romania achieved rapid industrial expansion during the 1960s and 1970s, and machinery, chemicals, and consumer goods, as well as agricultural produce, oil, and gas are major exports. The country was formed by the union of Walachia and Moldavia (1861), and achieved independence in 1878. After World War II it became a Soviet satellite but under President Ceauçescu, since 1967 has pursued an increasingly independent course. Area, 237 500 square kilometres (91,699 square miles). Population 22,600,000. Capital, Bucharest.
Ro·ma·ni·an, Ru·ma·ni·an (roō-máyni-ən, roō-, rō-) *adj. Abbr.* **Rom.** Of or pertaining to Romania, its people, or their language.
~*n.* **1.** An inhabitant, native, or citizen of Romania. **2.** The Romance language of the Romanian people.
Ro·man·ic (rō-mánnik, rə-) *adj.* **1.** Of or derived from the ancient Romans or their language. **2.** Of or pertaining to the Romance languages.
~*n.* Romance. [Latin *Rōmānicus,* from *Rōmānus,* ROMAN.]
Ro·man·ise, Ro·man·ize (rōmən-īz) *v.* **-ised, -ising, -ises.** —*tr.* **1.** To convert (a person) to Roman Catholicism. **2.** To make (a ritual, for example) Roman Catholic in character. **3.** To make Roman in character: *Our laws were Romanised.* **4.** To write or transliterate (a language, for example) into the Roman alphabet. —*intr.* **1.** To be converted to Roman Catholicism. **2.** To adopt Roman Catholic practices. —**Ro·man·i·sa·tion** (-ī-záysh'n ‖ *U.S.* -i-) *n.*
Ro·man·ism (rōmən-iz'm) *n.* **1.** Roman Catholicism. Usually used derogatorily. **2.** Admiration for the spirit of ancient Rome.
Ro·man·ist (rōmən-ist) *n.* **1. a.** A Roman Catholic. Usually used derogatorily. **b.** A member of the Church of England who favours

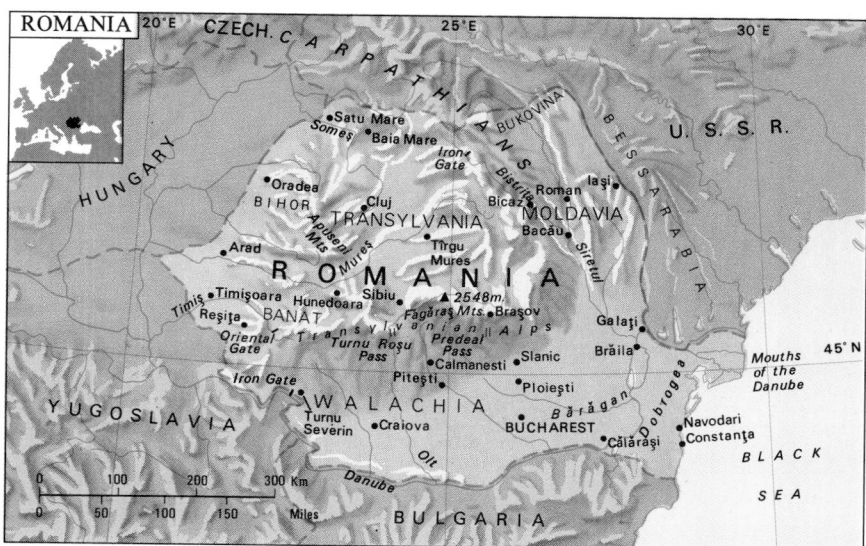

ROMANIA

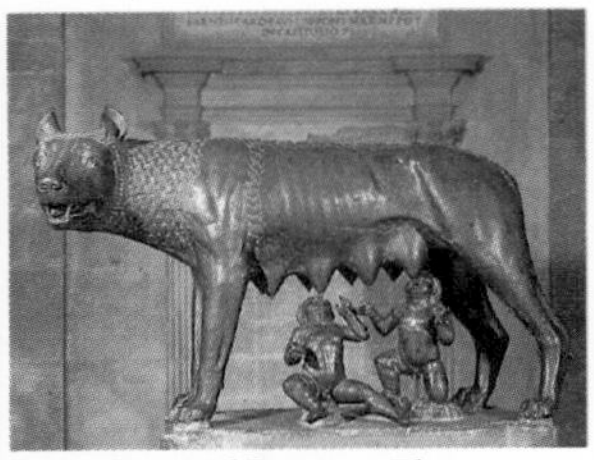

Romulus and Remus *These legendary twins were abandoned at birth but, as this fifth-century Roman statue shows, they were suckled and reared by a wolf.*

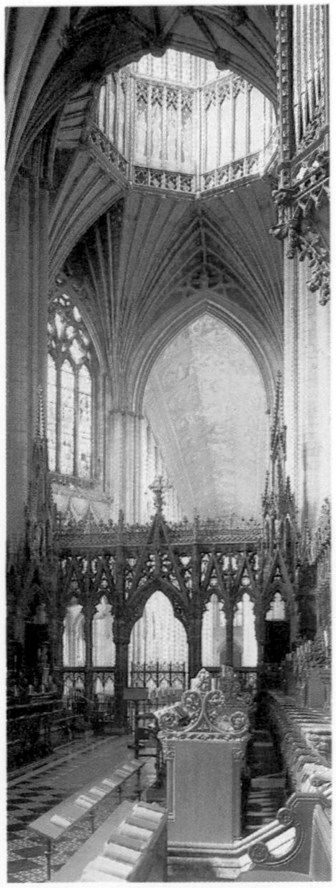

rood screen *The choir is separated from the nave in many English churches by the rood screen, which rises from the floor to a beam which was called the rood (cross) beam.*

Catholic ritual. **2.** A student of or authority on Roman law, culture, and institutions.
~adj. **1.** Of, belonging to, or designating the Roman Catholic Church. Usually used derogatorily. **2.** Favouring Catholic ritual.

Roman law *n.* The system of laws of ancient Rome, upon which the legal systems of many countries are based. See **civil law.**

Roman nose *n.* A nose with a high, prominent bridge.

Roman numerals *pl.n.* Certain letters of the Roman alphabet used as numerical symbols by the ancient Romans and still used today in certain formal contexts. In this system I stands for 1, V for 5, X for 10, L for 50, C for 100, D for 500, and M for 1000. Compare **Arabic numerals.**

Romano- *comb. form.* Indicates Roman; for example, *Romano-Celtic.*

Ro·ma·nov (rṓmən-off; *Russian* ra-ma̋anəf). The imperial dynasty (1613–1917) in Russia. The line began with the accession of Tsar Michael and ended with the abdication of Nicholas II during the Russian Revolution.

Ro·mans (rṓmənz) *n. Used with a singular verb. Abbr.* **Rom.** A book of the New Testament, an epistle of Saint Paul to the Christians of Rome.

Ro·mansch, Ro·mansh (rō-mánsh, rə- || *U.S. also* -ma̋ansch) *n.* The Rhaeto-Romanic dialects spoken in eastern Switzerland and in neighbouring parts of Italy. [Romansch *Ruman(t)sch, Roman(t)sch,* "Roman", "Romance language", from Vulgar Latin *Rōmānicē* (unattested), in the Roman manner, in the Roman tongue. See **romance.**]

Roman snail *n.* A large snail, *Helix pomatia,* that is the more commonly used edible species.

ro·man·tic (rō-mántik, rə-) *adj.* **1. a.** Of, pertaining to, designating, characterised by, or evoking feelings of love, especially of a passionate or sentimental nature: *romantic lighting.* **b.** Given or inclined to such feelings or thoughts: *a romantic young girl.* **2.** Of or pertaining to a sexual relationship. **3. a.** Of or pertaining to a literary romance. **b.** Characteristic of the atmosphere or mood or such romances; idealistic, heroic, exciting, and noble. **4.** Imaginative but impractical: *romantic notions.* **5.** Not based on fact; fictitious. **6.** *Often capital* **R.** Of or characteristic of romanticism in the arts.
~n. **1.** A person whose mind and emotions are orientated towards love, adventure, or high ideals; a romantic person. **2.** A person who enjoys the artistic products of Romanticism more than those of other movements and styles; a romanticist. **3.** *Often capital* **R.** A writer or other artist creating works of art in the style or spirit of Romanticism; especially, one who lived in the romantic era; a romanticist. [French *romantique,* from Old French *romant, romanz,* ROMANCE.] **—ro·man·ti·cal·ly** *adv.*

ro·man·ti·cise, ro·man·ti·cize (rō-mánti-sīz, rə-) *v.* **-cised, -cising, -cises.** *—tr.* **1.** To make romantic in style or character. **2.** To consider or portray in an often inappropriately romantic way: *Don't romanticise crime.* *—intr.* **1.** To think or speak in a romantic way; fantasise. **2.** To act in a romantic way; flirt. **3.** To render the account of some event more interesting; exaggerate.

ro·man·ti·cism (rō-mánti-siz'm, rə-) *n.* **1.** *Often capital* **R.** A literary and artistic movement originating in Europe towards the end of the 18th century that sought to assert the validity of subjective experience and to escape from the prevailing subordination of content and feeling to classical forms. Also called "Romantic Movement". **2.** The spirit and attitudes characteristic of this movement. **—ro·man·ti·cist** *n.*

Rom·a·ny, Rom·ma·ny (rómməni, rṓməni) *n., pl.* **-nies** or collectively **Romany. 1.** A Gypsy. **2.** The Indic language of the Gypsies.
~adj. Of or pertaining to the Gypsies, their culture, or their language. [Romany *romani,* plural of *romano,* gypsy, from *rom,* man, husband, gypsy man, from Sanskrit *ḍomba, ḍoma,* man of a low caste of musicians, from Dravidian.]

ro·maunt (rō-máwnt, rə-, -ma̋ant) *n. Archaic.* A medieval romance in verse or prose. [Middle English, from Old French *romant, romanz,* ROMANCE.]

Rom. Cath. Roman Catholic.

Rome[1] (rōm), *Italian* **Ro·ma** (rṓmaa). Capital of Italy and of the Latium region, known as the Eternal City. Situated on the river Tiber, it is built on and around seven hills and was founded, according to legend, by Romulus, on the Palatine hill (753 B.C.). Once the centre of the Roman Empire, it has many ancient remains, including the Forum and Colosseum. Rome fell to the Goths in the 5th century, and to the Byzantines in 552, and was later sacked by the Arabs (846) and Normans (1084). Gradually it came under papal control, its fortunes following those of the papacy until it was annexed to Italy (1870). During the Renaissance it was a flourishing art centre, and it is rich in buildings and works of art of the period. Rome became Italy's capital in 1871. It is also a cultural, tourist, and manufacturing centre.

Rome[2] *n.* **1.** The ancient Roman kingdom, republic, and empire. **2.** The Roman Catholic Church or Roman Catholicism.

Ro·me·o (rṓmi-ō) *n., pl.* **-os.** An ardent male lover. [After the tragic hero of Shakespeare's *Romeo and Juliet.*]

Rom·ish (rṓmish) *adj.* Of or pertaining to the Roman Catholic Church. Often used derogatorily.

Rom·mel (rómm'l), **Erwin** (1891–1944). German general, nicknamed the Desert Fox, famous for his desert campaigns of World War II. In 1941 he was made commander in chief of the newly formed Afrika Korps. Following victories at Tobruk and Benghazi (1942), he invaded Egypt, but was forced to withdraw after the battle of El Alamein (1942) and recalled to Europe in 1943. He was implicated in the July Plot (1944) to assassinate Hitler, and committed suicide when his complicity was discovered.

Rom·ney (róm-ni, rúm-), **George** (1734–1802). British portrait painter. A Lancashire cabinetmaker's son, he trained under an itinerant artist and later set up as a commercial portrait painter. In 1762 he moved to London, where he acquired a fashionable clientele to rival that of Reynolds.

romp (romp) *intr.v.* **romped, romping, romps. 1.** To play or frolic boisterously. **2.** *British Informal.* To succeed in some venture without effort. Used with *through*: *He romped through his exams.* **3.** To proceed easily or effortlessly. Often used with *about* or *along.* **—romp home** or **in.** To win a race or other competition with ease.
~n. **1.** An occasion of lively, merry play; a frolic. **2.** *Archaic.* One who sports and frolics, especially a girl. **3.** An easy win. [Variant of RAMP (to rage).]

romp·ers (rómpərz) *pl.n.* **1.** A one-piece baby's playsuit, usually with short legs. **2.** *N.Z.* Baggy gym shorts worn by schoolgirls.

Rom·u·lus (rómmewləss). *Roman Mythology.* The son of Mars and a vestal virgin, who, with his twin brother Remus, was abandoned as an infant to die but was suckled by a she-wolf. He later killed Remus and founded Rome in 753 B.C.

Romulus Au·gus·tu·lus (aw-gústewləss) (born *c.* A.D. 460). The last Roman emperor in the West (A.D. 475–6). As a youth he was deposed by the German ruler Odoacer who spared his life. He died in retirement at an unknown date.

Ron·ces·valles (rón-sə-válz; *Spanish* -thess-vál-yess). *French* **Ronce·vaux** (roɴss-vṓ). Mountain pass and village of Navarra, northern Spain. It was the site of the defeat and massacre of the rearguard of Charlemagne's army, under Roland, by the Saracens (778).

ron·da·vel (rón-da̋av'l) *n. South African.* A round house, hut, or outbuilding with a conical roof. Originally a one-roomed native hut with a thatched roof, it now often has several rooms and can be made of modern materials. [Afrikaans *rondawel*†.]

rond de jambe (róɴ də zhóɴb) *n., pl.* **ronds de jambe.** In ballet, a circular movement of the leg from below the knee, executed either in the air or on the ground.

ron·deau (róndō || *U.S. also* ron-dṓ) *n., pl.* **-deaux** (-z). **1.** A lyrical poem of French origin having 13, or sometimes 10, lines with two rhymes throughout and with the opening phrase repeated twice as a refrain. Also called "roundel". **2.** *Music.* **a.** An originally monophonic medieval song of the trouvères or troubadours. **b.** An early rondo. [French, variant of RONDEL.]

ron·del (rónd'l || *U.S. also* ron-dél) *n.* A rondeau that usually has 14 lines. Also called "roundel". [Middle English, from Old French, "small circle" (from the repetition of the first lines at the end of the poem), from *ronde, rounde,* ROUND.]

ron·de·let (róndə-let) *n.* A short rondeau having five or seven lines and one refrain in one stanza. [Old French, diminutive of RONDEL.]

ron·do (róndō || *U.S. also* ron-dṓ) *n., pl.* **-dos.** A musical composition having a refrain that occurs at least three times in its original key. [Italian *rondò,* from French *rondeau,* RONDEAU.]

ron·dure (rón-dewr, -jər) *n. Archaic.* Something circular or gracefully rounded. [Old French *rondeur,* from *rond, rounde,* ROUND.]

rone (rōn) *n. Scottish.* A gutter or drainpipe on a house. [19th century : origin obscure.]

Ro·ne·o (rṓni-ō) *n., pl.* **-os.** *British.* **1.** A trademark for a machine that copies documents from a stencil. **2.** A copy made on such a machine.
~tr.v. **Roneod, -neoing, -neos.** *British. Often small* **r.** To copy (a document, for example) using such a machine.

Ron·sard (róɴ-saar, *French* roɴ-sár), **Pierre de** (1524–85). French lyric poet. His love poems are his most highly regarded works, among them *Les Amours* (1552) and *Sonnets pour Heléne* (1578).

röntgen. Variant of **roentgen.**

roo, 'roo (rōō) *n. Australian Informal.* A kangaroo. [Shortening.]

rood (rōōd) *n.* **1.** A cross or crucifix, especially: **a.** One representing the cross on which Christ was crucified. **b.** One surmounting a rood screen in a medieval church. **2.** *Archaic.* The cross on which Christ was crucified. **3.** *Abbr.* **ro.** A British Imperial unit of length that varies from 5½ to 8 yards. **4.** *Abbr.* **ro.** A British Imperial unit of area usually equal to ¼ acre or 40 square rods. [Middle English *ro(o)d,* Old English *rōd,* rod, cross.]

rood arch *n.* An arch in a church, between the choir and the nave.

rood beam *n.* A beam in a church across the entrance to the choir, where it supports the rood and usually forms the head of the rood screen.

rood loft *n.* A gallery above a rood screen.

rood screen *n.* An ornamented wooden or stone altar screen, usually surmounted by a crucifix, separating the choir of a church from the nave.

roof (rōōf || rŏŏf) *n.* **1.** An exterior surface and its supporting structures on the top of a building. **2.** The top covering of anything. **3.** Anything resembling or compared to a roof, such as the sky or overhead foliage. **4.** *Anatomy.* The upper covering structure of any part of the body: *roof of the mouth.* **5.** The highest point; the summit: *the roof of the world.* **—a roof over (one's) head.** Somewhere to live. **—go through** or **hit the roof.** *Slang.* To lose one's temper suddenly. **—raise the roof.** *Informal.* **1.** To be extremely noisy and boisterous. **2.** To complain loudly and bitterly.
~tr.v. **roofed, roofing, roofs.** To furnish or cover with a roof. Often used with *in* or *over.* [Middle English *ro(o)f,* Old English *hrōf.*]

roof·er (ro͞of-ər || ro͝of-) *n.* One who makes or repairs roofs.
roof garden *n.* A garden on a flat roof of a building.
roof·ing (ro͞of-ing || ro͝of) *n.* **1.** The act of constructing a roof. **2.** A roof of a building. **3.** Materials used in building a roof.
roof·less (ro͞of-ləss, -liss || ro͝of-) *adj.* **1.** Lacking a roof. **2.** Having no home or shelter; homeless.
roof rack *n. Chiefly British.* A metal rack fixed to the top of a motor vehicle for carrying luggage or other objects.
roof·top (ro͞of-top || ro͝of-) *n.* The upper surface of a roof of a building.
roof·tree (ro͞of-tree || ro͝of-) *n.* A long horizontal beam extending along the ridge of a roof; a ridgepole.
rooi·nek (róy-nek) *n. South African.* An Englishman or English South African. Formerly used derogatorily. [Afrikaans, "red neck".]
rook[1] (ro͝ok || ro͞ok) *n.* **1.** A crowlike Old World bird, *Corvus frugilegus,* with white patches at the base of its bill, that nests in colonies near the tops of trees. **2.** *Slang.* A swindler; especially, one who cheats when gambling.
~*tr.v.* **rooked, rooking, rooks.** *Slang.* To swindle, especially by overcharging or by cheating when gambling. [Middle English *rok, ruke,* Old English *hrōc.*]
rook[2] *n. Abbr.* **R** A chess piece that may move in a straight line over any number of empty squares in a rank or file. Also called "castle". [Middle English *rok(e),* from Old French *roc(k),* from Arabic *rukh,* from Persian *rukh*†.]
rook·er·y (ro͝ok-əri || ro͞ok-) *n., pl.* **-ies. 1. a.** A place where rooks nest and breed. **b.** A colony of rocks or their nests. **2. a.** The breeding ground of certain other birds and animals, such as seals. **b.** A colony of such birds or animals. **3.** *Informal.* A crowded tenement.
rook·ie (ro͝oki) *n. Slang.* **1.** An untrained recruit, especially in an army. **2.** Any inexperienced person. [Alteration of RECRUIT (influenced by the bird ROOK).]
room (ro͞om, ro͝om) *n. Abbr.* **rm. 1.** Space that is or may be occupied by something; open space: *a desk that takes up too much room.* Sometimes used in combination: *Shelf-room.* **2.** An area or part inside a building enclosed by a floor, a ceiling, and walls. **3.** The people present in such an area: *The whole room was amazed.* **4.** *Plural.* Living quarters; lodgings. **5.** Scope; opportunity. Used with *for* or *to*: *room for error.* **—make room.** To make more space available, usually by giving way or removing something.
~*intr.v.* **roomed, rooming, rooms.** *U.S.* To occupy a room; lodge. [Middle English *roum,* Old English *rūm.*]
room divider *n.* A partition dividing up a room.
room·ful (ro͞om-fo͝ol, ro͝om-) *n., pl.* **-fuls. 1.** As much or as many as a room will hold. **2.** The number of people in a room.
room·ing house (ro͞om-ing, ro͝om-) *n. U.S.* A lodging house.
room·mate (ro͞om-mayt, ro͝om-) *n.* **1.** A person with whom one shares a room. **2.** *U.S.* A flatmate.
room service *n.* **1.** A service in a hotel attending to guests' requirements, especially for refreshments, in their rooms. **2.** The staff providing this service.
room temperature *n.* A temperature of about 20° C; a comfortable living temperature inside a room.
room·y (ro͞omi, ro͝omi) *adj.* **-ier, -iest.** Having plenty of room; spacious; large. **—room·i·ly** *adv.* **—room·i·ness** *n.*
Roo·se·velt (rōzə-vəlt, -velt, *also* ro͞oss-), **Franklin D(elano).** (1882–1945). U.S. statesman, Democratic president (1933–45). His career was interrupted in 1921 when he was crippled by polio, but he went on to become governor of New York (1928–32). As president he fulfilled his promise of a New Deal for the American people by initiating relief programmes, measures to aid employment, and assist industrial and agricultural recovery from the Depression. He was the only U.S. president to be re-elected three times (1936, 1940, 1944). His wife, Eleanor Roosevelt (1884–1962), was an active crusader for human rights and a delegate to the United Nations.
Roosevelt, Theodore (1858–1919). U.S. statesman, Republican president (1901–09). As president, he won, through forceful diplomacy, the United States' concession to build the Panama Canal (1903). His foreign policy exemplified his principle "speak softly and carry a big stick," and in 1906 he won the Nobel Peace prize for his mediation in the Russo-Japanese War (1904-5).
roost (ro͞ost) *n.* **1.** A perch on which domestic fowls or other birds rest or sleep. **2.** A place with perches for fowls or other birds. **3.** A place for temporary rest or sleep. **—come home to roost.** To recoil unpleasantly upon the doer: *His corrupt practices came home to roost.* **—rule the roost.** To be in charge; be in a dominant position.
~*v.* **roosted, roosting, roosts.** *—intr.* **1.** To rest or sleep on a perch or roost. **2.** To settle down for the night. *—tr.* To supply with a sleeping place for the night. [Middle English *rooste,* Old English *hrōst.*]
roost·er (ro͞ostər) *n. Chiefly U.S.* **1.** The adult male of the common domestic fowl; a cock. **2.** A pugnacious and cocky person.
root[1] (ro͞ot || ro͝ot) *n.* **1. a.** The usually underground portion of a plant that serves as support, draws water and mineral ions from the surrounding soil, and in some plants stores food. **b.** Any similar underground plant part, such as a rhizome, corm, or tuber. **c.** Any of numerous small, hairlike growths that serve to attach and support plants such as the ivy and other vines. **2.** *Anatomy.* **a.** The embedded part of an organ or structure such as a hair or tooth. **b.** The point of emergence of a nerve from the spinal cord, consisting of a bundle of nerve fibres. **3. a.** Any base or support. **b.** A part of an object by which it is attached to a base or larger object: *the root of a propeller.* **4.** Any base or support. **5.** An essential part or element; a basic core or fundamental nature: *strikes at the roots of our democracy.* **6.** A primary source or cause; an origin: *money is the root of all evil.* Also used adjectivally: *the root cause.* **7.** An antecedent or ancestor. **8.** An emotional or psychological attachment or historical association with a particular place or society: *Her roots lie in Antrim.* **9.** *Linguistics.* **a.** In etymology, a word or word element from which other words are formed. **b.** In morphology, a base to which prefixes and suffixes may be added. Also called "radical". **10.** *Mathematics.* **a.** A number that when multiplied by itself a specified number of times forms a product equal to a given number: *a fourth root of 16 is 2.* Also called "numerical root". **b.** A number or quantity that when substituted for the variable, satisfies the polynomial equation $f(x)=0$. See **function. c.** A **multiple root** *(see).* **11.** *Music.* **a.** The note from which a chord is built. **b.** The first or lowest note of a triad or chord. **12.** *Australian Vulgar Slang.* An act of sexual intercourse. —See Synonyms at origin. **—put down roots.** To settle; become established, as by taking up permanent residence in a place. **—take root. 1.** To put out roots and grow. **2.** To become fixed, established, or recognised. **—root and branch.** Entirely; utterly; radically: *overhauled the vetting procedures root and branch.*
~*v.* **rooted, rooting, roots.** *—intr.* **1.** To grow a root or roots. **2.** To become firmly established, settled, or entrenched. *—tr.* **1.** To cause to put out roots and grow. **2.** To implant by or as if by the roots; fix: *stood rooted to the spot.* **3.** To pull or dig up by or as if by the roots. Used with *up* or *out.* **4.** To eliminate; remove totally. Used with *out*: *root out abuses.* **5.** *Australian Vulgar Slang.* To have sexual intercourse with. [Middle English *rot(e),* Old English *rōt,* from Old Norse.] **—root·er** *n.*
root[2] *v.* **rooted, rooting, roots.** *—tr.* **1.** To dig (the ground, for example) with or as with the snout or nose. **2.** To bring to light or turn up by searching. Often used with *out*: *rooted out dark secrets from his past.* *—intr.* **1.** To dig in the ground with or as with the snout or nose. Used chiefly of pigs. **2.** To search about or rummage for something. Often used with *about* or *around.* [Alteration (influenced by ROOT of a plant) of earlier *wroot,* Middle English *wroten,* Old English *wrōtan.*] **—root·er** *n.*
root[3] *intr.v.* **rooted, rooting, roots.** *Chiefly U.S.* To give encouragement or support, especially to a team or contestant. Used with *for.* [Perhaps from ROOT (to dig with the snout).] **—root·er** *n.*
root·age (ro͞ot-ij || ro͝ot-) *n.* **1.** A system or growth of roots. **2.** Establishment or fixing by or as if by roots.
root·ball (ro͞ot-bawl || ro͝ot-) *n.* The tightly packed mass of roots and soil produced by a plant grown in a container.
root beer *n. U.S.* A carbonated soft drink made from extracts of the roots of several plants.
root canal *n.* The pulp-filled cavity in a root of a tooth.
root cap *n. Botany.* A thimble-shaped mass of cells that covers and protects the tip of a growing root.
root·ed (ro͞ot-id || ro͝ot-) *adj.* **1.** Deep-seated or deeply felt. **2.** *Australian Slang.* Exhausted. **—get rooted!** *Australian Vulgar Slang.* Go away!
root hair *n. Botany.* A thin, hairlike outgrowth of a plant root that absorbs water and minerals from the soil.
root·less (ro͞ot-ləss, -liss || ro͝ot-) *adj.* **1.** Having no roots: *a rootless tooth.* **2.** Not belonging to any particular place or society: *the rootless refugees in a strange country.* **—root·less·ness** *n.*
root·let (ro͞ot-lət, -lit || ro͝ot-) *n.* A small root or division of a root.
root mean square *n. Abbr.* **rms** The square root of the arithmetic mean of the squares of a set of numbers.
root mean square deviation *n. Statistics.* **Standard deviation** *(see).*
root·stock (ro͞ot-stok || ro͝ot-) *n.* **1.** A rootlike underground stem, such as a **rhizome** *(see).* **2.** A root or part of a root used as a stock for grafting. **3.** A source of origin.
root vegetable *n.* A vegetable, such as a carrot or beetroot, that is grown for its edible root.
root·y (ro͞oti || ro͝oti) *adj.* **-ier, -iest. 1.** Full of roots. **2.** Consisting of or resembling roots. **—root·i·ness** *n.*
rop·a·ble, rope·a·ble (rōpəb'l) *adj.* **1.** Able to be roped. **2.** *Australian.* Wild and untamable. Said of an animal. **3.** *Australian Informal.* Angry and often violent. Said of a person.
rope (rōp) *n.* **1. a.** Flexible, heavy cord of twisted hemp, flex, nylon, wire or other material. **b.** A section of such cord. **c.** Any strand or other object resembling a rope, especially one consisting of braided or wound material. **2.** A cord with a noose at one end for hanging a person. **3.** Death by hanging. Preceded by *the.* **4.** *Plural.* Several cords strung between poles to enclose a boxing ring. Preceded by *the.* **5.** Any string of items attached in one line by twisting or braiding: *a rope of onions.* **6.** *Plural.* The special procedures, details, or conditions of a field of activity: *Please show me the ropes.* **—give (someone) enough rope to (hang himself).** To deliberately allow (someone) sufficient freedom of action to cause his own downfall. **—on the ropes.** *Informal.* Nearing total collapse, defeat, or ruin.
~*v.* **roped, roping, ropes.** *—tr.* **1.** To tie or fasten with or as with rope. **2.** To enclose, mark off, or divide with a rope. Usually used with *off.* **3.** *British Informal.* To persuade or force (a person) to help or become involved in an activity. Used with *in*: *roped them in to paint the house.* **4.** To join or connect (mountaineers) securely with a rope. Used with *up*: *The guide roped the party up.* **5.** *Chiefly U.S.* To catch with a rope. **6.** *U.S. Informal.* To trick or deceive. Usually used with *in.* *—intr.* In mountaineering, to tie oneself to the other climbers. Used with *up.* [Middle English *rop(e),* Old English *rāp.*]

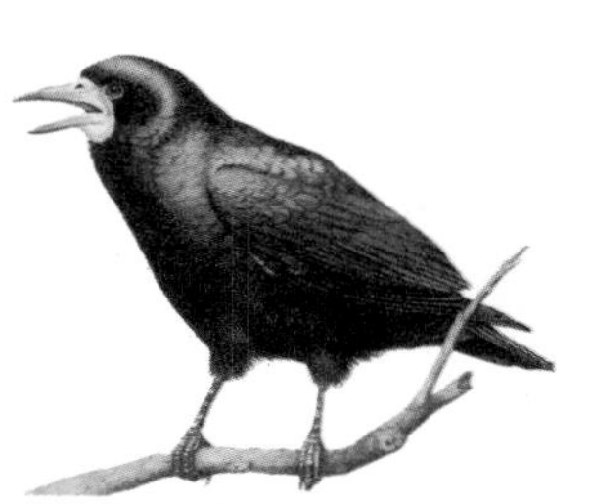

rook Corvus frugilegus, *the common rook of Europe and Asia, is among the most sociable of birds. It feeds in flocks, mainly on insects in the soil, and nests in large rookeries high up in tall trees. Some rookeries may contain as many as 9,000 pairs, and the birds' incessant cawing has given rise to the collective names by which they are sometimes known – a clamour or a parliament of rooks.*

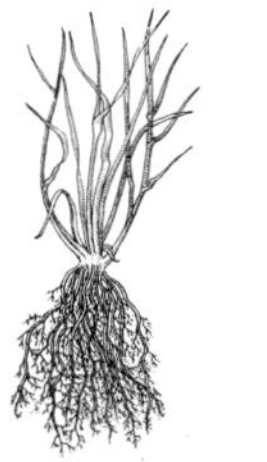

Fibrous roots (grass)

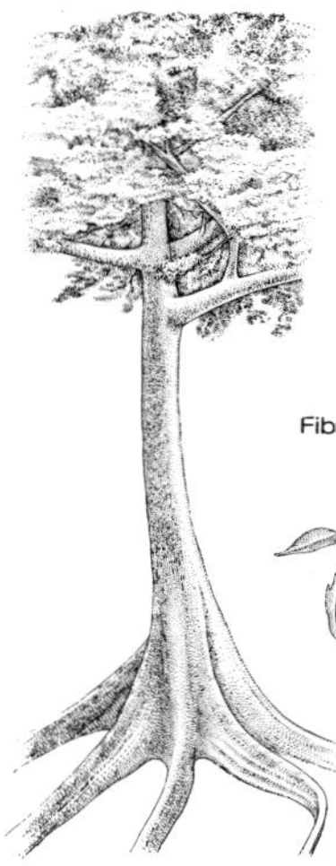

Buttress roots (kapok tree)

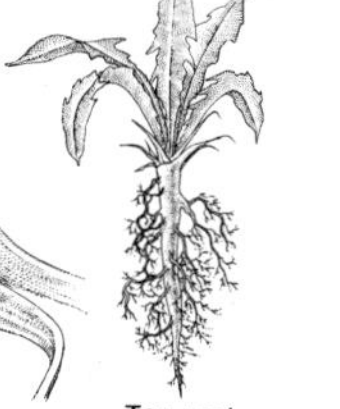

Tap-root (dandelion)

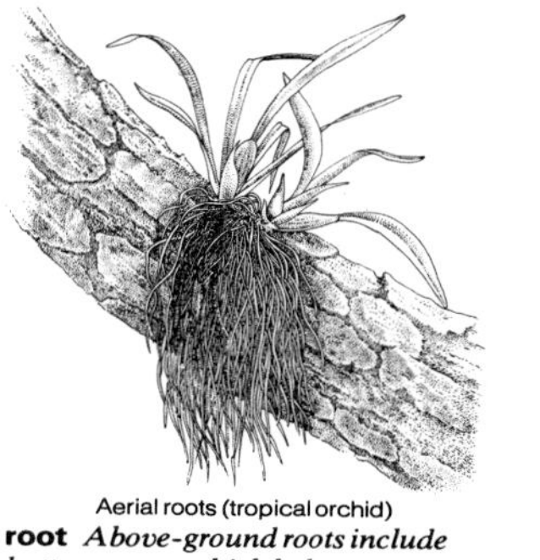

Aerial roots (tropical orchid)

root *Above-ground roots include buttress roots, which help to support tree trunks, and aerial roots, which absorb moisture from the air. The two major types of underground roots are fibrous roots – masses of slender tendrils of roughly equal size – and tap roots – large central roots through which the plant draws the bulk of its water supply.*

rope ladder *n.* A flexible ladder made from two ropes linked by rungs.

rope's end *n.* A short length of usually thick rope formerly used on ships for flogging sailors.

rope-walk (rōp-wawk) *n.* A long, narrow path or building where ropes are manufactured by twisting fibres together.

rope-way (rōp-way) *n.* A system of overhead cables and supporting towers used to transport goods or passengers in containers or cabins suspended from the cables, as at a ski resort.

rope yarn *n.* The fibres of hemp, nylon, or other material from which rope is made.

rop-y (rōpi) *adj.* **-ier, -iest. 1.** Resembling a rope or ropes. **2.** *British Informal.* Of poor or inferior quality. **3.** Forming sticky glutinous strings or threads. —**rop-i-ly** *adv.* —**rop-i-ness** *n.*

roque (rōk) *n.* A form of croquet played in the United States on a hard court. [Alteration of CROQUET.]

Roque-fort (rōk-fawr ‖ *U.S.* rōk-fərt) *n.* A French cheese made from ewes' and goats' milk, and containing a blue mould, *Penicillium roqueforti.* [After *Roquefort*-sur-Soulzon, village in southeast France.]

roqu-e-laure (rócka-lawr, rōka-) *n.* A man's knee-length cloak popular during the 18th and early 19th centuries. [After the Duc de Roquelaure (1656–1738), French marshal.]

ro-quet (rō-ki, -kay) *v.* **-queted, -queting, -quets.** —*tr.* In croquet: **1.** To cause one's ball to strike (another player's ball). **2.** To strike (another ball). Used of a ball. —*intr.* In croquet, to strike another player's ball with one's own.
~*n.* The act of roqueting. [Arbitrarily formed from CROQUET.]

ror-qual (rórkwal) *n.* Any of several whalebone whales of the genus *Balaenoptera*, having longitudinal grooves on the throat, and a small, pointed dorsal fin. Also called "finback","razorback". [French, from Norwegian *rørhval*, from Old Norse *reytharhvalr* : *reythr*, rorqual, "red whale" (from its red streaks), from *rauthr*, red + *hvalr*, whale.]

Ror-schach test (rór-shaak, -shak, -shaakh; *German* -shakh) *n.* *Psychology.* A type of projective test of personality in which a subject's interpretations of ten abstract inkblot designs are analysed as a measure of emotional and intellectual functioning and integration. [Devised by Hermann *Rorschach* (1884–1922), Swiss psychiatrist.]

Ro-ry O'Con-nor (ráw-ri ō-kónnər, ə- ‖ rō-), also known as Roderic O'Connor. (c. 1116–98). King of Connaught (1156–98) and the last High King of Ireland (1166–98). In 1175 Rory was forced to accept vassalage under Henry II of England, though he remained overlord within Ireland. He retired to a monastery in 1191.

Ro-sa (rōza), **Salvator** (1615–73). Italian painter, born near Naples. He developed a distinctive preoccupation with wild landscapes and battle scenes. He was also a poet, actor, and musician.

ro-sa-ceous (rōz-áyshəss) *adj.* **1.** *Botany.* Of or belonging to the Rosaceae, the plant family that includes the roses. **2.** Resembling the flower of a rose. [New Latin *Rosaceae*, from Latin *rosáceus*, made of roses : ROSE + -ACEOUS.]

ros-an-i-line (rōz-ánni-leen, -lin) *n.* Also **ros-an-i-lin** (-lin). A brownish-red crystalline organic compound, $C_{20}H_{19}N_3$, derived from aniline and used in the manufacture of dyes. [ROSE (flower) + ANILINE.]

Ro-sa-ri-o (rō-zaári-ō, -saári-). Chief port of east central Argentina, situated on the river Paraná.

ro-sa-ry (rōzəri) *n., pl.* **-ries. 1.** *Roman Catholic Church.* **a.** A form of devotion to the Virgin Mary, consisting of a recitation of any of three sets of five decades each of the Ave Maria, each decade preceded by a Lord's Prayer, ending with a Gloria Patri, and commemorating an event in the life of Christ or Our Lady. See **mystery. b.** A string of beads on which these prayers are counted. **2.** Similar beads used by other religious groups. [Middle English, from Medieval Latin *rosárium*, from Latin *rosa*, ROSE.]

rosary pea *n.* A woody vine, **Indian liquorice** *(see).*

Rosce-lin (ross-lán) (c. 1050–c. 1120). Also called Roscellinus. French philosopher and theologian, a pioneer of nominalism. He taught that universal concepts are mere expressions of speech; each component is in reality an independent entity, and a "whole" cannot thus be divided into "parts". He was ordered to recant at the synod of Soissons (1092). His notion of the Trinity challenged orthodox teaching.

Ros-ci-us (róssi-əss, róshi-), born Quintus Roscius Gallus (c. 126–62B.C.). The most celebrated Roman comic actor. A friend of Cicero, he wrote a treatise on the relative merits of acting and oratory as means of expression.

Ros-com-mon (ross-kómmən). County of Connaught province, north central Republic of Ireland. Bounded by the river Shannon in the east, it is largely boggy and has several lakes. Its county town is Roscommon.

rose¹ (rōz) *n.* **1.** Any of numerous shrubs or vines of the genus *Rosa*, usually having prickly stems, compound leaves, and variously coloured, often fragrant flowers. **2.** The flower of any of these plants, occurring in a wide variety of colours, such as pink, red, yellow, and white. **3.** Any of various plants related to or resembling the rose. **4.** A dark pink to purplish pink, to moderate red or purplish red. **5.** *Usually plural.* A rosy colour of the cheeks. **6.** An ornament resembling a rose in form; a rosette. **7.** A perforated nozzle for spraying water from a hose or watering can. **8. a.** A form of gem cut, marked by a flat base and a faceted, hemispheric upper surface. **b.** A diamond so cut. **9.** A **rose window** *(see).* **10.** A **compass card** *(see).*
~*adj.* Rose-coloured. [Middle English *rose*, Old English *rose*, *rōse*, from Latin *rosa*.]

rose². Past tense of **rise.**

ro-sé (rōzay, rō-záy) *n.* A pink, light wine, traditionally made from red grapes from which the skins are removed during fermentation. [French "pink", from Old French *rose*, rosy, a rose, from Latin *rosa*, ROSE.]

rose apple *n.* An East Indian tree, *Eugenia jambos*, cultivated in the tropics for its edible fruit and ornamental flowers.

ro-se-ate (rōzi-ət, -it, -ayt) *adj.* **1.** Rose-coloured. **2.** Cheerful; optimistic; rosy. [Latin *roseus*, from *rosa*, ROSE.] —**ro-se-ate-ly** *adv.*

rose-bay (rōz-bay) *n.* **1.** Any of several American rhododendrons. **2.** A shrub, the oleander *(see).* **3.** See **willowherb.**

Rose-be-ry (rōz-bri, -bəri ‖ -berri), **Archibald Philip Primrose, 5th Earl of** (1847–1929). British statesman, Liberal prime minister (1894–95). A strong imperialist, he was also popular as a witty speaker and successful racehorse owner, his horses winning the Derby on three occasions (1894, 1895, 1905).

rose-bud (rōz-bud) *n.* The bud of a rose.

rose-bush (rōz-bŏŏsh) *n.* A shrub that bears roses.

rose campion *n.* A widely naturalised European plant, *Lychnis coronaria*, that is covered with white, woolly down and has rose-red flowers. Also called "dusty miller".

rose chafer *n.* A golden-green beetle, *Catonia aurata*, that causes damage to garden plants, especially roses. Also called "rose beetle".

rose geranium *n.* A woody plant, *Pelargonium graveolens*, having rose-pink flowers and fragrant leaves used for flavouring and in perfumery.

rose-hip (rōz-hip) *n.* The fruit of the rose, a **hip** *(see).*

ro-sel-la (rō-zéllə) *n.* Any of various brightly coloured, Australian parrots of the genus *Platycercus*. [Alteration of *Rosehiller*, after *Rosehill*, New South Wales, where the parrots were first found.]

ro-selle (rō-zél) *n.* A tropical Old World plant, *Hibiscus sabdariffa*, with yellow flowers. Its immature floral bracts are used to make jelly and beverages. [Origin uncertain.]

rose-mar-y (rōz-məri, -mri ‖ -mair-i) *n., pl.* **-ies.** An aromatic evergreen shrub, *Rosmarinus officinalis*, native to southern Europe but widely cultivated, having light-blue flowers and greyish-green leaves that are used in cooking and perfume manufacture. [Middle English, alteration (influenced by ROSE and MARY) of *rosmarine*, from Latin *rōs marīnus*, "sea dew" : *rōs*, dew + *marīnus*, of the sea, from *mare*, sea.]

rose moss *n.* **1.** Any moss of the genus *Rhodobryum*; especially, *R. roseum*, characterised by conspicuous terminal leaf rosettes. **2.** A garden plant, **portulaca** *(see).*

Ro-sen-berg (rōz'n-berg), **Julius** (1918–53). U.S. government weapons inspector who helped to transmit nuclear secrets to the Russian vice-consul in New York. He was executed with his wife, Ethel Rosenberg, in 1953. Their deaths caused much controversy, as they were the first U.S. civilians to be executed for espionage.

rose of Jericho *n.* A fernlike desert plant, *Anastatica hierochuntica*, that forms a tight ball when dry, and unfolds and blooms under moist conditions. Also called "resurrection plant".

rose of Sharon *n.* **1.** A tall shrub, *Hibiscus syriacus*, having large reddish, purple, or white. flowers. Also called "alathea". **2.** A shrubby plant, *Hypericum calycinum*, native to Eurasia, having evergreen leaves and yellow flowers. Also called "St. John's wort".

ro-se-o-la (rō-zée-ələ, rə-) *n.* Any red skin rash, such as that associated with measles. [New Latin, diminutive of Latin *roseus*, rosy, from *rosa*, ROSE.]

rose pink *n.* A light purplish pink to moderate or strong pink. —**rose-pink** (rō-pĭngk) *adj.*

rose quartz *n.* A pinkish quartz used as a gemstone.

rose-root (rōz-rŏŏt ‖ -rŏōt) *n.* A plant, *Sedum roseum*, of the Northern Hemisphere, having fleshy leaves and greenish-yellow or purple flowers.

Roses, Wars of the *pl.n.* A sporadic dynastic war (1455–85) in England between the supporters of the House of York (white rose) and of the House of Lancaster (red rose) for possession of the English Crown.

Rose's metal *n.* An alloy with a low melting point (94°C) consisting of bismuth, lead, and tin. Also called "Rose's alloy".

Ro-set-ta stone (rō-zéttə, rə-) *n.* A basalt tablet now in the British museum, inscribed with a decree of Ptolemy V of 196 B.C. in Greek, Egyptian hieroglyphics, and demotic characters, that was discovered in 1799 near the town of Rosetta (*Arabic* Rashid), Egypt, and provided the key to the decipherment of hieroglyphics.

ro-sette (rō-zét, rə-) *n.* **1.** An ornament made of ribbons gathered into a shape resembling a rose, especially: **a.** One worn as a badge showing the wearer's support for a particular political party or football club, for example. **b.** One given as a prize in a competition, as at a showjumping or agricultural event. **2.** Any roselike marking or formation, such as one of the clusters of spots on a leopard's fur. **3.** *Architecture.* A painted, carved, or sculptured ornament in a stylised circular pattern resembling a rose. **4.** *Botany.* A circular cluster of leaves or other plant parts. [French, "small rose", from Old French, from *rose*, rose, from Latin *rosa*, ROSE.]

Rose-wall (rōz-wawl), **Ken(neth Ronald)** (1934–). Australian tennis player. In an outstanding career, he took most major titles, but as a British professional from 1956 he was barred at Wimbledon until 1968, and never took the Wimbledon singles title.

rose-wa-ter (rōz-wawtər ‖ *U.S. also* -wottər) *n.* A fragrant preparation made by steeping or distilling rose petals in water, used in cosmetics and in cookery.

rose window n. A circular window, usually of stained glass, with radiating tracery in the form of a rose.

rose·wood (róz-wŏŏd) n. **1.** Any of various tropical or semitropical trees, chiefly of the genus *Dalbergia*, having hard reddish or dark wood with a strongly marked grain. **2.** The wood of any of these trees, used in cabinetmaking.

Rosh Ha·sha·nah (rósh hə-sháanə, rósh; *Hebrew* hasha-naá) n. The Jewish New Year, a solemn occasion celebrated on the first or first and second of Tishri (usually late September or early October). [Hebrew *rōsh hasshānāh*, beginning of the year : *rōsh*, head + *hash-shānāh*, the year.]

Ro·si·cru·cian (rŏzi-krŏŏsh-'n, rózzi-, -iən) n. **1.** A member of a secret religious organisation active in the 17th and 18th centuries and claiming to have esoteric and magical knowledge. **2.** A member of a modern international fraternity, the Rosicrucian Order, supposedly descended from the Rosicrucians and devoted to the application of esoteric religious doctrine to modern life. [Medieval Latin *(Frater) Rosae Crucis*, translation of the German name (Friar) Christian *Rosenkreutz*, supposed founder of the society in the 15th century.] **—Ro·si·cru·cian** adj. **—Ro·si·cru·cian·ism** n.

ros·in (rózzin) n. A translucent yellowish to dark-brown resin derived from the sap of various pine trees, and used to increase sliding friction on the bows of certain stringed instruments and in a wide variety of manufactured products including varnishes, inks, linoleum, and soldering fluxes. Also called "colophony". ~tr.v. **rosined, -ining, -ins.** To coat or rub with rosin. [Middle English *rosyn, rosine,* variants of RESIN.] **—ros·in·y** adj.

rosin oil n. A white to brown viscous liquid obtained by fractional distillation of rosin and used in lubricants, electrical insulation, and printing inks. Also called "retinol", "rosinol".

Ros·kil·de (*Danish* róskilə). Town of east Zealand, Denmark. Situated on the Roskilde Fjord, it was the Danish capital until 1443, and its cathedral (begun in the 12th century) has many royal tombs.

RoS·PA (róspə). Royal Society for the Prevention of Accidents (in Britain).

Ross (ross ‖ rawss), **Sir James Clark** (1800–62). British polar explorer. Having entered the navy he explored the Arctic with his uncle, Sir John Ross (1777–1856), discovering the north magnetic pole in 1831. On a voyage to the Antarctic (1839–43), he discovered the sea later named after him.

Ross and Crom·ar·ty (krómmərti). Former county of northern Scotland. It included Lewis in the outer Hebrides, which became part of the Western Isles (1975), and a part of the mainland which was absorbed into the Highland Region (1975).

Rosse (ross ‖ rawss), **William Parsons, 3rd Earl of** (1800–67). Irish astronomer. He developed one of the first large-scale reflecting telescopes. Its 183-centimetre (72-inch) reflector was in operation by 1845, and with it he pioneered the study of nebulae.

Ros·sel·li·ni (róss-i-léeni, -e-), **Roberto** (1906–77). Italian film director. With de Sica he pioneered the neorealist school of cinema, characterised by informal camera technique and concern with the underprivileged. His films include *Rome, Open City* (1945), describing conditions in Rome under the German occupation.

Ros·set·ti (rə-zétti, ro-, -sétti), **Christina (Georgina)** (1830–94). British poet, the sister of Dante Gabriel Rossetti. Her first publication, *Goblin Market and Other Poems,* appeared in 1862 and a posthumous volume, *New Poems,* in 1896.

Rossetti, Dante Gabriel (1828–82). British painter and poet. He was a leading member of the Pre-Raphaelite Brotherhood which he helped to found (1848) with Millais and Holman Hunt. His paintings include many portraits of Elizabeth Siddal, whom he married in 1860 and who died two years later of an overdose of laudanum. He buried the manuscripts of many early poems in his wife's coffin, but later disinterred them, and published them as *Poems* (1870).

Ross Ice Shelf. A mass of floating ice, the largest in the world, situated at the head of the Ross Sea on the Pacific coastline of Antarctica. Its estimated size ranges from 496 000–540 000 square kilometres (192,000-208,000 square miles).

Ros·si·ni (ro-séeni, rə-), **Gioacchino Antonio** (1792–1868). Italian composer. He established his reputation with a series of 36 operas, all written in the space of 19 years. They include *Tancredi* (1813), *The Barber of Seville* (1816), and *William Tell* (1829).

Ross Island. Island in the Ross Sea, Antarctica. It is the site of Mount Terror, and the active volcano Mount Erebus.

Ross Sea. Area of the South Pacific Ocean lying east of Victoria Land, Antarctica.

Ros·tand (ro-stón), **Edmond** (1868–1918). French playwright. He is chiefly remembered for the verse drama *Cyrano de Bergerac* (1897), a chivalric comedy based loosely on the 17th-century French writer and adventurer of that name.

ros·tel·late (róstə-layt, ross-téllayt) adj. Having a rostellum. [New Latin *rostellatus,* from ROSTELLUM.]

ros·tel·lum (ross-télləm) n., pl. **-tella** (-téllə). *Biology.* A small, beak-like part, such as a projection on the stigma of an orchid, a tubular mouth part on some insects, or the hooked projection on the head of a tapeworm. [New Latin, from Latin, diminutive of *rostrum,* beak, ROSTRUM.] **—ros·tel·lar** adj.

ros·ter (róstər) n. A plan or list showing the order in which each member of an organisation, military unit, or other group becomes liable for a particular duty. ~tr.v. **rostered, -tering, -ters.** To place on a roster. [Dutch *rooster,*

gridiron, list (on a ruled sheet), from Middle Dutch, gridiron, from *roosten,* to roast, from *roost,* gridiron, from Germanic *raust* (unattested). See roast.]

Ros·tock (róss-tok). Baltic industrial port of East Germany. Situated on the estuary of the river Warnow 18 kilometres (8 miles) from the Baltic Sea, it was an important member of the Hanseatic League (14th century) and has many medieval remains.

Ros·tov-na-Do·nu (rəstóf-nə-dənóo). *English* **Rostov-on-Don.** Industrial port in southeast European U.S.S.R. It lies on the river Don near the Sea of Azov, and is also a cultural and scientific centre.

Ros·tro·po·vich (róstrə-póvish; *Russian* rəstra-), **Mstislav (Leopoldovich)** (1927–). Russian cellist, noted for his outstanding range of tone. He travelled widely in the West from 1947 and had works written for him by Khachaturian, Prokofiev, Shostakovich, and Britten. In 1975 he left the U.S.S.R.

ros·trum (róss-trəm) n., pl. **-trums** or **-tra** (-trə) (the only form for sense 2). **1.** A dais, platform, or similar raised place used, for example, by public speakers or conductors. **2.** *Often plural.* In ancient Rome, the speakers' platform in the Forum, which was decorated with the prows of captured enemy ships. **3.** *Biology.* A beaklike or snoutlike projection. [Latin, beak, ship's prow.] **—ros·tral** (-trəl) adj. **—ros·trate** (-trayt) adj.

ros·y (rŏzi) adj. **-ier, -iest. 1.** Having the characteristic pink or red colour of a rose. **2.** Flushed with a healthy glow. **3.** Optimistic or giving cause for optimism. **—ros·i·ly** adv. **—ros·i·ness** n.

rosy pastor n. A bird, the **pastor** *(see).*

Ro·syth (rə-síth). Port on the Firth of Forth, Fife Region, eastern Scotland. It is also a naval base for nuclear-powered submarines.

rot¹ (rot) v. **rotted, rotting, rots. —intr. 1.** To undergo decomposition, especially organic decomposition; decay. **2.** To disappear or fall by decaying. Used with *off* or *away.* **3.** To undergo moral or intellectual decay; become decadent or degenerate. **4.** To waste away, as from neglect or inactivity. **—tr.** To cause to decompose, deteriorate, or decay. **—See Synonyms at decay.** ~n. **1.** The process of rotting or the condition of being rotten. **2.** A condition of degeneration or decline: *brought in a new director in an attempt to stop the rot.* **3.** Foot rot *(see).* **4.** Any of several plant diseases characterised by the breakdown of tissue, and caused by various bacteria, fungi, or other microorganisms. See **dry rot, wet rot. 5.** *Medicine. Archaic.* Any disease causing the decay of flesh. **6.** *Informal.* Foolish talk; nonsense. ~interj. Used to express contempt or impatience, especially in reaction to foolish talk. [Middle English *roten, rotyen,* Old English *rotian,* from Germanic *rutjan* (unattested).]

rot². Variant of **ret.**

rot. rotating; rotation.

ro·ta (rŏtə) n., pl. **-tas. 1.** *Chiefly British.* A roster, especially one regulating unofficial activities: *a rota for driving the children to school.* **2.** *Capital* R. The supreme court of the Roman Catholic Church, called in full the Sacred Roman Rota and functioning as a court of final appeal, especially in cases regarding the dissolution of marriages. [Latin, wheel.]

Ro·tar·i·an (rō-taír-i-ən) n. A member of a Rotary Club.

ro·ta·ry (rŏtəri) adj. **1.** Of, pertaining to, causing, or characterised by rotation, especially rotation round an axis. **2.** Operating by means of a rotary part or parts: *a rotary mower.* ~n., pl. **rotaries. 1.** A part or device that rotates round an axis. **2.** *U.S.* A traffic roundabout. [Medieval Latin *rotārius,* from Latin *rota,* wheel.]

Rotary Club n. Any club belonging to *Rotary International,* an organisation pledged to give service to the community.

rotary engine n. An engine, such as a turbine, in which power is supplied directly to vanes or other rotary parts.

rotary harrow n. A harrow, consisting of a series of freely turning wheels rimmed with spikes. Also called "rotary hoe".

rotary plough n. A plough having a series of hoes arranged on a revolving power-driven shaft. Also called "rotary tiller".

rotary press n. A printing press having a cylinder to which curved plates are attached so that, when revolving, they will print onto a continuous roll of paper.

ro·tate (rō-táyt, rə- ‖ *chiefly U.S.* rṓ-tayt) v. **-tated, -tating, -tates. —intr. 1.** To turn or spin on an axis. **2.** To proceed in sequence; alternate. **—tr. 1.** To cause to rotate. **2.** To plant or grow (crops) in a fixed order of succession. **3.** To perform in a fixed order of succession; alternate. **—See Synonyms at turn.** ~adj. *Botany.* Having radiating parts; wheel-shaped. [Latin *rotāre,* to revolve, from *rota,* wheel.] **—ro·tat·a·ble** adj.

ro·ta·tion (rō-táysh'n, rə-) n. *Abbr.* **rot. 1.** Motion in which the path of every point in the moving object is a circle or circular arc centred on a specific axis, especially on an internal axis: *the axial rotation of the earth.* **2.** A single complete cycle of such motion; a revolution. **3.** *Geometry.* A coordinate transformation consisting of an angular displacement, or successive angular displacements, of coordinate axes with the origin remaining fixed. **4. a.** A regularly recurring sequence: *The chairmanship goes to each member in strict rotation.* **b.** The use or application of a planned sequence, as in the growing of crops. **—ro·ta·tion·al** adj.

ro·ta·tive (rŏtətiv, rō-táytiv) adj. **1.** Of, pertaining to, causing, or characterised by rotation. **2.** Characterised by or occurring in alternation or succession. **—ro·ta·tive·ly** adv.

ro·ta·tor (rō-táytər) n. **1.** One that rotates. **2.** Any of several muscles that effect rotation of a part of the body.

ro·ta·to·ry (rṓtə-tri, -təri, rō-táytəri) *adj.* **1.** Of, pertaining to, causing, or characterised by rotation. **2.** Occurring or proceeding in alternation or succession.

Ro·ta·va·tor (rṓtə-vaytər) *n. British.* A trademark for a motor-driven machine with rotating blades, used for breaking up and turning over soil in preparation for cultivation. **—ro·ta·vate** (-vayt) *tr.v.*

rote[1] (rōt) *n.* **1.** Memorisation by means of repetition and with little or no comprehension: *learn by rote.* **2.** Mechanical routine; unthinking repetition. [Middle English *rote*†.]

rote[2] *n.* A medieval stringed instrument. [Middle English, from Old French, from Germanic.]

ro·te·none (rṓti-nōn) *n.* A white crystalline compound, $C_{23}H_{22}O_6$, extracted from the roots of derris and cubé, and used as an insecticide. [Japanese *rōten,* derris plant + -ONE.]

rot·gut (rót-gut) *n. Slang.* Alcoholic drink of a very inferior kind.

Roth·er·ham (rót͟hərəm). Town of South Yorkshire, northern England. Situated on the river Don in a coalmining area, its industries include iron and steel, brass, glassware, pottery, and machinery.

Roth·er·mere (rót͟hər-meer), **Harold Sydney Harmsworth, 1st Viscount** (1868–1940). British newspaper magnate and politician. The younger brother of Lord Northcliffe, he assisted in the founding and purchase of several papers, and was Air Minister (1917–18). He acquired the *Daily Mirror* (1914) from his brother, and bought the *Daily Mail* (1922) on Northcliffe's death.

Rothe·say (róth-si, -say). Port and capital of the Isle of Bute, west Scotland. Incorporated into Strathclyde Region (1975), it is a tourist centre and fishing town.

Roth·ko (róth-kō), **Mark,** born Marcus Rothkovitch (1903–1970). In the late 1940s and early 1950s he produced a series of large, abstract canvasses employing horizontal bands of colour with blurred edges. *Number 10* (1950) is characteristic of his style.

Roth·schild (róth-chīld, róss-, róths-). A banking family of German Jewish origin. The Rothschild bank was founded at Frankfurt by Mayer Amschel Rothschild (1743–1812). His eldest son took over the Frankfurt business, and four younger sons set up branches in Vienna, London, Naples and Paris. All of the founding members were created Austrian barons, and the family won international fame by negotiating major loans to European governments.

ro·ti (rṓti) *n.* A flat, usually circular, piece of unleavened bread, similar to a chapatti. [Hindi, bread.]

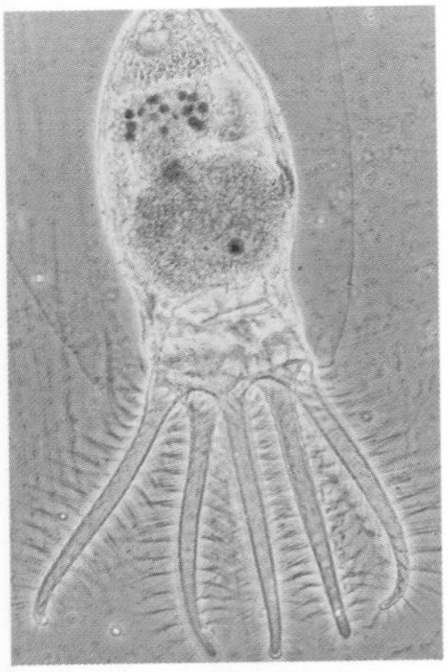

rotifer *These minute and almost transparent freshwater animals are members of the scientific group* Rotifera *– so called because they have a wheel-like ring of microscopic tentacles or cilia (seen here from the side) with which they propel themselves through the water and gather food particles.*

ro·ti·fer (rṓtifər) *n.* Any of various minute, multicellular aquatic organisms of the phylum Rotifera, having at the anterior end a wheel-like ring of cilia used for feeding and locomotion. Also called "wheel animalcule". [New Latin *Rotifera* : Latin *rota,* wheel (see **rotate**) + -FER.] **—ro·tif·er·al** (rō-tíffərəl), **ro·tif·er·ous** (rō-tíffərəss) *adj.*

ro·tis·se·rie (rō-tíssəri) *n.* **1.** A cooking device equipped with a rotating spit on which meat or other food is roasted. **2.** A shop or restaurant specialising in meats roasted in this way. [French *rôtisserie,* from Old French *rostisserie,* from *rostir* (present stem *rostiss-*), to ROAST.]

rot·l (rótt'l) *n.* Any of various units of weight used in countries bordering on the eastern Mediterranean, varying in amount from about half a kilogram to two and a half kilograms (one to five pounds). [Arabic *raṭl, riṭl,* perhaps altered by metathesis from Greek *litra.* See **litre.**]

ro·to·gra·vure (rṓt-ō-grə-véwr, -ə-) *n.* **1.** An intaglio printing process in which letters and pictures are transferred from an etched copper cylinder to a web of paper, plastic, or similar material in a rotary press. **2.** Printed material, such as a newspaper section, produced by this process. [Latin *rota,* wheel + GRAVURE.]

ro·tor (rṓtər) *n.* **1.** A rotating part of a mechanical device; especially, the moving part of an electric motor or generator. Compare **stator.** **2.** An assembly of rotating horizontal aerofoils, such as that of a helicopter. **3.** The rotating part of the distributor in an internal-combustion engine. In this sense, also called "rotor arm". [Short for ROTATOR.]

rotor ship *n.* A ship propelled by one or more tall cylindrical rotors operated by wind power.

Ro·to·ru·a (rṓtə-rōō-ə). City of central North Island, New Zealand. It is a spa resort situated on a picturesque volcanic plateau in a region of mudpools, hot springs, lakes, and active volcanoes.

rot·ten (rótt'n) *adj.* **-tener, -tenest.** **1.** In a state of putrefaction or decay; decomposed. **2.** Having a foul odour resulting from or suggestive of decay; putrid. **3.** Made weak or unsound by rot. **4.** Morally corrupt or despicable. **5.** *Informal.* Very bad; wretched, as by being: **a.** Disagreeable; unpleasant: *had a rotten time.* **b.** Unkind: *a rotten thing to do.* **c.** Unwell. **d.** Ashamed: *felt a bit rotten about letting them down.* **e.** Inferior; of a poor standard: *a rotten actor.* [Middle English *roten, rotin,* from Old Norse *rotinn,* from Germanic *ruteno-* (unattested), akin to *rutjan* (unattested), to ROT.] **—rot·ten·ly** *adv.* **—rot·ten·ness** *n.*

rotten borough *n.* In England prior to the Parliamentary reform of 1832, a constituency entitled to send a representative to Parliament despite having hardly any voters. Compare **pocket borough.**

rot·ten·stone (rótt'n-stōn) *n.* A friable variety of tripoli, the product of decomposed siliceous limestone, used for polishing.

rot·ter (róttər) *n. Chiefly British Informal.* An objectionable or despicable person. [ROT + -ER.]

Rot·ter·dam (róttər-dam, -dám). Seaport and industrial city of South Holland province, Netherlands. It lies on the Nieuwe Maas river near its mouth on the North Sea, and is a major world port, and the heart of the largest conurbation in the Netherlands. The city's inner port is connected to the Hook of Holland, its outer port, by the New Waterway (constructed 1866–90). Adjoining Europoort, built in the 1960s, handles mostly petroleum. Rotterdam is also the main seaport for the heavily industrialised Ruhr district of West Germany. The city's industries include shipbuilding, petrochemicals, engineering, paper, and foodstuffs.

Rott·wei·ler (rót-wīlər, -vīlər) *n.* A dog of an ancient German breed, having a stocky body, a short black coat, and tan face markings. [Originally bred in *Rottweil,* town in southwestern Germany.]

ro·tund (rō-túnd, rə- || rṓ-tund) *adj.* **1.** Rounded; plump. **2.** Sonorous in delivery or grandiloquent in style. —See Synonyms at **fat.** [Latin *rotundus,* round.] **—ro·tund·ly** *adv.* **—ro·tund·i·ty** (rō-túndəti, rə-), **ro·tund·ness** *n.*

ro·tun·da (rō-túndə, rə-) *n.* A circular building, hall, or room, especially one with a dome. [Italian *rotonda,* from Latin *rotunda,* feminine of *rotundus,* round.]

ro·tu·ri·er (rō-téwr-i-ay || -tóor-) *n.* A person of low rank; a commoner. [French, from Old French, from *roture,* newly broken land, obligation to a lord for land, hence, a commoner, from Vulgar Latin *ruptūra,* from Latin, a RUPTURE.]

Rou·ault (rōō-ṓ), **Georges (Henri)** (1871–1958). French artist. Apprenticed to a glazier in his youth, he worked on stained glass windows and retained as an artist a fondness for flat areas of luminous colour enclosed by strong, dark outlines. His works include *The Clown* (1905) and a series of 60 prints *Miserere* (1916–27).

Rou·bil·lac (rōō-bee-yak, -yák), **Louis François** (1695–1762). French sculptor who worked chiefly in England. His works include several statues in Westminster Abbey. His statue of Handel stands in Poets' Corner.

rou·ble, ru·ble (rōōb'l) *n. Abbr.* **r., R.** **1.** The basic monetary unit of the U.S.S.R., equal to 100 kopecks. **2.** A coin or note worth one rouble. [Russian *rubl',* "silver bar", from Old Russian, "bar", "block", from *rubiti,* to cut up, build, from Balto-Slavic *romb-* (unattested).]

rouche. Variant of **ruche.**

rou·é (rōō-ay || *U.S.* rōō-áy) *n.* A debauched and dissipated man; a profligate. [French, "broken on the wheel", completely tired, from the past participle of *rouer,* to break on the wheel, from Medieval Latin *rotāre,* to turn, from Latin, to ROTATE.]

Rou·en (rōō-ON; *French* rwON). Capital of the Seine-Maritime département, northern France. Situated on the river Seine, it is a port handling trade for Paris. It is also a cultural and industrial centre, and a centre for the wine trade. Once the capital of Normandy, it was held by England between 1419 and 1449. It has fine Gothic architecture, including a cathedral (12th-15th century).

rouge (rōōzh) *n.* **1.** A red or pink cosmetic for colouring the cheeks. **2.** A form of iron oxide, **jeweller's rouge** *(see).*
~*v.* **rouged, rouging, rouges.** —*tr.* To put rouge on; colour with rouge. —*intr.* To use rouge as a cosmetic. [French, from Old French, red, from Latin *rubeus.*]

rouge et noir (rōōzh ay nwár) *n.* A gambling card game played at a table marked with two red and two black diamond-shaped spots, on which bets are placed. Also called "trente et quarante". [French, "red and black".]

rough (ruf) *adj.* **rougher, roughest.** **1.** Having an uneven surface; full of bumps, ridges, or other irregularities; not smooth. **2.** Rugged, uneven, or uncultivated. Said of land. **3.** Coarse, shaggy, or uneven in texture: *a rough bearskin.* **4.** Characterised by violent motion; turbulent; agitated: *rough waters.* **5.** Severely inclement; stormy; tempestuous: *rough weather.* **6.** Characterised by rowdy, unruly, or boisterous behaviour: *a rough neighbourhood.* **7. a.** Marked by lack of care, gentleness, or consideration; harsh or brutal: *rough treatment.* **b.** Lacking amenities or comforts: *a rough hotel.* **8.** Lacking refinement; uncouth; unmannerly. **9. a.** Produced, performed, or dispensed without attention to precision, elaboration, or completeness: *a rough translation; rough justice.* **b.** Tentative or approximate: *a rough idea of the cost.* **c.** Used in doing work of a preliminary kind: *rough paper.* **d.** *Informal.* Of low quality; substandard. **10.** Harsh to the ear. **11.** Harsh or sharp to the taste: *a rough wine.* **12.** In a natural state: *rough diamonds.* **13.** Requiring physical strength rather than intelligence; unskilled: *rough work.* **14.** *Informal.* Difficult, unpleasant, or unfair. **15.** *Informal.* Unwell: *feeling a bit rough.*
~*n.* **1.** Uneven or overgrown ground. **2.** The part of a golf course left unmown and uncultivated, as distinguished from the fairway and the greens. **3.** A rough, disagreeable, or difficult aspect or condition: *take the rough with the smooth.* **4.** Something in an unfinished or hastily worked-out state. **5.** A rough, unruly, or violent person; a hooligan. **—in the rough.** In a crude or unfinished state.
~*tr.v.* **roughed, roughing, roughs.** **1.** To make rough; roughen. **2.** To subject to rough treatment or physical violence. Used with *up.* **3.** To prepare or indicate in a rough or unfinished form: *rough in the illustrations for a book.* **—rough it.** To get along without the usual comforts: *rough it on a camping trip.*
~*adv.* In a rough manner; roughly: *slept rough.* [Middle English *ruch, r(o)wgh,* Old English *rūh.*] **—rough·er** *n.* **—rough·ly** *adv.* **—rough·ness** *n.*

Synonyms: *rough, jagged, rugged, scabrous, uneven.*

rough·age (rúffij) *n.* **1.** Any rough or coarse material. **2.** The relatively coarse, indigestible parts of certain foods and fodder that contain cellulose and stimulate peristalsis; dietary fibre.

rough-and-read·y (rúf-ən-réddi, -ənd-) *adj.* Rough or crude but effective or usable.

rough-and-tum·ble (rúf-ən-túmb'l, -ənd-) *adj.* Characterised by roughness and disregard for order or rules.
~*n.* **1.** A disorderly scuffle. **2.** A rough-and-tumble quality: *enjoyed the rough-and-tumble of a game of rugger.*
rough breathing *n.* **1.** An aspirate sound in ancient Greek like that of the letter *h* in English. **2. a.** The mark (‘) placed over initial sounds in Greek to indicate a preceding aspirate. **b.** This mark in Modern Greek as an orthographic feature.
rough·cast (rúf-kaast || -kast) *n.* **1.** A coarse plaster used for outside wall surfaces. Also called "slapdash". **2.** A rough, preliminary model or form.
~*tr.v.* **roughcast, -casting, -casts. 1.** To plaster (a wall, for example) with roughcast. **2.** To shape or work into a rough or preliminary form. **—rough·cast·er** *n.*
rough diamond *n.* A coarse-mannered but basically decent and likable person.
rough·dry (rúf-drí) *tr.v.* **-dried, -drying, -dries.** To dry (something laundered) without ironing or smoothing out.
~*adj.* Laundered but not ironed.
rough·en (rúff'n) *v.* **-ened, -ening, -ens.** *—tr.* To make rough. *—intr.* To become rough.
rough·hew (rúf-héw) *tr.v.* **-hewed** or **-hewn** (-héwn), **-hewing, -hews. 1.** To hew or shape (timber or stone, for example) roughly, without finishing. **2.** To make in rough form; roughcast.
rough·house (rúf-howss) *n.* Rowdy, uproarious play or behaviour.
~*v.* **roughhoused, -housing, -houses.** *—intr.* To engage in boisterous or rowdy activity. *—tr.* To handle or treat roughly, usually in fun.
rough-leg·ged buzzard (rúf-leggid, -legd) *n.* A buzzard, *Buteo lagopus,* having dark plumage and whitish feathers covering the legs.
rough·neck (rúf-nek) *n.* **1.** A rough, pugnacious man. **2.** *Chiefly U.S.* A worker on an oil rig.
rough·shod (rúf-shod) *adj.* Shod with horseshoes having projecting nails or points to prevent slipping.
rough trade *n. Slang.* Men of aggressively masculine but unpolished appearance considered as potential homosexual partners.
roul. *Philately.* roulette.
rou·lade (rōō-laád) *n.* **1.** A musical embellishment consisting of a rapid run of several notes sung to one syllable. **2.** A slice of meat rolled around a filling and cooked. [French, "a rolling", from *rouler,* to roll, from Old French *roller,* to ROLL.]
rou·leau (rōō-lō, rōō-lṓ) *n., pl.* **-leaux** (-z) or **-leaus. 1.** A small roll, especially of coins wrapped in paper. **2.** A roll or fold of ribbon used for piping. [French, from Old French *rolel,* diminutive of *rol(l)e,* a roll, from Latin *rotulus,* small wheel. See **roll.**]
rou·lette (rōō-lét, rōō-) *n.* **1.** A gambling game played with a shallow bowl enclosing a rotating disc, that has numbered slots alternately coloured red and black, the players betting on which slot, or which colour, a small ball will come to rest in. **2.** A small, toothed disc of tempered steel attached to a handle and used to make rows of dots, slits, or perforations, as in engraving or on a sheet of postage stamps. **3.** *Abbr.* **roul.** In stamp-collecting, any of the short consecutive incisions made between individual stamps in a sheet for easy separation. Compare **perforation. 4.** *Geometry.* A curve, such as a cycloid or epicycloid, that is generated by the motion of a point on one curve as it rolls along another.
~*tr.v.* **rouletted, -letting, -lettes.** To mark or divide with a roulette. [French, from Old French, from *rouelle,* from Late Latin *rotella,* diminutive of Latin *rota,* a wheel.]
Roumania. See **Romania.**
Roumelia. See **Rumelia.**
round[1] (rownd || *West Indies also* rungd) *adj. Abbr.* **rd. 1.** Spherical; globular; ball-shaped. **2.** Circular, or circular in cross-section. **3. a.** Having a curved edge or surface; not flat or angular: *a round arch.* **b.** Full; plump: *round cheeks.* **4.** Formed or articulated with the lips assuming an oval shape: *a round vowel.* **5.** Whole or complete; full; entire: *a round dozen.* **6. a.** Expressed or designated as a whole number or integer; not fractional; integral. **b.** Adjusted so as to express an exact number in an approximate, more convenient form: *That's a thousand pounds in round figures.* **c.** Approximate; rough; not exact: *a round estimate.* **7.** Large; ample; considerable: *a round sum.* **8. a.** Fully characterised or drawn; substantial; developed: *the novel lacks round characters.* **b.** Brought to a satisfying perfection; finished: *a round, polished writing style.* **9. a.** Sonorous; full in tone. **b.** Full-bodied; satisfying: *a round taste.* **10.** Brisk; rapid; smart: *a round pace.* **11.** Outspoken; candid; blunt. **12.** Made with full force; unrestrained: *a round thrashing.*
~*n.* **1.** The state of being round. **2.** Something round, as a circle, disc, globe, or ring; a curved or rounded form or part. **3.** A rung or crossbar, as on a ladder or chair. **4.** The part of the thigh on a beef animal between the rump and shank, considered as a joint of meat. **5.** A distinct set, group, or session: *a round of negotiations.* **6.** Movement around a circle, or about an axis. **7.** A round dance. **8.** A complete course, succession, or series, often ending at the starting point: *a round of parties.* **9.** *Often plural.* **a.** A course of customary or prescribed actions, duties, or places: *the daily round; a sentry's rounds.* **b.** A set of calls or visits for a particular purpose: *a doctor's round; delivery rounds.* **10.** A complete range or extent. **11. a.** Drinks for a group of people, bought at one time: *I'll buy a round.* **b.** One's turn to buy these drinks: *It's my round.* **12.** A single outburst of applause or cheering. **13. a.** A single shot or volley from a gun or guns. **b.** Ammunition for a single shot. **14. a.** A whole slice of bread. **b.** A sandwich made with two whole slices of bread. **15.** *Archery.* A specified number of arrows shot from a specified distance to a target. **16. a.** An interval of play in various games and sports that occupies a specific time, comprises a certain number of plays, or allows each player a turn. **b.** A stage or set of games, as in a knockout competition. **c.** A playing of all the holes in golf. **17.** *Music.* A short, rhythmical canon in which each part enters in unison at equal time intervals. **—go the rounds.** To be widely circulated. Used of news. **—in the round. 1.** With the stage in the centre of the audience: *theatre in the round.* **2.** Not attached to a background; freestanding. Said of sculpture.
~*v.* **rounded, rounding, rounds.** *—tr.* **1.** To make round. **2.** To pronounce with rounded lips; labialise. **3.** To lessen in angularity; fill out; make plump. **4.** To bring to completion or perfection; finish. **5.** To make a complete circuit of; go or pass around. **6.** To make a turn about or to the other side of: *rounded a bend in the road.* **7.** To encompass; surround. **8.** To move or cause to proceed in a circular course. **9.** To bring (a number) to the nearest whole or round number. Used with *up* or *down*: *Round it up to the nearest £100.* *—intr.* **1.** To become round. **2.** To take a circular course; complete or partially complete a circuit. **3.** To turn about, as on an axis; reverse. **4.** To become curved, filled out, or plump. Often used with *out.* **—round off. 1.** To express (a number) approximately, or only to a specified number of decimals. **2.** To bring or come to completion or perfection: *round off the meal.* **—round on.** To attack suddenly; turn on angrily.
~*adv.* **1.** On or to all sides or in all directions: *pass the word round.* **2.** In a circle or circular motion: *spinning round.* **3.** In a cycle or cyclic motion: *Payday comes round soon.* **4.** Taking a particular, often circuitous, route: *Go round by the pond and see the ducks.* **5.** In or towards the opposite direction, position, or attitude: *switch them round; turn round.* **6.** Measuring in circumference: *one metre round.* **7.** From one place to another; here and there: *wander round.* **8.** To each member of a group; to every one of a set: *enough to go round.* **9.** To a specific place or area, such as one's home: *when you come round again.* **10.** To a normal or desired state: *He'll come round eventually.* **—get round to.** To find time or occasion to give one's attention to. See Usage note at **around.**
~*prep.* **1.** On all sides of. **2.** So as to enclose, surround, or envelop. **3.** About the circumference or periphery of; encircling. **4.** About the central point of: *the Earth's motion round the Sun.* **5.** In or to various places within, from, or near: *drive round the town; the countryside round Brighton.* **6.** On or to the farther side of: *the house round the corner.* **7.** In the area of; near: *Do you live round here?* **8.** From the beginning to the end of; throughout: *a plant that grows round the year.* **—round about.** Approximately at or equal to: *round about 5.30; round about £5.* See Usage note at **about.** [Middle English, from Old French *ronde,* from Latin *rotundus.*] **—round·ness** *n.*
round[2] *tr.v.* **rounded, rounding, rounds.** *Archaic.* To say in a whisper. [Middle English *r(o)unen,* Old English *rūnian.*]
round·a·bout (równd-ə-bowt) *n.* **1.** *British.* A circular one-way road round a central island at the junction of three or more roads, around which traffic flows to move from one road to another. Also *U.S.* "traffic circle", "rotary". **2.** A **merry-go-round** *(see).*
~*adj.* Indirect; oblique; circuitous: *in a roundabout way.*
round angle *n.* An angle of 360°.
round-arm (równd-aarm) *adj.* **1.** In cricket, designating a now illegal form of bowling, with the arm swung horizontally or not going much higher than the shoulder. **2.** Performed with a circular, horizontal swing of the arm: *a round-arm blow.* **—round-arm** *adv.*
round bracket *n. British.* A **parenthesis** *(see).*
round dance *n.* **1.** A folk dance performed with the dancers arranged in a circle. **2.** A ballroom dance performed with circular movements around the room. Also called "round".
round·ed (równdid) *adj.* **1.** Made round; shaped in a circle or sphere. **2.** Pronounced with the lips shaped ovally; labialised. **3.** Complete; balanced.
roun·del (równd'l) *n.* **1.** A curved form; especially: **a.** A semicircular panel, window, or recess. **b.** *Heraldry.* A circular design or symbol. **2.** In poetry: **a.** A **rondel** *(see).* **b.** A **rondeau** *(see).* **c.** An English variation of the rondeau, consisting of three triplets with a refrain after the first and third. [Middle English, from Old French *rondel,* "small circle", RONDEL.]
roun·de·lay (równdə-lay) *n.* **1.** A poem or song with a regularly recurring refrain. **2.** A dance in a circle; a round dance. [Old French *rondelet,* diminutive of *rondel,* ROUNDEL.]
round·er (równdər) *n.* **1.** One that rounds; specifically, a tool for rounding corners and edges. **2.** One who makes rounds, such as a watchman. **3.** A complete circuit, made without stopping, of all the bases in rounders.
round·ers (równdərz) *n. Used with a singular verb.* A ball game played with a rounded bat or stick between two teams, usually of nine players, in which members of the batting side successively attempt to hit the ball and run round all the bases without stopping before the ball is retrieved, thus scoring rounders.
round game *n.* Any game in which players play individually, as opposed to in teams or with partners.
round hand *n.* A style of handwriting in which the letters are rounded and full, rather than angular.
Round·head (równd-hed) *n.* A member or supporter of the Parliamentary or Puritan party during the English Civil War (1642–49).

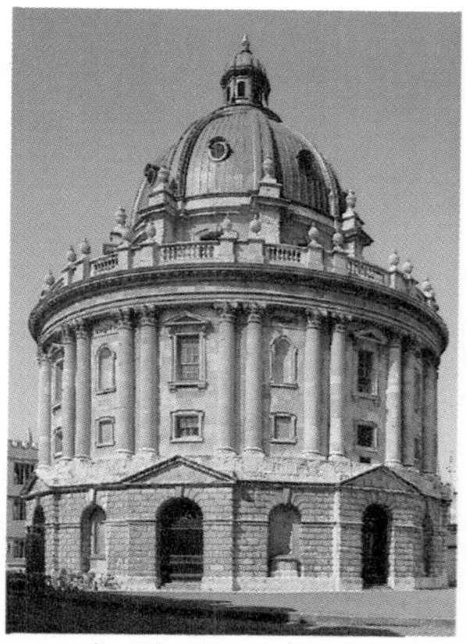

rotunda *The domed cylinder of the Radcliffe Camera, a rotunda in Oxford, England. The building was designed by the 18th-century architect James Gibbs.*

PRONUNCIATION KEY

a, trap; aa, father; ai, fair;
ar, star; aw, lawn; ay, play;
b, bb, stab; rubber;
ch, church; ck, ticket;
d, dd, dead; ladder; e, dress;
ee, bee; er, defer; ew, few;
ewr, pure; ə, about;
ər, letter; f, ff, fife; differ;
g, gg, giggle; h, hat; i, kit;
ī, price; īr, fire; j, judge;
k, kick; l, ll, let; 'l, needle;
m, mm, man; n, nn, no;
'n, sudden; ng, thing; o, lot;
ō, no; ōō, foot; ōō, shoe;
oor, poor; ow, cow;
owr, hour; oy, boy;
p, pp, pepper; r, rr, red;
s, ss, sauce; sh, ship;
t, tt, totter; th, thick; th, this;
smooth; u, cut; ur, turn;
v, vv, valve; w, wet; y, yes;
z, zz, zebra; zh, vision;
pleasure

IN FOREIGN WORDS:

aN, oN, Saint-Saëns;
hl, Llanelli; Hluhluwe;
kh, loch; lough; Khaled

STRESS MARK:

ín-sīt, insight; in-sít, incite

Used as a term of derision by the Royalists in reference to the Puritans' close-cropped hair. Compare **Cavalier.**

round·house (równd-howss) *n.* **1.** A circular building for housing and repairing locomotives, having radial tracks converging on a large turntable. **2.** A cabin on the after part of the quarter-deck of a ship.

round·ish (równdish) *adj.* Rather round. —**round·ish·ness** *n.*

round·let (równd-lət, -lit) *n.* A little circle or a small circular object. [Middle English *roundelet,* from Old French *rondelet,* diminutive of *rondel,* small circle, RONDEL.]

round·ly (równdli) *adv.* **1.** In the form of a circle or sphere. **2.** In a forceful manner; bluntly; candidly. **3.** Fully; thoroughly.

round robin *n.* **1.** A petition or protest on which the signatures are arranged in the form of a circle in order to conceal the order of signing. **2.** A letter sent among members of a group, often with comments added by each person in turn. **3.** *U.S.* A tournament in which each contestant is matched against every other contestant.

round-shoul·dered (równd-shóldərd, -shōldərd) *adj.* Having the shoulders bent forward and drooping and the upper back rounded.

rounds·man (równdz-mən) *n., pl.* **-men** (-mən). One who makes rounds, such as a deliveryman.

Round Table *n.* **1.** The table of King Arthur, made circular in order to avoid disputes about precedence among his knights. **2.** King Arthur and his knights as a group. **3.** An organisation of local associations of business and professional men who meet as a club and do charitable work. **4.** *Small* r, *small* t. A conference or discussion with several participants all on an equal footing.

round-the-clock (równd-thə-klók, równ-) *adj.* Throughout the entire day and night; continuous. —**round the clock** *adv.*

round trip *n.* A trip from one place to another, and back again, often by a different route.

round up *tr.v.* **1.** To seek out and bring together; gather. **2.** To herd together for inspection, branding, or shipping.

round-up (równd-up) *n.* **1. a.** The herding together of cattle for inspection, branding, or shipping. **b.** The cattle that are herded together. **c.** The cowboys and horses employed in such herding. **2.** Any similar gathering up, as of persons under suspicion by the police. **3.** A summing up; a summation; a résumé.

round-worm (równd-wurm) *n.* A **nematode** (*see*).

roup¹ (rōōp) *n.* An infectious disease of poultry and pigeons characterised by inflammation and discharge from the mouth and eyes. [16th century : origin obscure.]

roup² (rowp) *n.* *Chiefly Scottish.* A sale by auction. ~*tr.v.* **rouped, rouping, roups.** To sell by auction. [Middle English *roupen,* to shout, from Scandinavian.]

rouse (rowz) *v.* **roused, rousing, rouses.** —*tr.* **1.** To cause to come out of a state of slumber, calmness, complacency, apathy, or depression. **2. a.** To excite, as to anger or action; spur. **b.** To provoke (an emotion): *roused her fury.* **3.** To startle (game) from a covert or lair. —*intr.* **1.** To awaken, as from sleep, repose, or unconsciousness. **2.** To stir; become active. **3.** To rise or start from cover, as game birds do. —See Synonyms at **provoke.** [Originally "to startle (game) from cover", Middle English *rowsen†,* to shake feathers or body.] —**rous·er** *n.*

Usage: Rouse and *arouse* are usually distinguishable. *Arouse* generally refers to an immediate and often brief response (*arouse interest, fear, criticism.* . .); *rouse* implies a deeper, stronger response (*rouse to anger, action.* . .).

rouse·a·bout (rówss-ə-bowt) *n.* *Australian & N.Z.* A person who works on a sheep station, especially during the shearing season; a farmhand. Also called "roustabout", informally "rousie", "rouser". [Variant of ROUSTABOUT.]

rous·ing (rówzing) *adj.* **1.** Inducing enthusiasm or excitement; stirring: *a rousing sermon.* **2.** Active; lively; vigorous: *a rousing march tune.* —**rous·ing·ly** *adv.*

Rous sarcoma (rowss) *n.* A malignant tumour that can be produced on chickens by inoculation with the specific viral causative agent (*Rous sarcoma virus*). [After Francis Peyton *Rous* (1879–1970), U.S. pathologist.]

Rous·seau (rōō-sō; *French* rōō-sṓ), **Henri,** also known as Le Douanier (the customs official) (1844–1910). French primitive painter. A collector of tolls, he retired at 41 to take up painting full time. His early work was mocked for its naive style and apparently inept draughtsmanship. However a few artists, including Picasso, were impressed by his work. His paintings include the apocalyptic *War* (1894), jungle scenes such as *The Snake Charmer* (1907), and group portraits such as *The Cart of Père Juniet* (1908).

Rousseau, Jean-Jacques (1712–78). French philosopher, born in Geneva. Rousseau held that mankind is essentially good but corrupted by society, and his novel *The New Héloïse* (1761) proposed spiritual refreshment through a return to nature. In his major political work *On the Social Contract* (1762) he argued that individuals surrendered their natural rights to society and that these should find expression through the general will.

Rousseau, Théodore (1812–67). French painter, a leading member of the Barbizon group. He sketched direct from nature, but usually reworked his canvasses before submitting them for exhibition. His many rural scenes, often muted in tone, include *Sortie de la Forêt de Fontainebleau* (1848).

roust (rowst) *tr.v.* **rousted, rousting, rousts.** To force or drive out, especially out of bed. [Alteration of ROUSE.]

roust·a·bout (rówstə-bowt) *n.* **1.** A general labourer on an oil instal-

lation. **2.** *U.S.* An unskilled labourer. **3.** *Australian & N.Z.* A rouseabout. [ROUST + ABOUT.]

rout¹ (rowt) *n.* **1.** A disorderly retreat or flight following defeat. **2.** An overwhelming defeat. **3.** A disorderly crowd of persons; a boisterous mob; a rabble. **4.** A public disturbance; a riot. **5.** *Archaic.* A company of people or animals, especially of knights or wolves. **6.** *Archaic.* A large evening party. ~*tr.v.* **routed, routing, routs.** **1.** To put to disorderly flight or retreat. **2.** To defeat overwhelmingly. —See Synonyms at **defeat.** [Middle English *route,* troop, disorderly crowd (influenced by French *deroute,* defeat), from Old French, dispersed group, troop, from Vulgar Latin *rupta* (unattested), from Latin *rumpere* (past participle *ruptus*), to break.]

rout² *v.* **routed, routing, routs.** —*intr.* **1.** To dig for food with the snout; root. **2.** To search; poke around; rummage. —*tr.* **1.** To dig up with the snout. **2.** To expose to view or uncover. **3.** To hollow, scoop, or gouge out. **4.** To fetch, force, or drive out after searching. Often used with *out.* **5.** To cut grooves or shapes in (wood, metal, or the like). Often used with *out.* [Variant of ROOT (to dig up).]

route (rōōt; *militarily also* rowt ‖ rowt) *n. Abbr.* **rte. 1.** A road, course, or way for travel from one place to another. **2.** A regular way taken from one place to another; a customary line of travel. **3.** *Medicine.* The means by which a drug is introduced into the body: *the intravenous route.* —See Synonyms at **way.** ~*tr.v.* **routed, routing, routes.** **1.** To send along; forward. **2.** To schedule or dispatch on a particular route: *The travel agency routed them to Paris by way of Luxembourg.* [Middle English, from Old French, from unattested Vulgar Latin *rupta (via),* "broken or beaten (way)". See **rout** (retreat).]

route-march, route march (rōōt-march) *n.* A long and hard march by soldiers in training. —**route-march** *intr.v.*

rout·er¹ (rōōtər ‖ rówtər) *n.* One that routes.

rout·er² (rówtər) *n.* One that routs; specifically, a machine tool for cutting grooves or shapes.

rou·tine (rōō-téen, rōō-) *n.* **1.** A prescribed and detailed course of action to be followed regularly; a standard procedure. **2.** A set of customary and often mechanically performed procedures or activities. **3. a.** A particular sequence of dance steps. **b.** A set piece of entertainment, especially in a nightclub or theatre. **4.** A computer program, or part of a program, for performing a particular task. —See Synonyms at **method.** ~*adj.* **1.** In accordance with established procedure. **2.** Habitual; regular. **3.** Lacking in interest or originality. [French, from Old French, from ROUTE (beaten path).] —**rou·tine·ly** *adv.* —**rou·tin·ism** *n.* —**rou·tin·ist** *n.*

rou·tin·ise, rou·tin·ize (rōō-téen-īz) *tr.v.* **-ised, -ising, -ises. 1.** To establish a routine for. **2.** To reduce to a routine. —**rou·tin·is·a·tion** (-ī-záysh'n ‖ *U.S.* -i-) *n.*

roux (rōō) *n., pl.* **roux** (rōōz, rōō). A mixture of flour and butter or other fat, heated together and used as a basis for many sauces. [French (*beurre*) *roux,* browned (butter), from *roux,* reddish brown, from Old French *rous,* from Latin *russus,* red.]

Roux (rōō), **(Paul) Emile** (1853–1933). French bacteriologist. He worked closely with Pasteur, helped produce a vaccine against anthrax and developed an antitoxin for diphtheria.

rove¹ (rōv) *v.* **roved, roving, roves.** —*intr.* **1.** To wander about at random, especially over a wide area; roam. **2.** To move or look around without settling: *his gaze roved around the room.* —*tr.* To roam or wander over or through. —See Synonyms at **wander.** ~*n.* An act of roaming; a ramble. [Middle English *roven,* (in archery) to shoot at a random mark (sense influenced by ROVER, a pirate), probably from Scandinavian, akin to Icelandic *râfa,* to wander, loiter.]

rove² *tr.v.* **roved, roving, roves. 1.** To card (wool). **2.** To stretch and twist (fibres), before spinning; ravel out. ~*n.* A slightly twisted and extended fibre or sliver. [18th century : origin obscure.]

rove³. Alternative past tense and past participle of **reeve.**

rove⁴ *n.* A metal ring or small plate over which the end of a rivet is flattened. [Old Norse *ró.*]

rove beetle *n.* Any of numerous beetles of the family Staphylinidae, often found in decaying matter and having slender bodies and short wing covers. [Perhaps from ROVE (to wander about).]

rov·er¹ (rōvər) *n.* **1.** One who roves; a wanderer; a nomad. **2. a.** In croquet, a ball that has gone through all the hoops but has not hit the winning peg. **b.** A player of such a ball. **3.** *Archery.* A mark selected by chance. **4.** In Australian Rules football, a player who takes and clears the ball after a ruck. [Middle English, from *roven,* to shoot at a random mark. See **rove** (to wander about).]

rov·er² *n.* **1.** A pirate. **2.** A pirate vessel. [Middle English, from Middle Dutch *rôver,* robber, from *rôven,* to rob.]

rov·ing (rōving) *adj.* **1.** Wandering or having a tendency to wander or roam. **2.** Not limited to a specific area or sphere of activity: *a roving commission; a roving ambassador.*

row¹ (rō) *n.* **1. a.** A horizontal linear arrangement or array. **b.** A line of things or people placed or occurring side by side. **2.** A line of adjacent seats, as in a theatre, auditorium, or classroom. **3.** A street flanked by a continuous line of buildings on one or both sides. **4.** *Mathematics.* A horizontal line of quantities in a determinant or matrix. —**in a row.** In succession: *That's the third bill in a row.* [Middle English *raw, row,* Old English *rāw, rǣw.*]

row² (rō) *v.* **rowed, rowing, rows.** —*intr.* **1.** To propel a boat with or as if with oars. **2.** To race in rowing boats as a sport. —*tr.* **1.** To

propel (a boat) with or as if with oars. **2.** To carry in or on a boat propelled by oars. **3.** To propel or convey in a manner resembling rowing. **4.** To employ (a specified number of oars or oarsmen). **5.** To pull (an oar) as part of a racing crew. **6.** To race against by rowing.
~*n.* **1.** An act of rowing. **2.** A trip or excursion in a rowing boat. [Middle English *rowen*, Old English *rōwan*.] —**row·er** *n.*

row³ (row) *n.* **1.** A boisterous disturbance or quarrel; a brawl. **2.** Noise; clamour; uproar. **3.** A loud or strong protest; trouble. Used chiefly in the phrases *make a row* or *kick up a row.*
~*intr.v.* **rowed, rowing, rows.** To take part in a row. [18th century (slang) : origin obscure.]

R.O.W. 1. right of way. **2.** Rights of Women.

row·an (rō-ən, rów-) *n.* See **mountain ash.** [Of Scandinavian origin, akin to Old Norse *reynir.*]

row·dy (rówdi) *n., pl.* **-dies.** A rough, disorderly person.
~*adj.* **rowdier, -diest.** Disorderly; rough and noisy. [Probably from ROW (quarrel).] —**row·di·ly** *adv.* —**row·di·ness, row·dy·ism** *n.*

row·el (rów-əl) *n.* **1.** A sharp-toothed wheel inserted into the end of the shank of a spur. **2.** A disc of leather or other material with a central hole, which is inserted beneath the skin of a horse in order to drain an abscess, for example.
~*tr.v.* **rowelled** or *U.S.* **roweled, -elling** or *U.S.* **-eling, -els.** To spur; urge with a rowel. [Middle English *rowelle,* from Old French *roele,* from Late Latin *rotella,* diminutive of Latin *rota,* a wheel.]

row·en (rów-ən) *n.* A second crop of hay in a season; an aftermath. [Middle English *rewayn,* from Old Northern French, Old French *regain* : *re-,* again + *gain,* rowen, from *gaaignier,* to till, "to obtain food", "gain".]

row·ing boat (rō-ing) *n.* A small boat propelled by oars. Also *U.S.* "rowboat".

rowing machine *n.* An exercise apparatus resembling the bottom and sides of a rowing boat with oars and a sliding seat.

Row·land·son (rōlənd-s'n), **Thomas** (1756–1827). British caricaturist. He delighted particularly in satirising grossness and sensuality in crowded social scenes. His *Tour of Dr. Syntax* (1812–21) was especially popular, and he also illustrated works by Sterne, Smollett, Swift, and Goldsmith.

Row·ley (rōli), **William** (c. 1585–c. 1642). British playwright. Much of his best work was produced in collaboration with other dramatists, notably *The Changeling* (1622), written with Middleton.

row·lock (róllək, *also* rúllək *or as a spelling pronunciation* rō-lok) *n.* A device used as a fulcrum to hold an oar in place while rowing, usually a U-shaped metal hoop on a swivel fixed to the side of the boat. Also *U.S.* "oarlock".

Rowse (rowss), **A(lfred) L(eslie)** (1903–). British historian and man of letters. He is especially known as a scholar of the Tudor period, which he has described in *The Elizabethan Renaissance* (1971–72) and other works.

Rox·burgh·shire (róks-brə-shər, -bərə-, -sheer ‖ -shīr). Former county of southern Scotland. Incorporated into the Borders Region (1975), it is largely hilly sheep pastureland.

Roy (roy) *n. Australian.* A young, trendy, middle-class man, typically portrayed as a middlebrow, sports-car-owning executive. Compare **Alf, ocker.** [From the name *Roy.*]

roy·al (róy-əl, royl) *adj. Abbr.* **R. 1.** Of or pertaining to a king, queen, or other monarch. **2.** Of the rank of a king or queen. **3.** Of, pertaining to, or designating the family of a monarch. **4.** Issued or performed by a monarch. **5.** Founded, chartered, or authorised by a monarch. **6.** Befitting a king; stately; majestic. **7.** Superior in size or quality. **8.** Magnificent; first-rate: *a royal welcome.*
~*n.* **1.** A sail set on the royal mast. **2.** A paper size, 20 by 25 inches for printing, 19 by 24 inches for writing. **3.** *Informal.* A member of a royal family. **4.** A stag having antlers with at least 12 branches. Also called "royal stag". [Middle English *roial,* from Old French, from Latin *rēgālis,* from *rēx* (stem *rēg-*), king.] —**roy·al·ly** *adv.*

Royal Academy of Arts *n.* An art society founded in 1768 by George III to support and encourage the visual arts in Britain by instruction and the holding of exhibitions. The number of academicians is limited to 40.

Royal Air Force *n. Abbr.* **R.A.F.** The air force of the United Kingdom.

royal assent *n.* The consent given by a monarch to a parliamentary bill, after which it becomes an act.

royal blue *n.* Deep to strong blue. —**roy·al-blue** *adj.*

Royal British Legion. The official name for the British Legion *(see).*

Royal Canadian Mounted Police *n. Abbr.* **R.C.M.P.** The Canadian federal police force. Also called "Mounties".

Royal Commission *n.* A group of people formally commissioned by the monarch on the recommendation of the government to inquire into and report on issues, laws, institutions, and the like.

Royal Engineers *n.* The branch of the British army in charge of military engineering works such as the building of fortifications and bridges.

royal fern *n.* A deep-rooted fern, *Osmunda regalis,* of worldwide distribution, having tall, upright fronds.

royal flush *n.* The highest hand attainable in poker, consisting of the five highest cards of one suit.

Royal Highness *n.* A title of or form of address for a member of a royal family. Used with *His, Her,* or *Your.*

ryal icing *n.* A type of hard icing made from icing sugar and egg whites and used to decorate rich fruit cakes, such as wedding cakes.

Royal Institution of Great Britain *n.* A British scientific society, founded in London in 1799 as a research centre.

roy·al·ist (róy-əl-ist) *n.* **1.** A supporter of a monarch or of the principle of monarchy. **2.** *Capital* R. An Englishman loyal to Charles I; a Cavalier. **3.** *Capital* R. A supporter of the House of Bourbon's claims to the French throne since the French Revolution. **4.** *Capital* R. A Colonial American loyal to British rule. —**roy·al·ist, roy·al·is·tic** (-ístik) *adj.* —**roy·al·ism** *n.*

royal jelly *n.* A nutritious substance secreted in the pharyngeal glands of worker bees, serving as food for the young larvae, and as the only food for those that develop into queen bees.

Royal Leamington Spa. See **Leamington Spa.**

Royal Marines *n.* A corps of troops serving on land, sea, or in the air, administered by the Royal Navy but having ranks corresponding to those of the army.

royal mast *n.* The small mast immediately above the topgallant mast.

Royal Navy *n. Abbr.* **R.N.** The navy of the United Kingdom.

royal palm *n.* Any of several palm trees of the genus *Roystonea,* mostly from the West Indies; especially, *R. regia,* having a tall, naked trunk surmounted by a large tuft of pinnate leaves.

royal penguin *n.* A crested penguin, *Eudyptes schlegeli,* having white cheeks and throat, found on Macquarie Island, off Tasmania.

royal poinciana *n.* A tropical and semitropical tree, *Delonix regia,* native to Madagascar, having clusters of large scarlet and yellow flowers and long pods. Also called "flamboyant".

Royal prerogative *n.* The special powers and rights belonging to a monarch. They include personal prerogatives, such as immunity from legal action, and political prerogatives (now exercised on the advice of the government), such as the dissolution of Parliament or the appointment of ministers.

royal purple *n.* A moderate or strong violet to deep purple or dark reddish purple. —**roy·al-pur·ple** *adj.*

Royal Society *n. Abbr.* **R.S.** The oldest and most prestigious British scientific society, incorporated by royal charter in 1662 by Charles II.

royal tennis *n.* Real tennis *(see).*

roy·al·ty (róy-əlti, róylti) *n., pl.* **-ties. 1. a.** A king, queen, or other person of royal lineage. **b.** Monarchs and their families collectively. **2.** The lineage or rank of a king or queen. **3.** The power, status, or authority of monarchs. **4.** Royal quality or bearing. **5.** A right or prerogative of the crown, as that of receiving a percentage of the proceeds from mines in the royal domain. **6. a.** The granting of a right by a sovereign to a business enterprise or individual to exploit natural resources. **b.** The payment for such a right. **7. a.** A share paid to an author or composer out of the proceeds resulting from the sale or performance of his work. **b.** A share in the proceeds paid to an inventor or proprietor for the right to use his invention or services.

Royce (royss), **Sir (Frederick) Henry** (1863–1933). British car designer and manufacturer. Working in Manchester, he founded the engineering firm of Royce Ltd (1884), later merging it with the company of Charles Rolls to form Rolls Royce Ltd (1906). Royce designed the first of the famous Silver Ghost cars in the same year. During World War I he designed aeroengines. The first transatlantic flight (1919) by Alcock and Brown was made in a plane with Rolls Royce engines.

roz·zer (rózzər) *n. British Slang.* A policeman. [19th century : origin obscure.]

R.P., RP 1. Received Pronunciation. **2.** Reformed Presbyterian. **3.** Regius Professor.

R.P.C. Royal Pioneer Corps.

r.p.m. revolutions per minute.

R.P.M resale price maintenance.

r.p.s. revolutions per second.

rpt. report.

R.Q. respiratory quotient.

R.R. Right Reverend (title).

–rrhagia *n. comb. form. Pathology.* Indicates an abnormal or excessive flow or discharge; for example, **menorrhagia.** [New Latin, from Greek, from *rhēgnunai,* to burst forth.]

–rrhoea *n. comb. form.* Also *chiefly U.S.* **-rrhea.** *Pathology.* Indicates a flow or discharge; for example, **seborrhoea, amenorrhoea.** [Middle English *-ria,* from Late Latin *-rrhoea,* from Greek *-rrhoia,* from *rhoia,* a flowing, flux, from *rhein,* to flow.]

RR Lyrae variable *n. Astronomy.* A type of pulsating variable star characterised by periods that range from several hours to about one day and having absolute magnitudes close to 0.6.

rRNA *n.* **Ribosomal RNA** *(see).*

RRP retailers' recommended price.

R.S. Royal Society.

R.S.F.S.R. Russian Soviet Federated Socialist Republic.

RSJ *n.* A rolled-steel joist: a steel beam, usually an H- or I-beam, used in building construction.

R.S.M. 1. Regimental Sergeant-Major. **2.** Royal Society of Medicine.

R.S.P.B. Royal Society for the Protection of Birds.

R.S.P.C.A. Royal Society for the Prevention of Cruelty of Animals.

R.S.V. Revised Standard Version (of the Bible).

R.S.V.P. répondez s'il vous plaît (English *please reply*).

rt. right.

rte. route.

royal palm *One of about 2,600 species of palm, the royal palm is native to tropical and subtropical America. It grows to a height of about 30 metres (100 feet).*

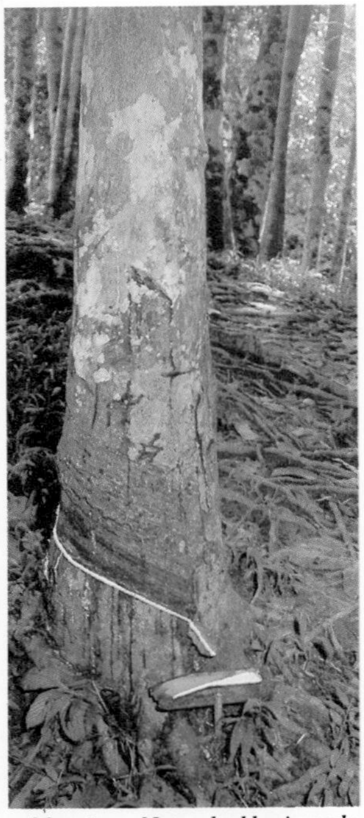

rubber tree *Natural rubber is made from the milky juice, or latex, of this tropical tree, which is native to South America. The latex is extracted by tapping the tree, as seen here on a Borneo plantation.*

Rt. Hon. Right Honourable (title).
Rt. Rev. Right Reverend (title).
Ru The symbol for the element ruthenium.
R.U. Rugby Union.
Ruanda-Urundi. See **Rwanda, Burundi.**
Ru·a·pe·hu, Mount (rŏŏ-ə-páy-hōō). Intermittently active volcano and highest peak of North Island, New Zealand. Situated in Tongariro National Park, it is 2 797 metres (9,175 feet) high.
rub (rub) *v.* **rubbed, rubbing, rubs.** *—tr.* **1.** To apply pressure and friction to (a surface), manually or mechanically. **2.** To clean, polish, or manipulate by applying pressure and friction. **3.** To apply firmly and with friction upon a surface. **4.** To move (an object or objects) against another or each other repeatedly and with friction. **5.** To cause to become worn, chafed, or irritated. **6.** To remove or erase. Used with *out, off,* or *away.* *—intr.* **1.** To exert pressure and friction on something. **2.** To move along in contact with a surface; graze or scrape. **3.** To become worn or chafed from friction. **4.** To be removed by pressure and friction. Used with *off* or *out.* **5.** In bowls, to be diverted or slowed down by unevenness on the green. Used of a bowl. **—rub along.** *Informal.* **1.** To manage or proceed despite difficulties. **2.** To maintain a reasonably friendly relationship. **—rub it in.** To remind someone repeatedly of some mistake, shortcoming, or failure. **—rub off.** To be communicated or transferred; be infectious: *Her enthusiasm rubbed off on me.* **—rub out.** *Slang.* To murder. **—rub up.** To refresh one's memory of. **—rub (someone) up the wrong way.** *Informal.* To arouse hostility or irritation in; antagonise.
~n. **1.** An act of rubbing. **2.** An unevenness on a surface. **3.** Difficulty: *"Aye, there's the rub"* (Shakespeare). [Middle English *rubben,* perhaps from Middle Low German *rubben*†.]
Rub'al Kha·li (rŏŏb-al-k͟háali). Vast desert area in southern Saudi Arabia. The name is Arabic for "Empty Quarter".
ru·basse (rōō-báss, -baass) *n.* A dark red variety of quartz containing iron oxide. [French *rubace,* from Old French *rubi, rubis,* RUBY.]
ru·ba·to (rōō-baatō, rōō-) *n., pl.* **-tos.** *Music.* Variation of tempo within a phrase or measure without altering its length.
~adj. Characterised by rubato. [Italian, *(tempo) rubato,* "stolen (time)", from the past participle of *rubare,* to rob, from Germanic.]
rub·ber[1] (rúbbər) *n.* **1.** A light cream to dark amber, amorphous, elastic, solid polymer of isoprene, $(C_5H_8)_n$, generally prepared by coagulation and drying of the milky sap, or latex, of various tropical plants, especially the **rubber tree** *(see).* Also called "caoutchouc", "India rubber". **2.** Any of various materials made from natural rubber by curing, vulcanising, adding pigment, and otherwise modifying for use in a wide variety of manufactured products including electric insulation, elastic bands and belts, tyres, and containers. **3.** Any of numerous synthetic elastic materials of varying chemical composition, with properties similar to those of natural rubber. **4.** *Chiefly U.S. Slang.* A condom. **5. a.** One who rubs. **b.** One who gives a massage; a masseur or masseuse. **6.** Something used for rubbing or erasing; specifically, an eraser made of rubber.
~adj. Made of or pertaining to rubber. [RUB + -ER (sense 1, from its original use in erasing pencil marks).]
rubber[2] *n. Abbr.* **r. 1.** In bridge, whist, and other games and sports, a series of games of which two out of three or three out of five must be won to terminate the play. **2.** The game that breaks a tie and ends such a series. [17th century (in bowls) : origin obscure.]
rubber band *n.* An elastic loop of natural or synthetic rubber, used to hold papers or objects together. Also called "elastic band".
rub·ber-base paint (rúbbər-bayss) *n.* **Latex paint** *(see).*
rubber cement *n.* A solution of rubber in a volatile solvent, used as an adhesive.
rubber cheque *n.* A cheque returned by a bank because of insufficient funds in the account on which it is drawn. Used humorously.
rub·ber·ise, rub·ber·ize (rúbbər-īz) *tr.v.* **-ised, -ising, -ises.** To coat, treat, or impregnate with rubber.
rub·ber·neck (rúbbər-nek) *n. U.S. Slang.* A gawking tourist or sightseer.
rubber plant *n.* **1.** Any of several tropical plants yielding sap that can be coagulated to form crude rubber. **2.** A plant, *Ficus elastica,* that has large, glossy, leathery leaves, and is popular as a house plant. It grows as a tall tree in its native India and Malaysia but is not a source of commercial rubber.
rubber stamp *n.* **1.** A piece of rubber affixed to a handle and bearing raised characters, used to make ink impressions of names, dates, and the like. **2.** A person or body that gives perfunctory approval or endorsement of a policy without assessing its merit. **3.** A perfunctory authorisation or endorsement.
rub·ber-stamp (rúbbər-stámp) *tr.v.* **-stamped, -stamping, -stamps. 1.** To mark with the imprint of a rubber stamp. **2.** To endorse, vote for, or approve without question or deliberation.
rubber tree *n.* A tree, *Hevea braziliensis,* native to tropical America but widely cultivated throughout the tropics, yielding a milky juice, or latex, that is a major source of commercial rubber.
rub·ber·y (rúbbəri) *adj.* Of or like rubber; elastic; resilient.
rub·bing (rúbbing) *n.* A representation of a raised or indented surface made by placing paper over the surface and rubbing the paper gently with a marking agent such as charcoal or chalk.
rub·bish (rúbbish) *n.* **1.** Something discarded as refuse; debris; litter. **2.** Worthless material. **3.** Foolish talk or writing; nonsense.
~tr.v. **rubbished, -bishing, -bishes.** *Informal.* To dismiss or reject (something or something) as being worthless, foolish, or hopeless. [Middle English *robishe, robys, robous,* from Anglo-French *robbous,* plural of *robel* (unattested), RUBBLE.] **—rub·bish·y** *adj.*
rub·ble (rúbb'l) *n.* **1.** Fragments of rock or masonry crumbled by natural or manmade forces. **2. a.** Irregular fragments or pieces of rock used in masonry. **b.** The masonry made with such rocks. In this sense, also called "rubblework". [Middle English *robyl,* from Anglo-French *robel* (unattested), from Old French *robe,* booty; see **robe.**] **—rub·bly** *adj.*
Rub·bra (rúbbrə), **Edmund** (1901–). British composer. He made his reputation as a symphonic composer with eleven symphonies and is also noted for his chamber music, which often employs polyphonic effects.
rub down *tr.v.* **1.** To clean and dry (oneself, or a horse, for example) by rubbing vigorously. **2.** To massage.
rub·down (rúb-down) *n.* **1.** An energetic massage of the body. **2.** An act or instance of cleaning or drying by rubbing.
ru·be·fa·cient (rŏŏbi-fáy-shənt, -si-ənt || réwbi-) *adj.* Producing redness and warmth of the skin.
~n. A substance that irritates the skin, causing redness, and often used as a counterirritant. [Latin *rubefaciēns* (stem *rubefacient-*), present participle of *rubefacere,* to redden : *rubeus,* red, reddish + *facere,* to make.] **—ru·be·fac·tion** (-fáksh'n) *n.*
ru·bel·la (rōō-béllə, rōō- || rew-) *n.* A disease, **German measles** *(see).* [New Latin, from Latin, feminine of *rubellus,* reddish, from *rubeus,* red, reddish.]
ru·bel·lite (rōō-béllīt, rŏŏbi-līt || rew-) *n.* A pink or red variety of tourmaline used as a gemstone. [Latin *rubellus,* reddish (see **rubella**) + -ITE.]
Ru·bens (rŏŏ-binz, -bənz, -benz; *Dutch* rü-bənss), **Peter Paul** (1577–1640). Flemish baroque painter. Appointed court painter (1609) to the Archduke Albert, he set up a studio in Antwerp and, aided by assistants, produced many paintings often with religious, historical, or allegorical themes. *An Allegory of War and Peace* (1629) is among examples of his grand style, while *The Straw Hat* (1622–5) shows his more tender and intimate portraiture. He was knighted by Charles I of England (1629), who commissioned from him the ceiling of the Banqueting House in Whitehall.
ru·be·o·la (rōō-bée-ə-lə, rōō-, -ō- || rew-) *n.* A disease, **measles** *(see).* [New Latin, neuter plural diminutive of Latin *rubeus,* red.] **—ru·be·o·lar** *adj.*
ru·bes·cent (rōō-béss'nt, rōō- || rew-) *adj.* Reddening. [Latin *rubescēns* (stem *rubescent-*), present participle of *rubescere,* to grow red, inchoative of *rubēre,* to be red.] **—ru·bes·cence** *n.*
Ru·bi·con (rŏŏ-bi-kən || réw-, -kon). A small river in northern Italy rising just north of San Marino and flowing northeast to the Adriatic Sea. Caesar's crossing it with his army in 49 B.C. constituted an illegal entry into Italy and thereby initiated civil war. **—cross** or **pass the Rubicon.** To embark on an undertaking from which one cannot turn back.
ru·bi·cund (rŏŏ-bi-kənd || réw-, -kund) *adj.* Having or showing a healthy rosiness; ruddy. [Latin *rubicundus,* from *rebēre,* to be red.] **—ru·bi·cun·di·ty** (-kúndəti) *n.*
ru·bid·i·um (rōō-bíddi-əm, rōō- || rew-) *n. Symbol* **Rb** A soft, silvery-white alkali-metal element that ignites spontaneously in air and reacts violently with water. It is used in photocells and in the manufacture of vacuum tubes. Atomic number 37, atomic weight 85.47, melting point 38.89°C, boiling point 688°C, relative density (solid) 1.532, valency 1. [New Latin, from Latin *rubidus,* red (from the red lines in its spectrum).]
ru·bid·i·um-stron·ti·um dating (rōō-bíddi-əm-strónti-əm || rew-, -strónsh-) *n.* A method of dating rocks and minerals by measuring the amount of the isotope strontium-87 present as a result of the radioactive decay of rubidium-87. It is used for ages up to 10^9 (a thousand million) years.
ru·big·i·nous (rōō-bíjinəss, rōō- || rew-) *adj.* Rust-coloured; reddish-brown. [Latin *rūbīginōsus,* from *rūbīgo, rōbīgo,* rust.]
Ru·bik's cube (rŏŏ-biks || réw-) *n.* Also **Rubik cube.** A puzzle consisting of a cube with each face made up of nine smaller coloured cubes joined by internal connections so that the faces can be rotated. The test of skill is to rearrange the puzzle so that each face has a different single colour, starting from a position in which each face is randomly made up of different colours. [After Ernő *Rubik,* 20th-century Hungarian teacher of architecture.]
Ru·bin·stein (rŏŏbin-stīn), **Anton Grigoryevich** (1829–94). Russian composer and pianist. Of German-Jewish extraction, he was, in his time, considered a rival to Liszt. He helped found (1862) the St. Petersburg Conservatoire.
Rubinstein, Artur (1887–1982). Polish born U.S. pianist. Performing in public by the time he was eleven years old, he went on to acquire an international reputation for his interpretations of the works of Chopin. He became a U.S. citizen in 1946.
ru·bi·ous (rŏŏ-bi-əss || réw-) *adj.* Having the colour of a ruby; red.
ruble. Variant of **rouble.**
Ru·blyov (rōō-blyóff), **Andrey,** also known as Rublev (*c.* 1370–*c.* 1430). Russian artist. He trained as an iconographer in the Byzantine tradition before retiring to the monastic life.
ru·bric (rŏŏ-brik || réw-) *n.* **1.** A part of a manuscript or book, such as a title, heading, or initial letter, that appears in decorative red lettering, or is in some other way distinguished from the rest of the text. **2.** A title or heading of a statute or chapter in a code of law, originally written or printed in red. **3.** A name for a class or category; a title. **4.** *Ecclesiastical.* A direction in a missal, hymnal, or other liturgical book. **5.** Any brief, authoritative rule or direction.

PRONUNCIATION KEY

a, trap; aa, father; ai, fair; ar, star; aw, lawn; ay, play; b, bb, stab; rubber; ch, church; ck, ticket; d, dd, dead; ladder; e, dress; ee, bee; er, defer; ew, few; ewr, pure; ə, about; ər, letter; f, ff, fife; differ; g, gg, giggle; h, hat; i, kit; ī, price; īr, fire; j, judge; k, kick; l, ll, let; 'l, needle; m, mm, man; n, nn, no; 'n, sudden; ng, thing; o, lot; ō, no; ŏŏ, foot; ōō, shoe; oor, poor; ow, cow; owr, hour; oy, boy; p, pp, pepper; r, rr, red; s, ss, sauce; sh, ship; t, tt, totter; th, thick; t͟h, this; smooth; u, cut; ur, turn; v, vv, valve; w, wet; y, yes; z, zz, zebra; z͟h, vision; pleasure

IN FOREIGN WORDS:

aN, oN, Saint-Saëns; h͟l, Llanelli; Hluhluwe; k͟h, loch; lough; Khaled

STRESS MARK:

ín-sīt, insight; in-sī́t, incite

6. A short commentary or explanation covering a broad subject. **7.** The instructions to the candidate in an examination paper. **8.** *Archaic.* Red ochre. [Middle English *rubrike,* from Old French *rubriche,* from Latin *rubrīca (terra),* "red earth", "red ochre", from *ruber,* red.] **—ru·bri·cal** *adj.*

ru·bri·cate (ro͞o-bri-kayt || réw-) *tr.v.* **-cated, -cating, -cates. 1.** To arrange, write, or print as a rubric. **2.** To provide with rubrics. **3.** To establish rules for. [Late Latin *rubrīcāre,* from *rubrīca,* RUBRIC.] **—ru·bri·ca·tor, ru·bri·ca·tion** (-káysh'n) *n.*

ru·bri·cian (ro͞o-brísh'n || rew-) *n.* A person learned in the rubrics of ecclesiastical ritual.

ru·by (ro͞obi || réwbi) *n., pl.* **-bies. 1.** A deep red, transparent form of corundum, highly valued as a precious stone. Also called "Oriental ruby", "true ruby". **2.** Something made from a ruby, as a watch bearing. **3.** A dark or deep red to deep purplish red.
~*adj.* **1.** Of or having the colour of rubies. **2.** Designating a fortieth anniversary: *a ruby wedding.* [Middle English, from Old French *rubi,* from Medieval Latin *rubīnus (lapis),* "red stone", from Latin *rubeus,* red.]

ruby silver *n.* A mineral, **pyrargyrite** *(see).*

ruby spinel *n.* A red form of **spinel** *(see)* used as a gemstone.

R.U.C. Royal Ulster Constabulary.

ruche, rouche (ro͞osh) *n.* A ruffle, gather, or pleat of lace, muslin, or other fine fabric used for trimming women's garments.
~*tr.v.* **ruched, ruching, ruches.** To decorate with ruches. [French, beehive, frill (pleated like a straw beehive), from Old French *ruche,* bark of a tree, beehive made of barks, from Medieval Latin *rūsca,* from Gaulish *rūska* (unattested), akin to Old Irish *rūsc*†, bark.]

ruch·ing (ro͞oshing) *n.* **1.** Ruches collectively. **2.** Fabric for ruches.

ruck¹ (ruk) *n.* **1.** A large number mixed together; a jumble. **2.** The multitude of ordinary people. **3.** In Rugby football, a loose scrum occurring when the ball is on the ground. **4.** In Australian Rules football, three players who play all over the field, following the ball.
~*v.* **rucked, rucking, rucks.** *—tr.* In Rugby football, to extract (the ball) from a ruck by clawing backwards using the foot. *—intr.* To ruck a ball. [Middle English *ruke*†, heap, stack.]

ruck² *v.* **rucked, rucking, rucks.** Also **ruck·le** (rúck'l). *—tr.* To make a fold in; crease. Often used with *up.* *—intr.* To become creased. Often used with *up.*
~*n.* Also **ruckle.** A crease or pucker, as in cloth. [Ultimately from Old Norse *hrukka,* wrinkle, crease.]

ruck·sack (rúk-sak, ro͞ok-) *n.* A bag with straps fitting round the shoulders, worn on the back and often supported by a light frame, used by hikers or travellers for carrying equipment, supplies, or the like. [German *Rucksack* : *Rücken,* back, from Old High German *hrukki* + *Sack,* sack, from Old High German *sac,* from Latin *saccus,* SACK.]

ruck·us (rúckəss) *n. Informal.* A noisy disturbance; a commotion. [Probably RUC(TION) + (RUMP)US.]

ruc·tion (rúcksh'n) *n. Informal.* A riotous disturbance; a noisy quarrel. [19th century : origin obscure.]

ru·da·ce·ous rock (ro͞o-dáyshəss) *n.* A sedimentary rock composed of fragments of disintegrated rock material 2 millimetres (0.08 inch) or more in diameter. [New Latin, from Latin *rūdus,* rubble + -ACEOUS.]

rud·beck·i·a (rud-bécki-ə) *n.* Any plant of the genus *Rudbeckia,* native to North America but widely cultivated for their showy, yellow, daisy-like flowers. See **black-eyed Susan.** [New Latin, after Olaus *Rudbeck* (1630–1702), Swedish botanist.]

rudd (rud) *n.* A European freshwater fish, *Scardinius erythrophthalmus,* having a brownish body and red fins. [Probably from obsolete *rud,* a ruddy colour. See **ruddle.**]

rud·der (rúddər) *n.* **1.** A vertically hinged plate mounted at the stern of a vessel for directing its course. **2.** A similar structure at the tail of an aircraft, used for effecting horizontal changes in course. **3.** Anything that controls direction; a guide. [Middle English *rother, rodyr,* Old English *rōther,* steering oar.]

rud·der·post (rúddər-pōst) *n.* The vertical shaft of a rudder, allowing it to pivot when the tiller or steering gear is operated. Also called "rudderstock".

rud·dle (rúdd'l) *n.* Also **red·dle** (rédd'l), **rad·dle** (rádd'l). Red ochreous iron ore, an earthy variety of haematite, used in dyeing and marking.
~*tr.v.* **ruddled, -dling, -dles.** Also **red·dle, rad·dle.** To dye or mark with red ochre: *ruddle sheep.* [Diminutive of obsolete *rud,* a ruddy colour, Middle English *rud(d)e,* Old English *rudu.*]

rud·dle·man (rúdd'l-mən, -man) *n., pl.* **-men** (-mən, -men). A man who sells ruddle, or red ochre.

rud·dock (rúddək) *n. British Regional.* The robin. [Middle English *ruddok,* Old English *rudduc* : *rudu* (see **ruddle**) + *-uc,* -OCK.]

rud·dy (rúddi) *adj.* **-dier, -diest. 1.** Having a healthy, reddish colour. **2.** Reddish; rosy. **3.** *Informal.* Damned; bloody. Used euphemistically.
~*adv. Informal.* Used as an intensive: *ruddy awful play.* [Middle English *rudie,* Old English *rudig,* from *rudu,* red colour.] **—rud·di·ly** *adv.* **—rud·di·ness** *n.*

rude (ro͞od || rewd) *adj.* **ruder, rudest. 1.** Ill-mannered; uncivil; discourteous. **2.** Lacking the graces of civilised life; unrefined; uncouth. **3.** Lowly; humble: *a rude thatched hut.* **4.** Primitive; uncivilised. **5.** Formed without skill or precision; makeshift; crude: *made a rude shelter.* **6.** Approximate; rough: *"the height of the cliffs thus affording a rude measure of the age of the streams"* (Charles Darwin). **7.** Vigorous; robust. **8. a.** Harsh; severe: *rude winters.* **b.** Violent and upsetting: *a rude shock.* **9.** Discordant: *"rude harsh-sounding rhymes"* (Shakespeare). **10.** Sexually titillating or obscene. Used euphemistically or humorously. [Middle English, from Old French, from Latin *rudis,* rough, raw, akin to *rūdus*†, broken stone.] **—rude·ly** *adv.* **—rude·ness** *n.*

ru·der·al (ro͞o-dərəl || réw-) *adj. Botany.* Growing in rubbish, poor land, or waste places.
~*n. Botany.* A ruderal plant. [New Latin *rūderālis,* from Latin *rūdera,* ruins, rubbish, plural of *rūdus*†, broken stone.]

ru·di·ment (ro͞o-di-mənt || réw-) *n.* **1.** *Often plural.* A fundamental element, principle, or skill, as of a field of learning. **2.** *Often plural.* Something in an incipient or undeveloped form; beginnings: *the rudiments of social behaviour in children.* **3.** *Biology.* An initial group of cells which gives rise to a structure; a vestige. [French, from Latin *rudīmentum,* beginning (formed after *elementum,* ELEMENT), from *rudis,* RUDE.]

ru·di·men·ta·ry (ro͞o-di-méntri, -méntəri || réw-) *adj.* Also **ru·di·men·tal** (-mént'l). **1.** Of, pertaining to, or involving basic facts or principles that must be learned first; elementary. **2.** In the earliest stages of development; incipient. **3.** *Biology.* Imperfectly or incompletely developed; vestigial: *a rudimentary organ.* **—ru·di·men·ta·ri·ly** (-méntrəli || -men-térrəli) *adv.* **—ru·di·men·ta·ri·ness** *n.*

Ru·dolf I (ro͞o-dolf), also known as Rudolph of Habsburg (1218–91). German king. In 1273 he became the first Habsburg to be elected Holy Roman Emperor. His conquest of Austria and the surrounding territories formed the power base for his descendants until 1918.

Rudolf. See **Turkana, Lake.**

rue¹ (ro͞o || rew) *v.* **rued, ruing, rues.** *—tr.* To feel remorse or sorrow because of; regret; repent. *—intr.* To feel remorse or sorrow; be penitent or regretful.
~*n. Archaic.* Sorrow; regret. [Middle English *ruen,* Old English *hrēowan,* to make penitent, distress.] **—ru·er** *n.*

rue² *n.* An aromatic Eurasian plant of the genus *Ruta;* especially, *R. graveolens,* having evergreen leaves that yield an acrid, volatile oil formerly used in medicine. Formerly called "herb-of-grace". [Middle English, from Old French, from Latin *rūta,* from Greek *rhutē.*]

Rue·il-Mal·mai·son (rö-i-mal-me-zóɴ). Western suburb of Paris, in the Hauts-de-Seine département, France. Once a separate town, its Château de Malmaison was a favourite residence of Napoleon.

rue·ful (ro͞o-f'l || réw-) *adj.* **1.** Inspiring pity or compassion. **2.** Causing, feeling, or expressing sorrow or regret. **3.** Expressive of a faintly sardonic regret; wry. **—rue·ful·ly** *adv.* **—rue·ful·ness** *n.*

ru·fes·cent (ro͞o-féss'nt || rew-) *adj. Botany.* Tinged with red. [Latin *rūfēscēns* (stem *rūfēscent-*), present participle of *rūfēscere,* to become reddish, from *rūfus,* reddish.] **—ru·fes·cence** *n.*

ruff¹ (ruf) *n.* **1.** A stiffly starched, frilled or pleated circular collar of lace, muslin, or other fine fabric, worn by men and women especially in Europe in the 16th and 17th centuries. **2.** A distinctive collar-like projection around the neck, as of feathers on a bird or of fur on a mammal. **3. a.** A Eurasian sandpiper, *Philomachus pugnax,* the male of which has collar-like, erectile feathers around the neck during the breeding season. **b.** The male of this bird. The female is called a "reeve". [Short for RUFFLE (frill).] **—ruffed** *adj.*

ruff² *n.* In card games: **1.** The playing of a trump card when one cannot follow suit. **2.** An old game resembling whist.
~*v.* **ruffed, ruffing, ruffs.** In card games: *—tr.* To trump. *—intr.* To play a trump. [Old French *roffle,* name of a card game, earlier *ronfle,* probably from Italian *ronfa,* perhaps alteration of *trionfa,* "triumph", trump card, from Latin *triumphus,* TRIUMPH.]

ruffe, ruff (ruf) *n.* A European freshwater fish, *Acerina cernua,* related to the perches. Also called "pope". [Middle English *ruf, ruffe,* sea bream, perhaps from *ruch, r(o)wgh,* ROUGH (from its rough scales).]

ruf·fi·an (rúf-yən, -i-ən) *n.* **1.** A tough, violent man. **2.** A thug or gangster. [French *rufien, ruf(f)ian,* from Italian *ruffiano,* pander, "filthy or scabby person", from *roffia, ruffia,* scab, filth, probably from Germanic.] **—ruf·fi·an·ism** *n.* **—ruf·fi·an, ruf·fi·an·ly** *adj.*

ruf·fle¹ (rúff'l) *n.* **1.** A strip of frilled or closely pleated fabric used for trimming or decoration. **2.** Something resembling such trimming, such as a bird's ruff. **3.** A slight discomposure; an agitation. **4.** An irregularity in smoothness; a slight disturbance. **5.** A low continuous beating of a drum that is not as loud as a roll.
~*v.* **ruffled, -fling, -fles.** *—tr.* **1.** To disturb the smoothness or regularity of; ripple: *wind ruffled the surface of the water.* **2.** To pleat or gather (fabric) into a ruffle. **3.** To erect (the feathers). Often used with *up.* **4.** To discompose; fluster. **5.** To flip through (the pages of a book). **6.** To beat a ruffle on (a drum). **7.** To shuffle (cards). *—intr.* **1.** To become irregular or rough. **2.** To flutter. **3.** To become flustered. [Middle English *ruffelen*†.]

ruffle² *intr.v.* **-fled, -fling, -fles.** To behave arrogantly or roughly; swagger. [Middle English *ruffelen*†.] **—ruf·fler** *n.*

ru·fous (ro͞o-fəss || réw-) *adj. Zoology.* Reddish brown. [Latin *rūfus,* red, reddish.]

rug (rug) *n.* **1.** A piece of heavy, usually woollen, fabric, used to cover a portion of a floor and typically smaller than a carpet. **2.** An animal skin used as a floor covering. **3.** *Chiefly British.* A blanket or piece of thick, warm fabric or fur used as a coverlet or wrap. [Probably from Scandinavian; akin to Swedish *rugg,* ruffled hair, and to Old Norse *rogg,* tuft. See **rugged.**]

ru·ga (ro͞o-gə || réw-) *n., pl.* **-gae** (-jee, -gī). *Biology & Anatomy.* A fold, crease, or wrinkle, as in the lining of the stomach. [Latin *rūga,* fold.]

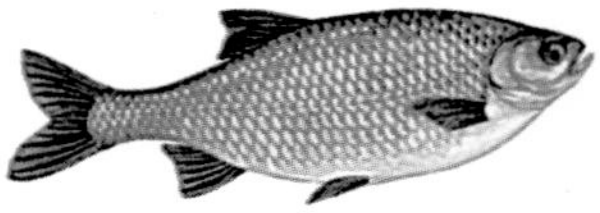

rudd *Found in both still and flowing water, the rudd is a favourite target for anglers in Europe; it is also fished commercially in eastern Europe.*

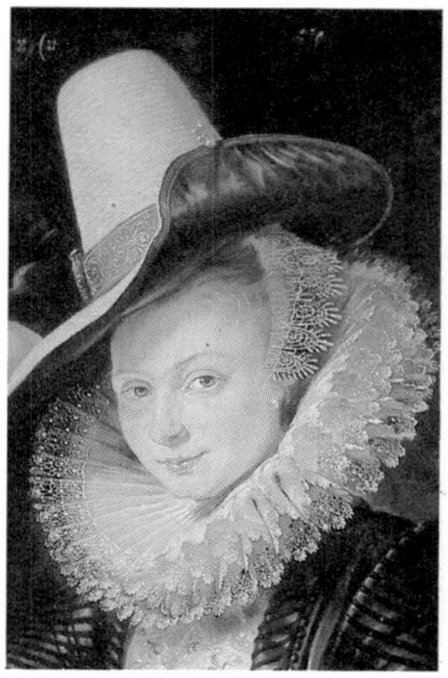

ruff *Isabella Brant wearing a ruff; a detail from a painting by Rubens, who married her in 1609.*

rugby football

THE GAME WITH SCRUMS, LINE-OUTS, AND AN OVAL BALL
According to tradition, Rugby football was born during a school game

Rugby is a ball game that mixes skill with aggressive physical contact. Teams of 15 or 13 a side battle in scrums and line-outs for possession of an oval ball. Then, by powerful kicking, running while holding the ball, and skilful passing, they aim to place the ball behind a goal line defended by their opponents.

Traditionally, the game began at Rugby School in 1823, when, during a game of football, a boy called William Webb Ellis picked up the ball and ran with it. The skipper apologised for

Ellis's behaviour, but the idea of carrying the ball caught on – and launched a new game. Other schools began playing it.

Teams were formed at Liverpool (1857) and the following year at Edinburgh and at Blackheath in Kent. In 1871, the Rugby Football Union was founded to standardise rules. Rugby Union, strictly amateur, is played in many countries with 15 players on each side. A mainly professional game – Rugby League – with 13 a side and slightly different rules is also played.

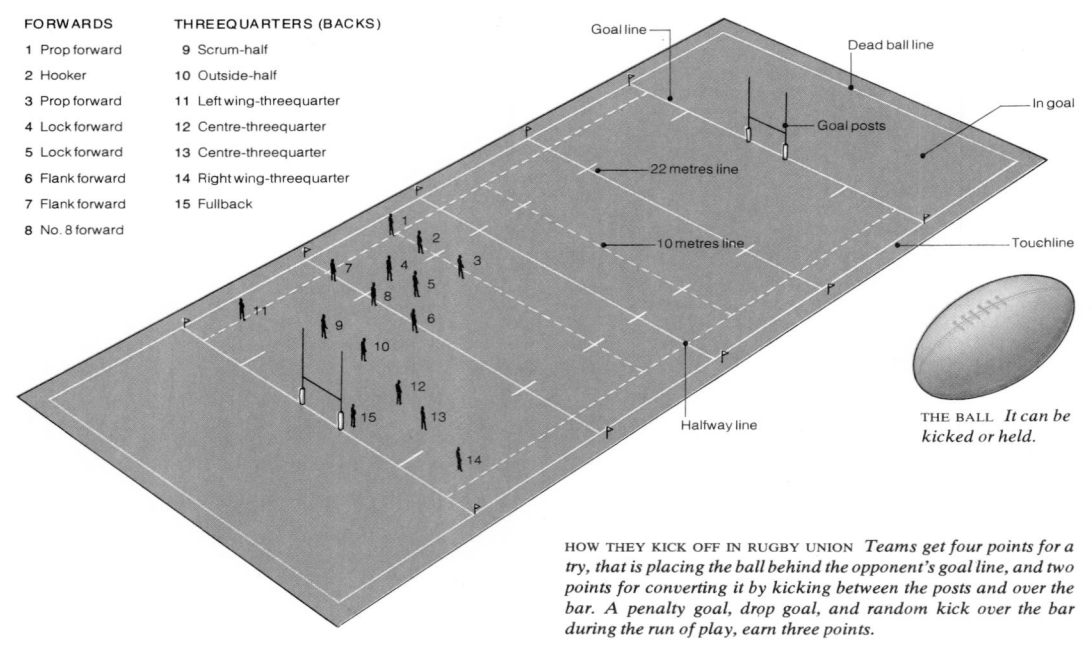

FORWARDS	THREEQUARTERS (BACKS)
1 Prop forward	9 Scrum-half
2 Hooker	10 Outside-half
3 Prop forward	11 Left wing-threequarter
4 Lock forward	12 Centre-threequarter
5 Lock forward	13 Centre-threequarter
6 Flank forward	14 Right wing-threequarter
7 Flank forward	15 Fullback
8 No. 8 forward	

Goal line
Dead ball line
In goal
Goal posts
22 metres line
10 metres line
Touchline
Halfway line

THE BALL *It can be kicked or held.*

HOW THEY KICK OFF IN RUGBY UNION *Teams get four points for a try, that is placing the ball behind the opponent's goal line, and two points for converting it by kicking between the posts and over the bar. A penalty goal, drop goal, and random kick over the bar during the run of play, earn three points.*

Rug·by (rúg-bi). Town of Warwickshire, central England, an important railway junction and manufacturing centre.

Rugby fives *n.* See **fives**.

Rugby football *n.* Either of two types of football played with an oval ball which players are allowed to handle. *Rugby Union* is a strictly amateur game, played between two teams of 15 players. Also called "rugger". *Rugby League* is both amateur and professional and is played between two teams of 13 players. [After *Rugby* School, in RUGBY, where it originated.]

rug·ged (rúggid) *adj.* **1.** Having a rough, irregular surface. **2.** Having strong features marked with furrows or wrinkles. **3.** Austere; stern. **4.** Demanding great effort, ability, or endurance. **5.** Lacking culture or polish. **6.** Vigorous; sturdy; hardy. —See Synonyms at **rough.** [Middle English, shaggy, probably from Scandinavian; akin to Old Norse *rögg*, tuft, from Germanic *rawwō* (unattested).] —**rug·ged·ly** *adv.* —**rug·ged·ness** *n.*

rug·ger (rúggər) *n. British.* Rugby Union. See **Rugby football.**

ru·gose (róo-gōz, -gŏss ‖ réw-) *adj.* Also **ru·gous** (-gəss), **ru·gate** (-gayt). **1.** Having many wrinkles or creases. **2.** *Botany.* Having a rough and ridged surface, as certain prominently veined leaves do. [Latin *rūgōsus*, creased, from *rūga*, fold.] —**ru·gose·ly** *adv.* —**ru·gos·i·ty** (-góssəti) *n.*

Ruhr (roor). A major industrial region of the world, lying in West Germany. It comprises the valley of the river Ruhr, which rises in Sauerland and flows west to the Rhine at Duisburg, and the Lippe valley to the north. The Ruhr provides most of West Germany's coal, and nearly half its electricity supply. Raw materials are imported via Rotterdam and the Rhine, and the region's products include iron, steel, chemicals, and glass.

ru·in (róo-in ‖ réw-) *n.* **1.** Total destruction or disintegration, rendering something formless, useless, or valueless. **2.** The cause of such destruction: *A single flaw is the ruin of a diamond.* **3.** *Often plural.* A condition of total destruction or collapse. **4.** *Often plural.* The remains of something destroyed, disintegrated, or decayed. **5.** A person whose physical or mental capacities have been destroyed. **6. a.** The loss or severe impairment of one's health, position, or honour. **b.** *Archaic.* Loss of virginity in an unmarried woman. **7.** The cause of such loss.
~*v.* **ruined, -ining, -ins.** —*tr.* **1.** To destroy or demolish; reduce to ruin or disintegrate. **2.** To harm, damage, or spoil irreparably. **3.** To reduce to poverty or bankruptcy. **4.** *Archaic.* **a.** To deprive of chastity. **b.** To seduce and abandon (a woman). —*intr. Archaic.*

To fall into ruin. [Middle English *ruine*, from Old French, from Latin *ruīna*, "fall", from *ruere*, to fall, crumble.] —**ru·in·a·ble** *adj.* —**ru·in·er** *n.*

Synonyms: ruin, raze, demolish, destroy, devastate, damage, wreck.

ru·in·a·tion (róo-i-náysh'n ‖ réw-) *n.* **1. a.** The act of ruining. **b.** The condition of being ruined. **2.** The cause of ruin.

ru·in·ous (róo-inəss ‖ réw-) *adj.* **1.** Causing or apt to cause ruin; destructive. **2.** Falling to ruin; dilapidated or decayed. **3.** *Informal.* Very expensive. —**ru·in·ous·ly** *adv.* —**ru·in·ous·ness** *n.*

Ruis·dael (réez-daal, rĭz-, -dayl; *Dutch* rŏ-iz-daal), **Jacob van** (*c.* 1628–82). Dutch artist. Possibly the greatest Dutch landscape painter, he composed baroque, tranquil works which proved profoundly influential on Western European landscape painting.

rule (rool ‖ rewl) *n.* **1. a.** Governing power, or its possession or use; authority; control: *under the rule of Henry VIII.* **b.** The period of time that such authority lasts: *the nineteen-year rule of Henry VIII.* **2.** An authoritative direction for conduct or procedure, specifically: **a.** Any of the regulations governing procedure in a legislative body. **b.** A principle of conduct observed by the members of a group. **c.** A regulation observed by the players in a game, sport, or contest. **3.** A code of principles for the conduct of religious services or activities. **4.** An established standard or habit of behaviour. **5.** Something that generally prevails or obtains. **6.** A standard method or procedure for solving a class of mathematical problems. **7.** *Law.* **a.** A court order limited in application to a specific case. **b.** A subordinate regulation governing a particular matter. **8.** A straight-edged measuring or drawing device; a ruler. **9.** *Printing.* **a.** A thin, straight line used to make a border or to separate columns. **b.** A dash used as a punctuation mark: *an em rule; an en rule.* **c.** A thin metal strip of various widths and designs, used to print rules. **10.** The discipline and regulations under which a religious order lives: *the Benedictine rule.* —**as a rule.** Usually; normally.
~*v.* **ruled, ruling, rules.** —*tr.* **1.** To exercise control over; govern. **2.** To dominate by powerful influence; hold sway over. **3.** To keep within proper limits; restrain. **4.** To decide or declare as a judgment; decree. **5. a.** To mark with straight parallel lines: *ruled notepaper.* **b.** To mark (a straight line), as with a ruler. —*intr.* **1.** To exercise authority; be in control or command. **2.** To formulate and issue a decree or decision. —**rule out. 1.** To make impossible. **2.** To exclude as a possibility; dismiss. —See Synonyms at **decide.**

[Middle English *riule, reule,* from Old French, from Latin *rēgula,* straight stick, ruler, rule, pattern.] **—rul·a·ble** *adj.*
ruled surface (ro͞old ‖ rewld) *n.* A surface, such as a cone or a cylinder, generated by the motion of a straight line.
rule of thumb *n.* A useful principle with wide application, not intended to be strictly accurate. [From the use of the thumb in measuring.]
rul·er (ro͞ol-ər ‖ réwl-) *n.* **1.** One that rules or governs; especially, a sovereign. **2.** A straight-edged strip, as of wood or metal, for drawing straight lines and measuring lengths.
rules (ro͞olz ‖ rewlz) *n. Used with a singular verb.* **1.** Formerly, areas around the King's Bench, Marshalsea, and Fleet prisons in London in which some prisoners, mainly debtors, were allowed to live subject to certain regulations and restrictions. **2.** *Capital* **R. Australian Rules** *(see).*
rul·ing (ro͞ol-ing ‖ réwl-) *adj.* Exercising control or dominion; predominant.
∼n. **1.** An authoritative or official decision. **2.** A ruled line or ruled lines.
rum¹ (rum) *n.* **1.** An alcoholic drink distilled from fermented molasses or sugar cane. **2.** Intoxicating beverages. [17th century : perhaps shortened from *rumbullion*†.]
rum² *adj.* Also **rum·my** (rúmmi). *British Informal.* Odd; strange. [16th century (cant) : originally "fine", "lively", perhaps from Romany *rom,* man.]
Rum. See **Byzantine Empire.**
Rum or **Rhum** (rum). Mountainous island of the Inner Hebrides, in Highland Region, northwest Scotland.
Rumania. See **Romania.**
Rumanian. Variant of **Romanian.**
rum·ba, rhum·ba (rúm-bə ‖ ro͝om-) *n.* **1.** A complex syncopated dance that originated among black Cubans. **2.** A modern ballroom adaptation of this dance. **3.** A piece of music composed in the rhythm of this dance. [American Spanish, from *rumbo,* carousel, from Spanish, pomp, perhaps extended use of *rumbo,* bearing, rhumb line, from Middle Dutch *rume.*]
rum baba *n.* A **baba** *(see).*
rum·ble (rúmb'l) *v.* **-bled, -bling, -bles.** *—intr.* **1.** To make a continuous, deep, heavy, reverberating sound, as thunder does. **2.** To move or proceed with such a sound. *—tr.* **1.** To utter with a rumbling sound. **2.** To polish or mix (metal parts) in a tumbling box. **3.** *Informal.* To bring to light; uncover; find out: *rumbled our plot.*
∼n. **1.** A continuous, deep, heavy, rolling sound. **2.** A **tumbling box** *(see).* **3.** A luggage compartment or servant's seat in the rear of a carriage or of an early motor car. **4.** *U.S. Slang.* A gang fight. [Middle English *romblen,* probably from Middle Dutch *rommelen* (imitative).] **—rum·bler** *n.* **—rum·bling·ly** *adv.* **—rum·bly** *adj.*
rum·bus·tious (rum-búss-chəss, -bústi-əss) *adj.* Lively and noisy; boisterous. [Probably variant of ROBUSTIOUS.]
Ru·me·li·a or **Rou·me·li·a** (ro͞o-méeli-ə, ro͞o-). The possessions of the former Ottoman Empire in the Balkan Peninsula, including Macedonia, Albania, and Thrace.
ru·men (ro͞o-men ‖ réw-) *n., pl.* **-mina** (-minə) or **-mens.** The first division of the stomach of a ruminant animal, in which food is partly digested before being regurgitated for further chewing. [Latin *rūmen*†, throat, gullet.]
Rum·ford (rúmfərd), **Benjamin Thompson, Count** (1753–1814). U.S. born British scientist and diplomat. After serving as a spy and administrator in America, Britain, and France, he became a minister of the Elector of Bavaria. His observations of the Elector's artillery growing hot with sustained firing helped him to establish, on his return to England, the motive theory of heat.
ru·mi·nant (ro͞o-minənt ‖ réw-) *n.* Any of various hoofed, even-toed, usually horned mammals of the suborder Ruminantia, such as cattle, sheep, goats, deer, and giraffes, characteristically having a stomach divided into four compartments, and chewing a cud consisting of regurgitated, partially digested food.
∼adj. **1.** Characterised by the chewing of cud. **2.** Of or belonging to the Ruminantia. **3.** Meditative; contemplative. [Latin *rūminans* (stem *rūminant-*), present participle of *rūminārī,* to chew cud, RUMINATE.]
ru·mi·nate (ro͞o-mi-nayt ‖ réw-) *v.* **-nated, -nating, -nates.** *—intr.* **1.** To chew cud. **2.** To meditate at length; muse. Often used with *on* or *upon.* *—tr.* To meditate or reflect on. —See Synonyms at **ponder.** [Latin *rūminārī,* from *rūmen,* RUMEN.] **—ru·mi·nat·ing·ly, ru·mi·na·tive·ly** *adv.* **—ru·mi·na·tive** (-nətiv, -naytiv) *adj.* **—ru·mi·na·tor** (-naytər) *n.* **—ru·mi·na·tion** (-náysh'n) *n.*
rum·mage (rúmmij) *v.* **-maged, -maging, -mages.** *—tr.* **1.** To search thoroughly by handling, turning over, or disarranging the contents of. **2.** To discover by searching thoroughly. Used with *up* or *out.* *—intr.* To make a thorough, energetic search.
∼n. **1.** An act of rummaging; a thorough search among a number of things. **2.** A confusion of miscellaneous articles. [Originally "arrangement of cargo in a ship's hold", odds and ends, from Anglo-French *rumage* (unattested), variant of Old French *arrumage,* from *arrumer,* to put in a ship's hold : *a-,* from Latin *ad-,* to, at + *run,* ship's hold, from Middle Dutch *ruim,* ROOM.] **—rum·mag·er** *n.*
rummage sale *n.* **1.** A sale of unclaimed or excess goods, as at a warehouse or docks. **2.** *U.S.* A **jumble sale.** *(see).*
rum·mer (rúmmər) *n.* A large drinking glass. [Perhaps from German *Römer,* from Dutch *roemer,* "glass for drinking toasts", from *roemen,* to praise, extol.]
rum·my¹ (rúmmi) *n.* A card game, played in many variations, in which the object is to obtain sets of three or more cards of the same denomination or suit. [20th century : origin obscure.]
rummy². *British Slang.* Variant of **rum** (odd).
ru·mour, *U.S.* **ru·mor** (ro͞o-mər ‖ réw-) *n.* **1.** Unverified information of uncertain origin usually spread by word of mouth; gossip; hearsay. **2.** An instance of this; a current but unverified report or assertion.
∼tr.v. **rumoured** or *U.S.* **rumored, -mouring** or *U.S.* **-moring, -mours** or *U.S.* **-mors.** To spread or tell by rumour. [Middle English *rumo(u)r,* from Old French, from Latin *rūmor.*]
ru·mour·mon·ger (ro͞o-mər-mung-gər ‖ réw-, -mong-) *n.* One who spreads rumours.
rump (rump) *n.* **1.** The fleshy hindquarters of an animal. **2.** A cut of beef or veal from this part. **3.** The human buttocks. **4.** The part of a bird's back nearest the tail. **5.** The part that remains after the removal or departure of a larger, more valuable, or more important part; a worthless, insignificant, or unrepresentative remnant. **6.** A legislature having only a small part of its original membership and so unrepresentative or lacking authority. **—the Rump.** The Rump Parliament. [Middle English *rumpe,* from Scandinavian, akin to Danish *rumpe*†, buttocks.]
rum·ple (rúmp'l) *v.* **-pled, -pling, -ples.** *—tr.* To wrinkle, tousle, or form into folds or creases. *—intr.* To become rumpled.
∼n. An uneven fold; an irregular or untidy crease. [Obsolete *rumple* (noun), from Middle Dutch *rompelen, rumpelen,* from *rompe,* wrinkle.] **—rum·ply** *adj.*
Rump Parliament *n.* The part of the **Long Parliament** *(see)* that remained after Pride's Purge (1648) until dismissed by Cromwell (1653). It was recalled (1659), but again disbanded at the restoration of Charles II (1660). Also called the "Rump".
rum·pus (rúmpəss) *n.* A noisy clamour. [18th century : probably fanciful coinage.]
rumpus room *n. U.S.* A room for play and parties.
run (run) *v.* **ran** (ran), **running, runs.** *—intr.* **1. a.** To move on foot at a pace faster than the walk and in such a manner that both feet leave the ground during each stride. **b.** To move at a gait faster than the canter; gallop. Used of a horse. **2.** To retreat rapidly; flee: *turn and run.* **3.** To move freely and without restraint: *children running about in the park.* **4.** To move or roll forward, as if out of control: *The car ran down the hill and into a wall.* **5.** To make a short, quick trip or visit: *run down to the shops.* **6. a.** To swim rapidly: *A trout took the fly and ran upstream.* **b.** To shoal or migrate inshore or upstream, especially prior to spawning. **7.** To move or act quickly or hurriedly: *Her eye ran down the list.* **8.** To have frequent recourse: *always running to the doctor.* **9.** To take part in a race. **10.** To compete for elected office; stand: *running for parliament.* **11.** To finish a race in a specified position: *He ran second.* **12. a.** To be in operation: *The car's engine is running.* **b.** To be powered in the specified way: *runs on 2-star petrol.* **13.** To provide regular transport from one place to another; ply: *The ferry runs every hour.* **14.** *Nautical.* To sail or steer before the wind or on a specified course: *run before the storm; run into port.* **15.** To operate or progress in the specified way in relation to a schedule: *Tonight's programmes are running an hour late; made the trains run on time.* **16.** To flow in a steady stream, as fluids or loose particles do. **17.** To melt and flow: *Tin must be hot for the solder to run.* **18.** To flow and spread, as dyes in a fabric sometimes do: *The colours ran.* **19.** To be wet; flow with liquid; stream: *The street ran with blood.* **20.** To discharge liquid or reach a specified state by discharging liquid: *left the hot tap running; The well has run dry.* **21.** To discharge pus or mucus: *a running sore; a running nose.* **22.** To surge, as waves or the tides do: *A heavy surf was running.* **23.** To extend in space; stretch or reach: *a line running down the middle of the road; The pipes run under the floorboards.* **24.** To spread or climb. Used of a creeping plant. **25.** To spread rapidly: *A rumour ran through the crowd.* **26.** To impress itself persistently on one's consciousness: *a tune running through my head all day.* **27.** *Chiefly U.S.* To unravel; ladder: *Her stocking ran.* **28.** To continue to have legal force; remain valid: *The lease has two years to run.* **29.** To continue to be performed or shown. Used of a play or film. **30.** To pass: *Days ran into weeks.* **31.** To persist or recur: *Gout runs in the family.* **32.** *Law.* To be concurrent: *Fishing rights run with ownership of the land.* **33. a.** To accumulate or accrue. **b.** To become payable: *Your note runs, with interest, to June 1st.* **34.** To be or have enough: *I don't think our budget will run to a new car.* **35.** To be expressed in a given way: *His reasoning ran thus.* **36.** To tend or incline: *His tastes run to the macabre.* **37.** To vary or range in quality, price, size, proportion, or the like: *House prices were running high.* **38.** To come into or out of a specified condition: *We ran into debt.* *—tr.* **1. a.** To traverse on foot at a pace faster than the walk: *run the entire distance.* **b.** To cause (a horse) to move at a gait faster than the canter. **2.** To allow to move without restraint: *He runs his sheep on hill pasture.* **3.** To do or accomplish by or as if by running: *run errands.* **4.** To hunt or pursue: *Wolves ran the sheep in the night.* **5.** To bring to a specified condition by or as if by running: *ran himself into the ground.* **6.** To cause to pass, move, or go lightly or quickly: *ran his fingers over the keyboard; ran a comb through her hair.* **7.** To compel to leave: *They ran him out of town.* **8. a.** To compete in (a race). **b.** To cause to compete in or as if in a race: *He ran two horses in the Derby.* **c.** To cause (a race) to take place: *the last Grand National to be run at Aintree.* **9.** *Chiefly U.S.* To present or nominate for elective office: *They ran him for mayor.* **10.** To compete in a given manner against: *He ran them a close second.* **11.** To cause to move or progress freely:

PRONUNCIATION KEY

a, trap; aa, father; ai, **fair**;
ar, **star**; aw, **lawn**; ay, **play**;
b, bb, **stab**; **rubber**;
ch, **church**; ck, **ticket**;
d, dd, **dead**; **ladder**; e, **dress**;
ee, **bee**; er, **defer**; ew, **few**;
ewr, **pure**; ə, about;
ər, letter; f, ff, **fife**; **differ**;
g, gg, **giggle**; h, **hat**; i, **kit**;
ī, price; īr, fire; j, **judge**;
k, **kick**; l, ll, **let**; 'l, **needle**;
m, mm, **man**; n, nn, **no**;
'n, **sudden**; ng, **thing**; o, **lot**;
ō, no; o͝o, **foot**; o͞o, **shoe**;
oor, **poor**; ow, **cow**;
owr, **hour**; oy, **boy**;
p, pp, **pepper**; r, rr, **red**;
s, ss, **sauce**; sh, **ship**;
t, tt, **totter**; th, **thick**; th, **this**;
smooth; u, **cut**; ur, **turn**;
v, vv, **valve**; w, **wet**; y, **yes**;
z, zz, **zebra**; zh, **vision**;
pleasure

IN FOREIGN WORDS:

aN, oN, **Saint-Saëns**;
hl, **Llanelli**; **Hluhluwe**;
kh, **loch**; **lough**; **Khaled**

STRESS MARK:

in-sīt, insight; in-sī́t, incite

run up the jib. **12.** To cause to function; operate: *He ran his engine.* **13.** To convey or transport: *Run me into town.* **14.** To cause to ply: *They don't run the ferries here in winter.* **15.** To cause (a boat or car, for example) to move on a specified course: *ran our boat into a cove; ran the car into a tree.* **16. a.** To smuggle: *run rifles.* **b.** To evade and pass through (a blockade, for example). **17.** To move swiftly down or through: *run the rapids.* **18. a.** To cause to flow: *run water into a bath.* **b.** To fill (a bath) with water. **19.** To emit or flow with: *The fountains ran wine.* **20. a.** To melt, fuse, or smelt (metal). **b.** To mould or cast (molten metal): *run gold into ingots.* **21.** To cause to extend in a specified way: *run a road into the hills.* **22.** To mark or trace on a surface: *run a pencil line between two points.* **23.** To sew with a continuous line of stitches: *run a seam.* **24.** *Chiefly U.S.* To cause to unravel; ladder. **25.** To cause to penetrate: *She ran a pin into her thumb.* **26.** To cause to continue being shown or performed: *They ran the film for a month.* **27.** To publish in a periodical: *They're running a special feature on European cookery.* **28.** To cause or allow (an account, for example) to accumulate. **29.** To expose oneself or be subjected to (risk, for example). **30.** To have (a fever) as a symptom. **31.** In cricket, to score (one or more runs). **32.** To score (balls or points) consecutively in billiard games: *run 15 balls.* **33.** To carry out or perform (a test or experiment, for example). **34. a.** To be the manager or proprietor of: *runs a greengrocer's.* **b.** To be in charge of; conduct, control, or direct: *What a way to run a business!* **35.** To own and drive (a vehicle). **36.** To unite or combine: *We ran two companies into one.* **—run across.** To meet or find by chance. **—run after. 1.** To pursue; chase. **2.** *Informal.* To seek the company or attentions of. **—run away with. 1. a.** To make off with. **b.** To elope with. **2.** To cause to lose control; get the better of: *His ambition ran away with him.* **3.** To win (an election or competition) by a large margin. **4.** To form (an impression or opinion) too hastily: *Don't run away with the idea that it'll be easy.* **—run for it.** To attempt to escape. **—run into. 1.** To meet by chance. **2.** To encounter; be faced with: *ran into difficulties.* **3.** To collide with. **4.** To reach as far as; add up to: *The cost could run into millions.* **—run over. 1.** To knock down or drive over, as in a car. **2.** To overflow. **3.** To examine, review, or rehearse. **4.** To extend beyond.

~n. **1. a.** A pace faster than the walk. **b.** A gait faster than the canter. **2. a.** An act of running. **b.** A running race: *a cross-country run.* **c.** An act of running away; a bolt: *made a run for it.* **3. a.** A distance covered by or as if by running. **b.** The time taken to cover it: *a two minute run from the station.* **4.** A quick trip or visit, especially by car: *a run into town.* **5.** In cricket: **a.** A successful act of running from one popping crease to the other by both batsmen. **b.** The point so scored. **6.** In baseball, an act of successfully completing a circuit of the bases and returning to home plate. **7.** The distance a golf ball rolls after hitting the ground. **8.** A migration of fish inshore or upstream, especially prior to spawning: *the shad run.* **9.** Unrestricted freedom or use: *I had the run of their library.* **10.** A stretch or period of riding, as in a race or to hounds. **11.** A track or slope along or down which something can travel: *a ski run.* **12. a.** A journey between points on a scheduled or regular route. **b.** The distance so covered. **c.** The time taken to cover this distance. **13. a.** A continuous period of operation, as by a machine or factory. **b.** The production achieved during such a period. **14.** The final approach of a military aircraft to its target: *a bombing run.* **15.** A transit of smuggled goods. **16. a.** A movement or flow, as of fluid or sand. **b.** The duration of such a flow. **c.** The amount of such a flow. **17.** A pipe or channel through which something flows: *a mill run.* **18.** *U.S.* A small, fast-flowing stream or brook. **19.** *Mining.* A fall or slide, as of sand or mud. **20.** A continuous length or extent of something: *a ten-foot run of tubing.* **21.** *Mining.* A vein or seam, as of ore or rock. **22.** The direction, configuration, or lie of something: *the run of the grain in leather.* **23.** A trail or burrow made or frequented by animals: *a rabbit run.* **24. a.** An outdoor enclosure for domestic animals or poultry. **b.** *Australian.* A large stretch of grazing land; a station. **25.** *Chiefly U.S.* A length of unravelled stitches; a ladder. **26.** An unbroken series or sequence: *a run of dry summers.* **27.** An unbroken sequence of theatrical performances. **28.** *Music.* A rapid sequence of notes; a roulade. **29. a.** Urgent and heavy demand for a product. **b.** Urgent and heavy demand by depositors, creditors, or the like: *a run on the bank.* **c.** Pressure on a currency caused by widespread selling. **30. a.** In certain games, a continuous set or sequence, as of playing cards in one suit. **b.** A successful sequence of shots or points. **31.** A sustained state or condition: *a run of good luck.* **32.** A trend or tendency: *the run of events.* **33.** The average type, group, or category; majority: *The broad run of voters want him to win.* **—a run for (one's) money. 1.** Strong competition. **2.** A degree of satisfaction or enjoyment derived from an expenditure of money or effort. **—in the long run.** In the final analysis or outcome. **—on the run. 1. a.** In rapid retreat. **b.** In hiding, as a fugitive might be. **2.** Hurrying busily from place to place. **—the runs.** *Slang.* Diarrhoea.

~adj. **1.** In a liquid state; melted. **2.** Poured into a mould while liquid: *run metal.* **3.** Drained; extracted: *run honey.* [Run, ran, run; Middle English *runnen, ran, runnen,* Old English *rinnan* (but influenced by the past participle), *ran(n), gerunnen,* reinforced by Old Norse cognate verb *rinna.*]

run·a·bout (rún-ə-bowt) *n.* **1. a.** A usually small car used for short journeys. **b.** A light aircraft. **c.** *Chiefly U.S.* A small motorboat. **2.** A vagabond or wanderer.

run·a·gate (rúnnə-gayt) *n. Archaic.* **1.** A renegade or deserter. **2.** A vagabond. [Variant of RENEGADE (influenced by RUN).]

run·a·round (rún-ə-rownd) *n.* **1.** *Informal.* Deception, evasion, or delaying tactics. Used chiefly in the phrase *give someone the run-around.* **2.** *Printing.* Type set in a column narrower than the body of the text, as on either side of a picture.

run·a·way (rún-ə-way) *n.* **1.** One that runs away, such as a fugitive or a horse that has bolted. **2.** An act of running away.

~adj. **1.** Escaping or having escaped. **2.** Of or done by running away. **3.** Easily won, as a victory in a race. **4.** Completely out of control: *a runaway train; runaway inflation.*

run·ci·ble spoon (rúnssib'l) *n.* A three-pronged fork, such as a pickle fork, curved like a spoon and having a cutting edge. [*Runcible,* a nonsense word coined by Edward Lear.]

run·ci·nate (rún-si-nət, -nit, -nayt) *adj. Botany.* Having saw-toothed divisions directed backwards: *runcinate leaves.* [Latin *runcinātus,* past participle of *runcināre,* to plane, from *runcina,* carpenter's plane (formerly taken also to mean a saw), from Greek *rhukanē*†.]

Run·corn (rúng-kawrn). Industrial port and new town of Cheshire, northwest England, situated on the river Mersey.

run down *intr.v.* **1.** To lose power and stop working: *The battery has run down.* **2.** To grow gradually weaker; suffer a loss of health or vigour. *—tr.v.* **1. a.** To pursue and capture. **b.** To find by diligent searching; track down: *ran down the source of the trouble.* **2.** To hit with a moving vehicle. **3.** To disparage; denigrate. **4.** To cause to decline in numbers, size, output, or the like: *running down the firm's South African operations.*

run-down (rún-down) *n.* A summary or résumé.

~adj. (rún-dówn) **1. a.** In poor physical condition; weak or exhausted. **b.** In a poor state of repair; dilapidated. **2.** Unwound and not running.

rune (rōōn || rewn) *n.* **1.** Any of the letters of an alphabet used by ancient Germanic peoples, especially by the Scandinavians and Anglo-Saxons. **2.** Any poem, riddle, or the like written in runic characters. **3.** Any character or symbol supposed to have magical powers or significance. **4.** A Finnish poem or canto. [In sense 4, from Finnish *runo.* In other senses, Middle English *roun, rune,* secret writing, rune, from Old Norse *rūn* (unattested).]

rung[1] (rung) *n.* **1. a.** A rod or bar forming a step of a ladder. **b.** Anything resembling this. **2.** A crosspiece supporting the legs or back of a chair. **3.** A point or level in a hierarchy or similar series of ascending stages. **4.** *Nautical.* Any of the spokes or handles on a ship's steering wheel. [Middle English *rung, rong,* Old English *hrung,* akin to Old High German *runga,* Gothic *hrugga*†.]

rung[2]. Past tense and past participle of **ring.**

ru·nic (rōō-nik || réw-) *adj.* **1.** Consisting of, inscribed with, or written in runes. **2.** Made in the ornate interlacing style characteristic of rune-bearing monuments. **3.** Having a cryptic or magical significance.

run in *tr.v.* **1.** To insert or include as something extra. **2.** *Printing.* To make (a body of text) solid without a paragraph or other break. **3.** *Slang.* To take into legal custody. **4.** To run (an engine or car) for a certain period at low speed when new so that engine parts in contact become smooth.

run-in (rún-in) *n.* **1.** *Chiefly U.S.* A quarrel; an argument; a fight. **2.** *Printing.* Matter added to a text.

run·let (rún-lət, -lit) *n.* A rivulet. [Diminutive of RUN (stream).]

run·nel (rúnn'l) *n.* **1.** A rivulet; a brook. **2.** A narrow channel or course, as for water. **3.** On a beach, a long narrow hollow between two shingle ridges running parallel to the coastline. [Middle English *rynel,* Old English *rynel,* from *rinnan,* to run, flow.]

run·ner (rúnnər) *n.* **1.** One that runs, as: **a.** One that competes in a race. **b.** A messenger or errand boy. **c.** In cricket, a player who takes runs on behalf of a batsman who is unable to run himself. **2.** An agent or collector, as for a bank or brokerage house. **3.** One who solicits business for others. **4.** A smuggler or a vessel engaged in smuggling. Often used in combination: *a gun-runner.* **5.** An antique dealer who has no retail outlet but acts as a go-between for other dealers. **6.** A device in or on which a mechanism slides or moves, as: **a.** The blade of a skate. **b.** Either of the pieces of wood or metal on which a sledge runs. **c.** The supports on which a drawer slides. **7.** A long narrow carpet. **8.** A long narrow tablecloth. **9.** A channel along which molten metal is poured into a mould; a gate. **10. a.** A slender, creeping stem that puts forth roots and shoots either from nodes along its length or at the tip. **b.** A plant, such as the strawberry, having such a stem. **c.** A twining vine.

runner bean *n.* **1.** A widely cultivated tropical American climbing bean plant, *Phaseolus coccineus,* with typically scarlet flowers and long, green, edible pods. **2.** A pod of this plant, eaten as a vegetable. Also called "scarlet runner".

run·ner-up (rúnnər-úp) *n.* One that takes second place in a race, competition, or election.

run·ning (rúnning) *n.* **1.** The act or sport of one that runs. **2. a.** The act or skill of managing something. **b.** The act or process of operating something. Also used adjectivally: *high running costs.* **—in** (or **out of**) **the running.** Still in (or no longer in) serious contention, as in a race or other competitive situation. **—make the running.** To determine the speed at which something progresses or develops; set the pace.

~adj. **1.** Performed while running: *a running jump.* **2.** Intended for the use of runners: *a running track; running shoes.* **3.** Piped and

supplied by taps: *running water.* **4.** Continuous: *A running battle.* **5.** Describing events as they happen: *a running commentary.*
~*adv.* Consecutively: *four years running.*

running board *n.* A narrow footboard extending under and beside the doors of some cars and other vehicles.

running gear *n.* **1.** The working parts of a car, locomotive, or other vehicle. **2.** Running rigging.

running hand *n.* A type of handwriting done rapidly without lifting the pen from the paper.

running head *n. Printing.* A title printed at the top of every page or every other page. Also called "running headline", "running title".

running knot *n.* A **slipknot** *(see).*

running light *n.* **1.** Any of several lights on a boat or ship kept lighted between dusk and dawn. **2.** Any of several similar lights on an aircraft; a navigation light.

running mate *n. Chiefly U.S.* **1.** A horse used as a pacemaker for another horse of the same stable. **2.** The candidate or nominee for the lesser of two closely associated political offices, such as the vice-presidency.

running rigging *n.* The part of a ship's rigging that comprises the ropes with which sails are raised, lowered, or trimmed, and booms and gaffs are operated. Also called "running gear".

running stitch *n.* Any of a series of small, even stitches.

run·ny (rúnni) *adj.* **-nier, -niest. 1.** Inclined to run or flow. **2.** Discharging mucus. Said of the nose.

Run·ny·mede (rúnni-meed). A meadow on the south bank of the river Thames, near Egham, Surrey, where King John sealed the Magna Carta in 1215. [Middle English *Runimede,* "meadow on the council island" : Old English *Rūnīeg,* council island : *rūn,* secret, secret council + *īeg, īg,* ISLAND + *mede,* MEAD (meadow).]

run off *intr.v.* **1.** To run away, abscond, or elope. **2.** To flow off or drain away. —*tr.v.* **1.** To cause to flow off or drain away. **2.** To decide (a contest or competition) by a run-off. **3.** To produce (a copy), as with a printing or duplicating machine.

run-off (rún-off, -awf) *n.* **1. a.** The overflow of a fluid from a container. **b.** The amount of precipitation that reaches streams and rivers, and flows away to the sea. **2.** Eliminated waste products from manufacturing processes. **3.** A final round or contest to decide the winner in the event of a tie.

run-of-the-mill (rún-əv-thə-míl) *adj.* Ordinary; not special; average. See Synonyms at **average.** [From *run of (the) mill,* products of a mill that are not graded for quality.]

run on *intr.v.* **1.** To continue on and on. **2.** To talk at length and without a break. —*tr.v. Printing.* To continue (a text) without a formal break.

run-on (rún-on || -awn) *n. Printing.* Matter that is appended or added without a formal break.

run out *intr.v.* **1.** To become completely used up. Used of a supply or allocation of something. **2.** To exhaust one's supply of something. Often used with *of.* —*tr.v.* In cricket, to dismiss (a batsman who is taking a run) by hitting the wicket with the ball before he has completed his run.

run-out (rún-owt) *n.* An instance of running a batsman out in cricket.

runt (runt) *n.* **1.** An undersized animal; especially, the smallest animal of a litter. **2.** A person of small stature. Used derogatorily. [16th century : origin obsucre.] **—runt·i·ness** *n.* **—runt·ish, runt·y** *adj.*

run through *tr.v.* **1.** To pierce: *ran him through with my sword.* **2.** To use up (money, for example) wastefully; fritter away. **3.** To examine, review, or rehearse quickly.

run-through (rún-thrōō) *n.* A complete but rapid review or rehearsal of something, such as a theatrical work.

run up *tr.v.* **1.** *Informal.* To make quickly by sewing. **2.** To raise (a flag) on a flagpole. **3.** *Informal.* To allow (a debt, for example) to accumulate.

run-up (rún-up) *n.* **1.** *Informal.* The time leading up to a particular event; a preliminary period. **2.** *Sports.* A player's running approach, such as that of a fast bowler gaining speed prior to delivering a cricket ball.

run·way (rún-way) *n.* **1.** A strip of level ground, usually paved, on which aircraft take off and land. **2.** A path, channel, or track over which something runs. **3.** *Chiefly U.S.* A chute down which logs are skidded. **4.** A narrow walkway extending from a stage into an auditorium.

Run·yon (rún-yən), **(Alfred) Damon** (1884–1946). U.S. writer. From his experiences as a journalist of New York low-life, he wrote many popular stories in collections such as *Guys and Dolls* (1931), later the subject for a hit musical of the same name.

ru·pee (rōō-pée, rōō- || rew-, *U.S. also* rōōpi) *n. Abbr.* **Re., r., R. 1. a.** The basic monetary unit of India, equal to 100 paise. **b.** The basic monetary unit of Nepal, equal to 100 paisa or pice. **c.** The basic monetary unit of Pakistan, equal to 100 paisa. **d.** The basic monetary unit of Sri Lanka, the Seychelles, and Mauritius, equal to 100 cents. **e.** The basic monetary unit of the Maldives, equal to 100 laris. **2.** A coin or note worth one rupee. [Hindi *rupaīyā,* from Sanskrit *rūpya,* wrought silver, from *rūpa*†, shape, image.]

Ru·pert (rōō-pərt || réw-), **Prince, Duke of Cumberland.** (1619–82). German-born British general. A maternal grandson of James I, he was the senior Royalist cavalry commander in the Civil War. Following the Restoration, he served as an admiral in the Dutch Wars. He was also a patron of the art and sciences.

Rupert's Land *n.* The Canadian territory granted the Hudson's Bay Company in 1670, most of which was incorporated in the Northwest Territories after its purchase by Canada in 1869. Also known as Prince Rupert's Land.

ru·pi·ah (rōō-pée-ə, -aa) *n., pl.* **rupiah** or **-ahs. 1.** The basic monetary unit of Indonesia, equal to 100 sen. **2.** A note worth one rupiah. [Hindi *rupaīyā,* RUPEE.]

rup·ture (rúpchər) *n.* **1. a.** The act of breaking open or bursting. **b.** The state of being broken open or burst. **2.** A break in friendly relations between individuals or nations. **3.** *Pathology.* **a.** A **hernia** *(see),* especially of the groin or intestines. **b.** A tear in bodily tissue.
~*v.* **ruptured, -turing, -tures.** —*tr.* **1.** To break open; burst. **2.** To cause a break in (friendly relations). **3.** To cause to suffer a hernia. —*intr.* To undergo or suffer a rupture. —See Synonyms at **break.** [Middle English *ruptur,* from Old French *rupture,* from Latin *ruptūra,* from *rumpere* (past participle *ruptus*), to break.] **—rup·tur·a·ble** *adj.*

ru·ral (rŏor-əl || réwr-) *adj.* **1.** Of, pertaining to, or characteristic of the country as opposed to the city; rustic. **2.** Of or pertaining to people who live in the country. **3.** Of or pertaining to farming; agricultural. [Middle English, from Old French, from Latin *rūrālis,* from *rūs* (stem *rūr-*), country.] **—ru·ral·ism** *n.* **—ru·ral·ist** *n.* **—ru·ral·i·ty** (roor-rál-əti || rōō-, rew-) *n.* **—ru·ral·ly** *adv.*

Synonyms: *rural, arcadian, bucolic, rustic, pastoral, sylvan.*

rural dean *n.* In the Church of England, a clergyman who supervises the running of a number of parishes.

rural district *n.* Before April 1974, a subdivision of a county in England and Wales for purposes of local government.

Ru·ri·ta·ni·a (rŏor-i-táyn-i-ə || réwr-) *n.* An imaginary central European kingdom used as a setting for tales of romance, adventure, and suspense. [After the setting of Anthony Hope's novels *The Prisoner of Zenda* (1894) and *Rupert of Hentzau* (1898).] **—Ru·ri·ta·ni·an** *adj.*

Rus. Russia; Russian.

ruse (rōōz || rewz) *n.* An action meant to confuse or mislead; a clever trick. See Synonyms at **artifice.** [Middle English, detour of a hunted animal, from Old French, from *ruser,* to repulse, detour. See **rush** (to dash off).]

rush[1] (rush) *v.* **rushed, rushing, rushes.** —*intr.* **1.** To move, act, or proceed with great speed and vigour. **2.** To act or proceed with impetuous haste: *rushed into marriage.* **3.** To make a sudden or swift attack or charge. Used with *on* or *upon.* —*tr.* **1.** To cause to move, act or proceed with unusual haste or vigour: *Medical supplies were rushed to the scene.* **2.** To pressurise into hasty action. **3.** To perform with great haste. **4.** To attack swiftly and suddenly. **5.** *British Informal.* To charge (a customer) excessively: *rushed us £5 for two coffees.* **6.** *U.S.* To attempt to impress or seek the favour of.
~*n.* **1.** The act of rushing; a sudden forward motion or turbulent movement. **2.** An eager, often competitive movement of people in pursuit of some object: *a rush for the best seats; a gold rush.* **3.** Urgency; need for haste: *There's no rush.* **4.** A sudden attack; an onslaught. **5.** A great flurry of activity or press of business: *the usual last-minute rush.* **6.** *Slang.* A sudden, pleasurable rushing sensation induced by taking certain drugs. **7.** *Often plural.* The first, unedited print of a scene in a cinema film.
~*adj.* Requiring or marked by haste or urgency: *a rush job.* [Middle English *russhen,* from Anglo-French *russher,* variant of Old French *ruser,* to repulse, from Latin *recusāre,* to object to (in Vulgar Latin, "to repel") : *re-,* back + *causārī,* to plead, give as a reason, from *causa,* CAUSE.] **—rush·er** *n.*

rush[2] *n.* **1.** Any of various grasslike marsh plants of the genus *Juncus,* having pliant, hollow, or pithy stems and clusters of small, brownish flowers. **2.** Any of various similar, usually aquatic plants, such as the woodrush. **3.** The stem of a rush, used in making baskets, mats, and chair seats. [Middle English *rush, rish,* Old English *rysc.*]

rush hour *n.* Either of the two periods in the working day when most people are travelling to or from work. **—rush-hour** *adj.*

rush·light (rúsh-līt) *n.* A candle consisting of a rush wick in tallow. Also called "rush candle".

rush·y (rúshi) *adj.* **-ier, -iest. 1.** Resembling or characteristic of rushes; rushlike. **2.** Abounding in rushes: *a rushy marsh.*

rusk (rusk) *n.* A piece of sweet or plain bread that has been dried and browned in an oven, often given to babies. [Spanish and Portuguese *rosca*†, a coil, twisted roll.]

Rus·kin (rúskin), **John** (1819–1900). English art critic. He developed a philosophy in which art, morality, economics, and religion are interrelated, and which is expressed in works such as *The Stones of Venice* (1851–53) and *Sesame and Lilies* (1865).

Rus·sell (rúss'l), **Bertrand (Arthur William), 3rd Earl** (1872–1970). British philosopher. In his *Principia Mathematica* (1910–1913) he attempted to show that mathematics was an extension of logic. He later developed interests in social morality, epistomology, languages, and education. He was a prominent pacifist in both World Wars and, as the doyen of British philosophy, he was an important figure in the CND movement. In 1950 he was awarded the Nobel prize for literature.

Russell, John, 1st Earl (1792–1878). British politician. A champion of Parliamentary reform throughout his career, he was elected to parliament in 1813, and held cabinet posts in Whig governments from 1835. He served two terms as Prime Minister (1846–52, 1865–66). He was also a writer and a biographer.

Russell, Ken (1927–). British film and television director. His films, such as *Women in Love* (1969), *The Music Lovers* (1970),

PRONUNCIATION KEY

a, trap; aa, father; ai, fair; ar, star; aw, lawn; ay, play; b, bb, stab; rubber; ch, church; ck, ticket; d, dd, dead; ladder; e, dress; ee, bee; er, defer; ew, few; ewr, pure; ə, about; ər, letter; f, ff, fife; differ; g, gg, giggle; h, hat; i, kit; ī, price; īr, fire; j, judge; k, kick; l, ll, let; 'l, needle; m, mm, man; n, nn, no; 'n, sudden; ng, thing; o, lot; ō, no; ŏŏ, foot; ōō, shoe; oor, poor; ow, cow; owr, hour; oy, boy; p, pp, pepper; r, rr, red; s, ss, sauce; sh, ship; t, tt, totter; th, thick; th, this; smooth; u, cut; ur, turn; v, vv, valve; w, wet; y, yes; z, zz, zebra; zh, vision; pleasure

IN FOREIGN WORDS:

aN, oN, Saint-Saëns; hl, Llanelli; Hluhluwe; kh, loch; lough; Khaled

STRESS MARK:

ín-sīt, insight; in-sīt, incite

russet *Most of this group of dessert apple varieties are related to a crab apple,* Malus sylvestris mitis. *This variety is "Rosemary russet".*

Mahler (1974), and *Valentino* (1977) are notable for their use of spectacular visual effects.

Russell diagram *n. Astronomy.* A **Hertzsprung-Russell diagram** *(see).*

rus·set (rússit) *n.* **1.** Moderate to deep reddish brown. **2.** A coarse reddish-brown to brown homespun cloth. **3.** An eating apple with a rough reddish-brown skin. [Middle English, from Old French *rousset,* from *rous,* red, from Latin *russus.*] —**rus·set** *adj.*

Rus·sia (rúshə). **1.** See **Russian Soviet Federative Socialist Republic. 2.** See **Union of Soviet Socialist Republics.**

Rus·sian (rúsh'n) *n. Abbr.* **Rus., Russ. 1. a.** A native or inhabitant of the U.S.S.R. **b.** A native or inhabitant of the Russian Soviet Federated Socialist Republic. **c.** A native or inhabitant of the former Russian Empire. **2.** One who is of Russian descent. **3.** The Slavonic language of the Russian people that is the official language of the U.S.S.R.

~*adj.* **1.** Of or pertaining to Russia, its people, or their language. **2.** Loosely, of or pertaining to the U.S.S.R., especially when considered as a political power.

Russian Orthodox Church *n.* **1.** An independent branch of the Eastern Orthodox Church in Russia headed by the Patriarch of Moscow. **2.** A branch of this church outside Russia.

Russian Revolution *n.* **1.** The seizure of the central organs of state power in Petrograd by the Bolsheviks under the leadership of Lenin on November 7, 1917 (October 25, Old Style). Also called "October Revolution". **2.** The entire sequence of events in Russia that began with the overthrow of tsarism by the uprising of March 1917 (the *February Revolution*), continued with the removal of the provisional government and the inauguration of socialist revolution led by the Bolsheviks, and ended with the defeat of counterrevolution in the civil war (1918–22).

Russian roulette *n.* **1.** An act of bravado, traditionally done as a wager, in which a person spins the cylinder of a revolver loaded with one bullet, aims the muzzle at his head, and pulls the trigger. **2.** Any exceptionally hazardous or foolhardy venture.

Russian salad *n.* A salad of diced cooked vegetables mixed with a piquant mayonnaise dressing *(Russian dressing).*

Russian Soviet Federated Socialist Republic. Formerly **Russian Soviet Federated Socialist Republic.** The largest constituent republic of the U.S.S.R. It stretches from the Baltic Sea to the Pacific Ocean, and from the Arctic Ocean to the Black Sea. It covers some 76 per cent of the country, and has 52 per cent of its people. More than 80 per cent of the republic's inhabitants are Russian. It includes 16 autonomous soviet socialist republics and accounts for some 70 per cent of the country's total agricultural and manufacturing output. Moscow is the capital.

Russian wolfhound *n.* A dog, the **borzoi** *(see).*

Russian wedding ring *n.* A ring consisting of three interlaced loops, each made of a different type of gold.

russ·ki, russ·ky (rúski) *n. pl.* **-kies.** *Informal.* A native or inhabitant of Russia. Often considered offensive.

Russo– *comb. form.* Indicates Russia; for example, **Russophilia.** [From RUSSIA.]

Rus·so-Jap·a·nese War (rússō-jáppə-néez ‖ -néess) *n.* A war (1904–05) between Russia and Japan arising out of their conflicting interests in Manchuria and resulting in defeat for Russia.

Rus·so·phil·i·a (rúss-ō-fílli-ə, -ə-) *n.* Interest in or enthusiasm for Russia, its culture, people, government, or language. [RUSSO- + -PHILIA.] —**Rus·so·phile** (-fīl ‖ -fil) *n.*

Rus·so·pho·bi·a (rúss-ō-fṓbi-ə, -ə-) *n.* Dislike or fear of Russia or its policies. [RUSSO- + -PHOBIA.] —**Rus·so·phobe** (-fōb) *n.*

rust (rust) *n.* **1.** Any of various powdery or scaly reddish-brown or reddish-yellow hydrated ferric oxides formed on iron and steel by low-temperature oxidation in the presence of water. **2.** Any of various metallic coatings, especially oxides, formed by corrosion. **3.** A stain or coating resembling iron rust. **4.** Any deterioration of ability or character resulting from inactivity or neglect. **5.** *Botany.* **a.** Any of various parasitic fungi of the order Uredinales, that are injurious to a wide variety of plants, including cereals. **b.** A plant disease caused by such fungi, characterised by reddish or brownish spots on leaves, stems, and other parts. **6.** Strong reddish brown.

~*v.* **rusted, rusting, rusts.** —*intr.* **1.** To become corroded; form rust. **2.** To deteriorate or degenerate through inactivity or neglect. **3.** To become the colour of rust. **4.** To develop a disease caused by a rust fungus. —*tr.* **1.** To corrode or subject (a metal) to rust formation. **2.** To impair or spoil by misuse, inactivity, and the like. ~*adj.* Rust-coloured. [Middle English *rust,* Old English *rŭst.*] —**rust·a·ble** *adj.* —**rust·less** *adj.*

rus·tic (rústik) *adj.* **1.** Of, pertaining to, or characteristic of country life. **2. a.** Charmingly simple and unsophisticated. **b.** Lacking refinement or polish; uncouth. **3.** Made of rough tree branches: *rustic furniture.* **4.** Having a rough surface with deep or chamfered joints. Said of masonry. —See Synonyms at **rural.**

~*n.* **1.** A rural person. **2.** An awkward or unpolished simpleton. [Middle English *rustyk,* from Old French *rustique,* from Latin *rŭsticus,* from *rŭs,* country.] —**rus·ti·cal·ly** *adv.* —**rus·tic·i·ty** (russ-tíssəti) *n.*

rus·ti·cate (rústi-kayt) *v.* **-cated, -cating, -cates.** —*intr.* **1.** To go to or live in the country. **2.** To lead a simple, rustic life. —*tr.* **1.** To send to the country. **2.** To impart a rustic character to. **3.** *British.* To suspend (a student) from a university or school. **4.** To construct (masonry) in the rustic style. [Latin *rŭsticārī,* from *rŭsticus,* RUSTIC.] —**rus·ti·ca·tion** (-káysh'n) *n.* —**rus·ti·ca·tor** (-kaytər) *n.*

rus·tle[1] (rúss'l) *v.* **-tled, -tling, -tles.** —*intr.* To move with soft whispering sounds. —*tr.* To cause to make such sounds.

~*n.* A soft whispering sound: *The gentle rustle of a silken gown.* [Middle English *rustlen, rustelen,* akin to Frisian *russelje,* Dutch *ridselen* (imitative).] —**rus·tler** *n.* —**rus·tling·ly** *adv.*

rustle[2] *v.* **-tled, -tling, -tles.** —*tr. Chiefly U.S.* To steal (cattle or other livestock). —*intr. Chiefly U.S.* **1.** To steal livestock. **2.** *Informal.* To act or proceed energetically; hustle. —**rustle up.** To prepare or produce, especially hastily or in an improvised fashion. [Probably from RUSTLE (to move with soft sounds).] —**rus·tler** (rússlar) *n.*

rust·proof (rúst-proof ‖ -prōof) *adj.* Specially treated so as to be incapable of rusting. —**rust·proof** *tr.v.*

rust·y (rústi) *adj.* **-ier, -iest. 1.** Covered with or affected by rust; corroded. **2.** Consisting of or produced by rust. **3.** Rust-coloured. **4.** Working or operating stiffly or incorrectly because of or as if because of rust. **5.** Weakened or impaired by neglect, disuse, or lack of practice. —**rust·i·ly** *adv.* —**rust·i·ness** *n.*

rut[1] (rut) *n.* **1.** A sunken track or groove made by the passage of vehicles. **2.** A fixed, monotonous routine of thought or action.

~*tr.v.* **rutted, rutting, ruts.** To furrow. [Old French *rote, route,* way, ROUTE.]

rut[2] *n.* **1.** A cyclically recurring condition of sexual excitement and reproductive activity in male mammals, such as deer. **2.** The comparable condition of female mammalian sexual activity; oestrus. ~*intr.v.* **rutted, rutting, ruts.** To be in rut. [Middle English *rutte,* from Old French *rut, ruit,* "bellowing (of stags in rut)", from Late Latin *rūgitus,* from Latin *rūgīre,* to roar.]

ru·ta·ba·ga (rōōtə-báygə, rōōtə-, -béggə) *n. U.S.* A vegetable, the

Russian Revolution

THREE UPHEAVALS THAT BROUGHT LENIN TO POWER

War provides the catalyst for the Bolshevik revolution

The revolution which put the Bolshevik party into power in Russia came after the age-old tyranny of Tsardom had disintegrated; it was the third in a sequence of three. The revolution of 1905 broke out after government troops had fired on demonstrators in St. Petersburg (now Leningrad) weary of the Russo-Japanese War. In its wake came a parliament (Duma) elected by popular vote for the first time. However, the Duma's authority was soon dissipated by the Tsar, and Russia drifted into World War I, a conflict which would break the backbone of the tsarist regime.

Military defeat, heavy losses, and poor leadership at the front, coupled with famine and administrative chaos at home, intensified the pressure. To make matters worse, Tsar Nicholas II had made himself commander in chief of the army, thereby assuming total responsibility for military reversals. The February Revolution (1917) was an explosion of riots and strikes that

eventually forced the Tsar to abdicate. A provisional government, dominated by Kerensky, sought to continue the war but received little support. Mass desertion at the front followed and the army was by now ripe for revolution. The German government, intent on sabotaging Russia's war effort, helped Lenin and other Bolsheviks to return from exile in Switzerland by providing them with a sealed train to cross Europe.

In October 1917, Lenin and his chief associate Trotsky organised revolutionary soviets (councils of workers and soldiers) whose "Red Guards" stormed the headquarters of the provisional government in the Winter Palace at St. Petersburg and seized power. Local Bolsheviks established similar soviets in other key cities, taking Russia out of the war and into a Communist revolution. But their triumph was far from complete, for a bloody three-year civil war was to follow.

MAN OF THE PEOPLE *Lenin roused the workers and soldiers by advocating actions that were simplified into powerful slogans such as "all power to the Soviets" and "Peace, Land, Bread".*

swede (*see*). [Swedish (dialectal) *rotabagge*, "baggy root" : *rot*, root, from Old Norse *rōt* + *bagge*, from Old Norse *baggi*, BAG.]

ruth (rōoth ‖ rewth) *n. Archaic.* **1.** Compassion or pity. **2.** Sorrow; misery; grief. [Middle English *ruthe, rewthe*, from *rewen*, to rue, from Old English *hrēowan*.]

Ruth[1] (rōoth ‖ rewth). In the Old Testament, a Moabite widow who went to Bethlehem where she later married Boaz.

Ruth[2] *n.* A book of the Old Testament in which the story of Ruth is told.

Ru·the·ni·a (rōo-théeni-ə, rōo- ‖ rew-). Region of eastern Europe, in western Ukraine, west of the Carpathian Mountains. Part of it constituted a province of Czechoslovakia (1918–39) and all of it was annexed by the U.S.S.R. in 1945, becoming the Zakarpatskaya Oblast, also known as Transcarpathian Ukraine. [Medieval Latin, Russia, from *Rut(h)enī*, Russians, from Russian *Rusin*, from Old Russian *Rus'*, "Norsemen".]

Ru·the·ni·an (rōo-théeni-ən, rōo- ‖ rew-) *n.* **1.** A member of a group of Ukrainians living in Ruthenia. **2.** A Ukrainian dialect spoken by these people. —**Ru·the·ni·an** *adj.*

ru·then·ic (rōo-thénnik, rōo-, -théenik ‖ rew-) *adj. Chemistry.* Of or pertaining to ruthenium. Said especially of a compound that contains ruthenium with a high valency.

ru·the·ni·um (rōo-théeni-əm, rōo- ‖ rew-) *n. Symbol* **Ru** A hard white acid-resistant metallic element found in platinum ores. It is used to harden platinum and palladium for jewellery and in alloys for nonmagnetic wear-resistant instrument pivots and electrical contacts. Atomic number 44, atomic weight 101.07, melting point 2,250°C, boiling point 3,900°C, relative density 12.41, valencies 1, 2, 3, 4, 5, 6, 7, 8. [New Latin; discovered in the Ural Mountains in Russia, from Medieval Latin *Ruthenia*, Russia. See **Ruthenia**.]

ru·then·i·ous (rōo-théeni-əss, rōo- ‖ rew-) *adj. Chemistry.* Of or pertaining to ruthenium. Said especially of a compound that contains ruthenium with a low valency.

ruth·er·ford (rúthər-fərd) *n.* A unit of radioactivity equal to the quantity of radioactive material that undergoes one million disintegrations per second. [After Ernest RUTHERFORD.]

Rutherford (rúthər-fərd), **Ernest, 1st Baron** (1871–1937). New Zealand-born British scientist. He classified radiation into alpha, beta, and gamma types; his discovery that alpha radiation consists of positive charged helium atoms led to his discovery (1906) of the atomic nucleus. He was awarded the Nobel prize for chemistry (1908).

Rutherford, Dame Margaret (1892–1972). British actress. Starting her film career in 1936, she appeared in more than 40 films, mostly comedies, in parts characterised by a uniquely British eccentricity. In *Murder She Said* (1962) and its sequels, she played Agatha Christie's detective, Miss Marple.

ruth·er·for·di·um (rúthər-fórdi-əm ‖ -fórdi-) *n.* The element **unnilquadium** (*see*). Not in current technical usage. [After Ernest RUTHERFORD.]

ruth·ful (rōoth-f'l ‖ rewth-) *adj. Archaic.* **1.** Full of or causing sorrow. **2.** Compassionate. —**ruth·ful·ly** *adv.* —**ruth·ful·ness** *n.*

ruth·less (rōoth-ləss, -liss ‖ rewth-) *adj.* Having or showing no compassion, pity, or leniency; merciless. See Synonyms at **cruel**. —**ruth·less·ly** *adv.* —**ruth·less·ness** *n.*

ru·ti·lant (rōoti-lənt ‖ rewti-) *adj. Archaic.* Having a reddish glow or gleam. [Middle English *rutilaunt*, from Latin *rutilāns* (stem *rutilant-*), from *rutilāre*, to make reddish, from *rutilus*, reddish.]

ru·tile (rōo-tīl ‖ rew-, -teel) *n.* The lustrous red, reddish-brown, yellowish, or black natural mineral form of titanium dioxide, TiO_2, used as a gemstone, as a source of titanium, and in paints and fillers. [German *Rutil*, from Latin *rutilus*, reddish. See **rutilant**.]

Rut·land (rút-lənd). Former county of central England. Absorbed into Leicestershire (1974) despite local opposition, it was the smallest county of England. Its county town was Oakham.

rut·tish (rúttish) *adj.* Lustful; libidinous.

rut·ty (rútti) *adj.* **-tier, -tiest.** Full of ruts. —**rut·ti·ness** *n.*

Ru·wen·zo·ri Mountains (rōo-en-záw-ri, -ən- ‖ -zó-). Mountain range between Uganda and Zaire, central Africa. Extending from Lake Albert to Lake Edward, the range rises to 5 120 metres (16,798 feet) at Mount Ngaliema (Mount Stanley). The peaks are snow-capped, and are thought to be Ptolemy's Mountains of the Moon.

R.V. Revised Version (of the Bible).

Rwan·da (roo-ándə), **Republic of.** Small republic of central Africa. It is chiefly mountainous with part of Lake Kivu to the west, and the volcanic Virunga mountains in the northwest. Densely populated, it was a refuge in the days of the slave trade and was administered with Burundi by Belgium as Ruanda-Urundi from 1919 until independence (1962). There has been sporadic violence between the two main ethnic groups, the Hutu and Tutsi, since 1959. A poor, predominantly agricultural country, Rwanda relies on exports of coffee and tea, but its considerable mineral resources are now being developed. Area 26 338 square kilometres (10,169 square miles). Population 5,400,000. Capital, Kigali. See map at **Tanzania**.

Rwy., Ry. railway.

-ry. Variant of **-ery.**

ryd·berg (ríd-berg) *n.* A unit of energy, the **hartree** (*see*). [After Johannes Robert *Rydberg* (1854–1919), Swedish physicist.]

Rydberg constant *n. Physics. Symbol* **R.** A constant used in formulae for series of lines in atomic spectra, equal to $1.09737 \times 10^7 m^{-1}$.

Ry·der (rídər), **Baroness Sue** (1923–). British philanthropist. The wife of Group Captain Leonard Cheshire, she founded the Sue Ryder Foundation for the Sick and Disabled of All Age Groups, which grew from her work with refugees after World War II.

rye[1] (rī) *n.* **1.** A widely cultivated cereal grass of the genus *Secale*, the seeds of which are valued as grain. **2.** The grain of this plant, used in making flour and whiskey and for livestock feed. **3.** Rye bread. **4.** Rye whiskey. [Middle English *rye, ruge*, Old English *ryge*.]

rye[2] *n.* A gentleman among Gypsies. [Romany *rai*, from Sanskrit *rājan*, king.]

Rye (rī). Market town and resort of East Sussex, southeast England. It is one of the Cinque Ports but silt deposits have moved the coastline 3 kilometres (2 miles) from the town.

rye bread *n.* Bread made partially or entirely from rye flour.

rye brome *n.* A Eurasian grass, *Bromus secalinus*, widely introduced, having rough leaves and wheatlike ears. Also *U.S.* "chess".

rye grass *n.* Any of several pasture or meadow grasses of the genus *Lolium*, native to Eurasia, some species of which are cultivated for forage.

rye whiskey *n.* Whiskey distilled from rye.

Ry·kov (rée-kof; *Russian* -kəf), **Aleksei Ivanovich** (1881–1938). Russian politician. He succeeded Lenin as chairman of the Council of Peoples' Commissars, but was obliged to resign (1930) for his opposition to Stalin's disastrous collectivisation of agriculture. He was eventually executed after a public trial for treason.

Ryle (rīl), **Sir Martin** (1918–). British astronomer. He is best known for pioneering the technique of setting up a line of two or more radio telescopes and using the Earth's rotation to multiply their effective aperture. In 1974 he shared with Antony Hewish (1924–) the Nobel prize for physics.

ry·ot (rī-ət) *n.* A peasant or tenant farmer in India. [Hindi *ra'iyat*, from Arabic *ra'īyah*, herd, peasants, from *ra'ā*, pasture.]

Ryu·kyu Islands (ri-ōo-kew; *Japanese* réw-). Island group of the west Pacific Ocean. Forming an arc between Kyushu Island (Japan) and Taiwan, they were seized from China by Japan (1879) and were occupied by the United States from 1945, returning to Japan in 1953 and 1972. Okinawa is the main island. See map at **Japan**.

rye *This cereal, which will grow even on poor soil, is cultivated mainly for animal fodder. Flour made from it produces a dark bread – the black bread of eastern Europe – and it is sometimes used in place of barley in whisky distilling.*

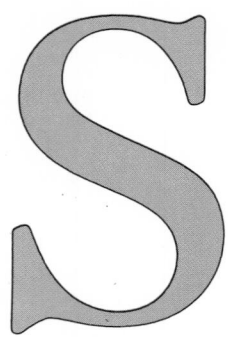

s, S (ess) *n., pl.* **s's, S's** or **Ss. 1.** The 19th letter of the modern English alphabet. **2.** Any of the speech sounds represented by this letter. **3.** Anything shaped like the letter **S**.

s, S, s., S. *Note:* As an abbreviation or symbol, *s* may be a small or a capital letter, with or without a full stop. Established forms or those generally preferred precede the definition. When no form is given, all four forms are in general use in that sense. **1. S.** Sabbath. **2. S.** saint. **3. S.** Saturday. **4. S.** Saxon. **5. s., S.** school. **6. s., S.** sea. **7. s** second (unit of time). **8. s** second of arc. **9. s.** see. **10. s.** semi-. **11. S.** September. **12. s.** shilling. **13. S.** *Medicine.* signature. **14. S.** signor; signore. **15. s.** singular. **16. s.** sire. **17. s.** sister. **18. s.** small. **19. s., S.** society. **20. s.** son. **21.** south; southern. **22. s** stere. **23. S** *Physics.* strangeness. **24. s.** substantive. **25. S** The symbol for the element sulphur. **26. S.** Sunday.

–s¹ *n. suffix.* Indicates the plural form, for which it is used: **a.** In most nouns not ending in a sibilant (such as *s* or *sh*), an affricate (such as *ch*), or a postconsonantal *y*; for example, *charms, toys.* **b.** In abbreviations, numbers, or symbols used as nouns; for example, *MAs, D.T.s, 1960s, As.* Compare **-es** (in nouns). [Middle English *-es, -s,* Old English *-as,* nominative and accusative plural ending of some nouns.]

–s² *v. suffix.* Indicates the third person singular form of the present indicative, for which it is used in most verbs not ending in a sibilant, an affricate, or a postconsonantal *y*; for example, she *sleeps,* one *stays.* Compare **-es** (in verbs). [Middle English *-es,* Old English *-es, -as.*]

–s³ *adv. suffix.* **1.** Used in the formation of certain adverbs; for example, **unawares. 2.** Used, especially in American English, to form adverbs indicating regular repetition of action; for example, *mornings,* (in *Mornings he takes the train*), *nights* (in *She works nights*). [Middle and Old English *-es,* genitive singular ending was used to form adverbs from some nouns and adjectives.]

–'s¹ *n. & pron. suffix.* Indicates the possessive case, for which it is used in singular nouns, in some pronouns, and in irregularly formed plural nouns; for example, **nation's, somebody's, men's.** [Middle and Old English *-es,* genitive singular ending.]

–'s² *n. suffix.* Indicates the plural form in abbreviations, numbers, or symbols used as nouns; for example, *MA's, D.T.'s, 1960's, A's.* [From **-s** (plural suffix).]

–'s³. 1. Contraction of *is: She's here.* **2.** Contraction of *has: He's been eating.* **3.** Contraction of *us: Let's go.* **4.** *Nonstandard.* Contraction of *does: What's it mean?*

s.a. without date [Latin *sine anno.*]

S.A. 1. Salvation Army. **2.** South Africa. **3.** South America. **4.** South Australia. **5.** Sturmabteilung.

Saa·nen (sáʼanən) *n.* A dairy goat of a breed developed in Switzerland, having a white, short-haired coat and no horns. [After *Saanen,* a town in southwest Switzerland.]

Saar·brück·en (sár-brŏockən; *German* zaar-brúckən). *French* **Sarre·bruck** (saar-brúk). Capital of Saarland, southwest West Germany. Situated on the river Saar near the French border, it is the industrial centre of the Saar coalfield.

Saa·ri·nen (sáari-nən; *Finnish* -nen), **Eero** (1910–61). Finnish-born U.S. architect. His innovative designs include the General Motors Technical Center at Warren, Michigan, and the Trans World Airlines terminal at Kennedy Airport.

Saar·land (sár-land; *German* zár-lant) Formerly **Saar·ge·biet** (-gə-beet) or **Saar (Territory)** *French* **Sarre** (sar). State of southwest West Germany, bordered by Luxembourg and France. With rich coal deposits, it has heavy industries including iron and steel and metal goods, and also glass and textiles. A German-speaking border territory, Saarland became the Saar Territory, administered by France under the League of Nations (1919). After a plebiscite, the territory was constituted the German province of Saarland (1935). It became part of the French zone of occupied Germany in 1945, and joined a customs union with France (1948). A referendum (1955) rejected plans for an autonomous, neutral state and the area gained its present status (1957). Saarbrücken is the capital.

Sab. Sabbath.

sab·a·dil·la (sábbə-díllə) *n.* **1.** A tropical American plant, *Schoenocaulon officinale,* having poisonous seeds used in insecticides. **2.** The dry, ripe seeds of this plant. [Spanish *cebadilla,* diminutive of *cebada,* barley, from *cebo,* feed, from Latin *cibus,* food, probably of non-Indo-European origin.]

Sa·bah (sáʼa-baa, -bə). State of East Malaysia, on the island of Borneo. It was the British protectorate of North Borneo from 1882 and joined the Federation of Malaysia (1963). It has been claimed by the Philippines. Sabah produces rubber, copra, cocoa, rice, and wood, and has oil and copper resources. Its capital is Kota Kinabalu.

Sab·a·oth (sábbay-oth, sa-báy-, sə-, -əth) *pl.n.* Hosts; armies: *the Lord of Sabaoth.* Romans 9:29; James 5:4. [Latin *Sabaōth,* from Greek, from Hebrew *ṣəbhā'ōth,* from *ṣābhā',* host, army.]

sa·ba·yon (sábbī-ón) *n.* A dessert sauce made with beaten egg yolks. [French, from Italian *zabaione,* ZABAGLIONE.]

sab·bat (sábbət, sa-báʼa) *n.* The witches' Sabbath *(see).* [French, "Sabbath", from Latin *sabbatum,* SABBATH.]

Sab·ba·tar·i·an (sábbə-taír-i-ən) *n.* **1.** A person who observes Saturday as the Sabbath, as in Judaism and some sects of Christianity. **2.** A person who believes in strict observance of the Sabbath. *~adj.* Of the Sabbath or Sabbatarians. [Late Latin *sabbatārius,* from Latin *sabbatum,* SABBATH.] **—Sab·ba·tar·i·an·ism** *n.*

Sab·bath (sábbəth) *n. Abbr.* **S., Sab. 1.** Saturday, taken as the seventh day of the week, named in the Ten Commandments as the day of rest and worship and observed as such by the Jews and some Christian sects. **2.** Sunday, taken as the first day of the week, observed as the day of rest by most Christian churches. [Middle English *sabat(h),* from Old English *sabat* and Old French *sab(b)at,* both from Latin *sabbatum,* from Greek *sabbaton,* from Hebrew *shabbāth,* from *shābhath,* to rest.]

sab·bat·i·cal (sə-báttik'l) *adj.* Also **sab·bat·ic** (sə-báttik). **1.** *Sometimes capital* **S.** Pertaining or appropriate to the Sabbath as the day of rest. **2.** Designating a period of paid leave granted, as to a university lecturer, for travel, research, or rest: *sabbatical leave.* *~n.* A sabbatical year. [Late Latin *sabbaticus,* from Greek *sabbatikos,* from *sabbaton,* SABBATH.]

sabbatical year *n.* **1.** A year's sabbatical leave, usually granted every seventh year. **2.** *Often capital* **S.** A year during which land remained fallow, observed every seven years by the ancient Jews.

S.A.B.C. South African Broadcasting Corporation.

Sa·be·an, Sa·bae·an (sə-bée-ən, sa-) *n.* **1.** An inhabitant of ancient Sheba. **2.** The Semitic language of ancient Sheba. [Latin *Sabaeus,* from Greek *Sabaios,* from *Saba,* SHEBA.] **—Sa·be·an** *adj.*

Sa·bel·li·an (sə-bélli-ən) *n.* **1.** An extinct division of the subfamily of Italic Indo-European languages, including ancient Aequian, Sabine, and Volscian. **2.** A member of any of the Sabellian-speaking peoples of ancient Italy, who included the Sabines and the Samnites. [Latin *Sabellus†,* Sabine.] **—Sa·bel·li·an** *adj.*

saber. *Chiefly U.S.* Variant of **sabre.**

sa·bin (sáybin, sábbin) *n.* A unit of acoustic absorption, equivalent to the absorption by one square foot of a surface that absorbs all incident sound. [After W.C.W. Sabine (1868–1919), U.S. physicist.]

Sab·ine (sáb-īn ‖ *chiefly U.S.* sáy-bīn) *n.* **1.** A member of an ancient tribe of central Italy, conquered and assimilated by the Romans in 290 B.C. **2.** The Sabellian language of this people. [Middle English *Sabyn,* from Latin *Sabīnus†.*] **—Sab·ine** *adj.*

Sa·bin vaccine (sáybin) *n.* A live but nonvirulent form of the polio virus taken orally to immunise against poliomyelitis. [After A.B. Sabin (born 1906), U.S. microbiologist.]

sa·ble (sáyb'l) *n.* **1. a.** A carnivorous mammal, *Martes zibellina,* of northern Europe and Asia, having soft, dark fur. **b.** The highly valued pelt or fur of this animal. **2.** The similar fur of other species of martens; especially, the fur of the American marten, *Martes americana.* In this sense, also called "American sable". **3. a.** The colour black, especially in heraldry. **b.** *Usually plural. Literary.* Black clothing worn in mourning. **4.** Greyish yellowish brown. *~adj.* **1.** Made of or trimmed with sable fur. **2.** Having the colour of sable fur. **3. a.** Of the colour black, as in heraldry or mourning.

b. *Literary.* Dark; sombre. [Middle English, from Old French, from Medieval Latin *sabelum,* from Slavic, akin to Russian *sobol†.*]

sable antelope *n.* A large African antelope, *Hippotragus niger,* having a usually dark coat and backward-curving horns.

sab·ot (sáb-ō || -ət) *n.* **1.** A shoe carved from a single piece of wood, worn in several European countries. **2.** A wooden-soled sandal or shoe having a leather upper. [French, from Old French, perhaps blend of *savate,* shoe, akin to Spanish *zapáto,* shoe, perhaps of Oriental origin, + *bot, bote,* BOOT.]

sab·o·tage (sábbə-taazh, -taaj) *n.* **1.** The deliberate damaging of property or disruption of procedure carried out, as by enemy agents or dissatisfied workers, with the intention of obstructing productivity or normal functioning. **2.** Any underhand action intended to defeat or frustrate an endeavour; deliberate subversion.
∼*tr.v.* **sabotaged, -taging, -tages.** To deliberately and maliciously damage or frustrate. [French, from *saboter,* "to clatter shoes", work clumsily, deliberately wreck, from SABOT.]

sab·o·teur (sábbə-tér, -ter, -tőr) *n.* A person who commits sabotage. [French, from *saboter,* to work clumsily, SABOTAGE.]

sa·bra (saábrə) *n.* A native-born Israeli. [Modern Hebrew *sābrāh,* "prickly pear", a plant widespread in the Negev.]

sa·bre, *U.S.* **sa·ber** (sáybər) *n.* **1.** A heavy cavalry sword with a one-edged, slightly curved blade. **2. a.** A fencing sword having a tapering two-edged blade and a guard that covers the back of the hand. **b.** The art of fencing with the sabre.
∼*tr.v.* **sabred** or *U.S.* **sabered, -bring** or *U.S.* **-bering, -bres** or *U.S.* **-bers.** To strike, wound, or kill with a sabre. [French, earlier *sable,* from German *Sabel, Säbel,* from Hungarian *száblya* or Polish *szabla.*]

sabre rattling *n.* An ostentatious display of military power or the threatening of war.

sa·bre-toothed tiger (sáybər-tōōtht) *n.* Any of various extinct cats of the Oligocene to the Pleistocene epoch, characterised by long upper canine teeth; especially, one of the larger members of the genus *Smilodon.* Also called "sabre-toothed cat".

sab·u·lous (sábbew-ləss) *adj.* Gritty; sandy. [Latin *sabulōsus,* from *sabulum,* coarse sand.] **—sab·u·los·i·ty** (-lóssəti) *n.*

sac (sak) *n.* A pouchlike part in a plant or animal, sometimes filled with fluid. [French, a bag, from Latin *saccus,* a SACK.]

S.A.C. senior aircraftman.

sac·cate (sák-ayt, -ət, -it) *adj.* Shaped like or having a pouch or sac. [New Latin *saccatus,* from Latin *saccus,* a bag, SACK.]

sac·cha·rase (sáckər-ayz, -ayss) *n.* An enzyme, **invertase** *(see).* [SACCHAR(O)- + -ASE.]

sac·cha·rate (sáckə-rayt) *n.* A salt or ester of saccharic acid. [SACCHAR(IC ACID) + -ATE.]

sac·char·ic acid (sə-kárrik) *n.* A white crystalline acid, $COOH(CHOH)_4COOH$, formed by the oxidation of glucose. [SACCHAR(O)- + -IC.]

sac·cha·ride (sáckə-rīd || -rid) *n.* Any of a series of compounds of carbon, hydrogen, and oxygen in which the atoms of the latter two elements are in the ratio of 2:1, especially sugars and other carbohydrates containing the group $C_6H_{10}O_5$. [SACCHAR(O)- + -IDE.]

sac·char·i·fy (sə-kárri-fī, sa-) *tr.v.* **-fied, -fying, -fies.** Also **sac·cha·rise** (sáckə-rīz), **-rised, -rising, -rises.** To convert (starch, for example) into sugar. [SACCHAR(O)- + -FY.] **—sac·char·i·fi·ca·tion** (-fi-káysh'n) *n.*

sac·cha·rim·e·ter (sáckə-rímmitər) *n.* **1.** A polarimeter that indicates the concentration of sugar in a solution. **2.** An instrument that determines the sugar content of a fermenting sample from carbon dioxide measurements. [SACCHAR(O)- + -METER.]

sac·cha·rin (sáckə-rin, -reen) *n.* A white crystalline powder, $C_7H_5NO_3S$, having a taste about 500 times sweeter than cane sugar, used as a calorie-free sweetener. [SACCHAR(O)- + -IN.]

sac·cha·rine (sáckə-rin, -reen, -rīn) *adj.* **1.** Pertaining to, or of the nature of sugar or saccharin; sweet. **2.** Ingratiatingly or cloyingly sweet: *a saccharine smile.* [SACCHAR(O)- + -INE.] **—sac·cha·rine·ly** *adv.* **—sac·cha·rin·i·ty** (-rínnəti) *n.*

saccharo-, sacchar- *comb. form.* Indicates sugar; for example, **saccharometer, saccharide, saccharin.** [Latin *saccharum,* sugar, from Greek *sakkharon,* from Pali *sakkharā,* from Sanskrit *śarkarā,* gravel, SUGAR.]

sac·cha·roid (sáckə-royd) *adj.* Also **sac·cha·roi·dal** (-róyd'l). Designating rocks and minerals having a granular structure similar to that of loaf sugar. [SACCHAR(O)- + -OID.]

sac·cha·rom·e·ter (sáckə-rómmitər) *n.* A hydrometer that determines the amount of sugar in a solution from relative density measurements. [SACCHARO- + -METER.]

sac·cha·ro·my·cete (sáckərō-mī́-seet) *n.* Any of the yeast fungi, many of which ferment sugar. [SACCHARO- + -MYCETE.] **—sac·cha·ro·my·ce·tic** (-séttik), **sac·cha·ro·my·ce·tous** (-séetəss) *adj.*

sac·cha·rose (sáckə-rōz, -rōss) *n.* A sugar, **sucrose** *(see).* [SACCHAR(O)- + -OSE.]

sac·cu·late (sáckew-layt, -lət, -lit) *adj.* Also **sac·cu·lat·ed** (-laytid), **sac·cu·lar** (-lər). **1.** Formed of or divided into a series of saclike dilations or pouches. **2.** Possessing a saccule or saccules. [New Latin *sacculus,* SACCULE + -ATE.]

sac·cule (sáckewl) *n.* Also **sac·cu·lus** (sáckew-ləss) *pl.* **-li** (-lī). **1.** A small sac. **2.** The smaller of two membranous sacs in the vestibule of the labyrinth of the ear. [New Latin *sacculus,* from Latin, diminutive of *saccus,* bag, SACK.]

sac·er·do·tal (sássər-dṓt'l, sáckər-) *adj.* **1.** Of or pertaining to priests or the priesthood; priestly. **2.** Of or pertaining to sacerdotalism. [Middle English, from Old French, from Latin *sacerdōtālis,* from *sacerdōs* (stem *sacerdōt-*), a priest.] **—sac·er·do·tal·ly** *adv.*

sac·er·do·tal·ism (sássər-dṓt'l-iz'm, sáckər-) *n.* **1.** The belief that ordained priests are invested with supernatural powers and are the indispensable mediators between God and man. **2.** The assumption of excessive authority by the priesthood over the laity, based on such a belief.

sa·chem (sáychəm) *n.* **1.** The chief of a tribe or confederation among some North American Indian peoples. Also called "sagamore". **2.** *U.S.* Any of the high officials of the Tammany Society. [Narraganset *sâchim,* "chief", from Proto-Algonquian *saakimaawa* (unattested). See also **sagamore.**]

sa·cher·tor·te (zákhər-tawrtə) *n.* A rich chocolate cake filled with jam and chocolate and coated in chocolate icing. [German *Sachertorte* : *Sacher,* 19th- and 20th-century family of hotel owners + TORTE.]

sa·chet (sáshay || *U.S.* sa-sháy) *n.* **1.** A small bag or packet containing perfumed powder and used to scent clothes, as in trunks or wardrobes. **2.** A small sealed packet containing a quantity of a product, such as shampoo or dried yeast, that is enough for use on a single occasion. [French, from Old French, a small bag, diminutive of *sac,* a bag, from Latin *saccus,* SACK.]

Sachs (zaks), **Hans** (1494–1576). German poet and dramatist. A cobbler by trade, he became a Meistersinger of Nuremberg. Though much of his vast output of songs seems dull by modern standards, his shorter plays and verse anecdotes still amuse. His life inspired Wagner's opera, *Die Meistersinger von Nürnberg.*

Sachsen. See **Saxony.**

sack[1] (sak) *n.* Also **sacque** (for sense 2). **1.** *Abbr.* **sk. a.** A large bag of strong, coarse material for holding foodstuffs or other objects in bulk. **b.** The contents of such a bag. **c.** The amount a sack will hold, used as a unit of measure for various commodities. **2. a.** A short, loose-fitting coat for women and children. **b.** A woman's loose-fitting dress. **3.** *Informal.* Dismissal from employment: *His boss finally gave him the sack.* **4.** *Chiefly U.S. Slang.* A bed, mattress, or sleeping bag. **—hit the sack.** *Informal.* To go to bed.
∼*tr.v.* **sacked, sacking, sacks. 1.** To place in a sack or sacks. **2.** *Informal.* To discharge from employment. [Middle English *sack, sak,* Old English *sæcc, sacc,* from Latin *saccus,* from Greek *sakkos,* from Semitic; akin to Hebrew *śaq,* sack, sackcloth.]

sack[2] *tr.v.* **sacked, sacking, sacks.** To loot or pillage (a captured city, for example).
∼*n.* **1.** The looting or pillaging of a captured town. **2.** Plunder; loot. [French *(mettre à) sac,* (to put in) a sack, to plunder, from Italian *sacco,* bag, from Latin *saccus,* SACK.]

sack[3] *n.* Any of various strong white wines from Spain and the Canary Islands, imported to England in the 16th and 17th centuries. [16th-century *wyne seck,* from Old French *(vin) sec,* dry (wine), from Latin *siccus,* dry.]

sack·but (sák-but, -bət) *n.* A medieval musical instrument resembling the trombone. [French *saquebute, saqueboute,* "hooked lance" : *saquer, sachier†,* to pull, draw + *bouter,* to push, thrust against, from Common Romance *bottāre* (unattested), from Germanic.]

sack·cloth (sák-kloth || -klawth) *n.* **1.** Sacking. **2. a.** A rough cloth of camel's hair, goat hair, hemp, cotton, or flax. **b.** Garments made of this cloth, worn as a symbol of mourning or penitence.

sackcloth and ashes *n.* An outward show of repentance. [From the traditional symbols of mourning or penitence, of Biblical origin (in numerous passages, for example Matthew 11:21).]

sack·ful (sák-fōōl) *n., pl.* **-fuls.** The amount a sack will hold; a sack.

sack·ing (sácking) *n.* A coarse, stout woven cloth, made of jute, hemp, or the like, used for making sacks.

sack race *n.* A race in which the competitors, whose legs are enclosed in sacks, proceed by short jumps.

Sack·ville-West (sák-vil-wést), **Vita.** See Sir Harold **Nicolson.**

sa·cral[1] (sáykrəl || *U.S. also* sáckrəl) *adj.* Of, near, or pertaining to the sacrum. [New Latin *sacralis,* from SACRUM.]

sacral[2] *adj.* Pertaining to sacred rites or observances. [Latin *sacer* (stem *sacr-*), SACRED.]

sac·ra·ment (sáckrəmənt) *n.* **1.** Any of various religious rites considered to have been instituted or observed by Jesus as a visible sign of inner grace or a means of achieving grace, specifically: **a.** In the Roman Catholic and Eastern Churches, the rites of baptism, confirmation, the Eucharist, matrimony, holy orders, penance, and the Sacrament of the Sick. **b.** In the Protestant Churches, baptism and the Eucharist. **2.** *Often capital* **S. a.** The Eucharist. **b.** The consecrated elements of the Eucharist; especially, the bread or Host. **3.** Something considered to have sacred or mystical significance; a spiritual symbol or bond. [Middle English, from Old French *sacrement,* from Latin *sacrāmentum,* from Latin, oath, solemn obligation, from *sacrāre,* to consecrate, from *sacer* (stem *sacr-*), SACRED.]

sac·ra·men·tal (sáckrə-mént'l) *adj.* **1.** Pertaining to, of the nature of, or used in a sacrament. **2.** Having the force and sacred character of a sacrament: *a sacramental obligation.*
∼*n.* Any rite, action, or sacred object instituted by some Christian churches for use in worship. **—sac·ra·men·tal·ly** *adv.*

sac·ra·men·tal·ism (sáckrə-mént'l-iz'm) *n.* **1.** The doctrine that observance of the sacraments is necessary for salvation and that such participation can confer grace. **2.** Emphasis upon the efficacy of a sacramental. **—sac·ra·men·tal·ist** *n.*

sac·ra·men·tar·i·an (sáckrə-men-taír-i-ən) *n. Often capital* **S.** A person who regards the sacraments, especially the Eucharist, as merely

sable antelope *The plains of Africa are the home of this black-skinned antelope. Like its northern fur-bearing namesake, the sable, it has been hunted – but for its curved and ringed horns rather than its skin.*

visible symbols, not inherently efficacious nor corporeally manifesting Christ.

~adj. **1.** *Often capital* **S.** Of or pertaining to sacramentarians. **2.** Of or pertaining to sacramentalism. [Translation of German *Sakramenter, Sakramentierer.*] **—sac·ra·men·tar·i·an·ism** *n.*

Sac·ra·men·to (sáckrə-méntō). Capital of California, western United States. Situated on the Sacramento river, it was founded as Fort Sutter (1839) and expanded with the gold rush of 1848. It became the state capital (1854) and terminus of the Pony Express (1860). It has a deep-water port connected to the Pacific by the Suisun canal.

Sacrament of the Sick *n. Roman Catholic Church.* A sacrament in which a priest anoints and prays for a sick person, especially one in danger of death. Also called "extreme unction".

sa·crar·i·um (sa-kráir-i-əm, sə-) *n., pl.* **-ia** (-i-ə). **1.** The sanctuary of a church. **2.** In the Roman Catholic Church, a **piscina** *(see).* [Medieval Latin *sacrārium,* from Latin, a place for keeping holy things, from *sacer,* SACRED.]

sa·cred (sáykrid) *adj.* **1.** Dedicated, consecrated, or set apart for the worship of a deity. **2.** Dedicated or devoted exclusively to a single use, purpose, or person. **3.** Worthy of reverence or respect; venerable: *the sacred teachings of Buddha.* **4.** Entitled, because of religious or quasi-religious feeling, to immunity from violation; sacrosanct: *a football match at Lord's —is nothing sacred?* **5.** Of or pertaining to religious objects, rites, or practices. [Middle English, from the past participle of *sacren,* to consecrate, from Old French *sacrer,* from Latin *sacrāre,* from *sacer* (stem *sacr-*), dedicated, holy, sacred.] **—sa·cred·ly** *adv.* **—sa·cred·ness** *n.*

Sacred College *n.* The **College of Cardinals** *(see).*

sacred cow *n.* A person, idea, institution, or object regarded as immune from reasonable criticism. [Referring to the veneration of cows as sacred by Hindus.]

Sacred Heart *n. Roman Catholic Church.* **1. a.** The heart of Christ, regarded as a symbol of his sacrifice and an object of devotion. **b.** Christ himself so symbolised. **2.** A picture of the Sacred Heart.

sacred mushroom *n.* Any of various mushrooms, such as species of *Psilocybe* and *Amanita,* that are ritually eaten for their hallucinogenic effects in various parts of the world.

sac·ri·fice (sáckri-fīss) *n.* **1. a.** The act of offering something to a deity in propitiation or homage; especially, the ritual slaughter of an animal or person for this purpose. **b.** That which is so offered. **2. a.** The forfeiture of something highly valued, as an idea, object, or friendship, for the sake of someone or something considered to have a greater value or claim. **b.** Something so forfeited. **3. a.** A relinquishing of something at less than its presumed value. **b.** Something so relinquished. **c.** A loss so sustained.

~v. **sacrificed, -ficing, -fices.** *—tr.* **1.** To offer as a sacrifice to a deity. **2.** To forfeit (something of value) for something considered to have a greater value or claim. **3.** To sell at a loss. **4.** In chess, to allow one's opponent to capture (a piece) without the loss of an equivalent piece, as for tactical reasons. *—intr.* To make or offer a sacrifice. [Middle English, from Old French, from Latin *sacrificium* : *sacer,* holy, SACRED + *facere,* to do, make.] **—sac·ri·fic·er** *n.*

sac·ri·fi·cial (sáckri-físh'l) *adj.* Pertaining to, intended as, or concerned with a sacrifice: *a sacrificial lamb.* **—sac·ri·fi·cial·ly** *adv.*

sacrificial anode *n. Metallurgy.* A piece of electropositive metal, such as magnesium or zinc, connected by a wire to a steel structure and buried in the ground, used to inhibit corrosion of the steel. [The magnesium corrodes instead (sacrifices itself for the steel).]

sac·ri·lege (sáckri-lij) *n.* **1.** The misuse, theft, desecration, or profanation of anything consecrated to a deity. **2.** An act of gross disrespect towards something regarded as sacred: *thought it sacrilege to put milk in China tea.* [Middle English, from Old French, from Latin *sacrilegium,* from *sacrilegus,* one who steals sacred things : *sacer,* SACRED + *legere,* to gather, pluck, steal.] **—sac·ri·le·gist** (-líj-ist || *chiefly U.S.* -léej-) *n.*

sac·ri·le·gious (sáckri-líj-əss, *rarely* -líji- || *chiefly U.S.* -léej-) *adj.* **1.** Disrespectful or irreverent towards anything regarded as sacred; impious; profane. **2.** Guilty of sacrilege. —See Synonyms at **profane.** **—sac·ri·le·gious·ly** *adv.* **—sac·ri·le·gious·ness** *n.*

sa·cring bell (sáykring) *n.* A bell rung at the elevation of the Host in the Mass. [Middle English *sacringe belle* : *sacringe,* gerund of *sacren,* to consecrate (see **sacred**) + BELL.]

sac·ris·tan (sáckristən) *n.* Also **sa·crist** (sáckrist, sáykrist) **1.** A person in charge of a sacristy. **2.** *Archaic.* A sexton. [Middle English, from Medieval Latin *sacristānus,* from *sacrista,* "one in charge of sacred vessels", from Latin *sacer* (stem *sacr-*), SACRED.]

sac·ris·ty (sáckristi) *n., pl.* **-ties.** A room in a church housing the sacred vessels and vestments; a vestry. [French *sacristie,* from Medieval Latin *sacristia,* from *sacrista,* SACRISTAN.]

sac·ro·il·i·ac (sáykrō-ílli-ak, sáckrō-) *adj. Anatomy.* Of, pertaining to, or affecting the sacrum and ilium, their articulation, or associated ligaments.

~n. The sacroiliac joint or region. [SACR(UM) + ILI(UM) + -AC.]

sac·ro·sanct (sák-rə-sangkt, -rō-) *adj.* Regarded as sacred and inviolable. Often used to imply undeserved immunity to questioning, change, or attack. [Latin *sacrōsanctus,* consecrated with religious ceremonies : *sacrō,* by a sacred rite, ablative of *sacrum,* a holy thing, religious rite, from *sacer,* SACRED + *sanctus,* past participle of *sancīre,* to consecrate.] **—sac·ro·sanc·ti·ty** (-sángktəti) *n.*

sa·crum (sáy-krəm || *U.S. also* sá-) *n., pl.* **-cra** (-krə). **1.** A triangular bone consisting, in humans, of five fused vertebrae and forming the posterior section of the pelvis. **2.** The corresponding bone in other vertebrates. [New Latin, from Late Latin *(os) sacrum* (translation of Greek *hieron osteron,* "sacred bone", because it was used in sacrifice), from Latin, a sacred thing, from *sacer,* SACRED.]

sad (sad) *adj.* **sadder, saddest.** **1.** Low in spirits; dejected; sorrowful. **2.** Expressive of or characterised by sorrow or gloom. **3.** Causing sorrow or gloom; depressing. **4.** Deplorable; sorry. **5.** Dark-hued; sombre. [Middle English *sad,* grave, sad, full (of something), Old English *sæd,* sated, weary, from Germanic.] **—sad·ly** *adv.* **—sad·ness** *n.*

Synonyms: *sad, melancholy, depressed, dejected, downcast, sorrowful, doleful, desolate, miserable, wretched.*

Sadat (sə-dát, -daát), **Muhammad Anwar El** (1918–81). Egyptian politician, who succeeded to the presidency on Nasser's death (1970). He distanced his country from Soviet influence and turned more to the United States, but is best remembered for his dramatic visit to Israel and his attempts to initiate a lasting settlement between the two countries. For this he was awarded the Nobel peace prize jointly with Menachem Begin. He was assassinated by Muslim fundamentalists.

sad·den (sádd'n) *v.* **-dened, -dening, -dens.** *—tr.* To make sad. *—intr.* To grow sad.

saddhu. Variant of **sadhu.**

sad·dle (sádd'l) *n.* **1.** A leather seat for a rider, secured on an animal's back by a girth. **2.** The padded part of a driving harness fitting over a horse's back. **3.** The part of an animal's back upon which a saddle is placed. **4.** Something resembling or suggestive of a saddle in position, function, or shape, as: **a.** The seat of a bicycle, motorcycle, or similar vehicle. **b.** A cut of meat, especially lamb or mutton, consisting of part of the backbone and both loins. **c.** The lower part of a male fowl's back. **d.** A saddle-shaped depression in the ridge of a hill; a col. **e.** A ridge between two peaks. **f.** The **clitellum** *(see)* of an earthworm. **5.** *Geometry.* A saddle-shaped surface. **—in the saddle.** In a position of control or dominance.

~v. **saddled, -dling, -dles.** *—tr.* **1.** To put a saddle on (a horse, for example). **2.** *Informal.* To load or burden; encumber: *saddled with ten children.* **3.** *Informal.* To impose (a burdensome responsibility) upon another: *She saddled her debts on him.* *—intr.* To saddle a horse or get into a saddle. Often used with *up.* [Middle English *sadel,* Old English *sadol,* from Germanic.]

sad·dle·back (sádd'l-bak) *n.* **1.** A roof having a gable at each end connected by a ridge. Also called "saddle roof". **2.** A rare New Zealand songbird, *Philesturnus carunculatus,* having black plumage with a brown back patch and orange wattles.

sad·dle·bag (sádd'l-bag) *n.* A bag or pouch, usually one of a pair, hung across the saddle of an animal or behind the saddle of a bicycle or motorcycle.

sad·dle·bill (sádd'l-bil) *n.* A tropical African stork, *Ephippiorhynchus senegalensis,* having a black and white plumage and a large red bill with a black band round the middle.

sad·dle·bow (sádd'l-bō) *n.* The arched upper front part of a saddle; a pommel. [Middle English *sadelbowe,* Old English *sadulboga* : SADDLE + BOW (arch).]

sad·dle·cloth (sádd'l-kloth || -klawth) *n.* A cloth placed between a saddle and a horse's back to prevent rubbing.

saddle horse *n.* A horse bred or schooled for riding.

sad·dler (sáddlər) *n.* One who makes, repairs, or sells saddles and other riding equipment.

sad·dler·y (sáddləri) *n., pl.* **-ies.** **1.** Saddles, harnesses, and other equipment for horses; tack. **2.** A shop selling such equipment. **3.** The craft or business of a saddler.

saddle soap *n.* A preparation containing mild soap and neat's-foot oil, used for cleaning and softening leather.

sad·dle·sore (sádd'l-sōr) *adj.* **1.** Having sores caused by an improperly fitted saddle. **2.** Sore as a result of riding.

saddle stitch *n.* **1.** A simple running stitch used primarily as ornament on the edges of clothing and accessories, and usually done in a thread contrasting in colour with the fabric of the garment. **2.** *Bookbinding.* A stitch used in sewing together the leaves of a book at the fold lines. **—sad·dle-stitch** *tr.v.*

sad·dle·tree (sádd'l-tree) *n.* The frame of a saddle.

Sad·du·cee (sáddew-see) *n.* A member of a Jewish sect flourishing from the second century B.C. to the first century A.D., that retained the older interpretation of the written Mosaic law against the oral tradition and denied the resurrection of the dead. Compare **Pharisee.** [Middle English *Saducee,* Old English *Sadducēas* (plural), from Late Latin *Saddūcaeus,* from Late Greek *Saddoukaios,* from Hebrew *Ṣəddūqī,* probably "descendant of *Ṣādōq*", Zadok, "righteous", high priest of Israel in King David's time (II Samuel 8:17).] **—Sad·du·ce·an** (-sée-ən) *adj.* **—Sad·du·cee·ism** *n.*

sa·de, sa·dhe, tsa·de (saá-di, tsaá-, -də) *n.* The 18th letter of the Hebrew alphabet. [Hebrew *ṣadhe.*]

Sade (saad), **Donatien Alphonse François, Comte de,** known as the Marquis de Sade (1740–1814). French novelist. While imprisoned during the 1780s and 1790s for prohibited sexual practices, he wrote several pornographic fantasies, whose preoccupation with sexual violence led to the term sadism.

sad·hu, sad·dhu (saádōō) *n.* A Hindu ascetic holy man. [Sanskrit *sādhu,* from adjective, "straight", right, holy, from Indo-Iranian *sādh* (unattested).]

sad·i·ron (sád-īrn, -ī-ərn) *n.* A heavy flatiron, having points at both ends and a removable handle. [SAD (in the dialectal sense of "heavy") + IRON.]

sa·dism (sáyd-iz'm, *rarely* sád-) *n.* **1.** *Psychology.* An abnormal con-

PRONUNCIATION KEY

a, trap; aa, father; ai, fair; ar, star; aw, lawn; ay, play; b, bb, stab; rubber; ch, church; ck, ticket; d, dd, dead; ladder; e, dress; ee, bee; er, defer; ew, few; ewr, pure; ə, about; ər, letter; f, ff, fife; differ; g, gg, giggle; h, hat; i, kit; ī, price; īr, fire; j, judge; k, kick; l, ll, let; 'l, needle; m, mm, man; n, nn, no; 'n, sudden; ng, thing; o, lot; ō, no; ŏŏ, foot; ōō, shoe; oor, poor; ow, cow; owr, hour; oy, boy; p, pp, pepper; r, rr, red; s, ss, sauce; sh, ship; t, tt, totter; th, thick; th, this; smooth; u, cut; ur, turn; v, vv, valve; w, wet; y, yes; z, zz, zebra; zh, vision; pleasure

IN FOREIGN WORDS:

aN, oN, Saint-Saëns; hl, Llanelli; Hluhluwe; kh, loch; lough; Khaled

STRESS MARK:

ín-sīt, insight; in-sít, incite

dition in which a person derives sexual gratification from inflicting pain and humiliation on others. **2.** Broadly, delight in mental or physical cruelty. [After Comte Donatien de SADE.] **—sa•dist** *n.* **—sa•dis•tic** (sə-dístik, sa-) *adj.* **—sa•dis•ti•cal•ly** *adv.*

sa•do-mas•och•ism (sáydō-mássə-kiz'm) *n.* The combination of sadism and masochism in one person, marked by the gaining of pleasure from both inflicting and submitting to pain. [SAD(ISM) + MASOCHISM.] **—sa•do-mas•och•ist** *n.* **—sa•do-mas•o•chis•tic** (-kístik) *adj.*

sad sack *n. U.S. Informal.* An extremely inept or clumsy person.

s.a.e. stamped addressed envelope.

Sa•far, Sa•phar (sə-fár) *n.* The second month of the Muslim calendar. [Arabic.]

sa•fa•ri (sə-fáari) *n., pl.* **-ris. 1.** An overland expedition, especially for hunting or observing wild animals in Africa. **2.** The people, animals, and equipment of such an expedition. [Arabic *safarīy,* a journey, from *safara,* to travel, set out.]

safari park *n.* A type of zoo in which wild animals are allowed to roam over an extensive area and can be viewed by the public from cars or buses.

safari suit *n.* A lightweight outfit consisting of a loose, shirtlike jacket and matching trousers or skirt.

safe (sayf) *adj.* **safer, safest. 1.** Free from harm or injury; unhurt: *safe and sound after their ordeal.* **2. a.** Free from the threat of harm or danger. **b.** Affording protection against harm or danger: *a safe place.* **c.** Unable or unlikely to cause harm or danger: *a safe drug.* **3.** Free from the risk of loss or failure: *a safe parliamentary seat; a safe investment.* **4. a.** Cautious; disinclined to provoke controversy or take risks: *a safe speech; better safe than sorry.* **b.** Reliable; dependable: *a safe pair of hands.*

~n. **1.** A metal container usually having a lock, used for storing valuables; a strongbox or safe-deposit box. **2.** Any repository for protecting stored items, such as a **meat safe** *(see).* **3.** *U.S. Slang.* A condom. [Middle English *sauf,* from Old French, from Latin *salvus,* healthy, uninjured, safe.] **—safe•ly** *adv.* **—safe•ness** *n.*

safe-blow•er (sáyf-blō-ər) *n.* A safe-breaker who uses explosives.

safe-break•er (sáyf-braykər) *n.* A criminal skilled in breaking open safes. **—safe-break•ing** *n.*

safe-con•duct (sáyf-kón-dukt) *n.* **1.** An official document assuring unmolested passage, as through enemy territory. **2.** The protection thus afforded.

~tr.v. (*also* -kən-dúkt || -kon-) **safe-conducted, -ducting, -ducts. 1.** To grant a safe-conduct to. **2.** To escort with a safe-conduct.

safe-de•pos•it (sáyf-di-pozzit, -də-, -pózzit) *n.* A vault or strongroom usually containing rows of small safes *(safe-deposit boxes)* for individual use for storing papers, jewellery, or other valuables.

safe•guard (sáyf-gaard) *n.* **1.** One that serves as a protection or precaution, as: **a.** A mechanical device or technical improvement designed to prevent accidents. **b.** A protective stipulation, as in a contract. **2.** A safe-conduct.

~tr.v. **safeguarded, -guarding, -guards.** To keep safe or secure, as from danger, attack, or violation; protect. See Synonyms at **defend.**

safe house *n.* A house or flat offering safe conditions for clandestine activities, such as: **1.** One used by intelligence officers, as for the debriefing of a person seeking political asylum. **2.** One in which an escaped prisoner, especially a prisoner of war, may seek refuge.

safe•keep•ing (sáyf-kéeping) *n.* The act of keeping in safety or the state of being kept safe; protection; care.

safe•light (sáyf-līt) *n.* A lamp having one or more colour filters capable of permitting moderate darkroom illumination without exposure of photosensitive film or paper.

safe period *n.* The days of a woman's menstrual cycle during which sexual intercourse is considered least likely to result in pregnancy. See **rhythm method.**

safe•ty (sáyfti) *n., pl.* **-ties. 1.** Freedom from or prevention of danger, risk, or injury. **2.** Any of various devices designed to prevent accident; specifically, a lock on a firearm preventing accidental firing. Also called "safety catch". **3.** In American football: **a.** A touchdown behind one's own goal line. **b.** Either of two defensive backs, usually positioned closest to the goal line they defend.

~adj. Contributing to or insuring safety; protective.

safety belt *n.* A **seat belt** *(see).*

safety curtain *n.* A fireproof curtain or screen lowered between the stage and auditorium in a theatre when no performance is taking place to contain any possible outbreak of fire.

safety factor *n.* A **factor of safety** *(see).*

safety film *n.* Nonflammable photographic film.

safety fuse *n.* **1.** A slow-burning fuse used for detonating an explosive from a safe distance. **2.** An electrical **fuse** *(see).*

safety glass *n.* Glass that has been toughened, reinforced, or otherwise modified so as to diminish the risk of breakage or to reduce the risk of injury should breakage occur. The main types either have a laminated structure including wire or plastic sheet (*laminated glass*), or are strained so that they can break into small pieces without sharp edges (*toughened glass*).

safety helmet *n.* A reinforced hat made of plastic or metal worn especially by workers on building sites.

safety lamp *n.* **1.** A miner's lamp with a protective wire gauze surrounding the flame to prevent ignition of flammable gases. **2.** Any specially protected lamp.

safety match *n.* A match that can be lighted only by being struck against a chemically prepared friction surface. See **match.**

safety net *n.* **1.** A net held above the ground to break a person's fall, especially one for acrobats and similar performers. **2.** Any arrangement or measure providing for an emergency.

safety pin *n.* **1.** A pin in the form of a clasp, having a sheath to enclose the point, thus giving protection to the user. **2.** A pin that prevents the premature or accidental detonation of a bomb, grenade, or other explosive.

safety razor *n.* A razor in which the blade is fitted into a holder with guards to prevent cutting of the skin.

safety valve *n.* **1.** A valve in a pressure container, as in a steam boiler, that automatically opens when pressure reaches a dangerous level. **2.** Any outlet for the release of an excess, as of emotion.

saf•flow•er (sáf-lowr, -low-ər) *n.* **1.** A plant, *Carthamus tinctorius,* native to Asia, having orange flowers that yield a dyestuff and seeds that are the source of an oil used in cooking, cosmetics, paints, and medicine. **2.** The dried flowers of this plant. **3.** Any of the products of this plant. [Earlier *safflore,* from Dutch *saffloer* or German *Safflor,* from Old French *saffleur,* from obsolete Italian *saffiore*†.]

saf•fron (sáffrən) *n.* **1.** A plant, *Crocus sativus,* native to the Old World, having purple or white flowers with orange stigmas. **2.** The dried stigmas of this plant, used to colour foods and as a cooking spice and a dyestuff. **3.** Any of various similar or related plants, such as the meadow saffron. See **autumn crocus. 4.** Moderate orange-yellow to moderate orange. In this sense, also called "saffron yellow". [Middle English *saffran,* from Old French *safran,* from Medieval Latin *safranum,* from Arabic *za'farān.*] **—saf•fron** *adj.*

S.Afr. South Africa.

saf•ra•nine (sáffrən-een, -in) *n.* Also **saf•ra•nin** (-in). Any of a family of dyes based on phenazine, used in the textile industry and as a biological stain. [French *safran,* SAFFRON + -INE.]

saf•role (sáffrōl) *n.* A colourless or pale yellow oily liquid, $C_{10}H_{10}O_2$, derived from oil of sassafras and other essential oils and used in making flavourings, perfume, and soap. [French *safran,* SAFFRON + -OLE.]

sag (sag) *v.* **sagged, sagging, sags.** *—intr.* **1.** To sink, curve, or bulge downwards, as from pressure, weight, or slackness. **2.** To hang loosely or unevenly; droop. **3.** To diminish in firmness, strength, or vigour; weaken: *Morale is sagging.* **4.** To decline in value or price. **5.** *Nautical.* To drift to leeward. *—tr.* To cause to sag or curve in the middle.

~n. **1.** The act, degree, or extent of sagging. **2.** A sunken place or area; a depression. **3.** A decline, as in price or value. **4.** *Nautical.* A drift to leeward. [Middle English *saggen,* from Middle Low German *sacken,* to settle, ultimately of Scandinavian origin.]

sa•ga (sáagə || *U.S. also* sággə) *n.* **1.** An Icelandic prose narrative of the 12th and 13th centuries recounting historical and legendary events and exploits. **2.** Broadly, any long, heroic narrative. **3.** A novel or series of novels relating the history of a family. **4.** A series of events occurring over a relatively long time, such as one concerning an involved domestic drama: *the saga of our washing machine.* [Old Norse, a story, legend; akin to SAW (saying).]

sa•ga•cious (sə-gáyshəss) *adj.* Possessing or showing sound judgment and keen perception; wise. See Synonyms at **shrewd.** [Latin *sagāx* (stem *sagāc-*).] **—sa•ga•cious•ly** *adv.* **—sa•ga•cious•ness** *n.*

sa•gac•i•ty (sə-gássəti) *n.* Keen intelligence; shrewdness.

sag•a•more (sággə-mawr || -mōr) *n.* **1.** A subordinate chief among the Algonquian Indians of North America. **2.** A North American Indian chief, a **sachem** *(see).* [Eastern Abnaki *sàkama,* from Proto-Algonquian *saakimaawa* (unattested). See also **sachem.**]

Sa•gan (sa-góN), **Françoise,** pen name of Françoise Quoirez (1935–). French novelist and playwright. Her work generally deals with sexual ennui amongst prosperous, middle-class characters. Her works include the popular success, *Bonjour Tristesse* (1954).

saga novel *n.* A **roman-fleuve** *(see).*

sage[1] (sayj) *n.* A person, usually an elderly man, who is venerated for his experience, judgment, and wisdom.

~adj. **sager, sagest. 1.** Having, proceeding from, or showing wisdom and calm judgment; judicious; wise. **2.** *Obsolete.* Serious; solemn: *"a sage Requiem"* (Shakespeare). [Middle English, from Old French, from Vulgar Latin *sapius* (unattested), from Latin *sapere,* to be sensible, be wise.] **—sage•ly** *adv.* **—sage•ness** *n.*

sage[2] *n.* **1.** Any of various plants and shrubs of the genus *Salvia;* especially, *S. officinalis,* having aromatic greyish-green leaves used as a cooking herb. See **salvia. 2.** The leaves of this plant. **3.** Sage green. [Middle English *sauge,* from Old French *sauge,* from Latin *salvia,* "the healing plant", from *salvus,* healthy, safe.]

sage•brush (sáyj-brush) *n.* Any of several aromatic American plants of the genus *Artemisia;* especially, *A. tridentata,* a shrub of arid regions of western North America, having silver-green leaves and large clusters of small white flowers.

sage Derby *n.* A hard yellow cheese, flavoured with sage and streaked with green colouring, originally made in Derby.

sage green *n.* Greyish green. **—sage-green** *adj.*

sage grouse *n.* A bird *Centrocercus urophasianus,* of western North America, the male of which has long, pointed tail feathers that can be spread in a fan during courtship displays.

sage grouse *During courtship, the male sage grouse spreads its long tail feathers into a spiky fan (above). Sage grouse are the largest of North America's game birds, and live in the western sagebrush plains where they feed on insects, berries, and shoots.*

sag•gar, sag•ger (sággər) *n.* **1.** A protective casing of fire clay in which delicate ceramic articles are fired. **2.** Clay used to make such casings.

~tr.v. **saggared, -garing, -gars.** To place or bake in a saggar. [Perhaps a contraction of SAFEGUARD.]

Sa•git•ta (sə-jíttə) *n.* A constellation in the Northern Hemisphere near Aquila and Cygnus. [Latin *sagitta*†, Sagitta, arrow.]

saguaro *Native to Mexico, Arizona, and California, the saguaro cactus lives for 150–200 years and can grow to 15 metres (50 feet) high. When fully grown, the plant may weigh several tonnes.*

saiga *This antelope of the dry, cold steppes of Eurasia has a large downward-pointing nose which may help to warm the air it breathes and minimise water loss.*

sag·it·tal (sájit'l) *adj.* **1.** Of or like an arrow or arrowhead. **2.** *Anatomy.* Of or designating the suture uniting the two parietal bones of the skull. **3.** *Zoology & Anatomy.* Of or designating the vertical plane that divides the body of a symmetrical animal into right and left halves. [Latin *sagitta*†, arrow.] **—sag·it·tal·ly** *adv.*

Sag·it·ta·ri·an (sáji-táir-i-ən, *rarely* sággi-, -táar-) *n.* One born under the sign of Sagittarius. **—Sag·it·ta·ri·an** *adj.*

Sag·it·ta·ri·us (sáji-táir-i-əss, *rarely* sággi-, -táar-) *n.* **1.** A constellation in the Southern Hemisphere near Scorpius and Capricornus. **2. a.** The ninth sign of the **zodiac** *(see).* Also called the "Archer". **b.** A Sagittarian. [Middle English, from Latin *sagittārius,* an archer, Sagittarius, from *sagitta*†, arrow.]

sag·it·tate (sáji-tayt) *adj.* Also **sa·git·ti·form** (sa-jítti-fawrm, sə-). *Botany.* Having the shape of an arrowhead: *sagittate leaves.* [Latin *sagitta*†, arrow.]

sa·go (sáygō) *n.* **1.** A powdery starch obtained from the trunks of the sago palm and used in puddings and as a thickener in sauces. **2.** A milk pudding made from this. [Malay *sāgū.*]

sago palm *n.* **1.** Any of various tropical Asian palm trees, especially of the genus *Metroxylon,* yielding starch from their trunks. **2.** A palmlike cycad, *Cycas revoluta,* which yields starch from its stem.

sa·gua·ro (sə-gwáarō, -wáarō) *n., pl.* **-ros. 1.** A very large cactus, *Carnegiea gigantea,* of the southwestern United States and northern Mexico, having upward-curving branches, white flowers, and edible red fruit. **2.** The fruit of this cactus. [Mexican Spanish, probably of Piman origin.]

Sa·gun·to (sa-gŏŏntō). Formerly **Mur·vie·dro** (moorv-yáydrō). Latin name **Sa·gun·tum** (sə-gúntəm). Town in the Spanish province of Valencia, situated in a major orange-producing region. Its industries include iron and steel founding and oil refining. The siege and capture of Saguntо by Hannibal (219–218 B.C.) signalled the start of the Second Punic War, and it later fell to the Romans (214 B.C.). The city was taken by the Moors (A.D. 713), and reconquered by Aragon (1238). The city is noted for Roman remains.

Sa·hap·tin (sə-háp-tin, saa-) *n., pl.* **-tins** or collectively **Sahaptin.** Also **Sha·hap·tin** (shə-, shaa-). **1.** A member of a North American Indian people of Idaho, Washington, and Oregon. **2.** The language of this people.

Sa·ha·ra (sə-háarə || *U.S.* -háarrə). The largest desert in the world, covering some 9 065 000 square kilometres (*c.*3,500,000 square miles) of North Africa. It extends from the Atlantic Ocean to the Red Sea, and merges with the Sahel to the south. With one of the harshest climates in the world, much of it averages less than 125 millimetres (*c.* 5 inches) of rain a year, has a daily temperature range of up to 30°C (86°F), and is swept by sandstorms. Stone deserts, tracts of bare rock (hamada), and of gravel (reg) cover some 70 per cent of the Sahara, and sand dunes (erg) another 15 per cent. Desert peoples include the Tuareg of the central mountains, those of largely Negroid descent in the Tibesti Massif, and people of mixed Berber and Arab origin. Of the Sahara's traditional inhabitants, some 60 per cent farm in the oases, both natural and those irrigated by water pumped from great depths. The rest rely on the herding of goats, camels, and sheep. The desert is rich in minerals, including deposits of oil, gas, phosphates, manganese, zinc, iron ore, and salt. **—Sa·ha·ran** *adv.*

Saharan Arabic Republic. See **Western Sahara.**

Sa·hel (sáa-hel, -hél). Semidesert and dry grassland region fringing the south of the Sahara. It stretches across eight countries from Senegal eastwards into Sudan. In the late 1960s and throughout the 1970s it suffered drought, with 12 consecutive years when the rainfall was below normal.

sa·hib (sáab, sáa-ib, -hib) *n.* In India, a title of respect or form of address equivalent to *master* or *sir.* Used especially for European colonials. [Hindi *ṣāḥib,* master, lord, from Arabic, friend, companion, master.]

said (sed || sayd). Past tense and past participle of **say.**
~*adj.* Named or mentioned before; aforementioned. Used especially in legal proceedings or documents.

sai·ga (sīgə) *n.* A Eurasian antelope, *Saiga tatarica,* having a stubby, proboscis-like nose. [Russian *saĭga,* from Chagatai *saigak.*]

Saigon. See **Ho Chi Minh City.**

Sai·go Ta·ka·mo·ri (sīgō táckə-máwri, táakə-) (1828–77). Japanese soldier and statesman. A samurai, he was instrumental in the overthrow of the Shogunate and the establishment of the Meiji restoration (1867), but he left the government (1873) in protest at the reform of the feudal system. He committed ritual suicide.

sail (sayl) *n.* **1.** A length of shaped canvas or other strong material attached to a ship, boat, or other vessel to catch the wind and propel it through the water. **2.** A sailing vessel. **3. a.** Sails collectively. **b.** Sailing vessels collectively. **4.** A trip or voyage in a sailing vessel. **5.** Something resembling a sail in form or function; especially, the blade of a windmill, turned by the wind. **—in sail.** Having the sails set. **—make sail. 1.** To unfurl a ship's sail or sails. **2.** To begin a voyage. **—set sail. 1.** To hoist the sails preparatory to a voyage. **2.** To begin a trip or voyage. **—take in sail. 1.** To reduce the area of sail exposed to the wind; reef. **2.** To modify one's ambitions or aims. **—under sail** or **sails.** With sails set and catching the wind; sailing.
~*v.* **sailed, sailing, sails.** —*intr.* **1.** To move across the surface of water, especially by means of a sail. **2.** To travel by water in a vessel. **3.** To start out on a voyage; set sail. **4.** To operate a sailing craft, especially for sport. **5.** To glide smoothly and easily: *skiers sailing down the slopes.* **6.** To move in a stately, self-confident manner, like a ship in full sail. —*tr.* **1.** To navigate or manage (a vessel). **2.** To voyage upon or across (a body of water): *sail the Pacific.* **—sail through.** To accomplish (a task, for example) with great ease: *sailed through his finals.* [Middle English *sail(le),* Old English *segl,* from Germanic *seglam* (unattested).]

sail·cloth (sáyl-kloth || -klawth) *n.* **1.** Cotton canvas or other strong fabric suitable for making sails, tents, or the like. **2.** A light canvas fabric used for making clothing.

sailed (sayld) *adj.* Having sails, especially of a specified type or number. Used chiefly in combination: *white-sailed.*

sail·fish (sáyl-fish) *n., pl.* **-fishes** or collectively **sailfish. 1.** Any of various large marine fishes of the genus *Istiophorus,* having the upper jaw prolonged into a spearlike bone and a large, sail-like dorsal fin. **2.** A **basking shark** *(see).*

sail·ing (sáyling) *n.* **1.** The act, skill, or sport of sailing a vessel, especially a sailing boat. **2.** The skill required to operate and navigate a sailing vessel; navigation. **3.** The departure or time of departure of a vessel: *The sailing is at 2:00 p.m.*

sailing boat *n.* A boat propelled by wind in her sails rather than by oars or an engine. Also *U.S.* "sailboat".

sailing ship *n.* A large vessel powered by the wind.

sail·or (sáylər) *n.* **1.** One who serves in a navy or who earns his living by working on a ship; especially, an ordinary seaman. **2.** One travelling by water, especially with reference to his susceptibility to seasickness: *a poor sailor.* **3.** A sailor hat. [Variant of earlier *sailer,* from SAIL (verb).] **—sail·or·ly** *adj.*

sailor hat *n.* A low-crowned straw hat with a flat top and a flat brim.

sailor suit *n.* A suit imitating the uniform of a sailor, worn especially by a child.

sain·foin (sán-foyn || *chiefly U.S.* sáyn-) *n.* A plant, *Onobrychis viciifolia,* native to Eurasia, that has compound leaves and pink flowers and is often used as fodder. [French, from Old French, from Medieval Latin *sānum faenum,* "wholesome hay" (formerly used as a medicinal herb) : Latin *sānum, sānus,* healthy, whole + *faenum, fēnum,* hay.]

saint (sáynt, *weak forms* sənt, sən) *n.* **1.** *Abbr.* **S., St.** *Theology.* **a.** A person, whose life on earth was exceptionally holy, officially recognised by the Roman Catholic Church and certain other Christian churches as being entitled to public veneration and as being capable of interceding for men on earth; one who has been canonised. **b.** Any person who has died and gone to heaven. **c.** Any baptised believer in Christ, according to the New Testament. **d.** *Capital* **S.** A member of any of various religious groups; especially, a **Latter-Day Saint** *(see).* **2.** A very holy person. **3.** A charitable, unselfish, or patient person.
~*tr.v.* **sainted, sainting, saints.** To name, recognise, or venerate as a saint; canonise. [Middle English, from Old French, from Latin *sanctus,* sacred, from the past participle of *sancīre,* to sanctify.]

Saint. Entries not found under **Saint** may appear at **St.** Biographies of Saints appear at the name of the individual Saint; for **Saint Paul,** see **Paul.**

Saint Agnes' Eve *n.* The night of January 20th, when, according to legend, a woman will dream of her future husband. [After St. *Agnes* (died A.D. 304), Christian child martyr, who was beheaded for refusing to marry.]

Saint Andrew's cross *n.* A cross shaped like the letter X.

Saint Anthony's cross *n.* A cross in the shape of a T. Also called "tau cross".

Saint Bernard *n.* A large, strong dog of a breed developed in Switzerland, having a thick brown and white coat, and originally used by monks of the hospice of St. Bernard in the Swiss Alps to help patrol the snow-covered region for travellers in distress.

saint·dom (sáynt-dəm) *n.* The condition or quality of being a saint.

Sainte-Beuve (saNt-bérv, -bőv), **Charles-Augustin** (1804–69). French writer. He is best known for his criticism, wide-ranging in interest, which encouraged the Romantic movement.

Saint Chris·to·pher (krístəfər) *n.* A medallion, or sometimes a small statuette, representing Christ as a child being carried on the shoulders of St. Christopher, worn by travellers as a supposed protection against danger. [After *St. Christopher,* the patron saint of travellers.]

saint·ed (sáyntid) *adj.* **1.** Enrolled among the saints; canonised. **2.** Of saintly character; holy.

Saint-Ex·u·péry (sáN-teg-zŏŏpəri; *French* -zü-pay-rée), **Antoine de** (1900–44). French writer. His novels, and his famous children's book, *Le Petit Prince* (1943), were inspired by his career as an pilot, particularly on the mail routes of North Africa and South America. He died on an air force mission in World War II.

Saint George's cross *n.* A red cross on a white background, as used in the Union Jack.

Saint George's Day *n.* April 23, observed in honour of St. George, the patron saint of England.

Saint He·le·na (sénti-léenə, *also* sáynt hi-). Volcanic island in the South Atlantic Ocean, 122 square kilometres (47 square miles) in area. Jamestown is the main port and seat of government. Napoleon died there in exile (1821). See map at **Atlantic Ocean.**

saint·hood (sáynt-hŏŏd) *n.* **1.** The status, character, or condition of being a saint. **2.** Saints collectively.

Saint John (jon). City and port in New Brunswick, eastern Canada, situated at the mouth of the Saint John river. Founded by the French as a trading post (1635), it became the eastern terminus of the Canadian Pacific Railway. It has an ice-free port.

Saint John's wort *n.* Any of various plants of the genus *Hypericum,* having yellow, five-petalled flowers with many stamens. See **rose of Sharon, tutsan.** [After *St. John the Baptist*; the plants were formerly gathered on St. John's Eve for magical and medicinal use.]

Saint-Just (saN-<u>zh</u>üst), **Louis (Antoine Léon) de** (1767–94). French politician and soldier. He was the Committee of Public Safety's military supervisor, and led the French at Fleurus (1794), but was executed with Robespierre that same year.

Saint-Laurent (sáN-law-róN), **Yves** (1936–). French fashion designer. Becoming Dior's assistant at the age of 17, he eventually succeeded him, but lost control of the fashion house in 1960. He subsequently founded (1962) his own house, and has become one of Paris' most important designers.

saint·ly (sáyntli) *adj.* **-lier, -liest.** Resembling, pertaining to, or befitting a saint. **—saint·li·ness** *n.*

Saint Nicholas. See **Santa Claus.**

Saint Patrick's Day *n.* March 17, observed in honour of St. Patrick, the patron saint of Ireland.

saint·pau·li·a (sənt-páwli-ə ‖ saynt-) *n.* A plant, **African violet** *(see).* [New Latin, after W. von *Saint Paul* (died 1970), German soldier who discovered it.]

Saint-Saëns (sáN-sóNss), **(Charles) Camille** (1835–1921). French composer and critic. The light-hearted orchestral suite *Carnival of the Animals* (1922) is still his most popular work. As a critic, he championed Liszt, Wagner, and Berlioz. He wrote 12 operas, of which the most famous is *Samson and Delilah* (1877), 5 symphonies, and 5 piano concertos.

saint's day *n.* A day nominated by the church for the commemoration of a particular saint.

Saint-Si·mon (sáN-see-móN), **Claude Henri de Rouvroy, Comte de** (1760–1825). French political philosopher. He envisaged an industrial state run by technocrats, in which poverty would be abolished and religion replaced by rationalism. His ideas greatly influenced the development of socialism, particularly in France.

Saint-Simon, Louis de Rouvroy, Duc de (1675–1755). French courtier and writer. His *Mémoires* for the years 1694 to 1723 provide a personal and prejudiced picture of the court of Louis XIV, whom he particularly disliked.

Saint Valentine's Day *n.* February 14, on which valentines are traditionally exchanged. [Birds were believed to pair on this day.]

Sa·is (sáy-iss). Ancient Egyptian city on the Nile delta; a capital of Lower Egypt in the seventh and sixth centuries B.C.. **—Sa·ite** (-īt) *n.* **—Sa·it·ic** (-ittik) *adj.*

saith (seth ‖ sayth, say-ith). *Archaic.* Third person singular present indicative of **say.**

saithe (sayth, *also* say<u>th</u>) *n.* The **coalfish** *(see).* [Old Norse *seithr.*]

Sai·va (sī-və, shī-) *n.* In Hinduism, a member of the cult of the god Siva. **—Sai·vism** *n.* **—Sai·vite** *n. & adj.*

sake¹ (sayk) *n.* **1.** The purpose, motive, or end: *a quarrel only for the sake of argument.* **2.** Advantage; good: *for the sake of her health.* **3.** Personal benefit or interest; welfare: *for his own sake.* **4.** Used in combination in various expressions of anger, irritation, impatience, or the like: *for Pete's sake; for God's sake.* [Middle English *sake,* contention, lawsuit, guilt (the phrase "for the sake of" probably originated in legal usage), Old English *sacu,* lawsuit, from Germanic *sakō,* (unattested), charge, accusation.]

sa·ke², sa·ki (saáki) *n.* A Japanese alcoholic drink made from fermented rice. [Japanese, "alcohol".]

sa·ker (sáykər) *n.* A southern Eurasian falcon, *Falco cherrug,* having brown plumage and often trained for falconry. [Middle English *sagre,* from Old French *sacre,* from Arabic *ṣaqr.*]

Sakh·a·rov (sáckə-rov, -roff; *Russian* sákhərəf), **Andrei Dimitrievich** (1921–). Soviet physicist. After working on nuclear power in the 1940s and 1950s, he became an outspoken critic of his government's part in the arms race. He was exiled to Gorky. In 1975 he was awarded the Nobel peace prize.

sa·ki (saáki) *n.* Any small South American monkey belonging to either of two genera, *Pithecia* or *Chiropotes,* and having curly hair and a long, bushy tail. [French, from Tupi *saqi.*]

Saki. See H.H. Munro.

Sakkara. See **Saqqara.**

Sakta. Variant of **Shakta.**

Sakti. Variant of **Shakti.**

sal (sal) *n.* Salt. Used chiefly in compounds: *sal volatile.* [Latin *sāl.*]

sa·laam (sə-laám) *n.* **1.** A Muslim salutation or ceremonial greeting performed by bowing low while placing the right palm on the forehead. **2.** In the East, a respectful or ceremonial greeting. **~***v.* **salaamed, -laaming, -laams.** *—tr.* To greet with a salaam. *—intr.* To perform a salaam. [Arabic *salām,* "peace" (part of *assalām 'alaikum,* "peace to you").]

salable. Variant of **saleable.**

sa·la·cious (sə-láyshəss) *adj.* **1.** Stimulating to the sexual imagination; especially, morbidly appealing to lust: *salacious writing.* **2.** Lustful; lecherous. [Latin *salāx* (stem *salāc-*), fond of leaping (said of male animals), lustful, from *salīre,* to leap.] **—sa·la·cious·ly** *adv.* **—sa·la·cious·ness, sa·lac·i·ty** (sə-lássəti) *n.*

sal·ad (sál-əd) *n.* **1.** A cold dish typically consisting of green, leafy raw vegetables, such as lettuce, often with radish, cucumber, or tomato, often tossed with a dressing. **2.** A dish consisting of this as an accompaniment to a main food such as meat or fish. **3.** A cold dish of chopped fruit, vegetables, meat, fish, eggs, or other food, usually prepared with mayonnaise or other dressing. **4.** Any green vegetable or herb eaten raw or used in salad. [Middle English *sa-*

sail

COMBINING SAILS TO HARNESS THE POWER OF THE WIND
The triangular sail that revolutionised sea-going

Wind power has been used to drive sailing vessels since at least 3000 B.C., when Egyptian trading ships used square sails to supplement their rowers when the wind was behind them. The wind's energy was trapped in this way almost unaltered for 4,000 years. The square sail receives wind only from the rear, but can be angled to obtain maximum thrust. Sailing was revolutionised in the 9th century A.D. by the lateen sail, probably invented by Arab seamen. This triangular sail, slung fore and aft from the masthead on a loose-fitted boom, could accept the wind on either side. Some of its effectiveness was due to a principle unknown to its inventors – air passing over the leading edge of a billowing sail creates a vacuum in front of the sail, drawing it forwards in the same way an aeroplane wing is lifted. The resulting airflow increased a ship's speed. The combination of lateen sails with square sails on three-masted ships, adopted by the British, Dutch, and Portuguese in the 15th and 16th centuries, was probably the crucial development that launched the great age of sail and exploration.

In the early 18th century, the triangular headsail was introduced on large vessels. The steering wheel was being installed in ships by then and the greater degree of control it gave made it safer to sail close to the wind at speed, as the triangular headsails allowed.

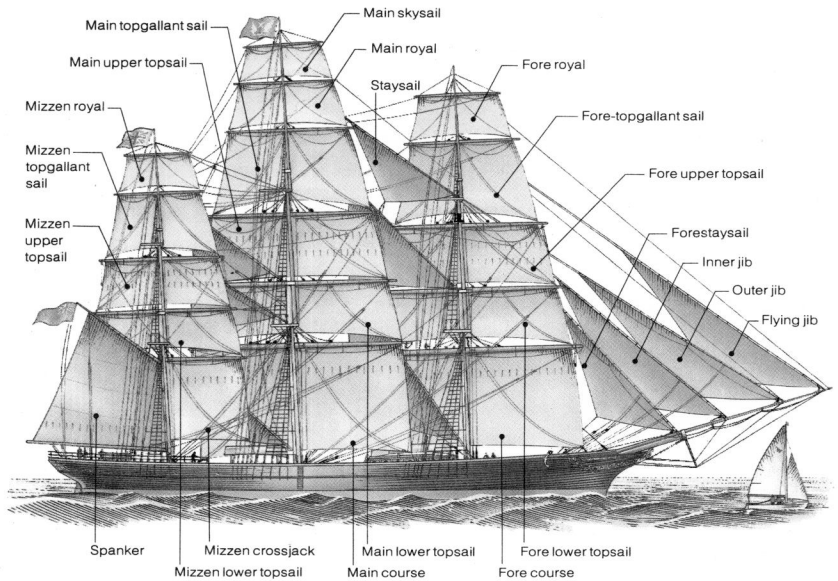

Labels: Main topgallant sail · Main upper topsail · Mizzen royal · Mizzen topgallant sail · Mizzen upper topsail · Main skysail · Main royal · Staysail · Fore royal · Fore-topgallant sail · Fore upper topsail · Forestaysail · Inner jib · Outer jib · Flying jib · Spanker · Mizzen lower topsail · Mizzen crossjack · Main lower topsail · Main course · Fore lower topsail · Fore course

FULL-RIGGED SAILING SHIP *Once the lateen sail had been combined with the square sail, the might of the wind had been harnessed by man. Great ships, fitted with this typical clipper rigging, a mass of sails, masts, and shrouds, could race along with large cargoes for thousands of miles at speeds of about 15 knots (about 17 miles an hour), occasionally reaching 20 knots.*

lade, from Old French, from Provençal *salada,* from Vulgar Latin *salāta* (unattested), from the feminine past participle of *salāre* (unattested), to salt, from Latin *sāl,* salt.]

salad burnet *n.* A short perennial plant, *Sanguisorba minor,* with compound leaves sometimes used in salads, and petal-less flowers borne in round heads.

salad cream *n.* A sauce resembling mayonnaise in consistency, but having a more pungent taste, used especially in Britain to accompany salad.

salad days *pl.n.* The time of youth, innocence, and inexperience. [From Shakespeare: "my salad days when I was green in judgment, cold in blood" (*Antony and Cleopatra,* Act 1, scene 5).]

salad dressing *n.* A sauce, as of mayonnaise or oil and vinegar, served on salad.

Sal·a·din (sál-ə-din), Arabic name Salah ad-Din Yusuf ibn-Aiyub (c. 1137–93). Kurdish general and Sultan of Egypt. As a vizir he conquered Egypt (1169), founded a dynasty (1175), conquered Syria, and took Jerusalem (1187), thereby precipitating the Third Crusade. He became renowned throughout Islam and Christendom for his chivalry and generosity to the poor of all faiths.

Sa·lam (sa-laám), **Abdus** (1926–). Pakistani physicist. The director of the International Centre for Theoretical Physics in Trieste, he won a Nobel prize (1979) for work done at Imperial College, London, on weak interaction and electromagnetic interaction.

Sal·a·man·ca (sál-ə-mángkə). Capital of Salamanca province in central Spain, situated on the river Tormes. Conquered by Hannibal (220 B.C.), it prospered as a cultural centre following the founding of its university (1230), which is the oldest in Spain. The city's many historic sites include the old university buildings, a 12th-century cathedral, and a fine 18th-century plaza.

sal·a·man·der (sál-ə-mandər, *rarely* -maandər) *n.* **1.** Any of various small, lizard-like amphibians of the order Caudata, having porous,

sailing ship *The Portuguese barque Sagres II, a modern descendant of the square-rigged sailing ships that dominated world trade before the age of steam.*

salamander *Giant salamanders – native to China and Japan – can grow to about 1.5 metres (5 feet) in length. The smaller European type (above) is sometimes called the fire salamander, from the old belief that it could withstand flames.*

PRONUNCIATION KEY

a, trap; aa, father; ai, fair; ar, star; aw, lawn; ay, play; b, bb, stab; rubber; ch, church; ck, ticket; d, dd, dead; ladder; e, dress; ee, bee; er, defer; ew, few; ewr, pure; ə, about; ər, letter; f, ff, fife; differ; g, gg, giggle; h, hat; i, kit; ī, price; īr, fire; j, judge; k, kick; l, ll, let; 'l, needle; m, mm, man; n, nn, no; 'n, sudden; ng, thing; o, lot; ō, no; o͝o, foot; o͞o, shoe; oor, poor; ow, cow; owr, hour; oy, boy; p, pp, pepper; r, rr, red; s, ss, sauce; sh, ship; t, tt, totter; th, thick; th, this; smooth; u, cut; ur, turn; v, vv, valve; w, wet; y, yes; z, zz, zebra; zh, vision; pleasure

IN FOREIGN WORDS:

aN, oN, Saint-Saëns; hl, Llanelli; Hluhluwe; kh, loch; lough; Khaled

STRESS MARK:

ín-sīt, insight; in-sít, incite

scaleless skin and four legs that are often weak or rudimentary. **2. a.** A mythical creature, generally resembling a lizard, once thought capable of living in or withstanding fire. **b.** One who is capable of enduring fire, heat, or the like. **c.** According to Paracelsus, an elemental spirit supposed to live in fire. **3.** An object used in fire or capable of withstanding heat, such as a poker. **4.** *Metallurgy.* A mass of solidified material, largely metallic, left in a blast-furnace hearth. **5.** A portable stove used to heat or dry buildings under construction. [Middle English *salamandre,* from Old French, from Latin *salamandra,* from Greek *salamandra*†.]

sa·la·mi (sə-láami) *n.* A highly spiced and salted sausage, flavoured with garlic, that originated in Italy. [Italian, plural of *salame,* "salted pork", from *salare,* to salt, from Vulgar Latin *salāre* (unattested). See **salad**.]

Sal·a·mis (sál-ə-miss). Greek island in the Aegean Sea west of Athens. The Battle of Salamis (480 B.C.) was a major Greek naval victory over the Persians. It was fought in the narrow straits which separate the island from the coast of Attica, allowing the Greeks' smaller ships to overcome the Persians' superior numbers.

sal ammoniac *n.* A chemical, **ammonium chloride** *(see).* [Middle English *sal armoniak,* from Medieval Latin *sāl armōniacus,* from Latin *sāl ammōniacus* : SAL + AMMONIAC.]

sal·a·ried (sál-ə-rid || -reed) *adj.* Earning or yielding a regular salary: *a salaried job; a salaried worker.*

sal·a·ry (sál-əri || -ri) *n., pl.* **-ries.** A fixed amount of money, usually for nonmanual services, paid to a person on a regular, often monthly or quarterly, basis. Compare **wage.** [Middle English *salarie,* from Anglo-French, Old French *salaire,* from Latin *salārium,* originally "money given to Roman soldiers to buy salt", from *salārius,* of salt, from *sāl,* salt.]

Sa·la·zar (sál-ə-záar; *Portuguese* səl-), **Antonio de Oliveira** (1889–1970). Portuguese politician. Following a military coup, he twice served as finance minister (1926, 1928), and in 1932 became prime minister. His corporatist policies stabilised the country but repressed opposition, and his attempts to retain Portugal's colonies led to numerous wars and much international criticism. His dictatorship lasted until 1968.

sal·chow (sál-kō) *n.* A jump in ice-skating performed by taking off from the back inside edge of one skate, making a complete turn, and landing on the back outside edge of the other skate. [After Ulrich *Salchow* (1877–1949), Swedish skater who introduced it.]

Sal·da·nha Bay (sal-daánə). Large bay on the southwestern coast of South Africa, roughly 90 kilometres (56 miles) north of Cape Town, offering a fine natural harbour.

sale (sayl) *n.* **1. a.** The exchange of property or services for a given amount of money or its equivalent; the act or an instance of selling. **b.** An amount or quantity sold. **2.** An opportunity for selling; a market; a demand. **3.** Availability for purchase. Often preceded by *for* or *on*: *a flat for sale.* **4.** A selling of goods to the highest bidder; an auction. **5.** A special disposal of goods at lowered prices, especially a seasonal one held to clear stock. **6.** *Plural.* The branch of a business enterprise that deals with the selling and marketing of its goods or services: *She's head of sales.* Also used adjectivally: *a sales conference.* [Middle English *sale,* Old English *sala,* from Old Norse.]

Sa·lé (sál-i, sə-láy). *Arabic* **Sla** (slaa). Port on the Atlantic coast of Morocco. A Muslim trading centre in medieval times, it became an independent republic in the 17th century and won notoriety as a haunt of the Barbary pirates known as the Sallee Rovers.

sale·a·ble, sal·a·ble (sáylə-b'l) *adj.* **1.** Offered or suitable for sale. **2.** Easily sold. **—sale·a·bil·i·ty** (-bílləti) *n.*

sale or return *n.* A business agreement in which a retailer has the right to return to the wholesaler those goods which he has been unable to sell, without having to pay for them.

sal·ep (sál-ep, sə-lép) *n.* A starchy meal ground from the dried roots of various Old World orchids of the genus *Orchis* and used for food and formerly as a medicine. [French or Spanish, from Turkish *sālep,* from Arabic *saḥleb,* variant of *khasyu aththa'lab,* "the fox's testicles", a kind of orchid.]

sal·e·ra·tus (sál-ə-ráytəss) *n.* Sodium or potassium bicarbonate used as a leavening agent; baking soda. [New Latin *sal aeratus,* "aerated salt".]

Sa·ler·no (sə-lér-nō, -láir-). Latin name **Sa·ler·num** (-nəm). Port in Campania, southwestern Italy, capital of Salerno province. Originally a Roman colony, the town came under Norman rule from 1076. During the Norman period a magnificent cathedral was founded, and Salerno won fame for its medical school around which one of Europe's earliest universities developed. Salerno was the site of major Allied landings (1943).

sale·room (sáyl-ro͞om, -ro͝om) *n.* A room in which articles to be auctioned are put on show. Also *U.S.* "salesroom".

sales·clerk (*U.S.* sáylz-klerk || -klark) *n. U.S.* A shop assistant.

Sa·le·si·an (sə-léez-i-ən, -léezh- || saa-) *n.* A member of the Society of St. Francis de Sales, a Roman Catholic order founded in Turin in 1845 and dedicated chiefly to education and missionary work. **—Sa·le·sian** *adj.*

sales·man (sáylz-mən) *n., pl.* **-men** (-mən, -men). A man employed to sell merchandise, either in a shop or direct to domestic or business customers in a designated area.

sales·man·ship (sáylz-mən-ship) *n.* **1.** The work or occupation of a salesman. **2.** Skill or ability in selling, as by persuasive speaking.

sales·per·son (sáylz-perss'n) *n.* A salesman or saleswoman.

sales resistance *n.* A lack of interest in or willingness to buy a product, on the part of a person or the public.

sales talk *n.* Argument or other persuasion intended to induce a person to purchase a product or service or accept an idea or suggestion. Also called "sales pitch".

sales tax *n.* A tax levied as a percentage of the retail price of goods and services.

sales·wom·an (sáylz-wo͝omən) *n., pl.* **-women** (-wimmin). A woman or girl employed to sell goods, especially in a department store. Also called "salesgirl", "saleslady".

Sal·ford (sáwl-fərd || sól-, sál-; *locally* sól-). City in Greater Manchester, northwestern England, on the river Irwell. A cotton town, it expanded from 1894 after the opening of the Manchester Ship Canal. Salford today is Manchester's docking centre, with industries which include textiles, chemicals, electrics, and engineering.

sali- *comb. form.* Indicates salt; for example, **salimeter.** [Latin *sāl* (stem *sali-*), salt.]

Sa·li·an (sáyli-ən) *n.* A member of a tribe of Franks, the Salii, who settled in the Rhine region of the Netherlands in the fourth century A.D. [Late Latin *Saliī*†, the Salian Franks.] **—Sa·li·an** *adj.*

sal·ic (sál-ik) *adj.* Pertaining to or designating minerals, such as quartz and the feldspars, containing large amounts of silica and alumina. [S(ILICA) + AL(UMINA) + -IC.]

Sal·ic (sál-ik || sáyl-) *adj.* Also **Sal·ique** (*also* sə-léek). **1.** Pertaining to the Salian Franks. **2.** Pertaining to the Salic law or to the legal code of the Salian Franks. [Old French *salique,* from Medieval Latin *Salicus,* from Late Latin *Saliī*†, the Salian Franks.]

sal·i·cin (sál-i-sin) *n.* A bitter glucoside, $C_{13}H_{18}O_7$, obtained mainly from the bark of poplar and willow trees and formerly used as an analgesic and antipyretic. [French *salicine* : Latin *salix* (stem *salic-*), willow + -IN.]

Salic law *n.* A law, thought to derive from the code of the Salic Franks, prohibiting a woman from succession to the throne and later used to exclude women from the thrones of France and Spain.

sal·i·cyl·ate (sə-líssi-layt, -lət, -lit) *n.* A salt or ester of salicylic acid. [SALICYL(IC ACID) + -ATE.]

sal·i·cyl·ic acid (sál-i-síllik) *n.* A white crystalline acid, $C_7H_6O_3$, used in making aspirin, as a preservative, and in the external treatment of certain skin conditions such as eczema. [French *salicyle,* the radical of salicylic acid : SALIC(IN) + -YL.]

sal·i·cyl·ism (sál-i-síl-iz'm, sə-líssil-) *n.* Poisoning caused by an overdose of aspirin or other drug containing salicylic acid, characterised by headache, dizziness, vomiting, collapse, and, in many cases, kidney failure. [SALICYL(IC ACID) + -ISM.]

sa·li·ence (sáyli-ənss) *n.* Also **sa·li·en·cy** (-ən-si). **1.** The quality or condition of being salient. **2.** A pronounced feature or part.

sa·li·ent (sáyli-ənt) *adj.* **1.** Projecting or jutting beyond a line or surface; protruding up or out: *a salient angle.* **2.** Striking; outstanding; conspicuous: *the salient point in her lecture.* **3.** *Zoology.* Springing; jumping: *salient tree toads.*
~*n.* **1.** The part of a battle line, trench, fortification, or other military defence that projects out towards the enemy. **2.** A salient angle or part. [Latin *saliēns* (stem *salient-*), present participle of *salīre,* to leap, jump.] **—sa·li·ent·ly** *adv.* **—sa·li·ent·ness** *n.*

sa·li·en·ti·an (sáyli-énshi-ən) *n.* A type of amphibian, an **anuran** *(see).* [New Latin *Salientia,* from Latin, neuter plural of *saliēns,* leaping, SALIENT.]

Sa·lie·ri (sal-yáir-i, sál-i-áir-i), **Antonio** (1750–1825). Italian composer. A teacher to Beethoven, Schubert, and Liszt, he became (1788) composer to the Imperial Court of Austria. He was more popular (but less talented) than his rival, Mozart, who accused him of trying to poison him. This allegation inspired Rimsky-Korsakov's opera *Mozart and Salieri* (1898) and Peter Shaffer's play *Amadeus* (1979).

sa·lif·er·ous (sa-líffərəss, sə-) *adj.* Containing or yielding salt. [SALI- + -FEROUS.]

sal·i·fy (sál-i-fī) *tr.v.* **-fied, -fying, -fies. 1.** To form or convert into a salt, as by chemical combination. **2.** To mix or impregnate with a salt. [French *salifier* : SALI- + -FY.] **—sal·i·fi·a·ble** *adj.* **—sal·i·fi·ca·tion** (-fi-káysh'n) *n.*

sa·lim·e·ter (sa-límmitər, sə-) *n. Chemistry.* A specially graduated hydrometer that indicates directly the percentage of a salt in a salt solution. [SALI- + -METER.] **—sal·i·met·ric** (sál-i-méttrik) *adj.* **—sal·im·e·try** (-límmətri) *n.*

sa·li·na (sə-līnə) *n.* A salt marsh, spring, pond, or lake. [Spanish, from Latin *salīnae,* salt pits, feminine plural of *salīnus,* SALINE.]

sa·line (sáy-līn, *rarely* sál-īn, sə-līn || *U.S. also* -leen) *adj.* **1.** Of, pertaining to, or containing salt; salty. **2.** Of or pertaining to mineral salts having the characteristics of common salt.
~*n.* **1.** Any salt of the alkali or alkaline-earth metals, used in medicine as a cathartic. **2.** A saline solution, especially one that is isotonic with blood and is used in medicine. In this sense, also called "physiological saline". [Middle English *salyne,* from Latin *salīnus,* from *sāl,* salt.] **—sa·lin·i·ty** (sə-línnəti, sa-) *n.*

Sal·in·ger (sál-in-jər), **J(erome) D(avid)** (1919–). U.S. author. He achieved recognition for his novel about adolescence, *The Catcher in the Rye* (1951). His other works concentrate mainly on the lives and times of the Jewish Glass family; these stories include *Raise High the Roofbeam* and *Seymour: an Introduction* (1963).

sal·i·nom·e·ter (sál-i-nómmitər) *n.* Any of various instruments, especially a salimeter, used to measure the amount of salt in a solution. [SALIN(E) + -METER.] **—sal·i·no·met·ric** (-nə-méttrik) *adj.* **—sal·i·nom·e·try** (-nómmətri) *n.*

Salique. Variant of **Salic.**
Salis·bur·y[1] (sáwlz-bri, -bəri || sólz-, -berri). Also **New Sarum** (sáir-əm). City in Wiltshire, southeast England, situated at the confluence of the rivers Avon and Wylye. Old Sarum nearby is the site of an Iron Age fort whose earthworks survive. Salisbury cathedral (1220–58) is a magnificent example of Early English architecture, with the tallest spire in England (123 metres; 404 feet). The town, a market centre, attracts many tourists, and has some light industry. It is the Melchester of the Wessex novels of Thomas Hardy.
Salisbury[2]. See **Harare.**
Salisbury, Robert Arthur Talbot Gascoyne-Cecil, 3rd Marquess of (1830–1903). British politician. Before becoming a peer he was a Conservative M.P. (1853–1868). His isolationist diplomacy favouring non-alignment dominated British foreign policy from 1878 until his death. He served three terms as prime minister: 1885–86, 1886–92, and 1895–1902.
Salisbury Plain. Chalk plateau in Wiltshire, situated to the north of Salisbury in southern England. The area is rich in prehistoric remains which include the megalithic monument of Stonehenge.
Sa·lish (sáy-lish) *n.* **1.** A family of languages spoken by North American Indian tribes, including the Flathead, in the northwestern United States and British Columbia. **2.** *Used with a plural verb.* The Indians speaking languages of this family. **—Sa·lish·an** (-'n, sál-ish'n) *adj.*
sa·li·va (sə-lívə) *n.* The watery, tasteless liquid mixture of salivary and oral mucous gland secretions that lubricates chewed food, moistens the oral walls, and contains the enzyme ptyalin, which functions in the predigestion of starches. [Latin *salīva*†.] **—sal·i·var·y** (sál-i-vəri, sə-lí- || -verri) *adj.*
salivary gland *n.* A gland that secretes saliva; especially, any of three pairs of large glands, the parotid, submandibular, and sublingual, the secretions of which enter the mouth and mingle in saliva.
sal·i·vate (sál-i-vayt) *v.* **-vated, -vating, -vates.** *—intr.* To secrete or produce saliva. *—tr.* To produce an excessive salivation in (a person or animal). [Latin *salīvāre,* to spit out, from *salīva,* SALIVA.]
sal·i·va·tion (sál-i-váysh'n) *n.* **1.** The act or process of secreting saliva. **2.** An abnormally abundant flow of saliva.
Salk vaccine (sawlk) *n.* A vaccine made from a deactivated (or killed) virus, formerly used to immunise actively against poliomyelitis. [After by Jonas *Salk* (born 1914), U.S. microbiologist.]
sal·lee, sal·ly (sál-i) *n. Australian.* Any of various species of acacia or eucalyptus. [From a native Australian language.]
sal·let (sál-it) *n.* A light medieval helmet, sometimes fitted with a visor and with a piece at the back to protect the neck. [Middle English *sal(l)et,* from Old French *salade,* from Old Italian *celata,* perhaps from Vulgar Latin *caelāta* (unattested), from Latin, feminine past participle of *caelāre,* to engrave (as on the metal of a helmet), from *caelum,* chisel.]
sal·low[1] (sál-ō) *adj.* **-lower, -lowest.** Of a pale, sickly yellowish hue or complexion.
~tr.v. **sallowed, -lowing, -lows.** To make sallow. [Middle English *salowe,* Old English *salo,* dusky, from Germanic.] **—sal·low·ish** *adj.* **—sal·low·ness** *n.*
sal·low[2] *n.* Any of several of the broader-leaved European willows, especially the three common species *Salix caprea, S. cinerea,* and *S. aurita.* [Middle English *salwe,* Old English *sealh,* from Germanic.]
Sal·lust (sál-əst). Latin name Gaius Sallustius Crispus (*c.* 86–*c.* 34 B.C.). Roman politician and historian. He became governor of Numidia, but resigned after being implicated in corruption. He then turned to historical writing, producing his well-known accounts of the Catilinarian conspiracy and the Jugurthine war.
sal·ly[1] (sál-i) *intr.v.* **-lied, -lying, -lies. 1.** To rush or leap forth suddenly; especially, to issue suddenly from a defensive or besieged position to make an attack upon an enemy. **2.** To set out on a trip or excursion. Often used with *forth.*
~n., pl. **sallies. 1.** A sudden rush forward; a leap. **2.** An assault from a defensive position; a sortie. **3.** A sudden emergence, as from rest to action or from silence to comment; an outburst. **4.** A quick witticism or bantering remark; a quip. **5.** A venturing forth; an excursion; a jaunt. —See Synonyms at **joke.** [Old French *saillie,* a sally, from the feminine past participle of *salir, saillir,* to leap or rush forward, from Latin *salīre,* to leap.]
sally[2] *n.* The woollen covering of the end of a bellrope. [Perhaps from SALLY; referring to the sudden movement of the bell.]
sally[3]. Variant of **sallee.**
Sal·ly Army (sál-i) *n. Informal.* The **Salvation Army** *(see).*
Sally Lunn (lun) *n.* A round, light tea cake, similar to a muffin. [Perhaps from the name of a girl who sold them in Bath about 1800.]
sal·ma·gun·di (sál-mə-gúndi) *n.* **1.** A salad of chopped meat, anchovies, eggs, and onions, often arranged in rows on lettuce, and served with vinegar and oil. **2.** Any mixture or assortment; a potpourri. [French *salmigondis, salmigondin*†.]
sal·mi, sal·mis (sál-mi, sal-mée) *n.* A highly spiced dish consisting of a roasted game bird, minced and stewed in wine. [French *salmis,* short for *salmigondis,* SALMAGUNDI.]
salm·on (sámmən || *Scottish also* sáamən) *n., pl.* **-mons** or collectively **salmon. 1.** Any of various large food and game fishes of the genera *Salmo* and *Oncorhynchus,* of northern waters, characteristically swimming from salt to fresh water to spawn, and having a delicate pinkish flesh. **2.** *Australian.* Any of various similar unrelated fishes, such as the barramundi. **3.** Salmon pink. [Middle English *samoun, salmon,* from Anglo-French, Old French *saumon,* from Latin *salmo* (stem *salmon-*), probably akin to *salīre,* to leap.] **—salm·on** *adj.*
sal·mo·nel·la (sál-mə-néllə) *n., pl.* **salmonella** or **-nellas** or **-nellae** (-néllee). **1.** Any of various rod-shaped bacteria of the genus *Salmonella,* many of which are pathogenic. **2.** Salmonellosis. In this sense, not in technical usage. [New Latin, after Daniel E. *Salmon* (1850–1914), U.S. veterinary surgeon.]
sal·mo·nel·lo·sis (sál-mə-nel-ṓ-siss) *n.* Food poisoning caused by salmonella. [SALMONELL(A) + -osis.]
sal·mo·noid (sámmən-oyd) *adj.* **1.** Resembling or characteristic of a salmon. **2.** Of or belonging to the family Salmonidae, which includes the salmon, trout, and whitefishes. **—sal·mo·noid** *n.*
salmon pink *n.* Yellowish pink. **—salmon-pink** *adj.*
salmon trout *n.* Any of various salmon-like fish, especially the sea trout.
Sa·lò, Republic of (sə-lṓ, sa-). Puppet regime in northern Italy (1943–45), set up by Mussolini after Italy's surrender in World War II. The regime was named after the town of Salò, on Lake Garda, and ended with the German withdrawal and Mussolini's death at the hands of Italian partisans.
sal·ol (sál-ol || -ōl) *n.* A white crystalline powder, $C_{13}H_{10}O_3$, derived from salicylic acid, and used in the manufacture of plastics and sun-tan oils and medicinally as an analgesic and antipyretic. [Originally a trademark : SAL(ICYLIC ACID) + -OL.]
Sa·lo·me (sə-lṓmi). Daughter of Herodias and niece of Herod Antipas, who granted her the head of John the Baptist in return for her dancing. Matthew 14:6-11.
sa·lon (sál-ON, -on || *U.S.* sə-lón; *French* sa-lóN) *n.* **1.** A drawing room or other large room or hall for receiving and entertaining guests, especially one in a French mansion. **2.** A reception held in such a room for a group of people, especially of social, artistic, or intellectual distinction, as in France in the 18th century. **3.** A hall or gallery for the exhibition of works of art. **4.** *Often capital* **S.** Any of various exhibitions of works by living artists held annually in France. **5.** A commercial establishment offering some product or service related to fashion or beauty. [French, from Italian *salone,* augmentative of *sala,* a hall, room, from Germanic.]
Salonika. See **Thessaloniki.**
sa·loon (sə-lóon) *n.* **1.** A large room or hall for receptions, public entertainment, or exhibitions, or for a particular use, such as dancing. **2.** A large, comfortable social lounge for passengers on a ship. **3.** An enclosed car having two or four doors and front and rear seats. Also *U.S.* "sedan". **4. a.** *British.* A saloon bar. **b.** *U.S.* Any place where alcoholic drinks are sold and drunk. [French *salon,* SALON.]
saloon bar *n. British.* A bar in a public house or hotel that is usually more luxuriously furnished and where drinks are more expensive than in the public bar. Also called "lounge bar", "saloon".
sa·loop (sə-lóop) *n.* A hot drink, formerly used medicinally, made from salep, sassafras, or similar aromatic herbs. [Variant of SALEP.]
Salop. See **Shropshire.**
salp (salp) *n.* Any of various free-swimming primitive chordates of the genus *Salpa,* of warm seas, having a translucent, somewhat flattened, keglike body. Also called "salpa". [New Latin *salpa,* from Latin, a kind of stockfish, from Greek *salpē*†.] **—sal·pi·form** (sál-pi-fawrm) *adj.*
sal·pi·glos·sis (sál-pi-glóssiss) *n.* Any of various plants of the Chilean genus *Salpiglossis,* especially those grown as garden ornamentals for their showy tubular flowers. [New Latin, "trumpet-tongue", irregularly from Greek *salpinx* (stem *salping-*), trumpet + *glōssa,* tongue.]
sal·pin·gec·to·my (sál-pin-jéktəmi) *n., pl.* **-mies.** The surgical removal of a Fallopian tube. [New Latin *salpinx* (stem *salping-*), SALPINX + -ECTOMY.]
sal·pin·gi·tis (sál-pin-jítiss) *n. Pathology.* Inflammation of a Fallopian or Eustachian tube. [New Latin : *salpinx* (stem *salping-*), SALPINX + -ITIS.]
sal·pinx (sál-pingks) *n., pl.* **salpinges** (sal-pín-jeez). **1.** The Fallopian tube. **2.** The Eustachian tube. [New Latin, from Greek *salpinx*†, trumpet.] **—sal·pin·gi·an** (sal-pínji-ən) *adj.*
sal·sa (sál-sə) *n.* **1.** A type of music of Latin-American origin, combining elements of rock and jazz. **2.** A dance performed to this music. [Spanish, SAUCE (alluding to the blending of styles).]
sal·si·fy (sál-si-fi, sáwl- || sól-, *U.S. also* -fī) *n.* **1.** A plant, *Tragopogon porrifolius,* native to Europe, having grasslike leaves, purple flowers, and an edible taproot. **2.** The oyster-flavoured root of this plant, eaten as a vegetable. Also called "vegetable oyster", "oyster plant". [French *salsifis,* from (obsolete) Italian *salsifica*†.]
sal soda *n.* A cleansing agent, **washing soda** *(see).*
salt (sawlt || solt) *n.* **1.** A colourless or white crystalline solid, chiefly **sodium chloride** *(see),* used as a food seasoning and preservative. **2.** A chemical compound formed by replacing all or part of the hydrogen atoms of an acid with one or more metal ions or other positive ions from a base. **3.** *Often plural.* Any of various mineral salts used medicinally, such as **Epsom salts** or **Glauber's salts** *(both of which see).* **4.** *Plural.* **Smelling salts** *(see).* **5.** An element that gives flavour, piquancy, or zest. **6.** Sharp, lively wit; pungency of expression. **7.** *Informal.* A sailor, especially when old or experienced. **8.** A saltcellar. **—rub salt in the wound.** To make a painful situation worse, as by a further act of humiliation or mockery. **—salt of the earth.** A person or group regarded as worthy and admirable. [Matthew 5:13.] **—take with a grain** or **pinch of salt.** To treat with sceptical reserve. **—worth (one's) salt.** Of some merit or

salmon *Salmo salar (above) is the Atlantic salmon; several other species are native to the Pacific. Salmon spend most of their lives at sea, but they return to rivers to spawn. Pacific salmon die after spawning; the Atlantic salmon, however, often returns to the sea and spawns again in a year or two.*

salsify *The long, white, fleshy root of this vegetable plant has an oyster-like flavour.*

competence: *Any plumber worth his salt could do it.* [From the former custom of paying for some jobs in salt rather than money.]
~*adj.* **1.** Tasting of, containing, or filled with salt; salty. **2.** Preserved in salt or a salt solution. **3. a.** Flooded with sea water. **b.** Found in or near such a flooded area: *salt grasses.* **4.** Sharp or pungent.
~*tr.v.* **salted, salting, salts. 1. a.** To add salt to; season with salt. **b.** To sprinkle salt on (snow) to melt it. **2.** To cure or preserve by treating with salt or a salt solution. **3.** *Informal.* To stock up or store away (money, for example); hoard. Often used with *away* or *down.* **4.** *U.S.* To provide salt for (livestock). **5.** To add zest or liveliness to; season: *salt a lecture with anecdotes.* **6.** To give an appearance of value to by fraudulent means; especially, to place valuable minerals in (a mine, for example) for the purpose of deceiving. **—salt out.** To separate (a dissolved substance) by adding a salt to the solution so as to increase the number of ions. [Middle English *salt,* Old English *sealt.*] **—salt•ish** *adj.* **—salt•ness** *n.*

SALT (sawlt || solt) *n.* Strategic Arms Limitation Talks.

salt-and-pepper *n.* See **pepper-and-salt.**

sal•tant (sál-tənt, sáwl- || sól-) *adj. Biology.* Differing from other organisms of the same species because of saltation. [Latin *saltāns* (stem *saltant-*), present participle of *saltāre,* to leap, frequentative of *salīre* (past participle *saltus*), to jump.]

sal•ta•rel•lo (sál-tə-réllō) *n., pl.* **-relli** (-réllee). **1.** A lively Italian dance with a skipping step at the beginning of each measure. **2.** Music for this dance, generally in triple or sextuple time. [Italian, from *saltare,* to leap, from Latin *saltāre.* See **saltant.**]

sal•ta•tion (sal-táysh'n, sawl- || sol-) *n.* **1.** The act of leaping, jumping, or dancing. **2.** An abrupt, discontinuous movement, transition, or development. **3.** *Biology.* Abrupt variation within a species, usually caused by mutation. [Latin *saltātiō* (stem *saltātiōn-*), from *saltātus,* past participle of *saltāre,* to leap. See **saltant.**]

sal•ta•to•ri•al (sál-tə-táwri-əl, sáwl- || sól-, -tōri-) *adj.* **1.** Of or relating to leaping or dancing. **2.** *Zoology.* Adapted for or characterised by leaping.

sal•ta•to•ry (sál-tə-tri, sáwl-, -təri; sal-táytəri, sawl- || sól-) *adj.* **1.** Of, pertaining to, or adapted for leaping or dancing. **2.** Proceeding by leaps, hops, or abrupt movements. [Latin *saltātōrius,* from *saltātus,* past participle of *saltāre,* to leap. See **saltant.**]

salt cake *n.* Impure sodium sulphate, used in making paper pulp, soaps and detergents, glass, ceramic glazes, and dyes.

salt•cel•lar (sáwlt-sellər || sólt-) *n.* **1.** A small container or shaker for holding and dispensing salt. **2.** *Informal.* Either of the two hollows above the collarbones, especially noticeable in very thin people. [Variant (influenced by CELLAR) of Middle English *salt saler* : SALT + *saler,* saltcellar, from Old French *saliere,* from Latin *salārius,* of salt, from *sāl,* salt.]

salt dome *n. Geology.* A dome-shaped formation in stratified rock with a core of salt. Oil and gas are often found in association with salt domes. Also called "salt plug".

salt•ed weapon (sáwltid || sóltid) *n.* A type of nuclear weapon designed to capture neutrons on exploding, so as to produce higher levels of radiation.

salt•er (sáwltər || sóltər) *n.* **1.** A person who manufactures or sells salt. **2.** A person who treats meat, fish, or other foods with salt.

salt•ern (sáwl-tərn || sól-) *n.* **1.** A building or place of salt manufacture; a saltworks. **2.** A series of salt-water pools producing salt by natural evaporation. [Ultimately from Old English *sealtærn, sealtern* : *sealt,* SALT + *ærn, ern,* house.]

salt flat *n.* A wide, flat, stretch of country that has very salty soil, owing to the former presence of water.

salt glaze *n.* A glaze given to stoneware by burning salt in the kiln when the ware is fired. **—salt-glaze** (sáwlt-glayz || sólt-) *tr.v.*

salt grass *n.* Any of various grasses, such as those of the genus *Distichlis,* that grow in salt marshes and alkaline regions.

sal•ti•grade (sál-ti-grayd, sáwl- || sól-) *adj.* Adapted for or proceeding by leaping. Said of certain insects and spiders. [New Latin *Saltigradae,* former designation for saltigrade spiders : Latin *saltus,* a leap, from the past participle of *salīre,* to leap + *gradī,* to step.]

sal•tim•boc•ca (sál-tim-bóckə) *n.* An Italian dish consisting of thin slices of veal, each rolled round a slice of ham and a sage leaf and cooked in Marsala or white wine.

sal•tire (sáwl-tīr, sál- || sól-) *n. Heraldry.* An ordinary in the shape of a St. Andrew's cross, formed by the crossing of a bend and a bend sinister. [Middle English *sawturoure, sawtire,* from Old French *sau(l)toir,* originally a cross-shaped stile to keep cattle from straying, but which people could jump over, from *sau(l)ter,* to jump, from Latin *saltāre.* See **saltant.**]

Salt Lake City. Capital of Utah in the central western United States, situated near the Great Salt Lake. Founded by a party of Mormons led by Brigham Young, it is today the headquarters of the Mormon Church.

salt lick *n.* **1.** A natural deposit of exposed salt that animals lick. **2.** A block of salt or an artificial medicated saline preparation set out for cattle, sheep, or deer to lick.

salt marsh *n.* Low coastal grassland frequently inundated by the tide. Also called "salt meadow", "marsh".

Salto Angel. See **Angel Fall.**

salt pan *n.* **1.** A depression in the ground from which sea water evaporates to leave a salt deposit. **2.** A shallow vessel used for the same process.

salt•pe•tre, *U.S.* **salt•pe•ter** (sáwlt-péetər, -peetər || sólt-) *n.* **1. Potassium nitrate** *(see).* **2. Sodium nitrate** *(see).* [Variant of earlier *salpetre,* from Middle English, from Old French, from Medieval Latin *salpetra,* probably "salt rock" (so called because it appears as a saltlike crust on rocks) : Latin *sāl,* salt + *petra,* rock, from Greek.]

sal•tus (sál-təss) *n., pl.* **-tuses.** A sudden break in a sequence, as in the logical steps in an argument. [Latin, leap.]

salt•water (sáwlt-wawtər || sólt-, *U.S. also* -wottər) *adj.* Pertaining to, consisting of, or inhabiting salt water.

salt•works (sáwlt-wurks || sólt-) *n. Used with a singular or plural verb.* A place or building where salt is manufactured commercially.

salt•wort (sáwlt-wurt || sólt-, -wawrt) *n.* **1.** Any of several plants of the genus *Salsola;* especially, *S. kali,* native to the Old World, having stiff, prickly leaves, and growing on sandy seashores. Also called "glasswort". **2.** A plant, the **sea milkwort** *(see).*

salt•y (sáwlti || sólti) *adj.* **-ier, -iest. 1.** Pertaining to, containing, or tasting of salt. **2.** Suggesting of the sea or sailing life. **3. a.** Piquant; witty **b.** Racy; risqué. **—salt•i•ly** *adv.* **—salt•i•ness** *n.*

sa•lu•bri•ous (sə-lōō-bri-əss, -lēw-) *adj.* Conducive or favourable to health or well-being; wholesome: *a salubrious climate.* [Latin *salūbris,* from *salūs,* health.] **—sa•lu•bri•ous•ly** *adv.* **—sa•lu•bri•ous•ness, sa•lu•bri•ty** (-brəti) *n.*

sa•lu•ki (sə-lōō-ki, -lēw-) *n., pl.* **-kis.** *Often capital* **S.** A tall, slender dog of an ancient breed developed in Arabia and Egypt, having a smooth, silky, variously coloured coat. [Arabic *salūqīy,* (dog) of *Salūq,* ancient southern Arabian city.]

sal•u•tar•y (sál-yoo-tri, -təri || -terri) *adj.* **1.** Effecting or intended to effect an improvement; beneficially corrective: *salutary advice.* **2.** Favourable or conducive to health or recovery; wholesome or curative. [Middle English, Old French *salutaire,* from Latin *salūtāris,* of health, from *salūs* (stem *salūt-*), health.] **—sal•u•tar•i•ly** *adv.* **—sal•u•tar•i•ness** *n.*

sal•u•ta•tion (sál-yoo-táysh'n) *n.* **1. a.** A polite expression of greeting or good will. **b.** A gesture of greeting, such as a bow or kiss. **2.** Words of greeting, such as *Dear Sir* in a letter or *Ladies and Gentlemen* in a speech. [Middle English *salutacioun,* from Latin *salūtātiō* (stem *salūtātiōn-*), from *salūtātus,* past participle of *salūtāre,* to SALUTE.] **—sa•lu•ta•to•ry** (-táytəri, sə-lōōt-ə-tri) *adj.*

sa•lute (sə-lōōt, -lēwt) *v.* **-luted, -luting, -lutes.** *—tr.* **1.** To greet or address with an expression of welcome, goodwill, or respect. **2. a.** To recognise (a military superior) with a gesture prescribed by regulations, as by raising the hand to the cap. **b.** To honour formally and ceremoniously. **3.** To express appreciative acknowledgment of; commend. *—intr.* To perform a salute.
~*n.* **1.** An act, gesture, or expression of welcome, honour, respect, or courteous recognition: *They stood in silence as a salute to his courage.* **2. a.** An act of respect towards a military superior, normally performed by raising the outstretched hand, palm forwards, to the cap. **b.** A similar act made by a superior officer to return another's salute. **c.** Any formal military display of honour or greeting, as firing cannon or presenting arms. [Middle English *saluten,* from Latin *salūtāre,* to preserve, salute, wish health to, from *salūs* (stem *salūt-*), health, safety.] **—sa•lut•er** *n.*

sal•va•ble (sál-vəb'l) *adj.* **1.** Capable of being saved. **2.** Able to be salvaged. [Late Latin *salvāre,* to save, SALVAGE.]

Sal•va•dor (sál-və-dawr, *Brazilian Portuguese* sów-). Formerly **São Salvador** or **Bahia.** Seaport and capital of Bahia State, northeastern Brazil. It is also a major industrial centre. Founded by the Portuguese in 1549, it was the capital of Portuguese America until this was transferred to Rio de Janeiro (1763).

Sal•va•do•ri•an (sál-və-dáwri-ən || -dōri-) *n.* Also **Sal•va•do•ran** (-dáwr- || -dōr-). A native or inhabitant of Salvador or El Salvador. **—Sal•va•do•ri•an** *adj.*

sal•vage (sál-vij) *tr.v.* **-vaged, -vaging, -vages. 1.** To save (a ship or its cargo, for example) from loss or destruction. **2.** To save (discarded or damaged material) for further use. **3.** To save as if from disaster or loss: *salvage the project.* **4.** To retrieve (something liable to be included in a loss or disaster): *Most of the orders were cancelled but we salvaged a few.*
~*n.* **1. a.** The rescue of a ship or its crew or cargo from fire, shipwreck, or the like. **b.** That which has been thus rescued. **2.** Compensation given to those who voluntarily aid in such a rescue. **3. a.** The act of saving anything in danger. **b.** That which is saved. [French, the act of saving, from Old French, from *salver,* to save, from Late Latin *salvāre,* from Latin *salvus,* unharmed, safe.] **—sal•vage•a•ble** *adj.* **—sal•vag•er** *n.*

Sal•var•san (sál-vər-s'n, -san) *n.* A trademark for an arsenic compound, **arsphenamine** *(see),* used to treat syphilis.

sal•va•tion (sal-váysh'n) *n.* **1.** Preservation or deliverance from evil or difficulty. **2.** A source, means, or cause of such deliverance or preservation. **3.** The deliverance, through Christ, of man or his soul from the power of sin and consequent penalties; redemption. [Middle English, from Old French, from Late Latin *salvātiō* (stem *salvātiōn-*), from *salvāre,* to save, to SALVAGE.] **—sal•va•tion•al** *adj.*

Salvation Army *n. Abbr.* **S.A.** An international evangelical and charitable organisation founded (1865) by William Booth and organised on military lines.

sal•va•tion•ist (sal-váysh'n-ist) *n.* **1.** *Usually capital* **S.** A member of the Salvation Army. **2.** An evangelist, especially one emphasising salvation. **—sal•va•tion•ism** *n.*

salve¹ (salv, saav || *U.S. also* sav) *n.* **1.** An analgesic or medicinal ointment. **2.** Anything that soothes or heals; a balm: *Bach was her salve for depression.*
~*tr.v.* **salved, salving, salves. 1.** To soothe as if with salve; quiet;

PRONUNCIATION KEY

a, trap; aa, father; ai, fair; ar, star; aw, lawn; ay, play; b, bb, stab; rubber; ch, church; ck, ticket; d, dd, dead; ladder; e, dress; ee, bee; er, defer; ew, few; ewr, pure; ə, about; ər, letter; f, ff, fife; differ; g, gg, giggle; h, hat; i, kit; ī, price; īr, fire; j, judge; k, kick; l, ll, let; 'l, needle; m, mm, man; n, nn, no; 'n, sudden; ng, thing; o, lot; ō, no; ŏŏ, foot; ōō, shoe; oor, poor; ow, cow; owr, hour; oy, boy; p, pp, pepper; r, rr, red; s, ss, sauce; sh, ship; t, tt, totter; th, thick; th, this; smooth; u, cut; ur, turn; v, vv, valve; w, wet; y, yes; z, zz, zebra; zh, vision; pleasure

IN FOREIGN WORDS:

aN, oN, Saint-Saëns; hl, Llanelli; Hluhluwe; kh, loch; lough; Khaled

STRESS MARK:

ín-sīt, insight; in-sīt, incite

appease. **2.** To dress (a wound or sore) with salve. [Middle English *salf, salve,* Old English *salf, sealf,* from Germanic.]

salve² (salv) *tr.v.* **salved, salving, salves.** To save (a ship, for example) from danger, loss, or destruction. [Back-formation from SALVAGE.]

sal·ver (sál-vər) *n.* A tray or platter, usually made of or plated with silver or gold, and used to present food or visiting cards, for example. [French *salve* (influenced by *platter*), a tray for presenting food (to the king), from Spanish *salva,* originally "foretasting of food to detect poison", from *salvar,* to foretaste food or drink, "to save", from Late Latin *salvāre,* to save, to SALVAGE.]

sal·vi·a (sál-vi-ə) *n.* Any of various plants and shrubs of the genus *Salvia;* especially, *S. splendens,* native to South America and widely cultivated for its showy scarlet flowers. [New Latin, from Latin, "the healing plant", SAGE.]

sal·vo¹ (sál-vō) *n., pl.* **-vos** or **-voes. 1.** A simultaneous discharge of firearms. **2. a.** The simultaneous release of a rack of bombs or rockets, as from an aircraft. **b.** The projectiles thus released. **3.** A sudden outburst of cheers, applause, or the like. [Earlier *salve, salva,* from Italian *salva,* salute, volley, from Latin *salvē,* hail, imperative of *salvēre,* to be in good health, from *salvus,* safe, well.]

salvo² *n., pl.* **-vos. 1.** A reservation or saving clause, as in a document; a proviso. **2.** An excuse, evasion, or other means of saving face or allaying a guilty conscience. Sometimes used derogatorily. [(Medieval) Latin, ablative of *salvus,* SAFE, in such phrases as *salvō iure,* with (someone's) right kept safe.]

sal vol·a·ti·le (və-láttəli, võ-) *n.* **1.** A preparation used for smelling salts, consisting of ammonium carbonate and aromatic oils dissolved in alcohol and aqueous ammonia. Also called "spirits of ammonia". **2. Ammonium carbonate** *(see).* [New Latin, volatile salt.]

sal·vor (sál-vər) *n.* A person or ship involved in salvaging a ship or cargo at sea. [From SALVE (to salvage).]

Salz·burg (sálts-burg, saálts-; *German* zálts-boork). Capital of Salzburg state, Austria, situated on the river Salzach near the West German border. It is one of Austria's main tourist centres, and its many historic buildings include the 11th-century fortress of Hohensalzburg and a fine 17th-century cathedral. Mozart was born in the city, and a Salzburg Festival of music is held annually. Salzburg University (1623) was refounded in 1963. Originally a Celtic settlement and then a Roman trading post, Salzburg developed in the eighth century around a Benedictine monastery. For nearly a thousand years from *c.* 800, it was governed by its autocratic archbishops, princes of the Holy Roman Empire from 1278.

SAM (sam) *n.* A surface-to-air missile.

Sam. Samuel (Old Testament).

sam·a·ra (sə-maárə ‖ -márrə, sámmərə) *n. Botany.* A winged, one-seeded fruit that does not split open, such as that of the ash or sycamore. Also called "key fruit". [New Latin, from Latin *samara†,* seed of the elm.]

Samara. See **Kuybyshev.**

Sa·ma·ri·a¹ (sə-maír-i-ə). Region of the Middle East, now in Israel and Jordan. In ancient times it was the centre of Palestine, between Galilee in the north and Judah in the south.

Samaria² Modern **Sabastiya.** Hill city in ancient Palestine, now a village in Jordan (occupied by the Israelis in 1967). It was built by King Omri as the capital of the Northern Kingdom (Israel) in the early ninth century B.C., but later fell to Sargon of Assyria (721 B.C.). Its people were deported to Babylon, and foreign settlers, many from Syria and Mesopotamia, were brought in. Most of these non-Jewish settlers adopted Judaism, but recognised only the Pentateuch, causing hostility with the Jews. Samaria was destroyed by John Hyrcanus (one of the Macabees) in 120 B.C. and restored by Herod the Great as **Sebaste.** It has Roman remains, and excavations in the 20th century have revealed remnants of Omri's palace.

Sa·mar·i·tan (sə-márrit'n) *n.* **1. a.** A native or inhabitant of ancient Samaria. **b.** A member of a people descended from the ancient non-Jewish inhabitants of Samaria, now inhabiting the area around Tel Aviv in Israel and in Jordan. **c.** The Semitic language of this people, a variety of Aramaic. **2.** A member of an organisation, *the Samaritans,* for helping those in a state of emotional distress and suicidal despair. **3.** A **Good Samaritan** *(see).* —**Sa·mar·i·tan** *adj.*

sa·mar·i·um (sə-maír-i-əm) *n.* Symbol **Sm** A silvery or pale-grey metallic rare-earth element found in monazite and bastnaesite and used as a dopant for laser materials, in infrared absorbing glass, and as a neutron absorber in certain nuclear reactors. Atomic number 62, atomic weight 150.35, melting point 1,072°C, boiling point 1,900°C, relative density (approximately) 7.50, valencies 2, 3. [New Latin : SAMAR(SKITE) + -IUM.]

Sam·ar·kand or **Sam·ar·qand** (sám-aar-kánd, -ər-). City in the Uzbek S.S.R., southern central U.S.S.R. A key station on the ancient Silk Road, it was taken by the Arabs (A.D. 712) and became a great centre of Islamic culture. Pillaged by Genghis Khan (1220), it became prominent again from 1365 as the royal city of the Mongol ruler, Timur. The Russians conquered the city in 1868.

Sa·mar·ra (sə-maárə). City in central Iraq, situated on the river Tigris. From 836 to 892 it replaced Baghdad as the capital of the Abbasid caliphs, and it is today an important centre of pilgrimage for Shiite Muslims.

sa·mar·skite (sə-maár-skīt) *n.* A black mineral oxide with red-brown streaks that is a source of several rare-earth elements. [After Colonel von *Samarski,* 19th-century Russian mine official.]

sam·ba (sámbə ‖ *U.S. also* saámbə) *n.* **1.** A dance, originating in Africa, that was modified in Brazil as a ballroom dance. **2.** Music in 4/4 time for dancing the samba. [Portuguese, of African origin.] —**sam·ba** *intr.v.*

sam·bal (sám-bal, -bəl) *n.* A sharp, spicy, and vinegary sauce or chutney of raw vegetables or fruit, used as a relish or in cookery. [Malay, condiment.]

sam·bar (saám-bər, sám-, -baar) *n.* Also **sam·bur** (-bər). A large deer, *Cervus (or Rusa) unicolor,* of southeastern Asia, having a reddish-brown coat and three-pronged antlers. [Hindi *sābar, sāmbar,* from Sanskrit *śambara†.*]

Sam Browne belt (sám brówn) *n.* A belt worn as part of a military officer's uniform, supported by a shoulder strap that runs diagonally across the chest. [Modelled after the sword belt invented by Sir *Samuel James Browne* (1824–1901), British general who having lost his left arm could not support his sword with his left hand.]

same (saym) *adj.* **1.** Being the very one; not different; identical: *went to the same school.* **2.** Exhibiting close similarity with another; being alike in every or almost every respect: *We were both wearing the same dress.* **3.** Conforming absolutely; unaltered; unchanged. Often used with *as: playing according to the same rules as before.* **4.** Being the one previously mentioned or indicated; aforesaid: *This same man turned out to be my old school friend.* ~*pron.* **1.** The person, thing, or event identical with or similar to another: *Let's do the same as we did last week.* **2.** The person or thing previously mentioned or described. See Usage note. —**all the same. 1.** Nevertheless. **2.** Of no importance; of little significance: *It's all the same to me what we do.* —**just the same.** Nevertheless. —**not the same without.** Less pleasant without the presence of: *It's just not the same without Faye and Sarah.* ~*adv.* In like manner; in the identical way: *He walks the same as his father.* [Middle English, from Old Norse *samr.*]

Synonyms: same, selfsame, identical, equal, equivalent.

Usage: The use of *same,* with or without the article, to replace another pronoun in the sense of "aforesaid thing or person" is most common in formal legal or commercial contexts *(We hope to receive same next week),* and even there it is increasingly less commonly used. It is usually considered inappropriate outside such contexts, unless used humorously. The elliptical omission of *the,* in such sentences as *He goes by train, same as I do,* is a feature of informal British English.

sa·mekh (saá-mek, -mekh) *n.* The 15th letter of the Hebrew alphabet. [Hebrew *sāmekh.*]

same·ness (sáym-nəss, -niss) *n.* **1.** The condition of being the same; identity. **2.** A lack of variety or change; monotony.

same·y (sáymi) *adj. Informal.* Monotonously alike. [SAME + -Y (adjective suffix)]

sam·foo, sam·fu (sám-fõo) *n.* A type of loose suit consisting of an jacket and trousers, worn by Chinese women, especially in Southeast Asia. [Cantonese *saam foo,* "shirt and trousers".]

Sa·mi·an (sáymi-ən) *adj.* Of or pertaining to the island of Samos or its inhabitants. ~*n.* A native or inhabitant of Samos.

Samian ware *n.* A type of pottery produced in southern Gaul in the first three centuries A.D., and commonly found in Roman sites in Britain. [From the type of earth, similar to that found in SAMOS.]

sam·iel (sám-yel) *n.* A wind, simoom *(see).* [Turkish *samyeli : sam,* poisonous + *yel,* wind.]

sam·i·sen (sámmi-sen) *n.* A Japanese musical instrument resembling a banjo, having a very long neck and three strings played with a plectrum. [Japanese, "three-stringed" : *sam,* three + *-mi,* taste, touch + *sen,* string, chord, from Chinese *sān, wèi, xiàn.*]

sam·ite (sám-īt, sáym-) *n.* A heavy silk fabric, often interwoven with gold or silver, worn in the Middle Ages. [Middle English *samit,* from Old French, from Medieval Latin *examitum,* from Medieval Greek *hexamiton,* from Greek *hexamitos,* of six threads : HEXA- (six) + *mitos,* thread of the warp.]

sam·iz·dat (sámmiz-dát) *n.* In the U.S.S.R., the printing and distributing of literature that has been officially banned by the government. [Russian, from *sam,* self + *izdatel'stvo,* publisher, from *izdat',* to publish (iz, out + *dat',* to give).]

Sam·nite (sám-nīt) *n.* **1.** In ancient Italy, a member of a people, related to the Sabines, who inhabited Samnium. **2.** The Oscan language spoken by this people. —**Sam·nite** *adj.*

Sam·ni·um (sám-ni-əm) *n.* An ancient region of southern central Italy that was eventually absorbed into the Roman commonwealth in the third century B.C., after a series of wars against Rome.

Sa·mo·a (sə-mṓə, saa-). Mainly volcanic archipelago in the South Pacific. Discovered by the Dutch in 1722, the tropical islands were disputed by the United States, Britain, and Germany in the 19th century, and there were rivalries among native chiefs. Finally a treaty of 1899 assigned the smaller eastern group of islands to the United States and the western group to Germany.

Samoa, American. Territory of the United States, comprising eight islands of the archipelago of **Samoa.** It has a land area of 197 square kilometres (76 square miles). Tutuila is the largest island, with the capital and port of Pago Pago.

Samoa, Western. Independent state, part of the archipelago of Samoa. It was controlled by Germany (1900–19) and then by New Zealand until 1962, when it became the first independent Polynesian state. It formally joined the Commonwealth in 1970 and in 1976 became a member of the United Nations. The largest island is Savaii. The second largest, Upolu, has about two-thirds of the population. Exports include copra, taro, and timber, and tourism is

sampler *A sampler by Hannah Taylor, made in 1774 in Newport, Rhode Island; it is now in the American Museum, Bath, England. Samplers were so called because they were used to display a variety, or "sample", of stitches.*

samurai *As the warrior caste of feudal Japan, the samurai were the only class permitted to bear arms. This armour was made for the Akita family of samurai overlords in about 1741.*

increasingly important. Area, 2 842 square kilometres (1,097 square miles). Population, 200,000. Capital, Apia, on Upolu. See map **Pacific Ocean.**

Sa·mo·an (sə-mṓ-ən, saa-) *adj.* Of or pertaining to Samoa, its Polynesian inhabitants, or their language.
~*n.* **1.** A native or inhabitant of Samoa. **2.** The Polynesian language of the Samoans.

Sa·mos (sáy-moss; *Greek* saá-). *Turkish* **Susam Adası.** Greek island in the Aegean Sea, lying close to mainland Turkey. In the seventh century B.C. it became an important Greek commercial centre, reaching its cultural zenith under the sixth-century tyrant, Polycrates. Pythagoras was born here. Held by Persia (522–479 B.C.), Athens, Sparta, Rome, Byzantium, and Genoa, Samos fell to the Ottoman Turks in 1475. It was restored to Greece in 1912. The island is fertile and produces citrus fruit, grapes, olives, and tobacco.

sa·mo·sa (sə-mṓ-sə) *n.* Also **sa·moo·sa, sa·mou·sa, sa·mu·sa** (sə-mo͞o-sə). A snack or savoury food of Indian origin, consisting of a triangular envelope of crisp pastry with a spicy meat or vegetable filling.

Sam·o·thrace (sám-ə-thrayss, -ō-). *Modern Greek* **Samothraki;** *Turkish* **Semadrek.** Mountainous Greek island in the northern Aegean Sea. It was a centre of worship in ancient times. The statue of *Winged Victory* (now in the Louvre, Paris) dating back to the fourth century B.C., was found here in 1863.

sam·o·var (sám-ə-vaar, -ō-, -vár) *n.* A metal urn originating in Russia, having a heating device inside to boil water for tea. [Russian, "self-boiler" : *samo-,* self + *varit',* to boil, cook, probably from Old Church Slavonic *variti.*]

Sam·o·yed (sám-oy-éd, -ə-yed; *for sense 3 also* sə-móy-ed) *n.* **1.** A member of a Ural-Altaic people inhabiting the tundra lands of the northeastern European U.S.S.R. and northwestern Siberia. **2.** A branch of the Uralic family of languages represented by four living languages spoken by the Samoyed tribes inhabiting this region. **3.** A dog of a breed originally developed by the Samoyed people, having a thick, long white coat. [Russian *samoed,* from Lapp *Sāme-Ǣdnàma,* "of Lapland".] **—sam·o·yed·ic** (sám-oy-éddik, -ə-yéddik) *adj.*

samp *n. U.S., Canadian, & South African.* **1.** Crushed maize kernels, a staple food among poor indigenous peoples. **2.** A boiled porridge made from samp. [Narraganset *nasaump,* "softened by water", samp, soup.]

sam·pan (sám-pan) *n.* Any of various flat-bottomed skiffs, usually propelled by oars, used on the waterways of the Orient. [Chinese, *sān bǎn,* "three board".]

sam·phire (sám-fīr) *n.* Any of several Old World plants of coastal areas; especially: **1.** *Crithmum maritimum,* having fleshy divided leaves and small yellow flowers. Also called "rock samphire". **2.** *Inula crithmoides,* having linear fleshy leaves and yellow daisy-like flowers. Also called "golden samphire". **3.** The marsh samphire or **glasswort** *(see).* [Variant (perhaps influenced by earlier *camphire,* camphor) of earlier *sampere,* from Old French *(herbe de) Saint Pierre,* "Saint Peter's herb".]

sam·ple (saámp'l || sámp'l) *n.* **1.** A portion, piece, entity, or segment regarded as representative of a whole or of a group; a specimen. Also used adjectivally: *a sample copy; a sample question.* **2.** *Statistics.* A set of elements drawn from and analysed to estimate the characteristics of a population. In this sense also called "sampling". —See Synonyms at **example.**
~*tr.v.* **sampled, -pling, -ples.** To take a sample of; especially, to evaluate or examine by a sample. [Middle English, short for Old French *essample,* EXAMPLE.]

sam·pler (saám-plər || sám-) *n.* **1.** One that takes, appraises, or analyses a sample, such as a machine for testing food products. **2.** A piece of cloth embroidered with various designs or mottoes so as to show the skill of the sewer.

sam·pling (saám-pling || sám-) *n.* **1.** *Statistics.* A sample. **2.** The process of selecting a sample.

sam·sa·ra (səm-saárə) *n.* **1.** In Hinduism, the eternal cycle of birth, suffering, death, and rebirth. **2.** In Buddhism, the world and existence as experienced by unenlightened beings, characterised by insubstantiality, impermanence, and the endless round of birth, old age, disease, and death. [Sanskrit *saṁsāra,* "a passing through" : *sam,* together, completely + *sarati,* it runs, it flows.]

Sam·son¹ (sám-s'n, sámps'n). An Israelite judge of extraordinary strength, betrayed to the Philistines by Delilah. Judges 14–16. [Hebrew *Shimshōn,* "like the sun", from *shemesh,* sun.]

Samson² *n.* A man of great physical strength. [After SAMSON.]

Sam·u·el¹ (sámmew-əl || sámmewl). Hebrew judge and prophet of the 11th century B.C.

Samuel² *n. Abbr.* **Sam.** Either of two books, I and II Samuel, of the Old Testament.

sam·u·rai (sámmoo-rī, sámmew-) *n., pl.* **samurai.** *Often capital* **S. 1.** A warrior belonging to the military aristocracy of feudal Japan. **2.** A modern descendant of a samurai. [Japanese, "warrior".]

Sa·n'ā or **Sa·naa** (san-aá, saan-). Capital of Yemen. It lies in the centre of the country on a high plain (2,210 metres; 7,250 feet). A walled city celebrated in the early Islamic period, it has many fine buildings, chief of which is the Jami' Masjid (Great Mosque).

San An·dre·as Fault (sán-an-dráy-əss). Fracture in the Earth's crust running through California, western United States. More than 960 kilometres (600 miles) long, it is a strike-slip fault where two of the Earth's tectonic plates are moving slowly past each other in the horizontal plane. At irregular intervals, the immense strain is released in tremors and earthquakes which have included the major earthquake that devastated San Francisco in 1906.

San An·to·ni·o (sán-an-tṓ-ni-ō, -tṓn-yō). City in Texas, southern United States, situated on the San Antonio river. A Catholic mission was founded here in 1718 and its chapel, the Alamo, was the site of a famous Mexican attack (1836) during the struggle for Texan independence. Its ruins are a major tourist attraction, and there are also military and air force establishments, the city being one of the largest U.S. military centres.

san·a·tive (sánnətiv) *adj.* Able to cure or heal; curative. [Middle English, from Old French *sanatif* or Late Latin *sānātīvus,* from *sānāre,* to cure, from *sānus,* sound, SANE.]

san·a·to·ri·um (sánnə-táwri-əm || -tṓri-) *n., pl.* **-ums** or **-toria** (-táwri-ə). Also *U.S.* **san·i·ta·ri·um** (-taír-i-əm || -tṓri-). **1.** An institution for the treatment of chronic diseases, such as tuberculosis, or for medically supervised convalescence. **2.** *British.* A building or part of a building at a college or boarding school reserved for those who are sick. [New Latin, from Late Latin *sānātōrium,* neuter of *sānātōrius,* from Latin *sānātus,* past participle of *sānāre,* to heal, from *sānus,* healthy, SANE.]

san·be·ni·to (sán-bə-néetō, -be-) *n., pl.* **-tos.** A yellow garment with Saint Anthony's cross on its front and back, worn by a penitent under the Spanish Inquisition. **2.** A similar but black garment with painted flames and devils on it, for impenitents at an auto-da-fé. [Spanish *sambenito,* after *San Benito,* Saint BENEDICT (from its resemblance to the Benedictine scapular).]

San·cho Pan·za (sánchō pánzo) *n.* A companion who is simple and down-to-earth. [After the squire in Cervantes' *Don Quixote.*]

sanc·ti·fied (sángkti-fīd) *adj.* **1.** Made holy; dedicated to sacred use; consecrated. **2.** *Archaic.* Sanctimonious.

sanc·ti·fy (sángkti-fī) *tr.v.* **-fied, -fying, -fies. 1.** To reserve for sacred use; consecrate. **2.** To make holy; purify. **3.** To give religious sanction or legitimacy to: *sanctify a marriage.* **4.** To make productive of holiness or blessing. [Middle English *sanctifien,* from Old French *sanctifier,* from Late Latin *sanctificāre* : Latin *sanctus,* holy, sacred, from the past participle of *sancīre,* to consecrate + *facere,* to make.] **—sanc·ti·fi·ca·tion** (-fi-káysh'n) *n.* **—sanc·ti·fi·er** *n.*

sanc·ti·mo·ni·ous (sángkti-mṓni-əss) *adj.* Making a pretence of sanctity, piety, or righteousness. [Latin *sanctimōnia,* sanctity, from *sanctus,* sacred (see **sanctify**) + *mōnia,* -MONY + -OUS.] **—sanc·ti·mo·ni·ous·ly** *adv.* **—sanc·ti·mo·ni·ous·ness, sanc·ti·mo·ny** (-mən-i || *U.S.* -mōni) *n.*

sanc·tion (sángksh'n) *n.* **1. a.** Authoritative permission or approval that makes a course of action valid. **b.** The ratification or confirmation of a law or other measure. **2.** Support or encouragement, as from public opinion or established custom. **3.** The penalty for non-compliance or the reward for compliance with a law or decree. **4.** Any consideration or principle that influences ethical choices or otherwise acts to ensure compliance or conformity. **5.** A coercive measure adopted usually by several nations acting together against a nation violating international law: *Trade sanctions were implemented against the Boggato Republic.* **6.** *Archaic.* A law or decree, especially an ecclesiastical decree.
~*tr.v.* **sanctioned, -tioning, -tions. 1.** To authorise; legitimise; ratify. **2.** To approve, support, or encourage: *sanctioned by the frequency of its occurrence.* —See Synonyms at **approve.** [French, from Latin *sanctiō* (stem *sanctiōn-*), an ordaining, a sanction, from *sanctus,* sacred. See **sanctify.**]

sanc·ti·ty (sángktəti) *n., pl.* **-ties. 1.** Saintliness, holiness, or godliness. **2.** The quality or condition of being considered hallowed or sacred; inviolability. **3.** Anything considered sacred. [Middle English *saunctite,* from Old French *sainctite,* from Latin *sanctitās* (stem *sanctitāt-*), from *sanctus,* sacred. See **sanctify.**]

sanc·tu·ar·y (sángk-tew-əri, -chəri || *U.S.* -choo-erri) *n., pl.* **-ies. 1.** A sacred place, such as a church, temple, or mosque. **2.** The most holy part of a sacred place, such as the area around the altar in a church. **3.** A church or other sacred place in which fugitives formerly were safe from arrest or punishment. **4.** Immunity from arrest or punishment, by taking refuge in or as if in a sacred place: *sought sanctuary at the French embassy in Prague.* **5.** Any place of refuge or asylum. **6.** A reserved area in which wildlife is protected from hunting or other molestation. —See Synonyms at **shelter.** [Middle English *sanctuarie,* from Old French *saintuarie,* from Late Latin *sanctuārium,* from Latin *sanctus,* sacred. See **sanctify.**]

sanc·tum (sángk-təm) *n., pl.* **-tums** or **-ta** (-tə). **1.** A sacred or holy place. **2.** A private room or study where one is not to be disturbed. [Latin, neuter of *sanctus,* sacred. See **sanctify.**]

sanctum sanc·to·rum (sángk-táwrəm || -tṓrəm) *n.* **1.** The **holy of holies** *(see).* **2.** An inviolably private place. Often used humorously. [Late Latin, "the holy of holies" (translation of Greek *to hagion tōn hagiōn,* translation of Hebrew *qōdesh ha-qqodashīm*).]

Sanc·tus (sángktəss) *n.* **1.** The hymn of praise that follows on from the Preface in many eucharistic liturgies. **2.** A musical setting of this. [Middle English, from Medieval Latin, first word of the hymn, from Late Latin, "holy" (first word of the hymn sung by the angels in Isaiah 6:3), from Latin. See **sanctify.**]

sand (sand) *n.* **1.** Loose, granular, gritty particles of worn or disintegrated rock, especially quartz, finer than gravel and coarser than dust. **2.** *Usually plural.* A tract or stretch of land covered with this material, as a beach or desert. **3. a.** This material in an hourglass. **b.** *Plural.* Moments of allotted time or duration: *"The sands are number'd that make up my life"* (Shakespeare). **4.** *U.S. Slang.* Grit;

San Andreas fault

THE FRACTURE THAT DIVIDES SAN FRANCISCO
Displaced orange trees reveal movements in the Earth's crust

The dark streaks of the San Andreas fault system, which fractures coastal California in the United States, is one of the few places in the world where the meeting of two plates of the lithosphere, formed from the Earth's crust and upper mantle, is visible. The Pacific plate to the west of the fault is drifting northwestwards past the slower-moving North American plate. In the process a narrow strip of the California coast is gradually being sheared off from the mainland. Every so often, the plates bind, but the underground pressures causing them to move continue, making the boundary rock bend and tense. Eventually it gives under the accumulated strain, causing an earthquake.

San Francisco straddles the San Andreas fault and is therefore at risk from earthquakes. The worst in living memory happened just before dawn on April 18, 1906. Buildings collapsed and fires roared through the city, unchecked because water mains had burst. Ten square kilometres (4 square miles) were devastated and almost 700 people died. The city was rebuilt, but it could be destroyed again unless a way is found of preventing earthquakes. Prediction is still far from reliable and methods of control are in their infancy. For the time being the worst effects of earthquakes can be avoided by careful siting of communities and the construction of shock-resistant buildings.

RELATIVE MOTION OF PLATES

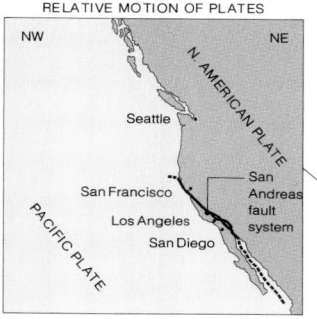

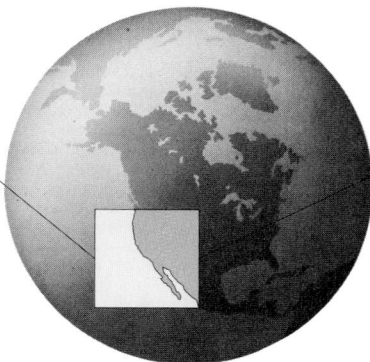

EFFECTS OF PLATE MOVEMENT

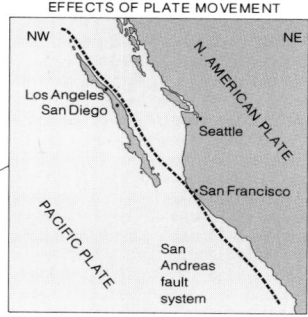

Both plates are moving northwest, but because the Pacific plate is moving faster than the North American, their relative movement is in opposite directions.

If the San Andreas fault continues to slip at its present rate, in 50 million years Los Angeles will be an island off the west coast of Canada.

FAULT IN AN ORANGE GROVE *An aerial photograph shows the displacement of trees in a Californian orange grove. The earthquake of 1940 in the Imperial Valley of southeast California* *shifted the two sides of this sub-fault of the San Andreas system 3 metres (10 feet). It is now stationary, but the main fault is moving irregularly at an average of a few centimetres a year.*

---

courage. **5.** Light greyish brown to yellowish grey. **—build on sand.** To base on a foundation that is insecure or uncertain. *~tr.v.* **sanded, sanding, sands. 1.** To sprinkle or cover with sand or similar particles: *sanded the icy road.* **2.** To polish or scrape with sand or sandpaper. **3.** To mix or adulterate with sand. [Middle English *sand,* Old English *sand,* from Germanic *sandam, sandaz* (unattested).]

Sand (sond), **George,** pen name of Amandine Aurore Lucie Dupin; also known as Baronne Dudevant (1804–76). French writer. She married Casimir Dudevant in 1822 and her first novel, *Indiana,* which was a plea for feminine independence, was published in 1832, a year after she had left her husband and gone to live with Jules Sandeau. She wrote many successful novels, including *la Mare au diable* (1846), and could count Alfred de Musset and Frédéric Chopin among her lovers.

san·dal¹ (sánd'l) *n.* **1.** A light shoe consisting of a sole fastened to the foot by thongs or straps, and worn especially in warm weather.

2. A lightweight shoe, typically having a perforated design in the upper and a flat, spongy sole, worn especially by children. **3.** A strap or band for fastening a low shoe or slipper on the foot. [Middle English *sandalie,* from Latin *sandalium,* from Greek *sandalion,* diminutive of *sandalon,* sandal, probably of Asiatic origin.]

sandal² *n.* Sandalwood. [Middle English, from Old French, from Medieval Latin *sandalum, santalum,* from Greek *santalon, sandanon,* probably from Sanskrit *candanaḥ.*]

san·dal·wood (sánd'l-wŏŏd) *n.* **1.** Any of several south Asian or Australasian evergreen trees of the genus *Santalum;* especially, *S. album,* having aromatic yellowish heartwood that is used in cabinet-making and wood carving, and that yields an oil used in perfumery. Also called "sandal". **2.** The wood of this tree or of similar trees. **3.** Any of various similar trees; especially, red sandalwood, *Pterocarpus santalinus,* the dark-red wood of which yields a dye. **4.** Light to moderate or greyish brown.

san·da·rac, san·da·rach (sánda-rak) *n.* **1.** A tree, *Tetraclinis articu-*

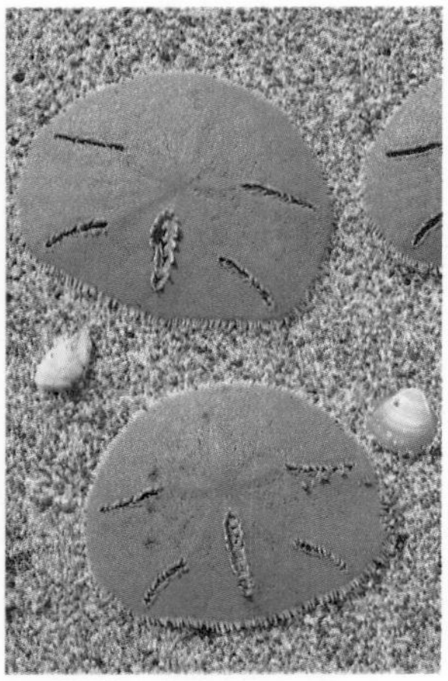

sand dollar *Found on sandy ocean beds throughout the world, sand dollars are flat circular sea urchins belonging to the scientific order* Exocycloida.

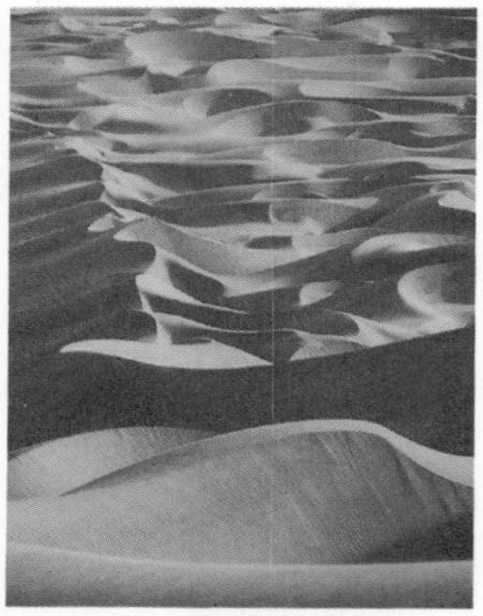

sand dune *The world's largest areas of sand dunes are in deserts. These huge wind-shaped dunes are on the arid coastal strip of Peru near the Atacama Desert, the driest region in the world.*

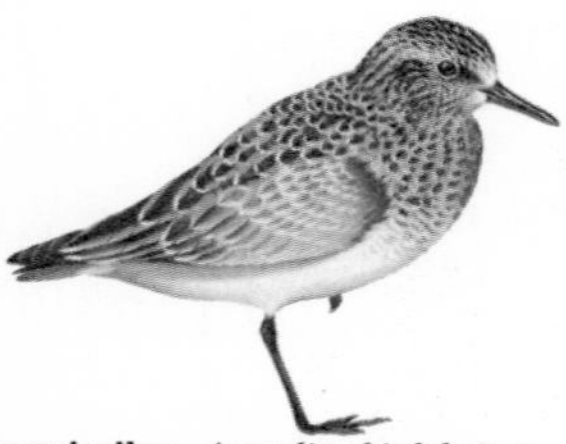

sanderling *A wading bird that breeds in the Arctic and spends its winter in flocks along the shores of southern Europe. It feeds on tiny sea creatures along the water's edge.*

lata (or *Callitris quadrivalvis*), of northern Africa, having wood yielding a brittle, translucent resin used in varnishes. **2.** The resin of this tree. [Latin *sandaraca,* red pigment, beebread, from Greek *sandarak(h)ē,* (red pigment derived from) realgar.]

sand·bag (sánd-bag) *n.* **1.** A bag filled with sand, used, especially: **a.** In piles to form protective walls, as against flooding or gunfire. **b.** As a ballast in a balloon or boat. **2.** A small, narrow bag partially filled with sand, used as a weapon to hit someone.
~*tr.v.* **sandbagged, -bagging, -bags. 1.** To put sandbags in, on, or around as a means of protection. **2. a.** To hit with a sandbag. **b.** *U.S.* To force by crude means.

sand·bank (sánd-bangk) *n.* A bank of sand in a sea or river formed by currents and often exposed at low tide.

sand·bar (sánd-baar) *n.* An offshore shoal of sand built up by the action of waves or currents.

sand·blast (sánd-blaast || -blast) *n.* **1.** A blast of air or steam carrying sand at high speed to etch glass or to clean stone or metal surfaces. **2.** A machine used to apply such a blast.
~*tr.v.* **sandblasted, -blasting, -blasts.** To apply a sandblast to for the purpose of cleaning or engraving. **—sand·blast·er** *n.*

sand-blind (sánd-blīnd) *adj. Archaic.* Partially blind; dim-sighted. [Middle English *sand-blind,* Old English *sāmblind* (unattested) : *sām-,* half + BLIND.] **—sand-blind·ness** *n.*

sand·box (sánd-boks) *n.* A box or receptacle for sand, especially: **1.** A small vessel formerly used to sprinkle sand on wet ink. **2.** A container on a locomotive for sprinkling sand on icy rails. **3.** *U.S.* A **sandpit** *(see)* a boxlike enclosure.

sandbox tree *n.* A tropical American tree, *Hura crepitans,* having a spiny trunk and woody seed capsules that split explosively when ripe. [So called because the capsules were formerly used to hold sand for drying ink.]

sand-cast (sánd-kaast || -kast) *tr.v.* **-cast, -casting, -casts.** To make (a casting) by pouring molten metal into a sand mould.

sand·cas·tle (sánd-kaass'l || -kass'l) *n.* A mound of sand built up to resemble a castle, especially by children at the seaside.

sand crack *n.* A fissure in the side of a horse's hoof, often causing lameness.

sand dollar *n.* Any of various thin, circular echinoderms; especially, *Echinarachnius parma,* of sandy ocean bottoms of the northern Atlantic and Pacific.

sand dune *n.* A **dune** *(see).*

sand eel *n.* Any of several small marine fishes of the genus *Ammodytes,* having a slender body with a forked tail fin, and often burrowing in coastal sand or shingle. Also called "launce", "sand launce".

sand·er (sándər) *n.* **1.** One that spreads sand. **2.** One that sands surfaces; especially, a machine with an abrasive-covered disc or belt, used for smoothing or polishing.

san·der·ling (sándər-ling) *n.* A small shore bird, *Crocethia (*or *Calidris) alba,* having predominantly grey and white plumage. [Perhaps from SAND + -LING.]

sand flea *n.* Any of various small crustaceans living on sandy beaches, such as the sand hopper.

sand fly *n.* **1.** Any of various small biting flies of the genus *Phlebotomus,* of tropical areas, some of which transmit diseases. **2.** Any of various similar or related flies.

sand glass *n.* An instrument, such as an hourglass, consisting of two glass chambers with a narrow connecting channel, and containing sand that takes a definite time to trickle from one chamber to the other.

sand·grouse (sánd-growss) *n.* Any of various sandy-coloured pigeon-like birds of the genera *Pterocles* and *Syrrhaptes,* of arid and semiarid regions of the Old World.

san·dhi (sánd-i, súnd-, -ee, -hee) *n. Linguistics.* The modification of the sound or form of a word because of its position in certain contexts; for example, the difference between the pronunciation of *the* in *the house* and in *the other house* is an instance of sandhi. [Sanskrit *saṁdhi,* "a placing together" : *sam,* together + *dadhāti,* he places.]

sand·hog (sánd-hog || -hawg) *n. U.S.* A labourer who works in a pressure chamber, as in the construction of underwater tunnels.

sand hopper *n.* Any small, jumping crustacean of the genera *Orchestia* and *Talitrus,* common in intertidal zones. Also called "beach flea".

Sand·hurst (sánd-hurst). Village in Berkshire in south central England. It is famous as the site of the Royal Military Academy (founded 1790) where many British and Commonwealth army officers are trained.

San Di·e·go (sándi-áygō). City and seaport in southern California, western United States, situated on San Diego Bay. The city has an oceanographic institute, a major naval and marine base, and shipbuilding, aviation, and aerospace industries.

sand launce *n.* The **sand eel** *(see).*

sand lizard *n.* A light brown to greyish European lizard, *Lacerta agilis,* which has, in the male, bright green underparts.

sand·man (sánd-man) *n.* A character in fairy tales and folklore who puts children to sleep by sprinkling sand in their eyes.

sand martin *n.* A small European martin, *Riparia riparia,* which has white underparts with a brown breast band and nests in sand and gravel banks.

sand mould *n.* A mould used in a foundry, made from sand in which a design has been impressed.

sand painting *n.* **1.** A ceremonial design of the Navaho Indians of North America made by trickling fine coloured sand onto a base of neutral sand. **2.** The art of making such designs.

sand·pa·per (sánd-paypər) *n.* Paper coated on one side with sand or other abrasive material, used for smoothing.
~*tr.v.* **sandpapered, -pering, -pers.** To rub with sandpaper for the purpose of smoothing, polishing, or finishing.

sand·pi·per (sánd-pīpər) *n.* Any of various small wading birds of the family Scolopacidae, usually having a long, straight bill, and characteristically frequenting the seashore in flocks.

sand·pit (sánd-pit) *n.* **1.** A pit from which sand can be excavated. **2.** *British.* A pit or low container filled with sand, used by children for play and by athletes in the high and long jump.

San·dring·ham (sándring-əm). Village in Norfolk, in eastern England. Sandringham House, with its estate, has been a country residence of English royalty since 1863.

sand·shoe (sánd-shōō) *n. British.* A light summer or sports shoe, often made of canvas with a rubber sole.

sand smelt A widely distributed fish of the genus *Atherina,* closely related to the grey mullet and found in inshore waters, especially estuaries.

sand·stone (sánd-stōn) *n.* Variously coloured sedimentary rock composed predominantly of sandlike quartz grains cemented by lime, silica, or other materials.

sand·storm (sánd-stawrm) *n.* A strong wind carrying clouds of sand through the air near the ground, especially in a desert.

sand table *n.* A table on which a relief model of a town or terrain is built out of sand and used for the study of military tactics and manoeuvres.

sand trap *n. Chiefly U.S.* In golf, a **bunker** *(see).*

sand viper *n.* Any of various snakes of sandy areas, such as *Vipera ammodytes,* a venomous species of southern Europe and Asia Minor, or the **horned viper** *(see).*

sand·wich (sán-wij, sánd-, -wich) *n.* **1.** Two or more slices of bread with meat, cheese, jam, or other filling placed between them. **2.** Any arrangement resembling a sandwich.
~*tr.v.* **sandwiched, -wiching, -wiches. 1.** To insert between two things of another type. **2.** To fit with difficulty between two other things; make room or time for: *sandwich a meeting between lunch and leaving the office.* [After the 4th Earl of SANDWICH .]

Sand·wich (sán-wich, sánd-, -wij, sánnij). Market town in Kent, southeastern England. It was one of the original Cinque Ports, though its harbour later silted up and it now lies some 3 kilometres (2 miles) from the sea. Sandwich is a tourist resort.

Sandwich, John Montagu, 4th Earl of (1718–92). He is said to have sustained long periods at the gaming table by eating cold beef placed between slices of bread, so giving rise to the word sandwich.

sandwich board *n.* Either of two large boards bearing advertising placards, hinged at the top by straps for hanging on a carrier's shoulders.

sandwich cake *n. British.* A layer cake consisting of a filling, such as jam and cream, sandwiched between two round thick slices of sponge.

sandwich compound *n.* A type of chemical compound, such as fenocene, in which a metal atom or ion is sandwiched between two parallel organic rings.

sandwich course *n. British.* An educational course, especially a vocational one, in which periods of academic study alternate with periods of practical experience.

sandwich man *n.* A man hired to carry sandwich boards.

sand·worm (sánd-wurm) *n.* Any of various segmented worms, especially of the genera *Nereis* and *Arenicola,* generally inhabiting coastal mud or sand, and often used as fishing bait.

sand·wort (sánd-wurt || -wawrt) *n.* Any of numerous low-growing plants of the genera *Arenaria, Minuartia,* and *Moehringia,* having small, usually white flowers.

sand·y (sándi) *adj.* **-ier, -iest. 1.** Covered with, consisting of, or containing a high proportion of sand: *sandy soil.* **2.** Like sand, as in being unstable. **3. a.** Having the colour of sand; yellowish red. **b.** Having hair of this colour. **—sand·i·ness** *n.*

sand yacht *n.* A vehicle with wheels and sails, designed to be propelled across flat stretches of sand, as on a beach, by the wind. **—sand-yacht·ing** *n.*

sane (sayn) *adj.* **saner, sanest. 1.** Mentally healthy; of sound mind. **2.** Having or showing sound judgment; reasonable; rational. [Latin *sānus,* sound, whole, healthy.] **—sane·ly** *adv.* **—sane·ness** *n.*

San·for·ized (sán-fər-īzd) *adj.* A trademark designating fabrics preshrunk by a patented mechanical process before being made into clothing so as to minimise later shrinkage.

San Fran·cis·co (sán-frən-sískō, -fran-). Major city and seaport in California, western United States, situated on a peninsula between San Francisco Bay and the Pacific Ocean, which are linked by the strait known as the Golden Gate. Founded as a Spanish mission in 1776, it boomed during the Californian gold rush of 1848 and further expanded after the opening of the transcontinental railway (1869). Lying on the **San Andreas Fault,** it was partially destroyed in an earthquake and fire in 1906, and has been subject to lesser tremors at irregular intervals. The city is the financial centre of the West Coast, and also serves a prosperous agricultural and mining region. Among its famous sights are the Golden Gate Bridge, the municipal cable car system, Chinatown, and the island of **Alcatraz,** which lies in the Bay. The Haight-Ashbury district of San Francisco won fame in the 1960s as the centre of hippy counterculture. **—San Fran·cis·can** *adj. & n.*

sang. Past tense of **sing.**

san·ga·ree (sáng-gə-rée) *n.* A cold drink usually made of wine, often Madeira, and grated nutmeg. [Spanish *sangría,* "a bleeding", from *sangre,* blood, from Latin *sanguis.* See **sanguine.**]

Sang·er (sáng-ər), **Frederick** (1918–). British biochemist. He determined the order of amino acids in the insulin molecule and was awarded the Nobel prize for chemistry in 1958 and 1980.

sang-froid (sóɴ-frwáa, sáng-) *n.* Composure; coolness; imperturbability. See Synonyms at **equanimity.** [French, "cold blood".]

sangh (sungg) *n.* An association in India that promotes the consolidation of the different groups in Hinduism. [Hindi *sãg,* from Sanskrit *saṅga,* association, from *sajati,* he adheres.]

san·gha (sáng-gə, súng-, -g-hə) *n.* The community of monks in Buddhism, considered collectively. [Sanskrit. See **sangh.**]

San·graal (sang-gráyl) *n.* The **grail** *(see).* [Old French, "holy grail".]

san·gri·a (sang-grée-ə) *n.* A cold drink made of red or white wine mixed with fruit juice or lemonade, and sometimes brandy, and garnished with fruit. [Spanish *sangría,* "bleeding", from *sangre,* blood, from Latin *sanguis.* See **sanguine.**]

san·gui·na·ri·a (sáng-gwi-náir-i-ə) *n.* A North American plant of the genus *Sanguinaria;* especially, *S. candensis,* the bloodroot, the dried rhizome of which is used as an emetic. [New Latin, from Latin *sanguinarius,* bloody, from *sanguis* (stem *sanguin-*), blood.]

san·gui·nar·y (sáng-gwin-əri || -erri) *adj.* **1.** Accompanied by bloodshed and carnage. **2.** Bloodthirsty. **3.** Consisting of or stained with blood. [Latin *sanguinārius,* of blood, from *sanguis* (stem *sanguin-*), blood.] **—san·gui·nar·i·ly** *adv.* **—san·gui·nar·i·ness** *n.*

san·guine (sáng-gwin) *adj.* **1. a.** *Archaic.* Of the colour of blood; red. **b.** Ruddy; florid. Said of the complexion. **2.** Dominated by the humour of blood in terms of medieval physiology. See **humour. 3.** Having the courageous or passionate temperament and ruddy complexion formerly thought to be characteristic of one dominated by this humour. **4.** Eagerly optimistic; cheerful; hopeful. [Middle English *sanguin,* from Old French, from Latin *sanguineus,* of blood, bloody, from *sanguis*† (stem *sanguin-*), blood.] **—san·guine·ly** *adv.* **—san·guine·ness, san·guin·i·ty** (sang-gwínnəti) *n.*

san·guin·e·ous (sang-gwínni-əss) *adj.* **1. a.** Pertaining to or involving blood or bloodshed. **b.** Bloodthirsty; sanguinary. **2.** Blood-red. **3.** Cheerful; optimistic; sanguine. [Latin *sanguineus,* SANGUINE.]

san·guin·o·lent (sang-gwínnələnt) *adj.* Of, mixed with, or tinged with blood. [Latin *sanguinolentus,* full of blood, from *sanguis* (stem *sanguin-*), blood. See **sanguine.**]

San·he·drin (sán-i-drin, -ə-, -e-, *also* san-hé-) *n.* Also **San·he·drim** (-drim). **1.** The highest judicial and ecclesiastical council of the ancient Jewish nation, composed of from 70 to 72 members. Also called "Great Sanhedrin". **2.** A similar but less important assembly with 23 members. [Hebrew *sanhedhrīn,* from Greek *sunedrion,* a council, from *sunedros,* sitting within council : SYN- (together) + *hedra,* a seat, a sitting.]

san·i·cle (sánnik'l) *n.* Any of various plants of the genus *Sanicula,* having clusters of small, greenish-white or pale pink flowers and reputedly having medicinal value as an astringent. [Middle English, from Old French, from Medieval Latin *sanicula,* probably from Latin *sānus,* healthy, SANE (because the plant was once thought to have healing powers).]

sa·ni·es (sáyni-eez) *n.* A thin, fetid, greenish fluid consisting of serum and pus discharged from a wound, ulcer, or fistula. [Latin *saniēs*†.] **—sa·ni·ous** (-əss) *adj.*

sanitarium. Variant of **sanatorium.**

san·i·tar·y (sánni-tri, -təri || -terri) *adj.* **1. a.** Pertaining to or used for the preservation of health. **b.** Pertaining to or concerned with sanitation: *sanitary ware; the sanitary department.* **2.** Free from dirt and infection; clean; hygienic. [French *sanitaire,* from Latin *sānitās,* health, SANITY.] **—san·i·tar·i·ly** *adv.*

sanitary belt *n.* A band, usually of elastic, for holding a sanitary towel in place.

sanitary engineer *n.* An engineer specialising in the maintenance of services and conditions conducive to the preservation of public health, such as the disposal of sewage and provision of pure water. **—sanitary engineering** *n.*

sanitary towel *n.* A usually disposable pad of absorbent material worn to absorb menstrual flow. Also *chiefly U.S.* "sanitary napkin".

san·i·ta·tion (sánni-táysh'n) *n.* **1.** The formulation and application of measures designed to protect public health. **2.** The disposal of sewage and refuse. [From SANITARY.]

san·i·tise, san·i·tize (sánni-tīz) *tr.v.* **-tised, -tising, -tises. 1.** To make sanitary. **2.** To make innocuous or inoffensive.

san·i·ty (sánnəti) *n.* **1.** The condition of having sound mental health; saneness. **2.** Soundness of judgment or reason. [Middle English *sanite,* from Old French, from Latin *sānitās* (stem *sānitāt-*), health, sanity, from *sānus,* healthy, SANE.]

san·jak (sán-jak) *n.* In the Ottoman Empire, an administrative district that was a subdivision of a vilayet. [Turkish *sancak,* "banner".]

San Jo·se (sán-hō-záy, -ə-). City in California, western United States. It is an important centre for fruit canning and drying, and wine production, along with some light industry.

San José (sán hō-záy, ə-, *Spanish* -sáy). Capital of Costa Rica, situated in the centre of the country. Founded in 1738, it became the capital in 1823. The city lies on a temperate upland plateau and is a centre for coffee processing and distribution.

San Jose scale *n.* A destructive scale insect, *Quadraspidiotus perniciosus,* that does considerable damage to fruit trees and fruit-bearing plants. [First seen in the United States in SAN JOSE.]

San Juan (sán wáan, hwáan). Capital and chief port of Puerto Rico, situated on the northeastern coast of the island. Developed by the Spaniards from 1533, the city was taken by U.S. troops in 1898. San Juan is a tourist centre, with industries which include food processing and machinery.

sank. Past tense of **sink.**

San·khya (sáangk-yə) *n.* A system of Hindu philosophy based on the distinction between spirit and matter. [Sanskrit *sāṁkhya-,* "based on calculation", from *saṁkhyā-,* calculation, from *saṁkhyāti*†, he counts up.]

San Ma·ri·no, Republic of (sán mə-réenō). Small republic situated in the Apennine mountains of central Italy. Traditionally founded in the fourth century, it became a city-state whose independence was recognised by the Pope in 1631. In 1862 it joined a customs union with Italy, and a treaty of mutual friendship was signed in 1897. The main agricultural products are wine, cereals, and cattle. Tourism and ceramics are among the chief industries. Area, 61 square kilometres (24 square miles). Population, 22,000. Capital, San Marino. See map at **Italy. —San Mar·i·nese** (marri-néez) *n. & adj.*

San Mart·ín (sán maar-téen), **José de.** (1778–1850) South American soldier and statesman, born in Argentina. He devoted himself to the struggle of South American countries to throw off the authority of Spain and played a major part in freeing Chile (1817–18) and Peru (1821).

san·nup (sánnəp) *n.* A married male North American Indian. [From a Massachusetts word akin to Eastern Abnaki *sénape,* "man".]

san·nya·si (sun-yáa-si) *n.* Also **san·nya·sin** (-sin). An ascetic Hindu holy man or mendicant. [Hindi and Urdu, from Sanskrit *saṁnyāsin,* setting aside : *sam,* together + *ni,* down + *as,* throw.]

sans (sanz; *French* sᴏɴ) *prep. Archaic.* Without. [Middle English *saunz, san(s),* from Old French *san(s), sen(s),* from Vulgar Latin *sene* (unattested), from Latin *sine* (influenced by Latin *absentiā,* in the absence of).]

San Sal·va·dor (san sálvə-dawr; *Spanish* -dór). Capital of El Salvador, situated in the interior of the country Founded in 1528 on high volcanic slopes, it has been repeatedly damaged by severe earthquakes. The city witnessed frequent shootings by left-wing guerrillas and right-wing death squads after the military coup in El Salvador (1979). Products include textiles, cigars, and processed food.

San Salvador Island. Formerly **Watling Island.** Island in the Bahamas group of the West Indies. It was Columbus's first landfall (1492) during his first voyage to the Americas.

sans-cu·lotte (sánz-kew-lót, sóɴ-, -kü-) *n., pl.* **sans-culottes. 1.** An extreme republican during the French Revolution. **2.** Broadly, any revolutionary extremist. [French *sans-culotte,* "without breeches" (the revolutionaries wore pantaloons instead of the kneebreeches worn by members of the upper classes) : SANS + CULOTTES.] **—sans-cu·lot·tic** *adj.* **—sans-cu·lot·tism** *n.*

San Se·bas·tián (sán si-bást-yən; *Spanish* se-bast -yáan). Coastal resort and capital of Guipúzcoa province, northern Spain, situated on the Bay of Biscay. Overlooked by the fortress of Castillo de la Mota, the city was the summer residence of the Spanish court. The city also has fishing, paper, and steel industries.

san·se·vie·ri·a (sán-sə-véer-i-ə) *n.* Any of various tropical Old World plants of the genus *Sansevieria,* having thick, lance-shaped leaves and often cultivated as a house plant. Also called "mother-in-law's tongue". [New Latin, after Raimondo di Sangro (1710–71), Prince of *San Severo,* Italy.]

San·skrit, San·scrit (sán-skrit) *n. Abbr.* **Skt., Skr. 1.** An ancient language of India, belonging to the Indic branch of the Indo-Iranian subfamily of Indo-European languages, of which it is the oldest known member. It is the language of the Vedas and of Hinduism. **2.** The literary language of ancient and medieval India, classical Sanskrit, the grammar of which was fixed by Indian grammarians before the fourth century B.C., now used only for sacred or scholarly writings. [Sanskrit *saṃskṛta,* put together, well-formed, refined : *saṃ,* together + *kṛ,* to make.] **—San·skrit·ist** *n.*

San·skrit·ic (san-skríttik) *adj.* **1.** Designating or belonging to a large group of Indian languages and dialects, both ancient and modern, such as Hindi, Pali, Bengali, and Punjabi. **2.** Of, relating to, or written in Sanskrit.

~*n.* The Sanskritic group of languages.

sans serif, san·ser·if (sán-sérrif) *n.* Any of a number of typefaces without serifs.

San·ta An·na (sántə ánnə), **Antonio López de** (1794–1876). Mexican general and statesman. He led revolts against Iturbide (1823), Guerrero (1828), and Bustamante (1832) before becoming president of Mexico (1833–36). He tried to crush the Texan revolt at the Alamo (1836) but was defeated and captured at San Jacinto (1836). He was made dictator in 1841, deposed in 1845, and recalled in 1846, only to be driven from Mexico City by the U.S. army before being exiled in 1848. He was recalled once more to be president (1853–55) before being exiled again, returning at last to Mexico City in 1874 to die in poverty.

San·ta Claus (sántə kláwz, klawz) *n.* A mythological person or personification of the spirit of Christmas, based originally on Saint **Nicholas** and represented as a jolly, fat old man with a white beard and a red suit, who is supposed to come down chimneys on Christmas Eve to bring presents for children. Also called "Father Christ-

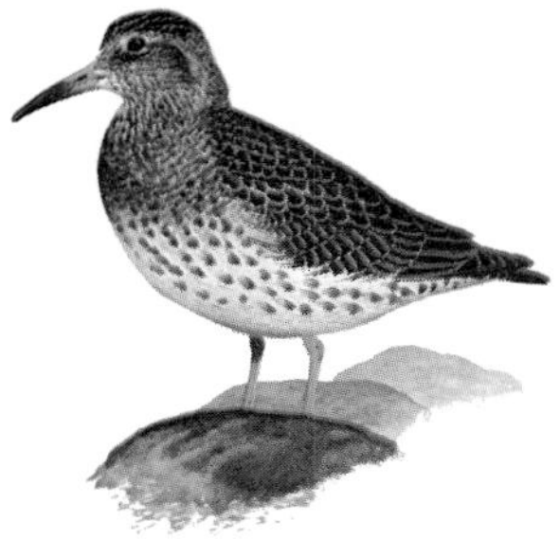

sandpiper *Found mainly in the Northern Hemisphere, the wading sandpiper is a relative of the dunlin. It lives chiefly on rocky shores feeding on insects and other invertebrates and has a shrill piping call. This is the purple sandpiper.*

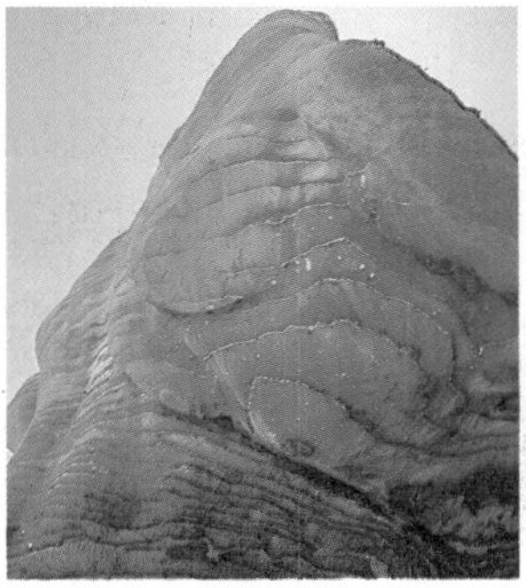

sandstone *This variously coloured, soft sedimentary rock is generally formed from quartz crystals.*

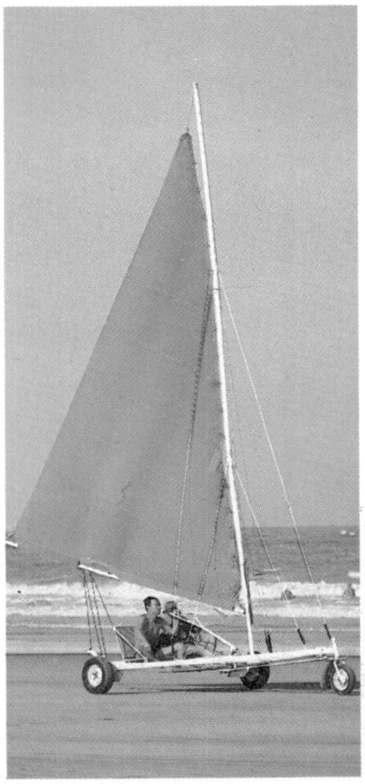

sand yacht *An ingenious recreational vehicle, seen here on a beach near Malindi, Kenya.*

mas". [Variant (U.S.) of Dutch (dialectal) *Sante Klaas,* unexplained shortening of *Sint Nicolaes,* Saint Nicholas.]

San·ta Fe (sántə fáy). Capital of New Mexico, in the southwestern United States, on the Santa Fe river. It was founded at the terminus of the Santa Fe Trail, which led from Missouri. Surviving examples of Spanish colonial architecture include the original governor's palace (1610). Santa Fe is a market centre, and a major tourist resort noted for its Indian and Mexican crafts.

San·ta Fé (sántə fáy). River port on the Salado river in northeastern Argentina, and capital of Santa Fé province. Founded in 1573, it is the centre of a grain-growing and stock-rearing area. Its port was opened to oceangoing ships in 1911, and is linked to the Parana river by canal.

San·tan·der (sán-tan-daír ‖ U.S. *also* saʹan-taan-). Port and capital of Santander province in northern Spain, situated on the Bay of Biscay. A major port for the Americas in colonial days, it is now an important tourist centre, and its industries include fishing and fish processing, shipbuilding, and iron working. Nearby are the famous caves of Altamira, with prehistoric paintings.

San·ta·ya·na (sántə-yáänə ‖ -yánnə), **George** (1863–1952). Spanish-born philosopher. He moved to the U.S. in 1872 and gained a degree at Harvard, where he lectured for a while before going to live in Europe. He wrote volumes of verse and novels as well as many works of philosophy, of which the keystone was the largely materialist series *Realms of Being* (1927–40).

San·ti·a·go (sánti-áägō; *Spanish* sant-yaʹagō). Also **Santiago de Chile.** Capital city of Chile and of Santiago province. It lies on the river Mapocho, and was founded by the Spanish conquistador Pedro de Valdivia in 1541. Greater Santiago contains nearly a third of Chile's population and produces half the nation's total industrial output.

Santiago de Com·po·ste·la (kóm-poss-téllə, -pəss-). City in Galicia, northwest Spain. Its Romanesque cathedral is reputedly sited over the tomb of Saint James (*Santiago* in Spanish), patron saint of Spain. Santiago has been one of the most important centres of pilgrimage in Europe since the ninth century.

Santiago de Cuba. Seaport and capital of Oriente province in southern Cuba. It is Cuba's second largest city, and has the largest cathedral in Cuba and a university. On July 26, 1953 Fidel Castro began his revolt here by leading a guerrilla attack on the Moncada army barracks.

San·to Do·min·go (sántō də-míng-gō, do-). Formerly (1936–1961) **Ciudad Trujillo.** Capital city and chief port of the Dominican Republic, situated on its south coast at the mouth of the river Ozama. It is the oldest continuously inhabited settlement established by Europeans in the Western Hemisphere, having been founded by Bartholomew Columbus, brother of Christopher, in 1496. Its cathedral (1514) is the oldest in the New World. The city has been the country's capital since 1844, and is a major manufacturing and tourist centre.

san·ton·i·ca (san-tónnikə) n. **1.** A wormwood, *Artemisia maritima* (or *A. cina*), of the Old World, having flowers that yield santonin. **2.** The dried unopened flowers of this plant. Also called "wormseed". [New Latin, from Latin *(herba) santonica,* from the feminine of *santonicus,* of the *Santoni,* a people of Aquitania.]

san·to·nin (sántə-nin) n. A colourless crystalline compound, $C_{15}H_{18}O_3$, obtained from species of wormwood, especially santonica, and used as a vermifuge. [SANTON(ICA) + -IN.]

Santorini. See **Thíra.**

San·tos (sán-toss, *Portuguese* -tōōsh). Seaport of São Paulo state, southeast Brazil. It is the world's largest coffee-exporting port, and also a fashionable residential and resort area.

São Pau·lo (sown pów-lō, -lōō). Largest city in Brazil and capital of São Paulo state. It was founded on the river Tiete by Portuguese Jesuits in 1554. Brazilian independence from Portugal was proclaimed here in 1822. The spread of coffee growing in the state stimulated rapid growth of the city from the 1880s. Today the ultramodern metropolis is the biggest financial, commercial, and industrial centre in South America.

São To·mé and Prin·ci·pe, Democratic Republic of (sówn tōō-máy; prín-si-pə). Small country consisting of four islands off the coast of West Africa in the Gulf of Guinea. The two main islands (São Tomé and Principe) and the islets of Pedras Tinhosas and Rôlas make up the group. The archipelago was discovered by the Portuguese in 1471 and proclaimed a colony of Portugal (1522). The Dutch held the islands from 1641 until 1740, when they were recovered by the Portuguese who ruled them until their independence (1975). The economy is almost entirely agricultural, and cocoa, coffee, palm oil, and bananas are exported. Area, 964 square kilometres (372 square miles). Population 100,000. Capital, São Tomé. See map at **Cameroon.**

sap[1] (sap) n. **1. a.** The watery fluid that circulates through a plant, carrying food and other substances to the tissues. **b.** Any plant juice or fluid. **2.** Any essential bodily fluid. **3.** Health and energy; vitality. **4.** *Informal.* A weak, foolish, or gullible person. **5.** *Chiefly U.S. Slang.* A small club or bludgeon; a cosh.
~*tr.v.* **sapped, sapping, saps.** *Chiefly U.S. Slang.* To hit with a sap; cosh. [Middle English *sap,* Old English *sæp.*] —**sap·less** *adj.*
sap[2] n. **1.** The process of making a covered trench or tunnel to a point near to, inside, or underneath an enemy position that is under siege. **2.** A narrow trench dug for protection against enemy fire while approaching enemy positions.
~*v.* **sapped, sapping, saps.** —*tr.* **1.** To undermine the founda-

tions of (a fortification). **2.** To deplete or weaken gradually or insidiously: *Strength and energy were sapped by the hot sun.* —*intr.* To dig a sap. [Earlier *sappe,* trench, from French *sappe,* "an undermining", or Italian *zappa,* probably from Arabic.]

sap·a·jou (sáppə-jōō) n. A monkey, the **capuchin** (see). [French, from Tupi.]

sapanwood. Variant of **sappanwood.**

sa·pe·le (sə-péeli, sa-) n. **1.** Any of several West African trees of the genus *Entandrophragma,* yielding a hard, dark wood resembling mahogany. **2.** The wood of such a tree used in furniture making. [West African name.]

Saphar. Variant of **Safar.**

sap·head (sáp-hed) n. *Chiefly U.S. Slang.* A fool. [SAP (dupe) + HEAD.] —**sap·head·ed** *adj.*

sa·phe·na (sə-fée-nə) n., *pl.* **-nae** (-nee). Either of two large superficial veins on the inner and outer sides of the leg and foot. [Middle English, from Medieval Latin, from Arabic *ṣāfīn.*] —**sa·phe·nous** *adj.*

sap·id (sáppid) *adj. Rare.* **1.** Having a distinctive, usually pleasant flavour; savoury. **2.** Pleasing to the mind; engaging. [Latin *sapidus,* tasty, from *sapere,* to taste, savour.] —**sa·pid·i·ty** n.

sa·pi·ent (sáypi-ənt) *adj.* Having wisdom; wise; discerning. Sometimes used ironically. [Middle English, from Old French, from Latin *sapiēns* (stem *sapient-*), present participle of *sapere,* to taste, to have good taste, to be sensible or wise.] —**sa·pi·ence** n. —**sa·pi·ent·ly** *adv.*

Sa·pir (sə-péer), **Edward** (1884–1939). U.S. anthropologist and linguist, born in Germany. He was a professor at Chicago (1925–31) and then Yale. He is renowned for his studies of the ethnology and languages of the American Indians of the northwest and for his interest in the ways that language shapes thought.

sap·ling (sáp-ling) n. **1.** A young tree. **2.** A youth. **3.** A greyhound less than one year old. [SAP (juice) + -LING.]

sap·o·dil·la (sáppə-dillə) n. **1.** An evergreen tree, *Achras zapota,* of tropical America, having latex that yields chicle. **2.** The edible russet fruit of this tree. Also called "sapodilla plum". Also called "naseberry", "sapota". [Spanish *zapotillo,* diminutive of *zapote,* sapodilla fruit, from Nahuatl *tzapotl.*]

sap·o·na·ceous (sáp-ə-náyshəss, -ō-) *adj.* Having the qualities of soap. [New Latin *saponaceus* : Latin *sāpō* (stem *sāpōn-*), soap + -ACEOUS.] —**sap·o·na·ceous·ness** n.

sa·po·na·ted (sáp-ə-naytid, -ō-) *adj.* Combined or treated with a soap. [Latin *sāpō* (stem *sāpōn-*), soap.]

sa·pon·i·fi·ca·tion (sə-pónnifi-káysh'n, sa-) n. *Chemistry.* The hydrolysis of an ester by an alkali, producing a free alcohol and an acid salt; especially, alkaline hydrolysis of fats to make soap.

sa·pon·i·fy (sə-pónni-fī, sa-) v. **-fied, -fying, -fies.** *Chemistry.* —*tr.* **1.** To convert (an ester) by saponification. **2.** To convert (fats) into soap. —*intr.* To undergo saponification. [French *saponifier* : Latin *sāpō* (stem *sāpōn-*), soap.] —**sa·pon·i·fi·a·ble** (-fī-əb'l, -fī-) *adj.* —**sa·pon·i·fi·er** n.

sap·o·nin (sáppənin) n. Any of various plant glucosides that form soapy colloidal solutions when mixed and agitated with water, used in detergents, synthetic sex hormones, foaming agents, and emulsifiers. [French *saponine* : Latin *sāpō* (stem *sāpōn-*), soap + -IN.]

sap·o·nite (sáppə-nīt) n. An amorphous, hydrous silicate of aluminium and magnesium, occurring as a soaplike mass in the cavities of certain rocks, such as diabase. [Swedish *saponit* : Latin *sāpō* (stem *sāpōn-*), soap + -ITE.]

sa·por (sáy-pər, -pawr) n. A quality perceptible to the sense of taste; flavour. [Middle English, from Latin *sapor,* taste, from *sapere,* to taste.] —**sap·o·rif·ic** (-pə-riffik), **sap·o·rous** *adj.*

sap·pan·wood, sa·pan·wood (sáppan-wood, sə-pán-) n. **1.** A tree, *Caesalpinia sappan,* of tropical Asia, having wood that yields a red dye. **2.** The wood of this tree. [Malay *sapang* + WOOD.]

sap·per (sáppər) n. **1.** A soldier skilled in sapping. **2.** In the British army, a member, especially a private, of the Royal Engineers.

Sap·per (sáppər), pen name of Herman Cyril McNeile (1888–1937). British author. He achieved popular success with his novel *Bulldog Drummond* (1920) and its numerous sequels.

Sap·phic (sáffik) *adj.* **1.** Of or pertaining to the Greek poet Sappho. **2. a.** Designating a verse meter of 11 syllables with a dactyl at the third foot; for example, the line *Trumpet, cello, timpani join together* exhibits Sapphic meter. **b.** Designating a stanza of three lines in such meter followed by a shorter line of a dactyl and spondee. **3.** *Usually small* **s.** Of, pertaining to, or designating homosexuality among women; lesbian.
~n. A Sapphic meter, line, stanza, or poem.

sap·phire (sáffīr) n. **1.** Any of several relatively pure forms of corundum, especially a blue form used as a gemstone. **2.** A corundum gem. **3.** The deep blue colour of a gem sapphire.
~*adj.* Having the colour of a blue sapphire. [Middle English *saphir, safir,* from Old French *safir,* from Latin *sapphīrus,* from Greek *sappheiros;* perhaps akin to Sanskrit *śanipriya,* "precious to the planet Saturn" : *Sani†,* the planet Saturn + *priya,* precious.]

sap·phi·rine (sáffə-reen, -rin) *adj.* Of or resembling sapphire.
~n. *Mineralogy.* A rare light blue or green aluminium-magnesium silicate mineral.

sap·phism (sáffiz'm) n. Lesbianism. [After SAPPHO, referring to her supposed homosexuality.]

Sap·pho (sáffō) (c. 612–c. 580 B.C.). Greek lyric poet. She lived on Lesbos and her passionate poetry appears to have been directed at her coterie of female admirers. Only fragments of her work have survived, but it was ranked very highly by the ancients.

Sap·po·ro (sə-páw-rō, saa- ‖ -pŏ-). City in Japan, capital of the island of Hokkaido. It is a popular winter resort with an annual festival in which giant figures of carved ice are displayed.

sap·py (sáppi) adj. -pier, -piest. 1. Full of sap; juicy. 2. Vital; vigorous. 3. Chiefly U.S. Informal. Silly or foolish. —**sap·pi·ly** adv. —**sap·pi·ness** n.

sa·prae·mi·a (sa-préemi-ə, sə-) n. A form of toxaemia, caused by saprophytic bacteria, in which the bacterial toxins poison the bloodstream but the bacteria themselves do not invade the blood. [New Latin : SAPR(O)- + -AEMIA.] —**sa·prae·mic** adj.

sapro-, sapr– comb. form. Indicates dead or decaying material; for example, **saprophyte, sapraemia**. [Greek, from sapros, rotten, putrid, akin to sēpein, to rot. See **septic**.]

sap·robe (sápprōb) n. An organism that derives its nourishment from nonliving or decaying organic matter. [SAPRO- + Greek bios, life.] —**sa·pro·bic** (sa-prōbik) adj. —**sa·pro·bi·cal·ly** adv.

sap·ro·gen·ic (sápprō-jénnik, sáppra-) adj. Also **sa·prog·e·nous** (sa-prójənəss, sə-). 1. Producing decay or putrefaction: saprogenic bacteria. 2. Resulting from decay or putrefaction. [SAPRO- + -GENIC.] —**sap·ro·ge·nic·i·ty** (-jə-níssəti, -je-) n.

sap·ro·lite (sápprō-līt, sáppra-). n. Clay, silt, or other remnants remaining in the site of a disintegrated rock. [SAPRO- + -LITE.]

sap·ro·pel (sápprō-pel, sáppra-) n. An organic sludge that accumulates on the beds of lakes or seas. It consists of the decomposed remains of aquatic organisms, mainly algae. [SAPRO- + Greek pēlos, clay, mud.] —**sa·pro·pel·ic** (-péllik) adj.

sa·proph·a·gous (sa-próffəgəss, sə-) adj. Feeding on decaying matter. [SAPRO- + -PHAGOUS.]

sap·ro·phyte (sápprə-fīt, sáppro-) n. Biology. A living organism, such as a fungus or bacterium, that lives on and derives its nourishment from dead or decaying organic matter. [SAPRO- + -PHYTE.] —**sap·ro·phyt·ic** (-fíttik) adj.

sap·ro·zo·ic (sápprə-zṓ-ik, sáppro-) adj. 1. Pertaining to or designating nutrition by absorption of dissolved organic materials, as in protozoans and some fungi. 2. Feeding on dead or decaying organic matter. [SAPRO- + -ZOIC.]

sap·wood (sáp-wŏŏd) n. Newly formed living wood that lies just inside the bark of a tree or woody plant, is actively involved in food and water transport, and is lighter in colour than the heartwood. Also called "alburnum".

Saq·qa·ra or **Sak·ka·ra** (sáckərə). Historical site near the village of Saqqara in lower Egypt. It lies close to the site of the ancient city of Memphis, and its most prominent monument is the stone-built stepped pyramid of King Zoser (or Djoser).

sar·a·bande, sar·a·band (sárrə-band) n. 1. A stately court dance, originally from Spain, of the 17th and 18th centuries, in slow triple time. 2. The music for this dance, usually forming one of the movements of the classical suite. [French, from Spanish zarabanda†.]

Sar·a·cen (sárrə-s'n, rarely -sen, -sin) n. 1. A member of a pre-Islamic nomadic people of the Syrian-Arabian deserts. 2. An Arab. 3. Any Muslim of the time of the Crusades. [Middle English, from Old French Saracin, from Late Latin Saracēnus, from Late Greek Sarakēnos, probably from Arabic sharqīyīn, "Easterners", from sharq, sunrise, east, from shāraqa, to rise.] —**Sar·a·cen, Sar·a·cen·ic** (-sénnik) adj.

Saragossa. See **Zaragoza**.

Sa·rah (saír-ə). The wife of Abraham and mother of Isaac. Genesis 7:15. [Hebrew Sārāh, "princess".]

Sa·ra·je·vo (sárrə-yáyvō, saára-). Also **Se·ra·je·vo** (sérrə-). Industrial city in central Yugoslavia. It is the capital of the republic of Bosnia and Hercegovina. In 1914 the Archduke Francis Ferdinand, heir apparent to the throne of Austria-Hungary, was assassinated here by Gavrilo Princip, a Serbian nationalist, an event which precipitated World War I.

sa·ran (sə-rán) n. Any of various thermoplastic resins derived from vinyl compounds and used to make packaging films, corrosion-resistant pipes, fittings, and bristles, and as a fibre in screens, carpets, curtain materials, and other heavy textiles. [From the trademark Saran, coined by Dow Chemical Co., by which it was first developed.]

sarape. Variant of **serape**.

Saratoga. See **Schuylerville**.

Sa·ra·wak (sə-ráa-wak, -wək, -wə, also sárrə-wák). State of Malaysia on the northwest coast of the island of Borneo. It has a mountainous interior, and a swampy coastal plain where rubber, pepper, and rice are grown. It is rich in oil, its main export. Sarawak was given to the English adventurer Sir James (Rajah) Brooke by the Sultan of Brunei in 1841 and ruled by the Brooke family, under British protection, until the Japanese occupation of 1941–45. In 1946 it was ceded to the British Crown but joined Malaysia in 1963. Kuching is the capital.

sar·casm (sár-kaz'm) n. 1. Sharply mocking or contemptuous language, typically using statements or implications pointedly opposite or irrelevant to the meaning that the speaker wishes to convey; for example, to say "congratulations" to someone who has dropped a plate, would be an instance of sarcasm. 2. The use of such language. —See Synonyms at **wit**. [French sarcasme, from Greek sarkasmos, from sarkazein, "to tear flesh", bite the lips in rage, speak bitterly, from sarx (stem sark-), flesh.]

sar·cas·tic (saar-kástik) adj. 1. Characterised by or full of sarcasm.

2. Given to using sarcasm. [French sarcastique, from sarcasme, SARCASM.] —**sar·cas·ti·cal·ly** adv.

Usage: sarcastic, ironic, caustic, satirical, sardonic. These adjectives apply to language or remarks that are bitter, cutting, or derisive. Sarcastic and ironic both pertain to a form of expression in which meanings are conveyed obliquely. Sarcastic suggests taunting and ridicule; ironic suggests a milder and subtler form of mockery. Caustic can apply to any expression that is mocking or ironic in a harsh or cutting way. Satirical refers to expression that seeks to expose wrong or folly to ridicule, often by means of sarcasm or irony. Sardonic can describe both the content and manner of expression and implies scorn or mockery overlaid with cynicism.

sarce·net, sarse·net (sárss-nit) n. A fine, soft silk cloth. [Middle English sarsenet, from Anglo-French sarzinett, perhaps diminutive of (drap) Sarzin, Saracen (cloth), from Latin Saracēnus, SARACEN.]

sarco–, sarc– comb. form. Indicates flesh; for example, **sarcoma, sarcophagus**. [Greek sarx (stem sark-), flesh.]

sar·co·carp (sár-kō-kaarp, -kə-) n. Botany. The fleshy pulp surrounding the seed of a drupaceous fruit such as a peach or plum. [French sarcocarpe : SARCO- + -CARP.]

sar·coid (sár-koyd) adj. Pertaining to or resembling flesh. ~n. A fleshy tumour. [Greek sarkoeidēs : SARC(O)- + -OID.]

sar·co·ma (saar-kṓmə) n., pl. -mas or -mata (-tə). A malignant tumour arising from non-epithelial connective tissues, such as muscle, blood, fat, or the like. [New Latin, from Greek sarkōma, fleshy excrescence : sarkoun, to make fleshy, from sarx (stem sark-), flesh + -OMA.] —**sar·co·ma·toid, sar·co·ma·tous** adj.

sar·co·ma·to·sis (saar-kṓmə-tṓ-siss) n. Pathology. A condition characterised by the formation of numerous sarcomas in the body. [New Latin : sarcoma (stem sarcomat-), SARCOMA + -OSIS.]

sar·co·mere (sár-kō-meer, -kə-) n. A contractile unit in a striated muscle fibril. [SARCO- + -MERE.]

sar·coph·a·gus (saar-kóffə-gəss) n., pl. -gi (-gī, -jī). A stone coffin, often inscribed or decorated with sculpture. [Latin sarcophagus (lapis), "flesh-eating (stone)", from Greek (lithos) sarkophagos : SARCO- + -PHAGOUS.]

sar·co·plasm (sár-kō-plaz'm, -kə-) n. The cytoplasm of striated muscle fibres occurring between the muscle fibrils. [SARCO- + -PLASM.] —**sar·co·plas·mic** (-plázmik) adj.

sar·cous (sárkəss) adj. Of, pertaining to, or consisting of flesh or muscle. [Greek sarx (stem sark-), flesh.]

sard (sard) n. A clear or translucent deep orange-red to brownish red **chalcedony** (see). Also called "sardius". [French sarde, from Latin sarda, perhaps variant of Greek sardion, "the Sardian stone", from Sardeis, SARDIS.]

sardar. Variant of **sirdar**.

sar·dine (sár-déen) n. 1. Any of various small or half-grown edible herrings or related fishes of the family Clupeidae, especially a young pilchard, frequently canned in oil. 2. Any of numerous unrelated small, silvery freshwater or marine fishes that are similarly processed. 3. Plural. A game, similar to hide-and-seek, in which one person hides and others seek him. If a seeker discovers the hider, he must join him until all the seekers but one have gathered at the hiding-place, at which point the game is over. —**like sardines**. Closely packed together. [Middle English sardeyn, from Old French sardine, from Latin sardīna, from Greek sardinos, possibly from Sardō, SARDINIA.]

Sar·din·i·a (saar-dínni-ə). Italian **Sar·de·gna** (-dáyn-ya). Island in the Mediterranean, which with some small neighbouring islands constitutes the Italian autonomous region of Sardinia. It is largely mountainous, its chief agricultural area being the fertile Campidano plain in the southwest. Cereals, olives, and vines are grown, and sheep and goats are raised. Sardinia is rich in minerals, including zinc, lead, coal, and copper. The island was ceded to Savoy (1720) and became part of the kingdom of Piedmont, which was the basis of a united Italy. Cagliari is the capital.

Sar·din·i·an (saar-dínni-ən) n. 1. A native or inhabitant of Sardinia. 2. A Romance language spoken in Sardinia. —**Sar·din·i·an** adj.

Sar·dis (sár-diss). Also **Sar·des** (-deez). Capital city of ancient Lydia, now a small village in west Turkey. When Lydia was absorbed into the Persian empire following the defeat of Croesus (c. 550 B.C.), Sardis remained the provincial capital of Asia Minor. It later became an early centre of Christianity–one of the Seven Churches of Asia (Minor). Extensive excavations of the site have yielded the earliest known coins, dating from c. 700 B.C.

sar·don·ic (saar-dónnik) adj. Scornful or mocking, especially in a cynical way. See Usage note at **sarcastic**. [French sardonique, from Latin Sardonius (rīsus), bitter (laugh), from Late Greek Sardonios, Sardinian, alteration (influenced by Latin herba Sardonia, "Sardinian herb", a poisonous plant supposed to distort the face of the eater) of sardanios, bitter, scornful.] —**sar·don·i·cal·ly** adv. —**sar·don·i·cism** (saar-dónni-siz'm) n.

sar·do·nyx (sárd-əniks, -onniks, -ónniks) n. A variety of chalcedony with alternating brown and white bands. [Middle English sardonix, from Latin sardonyx, from Greek sardonux : probably sardion, SARD + onux, ONYX.]

sar·gas·so (saar-gássō) n. A seaweed, **gulfweed** (see). [Portuguese sargaço†.]

Sar·gas·so Sea (saar-gássō). Large area of the North Atlantic between latitudes 20° and 35°N and longitudes 30° and 70°W. Ocean currents sweep clockwise round it, leaving its centre relatively still. The sea is named after the floating seaweed, Sargassum bacciferum, found there in abundance.

sarge (sarj) *n. Informal.* A sergeant. Often used as a term of address.

Sar·gent (sárjənt), **John Singer** (1856–1925). U.S. portrait painter. He is famous for his portraits and watercolours, including his celebrated World War I landscape *Gassed* (1918).

Sargent, Sir Malcolm born Harold Malcolm Watts-Sargent (1895–1967). British conductor. He was the chief conductor of the BBC Symphony Orchestra (1950–57) and a popular conductor-in-chief of the London Promenade Concerts (1957-67).

Sar·gon (sár-gon), also known as Sargon II (erroneously) (722–705 B.C.). King of Assyria, founder of the last major Assyrian dynasty. He continued his predecessor's war against the northern Jewish kingdom of Israel (later known as Samaria) and destroyed it utterly (721), taking many Israelite captives. Sargon also conquered Carchemish, Babylonia, and part of Kurdistan.

Sargon of Akkad, also known as Sargon I (erroneously) (c. 2335–c.2280 B.C.). Semi-legendary king in Mesopotamia. He usurped royal power and founded the Semitic dynasty of Akkad, building an empire that stretched from the Persian Gulf to the Mediterranean.

sa·ri (sáari) *n., pl.* **-ris.** An outer garment, worn as traditional dress chiefly by Hindu women, consisting of a length of lightweight cloth with one end wrapped about the waist to form a skirt and the other draped over the shoulder or covering the head. [Hindi *sārī,* from Sanskrit *śāṭī†,* "cloth", sari.]

sark (sark) *n. Chiefly Scottish.* A shirt. [Middle English *serk,* from Old Norse *serkr,* from Germanic.]

Sark (sark). One of the Channel Islands in the English Channel, and part of the bailiwick of Guernsey. Sark comprises Great Sark and Little Sark, connected by a narrow isthmus called the Coupée. Created a seigneury by Elizabeth I, the island is still ruled in a semi-feudal manner by a seigneur or dame. No motor cars are allowed here.

sark·y (sárki) *adj.* **-ier, -iest.** *British Informal.* Sarcastic or sardonic. [SARC(ASTIC) + -Y.] —**sark·i·ly** *adv.*

Sar·ma·ti·a (saar-máyshə, -máyshi-ə). An ancient region in eastern Europe between the Vistula and the Volga in present-day Poland and the U.S.S.R.

sar·men·tose (saar-mént-ōss) *adj.* Also **sar·men·tous** (-əss). *Botany.* Having slender, prostrate stems or runners that root at intervals, as the strawberry does. [Latin *sarmentōsus,* full of twigs, from *sarmentum,* twigs, from *sarpere,* to cut off, prune.]

Sar·nath (sarnát). Archaeological site near Varanasi (Benares) in Uttar Pradesh, north India. It was in the deer park here that, according to tradition, Gautama Buddha first taught.

sarod (sarród) *n.* An Indian musical instrument having two sets of strings, one of which provides a drone while the strings of the other are plucked. [Hindi.]

sa·rong (sə-róng ‖ *U.S. also* sə-ráwng) *n.* A length of brightly coloured cloth wrapped about the waist and hanging as a skirt, worn by both men and women of the Malay Archipelago and the Pacific islands. [Malay, sheath, covering, sarong.]

sa·ros (sáir-oss) *n.* A cycle of 6585.32 days during which solar and lunar eclipses occur at regular intervals in the same sequence. [Greek, from Babylonian *šāru,* 3600 (years); the modern use is apparently based on a misinterpretation of the original cycle as one of 18.5 years.]

Sa·roy·an (sə-róy-ən), **William** (1908–81). U.S. writer. He achieved success as a short-story writer with *The Daring Young Man on the Flying Trapeze* (1934). He also produced novels and plays.

Sar·raute (sa-rṓt, sa-), **Nathalie** (1900-). French novelist. Her work, which includes *Tropismes* (1939) and *Les Fruits d'Or* (1963), is less concerned with style, plot, and characterisation than with the impersonal psychological analysis of human reactions.

sar·rus·o·phone (sə-rṓo-sə-fōn, -zə- ‖ -réw-) *n.* A wind instrument made of brass with a double reed, played like a bassoon. [After *Sarrus,* 19th-century French bandmaster who invented it (1856).]

sar·sa·pa·ril·la (sárspə-ríllə, sár-səpə- ‖ sáspə-) *n.* **1.** Impudent. roots of any of several tropical American plants of the genus *Smilax,* especially *S. aristolochiaefolia,* of Mexico, used as a flavouring and, formerly, as an emetic and to treat psoriasis. Also called of the plants from which sarsaparilla is obtained. **4.** Either of two North American plants, *Aralia hispida* or *A. nudicaulis,* having small white flowers. [Spanish *zarzaparrilla* : *zarza,* bramble, from Arabic *sharaṣ,* thorny plant + *parrilla,* diminutive of *parra†,* vine.]

sar·sen (sárss'n) *n.* A sandstone boulder of Tertiary age, found mainly on the chalk lands of southern England. [17th century : from earlier *Sardens, Saracen's stones,* probably from SARACEN.]

sarsenet. Variant of **sarcenet.**

Sarto, Andrea del. See **Andrea del Sarto.**

sar·to·ri·al (saar-táw-ri-əl ‖ -tṓ-) *adj.* **1.** Of or pertaining to a tailor or tailoring. **2.** Of or pertaining to clothing or fashion, especially men's. **3.** *Anatomy.* Of or pertaining to the sartorius. [Latin *sartor,* a tailor. See **sartorius.**] —**sar·to·ri·al·ly** *adv.*

sar·to·ri·us (saar-táw-ri-əss ‖ -tṓ-) *n.* A flat, narrow thigh muscle, the longest of the human body, crossing the front of the thigh obliquely from the hip to the inner side of the tibia. [New Latin *sartorius (musculus),* "tailor's (muscle)" (because it enables one to sit in a cross-legged position like a tailor at work), from Latin *sartor,* a tailor, from *sartus,* past participle of *sarcīre,* to mend.]

Sar·tre (sártrə, sartr), **Jean-Paul** (1905–80). French philosopher and writer. A friend of Simone de Beauvoir and a Marxist sympathiser, he was a founder and leading exponent of the existentialist

school. He worked for the French Resistance in World War II. His work includes novels such as the *Roads to Freedom* trilogy (1945–49), philosophical essays such as *Being and Nothingness* (1943), and many plays, including *In Camera* (1944). In 1964 he refused the Nobel prize for literature, for "personal reasons".

Sarum. See **Salisbury.**

SAS *n.* Special *Air* Service: a British army regiment of highly trained troops used on special assignments.

sash¹ (sash) *n.* A band or ribbon worn about the waist of a dress, as for ornament, or over the shoulder, as a symbol of military or other rank. [Earlier *shash,* from Arabic *shāsh,* muslin.]

sash² *n.* A frame in which the panes of a window or door are set; especially, either of the two movable frames in a sash window. —*tr.v.* **sashed, sashing, sashes.** To furnish with a sash. [Variant of earlier *shashes* (plural), from French *châssis,* a frame, CHASSIS.]

sash·ay (sásh-ay, sa-sháy) *intr.v.* **-shayed, -shaying, -shays.** *Chiefly U.S. Informal.* **1. a.** To flounce and sway. **b.** To glide. **2.** To perform the chassé in dancing. —*n. Chiefly U.S. Informal.* An excursion; a sally. [Variant of CHASSÉ.]

sash window *n.* A window consisting of a fixed frame enclosing two movable frames (sashes) set in grooves one above the other, which can slide up and down; they are held in position by a *sash cord* running over a pulley attached to the outer frame, and a counterbalancing weight (a *sash weight*).

sas·in (sássin) *n.* The **black buck** (see).

Sas·katch·e·wan¹ (sass-kácha-wən, səss-, -won). Province of south central Canada. Its southern prairies provide two-thirds of Canada's wheat, and the province is also rich in minerals, including uranium, copper, zinc, coal, potash, oil, and natural gas. The area was under the control of the Hudson's Bay Company (1670–1869), and became a province in 1905. Regina is the capital.

Saskatchewan². River, in central Canada. It is formed by the confluence of the North and South Saskatchewan rivers just east of Prince Albert, and flows east to Lake Winnipeg. The Qu'Appelle and Gardiner dams are major elements in the South Saskatchewan river project for hydroelectric power and irrigation.

Sas·ka·toon (sáskə-tōon). City in central Saskatchewan, Canada. Founded in 1883 on the South Saskatchewan river, it is a major rail junction and distribution centre for a large agricultural area.

sass (sass) *n. Chiefly U.S. Informal.* Impertinence; backchat. —*tr.v.* **sassed, sassing, sasses.** *U.S. Informal.* To argue impudently with; answer back. [Back-formation from SASSY (impudent).]

sas·sa·by (sássəbi) *n., pl.* **-bies** or collectively **sassaby.** Also **tses·se·be** (tséssəbi) *pl.* **-bes** or collectively **tsessebe.** An African antelope, *Damaliscus lunatus,* having curved, ridged horns. [Bantu (Tswana) *tshêsêbê.*]

sas·sa·fras (sássə-frass) *n.* **1.** A North American tree, *Sassafras albidum,* having irregularly lobed leaves and aromatic bark. **2.** The dried root bark of this tree, used as flavouring and as a source of a volatile antiseptic oil containing camphor, safrole, and pinene. **3.** Any of various other trees with aromatic bark, such as the Australian species *Doryphora sassafras* and *Atherosperma moschatum.* [New Latin, from Spanish *sasafrás†.*]

Sas·sa·nid (sássənid) *n., pl.* **-nids** or **-nidae** (sə-sánni-dee). Also **Sas·sa·ni·an** (sə-sáyni-ən). A member of the dynasty of Persian kings ruling from the third to the middle of the seventh century A.D. [Medieval Latin *Sassanidae* (plural), from *Sassan,* grandfather of Ardashir I, founder of the dynasty.] —**Sas·sa·nid** *adj.*

Sas·se·nach (sássə-nak, -nakh) *n. Chiefly Scottish.* An English person. Used derogatorily. [Irish *Sasanach,* from *Sasan-,* Saxon, from Late Latin *Saxonēs,* SAXON(S).] —**Sas·se·nach** *adj.*

Sas·soon (sa-sōon), **Siegfried** (1886–1967). British poet and writer. He served in the army with distinction in Palestine and France until 1917, when disgust at the course of World War I led him to make a public refusal to serve further. His work includes *War Poems* (1919) and several largely autobiographical novels.

sas·sy¹ (sássi) *adj.* **-sier, -siest.** *U.S. Informal.* **1.** Impudent. **2.** Jaunty. [Variant of SAUCY.] —**sas·si·ly** *adv.* —**sas·si·ness** *n.*

sassy² *n.* A tree, *Erythrophloeum guineense,* of west Africa, having bark that yields a poison. Also called "sasswood", "sassy bark". [Probably of African origin.]

sas·tru·ga (sə-strōō-gə, sa-) *n., pl.* **-gi** (-gee, -jee). Also **zas·tru·ga** (zə-, za-). A long, wavelike ridge of snow formed by the wind and found on the polar plains. [Russian *zastruga,* groove.]

sat. Past tense and past participle of **sit.**

Sat. Saturday.

Sa·tan (sáyt'n) *n.* In Judaism and Christianity, the chief adversary of God and mankind; the Devil. [Middle English, Old English, from Late Latin *Satān,* from Greek *Satan,* from Hebrew *śāṭān,* devil, adversary, from *śāṭan,* to accuse.]

sa·tang (sa-táng, sə- ‖ *U.S.* -táang) *n., pl.* **satang.** A coin equal to 1/100 of the baht of Thailand. [Thai *satăŋ.*]

sa·tan·ic (sə-tánnik, say-) *adj.* Also **sa·tan·i·cal** (-'l). **1.** Pertaining to or suggestive of Satan or Satanism. **2.** Profoundly cruel or evil; fiendish. —**sa·tan·i·cal·ly** *adv.*

Sa·tan·ism (sáyt'n-iz'm) *n.* **1.** Worship of Satan, especially in the form of a travesty of Christian ritual. **2.** Evil or satanic practices or tendencies. —**Sa·tan·ist** *n.*

sat·ay (sát-ay, sáat) *n.* A Malaysian and Indonesian dish consisting of pieces of meat barbecued on skewers and usually eaten with a spicy peanut sauce. [Malay.]

S.A.T.B. soprano, alto, tenor, bass. Used in choral music.

satch·el (sáchəl) *n.* A small bag, often having a shoulder strap, and used especially by schoolchildren for carrying books. [Middle English *sachel*, from Old French, from Latin *saccelus*, diminutive of *saccus*, a bag, SACK.]

sate[1] (sayt) *tr.v.* **sated, sating, sates. 1.** To indulge (a person or his appetite or desire) fully. **2.** To indulge to excess; glut. —See Synonyms at **satiate.** [Probably variant (influenced by SATIATE) of obsolete *sade*, Middle English *sad(d)en*, Old English *sadian*.]

sate[2]. *Archaic.* Past tense of **sit.**

sa·teen (sa-téen, sə-) *n.* A cotton fabric with a satin weave and a glossy sheen. [Variant of SATIN (influenced by VELVETEEN).]

sat·el·lite (sátt'l-īt) *n.* **1.** *Astronomy.* A relatively small body orbiting a planet; a moon. **2.** *Aerospace.* A man-made object that orbits the Earth, Moon, or another planet. Also called "artificial satellite". **3.** One who attends a powerful dignitary. **4.** One that is dependent on another, as: **a.** A subservient follower. **b.** A nation that is dominated politically by another. **c.** A small town, such as a dormitory town, that is economically dependent on a larger neighbouring town or city. [French, from Latin *satelles* (stem *satellit-*), an attendant, escort, probably from Etruscan *śatnal*.]

sa·tem (sáttəm, sáʹatəm) *adj.* Of, pertaining to, or constituting the group of those Indo-European languages in which the velar *k* of primitive Indo-European became *s* and the labiovelar *kw* became *k*. Compare **centum.** [Avestan *satəm*, hundred (an arbitrarily chosen word in which initial *s* represents initial Indo-European *k*).]

Sati *n. Hinduism.* The goddess Devi as a self-sacrificing mother.

sa·ti·a·ble (sáyshi-əb'l, sáysh-) *adj.* Capable of being satiated. [Latin *satiābilis*, from Latin *satiāre*, SATIATE.] —**sa·ti·a·bil·i·ty** (-ə-bílləti), **sa·ti·a·ble·ness** *n.* —**sa·ti·a·bly** *adv.*

sa·ti·ate (sáyshi-ayt) *tr.v.* **-ated, -ating, -ates. 1.** To gratify to excess; surfeit. **2.** To satisfy (an appetite or desire) fully; sate.
~*adj. Archaic.* Filled to satisfaction; satiated. [From Latin *satiāre*, from *satis*, sufficient, enough.] —**sa·ti·a·tion** (-áysh'n) *n.*
        Synonyms: satiate, sate, glut, gorge, surfeit.

Sa·tie (sa-tée), **Erik,** born Alfred Erik Leslie-Satie (1866–1925). French composer, chiefly of piano works and ballets, noted for his eccentricity and humour. He used simplicity of technique to achieve surreal effects, as in the *Gymnopédies* (1888), which have had some influence on younger composers.

sa·ti·e·ty (sə-tíʹəti, sáyshi-əti) *n.* **1.** The condition of being full to satisfaction, as with food. **2.** The condition of being gratified beyond the point of satisfaction; surfeit. [Obsolete French *societé*, from Latin *satietās* (stem *satietāt-*), sufficiency, from *satis*, sufficient, enough.]

sat·in (sáttin ‖ sátt'n) *n.* A smooth silk, cotton, rayon, or nylon fabric woven with a glossy face and a dull back.
~*adj.* **1.** Made of satin. **2.** Resembling satin, as in texture or appearance. [Middle English, from Old French, from Arabic possibly ultimately from Chinese.] —**sat·in·y** *adj.*

sat·i·net, sat·i·nette (sátti-nét) *n.* A thin satin or an imitation satin, such as a blend of cotton with silk or cotton and wool. [French, from Old French, diminutive of SATIN.]

sa·tin·flow·er (sáttin-flowr) *n.* A European plant, *Stellaria holostea*, with white flowers.

satin stitch *n.* An embroidery stitch worked in close parallel lines to give a smooth finish.

satin weave *n.* A basic weave construction with the interlacing of the threads so arranged that the face of the cloth is covered with warp yarn or filling yarn and no twill line is distinguishable.

sat·in·wood (sáttin-wŏŏd) *n.* **1. a.** A tree, *Chloroxylon swietenia*, of southern Asia, having hard, yellowish, close-grained wood. **b.** The wood of this tree, used in cabinetwork. **2. a.** Any of several other trees having similar wood. **b.** The wood of any of these trees.

sat·ire (sáttīr) *n.* **1.** A dramatic or literary work or entertainment in which irony, derision, caricature or wit in any form is used to expose folly or wickedness, especially by ridiculing aspects of and personalities in contemporary society. **2.** The branch of entertainment or art, especially literature, comprising such works. **3.** The use of derisive wit in any context to attack or ridicule folly or wickedness. —See Synonyms at **caricature.** [French, from Latin *satira*, *satura*, satire, medley, mixture, mixed fruits, from the feminine of *satur*, full of food, sated.]

sa·tir·i·cal (sə-tírrik'l) *adj.* Also **sa·tir·ic** (-tírrik). Constituting, characteristic of, or inclined to the use of satire. See Usage note at **sarcastic.** —**sa·tir·i·cal·ly** *adv.* —**sa·tir·i·cal·ness** *n.*

sat·i·rise, sat·i·rize (sáttə-rīz, sátti-) *tr.v.* **-rised, -rising, -rises.** To ridicule or attack by means of satire.

sat·i·rist (sáttə-rist, sátti-) *n.* **1.** A writer of satirical works. **2.** One who uses or tends to use satire.

sat·is·fac·tion (sáttiss-fáksh'n) *n.* **1.** The fulfilment or gratification of a desire, need, or appetite. **2.** Pleasure or contentment, as derived from the gratification of a desire or from a personal achievement or attainment: *gets a lot of satisfaction from her work.* **3.** Reparation in the form of penance for sin; atonement. **4.** Compensation for injury or loss, as to one's honour or reputation; amends. **5.** A source of gratification. **6.** Assurance; certainty.

sat·is·fac·to·ry (sáttiss-fáktri, -fáktəri) *adj.* **1.** Giving satisfaction; sufficient to meet a demand or requirement; adequate: *a satisfactory reason.* **2.** Warranting some pleasure; gratifying. **3.** Serving to atone for sin. —**sat·is·fac·to·ri·ly** *adv.* —**sat·is·fac·to·ri·ness** *n.*

sat·is·fy (sáttiss-fī) *v.* **-fied, -fying, -fies. 1.** To gratify the need, desire, or expectation of. **2.** To fulfil (a need or desire). **3.** To relieve of doubt or question; assure. **4.** To suffice to dispel (a doubt

or question). **5.** To fulfil or discharge (an obligation, contract, or debt). **6.** To discharge an obligation to (a creditor). **7.** To conform to the requirements of (a standard or rule, for example). **8.** To make reparation to (a wronged party). **9.** *Mathematics.* To fulfil the conditions of (a theorem, equation, or the like). —*intr.* To give satisfaction. [Middle English *satisfien*, from Old French *satisfier*, from Latin *satisfacere* : *satis*, sufficient, enough + *facere*, to do, make.] —**sat·is·fi·er** *n.* —**sat·is·fy·ing·ly** *adv.*

Sa·to (sáa-tō), **Eisaku** (1901–75). Japanese Conservative politician. He was prime minister from 1964 to 1972, presiding over Japan's economic expansion and pursuing an independent foreign policy. In 1974 he shared the Nobel prize for peace for his opposition to nuclear weapons.

---

satellite

TRANSMITTERS IN ORBIT
Relaying signals and monitoring the weather

Artificial satellites for communications purposes can relay television programmes, telephone calls, telex, computer data, and printed matter. They operate by receiving radio signals from the Earth, amplifying them, and transmitting them to other points on Earth. Such satellites must orbit hundreds of kilometres above the Earth; at low levels their range would be severely limited by the Earth's curvature.

Weather satellites record information on cloud, snow, ice cover, and temperature, and transmit it by infrared TV pictures. They are particularly vital for giving advance warning of hurricanes and other storm systems, and their information, shared internationally, has led to the saving of lives and property that has more than repaid their cost.

The first weather satellites, codenamed Tiros, were launched in 1960 by the United States. Tiros was followed by increasingly involved series in many different orbits: ESSA (Environmental Science Services Administration) satellites, the Nimbus series, and the National Oceanic and Atmospheric Administration series (NOAA). Another series in geostationary orbits – that is, maintaining position above the same point of the Earth – provide permanent monitoring of selected areas. Most of these are U.S. satellites, but Russia has its own series, Meteor.

In the 1970s, three other U.S. satellites, Landsats (originally called Earth Resources and Technology satellites), were placed in orbits that scan the whole Earth every 18 days, and can stay in operation indefinitely. Landsats use both still and TV cameras, and work in four wavelengths, each revealing a different type of information – on forest cover, crops, water and air pollution, and marine resources.

DEVELOPMENT AID *Computer-aided photography by a U.S. satellite provides information on land cover to help in making decisions about land development. Different colours indicate different features: red areas show urban complexes, green, forest land, and blue marsh areas and water. The deeper the intensity of the colour, the more concentrated is the feature.*

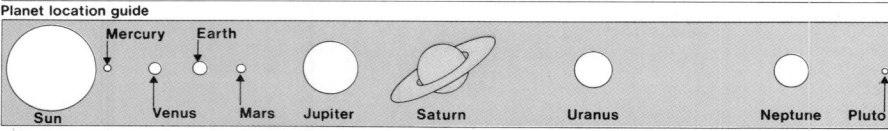

saturated *Ethane (C₂H₆) – a colourless, odourless gas – is known as a saturated compound; its atoms are linked only by single bonds (upper drawing). Unsaturated compounds – such as the flammable gas ethene or ethylene, C₂H₄ (lower drawing) – contain double or triple bonds and combine with other chemicals more readily than saturated compounds. Ethane and ethylene are both used in the manufacture of plastics.*

sa·to·ri (sə-táwri, saa- ‖ -tőri) *n.* A state of spiritual enlightenment sought in Zen Buddhism. [Japanese, "insight".]

sa·trap (sáttrap, sáttrəp ‖ *U.S. also* sáy-trap) *n.* **1.** A governor of a province in ancient Persia. **2.** Any colonial governor or subordinate ruler. [Middle English *satrape*, from Old French, from Latin *satrapēs*, from Greek, from Old Persian *khshathrapāvan*, "protector of the country" : *khshathra-*, province, country + *-pāvan*, protector.]

sa·trap·y (sáttrəpi ‖ sáytrəpi) *n., pl.* **-ies. 1.** The territory or sphere under the rule of a satrap. **2.** The office of satrap. **3.** The period of rule of a satrap. [French *satrapie*, from Latin *satrapia*, from Greek *satrapeia*, from *satrapēs*, SATRAP.]

sat·su·ma (sat-sŏŏmə, sátsŏŏmə) *n.* **1.** A variety of the small citrus tree, *Citrus reticulata*, native to Japan, grown widely for its sweet mandarin-like fruit. **2.** The fruit of this tree, having a loose orange rind and segmented pulp. [After *Satsuma*, former province of Kyushu, Japan, where it was originally grown.]

Sa·tsu·ma ware (sat-sŏŏmə) *n.* A yellow porcelain ware originally made at Satsuma, a former province of Kyushu, Japan.

sat·u·rant (sáchər-ənt, sáttewr-) *n.* A substance used to saturate a solution. [Latin *saturāns* (stem *saturānt-*), present participle of *saturāre*, SATURATE.] **—sat·u·rant** *adj.*

sat·u·rate (sáchər-ayt, sáttewr-) *tr.v.* **-rated, -rating, -rates. 1.** To wet thoroughly; fill with moisture. **2.** To steep, imbue, or impregnate thoroughly. **3.** To fill to capacity or beyond; surfeit; sate. **4.** *Chemistry.* **a.** To cause (a solution) to be saturated. **b.** To cause (a compound) to be saturated. **5.** *Military.* To subject (a target) to heavy bombardment with the aim of totally destroying enemy defences. [Latin *saturāre*, to fill, satiate, from *satur*, full of food, sated.] **—sat·u·ra·bil·i·ty** (-ə-bílləti) *n.* **—sat·u·ra·ble** (-əb'l) *adj.* **—sat·u·ra·tor** (-aytər) *n.*

sat·u·rat·ed (sáchər-aytid, sáttewr-) *adj.* **1.** Unable to hold or contain more of a substance; full. **2.** *Chemistry.* **a.** Containing all the solute that can normally be dissolved at a given temperature. Said of a solution. **b.** Containing all the water vapour or other vapour that can normally be present at a given temperature. Said of a gas. **c.** Having all available valency bonds filled. Said especially of organic compounds. **3.** *Geology.* Of or designating minerals that can crystallise from magmas even in the presence of excess silica. **4.** In a state of saturation. Said of a colour.

sat·u·ra·tion (sáchər-áysh'n, sáttewr-) *n.* **1. a.** The act or process of saturating. **b.** The condition of being saturated. **2.** *Physics.* A state of a ferromagnetic substance in which an increase in applied magnetic field strength does not produce an increase in magnetic field strength. **3.** *Chemistry.* The state of a compound or solution that is fully saturated. **4.** *Meteorology.* A condition in which air at a specific temperature contains all the moisture vapour possible without precipitating; 100 per cent relative humidity. **5.** Vividness of hue; degree of difference of a colour from a grey of the same lightness or brightness. **6.** *Military.* The striking of a target with so many missiles that it is totally destroyed. Also used adjectivally: *saturation bombing.* **7.** The flooding of a market with all of a commodity that its consumers can possibly purchase.

saturation point *n.* **1.** *Chemistry.* The point at which a substance will receive no more of another substance in solution. **2.** The point at which no more can be absorbed, assimilated, or incorporated.

saturation zone *n.* The layers of rock below the water table which are saturated with water.

Sat·ur·day (sáttər-di, -day ‖ sát-) *n.* *Abbr.* Sat. The day of the week following Friday; the first day of the weekend. [Middle English *Saterday*, Old English *Sæterdæg*, short for *sæternesdæg*, "Saturn's day" : *Sætern*, *Saturnus*, SATURN + *dæg*, DAY.]

Sat·urn¹ (sátturn, sátt'n) An Italic and Roman deity identified with the Greek god Cronos. [Middle English *Saturnus*, *Satourn*, Old English *Saturnus*, from Latin *Sāturnus*, Saturn (the god), Saturn (the planet), probably of Etruscan origin.]

Saturn² *n.* **1.** The sixth planet from the Sun and the second-largest

---

Saturn

A GASEOUS GIANT AND ITS MYSTERIOUS RINGS
The complex of icy circles seen by Voyager space probes

Saturn, one of the outer planets of the Solar System and second in size only to Jupiter, is visible to the naked eye as a bright, yellowish star. Saturn's overall density is less than that of water, and it probably has a rocky core surrounded by layers of liquid hydrogen, which are in turn overlaid by a gaseous atmosphere – the actual surface that we can see. The cloud tops are very cold, at a temperature of about − 180°C (− 292°F). But the core must be hot since Saturn radiates more energy than it receives from the Sun.

The main glory of Saturn is its magnificent system of rings, visible with a small telescope, which are composed of icy particles. There are two main rings, separated by a gap known as Cassini's Division, and various less conspicuous rings. The Voyager space probes have shown that the rings are very complex, and are made up of thousands of individual thin rings separated by gaps.

Saturn has a wealth of satellites; nine were known before the flights of the Pioneer and Voyager space probes, and today at least 20 are known. Most of them are comparatively small, but there is one large satellite, Titan, which is 5800 kilometres (3,600 miles) in diameter – bigger than the planet Mercury. Titan has a dense atmosphere composed chiefly of nitrogen, with considerable quantities of methane. On Titan's surface, hidden by a reddish photochemical smog, there may be cliffs of solid methane, rivers of liquid methane, and a methane drizzle from the clouds.

Planet location guide

Sun   Mercury   Venus   Earth   Mars   Jupiter   Saturn   Uranus   Neptune   Pluto

VOYAGER'S VIEW OF SATURN *Colour pictures sent back to the Earth by Voyager 2 revealed among the yellow and pastel hues of the planet's surface many dark and light bands in both hemispheres. The contrasts are believed to be caused by Saturn's weather system. Three of Saturn's moons – Tethys, Dione, and Rhea – show as bright spots below Saturn, and Tethys casts its shadow on the planet.*

SATURN'S RINGS *Computer-enhanced colour pictures of Saturn's rings record differences that may be caused by chemical variations from one part to another. The lumps of icy material which make up the rings range from the size of a house down to that of coins. The outermost ring contains two strands twisted round each other and this braided effect is believed to be caused by Saturn's magnetic field.*

in the Solar System, having an equatorial diameter of about 120 000 kilometres (75,000 miles), a mass 95 times that of Earth, and an orbital period of 29.5 years at a mean distance from the Sun of about 1 427 million kilometres (886 million miles). It has nine major and numerous minor satellites and is encircled by a system of rings composed of many small, solid, icy bodies. **2.** In alchemy, the element lead.

sat·ur·na·li·a (sáttər-náyli-ə) *n., pl.* **-lias** or **saturnalia.** An occasion or period of unrestrained or orgiastic revelry and licentiousness. [Latin *sāturnālia,* festival of SATURN (celebrated in December in ancient Rome and marked by wild revelry.] —**sat·ur·na·li·an** *adj.*

Sa·tur·ni·an (sə-túrni-ən) *adj.* **1.** Of or pertaining to the planet Saturn or to its supposed astrological influence. **2.** Of or pertaining to the god Saturn or to the golden age of his reign.

sa·tur·ni·id (sə-túrni-id) *n.* Any of various often large and colourful moths of the mainly tropical family Saturniidae. [New Latin *Saturniidae,* from *Saturnia* (type genus), from Latin *Sāturnia,* daughter of SATURN.] —**sa·tur·ni·id** *adj.*

sat·ur·nine (sáttər-nīn) *adj.* **1.** Having a gloomy, taciturn, and somewhat sinister character; having or showing the temperament of one born under the supposed astrological influence of the planet Saturn. **2.** *Archaic.* Pertaining to or resembling lead or produced by the absorption of lead.

sat·urn·ism (sáttər-niz'm) *n. Pathology.* **Lead poisoning** (see). [Middle English *saturne,* from Medieval Latin *sāturnus,* lead, from Latin *Sāturnus,* SATURN + -ISM.]

sat·ya·gra·ha (sət-yáagrə-hə) *n. Often capital* **S.** The policy of non-violent resistance initiated in India by Mahatma Gandhi as a means of pressing for political reform. [Sanskrit *satyāgraha,* "insistence on truth" : *satya,* truth, reality, from *sat, sant,* existing, true + *āgraha,* the act of holding firmly to, insistence : *ā,* to + *grbhṇāti,* he seizes.]

sat·yr (sáttər ‖ *U.S. also* sáytər) *n.* **1.** *Greek Mythology.* Any of a class of manlike woodland gods or demons often having the pointed ears, legs, and short horns of a goat. **2.** A lecher. **3.** A man afflicted with satyriasis. **4.** Any of various butterflies of the subfamily Satyridae, having brown wings marked with eyelike spots. In this sense, also called "brown", "satyrid". [Middle English, from Latin *satyrus,* from Greek *saturos†.*] —**sa·tyr·ic** (sə-tírrik), **sa·tyr·i·cal** *adj.*

sat·y·ri·a·sis (sátti-rī-ə-siss, sáttə-) *n.* Abnormally strong sexual drive in the heterosexual male. Also called "satyromania". Compare **nymphomania.** [Late Latin, from Greek. See **satyr, -iasis.**]

satyr play *n.* A comic drama in a burlesque style, having a chorus of satyrs, traditionally staged following a series of tragic plays at ancient Greek dramatic festivals. See **tetralogy.**

sauce (sawss) *n.* **1.** Any soft or liquid dressing or relish, usually cooked, served as an accompaniment to food. **2.** *U.S.* Stewed or puréed sweetened fruit, eaten as a dessert. **3.** *U.S. Regional.* Vegetables; greens. **4.** Anything that adds zest, flavour, or piquancy to something. **5.** *Informal.* Impudence; sauciness.
~*tr.v.* **sauced, saucing, sauces. 1.** To season or flavour with sauce. **2.** To add piquancy or zest to. **3.** *Informal.* To be impertinent or impudent to. [Middle English, from Old French, from Latin *salsa,* feminine of *salsus,* salted, from the past participle of *sallere,* to salt, from *sāl,* salt.]

sauce béarnaise. See **béarnaise sauce.**

sauce béchamel. See **béchamel sauce.**

sauce-boat (sáwss-bōt) *n.* A low, boat-shaped vessel with a wide lip at one end and a handle at the other end, used chiefly for serving gravies and sauces.

sauce bordelaise *n.* See **bordelaise sauce.**

sauce-box (sáwss-boks) *n. Informal.* An impertinent person.

sauce-pan (sáwss-pən ‖ sóss-, -pan) *n.* A long-handled cooking pan of medium depth, usually having a lid.

sau·cer (sáwssər) *n.* **1.** A small, round, shallow dish having a slight circular depression in the centre for holding a cup. **2.** Any dish or other object having a similar shape: *a flying saucer.* **3.** As much as a saucer can hold: *a saucer of milk.* In this sense, also called "saucerful". [Middle English, sauce dish, from Old French *saussier,* from *sausse, sauce,* SAUCE.]

sau·cy (sáwssi) *adj.* **-cier, -ciest. 1.** Impertinent or disrespectful; impudent. **2.** Piquant; pert. **3.** Risqué; racy. —**sau·ci·ly** *adv.* —**sau·ci·ness** *n.*

Saud (sowd; *Arabic* sa-ōōd), born Saud ibn Abd al-Aziz (1902–69). King of Saudi Arabia (1953–64). He was deposed by his brother Faisal following his failure to deal with the difficulty of using his country's wealth from oil to modernise a conservative nation.

Sau·di Arabia, Kingdom of (sówdi, *also* sáwdi). *Arabic* **Al-Mamla-kah al-'Arabiyah as-Sa'udiyah.** Country in southwest Asia. The kingdom, which covers most of the Arabian peninsula, was founded in 1932 by Ibn Saud, a descendant of the puritanical Wahhabi Muslim rulers of the 18th century. The rulers of the country are the guardians of the holiest shrines of Islam at Mecca and Medina, and these attract many hundreds of thousands of pilgrims annually. Saudi Arabia is mostly desert and includes the world's largest continuous sand area—the Rub al-Khali, or Empty Quarter. Only Asir in the southwest and the various oases are cultivated. Food and consumer goods are imported on a lavish scale made possible by the country's enormous wealth in oil. The country is the world's greatest exporter of oil and possesses a significant proportion of the world's proven reserves. Area, 2 149 690 square kilometres (830,000 square miles). Population, 11,100,000. Capital, Riyadh.

sauer·kraut (sówr-krowt) *n.* Chopped or shredded cabbage that is salted and fermented in its own juice. [German *Sauerkraut* : *sauer,* sour + *Kraut,* cabbage.]

sau·ger (sáwgər) *n.* A small North American freshwater fish, *Stizostedion canadense,* having a spotted, spiny dorsal fin.

Saul (sawl). First king of Israel (11th century B.C.); proclaimed by Samuel; succeeded by David. [Hebrew *Shā-ul,* "asked for".]

Saul of Tarsus. See Saint Paul.

sau·na (sáwnə, sównə) *n.* **1.** A steam-bath treatment or recreation originating in Finland, in which the bather is first subjected to steam produced originally by running water over heated rocks, and then to a cold bath and sometimes a light beating with twigs. **2.** A room or building in which this bath is taken. [Finnish.]

saun·ter (sáwntər) *intr.v.* **-tered, -tering, -ters.** To walk at a leisurely pace; stroll.
~*n.* A leisurely pace; a stroll. [Probably Middle English *santerent,* to muse.]

saur-, sauro- *comb. form.* Indicates lizard-like; for example, **sauropod.** [New Latin *saurus,* lizard, from Latin, from Greek, *savros†.*]

-saur, -saurus *n. comb. form.* Indicates a lizard-like creature; for example, **brontosaur.** [New Latin *saurus,* lizard. See **saur-.**]

sau·ri·an (sáwri-ən) *n.* Any of various reptiles of the former order Sauria (now the Lacertilia), which includes the true lizards.
~*adj.* Of, belonging to, or characteristic of the Sauria; lizard-like. [New Latin *Sauria,* from *saurus,* lizard. See **saur-.**]

sau·ro·pod (sáwr-ə-pod, -ō-) *n.* Any of various large, semiaquatic, herbivorous dinosaurs of the suborder Sauropoda, of the Jurassic and Cretaceous periods. [New Latin *Sauropoda* : SAUR- + -POD.] —**sau·ro·pod, sau·rop·o·dous** (saw-róppədəss) *adj.*

sau·ry (sáwri) *n., pl.* **-ries.** Any of several offshore marine fishes of the family Belonidae, found in tropical and temperate waters and related to the needlefishes. Also called "skipper". [New Latin *saurus,* saury, lizard. See **saur-.**]

sau·sage (sóssij ‖ *U.S.* sáwssij) *n.* **1.** An item of food, consisting of seasoned minced meat and other filling that has been stuffed into a prepared animal intestine or similar cylindrical casing, and usually cooked before serving. **2. a.** A similar item of food, usually larger, in which the meat is cured or precooked, slices of which are eaten, usually cold, and an hors d'oeuvre or in sandwiches, for example. **b.** A piece, or pieces collectively, cut off from such a sausage: *Do you want cheese or sausage on your roll?* **3.** *Informal.* Any sausage-shaped object, such as an observation balloon. —**not a sausage.** *Informal.* Nothing. [Middle English *sausige,* from Old North French *saussiche,* from Late Latin *salsīcia,* from *salsīcius,* prepared by salting, from Latin *salsus,* salted. See **sauce.**]

sausage dog *n. British Informal.* A **dachshund** (see). [Referring to its elongated body.]

sausage meat *n.* Finely minced meat with bread, cereal, or other filling, seasoned and used in sausages or as a stuffing.

sausage roll *n.* A cylindrical piece of sausage meat covered in flaky or puff pastry.

Saus·sure (sō-séwr, *French* -súr), **Ferdinand de** (1857–1913). Swiss linguist. He was professor of Sanskrit at Geneva from 1901, but his greatest contribution to modern linguistics was made in his *Cours de linguistique générale* (1916), which was posthumously assembled from his students' lecture notes. Saussure developed a number of concepts that have been highly influential, notably the distinction between **langue** and **parole** (*both of which* see).

satyr *Half man and half goat, the satyr of Greek mythology is mischievous, drunken, and lecherous. This 2,000-year-old Roman sculpture shows a satyr's head with its pointed goatlike ears and budding horns.*

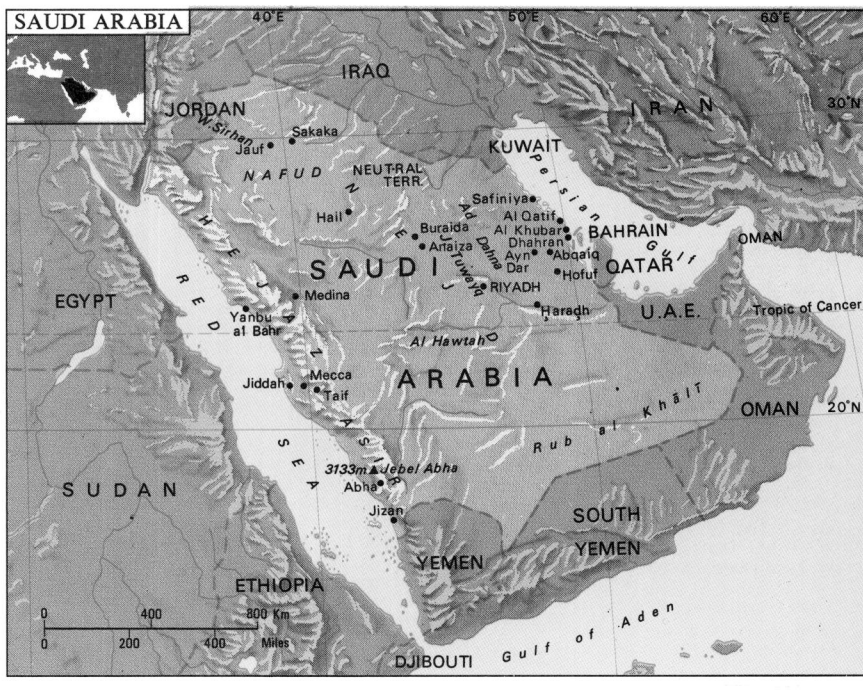

sau·té (sṓ-tay || sáw-, -ti, sō-táy) *tr.v.* **-téed, -téing, -tés.** To fry lightly in fat in a shallow, open pan.
~n. Sautéed food.
~adj. Sautéed. [French, "tossed (in a pan)", from the past participle of *sauter,* to leap, from Old French, from Latin *saltāre,* frequentative of *salīre* (past participle *saltus*), to leap.]

Sau·ternes, Sau·terne (sō-térn, -táirn) *n. Sometimes small* **s.** A delicate, sweet white dessert wine. [French, made in *Sauternes,* commune in southwest France.]

sau·vi·gnon (sṓveen-yóɴ) *n.* A variety of white grape widely used in western France for making white wine. [French, of obscure origin.]

sav·age (sávvij) *adj.* **1.** Not domesticated; wild; untamed. **2.** Not civilised; in a primitive state. **3.** Ferocious; fierce. **4.** Vicious or merciless; brutal: *savage cuts in spending.* **5.** Lacking polish or manners; rude. **6.** Rugged; desolate: *savage terrain.*
~n. **1.** A primitive or uncivilised person. **2.** A brutal, fierce, or vicious person. **3.** A rude person; a boor.
~tr.v. **savaged, -aging, -ages. 1.** To attack violently. **2.** To bite or maul ferociously. [Middle English *sauvage,* from Old French, from Vulgar Latin *salvāticus* (unattested), from Latin *silvāticus,* of the woods, wild, from *silva,* woods, forest. See **sylvan.**] **—sav·age·ly** *adv.* **—sav·age·ness** *n.*

Sav·age (sávvij), **Michael Joseph** (1872–1940). New Zealand politician. Born in Australia, he went to New Zealand in 1907 and worked as a miner. He entered Parliament in 1919 and led his country's first Labour government in 1935 when he became prime minister.

sav·age·ry (sávvij-ri, -əri) *n., pl.* **-ries. 1.** The condition or quality of being savage. **2.** A cruel or barbarous action.

sa·van·nah, sa·van·na, sa·van·a (sə-vánnə) *n.* Open grassland with tall grasses, scattered trees, and bushes, of drier tropical or subtropical regions. [Earlier *zavana,* from Spanish, from Taino *zabana.*]

sa·vant (sávv'nt, *French* sa-vóɴ) *n. Feminine* **sa·vante** (*French* -vóɴt). A learned, scholarly person. [French, from the present participle of *savoir,* to know, from Vulgar Latin *sapēre* (unattested), from Latin *sapere,* to be sensible, be wise.]

sav·a·rin (sávvə-rin, -ráɴ) *n.* A yeast-leavened cake baked in a ring-shaped mould and served moistened with liqueur or fruit syrup and with fruit or other filling in the centre. [After Anthelme Brillat-*Savarin* (1755–1826), French writer and gourmet.]

save[1] (sayv) *v.* **saved, saving, saves.** *—tr.* **1.** To deliver or preserve from disaster, harm, danger, or loss. **2.** To keep in a safe, intact condition; safeguard. **3.** To prevent or reduce the waste, loss, or expenditure of: *Save energy—insulate your home.* **4.** To keep for future use or enjoyment; store. Often used with *up.* **5.** To treat with care in order to avoid fatigue, wear, or damage; spare: *Save your legs and travel by bus.* **6.** To make unnecessary; obviate: *This will save you an extra trip.* **7.** *Theology.* To deliver from sin its consequences; redeem. **8.** In sports such as football and hockey: **a.** To stop (a ball, puck, or the like) going into the goal. **b.** To prevent (a goal). *—intr.* **1.** To avoid wasting, losing, or spending something, especially habitually; be economical: *drove slowly to save on petrol.* **2.** To accumulate money for future use. **3.** To preserve a person or thing from harm or loss.
~n. An act or instance of saving a goal. [Middle English *saven, salven,* from Old French *sauver,* from Late Latin *salvāre,* from Latin *salvus,* safe.] **—sav·a·ble, save·a·ble** *adj.* **—sav·a·ble·ness** *n.*
Synonyms: *save, rescue, reclaim, redeem, deliver.*

save[2] *prep.* With the exception of; except; but: *all save one.*
~conj. Archaic. **1.** Were it not; except; but. Usually used with *that.* **2.** Unless. [Middle English *save, sa(u)f,* from Old French *sa(u)f, salf,* from Latin *salvō,* without injury or prejudice to, except, ablative singular of *salvus,* safe, sound, healthy.]

save-all (sáyv-awl) *n.* Any device or contrivance that prevents the waste, damage, or loss of something, or that catches the waste products of a process for further use in manufacture.

sav·e·loy (sávvə-loy, -lóy) *n.* A highly seasoned smoked pork sausage. [Variant of obsolete French *cervelat,* from Italian *cervellato,* from *cervello,* brain (the sausage is sometimes made from the brain of pigs), from Latin *cerebellum,* diminutive of *cerebrum,* brain.]

sav·er (sáyvər) *n.* **1.** One that saves; especially, a person who saves money regularly. **2.** Something that prevents loss, waste, or expenditure. Usually used in combination: *money-saver; time-saver.*

sav·in, sav·ine (sávvin) *n.* **1.** An evergreen Eurasian shrub, *Juniperus sabina,* the young shoots of which yield an oil formerly used medicinally. **2.** *U.S.* Any of several similar or related shrubs or trees; especially, the **red cedar** *(see).* [Middle English *savin,* from Old English *safīne* and Old French *savine,* both from Latin *(herba) Sabīna,* "Sabine (plant)", from *Sabīnus,* SABINE.]

sav·ing (sáyving) *adj.* **1.** Redeeming; compensating: *saving graces.* **2.** Making or containing a reservation; qualifying: *a saving clause.*
~n. **1.** Preservation or rescue from harm, danger, or loss. **2.** Avoidance of wastage; economy. **3.** A reduction in expenditure or cost: *a saving of £20.* **4.** *Plural.* A sum of money saved. **5.** Anything that is saved. **6.** *Law.* An exception or reservation.
~prep. With the exception of.
~conj. Archaic. Except; save.

sav·ings account (sáyvingz) *n.* An account, held in a savings bank, into which individual depositors pay their savings and usually receive a higher rate of interest than on deposit accounts.

savings bank *n.* A bank that receives and invests the savings of private depositors and pays interest on the deposits. In Britain these are either the National Savings Bank, which is run by the government, or the Trustee Savings Banks, which are non-profit-making organisations managed by trustees.

sav·iour, *U.S.* **sav·ior** (sáyv-yər) *n.* **1.** One that rescues someone or something from dire circumstances. **2.** *Capital* **S.** Christ. Usually preceded by *the.* [Middle English *saviour, sauveur,* from Old French *sauveour,* from Late Latin *salvātor,* from *salvāre,* to SAVE.]

sa·voir-faire (sávwaar-fáir) *n.* The ability to say and do the right thing in any situation; social adroitness; tact. See Synonyms at **tact.** [French, "knowing how to do".]

sa·voir-vivre (sávwaar-véevrə, -véevr) *n.* Worldly knowledge and sophistication. [French, "knowing how to live".]

Sav·o·na·ro·la (sávvənə-rṓlə), **Girolamo** (1452–98). Italian religious reformer. A Dominican friar, he gained a vast popular following with his fervent preaching, which enabled him to lead a revolt that turned the Medici family out of Florence in 1494. He became the virtual ruler of Florence, but after criticising Pope Alexander VI he was excommunicated in 1497 and later executed.

sa·vor·y (sáyvəri) *n., pl.* **-ies. 1.** Either of two aromatic herbs, *Satureja hortensis* or *S. montana,* native to the Old World. The former species is also called "summer savory" and the latter "winter savory". **2.** The leaves of either of these plants, used as seasoning. [Middle English *saverey,* variant (perhaps influenced by SAVOURY) OF OLD ENGLISH *sætherie,* from Latin *saturēia*†.]

sa·vour, *U.S.* **sa·vor** (sáyvər) *n.* **1.** The quality of a thing which affects the sense of taste or smell; taste or aroma. **2.** A specific taste or smell. **3.** A distinctive or typical quality. **4.** Power or the quality of exciting interest; zestfulness. —See Synonyms at **smell.**
~v. **savoured** or *U.S.* **savored, -vouring** or *U.S.* **-voring, -vours** or *U.S.* **-vors.** *—intr.* **1.** To have a specified savour. Used with *of*: *The kitchen savoured of fresh bread.* **2.** To have an implication or suggestion; smack. Used with *of*: *savours of corruption.* *—tr.* **1.** To impart a flavour or scent to. **2.** To taste, smell, or experience with appreciation and enjoyment; relish. [Middle English *savour,* from Old French, from Latin *sapor,* taste, savour, from *sapere,* to taste, savour.] **—sa·vour·er** *n.* **—sa·vour·less** *adj.* **—sa·vor·ous** *adj.*

sa·vour·y, *U.S.* **sa·vor·y** (sáyvəri) *adj.* **1.** Appetising to the taste or smell. **2.** Piquant, pungent, or salty to the taste; not sweet. **3.** Pleasant or inoffensive. **4.** Morally respectable.
~n., pl. **savouries.** A savoury dish, such as Welsh rabbit or anchovies on toast, sometimes served in Britain as an hors d'oeuvre or at the end of a meal instead of a dessert. [Middle English *savory, savure,* from Old French *savoure,* from the past participle of *savourer,* to savour, from Late Latin *sapōrāre,* from Latin *sapor,* SAVOUR.] **—sa·vour·i·ly** *adv.* **—sa·vour·i·ness** *n.*

sa·voy (sə-vóy) *n.* A variety of cabbage with crinkled leaves and a compact head. [After SAVOY, where it was cultivated.]

Sa·voy (sə-vóy). *French* **Sa·voie** (sa-vwáa); *Italian* **Sa·voi·a** (sa-vóy-ə). Region on the French-Italian border in the western Alps, ruled by the House of Savoy from the 11th century. Savoy grew to include Nice in France and Piedmont in Italy, and became a duchy in 1416. The House of Savoy gained control of Sardinia in 1713, and Savoy, with Piedmont and the island of Sardinia, formed the kingdom of Sardinia. Genoa was added in 1815. On the unification of Italy in 1860, French Savoy was ceded to France. Today, Savoy comprises mainly the French départements of Haute-Savoie and Savoie. Chambéry is the chief city.

Sa·voy·ard (sə-vóy-aard, sávvoy-árd) *n.* **1.** A native or inhabitant of Savoy. **2.** A dialect of French spoken in Savoy. **3.** Any performer in or enthusiastic admirer of Gilbert and Sullivan operas, most of which were first staged at London's Savoy Theatre.
~adj. Of or pertaining to Savoy, its inhabitants, or their dialect.

sav·vy (sávvi) *intr.v.* **-vied, -vying, -vies.** *Slang.* To understand or know; comprehend. **—no savvy.** *Slang.* To fail to understand. Often used without the relevant pronoun.
~n. Slang. Practical understanding or knowledge; common sense. [Probably from West African pidgin or Atlantic creole, from phonetic approximation to Spanish *sabe (usted),* (you) know, from *saber,* to know, from Latin *sapere,* to be sensible, be wise.]

saw[1] (saw) *n.* **1.** A tool, usually portable and either hand-operated or power-operated, having a thin metal blade or disc with a sharp-toothed edge, used for cutting wood, metal, or other hard materials. **2.** A powered disc tool lacking teeth, used for cutting metal. **3.** A fixed machine for the operation of a saw or series of saws.
~v. **sawed, sawn** (sawn) or **sawed, sawing, saws.** *—tr.* **1.** To cut or divide with or as if with a saw. **2.** To produce or shape with or as if with a saw. *—intr.* **1.** To use a saw. **2.** To cut. Used of a saw. **3.** To admit of cutting with a saw: *This board saws evenly.* [Middle English *sawe,* Old English *sagu* (unattested), *saga.*] **—saw·er** *n.*

saw[2] *n.* A familiar, proverbial saying, especially when trite. See Synonyms at **saying.** [Middle English *sawe,* Old English *sagu,* speech, talk, from Germanic *sagō* (unattested); akin to SAGA.]

saw[3]. Past tense of **see.**

saw·bill (sáw-bil) *n.* A duck, the **merganser** *(see).* [Referring to the serrated edges of its bill.]

saw·bones (sáw-bōnz) *n. Slang.* A surgeon. Used humorously.

saw·dust (sáw-dust) *n.* The small particles of wood that fall from a wooden object as a result of sawing.

saw-edged (sáw-ejd, *often* sáwr-) *adj.* Having jagged, serrated edges.

saw·fish (sáw-fish) *n., pl.* **-fishes** or collectively **sawfish.** Any of various marine fishes of the genus *Pristis,* related to the rays and skates, and having a bladelike snout with teeth along both sides.

PRONUNCIATION KEY

a, trap; aa, father; ai, fair;
ar, star; aw, lawn; ay, play;
b, bb, stab; rubber;
ch, church; ck, ticket;
d, dd, dead; ladder; e, dress;
ee, bee; er, defer; ew, few;
ewr, pure; ə, about;
ər, letter; f, ff, fife; differ;
g, gg, giggle; h, hat; i, kit;
ī, price; īr, fire; j, judge;
k, kick; l, ll, let; 'l, needle;
m, mm, man; n, nn, no;
'n, sudden; ng, thing; o, lot;
ō, no; ŏŏ, foot; ōō, shoe;
oor, poor; ow, cow;
owr, hour; oy, boy;
p, pp, pepper; r, rr, red;
s, ss, sauce; sh, ship;
t, tt, totter; th, thick; th, this;
smooth; u, cut; ur, turn;
v, vv, valve; w, wet; y, yes;
z, zz, zebra; zh, vision;
pleasure

IN FOREIGN WORDS:

aɴ, oɴ, Saint-Saëns;
hl, Llanelli; Hluhluwe;
kh, loch; lough; Khaled

STRESS MARK:

ín-sīt, insight; in-sī́t, incite

saw·fly (sáw-flī) *n., pl.* **-flies.** Any of various destructive insects, chiefly of the family Tenthredinidae, the females of which have sawlike ovipositors used for cutting into plant tissue to deposit eggs.
saw·horse (sáw-hawrss) *n.* A rack or trestle used to support a piece of wood being sawn.
saw·mill (sáw-mil) *n.* **1.** A plant where timber is machine-cut into boards. **2.** A large machine for sawing timber.
sawn. Past participle of **saw.**
sawn-off (sáwn-óff, -áwf) *adj.* Also *U.S.* **sawed-off** (sáwd-). **1.** Designating a shotgun that has the barrels shortened by sawing to make it less conspicuous and increase the spread of shot over short ranges. **2.** *Informal.* Shorter than average. Said of a person.
saw set *n.* An instrument used to deflect the teeth of a saw by bending each tooth slightly, alternate teeth being bent in the same direction.
saw-toothed (sáw-tōōtht || -tōōtht) *adj.* Having teeth resembling the teeth of a saw; serrate.
saw-wort (sáw-wurt || -wawrt) *n.* Either of two thistle-like plants, *Serratula tinctoria* of moist meadows and *Saussurea alpina* of mountain grassland. [Referring to its serrated leaves.]
saw·yer (sáw-yər) *n.* **1.** One employed at sawing wood, as in a sawmill. **2.** *U.S.* Any of several longicorn beetles having larvae that bore holes in wood. [Middle English *sawier,* from *sawen,* to SAW.]
sax[1] (saks) *n.* Also **zax** (zaks). A hatchet-like tool used for trimming roofing slates. [Middle English, Old English *seax,* knife, from Germanic *sahsam* (unattested).]
sax[2] *n. Informal.* A saxophone.
Sax. Saxon; Saxony.
saxe blue (saks) *n.* A light greyish blue. [French *Saxe,* SAXONY, origin of a dye of this colour.] **—saxe-blue** *adj.*
sax·horn (sáks-hawrn) *n.* Any of a family of valved brass wind instruments, resembling the bugle and having a full, even tone and wide range. [Invented (1845) by Adolphe *Sax* (1814-94), Belgian musical instrument maker.]
sax·ic·o·lous (sak-síckə-ləss) *adj.* Also **sax·ic·o·line** (-līn). Growing on or living among rocks. [Latin *saxum,* rock + -COLOUS.]
sax·i·frage (sáksi-frij, -frayj, -frayzh) *n.* Any of numerous plants of the genus *Saxifraga,* of temperate regions, having small flowers and leaves often forming a basal rosette. [Middle English, from Old French, from Late Latin *saxifraga (herba),* "rock-breaking (herb)" (because it grows in rock crevices), from Latin *saxifragus* : *saxum,* rock + *frangere* (stem *frag-*), to break.]
Sax·on (sáks'n) *n. Abbr.* **S., Sax. 1.** A member of a West Germanic people that inhabited north Germany and invaded England in the fifth and sixth centuries with the Angles and Jutes. See **Anglo-Saxon. 2.** A native or inhabitant of Saxony. **3.** The West Germanic language or dialect spoken by any Saxon people. **4.** The Germanic elements present in Modern English as distinguished from French or Latin elements.
~*adj.* **1.** Of or pertaining to the Saxons or their language. **2.** Of Anglo-Saxon origin. **3.** Of or pertaining to Saxony, the German Saxons, or their language. [Middle English, from Old French, from Late Latin *Saxō* (stem *Saxon-*), from Greek *Saxones* (plural), from West Germanic *Saxon-* (unattested), probably from Germanic *sahsam* (unattested), knife (perhaps considered as their typical weapon); compare Old English *Seaxan,* Saxon, and *seax,* knife, SAX (tool).]
Saxon blue *n.* A dye made from indigo dissolved in a sulphuric acid solution. [After SAXONY, where it originated.]
sax·o·ny (sáksəni) *n. Often capital* **s. 1.** A high-grade wool, of a type originally from sheep raised in Saxony. **2.** A fine soft woollen fabric made from this wool.
Sax·o·ny (sáksəni). *German* **Sach·sen** (záks'n). Area of north Germany, the original home of the Saxons. Conquered by Charlemagne in the eighth century, it became a duchy after his death. This was frequently divided after 1180, and re-formed in various ways, moving generally southeastwards. The dukes became electors of the Holy Roman Empire (1356), and made Dresden their capital. Raised to kingship (1806), the elector lost half his territory to Prussia (1815). This province of Prussia later became part of East Germany (1949). The kingdom of Saxony was part of the German Empire (1871–1918), and, as the state of Saxony, part of pre-war Germany. This too became part of East Germany (1949). [See **Saxon.**]
sax·o·phone (sáksə-fōn) *n.* A wind instrument having a single-reed mouthpiece, a conical usually metal bore, and finger keys, and made in a variety of sizes. [Invented (1846) by Adolphe *Sax.* See **saxhorn.**] **—sax·o·phon·ist** (sak-sóffənist, sáksə-fōnist) *n.*
sax·tu·ba (sáks-téwbə || -tōōbə) *n.* A large bass saxhorn. [SAX(HORN) + TUBA.]
say (say) *v.* **said** (sed || sayd), **saying, says** (sez || sayz). *—tr.* **1.** To utter aloud; pronounce; speak. **2.** To express in words; state; declare. **3.** To state (an opinion, for example) with positive assurance or conviction. **4.** To repeat or recite: *say grace.* **5.** To report or maintain; allege: *They say she's won.* **6.** To estimate or suppose; assume: *Let's say that you're right.* **7.** To classify or describe. Usually used in the passive: *The player is then said to be offside.* **8.** To mean to express or convey; signify: *What is Picasso saying in this painting?* **9.** To indicate; show: *When I woke, the clock said midnight.* **10.** To adduce in favour or defence of something: *There's a lot to be said for the system.* **11.** To state by way of instruction. Used with an infinitive: *He said to start without him if he was late. —intr.* To make a statement or express an opinion. **—go without saying.** To be so self-evident as to need no justification or explanation. **—I say.** Used to express surprise or dismay, or to call for attention. **—not to say.** Indeed; perhaps in fact: *seemed unwelcoming, not to say hostile.* **—that is to say.** In other words; meaning.
~*n.* **1.** One's turn or chance to speak. **2.** What one has to say; one's opinion. **3.** The right or power to influence a decision; voice; authority: *have a say in the matter.*
~*adv.* **1.** Approximately: *There were, say, 500 people present.* **2.** For instance: *a woodwind, say an oboe.*
~*interj. U.S.* Used to gain the attention of someone. [Say, said (past tense and past participle); Middle English *seggen* (later *sayen*), *saide,* Old English *secgan, sægde* (past tense), *(ge)sægd* (past participle).] **—say·er** *n.*
S.A.Y.E. *n.* Save as you earn: a government saving scheme in Britain in which monthly deposits earn tax-free interest.
Say·ers (sáy-ərz, sairz), **Dorothy L(eigh)** (1893–1957). British novelist and translator. She is best known for her detective stories, usually featuring Lord Peter Wimsey, the gentlemanly, amateur investigator, who made his first appearance in *Whose Body?* (1923). For the last 20 years of her life she concentrated on religious books and drama, particularly her cycle of radio plays, *The Man Born To Be King.*
say·ing (sáy-ing) *n.* **1.** An adage; a maxim. **2.** A word of wit or wisdom.
Synonyms: *saying, maxim, adage, saw, motto, epigram, proverb, aphorism.*
say-so (sáy-sō) *n., pl.* **-sos.** *Informal.* **1.** An unsupported statement or assurance. **2.** An authoritative assertion; a dictum. **3.** The right of final decision; authority.
say·yid, say·id (sī-id) *n.* A Muslim claiming descent from Muhammad. Used as a title of respect. [Arabic, "lord".]
Sb The symbol for the element antimony [Latin *stibium*].
S-bend (éss-bend) *n.* An S-shaped bend, as in a road or pipe.
'sblood (zblud) *interj. Archaic.* Used as an oath. [Contraction of *God's blood.*]
Sc The symbol for the element scandium.
sc. 1. scene. **2.** scilicet. **3.** scruple (weight). **4.** sculpsit.
Sc. Scotch; Scots; Scottish.
s.c. *Printing.* small capitals.
S.C. Signal Corps.
scab (skab) *n.* **1. a.** The crustlike material that covers a healing wound. **b.** A small patch of such material. **2.** Scabies or mange in domestic animals or livestock. **3. a.** Any of various plant diseases caused by fungi or bacteria and resulting in crustlike spots on fruit, leaves, or roots. **b.** A spot or the spots caused by such a disease. **4.** *Informal.* **a.** A worker who refuses to join a trade union. **b.** An employee who works while others are on strike; a strikebreaker; a blackleg. Also used adjectivally: *scab labour.* **5.** *Informal.* A low or contemptible person. Not in current usage.
~*intr.v.* **scabbed, scabbing, scabs. 1. a.** To form a scab. **b.** To become covered with a scab. **2.** *Chiefly U.S. Informal.* To take a job held by a worker on strike; act as a scab. [Middle English *scabbe,* from Old Norse *skabb.*]
scab·bard (skábbərd) *n.* A sheath or container for a dagger, sword, or other similar weapon. [Middle English *scauberc,* from Anglo-French *escaubers* (plural) : probably Old High German *scār,* scissors, sword + *-berc,* protection, from *bergan,* to protect.]
scabbard fish *n.* Any of several narrow-bodied marine fishes of the family Trichiuridae; especially, *Lepidopus caudatus,* of Mediterrantan waters. [From its narrow, sheathlike body.]
scab·ble (skább'l) *tr.v.* **-bled, -bling, -bles.** To work or dress (stone) roughly. [Earlier *scapple,* Middle English *scaplen,* from Old French *eschapler,* "to cut off", dress timber : *es-,* from Latin *ex-,* off + *chapler,* to cut, from Late Latin *capulāre.*]
scab·by (skábbi) *adj.* **-bier, -biest. 1.** Having, consisting of, or covered with scabs or something resembling scabs. **2.** Suffering from scabies. **3.** *Informal.* Low; mean; vile: *a scabby trick.* **—scab·bi·ly** *adv.* **—scab·bi·ness** *n.*
sca·bi·es (skáy-bi-eez, -beez) *n. Used with a singular verb.* **1.** A contagious skin disease caused by a mite, *Sarcoptes scabiei,* and characterised by intense itching. **2.** A similar disease in animals, especially sheep. [Latin *scabiēs,* roughness, scurf, itch, from *scabere,* to scratch.] **—sca·bi·et·ic** (-bi-éttik) *adj.*
sca·bi·ous[1] (skáybi-əss || skábbi-) *adj.* **1.** Of or pertaining to scabies. **2.** Having scabs. [Latin *scabiōsus,* scabby, from SCABIES.]
scabious[2] *n.* **1.** Any of various plants of the genera *Knautia, Succisa,* or *Scabiosa;* especially, *K. arvensis* and *Scabiosa columbaria,* having opposite leaves and blue compound flower heads. See **devil's bit scabious. 2. Sheep's bit scabious** *(see).* [Middle English *scabiose,* from Medieval Latin *scabiōsa (herba),* "(herb) for scabies", from Latin, feminine of *scabiōsus,* SCABIOUS.]
scab·rous (skáyb-rəss || *chiefly U.S.* skáb-) *adj.* **1.** Roughened with small projections; rough to the touch; scaly. **2.** Difficult to handle tactfully; thorny. **3.** Indelicate or salacious; indecent: *a scabrous novel.* —See Synonyms at **rough.** [Latin *scabrōsus,* rough, from *scaber,* rough, scurfy.] **—scab·rous·ly** *adv.* **—scab·rous·ness** *n.*
scad (skad) *n., pl.* **scads** or collectively **Scad.** Any of several marine fishes of the family Carangidae; especially, the **horse mackerel** *(see).* [17th century : origin obscure.]
scads (skadz) *pl.n. Chiefly U.S. Informal.* A large number or amount: *scads of people.* [19th century : origin obscure.]
Sca·fell Pikes (skáw-fél). Highest point in England, situated in Cumbria's Lake District. Its height is 977 metres (3,205 feet).

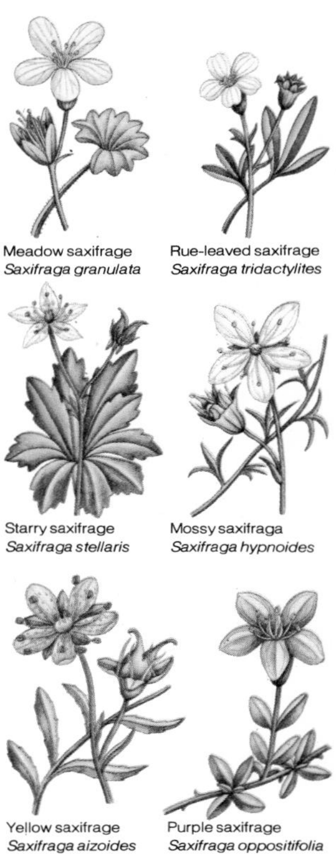

Meadow saxifrage
Saxifraga granulata
Rue-leaved saxifrage
Saxifraga tridactylites
Starry saxifrage
Saxifraga stellaris
Mossy saxifraga
Saxifraga hypnoides
Yellow saxifrage
Saxifraga aizoides
Purple saxifrage
Saxifraga oppositifolia

saxifrage *Most saxifrages are mountain plants which root in cracks between the rocks. It was once thought that saxifrage roots could penetrate rock, and the name means "rock breaking".*

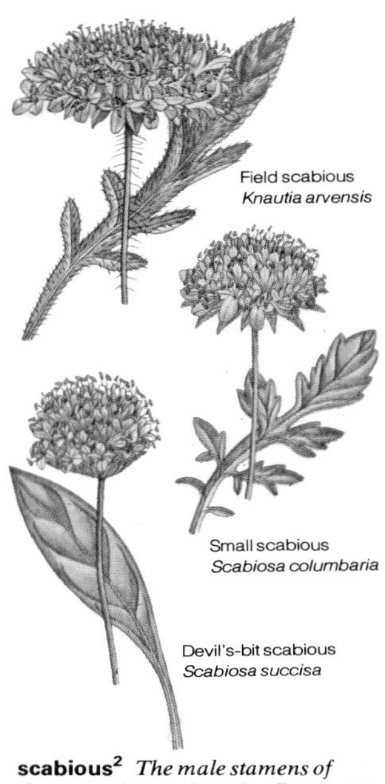

Field scabious
Knautia arvensis
Small scabious
Scabiosa columbaria
Devil's-bit scabious
Scabiosa succisa

scabious[2] *The male stamens of these meadow and garden flowers jut above the broad heads like pins, giving the plant a second common name in parts of Britain: pincushion flower. The plant was named scabious because its juice was once thought to be a cure for the skin complaint, scabies.*

scaf·fold (skáff'ld, skáffōld) *n.* **1.** A raised wooden framework or platform. **2.** A platform for the execution of condemned prisoners. Usually preceded by *the.* **3.** Scaffolding.
~*tr.v.* **scaffolded, -folding, -folds.** To provide or support with scaffolding. [Middle English, from Old North French *escafaut,* variant of Old French *eschafaud,* from *chafaud,* scaffold, from Vulgar Latin *catafalicum* (unattested), CATAFALQUE.] **—scaf·fold·er** *n.*
scaf·fold·ing (skáff'ld-ing || skáffōld-) *n.* **1.** A temporary platform or system of platforms, usually made of planks and tubular metal poles, used by workmen when constructing, repairing, or cleaning a building. **2.** The materials for scaffolding.
sca·glio·la (skal-yṓlə) *n.* Plasterwork in imitation of ornamental marble, consisting of ground gypsum and glue coloured with marble or granite dust. [Italian, diminutive of *scaglia,* scale, chip, small piece of marble, from Germanic.]
sca·lar (skáy-lər, *also* -laar) *n.* A quantity, such as mass, length, or time, completely described by a number on an appropriate scale. Scalars have magnitude but not direction. Compare **vector.** [Latin *scālāris,* of a staircase, from *scālae,* stairs, SCALE.] **—sca·lar** *adj.*
sca·la·re (skə-láir-i, -laár-) *n.* The **angelfish** *(see).* [New Latin, "ladder-like" (from its parallel stripes), from Latin, neuter of *scālāris,* of a staircase, from *scālae,* stairs, SCALE.]
sca·lar·i·form (skə-lárri-fawrm) *adj. Biology.* Ladder-like; having rungs: *scalariform xylem vessels.* [New Latin *scalariformis* : Latin *scālāris,* of a ladder (see **scalar**) + FORM.]
scalar product *n.* The numerical product of the lengths of two vectors and the cosine of the angle between them. Also called "dot product", "inner product". Compare **vector product.**
scalawag. *Chiefly U.S.* Variant of **scallywag.**
scald[1] (skawld || skold) *v.* **scalded, scalding, scalds.** *—tr.* **1.** To burn with or as if with hot liquid or steam. **2.** To subject to or treat with boiling water; especially: **a.** To blanch or partly cook vegetables in boiling water. **b.** To sterilise (instruments, for example). **3.** To heat (a liquid) almost to the boiling point. *—intr.* To be or become scalded.
~*n.* **1.** A burn or injury caused by scalding. **2. a.** A superficial discoloration on fruit, vegetables, leaves, or tree trunks caused by sudden exposure to intense sunlight or the action of gases. **b.** A disease of some cereal grasses, caused by a fungus of the genus *Rhynchosporium.* [Middle English *scalden,* from Old North French *escalder,* from Late Latin *excaldāre,* to wash in hot water : Latin *ex-,* to bring into a certain condition + *cal(i)da,* hot water, from the feminine of *calidus,* warm.]
scald[2]. **1.** Variant of **skald. 2.** Variant of **scall.**
scald head *n.* Any of various scaly disorders of the scalp. Not in current technical usage. [From SCALL.]
scald·ing (skáwld-ing || skóld-) *adj.* **1.** Burning hot to the touch or taste. **2.** Cutting; biting: *a scalding review.*
scale[1] (skayl) *n.* **1. a.** Any of the small, flattened, hard plates characteristically forming the external covering of fishes, reptiles, and certain mammals. **b.** A similar part, such as any of the minute structures overlapping to form the covering on the wings of butterflies and moths. **2.** *Pathology.* A dry, thin flake of epidermis shed from the skin. **3.** A small, thin, platelike piece of anything that flakes off from a surface. **4.** *Botany.* Any of various thin, often overlapping parts, such as any of the protective rudimentary leaves covering the buds of certain trees, or a membranous bract. **5. a.** A scale insect. **b.** A plant disease or infestation caused by scale insects. **6. a.** A flaky oxide film formed on a metal, as on iron, heated to high temperatures. **b.** A flake of rust. **7.** A coating of calcium carbonate formed inside boilers, kettles, and similar hot-water devices in hard-water regions; fur.
~*v.* **scaled, scaling, scales.** *—tr.* **1.** To clear or strip of scale or scales. **2.** To remove in layers or scales. **3.** To cover with scales; cause incrustation to form on. *—intr.* **1.** To come off in layers or scales; flake. **2.** To become covered with incrustation. [Middle English, from Old French *escale,* "shell", "husk", from Germanic.]

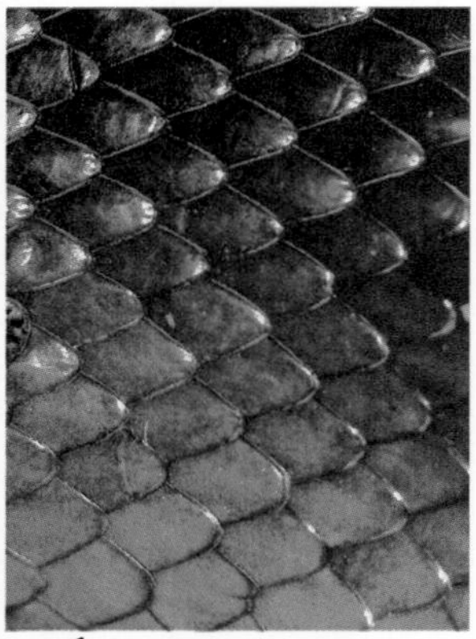

scale[1] *The scale-covered skin of the water python,* Liasis fuscus.

scale[2] *n.* **1.** A system of ordered marks at fixed intervals used as a reference standard in measurement. **2.** An instrument or device bearing such marks. **3. a.** The proportion used in determining the relationship of a representation to that which it represents. Also used adjectivally: *a scale drawing.* **b.** A calibrated line, as on a map or architectural plan, to indicate such a proportion. **4.** A progressive classification, as of size, amount, importance, or rank: *a salary scale; the social scale.* **5.** A relative level or degree: *entertain on a lavish scale.* Also used adjectivally in combination: *a small-scale exporter.* **6.** *Mathematics.* A system of notation in which the value of numbers is determined by their place relative to the fixed constant of the system: *decimal scale.* **7.** *Music.* An ascending or descending series of notes proceeding by a particular scheme of intervals and varying in pitch arrangement and interval size. In this sense, see **chromatic, diatonic. —to scale.** According to or in a uniform proportion or ratio.
~*v.* **scaled, scaling, scales.** *—tr.* **1.** To climb up to the top of or over, with or as if with a ladder, rope, or other device. **2.** To draw or reproduce in accordance with a particular proportion or scale. **3.** To adjust according to a proportion; regulate. **4.** To increase or decrease the size or importance of in fixed proportions. Used with *up* or *down.* *—intr.* **1.** To go up; climb; ascend. **2.** To ascend in steps or stages. [Middle English, ladder, graduation, from Late Latin *scāla,* ladder, from Latin *scālae,* stairs.]
scale[3] *n.* **1.** *Often plural.* Any instrument or machine for weighing: *bathroom scales.* **2.** Either of the pans, trays, or dishes of a balance. **—turn** or **tip the scales. 1.** To exercise a decisive effect. **2.** To amount in weight to; weigh. Used with *at.*
~*tr.v.* **scaled, scaling, scales. 1.** To weigh with scales. **2.** To have a weight of. [Middle English, from Old Norse *skāl,* bowl, scale of a balance.]
scale armour *n.* Armour made of small overlapping plates of metal or other hard material sewn or riveted to a strong backing of fabric or leather.
scale·board (skáyl-bawrd || -bōrd) *n.* **1.** Thin sheets of wood used as a veneer or a backing for pictures, mirrors, and the like. **2.** A wooden strip used for aligning hand-set type.
scale insect *n.* Any of various destructive sucking insects of the family Coccidae, the females of which secrete and remain under waxy scales on plant tissue.
scale leaf *n.* A membranous, often small, modified leaf, such as one that protects flower buds.
scale moss *n. Botany.* Any of various leafy liverworts of the order Jungermanniales.
sca·lene (skáy-leen, skay-léen, ska-) *adj.* **1.** Having unequal sides. Said of geometrical figures, especially triangles. **2.** *Anatomy.* Designating or pertaining to the scalenus. [Late Latin *scalēnus,* from Greek *skalēnos,* uneven.]
sca·le·nus (skə-léé-nəss, skay-) *n., pl.* **-ni** (-nī). Any one of four paired muscles in the neck, responsible for bending the neck and for raising the top two ribs when breathing in. Also called "scalene muscle". [New Latin. See **scalene.**]
scal·er (skáylər) *n.* **1.** An electronic circuit that records the aggregate of a specific number of signals that occur too rapidly to be recorded individually. **2.** A dental instrument used for removing tartar from teeth.
Scales (skaylz) *pl.n.* The constellation and sign of the zodiac, **Libra** *(see).* Preceded by *the.*
Scal·i·ger (skál-ijər), **Julius Caesar** (1484–1558). Italian scholar. He wrote commentaries on classical texts, the most famous being *Poetice* (1561). This analysis of Aristotelian theories of tragedy inspired later generations of French dramatists.
scall (skawl) *n.* Also **scald** (skawld || skold). A scaly eruption of the skin or scalp. Not in current technical usage. [Middle English *scalle,* from Old Norse *skalli,* baldhead.]
scal·li·on (skál-i-ən) *n. Chiefly U.S.* **1.** A young onion before the enlargement of the bulb, such as a spring onion. **2.** A **shallot** *(see).* [Middle English *scalo(u)n,* from Anglo-French, from Vulgar Latin *escalōnia* (unattested), from Latin *Ascalōnia (caepa),* "Ascalonian (onion)", from *Ascalō,* Ascalon, ancient port in southern Palestine.]
scal·lop (skól-əp, *also* skál-) *n.* Also **scol·lop** (skól-). **1.** Any of various marine bivalve molluscs of the family Pectinidae, having fan-shaped shells with a radiating fluted pattern. **2.** The edible adductor muscle of a scallop. **3.** A scallop shell, or a similarly shaped dish, used for baking and serving seafood. **4.** Any of a series of variously curved projections forming an ornamental border, as on fabrics or lace.
~*tr.v.* **scalloped, -loping, -lops.** Also **scol·lop. 1.** To design or border (material or part of a garment, for example) with scallops. **2.** To bake in a scallop shell or in a casserole with milk or a sauce and often with breadcrumbs. [Middle English *scalop,* from Old French *escalope,* shell, probably from Germanic.] **—scal·lop·er** *n.*

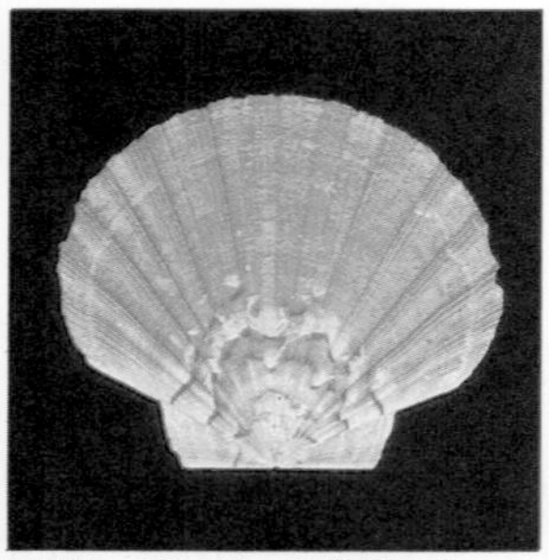

scallop *The twin-shelled scallop filters its food from seawater on the ocean bed. It detects predators such as starfish by means of a row of tiny eyes along its mantle – and escapes by clapping its shell shut, jetting itself away from danger.*

scal·ly·wag (skál-i-wag) *n.* Also *chiefly U.S.* **scal·ca·wag, scal·la·wag** (-ə-). **1.** A rascal; a reprobate; a good-for-nothing. **2.** *U.S.* A white Southerner supporting the policies of the Republican party, especially the abolition of slavery, after the American Civil War. Used derogatorily by U.S. Southern Democrats. [19th century (U.S. slang) : origin obscure.]
sca·lop·pi·ne, sca·lop·pi·ni (skál-ə-péeni || *U.S. also* skaál-) *pl.n.* **1.** Small, thin slices of veal or other meat, especially when cooked in a sauce of wine or tomatoes and seasonings. **2.** *Used with a singular verb.* A dish of scaloppine. [Italian *scaloppine,* plural of *scaloppina,* diminutive of *scaloppa,* fillet of meat, from Old French *escalope,* shell (the fillets are served curled like shells). See **scallop.**]
scalp (skalp) *n.* **1.** *Anatomy.* The skin covering the top of the human head. **2.** This skin with attached hair formerly cut or torn from an enemy as a battle trophy by certain North American Indians. **3.** Any trophy of victory.
~*tr.v.* **scalped, scalping, scalps. 1.** To cut or tear the scalp from. **2.** *Informal.* To defeat, especially in a humiliating or spectacular manner. **3.** *U.S.* **a.** To buy and resell (securities and commodities) to make a small but quick profit. **b.** To buy (tickets) and resell at inflated prices. **c.** To take advantage of or cheat (a customer, for example) by selling at inflated prices. [Middle English, probably from Scandinavian; akin to Old Norse *skalpr,* sheath, "shell".] **—scalp·er** *n.*
scal·pel (skál-p'l || *U.S. also* skal-pél) *n.* A small straight knife with a very thin, sharp, sometimes removable blade, used especially in surgery and dissection. [Latin *scalpellum,* diminutive of *scalper,* knife, from *scalpere,* to cut, scratch.]
scalp lock *n.* A long lock of hair left on the shaven head by certain North American Indians as a challenge to an enemy.
scal·y (skáyli) *adj.* **-ier, -iest. 1.** Covered or partially covered with scales or scale. **2.** Shedding scales; flaking. **—scal·i·ness** *n.*
scaly anteater *n.* A mammal, the **pangolin** *(see).*
scam (skam) *n. Chiefly U.S. Informal.* A fraudulent business operation; a swindle. [20th century : origin obscure.]
scam·mo·ny (skámməni) *n., pl.* **-nies. 1.** A plant, *Convolvulus scammonia,* of the eastern Mediterranean region, having large roots for-

merly used as a purgative. **2.** A resinous preparation made from the roots of this plant. [Middle English *scamonie,* from Latin *scammōnea,* from Greek *skammōnia*†.]

scamp¹ (skamp) *n.* **1.** A rogue; a rascal. **2.** A mischievous or prankish child or youth. [Originally "highwayman", "robber", from obsolete *scamp,* to slip away, bolt, probably from Middle Dutch *schampen,* from Old French *escamper,* to SCAMPER.]

scamp² *tr.v.* **scamped, scamping, scamps.** To perform in a careless or perfunctory way. [Probably a blend of SCANT and SKIMP.] —**scamp·er** *n.*

scam·per (skámpər) *intr.v.* **-pered, -pering, -pers.** To run or go hurriedly or playfully.
~*n.* A hasty or playful run or departure. [Flemish *scamperen,* to decamp, from Old French *escamper,* from Vulgar Latin *excampāre* (unattested) : Latin *ex-,* out of, away + *campus,* field (see **camp**).] —**scam·per·er** *n.*

scam·pi (skámpi) *n., pl.* **scampi.** Large prawns, especially when fried in batter. [Italian *scampi*†.]

scan (skan) *v.* **scanned, scanning, scans.** —*tr.* **1.** To examine or consider in close detail; scrutinise. **2.** To look over (a wide area) quickly but thoroughly, as from one end to another. **3.** To analyse (verse) into metrical feet and rhythm patterns. **4.** *Electronics.* **a.** To move a finely focused beam of light or electrons in a systematic pattern over (a surface) in order to reproduce, or sense and subsequently transmit, an image. **b.** To move a radar beam over (a sector of sky) in search of a target. **c.** *Computing.* To search (a series of punched cards or a magnetic tape) automatically for specific data. **d.** *Medicine.* To examine (a part of the body) using a scanner. **5.** To look over or leaf through hastily. —*intr.* **1.** To analyse verse into metrical feet. **2.** To conform to a metrical pattern. Used of verse. **3.** *Electronics.* To undergo electronic scanning. **4.** To use a scanner to examine a part of the body. —See Synonyms at **see.**
~*n.* An act or instance of scanning. [Middle English *scannen,* from Late Latin *scandere,* "to analyse the rising and falling rhythm in verses", from Latin, to climb.] —**scan·na·ble** *adj.*

Usage: The transitive use of *scan* is noteable in that it expresses two meanings which are opposites. On the one hand, it may mean "to examine closely" *(He scanned the examination paper for misprints);* on the other hand, it may mean "to make a quick inspection of" *(He scanned the newspaper for news of the battle).* The latter sense is somewhat more informal. Ambiguity is often possible.

Scand. Scandinavia; Scandinavian.

scan·dal (skánd'l) *n.* **1.** Any act or set of circumstances that brings about disgrace or offends accepted standards of morality or propriety; a public disgrace. **2.** The reaction caused by such an act or set of circumstances; outrage; shame. **3.** Any talk damaging to the character; malicious gossip. **4.** Damage to reputation or character caused by offensive or grossly improper behaviour; disgrace. **5.** One whose conduct brings about disgrace or defamation. —See Synonyms at **disgrace.**
~*tr.v.* **scandalled** or *U.S.* **scandaled, -dalling** or *U.S.* **-daling, -dals.** *Archaic.* To spread scandal about; defame. [French *scandale,* from Late Latin *scandalum,* from Greek *skandalon,* trap, snare, stumbling block.]

scan·dal·ise, scan·dal·ize (skándə-līz) *tr.v.* **-ised, -ising, -ises.** To shock the moral sensibilities of. —**scan·dal·is·er** *n.*

scan·dal·mong·er (skánd'l-mung-gər ‖ -mong-) *n.* A person who spreads scandal or gossip.

scan·dal·ous (skándələss) *adj.* **1.** Causing scandal; shocking; offensive. **2.** Containing defamatory or libellous material. —**scan·dal·ous·ly** *adv.* —**scan·dal·ous·ness** *n.*

scandal sheet *n.* A newspaper or other periodical that habitually prints stories of a sensational or defamatory nature.

scan·dent (skándent) *adj. Botany.* Climbing: *a scandent vine.* [Latin *scandēns* (stem *scandent-*), present participle of *scandere,* to climb.]

Scanderbeg. See **Skanderbeg.**

scan·di·a (skándi-ə) *n.* Scandium oxide. [From SCANDIUM.]

Scan·di·an (skándi-ən) *adj.* Scandinavian. [Latin *Scandia,* variant of *Scandinavia,* SCANDINAVIA.] —**Scan·di·an** *n.*

scan·dic (skándik) *adj.* Of, pertaining to, or containing scandium.

Scan·di·na·vi·a (skándi-náyvi-ə) *n. Abbr.* **Scand.** Region of north Europe. Strictly it is the peninsula comprising the kingdoms of Norway and Sweden, but culturally it also takes in Denmark, Finland, Iceland, and the Faeroe Islands are often included.

Scan·di·na·vi·an (skándi-náyvi-ən) *n. Abbr.* **Scand. 1.** A native or inhabitant of Scandinavia. **2.** The North Germanic languages; the languages spoken in Scandinavia. —**Scan·di·na·vi·an** *adj.*

Scandinavian Peninsula. The peninsula in northwest Europe comprising Norway and Sweden. See **Scandinavia.**

scan·di·um (skándi-əm) *n. Symbol* **Sc** A silvery-white, very lightweight metallic element found in various rare minerals. An artificially radioactive isotope of it is used as a tracer in oil-well and pipeline studies. Atomic number 21, atomic weight 44.956, melting point 1,539°C, boiling point 2,727°C, relative density 2.992, valency 3. [New Latin, from Latin *Scandia,* ancient name for Scandinavia, where it was discovered.]

scandium oxide *n.* A white amorphous powder, Sc_2O_3, used as a source of scandium and in the manufacture of ceramics. Also called "scandia".

scan·ner (skánnər) *n.* One that scans; specifically: **1.** An electronic device that provides a visual representation on a cathode-ray screen of the distribution of a radioactive compound in a particular system, such as the human body. **2.** A device that transmits or receives

a radar signal within a predetermined solid angle. See **optical scanner.**

scan·ning (skánning) *n.* Any of various electronic or optical techniques by which images or recorded information are sensed for subsequent modification, integration, or transmission. Also used adjectively: *a scanning device.*

scanning electron microscope *n.* An electron microscope capable of forming a three-dimensional image on a cathode-ray screen by means of a focused beam of electrons that is scanned across the object to be viewed; the image is formed both by the electrons which by the object scatters and by the secondary electrons produced.

scan·sion (skánsh'n) *n.* **1.** The analysis of verse into metrical feet and rhythm patterns. **2.** The way a line or verse scans. [Late Latin *scansiō* (stem *scansiōn-*), from Latin, a climbing, from *scandere* (past participle *scansus*), to climb.]

scan·so·ri·al (skan-sáw-ri-əl ‖ -sṓ-) *adj. Zoology.* Adapted to or specialised for climbing. [Latin *scansōrius,* from *scandere* (past participle *scansus*), to climb.]

scant (skant) *adj.* **scanter, scantest. 1.** Deficient in quantity or amount; meagre; inadequate. **2.** Being only just, or just short of, a specified measure: *a scant three miles.* **3.** Inadequately supplied. Used with *of: scant of breath.* —See Synonyms at **meagre.**
~*tr.v.* **scanted, scanting, scants. 1.** To provide with an inadequate portion or allowance; skimp. **2.** To limit, as in amount or share; stint. **3.** To reduce the size or amount of; cut down. **4.** To deal with or treat inadequately or neglectfully. [Middle English, from Old Norse *skamt,* neuter of *skammr,* short.] —**scant·ly** *adv.* —**scant·ness** *n.*

scant·ling (skánt-ling ‖ -lin) *n.* **1.** A small piece of timber, usually one having a cross-section no more than five inches square. **2.** Such pieces of timber collectively. **3.** The dimensions of building materials such as stone or timber, especially in breadth and thickness. **4.** *Usually plural. Nautical.* The dimensions of the structural parts of a vessel, such as its frames, plates, and girders. **5.** A very small amount. [Alteration of obsolete *scantlon,* Middle English *scantilon,* carpenter's gauge, dimension, from Old French *escantillon, eschandillon,* probably from Vulgar Latin *scandilia* (unattested), measure, scale, from Latin *scandere,* to climb.]

scant·y (skánti) *adj.* **-ier, -iest. 1.** Barely sufficient or adequate. **2.** Deficient in extent or degree; small; insufficient. —See Synonyms at **meagre.** —**scant·i·ly** *adv.* —**scant·i·ness** *n.*

Scap·a Flow (skáppə, skáapə). Sheltered stretch of sea in the Orkney Islands, north Scotland. It was the base of the British home fleet in both World Wars. In June 1919, 71 surrendered German warships were scuttled here. Following the sinking of the *Royal Oak* by a German submarine within Scapa Flow (1939), a barrier was built to seal off the eastern entrances.

scape¹ (skayp) *n.* **1.** *Botany.* A leafless flower stalk growing from a basal rosette of leaves. **2.** A similar stalklike part, such as a feather shaft or a segment of an insect's antenna. **3.** *Architecture.* The shaft of a column. [Latin *scāpus*†, stalk.]

scape². *Archaic.* Variant of **escape.**

-scape *n. comb. form.* Indicates scene or view; for example, **seascape.** [Back-formation from LANDSCAPE.]

scape·goat (skáyp-gōt) *n.* **1.** A person or group made to bear the blame for others, or unjustly regarded as being responsible for hardship or disaster, and often persecuted as a result. **2.** A live goat over whose head Aaron confessed all the sins of the children of Israel and which was sent into the wilderness symbolically bearing their sin on the Day of Atonement. Leviticus 16. [(E)SCAPE + GOAT (improper translation of Hebrew *azāzel,* probably "goat for Azazel" (desert demon), misconstrued as *ēz-ōzēl,* "goat that escapes".]

scape·grace (skáyp-grayss) *n.* An unprincipled or incorrigible person; a rascal. [(E)SCAPE + GRACE.]

scaph·oid (skáf-oyd) *adj.* Boat-shaped.
~*n. Anatomy.* The **navicular** *(see).* [New Latin *scaphoides,* from Greek *skaphoeidēs : skaphē,* tub, boat + -OID.]

sca·pho·pod (skáf-ə-pod, -ō-) *n. Zoology.* A **tusk shell** *(see).* [New Latin *scaphopoda :* Greek *skaphos,* boat + -POD.]

scap·o·lite (skáppə-līt) *n.* Any of a series of variously coloured mineral silicates of aluminium, calcium, and sodium. Also called "wernerite". [French : Latin *scāpus,* stalk, SCAPE (from its prismatic crystals) + -ITE.]

sca·pose (skáyp-ōz, -ōss) *adj. Botany.* Resembling or consisting of a scape.

scap·u·la (skáppew-lə) *n., pl.* **-las** or **-lae** (-lee). **1.** *Anatomy.* Either of two large, flat, triangular bones forming the back part of the shoulder. Also called "shoulder blade". **2.** The corresponding bone in other vertebrates. [Latin, shoulder blade, shoulder.]

scap·u·lar (skáppew-lər) *n.* Also **scap·u·lar·y** (-ləri ‖ -lerri) *pl.* **-ies. 1.** A monk's sleeveless outer garment hanging from the shoulders and sometimes having a cowl. **2.** Two pieces of cloth joined by strings and worn under the clothing about the shoulders as a badge or token of affiliation to certain religious orders. **3.** Any of the feathers covering the shoulder of a bird.
~*adj. Anatomy.* Of or pertaining to the shoulder or scapula. [Middle English *scapulare,* from Medieval Latin *scapulāre, scapulārium,* "shoulder cloak", from Latin *scapula,* shoulder, SCAPULA.]

scar¹ (skar) *n.* **1.** A mark left on the skin or other tissue following the healing of a surface injury or wound. **2.** Any impression or sign of damage caused by or remaining as evidence of mental or physical injury. **3.** *Botany.* A mark indicating a former attachment, as of a

---

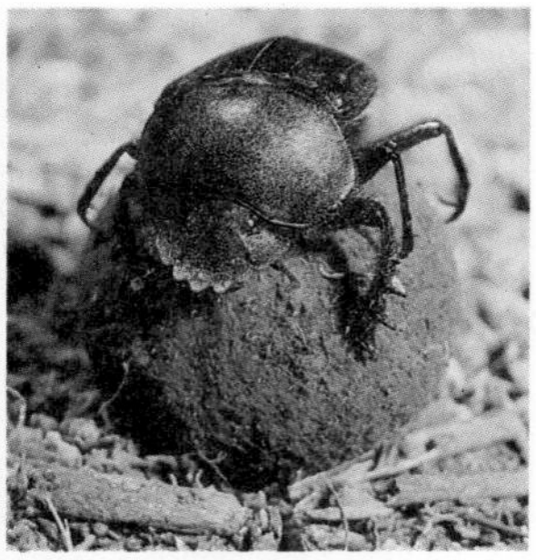

scarab *Regarded by the ancient Egyptians as a symbol of resurrection and immortality, the scarab or dung beetle (above) is native to Mediterranean countries. The Egyptian god of dawn, Khepera, was conventionally portrayed as a scarab. Khepera is shown below receiving the sun in a detail from the Papyrus of Anhai, painted in about 1150* B.C.

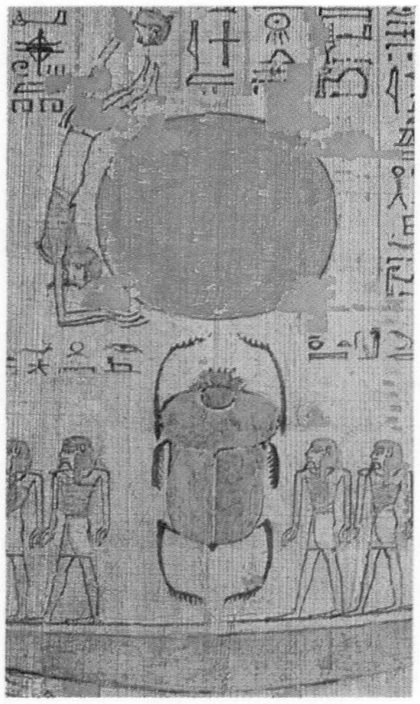

leaf to a stem. **4.** A mark, dent, or other blemish made by use, motion, or contact.
~*v.* **scarred, scarring, scars.** —*tr.* To mark with or as if with a scar. —*intr.* To form a scar. [Middle English *(e)scare,* from Old French *esc(h)are,* scab, from Late Latin *eschara,* from Greek *eskhara*†, hearth, scab caused by burning.]

scar² *n.* Also *Scottish* **scaur** (skawr). *Geology.* A bare rock-face, especially in northern England, where it indicates a limestone cliff. [Middle English *skerre,* from Old Norse *sker,* low reef.]

scar·ab (skárrəb) *n.* Also **scar·a·bae·us** (skárrə-bée-əss) *pl.* **-uses** or **-baei** (-bée-ī). **1.** Any scarabaeid beetle; especially, *Scarabaeus sacer,* regarded as sacred by the ancient Egyptians. **2.** A representation of a scarab beetle, especially one cut from a stone or gem, used in ancient Egypt as a talisman and a symbol of the soul. [Latin *scarabaeus*†.]

scar·a·bae·id (skárrə-bée-id) *n.* Any of the numerous beetles of the family Scarabaeidae, which includes the chafers and dung beetles. [New Latin *Scarabaeidae,* from Latin *scarabaeus,* SCARAB.] **—scar·a·bae·id, scar·a·bae·oid** (-bée-oyd), **scar·a·boid** (-boyd) *adj.*

Scar·a·mouch, Scar·a·mouche (skárrə-mo͞osh, -mo͞och, -mowch) *n.* A stock character in old Italian comedy and pantomime, depicted as a boastful, cowardly braggart or buffoon. [French *Scaramouche,* from Italian *Scaramuccia,* jocular use of *scaramuccia,* SKIRMISH.]

Scar·bo·rough (skár-brə, -bərə || -burrə). Seaside resort of North Yorkshire. There are remains of a fourth-century Roman signalling station above the town.

scarce (skairss) *adj.* **scarcer, scarcest. 1.** Uncommonly or infrequently seen or found. **2.** Insufficient to meet a demand or requirement; not plentiful or abundant. **—make (oneself) scarce.** *Informal.* To leave hurriedly or surreptitiously.
~*adv. Literary.* Scarcely. [Middle English *scars,* from Anglo-French *escars,* from Vulgar Latin *excarpsus* (unattested), "picked", "choice", hence "rare", variant of Latin *excerptus,* past participle of *excerpere,* to pick out, select : *ex-,* out + *carpere,* to pick, pluck.] **—scarce·ness** *n.*

scarce·ly (skáirssli) *adv.* **1.** By a small margin; just; barely. **2.** Almost not; hardly. **3.** Certainly not. —See Synonyms at **hardly.**

Usage: Because *scarcely* has a negative meaning, formal English disapproves of its use with another negative word in the same clause: *He could scarcely hear her* is preferable to *He couldn't scarcely hear her,* or *She departed with scarcely a word* is preferable to *She departed without scarcely a word.* Standard English also prefers the use of *when* rather than *than* with a following clause: *Scarcely had he entered when the telephone rang.*

scar·ci·ty (skáirssəti) *n., pl.* **-ties. 1.** An insufficient amount or supply; a shortage. **2.** Infrequency of appearance or occurrence; rarity.

scare (skair) *v.* **scared, scaring, scares.** —*tr.* **1.** To startle with fear; frighten; alarm; terrify. **2.** To force or drive by frightening. Used with *away, off, out,* or other adverbs. **3.** *Informal.* To cause to be in a specified state by frightening: *It scared him silly.* —*intr.* To become frightened. —See Synonyms at **frighten. —scare up.** *Chiefly U.S. Informal.* To gather or prepare hurriedly; improvise.
~*n.* **1.** A condition or sensation of sudden fear. **2.** A general state of alarm, especially when exaggerated or groundless; a panic. **3.** Something that causes unreasonable or exaggerated alarm. Also used adjectivally: *scare stories.* [Middle English *skerren,* from Old Norse *skirra,* from *skjarr,* shy, timid, from North Germanic *skerza-* (unattested).] **—scar·er** *n.* **—scar·ing·ly** *adv.*

scare·crow (skáir-krō) *n.* **1.** An object, usually a crude figure of a man, set up in a field to scare birds away from crops. **2.** Something frightening but not inherently dangerous. **3.** A person resembling a scarecrow, especially in being shabbily dressed or very thin.

scared (skaird) *adj.* Frightened or alarmed.

scared·y-cat (skáirdi-kat) *n. Informal.* One who is timid or easily scared.

scare·mon·ger (skáir-mung-gər || -mong-) *n.* A person who spreads frightening rumours; an alarmist.

scarf¹ (skarf) *n., pl.* **scarves** (skarvz) or **scarfs.** A rectangular or triangular piece of cloth, worn about the neck, shoulders, or head for protection, warmth, or decoration. [Probably from Old North French *escarpe,* variant of Old French *escherpe,* originally "pilgrim's wallet suspended from the neck", from Frankish *skirpja* (unattested), from Latin *scirpea,* basket made of rushes, from *scirpeus,* of rushes, from *scirpus*†, rush, bulrush. See also **scrip** (wallet).]

scarf² *n., pl.* **scarfs. 1.** A joint made by cutting and notching the ends of two timbers and strapping or bolting them together to make a continuous piece. Also called "scarf joint". **2.** The end of a timber notched in this fashion. **3.** A cut made into the body of a whale in order to remove the blubber.
~*tr.v.* **scarfed, scarfing, scarfs. 1.** To join by means of a scarf joint. **2.** To cut a scarf in. [Middle English *skarf*†.]

Scarfe (skarf), **Gerald** (1936–). British cartoonist. His caricatures are noted for their violent but recognisable distortions.

scarf·skin (skárf-skin) *n.* The epidermis or outermost layer of skin.

scar·i·fi·ca·tor (skárri-fi-kaytər, skáir-i-) *n.* A surgical instrument with several spring-operated lancets, used for skin scarification.

scar·i·fy (skárri-fī, skáir-i-) *tr.v.* **-fied, -fying, -fies. 1.** To make superficial incisions in (the skin), as when vaccinating. **2.** To break up the surface of (topsoil, for example). **3.** To wound with severe criticism. **4.** *Botany.* To slit or soften the outer coat of (seeds) to speed germination. [Middle English *scarifien,* to make incisions on the bark of a tree, from Old French *scarifier,* from Late Latin *scarīficāre,* variant of Latin *scarīfāre,* from Greek *skariphasthai,* to scratch an outline, sketch, from *skariphos,* stylus.] **—scar·i·fi·ca·tion** (-fi-káysh'n) *n.* **—scar·i·fi·er** (-fīər) *n.*

scar·i·ous (skáir-i-əss) *adj.* Also **scar·i·ose** (-ōz, -ōss). *Botany.* Thin, membranous, and dry: *scarious bracts.* [New Latin *scariosus*†.]

scar·la·ti·na (skárlə-téenə) *n.* Scarlet fever. [New Latin, from Italian *(febbre) scarlattina,* scarlet (fever), diminutive of *scarlatto,* SCARLET.] **—scar·la·ti·noid** (skárlə-téen-oyd) *adj.*

Scar·lat·ti (skaar-látti || *U.S.* -láati), **Domenico** (1685–1757). Italian composer, son of the prolific composer, Alessandro Scarlatti (1660–1725), He was a virtuoso harpsichordist, and his numerous works for the instrument were influential in the development of keyboard music generally, and of the sonata form.

scar·let (skár-lət, -lit) *n.* **1.** Strong to vivid red or reddish orange. **2.** Clothing or cloth having this colour. [Middle English, from Old French *escarlate*†.] **—scar·let** *adj.*

scarlet fever *n.* An acute contagious disease caused by a haemolytic streptococcus, occurring mainly in children and characterised by a scarlet skin rash and high fever. Also called "scarlatina".

scarlet pimpernel *n.* See **pimpernel.**

scarlet runner *n.* The **runner bean** *(see).*

scarlet woman *n.* **1.** A sexually promiscuous woman. **2.** *Capital* **S,** *capital* **W.** The Roman Catholic Church. Used derogatorily by some Protestants. [Biblical allusion (Revelation 17).]

scarp (skarp) *n.* An escarpment. Not in current technical usage.
~*tr.v.* **scarped, scarping, scarps.** To cut or make into a steep slope. [Italian *scarpa,* probably from Gothic *skarpō* (unattested), pointed object.]

scar·per (skárpər) *intr.v.* **-pered, -pering, -pers.** *British Slang.* To run away; leave hastily. [Perhaps from Italian *scappare,* to ESCAPE, associated with SCAPA FLOW, rhyming slang for *go.*]

Scar·ron (ska-RÓN, skaa-), **Paul** (1610–60). French writer. Though a noted dramatist, his best-known work is the burlesque epic and novel, *Le Roman comique* (1651–57).

scar tissue *n.* A dense, often hard layer of connective tissue formed over a healing wound or cut.

scarves. Alternative plural of **scarf.**

scar·y (skáir-i) *adj.* **-ier, -iest.** *Informal.* Frightening; alarming.

scat¹ (skat) *intr.v.* **scatted, scatting, scats.** *Informal.* To go away hastily; leave at once. Usually used in the imperative. [Perhaps short for SCATTER.]

scat² *n.* A type of jazz singing consisting of the improvisation and repetition of meaningless syllables sung to a melody. Also used adjectivally: *a scat singer.*
~*intr.v.* **scatted, scatting, scats.** To sing scat. [Perhaps imitative.]

scat³ *n.* Any of several fishes of the genus *Scatophagus,* of tropical Asia and adjacent areas; especially, *S. argus,* having a flat, rounded, spotted or striped body, and popular as an aquarium fish. [Shortened from New Latin *Scatophagus,* from Greek *skatophagos,* SCATOPHAGOUS.]

scat⁴ *n. Often plural.* The faeces of animals, especially animals being hunted; droppings. [Greek *skōr* (stem *skat-*).]

scathe (skayth) *tr.v.* **scathed, scathing, scathes. 1.** To criticise severely. **2.** To harm or injure severely especially by fire or heat; wither; sear.
~*n. Archaic.* Harm; injury. [Middle English *skathen,* from Old Norse *skadha.*]

scath·ing (skáything) *adj.* **1.** Extremely severe or harsh; bitterly denunciatory: *scathing criticism.* **2.** Harmful or painful; injurious. **—scath·ing·ly** *adv.*

scato– *comb. form.* Indicates faeces or excrement; for example, **scatology.** [Greek *skato-,* from *skōr* (stem *skat-*), dung, ordure.]

sca·tol·o·gy (ska-tólləji, skə-) *n.* **1.** The study of faecal excrement, as in medicine or palaeontology. **2.** An obsession with excrement or excretory functions. **3.** Preoccupation with obscenity, as in literature. [SCATO- + -LOGY.] **—scat·o·log·ic** (skáttə-lójik), **scat·o·log·i·cal** (-'l) *adj.* **—sca·tol·o·gist** (-tólləjist) *n.*

sca·toph·a·gous (ska-tóffəgəss, skə-) *adj.* Feeding on dung, as a beetle or fly might be. [Greek *skatophagos* : SCATO- + -PHAGOUS.]

scat·ter (skáttər) *v.* **-tered, -tering, -ters.** —*tr.* **1.** To cause to separate and go in various directions; disperse. **2. a.** To distribute widely or loosely by or as if by sprinkling or throwing or dropping randomly. **b.** To cover or strew (a surface) by scattering. **3.** *Physics.* To deflect (radiation or particles). —*intr.* **1.** To separate and go in several directions; disperse. **2.** To appear, occur, or fall over a wide area and at widely spaced intervals.
~*n.* **1.** The act of scattering. **2.** The condition or extent of being scattered. **3.** That which is scattered. [Middle English *scateren,* probably variant of *schateren,* SHATTER.] **—scat·ter·er** *n.*

scat·ter·brained (skáttər-braynd) *n. Informal.* Lacking in power of concentration or attention; forgetful, disorganised, or thoughtless. **—scat·ter·brain** *n.*

scatter cushion *n.* A small cushion, typically any one of several that are strewn here and there on the furniture in a room. Also *U.S.* "throw pillow".

scat·ter·ing (skáttəring) *n.* **1.** A sparse distribution or irregular occurrence of something: *a scattering of applause.* **2.** *Physics.* The dispersal of a beam of particles or of radiation into a range of directions resulting from physical interactions.
~*adj. Chiefly U.S.* Placed at intervals or occurring irregularly.

scat·ty (skátti) *adj.* **-tier, -tiest.** *British Informal.* **1.** Slightly crazy. **2.** Scatterbrained. [From SCATTERBRAINED.] **—scat·ti·ly** *adv.* **—scat·ti·ness** *n.*

scaup (skawp) *n.* Either of two diving ducks, *Aythya marila* or *A. affinis,* having predominantly black and white plumage. Also called "scaup duck". [Perhaps from Scottish *scaup,* variant of SCALP (rare sense "bed of mussels"), because these ducks feed on shellfish.]

scaur. *Scottish.* Variant of **scar** (rock).

scav·enge (skávvinj) *v.* **-enged, -enging, -enges.** —*tr.* **1.** To collect and remove refuse from; clean up. **2.** To search through (rubbish, discarded matter, or the like) for reusable material, such as food. **3.** To collect (reusable material) by searching. **4.** To expel (exhaust gases) from a cylinder of an internal-combustion engine. **5.** *Metallurgy.* To clean (molten metal) by chemically removing impurities. —*intr.* To act as a scavenger; especially, to search through discarded material for edible or useful things. [Back-formation from SCAVENGER.]

scav·en·ger (skávvinjər) *n.* **1.** Any organism that feeds on dead animal flesh or other decaying organic matter. **2.** One who scavenges. **3.** *Chemistry.* A substance added to a mixture to remove impurities or to counteract the undesirable effects of other constituents. **4.** *Metallurgy.* A metal added to a molten metal or alloy that acts, by combining with oxygen or nitrogen, to remove impurities, which then remain behind the slag. [Middle English *scavager,* collector of tolls (later, street cleaner), from Anglo-French *scawager,* from *scawage,* a toll levied on foreign merchants, variant of Old North French *escauwage,* inspection, from *escauwer,* to inspect, from Flemish *scawuen,* to look at, SHOW.]

S.C.E. Scottish Certificate of Education.

sce·nar·i·o (si-naár-i-ō, se-, sə- || -náir-) *n., pl.* **-os.** **1.** An outline of the plot of a dramatic or literary work. **2.** A **screenplay** *(see).* **3.** An outline of an imagined chain of events; a possible state of affairs or course of action. [Italian, "scenery", from Late Latin *scaenārius,* of the stage, from Latin *scaena,* stage, SCENE.]

sce·nar·ist (séenər-ist, si-naár- || -náir-) *n.* A writer of scenarios.

scend, send (send) *intr.v.* **scended** or **sended, scending** or **sending, scends** or **sends.** *Nautical.* To rise upwards or plunge downwards on a wave or swell.
∼*n.* The rising and falling movement of a ship on a wave or swell. [Perhaps from earlier *'scend,* short for DESCEND or ASCEND.]

scene (seen) *n.* **1.** A locality as seen by a viewer; a view. **2. a.** The surroundings and place where an action or event occurs: *The police arrived at the scene of the accident.* **b.** Such a place or setting marked by a specified feature or characteristic: *The road was a scene of carnage following the accident.* **3.** *Abbr.* **sc.** The place in which the action of a play, film, novel, or other narrative occurs; a setting; a locale. **4.** *Abbr.* **sc.** A subdivision of an act in a dramatic presentation in which the setting is fixed and the time continuous. **5.** *Abbr.* **sc.** A shot or series of shots in a film constituting a unit of continuous related action. **6.** The scenery and properties for a dramatic presentation. **7.** *Archaic.* A theatre stage. **8.** A real or fictitious episode, especially when described. **9.** A public display of passion or temper. **10.** *Informal.* A place or realm of a particular activity or interest: *The battle for promotion has livened up the football scene.* **11.** *Informal.* What one likes or is interested in: *Opera is more your scene than mine.* **—behind the scenes. 1.** Backstage. **2.** In private. **—set the scene.** To describe the events leading up to, or the surrounding location of, a particular scene or event. **—steal the scene.** To draw favourable attention on to oneself and away from others. [French *scène,* from Old French *scene,* stage, from Latin *scaena,* stage, theatre, from Greek *skēnē*†, "tent".]

scen·er·y (séenəri) *n.* **1.** The overall appearance of the natural surroundings of an area, especially when considered aesthetically; the landscape. **2.** Painted backdrops and similar properties on a theatrical stage. [Italian *scenario,* SCENARIO.]

scene-shift·er (séen-shiftər) *n.* A stagehand who moves scenery.

sce·nic (séenik) *adj.* **1.** Of, pertaining to, or having picturesque natural landscapes: *a scenic route.* **2.** Of or pertaining to theatrical scenery. **3.** Representing an event, piece of action, or the like. Said of a work of art. **—sce·ni·cal·ly** *adv.*

scenic railway *n.* **1.** A miniature railway as at a fairground. **2.** A railway that extends through picturesque natural scenery.

scent (sent) *n.* **1.** A distinctive odour or smell, especially a pleasant one. **2.** A perfume. **3.** An odour left by the passing of an animal. **4. a.** The trail of a hunted animal or fugitive. **b.** Any trail, set of clues, or the like that may be followed. **5. a.** The sense of smell. **b.** The power of following a trail, set of clues, or the like. **6.** A hint of something imminent; a suggestion. —See Synonyms at **smell.**
∼*v.* **scented, scenting, scents.** —*tr.* **1.** To perceive or identify by the sense of smell. **2.** To suspect or detect as if by smelling: *scent danger.* **3.** To perfume. —*intr.* To hunt by means of the sense of smell. Used of hounds. [Middle English *sent,* from *senten,* to smell, scent, from Old French *sentir,* from Latin *sentīre,* to feel.]

scent gland *n.* A specialised exocrine gland in many mammals that secretes a strong-smelling substance.

scep·tic, *U.S.* **skep·tic** (sképtik) *n.* **1.** One who instinctively or habitually doubts, questions, or disagrees with assertions or generally accepted conclusions. **2.** One inclined to scepticism in religious matters. **3. a.** *Often capital* **S.** An adherent of any philosophical school of scepticism. **b.** *Capital* **S.** A member of an ancient Greek school of philosophical scepticism, especially that of Pyrrho of Elis. [Latin *Scepticus,* singular of *Scepticī,* followers of Pyrrho of Elis, from Greek *Skeptikoi,* from *skeptesthai,* to examine, consider.]

scep·ti·cal (sképtik'l) *adj.* **1.** Doubting; disbelieving. **2.** Pertaining to or characteristic of sceptics or scepticism. **—scep·ti·cal·ly** *adv.*

scep·ti·cism (sképti-siz'm) *n.* **1.** A doubting or questioning attitude or disposition; a critical, often reasoned, uncertainty. **2.** The philosophical doctrine that absolute knowledge is impossible and that inquiry must be a process of doubting in order to acquire approximate or relative certainty. **3.** Doubt or disbelief about religion, especially Christianity. —See Synonyms at **uncertainty.**

scep·tre, *U.S.* **scep·ter** (séptər) *n.* **1.** A staff held by a sovereign on ceremonial occasions as an emblem of authority. **2.** Sovereign office or power.
∼*tr.v.* **sceptred** or *U.S.* **sceptered, -tring** or *U.S.* **-tering, -tres** or *U.S.* **-ters.** To invest with royal authority. [Middle English *(s)ceptre,* from Old French, from Latin *scēptrum,* from Greek *skēptron*†, "staff", "stick".]

sch. school.

Scha·den·freu·de (shaád'n-froydə) *n.* A feeling of pleasure caused by another's unhappiness or misfortune; malicious delight. [German : *Schade,* harm + *Freude,* joy.]

sched·ule (shéddewl || *U.S.* skéj-əl, -ōōl, *Canadian* shéj-) *n.* **1.** A written list or statement, usually in tabular form, such as: **a.** A listing of rates or prices. **b.** An agenda. **c.** *U.S.* A timetable, as for buses or trains. **2.** A programme of forthcoming events or appointments. **3.** A production plan allotting work to be done and specifying deadlines. **4.** A supplementary statement of details appended to a document.
∼*tr.v.* **scheduled, -uling, -ules.** **1.** To enter on a schedule. **2.** To make up a schedule for. **3.** To plan or appoint for a certain time or date. [Middle English *cedule, sedule,* slip of parchment or paper, short note, from Old French *cedule,* from Late Latin *schedula,* diminutive of Latin *scheda, scida,* papyrus leaf, from Greek *skhedē.*]

sched·uled castes (shéddewld || skéj-əld, shéj-, -ōōld) *pl.n.* The **harijans** *(see).*

scheduled territories *pl.n.* Those territories using sterling or currencies linked to sterling and subject to United Kingdom exchange controls. They are the United Kingdom, the Channel Islands, the Isle of Man, Gibraltar, and formerly the Republic of Ireland. Also called "sterling area", "sterling bloc".

Scheel (shayl), **Walter** (1919–). West German politician. He entered the Bundestag (1953), and became minister for economic cooperation (1961), vice-president (1967), and vice-chancellor and foreign minister (1969). He was federal president from 1974 to 1979.

schee·lite (shée-līt, sháy-) *n.* A variously coloured natural form of calcium tungstate, $CaWO_4$, found in igneous rocks and used as a source of tungsten. [After K. *Scheele* (1742–86), Swedish chemist.]

Sche·her·a·za·de (shə-hérrə-zaádə, -héer-ə-, -zaád). The fictional narrator of the tales in *The Arabian Nights.*

Scheldt (shelt, skelt). *French* **Escaut** (ess-kṓ); *Dutch* **Schelde** (s<u>kh</u>éldə). River in northwestern Europe. Rising in Aisne département, France, it flows 435 kilometres (270 miles) through Belgium and the port of Antwerp to join the North Sea in the Netherlands via the West Scheldt estuary (Westerschelde). The river was cut off from its East Scheldt outlet (Oosterschelde) by dykes built in the 19th century. The Scheldt is navigable for most of its length, and connects with the Belgian and Dutch canal systems.

sche·ma (skée-mə) *n., pl.* **-mata** (-mətə, *also* skee-maátə). **1.** A summarised or diagrammatic representation of something; an outline. **2.** A pattern or structure, especially of a logical proof or argument. [German *Schema,* from Greek *skhēma,* form. See **scheme.**]

sche·mat·ic (skee-máttik, ski-) *adj.* Pertaining to or in the form of a scheme or schema; diagrammatic.
∼*n.* A structural or procedural diagram, especially of an electrical or mechanical system.

sche·ma·tise, sche·ma·tize (skéemə-tīz) *tr.v.* **-tised, -tising, -tises.** To form into, or express by means of, a scheme or schema. [Greek *skhēmatizein,* to give a form to, from *skhēma,* form, manner. See **scheme.**] **—sche·ma·ti·sa·tion** (-tī-záysh'n || *U.S.* -ti-) *n.*

sche·ma·tism (skéemə-tiz'm) *n.* The patterned disposition or arrangement of constituents within a given system.

scheme (skeem) *n.* **1.** A systematic plan of action. **2.** An orderly combination of related or successive parts or things; a system. **3.** An underhand or secret plan; a plot; an intrigue. **4.** An official or commercial plan, policy, or project: *an insurance scheme.* **5.** A chart, diagram, or outline of a system or object. **6.** *Scottish.* A housing estate, especially a council estate.
∼*v.* **schemed, scheming, schemes.** —*tr.* **1.** To contrive a plan or scheme for. **2.** To plot. —*intr.* To make devious plans. [Latin *schēma,* form, figure, manner, from Greek *skhēma.*] **—schem·er** *n.*

schem·ing (skéeming) *adj.* Given to plotting or intrigue.

schemozzle. Variant of **shemozzle.**

scher·zan·do (skairt-sándō, skert- || *U.S.* -saándō) *adv. Music.* In a playful or sportive manner. Used as a direction to the performer.
∼*n., pl.* **scherzandos.** *Music.* A scherzando passage or movement. [Italian, gerund of *scherzare,* to joke, from *scherzo,* joke, SCHERZO.] **—scher·zan·do** *adj.*

scher·zo (skáirt-sō, skért-) *n., pl.* **-zos** or **-zi** (-see). *Music.* A lively movement commonly in 3/4 time. [Italian, joke, from Middle High German *scherz,* from *scherzen,* to joke, leap with joy.]

Schia·pa·rel·li (skyáppə-rélli), **Elsa** (1896–1973). Italian-born French fashion designer. She did much to make Paris the world centre of fashion design.

Schiaparelli, Giovanni Virginio (1835–1910). Italian astronomer. He is best known for his discovery of linear markings on the surface of Mars, which he thought were water channels. His theory that Mercury and Venus rotate on their axes as they travel around the

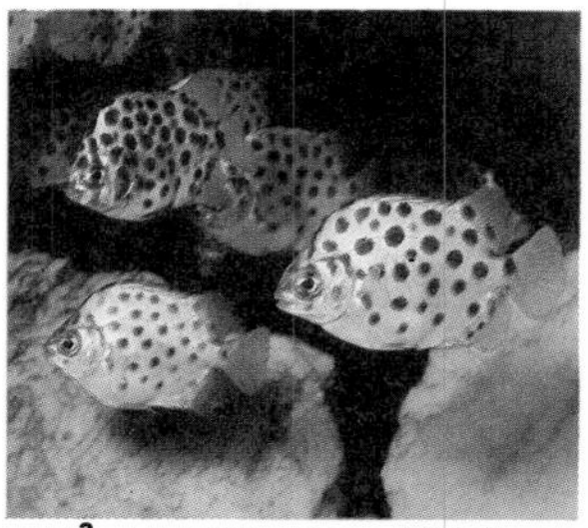

scat[3] *A brightly coloured fish found in fresh and estuarine waters along the coasts of Asia and Indonesia.*

PRONUNCIATION KEY

a, trap; aa, father; ai, fair;
ar, star; aw, lawn; ay, play;
b, bb, stab; rubber;
ch, church; ck, ticket;
d, dd, dead; ladder; e, dress;
ee, bee; er, defer; ew, few;
ewr, pure; ə, about;
ər, letter; f, ff, fife; differ;
g, gg, giggle; h, hat; i, kit;
ī, price; īr, fire; j, judge;
k, kick; l, ll, let; 'l, needle;
m, mm, man; n, nn, no;
'n, sudden; ng, thing; o, lot;
ō, no; ŏŏ, foot; ōō, shoe;
oor, poor; ow, cow;
owr, hour; oy, boy;
p, pp, pepper; r, rr, red;
s, ss, sauce; sh, ship;
t, tt, totter; th, thick; <u>th</u>, this;
smooth; u, cut; ur, turn;
v, vv, valve; w, wet; y, yes;
z, zz, zebra; <u>zh</u>, vision;
pleasure

IN FOREIGN WORDS:

aɴ, oɴ, Saint-Saëns;
<u>hl</u>, Llanelli; Hluhluwe;
<u>kh</u>, loch; lough; Khaled

STRESS MARK:

ín-sīt, insight; in-sít, incite

Sun, so that they always have the same side facing the Sun, was not refuted until the 1960s.

Schick test (shik) *n.* A test of susceptibility to diphtheria in which diphtheria toxin is injected into the skin. A red patch indicates the absence of antibodies and therefore the need for immunisation. [After Bela *Schick* (1877-1967), U.S. paediatrician.]

Schiele (shéelə), **Egon** (1890-1918). Austrian painter, a leader of the Austrian expressionist movement. His paintings, erotic and disturbing, were influenced by Freudian psychology.

Schiff's reagent (shifs) *n.* An aqueous solution of rosaniline and sulphurous acid used to test for the presence of aldehydes, which oxidise the reduced form of the dye rosaniline back to its original magenta colour. [After Hugo *Schiff* (1834-1915), German chemist.]

schil·ler (shíllər) *n.* A lustrous, almost metallic sheen on certain minerals caused by internal reflections from microscopic inclusions. [German *Schiller*, iridescence, from Middle High German *schilher*, iridescent taffeta, from *schilhen*, to wink, blink, from Old High German *scilihen*.]

Schil·ler (shíllər), **(Johann Christoph) Friedrich (von)** (1759-1805). German poet and dramatist. His historical plays include *Wallenstein* (1798-99), *Mária Stuart* (1800), and *Wilhelm Tell* (1804), and he also wrote a study of aesthetics. He is an important figure in the Romantic movement.

schil·ling (shílling) *n.* **1.** The basic monetary unit of Austria, equal to 100 gröschen. **2.** A coin worth one schilling. [German *Schilling*, from Middle High German *schillinc*, from Old High German *skilling*, from Germanic *skillingaz* (unattested), SHILLING.]

schip·per·ke (shíppər-ki, skíppər- ‖ -kə) *n.* A small dog of a breed developed in Belgium, having a dense, long, black coat. [Flemish, "little skipper" (it is often trained as a watchdog on a boat), from *schipper*, skipper, from Middle Dutch, from *schip*, ship.]

schism (síz'm, *also* skíz'm) *n.* **1.** A separation or division into hostile, opposing groups or factions; especially, a formal breach of union within a Christian church. **2.** The offence of attempting to promote or perpetuate such a split within a church or religious group. **3.** A body or sect that has brought about, or is the result of, a separation or division. [Middle English *(s)cisme*, from Old French, from Late Latin *schisma*, from Greek *skhisma*, a split, division, from *skhizein*, to split.] —**schis·mat·ic** (siz-máttik, skiz-) *n. & adj.* —**schis·mat·i·cal·ly** *adv.*

schist (shist) *n.* Any of various medium- to coarse-grained metamorphic rocks composed of parallel layers, which are often wavy and flaky. [French *schiste*, from Latin *(lapis) schistos*, "fissile (stone)", from Greek *skhistos (lithos)*, talc, from *skhizein*, to split.] —**schis·tose** (-ōz, -ōss), **schis·tous** (-əss) *adj.* —**schis·tos·i·ty** (shi-stóssəti) *n.*

schis·to·some (shíst-ə-sōm, -ō-) *n.* Any of several chiefly tropical trematode worms of the genus *Schistosoma*, many of which are parasitic in the blood of humans and other mammals. Also called "bilharzia", "blood fluke". [New Latin *Schistosoma*, "cleft body" : Greek *skhistos*, cleft, from *skhizein*, to split + -SOME (body).]

schis·to·so·mi·a·sis (shíst-ə-sō-mí-ə-siss, -ō-) *n.* Any of various generally tropical diseases caused by infestation with schistosomes. Also called "bilharziasis". [New Latin : *Schistosoma*, SCHISTOSOME + -IASIS.]

schiz·o (skítsō) *adj. Informal.* Schizophrenic.
~*n., pl.* **schizos.** *Informal.* A schizophrenic. [Shortening.]

schizo–, schiz– *comb. form.* Indicates division, split, or cleavage; for example, **schizophrenia**, **schizont**. [New Latin, from Greek *skhizo-*, from *skhizein*, to split.]

schiz·o·carp (skíz-ə-kaarp, skíts-, -ō-) *n.* A dry fruit that splits at maturity into two or more closed carpels, each usually containing one seed, as in the mallow. [SCHIZO- + -CARP.] —**schiz·o·car·pic** (-kárpik), **schiz·o·car·pous** (-kárpəss) *adj.*

schiz·o·gen·e·sis (skíts-ō-jénnə-siss, skíz-, -ə-) *n. Biology.* Reproduction by fission. [New Latin : SCHIZO- + -GENESIS.] —**schiz·o·ge·net·ic** (-jə-néttik, -je-) *adj.*

schi·zog·o·ny (skit-sóggəni, ski-zóggəni) *n. Biology.* Reproduction by multiple asexual fission, characteristic of many protozoans. [New Latin *schizogonia* : SCHIZO- + -GONY.] —**schi·zog·o·nous**, **schiz·o·gon·ic** (skíz-ə-gónnik, skízə-) *adj.*

schiz·oid (skítsoyd) *adj.* **1.** Characteristic of, tending to, or resembling schizophrenia. **2.** Loosely, marked by extremes of mood or temperament.
~*n.* A schizoid person. [SCHIZ(O)- + -OID.]

schiz·o·my·cete (skíts-ō-mi-séet, skíz-, -ə-, -mí-seet) *n.* Any of numerous single-celled microorganisms of the class Schizomycetes, which includes the bacteria. [New Latin *Schizomycetes*, "fission fungi" (from their multiplying by fission) : SCHIZO- + -MYCETE.] —**schiz·o·my·ce·tous** (-séetəss) *adj.*

schiz·ont (skíts-ont, skíz-) *n.* A protozoan cell produced by schizogony in the life cycle of a sporozoan. [SCHIZO- + -ont, being, from Greek *ōn* (stem *ont-*), present participle of *einai*, to be.]

schiz·o·phre·ni·a (skíts-ō-fréeni-ə, skidz-, -ō-) *n.* Any of a group of psychotic conditions characterised by withdrawal from reality and accompanied by highly variable affective, behavioural, and intellectual disturbances. Formerly called "dementia praecox". [New Latin, "split mind" : SCHIZO- + -PHRENIA.] —**schiz·o·phren·ic** (-frénnik) *adj. & n.*

schiz·o·phyte (skíts-ə-fīt, skíz-, -ō-) *n.* Any of various single-celled or simple colonial organisms of the division Schizophyta, including bacteria and the blue-green algae, reproducing asexually, usually by

fission. [New Latin *Schizophyta* : SCHIZO- + -PHYTE.] —**schiz·o·phyt·ic** (-fíttik) *adj.*

schiz·o·pod (skíts-ə-pod, skíz-, -ō-) *n.* Any of various shrimplike crustaceans of the orders Euphausiacea and Mysidacea (formerly included in the single order Schizopoda). [New Latin *Schizopoda*, "split-footed ones" (from the splitting of the thoracic limbs) : SCHIZO- + -POD.] —**schiz·op·o·dous** (skit-sóp-ədəss, ski-zóp-) *adj.*

schiz·o·thy·mi·a (skíts-ə-thími-ə, -ō-) *n.* Schizoid behaviour that resembles schizophrenia in the tendency to withdrawal and introversion but remains within the limits of normality. [New Latin, "split spirit" : SCHIZO- + -THYMIA.] —**schiz·o·thy·mic** (-thímik) *adj.*

Schle·gel (shláyg'l), **August Wilhelm von** (1767-1845). German critic and translator. Best known for his translations of the works of Shakespeare, he also translated other foreign authors, and contributed critical work to the Romantic movement.

Schlegel, (Carl Wilhelm) Friedrich von (1772-1829). German writer and critic. A Sanskrit scholar, he was a leader of the Romantic movement, formulating its aims and publishing his poetry and philosophy in the magazine *Das Athenäum.*

schle·miel (shlə-méel) *n. Chiefly U.S. Slang.* An unlucky and habitual bungler; a dolt. [Yiddish, perhaps from Hebrew *Shelūmīel*, character in the Bible.]

schlen·ter (shlén-tər, slén-) *n. South African.* A counterfeit diamond.
~*adj.* Fake or counterfeit. [Dutch *slenter*, a trick.]

schlep (shlep) *v.* **schlepped, schlepping, schleps.** *Chiefly U.S. Slang.* —*tr.* To carry clumsily or with difficulty; lug. —*intr.* **1.** To carry something clumsily. **2.** To go or travel.
~*n. Chiefly U.S. Slang.* **1.** An arduous journey. **2.** A clumsy or stupid person. **3.** A boring event or period of time. [Yiddish *shlep-pen*, to drag, trail, from Middle Low German *slēpen*.]

Schles·in·ger (shléssinjər, sléssinjər), **John (Richard)** (1926-). British theatre and film director. His films, often dourly naturalistic, include *Billy Liar* (1963), *Midnight Cowboy* (1969), and *Sunday Bloody Sunday* (1970).

Schles·wig (shléz-wig, -vig; German shláyss-vikh). Former duchy on the Jutland peninsula, north Europe, to the north of the river Eider. The greater part of it is now incorporated in the West German state of **Schleswig-Holstein.**

Schles·wig-Hol·stein (shléz-wig-hól-shtīn, -vig-, -hól-, -stīn; German shláyss-vikh-hól-shtīn). State of West Germany. It comprises most of the two former duchies of **Schleswig** and **Holstein.** These were inherited by the Danish royal house in 1460. Centuries of conflict ensued as the Danes periodically sought to make them part of Denmark, while their predominantly German populations resisted or sought union with German states, later the German Confederation. Eventually (1866) Prussia annexed both duchies. The northern part of Schleswig was awarded to Denmark after a plebiscite (1920), and it now forms the Danish county of Sønderjylland (South Jutland). Schleswig-Holstein is a low-lying, largely fertile area. There are good harbours along the coast, and tourist resorts on offshore islands. The port of Kiel is the state capital.

Schlick (shlik), **Moritz** (1882-1936). German-born Austrian philosopher. He organised (1928) a group of philosophers, the Vienna circle, which developed the theories of logical positivism. He held that the meaning of a statement lies in its experimental verification.

Schlie·mann (shlée-man, -mən), **Heinrich** (1822-90). German archaeologist. Retiring from business (1863), he began to excavate at Homer's Troy at Hissarlik in Turkey. His carelessness and determination to prove the existence of the city somewhat devalued the veracity of his results. From Troy, he went on to excavate most of the sites of Mycenaean Greece.

schlie·ren (shléer-ən) *pl.n.* **1.** *Geology.* Irregular tabular bodies occurring as essential components of plutonic rock but differing in structure or composition from the principal mass. **2.** *Physics.* Regions of a transparent medium, as of a flowing gas, that exhibit densities different from that of the bulk of the medium. [German *Schlieren*, plural of *Schliere*, streak, from dialectal German *Schlier*, "slimy mass", from Middle High German *slier*, mud, slime.]

schli·ma·zel (shli-máaz'l) *n. U.S. Slang.* An extremely unlucky or inept person, a habitual failure. [Yiddish, "bad luck".]

schlock (shlok) *n. Chiefly U.S. Slang.* Goods, creative artefacts, entertainments, or the like, that are of meretricious or obviously inferior quality. [Yiddish, "broken merchandise", perhaps from German *Schlag*, a blow, from Middle High German *slac*, from Old High German *slag*.] —**schlock** *adj.*

schm-, shm- (shm-) *prefix & infix. Slang.* Inserted before the dismissive repetition of all or part of a word: *Oedipus-Schmoedipus, who cares? Graffiti-graschmiti, it's vandalism.* [Abstracted from Yiddish words in *schm-*, such as SCHMUK.]

schmaltz, shmalz (shmawlts, shmolts) *n.* **1.** *Informal.* Excessive sentimentality, especially in art or music. **2.** *Informal.* Excessively profuse flattery or praise. **3.** Animal fat used as food, especially chicken fat. [German, "melted fat", from Middle High German *smalz*, from Old High German.] —**schmaltz·y** *adj.*

Schmidt (shmit), **Helmut** (1918-). German politician. A member of the Social Democrat party, he was minister of defence (1969-72) and minister of finance (1972-74). From 1974 to 1982 he was federal chancellor.

Schmidt telescope *n.* A reflecting telescope consisting of a concave spherical mirror and a transparent plate of glass at its centre of curvature, used to offset spherical aberration, coma, and astigmatism. [After Bernhard *Schmidt* (1879–1935), Swedish-born German astronomer, who invented it.]

schmo, schmoe (shmō) *n., pl.* **schmoes.** *Chiefly U.S. Slang.* A dull or stupid person. [Yiddish *shmok*, from Slovene *šmok*.]

schmuck (shmuk) *n. Chiefly U.S. Slang.* A clumsy or stupid person; an oaf. [Yiddish *schmuck*, "penis", from German *Schmuck*, ornament, from Middle Low German *smuck*.]

Schna·bel (shnaáb'l), **Artur** (1882–1951). Austrian pianist. Performing mostly in the United States, he was regarded as the leading interpreter of Beethoven's piano sonatas.

schnap·per (snáppər) *n.* Australian. A fish, the **snapper** *(see)*. [Pseudo-German spelling of SNAPPER (fish).]

schnapps (shnaps ‖ *U.S. also* shnaaps) *n.* Any of various strong alcoholic spirits; especially, a kind of Dutch gin. [German *Schnaps*, from Low German *snaps*, mouthful, dram, from *snappen*, to snap, from Middle Low German, SNAP.]

schnau·zer (shnówtsər ‖ *U.S.* shnóvzər) *n.* A dog of a breed developed in Germany, having a wiry grey or black coat and a blunt muzzle. [German *Schnauzer*, from *Schnauze*, snout.]

schnit·zel (shníts'l) *n.* A thin cutlet of veal coated with breadcrumbs, fried lightly in butter. [German *Schnitzel*, diminutive of *Schnitz*, slice, from Middle High German *sniz*.]

Schnitz·ler (shnítslər), **Arthur** (1862–1931). Austrian playwright and novelist. His work portrays Viennese cafe society. His best-known work, *Reigen* (1900), also known as *La Ronde*, met with such controversy for its sexual explicitness that he forbade it to be performed until 50 years after his death.

schnook (shnōōk) *n. U.S. Slang.* A stupid or easily victimised person; a dupe. [Yiddish *shnok*, variant of *shmok*, SCHMO.]

schnor·rer (shnáw-rər ‖ shnô-) *n. Chiefly U.S. Slang.* One who takes advantage of the generosity of friends; a parasite; a sponger. [Yiddish, from *schnorren*, to beg (while playing a pipe or harp), from Middle High German *snurren*, to hum, whirr.]

schnoz·zle (shnózz'l) *n. Chiefly U.S. Slang.* The nose. [Probably alteration (influenced by NOZZLE) of Yiddish *shnoitsl*, diminutive of *shnoits*, snout, from German *Schnauze*.]

Schoen·berg (shúrn-berg; *German* shŏn-bairk), **Arnold,** born Arnold Schönberg (1874–1951). Austrian composer and teacher. His style is usually called "atonal", a term he disliked. An example is *Pierrot Lunaire* (1912), a set of recitations with chamber accompaniment which also makes use of **Sprechgesang** *(see).* He emigrated to the United States in 1933 to escape Nazi persecution.

schol·ar (skóllər) *n.* **1. a.** A learned or erudite person. **b.** A specialist in some given branch of the humanities. **2. a.** One who studies; especially, a school pupil. **b.** One considered in the light of his ability to learn: *a poor scholar.* **3.** A student who holds a scholarship. [Middle English *scoler*, from Old French *escoler*, from Late Latin *scholāris*, of a school, from Latin *schola*, SCHOOL.]

schol·ar·ly (skóllərli) *adj.* Pertaining to, characteristic of, or befitting scholars or scholarship. —**schol·ar·li·ness** *n.*

schol·ar·ship (skóllər-ship) *n.* **1.** The methods, qualities, and attainments of a scholar; learning; erudition. **2.** Existing knowledge resulting from scholarly research in a particular field. **3. a.** An award of financial aid to a student or pupil, usually gained through competitive examination, that is given by a fund or endowment set up for such a purpose. **b.** The position of a student or pupil who has won such an award. —See Synonyms at **knowledge.**

scho·las·tic (skə-lástik, sko-) *adj.* **1.** Of or pertaining to schools, scholars, or education. **2.** *Usually capital* **S.** Pertaining to or characteristic of the medieval Schoolmen or Scholasticism: *Scholastic theology.* **3.** Pedantic; dogmatic.
~*n.* **1.** *Usually capital* **S.** A Schoolman. **2.** A dogmatist; a pedant. **3.** A formalist in art. **4.** A Jesuit student at a scholasticate, between the novitiate and the priesthood. [Latin *scholasticus*, from Greek *skholastikos*, academic, from *skholazein*, to study, attend lectures, from *skholē*, SCHOOL.] —**scho·las·ti·cal·ly** *adv.*

scho·las·ti·cate (skə-lásti-kayt, sko-, -kət, -kit) *n.* In the Roman Catholic Church: **1.** An institution where Jesuit scholastics undergo a period of general study before beginning their theological studies and entering the priesthood. **2. a.** A scholastic. **b.** The status or period of being a scholastic. [New Latin *scholasticātus*, from Latin *scholasticus*, SCHOLASTIC.]

scho·las·ti·cism (skə-lásti-siz'm, sko-) *n.* **1.** *Usually capital* **S.** The dominant theological and philosophical school of medieval western Europe, based on the authority of the Latin Fathers and of Aristotle and his commentators. **2. a.** Close adherence to the traditional doctrines of a school or religious order. **b.** Pedantry.

scho·li·ast (skóli-ast) *n.* Any of the ancient commentators who annotated the classical authors. [Late Greek *skholiastēs*, from *skholiazein*, to comment on, from *skholion*, SCHOLIUM.]

scho·li·um (skō-li-əm) *n., pl.* **-ums** or **-lia** (-li-ə). **1.** An explanatory note or commentary, as on a Greek or Latin text. **2.** A note amplifying a proof or process, as in mathematics. [New Latin, from Greek *skholion*, diminutive of *skholē*, lecture, SCHOOL.]

school[1] (skōōl) *n. Abbr.* **s., S., sch. 1.** An institution for the instruction or education of children or young people. Often used adjectivally or in combination: *school fees; schoolboy.* **2.** An institution within a college or university for instruction in a specialised field: *medical school.* **3.** Any institution that provides instruction, especially of a practical or technical nature: *a driving school; drama school.* **4.** The pupils and sometimes the teachers of a school. **5.** The building or group of buildings housing a school, in which instruction is given or in which pupils work and live. **6.** *U.S. A* college or university. **7.** The process of being educated; especially, formal education comprising a planned series of courses over a number of years. **8.** A session or period of instruction at a school: *went swimming before school.* **9.** A group of persons, especially intellectuals or artists, whose thought, work, or style demonstrates some common influence or unifying belief. **10.** A class of people distinguished by shared values, opinions, or principles: *a politician of the old school.* **11.** The education provided by a set of circumstances or experiences. **12.** *Plural. Often capital* **S.** The medieval universities and Schoolmen. **13.** *Plural. British.* At Oxford University, the final examinations of an honours course for the degree of Bachelor of Arts. **14.** *British Slang.* A group of people playing cards, usually for money: *a poker school.*
~*tr.v.* **schooled, schooling, schools. 1.** To instruct; educate. **2.** To train; discipline. —See Synonyms at **teach.** [Middle English *scole*, Old English *scōl*, from Medieval Latin *scōla*, from Latin *schola*, leisure, school, from Greek *skholē*, leisure (devoted to learning), lecture, school.]

school[2] *n.* A large group of aquatic animals, especially fish, swimming together; a shoal. See Synonyms at **flock.**
~*intr.v.* **schooled, schooling, schools.** To swim in, or form into, a school. [Middle English *scole*, from Middle Dutch *schōle*, troop, group.]

school board *n.* **1.** In Britain, a local education authority formerly empowered to establish and maintain elementary schools. **2.** *U.S.* A local education authority.

school·boy (skōōl-boy) *n.* A boy attending school.

school·child (skōōl-chīld) *n., pl.* **-children** (-children). A child attending school.

school·girl (skōōl-gurl) *n.* A girl attending school.

school·house (skōōl-howss) *n.* **1.** A building used as a school, especially in a rural area. **2.** A house provided for a head teacher, usually attached to a school.

school·ing (skōōling) *n.* **1.** Instruction or training given at school; especially, a programme of formal education. **2.** The training of a horse or of a horse and rider in dressage.

school·man (skōōl-mən, -man) *n., pl.* **-men** (-mən, -men) **1.** *Often capital* **S.** A philosopher or theologian of a medieval university; an adherent of Scholasticism. **2.** *Chiefly U.S.* A professional teacher or scholar.

school·marm (skōōl-maarm) *n. Informal.* **1.** A woman schoolteacher, especially one who is pedantic, old-fashioned, or a priggish disciplinarian. **2.** A woman who resembles a schoolmarm in being prim, old-fashioned, and priggish. [Dialectal *marm*, variant of *ma'am*, MADAM.] —**school·marm·ish** *adj.*

school·mas·ter (skōōl-maastər ‖ -mastər) *n.* **1.** A male teacher or headmaster. **2.** A reddish-brown food fish, the snapper *Lutjanus apodus*, of the tropical Atlantic and the Gulf of Mexico.

school·mate (skōōl-mayt) *n.* A school companion or associate. Also called "schoolfellow".

school·mis·tress (skōōl-miss-triss, -trəss) *n.* **1.** A woman teacher. **2.** A headmistress of a school.

school of thought *n.* A number of people who share an opinion or view.

school·room (skōōl-rōōm, -rŏŏm) *n.* A classroom.

school ship *n.* **1.** A ship on which training in seamanship is given, especially for persons entering the navy. **2.** A ship that is made available for educational cruises.

school·teach·er (skōōl-teechər) *n.* One who teaches in a school.

school year *n.* The period of a year that constitutes a complete annual session of school.

schoo·ner (skōōnər) *n.* **1.** A ship with two or more masts, all of which are fore-and-aft-rigged, the mainmast being abaft of and taller than the foremast. **2.** *British.* A measure of or large glass for sherry. **3.** *U.S. & Australian.* A large beer glass, generally holding a pint or more. [18th century : origin obscure.]

Scho·pen·hau·er (shōpən-how-ər, shóppən-), **Arthur** (1788–1860). German philosopher. Rejecting the theories of Hegel, he held that primordial reality—the will to live—is irrational, and that attempts to understand the world rationally are doomed to failure. His major work was the *The World as Will and Idea* (1818).

schorl (shorl) *n.* A black, opaque variety of tourmaline. [German *Schörl†*.] —**schor·la·ceous** (shawr-láyshəss) *adj.*

schot·tische (sho-teesh ‖ shóttish) *n.* **1.** A German round dance in ²/₄ time, resembling a slow polka. **2.** A piece of music for this dance. [German *Schottische*, short for *(der) schottische (Tanz)*, (the) Scottish (dance).]

Schrei·ner (shrínər), **Olive (Emilie Albertina)** (1855–1920). South African novelist. She is best known for *The Story of An African Farm* (1883), a thinly-veiled autobiographical work.

Schrö·ding·er (shrúr-ding-ər, shrō-; *German* shró-), **Erwin** (1887–1961). Austrian physicist. He won the Nobel prize (1933) for his work on the development of the quantum theory. He left Austria after the Nazi Anschluss.

Schrödinger wave equation *n. Physics.* A partial differential equation, fundamental to wave mechanics, describing the behaviour of a particle in a potential, based on the de Broglie hypothesis of wave-particle duality: $(h/2\pi)(\partial\psi/\partial t) = H\psi$, where h is Planck's constant, H is the Hamiltonian, ψ is the wave function of the particle, and ∂t is the partical differential operator. Also called "wave equation".

Schu·bert (shōŏbərt), **Franz (Peter)** (1797–1828). Austrian composer. In addition to his 600 songs, which established the tradition of the German *lied,* his genius for the lyrical is evident in his eight surviving symphonies, and his many other choral and orchestral works. **—Schu·bert·i·an** (shōō-bárti-ən) *adj.*

Schu·man (shōō-mən, -man), **Robert** (1886–1963). French statesman. He was prime minister (1947–48), and president of the Assembly of the European Economic Community (1958–60). While foreign minister (1948–53), he prepared the Schuman Plan which led to the establishment of the European Coal and Steel Community.

Schu·mann (shōō-man, -mən), **Clara (Josephine),** born Clara Wieck (1819–96). German pianist. The daughter of Friedrich Wieck (1788–1873), she married his pupil Robert Schumann in 1840, and became the foremost interpreter and editor of his works.

Schumann, Elisabeth (1885–1952). German-born U.S. singer. From 1938 she won great popularity in the United States for her interpretation of the works of Mozart and Richard Strauss.

Schumann, Robert (Alexander) (1810–56). German composer. One of the earliest composers of the Romantic movement, he started by writing for the piano only, but later moved to emotional and inventive works for full orchestra.

Schusch·nigg (shŏŏsh-nig; *German* -nik), **Kurt von** (1897–1977). Austrian politician. He became chancellor (1934) after the assassination of Dollfuss. After Austria was annexed by Germany in the Anschluss of 1938, Schuschnigg resigned and was later imprisoned by the Germans.

schuss (shŏŏss) *intr.v.* **schussed, schussing, schusses.** To make a fast straight run in skiing.
~*n.* **1.** A straight, steep course for skiing. **2.** The act of skiing such a course. [German *Schuss,* shot, from Middle High German *schuz,* from Old High German *scuz.*]

Schutz·staf·fel (*German* shŏŏts-shtaff'l) *n., pl.* **-feln** (-shtaff'ln). *German.* The **SS** *(see).*

schwa (shwaa; *German* shvaa) *n.* **1.** A mid-central vowel sound. In English it occurs in many unstressed syllables, as in those of the words *mother* and *about.* **2.** The symbol (ə) used to represent this sound. [German *Schwa,* from Hebrew *shəwā',* probably from *shaw',* emptiness.]

Schwaben. See **Swabia.**

Schwann (shvan), **Theodor** (1810–82). German physiologist. He developed cell theory, showing that animals are formed of cells and coining the term "metabolism".

Schwann cell (shwon, shvan) *n.* A cell responsible for the formation of a myelin sheath around certain nerve fibres. [After Theodor SCHWANN.]

Schwarz·kopf (shvárts-kopf), **Elizabeth** (1915–). German soprano. She is noted for her interpretation of lieder and of operas by Mozart and Richard Strauss.

Schwarz·wald (shvárts-valt). Also **Black Forest.** Highland region of southwest West Germany, extensively forested. It stretches from the Swiss border northwards to the river Main.

Schweit·zer (shwī́t-sər, shvī́t-), **Albert** (1875–1965). German-born French missionary. From 1913 he ran a hospital in the Gabon village of Lambaréné, financed by his organ recitals of the music of Bach. His books include *The Quest for the Historical Jesus* (1906). His own theology was based on "reverence for life". He was awarded the Nobel prize for peace (1952).

Schweiz. See **Switzerland.**

Schwit·ters (shvíttərz), **Kurt** (1887–1948). German artist and poet. He founded his own version of the Dada movement in Hanover. His work, for which he coined the nonsense word "Merz", consists mainly of collages of random words and objects.

sci. science; scientific.

sci·a·gram, ski·a·gram (sī́-ə-gram, skī́-) *n.* Also **sci·a·graph** (-graaf || -graff). A picture or photograph made up of shadows or outlines. [Greek *skia,* shadow + -GRAM.]

sci·ag·ra·phy, ski·ag·ra·phy (sī-ággrəfi, skī-) *n.* The art or technique of making sciagrams. [SCIA(GRAM) + -GRAPHY.]

sci·am·a·chy, ski·am·a·chy (sī-ámməki, skī-) *n.* Fighting with shadows or imaginary enemies. [Greek *skiamakhia* : *skia,* shadow + *-makhia,* -fighting.]

sci·at·ic (sī-áttik) *adj.* **1.** *Anatomy.* Of or pertaining to the **ischium** *(see).* **2.** Of or pertaining to sciatica. [French *sciatique,* from Late Latin *(i)sc(h)iaticus,* variant of Latin *ischiadicus,* from Greek *iskhiadikos,* from *iskhion,* hip joint, ISCHIUM.]

sci·at·i·ca (sī-áttikə) *n.* Neuralgia of the sciatic nerve, characterised by pain down the back of the leg, often caused by pressure from a slipped disc. [Middle English, from Medieval Latin *sciatica (passiō),* "(suffering) in the hip", from Late Latin *sciaticus,* SCIATIC.]

sciatic nerve *n. Anatomy.* A sensory and motor nerve originating in the sacral plexus and running through the pelvis and down the leg.

sci·ence (sī́-ənss) *n. Abbr.* **sci. 1.** Learning or study concerned with demonstrable truths or observable phenomena, and characterised by the systematic application of scientific method. **2.** Such learning or study concerned with the phenomena of the physical universe; any or all of the natural sciences: *the biological sciences.* **3.** Any branch of knowledge conducted according to scientific method: *forensic science.* **4.** Any methodological activity, discipline, or study. **5.** Any skill or technique that may be developed through systematic learning: *the science of drawing.* **6.** *Archaic.* Knowledge; especially, knowledge gained through experience. **—blind with science.** To confuse or overawe with a display of specialist knowledge. [Middle English, knowledge, learning, from Old French, from Latin *scientia,* from *sciēns* (stem *scient-*), present participle of *scīre,* to know.]

science fiction *n. Abbr.* **SF** A literary or cinematic genre in which fantasy, typically based on speculative scientific discoveries and developments, forms an element of plot or background; especially, imaginative work based on prediction of future scientific discoveries, environmental changes, space travel, and life on other planets. **—sci·ence-fic·tion** (sī́-ənss-fíksh'n) *adj.*

sci·en·ter (sī-éntər) *adv. Law.* Deliberately or knowingly. [Latin, from *scīre,* to know.]

sci·en·tial (sī-énsh'l) *adj.* **1.** Of or producing knowledge or science. **2.** Having knowledge or skill.

sci·en·tif·ic (sī-ən-tíffik) *adj. Abbr.* **sci. 1.** Of, pertaining to, or used in science. **2.** Broadly, having or appearing to have an exact, objective, factual, systematic, or methodological basis. [Medieval Latin *scientificus,* "producing knowledge" : Latin *scientia,* knowledge, SCIENCE + -FIC.] **—sci·en·tif·i·cal·ly** *adv.*

scientific method *n.* The totality of principles and processes regarded as characteristic of or necessary for scientific investigation, generally taken to include rules for concept formation, conduct of observations and experiments, and validation of hypotheses by observations or experiments.

sci·en·tism (sī́-ən-tiz'm) *n.* **1.** The theory that investigational methods used in the natural sciences should be applied in all fields of inquiry. **2.** The application of quasi-scientific techniques or justifications to unsuitable subjects or topics. **—sci·en·tis·tic** (-tístik) *adj.*

sci·en·tist (sī́-əntist) *n.* **1.** A student of or expert in a science, especially one or more of the natural sciences. **2.** *Capital* **S.** A Christian Scientist.

sci·en·tol·o·gy (sī́-ən-tólləji) *n. Often capital* **S.** The church and religious system founded by L. Ron Hubbard and based on his system of **dianetics** *(see).* [Latin *scientia,* knowledge, SCIENCE + -LOGY.] **—sci·en·tol·o·gist** *n.*

sci-fi (sī́-fī́) *n. Informal.* Science fiction.

scil·i·cet (sī́li-set, sílli-, skéeli-ket) *adv. Abbr.* **sc., scil., ss** That is to say; namely. Used when introducing an explanation of an obscure or ambiguous part of a text or when supplying a missing word. [Latin, short for *scīre licet,* "it is permitted to know", it is evident, of course, namely : *scīre,* to know + *licet,* third person singular present of *licēre,* to be allowed (see **leisure**).]

scil·la (síllə) *n.* Any bulbous plant of the genus *Scilla;* a **squill** *(see).* [New Latin, from Greek *skilla,* SQUILL.]

Scil·ly, Isles of (sílli). Also **Scil·lies** (sílliz). Archipelago in the northeast Atlantic, lying approximately 40 kilometres (25 miles) off the southwest tip of mainland England and forming part of the county of Cornwall. Five of the 140 islands are inhabited. Hugh Town, on St. Mary's, is the chief town and administrative centre.

scim·i·tar (símmi-tər, -taar) *n.* A curved Oriental sword with an edge on the convex side. [French *cimeterre,* from Italian *scimitarra,* from Persian *šimšīr*†.]

scin·tig·ra·phy (sin-tíggrəfi) *n.* A technique used in medical diagnosis, in which the distribution of a radioactive tracer in a part of the body is measured by a scintillation counter and recorded on a *scintigram.* See **scintiscan.** [SCINTI(LLATION) + -GRAPHY.]

scin·til·la (sin-tíllə) *n.* A minute amount; a trace. [Latin, spark.]

scin·til·late (sínti-layt) *v.* **-lated, -lating, -lates.** —*intr.* **1.** To throw off sparks; flash. **2.** To sparkle or shine. **3.** To be animated and witty. —*tr.* To give off (sparks or flashes). **—**See Synonyms at **flash.** [Latin *scintillāre,* from *scintilla,* spark.] **—scin·til·lant** *adj.* **—scin·til·lat·ing·ly** *adv.*

scin·til·la·tion (sínti-láysh'n) *n.* **1.** The action of scintillating. **2.** A spark; a flash. **3.** *Astronomy.* Rapid variation in the light of a celestial body caused by turbulence in the earth's atmosphere; a twinkling. **4.** *Physics.* A flash of light produced in certain media by absorption of an ionising particle or photon.

scintillation counter *n.* A device for detecting and counting scintillations produced by ionising radiation.

scin·til·la·tor (sínti-laytər) *n. Physics.* A substance that scintillates when hit by high-energy particles or photons.

scin·ti·scan (sínti-skan) *n.* A diagram of the distribution of radiation produced when the body is scanned using the technique of scintigraphy. [SCINTI(GRAPHY) + SCAN.]

sci·o·lism (sī́-ə-liz'm) *n.* A pretentious attitude of scholarship; superficial knowledgeability. [Late Latin *sciolus,* smatterer, diminutive of *scius,* knowing, from *scīre,* to know + -ISM.] **—sci·o·list** *n.* **—sci·o·lis·tic** (-lístik) *adj.*

sci·o·man·cy (sī́-ə-man-si) *n.* Divination by the apparent consulting of ghosts. [Late Latin *sciomantia,* from Greek *skia,* shade, ghost + -MANCY.] **—sci·o·man·cer** *n.* **—sci·o·man·tic** (-mántik) *adj.*

sci·on (sī́-ən) *n.* **1.** A descendant, heir, or young member of a family. **2.** A detached shoot or twig containing buds from a woody plant and used in grafting. [Middle English, from Old French *ciun, cion,* twia, sprout, from Germanic.]

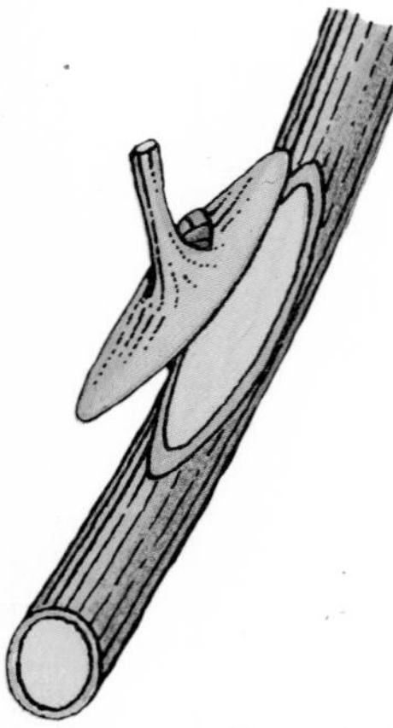

scion *Woody plants and shrubs such as roses and fruit trees are often propagated by grafting. In this technique a scion bud – a section containing a bud – is cut from the plant and bound firmly to the stem of another plant known as the rootstock. The rootstock is usually a different variety of the same species. If the graft takes, the bud breaks into growth and the scion and rootstock fuse, effectively becoming a single new plant. The new plant will have the flowers and fruit of the scion variety, but often the growth habit of the rootstock.*

Scip·i·o[1] (skíppi-ō || síppi-ō), full name Publius Cornelius Scipio Aemilianus Africanus Minor (*c.* 185–129 B.C.). Roman general. In the Third Punic War he was responsible for the final destruction of Carthage (146 B.C.).

Scipio[2], full name Publius Cornelius Scipio Africanus Major (234–183 B.C.). Roman general. In 204 he invaded North Africa, and ended the Second Punic War by defeating Hannibal in 202.

sci·re fa·ci·as (sī́r-i fáyshi-əss, -ass) *n. Law.* **1.** Formerly, a writ requiring the party against whom it is issued to appear and show cause why a judicial record should not be enforced, repealed, or annulled. **2.** A judicial proceeding under such a writ. [Latin *scīre facias,* "you are to cause (him) to know" (phrase commonly used in the writ) : *scīre*, to know + *facias*, second person singular present subjunctive of *facere*, to make, do.]

scirocco. Variant of **sirocco**.

scir·rhus (sírrəss, skírrəss) *n., pl.* **-rhi** (sírrī, skírrī) or **-rhuses**. A hard cancerous growth. [New Latin, from Greek *skirros*, *skiros†*, hard.] —**scir·rhous, scir·rhoid** (sírroyd, skírroyd) *adj.*

scis·sel (síss'l, skíss'l) *n.* The scrap metal left when discs are punched out of a sheet of metal. [French *cisaille*, "clippings", from *cisailler*, to clip.]

scis·sile (sissīl ‖ *U.S. also* síss'l) *adj.* Capable of being cut or split easily. [French, from Latin *scissilis*, from *scindere* (past participle *scissus*), to cut. See **scission**.]

scis·sion (sízh'n, sísh'n) *n.* The act of cutting or severing; division; fission. [French, from Late Latin *scissiō* (stem *scissiōn-*), from Latin *scindere* (past participle *scissus*), to cut.]

scis·sor (sízzər) *tr.v.* **-sored, -soring, -sors.** To cut or clip with scissors or shears.

scis·sors (sízzərz) *n., pl.* **scissors. 1.** *Used with a plural verb.* A cutting implement consisting of two blades, each with a loop handle, joined by a swivel pin that allows the cutting edges to be opened and closed. Also called "pair of scissors". **2.** *Used with a singular verb.* A movement in certain sports, as: **a.** In wrestling, a hold in which the legs are locked about the head or body of the opponent. **b.** A movement of the legs, as in swimming, jumping, or gymnastics, that suggests the opening and closing of scissors. [Middle English *sisoures*, from Old French *cisoires*, from Medieval Latin *cīsōria*, plural of Late Latin *cīsōrium*, cutting instrument, from Latin *caedere* (past participle *caesus*, in compounds *-cīsus*), to cut.]

scis·sor·tail (sízzər-tayl) *n.* A bird, *Muscivora forficata*, of the southwestern United States, Mexico, and Central and South America, having a long, forked tail. Also called "scissor-tailed fly-catcher".

sci·u·rine (sī-yoor-īn, -in) *adj.* **1.** Of pertaining to, or belonging to the rodent family Sciuridae, which includes the squirrels and marmots. **2.** Resembling a squirrel. [Latin *sciūrus*, squirrel, from Greek *skiouros*, "shadow tail", squirrel, (*skia*, shadow + *oura*, tail) + -INE.] —**sci·u·rine** *n.*

sci·u·roid (sī-yoor-oyd, sī-yóor-oyd) *adj.* **1.** Resembling or characteristic of a squirrel; sciurine. **2.** *Botany*. Similar in shape to a squirrel's tail; bushy and curved. [Latin *sciūrus*, SQUIRREL + -OID.]

sclaff (sklaf) *v.* **sclaffed, sclaffing, sclaffs.** —*intr.* In golf, to scrape or strike the ground with the club behind the ball before hitting it. —*tr.* **1.** To strike (the ground) with the club before hitting the ball. **2.** To hit (a ball) in this way. —*n.* A golf stroke made in this manner. [Scottish, to strike with a flat surface (imitative).] —**sclaff·er** *n.*

scle·ra (skléer-ə) *n.* Also **scle·rot·ic** (sklə-róttik, skleer-, skle-), **scle·rot·i·ca** (-ə). The tough, white, fibrous outer envelope of tissue covering all of the eyeball except the cornea. [New Latin, from Greek *sklēros*, hard.] —**scle·ral** (skléer-əl) *adj.*

scle·re·id (skléer-i-id) *n.* Any of various cells (except fibres) that make up sclerenchyma. [Greek *sklēros*, hard.]

scle·ren·chy·ma (skleer-éng-kimə, sklə-réng-) *n.* Supportive or protective plant tissue consisting of thick-walled, usually lignified cells. [New Latin : SCLER(O)- + -ENCHYMA.] —**scle·ren·chym·a·tous** (skléer-eng-kímmətəss) *adj.*

scle·rite (skléer-īt) *n.* Any of the hard outer plates forming part of the exoskeleton of an arthropod, especially an insect. [SCLER(O)- + -ITE.] —**scle·rit·ic** (sklə-ríttik, skleer-, skle-) *adj.*

scle·ri·tis (skleer-ítiss, sklə-rítiss) *n.* Also **scle·ro·ti·tis** (skléer-ō-títiss). Inflammation of the sclera. [New Latin : SCLER(O)- + -ITIS.]

sclero-, scler- *comb. form.* Indicates: **1.** Hardness; for example, **scleroderma, sclerite. 2.** Of or affecting the sclera; for example, **sclerotomy, scleritis.** [New Latin, from Greek *sklēros*, hard.]

scle·ro·der·ma (skléer-ō-dérmə) *n.* Pathological thickening and hardening of the skin or other connective tissue. [New Latin : SCLERO- + -DERMA.]

scle·ro·der·ma·tous (skléer-ō-dérmətəss) *adj.* **1.** Characterising or afflicted with scleroderma. **2.** *Zoology*. Having an outer covering of hard plates or bony scales.

scle·roid (skléer-oyd) *adj. Biology*. Hard or hardened; indurated. [SCLER(O)- + -OID.]

scle·ro·ma (skleer-rōmə, sklə-) *n., pl.* **-mata** (-mətə). An abnormally hard patch of skin or mucous membrane. [New Latin, from Greek *sklērōma*, hardening, from *sklēroun*, to harden, from *sklēros*, hard.]

scle·rom·e·ter (skleer-rómmitər, sklə-) *n.* An instrument used to determine relative hardness of solids, especially minerals and metals, by measurement of the pressure required on a standard diamond stylus to achieve penetration. [SCLERO- + -METER.]

scle·ro·phyll (skléerrə-fil) *n.* Any woody plant with leathery, evergreen leaves that are specialised to reduce water loss. [SCLERO- + -PHYLL.]

scle·ro·pro·tein (skléer-ō-pró-teen, -tee-in) *n.* Any of a large class of proteins, such as keratin, elastin, and collagen, found in skeletal and connective tissue. Also called "albuminoid".

scle·rosed (skléer-ōst, -ōzd) *adj.* **1.** Affected with sclerosis; hardened. **2.** Lignified. [From SCLEROSIS.]

scle·ro·sis (skleer-rō-siss, sklə-, skle-) *n., pl.* **-ses** (-seez). **1. a.** *Pathology*. A thickening or hardening of a body part, as of an artery or the spinal cord, especially from tissue overgrowth or disease. **b.** A disease characterised by sclerosis. See **arteriosclerosis, atherosclerosis, multiple sclerosis. 2.** *Botany*. The hardening of an outer cell wall by formation or deposit of lignin. [Middle English *sclirosis*, from Medieval Latin *sclīrōsis*, from Greek *sklērōsis*, hardening, from *sklēroun*, to harden, from *sklēros*, hard.] —**scle·ro·sal** (-róss'l) *adj.*

scle·rot·ic (skleer-róttik, sklə-, skle-) *adj.* **1.** Affected or characterised by sclerosis. **2.** *Anatomy*. Of or pertaining to the sclera. ~*n.* Variant of **sclera**. [New Latin *scleroticus*, from SCLEROSIS and SCLERA.]

sclerotica. Variant of **sclera**.

sclerotitis. Variant of **scleritis**.

scle·ro·ti·um (skleer-rō-shi-əm, sklə-) *n., pl.* **-tia** (-shi-ə). A dense mass of branching filaments, or hyphae, in certain fungi, containing stored food and capable of remaining dormant for long periods. [New Latin, from Greek *sklērotēs*, hardness, from *sklēros*, hard.] —**scle·ro·ti·al** *adj.*

scle·rot·o·my (skleer-róttə-mi, sklə-, skle-) *n., pl.* **-mies**. Surgical incision into the sclera. [SCLERO- + -TOMY.]

scle·rous (skléer-əss) *adj.* Hardened; toughened; bony. [Greek *sklēros*, hard.]

S.C.M. 1. State Certified Midwife (in Britain). **2.** Student Christian Movement.

scoff¹ (skof ‖ skawf) *intr.v.* **scoffed, scoffing, scoffs.** To jeer or mock; speak derisively. Often used with *at*. ~*n.* An expression of derision or scorn; a jeer. [Middle English *scoffen*, from *scof*, mockery, probably from Scandinavian, akin to Danish *skof*, jest.] —**scoff·er** *n.* —**scoff·ing·ly** *adv.*

scoff² *v.* **scoffed, scoffing, scoffs.** *British Informal.* —*tr.* To eat (food) quickly and greedily —*intr.* To eat greedily. ~*n. British Informal.* **1.** A meal. **2.** Food. [Variant of dialect *scaff*, associated with Afrikaans *schoff*, Dutch *schoft*, a quarter of a day, hence, a meal.]

Sco·field (skō-feeld), **(David) Paul** (1922–). British actor. A member of the National Theatre, he has played many Shakespearean roles. His performance as Sir Thomas More in the film version of *A Man For All Seasons* (1967) won him an Academy Award.

scold (skōld) *v.* **scolded, scolding, scolds.** —*tr.* To reprimand harshly or noisily. —*intr.* To find fault angrily or persistently. ~*n.* A person, especially a woman, who persistently nags or criticises. [Middle English *scalden, scolden*, from *scald, scold*, ribald or abusive person, perhaps from Old Norse *skāld*, poet.] —**scold·er** *n.* —**scold·ing·ly** *adv.*

Synonyms: scold, upbraid, berate, revile, nag.

scold·ing (skōlding) *n.* A sharp or rude reprimand.

scol·e·cite (skólli-sīt, skóli-) *n.* A white zeolite mineral, $Ca\,Al_2\,Si_3\,O_{10}$.$3H_2$ O, consisting of monoclinic crystals. [Greek *skōlēx* (stem *skōlek-*), worm (from its appearance).]

sco·lex (skō-leks) *n., pl.* **-leces** or **-lices** (-li-seez). The knoblike anterior end of a tapeworm, having suckers or hooklike parts that serve as organs of attachment to the host. [New Latin, from Greek *skōlēx*, worm, grub.]

sco·li·o·sis (skólli-ō-siss ‖ skóli-) *n.* Also **sco·li·o·ma** (-ōmə). Abnormal lateral curvature of the spine. [New Latin, from Greek *skiliōsis*, crookedness, from *skolios*, crooked.] —**sco·li·ot·ic** (-óttik) *adj.*

scollop. Variant of **scallop**.

scol·o·pen·drid (skóllə-pén-drid) *n.* Any of various centipedes of the family Scolopendridae, which includes some large, poisonous, tropical species. [New Latin *Scolopendridae*, from Latin *scolopendra*, millipede, from Greek *skolopendra†*.] —**scol·o·pen·drid, scol·o·pen·drine** (-drīn, -drin) *adj.*

scom·broid (skóm-broyd) *adj.* Of or belonging to the suborder Scombroidei, which includes marine fishes such as the mackerel. ~*n.* A scombroid fish. [New Latin *Scombroidei*, from Latin *scomber*, mackerel, from Greek *skombros†*.]

sconce¹ (skonss) *n.* A small earthwork or fort for defence. [Dutch *schans*, from Middle High German *Schanze*, fortification originally made of latticework, from Italian *scanso*, defence, from *scansare*, to turn off, ward off, from Vulgar Latin *excampsāre* (unattested) : Latin *ex-*, out + *campsāre*, to turn around, sail by, from Greek *kamptein* (aorist stem *kamps-*), to bend, curve, turn.]

sconce² *n.* **1.** A decorative wall bracket for candles or lights. **2.** A flattened candlestick that has a handle. [Middle English, from Old French *esconse*, lantern, hiding place, from Medieval Latin *(a)sconsa*, from *absconsus*, past participle of *abscondere*, to hide away : *(ab)s-*, away + *condere*, to hide.]

sconce³ *n. Archaic*. **1.** The head or skull. **2.** Sense or wit. [Jocular use of SCONCE (wall bracket).]

sconce⁴ *tr.v.* **sconced, sconcing, sconces.** Formerly, at Oxford and Cambridge Universities, to challenge (a fellow student) to drink a large amount of beer for having committed an offence against table etiquette. **2.** Broadly, to subject to exaction or extortion. ~*n.* An act or instance of sconcing. [Perhaps from SCONCE (head), jocular reference to a head tax.]

scone (skon, skōn) *n.* **1.** A round, soft, plain, doughy cake made with very little fat. **2.** See **drop scone**. [Short for Dutch *schoonbrood*, fine white bread, from Middle Dutch *schoonbroot*, from *schoon*, beautiful, bright, white + *broot*, bread.]

Scone (skōōn). Village in central Scotland, now in Tayside Region. Pictish and Scottish kings were crowned in Old Scone until 1651. Early kings sat on the Stone of Scone (or Stone of Destiny), but this was captured by the English (1297), and is now incorporated in the coronation chair in Westminster Abbey, London.

scoop (skōōp) *n.* **1.** A shovel-like utensil, usually having a deep, curved dish and short handle, used for taking up and transferring loose material such as grain or sugar. **2.** A long-handled utensil with a round bowl, especially one for liquids; a ladle. **3.** An implement for bailing water from a boat. **4.** A narrow, spoon-shaped instrument for surgical extraction in cavities or cysts. **5. a.** A thick-handled kitchen utensil for dispensing balls of ice cream, mashed potatoes, or the like, usually having a sweeping band in the dish which is levered by the thumb to free the contents. **b.** A portion gathered in such a scoop. **6.** The bucket or shovel of a steam shovel or dredge. **7.** A scooping movement or action; a sweep. **8.** A wide hole or bowl-shaped cavity. **9.** *Informal.* A large, sudden profit, especially one gained through speculation. **10.** *Informal.* A usually sensational story acquired by luck or initiative and reported by a paper in advance of its competitors.

~*tr.v.* **scooped, scooping, scoops. 1.** To take up or dip into with or as if with a scoop; spoon. **2.** To hollow out or excavate; form by digging. Used with *out.* **3.** To gather or collect swiftly and unceremoniously; grab. Used with *up.* **4.** *Informal.* To forestall or outmanoeuvre (a competitor), especially in acquiring and publishing an important news story. **5.** To make (a large profit) suddenly or by luck. **6.** In hockey, golf, or the like, to hit (the ball) from underneath so that it rises steeply. [Middle English, from Middle Low German and Middle Dutch *schōpe.*] **—scoop·er** *n.*

scoot (skōōt) *intr.v.* **scooted, scooting, scoots.** To go speedily; dart or scurry off; hurry.

~*n.* A darting or scurrying off; a hurried departure. [19th century (U.S.) : earlier *scout,* origin obscure.]

scoot·er (skōōtər) *n.* **1.** A child's vehicle consisting of a long footboard between two small end wheels, the front wheel being controlled by an upright steering handle. **2.** A **motor scooter** *(see).* [From SCOOT.]

scop (skop) *n.* A bard or minstrel of Anglo-Saxon England. [Middle English *scop(e),* Old English *scop,* from Germanic.]

scope (skōp) *n.* **1.** Range of perceptions or mental activity. **2.** Breadth or opportunity to function or extend; outlet. **3. a.** The area covered by a given activity or subject. **b.** Agreed or stipulated limits of application or treatment. **4.** The length or sweep of a mooring cable. **5.** *Informal.* A microscope, periscope, telescope, or the like. [Originally "something aimed at", "purpose", from Italian *scopo,* from Greek *skopos,* watcher, goal, aim.]

-scope *n. comb. form.* Indicates an instrument for observing or detecting; for example, **oscilloscope, telescope, microscope.** [Latin *-scopium,* from Greek *-skopion,* from *skopein,* to see.]

sco·pol·a·mine (skə-póllə-meen, -min || skō-, skōpə-lámmin) *n.* A thick, syrupy, colourless alkaloid, $C_{17}H_{21}NO_4$, extracted from such plants as henbane and used as a mydriatic, smooth-muscle relaxant, sedative, and truth serum. Also called "hyoscine". [German *Scopolamin* : New Latin *Scopolia,* genus of plants from which the alkaloid is extracted, named after Giovanni *Scopoli* (1723–88), Italian naturalist + -AMINE.]

sco·po·phil·i·a (skōpə-filli-ə) *n.* Also **scop·to·phil·i·a** (skóptə-). The derivation of sexual pleasure from viewing sexual organs or erotic scenes; voyeurism. [New Latin : Greek *skopein,* to see + -PHILIA.]

scop·u·la (skóppew-lə) *n., pl.* **-lae** (-lee). A dense, brushlike tuft of hairs, as on the legs of certain spiders. [Late Latin *scōpula,* diminutive of Latin *scopa*†, twigs, broom.] **—scop·u·late** (-layt) *adj.*

-scopy *n. comb. form.* Indicates viewing, examining, or observing; for example, **microscopy, telescopy.** [Greek *-skopia,* from *skopein,* to look into, behold.]

scor·bu·tic (skawr-béwtik) *adj.* Related to, resembling, or suffering from scurvy. [New Latin *scorbuticus,* from Late Latin *scorbūtus,* scurvy, from Russian *skrobota,* "scratch", from *skrest',* to scratch, scrape.] **—scor·bu·ti·cal·ly** *adv.*

scorch (skorch) *v.* **scorched, scorching, scorches.** *—tr.* **1.** To burn slightly so as to alter the colour or taste. **2.** To wither or parch with intense heat; char. **3.** To subject to severe censure or anger; excoriate. *—intr.* **1.** To become scorched or singed. **2.** *British Informal.* To move at a very fast pace. —See Synonyms at **burn.**

~*n.* **1.** A slight or surface burn. **2.** A discoloration caused by heat. Also used adjectivally: *a scorch mark.* **3.** Brown spotting on plant leaves caused especially by fungi, heat, or lack of water. [Middle English *scorchen, scorcnen,* perhaps from Old Norse *skorpna,* to shrivel.] **—scorch·ing·ly** *adv.*

scorched-earth policy (skórcht-érth) *n.* A military policy of devastating all land and buildings in the course of an advance or retreat, so as to leave nothing of use to the enemy.

scorch·er (skórchər) *n.* **1.** One that scorches. **2.** *Informal.* An extremely hot day. **3.** *British Informal.* Something that is outstanding or remarkable, especially in terms of speed, excitement, or severity.

scorch·ing (skórching) *adj. Informal.* **1.** Very hot. Said of the weather. **2.** Biting; scathing: *scorching criticism.*

~*adv. Informal.* Used as an intensive: *scorching hot.* **—scorch·ing·ly** *adv.*

score (skor || skōr) *n., pl.* **scores** or (for sense 7) **score. 1.** A notch or incision, made by or as if by a sharp instrument. **2.** An evaluative record, usually numerical, of any competitive event: *keeping score.* **3. a.** The total number of points, goals, or the like made by each competitor or side in a contest, either finally or at a given stage. **b.** The number of points, goals, or the like attributed to any one competitor or team. **c.** The act of scoring a point, goal, or the like. **4.** *Chiefly U.S.* A result, usually expressed numerically, of a test or examination. **5. a.** An amount due, as on a customer's account. **b.** A harboured grievance; a grudge: *I have a score to settle with him.* **6.** A ground; a reason: *I've no grudge against her on that score.* **7.** A group of 20 items. Sometimes used in combination: *threescore years and ten.* **8.** *Plural.* A large number. **9.** The written form of a musical composition for orchestral or vocal parts, either complete or for a particular instrument or voice. **10.** The music composed for a musical or film. **—know the score.** *Informal.* To be aware of the true facts of a situation.

~*v.* **scored, scoring, scores.** *—tr.* **1. a.** To mark with lines, notches, or incisions. **b.** To make (lines, notches, or incisions) on a surface. **2.** To cancel or eliminate by or as if by superimposing lines. Used with *out.* **3.** In cooking, to mark the surface of (meat, for example) with cuts that are usually parallel. **4. a.** To gain (a point or points) in a game or contest: *scored a goal in the last minute.* **b.** To achieve or win in total: *had scored 300 by close of play.* **5. a.** To award (a certain number of points) in a competition: *The judge scored 19 to the English skaters.* **b.** To award a number of points to: *scored him 19.* **6.** To count as or be worth: *A try scores four points.* **7.** To keep a record of (a debt or offence, for example). Used with *against* or *to.* **8.** To achieve or gain (a success or advantage, for example). **9.** *U.S.* To evaluate and assign a mark to. **10.** *Music.* **a.** To orchestrate or arrange (music) for a particular instrument or voice. **b.** To compose music for (a film, for example). **11.** *U.S.* To criticise cuttingly; berate. **12.** *Slang.* To be successful in obtaining (something, especially an illicit drug): *score heroin.* *—intr.* **1.** To gain points in a game or contest. **2.** To keep the score of a game or contest. **3.** To achieve a purpose or advantage, often at another's expense. **4.** To succeed in obtaining illicit drugs. **5.** *Slang.* To seduce a woman. Used of a man. [Middle English *scor,* Old English *scoru* (attested only in plural *scora*), twenty, from Old Norse *skor,* notch, twenty.] **—score·less** *adj.*

score·board (skór-bawrd || skōr-bōrd) *n.* A large board, used especially in sports, that records and displays a score.

score·card (skór-kaard || skōr-) *n.* **1.** A printed card enabling a spectator to identify players and record the progress of a game. **2.** A small card used by an individual player, as in golf, to record his own performance.

score draw *n.* A soccer match in which each side has scored the same number of goals, distinguished from a goalless draw and scoring more points on a football-pools coupon.

scor·er (skáwrər || skōrər) *n.* **1.** One who keeps an official record of the score of a game. **2.** A player who scores a point, goal, or the like.

sco·ri·a (skáwri-ə || skōri-ə) *n., pl.* **-riae** (-ee). **1.** *Geology.* Rough fragments of burnt, basic lava, darker and more cindery than pumice. Also called "cinders", "slag". **2.** *Metallurgy.* The refuse of a smelted metal or ore; slag. [Middle English, slag, dross, from Latin *scōria,* from Greek *skōria,* from *skōr,* excrement.] **—sco·ri·a·ceous** (-áyshəss) *adj.*

sco·ri·fy (skáwri-fī || skōri-) *tr.v.* **-fied, -fying, -fies.** To separate (an ore) into scoria and a precious metal. [SCORI(A) + -FY.] **—sco·ri·fi·ca·tion** (-fi-káysh'n) *n.* **—sco·ri·fi·er** *n.*

scorn (skorn) *n.* **1.** Contempt or disdain, as felt towards a person or thing considered despicable or inferior. **2.** An object of scorn or contempt. **3.** *Archaic.* An expression of scorn; a taunt.

~*v.* **scorned, scorning, scorns.** *—tr.* **1.** To consider or treat as contemptible or unworthy. **2.** To reject with derision. *—intr. Archaic.* To express contempt. [Middle English *scornen, schornen,* to despise, from Old French *escharnir,* from Vulgar Latin *escarnīre* (unattested), from Germanic *skarnjan* (unattested).] **—scorn·er** *n.* **—scorn·ful** *adj.* **—scorn·ful·ly** *adv.* **—scorn·ful·ness** *n.*

scor·pae·noid (skawr-péenoyd) *adj.* Of or belonging to the suborder Scorpaenoidei, which includes the scorpion fishes and gurnards.

~*n.* A scorpaenoid fish. [New Latin *Scorpaenoidei* : *Scorpaena* (genus), from Latin, a fish, from Greek *skorpaina,* feminine of *skorpios,* a sea fish, SCORPION + *-oidei,* plural of Latin *-oidēs,* -OID (likeness).]

Scor·pi·o (skórpi-ō) *n.* **1.** The eighth sign of the **zodiac** *(see).* Also called the "Scorpion". **2.** One born under this sign. **3.** Variant of **Scorpius.** [Latin, scorpion.]

scor·pi·oid (skórpi-oyd) *adj.* **1.** Pertaining to or resembling a scorpion. **2.** *Botany.* Curved or curled like the tail of a scorpion: *a scorpioid inflorescence.* [Greek *skorpioeidēs,* scorpion-like : *skorpios,* SCORPION + -OID.]

scor·pi·on (skórpi-ən) *n.* **1.** Any of various arachnids of the order Scorpionida, of warm, dry regions, having a segmented body and an erectile tail tipped with a venomous sting. **2.** Any of various similar arachnids, such as the **whip scorpion** *(see).* **3.** *Capital* **S. a.** The constellation Scorpius. **b.** A sign of the zodiac, Scorpio. **4.** A type of whip usually thought to have been armed with knotted cords or steel spikes. I Kings 12:11. [Middle English *scorpioun,* from Old French *scorpion,* from Latin *scorpiō* (stem *scorpiōn-*), from Greek *skorpios*†.]

scorpion fish *n.* Any of numerous small, often brilliantly coloured marine fishes of the family Scorpaenidae, having poisonous spines in the dorsal fin in most species.

scorpion fly *n.* Any insect of the order Mecoptera, having in the male of most species a curved genital structure that resembles the sting of a scorpion.

scorpion grass *n.* The **forget-me-not** *(see).*

Scor·pi·us (skórpi-əss) *n.* Also **Scor·pi·o** (-ō), **Scor·pi·on** (-ən). A constellation in the Southern Hemisphere near Libra and Sagittarius. It contains the star Antares. Also called "Scorpion". [New Latin, from Latin *scorpius, scorpiō,* SCORPION.]

PRONUNCIATION KEY

a, trap; aa, father; ai, fair; ar, star; aw, lawn; ay, play; b, bb, stab; rubber; ch, church; ck, ticket; d, dd, dead; ladder; e, dress; ee, bee; er, defer; ew, few; ewr, pure; ə, about; ər, letter; f, ff, fife; differ; g, gg, giggle; h, hat; i, kit; ī, price; īr, fire; j, judge; k, kick; l, ll, let; 'l, needle; m, mm, man; n, nn, no; 'n, sudden; ng, thing; o, lot; ō, no; ŏŏ, foot; ōō, shoe; oor, poor; ow, cow; owr, hour; oy, boy; p, pp, pepper; r, rr, red; s, ss, sauce; sh, ship; t, tt, totter; th, thick; th, this; smooth; u, cut; ur, turn; v, vv, valve; w, wet; y, yes; z, zz, zebra; zh, vision; pleasure

IN FOREIGN WORDS:

aN, oN, Saint-Saëns; hl, Llanelli; Hluhluwe; kh, loch; lough; Khaled

STRESS MARK:

ín-sīt, insight; in-sīt, incite

scor·zo·ner·a (skórzə-néer-ə) n. Any of several Eurasian plants of the genus *Scorzonera,* similar and related to the salsify; especially, the Mediterranean species *S. hispanica,* the roots of which are eaten as a vegetable. [Italian, from *scorzone,* a poisonous snake, alteration of Medieval Latin *curtio†* (stem *curtiōn-*), poisonous snake; the plant was perhaps used as an antidote.]

Scot (skot) n. **1.** A native or inhabitant of Scotland. **2.** A member of the ancient Gaelic tribe that migrated to the northern part of Britain from Ireland in about the sixth century A.D. [Middle English, from Old English (attested in plural, *Scottas*), from Late Latin *Scottus†.*]

Scot. Scotch; Scotland; Scottish.

scot and lot (skot) n. A municipal tax formerly levied in Great Britain on the members of a community proportionate to their ability to pay. **—pay scot and lot.** To pay in full; settle all obligations. [Middle English *scot,* tax, contribution, partly from Old Norse *skot* and partly from Old French *escot,* from Frankish *skot* (unattested).]

scotch¹ (skoch) tr.v. **scotched, scotching, scotches. 1.** To put an abrupt and decisive end to; crush; stifle: *scotch a rumour.* **2.** *Archaic.* To cut or score; scratch. **3.** *Archaic.* To injure so as to render harmless; cripple.
~n. **1.** A surface cut or abrasion; a gash or scratch. **2.** A line drawn on the ground, such as one used in playing hopscotch. [Middle English *scocchen,* from Anglo-French *escocher,* to cut a notch: *es-,* from Latin *ex-* (intensifier) + Old French *coche,* notch, from Vulgar Latin *cocca†* (unattested).]

scotch² tr.v. **scotched, scotching, scotches.** To hold (a wheel or log, for example) with a wedge to prevent rolling or slipping.
~n. A block or wedge used as a prop behind or under a wheel or other object likely to roll. [Perhaps variant of *scatch,* stilt, from Old French *escache,* "wooden leg", from Frankish *skakkja* (unattested), from *skakan* (unattested), to run fast, from Germanic *skakan* (unattested), to SHAKE.]

Scotch (skoch) n. *Abbr.* **Sc., Scot. 1.** *Used with a plural verb.* The people of Scotland; the Scots. Preceded by *the.* **2.** Their language; Scots. **3.** Scotch whisky. [Contraction of SCOTTISH.] **—Scotch** adj.
Usage: The people of Scotland are variously referred to as *Scotsmen* and *Scotswomen,* with *Scots* being used as a more informal and neutral term. *Scotchman/woman* are forms sometimes heard outside of Scotland, but many people find them mildly offensive. *The Scottish* is a generally acceptable collective term. Of the corresponding adjectives, *Scotch,* though fairly common, is now used chiefly of products originating in or associated with Scotland (*Scotch whisky, Scotch broth, Scotch wool*). *Scottish* is used most frequently when the sense of "located in or pertaining to Scotland" is referred to (*Scottish universities, Scottish newspapers*); and *Scots* is most commonly used of people.

Scotch broth n. A nourishing soup made from vegetables, pearl barley, and stock.

Scotch catch n. *Music.* A short note on the beat followed by a longer one, found, for example, in Scottish dance music. Also called "Scotch snap".

Scotch egg n. A cold snack or savoury consisting of a hard-boiled egg wrapped in sausage meat that is coated with breadcrumbs and deep-fried.

Scotch·man (skóch-mən) n., pl. **-men** (-mən). A male Scot.

Scotch mist n. **1.** A dense, wet mist. **2.** A mizzle (see).

Scotch pancake n. A drop scone (see).

Scotch tape n. U.S. A trademark for a cellulose adhesive tape of a type similar to Sellotape (see).

Scotch terrier n. A Scottish terrier (see).

Scotch whisky n. Whisky distilled in Scotland from malted barley, and often blended with grain spirit.

Scotch·wom·an (skóch-wŏŏmən) n. pl. **-women** (-wimmin). A female Scot.

Scotch woodcock n. A savory dish consisting of scrambled eggs on toast with anchovies or anchovy paste. [By humorous analogy with WELSH RABBIT.]

sco·ter (skŏtər) n. Any of several dark-coloured marine diving ducks of the genera *Oidemia* and *Melanitta,* of northern coastal areas. [Perhaps related to Old Norse *skoti,* shooter, and *skjōta,* to shoot (from its swiftness).]

scot-free (skót-frée) adv. **1.** Without having to pay; free from obligation. **2.** Without incurring any penalty; unpunished. [Middle English *scot,* tax. See scot and lot.] **—scot-free** adj.

sco·tia (skŏshə) n. A hollow concave moulding at or near the base of a column. [Latin, from Greek *skotia,* from *skotos,* darkness (referring to the shadow produced by the cavity).]

Sco·tia (skŏshə) n. *Poetic.* Scotland. [Medieval Latin, from Late Latin *Scottus,* Scotsman, Irishman. See **Scot.**]

Sco·tism (skŏt-iz'm) n. The scholastic philosophy of John **Duns Scotus** (see). **—Sco·tist** n.

Scot·land (skótlənd). Country in northwest Europe. It is part of the United Kingdom and occupies the northern part of the island of Great Britain. The population is concentrated in the heavily industrialised Central Lowlands, which occupy the valleys of the Clyde and Forth between the Southern Uplands and the Highlands of the north. The Scots themselves were immigrants from Ireland, who together with the native Picts and with immigrants from Scandinavia formed a kingdom by the ninth century. Frequent wars with England ended when the two crowns were united (1603) under James I of England (James VI of Scotland). In a referendum (1979) the Scots rejected devolution for their country. Tourism is a major industry and the discovery of North Sea oil has brought new prosperity to some parts of the country. Area, 78 749 square kilometres (30,405 square miles). Capital, Edinburgh.

Scotland Yard n. **1.** The headquarters of the London Metropolitan Police, formerly housed at New Scotland Yard on the Thames embankment, now at Broadway, Victoria. **2.** The London Metropolitan Police, especially the Criminal Investigation Department (C.I.D.). Also called "New Scotland Yard" and informally the "Yard".

sco·to·ma (sko-tŏmə, skə-) n., pl. **-mas.** An area of pathologically diminished vision within the visual field. [New Latin, from Medieval Latin, dim sight, from Greek *skotōma,* dizziness, vertigo, from *skotoun,* to darken, from *skotos,* darkness.]

sco·to·pi·a (sko-tŏpi-ə, skə-, skō-) n. The ability of the eyes to adapt to dim light. [New Latin : Greek *skotos,* darkness (see **scotoma**) + -OPIA.] **—sco·to·pic** (-tŏpik, -tóppik) adj.

Scots (skots) adj. *Abbr.* **Sc.** Scottish. See Usage note at **Scotch.**
~n. Any of the dialects of English spoken in Scotland.

Scots·man (skóts-mən) n., pl. **-men** (-mən). A male Scot.

Scots pine n. **1.** A Eurasian pine tree, *Pinus sylvestris,* having prickly cones and needle-like leaves, and valued for its timber. **2.** The wood of this tree.

Scots·wom·an (skóts-wŏŏmən) n., pl. **-women** (wimmin). A female Scot.

Scott (skot), **Sir (George) Gilbert** (1811–78). British architect. He was a leading figure of the Gothic revival. Among the public buildings he designed are the Foreign Offices at Whitehall (1861), the Albert Memorial (1864), and St. Pancras station (1865).

Scott, Sir Peter (Markham) (1909–). British ornithologist. He has made a major contribution to public awareness of the need for wildlife conservation.

Scott, Robert (Falcon) (1868–1912). British Antarctic explorer. On his second expedition to Antarctica (1920–12) he attempted to be the first to reach the South Pole, but discovered that Amundsen had beaten him to it by a month. On the return journey, he and his four companions died of exposure.

Scott, Sir Walter (1771–1832). Scottish novelist and poet. His romantic ballads did much to popularise the history and folklore of Scotland, especially of the Borders. His historical novels, beginning with *Waverley* (1814), influenced the development of the form.

Scot·ti·cism (skótti-siz'm) n. An idiom or other expression characteristic of Scottish English.

Scot·tie, Scot·ty (skótti) n., pl. **-ties. 1.** *Informal.* A Scotsman. **2.** A Scottish terrier.

Scot·tish (skóttish) adj. *Abbr.* **Sc., Scot.** Of, pertaining to, or characteristic of Scotland, its people, or its dialects. See Usage note at **Scotch.**
~n. **1.** Any of the dialects of English spoken in Scotland. **2.** *Used with a plural verb.* The people of Scotland. Preceded by *the.*

Scottish Certificate of Education n. *Abbr.* **S.C.E.** An examination in Scotland, equivalent in level to the English General Certificate of Education.

Scottish Gaelic n. The Gaelic language of the Scottish Highlanders. Also called "Erse".

Scottish terrier n. A terrier of a breed originating in Scotland, having a heavy-set body, short legs, blunt muzzle, and a dark, wiry coat. Also called "Scotch terrier", and formerly "Aberdeen terrier".

scoun·drel (skówn-drəl ‖ *West Indies also* skúng-) n. A villain; a rogue. [16th century : origin obscure.] **—scoun·drel·ly** adj.

scour¹ (skowr) v. **scoured, scouring, scours.** *—tr.* **1. a.** To clean, polish, or wash by scrubbing vigorously, usually with an abrasive. **b.** To remove by scrubbing. **2.** To remove dirt or grease from (cloth or fibres) by means of a detergent. **3.** *Archaic.* To clear (an area) of someone or something undesirable. **4.** To clear (a channel or pipe) by removing obstructions or flushing with water. **5.** To cause (livestock) to purge their bowels. **6.** *Geology.* To erode by the action of a strong current. *—intr.* **1.** To scrub something in order to clean or polish it. **2.** To have diarrhoea. Used of livestock.
~n. **1.** A scouring action or effect. **2.** A place that has been scoured, as by flushing with water. **3.** A cleansing agent for wool or other cloth or fibres. **4.** *Usually plural.* Diarrhoea in livestock. [Middle English *scouren,* from Middle Dutch *scūren,* from Old French *escurer,* from Late Latin *excūrāre,* to clean out : Latin *ex-,* out + Late Latin *cūrāre,* to clean, from Latin, to take care of, from *cūra,* care, cure.] **—scour·er** n.

scour² v. **scoured, scouring, scours.** *—tr.* **1.** To range over (an area) quickly and energetically. **2.** To search through or over thoroughly. *—intr.* **1.** To range over or about an area, especially in a search. **2.** To move swiftly; scurry; run. [Middle English *scouren,* perhaps from Old Norse *skȳra,* to rush in.]

scourge (skurj) n. **1.** A whip used to inflict punishment. **2.** Any means of inflicting severe suffering, vengeance, or punishment. **3.** A cause of widespread affliction, as pestilence or war might be. *~tr.v.* **scourged, scourging, scourges. 1.** To flog. **2.** To chastise severely; excoriate. **3.** To afflict with severe or widespread suffering; devastate. [Middle English, from Old French *escorge,* from *escorgier,* to whip, from Vulgar Latin *excorrigiāre* (unattested) : Latin *ex-* (intensive) + *corrigia,* thong, shoelace, "whip", from Celtic.] **—scourg·er** n.

scour·ing rush (skówr-ing) n. Any of several species of horsetail; especially, *Equisetum hyemale,* having rough-ridged stems formerly used for scouring utensils.

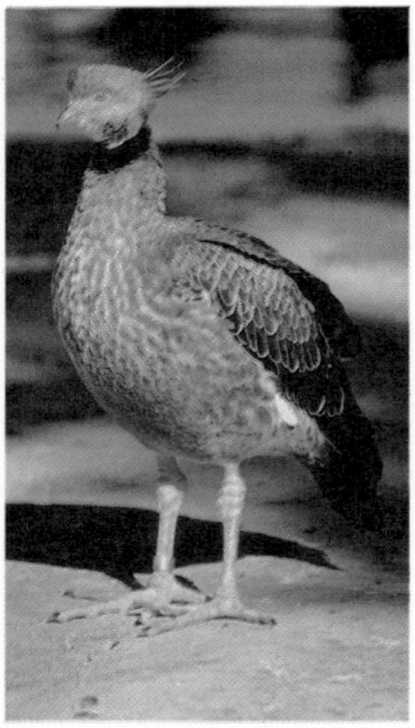

screamer *During the breeding season or when alarmed, the cry of a single screamer – a wading bird of South America – can be heard up to about 3 kilometres (2 miles) away. This is the crested screamer.*

PRONUNCIATION KEY

a, trap; aa, father; ai, fair; ar, star; aw, lawn; ay, play; b, bb, stab; rubber; ch, church; ck, ticket; d, dd, dead; ladder; e, dress; ee, bee; er, defer; ew, few; ewr, pure; ə, about; ər, letter; f, ff, fife; differ; g, gg, giggle; h, hat; i, kit; ī, price; īr, fire; j, judge; k, kick; l, ll, let; 'l, needle; m, mm, man; n, nn, no; 'n, sudden; ng, thing; o, lot; ō, no; ŏŏ, foot; ōō, shoe; oor, poor; ow, cow; owr, hour; oy, boy; p, pp, pepper; r, rr, red; s, ss, sauce; sh, ship; t, tt, totter; th, thick; th, this; smooth; u, cut; ur, turn; v, vv, valve; w, wet; y, yes; z, zz, zebra; zh, vision; pleasure

IN FOREIGN WORDS:

aN, oN, Saint-Saëns; hl, Llanelli; Hluhluwe; kh, loch; lough; Khaled

STRESS MARK:

ín-sīt, insight; in-sít, incite

scour·ings (skówr-ingz) *pl.n.* **1.** Refuse matter removed by scouring. **2.** Dregs; scum.

scouse (skowss) *n.* Also **scous·er** (-ər) (for sense 1). *British Informal.* **1.** A native of Liverpool. **2.** *Often capital* **S.** The dialect of English spoken in Liverpool. [Shortened from LOBSCOUSE (dish particularly associated with Liverpool).] **—scouse** *adj.*

scout[1] (skowt) *n.* **1. a.** A person, aircraft, or ship dispatched from a main body to gather information, as about the terrain or enemy ahead. **b.** The action so performed; a reconnoitring. **2.** A person employed to discover and recruit persons with talent, as in sports or entertainment: *a talent scout.* **3.** *Usually capital* **S.** A member of the Scout Association. **4.** *British.* A person employed by a college, especially one at Oxford University, to clean students' rooms. Compare **bedder. 5.** A companion; a fellow: *He's a good scout.*
~v. **scouted, scouting, scouts.** *—tr.* To spy upon or explore carefully in order to obtain information. *—intr.* **1.** To act as a scout, especially as a scout for talent. **2.** To search or look. Often used with *about* or *around.* [Middle English *scoute,* from Old French *escoute,* "listener", spy, from *escouter,* to listen, from Vulgar Latin *ascultāre* (unattested), variant of Latin *auscultāre.*] **—scout·er** *n.*

scout[2] *v.* **scouted, scouting, scouts.** *—tr.* To reject contemptuously; dismiss with disdain or derision. *—intr.* To scoff. Used with *at.* [Probably from Scandinavian; akin to Old Norse *skūta, skūti,* mockery, taunt.]

Scout Association *n.* A worldwide organisation of young men and boys, founded in England in 1908, for developing character, practical skills, and self-reliance.

scout car *n. Military.* A fast, armoured vehicle used for reconnoitring.

scout·ing (skówting) *n.* The activities of the Scout Association.

scout·mas·ter (skówt-maastər || -mastər) *n.* The adult leader in charge of a troop in the Scout Association.

scow (skow) *n. Chiefly U.S.* A large flat-bottomed boat with square ends, used chiefly for transporting cargo. [Dutch *schouw,* ferryboat, from Middle Dutch *scoude, scouwe,* akin to Old Saxon *skaldan*†, to push a boat from the shore.]

scowl (skowl) *n.* A look of anger, sullenness, or strong disapproval. *~intr.v.* **scowled, scowling, scowls.** To lower or contract the brows in an expression of anger, disapproval, or bitterness; frown angrily. [Middle English *scoulen,* probably from Scandinavian; akin to Danish *skule*†, to scowl.] **—scowl·er** *n.* **—scowl·ing·ly** *adv.*

SCP single-cell protein.

SCR silicon-controlled rectifier.

scr. scruple (unit of weight).

S.C.R. Senior Common Room.

scrab·ble (skrább'l) *v.* **-bled, -bling, -bles.** *—intr.* **1.** To scrape or grope about frenetically with or as if with the hands or claws. Often used with *about* or *around.* **2.** To struggle, especially in a frantic or confused manner. **3.** To make hasty, disordered markings; scribble. *—tr.* **1.** To make or obtain by scraping or scratching. **2.** To scribble on. **3.** To make scrabbling movements on or with.
~n. **1.** The act or an instance of scrabbling. **2.** A scribble; a doodle. **3.** A confused fight or struggle. [Middle Dutch *schrabbelen,* frequentative of *schrabben,* to scrape.]

Scrab·ble (skrább'l) *n.* A trademark for a board game in which players build words with small lettered blocks.

scrag (skrag) *n.* **1.** A bony or scrawny person or animal. **2.** A piece of inferior bony meat, especially from a neck of lamb. **3.** *Informal.* The human neck.
~tr.v. **scragged, scragging, scrags.** *Informal.* **1.** To wring the neck of; kill by strangling. **2.** To seize and manhandle roughly. [Variant of obsolete *crag(ge),* neck, throat, Middle English *crag, crage,* from Middle Dutch *crāghe.*]

scrag·gly (skrággli) *adj.* **-glier, -gliest.** Ragged; irregular; untended or unkempt. [From SCRAG.]

scrag·gy (skrággi) *adj.* **-gier, -giest. 1.** Bony and lean; scrawny. **2.** Jagged; ragged; rough. **—scrag·gi·ly** *adv.* **—scrag·gi·ness** *n.*

scram[1] (skram) *intr.v.* **scrammed, scramming, scrams.** *Slang.* To leave a scene at once; go abruptly. Usually used in the imperative. [Short for SCRAMBLE.]

scram[2] *n.* A rapid shutting down of a nuclear reactor, especially in an emergency. [From SCRAM (to leave hastily).]

scram·ble (skrámb'l) *v.* **-bled, -bling, -bles.** *—intr.* **1.** To move or climb hurriedly, especially on the hands and knees. **2.** To struggle urgently, as with competitors, in order to get something: *all scrambled for the best seat.* **3.** *Military.* To take off with all possible haste, as to intercept enemy aircraft. **4.** To ride a motorcycle across rough terrain, especially in a race. *—tr.* **1.** To mix or throw together confusedly. **2.** To gather together in a hurried or disorderly fashion. Often used with *up.* **3.** To cook (beaten eggs) until of a firm but soft consistency. **4.** *Electronics.* To distort or garble (a signal) so as to render it unintelligible without a special receiver. **5.** *Military.* To cause (aircraft) to scramble.
~n. **1.** The act or an instance of scrambling. **2.** An arduous hike over rough terrain. **3.** An unceremonious scuffle for something. **4.** A motorcycle race across rough terrain. [Imitative; compare dialect *scamble*†, to struggle for, and *cramble*†, to crawl.]

scram·bled eggs (skrámb'ld) *n.* Also **scrambled egg. 1.** Eggs or an egg beaten and cooked until of a firm but soft consistency. **2.** *Informal.* The gold braid worn on the peak of the cap of a high-ranking officer in the armed forces.

scram·bler (skrámblər) *n.* **1.** One that scrambles. **2.** An electronic device that scrambles telecommunication signals to make them unintelligible to an eavesdropper. **3.** A motorcycle with thick ridged tyres and strong suspension, designed for riding across rough terrain; a trail bike.

scran (skran) *n. Regional Slang.* Provisions; food. [18th century : origin obscure.]

scrap[1] (skrap) *n.* **1. a.** A small detached piece or bit; a fragment. **b.** A shred; a particle. **2.** An unincorporated fragment of writing. **3.** *Plural.* Leftover and unwanted bits of food. **4.** Material left over or discarded as refuse; especially, metal suitable for reprocessing. Also used adjectivally and in combination: *scrapyard.*
~tr.v. **scrapped, scrapping, scraps. 1.** To break down into parts for disposal or salvage. **2.** *Informal.* To discard as useless or worthless. [Middle English, from Old Norse *skrap,* trifles, remains.]

scrap[2] *n. Informal.* A fight; a scuffle. [Perhaps variant of SCRAPE.] **—scrap** *intr.v.* **—scrap·per** *n.*

scrap·book (skráp-bŏŏk || -bŏŏk) *n.* A book with blank pages for the mounting and preserving of pictures, cuttings, or the like.

scrape (skrayp) *v.* **scraped, scraping, scrapes.** *—tr.* **1.** To rub, scratch, or grate roughly over or against (a surface). **2.** To draw (a sharp or abrasive object) forcefully over a surface. **3.** To clean, abrade, or smooth by drawing a sharp edge or rough instrument over, especially repeatedly. **4.** To remove (an outer layer or adherent matter) by scraping. **5.** To injure the skin of by rubbing against something rough or sharp. **6.** To amass or produce with difficulty. Used with *together* or *up*: *scrape up a few pennies.* *—intr.* **1.** To come into sliding, abrasive contact. **2.** To rub or move with a harsh grating noise. **3.** To draw the foot backwards along the floor when bowing. **4.** To scrimp; be very thrifty. **5.** To proceed or manage precariously or with difficulty; succeed narrowly. Usually used with *along* or *through*: *She scraped through the test.*
~n. **1.** The act of scraping. **2.** The sound of scraping. **3.** An abrasion on the skin. **4.** *Informal.* **a.** An embarrassing predicament. **b.** A fight; a scuffle. **5.** A **dilatation and curettage** (*see*). [Middle English *scrapen,* from Old Norse *skrapa* or Middle Dutch *schrapen.*]

scrap·er (skráypər) *n.* **1.** One that scrapes. **2.** A tool for scraping off paint or other adherent matter.

scrap·er·board (skráypər-bawrd || -bōrd) *n.* A board covered with white clay and a black surface layer which is scraped away to produce white-line drawings.

scrap·heap (skráp-heep) *n.* **1.** A pile or heap of waste material. **2.** *Informal.* The state of being discarded, old, useless, or unemployable: *an executive on the scrapheap at 50.*

scra·pie (skráypi) *n.* A virus disease of sheep marked by progressive degeneration of the central nervous system. [From SCRAPE (extreme itching causes the sheep to rub against trees, and so on).]

scrap·ing (skráyping) *n.* **1.** *Often plural.* Something that is scraped, or left to be scraped. **2.** The sound made by something being scraped.

scrap·py[1] (skráppi) *adj.* **-pier, -piest.** Composed of scraps; fragmentary or disjointed. **—scrap·pi·ly** *adv.* **—scrap·pi·ness** *n.*

scrappy[2] *adj.* **-pier, -piest.** *Informal.* Quarrelsome; contentious. **—scrap·pi·ly** *adv.* **—scrap·pi·ness** *n.*

scratch (skrach) *v.* **scratched, scratching, scratches.** *—tr.* **1.** To make a thin, shallow cut or mark on (a surface) with a sharp instrument. **2.** To draw something abrasive, especially the nails, across (the skin) to relieve itching. **3. a.** To scrape or graze on an abrasive surface: *scratched my hand on the brambles.* **b.** To scrape or abrade (a surface). **4. a.** To form (words or pictures, for example) by scratching. **b.** To write or draw hurriedly or haphazardly. **5.** To strike out or cancel (a word, name, or passage) by or as if by drawing lines through. Often used with *out.* **6.** To withdraw (an entry) from a contest. *—intr.* **1.** To use the nails or claws to dig, scrape, or wound. **2. a.** To draw something abrasive, especially the nails, across the skin to relieve itching. **b.** To produce a chafing or itching sensation. **3.** To make a harsh, scraping sound. **4.** To claw and scrape the ground searching for food, as hens do. **5.** To withdraw from a contest. **6.** In billiards, to make a scratch. **7.** To get along or manage with difficulty, especially in making a living. Often used with *along.* **—scratch together** or **up.** To assemble or put together haphazardly or with difficulty.
~n. **1. a.** An act of scratching, as to relieve irritation. **b.** A linelike mark produced by scratching. **c.** A slight wound resembling a line or series of lines. **2.** A mark or scribble hastily made. **3.** A sound made by scratching, as on a gramophone record. **4.** *Sports.* **a.** A starting line for a race. **b.** A line formerly drawn across a prize ring at which the boxers began each round. **c.** The starting time or position or initial score of a competitor who has no handicap or allowance. **5.** A contestant who has been withdrawn or who has withdrawn from a contest. **6.** In billiards: **a.** A shot that results in a penalty, as when the cue ball falls into a pocket or jumps the cushion. **b.** A fluke or chance shot. **7.** Poultry feed. **8.** *Slang.* Money. **—from scratch.** From the very beginning. **—up to scratch.** *Informal.* **1.** Meeting the requirements or standards. **2.** In a fit condition.
~adj. **1.** Done haphazardly or by chance. **2.** Assembled hastily or at random. **3.** *Sports.* Without handicap or allowance. [Middle English, probably blend of *scrat, scratten*†, and *cratch, cracchen*†, both meaning "to scratch".] **—scratch·er** *n.*

scratch test *n.* A test for allergy performed by scratching the skin and applying an allergen to the wound.

scratch·y (skráchi) *adj.* **-ier, -iest. 1.** Characterised by or consisting of scratches. **2.** Making a harsh, scratching noise: *a scratchy record.*

3. Irregular; uneven: *played a scratchy stroke.* **4.** Harsh and irritating: *a scratchy fabric.* —**scratch·i·ly** *adv.* —**scratch·i·ness** *n.*

scrawl (skrawl) *v.* **scrawled, scrawling, scrawls.** —*tr.* To write hastily or illegibly. —*intr.* To write in a sprawling, irregular manner.
~*n.* **1.** Irregular, often illegible handwriting. **2.** Something, such as a note, written hastily or illegibly. [Perhaps blend of SPRAWL and CRAWL.] —**scrawl·er** *n.* —**scrawl·y** *adj.*

scraw·ny (skráwni) *adj.* **-nier, -niest.** Unattractively thin and bony; skinny. See Synonyms at **lean.** [Variant of dialect *scranny,* probably from Scandinavian; compare Norwegian *scran,* shrivelled.] —**scraw·ni·ness** *n.*

scream (skreem) *v.* **screamed, screaming, screams.** —*intr.* **1.** To utter a long, loud, piercing cry, as of pain. **2.** To make or move with a loud, piercing sound. Used of machinery, for example. **3.** To speak or write in a heated, hysterical manner. **4.** To be conspicuous or obvious; cry out. **5.** To laugh wildly or uncontrollably. —*tr.* **1.** To utter or say in or as if in a screaming voice. **2.** To cause to be in a specified state by screaming: *screamed herself sick.*
~*n.* **1.** A long, loud, piercing cry or sound. **2.** *Informal.* Someone or something hilariously or ridiculously funny. [Middle English *scremen,* from Old Norse *skræma.*]
Synonyms: scream, shriek, screech.

scream·er (skréemər) *n.* **1.** One that screams. **2.** *Slang.* An exclamation mark. **3.** *Slang.* Something that evokes screams or laughter. **4.** *Chiefly U.S. Slang.* A sensational headline. **5.** Any of several large aquatic birds of the family Anhimidae, of South America, having a harsh, resonant call.

scream·ing·ly (skréeming-li) *adv.* So as to produce uproarious, uncontrolled laughter: *screamingly funny.*

scree (skree) *n.* **1.** Loose rock debris, usually comprising coarse, angular fragments. Also called "talus". **2.** A slope of this at the base of a steep incline or cliff. [Back-formation from *screes* (plural), contraction of *screethes* (unattested), from Old Norse *skrídha,* landslide, from Germanic *skríth-* (unattested).]

screech (skreech) *n.* **1.** A high-pitched, harsh, piercing cry; a shriek. **2.** A sound resembling this.
~*v.* **screeched, screeching, screeches.** —*tr.* To say or utter in or as if in a screeching voice. —*intr.* **1.** To utter a high-pitched, strident sound, as in pain or fright. **2.** To make a prolonged, shrill, grating noise. —See Synonyms at **scream.** [Earlier *scritch,* Middle English *scrichen,* from Old Norse *skraekja* (imitative).] —**screech·er** *n.* —**screech·y** *adj.*

screech owl *n.* **1.** Any of various small owls of the genus *Otus;* especially, *O. asio,* of North America, having a whistle-like call. Compare **hoot owl. 2.** Any owl having a screeching call.

screed (skreed) *n.* **1. a.** A long, monotonous harangue or piece of writing. **b.** *Often plural.* Any lengthy piece of writing, such as a letter. **2. a.** A strip of wood, plaster, or metal placed on a wall or horizontal surface as a guide for the even application of plaster or concrete. **b.** A layer or strip of material used to level off a horizontal surface, such as a floor. **c.** A smooth, final surface, as of concrete, applied to a floor. **3.** *Scottish.* A rent; a tear. [Middle English, probably variant of SHRED.]

screen (skreen) *n.* **1. a.** A movable device, especially a framed construction such as a hinged or sliding room divider, designed to divide, conceal, or protect. **b.** A decorative partition, as one in a church. **2.** Anything that serves to divide, conceal, or protect. **3. a.** A coarse sieve used for sifting out fine particles, as of sand, gravel, or coal. **b.** A system for appraising and selecting personnel. **4.** An insertion of framed wire or plastic mesh used in windows and doors to keep out insects. **5.** The white or silver surface upon which a picture is projected for viewing. **6.** The film industry. Preceded by *the.* **7.** *Electronics.* **a.** The electrode placed between the anode and the control grid in a tetrode valve. Also called "screen grid". **b.** The phosphorescent surface upon which the image is formed in a cathode-ray tube. **8.** *Printing.* A glass plate marked off with crossing lines, placed before the lens of a camera when photographing for halftone reproduction. **9.** A body of troops or ships sent in advance of or surrounding a larger body, in order to warn of attack or protect. **10.a .** A **windscreen** *(see).* **b.** A **sightscreen** *(see).* **11.** *Meteorology.* A wooden, white-painted box with louvred sides which stands 1.25 metres (4 feet) above the ground, and in which meteorological instruments are kept so that readings unaffected by strong winds and direct sunshine may be taken.
~*tr.v.* **screened, screening, screens. 1. a.** To provide with a screen. **b.** To divide or separate with a screen. Often used with *off: screen off the porch.* **2. a.** To conceal from view. **b.** To protect, guard, or shield. **3. a.** To sift or sift out by means of a sieve or screen. **b.** To vet or examine (applicants or candidates, for example) systematically in order to determine suitability. **4.** To show (a film, for example) on a screen. **5.** To test or examine for the presence of disease, for example. —See Synonyms at **hide.** [Middle English *screne,* from Old Northern French *escren, escran,* from Frankish *skrank* (unattested), barrier.] —**screen·er** *n.*

screen·ing (skréening) *n.* **1.** *Plural.* Refuse, such as waste coal, separated out by a screen; siftings. **2.** The mesh material used to make door or window screens. **3.** A presentation of a film.

screening test *n.* A programme of diagnostic tests, such as mass X-rays or cervical smears, carried out as a routine in a large section of the population.

screen memory *n. Psychology.* A memory of something that is un-

consciously used to repress recollection of an associated but distressing event.

screen·play (skréen-play) *n.* The script for a film, including camera directions and descriptions of scenes. Also called "scenario".

screen-print (skréen-print) *tr.v.* **-printed, -printing, -prints.** To print using the silk-screen process. —**screen-print·er** *n.*

screen-print·ing (skréen-printing) *n.* The **silk-screen process** *(see).*

screen test *n.* A brief filmed sequence made to test the ability of an aspiring actor or actress. —**screen-test** (skréen-test) *tr.v.*

screen·writer (skréen-rítər) *n.* A writer of screenplays.

screw (skroo ‖ skrew) *n.* **1. a.** A cylindrical rod incised with one or more helical or advancing spiral threads, such as a lead screw or worm screw. **b.** The tapped collar or socket that receives this. **2.** A metal pin with incised thread or threads, having a broad slotted head so that it can be driven as a fastener by turning it with a screwdriver, especially: **a.** A tapered and pointed wood screw. **b.** A cylindrical and flat-tipped machine screw. **3.** A device having helical form, such as a corkscrew. **4.** A **propeller** *(see).* **5.** A twist or turn of or as if of a screw. **6.** *Vulgar Slang.* **a.** An act of sexual intercourse. **b.** A person considered as a partner in sexual intercourse. **7.** *British Slang.* Salary; wages. **8.** *British.* A small twisted paper packet, as of tobacco. **9.** *British Slang.* An old broken-down horse. **10.** *Chiefly British Slang.* A stingy or crafty bargainer. **11.** *Slang.* A prison warder. **12.** *Usually plural.* **a.** A former instrument of torture, a **thumbscrew** *(see).* **b.** Any means of coercion or intimidation. Used chiefly in the phrase *put the screws on.* **13.** In billiards, snooker, or the like: **a.** The curving or backward motion of the cue ball hit just below and to one side of the centre. **b.** A stroke imparting such motion to the cue ball. —**have a screw loose.** *Slang.* **1.** To behave in an eccentric or whimsical manner. **2.** To be insane.
~*v.* **screwed, screwing, screws.** —*tr.* **1.** To drive or tighten (a screw). **2. a.** To fasten, tighten, or attach by or as if by means of a screw. **b.** To attach (a tapped or threaded fitting or cap) by twisting into place. Used with *on* or *in.* **c.** To rotate (a part) on a threaded axis. **3. a.** To contort (one's face). Often used with *up.* **b.** To twist or crumple (paper, for example). Often used with *up.* **4.** *Slang.* To take unfair advantage of; cheat or exploit. **5.** To use force or pressure to obtain. **6.** *Vulgar Slang.* To have sexual intercourse with. **7.** *Slang.* To burgle. **8.** To give (a ball) a curving or backward motion, as in billiards or snooker. —*intr.* **1.** To turn or twist. Used with *around.* **2. a.** To become attached by means of screw threads. Used with *into, on,* or *to.* **b.** To be capable of such attachment. **3.** *Vulgar Slang.* To engage in sexual intercourse. —**screw up. 1.** *Informal.* To muster or summon up. **2.** *Slang.* **a.** To make a mess of; bungle. **b.** To fail in an undertaking as a result of bungling. **3.** *Slang.* To make neurotic and anxious. [Middle English *skrewe,* from Old French *escroue,* originally "screw socket", from West Germanic *scrūva* (unattested), from Latin *scrōfa,* sow (probably because screw threads coil like a sow's tail, and perhaps influenced in sense by Latin *scrobis,* ditch, pudenda, hence, in Vulgar Latin, screw socket).] —**screw·er** *n.* —**screw·like** *adj.*

screw·ball (skroo-bawl ‖ skréw-) *n. U.S. Slang.* An eccentric, impulsively whimsical, or irrational person.
~*adj. U.S. Slang.* Odd; eccentric; zany.

screw cap *n.* A cap that screws onto the threaded mouth of a container, such as a bottle, jar, or the like.

screw·driv·er (skroo-drivər ‖ skréw-) *n.* **1.** A tool used for turning screws. **2.** A cocktail of vodka and orange juice.

screwed (skrood ‖ skrewd) *adj. British Slang.* **1.** Drunk. **2.** In trouble or danger. [Past participle of SCREW, perhaps humorous allusion to *tight* (drunk) and *in a tight corner* (in trouble).]

screw eye *n.* A wood screw with an eyelet in place of a head.

screw jack *n.* A lifting device having a screw thread; especially, one used to raise a motor vehicle to change a wheel. Also called "jack".

screw log *n. Nautical.* A **patent log** *(see).*

screw pine *n.* A plant, the **pandanus** *(see).*

screw propeller *n.* A **propeller** *(see).*

screw thread *n.* **1.** The continuous helical groove on a screw or on the inner surface of a nut. **2.** One complete turn of a screw thread.

screw·worm (skroo-wurm ‖ skréw-) *n.* The parasitic larva of the screwworm fly which can cause injury or death to livestock.

screw·worm fly *n.* A blue-green fly, *Cochliomyia hominivorax,* of the New World, that breeds in the living tissue of mammals, having penetrated chiefly through open wounds.

screw·y (skroo-i ‖ skréw-i) *adj.* **-ier, -iest.** *Slang.* Eccentric; crackbrained or ludicrously odd.

Scria·bin (skréer-bin, skri-ábbin ‖ *U.S.* -áabin), **Alexandr** (1872-1915). Russian composer. He is noted for works for the keyboard that include chords on the interval of the fourth.

scrib·ble¹ (skríbb'l) *v.* **-bled, -bling, -bles.** —*tr.* **1.** To write hurriedly without heed to legibility or grammatical form. **2.** To cover with such writing or with meaningless marks. **3.** To draw hurriedly or carelessly. —*intr.* **1.** To write or draw in a hurried, careless way. **2.** To be a writer, as of novels or poetry. Used humorously or derogatorily.
~*n.* **1.** Careless, hurried writing or drawing. **2.** Meaningless marks and lines. [Middle English *scriblen,* from Medieval Latin *scrībillāre,* frequentative of Latin *scrībere,* to write.]

scrib·ble² *tr.v.* **-bled, -bling, -bles.** To card (wool or cotton) coarsely. [Probably from Low German and akin to SCRUB (rub hard).]

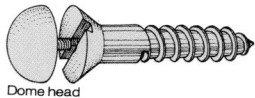
Dome head

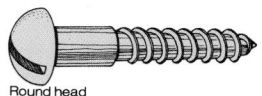
Round head

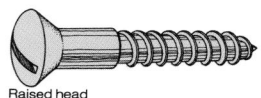
Raised head

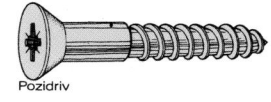
Pozidriv

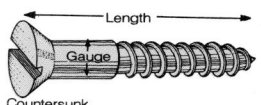
Length
Gauge
Countersunk

screw *A fixing pin used in woodworking. It has a raised, spiral surface that bites into the surrounding wood as it is driven in.*

scrib·bler (skrìbblər) *n.* **1.** One who scribbles. **2.** A very minor or untalented author.

scribe (skrīb) *n.* **1.** A public clerk or secretary, especially in ancient times. **2.** A professional copyist of manuscripts and documents, as in ancient or medieval times. **3.** A writer or journalist. Usually used humorously. **4.** A scriber. **5.** In ancient times, a scholar or teacher of the Jewish Law.
~*v.* **scribed, scribing, scribes.** —*tr.* To mark or produce with a scriber. —*intr. Archaic.* To work as a scribe. [Middle English, from Latin *scrība,* official writer, clerk, scribe, from *scrībere,* to write.] **—scrib·al** *adj.*

scrib·er (skrībər) *n.* A sharply pointed tool used for marking lines on wood, metal, ceramic, or the like.

scrim (skrim) *n.* **1.** A durable, loosely woven cotton or linen fabric used for curtains, upholstery lining, or in industry. **2.** *Chiefly U.S.* A similar fabric used in the theatre for creating special effects of light or atmosphere. [18th century : origin obscure.]

scrim·mage (skrímmij) *n.* **1.** A rough and confused struggle; a tussle. **2.** In American football: **a.** The contest between two teams from the time the ball is snapped back until it becomes out of play. **b.** A team's practice session. **3.** In Rugby football, a scrum. Not in current usage.
~*intr.v.* **scrimmaged, -maging, -mages.** In American football, to engage in a scrimmage. [Alteration of *scrimish,* obsolete variant of SKIRMISH.]

scrimp (skrimp) *v.* **scrimped, scrimping, scrimps.** —*intr.* To economise severely. Often used with *on* or the phrase *scrimp and save.*
~*tr.* **1.** To be excessively sparing with or of. **2.** To cut or make too small or scanty. [18th century (Scottish) : origin obscure.] **—scrimp·y** *adj.* **—scrimp·i·ness** *n.*

scrim·shank (skrím-shangk) *intr.v.* **-shanked, -shanking, -shanks.** *British Slang.* To avoid work or duty. [19th century : origin obscure.]

scrim·shaw (skrím-shaw) *v.* **-shawed, -shawing, -shaws.** —*tr.* To decorate (whale ivory, bone, or shells) with intricate carvings or designs. —*intr.* To produce such work.
~*n., pl.* **scrimshaws** or collectively **scrimshaw. 1.** A bone or ivory article so fashioned. **2.** The art of producing such articles. [19th century (nautical use) : perhaps from the surname *Scrimshaw.*]

scrimshaw *Usually carved on whalebone or ivory, scrimshaw is the traditional art of the seafarer. This sperm-whale tooth records part of a 19th-century voyage.*

scrip¹ (skrip) *n.* A small scrap of paper, especially one with writing, such as a list or a schedule. [Variant of SCRIPT (influenced by SCRAP).]

scrip² *n. Finance.* **1.** A provisional certificate entitling the holder to a fractional share of stock or of other jointly owned property. **2.** Such certificates collectively. [Short for *subscription (receipt),* receipt for portion of a loan.]

scrip³ *n. Archaic.* A wallet, small satchel, or bag. [Middle English *scrippe,* from Old French *escreppe,* variant of Old Northern French *escarpe,* "pilgrim's knapsack". See **scarf.**]

scrip issue *n. Finance.* An issue of shares made by a company free of charge to existing shareholders. Also called "bonus issue".

scrip·sit (skrípsit). *Latin.* He (or she) wrote (it). Placed after the author's name on a manuscript.

script (skript) *n.* **1. a.** Handwriting as distinguished from print. **b.** A style of writing with cursive characters. **c.** A particular system of writing: *cuneiform script.* **2. a.** A type that imitates handwriting. **b.** Matter printed with this type. **3.** *Law.* An original document, as distinguished from a copy. **4.** The text of a play, broadcast, or film; especially, a copy of a text used by a director or performer. **5.** *British.* An examinee's written paper.
~*tr.v.* **scripted, scripting, scripts.** To write a script for (a film or broadcast): *Perelman scripted several Marx Brothers movies.* [Middle English *skript,* from Old French *escript,* from Latin *scrīptum,* from *scrīptus,* past participle of *scrībere,* to write.]

Script. Scriptural; Scriptures.

scrip·to·ri·um (skrip-táw-ri-əm || -tṓ-) *n., pl.* **-riums** or **-ia** (-ri-ə). A room in a monastery set aside for the copying, writing, or illuminating of manuscripts and records. [Medieval Latin, from Latin *scrībere* (past participle *scrīptus*), to write.]

scrip·tur·al (skrípchərəl) *adj. Abbr.* **Script.** *Often capital* **S.** Of, pertaining to, based upon, or contained in the Scriptures. **—scrip·tur·al·ly** *adv.*

Scrip·ture (skrípchər) *n.* **1.** *Often plural. Abbr.* **Script. a.** A sacred writing or book; especially, the **Holy Scripture** *(see).* **b.** A passage from such a writing or book. **2.** *Small* **s.** A statement regarded as authoritative and definitive, such as a code of regulations. [Middle English, from Late Latin *scrīptūra,* from Latin, act of writing, from *scrībere* (past participle *scrīptus*), to write.]

script·writ·er (skrípt-rītər) *n.* A person who writes copy to be used by an announcer, performer, or director in a film or broadcast.

scrive·ner (skrívnər, skrívv'n-ər) *n. Archaic.* **1.** A professional copyist; a scribe. **2.** A notary. [Middle English *scriveiner,* from *scrivein,* scribe, from Old French *escrevein,* from Vulgar Latin *scrībānem* (unattested), accusative of Latin *scrība,* SCRIBE.]

scro·bic·u·late (skrō-bíckew-lət, -lit, -layt) *adj. Biology.* Marked with many shallow depressions, grooves, or pits. [Latin *scrobiculus,* diminutive of *scrobis,* trench.]

scrod (skrod) *n. U.S.* A young cod or haddock, especially one split and boned for cooking. [19th century : origin obscure.]

scrof·u·la (skróffewlə) *n.* Tuberculosis of the lymph nodes, a now rare condition chiefly affecting children and characterised by running sores in the neck region. Also called the "King's evil". [Middle English *scrophulas* (plural), from Medieval Latin *scrōfulae,* swelling of the glands, "small sows", from Latin *scrōfa,* sow (probably after Greek *khoirades,* scrofula, from *khoiras,* like a pig's back).]

scrof·u·lous (skróffewləss) *adj.* **1.** Pertaining to, affected with, or resembling scrofula. **2.** Morally degenerate; corrupt. **—scrof·u·lous·ly** *adv.* **—scrof·u·lous·ness** *n.*

scroll (skrōl) *n.* **1. a.** A roll of parchment, papyrus, or the like. **b.** An ancient book or volume written on a scroll. **2.** A list of names. **3.** Ornamentation resembling a partially rolled scroll of paper; especially: **a.** The volute in Ionic and Corinthian capitals. **b.** The curved head on an instrument of the violin family. **c.** *Heraldry.* A ribbon inscribed with a motto.
~*tr.v.* **scrolled, scrolling, scrolls. 1.** To inscribe on a scroll. **2.** To roll up into a scroll. **3.** To ornament with a scroll or scrolls. [Middle English *scrowle,* variant (influenced by *rowle,* a roll) of *scrow,* from Old French *escro(u)e,* strip of parchment, from Frankish *skrōda* (unattested), piece, shred.]

scroll saw *n.* A hand or power saw with a narrow ribbon-like blade for cutting curved or irregular shapes. See **fretsaw, jigsaw.**

scroll·work (skrṓl-wurk) *n.* Embellishment with a scroll motif; especially, ornamentation executed in wood with a scroll saw.

Scrooge (skrōōj) *n.* A mean-spirited, miserly person; a skinflint. [After Ebenezer *Scrooge* in Charles Dickens's *Christmas Carol.*]

scroop (skrōōp) *intr.v.* **scrooped, scrooping, scroops.** *Archaic.* To make a squeaking or grating sound. [Imitative.] **—scroop** *n.*

scro·tum (skrṓ-təm) *n., pl.* **-ta** (-tə) or **-tums.** The external sac of skin enclosing the testes in most mammals. [Latin *scrōtum.*] **—scro·tal** (skrṓt'l) *adj.*

scrounge (skrownj) *v.* **scrounged, scrounging, scrounges.** *Informal.* —*tr.* **1.** To sponge; cadge. **2.** To obtain by salvaging or foraging; round up. —*intr.* **1.** To obtain something by cadging or sponging. **2.** To forage about in an effort to acquire something at no cost. [Variant of dialectal *scrunge*†, to steal.] **—scroung·er** *n.*

scrub¹ (skrub) *v.* **scrubbed, scrubbing, scrubs.** —*tr.* **1.** To rub hard, as with a brush, soap, and water, in order to clean. **2.** To remove (dirt or stains) by such rubbing. **3.** To cleanse (a gas) in a scrubber. **4.** *Informal.* To cancel or abandon. —*intr.* To clean or wash something by hard rubbing. **—scrub up.** To wash the hands and arms thoroughly before an operation. Used of a surgeon.
~*n.* An act of scrubbing. [Middle English *scrobben,* from Middle Low German or Middle Dutch *schrobben, schrubben.*]

scrub² *n.* **1.** Vegetation characterised by straggly, stunted trees, shrubs, or brushwood. **2.** A growth or tract of stunted vegetation. Sometimes used in combination: *scrubland.* **3.** A domestic animal of inferior breeding or poor appearance. **4.** An undersized or insignificant person. **5.** *Australian.* Remote rural areas. Preceded by *the.* **6.** *Sports. U.S.* A player not in the first team.
~*adj.* **1.** Undersized, stunted, or inferior. **2.** *U.S.* Made up of or participated in by scrubs: *a scrub team.* [Middle English, variant of *schrubbe,* SHRUB.]

scrub·ber (skrúbber) *n.* **1.** One that scrubs. **2.** An apparatus for removing impurities from a gas. **3.** *Chiefly British Slang.* **a.** A sexually promiscuous woman. **4.** A prostitute. Used derogatorily.

scrub·bing brush (skrúbbing) *n.* A brush with strong, stiff bristles used for doing dirty cleaning jobs.

scrub bird *n.* Either of two rare Australian birds of the genus *Atrichornis,* having a brown plumage and long, pointed tails.

scrub·by (skrúbbi) *adj.* **-bier, -biest. 1.** Covered with or consisting of scrub or underbrush. **2.** Small; straggly; stunted. **3.** Shabby or paltry; wretched. **—scrub·bi·ness** *n.*

scrub fowl *n.* A **megapode** *(see).*

scrub oak *n.* Any of several shrubby or small oaks, such as *Quercus ilicifolia,* of eastern North America.

scrub pine *n.* Any of several small, straggling pine trees, such as *Pinus virginiana,* of the eastern United States.

scrub typhus *n.* An acute infectious disease common in southeast Asia and the western Pacific, caused by a parasitic microorganism, *Ricksettsia tsutsugamsushi,* and transmitted by a mite. Also called "tsutsugamushi disease", "Japanese river fever".

scrub wallaby *n.* A small wallaby, the **pademelon** *(see).*

scruff (skruf) *n.* The back of the neck; the nape. [Variant of obsolete *scuff,* perhaps from Old Norse *skoft,* hair on the head.]

scruf·fy (skrúffi) *adj.* **-fier, -fiest.** Shabby; untidy. [From *scruff,* variant of SCURF.]

scrum (skrum) *n.* A formation in Rugby football: **1.** A *set scrum,* in which the two sets of forwards must interlock together against each other, the ball is thrown in, and the opposing hookers try to kick the ball backwards out to their own team. **2.** A *loose scrum,* in which the players join together in the struggle to win the ball during play. Also called "scrummage" and formerly "scrimmage".
~*intr.v.* **scrummed, scrumming, scrums.** To engage in or form a scrum. Often used with *down.* [Shortened from SCRUMMAGE.]

scrum half *n.* **1.** In Rugby football, the player who throws the ball into a set scrum. **2.** The position of this player in a team.

scrum·mage (skrúmmij) *n.* In Rugby football, a scrum.
~*intr.v.* **scrummaged, -maging, -mages.** To engage in a scrum. [Variant of SCRIMMAGE.] **—scrum·mag·er** *n.*

scrump (skrump) *intr.v.* **scrumped, scrumping, scrumps.** *British Regional.* To steal fruit, especially apples. [From dialect *scrump*†, small apple. See **scrumpy.**]

scrump·tious (skrúmpshəss) *adj. Informal.* **1.** Delicious. **2.** Splendid; delightful. [19th century : origin obscure.]

scrump·y (skrúmpi) *n.* A rough, strong, cider brewed in southwest England. [From dialect *scrump*†, small apple.]

scrunch (skrunch || skrŏŏnch) *v.* **scrunched, scrunching, scrunches.** *—tr.* **1.** To crush or crunch. **2.** To crumple or squeeze. Often used with *up.* *—intr.* To move with or make a crunching sound: *scrunching along the gravel path.*
~n. A crunching sound. [Variant of CRUNCH.]

scru·ple (skrōṓp'l || skréwp'l) *n.* **1.** *Often plural.* A feeling of doubt or uncertainty as to whether a course of action is ethically right or justifiable; a dictate of conscience. **2.** *Abbr.* **sc., scr.** A unit of apothecary weight equal to 20 grains. **3.** *Archaic.* A minute part or amount. —See Synonyms at **qualm.**
~intr.v. **scrupled, -pling, -ples.** To hesitate through the demands of conscience or principle. [French *scrupule,* from Latin *scrūpulus,* small sharp stone, small weight, scruple, from *scrūpus*†, rough stone.]

scru·pu·lous (skrōṓ-pew-ləss || skréw-) *adj.* **1.** Having scruples; principled. **2.** Very conscientious and exacting; punctilious. —See Synonyms at **meticulous.** [Middle English, from Latin *scrūpulōsus,* from *scrūpulus,* SCRUPLE.] **—scru·pu·los·i·ty** (-lóssəti), **scru·pu·lous·ness** *n.* **—scru·pu·lous·ly** *adv.*

scru·ta·ble (skrōṓt-əb'l || skréwt-) *adj. Rare.* Comprehensible through scrutiny. [Medieval Latin *scrūtabilis,* searchable, from Latin *scrūtārī,* to search. See **scrutiny.**]

scru·ta·tor (skrōō-táytər || skrew-) *n.* A person who scrutinises; a scrutineer. [Latin, from *scrūtārī,* to search. See **scrutiny.**]

scru·ti·neer (skrōṓ-ti-néer, -t'n-éer || skréw-) *n.* A person who examines or checks; especially, a person who checks and counts votes. [SCRUTIN(Y) + -EER.]

scru·ti·nise, scru·ti·nize (skrōṓ-ti-nīz, -t'n-īz || skréw-) *tr.v.* **-nised, -nising, -nises.** To examine or observe with great care; inspect minutely or critically. **—scru·ti·nis·er** *n.* **—scru·ti·nis·ing·ly** *adv.*

scru·ti·ny (skrōṓ-ti-ni, -t'n-i || skréw-) *n., pl.* **-nies. 1.** A close, careful examination or study; a critical, sustained look. **2.** Close observation; surveillance. **3.** An official examination of the votes cast in an election. [Middle English, from Latin *scrūtinium,* from *scrūtārī,* to search, examine (originally said of ragpickers), "to rummage in a heap of rubbish", from *scrūta,* rubbish.]

scry (skrī) *intr.v.* **scried, scrying, scries.** To see or predict the future by means of a crystal ball. [Aphetic variant of DESCRY.]

scu·ba (skōṓbə, skéwbə) *n.* An apparatus containing compressed air used for underwater breathing. Also used adjectivally: *scuba diver.* [*S*elf-*c*ontained *u*nderwater *b*reathing *a*pparatus.]

scud (skud) *intr.v.* **scudded, scudding, scuds. 1.** To run or skim along swiftly and easily. **2.** *Nautical.* To run before a gale with little or no sail set.
~n. **1.** The act of scudding. **2.** *Sometimes plural.* **a.** A ragged mass of cloud, driven along by the wind at a lower level than the main cloud layer. **b.** Loosely, a sudden light shower or gust of wind. [Perhaps variant of SCUT (rabbit's tail, hence "run like a rabbit").]

scu·do (skōṓ-dō) *n., pl.* **-di** (-dee). A former monetary unit and coin of Italy and Sicily. [Italian, "shield", from Latin *scūtum.*]

scuff (skuf) *v.* **scuffed, scuffing, scuffs.** *—intr.* **1.** To scrape or drag the feet while walking; shuffle. **2.** To become scratched or scraped with wear: *These shoes scuff easily.* *—tr.* To scrape or scratch the surface of (shoes, for example) with use.
~n. **1.** The sound or act of scuffing. **2.** A worn or rough spot resulting from scuffing. **3.** *Chiefly U.S.* A flat, backless slipper. [Imitative.]

scuf·fle¹ (skúff'l) *intr.v.* **-fled, -fling, -fles. 1.** To fight or struggle confusedly at close quarters. **2. a.** To shuffle. **b.** To go or move about in a hurried and confused manner.
~n. **1.** A rough, disorderly struggle at close quarters. **2.** The action or sound of scuffling. —See Synonyms at **conflict.** [Probably from Scandinavian; akin to Old Norse *skūfa,* to push.] **—scuf·fler** *n.*

scuffle² *n. U.S.* A type of hoe manipulated by pushing rather than pulling. Also called "scuffle hoe". [Dutch *schoffel,* from Middle Dutch *schoffel, schuffel,* shovel.]

scull (skul) *n.* **1.** A long oar twisted from side to side over the stern of a boat to propel it. **2.** Either of a pair of short-handled oars used by a single rower. **3.** A small, light boat for sculling, especially a racing boat. **4.** *Plural.* A race between such boats.
~v. **sculled, sculling, sculls.** *—tr.* To propel (a boat) with a scull or sculls. *—intr.* To use a scull or sculls to propel a boat. [Middle English *sculle*†.] **—scull·er** *n.*

scul·ler·y (skúl-ri, skúlləri) *n., pl.* **-ies.** A small room adjoining a kitchen in which dishwashing and dirty kitchen chores are done. [Middle English, from Anglo-French *squillerie,* Old French *escuelerie,* from *escuelier,* keeper of dishes, from *escuele,* dish, from Vulgar Latin *scūtella* (unattested), variant (influenced by Latin *scūtum,* SCUTUM) of Latin *scutella,* salver, diminutive of *scutra*†, platter.]

Scul·lin (skúllin), **James Henry** (1876–1953). Australian politician. He was leader of the Labour Party (1928–35) and prime minister (1929–31).

scul·li·on (skúlli-ən, skúl-yən) *n. Archaic.* **1.** A servant employed to do menial tasks in a kitchen. **2.** A despicable or contemptible person. [Middle English *sculyon,* probably from Old French *escovillon,* dishcloth, diminutive of *escouve,* broom, from Latin *scopa.* See **scopula.**]

sculp. sculpsit.

scul·pin (skúlpin) *n., pl.* **-pins** or collectively **sculpin.** Any of various marine and freshwater fishes of the family Cottidae, of northern waters, having a large, flattened head and prominent spines. Also called "bullhead". [Perhaps variant of obsolete *scorpene,* from Latin *scorpaena,* sea scorpion. See **scorpaenoid.**]

sculp·sit (skúlpsit). *Latin. Abbr.* **sc., sculp., sculpt.** He (or she) sculptured (it). Placed after the artist's name.

sculpt (skulpt) *v.* **sculpted, sculpting, sculpts.** *—tr.* To sculpture. *—intr.* To be a sculptor. [French *sculpter, sculper,* from Latin *sculpere,* to carve. See **sculpture.**]

sculpt. sculpsit.

sculp·tor (skúlptər) *n.* **1.** One who sculptures; especially, an artist who works in stone, metal, or other hard or plastic material. **2.** *Capital* **S.** A constellation in the Southern Hemisphere near Cetus and Phoenix. Also called "Sculptor's Workshop". [Latin, from *sculpere* (past participle *sculptus*), to carve. See **sculpture.**]

sculp·tress (skúlp-triss, -trəss) *n.* A woman who sculptures.

sculp·ture (skúlpchər) *n. Abbr.* **sculp. 1.** The art or practice of shaping figures or designs, as by carving wood, chiselling marble, modelling clay, or casting in metal. **2. a.** A work of art created in this manner. **b.** Such works collectively. **3.** Ridges, indentations, or other markings, as on a shell, formed by natural processes.
~v. **sculptured, -turing, -tures.** *—tr.* **1.** To fashion (stone, bronze, wood, or the like) into a three-dimensional figure. **2.** To represent in sculpture. **3.** To ornament with sculpture. **4.** To give sculptural shape or contour to, as by erosion. *—intr.* To make sculptures. [Middle English, from Latin *sculptūra,* from *sculpere* (past participle *sculptus*), to carve.] **—sculp·tur·al** *adj.* **—sculp·tur·al·ly** *adv.*

sculp·tur·esque (skúlpchər-ésk) *adj.* Suggestive of sculpture; having the qualities of sculpture. **—sculp·tur·esque·ly** *adv.* **—sculp·tur·esque·ness** *n.*

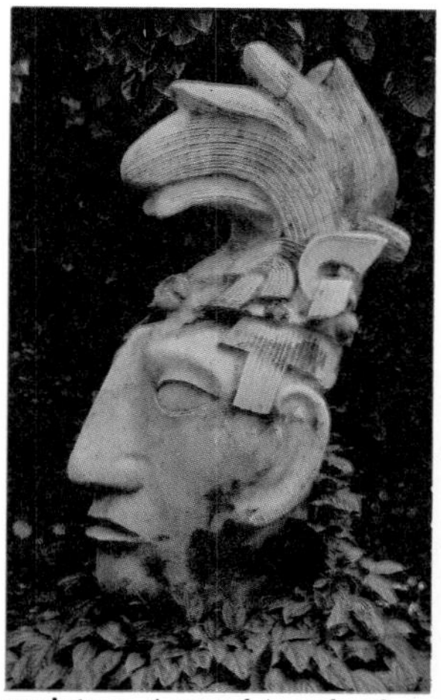

sculpture *A carved Aztec head protrudes from a cloak of encroaching vegetation. The Aztecs dominated central Mexico from the 12th century until the Spanish Conquest in the 16th century.*

scum (skum) *n.* **1.** A filmy layer of extraneous or impure matter that forms on or rises to the surface of a liquid or body of water. **2.** The refuse or dross of molten metals. **3.** Any refuse or worthless matter. **4.** *Informal.* An element of society or an individual regarded as being vile or worthless.
~v. **scummed, scumming, scums.** *—tr.* To remove the scum from; skim. *—intr.* To become covered with scum. [Middle English *scume, scome,* from Middle Dutch *schūm,* from Germanic *skūma-* (unattested), cover.] **—scum·mer** *n.* **—scum·my** *adj.*

scum·ble (skúmb'l) *tr.v.* **-bled, -bling, -bles.** In painting and drawing, to soften the colours or outlines of by covering with a film of opaque or semiopaque colour or by rubbing.
~n. **1.** The effect produced by scumbling. **2.** Material used for scumbling. [Probably frequentative of SCUM.]

scun·cheon (skúnchən) *n. Architecture.* The inside, vertical face of a door or window frame. [Middle English, from Old French *escoinson* (French *écoinçon*), a bevelled inside edge : *es-,* EX- + *coin,* corner, COIGN + *-son,* from Latin *-siōn-,* -TION.]

scun·gy (skúnji) *adj.* **-gier, -giest.** *Australian & N.Z. Informal.* Sordid or dingy. [Probably blend of SCUM + DINGY.]

scun·ner (skúnnər) *n. Chiefly Scottish.* **1.** A strong dislike; an aversion. **2.** A cause of vexation; a nuisance.
~v. **scunnered, -nering, -ners.** *Chiefly Scottish.* *—intr.* To feel aversion or dislike. *—tr.* To cause to feel aversion or dislike. [Middle English *skunner*†.]

Scun·thorpe (skún-thawrp). Town in Humberside, east England. It is an iron and steel manufacturing centre.

scup (skup) *n., pl.* **scups** or collectively **scup.** A food fish, *Stenotomus chrysops,* of western Atlantic waters, related to and resembling the porgies. [Short for Narraganset *mishcùp.*]

scup·per¹ (skúppər) *n.* **1.** *Nautical.* An opening in the side of a ship at deck level to allow water to run off. **2.** Any opening for draining off water, as on a building. [Middle English *skopper,* perhaps from Old French *escopir,* to spit (imitative).]

scupper² *tr.v.* **-pered, -pering, -pers.** *Chiefly British Slang.* **1.** To overwhelm or massacre. **2.** To ruin or destroy. [19th century (military use) : origin obscure.]

scup·per·nong (skúppər-nong || *U.S. also* -nawng) *n.* **1.** A grape, the **muscadine** *(see)*; especially, a cultivated American variety having sweet, yellowish fruit. **2.** A sweet American wine made from such grapes. [Short for *Scuppernong grape,* grown in the *Scuppernong* River basin, North Carolina.]

scurf (skurf) *n.* **1.** Scaly or shredded dry skin, as in dandruff. **2.** Any loose, scaly crust coating a surface, especially of a plant. [Middle English *scurf, scorf,* Old English *scurf,* variant (probably influenced by Old Norse *skurfóttr,* scurfy) of *sceorf, sceorfan,* to gnaw.] **—scurf·y** *adj.* **—scurf·i·ness** *n.*

scur·ril·i·ty (sku-rílləti, skə-) *n., pl.* **-ties. 1.** The quality of being scurrilous. **2.** A scurrilous remark or piece of writing.

scur·ri·lous (skúrriləss) *adj.* **1.** Given to the use of vulgar, obscene, or abusive language. **2.** Coarse, obscene, or abusive. [Latin *scurrīlis,* buffoon-like, jeering, from *scurra,* buffoon, perhaps from Etruscan.] **—scur·ri·lous·ly** *adv.* **—scur·ri·lous·ness** *n.*

scur·ry (skúrri) *intr.v.* **-ried, -rying, -ries. 1.** To go with light running steps; hurry; scamper. **2.** To flurry or swirl about.
~n., pl. **scurries. 1.** The act or noise of scurrying. **2.** A light whirling movement; a flurry. **3.** A short run or race on horseback. [Probably short for HURRY-SCURRY.]

scur·vy (skúrvi) *n.* A disease caused by deficiency of vitamin C, characterised by spongy and bleeding gums, bleeding under the skin, and extreme weakness.
~adj. **scurvier, -viest.** Mean; worthless; contemptible. [From SCURF (but used later to render like-sounding French *scorbut,* the skin disease, from Medieval Latin *scorbūtus.* See **scorbutic**).] **—scur·vi·ly** *adv.* **—scur·vi·ness** *n.*

scurvy grass *n.* A plant, *Cochlearia officinalis,* of northern regions, having bitter foliage, formerly used to cure scurvy.

PRONUNCIATION KEY

a, trap; aa, father; ai, fair; ar, star; aw, lawn; ay, play; b, bb, stab; rubber; ch, church; ck, ticket; d, dd, dead; ladder; e, dress; ee, bee; er, defer; ew, few; ewr, pure; ə, about; ər, letter; f, ff, fife; differ; g, gg, giggle; h, hat; i, kit; ī, price; īr, fire; j, judge; k, kick; l, ll, let; 'l, needle; m, mm, man; n, nn, no; 'n, sudden; ng, thing; o, lot; ō, no; ŏŏ, foot; ōō, shoe; oor, poor; ow, cow; owr, hour; oy, boy; p, pp, pepper; r, rr, red; s, ss, sauce; sh, ship; t, tt, totter; th, thick; th, this; smooth; u, cut; ur, turn; v, vv, valve; w, wet; y, yes; z, zz, zebra; zh, vision; pleasure

IN FOREIGN WORDS:

aN, oN, Saint-Saëns; hl, Llanelli; Hluhluwe; kh, loch; lough; Khaled

STRESS MARK:

ín-sīt, insight; in-sī́t, incite

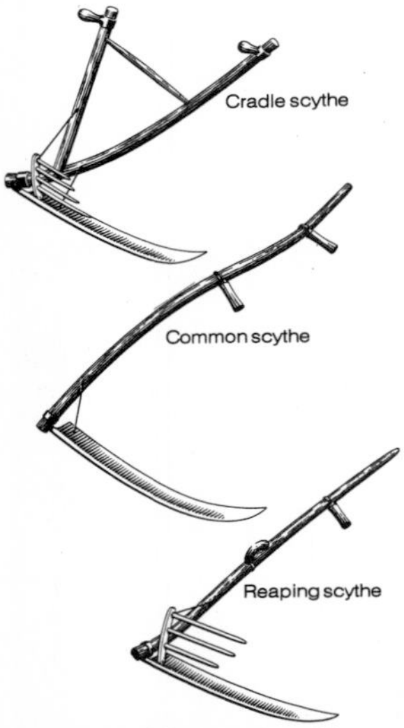

scythe *Until the invention of faster mechanical cutters and lawn mowers in the 19th century, scythes were the main tools used for cutting hay and grass, and for harvesting cereal crops.*

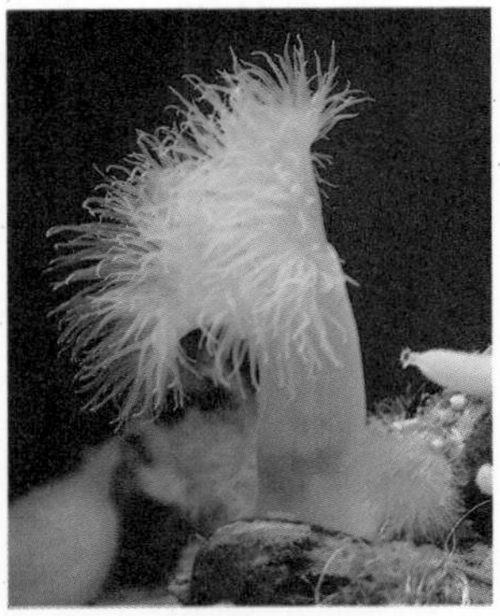

sea anemone *Found throughout the world, the flower-like anemone is actually an animal. It feeds on fish and other sea creatures, stunning its prey with stinging tentacles. There are over 1,000 species, some of which can grow to 1.5 metres (5 feet) across.*

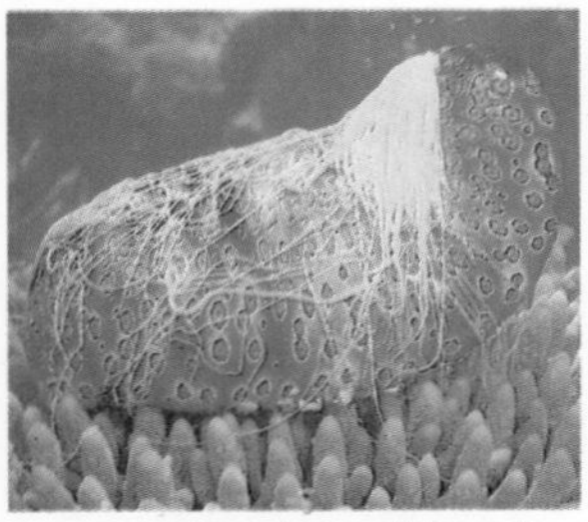

sea cucumber *Although it gets its name from its resemblance to a plant, the sea cucumber is actually an animal. When alarmed, some species – like the warm-water type shown here – exude sticky filaments to confuse or trap an attacker. Others can expel their own intestines, then grow a new set.*

scut (skut) *n.* A stubby erect tail, such as that of a hare, rabbit, or deer. [Middle English *scut*†, hare.]

scu·tage (skéwtij) *n.* In feudal times, a tax paid in lieu of military service. [Middle English, from Medieval Latin *scūtāgium,* "shield money", from Latin *scūtum,* shield, SCUTUM.]

Scutari. See **Shkodër** (Albania), **Üsküdar** (Turkey).

scu·tate (skéwt-ayt) *adj.* **1.** *Zoology.* Covered with bony plates or scales. **2.** *Botany.* Round in shape like a buckler or shield. [New Latin *scutatus,* from Latin *scūtātus,* equipped with a shield, from *scūtum,* shield, SCUTUM.]

scutch (skuch) *tr.v.* **scutched, scutching, scutches.** To separate the valuable fibres of (flax or other textile material) from the woody parts by beating.
~*n.* An implement for scutching. [Obsolete French *escoucher,* from Old French *escousser,* from Vulgar Latin *excussāre* (unattested), frequentative of Latin *excutere* (past participle *excussus*), to shake out : *ex-,* out + *quatere,* to shake.] **—scutch·er** *n.*

scutch·eon (skúchən) *n.* **1.** Variant of **escutcheon. 2.** A shield-shaped object, such as a scute.

scutch grass *n.* **1. Bermuda grass** *(see).* **2. Couch grass** *(see).*

scute (skewt) *n. Zoology.* A horny, chitinous, or bony external plate or scale, as on the shell of a turtle. [New Latin, SCUTUM.]

scu·tel·late (skew-tél-ayt, skéwtil-, -ət, -it) *adj.* Also **scu·tel·lat·ed** (skéwti-laytid) (for sense 1). **1.** *Zoology.* **a.** Covered with bony plates or scales. **b.** Having a scutellum. **2.** *Botany.* Shaped like a shield or platter. [From SCUTELLUM.]

scu·tel·la·tion (skéwti-láysh'n) *n.* An arrangement or covering of scales, as on a bird's leg.

scu·tel·lum (skew-téllәm) *n., pl.* **-tella** (-téllә). **1.** *Zoology.* A shield-like bony plate or scale, as on the thorax of some insects. **2.** *Botany.* Any of several shield-shaped structures, such as the cotyledon of a grass. [New Latin, diminutive of SCUTUM.]

scu·ti·form (skéwti-fawrm) *adj.* Shield-shaped: *scutiform leaves.* [New Latin *scutiformis* : Latin *scūtum,* SCUTUM + -FORM.]

scut·ter (skúttər) *intr.v.* **-tered, -tering, -ters.** *British Informal.* To scurry. [Variant (influenced by SCATTER) of SCUTTLE (to run).]

scut·tle[1] (skútt'l) *n.* **1.** A small opening or hatch with a movable lid in the deck, side, wall, or roof of a ship or in the roof, wall, or floor of a building. **2.** The lid or hatch for this.
~*tr.v.* **scuttled, -tling, -tles. 1.** To cut or open a hole or holes in (a ship's hull). **2. a.** To sink (a ship) by this means. **b.** To sink (a ship) by opening the seacocks. **3.** *Informal.* **a.** To scrap; discard. **b.** To undermine; sabotage. [Middle English *skottell,* from obsolete French *escoutille,* from Spanish *escotilla,* diminutive of *escota,* opening in a garment, "seam", probably from Gothic *skaut,* seam, hem.]

scuttle[2] *n.* **1.** See **coal scuttle. 2.** *Archaic.* A shallow open basket for carrying vegetables, flowers, grain, or the like. **3.** The part of a motor car connecting the bonnet with the rest of the body. [Middle English *scutel,* Old English *scutel,* ultimately from Latin *scutella,* salver. See **scullery.**]

scuttle[3] *intr.v.* **-tled, -tling, -tles.** To run with short hurried movements; scurry. [Variant of dialectal *scuddle,* frequentative of SCUD.] **—scut·tle** *n.*

scut·tle·butt (skútt'l-but) *n.* **1.** A drinking fountain on a ship. **2.** Formerly, a cask on a ship used to hold the day's supply of drinking water. **3.** *Slang.* Gossip; rumour. [SCUTTLE (hatch) + BUTT (cask).]

scu·tum (skéw-təm) *n., pl.* **-ta** (-tə). **1.** *Zoology.* A bony, calcareous, chitinous, or horny scale or plate, as on certain barnacles and on the thorax of an insect. **2.** *Capital* **S.** *Astronomy.* A constellation in the equatorial region of the southern sky near Sagittarius and Serpens Cauda. [Latin *scūtum,* shield.]

Scyl·la (síllə) *n.* A headland on the Italian side of the Strait of Messina, opposite the whirlpool Charybdis, personified by Homer as a female sea monster who devoured sailors. **—between Scylla and Charybdis.** In a position where avoidance of one danger exposes one to destruction by another.

scy·phis·to·ma (sī-fístə-mə) *n., pl.* **-mae** (-mee) or **-mas.** A sedentary polyp-like form in the life cycle of scyphozoans, which gives rise to free-swimming medusoid forms. [New Latin, from Greek *skuphos,* cup + *stoma,* mouth.]

scy·pho·zo·an (sīf-ə-zō-ən, -ō-) *n.* Any of various marine coelenterates of the class Scyphozoa, including the jellyfishes. [New Latin *Scyphozoa,* "cuplike creatures" : Greek *skuphos,* cup + -ZOA.] **—scy·pho·zo·an** *adj.*

scythe (sīth) *n.* An implement consisting of a long, curved single-edged blade with a long, bent handle, used for mowing or reaping.
~*tr.v.* **scythed, scything, scythes.** To cut with or as if with a scythe. [Middle English *sithe, sythe,* Old English *sīthe,* from Germanic.]

Scyth·i·a (síthi-ə, síthi-ə). An ancient region of Asia and southeast Europe, north of the Black Sea.

Scyth·i·an (síthi-ən, síthi-) *n.* **1.** A member of the ancient nomadic people inhabiting Scythia. **2.** The extinct Iranian language of these people. **—scyth·i·an** *adj.*

s.d. 1. sine die. **2.** *Statistics.* standard deviation.

S.D. *Statistics.* standard deviation.

SDP Social Democratic Party.

S.D.R., S.D.R.s special drawing rights (from the International Monetary Fund).

Se The symbol for the element selenium.

SE southeast; southeastern.

sea (see) *n.* **1.** *Abbr.* **s., S. a.** The continuous body of salt water covering most of the earth's surface; especially, this body regarded as a geophysical entity distinct from earth and sky. Usually preceded by *the.* **b.** A tract of water within an ocean, such as the North Sea. **c.** A relatively large body of salt water completely or partly landlocked, such as the Caspian Sea. **d.** A body of fresh water, such as the Sea of Galilee. **2.** *Sometimes plural.* The condition of the ocean's surface with regard to its course, flow, swell, or turbulence: *a high sea.* **3.** Something that suggests the sea in extent or quantity. **4.** Seafaring as a way of life. **5.** A lunar **mare** *(see).* **—at sea. 1.** On the open waters of the ocean. **2.** At a loss; perplexed. **—go to sea. 1.** To become a sailor. **2.** To set out on an ocean voyage. **—put (out) to sea.** To leave port. [Middle English *se(e),* Old English *sǣ,* from Common Germanic *saiwa-* (unattested).]

sea anchor *n. Nautical.* A drag, usually in the form of a canvas-covered conical frame, floating behind a vessel to prevent drifting or to maintain a heading into the wind. Also called "drag anchor", "drift anchor", "drogue".

sea anemone *n.* Any of numerous flower-like marine coelenterates of the order Actiniaria.

sea bag *n.* A strong canvas bag, usually with a drawstring at the top, in which a sailor carries his belongings.

sea bass *n.* Any of various marine food fishes of the genus *Centropristes* and related genera; especially, *C. striatus,* of coastal Atlantic waters of the United States. Also called "sea perch".

sea·bed (sée-bed) *n.* The floor of the sea or the ocean.

Sea·bee (sée-bee) *n.* A member of one of the U.S. Navy's construction battalions, established to build naval aviation bases. [Variant of *cee bee,* from the initials of *C*onstruction *B*attalion.]

sea bird *n.* A bird, such as a petrel or albatross, that frequents the sea, especially far from shore.

sea biscuit *n.* Hardtack.

sea·board (sée-bawrd || -bōrd) *n.* **1.** The seacoast. **2.** Land near the sea. [SEA + BOARD (obsolete sense "border").] **—sea·board** *adj.*

sea·borne (sée-bawrn || -bōrn) *adj.* **1.** Conveyed by sea; transported by ship. **2.** Carried on or over the sea.

sea bream *n.* Any of various marine food fishes of the family Sparidae; especially, *Pagellus centrodontus,* of European waters.

sea breeze *n.* A cool breeze blowing inland from the sea during the afternoon, especially in equatorial regions.

sea buckthorn *n.* A Eurasian coastal shrub, *Hippophae rhamnoides,* having narrow leaves, greenish flowers, and orange fruits.

sea butterfly *n.* A marine organism, a **pteropod** *(see).*

sea·coast (sée-kōst) *n.* Land bordering the sea.

sea·cock (sée-kok) *n.* A valve through which water can be let into or pumped out of the interior of a ship.

sea cow *n.* **1.** Any of several marine mammals of the order Sirenia, such as a manatee or dugong. **2.** *Archaic.* Any of several other aquatic animals, such as a walrus.

sea cucumber *n.* Any of various cucumber-shaped echinoderms of the class Holothuroidea. See **trepang.**

sea dog *n.* A sailor with long experience of the sea.

sea·dog (sée-dog || -dawg) *n.* A **fogbow** *(see).*

sea duck *n.* Any of various diving ducks, such as the eider or scoter, of coastal areas.

sea eagle *n.* Any of various fish-eating eagles or similar birds, especially any of the genus *Haliaetus.*

sea ear *n.* A mollusc, the **ormer** *(see).*

sea elephant *n.* The **elephant seal** *(see).*

sea fan *n.* Any of various yellowish to reddish fan-shaped corals of the genus *Gorgonia.*

sea·far·er (sée-fairər || *U.S.* -farrər, -ferrər) *n.* A sailor or mariner.

sea·far·ing (sée-fairing) *n.* **1.** Travel by sea. **2.** The calling of a sailor.
~*adj.* **1.** Following a life at sea. **2.** Travelling by sea.

sea feather *n.* Any of several anthozoans of the family Pennatulidae, having a feather-like shape.

sea·food, sea food (sée-fo͞od) *n.* Edible fish, shellfish, and the like, from the sea.

sea·fowl (sée-fowl) *n.* **1.** A sea bird. **2.** Sea birds collectively.

sea·front (sée-front) *n.* A strip of land at the very edge of the sea, especially when part of a town.

sea·girt (sée-gurt) *adj. Literary.* Surrounded by the sea.

sea·go·ing (sée-gō-ing) *adj.* **1.** Designed or used for ocean voyages. **2.** Seafaring.

sea gooseberry *n.* A marine organism of the genus *Pleurobrachia.* See **ctenophore.** [From its round, berry-like shape.]

sea green *n.* Moderate bluish green. **—sea-green** *adj.*

sea·gull (sée-gul) *n.* A gull, especially any appearing near coastal areas.

sea hare *n.* Any of various marine gastropod molluscs of the family Aplysiidae, having a soft body and two earlike tentacles.

sea holly *n.* An Old World plant, *Eryngium maritimum,* growing on seashores and having prickly leaves and blue or purplish flowers.

sea horse *n.* **1.** Any small marine fish of the genus *Hippocampus,* characteristically swimming in an upright position, and having a prehensile tail, a horselike head, and a body covered with bony plates. **2.** Loosely, a walrus. **3.** A mythical animal, half fish and half horse, ridden by Neptune and other sea gods.

Sea Island cotton *n.* **1.** A species of cotton, *Gossypium barbadense,* native to tropical America and widely cultivated for its fine, long-staple fibres. **2.** The fibres or fabric derived from this plant. [After the *Sea Islands* off South Carolina and Georgia, United States, where it was originally cultivated.]

UNCHANGING ZONES AND CURRENTS IN THE EVER-MOVING SEA

Life in the different layers of the sea's depths

Although seawater circulates ceaselessly between the poles and the equator and its surface is continuously disturbed by the pull of the Moon and the wind, it is not consistent in temperature but varies greatly from place to place and from top to bottom. It is forced by the shape of land masses and the ocean bed into a number of vast currents and drifts, all of which have an effect on climate.

The best-known current is the Gulf Stream, which carries water warmed by the tropical sun almost to Newfoundland, beyond which it widens and branches. One branch is the North Atlantic Drift, which warms the northwest shores of Europe in winter. All currents have a typical but remarkable integrity because seawater at a certain temperature and density does not easily mingle with different seawater around it. Some seawater may have been carried along in the same current for centuries – never mixing with the water that surrounds it.

Just as the sea maintains differences at the surface, so different layers are maintained from top to bottom in the warmer seas. The euphotic zone, the upper 200 metres (656 feet), is aerated and sunlit enough for minute plant and animal life such as algae and plank-ton to flourish. They are the first link in the food chain that sustains all sea creatures.

Besides the algae and plankton, the euphotic zone holds a concentration of sea creatures of greater size. There are both carnivores and herbivores and they are predominantly either colourless or blue – the best camouflage in the sea.

The bathyal zone below contains carnivores and creatures which live off the dead matter that sinks down from above. In the total darkness of the depths, the variety of living things decreases as does the food dropping from above.

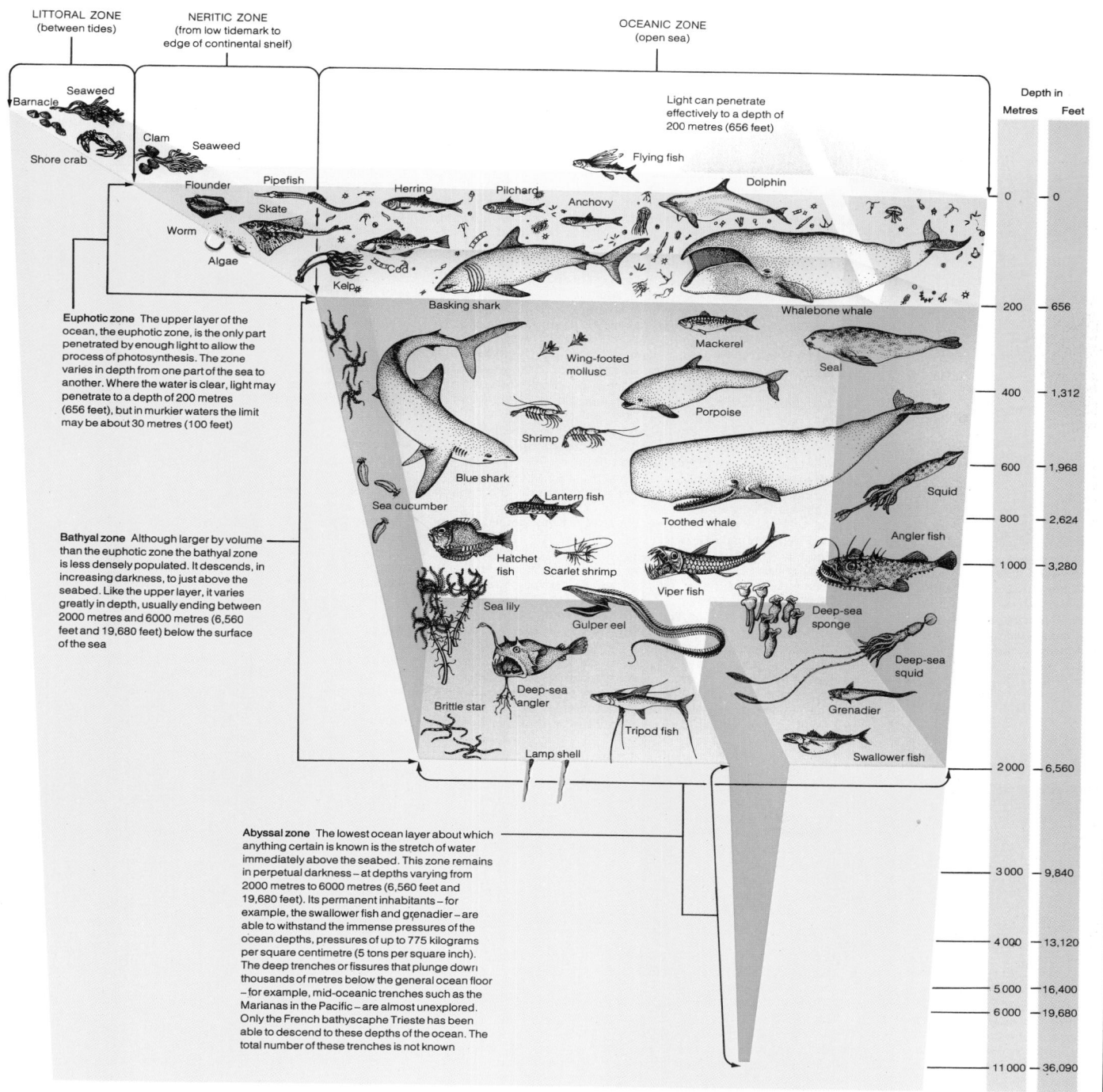

LITTORAL ZONE (between tides)

NERITIC ZONE (from low tidemark to edge of continental shelf)

OCEANIC ZONE (open sea)

Light can penetrate effectively to a depth of 200 metres (656 feet)

Depth in Metres / Feet

Barnacle — Seaweed — Shore crab — Clam — Seaweed — Flounder — Pipefish — Skate — Worm — Algae — Kelp — Cod — Herring — Pilchard — Anchovy — Flying fish — Dolphin — Basking shark — Whalebone whale

Euphotic zone The upper layer of the ocean, the euphotic zone, is the only part penetrated by enough light to allow the process of photosynthesis. The zone varies in depth from one part of the sea to another. Where the water is clear, light may penetrate to a depth of 200 metres (656 feet), but in murkier waters the limit may be about 30 metres (100 feet)

Mackerel — Wing-footed mollusc — Seal — Porpoise — Shrimp — Squid — Blue shark — Sea cucumber — Lantern fish — Toothed whale — Angler fish

Bathyal zone Although larger by volume than the euphotic zone the bathyal zone is less densely populated. It descends, in increasing darkness, to just above the seabed. Like the upper layer, it varies greatly in depth, usually ending between 2000 metres and 6000 metres (6,560 feet and 19,680 feet) below the surface of the sea

Hatchet fish — Scarlet shrimp — Viper fish — Sea lily — Gulper eel — Deep-sea sponge — Deep-sea squid — Brittle star — Deep-sea angler — Tripod fish — Grenadier — Lamp shell — Swallower fish

Abyssal zone The lowest ocean layer about which anything certain is known is the stretch of water immediately above the seabed. This zone remains in perpetual darkness – at depths varying from 2000 metres to 6000 metres (6,560 feet and 19,680 feet). Its permanent inhabitants – for example, the swallower fish and grenadier – are able to withstand the immense pressures of the ocean depths, pressures of up to 775 kilograms per square centimetre (5 tons per square inch). The deep trenches or fissures that plunge down thousands of metres below the general ocean floor – for example, mid-oceanic trenches such as the Marianas in the Pacific – are almost unexplored. Only the French bathyscaphe Trieste has been able to descend to these depths of the ocean. The total number of these trenches is not known

Metres	Feet
0	0
200	656
400	1,312
600	1,968
800	2,624
1 000	3,280
2 000	6,560
3 000	9,840
4 000	13,120
5 000	16,400
6 000	19,680
11 000	36,090

seal² *Like other seals, the Weddell seal (above), which is found around Antarctica, feeds largely on fish. Clumsy on land, it is an accomplished swimmer, capable of staying submerged for half an hour at a time and of diving to depths of more than 450 metres (about 1,500 feet).*

seaplane *Seaplanes are most widely used in thickly forested regions such as Canada and the Scandinavian countries where open water provides an abundance of ready-made landing strips. This plane operates in northern Finland.*

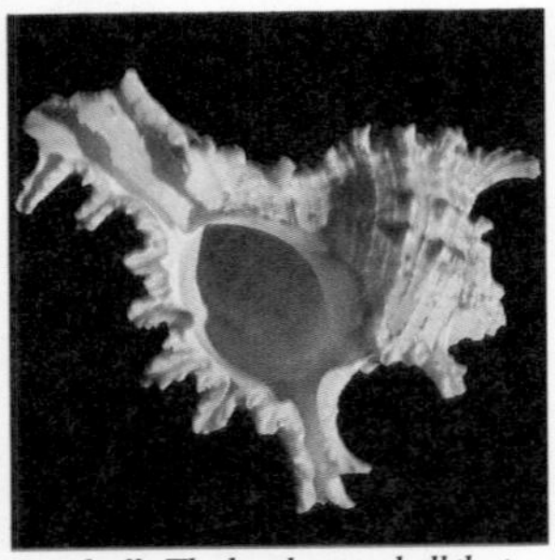

seashell *The hard outer shell that protects the soft boneless body of many marine molluscs. There are about 80,000 species of mollusc, though not all produce shells. This elaborate Pacific shell was found on a beach in California.*

sea kale *n.* A European plant, *Crambe maritima,* having cabbage-like leaves and young shoots that are edible.

sea king *n. Literary.* A piratical Scandinavian chief of the early Middle Ages.

seal¹ (seel) *n.* **1. a.** A die or signet having a raised or incised emblem, used to stamp an impression upon a receptive substance such as wax or lead. **b.** The impression made. **c.** The design or emblem itself, belonging exclusively to the user: *the king's seal.* **d.** A small disc or wafer of wax, lead, or paper bearing such an imprint and affixed to a document to prove authenticity or to seal it. **2.** Any act, event, or sign that is regarded as a confirmation or guarantee. **3.** An adhesive agent such as wax, paraffin, or putty used to close or secure something or to prevent seepage of moisture or air. **4.** A device or fluid in a drainpipe preventing the upward passage of gas. **5.** An airtight closure. **6.** A small decorative paper sticker: *a Christmas seal.* **—set (one's) seal on. 1.** To impart something of one's personal character to: *set his seal on the magazine.* **2.** To approve; endorse. **—set the seal on. 1.** To sanction in a formal or authoratative way. **2.** To bring to an end, especially in an appropriate manner. **—under seal of.** In confidence or secrecy on specified grounds: *under seal of confession.*
~*tr.v.* **sealed, sealing, seals. 1.** To affix a seal to so as to prove authenticity or attest to accuracy, quality, or conformity to an appropriate standard. **2. a.** To close with or as if with a seal: *seal an envelope; seal one's lips.* **b.** To close hermetically. **c.** To make fast or fill up as with plaster or cement. **d.** To give a protective coating to (a porous surface, for example). **3.** To grant, certify, or designate under seal or authority. **4.** To establish or determine irrevocably. **5.** To settle or agree upon; confirm: *sealed the bargain.* **6.** To provide (a road) with a hard surface. **—seal off.** To close off or enclose (a road or area) so as to prevent entry or exit. [Middle English, from Anglo-French, Old French, from Latin *sigillum,* seal, diminutive of *signum,* sign.] **—seal·a·ble** *adj.*

seal² (seel) *n.* **1.** Any of various aquatic, fish-eating mammals of the families Phocidae *(earless seals)* and Otariidae *(eared seals),* having a sleek, torpedo-shaped body and limbs that are modified into paddle-like flippers. **2.** The pelt or fur of a seal, especially a fur seal. **3.** Leather made from the hide of a seal.
~*intr.v.* **sealed, sealing, seals.** To hunt seals. [Middle English *selch, seel,* Old English *seolh,* from Germanic.]

sea lamprey *n.* A common marine lamprey, *Petromyzon marinus.*

sea lane *n.* An established course along which sea traffic moves, as when leaving or entering port.

seal·ant (séelənt) *n.* A sealing agent.

sea lavender *n.* Any of several salt-marsh plants of the genus *Limonium,* having clusters of small lavender or pinkish flowers.

sea lawyer *n. Nautical Slang.* An argumentative or fault-finding sailor.

sealed-beam (séeld-béem) *adj.* Designating a motor vehicle headlamp in which the lens is sealed to the prefocused reflector in order to maintain a vacuum in the lamp cavity.

sealed move (seeld) *n.* In chess, the last move by a player before an adjournment, written down and kept secret from the other player until the game is resumed.

sealed orders *pl.n.* Written orders that are not to be read or opened until a stipulated time.

sea legs *pl.n. Informal.* The ability to walk on board ship with steadiness, especially in rough seas. **—get (one's) sea legs.** To become accustomed to the motion of a ship at sea; especially, to be unaffected by seasickness.

seal·er¹ (séelər) *n.* **1.** One that seals. **2.** An undercoat of paint or varnish used to size a surface. **3.** An officer who inspects, tests, and certifies weights and measures.

sealer² *n.* A person or ship engaged in seal hunting.

seal·er·y (séeləri) *n., pl.* **-ies.** A place where seals are hunted.

sea lettuce *n* Any of several green seaweeds of the genus *Ulva,* having thin, irregularly shaped fronds sometimes used as food.

sea level *n.* The level of the ocean's surface; especially, the **mean sea level** *(see).*

sea lily *n.* Any of various marine crinoids having a flower-like body supported by a long stalk.

seal·ing wax (séeling) *n.* A resinous preparation of shellac, turpentine, a filler, and a dye that is soft and fluid when heated but solidifies upon cooling, used to seal letters, jars, or other objects.

sea lion *n.* Any of several seals of the family Otariidae, having distinct external ears, especially *Zalophus californianus,* of the northern Pacific.

sea loch *n.* An arm of the sea extending inland.

Sea Lord *n. British.* A naval officer who is a member of the Admiralty Board of the Ministry of Defence.

seal point *n.* A type of Siamese cat having dark brown ears, muzzle, paws, and tail.

seal ring *n.* A finger ring bearing a seal.

seal·skin (séel-skin) *n.* **1.** The pelt or fur of a fur seal, especially the underfur. **2.** A garment made of this skin. **—seal·skin** *adj.*

Sea·ly·ham terrier (séeli-əm || -ham) *n.* A terrier of a breed developed in Wales, having a wiry white coat, a long head, and short legs. [Originally bred at *Sealyham,* Dyfed, Wales.]

seam (seem) *n.* **1. a.** A line of junction formed by sewing together two pieces of material along their edges. **b.** A similar line, ridge, or groove made by fitting, joining, or lapping together two sections along their edges. **c.** A suture or scar, as left on the skin after surgery. **2.** Any line across a surface, such as a crack, fissure, or wrinkle. **3.** A thin layer or stratum, as of coal or rock. **—bursting at the seams.** Overcrowed or too full.
~*v.* **seamed, seaming, seams.** *—tr.* **1.** To fasten or join with or as if with a seam. **2.** To mark with a groove, wrinkle, scar, or other seamlike line. **3.** In cricket, to bowl (the ball) so that it changes direction as it pitches on the stitched seam. *—intr.* To crack open; become fissured or furrowed. [Middle English *se(e)m,* Old English *sēam,* from Germanic.] **—seam·er** *n.*

sea·maid·en (sée-mayd'n) *n.* Also **sea-maid** (-mayd). A mermaid or sea nymph.

sea·man (sée-mən) *n., pl.* **-men** (-mən, -men). **1.** A mariner or sailor. **2.** In the British Navy and certain other navies, a sailor ranking below a petty officer.

sea·man·ship (séemən-ship) *n.* Skill in managing or navigating a boat or ship.

sea·mark (sée-maark) *n.* **1.** A landmark visible from the sea, used as a guide in navigation. **2.** The mark along a coastline indicating the upper tidal limits.

seam bowler *n.* In cricket, a bowler, usually of fast or medium pace, who uses the stitched seam of the ball to make it change direction as it pitches. Also called "seamer".

sea mew *n.* Any of various gulls frequenting coastal areas, especially *Larus canus,* of Europe.

sea mile *n.* A former unit of length equal to 6,000 feet or 1,000 fathoms. Compare **nautical mile.**

sea milkwort *n.* A fleshy plant, *Glaux maritima,* of shores and brackish marshes, having pink flowers. Also called "saltwort".

seam·less (séem-ləss, -liss) *adj.* **1.** Without seams; woven without a seam: *seamless stockings.* **2.** Having a steady or rhythmic flow; harmonious: *seamless prose.* **—seam·less·ness** *n.*

sea·mount (sée-mownt) *n.* A submerged submarine mountain rising at least 1 000 metres (3,300 feet) above the ocean floor.

sea mouse *n.* Any of various segmented marine worms of the genus *Aphrodite*; especially, *A. aculeata,* having a flattened elliptical body with overlapping scales covered by long hairs.

seam·ster (sém-stər, sémp- || séem) *n. Archaic.* A tailor. [Middle English *semester,* Old English *sēamestre* : *sēam,* SEAM + -STER.]

seam·stress (sém-striss, sémp-, -strəss || séem-) *n.* A woman who sews, especially for a living.

seam·y (séemi) *adj.* **-ier, -iest. 1.** Having, marked with, or showing a seam or seams. **2.** Unattractively or unpleasantly rough and raw; sordid: *the seamy side of life.* **—seam·i·ness** *n.*

Sean·ad Éir·eann (sánnaad aáirən; *Irish* shánnaad) *n.* The Senate, or upper house of parliament, in the Republic of Ireland. [Irish *seanad,* senate, from Latin *senātus,* SENATE + *Éireann,* of Ireland.]

sé·ance (sáy-ONSS) *n.* **1.** A meeting of persons to receive messages from or communicate with the spirits of the dead. **2.** A meeting, session, or sitting. [French, "a sitting", from Old French, from *seoir,* to sit, from Latin *sedēre,* to sit.]

sea onion *n.* A plant, *Urginea maritima,* of the Mediterranean area, cultivated for its bulb that yields a powder used medicinally and as a rat poison. Also called "sea squill", "red squill".

sea otter *n.* A large marine otter, *Enhydra lutris,* of northern Pacific coasts, formerly hunted for its soft dark-brown coat.

sea parrot *n.* A bird, the **puffin** *(see).*

sea pen *n.* Any of various marine anthozoans of the families Stylatulidae and Funiculinidae. [From its resemblance to a quill pen.]

sea perch *n.* A fish, the **sea bass** *(see).*

sea pink *n.* A plant, the **thrift** *(see).*

sea·plane (sée-playn) *n.* An aircraft equipped with floats for landing on or taking off from a body of water.

sea·port (sée-port || -pōrt) *n.* A harbour or town having facilities for seagoing ships.

sea power *n.* **1.** A nation having naval strength. **2.** Naval strength.

sea purse *n.* A **mermaid's purse** *(see).*

sea purslane *n.* A small Eurasian shrub, *Halimione portulacoides,* that grows on salt marshes and has small, greenish flowers.

sea·quake (sée-kwayk) *n.* An earthquake under the sea floor.

sear¹ (seer) *v.* **seared, searing, sears.** *—tr.* **1.** To make withered; dry up or shrivel. **2.** To char, scorch, or burn the surface of with or as if with a hot instrument. *—intr.* To become withered or dried up; shrivel. —See Synonyms at **burn.**
~*n.* Any condition, such as a scar, produced by searing. [Middle English *seren,* Old English *sēarian,* from *sēar,* withered.]

sear² *n.* The catch in a gunlock that keeps the hammer halfcocked or fully cocked. [Probably from Old French *serre,* grasp, lock, from *serrer,* to grasp. See **serried.**]

sea raven *n.* A large sculpin, *Hemitripterus americanus,* of the western Atlantic.

search (serch) *v.* **searched, searching, searches.** *—tr.* **1.** To make a thorough examination of (a place, building, or receptacle, for example) in order to find something; look over; explore. **2.** To make a careful examination or investigation of; probe: *search one's conscience.* **3.** To make a thorough check of (a legal document or records, for example); scrutinise: *search a title.* **4.** To examine the person or personal effects of in order to find something concealed, especially as part of a police procedure. **5.** To come to know by investigation; learn. Used with *out.* **6.** To probe (a wound) so as to remove a foreign body. **7.** *Military.* To penetrate every part of (an area), as with gunfire. *—intr.* To conduct a thorough investigation; seek. Often used with *for.* **—search me.** *Informal.* Used to indicate that one is perplexed or unable to answer a question.
~*n.* **1.** An act of searching; an investigation, examination, or

probe. **2.** The exercise of **right of search** *(see).* [Middle English *serchen,* from Anglo-French *sercher,* Old French *cerchier,* "to go round", from Late Latin *circāre,* from Latin *circus,* circle.] **—search·a·ble** *adj.* **—search·er** *n.*

search·ing (sérching) *adj.* Penetrating; keen: *a searching gaze.* **—search·ing·ly** *adv.*

search·light (sérch-līt) *n.* **1.** An apparatus containing a light source and a reflector for projecting a bright beam of approximately parallel rays of light. **2.** The beam of light so projected.

search party *n.* A group of persons who make a search, as for a missing person or a fugitive.

search warrant *n.* A warrant, issued in Britain by a Justice of the Peace, giving legal authorisation to a policeman or other officer to make a search.

sear·ing (seér-ing) *adj.* **1.** Scorching. **2.** Intense; withering.

Searle (serl), **Ronald (William Fordham)** (1920–). British cartoonist. His grotesque draughtsmanship, popular in both the United Kingdom and France, combines wickedness with humour.

sea robin *n.* Any of various American marine fishes of the family Triglidae, having extremely long pectoral fins with finger-like rays.

sea room *n.* Space at sea adequate for manoeuvring a ship.

sea·scape (seé-skayp) *n.* A view or picture of the sea. [SEA + -SCAPE.]

sea scorpion *n.* Any of various marine fishes of the family Cottidae, having a tapering body and a large bony or spiny head.

Sea Scout *n.* A member of a Scout unit that gives training in seamanship.

sea serpent *n.* A large snakelike or dragon-like legendary marine animal.

sea·shell (seé-shel) *n.* The calcareous shell of a marine mollusc or similar marine organism.

sea·shore (seé-shawr || -shōr) *n.* **1.** Land immediately adjoining the sea. **2.** *Law.* Ground lying between high-water and low-water marks; foreshore.

sea·sick·ness (seé-sik-nəss, -niss) *n.* Nausea and vomiting provoked by the motion of a vessel at sea. **—sea·sick** *adj.*

sea·side (seé-sīd) *n.* **1.** The seashore. **2.** Any coastal area as a place of resort or recreation. Also used adjectivally: *a seaside hotel.*

sea slug *n.* Any of various shell-less marine gastropods of the suborder Nudibranchia. Also called "nudibranch".

sea snail *n.* Any of various small marine fishes of the family Liparidae, especially *Liparis liparis,* having a soft, tadpole-shaped body with a ventral sucker.

sea snake *n.* Any of various venomous tropical marine snakes of the family Hydrophidae, chiefly of the Pacific and Indian oceans.

sea·son (seéz'n) *n.* **1. a.** Any of the four equal divisions of the year, spring, summer, autumn, and winter, indicated by the passage of the sun through an equinox or solstice and derived from the apparent north-south movement of the sun caused by the fixed direction of the earth's axis in solar orbit. **b.** Any division of the year, rainy or dry, in tropical climates. **2.** A recurrent period that is characterised by certain occupations, events, festivities, or crops: *the Christmas season.* **3. a.** The time of year during which a tourist resort is at its busiest; the holiday season: *It's quieter out of season.* **b.** The time of year, especially formerly, when fashionable society assembled in a place for a period of intense social activity: *the London season.* **4.** A suitable, natural, or convenient time. **5.** Any period of time. **6.** The period of year during which a certain activity may legally take place, such as the hunting of a certain species of animal. **7.** A sequence of showings or performances having a common theme or feature: *a season of Polish films.* **—in season. 1.** Available or ready for eating or other use. **2.** Legally permitted to being hunted or fished during a stipulated time. **3.** At the right moment; opportunely. **4.** On heat. Said of animals. **—out of season. 1.** Not available or ready for eating or hunting. **2.** Not at the right or proper moment; inopportunely.
~*v.* **seasoned, -soning, -sons.** *—tr.* **1.** To improve or enhance the flavour of (food) by adding salt, spices, or other flavourings. **2.** To add zest, piquancy, or interest to. **3.** To dry (timber) until it is usable; cure. **4.** To render competent through trial and experience. **5.** To accustom; inure. **6.** To moderate; temper. *—intr.* To become seasoned. [Middle English *sesoun,* from Old French *seson,* from Latin *satiō* (stem *satiōn-*), act of sowing (in Vulgar Latin, "sowing time"), from *serere* (past participle *satus*), to sow, plant.]

sea·son·a·ble (seéz'n-əb'l) *adj.* **1.** In keeping with the time or the season: *very seasonable weather.* **2.** Occurring or performed at the proper time; timely. **—sea·son·a·bly** *adv.*

sea·son·al (seéz'n'l) *adj.* Of or dependent upon a particular season: *seasonal variations in employment.* **—sea·son·al·ly** *adv.*

sea·son·ing (seéz'n-ing) *n.* **1.** Anything used to flavour food, especially salt and pepper. **2.** The act or process by which something, such as timber, is seasoned.

season ticket *n.* A ticket entitling the holder to some service, such as travel or admission, over a stipulated period of time.

sea spider *n.* Any of various marine arachnids of the class Pycnogonida, having long legs and a relatively small body.

sea squill *n.* A plant, the **sea onion** *(see).*

sea squirt *n.* Any of various sedentary marine animals of the class Ascidiacea. [It squirts water when disturbed.]

seat (seet) *n.* **1.** Something that may be sat upon, such as a chair, bench, or the like. **2.** A place in which one may sit; especially, a place in which one is entitled to sit, as by the purchase of a ticket. **3.** The part of something on which one rests in sitting. **4. a.** The buttocks. **b.** That part of a garment covering the buttocks. **5. a.** A part serving as the base of something. **b.** The surface or part upon which another part sits or rests. **6. a.** The place where anything is or is held to be located or based: *the seat of the emotions.* **b.** A centre of authority; a capital: *the seat of government.* **7.** A place of abode or residence; especially, a large house that is part of an estate. **8. a.** Membership of an official or controlling body, as of a board of directors. **b.** Membership or the right of membership in a legislative body, obtained by election, appointment, or inheritance. **c.** *Chiefly British.* A constituency for parliament. **9.** The manner in which one sits and grips the saddle on a horse: *She has a good seat.*
~*tr.v.* **seated, seating, seats. 1. a.** To place in or on a seat. **b.** To cause or assist to sit down. **2.** To have or provide seats for: *We can seat 300.* **3.** To repair or replace the seat of (a chair or pair of trousers, for example). **4.** To install in a position of authority or eminence. **5.** To fix firmly in place. [Middle English *sete,* from Old Norse *sæti,* from Germanic.]

sea tangle *n.* Any of various brown seaweeds, especially of the genus *Laminaria.*

seat belt *n.* A safety strap to secure the occupant of a seat in a vehicle or aircraft. Also called "safety belt".

seat·ing (seéting) *n.* **1.** The arrangement or provision of seats in a room, auditorium, or the like. **2.** The member or part upon or within which another part is seated. **3.** Material for upholstering seats.

SEA·TO (seétō) *n.* Southeast Asia Treaty Organisation.

sea trout *n.* **1.** Any of several trouts or similar fishes that live in the sea but migrate to fresh water to spawn. **2.** Any of several marine fishes of the genus *Cynoscion,* especially the **weakfish** *(see).*

Se·at·tle (si-átt'l). Port in the northwest of the United States. It is the major port of Washington State.

sea urchin *n.* Any of various echinoderms of the class Echinoidea, having a soft body enclosed in a round, spiny casing.

sea wall *n.* An embankment to prevent erosion of a shoreline.

sea walnut *n.* Any of several ctenophores of the genus *Mnemiopsis* and related genera, having a translucent, ovoid body with lengthways ridges and rows of hairlike cilia.

sea·ward (seé-wərd) *adj.* Moving towards or lying in the direction of the sea.

sea·wards (seé-wərdz) *adv.* Also *Chiefly U.S.* **sea·ward** (-wərd). Towards the sea.

sea·ware (seé-wair) *n.* Seaweed that has been cast ashore and is collected for use as fertiliser. [SEA + *ware,* seaweed, Middle English *ware,* Old English *wār.*]

sea·way (seé-way) *n.* **1.** A sea route. **2.** An inland waterway for ocean shipping. **3.** A ship's progress through the water; headway. **4.** A rough sea.

sea·weed (seé-weed) *n.* **1.** Any of numerous marine algae, such as a kelp, rockweed, or gulfweed. **2.** Any of various other marine plants.

sea wormwood *n.* A wormwood, *Artemisia maritima,* of the Old World, having flowers that yield **santonin** *(see).*

sea·wor·thy (seé-wurthi) *adj.* Designating a vessel that is fit to sail or make a sea voyage. **—sea·wor·thi·ness** *n.*

sea wrack *n.* Any material cast ashore, especially seaweed.

se·ba·ceous (si-báyshəss) *adj. Physiology.* **1.** Of, pertaining to, or resembling fat or sebum; fatty. **2.** Secreting fat or sebum. [Latin *sēbāceus* : *sēbum,* tallow (see **sebum**) + -ACEOUS.]

sebaceous gland *n.* Any of various glands in the dermis of the skin that open into a hair follicle and produce and secrete sebum.

se·bac·ic acid (si-bássik, -báy-sik) *n.* A white crystalline acid, $C_{10}H_{18}O_4$, used in the manufacture of certain synthetic resins and fibres, various plasticisers, and polyester rubbers. Also called "decanedioic acid". [*Sebacic,* from SEBACEOUS (because originally obtained from melted suet).]

Se·bas·ti·an (si-básti-ən, se-, sə-), **Saint** (third century A.D.). Roman martyr. Believed to have been an officer of the Praetorian Guard, he was executed by a squad of archers. Other legends allege that he survived to be beaten to death by Diocletian.

Se·bas·ti·a·no del Pi·om·bo (si-básti-aánō del pi-ómbō), born Sebastiano Luciano (*c.* 1485–1547). Venetian painter. Securing the patronage of Pope Clement VII, he was appointed Keeper of the Papal Seals (*Piombi*), hence his adopted name.

Sebastopol. See **Sevastopol.**

Se·be (séb-ay, -e), **Lennox (Leslie Wongama)** (1926–). Founder of the Ciskei National Independence Party and the first chief minister of **Ciskei.**

sebi–, sebo– *comb. form.* Indicates fat or fatty material; for example, **sebiferous, seborrhoea.** [New Latin, from Latin *sēbum,* tallow. See **sebum.**]

se·bif·er·ous (si-bíffərəss, se-) *adj.* Producing or secreting fatty, oily, or waxy matter; sebaceous. [SEBI- + -FEROUS.]

seb·or·rhoe·a (sébbə-reé-ə) *n.* A disease of the sebaceous glands characterised by excessive secretion of sebum or an alteration in its quality, resulting in an oily coating, crusts, or scales on the skin. [SEBO- + -RRHOEA.] **—seb·or·rhoe·al, seb·or·rhoe·ic** *adj.*

se·bum (seébəm) *n.* The oily secretion of the sebaceous glands, which protects the skin from desiccation. Also called "smegma". [Latin *sēbum*†, tallow.]

sec¹ (sek) *adj.* **1.** Dry. Said of wines. **2.** Somewhat sweet. Said of champagne. Compare **brut.** [French.]

sec² *n. Informal.* A second or moment: *Just a sec!*

sec³ **1.** secant. **2.** second (unit of time). **3.** second (unit of angular measure).

sea snake *The powerful venom of this tropical marine reptile is used to stun or paralyse the fish on which it feeds.*

sea urchin *In death, the sea urchin's skeleton is a hollow spherical shell (above). When the urchin is alive, the shell protects the digestive and reproductive organs, and the outside is covered with spines and with five bands of tubular feet. When the animal dies, the spines and feet drop off, leaving a pattern of white scars. Sea urchins, some species of which are edible, are found worldwide.*

SEC Securities and Exchange Commission (in the United States).

sec. 1. secondary. 2. secretary. 3. sector.

SE·CAM (sée-kam) *n.* Système électronique couleur avec mémoire: a system of colour-television broadcasting used in France.

se·cant (sée-kənt ‖ *U.S. also* -kant) *n. Abbr.* **sec** 1. In geometry: **a.** A straight line intersecting a curve at two or more points. **b.** The straight line drawn from the centre through one end of a circular arc and intersecting the tangent to the other end of the arc. 2. In trigonometry: **a.** The reciprocal of the cosine of an angle. **b.** For an acute angle, the ratio of the hypotenuse to the side of a right-angled triangle adjacent to the acute angle. [French *(ligne) secante,* "cutting line", from Latin *secāns* (stem *secant-*), present participle of *secāre,* to cut.]

sec·a·teurs (séckə-térz, -tərz) *pl.n. Chiefly British.* Pruning shears made to be used with one hand, often spring-assisted.

sec·co (séckō) *n., pl.* **-cos.** The art or an example of painting on dry plaster. Compare **fresco.** [Italian, "dry", from Latin *siccus.*]

se·cede (si-séed) *intr.v.* **-ceded, -ceding, -cedes.** To withdraw formally from membership in an organisation, association, or alliance. [Latin *sēcēdere,* to go away : *sē,* apart + *cēdere,* to go.]

se·cern (si-sérn) *tr.v.* **-cerned, -cerning, -cerns.** 1. To discern as separate; distinguish. 2. *Physiology.* To secrete. Used of a gland or follicle. [Latin *sēcernere,* to separate : *sē,* apart + *cernere,* to separate, discern.] **—se·cern·ment** *n.*

se·ces·sion (si-sésh'n) *n.* 1. The act or an instance of seceding. 2. *Usually capital* **S.** *U.S.* The withdrawal of 11 Southern states from the Federal Union in 1860–61, precipitating the American Civil War. [Latin *sēcessiō* (stem *sēcessiōn-*), from *sēcēdere* (past participle *secessus*), SECEDE.] **—se·ces·sion·al** *adj.*

se·ces·sion·ism (si-sésh'n-iz'm) *n.* The policy of those maintaining the right of secession. **—se·ces·sion·ist** *adj. & n.*

se·clude (si-kloōd ‖ -kleewd) *tr.v.* **-cluded, -cluding, -cludes.** 1. To remove or set apart from others; place in solitude. 2. To screen from view; make private. [Middle English *secluden,* to shut off, keep away, from Latin *sēclūdere* : *sē,* apart + *claudere,* to shut.]

se·clud·ed (si-kloōd-id ‖ -kléwd-) *adj.* 1. Removed or remote from others; solitary. 2. Screened from view; hidden or private. **—se·clud·ed·ly** *adv.* **—se·clud·ed·ness** *n.*

se·clu·sion (si-kloō-zh'n ‖ -kléw-) *n.* 1. **a.** The act of secluding. **b.** The state of being secluded. 2. A secluded place or abode. **—See** Synonyms at **solitude.** [Medieval Latin *sēclūsiō* (stem *sēclūsiōn-*), from *sēclūdere* (past participle *sēclūsus*), SECLUDE.]

se·clu·sive (si-kloō-siv ‖ -kléw-, -ziv) *adj.* Fond of, seeking, or tending to seclusion. **—se·clu·sive·ly** *adv.* **—se·clu·sive·ness** *n.*

sec·ond[1] (séckənd ‖ séckənt) *n.* 1. *Abbr.* **s, sec** *Symbol* **″ a.** A unit of time equal to 1/60 of a minute. **b.** The SI unit of time equal to the duration of 9,192,631,770 periods of the radiation produced by the transition between two hyperfine levels in the ground state of caesium-133. 2. *Informal.* A brief lapse of time; a moment. 3. *Abbr.* **s, sec** *Symbol* **″** In geometry, a unit of angular measure equal to 1/60 of a minute of arc. **—See** Synonyms at **moment.** [Middle English *seconde,* unit in geometry, from Old French, from Medieval Latin *(pars minūta) secunda,* "second (small part)" (after the second sexagesimal division), from Latin, feminine of *secundus,* SECOND (in number).]

sec·ond[2] (séckənd) *adj.* 1. **a.** Coming next after the first in order, place, rank, time, or quality. **b.** Graded or judged to be between the first and third grades or levels. 2. **a.** Repeating an initial instance; another: *a second chance.* **b.** Alternate: *every second year.* **c.** Similar to or evoking the memory of a specified person or event from the past: *a second Hitler.* 3. Inferior to another; subordinate: *second to none.* 4. *Music.* **a.** Having a lower pitch. **b.** Singing or playing a part having a lower range. **c.** Singing or playing a part subordinate to the principal one. 5. Designating the next-to-lowest forward gear, as in a motor vehicle or bicycle.

~n. 1. The ordinal number two in a series. 2. One that is next in order, place, time, or quality after the first. 3. An article of merchandise that is imperfect in some way. 4. The official attendant of a contestant in a duel or boxing match. 5. *Music.* **a.** The interval between consecutive notes on the diatonic scale. **b.** A note separated by this interval from another note. **c.** A combination of two such notes in notation or in harmony. **d.** The second part, instrument, or voice in a harmonised composition. 6. An utterance of endorsement of a proposal or nomination, as in debating procedure. 7. The next-to-lowest forward gear, as in a motor vehicle or bicycle, having the second-highest ratio. 8. *Plural. Informal.* A second helping of a dish or a second or pudding course of a meal. 9. *British.* A second-class honours degree.

~tr.v. **seconded, -onding, -onds.** 1. To attend (a duellist, for example) as an aide or assistant. 2. To promote or encourage; reinforce. 3. To endorse (a motion or nomination) as a required preliminary to discussion or vote.

~adv. 1. In the second order, place, or rank. 2. But for one other; save one. Sometimes used in combination: *the second-highest peak.* [Middle English, from Old French, from Latin *secundus,* following, coming next.]

se·cond[3] (si-kónd, sə-) *tr.v.* **-conded, -conding, -conds.** *British.* 1. To transfer (an employee) temporarily to another department, branch, or task. 2. *Military.* To remove (an officer) from service with a view to transferral to another post, such as a staff or nonregimental post. [French *en second,* in second rank (or position).]

Second Advent *n.* The **Second Coming** (see).

sec·on·dar·y (séckən-dəri, -dri ‖ -derri) *adj. Abbr.* **sec.** 1. **a.** One step removed from the first; of the second rank; not primary. **b.** Inferior; lesser. 2. Derived from what is primary or original: *a secondary source.* 3. Of, pertaining to, or designating the shorter flight feathers projecting along the inner part of the edge of a bird's wing. 4. *Electricity.* Having an induced current that is generated by an inductively coupled primary. Said of a circuit or coil. 5. *Chemistry.* **a.** Designating a compound in which two hydrogen atoms have been replaced by a metal, radical, or alkyl group. **b.** Designating an organic compound having a functional group attached to a carbon that is attached to one hydrogen and two other groups. 6. *Geology.* Resulting from changes in the pre-existing minerals. 7. Of, pertaining to, or designating education received at secondary school. 8. Designating an industry that uses the raw materials gathered by a primary industry and processes or manufactures products from them. 9. *Linguistics.* Having been derived from a word that was itself derived from another word, such as *hauntingly,* from *haunting,* from *haunt.* 10. *Botany.* Designating plant growth of a type caused by activity of the cambium and resulting in an increase in the width of stems and branches.

~n., pl. secondaries. 1. One that acts in an auxiliary, subordinate, or inferior capacity. 2. Any of the shorter flight feathers projecting along the inner part of the edge of a bird's wing. 3. *Electricity.* A coil or circuit having an induced current. 4. *Astronomy.* A body that orbits a primary; a satellite. 5. A secondary colour. [Middle English, from Latin *secundārius,* from *secundus,* SECOND.] **—sec·on·dar·i·ly** *adv.* **—sec·on·dar·i·ness** *n.*

secondary accent *n.* An accent weaker than a primary accent, but stronger than a tertiary or weak stress. Also called "secondary stress". Compare **primary accent, tertiary accent.**

secondary battery *n. Electricity.* A **storage battery** (see).

secondary cell *n.* A rechargeable electric cell that converts chemical energy into electrical energy by a reversible chemical reaction. Also called "storage cell". Compare **primary cell.**

secondary colour *n.* A colour produced by mixing two primary colours in approximately equal proportions.

secondary depression *n.* A small, concentrated area of low atmospheric pressure on the margin of a main depression.

secondary electron *n.* An electron produced in secondary emission.

secondary emission *n. Physics.* The emission of electrons from the surface of a substance bombarded by electrons or ions.

secondary group *n. Sociology.* An association of people on the basis of some shared formal characteristic, often a large group involving little contact between members, such as a professional or sporting body. Compare **primary group.**

secondary modern school *n.* Formerly in Britain, a secondary school for students who failed their eleven-plus, specialising in more technical or practical subjects than a grammar school. Compare **comprehensive, grammar school, public school.**

secondary picketing *n.* Action taken in support of a picket by persons other than those directly involved in the dispute in question. **—secondary picket** *n.*

secondary school *n.* Any school providing education for young people, usually between the ages of 11 and 18, after primary school but preceding university or an occupation.

secondary sexual characteristic *n.* Any of various anatomical, physiological, or behavioural characteristics, such as voice quality, abundance of facial hair, or breast development, that first appear in humans at puberty and differentiate between the sexes without having a direct reproductive function.

second best *n.* One that is slightly or just below the best, as in quality, value, or importance. **—sec·ond-best** (séckənd-bést) *adj.*

second chamber *n.* The upper house in a bicameral legislative body.

second childhood *n.* Senility; dotage.

second class *n.* 1. The group or class that is next below the first or highest, as in quality, rank, or value. 2. The class on a train or other means of transport ranking next below first class.

sec·ond-class, second class (séckənd-klaáss ‖ séckənt-, -klass) *adj.* 1. **a.** In the rank or class that is next below the first or best. **b.** Inferior; second-rate. **c.** Socially, economically, or politically disadvantaged: *a second-class citizen.* 2. Of, pertaining to, or designating travel accommodation ranking below the highest or first class. 3. Of, pertaining to, or designating a class of mail in the United Kingdom that is handled and delivered more slowly than first-class mail. 4. *British.* Pertaining to or designating an honours degree or examination result in the class below a first. **—sec·ond-class** *adv.*

Second Coming *n.* The return of Christ as judge upon the last day. Also called "Second Advent", "parousia".

second cousin *n.* See **cousin.**

sec·ond-de·gree burn (séckənd-di-grée) *n.* A burn that damages underlying skin tissue. Not in current technical usage.

Second Empire *n.* 1. The French empire and government of Napoleon III. 2. The period of Napoleon III's reign (1852–70).

~adj. Of, resembling, or pertaining to the ornate style of furniture and architecture developed in the Second Empire.

second estate *n. Often capital* **S,** *capital* **E.** The aristocracy, especially as distinguished from other classes. See **first estate, third estate, fourth estate.**

sec·ond-gen·e·ra·tion (séckənd-jénnə-ráysh'n) *adj.* Pertaining or belonging to a generation whose grandparents were original migrants: *second-generation Australians.*

second growth *n.* Trees that cover an area after the removal of the original forest growth as by cutting or fire.

sec·ond-guess (séckənd-géss) *v.* **-guessed, -guessing, -guesses.** *Chiefly U.S.* —*tr.* **1.** To criticise (a decision) after the outcome is known. **2.** To anticipate the moves of; outwit. —*intr.* To criticise a decision in retrospect. **—sec·ond-guess·er** *n.*

second hand¹ *n.* The hand of a timepiece that marks the seconds.

second hand² *n.* An intermediary person or source. Usually preceded by *at: heard at second hand.*

sec·ond·hand, sec·ond-hand (séckənd-hánd || séckənt-) *adj.* **1.** Previously used or owned by another; not new. **2.** Dealing in previously used goods. **3.** Obtained or derived from another; not original. **—sec·ond·hand, sec·ond-hand** *adv.*

sec·ond-in-com·mand (séckənd-in-kə-ma̋and || -mánd) *n., pl.* **seconds-in-command.** The person next in authority to someone in charge; especially, a military officer ranking second to a commanding officer.

second lieutenant *n.* An officer of the British Army of the lowest commissioned grade, ranking below a lieutenant, equivalent in rank to a sublieutenant in the Navy and a pilot officer in the Air Force.

sec·ond·ly (séckəndli) *adv.* In the second place; second. Used chiefly to introduce a second enumerated point.

second mate *n.* The officer on a merchant ship ranking below the first mate. Also called "second officer".

se·cond·ment (si-kóndmənt, sə-) *n. British.* A transfer, as of an officer or employee, to a different position or department, where his expertise is needed temporarily, or where he may gain experience.

second mortgage *n.* A mortgage on property that is already mortgaged and that has a claim secondary to the first mortgage.

second nature *n.* An acquired personal disposition, tendency, or habit so long practised as to seem innate.

se·con·do (se-kón-dō, si-) *n., pl.* **-di** (-dee). *Music.* **1.** The second part in a concert piece; especially, the lower part in a piano duet. **2.** One who performs such a part. [Italian, "second", from Latin *secundus,* SECOND (next).]

second person *n. Grammar.* The form of a pronoun, verb, or verb inflection used in referring to the person or persons addressed; for example, *you* and *shall* in *you shall not enter.*

sec·ond-rate (séckənd-ráyt) *adj.* Not of the best quality; mediocre; inferior. **—sec·ond-rat·er** *n.*

second reading *n.* The intermediate stage in the enactment of a law in a legislative body, especially: **1.** In Britain, the debate and vote on a bill's general features. **2.** In the United States, the debate and vote on a bill, sometimes with amendments, after a committee has reported on it.

Second Republic *n.* **1.** The French republic and government from 1848 to 1852. **2.** The period of this republic's existence.

second sex *n.* Women collectively; the female sex. Preceded by *the.* Usually considered offensive.

second sight *n.* The ability to perceive future or remote events or things; clairvoyance.

sec·ond-strike (séckənd-strīk) *adj.* Designating, based on, or employing nuclear weapons capable of retaliating after an initial enemy attack: *a second-strike force; second-strike capability.*

second string *n. British.* A person or thing held in reserve.
~*adj.* Also **sec·ond-string** (séckənd-stríng). *Chiefly U.S.* **1.** Designating or pertaining to a reserve player or team. **2.** Second-rate; inferior.

second thought *n. Usually plural.* A revised opinion on a matter, especially when it has previously been considered too quickly. **—on second thoughts.** Used to introduce a revised opinion.

second wind *n.* Renewed energy or ability to function, as after fatigue or breathlessness through exertion.

Second World *n.* The countries of the Soviet bloc. See **First World.**

Second World War *n.* **World War II** *(see).*

se·cre·cy (seékrə-si) *n.* **1.** The fact or condition of being secret or hidden. **2.** The ability to keep secrets. **3.** A tendency to be secretive or to conceal things. [Middle English, variant of *secretee,* from *secre(t),* SECRET.]

se·cret (seé-krit, -krət) *adj.* **1.** Kept from general knowledge or view; kept hidden. **2.** Tending not to disclose information; discreet. **3.** Operating in a clandestine or confidential manner. **4.** Not visibly expressed or acknowledged. **5.** Not frequented; secluded. **6.** Known or shared only by the initiated: *secret rites.* **7.** Beyond ordinary understanding; mysterious. **8.** Of, pertaining to, or containing information whose secrecy is important to national security.
~*n.* **1.** Something kept hidden from others or known only to oneself or to a few. **2.** Something that remains beyond understanding or explanation; a mystery. **3.** A factor or element needed to achieve a particular end or state: *the secret of her success.* **4.** *Capital* **S.** A variable prayer said after the Offertory and before the Preface in the Tridentine Mass. **—in secret.** In a manner or place not known to others; in secrecy. [Middle English *secre(t),* from Old French, from Latin *sēcrētus,* separate, out of the way, secret, from the past participle of *sēcernere,* to put apart, separate : *sē,* apart + *cernere,* to separate.] **—se·cret·ly** *adv.*

Synonyms: *secret, stealthy, covert, clandestine, furtive, surreptitious, underhand.*

secret agent *n.* A spy.

se·cret·a·gogue (si-kreétə-gog || -gōg) *n. Physiology.* An agent that stimulates glandular secretion. [SECRET(E) + -AGOGUE.]

sec·re·taire (séckrə-tair) *n.* Also *U.S.* **secretary.** A writing desk with a compartment that can be closed. [French, secretary.]

sec·re·tar·i·at (séckrə-tair-i-ət, -at) *n.* **1. a.** A department of an international or public organisation that administers and executes the organisation's decisions and programmes under the direction of a secretary-general or secretary. **b.** The premises or staff of such a department. **2.** The position of a secretary. **3.** A group of secretaries in a company or other organisation.

sec·re·tar·y (séckrə-tri || -terri) *n., pl.* **-ies.** *Abbr.* **sec., secy. 1. a.** A person employed to handle correspondence, keep files, and do clerical work for an individual or company. **b.** An officer who keeps records of meetings and legal transactions and is responsible for the day-to-day business of a club, society, or similar organisation. **c.** A **company secretary** *(see).* **2.** *Often capital* **S. a.** In Britain, a secretary of state. **b.** In the United States, Australia, and certain other countries, a minister who is the head of a government department: *Secretary Shultz.* **3.** A diplomatic officer assisting an ambassador or minister. **4.** Variant of **secretaire.** [Middle English *secretarie,* from Medieval Latin *sēcrētārius,* confidential officer, secretary, from Latin *sēcrētus,* SECRET.] **—sec·re·tar·i·al** (-tair-i-əl) *adj.*

secretary bird *n.* A large southern African bird of prey, *Sagittarius serpentarius.* [The quills on its crest resemble quill pens.]

sec·re·tar·y-gen·er·al (séckrə-tri-jén-rəl, -jénnə- || -terri-) *n., pl.* **secretaries-general.** *Sometimes capital* **S,** *capital* **G.** A principal administrative officer, as in certain political parties or international bodies: *the secretary-general of NATO.*

secretary of state *n., pl.* **secretaries of state.** *Often capital* **S,** *capital* **S. 1.** A British minister who heads any of several government departments. **2.** The foreign minister of the United States.

se·crete¹ (si-kreét) *tr.v.* **-creted, -creting, -cretes.** To generate and separate out (a substance) from cells or bodily fluids. [Back-formation from SECRETION.] **—se·cre·tor** *n.*

se·crete² *tr.v.* **-creted, -creting, -cretes. 1.** To conceal. **2.** To appropriate (money, for example) secretly. —See Synonyms at **hide.** [From obsolete *secret,* to conceal, keep secret, from SECRET.]

se·cre·tin (si-kreétin) *n.* A hormone secreted in the duodenum to stimulate the flow of pancreatic juice. [SECRET(ION) + -IN.]

se·cre·tion (si-kreésh'n) *n.* **1.** The process of secreting a substance, especially one that is not a waste, from blood or cells. **2.** A substance so secreted. [Latin *sēcrētiō* (stem *sēcrētiōn-*), separation, from *sēcernere,* to separate. See **secret.**]

se·cre·tive (seékrətiv, si-kreétiv) *adj.* **1.** Tending not to disclose information; uncommunicative. **2.** Secretory. **—se·cre·tive·ly** *adv.* **—se·cre·tive·ness** *n.*

se·cre·tor (si-kreétər) *n.* A person in whose saliva and other body fluids the A or B antigens determining blood group can be detected.

se·cre·to·ry (si-kreétəri) *adj.* Pertaining to or performing the function of secretion.

secret police *n.* A police force, operating largely in secrecy and often with illegal methods, serving to control dissidents and ensure the security of the state.

secret service *n.* **1.** A government agency pursuing intelligence and counterintelligence activities. **2.** The activities of such an agency. **3.** *Capital* **S,** *capital* **S.** The branch of the U.S. Treasury Department concerned with the protection of the President, other leading public figures, and their families, and with the suppression of counterfeiting. In this sense, preceded by *the.*

sect (sekt) *n.* **1.** A group of people forming a distinct unit within a larger group by virtue of certain refinements or distinctions of belief or practice. **2. a.** A breakaway religious body; especially, one regarded as extreme, intolerant, or exclusive by the larger group from which it has separated. **b.** Any religious denomination, especially one regarded as exclusive or outlandish. **3.** Any small faction united by common interests or beliefs: *a Maoist sect.* [Middle English *secte,* from Old French, from Latin *secta,* "following", from *sectus,* archaic past participle of *sequī,* to follow.]

sect. sector.

-sect *v. comb. form.* Indicates cut or divide; for example, **trisect, bisect.** [Latin *sectus,* past participle of *secāre,* to cut.]

sec·tar·i·an (sek-tair-i-ən) *adj.* **1.** Pertaining to, characteristic of, or involving a sect or faction or its members. **2.** Adhering or confined to the dogmatic views of a sect.
~*n.* **1.** A member of a sect. **2.** One characterised by bigoted adherence to a factional viewpoint. **—sec·tar·i·an·ise** *v.* **—sec·tar·i·an·ism** *n.*

sec·ta·ry (séktəri) *n., pl.* **-ries. 1.** A sectarian. **2.** A dissenter from an established church; specifically, a Protestant nonconformist in the 17th and 18th centuries. [Medieval Latin *sectārius,* from Latin *secta,* SECT.]

sec·tile (sék-tīl || *U.S. also* -t'l) *adj.* Capable of being cut or severed smoothly by a knife. [Latin *sectilis,* from *secāre,* to cut.] **—sec·til·i·ty** (sek-tílləti) *n.*

sec·tion (séksh'n) *n.* **1. a.** Any of several component or constituent parts or groups; a portion. **b.** A part separated from a main body by or as if by cutting. **2.** Any division or grouping within an organised whole: *the accounts section.* **3.** A subdivision of a written work. **4.** A division of a statute or legal code. **5.** A grouping in an orchestra or band, consisting of members who play the same type of instrument. **6.** In printing, a **signature** *(see).* **7.** The act or process of separating or cutting; especially, the surgical separation of tissue. **8.** A thin slice, as of tissue, suitable for microscopic examination. **9.** A segment of a fruit, especially a citrus fruit. **10.** The representation of a solid object as it would appear if cut by an intersecting plane, so that the internal structure is displayed. **11.** In geometry, the planar configuration formed by the intersection of a solid by a

secretary bird *Snakes, mice, and lizards are the main prey of the secretary bird, which hunts on foot in the African savannah. The bird was named because of the quills on its crest – like the quill pens 19th-century secretaries pushed into the backs of their wigs.*

plane. Also called "plane section". **12.** *U.S.* A district or area with some particular characteristic. **13. a.** *N.Z.* A plot of land. **b.** *U.S.* A land unit of one square mile. **14. a.** *Military.* An army tactical unit smaller than a platoon and larger than a squad. **b.** A unit of vessels or aircraft within a division. **15. a.** A character (§) used in printing to mark the beginning of a section. **b.** This character used as the fourth in a series of reference marks for footnotes. In both senses, also called "section mark". **—in section.** In the view revealed by taking a section.
~tr.v. **sectioned, -tioning, -tions. 1.** To separate or divide into parts. **2.** To separate (tissue) surgically. **3.** To cut so as to reveal a section. [French, from Latin *sectiō* (stem *sectiōn-*), a cutting, from *sect-*, past participial stem of *secāre,* to cut.]

-section *n. comb. form.* Indicates the act or process of dividing or cutting; for example, **vivisection.** [From SECTION.]

sec·tion·al (séksh'n'l) *adj.* **1.** Pertaining to or characteristic of a particular section: *sectional prejudice in society.* **2.** Composed of or divided into component sections. **—sec·tion·al·ly** *adv.*

sec·tion·al·ise, sec·tion·al·ize (séksh'n'l-īz) *tr.v.* **-ised, -ising, -ises. 1.** To divide into sections, especially into geographical sections. **2.** To make sectional in nature or outlook. **—sec·tion·al·i·sa·tion** (-ī-záysh'n || *U.S.* -i-) *n.*

sec·tion·al·ism (séksh'n'l-iz'm) *n.* Excessive devotion to sectional interests. **—sec·tion·al·ist** *n. & adj.*

sec·tor (sék-tər || -tawr) *n. Abbr.* **sec., sect. 1.** In geometry, the portion of a circle bounded by two radii and one of the intercepted arcs. **2.** A measuring instrument consisting of two graduated arms hinged together at one end. **3.** *Military.* **a.** A division of a defensive position for which one unit is responsible. **b.** A division of an offensive position; a zone of action. **4.** A part or division of something, such as a specialised field of activity or interest: *the public sector of the economy.* [Late Latin, from Latin, cutter, from *secāre,* to cut.] **—sec·tor·al, sec·tor·i·al** (sek-táwr-i-əl || -tōr-) *adj.*

sec·u·lar (séckewlər) *adj.* **1.** Of or pertaining to temporal rather than to spiritual matters; worldly. **2.** Not pertaining to or concerned with religion or a religious body: *secular schools.* **3.** Advocating or characterised by secularism: *a secular outlook.* **4.** Not following monastic vows or living in a religious community. Said of the clergy. Compare **regular. 5.** Occurring or observed once in an age or century. **6.** Lasting for centuries.
~n. **1.** A secular clergyman. **2.** A layman. [Middle English *seculer,* from Old French, from Latin *saeculāris,* from *saeculum*†, generation, age.] **—sec·u·lar·ly** *adv.*

sec·u·la·rise, sec·u·la·rize (séckewlə-rīz) *tr.v.* **-rised, -rising, -rises. 1.** To transfer from ecclesiastical or religious to civil or lay use or ownership. **2.** To draw away from religious influences or orientation; make worldly. **3.** To lift the monastic rules from (a cleric); make secular. **—sec·u·lar·i·sa·tion** (-rī-záysh'n || *U.S.* -ri-) *n.* **—sec·u·la·ris·er** *n.*

sec·u·lar·ism (séckewlə-riz'm) *n.* **1.** Religious scepticism or indifference. **2.** The view that religious considerations should be excluded from civil affairs or public education. **—sec·u·lar·ist** *n.* **—sec·u·lar·is·tic** (-rístik) *adj.*

sec·u·lar·i·ty (séckew-lárrəti) *n., pl.* **-ties. 1.** The condition or quality of being secular. **2.** Something secular.

secular parallax *n. Astronomy.* The continuously increasing angular displacement in the position of stars resulting from the motion of the sun through space. See **parallax.**

se·cund (si-kúnd, sée-kund, sé-) *adj. Botany.* Arranged on or turned to one side of an axis. [Latin *secundus,* following, second.]

sec·un·dines (séckən-dīnz, -dinz, si-kúndinz) *pl.n. Physiology.* The **afterbirth** *(see).* [Late Latin *secundīnae,* from Latin *secundus,* second, following. See **secund.**]

se·cure (si-kéwr, sə-) *adj.* **-curer, -curest. 1.** Free from danger or risk of loss or escape; safe. **2.** Free from fear or doubt; not anxious or unsure. **3. a.** Not likely to fail or give way; stable; strong. **b.** Well-fastened. **4.** Assured; certain; guaranteed. **5.** *Archaic.* Careless or overconfident.
~v. **secured, -curing, -cures.** *—tr.* **1.** To guard from danger or risk of loss; specifically, to fortify or consolidate (a military position). **2.** To make firm or tight; fasten. **3.** To make certain; guarantee; ensure. **4. a.** To guarantee payment to (a creditor). **b.** To guarantee payment of (a loan, for example) with a pledge. **5.** To confine or lock up. **6.** To get possession of; acquire; procure. **7.** To bring about; effect. *—intr.* To become or make oneself safe. Used with *against.* [Latin *sēcūrus,* "without care" : *sē,* without + *cūra,* care.] **—se·cur·a·ble** *adj.* **—se·cure·ly** *adv.* **—se·cure·ment** *n.* **—se·cure·ness** *n.* **—se·cur·er** *n.*

Securities and Exchange Commission *n. Abbr.* **SEC** A U.S. governmental agency that supervises the issue and exchange of securities so as to protect investors against malpractice.

se·cu·ri·ty (si-kéwr-əti-, sə-) *n., pl.* **-ties. 1.** The state of being secure; especially: **a.** Freedom from risk or danger. **b.** Freedom from doubt, anxiety, or fear. **2.** Anything that gives or assures safety. **3.** Something deposited or given as assurance of the fulfilment of an obligation; a pledge. **4.** One who undertakes to guarantee the obligation of another; a surety. **5. a.** A document that guarantees the right of the holder to repayment, as of a debt or claim. **b.** *Plural.* Broadly, investments in the form of stocks, shares, and bonds. **6. a.** Measures adopted to thwart theft, espionage, escape, or attack. **b.** An organisation or department entrusted with such operations. [Middle English *securite,* from Latin *sēcūritās* (stem *sēcūritāt-*), from *sēcūrus,* SECURE.]

security blanket *n. Chiefly U.S.* A blanket or other familiar object carried about by a child to give a feeling of security.

security clearance *n.* **1.** The investigation of persons or groups to ensure that they are not a security risk, before allowing them access to confidential information or to people or places requiring protection. **2.** The permission or clearance subsequently granted.

Security Council *n. Abbr.* **SC** The permanent peace-keeping organ of the United Nations, composed of five permanent members and ten elected members.

security risk *n.* **1.** A government servant or candidate for government service thought to be a danger to national security because of dissident political beliefs, liability to blackmail, or unreliability of character. **2.** Any person thought likely to be disloyal.

secy. secretary.

se·dan (si-dán, sə-) *n.* **1.** A sedan chair. **2.** *U.S.* A saloon car. [Perhaps obscurely from Vulgar Latin *sedda* (unattested), variant of Latin *sella,* seat, chair.]

sedan chair *n.* A portable enclosed chair for one person, fashionable in Britain in the 17th and 18th centuries, having poles front and rear and carried by two men. Also called "sedan".

se·date¹ (si-dáyt) *adj.* Serenely deliberate in character or manner; composed; collected. See Synonyms at **serious.** [Latin *sēdātus,* past participle of *sēdāre,* to settle, calm, compose, from *sedēre,* to sit.] **—se·date·ly** *adv.* **—se·date·ness** *n.*

se·date² *tr.v.* **-dated, -dating, -dates.** To administer a sedative to (a patient). [Back-formation from SEDATIVE.]

se·da·tion (si-dáysh'n) *n.* **1.** The reduction of stress or excitement by administration of a sedative. **2.** The calm relaxed condition induced by a sedative.

sed·a·tive (séddətiv) *adj.* Having a soothing, calming, or tranquillising effect.
~n. A sedative agent or drug. [Middle English, from Medieval Latin *sēdātīvus,* from *sedāre,* to calm, settle; see **sedate** (adjective).]

Sed·don (sédd'n), **Richard (John),** also known as King Dick (1845–1906). British-born New Zealand politician. He became a Liberal cabinet minister in 1891 and was prime minister (1893–1906).

sed·en·tar·y (sédd'n-təri, -tri || *U.S.* -terri) *adj.* **1.** Characterised by or requiring much sitting: *a sedentary job.* **2.** Accustomed to sitting or to taking little exercise. **3.** Remaining in one area; not migratory: *sedentary birds.* **4.** Seated or in a sitting posture: *a sedentary statue.* **5.** *Zoology.* Attached to a surface and not free-moving. Said of a barnacle, for example. [French *sédentaire,* from Latin *sedentārius,* from *sedēns* (stem *sedent-*), present participle of *sedēre,* to sit.] **—sed·en·tar·i·ly** *adv.* **—sed·en·tar·i·ness** *n.*

Se·der (sáydər) *n., pl.* **-ders** or **Sedarim** (si-daárim, sáydər-éem). *Sometimes small* **s.** *Judaism.* The feast commemorating the exodus of the Israelites from Egypt, celebrated on the first evening or first two evenings of Passover. [Hebrew *sēdher,* "order", "arrangement".]

se·de·runt (si-déer-ənt, say-, -dáir-, -ōōnt) *n. Scottish.* **1.** A session or sitting, especially of an ecclesiastical assembly. **2.** The people present at such a session. **3.** Any session of talking or drinking. [Latin, they (the persons named below) sat, from *sedēre,* to sit.]

sedge (sej) *n.* Any of numerous plants of the family Cyperaceae, especially of the genus *Carex,* resembling grasses but having solid rather than hollow stems and often found near water. [Middle English *segge,* Old English *secg,* from Germanic.] **—sedg·y** *adj.*

sedge *Related to the grass family, sedge is a rushlike plant with a solid and usually three-sided stem. It grows in bogs and marshes.*

sedge warbler *n.* A small bird, *Acrocephalus schoenobaenus,* commonly found near water, having a brown streaked plumage.

se·dil·i·a (si-díli-ə, se-, -dée-, -dí-) *pl.n. Singular* **sedile** (-li). *Usually used with a plural verb.* The seats or set of seats, generally three, in the sanctuary of a church for the use of the celebrant and his ministers. [Latin *sedīlia,* plural of *sedīle,* seat, from *sedēre,* to sit.]

sed·i·ment (séddi-mənt) *n.* **1.** Material that settles to the bottom of a liquid; dregs; lees. **2.** Material comprising weathered particles of pre-existing rock, or particles of chemical or organic origin, deposited by wind, water, or glacial ice. [French, from Latin *sedimentum,* a settling, from *sedēre,* to sit, settle.]

sed·i·men·ta·ry (séddi-méntəri, -tri) *adj.* **1.** Of, containing, resembling, or derived from sediment. **2.** *Geology.* Of, designating, or pertaining to rocks formed from sediment.

sed·i·men·ta·tion (séddi-men-táysh'n, -mən-) *n.* The act or process of depositing sediment; especially, the process of forming sedimentary rocks.

sed·i·men·tol·o·gy (séddi-men-tólləji, -mən-) *n.* The study of the classification and origin of sedimentary rocks and associated geological deposits. [SEDIMENT + -LOGY.] **—sed·i·men·tol·o·gic·al** (-méntə-lójik'l) *adj.* **—sed·i·men·tol·o·gist** (-tólləjist) *n.*

se·di·tion (si-dísh'n, sə-) *n.* **1.** Conduct or language inciting to rebellion against the authority of the state. **2.** *Archaic.* An insurrection; a rebellion. [Middle English *sedicioun,* from Old French *sedition,* from Latin *sēditiō* (stem *sēditiōn-*), "a going apart", separation : *sē, sēd,* apart + *itiō,* act of going, from *īre* (past participle *itus*), to go.]

se·di·tious (si-díshəss, sə-) *adj.* **1.** Of, resembling, or characterised by sedition. **2.** Engaged in or inclined to sedition. —See Synonyms at **insubordinate. —se·di·tious·ly** *adv.* **—se·di·tious·ness** *n.*

se·duce (si-déwss || -dōōss) *tr.v.* **-duced, -ducing, -duces. 1. a.** To lead (a person) away from duty or proper conduct. **b.** Broadly, to entice into wrongful behaviour; corrupt. **2.** To induce to have sexual intercourse with one. **3. a.** To persuade or beguile. Often used with *into.* **b.** To win over; attract. —See Synonyms at **lure.** [Middle English *seduisen,* from Old French *seduire* (present stem *seduis-*), from Latin *sēdūcere,* to lead away : *sē,* apart + *dūcere,* to lead.] **—se·duc·er** *n.* **—se·duce·a·ble, se·duc·i·ble** *adj.*

se·duc·tion (si-dúksh'n) *n.* Also *archaic* **se·duce·ment** (si-déwss-mənt || -dóoss-). **1.** The act of seducing or the condition of being seduced. **2.** Something that seduces or has the qualities to seduce to wrongdoing; a temptation. **3.** *Often plural.* Something that attracts; an enticement. [French *séduction,* from Latin *sēductiō* (stem *sēductiōn-*), from *sēdūcere* (past participle *sēductus),* SEDUCE.]

se·duc·tive (si-dúktiv) *adj.* Tending to seduce; alluring; beguiling. **—se·duc·tive·ly** *adv.* **—se·duc·tive·ness** *n.*

se·duc·tress (si-dúk-triss, -trəss) *n.* A female seducer.

sed·u·lous (séddewləss) *adj.* **1.** Diligent; assiduous. **2.** Deliberate and industrious; painstaking: *sedulous flattery.* —See Synonyms at **busy.** [Latin *sēdulus,* diligent, zealous, from *sē dolō,* "without guile", hence with zeal : *sē,* without + *dolus,* guile.] **—se·du·li·ty** (si-déw-ləti || -dóo-), **sed·u·lous·ness** *n.* **—sed·u·lous·ly** *adv.*

se·dum (séedəm) *n.* Any of numerous rock plants of the genus *Sedum,* having thick, fleshy leaves and clusters of starlike flowers. See **orpine, stonecrop.** [Latin *sedum*†, houseleek.]

see[1] (see) *v.* **saw** (saw), **seen** (seen), **seeing, sees.** *—tr.* **1.** To perceive with the eye. **2.** To realise or come to know by seeing: *saw that the driver was in difficulties.* **3.** To have a mental image of; visualise. **4.** To understand; comprehend. **5.** To regard in a particular way; view: *Sees things differently now.* **6. a.** To imagine; believe possible: *I don't see him as a teacher.* **b.** To consider as likely: *I can see her getting angry when she finds out.* **7.** To foresee. **8.** To know through first-hand experience; undergo: *He saw some service in North Africa.* **9.** To be characterised by, be the occasion of, or bring forth: *Her long reign saw the heyday of colonialism.* **10.** To find out; ascertain: *See if he's ready.* **11.** *Abbr.* **s.** To refer to; read: *See page xi of the Introduction.* **12.** To discern; recognise: *saw the snags straight away.* **13. a.** To meet socially, especially often or regularly. **b.** To visit socially or for consultation: *see a doctor.* **c.** To receive, as for consultation. **14.** To cause to undergo something unpleasant. Used only in expressions of defiant anger: *I'll see him in hell before I agree.* **15.** To find attractive: *What do you see in him?* **16.** To watch without taking action: *How can you see a dog being kicked?* **17.** To watch or view as a spectator or tourist: *seeing the sights of London.* **18.** To escort; attend: *saw them home.* **19.** To make sure; take care: *See that it gets done right away.* **20.** To learn, as by reading or hearing on the radio: *I see that the railway strike has been called off.* **21.** In card games: **a.** To match (a bet). **b.** To match the bet of (another player). *—intr.* **1. a.** To have the power to see objects. **b.** To exercise that power. **c.** To perceive things with any of the senses, as if by the power of sight: *see with one's fingers.* **2.** To understand; comprehend. **3.** To consider; think a matter over: *Let's see, which should we take?* **4.** To have foresight: *We can see only to the end of the year.* **—see about. 1.** To attend to. **2.** To investigate. **—see here.** Used to demand a more reasonable attitude. **—see off. 1.** To be present to wish goodbye to (a person leaving on a journey). **2.** To be rid of, as by outlasting, ousting, or defeating. **—see out.** To last until the end, departure, or death of. **—see over.** To inspect by visiting. **—see (someone) right.** *Informal.* To make sure that (someone) is well looked after or properly rewarded. **—see to.** To attend to. **—See you.** *Informal.* Used as a farewell. [See, saw, seen; Middle English *se(e)n, sauh, seyen,* Old English *sēon, seah* (plural *sāwon*), *gesewen.*]

Synonyms: *see, behold, note, notice, espy, descry, observe, contemplate, survey, view, perceive, discern, remark, scan.*

see[2] *n.* **1.** The official seat, centre of authority, jurisdiction, or office of a bishop. **2.** A diocese. [Middle English, from Anglo-French *se, sed,* from Vulgar Latin *sedem* (unattested), from Latin *sēdem,* accusative of *sēdes,* "seat", "residence".]

See·beck effect (sée-bek; *German* záy-) *n.* The production of an electric current in a circuit consisting of two wires of different metals joined at their ends, when the junctions so formed are maintained at different temperatures. Compare **Peltier effect.** [After Thomas *Seebeck* (1770–1831), German physicist.]

seed (seed) *n.* **1.** A fertilised and ripened plant ovule containing an embryo and its food source. **2.** The hard, seedlike fruit of certain plants, such as grasses. **3.** Broadly, any propagative part of a plant, such as a tuber or spore. **4.** Seeds collectively. **5.** Anything resembling a seed in size or shape. **6.** A source or beginning; a germ. **7.** *Formal.* Offspring; progeny. **8.** *Archaic.* Sperm; semen. **9.** A **seed oyster** *(see).* **10.** A small crystal added to a supersaturated solution or a supercooled liquid to cause crystallisation. **11.** *Sports.* A seeded player. **—go** or **run to seed. 1.** To pass into the seed-bearing stage. **2.** To become weak or devitalised; deteriorate. **—in seed.** Bearing seeds. Said of a plant.

~v. **seeded, seeding, seeds.** *—tr.* **1.** To plant seeds in (land); sow. **2.** To plant in soil. **3.** To remove the seeds from (fruit). **4. a.** To add a small crystal to (a supersaturated solution or a supercooled liquid) to cause crystallisation. **b.** To sprinkle (a supercooled cloud) with particles, as of silver iodide, in order to produce rain by condensation and precipitation. **5.** *Sports.* **a.** To arrange (the drawing for positions in a tournament) so that the more skilled contestants meet only in the later rounds. **b.** To rank (a contestant) in this way. *—intr.* **1.** To sow seed. **2.** To produce or shed seed. [Middle English *seed, seid,* Old English *sǣd.*] **—seed·less** *adj.* **—seed·like** *adj.*

seed bank *n.* A place where plant seeds are stored at low temperatures.

seed·bed (séed-bed) *n.* **1.** A piece of land prepared for seeding. **2.** A place favourable to the development of something.

seed cake *n.* A sweet cake containing aromatic seeds, usually caraway seeds.

seed capsule *n.* The part of a fruit surrounding the seeds; the pericarp. Also called "seed case".

seed coat *n.* The outer protective covering of a seed; the testa.

seed corn *n.* **1.** Cereal grain that is kept or sold for sowing. **2.** Someone or something that forms a basis for future development.

seed·er (séedər) *n.* **1.** A machine or implement used for planting seeds. **2.** A machine used to remove the seeds from fruit.

seed fern *n.* Any seed-bearing fernlike plant of the extinct group Pteridospermae. Also called "pteridosperm".

seed leaf *n. Botany.* A **cotyledon** *(see).*

seed·ling (séedling) *n.* A young plant that develops by germination of a seed.

seed money *n.* Money needed or provided to start a new project.

seed oyster *n.* A young oyster; especially, one suitable for transplanting to another bed. Also called "seed".

seed pearl *n.* A very small, often imperfect, pearl.

seed plant *n.* A seed-bearing plant; a spermatophyte.

seed·pod (séed-pod) *n.* A **pod** *(see).*

seed potato *n.* A small potato tuber used for planting.

seeds·man (séedz-mən) *n., pl.* **-men** (-mən, -men). A dealer in seed.

seed·y (séedi) *adj.* **-ier, -iest. 1.** Having many seeds. **2.** Shabby-looking; disreputable in appearance. **3.** Tired or sick; out of sorts. **—seed·i·ly** *adv.* **—seed·i·ness** *n.*

see·ing (sée-ing) *conj.* Also **seeing that,** *informal* **seeing as.** Inasmuch as; in view of the fact that.

~n. Astronomy. The state of the atmosphere with respect to observation through telescopes.

seeing eye dog *n. U.S.* A **guide-dog** *(see).*

seek (seek) *v.* **sought** (sawt), **seeking, seeks.** *—tr.* **1.** To try to locate or discover; search for. **2.** To endeavour to obtain or reach. **3.** To move to; go to or towards: *Water seeks its own level.* **4.** To ask for; request: *seek professional advice.* **5.** To try; endeavour. Used with an infinitive: *sought to persuade them.* **6.** *Archaic.* To explore. *—intr.* To make a search or investigation. Often used with *after* or *for.* **—seek out.** To search determinedly for and find. [Seek, sought, sought; Middle English *seken, so(u)hte, soht,* Old English *sēcan, sōhte, sōht.*] **—seek·er** *n.*

seel (seel) *tr.v.* **seeled, seeling, seels.** To stitch closed the eyes of (a falcon, for example). [Middle English *silen,* from Old French *ciller,* from Medieval Latin *ciliāre,* from Latin *cilium,* eyelid.]

seem (seem) *intr.v.* **seemed, seeming, seems. 1.** To give the impression of being; appear. **2.** To appear, according to one's perception of the situation: *I can't seem to get the story straight.* **3.** To appear to be so; be evident: *It seems you object to the plan.* **4.** To appear to exist: *There seems no reason to postpone it.* [Middle English *semen,* to beseem, seem, from Old Norse *sœma,* to conform to, honour, from *sœmr,* fitting.]

Usage: Constructions like *can't seem* and *won't seem,* followed by an infinitive, are common in speech and informal writing: *I can't seem to find the key; He won't seem to learn.* They have sometimes attracted criticism, however, usually on the grounds that auxiliary verbs such as *can't/won't* apply to the main verb, and should not be made to apply to *seem.* Formal English would prefer alternative constructions, such as *do not seem able, seems that he won't.*

seem·ing (séeming) *adj.* Apparent, but usually not real; ostensible.

~n. Outward appearance; semblance. **—seem·ing·ly** *adv.* **—seem·ing·ness** *n.*

seem·ly (séemli) *adj.* **-lier, -liest. 1.** Conforming to accepted standards of conduct and good taste; proper; suitable. **2.** *Archaic.* Of pleasing appearance; handsome.

~adv. In a seemly manner. [Middle English *semely, semeliche,* from Old Norse *sœmiligr,* from *sœmr,* fitting.] **—seem·li·ness** *n.*

seen. Past participle of **see.**

seep (seep) *intr.v.* **seeped, seeping, seeps. 1.** To pass slowly through small openings or pores; ooze. **2.** To become gradually diffused: *The news seeped out.*

~n. **1.** A spot where water or petroleum oozes out of the ground. **2.** A seepage. [Perhaps variant of dialectal *sipe,* from Middle English *sipen,* Old English *sipian..*]

seep·age (séepij) *n.* **1.** The act or process of seeping or oozing; a leakage. **2.** A quantity of something that has seeped.

seer[1] (seer, sée-ər) *n.* **1.** One that sees; specifically, someone able to see into the future; a clairvoyant. **2.** Someone possessing spiritual insight; a sage. [Middle English, from *seen,* to SEE.]

seer[2] (seer) *n.* Any of several varying Indian units of weight; especially, a unit of weight equivalent to one kilogram (2.2 pounds). [Hindi *ser.*]

seer·ess (séer-iss, sée-ər-, -ess) *n.* A female seer.

seer·suck·er (séer-suckər) *n.* A light, thin fabric, generally cotton or rayon, with a crinkled surface and often a striped pattern. [Hindi *sirsakar,* from Persian *shīr-o-shakar,* "milk and sugar" : *shīr,* milk, from Avestan *khshīra,* perhaps from Dravidian + *shakar,* sugar, akin to Sanskrit *śarkāra,* SUGAR.]

see·saw, see-saw (sée-saw, -sáw) *n.* **1.** A long plank balanced on a central fulcrum so that, sitting with a person on either end, one end goes up as the other goes down. Also *U.S.* "teeter", "teeter-totter". **2.** The act or game of riding a seesaw. **3.** A back-and-forth or up-and-down movement. Also used adjectively: *a seesaw motion.* **4.** An alternation between two situations or positions.

seed *The individual seeds of* Clematis vitalba, *or old man's beard, are attached to the hairy plumes which give the plant its name. The seeds are spread by the wind.*

PRONUNCIATION KEY

a, trap; aa, father; ai, fair; ar, star; aw, lawn; ay, play; b, bb, stab; rubber; ch, church; ck, ticket; d, dd, dead; ladder; e, dress; ee, bee; er, defer; ew, few; ewr, pure; ə, about; ər, letter; f, ff, fife; differ; g, gg, giggle; h, hat; i, kit; ī, price; īr, fire; j, judge; k, kick; l, ll, let; 'l, needle; m, mm, man; n, nn, no; 'n, sudden; ng, thing; o, lot; ō, no; ŏŏ, foot; ōō, shoe; oor, poor; ow, cow; owr, hour; oy, boy; p, pp, pepper; r, rr, red; s, ss, sauce; sh, ship; t, tt, totter; th, thick; th, this; smooth; u, cut; ur, turn; v, vv, valve; w, wet; y, yes; z, zz, zebra; zh, vision; pleasure

IN FOREIGN WORDS:

aN, ON, Saint-Saëns; hl, Llanelli; Hluhluwe; kh, loch; lough; Khaled

STRESS MARK:

in-sīt, insight; in-sít, incite

~intr.v. **seesawed** or **see-sawed, -sawing, -saws. 1.** To play on a seesaw. **2.** To move back and forth or up and down. **3.** To alternate or oscillate. [Reduplication of SAW (to cut), from the up-and-down movement of sawing.]

seethe (see͟th) v. **seethed, seething, seethes.** —intr. **1.** To churn and foam as if boiling. Used of a liquid. **2.** To move in agitated confusion. **3.** To be violently excited or agitated. Often used with with: seething with fury. **4.** Archaic. To come to a boil. —tr. Archaic. **1.** To boil. **2.** To soak; steep. [Middle English sethen, Old English sēothan.] —**seethe** tr.

see through tr.v. **1.** To understand the true character or nature of. **2.** British. To help or provide for in time of trouble or need. **3.** To stay with (something) until completion: see the job through.

see-through, see·through (see-thrōō) adj. Partially or completely transparent.

Se·fer·is (sə-fáir-iss, se-), **George,** pen name of Georgios Seferiadis (1900–71). Greek poet. A diplomat by profession, he was hailed as the poet of the future on the publication of such works as Strophé (1931). He won the Nobel prize for literature (1963).

seg·ment (ségmənt) n. **1.** Any of the parts into which something is or can be divided. **2.** In geometry, a portion of a figure cut off by a line or plane; especially: **a.** The area bounded by a chord and the arc of a curve subtended by the chord. **b.** The portion of a curve between any two points on the curve. **c.** The portion of a sphere bounded by two parallel planes intersecting or tangent to the sphere. **3.** Biology. A clearly differentiated, repeated subdivision of an organism or part, such as a metamere. ~v. (seg-mént, səg-) **segmented, -menting, -ments.** —tr. To divide into segments. —intr. To become divided into segments. [Latin segmentum, from secāre, to cut.] —**seg·men·tal** (seg-mént'l, səg-), **seg·men·tar·y** (ségmən-təri, -tri ‖ U.S. -terri) adj. —**seg·men·tal·ly** adv.

seg·men·ta·tion (ség-men-táysh'n, -mən-) n. **1.** Division into segments. **2.** Biology. **Cleavage** (see). **3.** Zoology. **Metameric segmentation** (see).

segmentation cavity n. Biology. A **blastocoel** (see).

se·gno (sénn-yō, sáyn-) n., pl. **-gni** (-yee). Music. A notational sign; especially, the sign marking the beginning or end of a repeat. [Italian, sign, from Latin signum.]

se·go lily (sée-gō) n. A plant, Calochortus nuttallii, of western North America, having showy flowers. [Sego, from Paiute.]

Se·go·vi·a (si-gṓvi-ə, se-). Capital of Segovia province, central Spain. Built on a hill above the river Eresma, it is still supplied with the river by a Roman aqueduct.

Segovia, Andrés (1893–). Spanish guitarist. Segovia stimulated new interest in the guitar as an instrument for serious music through his arrangements of Bach, Handel, and others.

Se·grè (sə-gráy, say-), **Emilio Gino** (1905–). Italian-born U.S. physicist. In 1937 he produced the first artificial element, technetium. He discovered antiprotons with Owen Chamberlain (1955), and they were jointly awarded the 1959 Nobel prize.

seg·re·gate (séggri-gayt) v. **-gated, -gating, -gates.** —tr. **1.** To separate or isolate from others or from a main body or group. **2.** To enforce the separation of (a race, class, or minority) from the rest of society. **3.** To divide (a society or community) along racial lines. —intr. **1.** To become separated from a main body or mass. **2.** To practise a policy of racial segregation. **3.** Genetics. To undergo segregation. [Latin sēgregāre, "to separate from the flock" : sē, apart + grex (stem greg-), flock.] —**seg·re·gate** (-gət, -git, -gayt) adj. —**seg·re·ga·tive** (-gaytiv), adj. —**seg·re·ga·tor** n.

seg·re·gat·ed (séggri-gaytid) adj. **1.** Practising or characterised by segregation, especially along racial lines. **2.** Restricted to the members of one race or other group: a segregated school. **3.** Providing separate facilities or divided for members of different races or other groups: segregated buses.

seg·re·ga·tion (séggri-gáysh'n) n. **1.** The act or process of segregating or the condition of being segregated. **2.** The policy and practice of imposing separation of races, as in schools, housing, and industry; especially, discriminatory practices against nonwhites in a society dominated by whites. **3.** Genetics. The separation into different gametes of paired alleles in meiosis.

seg·re·ga·tion·ist (séggri-gáysh'n-ist) n. One who advocates or practices a policy of racial segregation. —**seg·re·ga·tion·ist** adj.

seg·ue (ség-way, sáyg-) v. Music. An uninterrupted transition from one movement or piece of music to another. Also used as a direction to proceed to the next movement without a pause. ~intr.v. **segued, -gueing, -gues.** To proceed from one movement or piece of music to the next without a pause. [Italian, "it follows", from sequire, to follow, from Latin sequī.]

se·gui·di·lla (séggi-déel-yə, -dée-) n. **1.** A Spanish stanza form of four to seven short verses. **2.** A lively Spanish dance. **3.** The music for this dance, in triple time. [Spanish, from seguida, "sequence", from the feminine past participle of seguir, to follow, from Vulgar Latin sequere (unattested), from Latin sequī.]

sei·cen·to (say-chéntō) n. The 17th century, especially with regard to the Italian literature and art of the period. [Italian (mil) seicento, (one thousand) six hundred : sei, six, from Latin sex + cento, hundred, from Latin centum.]

seiche (saysh) n. A vibration of the surface of lakes, bays, channels, or inland seas as a result of seismic or atmospheric disturbances. [Swiss French seiche†.]

Seid·litz powder (sédlits) n. Sometimes plural. A cathartic consisting of Rochelle salts, sodium bicarbonate, and tartaric acid. Also

called "Rochelle powder". [So called because it has laxative properties similar to those of the spring water of Seidlitz, the German name of Sedlice, village in Bohemia.]

seif·dune n. A ridge of sand, often many miles long, crossing the desert parallel to the direction of the prevailing wind. [Seif, Arabic, sword.]

sei·gneur (sen-yúr, seen-; French se-nyór n. **1.** Formerly, a feudal lord or landowner, especially in France. **2.** Formerly in Çanada, the landlord of a large estate subdivided into smallholdings. **3.** The hereditary civil head of government of the island of Sark. [French, from Old French, from Vulgar Latin senior. See **seignior.**] —**sei·gneur·i·al** adj.

sei·gneur·y, sei·gneur·ie (sáyn-yəri, sén-, séen-) n., pl. **-ies. 1.** The power, status, estate, or house of a seigneur. **2.** The official designation of the island of Sark.

seign·ior (sáyn-yər ‖ -yawr) n. A man of rank; specifically, a feudal lord. [Middle English seignour, from Old French seigneur, from Medieval Latin senior, from Latin, older, comparative of senex, old.] —**sei·gnio·ri·al** (sayn-yáwr-i-əl ‖ -yór-) adj.

seign·ior·age (sáyn-yərij) n. A profit or revenue raised by the Crown from the minting of coins, usually by means of the difference between the value of the bullion used and the face value of the coin. [Middle English seigneurage, duty imposed by a lord as his prerogative, from Old French, from seigneur, **SEIGNIOR.**]

seign·ior·y (sáyn-yəri) n., pl. **-ies. 1.** The estate of a feudal lord; a manor. **2.** The authority and power of a feudal lord.

seine (sayn) n. A large fishing net made to hang vertically in the water by weights at the lower edge and floats at the top. ~v. **seined, seining, seines.** —intr. To fish with a seine. —tr. To fish for or catch with a seine. [Middle English seine, Old English segne, from West Germanic sagina (unattested), from Latin sagēna, from Greek sagēnē.]

Seine (sayn; French sen) River of north France rising in the Langres Plateau. It flows approximately 770 kilometres (480 miles), passing through Paris and reaching the English Channel at Le Havre. The Seine channel is dredged to allow ocean-going vessels to reach Rouen.

seise. Law. Variant of **seize.**

sei·sin (séezin) n. Law. Also chiefly U.S. **sei·zin.** Legal possession of a freehold estate. [Middle English, from Anglo-French sesine, Old French seisine, from seisir, to **SEIZE.**]

seism (síz'm) n. An **earthquake** (see). [Greek seismos, from seiein, to shake.]

seis·mic (sízmik) adj. Of, subject to, or caused by an earthquake or a natural or man-made earth vibration. [SEISM(O)- + -IC.] —**seis·mi·cal·ly** adv. —**seis·mic·i·ty** (sīz-míssəti) n.

seismic wave n. A vibration emitted by an earthquake or a man-made explosion.

seis·mism (síz-miz'm) n. The collective phenomena involved in earthquakes. [SEISM(O)- + -ISM.]

seismo-, seism– comb. form. Indicates earthquake; for example, **seismograph, seismism.** [Greek seismos, **SEISM.**]

seis·mo·gram (síz-mə-gram, -mō-) n. The record of an earth tremor made by a seismograph. [SEISMO- + -GRAM.]

seis·mo·graph (síz-mə-graf, -mō-, -graaf) n. An instrument for automatically detecting and recording the intensity, direction, and duration of any movement of the ground, especially that caused by an earthquake or man-made explosion. [SEISMO- + -GRAPH.] —**seis·mo·graph·ic** (-gráffik) adj. —**seis·mog·ra·pher** (sīz-móggrəfər) n. —**seis·mog·ra·phy** n.

seis·mol·o·gy (sīz-móllǝji) n. The geophysical science of earthquakes and of the mechanical properties of the earth's interior. [SEISMO- + -LOGY.] —**seis·mo·log·ic** (-mǝ-lójik), **seis·mo·log·i·cal** adj. —**seis·mo·log·i·cal·ly** adv. —**seis·mol·o·gist** (-móllǝjist) n.

seis·mom·e·ter (sīz-mómmitər) n. A detecting device that receives seismic waves. [SEISMO- + -METER.] —**seis·mo·metric** (sīzmǝ-méttrik), **seis·mo·met·ri·cal** adj.

seis·mo·scope (sízmǝ-skōp) n. An instrument that indicates the occurrence or time of occurrence of a seismic wave. [SEISMO- + -SCOPE.] —**seis·mo·scop·ic** (-skóppik) adj.

sei whale (say) n. A widely distributed, dark blue rorqual, Balaenoptera borealis, valued for its whalebone. [Partial translation of Norwegian sei-val : sei, coalfish + val, whale.]

seize (seez) v. **seized, seizing, seizes.** Also **seise** (for sense 5c). —tr. **1.** To grasp suddenly and forcibly; lay hold of; clutch or grab. **2.** To grasp with the mind; comprehend. **3.** To have a sudden and overpowering effect upon; possess or overwhelm. **4.** To take into custody; make a prisoner of; arrest. **5. a.** To take quick and forcible possession of; capture. **b.** To take possession of by legal authority or process; confiscate. **c.** Law. To put in legal possession, as of an estate or other property. Used chiefly in the passive with of. **6.** To avail oneself eagerly and immediately of (an opportunity). **7.** Nautical. To bind with turns of small line. —intr. **1.** To take up or lay hold eagerly or forcibly. Used with on or upon. **2. a.** To cohere or fuse with another part as a result of high pressure or temperature, restricting or preventing further motion. Often used with up. **b.** To come to a halt. Used with up: The talks seized up. [Middle English saisen, seisen, from Old French seisir, saisir, from Gallo-Latin sacīre (unattested), to claim, from Germanic.] —**seiz·a·ble** adj.

seizin. Variant of **seisin.**

seiz·ing (séezing) n. Nautical. A binding of larger lines made with multiple turns of smaller line.

sei·zure (séezhər) n. **1.** The act or an action of seizing or the state of

seismograph

MEASURING EARTHQUAKES
Needles to detect the Earth's faintest jolt

The needle of a delicate seismograph can pick up and define any movement in the ground, detecting and recording its direction, duration, and intensity. All earthquakes, however faint, emit shock waves, known as seismic waves, which radiate in all directions. These waves trigger the movement of the seismograph needle, and a pen fixed to its head traces the movement on a graph.

Modern seismographs consist of a rigid frame, with a weight suspended from a horizontal boom. Shock waves jolt the frame but the weight remains still, and the needle fixed to the weight traces the relative motion of the frame. The size of the shock waves, indicating the size of the earthquake, are measured on a scale created by an American, Charles F. Richter, in 1935. The scale is logarithmic; in it, a shock magnitude of 8, for example, is 10 times greater than 7, and 100 times greater than 6.

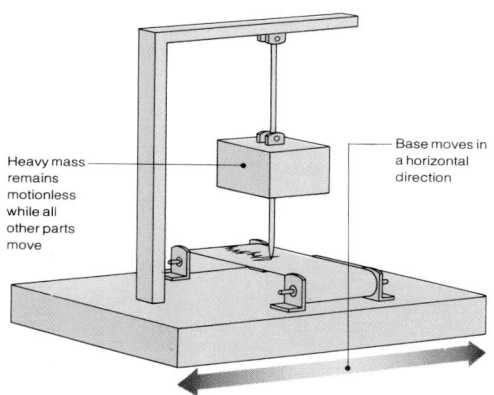

Heavy mass remains motionless while all other parts move

Base moves in a horizontal direction

HORIZONTAL MOVEMENT *Shock waves radiating vertically or horizontally can be measured by a seismograph. This one, its weight held on a pendulum and the needle pointing down, records horizontal movement in the Earth.*

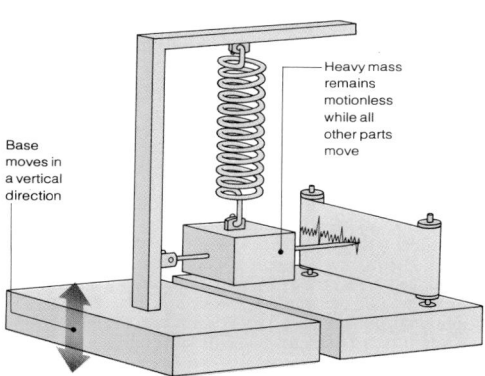

Heavy mass remains motionless while all other parts move

Base moves in a vertical direction

VERTICAL MOVEMENT *In this seismograph, the weight is suspended from the rigid boom by a spring, and the needle and pen are held horizontally. The base holding the boom will jolt vertically and the pen record vertical movement.*

being seized. **2.** A sudden paroxysm, such as an epileptic convulsion or heart attack.

se·jant (sée'jənt) *adj. Heraldry.* In a sitting position with forepaws extended to the ground: *a lion sejant.* [Variant of *seant,* from Old French, present participle of *seoir,* to sit, from Latin *sedere.*]

Sejm (saym) *n.* The unicameral legislative body of the Polish People's Republic. [Polish, assembly.]

se·la·chi·an (si-láyki-ən) *adj.* Of or belonging to the order Selachii, which includes the sharks and rays.
~*n.* A member of the Selachii. [New Latin *Selachii,* from Greek *selakhē,* plural of *selakhos†,* cartilaginous fish.]

sel·a·gi·nel·la (séllʒji-néllʒ) *n.* Any of numerous fernlike, usually prostrate plants of the genus *Selaginella,* having small scalelike leaves and bearing spores in cones. [New Latin, from Latin *selāgō†* (stem *selāgin-*), plant resembling the savin.]

se·lah (sée'lə) *n.* A Hebrew word of unknown meaning often marking the end of a verse in the Psalms and thought to be a term indicating a pause or rest. [Hebrew *selāh.*]

Se·lan·gor (si-láng-ər, sə-, -awr). State in the west of Peninsular Malaysia. Lying on the Strait of Malacca, it was a sultanate before becoming a British protectorate (1874). It has chemical, rubber, tin, and coal industries. Shah Alum is the capital.

sel·dom (séldəm) *adv.* Not often; infrequently; rarely.
~*adj. Archaic.* Infrequent; rare. [Middle English *selden, seldom,* Old English *seldan,* from Common Germanic *seldo-* (unattested).] —**sel·dom·ness** *n.*
Usage: Acceptable idioms include *seldom if ever* and *seldom or never,* but not *seldom or ever* or *seldom ever,* though the latter pair are sometimes encountered in informal speech. See also **rarely.**

se·lect (si-lekt, sə-) *v.* **-lected, -lecting, -lects.** —*tr.* To choose from among several; take in preference; pick out. —*intr.* To make a choice or selection; choose. —See Synonyms at **choose.**
~*adj.* **1.** Singled out in preference; chosen; picked out. **2.** Of special value or quality; choice. **3.** Open to or made up of a limited number of people, especially those of high social or economic status: *select company.* [Latin *sēligere* (past participle *sēlectus*), to choose out: *sē,* apart + *legere,* to choose.] —**se·lect·ness** *n.*

select committee *n.* In the British Parliament, a committee appointed by either of the two Houses to investigate a matter.

se·lec·tion (si-léksh'n, sə-) *n.* **1. a.** The act of selecting or the fact of being selected; choosing; choice. **b.** That which is selected. **2.** A carefully chosen or representative collection of persons or things. **3.** *Sports.* A contestant or runner singled out, as by a sports writer, as being likely to win or gain a place in a contest or race. **4.** A range of items of the same kind, as of goods for sale: *a good selection of wines.* **5.** *Biology.* A process that favours or induces the survival and perpetuation of one kind of organism in competition with others. See **natural selection. 6.** In Australia, a piece of farmland provided under a government scheme (*free selection*) that offered favourable terms of purchase to early settlers. —See Synonyms at **choice.** [Latin *sēlectiō* (stem *selectiōn-*). See **select.**]

se·lec·tive (si-léktiv, sə-) *adj.* **1.** Of or characterised by selection or discrimination; tending to select or empowered to select: *selective import controls.* **2.** Careful in selecting; fastidious; particular. **3.** *Electronics.* Capable of rejecting frequencies other than those selected or tuned. —**se·lec·tive·ly** *adv.* —**se·lec·tive·ness** *n.*

se·lec·tiv·i·ty (si-lék-tívvəti, sillek-, séelek-) *n.* **1.** The state or quality of being selective. **2.** *Electronics.* The degree to which an electronic receiver or other circuit is selective.

se·lect·man (si-lékt-mən, sə-, -mán) *n., pl.* **-men** (-mən, -men). A member of a board of town officers chosen annually in New England communities to manage local affairs.

se·lec·tor (si-léktər, sə-) *n.* **1.** One that selects; specifically, a member of a committee that selects a sports team. **2.** A device forming part of an automatic telephone switching system that connects one circuit to one or more other circuits.

sel·e·nate (sélli-nayt) *n.* A salt or ester of selenic acid. [From SELENIUM.]

Se·len·e (si-léeni, sə-). The Greek goddess of the Moon. [Greek *selēnē,* Moon.]

se·le·nic acid (si-léenik, -lénnik) *n.* A highly corrosive, hygroscopic, white solid acid with composition H_2SeO_4. [From SELENIUM.]

sel·e·nite (sélli-nīt) *n.* Gypsum in the form of colourless clear crystals. [Latin *selēnītēs,* from Greek *selēnītēs (lithos),* "moon (stone)" (because its brightness supposedly waxed and waned with the Moon), from *selēnē,* Moon.]

se·le·ni·um (si-léeni-əm) *n. Symbol* **Se** A nonmetallic element, red in powder form, black in vitreous form, and metallic grey in crystalline form, resembling sulphur and obtained primarily as a byproduct of electrolytic copper refining. It is widely used in rectifiers, as a semiconductor, and in xerography, and certain forms exhibit photovoltaic and photoconductive action, making it useful in photocells, photographic exposure meters, and solar cells. Atomic number 34, atomic weight 78.96, melting point (of grey selenium) 217°C, boiling point (grey) 684.9°C, relative density (grey) 4.79, (vitreous) 4.28, valency 2, 4, or 6. [New Latin, from Greek *selēnē,* Moon (named by analogy to a related element, tellurium, which is from Latin *tellus,* Earth).]

selenium cell *n.* A photoconductive cell consisting of an insulated selenium strip between two suitable electrodes.

sel·e·nod·e·sy (sélli-nóddəsi) *n.* The study or mapping of the physical characteristics of the Moon, such as its exact shape, size, and gravity; lunar geodesy. [Greek *selēnē,* Moon + (GEO)DESY] —**sel·e·nod·e·sist** *n.* **sel·e·no·det·ic** (-nə-déttik) *adj.*

se·le·no·dont (si-léenə-dont, sə-) *adj.* Having crescent-shaped ridges on the crowns of the teeth, as deer do.
~*n.* A selenodont mammal. [Greek *selēnē,* moon + -ODONT.]

sel·e·nog·ra·phy (sélli-nóggrəfi, séeli-) *n.* The study of the physical features of the moon. [New Latin *selenographia* : Greek *selēnē,* Moon + -GRAPHY.] —**sel·e·nog·ra·pher, sel·e·nog·ra·phist** *n.* —**sel·e·no·graph·ic** (-nə-gráffik, si-lée-), **sel·e·no·graph·i·cal** *adj.* —**sel·e·no·graph·i·cal·ly** *adv.*

sel·e·nol·o·gy (sélli-nólləji, séeli-) *n.* The astronomical study of the moon. [Greek *selēnē,* Moon + -LOGY.] —**se·le·no·log·i·cal** (-nə-lójik'l, si-lée-) *adj.* —**sel·e·nol·o·gist** (-nólləjist) *n.*

se·le·no·mor·phol·o·gy (si-léenō-mawr-fólləji, sə-) *n.* The study of the surface and landscape of the moon. [Greek *selēnē,* Moon + MORPHOLOGY.]

se·le·nous acid (si-léenəss, séllinəss) *n.* Also **se·le·ni·ous acid** (si-léeni-əss). A transparent, colourless crystalline acid, H_2SeO_3, used as a chemical reagent. [From SELENIUM.]

Se·leu·ci·a[1] (si-lóo-shi-ə, -léw-, -si-) Ancient city of Mesopotamia, on the Tigris southeast of modern Baghdad. It was the eastern capital of the Seleucid empire.

Seleucia[2] or **Seleucia Pi·e·ri·a** (pī-írriə). Ancient city on the Orontes river, Syria. It was founded by Seleucus I as the seaport for Antioch, and was visited by St. Paul (Acts 13:4).

Se·leu·cid (si-lóo-sid, -léw-) *n., pl.* **Seleucids** or **-cidae** (-si-dee). A member of a Hellenistic dynasty founded by Seleucus I after the death of Alexander, and ruling in Babylonia from 312 B.C. and in Syria from 301 B.C. to 64 B.C. —**Se·leu·cid, Se·leu·ci·dan** *adj.*

self (self) *n., pl.* **selves** (selvz). **1.** The total, essential, or particular being of one person; the individual. **2.** The qualities of one person distinguishing him from another; a person's typical personality or character: *not his usual cheerful self.* **3.** An individual's consciousness of his own being or identity; subjectivity; ego. **4.** One's own interests, welfare, or advantage; selfish concerns.
~*pron.* Myself, yourself, himself, or herself: *a living wage for self.*
~*adj.* **1.** *Obsolete.* Same or identical. **2. a.** Uniform throughout. Said of a colour. **b.** Self-coloured. **3.** Homogeneous, as in colour, design, or material; matching. Said especially of clothes: *a self scarf.* [Middle English *se(o)lf, silf,* noun, pronoun, and adjective, Old English *self, silf.*]
   Usage: The use of a reflexive pronoun as a means of emphasising a previously stated pronoun is often criticised, though it is very common in spoken English: *I myself believe him.* The use of *self* alone, as a pronoun, is found only in commercial English (*sold to self three boxes*), especially in certain fixed phrases (*your good self/selves*) which business usage these days tends to avoid.

self– *comb. form.* Indicates: **1.** Oneself or itself; for example, **self-correcting, self-perpetuating. 2.** Of the self, oneself, or itself; for example, **self-control, self-government, self-knowledge. 3.** With regard to oneself; for example, **self-assurance, self-interest. 4.** By, by means of, or relying solely upon, oneself; for example, **self-appointed, self-educated, self-help. 5.** Acting on or directed towards oneself or itself; for example, **self-addressed, self-pity. 6.** In oneself or itself; inherently: for example, **self-contradictory, self-evident. 7.** Autonomous, automatic, or automatically; for example, **self-propelled, self-winding.** *Note:* Many compounds other than those entered here may be formed with *self-*. When *self-* is joined with a word that can stand alone, it is joined by a hyphen: *self-deception.* In the rare cases when *self-* is joined with a form that cannot stand alone as a word, it is joined without space or hyphen: *selfhood.* [Middle English, Old English, from SELF.]

self-a·base·ment (sélf-ə-báyssmənt) *n.* Degradation or humiliation of oneself, especially because of feelings of guilt or inferiority.

self-ab·ne·ga·tion (sélf-ábni-gáysh'n) *n.* The setting aside of self-interest for the sake of others or for a belief or principle. —**self-ab·ne·gat·ing** (-gayting) *adj.*

self-a·buse (sélf-ə-béwss) *n.* **1.** Criticism of oneself or one's abilities. **2.** Masturbation. Not in current usage.

self-act·ing (sélf-ákting) *adj.* Capable of acting or working automatically.

self-ad·dressed (sélf-ə-drést) *adj.* Addressed to oneself.

self-ag·gran·dise·ment (sélf-ə-grándizmənt) *n.* The act or practice of enhancing one's own importance, power, or reputation. —**self-ag·gran·dis·ing** (-grándīzing) *adj.*

self-an·neal·ing (sélf-ə-néeling) *adj.* Designating those metals, such as lead and tin, that do not harden as a result of cold-working.

self-an·ni·hi·la·tion (sélf-ə-ní-ə-láysh'n, -i-, -hi-) *n.* **1.** Self-destruction. **2.** Complete loss of the ego or consciousness of self, as in a mystical state.

self-ap·point·ed (sélf-ə-póyntid) *adj.* Designated or chosen by oneself rather than by due authority; unsanctioned and usually ill-qualified: *a self-appointed authority on English grammar.*

self-as·ser·tion (sélf-ə-sérsh'n) *n.* Forceful assertion of one's own personality, wishes, claims, or views. —**self-as·ser·tive** *adj.* —**self-as·ser·tive·ly** *adv.*

self-as·sured (sélf-ə-shoórd ‖ -shéwrd) *adj.* Having or showing confidence and sureness. —**self-as·sur·ance** *n.*

self-a·ware (sélf-ə-waír) *adj.* Aware of one's own personality or individual qualities. —**self-a·ware·ness** *n.*

self-cen·tred (sélf-séntərd) *adj.* Engrossed in oneself and one's affairs. —**self-cen·tred·ly** *adv.* —**self-cen·tred·ness** *n.*

self-cert·i·fi·ca·tion (sélf-sértifi-káysh'n, -sər-tíffi-) *n.* In Britain, a procedure whereby a sick person personally gives notice of absences from work, rather than producing a doctor's certificate.

self-col·oured (sélf-kúllərd) *adj.* **1.** In the natural or original colour. **2.** Of only one colour.

self-com·mand (sélf-kə-maánd ‖ -mánd) *n.* Full presence of mind; self-control.

self-con·fessed (sélf-kən-fést ‖ -kon-) *adj.* According to one's own admission; avowed.

self-con·fi·dence (sélf-kónfidənss) *n.* Confidence in oneself or one's abilities. —**self-con·fi·dent** *adj.* —**self-con·fi·dent·ly** *adv.*

self-con·scious (sélf-kónshəss) *adj.* **1.** Conscious to the point of discomfort or embarrassment of one's appearance or manner; socially ill at ease. **2.** Having or showing an excessive concern for one's impact upon others; unnatural or contrived: *a very self-conscious style of poetry.* **3.** Aware of oneself or one's own being, actions, or thoughts. —See Synonyms at **humble.** —**self-con·scious·ly** *adv.* —**self-con·scious·ness** *n.*

self-con·tained (sélf-kən-táynd ‖ -kon-) *adj.* **1.** Constituting a complete and independent unit: *a self-contained flat.* **2. a.** Not dependent on others; self-sufficient. **b.** Keeping to oneself; reserved.

self-con·tent (sélf-kən-tént ‖ -kon-) *n.* Also **self-con·tent·ment** (-mənt). Satisfaction, especially complacent satisfaction, with oneself and one's condition. —**self-con·tent·ed** *adj.* —**self-con·tent·ed·ly** *adv.*

self-con·tra·dic·tion (sélf-kóntrə-díksh'n) *n.* **1.** The act, state, or fact of contradicting oneself or itself. **2.** An idea or statement containing contradictory elements. —**self-con·tra·dic·to·ry** (-dík-təri, -tri) *adj.*

self-con·trol (sélf-kən-trốl ‖ -kon-) *n.* Control of one's emotions, desires, or actions by one's own will. —**self-con·trolled** *adj.*

self-cor·rect·ing (sélf-kə-rékting) *adj.* Correcting its or one's own mistakes; especially, designating a typewriter with a mechanism facilitating correction of typing errors.

self-crit·i·cal (sélf-krítik'l) *adj.* Critical of oneself; watchful for one's own faults and weaknesses. —**self-crit·i·cal·ly** *adv.* —**self-crit·i·cism** *n.*

self-de·ceived (sélf-di-séevd, -də-) *adj.* Deceived by one's own illusion or error.

self-de·cep·tion (sélf-di-sépsh'n, -də-) *n.* Also **self-de·ceit** (-séet). The act of deceiving oneself or the state of being deceived by oneself. —**self-de·cep·tive** *adj.*

self-de·feat·ing (sélf-di-féeting, -də-) *adj.* Conflicting with or going against one's or its own purposes or welfare.

self-de·fence (sélf-di-fénss, -də-) *n.* **1.** The act or skill of defending oneself against physical attack. **2.** Defence of what belongs to oneself, as of one's rights or beliefs. **3.** *Law.* The right to protect oneself against violence or threatened violence with whatever force or means are reasonably necessary. —**self-de·fen·sive** *adj.*

self-de·ni·al (sélf-di-ní-əl, -də-) *n.* Sacrifice of one's own comfort or gratification; restraint of one's natural desires. See Synonyms at **abstinence.** —**self-de·ny·ing** *adj.* —**self-de·ny·ing·ly** *adv.*

self-dep·re·cat·ing (sélf-déppri-kayting) *adj.* Tending to undervalue oneself and one's abilities. —**self-dep·re·cat·ing·ly** *adv.* —**self-dep·re·ca·tion** (-káysh'n) *n.*

self-de·struct (sélf-di-strúkt, -də-) *n.* A mechanism forming part of a missile or other device that enables it to destroy itself under predetermined circumstances or on command. Also used adjectivally: *a self-destruct mechanism.*
~*intr.v.* **self-destructed, -structing, -structs.** To destroy oneself, especially automatically.

self-de·struc·tive (sélf-di-strúktiv, -də-) *adj.* Marked by an impulse or tendency to harm or kill oneself. —**self-de·struc·tion** *n.* —**self-de·struc·tive·ly** *adv.* —**self-de·struc·tive·ness** *n.*

self-de·ter·mi·na·tion (sélf-di-térmi-náysh'n, -də-) *n.* **1.** Determination of one's own fate or course of action without compulsion; free will. **2.** Freedom of a people or area to determine its own political status and alignment; independence.

self-dis·ci·pline (sélf-díssiplin) *n.* Training and control of one's impulses and conduct, usually for personal improvement.

self-dis·cov·er·y (sélf-di-skúvvəri) *n.* The act or process of achieving understanding or knowledge of oneself.

self-drive (sélf-drîv) *adj.* Designating a hired car to be driven by the hirer.

self-doubt (sélf-dówt) *n.* A lack of faith or confidence in oneself. —**self-doubt·ing** *adj.*

self-ed·u·cat·ed (sélf-éddew-kaytid) *adj.* Educated by one's own efforts, not by formal instruction. —**self-ed·u·ca·tion** (-káysh'n) *n.*

self-ef·fac·ing (sélf-i-fáy-sing, -ə-) *adj.* Not drawing attention to oneself; modest or shy. —**self-ef·face·ment** *n.*

self-em·ployed (sélf-im-plóyd, -em-) *adj.* Earning one's livelihood directly from one's own trade or business, not as an employee.

self-es·teem (sélf-i-stéem, -ə-) *n.* Pride in oneself; self-respect.

self-ev·i·dent (sélf-évvi-dənt ‖ -dent) *adj.* Requiring no proof or explanation. —**self-ev·i·dence** *n.*

self-ex·am·i·na·tion (sélf-ig-zámi-náysh'n ‖ -eg-, -ik-) *n.* **1.** Careful, introspective consideration of one's own thoughts, feelings, or motives. **2.** Examination of one's own body for medical reasons; especially, examination by a woman of her breasts as a precaution against cancer.

self-ex·cit·ed (sélf-ik-sítid, -ek-) *adj.* *Electricity.* **1.** Designating an oscillator that provides its own energy source. **2.** Designating an electrical machine in which the current that excites the magnetic field is generated by the machine itself.

self-ex·plan·a·to·ry (sélf-ik-splánnə-tri, -ek-, -təri) *adj.* Needing no explanation; obvious in meaning.

self-ex·pres·sion (sélf-ik-sprésh'n, -ek-) *n.* Expression of one's own personality, feelings, or ideas, as through speech or art.

self-fer·til·i·sa·tion (sélf-fértilī-záysh'n ‖ U.S. -fért'l-i-) *n.* Fertilisation by sperm from the same animal, as in some hermaphrodites, or by pollen from the same flower. See **autogamy.** —**self-fer·ti·lised, self-fer·ti·lis·ing, self-fer·tile** (-fértīl ‖ U.S. -fért'l-) *adj.*

self-ful·fill·ing (sélf-fŏŏl-filling) *adj.* Achieving fulfilment as a result of having been predicted or expected: *a self-fulfilling prophecy.*

self-gov·ern·ment (sélf-gúvvərnmənt) *n.* **1.** Political independence; autonomy. **2.** *Archaic.* Self-control. —**self-gov·erned, self-gov·ern·ing** *adj.*

self-hard·en·ing (sélf-hárd'n-ing) *adj.* Of, designating, or pertaining to materials, such as certain steels, that harden without special treatment.

self-heal (sélf-heel) *n.* Any of several plants reputed to have healing powers; especially, *Prunella vulgaris,* a plant native to Europe, having violet-blue flowers. Also called "heal-all", "all-heal".

self-help (sélf-hélp) *n.* The act or an instance of helping or providing for oneself without assistance from others. Also used adjectivally: *a self-help project.*

self·hood (sélf-hŏŏd) *n.* **1.** The state of having a distinct identity; individuality. **2.** The fully developed self; achieved personality. **3.** Self-centredness. [Translation of German *Selbheit.*]

self-im·age (sélf-ímmij) *n.* One's mental concept of oneself or one's position in relation to others; how one sees oneself.

self-im·por·tance (sélf-im-pórtənss) *n.* Excessively high opinion of one's own importance or station; pomposity; conceit. **—self-im·por·tant** *adj.* **—self-im·por·tant·ly** *adv.*

self-im·posed (sélf-im-pṓzd) *adj.* Imposed by oneself on oneself; voluntarily assumed or endured.

self-im·prove·ment (sélf-im-prŏŏvmənt) *n.* Improvement of one's condition through one's own efforts.

self-in·duced (sélf-in-déwst || -dŏŏst) *adj.* **1.** Induced by oneself or itself; wilfully acquired or brought on. **2.** *Electricity.* Produced by self-induction.

self-in·duct·ance (sélf-in-dúktənss) *n. Electricity.* The ratio of the electromotive force produced in a circuit by self-induction to the rate of change of current producing it. It is expressed in henries. Also called "coefficient of self-induction".

self-in·duc·tion (sélf-in-dúksh'n) *n.* The generation by a changing current of an electromotive force in the same circuit that tends to counteract such change. **—self-in·duc·tive** *adj.*

self-in·dul·gence (sélf-in-dúljənss) *n.* Excessive indulgence of one's own appetites, desires, or attitudes. **—self-in·dul·gent** *adj.* **—self-in·dul·gent·ly** *adv.*

self-in·flict·ed (sélf-in-flíktid) *adj.* Inflicted or imposed upon oneself: *a self-inflicted punishment.* **—self-in·flic·tion** *n.*

self-in·ter·est (sélf-ín-tərəst, -trist, -tə-rest) *n.* **1.** Personal advantage or interest; selfish motive or gain. **2.** Pursuit of or excessive regard for such advantage or interest. **—self-in·ter·est·ed** *adj.*

self·ish (sélfish) *adj.* **1.** Concerned chiefly or only with one's own welfare, pleasure, or advantage, without regard for the well-being of others; egoistic. **2.** Arising from, characterised by, or showing such concern: *a selfish whim.* **—self·ish·ly** *adv.* **—self·ish·ness** *n.*

self-jus·ti·fy·ing (sélf-jústi-fī-ing) *adj.* **1.** Making excuses for one's behaviour. **2.** Automatically arranging type to fill a full line.

self-knowl·edge (sélf-nóllij) *n.* Knowledge of one's own nature, abilities, and limitations; insight into oneself.

self·less (sélf-ləss, -liss) *adj.* Without concern for oneself; unselfish. **—self·less·ly** *adv.* **—self·less·ness** *n.*

self-liq·ui·dat·ing (sélf-líkwi-dayting) *adj.* **1.** Designating a loan advanced to finance the purchase or production of goods that can be quickly converted into cash. **2.** Producing a return equal to the sum invested to create or maintain it: *a self-liquidating toll-bridge project.*

self-load·ing (sélf-lṓding) *adj.* Automatically ejecting the shell and chambering the next round from the magazine; automatic or semi-automatic. Said of a firearm.

self-loc·king (sélf-lócking) *adj.* Locking automatically when shut.

self-love (sélf-lúv) *n.* The instinct or desire to promote one's own well-being; regard for or love of self. **—self-lov·ing** *adj.*

self-made (sélf-máyd) *adj.* **1.** Having achieved success purely by one's own efforts: *a self-made man.* **2.** Made by oneself or itself.

self-man·age·ment (sélf-mánnijmənt) *n.* Management, as of a factory or other enterprise, by those employed in it.

self-o·pin·ion·at·ed (sélf-ə-pín-yənaytid) *adj.* Given to forceful, sometimes obstinate, assertion of one's own opinions.

self-per·pet·u·at·ing (sélf-pər-péttew-ayting) *adj.* Having the power to renew or perpetuate itself indefinitely.

self-pit·y (sélf-pítti) *n.* Pity for oneself, especially of an exaggerated or self-indulgent kind. **—self-pit·y·ing** *adj.* **—self-pit·y·ing·ly** *adv.*

self-pol·li·na·tion (sélf-pólli-náysh'n) *n.* The transfer of pollen from an anther to a stigma of the same flower. **—self-pol·li·nat·ed, self-pol·li·nat·ing** *adj.*

self-por·trait (sélf-pór-trit, -trət, -trayt || -pṓr-) *n.* A portrait, pictorial or literary, of oneself created by oneself.

self-pos·ses·sion (sélf-pə-zésh'n || -pō-) *n.* Full command of one's faculties, feelings, and behaviour, especially in difficult circumstances; presence of mind; poise. **—self-pos·sessed** *adj.*

self-pres·er·va·tion (sélf-prézzər-váysh'n) *n.* **1.** Protection of oneself from harm or destruction. **2.** The instinct for such individual preservation; the innate desire to stay alive.

self-pro·claimed (sélf-prə-kláymd, -prō-) *adj.* So called by oneself; self-styled.

self-pro·pelled (sélf-prə-péld || -prō-) *adj.* Containing its own means of propulsion. Said of a vehicle, for example.

self-rais·ing flour (sélf-ráyzing) *n.* A commercially produced mixture of flour and a leavening agent, usually baking powder. Also *U.S.* "self-rising flour".

self-re·al·i·sa·tion (sélf-réer-lī-záysh'n, -rée-ə- || *U.S.* -li-) *n.* The complete development or fulfilment of the self's potential.

self-re·cord·ing (sélf-ri-kórding, -rə-) *adj.* Automatically recording its own functions or operations. Said of a machine or instrument.

self-re·gard (sélf-ri-gárd, -rə-) *n.* **1.** Consideration of oneself or one's interests. **2.** Self-respect.

self-reg·u·lat·ing (sélf-réggew-layting) *adj.* Regulating itself automatically.

self-re·li·ance (sélf-ri-lī́-ənss, -rə-) *n.* Reliance upon one's own capabilities, judgment, or resources. **—self-re·li·ant** *adj.* **—self-re·li·ant·ly** *adv.*

self-re·proach (sélf-ri-prṓch, -rə-) *n.* The act or habit of blaming or finding fault with oneself. **—self-re·proach·ful** *adj.* **—self-re·proach·ful·ly** *adv.*

self-re·spect (sélf-ri-spékt, -rə-) *n.* Due respect for oneself and one's personal worth. **—self-re·spect·ing** *adj.*

self-re·straint (sélf-ri-stráynt, -rə-) *n.* Restraint of one's emotions, desires, or inclinations; self-control.

self-right·eous (sélf-rī́chəss, -rī́t-yəss) *adj.* Piously sure of one's righteousness. **—self-right·eous·ly** *adv.* **—self-right·eous·ness** *n.*

self-right·ing (sélf-rī́ting) *adj.* Able to right itself when overturned.

self-rule (sélf-rŏŏl || -réwl) *n.* Self-government.

self-sac·ri·fice (sélf-sáckri-fīss) *n.* Sacrifice of one's personal interests or well-being for the sake of others or for a cause. **—self-sac·ri·fic·ing** *adj.*

self·same (sélf-saym, sáym) *adj.* Exactly identical; the very same. See Synonyms at **same.** [Middle English *selve same* : *self,* SELF (obsolete sense "same") + SAME.] **—self·same·ness** *n.*

self-sat·is·fac·tion (sélf-sáttiss-fáksh'n) *n.* Satisfaction, especially complacent satisfaction, with oneself or one's own accomplishments. **—self-sat·is·fied** *adj.*

self-seal·ing (sélf-seeling) *adj.* Able to be sealed without the application of moisture: *a self-sealing envelope.*

self-seed·ed (sélf-seedid) *adj.* Self-sown.

self-seek·ing (sélf-seeking) *n.* The determined pursuit of one's own ends or interests. **—self-seek·er** *n.* **—self-seek·ing** *adj.*

self-serv·ice (sélf-sérviss) *adj.* Designating a retail commercial enterprise in which the customers serve themselves and pay a cashier.

self-serv·ing (sélf-sérving) *adj.* Serving one's own interests, especially without consideration for the needs or interests of others.

self-sown (sélf-sṓn) *adj.* Growing from seed dispersal by natural means rather than sown by man; self-seeded. Said of plants.

self-start·er (sélf-stártər) *n.* **1.** A device for starting an engine, a **starter** *(see).* **2.** A person with initiative.

self-stud·y (sélf-stúddi) *n.* A form of study in which the student is to a large extent responsible for his own instruction. Also used adjectivally: *a self-study course.*

self-styled (sélf-stī́ld) *adj.* As characterised by oneself, often without right or justification: *the self-styled "Voice of Britain".*

self-suf·fi·cient (sélf-sə-físh'nt) *adj.* **1.** Able to provide for oneself without the help of others; not dependent on others for food, energy, or the like. **2.** *Archaic.* Having undue confidence; smug or overbearing. **—self-suf·fi·cien·cy** *n.*

self-sup·port (sélf-sə-pórt || -pṓrt) *n.* The act of or capacity for supporting oneself, especially financially, without the help of others. **—self-sup·port·ed, self-sup·port·ing** *adj.*

self-taught (sélf-táwt) *adj.* Having taught oneself without formal instruction or the help of others.

self-will (sélf-wíl) *n.* Wilfulness, especially in satisfying one's own desires or adhering to one's own opinions. **—self-willed** *adj.*

self-wind·ing (sélf-wī́nding) *adj.* Having a mechanism that does not need winding. Said of watches in which the spring is wound by a weight activated by the movement of the wearer's hand.

Sel·juk (sel-jŏŏk, sél-jŏŏk) *n.* A member of any of several Turkish dynasties ruling over central and western Asia from the 11th to the 13th century. [Turkish, after *Seljūk,* the reputed eponymous ancestor.] **—Sel·juk** *adj.*

Sel·kirk (sél-kurk). Also **Sel·kirk·shire** (-shər, -sheer). A former county of southern Scotland, now part of the Borders Region. Its administrative centre was Selkirk, a royal burgh on Ettrick Water.

Selkirk, Alexander (1676–1721). Scottish sailor whose experiences inspired Defoe's *Robinson Crusoe.* In 1704 he was marooned on the uninhabited island of Juan Fernández. He was discovered there in 1709.

Selkirk bannock *n.* A sweet Scottish bread containing dried fruit. [After SELKIRK, Scottish county, where it originated.]

sell (sel) *v.* **sold** (sōld), **selling, sells.** *—tr.* **1.** To exchange or deliver for money or its equivalent, as goods, services, or property; dispose of for a price. **2.** To deal in; offer for sale as one's business: *sells computers for an American company.* **3.** To give up or surrender, often treacherously or dishonourably, in exchange for a price or reward: *witches who had sold themselves to Satan.* **4.** To promote the sale of; cause to be sold: *Publicity sold that product.* **5. a.** To convince of the worth or desirability of something. Used with *on*: *He's completely sold on the idea.* **b.** To convince someone of the worth or desirability of (an idea or product, for example): *made efforts to sell their policy to the electorate.* **6.** To achieve sales of: *has already sold half a million copies in hardback.* **7.** *Informal.* To cheat or dupe. *—intr.* **1.** To exchange ownership for money or its equivalent; engage in selling goods or services. **2.** To be sold or be on sale. **3.** To attract prospective buyers; be popular on the market: *an item that sells well.* **4.** To be approved of; gain acceptance. **—sell off.** To get rid of by selling, often at reduced prices; deplete. **—sell short. 1.** *Finance.* To contract for the sale of securities or commodities one expects to own at a later date and on more advantageous terms. **2.** To undervalue (oneself or another); fail to appreciate the worth of. **—sell up.** *Chiefly British.* **1.** To sell (one's business, for example). **2.** To dispose of the assets of (a bankrupt or insolvent person) in order to pay creditors.

self-heal Prunella vulgaris, *or self-heal, is native to Europe, growing on waste ground or grassland. It was formerly thought to be of value in the treatment of a sore throat.* Prunella *comes from a German word meaning "sore throat".*

~n. 1. The act of selling. **2.** A sales presentation of a specified type. See **hard sell, soft sell. 3.** *Slang.* A hoax or swindle. [Sell, sold, sold; Middle English *sellen, sold, sold,* Old English *sellan, sealde, seald,* to give, betray, sell.] **—sel·la·ble** *adj.*

sell·er (séllər) *n.* **1.** A person who sells; a salesman or vendor. **2.** An item that sells in a particular manner: *a best seller.*

Sel·lers (séllərz), **Peter** (1925–80). British comic actor, noted for the brilliance and variety of his characterisations. He won fame in the 1950s radio series *The Goon Show* and established an international reputation in films such as *Dr. Strangelove* (1963) and the *Pink Panther* series (1963–77).

sellers' market *n. Economics.* A market condition characterised by relatively high prices, occurring when the supply of commodities falls short of market demand. Compare **buyers' market.**

sell·ing point (sélling) *n.* A particularly attractive aspect, as of a product or idea, that is stressed in order to promote its sale.

Sel·lo·tape (sél-ə-tayp, -ō-) *n.* A trademark for a type of transparent adhesive tape. **—Sel·lo·tape** *tr.v.*

sell out *tr.v.* **1.** To sell the whole of (one's stock). **2.** To sell (one's share in a business). **3.** To betray (a cause, a principle, or a colleague), especially for the sake of gain: *sold out his artistic principles.* —*intr.v.* **1.** To sell the whole of one's stock: *We've sold out of bread.* **2.** To sell one's share in a business. **3.** To betray one's principles, colleagues, or other loyalties.

sell·out (sél-owt) *n.* **1.** A betrayal. **2.** An event for which all the tickets are sold. **3.** One who has betrayed principles or a cause.

sel·syn (sél-sin) *n.* A device for the instantaneous transmission and reception, from a generator to a motor, of the angular movement of rotating parts. Also called "synchro". [Short for *self-synchronous.*]

selt·zer (séltsər) *n.* **1.** A natural effervescent spring water of high mineral content. **2.** Such water artificially prepared and containing carbon dioxide. Also called "seltzer water". [German *Selterser (Wasser),* "(water) of Nieder Selters", a district near Wiesbaden, West Germany, locality of the springs.]

sel·va (sélvə) *n.* **1.** Dense tropical rain forest occurring in the Amazon basin. **2.** Any area of such forest. [Portuguese, from Latin *silva,* forest.]

sel·vage, sel·vedge (sélvij) *n.* **1.** The edge of a fabric woven so that it will not unravel; especially, an ornamental fringe at either end of an oriental carpet. **2.** Any edge similar to this, usually a tapelike one. **3.** The edge plate of a lock with a slot for a bolt. [Middle English : *selve, self,* SELF + *egge,* EDGE (after obsolete Dutch *selfegghe*).]

selves. Plural of **self.**

Sel·wyn-Lloyd (sélwin-lóyd), **John, Baron** (1904–78). British Conservative politician. He was foreign secretary (1955–60) at the time of the Suez crisis, and Chancellor of the Exchequer (1960–62) under Macmillan. He was Speaker of the House of Commons (1971–76).

Selz·nick (sélznik), **David O(liver)** (1902–65). U.S. film producer. He established his reputation as a producer with films such as *David Copperfield* (1935) and *A Star is Born* (1937). *Gone With the Wind* (1939) became one of the world's greatest box office successes.

sem. seminary.

se·man·tic (si-mántik, sə-) *adj.* **1.** Pertaining to meaning in language. **2.** Of, pertaining to, or according to the science of semantics. [Greek *sēmantikos,* significant, from *sēmainein,* to signify, show by a sign, from *sēma,* sign.]

se·man·ti·cist (si-mánti-sist, sə-) *n.* A specialist in semantics.

se·man·tics (si-mántiks, sə-) *n. Used with a singular verb.* **1.** *Linguistics.* The study or science of meaning in language forms, particularly with regard to its historical change. **2.** *Logic.* The study of relationships between signs and symbols and what they represent. **3.** Subtleties in meaning. Often used derogatorily.

sem·a·phore (sémmə-fawr ‖ -fōr) *n.* **1.** Any visual signalling apparatus with flags, lights, or mechanically moving arms, as on a railway. **2.** A visual system of sending information by means of two flags, one in each hand, using an alphabetic code based on the positions of the signaller's arms.
~v. semaphored, -phoring, -phores. —*tr.* To send (a message) by semaphore. —*intr.* To signal with a semaphore. [Greek *sēma,* sign + -PHORE.]

se·ma·si·ol·o·gy (si-máy-si-óllǝji, -zi-) *n.* Semantics, especially the study of semantic development. [Greek *sēmasia,* meaning, from *sē-mainein,* to signify, mean (see **semantic**) + -LOGY.] **—se·ma·si·o·log·i·cal** (-ə-lójik'l) *adj.* **—se·ma·si·o·logist** (-óllǝjist) *n.*

se·mat·ic (si-máttik) *adj.* Serving as a warning or signal of danger, particularly to predators. Said especially of the colouring of certain animals. [Greek *sēma* (stem *sēmat-*), sign.]

sem·bla·ble (sémblǝb'l) *adj. Archaic.* Appearing real; apparent. [Middle English, from Old French, from *sembler,* to resemble, seem, from Latin *similāre, simulāre,* to SIMULATE.] **—sem·bla·bly** *adv.*

sem·blance (sémblǝnss) *n.* **1.** An outward or token appearance. **2.** A representation or resemblance. **3.** The barest trace; a modicum. [Middle English, from Old French, from *semblant,* present participle of *sembler,* to resemble, seem. See **semblable.**]

se·mé (sémmay, sémmi ‖ se-máy) *adj. Heraldry.* Having a design embellished with small, delicate figures, as a lacing of stars or flowers. [French, past participle of *semer,* to sow, scatter, from Latin *sēmināre,* from *sēmen,* seed.]

semeiology. Variant of **semiology.**

semeiotic. Variant of **semiotic.**

se·meme (sée-meem) *n.* The meaning expressed by a morpheme. [SEM(ANTIC) + -EME.]

se·men (sée-men, -mən) *n.* **1.** The viscous whitish fluid that is ejaculated from the male reproductive organs of animals and transports the spermatozoa. **2.** Sperm. [Middle English, from Latin *sēmen,* "seed.]

se·mes·ter (si-méstər, sə-) *n.* Either of the two 15 to 18 week sessions into which an academic year is divided; especially in U.S. universities. [German *Semester,* from Latin *(cursus) sēmēstris,* "(period) of six months" : *sex,* six + *mēnsis,* month.]

sem·i (sémmi ‖ *U.S. also* sémmī) *n., pl.* **semis.** *Informal.* **1.** *British.* A semidetached house. **2.** A semifinal. **3.** *U.S. & Australian.* A semitrailer.

semi– *prefix. Abbr.* **s.** Indicates: **1.** Partly, partially, or incompletely; for example, **semiaquatic, semiliterate. 2.** Half of; for example, **semicircle. 3.** Occurring twice within a particular period of time; for example, **semimonthly.** *Note:* Many compounds other than those entered here may be formed with *semi-.* In this dictionary, in forming compounds, *semi-* is normally joined with the following element without space or hyphen: *semiannual.* However, many users prefer the hyphenated form, especially if the second element begins with a capital letter or with *i: semi-Americanised, semi-idle.* The prefix is often pronounced (sémmī-) in the United States; this variant is not shown in entries below. [Latin *sēmi-.*]

sem·i·an·nu·al (sémmi-ánnew-əl) *adj.* Happening or issued twice a year. **—sem·i·an·nu·al·ly** *adv.*

sem·i·a·quat·ic (sémmi-ə-kwáttik ‖ -kwóttik) *adj.* Adapted for living or growing in or near water; not entirely aquatic.

sem·i·ar·id (sémmi-árrid) *adj.* Designating regions often found in continental interiors, that are transitional between Savannah grassland and the desert, having relatively low rainfall and scrubby vegetation with coarse grasses; partly arid.

sem·i·au·to·mat·ic (sémmi-áwtə-máttik) *adj.* **1.** Partially automatic. **2.** Having an automatic reloading mechanism but requiring a pull of the trigger for each shot; autoloading. Said of a firearm. Compare **automatic. —sem·i·au·to·mat·ic** *adj.*

sem·i·au·ton·o·mous (sémmi-aw-tónnəməss) *adj.* Partially self-governing; especially, having powers of self-government within a larger organisation or structure.

sem·i·breve (sémmi-breev ‖ *U.S. also* -brev) *n. Music.* The longest note in ordinary use, having a time value equal to two minims. Also *U.S.* "whole note".

sem·i·cir·cle (sémmi-surk'l) *n.* **1.** A half of a circle as divided by a diameter. **2.** An object or arrangement of objects or people in the shape of a half-circle. **—sem·i·cir·cu·lar** (-súrkewlər) *adj.*

semicircular canal *n.* One of the three tubular and looped structures in the labyrinth of the inner ear, together functioning in the maintenance of a sense of balance and orientation.

sem·i·civ·i·lised (sémmi-sívvilīzd) *adj.* Partly civilised.

sem·i·co·lon (sémmi-kǒ-lən, -kō-, -lon) *n.* A mark of punctuation (;) indicating a degree of separation intermediate in value between the comma and the full stop.

sem·i·con·duc·tor (sémmi-kən-dúktər ‖ -kon-) *n.* Any of various solid crystalline substances, such as germanium or silicon, having electrical conductivity greater than insulators but less than good conductors.

sem·i·con·scious (sémmi-kónshəss) *adj.* Half-conscious; not fully conscious or aware. **—sem·i·con·scious·ly** *adv.* **—sem·i·con·scious·ness** *n.*

sem·i·des·ert (sémmi-dézzərt) *n.* A semiarid area. **—sem·i·des·ert** *adj.*

sem·i·de·tached (sémmi-di-tácht) *adj.* Attached to another building on one side only. Said of either of a pair of houses joined by a common wall. **—sem·i·de·tached** *n.*

sem·i·di·am·e·ter (sémmi-dī-ámmitər) *n.* The apparent angular radius of a celestial body when viewed as a disc from the Earth.

sem·i·di·ur·nal (sémmi-dī-úrn'l) *adj.* **1.** Of, pertaining to, occurring, or performed during a half-day. **2.** Occurring or coming approximately once every 12 hours, as the tides do. **3.** Designating the arc described by a celestial body between its meridian passage and its points of rising or setting.

sem·i·dome (sémmi-dōm) *n.* A roof covering a semicircular space; half a dome.

sem·i·el·lip·ti·cal (sémmi-i-líptik'l) *adj.* Having the form or shape of half of an ellipse, especially when divided along the major axis.

sem·i·fi·nal (sémmi-fīn'l) *n.* **1.** One of the two competitions of the next to the last round in an elimination tournament. **2.** A match, competition, or other event that precedes the final event. **—sem·i·fi·nal** *adj.* **—sem·i·fi·nal·ist** *n.*

sem·i·flu·id (sémmi-flōo-id ‖ -flew-) *adj.* Also **sem·i·flu·id·ic** (-floo-íddik). Intermediate in flow properties between solids and liquids; highly viscous. **—sem·i·flu·id** *n.* **—sem·i·flu·id·i·ty** (-íddəti) *n.*

sem·i·for·mal (sémmi-fórm'l) *adj.* Somewhat formal.

sem·i·group (sémmi-grōop) *n. Algebra.* A non-empty set with an associative binary multiplication.

sem·i·liq·uid (sémmi-líkwid) *adj.* Intermediate in properties, especially flow properties, between liquids and solids.
~n. A semiliquid substance.

sem·i·lit·er·ate (sémmi-líttər-ət, -it) *adj.* **1.** Having achieved an elementary level of literacy. **2.** Having limited knowledge or understanding, as of a technical subject.

sé·mi·llon (sémmi-yón, sáymi-) *n.* A variety of white grape used in making sauternes. [French, diminutive of Old French *seme*, seed, from Latin *semen* (stem *semin-*), seed.]

sem·i·log·a·rith·mic (sémmi-lóggə-ríth-mik ‖ -ríth-) *adj*. 1. Having one logarithmic and one arithmetic scale: *semilogarithmic graph paper*. 2. Characteristic of a relationship expressed using such scales.

sem·i·lu·nar (sémmi-lóō-nər, -léw-) *adj*. Also **sem·i·lu·nate** (-nayt-). Shaped like a half-moon; crescent.

semilunar bone *n. Anatomy*. The **lunate bone** *(see)*.

semilunar valve *n*. Either of two crescent-shaped valves, each having three cusps, located in the aorta and in the pulmonary artery and preventing blood from flowing back into the heart.

sem·i·month·ly (sémmi-múnthli) *adj*. Occurring or issued twice a month.
~*n., pl.* **semimonthlies**. A semimonthly publication.
~*adv.* Twice monthly; at half-monthly intervals. See Usage note at **bimonthly**.

sem·i·nal (sémmin'l, séemin'l) *adj*. 1. Of, relating to, or containing semen or seed. 2. Highly influential in an original way; constituting or providing a basis for further development. [Middle English, from Old French, from Latin *sēminālis*, from *sēmen* (stem *sēmin-*), seed, SEMEN.] **—sem·i·nal·ly** *adv*.

sem·i·nar (sémmi-naar) *n*. 1. **a**. A small group, usually of advanced students, engaged in original research and meeting regularly, under the guidance of a tutor, to exchange and discuss their views and findings. **b**. A course of study so pursued. **c**. A scheduled meeting of such a group. 2. A meeting for an exchange of ideas on a particular topic; a conference. [German *Seminar*, from Latin *sēminārium*, seed plot, nursery. See **seminary**.]

sem·i·nar·i·an (sémmi-naír-i-ən) *n*. Also **sem·i·nar·ist** (-nərist). A seminary student.

sem·i·nar·y (sémmi-nəri ‖ *U.S.* -nerri) *n., pl.* **-ies**. *Abbr.* **sem**. 1. A place of education, especially: **a**. A theological school for the training of priests, ministers, or rabbis. **b**. *Archaic*. A private secondary school for girls. 2. A place or environment in which something is developed or nurtured. [Middle English, seed plot, place for cultivation, nursery garden, from Latin *sēminārium*, garden, seed plot, nursery, from *sēminārius*, of seeds, from *sēmen* (stem *sēmin-*), seed.]

sem·i·na·tion (sémmi-náysh'n) *n. Rare*. The dispersal or production of seed. [Latin *sēminātiō* (stem *sēminātiōn-*), propagation, from *sēminātus*, past participle of *sēmināre*, to sow, from *sēmen* (stem *sēmin-*), seed.]

sem·i·nif·er·ous (sémmi-níffərəss) *adj. Biology*. 1. Conveying or producing sperms: *the seminiferous tubules of the testis*. 2. Bearing seed. [Latin *sēmen* (stem *sēmin-*), SEMEN + -FEROUS.]

Sem·i·nole (sémmi-nōl) *n., pl.* **-noles** or collectively **Seminole**. 1. A member of a Muskhogean-speaking North American Indian people, now living chiefly in Oklahoma. 2. The language of this people. [Creek *simanóli, simalóni*, from American Spanish *cimarrón*, wild, runaway. See **maroon** (to abandon).] **—Sem·i·nole** *adj*.

sem·i·no·mad (sémmi-nő-mad) *n*. One of a people whose living habits are largely nomadic but who plant some crops. **—sem·i·no·mad·ic** (-nő-máddik) *adj*.

sem·i·of·fi·cial (sémmi-ə-físh'l ‖ -ō-) *adj*. Having some official authority or sanction. **—sem·i·of·fi·cial·ly** *adv*.

se·mi·ol·o·gy, se·mei·ol·o·gy (sémmi-ólləji, séemi- ‖ *U.S. also* séemī-, sémmī-) *n*. 1. The science dealing with signs, sign language, or systems of signalling. 2. *Medicine*. **Symptomatology** *(see)*. [New Latin *semaeologia* : Greek *sēmeion*, mark, sign, from *sēma*, sign, signal + -LOGY.]

se·mi·ot·ic, se·mei·ot·ic (sémmi-óttik, séemi- ‖ *U.S. also* séemī-, sémmī-) *adj*. 1. Of or relating to semiotics. 2. *Medicine*. Relating to symptomatology. [Greek *sēmeiōtikos*, observant of signs, from *sēmeioun*, to mark; give signals, note, from *sēmeion*, sign. See **semiology**.]

se·mi·ot·ics, se·mei·ot·ics (sémmi-óttiks, séemi- ‖ *U.S. also* séemī-, sémmī-) *n*. Used with a singular verb. 1. The study of all forms of human communicative behaviour, especially of signs and symbols. 2. *Medicine*. **Symptomatology** *(see)*. **—se·mi·o·ti·cian** (-ə-tísh'n) *n*.

sem·i·pal·mate (sémmi-pál-mət, -paál-, -mit, -mayt) *adj*. Also **sem·i·pal·mat·ed** (-máytid, -maytid). Having partial or reduced webbing between the toes, as some wading birds do.

sem·i·par·a·site (sémmi-párrə-sīt) *n. Biology*. A **hemiparasite** *(see)*. **—sem·i·par·a·sit·ic** (-síttik) *adj*. **—sem·i·par·a·sit·ism** (-sit-iz'm) *n*.

sem·i·per·me·a·ble (sémmi-pérmi-əb'l ‖ *U.S. also* sémmī-) *adj*. 1. Partially permeable. 2. Of or relating to a natural or artificial membrane that is permeable to some molecules in a mixture or solution but not to all. See **osmosis**.

sem·i·po·lar bond (sémmi-pólər) *n. Chemistry*. A **coordinate** *(see)*.

sem·i·por·ce·lain (sémmi-pór-səlin, -slin ‖ *U.S.* -pőr-) *n*. Any of several glazed ceramic wares resembling porcelain but having little or no translucency.

sem·i·pre·cious (sémmi-préshəss) *adj*. Designating stones of less value than precious stones, such as the topaz.

sem·i·pro (sémmi-prő) *adj. Informal*. Semiprofessional. **—sem·i·pro** *n*.

sem·i·pro·fes·sion·al (sémmi-prə-fésh'n'l ‖ -prō-) *adj*. 1. Taking part in a sport or other activity for pay, but not on a full-time basis. 2. Composed of or engaged in by semiprofessional players. ~*n*. A semiprofessional person.

sem·i·qua·ver (sémmi-kwayvər) *n. Music*. A note having a time value equal to half a quaver. Also *U.S.* "sixteenth note".

Se·mir·a·mis (se-mírrəmiss). The legendary founder of Babylon and wife of Ninus.

sem·i·rig·id (sémmi-ríjid) *adj*. 1. Moderately rigid. 2. Having some rigid components.

sem·i·round (sémmi-rőwnd) *adj*. Having a round side and a flat side. **—sem·i·round** *n*.

sem·i·skilled (sémmi-skild) *adj*. Possessing or requiring some skills or training, but less than those required for specialised work.

sem·i·sol·id (sémmi-sóllid) *adj*. Intermediate in properties, especially in rigidity, between solids and liquids.

---

semaphore

ONE OF THE FIRST SIGNALLING SYSTEMS
Arms that point out messages

The semaphore machine, which spelt out messages by moving its arms to indicate letters, words, and numbers, was invented by a French clergyman, Claude Chappe, in 1793. Semaphores were installed along the French coast to relay warnings of British naval activity during the Napoleonic war.

The British Admiralty had semaphore systems operating from 1816 between London and its naval bases. Even though the electric telegraph largely ousted them by 1848, semaphore signalling continued from towers to ships offshore until wireless telegraphy was introduced in Britain by Guglielmo Marconi in 1898.

SEMAPHORE ALPHABET *Signals can be sent by arm movements, with or without flags, as well as by machine. The receiver may be in front of or behind the signaller, so the direction sign – with left arm horizontal – is given first to show which way round the signs are to be read.*

~*n.* A semisolid substance, such as a stiff dough or firm gelatine.

Sem·ite (sée-mīt, sémmīt) *n.* Also **Shem·ite** (shémmīt). A member of a people of Caucasian stock comprising chiefly Jews and Arabs but in ancient times also including Babylonians, Assyrians, Phoenicians, and others of the eastern Mediterranean area. [New Latin *semita*, from Late Latin *Sēm*, Shem (traditional ancestor of the Semites), from Greek, from Hebrew *Shem.*]

Se·mit·ic (si-míttik, sə-, se-) *adj.* **1.** Of, pertaining to, or designating a subfamily of the Afro-Asiatic family of languages including Arabic, Hebrew, Ethiopic, Amharic, and Aramaic. **2.** Of, pertaining to, or designating any of the people who speak a Semitic language; especially, the Jewish.
~*n.* **1.** The Semitic subfamily of languages. **2.** Any one of these languages.

Se·mit·ics (si-míttiks, sə-, se-) *n. Used with a singular verb.* The study of the history, languages, and cultures of the Semitic peoples.

Sem·i·tism (sémmitiz'm) *n.* **1.** A Semitic word, idiom, or characteristic. **2.** A policy of favouring Jewish interests.

Sem·i·to-Ham·it·ic (sémmitō-ha-míttik) *n.* A family of languages, **Afro-Asiatic** (see). —**Sem·i·to-Ham·it·ic** *adj.*

sem·i·tone (sémmi-tōn) *n. Music.* The smallest interval normally used in Western music, equal to half a tone in the standard diatonic scale. Also *U.S.* "half tone". —**sem·i·ton·ic** (-tónnik) *adj.*

sem·i·trail·er (sémmi-traylər) *n.* A trailer with wheels at the rear only, the forward end being supported by the towing vehicle.

sem·i·trans·par·ent (sémmi-transs-párrənt, -tranz-, -paír-ənt) *adj.* Not completely transparent.

sem·i·trop·i·cal (sémmi-tróppik'l) *adj.* Partly tropical; subtropical.

sem·i·vow·el (sémmi-vow-əl, -vów-) *n. Phonetics.* A speech sound that from the articulatory viewpoint is a vowel but that functions as a consonant in the sound system of a particular language; for example, (w) and (y) in English are semivowels. Also called "glide".

sem·i·week·ly (sémmi-wéekli) *adj.* Issued or happening twice a week.
~*n., pl.* **semiweeklies.** A semiweekly publication.
~*adv.* Twice weekly. See Usage note at **bimonthly.**

Semmelweis (zémmǝl-vīs), **Ignaz Philipp** (1818–65). Hungarian physician. He discovered that puerperal fever was an infectious disease transmitted by medical staff after carrying out post-mortems. His theory was not heeded and it was left to Joseph Lister to pioneer antiseptic techniques.

sem·mit (sémmit) *n. Scottish.* A vest. [Middle English *semmit*†.]

sem·o·li·na (sémmə-léenə) *n.* **1.** The gritty, coarse particles of wheat left after flour has been sifted. **2.** A milk pudding prepared from this. [Variant of Italian *semolino*, diminutive of *semola*, bran, from Latin *simila*, fine flour. See **simnel.**]

sem·pi·ter·nal (sémpi-térn'l) *adj.* Eternal; perpetual. [Middle English, from Old French *sempiternel*, from Late Latin *sempiternālis*, from Latin *sempiternus* : *semper*, always + *aeternus*, eternal.] —**sem·pi·ter·ni·ty** (-térnəti) *n.*

sem·pli·ce (sémplichi) *adv. Music.* Simply; plainly. Used as a direction. [Italian, from Latin *simplex* (stem *simplic-*), simple.] —**sem·pli·ce** *adj.*

sem·pre (sémpri, sémpray) *adv. Music.* In the same manner throughout. Used as a direction. [Italian, "always", from Latin *semper.*]

semp·stress (sémp-striss, -strəss) *n.* A seamstress. [Variant of SEAMSTRESS.]

sen (sen) *n., pl.* **sen.** **1. a.** A former monetary unit equal to ¹/₁₀₀ of the yen of Japan. **b.** A monetary unit equal to ¹/₁₀₀ of the dollar of Brunei. **c.** A monetary unit equal to ¹/₁₀₀ of the rupiah of Indonesia. **d.** A monetary unit equal to ¹/₁₀₀ of the riel of Kampuchea. **e.** A monetary unit equal to ¹/₁₀₀ of the dollar or ringgit of Malaysia. **2.** A coin worth one sen. [Japanese, from Chinese (Mandarin) *qián*, money, coin.]

SEN, S.E.N. State Enrolled Nurse (in Britain).

sen., Sen. **1.** senate; senator. **2.** senior.

Sen·a·nay·a·ke (sénnə-nī́-əkə), **D(on) S(tephen)** (1884–1952). Ceylonese statesman, prime minister (1947–52). He headed the movement for constitutional reform which led to independence and was the first prime minister of Ceylon (now Sri Lanka).

Senanayake, Dudley (1911–73). Ceylonese statesman, prime minister (1952–3, 1960, 1965-70). The son of D.S. Senanayake, he succeeded his father as premier.

se·nar·i·us (si-naár-i-əss, -naír-) *n., pl.* **-narii** (-naír-i-ī). A Greek or Latin verse consisting of six feet. [Latin *sēnārius*, from adjective, SENARY.]

sen·ar·mon·tite (sénnaar-món-tīt) *n.* A white or greyish mineral, Sb₂O₃, that occurs in cubic crystalline form. [After Henri de *Sénarmont* (died 1862), French mineralogist.]

sen·a·ry (séenəri, sénnəri) *adj.* Of or pertaining to the number six; having six things or parts. [Latin *sēnārius*, from *sēnī*, six each, from *sex*, six.]

sen·ate (sénnit, sénnət) *n. Abbr.* **sen., Sen.** **1.** An assembly or council of citizens having the highest deliberative and legislative functions in a government, especially: **a.** *Capital* **S.** The upper house of Congress in the United States, to which two members are elected from each state. **b.** *Capital* **S.** The upper legislative house in Australia, Canada, France, and other countries. **c.** The supreme council of state of the ancient Roman republic and, nominally, of the empire. **2.** The building or hall in which a senate meets. **3.** The governing body of some universities, composed of faculty members and sometimes student representatives. [Middle English *senat*, from Old

French, from Latin *senātus*, from *senex*, old, an old man, an elder.]

sen·a·tor (sénnətər) *n. Often capital* **S.** *Abbr.* **Sen., sen.** A member of a senate. —**sen·a·tor·ship** *n.*

sen·a·to·ri·al (sénnə-táwr-i-əl ‖ -tór-) *adj.* **1.** Of, concerning, or befitting a senator or a senate. **2.** Composed of senators. **3.** *U.S.* Designating a district from which a senator is elected. —**sen·a·to·ri·al·ly** *adv.*

se·na·tus con·sul·tum (se-naá-təss kon-súl-tōōm, si-, -náy-, -sōōl-, -təm ‖ *U.S. also* kōn-) *n., pl.* **senatus consulta** (-súltə). *Latin.* A decree of the ancient Roman senate.

send¹ (send) *v.* **sent** (sent), **sending, sends.** —*tr.* **1. a.** To cause to be conveyed to a destination by an intermediary or means of communication: *sent his reply by telegram.* **b.** To express for conveyance: *She sends her love.* **2.** To cause or order to go, especially: **a.** To direct to go on a mission or errand. **b.** To enable or arrange for (someone) to go: *sent all their children to private schools.* **c.** To command or request to depart; dismiss: *Send the guard away.* **d.** To direct or require to go or be taken; consign:*sent them to the gallows.* **e.** To cause to go or move in a specified way or direction: *The rain sent them hurrying indoors.* **f.** To direct (a person) to a source of information; refer. **3. a.** To give off; emit (heat or smoke, for example). Often used with *forth* or *out.* **b.** To produce; cause to grow: *sending forth new roots.* **4.** To direct or propel with force: *an explosion that sent glass flying everywhere.* **5.** To cause to take place or befall; bestow or inflict: *a punishment sent by the gods.* **6. a.** To put or drive into some state or condition: *His lecture sent me to sleep.* **b.** *Slang.* To transport with delight; carry away. —*intr.* To dispatch a messenger or message. —**send away for.** To order by mail. —**send down.** *British.* **1.** To suspend or dismiss from a university. **2.** *Informal.* To send to prison. —**send for.** **1.** To order. **2.** To summon —**send packing.** *Informal.* To dismiss summarily or abruptly. [Send, sent, sent; Middle English *senden, sente, sent,* Old English *sendan, sende, sended.*] —**send·er** *n.*

send² Variant of **scend.**

sen·dal (sénd'l) *n.* A light, thin silk used in the Middle Ages. [Middle English *cendal*, from Old French, obscurely akin to Greek *sindōn*†, a fine linen cloth.]

send off *tr.v.* **1.** *Sports.* To order (a player) to leave the field because of a serious violation of the rules. **2.** To give a send-off to.

send-off (sénd-off, -awff) *n.* **1.** A demonstration of affection and good wishes for one about to leave on a.journey or to begin a new undertaking. **2.** A start given to someone or something.

send up *tr.v.* **1.** *Chiefly British.* To satirise or make fun of, especially by mimicry or parody. **2.** *U.S. Informal.* To send to prison.

send-up (sénd-up) *n.* An amusing imitation or parody.

Sen·e·ca¹ (sénnikə) *n., pl.* **Seneca** or **-cas.** **1.** A member of an Iroquoian-speaking North American Indian people formerly inhabiting western New York. **2.** The language of this people.

Seneca². Latin name Marcus Annaeus Seneca; known as Seneca the Elder (c. 55 B.C.–c. A.D. 39). Roman writer on rhetoric. His works include the *Controversiae*, a series of imaginary legal cases which illustrate various approved methods of oratorical presentation.

Seneca³. Latin name Lucius Annaeus Seneca; known as Seneca the Younger (c. 4 B.C.–A.D. 65). Roman writer, philosopher, and politician. The son of Seneca the Elder, he was tutor to the young Nero and became one of the emperor's chief advisors on his accession. He produced several works of moral philosophy, advocating Stoicism, and also wrote nine tragedies. Seneca was forced to commit suicide for alleged conspiracy against Nero.

se·nec·ti·tude (si-nékti-tewd, sə- ‖ -tōōd) *n.* Old age. [Medieval Latin *senectitūdō*, from Latin *senectūs*, from *senex*, old.]

sen·e·ga (sénnigə) *n.* The dried root of a North American plant, *Polygala senega*, used as an expectorant. [Variant of SENECA.]

Sé·né·gal (sénni-gáwl; *French* -gál). A river of west Africa. Formed by the confluence of the Bafing and Bakoy rivers, both of which rise in the Fouta Djallon in northern Guinea, it flows 1 690 kilometres (1,050 miles) to the Atlantic at St. Louis in Senegal.

Sen·e·gal, Republic of (sénni-gáwl). *French* **Sé·né·gal** (-gál). A state of West Africa, which takes its name from the Sénégal river. Consisting mainly of lowland plains it has important phosphate and iron ore deposits. Following the Sahel droughts of the 1970s, groundnuts, which accounted for over three-quarters of the country's total exports, now accounts for only a quarter. Fishing and tourism are increasingly also important. Senegal is one of West Africa's most industrialised countries, producing textiles, beer, foodstuffs, tobaccos, and cement. By 1887, the French had conquered all of Senegal. It gained independence in 1960, but maintains close ties with France. In 1981, it joined with Gambia to form the Confederation of Senegambia. Area, 196 722 square kilometres (75,934 square miles). Population, 5,900,000. Capital, Dakar. See map at **West African States.**

Sen·e·gam·bi·a, Confederation of (sénni-gámbi-ə). Union formed in December 1981 by the states of Senegal and Gambia. It is not a political union, but does involve some economic integration and close ties in foreign policy matters.

se·nes·cence (si-néss'nss, sə-) *n.* The state associated with advancing age of an organism or part, usually characterised by a reduced capacity to repair and maintain tissues. —**se·nes·cent** *adj.*

sen·e·schal (sénnish'l) *n.* An official in a royal or noble medieval household in charge of domestic arrangements and the administration of servants; a steward. [Middle English, from Old French, from Medieval Latin *siniscalcus*, from Germanic.]

Sen·ghor (seng-gór, saN-), **Léopold Sédar** (1906–). Senegalese writer and statesman, president (1960–80). A noted poet whose collections include *Chants d'Ombre* (1945), led his country to independence in 1960 as head of the Senegalese Progressive Union. He became Senegal's first president.

se·nile (séenīl || *U.S. also* sénnīl) *adj.* **1.** Pertaining to, characteristic of, or proceeding from old age. **2.** Exhibiting senility. **3.** *Geology.* Worn away nearly to the base level, as at the end of an erosion cycle. [French *sénile,* from Latin *senīlis,* from *senex* (stem *sen-*), old.] **—se·nile·ly** *adv.*

senile dementia *n.* Progressive deterioration of mental faculties in old age. See **presenile dementia.**

se·nil·i·ty (si-nílləti, se-) *n.* **1.** The state of being senile. **2.** Mental and physical deterioration with old age.

sen·ior (séen-yər, séeni-ər) *adj. Abbr.* **Sr., sr., Sen., sen., Snr.** **1.** More advanced in age. Used especially after a name to denote the older of two persons who share the same name, such as a father and son: *Douglas Fairbanks Senior.* **2. a.** Pertaining to or having a high or higher rank: *senior levels of management.* **b.** Above others in terms of length of service or appointment. **3.** Of, designating, or intended for older or more advanced students or pupils.
~n. A senior person, especially: **1.** One who is older: *He is three years my senior.* **2.** *U.S.* A final-year student at university or high school. [Latin, comparative of *senex,* old.]

senior citizen *n.* A person of or over the age of retirement.
Usage: The phrase *senior citizen* is now widely used as a euphemism for "elderly person", especially in the fields of politics and advertising. While many people find it unobjectionable, the phrase has attracted criticism on the grounds that it lacks any real meaning, and that it distracts people's attention from the problems involved in society's care (or lack of care) of the aged.

senior common room *n. Abbr.* **S.C.R.** A common room for faculty members, especially at a British university.

Senior Executive Officer *n. Abbr.* **S.E.O.** An administrative officer in the British Government service in the grade between a Principal and a Higher Executive Officer.

se·ni·or·i·ty (sée-ni-órrəti) *n., pl.* **-ties.** **1.** The state of being older or higher in rank. **2.** Precedence of position; especially, precedence over others of the same rank by reason of a longer span of service.

senior nursing officer *n.* In Britain, a senior nurse in charge of all the nurses and ancillary staff (but not the doctors) in a hospital, or in one department of a hospital. Formerly called "matron".

senior service *n. British.* The Royal Navy. Preceded by *the.*

sen·na (sénnə) *n.* **1.** Any of various plants of the genus *Cassia,* having compound leaves and usually yellow flowers. **2.** The dried leaves or pods of *C. angustifolia* or *C. acutifolia,* used medicinally as a cathartic. [New Latin, from Arabic *sanā'.*]

Sen·nach·er·ib (se-náckərib, si-, sə-) (died 681 B.C.). King of Assyria (704–681). The son of Sargon II, he is especially remembered for his building works which included the restoration of Nineveh.

sen·net (sénnit) *n.* A call on a trumpet or cornet signalling the ceremonial exits and entrances of actors in Elizabethan drama. [Perhaps variant of SIGNET.]

Sen·nett (sén-it, -ət), **Mack,** born Michael Sinott (1884–1960). U.S. film producer and director, born in Canada. His many slapstick films, included the Keystone comedies (1912–16).

sen·night, se'n·night (sénnīt) *n. Archaic.* A week. [Middle English *seoveniht, sennet,* Old English *seofon nihta* : *seofon,* SEVEN + *nihta,* plural of *niht,* NIGHT.]

sen·nit (sénnit) *n.* Also **sin·net** (sínnit). *Nautical.* Braided cordage formed by plaiting several strands of rope fibre or similar material. [17th century : origin obscure.]

sen·o·pi·a (sen-ōpi-ə) *n.* Improvement of near vision sometimes occurring in the aged because of swelling of the crystalline lens in incipient cataract. [Latin *senex,* old + -OPIA.]

se·ñor (sen-yór) *n., pl.* **señores** (-ayz; *Spanish* -ayss). *Abbr.* **Sr.** **1.** The Spanish title of courtesy for a man, equivalent to the English *Mr.* or *sir.* It may be used alone or prefixed to a name. **2.** A Spanish or Spanish-speaking man.

se·ño·ra (sen-yáw-rə; *Spanish* -ra) *n., pl.* **señoras** (-z; *Spanish* -ss). *Abbr.* **Sra.** **1.** The Spanish title of courtesy for a married woman, equivalent to the English *Mrs.* or *madam.* It may be used alone or prefixed to a name. **2.** A Spanish or Spanish-speaking woman.

se·ño·ri·ta (sényaw-rée-tə; *Spanish* -ta) *n., pl.* **-tas** (-z; *Spanish* -ss). *Abbr.* **Srta.** **1.** The Spanish title of courtesy for an unmarried young woman or a girl, equivalent to the English *Miss.* It may be used alone or prefixed to a name. **2.** A Spanish or Spanish-speaking unmarried woman or girl.

sen·sate (sén-sayt) *adj.* Perceived by the senses. [Late Latin *sēnsātus,* gifted with sense, from Latin *sēnsus,* SENSE.] **—sen·sate·ly** *adv.*

sen·sa·tion (sen-sáysh'n, sən-) *n.* **1. a.** A perception associated with stimulation of a sense organ or with a specific bodily condition: *the sensation of heat.* **b.** The faculty to feel or perceive; physical sensibility: *He had little sensation left in his leg.* **2.** An emotional state that is hard to define but is associated with particular conditions or circumstances: *a strange sensation of relief.* **3. a.** A condition of intense public interest and excitement. **b.** An event, person, or object causing such public excitement. [Medieval Latin *sēnsātiō* (stem *sēnsātiōn-*), from Late Latin *sēnsātus,* SENSATE.]

sen·sa·tion·al (sen-sáysh'n'l, sən-) *adj.* **1.** Of or pertaining to sensation. **2.** Arousing or intended to arouse strong curiosity, interest, or reaction, especially by exaggerated or lurid details. **3.** Outstanding; wonderful. **—sen·sa·tion·al·ly** *adv.*

sen·sa·tion·al·ism (sen-sáysh'n'l-iz'm, sən-) *n.* **1. a.** The use of sensational matter or methods, as in writing, art or politics. **b.** Sensational subject matter. **c.** Interest in or the effect of such subject matter. **2.** *Philosophy.* The theory that sensation is the only source of knowledge. Also called "sensualism". **3.** The ethical doctrine that feeling is the only criterion of good. **—sen·sa·tion·al·ist** *n.* **—sen·sa·tion·al·is·tic** (-ístik) *adj.*

sense (senss) *n.* **1.** Any of the animal functions of hearing, sight, smell, touch, and taste. **2.** The faculty of external perception exemplified by these functions. **3.** *Plural.* The faculties of sensation as means of providing physical gratification and pleasure. **4. a.** Intuitive or acquired perception or ability to make appropriate judgments: *good dress sense.* **b.** A capacity to appreciate or understand: *a sense of humour.* **c.** A vague feeling, impression, or presentiment: *a sense of impending trouble.* **d.** Recognition or awareness of moral issues and their relevance to one's own conduct: *a sense of duty.* **5. a.** *Usually plural.* One's normal conscious or rational state: *Come to your senses.* **b.** A capacity for sound practical judgments; common sense: *hasn't got an ounce of sense.* **c.** The quality of being consistent with good judgment: *There's no sense in waiting.* **6. a.** Import; point; intended meaning. **b.** Lexical meaning. **c.** The meaning of a word in a particular context. **7.** The prevailing view; the consensus. **—make sense.** **1.** To be coherent or intelligible. **2.** *Informal.* To be practical or advisable. —See Synonyms at **meaning, mind.**
~tr.v. **sensed, sensing, senses.** **1.** To become aware of, often on the basis of intuition rather than explicit information; perceive. **2.** To detect something automatically: *sense radioactivity.* **3.** *Chiefly U.S. Informal.* To grasp; understand. [Latin *sēnsus,* the faculty of perceiving, from the past participle of *sentīre,* to perceive by senses, to feel.]

sense datum *n.* A basic unanalysable experience resulting from the stimulation of a sense organ.

sense·less (sénss-ləss, -liss) *adj.* **1.** Without sense or meaning; meaningless. **2.** Foolish; lacking sense: *a senseless boy.* **3.** Insensate; unconscious. **—sense·less·ly** *adv.* **—sense·less·ness** *n.*

sense organ *n.* A specialised organ or structure, such as the eye, the stimulation of which initiates a process of sensory perception.

sense perception *n.* Perception by the bodily senses.

sen·si·bil·i·ty (sén-si-bílləti, -ə-) *n., pl.* **-ties.** **1.** The ability to feel or perceive. **2. a.** Keen intellectual or aesthetic perception: *the sensibility of a painter to colour.* **b.** The capacity for sensitive emotional response, as to the feelings of another; sensitiveness. **3.** *Often plural.* **a.** Receptiveness to impression, whether pleasant or unpleasant; acuteness of feeling. **b.** Acute susceptibility to emotional influences; oversensitiveness. **4.** *Botany.* The susceptibility of plants to environmental influences.

sen·si·ble (sén-sib'l, -səb'l) *adj.* **1.** Perceptible by the senses or by the mind. **2.** Readily perceived; appreciable. **3.** Having the faculty of sensation; able to feel or perceive. **4.** Having a perception of something; cognisant; aware. **5.** Acting with or showing good sense: *a sensible choice.* **6.** Practical and unpretentious: *sensible shoes.* —See Synonyms at **aware.** —See Usage note at **sensitive.** [Middle English, from Old French, from Latin *sēnsibilis,* from *sēnsus,* SENSE.] **—sen·si·ble·ness** *n.* **—sen·si·bly** *adv.*

sen·si·tise, sen·si·tize (sén-si-tīz, -sə-) *v.* **-tised, -tising, -tises.** *—tr.* **1.** To make sensitive. **2.** *Photography.* To make (a film or plate) sensitive to light, especially to light of a specific wavelength. *—intr.* To become sensitive. **—sen·si·ti·sa·tion** (-tī-záysh'n || *U.S.* -ti-) *n.* **—sen·si·tis·er** *n.*

sen·si·tive (sén-si-tiv, -sə-) *adj.* **1.** Capable of perceiving with a sense or senses. **2.** Responsive to and readily affected by external conditions or emotional stimulation: *a sensitive part of the body; a sensitive child.* **3.** Susceptible to the attitudes, feelings, or circumstances of others; acutely or sympathetically aware. **4. a.** Easily upset. **b.** Quick to take offence; touchy. **5.** Easily irritated: *sensitive skin.* **6.** Readily altered by the action of some agent: *sensitive to light.* **7.** Registering very slight differences or changes of condition. Said of an instrument. **8.** Unusually susceptible to external conditions and tending to fluctuate. Said of stock market prices. **9. a.** Dealing with classified information, usually involving national security: *a sensitive post in the Foreign Office.* **b.** Liable to arouse controversy or strong feelings: *a sensitive issue.* [Middle English, from Old French *sensitif,* from Medieval Latin *sēnsitīvus,* from Latin *sēnsus,* SENSE.] **—sen·si·tive·ly** *adv.* **—sen·si·tive·ness** *n.*
Usage: *Sensitivity* can be used as the noun relating to any of the senses of *sensitive,* but *sensitiveness* is the form usually employed for the personal tendency to be offended easily or to react readily to criticism. *Sensitive* should also be clearly distinguished from *sensible, sensual,* and *sensuous. Sensitive* refers primarily to the delicate nature of someone's feelings (*he's very sensitive about that issue*); *sensible* emphasises one's conscious awareness of something (*he was sensible that a lot remained to be done*); *sensual* applies specifically to gratification of the physical senses, especially those associated with sexual activity (*sensual pleasures*); *sensuous* refers to satisfaction of any of the senses, especially through the aesthetic enjoyment of nature, art, and so on (*sensuous colours/music*).

sensitive plant *n.* **1.** A woody tropical American plant, *Mimosa pudica,* having leaflets and stems that fold and droop when touched. **2.** Any of various similar plants.

sen·si·tiv·i·ty (sén-si-tívvəti, -sə-) *n., pl.* **-ties.** **1.** The quality or condition of being sensitive. **2.** *Electronics.* The minimum input signal required to produce a specific output signal. **3.** *Photography.* The

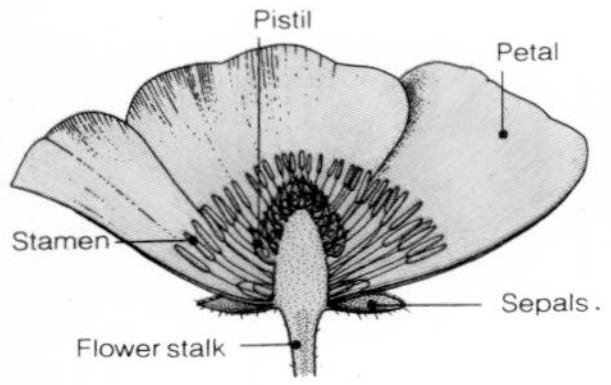

sepal *The sepals on a plant – as in the meadow buttercup shown here in cross-section – are the protective casing which encloses and shelters the flower in bud. They fold back as the petals unfurl. The flower's reproductive organs are in the centre: the pollen-producing stamens; and the pistils containing the embryonic seeds which are fertilised by pollen.*

degree of response of a plate or film to light, especially to light of a particular wavelength.

sen·si·tom·e·ter (sén-si-tómmitər) *n.* A device used for measuring the sensitivity of photographic film to light. [SENSIT(IVE) + -METER.] **—sen·si·tom·e·try** *n.*

sen·sor (sén-sər, -sawr) *n.* A device, such as a photoelectric cell, that receives and responds to a signal or stimulus. [Latin *sēnsus,* SENSE.]

sen·so·ri·mo·tor (sén-səri-mṓtər) *adj.* Of, pertaining to, or combining the functions of the sensing and motor activities. Said of nerves. [*sensory* + *motor.*]

sen·so·ri·um (sen-sáwr-i-əm || -sṓr-) *n., pl.* **-ums** or **-soria** (sáwr-i-ə). **1.** The part of the brain that receives and correlates the impressions conveyed from various sensory areas. **2.** The entire sensory system. [Late Latin *sēnsōrium,* organ of sensation, from Latin *sēnsus,* SENSE.]

sen·so·ry (sén-səri) *adj.* Also **sen·sor·i·al** (sen-sáwr-i-əl || -sṓr-). **1.** Of or pertaining to the senses or sensation. **2.** Transmitting impulses from sense organs to nerve centres; afferent.

sensory deprivation *n.* A situation in which a subject undergoes complete deprivation of sensory stimulation, so that his physical and psychological reactions may be observed.

sen·su·al (sénssew-əl, -shoo-əl) *adj.* **1.** Pertaining to or affecting any of the senses or a sense organ; sensory. **2. a.** Pertaining to, consisting in, or excessively fond of the gratification of the physical appetites, especially sexual appetites. **b.** Suggesting sexuality or a sensual disposition; voluptuous. **c.** Carnal rather than spiritual or intellectual; worldly. —See Synonyms at **sensuous.** —See Usage note at **sensitive.** [Middle English, from Latin *sēnsuālis,* from *sēnsus,* SENSE.] **—sen·su·al·ly** *adv.* **—sen·su·al·ness** *n.*

sen·su·a·lise, sen·su·al·ize (sénssew-ə-līz, -shoo-) *tr.v.* **-ised, -ising, -ises.** To make sensual. **—sen·su·al·i·sa·tion** (-lī-záysh'n || *U.S.* -li-) *n.*

sen·su·al·ism (sénssew-ə-liz'm, -shoo-) *n.* **1.** Sensuality. **2.** The ethical doctrine that the pleasures of the senses are the highest good. **3.** *Philosophy.* **Sensationalism** *(see).* **—sen·su·al·ist** *n.* **—sen·su·al·is·tic** (-lístik) *adj.*

sen·su·al·i·ty (sénssew-ál-əti, -shoo-) *n., pl.* **-ties. 1.** The quality or state of being sensual. **2.** Excessive devotion to sensual pleasures.

sen·su·ous (sén-əss, -shoo-) *adj.* **1.** Pertaining to or derived from the senses. **2.** Having qualities that appeal to the senses, especially on an aesthetic level. **3.** Readily susceptible to influences perceived by the senses; highly appreciative of the pleasures of sensation. —See Usage note at **sensitive.** [Latin *sēnsus,* SENSE + -OUS.] **—sen·su·ous·ly** *adv.* **—sen·su·ous·ness** *n.*

Synonyms: *sensuous, sensual, luxurious, sybaritic, epicurean.*

sent. Past tense and past participle of **send.**

sen·tence (séntənss) *n.* **1.** A complete and independent grammatical unit comprising a word or a group of words, and usually consisting of at least one subject with its predicate, containing a finite verb or verb phrase; for example, *The door is open* and *Go!* are sentences. **2. a.** A judicial decision of what punishment is to be inflicted on a convicted person. **b.** The punishment so meted out. **3.** *Archaic.* An opinion; especially, one given formally after deliberation. **4.** *Archaic.* An aphorism.
~*tr.v.* **sentenced, -tencing, -tences. 1.** To pass sentence upon (a convicted person). **2.** To cause to undergo something undesirable; condemn. [Middle English, opinion, judgment, thought, from Old French, from Latin *sententia,* a way of thinking, opinion, from *sentīre,* to feel.] **—sen·tenc·er** (sentən-sər) *n.* **—sen·ten·tial** (sen-ténsh'l) *adj.* **—sen·ten·tial·ly** *adv.*

sen·ten·tious (sen-ténshəss) *adj.* **1.** Terse, pithy, and aphoristic in expression. **2.** Fond of using maxims. **3.** Given to pompous moralising. [Latin *sententiōsus,* full of meaning, from *sententia,* opinion, SENTENCE.] **—sen·ten·tious·ly** *adv.* **—sen·ten·tious·ness** *n.*

sen·ti·ence (sén-sh'nss, -shi-ənss || -ti-ənss) *n.* Also **sen·ti·en·cy** (-ən-si). **1.** The quality or state of being sentient; consciousness. **2.** Feeling as distinguished from perception or thought.

sen·ti·ent (sén-sh'nt, -shi-ənt || -ti-ənt) *adj.* Having the power of sensation; conscious.
~*n.* A sentient being. [Latin *sentiēns* (stem *sentient-*), present participle of *sentīre,* to feel.] **—sen·ti·ent·ly** *adv.*

sen·ti·ment (séntimənt) *n.* **1. a.** A thought, attitude, or general mental disposition modified or coloured by emotion: *a certain amount of anti-American sentiment.* **b.** *Often plural.* An opinion about a specific matter; a view. **2.** The emotional import of a passage, work of art, or the like, as distinguished from the form of expression. **3. a.** Susceptibility to delicate or refined feeling. **b.** An expression of this, especially in art or literature. **4.** Excessive susceptibility to such feeling; emotion that borders on mawkishness. —See Synonyms at **opinion.** [Middle English *sentement,* from Old French, from Medieval Latin *sentīmentum,* from Latin *sentīre,* to feel.]

sen·ti·men·tal (sénti-mént'l) *adj.* **1. a.** Characterised by, influenced by, or exhibiting delicate or refined feeling. **b.** Affectedly or extravagantly emotional; mawkish. **2.** Based on or influenced by emotional considerations rather than reason: *kept the watch for sentimental reasons.* **3.** Appealing to the sentiments, especially to romantic feelings: *sentimental music.* **—sen·ti·men·tal·ly** *adv.*

sen·ti·men·tal·ise, sen·ti·men·tal·ize (sénti-mént'l-īz) *v.* **-ised, -ising, -ises.** —*tr.* To be sentimental about or impart a sentimental quality to. —*intr.* To behave in a sentimental manner. **—sen·ti·men·tal·i·sa·tion** (-lī-záysh'n || *U.S.* -li-) *n.*

sen·ti·men·tal·ism (sénti-mént'l-iz'm) *n.* **1.** A predilection for the sentimental. **2.** An idea or expression marked by excessive sentiment. **—sen·ti·men·tal·ist** *n.*

sen·ti·men·tal·i·ty (sénti-men-tál-əti, -mən-) *n., pl.* **-ties. 1.** The condition or quality of being excessively or affectedly sentimental. **2.** Any expression of this.

sen·ti·nel (séntin'l) *n.* One that keeps guard; a sentry.
~*tr.v.* **sentinelled** or *U.S.* **sentineled, -nelling** or *U.S.* **-neling, -nels. 1.** To watch over as a sentinel. **2.** To provide with a sentinel. **3.** To post as a sentinel. [French *sentinelle,* from Italian *sentinella,* perhaps from *sentire,* to perceive, watch, from Latin *sentīre,* to perceive, feel.]

sen·try (séntri) *n., pl.* **-tries. 1.** A guard, especially a soldier posted at some spot to prevent the passage of unauthorised persons. **2.** The duty of a sentry; a watch. [Perhaps short for obsolete *centrinell,* variant of SENTINEL.]

sentry box *n.* A small shelter for a sentry at his post.

sentry palm *n.* The **Kentia palm** *(see).*

S.E.O. Senior Executive Officer.

Se·oul (sōl). *Japanese* **Keijo.** Also **Kyongsong.** The capital of the Republic of Korea, and also of Kyonggi province. The capital of Korea since 1392, it became the capital of South Korea on partition of the country in 1948. It suffered severe damage during the Korean War. Its industries include cotton, flour, paper, chemicals, and engineering. Inchon serves as the city's port.

se·pal (sépp'l, seép'l) *n.* One of the usually green segments forming the calyx of a flower. Compare **petal.** [French *sépale,* from New Latin *sepalum* : *sepa,* sepal, variant of Greek *skepē*†, covering + (PET)AL, misnamed by N.J. de Necker (died 1790), who combined the terms petal and sepal, not distinguishing between the corolla and calyx.] **—se·palled, se·paled, sep·a·lous** (sépp'l-əss) *adj.*

se·pal·oid (sépp'l-oyd, seép'l-) *adj.* Also **se·pal·ine** (-īn, -in). Resembling or characteristic of a sepal.

-sepalous *adj. comb. form.* Indicates sepals of a certain type or number; for example, **polysepalous.**

sep·a·ra·ble (séppərə-b'l, séppra-) *adj.* Capable of being separated. [French *séparable* or Latin *sēparābilis,* from *sēparāre,* to SEPARATE.] **—sep·a·ra·bil·i·ty** (-bílləti) *n.* **—sep·a·ra·bly** *adv.*

sep·a·rate (séppə-rayt) *v.* **-rated, -rating, -rates.** —*tr.* **1. a.** To set apart; disunite or disjoin. **b.** To occupy the space or time between; keep or cause to be apart: *separates the ancient and modern parts of the city.* **c.** To space apart. **2.** To differentiate or discriminate between; distinguish. **3.** To remove from a compound or complex whole; isolate, extract, or sort into constituent elements. **4.** To part (a married couple) by decree. **5.** *U.S.* To terminate a contractual relationship with; discharge. —*intr.* **1.** To become disconnected or severed; come apart; part. **2.** To withdraw or secede. **3.** To part company; disperse. **4.** To cease living together in a conjugal relationship. **5.** To become divided into components or parts.
~*adj.* (-rət, -rit, sépprət, sépprit). **1.** Set apart from the rest; not connected; disjoined; detached. **2.** Existing as a distinct and independent entity: *on three separate occasions.* **3.** Dissimilar; peculiar to oneself or itself: *went their separate ways.* **4.** Not shared; individual. **5.** *Archaic.* Withdrawn from others; solitary; isolated.
~*n.* (-rət, -rit, sépprət, sépprit). A garment, such as a skirt, jacket, or pair of slacks, that may be purchased separately and worn in various combinations with other garments. Usually used in the plural. [Middle English *separaten,* from Latin *sēparāre* (past participle *sēparātus*) : *sē,* apart + *parāre,* to make ready, prepare.] **—sep·a·rate·ly** *adv.* **—sep·a·rate·ness** *n.*

Synonyms: *separate, divide, part, sever, sunder, divorce, diverge.*

separate development *n.* The South African policy of apartheid, especially as it envisages the establishment of black homelands.

sep·a·ra·tion (séppə-ráysh'n) *n.* **1. a.** The act or process of separating. **b.** The state of being separated. **2.** The place where a division or parting occurs. **3.** An interval or space that separates; a gap. **4.** *Law.* An agreement or court decree terminating the conjugal relationship of a husband and wife. See **judicial separation.**

sep·a·ra·tist (séppə-rət-ist, sép- || -rayt-) *n.* Also **sep·a·ra·tion·ist** (séppə-ráysh'n-ist). One who secedes or advocates separation, as from an established church or political unit; a secessionist. **—sep·a·ra·tism** *n.* **—sep·a·ra·tist, sep·a·ra·tis·tic** (-ístik) *adj.*

sep·a·ra·tive (séppə-rət-iv, sép- || -rayt-) *adj.* Tending to separate or causing separation.

sep·a·ra·tor (séppə-raytər) *n.* **1.** One that separates. **2.** A device for separating cream from milk.

Se·phar·di (se-fár-di, si-) *n., pl.* **-dim** (-dim). A member of one of the two main divisions of Jews; a Spanish or Portuguese Jew or a descendant from one of these. Compare **Ashkenazi.** [Modern Hebrew *Səphāradhī,* Spaniard, from *Səphāradh,* Spain.] **—Se·phar·dic** *adj.*

se·pi·a (seépi-ə) *n.* **1.** A dark-brown ink or pigment originally prepared from the secretion of the cuttlefish. **2. a.** A drawing or picture done in this pigment. **b.** A photograph in a brown tint. **3.** Dark greyish yellowish brown to dark or moderate olive brown.
~*adj.* **1.** Of the colour sepia. **2.** Done in sepia. [Italian *seppia,* from Latin *sēpia,* cuttlefish, dark-brown pigment prepared from its secretion, from Greek, akin to *sēpein,* to rot. See **septic.**]

se·pi·o·lite (seépi-ə-līt) *n. Mineralogy.* **Meerschaum** *(see).* [German *Sepiolith* : Greek *sēpion,* cuttlebone, from *sēpia,* cuttlefish (see **sepia**) + -LITE.]

se·poy (seé-poy) *n.* Formerly, a native of India serving as a soldier under European, especially British, command. [Perhaps from Portuguese *sipae,* from Urdu *sipāhī,* from Persian, from *sipāh,* army, from Old Persian *śpāda*†.]

sep·pu·ku (sep-pŏŏkŏŏ) n. Japanese. **Hara-kiri** (see). [Japanese, "to cut open the stomach".]

sep·sis (sépsiss) n. **1.** The presence of pus-forming microorganisms in the blood or tissues. **2.** Archaic. A putrefactive process in the body. [New Latin, from Greek sēpsis, putrefaction, from sēpein, to make rotten. See **septic**.]

sept (sept) n. A division of a tribe or clan, especially in medieval Ireland or Scotland. [Perhaps variant of SECT.]

Sept. September.

sep·ta. Plural of **septum**.

sep·tal (séptəl) adj. Of or pertaining to a septum.

sep·tar·i·um (sep-taír-i-əm) n., pl. **-ia** (-i-ə). An irregular polygonal system of calcite-filled cracks occurring in certain rock concretions. [New Latin : SEPT(I)- (partition) + -ARIUM.] —**sep·tar·i·an** adj.

sep·tate (séptayt) adj. Having a septum or septa. [New Latin septatus, from SEPTUM.]

Sep·tem·ber (sep-témbər, səp-, sip-) n. Abbr. **Sept.** The ninth month of the year, according to the Gregorian calendar. September has 30 days. [Middle English Septembre, from Old French, from Latin September, the seventh month (of the Roman calendar), from septem, seven.]

sep·te·nar·i·us (séptə-naír-i-əss) n., pl. **-narii** (-naír-i-ee). A Greek or Latin verse consisting of seven feet. [Latin septēnārius, SEPTENARY.]

sep·te·nar·y (sep-téenəri, séptĭ-nəri ‖ U.S. -nerri) adj. Of, pertaining to, or based on the number seven.

~n., pl. **septenaries.** A set or group of seven. [Latin septēnārius, from septēnī, seven each, from septem, seven.]

sep·ten·ni·al (sep-ténni-əl) adj. **1.** Occurring every seven years. **2.** Lasting for or containing seven years. [Latin septennium, period of seven years, from septennis, of seven years : septem, seven + annus, year.] —**sep·ten·ni·al·ly** adv.

sep·ten·tri·on (sep-téntri-ən ‖ -on) n. Archaic. The north; northern regions. [Middle English septentrioun, from Old French septentrion, from Latin septentriōnēs, "seven plough-oxen", northern constellation : septem, seven + triōnēs, plough-oxen.] —**sep·ten·tri·o·nal** (-ən'l) adj.

sep·tet, sep·tette (sep-tét, sép-) n. **1.** A group of seven. **2.** Music. **a.** A composition for seven voices or instruments. **b.** The musicians performing such a composition. [German Septet, from Latin septem, seven.]

septi–[1] comb. form. Indicates seven; for example, **septilateral**. [Latin, from septem, seven.]

septi–[2], **sept–** comb. form. Indicates partition or septum; for example, **septarium**, **septifragal**. [From SEPTUM.]

sep·tic (séptik) adj. **1.** Of, pertaining to, characterised by or of the nature of sepsis. **2.** Causing sepsis; putrefactive. [Latin sēpticus, putrefying, septic, from Greek sēptikos, from sēptos, rotten, from sēpein†, to make rotten.] —**sep·tic·i·ty** (sep-tíssiti) n.

sep·ti·cae·mi·a (sépti-séemi-ə) n. A systemic disease caused by pathogenic organisms or their toxins in the bloodstream. Also called "blood poisoning". [New Latin : Latin sēpticus, SEPTIC + -AEMIA.] —**sep·ti·cae·mic** (-séemik) adj.

sep·ti·ci·dal (sépti-sĭd'l) adj. Botany. Splitting along the junctions of the carpels. Said of a seed capsule. [SEPTI- (partition) + -cidal, from -CIDE.] —**sep·ti·ci·dal·ly** adv.

septic tank n. A sewage disposal tank in which a continuous flow of waste material is decomposed by anaerobic bacteria.

sep·tif·ra·gal (sep-tíffrəg'l) adj. Botany. Characterised by the breaking apart of fruits along natural dividing walls. [From SEPTI- (partition) + Latin frangere, to break.]

sep·ti·lat·er·al (sépti-láttrəl, -láttərəl) adj. Seven-sided. [SEPTI- (seven) + LATERAL.]

sep·til·li·on (sep-tíllian, -tíl-yən) n. **1.** In British usage, the cardinal number represented by 1 followed by 42 zeros, usually written 10[42]. **2.** In U.S. usage, the cardinal number represented by 1 followed by 24 zeros, usually written 10[24]. Called in British usage "quadrillion". [French : SEPTI- (seven) + (MI)LLION.] —**sep·til·li·onth** n. & adj.

Septimius. See Severus.

sep·tu·a·ge·nar·i·an (sép-tew-əji-naír-i-ən ‖ -too-) adj. **1.** Being seventy years old or between seventy and eighty years old. **2.** Of or like someone of this age.

~n. A person of seventy or between seventy and eighty years of age. [Latin septuāgēnārius, noun and adjective, from septuāgēnī, seventy each, from septuāgintā, seventy. See **Septuagint**.]

Sep·tu·a·ges·i·ma (sép-tew-ə-jéssimə ‖ -too-) n. The third Sunday before Lent. Also called "Septuagesima Sunday". [Middle English Septuagesime, Septuagesima, the seventy days following it, from Old French, from Late Latin septuāgēsima, feminine of septuāgēsimus, seventieth, from septuāgintā, seventy. See **Septuagint**.]

Sep·tu·a·gint (sép-tew-ə-jint ‖ -too-) n. Abbr. **LXX.** A Greek translation of the Old Testament made in the third century B.C. [Latin septuāgintā, seventy, "the Seventy", designation of the 70 or 72 Jewish scholars who, according to an unhistorical tradition, completed the translation in 72 days on the island of Pharos : septem, seven + -gintā, decimal suffix, ten times.]

sep·tum (séptəm) n., pl. **-ta** (-tə). **1.** A thin partition or membrane between two cavities or soft masses of tissue in a plant or animal. **2.** In filamentous organisms, a cell wall at right angles to the length of the filament. [Latin septum, saeptum, partition, from sēpīre, saepīre, to surround with a hedge, from sēpes, saepes†, hedge.]

sep·tu·ple (sép-tyŏŏ-p'l ‖ sep-tyŏŏ-p'l, -tŏŏ-) adj. **1.** Consisting of or having seven parts, members, or copies. **2.** Multiplied by seven; seven times as such, as many, or as large.

~n. A sevenfold amount or number.

~v. **septupled, -pling, -ples.** —tr. To multiply or increase by seven. —intr. To be multiplied sevenfold. [Late Latin septuplus, sevenfold : Latin septem, seven + -plex, -fold.]

se·pul·chral (si-púlkrəl, sə-, sə-) adj. **1.** Of or pertaining to a sepulchre. **2.** Suggestive of the grave; gloomy. —**se·pul·chral·ly** adv.

sep·ul·chre, U.S. **sep·ul·cher** (sépp'lkər) n. A burial vault.

~tr.v. **sepulchred** or U.S. **sepulchered, -chring** or U.S. **-chering, -chres** or U.S. **-chers.** To place in a sepulchre; inter. [Middle English sepulcre, from Old French, from Latin sepulcrum, from sepultus, past participle of sepelīre, to bury.]

seq. 1. sequel. **2.** the following (Latin sequēns).

seqq. the following (ones) (Latin sequentes, sequentia).

se·qua·cious (si-kwáyshəss, se-, sə-) adj. **1.** Archaic. Disposed to follow others in a slavish unquestioning way. **2.** Following in logical sequence and regularity. [Latin sequāx (stem sequāc-), pursuing, sequacious, from sequī, to follow.] —**se·qua·cious·ly** adv. —**se·quac·i·ty** (-kwássəti) n.

se·quel (séekwəl) n. Abbr. **seq. 1.** Anything that follows; a continuation. **2.** A film, play, or literary work complete in itself but continuing the narrative of an earlier work. **3.** A result or consequence. —See Synonyms at **effect**. [Middle English sequele, from Old French sequelle, from Latin sequēla, from sequī, to follow.]

se·que·la (si-kwée-lə, -kwé-) n., pl. **-lae** (-lee). Something that follows; especially, a pathological condition or the various complications resulting from a disease. [Latin sequēla, SEQUEL.]

se·quence (séekwənss) n. **1.** A following of one thing after another; succession. **2.** An order of succession. **3.** A related or continuous series. **4.** Three or more playing cards in consecutive order; a run. **5.** A series of single shots in a film, so edited as to constitute an aesthetic or dramatic unit; an episode. **6.** Music. A melodic or harmonic pattern successively repeated at different pitches, with or without a key change. **7.** Roman Catholic Church. In the Tridentine Mass, a hymn read or sung between the gradual and the gospel. **8.** Mathematics. An ordered set of quantities, as x, $2x^2$, $3x^3$, $4x^4$. **9.** A subsequent or consequent event or development. —See Synonyms at **series**. [Middle English, from Late Latin sequentia, from Latin sequēns (stem sequent-), present participle of sequī, to follow.]

se·quenc·er (séekwənssər) n. **1.** A device for sorting information into a predetermined order for data processing. **2.** An electronic device that sets into a predetermined order a sequence of operations. [SEQUENC(E) + -ER.]

se·quent (séekwənt) adj. **1.** Following in order or time; subsequent. **2.** Following as a result; consequent.

~n. That which follows, in sequence or in consequence. [Latin sequēns. See **sequence**.]

se·quen·tial (si-kwén-sh'l, sə-) adj. **1.** Forming a sequence or characterised by ordered sequence, as of notes or units. **2.** Sequent. —**se·quen·ti·al·i·ty** (-shi-ál-əti) n. —**se·quen·tial·ly** adv.

sequential access n. A method of obtaining information from a computer file by reading through it from the start. Compare **random access**.

se·ques·ter (si-kwéstər, sə-) v. **-tered, -tering, -ters.** —tr. **1.** To remove or set apart; segregate. **2.** Law. To take temporary possession of (property) as security against legal claims. **3.** To requisition or confiscate, especially by legal authority. **4.** To isolate or withdraw into seclusion. Usually used reflexively or in the passive: to sequester oneself; a sequestered spot. —intr. Chemistry. To undergo sequestration. [Middle English, from Late Latin sequestrāre, to separate, give up for safekeeping, from Latin sequester, depository.]

se·ques·trant (si-kwéstrənt, sə-) n. A chemical that promotes sequestration. [From SEQUESTER.]

se·ques·trate (sée-kwiss-trayt, -kwess-, si-kwéss-) tr.v. **-trated, -trating, -trates. 1.** Law. To seize. **2.** Archaic. To set apart. [Late Latin sequestrāre, to SEQUESTER.] —**se·ques·tra·tor** (-traytər) n.

se·ques·tra·tion (sée-kwiss-tráysh'n, -kwess-) n. **1.** The act of sequestering or state of being sequestered; segregation or separation. **2.** Law. **a.** Seizure of property. **b.** A writ authorising seizure of property. **3.** Chemistry. The inhibition or prevention of normal ion behaviour by combination with added materials; especially, the prevention of metallic ion precipitation from solution by formation of a coordination complex with a phosphate.

se·ques·trum (si-kwéss-trəm) n., pl. **-tra** (-trə). A dead bone fragment that has separated from healthy bone. [New Latin, from Latin, deposit, "something separated", from sequester, depository.]

se·quin (séekwin) n. **1.** A small shiny ornamental disc, often sewn on cloth; a spangle. **2.** A gold coin of the Venetian Republic. In this sense, also called "zecchino". [French, from Italian zecchino, from zecca, the mint, from Arabic sikkah, coin die.] —**se·quinned, se·quined** adj.

se·quoi·a (si-kwóy-ə, se-) n. Any very large evergreen tree of the genus Sequoia, which includes the **redwood** and the **giant sequoia** (both of which see). [New Latin, after Sequoiah, a Cherokee Indian who wrote a syllabary for Cherokee.]

se·ra. Alternative plural of **serum**.

sé·rac (sérrak) n. An ice pinnacle between intersecting crevasses in an icefall in a glacier. [Swiss French, piece of white cheese (which the ice resembles), perhaps from Latin serum, whey.]

se·ra·gli·o (si-raáli-ō, se-, sə-, -raál-yō ‖ -rál-yō) n., pl. **-glios. 1.** A large harem. **2.** A sultan's palace. [Italian serraglio, probably from Turkish serai†, a palace, lodging, from Persian.]

se·ra·pe, sa·ra·pe (sə-ráppi, -ráapi) n. A woollen cloak or poncho worn by Latin-American men. [Mexican Spanish *sarape†*.]

ser·aph (sérrəf) n., pl. **-aphs** or **seraphim** (sérrəfim). 1. A celestial being having three pairs of wings. Isaiah 6:2. 2. One of the nine orders of angels. See **angel**. [Back-formation from plural *seraphim*, from Middle English *seraphin*, Old English *seraphin*, from Late Latin *seraphim, seraphin*, from Hebrew *Sərāphim*, plural of *sārāph*.] —**se·raph·ic** (si-ráffik, se-, sə-) adj. —**se·raph·i·cal·ly** adv.

Se·ra·pis (sérrəpiss ‖ U.S. sə-ráypiss). A god combining features of Egyptian and Greek deities, whose worship became widespread in the ancient world from the Hellenistic period onwards.

Serb (serb) n. A Serbian. [Serbo-Croatian *Srb†*.] —**Serb** adj.

Ser·bi·a (sérbi-ə). *Serbo-Croat* **Sr·bi·ja**; *English (before 1918)* **Ser·vi·a** (sérvi-ə). Largest constituent republic of Yugoslavia, lying in the northeast of the country. Largely mountainous in the west and south, it descends to the fertile Danubian plain in the north. It has large mineral deposits, and is also the country's main agricultural producer. Settled by the Serbs in the seventh century A.D., it was established as an independent kingdom in the 12th century, but was subsequently held by the Turks (1389–1829). After World War I, the Kingdom of the Serbs, Croats, and Slovenes under Peter I of Serbia was proclaimed (1918), but was later renamed Yugoslavia (1929). In 1946 Serbia became a constituent republic of Yugoslavia under the new constitution.

Ser·bi·an (sérbi-ən) n. 1. A member of a southern Slavic people that is the dominant ethnic group of Serbia. 2. A Serbo-Croatian. —**Ser·bi·an** adj.

Ser·bo-Cro·at (sérbō-krố-at) n. Also **Ser·bo-Cro·a·tian** (-krō-áysh'n). The Slavonic language of the Serbs and Croats of Yugoslavia, usually written in Cyrillic letters in Serbia and in Roman letters in Croatia. Also called "Croatian". —adj. Of or pertaining to this language or those who speak it.

sere¹ (seer) adj. *Literary*. Withered; dry. [Middle English *sere*, Old English *sēar*.]

sere² n. The entire sequence of ecological communities successively occupying an area. [From SERIES.]

ser·e·nade (sérrə-náyd, sérri-) n. 1. a. A musical performance given outdoors in the evening, especially, one given by a lover for his sweetheart. b. A piece of music so performed. 2. An instrumental form comprising characteristics of the suite and the sonata. —v. **serenaded, -nading, -nades**. —tr. To perform a serenade for. —intr. To perform a serenade. [French *sérénade*, from Italian *serenata*, evening serenade, from *sereno*, serene (influenced in meaning by *sera*, evening), from Latin *serēnus*, SERENE.] —**ser·e·nad·er** n.

ser·en·dip·i·ty (sérrən-díppəti, sérren-) n. The faculty of making fortunate and unexpected discoveries by accident. [Coined (1754) by Horace Walpole after the characters in the fairy tale *The Three Princes of Serendip* (that is, Sri Lanka), who made such discoveries.] —**ser·en·dip·i·tous** adj.

se·rene (si-réen, sə-) adj. 1. Unruffled; tranquil; dignified. 2. Unclouded; fair; bright. 3. *Often capital* **S**. August. Used as part of a title of respect for certain royal personages: *His Serene Highness.* —See Synonyms at **calm**. [Latin *serēnus*, serene, bright, clear.] —**se·rene·ly** adv. —**se·rene·ness** n.

Se·ren·ge·ti (sérrən-gétti) National park on the southeast shores of Lake Victoria, Tanzania. It covers about 14 500 square kilometres (5,600 square miles), and is noted for its wildlife.

se·ren·i·ty (si-rénnəti, sə-) n., pl. **-ties**. 1. The state or quality of being serene; dignified calm; quiet. 2. Clearness, brightness, and stillness, as of the air and sky. —See Synonyms at **equanimity**.

serf (serf) n. 1. A person in a condition bordering on slavery, especially a member of the lowest feudal class in medieval Europe, bound to the land and subject to the control of a lord. 2. Anyone in a state of servitude or oppression. [Old French, from Latin *servus*, slave.] —**serf·dom** n.

serge (serj) n. A twilled cloth of worsted or worsted and wool, often used for suits. [Middle English *sarge, serge*, from Old French, from Vulgar Latin *sārica* (unattested), from Latin *sērica (lāna)*, (wool) of the Seres (a people), that is, silk, from Greek *sērikos*, of silk, originally "pertaining to the Seres". See **silk**.]

ser·geant (sárjənt) n. 1. a. A noncommissioned officer in the British Army, the Royal Air Force, and the Royal Marines, ranking above a corporal. b. A noncommissioned officer of equivalent rank in certain similar forces elsewhere. 2. A police officer of middle rank, especially: a. An officer in a British force ranking above a constable and below an inspector. b. An officer in a U.S. force ranking below a captain, or sometimes a lieutenant. —See **serjeant at arms, serjeant at law**. [Middle English *sergeaunte, sergant*, from Old French *sergent*, from Latin *serviēns* (stem *servient-*), present participle of *servīre*, to serve, from *servus*, slave, servant.] —**ser·gean·cy, ser·geant·ship** n.

sergeant at arms. Variant of **serjeant at arms**.

sergeant at law. Variant of **serjeant at law**.

sergeant major n. *Abbr.* **Sgt. Maj., S.M.** 1. A warrant officer in the British Army and the Royal Marines. 2. A noncommissioned officer of the highest rank in the U.S. and other armed forces. 3. A fish, *Abudefduf saxatilis*, of warm seas, having a flattened body with dark vertical stripes.

se·ri·al (séer-i-əl) adj. 1. Of, forming, or arranged in a series. 2. Published or produced in instalments, as a novel might be. 3. Pertaining to such publication or production. 4. *Music*. Designating or pertaining to music based on a series of intervals chosen by the composer, especially in a 12-note row, rather than on the diatonic scale. See **Schoenberg**. 5. *Computing*. Designating or pertaining to a system of computer operation is which processing is carried out sequentially. In this sense compare **parallel**. —n. A literary or dramatic work published or produced in instalments. [From SERIES.] —**se·ri·al·ly** adv.

se·ri·al·ise, se·ri·al·ize (séer-i-ə-līz) tr.v. **-ised, -ising, -ises**. To write, publish, or produce in serial form. —**se·ri·al·i·sa·tion** n.

se·ri·al·ism (séer-i-ə-liz'm) n. 1. Serial music. 2. The theory or composition of serial music.

serial number n. A number that is one of a series, used for identification, as of a machine or banknote, for example.

se·ri·ate (séer-i-ət, -it, -ayt) adj. Arranged or occurring in a series or in rows. [From SERIES.] —**se·ri·ate·ly** adv.

se·ri·a·tim (séer-i-áytim, sérri-, -áatim) adv. One after another; in a series. [Medieval Latin, from Latin *seriēs*, SERIES.]

se·ri·ceous (si-ríshəss, se-) adj. *Biology*. Covered with soft, silky hairs. [Late Latin *sēriceus*, from *sēricus*, of Seres. See **serge**.]

ser·i·cin (sérri-sin) n. A viscous, gelatinous protein that forms on the surface of raw-silk fibres. [Latin *sēricus*, silken, of Seres (see **serge**) + -IN.]

ser·i·cul·ture (sérri-kulchər) n. The production of raw silk and the breeding of silkworms for this purpose. [French *sériculture* : Latin *sēricus*, silken, of Seres (see **serge**) + CULTURE.] —**ser·i·cul·tur·al** (-kúlchərəl) adj. —**ser·i·cul·tur·ist** n.

ser·i·e·ma (sérri-éemə) n. Either of two cranelike South American birds, *Cariama cristata* or *Chunga burmeisteri*, having a tuftlike crest at the base of the bill. [Tupi *seriema, çariama*, "crested".]

se·ries (séer-iz, -eez, *rarely* -i-eez) n., pl. **series**. 1. A number of things, events, or people having some common characteristic and following one another in order of their occurrence in space or time. 2. A set of publications, typically in a uniform format, having some common theme or feature: *a series of phrase books*. 3. A set of sporting games played between two teams, especially at international level. 4. A group of thematically connected performances; especially, a set of radio or television programmes featuring the same fictional characters in a succession of self-contained episodes. 5. A group of objects related in terms of their composition, structure, or properties: *the paraffin series*. 6. *Mathematics*. A finite or sequentially ordered infinite set of terms expressed in the form $x_1 + x_2 + x_3 + \ldots\ldots$ where x_i is a real or complex number. 7. *Grammar*. A succession of coordinate elements in a sentence. 8. An arrangement of electrical components such that the current flows through each in turn. Compare **parallel**. 9. *Geology*. A subdivision of a system that represents the rocks formed during an epoch. [Latin *seriēs*, from *serere*, to join.]

Synonyms: series, succession, progression, sequence, chain, train, string.

series circuit n. An electrical circuit connected so that current passes through each circuit element in turn without branching. See **parallel** (sense 6).

se·ries-wound (séer-iz-wownd, -eez-) adj. Designating an electric motor or dynamo with its armature circuit and field circuit connected in series with the external circuit. Compare **shunt-wound**.

ser·if (sérrif) n. *Printing*. A fine line finishing off the main strokes, as at the top and bottom of *M* or ending the cross stroke of *T*. [Perhaps from Dutch *schreef*, line, from Middle Dutch *scrēve*.]

ser·i·graph (sérri-graaf, -graf) n. A print made by the silk-screen process. [Latin *sēri(cum)*, SILK + -GRAPH.] —**se·rig·ra·phy** (sə-ríggrəfi) n.

ser·in (sérrin) n. Any of several Old World finches of the genus *Serinus*, having yellowish streaked plumage. See **canary**. [French, from Old French, perhaps from Old Provençal *serena*, bee-eater, from Latin *sīrēn*, a kind of bird, from *Sīrēn*, SIREN.]

ser·ine (sérrin, séer-in, -een) n. An amino acid, $C_3H_7NO_3$, that is a common constituent of many proteins. [SER(ICIN) + -INE.]

se·rin·ga (sə-ring-gə, si-) n. 1. **Syringa** (see). 2. Any of several rubber trees of the Brazilian genus *Hevea*.

se·ri·o·com·ic (séer-i-ō-kómmik) adj. Combining serious and comic characteristics. [SERIO(US) + COMIC.]

se·ri·ous (séer-i-əss) adj. 1. Grave in character or manner; responsible. 2. Said, done, or acting in earnest; marked by sincerity or commitment. 3. Concerned with important rather than trivial matters. 4. Requiring or employing considerable thought, effort, or concentration: *serious music*. 5. Causing anxiety; critical; dangerous. 6. Not to be taken lightly; of considerable significance, gravity, or effect: *serious damage*. —See Synonyms at **critical**. [Middle English *seryous*, from Old French *serieux*, from Late Latin *sēriōsus*, from Latin *sērius*.] —**se·ri·ous·ly** adv. —**se·ri·ous·ness** n.

Synonyms: serious, sober, grave, solemn, earnest, sedate, staid.

ser·jeant at arms, sergeant at arms (sárjənt) n. An officer responsible for the maintenance of order in a legislative body, court of law, or other organisation.

serjeant at law, sergeant at law n. Formerly in Britain, a member of a class of barristers of the highest rank.

ser·mon (sérmən) n. 1. A religious discourse delivered as part of a church service. 2. Any discourse or speech; especially, a lengthy and tedious reproof or exhortation. [Middle English *sermun*, from Anglo-French, from Latin *sermō* (stem *sermōn-*), a speaking, a discourse.] —**ser·mon·ic** (ser-mónnik) adj.

ser·mon·ise, ser·mon·ize (sérmən-īz) v. **-ised, -ising, -ises**. —tr. To preach to. —intr. To deliver, or speak as though delivering, a sermon. —**ser·mon·is·er** n.

Sermon on the Mount *n.* A discourse of Jesus, delivered on the Mount of Olives. Matthew 5–7.

sero– *comb. form.* Indicates serum, as **serology.** [From SERUM.]

se·rol·o·gy (si-róllәji, seer-) *n.* The medical study of serum. [SERO- + -LOGY.] **—ser·o·log·ic** (séer-ә-lójik || *U.S.* sírr-), **ser·o·log·i·cal** *adj.* **—se·rol·o·gist** *n.*

se·ro·sa (si-rṓ-sә, seer- || -zә) *n., pl.* **-sas** or **-sae** (-see || -zee). A serous membrane. [New Latin, feminine of *serosus,* SEROUS.]

se·ro·ther·a·py (séer-ō-thérrәpi) *n.* Treatment of disease by administration of a serum or antitoxin. [SERO- + THERAPY.]

ser·o·tine (sérrә-tīn) *adj.* Also **se·rot·i·nous** (si-róttinәss), **se·rot·i·nal** (-róttin'l). *Biology.* Late in developing or blooming.
~n. A European insectivorous bat, *Eptesicus Serotinus.* [Latin *sērōtinus,* late, from *sērō,* late, from *sērus,* late.]

se·ro·to·nin (séer-ә-tṓnin, -ō-, sérrә-) *n.* An organic compound, $C_{10}H_{12}N_2O$, found in animal and human tissue, especially the brain, blood serum, and gastric mucosa, and capable of raising the body temperature, contracting smooth muscle, and changing behaviour. Also called "hydroxytryptamine". [SERO- + TON(IC) + -IN.]

se·ro·type (séer-ә-tīp, -ō-, sérrә-) *n.* A subspecific category of microorganisms, distinguished by having the same serological activity. Also called "serological type". [*Sero*logical *type.*]

se·rous (séer-әss) *adj.* Containing, secreting, or resembling serum. [New Latin *serosus,* from SERUM.]

serous cavity *n.* A body cavity lined with serous membrane.

serous membrane *n.* A thin membrane lining a closed bodily cavity. Also called "serosa".

se·row (sérrō, sә-rṓ) *n.* Any of several goatlike antelopes of the genus *Capricornis,* of mountainous regions of eastern Asia, having short horns and a dark coat. [Lepcha *să-ro,* Tibetan goat.]

Ser·pens (sér-penz, -pәnz) *n.* A constellation in the equatorial region of the northern sky, made up of two parts: *Serpens Cauda,* the "tail", and *Serpens Caput,* the "head", both near Hercules and Ophiuchus. Also called the "Serpent." [Latin *serpēns,* SERPENT.]

ser·pent (sérpәnt) *n.* **1.** A snake, especially a large one. **2.** *Often capital* **S.** The creature that tempted Eve; Satan. Genesis 3. **3.** A sly or treacherous person. **4.** A kind of firework that writhes while burning. **5.** *Music.* A deep-toned wind instrument of serpentine shape, used principally in the 18th century. [Middle English, from Old French, from Latin *serpēns* (stem *serpent-*), "crawling thing", from the present participle of *serpere,* to crawl, creep.]

ser·pen·tine (sérpәn-tīn || -teen) *adj.* **1.** Of or resembling a serpent, as in form or movement; sinuous. **2.** Subtle, sly, and treacherous.
~n. A greenish, brownish, or spotted mineral, $Mg_6(Si_4O_{10})(OH)_8$, used as a source of magnesium and in architecture as a decorative stone. [Middle English, from Old French *serpentin,* from Late Latin *serpentīnus,* from Latin *serpēns,* SERPENT.]

ser·pi·go (ser-pī́gō, sәr-) *n.* A spreading skin eruption or lesion, such as ringworm. [Middle English, from Medieval Latin *serpīgo,* from Latin *serpere,* to creep.] **—ser·pig·i·nous** (-píjinәss) *adj.*

ser·pu·la (sérpew-lә) *n.* Any of various polychaete worms of the family Serpulidae, especially of the genus *Serpula,* that live in specially secreted calcareous tubes attached to stone. [New Latin, from Late Latin, small serpent, from Latin *serpere,* to creep.]

ser·ra·nid (sә-rránnid, se-, sérrәnid) *n.* Also **ser·ra·noid** (sérrә-noyd), **ser·ran** (sérrәn). Any of various fishes belonging to the family Serranidae, which includes the sea basses and groupers. [New Latin *Serranidae,* from *Serranus* (genus), from Latin *serra,* saw (perhaps from its serrated dorsal fin). See **serrate.**] **—ser·ra·nid, ser·ra·noid** *adj.*

ser·rate (sérr-әt, -it, -ayt) *adj.* **1.** Having notched, toothlike projections. **2.** Having the edge or margin notched with toothlike projections: *serrate leaves.*
~tr.v. (se-ráyt, si-, sә- || sérrayt) **serrated, -rating, -rates.** To provide or mark with notched, toothlike projections. [Latin *serrātus,* saw-shaped, from Latin *serra*†, saw.]

ser·ra·tion (se-ráysh'n, si-, sә-) *n.* **1.** The state of being serrate. **2.** A series or set of teeth or notches. **3.** A single such tooth or notch.

ser·ried (sérrid) *adj.* Pressed together in rows; in close order: *"Troops in serried ranks assembled"* (W.S. Gilbert). [From past participle of obsolete *serry,* to press together, from Old French *serré,* past participle of *serrer,* to close, from Vulgar Latin *serrāre* (unattested), from Latin *sērāre,* to fasten with a bolt, from *sera,* lock.]

ser·ru·late (sérrōōlәt, sérrew-, -lit, -layt) *adj.* Also **ser·ru·lat·ed** (-laytid). Having small, toothlike notches along the edge; minutely serrate. [New Latin *serrulatus,* from Latin *serrula,* diminutive of *serra,* saw. See **serrate.**]

ser·tu·lar·i·an (sértew-láir-i-әn) *n.* Any of various colonial hydroids of the genus *Sertularia,* having stalkless polyps arranged in pairs along a long, branching stem. [New Latin *Sertularia,* from Latin *sertula,* diminutive of *serta,* melilot, garland, from the feminine past participle of *serere,* to join, entwine.]

se·rum (séer-әm) *n., pl.* **-rums** or **sera** (séer-ә). **1.** The clear yellowish fluid obtained upon separating blood into its solid and liquid components. Also called "blood serum". **2.** The fluid from the tissues of immunised animals, used especially as an antitoxin. **3.** Any watery fluid from animal tissue, as is found in oedema. **4. Whey** *(see).* [Latin, whey, serum.]

serum albumin *n.* The main protein fraction of blood serum that is involved in maintaining osmotic pressure, and that is used in the treatment of shock.

serum globulin *n.* A protein fraction of blood serum chiefly containing antibodies.

serum hepatitis *n.* See **hepatitis.**

serum sickness *n.* An allergic reaction, such as a skin eruption, vomiting, or fever, that may follow injection of serum.

serv. **1.** servant. **2.** service.

serum therapy *n.* **Serotherapy** *(see).*

ser·val (sérv'l || sәr-vál) *n.* A long-legged wild cat, *Felis serval,* of Africa, having a yellowish coat with black spots. [French, from Portuguese *(lobo) cerval,* deerlike (wolf), from *cervo,* deer, from Latin *cervus.*]

ser·vant (sérvәnt) *n. Abbr.* **serv. 1.** One that serves another or others. **2.** Someone privately employed to perform domestic services. **3.** Someone publicly employed to perform services, as for a government. **—your humble** or **obedient servant.** Used chiefly in letters as a conventional expression of politeness. [Middle English, from Old French, from the present participle of *servir,* to SERVE.]

serve (serv) *v.* **served, serving, serves.** *—tr.* **1.** To be a servant to or of; work for (an employer or company, for example): *served the firm for 30 years.* **2. a.** To prepare and offer (food or drink): *serve tea.* **b.** To place food or drink before (someone); wait on. **c.** To attend to (a customer in a shop): *Are you being served?* **d.** To assist the celebrant during (Communion or Mass). **3.** To meet the requirements of; provide with something useful or needed: *a bus serving the rural areas; served the public for 100 years.* **4.** To be useful or adequate for fulfilling (a need or purpose); suffice for: *not quite big enough, but it will serve the purpose.* **5.** To be of assistance to; promote the interests of; aid: *serving the national interest.* **6.** To perform or complete (a stipulated term), as in prison, elective office, or an apprenticeship. **7.** To fight or undergo military service for: *served his country in two World Wars.* **8.** To give homage and obedience to. **9. a.** To treat in a specified, usually unpleasant way; requite: *It will serve her right.* **b.** To perform a function for in a specified way; avail: *if my memory serves me well.* **10.** To copulate with. Used of male animals: *The buck served the doe.* **11.** To be used in common by: *One phone serves the whole office.* **12.** To enable (a cannon, for example) to keep firing: *serve the guns.* **13.** *Law.* **a.** To deliver or present (a legal writ or summons). **b.** To present such a writ to. **14.** To put (the ball or shuttlecock) in play in games such as tennis or badminton. **15.** To bind (a rope) with fine cord or wire.
—intr. **1.** To be employed as a servant. **2. a.** To do military service: *served under Montgomery.* **b.** To perform or discharge an official duty; hold office: *served under four prime ministers.* **3. a.** To be of service or use; function: *serve as a reminder.* **b.** To be reliable or safe: *if memory serves.* **c.** To function so as to produce a specified effect: *a repressive measure that merely served to increase opposition to the government.* **4. a.** To meet requirements or needs; satisfy; suffice: *"'Tis not so deep as a well . . . but 'twill serve"* (Shakespeare). **b.** To be suitable or favourable. Used of a tide, weather conditions, and the like. **5.** To wait at table; provide people with food or drink: *Shall I serve?* **6.** To put a ball or shuttlecock into play in games such as tennis or badminton. **7.** To assist the celebrant during Mass or a Communion service.
~n. In many games played on a court: **1.** The manner or act of serving. **2.** One's turn or right to serve which, in tennis, lasts throughout a game. **3.** In tennis, the game in which a particular player serves: *lost her serve.* [Middle English *serven,* from Old French *servir,* from Latin *servīre,* from *servus,* slave.]

serv·er (sérvәr) *n.* **1.** One that serves. **2.** Something used in serving food or drink, such as a tray or utensil: *salad servers.* **3.** An attendant to the celebrant at a Communion service or Mass. **4.** The player who serves, as in tennis or badminton.

serv·ice (sérviss) *n. Abbr.* **serv. 1.** The occupation, condition, or duties of a servant. **2.** Employment in duties or work for another; especially, such employment for a government: *in the service of the Crown.* **3.** A branch or department of an organisation or government, together with its employees: *the diplomatic service.* **4.** Any branch of the armed forces of a nation. **5. a.** Useful work or duty performed by a person or thing: *has done good service.* **b.** The performance of work or duty, as of an official or military nature: *jury service; killed on active service.* **c.** The condition of being used for the performance of work: *Some of the old planes are still in service.* **6. a.** The action of helping others; assistance: *if I may be of service.* **b.** An act of helping others; a favour: *did us all a great service.* **7.** Power to control or make use of some resource; disposal: *My staff is at your service.* **8. a.** Installation, maintenance, or repairs provided or guaranteed by a dealer or manufacturer: *after-sales service.* **b.** A regularly-performed inspection and carrying out of repairs, as of a car or other machine, for the purpose of routine maintenance. **9.** *Often plural.* Work done for others as an occupation or business: *needed the services of a good accountant.* **10.** An organisation or system providing the public with something useful or necessary: *a bus service; the BBC World Service.* **11.** A nonmaterial commodity produced by human labour, especially as distinguished from a manufactured product. **12. a.** A meeting for public worship. **b.** A particular religious rite: *the burial service.* **13.** The act or manner of serving food, attending to customers, or the like: *fast, friendly service.* **14.** A set of dishes or utensils: *a silver tea service.* **15.** The act, manner, turn, or right of serving in racket games; a serve. **16.** Copulation by a male animal with a female. **17.** *Law.* The serving of a writ or summons. **18.** Any material, such as cord, used in binding or wrapping rope.
~adj. **1.** Concerned with the provision of services rather than the production of goods: *service industries.* **2.** Not for use by the gen-

serow *The shaggy-haired serow has short horns and is a distant relative of the mountain goat. It lives in the hill forests of eastern Asia.*

eral public; reserved for employees, deliveries, or the like: *a service lift.* **3.** Of or pertaining to the armed forces.
~*tr.v.* **serviced, -vicing, -vices. 1.** To perform routine maintenance on so as to ensure effective operation: *service a car.* **2.** To provide with services. **3.** To copulate with. Used of a male animal. **4.** To meet the interest payments on (a loan). [Middle English *servis(e),* from Old French *service,* from Latin *servitium,* servitude, slavery, from *servus,* slave.]

serv·ice·a·ble (sérvi-sə-b'l) *adj.* **1.** Ready or suitable for service; useful or usable. **2.** Able to give good service; long-wearing. **—serv·ice·a·bil·i·ty** (-bílləti), **serv·ice·a·ble·ness** *n.* **—serv·ice·a·bly** *adv.*

service area *n.* An area adjoining a motorway in which garage facilities, restaurants, and lavatories are provided.

serv·ice·ber·ry (sér-viss-berri || *U.S. also* sár-) *n., pl.* **-ries. 1.** The fruit of the service tree. **2.** The **shadbush** *(see),* or one of its fruit. [SERVICE (TREE) + BERRY.]

service break *n.* A game won during an opponent's serve, as in tennis.

service car *n.* **1.** *Australian.* A minibus or large car providing public transport in rural areas, and sometimes also carrying mail. **2.** *N.Z.* A coach.

service charge *n.* **1.** A charge added to a customer's bill, as at a restaurant, to pay for service. **2.** An additional charge for a service for which there is often already a basic fee.

service flat *n. British.* A flat for which certain services, such as cleaning and porterage, are automatically provided for a charge.

serv·ice·man (sérviss-man, -mən) *n., pl.* **-men** (-mən, -men). A male member of the armed forces.

service module *n.* The part of the third stage of an Apollo spacecraft containing the rocket motor, fuel supply, and various service facilities, which is jettisoned prior to reentry into the earth's atmosphere.

service road *n.* A narrow road running parallel to a main road to provide access to houses, shops, and the like, along its length.

service station *n.* A place that supples petrol, oil, and similar products for motor vehicles, often also having facilities for carrying out repairs and services.

service tree *n.* Either of two Old World trees, *Sorbus domestica* or *S. torminalis,* having clusters of white flowers and brownish, edible fruit. [Middle English *serves,* plural of *serve,* Old English *syrfe,* from Vulgar Latin *sorbea* (unattested), from Latin *sorbus*†.]

ser·vice·wom·an (sérviss-wŏŏmən) *n., pl.* **-women** (-wimmin). A female member of the armed forces.

ser·vi·ette (sérvi-ét) *n.* A table napkin. [French, from Old French, towel, napkin, from *servir,* to SERVE.]

ser·vile (sér-vīl || *U.S. also* -v'l) *adj.* **1.** Slavish in character or attitude; obsequious; submissive. **2.** Of or suitable to a slave or servant: *"freed from servile bands"* (John Bunyan). —See Synonyms at **obedient.** [Middle English, from Latin *servīlis,* from *servus,* slave.] **—ser·vile·ly** *adv.* **—ser·vile·ness, ser·vil·i·ty** (ser-víllәti) *n.*

serv·ing (sérving) *n.* An individual portion or helping of food or drink.
~*adj.* Pertaining to or used for serving.

ser·vi·tor (sérvi-tər || -tawr) *n. Archaic.* A servant; an attendant. [Middle English, from Old French, from Latin *servītor,* from Latin *servīre,* to SERVE.] **—ser·vi·tor·ship** *n.*

ser·vi·tude (sérvi-tewd || -tōōd) *n.* **1.** Submission to the control, will, or political domination of another; slavery. **2.** Forced labour imposed as a punishment for crime: *penal servitude.* **3.** *Law.* A right that grants use of another's property for certain purposes. [Middle English, from Old French, from Latin *servitūdō,* from *servus,* slave.]
Synonyms: *servitude, bondage, slavery.*

ser·vo·mech·a·nism (sérvō-meckə-niz'm, -méckə-) *n.* A feedback system that consists of a sensing element, an amplifier, and a servomotor, and is used in the automatic control of a mechanical device. Also called "servo". [SERVO(MOTOR) + MECHANISM.]

ser·vo·motor (sérvō-mōtər) *n.* An electric motor or hydraulic piston that supplies power to a servomechanism. Also called "servo". [French *servo-moteur* : *servo-,* from Latin *servus,* slave + French *moteur,* MOTOR.]

ses·a·me (séssəmi) *n.* **1.** A plant, *Sesamum indicum,* of tropical Asia, bearing small, flat seeds used as food and as a source of oil. **2.** The seeds of this plant. Also called "benne". [Latin *sēsamum, sīsamum,* from Greek *sēsamon, sēsamē,* of Semitic origin; akin to Arabic *simsim,* Akkadian *shamashshamu.*]

ses·a·moid (séssə-moyd) *adj.* Of or designating a small bone, such as the kneecap, that develops in a tendon. [Greek *sēsamoeidēs,* shaped like a sesame seed : SESAME + -OID.] **—ses·a·moid** *n.*

Se·so·tho (si-sŏŏtōō) *n.* The dialect of **Sotho** *(see)* spoken in Lesotho. Formerly called "Basuto".

sesqui- *comb. form.* Indicates one and a half; for example, **sesquicentennial.** [Latin, from *semisque* (unattested), one-half more : *sēmis,* half + *-que* (enclitic), and.]

ses·qui·car·bon·ate (séskwi-kárbə-nayt, -nət, -nit) *n.* A mixed salt consisting of a carbonate and a hydrogen carbonate, such as sodium sesquicarbonate, $NaCO_3NaHCO_3$.

ses·qui·cen·ten·ni·al (séskwi-sen-ténni-əl) *adj.* Of or pertaining to a period of 150 years.
~*n.* A 150th anniversary or its celebration. [SESQUI- + CENTENNIAL.]

ses·qui·ox·ide (séskwi-ók-sīd) *n.* An oxide that contains three oxygen atoms for every two atoms of the element, such as Cr_2O_3.

ses·qui·pe·da·li·an (séskwi-pi-dáyli-ən, -pe-) *adj.* **1.** Long and ponderous; polysyllabic. **2.** Given to using long words.
~*n.* A long word. [Latin *sesquipedalis,* of a foot and a half in length : SESQUI- + *pes* (stem *ped-*), foot.]

Ses·shu (sésh-shōō), also called Sesshu Toyo (1420–1506). Japanese painter, known for his landscapes and Zen Buddhist pictures. He visited China, and his work combines Chinese with Japanese influences.

ses·sile (séssīl || *U.S. also* séss'l) *adj.* **1.** *Botany.* Stalkless and attached directly at the base: *sessile leaves.* **2.** *Zoology.* Permanently attached or fixed; not free-moving. [Latin *sessilis,* of sitting, low (said of plants), from *sessus,* past participle of *sedēre,* to sit.]

sessile oak *n.* An oak, the **durmast** *(see).*

ses·sion (sésh'n) *n.* **1.** A meeting of a legislative or judicial body for the purpose of transacting business. **2.** The term or period during which such meetings are held. **3.** *Chiefly U.S. & Scottish.* The part of a year during which teaching is given at a university or college; an academic year. **4.** *Plural.* A sitting or sittings of justices of the peace. See **petty sessions, quarter sessions. 5. a.** Any period of time devoted to a specific activity. **b.** A period of time spent singing or playing and recording music in a studio; a recording session. **6.** The ruling body of a Presbyterian church.
~*adj.* Designating a professional musician who provides instrumental or vocal accompaniment during recording sessions for other people's records: *a session guitarist.* [Middle English *sessioun,* a session, a sitting, from Old French *session,* from Latin *sessiō* (stem *sessiōn-*), from *sessus,* past participle of *sedēre,* to sit.] **—ses·sion·al** *adj.* **—ses·sion·al·ly** *adv.*

Ses·sions (sésh'nz), **Roger (Huntington)** (1896–). U.S. composer. His early works show the influence of Stravinsky, but with his *Violin Sonata* (1953) he began to introduce serialism into his work.

ses·terce (séss-tərss, -terss) *n.* A silver or bronze coin of ancient Rome, equivalent to ¼ denarius. [Latin *sestertius,* (coin) worth two and a half (asses) (i.e., two plus a half of a third ass) : *sēmis,* a half + *tertius,* a third.]

ses·ter·ti·um (sess-tér-shi-əm, -ti-) *n., pl.* **-tia** (-shi-ə, -ti-ə). A money of account in ancient Rome, equivalent to 1,000 sesterces. [Latin *(mille) sestertium,* (a thousand) sesterces, from the genitive plural of *sestertius,* SESTERCE.]

ses·tet (sess-tét) *n.* A stanza constituting the last six lines of a sonnet. Compare **octet.** [Italian *sestetto,* from *sesto,* sixth, from Latin *sextus.*]

ses·ti·na (sess-téenə) *n.* An originally Provençal verse form consisting of six six-line stanzas and a three-line envoi, repeating the end words of the first stanza in the other five stanzas according to an elaborate pattern. [Italian, from *sesto,* sixth, from Latin *sextus.*]

set[1] (set) *v.* **set, setting, sets.** *—tr.* **1.** To put or cause to be situated in a specified place or position: *Set the box on the table.* **2.** To put (a broken or dislocated bone) into a position that will restore a proper and normal state. **3. a.** To adjust according to a standard: *set one's watch by the station clock.* **b.** To adjust to a specified point or calibration: *set the alarm for six o'clock.* **4.** To fix (the hair) in position while wet so as to achieve a particular style. **5.** To arrange scenery upon (a theatre stage) or in (a television or film studio). **6. a.** To put (a precious stone, for example) in a setting; mount. **b.** To apply jewels to; stud. **7. a.** To arrange (type or filmset characters) preparatory to printing; compose. **b.** To transpose (text) into filmset characters or type. **8.** To place in a sitting position; seat: *set the child on his knee.* **9. a.** To put (a hen) on eggs for the purpose of hatching them. **b.** To put (eggs) beneath a hen or in an incubator. **10.** To bring into or cause to be in a specified condition or relation: *sets her apart from others.* **11.** To cause to be taken into account so as to offset or compensate for something else; balance: *set these losses against tax.* **12.** To cause to take up a hostile position or attitude; pit (one person) against another. **13.** To focus (one's hopes or attention, for example) towards a particular purpose. **14.** To put into a rigid position showing defiance or determination: *set one's jaw.* **15. a.** To put an edge or point on (a cutting instrument). **b.** To adjust (a saw) by deflecting the teeth. **16.** To prepare for effective use or action, as: **a.** To make (a table) ready for a meal. **b.** To make (a trap) ready to operate. **17.** To detail or assign to a particular duty, task, or station: *set them to work cleaning up.* **18.** To allot or prescribe (a task): *set some homework.* **19.** To determine, fix, or assign: *set a date.* **20.** To establish (a record). **21.** To present as a model for emulation: *set an example.* **22.** To consider as having a particular value or worth; rate: *set great store by punctuality.* **23.** To provide (a scene or story) with a specified background in space and time: *a novel set in 18th-century England.* **24.** To compose music to fit (a given text). **25.** To cause (a liquid or a soft substance) to become firm or solid. **26.** To incite to make an attack: *set his dogs on us.* **27.** To point to the location of (game) by holding a fixed attitude. Used of a hunting dog. **28.** *Horticulture.* To produce, as after pollination: *set seed.* **29.** To sink (a nail) so that its head lies below the surrounding surface. *—intr.* **1.** To go down towards and below the horizon. Used of the sun or any other heavenly body. **2.** To diminish or decline; wane. **3.** To sit on eggs. Used of a hen. **4.** To solidify, harden, or congeal. **5.** To embark upon a journey. Used with *out, forth,* or *off.* **6.** To become restored to a normal state; knit. Used of a broken bone. **7.** To have or follow a specified course or direction. Used of a wind, current, or the like. **8.** *Horticulture.* To mature or develop, as after pollination. **9.** To point to the position of game by holding a fixed attitude. Used of a hunting dog. **10.** *Regional.* To sit. **—set about.** To start

PRONUNCIATION KEY

a, trap; aa, father; ai, fair;
ar, star; aw, lawn; ay, play;
b, bb, stab; rubber;
ch, church; ck, ticket;
d, dd, dead; ladder; e, dress;
ee, bee; er, defer; ew, few;
ewr, pure; ə, about;
ər, letter; f, ff, fife; differ;
g, gg, giggle; h, hat; i, kit;
ī, price; īr, fire; j, judge;
k, kick; l, ll, let; 'l, needle;
m, mm, man; n, nn, no;
'n, sudden; ng, thing; o, lot;
ō, no; ŏŏ, foot; ōō, shoe;
oor, poor; ow, cow;
owr, hour; oy, boy;
p, pp, pepper; r, rr, red;
s, ss, sauce; sh, ship;
t, tt, totter; th, thick; th, this;
smooth; u, cut; ur, turn;
v, vv, valve; w, wet; y, yes;
z, zz, zebra; zh, vision;
pleasure

IN FOREIGN WORDS:

aɴ, oɴ, Saint-Saëns;
hl, Llanelli; Hluhluwe;
kh, loch; lough; Khaled

STRESS MARK:

ín-sīt, insight; in-sít, incite

or begin doing. **—set aside.** 1. To separate and reserve for a special purpose or later consideration. 2. To dismiss or discard. 3. To declare invalid or void; annul. **—set down.** 1. To put into written or printed form; record. 2. To regard or consider. 3. To attribute. 4. To allow (a passenger) to alight. 5. To land (an aircraft), especially in abnormal circumstances. **—set forth.** To make known or propound (plans or ideas, for example). **—set in.** To begin to happen and become established. **—set out.** 1. To display for exhibition or sale. 2. To describe or expound; put forward in detail. 3. To lay out (a room, town, or garden, for example); plan. 4. To plant out (seedlings, for example).

~adj. 1. Fixed or prescribed by authority, agreement, or convention: *set mealtimes.* 2. Consisting of or offering a fixed number and combination of dishes for one price: *a set menu.* 3. Fixed, rigid, or unmoving: *a set smile.* 4. Clichéd or stereotyped: *set phrases.* 5. Rigid and unchanging in disposition: *set in one's ways.* 6. Holding resolutely to a particular attitude or intention: *set on going; dead set against it.* 7. Ready for action: *get set.*

~n. 1. a. The act or process of setting. b. The condition resulting from setting. 2. A permanent firming or hardening of a substance, as by cooling. 3. The manner in which something is positioned. 4. The carriage or bearing of a part of the body. 5. An inclination or tendency, as of the mind or character, in a particular direction. 6. The direction or course of wind or water. 7. An act of styling the hair by setting it: *a shampoo and set.* 8. A seedling, slip, or cutting that is ready for planting. 9. Variant of **sett.** [Set (infinitive, past tense, past participle); Middle English *setten, sette,* to cause to sit, place, Old English *settan, sette, sett.*]

set² *n.* 1. A group of persons, things, or circumstances that belong together by virtue of similarities, as in appearance, character, or function, especially: a. A group of persons who associate with each other and share a common lifestyle and common interests: *the jet set.* b. A group of related objects having the same or a similar function and often used together in a particular activity: *a chess set; a set of wine glasses.* c. A group of situations, events, or the like considered collectively or as forming a whole: *a set of lectures.* 2. A part of a programme or a session of music, typically popular music or jazz, performed at one time: *played a relaxed set.* 3. a. A basic configuration of dancers, as in a country dance or a square dance. b. The series of movements constituting such a dance. 4. a. The scenery constructed for a dramatic performance. b. The area, as in a studio or on location, in which a film is shot. 5. An apparatus that receives radio or television signals; a receiver. 6. *Mathematics & Logic.* A collection or group specified in such a way that, given any object, it can be determined whether that object does or does not belong to that collection or group: *the empty set; the set of positive integers.* 7. In tennis and other games, a group of games constituting one division or unit of a match. 8. *British.* A grouping of pupils whose ability in a particular subject is similar, and who are taught that subject as a group. —See Synonyms at **circle.**

~v. **set, setting, sets.** *—tr.* 1. To group (pupils) into sets. 2. To teach (a subject) in sets. *—intr.* To do a series of country-dance or square-dance steps facing one's partner. Used with *to.* [Middle English *sette,* sect, set, from Old French, from Latin *secta,* SECT (later confused with *set,* to place, taken as "a group or number set together").]

se·ta (séetə) *n., pl.* **setae** (séetee). *Biology.* 1. A stiff hair, bristle, or bristle-like growth or organ. 2. *Botany.* The stalk that bears the capsule in mosses. [New Latin, from Latin *sēta, saeta*†, bristle.] **—se·tal** *adj.*

se·ta·ceous (si-táyshəss, se-) *adj.* 1. Having or consisting of bristles; bristly. 2. Resembling a bristle or bristles; bristle-like. [New Latin *setaceus* : SET(A) + -ACEOUS.]

set back *tr.v.* 1. To impede the progress or advance of. 2. *Informal.* To cost (a person) a specified amount.

set·back (sét-bak) *n.* 1. An unanticipated or sudden check in progress; a reverse. 2. a. A steplike recession in a wall. b. Any of a series of such recessions in the rise of a tall building.

set book *n.* A text prescribed for study as part of an examination syllabus.

set chisel *n.* A chisel with a cutting edge on a tapered shaft; a cold chisel.

Seth (seth). The third son of Adam. Genesis 4:25.

se·tif·er·ous (si-tíffərəss, se-) *adj.* Also **se·tig·er·ous** (-tíjərəss). Setose. [From Latin *seta,* bristle + -FEROUS.]

se·ti·form (séeti-fawrm) *adj.* Having the shape of a seta or bristle. [SET(A) + -FORM.]

set·line (sét-līn) *n.* A long fishing line towed by a boat and supporting many smaller lines bearing baited hooks. Also *U.S.* "trawl", "trawl line".

set off *tr.v.* 1. To show to best advantage; enhance by contrast. 2. To cause to explode. 3. a. To cause (sudden or hurried activity); spark off: *set off a wave of selling.* b. To cause (a person) to start some activity: *set him off on one of his boring stories.*

set·off (sét-off, -awff) *n.* 1. Anything that has the effect of enhancing something else, especially by contrast. 2. Anything that offsets or compensates for something else. 3. A counterbalancing debt. 4. An **offset** *(see).*

se·tose (sée-tōss || -tōz) *adj.* Bristly or bristle-like; setaceous. [Latin *sētōsus,* from *sēta,* bristle, SETA.]

set piece *n.* 1. An often brilliantly executed artistic or literary work, or part of a work, characterised by a formal pattern. 2. A realistic piece of stage scenery constructed to stand by itself. 3. An elaborate firework display that forms a pattern. 4. A carefully planned and executed operation, especially a military operation. 5. In soccer, hockey, and similar games, a specially rehearsed plan of action put into effect by a team in a situation, such as a free kick or corner, outside the run of normal play.

set point *n.* A point that, if won, wins a set, as in tennis.

set·screw (sét-skrōō || -skrew) *n.* 1. A screw, often without a head, used to hold two parts in a position relative to each other without motion. 2. A screw used to regulate the tension of a spring.

set square *n.* A device used in technical drawing consisting of a flat sheet, usually of plastic or wood, in the shape of a right-angle triangle, used to draw vertical lines in conjunction with a T-square and also to construct angles of 30°, 45°, and 60°.

sett, set (set) *n.* 1. A badger's burrow. 2. A small square or rectangular block, usually made of granite, used especially formerly as a paving stone. 3. a. A square section in a tartan pattern. b. The pattern itself. 4. An adjustment made to the reeds in a loom so as to weave a particular pattern.

set·tee (se-tée, sə-) *n.* A long seat with a back and usually arms; a sofa. [Perhaps variant of SETTLE (bench).]

set·ter (séttər) *n.* 1. One that sets. 2. A dog of any of several long-haired breeds, originally trained to indicate the presence of game by crouching in a set position. See **English setter, Irish setter, red setter.**

set theory *n.* The study of the mathematical properties of sets.

set·ting (sétting) *n.* 1. The context or surroundings in which an event, story, or the like is set. 2. A mounting, as for a jewel. 3. The scenery constructed for a theatrical, film, or television performance. 4. Music composed or arranged to fit a text. 5. Any of the positions in which a machine or instrument can be set. 6. The cutlery, glassware, and the like for one person at table.

set·tle (sétt'l) *v.* **-tled, -tling, -tles.** *—tr.* 1. To place, dispose, or establish in a desired position; especially, to place (oneself) in a comfortable position. 2. To put in order; arrange in a final or satisfactory form. 3. To reach decisive agreement regarding (a course of action, for example); decide on: *settled the details.* 4. To conclude or resolve (a dispute, for example). 5. To decide (a lawsuit) by mutual agreement of the involved parties, usually without court action: *settled the affair out of court.* 6. a. To cause to take up residence in a place. b. To colonise or otherwise provide (a place) with inhabitants or settlers. 7. To fix or establish in a more or less permanent and unvarying form: *a settled life.* 8. To cause to become less disturbed or agitated; restore calmness or quiet to: *settle one's stomach.* 9. To pay or pay back (what is owing): *settle an account; a few old scores to settle.* 10. a. To cause to come to rest, sink, or become compact. b. To cause (a liquid) to become clear by forming a sediment. 11. *Law.* To secure or assign (property or title, for example) to another by a legal settlement. Used with *on* or *upon.* *—intr.* 1. To discontinue moving and come to rest in one place. 2. To subside gradually; shift to a lower level. 3. To sink and become more compact: *The dust settled.* 4. a. To become clear. Used of liquids. b. To be separated from a solution or mixture as a sediment. 5. To become less agitated or restless; regain calmness or composure. Often used with *down.* 6. To take up permanent residence. 7. To reach a decision; determine. Used with *on, upon,* or *with.* 8. To decide a lawsuit by mutual agreement: *settled out of court.* 9. To pay what is owing. Often used with *up.* —See Synonyms at **decide.** **—settle down.** 1. To begin living a more ordered life, as by marrying or taking a permanent job. 2. To apply one's attention purposefully and diligently. **—settle for.** To accept in spite of incomplete satisfaction. **—settle in.** 1. To become comfortably adapted to a new environment or situation. 2. To help (someone) to settle in.

~n. A long wooden bench with a high back, often including storage space beneath the seat. [Middle English *setlen,* to place in order, seat, Old English *setlan,* from *setl,* seat.]

set·tle·ment (sétt'lmənt) *n.* 1. The act or process of settling. 2. a. The establishment of a new population in a place. b. A newly colonised region. 3. A small community, especially in a thinly-populated or newly-settled area. 4. An understanding or agreement by which differences are resolved. 5. a. An arrangement or legal instrument by which property is settled on a person. b. Property thus transferred. 6. A welfare centre providing community services in a deprived inner city area. Also called "settlement house". 7. Slow sinking, as of a wall or building, due to subsidence.

set·tler (sétt'l-ər, séttlər) *n.* One that settles; especially, a person who settles in a new and previously uncolonised region.

set·tlings (sétt'l-ingz, séttlingz) *pl.n.* Sediment; dregs.

set to *intr.v.* 1. To begin working actively or eagerly. 2. To begin fighting.

set-to (sét-tōō, -tóō) *n., pl.* **-tos.** A brief but usually heated fight or contest.

set up *tr.v.* 1. To place in a raised or upright position; erect or elevate. 2. To establish in a position of power: *set up a dictator.* 3. To cause or produce: *set up a din.* 4. To restore or improve the health and well-being of. 5. To establish; found. 6. To establish (a person) in business by providing capital, equipment, and the like. 7. To put forward or propose. 8. To put (especially oneself) forward, often without justification, as having some quality: *sets himself up as an expert on wine.* 9. To create conditions favourable for the scoring of (a goal, try, or the like). 10. *Informal.* To provide (drinks) for a person or group. 11. *Informal.* To arrange for (someone) to be discovered in incriminating or embarrassing circum-

seventeen-year locust *This sap-sucking cicada of North America gets its name because its nymphs live for up to 17 years before metamorphosing into the winged adult form (above). The nymphs feed underground on the sap of tree roots.*

Sèvres plate *Porcelain ware which takes its name from the suburb of Paris where it has been manufactured since 1756. This example is* The Sphinx *from the "Egyptian Service" painted by Swebach in 1811.*

stances. —*intr.v.* To start in business: *has set up as a decorator.*

set-up (sét-up) *n. Informal.* **1.** The way in which anything operates or is constituted or arranged. **2.** A situation prearranged to place someone in an incriminating or embarrassing position. **3.** *Chiefly U.S.* A task, undertaking, or contest prearranged so that it is accomplished or won without any real difficulty.
~*adj.* Of or having a physically developed body or bearing: *a well set-up man.*

Seu·rat (súr-raa; *French* sö-raá), **Georges (Pierre)** (1859–91). French painter, the founder of pointillism. Developing the impressionist concerns with light and atmosphere, he evolved a distinctive technique for rendering appearances through innumerable dots of pure colour, which produced a number of masterpieces, including *Une Baignade* (1884) and *La Grande Jatte* (1886).

Se·vas·to·pol (*Russian* si-vuss-tóppəl). *English* **Se·bas·to·pol** (si-bástə-p'l, se-, sə-, -pol). Seaport in the Crimea, in southwest U.S.S.R. It became the main base of the Russian Black Sea fleet (1804). It was twice captured after prolonged sieges: 322 days (1854–55) by the Allies in the Crimean War, and 250 days (1941–42) by the Germans in World War II.

sev·en (sévv'n) *n.* **1. a.** The cardinal number that is one more than six. **b.** A symbol representing this, such as 7, VII, or vii. **2.** A set made up of seven persons or things. **3. a.** The seventh in a series. **b.** A playing card marked with seven pips. **4.** Seven parts: *cut in seven.* **5.** A size, as in clothing, designated as seven. **6.** Seven hours after midnight or midday. [Middle English *seven,* Old English *seofon.*] —**sev·en** *adj.* —**sev·en·fold** (-fōld) *adj. & adv.*

seven deadly sins *pl.n.* The sins of pride, lust, envy, anger, covetousness, gluttony, and sloth. Also called "cardinal sins".

seven seas *pl.n.* All the oceans of the world.

Seven Sisters *pl.n. Astronomy.* The **Pleiades** *(see).*

sev·en·teen (sévv'n-teén), *n.* **1. a.** The cardinal number that is one more than 16. **b.** A symbol representing this, such as XVII. **2.** A set made up of 17 persons or things. **3.** The seventeenth in a series. **4.** A size, as in clothing, designated 17. [Middle English *seventene,* Old English *seofontīne* : SEVEN + -TEEN.] —**sev·en·teen** *adj.*

sev·en·teenth (sévv'n-teénth) *n.* **1.** The ordinal number 17 in a series. Also written 17th. **2.** One of 17 equal parts. —**sev·en·teenth** *adj. & adv.*

sev·en·teen-year locust (sévv'n-teen-yeér, -yér) *n.* A cicada of the genus *Magicicada,* of the eastern United States, which as a nymph remains underground for 17 or sometimes 13 years.

sev·enth (sévv'nth) *n.* **1.** The ordinal number seven in a series. Also written 7th. **2.** One of seven equal parts. **3.** *Music.* **a.** A note that is on the seventh diatonic degree with respect to another given note. **b.** The interval encompassing two such notes. **c.** A chord consisting of a note together with its third, fifth, and seventh. In this sense, also called "seventh chord". —**sev·enth** *adj. & adv.*

Sev·enth-Day Adventist (sévv'nth-day) *n.* A member of a sect of Adventism distinguished chiefly for its observance of the Sabbath on Saturday. See **Adventist.**

seventh heaven *n.* **1.** A state of great joy and satisfaction. **2.** The furthest of the concentric spheres containing the stars and comprising the dwelling place of God and the angels in the Muslim and cabbalist systems.

sev·en·ti·eth (sévv'nti-əth, -ith) *n.* **1.** The ordinal number 70 in a series. Also written 70th. **2.** One of 70 equal parts. —**sev·en·ti·eth** *adj. & adv.*

sev·en·ty (sévv'nti) *n., pl.* **-ties 1. a.** The cardinal number that is 10 more than 60. **b.** A symbol representing this, such as 70 or LXX. **2.** A set made up of 70 persons or things. **3.** The seventieth in a series. **4.** A size, as in clothing, desigated as 70. **5.** *Plural.* **a.** The range of numbers from 70 to 79 considered as a range of age, price, temperature, or the like. **b.** *Often capital* **S.** The years numbered 70 to 79 in a century. In this sense, also used adjectivally: *a well-known seventies group.* —**sev·en·ty** *adj. & pron.*

sev·en-up (sévv'n-úp) *n. U.S.* A card game, **all fours** *(see).*

Seven Wonders of the World *pl.n.* Seven monuments of the ancient world that appeared on various lists of late antiquity. Most commonly, they are: the Colossus of Rhodes, the Pharos at Alexandria, the Hanging Gardens (and Walls) of Babylon, the temple of Artemis at Ephesus, the pyramids of Giza, the tomb of Mausolus at Halicarnassus, and the statue of Zeus at Olympia. Preceded by *the.*

sev·en-year itch (sévv'n-yeer, -yer) *n.* A tendency towards infidelity that is supposed to develop after seven years of marriage.

sev·er (sévvər) *v.* **-ered, -ering, -ers.** —*tr.* **1.** To divide or separate into parts; keep apart or make distinct. **2.** To cut or break off forcibly; remove by cutting. **3.** To break off (a relationship, for example); dissolve. —*intr.* **1.** To become cut or broken apart. **2.** To divide; separate or go apart. —See Synonyms at **separate, tear.** [Middle English *severen,* from Anglo-French *severer,* from Vulgar Latin *sēperāre* (unattested), from Latin *sēparāre,* to SEPARATE.] —**sev·er·a·ble** (sévvərəb'l) *adj.*

sev·er·al (sévvrəl, sévvərəl) *adj.* **1.** More than two but not many; of an indefinitely small number. **2.** Single; distinct. **3.** Respectively different; diverse; various. **4.** *Law.* Pertaining separately to each party involved.
~*pron.* Several persons or things; a few. [Middle English *severall,* separate, distinct, from Anglo-French *several,* from Medieval Latin *sēparālis,* from Latin *sēpār,* separate, from *sēparāre,* to SEPARATE.] —**sev·er·al·ly** *adv.*

sev·er·ance (sévvərənss) *n.* **1.** The act or process of severing, division, or separation. **2.** The condition of being severed.

severance pay *n.* Money paid by an employer to an employee who has lost his job through no fault of his own.

se·vere (si-veér, sə-) *adj.* **-verer, -verest. 1.** Having or showing a harsh, unsparing, and inflexible disposition in one's treatment of or attitude towards others; stern; strict. **2.** Adhering to or based on stringent and exacting rules or standards: *severe discipline.* **3.** Grave and austere in appearance, manner, or temperament; forbidding. **4.** Extremely plain and unadorned, as in dress or style; sober and restrained. **5.** Causing intense pain or distress; hard; grievous: *a severe winter; severe depression.* **6.** Extremely difficult to perform or accomplish; arduous. [French *severe,* from Latin *sevērus.*] —**se·vere·ly** *adv.* —**se·vere·ness, se·ver·i·ty** (si-vérrəti, sə-) *n.*

Synonyms: *severe, stern, austere, ascetic, strict, exacting.*

Sev·ern (sévvərn). *Welsh* **Haf·ren** (háv-ren). Britain's longest river. It rises on the northeastern slopes of Plynlimon and flows for 340 kilometres (211 miles) through the Vale of Powys, and to the Bristol Channel via an exceptionally long estuary; the tidal bore can reverse the flow of the river as far up as Gloucester. The Severn Road Bridge (opened 1966), linking South Wales and England, is one of the world's longest suspension bridges.

Se·ve·rus (se-vaírəss), full name Lucius Septimius Severus (A.D. 146–211). Roman emperor (193–211) born in Roman North Africa. He restored order to the empire after a turbulent period, and consolidated the eastern frontier. He died at York while planning a major campaign into Scotland.

Se·ve·so (sáyv-sō; *Italian* sévve-zō). A town near Milan, northern Italy. Between July 1976 and September 1977, it was evacuated after an escape of poisonous dioxin gas from a factory.

Sé·vi·gné (sáyveen-yáy), **Marie de Rabutin-Chantal, Marquise de** (1626–96). French writer. A widow from the age of 25, she is remembered for her prolific correspondence. Her letters, including many to her daughter, radiate lively wit and understanding and vividly depict aristocratic life in the age of Louis XIV.

Se·ville (sə-víl, se-, si-, *also* sévvil). *Spanish* **Se·vi·lla** (se-veél-ya). A port of southwest Spain, the capital of Sevilla province. It was an important Moorish stronghold and centre of culture and learning (712–1248), and prospered as the main port for the Spanish colonies in the New World from 1492 until eclipsed by Cádiz in the late 17th century. Seville is also noted for its school of painting, whose artists included Velásquez and Murillo.

Seville orange *n.* **1.** A citrus tree, *Citrus aurantium,* that bears bitter oranges, used to make marmalade. **2.** The fruit of this tree. Also called "bitter orange". [After SEVILLE where it is cultivated.]

Sè·vres (sáyvrə, sayvr; *French* sévvrə) *n.* A fine porcelain made in Sèvres, northern France. Also called "Sèvres ware".

sew (sō) *v.* **sewed, sewn** (sōn) or **sewed, sewing, sews.** —*tr.* **1.** To make, repair, or fasten using a needle and thread. **2.** To close, enclose, or attach by means of stitches. —*intr.* To work with a needle and thread or with a sewing machine. —**sew up.** *Informal.* **1.** To bring (a business deal) to a successful close. **2.** *Chiefly U.S.* To gain control of. [Middle English *sewen,* Old English *seowian.*]

sew·age (séw-ij, sóō-) *n.* Liquid and solid waste carried off with ground water in sewers or drains. [SEW(ER) + -AGE.]

sewage farm *n.* A place where sewage is so that the solid constituents may be used as fertiliser, or so as to render it nontoxic.

Sew·all Wright effect (sóō-əl) *n.* **Genetic drift** *(see).* [After *Sewall Wright* (born 1889), U.S. geneticist and statistician.]

Sew·ell (séw-əl, sóō-), **Anna** (1820–78). British author of the children's classic, *Black Beauty* (1877). Partially crippled from childhood, she wrote her one novel, set in the form of the autobiography of a horse, to expose the maltreatment of animals in her day.

se·wel·lel (si-wélləl) *n.* A **mountain beaver** *(see).* [Probably from Chinook.]

sew·er[1] (séw-ər, sóō-) *n.* An artificial, usually underground conduit for carrying off sewage or rainwater. [Middle English *sewer,* from Anglo-French *sever(e),* from Vulgar Latin *exaquāria* (unattested) : Latin *ex-,* out of + *aqua,* water.]

sew·er[2] (séw-ər, sóō-) *n.* A medieval servant who supervised the serving of meals. [Middle English *sewer,* from Anglo-French *asseour,* from Old French *asseoir,* to cause to sit (seating of guests was a sewer's responsibility), from Latin *assidēre,* to sit down.]

sew·er[3] (sō-ər) *n.* One that sews.

sew·er·age (séw-ərij, sóō-) *n.* **1.** A system of sewers. **2.** The removal of waste materials by means of a sewer system. **3.** Sewage.

sew·in, sew·en (séw-in, sóō-) *n.* A salmon trout found along the west coast of Britain and in Ireland. [16th century : origin obscure.]

sew·ing (sō-ing) *n.* **1.** The act, skill, or hobby of one who sews. **2.** An article that is or is to be worked on with needle and thread; needlework.

sewing machine *n.* A machine that sews, often having additional attachments for special stitching.

sewn. Past participle of **sew.**

sex (seks) *n.* **1. a.** The sum of properties by which organisms are classified according to their reproductive functions. **b.** Either of two divisions, designated *male* and *female,* of this classification. **2.** Males or females collectively. **3.** The condition or character of being male or female; the physiological, functional, and psychological differences that distinguish the male and the female. **4.** The sexual urge or instinct or sexual desire as it manifests itself in behaviour. **5.** Sexual intercourse.
~*adj.* Of, based on, or concerned with sex or sexual intercourse.
~*tr.v.* **sexed, sexing, sexes.** To determine the sex of. [Middle English, from Old French *sexe,* from Latin *sexus*†.]

Seven Deadly Sins

THOUGHTS AND DEEDS THAT CARRIED THE PROSPECT OF ETERNAL DAMNATION

Mortal sins for Christians to shun

From the earliest Christian times, converts were received into the Church by the rite of baptism. The water used in the ceremony symbolised the cleansing of the convert from the sins he had committed before becoming a Christian. There was no ritual for absolving believers from sins committed after baptism because of a strong belief that such lapses ought not to occur.

As the Christian congregation grew, these high standards could not be maintained and methods of punishment, or "penance", for different categories of sin were established. The majority of sins were regarded as comparatively minor, or "venial", and, although they could not be committed with impunity, they were not as damaging to the soul and its prospects

in the afterlife as the few, worst sins. These were the "deadly" or "mortal" sins which carried a penalty of eternal damnation in hell for the sinner unless the sin was sincerely repented of and adequate penance was done.

The seven sins usually listed as deadly are pride, covetousness, lust, anger, gluttony, envy, and sloth. Committing them in spirit was as sinful as committing them in actual deed. Suppressed anger, for instance, was quite as reprehensible as the curses or blows that might result from a vigorously expressed bout of rage. To avoid damnation, Christians had to watch for any sign of weakness in thought or deed – a merely outward show of righteousness was not enough.

GRAPHIC PAINTINGS *The seven deadly sins have been a favourite theme of artists. The table top above, painted by Hieronymus Bosch, uses the cartwheel design much favoured in his time to illustrate virtues and vices. Each division is devoted to a particular sin and, at the hub is the all-seeing eye of God. Within it is Christ above a Latin inscription meaning "Beware, the Lord sees".*

sex– *comb. form.* Indicates six; for example, **sexpartite.** [Latin *sex*, six.]

sex·a·ge·nar·i·an (séksə-ji-naír-i-ən, -jə-) *adj.* **1.** Being sixty years old or between sixty and seventy years old. **2.** Of or like someone of this age.
~*n.* A person of sixty or between sixty and seventy years of age. [Latin *sexāgēnārius*, from *sexāgēni*, sixty each, from *sexāgintā*, sixty : SEX + -*ginta*, ten times.]

Sex·a·ges·i·ma (séksə-jéssimə) *n.* The second Sunday before Lent. Also called "Sexagesima Sunday". [Late Latin *sexāgēsima*, sixtieth (day before Easter), from Latin, feminine of *sexāgēsimus*, sixtieth, from *sexāgintā*, sixty. See **sexagenarian.**]

sex·a·ges·i·mal (séksə-jéssim'l) *adj.* Relating to or based upon the

number 60. [From Latin *sexāgēsimus*, sixtieth, from *sexāgintā*, sixty. See **sexagenarian.**]

sex appeal *n.* Attractiveness that arouses sexual desire; the possession of qualities that are sexually attractive.

sex·cen·te·nar·y (sék-sen-téenəri, -sin-, -ténnəri, -sénti-nəri ‖ -nerri) *adj.* Pertaining to 600 or to a 600-year period.
~*n., pl.* **sexcentenaries.** A 600th anniversary or its commemoration. [From Latin *sexcentēni*, six hundred each : SEX- + *centēni*, a hundred each, from *centum*, hundred.]

sex chromosome *n.* Either of a pair of chromosomes, usually designated X or Y, that combine to determine the sex of an individual. In humans, XX results in a female and XY in a male. See **X chromosome, Y chromosome.**

sex·en·ni·al (sek-sénni-əl) *adj.* **1.** Occurring every six years. **2.** Of or for six years. [Latin *sexennium,* (period of) six years : SEX- + *annus,* year.] —**sex·en·ni·al·ly** *adv.*

sex hormone *n.* Any of various animal hormones, such as oestrogen and androgen, affecting the growth or function of the reproductive organs and the development of secondary sex characteristics.

sex·ism (séksiz'm) *n.* **1.** Discrimination based on sex; especially, prejudice against the female sex. **2.** Any arbitrary stereotyping of males and females on the basis of their gender. [SEX + -ISM, after RACISM.] —**sex·ist** *adj.* & *n.*

sex·less (séks-ləss, -liss) *adj.* **1.** Lacking sexual characteristics; asexual; neuter. **2.** Arousing or exhibiting no sexual interest or desire. —**sex·less·ly** *adv.* —**sex·less·ness** *n.*

sex linkage *n.* The condition in which a gene responsible for a specific phenotypic trait is located on a sex chromosome, usually on the X chromosome but not on the Y chromosome, resulting in sexually dependent inheritance of the trait.

sex·linked (séks-lingkt) *adj.* **1.** Carried by a sex chromosome, especially an X chromosome. Said of genes. **2.** Broadly, sexually determined. Said especially of inherited traits.

sex object *n.* One who is valued, or is portrayed as having value, purely for her or his sexual attributes.

sex·ol·o·gy (sék-sólləji) *n.* The study of human sexual behaviour. [SEX + -LOGY.] —**sex·o·log·ic** (-sə-lójik), **sex·o·log·i·cal** *adj.* —**sex·ol·o·gist** (-sólləjist) *n.*

sex·par·tite (séks-pártīt) *adj.* Composed of or divided into six parts. [SEX- + PARTITE.]

sex·pot (séks-pot) *n. Informal.* A woman who is sexually attractive in an uninhibited way.

sext (sekst) *n.* **1.** The fourth of the seven **canonical hours** *(see).* **2.** The time of day set aside for this prayer, usually the sixth hour, or noon. [Middle English *sexte,* from Latin *sexta (hora),* sixth (hour), from the feminine of *sextus,* sixth.]

Sex·tans (séks-tanz, -tənz) *n.* A constellation in the equatorial region of the sky near Leo and Hydra. Also called the "Sextant". [New Latin, SEXTANT.]

sex·tant (sékstənt) *n.* **1.** An instrument used in navigation for measuring the altitudes of celestial bodies and hence determining the position of the observer. **2.** *Capital* **S.** The constellation Sextans. [New Latin *sextans* (stem *sextant-*), from Latin, a sixth part (the instrument has an arc graduated in sixths of a circle).]

sex·tet (séks-tét) *n.* **1. a.** A group of six vocalists or musicians. **b.** A musical composition written for six performers. **2.** Any group of six persons or things. [Respelling of SESTET, after Latin *sex,* six.]

sex·tile (sékstīl) *adj.* Designating the position of two celestial bodies when they are 60 degrees apart. [Latin *sextīlis,* one sixth (of a circle), from *sextus,* sixth.]

sex·til·li·on (séks-tílliən, -tíl-yən) *n.* **1.** In British usage, the cardinal number represented by 1 followed by 36 zeros, usually written 10^{36}. **2.** In U.S. usage, the cardinal number represented by 1 followed by 21 zeros, usually written 10^{21}. [French : SEX- + (M)ILLION.] —**sex·til·li·onth** *n.* & *adj.*

sex·to·dec·i·mo (sékstō-déssimō) *n., pl.* **-mos. 1.** The page size of a book composed of printer's sheets folded into 16 leaves or 32 pages. **2.** A book composed of pages of this size. Also called "sixteenmo". Also written *16 mo, 16°.* [Latin *sextōdecimō,* ablative of *sextusdecimus,* a sixteenth : *sextus,* sixth + *decimus,* tenth, from *decem,* ten.] —**sex·to·dec·i·mo** *adj.*

sex·ton (sékstən) *n.* A church officer responsible for the care and upkeep of the church, its furnishings and vestments, the churchyard, and sometimes for bell-ringing or gravedigging. [Middle English *segerstone, sexton,* from Anglo-French *segerstaine,* from Medieval Latin *sacristānus,* SACRISTAN.]

sexton beetle *n.* The **burying beetle** *(see).*

sex·tu·ple (séks-tewp'l ‖ -téwp'l, -too͞o'l, -tupp'l, -túpp'l) *adj.* **1.** Consisting of or having six parts, members, or copies. **2.** Multiplied by six; six times as much, as many, or as large. —*n.* A sixfold amount or number. —*v.* **sextupled, -pling, -ples.** —*tr.* To multiply or increase by six. —*intr.* To be multiplied sixfold. [Medieval Latin *sextuplus,* irregularly (influenced by *quintuplus,* QUINTUPLE) from Latin *sex,* six.] —**sex·tu·ply** *adv.*

sex·tu·plet (séks-tew-plət, -téw-, -plit ‖ -to͞o-, -tú-) *n.* **1.** One of six offspring delivered at one birth. **2.** A collection or set of six similar persons or things; a sextet. **3.** *Music.* A set of six equal notes to be performed in the time normally given for four notes of the same value. [SEXTU(PLE + TRI)PLET.]

sex·tu·pli·cate (séks-téw-pli-kət, -kit ‖ -to͞o-, -túppli-) *adj.* **1.** Six times as many or as much; sixfold. **2.** Sixth in a group or set. —*n.* One of six similar things. [SEXTU(PLE + DU)PLICATE.] —**sex·tu·pli·cate·ly** *adv.* —**sex·tu·pli·ca·tion** (-káysh'n) *n.*

sex·u·al (sék-sew-əl, -sewl, -shoo-əl, -shoo͞ol) *adj.* **1.** Pertaining to, affecting, or associated with sex, the sexes, or the sex organs and their functions. **2.** Of or pertaining to the desire or urge for physical contact and stimulation with another person that, typically, is satisfied by sexual intercourse. **3.** Having a sex or sexual organs. [From Late Latin *sexuālis,* from Latin *sexus,* SEX.] —**sex·u·al·ly** *adv.*

sexual intercourse *n.* **1.** Copulation between a man and a woman, involving the insertion of the erect penis into the vagina. **2.** Intercourse between two or more individuals involving genital stimulation. Also called "intercourse".

sexual reproduction *n.* Reproduction involving the union of male and female gametes.

sex·u·al·i·ty (sék-sew-al-əti, -shoo͞o-) *n.* **1.** The condition of being characterised and distinguished by sex. **2.** Concern or preoccupation with sex. **3.** The quality of possessing a sexual character or potency. **4.** The condition of having sexual feelings and desires of a certain kind; a particular sexual nature.

sexual selection *n.* A Darwinian adjunct of natural selection hypothesising the selection by females of characteristics involved in male courtship displays and combat and hence the retention of such characteristics in future generations.

sex·y (séksi) *adj.* **-ier, -iest.** *Informal.* Arousing or intended to arouse sexual desire or interest.

Sey·chelles, Republic of (sáy-shélz, say-). A state of the northwestern Indian Ocean, comprising an archipelago of some 85 coral or volcanic islands, northeast of Madagascar. It was discovered by Vasco da Gama (1502), settled by the French (1770s), and seized by the British (1794). The Seychelles became an independent republic within the Commonwealth in 1976. Its economy rests on tropical produce, particularly copra and cinnamon, and, increasingly, on tourism and fishing. Mahé is the largest island, with more than 60 per cent of the population. Area, 278 square kilometres (107 square miles). Capital, Victoria (on Mahé). Population, 100,000. See map at **Indian Ocean.** —**Sey·chel·lois** (sáy-shel-wáa) *n.* & *adj.*

Sey·fert galaxy (sī-fərt, sée-) *n.* Any of a number of spiral galaxies with an exceptionally bright nucleus. [After Carl K. *Seyfert* (1911–60), U.S. astronomer.]

Sey·mour (sée-mawr ‖ -mōr), **Jane** (c. 1509–37). English noblewoman, the third wife of Henry VIII and the mother of Edward VI. A lady-in-waiting to Anne Boleyn, she married Henry in 1536 soon after Anne's execution. She died shortly after providing the king with his only male heir.

sez (sez). *Nonstandard.* Variant of **says.**

SF science fiction.

sferics. *U.S.* Variant of **spherics.**

sfor·zan·do (sfawrt-sán-dō ‖ -sáan-) *adv.* Also **for·zan·do** (fawrt-). *Abbr.* **sf., sfz.** Suddenly and strongly accented. Used as a musical direction. —*n.* Also **forzando.** A sforzando note or chord. [Italian, gerund of *sforzare,* to use force : *s-,* from Latin *ex-,* out of + *forzare,* to force, from Vulgar Latin *fortiāre* (unattested), from *fortia* (unattested), FORCE.] —**sfor·zan·do** *adj.*

S.G. solicitor general.

sgd. signed.

sgraf·fi·to (sgrə-féetō, sgra-; *Italian* zgra-) *n., pl.* **-fiti** (-féetee). **1.** Decoration, as on a wall or piece of pottery, produced by scratching through a surface of plaster or glazing to reveal a different colour beneath. **2.** Something decorated in this way. [Italian, from the past participle of *sgraffire,* to scratch, from *sgraffio,* a scratch, from *sgraffiare,* to produce sgraffito : *s-,* from Latin *ex-,* out of + *graffiare,* to scratch (see **graffito**).]

's Gravenhage. See **Hague, The.**

Sgt. sergeant.

Sgt. Maj. sergeant major.

sh (sh) *interj.* Used to urge silence.

sh. 1. share. **2.** sheet. **3.** shilling.

Shaan·xi or **Shan·hsi** or **Shen·si** (shán-sée). Province in north central China, lying to the south of the Huang-He. It is crossed by the Wei river valley, one of the earliest cultural and political centres of northern China, and today a rich agricultural region and the most densely populated part of the province. Since the 1960s Shaanxi has developed industrially. Following the "long march", the province was the headquarters of the Chinese Communist party (1935–49). Xi'an is the capital.

Sha·ba (sháabə). Formerly **Ka·tan·ga** (kə-táng-gə, ka-) Province of southeast Zaire. Its extensive mineral deposits, particularly copper, have made it the country's richest province. Shortly after Zaire's independence (1960), Katanga seceded and was not reconstituted a province until 1967. Lubumbashi is the capital.

Sha·ban, shaa·ban (shə-báan, shaa-) *n.* The eighth month of the year on the Muslim calendar. [Arabic *sha'bān.*]

Shab·bat (shaa-báat, shə-, sháabəss) *n., pl.* **-batim** (-báatim, -báw-sim). The Jewish Sabbath. [Hebrew *shabbāth,* SABBATH.]

shab·by (shábbi) *adj.* **-bier, -biest. 1.** Threadbare; worn-out. **2.** Wearing worn-out clothes; seedy. **3.** Dilapidated; in poor repair. **4.** Despicable; mean. **5.** Unfair. [Obsolete *shab,* a scab, from Middle English *schab(be),* Old English *sceabb,* from Old Norse *skabbr* (unattested). See **scab**.] —**shab·bi·ly** *adv.* —**shab·bi·ness** *n.*

Shabuoth. Variant of **Shavuot.**

shack (shak) *n.* A small, crudely built cabin; a shanty. —**shack up.** *Informal.* To live together or with another in a sexual relationship while unmarried. Usually used with *with.* [Short for Mexican Spanish *jacal,* from Aztec *xacatti,* thatched cabin.]

shack·le (shák'l) *n.* **1.** A metal fastening, usually one of a pair, for encircling and confining the ankle or wrist of a prisoner or captive; a fetter; a manacle. **2.** Any of several devices, such as a clevis, used to fasten or couple. **3.** Anything that confines or restrains. —*tr.v.* **shackled, -ling, -les. 1.** To put shackles on; fetter. **2.** To fasten or connect with a shackle. **3.** To restrict; confine; hamper. [Middle English *schackle,* Old English *sceacel,* fetter, from Germanic *skakulo-* (unattested).] —**shack·ler** *n.*

Shack·le·ton (shák'ltən), **Sir Ernest Henry** (1874–1922). British Antarctic explorer. In 1907-9 he led an expedition which came within 161 kilometres (100 miles) of the South Pole. On a second expedition, Shackleton's ship *Endurance* became ice-bound and he made a gruelling journey to South Georgia to get help. He died on South Georgia, leading his third expedition (1921–22).

shad (shad) *n., pl.* **shads** or collectively **shad.** **1.** Any of several food fishes of the genus *Alosa,* related to the herrings but atypical in swimming to estuaries or up streams from marine waters to spawn. **2.** Broadly, any of various unrelated silvery fishes. [Middle English *shad,* Old English *sceadd*†.]

shad·ber·ry (shád-berri) *n., pl.* **-ries.** **1.** The fruit of the shadbush. **2.** The fruit of the service tree.

shad·bush (shád-bŏŏsh) *n.* Any of various North American shrubs or trees of the genus *Amelanchier,* having white flowers and edible blue-black or purplish fruit. Also called "shadblow", "serviceberry", "Juneberry". [So called because the flowers bloom at about the same time shad appear in U.S. rivers.]

shad·dock (sháddək) *n.* **1.** A tropical tree, *Citrus maxima* (or *C. grandis*), closely related to the grapefruit. **2.** The edible yellow, pear-shaped fruit of this tree. Also *chiefly U.S.* "pomelo". [After Captain *Shaddock,* commander of an East India Company ship, who took the seed to Jamaica in 1696.]

shade (shayd) *n.* **1.** Light diminished in intensity as a result of the interception of the rays; comparative darkness. **2.** Cover or shelter from the sun provided by an object's interception of its rays. **3.** A place or area sheltered from the sun. **4.** Any of various devices, such as a lampshade, used to reduce or screen light or heat. **5.** *Plural. Slang.* Sunglasses. **6.** Relative obscurity or inconspicuousness. **7.** *Plural.* Dark shadows occurring at dusk: *shades of evening.* **8.** The part of a picture or photograph depicting darkness or shadow. **9.** The degree to which a colour is mixed with black or is decreasingly illuminated; gradation of darkness. **10.** A colour that resembles a standard colour but is slightly different in saturation, hue, or luminosity: *a shade of red.* **11.** A slight difference or variation; a nuance. **12.** A small amount; a trace; a jot. **13.** A disembodied spirit; a ghost. **—shades of.** Used humorously to suggest some association with or evocation of the person or thing specified.
~*v.* **shaded, shading, shades.** —*tr.* **1.** To screen from light or heat. **2.** To obscure or darken. **3. a.** To represent the effect of shade in (a picture). **b.** To produce gradations of light or colour in (a picture). **c.** To cover in (part of a picture) with fine pencil lines, brushstrokes, or the like. **4.** To change or vary by slight degrees: *shade the meaning.* —*intr.* To change gradually or imperceptibly, as from one state or colour into another. Often used with *off.*
~*adj.* Providing or intended to provide shade: *a shade tree.* [Middle English *schade,* Old English *sceadu, scead.*]

shad·ing (sháyding) *n.* **1.** Screening against light or heat. **2.** The lines or other marks used in a sketch, engraving, or painting to represent gradations of light or colour. **3.** Any small variation, gradation, or difference.

shad·ow (sháddō) *n.* **1.** An area that is not, or is only partially, irradiated or illuminated because of the interception of radiation by an opaque object between the area and the source of radiation. **2.** The rough image of the intervening object, especially the umbral image, that delimits the shaded area. **3.** An imperfect, insubstantial, or delusive imitation; a semblance. **4.** *Plural.* The darkness following sunset. **5.** Gloom or unhappiness or an influence that causes such feeling. **6.** A shaded area in a picture or photograph. **7.** A mirrored image or reflection. **8.** A phantom; a ghost. **9.** One who constantly follows another around, such as: **a.** A constant companion. **b.** A detective. **10.** A faint indication; a premonition. **11.** A vestige; a remnant. **12.** An insignificant portion or amount; a slight trace. **13.** Shelter; protection. **14.** An influence that dominates or overshadows: *grew up in his brother's shadow.*
~*adj.* Belonging to a shadow cabinet and acting as the counterpart in opposition of a particular member of the government.
~*tr.v.* **shadowed, -owing, -ows.** **1.** To cast a shadow upon; shade. **2.** To make gloomy or dark; to cloud. **3.** To represent vaguely, mysteriously, or prophetically. **4.** To follow after, especially in secret; trail. [Middle English *schadow,* Old English *sceaduwe,* oblique case of *sceadu,* SHADE.] **—shad·ow·er** *n.*

shad·ow·box (sháddō-boks) *intr.v.* **-boxed, -boxing, -boxes.** To spar with an imaginary opponent, as in training.

shadow cabinet *n.* The members of the main opposition party in Parliament who act as spokesmen for their party on the issues dealt with by their ministerial counterparts in government, and who are expected to hold positions in the cabinet when their party is returned to power.

shad·ow·graph (sháddō-graaf, -graf) *n.* An image produced by casting a shadow on a screen.

shadow play *n.* A play presented by casting shadows of puppets or actors on a screen.

shad·ow·y (sháddō-i) *adj.* **-ier, -iest.** **1.** Resembling a shadow; insubstantial; unreal. **2.** Full of shadows; dark; shady. **3.** Barely perceptible; indistinct; dim. —See Synonyms at **dark.** **—shad·ow·i·ness** *n.*

Sha·drach (sháy-drak, shá-). A Hebrew captive who miraculously escaped death in Nebuchadnezzar's fiery furnace. Daniel 3.

shad·y (sháydi) *adj.* **-ier, -iest.** **1.** Full of shade; shaded. **2.** Providing shade. **3. a.** Of dubious character or honesty. **b.** Legally or morally questionable. —See Synonyms at **dishonest, dark.** **—shad·i·ly** *adv.* **—shad·i·ness** *n.*

Shaf·fer (sháffər), **Peter** (1926–). British playwright. His works include *Equus* (1973) and the historical dramas *The Royal Hunt of the Sun* (1964) and *Amadeus* (1979).

shaft[1] (shaaft || shaft) *n.* **1.** The long, narrow stem or body of a spear or arrow. **2.** A spear, arrow, or the like. **3.** Something suggestive of an arrow in appearance or effect: *shafts of satire.* **4.** A ray or beam of light. **5.** The handle of any of various tools or implements. **6.** The rib of a feather. **7.** *Anatomy.* **a.** The midsection of a long bone; the diaphysis. **b.** The section of a hair projecting from the surface of the body. **c.** Any elongated cylindrical body part. **8.** The section of a column or pillar between the capital and base. **9.** One of two parallel poles between which an animal is harnessed. **10.** *Machinery.* A long, generally cylindrical bar, especially one that rotates and transmits power: *a drive shaft.* [Middle English *shaft,* Old English *sceaft,* from Germanic *skaftaz* (unattested).]

shaft[2] *n.* **1.** A long, narrow passage sunk into the earth; a tunnel. **2.** A vertical passage housing a lift. **3.** A duct or conduit for the passage of air, as for ventilation or heating.

Shaftes·bur·y (shaáfts-bri, -bəri || sháfts-, -berri), **Anthony Ashley Cooper, 1st Earl of** (1621–83). English politician, the father of the Whig party. Shaftesbury came over to the Parliamentarians in early 1644, during the English Civil War, and was appointed to official posts in 1648–49 by Cromwell's government. In 1654 he withdrew his support from Cromwell and took part in the restoration of Charles II in 1660. In 1667 he became one of the five ministers in the so-called **cabal** (after the initials of the five leaders) administration, rising to be Lord Chancellor as the Earl of Shaftesbury in 1672. Dismissed from office in the following year, he organised an oppositon faction, which was the origin of the Whig party.

Shaftesbury, Anthony Ashley Cooper, 7th Earl of (1801–85). British politician. An M.P. from 1826, he pioneered social and industrial reform. He helped to introduce laws that banned sweeps from using climbing boys (1840), excluded women and children from the mines (1842), and established the 10-hour day for factory workers (1847).

shaft·ing (shaáft-ing || sháft-) *n.* **1.** A system of shafts, as in a mechanical device, for transmitting motion or power. **2.** Material from which shafts are made.

shag[1] (shag) *n.* **1.** A tangle or mass, especially of rough, matted hair. **2. a.** A coarse long nap, as on some woollen cloth. **b.** Cloth having such a nap. **3.** Coarse shredded tobacco.
~*tr.v.* **shagged, shagging, shags.** To make shaggy; roughen. [Middle English *shagge* (unattested), Old English *sceacga,* beard, from Germanic *skag-* (unattested).] **—shag** *adj.*

shag[2] *n.* A dance step of the 1930s consisting of a hop on each foot in alternation. [20th century : origin obscure.] **—shag** *intr.v.*

shag[3] *n.* A marine bird, of the genus *Phalacrocorax (P.aristotelis)* which also includes the cormorants. The mature bird is black and has a short crest and yellow beak. [Perhaps from its shaggy crest.]

shag[4] *tr.v.* **shagged, shagging, shags.** *Slang.* **1.** *Vulgar.* To have sexual intercourse with. **2.** To tire; exhaust. Usually used with *out.*

shag·bark (shág-baark) *n.* A North American hickory tree, *Carya ovata,* having shaggy bark, compound leaves, and edible nuts with a hard shell. Also called "shellbark".

shag·gy (shággi) *adj.* **-gier, -giest.** **1.** Having, covered with, or resembling long, rough hair or wool. **2.** Bushy and matted. **3.** Poorly groomed; unkempt. **—shag·gi·ly** *adv.* **—shag·gi·ness** *n.*

shaggy cap *n.* An edible ink cap fungus, *Coprinus comatus,* having a long white stalk and a greyish-white flaking cap.

shag·gy-dog story (shággi-dóg || -dáwg) *n.* A long, drawn-out anecdote depending for humour upon an absurd or anticlimactic punch line.

shaggy parasol *n.* A basidiomycete fungus, *Lepiota rhacodes,* having a broad, pale brown cap covered in brown scales.

sha·green (sha-gréen, shə-) *n.* **1.** The rough hide of a shark or ray, covered with numerous bony denticles, and used as an abrasive and as leather. **2.** Leather with a granular surface, prepared from the skins of various animals. [From French *chagrin,* "rough hide". See **chagrin.**] **—sha·green** *adj.*

shag·pile (shágg-pīl) *n.* A long shaglike or soft pile on a carpet.

shah (shaa) *n.* The monarch of certain lands of the Middle East, especially, formerly, Iran. [Persian *shāh,* from Old Persian *khshāya-thiya.*]

Shah Ja·han (jə-haán) (1592–1666). Mogul emperor of India (1628-58), who brought the Mogul Empire to its golden age. A noted patron of the arts, he was also a great builder and had the Taj Mahal erected (1638–48). He was deposed by his son, Aurangzeb.

shai·tan, shei·tan (shī-taán) *n.* **1.** *Often capital* **S.** *Islam.* Satan; the Devil. **2.** An evil spirit; a fiend. [Arabic *shaiṭān,* from Hebrew *śāṭān,* SATAN.]

Shak. Shakespeare.

Sha·ka (shaá-gə, -kə) (*c.* 1787–1828). Chief of the Zulu (1816–28) who made the Zulu state the strongest in southern Africa. An outstanding war leader, he built a disciplined, mobile, and highly successful army.

shake (shayk) *v.* **shook** (shŏŏk || shōōk), **shaken** (sháykən), **shaking, shakes.** —*tr.* **1.** To cause to move to and fro with short jerky movements. **2.** To cause to quiver or tremble; vibrate or rock: *A severe tremor shook the ground.* **3.** To cause to stagger or waver; upset; unsettle. **4.** To remove or dislodge by jerky movements: *shake the dust out.* **5.** To bring to a specified condition by or as if by jerky movements: *shook her out of her complacency.* **6.** To disturb or agitate; unnerve. Often used with *up.* **7.** To brandish or wave: *shake one's fist.* **8.** To clasp (hands or another's hand) in greeting or leave-taking or as a sign of agreement. **9.** To free oneself from; get rid of. Usually used with *off.* **10.** *Music.* To trill (a note). **11.** To rattle and mix (dice) before casting. **12.** To make unstable; weaken:

shag[3] *In spring the shag's erect crest distinguishes it from its larger relative, the cormorant. Both birds dive for fish in deep coastal waters and nest on remote cliffs.*

His convictions were shaken. **13.** *Australian Slang.* To rob; steal. —*intr.* **1.** To move to and fro in short jerky movements. **2.** To tremble, as from cold or in anger. **3.** To totter or waver; become unsteady. **4. a.** *Music.* To trill. **b.** To change pitch rapidly or tremulously because of emotion. Used of the voice. **5.** To shake hands. ~*n.* **1.** An act of shaking. **2.** A trembling or quivering movement. **3.** *Informal.* An earthquake. **4.** A fissure in rock. **5.** A crack in timber caused by wind or frost. **6.** *Music.* A trill. **7.** A drink in which the ingredients are mixed by shaking: *a milk shake.* **8.** *Informal.* An instant; a moment: *She'll be here in two shakes.* **—no great shakes.** *Informal.* Unexceptional; ordinary; mediocre. **—the shakes.** *Informal.* **1.** The chill accompanying intermittent fever. **2.** Uncontrollable trembling, especially as a symptom of alcoholism or metal poisoning. [Shake, shook, shaken; Middle English *schaken, schook, schaken,* Old English *sceacan, sceōc, sceacen,* from Germanic *skakan* (unattested).] **—shak·a·ble, shake·a·ble** *adj.*

Synonyms: *shake, tremble, quake, quiver, shiver, shudder.*

shake down *intr.v.* **1.** To put together hurriedly, or settle down on, a makeshift bed. **2.** To settle down or settle in comfortably. —*tr.v.* *U.S. Informal.* **1.** To extort money from. **2.** To make a thorough search of. **3.** To subject to a shakedown cruise.

shake·down (sháyk-down) *n.* **1.** A hastily made up resting place; a makeshift bed. **2.** *U.S. Informal.* An extortion of money by blackmail or other means. **3.** *U.S. Informal.* A thorough search of a place or person. **4.** *U.S. Informal.* A test run for appraising operating performance, as of a new ship or plane, followed by adjustments to improve efficiency or functioning. Also used adjectivally.

shak·er (sháykər) *n.* **1.** One that shakes. **2.** A container used for shaking something out: *a salt shaker.* **3.** A container used to mix or blend by shaking: *a cocktail shaker.*

Shaker *n.* A member of a millenarian religious sect originating in England in 1747, practising communal living and observing celibacy. [From the former custom of dancing with shaking movements during ceremonies.]

Shake·speare (sháyk-speer), **William** (1564–1616). English dramatist and poet, the greatest writer in English literature. He was born at Stratford-on-Avon, the son of a tradesman, was educated at the free grammar school, and in 1582 married Anne Hathaway. By 1592 he had established a reputation in London both as an actor and playwright. His first play, *Henry VI* (in three parts) dates from 1590–91, while his first major poem, *Venus and Adonis,* appeared in 1593 and was dedicated to his patron, the Earl of Southampton. Shakespeare's prolific dramatic output for the open-air Globe Theatre includes such historical plays as *Julius Caesar* and *Henry V* (1598–1600), and such comedies as *As You Like It* and *Twelfth Night* (1598–1600). His tragedies begin with *Romeo and Juliet* (1594–5) and include *Hamlet* (1600–01), *Othello* (1604–05), *King Lear* (1605), and *Macbeth* (1605–06). Shakespeare's later fantasy plays *The Winter's Tale* (*c.* 1610) and *The Tempest* (*c.* 1611) were written for an indoor theatre at Blackfriars. The first collected edition of his works, known as the First Folio, contained 36 plays and was published posthumously in 1623.

shallot A small, onion-like bulb that grows in clusters. It is generally used for pickling.

Shake·spear·e·an, Shake·spear·i·an (shayk-spéer-i-ən) *adj.* Of, pertaining to, or like Shakespeare, his works, or his style. ~*n.* A scholar of Shakespeare or his works.

Shakespearean sonnet *n.* The sonnet form used by Shakespeare, composed of three quatrains and a final couplet with the rhyme pattern *abab cdcd efef gg,* and retaining the break or pause in theme that falls between the octave and sestet in earlier sonnet forms. Also called "Elizabethan sonnet", "English sonnet".

shake up *tr.v. Informal.* To reorganise or rearrange drastically.

shake·up (sháyk-up) *n.* A thorough or drastic reorganisation, as in the personnel of a business or government.

shak·ing palsy (sháyking) *n.* **Parkinson's disease** *(see).*

shak·o (sháckō || shaáa-kō, sháy-) *n., pl.* **-os** or **-oes.** A stiff, cylindrical military dress hat with a metal plate in front, a short visor, and a plume. [French *schako,* from Hungarian *csákó,* from *csákó (süveg),* pointed (cap), from *csák,* peak, from German *Zacken,* point, from Middle High German *zacke.*]

Shak·ta (shaák-tə, shúk-) *n.* Also **Sak·ta** (saák-, súk-). A member of a Hindu sect that worships Shakti. [Sanskrit *śākta,* from *śakti,* SHAKTI.] **—Shak·tism** *n.* **—Shak·tist** *n.*

Shak·ti (shaák-ti, shúk-). Also **Sak·ti** (saák-, súk-). *Hinduism.* **1.** The female principle, especially as personified by the wife of the god Shiva. **2.** The personification of nature and generative power. [Sanskrit *śakti,* from *śaknōti,* is strong.]

shak·y (sháyki) *adj.* **-ier, -iest.** **1.** Trembling or quivering; tremulous; shaking. **2.** Unsteady or unsound; weak: *a shaky table.* **3.** Not to be depended upon; insecure. **—shak·i·ly** *adv.* **—shak·i·ness** *n.*

shale (shayl) *n.* A sedimentary rock produced from clay, which has a fine-grained structure in well-defined narrow strata 0.1. to 0.4 millimetre (0.004 to 0.016 inch) thick. [Probably from German *Schale,* from Old English *sc(e)alu.* See **scale.**]

shale oil *n.* A fuel oil obtained from oil shales.

shall (shal, *weak forms* sh'l, shə, sh) *v.* past **should** (shŏŏd, *weak forms* shəd, shd) or *archaic* **shouldst** (shŏŏdst) or **shouldest** (shŏŏddist) for second person singular, present **shall** or *archaic* **shalt** (shalt, *weak form* sh'lt) for second person singular. Used as an auxiliary followed by a simple infinitive or, in reply to a question or suggestion, with the infinitive understood. It can indicate: **1.** In the first person singular or plural, simple futurity: *I shall be twenty-eight tomorrow.* **2.** In the second and third persons: **a.** Determination or promise: *Your services shall be rewarded.* **b.** Inevitability: *That day shall come.* **c.** Command: *Thou shalt not kill.* **d.** Compulsion, with the force of *must,* in statutes, deeds, and other legal documents: *The penalty shall not exceed two years in prison.* **3.** *Formal.* In all persons, indefinite futurity, in conditional clauses and in clauses expressing doubt, anxiety, or desire: *If you shall ever change your opinion, come to me again.* [Shall, shalt, should; Middle English *schal, schalt, scholde,* Old English *sceal, scealt, sceolde.*]

Usage: Traditional grammars and manuals of usage have insisted on a systematic distinction between the use of *shall* and *will* since the 18th century. It is recommended that *shall* be used in the first person to express simple futurity *(I shall visit you next week),* and in the second and third persons to express such meanings as obligation or determination *(You shall go to the ball). Will,* by contrast, is supposed to be used to express simple futurity in the second and third persons *(He will see you next week),* and such meanings as obligation or determination in the first person. The two verbs are thus thought to complement each other nicely, and many people try to speak and write according to these rules, especially in British English. However, these distinctions are not closely observed in speech, and often not in writing, and it is questionable whether the language ever maintained such a systematic distinction. In modern English speech, contracted forms are in such common use that it is impossible to say which verb is involved *(I'll, You'll,* etc.); extra emphasis is hence largely a matter of extra stress (*I* SHALL *go* and *I* WILL *go* seem to be semantically indistinguishable). American English has largely dropped the distinction, and uses *will* in all except the most formal styles; similarly, *won't* is standard usage for all persons, *shan't* being extremely rare. The distinction is more often maintained in British English, especially in formal styles. In England it is in standard use in most first-person question forms *(Shall I answer? Shall we go? I'll answer, shall I?),* though here American English prefers *should. Shall* is also avoided in Scottish and Irish English, *will* being used instead *(Will I drop you here or at your house?).* In standard English, *will* is used rather than *shall* in first-person question forms if a prediction or specific information about the future is required *(Will I look awful if I cut my hair?).*

shal·loon (sha-lo͞on) *n.* A lightweight wool or worsted twill fabric, used chiefly for coat linings. [French *chalon,* after *Châlons*-sur-Marne, France.]

shal·lop (shál-əp) *n.* An open boat fitted with oars, sails, or both. [French *chaloupe,* from Dutch *sloep,* SLOOP.]

shal·lot (shə-lót) *n.* **1.** A plant, *Allium ascalonicum,* closely related to the onion, cultivated for its edible bulb that divides into smaller sections. Also called "scallion". **2.** The mildly flavoured bulb of this plant, used in cookery. [Obsolete *eschalot,* from obsolete French *eschalotte,* from Old French *eschaloigne,* from Vulgar Latin *iscalōnia* (unattested), from Latin *Ascalōnia (caepa),* (onion) of Ascalon. See **scallion.**]

shal·low (shál-ō) *adj.* **-lower, -lowest.** **1. a.** Measuring little from bottom to top or surface; not deep. **b.** Gently sloping or curved; not steep. **2.** Lacking depth, as in intellect, character, or significance: *shallow criticism.* —See Synonyms at **superficial.** ~*n. Usually plural.* A shallow part of a body of water; a shoal. ~*v.* **shallowed, -lowing, -lows.** —*tr.* To make shallow. —*intr.* To become shallow. [Middle English *schalowe,* akin to Old English *sceald,* shallows. See **shoal.**] **—shal·low·ly** *adv.* **—shal·low·ness** *n.*

shal·low-fry (shállō-fry) *tr.v.* **-fried, -frying, -fries.** To cook in a small amount of fat or oil, so that only part of the food being fried is in contact with the fat or oil at one time.

sha·lom (shə-lóm, sha- || -lōm) *interj. Hebrew.* Used as a greeting or farewell. [Hebrew "peace".]

shalom a·lei·chem (ə-láy-kəm, a-, -khəm) *interj. Hebrew.* Used as a greeting or farewell. [Hebrew, "peace be with you".]

shalt. *Archaic.* Second person singular present tense of **shall.** Used with *thou.*

sham (sham) *n.* **1.** Something false or empty purporting to be genuine; a spurious imitation. **2.** The quality of deceitfulness; empty pretence. **3.** A person who assumes a false character; an impostor. **4.** *Archaic.* A decorative cover made to simulate an article of household linen and used over or in place of it: *a pillow sham.* ~*adj.* Not genuine; fake, pretended, or counterfeit. ~*v.* **shammed, shamming, shams.** —*tr.* To simulate; feign. —*intr.* To assume a false appearance or character; dissemble. [Perhaps northern dialect of SHAME.] **—sham·mer** *n.*

sham·an (shámmən || sháy-mən, shaá-) *n.* **1.** A priest of shamanism. **2.** A medicine man among certain North American Indians. [German *Schamane,* from Russian *shaman,* from Tungus *šaman,* from Tocharian *ṣamāne,* from Prakrit *samaṇa,* from Sanskrit *śramaṇás*†, "ascetic".]

sham·an·ism (shámmə-niz'm || sháymə-, shaámə-) *n.* **1.** The religious practices of certain peoples of northern Asia who believe that good and evil spirits pervade the world and can be summoned or heard through inspired priests acting as mediums. **2.** Any similar form of spiritualism, such as that practised among certain North American Indian tribes. **—sha·man·ist** *n.* **—sha·man·is·tic** (-nístik) *adj.*

Sha·mash (shaámash). The sun-god of Assyro-Babylonian religion, worshipped as the author of justice and compassion. [Akkadian, "sun", akin to Hebrew *shémesh.*]

sham·a·teur (shámmə-tər, -ter, -tewr, -chər || -toor) *n.* A sports player who professes to be, and plays as, an amateur but who receives large financial rewards from participating in the sport. [SHAM + (AM)ATEUR.]

sham·ble (shámb'l) *intr.v.* **-bled, -bling, -bles.** To walk in an awkward, lazy, or unsteady manner, shuffling the feet.
~*n.* A shambling walk; a shuffling gait. [From earlier *shamble,* ungainly, perhaps from *shamble legs,* probably referring to legs which were ungainly like those of a meat table. See **shambles.**]

sham·bles (shámb'lz) *n. Used with a singular verb.* **1.** A scene or condition of complete disorder or ruin: *left the room in a shambles.* **2.** A place or scene of bloodshed or carnage. **3.** *Archaic.* A meat market or slaughterhouse. **4.** *British. Archaic.* A row of covered market tables or stalls. [From plural of earlier *shamble,* table for display or sale of meat, Middle English *shamel,* Old English *sc(e)amul,* table, from West Germanic *skamel* (unattested), from Latin *scamellum,* diminutive of *scamnum,* bench.]

sham·bo·lic (shamm-bóllik) *adj.* Hopelessly disorganised or inept.

shame (shaym) *n.* **1.** A painful emotion caused by a strong sense of guilt, embarrassment, unworthiness, or disgrace. **2.** Capacity for such a feeling: *Have you no shame?* **3.** A person or thing that brings dishonour, disgrace, or condemnation. **4.** A condition of disgrace or dishonour; ignominy. **5.** A great disappointment or an occasion for pity or regret. —See Synonyms at **disgrace.** —**put to shame. 1.** To fill with shame; disgrace. **2.** To outdo thoroughly; surpass.
~*tr.v.* **shamed, shaming, shames. 1.** To cause to feel shame. **2.** To bring dishonour or disgrace upon. **3.** To force by making ashamed. Used with *into* or *out of*: *He was shamed into an apology.*
~*interj.* **1.** Used to express strong disapproval. **2.** *South African* Used to express sympathy or tender admiration. [Middle English *s(c)hame,* Old English *sc(e)amu,* from Germanic *skamō.*]

shame·faced (sháym-fayst, -fáyst) *adj.* **1.** Indicative of shame; ashamed: *a shamefaced explanation.* **2.** Extremely modest or shy; bashful. [Variant (influenced by FACE) of earlier *shamefast,* from Middle English *sham(e)fast,* Old English *sceamfæst* : *sceamu,* SHAME + *fæst,* FAST (firm), as if held firm by shame.] —**shame·fac·ed·ly** (*also* -fáyssid-li) *adv.* —**shame·fac·ed·ness** *n.*

shame·ful (sháymf'l) *adj.* **1.** Bringing or deserving shame; disgraceful; indecent. **2.** *Archaic.* Full of shame; shamefaced; ashamed. —**shame·ful·ly** *adv.* —**shame·ful·ness** *n.*

shame·less (sháym-ləss, -liss) *adj.* **1.** Not subject to the restraint of shame; impudent or immodest; brazen. **2.** Done without shame: *a shameless lie.* —**shame·less·ly** *adv.* —**shame·less·ness** *n.*
Synonyms: *shameless, brazen, barefaced, brash, bold, impudent, unblushing, forward.*

sham·mes (shaáməss) *n., pl.* **shammosim** (shaa-máw-sim). *Judaism.* **1.** A sexton in a synagogue. Also called "beadle". **2.** The candle used to light the other eight candles of the Chanukah Menorah. [Yiddish *shames,* from Hebrew *shammāsh,* from Aramaic *shəmmāsh,* to serve.]

shammy. Variant of **chamois.**

sham·poo (sham-pōō, shán-) *n., pl.* **-poos. 1.** Any of various liquid or cream preparations of soap or detergent used to wash the hair and scalp. **2.** Any of various cleaning agents, as for rugs, upholstery, or cars. **3.** An act of washing or cleaning with shampoo.
~*v.* **shampooed, -pooing, -poos.** —*tr.* To wash or clean with shampoo. —*intr.* To wash the hair with shampoo. [From Hindi *chāmpo,* from *chāmpnā,* massage, press, mark.]

sham·rock (shám-rok) *n.* Any of several plants, such as a trefoil, medick, clover, or wood sorrel, having compound leaves with three small leaflets, considered the national emblem of Ireland. [From Irish *seamrog,* diminutive of *seamar,* clover, from Old Irish *semar*†.]

sha·mus (shaá-məss, sháy-) *n. U.S. Slang.* A policeman or private detective. [Perhaps variant of SHAMMES.]

Shan (shaan || shan) *n.* **1.** A member of a group of Mongoloid tribes living in Burma, Thailand, and southern China. **2.** The northern Tai language spoken by these tribes. —**Shan** *adj.*

Shan·dong or **Shan·tung** or **Shan-tung** (shán-dóng || -túng). Densely populated maritime province of northeast China. It is crossed by the lower Huang-He and the Grand Canal, and has mountains in the east, and centre, where the sacred Tai Shan mountains reach 1 500 metres (5,000 feet). The lowlands are highly fertile, but with low, unreliable rainfall, famines used to occur. Settled by Chinese farmers since earliest times, Shandong became a province under the Ming dynasty.

shan·dy (shándi) *n.* A drink of beer and lemonade or ginger beer. Also *chiefly U.S.* "shandygaff". [19th century : origin obscure.]

Shang (shang) *n.* A Chinese dynasty (*c.*1525–*c.*1027 B.C.). Its capital was Yin, present-day **Anyang** *(see).*

shang·hai (sháng-hī) *tr.v.* **-haied, -haiing, -hais.** *Informal.* **1.** To kidnap (a man) for compulsory service aboard a ship, especially after rendering him insensible. **2.** To trick or coerce (a person) into some action. [After SHANGHAI, from the former custom of kidnapping sailors to man ships going to that city.]

Shang·hai or **Shang-hai** (sháng-hī). Largest city in China, lying within, but independent of, the eastern province of Jiangsu, on the river Huangpu at its confluence with the Chang Jiang (Yangtze) estuary. One of the world's leading seaports, it is also the most important industrial centre in China. Its commercial and industrial importance dates from 1842, when the Treaty of Nanking opened the port to western trade. In the 19th century much of the city was ceded to Britain (1843) and the United States (1862), the two cessions being merged into the International Settlement in 1863. The French maintained a separate cession (1849). Great Britain and the United States gave up their claims during World War II and France withdrew in 1946. Shanghai is surpassed only by Beijing as a leading educational and cultural centre of China.

Shan·gri-la (sháng-gri-laá) *n.* An imaginary, remote paradise on earth; utopia. [After *Shangri-La,* the imaginary land in *Lost Horizon* (1933) by James Hilton (1900–54).]

shank (shangk) *n.* **1.** *Anatomy.* The part of the human leg between the knee and ankle or the corresponding part in other vertebrates. **2.** The whole leg of a human being. **3.** A cut of meat from the leg of an animal. **4.** The long, narrow part of a nail or pin. **5.** A stem, stalk, or similar part. **6.** The stem of an anchor. **7.** The long shaft of a fishhook. **8.** That part of a tobacco pipe between the bowl and stem. **9.** The shaft of a key. **10.** The narrower section of a spoon's handle. **11. a.** The narrow part of a shoe's sole under the instep. **b.** A piece of metal or other material used to reinforce or shape this part. **12.** The ring or other projection on the back of some buttons by which they are sewn to the cloth. **13. a.** The part of a drill or other tool that connects the functioning head to the handle. **b.** A **tang** *(see).* **14.** Any of various long-legged wading birds of the genus *Tringa;* especially, the redshank and greenshank. [Middle English *shanke,* Old English *sc(e)anca.*]

Shan·kar (sháng-kər, -kaar), **Ravi** (1920–). Indian sitar player who has stimulated appreciation of Indian classical music throughout the western world.

shank·piece (shángk-peess) *n.* An arch support inserted into the shank of a shoe.

shanks's pony (shangks, shángksiz). *n. Informal.* One's own legs as a means of transport. Also *U.S.* "shank's mare".

Shan·non (shánnən). Chief river of the Republic of Ireland, and the longest river in the British Isles. About 390 kilometres (240 miles) long, it rises in northwest Cavan, and flows south to Limerick, where it broadens into a long, wide estuary, which empties into the Atlantic. Shannon International Airport lies on the north bank of the estuary, some 24 kilometres (15 miles) west of Limerick.

shan·ny (shánni) *n., pl.* **-nies.** A goby-like marine fish, the common blenny, *Blennius pholis.* See **blenny.** [19th century : origin obscure.]

Shansi. See **Shanxi.**

shan't (shaant || shant). Contraction of *shall not.*

shan·tung (shán-túng) *n.* **1.** A heavy silk fabric with a rough, nubby surface, made of spun wild silk. **2.** An imitation of this fabric, made of rayon or cotton. [Manufactured in SHANDONG.]

Shantung. See **Shandong.**

shan·ty¹ (shánti) *n., pl.* **-ties. 1.** A roughly built or ramshackle cabin; a shack. **2.** *Australian.* A rough or shabby, usually unlicensed, hotel. [19th century (originally American, often used of houses of Irish immigrants) : perhaps from Irish *sean tig,* "old house" : *sean,* old + *tig,* house, from Old Irish *tech.*]

shan·ty² (shánti) *n., pl.* **-ties.** Also **chan·ty** (chaánti || chánti), *chiefly U.S.* **chan·tey** (chánti), **shan·tey** (shánti) *pl.* **-teys.** A song sung, especially formerly, by sailors to the rhythm of their work movements. [Probably from French *chantez,* imperative plural of *chanter,* to sing.]

shan·ty·town (shánti-town) *n.* A town or district of a town consisting of ramshackle huts or shanties.

Shan·xi or **Shansi-hsi** or **Shan·si** (shán-seé). Strategic province of northeast China. Much of it is a high plateau cut by the Fen He, a tributary of the Huang He. With fertile loess soils, Shansi was part of the Chinese "heartland". Its low rainfall is now offset by irrigation and reafforestation. Taiyuan is the capital.

shape (shayp) *n.* **1.** The outline or characteristic surface configuration of a thing; a contour; a form. **2.** The contour of a person's body; a figure. **3.** Developed, definite, or proper form. **4.** Any form or condition in which something may exist or appear; an embodiment. **5.** Assumed or false appearance; guise. **6.** An imaginary or ghostly form; a phantom. **7. a.** Something used to give or determine form, such as a mould or pattern. **b.** Something formed by a pattern or set in a mould. **8.** *Informal.* Condition as regards health, efficiency, state of repair, or the like: *in good shape.* —**lick into shape.** To put right or in a better state or condition. —See Synonyms at **form.**
~*v.* **shaped, shaped** or *archaic* **shapen** (sháypən), **shaping, shapes.** —*tr.* **1.** To give a particular form to. **2.** To cause to conform to a particular form or pattern; modify; adapt to fit. **3.** To plan and supervise. —*intr.* **1.** *Informal.* To take a definite form; develop. Often used with *into* or *up.* **2.** *Informal.* To proceed or develop in a satisfactory or desirable manner. Used with *up.* [Middle English *schap, shape,* Old English *(ge)sceap.*]

SHAPE (shayp). Supreme Headquarters Allied Powers, Europe.

shaped (shaypt) *adj.* **1.** Formed by shaping: *shaped clay.* **2.** Having the shape of or possessing a similar shape to something specified. Often used in combination: *egg-shaped.*

shape·less (sháyp-ləss, -liss) *adj.* **1.** Having no distinct shape. **2.** Lacking symmetrical or attractive form; not shapely. —**shape·less·ly** *adv.* —**shape·less·ness** *n.*

shape·ly (sháypli) *adj.* **-lier, -liest.** Having a pleasing or attractive shape; well-proportioned. —**shape·li·ness** *n.*

shard (shard) *n.* Also **sherd** (sherd). **1.** A piece of broken pottery; a **potsherd** *(see).* **2.** A fragment of a brittle substance, as of glass or metal. **3.** *Zoology.* A tough sheath; especially, the outer wing covering of a beetle. [Middle English *sherd,* Old English *sceard.*]

share¹ (shair) *n.* **1.** A part or portion belonging to, distributed to, contributed by, or owed by a person or group. **2.** An equitable, reasonable, or full amount. **3.** *Abbr.* **sh., shr.** Any of the equal parts into which the capital stock of a company is divided. —**go shares.** To be involved equally or jointly, as in a business venture.
~*v.* **shared, sharing, shares.** —*tr.* **1.** To divide and parcel out in

PRONUNCIATION KEY

a, trap; aa, father; ai, fair; ar, star; aw, lawn; ay, play; b, bb, stab; rubber; ch, church; ck, ticket; d, dd, dead; ladder; e, dress; ee, bee; er, defer; ew, few; ewr, pure; ə, about; ər, letter; f, ff, fife; differ; g, gg, giggle; h, hat; i, kit; ī, price; īr, fire; j, judge; k, kick; l, ll, let; 'l, needle; m, mm, man; n, nn, no; 'n, sudden; ng, thing; o, lot; ō, no; ŏŏ, foot; ōō, shoe; oor, poor; ow, cow; owr, hour; oy, boy; p, pp, pepper; r, rr, red; s, ss, sauce; sh, ship; t, tt, totter; th, thick; th, this; smooth; u, cut; ur, turn; v, vv, valve; w, wet; y, yes; z, zz, zebra; zh, vision; pleasure

IN FOREIGN WORDS:

aN, oN, Saint-Saëns; hl, Llanelli; Hluhluwe; kh, loch; lough; Khaled

STRESS MARK:

ín-sīt, insight; in-sít, incite

shark *The blue shark (above) is a native of tropical and temperate waters the world over. It grows to a maximum length of about 4 metres (13 feet) and is considered dangerous, although there are no recorded reports of attacks by blue sharks on man.*

shearwater *In its long flights, this seabird skims the wavetops and appears to shear the water. Shearwaters are capable of flying vast distances; Manx shearwaters, such as the one shown here, have been known to fly nearly 5000 kilometres (3,000 miles) in 12 days.*

PRONUNCIATION KEY

a, trap; aa, father; ai, fair; ar, star; aw, lawn; ay, play; b, bb, stab; rubber; ch, church; ck, ticket; d, dd, dead; ladder; e, dress; ee, bee; er, defer; ew, few; ewr, pure; ə, about; ər, letter; f, ff, fife; differ; g, gg, giggle; h, hat; i, kit; ī, price; īr, fire; j, judge; k, kick; l, ll, let; ’l, needle; m, mm, man; n, nn, no; ’n, sudden; ng, thing; o, lot; ō, no; ŏŏ, foot; ōō, shoe; oor, poor; ow, cow; owr, hour; oy, boy; p, pp, pepper; r, rr, red; s, ss, sauce; sh, ship; t, tt, totter; th, thick; th, this; ts, tsetse; u, cut; ur, turn; v, vv, valve; w, wet; y, yes; z, zz, zebra; zh, vision; pleasure

IN FOREIGN WORDS:

aN, oN, Saint-Saëns; hl, Llanelli; Hluhluwe; kh, loch; lough; Khaled

STRESS MARK:

ín-sīt, insight; in-sít, incite

shares; apportion. **2.** To participate in, use, or experience in common with others. *—intr.* To have or take a part or share. **—share and share alike.** To share equally; have equal shares. [Middle English *share,* division, share, Old English *scearu,* division or fork of the body, tonsure.] **—shar·er** *n.*

Synonyms: *share, participate, partake.*

share² *n.* A ploughshare. [Middle English *shaar,* Old English *scēar.*]

share certificate *n.* A legal document, issued to a shareholder by a company, declaring ownership of shares and specifying their class, quality, and serial numbers.

share·crop·per (sháir-kroppər) *n.* A tenant farmer, especially in the United States, who gives a share of his crop to the landlord in lieu of rent. **—share·crop** *v.*

share·hold·er (sháir-hōldər) *n.* A person or institution that owns or holds a share or shares in a company.

share out *tr.v.* To distribute; give out in shares. **—share·out** (sháir-owt) *n.*

share-push·er (sháir-pŏŏshər) *n.* A broker who deals dishonestly in worthless stocks and shares. Also called "share-hawker".

sharif. Variant of **sherif.**

shark¹ (shark) *n.* Any of numerous chiefly marine, sometimes ferocious, fishes of the order Pleurotremata, having a cartilaginous skeleton and tough skin covered with small, toothlike scales. [16th century : origin obscure.]

shark² *n.* **1.** A ruthless, greedy, or dishonest person; a swindler. **2.** *U.S. Slang.* A person with unusually great skill in some field of activity. [Perhaps from SHARK (fish).]

shark·skin (shárk-skin) *n.* **1.** A shark's skin. **2.** Leather made from a shark's skin. **3.** A rayon and acetate fabric having a smooth, somewhat shiny surface.

shark sucker *n.* A **remora** *(see).*

sharp (sharp) *adj.* **sharper, sharpest. 1.** Having a thin, keen edge or a fine, acute point; suitable for or capable of cutting or piercing: *a sharp knife.* **2.** Having an acute edge or point; not rounded or blunt; peaked: *a sharp nose.* **3.** Abrupt or acute; not gradual; sudden. **4.** Clear or marked; distinct. **5.** Shrewd; astute. **6.** Artful; underhand. **7.** Vigilant; alert. **8.** Brisk; vigorous. **9. a.** Harsh; biting; acrimonious. **b.** Stinging; bitter; pungent: *a sharp taste.* **c.** Bitterly cold. **10.** Fierce or impetuous; violent. **11. a.** Intense; severe. **b.** Painful. **12.** Sudden and shrill. **13.** Composed of hard, angular particles: *sharp sand.* **14.** *Music.* **a.** Raised in pitch by a semitone. **b.** Above the proper pitch. **c.** Having the key signature in sharps. Compare **flat. 15.** *Phonetics.* Voiceless. Said of a consonant. **16.** Attractively stylish; snappy: *a sharp dresser.*

~adv. **1.** In a sharp manner. **2.** Punctually; exactly. **3.** *Music.* Above the true or proper pitch.

~n. **1. a.** A musical note raised one semitone above its normal pitch. **b.** A sign (#) indicating this. Compare **flat. 2.** A slender sewing needle with a very fine point. **3.** *Informal.* A sharper.

~v. **sharped, sharping, sharps.** *U.S. Music.* *—tr.* To raise by a semitone. *—intr.* To sound above the proper pitch. [Middle English *s(c)harp,* Old English *scearp.*] **—sharp·ly** *adv.* **—sharp·ness** *n.*

Synonyms: *sharp, keen, acute.*

Sharp (sharp), **Cecil (James)** (1859–1924). British musician and collector of folk music. He founded the English Folk Dance and Song Society (1911) and is chiefly remembered for his collections and arrangements of English folk songs and dances.

sharp·en (shárpən) *v.* **-ened, -ening, -ens.** *—tr.* To make sharp or sharper. *—intr.* To become sharp or sharper. **—sharp·en·er** *n.*

sharp end *n. Informal.* The point of direct action, confrontation, or decision-making.

sharp·er (shárpər) *n.* One who deals dishonestly with others; especially, a gambler who cheats.

sharp-eyed (shárp-íd) *adj.* **1.** Having keen eyesight. **2.** Keenly perceptive or observant; alert.

sharp·shoot·er (shárp-shōōtər) *n.* An expert marksman.

sharp-tongued (shárp-túngd || -tóngd) *adj.* Harsh, critical, or sarcastic.

shash·lik, shash·lick (sháshlik, sháash-, -lík) *n.* A kind of kebab of Russian origin. [Russian *shashlyk,* of Turkic origin.]

Shas·ta daisy (shástə) *n.* A cultivated variety of *Chrysanthemum* (or *Leucanthernum*) *maximum,* of the Pyrenees, having large, white, daisy-like flowers. [After Mt. *Shasta,* California; named by Luther Burbank, who lived in California.]

Shas·tri (shass-tri, sháass-), **Shri Lal Bahadur** (1904–66). Indian statesman. He succeeded Nehru as prime minister (1964–66), and his major achievement was to negotiate, with Ayub Khan, a cease-fire in the war between India and Pakistan.

shat. *Vulgar.* Past tense and past participle of **shit.**

Shatt al Ar·ab (shát al árrəb). Tidal river flowing for about 195 kilometres (121 miles) into the northern end of the Gulf, and formed by the confluence of the rivers Tigris and Euphrates. It is navigable as far up as Basra, the chief port of Iraq. Across from Basra are the Iranian ports of Khorramshahr and Abadan. Control of the river has been in dispute between Iran and Iraq since 1935, when an international commission awarded it to Iraq.

shat·ter (sháttər) *v.* **-tered, -tering, -ters.** *—tr.* **1.** To cause to break or burst suddenly into pieces, as with a violent blow. **2.** To damage seriously; disable; ruin. **3.** To disturb or severely upset. **4.** *Informal.* To tire completely; exhaust. *—intr.* To break into pieces; smash or burst. —See Synonyms at **break.**

~n. Usually plural. Rare. A splintered or fragmented condition. [Middle English *schateren,* akin to SKATTER.]

shat·ter·proof (sháttər-prōōf || -prŏŏf) *adj.* **1.** Designed to resist shattering. **2.** Designed to break into small, round granules rather than sharp, jagged pieces.

shave (shayv) *v.* **shaved, shaved** or **shaven** (shayv'n), **shaving, shaves.** *—tr.* **1.** To remove the beard or other body hair from. **2.** To cut (the beard, for example) at the surface of the skin with a razor. Often used with *off.* **3.** To crop, trim, or mow closely. **4.** To remove thin slices from. **5.** To cut into thin slices; shred. **6.** To come close to or graze in passing. **7.** *Informal.* To take off or away. *—intr.* To remove one's own beard or hair with a razor.

~n. **1.** The act, process, or result of shaving. **2.** A thin slice or scraping; a shaving. **3.** Any of various tools used for shaving. [Middle English *shaven,* to scrape, shave, Old English *sceafan.*]

shav·er (sháyvər) *n.* **1. a.** A person who shaves. **b.** An electric or mechanical device used to shave, especially an electric razor. **2.** *Informal.* A young person, especially a boy.

Sha·vi·an (sháyvi-ən) *adj.* Of or characteristic of George Bernard Shaw or his works: *Shavian wit.*

~n. An admirer or disciple of George Bernard Shaw. [From *Shavius,* pseudo-Latin form of the name *Shaw.*]

shav·ing (sháyving) *n.* A thin slice; a sliver: *wood shavings.*

~adj. Used in or for shaving the face: *a shaving mirror.*

Sha·vu·ot, Sha·bu·oth (shə-vōō-əss, -ot, -oth) *n.* A Jewish holiday commemorating the revelation of the Law on Mount Sinai and the celebration of the wheat festival in ancient times, observed on the sixth and seventh of Sivan. Also called "Feast of Weeks". [Hebrew *shābhū'ōth,* from *shābhūa',* week.]

Shaw (shaw), **Artie,** born Arthur Arshawsky (1910–). U.S. jazz clarinettist, composer, and band leader. From 1935 he headed various bands organised around his virtuosity on the clarinet.

Shaw, George Bernard (1856–1950). Irish dramatist and writer. He established a reputation in London as a controversial music and theatre critic and an idiosyncratic spokesman for socialism. Shaw was a founder member of the Fabian Society (1884) and an early enthusiast of Wagner and Ibsen. He won further recognition through his many plays, often satirical in theme, which include *Man and Superman* (1905), *Pygmalion* (1912), and *St. Joan* (1924). His prolific writings on social, political, and religious issues include *The Intelligent Woman's Guide to Socialism and Capitalism* (1928). He was awarded the Nobel prize for literature in 1925.

shawl (shawl) *n.* A square or oblong piece of cloth, knitted fabric, or the like worn especially by women as a covering for the head, neck, and shoulders.

~tr.v. **shawled, shawling, shawls.** To cover with a shawl. [Earlier *shal, shaul,* from Urdu, from Persian *shāl†.*]

shawm (shawm) *n.* Any of various early double-reed wind instruments, forerunners of the modern oboe. [Middle English *schallemele, schalme,* from Old French *chalemel,* from Vulgar Latin *calamellus* (unattested), diminutive of Latin *calamus,* reed, from Greek *kalamos.*]

Shaw·nee (shaw-née) *n., pl.* **Shawnee** or **-nees. 1.** A member of an Algonquian-speaking North American Indian people, formerly living in the Tennessee Valley and adjacent areas, now surviving in Oklahoma. **2.** The language of this people.

Shaw·wal (shə-wáal) *n.* The tenth month of the year in the Muslim calendar. [Arabic *Shawwāl.*]

she (shee, *weak form* shi) *pron.* The third person singular pronoun in the nominative case, feminine gender. **1.** Used to represent the female person, animal, or other being last mentioned or implied. **2.** Used traditionally of certain objects and institutions such as ships, cars, and nations. **3.** *Australian.* Applied to the circumstances or events in question; it: *She'll be right!*

~n. A female animal or person. Often used in combination: *a she-cat.* [Middle English *s(c)ho, s(c)he,* Old English *sēo,* she (Old English *hēo,* she, remained in Middle English dialects but only appears in Modern English HER). See Usage note at **me.**]

s/he. She or he.

she·a (shée-ə, sheer, shee) *n.* The **shea tree** *(see).*

shea butter *n.* A whitish or yellowish fat obtained from the nut of the **shea tree** *(see),* used as food and for making soap and candles.

shead·ing (shéeding) *n.* Any of the six administrative divisions of the Isle of Man.

sheaf (sheef) *n., pl.* **sheaves** (sheevz). **1.** A bundle of cut stalks of grain or similar plants, usually laid lengthways, bound with straw or twine. **2.** Any gathering or collection of articles, especially papers, held or bound together. **3.** An archer's quiver of arrows.

~tr.v. **sheafed, sheafing, sheafs.** To bind into a sheaf. [Middle English *sheef, shefe,* Old English *scēaf.*]

shear (sheer) *v.* **sheared** or *archaic* **shore** (shor), **shorn** (shorn), or **sheared, shearing, shears.** *—tr.* **1.** To remove (fleece, hair, or the like) by cutting or clipping with a sharp instrument. **2.** To remove the hair or fleece from. **3.** To cut with or as if with shears. **4.** To strip, divest, or deprive of something. **5.** To cause to break or fracture, especially as a result of shearing strain. *—intr.* **1.** To use shears or a similar cutting tool. **2.** To move or proceed by or as if by cutting. Used with *through.* **3.** *Physics.* To become deformed by forces tending to produce a shearing strain. **4.** To break or fracture, especially as a result of shearing strain.

~n. **1.** The act, process, or result of shearing. **2.** Something cut off by shearing. **3.** A shearing. Used to indicate a sheep's age: *a two-shear ram.* **4.** *Physics.* **a.** An applied force or system of forces that tends to produce a shearing strain. Also called "shear stress", "shearing stress". **b.** Shearing strain. **5.** Any device for cutting ma-

terial by means of a knife blade. [Shear, shore, shorn; Middle English *sc(h)eren, share, shorn,* Old English *sceran, scǣron* (third person plural), *scoren.*] **—shear·er** *n.*

shear·ing strain (sheering) *n.* A condition in or deformation of an elastic body caused by forces that tend to produce an opposite but parallel sliding motion of the body's planes.

shear legs *n.* Also **sheer·legs** (shéer-legz). An apparatus used to lift heavy weights, consisting of two or more spars joined at the top and spread at the base, the tackle being suspended from the top. Also called "shears", "sheers".

shear·ling (shéerling) *n.* **1.** A year-old sheep that has been shorn once. **2.** The skin of such a sheep, or of any newly shorn sheep, tanned and with the wool on. [Middle English *scherling* : *scheren,* to SHEAR + -LING.]

shear modulus *n.* A **rigidity modulus** *(see).*

shear pin *n.* A replaceable pin placed in a machine in such a position that it will shear and arrest the movement of the machine if the stress exceeds a predetermined value.

shears (sheerz) *pl.n.* **1.** Large-sized scissors. **2.** Any of various other implements or machines that cut with scissor-like action. **3.** *Used with a singular verb.* A lifting crane, a shear legs. [Middle English *s(c)here* (singular), scissors, Old English *scēara* (plural).]

shear·wa·ter (shéer-wawtər || *U.S. also* -wottər) *n.* Any of various oceanic birds of the family Procellariidae, especially of the genus *Puffinus,* having long wings and a hooked bill. See **Manx shearwater.** [From its habit of skimming close to the water.]

sheat·fish (shéet-fish) *n., pl.* **-fishes** or collectively **sheatfish.** A large freshwater catfish, *Silurus glanis,* of Eurasia. [Variant of obsolete *sheath-fish* : SHEATH (probably from its shell-like covering or its sheathlike shape) + FISH.]

sheath (sheeth) *n., pl.* **sheaths** (sheethz || sheeths). **1.** A case for the blade of a knife, sword, or similar instrument. **2.** Any of various coverings applied like or resembling a sheath. **3.** *Biology.* An enveloping structure or part, such as the tubular base of a leaf surrounding a stem. **4.** A close-fitting dress, usually having a straight skirt and no belt. **5.** A protective covering for an electric cable. **6.** A **condom** *(see).* [Middle English *s(c)hethe,* Old English *scēath, scǣth.*]

sheath·bill (shéeth-bil) *n.* Either of two shore birds, *Chionia alba* or *C. minor,* of Antarctic regions, having white plumage and a horny covering on the base of the bill.

sheathe (sheeth) *tr.v.* **sheathed, sheathing, sheathes. 1.** To insert into or provide with a sheath. **2.** To retract into a sheath or sheaths: *sheathed its claws.* **3.** To encase in sheathing. **—sheath·er** *n.*

sheath·ing (shéething) *n.* **1.** A layer of boards or of other wood or fibre materials applied to the outer studs, joists, and rafters of a building to strengthen the structure and serve as a base for an exterior weatherproof cladding. **2.** An exterior covering, usually metal, on the underwater part of a ship's hull, to protect against marine growths. **3.** The action of providing sheathing for something.

sheath knife *n.* A knife having a fixed blade and fitting into a sheath.

shea tree *n.* An African tree, *Butyrospermum parkii,* having fruit containing oily seeds that yield an edible fat called shea butter. Also called "shea". [From Bambara *si.*]

sheave[1] (sheev) *tr.v.* **sheaved, sheaving, sheaves.** To bind into a sheaf or sheaves; gather; collect.

sheave[2] *n.* A wheel with a grooved rim, especially one used as a pulley. [Middle English *shive, sheve,* Old English *scīfe* (unattested).]

sheaves (sheevz) **1.** Plural of **sheaf. 2.** Plural of **sheave.**

She·ba (shéebə). *Arabic* **Sa·ba** (sáabaa). Biblical name for an ancient region of southern Arabia, encompassing present-day Yemen and the Hadhramaut region of South Yemen. Situated on the trade route between India and Africa, it became a region of great wealth at its height in the sixth and fifth centuries B.C.

Sheba, Queen of. A queen who came from southern Arabia to test the wisdom of King Solomon. I Kings 10:1.

she·bang (shi-báng, shə-) *n. Chiefly U.S. Informal.* A situation, organisation, contrivance, or set of facts or things. Used chiefly in the phrase *the whole shebang.* [19th century : origin obscure.]

Shebat. Variant of **Shevat.**

she·been (shi-béen) *n. Chiefly Irish & South African.* A place where alcohol is sold and drunk illegally. [Anglo-Irish *síbín;* akin to *séibe,* mugful.]

shed[1] (shed) *v.* **shed, shedding, sheds.** *—tr.* **1.** To pour forth or cause to pour forth: *shed a tear.* **2.** To send forth; diffuse or radiate: *shed light; shed confidence.* **3.** To repel without allowing penetration: *A duck's feathers shed water.* **4.** To lose by natural process: *shedding leaves in winter.* **5.** To drop; cause to fall or fall off: *A lorry has shed its load on the A23.* *—intr.* **1.** To lose a natural growth or covering by natural process: *Trees shed in winter.* **2.** To pour forth, fall off, or drop out: *All the leaves have shed.*
~n. An elevation in the earth's surface from which water flows in two directions; a watershed. [Shed, shed (past tense and past participle); Middle English *sheden, schede, scheden,* shed, divide, Old English *scēadan, scēad, sceādan,* to divide.]

shed[2] *n.* **1.** A small, usually low, structure, either freestanding or attached to a larger structure, serving for storage or shelter. **2.** A large structure, often open on all sides, for storage, locomotive repair, sheepshearing, shelter, or the like. [Earlier *shadde,* perhaps specialised use of SHADE.]

she'd (sheed, shid). **1.** Contraction of *she had.* **2.** Contraction of *she would.*

shed·der (shéddər) *n.* One that sheds by a natural process, such as a long-haired animal, a crab, or a lobster.

she-dev·il (shée-devv'l) *n.* A malicious or cruel woman.

shed·hand (shéd-hand) *n. Australian.* An unskilled worker who moves the shorn wool in a sheepshearing shed.

sheen (sheen) *n.* **1.** A smooth, glossy shine on a surface. **2.** Glistening brightness; radiance. **2.** *Poetic.* Splendid attire. [From obsolete *sheen,* beautiful, bright, Old English *scīene, scēne.*]

Sheene (sheen), **Barry** born Stephen Frank Sheene (1950–). British racing motorcyclist. He was 500 cc world champion in 1976 and 1977.

sheep (sheep) *n., pl.* **sheep. 1.** Any of various usually horned, ruminant mammals of the genus *Ovis;* especially, the domesticated species *O. aries,* raised in many breeds for its wool, edible flesh, or skin. **2.** The skin of a sheep or leather made from it. **3.** One who is meek, submissive, or easily led. **—separate the sheep from the goats.** To distinguish or discriminate between the worthy and the unworthy. [Middle English *she(e)p,* Old English *scē(a)p,* from West Germanic *skǣpa* (unattested).]

sheep·back (shéep-bak) *n. Geology.* **Roche moutonnée** *(see).*

sheep·cote (shéep-kōt) *n.* A sheepfold. [Middle English *shepcote* : SHEEP + COTE.]

sheep dip *n.* **1.** Any of various liquid disinfectants used to destroy parasites in the wool of sheep prior to shearing. **2.** A deep trough containing a disinfectant in which sheep are dipped.

sheep·dog (shéep-dog || -dawg) *n.* A dog trained to guard and herd sheep. See **Old English sheepdog, Shetland sheepdog.**

sheep·fold (shéep-fōld) *n.* A pen for sheep.

sheep·herd·er (shéep-herdər) *n. U.S.* A shepherd.

sheep·ish (shéepish) *adj.* **1.** Embarrassed or bashful, as by consciousness of a fault: *a sheepish grin.* **2.** Resembling a sheep in meekness or stupidity. **—sheep·ish·ly** *adv.* **—sheep·ish·ness** *n.*

sheep ked *n.* See **ked.**

sheep's-bit scabious (shéeps-bit) *n.* A plant, *Jasione montana,* with blue flowers in a globular head that superficially resemble those of a scabious. Also called "sheepsbit".

sheep's eyes *pl.n.* Bashful, amorous glances.

sheep's fescue *n.* A forage grass, *Festuca ovina,* with narrow leaves that roll inwards.

sheep·shank (shéep-shangk) *n.* A knot used to shorten a line.

sheep·shear·ing (shéep-sheer-ing) *n.* **1.** The act of shearing sheep. **2. a.** The time or season when sheep are sheared. **b.** The festivities held at this time. **—sheep·shear·er** *n.*

sheep·skin (shéep-skin) *n.* The skin of a sheep either tanned with the fleece left on or in the form of leather or parchment.

sheep's sorrel *n.* A sorrel, *Rumex acetosella,* common on dry heaths and acid soils.

sheep station *n. Australian.* A large sheep farm.

sheep tick *n.* A tick, *Ixodes ricinus,* parasitic on many mammals and birds, which carries the virus causing louping ill in sheep and cattle.

sheep·walk (shéep-wawk) *n. British.* A piece of pastureland where sheep are grazed.

sheep·wash (shéep-wosh || -wawsh) *n.* A **sheep dip** *(see).*

sheer[1] (sheer) *v.* **sheered, sheering, sheers.** *—intr.* To swerve or deviate from a course. Usually used with *away* or *off.* *—tr.* To cause to swerve or deviate. Usually used with *away* or *off.*
~n. **1.** A swerving or deviating course. **2.** *Nautical.* **a.** The upward curve, or the amount of upward curve, of the longitudinal lines of a ship's hull as viewed from the side. **b.** The position in which a ship is placed to enable it to keep clear of a single bow anchor. [Perhaps a variant of SHEAR.]

sheer[2] *adj.* **sheerer, sheerest. 1.** Thin, fine, and transparent; diaphanous. Said of a fabric. **2.** Not mixed or blended with anything; undiluted; pure: *sheer luck.* **3.** Perpendicular or nearly perpendicular; steep: *sheer rocks; a sheer drop.*
~adv. **1.** Perpendicularly or nearly perpendicularly. **2.** Absolutely; outright. [Perhaps Middle English *schir,* bright, shining, Old English *scīr.*] **—sheer·ly** *adv.* **—sheer·ness** *n.*

sheerlegs, sheers. Variants of **shear legs.**

sheet[1] (sheet) *n. Abbr.* **sh. 1.** A rectangular piece of linen, cotton, or similar material serving as a basic article of bedding, commonly used in pairs, one above and one below the body of the sleeper. **2.** A broad, thin, usually rectangular mass or piece of any material, such as paper, metal, glass, or plywood. **3.** A broad, flat, continuous surface or expanse: *a sheet of rain.* **4.** A newspaper; especially, a tabloid: *a scandal sheet.* **5.** *Geology.* A broad, relatively thin deposit or layer of igneous or sedimentary rock. **6.** The large block of stamps printed by a single impression of a plate before the individual stamps have been separated. **7. a.** A piece of paper. **b.** A piece of paper printed and folded ready to be bound as pages in a book.
~v. **sheeted, sheeting, sheets.** *—tr.* To cover with, wrap in, or provide with a sheet or sheets. *—intr.* To fall in sheets, as heavy rain does. [Middle English *s(c)hete,* cloth, sheet, towel, Old English *scēte.*]

sheet[2] (sheet) *n. Nautical.* A rope or chain attached to one or both of the lower corners of a sail, serving to move or extend it. **—three sheets to the wind.** *Informal.* Drunk.
~intr.v. **sheeted, sheeting, sheets.** *Nautical.* To extend in a certain direction. Used of the sheets of a sail. [Middle English *s(c)hete,* Old English *scēata,* corner of a sail.]

sheet anchor *n.* **1.** A large extra anchor intended for use in emer-

sheep *Six species of wild sheep live in Asia and North America. None has the long woolly coat characteristic of many domestic sheep such as the German breed shown here.*

sheepdog *Dogs have been used by shepherds for centuries to help control flocks. This is a Briard, one of an old race of sheepdogs from the Brie district of France.*

sheepshank *A knot used to shorten a rope.*

gency. **2.** A person or thing that can be turned to in time of emergency, especially one that can be relied on if all else fails.

sheet bend *n.* A knot in which one rope or piece of string is made fast to the bight of another.

sheet glass *n.* Molten glass drawn into a wide sheet which, after annealing and hardening, is cut into required lengths.

sheet·ing (shéeting) *n.* Any material, such as metal or cloth, in the form of or used to make a sheet.

sheet lightning *n.* Lightning that appears as a broad, sheetlike illumination, caused by diffusion of a lightning flash by a thunder cloud.

sheet metal *n.* Metal that has been rolled into a sheet thinner than plate but thicker than foil.

sheet music *n.* Music printed on unbound sheets of paper.

sheets (sheets) *pl.n. Nautical.* The spaces at the bow and stern of an open rowing boat that are not occupied by oarsmen.

Shef·field (shéffeeld). Industrial city in South Yorkshire, northern England, lying at the confluence of the river Don and four tributaries. Since the 14th century it has been the most important centre for cutlery manufacture in the country. It is also a leading centre for silver and for heavy steel manufacture.

Sheffield plate *n.* An article or articles of tableware made of copper and coated with a thin layer of silver by a former process now replaced by electroplating. [After SHEFFIELD where it was made.]

sheik, sheikh (sháyk || sheek) *n.* **1.** A Muslim religious official. **2.** The leader of an Arab family, village, or tribe. [Arabic *shaikh,* old man, from *shākha,* to be old.]

sheik·dom (sháyk-dəm || shéek-) *n.* The area ruled by a sheik.

shei·la (shéelə) *n. Australian & N.Z. Informal.* A woman. [Earlier *shaler*†, assimilated to the name *Sheila.*]

sheitan. Variant of **shaitan.**

shek·el (shéck'l) *n.* **1.** The basic monetary unit of Israel, equal to 100 new agora. **2. a.** Any of several ancient units of weight; especially, an ancient Hebrew unit equal to about half an ounce. **b.** A gold or silver coin equal in weight to one of these units; especially, the chief silver coin of the Hebrews. **3.** *Plural. Slang.* Cash; money. [Hebrew *sheqel,* from *shāqal,* to weigh.]

She·ki·nah (she-kī́nə, shi-; *Hebrew* -khee-naá) *n.* A visible manifestation of the divine presence as described in Jewish theology. [Hebrew *shəkhīnāh,* from *shākhan,* to dwell.]

shel·duck (shél-duk) *n., pl.* **-ducks** or collectively **shelduck. 1.** Any of various large Old World ducks of the genus *Tadorna;* especially, *T. tadorna,* having predominantly black and white plumage. **2.** Any of several other ducks. [Middle English : *sheld-,* variegated, perhaps of Low German origin, akin to Middle Dutch *schillede* + DUCK.]

shelduck *The large waterfowl known as the shelduck – this is a male bird – is native to Europe and parts of Asia, and feeds on water snails, shellfish, insects, and fish. It frequently nests in rabbit burrows on sand dunes.*

shel·drake (shél-drayk) *n., pl.* **-drakes** or collectively **sheldrake.** The shelduck, especially the male shelduck.

shelf (shelf) *n., pl.* **shelves** (shelvz). **1.** A flat, usually rectangular structure of a rigid material, such as wood, glass, or metal, fixed at right angles to a wall or other vertical surface and used to hold or store objects. **2.** The contents or capacity of such a structure. **3.** Anything resembling such an object, such as a balcony or a ledge of rock. **4.** A **continental shelf** *(see).* **5.** *Mining.* Bedrock. **—on the shelf. 1.** In a state of disuse; put aside. **2.** *Informal.* Unmarried and likely to remain so. [Middle English *shelf(e),* perhaps from Middle Low German *schelf.*]

shelf ice *n.* An extension of glacial ice floating on coastal waters. Also called "barrier ice".

shelf life *n.* The amount of time that something, such as a drug or packaged food, may be stored without deteriorating.

shell (shel) *n.* **1. a.** The usually hard outer covering that encases certain organisms such as molluscs, certain insects, or tortoises. **b.** A similar outer covering on an egg, fruit, or nut. **2.** The material composing such a covering. **3.** Anything resembling such a covering, especially: **a.** A framework, case, or exterior, as of a building, motor vehicle, or machine. **b.** A thin layer of pastry. **c.** The hull of a ship. **d.** The external part of the ear. **e.** A long, narrow racing boat propelled by oarsmen. **4. a.** A projectile or piece of ammunition; especially, the hollow tube containing explosives used to propel such a projectile. **b.** A metal or cardboard case, containing the charge, primer, and shot, fired from a shotgun; a cartridge. **5. a.** An attitude or manner adopted to mask one's true feelings. **b.** *Informal.* A state of shyness or reserve: *brought her out of her shell.* **6.** *Physics.* **a.** Any of the set of hypothetical spherical surfaces centred on the nucleus of an atom that contain the orbits of electrons having the same principal quantum number; hence, all the electrons in an atom that have the same principal quantum number. **b.** Any of a set of groupings of nucleon energy states in a nucleus, or of nucleons occupying such states, in which the binding energies of states differ from one another by much less than from the binding energies of states in another grouping.
~*v.* **shelled, shelling, shells.** *—tr.* **1. a.** To remove the shell of. **b.** To remove from a shell, pod, or the like. **2.** To separate (grains, kernels of maize, or the like) from the ear, husk, or cob. **3.** To fire artillery shells at; bombard. *—intr.* To shed or become free of a shell. **—shell out.** *Informal.* To pay or hand out (money). [Middle English *shell,* Old English *scell, scill.*] **—shell·er** *n.* **—shell·y** *adj.*

she'll (sheel, shil). **1.** Contraction of *she will.* **2.** Contraction of *she shall.*

shel·lac (shə-lák, she-, shéllak) *n.* **1.** A purified resin formed into thin yellow or orange flakes or buttons and widely used in varnishes, paints, stains, inks, and sealing wax. **2.** A thin varnish made by dissolving shellac in denatured alcohol, used as a wood coating. ~*tr.v.* **shellacked, -lacking, -lacs.** To apply shellac to. [SHEL(L) + LAC (lacquer), translation of French *laque en écailles,* lac (melted) in thin plates.]

shell·back (shél-bak) *n.* A veteran sailor; especially, one who has crossed the equator. [Referring to a sailor hardened by experience.]

shell·bark (shél-baark) *n.* A tree, the **shagbark** *(see).*

Shel·ley (shélli), **Mary Wollstonecraft,** born Mary Godwin. (1797–1851). British novelist, the daughter of the feminist writer Mary Wollstonecraft and the philosopher William Godwin, and the wife of Percy Bysshe Shelley. She eloped with Shelley in 1814 and married him two years later. She is famous as the author of *Frankenstein, or the Modern Prometheus* (1818).

Shelley, Percy Bysshe (1792–1822). British Romantic poet. In 1811 he was sent down from Oxford University for circulating an atheist pamphlet; in 1813, *Queen Mab,* a poem that virulently attacked the monarchy, church, and other established institutions, was privately printed. His works include the verse dramas *The Cenci* (1819) and *Prometheus Unbound* (1820), and several odes, among them *To the West Wind* and *To a Skylark.*

shell·fire (shél-fīr) *n.* The firing of artillery projectiles at, or their reception in, a target area.

shell·fish (shél-fish) *n., pl.* **-fishes** or collectively **shellfish.** Any aquatic animal having a shell or shell-like exoskeleton, as a mollusc or crustacean, especially those having edible flesh.

shell pink *n.* Pinkish white to strong yellowish pink, including greyish and light yellowish pinks. **—shell-pink** (shél-píngk) *adj.*

shell·proof (shél-proŏf || -proŏf) *adj.* Able to withstand shellfire.

shell shock *n.* Any of various usually acute, often hysterical neuroses originating in trauma suffered under fire in modern warfare. **—shell-shocked** (shél-shokt) *adj.*

Shel·ta (shéltə) *n.* An ancient secret language based on Gaelic and used by itinerant tinkers and Gypsies in Ireland and some parts of Britain. [19th century : origin obscure.]

shel·ter (shéltər) *n.* **1. a.** Something that provides cover or protection, as from the weather or bombardment. **b.** The cover or protection so provided. **2.** A refuge; a haven. **3.** The state of being covered or protected.
~*v.* **sheltered, -tering, -ters.** *—tr.* To provide cover or protection for. *—intr.* To take cover; find refuge. **—shel·ter·er** *n.*
Synonyms: *shelter, cover, retreat, refuge, asylum, sanctuary, haven.*

shel·tered (shéltərd) *adj.* **1.** Protected or overprotected from harm or harsh realities: *a sheltered life.* **2.** Designating accomodation for the elderly or disabled where they may live alone, or as independently as possible, in separate autonomous units, but under the care of a supervisor: *sheltered housing.* **3.** Designating a workplace that has special facilities and provides work for the disabled.

shel·tie, shel·ty (shélti) *n. pl.* **-ties. 1.** A **Shetland pony** *(see).* **2.** A **Shetland sheepdog** *(see).* [Norse *sjalti,* Shetland pony, Shetlander, from Old Norse *Hjalti,* Shetlander, from *Hjaltland,* Shetland, probably from *hjalt,* hilt, from Germanic *heltaz* (unattested), HILT.]

shelve (shelv) *v.* **shelved, shelving, shelves.** *—tr.* **1.** To place or arrange on a shelf or shelves. **2.** To put away as though on a shelf; put aside; postpone: *"as usual, Dixon shelved this question"* (Kingsley Amis). **3.** To cause to retire from service; dismiss. **4.** To furnish with shelves. *—intr.* To slope gradually; incline. [From SHELVES.]

shelves. Plural of **shelf.**

shelv·ing (shélving) *n.* **1.** Shelves collectively. **2.** Material for shelves.

Shem (shem). The eldest son of Noah. Genesis 5:32.

Shemite. Variant of **Semite.**

she·moz·zle, sche·moz·zle (shi-mózz'l) *n.* **1.** A muddle; a state of chaos. **2.** An uproar; a noisy row. [Yiddish.]

Shen·an·do·ah Valley (shénnən-dṓ-ə || shánnə-). Part of the Great Appalachian Valley in Virginia, eastern United States, lying between the Allegheny Mountains to the west and the Blue Ridge Mountains to the east. In the American Civil War (1861–65) the valley was the scene of several of Thomas J. "Stonewall" Jackson's Valley Campaigns.

she·nan·i·gans (shi-nánnigənz) *pl.n. Informal.* **1.** Prankishness; mischief. **2.** Treachery; deceit. [19th century : origin obscure.]

Shensi. See **Shaanxi.**

Shen·yang or **Shen-yang** (shə̂n-yáng), formerly **Muk·den** (mŏŏk-dən). City in northeastern China, the capital of Liaoning province. The fourth-largest city in China, it is the centre of a highly developed industrial region. The city, a major strategic centre, fell to the Japanese in the Russo-Japanese War (1904–05). It was there also that the Mukden, or Manchurian, Incident took place (1931), when the Japanese used an explosion on the railway as an excuse to occupy the city and begin the occupation of Manchuria.

she-oak (shée-ōk) *n.* Any of various Australian trees of the genus *Casuarina,* such as the beefwood. See **Casuarina.** [SHE (used in the obsolete sense of a lesser plant) + OAK.]

she·ol (shée-ol, -ōl) *n.* **1.** Hell. **2.** *Capital* **S.** A place described in the Old Testament as the abode of the dead. [Hebrew *shəʼōl.*]

Shep·ard (shéppərd), **Allan Bartlett, Jr.** (1923–). U.S. astronaut. On 5 May 1961, he became the first American in space, and commanded the Apollo 14 mission to the Moon in 1971.

Shepard, Ernest H(oward) (1879–1976). British cartoonist and illustrator. He worked for *Punch,* and is remembered for his illustrations to A.A. Milne's Winnie the Pooh books.

shep·herd (shéppərd) *n.* **1.** One who herds, guards, and cares for

PRONUNCIATION KEY

a, trap; aa, father; ai, fair; ar, star; aw, lawn; ay, play; b, bb, stab; rubber; ch, church; ck, ticket; d, dd, dead; ladder; e, dress; ee, bee; er, defer; ew, few; ewr, pure; ə, about; ər, letter; f, ff, fife; differ; g, gg, giggle; h, hat; i, kit; ī, price; īr, fire; j, judge; k, kick; l, ll, let; 'l, needle; m, mm, man; n, nn, no; 'n, sudden; ng, thing; o, lot; ō, no; ŏŏ, foot; ōō, shoe; oor, poor; ow, cow; owr, hour; oy, boy; p, pp, pepper; r, rr, red; s, ss, sauce; sh, ship; t, tt, totter; th, thick; th, this; smooth; u, cut; ur, turn; v, vv, valve; w, wet; y, yes; z, zz, zebra; zh, vision; pleasure

IN FOREIGN WORDS:

aN, oN, Saint-Saëns; hl, Llanelli; Hluhluwe; kh, loch; lough; Khaled

STRESS MARK:

ín-sīt, insight; in-sī́t, incite

NATURE'S OWN COATS OF ARMOUR
The remains of tiny creatures decorate the seashore

The shells found on the seashores of the world are the hard outer skeletons of soft-bodied animals known as molluscs. They consist largely of calcium carbonate, which is secreted by glands contained in a fleshy part of the mollusc known as the mantle. These glands also produce the exquisite colours with which the shells are tinted. Shells, in all their variety of shapes and sizes, are built up in three layers – a horny outer layer, a chalky middle layer, and a glossy inner layer.

Shell-bearing molluscs are mostly univalves or bivalves. Univalves have one spiral shell shaped like a cone or a bowl. They include snails, cowries, winkles, ormers, and whelks. Bivalves have a pair of flattish shells, and include oysters, clams, mussels, scallops, and shipworms.

The two shells of bivalves may be the same size (as in mussels), of unequal size (as in scallops), or extremely small in relation to the animal's body (as in shipworms, which have a pair of small shells at the front end of a long worm-like body). Many bivalve shells have a thick lining of nacre – mother-of-pearl.

Although hundreds of different species of mollusc are found on beaches, every beach – whether sandy or rocky, sheltered or exposed – has its own characteristic inhabitants, and so is able to produce a fascinating variety of shells.

The best time to collect shells is at low tide, when more beach is exposed. It is especially good during the spring tides, which occur for a few days every fortnight at the time of a full or new moon.

SOME COMMON SHELLS, AND WHERE THEY ARE FOUND

Ormer (univalve)
Haliotis tuberculata
80–100 millimetres
(3–4 inches)
Lives on and under stones

Edible winkle (univalve)
Littorina littorea
15–40 millimetres (½–1½ inches)
Found on rocks and beneath seaweeds

Hump-back cowrie
(univalve)
Cypraea mauritiana
70–110 millimetres (2¾–4⅜ inches)
Lives on rocks

Pullet carpet shell (bivalve)
Venerupis pullastra
40–65 millimetres (1½–2½ inches)
Found in sand and muddy gravel

Giant clam (bivalve)
Tridacna gigas
Up to 1.2 metres (4 feet)
Lives on coral reefs in pools

Horse mussel (bivalve)
Modiolus modiolus
180–220 millimetres (7–8½ inches)
Lives among brown seaweed

Curved razor (bivalve)
Ensis ensis
80–130 millimetres
(3–5 inches)
Lives in sand

Grooved razor (bivalve)
Solen marginatus
130 millimetres (5 inches)
Lives in sandy mud

Common whelk (univalve)
Buccinum undatum
50–100 millimetres (2–4 inches)
Found in muddy gravel, sand, and on
rocky shores

Common otter shell (bivalve)
Lutraria lutraria
100–130 millimetres (4–5 inches)
Lives in sand and sandy mud

Prickly cockle (bivalve)
Cardium echinata
65 millimetres (2½ inches)
Lives in sand and muddy sand

Argonaut or paper nautilus (univalve)
Argonauta nodosa
150–180 millimetres (6–7 inches)
Found on rocks on sea floor

Sand gaper or old maid (bivalve)
Mya arenaria
120–150 millimetres (4¾–6 inches)
In clay, sand, and sandy mud

Common limpet (univalve)
Patella vulgaris
20–50 millimetres (¾–2 inches)
Lives on rocks

Great scallop or escallop (bivalve)
Pecten maximus
70–160 millimetres (2¾–6¼ inches)
Lives in coarse sand

Queen scallop (bivalve)
Chlamys opercularis
40–90 millimetres (1½–3½ inches)
Lives in coarse sand and gravel

Queen conch (univalve)
Strombus gigas
150–300 millimetres
(6–12 inches)
Found in sand and
muddy sand

Smooth buckle or spindle shell (univalve)
Neptunea antiqua
130 millimetres (5 inches)
Lives in sand and mud

shepherd's-purse *A weed that thrives in all sorts of soil. The tiny white flowers are self-pollinating, and the pods, like wallets, open to shower seeds.*

shield *This 15th-century Flemish shield was made for a medieval tournament. It represents a courtly love scene: the knight kneeling before his lady is vowing: "Vous ou la Mort" ("You or Death"), and it is possible that the figures are actual portraits. The socket at the top of the gilded wooden shield was designed to hold a lance.*

sheep. **2.** One who cares for a group of people, such as a priest or teacher. **3.** *Australian.* One who owns the rights to a mine or mining claim but does not work it.
~*tr.v.* **shepherded, -herding, -herds. 1.** To herd, guard, or care for as or in the manner of a shepherd. **2.** *Australian.* To own the right to, but not to work, (a mine or mining claim). [Middle English *sheepherde,* Old English *scēaphirde* : *scēap,* SHEEP + *hirde,* HERD (herdsman).]

shepherd dog *n.* A sheepdog.

shep·herd·ess (shéppər-diss, -dess, -déss) *n.* A woman shepherd.

shepherd's needle *n.* A European plant, *Scandix pecten-veneris,* with finely divided leaves and conspicuous needle-like fruit.

shepherd's pie *n.* A dish of minced beef or lamb with gravy, topped by a layer of mashed potatoes. Also called "cottage pie".

shep·herd's-purse (shéppərdz-púrss) *n.* A common weed, *Capsella bursa-pastoris,* having small white flowers and flat, heart-shaped fruit. [From its pouchlike pods.]

shepherd's weatherglass *n.* A plant, the **pimpernel** *(see).*

sher·ard·ise, sher·ard·ize (shérrər-dīz) *tr.v.* **-ised, -ising, -ises.** To form a layer of zinc on (iron or steel) by heating with zinc dust. [After *Sherard* Cowper-Coles (died 1936), British inventor.] **—sher·ard·i·sa·tion** (-dī-záysh'n || *U.S.* -di-) *n.*

Sher·a·ton (shérrətən) *adj.* Of or designating a style of English furniture originated by Thomas Sheraton, and characterised by straight lines and graceful proportions.

Sheraton, Thomas (1751–1806). British furniture designer. His four-volume *Cabinet-Maker and Upholsterer's Drawing Book* (1791–94) provides an elegant and influential survey of contemporary taste.

sher·bet (shérbət) *n.* **1.** An effervescent powder eaten as a sweet, or used to make fizzy drinks. **2.** *Chiefly U.S.* **Solbet** *(see).* [Turkish *sherbet* and Persian *sharbat,* from Arabic *sharbah,* drink, from *shariba,* to drink. See also **syrup, shrub.**]

sherd. Variant of **shard.**

Sher·i·dan (shérrid'n), **Richard Brinsley (Butler)** (1751–1816). British dramatist and politician, born in Ireland. He is known for his comedies of manners, especially *The Rivals* (1775) and *The School for Scandal* (1777). Elected an M.P. in 1780, he became an outstanding Whig orator, and was treasurer of the Navy (1806–07).

she·rif (she-reéf, shə-) *n.* Also **sha·rif** (sha-, shə-). **1. a.** A descendant of the prophet Muhammad through his daughter Fatima. **b.** The title of certain Arab princes claiming such descent. **2.** The chief magistrate of Mecca. Also called "grand sherif". **3.** A Moroccan prince or ruler. [Arabic *sharīf,* "noble", from *sharafa,* to be high-born.]

sher·iff (shérrif) *n.* **1.** In England and Wales, the chief officer of the Crown in every county, whose powers are now mainly ceremonial, but include some legal powers such as the summoning of juries in some courts, and acting as returning officer in parliamentary elections. Also officially called "high sheriff". **2.** In Scotland, a judge presiding over a *sheriff court* (roughly equivalent to an English county court and the middle tier of a Crown court). **3.** The chief executive of the courts of superior jurisdiction in a U.S. county; the chief law-enforcement officer in a county. [Middle English *shir(r)eve, shirrif,* Old English *scīrgerēfa* : *scīr,* SHIRE + *gerēfa,* officer, REEVE.]

sher·iff-dep·ute (shérrif-déppewt) *n., pl.* **sheriffs-depute.** In Scotland, a judge carrying out various administrative duties and hearing both civil and criminal cases. Also called "sheriff principal".

Sher·lock Holmes (shérlok hōmz). English detective with superb powers of observation and deduction, a central character in stories and novels by Sir Arthur Conan Doyle.

Sher·man (shérmən), **William Tecumseh** (1820–91). U.S. soldier, a Union general in the Civil War. As commander of all Federal forces in the west from 1864, he helped secure Union victory through his capture of Atlanta and march through the Carolinas (1864–65).

Sher·pa (shérpə) *n., pl.* **-pas** or collectively **Sherpa.** A member of a Tibetan people living in northern Nepal.

Sher·ring·ton (shérringtən), **Sir Charles Scott** (1857–1952). British physiologist, known for his pioneering work on the nervous system. His research into the function of the neuron won him the Nobel prize for physiology or medicine in 1932, jointly with Lord Adrian.

sher·ry (shérri) *n., pl.* **-ries. 1.** A fortified Spanish wine ranging from very dry to sweet, and usually drunk as an apertif. **2.** A similar wine made outside Spain. [Earlier *sherris,* "wine of Jerez", from *Xeres,* older form of JEREZ.]

sher·wa·ni (shair-waáni) *n.* A tight-fitting, knee-length formal coat with a high collar, worn by men in India. [Hindi *shērwānī.*]

Sher·wood Forest (shér-wŏŏd). Ancient royal forest, mainly in Nottinghamshire, central England, famous as the scene of Robin Hood's exploits. Today only parts of it remain, near Mansfield.

she's (sheez, shiz). **1.** Contraction of *she is.* **2.** Contraction of *she has.*

Shet·land (shéttlənd) *adj.* Of or from the Shetland Islands.
~*n.* **1.** A fine, loosely twisted yarn made from the wool of Shetland sheep and used for knitting and weaving. Also called "Shetland wool". **2.** A garment, especially a sweater, made of this wool.

Shetland Islands. Also **Shetlands.** The most northerly part of Britain, comprising about 100 islands off northern Scotland. They lie northeast of the Orkney Islands, and constitute the county of **Shetland** or **Zetland.** The largest of them are Mainland, Yell, Unst, Fetlar, and Whalsey, and 19 are inhabited. The poor soil supports some crops, chiefly oats and barley, but the main economic activities are the raising of sheep, cattle, and Shetland ponies, fishing and tourism, and the islands are noted for their wool, knitwear, and knitted lace. Under Norse rule from the late 9th century, the Shetland Islands were annexed to the Scottish crown in 1472. Lerwick on Mainland is the administrative centre. **—Shet·land·er** *n.*

Shetland pony *n.* A small, compactly built pony of a breed originating in the Shetland Islands. Also called "sheltie".

Shetland sheepdog *n.* A dog of a breed developed in the Shetland Islands, having a rough coat and resembling a small collie. Also called "sheltie".

She·vat (shə-vaát) *n.* Also **She·bat** (-baát, -vaát). The fifth month of the Hebrew calendar. [Hebrew *shəbhāṭ.*]

shew (shō) *v.* **shewed, shewing, shews.** *Archaic.* To show.

shew·bread, show·bread (shō-bred) *n.* The 12 loaves of blessed, unleavened bread placed every Sabbath in the sanctuary of the Tabernacle by the ancient Hebrew priests. Exodus 25:20. Leviticus 24:5-9. [16th century (Tindale) : translating German *Schaubrot,* from Hebrew *lēchem pānim,* "bread of presence" (that is, the bread left in the presence of God in the temple).]

shf, SHF superhigh frequency.

Shi·ah, Shi·a (sheé-ə) *n.* **1.** The principal minority sect of Islam, composed of the followers of Ali, the cousin and son-in-law of Muhammad, who regard the heirs of Ali as the legitimate successors to the Prophet and reject the other caliphs and the Sunnite legal and political institutions. Compare **Sunni. 2.** A **Shiite** *(see).*
~*adj.* Shiite. [Arabic *shī'ah,* following (of Ali), from *shā'a,* to follow, accompany.]

shib·bo·leth (shíbbə-leth, shíbbō- || -ləth, -lith) *n.* **1.** A password, phrase, custom, or usage that reliably distinguishes the members of one group or class from another. **2.** A slogan, catchword, or saying, especially one distinctive of a particular group. **3.** An outmoded custom, doctrine, slogan or the like that was once thought to be important or even fundamental to the existence of the group that adhered to or used it. [Hebrew *shibbōleth,* an ear of corn, stream (password used by the Gileadites in the Bible, Judges 12:6).]

shield (sheeld) *n.* **1.** An article of protective armour made of metal or other rigid material carried on the forearm to ward off blows or missiles. **2.** A means of defence; protection. **3.** Something resembling a shield in shape, such as a trophy or badge. **4. a.** Something such as a protective plate that screens off potentially dangerous machinery or equipment. **b.** *Military.* A steel sheet attached to a gun to protect the gunners from small-arms fire. **5.** *Zoology.* A protective plate or similar hard outer covering. **6.** *Heraldry.* A design or drawing of a shield on which a coal of arms is displayed. **7.** *Physics.* A mass of material, such as lead or cement, that encloses a nuclear reactor in order to reduce the amount of radiation that escapes into the surrounding area. **8.** *Geology.* A **craton** *(see).* —*v.* **shielded, shielding, shields.** —*tr.* **1.** To protect or defend with or as if with a shield; guard. **2.** To cover up; conceal. —*intr.* To act or serve as a shield or safeguard. —See Synonyms at **defend.** [Middle English *shild, sheld,* Old English *scild, sceld.*] **—shield·er** *n.*

shield·bug (sheéld-bug) *n.* Any of numerous flattened, shield-shaped, plant-eating insects.

shield-fern (sheéld-fern) *n.* Either of two large tufted ferns, *Polystichum aculeatum* of *P. setiferum,* having round, shield-shaped indusia (spore-protecting coverings).

Shield of David *n.* A six-pointed star, the **Star of David** *(see).*

shiel·ing (sheéling) *n. Scottish.* A shepherd's hut. [Scottish *shiel,* shed, hut, Middle English *schele, shale,* probably from Scandinavian; akin to Old Norse *skjol,* shelter, hut.]

shift (shift) *v.* **shifted, shifting, shifts.** —*tr.* **1.** To move or transfer from one place or position to another. **2.** To exchange for or replace with something similar in quality or kind; switch. **3.** *U.S.* To change (gear) in a car. **4.** *Linguistics.* To alter phonetically or as part of a systematic change. **5.** *Informal.* To remove: *I can't shift this dirty mark.* —*intr.* **1.** To change position, direction, place, form, or the like. **2. a.** To provide for one's needs; get along; manage: *I can shift for myself.* **b.** To get along by resourceful or evasive means. **3.** *U.S.* To change gear, as when driving a car. **4.** *Informal.* To be removed: *That mark won't shift.*
~*n.* **1.** A change, transference, or displacement from one individual, position, or configuration to another. **2.** A change of direction or form. **3. a.** A group of workers who work for a particular period, and are replaced by the next group. **b.** The working period or time of such a group: *The night shift ends at six.* **4.** *Music.* A change of the position of the hand in playing the violin or a similar instrument. **5.** *Linguistics.* **a.** A systematic change of the phonetic or phonemic structure of a language. **b. Functional shift** *(see).* **6. a.** A woman's dress hanging straight from the shoulders. Also called "chemise". **b.** A woman's undergarment; a slip; a chemise. **7.** An ingenious, evasive, or fraudulent expedient; a trick. [Middle English *shiften,* to arrange, apportion, change, Old English *sciftan,* to arrange, from Germanic *skip-* (unattested).] **—shift·er** *n.*

shift·less (shíft-ləss, -liss) *adj.* **1.** Showing a lack of ambition or purpose; lazy. **2.** Showing a lack of resourcefulness or efficiency; not capable. [From SHIFT (archaic sense "resourcefulness").] **—shift·less·ly** *adv.* **—shift·less·ness** *n.*

shift·y (shífti) *adj.* **-ier, -iest. 1.** Tricky; crafty. **2.** Suggesting craft, guile, or deceitfulness; furtive. **—shift·i·ly** *adv.* **—shift·i·ness** *n.*

shi·gel·la (shi-géllə) *n.* Any bacterium of the genus *Shigella,* some species of which cause dysentery in humans. [New Latin, after K. *Shiga* (1870–1957), Japanese bacteriologist who discovered it.]

shih-tzu (shée-tsōō) *n.* A small long-haired dog of a breed originating in Tibet, resembling a terrier or pekingese. [Chinese, "Lion".]

Shi·ism, Shi'·ism (shée-iz'm) *n.* The religion or doctrines of the **Shiah** *(see).*

Shi·ite, Shi'·ite (shée-īt) *n.* A member of the **Shiah** *(see)* branch of Islam. Also called "Shiah". **—Shi·ite, Shi·it·ic** (shee-íttik) *adj.*

shi·ka·ree, shi·ka·ri (shi-kaári) *n. Anglo-Indian.* A big-game hunting guide. [Hindi, from Persian *shikārī,* from *shikār,* hunting, from Middle Persian *shkārt.*]

Shi·ko·ku (shi-kō-kōō). Smallest of the four main islands of Japan. It covers 18 770 square kilometres (7,247 square miles) and lies across the Inland Sea from Kyushu and Honshu.

shik·sa, shik·se, shick·sa (shíksə) *n.* **1.** A non-Jewish girl or young woman. Usually used derogatorily. **2.** A Jewish girl or young woman who fails to live up to traditional Jewish teachings or practices. Usually used derogatorily. [Yiddish *shikse,* feminine of *sheygets,* from Hebrew *sheqeṣ,* blemish.]

shil·le·lagh, shil·la·lah (shi-láy-li, -lə) *n.* In Ireland, a club or cudgel, especially one of oak or blackthorn. [Such clubs were originally made in *Shillelagh,* town in County Wicklow, Ireland.]

shil·ling (shílling) *n. Abbr.* **s., sh. 1.** Formerly, a coin equal to $^1/_{20}$ of the pound of the United Kingdom, the Republic of Ireland, and a number of former British dominions. **2.** The basic monetary unit of Kenya, the Somali Republic, Tanzania, and Uganda, equal to 100 cents. [Middle English *shilling,* Old English *scilling,* from Germanic *skillingaz* (unattested).]

shilling mark *n.* A **solidus** *(see).*

shil·ly-shal·ly (shílli-shal-i) *intr.v.* **-lied, -lying, -lies. 1.** To put off acting; hesitate or waver. **2.** To idle or dawdle.
~*adj.* Hesitant; vacillating.
~*n., pl.* **shilly-shallies.** Procrastination; hesitation.
~*adv.* In a hesitant manner; irresolutely. [Originally in phrases such as *stand* (or *go*), *shill I? shall I?* reduplication of *shall I?*] **—shil·ly-shal·li·er** *n.*

shim (shim) *n.* A thin washer or tapered piece of metal, wood, stone, or other material, used to adjust a space or as a filler between materials or to make parts of it.
~*tr.v.* **shimmed, shimming, shims.** To make (parts) fit by inserting a shim or shims. [18th Century : origin obscure.]

shim·mer (shímmər) *intr.v.* **-mered, -mering, -mers.** To shine with a soft tremulous or flickering light. See Synonyms at **flash.**
~*n.* A flickering or tremulous light; a glimmer. [Middle English *schimeren,* Old English *scimerian, scimrian,* from Germanic; akin to SHINE.] **—shim·mer·y** *adj.*

shim·my (shímmi) *n., pl.* **-mies.** *Chiefly U.S.* **1.** A dance popular in the 1920s, characterised by rapid shaking of the body. Also called "shimmy shake". **2.** Abnormal vibration or wobbling, as in the chassis of a car. **3.** *Regional.* A chemise.
~*intr.v.* **shimmied, -mying, -mies. 1.** To vibrate or wobble. **2.** To shake the body in or as if in dancing the shimmy. [Short for *shimmy-shake,* perhaps "to shake one's chemise", from *shimmy,* incorrect form of CHEMISE.]

shin¹ (shin) *n.* **1.** *Anatomy.* **a.** The front part of the leg below the knee and above the ankle. **b.** The front of the tibia. **2.** A cut of meat from the lower part of the foreleg in beef cattle, as opposed to the upper foreleg or shank.
~*v.* **shinned, shinning, shins.** *—tr.* **1.** To climb (a rope or pole, for example) by gripping and pulling alternately with the hands and legs. Usually used with *up.* **2.** To kick or hit in the shins. *—intr.* To climb something by shinning. Usually used with *up.* [Middle English *shine,* Old English *sinu.*]

shin² (shin, sheen) *n.* The 22nd letter in the Hebrew alphabet. [Hebrew *shīn,* variant of *shēn,* tooth (from the shape of the letter).]

Shi·nar (shī́-nər, -naar). The Biblical name for an ancient country on the lower courses of the Tigris and Euphrates. Genesis 10:10.

shin·bone (shín-bōn) *n. Anatomy.* The **tibia** *(see).*

shin·dig (shín-dig) *n. Slang.* **1.** A noisy party or celebration. Also called "shindy". **2.** A shindy. [Probably an alteration of SHINDY.]

shin·dy (shíndi) *n., pl.* **-dies.** *Slang.* **1.** A commotion; a row; an uproar. Also called "shindig". **2.** A shindig. [Alteration of SHINTY.]

shine (shīn) *v.* **shone** (shon || *U.S.* shōn) or **shined** (for transitive sense 2), **shining, shines.** *—intr.* **1.** To emit light; be radiant; beam. **2.** To reflect light; glint or glisten. **3.** To distinguish oneself in some sphere; excel: *shine at tennis.* **4.** To become clearly apparent. *—tr.* **1.** To aim or cast the beam or glow of: *Shine the torch over here.* **2.** To make glossy or bright by polishing.
~*n.* **1.** Brightness; radiance; lustre. **2.** An act of shining something: *gave her shoes a shine.* **3.** Fair weather. Used in the phrase *rain or shine.* **—take a shine to.** *Informal.* To like spontaneously. [Shine, shone (past tense); Middle English *shinen, schon,* Old English *scīnan, scān* (past singular). The past participle *shone* is formed in Modern English from the past tense *shone.*]

shin·er (shī́nər) *n.* **1.** One that shines. **2.** *Slang.* A black eye. **3. a.** Any of numerous small, often silvery North American freshwater fishes of the family Cyprinidae, especially one of the genus *Notropis.* **b.** Any of various other small silvery fishes, especially the mackerel.

shin·gle¹ (shíng-g'l) *n.* **1.** A thin oblong piece of wood, asbestos, or other material, laid in overlapping rows to cover the roofs and sides of houses. **2.** A woman's close-cropped layered haircut.
~*tr.v.* **shingled, -gling, -gles. 1.** To cover (a roof or building) with shingles. **2.** To cut (a woman's hair) short and in layers so that the hair is full out at the back of the head and tapers in to the nape of the neck. [Middle English *scincle, scingle,* from Latin *scindula,* variant of *scandula,* a roofing shingle, from *scandere,* to ascend.] **—shin·gler** *n.*

shingle² A mass of rounded, water-worn stones of various sizes, often found on beaches. [16th century : origin obscure.] **—shin·gly** *adj.*

shingle³ *tr.v.* **-gled, -gling, -gles.** To hammer the slag out of (puddled iron) during the manufacture of wrought iron. [French *cingler,* from German *zängeln,* from *Zange,* TONG(S).]

shin·gles (shíng-g'lz) *n.* *Usually used with a singular verb. Pathology.* A viral infection caused by chickenpox viruses and characterised by skin eruptions along the routes of cutaneous nerves on one side of the body, often accompanied or followed by severe neuralgia. The virus may remain latent within the body between outbreaks. Also called "herpes zoster", "zoster". [Middle English, from Medieval Latin *cingulus,* from Latin *cingulum,* girdle, from *cingere,* to gird.]

shin·ny¹ (shínni) *v.* **-nied, -nying, -nies.** *Informal. —intr.* To climb by shinning. *—tr.* To climb (a rope, for example) by shinning.

shinny². *U.S.* Variant of **shinty.**

shin·plas·ter (shín-plaastər || -plastər) *n.* **1.** *U.S.* A note of paper currency issued privately; especially, such a note devalued by lack of backing or by inflation. **2.** *Australian.* A promissory note used in the outback as currency. [From the comparison of such notes to small squares of brown paper soaked with vinegar or tobacco juice and used by poor people to treat sore legs.]

Shin·to (shíntō) *n.* Also **Shin·to·ism** (-iz'm). The indigenous religion of Japan, marked by the veneration of nature spirits and of ancestors. [Japanese *shintō,* "the way of the gods" : *shin,* from Chinese *shén,* god(s), + *tō,* for *do,* way, from Chinese (Mandarin) *dào,* way.] **—Shin·to·ist** *n. & adj.*

shin·ty (shínti) *n.* Also *U.S.* **shinny. 1.** A vigorous game similar to hockey. **2.** The curved stick used in this game. [Perhaps from the cry of *shin ye* used in the game.]

shin·y (shī́ni) *adj.* **-ier, -iest.** Having a surface that reflects light, as: **1.** Glossy; glistening: *shiny satin.* **2.** Bright; polished: *shiny shoes.* **3.** Clear; shining: *shiny-eyed.* **4.** Worn away so as to appear smooth and glossy. Said of fabric. **—shin·i·ness** *n.*

ship (ship) *n.* **1.** Any vessel of considerable size adapted for deep-water navigation and powered by wind or engines. **2.** A three-masted sailing vessel with square mainsails on all masts. **3.** *Maritime Law.* A vessel intended for marine transport without regard to form, rig, or means of propulsion. **4.** A ship's company. **5.** A spaceship or airship. **—dress ship.** To display the ensign, signal flags, and bunting on a ship.
~*v.* **shipped, shipping, ships.** *—tr.* **1.** To place or take on board a ship. **2. a.** To send or transport. **b.** *Informal.* To dispatch to a specified destination. **3.** To bring into a vessel; especially, to lift (oars) from the water and place inside the boat without removing them from the rowlocks. **4.** To take in (water) over the side. **5.** To set (a mast or rudder, for example) in place for use. *—intr.* **1.** To go or travel by means of a ship. **2.** To hire oneself out or enlist for service on a ship. [Middle English *s(c)hip,* Old English *scip.*]

-ship *n. suffix.* Indicates: **1.** The quality or condition of; for example, **friendship, scholarship. 2.** The status, rank, or office of; for example, **professorship, authorship. 3.** The art or skill of; for example, **penmanship, leadership.** [Middle English *-s(c)hip(e),* Old English *-scipe.*]

ship·board (shíp-bawrd || -bōrd) *n. Obsolete.* The side of a ship. **—on shipboard.** On board a ship.
~*adj.* Occurring on board a ship: *a shipboard romance.*

ship·build·ing (shíp-bilding) *n.* The industry or occupation of constructing ships. **—ship·build·er** *n.*

ship canal *n.* A canal deep enough for ships. Also "shipway".

ship chandler *n.* A person who deals in equipment for ships.

ship fever *n.* **Typhus** *(see),* especially as it formerly occurred on overcrowded ships.

ship·load (shíp-lōd) *n.* **1.** The cargo or passengers carried by a ship. **2.** A capacity cargo for a ship.

ship·man (shíp-mən) *n., pl.* **-men** (-mən, -men). *Archaic.* **1.** A sailor. **2.** A shipmaster.

ship·mas·ter (shíp-maastər || -mastər) *n.* The master or captain of a ship.

ship·mate (shíp-mayt) *n.* A sailor serving on the same ship as another; a fellow sailor.

ship·ment (shípmənt) *n. Abbr.* **shpt. 1.** The act of sending or transporting goods. **2.** A quantity of goods or cargo transported.

ship money *n.* A former tax on English maritime towns and shires to provide revenue for the construction of warships.

ship of state *n.* A country or its affairs symbolised as a ship bound on a course.

ship of the line *n.* Formerly, a warship large enough to take a position in the line of battle.

ship·per (shíppər) *n.* A person or company that consigns or receives goods for shipping; a shipping agent.

ship·ping (shípping) *n.* **1.** The act or business of transporting goods, especially by ship. **2.** The body of ships belonging to one port, industry, or country, often referred to in aggregate tonnage. **3.** Ships collectively.

shipping clerk *n.* A person employed to manage the shipment or receipt of goods.

shipping lane *n.* A regular or prescribed route for ships.

shieldbug *There are about 2,500 species of these sap-sucking insects, which are found all over the world and named because of their shield-shaped bodies. When alarmed, shieldbugs give off an offensive smell as a defence mechanism.*

ship canal *A man-made canal large enough to carry ocean-going vessels. Some – such as Britain's Manchester Ship Canal – link the sea to an inland port. Others – such as the Corinth ship canal, shown here – link two seas. The canal, which is about 6 kilometres (4 miles) long, cuts through the Isthmus of Corinth in Greece to join the Ionian Sea and the Mirtoan Sea.*

shire horse These large English-bred horses are still used as draught horses on farms in some parts of the country. But they are more often seen at shows in decorative livery, as here. Shires usually have a white blaze and white "feathered" feet, and can be up to 17.3 hands tall at the shoulder – almost 1.8 metres (6 feet).

PRONUNCIATION KEY

a, trap; aa, father; ai, fair; ar, star; aw, lawn; ay, play; b, bb, stab; rubber; ch, church; ck, ticket; d, dd, dead; ladder; e, dress; ee, bee; er, defer; ew, few; ewr, pure; ə, about; ər, letter; f, ff, fife; differ; g, gg, giggle; h, hat; i, kit; ī, price; īr, fire; j, judge; k, kick; l, ll, let; 'l, needle; m, mm, man; n, nn, no; 'n, sudden; ng, thing; o, lot; ō, no; o͝o, foot; o͞o, shoe; oor, poor; ow, cow; owr, hour; oy, boy; p, pp, pepper; r, rr, red; s, ss, sauce; sh, ship; t, tt, totter; th, thick; th, this; smooth; u, cut; ur, turn; v, vv, valve; w, wet; y, yes; z, zz, zebra; zh, vision; pleasure

IN FOREIGN WORDS:

aN, oN, Saint-Saëns; hl, Llanelli; Hluhluwe; kh, loch; lough; Khaled

STRESS MARK:

ín-sīt, insight; in-sī́t, incite

ship-rigged (shíp-rigd) *adj. Nautical.* Rigged as a ship, with three or more masts and square sails.

ship's biscuit *n.* A type of bread, **hardtack** *(see).*

ship·shape (shíp-shayp) *adj.* Neatly arranged; orderly; tidy. [Originally, "arranged in a manner befitting a ship" (said of rigging).] **—ship·shape** *adv.*

ship's papers *pl.n.* The documents giving details of ownership, nationality, destination, or the like that international law requires a ship to carry and be able to provide on demand for inspection.

ship-to-shore (shíp-tə-shór || -shṓr) *adj.* In operation between a ship and the shore. Said of a radio system. **—ship-to-shore** *adv.*

ship·way (shíp-way) *n.* **1.** The structure supporting a ship during construction or in dry dock. **2.** A **ship canal** *(see).*

ship·worm (shíp-wurm) *n.* Any of various wormlike marine molluscs of the genera *Teredo* and *Bankia,* having rudimentary shells with which they bore into wood, often doing extensive damage.

ship·wreck (shíp-rek) *n.* **1.** The destruction of a ship, as by storm or collision. **2.** The remains of a wrecked ship. **3.** Complete failure or ruin.
~tr.v. **shipwrecked, -wrecking, -wrecks. 1.** To cause (a ship or its passengers) to suffer shipwreck. **2.** To ruin utterly. [Earlier *shipwrack,* Middle English *shipwrak,* Old English *scipwræc,* cargo thrown overboard to lighten a ship in danger : SHIP + *wræc,* thing driven by the sea, WRACK.]

ship·wright (shíp-rīt) *n.* A skilled worker, such as a carpenter, employed in the construction or maintenance of ships.

ship·yard (shíp-yaard) *n.* A place where ships are built or repaired.

shi·ra·lee (shírrə-lée, -lee) *n. Australian.* A bag or bundle of personal belongings carried by a traveller or swagman; a swag. [20th century : origin obscure.]

Shi·raz (shéer-ráaz). City in southwestern Iran, the capital of Fars province. It has been a leading commercial and administrative town since the eighth century. It is noted especially for its metalwork, wines, and carpets.

shire (shīr) *n.* **1.** Any of the counties of the United Kingdom. Used chiefly in combination: *Lancashire.* **2.** *Australian.* A division of a state, often rural, having its own elected administration. **—the Shires.** The counties of the Midlands, especially those renowned for foxhunting, such as Leicestershire. [Old English *scir*†.]

shire horse *n.* A large, powerful draught horse of a breed originating in the shires of Lincoln, Cambridge, or Huntingdon.

shirk (shurk) *v.* **shirked, shirking, shirks.** *—tr.* To put off or avoid discharging (work or duties). *—intr.* To avoid work or duty.
~n. A person who avoids work or duty. Also called "shirker". [From obsolete *shirk,* parasite, rogue, probably from German *Schurke,* scoundrel, perhaps from Old High German *(fiur)-scurgo,* "fire stirrer", stoker, hence devil (as an infernal stoker), from *scurigen,* to poke.]

Shir·ley poppy (shúrli) *n.* A variety of the field poppy having scarlet, pink, or salmon single or double flowers. [After *Shirley* Vicarage, Croydon, Surrey, where it was first grown.]

shirr (shur) *tr.v.* **shirred, shirring, shirrs. 1.** To gather (cloth) into decorative parallel rows using fine elastic thread. **2.** *U.S.* To cook (eggs) by baking unshelled in moulds.
~n. A decorative gathering of cloth into parallel rows. Also called "shirring". [19th century : origin obscure.]

shirt (shurt) *n.* A garment for the upper part of the body, especially a man's, typically made of light fabric and having a collar, long or short sleeves, and a buttoned front opening. **—keep (one's) shirt on.** *Informal.* To remain calm or patient. **—lose (one's) shirt.** *Informal.* To lose everything one has or owns. **—put (one's) shirt on.** To bet or gamble everything one has on. [Middle English *sherte, scurte,* Old English *scyrte;* akin to Old Norse *skyrta* (whence SKIRT), from Germanic *skurt-* (unattested), SHORT.]

shirt·ing (shúrting) *n.* Fabric suitable for making shirts.

shirt·sleeve (shúrt-sleev) *n.* A sleeve of a shirt. **—in (one's) shirt-sleeves.** Informally dressed. **—shirt·sleeved** *adj.*

shirt·waist·er (shúrt-waystər) *n.* A woman's dress with the bodice styled like a tailored shirt. Also *U.S.* "shirtwaist".

shirt·y (shúrti) *adj.* **-tier, -tiest.** *Chiefly British Informal.* Annoyed and rude; bad-tempered. [See idioms at **shirt.**]

shish ke·bab (shísh ki-báb, -bab) *n.* Also *U.S.* **shish ke·bob, shish ka·bob** (-bob). A dish consisting of pieces of seasoned marinated meat cooked on skewers, often over charcoal. Also called "kebab". [Turkish *şiş kebabiu* : *şiş,* skewer + *kebap,* roast meat.]

shit (shit) *v.* **shat** or **shitted, shitting, shits.** *Vulgar.* *—intr.* To excrete faeces; defecate. *—tr.* **1.** To excrete (faeces). **2.** To soil by defecating on.
~n. **1.** *Vulgar.* Faeces. **2.** *Vulgar.* An act of defecating. **3.** *Vulgar. Slang.* Nonsense; rubbish. **4.** *Vulgar Slang.* A thoroughly unpleasant person. **5.** *Vulgar Slang.* An unpleasant situation; trouble. Used in the phrase *in the shit.* **6.** *Vulgar Slang.* Business: *She's really got her shit together.*
~interj. Vulgar Slang. Used as an expression of annoyance, anger, or amazement.
~adv. Vulgar Slang. Used as an intensive: *shit-scared.* [Old English *scite, scītan* (unattested), from Germanic *skit-, skīt-* (unattested); compare Middle Dutch *schitte,* dung, Old Norse *skīta,* to defecate.] **—shit·ti·ly** *adv.* **—shit·ty** *adj.*

shit-hot (shít-hót shít-hot) *adj. Vulgar Slang.* Excellent.

shit·less (shít-ləss, -liss) *adj. Vulgar Slang.* Terrified. Used especially in the phrases *scare someone shitless, scared shitless.*

shit·tim·wood (shíttim-wo͝od) *n.* **1.** A tree, probably a species of acacia, that was a source of a wood mentioned frequently in the Bible. Also called "shittah tree". **2.** The wood of this tree, used to make the ark of the Tabernacle. Exodus 25:10. [Hebrew *shiṭṭīm,* plural of *shiṭṭāh,* related to Egyptian *sont,* acacia.]

shiv (shiv) *n. Slang.* A knife or razor, especially when considered as a weapon. [Romany *chiv*†, "blade".]

shi·va, shi·vah (shívvə) *n. Judaism.* A seven-day period of formal mourning observed after the funeral of a close relative. [Yiddish, from Hebrew *shiv'āh,* seven.]

Shiva. Variant of **Siva.**

shivaree. *U.S.* Variant of **charivari.**

shive (shīv) *n.* **1.** A thin, flat cork used to stop wide-mouthed bottles. **2.** *Archaic.* A slice. [Middle English, slice, probably from Middle Dutch or Middle Low German *schīve.*]

shiv·er[1] (shívvər) *v.* **-ered, -ering, -ers.** *—intr.* **1.** To shudder or shake, as from cold or excitement; tremble. **2.** To quiver or vibrate, as by the force of wind. *—tr. Nautical.* To cause (a sail) to flutter in the wind. **—**See Synonyms at **shake.**
~n. **1.** An act of shivering; a tremble. **2.** *Often plural.* A tingling sensation caused by fear, excitement, or the like: *It sent shivers up my spine.* [Middle English *shiveren,* earlier *chiveren,* perhaps alteration of *chevelen,* to shiver, originally "to chatter" (used of teeth), from Old English *ceafl,* the jaw.]

shiver[2] *v.* **-ered, -ering, -ers.** *—intr.* To break into fragments or splinters; shatter. *—tr.* To cause to break into fragments. **—**See Synonyms at **break.** [Middle English, from *scivre,* fragment, perhaps of Low German origin, akin to Middle Low German *schever.*]

shiv·er·y[1] (shívvəri) *adj.* **1.** Trembling, as from cold or fear. **2.** Making one shiver with cold or fear; chilling.

shivery[2] *adj. Archaic.* Easily broken; brittle.

Shko·dër (shkṓ-dər) or **Shko·dra** (-draa). *Italian* **Scu·ta·ri** (sko͞o-táari; *Italian* sko͞otəri). City in Albania, capital of Shkodër province. It is the manufacturing and cultural centre of northern Albania.

shm–. Variant of **schm–.**

S.H.M. simple harmonic motion.

shmo. Variant of **schmo.**

shoal[1] (shōl) *n.* **1.** A shallow area in any body of water. **2.** An elevation of the bottom of a body of water, constituting a hazard to navigation; a sandbank, mudbank, or pebble bank.
~ v. **shoaled, shoaling, shoals.** *—intr.* To become shallow. *—tr.* **1.** To make shallow. **2.** To come or sail into a shallower area of (water): *The ship shoaled water.*
~adj. Having little depth; shallow. [Middle English *schald, sholde,* originally "shallow", Old English *sc(e)ald,* from Germanic *skaldaz* (unattested).] **—shoal·y** *adj.*

Usage: *shoal, reef, bar, bank.* These nouns have reference to elevations of ground under water. A *shoal* is an elevation coming close to but not above the surface of the water. The term is also applied to the shallow area thus formed. A *reef* is a ridge, usually of rock or coral, or slightly above the low-tide mark. A *bar* is a ridge, usually of sand, near the surface and often exposed at low water. A *bank* in this comparison is a large, totally submerged plateau of mud or sand that is not a danger to shipping.

shoal[2] *n.* **1.** A large group; a crowd. **2.** A school of fish or other marine animals.
~intr.v. **shoaled, shoaling, shoals.** To come together in a shoal. [Probably from Middle Dutch or Middle Low German *schōle.* See **school** (of fish).]

shoat, shote (shōt) *n.* A young pig just after weaning. [Middle English *shote,* probably Low German origin, akin to West Flemish *schote.*]

shock[1] (shok) *n.* **1.** A violent collision or impact; a heavy blow. **2.** Something that jars the mind or emotions as if with a violent, unexpected blow. **3.** The disturbance of function, equilibrium, or emotional and mental state caused by such a blow. **4.** *Pathology.* A generally temporary state of massive physiological reaction to bodily damage or emotional trauma, usually characterised by a cold sweat, marked loss of blood pressure, and the depression of vital processes such as respiration. **5.** The sensation and muscular spasm caused by an electric current passing through the body or through a bodily part. Also called "electric shock". **6. Shock therapy** *(see).*
~v. **shocked, shocking, shocks.** *—tr.* **1.** To fill with a powerful feeling of disgust, incredulity, horror, or the like. **2.** To outrage; scandalise. **3.** To induce a state of shock in (a person). **4.** To subject (an animal or person) to an electric shock. *—intr.* **1.** To be susceptible to shock. **2.** *Archaic.* To come into contact violently, as in battle; collide. [French *choc,* from *choquer*†, to strike (with fear).] **—shock·a·ble** *adj.*

shock[2] *n.* A number of sheaves of corn stacked upright in a field for drying.
~tr.v. **shocked, shocking, shocks.** To gather (sheaves of corn) into shocks. [Middle English *shokke,* probably from Middle Dutch or Middle Low German *schok,* shock, group of sixty, akin to Old Saxon *scok*†.]

shock[3] *n.* A thick, shaggy, heavy mass: *a shock of hair.*
~adj. Thick and shaggy. [Perhaps from SHOCK (stack).]

shock absorber *n.* Any of various devices used to absorb mechanical shocks; especially, a hydraulically damped coupling used to absorb impulsive forces generated by the contact of the wheels of a motor vehicle with irregular road surfaces.

shock·er (shóckər) *n.* **1.** One that startles, shocks, or horrifies; especially, a sensational story or novel. **2.** *Informal.* A thoroughly unpleasant person.

shock-head-ed (shók-héddid) *adj.* Having thick, shaggy hair.

shock-ing (shócking) *adj.* **1.** Highly disturbing emotionally. **2.** Highly offensive; indecent or distasteful. **3.** Very vivid or intense in tone: *shocking pink.* **4.** *Informal.* Nasty; very bad. —**shock-ing-ly** *adv.*

Shock-ley (shóckli), **William Bradford** (1910–). U.S. physicist, born in England. He directed U.S. naval research into antisubmarine warfare during World War II, and in 1948 developed the transistor jointly with Bardeen and Brattain. The three were awarded the 1956 Nobel physics prize for their work. Latterly he has expressed controversial views on the inheritance of intelligence.

shock-proof (shók-prōōf) *adj.* Able to withstand the effects of collisions or blows.

shock stall *n. Aeronautics.* Air resistance on an aircraft when it is close to the speed of sound that may lead to stalling.

shock therapy *n.* The inducing of shock by electric current or drugs, sometimes causing convulsions, as a therapy for mental illness. Also called "shock treatment".

shock treatment *n.* **1.** Shock therapy. **2.** Any brutally direct approach to a problem.

shock troops *pl.n. Military.* Highly experienced and capable soldiers specially trained to lead attacks.

shock tube *n. Physics.* A long tube in which a shock wave can be produced for spectrosopic investigation of radicals and excited molecules formed by the high temperature of the wave.

shock wave *n.* A large-amplitude compression wave, such as that produced by an explosion or by supersonic motion of a body in a medium.

shock workers *pl.n.* Labourers and skilled workers in Communist countries such as the U.S.S.R. and Poland who performed extremely arduous tasks, such as constructing buildings and roads in record time, particularly in the 1950s.

shod-dy (shóddi) *n., pl.* **-dies. 1.** Wool fibres obtained by shredding unfelted woollen or worsted rags or worn garments. **2.** Yarn, fabric, or garments made from or containing such recycled wool fibres. **3.** Inferior or imitation goods; cheap, derivative material. ~*adj.* **shoddier, -iest. 1.** Transparently imitative or inferior. **2.** Of poor quality or workmanship; trashy. **3.** Made of or containing shoddy or other inferior material. [19th century : of obscure (dialectal) origin.] —**shod-di-ly** *adv.* —**shod-di-ness** *n.*

shoe (shōō) *n., pl.* **shoes** or *archaic* **shoon** (shōōn). **1. a.** A durable covering for the human foot; especially, either of a matched pair made of leather or similar material and having a rigid sole and a heel of variable height. **b.** *British.* Such a foot covering reaching to just below the ankle. **c.** *U.S.* Such a foot covering reaching to just below or just above the ankle. **2.** A horseshoe. **3.** A part or device placed at an end, foot, or bottom, especially: **a.** A strip of metal fitted onto the bottom of a sledge runner. **b.** A skid placed under the wheel of a vehicle to retard its motion. **c.** A metal or rubber rim or casing protecting the bottom end of a walking stick, cane, or the like. **4.** The part of a brake that presses against the wheel or drum to retard its motion. **5. a.** The sliding contact plate on an electric train or tram that conducts electricity from the third rail. **b.** An oblong box used for holding and dealing cards in some gambling card games in which several packs of cards are used. —**fill (someone's) shoes.** To take the place of; succeed (another). —**in (someone's) shoes.** In someone else's position or predicament. ~*tr.v.* **shod** (shod), **shod** or **shodden** (shódd'n), **shoeing, shoes. 1.** To furnish or fit with shoes. **2.** To cover with a wooden or metal guard to protect against wear. [Middle English *sho(o),* Old English *scōh,* from Germanic *skōhaz* (unattested).]

shoe-bill (shōō-bil) *n.* A tall wading bird, *Balaeniceps rex,* native to swampy regions of eastern tropical Africa, and having slaty plumage, long black legs, a stubby neck, and a large shoelike bill with a hook on the upper mandible.

shoe-black (shōō-blak) *n.* A bootblack *(see).*

shoe-horn (shōō-hawrn) *n.* A curved implement, often of horn or smooth metal, inserted at the heel to help slip on a shoe.

shoe-lace (shōō-layss) *n.* A string or cord used for lacing and fastening a shoe.

shoe-mak-er (shōō-maykər) *n.* A person who makes or repairs shoes and boots as an occupation. —**shoe-mak-ing** *n.*

sho-er (shōō-ər) *n.* A person who shoes horses; a blacksmith.

shoe-string (shōō-string) *n.* **1.** A shoelace. **2.** A small sum of money; barely adequate funds: *living on a shoestring.* ~*adj.* **1.** Having or using a barely adequate amount, especially of money. **2.** *Chiefly U.S.* Cut to or in the shape of a shoestring; long and slender: *shoestring potatoes.*

shoe-tree (shōō-tree) *n.* A foot-shaped form inserted into a shoe when it is not being worn to preserve its shape.

sho-far, sho-phar (shō-faar) *n., pl.* **-fars** or **sho-froth** (shō-fráwt). *Judaism.* A trumpet made of a ram's horn, blown for warning, summoning, and ritual purposes by the ancient Hebrews, and now sounded in the synagogue at Rosh Hashanah and Yom Kippur. [Hebrew *shōphār,* "ram's horn".]

sho-gun (shō-gōōn, -gun) *n.* Any of a line of military leaders of Japan who, until 1867, exercised absolute rule under the nominal leadership of the emperor. [Japanese *shōgun,* "general", from Chinese *jiāng jūn : jiāng,* to lead, command + *jūn,* army.]

sho-gun-ate (shōgə-nət, -nit, -nayt) *n. Sometimes capital* **S.** The government of a shogun.

sho-ji (shōji) *n., pl.* **shoji** or **-jis.** A translucent paper screen forming a sliding door or partition in a Japanese house. [Japanese *shōji,* from Chinese *zhàngzi.*]

Sho-lem A-lei-chem (shōl-əm ə-láykhəm, sháwl-), pen name of Sholem Yakov Rabinowitz (1859–1916). Russian writer, known for his Yiddish tales, which are celebrated for their homespun wisdom. He settled in the United States at the outbreak of World War I.

Sho-lo-khov (shóllə-kov; *Russian* -khəf), **Mikhail Alexandrovich** (1905–). Russian novelist. The four-part novel by which he is best known is published in English as *And Quiet Flows the Don* (1934) and *The Don Flows Home to the Sea* (1940); the work spans the pre- and post-revolutionary periods and has been acclaimed in the U.S.S.R. as an outstanding example of socialist realism. Sholokhov was awarded the 1965 Nobel prize for literature.

Sho-na (shónnə) *n., pl.* **nas** or collectively **Shona.** Also **Ma-sho-na** (mə-shónnə). **1.** A member of any of various closely related groups of southern African people, living chiefly in Zimbabwe. **2.** The Bantu language of this people. —**Sho-na** *adj.*

shone. Past tense and past participle of **shine.**

shoo (shōō) *interj.* Used to scare away animals or birds. ~*v.* **shooed, shooing, shoos.** —*tr.* To drive or scare away, as by crying "shoo". —*intr.* To cry "shoo". [Middle English *schowe* (imitative).]

shoo-in (shōō-in) *n. U.S. Informal.* A contestant or candidate who seems certain of winning.

shook¹ (shōōk) *n.* A set of parts for assembling a barrel or packing case. [18th century : origin obscure.]

shook². Past tense of **shake.**

shook-up (shōōk-úp ‖ shōōk-) *adj. U.S. Slang.* Emotionally upset.

shoot (shōōt) *v.* **shot** (shot), **shooting, shoots.** —*tr.* **1.** To hit, wound, or kill with a missile fired from a weapon; especially, to kill with a bullet. **2.** To fire or let fly (a missile) from a weapon. **3.** To discharge or fire (a weapon). **4.** To cause to move directly and swiftly by or as if by a sudden release of tension. **5.** To send forth swiftly or dartingly: *She shot a look of contempt at him.* **6.** To pass over or through swiftly: *shoot the rapids.* **7.** To cover (country) in hunting for game. **8.** To record in photographs or on film. **9.** To record (a film sequence). **10.** To put forth; begin to grow or produce; generate. Used especially of a plant. **11.** To pour, empty out, or discharge down or as if down a chute. **12.** In golf, to make (a specified number of strokes). **13.** *Sports.* **a.** To move or propel (a ball), as by hitting or kicking, towards a goal. **b.** To score (a goal). **c.** *U.S.* To play (golf, craps, or pool). **14.** To slide into or out of a fastening: *shoot a door bolt.* **15.** To measure the altitude of with a sextant or other instrument: *shoot a star.* **16.** *Slang.* To inject (a narcotic drug) directly into a vein. —*intr.* **1.** To discharge a missile from a weapon. **2.** To discharge fire; go off. **3.** To move swiftly, as if discharged from a weapon; dart: *shot past in a car; pain shot through his leg.* **4.** To protrude; extend; project. **5.** To hunt game, for example, with a weapon: *shoot in the marshes.* **6.** To put forth new growth; germinate; sprout. **7. a.** To take pictures; film. **b.** To start filming. **8.** To propel a ball, as by kicking or hitting, towards the goal. **9.** To move fast and low after pitching. Used of a ball. **10.** To begin questioning someone. Used in the imperative. —**shoot down. 1.** To bring down (an aircraft, for example) by hitting and damaging with a missile. **2.** *Informal.* **a.** To ruin the plans, hopes, aspirations of, as by penetrating argument. **b.** To show (a plan or idea, for example) to be impractical or invalid. —**shoot through.** *Australian Informal.* To go away; depart. —**shoot up. 1.** *Informal.* **a.** To grow or get taller rapidly. **b.** To rise or increase rapidly. **2.** *Informal.* To hit many times with shot or other projectiles. **3.** *Informal.* To terrorise (an area) by lawless, wild shooting. **4.** *Slang.* To inject a narcotic drug directly into a vein. ~*n.* **1.** The motion or movement of something that is shot; a forward or upward advance. **2. a.** The young growth arising from a germinating seed; a sprout. **b.** A bud or young leaf on a plant. **3.** Any new growing part. **4.** A narrow and swift or turbulent section of a stream; a rapid. **5.** See **chute. 6. a.** A party or expedition engaged in shooting game. **b.** Land where game may be shot. **7.** *Informal.* The launching of a rocket or similar missile. **8.** An act of or occasion for filming. **9.** In rowing, the interval between strokes. —**the whole shoot.** Everything. [Middle English *shoten,* past *shote,* past participle *shote(n),* Old English *scēotan, scēat* (past singular), *scoten.*]

shoot-er (shōōtər) *n.* **1.** One that shoots. **2.** *Slang.* A firearm.

shoot-ing box (shōōting) *n. British.* A small house for the use of those engaged in shooting game. Also called "shooting lodge".

shooting brake *n. British.* An **estate car** *(see).*

shooting gallery *n.* An enclosed target range for shooting practice or competition.

shooting iron *n. U.S. Informal.* A firearm, such as a pistol.

shooting star *n.* A briefly visible **meteor** *(see).*

shooting script *n.* A script giving details of camerawork, including the order in which sequences are to be shot.

shooting stick *n.* A type of walking stick opening into a seat at one end, typically used by spectators at a shoot.

shooting war *n.* A war in which hostilities have reached the point of open military aggression as opposed to the use of diplomatic or economic sanctions, for example.

shoot-out (shōōt-owt) *n.* A confrontation in which armed opponents fire guns at one another.

shop (shop) *n.* **1.** A place, such as a building or room, where retail goods or certain services may be obtained. **2.** A workshop for the

shoebill *The capacious beak of the shoebill, also known as the shoebilled stork, helps the bird to forage for lungfish, frogs, and baby crocodiles in the swamps of East Africa, where it lives.*

shofar *An ancient Hebrew instrument made from a ram's horn and used originally to sound a warning or summons. Today, it is used ceremonially at Jewish religious festivals.*

manufacture or repair of machinery, for example: *a machine shop*. **3.** *Informal.* **a.** Any commercial or industrial establishment. **b.** A business or other similar activity: *set up shop; close up shop*. —**all over the shop.** *British Informal.* **1.** In a state of confusion or disarray. **2.** In every place; everywhere. —**talk shop.** To talk about one's business or occupation, especially to the exclusion of other topics. —See Usage note at **store.**
~*v.* **shopped, shopping, shops.** —*intr.* To visit shops for the purpose of looking for and buying goods. Often used with *for*. —*tr. British Slang.* To betray to the police. —**shop around. 1.** To investigate the different prices and quality of certain goods before deciding on a purchase. **2.** To investigate a number of possibilities before deciding on a course of action. [Middle English *shoppe*, Old English *sceoppa*, booth, stall, from Germanic *skupp-* (unattested).]
shop floor *n.* **1.** The area, in a factory for example, where manual workers, as opposed to management, operate. **2.** These workers, especially when organised as a union. —**shop-floor** (shóp-flór) *adj.*
shophar. Variant of **shofar.**
shop·keep·er (shóp-keepər) *n.* An owner or manager of a shop.
shop·lift·er (shóp-liftər) *n.* One who steals goods on display in a shop. —**shop·lift** *v.* —**shop·lift·ing** *n.*
shop·per (shóppər) *n.* One who buys goods at shops; a customer.
shop·ping (shópping) *n.* Items purchased from shops.
shopping centre *n.* The part of a town or suburban area providing a group of shops situated close together.
shop·soiled (shóp-soyld) *adj. British.* **1.** Faded, worn, or in some other state of deterioration as a result of being on display in a shop. **2.** Unfavourably marked by experience.
shop steward *n.* A union member chosen by fellow workers to represent them in their dealings with the management.
shop·talk (shóp-tawk) *n. Chiefly U.S.* Talk or conversation concerning one's business or occupation.
shop·walker (shóp-wawkər) *n. British.* An employee of a department store who supervises sales personnel and assists customers. Also *U.S.* "floor walker".
shop·worn (shóp-wawrn) *adj. U.S.* **1.** Shopsoiled; faded or worn. **2.** Trite; hackneyed: *shopworn anecdotes.*
sho·ran (sháwr-an ‖ shór-) *n.* A relatively short-range radar navigation system by which a ship or aircraft can determine its position with high precision by measuring the times required for a radio signal to reach each of two ground stations of known position and to return. [*Sho*rt *ra*nge *n*avigation.]
shore¹ (shor ‖ shōr) *n.* **1.** The land along the edge of an ocean, sea, lake, or river. **2.** Land: *set foot on shore.* **3.** *Often plural.* A country: *When will you see these shores again?* **4.** *Law.* See **foreshore.**
~*tr.v.* **shored, shoring, shores.** To put or set on shore. [Middle English, from Middle Dutch and Middle Low German *schore†*.]
shore² *tr.v.* **shored, shoring, shores.** To prop up or support with or as if with an inclined timber. Usually used with *up*.
~*n.* A beam or timber propped against a ship, wall, or other structure as a temporary support. [Middle English, *shoren*, from Middle Dutch *schōren†*.]
shore³. *Archaic.* Past tense of **shear.**
shore bird *n.* Any of various birds, such as the sandpiper, plover, or snipe, that frequent the shores of coastal or inland waters. Also called "wader".
shore leave *n.* **1.** Permission granted to a sailor to spend time ashore. **2.** The amount of time so allowed.
shore·line (shór-līn ‖ *U.S.* also shōr-) *n.* The line marking the edge of a body of water.
shor·ing (shór-ing ‖ shōr-) *n.* A system of shores or props used for supporting something.
shorn. Alternative past participle of **shear.**
short (short) *adj.* **shorter, shortest. 1.** Having little length; not long: *a short corridor; short arms.* **2.** Having little height; not tall; low: *Jockeys must be short.* **3.** Having a small extent in time; brief. **4.** Not attaining that which is required; inadequate; insufficient: *in short supply.* **5.** Lacking the required length, extent, or amount: *a plank two inches short.* **6.** Lacking; inadequately supplied with something: *I'm short of cash.* **7.** Not lengthy; concise; succinct: *short and to the point.* **8.** *Finance.* **a.** Not owning the stocks or commodities one is selling. **b.** Pertaining to or designating a sale of stocks or goods not yet owned by the seller, but which he must produce to meet the terms of a contract. **9.** Lacking in retentiveness: *a short memory.* **10.** Rudely brief; abrupt; curt. **11.** Containing shortening; crisp; friable: *short pastry.* **12.** In prosody, designating a syllable that is of relatively brief duration in classical verse and unstressed in English verse. **13.** *Phonetics.* **a.** Designating a particular pronunciation of the letters for the vowel sounds, such as the sound of (a) in *pan*, of (e) in *pen*, of (i) in *pin*, of (o) in *pond*, of (ŏŏ) in *put*, and of (u) in *putt*, as distinguished from the sound of (ay) in *pane*, of (ee) in *penal*, of (ī) in *pine*, of (ō) in *post*, and of (ōō) in *poop*. **b.** Designating a speech sound of relatively brief duration, as opposed to the same or similar sound of relatively long duration. **14.** In cricket: **a.** Designating a fielder or fielding position close to the batsman. **b.** Designating a bowled ball that lands some distance from the batsman. —See Usage note at **brief.** —**for short.** As an abbreviated form: *My name is Robert, but call me Rob for short.* —**in short.** To sum up concisely. —**short and sweet.** Brief and to the point, especially when contrary to expectation: *Fortunately, the negotiations were short and sweet.* —**short for.** In shortened form: *"Jim" is short for "James".* —**short of. 1.** Not equivalent to; less than: *something short of a mile.* **2.** Lacking a sufficient amount of:

short of breath. **3.** Without reaching an extreme of; almost including: *took every step short of mining his back garden.* **4.** Except for; apart from: *Short of buying a car, I don't know how I'll get in to work.* —**short on.** Lacking in: *short on ideas.*
~*adv.* **1.** Abruptly; suddenly: *stop short.* **2.** Rudely; crossly. **3.** Concisely. **4.** Without owning what one is selling: *sell short.* —**caught** or **taken short. 1.** Unexpectedly lacking what is necessary. **2.** Having a sudden need to urinate or defecate. —**fall short.** To fail to meet expectations or requirements.
~*n.* **1.** Anything that is short, especially: **a.** A briefly articulated or unaccented syllable. **b.** A short vowel. **c.** A short sale, or a person who sells short. **d.** *Plural.* Short trousers extending to the knee or above. **e.** *Plural. U.S.* Men's underpants. **f.** A short film shown before the main feature film. **2.** *Plural.* A by-product of wheat processing, consisting of bran mixed with coarse meal or flour. **3.** A strong drink of an alcoholic spirit, especially one that is undiluted. **4. a.** A short circuit. **b.** A malfunction caused by a short circuit.
~*v.* **shorted, shorting, shorts.** —*tr.* To cause a short circuit in. ~*intr.* To short-circuit. [Middle English *short*, Old English *sceort*, from Germanic *skurtaz* (unattested).] —**short·ish** *adj.* —**short·ness** *n.*
short account *n.* The account of a person who sells short.
short·age (shórtij) *n.* A deficiency in amount; a deficit.
short-arm (shórt-aarm) *adj.* Designating a blow in which the arm is kept in a bent position rather than punched out straight.
short·bread (shórt-bred) *n.* A type of rich, crumbly biscuit made with flour, sugar, and butter.
short·cake (shórt-kayk) *n.* **1.** A type of rich semisweet biscuit, similar to shortbread. **2.** A dessert consisting of a cake made with rich biscuit dough, split and filled with strawberries or other fruit, and topped with cream.
short-change (shórt-cháynj) *tr.v.* **-changed, -changing, -changes. 1.** To give less change than is due. **2.** *Informal.* To swindle, cheat, or trick. —**short-chang·er** *n.*
short circuit *n.* An accidentally established low-resistance connection between two points in an electric circuit that bypasses the load and causes an excessive current to flow. Also called "short".
short-cir·cuit (shórt-súrkit ‖ -surkit) *v.* **-cuited, -cuiting, -cuits.** —*tr.* **1.** To cause to have a short circuit. **2.** To avoid; bypass. —*intr.* To become affected with a short circuit.
short·com·ing (shórt-kumming, -kúmming) *n.* A deficiency or flaw.
short covering *n.* The buying of securities, stocks, or commodities to make provision for a short sale.
short·crust pastry (shórt-krust) *n.* Pastry made from flour and a shortening, such as fat or butter, which, when cooked, has a brittle, dense texture, as opposed to flaky or puff pastry.
short cut *n.* **1.** A quicker, more direct route than the customary one. **2.** Any means of speeding up a process: *Becoming famous is a short-cut to getting your book published.*
short-dat·ed (shórt-dáytid) *adj. Finance.* Designating gilt-edged securities redeemable after a time less than five years away. Compare **long-dated, medium-dated.**
short-day (shórt-dáy) *adj.* Designating or producing plants that will flower only when exposed to periods of daylight of less than 12 hours: *short-day seeds.* Compare **long-day.**
short division *n.* A division of one number by another, usually no more than two digits, without writing out the remainders.
short·en (shórt'n) *v.* **-ened, -ening, -ens.** —*tr.* **1.** To make short or shorter. **2.** To take in (a sail) so that less canvas is exposed to the wind. **3.** To cause to come down or decrease: *shortened the odds.* **4.** To add shortening to (dough) so as to produce a crumbly texture. —*intr.* **1.** To become short or shorter. **2.** To decrease; lessen.
short·en·ing (shórt'n-ing) *n.* A fat, such as butter, lard, or vegetable oil, used to make cake or pastry light or flaky.
short·fall (shórt-fawl) *n.* **1.** A failure to attain a required amount or level; a shortage; a deficiency. **2.** The amount by which a supply falls short of expectation, need, or demand.
short·hand (shórt-hand) *n.* **1. a.** A system of rapid handwriting employing symbols to represent words, phrases, and letters; stenography. **b.** The handwriting itself. **2.** Any system, form, or instance of abbreviated or formulaic reference: *"The classical error is to regard a scientific law as only a shorthand for its instances."* (Jacob Bronowski). —**short·hand** *adj.*
short·hand·ed (shórt-hándid) *adj.* Lacking the usual or necessary number of workmen, employees, or assistants.
shorthand typist *n.* A typist who records speech in shorthand and then transcribes it on a typewriter. Also *U.S.* "stenographer".
short-haul (shórt-háwl) *adj.* Involving or designating the transport of goods or passengers over short distances.
short·horn (shórt-hawrn) *n.* Any of a breed of beef or dairy cattle originating in northern England and having short, curved horns. Also called "Durham".
short hundredweight *n.* A hundredweight (see).
shor·tie, shor·ty (shórti) *n. Informal.* A short person or thing. ~*adj. Informal.* Short in length: *a shortie jacket.*
short list *n. British.* A list of names of the most likely candidates, as for a job or position, who have been selected from the larger number of original applicants.
short-list (shórt-líst-, -list) *tr.v.* **-listed, -listing, -lists.** *British.* To put (a person) on a short list.
short-lived (shórt-lívd ‖ *U.S.* also -lĭvd) *adj.* Living or lasting only a short time; ephemeral.

short·ly (shórtli) adv. **1.** In a short time; soon; presently. **2.** In a few words; concisely. **3.** Abruptly or curtly.

short-range (shórt-ráynj) adj. Of or having a limited range in distance or time: a short-range forecast.

short shrift n. **1.** Summary and unsympathetic treatment or dismissal. **2.** Archaic. The short space of time granted a condemned prisoner for his confession before execution. —**make short shrift of** or **give short shrift to. 1.** To dispose of summarily or without consideration. **2.** To make quick work of; dispatch.

short·sight·ed (shórt-sítid) adj. **1.** Suffering from myopia; near-sighted. **2.** Lacking foresight. **3.** Resulting from a lack of foresight. —**short·sight·ed·ly** adv. —**short·sight·ed·ness** n.

short·spo·ken (shórt-spóken) adj. Given to shortness or abruptness in manner or speech; curt.

short story n. A piece of fictional prose much shorter than a novel and typically concentrating on a single event, situation, or character.

short-tem·pered (shórt-témpərd) adj. Easily moved to anger.

short-term (shórt-térm) adj. **1.** Lasting or extending for a relatively short period of time: short-term measures. **2.** Payable or reaching maturity within a relatively short time: a short-term loan.

short ton n. A unit of weight, a **ton** (see).

short-waisted (shórt-wáystid) adj. Having or being of less than average length from shoulders to waist: a short-waisted dress.

short wave n. Abbr. **sw** An electromagnetic wave with wavelength in the short-wave region.

short-wave (shórt-wáyv) adj. Abbr. **sw 1.** Having a wavelength in the range 10 to 100 metres. **2.** Capable of receiving or transmitting at such wavelengths.

short-wind·ed (shórt-windid) adj. **1.** Having shortness of breath; easily winded. **2.** Not discursive; brief: a short-winded speech.

shorty. Variant of **shortie**.

Sho·sho·ne (shō-shóni, shə-) n., pl. **-nes** or collectively **Shoshone**. Also **Sho·sho·ni. 1.** A member of a Uto-Aztecan-speaking North American Indian people, formerly occupying parts of the American West. **2.** The language of this people.

Sho·sho·ne·an (shō-shóni-ən, shə-, shóshə-née-ən) n. An Indian linguistic group in western North America, comprising most of the Uto-Aztecan languages found in the United States. —**Sho·sho·ne·an** adj.

Shos·ta·ko·vitch (shóstə-kóvich), **Dmitri Dmitrievich** (1906–75). Russian composer, one of the most prolific and most widely acclaimed of the 20th century. He wrote in all forms, but is perhaps best known for his 15 symphonies and his chamber music.

shot[1] (shot) n., pl. **shots** or **shot** (for sense 2). **1.** A firing or discharge of a weapon, such as a gun or bow. **2. a.** Tiny pellets, especially made of lead, discharged from a shotgun in one charge. **b.** Any of these pellets. **c.** A projectile, such as an iron ball, fired from a cannon, for example. **3.** In certain games, such as soccer, snooker, golf, or tennis, a hit or kick of the ball. **4.** One who shoots, considered with regard to the accuracy of his aim: a good shot. **5.** The distance over which something is shot; range. **6.** An attempt to hit or land on something with a weapon or rocket: a moon shot. **7.** Informal. An attempt, guess, or opportunity: had a shot at playing bridge. **8.** The heavy metal ball that an athlete throws in the shot-put. **9.** Mining. A charge of explosives used in blasting. **10. a.** A photograph or one in a series of photographs. **b.** A single cinematic view or take. **11.** Informal. A hypodermic injection. **12.** Informal. A drink of spirits, especially a jigger. **13.** Nautical. A unit designating chain length, in the United Kingdom equal to 12½ fathoms and in the United States equal to 15 fathoms. —**by a long shot.** By a considerable extent or margin. —**get shot of.** Informal. To lose, shake off, or get rid of. —**like a shot.** Quickly; in an instant. —**shot in the arm.** That which revives or stimulates: a shot in the arm for the industry. —**shot in the dark.** A completely wild guess. ~tr.v. **shotted, shotting, shots.** To load or weight with shot. [Middle English shot, Old English sceot.]

shot[2] adj. **1.** Of changeable, variegated, or iridescent colour. Said of fabric having different-coloured warp and weft. **2.** Informal. Worn-out; ruined; exhausted. —**shot through with.** Filled or riddled with: a poem shot through with vivid imagery.

shot[3]. Past tense and past participle of **shoot**.

shote. Variant of **shoat**.

shot·gun (shót-gun) n. A shoulder-held firearm that fires multiple pellets through a smooth bore.

shotgun wedding n. A wedding which one or both of the partners are forced to enter into, especially as a consequence of the woman becoming pregnant. Also called "shotgun marriage". [Alluding to the bride's father or relatives armed to force the groom to marry.]

shot hole n. A hole drilled into rock or other material into which an explosive charge is inserted for blasting purposes.

shot-put (shót-pòot) n. **1.** An athletic event in which the contestants attempt to throw or put a shot or heavy ball as far as possible. **2.** One such throw. —**shot-put·ter** n.

shott (shot) n. Also **chott** (chott). **1.** A shallow intermittent salt lake or salt marsh in a hot desert. **2.** The depression or hollow occupied by such a salt lake or salt marsh.

shot·ten (shótt'n) adj. **1.** Having recently spawned and being thus less desirable as food. Said of fish, especially herring. **2.** Archaic. Of no value; worthless. [Archaic past participle of **shoot** (specialised sense "to spawn").]

shot tower n. A tower formerly used for making lead shot by dropping molten lead from the top into water at the bottom.

should (shōod; weak forms shəd, shd, sht). Past tense of **shall**, but more often used as an auxiliary verb expressing various shades of attendant meaning indicating: **1.** Obligation; duty; necessity: They should tell him the bad news. **2.** Anticipation of a probable occurrence; expectation: They should arrive at noon. **3.** Condition; contingency of one condition upon another: Should he so much as move, shoot him dead. **4.** Moderation of the directness or bluntness of a request or statement: I should like to query that figure. **5.** An implication of the unusual or surprising: Who should I bump into in the street but my ex-husband! **6.** A piece of advice: I should apologise if I were you. **7.** Informal. An ironic negative, asserting the negative in a positive way: With his talent, he should worry (meaning should not worry) about winning!

Usage: Traditional grammars argue that a distinction needs to be maintained between would and should parallel to that recommended for will and shall: should is to be used in first person forms for the expression of simple conditionality, would in second and third person forms; and the opposite situation obtains when other meanings (such as determination or compulsion) are to be expressed. In practice, this distinction is hardly ever maintained. American English uses would with all three persons for expressing conditionality, and prefers this form to should. British English usage is mixed: older people and more formal styles still maintain should, especially in the first person; younger people generally use would. Thus we find If I had the money, I would go or I would like to go (American English and some British English) and If I had the money, I should go or I should like to go (more formal British English). In referring to past time, both the following constructions occur without any difference in meaning: I would/should like to have gone, I would/should have liked to go. The double use of have, as in I would/should have liked to have gone, is not standard though it will sometimes be heard in casual speech. If I would have found it . . . is a possible construction in informal American English, but in British English a construction with had is standard (If I had found it . . .). See also Usage notes at **shall, ought**.

shoul·der (shóldər) n. **1.** Anatomy. **a.** The part of the human body between the neck and upper arm. **b.** The joint connecting the arm with the trunk. **2.** The corresponding part of an animal. **3.** Plural. **a.** The two shoulders and the area of the back between them. **b.** This area of the back considered as the part to bear burdens. **4.** The forequarter of some animals. **5.** The part of a garment that covers the shoulder. **6.** The angle between the face and the flank of a bastion in fortifications. **7.** Printing. The extended flat surface on the body of type beyond the letter or character. **8.** A cut of meat, as lamb, consisting of the top part of the foreleg. **9. a.** The edge or ridge running on either side of a main road. **b.** Any projection or slope that resembles a shoulder in shape. —**rub shoulders with.** Informal. To meet or associate with. —**shoulder to shoulder.** United in a common cause or effort. —**straight from the shoulder.** With utter frankness.

~v. **shouldered, -dering, -ders.** —tr. **1.** To carry (a burden, for example) on or as on the shoulders; bear or support; assume. **2.** To push (one's way) through, with or as if with the shoulder. **3.** To apply force to with or as if with the shoulder. —intr. To push with the shoulder or shoulders. [Middle English shulder, Old English sculdor, from Germanic skuldra- (unattested).]

shoulder bag n. A handbag or travelling bag that is supported by means of a long strap passing over the shoulder.

shoulder blade n. The **scapula** (see).

shoulder girdle n. The **pectoral girdle** (see).

shoulder patch n. A military identification patch worn on the upper portion of the sleeve to designate one's regiment, for example.

shoulder strap n. **1.** A strap attached to the shoulder of a military uniform to show rank. **2.** A strap that fits over the shoulder, such as one that supports a garment.

should·n't (shōod'nt). Contraction of should not.

shouldst (shōodst). Also **should·est** (shōodist). Archaic. Second person singular past tense of **shall**. Used with thou.

shout (showt) n. **1.** A loud, vigorous, cry, often expressing strong emotion or a command. **2.** Chiefly Australian Informal. A person's turn to buy drinks; a round.

~v. **shouted, shouting, shouts.** —tr. **1.** To utter with a shout. **2.** Chiefly Australian Informal. **a.** To treat (a person) to a round of drinks, for example. **b.** To treat a person to (a round of drinks). —intr. **1.** To utter a loud cry; yell. **2.** To speak or laugh loudly. —**shout down.** To overwhelm or silence by shouting loudly. [Middle English shouten†.] —**shout·er** n.

shove (shuv) v. **shoved, shoving, shoves.** —tr. **1.** To cause to move with a sudden push or thrust. **2.** To push roughly or rudely; jostle. **3.** Informal. To put or place somewhere. —intr. To push rudely or roughly or with sudden force. —**shove off. 1.** To set a beached boat afloat. **2.** Informal. To leave. Often used in the imperative. ~n. The act of shoving; especially, a rude push. [Middle English sho(u)ven, Old English scūfan, from Germanic.] —**shov·er** n.

shove-half·pen·ny (shóv-háyp-əni) n. British. A game in which players try to propel old halfpennies along a marked wooden board so that they land between any two parallel lines.

shov·el (shúvv'l) n. **1.** A tool with a handle and a somewhat flattened scoop for picking up earth, coal, or other materials. **2.** A large mechanical device for heavy digging or excavation, usually a jawed scoop suspended from a boom or crane. **3.** Informal. A shovel hat.

~v. **shovelled** or U.S. **shoveled, -elling** or U.S. **-eling, -els.** —tr.

shoveler *Named for its spadelike bill, the shoveler uses the beak as a sieve, straining weeds and insects from the water in ponds and lakes. Unlike most dabbling ducks, the shoveler rarely up-ends its body to pick up food under the water, but it may dive when alarmed. The birds breed in Europe, Asia, and North America, and some migrate for part of the year to Central America and southern Africa.*

shrew *Although shrews are the smallest of mammals, they have big appetites: some species have to eat their own body-weight in food every day, and will resort to cannibalism. Their main defence against predators – a foul-smelling secretion – deters carnivorous mammals, but not birds of prey. This is the greater white-toothed shrew,* Crocidura russula.

1. To dig into or move with a shovel. **2.** To clear or make (a path, for example) with a shovel. **3.** To convey roughly or in large quantities, as with a shovel: *shovelled cake into her mouth.* —*intr.* To dig or work with a shovel. [Middle English *shovel,* Old English *scofl,* from Germanic.] —**shov·el·ler** *n.*

shovelboard. Variant of **shuffleboard.**

shov·el·er (shúvv'l-ər, shúvvlər) *n.* A widely distributed duck, *Anas clypeata,* having a long, broad bill.

shov·el·ful (shúvv'l-fo͝ol) *n., pl.* **-fuls.** The amount a shovel will hold.

shovel hat *n.* A stiff, broad-brimmed, low-crowned hat, turned up at the sides and projecting in front, formerly worn by some clergymen. Also informally called "shovel".

shov·el·head (shúvv'l-hed) *n.* A shark, *Sphyrna tiburo,* of Atlantic and Pacific waters.

shov·el-nosed (shúvv'l-nōzd) *adj.* Having a broad, flattened snout, bill, or head.

show (shō) *v.* **showed, shown** (shōn || shṓ-ən) or **showed, showing, shows.** —*tr.* **1. a.** To cause or allow to be seen; make visible: *a white carpet shows the dirt; showed her talent.* **b.** To present to the view of: *She showed me her operation scar.* **c.** To exhibit or present to the public: *Which film is being shown at the Plaza?* **d.** To present (an animal of a recognised breed) for judging in a competitive exhibition. **2.** To conduct; guide: *Show me round your garden.* **3. a.** To point out; demonstrate. **b.** To make clear; prove. **c.** To teach by practical demonstration: *Show me how to knit.* **4. a.** To manifest; reveal. **b.** To indicate; register. **5.** To grant; confer; bestow: *showed great devotion to the cause.* **6.** *Law.* To plead; allege: *show cause.* —*intr.* **1.** To be or become visible or evident: *If you're nervous, it certainly doesn't show.* **2.** To appear: *His face showed red.* **3.** To be exhibited; run: *The film will show for three days.* **4.** *Informal.* To make an appearance; show up. **5.** *Sports. U.S.* To finish third or better for betting purposes. —**show for.** As evidence of gain, as from a course of action: *nothing to show for my efforts.* —**show up. 1.** To expose or reveal (faults, flaws, or the like). **2.** To be clearly or ultimately visible: *The white shows up well against the dark background..* **3.** *Informal.* To put in an appearance; arrive. **4.** *Informal.* To cause to feel shame or inferiority.

~*n.* **1.** The act of showing or revealing. **2. a.** A display; a manifestation; a demonstration: *a show of force.* **b.** An outward appearance; a semblance: *A show of kindness concealed her diabolical motives.* **4.** A striking appearance or display; a spectacle. **5.** A pompous or ostentatious display: *It's all done for show.* **6. a.** A public exhibition or competition: *a flower show.* **b.** An entertainment such as a play or film: *a television show.* **7. a.** A trace; an indication. **b.** In obstetrics, a discharge of blood occurring at the start of labour. **8.** *Informal.* Any affair or undertaking: *Who is supposed to be running this show?* **9.** *Informal.* An attempt or try; an effort: *put up a bad show.* **10.** *Sports. U.S.* Third place or better for betting purposes: *win, place, and show.* —**good** (or **bad**) **show.** Used to express approval (or disapproval). —**show of hands.** A raising of hands among the members of a group so that a vote may be taken. —**steal the show.** *Informal.* To gain the greatest amount of adulation or applause.

~*adj.* Of, in, or used for a show or shows. [Middle English *shewen, showen,* to look at, cause to look at, show, Old English *scēawian,* to look at, see, from Germanic.] —**show·er** (shṓ-ər) *n.*

Synonyms: *show, display, expose, parade, exhibit, flaunt.*

show bill *n.* An advertising poster.

show biz *n. Slang.* Show business.

show·boat (shṓ-bōt) *n.* Especially in the United States, a river steamboat having a troupe of actors and a theatre on board giving performances on the river.

showbread. Variant of **shewbread.**

show business *n.* The entertainment business, especially that part of it concerned with theatre and films.

show·case (shṓ-kayss) *n.* **1.** A display case or cabinet, as in a shop or museum. **2.** A setting in which something may be displayed to advantage: *The Great War was a showcase for the effectiveness of tanks.*

show·down (shṓ-down) *n.* **1.** *Informal.* A confrontation that forces a disputed issue to a conclusion. **2.** In card games such as poker, the laying down of the players' hands of cards for the purpose of determining the winner.

show·er (showr, shów-ər) *n.* **1.** A brief fall of rain, hail, snow, or sleet. **2.** Any brief or sudden fall resembling a spray or shower: *a meteor shower.* **3.** An abundant flow; an outpouring: *a shower of abuse.* **4.** A stream of elementary particles resulting from the impact of a high-energy particle, especially a cosmic-ray particle, on a target particle **5.** *British Slang.* A group of untidy, ill-assorted people. **6.** *U.S.* A party held to honour and present gifts to someone, especially a bride-to-be. **7. a.** A bath in which water is sprayed onto the bather by means of a device, usually situated overhead. **b.** A device so used to spray water, usually having a nozzle through which fine jets of water may pass. **c.** A room or cubicle equipped for such baths. Also called "shower bath".

~*v.* **showered, -ering, -ers.** —*tr.* **1.** To sprinkle; spray. **2. a.** To bestow on abundantly: *showered her with gifts.* **b.** To present in abundance: *showered gifts on her.* —*intr.* **1.** To fall or pour down in a shower. **2.** To have a shower bath. [Middle English *shour,* Old English *scūr,* from Germanic.] —**show·er·y** *adj.*

show·er·proof (shów-ər-pro͞of) *adj. British.* Able to repel water, though not fully waterproof. —**show·er·proof** *tr.v.*

show·girl (shṓ-gurl) *n.* A chorus girl or similar entertainer as opposed to a serious actress.

show·ing (shṓ-ing) *n.* **1.** A performance, as in a competition or test of skill: *a poor showing.* **2.** A presentation of evidence, facts, or figures: *On the present showing he will pass easily.*

show·jump·ing (shṓ-jumping) *n.* A horseriding competition in which competitors must complete a course of fences and obstacles and are judged on the number of errors committed and sometimes on time taken. —**show·jump·er** *n.*

show·man (shṓ-mən) *n., pl.* **-men** (-mən, -men). **1.** A theatrical producer. **2.** A person whose behaviour displays a flair for showiness or the dramatic. —**show·man·ship** *n.*

shown. Past participle of **show.**

show off *tr.v.* To display in such a way as to invite admiration. —*intr.v. Informal.* To behave like a show-off.

show-off (shṓ-off, -awf) *n. Informal.* One who self-confidently displays his talent or ability, especially to an excessive degree.

show·piece (shṓ-peess) *n.* **1.** An exhibition piece. **2.** That which is exemplary of its kind.

show·place (shṓ-playss) *n.* A place that is visited for its beauty, historical interest, or the like.

show·room (shṓ-ro͞om, -ro͝om) *n.* A room in which goods are on display.

show stopper *n. Informal.* **1.** A person or event, such as a theatrical act, that receives enthusiastic applause and so causes a short interruption in the proceedings. **2.** Broadly, anything that receives instant and enthusiastic admiration or approval.

show trial *n.* A public judicial trial that is primarily designed to serve the propaganda needs of a regime.

show·y (shṓ-i) *adj.* **-ier, -iest. 1.** Making a conspicuous display; striking: *showy flowers.* **2.** Displaying brilliance and virtuosity of ability or performance. **3.** Ostentatious; gaudy; flashy. —See Synonyms at **ornate.** —**show·i·ly** *adv.* —**show·i·ness** *n.*

shpt. shipment.

Shquiperi. See **Albania, Socialist People's Republic of.**

shr *Finance.* share.

shrank. Past tense of **shrink.**

shrap·nel (shrápnəl) *n. Military.* **1. a.** An antipersonnel projectile containing metal balls, fused to explode in the air above enemy troops. **b.** These projectiles collectively. **2.** Shell fragments from any high-explosive shell. [After Henry *Shrapnel* (1761–1842), British artillery officer who invented it.]

shred (shred) *n.* **1.** A long, thin, irregular strip cut or torn off. **2.** A small amount; a particle; a scrap: *not a shred of evidence.*

~*tr.v.* **shredded** or **shred, shredding, shreds.** To cut or tear into shreds. [Middle English *shrede,* Old English *scrēade.*] —**shred·der** *n.*

shrew (shro͞o || shrew) *n.* **1.** Any of various small, chiefly insectivorous mammals of the family Soricidae, having a long, pointed nose and small, often poorly developed eyes. Sometimes called "shrewmouse". **2.** A woman with a violent, scolding, or nagging temperament; a scold. [Middle English *shrewe* (unattested), Old English *scrēawa.*]

shrewd (shro͞od || shrewd) *adj.* **shrewder, shrewdest. 1.** Having or showing keen insight; sharp; astute: *a shrewd political commentator.* **2.** Having experience, cleverness, and cunning, especially in practical affairs: *a shrewd businessman.* —See Synonyms at **clever.** [Middle English *shrewed(e),* wicked, dangerous, serious, from SHREW (evil person).] —**shrewd·ly** *adv.* —**shrewd·ness** *n.*

Synonyms: *shrewd, sagacious, astute, quick-witted.*

shrew·ish (shro͞o-ish || shréw-) *adj.* Like a shrew in temperament; ill-tempered; nagging. —**shrew·ish·ly** *adv.* —**shrew·ish·ness** *n.*

shrew mole *n.* Any of several shrewlike moles of the family Talpidae; especially, *Neurotrichus gibbsi,* of western North America, or *Uropsilus soricipes,* of eastern Asia.

Shrews·bur·y (shrṓz-bri, -bəri || shro͞oz-, shréwz-). County town of Shropshire in western England, lying on the river Severn.

shriek (shreek) *n.* **1.** A shrill outcry; a high-pitched scream; a screech. **2.** Any sound suggestive of a shriek.

~*v.* **shrieked, shrieking, shrieks.** —*intr.* **1.** To utter a shriek. **2.** To make a shrill sound similar to a shriek: *"the winds shriek through the clouds"* (Ezra Pound). —*tr.* To utter with a shriek. —See Synonyms at **scream.** [Middle English *shriken* (imitative), probably from Old Norse *skrækja.*] —**shriek·er** *n.*

shriev·al·ty (shréev'lti) *n.* The office, tenure, or jurisdiction of a sheriff. —**shrie·val** *adj.*

shrift (shrift) *n. Archaic.* **1.** The act of shriving. **2.** Confession or absolution given by a priest. **3.** See **short shrift.** [Middle English *shrift(e),* Old English *scrift,* from *scrīfan,* to SHRIVE.]

shrike (shrīk) *n.* **1.** Any of various carnivorous birds of the genus *Lanis,* having a hooked bill, and often impaling its prey on sharp-pointed thorns or barbs of wire fencing. Some species are also called "butcherbird". **2.** Any of various similar but unrelated birds. [Probably from Middle English *shrik* (unattested), from Old English *scrīc,* thrush (imitative).]

shrill (shril) *adj.* **shriller, shrillest. 1.** High-pitched and piercing. **2.** Producing a sharp, high-pitched tone or sound. **3.** Insistently nagging or sharp in tone: *shrill attacks on the government.*

~*v.* **shrilled, shrilling, shrills.** —*tr.* To utter in a shrill manner; scream; shriek. —*intr.* To produce a shrill cry or sound. [Middle English *shrille,* from *shrillen,* to shriek, perhaps from Scandinavian; akin to Norwegian *skrylla.*] —**shrill·ness** *n.* —**shril·ly** *adv.*

shrimp (shrimp) *n., pl.* **shrimps** or collectively **shrimp. 1. a.** Any of various small, slender-bodied, chiefly marine decapod crustaceans of the order Crangon, many species of which are edible. **b.** Any of various similar unrelated crustaceans. **2.** *Informal.* A diminutive or unimportant person.

~intr.v. **shrimped, shrimping, shrimps.** To fish for shrimps. [Middle English *shrimpe,* pigmy, shrimp, perhaps of Low German origin; akin to Middle Low German *schrempen,* to shrink, wrinkle.]

shrimp plant *n.* A shrubby plant, *Beloperone guttata,* having inconspicuous flowers borne between shrimp-like reddish bracts.

shrine (shrīn) *n.* **1.** A container or receptacle for sacred relics; a reliquary. **2.** The tomb of a saint or other venerated person. **3.** A site, as a church, or an object, as an altar, devoted to a holy person. **4.** Any place hallowed by a venerated person or object, or their associations.

~tr.v. **shrined, shrining, shrines.** To enshrine. [Middle English *shrin(e),* box, chest, reliquary, Old English *scrīn,* from Latin *scrīnium*†, box, bookcase.]

shrink (shringk) *v.* **shrank** (shrangk) or **shrunk** (shrungk), **shrunk** or **shrunken** (shrúngkən), **shrinking, shrinks.** *—intr.* **1.** To draw together or constrict from heat, moisture, or cold; contract. Used especially of fabrics. **2.** To become reduced in amount or value; dwindle. **3.** To draw back; recoil, as through shyness: *shrank into the corner.* **4.** To be reluctant; flinch: *Shrank from the task of leading the charge.* *—tr.* To cause to shrink. —See Synonyms at **contract, decrease.**

~n. **1.** A shrinking or shrinkage. **2.** *Slang.* A psychiatrist or psychoanalyst. [Shrink, shrank, shrunk; Middle English *shrinken, shrank* (also *shrunk*), *shrunken,* Old English *scrincan, scranc* (plural *scruncon*), *(ge)scruncen.*] **—shrink·a·ble** *adj.* **—shrink·er** *n.*

Usage: This verb has two past tenses, *shrank* and *shrunk,* the former being more common. The past participle form is *shrunk. Shrunken* is occasionally used in this way, but generally this form is restricted to adjectival use *(a shrunken figure).*

shrink·age (shríngkij) *n.* **1.** The act or process of shrinking. **2.** A reduction or depreciation, as in value. **3.** The amount of weight lost by livestock, as during shipment, before being marketed.

shrink·ing violet (shríngking) *n. Informal.* A shy or retiring person.

shrink wrapping *n.* A transparent form-fitting plastic wrapping, especially of polythene or polyvinyl chloride, used to protect a commodity from dust, moisture, and abrasion.

shrink-wrap (shríngk-ráp, -rap) *tr.v.* **-wrapped, -wrapping, -wraps.** To enclose (an article) in shrink wrapping.

shrive (shrīv) *v.* **shrove** (shrōv) or **shrived, shriven** (shrívv'n) or **shrived, shriving, shrives.** *Archaic.* *—tr.* **1.** To hear the confession of and give absolution to (a penitent). **2.** To obtain absolution for (oneself) by confessing and doing penance. *—intr.* **1.** To make or go to confession. **2.** To hear confessions. [Shrive, shrove, shriven; Middle English *shriven, shrove, shriven,* Old English *scrīfan, scrāf* (past singular), *scrifen(e),* from West Germanic *skrīban* (unattested), to write, "prescribe (penance)", from Latin *scrībere,* to write.] **—shriv·er** *n.*

shriv·el (shrívv'l) *v.* **-elled** or *U.S.* **-eled, -elling** or *U.S.* **-eling, -els.** *—intr.* **1.** To shrink and wrinkle, often in drying. Often used with *up.* **2.** To lose vitality; become wasted and useless. *—tr.* To cause to become shrivelled. [Perhaps from Old Norse *skrīfla* (unattested), to wrinkle.]

Shrop·shire (shróp-shər, -sheer || -shīr). Formerly **Sal·op** (sáləp). Nonmetropolitan county of western England, lying on the Welsh border. It is predominantly agricultural, with plains to the north and east of the river Severn, and hills to the southwest. Shrewsbury is the county town.

shroud (shrowd) *n.* **1.** A cloth used to wrap a body for burial; a winding sheet. **2.** Something that conceals, protects, or screens: *a shroud of darkness.* **3.** *Plural.* A set of ropes or wire cables stretched from the masthead to a vessel's sides to support the mast. **4.** A similar support for a chimney or comparable structure. **5.** The ropes connecting the harness and canopy of a parachute.

~v. **shrouded, shrouding, shrouds.** *—tr.* **1.** To wrap (a corpse) in burial clothing. **2.** To envelop; screen; hide. **3.** *Archaic.* To shelter; protect. *—intr. Archaic.* To take cover; find shelter. [Middle English *sc(h)rud,* garment, clothing, Old English *scrūd,* from Germanic.]

shroud-laid (shrówd-layd) *adj.* Designating a rope made from four strands twisted to the right, usually round a core.

Shrove·tide (shrṓv-tid) *n.* The three days, Shrove Sunday, Shrove Monday, and Shrove Tuesday, preceding Ash Wednesday. [Middle English *schroftyde* : *schrof-,* "shriving", irregularly from *schrov-,* past stem of *shriven,* SHRIVE + *tyde, tid(e),* TIDE (time).]

Shrove Tuesday (shrōv) *n.* The day before Ash Wednesday, on which, in Britain, pancakes are traditionally eaten.

shrub[1] (shrub) *n.* A woody plant of relatively low height, distinguished from a tree by having several stems rather than a single trunk; a bush. [Middle English *schrubbe,* Old English *scrybb.*]

shrub[2] *n.* A drink made from fruit juice, sugar, and a spirit such as rum or brandy. [Arabic *shurb,* a drink, from *shariba,* to drink. See also **sherbet, syrup.**]

shrub·ber·y (shrúbbəri) *n., pl.* **-ies.** **1.** A group or plantation of shrubs. **2.** Shrubs collectively.

shrub·by (shrúbbi) *adj.* **-bier, -biest.** **1.** Consisting of, planted with, or covered with shrubs. **2.** Of or resembling a shrub; shrublike. **—shrub·bi·ness** *n.*

shrug (shrug) *v.* **shrugged, shrugging, shrugs.** *—tr.* To raise (the shoulders) as a gesture of doubt, disdain, or indifference. *—intr.* To make this gesture. **—shrug off.** **1.** To minimise the importance of. **2.** To get rid of without trouble: *shrug off a cold.*

~n. **1.** An act of shrugging. **2.** *U.S.* A short jacket or sweater, open down the front. [Middle English *shruggen*†.]

shrunk. Past participle and alternative past tense of **shrink.**

shrunken. Alternative past participle of **shrink.**

shtick (shtik) *n. U.S. Slang.* A characteristic talent or act of an entertainer. [Yiddish, probably from Middle High German *stich,* a thrust, puncture, from Old High German *stih.*]

shuck (shuk) *n. U.S.* The outer covering of something, such as a pea pod, maize husk, or oyster shell.

~tr.v. **shucked, shucking, shucks.** *U.S.* **1.** To remove the husk or shell from. **2.** *Informal.* To cast off (clothing, for example). [17th century : origin obscure.] **—shuck·er** *n.*

shucks (shuks) *interj. U.S.* Used to express disappointment, disgust, or annoyance. [From SHUCK (in U.S. sense "thing of no value").]

shud·der (shúddər) *intr.v.* **-dered, -dering, -ders.** **1.** To tremble or shiver convulsively, as from fear, cold, or aversion. **2.** To vibrate; quiver: *The engine shuddered to a halt.* —See Synonyms at **shake.**

~n. A convulsive shiver, as from fear or cold. [Middle English *shoddren, shudren,* from Middle Low German *schōderen.*] **—shud·der·ing·ly** *adv.*

shuf·fle (shúff'l) *v.* **-fled, -fling, -fles.** *—tr.* **1.** To move (the feet) in short dragging movements along the floor or ground while walking or dancing. **2.** To move back and forth or from one place to another. **3.** To mix together or otherwise handle (papers, for example) in a disordered, haphazard fashion. **4.** To put aside or conceal hastily; cover up: *Important issues were quickly shuffled off.* **5.** To mix together (playing cards, for example) to change the order of arrangement. *—intr.* **1.** To move by shuffling one's feet. **2.** To dance the shuffle. **3.** To shift about from side to side. **4.** To act in a shifty or deceitful manner; equivocate. **5.** To shuffle playing cards.

~n. **1.** The act or an instance of shuffling. **2.** A dance in which the feet scrape along the floor at each step. **3.** An evasive or deceitful action; a dodge. **4. a.** The act of mixing cards. **b.** A player's turn to do this. [Probably from Low German *schüffeln,* to walk clumsily, shuffle cards.] **—shuf·fler** *n.*

shuf·fle·board (shúff'l-bawrd || -bōrd) *n.* Also **shov·el·board** (shúvv'l-). **1.** A game, played especially on a ship, in which discs are pushed or slid along a smooth, level surface towards numbered squares with a pronged cue. **2.** The surface on which this game is played. [Alteration (influenced by SHUFFLE) of earlier *shove-board* : SHOVE + BOARD.]

shuf·ti (shŏŏfti) *n., pl.* **-tis.** *British Slang.* A look: *took a quick shufti at the paper.* [Arabic.]

shul (shōōl, shŏŏl) *n.* A synagogue. [Yiddish.]

shun (shun) *tr.v.* **shunned, shunning, shuns.** To avoid (a person, group, or thing) deliberately and consistently; keep away from. See Synonyms at **escape.** [Middle English *shun(n)en,* Old English *scunian*†, to avoid, be afraid, abhor.] **—shun·ner** *n.*

shunt (shunt) *n.* **1.** The act or an instance of shunting. **2.** A railway point. **3.** A low-resistance connection between two points in an electric circuit that forms an alternative path for a portion of the current. Also called "bypass". **4.** *Slang.* A collision between two cars, especially racing cars. **5.** *Medicine.* A passage through which blood passes from one part or organ to another. It may be created by surgery or occur as a congenital abnormality.

~v. **shunted, shunting, shunts.** *—tr.* **1.** To turn or move (something) aside or onto another course. **2.** To move or switch (a train or carriage) from one track to another. **3.** *Electricity.* To provide or divert (current) by means of a shunt. **4.** To evade or avoid (a task, for example) by refusing or putting aside. **5.** *Informal.* To transfer to a different position or task, usually a less demanding or important one. *—intr.* **1.** To move or turn aside. **2.** To move from one track to another. Used of a train. **3.** *Electricity.* To become diverted by means of a shunt. Used of a circuit. [Middle English *shunten,* to flinch, shy, run away, perhaps from *shun(n)en,* SHUN.]

shunt·er (shúntər) *n.* A railway locomotive used in shunting rather than in pulling trains on journeys.

shunt-wound (shúnt-wownd) *adj.* Of or designating a direct-current motor or generator in which the field coil is connected in parallel with the armature so that the same voltage appears across each. Compare **series-wound.**

shush (shŏŏsh, shush) *interj.* Used to express a demand for silence.

~tr.v. **shushed, shushing, shushes.** To demand silence from by saying "shush": *"Simon shushed him quickly as though he had spoken too loudly in church."* (William Golding). [Imitative.]

shut (shut) *v.* **shut, shutting, shuts.** *—tr.* **1. a.** To move (a door, lid, or valve, for example) into closed position over or within an opening. **b.** To bring (something that extends or opens out) into a folded or compact state: *shut the book.* **c.** To bring the two edges of together: *shut your eyes.* **2.** To block passage or access to; close: *shut the garage.* **3.** To fasten or secure with a lock, catch, or latch. Often used with *up.* **4.** To deny (someone) access to a place; bar: *She was shut out of her house.* **5.** To keep from leaving a place; confine: *I was shut in the cellar.* **6.** To cause to reject or ignore: *shut his mind to criticism.* **7.** To catch something as it is being shut: *shut my sleeve in the door.* **8.** To close (a business establishment). Often used with *up.* **—get shut of.** *Informal.* To dispose of (an unwanted person or thing); rid oneself of. *—intr.* **1.** To become shut; close. **2.** To admit of being shut: *The door shuts easily now you've oiled the hinges.*

shrike Found in North America, Eurasia, and Africa, the shrike supplements its diet of insects with small birds, catching and killing them with its talons in mid-flight. From its habit of then impaling the corpses on thorn bushes, it is also called the butcherbird. This is the great grey shrike.

PRONUNCIATION KEY

a, trap; aa, father; ai, fair; ar, star; aw, lawn; ay, play; b, bb, stab; rubber; ch, church; ck, ticket; d, dd, dead; ladder; e, dress; ee, bee; er, defer; ew, few; ewr, pure; ə, about; ər, letter; f, ff, fife; differ; g, gg, giggle; h, hat; i, kit; ī, price; īr, fire; j, judge; k, kick; l, ll, let; 'l, needle; m, mm, man; n, nn, no; 'n, sudden; ng, thing; o, lot; ō, no; ŏŏ, foot; ōō, shoe; oor, poor; ow, cow; owr, hour; oy, boy; p, pp, pepper; r, rr, red; s, ss, sauce; sh, ship; t, tt, totter; th, thick; th, this; smooth; u, cut; ur, turn; v, vv, valve; w, wet; y, yes; z, zz, zebra; zh, vision; pleasure

IN FOREIGN WORDS:

aN, oN, Saint-Saëns; hl, Llanelli; Hluhluwe; kh, loch; lough; Khaled

STRESS MARK:

ín-sīt, insight; in-sīt, incite

Siamese cat *Originally from Southeast Asia, the Siamese breed of domestic cat is characterised by pointed ears, a long tail and blue eyes.*

—shut up. **1.** *Informal.* To silence (a person). **2.** *Informal.* To be or become silent: *I'll have my say and then I'll shut up.*
~*n.* **1.** The line of connection between welded pieces of metal. **2.** *Archaic.* The act or time of closing or shutting.
~*adj.* Closed. [Middle English *shutten,* originally a West Midland form of *shitten, shetten,* Old English *scyttan.*]

shut down *tr.v.* **1. a.** To cause (an industrial plant, for example) to close. **b.** To stop the operation of (a machine, for example). **2.** To put a check on or stop to. *—intr.v.* To stop working; close. Used of a factory, machine, or the like.

shut·down (shút-down) *n.* **1.** A temporary or permanent closing of an industrial plant. **2.** The failure or intentional cessation of operation of any apparatus or enterprise.

Shute (sho͞ot), **Nevil,** born Nevil Shute Norway (1899–1960). British novelist, who lived in Australia after 1950. His many internationally popular novels include *A Town Like Alice* (1950) and *On The Beach* (1957).

shut·eye (shút-ī) *n. Slang.* Sleep.

shut-in (shút-in) *n. U.S.* An invalid.
~*adj.* (-ín). *U.S.* Confined to a house or hospital, as by illness.

shut off *tr.v.* **1.** To stop or prevent from flowing or working: *shut off the water supply.* **2.** To separate or isolate.

shut-off (shút-off, -awf) *n. Chiefly U.S.* **1.** A device that shuts something off. **2.** A stoppage or interruption.

shut out *tr.v.* **1.** To forbid access to; bar; exclude. **2.** To keep from being seen: *shut out the view of the gasworks.*

shut·out (shút-owt) *n.* **1.** A **lockout** *(see).* **2.** *Sports. U.S.* A game in which one side does not score.

shut·ter (shúttər) *n.* **1.** One that shuts. **2.** A hinged window cover, usually made of wood and fitted with louvres, and used to exclude light but not necessarily air. **3.** Any of the movable louvres on a pipe organ, controlled by pedals, that open and close the swell box. **4.** A mechanical device that opens and shuts the lens aperture of a camera to expose a plate or film. **5.** A similar device in a film projector that enables an image to be thrown onto the screen only when the film is momentarily stationary.
~*tr.v.* **shuttered, -tering, -ters.** To furnish or close with a shutter or shutters.

shut·tle (shútt'l) *n.* **1.** A device used in weaving to carry the woof thread back and forth between the warp threads. **2.** A device for holding the thread in tatting, in netting, and in a sewing machine. **3. a.** A train, bus, or aircraft making short, frequent trips to and fro between two points. Also used adjectivally: *a shuttle service.* **b.** A space shuttle. **4.** The act of shuttling.
~*v.* **shuttled, -tling, -tles.** *—intr.* To go, move, or travel back and forth by or as if by a shuttle. *—tr.* To move or transport by or as if by a shuttle. [Middle English *schutylle,* Old English *scytel,* dart.]

shut·tle·cock (shútt'l-kok) *n.* **1.** A small rounded piece of cork or similar material with a crown of feathers, used in the games of badminton and battledore. **2.** The game of battledore.
~*tr.v.* **shuttlecocked, -cocking, -cocks.** To send or bandy back and forth like a shuttlecock. [SHUTTLE + COCK (bird).]

shuttle diplomacy *n.* A type of diplomacy in which a statesman of a country neutral to two others in dispute travels back and forth between them as mediator.

shy¹ (shī) *adj.* **shier** or **shyer, shiest** or **shyest.** **1.** Easily startled; timid. Said especially of an animal. **2.** Nervous in company; unsure of oneself; reserved. **3.** Distrustful; wary; cautious. **4.** *Informal.* Not having paid an amount due, as one's ante in poker. **5.** *Informal.* Short; lacking: *We're still £5 shy.* **6.** Reluctant to engage in or associate with a specified thing, activity, or group. Usually used in combination: *work-shy.*
~*intr.v.* **shied, shying, shies.** **1.** To move suddenly, as if startled: *The horse shied at the noise.* **2.** To draw back, as through fear or caution: *He shied away from responsibility.*
~*n., pl.* **shies.** A sudden movement, as from fright; a start. [Middle English *schey,* timid, Old English *scēoh,* from Germanic *skiuhwaz* (unattested).] **—shy·er** *n.* **—shy·ly** *adv.* **—shy·ness** *n.*
Synonyms: *shy, bashful, timid, self-conscious, diffident, retiring, modest, coy, demure.*

shy² *v.* **shied, shying, shies.** *—tr.* To throw with a swift sideways motion. *—intr.* To throw something in this manner.
~*n., pl.* **shies.** **1.** A quick throw; a fling. **2.** *Informal.* A gibe; a sneer. **3.** *Informal.* An attempt; a try. [Earliest senses, "to take sudden fright", "shrink", "flinch", probably from SHY (timid).]

Shy·lock (shī́-lok) *n.* A heartless, exacting creditor. [After *Shylock,* the ruthless usurer in Shakespeare's *Merchant of Venice* (1596).]

shy·ster (shī́stər) *n. Chiefly U.S. Slang.* A person given to unethical or unscrupulous practices, especially in business, law, or politics. [Perhaps after *Scheuster,* an unscrupulous 19th-century New York lawyer.]

si (see) *n. Music.* The former name for **ti** *(see).*

Si The symbol for the element silicon.

SI International System of measurement. See **SI unit.** [French *Système international.*]

si·al (sī́-al) *n.* The silicon and aluminium-rich rocks which form the earth's continental upper crust. Compare **sima.** [*Si*lica + *al*umina.] **—si·al·ic** *adj.*

si·al·a·gogue, si·al·o·gogue (sī́-əl-ə-gog, sī-ál-) *n. Medicine.* Any drug or agent that stimulates the flow of saliva. [New Latin *sialagōgus,* from Greek *sialon,* saliva + -AGOGUE.] **—si·al·a·gog·ic** (-gójik), **si·al·o·gog·ic** *adj.*

Si·am (sī-ám). See **Thailand.**

si·a·mang (seé-ə-mang, sī́-) *n.* A large black gibbon, *Symphalangus syndactylus* (or *Hylobates syndactylus*), of Sumatra and the Malay Peninsula, having an inflatable throat sac and webbing joining the second and third toes. [Malay.]

Si·a·mese (sī́-ə-meéz || -meéss) *adj.* Thai.
~*n., pl.* **Siamese.** **1.** A **Thai** *(see).* **2.** The language, **Thai** *(see).*

Siamese cat *n.* A short-haired cat of a breed developed in the Orient, having blue eyes and a pale fawn or grey coat with darker ears, face, tail, and feet.

Siamese fighting fish *n.* A small, often brightly coloured freshwater fish, *Betta splendens,* native to tropical Asia and popular in home aquariums.

Siamese twin *n.* Either of a pair of twins born with their bodies joined together in any manner. [After Chang and Eng (1811–74), joined twins born in *Siam.*]

Sian. See **Xi'an.**

sib (sib) *n.* **1. a.** A blood relation; a kinsman. **b.** Relatives collectively. **2.** A brother or sister; a sibling. **3.** A plant that is the product of a self-pollination, especially one in a group of plants that are mainly the products of cross-pollinations. Also called "sibling".
~*adj.* Related by blood; akin. Used with *to.* [Middle English *sib(be),* Old English *sibb.*]

Sib·bald's rorqual (síbb'ldz) *n.* The **blue whale** *(see).* [After Sir R. *Sibbald* (1644–1722), Scottish scientist and physician.]

Si·be·li·us (si-báyli-əss), **Jean (Julius Christian)** (1865–1957). Finnish composer, the most famous of his country. Often looked upon as a nationalist composer, he is best known popularly for the symphonic tone poem, *Finlandia* (1900). He also wrote seven symphonies and a violin concerto (1903–05).

Si·be·ri·a (sī-beér-i-ə). Vast geographical region of the U.S.S.R. comprising the northern third of Asia, stretching from the Urals in the west to the Pacific Ocean in the east, and south from the Arctic Ocean to the Mongolian border. About two fifths of the region is covered in forest. Most of the population lives in the southwest, which is now one of the most densely industrialised parts of the U.S.S.R. owing largely to the Kuznetsk Basin, rich in coal and iron deposits. Large petroleum and natural gas fields are also exploited in the western lowlands, and huge hydroelectric stations are located on the river Angara at Irkutsk and Bratsk. The chief city of western Siberia is Novosibirsk. **—Si·be·ri·an** *adj. & n.*

Siberian husky *n.* A husky of a breed from northeast Asia.

sib·i·lant (síbbilənt) *adj.* **1.** Producing a hissing sound. **2.** *Phonetics.* Characterised by the sound of (s) or (sh).
~*n. Phonetics.* **1.** A speech sound that suggests hissing, such as (s), (sh), (z), or (zh). **2.** A sibilant consonant. [Latin *sībilāns* (stem *sībilant-*), present participle of *sībilāre,* to hiss, whistle, SIBILATE.] **—sib·i·lance, sib·i·lan·cy** *n.* **—sib·i·lant·ly** *adv.*

sib·i·late (síbbi-layt) *v.* **-lated, -lating, -lates.** *—intr.* To utter a hissing sound; hiss. *—tr.* To pronounce with a hissing sound. [Latin *sībilāre,* to hiss, whistle.] **—sib·i·la·tion** (-láysh'n) *n.*

Si·bi·u (si-beé-o͞o, -béw). *German* **Her·mann·stadt** (háir-man-shtat); *Hungarian* **Nagy·sze·ben** (nóch-sebben). City in central Romania, lying at the foot of the Transylvanian Alps.

sib·ling (síbbling) *n.* **1.** One of two or more persons having one or normally both parents in common; a brother or sister. **2.** A plant, a sib. [Middle English *siblyng,* Old English *sibling* : SIB + -LING.]

sib·yl (síbbil, síbb'l) *n.* **1.** Any of various women regarded as oracles or prophetesses in the ancient world. **2. a.** A prophetess. **b.** A witch; a sorceress. [Middle English *Sibile, Sybylle,* from Old French *Sibile, Sebile,* from Latin *Sibylla,* from Greek *Sibulla*†.] **—sib·yl·line** (-īn), **si·byl·ic** (si-bíllik) *adj.*

sic¹ (sik || seek) *adv. Latin.* Thus; so. Used in written texts to indicate that a surprising or dubious word, phrase, or fact is not a mistake and is to be read as it stands. [Latin *sīc.*]

sic², sick (sik) *tr.v.* **sicked, sicking, sics** or **sicks.** **1.** To urge to attack or chase. **2.** To set upon or chase. Used only in the imperative, as a command to a dog. [Dialectal variant of SEEK.]

Si·ca·ni·an (si-káyni-ən) *adj.* Sicilian.

sic·ca·tive (síckətiv) *n.* A substance added to paints and some medicines to promote drying; a drier. [Latin *siccātīvus,* drying, from *siccāre,* to dry, from *siccus,* dry.] **—sic·ca·tive** *adj.*

sice. Variant of **syce.**

Si·chuan (sích-waán). Also **Sze·chwan** (séch-). Province in southwestern China, lying to the east of Tibet. The capital is Chengdu. It forms a natural geographical region, being entirely ringed by mountains. It is China's leading producer of rice, and is also important for its sugar cane, cotton, and cattle-farming.

Sic·i·ly (síssili, siss'l-i). *Italian* **Si·ci·lia** (see-cheél-ya). Region of southern Italy, consisting mainly of the island of Sicily, separated from the extreme southwestern tip of the mainland by the narrow Strait of Messina. The region also includes the Egadi, Lipari, and Pelagie island groups, and the islands of Pantelleria and Ustica. The main island is the largest in the Mediterranean. It is almost entirely hilly and mountainous, the highest point being Mount Etna, an active volcano, which rises to 3 323 metres (10,902 feet). Palermo is the capital. **—Si·cil·i·an** (si-síl-i-ən) *adj. & n.*

sick¹ (sik) *adj.* **sicker, sickest.** **1. a.** Not in normal health physically or psychologically; ill; unwell. **b.** Wishing to vomit or in the act of vomiting: *She was sick in the sink.* **2.** Of or for sick persons: *sick leave.* **3. a.** Producing or characterised by black humour; unwholesome; in deliberately bad taste: *a sick joke.* **b.** Culturally ailing or unsound; rotten; decadent: *a sick society.* **4.** *Informal.* **a.** Deeply distressed; chagrined; upset: *felt sick at losing the game.* **b.** Dis-

gusted; revolted. **c.** Weary; tired. Usually used with *of*: *sick of it all.* **d.** Pining; longing. Used with *for.* **5.** In need of repairs. Said of a ship. **6.** Unable to produce a profitable yield of crops, especially as a result of excessive cultivation of a single crop. Often used in combination: *rose-sick soil.* **7.** *Informal.* In a position of obvious embarrassment, humiliation, or inferiority: *Now that she's walked out on him, he looks pretty sick.* **—sick up.** *Informal.* To vomit.
~n. Informal. Vomit. [Middle English *sēk, sīk,* Old English *sēoc,* from Germanic *siukaz* (unattested).] **—sick·ish** *adj.*
Synonyms: *sick, ill, indisposed, poorly, unwell.*

sick². Variant of **sic** (to urge to attack).

sick·bay (sík-bay) *n.* An area, as on a ship, used as a hospital or infirmary.

sick·bed (sík-bed) *n.* A sick person's bed.

sick call *n. Military.* **1. a.** The daily line-up of personnel requiring medical attention. **b.** The signal announcing this. **2.** A call made by a doctor to a sick person.

sick·en (síckən) *v.* **-ened, -ening, -ens.** *—tr.* To make sick; fill with nausea or revulsion. *—intr.* To become sick or show signs of sickness. **—sick·en·er** *n.*

sick·en·ing (síckəning) *adj.* **1.** Causing sickness or nausea. **2.** Revolting or disgusting; loathsome. **3.** *Informal.* Very annoying or disagreeable. **—sick·en·ing·ly** *adv.*

Sick·ert (síckərt), **Walter (Richard)** (1860–1942). British painter, born in Munich. He studied with Whistler, then with Degas in Paris in 1883, and did not live permanently in England until after 1905. His studio in Bloomsbury became a centre for the transmission to England of influences from the impressionist movement. Sickert was at his best in painting figures from the world of the theatre.

sick headache *n.* **1.** A headache accompanied by nausea. **2.** An attack of migraine.

sick·le (síck'l) *n.* An implement having a semicircular blade attached to a short handle, for cutting grain or tall grass.
~tr.v. **sickled, -ling, -les.** *Chiefly U.S.* To cut with a sickle. [Middle English *sikel,* Old English *sicol, sicel,* from West Germanic, from Vulgar Latin *sicila* (unattested), variant of Latin *sēcula.*]

sick leave *n.* Leave of absence given because of sickness.

sick·le·bill (síck'l-bil) *n.* Any of several birds having sharply curved bills; especially, *Falculea palliata,* of Madagascar.

sickle cell *n.* An abnormal crescent-shaped red blood cell.

sickle cell anaemia *n.* A hereditary anaemia mainly affecting black people, characterised by the presence of oxygen-deficient sickle-shaped red blood cells.

sickle feather *n.* Any of the long, curving feathers of a cock's tail.

sick list *n.* A list of sick personnel, as in the army.

sick·ly (síckli) *adj.* **-lier, -liest. 1.** Prone to sickness; ailing. **2.** Of, caused by, or associated with sickness: *a sickly pallor; a sickly shade of green.* **3.** Conducive to ill health; unhealthy. **4.** Inducing vomit; nauseating; sickening: *sickly, rich food.* **5.** Mawkish; weak.
~adv. U.S. In a sick manner.
~tr.v. **sicklied, -lying, -lies.** *Archaic.* To make sickly, as in colour. **—sick·li·ness** *n.*

sick·ness (sík-nəss, -niss) *n.* **1.** The condition of being sick; illness. **2.** A disease; a malady. **3.** Nausea.

sickness benefit *n.* Money paid by the state, in weekly instalments, to one who is unable to work through being ill.

sick·room (sík-rōōm, -rŏŏm) *n.* A room occupied by a sick person.

sic pas·sim (sík pássim || seék). *Latin.* Thus everywhere. Used in textual annotation to indicate that a term or idea is to be found throughout the work cited.

Sid·dons (sídd'nz), **Sarah (Kemble)** (1755–1831). British actress, the most illustrious member of the theatrical Kemble family. From 1785, when she first played Lady Macbeth, to 1812, when she gave her last performance in the same role, she was acknowledged as the finest Shakespearean actress of her day.

Sid·dhar·tha (si-dártə). See **Buddha.**

sid·dur (síddər, síddoor) *n., pl.* **siddurim** (síddoo-reém) or **-durs.** A Jewish prayer book containing prayers for the various days of the year. Compare **machzor.** [Hebrew *siddūr,* "order", "arrangement (of prayers)", from *siddēr,* to arrange.]

side (sīd) *n.* **1.** *Geometry.* **a.** A line bounding a plane figure. **b.** A surface bounding a solid figure. **2.** A surface of an object; especially, a surface joining a top and bottom: *Hold the box by its sides.* **3.** A surface of an object that extends more or less perpendicularly from an observer standing in front of it: *the side of the mountain.* **4. a.** Either of the two surfaces of a flat object, such as a piece of paper. **b.** The amount of writing it takes to fill a side of paper: *wrote four sides in the exam.* **5. a.** The area to the left or right of the observer, or of an axis: *played on the left side of the field.* **b.** The left or right half of the trunk of a human or the corresponding part of an animal body: *a side of mutton.* **6.** The space immediately next to someone or something: *stood at her side.* Often used in combination: *roadside.* **7.** One of two or more contrasted parts or places within an area, identified by its location with respect to a centre: *the north side of the park.* **8. a.** An area separated from another area by some intervening line, barrier, or other feature: *on this side of the Atlantic.* **b.** That which comes before some dividing line: *this side of madness.* **9. a.** One of two or more opposing groups, teams, or sets of opinions. **b.** A sports team: *one of the best sides in Europe.* **c.** Any of the positions maintained as in a dispute or debate: *He always takes her side in arguments.* **10.** A distinct aspect or quality: *the cruel side of her nature.* **11.** A line of descent: *my aunt on my mother's side.* **12.** *British Slang.* Arrogance or affected superiority: *has got too much side.* **13.** *Informal.* A television channel: *What's on the other side?* **14.** In certain games, such as snooker, tennis, or table tennis, a spin imparted to the ball by a sideways motion of the bat or cue, usually causing a variation in the ball's movement. **—let the side down.** To fail or disappoint one's comrades. **—on the side.** *Informal.* **1.** In addition to a main activity, occupation, or arrangement, often with a suggestion of illegality: *was making a bit of money on the side.* **2.** *U.S.* Served as a side dish. **—on the (specified) side.** Tending towards a specified condition, quality, or amount: *she's a bit on the slow side.* **—put to** or **on one side.** To set apart from the main subject under consideration. **—side by side.** Next to each other; close together. **—split (one's) sides.** To be convulsed with laughter. **—take sides.** To associate oneself with a faction, contested opinion, or cause. **—the other side.** To realm of the dead; the spirit world.
~adj. **1.** Located on a side: *a side chapel.* **2.** From or to one side; oblique: *a side view.* **3.** Minor; incidental: *a side interest.* **4.** In addition to the main part; supplementary: *a side benefit.*
~intr.v. **sided, siding, sides.** To align oneself. Used with *with* or *against*: *sided with Peter against Paul.* [Middle English *side,* Old English *sīde,* from Germanic.]

-side *n. comb. form.* Indicates a region bordering a river or estuary, especially when heavily industrialised—for example, *Clydeside, Humberside.*

side arms *pl.n.* Weapons carried at the side or waist, such as swords or pistols.

side·band (sīd-band) *n.* Either of the two bands of frequencies, one just above and one just below a carrier frequency, that result from modulation of a carrier wave.

side·board (sīd-bawrd || -bōrd) *n.* A piece of dining-room furniture originally for holding dishes of food and usually having drawers and shelves for storing tableware.

side·boards (sīd-bawrdz || -bōrdz) *pl.n.* Growths of hair or whiskers down the sides of a man's face in front of the ears. Also *chiefly U.S.* "sideburns".

side·car (sīd-kaar) *n.* **1.** A one-wheeled car for a single passenger, attached to the side of a motorcycle. **2.** A cocktail combining brandy, an orange-flavoured liqueur, and lemon juice.

side chain *n. Chemistry.* A radical, group, or chain of atoms attached to a carbon atom in the main chain of an organic molecule or to the cyclic nucleus of such a molecule.

sid·ed (sīdid) *adj.* Having sides usually of a specified number or kind. Used in combination: *straight-sided.*

side dish *n.* A small dish, as of salad, served with a main course.

side-dress (sīd-dress) *tr.v.* **-dressed, -dressing, -dresses.** To treat (plants) by placing fertiliser near their roots, on or in the soil.

side drum *n.* A small double-headed snare drum, traditionally worn at the side by soldiers.

side effect *n.* A peripheral or secondary effect; especially, an undesirable secondary effect of a drug or therapy.

side issue *n.* An issue that is not directly relevant to the main point under consideration.

side·kick (sīd-kik) *n. Informal.* A close friend or associate. [Earlier *sidekicker,* perhaps from *kicker* (in draw poker), an unmatched card held with a pair or three of a kind for purposes of bluffing or improving the hand.]

side·light (sīd-līt) *n.* **1.** A light coming from the side. **2.** Either of two small lights on the front of a motor vehicle used to indicate its presence when parked or when moving on well-lit streets at night. **3.** *Nautical.* Either of two lights, red to port, green to starboard, shown by ships at night. **4.** Incidental information.

side·line (sīd-līn) *n.* **1. a.** A line along either of the two sides of a playing court or field, marking its limits. **b.** *Plural.* The space outside such limits, occupied by spectators. **c.** *Plural.* The position or point of view of those who observe and do not participate in some activity. **2.** A subsidiary line of merchandise. **3.** An activity pursued in addition to one's regular occupation.
~tr.v. **sidelined, -lining, -lines.** *Chiefly U.S.* To remove or keep (a player) from active participation, as in athletic contests.

side·ling (sīdling) *adj.* **1.** Directed to one side; oblique. **2.** Sloping.
~adv. Obliquely; sideways. [Middle English *sideling* : SIDE + -LING (adverbial suffix).]

side·long (sīd-long || -lawng) *adj.* Directed to one side; sideways.
~adv. On, from, or towards the side; obliquely; sideways. [Alteration of SIDELING.]

side·man (sīd-man) *n., pl.* **-men** (-men). *U.S.* Any player in a jazz band who is not the leader of it.

si·de·re·al (sī-deér-i-əl, si-) *adj.* **1.** Of, pertaining to, or concerned with the stars or constellations; stellar. **2.** Measured or determined in relation to the stars: *sidereal time.* [Latin *sīdereus,* from *sīdus* (stem *sīder-*), constellation.]

sidereal day *n.* The time required for a complete rotation of the Earth, measured as the interval between two successive transits of a star over the same meridian, or 23 hours, 56 minutes, 4.09 seconds of solar time.

sidereal hour *n.* A 24th part of a sidereal day.

sidereal month *n.* See **month.**

sidereal time *n.* Time based upon the axial and orbital rotation of the Earth with reference to the background of stars.

sidereal year *n.* The time required for one complete revolution of the Earth about the Sun, relative to the fixed stars, or 365.256 mean solar days.

sid·er·ite (sīdə-rīt || síddə-) *n.* **1.** An impure yellowish-brown iron

PRONUNCIATION KEY

a, trap; aa, father; ai, fair; ar, star; aw, lawn; ay, play; b, bb, stab; rubber; ch, church; ck, ticket; d, dd, dead; ladder; e, dress; ee, bee; er, defer; ew, few; ewr, pure; ə, about; ər, letter; f, ff, fife; differ; g, gg, giggle; h, hat; i, kit; ī, price; īr, fire; j, judge; k, kick; l, ll, let; 'l, needle; m, mm, man; n, nn, no; 'n, sudden; ng, thing; o, lot; ō, no; ŏŏ, foot; ōō, shoe; oor, poor; ow, cow; owr, hour; oy, boy; p, pp, pepper; r, rr, red; s, ss, sauce; sh, ship; t, tt, totter; th, thick; th, this; smooth; u, cut; ur, turn; v, vv, valve; w, wet; y, yes; z, zz, zebra; zh, vision; pleasure

IN FOREIGN WORDS:

aN, oN, Saint-Saëns; hl, Llanelli; Hluhluwe; kh, loch; lough; Khaled

STRESS MARK:

ín-sīt, insight; in-sīt, incite

carbonate mineral. **2.** An iron meteorite. [SIDER(O)- + -ITE.] —**sid·er·it·ic** (-rĭttĭk) *adj.*

sidero-, sider– *comb. form.* Indicates iron; for example, **siderolite, siderosis.** [Greek *sidēros†*, iron.]

side road *n.* A road that joins and is subsidiary to a main road.

si·der·o·lite (sĭdərə-līt ‖ sĭddərə-) *n.* A meteorite that contains iron, nickel, silicon, magnesium, and small amounts of other elements. [SIDERO- + -LITE.]

si·der·o·sil·i·co·sis (sĭdərə-sĭlli-kŏ-siss) *n.* A lung disease caused by excessive inhalation of dust containing silica and iron oxide.

si·der·o·sis (sĭdə-rŏ-siss ‖ sĭddə-) *n.* A chronic disease of the lungs caused by excessive inhalation of dust containing iron oxide or iron particles. [SIDER(O)- + -OSIS.] —**sid·er·ot·ic** (sĭdə-rŏttik) *adj.*

si·der·o·stat (sĭdər-ō-stat, -ə- ‖ sĭddər-) *n.* An optical system consisting of a rotating clock-driven mirror that reflects light from a celestial body in a relatively fixed direction to a fixed telescope or other bulky instrument. [Latin *sīdus* (stem *sīder-*), constellation (see **sidereal**) + -STAT.] —**sid·er·o·stat·ic** (-ə-státtik) *adj.*

side·sad·dle (sĭd-sadd'l) *n.* A saddle designed so that a woman may sit with both legs on one side of the horse. ~*adv.* On or as if on a sidesaddle.

side show *n.* **1.** A small show offered in addition to the main attraction, as at a circus. **2.** A diverting incident or spectacle.

side-slip (sĭd-slip) *intr.v.* -**slipped,** -**slipping,** -**slips.** To slip or skid to one side. ~*n.* **1.** A sideways skid, as of a motor vehicle. **2.** *Aeronautics.* Movement sideways and downwards along the lateral axis as the result of banking too steeply, or caused deliberately in order to reduce altitude steeply without gaining speed.

sides·man (sĭdz-mən) *n., pl.* -**men** (-mən, -men). In the Church of England, one whose task is to help the parish churchwarden.

side·split·ting (sĭd-splitting) *adj.* Causing convulsions of laughter. —**side·split·ting·ly** *adv.*

side step *n.* A step to one side, as in dancing or to avoid something.

side-step (sĭd-step) *v.* -**stepped,** -**stepping,** -**steps.** —*intr.* **1.** To step aside. **2.** To dodge an issue or responsibility. —*tr.* **1.** To step out of the way of (an opponent in a sports match, for example). **2.** To evade (an issue, for example); skirt. —**side-step·per** *n.*

side street *n.* A relatively minor and quiet street, usually providing access to residential areas rather than serving as a main thoroughfare.

side stroke *n.* A swimming stroke in which a person swims on one side and thrusts the arms backwards and downwards while performing a scissors kick with the legs.

side·swipe (sĭd-swīp) *tr.v.* -**swiped,** -**swiping,** -**swipes.** To deal a sideswipe to (a person). ~*n.* **1.** A glancing blow on or along the side. **2.** A caustic remark made in the course of other comments.

side·track (sĭd-trak) *tr.v.* -**tracked,** -**tracking,** -**tracks.** To divert from a main issue or course. ~*n.* **1.** An instance of sidetracking. **2.** *U.S.* A railway siding.

side-valve (sĭd-valv) *adj.* Designating an internal-combustion engine with the inlet and outlet valves located within the cylinder block rather than the cylinder head. Compare **overhead valve.**

side·walk (sĭd-wawk) *n. U.S.* A pavement *(see).*

side wall *n.* A side surface of a pneumatic tyre.

side·ward (sĭd-wərd) *adj.* Moving or directed towards one side. ~*adv. Chiefly U.S.* Variant of **sidewards.**

side·wards (sĭd-wərdz) *adv.* Also *chiefly U.S.* **side·ward.** Towards or from one side.

side·ways (sĭd-wayz) *adv.* Also **side·wise** (-wīz). **1.** Towards one side; leaning or moving in a sideward direction. **2.** From one side. **3.** Presenting the side instead of the front or back. ~*adj.* Also **side·wise.** Towards or from one side.

side wheel *n.* A paddle wheel on the side of a steamboat. —**side-wheel** (sĭd-weel, -hweel) *adj.* —**side-wheel·er** *n.*

side·whis·kers (sĭd-wiskərz, -hwiskərz) *pl.n.* Whiskers growing on the sides of the face.

side·wind·er (sĭd-wīndər) *n.* **1.** A small rattlesnake, *Crotalus cerastes,* of the southwestern United States and Mexico, that moves by a distinctive sideways looping motion of its body. **2.** *U.S.* A powerful blow by the fist delivered from the side. **3.** *Military.* A short-range supersonic air-to-air missile.

Si·di-bel-Ab·bès (sĭddi-bel-ábbess, -a-béss). City in northwest Algeria, the headquarters of the French Foreign Legion until Algeria gained its independence in 1962.

sid·ing (sĭding) *n.* **1.** A short section of railway line connected to a main line either to provide access, as to a factory or mine, or to provide storage space for rolling stock. **2.** *U.S.* Material, such as planks or shingles, used for surfacing the outside of a building.

Siding Spring Mountain. Mountain peak in the Warrumbungle range of New South Wales, Australia, the site of the Siding Spring Observatory. This technically sophisticated observatory has a 3.9-metre (153-inch) reflecting telescope, one of the world's largest.

si·dle (sĭd'l) *intr.v.* -**dled,** -**dling,** -**dles.** To move sideways; edge along. **2.** To move in a nervous, furtive manner: *sidled into the office late.* ~*n.* A sidling movement. [Back-formation from SIDELING and SIDELONG.] —**sid·ling·ly** *adv.*

Sid·ney or **Syd·ney** (sĭd-ni), **Sir Philip** (1554-86). English poet, critic, soldier, and courtier. His most important works are a collection of pastoral idylls, *Arcadia,* a sonnet sequence, *Astrophel and Stella,* and two essays of criticism, *The Defence of Poesie* and *An Apology for Poetry* (all published posthumously).

Si·don (sĭd'n, *rarely* sī-don). Ancient Phoenician seaport, on the Mediterranean coast, occupying the site of present-day Saida, in Lebanon. It was one of the oldest Phoenician trading centres, famous for its glass and purple dyes.

siege (seej, *also* seezh) *n.* **1.** The surrounding and blockading of a town or fortress by an army intent on capturing it. **2.** A prolonged attempt to break the resistance of a person or group, as by force or psychological pressure: *The siege began when the police surrounded the terrorist hideout.* **3.** *Obsolete.* **a.** A seat. **b.** A seat of rule. —**lay siege to.** To begin a siege against. ~*tr.v.* **sieged, sieging, sieges.** To lay siege to; besiege. [Middle English *sege,* from Old French, "seat", from Vulgar Latin *sedicum* (unattested), from *sedicāre* (unattested), "to seat oneself", from Latin *sedēre.*]

Sieg·fried (seeg-freed; *German* zeek-freet). The hero of the first part of the **Nibelungenlied** *(see)* and other medieval epics. [German, from Old High German *Sigifrith : sigu, sigo,* victory + *fridu,* peace.]

sie·mens (seemənz) *n.* The SI unit of electrical conductance equal to the conductance of a device that has a resistance of one ohm. Formerly called "mho", "reciprocal ohm". [After Ernst Werner von SIEMENS.]

Siemens (seemənz), **Ernst Werner von** (1816-92). German electrical engineer. He installed the first telegraph line between Frankfurt and Berlin in 1848-49 and the first lines in Russia in 1850. With his brothers Wilhelm and Karl he went on to install lines between India and Europe, as well as across the Atlantic. The Siemens unit of electrical conductance is named after him.

Siemens, Sir William, born Karl Wilhelm Siemens (1823-83). British electrical engineer, born in Germany. After developing an electroplating method with his brother, Ernst, he settled in England in 1844 and for the rest of his life managed the English division of their joint telegraphic and electrical firm.

Si·en·a (si-énnə). City in north central Italy, the capital of Siena province. In the 13th and 14th centuries it boasted the finest painters in Italy, known as the Sienese School. The city is rich in fine architecture. The Palio festival, with its horse race through the streets of the town centre, is held twice each summer. —**Si·en·ese** (-ənéez) *n. & adj.*

Sien·kie·wicz (shenk-yáy-vich), **Henryk** (1846-1916). Polish novelist. Although he is most widely known for his historical novel, *Quo Vadis?* (1895), his critical reputation rests on his trilogy dealing with Poland's struggle for national liberation, *With Fire and Sword* (1883), *The Deluge* (1886), and *Pan Michael* (1888). He was awarded the Nobel prize for literature in 1905.

si·en·na (si-énnə) *n.* **1.** A special clay containing iron and manganese oxides, used as a pigment for oil and water-colour painting. **2. Raw sienna** *(see).* **3. Burnt sienna** *(see).* [From *terra-sienna,* from Italian *terra di Sienna,* "earth of SIENA."]

si·er·ra (si-érrə, séer-ə) *n.* **1.** A rugged range of mountains having an irregular or serrated profile. **2.** Any of several mackerel-like fishes of the genus *Scomberomorus,* of tropical seas. [Spanish, "a saw", from Latin *serra.* See **serrate.**] —**si·er·ran** *adj.*

Sierra Le·o·ne (li-ŏn, -ŏni). Republic on the west coast of Africa. Although the economy is predominantly agricultural, the country has an important mining industry, with diamonds, bauxite, and titanium accounting for some 70 per cent of the country's exports by value. Freetown was founded as a British colony for ex-slaves in 1787 and thereafter British control gradually extended into the interior, over which a protectorate was proclaimed in 1896. The country gained its independence within the Commonwealth in 1961. Area, 71 740 square kilometres (27,699 square miles). Population, 3,700,-000. Capital, Freetown. See map at **West African States.**

Sierra Ma·dre (maa-dray, -dri). Chief mountain system of Mexico, comprising three principal ranges: the Sierra Madre Oriental, running roughly parallel to the coast of the Gulf of Mexico, the Sierra Madre Occidental, running parallel to the Pacific coast, and the Sierra Madre del Sur, a continuation of the latter range, running south from Guadalajara. The two highest peaks, Orizaba and Popocatépetl, are both above 5 000 metres.

Sierra Nevada¹. Chief mountain range in southern Spain, in the Granada region, extending for about 100 kilometres (60 miles) parallel to the Mediterranean coast. It contains the highest peak in Spain, Mulhacen, which rises to 3 487 metres (11,440 feet).

Sierra Nevada². Range in eastern California containing the highest peak in the United States (excluding Alaska), Mount Whitney, which rises to 4 418 metres (14,495 feet).

si·es·ta (si-éstə) *n.* A short sleep or rest, usually taken after the midday meal, especially in hot countries. [Spanish, from Latin *sexta (hora),* sixth (hour after sunrise), noon, from *sextus,* sixth.]

sieve (siv) *n.* **1.** Any meshwork, especially a utensil of wire mesh or closely perforated metal, used for straining, sifting, or separating. **2.** *Informal.* One who is prone to give away secrets. ~*tr.v.* **sieved, sieving, sieves.** To pass through a sieve; sift. [Middle English *sive,* Old English *sife.*]

sieve tube *n.* A series of cells joined end to end, with pores in their connecting walls, forming a tube through which nutrients are conducted in vascular plants.

Sie·yès (si-ay-yéss), **Emmanuel Joseph** (1748-1836). French clergyman and revolutionary leader, usually known as Abbé Sieyès. His pamphlet, *What is the Third Estate* (1789), was one of the most influential attacks on the ancien régime. After helping to bring

Napoleon to power, he served for a few months as one of the consular triumvirate with Napoleon and Ducos (1799), but thereafter his political influence waned.

si·fa·ka (si-faákə) *n.* Either of two Madagascan primates, *Propithecus diadema* or *P. verreauxi,* that are related to lemurs and have long, often brightly coloured fur. [From Malagasy.]

sift (sift) *v.* **sifted, sifting, sifts.** *—tr.* **1.** To put through a sieve or other straining device in order to separate the fine from the coarse particles. **2.** To apply by scattering with a sieve: *Sift icing sugar on the cake.* **3.** To separate by or as if by using with a sieve; screen. **4.** To examine closely and carefully: *sift the evidence.* *—intr.* **1.** To sift something. **2.** To fall through or as if through a sieve: *White light sifted through the spreading cedar tree.* **3.** To make a careful and critical examination. Used with *through.* [Middle English *siften,* Old English *siftan.*] **—sift·er** *n.*

sift·ings (síftingz) *pl.n.* Material removed or separated with or as if with a sieve.

sig. **1.** signal. **2.** signature. **3.** signor; signore.

Sig. **1.** signor; signore. **2.** *Medicine.* signature.

sigh (sī) *v.* **sighed, sighing, sighs.** *—intr.* **1.** To exhale audibly in a long, deep breath, as from sorrow, weariness, or relief. **2.** To produce a similar sound: *willows sighing in the wind.* **3.** *Literary.* To feel yearning, longing, or grief; mourn. *—tr.* **1.** To express with or as if with an audible exhalation. **2.** *Archaic.* To lament; mourn. *~n.* An act or a sound of sighing. [Middle English *sighen,* probably altered from *siken* (weak past tense *sighte*), Old English *sīcan,* from West Germanic *sīk-* (unattested).]

sight (sīt) *n.* **1.** The ability to see; the faculty of vision: *Surgeons saved her sight.* **2.** The act or fact of seeing. **3.** The field or range of one's vision: *Get out of my sight!* **4.** The way in which one sees and evaluates experience; a point of view; an estimation: *In his sight she was perfect.* **5.** Something that is seen; an object of vision; a view: *The garden is a lovely sight.* **6.** Something worth seeing; an attraction or spectacle: *the sights of London.* **7.** *Informal.* Something unsightly: *Her hair was a sight.* **8. a.** A device used to assist aim by guiding the eye, as on a firearm or surveying instrument. **b.** *Often plural.* An aim or observation taken with such a device: *A rabbit came into his sights.* **c.** *Plural.* An aim; a goal; an ambition: *set his sights on promotion.* **9.** *Informal.* A considerable amount; a lot: *a sight more than what he's earning.* **—sight for sore eyes.** Something pleasurable to behold; a welcome sight. **—at first sight.** **1.** Immediately; at once: *love at first sight.* **2.** Without a close examination; according to initial impressions. **—at** or **on sight.** As soon as seen: *shoot on sight.* **—catch sight of.** To manage to see; glimpse. **—in sight.** **1.** Able to be seen. **2.** Coming closer; approaching: *The end is in sight.* **—know by sight.** To recognise (a person) by his appearance rather than by his name or any other personal detail. **—lose sight of.** To allow to be neglected or remain unconsidered: *mustn't lose sight of our objectives.* **—out of sight.** **1.** Not able to be seen; concealed; hidden. **2.** *Informal.* To a very great extent; with much severity: *They were beaten out of sight by a superior team.* **3.** *Chiefly U.S. Slang.* Incredible; marvellous.

~tr.v. **sighted, sighting, sights.** **1.** To see or observe within one's field of vision: *sight land.* **2.** To observe or take a sight of with an instrument: *sight a target.* **3.** To adjust the sights of (a rifle, for example). **4.** To provide with sights. **5.** To take aim with (a firearm). [Middle English *si(g)ht,* Old English *sihth, gesiht,* eyesight, vision, thing seen.]

sight bill *n.* A bill payable upon demand or presentation. Also *chiefly U.S.* "sight draft".

sight·ed (sītid) *adj.* **1.** Having sight; not blind. **2.** Having eyesight of a specified kind. Used in combination: *short-sighted.*

sight·less (sīt-ləss, -liss) *adj.* **1.** Blind. **2.** Invisible. **—sight·less·ly** *adv.* **—sight·less·ness** *n.*

sight·ly (sītli) *adj.* **-lier, -liest.** Pleasing to see; handsome.

sight-read (sīt-reed) *v.* **-read** (-red), **-reading, -reads.** *—tr.* To read or perform (music) at first sight without preparation. *—intr.* To sight-read music. **—sight-read·er** *n.*

sight rule *n.* An **alidade** *(see).*

sight screen *n.* In cricket, a large, white screen placed on the boundary behind the bowler to facilitate the batsman's view of the bowled ball. Also called "screen", *Australian* "sightboard".

sight·see·ing (sīt-see-ing) *n.* The act or pastime of touring places of interest. **—sight·see** *intr.v.* **—sight·se·er** *n.*

sig·il (sijil, siggil) *n.* **1.** A seal; a signet. **2.** A supposedly magical sign or image. [Latin *sigillum,* diminutive of *signum,* SIGN.]

sigill. seal. [Latin *sigillum.*]

Sig·int (síg-int) *n.* **1.** A department in Britain monitoring and gathering intelligence from broadcasts and other communications from foreign countries. **2.** The intelligence gathered by this department. [*Sig*nal + *int*elligence.]

sig·lum (síg-ləm) *n., pl.* **-gla** (-lə). A letter, especially an initial, used for identification. [From Late Latin *sigla* (plural), perhaps from *singula,* neuter plural of *singulus,* single.]

sig·ma (síg-mə) *n.* **1.** The 18th letter in the Greek alphabet, written Σ,σ. Transliterated in English as *S, s.* **2.** *Physics. Symbol* Σ. Any of three elementary particles in the baryon family. [Greek, from Semitic, akin to Hebrew *sāmekh,* SAMEK.] **—sig·mate** (-mayt) *adj.*

sig·moid (síg-moyd) *adj.* Also **sig·moi·dal** (sig-móyd'l). **1.** Having the shape of the letter S. **2.** Of or pertaining to the sigmoid colon. [Greek *sigmoeidēs* : SIGMA + -OID.]

sigmoid colon *n. Anatomy.* An S-shaped bend in the final part of the colon between the descending section and the rectum. Also called "sigmoid flexure".

sig·moid·o·scope (sig-móydə-skōp) *n.* An instrument equipped with a light that is inserted into the anus in order to inspect the rectum and sigmoid colon. [SIGMOID + -SCOPE.] **—sig·moid·os·co·py** (síg-moyd-óskəpi) *n.*

sign (sīn) *n., pl.* **signs** or **sign** (for sense 8 only). **1.** Something that points to the presence or existence of a fact, condition, or quality not immediately evident; an indication: *showed no sign of life.* **2.** An action or gesture used to convey an idea, command, or the like: *blew a kiss as a sign of her affection.* **3.** A board, poster, or placard displayed in a public place to advertise or to convey information or a direction: *a road sign; a stop sign.* **4.** A conventional figure or device that stands for a word, phrase, or operation; especially, a symbol, as in mathematics or musical notation: *the plus and minus signs.* **5.** *Medicine.* Any bodily manifestation that indicates the presence of a malfunction or disease to an observer but is not apparent to the patient. Compare **symptom.** **6.** A portentous incident or event; especially, something that indicates a supernatural existence. **7.** *U.S.* An indicator, such as a spoor or scent, of the presence or trail of an animal: *deer sign.* **8.** *Astrology.* Any of the 12 divisions of the zodiac, each named after a constellation and represented by a symbol. Also called "sign of the zodiac".

~v. **signed, signing, signs.** *—tr.* **1.** To affix one's signature to: *signed the letter.* **2.** To write (one's signature). **3.** To approve, authorise, or ratify by affixing a signature, seal, or other mark: *signed the petition.* **4.** To engage by means of obtaining a signature on a contract: *sign a new player.* **5.** To relinquish or transfer (title or ownership, for example) to by signature. Used with *away, off,* or *over.* **6.** To express or signify with a sign; signal. **7.** To make a mark with a sign; especially, to consecrate with the sign of the cross. *—intr.* **1.** To make a sign or signs; signal. **2.** To write one's signature. **—sign in.** To sign one's signature in a book upon arriving at a destination. **—sign off.** **1.** In broadcasting, to announce the end of transmission, as at the end of the day. **2.** To end a letter, as with a signature or a message of affection. **3.** *Informal.* In Britain, to cease drawing unemployment or supplementary benefit. **—sign on.** **1.** In broadcasting, to announce the beginning of transmission, as at the start of the day. **2.** To join or enlist; sign up: *signed on as a midshipman.* **3.** *Informal.* In Britain, to register with the Department of Health and Social Security so as to draw unemployment or supplementary benefit. **4.** To engage the services of; employ. **—sign out.** To sign one's signature in a book before leaving to go elsewhere. **—sign up.** **1.** To join or enlist; sign on. **2.** To engage the services of; employ: *signed up two players.* [Middle English *signe,* from Old French, from Latin *signum,* distinctive mark or figure, seal, signal.]

Synonyms: *sign, badge, mark, token, indication, symptom.*

Si·gnac (seenyáck), **Paul** (1863–1935). French neoimpressionist painter and theoretician, a disciple of Georges Seurat. He painted mainly landscapes and marines, like the *Port of St. Tropez* (1916). He was an exponent of pointillism.

sig·nal (síg-n'l) *n. Abbr.* **sig.** **1. a.** A sign, gesture, mechanical device, or other indicator serving as a means of communication: *Tears are a signal of grief; The railway signal was green.* **b.** A message communicated by such means. **2.** That which is the occasion for or incites action: *The execution was the signal for mass protests.* **3.** *Electronics.* An impulse or fluctuating electric quantity, such as voltage, current, or electric field strength, the variations of which represent coded information. **4.** The sound, image, or message transmitted or received in telegraphy, telephony, radio, television, or radar.

~adj. **1.** Out of the ordinary; remarkable; conspicuous: *a signal feat.* **2.** Used or acting as a signal: *a signal flare.*

~v. **signalled** or *U.S.* **-naled, -nalling** or *U.S.* **-naling, -nals.** *—tr.* **1.** To make a signal or signals to (a person or thing); communicate with by signals: *signalled her to stop her car.* **2.** To relate or make known, as by signals; herald: *Gunfire signalled the start of the battle.* *—intr.* To make a signal or signals. [French, from Old French *s(e)ignal,* from Medieval Latin *signāle,* from Latin *signālis,* of a sign, from *signum,* SIGN.] **—sig·nal·ler** *n.*

signal box *n.* A building containing manually operated levers or the automatic control system operating the signals on a railway network in a particular area.

sig·nal·ise, sig·nal·ize (signə-līz) *tr.v.* **-ised, -ising, -ises.** **1.** To make remarkable or conspicuous. **2.** To point out particularly.

sig·nal·ly (síg-nəli) *adv.* Conspicuously; noticeably; especially.

sig·nal·man (síg-n'l-mən, -man) *n., pl.* **-men** (-mən, -men). **1.** One whose job it is to operate railway signals. **2.** A soldier trained to communicate by signals. In this sense, also called "signaller".

sig·nal·ment (síg-n'l-mənt) *n. U.S.* A detailed description of the appearance of a person, as for police files. [French *signalement,* from *signaler,* to mark out, describe, from *signal,* SIGNAL.]

signal-to-noise ratio (síg-n'l-tə-nóyz, -tōō-) *n.* The ratio of the amplitude of the signal in an electronic device to the amplitude of the noise in that device.

sig·na·to·ry (sig-nə-tri, -təri) *adj.* Bound by signed agreement.

~n., pl. **signatories.** A person or nation that has signed a treaty or other document. [Latin *signātōrius,* from *signāre,* to mark, affix one's seal to, from *signum,* SIGN.]

sig·na·ture (síg-ni-chər, -nə- || *chiefly U.S.* -choor) *n. Abbr.* **sig.** **1. a.** The name of a person as written by himself, especially to approve a document. **b.** The act of signing one's name. **2.** Any sign

sign language

SOUNDS IN SILENCE
Words that are spoken by the hands alone

Before man learned to speak, he had to communicate with his companions by means of grunts, cries, facial expressions, and gestures. Even when spoken language developed, however, sign language survived. Today it is used by some primitive peoples, such as Australia's Aborigines, and in modern societies as an extra way of expressing moods and commands. The most widely known sign languages are those used by the deaf, but deep-sea divers, air traffic controllers, bookmakers, and broadcasters also have their own specialised vocabularies of gestures.

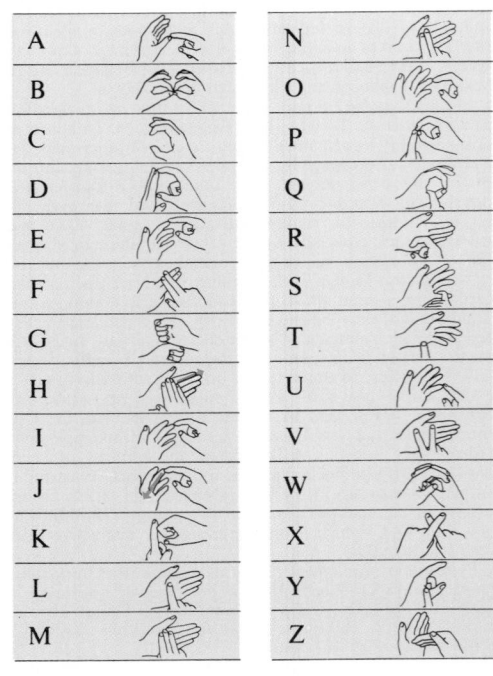

FINGER TALK *One common deaf-and-dumb language is based on the alphabet. The consonant signs are mostly copies of the letters; the vowels are represented by the five fingers.*

that indicates the presence or activity of a person, group, or thing: *The robbery bore the signature of a professional.* **3.** *Music.* **a.** A key **signature** *(see).* **b.** A **time signature** *(see).* **4.** In printing: **a.** A group of printed pages, most commonly 16 or 32, folded from a single sheet, that is bound together with others to make up a book. Also called "gather", "section". **b.** A letter, number, or symbol placed at the bottom of the first page of such a group of printed pages of a book as a guide to the proper sequence of the sheets in binding. **5.** *Abbr.* **S., Sig.** That part of a medical prescription giving the doctor's instructions to the patient. [Medieval Latin *signātūra*, from Latin *signāre*, to mark with a sign, from *signum*, SIGN.]

signature tune *n.* A short, distinctive tune that is used to signify the beginning or end of a particular television or radio programme or to accompany the appearance of an individual performer.

sign-board (sīn-bawrd ‖ -bōrd) *n.* A board that bears a sign giving information.

sign-er (sīnər) *n.* **1.** One that signs. **2.** A person skilled in sign language, especially as an interpreter for the deaf.

sig-net (sig-nit) *n.* **1.** A small seal; especially, an official seal used on a document. **2.** The impression made with such a seal.
~*tr.v.* **signeted, -neting, -nets.** To mark or endorse with a signet. [Middle English, from Old French, diminutive of *signe*, SIGN.]

signet ring *n.* A finger ring bearing a signet or set of initials.

sig-nif-i-cance (sig-niffi-kənss, -nívvi-) *n.* Also **sig-nif-i-can-cy** (-kən-si). **1.** The state or quality of being significant; meaning. **2.** Importance; consequence: *an event of great significance.* **3.** Implied or underlying meaning: *I understand the words, but not their significance.* —See Synonyms at **importance, meaning.**

sig-nif-i-cant (sig-niffikənt, -nívvikənt) *adj.* **1.** Having or expressing a meaning; meaningful. **2.** Having or expressing a covert meaning: *She darted me a significant glance.* **3.** Important; notable; valuable. [Latin *significāns* (stem *significant-*), present participle of *significāre*, to SIGNIFY.] —**sig-nif-i-cant-ly** *adv.*

significant figures *pl.n. Mathematics.* The digits of the decimal

form of a number beginning with the digit farthest to the left and higher than zero and extending to the right to include all digits warranted by the accuracy of measuring devices used to obtain the numbers or to include a specific number of digits after rounding up or down. Also called "significant digits".

sig-ni-fi-ca-tion (síg-nifi-káysh'n) *n.* **1.** Intended meaning; sense. **2.** The act or process of signifying. —See Synonyms at **meaning.**

sig-nif-i-ca-tive (sig-niffi-kətiv, -nívvi-, -kaytiv) *adj.* **1.** Indicative; significant. **2.** Signifying; symbolic.

sig-ni-fy (signi-fī) *v.* **-fied, -fying, -fies.** —*tr.* **1.** To serve as a sign or symbol of; betoken; denote. **2.** To make known; intimate: *signified her approval with a gesture.* —*intr.* To have meaning or importance. —See Synonyms at **mean** (convey sense). [Middle English *signifien*, from Old French *signifier*, from Latin *significāre* : *signum*, SIGN + *facere*, to make.] —**sig-ni-fi-er** *n.*

sign language *n.* A system of communication by means of hand gestures, as used by deaf and dumb people.

sign manual *n., pl.* **signs manual.** A person's signature; especially, the signature of a monarch at the top of a royal decree.

sign of the cross *n.* A gesture in the form of a cross, made in token of faith in Christ or as an invocation of blessing or divine protection; especially, such a gesture of the right hand from the forehead to the breast and then from the left to the right shoulder.

sign of the zodiac *n. Astrology.* A **sign** *(see).*

si-gnor (seen-yawr ‖ -yōr, *chiefly U.S.* seen-yór, -yōr) *n., pl.* **signori** (seen-yáwr-ee ‖ -yōr-) or **-gnors.** Also **si-gnior.** *Abbr.* **S., sig., Sig.** **1.** The Italian title of courtesy for a man used before a surname and equivalent to the English *Mr.* **2.** In an Italian-speaking country, a gentleman. [See **signore.**]

si-gno-ra (seen-yór-ə ‖ -yōr-) *n., pl.* **signore** (-ay) or **-ras.** The Italian title of courtesy for or form of address to a married woman, equivalent to the English *Mrs.* or *madam.* [See **signore.**]

si-gno-re (seen-yór-ay ‖ -yōr-) *n., pl.* **signori** (-ee). *Abbr.* **S., sig., Sig.** **1.** The Italian form of address to a man, equivalent to the English *sir.* **2.** In an Italian-speaking country, a gentleman. [Italian, from Latin *senior,* older, SENIOR.]

Si-gno-rel-li (seen-yaw-rélli), **Luca** (*c.*1441–1523). Italian painter of the Umbrian school. His masterpiece is the fresco cycle at or Orvieto cathedral depicting the end of the world and the last judgment.

si-gno-ri-na (seen-yaw-rée-nə) *n., pl.* **-ne** (-nay) or **-nas.** The Italian title of courtesy for or form of address to an unmarried woman, equivalent to the English *Miss.* [Italian, diminutive of SIGNORA.]

sign-post (sīn-pōst) *n.* **1.** A post supporting a sign. **2.** Anything that serves as an indication, sign, or guide.
~*tr.v.* **signposted, -posting, -posts.** *Chiefly British.* **1.** To equip with signposts. **2.** To make obvious; indicate; show: *She signposted her intentions.*

Sig-urd (síg-oord, -urd). *Norse Mythology.* The hero who slew the dragon Fafnir. He corresponds to Siegfried of the *Nibelungenlied.*

Si-ha-nouk (sée-ə-nōōk, -nōōk), **Prince (Samdech Preah) Norodom** (1922–). Former king of Cambodia, son of King Norodom Suramarit. He was elected king in 1941 and abdicated in March, 1955 to become prime minister and minister of foreign affairs in the following October. In 1960 he was elected head of state, a position which he held until he was deposed by a right-wing faction which opposed his policy of allowing the Vietcong troops to use Cambodian territory. He was restored in 1975 when the Khmer Republic was overthrown, but resigned in 1976. In 1979 he was made a special envoy of the Khmer Rouge to the United Nations.

si-ka (sééka) *n.* A deer, *Cervus nippon,* of southern Asia and Japan, having a white-spotted brown coat in summer and, in the male, slender antlers. [Japanese *shika.*]

Sikh (seek) *n.* An adherent of Sikhism.
~*adj.* Of or pertaining to the Sikhs or Sikhism. [Hindi, from Sanskrit *śiṣya,* "disciple", from *śikṣati,* he helps, pays homage, learns, serves, desiderative of *śaknoti,* he can, is able to do.]

Sikh-ism (séek-iz'm) *n.* The doctrines and practices of a monotheistic religious sect that broke away from orthodox Hinduism in the 16th century.

Si Kiang. See **Xi Jiang.**

Sik-kim (síckim, síckim). State of northern India. It was formerly a constitutional monarchy (controlled by India), but was incorporated into India in 1975. Almost the entire state lies within the eastern Himalayas. Most of the people are subsistence farmers, but spices and tea•are grown for sale. The capital is Gangtok. —**Sik-kim-ese** (síckim-éez) *adj. & n.*

Si-kor-ski (si-kórski; *Polish* shi-), **Władysław** (1881–1943). Polish general and politician. He served in several Cabinet posts in the 1920s before his dismissal from public office by the prime minister, Piłsudski, in 1928. After 1939 he was prime minister of the Polish government-in-exile and commander in chief of the Polish forces in World War II. He was killed in an air crash.

si-lage (sílij) *n.* Fodder prepared by storing and fermenting green forage plants in a silo or pit. [Alteration (influenced by SILO) of ENSILAGE.]

si-lane (sí-layn) *n.* Any of a class of silicon hydrides with the general formula Si_nH_{2n+2}. They are similar to the alkanes and are named by the number of silicon atoms in the molecule (as disilane, Si_2H_6). [*Silicon* + -ANE.]

sild (sild) *n.* Any of various small Norwegian herrings, especially when canned or otherwise prepared for eating. [Norwegian.]

si-lence (sílənss) *n.* **1.** The condition or quality of being or keeping silent; avoidance of speech or noise. **2.** The absence of sound; still-

ness. **3.** A period of time without communication by word or noise: *two minutes' silence.* **4.** Refusal or failure to speak out.
~*tr.v.* **silenced, -lencing, -lences. 1.** To make silent or bring to silence. **2.** To curtail the expression of; suppress. [Middle English, from Old French, from Latin *silentium,* from *silēre,* to be silent.]
si·lenc·er (sī́lən-sər) *n.* **1.** One that silences. **2.** A device in the exhaust system of an internal-combustion engine, especially one fitted to a motor vehicle, in which the sound is deadened by making the exhaust gases pass through a system of baffle plates. **3.** A device attached to the muzzle of a firearm to muffle the report.
si·lent (sī́lənt) *adj.* **1. a.** Making no sound or noise; quiet. **b.** Free of all sound. **2.** Not disposed to speak; taciturn. **3.** *Chiefly U.S.* Unable to speak; mute. **4.** Refusing or failing to give information or an opinion: *remained silent on the matter.* **5.** Not voiced or expressed; tacit: *silent declarations of love.* **6.** Inactive or undisturbed; quiescent: *a silent volcano.* **7.** Having no phonetic value; unpronounced; for example, the letter *b* in *subtle* is silent. **8.** Having no sound track: *a silent film.* —See Synonyms at **still.**
~*n.* A silent film. [Latin *silēns* (stem *silent-*), present participle of *silēre,* to be silent.] —**si·lent·ly** *adv.* —**si·lent·ness** *n.*
silent majority *n.* A group, held to represent the majority of a population or membership, that does not normally express its views but may be taken to favour the status quo.
silent partner *n. Chiefly U.S.* A **sleeping partner** *(see).*
si·le·nus (sī-leé-nəss) *n., pl.* **-ni** (-nī). *Greek Mythology. Sometimes capital* **S.** Any of various minor woodland deities or spirits and companions of Dionysus.
Si·le·nus (sī-leénəss). *Greek Mythology.* A satyr, the foster father of Bacchus.
si·le·si·a (sī-leézi-ə, -leézhə, -leé-si-ə, -leé-shə) *n.* A thin, light, twilled cotton fabric used for linings. [After SILESIA, where it was first produced.]
Si·le·si·a (sī-leézi-ə, -leézhə, -leé-si-ə, -leéshə). *Polish* **Śląsk** (shlonsk); *Czech* **Slez·sko** (sléskō); *German* **Schle·si·en** (shláyzi-ən). Region of east central Europe, extending along the foot of the Sudeten mountains and the west Carpathians, and into the Oder valley. Most of it now lies in Poland, with the rest in Czechoslovakia and East Germany. The area is mostly agricultural land and forest, but the south forms one of Europe's main coal-mining and manufacturing regions. —**Si·le·si·an** *n. & adj.*
sil·hou·ette (sílloo-ét, -et) *n.* **1.** A representation of the outline of something, especially a person's profile, usually filled in with black or another solid colour. **2.** The shadow image or outline of something, such as one produced on a white, illuminated screen by an object interposed between the screen and the source of light.
~*tr.v.* **silhouetted, -etting, -ettes.** To represent or cause to be seen as a silhouette. [French, short for *portrait à la silhouette,* from *silhouette,* object intentionally marred or incomplete, after Étienne de *Silhouette* (1709–67), French controller-general.]
sil·i·ca (síllikə) *n.* A white or colourless crystalline compound, SiO_2, occurring abundantly as quartz, sand, flint, agate, and many other minerals, and used to manufacture a wide variety of materials, notably glass and concrete. Also called "silicon dioxide". [New Latin, from Latin *silex* (stem *silic-*), flint.]
silica gel *n.* Amorphous silica that resembles white sand and is used as a drying and dehumidifying agent, a catalyst and catalyst carrier, an anticaking agent in cosmetics, and in chromatography.
sil·i·cate (sílli-kət, -kit, -kayt) *n.* Any of numerous compounds containing silicon, oxygen, and a metallic or organic radical, occurring in many rocks, and with silicon dioxide (quartz) forming at least 95 per cent of the earth's crust. [SILIC(A) + -ATE.]
si·li·ceous (si-líshəss) *adj.* Containing, resembling, pertaining to, or consisting of silica. [Latin *siliceus,* of flint, from *silex,* flint.]
silici-, silic- *comb. form.* Indicates silica or silicon; for example, **siliciferous, silicide.** [From SILICA.]
si·lic·ic (si-líssik) *adj.* Pertaining to, resembling, or derived from silica or silicon. [SILIC- + -IC.]
silicic acid *n.* A jelly-like substance, $SiO_2.nH_2O$, produced when sodium silicate solution is acidified and used for the same purposes as silica gel.
sil·i·cide (sílli-sīd) *n.* A compound of silicon with another element or radical. [SILIC(I)- + -IDE.]
sil·i·cif·er·ous (sílli-sífərəss) *adj.* Bearing, producing, or in partial combination with silica. [SILICI- + -FEROUS.]
si·lic·i·fy (si-líssi-fī) *v.* **-fied, -fying, -fies.** —*tr.* To convert into silica. —*intr.* To be converted into silica. [SILICI- + -FY.] —**si·lic·i·fi·ca·tion** (-fi-káysh'n) *n.*
sil·i·cle (síllik'l) *n.* Also **si·lic·u·la** (si-líckew-lə). *Botany.* A short, flat siliqua, such as the fruit of the plant honesty. [Latin *silicula,* diminutive of *siliqua,* seed pod, SILIQUA.]
sil·i·con (sílli-kən ‖ -kon) *n. Symbol* **Si** A nonmetallic element occurring extensively in the earth's crust in silica and silicates, having both an amorphous and a crystalline allotrope, and used in combination with other materials in glass, semiconducting devices, concrete, brick, refractories, pottery, and silicones. Atomic number 14, atomic weight 28.086, melting point 1 410°C, boiling point 2 355°C, relative density 2.33, valency 4. [From SILICA.]
silicon carbide *n.* A bluish-black crystalline compound, SiC, one of the hardest known substances, used as an abrasive and heat-refractory material, and in single crystals as a semiconductor, especially in high-temperature applications.
silicon chip *n.* A **chip** based on a silicon wafer, used in microprocessors.
sil·i·con-con·trolled rectifier (síllikən-kən-trṓld ‖ -kon-) *n. Abbr.* **SCR.** An electronic device consisting of a four-layer chip of semiconducting material in which the anode-cathode current is controlled by the signal applied to a third electrode, called the gate.
silicon dioxide *n. Chemistry.* **Silica** *(see).*
sil·i·cone (sílli-kōn) *n.* Any of a group of semi-inorganic polymers based on the structural unit R_2SiO, where R is an organic group, characterised by thermal stability, water repellence, and physiochemical inertness. They are used in adhesives, lubricants, protective coatings, paints, electrical insulation, synthetic rubber, and prosthetic replacements for bodily parts. Compare **siloxane.** [SILIC(I)- + -ONE.]
sil·i·co·sis (sílli-kṓ-siss) *n.* Fibrosis of the lungs caused by long-term inhalation of silica dust and resulting in a chronic shortness of breath. [New Latin : SILIC(I)- + -OSIS.]
si·li·qua (síllikwə, si-leékwə) *n.* Also **si·lique** (si-leék). A long pod that is divided by a membranous partition and splits at both seams, characteristic of fruit of the mustards and related plants. [French, from Latin *siliqua*†, pod.] —**sil·i·quous** (sílli-kwəss), **sil·i·quose** (-kwōz, -kwōss) *adj.*
silk (silk) *n.* **1.** The fine, lustrous fibre produced by certain insect larvae and spiders; especially, fibre produced by a silkworm to form its cocoon. **2.** Thread or fabric made from this fibre. **3. a.** A garment made from this fabric, such as a gown. **b.** *Plural.* Brightly coloured silk garments used to identify a jockey. **4.** Any silky, filamentous material, such as the styles forming a tuft on an ear of maize. **5.** *British Informal.* A Queen's or King's Counsel. —**take silk.** *British.* To become a Queen's or King's Counsel.
~*adj.* Of, resembling, or pertaining to silk. [Middle English *silk, selk,* Old English *sioloc, seolec,* from Late Latin *sericum* (noun), Latin *sericus* (adjective), from *seres,* from Greek *Sēres,* an oriental people (probably originally meaning "the silk people"), from Chinese *sī,* silk. See also **serge, sericeous.**]
silk cotton *n.* Any of several silky fibres of plant origin; especially, **kapok** *(see).*
silk-cot·ton tree (sílk-kótt'n) *n.* Any of several trees of the family Bombacaceae; especially, *Ceiba pentandra,* native to tropical America, cultivated for its leathery fruit containing the fibre **kapok** *(see).* Also called "cotton tree".
silk·en (sílkən) *adj.* **1.** Made of silk. **2.** Resembling silk in texture or appearance; smooth and lustrous: *silken hair.* **3.** Delicately pleasing or caressing in effect: *a silken voice.* **4.** Dressed in or wearing silk.
silk hat *n.* A man's silk-covered top hat.
Silk Road. Ancient trade route between China and the Mediterranean, linking China to the Roman Empire. Its length was about 6 400 kilometres (4,000 miles). It was the route followed by Marco Polo on his historic trip to Cathay.
silk-screen process (sílk-skreen) *n.* A method of producing a stencil for printing in which a design is imposed upon a screen of silk or other fine fabric, coated on areas to be left blank with an impermeable substance. Ink is forced through the cloth onto the printing surface. Also called "screen printing".
silk·worm (sílk-wurm) *n.* Any of various caterpillars that produce silk cocoons; especially, the larva of a Chinese moth, *Bombyx mori,* that spins a cocoon of fine, lustrous fibre that is the source of commercial silk.
silk·y (sílki) *adj.* **-ier, -iest. 1.** Resembling silk; soft and smooth; lustrous. **2.** *U.S.* Made of silk; silken. **3.** Having long, silklike hairs or a silky covering: *a silky leaf.* **4.** Ingratiatingly smooth; seductive. —**silk·i·ly** *adv.* —**silk·i·ness** *n.*
silky oak *n.* A tree, *Grevillea robusta,* native to Australia, having divided leaves and showy clusters of orange flowers.
sill (sil) *n.* **1.** The horizontal member, often of wood or stone, that bears the upright portion of a frame; especially, the base of a window or door frame. **2.** The horizontal member at the base of a window protruding beyond the frame. **3.** *Geology.* A relatively thin sheet of igneous rock intruded between beds of other rock. [Middle English *sille, selle,* Old English *syll(e),* threshold, sill.]
sillabub. Variant of **syllabub.**
sil·li·ma·nite (síllimə-nīt) *n.* A grey, brown, or green mineral, Al_2SiO_5, that occurs in metamorphic rocks. [After Benjamin *Silliman* (1779–1864), U.S. chemist.]
Sil·li·toe (sílli-tō), **Alan** (1928–). British novelist, one of the leading figures in the kitchen-sink movement of the 1950s and 1960s. His two most famous novels of working-class life, *Saturday Night and Sunday Morning* (1958) and *The Loneliness of the Long Distance Runner* (1959), were both made into successful films.
Sills (silz), **Beverly,** born Belle Silverman (1929–). U.S. coloratura soprano. She made her debut with the New York City Opera in 1955 and became its general director in 1979.
sil·ly (sílli) *adj.* **-lier, -liest. 1.** Showing a lack of good sense; unreasoning; foolish. **2.** Showing a lack of or disregard for intelligence; fatuous. **3.** *Informal.* Semiconscious; dazed: *knocked me silly.* **4.** Extremely close to the facing batsman. Said of a fielder in cricket: *silly point.* **5.** *Archaic.* Innocent; harmless; helpless.
~*n., pl.* **sillies.** *Informal.* A silly person. —See Synonyms at **foolish.** [Middle English, "pitiable", originally variant of *seely,* happy, blessed, Old English *gesǣlig.*] —**sil·li·ly** *adv.* —**sil·li·ness** *n.*
sil·ly-bil·ly (sílli-billi) *n., pl.* **-billies.** *Informal.* A silly person. Used affectionately or humorously.
silly season *n.* A period during the summer months when an ab-

silkworm *A woman employed in a spinning factory in China sorts the cocoons produced by the silkworm. The worms – the larvae of* Bombyx mori, *a species of moth – feed on the leaves of the mulberry tree.*

sence of serious news is supposed to lead newspapers to publish frivolous articles. Preceded by *the.*

si·lo (sílō) *n., pl.* **-los. 1. a.** A tall, cylindrical, airtight structure in which fodder is stored. **b.** A pit dug for the same purpose. **2.** *Military.* A sunken missile shelter with facilities either for lifting the missile to a launch position or for launching from underground. ~*tr.v.* **siloed, -loing, -los.** To store in a silo. [Spanish, from Latin *sirus,* from Greek *sirost*†, pit for the storage of grain.]

si·lox·ane (si-lóks-ayn) *n.* Any of a class of organic or inorganic chemical compounds of silicon, oxygen, and usually carbon and hydrogen, based on the structural unit R_2SiO, where R is CH_3, H, C_2H_5, or a more complex group. Compare **silicone.** [*Sil*icon + *ox*ygen + -ANE.]

silt (silt) *n.* A sedimentary material consisting of fine mineral particles intermediate in size between sand and clay.
~*v.* **silted, silting, silts.** —*intr.* To become filled with silt. Usually used with *up.* —*tr.* To fill with silt. Usually used with *up.* [Middle English *cylte,* probably from Scandinavian, akin to Danish and Norwegian *sylt,* salt marsh.] —**sil·ta·tion** (sil-táysh'n) *n.*

silt·stone (sílt-stōn) *n.* A sandstone formed from consolidated silt.

Si·lu·res (sī-lóor-eez, -léwr-, -ayz || *U.S.* síllewr-) *pl.n.* A people described by the Roman historian Tacitus as occupying southwestern Britain at the time of the Roman invasion.

Si·lu·ri·an (sī-lóor-i-ən, si-, -léwr-) *adj.* **1.** Of, belonging to, or designating the geological time or system of rocks of the third period of the Palaeozoic era, characterised by the appearance of land plants. **2.** Of or pertaining to the Silures or their culture.
~*n. Geology.* The Silurian period or system of rocks. Preceded by *the.* [After the SILURES, the rocks having been first identified in the part of Wales supposed to have been inhabited by them.]

si·lu·rid (sī-lóor-id, si-, -léwr-) *adj.* Of or belonging to the family Siluridae, which includes various freshwater catfishes of Europe and Asia.
~*n.* A silurid fish. [New Latin *Siluridae,* from Latin *silurus,* a large freshwater fish, probably the sheatfish, from Greek *silouros.*]

sil·va, syl·va (sílvə) *n.* The trees or forests of a region. [Latin, forest. See **sylvan.**]

silvan. Variant of **sylvan.**

sil·ver (sílvər) *n.* **1.** *Symbol* **Ag** A lustrous white, ductile, malleable metallic element, occurring both uncombined and in ores such as argentite, having the highest thermal and electrical conductivity of the metals. It is highly valued for jewellery, tableware, and other ornamental use, and is widely used in coinage, photography, dental and soldering alloys, electrical contacts, and printed circuits. Atomic number 47, atomic weight 107.870, melting point 960.8°C, boiling point 2 212°C, relative density 10.50, valencies 1, 2. See **sterling silver. 2.** This metal as a commodity or medium of exchange. **3.** Coins made of this metal or a metal similar in colour. **4. a.** Tableware, especially cutlery, and other domestic articles made of or plated with this metal. **b.** Any tableware. **5.** Lustrous light grey to white. **6.** *Photography.* A silver salt, especially silver nitrate, used to sensitise paper. **7.** A silver medal.
~*adj.* **1.** Made of, containing, or coated with silver. **2.** Of, pertaining to, or based on silver: *the silver standard.* **3.** Having a lustrous medium-grey colour: *silver hair.* **4.** Having a sonorous, ringing sound. **5.** Eloquent; persuasive: *a silver tongue.* **6.** Of or designating a 25th anniversary: *a silver jubilee.*
~*v.* **silvered, -vering, -vers.** —*tr.* **1.** To cover, plate, or adorn with silver or a similar lustrous substance, usually by chemical reduction of silver nitrate solution or by deposition of an evaporated metal film in vacuum. **2.** To cause to resemble silver: *Moonlight silvered the waves.* **3.** To coat (photographic paper) with a film of silver nitrate or other silver salt. —*intr.* To become silvery. [Old English *siolfor, seolfor,* Common Germanic *silubhra*-† (unattested).]

silverfish *Flour, paper, and cloth are the favourite foods of the silverfish, a wingless insect which lives in damp, cool places.*

silver age *n. Classical Mythology.* The second of the great periods of the world's history characterised by the diminishing awareness and practice of morality and religion. Compare **golden age, iron age.**

silver band *n.* A group of musicians, a brass band, whose instruments are silver plated.

silver birch *n.* A Eurasian birch tree, *Betula pendula,* having silvery-white, peeling bark.

silver bromide *n.* A pale-yellow powder, AgBr, that darkens on exposure to light, and is used as the light-sensitive component on ordinary photographic films and plates.

silver chloride *n.* A white granular powder, AgCl, that darkens on exposure to light and is used in photography and optics.

silver-eye (sílvər-ī) *n.* An Australian songbird, the **white-eye** *(see).*

silver fir *n.* Any of various coniferous trees of the genus *Abies,* the leaves of which have a silvery undersurface. See **fir.**

sil·ver·fish (sílvər-fish) *n., pl.* **-fishes** or collectively **silverfish. 1.** A silvery, wingless insect, *Lepisma saccharina,* that often causes extensive damage to bookbindings, starched clothing, and similar material. **2.** Any of various fishes having silvery scales, such as a variety of the goldfish *Carassius auratus.*

silver fox *n.* **1.** A variety of the red fox in a colour phase in which it has black fur tipped with white. **2.** The fur of this animal.

silver frost *n.* **Glaze ice** *(see).*

silver iodide *n.* A pale yellow powder, AgI, that darkens on exposure to light and is used in artificial rainmaking, in photography, and as an antiseptic.

silver medal *n.* A medal awarded for achieving second place in a race or similar competition.

sil·vern (sílvərn) *adj. Poetic.* Like silver; silvery.

silver nitrate *n.* A poisonous, colourless crystalline compound, $AgNO_3$, that darkens when exposed to light in the presence of organic matter and is used in photography, mirror manufacturing, hair dyeing, silver plating, and as an external medicine.

silver paper *n.* Thin paper backed with silver-coloured foil, used especially for wrapping confectionery.

silver plate *n.* **1.** Tableware or other household articles made of metal plated with silver. **2.** The thin layer of silver used to plate such articles.

sil·ver-plate (sílvər-pláyt) *tr.v.* **-plated, -plating, -plates.** To cover (a base metal or article) with a thin layer of silver.

sil·ver·point (sílvər-poynt) *n.* **1.** A sketching process using a silver-tipped stylus and specially prepared paper. **2.** The stylus used in this process.

silver salmon *n.* The **coho salmon** *(see).*

silver screen *n.* **1.** *Informal.* Cinematic films collectively. Preceded by *the.* **2.** A screen used for showing a film.

sil·ver·side (sílvər-sīd) *n.* Also **sil·ver·sides** (-sīdz) (for sense 2). **1.** *British.* A boned joint of beef cut from the outer side of the round (the top part of the leg), and often salted and boiled, or roasted. **2.** Any of various marine and freshwater fishes of the family Atherinidae, having a silvery band along each side.

sil·ver·smith (sílvər-smith) *n.* A person who makes, repairs, or replates articles of silver or silver plate. —**sil·ver·smith·ing** *n.*

silver standard *n.* A monetary standard under which a fixed quantity of silver constitutes the basic unit of currency.

silver thaw *n.* **Glaze ice** *(see).*

sil·ver-tongued (sílvər-túngd) *adj.* Fluent and persuasive in speech; eloquent.

sil·ver·ware (sílvər-wair) *n.* Articles, especially cutlery, made of or plated with silver.

sil·ver·weed (sílvər-weed) *n.* **1.** A plant, *Potentilla anserina,* having yellow flowers and leaves that often have silvery hairs. **2.** Any of various twining shrubs of the genus *Argyreia* of southeastern Asia, having purple flowers and silvery leaves.

sil·ver·y (sílvəri) *adj.* **1.** Like silver in colour or lustre. **2.** Having a clear, ringing sound. **3.** Containing or coated with silver. —**sil·ver·i·ness** *n.*

sil·vi·cul·ture (sílvi-kulchər) *n.* The care and cultivation of forest trees; forestry. [French : Latin *silva, sylva,* forest, SILVA + CULTURE.] —**sil·vi·cul·tur·al** (-kúlchərəl) *adj.* —**sil·vi·cul·tur·ist** *n.*

si·ma (sīmə) *n.* The lower layer of the earth's outer crust, rich in silica and magnesium, that underlies the **sial** *(see).* [German *Sima* : New Latin *si*lica + *ma*gnesium.]

sim·ba (símbə) *n. East African.* A name for a lion, especially as used in folktales.

Sim·chath To·rah (sím-kaass táwrə, -kəss || tṓrə, *Hebrew* -khass) *n.* A Jewish holiday celebrated on the 23rd day of Tishri, marking the end of the cycle of reading the Torah, and coinciding with the last day of Succoth. [Hebrew *shimḥath tōrāh,* "rejoicing over the Law" : *śimḥath,* inflectional form of *śimḥāh,* joy, merriment, from *śāmaḥ,* he rejoiced + TORAH.]

Si·me·non (séemə-NON; *French* -nóN), **Georges (Joseph Christian)** (1903–). Belgian novelist and short-story writer. He began to publish in 1922 and during the next 14 years produced more than 1500 short stories, writing under more than a dozen pseudonyms. The first novel introducing his famous detective, Inspector Maigret, was published in 1931. He has published 212 novels, including 80 in the Maigret series.

Sim·e·on (símmi-ən). **1.** In the Old Testament, the second son of Jacob and Leah and the name of the tribe of Israel descended from him. Genesis 29:33. **2.** The man who, upon seeing the infant Jesus, spoke the **Nunc Dimittis** *(see).* Luke 2:25–35.

Simeon Sty·li·tes (stī-lī́t-eez || *U.S. also* sti-), **Saint** (*c.* 390–459). Syrian monk. He entered a monastery near Aleppo, but was forced to leave it and became a hermit. He then spent 40 years on a high column, from *c.* 420, and thus became the first-known Christian stylite, or "column-dweller".

sim·i·an (símmi-ən) *adj.* Also **sim·i·ous** (-əss). Pertaining to, characteristic of, or resembling an ape or monkey.
~*n.* An ape or monkey. [Latin *sīmia,* ape, perhaps from *sīmus,* snub-nosed, from Greek *simos*†, bent upwards, snub-nosed.]

sim·i·lar (sím-i-lər, -ə-) *adj.* **1.** Showing some resemblance; related in appearance or nature; alike though not identical. **2.** *Geometry.* Designating figures having corresponding angles equal and corresponding line segments proportional. [French *similaire,* from Latin *similis,* like.] —**sim·i·lar·ly** *adv.*
Usage: *Similar* is an adjective only, and is not used adverbially in standard English. *X is similar to Y* is acceptable, but *X works similar to Y* is nonstandard.

sim·i·lar·i·ty (sím-i-lárrəti, -ə-) *n., pl.* **-ties. 1.** The condition or quality of being similar; resemblance. **2.** A respect in which persons or things are similar. —See Synonyms at **likeness.**

sim·i·le (sím-i-li, -ə- || -lee) *n.* A figure of speech in which two different things are compared, the comparison usually being made explicit by being introduced with *like* or *as*; for example, *"saw the crowd race away like scattered sheep"* (Saki). Compare **metaphor.** [Latin, neuter of *similis,* SIMILAR.]

si·mil·i·tude (si-mílli-tewd || -tōōd) *n.* **1.** Similarity. **2.** Something closely resembling another; a counterpart; a double. **3.** A simile, allegory, or parable. —See Synonyms at **likeness.** [Middle English, from Old French, from Latin *similitūdo,* from *similis,* SIMILAR.]

Sim·la (símmlə). City in northwest India, capital of Himachal Pradesh state. Situated in the foothills of the Himalayas, its pleasant climate made it a popular holiday and health resort, and it was India's summer capital from 1865 to 1939.

Sim·men·tal (símmən-taal; *German* zímmən-) *n.* Any of a breed of European cattle reared for milk, meat, and as draught animals, having a reddish or yellowish coat. —**Sim·men·tal** *adj.*

sim·mer (símmər) *v.* **-mered, -mering, -mers.** —*intr.* **1.** To cook gently just below or at the boiling point. **2.** To be filled with barely controlled anger or resentment; seethe. —*tr.* To cook just below or at the boiling point. —**simmer down. 1.** To reduce the liquid volume of by boiling slowly. **2.** To become calm after excitement or anger.
~*n.* The state or process of simmering. [Earlier *simper*, Middle English *simperen* (imitative).]

sim·nel (sím-n'l) *n. British.* A rich fruit cake, often covered with marzipan, traditionally eaten at Eastertide. Also called "simnel cake". [Middle English *simenel*, from Old French, from Latin *simila*, fine flour, or Greek *semidalis*, perhaps from Semitic, akin to Akkadian *samīdu*. See also **semolina**.]

Sim·nel (sím-n'l), **Lambert** (c. 1475–1525). Fraudulent pretender to the English throne. He was then trained to impersonate Edward, Earl of Warwick. In 1487, supported by some Yorkists, he made his bid for the throne, but was defeated by Henry VII's forces at Stoke. He was pardoned and sank into obscurity.

si·mo·ni·ac (sī-mǒni-ak, si-) *n.* One who practises simony. —**sim·o·ni·a·cal** (símə-nī-ək'l ‖ símmə-) *adj.* —**sim·o·ni·a·cal·ly** *adv.*

Simon Peter. See **Saint Peter.**

si·mon-pure (símən-péwr) *adj. Literary.* Genuine; thoroughgoing; real. [From the *real Simon Pure*, after *Simon Pure*, a character who is impersonated by a rival in Susanna Centlivre's play *A Bold Stroke for a Wife* (1717).]

Si·mons·town (símənz-town). Town in South Africa, lying on False Bay, just south of Cape Town. It was the headquarters of the British Atlantic fleet from 1814 to 1957.

sim·o·ny (síməni ‖ *U.S. also* símməni) *n.* The buying or selling of ecclesiastical pardons, offices, or emoluments. [Middle English *simonie*, from Old French, from Late Latin *sīmōnia*, after *Simon Magus*, a Samaritan who offered money to the Apostles Peter and John for the power of conferring the Holy Ghost on whomsoever he wished. Acts 8:18–19.] —**sim·o·nist** *n. & adj.*

Simon Ze·lo·tes (zi-lǒ-teez). Christian leader of the first century A.D.; one of the Twelve Apostles. He was a former Zealot.

si·moom (si-moom) *n.* Also **si·moon** (-moon). A strong hot sandladen wind of the Sahara and Arabian deserts. Also called "samiel". [Arabic *samūm*, "poisonous", from *samma*, "he poisoned", from *sam*, poison, from Aramaic *sammā*, drug, poison.]

simp (simp) *n. U.S. Slang.* A simpleton; a fool. [From **SIMPLE.**]

sim·pa·ti·co (sim-pátti-kō, -páati-) *adj. Informal.* **1.** Of like mind or temperament; compatible. **2.** Having attractive qualities; likeable. [Italian, from *simpatia*, sympathy, from Latin *sympathīa*, **SYMPATHY.**]

sim·per (símpər) *v.* **-pered, -pering, -pers.** —*intr.* To smile in a silly, coy, self-conscious manner. —*tr.* To utter or express with a simper.
~*n.* A silly or self-conscious smile. [Scandinavian, akin to Danish dialectal *simper†*, affected.] —**sim·per·er** *n.* —**sim·per·ing·ly** *adv.*

sim·ple (simp'l) *adj.* **-pler, -plest. 1.** Having or composed of one thing or part only; not combined or compound: *a simple device.* **2.** Not involved or complicated; easy. **3.** Without additions or modifications; bare; mere: *the simple facts.* **4.** Without embellishment; not ornate or adorned: *a simple black dress.* **5.** Not elaborate, elegant, or luxurious: *a simple dwelling.* **6.** Not affected; unassuming or unpretentious. **7.** Not guileful or deceitful; sincere. **8.** Humble or lowly in condition or rank: *a simple peasant.* **9.** Ordinary or common: *not migraine, just a simple headache.* **10.** Not important or significant; trivial. **11. a.** Having or manifesting little sense or intellect; stupid. **b.** Mentally subnormal: *a bit simple in the head.* **12.** *Biology.* Having no divisions or subdivisions; not compound: *a simple leaf.* **13.** *Chemistry.* Consisting of only one compound; not complex or mixed: *a simple salt.* **14.** *Music.* Without figuration or ornamentation: *simple harmony.* —See Synonyms at **naive.**
~*n. Archaic.* **1.** A fool; a simpleton. **2.** A person of humble birth or condition. **3.** A medicinal plant or the medicine obtained from it. [Middle English, from Old French, from Latin *simplus*.]

simple fraction *n.* A fraction in which both the numerator and denominator are integers. Also called "common fraction", "vulgar fraction".

simple fracture *n.* See **fracture.**

simple fruit *n. Botany.* A fruit developed from a single pistil that may consist of one carpel or several united carpels.

simple harmonic motion *n. Abbr.* **S.H.M.** *Physics.* A periodic motion that may be described as a sinusoidal function of time; specifically, the motion of a particle that obeys the equation $x = A\cos(kt + \phi)$, where x is the displacement of the particle from the origin at any time t, A is the maximum displacement, ϕ is the initial phase or angular displacement at $t = 0$, and k is a constant equal to 2π times the frequency of the oscillation.

simple interest *n.* Interest paid only on the original principal, not on the interest accrued. Compare **compound interest.**

simple machine *n.* A device for changing the magnitude or direction of a force, a **machine** (see).

simple microscope *n.* A microscope having one lens or lens system, such as a magnifying glass or hand lens.

sim·ple-mind·ed (simp'l-míndid) *adj.* **1.** Not sophisticated; artless. **2.** Stupid or silly. **3.** Mentally subnormal. —**sim·ple-mind·ed·ly** *adv.* —**sim·ple-mind·ed·ness** *n.*

simple pendulum *n.* A pendulum *(see)*.

simple sentence *n.* A sentence having no coordinate or subordinate clauses; for example, *The cat purred.* Compare **complex sentence.**

Simple Simon *n. Informal.* A foolish fellow; a simpleton. [After the title character of a nursery rhyme.]

simple sugar *n.* A monosaccharide *(see)*.

simple tense *n. Grammar.* A tense in which the verb is expressed without an auxiliary; for example, the simple past tense of "go", *I went*, as opposed to the perfect (or present perfect) tense, *I have gone.* Compare **compound tense.**

simple time *n. Music.* A time in which each beat in the bar is divisible into two. Compare **compound time.**

sim·ple·ton (simp'l-tən) *n.* A silly or feeble-minded person; a fool. [SIMPLE + *-ton*, "town" (as in surnames derived from place names).]

sim·plex (sím-pleks) *adj.* Designating a system of telegraphy in which only one message may be sent in either direction at one time. Compare **duplex, multiplex.**
~*n.* A simplex system. [Latin *simplex*, simple, single.]

sim·plic·i·ty (sim-plíssəti) *n., pl.* **-ties.** The state or quality of being simple, especially: **1.** Absence of complexity, adornment, or artificiality. **2.** Lack of good sense or intelligence; foolishness. [Middle English *symplicite*, from Old French, from Latin *simplicitās*, from *simplex*, simple.]

sim·pli·fy (símpli-fī) *tr.v.* **-fied, -fying, -fies.** To make simple or simpler; render less complex or intricate. [French *simplifier*, from Medieval Latin *simplificāre* : Latin *simplus*, SIMPLE + *facere*, to make.] —**sim·pli·fi·ca·tion** (-fi-káysh'n) *n.* —**sim·pli·fi·er** *n.*

sim·plis·tic (sim-plístik) *adj.* **1.** Showing a tendency to oversimplify an issue or problem by ignoring complexities or complications. **2.** *Informal.* Extremely simple or uncomplicated. —**sim·plism** (sím-pliz'm) *n.* —**sim·plis·ti·cal·ly** (sim-plístik'l-i, -plístikli) *adv.*

Sim·plon Pass (sán-plon; *French* saN-plóN). Pass in the Lepontine Alps, southern Switzerland, at an altitude of 2 010 metres (6,590 feet). It is crossed by a railway connecting Brig in Switzerland with Iselle in Italy through the Simplon Tunnel, which runs for 19.8 kilometres (12.3 miles) and is the longest in the world.

sim·ply (símpli) *adv.* **1.** In a simple manner; plainly. **2.** Merely; only: *I left simply to avoid her.* **3.** Absolutely; altogether: *a simply marvellous film.* **4.** Speaking frankly; candidly: *You are, quite simply, inadequate for this job.*

Simp·son Desert (símps'n). Uninhabited, arid wilderness in central Australia, lying mainly in Northern Territory, but extending slightly into Queensland and South Australia. It occupies about 145 000 square kilometres (56,000 square miles).

sim·u·la·crum (símmew-láy-krəm, -lá-) *n., pl.* **-cra** (-krə). Also *archaic* **sim·u·la·cre** (-kər) *pl.* **-cres. 1.** An image or representation of something. **2.** An unreal or false semblance of something. [Latin, from *simulāre*, to SIMULATE.]

sim·u·lar (símmew-lər ‖ -laar) *n. Archaic.* One that simulates.
~*adj. Archaic.* Simulated; sham.

sim·u·late (símmew-layt) *tr.v.* **-lated, -lating, -lates. 1. a.** To have or take on the appearance, form, or sound of; imitate. **b.** To make so as to resemble the real or genuine thing: *simulated diamonds.* **2.** To make a pretence of; feign: *simulate an interest.* **3.** To imitate or create the conditions of, as for an experiment or for training. —See Synonyms at **imitate, pretend.**
~*adj.* (-lət, -lit, -layt). *Archaic.* Simulated; assumed; pretended. [Latin *simulāre*, from *similis*, SIMILAR.] —**sim·u·la·tive** (-lətiv, -laytiv) *adj.* —**sim·u·lant** (-lənt) *adj. & n.*

sim·u·la·tion (símmew-láysh'n) *n.* **1.** The act or process of simulating. **2.** An imitation. **3.** The assumption of a false appearance; a feigning or pretending. **4.** A process for studying or finding a solution for a problem or for calculating the effects of a course of action, by representing it in mathematical terms, especially using a computer.

sim·u·la·tor (símmew-laytər) *n.* One that simulates; especially, an apparatus that generates test conditions approximating actual or operational conditions.

si·mul·cast (símm'l-kaast ‖ -kast, *U.S.* sím'l-) *tr.v.* **-casted, -casting, -casts.** To broadcast simultaneously by radio and television.
~*n.* A broadcast so transmitted. [*Simul*taneous + broad*cast*.]

si·mul·ta·ne·ous (símm'l-táyni-əss ‖ *chiefly U.S.* sím'l-) *adj.* **1.** Happening, existing, or done at the same time. **2.** *Mathematics.* Collectively restricting the values of a set of variables: *simultaneous equations.* —See Synonyms at **contemporary.** [Formed by analogy with INSTANTANEOUS from Latin *simul*, at the same time.] —**si·mul·ta·ne·i·ty** (-tə-née-əti, -náy-), **si·mul·ta·ne·ous·ness** *n.* —**si·mul·ta·ne·ous·ly** *adv.*

sin[1] (sin) *n.* **1.** A transgression of a religious or moral law, especially when deliberate. **2.** *Theology.* A condition of estrangement from God resulting from a transgression of His known will. **3.** Any course of action regarded as shameful or deplorable: *It's a sin the way they treat that dog.* —**live in sin.** To cohabit as wife and husband without being married.
~*intr.v.* **sinned, sinning, sins. 1.** To commit a sinful act; violate a religious or moral law. **2.** To commit an offence or violation; do wrong. Usually used with *against.* [Middle English *sinne, sunne*, Old English *syn(n)*.]

sin² (seen) *n.* The 21st letter of the Hebrew alphabet. [Hebrew *sin*, variant of *shīn*, "tooth", SHIN (letter).]

sin³ (sīn). *Trigonometry.* sine.

Si·na·i (sī-ni-ī, -nay-, -nī). Triangular peninsula forming the north-eastern part of Egypt and providing a land bridge between Africa and Asia. It lies between the Suez Canal and the Gulf of Suez on the west and Israel and the Gulf of Aqaba on the east. Mount Sinai, of sacred importance in the Jewish, Christian, and Islamic traditions, has usually been identified with Mount Musa in the southern mountainous region of the peninsula. Sinai has rich deposits of manganese and petroleum and has been of central strategic significance in the Arab-Israeli hostilities since 1956.

sin·an·thro·pus (sī-nánthrə-pəss, si-, sīn-an-thrŏ-, sin-an-) *n.* An extinct humanlike primate, *Sinanthropus pekinensis,* known as Peking man. It is now designated as *Homo erectus.* [New Latin *Sinanthropus,* "Chinese human" : SIN(O)- + -ANTHROPUS.]

sin·a·pism (sínnə-piz'm) *n.* A mustard plaster. [French *sinapisme,* from Late Latin *sināpismus,* from Greek *sinapismos,* use of a mustard plaster, from *sinapizein,* to apply a mustard plaster, from *sinapi,* mustard, related to earlier *napu,* probably from Egyptian.]

Si·na·tra (si-naátrə), **Frank,** born Francis Albert Sinatra (1915–). U.S. popular singer of the late 1930s and 1940s and screen actor. After World War II he began a long and successful film career, appearing in such films as *On The Town* (1949) and *Guys and Dolls* (1955). He won an Academy Award as best actor for his performance in *From Here to Eternity* (1953).

sin bin *n.* **1.** In sports such as ice hockey, a place for players to wait at the side of a playing area when they have been sent off temporarily for rule infringements. **2.** *Informal.* A place of temporary detention or punishment.

since (sinss) *adv.* **1.** From a time in the past up to the present; from then until now. Often preceded by *ever: She arrived last week and has been here ever since.* **2.** At a time between a past time or event and the present; between then and now. **3.** At some past time; before now; ago: *long since forgotten.*
~*prep.* **1.** During the time following: *She has not been home since Easter.* **2.** Continuously throughout the time following: *up since seven.*
~*conj.* **1.** During the time after which: *She hasn't been home since she graduated.* **2.** Continuously from the time when: *She hasn't spoken since she sat down.* **3.** As a result of the fact that; inasmuch as. [Middle English *sin(ne)s,* contraction of *sithen(es),* Old English *siththan,* "after that".]

sin·cere (sin-seér) *adj.* **-cerer, -cerest. 1.** Not feigned or affected; true: *sincere indignation.* **2.** Presenting no false appearance; not hypocritical; honest: *a sincere believer.* **3.** *Archaic.* Pure; unadulterated. [Latin *sincērus,* clean, pure, genuine, honest.] —**sin·cere·ly** *adv.* —**sin·cere·ness** *n.*

    Synonyms: *sincere, natural, unaffected, unfeigned, wholehearted, heartfelt.*

sin·cer·i·ty (sin-sérrəti ‖ *U.S. also* -seér-əti) *n., pl.* **-ties. 1.** The quality or condition of being sincere; sincereness. **2.** A sincere feeling or expression.

sin·ci·put (sín-si-put, -pət) *n., pl.* **-puts** or **sincipita** (sin-síppitə). *Anatomy.* **1.** The upper half of the cranium, especially the anterior portion above and including the forehead. **2.** The forehead. [Latin, from earlier *sēmicaput* (unattested) : SEMI + *caput,* head.] —**sin·cip·i·tal** (sin-síppit'l) *adj.*

Sin·clair (síng-klair, sín-, sin-kláir ‖ *chiefly Scottish* -klər), **Upton** (1878–1968). U.S. novelist. His first novel, *The Jungle* (1906), exposed the insanitary conditions in the Chicago stockyards and helped to form the wave of public protest which led to reform legislation. He won a Pulitzer prize for *Dragon's Teeth* in 1942.

Sind (sind). Province of southeastern Pakistan, bordering on the Arabian Sea and on India to the south and east. It occupies the lower Indus valley. The capital is Karachi. The leading industrial centre in this chiefly agricultural province is Hyderabad.

Sin·dhi (sindi, sínd-hi) *n., pl.* **-dhis** or collectively **Sindhi. 1.** A member of the predominantly Muslim people of Sind. **2.** The Indic language of Sind. —**Sin·dhi** *adj.*

sine (sīn) *n. Abbr.* **sin 1.** The ordinate of the endpoint of an arc of a unit circle centred at the origin of a Cartesian coordinate system, the arc being of length x and measured anticlockwise from the point $(1, 0)$ if x is positive, or clockwise if x is negative. **2.** In a right-angled triangle, the function of an acute angle that is the ratio of the opposite side to the hypotenuse. [Medieval Latin *sinus,* "fold of a garment" (mistranslation of Arabic *jayb,* chord of an arc, sine, through confusion with Arabic *jayb,* fold of a garment), from Latin, curve, fold, hollow. See **sinus.**]

si·ne·cure (sīni-kewr, sínni-) *n.* **1.** An office, position, or charge that is remunerated but requires little or no work. **2.** An ecclesiastical benefice not involving any of the spiritual duties of a parish. [Medieval Latin (*beneficium*) *sine cūrā,* (benefice) without care (of souls) : *sine,* without + *cūrā,* ablative of *cūra,* cure, care.] —**si·ne·cur·ism** *n.* —**si·ne·cur·ist** *n.*

sine curve (sīn) *n.* The graph of the equation $y = \sin x$. Also called "sinusoid".

si·ne di·e (sīni dī-ee, sínni dée-ay) *adv. Abbr.* **s.d.** Indefinitely: *Parliament was dismissed sine die.* [Latin, "without a day (fixed)".]

si·ne qua non (sīni kway nón, sínni kwaa, nŏn) *n.* An essential element or condition. [Latin, "without which not".]

sin·ew (sínnew) *n.* **1.** A tendon. **2.** Vigorous strength; muscular power. **3.** *Often plural.* The source or mainstay, as of vitality or strength. [Middle English *sin(e)we, sen(e)ue,* Old English *sinu, seonu,* from Germanic.]

sin·ew·y (sínnew-i) *adj.* **1.** Like or consisting of sinews. **2.** Lean and muscular. **3.** Strong; vigorous.

sin·fo·ni·a (sin-fə-néer, -née-ə, sin-fŏn-i-ə) *n., pl.* **-nias** or **-nie** (-née-ay). *Music.* **1.** A symphonic work. Sometimes used as part of the name of an orchestra. **2.** An overture, especially to an early Italian opera. [Italian, symphony.]

sin·fo·ni·et·ta (sin-fən-yéttə, -fŏn-i-éttə) *n., pl.* **-tas.** *Music.* A small-scale symphony, either one that is short in length or one that uses a small orchestra. Sometimes used as part of the name of a small orchestra. [Italian, diminutive of SINFONIA.]

sin·ful (sín-f'l) *adj.* Marked by or full of sin; wicked. —**sin·ful·ly** *adv.* —**sin·ful·ness** *n.*

sing (sing) *v.* **sang** (sang) or *rare* **sung** (sung), **sung, singing, sings.** —*intr.* **1.** To utter a series of words or sounds in musical tones. **2. a.** To perform songs for an audience, especially as a profession. **b.** To render a song or songs to an accompaniment. Used with *to: sing to the guitar.* **3. a.** To make noises that are melodious or sound like music. Used chiefly of birds. **b.** To give or have the effect of melody; lilt. **4.** To produce musical sounds when played. **5.** To make a high whine or hum. **6.** To be filled with a buzzing sound. Used chiefly of the ears or head. **7. a.** To proclaim or extol something in verse. **b.** To relate a tale in a song. Used with *of: sang of ancient heroes.* **8.** *Chiefly U.S. Slang.* **a.** To give information or evidence against someone. **b.** To confess to a crime. —*tr.* **1.** To utter (a song or lyrics, for example) with musical inflections of the voice. **2.** To intone; chant. **3.** To proclaim or extol, often in verse: *sings your praises.* **4.** To bring to a specified state by singing: *Sing me to sleep.* —**sing out. 1.** To sing loudly. **2.** To shout out.
~*n.* **1.** *Informal.* An act of singing. **2.** *U.S.* A gathering of people for group singing. [Middle English *singen, sang, sungen,* Old English *singan, sang* (past singular), *sungen.*] —**sing·a·ble** *adj.*

sing. singular.

Sin·ga·pore (síng-ə-pór, -gə- ‖ -pŏr, *chiefly U.S.* -pawr, -pōr). Independent republic lying off the southern tip of the Malay peninsula. In addition to the main island of Singapore it includes about 60 smaller islands. A major commercial centre with a large shipping and shipbuilding industry, Singapore has one of the highest standards of living in southeast Asia. It is highly industrialised, petroleum products, electronics, and rubber accounting for half its exports, and tourism is also important. Three quarters of the population is Chinese. In 1963 Singapore joined the Federation of Malaysia, but withdrew two years later to become an independent republic. Area, 581 square kilometres (224 square miles). Population, 2,500,000. Capital, Singapore.

singe (sinj) *tr.v.* **singed, singeing, singes. 1.** To burn superficially; scorch. **2.** To burn the ends of. **3.** To burn off the feathers or bristles of by subjecting briefly to flame. —See Synonyms at **burn.**
~*n.* A burn that is superficial. [Middle English *sengen,* Old English *sencgan,* from Germanic.] —**sing·er** (sínjər) *n.*

sing·er (síng-ər) *n.* **1.** A person who sings, especially a trained or professional vocalist. **2.** A poet, especially in ancient or medieval times. **3.** A songbird.

Sing·er (síng-ər), **Isaac Bashevis** (1904–). U.S. novelist and short-story writer, born in Poland. He has published such collections as *Gimpel the Fool and Other Stories* (1961) and *A Crown of Feathers* (1973). He was awarded the Nobel prize for literature in 1978.

Singhalese. Variant of **Sinhalese.**

sin·gle (síng-g'l) *adj.* **1. a.** Not accompanied by another or others; solitary. **b.** Even one, not to mention others. Used with a negative:

Not a single person offered to help. **2.** Consisting of one form or part; not double or multiple. **3.** One throughout; undiversified; uniform. **4.** Separate from others; distinct; individual: *every single day.* **5.** Designed to accommodate or be sufficient for one person: *a single bed.* **6.** *Chiefly British.* Of or designating a ticket entitling the holder to travel to a destination but not back again. Compare **return. 7. a.** Unmarried. **b.** Of or associated with the state of being unmarried: *living in single bliss.* **8.** Without a partner: *a single parent.* **9.** *Botany.* Having only one rank or row of petals: *a single flower.* **10.** One-against-one: *single combat.*
~*n.* **1.** A separate unit; an individual. **2.** Something, such as a room or bed, intended for use by one person. **3.** An unmarried person. **4.** A one-pound note or a one-dollar bill. **5.** A single ticket. **6.** In cricket, a single run. **7. a.** A small record, often with only one piece of music or track on each side, usually to be played at 45 revolutions per minute. Also called "forty-five". **b.** A piece of music or track on one side of such a record. **8.** See **singles.**
~*tr.v.* **singled, -gling, -gles.** To choose or distinguish from among others. Used with *out.* [Middle English *sengle,* from Old French, from Latin *singulus.*] —**sin·gle·ness** *n.*
  Synonyms: *single, sole, unique, solitary, individual.*
sin·gle-act·ing (síng-g'l-ákting) *adj.* Designating a steam engine or pump in which the pistons are pressurised on one side only. Compare **double-acting.**
sin·gle-ac·tion (síng-g'l-áksh'n) *adj.* Having a hammer that must be cocked by hand after each shot. Said of a firearm.
single-blind (síng-g'l-blínd) *adj.* Pertaining to or designating an experimental procedure, such as one to test reactions to medicinal drugs, in which the experimenters know the composition of the test items and control substances but the subjects do not. Compare **double-blind.**
single bond *n. Chemistry.* A type of chemical bond formed by one pair of shared electrons.
sin·gle-breast·ed (síng-g'l-bréstid) *adj.* Closing with a narrow overlap and a single row of fasteners. Said of a coat or jacket.
single-cell protein (síng-g'l-sel) *n.* Any protein produced by a mass of cells that have been cultured from a single cell.
single crochet *n.* A stitch or method of stitching in crochet. See **slip stitch.**
single cross *n. Genetics.* A first-generation hybrid produced by a cross between two inbred lines.
sin·gle-deck·er (sing-g'l-déckər) *n.* A bus with only one floor to accommodate passengers. —**sin·gle-deck·er** *adj.*
single entry *n.* A system of bookkeeping in which a business keeps only a single account showing amounts due and amounts owed. Compare **double entry.** —**sin·gle-en·try** *adj.*
single eye *n.* Sole devotion: *has a single eye for her work.*
single file *n.* A line of people, animals, or things standing or moving one behind the other. Also called "Indian file".
~*adv.* In single file.
sin·gle-foot (síng-g'l-fŏŏt) *n.* A horse's gait, the **rack** (see).
~*intr.v.* **single-footed, -footing, -foots.** To go at this gait.
sin·gle-hand·ed (síng-g'l-hándid) *adj.* **1.** Working or done without help; unassisted. **2.** Designed for use with one hand. **3.** Having or using only one hand. —**sin·gle-hand·ed, sin·gle-hand·ed·ly** *adv.* —**sin·gle-hand·ed·ness** *n.*
single knot *n.* An **overhand knot** (see).
sin·gle-lens reflex (síng-g'l-lénz) *adj. Abbr.* **SLR** Designating a form of reflex camera in which the lens through which light enters the camera to expose the film also serves to illuminate the viewfinder screen after the light has been reflected by a retractable viewfinder mirror.
~*n.* A single-lens reflex camera.
single malt *n.* A Scotch whisky distilled from a single batch of fermented malted barley.
sin·gle-mind·ed (síng-g'l-míndid) *adj.* **1.** Having one overriding purpose or opinion. **2.** Steadfast. —**sin·gle-mind·ed·ly** *adv.* —**sin·gle-mind·ed·ness** *n.*
sin·gle-phase (síng-g'l-fáyz) *adj.* Producing, carrying, or powered by a single alternating voltage.
sin·gles (síng-g'lz) *n.* Used with a singular verb. A match, as in tennis, between two players only.
singles bar *n. Chiefly U.S.* A bar used mostly by single people, especially with the aim of pairing off.
sin·gle-sex (síng-g'l-séks) *adj.* Of, pertaining to, or accepting members of one sex only: *single-sex schools.*
sin·gle-space (síng-g'l-spáyss) *v.* **-spaced, -spacing, -spaces.** —*tr.* To type (copy) without leaving a blank line between the lines of print. —*intr.* To type copy without line spaces.
sin·gle-stick (síng-g'l-stik) *n.* **1.** A one-handed fencing stick fitted with a hand guard. Also called "backsword". **2.** The art, sport, or exercise of fencing with such a stick.
sin·glet (síng-glit, -glət) *n.* **1.** *Chiefly British.* **a.** A man's sleeveless vest. **b.** *Australian & N.Z.* Any, usually sleeveless, undershirt. **c.** *Chiefly British.* A sleeveless vest worn for running or other sports. **2.** *Physics.* A multiplet with a single member. **3.** *Chemistry.* A single, shared electron in a chemical bond. [From *single* (in sense 1, referring to an unlined garment), after DOUBLET.]
single tax *n. U.S. Economics.* A system by which all revenue is derived from a tax on one object, especially on land.
sin·gle·ton (síng-g'l-tən) *n.* **1.** A playing card that is the only one of its suit in a player's hand. **2.** An individual as distinguished from a pair or group. [From *single* (by analogy with SIMPLETON).]

sin·gle-tongu·ing (síng-g'l-túng-ing ‖ *Northern English* -tóng-) *n.* The playing of a wind instrument, interrupting the wind stream by moving the tongue as if to pronounce a *t* sound repeatedly. Compare **double-tonguing, triple-tonguing.** —**single-tongue** *v.*
sin·gle-tree (síng-g'l-tree) *n. Chiefly U.S.* A **swingletree** (see).
sin·gly (síng-gli) *adv.* **1.** Without company or help; alone. **2.** One by one; individually.
Sing Sing. See **Ossining.**
sing·song (síng-song ‖ *U.S. also* -sawng) *n.* **1.** Verse characterised by mechanical regularity of rhythm and rhyme. **2.** Enunciation marked by a repetitive rise and fall in pitch. **3.** *Chiefly British.* An impromptu or informal session of singing or a meeting to sing.
~*adj.* Characterised by repetitive rise-and-fall tone.
Sing·spiel (zíng-shpeel) *n. German.* A type of opera consisting of spoken dialogue with songs interspersed, popular in the 18th century, especially in Germany. ["Singing play".]
sin·gu·lar (síng-gew-lər) *adj.* **1.** Being only one; separate; individual. **2. a.** Remarkable; extraordinary; rare. **b.** Deviating strongly from a norm; peculiar; odd. **3.** *Abbr.* **s., sing.** *Grammar.* Of, pertaining to, or being the grammatical number denoting a single person or thing or several considered as a single unit. Compare **plural. 4.** *Logic.* Of or pertaining to the specific as distinguished from the general; individual. —See Synonyms at **strange.**
~*n. Abbr.* **s., sing.** *Grammar.* The singular number, a form denoting it, or a word having a singular number. [Middle English *singuler,* solitary, single, from Old French, from Latin *singulāris,* from *singulus,* SINGLE.] —**sin·gu·lar·ly** *adv.* —**sin·gu·lar·ness** *n.*
sin·gu·lar·ise, sin·gu·lar·ize (síng-gewlər-īz) *tr.v.* **-ised, -ising, -ises.** To make conspicuous; distinguish from others. —**sin·gu·lar·i·sa·tion** (-ī-záysh'n ‖ *U.S.* -i-) *n.*
sin·gu·lar·i·ty (síng-gew-lárrəti) *n., pl.* **-ties. 1.** The condition or quality of being singular. **2.** A trait marking out a person or thing as distinct from others; a peculiarity. **3.** Something uncommon or unusual. **4.** *Physics.* A point in space-time at which there is an infinite density of matter, theoretically the ultimate fate of matter within the event horizon of a black hole. A singularity without an event horizon is a **naked singularity** (see).
sin·gul·tus (sing-gúl-təss) *n.* A **hiccup** (see). [Latin, sob.]
sinh (shīn, *also* sinsh) hyperbolic sine.
Sin·ha·lese (sing-hə-léez, -gə-, *also* sín-hə-, sínnə- ‖ -leess) *n., pl.* **Sinhalese.** Also **Sin·gha·lese. 1.** A member of a people constituting the major portion of the population of Sri Lanka. **2.** The Indic language of this people.
~*adj.* Also **Sin·gha·lese.** Of or pertaining to the Sinhalese or their language. [Sanskrit *sinhalam,* Sri Lanka.]
Sin·i·cism (sĭni-siz'm, sínni-) *n.* A custom or trait peculiar to the Chinese. [Medieval Latin *Sinicus,* Chinese, from Late Latin *Sinae,* the Chinese. See *Sino-.*]
sin·is·ter (sínnistər) *adj.* **1. a.** Suggesting an evil force or motive: *a sinister smile.* **b.** Evil or base. **2.** Presaging trouble; ominous. **3.** *Archaic.* On the left side; left. **4.** *Heraldry.* On the left of the bearer and hence on the right of the observer. Compare **dexter.** [Middle English *sinistre,* from Old French, from Latin *sinister†,* left, on the left, hence evil, unlucky (in augury the left side being regarded as inauspicious).] —**sin·is·ter·ly** *adv.* —**sin·is·ter·ness** *n.*
sin·is·tral (sínnistrəl) *adj.* **1.** Of, facing, or situated on the left side. **2.** Left-handed. Compare **dextral. 3.** *Zoology.* Designating or pertaining to a gastropod shell that has its aperture to the left when facing the observer with the apex upwards. —**sin·is·tral·ly** *adv.*
sin·is·tro·dex·tral (sínnistro-dékstrəl, -trə-) *adj.* Moving or directed from left to right: *a sinistrodextral text.* [Sinistro-, from Latin *sinister,* left + DEXTRAL.]
sin·is·trorse (sínniss-trawrss, -trórss) *adj.* Growing upwards in a spiral that turns from right to left: *a sinistrorse vine.* Compare **dextrorse.** [New Latin *sinistrorsus,* turned towards the left : SINISTER (left) + *versus,* past participle of *vertere,* to turn.] —**sin·is·trorse·ly** *adv.*
sin·is·trous (sínnistrəss) *adj. Archaic.* Sinister; ill-omened: *"The arrival of a beggar on an island is accounted a sinistrous event."* (Samuel Johnson). —**sin·is·trous·ly** *adv.*
Si·nit·ic (sī-níttik, si-) *n.* One of the two branches of the Sino-Tibetan linguistic group, comprising all the various Chinese languages and dialects, including Mandarin, Cantonese, and Fukien. —**Si·nit·ic** *adj.*
sink (singk) *v.* **sank** (sangk) *or* **sunk** (sungk), **sunk** *or* **sunken** (súngkən), **sinking, sinks.** —*intr.* **1.** To descend beneath the surface or to the bottom of a liquid or soft substance; especially, to cease to float through lack of buoyancy: *The ship sank.* **2.** To move to a lower level; go down slowly or in stages. **3.** To appear to move downwards or below the horizon. **4.** To slope downwards; incline. **5.** To pass into a worsened physical condition; approach death. **6. a.** To become weaker, quieter, or less forceful: *Her voice sank and died away.* **b.** To fall down or give way, as through weakness or fatigue: *sank into a chair.* **7.** To diminish, as in value or amount. **8. a.** To suffer a loss of morale, spirit, or vitality. Used with *in* or *into*: *sank into a deep depression.* **b.** To be depressed or dismayed: *My heart sank.* **c.** To decline, as in morality or reputation. Used with *in* or *into*: *sank into anonymity.* **9.** To penetrate or cut through something. Used with *in* or *into*: *The blade sank in.* **10.** *Informal.* To penetrate or be absorbed by the mind. Used with *in* or *into*: *The message finally sank in.* **11.** To seep or be soaked up. Used with *in* or *into.* **12.** To become hollowed or shrunken. Used of the cheeks.
—*tr.* **1.** To cause to descend beneath the surface; especially, to

cause (a vessel) to lose buoyancy and cease to float. **2.** To cause or allow to fall; drop or lower. **3. a.** To force into the ground: *sink piles into a river bed.* **b.** To cause to cut through or penetrate: *sank her fork into the steak.* **4.** To dig or drill (a mine or well) in the earth. **5.** To degrade; debase the character or reputation of. **6.** To cause to diminish, as in value or price. **7.** To suppress; hide; conceal: *sink our differences for the sake of appearances.* **8.** To cause to fail or suffer a reverse; defeat: *could sink the whole project.* **9.** To invest (money). Used with *in* or *into.* **10.** To lose (part or all of an investment). **11.** To pay off (a debt). **12.** To cause (a ball) to enter a target in games such as golf, snooker, or basketball. **13.** *Informal.* To drink. **—sink or swim.** To succeed through one's own efforts, or else fail completely.

~n. **1.** A water basin fixed to a wall or floor and having a drainpipe and generally a piped supply of water. **2.** A cesspool. **3.** A **sinkhole** *(see).* **4.** In thermodynamics, the part of a system from which heat or, more generally, energy is removed from the system. **5.** Any place regarded as an abode of wickedness and corruption. [Middle English *sinken, sank, sunken,* Old English *sincan, sanc* (past singular), *suncen.*] **—sink·a·ble** *adj.* **—sink·age** *n.*

Usage: The past tense of this verb is most commonly *sank,* though *sunk* is often heard, especially informally. The past participle is *sunk*; *sunken* is usually only adjectival *(sunken treasure).*

sink·er (síngkər) *n.* **1.** One that sinks. **2.** A weight used for sinking fishing lines, nets, or the like. **3.** *U.S. Slang.* A doughnut.

sink estate *n. British.* A dilapidated, squalid council housing estate, inhabited by those unable to be housed elsewhere, usually belonging to the poorest, most disadvantaged group of society.

sink·hole (síngk-hōl) *n.* **1.** A natural depression in a land surface communicating with a subterranean passage, generally occurring in limestone regions and formed by solution or by collapse of a cavern roof. **2.** A natural hole or hollow in limestone or chalk into which surface water disappears. In this sense, also called "swallow hole".

Sinkiang Uighur Autonomous Region. See **Xinjiang Uygur Zizhiqu.**

sink·ing feeling (síngking) *n.* A sensation in the pit of the stomach caused, for example, by hunger, fear, or anxiety.

sinking fund *n.* A fund accumulated over a period and invested for the paying off of a public or corporate debt.

sin·less (sín-ləss, -liss) *adj.* Free from or without sin or guilt. **—sin·less·ly** *adv.* **—sin·less·ness** *n.*

sin·ner (sínnər) *n.* Especially in Christianity, one who sins.

sinnet. Variant of **sennit.**

Sinn Fein (shín fáyn) *n.* An Irish nationalist organisation founded in about 1905, that constitutes the political branch of the **I.R.A.** *(see),* and is dedicated to the political and economic independence of a united Ireland. It split into the **Official** and **Provisional** wings *(both of which see),* after a similar split in the I.R.A. in 1969. [Irish *sinn féin,* "we ourselves".] **—Sinn Fein·er** *n.* **—Sinn Fein·ism** *n.*

Sino– *comb. form.* Indicates Chinese; for example, **Sinophile.** [French, from Late Latin *Sinae,* the Chinese, from Greek *Sinai,* from Arabic *Sīn,* China, from Chinese (Mandarin) *Qín,* dynastic name of the country. See also **China.**]

si·no·a·tri·al node (sīnō-áytri-əl) *n.* A group of specialised cells in the wall of the right atrium of the heart that initiates the heartbeat. Also called "pacemaker". [*Sino-,* from Latin *sinus,* cavity + ATRIAL.]

Sin·o·logue (sīnə-log, sínnə- || *U.S. also* -lawg) *n.* A student of Sinology. [French *sinologue* : SINO- + -LOGUE.]

Si·nol·o·gy (sī-nólləji, si-) *n.* The study of Chinese language, literature, or civilisation. [French *sinologie* : SINO- + -LOGY.] **—Sin·o·log·i·cal** (sīnə-lójik'l, sinnə-) *adj.* **—Si·nol·o·gist** *n.*

Sin·o·phile (sīn-ə-fīl, sín-, -ō-) *n.* One friendly to the Chinese and their interests. [SINO- + -PHILE.] **—Sin·o·phile** *adj.*

Sin·o-Ti·bet·an (sīnō-ti-bétt'n, sínnō-) *n.* A linguistic group that includes the Sinitic and Tibeto-Burman families. **—Sin·o-Ti·bet·an** *adj.*

sin·ter (síntər) *n.* **1.** *Geology.* A crust of porous silica, deposited by a hot spring or geyser. **2.** A mass formed by sintering.

~v. **sintered, -tering, -ters.** *—tr.* To weld together (metallic powder, for example) partially and without melting. *—intr.* To form a homogeneous mass by heating without melting. [German *Sinter,* iron dross, from Old High German *sintar.*]

Sin·tra (sín-trə, séen-). *Formerly* **Cin·tra.** Town in the Estremadura region of western Portugal, lying near the Atlantic coast just west of Lisbon. It was a Moorish centre until 1147.

sin·u·ate (sínnew-ət, -it, -ayt) *adj.* Also **sin·u·at·ed** (-aytid). Having a wavy indented margin. Said of a leaf. [Latin *sinuātus,* past participle of *sinuāre,* to bend, wind, from *sinus,* a bend, curve, fold. See **sinus.**] **—sin·u·ate·ly** *adv.* **—sin·u·a·tion** (-áysh'n) *n.*

sin·u·os·i·ty (sínnew-óssəti) *n., pl.* **-ties.** **1.** The quality of being sinuous. **2.** A bending or curving shape or movement.

sin·u·ous (sínnew-əss) *adj.* **1.** Supple and lithe in movement. **2.** Characterised by many curves or turns; winding. **3.** Devious and intricate. [Latin *sinuōsus,* from *sinus,* a bend, curve, fold. See **sinus.**] **—sin·u·ous·ly** *adv.* **—sin·u·ous·ness** *n.*

si·nus (sīnəss) *n.* **1.** A depression or cavity formed by a bending or curving. **2.** *Anatomy.* **a.** Any of various air-filled cavities in the cranial bones, especially one communicating with the nostrils. **b.** A wide channel for the passage of blood, especially venous blood. **3.** *Pathology.* A fistula or channel to a suppurating cavity. **4.** *Botany.* A notch or indentation between lobes of a leaf or corolla. [Latin *sinus*†, a bend, curve, fold, hollow.]

si·nus·i·tis (sīnə-sītiss || sīnew-) *n.* Inflammation of a sinus membrane, especially in the nasal region.

si·nus·oid (sīnə-soyd || sīnew-) *n.* **1.** *Mathematics.* A **sine curve** *(see).* **2.** *Anatomy.* A minute blood vessel occurring in such organs as the liver and adrenal gland. [Medieval Latin *sinus,* sine, from Latin, a curve + -OID.] **—si·nus·oi·dal** (-sóyd'l) *adj.*

sinusoidal projection *n.* A particular case of Bonne's projection, in which the standard parallel is the equator, the other parallels of latitude are drawn as horizontal lines spaced at true intervals, and the meridians of longitude, apart from the standard meridian, are drawn as sine curves. Like Bonne's it is an equal-area projection, but can be used for the whole globe. Also called "Sanson-Flamsteed Projection".

Sion. Variant of **Zion.**

Siou·an (sōō-ən) *n.* A large North American Indian language family spoken from Lake Michigan to the Rocky Mountains and southwards to Arkansas by many peoples, including the Omaha, Iowa, Winnebago, Sioux, and Crow groups. **—Siou·an** *adj.*

Sioux (sōō) *n., pl.* **Sioux** (-z, *or as singular*). **1.** A member of any of the various groups of Siouan-speaking North American Indian peoples, formerly occupying parts of the Great Plains in the Dakotas, Minnesota, and Nebraska. **2.** Any Siouan language. See **Dakota.** **—Sioux** *adj.*

sip (sip) *v.* **sipped, sipping, sips.** *—tr.* To drink delicately and in small quantities: *She sipped the hot tea.* *—intr.* To drink in sips. *~n.* **1.** The act of sipping. **2.** A small quantity of liquid sipped. [Middle English *sippen,* probably of Low German origin; akin to Low German *sippen,* to sip.]

si·phon, sy·phon (sīf'n) *n.* **1.** A pipe or tube fashioned or deployed in an inverted U shape and filled until atmospheric pressure is sufficient to force a liquid from a reservoir in one end of the tube over a barrier higher than the reservoir and out of the other end. **2.** A bottle from which soda water may be dispensed under pressure. **3.** *Zoology.* A tubular organ, especially of aquatic invertebrates such as squids, by which water is taken in or expelled.

~v. **siphoned, -phoning, -phons.** *—tr.* **1.** To draw off or convey through a siphon. **2.** To divert (money, for example) for another purpose. Used with *off.* *—intr.* To pass through a siphon. [French, from Latin *sīphō, sīphōn,* from Greek *siphōn*†, pipe, tube.] **—si·phon·al, si·phon·ic** (sī-fónnik) *adj.*

si·pho·no·phore (sīfənə-fawr, sī-fónnə- || -fōr) *n.* Any of various colonial marine coelenterates of the order Siphonophora, which includes the Portuguese man-of-war. [New Latin *Siphonophora,* "tube-bearers" (from their feeding tube) : Latin *sīphō(n),* tube, SIPHON + New Latin *-phora,* neuter plural of *-phorus,* -PHOROUS.]

si·pho·no·stele (sīfənə-steel, sī-fónnə-) *n.* A vascular tube surrounding the pith in the stems of certain plants. [SIPHON + STELE (vascular tissue).] **—si·pho·no·ste·lic** *adj.*

si·phun·cle (sī-fungk'l) *n. Zoology.* **1.** A tubelike structure in the body of a shelled cephalopod, such as a chambered nautilus, extending through each chamber of the shell. **2.** A dorsal tube in an aphid, secreting a waxy fluid. Formerly called "nectary". [Latin *sīphunculus,* diminutive of *sīphō, sīphōn,* tube, SIPHON.]

sip·pet (síppit) *n.* A small piece of toast or fried bread soaked in gravy or other juice or served as a garnish on soups or stews. [*Sip,* alteration of SOP + -ET.]

sir (sur, *weak form* sər) *n.* **1. a.** A respectful or polite form of address for a man. **b.** *Capital* **S.** A conventional form of address used instead of a man's name at the opening of a letter. **2.** *Capital* **S.** A title of honour used before the first name or the full name of baronets and knights. **3.** *Obsolete.* A form of address used with a noun indicating a man's profession, rank, or the like. Sometimes used humorously or derogatorily. **4.** *Archaic.* A gentleman of rank. [Middle English, unstressed variant of SIRE.]

Siracusa. See **Syracuse.**

sir·dar (súr-daar) *n.* Also **sar·dar** (sər-dár). **1.** A person of rank in India or Pakistan. **2.** A military chief or leader in India or Pakistan. **3.** Formerly, the British commander of the Egyptian army. [Hindi *sardār,* from Persian : *sar,* head + *dār,* possession, from Old Persian, from *dar-,* to hold, possess.]

Sir Ddinbych. See **Denbighshire.**

sire (sīr) *n.* **1.** *Poetic.* A father or forefather. **2.** *Abbr.* **s.** The male parent of an animal, especially a domesticated mammal, such as a horse. **3.** *Archaic. Capital* **S.** A title or form of address for a nobleman, especially for a king.

~tr.v. **sired, siring, sires.** **1.** To be the father of. Used especially of a stallion. **2.** *Poetic.* To give rise to; beget. [Middle English, from Old French, from Vulgar Latin *seior* (unattested), variant of Latin *senior,* older, from *senex,* old.]

si·ren (sīr-ən, -in) *n.* **1.** *Greek Mythology. Often capital* **S.** Any of a group of sea nymphs who, by their sweet singing, lured sailors to destruction on the rocks surrounding their island. **2.** A dangerously seductive woman; a temptress. **3.** A device in which compressed air or steam is driven against a rotating perforated disc to create a loud, penetrating whistle, wailing, or other sound as a signal or warning. **4.** Any instrument producing a similar sound as a signal or warning. **5.** Any of several North American amphibians of the family Sirenidae, having an eel-like body and no hind limbs.

~adj. Suggesting the effect of the mythological sirens; bewitching. [Middle English *ser(e)yne, siren,* from Old French *sereine,* from Late Latin *sīrēna,* from Latin *Sīrēn,* from Greek *Seirēn.*]

si·re·ni·an (sīr-réeni-ən, sī-, si-) *n.* Any herbivorous aquatic mammal of the order Sirenia, including the manatee and the dugong.

PRONUNCIATION KEY

a, trap; aa, father; ai, fair; ar, star; aw, lawn; ay, play; b, bb, stab; rubber; ch, church; ck, ticket; d, dd, dead; ladder; e, dress; ee, bee; er, defer; ew, few; ewr, pure; ə, about; ər, letter; f, ff, fife; differ; g, gg, giggle; h, hat; i, kit; ī, price; īr, fire; j, judge; k, kick; l, ll, let; 'l, needle; m, mm, man; n, nn, no; 'n, sudden; ng, thing; o, lot; ō, no; ŏŏ, foot; ōō, shoe; oor, poor; ow, cow; owr, hour; oy, boy; p, pp, pepper; r, rr, red; s, ss, sauce; sh, ship; t, tt, totter; th, thick; th, this; smooth; u, cut; ur, turn; v, vv, valve; w, wet; y, yes; z, zz, zebra; zh, vision; pleasure

IN FOREIGN WORDS:

aN, oN, Saint-Saëns; hl, Llanelli; Hluhluwe; kh, loch; lough; Khaled

STRESS MARK:

ín-sīt, insight; in-sīt, incite

~*adj.* Of or belonging to the Sirenia. [New Latin *Sīrēnia* (order), from Latin *Sīrēn,* SIREN.]
Sir·i·us (sírri-əss, *rarely* sīr-i-) *n.* A star in the constellation Canis Major. It appears as the brightest star in the sky, and is approximately 8.7 light years distant from Earth. Also called "Canicula", "Dog Star". [Latin, from Greek *Seirios,* from *seirios*†, burning, glowing.]
sir·loin (súr-loyn) *n.* A cut of beef from the upper part of the loin between the rump and the porterhouse. [Earlier *surloyn(e),* from Old French *surlonge* : *sur,* above, from Latin *super* + *longe, loigne,* loin, from Latin *lumbus* .]
si·roc·co (si-róckō) *n., pl.* **-cos.** Also **sci·roc·co** (shi-). A hot, humid south or southeast wind of southern Italy, Sicily, and the Mediterranean islands, originating in the Sahara as a dry, dusty wind but becoming moist as it passes over the Mediterranean. [Italian, from Arabic *sharuq,* "east (wind)", from *sharaqa,* (the sun) rose.]
sir·rah (sírrə) *n. Archaic.* Fellow. Used as a contemptuous form of address. [Probably alteration of Middle English SIRE (sir).]
sir·ree, sir·ee (sə-rée) *n. U.S. Informal.* Sir. Used with *yes* or *no* for emphasis.
Sir Rog·er de Cov·er·ley (sər rójər də kúvvərli) *n.* An English country dance performed by an unspecified number of couples initially facing each other in a long line. [After the fictitious character in a series of essays by Addison and Steele in the *Spectator.*]
sirup. *U.S.* Variant of **syrup.**
sir·vente (sər-vént, seer-, -vóNT) *n., pl.* **-ventes** (-s, *or pronounced as singular*). Also **sir·ventes.** A form of lyric verse used by the Provençal troubadours to satirise political, social, or moral themes. [French, from Provençal *sirventes,* "a servant's song", from *sirvent, servent,* servant, from Latin *serviēns* (stem *servient-*), present participle of *servīre,* to serve, from *servus,* servant.]
sis[1] (siss) *n. Informal.* Sister.
sis[2] *interj. South African.* Used to express disgust, revulsion, or strong disapproval. [Afrikaans *sies,* possibly from Hottentot *si, tsi.*]
si·sal (sī-s'l || -z'l) *n.* **1.** A fleshy plant, *Agave sisalana,* native to Mexico, widely cultivated for its large leaves that yield a stiff fibre used for cordage and rope. **2. a.** The fibre of this plant. **b.** The fibre of certain similar or related plants. [Mexican Spanish, after *Sisal,* town in Yucatán, Mexico.]
sis·kin (sískin) *n.* Any of several small birds of the family Fringillidae; especially, *Carduelis spinus,* of Eurasia, having a yellow and black plumage. [Middle Dutch *sīseken,* formed as diminutive of Middle Low German *sīsek,* from Slavonic; akin to Czech *čiž,* Russian *chizh* (imitative).]
sis·si·fied (síssi-fīd) *adj. Informal.* Womanish; effeminate. Said of a male.
sis·sy, cis·sy (síssi) *n., pl.* **-sies. 1.** An effeminate or weak boy or man; a milksop. **2.** A timid or cowardly person. [From *sis,* short for SISTER.] **—sis·sy** *adj.*
sis·ter (sístər) *n.* **1.** *Abbr.* **s.** A female having the same mother and father as another person *(full sister),* having one parent in common with another person *(half sister),* having one parent in common with another person by marriage rather than by blood *(stepsister),* or having a shared mother and father after adoption *(foster sister).* **2.** A female who shares a common ancestry, allegiance, character, or purpose with another or others, especially: **a.** A kinswoman. **b.** A female fellow member, as of a trade union. **c.** A female who shares feminist beliefs, principles, and aspirations. **d.** A fellow woman, friend, or companion. **3.** *U.S. Informal.* A girl or woman. Used as a form of direct address. **4.** *Capital* **S. a.** *Abbr.* **Sr.** A member of a religious order of women; a nun. **b.** A title or form of address for such a person. **5.** *British.* **a.** The nurse in charge of a hospital ward. **b.** A title or form of address for such a person. **6.** One identified as female and closely related to another.
~*adj.* Standing in the relationship of a sister; related by or as if by sisterhood: *sister souls.* [Middle English *suster, sister,* Old English *sweostor, swuster.*]
sis·ter·hood (sístər-hŏŏd) *n.* **1.** The state or relationship of being a sister or sisters. **2.** The quality of being sisterly. **3.** A society of women; especially, a religious society of women. **4. a.** The feminist movement. **b.** Feminists collectively. Preceded by *the.*
sis·ter-in-law (sístər-in-law) *n., pl.* **sisters-in-law. 1.** The sister of one's wife or husband. **2.** The wife of one's brother. **3.** The wife of the brother of one's spouse.
sis·ter·ly (sístərli) *adj.* Characteristic of or befitting a sister or sisters.
~*adv.* As a sister. **—sis·ter·li·ness** *n.*
Sis·tine (sís-teen) *adj.* Also **Six·tine** (síks-). **1.** Of or concerning any of the popes named Sixtus. **2.** Of or pertaining to the Sistine Chapel, built for pope Sixtus IV. [Italian *sistino,* from New Latin *sixtinus,* from the name *Sixtus.*]
sis·troid (síss-troyd) *adj.* Lying between the convex sides of two curves. Compare **cissoid.** [SISTR(UM) + -OID.]
sis·trum (síss-trəm) *n., pl.* **-trums** or **-tra** (-trə). An ancient Egyptian musical instrument consisting of a thin metal frame with rods or loops that rattle. [Middle English, from Latin, from Greek *seistron,* from *seiein,* to shake.]
si·Swa·ti (si-swáa-ti) *n.* The Bantu language, **Swazi** *(see).* **—si·Swa·ti** *adj.*
Sis·y·phe·an (síssi-fée-ən) *adj.* **1.** Of or pertaining to Sisyphus. **2.** *Often small* **s.** Endless and to no avail.
Sis·y·phus (síssifəss) *n. Greek Mythology.* A cruel king of Corinth who because of disrespect to Zeus was condemned forever to roll a huge stone up a hill in Hades, only to find it roll down again on nearing the top.
sit (sit) *v.* **sat** (sat) or *archaic* **sate** (sayt, sat), **sat, sitting, sits.** *—intr.* **1.** To rest with the body supported upon the buttocks and the torso vertical. **2.** To rest with the hindquarters lowered onto a supporting surface. Used of animals. **3.** To perch. Used of birds. **4.** To cover eggs for hatching; brood. **5.** To be situated; lie. **6.** To take and maintain a position for an artist or photographer; pose. **7. a.** To occupy a seat in an official capacity, as a judge, or as a member of a deliberative body: *sits on the transport committee.* **b.** To be in session. Used of a deliberative or judicial body. **8.** To remain inactive or unused. **9.** To lie or rest in a specified manner: *sat uneasily on the edge of the chair.* **10.** To affect one with or as if with a burden; weigh. Used with *on* or *upon*: *Official duties sat heavily on her.* **11. a.** To fit, fall, or hang in a specified manner. Used of clothing: *That dress sits well on her.* **b.** To be suitable or appropriate: *Arrogance does not sit well on them.* **12.** To lie, rest, or belong in a specified place: *Those sit on the top shelf.* **13.** To blow from a particular direction. Used of the wind. **14.** To baby-sit or keep watch over an invalid. **15.** To take an examination: *sitting for her A levels.* *—tr.* **1.** To cause to sit; to seat. Often used reflexively: *Sit yourself over there.* **2.** To keep one's seat upon (a horse or other animal). **3.** *Chiefly British.* To take (an examination), as for a degree. **—sit back.** To relax; not concern or worry oneself: *sit back and enjoy the film.* **—sit on** or **upon.** *Informal.* **1.** To suppress or delay publication of (information, news, or a decision, for example). **2.** To rebuke sharply; reprimand. **—sit out. 1.** To stay until the end of: *sit out a speech.* **2.** To remain seated throughout; take no part in (a dance or game, for example). **3.** To lean out over the side of a small sailing vessel with the back towards the water when sailing close to the wind, so as to keep the boat level. **—sit tight.** *Informal.* To be patient and await the next move. **—sitting pretty.** *Informal.* In an advantageous or favourable position. **—sit up. 1.** To sit straight or erect. **2.** To stay up later than one's customary bedtime. **3.** To become suddenly alert or attentive.
~*n.* An act, instance, or period of sitting. [Sit, sat (past); Middle English *sitten, sat(e),* Old English *sittan, sæt* (plural *sǣton*). Sat (past participle); Middle English *sat,* adopted from the past tense *sat(e)* and replacing the regular *seten,* Old English *(ge)seten.*]
si·tar (si-tár, sít-aar) *n.* A Hindu stringed instrument made of seasoned gourds and teak and having a track of 20 metal frets with 3 to 7 main playing strings above and 13 sympathetic resonating strings below. [Hindi *sitār,* "three-stringed" : Persian *si,* three + *tār,* string, from Avestan *tąthra-* (unattested).] **—si·tar·ist** *n.*
sit·com (sít-kom) *n. Informal.* A **situation comedy** *(see).* **—sit·com** *adj.*
sit down *intr.v.* To seat oneself; take a seat.
~*tr.v.* To seat (oneself or another).
sit-down (sít-down || *West Indies also* -dung) *adj.* Served to and eaten by people seated at a table. Said of a meal: *a sit-down dinner.*
~*n.* A sit-in.
sit-down strike *n.* A sit-in.
site (sīt) *n.* **1.** The place or plot of land where something was, is, or is to be situated, especially a place where construction work is taking place. **2.** The place or setting of an event.
~*tr.v.* **sited, siting, sites.** To situate or locate on a site: *siting a power plant.* [Middle English, from Old French, from Latin *situs,* place, locality, from *situs,* past participle of *sinere*†, to allow (to remain in a place), hence lay, put.]
site of special scientific interest *n. Abbr.* **SSSI** In Britain, a site defined, listed, and protected to some degree by the Nature Conservancy Council because of its interesting flora, fauna, or geology. There are also larger areas of special scientific interest.
sith (sith) *conj. Archaic.* Since. [Middle English *sith(th)e,* Old English *siththa, siththan,* SINCE.] **—sith** *adv. & prep.*
sit in *intr.v.* **1.** To participate in a sit-in. **2.** To take the place of an absent person: *sat in for me at the meeting.* **3.** To be present as an observer or guest: *sat in on the meeting.*
sit-in (sít-in) *n.* A form of industrial action in which workers strike while occupying their place of work. Also called "sit-down", "sit-down strike". **2.** A form of protest, as against racial discrimination or the policies of a government or company, in which demonstrators occupy appropriate premises to call attention to their views. Also called "sit-down". Compare **work-in.**
Sit·ka (sít-kə). Town on Baranof Island, in the Alexander archipelago of Alaska. From 1867 to 1900 it was the capital of Alaska.
Sitka spruce *n.* A North American spruce tree, *Picea sitchensis,* that is an important source of softwood.
si·tol·o·gy (sī-tólləji) *n. Rare.* The science of foods, nutrition, and diet. [Greek *sitos*†, food, grain + -LOGY.]
si·tos·ter·ol (sī-tóstə-rol || -rōl) *n.* Any of various sterols extracted from soya beans for the preparation of medicines, such as synthetic steroid hormones, and cosmetics. [Greek *sitos,* food + STEROL.]
sit·tel·la (si-téllə) *n.* Any of various Australian birds of the genus *Neositta,* some species of which use small twigs to draw out of concealment the grubs on which they feed. Also called "tree-runner". [New Latin, diminutive of Latin *sitta,* nuthatch.]
sit·ter (síttər) *n.* **1.** One that sits; especially, one who sits for an artist or photographer. **2.** A brooding hen. **3.** *Informal.* Something that is easy to do, such as an easy catch at cricket.
sit·ting (sítting) *n.* **1.** The act or position of one that sits. **2.** A period during which one is seated and occupied with a single activity, such as posing for a portrait or reading a book. **3.** A term or ses-

sion, as of a legislature or court. **4.** A time at which a meal is served, typically one of several such periods allocated in order to make full use of limited facilities. **5. a.** An act or period of incubation of eggs by a bird. **b.** The number of eggs under a brooding bird.

Sitting Bull (*c.* 1831–90). North American chief. He led the Indian forces during the Sioux war against the U.S. army (1876–77), defeating General Custer's cavalry at the Battle of the Little Big Horn (1876).

sitting duck *n. Informal.* An easy target or victim. Also called "sitting target".

sitting room *n.* A living room in a private house.

sitting tenant *n.* A tenant who is actually in occupation of rented premises.

sitting trot *n.* A slow trot during which the rider of the horse stays seated in the saddle.

sit·u·ate (síttew-ayt, síchoo- || *Welsh also* síttoo-) *tr.v.* **-ated, -ating, -ates. 1.** To place in a certain spot or position; locate. **2.** To place under particular circumstances or in a given condition.
~*adj.* (-ayt, -ət, -it). *Archaic & Law.* Situated. [Medieval Latin *situāre,* to put, place, from *situs,* place, SITE.]

sit·u·a·tion (síttew-áysh'n, síchoo- || *Welsh also* síttoo-) *n.* **1.** A place or position in which something is situated; a location. **2.** A position or status with regard to conditions and attendant circumstances; especially, a person's financial position or status. **3.** A combination of circumstances at a given moment; a state of affairs. **4.** A critical or problematic combination of circumstances. **5.** A position of employment; a post. —See Synonyms at **state.** [Middle English, from Medieval Latin *situātiō* (stem *situātiōn-*), from *situāre,* to SITUATE.] **—sit·u·a·tion·al** *adj.*

situation comedy *n.* **1.** A genre of comedy in which the humour is derived from the reactions of a regular cast of characters to unusual situations, such as misunderstandings or embarrassing coincidences. **2.** A radio or television programme or series using this type of comedy. In this sense, also called "sitcom".

si·tus (sítəss) *n., pl.* **situs.** Position; especially, the normal position of a bodily organ. [Latin *situs,* place, SITE.]

Sit·well (sít-wəl, -wel), **Dame Edith (Louisa)** (1887–1964). British poet, biographer, and critic. One of the most famous literary eccentrics of the 20th century, she wrote *English Eccentrics* (1933), by which time she had already established a reputation by her poetry, written in the obscure manner of the French symbolists. *Façade,* near-nonsense verse to be read against music composed by William Walton, was first performed by her in 1922. Her brother, Sir Osbert Sitwell (1892–1969), was a poet, novelist, and short-story writer.

sitz bath (sits) *n.* A type of bath in which one bathes in a sitting position. [Partial translation of German *Sitzbad* : *Sitz,* a sitting, from Old High German *siz,* from *sizzen,* to sit + *Bad,* bath.]

sitz·krieg (síts-kreeg, zíts-) *n.* A war in which very little actual fighting takes place; a nonaggressive war. [German, "sitting-war".]

SI unit (éss-ī) *n.* Any of the units that form part of the Système international d'unités, used for all scientific purposes. The seven base units are the metre, kilogram, second, ampere, kelvin, candela, and mole; the radian and the steradian are treated as supplementary units. All other units are derived from these units.

Si·va (shée-və, sée-). Also **Shi·va** (shée-). *Hinduism.* The god of destruction and reproduction, a member of the Hindu triad along with Brahma and Vishnu. [Sanskrit *Śíva,* "the auspicious (one)", from *siva,* auspicious, dear.] **—Si·va·ism** *n.* **—Si·va·ist** *n. & adj.*

Si·van (sivv'n, see-va'an) *n.* The ninth month of the Hebrew year. [Hebrew *Sīwān,* from Assyro-Babylonian *Simānu,* possibly related to Persian *Sefend,* an Iranian deity.]

six (siks) *n.* **1. a.** The cardinal number that is one more than five. **b.** A symbol representing this, such as 6, VI, or vi. **2.** A set made up of six persons or things. **3. a.** The sixth in a series. **b.** A playing card marked with six pips. **4.** Six parts: *cut into six.* **5.** A size, as in clothing, designated as six. **6.** Six hours after midnight or midday. **7. a.** In cricket, a ball hit beyond the boundary line that does not touch the ground and thus scores six runs. **b.** The six runs scored. **8.** A group of six Brownies or Cub Scouts constituting a division of a pack. **—at sixes and sevens.** *Informal.* In a state of confusion or disorder. **—knock (someone) for six.** *Informal.* To surprise or stun (someone) completely. **—six of one and half a dozen of the other.** A merely nominal difference; a situation in which neither choice is clearly preferable. **—six of the best.** Six strokes of the cane as a punishment. [Middle English *six, sex,* Old English *s(i)ex, six.*] **—six** *adj.* **—six·fold** *adj. & adv.*

six·ain (síks-ayn) *n.* A stanza consisting of six lines. [French, from *six,* SIX.]

Six Counties *pl.n.* The six counties of Northern Ireland: Antrim, Armagh, Down, Fermanagh, Londonderry, and Tyrone.

six·er (síksər) *n.* The leader of a six of Brownies or Cub Scouts.

six-foot·er (síks-fŏŏtər) *n.* A person who is six feet tall or more.

Six Nations. See **Iroquois.**

six-pack (síks-pak) *n.* A pack of six cans of a drink, especially beer.

six·pence (síks-pənss; *for sense 2, also* -pénss) *n. British.* **1.** A coin worth six old pennies or half a shilling (2.5 new pence), no longer in circulation. **2.** The sum of six pennies.

six·pen·ny (síks-pəni || *U.S. also* -penni) *adj.* **1.** Valued at, selling for, or worth sixpence (2.5 new pence). **2.** Of little worth; cheap; paltry. **3.** Designating a nail of a certain size, generally two inches.

six-shoot·er (síks-shŏŏtər) *n. Informal.* A six-chambered revolver. Also called "six-gun".

six·teen (síks-téen) *n.* **1. a.** The cardinal number that is one more than 15. **b.** A symbol representing this, such as 16 or XVI. **2.** A set made up of 16 persons or things. **3.** The sixteenth in a series. **4.** A size, as in clothing, designated as 16. [Middle English *sixtene,* Old English *sixtȳne* : SIX + -TEEN.] **—six·teen** *adj.*

six·teen·mo (siks-téen-mō) *n., pl.* **-mos. Sextodecimo** *(see).*

six·teenth (síks-téenth) *n.* **1.** The ordinal number 16 in a series. **2.** Any of 16 equal parts. **—six·teenth** *adj. & adv.*

sixteenth note *n. Music. U.S.* A **semiquaver** *(see).*

sixth (siksth) *n.* **1.** The ordinal number six in a series. **2.** One of six equal parts. **3.** *Music.* **a.** An interval of six degrees in a diatonic scale. **b.** A note separated by this interval from a given note. **c.** The chord consisting of two notes separated by this interval. **d.** The sixth note of a scale; the submediant. **—sixth** *adj. & adv.*

sixth form *n.* In the British secondary school system, the form containing the oldest pupils, normally preparing for A levels over two or more years. **—sixth-form·er** (síksth-fawrmər) *n.*

sixth-form college (síksth-fawrm) *n.* A college where students of 16 or over can follow A-level or, sometimes, vocational courses.

sixth sense *n.* A power of perception seemingly independent of and additional to the five senses.

six·ti·eth (síksti-əth, -ith) *n.* **1.** The ordinal number 60 in a series. **2.** Any of 60 equal parts. **—six·ti·eth** *adj. & adv.*

Sixtine. Variant of **Sistine.**

six·ty (síksti) *n., pl.* **-ties. 1. a.** The cardinal number that is ten more than fifty. **b.** A symbol representing this, such as 60 or LX. **2.** A set made up of sixty persons or things. **3.** The sixtieth in a series. **4.** A size, as in clothing, designated as sixty. **5.** *Plural.* **a.** The range of numbers from 60 to 69, considered as a range of age, price, temperature, or the like. **b.** *Sometimes capital* **S.** The years numbered 60 to 69 in a century. Also used adjectivally: *sixties music.* **—six·ty** *adj.*

six·ty-fourth note (síksti-fórth || -fōrth) *n. U.S. Music.* A **hemidemisemiquaver** *(see).*

sixty-four thousand dollar question (síksti-fór || -fōr) *n.* A question that is crucial or very difficult to answer. Also called "sixty-four dollar question". [Referring to the highest prize given in a U.S. television quiz.]

siz·a·ble (sízəb'l) *adj.* Also **size·a·ble.** Of considerable size; fairly large. **—siz·a·ble·ness** *n.* **—siz·a·bly** *adv.*

size[1] (sīz) *n.* **1.** The physical dimensions, proportions, magnitude, or extent of something. **2.** Any of a series of graduated categories of dimension whereby articles for sale are classified. **3.** Considerable extent, amount, or dimensions: *grown to quite a size.* **4.** Qualities or status with reference to relative importance or the capacity to meet certain requirements: *of no great size in her field.* **5.** The actual state of affairs or truth of the matter: *That's about the size of it.* **—cut down to size.** *Informal.* **1.** To reduce the self-importance of. **2.** To reduce to manageable proportions. **—try (out) for size.** *Informal.* To test out.
~*tr.v.* **sized, sizing, sizes. 1.** To arrange, classify, or distribute according to size. **2.** To make, cut, or shape to a required size. **—size up. 1.** *Informal.* To make an estimate or form a judgment of. **2.** To meet certain specifications or requirements. [Middle English *syse,* fixed amount, assize, from Old French *sise,* short for *assise,* ASSIZE.]

size[2] *n.* Any of several gelatinous or glutinous substances usually made from glue, wax, or clay and used as a glaze or filler for porous materials such as paper, cloth, or wall surfaces. Also called "sizing".
~*tr.v.* **sized, sizing, sizes.** To treat or coat with size or a similar substance. [Middle English *cyse, syse,* probably a specialised use of SIZE (dimension).] **—siz·y** *adj.*

sized (sīzd) *adj.* Having a particular or specified size. Often used in combination: *medium-sized.*

siz·ing (sízing) *n.* A glaze or filler; size.

siz·zle (sízz'l) *intr.v.* **-zled, -zling, -zles. 1.** To make the hissing sound characteristic of frying fat. **2.** *Informal.* To seethe with anger or indignation. **3.** *Informal.* To be extremely hot.
~*n.* A hissing sound. [Imitative.]

siz·zler (sízzlər) *n. Informal.* A very hot day.

S.J. Society of Jesus.

Sjæl·land (*Danish* syéllan). *English* **Zea·land** (zée-lənd). Denmark's largest island, lying off the extreme southwestern coast of Sweden. Low-lying and fertile, the island is the site of Copenhagen.

sjam·bok (shám-bok, *rarely* -buk) *n. South African.* A stiff whip made from the hide of a rhinoceros or hippopotamus.
~*tr.v.* **sjambokked, -bokking, -boks.** *South African.* To flog with such a whip. [Afrikaans, from Malay *chambok,* from Urdu *chābuk.*]

sk. sack.

ska (skaa || *Jamaican* skya) *n.* A type of West Indian popular music similar to reggae but lighter and with a more fluid rhythm. [20th century : origin obscure.] **—ska** *adj.*

Skag·er·rak (skággə-rak). Strait separating Norway and Denmark, linking the North Sea and the Baltic Sea by way of the Kattegat and extending for about 240 kilometres (150 miles). Here the British and German fleets engaged in the Battle of Jutland (1916).

skald, scald (skaald, skawld) *n.* An ancient Scandinavian poet; a bard. [Old Norse *skāld.*] **—skald·ic** *adj.*

Skar·a Brae (skárrə bráy). Stone-age village on the west coast of Mainland, Orkney, Scotland, dating from *c.* 2000 B.C.–1500 B.C. It is perhaps the most completely preserved in Europe.

skat (skat) *n.* **1.** A card game for three persons played with 32 cards, the sevens up to and including the aces. **2.** One of the combinations of cards occurring in this game. [German *Skat,* from Italian *scarto,* a discarded card, from *scartare,* to reject, discard : *s-,* negative pre-

PRONUNCIATION KEY

a, trap; aa, father; ai, fair; ar, star; aw, lawn; ay, play; b, bb, stab; rubber; ch, church; ck, ticket; d, dd, dead; ladder; e, dress; ee, bee; er, defer; ew, few; ewr, pure; ə, about; ər, letter; f, ff, fife; differ; g, gg, giggle; h, hat; i, kit; ī, price; īr, fire; j, judge; k, kick; l, ll, let; 'l, needle; m, mm, man; n, nn, no; 'n, sudden; ng, thing; o, lot; ō, no; ŏŏ, foot; ōō, shoe; oor, poor; ow, cow; owr, hour; oy, boy; p, pp, pepper; r, rr, red; s, ss, sauce; sh, ship; t, tt, totter; th, thick; th, this; smooth; u, cut; ur, turn; v, vv, valve; w, wet; y, yes; z, zz, zebra; zh, vision; pleasure

IN FOREIGN WORDS:

aN, ON, Saint-Saëns; hl, Llanelli; Hluhluwe; kh, loch; lough; Khaled

STRESS MARK:

ín-sīt, insight; in-sít, incite

fix, from Latin *ex-*, out of + *carta*, card, from Latin *charta*, leaf of papyrus (see **card**).]

skate[1] (skayt) *n.* **1. a.** An **ice skate** *(see).* **b.** The bladelike metal runner of an ice skate. **2.** A **roller skate** *(see).* **—get (one's) skates on.** *Informal.* To make haste; hurry.
~intr.v. **skated, skating, skates.** To glide or move along on or as if on skates. **—skate over.** To deal with (an important or complicated subject or matter) in a deliberately superficial manner. [Mistaken as singular of earlier *scates,* from Dutch *schaats,* a skate, from Old North French *escace,* stilt, from Frankish *skakkja* (unattested), from *skakan* (unattested), to run fast. See **scotch** (block).]

skate[2] *n.* Any of various marine cartilaginous fishes of the family Rajidae, having a flattened body with the pectoral fins forming winglike lateral extensions; a large ray. [Middle English *scate,* from Old Norse *skata*†.]

skate·board (skáyt-bawrd || -bōrd) *n.* An elongated oval or oblong board on wheels, designed to be ridden standing up.
~intr.v. **skateboarded, -boarding, -boards.** To ride on a skateboard, using one's feet and weight to propel oneself and change direction. **—skate·board·er** *n.* **—skate·board·ing** *n.*

skat·er (skáytər) *n.* **1.** One who skates. **2.** A **pond skater** *(see).*

skating rink *n.* An **ice rink** *(see).*

skat·ole, ska·tol (skát-ōl) *n.* A white crystalline organic compound, C_9H_9N, having a strong faecal odour, found naturally in faeces, beets, and coal tar, and used as a fixative in the manufacture of perfume. [Greek *skōr* (stem *skat-*), dung + -OLE.]

ske·an (skée-ən, shkée- || skeen, shkeen) *n.* A type of double-edged dagger formerly used in Ireland and Scotland. [Gaelic *sgian,* knife.]

skean dhu (dōō) *n.* A small dagger worn in a man's stocking with Highland dress. [Gaelic, black knife.]

ske·dad·dle (ski-dádd'l) *intr.v.* **-dled, -dling, -dles.** *Informal.* To run off or leave hastily.
~n. Informal. A hurried retreat. [19th century : origin obscure.]

skeet (skeet) *n.* A variety of clay-pigeon shooting in which clay targets are thrown from traps to simulate birds in flight and are fired at from eight different stations by the shooter. [Ultimately from Old Norse *skjōta,* to shoot.]

skeg (skeg) *n.* **1.** A timber that connects the keel and the sternpost of a ship. **2.** An arm extending to the rear of the keel to support the rudder and protect the propeller. **3.** A series of timbers attached to the stern of a small boat, serving as a keel to keep the boat on course. [Dutch *scheg(ge),* from Old Norse *skegg,* beard, projection.]

skein (skayn, skeen) *n.* **1.** A length of thread or yarn wound in a loose, elongated coil. **2.** Something like or suggestive of this; a tangle. **3.** A flock of geese or similar birds in flight. [Middle English *skeyne,* from Old French *escaigne*†.]

skel·e·tal (skéllit'l) *adj.* Pertaining to, forming, or resembling a skeleton. **—skel·e·tal·ly** *adv.*

skeletal muscle *n.* A **striated muscle** *(see).*

skel·e·ton (skéllit'n) *n.* **1. a.** The internal vertebrate structure composed of bone and cartilage that protects and supports the soft organs, tissues, and parts. **b.** Such a structure when the flesh has been removed after death. **c.** The hard external supporting and protecting structure in many invertebrates and certain vertebrates, such as turtles; the exoskeleton. **2.** Any supporting structure or essential framework, as of a building. **3.** A bare outline or sketch. **4.** *Informal.* A very thin or emaciated person or animal. **5.** A scandalous or humiliating fact that is kept secret from others. Used chiefly in the phrases *skeleton in the cupboard, family skeleton.*
~adj. **1.** Of or resembling a skeleton. **2.** Having or consisting only of an outline, essential parts, or the smallest practicable number: *a skeleton staff.* [New Latin, from Greek, neuter of *skeletos,* dried up, withered.]

Skeleton Coast. Remote and desolate stretch of the Namib desert that runs along the coast of Namibia (South West Africa). In former days anyone shipwrecked on this arid coast was virtually doomed to die of thirst.

skel·e·ton·ise, skel·e·ton·ize (skéllit'n-īz) *tr.v.* **-ised, -ising, -ises.** **1.** To create an outline of or framework for. **2.** To reduce to a minimum.

skeleton key *n.* A key with a large portion of the bit filed away so that it can open different locks. Also called "passkey".

skel·lum (skélləm) *n. Archaic.* A villain; a rogue. [Dutch; akin to Old High German *skelmo,* devil.]

skelm (skélləm, skelm) *n. South African Informal.* A mischievous or criminal person. [Afrikaans, from Dutch. See **skellum.**]

Skel·mers·dale (skélmərz-dayl). New town in northwestern England. It was designated as Lancashire's first new town in 1961 to alleviate overcrowding in Liverpool.

skelp[1] (skelp) *tr.v.* **skelped, skelping, skelps.** *Scottish.* To smack or hit.
~n. A slap or slapping noise. [Probably imitative.]

skelp[2] *n.* A sheet of metal used to make a pipe or tube. [Perhaps from Scottish Gaelic *sgealbh,* thin wooden strip.]

skep (skep) *n.* **1.** A beehive, especially one of straw. **2.** *Regional.* A large straw or wickerwork basket. [Middle English *skep(pe),* Old English *sceppe,* the quantity held by a skep, from Old Norse *skeppa*†, basket.]

skeptic. *U.S.* Variant of **sceptic.** **—skeptical** *adj.* **—skepticism** *n.*

sker·rick (skérrik) *n. Australian & U.S.* A tiny amount or small bit. Used chiefly in the phrase *not a skerrick.* [From northern English dialect, probably from Scandinavian.]

sker·ry (skérri) *n., pl.* **-ries.** *Chiefly Scottish.* A small, sometimes rocky isle. [Orkney dialect, from Old Norse *sker,* SCAR (crag).]

sketch (skech) *n.* **1.** A hasty or undetailed drawing or painting, often done as a preliminary study. **2.** A brief, general account or presentation; an outline. **3. a.** A brief, light, or informal short story, essay, or other literary composition. **b.** A short, usually humorous, scene or play in a revue or variety show. **c.** *Music.* A brief composition, especially for the piano.
~v. **sketched, sketching, sketches.** *—tr.* **1.** To make a rough drawing or sketch of. **2.** To outline; describe briefly. Often used with *out* or *in.* *—intr.* To make a sketch or sketches. [Dutch *schets* or German *Skizze,* from Italian *schizzo,* from *schizzare,* to sketch, from Vulgar Latin *schediāre,* from Latin *schedius,* hastily put together, from Greek *skhedios,* impromptu.] **—sketch·er** *n.*

sketch·book (skéch-bōōk || -bōōk) *n.* **1.** A pad consisting of sheets of paper used for sketching. **2.** A book of literary sketches.

sketch·y (skéchi) *adj.* **-ier, -iest.** **1.** Resembling a sketch; giving only an outline. **2.** Incomplete; slight; vague. **—sketch·i·ly** *adv.* **—sketch·i·ness** *n.*

skew (skew) *v.* **skewed, skewing, skews.** *—intr.* **1.** To take an oblique course or direction. **2.** To look obliquely or sideways. *—tr.* **1.** To turn or place at an angle. **2.** To give a bias to; distort.
~adj. **1.** Placed or turned to one side; asymmetrical. **2.** Distorted or biased in meaning or effect. **3.** Having a part that diverges, as from a straight line or a right angle, as in gearing. **4. a.** *Geometry.* Neither parallel nor intersecting. Said of straight lines in space. Compare **parallel. b.** *Statistics.* Not symmetrical about the mean. Said of distributions.
~n. An oblique or slanting movement, position, or direction. [Middle English *skewen,* to skew, escape, from Old North French *eskuer,* from Germanic *skiuhwan* (unattested). See **eschew.**] **—skew·ness** *n.*

skew arch *n. Architecture.* An arch whose line is not at right angles to the abutments.

skew·back (skéw-bak) *n. Architecture.* Either of two inset abutments sloped to support a segmental arch.

skew·bald (skéw-bawld) *adj.* Having spots or patches of white and a colour other than black on its coat: *a skewbald horse.* Compare **piebald.**
~n. A horse with this colouring. [From earlier *skued*† + BALD.]

skew·er (skéw-ər) *n.* **1.** A long metal or wooden pin used to secure meat during cooking or to hold pieces of meat and vegetables during grilling. **2.** Any of various picks or rods having a similar function or shape.
~tr.v. **skewered, -ering, -ers.** To hold together or pierce with or as if with a skewer. [Variant of dialectal *skiver*†.]

skew·whiff, skew·iff (skéw-wíf) *adj. Chiefly British Informal.* Lopsided; askew. [18th century (dialectal) : based on ASKEW.] **—skew·whiff, skew·iff** *adv.*

ski (skee, *rarely* shee) *n., pl.* **skis** or **ski.** **1.** Either of a pair of long, flat runners of wood, metal, or other material that curve upwards in front and may be attached to a boot for gliding or travelling over snow. **2.** A **water-ski** *(see).*
~adj. Of, pertaining to, or associated with skiing: *a ski resort.*
~v. **skied, skiing, skis.** *—intr.* To travel on skis, especially as a sport. *—tr.* To travel over on skis. [Norwegian *ski(d),* from Old Norse *skīth,* ski, snowshoe.] **—ski·er** *n.* **—ski·ing** *adj.*

skiagram. Variant of **sciagram.**

skiagraphy. Variant of **sciagraphy.**

skiamachy. Variant of **sciamachy.**

ski·a·scope (skī-ə-skōp) *n. Optometry.* A **retinoscope** *(see).* [Greek *skia,* shadow + -SCOPE.]

ski·as·co·py (skī-áskəpi) *n. Optometry.* **Retinoscopy** *(see).*

ski binding *n.* An attachment on a ski used to secure the ski to the skier's boot.

ski·bob (skée-bob) *n.* A kind of bicycle with two small skis instead of wheels, used for travelling downhill over snow by a rider wearing miniature skis for balance. [SKI + BOB(SLEIGH).] **—ski·bob·ber** *n.* **—ski·bob·bing** *n.*

skid (skid) *n.* **1.** An act or state of sliding or slipping over a surface, often uncontrollably and sideways. **2. a.** A plank, log, or timber, usually one of a pair, used as a support or as a track for sliding or rolling heavy objects. **b.** A small platform for stacking merchandise to be moved or temporarily stored. **c.** *U.S.* One of several logs or timbers forming a skid road. **3.** *Plural. Nautical.* A wooden framework attached to the side of a ship to prevent damage, as when unloading. **4.** A shoe or drag applying pressure to a wheel to brake a vehicle. **5.** A runner in the landing gear of certain aircraft. **—on the skids.** *Slang.* On a downward path to ruin, failure, or depravity. **—put the skids under.** *Slang.* To hasten the failure of.
~v. **skidded, skidding, skids.** *—intr.* **1.** To slip or slide sideways, usually out of control, while moving because of loss of traction. Used chiefly of a vehicle. **2.** To slide without revolving. Said of a wheel that does not turn while the vehicle is in motion. **3.** *Aviation.* To move sideways in a turn because of insufficient banking. *—tr.* **1.** To brake (a wheel) with a skid. **2.** *Chiefly U.S.* To haul on a skid or skids. [17th century : origin obscure.]

skid·lid (skíd-lid) *n. Chiefly British Slang.* A crash helmet.

skid pan *n. British.* A road or track that has been treated to make it slippery to enable road vehicle drivers to practise controlling skids.

skid road *n. U.S.* **1.** A track made of logs laid transversely, spaced about five feet apart, and used to haul logs to a loading platform or a mill. **2.** *Slang.* Skid row.

skiing *A skier demonstrates the slalom technique, weaving her way through a series of posts on a steep incline. Skiing became a popular sport only in the 19th century, but it has been familiar to Scandinavians since about 2500 B.C.*

skin

THE BODY'S PROTECTIVE TISSUE
Microscopic structures that are vital to life

Skin is the perfect protective wrapper for the body. Elastic and waterproof, no more than 0.3 millimetres (a hundredth of an inch) thick, it keeps moisture out and also prevents the body – which is 90 per cent water – from drying out. It acts as a barrier against dirt and germs, and provides a tough, resilient cover that withstands bumps and knocks. The skin also supplies much of the body's vitamin D, manufacturing it from sunlight.

Skin is made up of two main layers: the epidermis, the fine outer layer, only 0.1 millimetres (a 250th of an inch) thick, and the dermis, the relatively thick under layer.

The outermost part of the epidermis consists of flat, dead cells that are constantly being worn away by friction. The lower epidermis is made up of rapidly dividing cells that, every few weeks, build 1.59 square metres (17 square feet) of new skin to replace worn surface layers. Finger and toe nails grow from actively dividing skin cells at the nail bases.

All the skin's vital structures are in the dermis. Among them are millions of receptors sensitive to touch, pain, cold, and warmth. In the more sensitive areas – the fingertips and lips – there are as many as 200 touch receptors to every square centimetre (0.16 square inch). Less sensitive areas, such as the shoulders, have about four to each square centimetre. Blood vessels and sweat glands control body temperature. When the body is cold, blood vessels contract, reducing blood flow; when it is hot, they dilate and the sweat glands excrete moisture, which evaporates and cools the body.

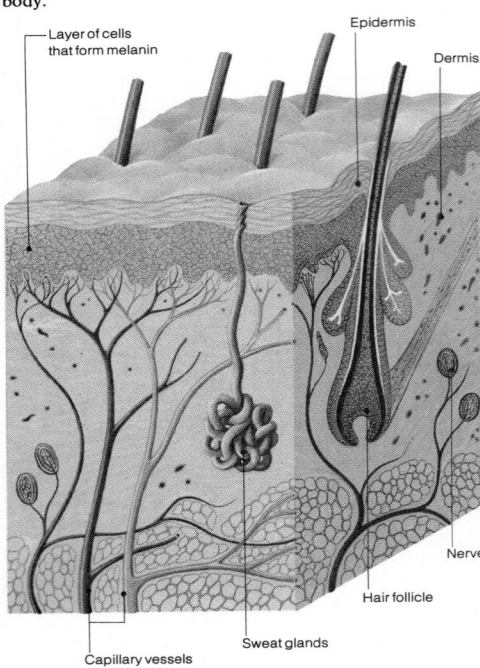

Layer of cells that form melanin

Epidermis

Dermis

Nerve

Hair follicle

Sweat glands

Capillary vessels

INSIDE THE SKIN *Embedded in the skin are sweat glands, hair follicles, and capillary vessels that control the blood supply. Each hair has a separate muscle that raises it on end, and an oil gland that helps to keep the skin waterproof, supple, and germ-resistant. Between the two main layers of skin, a layer of cells that form melanin pigment controls skin colour.*

skimmer *Trailing its long lower bill in the water, a skimmer swoops across a lake, scooping up fish as it flies. The birds live in large flocks on the fringes of lakes and rivers in Asia and Africa.*

skid row *n. Chiefly U.S. Slang.* A squalid area of a town, where down-and-outs gather. [Variant (influenced by ROW) of SKID ROAD.]

skiff (skif) *n. Nautical.* An open boat with a flat or rounded bottom having a pointed bow and a square stern and propelled by oars, sail, or motor. [French *esquif,* from Italian *schifo.*]

skif·fle (skiff'l) *n. Chiefly British.* A type of music, popular especially in the 1950s, that rendered folk songs or simple melodies to a fast, rhythmic beat, using improvised instruments, especially percussion instruments such as bottles or washboards. Also used adjectivally: *a skiffle band.* [Probably imitative.]

ski·jor·ing (skēé-jáwr-ing, -jawr- ‖ -jŏr-, -jŏr-) *n.* A sport in which a skier is drawn over ice or snow by a horse or vehicle. [Norwegian

skikjøring : SKI + *kjøring,* driving, from *kjøre,* to drive, from Old Norse *keyra.*] —**ski·jor·er** *n.*

ski jump *n.* **1.** A jump or leap made by a skier. **2.** A steep slope ending in a high ramp overhanging a slope, used for such a jump. **3.** A ramp used to assist the takeoff of a jump jet. —**ski-jump** (skēé-jump) *intr.v.* —**ski-jump·er** *n.*

skil·ful, *U.S.* **skill·ful** (skĭlf'l) *adj.* **1.** Possessing or exercising skill; able; expert. **2.** Characterised by, showing, or requiring skill. —See Synonyms at **proficient.** —**skil·ful·ly** *adv.* —**skil·ful·ness** *n.*

ski lift *n.* Any of various power-driven conveyors, usually with attached towing bars, suspended chairs, or gondolas, used to carry skiers to the top of a trail or slope.

skill (skĭl) *n.* **1.** The capacity to accomplish successfully something requiring special knowledge or ability; proficiency. **2.** An art, trade, or technique acquired through training or experience, particularly one requiring use of the hands or body. **3.** *Obsolete.* Understanding. —See Synonyms at **ability.** [Middle English *skil(e),* reason, skill, from Old Norse *skil.*]

skilled (skĭld) *adj.* **1.** Having or showing skill; expert. **2.** Having or requiring specialised ability or training, especially in a trade or craft: *a skilled occupation.* —See Synonyms at **proficient.**

skil·let (skĭllĭt) *n.* **1.** *Chiefly British.* A long-handled stewing pan or saucepan sometimes having legs. **2.** *Chiefly U.S.* A frying pan. [Middle English *skelet,* probably from *skele,* pail, from Scandinavian, akin to Old Norse *skjóla.*]

skil·li·on (skĭllĭ-ən) *n. Chiefly Australian.* An outhouse or lean-to with a roof that does not have a peak and slopes in one direction away from the main building. Also used adjectivally: *a skillion roof.* [From English dialect *skilling†,* outhouse.]

skil·ly (skĭllĭ) *n. British.* A thin broth or gruel, usually made with oatmeal. [Shortened from *skilligalee†.*]

skim (skĭm) *v.* **skimmed, skimming, skims.** —*tr.* **1.** To remove floating matter from (a liquid). **2.** To remove (floating matter, especially scum or cream) from a liquid. **3.** To coat or cover with or as if with a thin layer, as of scum or ice. **4. a.** To hurl across and close to the surface of water, ice, or the like, so as to bounce: *skimming stones.* **b.** To glide or pass quickly and lightly over. **5.** To read or glance through quickly or superficially; peruse hastily. —*intr.* **1.** To move or pass swiftly and lightly over or near a surface; glide; graze. **2.** To give a quick and superficial reading, scrutiny, or consideration. Used with *over* or *through.* **3.** To become coated with a thin layer. Used with *over.*
~*n.* **1.** The act of skimming. **2.** Something that has been skimmed, such as skim milk. **3.** A thin layer or film. [Middle English *skymen,* from Old French *escumer,* from *escume,* foam, from Old High German *scūm.*]

skim·mer (skĭmmər) *n.* **1.** One that skims. **2.** A flat utensil, usually perforated and resembling a ladle, used in skimming liquids. **3.** A wide-brimmed hat with a flat shallow crown. **4.** Any of several chiefly tropical coastal birds of the genus *Rynchops,* having long narrow wings and a long bill with a longer lower mandible for skimming the water's surface for food.

skim·mi·a (skĭmmi-ə) *n.* Any shrub of the genus *Skimmia,* native to south and southeast Asia but grown elsewhere for its ornamental foliage and red berries. [New Latin, from Japanese *mijama-skimmi.*]

skim milk *n.* Also **skimmed milk** (skĭmd). Milk from which the cream has been removed.

skim·ming (skĭmming) *n. Usually plural.* That which is skimmed off a liquid.

skimp (skĭmp) *v.* **skimped, skimping, skimps.** —*tr.* **1.** To do hastily, carelessly, or with poor material. **2.** To be extremely sparing with; scrimp. —*intr.* To be very or unduly thrifty. Usually used with *on: skimp on the budget.*
~*adj.* Scanty; skimpy. [Perhaps a variant of SCRIMP.]

skimp·y (skĭmpĭ) *adj.* **-ier, -iest. 1.** Inadequate in size, fullness, or amount; scanty. **2.** Unduly thrifty; stingy; niggardly. —See Synonyms at **meagre.** —**skimp·i·ly** *adv.* —**skimp·i·ness** *n.*

skin (skĭn) *n.* **1.** The tissue forming the external, protective covering of the body of a vertebrate. It consists of an outer **epidermis** and an inner **dermis** (both of which see). Also used adjectivally: *a skin graft.* **2.** An animal pelt, especially the comparatively pliable pelt of a small or young animal. Often used in combination: *pigskin; sheepskin.* **3.** Anything resembling skin in function or appearance; any outer layer, accretion, or protection, such as the rind of fruit, the surface film on boiled milk, or the plating on a ship or rocket. **4.** A container for liquid made of animal skin. **5.** *Often plural. Slang.* A drum. **6.** *Slang.* A cigarette paper used for rolling a cigarette, especially one containing cannabis. **7.** *Slang.* A skinhead *(see).* —**by the skin of (one's) teeth.** By the smallest margin; very closely; scarcely or barely. —**get under (someone's) skin. 1.** To anger or irritate. **2.** To be or become an obsession to. —**have a thick (or thin) skin.** To be unperturbed (or easily hurt) by criticism or insults. —**jump out of (one's) skin.** To be suddenly very startled or frightened. —**no skin off (someone's) nose.** *Informal.* Being a matter that does not adversely affect one. —**save (one's) skin.** To escape harm or avoid death.
~*v.* **skinned, skinning, skins.** —*tr.* **1.** To remove skin from; flay or peel. **2.** To cover with or as if with skin. Often used with *over.* **3.** To remove or peel off (skin or any outer covering). **4.** *Slang.* To fleece; swindle. **5.** To bruise, cut, or scrape the skin or surface of: *a skinned knee.* —*intr.* To become covered with or as if with skin.

Often used with *over.* **—skin up.** *Slang.* To roll a cigarette containing cannabis. [Middle English, from Old Norse *skinn.*]

skin-deep (skín-dḗep) *adj.* Superficial or shallow.
~adv. Shallowly; to a superficial degree.

skin-dive (skín-dīv) *intr.v.* **-dived, -diving, -dives.** To engage in skin diving.

skin diving *n.* Underwater swimming, exploration, or fishing in which the diver is equipped with goggles, flippers, and a snorkel or other breathing device. **—skin diver** *n.*

skin effect *n.* The tendency of electric current density in a conductor carrying alternating current to be greater at the surface than at the centre, producing an increase in resistance.

skin flick *n. Slang.* A cinematic film containing pornographic nudity. Also called "nudie".

skin•flint (skín-flint) *n.* A miser; a niggard. [From the notion that one would go so far as to try to skin a flint for money.]

skin friction *n.* Friction caused by a fluid crossing the surface of bodies, such as rockets, moving at high speeds. Also called "skin drag".

skin•ful (skín-fo͝ol) *n., pl.* **-fuls.** *Slang.* An amount of alcoholic drink that can make a person drunk: *I've had a skinful.*

skin graft *n.* A surgical graft of skin from one part of the body to another or from one individual to another. **—skin grafting** *n.*

skin•head (skín-hed) *n.* In Britain, a member of a gang of youths with shaven heads and usually wearing heavy, black, lace-up boots, drainpipe trousers worn off the ankle and with braces, and typically having rough and aggressive behaviour. Also called "skin".

skink (skingk) *n.* Any of numerous, mainly tropical, smooth, shiny lizards of the family Scincidae, having a cylindrical body and short or rudimentary legs. [Latin *scincus,* from Greek *skinkos*†.]

skinned (skind) *adj.* Having skin, especially of a specified kind. Used in combination: *fair-skinned.*

skin•ner (skínnər) *n.* A person who flays, dresses, or sells animal skins.

Skin•ner (skínnər), **B(urrhus) F(rederic)** (1904–). U.S. psychologist, the foremost representative of the Behaviourist school. His first important publication was *The Behaviour of Organisms* (1938). His most influential has been *Beyond Freedom and Dignity* (1971).

Skinner box *n.* A box used to study learning behaviour in animals. It is fitted with levers that the animal (usually a rat) can press to obtain a reward or punishment. [After B.F. SKINNER.]

skin•ny (skínni) *adj.* **-nier, -niest.** Very thin or slender; especially, unattractively thin. See Synonyms at **lean.** **—skin•ni•ness** *n.*

skin•ny-dip (skínni-dip) *intr.v.* **-dipped, -dipping, -dips.** *Informal.* To swim in the nude. **—skin•ny-dip•per** *n.*

skin•ny-rib (skínni-rib) *n.* A tight-fitting ribbed sweater.

skint (skint) *adj. British Slang.* Having or carrying no money. [Variant of *skinned,* past participle of SKIN.]

skin test *n.* A test for an allergy or infectious disease, performed by means of a **patch test, scratch test** *(both of which see),* or an injection beneath the skin of an allergen or extract of the disease-causing organism.

skin•tight (skín-tī́t, -tīt) *adj.* Fitting or clinging closely to the skin. Said of clothes.

skip[1] (skip) *v.* **skipped, skipping, skips.** *—intr.* **1. a.** To bound or trip lightly, especially by taking two steps at a time with each foot; hop and step; caper. **b.** To use a skipping rope. **2.** To bounce over or be deflected from a surface; skim or ricochet. **3.** To pass from point to point omitting or disregarding what intervenes. Often used with *through.* **4.** *Informal.* To leave hastily; abscond: *She skipped off somewhere.* *—tr.* **1.** To leap or jump lightly over. **2.** To pass over, omit, or disregard: *skipped the first page.* **3.** To cause to ricochet or skim. **4.** To deliberately avoid or not attend in: *skip classes.* **5.** *Chiefly U.S. Informal.* To leave hastily or secretly: *has skipped the country.* **—skip it.** *Informal.* To abandon or forget a subject, topic, or the like. Used in the imperative.
~n. **1.** A leaping or jumping movement; especially, a gait in which hops and steps alternate. **2.** A passing over or omission. [Middle English *skippen*†.]

skip[2] *n. Informal.* Used as a form of address for: **1.** A skipper, as of a boat or sports team. **2.** The leader of a Scout group.

skip[3] *n.* **1.** A large container for rubbish, as on a building site, that can be hoisted onto and taken away by a specially designed lorry. **2.** A large cage or bucket for lowering and raising people or material into or out of a mine. [Variant of SKEP.]

skip[4] *n. British.* A person employed at a college to clean students' rooms, especially at Trinity College, Dublin. [Probably from obsolete *skip-kennel,* from SKIP (jump, etc.) + KENNEL (gutter).]

skip distance *n.* The smallest separation between a transmitter and a receiver that permits radio signals of a specific frequency to travel from one to the other by reflection from the ionosphere.

skip•jack (skíp-jak) *n., pl.* **-jacks** or collectively **skipjack. 1.** Any of several tropical or subtropical marine food fishes of the genus *Euthynnus*; especially, *E. pelamis,* related to and resembling the tuna. **2.** Any of various other fishes, as certain herrings. **3.** The **click beetle** *(see).* [Originally "a fop" : SKIP + JACK (fellow).]

skip•per[1] (skíppər) *n.* **1.** The master of a ship, especially of a small one. **2.** The captain of an aeroplane or other aircraft. **3.** *Informal.* The captain of a side in sports. **4.** The leader of a Scout group.
~tr.v. **skippered, -pering, -pers.** To act as the skipper of. [Middle English *skypper,* from Middle Dutch *schipper,* from *schip,* ship.]

skipper[2] *n.* **1.** One that skips. **2.** Any of numerous butterflies of the family Hesperiidae, having a hairy, mothlike body and a darting flight pattern. **3.** Any of several related marine fishes; especially, a **saury** *(see).*

skip•pet (skíppit) *n.* A small box used, especially formerly, to enclose a seal attached to a document. [Middle English *skippet*†.]

skip•ping-rope (skípping-rōp) *n. Chiefly British.* A rope that has handles at either end and is swung over and over so that the person holding it or another person can jump over it.

skirl (skurl) *v.* **skirled, skirling, skirls.** *—intr.* To produce a shrill, piercing tone. Used of bagpipes. *—tr.* To play (music) on the bagpipes.
~n. **1.** The shrill sound made by the bagpipes. **2.** Any shrill, piercing sound. [Middle English *skirlen, skrillen,* probably of Scandinavian origin; akin to Norwegian dialectal *skrylla.*.]

skir•mish (skúrmish) *n.* **1.** A minor encounter in war between small bodies of troops, often unconnected with or at a distance from the main operations. **2.** Any minor or preliminary conflict or dispute.
~intr.v. **skirmished, -mishing, -mishes.** To engage in a skirmish. [Middle English *skirmisshe, skarmuch,* from Old French *eskermir* (present stem *eskirmiss-*), to fight with the sword, from Germanic.]

skirr (skur) *intr.v.* **skirred, skirring, skirrs.** To move or fly rapidly, especially with a whirring sound. Used with *away, off,* or other adverbs. [Perhaps variant of SCOUR (search).]

skir•ret (skírrit) *n.* An Old World plant, *Sium sisarum,* having a sweetish, edible root. [Middle English *skirwhite,* variant (influenced by *skir,* bright, and *whit,* white) of Old French *eschervi,* probably a variant of *carvi,* caraway, from Arabic *alkarawyā,* CARAWAY.]

skirt (skurt) *n.* **1.** That part of a garment, such as a dress or coat, that hangs from the waist down. **2.** A separate garment hanging from the waist, as worn by women and girls. **3. a.** One of the leather flaps hanging from the side of a saddle. **b.** The lower outer section of a rocket vehicle. **c.** A hanging part around the base of a hovercraft or certain racing cars. **4.** A border, margin, or outer edge. **5.** *Plural.* The edge or outskirts, as of a town. **6.** *Slang.* **a.** A woman or girl. **b.** Women collectively, considered as sexual objects. Used chiefly in the phrase *a bit of skirt.* Considered offensive. **7.** *British.* A cut of beef from the lower flank.
~v. **skirted, skirting, skirts.** *—tr.* **1.** To lie along, form the border of, or surround; bound. **2.** To move or pass around rather than across or through. **3.** To evade or elude (a topic of conversation, for example) by circumlocution. *—intr.* To be near or move along the edge or border of something. [Middle English, from Old Norse *skyrta,* SHIRT.]

skirt•ing (skúrting) *n.* Boarding that runs around the base of an interior wall next to the floor, to protect it from dirt, knocks, or damage.

skirting board *n.* A piece of skirting. Also *U.S.* "baseboard", "mopboard".

ski run *n.* A slope or course, usually marked, down which skiers ski.

ski-scoot•er (skḗe-sko͞otər) *n. British.* A motorised sledge with small skis at the front and moving on endless tracks at the back.

ski stick *n.* Either of a pair of sticks usually made of metal, with pointed ends, used by skiers to assist in turning and to gain momentum. Also called "ski pole".

skit (skit) *n.* **1.** A short, usually comic theatrical sketch. **2.** A short humorous or satirical piece of writing. [Perhaps from Old Norse; akin to *skjóta,* to SHOOT.]

skite[1] *intr.v.* **skited, skiting, skites.** *Scottish.* To slide or lose balance, as on a slippery suface. [Scottish and northern English dialect; akin to Old Norse *skjóta,* to shoot about, SHOOT.]

skite[2] *intr.v.* **skited, skiting, skites.** *Australian & N.Z. Informal.* To boast or show off.
~n. Australian & N.Z. Informal. A person who boasts or shows off. [Scottish and northern English dialect *skite*† (noun).]

ski tow *n.* A type of ski lift in which skiers cling to a continuous rope as they are hauled up a slope.

skit•ter (skíttər) *v.* **-tered, -tering, -ters.** *—intr.* **1.** To skip, scamper, or move lightly or rapidly along a surface; dart; flit. **2.** To fish by drawing a lure or baited hook over the surface of the water with a skipping movement. *—tr.* To cause to skitter. [Frequentative of dialectal *skite,* to run rapidly, shoot about, SKITE (slide).]

skit•tish (skíttish) *adj.* **1.** Excitable or nervous. **2. a.** Extremely lively or frivolous in action or character. **b.** Undependable or fickle. **3.** Shy, coy, or timid. [Middle English, perhaps ultimately from Old Norse *skjóta,* to shoot, shoot about.] **—skit•tish•ly** *adv.* **—skit•tish•ness** *n.*

skit•tle (skítt'l) *n. Chiefly British.* A wooden or plastic pin, wide at the base and tapering at the top, used in the game of skittles. Also called "ninepin".
~tr.v. **skittled, skittling, skittles.** In cricket, to get (batsmen) out in rapid succession and for very few runs. Usually used with *out.* [17th century : origin obscure.]

skit•tles (skítt'lz) *n. Used with a singular verb.* A game in which a wooden ball is bowled with the aim of knocking down nine pins. Also called "ninepins". **—all beer and skittles.** Nothing but pleasure and enjoyment.

skive[1] (skīv) *tr.v.* **skived, skiving, skives.** To shave or cut off the surface of (leather or rubber); pare. [Ultimately from Old Norse *skífa,* to slice.]

skive[2] *v.* **skived, skiving, skives.** *British Slang.* *—intr.* To shirk or avoid work or duty. Sometimes used with *off.* *—tr.* To shirk or avoid (work or duty). [20th century : origin obscure.]

skiv•er[1] (skī́vər) *n.* **1.** A soft, thin leather split off the outside of skin

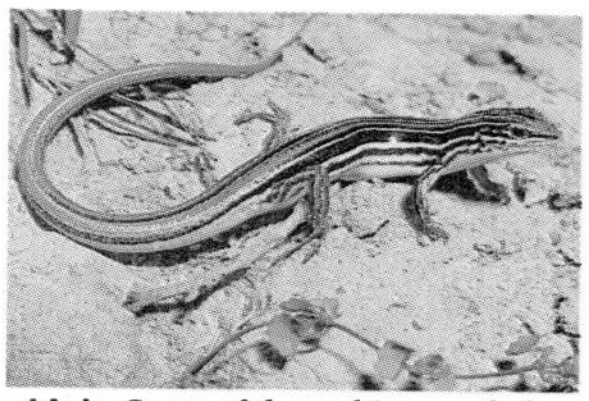

skink *Some of these shiny-scaled lizards are legless burrowers. The sandfish, for instance, which is a type of skink, spends much of its life underground. This species, which does have legs, is native to Australia.*

PRONUNCIATION KEY

a, trap; aa, father; ai, fair; ar, star; aw, lawn; ay, play; b, bb, stab; rubber; ch, church; ck, ticket; d, dd, dead; ladder; e, dress; ee, bee; er, defer; ew, few; ewr, pure; ə, about; ər, letter; f, ff, fife; differ; g, gg, giggle; h, hat; i, kit; ī, price; īr, fire; j, judge; k, kick; l, ll, let; 'l, needle; m, mm, man; n, nn, no; 'n, sudden; ng, thing; o, lot; ō, no; o͝o, foot; o͞o, shoe; oor, poor; ow, cow; owr, hour; oy, boy; p, pp, pepper; r, rr, red; s, ss, sauce; sh, ship; t, tt, totter; th, thick; th, this; smooth; u, cut; ur, turn; v, vv, valve; w, wet; y, yes; z, zz, zebra; zh, vision; pleasure

IN FOREIGN WORDS:

aN, oN, Saint-Saëns; hl, Llanelli; Hluhluwe; kh, loch; lough; Khaled

STRESS MARK:

ín-sīt, insight; in-sī́t, incite

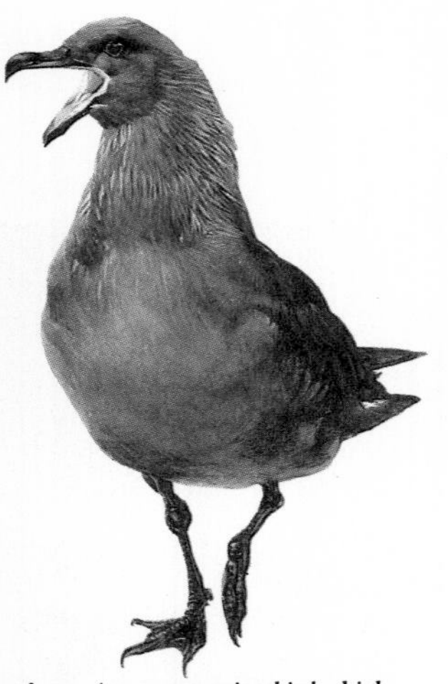

***skua** An ocean-going bird which lives in the regions around both Poles, the great skua is a skilful flyer and often harries other fishing birds to make them disgorge their catch, which it will often retrieve before the fish hits the water.*

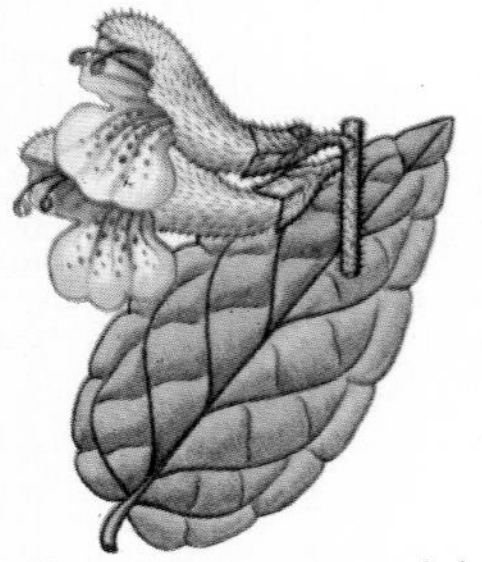

***skullcap** A square-stemmed plant with a pouchlike flower, the skullcap grows in marshes. Its name comes from the Latin* scutellum, *meaning "a disc-shaped pouch".*

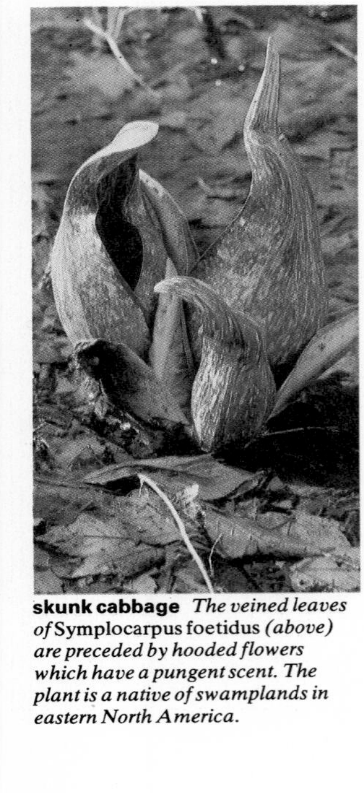

***skunk cabbage** The veined leaves of* Symplocarpus foetidus *(above) are preceded by hooded flowers which have a pungent scent. The plant is a native of swamplands in eastern North America.*

and used especially for bookbinding. **2.** A person who skives leather. **3.** A knife or other cutting device used in skiving.

skiver² *n. British Slang.* One who avoids work or duty.

skiv·vy (skívvi) *n., pl.* **-vies.** *British Slang.* A menial, usually female, servant, especially one who does washing and cleaning. Sometimes used derogatorily.
~intr.v. **skivvied, -vying, -vies.** *British Slang.* To work as a skivvy. [20th century : origin obscure.]

skoal, skol (skōl) *interj.* Used as a drinking toast. [Norwegian and Danish *skaal* and Swedish *skål,* from Old Norse *skāl,* drinking cup.]

skok·i·aan (skócki-aan, skáwki-) *n. South African.* A strong home-brew made with yeast, usually illicitly. [Afrikaans : origin obscure.]

Skop·je (skóp-yi; *Macedonian* -ye). *Serbo-Croat* **Skop·je.** City in southern Yugoslavia, the capital of Macedonia, lying on the river Vardar. From its capture by the Turks in 1392 until the fall of Constantinople in 1453, it was the most important Turkish city in Europe. Much of the city was destroyed by an earthquake in 1963.

Skr., Skt. Sanskrit.

sku·a (skéw-ə) *n.* Any of various predatory gull-like sea birds of the family Stercorariidae, of polar regions, having brownish plumage. [New Latin, from Faroese *skūvur,* Old Norse *skūfr*†, tassel.]

skul·dug·ger·y, skull·dug·ger·y (skul-dúggəri) *n. Informal.* Crafty deception or trickery. [From earlier (Scottish) *sculduddery*†, wantonness.]

skulk (skulk) *intr.v.* **skulked, skulking, skulks.** **1.** To lurk; lie in hiding. **2.** To move about stealthily or furtively. **3.** To evade work or obligations.
~n. One who skulks. [Middle English *skulken,* from Scandinavian; akin to Danish *skulke*†.] **—skulk·er** *n.*

skull (skul) *n.* **1.** The framework of the head of vertebrates, made up of the bones of the **cranium** *(see)* and face. **2.** This as a symbol of death. **3.** The head, especially regarded as the seat of thought or intelligence. Usually used derogatorily: *can't get it into your thick skull.* **3.** *Plural. Music.* A set of percussion instruments, consisting of inverted, fish-head-shaped, wooden objects that are hit with a stick to produce a clunking sound that varies in pitch according to size. [Middle English *schulle, skulle*†.]

skull and crossbones *n. Used with a singular or plural verb.* A representation of a human skull above two long crossed bones, a symbol of death once used by pirates, especially on their flag, and now often used as a warning label on poisons.

skull·cap (skúl-kap) *n.* **1. a.** A light, close-fitting, brimless cap sometimes worn indoors. **b.** A similar cap worn by Roman Catholic prelates and by male Jews. **2.** Any of various plants of the genus *Scutellaria,* having clusters of two-lipped, helmet-shaped flowers. **3.** *Anatomy.* The **calvaria** *(see).*

skunk (skungk) *n.* **1.** Any of several small, carnivorous New World mammals of the genus *Mephitis* and related genera; especially, *M. mephitis,* having a bushy tail and black fur with white markings and ejecting an unpleasant-smelling secretion from glands near the anus. **2.** *Slang.* A mean or despicable person.
~tr.v. **skunked, skunking, skunks.** *U.S. Slang.* **1.** To defeat overwhelmingly, especially by keeping from scoring in a game. **2.** To cheat, as by failing to pay. [Massachuset *squnck,* from Proto-Algonquian *shekākwa* (unattested) : *shek-* (unattested), to urinate + *-ākw-* (unattested), small mammal.]

skunk cabbage *n.* An ill-smelling swamp plant, *Symplocarpus foetidus,* of eastern North America, having minute flowers enclosed in a mottled greenish or purplish spathe.

sky (skī) *n., pl.* **skies.** **1. a.** The upper atmosphere, appearing as a hemisphere above the earth. **b.** The apparent hemispherical dome, as seen from the Earth's surface, upon which the celestial bodies seem to move; it appears blue in the daytime and almost black at night. **2.** The highest level or degree of something; the ultimate: *reaching for the sky.* **3.** The celestial or heavenly regions. **4.** *Often plural.* **a.** The appearance of the upper air: *blue skies.* **b.** The climate or weather, as indicated by the sky. **—praise to the skies.** To praise in an extravagantly enthusiastic way.
~tr.v. **skied, skying, skies.** **1.** To hit or throw (a ball, for example) high in the air. **2.** To hang (a painting, for example) above the line of vision. [Middle English, cloud, sky, from Old Norse *sky̆,* cloud, from Common Germanic *skewja-* (unattested).]

sky blue *n.* Light to pale blue. **—sky-blue** (skī-bloō) *adj.*

sky·borne (skī-bawrn ‖ -bōrn) *adj.* Airborne.

sky·dive (skī-dīv) *intr.v.* **-dived, -diving, -dives.** *Sports.* To jump from an aircraft, performing various manoeuvres before pulling the ripcord of one's parachute. **—sky·div·er** *n.* **—sky·div·ing** *n.*

Skye (skī). Largest and most northerly island of the Inner Hebrides, off west Scotland. It is part of the Highland Region and is some 80 kilometres (50 miles). Bonnie Prince Charlie took refuge there in 1746 after his defeat at Culloden Moor.

Skye terrier *n.* A small terrier of a breed native to the Isle of Skye, having a long, low body, short legs, and shaggy hair.

sky·ey (skī-i) *adj. Literary.* **1.** Of or from the skies: *skyey influences.* **2.** Blue like the sky. **3.** Lofty.

sky-high (skī-hī) *adv.* **1.** At or to an exceptionally high level: *the price of property has gone sky-high.* **2.** In a lavish or enthusiastic manner. **3.** In pieces or to pieces; apart: *blew it sky-high.*
~adj. **1.** High up in the air. **2.** Exorbitantly high.

sky·jack (skī-jak) *tr.v.* **-jacked, -jacking, -jacks.** To hijack (an aircraft, especially one in flight) through the use or threat of force. [SKY + (HI)JACK.] **—sky·jack·er** *n.*

Sky·lab (skī-lab) *n.* Any of several space stations launched into Earth orbit from the United States in the 1970s.

sky·lark (skī-laark) *n.* An Old World bird, *Alauda arvensis,* having brownish plumage and noted for its singing while in flight.
~intr.v. **skylarked, -larking, -larks.** To frolic or have fun.

sky·light (skī-līt) *n.* An overhead window admitting daylight.

sky·line (skī-līn) *n.* **1.** The line along which the surface of the earth and sky appear to meet; the horizon. **2.** An outline, as of a group of buildings or a mountain range, seen against the sky.

sky pilot *n. Slang.* A clergyman, especially a service chaplain.

sky·rock·et (skī-rockit) *n.* A firework, a **rocket** *(see).*
~intr.v. **skyrocketed, -eting, -ets.** To rise rapidly or suddenly, as in amount, position, or reputation.

sky·sail (skī-sayl, -s'l) *n.* A small square sail above the royal in a square-rigged vessel.

sky·scrap·er (skī-skraypər) *n.* A very tall building, especially a multistorey office block.

sky·ward (skī-wərd) *adj.* Moving or going towards the sky.

sky·wards (skī-wərdz) *adv.* Also **skyward.** Towards the sky.

sky wave *n.* A radio wave transmitted from one point on the earth's surface and received at another point after reflection by the ionosphere. Also called "ionospheric wave". Compare **ground wave.**

sky·writ·ing (skī-rīting) *n.* **1.** The process of writing in the sky by releasing a visible vapour from a flying aircraft. **2.** The letters or words thus formed. **—sky·writ·er** *n.*

s.l. without place. Used in book cataloguing. [Latin *sine loco.*]

slab¹ (slab) *n.* **1.** A broad, flat, somewhat thick piece, as of cake, stone, or cheese. **2.** An outside piece cut from a log when squaring it to make planks. **3.** *British Informal.* The table on which a corpse is put in a mortuary.
~tr.v. **slabbed, slabbing, slabs.** **1.** To make or shape into a slab or slabs. **2.** To cover or pave with slabs. **3.** To dress (a log) by cutting slabs. [Middle English *s(c)labbe*†.]

slab² *adj. Archaic.* Viscous. Used in the phrase *thick and slab.* [Probably of Scandinavian origin; akin to Danish *slab,* mud.]

Slab·bert (slábbərt), **Frederik van Zyl** (1940–). South African sociologist and politician. He has been leader of South Africa's Progressive Federal Party since 1979, and as such is leader of the opposition in the South African Parliament.

slab-sid·ed (sláb-sīdid) *adj. U.S. Informal.* **1.** Having flat sides. **2.** Tall and slim; lanky; lean.

slack¹ (slak) *adj.* **1.** Not lively or moving; slow; dull; sluggish. **2.** Not active or busy; lacking in work. **3.** Not tense or taut; loose. **4.** Lacking firmness; weak; relaxed: *a slack grip.* **5.** *Informal.* Lacking in diligence; idle or negligent. **6.** Flowing or blowing with little speed. Said of the wind or tide. **7.** *Phonetics.* Lax.
~v. **slacked, slacking, slacks.** *—tr.* To slacken. *—intr.* To be or become slack; especially, to be or become idle or inactive. **—slack off.** To decrease in activity or intensity; fall off; abate.
~n. **1.** A loose or slack part or portion of something, such as a rope or sail. **2.** A period of little activity; a lull. **3. a.** A cessation of movement in a current of air or water. **b.** An area of still water. **4.** *Plural.* A pair of trousers for casual wear.
~adv. In a slack manner. [Middle English *slak,* Old English *slæc.*] **—slack·ly** *adv.* **—slack·ness** *n.*

slack² *n.* A mixture of coal fragments, coal dust, and dirt that remains after screening coal. [Middle English *sleck,* probably from Middle Dutch *slacke.*]

slack³ *n.* **1.** A small dell or hollow. **2.** A bog; a morass. **3.** A depression between lines of sand dunes along a coast or in a desert. [Middle English *slak,* from Old Norse *slakki*†.]

slack·en (sláckən) *v.* **-ened, -ening, -ens.** *—tr.* **1.** To make slower; slow down. **2.** To lessen, as in vigour, intensity, firmness, or severity. **3.** To reduce the tension or tautness of; loosen. *—intr.* **1.** To slow down. **2.** To become slacker in some way, as by growing less energetic, active, firm, or strict. **3.** To become less tense or taut; loosen. In all senses, often used with *off.*

slack·er (sláckər) *n.* A person who shirks work or responsibility.

slack water *n.* **1.** The period at high or low tide when there is no visible flow of water. **2.** An area in a sea or river unaffected by currents; still water.

SLADE Society of Lithographic Artists, Designers, Engravers, and Process Workers (a trade union in Britain).

slag (slag) *n.* **1.** The vitreous mass left as a residue by the smelting of metallic ore. Also called "cinder". **2.** Volcanic refuse, **scoria** *(see).* **3.** A mixture of coal dust, shale, and other waste mineral matter produced during coalmining. **4.** *British Slang.* A vulgar, coarse, or sexually promiscuous woman or girl. Used derogatorily.
~v. **slagged, slagging, slang.** *—tr.* To change into slag. *—intr.* To form slag; become slaglike. **—slag (someone) off.** *British Slang.* To criticise or abuse (someone) verbally, in an extremely offensive or vulgar manner. [Middle Low German *slagge,* perhaps from *slagen,* to strike (alluding to fragments of rock).] **—slag·gy** *adj.*

slag heap *n.* A large mound consisting of slag deposited as a waste product from coalmining operations.

slain. Past participle of **slay.**

slàin·te (slaánjə) *interj. Scottish.* Used as a drinking toast, especially when drinking whisky. [Gaelic, health.]

slais·ter (sláystər) *n. Scottish.* A wet or slobbery mess. [18th century : origin obscure.]

slake (slayk) *v.* **slaked, slaking, slakes.** *—tr.* **1.** To quench; allay; satisfy. **2.** *Poetic.* To lessen the force or activity of; moderate. **3.** To cool or refresh by moistening. **4.** To combine (lime) chemically with water or moist air. *—intr.* To undergo a slaking process; crumble or disintegrate. Used of lime. [Middle English *slaken,* to lessen, Old English *slacian,* from *slæc,* SLACK (loose).]

slaked lime *n. Chemistry.* **Calcium hydroxide** *(see).*

sla·lom (slaaləm) *n.* **1.** Skiing in a zigzag course. **2.** A race, especially a skiing race, along a zigzag course, usually marked with poles. [Norwegian, "sloping path" : *sla(d)*†, sloping + *lom, låm,* path, from Northwest Germanic *lanu-* (unattested).]

slam[1] (slam) *v.* **slammed, slamming, slams.** *—tr.* **1.** To shut (a door or window, for example) with force and loud noise. **2.** To put, throw, or otherwise forcefully move so as to produce a loud noise. **3.** To hit or strike with great force. **4.** *Slang.* To criticise harshly; attack verbally. **5.** *Informal.* To beat easily and by a wide margin. **6.** To operate (brakes) suddenly and harshly. Used with *on.* *—intr.* **1.** To close or swing into place with force so as to produce a loud noise. **2.** To hit something with force; crash. **3.** To enter or leave a place violently or angrily: *slammed out of the house.*
∼n. **1.** A forceful closing or other movement that produces a loud noise. **2.** The noise so produced. [Perhaps from Scandinavian, akin to Old Norse *slam(b)ra,* to strike at.]

slam[2] *n.* In bridge, whist, or other card games derived from these, the winning of all the tricks *(grand slam)* or all but one *(little slam)* during the play of one hand. [Probably from SLAM (a stroke).]

slam-bang (slám-báng) *adv.* **1.** Loudly and violently. **2.** *U.S.* Recklessly.

s.l.a.n. without place, year, or name. Used in book cataloguing. [Latin *sine loco, anno, vel nomine.*]

slan·der (slaandər || slándər) *n.* **1.** *Law.* The utterance of defamatory statements that are injurious to the reputation or well-being of a person. Compare **libel. 2.** A malicious statement or report.
∼tr.v. **slandered, -dering, -ders.** To utter damaging or defamatory reports about. **—See Synonyms at malign.** [Middle English *s(c)laundre,* from Old French *esclandre,* variant of *escandle,* from Latin *scandalum,* SCANDAL.] **—slan·der·er** *n.* **—slan·der·ous** *adj.* **—slan·der·ous·ly** *adv.*

slang (slang) *n.* **1.** Language, typically of an ephemeral nature, whose use is usually restricted to informal contexts and among people familiar with or similar to one another. **2.** Language peculiar to a group; argot or jargon.
∼v. **slanged, slanging, slangs.** *—tr.* To direct abusive language at (somebody); insult. *—intr.* To use abusive or insulting language. [18th-century (cant) : origin obscure.] **—slang·i·ly** *adv.* **—slang·i·ness** *n.* **—slang·y** *adj.*

slang·ing match (sláng-ing) *n. British.* A quarrel or dispute in which abusive insults are exchanged.

Slán·ský (slaan-ski), **Rudolf** (1901–52). Czech Communist leader. In 1948 he became deputy premier in the new Communist government. In 1951 he was convicted for spying and Zionist activities; along with 13 others, and executed. In 1963 he was cleared of the charges.

slant (slaant || slant) *v.* **slanted, slanting, slants.** *—tr.* **1.** To give an oblique direction to. **2.** To present (information) so as to give it a particular bias, as by emphasising certain facts. *—intr.* **1.** To incline or move obliquely. **2.** To have a bias. Used with *towards.*
∼n. **1. a.** A sloping direction, plane, or course; an incline. **b.** Slope; obliquity. **2.** A particular bias, emphasis, or point of view.
∼adj. Slanting or sloping. [Earlier *slent,* from Middle English *slenten*†, from Old Norse *sletta,* to throw.] **—slant·ing·ly** *adv.*

slant·wise (slaant-wīz || slánt-) *adv.* Also **slant·ways** (-wayz). At a slant or slope; obliquely.
∼adj. Slanting; oblique.

slap (slap) *n.* **1. a.** A smacking blow, as made with the open hand. **b.** The sound so made. **2.** An injury, as to one's pride; a rebuff or rebuke. Used chiefly in the phrase *a slap in the face.*
∼v. **slapped, slapping, slaps.** *—tr.* **1.** To strike with a flat object, especially the palm of the hand. **2.** To put or place with a slapping sound: *slapped a fiver on the bar.* **3.** To set or apply in an emphatic manner: *slapped a tax on eggs.* **4.** To put or place carelessly or in a hurried manner: *slap a few pictures on the wall.* *—intr.* To strike or beat with the force and sound of a slap. **—slap down.** To put (a person) down; rebuff or reprimand.
∼adv. Informal. Directly and with force. [Low German *slapp* (imitative).] **—slap·per** *n.*

slap and tickle *n. Used with a singular verb. Informal.* Light-hearted sexual play.

slap-bang (sláp-báng) *adv. Chiefly British Informal.* **1.** Exactly or directly. **2.** In a careless, hasty, or violent manner.

slap·dash (sláp-dash) *adj.* Acting or done hastily or carelessly.
∼adv. In a reckless, haphazard manner.
∼n. **1.** Careless or hasty work. **2. Roughcast** *(see).*

slap·hap·py (sláp-happi) *adj. Informal.* **-pier, -piest. 1.** Dazed, silly, or incoherent from or as if from blows to the head. **2.** Reckless or casual in a jolly, cheerful manner.

slap·jack (sláp-jak) *n. U.S.* A pancake. [SLAP + (FLAP)JACK.]

slap·stick (sláp-stik) *n.* **1.** Comedy characterised by boisterous knockabout farce and broad visual humour. Also used adjectivally. **2.** A paddle designed to produce a loud whacking sound, formerly used in farces to simulate the sound of a heavy blow.

slap-up (sláp-up) *adj. British Informal.* Excellent and extravagant. Said especially of a meal.

slash (slash) *v.* **slashed, slashing, slashes.** *—tr.* **1.** To cut or form by violent sweeping strokes. **2.** To lash violently with sweeping strokes. **3.** To make a gash or gashes in. **4.** To cut a slit or slits in (a garment) to reveal the lining: *a slashed sleeve.* **5.** To criticise sharply: *a slashing attack.* **6.** To reduce or curtail drastically: *Profits were slashed.* *—intr.* To make violent and sweeping strokes with or as with a sharp instrument. **—See Synonyms at tear.**
∼n. **1.** A sweeping stroke made with a sharp instrument. **2.** A cut or other injury made by such a stroke; a gash; a slit. **3.** An ornamental slit in a fabric or article of clothing. **4.** *U.S.* **a.** Branches and other residue left on a forest floor after the cutting of timber. **b.** Wet or swampy ground overgrown with bushes and trees. **5.** *Printing.* A **solidus** *(see).* **6.** *British Slang.* An act of urinating. [Middle English *slaschen,* perhaps from Old French *esclaschier, esclachier,* to break (imitative).] **—slash·er** *n.*

Śląsk. See **Silesia.**

slat[1] (slat) *n.* **1.** A narrow strip of metal or wood, as in a Venetian blind. **2.** A movable auxiliary aerofoil running along the leading edge of the wing of an aircraft.
∼tr.v. **slatted, slatting, slats.** To provide or make with slats. [Middle English *s(c)lat,* from Old French *esclat,* splinter, fragment, from *esclater*†, to splinter.]

slat[2] *tr.v.* **slatted, slatting, slats.** *Archaic & Regional.* To throw or knock violently or carelessly.
∼n. Archaic & Regional. A blow or slap. [Middle English, from Scandinavian; akin to Old Norse *sletta,* to slap.]

slate[1] (slayt) *n.* **1.** A fine-grained metamorphic rock that splits into thin, smooth-surfaced layers. **2. a.** A piece of this rock cut for use as a roofing tile. **b.** A piece of slate or similar material, used, especially formerly, as a writing tablet. **3.** *U.S.* A list of the candidates of a political party running for various offices. **4.** Dark grey to purplish grey. **5.** An actual or imaginary record of money owed: *£5 on the slate.* **—start with a clean slate** or **wipe the slate clean.** To overlook past failures and make a fresh start.
∼tr.v. **slated, slating, slates. 1.** To cover (a roof, for example) with slates. **2.** *U.S.* To put on a list of candidates. **3.** *U.S.* To designate or destine: *"I was slated to amass wealth beyond the dreams of avarice"* (S.J. Perelman). [Middle English *s(c)late,* from Old French *esclate,* feminine of *esclat,* fragment, splinter. See **slat.**] **—slat·y** *adj.*

slate[2] *tr.v.* **slated, slating, slates.** *British Informal.* **1.** To criticise unfairly or harshly. **2.** To reprimand or scold. [Perhaps from SLATE (cover with slates).]

slate blue *n.* Greyish blue to dark bluish grey. **—slate-blue** (sláyt-bloo) *adj.*

slat·er (sláytər) *n.* **1.** One employed to lay slate roofs. **2.** Any of several small isopod crustaceans; especially, a woodlouse.

slath·er (sláthər) *tr.v.* **-ered, -ering, -ers.** *U.S. Informal.* **1.** To use great amounts of; lavish. **2. a.** To spread thickly with. **b.** To spread thickly.
∼n. Plural. Slang. A great amount; a lot: *slathers of money.* [19th century : origin obscure.]

slat·ing[1] (sláyting) *n.* **1.** The act, process, or occupation of laying slates. **2.** Slates collectively, used as a building material.

slating[2] *n. British Informal.* A harsh attack or reprimand.

slat·tern (sláttərn) *n.* A woman who is untidy or slovenly in person or habits; a slut. [Perhaps variant of dialectal *slattering,* present participle of *slatter*†, to spill awkwardly.]

slat·tern·ly (sláttərnli) *adj.* **1.** Slovenly; untidy. **2.** Characteristic of or befitting a slattern. **—See Synonyms at sloppy. —slat·tern·li·ness** *n.*

slaugh·ter (sláwtər) *n.* **1.** The killing of animals for food. **2.** The killing of a large number of persons; carnage; massacre.
∼tr.v. **slaughtered, -tering, -ters. 1.** To kill (animals) for food; butcher. **2. a.** To kill in large numbers; massacre. **b.** To kill in a violent or brutal manner. **3.** *Informal.* To defeat easily. [Middle English *slau(g)hter,* probably from Old Norse *slātr,* butchered meat.] **—slaugh·ter·er** *n.* **—slaugh·ter·ous** *adj.*

slaugh·ter·house (sláwtər-howss) *n.* **1.** A place where animals are butchered; an abattoir. **2.** A scene of massacre or carnage.

Slav (slaav || *U.S. also* slav) *n.* A member of any of the Slavonic-speaking peoples of eastern Europe. [Middle English *Sclave,* from Medieval Latin *S(c)lavus,* from Late Greek *Sklabos*†.]

Slav. Slavonic.

slave (slayv) *n.* **1.** One who is legally bound in absolute obedience and servitude to a person or household to perform labour. **2.** One who is submissive to or hopelessly in the power of a particular person or influence: *a slave to her eating habits.* **3.** One whose condition is likened to that of slavery, as through having to work extremely hard or under duress. **4.** A machine or component that is controlled, powered, or fed information by another machine or component. Also used adjectivally: *a slave cylinder.*
∼intr.v. **slaved, slaving, slaves.** To work like a slave; drudge. Often used with *away.* [Middle English *sclave,* from Old French *esclave,* slave, from Medieval Latin *sclavus,* from *Sclavus,* SLAV (the Slavs were reduced to slavery by conquest).]

slave-driv·er (sláyv-drīvər) *n.* **1.** A severely exacting employer or supervisor. **2.** An overseer of slaves at work, especially formerly.

slav·er[1] (slávvər, *rarely* sláyvər) *intr.v.* **-ered, -ering, -ers. 1.** To slobber. **2.** To fawn; drivel. Often used with *over.*
∼n. **1.** Saliva drooling from the mouth. **2.** Slobbering flattery or drivel. [Middle English *slaveren,* probably from Old Norse *slafra.*]

slav·er[2] (sláyvər) *n.* **1.** A ship engaged in slave traffic. **2.** One trading in slaves. **—slav·ing** *n.*

slav·er·y (sláyvəri) *n., pl.* **-ies. 1.** Bondage to a master or household as a slave. **2.** A mode of production in which slaves constitute the principal work force. **3.** The condition of being subject or addicted

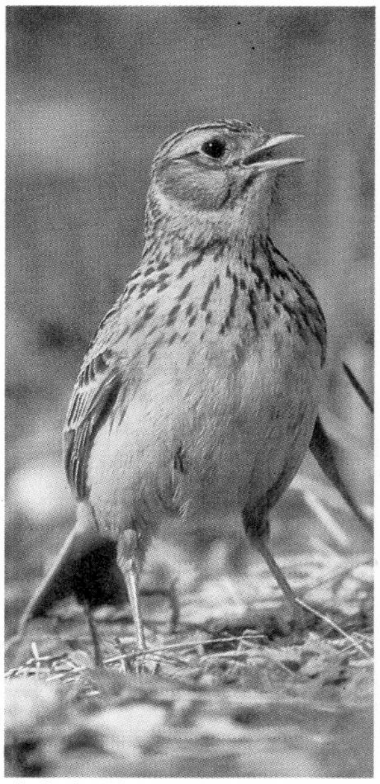

skylark *The male skylark marks out its territory by singing a clear, warbling song while hovering high in the air. Found throughout Europe, Asia, and North Africa, the skylark is considered a delicacy in some countries.*

PRONUNCIATION KEY

a, trap; aa, father; ai, fair; ar, star; aw, lawn; ay, play; b, bb, stab; rubber; ch, church; ck, ticket; d, dd, dead; ladder; e, dress; ee, bee; er, defer; ew, few; ewr, pure; ə, about; ər, letter; f, ff, fife; differ; g, gg, giggle; h, hat; i, kit; ī, price; īr, fire; j, judge; k, kick; l, ll, let; 'l, needle; m, mm, man; n, nn, no; 'n, sudden; ng, thing; o, lot; ō, no; ŏŏ, foot; ōō, shoe; oor, poor; ow, cow; owr, hour; oy, boy; p, pp, pepper; r, rr, red; s, ss, sauce; sh, ship; t, tt, totter; th, thick; th, this; smooth; u, cut; ur, turn; v, vv, valve; w, wet; y, yes; z, zz, zebra; zh, vision; pleasure

IN FOREIGN WORDS:

aN, oN, Saint-Saëns; hl, Llanelli; Hluhluwe; kh, loch; lough; Khaled

STRESS MARK:

ín-sīt, insight; in-sīt, incite

to a particular influence. **4.** A condition of subjection likened to that of a slave: *wage slavery.* **—**See Synonyms at **servitude.**

Slave State *n.* In the United States, any of the 15 southerly states in which slavery was legal before the Civil War.

slave trade *n.* Traffic in slaves; specifically, that of black Africans to America. **—slave-trad·er** *n.* **—slave-trad·ing** *n.*

slav·ey (sláyvi) *n., pl.* **-eys.** *British Informal.* A maidservant, especially one who is overworked.

Slavic. *Chiefly U.S.* Variant of **Slavonic.**

slav·ish (sláyvish) *adj.* **1.** Pertaining to or characteristic of a slave; servile. **2.** Pertaining to or characteristic of the institution of slavery; oppressive. **3.** Blindly dependent on or imitative of something: *a slavish copy of the original.* **4.** Extremely laborious or difficult. **—slav·ish·ly** *adv.* **—slav·ish·ness** *n.*

Slav·ism (slaáv-iz'm || *U.S. also* sláv-) *n.* Anything peculiar to or characteristic of the Slavs or the Slavonic languages.

Slavkov. See **Austerlitz.**

Sla·von·ic (slə-vónnik, sla-, slaa-) *adj. Abbr.* **Slav.** Also *chiefly U.S.* **Slav·ic** (slaávik, slávvik). Of or pertaining to the Slavs or their languages or cultures.
~*n. Abbr.* **Slav.** Also *chiefly U.S.* **Slavic.** A branch of the Indo-European language family, divided into East Slavonic, South Slavonic, and West Slavonic.

Slav·o·phile (slaáv-ə-fīl, sláv-, -ō-) *n.* Also **Slav·o·phil** (-fil). **1.** A person who admires the Slavs. **2.** *Sometimes small* **s.** In 19th-century Russia, one who advocated the supremacy of Slavonic, especially Russian, culture. [SLAV + -PHILE.] **—Slav·o·phile, Slav·o·phil** *adj.* **—Sla·voph·i·lism** (-iz'm, slə-vóffil-) *n.*

slaw (slaw) *n. Chiefly U.S.* **Coleslaw** *(see).*

slay (slay) *tr.v.* **slew** (sloō || slew) or (for sense 2) **slayed, slain** (slayn) or (for sense 2) **slayed, slaying, slays. 1.** To kill violently, as in battle. **2.** *Slang.* To overwhelm, as with admiration, laughter, or love: *He slays all the girls.* [Slay, slew, slain; Middle English *slen(en), slew, slayn,* Old English *slēan, slōh, slægen.*] **—slay·er** *n.*
Usage: The usual past tense form of this verb is *slew,* past participle *slain.* But regular variants have emerged in informal speech, with *slayed* being used for both past tense and participle, in the sense "overwhelm" *(I slayed them at the Empire last week).*

S.L.B.M. submarine-launched ballistic missile.

sld. 1. sailed. **2.** sealed.

sleave (sleev) *tr.v.* **sleaved, sleaving, sleaves.** *Archaic.* To separate or disentangle (a twisted mass of threads, for example).
~*n. Archaic.* Any tangled or knotted thread. [Middle English *sleven* (unattested), Old English *slǣfan,* to cut, cut up, akin to *-slīfan,* to splice. See **sliver.**]

sleave silk *n.* Raw untwisted silk; floss, as for embroidery.

sleaze (sleez) *n. Informal.* **1.** Squalidness or disreputableness; sleaziness. **2.** A sleazy person. [From SLEAZY.]

slea·zy (sleézi) *adj.* **-zier, -ziest. 1.** Having a sordid, squalid, or disreputable character: *a sleazy restaurant.* **2.** Flimsy or thin. Said of fabric. **3.** Made of low-quality materials; shoddy. [17th century : origin obscure.] **—slea·zi·ly** *adv.* **—slea·zi·ness** *n.*

sledge (slej) *n.* Also **sled** (sled). **1.** A vehicle mounted on low runners, drawn by horses, dogs, or other work animals, and used for transport or travel across ice and snow. **2.** A **toboggan** *(see).*
~*v.* **sledged, sledging, sledges.** *—tr.* To carry or convey on a sledge. *—intr.* **1.** To travel on a sledge. **2.** *Chiefly British.* To ride down slopes on a sledge; toboggan. [Dutch (dialectal) *sleeds,* from Middle Dutch *sleedse.*]

sledge·ham·mer (sléj-hammər) *n.* A long, heavy hammer, often wielded with both hands, used for driving wedges and posts and for other heavy work.
~*tr.v.* **sledgehammered, -mering, -mers.** To strike with or as if with such a hammer.
~*adj.* Ruthlessly severe; crushing. [Middle English *sleg(g)e,* Old English *slecg* + HAMMER.]

sledg·ing (sléj-ing) *n. Slang.* In cricket, a form of gamesmanship whereby a fielding side attempts to influence the umpire, especially by making repeated appeals. [Perhaps from SLEDGEHAMMER.]

sleek (sleek) *adj.* **sleeker, sleekest. 1. a.** Smooth and lustrous as if polished; glossy. **b.** Smooth, shiny, and healthy-looking. Said of the coat or fur of an animal. **2.** Appearing well-fed or well-groomed; prosperous-looking; thriving. **3.** Polished or smooth in behaviour, especially in an unctuous way; slick.
~*tr.v.* **sleeked, sleeking, sleeks. 1.** To make sleek; smooth or polish. **2. a.** To make calm or free from agitation. **b.** To cause to appear in a favourable light; gloss over. Used with *over.* [Variant of SLICK.] **—sleek·ly** *adv.* **—sleek·ness** *n.*

sleek·it (sleékit) *adj. Scottish.* **1.** Crafty; sly. **2.** Sleek. [From past participle of SLEEK.]

sleep (sleep) *n.* **1.** A natural, periodically recurring physiological state of rest, characterised by relative physical and nervous inactivity, unconsciousness, and lessened responsiveness to external stimuli. See **paradoxical sleep, orthodox sleep. 2.** A period of this form of rest. **3.** Any similar condition of inactivity, such as unconsciousness, dormancy, or hibernation. **4.** *Botany.* **Nyctinasty** *(see).* **5.** *Poetic.* Death. Often used euphemistically. **6.** *Informal.* The matter that collects in the corners of the eyes after a period of sleeping: *wipe the sleep from one's eyes.* **—go to sleep 1.** To fall asleep. **2.** To become numb because of pressure on a blood vessel. Used chiefly of limbs. **—put to sleep.** To kill (an animal) humanely.
~*v.* **slept** (slept || slep), **sleeping, sleeps.** *—intr.* **1.** To be in the state of sleep or to fall asleep. **2.** To be in a condition resembling sleep, such as hibernation, dormancy, or inattentiveness. **3.** To have sexual intercourse. Used with *with* or *together.* **4.** *Poetic.* To be dead. Often used euphemistically. *—tr.* **1. a.** To pass (time) by sleeping. **b.** To get rid of by sleeping: *went home to sleep it off.* **2.** To provide (a certain number of people) with accommodation for sleeping. **—sleep around.** *Informal.* To be sexually promiscuous. **—sleep in. 1.** To sleep at one's place of employment. **2.** *Chiefly British.* To sleep past one's usual hour of waking. **—sleep on.** To give (a matter) long consideration, especially by delaying one's decision until the next day. **—sleep out. 1.** To sleep at one's own home rather than at one's place of work. **2.** To sleep outdoors. [Middle English *slep(e), sleep,* Old English *slǣp, slǣpan.*]

sleep·er (sleépər) *n.* **1.** A person or animal that sleeps. **2.** A sleeping car or compartment on a railway train. **3.** Any of various usually small marine and freshwater fishes of the tropical family Eleotridae, related to the gobies. **4.** *British.* A heavy beam used as a support for rails on a railway. Also *U.S.* "tie". **5.** *British.* A thin ring, usually of gold, worn in a pierced ear in order to keep the hole open when earrings are not being worn. **6.** A person who is planted as a spy for future use. **7.** *Slang.* A sleeping pill. **8.** *Chiefly U.S. Informal.* One that achieves unexpected recognition or success, such as a racehorse, book, or marketed product.

sleep·ing-bag (sleéping-bag) *n.* A large, warmly lined bag, often having a zip, in which a person may sleep outdoors.

sleeping car *n.* A railway carriage providing bunks or beds.

sleeping draught *n.* A drink containing a sedative or hypnotic drug to induce sleep.

sleeping partner *n.* A person who makes a financial investment in a business enterprise but does not participate in its management. Also *U.S.* "silent partner".

sleeping pill *n.* A sedative or hypnotic drug in the form of a pill or capsule used to relieve insomnia.

sleeping policeman *n.* A small hump built across a road to restrict the speed of motorists, especially in built-up areas.

sleeping sickness *n.* **1.** An often fatal, endemic infectious disease of man and animals in tropical Africa, caused by either of two protozoans of the genus *Trypanosoma,* transmitted by the tsetse fly, and characterised by fever and lethargy. Also called "African trypanosomiasis". **2.** *Pathology.* **Encephalitis lethargica** *(see).*

sleep-learn·ing (sleép-lerning) *n.* A method of learning by listening to a tape recording while asleep, the information supposedly being absorbed by the unconscious. Also called "sleep-teaching".

sleep·less (sleép-ləss, -liss) *adj.* **1.** Without sleep; wakeful; restless; unquiet. **2.** Never sleeping or resting; always alert or active. **—sleep·less·ly** *adv.* **—sleep·less·ness** *n.*

sleep·walk·ing (sleép-wawking) *n.* Walking while asleep or in a sleep-like condition. Also called "noctambulation", "noctambulism", "somnambulance", "somnambulation", "somnambulism". **—sleep·walk** *intr.v.* **—sleep·walk·er** *n.*

sleep·y (sleépi) *adj.* **-ier, -iest. 1.** Ready for or needing sleep; drowsy. **2.** Sluggish, inattentive, or lethargic; dull. **3.** Inducing sleep; soporific. **4.** Quiet and without activity: *a sleepy little town.* **—sleep·i·ness** *n.* **—sleep·i·ly** *adv.*

sleep·y·head (sleépi-hed) *n. Informal.* **1.** A drowsy or sleepy person. **2.** A slow or dull person.

sleet (sleet) *n.* A mixture of rain and snow or melting snow.
~*intr.v.* **sleeted, sleeting, sleets.** To shower sleet. [Middle English *slete,* Old English *slēte* (unattested).] **—sleet·y** *adj.*

sleeve (sleev) *n.* **1.** The part of a garment that covers all or a part of the arm. **2.** Any encasement or shell into which a piece of equipment fits. **3.** A sleeve coupling. **4.** A paper or cardboard envelope for storing a gramophone record in. **—laugh up (one's) sleeve.** To be secretly amused, especially over the discomfiture of another. **—up (one's) sleeve.** Hidden but ready to be used when needed; in reserve. [Middle English *slefe, sleve,* Old English *slīf, slēf.*] **—sleeve·less** *adj.*

sleeve board *n.* A small ironing board used for ironing sleeves.

sleeve coupling *n.* A thin steel cylinder uniting two lengths of shafting or pipe. Also called "sleeve".

sleeved (sleevd) *adj.* Having a sleeve or sleeves, especially of a specified kind. Often in combination: *short-sleeved.*

sleeve notes *pl.n.* Notes printed on a record sleeve, giving details of its contents and the performers, and other information.

sleev·ing (sleéving) *n.* Flexible plastic tubing into which bare wires are inserted for insulation in electrical and electronic equipment.

sleigh (slay) *n.* A light vehicle mounted on runners for use on snow or ice, having one or more seats and usually drawn by a horse.
~*intr.v.* **sleighed, sleighing, sleighs.** To ride in or drive a sleigh. [Dutch *slee,* from *slede,* from Middle Dutch *slēde.*] **—sleigh·er** *n.*

sleight (slīt) *n. Archaic.* **1.** Deftness; dexterity; skill. **2. a.** Cunning; trickery. **b.** A skilful trick or deception; a stratagem. [Middle English *sle(i)ght,* from Old Norse *slœgdh,* from *slœgr,* sly.]

sleight of hand *n.* **1.** The skill, as in conjuring, of performing tricks or feats so quickly that their manner of execution cannot be observed; legerdemain. **2.** Any trick or feat so performed. **3.** Cunning deception or sophistry, or any act in which such skills are employed. **—sleight-of-hand** (slīt-əv-hánd) *adj.*

slen·der (sléndər) *adj.* **1.** Having little width in proportion to the height or length; elongated. **2.** Gracefully slim; willowy. **3.** Spare or small in amount or extent; meagre; inadequate: *slender wages.* **4.** Having little force, justification, or foundation; limited; feeble: *only a slender chance of success.* [Middle English *s(c)lendre*†.] **—slen·der·ly** *adv.* **—slen·der·ness** *n.*

slen·der·ise (sléndər-īz) *v.* **-ised, -ising, -ises.** —*intr.* To become slender or more slender. —*tr.* **1.** To make slender or more slender. **2.** To cause to appear slender. Used especially of a garment.

slept. Past tense and past participle of **sleep.**

sleuth (slo͞oth, slewth) *n.* **1.** *Informal.* A detective. **2.** A sleuthhound.
~*v.* **sleuthed, sleuthing, sleuths.** —*tr.* To track or follow. —*intr.* To act as a detective. [Short for SLEUTHHOUND.]

sleuth·hound (slo͞oth-hownd, sléwth-) *n.* **1.** Formerly, a dog used for tracking or pursuing, such as a bloodhound. Also called "sleuth". **2.** A detective. [Middle English : *sleuth,* track of an animal, from Old Norse *slōdh*† + HOUND.]

slew[1], **slue** (slo͞o || slew) *n. U.S. Informal.* A large amount or number; a lot: *a whole slew of her friends.* [Irish Gaelic *sluagh,* from Old Irish *slúag, slóg.*]

slew[2]. Past tense of **slay.**

slew[3], *U.S.* **slue** *v.* **slewed** or *U.S.* **slued, slewing** or *U.S.* **sluing, slews** or *U.S.* **slues.** —*tr.* **1.** To turn or twist (something) off course or sideways. **2.** To twist (a mast or boom) around on its axis. —*intr.* To turn, twist, veer, or skid off course or to the side.
~*n.* Also *U.S.* **slue. 1.** The act of slewing. **2.** The position or angle to which something has slewed. [18th century (verb sense 2) : origin obscure.]

slewed (slo͞od, slewd) *adj. Chiefly British Slang.* Drunk. [From SLEW (turn off course).]

slice (slīss) *n.* **1.** A thin, flat, or wedge-shaped piece cut from a larger object. **2.** A portion or share. **3. a.** A knife with a broad, thin, flexible blade, used for cutting and serving food. **b.** A similar implement for spreading printing ink. **c.** A wide serving spatula, often perforated to drain cooking liquid. **4.** *Sports.* **a.** A stroke that causes a ball to curve off course to the right or, if the player is left-handed, to the left. **b.** The course followed by such a ball.
~*v.* **sliced, slicing, slices.** —*tr.* **1.** To cut or divide into slices. **2.** To cut or remove from a larger piece. Often used with *off* or *away.* **3.** To cut through or across with or as if with a knife. **4.** To spread, work at, or clear away with a bladed tool such as a slice bar. **5.** *Sports.* To hit (a ball) with a slice. —*intr.* **1.** To cut with or as if with a knife; pass cleanly or effortlessly: *The wind sliced through us.* **2.** To slice a ball. [Middle English *s(c)lice,* slice, splinter, from Old French *esclice,* from *esclicer,* to reduce to splinters, from West Germanic *slītjan* (unattested), from Germanic *slītan* (unattested), to SLIT.] —**slice·a·ble** *adj.* —**slic·er** *n.*

slice bar *n.* An iron tool with a flat, broad end, used to loosen and clear out clinker from furnace grates.

slice of life *n.* A vividly realistic portrayal, as in drama or literature, of a segment of real life. —**slice-of-life** (slīss-əv-līf) *adj.*

slick (slik) *adj.* **1.** Deftly executed; neat. **2.** Superficially attractive or skilful but without real quality; glib. **3.** Shrewd; wily. **4.** Smooth and slippery, as if covered with oil or ice.
~*n.* **1.** A smooth or slippery surface or area. **2.** An **oil slick** *(see).* **3.** Any of various implements, especially a chisel, used for smoothing and polishing. Also called "slick chisel". **4.** A racing-car tyre with a smooth tread. **5.** *U.S.* A glossy magazine.
~*tr.v.* **slicked, slicking, slicks.** To make (hair, for example) sleek, smooth, or glossy. [Middle English *slike,* perhaps from Old English *slice* (unattested).]

slick·en·side (slíckən-sīd) *n.* A polished and striated rock surface caused by one rock mass sliding over another in a fault plane. [Dialectal *slicken,* glossy, variant of SLICK + SIDE.]

slick·er (slíckər) *n. Informal.* **1.** A stylish, sophisticated city-dweller: *a city slicker.* **2.** *Chiefly U.S.* A cheat; a swindler. **3.** *U.S.* A glossy raincoat, especially one made of oilskin.

slide (slīd) *v.* **slid** (slid), **sliding, slides.** —*intr.* **1.** To move in smooth, continuous contact with a surface. **2.** To move or pass smoothly and quietly; glide. **3.** To pass gradually into a new, often less desirable, state; drift: *slid into a life of crime.* **4.** To go unattended or unacted upon: *Let it slide.* **5.** To lose one's balance or intended direction on a slippery surface. **6.** To undergo a gradual decline. —*tr.* **1.** To cause to slide. **2.** To place quietly and unobtrusively: *slid his hand into the drawer.*
~*n.* **1.** A sliding movement, action, or progression: *a further slide in share prices.* **2.** A smooth surface or track for sliding. **3.** A playground apparatus for children to slide down, typically consisting of a smooth metal chute mounted by means of a ladder. **4.** A part or mechanism that operates by sliding, such as a sliding seat in a rowing boat, or the U-shaped section of tube on a trombone that is moved to produce different notes. **5.** An image on a transparent celluloid plate for use with a viewer or projector. **6.** A small glass plate for mounting specimens to be examined under a microscope. **7.** An avalanche of rock or soil. **8.** *Music.* **a.** A **portamento** *(see).* **b.** An ornament of two grace notes approaching the main note. **9.** A **hair-slide** *(see).* [Slide, slid, slid; Middle English *sliden, slydde, slide,* Old English *slīdan, -slād, -sliden.*] —**slid·er** *n.*

slide guitar *n.* **1.** A style of guitar playing, **bottleneck** *(see).* **2.** A guitar played in the bottleneck style.

slid·er (slīdər) *n. Scottish.* An ice cream between wafers.

slide rule *n.* A device consisting essentially of two logarithmically scaled rules mounted to slide along each other so that multiplication, division, and sometimes more complex calculations may be reduced to the mechanical equivalent of addition or subtraction.

slide valve *n.* A valve that slides back and forth over ports in the cylinder wall of a steam engine, permitting the intake and outflow of steam to move the piston.

sliding scale *n.* A scale in which indicated prices, taxes, or wages vary in accordance with some other factor, such as wages with the cost-of-living index or prices with a customer's income.

slight (slīt) *adj.* **slighter, slightest. 1.** Small in size, degree, or amount; meagre. **2.** Of small importance; inconsiderable; trifling. **3.** Slender or frail; delicate: *a slight figure.*
~*tr.v.* **slighted, slighting, slights. 1.** To treat with disdain or discourteous indifference; snub. **2.** To fail to give sufficient consideration or attention to; treat as unimportant.
~*n.* An act of pointed disrespect or discourtesy. [Middle English *sl(e)ight,* smooth, slight, from Old Norse *sléttr,* smooth, sleek.] —**slight·ness** *n.*

slight·ing (slīting) *adj.* Constituting or conveying a slight; disparaging; disrespectful. —**slight·ing·ly** *adv.*

slight·ly (slīt-li) *adv.* **1.** To a small degree or extent; somewhat. **2.** In a slight or delicate way: *She is slightly built.*

Sli·go (slīgō). County in the northwest of the Republic of Ireland. The county town is also called Sligo. The Atlantic coastline is indented and much of the interior is mountainous. Beef and dairy farming are the chief occupations of the people.

slily. Variant of **slyly.**

slim (slim) *adj.* **slimmer, slimmest. 1.** Small in girth or thickness in proportion to height or length: *a slim volume.* **2.** Pleasantly thin; slender: *a slim build.* **3.** Small in quality or amount; scant; meagre.
~*v.* **slimmed, slimming, slims.** —*tr.* To reduce in volume or amount. Often used with *down: slim down the work force.* —*intr.* **1.** To become slim. **2.** To diet for the purpose of losing weight. [Dutch, small, inferior, from Middle Dutch *slim,* slanting, bad.] —**slim·ly** *adv.* —**slim·ness** *n.*

Slim (slim), **William Joseph, 1st Viscount** (1891–1970). British field marshal. He commanded the army in Burma (1943–45). He served as Governor-General of Australia from 1953 to 1960.

slime (slīm) *n.* **1. a.** Viscous mud. **b.** Any substance having a runny or glutinous consistency, especially when considered unpleasant or offensive. **2.** A mucous substance secreted by certain animals, such as fish or slugs.
~*v.* **slimed, sliming, slimes.** —*tr.* **1.** To smear with slime. **2.** To remove slime from (fish, for example). —*intr. Informal.* To ingratiate oneself. Often used with *up to: slimed up to the boss.* [Middle English *slim(e),* Old English *slīm,* akin to Latin *limus,* mud.]

slime mould *n.* Any of various fungi of the class Myxomycetes, having both plant and animal characteristics, with a body consisting of a naked creeping mass of protoplasm. Also called "slime fungus", "myxomycete".

slim·line (slím-līn) *adj.* Slim or compact, especially by comparison with larger or more bulky objects of the same class: *a slimline diary for the handbag.* [SLIM + LINE, by analogy with STREAMLINE.]

slim·y (slīmi) *adj.* **-ier, -iest. 1.** Consisting of or resembling slime; viscous. **2.** Covered with or exuding slime. **3.** Vile; disgusting; foul. **4.** Sycophantic; ingratiating. —**slim·i·ly** *adv.* —**slim·i·ness** *n.*

sling[1] (sling) *n.* **1. a.** A weapon consisting of a looped strap with which a stone is whirled and then let fly. **b.** A catapult. **2.** A looped rope, strap, or chain for supporting, cradling, or hoisting something; especially: **a.** A strap used to carry a rifle over the shoulder. **b.** *Nautical.* A rope or chain for supporting a yard. **c.** *Nautical.* An arrangement, as of looped ropes or nets, for supporting cargo that is being transferred. **d.** A band suspended from the neck to support an injured arm or hand. **e.** A baglike device made of soft material, equipped with straps and worn over the back or chest and used for carrying a baby. **3.** An act of slinging.
~*tr.v.* **slung** (slung), **slinging, slings. 1.** To hurl from or as if from a sling; fling. **2.** To carry or support by means of a sling: *with his rifle slung over his shoulder.* **3.** To move by means of a sling; raise or lower in a sling. **4.** To cause to hang loosely or freely; let swing. —See Synonyms at **throw.** [Middle English, perhaps from Middle Low German *slinge.*] —**sling·er** (slíng-ər) *n.*

sling[2] *n.* A drink of brandy, whisky, or gin, sweetened and usually lemon-flavoured. See **gin sling** [18th century : origin obscure.]

sling·back (slíng-bak) *n.* An open-backed shoe held in place by a strap above the heel.

sling·shot (slíng-shot) *n. U.S.* A catapult.

slink (slingk) *v.* **slunk** (slungk), **slinking, slinks.** —*intr.* To move in a quiet, furtive manner; sneak. —*tr.* To give birth to prematurely. Used especially of a cow.
~*n.* **1.** An animal, especially a calf, born prematurely. **2.** The flesh or skin of a slink.
~*adj.* Born prematurely. [Middle English *slynken,* Old English *slincan.*] —**slink·ing·ly** *adv.*

slink·y (slíngki) *adj.* **-ier, -iest. 1.** Of feline sleekness and grace. **2.** Soft, close-fitting, and usually glamorous. Said of women's clothing. **3.** *Informal.* Stealthy; furtive. —**slink·i·ness** *n.*

slip[1] (slip) *v.* **slipped, slipping, slips.** —*intr.* **1.** To move lightly and smoothly; glide. **2.** To move or pass swiftly, stealthily, or imperceptibly: *The years slipped by.* **3. a.** To slide unexpectedly and by accident; lose one's balance. **b.** To slide out of place; shift position. **c.** To escape, as from a fastening or grip. **4.** To get away completely; escape; be lost: *let chances slip by.* **5.** To be said unintentionally, as through lack of discretion: *let slip that he'd had a rise.* **6.** To put on or take off clothing quickly or smoothly. Used with *into* or *out of.* **7.** To fall below a usual or prescribed standard; decline or deteriorate. **8. a.** To make a mistake. **b.** To fall into error; lapse. **9.** To slide sideways; sideslip. Used of an aircraft. **10.** To fail to engage. Used of the clutch of a motor or vehicle. —*tr.*

PRONUNCIATION KEY

a, trap; aa, father; ai, fair; ar, star; aw, lawn; ay, play; b, bb, stab; rubber; ch, church; ck, ticket; d, dd, dead; ladder; e, dress; ee, bee; er, defer; ew, few; ewr, pure; ə, about; ər, letter; f, ff, fife; differ; g, gg, giggle; h, hat; i, kit; ī, price; īr, fire; j, judge; k, kick; l, ll, let; 'l, needle; m, mm, man; n, nn, no; 'n, sudden; ng, thing; o, lot; ō, no; o͝o, foot; o͞o, shoe; oor, poor; ow, cow; owr, hour; oy, boy; p, pp, pepper; r, rr, red; s, ss, sauce; sh, ship; t, tt, totter; th, thick; th, this; smooth; u, cut; ur, turn; v, vv, valve; w, wet; y, yes; z, zz, zebra; zh, vision; pleasure

IN FOREIGN WORDS:

aN, oN, Saint-Saëns; hl, Llanelli; Hluhluwe; kh, loch; lough; Khaled

STRESS MARK:

ín-sīt, insight; in-sīt, incite

1. To cause to move in a smooth, easy, or sliding motion. **2.** To place, insert, or introduce smoothly. **3.** To put on or remove (clothing) quickly or smoothly. Used with *on* or *off.* **4.** To free oneself or itself from; get loose from: *slipped its moorings.* **5.** To pass out of (one's memory or attention) so as to be forgotten or unnoticed: *It slipped my mind.* **6.** To bring forth (young) prematurely. Used of an animal. **7.** To unleash or free (a dog or hawk, for example). **8.** To undo or unfasten: *slip the knot.* **9.** To dislocate (a bone), or suffer displacement of (an intervertebral disc). **10.** *Informal.* To give surreptitiously: *slipped me a fiver.* **11.** In knitting, to pass (a stitch) from one needle to the other without working it. **—slip one over on.** *Informal.* To hoodwink; trick.
~n. **1.** An act of slipping, sliding, or falling. **2. a.** An error in judgment or procedure; a fault or deviation. **b.** A slight mistake or oversight in speech or writing: *a slip of the pen.* **3. a.** A **slipway** *(see).* **b.** *U.S.* A space for a ship between two docks or wharves. **4.** A woman's loose, sleeveless undergarment serving as a lining for a dress or skirt. **5.** A pillowcase. **6.** A leash allowing quick release of the dog. **7.** In cricket: **a.** A fielder positioned closely behind and to the offside of the batsman, typically any of three or four. **b.** *Often plural.* The position of such a fielder: *fielding in the slips; caught at slip.* **8.** The difference between a vessel's actual speed through water and the speed at which the vessel would move if the screw were propelling against a solid. **9.** The difference between optimal and actual output in a mechanical device. **10.** *Geology.* A smooth crack at which rock strata have moved relative to each other. **11.** Movement between two parts where none should exist, as between the clutch plates of a motor vehicle. **12.** *Aeronautics.* The sliding movement of an aircraft in certain attitudes of the plane. See **sideslip. 13.** *Geology.* The relative movement along a fault plane. **—**See Synonyms at **error. —give (someone) the slip.** *Informal.* To escape or elude. [Middle English *slippen,* to slip, slip away, probably from Middle Low German.]

slip² *n.* **1.** A part of a plant cut or broken off for grafting or planting; a scion or cutting. **2.** Any long, narrow piece; a strip. **3.** A youthful, slender person: *a slip of a girl.* **4.** A small piece of paper; especially, a small form or list: *a sales slip.* **5. a.** *Plural. Chiefly British.* The area along the sides of the gallery in a theatre. **b.** *U.S.* A narrow pew in a church. **6.** *British.* A galley proof.
~tr.v. **slipped, slipping, slips.** To make a slip from (a plant or plant part). [Middle English *slippe*†, a strip.]

slip³ *n.* Thinned potter's clay used for decorating or coating ceramics. [Middle English *slyppe,* a soft mass, curds, mud, Old English *slypa,* slime.]

slip·case (slíp-kayss) *n.* An open-ended protective box for a book.

slip·cov·er (slíp-kuvvər) *n. U.S.* A **loose cover** *(see).*

slip·knot (slíp-not) *n.* **1.** A knot made with a loop so that it slips easily along the rope or cord around which it is tied. Also called "running knot". **2.** A knot made so that it can readily be untied by pulling one free end.

slip-on (slíp-on || -awn) *adj.* Designed to be easily put on or taken off: *slip-on shoes.*
~n. A slip-on garment or shoe.

slip·o·ver (slíp-ōvər) *adj.* Designed to be put on or taken off over the head.
~n. A slipover garment, such as a sweater.

slip·page (slíppij) *n.* **1.** A slipping. **2.** The amount or extent of slipping. **3.** Loss of motion or power due to slipping.

slipped disc (slipt) *n.* Protrusion of the inner pulp of an intervertebral disc through its fibrous wall, causing pressure on adjacent nerves and hence sciatica or back pain.

slip·per (slíppər) *n.* **1.** A light, low, slip-on shoe for indoor wear, having an upper made of soft material. **2.** A woman's light slip-on shoe for dancing or evening wear.

slipper bath *n. Chiefly British.* A bath in the shape of a slipper.

slipper orchid *n.* Any of various tropical orchids of the genus *Paphiopedilum* and related genera, having slipper-shaped flowers.

slip·per·wort (slíppər-wurt || -wawrt) *n.* A plant, the **calceolaria** *(see).*

slip·per·y (slíppəri) *adj.* **-ier, -iest. 1.** Causing or tending to cause sliding or slipping, as a waxed, greasy, or wet surface may. **2.** Tending to slip or slide, as from one's grasp or from a position of being secured. **3.** Elusive; evasive; untrustworthy: *a slippery customer.* [Perhaps coined by Miles Coverdale (1535) to translate German *schlipfferig,* based on dialect *slipper,* from Middle English *sli(p)per,* Old English *slipor.*] **—slip·per·i·ly** *adv.* **—slip·per·i·ness** *n.*

slippery elm *n.* A tree, *Ulmus rubra,* of eastern North America, having twigs and leaves with a mucilaginous, aromatic juice formerly used medicinally.

slip·py (slíppi) *adj.* **-pier, -piest.** *Informal.* **1.** Slippery. **2.** *British.* Quick; nimble; alert. Often used in the phrase *look slippy.*

slip ring *n.* A metal ring mounted on a rotating part of a machine to provide a continuous electrical connection through brushes on stationary contacts.

slip road *n. British.* A narrow road, usually having a one-way traffic flow, that gives access to a motorway or other main road.

slip-sheet (slíp-sheet) *n. Printing.* A blank sheet of paper slipped between newly printed sheets to prevent offsetting.
~tr.v. **slip-sheeted, -sheeting, -sheets.** *Printing.* To insert blank sheets between (printed sheets).

slip·shod (slíp-shod) *adj.* **1.** Made or done carelessly and unsystematically. **2.** Slovenly in appearance; shabby; seedy. [Originally "wearing slippers or loose shoes" : SLIP + SHOD.]

slip·slop (slíp-slop) *n.* **1.** *Archaic.* Sloppy, unappetising food; slops. **2.** Trivial or sentimental talk or writing; twaddle. **3.** *South African.* A simple, backless rubber sandle; a flip-flop. [Reduplication of SLOP.]

slip·stitch (slíp-stich) *n.* **1.** A stitch used wherever stitching must be invisible, as on hems and facings, made by picking up one or two threads of fabric and then passing the needle diagonally through the hem edge. **2.** The basic chain stitch used for edgings in crochet. In this sense also called "single crochet". **—slip·stitch** *v.*

slip·stream (slíp-streem) *n.* **1.** The turbulent flow of air driven backwards by the propeller or propellers of an aircraft. Also called "race". **2.** The stream of air behind any fast moving object.
~intr.v. **slip-streamed, -streaming, -streams.** In cycling or motor racing, to drive in the slip-stream of another vehicle as a way of maintaining a high speed while conserving energy or fuel.

slip up *intr.v. Informal.* To make a mistake; blunder.

slip-up (slíp-up) *n. Informal.* An error or oversight; a mistake.

slip·way (slíp-way) *n.* A sloping incline leading down to the water, on which ships are built or repaired. Also called "slip".

slit (slit) *n.* A long, narrow, usually straight cut, tear, or opening.
~tr.v. **slit, slitting, slits. 1.** To make a long, narrow incision in. **2.** To cut lengthways into strips; split. See Synonyms at **tear.**
~adj. Having or resembling a slit: *slit eyes; a slit skirt.* [Middle English *slitte,* perhaps Old English *geslit,* a tearing, akin to *slītan,* to slit, from Germanic *slītan* (unattested).]

slith·er (slíthər) *v.* **-ered, -ering, -ers.** *—intr.* **1.** To slip and slide, as on a loose or uneven surface. **2.** To move along by gliding, as a snake does. *—tr.* To cause to slither.
~n. A slithering movement or gait. [Middle English *slideren,* Old English *slid(o)rian,* frequentative of *slīdan,* to SLIDE.] **—slith·er·y** *adj.*

slit trench *n.* A narrow, shallow trench dug during combat for the protection of a single soldier or a small group.

sliv·er (slívvər; *also* slīvər *for sense 2*) *n.* **1.** A sharp, slender piece cut, split, or broken off; a splinter. **2.** A continuous strand of loose wool, flax, or cotton, ready for drawing and twisting.
~v. **slivered, -ering, -ers.** *—tr.* To split, cut, or form into slivers. *—intr.* To become split into slivers. [Middle English *slivere,* from *slyven,* to split, Old English *-slīfan*† (unattested). See **sleave.**]

sli·vo·vitz (slívvə-vits) *n.* A dry, colourless plum brandy common in southeastern Europe. [Serbo-Croat *šljivovica,* from *šljiva,* plum.]

Sloane (slōn), **Sir Hans** (1660–1753). English physician and botanist. He was secretary to the Royal Society (1693–1712) and president of the Royal College of Physicians (1719–35). He was also the founder of the Botanic Garden at Chelsea Manor.

Sloane Ranger *n.* In Britain, any of a group of young upper-middle-class people readily identified by characteristic styles of dress. [After *Sloane* Square (in an affluent area of southwest London, typical haunt of Sloane Rangers), by analogy with the *Lone Ranger,* character in old westerns.]

slob (slob) *n. Informal.* An obnoxious, uncouth, or slovenly person. [Irish *slab,* mud, probably from Scandinavian; akin to Old Danish *slab,* mud.]

slob·ber (slóbbər) *v.* **-bered, -bering, -bers.** *—intr.* **1.** To let saliva dribble from the mouth; slaver; drool. **2.** To indulge in mawkish sentimentality in speech or writing. *—tr.* To wet or smear with or as if with saliva or food dribbled from the mouth.
~n. **1.** Saliva or liquid running from the mouth; drivel; slaver. **2.** Drivelling, oversentimental speech or writing. [Middle English *sloberen,* perhaps of Low German origin, akin to Low German *slubberen* (imitative).] **—slob·ber·er** *n.* **—slob·ber·y** *adj.*

sloe (slō) *n.* **1.** A shrub, the **blackthorn** *(see).* **2.** The tart, blue-black, plumlike fruit of this shrub. [Middle English *slo(o),* Old English *slā(h).*]

sloe-eyed (slṓ-īd) *adj.* **1.** Having dark, blue-black eyes. **2.** Having slanted eyes.

sloe gin *n.* A liqueur made by steeping sloes in gin.

slog (slog) *v.* **slogged, slogging, slogs.** *—tr.* To strike powerfully, or wildly or unskilfully, as in cricket or boxing. *—intr.* **1.** To walk with a slow, plodding gait. **2.** To work doggedly; toil. Often used with *at* or *away.* **3.** To slog the ball in cricket.
~n. **1.** Hard, unremitting work, or a spell of this. **2.** A long, exhausting march or hike. **3.** A powerful swipe, as in cricket. [19th century : origin obscure.] **—slog·ger** *n.*

slo·gan (slṓgən) *n.* **1.** A catch phrase or motto expressing some characteristic quality, stance, or purpose, and typically used in political campaigning or advertising. **2.** A battle cry, as formerly used by a Scottish clan. [Earlier (Scottish) *slog(g)orne,* from Gaelic *sluagh-ghairm* : *sluagh,* host, army + *gairm,* shout, cry.]

sloop (sloop) *n. Nautical.* A single-masted, fore-and-aft-rigged sailing boat with a single headsail set from the forestay. Compare **cutter.** [Dutch *sloep(e)*†.]

sloop of war *n.* Formerly, a small, armed vessel larger than a gunboat, carrying guns on one deck only.

sloot (sloot, sloo-ət) *n. South African.* **1.** A furrow or channel dug for the conveyance of water. **2.** A natural ditch, as caused by rain. [Afrikaans, ditch, from Dutch.]

slop¹ (slop) *n.* **1.** Liquid spilled or splashed. **2.** Soft mud or slush. **3.** Unappetising, watery food or soup. **4.** *Usually plural.* Waste food used to feed pigs or other animals; swill. **5.** *Usually plural.* Liquid or semiliquid waste, such as: **a.** Liquid household refuse. **b.** Human excreta. **c.** Beer spilt while being drawn from a barrel. **6.** Repulsively effusive writing or speech.

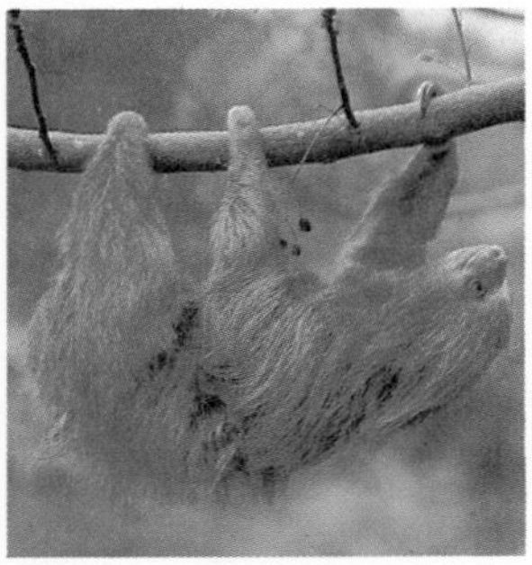

sloth *The toes of the two-toed sloth (above) – there are two on the forefeet and three on the hind limbs – are large claws which enable the animal to hang from tree branches. It is a native of South America and lives on the fruit and leaves of trees, spending so much time upside-down that its fur grows in the opposite direction from that of other animals.*

PRONUNCIATION KEY

a, trap; aa, father; ai, fair;
ar, star; aw, lawn; ay, play;
b, bb, stab; rubber;
ch, church; ck, ticket;
d, dd, dead; ladder; e, dress;
ee, bee; er, defer; ew, few;
ewr, pure; ə, about;
ər, letter; f, ff, fife; differ;
g, gg, giggle; h, hat; i, kit;
ī, price; īr, fire; j, judge;
k, kick; l, ll, let; 'l, needle;
m, mm, man; n, nn, no;
'n, sudden; ng, thing; o, lot;
ō, no; ŏŏ, foot; ōō, shoe;
oor, poor; ow, cow;
owr, hour; oy, boy;
p, pp, pepper; r, rr, red;
s, ss, sauce; sh, ship;
t, tt, totter; th, thick; th, this;
smooth; u, cut; ur, turn;
v, vv, valve; w, wet; y, yes;
z, zz, zebra; zh, vision;
pleasure

IN FOREIGN WORDS:

aN, ON, Saint-Saëns;
hl, Llanelli; Hluhluwe;
kh, loch; lough; Khaled

STRESS MARK:

ín-sīt, insight; in-sít, incite

~*v.* **slopped, slopping, slops.** —*intr.* **1.** To spill, splash, or overflow. **2.** To heave to and fro within a container. Usually used with *about.* **3.** To move in an awkward or slovenly manner as if plodding through mud. —*tr.* **1.** To spill (liquid). **2.** To spill liquid upon. **3.** To dish out or serve unappetisingly or clumsily. **4.** To feed slops to (animals). **—slop out.** To empty one's chamber pot, usually as part of a daily routine. Used of a prisoner. [Middle English *sloppe,* a muddy place, probably Old English *sloppe* (unattested).]

slop[2] *n.* **1.** *Plural.* Articles of clothing and bedding issued to sailors from a ship's stores. **2.** *Plural.* Short, full trousers or breeches as worn by men in the 16th century. **3.** A loose outer garment, such as a smock or overalls. **4.** *Plural. Chiefly British.* Cheap, ready-made garments. [Middle English *sloppe,* a kind of garment, perhaps Old English *(ofer)slop,* surplice.]

slop basin *n. British.* A small bowl used as a receptacle for tea leaves or coffee grounds from the bottoms of cups. Also called "slop bowl".

slope (slōp) *v.* **sloped, sloping, slopes.** —*intr.* **1.** To incline upwards or downwards; lie on a slant. **2.** To follow a sloping course; ascend or descend at an angle. **3.** *Informal.* To go surreptitiously. Usually used with *off.* —*tr.* **1.** To cause to slope. **2.** *Military.* To bring (a rifle) into a sloping position resting on the shoulder. Used chiefly in the command *slope arms.*

~*n.* **1.** Any inclined line, surface, plane, position, or direction. **2.** A stretch of ground forming a natural or artificial incline: *ski slopes.* **3.** Any deviation from the horizontal. **4.** The amount or degree of such deviation. **5.** *Mathematics.* The rate at which an ordinate of a point on a line on a plane containing the line changes with respect to a change in its abscissa. [Middle English *slope,* sloping, short for *aslope,* perhaps Old English *āslopen* (unattested), past participle of *āslūpan,* to slip away : *ā-,* away + *slūpan,* to slip.] **—slop·er** *n.* **—slop·ing·ly** *adv.*

slop·py (slóppi) *adj.* **-pier, -piest.** **1.** Wet, slushy, or muddy. **2.** Watery and unappetising: *a sloppy stew.* **3.** Spotted or splashed with liquid or slop. **4.** *Informal.* Careless; untidy or unsystematic. **5.** *Informal.* Loose or ill-fitting; baggy. **6.** *Informal.* Oversentimental; slushy. **—slop·pi·ly** *adv.* **—slop·pi·ness** *n.*

Synonyms: *sloppy, slovenly, slatternly, blowzy, frowzy, unkempt, untidy.*

sloppy joe *n.* A long, baggy sweater.

slop·work (slóp-wurk) *n.* **1.** The manufacture of cheap, ready-made clothes. **2.** Such clothes. **3.** Any work of inferior quality.

slosh (slosh) *v.* **sloshed, sloshing, sloshes.** —*tr.* **1.** To pour or splash (a liquid). **2.** To stir or agitate in a liquid: *slosh clothes in water.* **3.** *British Informal.* To hit or punch heavily. —*intr.* **1.** To splash or flounder in water or another liquid. **2.** To splash about or move through being agitated: *Water sloshed about the basin.*

~*n.* **1.** Slush. **2.** The sound of splashing liquid. **3.** *British Informal.* A punch or blow. [Variant of SLUSH.] **—slosh·y** *adj.*

sloshed (slosht) *adj. Chiefly British Informal.* Drunk.

slot[1] (slot) *n.* **1.** A long, narrow groove, opening, or notch, as for receiving coins in a vending machine. **2.** A gap between a main and an auxiliary aerofoil to provide space for airflow and facilitate the smooth passage of air over the wing. **3.** *Informal.* A place in a programme or schedule.

~*v.* **slotted, slotting, slots.** —*tr.* **1.** To cut or make a slot or slots in. **2.** To place or fit in or as if in a slot. —*intr.* To fit into a slot. Often used with *in: This board slots in easily.* [Middle English, hollow between the breasts, from Old French *esclot*†.]

slot[2] *n.* The track or trail of an animal, especially a deer. [Old French *esclot,* horse's hoofprint, probably from Old Norse *slōdh,* animal's track. See **sleuthhound.**]

sloth (slōth ‖ sloth, slawth) *n.* **1.** Aversion to work or exertion; laziness; indolence. **2.** Any of various shaggy, slow-moving, arboreal mammals of the family Bradypodidae, of tropical America, including: **a.** Any member of the genus *Bradypus.* Also called "ai". **b.** Any member of the genus *Choloepus.* Also called "unau". [Middle English *slowthe,* from *slow,* SLOW.]

sloth bear *n.* A bear, *Melursus ursinus,* of south-central Asia, having a long snout and dark, shaggy hair.

sloth·ful (slṓth-f'l ‖ slóth-, sláwth-) *adj.* Lazy; indolent; sluggish. **—sloth·ful·ly** *adv.* **—sloth·ful·ness** *n.*

slot machine *n.* **1.** A vending machine having a slot or slots through which coins are inserted in order to operate it. **2.** *Chiefly U.S.* A **fruit machine** *(see).*

slouch (slowch) *v.* **slouched, slouching, slouches.** —*intr.* **1.** To sit, stand, or walk with an awkward, drooping posture; assume an excessively relaxed position. **2.** To droop or hang down. —*tr.* To cause to slouch.

~*n.* **1.** A slouching movement, posture, or position. **2.** *Informal.* An ungainly, lazy, or incompetent person. [16th century : origin obscure.] **—slouch·i·ly** *adv.* **—slouch·i·ness** *n.* **—slouch·y** *adj.*

slouch hat *n.* A soft hat with a broad, flexible brim.

slough[1] (slow ‖ *chiefly U.S.* slo͞o) *n.* Also **slue** (slo͞o) (for sense 2). **1. a.** A depression or hollow, usually filled with mud. **b.** *U.S.* A stagnant inlet or backwater. **2.** A state of deep despair or degradation. [Middle English *slo(g)h,* Old English *slōh, slō(g).*] **—slough·y** *adj.*

slough[2] (sluf) *n.* **1.** The dead outer skin shed by a snake or amphibian. **2.** *Medicine.* Dead tissue separated from a living structure. **3.** Broadly, anything that can be shed, such as an outer layer.

~*v.* **sloughed, sloughing, sloughs.** —*intr.* **1.** To be cast off or shed; come off. **2.** To shed a slough. **3.** *Medicine.* To separate from surrounding tissue. Used of dead tissue. —*tr.* **1.** To shed; throw off. **2.** To get rid of; discard as undesirable or unfavourable. Often used with *off.* [Middle English *slugh(e), slouh,* perhaps of Low German origin, akin to Low German *slu(we),* husk, shell, from Common Germanic *slūhwō* (unattested).]

slough of despond (slow ‖ slo͞o) *n.* A state of depression or despair. [After the place in Bunyan's *Pilgrim's Progress* (1678).]

Slo·vak (slṓ-vak ‖ *chiefly U.S.* -vaak) *n.* Also **Slo·vak·i·an** (slə-vácki-ən, slō-, -vaáki-). **1.** A member of a Slavonic people living in Slovakia. **2.** The West Slavonic language of these people, closely related to Czech. **—Slo·vak, Slo·vak·i·an** *adj.*

Slo·vak·i·a (slō-vácki-ə, slə-, -vaáki-). Easternmost of the three natural regions which make up Czechoslovakia. The Slovak Socialist Republic is one of the two equal constituent republics of the country. Mining, shipbuilding, and metal processing are highly developed industries. Nearly 90 per cent of the population is of Slovak stock. Bratislava is the capital.

slov·en (slúvv'n) *n.* One who is careless and untidy in his behaviour, personal appearance, or work. [Middle English *sloveyn,* perhaps from Middle Dutch *slof*†, negligent.]

Slo·vene (slṓ-veen, *rarely* slō-veén) *n.* **1.** A native or inhabitant of Slovenia. **2.** The South Slavonic language spoken in Slovenia.

~*adj.* Of or pertaining to Slovenia, the Slovenes, or their language.

Slo·ve·ni·a (slō-veéni-ə, slə-). Constitutent republic of Yugoslavia, lying mainly in the Julian Alps and the Karst plateau in the north of the country. The capital is Ljubljana. It is the richest and most industrialised part of Yugoslavia. **—Slo·ve·ni·an** *n. & adj.*

slov·en·ly (slúvv'nli) *adj.* **-lier, -liest.** **1.** Having the habits or appearance of a sloven. **2.** Showing qualities associated with a sloven; specifically, **a.** Untidy; messy. **b.** Careless; marked by negligence; slipshod: *a slovenly piece of work.* —See Synonyms at **sloppy.** **—slov·en·li·ness** *n.* **—slov·en·ly** *adv.*

slow (slō) *adj.* **slower, slowest.** **1. a.** Not moving or able to move quickly; proceeding at a low speed: *a slow boat.* **b.** Marked by a low speed or tempo: *a slow waltz.* **2. a.** Taking or requiring a long time: *the slow job of making bread.* **b.** Taking more time than is necessary: *a slow worker.* **c.** Made or achieved over a long period of time; gradual: *a slow recovery.* **3.** Registering a time or rate behind or below the correct one: *a slow clock.* **4. a.** Lacking in promptness or willingness: *slow to accept; a slow response.* **b.** Not easily aroused; not precipitate: *slow to anger.* **5.** Sluggish; inactive: *Business was slow.* **6.** *Informal.* Lacking in interest; boring: *a slow film.* **7.** Mentally dull; obtuse: *a slow student.* **8. a.** Only moderately warm; low: *a slow oven.* **b.** Burning without strength: *a slow flame.* **9.** Not conducive to fast movement. Said of a sports surface: *a slow wicket.* —See Synonyms at **stupid.**

~*adv.* Slowly.

~*v.* **slowed, slowing, slows.** —*tr.* To make slow or slower. Often used with *up* or *down.* —*intr.* To become slow or slower; go or act slowly or more slowly. Often used with *up* or *down*: *The doctor told him to slow up for the sake of his health.* —See Synonyms at **delay.** [Middle English *slow, slaw,* Old English *slāw,* from Germanic *slǣwaz* (unattested).] **—slow·ly** *adv.* **—slow·ness** *n.*

Usage: *Slow* has an adverbial use, alongside *slowly,* but the two words are often not interchangeable. *Slowly* is the preferred form in written usage, and in formal speech; but spoken commands and exhortations generally use *slow (Go slow!),* and it is the expected form in certain idiomatic phrases *(my watch is running slow, the trains are running slow today),* with *how (How slow!),* and in some compound words *(slow-moving traffic).*

slow·coach (slṓ-kōch) *n. British Informal.* One who is excessively slow in action or movement. Also *U.S.* "slowpoke".

slow·down (slṓ-down) *n.* **1.** A slackening of pace. **2.** *U.S.* A **go-slow** *(see).*

slow handclap *n. British.* Slow and regular clapping used to express boredom or impatience, as by spectators at a sports match.

slow match *n.* A fuse that burns slowly, used to set off explosives.

slow motion *n.* **1.** In films, the technique whereby the action shown appears to be slower than the original action, achieved by projecting the sequence at a slower speed than that at which it was filmed. **2.** Broadly, a rate of action that is below normal. **—slow-mo·tion** (slṓ-mṓsh'n) *adj.*

slow neutron *n.* A **thermal neutron** *(see).*

slow virus *n.* Any infectious virus that has a long incubation period in the body before symptoms of disease appear.

slow·wit·ted (slṓ-wíttid) *adj.* Slow to comprehend; dull; stupid. **—slow·wit·ted·ly** *adv.* **—slow·wit·ted·ness** *n.*

slow-worm (slṓ-wurm) *n.* A limbless European lizard, *Anguis fragilis,* having a smooth, snakelike body. Also called "blindworm". [Middle English *slowurm,* Old English *slāwyrm* : *slā,* perhaps "slime" + *wyrm,* WORM.]

SLR single-lens reflex (camera).

slub (slub) *tr.v.* **slubbed, slubbing, slubs.** To draw out and twist (a sliver of silk or other textile fibre) in preparation for spinning.

~*n.* **1.** A soft, thick nub in yarn that is either an imperfection or purposely set for a desired effect. **2.** A slightly twisted roll of fibre, as of silk or cotton.

~*adj.* Having an uneven, irregular appearance. Said of material. [18th century : origin obscure.]

sludge (sluj) *n.* **1.** Mud, mire, or ooze covering the ground or forming a deposit, as on a river bed. **2.** Slushy matter or sediment such as that precipitated by the treatment of sewage or collected in a boiler. **3.** Finely broken or half-formed ice on a body of water.

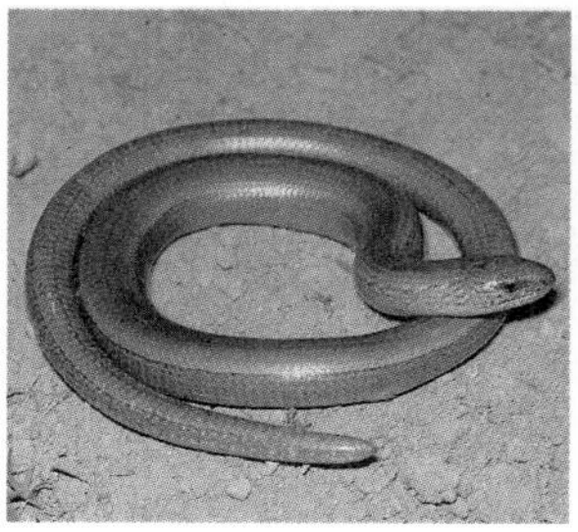

slow-worm *Although the slow-worm resembles a snake, it is actually a legless lizard and is not venomous. It is found mostly in European forests and lives on slugs, worms, and caterpillars.*

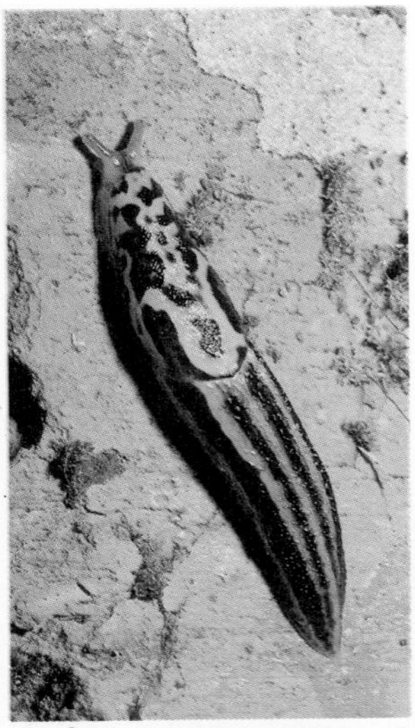

slug² *Slugs are relatives of the snail which have little or no shell. They live in damp places all over the world and feed mostly on plants.*

PRONUNCIATION KEY

a, trap; aa, father; ai, fair; ar, star; aw, lawn; ay, play; b, bb, stab; rubber; ch, church; ck, ticket; d, dd, dead; ladder; e, dress; ee, bee; er, defer; ew, few; ewr, pure; ə, about; ər, letter; f, ff, fife; differ; g, gg, giggle; h, hat; i, kit; ī, price; īr, fire; j, judge; k, kick; l, ll, let; 'l, needle; m, mm, man; n, nn, no; 'n, sudden; ng, thing; o, lot; ō, no; ŏŏ, foot; ōō, shoe; oor, poor; ow, cow; owr, hour; oy, boy; p, pp, pepper; r, rr, red; s, ss, sauce; sh, ship; t, tt, totter; th, thick; th, this; smooth; u, cut; ur, turn; v, vv, valve; w, wet; y, yes; z, zz, zebra; zh, vision; pleasure

IN FOREIGN WORDS:

aN, oN, Saint-Saëns; hl, Llanelli; Hluhluwe; kh, loch; lough; Khaled

STRESS MARK:

ín-sīt, insight; in-sī́t, incite

[17th century : origin obscure (probably akin to SLUSH).] —**sludg·y** *adj.*

slue¹. *U.S.* Variant of **slew** (to turn or twist).

slue². Variant of **slew** (a large number).

slue³. Variant of **slough** (backwater).

slug¹ (slug) *n.* **1.** A round bullet or pellet, as used in an airgun. **2.** *Informal.* A swig or measure of a drink, especially a spirit. **3.** A lump of metal or glass ready to be processed. **4.** *Printing.* **a.** A strip of type metal, less than type-high used for spacing. **b.** A line of cast type in a single strip of metal. **c.** A compositor's type line of identifying marks or instructions. **5.** *Physics.* A unit of mass equal to the mass accelerated at the rate of one foot per second per second when acted upon by a force of one pound weight. Also called "geepound". **6.** *U.S.* A small metal disc for use in a slot machine, especially one used illegally. [Probably from the animal SLUG (from its shape); sense 2, perhaps from Irish Gaelic *slog,* swallow.]

slug² *n.* **1.** Any of various terrestrial gastropod molluscs of the family Limacidae and other genera, having an elongated body with no shell. **2.** The smooth, soft larva of certain insects, especially the sawfly. Also called "slugworm". **3.** *Informal.* A lazy person; a sluggard. [Middle English *slugge,* slow person or animal, probably from Scandinavian; akin to Norwegian (dialectal) *slugg.*]

slug³ *tr.v.* **slugged, slugging, slugs.** *Chiefly U.S.* To strike heavily, especially with the fist.
~*n.* *Chiefly U.S.* A hard, heavy blow, as with the fist or a baseball bat; a slog. —**slug·ger** *n.* [19th century : origin obscure.]

slug·a·bed (slúggə-bed) *n.* One inclined to stay in bed out of laziness. [SLUG (sluggard) + ABED.]

slug·gard (slúggərd) *n.* A slothful, lazy person; an idler. [Middle English *sluggart,* probably from *sluggen,* to be lazy, from Scandinavian; akin to Swedish (dialectal) *slugga.*] —**slug·gard·ly** *adj.* —**slug·gard·ness** *n.*

slug·gish (slúggish) *adj.* **1.** Displaying little movement or activity; slow; inactive. **2.** Lacking in alertness, vigour, or energy; dull or lazy. **3.** Slow to perform or respond to treatment or stimulation. [Middle English, perhaps from *sluggen,* to be lazy. See **sluggard.**] —**slug·gish·ly** *adv.* —**slug·gish·ness** *n.*

sluice (slōōss || slewss) *n.* **1.** An artificial structure equipped with a valve or gate and used for holding back or regulating the flow of a body of water. **2.** The body of water so regulated or held back. **3.** The valve or gate used in a sluice. Also called "sluice gate", "sluice valve". **4.** A channel or drain, especially one for carrying off excess water. Also called "sluiceway". **5.** A long inclined trough, as for carrying logs or for washing gold ore.
~*v.* **sluiced, sluicing, sluices.** —*tr.* **1. a.** To flood or drench by means of a sluice. **b.** To pour or splash water over or upon. **c.** To wash with a sudden flow of water; flush. Often used with *out* or *away.* **2.** To draw off or let out by a sluice. **3.** To send (logs) down a sluice. **4.** To wash (gold ore) in a sluice. —*intr.* To flow out from or as if from a sluice. [Middle English *scluse,* from Old French *excluse,* from Gallo-Roman *exclūsa* (unattested), from the feminine past participle of Latin *exclūdere,* to shut out, EXCLUDE.]

slum (slum) *n.* **1.** *Often plural.* A heavily populated urban area characterised by poor housing and squalor: *the slums of Glasgow.* **2.** *Informal.* Any place that is uncared for, untidy, or squalid.
~*intr.v.* **slummed, slumming, slums.** To visit a slum or any place considered inferior to one's usual environment, as from curiosity. Usually used in the phrase *go slumming.* —**slum it.** *Informal.* To live below the standards to which one is accustomed. [19th century (cant) : origin obscure.]

slum·ber (slúmbər) *v.* **-bered, -bering, -bers.** —*intr.* **1.** To sleep or doze. **2.** To be dormant or quiescent. —*tr.* To pass (time) in sleep. Often used with *away.*
~*n.* **1.** *Often plural.* Sleep: *was woken from her slumbers.* **2.** A state of inactivity or dormancy. [Middle English *slum(b)eren,* perhaps frequentative of *slumen,* to doze, probably from *slume,* sleep, Old English *slūma.*] —**slum·ber·er** *n.* —**slum·ber·ing·ly** *adv.*

slum·ber·ous (slúmbərəss) *adj.* **1.** Sleepy; drowsy. **2. a.** Suggestive of or like sleep. **b.** Peaceful; tranquil. **3.** Causing or inducing sleep; soporific. —**slum·ber·ous·ly** *adv.* —**slum·ber·ous·ness** *n.*

slum·lord (slúm-lawrd) *n.* *Chiefly U.S. Informal.* A profiteering landlord of slum property.

slump (slump) *intr.v.* **slumped, slumping, slumps.** **1.** To fall or sink suddenly and heavily; plump; collapse. **2.** To decline suddenly; suffer a slump. **3.** To droop, as in sitting or standing; slouch.
~*n.* A sudden falling off or decline, as in interest, prices, or business. [17th century ("to sink in a bog") : perhaps from Scandinavian; akin to Norwegian *slumpa,* to fall, Low German *slump,* bog.]

slung. Past tense and past participle of **sling.**

slung·shot (slúng-shot) *n.* *U.S.* A small, heavy weight attached to a thong, used as a weapon.

slunk. Past tense and past participle of **slink.**

slur (slur) *tr.v.* **slurred, slurring, slurs.** **1.** To pass over lightly or carelessly; treat without due consideration. Often used with *over.* **2.** To pronounce (words or sounds) indistinctly. **3.** To speak slightingly of; disparage; slander. **4.** *Music.* **a.** To glide over (a series of notes) smoothly without a break. **b.** To mark with a slur. **5.** *Printing.* To blur or smudge.
~*n.* **1. a.** A disparaging remark; an aspersion. **b.** A blot or stain, as on one's reputation. **2.** A slurred utterance or manner of speech. **3.** *Music.* **a.** A curved line connecting notes on a score to indicate that they are to be played or sung legato. **b.** A group of notes so connected. **4.** Slurred written or printed matter. [Middle English *sloor, slore,* mud, perhaps from Middle Dutch; compare Low German *slūren,* Middle Dutch *sloren,* to drag, trail]

slurp (slurp) *v.* **slurped, slurping, slurps.** —*tr.* To eat or drink in a noisy manner. —*intr.* To eat or drink something noisily. [Dutch *slurpen,* to slurp, lap, from Middle Dutch *slorpen.*]

slur·ry (slúrri) *n., pl.* **-ries.** A thin mixture of a liquid, especially water, and a finely divided substance, such as cement, plaster of Paris, or clay particles. [Middle English *slory,* probably akin to *sloor,* mud. See **slur.**]

slush (slush) *n.* **1.** Partially melted snow or ice. **2.** Soft mud; mire. **3.** Refuse grease or fat from a ship's galley. **4.** Maudlin speech or writing; sentimental drivel.
~*v.* **slushed, slushing, slushes.** —*tr.* **1.** To splash or soak with slush. **2.** To fill (joints in masonry) with mortar. Usually used with *up.* —*intr.* **1.** To walk or proceed through slush. **2.** To make a splashing or slushy sound. [17th century : origin obscure.] —**slush·i·ness** *n.* —**slush·y** *adv.*

slush fund *n.* *Chiefly U.S.* A contingency fund kept, as by a political group, to finance corrupt practices such as bribing public officials. [From SLUSH (sense 3), alluding to greasing as bribery.]

slut (slut) *n.* **1.** A slovenly, dirty woman; a slattern. **2. a.** A woman of loose morals. **b.** A prostitute. [Middle English *slutte*†.] —**slut·tish** *adj.* —**slut·tish·ly** *adv.* —**slut·tish·ness** *n.*

sly (slī) *adj.* **slier** or **slyer, sliest** or **slyest.** **1.** Stealthily clever; crafty; cunning: *He was a sly old dog.* **2.** Secretive rather than open; underhand; deceitful. **3.** Playfully mischievous; roguish; arch. —**on the sly.** Secretively or surreptitiously. [Middle English *sli, sleih,* from Old Norse *slœgr,* cunning, clever, "able to strike", from *slōg-,* past stem of *slā,* to strike.] —**sly·ly, sli·ly** *adv.* —**sly·ness** *n.*
Synonyms: *sly, cunning, tricky, crafty, wily, foxy, artful.*

sly·boots (slī́-bōōts) *n.* *Informal.* A sly person.

slype (slīp) *n.* *Architecture.* A covered passage, especially one between the transept and chapter house of a cathedral. [Probably from Middle Flemish *slijpen,* to slip.]

Sm The symbol for the element samarium.

s.m. sadomasochism; sadomasochistic.

S.M. sergeant major.

smack¹ (smak) *v.* **smacked, smacking, smacks.** —*tr.* **1.** To strike, as with the flat of the hand, heartily and noisily. **2.** To make a sound by pressing together (the lips) and opening them again quickly. **3.** To move or place with force, causing a smacking sound: *smacked the money on the bar.* —*intr.* To make or give a smack.
~*n.* **1.** A sharp blow or slap. **2.** The loud, sharp sound of smacking. **3.** A noisy kiss. **4.** *Informal.* An attempt; a go. Used in the phrase *have a smack at.* —**smack in the eye** or **face.** *Informal.* A setback or rebuff.
~*adv.* **1.** With a smack: *fell smack on her head.* **2.** Directly; right: *went smack against the rules.* [Middle Low German or Middle Dutch *smacken* (imitative).]

smack² *n.* **1. a.** A distinctive flavour or taste. **b.** A suggestion or trace. **2.** A small amount; a smattering. **3.** *Slang.* Heroin.
~*intr.v.* **smacked, smacking, smacks.** **1.** To have a distinctive taste. Used with *of.* **2.** To give an indication; suggest. Used with *of*: *smacks of foul play.* [Middle English, Old English *smæc.*]

smack³ *n.* A single-masted boat, such as a sloop, used chiefly in fishing. [Dutch *smak,* from Middle Dutch *smacke*†.]

smack·er (smákər) *n.* *Slang.* **1.** A loud kiss. **2.** A resounding blow. **3.** A pound or, in the United States, a dollar.

smack·ing (smácking) *adj.* **1.** Given with a smacking sound: *a smacking kiss.* **2.** Brisk; vigorous; spanking: *a smacking breeze.*

small (smawl) *adj.* **smaller, smallest.** *Abbr.* **s.** **1.** Little or relatively little; of less than usual or average size, number, quantity, magnitude, or extent: *a small house; a small portion of pie.* **2.** Limited in importance or significance; trivial. **3.** Limited in degree, scope, or intensity: *paid small attention; had small hope.* **4.** Lacking position, influence, or status; minor. **5.** Engaged in commercial or other activity on a relatively limited scale: *small businesses.* **6.** Unpretentious; modest. **7.** Not fully grown; very young. **8.** Showing littleness of mind or character; petty: *very small of him to object.* **9.** Belittled; humiliated: *made him feel small.* **10. a.** Designating a letter written or printed in lower case. **b.** Lower-case in order to distinguish a specified word from the same word when capitalised: *catholic with a small c.* **11.** Soft; low: *a small voice.*
~*adv.* **1.** In small pieces: *Cut it up small.* **2.** In a small manner.
~*n.* **1.** A small, slender part: *the small of the back.* **2.** *Plural. British Informal.* Small items of laundry, such as underclothes. [Middle English *small(l),* Old English *smæl.*] —**small·ness** *n.*
Synonyms: *small, little, diminutive, minute, tiny, minuscule, infinitesimal.*

small ad *n.* A **classified advertisement** *(see).*

small arms *n.* Firearms small enough to be carried in the hand.

small beer *n.* Someone or something of little consequence. [Popularised by its use in Shakespeare's *Othello* ("To suckle fools and chronicle small beer", Act II, scene 1).]

small calorie *n.* A **calorie** *(see).*

small capital *n.* *Abbr.* **s.c.** A letter having the form of a capital letter but lower in height; for example, the words SMALL CAPITALS are printed in small capitals.

small change *n.* **1.** Coins of low denomination. **2.** Something of little value or significance.

small chop *n.* *West African.* Party snacks, such as olives and nuts.

small circle *n.* In geometry, a circle on the surface of a sphere with a radius that is not a radius of the sphere. Compare **great circle.**

small·clothes (smáwl-klōthz, -klōz) *pl.n. Archaic.* Men's close-fitting knee breeches worn in the 18th century.
small fry *pl.n.* **1.** Young or small fish. **2.** Young, unimportant, or insignificant persons or things.
small·hold·er (smáwl-hōldər) *n. Chiefly British.* One who owns or rents a smallholding.
small·hold·ing (smáwl-hōlding) *n. Chiefly British.* An area of agricultural land smaller than an average farm.
small hours *pl.n.* The early hours of the morning before dawn.
small intestine *n.* The part of the intestine in which digestion is completed, extending from the pylorus to the caecum and consisting of the duodenum, the jejunum, and the ileum.
small-mind·ed (smáwl-mīndid) *adj.* Having or characterised by a narrow, petty, or selfish attitude; lacking breadth of sympathy or interest. **—small-mind·ed·ly** *adv.* **—small-mind·ed·ness** *n.*
small·pox (smáwl-poks) *n.* An infectious disease, now eradicated, caused by a virus and characterised by widespread pimples which blister and form pockmarks. Also called "variola".
small print *n.* Small printed matter; especially, sections, as of contracts or guarantees, printed in small type and often containing important provisions or conditions that might easily be overlooked.
small-scale (smáwl-skáyl) *adj.* **1.** Small or limited in scope, range, or extent. **2.** Having a small scale. Said of a map.
small screen *n. Informal.* Television. Compare **big screen.**
small·sword (smáwl-sawrd || -sōrd) *n.* A lightweight, tapering sword used, especially in former times, for fencing.
small talk *n.* Casual, light, or trivial conversation.
small-time (smáwl-tīm) *adj. Informal.* Insignificant or unimportant; minor: *a small-time comedian.* **—small-tim·er** *n.*
smalt (smawlt || smolt) *n.* A deep-blue paint and ceramic pigment produced by pulverising a glass made of silica, potash, and cobalt oxide. [French, from Italian *smalto,* from Germanic; akin to SMELT.]
smalt·ite (smáwl-tīt || smól-) *n.* Also **smalt·ine** (-teen, -tin). A white to silver-grey mineral arsenide of cobalt and nickel, usually with some iron present. It is an important ore of cobalt. [Originally *smaltine,* from French : SMALT + -INE.]
sma·rag·dite (smə-rágdīt) *n.* A fibrous, green amphibole mineral occurring in rocks such as eclogite. [French, from Latin *smaragdus,* a kind of precious stone. See **emerald.**]
smarm (smarm) *v.* **smarmed, smarming, smarms.** *Informal.* *—tr.* To flatten (hair) by smoothing with grease. Often used with *down.* *—intr.v.* To act or behave in an unctuous, obsequious manner. Often used with *up to.* [19th century (dialect) : origin obscure.]
smarm·y (smármi) *adj.* **-ier, -iest.** *Informal.* Having or characterised by an unpleasantly smooth, obsequious manner.
smart (smart) *intr.v.* **smarted, smarting, smarts. 1. a.** To cause a sharp, usually superficial, stinging pain, as an acrid liquid or a slap may. **b.** To be the source of such a pain, as a wound may. **c.** To feel such a pain. **2.** To suffer acutely, as from mental distress, wounded feelings, or remorse: *smarting from wounded pride.* **3.** To suffer or pay a heavy penalty. Usually used with *for.*
∼n. Sharp mental or physical pain.
∼adj. **smarter, smartest. 1. a.** Characterised by sharp, quick thought; bright. **b.** Amusingly or impertinently clever; witty: *a smart answer.* **2.** Characterised by sharp, quick movement; specifically: **a.** Forceful; stinging: *a smart slap.* **b.** Brisk; energetic: *a smart pace.* **3.** Characterised by or involving astuteness or shrewdness. **4.** Neat, fresh, and spruce, as in dress or appearance. **5.** Associated with or consisting of persons of fashion and sophistication; fashionable. —See Synonyms at **intelligent.**
∼adv. In a smart manner: *play it smart.* [Middle English *smarten, smerten,* Old English *smeortan.*] **—smart·ly** *adv.* **—smart·ness** *n.*
smart al·eck (ál-ik, -ek). *Informal.* One who shows off his cleverness in a self-assertive and arrogant way. [SMART + *Aleck,* pet form of the name *Alexander.*] **—smart-al·eck·y** *adj.*
smart·en (smárt'n) *v.* **-ened, -ening, -ens.** *—tr.* **1.** To improve in appearance or stylishness; spruce up. Usually used with *up.* **2.** To make brighter or quicker: *smarten the pace.* *—intr.* To make oneself smart or smarter. Usually used with *up.*
smart money *n.* **1.** Compensation made for injury or disablement, especially when sustained on military service. **2.** Money paid to obtain discharge from the army. **3.** *U.S.* Compensation beyond the value of actual harm, awarded in cases of gross negligence or wilful misconduct. **4.** *Chiefly U.S.* Money gambled or invested by experienced gamblers or those having privileged information.
smart·weed (smárt-weed) *n.* A plant, the **water-pepper** *(see).*
smash (smash) *v.* **smashed, smashing, smashes.** *—tr.* **1.** To break into pieces suddenly, noisily, and violently; shatter: *smashed the glass.* **2. a.** To throw or dash (something) violently so as to shatter or crush: *smashed the vase against the wall.* **b.** To strike with a heavy blow; batter: *smashed the door in.* **3.** To hit (a ball or shuttlecock) with an aggressive overhead stroke. **4.** To crush or destroy completely; ruin. **5.** To break up; put an end to: *smash a drugs ring.* *—intr.* **1.** To move or be moved suddenly into violent contact with another object: *smashed into a wall.* **2.** To break into pieces, as from a violent blow or collision. **3.** To smash a ball or shuttlecock. **4.** To become wrecked or destroyed. **5.** To go bankrupt. Often used with *up.* —See Synonyms at **break.**
∼n. **1. a.** The act or sound of smashing. **b.** The condition of having been smashed. **2. a.** Total defeat, destruction, or ruin. **b.** Financial failure; bankruptcy. **3.** A collision or crash. **4.** An aggressive overhead stroke in tennis, badminton, or the like. **5.** *Informal.* A resounding success. **6.** *U.S.* A drink made of mint, sugar, soda-water, and alcoholic spirit, usually brandy.
∼adj. Informal. Of, pertaining to, or being a resounding success: *a smash hit.*
∼adv. With a sudden, violent crash. [Imitative; perhaps blend of SMACK and CRASH.] **—smash·er** *n.*
smash-and-grab (smásh'n-gráb) *adj.* Designating a robbery in which a shop window is smashed, as with a brick, and goods taken from the window display. **—smash-and-grab** *n.*
smashed (smasht) *adj. British Informal.* Intoxicated; drunk.
smash·er (smáshər) *n. British Informal.* One that is outstandingly fine or attractive.
smash·ing (smáshing) *adj. Informal.* Extraordinarily or unusually impressive, fine, or attractive; wonderful; admirable.
smash·up (smásh-up) *n.* **1.** A total collapse or defeat. **2.** A serious collision between vehicles; a crash.
smat·ter (smáttər) *v.* **-tered, -tering, -ters.** *Archaic.* *—tr.* **1.** To speak (a language) without fluency. **2.** To study or approach superficially; dabble in. *—intr.* To have a superficial knowledge; dabble.
∼n. A smattering. [Middle English *smat(e)ren* (probably imitative).] **—smat·ter·er** *n.*
smat·ter·ing (smáttəring) *n.* **1.** A fragmented or superficial knowledge. **2.** A small amount or number; a scattering. [From SMATTER.]
smear (smeer) *v.* **smeared, smearing, smears.** *—tr.* **1. a.** To spread or daub with a sticky, greasy, or dirty substance. **b.** To spread or daub (a sticky, greasy, or dirty substance) on a surface. **2.** To stain or blur by or as if by smearing. **3.** To stain or attempt to destroy the reputation of; vilify. *—intr.* To be or become smeared.
∼n. **1.** A mark made by smearing; a spot; a blot. **2.** A substance to be spread on a surface; especially, a substance or preparation placed on a slide for microscopic examination. **3.** A malicious, unsubstantiated charge made in an attempt to destroy someone's reputation; a slander. Also used adjectivally: *a smear campaign.* [Middle English *smeren,* to anoint, cover, daub, Old English *smierwan, smerian.*] **—smear·y** *adj.*
smear test *n.* A **Pap test** *(see).*
smec·tic (sméktik) *adj. Chemistry.* Of, pertaining to, or designating one of the two types of anisotropic melts characteristic of a liquid crystal, in which the molecules are linearly orientated in a planar arrangement. Compare **nematic.** [Greek *smēktikos,* cleansing, detergent, from *smēkhein,* to cleanse (referring to the soapy consistency of such substances).]
smeg·ma (smég-mə) *n.* **1. Sebum** *(see).* **2.** The sebaceous substance secreted under the foreskin. [Greek *smēgma* (stem *smēgmat-),* detergent, from *smēkhein,* to cleanse (referring to the soaplike consistency).] **—smeg·ma·tic** (smeg-máttik) *adj.*
smell (smel) *v.* **smelled** or **smelt** (smelt), **smelling, smells.** *—tr.* **1.** To perceive the scent of (something) by means of the olfactory nerves. **2. a.** To sense the presence of by or as if by the olfactory nerves; detect: *to smell danger.* **b.** To find or discover by smelling. Used with *out.* *—intr.* **1.** To use the sense of smell; perceive the scent of something. **2.** To have or emit an odour of a specified kind: *doesn't smell fresh; smells of old socks.* **3.** To be suggestive; smack of something. Used with *of*: *smells of dishonesty.* **4.** To have or emit an unpleasant odour; stink. **5.** *Chiefly U.S.* To appear to be dishonest; suggest evil or corruption.
∼n. **1.** The sense by which odours are perceived; the olfactory sense. **2. a.** That quality of something that may be perceived by the olfactory sense; odour; scent. **b.** An unpleasant odour. **3.** The act or an instance of smelling. **4.** A distinctive or pervasive quality; an aura: *the smell of corruption.* [Middle English *smellen, smullen*†.]
Synonyms: *smell, odour, scent, aroma, fragrance, perfume, bouquet, savour, stink, stench.*
Usage: The past tense and participle forms of this verb may be *smelled* (preferred in American English) or *smelt* (preferred in British English). The verb may be followed either by an adjective or by an adverb, but different senses are involved. With an adjective, the sense is "emit an odour": *The flowers smell beautiful today.* The adverb is used only in the context of "emit an unpleasant odour": *They smell terribly.*
smelling salts *pl.n.* Any of several preparations based on spirits of ammonia, sniffed as a restorative after dizziness and fainting.
smell·y (smélli) *adj.* **-ier, -iest.** *Informal.* Having an unpleasant or offensive odour. **—smell·i·ness** *n.*
smelt[1] (smelt) *v.* **smelted, smelting, smelts.** *—tr.* **1.** To extract the metallic constituents from (ore) by melting. **2.** To extract (metal) from ore in this way. *—intr.* To melt or fuse. Used of ores. [Dutch or Low German *smelten,* from Middle Dutch or Middle Low German.]
smelt[2] *n., pl.* **smelts** or **smelt. 1.** Any of various small marine and freshwater food fishes of the family Osmeridae; especially, *Osmerus eperlanus,* of Europe. Also called "sparling". **2.** The sand smelt, *Atherina presbyter.* [Middle English, Old English *smelt, smylt.*]
smelt[3]**.** Alternative past tense and past participle of **smell.**
smelt·er (sméltər) *n.* Also **smelt·er·y** (-i) (for sense 1b). **1. a.** Any apparatus for smelting, usually a furnace. **b.** An establishment for smelting. **2.** A person engaged in the smelting industry.
Sme·ta·na (sméttənə), **Bedřich** (1824–84). Czech composer. He played a leading part in the founding of the Czech national opera (1862), and was its principal conductor until 1874. His most famous works are the opera *The Bartered Bride* (1866), the tone poem *Ma Vlast* (1879), and two string quartets both called *From My Life* (1876, 1882).

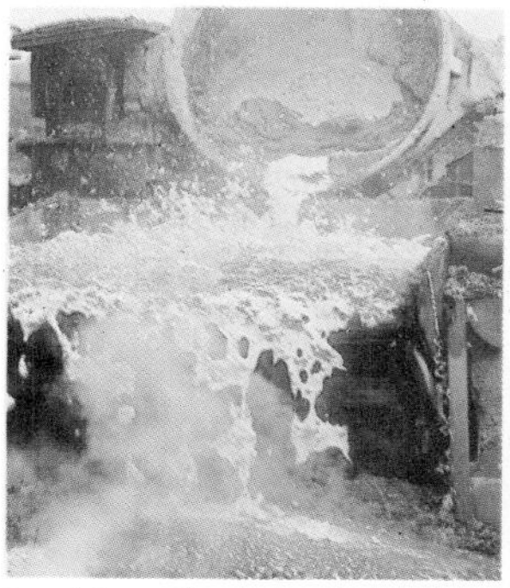

smelting *The process of extracting metal from its ore. Here the refined metal is being poured into troughs to cool.*

smew (smew) *n.* A small, crested Old World duck, *Mergellus albellus,* having a narrow bill and white and black plumage in the male. [17th century : origin obscure.]

smid·gen, smid·gin (smijin, smijən) *n. Chiefly U.S. Informal.* A very small quantity or portion; a bit. [Probably variant of dialectal *smitch,* probably variant of SMUTCH.]

smi·lax (smī-laks) *n.* **1.** Any plant of the genus *Smilax,* which mainly comprises climbing vines. The dried roots of certain species are also called "sarsaparilla". **2.** A vine, *Asparagus asparagoides,* that is popular as a floral decoration. [New Latin, from Latin *smilax,* a kind of oak, smilax, bindweed, from Greek *smilax†.*]

smile (smīl) *n.* **1.** A facial expression characterised by an upward curving of the corners of the mouth, typically expressing pleasant feelings such as amusement, affection, or approval, but sometimes arising from bitterness, cynicism, or derision. **2.** A pleasant or favourable disposition or aspect.
~*v.* **smiled, smiling, smiles.** —*intr.* **1.** To have or form a smile. **2. a.** To express approval or beneficence. Often used with *upon* or *on.* **b.** To regard with detached amusement or patient resignation. Often used with *at: smiled at misfortune.* —*tr.* **1.** To express with a smile. **2.** To act upon or change with or as if with a smile: *She smiled away her cares.* [Middle English *smilen,* perhaps from Scandinavian, akin to Swedish *smila.*] —**smil·er** *n.* —**smil·ing·ly** *adv.*

Smiles (smīlz), **Samuel** (1812–1904). British writer, the most famous populariser of the Victorian ethic of self-improvement and hard work, especially in *Self-Help* (1859) and *Thrift* (1875).

smirch (smurch) *tr.v.* **smirched, smirching, smirches. 1.** To soil, stain, or dirty, as with grime. **2.** To dishonour or defame. ~*n.* Something that smirches; a blot, smear, or stain. [Middle English *smorchen†.*]

smirk (smurk) *intr.v.* **smirked, smirking, smirks.** To smile in a self-conscious, knowing, or self-satisfied manner.
~*n.* A knowing, self-satisfied smile. [Middle English *smirken,* Old English *smearcian,* to smile.] —**smirk·er** *n.* —**smirk·ing·ly** *adv.*

Smirke (smurk), **Sir Robert** (1781–1867). British architect, a supporter of the early 19th-century Neoclassical movement. His best-known building is the British Museum, which was begun in 1823 and completed in 1855 by his brother, Sydney (1798–1877).

smite (smīt) *v.* **smote** (smōt) or *archaic* **smit** (smit), **smitten** (smitt'n) or **smit** or **smote, smiting, smites.** *Archaic & Literary.* —*tr.* **1.** To strike heavily with or as if with the hand, a tool, a weapon, or the like. **2.** To attack, damage, or destroy by or as if by blows. **3. a.** To affect, as with disease; afflict: *smitten with plague.* **b.** To strike down in retribution; chasten or chastise. Used of God. **c.** To affect sharply with deep feeling: *smitten with love.* —*intr.* To strike or beat: *smote upon the oaken door.* [Smite, smote or smit, smitten; Middle English *smiten, smot* or *smite, smitten,* Old English *smītan, smiton* (plural) or *smāt* (singular), *smiten.*] —**smit·er** *n.*

smith (smith) *n.* **1.** A metalworker; especially, one who works metal when it is hot and malleable. Often used in combination: *silversmith, goldsmith.* **2.** A blacksmith (*see*). **3.** A person who makes or creates something specified. Used in combination: *a wordsmith; a songsmith.* [Middle English, Old English.]

Smith (smith), **Adam** (1723–90). Scottish economist and moral philosopher. He came to prominence with his *Theory of Moral Sentiments* (1759), but is best known for his great work of political economy *An Inquiry into the Nature and Causes of the Wealth of Nations* (1776) which laid the foundations of classical "free-market" economic theory.

Smith, Bessie (*c.* 1894–1937). American jazz singer. She was known as the "Empress of the Blues", thanks to her recordings in the 1920s with leading jazz musicians such as Louis Armstrong.

Smith, F(rederick) E(dwin). See Birkenhead, 1st Earl of.

Smith, Ian (Douglas) (1919–). Rhodesian politician. He formed the Rhodesian Front party in 1961 to campaign for Southern Rhodesia's independence from Great Britain. In 1964 he became prime minister of Rhodesia and in 1965 he unilaterally declared its independence. In 1970 his rebel regime proclaimed Rhodesia a republic. For the next decade his white supremacist party fought a losing battle against Black guerrilla forces. He continues to lead the white minority in the new parliament of Zimbabwe.

Smith, Joseph (1805–44). U.S. religious leader, founder of the Mormon church, known as the Church of Jesus Christ of Latter-Day Saints. He alleged that a vision had shown him the hiding place of sacred tablets, which he unearthed in 1827 and transcribed in the publication the *Book of Mormon* (1830). The following year he founded his new church at Fayette, New York. In 1844 he was arrested with his brother on charges of treason and conspiracy, and was murdered by a mob at the prison in Carthage, Illinois.

Smith, Sir Keith Macpherson (1890–1955) and **Sir Ross Macpherson** (1892–1922). Australian aviators, brothers, who made the first flight from England to Australia (1919).

Smith, Maggie, born Margaret Natalie Smith (1934–). British actress. She joined the Old Vic company in 1959 and the National Theatre in 1963, establishing a reputation in both Shakespearean and modern roles. Among her many awards is an Academy Award as best actress in 1969 for *The Prime of Miss Jean Brodie.*

Smith, Stevie, pen name of Florence Margaret Smith (1902–1971). British poet, novelist, and artist. Her best-known collection of verse is *Not Waving but Drowning* (1957). Her novels include *Novel on Yellow Paper* (1936) and *The Holiday* (1949).

Smith, Wilbur (Addison) (1933–). South African novelist, born in Northern Rhodesia (now Zambia). Among his best-known works are *When the Lion Feeds* (1964) and *Shout at the Devil* (1968).

smith·er·eens (smithə-reenz) *pl.n. Informal.* Fragments or splintered pieces; bits: *The dish broke into smithereens.* [Perhaps from Irish *smidirīn,* diminutive of *smiodar†,* small fragment.]

smith·er·y (smithəri) *n., pl.* **-ies. 1.** The occupation or craft of a smith. **2.** A smithy.

Smith·field (smith-feeld). District in the northern part of the City of London, famous for its meat market. There has been a market on the site since the late 12th century. Smithfield is also the site of one of London's oldest hospitals, St. Bartholomew's, founded in 1137.

Smith·son (smith-s'n), **James** (1765–1829). British chemist and mineralogist. He was elected to the Royal Society at the age of 22. He endowed the U.S. Smithsonian Institution in his will.

smith·son·ite (smiths'n-īt) *n.* A white or yellow-to-brown mineral, chiefly zinc carbonate ($ZnCO_3$), used as a source of zinc. Also called "dry-bone ore", "hemimorphite"; formerly called "calamine". [After James SMITHSON.]

smith·y (smithi ‖ *U.S. also* smithi) *n., pl.* **-ies.** A blacksmith's workshop; a forge. [Middle English *smithy,* from Old Norse *smidhja.*]

smock (smok) *n.* **1.** A loose shirtlike outer garment worn, as by artists, to protect the clothes while working. **2.** A similar garment, usually knee-length and often decorated with smocking, as worn formerly by farm labourers. Also called "smock frock". **3.** A loose dress gathered in below the bust rather than at the waist, worn especially by pregnant women.
~*tr.v.* **smocked, smocking, smocks.** To decorate (fabric) with smocking. [Middle English *smok,* women's undergarment, smock, Old English *smoc.*]

smock·ing (smocking) *n.* Needlework decoration accomplished by stitching small regularly spaced gathers into a honeycomb or diamond-shaped pattern. [From SMOCK (verb).]

smock mill *n.* A type of windmill in which the top part only, rather than the entire body, turns in the wind.

smog (smog ‖ *U.S. also* smawg) *n.* A thick, yellow fog over a built-up area, where soot dust promotes condensation, and sulphur dioxide acidity. [Blend of SMOKE and FOG.] —**smog·gy** *adj.*

smoke (smōk) *n.* **1.** Small particles of carbonaceous matter in the air from the incomplete combustion of wood, coal, or the like. **2.** A suspension of particles in a gaseous medium. **3.** Anything insubstantial, unreal, or transitory. **4. a.** An act of smoking any form of tobacco. **b.** *Informal.* Tobacco in any form that can be smoked; especially, a cigarette. **5.** Greyish blue to dark grey. —**the Smoke.** *British Slang.* London. Compare **big smoke.**
~*v.* **smoked, smoking, smokes.** —*intr.* **1. a.** To emit smoke or a smokelike substance. **b.** To emit smoke excessively. **2. a.** To draw in and exhale smoke from a cigarette, cigar, pipe, or the like. **b.** To do this habitually. —*tr.* **1.** To draw in and exhale the smoke of (burning tobacco, for example). **2.** To preserve or cure (meat or fish) by exposure to the smoke of burning wood. **3.** To fumigate. **4.** To expose (glass) to smoke in order to darken or change its colour. —**smoke out. 1.** To force out of a place of hiding or concealment by the use of smoke. **2.** To detect and bring to public view; expose; reveal. [Middle English, Old English *smoca.*]

smoke bomb *n.* A bomb that is designed to give out thick smoke upon exploding, used especially to provide cover or concealment.

smoke-dried (smōk-drīd) *adj.* Cured in smoke. Said of fish or meat.

smoked rubber (smōkt) *n.* A crude, raw form of natural rubber made by coagulating latex with acid and drying sheets of it over wood fires.

smokeho. Variant of smoko.

smoke·house (smōk-howss) *n.* A structure in which meat or fish is cured with smoke.

smoke·jack (smōk-jak) *n.* A device for turning a roasting spit in a chimney, activated by the current of rising gases.

smoke·less (smōk-ləss, -liss) *adj.* **1.** Emitting little or no smoke: *smokeless fuel.* **2.** Designating an area in which emission of smoke is prohibited by law.

smokeless powder *n.* A propellant charge composed mainly of nitrocellulose, which produces little or no smoke, used in projectiles and small artillery rockets.

smok·er (smōkər) *n.* **1.** One that smokes. **2.** A section of a train carriage in which smoking is permitted. Also called "smoking compartment". **3.** An informal social gathering or entertainment.

smoker's cough *n.* A cough to which those who smoke are prone, characterised by a harsh, rasping sound and short convulsive movements of the body.

smoke screen *n.* **1.** A mass of dense artificial smoke used to conceal military areas or operations from an enemy. **2.** Any action or statement used to conceal plans or intentions.

smoke·stack (smōk-stak) *n.* A large chimney through which combustion vapours, gases, and smoke are discharged.

smoke tree *n.* Either of two trees, *Cotinus coggygria,* of Eurasia or *C. obovatus,* of the southern United States, having plumelike clusters of small yellowish flowers. The latter species is also called "chittamwood". [The flower clusters resemble puffs of smoke.]

smok·ing jacket (smōking) *n.* A man's evening jacket, often made of a fine fabric, elaborately trimmed, and usually worn at home.

smoking room *n.* A room, as in a hotel, reserved for those who wish to smoke.

smo·ko, smoke·ho (smōkō) *n. Australian and N.Z. Informal.* A tea or coffee break. [From SMOKE (noun).]

smok·y (smōki) *adj.* **-ier, -iest. 1.** Emitting smoke profusely. **2.** Full of smoke. 3. Resembling or suggestive of smoke, especially in taste or colour. 4. Darkened, stained, or discoloured by smoke. **—smok·i·ly** *adv.* **—smok·i·ness** *n.*

smoky quartz *n.* A mineral, **Cairngorm** *(see).*

smolder. *U.S.* Variant of **smoulder.**

Smo·lensk (smo-lénsk, smə-; *Russian* smul-yénsk). City in the Russian S.F.S.R., western U.S.S.R., on the river Dnepr. An important trade centre from the ninth century, it was held briefly by Poland (1611–54), France (1812), and Germany (1941–43). It is today a major railway junction with engineering and textile industries.

Smol·lett (smóllit), **Tobias (George)** (1721–71). Scottish novelist, one of the founders of the English novel. Among his works are *Peregrine Pickle* (1751) and *Humphrey Clinker* (1771).

smolt (smōlt) *n.* A young salmon at the stage at which it turns silvery and migrates from fresh water to the sea. [Middle English, obscurely related to Old English *smelt,* SMELT (fish).]

smooch (smōōch) *n. Slang.* A long, intimate kiss.
~*intr.v.* **smooched, smooching, smooches.** *Slang.* To kiss with a smooch. [From dialect *smouch* (imitative).]

smooth (smōōth) *adj.* **smoother, smoothest. 1. a.** Having a surface free from irregularities, roughness, or projections; even: *a smooth lawn.* **b.** Free from hair or bristles; soft. **2.** Having a surface whose roughness or projections have been worn level by use: *smooth tyres.* **3. a.** Having a fine, uniform consistency or texture; not lumpy: *smooth custard.* **b.** Free from harshness or acidity: *a smooth white wine.* **4. a.** Having an even or gentle motion: *a smooth drive.* **b.** Having flowing regularity: *smooth rhythm.* **5.** Having no obstructions or difficulties: *a smooth operation.* **6.** Having or showing an unruffled temperament; serene. **7.** Not harsh or coarse in sound; mellifluous. **8. a.** Polite and affable; polished. **b.** Excessively or suspiciously suave; plausible; persuasive: *a smooth talker.* **9.** *Phonetics.* Not aspirated. —See Synonyms at **level, suave.**
~*v.* **smoothed, smoothing, smoothes.** —*tr.* **1.** To make (something) even, level, unwrinkled, or the like. Sometimes used with *out* or *down: smoothed down his hair.* **2. a.** To rid of obstructions, hindrances, difficulties, or the like: *smooth the way for a settlement.* **b.** To remove (obstructions or difficulties): *smooth away a problem.* **3.** To soothe or alleviate; make calm. Sometimes used with *over: smoothed over hurt feelings.* **4.** *Archaic.* To make less harsh or crude; refine. —*intr.* To become smooth.
~*n.* **1.** A smooth part or surface. **2.** The act of smoothing. [Middle English *smoth(e),* Old English *smōth*; akin to Old Saxon *smōthi*†.] **—smooth·er** *n.* **—smooth·ly** *adv.* **—smooth·ness** *n.*

smooth·bore (smōōth-bawr || -bōr) *adj.* Having an unrifled barrel. Said of a firearm.
~*n.* Also **smooth bore.** A firearm having no rifling.

smooth breathing *n.* **1.** The symbol (') written over some initial vowels in Greek, that in classical Greek indicated that they were not aspirated. **2.** The absence of aspiration so indicated.

smooth·en (smōōth'n) *v.* **-ened, -ening, -ens.** —*tr.* To smooth. —*intr.* To become smooth.

smooth-hound (smōōth-hownd) *n.* A **hound shark** *(see).*

smooth·ie (smōōthi) *n. Informal.* One who is smooth and charming, sometimes excessively so, as when socialising with members of the opposite sex.

smooth muscle *n.* The unstriated involuntary muscle of the internal organs, as of the intestine, bladder, and blood vessels, excluding the heart.

smooth snake *n.* A common, small, European snake, *Coronella austriaca,* whose young hatch immediately from newly laid eggs.

smooth-talk (smōōth-tawk) *tr.v.* **-talked, -talking, -talks.** *Informal.* To make or bring about by means of plausible, persuasive talk.

smor·gas·bord (smór-gəss-bawrd, smúr- || -bōrd) *n.* Also *Swedish* **smör·gås·bord** (smörgawss-boord). A meal consisting of a varied number of dishes, such as salads, cheeses, and pâté, served buffet-style. [Swedish *smörgåsbord* : *smörgås,* (open-faced) sandwich, bread and butter : *smör,* butter, from Old Norse *smör, smjör,* fat + *gås,* goose, piece of butter, from Old Norse *gās* + *bord,* table, from Old Norse *bordh.*]

smote. Past tense and alternative past participle of **smite.**

smoth·er (smúthər || smóthər) *v.* **-ered, -ering, -ers.** —*tr.* **1. a.** To suffocate (a person or animal) by depriving of air. **b.** To deprive (a fire) of the oxygen necessary for it to burn. **2.** To conceal, suppress, or hide: *smothered a yawn; smothered the report.* **3.** To cover (a foodstuff) thickly with another foodstuff: *smothered the chips with vinegar.* **4.** To overwhelm, as with kisses or affection. —*intr.* **1.** To suffocate. **2.** To be concealed, stifled, or suppressed.
~*n.* **1.** Anything that smothers, such as a dense cloud of smoke or dust or a spray of spume. **2.** A disordered mass or confusion. **3.** *Archaic.* A state of smouldering, as in coals or ashes. [Middle English *smotheren, smortheren,* from *smorther,* a smother, from Old English *smorian*†, to suffocate, smother.] **—smoth·er·y** *adj.*

smoul·der, *U.S.* **smol·der** (smōldər) *intr.v.* **-dered, -dering, -ders. 1.** To burn or smoke slowly without flame. **2.** To exist in a hidden or suppressed state. **3.** To manifest repressed anger, hatred, or the like: *eyes smouldering with revenge.*
~*n.* A fire burning slowly with smoke but without flame.

smudge (smuj) *v.* **smudged, smudging, smudges.** —*tr.* **1.** To make a small, dirty mark on. **2.** To smear or blur (writing, for example). **3.** *U.S.* To fill (an orchard or other planted area) with dense smoke from a smudge pot in order to prevent damage from insects or frost. —*intr.* **1.** To make a smudge, as with dirt, soot, or ink. **2.** To become smudged.
~*n.* **1.** A dirty mark, blotch or smear. **2.** *U.S.* A smoky fire used as a protection against insects or frost. [Middle English *smogen*†.] **—smudg·i·ly** *adv.* **—smudg·i·ness** *n.* **—smudg·y** *adj.*

smudge pot *n. U.S.* A receptacle in which oil or other smoky fuel is burned, as to protect an orchard from insects or frost or to indicate wind direction.

smug (smug) *adj.* **smugger, smuggest.** Pleased with oneself; complacent; self-satisfied. [Probably from Low German *smuck,* neat, smooth, sleek, from Middle Low German, from *smucken,* to adorn.] **—smug·ly** *adv.* **—smug·ness** *n.*

smug·gle (smúgg'l) *v.* **-gled, -gling, -gles.** —*tr.* **1.** To import or export without paying lawful customs charges or duties. **2.** To bring in or take out illicitly or by stealth. **3.** To place in concealment; hide. Often used with *away.* —*intr.* To engage in smuggling. [Earlier *smuckle,* from Low German *smukkelen, smuggeln* and Dutch *smokkelen.*] **—smug·gler** *n.*

smut (smut) *n.* **1. a.** A particle or flake of soot or dirt. **b.** A dirty mark or smudge made by soot, smoke, or dirt. **2.** Obscenity, or obscene matter for reading or viewing. **3. a.** Any of various plant diseases, particularly affecting cereals, caused by fungi of the order Ustilaginales and producing black, powdery masses of spores on the affected parts. **b.** A fungus causing such a disease.
~*v.* **smutted, smutting, smuts.** —*tr.* **1.** To blacken or smudge, as with smoke or grime. **2.** To affect (a plant) with smut. **3.** To free (grain, for example) from smut. —*intr.* To become affected with smut, as a plant may. [Perhaps from Low German *smutt*†.] **—smut·ti·ly** *adv.* **—smut·ti·ness** *n.* **—smut·ty** *adj.*

smutch (smuch) *tr.v.* **smutched, smutching, smutches.** *Archaic.* To soil, stain, or besmirch.
~*n. Archaic.* A stain or spot of dirt. [Variant of SMUDGE.] **—smutch·y** *adj.*

Smuts (smuts, smöts), **Jan (Christiaan)** (1870–1950). South African statesman. He was a lawyer and political journalist before becoming a general in the Second Anglo-Boer War (1899–1902). He later became prime minister of the Union of South Africa (1919–24, 1939–48). He was an early proponent of a British Commonwealth, and a prime mover in the formation of The League of Nations; and he later drafted the preamble to the declaration of human rights that was included in the Charter for the United Nations Organisation.

Smyrna. See **Izmir.**

Sn The symbol for the element tin. [Latin *stannum.*]

snack (snak) *n.* **1.** A hurried or light meal. **2.** A small amount of food eaten between meals.
~*intr.v.* **snacked, snacking, snacks.** *U.S.* To eat a hurried or light meal. [Middle English *snake,* a snatch with the teeth, bite (especially of a dog), from Middle Dutch *snac(k)*; akin to SNAP.]

snack bar *n.* A café or counter where light meals are served.

snaf·fle (snáff'l) *n.* A bit for a horse, consisting of two bars jointed at the centre. Also called "snafflebit".
~*tr.v.* **snaffled, -fling, -fles. 1.** *British Informal.* To take, seize, or steal. **2.** To put a snaffle on or control with a snaffle. [Probably from Low Dutch; compare Middle Dutch *snavel,* beak, nose.]

sna·fu (sna-fōō) *adj. U.S. Slang.* In a state of complete confusion.
~*tr.v.* **snafued, -fuing, -fus.** *U.S. Slang.* To make confused.
~*n., pl.* **snafus.** *U.S. Slang.* Any chaotic or confused situation. [*S*ituation *n*ormal: *a*ll *f*ucked *u*p.]

snag (snag) *n.* **1.** Any rough, sharp, or jagged protuberance, such as: **a.** A tree or a part of a tree that protrudes above the surface in a body of water, and is hazardous to shipping. **b.** The stump of a broken off branch. **c.** An unaligned or broken tooth; a snaggletooth. **2.** A break, pull, or tear in a fabric that has been caught on a snag. **3.** An obstacle or difficulty, especially one that is unforeseen or hidden. —See Synonyms at **obstacle.**
~*tr.v.* **snagged, snagging, snags. 1. a.** To hinder, obstruct, or impede by or as if by a snag. **b.** To tear or catch on a snag. **2.** To free or clear of snags. **3.** *U.S. Informal.* To catch unexpectedly and quickly. [Probably from Scandinavian, akin to Old Norse *snagi*†, peg.] **—snag·gy** *adj.*

snag·gle·tooth (snágg'l-tōōth || -tōōth) *n., pl.* **-teeth** (-teeth). A tooth that is broken or out of alignment. [From dialectal *snaggled,* snaggletoothed, from SNAG.] **—snag·gle·toothed** (-t) *adj.*

snail (snayl) *n.* **1.** Any of numerous aquatic or terrestrial molluscs of the class Gastropoda, characteristically having a spirally coiled shell, a broad retractile foot, and a distinct head. **2.** A slow-moving or lazy person. [Middle English, Old English *snæg(e)l, sneg(e)l.*]

snail's pace *n.* A very slow pace or rate of progress.

snake (snayk) *n.* **1.** Any of various scaly, legless, sometimes venomous reptiles of the suborder Serpentes, having a long, tapering, cylindrical body. **2.** *Capital* **S.** The constellation **Hydra** *(see).* **3.** A treacherous person. **4.** A long, highly flexible metal wire used for cleaning drains. **—the Snake.** An agreement between member countries of the European Economic Community whereby the exchange rates of their respective currencies are allowed to fluctuate against each other only within relatively narrow limits. See feature, next page.
~*v.* **snaked, snaking, snakes.** —*tr.* To follow (a course) in the manner of a snake. —*intr.* To move with a sinuous, snakelike motion. [Middle English, Old English *snaca.*]

Snake (snayk). River in northwest United States. It rises in the Yellowstone National Park, Wyoming, and flows 1 670 kilometres (1,038 miles) westwards to join the Columbia river near Pasco. The largest and deepest of its many gorges is Hell's Canyon, some 160

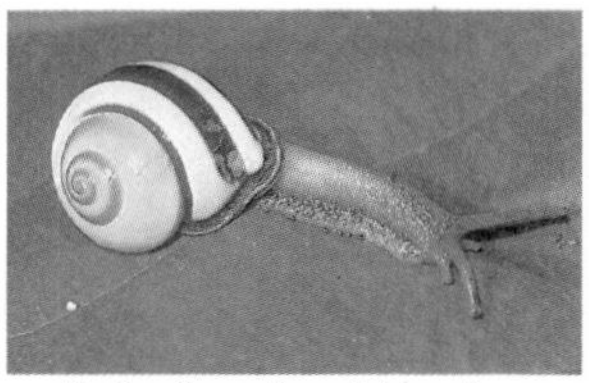

snail *Snails are found throughout the world on land and in the sea. Land snails are usually most active at night or in wet weather and feed on vegetation and sometimes small dead animals such as slugs. This striped snail is native to New Guinea.*

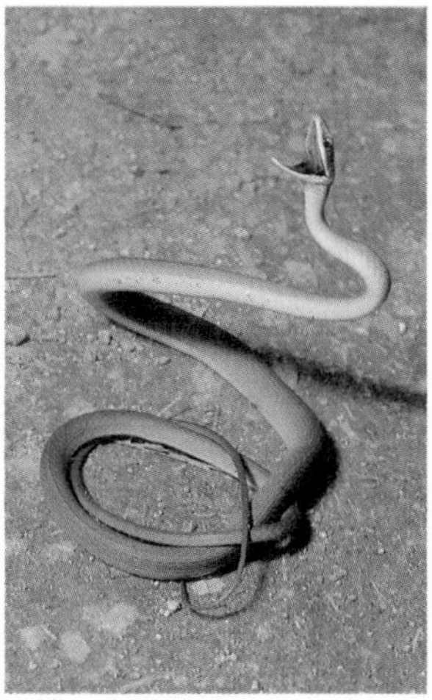

snake Opheodrys aestivus, *the rough green snake, lives on spiders and insects and is native to Mexico and the southern and eastern United States. Like many snakes, it rears up when alarmed.*

snake

THE REPTILE THAT MEN FEAR
The deaf snake that responds to the charmer's music

Snakes have no external ear openings and are, as far as we know, completely deaf to sounds in the air, but they react to vibrations passing through the ground. When they sway to the piping of a snake-charmer, they are mimicking the movements of the charmer himself.

Snakes are reptiles and there are 2,500 species of them divided into 11 families or main types. Only two whole families – cobras, which include seasnakes, and vipers – are venomous enough to poison man, but individual species of other families have venom fatal to man – the boomslang of the Colubridae family in Africa, for example. Other snakes produce enough poison to kill small animals.

All snakes are carnivorous. They have jawbones loosely attached to the skull so they can swallow their prey whole – an African snake with a neck the width of a man's finger can swallow a hen's egg.

POISONOUS SNAKES
The venomous cobra (right) and mamba have short fangs at the front of the mouth and inject poison as they bite to kill. The viper family have long, tubular fangs, and some species are so deadly that they need only to strike a victim once for the poison to squirt through those fangs and take its very rapid effect.

KILLING WITHOUT POISON *Although not poisonous the python, boa (above), and anaconda can be dangerous because they are constrictors. To kill they wrap themselves round their prey and squeeze it to death. A python has been known to swallow a leopard, and anacondas can grow to more than 11 metres (36 feet long).*

kilometres (100 miles) long, and reaching a maximum depth of 2 410 metres (about 7,900 feet).

snake-bird (snáyk-burd) *n.* Any of several long-necked, long-billed birds of the genus *Anhinga.* [From its elongated, snakelike neck.]

snake-bite (snáyk-bīt) *n.* **1.** The bite of a snake. **2.** Poisoning resulting from the bite of a venomous snake.

snake charmer *n.* An entertainer who, through music and bodily movements, causes a snake to dance or perform simple tricks.

snake dance *n.* **1.** A dance performed as part of a biennial religious ceremony of the Hopi Indians, in which the dancers carry live rattlesnakes in their mouths. **2.** *U.S.* An informal procession of persons who join hands and move forward in a zigzag line.

snake fly *n.* Any of various predatory insects of the family Raphidiidae having an elongated, snakelike neck.

snake in the grass *n.* A false friend or lurking danger.

snake mackerel *n.* A fish, the **escolar** (see).

snake plant *n.* Any of several tropical Old World plants of the genus *Sansevieria,* having narrow, rigid, often mottled leaves and widely cultivated as a house plant.

snake-root (snáyk-rōōt || -rŏŏt) *n.* Any of various plants having roots or rhizomes reputed to cure snakebite.

snakes and ladders *n. Used with a singular verb.* A board game in which each player throws dice to advance a counter to the finish. Landing on the foot or head of any of the pictured ladders and snakes speeds up or retards progress respectively.

snakes-head (snáyks-hed) *n.* A plant, the **fritillary** (see).

snake-skin (snáyk-skin) *n.* The skin of a snake, especially when prepared as leather.

snake-weed (snáyk-weed) *n.* Any of various plants reputed to cure snakebite; especially, **bistort** (see).

snak-y (snáyki) *adj.* **-ier, -iest. 1.** Pertaining to or characteristic of snakes. **2.** Having the form or movement of a snake; serpentine. **3.** Overrun with snakes. **4.** Treacherous; sly. **5.** *Australian Informal.* Annoyed; tetchy. **—snak-i-ly** *adv.* **—snak-i-ness** *n.*

snap (snap) *v.* **snapped, snapping, snaps. —intr. 1.** To make a brisk, sharp, cracking sound. **2.** To break suddenly with such a sound. **3.** To give way abruptly under pressure or tension: *The weight of responsibility made her nerves snap.* **4.** To bring the jaws briskly together, often with a clicking sound; bite or attempt to bite.

snake charmer *The snake cannot hear the sound of the flute, but is "charmed" by the instrument's to-and-fro movement.*

Often used with *at.* **5.** To snatch or grasp eagerly. Often used with *up* or *at.* **6.** To speak abruptly or irritably. Often used with *at.* **7.** To move swiftly and smartly: *snap to attention.* **8.** To open or close with a click: *The lock snapped shut.* **—tr. 1.** To snatch at with or as if with the teeth; bite. **2.** To cause to come apart or break with a snapping sound. **3.** To utter abruptly or irritably: *snapped out an order* **4. a.** To cause to emit a snapping sound: *snap a whip.* **b.** To cause to move into place or close with a snapping sound. **5.** To pick up or get hold of quickly and smartly. Often used with *up: snapped up a bargain.* **6. a.** To take (a photograph). **b.** To take a photograph of. **7.** In American football, to move (the ball) backwards to put it into play. **—snap out of it.** *Informal.* To recover quickly from a state of depression or a bad mood.

~n. 1. A sudden, sharp, cracking sound or the action producing such a sound. **2.** A sudden breaking of something brittle, such as a twig. **3.** A clasp, catch, or other fastening device that operates with a snapping sound. **4.** A sudden attempt to bite, snatch, or grasp. **5. a.** The sound produced by rapid movement of the second finger pressed down from the tip of the thumb to its base. **b.** The act of producing this sound. **6.** A curt or irritable retort or manner of speech: *answered me with a snap.* **7.** A thin, crisp biscuit: *a ginger snap.* **8.** *Informal.* Briskness, liveliness, or energy. **9.** A brief spell of cold weather. **10.** A snapshot. **11.** *British.* A card game in which the player who first notices that two cards, which have been turned up from two packs, have an equal value says "snap", and thus wins all the cards turned up. **12.** *U.S. Informal.* An effortless task; a snip.

~adj. 1. Made, done, or brought about on the spur of the moment, with little warning or consideration: *a snap decision; a snap election.* **2.** Fastening with a snap. Said of a locking device.

~interj. *British.* **1.** Used by a player in the game of snap. **2.** Used to express one's realisation of the similarity of two things.

~adv. With a snap. [Partly from Middle Low German or Middle Dutch *snappen,* to seize, speak hastily; partly imitative.]

snap bean *n. Chiefly U.S.* A bean, such as the **string bean** (see), cultivated for its unripe, crisp pods.

snap-brim (snáp-brim) *n.* A hat having a flexible brim, usually turned down in front and up at the back.

snap-drag-on (snáp-draggən) *n.* Any of several plants of the genera *Antirrhinum* or *Misopates;* especially, *A. majus,* of the Mediterranean region, having clusters of two-lipped, variously coloured flowers. [From a fanciful likening of the flower to a dragon's mouth.]

snap fastener *n. Chiefly U.S.* A **press stud** (see).

snap-per (snáppər) *n., pl.* **snappers** or collectively **snapper** (for senses 2, 3, and 4). **1.** One that snaps. **2.** Any of numerous widely distributed marine fishes of the family Lutjanidae. **3.** A large, red carnivorous Australian fish of the genus Pagrosomus. **4.** A snapping turtle.

snapping beetle *n.* The **click beetle** (see).

snap-pish (snáppish) *adj.* **1.** Liable to snap or bite, as a dog might be. **2.** Liable to speak sharply or curtly; irritable; curt. **—snap-pish-ly** *adv.* **—snap-pish-ness** *n.*

snap-py (snáppi) *adj.* **-pier, -piest. 1.** *Informal.* Lively or energetic; brisk. **2.** *Informal.* Smart or chic in appearance. **3.** Snappish. **—make it snappy.** *Informal.* Be quick; hurry up. **—snap-pi-ly** *adv.* **—snap-pi-ness** *n.*

snap ring *n.* In mountaineering, an oval-shaped or pear-shaped steel ring that is snapped to the eye of a piton and through which a rope is run.

snap roll *n.* An aerial manoeuvre in which an aircraft is put through a sharp roll of 360 degrees about its longitudinal axis.

snap-shot (snáp-shot) *n.* An informal photograph taken with a small hand-held camera.

snare¹ (snair) *n.* **1.** A trapping device, often consisting of a noose, used for capturing birds and small animals. **2.** Anything that serves to entangle, trap, or catch out the unwary. **3.** A surgical instrument with a wire loop controlled by a mechanism in the handle, used to remove growths, such as tumours and polyps.

~tr.v. snared, snaring, snares. 1. To trap (an animal) with a snare. **2.** To entrap or ensare. [Middle English, Old English *sneare,* from Old Norse *snara.*] **—snar-er** *n.*

snare² *n.* **1.** Any of the wires or cords stretched across the lower skin of a snare drum to increase reverberation. **2.** A snare drum. [Probably from Middle Dutch, string.]

snare drum *n.* A small double-headed drum having a snare or snares stretched across the lower head to increase reverberation.

snarl¹ (snarl) *v.* **snarled, snarling, snarls. —intr. 1.** To growl viciously while baring the teeth. **2.** To speak angrily or threateningly. **—tr.** To utter with anger or hostility.

~n. 1. A vicious growl. **2.** Any vicious or hostile utterance or expression. [From obsolete *snar,* to snarl, from Middle Low German *snarren.*] **—snarl-er** *n.* **—snarl-ing-ly** *adv.* **—snarl-y** *adj.*

snarl² *n.* **1.** A tangled mass, as of hair or yarn. **2.** Any confused, complicated, or tangled situation.

~v. snarled, snarling, snarls. —intr. To become tangled or confused. **—tr. 1.** To tangle or knot (hair or yarn, for example). **2.** To bring into a confused or tangled condition. Often used with *up: Traffic was snarled up at the lights.* [Middle English *snarle;* perhaps akin to SNARE (trap).] **—snarl-er** *n.* **—snarl-y** *adj.*

snarl-up (snárl-up) *n. British Informal.* A situation in which there is confusion, obstruction, or entanglement: *a traffic snarl-up.*

snatch (snach) *v.* **snatched, snatching, snatches. —tr. 1.** To grasp or seize abruptly or violently: *snatched her handbag.* **2.** To take, get,

or obtain hurriedly, unexpectedly, or improperly: *snatch a bite to eat; snatched a goal in the closing minutes.* **3.** To rescue or save opportunely: *snatched from death.* —*intr.* To seize or grasp, or attempt to seize or grasp. Used with *at: snatched at the chance.*
~*n.* **1.** The act or an action of snatching; a quick grasp or grab. **2.** A brief period of time: *slept in snatches.* **3.** A small amount; a bit or fragment: *a snatch of dialogue.* **4.** In weightlifting, a lift in which one raises the weight from the floor to above one's head in one movement. **5.** *British Informal.* A robbery: *a wages snatch.* **6.** *U.S. Slang.* A kidnapping. [Middle English *snacchen, snecchen*†, to make a sudden gesture.] **—snatch·er** *n.*

snatch block *n. Nautical.* A block that can be opened on one side to receive the looped part of a rope.

snatch·y (snáchi) *adj.* **-ier, -iest.** Occurring in snatches; intermittent; spasmodic.

snaz·zy (snázzi) *adj. Informal.* **-zier, -ziest.** Smooth, fashionable, or flashy. [Perhaps a blend of SNAPPY and JAZZY.]

sneak (sneek) *v.* **sneaked** or *U.S. nonstandard* **snuck** (snuk), **sneaking, sneaks.** —*intr.* **1.** To go or move in a quiet, stealthy way; slink: *sneaked out of the meeting.* **2.** To behave in a furtive or cowardly manner. **3.** *British Slang.* To tell tales or inform on others. —*tr.* **1.** To move, give, take, or put in a quiet, stealthy manner: *sneak a chocolate into one's mouth.* **2.** *Informal.* To steal.
~*n.* **1.** One who sneaks; a stealthy, cowardly, or underhand person. **2.** *Chiefly U.S.* An instance of sneaking, such as a stealthy movement. **3.** *British Slang.* One who tells tales or sneaks.
~*adj.* Acting with or involving secrecy, stealth, or surprise: *a sneak attack.* [Of dialectal origin, perhaps ultimately akin to Old English *snīcan,* to crawl, Old Norse *snīkja*†.]

sneak·er (snéekər) *n.* **1.** One who sneaks. **2.** *Chiefly U.S.* A canvas shoe with a soft rubber sole.

sneak·ing (snéeking) *adj.* **1.** Acting in a stealthy, furtive way. **2.** Unavowed; secret: *a sneaking affection.* **3.** Gradually growing or persistent: *a sneaking suspicion.* **—sneak·ing·ly** *adv.*

sneak preview *n.* **1.** *Informal.* A chance or opportunity to see something before it is on public view: *was given a sneak preview of her new dress.* **2.** *U.S.* A single showing of a film prior to its general release, usually as an addition to an announced programme.

sneak thief *n.* A burglar who enters without breaking in.

sneak·y (snéeki) *adj.* **-ier, -iest.** Furtive, underhand, or deceitful. **—sneak·i·ly** *adv.* **—sneak·i·ness** *n.*

sneer (sneer) *n.* **1.** A scornful facial expression characterised by a slight raising of one corner of the upper lip. **2.** Any contemptuous facial expression, sound, or statement.
~*v.* **sneered, sneering, sneers.** —*tr.* To utter with a sneer or in a sneering manner. —*intr.* **1.** To assume a sneer to express a scornful, contemptuous, or derisive attitude: *sneered at his amateur efforts.* **2.** To speak or write in a scornful, contemptuous, or derisive manner. [16th century : perhaps from Low Dutch *sneere*†.] **—sneer·er** *n.* **—sneer·ful** *adj.* **—sneer·ing·ly** *adv.*

sneeze (sneez) *intr.v.* **sneezed, sneezing, sneezes.** To expel air forcibly from the mouth and nose in an explosive, spasmodic, involuntary action resulting from irritation, as from dust, in the nose. **—sneeze at.** *Informal.* To dismiss lightly; consider as of little worth. Used in negative statements: *an offer not to be sneezed at.*
~*n.* An instance of sneezing. [Middle English *snesen,* misreading of obsolete *fnesen,* Old English *fnēosan* (unattested), from Old Norse *fnȳsa* (imitative).] **—sneez·er** *n.* **—sneez·y** *adj.*

sneeze·wort (snéez-wurt || -wawrt) *n.* A plant, *Achillea ptarmica,* native to Europe, having loosely clustered, daisy-like white flowers. [The dried leaves were used to induce sneezing.]

Snell's Law (snelz) *n. Physics.* The principle that in refraction of a light ray at a boundary between two mediums, the sine of the angle of incidence divided by the sine of the angle of refraction at the boundary is a constant for the given mediums. [After Willebrord *Snell* (1591–1626), Dutch physicist.]

snib (snib) *tr.v.* **snibbed, snibbing, snibs.** *Chiefly Scottish.* To bolt (a door).
~*n.* A latch or bolt. [Origin obscure.]

snick (snik) *tr.v.* **snicked, snicking, snicks.** **1.** To make a cut, incision, or notch in. **2.** In cricket, to hit (a ball) lightly, off the edge of one's bat.
~*n.* **1.** A small cut, notch or incision. **2.** In cricket, a hit in which the ball is snicked. [Perhaps from SNICKERSNEE, or perhaps from Scandinavian; compare Old Norse *snikka,* to whittle.]

snick·er (sníckər) *n.* **1.** A whinny or neigh. **2.** *Chiefly U.S.* A snigger.
~*intr.v.* **snickered, -ering, -ers.** To make a snicker. [Imitative.] **—snick·er·ing·ly** *adv.*

snick·er·snee (sníckər-snée || *chiefly U.S.* -snee) *n.* A large knife resembling a sword. Used humorously. [Earlier *stick or snee,* a fight with knives : Dutch *steken,* to stick, stab, from Middle Dutch + *snijden,* to cut, from Middle Dutch *snīden.*]

snide (snīd) *adj.* **1.** Derogatory in a malicious, superior way; sarcastic. **2.** Fake; counterfeit. [19th century (cant) : origin obscure.]

sniff (snif) *v.* **sniffed, sniffing, sniffs.** —*intr.* **1.** To inhale a short, audible breath through the nose, as in smelling something or stopping one's nose from running. **2.** To indicate ridicule, contempt, or doubt by or as if by sniffing. Often used with *at.* —*tr.* **1.** To inhale (a powdered drug, for example) forcibly through the nose. **2.** To smell or try to smell by sniffing. **3.** To perceive or detect by or as if by sniffing. **4.** To utter contemptuously, with or as if with a sniff.
~*n.* **1.** An instance or the sound of sniffing. **2.** Anything that is sniffed or perceived by sniffing; an odour; a whiff. [Middle English *sniffen* (imitative).]

snif·fle (sníff'l) *intr.v.* **-fled, -fling, -fles.** To breathe audibly through a congested nose, as when crying or suffering from a cold.
~*n.* **1.** An act or sound of sniffling. **2.** *Plural. Informal.* A condition, such as a head cold, accompanied by sniffles. Preceded by *the.* [Frequentative of SNIFF.]

snif·fy (sníffi) *adj.* **-fier, -fiest.** *Informal.* Disposed to showing arrogance or contempt; haughty; disdainful.

snif·ter (sníftər) *n.* **1.** *Slang.* A small amount of an alcoholic drink. **2.** *U.S.* A pear-shaped glass with a narrow top, as used in serving brandy. [From dialectal *snifter,* to sniff, perhaps from Scandinavian; compare Middle Swedish *snypta,* Middle Danish *snyfte.*]

snig·ger (sníggər) *n.* A snide, slightly stifled laugh.
~*v.* **sniggered, -gering, -gers.** —*intr.* To utter a snigger. —*tr.* To express by means of a snigger. [Variant of SNICKER.]

snip (snip) *v.* **snipped, snipping, snips.** —*tr.* To cut, clip, or separate in a short, quick stroke or strokes with scissors or shears. —*intr.* To cut or clip with short, quick strokes.
~*n.* **1.** An act of snipping or the sound produced by snipping. **2. a.** A small cut made with scissors or shears. **b.** A small piece cut or clipped off. **3.** *Informal.* **a.** Something accomplished without difficulty. **b.** *British.* A bargain. **4.** *Plural.* Small shears used in cutting sheet metal. Also called "tinsnips". **5.** *U.S. Informal.* A small, insignificant person or thing, especially one that is irritating. [Low German or Dutch *snippen,* to snap (imitative).]

snipe (snīp) *n., pl.* **snipe** or **snipes.** **1.** Any of various long-billed wading birds of the genus *Gallinago;* especially, the common, widely distributed species *G. gallinago.* **2.** Any of various similar or related birds. **3.** A shot or gunshot from a concealed place.
~*intr.v.* **sniped, sniping, snipes.** **1.** To shoot at individuals from a concealed place. Often used with *at.* **2.** To direct snide, carping criticism, especially from a safe position. Often used with *at.* [Middle English, perhaps from Old Norse *(mȳri)snīpa*†, (moor) snipe.]

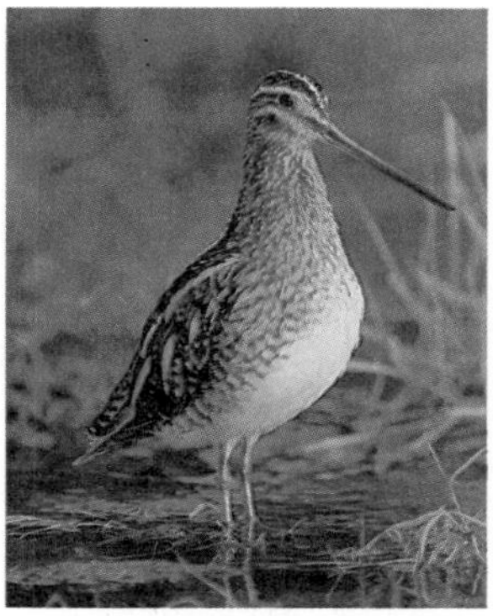

snipe *The long bill of this shore bird – which is found in warm and temperate regions around the world – enables it to forage for worms, beetles, and grubs among reeds and grasses along the water's edge. The species shown here is the common snipe,* Gallinago gallinago.

snipe fish *n.* Any fish of the family Macrorhamphosidae, having a long snout.

snipe fly *n.* Any of various two-winged predatory flies of the family Rhagionidae.

snip·er (snīpər) *n.* One who shoots at people from a concealed place, especially a marksman detailed to pick off enemy soldiers.

snip·pet (snípppit) *n.* A small piece; a fragment. [Diminutive of SNIP.]

snitch (snich) *v.* **snitched, snitching, snitches.** *Slang.* —*tr.* To steal (especially something of little value). —*intr.* To turn informer. Usually used with *on.*
~*n. Slang.* **1.** An informer; a sneak. **2.** The nose. [17th century (in the sense, nose, to strike the nose) : origin obscure.]

sniv·el (snívv'l) *intr.v.* **-elled** or *U.S.* **-eled, -elling** or *U.S.* **-eling, -els.** **1.** To cry or weep with sniffling. **2.** To speak or whine tearfully. **3.** To run at the nose. **4.** To sniffle.
~*n.* **1.** The act or an instance of sniffling or snivelling. **2.** Nasal mucus. [Middle English *snevelen,* Old English *snyflan* (unattested), akin to *snyflung, snofl,* mucus.] **—sniv·el·er, sniv·el·ler** *n.*

snob (snob) *n.* **1.** One who overvalues rank and status, and despises his supposed inferiors. **2.** An arrogant or affected person who strives to flatter, imitate, or associate with people of higher status or prestige. **3.** One who has or affects refined or esoteric tastes in cultural matters, and who despises anything that does not match these standards. [18th century (meaning "shoemaker", now dialect) : origin obscure.] **—snob·ber·y, snob·bism** *n.* **—snob·bish** *adj.* **—snob·bish·ly** *adv.* **—snob·bish·ness** *n.*

Sno-cat (snṓ-kat) *n.* A trademark for a type of snowmobile.

snoek (snōōk) *n. South African.* An edible fish, the **barracouta** *(see),* often dried and salted and eaten cold. [Afrikaans. See **snook**[1].]

snog (snog) *intr.v.* **snogged, snogging, snogs.** *British Informal.* To kiss and cuddle.
~*n.* An act of snogging. [20th century : origin obscure.]

snood (snōōd) *n.* **1.** A small netlike cap worn by women to keep the hair in place. **2.** A headband or fillet.
~*tr.v.* **snooded, snooding, snoods.** To hold (the hair) in place with a snood. [Middle English (unattested), Old English *snōd*†.]

snook[1] (snōōk || snōōk) *n., pl.* **snook** or **snooks.** Any of several chiefly marine fishes of the family Centropomidae; especially, *Centropomus undecimalis,* of warm Atlantic waters. Also called "robalo". [Dutch *snoek,* pike, from Middle Dutch *snoec*†.]

snook[2] (snōōk, snōōk) *n. British.* A deliberately offensive gesture signifying contempt or disrespect, made by putting the thumb to the nose, with the fingers stretched out; an act of thumbing the nose. **—cock a snook.** **1.** To make such a gesture. **2.** To show contempt or disrespect. [19th century : origin obscure.]

snoo·ker (snōōkər || *chiefly U.S.* snōōkər) *n.* **1.** A game played on a billiard table with 15 red balls and 6 others of different colours, each becoming, in a fixed order, the object ball which must be hit into one of the side pockets by the cue ball, which is white. **2.** A position in this game in which the cue ball is so placed that a player cannot hit the object ball directly. See feature, next page.
~*tr.v.* **snookered, -kering, -kers.** **1.** To make (one's opponent) play from the position of a snooker. **2.** To put in a difficult or impossible position; prevent from succeeding; thwart.

snoop (snōōp) *intr.v.* **snooped, snooping, snoops.** *Informal.* To pry into the private affairs of others, especially by prowling about.
~*n. Informal.* One who snoops. [Dutch *snoepen,* to eat on the sly.] **—snoop·er** *n.*

PRONUNCIATION KEY

a, trap; aa, father; ai, fair;
ar, star; aw, lawn; ay, play;
b, bb, stab; rubber;
ch, church; ck, ticket;
d, dd, dead; ladder; e, dress;
ee, bee; er, defer; ew, few;
ewr, pure; ə, about;
ər, letter; f, ff, fife; differ;
g, gg, giggle; h, hat; i, kit;
ī, price; īr, fire; j, judge;
k, kick; l, ll, let; 'l, needle;
m, mm, man; n, nn, no;
'n, sudden; ng, thing; o, lot;
ō, no; ōō, foot; ōō, shoe;
oor, poor; ow, cow;
owr, hour; oy, boy;
p, pp, pepper; r, rr, red;
s, ss, sauce; sh, ship;
t, tt, totter; th, thick; th, this;
smooth; u, cut; ur, turn;
v, vv, valve; w, wet; y, yes;
z, zz, zebra; zh, vision;
pleasure

IN FOREIGN WORDS:

aN, oN, Saint-Saëns;
hl, Llanelli; Hluhluwe;
kh, loch; lough; Khaled

STRESS MARK:

ín-sīt, insight; in-sīt, incite

snooker

MASTERING THE REACTIONS OF THE CUE BALL

A game invented to end the boredom of army officers

Snooker is a game played with 22 coloured balls on a billiard table. It was invented in 1875 by British Army officers at Ootacamund, southern India, who were bored playing billiards. The player uses his cue to strike the white, or cue, ball so that it pots a coloured ball without itself entering the pocket. The skill lies not in merely potting the balls but in making the cue ball take up position for the next pot. The balls have to be potted in order into any of the six pockets. Red balls that are potted are out of play but other colours are returned to the table until all the reds have been potted. It is possible to "snooker" an opponent by leaving the cue ball behind a coloured ball, making it difficult for the player to hit the correct ball. A sequence of successful strokes is called a break. A player continues until he fails to pot a ball. Striking the wrong ball is a foul which gives away points. The "frame", or game, ends when all balls are potted or one player concedes. There is no fixed number of frames in a match.

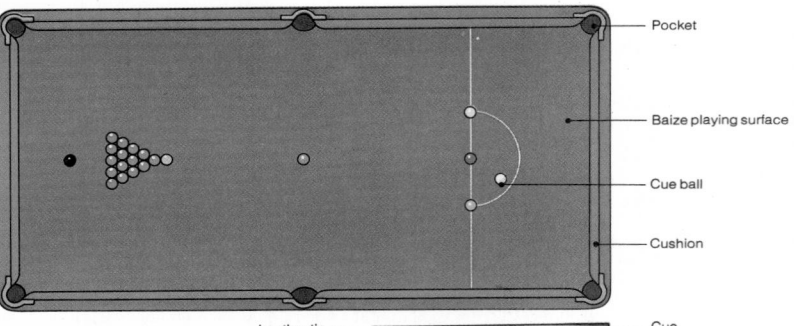

— Pocket

— Baize playing surface

— Cue ball

— Cushion

Leather tip — — Cue

SCORING *The players must pot first a red ball (1 point) then a colour until all 15 reds are potted. Then the colours are sunk in order: yellow (2 points), green (3), brown (4), blue (5), pink (6), black (7). The highest possible score for clearing all the balls in one break is 147.*

snoop·y (sno͞o'pi) *adj.* **-ier, -iest.** *Informal.* Tending to snoop; prying.

snoot (sno͞ot) *n. Slang.* The nose. [Variant of SNOUT.]

snoot·y (sno͞o'ti) *adj.* **-ier, -iest.** *Informal.* Snobbish or aloof; haughty. [20th century : origin obscure.]

snooze (sno͞oz) *intr.v.* **snoozed, snoozing, snoozes.** *Informal.* To take a light nap; doze.
~*n. Informal.* A brief light sleep. [18th century (cant) : origin obscure.]

snore (snor ‖ snôr) *intr.v.* **snored, snoring, snores.** To make snorting noises caused by the vibration of the soft palate, by breathing through both nose and mouth while sleeping.
~*n.* An instance of snoring or the noise produced by snoring. [Middle English *snoren*, to snort (probably imitative).] —**snor·er** *n.*

snor·kel (snôrk'l, *also* shnôrk'l) *n.* 1. A retractable vertical tube in a submarine, containing air-intake and exhaust pipes for the engines and for ventilation and which permits extended periods of submergence at periscope depth. 2. A breathing apparatus used by skin divers, consisting of a long tube held in the mouth which projects above the surface of the water.
~*intr.v.* **snorkelled** or *U.S.* **-keled, -kelling** or *U.S.* **-keling, -kels.** To swim under water using a snorkel. [German *Schnorchel*, from (dialectal) German, snout, from *schnarchen*, to snore, from Middle High German *snarche(l)n*.]

Snor·ri Stur·lu·son (snôrri stúrləss'n) (1178–1241). Icelandic chieftain and historian. His works include *Heimskringla*, a series of sagas, and the Younger or Prose *Edda*.

snort (snort) *v.* **snorted, snorting, snorts.** —*intr.* 1. **a.** To exhale forcibly and noisily through the nostrils, as a horse does. **b.** To inhale forcibly through the nose or mouth and so produce from the soft palate a vibratory snoring noise. 2. To express scorn, ridicule, or contempt with or as if with a snort. 3. *Informal.* To emit a loud outburst of laughter. —*tr.* 1. To express with a snort. 2. To eject from the nostrils with air or as with a snort. 3. *Slang.* To inhale (a powdered drug, such as cocaine) through the nose.
~*n.* 1. The act or sound of snorting. 2. *Slang.* A small alcoholic drink, especially when swallowed in one gulp. [Middle English *snorten* (imitative).]

snort·er (snôrtər) *n.* 1. One that snorts. 2. *Informal.* Anything that is outstanding, as in size, appearance, or severity.

snot (snot) *n.* 1. Nasal mucus; phlegm. Often considered vulgar. 2. *Slang.* A nasty or contemptible person. [Middle English *snot(te)*, from Low German or from Old English *gesnot;* akin to SNOUT.]

snot·rag (snót-rag) *n. British Slang.* A handkerchief.

snot·ty (snótti) *adj.* **-tier, -tiest.** *Slang.* 1. Dirtied with nasal mucus. 2. **a.** Nasty; unpleasant. **b.** Snooty; self-important.

snout (snowt) *n.* 1. The projecting nose, jaws, or front part of an animal's muzzle. 2. A similar extended front part of the head in certain insects, such as weevils. 3. A spout, nozzle, or similar projection likened to a snout. 4. *Slang.* The human nose. [Middle English *sn(o)ute*, probably from Middle Dutch *snūt(e).*]

snout beetle *n.* A weevil (see).

snow (sno) *n.* 1. **a.** Solid precipitation in the form of small white or translucent ice crystals of various shapes originating in the atmosphere as frozen particles of water vapour. **b.** A mass of fallen snow lying on the ground: *children playing in the snow.* 2. **a.** Anything resembling snow, such as frozen carbon dioxide. **b.** The white specks on a television screen resulting from weak reception. 3. A fall of snow. 4. *Slang.* Cocaine or heroin in powdered form.
~*v.* **snowed, snowing, snows.** —*intr.* To fall as snow. —*tr.* 1. To cover, shut off, or close in with snow. Used with *in, over, under,* or *up.* 2. *Chiefly U.S. Slang.* To overwhelm with insincere talk, especially with flattery. —**snow under.** To overwhelm, especially with work. [Middle English *snawe, snow,* Old English *snāw.*]

Snow (sno), **C(harles) P(ercy), Baron** (1905–80). British novelist, noted for his interest in the "two cultures" of science and the humanities. His long, semi-autobiographical novel sequence *Strangers and Brothers* includes such works as *The Masters* (1951) and *The Corridors of Power* (1964). He became a senior civil servant and parliamentary secretary in the ministry of technology (1964–66).

snow·ball (sno-bawl) *n.* 1. A mass of soft, wet snow packed into a ball that can be thrown, as in play. 2. A drink consisting of advocaat and lemonade.
~*v.* **snowballed, -balling, -balls.** —*intr.* 1. To throw snowballs. 2. To grow rapidly and uncontrollably, as in size or significance, like a snowball rolling over snow. —*tr.* To throw snowballs at.

snowball tree *n.* The cultivated variety of the guelder rose, having ball-like clusters of sterile flowers.

snow·ber·ry (sno-bri, -bəri, -berri) *n., pl.* **-ries.** Any of various shrubs of the genus *Symphoricarpos;* especially, *S. rivularis,* having small pinkish flowers and white berries.

snow·bird (sno-burd) *n.* 1. Any of several birds, such as the junco, seen mainly in winter conditions. 2. Any white or partly white bird, such as the snow bunting.

snow blindness *n.* Usually temporary conjunctivitis and deteriorated vision caused by sunlight reflected from snow or ice. —**snow·blind** (sno-blīnd) *adj.*

snow·blink (sno-blingk) *n.* A white glow in the sky reflected from snowfields.

snow·bound (sno-bownd) *adj.* Confined in one place by heavy snow; snowed-in.

snow·broth (sno-broth ‖ -brawth) *n.* Melted snow; slush.

snow bunting *n.* A bird, *Plectrophenax nivalis,* of northern regions, having black and white plumage in the male.

snow·cap (sno-kap) *n.* A cap of snow, as on a mountaintop. —**snow·capped** *adj.*

snow chain *n.* A linked metal covering for a tyre, used for improved grip on snowy or icy surfaces. Also called "tyre chain".

Snow·don (snod'n). *Welsh* **Yr Wydd·fa** (ər o͞o-ithvə). Highest peak in Wales, situated in northwestern Gwynedd, in the Snowdon range. The summit rises to 1 085 metres (3,560 feet) and can be reached by a rack and pinion railway. The scenic surrounding area has been a part of the Snowdonia National Park since 1951.

Snowdon, Anthony (Charles Robert) Armstrong-Jones, Earl of (1930–). British photographer. He married Princess Margaret in 1960. They were divorced in 1978.

snow·drift (sno-drift) *n.* A bank of snow heaped up by the wind.

snow·drop (sno-drop) *n.* Any of several bulbous plants of the genus *Galanthus,* native to Eurasia; especially *G. nivalis,* having solitary, nodding white flowers that bloom early in spring.

snow·fall (sno-fawl) *n.* 1. The amount of snow that falls during a given period or in a given area. 2. A fall of snow.

snow·field (sno-feeld) *n.* A large, permanently snow-covered area.

snow·flake (sno-flayk) *n.* 1. An aggregation of ice crystals which fall as snow. 2. Any of several bulbous plants of the genus *Leucojum,* native to Europe, having white or whitish flowers.

snow goose *n.* A goose, *Chen caerulescens,* that breeds in northern regions, having white plumage with black wing tips.

snow job *n. U.S. Slang.* An effort to overwhelm or deceive with insincere talk, especially flattery.

snow leopard *n.* A large feline mammal, *Uncia uncia,* of the highlands of central Asia, having long, thick, whitish fur with dark markings. Also called "ounce".

snow line *n.* The lower altitudinal boundary of a permanently snow-covered area, such as the snowcap of a mountain, higher in summer than in winter.

snow·man (sno-man) *n., pl.* **-men** (-men). A figure, usually intended to resemble a man, made of a packed mass of snow.

snow·mo·bile (sno-mo-beel, -mə-) *n.* A small vehicle with ski-like runners in front and tanklike treads, used for moving on snow. [SNOW + (AUTO)MOBILE.]

snow mould *n.* A plant disease affecting turf, forage grasses, and cereals caused by the fungus *Fusarium nivale* and occurring after snow or during prolonged cold weather.

snow·plough (sno-plow) *n.* 1. Any ploughlike device or vehicle used to remove snow, as from roads and railway tracks. 2. A skiing action in which the toes are turned inwards so that the skis meet in a V-shape, enabling the skier to slow down or stop.

snow·shoe (sno-sho͞o) *n.* A racket-shaped frame containing interlaced leather strips that can be attached to the foot to facilitate walking on deep snow.

snowberry *This garden shrub – originally native to North America, but which now grows wild in Europe, too – thrives in any soil and does not mind shade. Its large white berries, ignored by birds, can last all winter long.*

~intr.v. **snowshoed, -shoeing, -shoes.** To go or walk on snowshoes. **—snow·sho·er** *n.*
snow·storm (snṓ-stawrm) *n.* A storm marked by heavy snowfall and high winds; a blizzard.
snow-white (snṓ-wīt, -hwīt) *adj.* White as snow.
snow·y (snṓ-i) *adj.* **-ier, -iest. 1.** Abounding in snow; covered with or characterised by snow. **2.** Resembling or suggestive of snow; white; pure. **—snow·i·ly** *adv.* **—snow·i·ness** *n.*
Snowy Mountains. Mountain range in the Australian Alps of New South Wales, southeast Australia. Mount Kosciusko, Australia's highest mountain, is among its peaks. The Snowy Mountains Hydroelectric Scheme provides water for irrigation and hydroelectricity for Victoria and New South Wales.
snowy owl *n.* A large owl, *Nyctea scandiaca,* of tundra and high northern moorland regions, having predominantly white plumage with black or brownish markings on the upper parts.
S.N.P. Scottish National Party.
snr., Snr. senior.
snub (snub) *tr.v.* **snubbed, snubbing, snubs. 1.** To treat with scorn or contempt; slight by ignoring or behaving coldly towards. **2.** To reprove or stop short in a sharp, cutting manner; rebuke. **3. a.** To check suddenly the movement of (a rope or cable running out) by turning it about a post. **b.** To secure (a vessel or animal, for example) in this manner.
~n. **1.** A deliberate slight or affront. **2.** A sudden checking, as of a rope or cable running out.
~adj. Short and slightly flattened at the tip. Said of a nose. [Middle English *snubben,* to rebuke, from Old Norse *snubba.*] **—snub·ber** *n.*
snub-nosed (snúb-nōzd) *adj.* Having a short nose with a slightly flattened tip.
snuck. *U.S. Nonstandard.* Past tense and past participle of **sneak.**
snuff¹ (snuf) *v.* **snuffed, snuffing, snuffs.** *—tr.* **1.** To inhale through the nose; sniff. **2.** To sense, perceive, or examine by or as if by smelling. *—intr.* To snort or sniff.
~n. An act of snuffing or the sound produced in snuffing; a sniff. [Probably from Middle Dutch *snuffen.*]
snuff² *n.* The charred portion of a candlewick.
~tr.v. **snuffed, snuffing, snuffs. 1.** To cut off the charred portion of (a candlewick). **2.** To extinguish (a candle or lamp, for example), especially by smothering the flame. Often used with *out.* **3.** To put a sudden end to; destroy. Usually used with *out.* **4.** *Slang.* To kill. **—snuff it.** *Slang.* To die. [Middle English *snoffe*† (noun).]
snuff³ *n.* **1.** A preparation of finely pulverised tobacco that can be drawn up into the nostrils by inhaling. **2.** The quantity of this inhaled at a single time; a pinch of snuff. **3.** Any powdery substance, such as a medicine, taken by inhaling. **—up to snuff.** *Informal.* **1.** *Chiefly British.* Not easily deceived. **2.** *Chiefly U.S.* As good as usual or as expected; up to scratch.
~intr.v. **snuffed, snuffing, snuffs.** To take snuff. [Dutch *snuf,* short for *snuf(tabak),* (tobacco) for snuffing, from Middle Dutch *snuffen,* to SNUFF.]
snuff·box (snúf-boks) *n.* A small, often highly decorative box with a hinged lid that is used for carrying snuff in the pocket.
snuff·er¹ (snúffər) *n.* One who uses snuff.
snuffer² *n.* **1.** A small hollow cone with a handle, used to snuff out candles. **2.** *Plural.* An instrument resembling a pair of shears that is used for cutting the snuff from or for extinguishing candles.
snuf·fle (snúff'l) *v.* **-fled, -fling, -fles.** *—intr.* **1.** To breathe noisily, as through a congested nose or when crying; to sniffle. **2.** To talk whiningly or nasally; snivel. *—tr.* To utter in a snuffling tone or express by means of a snuffle.
~n. **1.** An act or the sound of snuffling. **2.** *Plural. Informal.* A condition, such as a head cold, accompanied by snuffles. Preceded by *the.* [Probably from Low German or Dutch *snuffelen.*] **—snuf·fler** *n.*
snug (snug) *adj.* **snugger, snuggest. 1.** Comfortably sheltered from the cold and the weather; cosy. **2.** Small but well-arranged; compact: *a snug little flat.* **3. a.** Closely secured and well-built; especially, adequately protected against bad weather. Said of a ship. **b.** Seaworthy. **4.** Close-fitting. Said of a garment. **5.** Providing adequate means for a relatively comfortable life: *a snug income.* —See Synonyms at **comfortable.**
~tr.v. **snugged, snugging, snugs. 1.** To make snug or secure. **2.** *Nautical.* To prepare (a vessel) to weather a storm, as by taking in sail or securing movable gear. Often used with *down.*
~n. British. A small, enclosed or private bar in a public house or inn. [16th century (a nautical term meaning neat, trim) : perhaps from Scandinavian; akin to Old Norse *snöggr,* "close-cropped".] **—snug, snug·ly** *adv.* **—snug·ness** *n.*
snug·ger·y (snúggəri) *n., pl.* **-ies. 1.** A snug position or place. **2.** A snug.
snug·gle (snúgg'l) *v.* **-gled, -gling, -gles.** *—intr.* To lie or press close together; nestle or cuddle. Often used with *together, with,* or *up.* *—tr.* To draw close or hold closely, as for comfort or in affection; hug. [Frequentative of SNUG (verb).]
so¹ (sō; *occasional weak form* sə) *adv.* **1. a.** In the manner described, shown, expressed, implied, or indicated; thus: *"She became his loyal friend and remained so to the end"* (Constantine Fitzgibbon). **b.** In such a manner: *The table was so arranged that I sat next to him.* **2. a.** To the amount or degree expressed or understood; in such quantity or to such an extent: *He was so weary that he fell.* **b.** To a certain degree or limit: *so far, so good; I can only do so much.* **c.** To the same degree or extent: *not quite so hot as yesterday.* **3.** To a great extent or degree; very or very much: *so kind of you to come; loved her so.* **4.** Because of the reason given; consequently; as a result: *He was weary and so he fell.* **5.** In the same way; also; likewise: *You were on time and so was I.* **6.** Then; apparently. Used in expressing astonishment, disapproval, or sarcasm: *So you think you've got troubles?* **7.** In truth; indeed: *"Your button's undone". "So it is!"* **—so as to.** In order to: *started early so as to avoid the rush.* **—so there.** My decision is final. Used to add force to expressions of defiance or refusal: *Well I'm going to do it anyway, so there* **—so what?** Also **so?** What relevance or importance does that have?
~adj. **1.** True; factual: *It is so.* **2.** Perfectly ordered or arranged. Usually used in the phrase *just so.*
~conj. **1.** With the purpose or reason that; in order that. Usually used with *that: I stopped so that you could catch up.* **2.** With the result or consequence that: *He agreed, so they went ahead.*
~pron. **1.** That; this; the same as has already been implied or specified: *I don't think so; Did he say so?* **2.** Approximately that quantity, amount, or number: *another ten minutes or so.*
~interj. Used to express surprise or comprehension. [Middle English *so, s(w)a,* Old English *swā.*]

Usage: *So,* used as a conjunction, is generally followed by *that* when it introduces a clause stating purpose or reason *(He stayed a day longer so that he could avoid the traffic),* but the *that* is often dropped in informal contexts. In the expression of result or consequence, the use of *so* without *that* is more widely acceptable *(The traffic was very heavy, so he stayed a day longer),* though some stylists prefer alternative constructions (such as *and therefore he stayed a day longer*). See also Usage note at **as.**

so². *Music.* Variant of **soh.**
So. *Chiefly U.S.* south; southern.
s.o. seller's option.
soak (sōk) *v.* **soaked, soaking, soaks.** *—tr.* **1.** To make thoroughly wet or saturated; drench; wet through. **2. a.** To immerse in liquid, often for a prolonged period; steep. **b.** To remove or draw out by immersion. Usually used with *out: soak out blood stains.* **3.** To absorb (liquid) through pores or interstices. Usually used with *up.* **4.** *Informal.* To take in eagerly or effortlessly, as if by absorption; absorb or assimilate. Used with *up: soaking up the sun; to soak up facts.* **5.** *Informal.* **a.** To drink (alcohol), especially to excess. **b.** To make (a person) drunk. **6.** *Informal.* To charge or tax excessively; force to pay too much. *—intr.* **1.** To be immersed until thoroughly saturated. **2.** To penetrate or permeate; seep. Often used with *in, into, through,* or *away.* **3.** *Slang.* To drink to excess.
~n. **1.** The act or process of soaking or the condition of being soaked. **2.** *Informal.* A drunkard. [Middle English *soken,* Old English *socian,* akin to *sūcan,* to SUCK.] **—soak·er** *n.*
soak·age (sṓkij) *n.* **1.** The process of soaking or the condition of being soaked. **2.** The amount of liquid that soaks into or through an object or seeps out of it.
soak·a·way (sṓk-ə-way) *n. Chiefly British.* A place, such as a pit or depression in the ground filled with broken bricks and covered with soil, through which water (usually rainwater conducted by a pipe) drains away.
Soames (sōmz), **(Arthur) Christopher (John), Baron** (1920–). British politician and diplomat. He held several posts in Conservative cabinets (1958–64), and was British ambassador to Paris (1968–72). From December 1979 to April 1980, he was governor of Southern Rhodesia, before its independence as Zimbabwe.
so-and-so (sṓ-ən-sō) *n., pl.* **-sos. 1.** A person or thing left unspecified. **2.** *Informal.* A very unpleasant person. Used euphemistically in place of various unsavoury epithets: *He's a real so-and-so.* Also used adjectivally: *her so-and-so father.*
soap (sōp) *n.* **1.** A cleansing agent, manufactured in bars, granules, flakes, or liquid form, consisting of a mixture of the sodium salts of various fatty acids made from natural oils and fats. Compare **detergent. 2.** *Chemistry.* A mixture of metallic salts of long chain fatty acids, especially: **a.** One containing sodium salts (*a hard soap*). **b.** One containing potassium salts (*a soft soap.*) **3.** *Slang.* Flattery. **4.** *Chiefly U.S. Informal.* A soap opera. **—no soap.** *U.S. Slang.* Impossible or without success; nothing doing: *tried to talk him out of it, but no soap.*
~tr.v. **soaped, soaping, soaps.** To treat or cover with soap. [Middle English *sope, saip,* Old English *sāpe.*]
soap·bark (sṓp-baark) *n.* **1.** A tree, *Quillaja saponaria,* of western South America, having bark used as soap and as a source of saponin. **2.** The bark of this tree. **3.** Any of several other trees or shrubs having similar bark.
soap·ber·ry (sṓp-berri) *n., pl.* **-ries. 1.** Any of various chiefly tropical New World trees of the genus *Sapindus,* having pulpy fruit that lathers like soap. **2.** The fruit of any of these trees.
soap·box (sṓp-boks) *n.* Also **soap box. 1.** A box or crate used as a temporary platform for making an impromptu or nonofficial public speech. **2.** A child's crude vehicle made of a wooden box mounted on a wheeled frame.
~adj. Designating speech-making or a public speaker characterised by ranting, fanaticism, or eccentricity. **—soap·box·er** *n.*
soap bubble *n.* **1.** A bubble formed from soapy water. **2.** Anything beautiful but transient, insubstantial, or illusory.
soap opera *n.* A broadcast serial, typically having a domestic theme and characterised by sentimentality and melodrama. [Many were originally sponsored in the United States by soap companies.]
soap plant *n.* **1.** A plant, *Chlorogalum pomeridianum,* of California,

snow leopard *Sheep, goats, and marmots are the chief prey of the snow leopard, which lives at altitudes of up to 6000 metres (20,000 feet) in the mountains of central Asia. The leopard hunts at night and is capable of leaping 9 metres (30 feet) in a single bound.*

snowplough *A modern snowplough in operation on an autobahn in West Germany. Beside its blade is a powerful blower to hurl the snow clear of the road.*

snuffbox *One of the souvenir enamelled snuffboxes made to commemorate the death of the British admiral Lord Nelson at the Battle of Trafalgar in 1805.*

FOOTBALL, THE WORLD'S FAVOURITE BALL GAME

The simple game of medieval towns that now has an international hold

Soccer has grown from a popular amateur sport of the 19th century into one of the world's great spectator entertainments, attracting crowds of 100,000 enthusiasts to major national and international matches. The game is played with a round ball between teams of 11 players each, one of whom must be a goalkeeper; he alone may handle the ball during play. The ten other players kick, head, pass to each other, and run with the ball. Their object is to place it in the opponents' goal. The winning team is the one that scores the most goals. Soccer is thought to have developed from simple contests between rival medieval towns. The Football Association was formed in England in 1863 to draw up the rules. Its cup was first played for in 1871. The Football League was formed in 1888. Football pools, a system of betting on matches, began in 1923. The first World Cup competition, won by Uruguay, was held in 1930.

1 Goalkeeper
2 Left back
3 Right back
4 Forward left back (centre back)
5 Forward right back (centre back)
6 Left midfield
7 Right midfield
8 Left wing
9 Left centre (central attacker)
10 Right centre
　　(central attacker)
11 Right wing

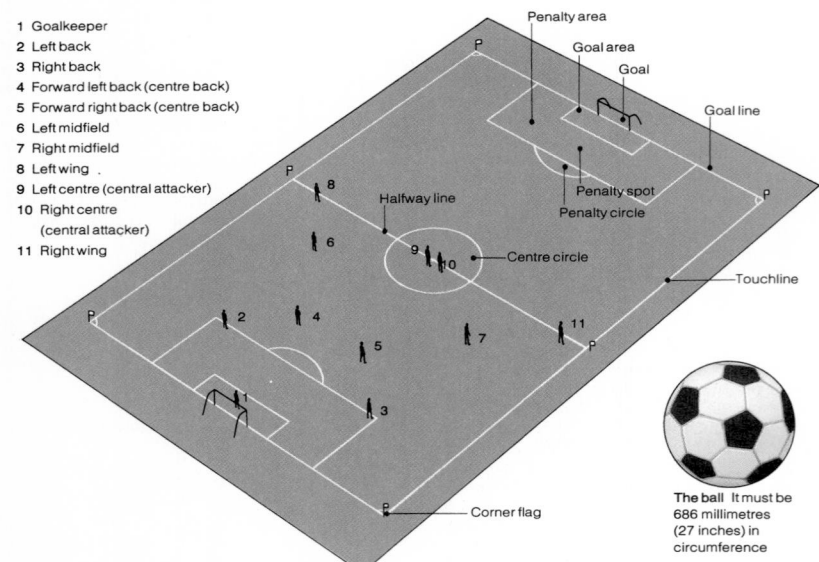

The ball It must be 686 millimetres (27 inches) in circumference

READY FOR KICK-OFF *A modern team might line up for a soccer match with, in addition to a goalkeeper, four defenders, two midfield players, and four attackers (known as 4:2:4). Many other combinations are possible – for example* 4:3:3, 3:4:3, 4:4:2, *and the like. The game is played on a marked out pitch 90–120 metres (100–130 yards) long and 45–90 metres (50–100 yards) wide. The goal is 7.3 metres (8 yards) wide, and 2.4 metres (8 feet) high.*

having small white flowers and a bulbous root formerly used as soap. **2.** Any of several other plants having parts used as soap.
soap·stone (sōp-stōn) *n.* **Steatite** *(see).* [From its soapy texture.]
soap·suds (sōp-sudz) *pl.n.* Lather or foam from soapy water.
soap·wort (sōp-wurt ‖ -wawrt) *n.* A Eurasian plant, *Saponaria officinalis,* with pale pink flowers, the leaves and stems of which make a lather when rubbed together. Also called "bouncing Bet".
soap·y (sōpi) *adj.* **-ier, -iest. 1.** Containing or consisting of soap; covered or filled with soap. **2.** Pertaining to or resembling soap. **3.** *Slang.* Unctuous; flattering in an oily way. **—soap·i·ly** *adv.* **—soap·i·ness** *n.*
soar (sor ‖ sōr) *intr.v.* **soared, soaring, soars. 1. a.** To fly upwards or rise high into the air; climb swiftly or powerfully. **b.** To rise steeply; be at a great height. **2.** To fly or glide high in the air without visibly moving the wings. **3.** *Aviation.* To glide while maintaining altitude. **4.** To rise suddenly above a normal or usual level; increase greatly. **5.** To rise to an exalted level; be inspired: *My heart soared.* **—See Synonyms at** **rise.**
~ *n.* **1.** The act of soaring. **2.** The altitude or scope attained in soaring. [Middle English *soren,* from Old French *esorer,* from Vulgar Latin *exaurāre* (unattested) : Latin *ex-,* out of + *aura,* the air, a breeze, from Greek, a breeze.] **—soar·er** *n.* **—soar·ing·ly** *adv.*
Soa·res (saʹar-ess, *Portuguese* -ish), **Mário Alberto Nobre Lopes** (1924–). Portuguese politician. Frequently imprisoned for his political views, he was eventually exiled (1970), but returned after a coup (1974) and as leader of the Socialist party became Prime Minister (1976–78). He resigned as leader in 1980.
so·a·ve (sō-aʹavay) *n.* A dry white Italian table wine. [Italian, "sweet", from Latin *suāvis,* pleasing.]
sob (sob) *v.* **sobbed, sobbing, sobs. —intr. 1.** To weep aloud with convulsing gasping and sniffling; cry uncontrollably. **2.** To make a sound resembling that of sobbing. **—tr. 1.** To utter with sobs. **2.** To put or bring (oneself) into a specified condition by sobbing: *sob oneself to sleep.* **—See Synonyms at** **cry.**
~ *n.* An act of sobbing or the sound produced in sobbing; a short, audible catch of the breath. [Middle English *sobben,* to catch

breath, probably imitative and of Low German origin; akin to Dutch dialectal *sabben†,* to suck.] **—sob·bing·ly** *adv.*
so·be·it (sō-bée-it) *conj. Archaic.* Provided that; if it be so that.
so·ber (sōbər) *adj.* **-berer, -berest. 1.** Habitually abstemious in the use of alcohol; temperate. **2.** Not intoxicated. **3.** Having or showing an earnest, dignified disposition; serious or grave. **4.** Plain or subdued; not garish or gay. Said of clothes or colours. **5.** Without frivolity, excess, exaggeration, or speculative imagination: *sober facts.* **6.** Characterised by self-control or sanity; reasonable; rational. **—See Synonyms at** **serious.**
~ *v.* **sobered, -bering, -bers. —tr.** To make sober, make less intoxicated or more serious and thoughtful. Often used with *up: a sobering experience.* **—intr.** To become sober. Often used with *up.* [Middle English *sobre,* from Old French, from Latin *sōbrius.*] **—so·ber·ly** *adv.* **—so·ber·ness** *n.*
So·bers (sōbərz), **Sir Garfield (St Auburn),** known as Garry Sobers (1936–). West Indian cricketer. He played for Barbados, Nottinghamshire, and the West Indies captaining the national side from 1965 to 1974. His many remarkable achievements include the record for the highest individual test score (365 not out).
sober·sides (sōbər-sīdz) *n., pl.* **sobersides.** *Informal.* A serious, sedate person lacking a sense of humour.
So·bran·je (sō-braʹan-yi, sə-) *n.* The Bulgarian national assembly. [Bulgarian, "assembly".]
so·bri·e·ty (sō-bríʹəti, sə-) *n.* **1.** Seriousness or gravity, as in manner or approach. **2.** Absence of drunkenness. [Middle English, from Old French *sobrieté* or Latin *sōbrietās,* from *sōbrius,* SOBER.]
so·bri·quet (sōbri-kay ‖ -káy, -ket, -két) *n.* Also **sou·bri·quet** (sōbri-, soōbri-). **1.** An affectionate or humorous nickname. **2.** An assumed name. [French *sobriquet,* earlier *soubriquet†,* (originally "a tap under the chin").]
sob sister *n.* A journalist, especially a woman, employed as a writer or editor of sob stories.
sob story *n.* A tale of personal hardship or misfortune intended to arouse pity or given as an excuse or rationalisation.
So·bu·kwe (sō-boō-kway), **Robert Mangaliso** (1924–78). Black South African political leader. He was leader of the African National Congress, and subsequently the more violence-orientated Pan-Africanist Congress. He was arrested and imprisoned by the South African government (1960–69).
soc., Soc. 1. socialist. **2.** society.
soc·age (sōckij) *n.* Feudal tenure of land by a tenant not a knight, in return for agricultural or other nonmilitary services or for payment. [Middle English *sokage,* from *soke,* SOKE.] **—soc·ag·er** *n.*
so-called (sō-káwld) *adj.* Designated thus or known by this term. Often used to imply that the thing or person so designated does not merit the term: *a so-called teetotaller.*
> *Usage:* The hyphen is used when the words are used before a noun *(these so-called friends),* and in these circumstances it is not usually felt to be necessary to add quotation marks as well. After a noun, the hyphen is not used: *his friends, so called.*
soc·cer (sōckər) *n.* The most common type of football, in which two teams of 11 players each play on a rectangular field with net goals at either end, manoeuvring a round ball mainly by kicking, heading, or by using any part of the body except the arms and hands in attempts to score points by getting the ball into the opposing team's goal. Also called "association football", "football". [From ASSOC., abbreviation of *Association (Football).*]
so·cia·bil·i·ty (sōsha-billəti) *n., pl.* **-ties. 1.** The disposition or quality of being sociable. **2.** An instance of being sociable.
so·cia·ble (sōshəb'l) *adj.* **1.** Pleasant, friendly, and enjoying good company. **2.** Providing occasion for conversation and conviviality. [French, from Latin *sociābilis,* from *sociāre,* to join, to share, from *socius,* partner.] **—so·cia·ble·ness** *n.* **—so·cia·bly** *adv.*
so·cial (sōsh'l) *adj.* **1. a.** Living or tending to live together in communities. **b.** Of, pertaining to, or characteristic of the activities of and the relations between human beings living in a community. **c.** Of or pertaining to human society and its modes of organisation: *social classes.* **2.** Living in an organised group or similar close aggregate: *social insects.* **3.** In Greek and Roman history, involving allies or members of a confederacy. **4.** Of or pertaining to fashionable or polite society: *social graces.* **5.** Sociable; fond of the company of others. **6. a.** Intended for convivial activities. **b.** Done or acting thus only in convivial circumstances rather than habitually: *social drinking.* **7.** Pertaining to or occupied with matters affecting human welfare: *a social worker.* **8.** Growing thickly in clumps, often covering a large area. Said of plant species.
~ *n.* An informal social gathering, as of the members of a club or church congregation. [From French or Latin *sociālis,* of companionship, from *socius,* companion, partner.]
social anthropology *n.* The branch of anthropology dealing with communal relationships and social customs and beliefs (such as kinship systems) in human societies, especially primitive societies.
social class. See **class** (sense 3).
social climber *n.* One striving to become a member of a higher social class.
social contract *n.* **1.** A theory of the ideal basis of political rule, advanced by political philosophers such as Hobbes, Locke, and especially Rousseau, which holds that government must rest on the consent of the governed, who freely give up certain individual rights and liberties in exchange for the advantages of having an organised government. **2.** Any reciprocal system whereby individuals or organisations give up certain freedoms in exchange for the benefits a

government can bestow; specifically, an agreement by trade unions to limit wage demands in return for other favourable government measures. Also called "social compact".

social credit *n.* **1.** An economic and political theory, formulated by the British engineer C.H. Douglas, holding that every person in a society should be paid dividends from the profits of industry and commerce. **2.** *Capital* **S,** *capital* **C.** A Canadian political party advocating this theory. **—Social Crediter** *n.*

Social Darwinism *n.* The application of some aspects of the Darwinian theory of biological evolution to the history and development of human society.

social democracy *n.* **1.** A political theory advocating a gradual advance towards socialism through democratic means. **2.** *Often capital* **S,** *capital* **D.** The aims or principles of the Social Democratic Party. **—social democrat** *n.* **—social democratic** *adj.*

Social Democratic Party *n. Abbr.* **SDP** A British political party of the centre, founded in 1981 chiefly by ex-members of the Labour Party, believing in a mixed economy, and strongly committed to Britain's membership of the European Economic Community.

social disease *n.* **1.** Venereal disease. Used euphemistically. **2.** A disease occuring especially among particular social classes predisposed to it by a given set of living or working conditions.

social engineering *n.* The attempt to adjust or manage institutional arrangements or patterns of behaviour in a society by applying principles of a social science. **—social engineer** *n.*

social insurance *n.* A national system of insurance, as against sickness, unemployment, or disability, usually financed jointly by employers, employees, and the government.

so•cial•ise, so•cial•ize (sṓsh'l-īz) *v.* **-ised, -ising, -ises.** *—tr.* **1.** To fit for companionship with others; train or bring up so as to be well adapted, as in attitude or manners, for life in society. **2.** To place under government or group ownership or control; establish on a socialistic basis. **3.** To convert or adapt to the needs of society. *—intr.* To enter into social relationships or social activities. **—so•cial•i•sa•tion** (-ī-záysh'n || *U.S.* -i-) *n.* **—so•cial•is•er** *n.*

socialised medicine *n. U.S.* The provision of medical and hospital care for all at a nominal cost, by means of government regulation of health services and subsidies derived from taxation.

so•cial•ism (sṓsh'l-iz'm) *n.* **1.** A social system in which the means of producing and distributing goods are owned collectively and political power is exercised by the whole community. **2.** The theory or practice of those who support such a social system. **3.** In Marxist-Leninist theory, the building, under the dictatorship of the proletariat, of the material base for communism, a transitional stage between capitalism and communism.

so•cial•ist (sṓsh'l-ist) *n.* **1.** An advocate of socialism. **2.** *Abbr.* **soc.** *Often capital* **S.** A member of a socialist party.
∼adj. **1.** Of, promoting, or practising socialism. **2.** *Capital* **S.** Of, belonging to, or constituting a socialist party.

so•cial•is•tic (sṓsh'l-ístik) *adj.* Of, advocating, or tending towards socialism. **—so•cial•is•ti•cal•ly** *adv.*

socialist realism *n.* An official Marxist theory of art, strongly held and propagated in the Soviet Union and other Communist countries, holding that the purpose of any art is to promote socialism.

so•cial•ite (sṓsh'l-īt) *n.* One prominent in fashionable society.

so•ci•al•i•ty (sṓshi-ál-əti) *n., pl.* **-ties.** **1. a.** The state or quality of being sociable; sociability. **b.** An instance of sociableness. **2.** The tendency to form communities and societies.

so•cial•ly (sṓsh'l-i) *adv.* **1.** In a social manner; with regard to social relations: *socially inept.* **2.** With regard to society: *socially important.* **3.** By society.

social mobility *n.* The movement of individuals from one social class to another, especially from a lower class to a higher one.

social psychology *n.* The branch of psychology concerned with the relationships between individuals and groups.

social realism *n.* *Sometimes capital* **S,** *capital* **R.** A movement in painting, literature, and other arts rejecting romanticism and concentrating on the realistic portrayal of contemporary political, economic, and social conditions.

social register *n.* In the United States, a directory listing persons of social prominence in the community.

social science *n.* **1.** The study of society and of individual relationships in and to society, generally regarded as including sociology, psychology, anthropology, economics, political science, and history. **2.** Any of these disciplines.

social security *n.* **1.** The provision by the state of financial and other assistance to those in need, such as the unemployed, the elderly, the disabled, and those with low incomes. **2.** *Often capital* **S,** *capital* **S.** The government system providing such assistance; this may be a single scheme or, as in Britain, a combination of social insurance schemes (such as unemployment benefit) and noncontributory schemes, both means-tested (such as payments to low-income families) and non-means-tested (such as child benefit).

social service *n.* **1.** *Usually plural.* **a.** Services and facilities that are government-funded and usually controlled by national or local government, such as health care, education, and social work. **b.** The staff running these services and facilities. **2.** Social work.

social studies *pl.n.* A course of study, often taught in schools, that includes sociology, geography, history, and politics.

social wage *n.* Benefits, especially government-provided ones such as health care and unemployment insurance, to which members of a society may be entitled in addition to their individual wages, and which should be considered in assessing their overall standard of living. Typically preceded by *the.*

social work *n.* The provision of welfare work, assistance, and advice to those in need such as the poor, the aged, and those with domestic and emotional problems. **—social worker** *n.*

so•ci•e•tal (sə-sī-ət'l || sō-) *adj.* Of or pertaining to the structure, organisation, or functioning of society. **—so•ci•e•tal•ly** *adv.*

so•ci•e•ty (sə-sī-əti || sō-) *n., pl.* **-ties.** *Abbr.* **S., s., Soc., soc.** **1. a.** The totality of social relationships among human beings. **b.** A group of human beings broadly distinguished from other groups by mutual interests, participation in characteristic relationships, shared institutions, and a common culture. **c.** The institutions and culture of a distinct self-perpetuating group. **2. a.** The rich, privileged, and fashionable social class. **b.** A particular section of a community or population, and its customs: *polite society; middle-class society.* **3. a.** Companionship; company. **b.** Participation in social or communal activity: *He's not much of a one for society.* **4.** *Biology.* A colony or community of organisms, usually of the same species. **5.** An organisation of people associated on the basis of common aims, beliefs, interests, or occupations. —See Synonyms at **circle.** [From Old French *societe,* from Latin *societās* (stem *societāt-*), fellowship, union, society, from *socius,* companion.]

Society Islands. Group of volcanic and coral islands in the central South Pacific, forming part of French Polynesia. They comprise the Windward Islands which include Tahiti, and the Leeward Islands.

Society of Friends *n.* The **Religious Society of Friends** *(see).*

Society of Jesus *n. Abbr.* **S.J.** The **Jesuits** *(see).*

So•cin•i•an (sō-sínni-ən, sə-) *n.* An adherent of a sect holding unitarian views, including denial of the divinity of Jesus, founded by Laelius and Faustus Socinus, Italian theologians of the 16th century. **—So•cin•i•an** *adj.* **—So•cin•i•an•ism** *n.*

socio– *comb. form.* Indicates: **1.** Society; for example, **sociometry. 2.** Social; for example, **socioeconomic.** [From French, from Latin *socius,* companion.]

so•ci•o•bi•ol•o•gy (sṓ-si-ō-bī-óllə-ji, -shi-) *n.* The study of the social behaviour and organisation of animal species and their relationship to human social evolution. **—so•ci•o•bi•o•log•i•cal** (-bī-ə-lójik'l) *adj.* **—so•ci•o•bi•o•log•i•cal•ly** *adv.* **—so•ci•o•bi•o•log•ist** (-jist) *n.*

so•ci•o•ec•o•nom•ic (sṓ-si-ō-éekə-nómmik, -shi-, -éckə-) *adj.* Of, based on, or influenced by a combination of social and economic considerations.

so•ci•o•lin•guis•tics (sṓ-si-ō-ling-gwístiks, -shi-) *n. Used with a singular verb.* The study of language in the context of its use in a particular society, and of the social and cultural factors that influence its acquisition and development. **—so•ci•o•lin•guis•tic** *adj.*

so•ci•ol•o•gy (sṓ-si-óllәji, -shi-) *n.* The study of human social behaviour; especially, the study of the origins, organisation, institutions, and development of human society. [French *sociologie* : SOCIO- + -LOGY.] **—so•ci•o•log•ic** (-ə-lójik), **so•ci•o•log•i•cal** *adj.* **—so•ci•o•log•i•cal•ly** *adv.* **—so•ci•ol•o•gist** (-óllәjist) *n.*

so•ci•om•e•try (sṓ-si-ómmətri, -shi-) *n.* The quantitative study of relationships between individuals in groups and populations, especially the study and measurement of preferences.

so•ci•o•po•li•ti•cal (sṓ-si-ō-pə-líttik'l, -shi-) *adj.* Of, based on, or influenced by a combination of social and political considerations.

sock[1] (sok) *n., pl.* **socks** (for all senses) or *U.S.* **sox** (for sense 1). **1.** A soft covering for the foot or foot and leg, reaching a point between the ankle and the knee and usually worn inside a shoe; a short stocking. **2. a.** A light shoe worn by comic actors in ancient Greek and Roman plays. Compare **buskin. b.** *Archaic.* Comic drama; comedy. **3.** A **windsock** *(see).* **—pull (one's) socks up.** *British Informal.* To make an effort to do better; sort oneself out; try harder. **—put a sock in it.** *British Informal.* To be quiet; shut up. **—socked in.** *U.S.* Closed because of bad weather. Said of an airport. [Middle English *socke,* Old English *socc,* a kind of light shoe, from Latin *soccus,* probably from Greek *sukkhos*†.]

sock[2] *v.* **socked, socking, socks.** *Slang. —tr.* To hit or strike forcefully; punch. *—intr.* To deliver a blow. **—sock it to (someone).** *Slang.* **1.** To impress (someone) forcefully. **2.** To attack vigorously.
∼n. Slang. A hard blow or punch. [18th century : origin obscure.]

sock•et (sóckit) *n.* **1.** An opening or cavity that acts as the receptacle for an inserted part. **2.** Any of various devices or fitments into which something is inserted, especially: **a.** An electrical power point in which a plug or light bulb fits. **b.** A recessed piece of metal used, in conjunction with a bar or wrench, to turn bolts or nuts. **3. a.** The hollow part of a joint that receives the end of a bone. **b.** A hollow or concavity into which a part, such as the eye, fits.
∼tr.v. **socketed, -eting, -ets.** To furnish with or insert into a socket. [Middle English *soket,* spearhead shaped like a ploughshare, socket, from Anglo-French *soket,* diminutive of Old French *soc,* ploughshare, probably from Celtic origin.]

sock•eye salmon (sók-ī) *n.* A salmon, *Oncorhynchus nerka,* of northern Pacific coastal waters. Also called "red salmon". [By folk etymology from Salish (dialectal) *suk-kegh.*]

so•cle (sṓk'l, sóck'l) *n.* A plain low block or plinth, serving as a pedestal, as for a vase or a column, or supporting a wall. [French *socle,* from Italian *zoccolo,* "wooden shoe", from Latin *socculus,* diminutive of *soccus,* a light shoe. See **sock** (stocking).]

soc•man (sók-mən, sṓk-) *n., pl.* **-men** (-men, -mən). Also **soke•man** (sṓk-). A tenant holding land under the system of socage. [Medieval Latin *sokemannus* : Old English *sōcn,* SOKE + *mann,* MAN.]

Soc•ra•tes (sóckrə-teez) (*c.* 469–399 B.C.). Greek philosopher. He initiated a method of teaching through question and answer

PRONUNCIATION KEY

a, trap; aa, father; ai, fair; ar, star; aw, lawn; ay, play; b, bb, stab; rubber; ch, church; ck, ticket; d, dd, dead; ladder; e, dress; ee, bee; er, defer; ew, few; ewr, pure; ə, about; ər, letter; f, ff, fife; differ; g, gg, giggle; h, hat; i, kit; ī, price; īr, fire; j, judge; k, kick; l, ll, let; 'l, needle; m, mm, man; n, nn, no; 'n, sudden; ng, thing; o, lot; ō, no; ŏŏ, foot; ōō, shoe; oor, poor; ow, cow; owr, hour; oy, boy; p, pp, pepper; r, rr, red; s, ss, sauce; sh, ship; t, tt, totter; th, thick; th, this; smooth; u, cut; ur, turn; v, vv, valve; w, wet; y, yes; z, zz, zebra; zh, vision; pleasure

IN FOREIGN WORDS:

AN, ON, Saint-Saëns; hl, Llanelli; Hluhluwe; kh, loch; lough; Khaled

STRESS MARK:

ín-sīt, insight; in-sī́t, incite

whereby man could get to know himself. He argued that virtue is knowledge, vice is ignorance, and no one wittingly does wrong. His stance led to his being charged with atheism and corrupting the minds of the youth. He was sentenced to death and drank hemlock and died in the presence of his pupils. His theories have survived only through the writings of Plato, his most important pupil, and to a lesser extent of Xenophon.

So·crat·ic (so-kráttik, sə-, sō-) *adj.* Also **So·crat·i·cal** ('l). Of, pertaining to, or characteristic of Socrates or his philosophical methods of instruction and argument.
~*n.* An adherent of the teachings of Socrates. **—So·crat·i·cal·ly** *adv.* **—So·crat·i·cism** (-krátti-siz'm) *n.*

Socratic irony *n.* Pretended ignorance, as used by Socrates as a method of instruction or to reveal inconsistencies in the arguments of an opponent. Also called "irony".

Socratic method *n.* A philosophical procedure used by Socrates as a form of instruction, using repeated and pointed questioning to elicit truths assumed to be innate in all rational beings.

sod[1] (sod) *n.* **1.** A section of grass-covered surface soil held together by matted roots; turf. **2.** The ground, especially when covered with grass. **3.** See **old sod.**
~*tr.v.* **sodded, sodding, sods.** To cover with sod. [Middle English *sod(de)*, from Middle Low German or Middle Dutch *sode,* akin to Old Frisian *sâda*†.]

sod[2] *n. Vulgar Slang* **1.** An obnoxious or contemptible person. **2.** A person; fellow. Used humorously. **3.** Something that is troublesome or infuriating.
~*tr.v.* **sodded, sodding, sods.** *Vulgar Slang.* To damn; curse. Used chiefly in an interjection: *Sod you! Sod it!* **—sod off.** *Vulgar Slang.* To go away or cease being annoying. Used in the imperative. [Shortened from SODOMITE.]

so·da (sōdə) *n.* **1. a.** Any of various forms of sodium carbonate, especially **washing soda** *(see).* **b.** Loosely, chemically combined sodium. **2. a.** Soda water. **b.** *U.S.* Any carbonated soft drink; pop. **3.** A beverage made from soda water, ice cream, and sometimes flavouring. **4.** In faro, the card turned face up at the beginning of the game. [Medieval Latin *soda*†, perhaps from *sodānum,* glasswort (a plant used to treat headaches), from Archaic *sudā,* headache, from *sada‘a,* to split.]

soda ash *n.* Crude anhydrous **sodium carbonate** *(see),* used especially as an industrial chemical.

soda bread *n.* Bread made with bicarbonate of soda, cream of tartar, and soured milk.

soda fountain *n. U.S.* **1.** An apparatus with taps for dispensing soda water and other soft drinks. **2.** A counter or café serving soft drinks, ice-cream dishes, and other snacks.

soda lime *n.* A mixture of calcium oxide and sodium or potassium hydroxide, used as a drying agent and carbon dioxide absorbent.

so·dal·ist (sōd'l-ist) *n.* A member of a sodality.

so·da·lite (sōdə-līt) *n.* A blue-white vitreous mineral, essentially $3(NaAlSiO_4)·NaCl$, found in igneous rocks.

so·dal·i·ty (sō-dál-əti, sə-) *n., pl.* **-ties. 1.** A society or association; especially, in the Roman Catholic Church, a devotional or charitable society. **2.** Brotherhood; fellowship. [From Latin *sodālitās,* fellowship, brotherhood, from *sodālis,* fellow, intimate.]

soda nitre *n. Chemistry.* **Sodium nitrate** *(see).*

soda pop *U.S. Informal.* A carbonated soft drink; pop.

soda water *n.* Effervescent water charged under pressure with purified carbon dioxide gas, used as a beverage or mixer. Also called "carbonated water", "soda".

sod·den (sódd'n) *adj.* **1.** Thoroughly soaked; saturated. **2.** Soggy and heavy from improper cooking; doughy. **3.** Bloated and dulled, especially from overindulgence in drink. **4.** *Archaic.* Boiled.
~*v.* **soddened, -dening, -dens.** *—tr.* To make sodden; saturate. *—intr.* To become sodden. [Middle English, Old English *soden,* from the past participle of *sethen, sēothan,* to SEETHE.] **—sod·den·ly** *adv.* **—sod·den·ness** *n.*

sod·ding (sódding) *adj. Slang.* Damned. Used as an intensive and often considered vulgar: *a sodding nuisance.* **—sod·ding** *adv.*

Sod·dy (sóddi), **Frederick** (1877–1956). British chemist and physicist. With Lord Rutherford he put forward the theory of atomic disintegration. His discovery that certain elements which possessed the same chemical properties differed in their nuclear mass *(Soddy's law),* laid the foundation of the isotope theory. He was awarded the Nobel prize for his work on radioactivity in 1921.

so·di·um (sōdi-əm) *n. Symbol* **Na** A soft, light, extremely malleable silver-white metallic element that reacts explosively with water. It is naturally abundant in combined forms, especially in common salt, and is present in a wide variety of industrially important compounds. Atomic number 11, atomic weight 22.99, melting point 97.8°C, boiling point 892°C, relative density 0.968, valency 1. [New Latin : $SOD(A)$ + -IUM.]

sodium ammonium phosphate *n.* A colourless, odourless crystalline compound, $NaNH_4HPO_4·4H_2O$, used as an analytical reagent.

sodium benzoate *n.* The sodium salt of benzoic acid, $C_6H_5COONa,$ used as a food preservative, antiseptic, and intermediate in dye manufacture, and in the production of pharmaceuticals. Also called "benzoate of soda".

sodium bicarbonate *n.* A white crystalline compound, $NaHCO_3,$ with a slightly alkaline taste, used in making effervescent salts and beverages, artificial mineral water, baking soda, pharmaceuticals, and in fire extinguishers. Also called "baking soda", "bicarbonate of soda", "sodium hydrogencarbonate", and informally "bicarb".

sodium borate *n.* A crystalline compound, $Na_2B_4O_7·10H_2O,$ used in the manufacture of glass, detergents, and pharmaceuticals. Also called "borax".

sodium carbonate *n.* A compound used in the manufacture of sodium bicarbonate, sodium nitrate, glass, ceramics, detergents, and soap, chiefly used as a white powder ($Na_2CO_3,$ sal soda) or a white crystalline decahydrate ($Na_2CO_3·IOH_2O,$ washing soda).

sodium chlorate *n.* A colourless crystalline compound, $NaClO_3,$ used as a bleaching and oxidising agent and in explosives.

sodium chloride *n.* A colourless crystalline compound, $NaCl,$ used in the manufacture of chemicals and as a food preservative and seasoning. Also called "common salt", "table salt".

sodium cyanide *n.* A poisonous white crystalline compound, $NaCN,$ used in extracting gold and silver from ores and in dye manufacture.

sodium cyclamate *n.* A soluble white crystalline powder, $C_6H_{11}NHSO_3Na,$ 30 times as sweet as sugar (sucrose) and formerly a major constituent of low-calorie sweetening agents.

sodium dichromate *n.* A red-orange crystalline compound, $Na_2Cr_2O_7·2H_2O,$ used as an oxidising agent.

sodium glutamate *n.* **Monosodium glutamate** *(see).*

sodium hydrogencarbonate *n.* Sodium bicarbonate.

sodium hydrosulphite *n.* A yellowish powder, $(NAO)_2S_2O_4·2H_2O,$ used as a bleaching and reducing agent. Also called "sodium hyposulphite", "sodium dithionite".

sodium hydroxide *n.* A strongly alkaline compound, $NaOH,$ used in the manufacture of chemicals and soaps and in petroleum refining. Also called "caustic soda", "lye".

sodium hypochlorite *n.* An unstable salt, $NaOCl,$ usually stored in solution and used as a fungicide and an oxidising bleach.

sodium hyposulphite *n.* **Sodium thiosulphate** *(see).*

sodium nitrate *n.* A white crystalline compound, $NaNO_3,$ used in solid rocket propellants and in the manufacture of explosives and tobacco. Also called "nitre", "saltpetre", "soda nitre", "Chile saltpetre", "caliche".

sodium pentobarbital *n.* **Pentobarbitone sodium** *(see).*

sodium pentothal *n. Chemistry.* **Thiopental sodium** *(see).*

sodium perborate *n.* A white odourless crystalline compound, $NaBO_2·H_2O_2·3H_2O,$ used as a mild alkaline oxidising agent in dentifrices, as a deodorant, and as an industrial reagent.

sodium peroxide *n.* A yellowish-white powder, $Na_2O_2,$ employed industrially as an oxidising and bleaching agent and medically as a germicide, antiseptic, and disinfectant.

sodium phosphate *n.* Any of the three sodium salts of phosphoric acid, $NaH_2PO_4,$ $Na_2HPO_4,$ and $Na_3PO_4,$ widely used in industry, pharmaceutical manufacturing, medicine, and chemistry.

sodium propionate *n.* A clear crystalline compound, $C_2H_5COONa,$ capable of retarding the growth of moulds and bacteria and used to prevent food spoilage.

sodium silicate *n.* Any of various water-soluble silicate glass compounds used as a preservative for eggs, in plaster and cement, and in various purification and refining processes. Also called "liquid glass", "soluble glass", "water glass".

sodium sulphate *n.* A white crystalline compound, $Na_2SO_4,$ used to manufacture paper, glass, dyes, and pharmaceuticals.

sodium sulphide *n.* A hygroscopic yellow compound, $Na_2S,$ used as a metal ore reagent and in photography, engraving, and printing.

sodium sulphite *n.* A white crystalline or powdered compound, $Na_2SO_3,$ used in preserving foods, silvering mirrors, developing photographs, and making dyes.

sodium thiosulphate *n.* A white crystalline compound, $Na_2S_2O_3·5H_2O,$ used as a photographic fixing agent and as a bleach. Also called "hypo", "hyposulphite", "sodium hyposulphite".

so·di·um-va·pour lamp (sōdi-əm-váypər) *n.* An electric lamp containing a small amount of sodium and neon gas, used in generating yellow light for street lighting.

Sod·om[1] (sóddəm). City of ancient Palestine, possibly located south of the Dead Sea, which, with nearby Gomorrah, was destroyed by "brimstone and fire from the Lord" (Genesis 19:24).

Sodom[2] *n.* Any place of exceptional wickedness or depravity.

sod·o·mise, sod·o·mize (sóddə-mīz) *tr.v.* **-ised, -ising, -ises.** To practise sodomy on.

sod·om·ite (sóddə-mīt) *n.* A person who indulges in sodomy. [Middle English, from Old French, from Late Latin, from Greek *Sodomitēs,* inhabitant of Sodom.]

sod·o·my (sóddəmi) *n.* **1.** *Law.* Anal sexual intercourse. **2.** Broadly, sexual intercourse between men, or any of various unnatural sexual acts, especially between humans and animals. [Middle English, from Medieval Latin *sodomia,* from Late Latin *peccatum sodomiticum,* the sin of Sodom.]

Sod's Law (sódz) *n.* Any of various satirically pessimistic observations propounded as quasi-scientific laws, such as: "The degree of failure is directly proportional to the effort made and to the need for success". [Personification of SOD (contemptible person, etc.).]

so·ev·er (sō-évvər) *adv.* At all; in any way. Used to generalise or emphasise a word or phrase, usually in combination, as with *how, what, when,* or *where: "Space to breathe, how short soever"* (Ben Jonson). [SO + EVER.]

so·fa (sōfə) *n.* A long upholstered seat with a back and arms. [Originally a raised dais with carpets and cushions, ultimately from Arabic *suffah;* perhaps akin to Hebrew *sapāh,* carpet, divan.]

sofa bed *n.* A sofa, the seat of which unfolds to form a bed.

so·far (sō-faar) *n.* A system for determining a position at sea, especially that of lost survivors, by the sound ranging of the explosion of an underwatercharge by three widely separated shore stations. [*Sound* *fixing* and *ranging*.]

sof·fi·o·ne (sóffi-ŏni ‖ *U.S. also* sŏfi-) *n., pl.* **sof·fi·o·ni** (-ŏ-nee). A jet of steam, and other vapours, that issues from the ground in volcanic regions. [Italian, augmentative form of *soffio*, a puff, from *soffiare*, to blow, from Latin *sufflare*, to blow upon.]

sof·fit (sóffit) *n.* The underside of a structural component, such as a beam, arch, staircase, or cornice. [French *soffite*, from Italian *soffito*, *soffitta*, from Vulgar Latin *suffictus* (unattested), from Latin *suffixus*, "something fastened beneath". See **suffix**.]

Sofia, Sophia (sŏfi-ə). Bulgarian **Sofiya**. Capital of Bulgaria, situated in the country's western mountains, and the chief industrial, communications, cultural and commercial centre. Its monuments include the ruined seventh century church of St. Sofia.

S. of Sol. Song of Solomon (Old Testament).

soft (soft ‖ sawft) *adj.* **softer, softest. 1. a.** Offering little resistance; easily moulded, cut, or worked; malleable; not hard. **b.** Yielding readily to pressure or weight; not firm. **c.** Marked by wet or sodden ground: *The going was soft.* **2.** Marked by or done with relatively little force; light: *a soft tap with a hammer.* **3. a.** Smooth or fine to the touch; not harsh or coarse. **b.** Lacking sharpness or acidity; bland; mellow. **4.** Not loud or strident; low-toned. **5.** Not brilliant or glaring; subdued: *soft lights.* **6.** Not sharply drawn or delineated: *soft contours.* **7.** Gentle; agreeable; mild; balmy: *soft weather; a soft breeze.* **8.** Having or showing a mild, gentle, or sympathetic disposition, as: **a.** Not stern or rigorous; lenient: *too soft on offenders.* **b.** Adopting a moderate rather than an aggressive approach or position: *the soft Left.* **c.** Easily moved; compassionate. **d.** Easily swayed; yielding; compliant. **9. a.** Tender; affectionate: *soft glances.* **b.** Amorously inclined; infatuated. Used with *on.* **10. a.** Lacking powers of endurance or exertion, especially as a result of prolonged ease or self-indulgence; weak; not robust. **b.** Out of condition; flabby. **11.** *Informal.* Simple; feeble-minded: *soft in the head.* **12.** *Military.* Lacking protection against bombs, missiles, or rockets: *a soft target.* **13.** Soft-core: *soft porn.* **14.** *Finance.* **a.** Designating a loan issued on very favourable terms. **b.** Fluctuating and tending to decline; not firm. Said of prices on a stock market. **15.** Having low dissolved mineral content. Said of water. **16. a.** Sibilant rather than guttural, as *c* in *certain* and *g* in *gem.* **b.** Voiced and weakly articulated: *a soft consonant.* **c.** Palatalised, as certain consonants in Slavonic languages are. **17.** *Physics.* **a.** Of low penetrating power. Said of radiation. **b.** Having a relatively high pressure. Said of a vacuum. ~*n.* A soft object or part. ~*adv.* Softly; gently. [Middle English *soft(e)*, agreeable, pleasant, Old English *sōfte*, *sēfte*, from Germanic *samfti-* (unattested).] **—soft·ly** *adv.* **—soft·ness** *n.*

sof·ta (sóftə ‖ sáwftə) *n.* A Muslim student of theology and religious law. [Turkish, from Persian *sōkhta*, "aflame, burning" (devoted to learning).]

soft·ball (sóft-bawl ‖ sáwft-) *n.* **1.** A variation of baseball played on a smaller diamond with a larger, softer ball that is pitched underhand. **2.** The ball used.

soft-boiled (sóft-bóyld ‖ sáwft-) *adj.* **1.** Boiled to a soft consistency. Said of an egg. **2.** *Informal.* Soft-hearted; lenient.

soft coal *n.* **Bituminous coal** (see).

soft-core (sóft-kór ‖ sáwft-, -kŏr) *adj.* Intended to be sexually titillating but not explicit; not hard-core: *soft-core pornography.*

soft-cov·er (sóft-kúvvər ‖ sáwft-) *n.* **1.** A paperback. **2.** A paperback format. Also used adjectivally: *a soft-cover edition.*

soft currency *n.* A currency that is not backed by government credit and so is not readily exchangeable for other currencies. Compare **hard currency.**

soft drink *n.* A nonalcoholic, usually fizzy, drink.

soft drug *n.* A drug, such as marijuana, that is considered not to be physically addictive, and hence to be less damaging to the health than a hard drug.

sof·ten (sóff'n ‖ sáwf'n, *also* sóftən, sáwftən) *v.* **-tened, -tening, -tens.** *—tr.* To make less severe or softer. *—intr.* To become soft or softer. **—soften up.** To weaken the defences and reduce the morale of (an enemy), as by bombardment prior to full-scale attack. **2.** To cajole, flatter, or otherwise reduce the resistance of (a potential customer, for example). **—sof·ten·er** *n.*

soft-finned (sóft-fínd ‖ sáwft-) *adj. Zoology.* Having fins supported by flexible cartilaginous rays. Compare **spiny-finned.**

soft focus *n.* A slightly blurred photographic effect, usually obtained by setting a lens slightly out of focus. **—soft-focus** *adj.*

soft fruit *n.* Soft, stoneless fruit such as raspberries, blackberries, and strawberries.

soft furnishings *pl.n. British.* Curtains, rugs, furniture covers, and similar textile items.

soft goods *pl.n.* Textiles, clothing, and similar items of trade. Also *U.S.* "dry goods".

soft grass *n.* A downy grass, *Holcus mollis*, found on acid soils.

soft hail *n.* A form of hail, **graupel** (see).

soft-head (sóft-hed ‖ sáwft-) *n.* A foolish or feeble-minded person; a simpleton.

soft-head·ed (sóft-héddid ‖ sáwft-) *adj.* Lacking judgment, realism, or firmness: *a soft-headed concession.* **—soft-head·ed·ly** *adv.*

soft-heart·ed (sóft-hártid ‖ sáwft-) *adj.* Easily moved; tender; merciful. **—soft-heart·ed·ly** *adv.* **—soft-heart·ed·ness** *n.*

soft landing *n.* The landing of a space vehicle on a celestial body in such a way as to prevent damage or destruction.

soft·ly-soft·ly (sóft-li-sóft-li ‖ sáwft-) *adj. Informal.* Cautious, tentative, and deliberate: *a softly-softly approach.*

soft mouthed shark *n.* A **hound shark** (see).

soft option *n.* A course of action open to one which is undemanding: *regarded History as a soft option.*

soft palate *n.* The movable fold, consisting of muscular fibres enclosed in mucous membrane, that is suspended from the rear of the hard palate and closes off the nasal cavity from the oral cavity during swallowing or sucking.

soft paste, soft-paste (sóft-payst ‖ sáwft-) *n.* Any of various ceramics containing frit and refined clay.

soft pedal *n.* A pedal on a piano operating a mechanism that softens or mutes the sound.

soft-ped·al (sóft-pédd'l ‖ sáwft-) *tr.v.* **-alled** or *U.S.* **-aled, -alling** or *U.S.* **-aling, -als. 1.** To soften or mute the tone of (a piano) by depressing the soft pedal. **2.** *Informal.* To make less emphatic or obvious; moderate; play down.

soft roe *n.* The spermatozoa or testes of a fish; milt. The soft roe of certain fish, such as cod and herring, is tinned and eaten.

soft rot *n.* Any of various bacterial plant diseases characterised by watery disintegration of the tissues. Compare **dry rot.**

soft sciences *pl.n. Informal.* The social sciences as opposed to the physical sciences.

soft sell *n. Informal.* A subtly persuasive, unaggressive method of selling or advertising. Compare **hard sell.**

soft-shell (sóft-shel ‖ sáwft-) *adj.* Also **soft-shelled** (-shéld). Having a soft, brittle, or unhardened shell.

soft-shell clam *n. U.S.* A **gaper** (see).

soft-shell crab *n.* A marine crab before its shell has hardened after moulting.

soft-shoe (sóft-shoo ‖ sáwft-) *adj.* Of or pertaining to a type of tap dancing performed without metal taps on the shoes.

soft soap *n.* **1.** A fluid or semifluid soap, usually consisting of potassium salts of fatty acids. **2. Green soap** (see). **3.** *Informal.* Cajolery.

soft-soap (sóft-sŏp ‖ sáwft-) *tr.v.* **-soaped, -soaping, -soaps.** *Informal.* To cajole or flatter. **—soft-soap·er** *n.*

soft sore *n.* A **chancroid** (see).

soft-spo·ken (sóft-spŏkən, -spŏkən ‖ sáwft-) *adj.* **1.** Speaking with a soft or gentle voice. **2.** Smooth; suave; ingratiating.

soft spot *n.* **1.** A place in one's heart or affections; a tender or sentimental feeling. **2.** In the skull of an infant, either of the points of juncture of the sagittal and lambdoid or the sagittal, coronal, and frontal sutures; the **fontanelle** (see).

soft top *n.* **1.** A car with a roof that folds back; a convertible. **2.** The folding top of such cars, normally made of leather, canvas, or similar material.

soft touch *n. Informal.* A person who is easily persuaded to donate or lend money.

soft verge *n.* A border of soft earth or grass running along the edge of a road. Also called "soft shoulder".

soft·ware (sóft-wair ‖ sáwft-) *n.* **1.** Written or printed data, such as programs, routines, and symbolic languages, essential to the operation of computers. **2.** Documents containing information on the operation and maintenance of computers, such as manuals, circuit diagrams, and flow charts. Compare **hardware, firmware.** [Coined after HARDWARE ("the machines").]

soft water *n.* Water containing little or no dissolved salts of calcium or magnesium, especially water containing less than 85.5 parts per million of calcium carbonate. Compare **hard water.**

soft·wood (sóft-wŏod ‖ sáwft-) *n.* **1.** The wood of a coniferous tree. **2.** A coniferous tree. Compare **hardwood.**

soft·y (sófti ‖ sáwfti) *n., pl.* **-ies.** *Informal.* A weak, effeminate, or sentimental person.

SOGAT (sŏ-gat). Society of Graphical and Allied Trades.

Sog·di·an (sógdi-ən) *n.* **1.** A member of an ancient Iranian people who inhabited Sogdiana. **2.** Their extinct Iranian language. **—Sog·di·an** *adj.*

Sog·di·a·na (sógdi-áynə, -áanə ‖ *U.S. also* -ánnə). Modern name **Trans·ox·i·a·na** (tránz-óksi-, tráanz-). An ancient region of central Asia and a province of the Persian Empire.

sog·gy (sóggi) *adj.* **-gier, -giest. 1.** Saturated or sodden with moisture; soaked. **2.** Lacking spirit; dull. **3.** Humid; sultry. [From dialectal *sog†*, a marsh.] **—sog·gi·ly** *adv.* **—sog·gi·ness** *n.*

soh, so (sŏ) *n.* Also **sol** (sol ‖ sŏl). *Music.* In tonic sol-fa, a syllable representing the fifth note of a diatonic scale. [Middle English *sol*, from Latin *solve*. See **gamut**.]

So·ho (sŏ-hŏ, -hŏ). District of central London, situated in the City of Westminster. A haunt of foreign emigrés from the 17th century, Soho is known today for its restaurants, theatres, cinemas, nightclubs, and sex shops.

soi-di·sant (swáa-dee-zón, -déezoN) *adj. French.* Self-styled; so-called.

soi·gné (swáan-yay ‖ *U.S.* swaan-yáy) *adj.* Feminine **soi·gnée.** *French.* **1.** Showing sophisticated care in performance, detail, or design. **2.** Well-groomed; polished; elegant.

soil¹ (soyl) *n.* **1.** The top layer of the earth's surface, suitable for the growth of plant life. **2.** A particular kind of earth or ground: *sandy soil.* **3.** Country; territory; region: *native soil.* **4.** Land, usually with agricultural or rural connotations: *a man of the soil.* [Middle English, from Anglo-French, from Latin *solium*, seat (influenced in meaning by *solum*, base, ground).]

soil

THE THIN FERTILE LAYER ABOVE THE BEDROCK
How living things and weathering create soil from rock

The layer of earth that covers much of the world's land surface began as rock. The exposed surface of this has been weathered into increasingly fine particles of rubble. The process exposes minerals which react with chemicals in the atmosphere and in the bodies of dead organisms such as insects. The reactions transform the rubble into a detritus that is fertile enough to be colonised by living organisms and which is recognised as soil.

Different soils have different structures but a highly productive agricultural or garden soil will have four main layers, called Horizons. Horizon A is the topsoil, which should be rich in the humus formed from decayed plant material such

as fallen leaves and deciduous plants. This topsoil is alive with microorganisms which break down dead plant and animal matter and also with soil invertebrates – beetles and mites feeding upon the microorganisms. Vertebrates such as lizards, mice, and moles also stir up the soil.

Horizon B, which is the coarser layer below the rich 150 millimetres (6 inches) or so of topsoil is also permeated and enriched by the excrement of burrowing worms and centipedes. This may be 600–900 millimetres (2–3 feet) thick. The subsoil below it – Horizon C – usually holds the water table; a permanently saturated soil layer which is largely infertile. Beneath this is the solid bedrock of Horizon D.

Arrow indicates direction and depth of the leaching of soil chemicals by the action of water

Horizon A Dark-coloured layer of decaying leaves, twigs, and animal remains mixed with weathered rock particles such as quartz and clay. In it there is intense biological activity ranging from insects and worms to rodents and plant roots. Most soluble chemicals have been leached or washed out by rainwater into lower layers

Horizon B Chiefly fine particles of rock but little organic matter, dead or alive. In regions of low rainfall this layer will contain some soluble chemicals. Where rainfall is high, however, soluble materials are washed down into the layer below. In tropical zones even the silica is dissolved out, allowing remaining iron oxides to give the soil a reddish-brown colour

Horizon C The subsoil lying below the soil proper (Horizons A and B). This layer consists of broken and partly decayed fragments from the solid rock layer lying below it, together with clay particles and soluble materials washed down from layers above

Horizon D Solid rock, known as the bedrock. The bedrock may be igneous, sedimentary, or metamorphic

soil² v. **soiled, soiling, soils.** —tr. **1.** To make dirty, particularly on the surface; begrime; smudge. **2.** To disgrace; tarnish: *It soiled his reputation.* **3.** To pollute with sin; defile. —intr. To become dirty, stained, or tarnished.
~n. **1. a.** The state of being soiled. **b.** A stain or discoloration caused by dirt and grime. **2.** Moral stain. **3.** Filth, sewage, or refuse matter. **4.** Manure, especially human faeces, used as fertiliser. [Middle English *soilen,* from Old French *souiller, suill(i)er,* from Vulgar Latin *suculāre* (unattested), from Latin *suculus, sucula,* diminutives of *sūs,* pig.]
soil³ tr.v. **soiled, soiling, soils. 1.** To feed (livestock) with soilage. **2.** To purge (livestock) by feeding with green food. [Perhaps from obsolete *soil,* to manure, from SOIL (manure).]
soil·age (sóylij) n. Green crops cut for feeding penned livestock.
soil erosion n. The removal of soil by wind, water, ice or gravity faster than the natural soil-forming process can replace it.
soil pipe n. A drain pipe that carries off waste from a lavatory.

soil·ure (sóyl-yər) n. *Archaic.* **1.** Soiling or the condition of being soiled. **2.** A blot, stain, or smudge.
soi·ree, soi·rée (swáa-ray, swó- ‖ *U.S.* swaa-ráy) n. A party of other social gathering held in the evening, often one featuring a musical or literary recital. [French *soirée,* from *soir,* evening, from Latin *sērum,* late hour, neuter of *sērus,* late.]
so·journ (sój-ərn, súj-, -urn ‖ *U.S.* sō-, sō-júrn) intr.v. **-journed, -journing, -journs.** To stay for a time; reside temporarily.
~n. A temporary stay; a brief residence. [Middle English *sojournen,* from Old French *sojorner,* from Vulgar Latin *subdiurnāre* (unattested) : Latin *sub-,* during, under + Late Latin *diurnum,* day, from Latin *diurnus,* daily, from *diēs,* day.] —**so·journ·er** n.
soke (sōk) n. **1.** In early English law, the right of local jurisdiction, generally one of the feudal rights of lordship. **2.** The district over which such jurisdiction was exercised. [Middle English, from Medieval Latin *sōca,* from Old English *sōcn,* inquiry, right of local jurisdiction, from Germanic *sōkniz* (unattested), akin to SEEK.]
sokeman. Variant of **socman.**
sol¹. Variant of **soh.**
sol² (sol) n. **1.** A former monetary unit of France, equal to 12 deniers. **2.** An old French coin of this value. [Middle English, from Old French, from Latin *solidus,* SOLIDUS.]
sol³ (sōl, sol) n., pl. **soles** (-ayss). **1.** The basic monetary unit of Peru, equal to 100 centavos. **2.** A coin or note worth one sol. [Spanish, "sun" (depicted on the coin), from Latin *sōl.*]
sol⁴ (sol ‖ sōl) n. *Chemistry.* A colloidal dispersion of a solid in a liquid medium. [Short for HYDROSOL.]
Sol (sol ‖ sōl) n. The sun personified. [Middle English, from Latin *sōl.*]
sol. solicitor.
so·la. 1. Feminine of **solus. 2.** A plural of **solum.**
sol·ace (sól-əss, -iss) n. Also **sol·ace·ment** (-mənt). **1.** Comfort in sorrow, misfortune, or distress; consolation. **2.** That which furnishes comfort or consolation.
~tr.v. **solaced, -acing, -aces. 1.** To comfort, cheer, or console, as in trouble or sorrow. **2.** To allay or assuage. [Middle English *solas,* from Old French, from Latin *sōlācium, sōlātium,* from *sōlārī,* to comfort, console.] —**sol·ac·er** n.
so·la·num (sə-láynəm, sō-, -láanəm) n. Any plant of the genus *Solanum,* which includes the potato, aubergine, and certain nightshades. [New Latin, from Latin, nightshade.]
so·lar (sōlər) adj. **1.** Of, pertaining to, or proceeding from the sun: *solar rays.* **2.** Utilising or operated by energy derived from the sun: *solar heating.* **3.** Determined or measured with respect to the sun. [Middle English, from Latin *sōlāris,* from *sōl,* sun.]
solar battery n. A system consisting of a large number of connected solar cells.
solar cell n. A semiconductor device that converts the energy of sunlight into electric energy.
solar constant n. The amount of solar radiation perpendicularly impinging on a surface of unit area at a distance of one astronomical unit from the sun in a unit interval of time, having an average value of 1388 watts per square metre.
solar day n. The interval between two successive meridian passages of the sun.
solar eclipse n. An **eclipse** (see) of the sun.
solar flare n. A temporary outburst of solar gases from a small area of the sun's surface, a source of intense radiation.
solar furnace n. A parabolic reflector that focuses solar radiation at a point to obtain high temperatures (up to 4 000°C.)
solar house n. A house having large quantities of heat-absorbing material behind large glass areas, designed to supplement or replace conventional heating methods.
so·lar·im·e·ter (sōlə-rímmitər) n. An instrument used to measure the flux of solar radiation through a surface. Also called "pyranometer". [SOLAR + -METER.]
so·lar·ise, so·lar·ize (sōlə-rīz) v. **-ised, -ising, -ises.** —tr. To expose (photographic film) briefly to the sun after developing and re-develop, so as to reverse some tones and increase highlights. —intr. *Photography.* To be overexposed. —**so·lar·i·sa·tion** (-rī-záysh'n ‖ *U.S.* -ri-) n.
so·lar·i·um (sə-laír-i-əm, sō-) n., pl. **-laria** or **-iums. 1.** A room, gallery, or glassed-in porch exposed to the sun, as in a sanitarium. **2.** A room or establishment with apparatus for artificial suntanning. [Latin *sōlārium,* sundial, terrace, balcony, from *sōl,* sun.]
solar month n. One-twelfth of a tropical year.
solar plexus n. The large network of sympathetic nerves and ganglia located in the peritoneal cavity behind the stomach and having branching tracts that supply nerves to the abdominal viscera. [From the branching ganglia resembling the sun's rays.]
solar power n. Power or energy obtained by direct conversion of radiation from the sun, either by its heating effect or by use of photoelectric cells to generate electricity. See feature, page 1588.
solar system n. Often capital **S**, capital **S**. The sun together with the nine planets, asteroids, comets, and all other celestial bodies that orbit the sun. See feature, page 1589.
solar wind n. The flow of charged particles from the sun, affecting the earth's magnetic field and causing the aurora.
solar year n. A **tropical year** (see).
so·la·ti·um (sō-láyshi-əm, sə-) n., pl. **-tia** (-ə). *Law.* Compensation for damage to the feelings as distinct from financial loss or physical suffering. [Late Latin *sōlātium,* SOLACE.]
sola topi n. A sun hat made from the pith of the sola; a pith helmet.

solar cell

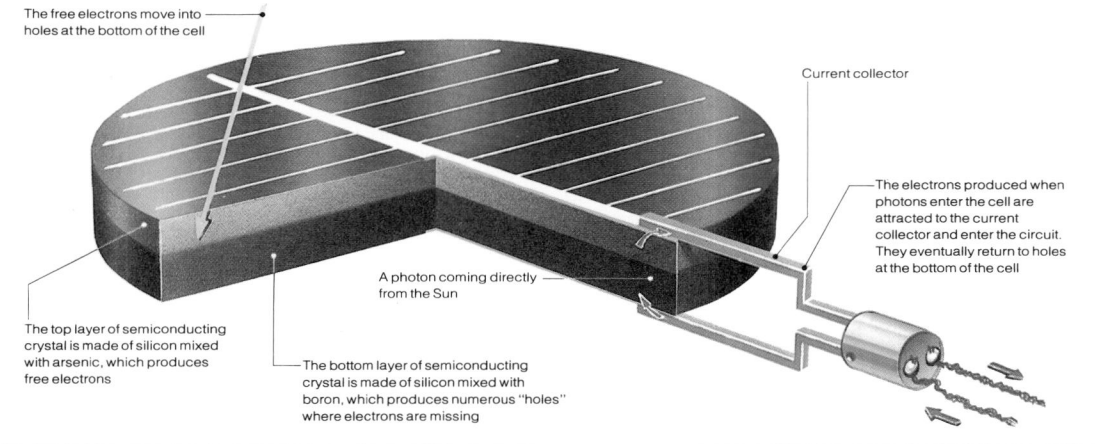

FROM SUNLIGHT TO ELECTRICITY
Solar cells are useful in space – but much less so on Earth

Solar cells, which convert sunlight directly into electricity, were first produced in 1954. Such cells are made from silicon, a semiconductor, in which a photon, or "packet" of light, can initiate a flow of electrons, producing an electric current. The flow is small, and many cells must be joined together to produce an appreciable current. Cells are no more than about 15 per cent efficient and are expensive. But they are also reliable, have no moving parts, and consume no fuel, all of which makes them ideal sources of energy for satellites. More efficient cells may be developed, but they are unlikely to be widely used on Earth for one reason: their power supply – sunlight – is highly variable, and their output is correspondingly erratic.

The free electrons move into holes at the bottom of the cell

Current collector

The electrons produced when photons enter the cell are attracted to the current collector and enter the circuit. They eventually return to holes at the bottom of the cell

A photon coming directly from the Sun

The top layer of semiconducting crystal is made of silicon mixed with arsenic, which produces free electrons

The bottom layer of semiconducting crystal is made of silicon mixed with boron, which produces numerous "holes" where electrons are missing

---

sold. Past tense and past participle of **sell.**

sol·dan (sól-dən ‖ sŏl-) *n. Archaic.* A sultan. [Middle English *soldan, soudan,* from Old French, from Arabic *sulṭān,* SULTAN.]

sol·der (sól-dər ‖ sŏl-, *chiefly U.S.* sóddər, sáwdər) *n.* **1.** Any of various fusible alloys used to join metallic parts when applied in the melted state to the solid metal. The two types are *soft solder,* which contains tin and lead and often flux and is used for electrical connections, and *hard solder,* which is an alloy of copper and zinc used for brazing. **2.** Anything that joins or cements. —*v.* **soldered, -dering, -ders.** —*tr.* **1.** To unite or repair with solder. **2.** To serve as a bond between; join closely. —*intr.* To be capable of being soldered. Used of metals. [Middle English *souldour, soudur,* from Old French *soudure, soldure,* from *souder, soulder,* to solder, from Latin *solidāre,* to make solid, from *solidus,* SOLID.] —**sol·der·er** *n.*

soldering iron *n.* A copper tip held in a handle, usually heated electrically, and used for applying soft solder.

sol·dier (sóljər, *rarely* sŏld-yər) *n.* **1.** One who serves in an army. **2.** A private or a noncommissioned officer as distinguished from a commissioned officer. **3.** One who possesses military skill and experience to a specified degree: *a fine soldier.* **4.** An active and loyal follower or worker. —*intr.v.* **soldiered, -diering, -diers.** **1.** To be or serve as a soldier. **2.** To make a show of working or to feign illness in order to avoid work; shirk or malinger. —**soldier on.** To persevere in face of adverse conditions; carry on doggedly. [Middle English *souldeour,* mercenary, from Old French *soud(i)er, soldier,* from *soulde,* pay, from Latin *solidus,* SOLIDUS.]

soldier ant *n.* A form of worker ant with a large head and large mandibles, usually performing particular functions such as guarding the nest and fighting off predators.

soldier beetle *n.* Any of various carnivorous beetles of the family Cantharidae commonly seen on flowers; especially, species of the genera *Cantharis* and *Rhagonycha.*

sol·dier·ly (sóljərli) *adj.* Befitting a good soldier.

soldier of fortune *n.* One who serves in a military capacity wherever there may be profit or adventure; a mercenary.

soldier orchid *n.* The **military orchid** (*see*).

sol·dier·y (sóljəri) *n., pl.* **-ies. 1.** Soldiers collectively. **2.** A body of soldiers. **3.** The military profession.

sole¹ (sōl) *n.* **1.** The undersurface of the foot. **2.** The under-surface of a shoe, sock, or boot. **3.** The part on which something rests while standing, especially: **a.** The bottom surface of a plough. **b.** The bottom surface of the head of a golf club. —*tr.v.* **soled, soling, soles. 1.** To furnish (a shoe or boot) with a sole. **2.** *Golf.* To put the sole of (a club) on the ground, as in preparing to make a stroke. [Middle English, from Old French *sole,* from Vulgar Latin *sola* (unattested), from Latin *solea,* sandal, from *solum,* bottom, ground, sole of the foot.]

sole² *adj.* **1.** Being the only one; existing or functioning without another or others; only. **2.** Of or pertaining to only one individual or group; exclusive: *The court has the sole right to decide.* **3.** *Archaic & Law.* Single or unmarried. **4.** *Archaic.* Solitary. —See Synonyms at **single.** [Middle English *soul(e), sole,* unmarried, alone, from Old French, from Latin *sōlus,* alone, single.]

sole³ *n., pl.* **sole** or **soles. 1.** Any of various chiefly marine flatfishes of the family Soleidae, related to and resembling the flounders; especially, the European species, *Solea solea,* the Dover sole, valued as a food fish. **2.** Any of various other flatfishes, such as the lemon sole. [Middle English, from Old French, sole (fish), SOLE (of the foot), from the shape of the fish.]

sol·e·cism (sól-i-siz'm, -e-, -ə- ‖ sŏl-) *n.* **1.** A nonstandard usage or grammatical construction. **2.** A violation of etiquette; an instance of bad manners or incorrect behaviour. **3.** Any impropriety, mistake, or incongruity. [From Latin *soloecismus,* from Greek *soloikismos,* from *soloikos,* speaking incorrectly, referring to the corrupt Attic dialect spoken by Athenian colonists at *Soloi,* in Cilicia.] —**sol·e·cist** *n.* —**sol·e·cis·tic** (-sístik) *adj.*

sole·ly (sól-li ‖ sóli) *adv.* **1.** Alone; singly. **2.** Entirely; exclusively.

sol·emn (sólləm) *adj.* **1.** Deeply earnest; serious; grave: *a solemn voice.* **2.** Of impressive and serious nature: *a solemn occasion.* **3.** Performed with full ceremony: *a solemn high Mass.* **4.** Invoking the force of religion; sacred: *a solemn vow.* **5.** Gloomy; sombre. —See Synonyms at **serious.** [Middle English *solem(p)ne,* from Old French, from Latin *sollemnis,* stated, established, appointed.] —**sol·emn·ness** *n.* —**sol·emn·ly** *adv.*

sol·em·nise, sol·em·nize (sólləm-nīz) *tr.v.* **-nised, -nising, -nises. 1.** To celebrate or observe (a religious occasion, for example) with formal ceremonies or rites. **2.** To perform with formal ceremony: *solemnise a marriage.* **3.** To make serious or grave. —See Synonyms at **observe.** —**sol·em·ni·sa·tion** (-nī-záysh'n ‖ *U.S.* -ni-) *n.*

so·lem·ni·ty (sə-lém-nəti, so-) *n., pl.* **-ties. 1.** The condition or quality of being solemn; gravity; seriousness. **2.** A solemn proceeding or observance, as of a religious feast.

so·len·o·don (sə-lénnə-don, so-, sō-) *n.* Either of two small insectivorous mammals, *Solenodon cubana,* of Cuba, or *Solenodon paradoxus,* of Haiti, which resemble shrews.

so·le·noid (sól-ə-noyd, sól-, -i-) *n.* **1.** A cylindrical coil of wire used to produce an axial magnetic field by a flow of electric current. **2.** An assembly consisting essentially of such a coil and a metal core free to slide along the coil axis under the influence of the magnetic field, often used as a switch as in connecting the battery to the starter motor in a motor vehicle. [From French *solénoïde,* from Greek *sōlēnoeidēs,* pipe-shaped, grooved, tubular : *sōlēn*†, channel, pipe + -OID.] —**so·le·noi·dal** (-nóyd'l) *adj.* —**so·le·noi·dal·ly** *adv.*

So·lent, The (sólənt) Strait in the English Channel, separating the Isle of Wight from the coast of Hampshire.

sole·plate (sól-playt) *n.* The undersurface of a clothes iron.

sol·fa (sól-fáa ‖ sŏl-) *n. Music.* **Tonic sol-fa** (*see*). [SOL (note) + FA.]

sol·fa·ta·ra (sól-fə-táarə ‖ sŏl-) *n.* A volcanic fissure that gently emits sulphurous vapours and water vapour. [Italian *Solfatara,* name of a sulphurous volcano near Naples, from *solfo,* SULPHUR.] —**sol·fa·ta·ric** *adj.*

sol·feg·gio (sol-féji-ō ‖ sŏl-, -féj-) *n., pl.* **-feggi** (-féjee) or **-gios.** Also **sol·fège** (-fáyzh, -fézh). *Music.* **1.** The study and use of the tonic sol-fa syllables based on solmisation to train the ear and voice, using a fixed system in which the lowest note is always C. **2.** A

---

solar power

DIRECT USE OF THE SUN'S ENERGY
Home heating and electricity from solar power

The Sun pours out energy at a phenomenal rate but only a minute fraction of it fuels life on Earth – and so indirectly provides us with fossil fuels. If solar energy could be used directly, it would exceed all our present needs many thousands of times over. As resources decline, research into solar power is intensifying.

There are many ways of harnessing solar power indirectly – through winds, tides, fossil fuels, and differences in ocean temperatures. But direct uses of solar energy involve just two main methods. In thermal methods, the Sun's heat is collected to heat water. The commonest system is the solar panel water heater shown below; another system uses mirrors to focus the Sun's rays. In nonthermal methods, solar cells produce electricity directly from sunlight. Such cells are vital for spacecraft, but too inefficient and expensive for commercial use on Earth.

SOLAR POWER STATION *In this power station near Mt. Etna, Sicily, mirrors on the ground follow the Sun and focus its rays on a tower-top collector, which heats water to generate electricity.*

PRINCIPLES BEHIND THE SOLAR PANEL

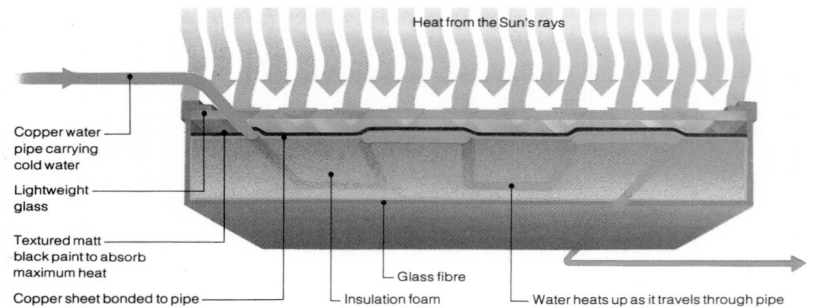

Heat from the Sun's rays

Copper water pipe carrying cold water

Lightweight glass

Textured matt black paint to absorb maximum heat

Copper sheet bonded to pipe

Glass fibre

Insulation foam

Water heats up as it travels through pipe

The principles of the domestic solar-powered water heater are extremely simple: water is heated as it flows through tubes in a flat container that is set to face the Sun. Efficiency depends partly on the rate of water flow and insulation, but principally on the climate. In some places, solar panels can provide all domestic hot water and central heating.

---

singing exercise using the tonic sol-fa syllables. [Italian, from *solfeggiare*, "to sol-fa", from *solfa*, sol-fa : SOL (note) + *fa*, FA.]

sol·fe·ri·no (sól-fə-réenō ‖ sŏl-) *n.* Moderate purplish red. [From a dye discovered in the year of the Battle of *Solferino* (1859). Compare **magenta**.] —**sol·fe·ri·no** *adj.*

so·lic·it (sə-líssit ‖ sō-) *v.* **-ited, -iting, -its.** —*tr.* **1.** To seek to obtain by persuasion, entreaty, or formal application: *solicit votes.* **2.** To petition (a person) persistently; importune. **3.** To entice or incite (a person) to action, particularly to an immoral or illegal action. **4.** To approach or accost (a person) with an offer of sexual services. —*intr.* **1.** To make an earnest or urgent request or petition for something desired. **2.** To approach someone with an offer of sexual services. [Middle English *soliciten*, to disturb, fill with concern, from Old French *solliciter*, from Latin *sollicitāre*, to disturb, agitate, from *sollicitus*, SOLICITOUS.] —**so·lic·i·ta·tion** (-áysh'n) *n.*

so·lic·i·tor (sə-líssitər ‖ sō-) *n. Abbr.* **sol. 1.** A lawyer who advises clients on legal matters, provides legal services such as the drawing up of conveyances or wills, and prepares a client's case for a barrister to represent the client in court. A solicitor may represent a client as an advocate, but only in certain lower courts. Compare **barrister. 2.** *Chiefly U.S.* One who solicits, as for a business or charity. **3.** The chief law officer of some U.S. cities, towns, or government departments. —See Usage note at **lawyer.**

Solicitor General *n., pl.* **Solicitors General.** *Abbr.* **S.G. 1.** In the United Kingdom, a Crown law officer ranking below the Attorney-General (in England, Wales, and Northern Ireland) or below the Lord Advocate (in Scotland). **2.** *Small* **s.**, *small* **g.** In the United States: **a.** A law officer assisting an attorney general. **b.** The chief law officer in a state not having an attorney general.

so·lic·i·tous (sə-líssitəss ‖ sō-) *adj.* **1.** Anxious and concerned; apprehensive. **2.** Taking or showing great care; meticulous or attentive. **3.** Full of desire; eager. —See Synonyms at **thoughtful.** [From Latin *sollicitus*, thoroughly moved, agitated : *sollus*, whole,

entire + *citus*, past participle of *ciēre*, to put in motion, move.] —**so·lic·i·tous·ly** *adv.* —**so·lic·i·tous·ness** *n.*

so·lic·i·tude (sə-lissi-tewd ‖ sō-, -tōōd) *n.* **1.** The state of being solicitous or concerned. **2. a.** Anxiety; concern. **b.** *Usually plural.* That which causes anxiety or concern. —See Synonyms at **anxiety.**

sol·id (sóllid) *adj.* **1.** Of definite shape and volume; not liquid or gaseous. **2.** Not hollowed out or having internal spaces; consisting of solid matter throughout: *a solid block of wood.* **3.** Being the same substance throughout: *solid gold.* **4. a.** Of or pertaining to three-dimensional geometric figures: *solid geometry.* **b.** Having three dimensions: *a solid angle.* **5. a.** Without gaps or openings; continuous: *a solid line of people.* **b.** Without breaks or interruptions: *three solid weeks.* **6.** Of good quality and substance; well-made: *solid foundations.* **7.** Having a close rather than loose consistency; hard and firm: *solid rock.* **8.** Substantial; satisfying: *a solid meal.* **9.** Sound; well-grounded; concrete: *solid facts.* **10.** Financially sound. **11.** Reputable and dependable: *a solid citizen.* **12.** Sensible, reliable, and consistent, but without brilliance or excellence; steady: *a solid worker.* **13.** Written or printed without a hyphen or space. Said of words. **14.** *Printing.* Without leads between the lines. **15. a.** Acting together; unanimous: *a solid voting bloc.* **b.** Firmly united: *a solid marriage.* **16.** *Geology.* Not superficial. ~*n.* **1.** A substance that is neither liquid nor gaseous, the atoms being packed more closely than in a liquid or gas; a solid substance. **2.** A geometric figure having three dimensions. **3.** *Plural.* Solid, rather than liquid, food. [Middle English *solide*, whole, solid, from Old French, from Latin *solidus.*] —**sol·id·ly** *adv.* —**sol·id·ness** *n.*

solid angle *n.* An angle subtended at a point by a surface, measured in steradians with respect to the area delimited on the unit sphere centred on that point by the locus of points of intersection of the sphere with the lines joining the point to the perimeter of the surface. Compare **polyhedral angle.**

sol·i·dar·i·ty (sólli-dárrəti) *n., pl.* **-ties. 1.** A feeling or quality of fellowship, arising from a union of interests, aspirations, or sympathies among members of a group: *A feeling of solidarity within the Women's Movement.* **2.** The firm holding together of such interests and fellow-feeling: *The solidarity of the campaign led to its success.*

sol·i·dar·y (sóllid-əri ‖ -erri) *adj.* Characterised by solidarity; united. [French *solidaire*, from *solide*, SOLID.]

solid fuel *n.* **1.** Fuel such as wood, coal, or coke, that is solid rather than liquid or gas. Also used adjectivally: *a solid-fuel heating system.* **2.** A solid propellant in a rocket.

so·lid·i·fy (sə-líddi-fī, so-) *v.* **-fied, -fying, -fies.** —*tr.* **1.** To make solid, compact or hard. **2.** To make strong or united. —*intr.* To become solidified. —**so·lid·i·fi·ca·tion** (-fi-káysh'n) *n.*

so·lid·i·ty (sə-líddəti, so-) *n., pl.* **-ties. 1.** The condition or property of being solid. **2.** Soundness, as of judgment, moral character, or finances; stability.

solid of revolution *n.* A volume generated by the rotation of a plane figure about an axis in its plane.

solid propellant *n.* A rocket propellant in solid form, combining both fuel and oxidiser in the form of a compact, cohesive grain.

solid solution *n. Chemistry.* A homogeneous crystalline structure in which one or more types of atoms or molecules may be partly substituted for the original atoms and molecules without changing the crystal structure.

sol·id-state (sóllid-stáyt) *adj.* **1.** Characteristic of or pertaining to the physical properties of solid materials, especially to the electromagnetic, thermodynamic, and structural properties of crystalline solids. **2.** Based on or consisting chiefly or exclusively of semiconducting materials, components, and related devices: *solid-state audio equipment, solid-state watches.*

sol·i·dus (sólli-dəss) *n., pl.* **-di** (-dī). **1.** A diagonal mark (/) used especially: **a.** To separate alternatives, as in *and/or.* **b.** To represent the word *per,* as in *kilometres/hour.* **c.** To separate the numerator from the denominator in writing fractions, as in *3/4.* **d.** To indicate the end of verse lines printed continuously, as in *"Let us honour if we can/The vertical man."* **e.** Formerly, to denote shillings, as in *5/–.* Also called "oblique", "shilling mark", "slash", "virgule". **2.** An ancient Roman coin used until the fall of the Byzantine Empire. [Middle English, from Latin, from adjective, SOLID.]

sol·i·fid·i·an (sólli-fiddi-ən ‖ sóli-) *n.* A person who believes that faith alone is sufficient to ensure salvation. [From New Latin *solifidius* : Latin *sōlus*, alone + *fidēs*, faith.] —**sol·i·fid·i·an·ism** *n.*

sol·i·fluc·tion (sōli-fluksh'n) *n.* The downhill flow of surface deposits, such as soil or clay, saturated with thaw water, over a slope that is still frozen.

so·lil·o·quise, so·lil·o·quize (sə-líllə-kwīz, so- ‖ sō-) *v.* **-quised, -quising, -quises.** —*intr.* To utter or deliver a soliloquy. —*tr.* To put into the form of a soliloquy. —**so·lil·o·quist, so·lil·o·quis·er** *n.*

so·lil·o·quy (sə-lílləkwi, so- ‖ sō-) *n., pl.* **-quies. 1.** A literary or dramatic form of discourse in which a character talks to himself or reveals his thoughts in the form of a monologue without addressing a listener. **2.** The act of speaking to oneself in or as if in solitude. [From Late Latin *sōliloquium* : Latin *sōlus*, alone + *loquī*, to speak.]

sol·ip·sism (sól-ipsiz'm, sŏl-) *n. Philosophy.* **1.** The theory that the self is the only thing that can be known and verified. **2.** The theory or view that the self is the only reality. Compare **objectivism.** [Latin *sōlus*, alone + *ipse*†, self + -ISM.] —**sol·ip·sist** *n.* —**sol·ip·sis·tic** (-ip-sístik) *adj.*

sol·i·taire (sólli-taír, -tair) *n.* **1.** A diamond or other gemstone set alone, as in a ring. **2.** A game for one person played on a special

Solar System

THE FAMILY OF THE SUN

A few large objects and thousands of small ones form patterns that suggest their origins

The Solar System consists of the Sun itself, nine planets, almost four dozen satellites, thousands of small, rocky asteroids, and an uncounted number of comets. The Sun makes up some 99.9 per cent of the Solar System's mass, and most of the remaining 0.1 per cent is taken up by the giant planet Jupiter.

The planets fall into two groups. The terrestrial planets are small, dense, and close to the Sun. They are separated by a belt of asteroids from the giant planets, which have gaseous surfaces and relatively small solid cores, most of their globes being liquid. The exception is Pluto, a frozen world with an orbit so eccentric that it is sometimes nearer the Sun than Neptune (as now, for a 20 year period 1979–99).

The planets, revolving in elliptical orbits that are nearly circular, are held to the Sun by gravity. The closer they are to the Sun, the faster they must move to counteract the Sun's greater pull. Mercury travels round the Sun in 88 days, moving at 48 kilometres (30 miles) a second. Pluto's year is 248 Earth years and it moves at three miles a second.

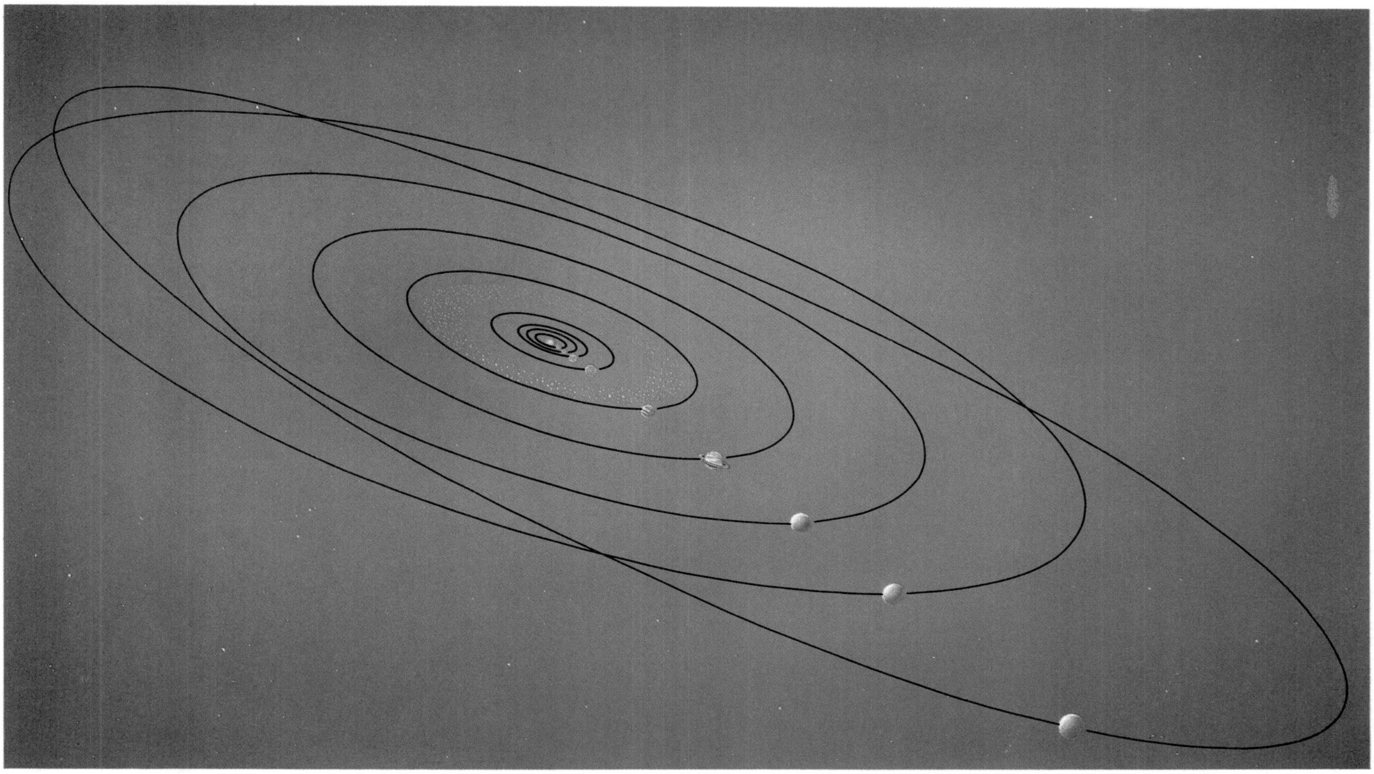

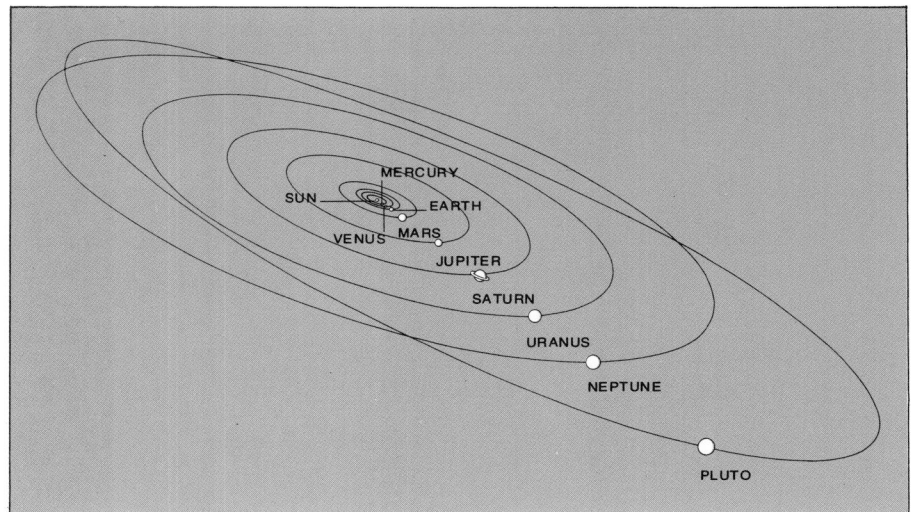

THE SOLAR SYSTEM

Planet	Mean distance from the Sun	
	million kilometres	million miles
Mercury	57.9	36
Venus	108.2	67
Earth	149.6	93
Mars	227.9	141.6
Jupiter	778.3	483.6
Saturn	1427	886.7
Uranus	2869.6	1,783
Neptune	4496.6	2,794
Pluto	5900	3,666

A FLAT, ORDERED SYSTEM *Taken as a whole, the Solar System's most noticeable feature is its flatness. All planets are in the same plane. Moreover, all orbit in the same direction. This suggests that the solar family condensed out of a revolving cloud of gas and dust. Several aggregations of matter came together, the biggest of them being the Sun.*

The Sun would have driven off the lighter-weight materials, including hydrogen and helium, from the inner planets – hence their density compared with the gaseous outer ones. This theory also suggests the notion that planetary formation would be a common result of the formation of any star.

board in which marbles or pegs are arranged in slots in a pattern, the object being to remove each marble or peg, save one, by jumping others over them. **3.** *U.S.* Any of a number of card games played by one person, **patience** *(see).* [French, from Old French, solitary, from Latin *sōlitārius,* SOLITARY.]
sol·i·tar·y (sólli-tri, -təri ‖ -terri) *adj.* **1. a.** Existing, living, or going without others; alone. **b.** Avoiding the company of others; not gregarious. **2.** Happening, done, or made alone. **3.** Remote; secluded; unfrequented: *a solitary retreat.* **4.** Having no companions; lonely. **5.** Single; sole. **6.** *Zoology.* Not living in groups or organised colonies: *solitary wasps.* —See Synonyms at **single.**
~*n., pl.* **solitaries. 1.** A person who lives alone; a recluse. **2.** *Informal.* Solitary confinement. [Middle English, from Latin *sōlitārius,* from *sōlus,* alone.] —**sol·i·tar·i·ly** *adv.* —**sol·i·tar·i·ness** *n.*

solitary confinement *n.* The confinement of a prisoner in a cell in which he is isolated from all others.

sol·i·tude (sólli-tewd ‖ -tōōd) *n.* **1.** The state of being alone or remote from others; isolation. **2.** A lonely or secluded place. [Middle English, from Old French, from Latin *sōlitūdo*, from *sōlus*, alone.]
    Synonyms: solitude, isolation, seclusion, retirement.

sol·ler·et (sólla-ret, -rét) *n.* A steel shoe made of overlapping plates, forming a part of a suit of armour. [Old French, diminutive of *soller*, shoe, from Medieval Latin *subtēlāris*, from Late Latin *subtēl*, hollow of the foot : Latin *sub-*, under + *tālus*, ankle (see **talus**).]

sol·mi·sa·tion (sólmi-záysh'n) *n. Music.* A system of using syllables to name the notes of a scale, as in **tonic sol-fa** *(see)*. [French *solmisation*, from *solmiser*, to sol-fa : **SOL** (note) + **MI**.]

soln solution.

so·lo (sṓlō) *n., pl.* **-los. 1.** A musical composition or passage for an individual voice or instrument, with or without accompaniment. **2.** Any performance or endeavour accomplished by a single individual, such as an aeroplane flight in which the pilot is unaccompanied. **3.** Any of various card games in which one player singly opposes others, such as *solo whist* in which each player plays independently, rather than as one of a pair.
  ~*adj.* **1.** Composed, arranged for, or performed by a single voice or instrument. **2.** Made or done by a single individual.
  ~*adv.* Unaccompanied; alone.
  ~*intr.v.* **soloed, -loing, -los.** To perform alone; especially, to fly an aeroplane without a companion or instructor. [Italian, from Latin *sōlus*, alone.]

so·lo·ist (sṓ-lō-ist) *n.* One who performs a solo or solos.

Solomon Islands. Also **Solomons.** Country comprising part of the Solomon Islands group in the southwestern Pacific. There are six main islands: Choiseul, New Georgia, Santa Isabel, Guadalcanal, Malaita, and San Cristobal, and many smaller islands and groups. (Bougainville and Buka, the northernmost islands, are part of Papua New Guinea.) Most of the islands are mountainous and wooded, and the chief products are timber, copra, and coconuts. A British protectorate was established over most of them by 1899. They witnessed fierce fighting in World War II, notably at Guadalcanal (1942–3). The Solomons became an independent state within the Commonwealth in 1978. Area, 28 446 square kilometres (10,983 square miles). Population, 200,000. Capital, Honiara (on Guadalcanal). See map at **Pacific Ocean.**

Solomon, King (*c.* 973–*c.* 933 B.C.). King of Israel. Succeeding his father, David, he built the Temple of Jerusalem. The Bible attributes him with great wisdom.

Solomon's seal *n.* **1.** A six-pointed star or hexagram, like a Star of David, supposed to possess mystical powers and sometimes used as a charm or amulet. **2.** Any of several plants of the genus *Polygonatum*, having paired, drooping, greenish white flowers. [The plant is probably so called from the seal-like markings on the root stocks.]

So·lon (sṓ-lon, -lən), (*c.* 638–*c.* 559). Athenian lawgiver and poet. His reforms preserved a class system based on wealth, but ended privilege by birth. The political franchise extended, and serfdom effectively abolished by outlawing the use of an individual's freedom as security for debt. The reforms were controversial but became the basis of Greek law.

so long *interj. Chiefly U.S. Informal.* Goodbye.

sol·stice (sól-stiss ‖ sṓl-) *n.* **1.** *Astronomy.* Either of two times of the year when the sun has no apparent northward or southward motion, at the most northern or most southern point of the ecliptic. In the Northern hemisphere, the summer solstice, the longest day of the year, when the sun is in the zenith at the tropic of Cancer, occurs about June 21 or 22, and the winter solstice, the shortest day, when it is over the tropic of Capricorn, occurs about December 21 or 22. The solstices are reversed in the Southern hemisphere. **2.** A turning point or culmination; a limit. [Middle English, from Old French, from Latin *sōlstitium* : *sōl*, sun + *sistere* (past participial stem *stit-*), to make stand.] —**sol·sti·tial** (-stish'l) *adj.*

Sol·ti (shólti), **Sir Georg,** (1912–). Hungarian born British conductor. He has been musical director, Royal Opera Covent Garden (1961–71) and conductor of the Chicago Symphony Orchestra.

sol·u·bil·ise, sol·u·bil·ize (sóllewb'l-īz) *tr.v.* **-ised, -ising, -ises.** To make (such substances as fats and lipids, which are not appreciably soluble under standard conditions) soluble in water by the action of a detergent or similar agent.

sol·u·bil·i·ty (sóllew-billəti) *n., pl.* **-ties. 1.** The quality or condition of being soluble. **2.** The maximum amount of a substance that can be dissolved in a given amount of solvent, usually expressed as the mass or volume of solute in a unit mass or volume of solvent at a given temperature.

sol·u·ble (sóllewb'l) *adj.* **1.** Capable of being dissolved; especially, having a high solubility. **2.** Capable of being solved or explained. [Middle English, from Old French, from Late Latin *solūbilis*, from *solvere*, to loosen.] —**sol·u·ble·ness** *n.* —**sol·u·bly** *adv.*

soluble glass *n. Chemistry.* **Sodium silicate** *(see).*

soluble RNA *n. Abbr.* **sRNA** *Genetics.* **Transfer RNA** *(see).*

so·lum (sṓ-ləm) *n., pl.* **-la** (-lə) or **-lums.** The surface layers of a soil profile in which topsoil formation occurs. [New Latin, from Latin, base, foundation. See **sole** (of a shoe).]

so·lus (sṓ-ləss) *adj. Feminine* **so·la** (-lə). *Latin.* Alone; by oneself. Used especially in stage directions.

sol·ute (sóllewt, so-léwt, -lōōt ‖ sṓ-lōōt) *n. Chemistry.* A substance dissolved in another substance, usually the component of a solution present in the lesser amount. Compare **solvent.** [From Latin *solūtus*, past participle of *solvere*, to loosen.] —**sol·ute** *adj.*

so·lu·tion (sə-lōōsh'n, -léwsh'n) *n.* **1.** *Abbr.* **soln** A homogeneous mixture of two or more substances, retaining its constitution in subdivision to molecular volumes, displaying no settling, and having various possible proportions of the constituents, which may be solids, liquids, gases, or intercombinations. **2.** The process of forming such a mixture. **3.** The state of being dissolved. **4.** The method or process of solving a problem. **5.** The answer to or explanation of a problem. **6.** *Law.* The payment of a claim or debt or the discharging of an obligation. **7.** The action of separating or breaking up; a dissolution. **8.** *Mathematics.* A number, function, or set of numbers or functions, that yields a true statement when substituted in a given equation. [Middle English, from Old French, from Latin *solūtiō* (stem *solūtiōn-*), from *solūtus*. See **solute.**]

solution set *n. Logic & Mathematics.* A **truth set** *(see).*

So·lu·tre·an, So·lu·tri·an (sə-lōō-tri-ən, -léw-) *adj. Anthropology.* Of or relating to an Upper Palaeolithic culture in Europe that succeeded the Aurignacian and was characterised by improved flint implements and stylised symbolic forms of art. [Classified from finds made at *Solutré*, Saône-et-Loire département France.]

solv·a·ble (sólv-əb'l ‖ *South of England also* sṓlv-) *adj.* Capable of being solved. —**solv·a·bil·i·ty** (-ə-billəti), **solv·a·ble·ness** *n.*

sol·va·tion (sol-váysh'n ‖ sṓl-) *n.* Any of a class of chemical reactions, such as the formation of hydrated copper sulphate in aqueous solution, in which solvent molecules combine with ions of the solvent. Compare **solvolysis.** [SOLV(ENT) + -ATION.]

Solvay process (sól-vay) *n.* A process used to manufacture sodium carbonate from salt, ammonia, carbon dioxide, and limestone. [Invented by Ernest *Solvay* (1838–1922), Belgian chemist.]

solve (solv ‖ *South of England also* sṓlv) *tr.v.* **solved, solving, solves. 1.** To find a solution to; answer; explain. **2.** To work out a correct solution to (a mathematical problem). [Middle English *solven*, to loosen, unbind, from Latin *solvere*.] —**solv·er** *n.*

sol·vent (sól-vənt ‖ sṓl-) *adj.* **1.** Able to meet financial obligations. **2. a.** Capable of dissolving another substance. **b.** Causing or promoting dissolution or disintegration.
  ~*n.* **1.** *Chemistry.* **a.** The component of a solution that is present in excess or that undergoes no change of state. **b.** A liquid capable of dissolving another substance. Compare **solute. 2.** Something that weakens, loosens, or dissipates. [Latin *solvēns* (stem *solvent-*), present participle of *solvere*, loosen. See **solve.**] —**sol·ven·cy** *n.*

solvent abuse *n.* **Glue-sniffing** *(see).*

sol·vol·y·sis (sol-vólla-siss ‖ sṓl-) *n.* Any of a class of ionic chemical reactions, such as hydrolysis, in which solute and solvent react to form other products. Compare **solvation.** [SOLV(ENT) + -LYSIS.]

Sol·way Firth (sól-way). Inlet of the Irish Sea, lying between the coast of Cumbria in England and Dumfries and Galloway region in Scotland. There is a tidal bore.

Sol·zhe·nit·syn (sól-zhə-nítsin ‖ sṓl-, -jə-), **Alexandr (Isayevich)** (1918–). Russian writer. He was sentenced for criticising Stalin to labour camps and exile in Siberia (1945–56), and works like *One Day in the Life of Ivan Denisovich* (1962) describe the experience. *The Gulag Archipelago*, published only outside the U.S.S.R., is a history of the labour camp system. He was awarded the Nobel prize for literature in 1970 and forcibly expelled from the U.S.S.R. in 1974.

so·ma¹ (sṓmə) *n., pl.* **-mata** (-tə) or **-mas.** *Biology.* The body of an organism, exclusive of the germ cells. [New Latin, from Greek.]

soma² *n.* **1.** An intoxicating drink prepared from the juice of an

Map: SOMALIA — YEMEN, S.YEMEN, 50°E, Gulf of Aden, DJIBOUTI (FTAI), Berbera, 2408m, Hargeisa, 10°N, ETHIOPIA, SOMALIA, Uebi Scebeli, Juba, INDIAN OCEAN, KENYA, MOGADISHU (MOGADISCIO), Merca, Kismayu, Equator, Km 0 400 800, Miles 0 200 400 unidentified plant, used in Vedic rituals in ancient India. **2.** The plant from which this drink is prepared. [Sanskrit *so̅ma.*]

So·ma·li (sə-maáli, so̅-) *n., pl.* **-lis** or collectively **Somali. 1.** A member of one of a group of Hamitic tribes of Somaliland. **2.** Their Hamitic language. **3.** A native or inhabitant of Somalia. —**So·ma·li** *adj.*

So·ma·li·a (sə-maáli-ə, so̅-). Official name **Somali Democratic Republic.** Country in East Africa. It is hot and arid, and one of the world's poorest states. The population is chiefly Muslim and largely nomadic. Livestock rearing is the main occupation, but settled farming and fishing are being developed. Livestock, bananas, and plantains are exported. The state was created (1960) from former British and Italian possessions in Somaliland. The armed forces seized power (1969) establishing a Revolutionary Council under Siad Barre. In 1977, Somalia invaded the Ogaden border region of Ethiopia to support Somali guerrillas. Though formal withdrawal took place in 1978, guerrilla activities persisted. Many Somali Ethiopians fled to Somalia, and in 1981 some 25 per cent of people in Somalia were refugees. Area, 637 657 square kilometres (246,201 square miles). Population, 4,600,000. Capital, Mogadishu.

So·ma·li·land (sə-maáli-land, so̅-). Region of northeast Africa, also known as the Horn of Africa. It is now divided between Djibouti, Ethiopia, and Somalia. The area is peopled mainly by Somali nomads, converted to Islam in the seventh to tenth centuries. Its strategic value after the opening of the Suez Canal (1869) led to European colonisation in the 19th century. French Somaliland became the French Territory of the Afars and Issas (1967), and gained independence as Djibouti (1977). Italian Somaliland with the Somali-speaking part of Ethiopia (the Ogaden) became a province of Italian East Africa (1936). This was taken by British forces in World War II. Italian Somaliland was made the U.N. Trust Territory of Somalia under Italian control (1950). The British returned the Ogaden to Ethiopia and Italy granted the trust territory internal self-government as Somalia (1956). British Somaliland and Somalia combined as the independent state of Somalia (1960).

so·mat·ic (so̅-máttik, sə-) *adj.* **1.** Of or pertaining to the body, especially as distinguished from a bodily part, the mind, or the environment; physical. **2.** Of or pertaining to the wall of the body cavity, especially as distinguished from the head, limbs, or viscera. **3.** Of or pertaining to the soma or somatoplasm. [From Greek *so̅matikos,* from *so̅ma,* body, SOMA.]

somatic cell *n.* Any cell other than a germ cell.

somato– *comb. form.* Indicates body; for example, **somatology.** [From Greek *so̅ma* (stem *so̅mat-*), body.]

so·ma·to·gen·ic (so̅mə-tə-jénnik, -to̅-, so̅-mátta-) *adj.* Arising within the body in response to environmental stimuli on somatic cells. [SOMATO- + -GENIC.]

so·ma·tol·o·gy (so̅mə-tóllə̇ji) *n.* **1.** The physiological and anatomical study of the body. **2. Physical anthropology** (see). [SOMATO- + -LOGY.] —**so·ma·to·log·i·cal** (-tə-lójik'l) *adj.*

so·ma·to·plasm (so̅mə-tə-plaz'm, -to̅-, so̅-mátta-) *n.* **1.** The entirety of specialised protoplasm, other than germ plasm, constituting the body. **2.** The protoplasm of a somatic cell. [SOMATO- + -PLASM.]

so·ma·to·pleure (so̅mə-tə-ploor, -to̅-, so̅-mátta-, -plur ‖ -plewr) *n.* A complex sheet of embryonic cells in certain vertebrates, formed by association of part of the mesoderm with the ectoderm and developing as the internal body wall. [SOMATO- + PLEURA.]

so·ma·to·tro·phin (so̅mə-tə-tro̅fin, -to̅-, so̅-mátta-) *n.* **Growth hormone** (see). [SOMATO- + Greek *trophe̅,* nourishment (from *trephein,* to feed) + -IN.]

so·ma·to·type (so̅mə-tə-tīp, -to̅-, so̅-mátta-) *n.* The morphological type of a human body; physique. See **endomorph, mesomorph, ectomorph.** —**so·ma·to·typ·ic** (-típpik) *adj.*

som·bre, *U.S.* **som·ber** (sómbər) *adj.* Also *archaic* **som·brous** (sómbrəss). **1. a.** Gloomy or shadowy; dim. **b.** Dark in colour; dull; sober. **2.** Melancholy; dismal. [French from Old French, shade, from Vulgar Latin *subombra̅re* (unattested), to shade : Latin *sub-,* under + *umbra,* shade.]

som·bre·ro (som-braír-o̅, -breér-) *n., pl.* **-ros.** A broad-brimmed Spanish or Mexican hat of felt or straw. [Spanish, hat, from *sombra,* shade, from Vulgar Latin *subombra̅re.* See **sombre.**]

some (sum; *weak form* səm) *adj.* **1.** Being an unspecified or unknown thing or things: *some people from the office; Some fool laughed.* **2.** Being an unspecified quantity; a certain part or number but not all: *I'll have some cake.* **3.** Being an appreciable amount; considerable: *some way to go yet.* **4.** At least a little of; a small amount of: *You might give me some idea.* **5.** Remarkable or impressive: *That was some party!* **6.** No sort of; no person or thing of the specified kind at all. Used ironically: *Some hope!*
~*pron.* **1.** An unspecified amount or part but not all: *Can I have some?* **2.** Certain, unspecified people or things: *Some like it hot.*
~*adv.* **1.** Approximately; about: *some 30 years ago.* **2.** *U.S. Informal.* To a certain degree: *She thought about him some.*

–some [1] (-səm) *adj. suffix.* Indicates: **1.** Being or tending to be; for example, **burdensome. 2.** Likely or inclined to; for example, **quarrelsome, tiresome. 3.** Tending or likely to produce; for example, **awesome.** [Middle English *-som,* Old English *-sum.*]

–some [2] (-so̅m) *n. comb. form.* Indicates body; for example, **chromosome.** [New Latin *-soma,* from Greek *so̅ma,* body.]

–some [3] (-səm) *n. suffix.* Indicates a group of. Used with numerals; for example, **threesome.** [Middle English *-sum,* from *sum, som,* SOME.]

some·bod·y (súm-bədi, -boddi) *pron.* An unspecified or unknown person; someone.
~*n., pl.* **somebodies.** *Informal.* A person of importance.
Usage: *Somebody* and *someone* are regarded as singulars, in formal usage: *Someone has left his coat.* Informally, especially in speech, plural pronouns are used, but the verb always remains in the singular: *Someone has left their coat.* There is a stress contrast between *someone* and some *one* (where a person or thing has been singled out of a *group*: *Some one of us will have to do it.*

some·day (súm-day) *adv.* At some time in the future.
Usage: *Someday* and *sometime* express indefinite future time: *I'll do it someday.* When a particular day or time is implied (but not made explicit), two word forms are used: *I want you to choose some day that won't be too busy.* Sometime also has an informal use in the sense of "occasional", but is critised as it allows confusion with the meaning "former": *He's a musician and sometime composer.*

some·how (súm-how, *occasionally* -ow) *adv.* In a way not specified, understood, or known.

some·one (súm-wun ‖ -wən, *North of England also* -won) *pron.* Some person; somebody. See Usage note at **somebody.**

some·place (súm-playss) *adv. U.S. Informal.* Somewhere.

som·er·sault, sum·mer·sault (súmmər-sawlt ‖ -solt) *n.* Also *archaic* **som·er·set, sum·mer·set** (-set). **1.** An acrobatic feat in which the body rolls in a complete circle, heels over head, either along the ground or in midair. **2.** Loosely, any complete reversal, as of sympathies or opinions.
~*intr.v.* **somersaulted, -saulting, -saults.** Also **sum·mer·sault,** *archaic* **som·er·set, sum·mer·set. -setted, -setting, -sets.** To execute a somersault. [From Old French *sombresau(l)t,* variant of *sobresault,* from Old Provençal *sobresaut* (unattested) : *sobre-,* over, above, from Latin *supra̅* + *saut,* leap, from Latin *saltus,* leap.]

Som·er·set (súmmər-set, -sit) Also **Som·er·set·shire** (-shər,- sheer). County in southwestern England. It borders the British Channel and comprises a lowland plain flanked by the uplands of Exmoor, the Quantocks, the Blackdown Hills and the Mendips. Dairy and fruit farming are important and the county is famous for its cider. Cheddar Gorge and the ancient Arthurian site of Glastonbury are among its tourist attractions. Taunton is the county town.

Somerset, Edward Seymour, Duke of (1506–1552). Lord Protector of England during the early part of the reign of Edward VI. He defeated a Scottish force at Pinkie (1547), but was later indicted by the Earl of Warwick. He was tried for felony and executed.

some·thing (súm-thing) *pron.* **1.** An undetermined or unspecified thing. **2.** A certain quantity, part, number, or quality: *There's something of her mother about her; something more than three weeks hence; I know something of French literature.* **3.** Used as a substitute for a name, word, or thing that has been forgotten or is not known: *She's something in publishing; Jane Something.* **4.** A thing, amount, or achievement of at least some value; a little more or better than nothing: *managed to salvage a few bits of furniture, which was something.* **5.** A person, thing, event, or achievement that is impressive or important: *That's really something!* —**make something of. 1.** To cause trouble over. **2.** To do well with; make effective or profitable use of. —**see something of.** To see occasionally. —**something of.** In someway; to some extent: *It's something of a mystery.*
~*adv.* **1.** Rather; to some extent: *She sounds something like me.* **2.** *British Nonstandard.* To a great degree. Used with an adjective to form an adverbial phrase: *messed it up something rotten.*

something else *pron. Chiefly U.S. Slang.* Something spectacular or impressive.

some·time (súm-tīm) *adv.* **1.** At an indefinite or unstated time. **2.** At an indefinite time in the future. **3.** *Archaic.* Sometimes. **4.** *Archaic.* Formerly.
~*adj.* Having been at some prior time; former: *a sometime secretary.* See Usage note at **someday.**

some·times (súm-tīmz) *adv.* **1.** On some occasions; at times; now and then. **2.** *Obsolete.* At some prior time; once; formerly.

some·what (súm-wot, -hwot ‖ *U.S. also* -wut, -hwut, *or with final stress*) *adv.* To some extent or degree; rather.
~*pron.* Some amount, part, or degree; something. Usually used with *of: He is somewhat of a fool.*

some·where (súm-wair, -hwair) *adv.* **1.** At, in, or to a place not specified or known; some place. **2.** At or to some unspecified point in time, amount, or degree. Usually used with *in* or *about.* —**get** or **go somewhere.** To achieve something or make progress.
~*pron.* An unknown or unspecified place.

so·mite (so̅m-īt) *n.* **1.** *Zoology.* A body segment, a **metamere** (see). **2.** *Embryology.* One of the segmental masses of mesoderm in the vertebrate embryo, occurring in pairs along the notochord. [SOM(A) + -ITE.] —**so·mit·ic** (so̅mittik) *adj.*

Somme (som). River in northern France. It rises in the Aisne départemente and flows west through Amiens and Abbeville to the English Channel. It is 243 kilometres (152 miles) long. The Battle of the Somme (1916) was one of the bloodiest engagements in history, in which tanks were used for the first time.

som·nam·bu·late (som-námbew-layt) *intr.v.* **-lated, -lating, -lates.** To walk while asleep. [SOMN(I)- + AMBULATE.]

som·nam·bu·lism (som-námbew-liz'm) *n.* Also **som·nam·bu·lance** (-láynss) **som·nam·bu·la·tion** (-láysh'n). The condition or practice of **sleepwalking** (see). —**som·nam·bu·list, som·nam·bu·la·tor** *n.* —**som·nam·bu·lis·tic** (-lístik), **som·nam·bu·lar** *adj.*

somni–, somn– *comb. form.* Indicates sleep; for example, **somnifacient, somnambulate.** [From Latin *somnus,* sleep.]

som·ni·fa·cient (sóm-ni-fáy-si-ənt, -shi- ‖ -fáysh'nt) *adj.* Tending to produce sleep; hypnotic. [SOMNI- + -FACIENT.]

som·nif·er·ous (som-níffərəss) *adj.* Also **som·nif·ic** (-níffik). Inducing sleep. [From Latin *somnifer:* SOMNI- + -FEROUS.]

som·no·lence (sóm-nələnss) *n.* Drowsiness; sleepiness.

som·no·lent (sóm-nələnt) *adj.* 1. Drowsy; sleepy. 2. Inducing or tending to induce sleep; soporific. [Middle English *sompnolent,* from Old French, from Latin *somnolentus,* from *somnus,* sleep.] —**som·no·lent·ly** *adv.*

son (sun) *n. Abbr.* **s.** 1. A male offspring. 2. Any male descendant. 3. **a.** An adopted male child. **b.** A son-in-law. 4. A male person associated with or considered as a product of something such as a place, activity, or cause: *sons of toil.* 5. A young man. Used as a familiar term of address. —**the Son.** The second person of the Trinity, Christ. [Middle English *son(e),* Old English *sunu.*]

so·nant (sónant, *also* sónnənt) *adj. Phonetics.* Voiced. ~*n. Phonetics.* 1. A voiced speech sound. 2. A syllabic consonant; a sonorant. [Latin *sonāns* (stem *sonānt-*), present participle of Latin *sonāre,* to sound.]

so·nar (só-naar) *n.* 1. A system using transmitted and reflected acoustic waves to detect and locate submerged objects. 2. An apparatus using such a system, as in a submarine. [*So*und *na*vigation *r*anging.]

so·na·ta (sə-naátə ‖ só-) *n.* A musical composition, as for the piano, violin, or other instrument, consisting of three or four independent movements varying in key, mood, and tempo. [Italian, from the feminine past participle of *sonare,* to sound, from Latin *sonāre.*]

sonata form *n.* A musical form consisting of three sections, the exposition, development, and recapitulation, often followed by a coda.

so·na·ti·na (sónnə-tée-nə ‖ sónə-) *n., pl.* **-nas** or **-ne** (-nay). A short sonata. [Italian, diminutive of SONATA.]

sonde (sond) *n.* A device, such as a **radiosonde** *(see),* launched into the atmosphere, used for making meteorological or other observations. [French. See **sound** (to measure water).]

sone (són) *n.* A subjective unit of loudness, equal to the loudness of a pure note having a frequency of 1,000 hertz at 40 decibels above the listener's threshold of hearing. [From Latin *sonus,* a sound.]

son et lu·mi·ère (són ay loómi-air, -aír; *French* soN-nay-lüm-yaír) *n.* A theatrical entertainment given at night in a historic, usually outdoor setting, using recorded sound, lighting, and other effects to present the history of the place. [French, sound and light.]

song (song ‖ *U.S. also* sawng *(and in compounds)*) *n.* 1. A usually brief musical composition consisting of words set to music, written or adapted for singing. 2. The act or art of singing. 3. A melodious utterance, such as a bird call. 4. **a.** *Poetic.* Poetry; verse. **b.** A lyric poem or ballad. 5. *Informal.* A small amount of money; a very low price: *picked it up for a song.* [Middle English *song, sang,* Old English *sang.*]

Song. See **Sung.**

Song (song, soong), **Mei-ling** (1897–). Wife of Nationalist Chinese president Jiang Jie-shi, and sister of T.V. Song. Educated in the United States, she introduced her husband to western culture and publicised his cause in the West.

Song Qing-Ling, also known as Soong, or Sung Ch'ing-Ling. (1892–1981). Chinese politician. The sister of T.V. Song, she married the Nationalist leader Sun Zhong-shan (Sun Yat-Sen), and became an active member of the movement. In modern China she has been honoured as a link between the original revolutionary movement and the present Communist regime.

Song, T.V. born Sung Tzu-Wen (1894–1971). Chinese financier and politician. He financed the Guomindang (Nationalist) Party of Sun Zhong-shan and established (1924) the Central Bank of China at Canton. He held various offices in the Guomindang governments and as foreign affairs minister negotiated (1945) the Sino-Soviet treaty of friendship. In 1949, he left China for the United States.

song and dance *n. Informal.* 1. A great fuss, commotion, display of anger, or rigmarole. 2. *Chiefly U.S.* An overelaborate effort to explain or justify.

song·bird (sóng-burd) *n.* A bird, especially one of the order Passeriformes, having a melodious song or call.

song form *n.* **Ternary form** *(see).*

song·ful (sóng-f'l) *adj.* Melodious; tuneful.

Song of Solomon *n. Abbr.* **S. of Sol.** A book of the Old Testament consisting of a dramatic love poem traditionally attributed to Solomon. Also called "Canticle of Canticles", "Song of Songs".

song·ster (sóng-stər) *n.* 1. One that sings. 2. A writer of songs or verses.

song thrush *n.* An Old World songbird, *Turdus philomelos,* having brown upper plumage and a spotted breast. Formerly also called "mavis", "throstle".

song·writ·er (sóng-rītər) *n.* One who writes lyrics or composes tunes, or both, for songs, especially popular songs.

son·ic (sónnik) *adj.* 1. Of or relating to audible sound: *a sonic wave.* 2. Having a speed approaching or being that of sound in air, approximately 332 metres per second (738 miles per hour) at sea level. [From Latin *son(us),* sound + -IC.]

sonic barrier *n.* The large increase in aerodynamic drag that acts on an aircraft as it approaches the speed of sound. Also called "sound barrier".

sonic boom *n.* A loud transient explosive sound caused by the shock wave preceding an aircraft travelling at supersonic speeds.

son-in-law (sún-in-law) *n., pl.* **sons-in-law** (súnz-). The husband of one's daughter.

son·net (sónnit) *n.* A 14-line poem usually in iambic pentameter and often made up either of a stanza of eight lines (an octet) followed by one of six lines (a sestet), or, in the Shakespearean form, three sets of four lines followed by a couplet, embodying the statement and the resolution of a single theme. [French, from Italian *sonetto,* from Old Provençal *sonet,* diminutive of *son,* song, from Latin *sonus,* sound.]

son·net·eer (sónni-téer) *n.* 1. A composer of sonnets. 2. An inferior poet.

son·ny (súnni) *n., pl.* **-nies.** Little boy; young man. Used as a familiar and sometimes contemptuous form of address. [Diminutive of SON.]

son of a bitch *n., pl.* **sons of bitches.** *Chiefly U.S. Slang.* A person for whom one feels intense dislike or contempt. Often considered vulgar.

son of a gun *n. pl.* **sons of guns.** *Chiefly U.S. Slang.* A man regarded with the admiring approval of his fellows, usually because of his macho qualities; a rogue. Often used as a term of address.

so·no·rant (sónnə-rənt, sónə- ‖ sə-nór-, -nôr-) *n. Phonetics.* 1. Any of a class of phonemes, such as (1), (r), (n), and (m), articulated without friction, being vocalic or consonantal in function according to context. 2. Either of the semivowels (w) and (y). [SONOR(OUS) + -ANT.]

so·nor·i·ty (sə-nórrəti, só- ‖ -náwrəti) *n.* The quality or state of being sonorous; resonance. [SONOR(OUS) + -ITY.]

so·no·rous (sónnə-rəss, sónə-, sə-náw- ‖ sə-nó-) *adj.* 1. Having or producing sound. 2. Having or producing a full, deep, or rich sound. 3. Rich and impressive, as in style or delivery; grandiloquent. [Latin *sonōrus,* from *sonor,* sound, from *sonāre,* to sound.] —**so·no·rous·ly** *adv.*

son·sy, son·sie (són-si) *adj. Chiefly Scottish.* 1. Plump. Used appreciatively. 2. Cheerful. 3. Bringing good luck. [Gaelic *sonas,* good luck, from *sona,* lucky.]

Soochow. See **Suzhou.**

soon (soon ‖ soon) *adv.* **sooner, soonest.** 1. Within a short time; not long after the present time or the time in question. 2. Without delay or hesitation; quickly; promptly: *came as soon as he got our message; the sooner the better.* 3. Before the usual or appointed time; early. 4. *Obsolete.* Immediately. —**as soon.** Willingly; by preference: *I'd as soon stay at home.* —**no sooner.** Immediately or immediately after. Used with *than.* —**sooner or later.** Inevitably. —**would sooner.** Would prefer to; would rather: *would sooner die than marry him.* [Middle English *sone, soon(e),* Old English *sōna,* from Germanic *sǣnō* (unattested).]

Usage: No sooner is generally followed by *than* in constructions such as *No sooner had she come in than the phone rang,* though *when* is a common alternative in informal speech.

soot (soot ‖ soot, sut) *n.* A fine dispersion of black particles, chiefly carbon, produced by the incomplete combustion of coal, oil, wood, or other fuels. ~*tr.v.* **sooted, sooting, soots.** To cover or smudge with soot. [Middle English *so(o)t,* Old English *sōt.*]

sooth (sooth) *adj. Archaic.* 1. True; truthful. 2. Soft; soothing. ~*n. Archaic.* Truth; reality. [Middle English *so(o)th,* Old English *sōth.*] —**sooth·ly** *adv.*

soothe (sooth) *v.* **soothed, soothing, soothes.** —*tr.* 1. To calm; mollify; placate. 2. To reduce the intensity of (pain or emotions, for example); assuage; alleviate. —*intr.* To bring comfort, composure, or relief. —See Synonyms at **relieve.** [Middle English *sothen,* to show to be true, Old English *sōthian,* from *sōth,* truth, SOOTH.] —**sooth·er** *n.* —**sooth·ing·ly** *adv.* —**sooth·ing·ness** *n.*

sooth·fast (sooth-faast ‖ -fast) *adj. Archaic.* 1. Truthful; honest. 2. True; real. [Middle English *sothfast,* Old English *sōthfæst : sōth,* SOOTH + *fæst,* FAST (firm).]

sooth·say (sooth-say) *intr.v.* **-said** (-sed), **-saying, -says** (-sez ‖ -sayz). To foretell future events; predict; prophesy. [Back-formation from SOOTHSAYER.]

sooth·say·er (sooth-say-ər) *n.* One who claims to predict future events; a prophet; a seer. [Middle English *sothsayer : soth,* SOOTH + *sayer,* one who says, from *sayen,* to SAY.]

soot·y (sootti ‖ sooti, sútti) *adj.* **-ier, -iest.** 1. Covered with soot. 2. Of or producing soot. 3. Black or dark like soot.

sooty mould *n.* 1. A fungal growth of mycelium and sooty spores on the surface of a leaf. 2. Any various epiphytic fungi, such as species of *Cladosporium,* producing such growths.

sooty tern *n.* An oceanic bird, *Sterna fuscata,* mainly from tropical Atlantic regions, having dark upper plumage.

sop (sop) *v.* **sopped, sopping, sops.** —*tr.* 1. To dip, soak, or drench in a liquid; saturate. 2. To take up by absorption. Usually used with *up.* —*intr.* To be or become thoroughly soaked or saturated. ~*n.* 1. A bit of bread or other food soaked in a liquid. 2. Something of little value offered in order to gain the favour or mollify the feelings of the recipient. [From Middle English *soppe,* dipped bread, Old English *sopp.*]

SOP standard operating procedure.

sop. soprano.

soph·ism (sóffiz'm) *n.* 1. A plausible but fallacious argument. 2. Any deceptive or fallacious form of argument; sophistry. [Middle English *sophime,* from Old French *sophi(s)me,* from Latin *sophisma,* from Greek, acquired skill, clever device, from *sophizesthai,* to play subtle tricks. See **sophist.**]

soph·ist (sóffist) *n*. **1.** *Capital* **S.** Any of a class of ancient Greek philosophers active during the second half of the fifth century B.C., who specialised in providing instruction in ethics and the art of public speaking, and came to be disparaged for their oversubtle, self-serving reasoning. **2.** A scholar or thinker, especially one skilful in devious argumentation. [From Latin *sophistēs*, from Greek, expert, deviser, from *sophizesthai*, to play subtle tricks, from *sophos†*, skilled, clever.]

so·phis·tic (sə-fístik, so-) *adj*. Also **so·phis·ti·cal** (-'l). **1.** Of, pertaining to, or characteristic of sophists, especially the ancient Sophists. **2.** Marked by or fond of sophistry; specious. **—so·phis·ti·cal·ly** *adv*.

so·phis·ti·cate (sə-físti-kayt) *v*. **-cated, -cating, -cates.** —*tr*. **1.** To cause to become less natural or simple; especially, to make less naive and more worldly-wise. **2.** To make less true, genuine, or honest; corrupt, pervert, or adulterate. **3.** To make more complex; refine. —*intr*. To use sophistry. ∼*n*. (-kət, -kit, -kayt). A sophisticated person. [From Medieval Latin *sophisticāre*, from Latin *sophisticus*, sophistic, from Greek *sophistikos*, from *sophistēs*, SOPHIST.] **—so·phis·ti·ca·tor** *n*. **—so·phis·ti·ca·tion** (-káysh'n) *n*.

so·phis·ti·cat·ed (sə-físti-kaytid) *adj*. **1. a.** Having acquired worldly knowledge; lacking natural simplicity or naiveté. **b.** Having acquired worldly refinement; urbane; cultured. **2.** Complex or complicated; elaborate. **3.** Suitable for or appealing to the tastes of sophisticated people. **—so·phis·ti·cat·ed·ly** *adv*.

soph·is·try (sóffistri) *n., pl.* **-tries. 1.** A plausible but misleading or fallacious argument. **2.** Plausible but fallacious argumentation; faulty reasoning.

Soph·o·cles (sóffə-kleez). (c. 495–406 B.C.). Greek dramatist. Together with **Euripides** and **Aeschylus**, he was one of the three greatest dramatists of ancient Greece. Of more than 100 plays written by him only seven survive. These include *Ajax*, probably the earliest, *Oedipus Rex*, considered his masterpiece, *Antigone*, and *Oedipus at Colonus*. **—Soph·o·cle·an** (-klée-ən) *adj*.

soph·o·more (sóffə-mawr ‖ -mōr, *U.S. also* sóff-) *n*. A second-year student in a four-year course at a U.S. university or high school. Also used adjectively: *a sophomore year*. [Probably from earlier *sophumer*, "arguer", from obsolete *sophum*, variant of SOPHISM.]

soph·o·mor·ic (sóffə-mórrik, -máwrik ‖ -mórik, *U.S. also* sóffi-) *adj*. Characteristic of a sophomore; especially, immature and overconfident. **—soph·o·mor·i·cal·ly** *adv*.

So·phy, so·phi (sófi) *n., pl.* **-phies.** A title formerly given to kings of Persia. [Persian *Safī*, surname of ruling Persian dynasty (1500–1736), from Arabic *Safī-ud-din*, "purity of religion."]

-sophy *n. comb. form*. Indicates knowledge or a system of thought; for example, **theosophy**. [From Greek *sophia*, wisdom, and *sophos*, wise. See **sophist**.]

so·por (só-pər, -pawr) *n*. An abnormally deep sleep; stupor. [Latin *sopor*, sleep.]

so·po·rif·er·ous (sóppə-rífferəss, sópə-) *adj*. Inducing sleep; soporific. [From Latin *soporifer* : SOPOR + -FEROUS.] **—so·po·rif·er·ous·ly** *adv*. **—so·po·rif·er·ous·ness** *n*.

so·po·rif·ic (sóppə-ríffik, sópə-) *adj*. **1.** Inducing or tending to induce sleep. **2.** Drowsy. ∼*n*. A sleep-inducing drug. [SOPOR + -FIC.]

sop·ping (sópping) *adj*. Soaked thoroughly; drenched. ∼*adv*. Used as an intensive in the phrase *sopping wet*.

sop·py (sóppi) *adj*. **-pier, -piest. 1.** Soaked; sopping. **2.** *Informal*. Oversentimental in a silly way. **—sop·pi·ness** *n*.

sop·ra·ni·no (sópprə-néenō ‖ sóprə-) *adj*. Having a pitch higher than a soprano. Said of a musical instrument. ∼*n., pl.* **sopraninos.** A sopranino instrument. [Italian, diminutive of SOPRANO.]

so·pran·o (sə-prá'a-nō ‖ *U.S. also* -prá'a-) *n., pl.* **-os** or **-prani** (-nee). *Abbr*. **sop.** *Music*. **1.** The highest natural human voice, found in some women and in young boys. **2.** A singer having such a voice. **3.** A part for such a voice in four-part harmony. **4.** The tonal range characteristic of a soprano. **5.** The highest-pitched musical instrument in certain families of instrument. ∼*adj*. Of, pertaining to, for, or in the range of a soprano: *a soprano saxophone*. [Italian, from *sopra*, above, from Latin *suprā*.]

sorb¹ (sorb) *tr.v.* **sorbed, sorbing, sorbs.** To take up and hold, as by absorption. [Back-formation from ABSORB.]

sorb² *n*. **1.** Any of several Old World trees of the genus *Sorbus* or related genera, such as the white beam or the rowan. **2.** The fruit of such a tree. In this sense, also called "sorb apple". [French *sorbe*, from Latin *sorbus*, SERVICE (tree).] **—sorp·tion** *n*.

Sorb (sorb) *n*. A Wend (see). [German *Sorbe*, perhaps variant of *Serbe*, Serb, from Serbian *Srb*, SERB.]

Sor·bi·an (sórbi-ən) *n*. **1.** A Wend (see). **2.** Wendish (see). [From SORB.] **—Sor·bi·an** *adj*.

sor·bic acid (sórbik) *n*. A white crystalline solid, $C_6H_8O_2$, found in the berries of the mountain ash and also synthesised and used as a food preservative and fungicide. [From SORB (tree).]

sor·bi·tol (sórbi-tol ‖ -tōl) *n*. A white sweet crystalline alcohol, $C_6H_8(OH)_6$, found in certain fruits and manufactured from sucrose for use as an artificial sweetener and raw material for making ascorbic acid and some plastics.

sor·bo rubber (sórbō) *n*. A form of spongy rubber. [*Sorbo*, from ABSORB.]

sor·bose (sórb-ōz, -ōss) *n*. A white crystalline sugar, $C_6H_{12}O_6$, used in the manufacture of ascorbic acid. [SORB (tree) + -OSE.]

sor·cer·er (sór-sərər) *n*. One who practices sorcery; a wizard or magician. [Middle English *sorser*, from Old French *sorcier*, from Vulgar Latin *sortiārius* (unattested), caster of lots, from *sors* (stem *sort-*), lot.]

sor·cer·ess (sór-sə-riss, -ress) *n*. A female sorcerer.

sor·cer·y (sór-səri) *n., pl.* **-ies.** The use of supernatural powers in order to produce supernatural effects, especially through the assistance of evil spirits; witchcraft; black magic. See Synonyms at **magic**. [Middle English *sorcerie*, from Old French, from *sorcier*, SORCERER.] **—sor·cer·ous** *adj*. **—sor·cer·ous·ly** *adv*.

sor·did (sórdid) *adj*. **1.** Filthy or dirty; foul: *a sordid sewer*. **2.** Depressingly squalid; wretched: *sordid shantytowns*. **3.** Morally degraded; vile; despicable: *sordid betrayal*. **4.** Exceedingly mercenary; grasping; selfish. [French *sordide*, from Latin *sordidus*, from *sordēre*, to be dirty.] **—sor·did·ly** *adv*. **—sor·did·ness** *n*.

sor·di·no (sawr-dée-nō) *n., pl.* **-ni** (-nee). Also **sor·dine** (sór-deen). A mute for a musical instrument. [Italian, from *sordo*, deaf, mute, from Latin *surdus*.]

sore (sor ‖ sŏr) *adj*. **sorer, sorest. 1.** Causing physical pain, as from injury or disease; aching or tender: *a sore foot*. **2.** Feeling physical pain; hurting: *I'm still sore today*. **3.** Causing or involving hardship misery, or distress; grievous: *sore need*. **4.** Causing embarrassment, irritation, or the like: *a sore subject*. **5.** Full of distress; grieved; sorrowful. **6.** *Chiefly U.S. Informal*. Angered; annoyed. ∼*adv. Archaic.* Sorely. ∼*n*. **1.** An open wound or ulcer on the skin or a mucous membrane. **2.** Any source of pain, distress, or irritation. [Middle English *sar, sor*, Old English *sār*.] **—sore·ness** *n*.

so·re·di·um (sə-réedi-əm, so-) *n*. A type of asexual spore produced by some lichens, consisting of a few algal cells enclosed in fungal hyphae. [New Latin, irregularly from Greek *sōros*, heap.]

sore·head (sór-hed ‖ sŏr-) *n*. *U.S. Informal*. A person who is easily offended, annoyed, or angered.

sore·ly (sór-li ‖ sŏr-) *adv*. **1.** Severely; painfully; grievously. **2.** Extremely; greatly: *His skill was sorely needed*.

sore throat *n*. Any of various inflammations of the tonsils, pharynx, or larynx characterised by pain in swallowing.

sor·ghum (sórgəm) *n*. **1.** An Old World grass of the genus *Sorghum*; especially, *S. vulgare*, several varieties of which are widely cultivated as grain and forage or as a source of syrup. **2.** Syrup made from the juice of this plant. [New Latin, from Italian *sorgo*, perhaps from Vulgar Latin *syricum (grāmen)* (unattested), Syrian (grass), from Latin *Syricum*, SYRIAN.]

sor·go, sor·gho (sórgō) *n., pl.* **-gos.** Any of various sorghums cultivated as a source of syrup. [Italian *sorgo*, SORGHUM.]

so·ri. Plural of **sorus**.

sor·i·cine (sórri-sīn ‖ sáwri-, sŏri-, -seen) *adj*. Of or belonging to the family Soricidae, which includes the shrews. [From Latin *sōricīnus*, from *sōrex* (stem *sōric-*), shrew, akin to Greek *hurax*, HYRAX.]

so·ri·tes (so-rīteez, sə-) *n., pl.* **sorites.** *Logic*. A form of argument in which a series of incomplete syllogisms is so arranged that the predicate of each premise forms the subject of the next. [Latin *sōrītēs*, from Greek *sōreitēs*, from *sōros*, heap, pile.]

so·ro·ral (sə-ráw-rəl, so- ‖ -rō-) *adj*. Pertaining to or like a sister; sisterly. [Latin *soror*, sister.]

so·ror·ate (sə-ráw-rət, so-, -rit ‖ -rō-) *n*. The custom of marriage of a man to his wife's sister or sisters, usually after the first wife has died or proved sterile. [From Latin *soror*, sister.]

so·ror·i·cide (sə-rórri-sīd, so- ‖ -ráwri-) *n*. **1.** The killing of one's sister. **2.** One who kills his own sister. [Medieval Latin *sororicidium* : Latin *soror*, sister + -CIDE.] **—so·ror·i·cid·al** (-sīd'l) *adj*.

so·ror·i·ty (sə-rórrəti, so- ‖ -ráwrəti) *n., pl.* **-ties. 1.** A sisterhood. **2.** *U.S.* A social club for female students, as at a university. Compare **fraternity**. [From Medieval Latin *sororitās*, from Latin *soror*, sister.]

so·ro·sis (sə-rō-siss, so-) *n., pl.* **-ses** (-seez). *Botany*. A fleshy composite fruit, such as a pineapple, formed from an enlarged spike or perianth. [From Greek *sōros*, heap.]

sorp·tion (sórpsh'n) *n*. *Chemistry*. **1.** The process of sorbing. **2.** The state of being sorbed. [Back-formation from ABSORPTION and ADSORPTION.]

sor·rel¹ (sórrəl ‖ sáwrəl) *n*. **1.** Any of several plants of the genus *Rumex*, having acid-flavoured leaves sometimes used as salad greens; especially, *R. acetosella*, a widely naturalised species native to Eurasia. **2.** Any of various plants of the genus *Oxalis*. See **wood sorrel**. [Middle English *sorel*, from Old French *surele*, from *sur*, sour, from Germanic.]

sorrel² *n*. **1.** Brownish orange to light brown. **2.** A horse of this colour. [Middle English *sorelle*, sorrel-coloured, from Old French *sorel*, from *sor*, red-brown, from Germanic.]

sor·row (sórrō ‖ sáwrō) *n*. **1.** Mental anguish or suffering, especially because of injury or loss; sadness. **2.** Something that causes such suffering; misfortune. **3.** The expression of such suffering; grieving. **—See Synonyms at regret.** ∼*intr.v.* **sorrowed, -rowing, -rows.** To feel or display sorrow;

sorrel *This widely distributed grassland plant flowers in summer and autumn. It is shown here growing among buttercups.*

grieve. [Middle English *sorge, sorow,* Old English *sorh, sorg,* anxiety, sorrow.] **—sor·row·er** *n.*

sor·row·ful (sórrō-f'l, sórrə- || sáwrō-, sáwrə-) *adj.* Causing, feeling, or expressing sorrow; mournful. See Synonyms at **sad.** **—sor·row·ful·ly** *adv.* **—sor·row·ful·ness** *n.*

sor·ry (sórri || *U.S. also* sáwri) *adj.* **-rier, -riest. 1. a.** Feeling sympathy, pity, or distress; sorrowful. **b.** Feeling regret or penitence. Often used to express apology: *I am sorry to be late.* **2.** Inspiring a mixture of pity and scorn; pitiful; deplorable: *a sorry sight.* **3.** Worthless or inferior; contemptible; paltry: *a sorry attempt at apology.* **4.** Causing sorrow or grief; sad; distressing.
~*interj.* Used to express apology or to ask someone to repeat what he has just said. [Middle English *sary, sory,* Old English *sārig,* painful, sad.] **—sor·ri·ly** *adv.* **—sor·ri·ness** *n.*

sort (sort) *n.* **1.** A particular class or kind of persons or things grouped together on the basis of some common characteristic. **2.** The character or nature of something; type; quality. **3.** Something that approximates to a certain, often inadequate, degree to the specific thing: *a job of a sort; lives in a sort of a penthouse.* **4.** *Informal.* **a.** A person: *a good sort.* **b.** *Australian.* A woman or girl. **5.** *Archaic.* Manner; way. **6.** *Usually plural. Printing.* One of the characters in a font of type. **—**See Synonyms at **type. —of sorts. 1.** Of a mediocre or inferior kind. **2.** Of one kind or another. **—out of sorts.** *Informal.* **1.** Somewhat ill; slightly sick. **2.** In a bad mood; irritable; cross. **—sort of.** *Informal.* Somewhat; rather.
~*v.* **sorted, sorting, sorts.** *—tr.* **1.** To classify, separate, or arrange according to quality, size, or some other criterion. **2.** *Scottish Informal.* To repair; restore to working order. *—intr. Formal.* To be in harmony; fit in; agree. Used with *with.* [Middle English, from Old French *sorte,* probably from Common Romance *sorta* (unattested), "kind", from Latin *sors* (stem *sort-*), lot, fortune.] **—sort·a·ble** *adj.* **—sort·er** *n.*

Usage: The numerical status of *sort of* and *kind of,* when used with a plural noun, has long been a source of controversy. The informal usage shown in *These sort of problems need to be solved* attracts criticism, on the grounds that the singular noun requires a singular modifier. In defence of the construction (which has literary precedent going back to Shakespeare), it is argued that the modifer *these/those* is used because of the collective plural sense of the whole noun phrase *(These (sort of) problems need to be solved).* However, many people prefer not to use the problematic construction, and use some other phrasing, such as *Problems of this sort . . .*

sor·tie (sór-ti, -tee) *n. Military.* **1.** A sally by besieged forces upon the besiegers. **2.** A single flight of an aircraft on a combat mission. [French, "a going out", from past participle of *sortir*†, go out.]

sor·ti·lege (sórtilij) *n.* The act or practice of foretelling the future by drawing lots. [Middle English, from Old French, from Medieval Latin *sortilegium,* from *sortilegus,* diviner : Latin *sors* (stem *sort-*), lot + *legere,* to read.]

sor·ti·tion (sawr-tísh'n) *n.* The drawing of lots, as in the selection of candidates for office. [Latin *sortitiō* (stem *sortitiōn-*), from *sortīrī,* to cast lots, from *sors,* lot.]

sort out *tr.v.* **1.** To separate or abstract (one kind, for example) from others. **2.** To resolve, deal with, or put to rights. **3.** *British Informal.* To punish or physically attack.

sort-out (sórt-owt) *n. British Informal.* An act of putting things in order.

so·rus (sáw-rəss || sṓ-) *n., pl.* **sori** (-rī). *Botany.* **1.** A cluster of spore cases borne by ferns on the undersides of the fronds. **2.** A similar structure in certain fungi and lichens. [New Latin, from Greek *sōros,* heap.]

S O S *n.* **1.** The letters represented by the radiotelegraphic signal •••–––•••, used internationally as a distress signal, particularly by ships and aircraft. **2.** Any call or signal for help.

so-so (sṓ-sō || -sṓ) *adj. Informal.* Neither very good nor very bad; mediocre; passable. See Synonyms at **average.**
~*adv. Informal.* Indifferently; tolerably; passably.

sos·te·nu·to (sóstə-nŏŏ-tō, sósti-, -néw-) *adv. Abbr.* **sost.** *Music.* In a sustained or prolonged manner. Used as a direction.
~*n., pl.* **sostenutos** or **-ti** (-tee). *Abbr.* **sost.** *Music.* A passage played or sung in this manner. [Italian, past participle of *sostenere,* to SUSTAIN.] **—sos·te·nu·to** *adj.*

sot (sot) *n.* A chronic drunkard. [Middle English *sot,* a fool, Old English *sott,* from Medieval Latin *sotius*†.]

so·te·ri·ol·o·gy (sō-téer-i-óllǝji) *n.* The theological doctrine of salvation as effected by Christ. [Greek *sōtērion,* deliverance, from *sōtēr,* saviour, from *sōzein,* to save, from *saos,* safe + -LOGY.] **—so·te·ri·o·log·i·cal** (-ə-lójik'l) *adj.*

So·thic (sṓthik, sóthik) *adj.* **1.** Designating the ancient Egyptian year, consisting of 365¼ days. **2.** Designating a cycle consisting of 1,461 years of 365 days in the ancient Egyptian calendar. [Greek *Sōthis,* the star Sirius, which appeared on the eastern horizon at sunrise when the year commenced.]

So·this (sṓthiss) *n.* Sirius, the Dog Star. [Greek *Sōthis,* the Egyptian, the star Sirius. See **Sothic.**]

So·tho (sŏŏ-tŏŏ, -tŏŏ, sṓtō) *n., pl.* **-thos** or collectively **Sotho. 1.** A group of Bantu languages spoken in Lesotho, Botswana, and South Africa. **2.** A member of a Sotho-speaking people. **3.** The dialect of Sotho spoken in Lesotho. In this sense also called "Sesotho".

sot·tish (sóttish) *adj.* **1.** Stupefied from or as if from drink. **2.** Tending to drink excessively; drunken. **—sot·tish·ly** *adv.*

sot·to vo·ce (sóttō vṓchi) *adv.* Very softly; especially, so as not to be overheard; in an undertone. [Italian, "under the voice".]

sou (sōō) *n.* **1.** A former French coin of very low value. **2.** A very small amount of money. [French, back-formation from Old French *sous,* plural of *sout,* from Latin *solidus,* SOLIDUS.]

Sou. southern.

sou·brette (sōō-brét) *n.* **1. a.** A saucy, coquettish, and intriguing lady's maid in comedies or comic opera. **b.** An actress or singer taking such a part. **2.** Any flirtatious or frivolous young woman. [French, from Provençal *soubreto,* feminine of *soubret,* coy, from *sobrar,* to be above, from Latin *superāre,* from *super,* above.]

soubriquet. Variant of **sobriquet.**

sou·chong (sōō-chóng, -shóng, -chong, -shong) *n.* One of several varieties of black tea native to China and adjacent regions. [Chinese *xiǎo zhǒng,* small kind.]

souf·fle (sōōf'l) *n. Medicine.* A blowing sound heard through a stethoscope, usually due to the movement of blood in vessels. [French, from *souffler,* to blow, ultimately from Latin *sufflāre* : *suf-,* SUB- + *flāre,* to blow.]

souf·flé (sōō-flay || *U.S.* sōō-fláy) *n.* A light, fluffy baked dish made with egg yolks and beaten egg whites combined with various other ingredients and served as a main dish or sweetened as a dessert.
~*adj.* Also **souf·fléed** (flayd || -fláyd). Made light and puffy by beating or cooking. [French, from the past participle of *souffler,* to blow, puff up. See **souffle.**]

sough (sow, suf) *intr.v.* **soughed, soughing, soughs.** To make a soft murmuring or rustling sound: *a gentle soughing wind.*
~*n.* A deep, soft murmuring sound, as of the wind or a gentle surf. [Middle English *swoghen,* Old English *swōgan.*]

sought. Past tense and past participle of **seek.**

sought-af·ter (sáwt-aaftər, -äaftər || -aftər, -áftər) *adj.* In great demand; highly-regarded.

soul (sōl) *n.* **1.** The animating and vital principle in humankind credited with the faculties of thought, action, and emotion and conceived as forming an immaterial entity distinguished from but temporally coexistent with the body. **2.** *Theology.* The spiritual nature of man considered in relation to God, regarded as immortal, separable from the body at death, and susceptible to happiness or misery in a future state. **3.** The disembodied spirit of a dead human being. **4.** The vital, central part or feature of something. **5.** A human being: *a village of 200 Souls.* **6.** A person considered as the perfect embodiment of some quality; a personification. **7.** A person considered as an inspiring force; a prime mover. **8.** The emotional nature in humankind as distinguished from the mind or intellect. **9.** Depth and sincerity of feeling, or the ability to convey this effectively. **10. a.** A capacity for intense and unhibited emotional feeling, especially considered as a characteristic quality of black American culture. **b.** Soul music. [Middle English *soul,* Old English *sāwol,* from Common Germanic *saiwalō* (unattested).]

soul brother *n. U.S. Slang.* A fellow black of the male sex.

soul-de·stroy·ing (sṓl-di-stróy-ing, -də-) *adj.* Monotonous and totally unstimulating; stultifying.

soul·food (sṓl-fōōd) *n. U.S.* Food that belongs to the traditional diet of blacks in the southern United States.

soul·ful (sṓl-f'l) *adj.* Full of or expressing deep feeling; profoundly emotional. **—soul·ful·ly** *adv.* **—soul·ful·ness** *n.*

soul·less (sṓl-ləss, -liss) *adj.* **1.** Devoid of sensitivity or the capacity for deep feeling. **2.** Devoid of human qualities; depressingly impersonal: *a big soulless office.* **—soul·less·ly** *adv.* **—soul·less·ness** *n.*

soul mate *n.* A person with whom one shares a deep empathy in terms of disposition, point of view, or sensitivity.

soul music *n.* Music derived from black American gospel music with elements of rhythm and blues, characterised by emotional fervour and earthiness.

soul-search·ing (sṓl-serching) *n.* The penetrating examination of oneself, one's motives, convictions, and feelings.

soul sister *n. U.S. Slang.* A fellow black of the female sex.

sound[1] (sownd || *West Indies also* sungd) *n.* **1. a.** A vibratory disturbance characterised by longitudinal waves in the pressure and density of a fluid, or in the elastic strain in a solid, with frequency in the approximate range between 20 and 20,000 hertz, and capable of being detected by the organs of hearing. **b.** Loosely, such a disturbance of any frequency. **2. a.** The sensation stimulated in the organs of hearing by such a disturbance. **b.** Such sensations collectively. **3.** A distinctive auditory effect produced by a particular cause: *the sound of the whistle.* **4.** The distance over which something can be heard; earshot: *within sound of cannon fire.* **5. a.** An articulation made by the vocal apparatus. **b.** The distinctive character of such an articulation. For example, *bear* and *bare* have the same sound. **6.** A mental impression conveyed; import; implication: *I don't like the sound of that.* **7.** Auditory material that is recorded, as for a film or television programme. **8.** A style of popular music associated with a particular place, person, or the like: *the Tamla-Motown sound.* **9.** *Archaic.* Rumour; report.
~*v.* **sounded, sounding, sounds.** *—intr.* **1.** To make or give forth a sound. **2. a.** To produce a particular effect when heard: *Your exhaust sounds very noisy.* **b.** To present a particular impression; seem to be: *That argument sounds reasonable; sounds as if we've lost.* *—tr.* **1.** To cause to give forth or produce a sound. **2.** To summon, announce, or signal by a sound: *sound a warning.* **3.** To articulate (a speech sound); pronounce. **4.** To make known; celebrate. **5.** To examine (a bodily organ or part) by causing to emit sound; auscultate. **—sound off.** *Informal.* To express one's opinions, complaints, or prejudices in a loud, vigorous tone. [Middle English *sun, soun,* from Old French *son,* from Latin *sonus.*]

PRONUNCIATION KEY

a, **trap**; aa, **father**; ai, **fair**; ar, **star**; aw, **lawn**; ay, **play**; b, bb, **stab**; **rubber**; ch, **church**; ck, **ticket**; d, dd, **dead**; **ladder**; e, **dress**; ee, **bee**; er, **defer**; ew, **few**; ewr, **pure**; ə, **about**; ər, **letter**; f, ff, **fife**; **differ**; g, gg, **giggle**; h, **hat**; i, **kit**; ī, **price**; īr, **fire**; j, **judge**; k, **kick**; l, ll, **let**; 'l, **needle**; m, mm, **man**; n, nn, **no**; 'n, **sudden**; ng, **thing**; o, **lot**; ō, **no**; ŏŏ, **foot**; ōō, **shoe**; oor, **poor**; ow, **cow**; owr, **hour**; oy, **boy**; p, pp, **pepper**; r, rr, **red**; s, ss, **sauce**; sh, **ship**; t, tt, **totter**; th, **thick**; th, **this**; **smooth**; u, **cut**; ur, **turn**; v, vv, **valve**; w, **wet**; y, **yes**; z, zz, **zebra**; zh, **vision**; **pleasure**

IN FOREIGN WORDS:

aɴ, oɴ, **Saint-Saëns**; hl, **Llanelli**; **Hluhluwe**; kh, **loch**; **lough**; **Khaled**

STRESS MARK:

ín-sīt, **insight**; in-sīt, **incite**

sound² *adj.* **sounder, soundest. 1.** Free from defect, decay, or damage; in good condition. **2.** Free from disease or injury; healthy: *sound in body and mind.* **3.** Having a firm basis; solid; substantial: *a sound foundation.* **4.** Financially secure or stable; reliable: *a sound economy.* **5. a.** Founded on valid reasoning; free from misapprehension or logical flaws; sensible and cogent: *a sound observation.* **b.** Marked by or showing common sense and good judgment; level-headed: *Sound advice.* **c.** Marked by or showing impressive breadth of learning; well-versed. **6.** Thorough; severe: *a sound flogging.* **7.** Deep and unbroken; undisturbed: *a sound sleep.* **8.** Free from moral defect; upright; honourable. **9.** Worthy of confidence; trustworthy. **10.** Compatible with an accepted point of view; orthodox, especially in a theological sense. **11.** *Law.* Legally valid. —See Synonyms at **healthy, valid.**
~*adv.* Deeply: *sound asleep.* [Middle English *sund,* Old English *gesund.*] —**sound·ly** *adv.* —**sound·ness** *n.*

sound³ *n.* **1.** A long, relatively wide body of water wider than a strait or a channel, connecting larger bodies of water. **2.** A long, wide ocean inlet. **3.** The air bladder of a fish. [Middle English *sound,* sound, swimming, Old English *sund,* swimming.]

sound⁴ *v.* **sounded, sounding, sounds.** —*tr.* **1.** To measure the depth of (water), especially by means of a weighted line; fathom. **2.** To try to find out the attitudes or intentions of (a person), especially by indirect questioning. Usually used with *out.* **3.** *Surgery.* To probe (a bodily cavity) with a sound. —*intr.* **1.** To measure depth. **2.** To dive swiftly downwards. Used of a whale or fish.
~*n.* *Surgery.* An instrument used to examine body cavities. [Middle English *sounden,* from Old French *sonder,* from *sonde,* a sounding line, probably from Old English *sund-,* from *sund,* sea.] —**sound·a·ble** *adj.*

Usage: **Sound out,** in the sense of 'search for an opinion', is now well-established as a transitive verb (*I'll sound them out and see what they think*), but it occasionally attracts criticism from purists who feel that the *out* is an unnecessary recent addition.

sound barrier *n.* The **sonic barrier** (see).

sound box *n.* A hollow chamber in the body of a musical instrument, such as a violin, that intensifies the resonance of the tone.

sound camera *n.* A cine camera equipped to record sound and image synchronously.

sound effects *pl.n.* Imitative sounds, as of thunder or an explosion, produced artificially for use in a film, play, or other performance. Also called "effects".

sound·er (sówndər ‖ *West Indies also* súngdər) *n.* One that sounds; specifically, a device for making soundings of the sea.

sound·ing¹ (sównding ‖ *West Indies also* súnding) *n.* **1.** Measurement or examination by sounding. **2.** An environmental probe for scientific observation. **3.** *Often plural.* **a.** The measurement of depth by a hand line or by sonic or ultrasonic means. **b.** A measured depth of water. **c.** Water shallow enough for depth measurements to be taken by a hand line. **4.** An investigation of opinions or attitudes; a probe.

sounding² *adj.* **1.** Emitting a full sound; resonant. **2.** Having a rich or impressive sound but little significance; high-sounding.

sounding balloon *n.* A **ballon sonde** (see).

sounding board *n.* **1.** A thin board forming the upper portion of the resonant chamber in a musical instrument, such as a violin or piano, and serving to increase resonance. Also called "sound board". **2.** A dome or other structure suspended behind or over a pulpit or platform to reflect the speaker's voice to the audience. **3.** Any person or group whose reactions to an idea, opinion, or point of view will serve as a measure of its effectiveness or acceptability. **4.** Any device or agency serving to spread or popularise an idea or point of view.

sounding lead *n.* The metal weight at the end of a sounding line.

sounding line *n.* A line marked at intervals of fathoms and weighted at one end, used to determine the depth of water.

sounding rocket *n.* A rocket used to make observations anywhere within the earth's atmosphere.

sound·less (sównd-ləss, -liss ‖ *West Indies also* súngd-) *adj.* Having or making no sound; silent. —**sound·less·ly** *adv.* —**sound·less·ness** *n.*

sound·proof (sównd-prōof ‖ -prōof, *West Indies also* súngd-) *adj.* Not penetrable by audible sound.
~*tr.v.* **soundproofed, -proofing, -proofs.** To make soundproof.

sound ranging *n.* The electronic location of a sound source, as of enemy weapons, by checking time intervals indicated by microphones of known position.

sound stage *n.* A room or studio, usually soundproof, used for the production of cinematic films.

sound system *n.* A set of equipment for playing back recorded sound usually consisting of a record deck, amplifier, speakers and often a cassette player and radio.

sound·track (sównd-trak ‖ *West Indies also* súngd-) *n.* **1.** The narrow strip at one side of a cine film that carries the sound recording. **2.** A recording of the music featured in a film.

sound wave *n.* A wave of sound (see).

soup (sōōp) *n.* **1.** A liquid food prepared from meat, fish, or vegetable stock with various other ingredients added, served either hot or cold. **2.** *Slang.* Anything suggestive of the consistency of soup, especially: **a.** Dense fog. **b.** Nitroglycerine. See **primordial soup.** —**in the soup.** *Informal.* In trouble; having difficulties. —**soup up.** *Informal.* **1.** To increase the power or speed potential of (an en-

gine). **2.** To improve; make more effective. [French *soupe,* from Old French, broth, sop, from Late Latin; from Germanic.]

soup·çon (sōōp-son ‖ *U.S.* sōōp-són) *n.* A very small amount; a trace; a touch. [French, SUSPICION.]

Sou·phan·ou·vong (sōō-fannoo-vóng), **Prince** (1902–). Laotian politician. He became first president of the republic of Laos in 1975.

soup kitchen *n.* A place where food is offered freely or at very low cost to the needy.

soup·spoon (sōōp-spōōn) *n.* A spoon used for eating soup, about the same size as a dessertspoon but with a more rounded bowl.

soup·y (sōōpi) *adj.* **-ier, -iest. 1.** Having the consistency or appearance of soup. **2.** Foggy. **3.** *Informal.* Inordinately sentimental.

soup·strain·er (sōōp-straynər) *n. Informal.* A bushy moustache that completely covers the upper lip.

sour (sowr) *adj.* *Rare* **sourer, sourest. 1.** Having a taste characteristic of that produced by acids; sharp, tart, or tangy, as lemons or vinegar are. **2.** Made acid or rancid by fermentation; spoiled. Said of milk for example. **3.** Having the characteristics of fermentation or rancidity; tasting or smelling of decay. **4.** Bad-tempered and morose; cross; peevish: *a sour temper.* **5. a.** Disagreeable; unpleasant. **b.** Turning out wrong; failing to fulfil expectations. **6.** Designating soil that is excessively acid and damaging to crops. **7.** Containing excessive amounts of sulphur compounds. Said of petrol.
~*n.* **1.** The sensation of sour taste, one of the four primary tastes. **2.** Anything that is sour. **3.** *Chiefly U.S.* A cocktail of spirits, such as whisky, with lime or lemon juice and sugar.
~*v.* **soured, souring, sours.** —*tr.* To make sour: "*Continued adversity had soured Johnson's temper*" (T.B. Macaulay). —*intr.* To become sour. [Middle English *so(u)r,* Old English *sūr,* from Germanic.] —**sour·ly** *adv.* —**sour·ness** *n.*

source (sorss ‖ sōrss) *n.* **1.** A spring, lake, or other body of water at which a stream or river originates. **2. a.** The place or thing from which something originates; the starting point: *the source of their quarrel.* **b.** That from which someting comes or is derived: *a source of income; alternative sources of energy.* **c.** One that causes, creates, or initiates something: *a source of continual annoyance.* **3.** A person or place that supplies information. Also used adjectivally: *a source book.* **4.** A book, document, or other record supplying primary or firsthand information. **5.** The electrode in a field-effect transistor from which the majority carriers flow into the interelectrode region. **6.** In thermodynamics, the part of a system at which heat, or more generally energy, is added to the system. In this sense, compare **sink.** —See Synonyms at **origin.**
~*tr.v.* **sourced, sourcing, sources.** To obtain (materials) from a producer: *sourcing steel from Germany.* [Middle English *sours,* source, from Old French *sourse,* from the feminine past participle of *sourdre,* to rise, from Latin *surgere,* to SURGE.]

source language *n.* A language out of which a translation is made. Compare **target language.**

source program *n.* A computer program as written in the original programming language for conversion into machine language by the computer.

sour cherry *n.* **1.** A tree, *Prunus cerasus,* native to Eurasia, having white flowers and tart red fruit. **2.** The edible fruit of this tree.

sour cream *n.* Also **soured cream.** A smooth, thick, cream, artificially soured by the use of lactic acid bacteria, widely used as an ingredient in soups, salads, and various meat dishes.

sour·dough (sówr-dō) *n.* **1.** *Regional.* Sour fermented dough used as leaven in making bread. **2.** *U.S. & Canadian Slang.* An old-time settler or prospector, especially in Alaska and northwest Canada.

sour grapes *n.* The adoption of a disparaging attitude towards something that one secretly wants or admires but cannot attain. [From Aesop's fable of the fox that, unable to reach the grapes it wants, decides that they are unripe.]

sour mash *n. U.S.* **1.** A mixture of new mash and mash from a preceding run used to distil certain malt whiskeys. **2.** The whiskey distilled from this mash.

sour·puss (sówr-pōoss) *n. Informal.* A person with a habitually gloomy or sullen expression or attitude. [SOUR + PUSS (face).]

sour·sop (sówr-sop) *n.* **1.** A tropical American tree, *Annona muricata,* bearing spiny fruit with tart, edible pulp. **2.** The fruit of this tree.

Sou·sa (sōō-zə, *also* -sə), **John Philip** (1854–1932). American bandmaster and composer. He wrote comic operas, as well as marches such as *Liberty Bell* and *Washington Post March.*

sou·sa·phone (sōō-zə-fōn, -sə-) *n.* A large brass wind instrument similar to the tuba, having a flaring bell. [After John Philip SOUSA.]

souse¹ (sowss) *v.* **soused, sousing, souses.** —*tr.* **1.** To plunge in a liquid. **2.** To make soaking wet; drench. **3.** To steep in a mixture, as in pickling. **4.** *Slang.* To make intoxicated. —*intr.* To become immersed or soaking wet.
~*n.* **1.** The act or process of sousing. **2. a.** *Chiefly U.S.* Food steeped in pickle; especially, the feet, ears, and head of a pig. **b.** The liquid used in pickling; brine. **3.** *Slang.* A drunkard. [Middle English *sousen,* to souse, from *souse,* pickled meat, from Old French *sous, souz,* from Old Saxon *sultia,* Old High German *sulza,* brine.]

souse² *v.* **soused, sousing, souses.** *Archaic.* —*tr.* To pounce upon; attack. —*intr.* To swoop down, as an attacking hawk does. Used with *on* or *upon.* [Middle English *souce,* swooping motion, perhaps variant of *sours,* SOURCE.]

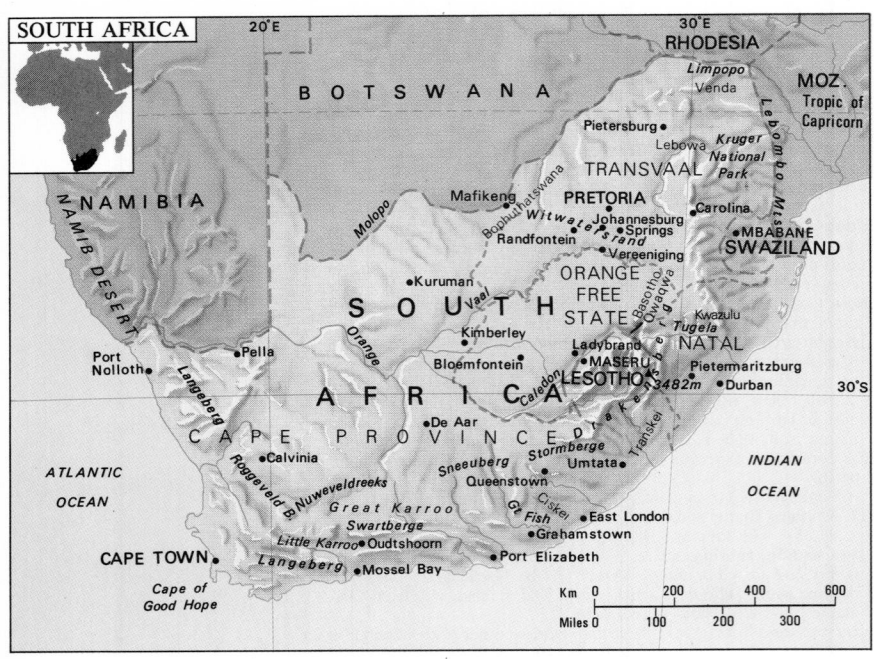

Natal (1843), but the other two territories became Boer republics. After the Anglo-Boer Wars (1880–81, 1899–1902), the British and former Boer territories were combined as the Union of South Africa (1910). In 1961, this became an independent republic and withdrew from the Commonwealth. Its ruling National Party's policy of apartheid, which provides for separate development of ethnic groups, has led to internal opposition and the hostility of many nations. Four black "homelands" have been granted independence: Transkei (1976), Bophuthatswana (1977), Venda (1979), and Ciskei (1981). However, they are not recognised by other countries. South Africa also administers Namibia. Area 1 221 037 square kilometres (471,445 square miles). Capitals, Pretoria (seat of government); Cape Town (seat of legislature); Bloemfontein (seat of judiciary). Population, 30,000,000 (mid-1982 est.).

South African n. A native or inhabitant of the Republic of South Africa, especially one of European descent. —**South African** adj.

South America. See **Americas, the.**

Southampton (sowth-ámp-tən, -hámp-, -ám-, -hám). City and major port in Hampshire, southern England, at the head of Southampton Water. Britain's largest passenger port, Southampton also has considerable freight trade and industries which include ship and yacht building, marine engineering, electronics, and aircraft.

Southampton, Henry Wriothesley, 3rd Earl of (1573–1624). English soldier and statesman. He was a patron of the Elizabethan poets, especially Shakespeare, who dedicated *Venus and Adonis* (1593), and *Rape of Lucrece* (1594) to him; several of the sonnets are probably addressed to him.

South Arabia, Federation of. See **South Yemen.**

South Australia. State in central southern Australia, much of which is inhospitable terrain, with deserts, mountains, salt lakes, and swampland. The Murray, in the extreme southeast, is the only important river. Some two thirds of the state's population are in the Adelaide metropolitan area. Agriculture, which produces cereals, vines, sheep, and livestock, is confined mostly to the Murray river area. There are valuable mineral deposits in the state; iron ore, salt, and gypsum are mined, and coal and natural gas are exploited. Adelaide, the capital, is the chief industrial centre, and Whyalla has steelworks and the largest shipyards in Australia.

south-bound (sówth-bownd) adj. Going towards the south.

south by east n. Abbr. **SbE** The direction, or point on the mariner's compass, halfway between due south and south-southeast. It is 168° 45′ east of due north. —**south by east** adj. & adv.

south by west n. Abbr. **SbW** The direction, or point on the mariner's compass, halfway between due south and south-southwest. It is 168° 45′ west of due north. —**south by west** adj. & adv.

South Carolina. State in the southeastern United States. Extensive coastal lowlands rise to inland plateaus, which flank the Appalachian Mountains. Traditionally known for its cotton and tobacco plantations, the state is also extensively forested and manufactures furniture, wood pulp, and paper. Other important industries include textiles and chemicals. Columbia is the capital.

south celestial pole n. Astronomy. The **South Pole** (see).

South China Sea. Arm of the western Pacific Ocean, lying off Southeast Asia and partially enclosed by Taiwan, the Philippines, and Borneo. It is subject to violent typhoons.

South Dakota. State in north central United States. It is bisected by the Missouri river, with fertile prairies to the east. The Great Plains to the west include the Black Hills and also the Badlands in the south. Gold and other minerals are mined, but the state's main products are cereals, soya beans, flax, and livestock. The Mount Rushmore National Memorial is a noted tourist attraction. Sioux Falls and Rapid City are the main urban areas. Pierre is the capital.

South Devon n. Any of a breed of red English cattle reared for milk and meat.

South-down (sówth-down) n. Any of a breed of small, hornless sheep of English origin, having dense, short, fine-textured wool. [From the *South Downs* in southern England.]

south-east (sówth-éest; nautical sow-éest) n. Abbr. **SE** 1. The direction, or point on the mariner's compass, halfway between south and east. It is 135° east of due north. 2. Sometimes capital **S.** The part of any country or region lying in this direction.

~adj. 1. Situated, towards, facing, or in the southeast. 2. Coming from the southeast. Said of a wind.

~adv. In, from, or towards the southeast. —**south-east-ern** adj.

Southeast Asia. Subcontinent comprising the ten modern states of Burma, Thailand, Laos, Kampuchea, Vietnam, Malaysia, Singapore, Brunei, Indonesia, and the Philippines. It covers 3 per cent of the world's land area and has 8 per cent of its people. The mainland is traversed by part of the Alpine-Himalayan mountain belt, which continues in the island arcs of the East Indies. Several major fertile valleys cross the area, including those of the Irrawaddy and Mekong. The region is the wettest of the major land areas, its equatorial lowlands having some 3 000 millimetres (about 120 inches) of rain a year, and temperatures averaging 27°C (81°F). Elsewhere there is a pronounced dry season. Rain forest with rich wildlife covered much of the region, and it still provides 18 per cent of the world's hardwoods. Soils are generally poor, but farming is important except in Singapore, and Southeast Asia produces more than 19 per cent of the world's rice and 27 per cent of its cassava. Commercial products include rice, palm oil, cane sugar, coffee, natural rubber (more than 85 per cent), and copra (over 70 per cent). The region is rich in minerals. It accounts for more than 50 per cent of the world's tin, and Singapore has a thriving import-ex-

souslik. Variant of **suslik.**

sou-tache (soō-tásh) n. A narrow flat braid in a herringbone effect, used for trimming and embroidery. [French, from Hungarian *sujtás*.]

sou-tane (soō-tán, -táan) n. A cassock worn by Roman Catholic priests. [French, from Italian *sottana*, garment worn under (religious vestments), from *sotto*, under, from Latin *subtus*, beneath, from *sub*, under.]

south (sowth) n. Abbr. **s, S, s., S., So., Sth.** 1. a. The direction along a meridian to the right of an observer facing in the direction of the earth's rotation; the direction to the right as one faces the rising sun. b. The cardinal point on the mariner's compass, 180° clockwise from north. 2. Any area or region lying in this direction. 3. Often capital **S.** a. One of the four positions at 90° intervals that lies in the south, points north, and stands at right angles to west and east. b. In games such as bridge and mah-jong, a player who occupies or is said to occupy this position. —**the South.** 1. The southern or Antarctic part of the Earth. 2. The southern part of any country or region, as: a. The southern part of England, as distinguished from the Midlands and the North. b. In the United States, the states lying south of Pennsylvania and east of the Mississippi. 3. The developing countries of the world, considered as chiefly occupying the southern regions of the earth; the Third World. 4. The Republic of Ireland as distinguished from Northern Ireland.

~adj. 1. To, towards, of, facing, or in the south. 2. Coming from or originating in the south. Said of a wind. 3. Capital **S.** Officially or conventionally designating the southern part of a country, continent, or other geographical area: *South America.*

~adv. In, from, or towards the south. [Middle English *south*, Old English *sūth*.]

South Africa, Republic of. Afrikaans **Republiek van Suid-Afrika.** Formerly **Union of South Africa.** Afrikaans **Urie van Suid-Afrika.** Southernmost, richest, most industrialised country of Africa. Its narrow coastal plains rise sharply to interior plateaus, flanked by the Drakensberg Mountains in the east. Desert areas in the northwest include part of the Kalahari. The population is chiefly Bantu-speaking Africans (67 per cent), with a ruling white minority (19) and Asians (3) and Coloureds (of mixed race) (11). The country has immense mineral resources, including gold, diamonds, chrome, platinum, phosphates, copper, iron, and coal. Mining accounts for some 13 per cent of the country's home production, manufacturing 24 per cent, and agriculture 8 per cent. Manufactures include steel and other metals, machinery, chemicals, and textiles. Only about 12 per cent of the land is cultivable, but 74 per cent is suited to grazing, and South Africa is noted for citrus fruits, apples, grapes, wines, cereals, cotton, beef, and wool. Forestry, fishing, and fish processing are also important. With no oil deposits, and following Middle Eastern conflicts and embargoes, South Africa now produces 47 per cent of its oil from coal. Johannesburg is the main industrial centre and Durban the chief port. The Portuguese were the first Europeans to reach South Africa (1488). Dutch settlers arrived in the 17th century and Britain eventually gained formal possession of the Cape (1814). Europeans from the Cape met the first African peoples at the Great Fish river, and the first major conflict between them occurred in 1781. Hostility between British and Dutch settlers (known as Boers or Africaaners) led to the Greak Trek (from 1835), a migration of Boers from the Cape who founded Natal, Orange Free State, and Transvaal. Britain seized port trade. Southeast Asia has some of the world's poorest countries, including Kampuchea and Laos.

Southeast Asia Treaty Organisation *n. Abbr.* **SEATO** The signatories to the Southeast Asian Collective Defence Treaty of 1954: Australia, France, New Zealand, Pakistan, the Philippines, Thailand, the United Kingdom, and the United States. The organisation was abolished in June 1977.

southeast by east *n. Abbr.* **SEbE** The direction, or point on the mariner's compass, halfway between southeast and east-southeast. It is 123° 45′ east of due north. —**southeast by east** *adj. & adv.*

southeast by south *n. Abbr.* **SEbS** The direction, or point on the mariner's compass, halfway between southeast and south-southeast. It is 146° 15′ east of due north. —**southeast by south** *adj. & adv.*

south·east·er (sówth-éestər; *nautical* sow-) *n.* A storm or wind blowing from the southeast.

south·east·er·ly (sówth-éestərli; *nautical* sow-) *adj.* **1.** Towards or in the southeast. **2.** Coming from the southeast. Said of a wind. ~*n., pl.* **south·east·er·lies.** A storm or wind blowing from the southeast. —**south·east·er·ly** *adv.*

south·east·ward (sówth-éest-wərd; *nautical* sow-) *adj.* Situated towards or facing the southeast. ~*n.* **1.** A direction or point towards the southeast. **2.** A region or part situated in or towards the southeast. ~*adv. Chiefly U.S.* Variant of **southeastwards.** —**south·east·ward·ly** *adj. & adv.*

south·east·wards (sówth-éest-wərdz) *adv.* Also *chiefly U.S.* **southeastward.** Towards the southeast.

south·er (sówthər) *n.* A strong wind coming from the south.

south·er·ly (súthərli) *adj.* **1.** Situated in or towards the south. **2.** Coming from the south. Said of a wind. ~*n., pl.* **southerlies.** A storm or wind blowing from the south. —**south·er·ly** *adv.*

southerly burster *n.* A strong dry wind bringing exceptionally low temperatures to New South Wales, Australia, when a mass of polar air pulled northwards behind a low "bursts" into warmer areas.

south·ern (súthərn) *adj. Abbr.* **s, S, s., S., So., Sou.** **1.** Situated towards, in, or facing the south. **2.** Coming from the south. Said of a wind. **3.** Native to or growing in the south. **4.** *Often capital* **S.** Of, pertaining to, or characteristic of southern regions or the South. [Middle English *southerne*, Old English *sūtherne*.]

Southern Alps. Mountain range in New Zealand, forming the backbone of South Island. It contains Mount Cook, at 3 763 metres (12,346 feet), the country's highest peak.

Southern Confederacy *n.* The **Confederate States of America** *(see).*

Southern Cross *n.* A constellation, **Crux** *(see).*

Southern Crown *n.* A constellation, **Corona Australis** *(see).*

South·ern·er (súthərnər) *n. Sometimes small* **s.** A native or inhabitant of the southern part of a country, especially of England or the United States.

Southern Hemisphere *n.* The half of the earth lying south of the equator.

southern lights *pl.n.* The **aurora australis** *(see).*

south·ern·most (súthərn-mōst) *adj.* Farthest south.

Southern Rhodesia. See **Zimbabwe, State of.**

south·ern·wood (súthərn-wŏŏd) *n.* A woody plant, *Artemisia abrotanum,* native to south Europe, having finely divided greyish, aromatic foliage. Also called "old man".

Sou·they (sówthi, *also* súthi), **Robert** (1774–1843). English poet and historian. He was one of the Lake poets and a pioneer of the Romantic movement, a friend of Coleridge and Wordsworth. In 1813 he became Poet Laureate.

South Georgia. See **Falkland Islands.**

South Glamorgan. Since 1974, a county in southern Wales, formed from southern Glamorgan and parts of Monmouthshire. The east of the county is dominated by the industrial centres of Cardiff and Barry, while the west consists of arable lowlands. Cardiff, the administrative centre, is also the capital of Wales.

South Holland. Also **Zuid-Holland** or **Zuidholland.** Province of southwestern Netherlands, bordering the North Sea. It is fragmented in the south by a network of rivers, canals, and channels. The province is densely populated, being both heavily industrialised and intensively farmed. It includes Rotterdam, Leiden, Delft, and Gouda. Its capital, The Hague, is also the nation's seat of government.

south·ing (sówthing) *n.* In navigation: **1.** The difference in latitude between two positions as a result of a movement to the south. **2.** Progress towards the south. **3.** *Astronomy.* A south declination.

South Island. Also **Middle Island.** The larger, but the less populous, of the two main islands of New Zealand. The principal cities are Christchurch and Dunedin. Much of the southwestern part of the island is taken up by the Fiordland National Park.

South Korea. See **Korea, South.**

South Orkney Islands. See **British Antarctic Territory.**

south·paw (sówth-paw) *n. Informal.* **1.** A boxer who leads with his right hand rather than with his left. **2.** A left-handed person. ~*adj. Informal.* Left-handed.

South Pole *n.* **1.** The southern end of the earth's axis of rotation. **2.** The celestial zenith of the heavens as viewed from the south terrestrial pole. Also called "south celestial pole". **3.** *Small* **s,** *small* **p.** The south-seeking **magnetic pole** *(see)* of a magnet.

south·ron (súthrən) *n. Chiefly Scottish. Often capital* **S.** A person who lives in the south, especially an Englishman.

~*adj. Chiefly Scottish.* Southern; English. [Middle English (Scottish), variant of *southren, southerne,* SOUTHERN.]

South Sandwich Islands. See **Falkland Islands.**

South Sea Bubble *n.* A scheme launched in 1720 by which the South Sea Company took partial responsibility for the national debt in exchange for a monopoly of trade with the South Sea Islands. The subsequent wild speculation was followed by a massive collapse in the same year.

South Shetland Islands. See **British Antarctic Territory.**

south-south-east (sówth-sowth-éest; *nautical* sów-sow-) *n. Abbr.* **SSE** The direction, or point on the mariner's compass, halfway between due south and southeast. It is 157° 30′ east of due north. ~*adj.* Situated towards, facing, or in this direction. ~*adv.* In, from, or towards this direction.

south-south-west (sówth-sowth-wést; *nautical* sów-sow-) *n. Abbr.* **SSW** The direction, or point on the mariner's compass, halfway between due south and southwest. It is 157° 30′ west of due north. ~*adj.* Situated towards, facing, or in this direction. ~*adv.* In, from, or towards this direction.

South·um·bri·an (sow-thúmbri-ən) *n.* A native or inhabitant of the northern part of the Anglo-Saxon kingdom of Mercia. —**South·um·bri·an** *adj.*

south·ward (sówth-wərd; *nautical* súthərd) *adj.* Situated towards, facing, or in the south. ~*n.* **1.** A direction towards the south. **2.** A region situated in or towards the south. ~*adv. Chiefly U.S.* Variant of **southwards.** —**south·ward·ly** *adj. & adv.*

south·wards (sówth-wərdz) *adv.* Also *chiefly U.S.* **southward.** Towards the south.

South·wark (súthərk). Borough of Greater London, England, lying across the river Thames from the City.

south·west (sówth-wést; *nautical* sow-) *n. Abbr.* **SW 1.** The direction, or point on the mariner's compass, halfway between south and west. It is 135° west of due north. **2.** *Sometimes capital* **S.** The part of any country or region lying in this direction. ~*adj.* **1.** To, towards, of, facing, or in the southwest. **2.** Coming from the southwest. Said of a wind. ~*adv.* In, from, or towards the southwest. —**south·west·ern** *adj.*

Southwest Africa. See **Namibia.**

southwest by south *n. Abbr.* **SWbS** The direction, or point on the mariner's compass, halfway between southwest and south-southwest. It is 146° 15′ west of due north. —**southwest by south** *adj. & adv.*

southwest by west *n. Abbr.* **SWbW** The direction, or point on the mariner's compass, halfway between southwest and west-southwest. It is 123° 45′ west of due north. —**southwest by west** *adj. & adv.*

south·west·er (sówth-wéstər, sow-) *n.* A storm or wind from the southwest.

south·west·er·ly (sówth-wéstərli; *nautical* sow-) *adj.* **1.** Towards or in the southwest. **2.** Comping from the southwest. Said of a wind. ~*n., pl.* **southwesterlies.** A storm or wind blowing from the southwest. —**south·west·er·ly** *adv.*

south·west·ward (sówth-wéstwərd; *nautical* sow-) *adj.* Situated towards, facing, or in the southwest. ~*n.* **1.** A direction towards the southwest. **2.** A region or part situated in or towards the southwest. ~*adv. Chiefly U.S.* Variant of **southwestwards.** —**south·west·ward·ly** *adj. & adv.*

south·west·wards (sówth-wést-wərdz) *adv.* Also *chiefly U.S.* **southwestward.** Towards the southwest.

South Yemen. Official name **People's Democratic Republic of Yemen.** Poor, desert country in the southwest of the Arabian peninsula, southwest Asia. The Hadhramaut valley is its only fertile area, yet 70 per cent of the people make a living from the land, producing millet, wheat, cotton, sheep, and goats. Aden's oil refinery accounts for more than 80 per cent of exports, petroleum being the main import. Yemenis working abroad are another important source of foreign exchange. The port of Aden was annexed by Britain (1839), and it was a British protectorate (1882–1914). Britain negotiated treaties with other rulers in the area, and the 17 sultanates combined in the Federation of South Arabia (1959). This was taken over by forces of the National Liberation Front during a civil war (1967). Britain withdrew, and the Southern Yemen People's Republic was proclaimed. It became the only Arab Marxist nation (1969), but receives development aid from both East and West. Area, 332 968 square kilometres (128,526 square miles). Population, 2,000,000 (mid-1982 estimate). Capital, Aden.

South Yorkshire. Metropolitan county in northern England. It was formed from parts of the former West Riding of Yorkshire and Nottinghamshire and the county boroughs of Barnsley, Doncaster, Rotherham, and Sheffield, and came into being in 1974.

Sou·tine (sŏŏ-téen), **Chaim** (1894–1943). French artist, born in Lithuania. His style is a vivid and turbulent expressionism; he is noted for his portraits. His works include *Choirboys* (1927) and *The Old Actress* (1924).

sou·ve·nir (sŏŏvə-néer) *n.* Something serving as a token of remembrance, as of a place, occasion, or experience; a memento. [French, "memory," from *souvenir,* come to mind, recall, from Latin *subvenīre,* come to aid, come to mind : *sub-,* up to + *venīre,* to come.]

sou'west·er (sow-wéstər) *n.* A waterproof hat worn especially by sailors, with a broad brim at the back to protect the neck. Also called "nor'wester". [From SOUTHWESTER.]

PRONUNCIATION KEY

a, trap; aa, father; ai, fair;
ar, star; aw, lawn; ay, play;
b, bb, stab; rubber;
ch, church; ck, ticket;
d, dd, dead; ladder; e, dress;
ee, bee; er, defer; ew, few;
ewr, pure; ə, about;
ər, letter; f, ff, fife; differ;
g, gg, giggle; h, hat; i, kit;
ī, price; īr, fire; j, judge;
k, kick; l, ll, let; 'l, needle;
m, mm, man; n, nn, no;
'n, sudden; ng, thing; o, lot;
ō, no; ōō, foot; ōō, shoe;
oor, poor; ow, cow;
owr, hour; oy, boy;
p, pp, pepper; r, rr, red;
s, ss, sauce; sh, ship;
t, tt, totter; th, thick; th, this;
smooth; u, cut; ur, turn;
v, vv, valve; w, wet; y, yes;
z, zz, zebra; zh, vision;
pleasure

IN FOREIGN WORDS:

aN, oN, Saint-Saëns;
hl, Llanelli; Hluhluwe;
kh, loch; lough; Khaled

STRESS MARK:

ín-sīt, insight; in-sít, incite

space shuttle

BACK AND FORTH TO OUTER SPACE

A replacement for expensive rockets

On April 14, 1981, the American space shuttle *Columbia* landed on a runway in the Mojave desert, California. Slowing to a halt it looked much like an ordinary aeroplane. In fact it had been rocketed from Cape Canaveral two days earlier and since then had orbited in space with a crew of two astronauts.

Columbia was the first reusable space craft to be launched and, as a result of the success of its mission, space shuttles are expected to replace expensive conventional rockets, which can be used only once.

The shuttle consists of a winged craft, or orbiter, the size of a DC-9 airliner, which is launched by reusable solid-fuel rocket boosters and a large external fuel tank. It is designed to launch satellites into space and to carry on board scientists who will be able to carry out experiments in the weightless conditions of space. Once its space mission has ended it re-enters the atmosphere to return to Earth and land on a runway. During this re-entry it is not a powered craft and it relies on its gliding ability to make a safe touch down.

It is hoped that the shuttle's reusability will halve the cost of space missions, but its novelty and complexity mean that it still has a lengthy maintenance time between flights. However, its performance on all proving missions has been impressive and it is hoped that it will be the key to a new American manned space effort into the next century.

LIFT-OFF *The space shuttle is dwarfed by its external fuel tank flanked by the rocket boosters, which will fall away at a height of 45 kilometres (28 miles). The boosters land in the sea to be recovered later but the fuel tank is discarded.*

sow thistle *A tall-growing flower, also known as milk thistle because of the white sap that exudes from a broken stem. The plant shown here is the perennial sow thistle.*

sov. sovereign.

sove·reign (sóv-rin, -rən ‖ sóvvə-) *n.* Also *literary* **sov·ran** (-rən) (for sense 1). **1.** The head of state in a monarchy; a king or queen; a monarch. **2.** *Abbr.* **sov.** A former British gold coin having a nominal value of one pound.
~*adj.* Also *literary* **sov·ran. 1.** Self-governing; independent: *a sovereign state.* **2.** Having supreme rank or power. **3.** Paramount; supreme. **4. a.** Of superlative quality or efficacy: *a sovereign remedy.* **b.** Unmitigated: *sovereign contempt.* [Middle English *souverein,* from Old French, from Vulgar Latin *superānus* (unattested), from Latin *super,* above.] —**sove·reign·ly** *adv.*

sove·reign·ty (sóv-rin-ti, -rən- ‖ sóvvə-) *n., pl.* **-ties. 1. a.** Supremacy of authority or rule, especially as exercised by the sovereign body in a state: *the sovereignty of Parliament.* **b.** The right to exercise such authority. **2.** Royal rank, authority, or power. **3.** The condition of political independence and self-government. **4.** A sovereign territory.

So·vetsk (səv-yétsk). *German.* **Til·sit** (tílzit). Town in the northwestern R.S.F.S.R., U.S.S.R., lying on the river Neman. Formerly in East Prussia, it is a marketing, cultural, and manufacturing centre.

so·vi·et (sóv-i-ət, sóv-, -yət, -yet) *n.* In the U.S.S.R., any of the popularly elected legislative assemblies existing at local, regional, and national levels, organised on the basis of the workers', soldiers', and peasants' councils of the revolutionary period. See **Supreme Soviet.** [Russian *sovet,* "council", from Old Russian *suvĕtu.*]

Soviet *adj.* Pertaining to the Union of Soviet Socialist Republics. ~*n. Plural.* The Russians, especially the Russian government.

so·vi·et·ise, so·vi·et·ize (sóv-i-ət-īz, sóv-, -yət-, -yet-) *tr.v.* **-ised, -ising, -ises.** *Sometimes capital* **S. 1.** To cause to come under Soviet control. **2.** To bring into line with the cultural, economic, or political norms of the U.S.S.R. —**so·vi·et·i·sa·tion** (-ī-záysh'n ‖ *U.S.* -i-) *n.*

Soviet Union. See **Union of Soviet Socialist Republics.**

sov·khoz (sóv-kóz, -koz; *Russian* saaf-<u>kh</u>áwss) *n., pl.* **-khozy** (kózi). A large state-owned farm in the U.S.S.R. that pays wages to its workers. [Russian, shortened from *sovetskoe khozyaistvo,* soviet economy.]

sow[1] (sō) *v.* **sowed, sown** (sōn) or **sowed, sowing, sows.** —*tr.* **1.** To scatter or plant (seed) over or in the ground for growing. **2.** To plant seed in (land). **3. a.** To implant and cause to arise; introduce: *sow doubts.* **b.** To disseminate; cause to spread: *sow rebellion.* **4.** To strew or cover with anything; spread thickly. —*intr.* To scatter seed for growing. —See Usage note at **sew.** [Middle English *sowen, sawan,* Old English *sāwan.*] —**sow·er** *n.*

sow[2] (sow) *n.* **1.** An adult female pig. **2. a.** A channel that conducts molten iron to the moulds in a pig bed. **b.** The mass of metal solidified in such a channel or mould. [Middle English *sow(e),* Old English *sugu.*]

So·we·to (sə-wéttō, sō-). Group of black African townships situated to the southwest of Johannesburg, South Africa. In June 1976, following the introduction of the compulsory use of Afrikaans for instruction in schools, students rioted in Soweto. Some 200 people were killed, and more than 1,000 were wounded. [*South Western Townships.*]

sow thistle *n.* The **milk thistle** (see).

sox. *U.S.* Alternative plural of **sock.**

soy·a bean (sóy-ə) *n.* Also *chiefly U.S.* **soy·bean** (sóy-been). **1.** A leguminous Asiatic plant, *Glycine max,* widely cultivated for forage and for its nutritious, edible seeds. **2.** The seed of this plant, used as a food and as a source of oil and flour.

soya sauce *n.* A salty brown liquid condiment made by fermenting soya beans in brine, and used in Chinese and Japanese cooking. Also called "soy sauce". [Japanese *shō-yu,* from Chinese *shi-yu : shi,* salted beans + *yu,* oil]

So·yin·ka (soy-íngkə, saw-yíngkə), **Wole** (1934–). Nigerian dramatist and poet. His works, which portray the experience of modern Africa, include plays (*Kongi's Harvest,* 1965), novels (*The Interpreters,* 1964), and memoirs (*The Man Died,* 1972).

soz·zled (sózz'ld) *adj. Informal.* Completely drunk. [Perhaps from dialect *sozzle,* to mix in a sloppy manner; akin to SOUSE (drench, make or become drunk).]

sp. 1. special. **2.** specialist. **3.** species. **4.** specific. **5.** spelling.

Sp. Spain; Spanish.

s.p. *Genealogy.* without issue. [Latin *sine prole.*]

S.P. starting price.

spa (spaa) *n.* **1.** A mineral spring. **2.** A resort area where such springs exist; a watering place. [After Spa (Belgium).]

Spaak (spaak), **Paul Henri** (1899–1972). Belgian statesman. He was the first president of the United Nations Assembly (1946), and of the Assembly of the Council of Europe (1949). He was also Secretary General of N.A.T.O. (1957–61).

space (spayss) *n.* **1. a.** A set of elements or points satisfying given geometric postulates: *a non-Euclidean space.* **b.** The infinite three-dimensional extent in which all matter exists. **2.** The expanse beyond the earth's atmosphere in which the Solar System, stars, and galaxies exist; the universe. **3. a.** A measurable interval or extent existing between two or more points or bounded by limits in three dimensions: distance, area, or volume. **b.** Such an interval or extent considered as being unoccupied; unfilled space: *clear a space in the cupboard; wide open spaces.* **c.** An amount of room available or designated for a particular purpose: *a parking space; used a smaller size of type to save space.* **4.** A period or interval of time. **5.** *Music.* Any of the intervals between the lines of a staff. **6.** *Printing.* Any of the blank pieces of type or other means used for separating words

or characters. **7.** Any of the intervals during the telegraphic transmission of a message when the key is open or not in contact.
~*tr.v.* **spaced, spacing, spaces. 1.** To place or arrange with spaces between. Often used with *out.* **2.** To separate or keep apart. [Middle English, time interval, from Old French *espace*, from Latin *spatium†*, space, distance.] —**spac·er** *n.*

space age *n.* The period, starting in the middle of the twentieth century, when humans have been able to travel in space.
~*adj.* Also **space-age** (spáyss-ayj). Extremely modern in design; based on or suggestive of the technology used in spacecraft.

space biology *n.* Exobiology *(see).*

space capsule *n.* A capsule *(see)* used in space flights.

space charge *n.* An electric charge in a vacuum or region of low gas pressure, as in an electronic valve or vacuum tube, carried by a stream of electrons or ions.

space·craft (spáyss-kraaft ‖ -kraft) *n., pl.* **spacecraft.** A vehicle designed to be launched into space. Also called "space vehicle", "spaceship".

spaced-out (spáyst-ówt) *adj. Slang.* **1.** Elated or stupefied as a result of taking a narcotic or hallucinogenic drug; high. **2.** Dazed or lacking concentration.

space flight *n.* A flight of a vehicle into space.

space heater *n.* A heater, especially a portable free-standing one, used to heat an enclosed area.

space lab *n.* A large manned satellite specially equipped for carrying out experimental work in space.

space lattice *n.* Any of the 14 possible geometric arrangements of points in three-dimensional space at which the components of a crystal may occur. Also called "Bravais lattice".

space·less (spáyss-ləss, -liss) *adj.* Having no spatial limits.

space·man (spáyss-man) *n., pl.* **-men** (-men). **1.** Someone who travels in outer space; an astronaut. **2.** In science fiction, one who comes to Earth from outer space.

space medicine *n.* The medical science of the biological, physiological, and psychological effects of space flight upon humans.

space·port (spáyss-pawrt ‖ -pōrt) *n.* An installation for testing and launching spacecraft.

space probe *n.* A spacecraft carrying instruments designed to explore the physical properties of outer space or of celestial bodies other than Earth. Also called "probe".

space science *n.* **1.** Any of several scientific disciplines, such as exobiology, that study phenomena occurring in the upper atmosphere, in space, or on celestial bodies other than Earth. **2.** Disciplines related to or dealing with the problems of space flight.

space shuttle *n.* A space vehicle capable of making repeated journeys to and from space.

space sickness *n.* Any of various ailments affecting humans during or as a result of space flight.

space station *n.* A large manned satellite designed for permanent orbit around Earth and used for scientific research, military reconnaissance, or as an assembly point for long-range spacecraft.

space suit *n.* A protective pressure suit having an independent air supply and other devices designed to permit the wearer relatively free movement in space.

space-time (spáyss-tīm) *n.* The four-dimensional continuum of one temporal and three spatial coordinates, in which any event or physical object is located. Also called the "space-time continuum".

space walk *n.* An excursion by an astronaut outside a spacecraft in space; extravehicular activity. —**space walker** *n.*

space writer *n.* A writer, especially a journalist, paid according to the amount of space his material occupies in print.

spacial. Variant of **spatial.**

spac·ing (spáyssing) *n.* **1.** The action or result of arranging with intervening spaces. **2.** A temporal or spatial interval, typically one forming part of a regular arrangement; a space.

spa·cious (spáyshəss) *adj.* **1.** Providing or having much space or room; roomy; extensive. **2.** Expansive in range or scope; all-inclusive. [Middle English, from Old French *spacios* or Latin *spatiōsus*; see space, -ous.] —**spa·cious·ly** *adv.* —**spa·cious·ness** *n.*

spade¹ (spayd) *n.* **1.** A sturdy digging tool having a long thick handle and a heavy, flat iron blade that can be pressed into the ground with the foot. **2.** Any of various digging or cutting tools resembling the spade. **3.** *Military.* A sharp metal piece at the back of a guncarriage trail that embeds into the ground to retard the backward motion of the carriage during recoil. —**call a spade a spade.** To call a thing by its proper name; speak frankly and directly.
~*tr.v.* **spaded, spading, spades.** To dig or cut with a spade. [Middle English *spade*, Old English *spadu*.] —**spad·er** *n.*

spade² *n.* **1.** The black symbol appearing on one of the four suits of playing cards, in the shape of an inverted heart with a short stalk at the fissure of the two lobes. **2.** A card bearing this symbol. [Italian *spada*, "broad sword" (from its flat, broad shape), from Latin *spatha*, spatula, from Greek *spathē*, broad blade.]

spade·fish (spáyd-fish) *n., pl.* **-fishes** or collectively **spadefish.** Any of several marine food fishes of the family Ephippidae, especially of the genus *Chaetodipterus.* [From their flat, spade-shaped bodies.]

spades *n.* Used with a singular or plural verb. One of the four suits of playing cards identified by the symbol of a spade.

spade·work (spáyd-wurk) *n.* The usually dull and arduous preparatory work necessary to a project or activity.

spa·dix (spáy-diks) *n., pl.* **spadices** (-di-seez). *Botany.* A clublike spike bearing minute flowers, usually enclosed within a sheathlike spathe, as in the calla and the cuckoopint. [Latin *spādīx*, broken-off

palm branch, from Greek *spadix*; akin to Greek *spasmos*, SPASM.]
—**spa·di·ceous** (spay-díshəss) *adj.*

spae·wife (spáy-wīf) *n. Scottish.* A woman thought to have clairvoyant powers; a fortuneteller. [Scottish *spae*, foretell, from Middle English, from Old Norse *spā.*]

spa·ghet·ti (spə-gétti) *n.* **1.** An Italian pasta consisting of long, solid strings of flour paste, cooked by boiling. **2.** *Electricity.* A slender tube of insulating material into which bare wire is inserted, especially in radio circuits. [Italian, plural diminutive of *spago†*, string.]

spa·ghet·ti·ni (spág-e-teeni, -i-) *n.* An Italian pasta, thinner than spaghetti. [Italian, diminutive of SPAGHETTI.]

spaghetti western *n.* A western made by the Italian film industry and filmed in Europe.

spa·gyr·ic (spə-jírrik) *adj.* Of or pertaining to alchemy; alchemical. [New Latin *spagiricus†*, coined by Paracelsus.]

Spain (spayn). *Spanish* **E·spa·ña** (ess-pánya). Country occupying most of the Iberian peninsula, southwest Europe. Most of it is a high plateau, the Meseta, which is broken by mountain ranges and great river valleys. Spain is industrialising steadily, and 25 per cent of its workers are in manufacturing, and 17 per cent in agriculture and fishing. With few fossil fuel resources, the country has an ambitious nuclear programme, and is a major uranium producer. The chief exports are fruit and vegetables, chemicals, engineering goods, footwear and leather goods, textiles, wine, olive oil, fish, and cork. Tourism is very important, with more than 35 million visitors a year. Spain, the ancient Roman province of Hispania, eventually emerged as a nation with the joining of the kingdoms of Aragon and Castile (1497), and the expulsion of its last Moorish conquerors (1492). The next two centuries were a golden age, in which a vast empire was built. However, most of this was lost in the 19th century, when the New World colonies gained independence. Spain remained neutral in both World Wars. After elections (1931) a republic was declared, but a bitter civil war (1936–39) brought the dictator General Franco to power. Following his death (1975), Juan Carlos, grandson of the last king, became head of state, and the Spaniards endorsed a parliamentary monarchy in a referendum (1978). The new government applied to join the European Economic Community, and sought the return of Gibraltar, ceded to Britain in 1713. The Catalan and Basque provinces became autonomous regions (1979), but separatist activity persists. Area, 504 782 square kilometres (194,846 square miles). Population, 37,900,000 (mid-1982 estimate). Capital, Madrid. See map, next page.

spake. *Archaic.* Past tense of **speak.**

spall (spawl) *n.* A chip or fragment from a piece of stone or ore.
~*v.* **spalled, spalling, spalls.** —*tr.* To break up into chips or fragments. —*intr.* To chip or crumble. [Middle English *spallet†.*]

spal·la·tion (spə-láysh'n, spaw-) *n.* A nuclear reaction in which many particles are ejected from an atomic nucleus by an incident particle of sufficiently high energy. [SPALL + -ATION.]

Spam (spam) *n.* A trademark for a type of tinned processed meat made mainly from ham.

span¹ (span) *n.* **1.** The full extent of space or time between two extremities: *the span of a bridge; a short life span.* **2.** The distance between the tips of an aircraft's wings. **3.** The section between two intermediate supports of a bridge. **4.** The length of time during or over which something functions effectively: *a child's attention span.* **5.** A former unit of measure equal to the length of the fully extended hand from the tip of the thumb to the tip of the little finger, generally considered as nine inches.
~*tr.v.* **spanned, spanning, spans. 1.** To measure by, or as if by, the fully extended hand. **2.** To encircle with the hand or hands, in or as if in measuring. **3.** To reach or extend over or across (an extent in space or time): *a life that spanned three reigns.* **4.** To provide with something that extends over; bridge. [Middle English *span(ne)*, short interval, distance, Old English *span(n).*]

span² *n.* **1.** *Nautical.* A stretch of rope made fast at either end. **2.** *Chiefly U.S.* A pair of animals, especially horses or oxen matched in size, strength, or colour and driven together. **3.** *Plural. South African Slang.* A large amount or number: *spans of teenagers.* [Middle Dutch *span*, from *spannen*, unite.]

span³. *Archaic.* Past tense and past participle of **spin.**

Span. Spanish.

Span·dau (shpán-dow, spán-). Industrial district of West Berlin, Germany, surrounding the canal port at the confluence of the rivers Havel and Spree. Its old fortress is a prison where the Nazi war criminal Rudolf Hess is detained.

span·drel, span·dril (spándrəl) *n. Architecture.* **1.** The triangular space between the left or right exterior curve of an arch and the rectangular framework surrounding it. **2.** The space between two adjacent arches and the horizontal moulding or cornice above them. [Middle English *spaundrell*, perhaps diminutive of Anglo-French *spaund(e)re*, from Old French *espandre*, to spread out, expand, from Latin *expandere*, EXPAND.]

spang (spang) *adv.* Precisely; squarely; firmly: *spang in the middle of the table.* [20th century : origin obscure.]

span·gle (spáng-g'l) *n.* **1.** A small, often circular piece of sparkling metal or plastic that may be sewn on clothing for decoration; a sequin. **2.** Any small sparkling object, drop, or spot.
~*v.* **spangled, -gling, -gles.** —*tr.* To adorn or cause to sparkle by covering with or as with spangles: *"the network of lights spangled the long, straight streets"* (Alec Waugh). —*intr.* To sparkle in the manner of spangles. [Middle English *spangele*, diminutive of *spange*, from Middle Dutch, ornament, clasp, buckle.] —**span·gly** *adv.*

Span·iard (spán-yərd) n. A native or inhabitant of Spain.

span·iel (spán-yəl, also spánn'l) n. 1. Any of several breeds of small to medium-sized dogs, originally bred as sporting dogs and usually having drooping ears, short legs, and a silky, wavy coat. 2. An obsequious or servile person. [Middle English spaynel, from Old French espaignol, "Spanish", from Vulgar Latin spāniōlŭs (unattested), from Latin Hispāniōlus, from Hispānia, SPAIN.]

Span·ish (spánnish) adj. Abbr. Sp., Span. Of or pertaining to Spain, its inhabitants, or their language or culture.
~n. 1. The Romance language of Spain and Spanish America. 2. Used with a plural verb. The people of Spain. Preceded by the.

Spanish America n. The parts of America inhabited mostly by Spanish-speaking people and including: 1. South America, except-ing Brazil, Guyana, Surinam, and French Guiana. 2. Central America, excepting Belize. 3. Mexico, Cuba, Puerto Rico, and the Dominican Republic.

Span·ish-A·mer·i·can (spánnish-ə-mérrikən) adj. 1. Of or pertain-ing to the countries or people of Spanish America. 2. Of or pertain-ing to people of Spanish descent residing in the United States.
~n. 1. A native or inhabitant of a Spanish-American country. 2. A person of Spanish descent who lives in the United States.

Spanish Armada n. A fleet sent against England by Philip II of Spain in 1588, considered invincible but defeated and subsequently destroyed by storms. Also called the "Armada".

Spanish bayonet n. Any of several New World plants of the genus Yucca; especially, Y. aloifolia, having a tall, woody stem, stiff, pointed leaves, and a large cluster of white flowers, or the similar species Y. filamentosa, which is also called "Adam's needle".

Spanish cedar n. 1. Any of several tropical American trees of the genus Cedrela; especially, C. odorata, having reddish, aromatic wood. 2. The wood of this tree.

Spanish chestnut n. See chestnut (sense 1).

Spanish Civil War n. The civil war (1936–39) in Spain in which nationalist forces under General Franco overthrew the legitimate republican government. The nationalists were aided by the fascist regimes of Italy and Germany, while the republicans attracted sup-port from socialists all over Europe.

Spanish flu n. A form of influenza that broke out in pandemic proportions in 1918 and caused millions of deaths. [Perhaps so called after a great epidemic in 1557, which appears to have begun in Spain.]

Spanish fly n. 1. A European blister beetle, Lytta vesicatoria. 2. A preparation, cantharides (see), produced from these beetles.

Spanish Guinea. See Equatorial Guinea.

Spanish Inquisition. The state tribunal of the Roman Catholic Church, instituted in Spain in 1480 to suppress heresy and infa-mous for its ruthless methods. It was abolished in 1834.

Spanish mackerel n. Any of various marine food fishes of the family Scombridae; especially, a commercially important species, Scomber colias, of European and east North American coastal wa-ter.

Spanish Main n. 1. In the 16th and 17th centuries, the Spanish possessions in the coastal regions of northern South America be-tween Panama and the Orinoco. 2. Those parts of the Caribbean traversed by Spanish ships in colonial times.

Spanish Morocco n. A former Spanish colony on the northern coast of Morocco, part of Morocco since 1956.

Spanish moss n. An epiphytic plant, Tillandsia usneoides, growing on trees of the southeastern United States and tropical America, having grey, threadlike stems drooping in long, matted clusters.

Spanish Netherlands. The southern part of the Netherlands which remained under Spanish Habsburg rule when the Dutch Nether-lands won independence in 1648. In 1714 it passed to the Austrian Habsburgs, and as the Austrian Netherlands declared its indepen-dence as Belgium in 1789.

Spanish omelette n. An omelette made by frying chopped vegeta-bles, such as onions, tomatoes, green peppers, and potatoes, before adding the beaten eggs.

Spanish onion n. A mild-flavoured, yellow-skinned onion, prob-ably derived from Allium fistulosum.

Spanish paprika n. A mild seasoning made from pimientos.

Spanish rice n. A dish consisting of rice, tomatoes, spices, chopped onions, and green peppers.

Spanish Sahara. See Western Sahara.

spank (spangk) v. spanked, spanking, spanks. —tr. To slap on the buttocks with a flat object or with the open hand, especially as punishment. —intr. To move briskly or spiritedly.
~n. Also spanking. A smart slap or series of slaps on the buttocks. [Perhaps imitative.]

spank·er (spángkər) n. 1. Nautical. A quadrilateral gaff sail set abaft the after mast of a square-rigged sailing ship. Also called "driver". 2. Informal. Something of exceptional quality or remark-able appearance.

spank·ing (spángking) adj. 1. Informal. Exceptional of its kind in

size, strength, quality, or, especially, smartness. **2.** Moving quickly and smartly; brisk; lively: *set off at a spanking pace.*
~*adv.* Splendidly: *spanking new.*
~*n.* A spank.

span·ner (spánnər) *n.* A hand tool with jaws or a ring at one end or both ends for tightening or slackening nuts and bolts. **—a spanner in the works.** *British Informal.* A source of trouble, confusion, or delay. [German *Spanner,* from *spannen,* to stretch, tighten, from Old High German *spannan.*]

span roof *n.* A roof which has two equal sloping sides.

span spek (span spek, spon-) *South African.* A sweet muskmelon, the cantaloupe, having a rough, ridged rind and orange flesh. [Afrikaans, from Dutch *spaenspek.*]

spar¹ (spar) *n.* **1.** *Nautical.* A wooden or metal pole, used as a mast, boom, yard, or bowsprit, or in any other way to support rigging. **2.** A similar pole, used as part of a crane or derrick. **3.** *Aeronautics.* A principal structural member in an aircraft wing that runs from tip to tip or from root to tip.
~*tr.v.* **sparred, sparring, spars.** **1.** To supply with spars. **2.** *Archaic.* To fasten with a bolt. [Middle English *sparre,* rafter, pole, from Old French *esparre* or from Old Norse *sperra,* beam, both from Germanic.]

spar² *intr.v.* **sparred, sparring, spars.** **1. a.** To box without exerting oneself to the full, as in a training session. **b.** To fight in any matched and generally indecisive contest. **2.** To bandy words about in argument; dispute. **3.** To fight by striking with the feet and spurs. Used of cocks.
~*n.* **1.** The act of sparring. **2.** A boxing match. **3.** A cock-fight. [Middle English *sparren,* to thrust or strike rapidly, Old English *sperran*†, to strike.]

spar³ *n.* **1.** Any of various bright, nonmetallic, readily cleavable minerals with a vitreous lustre, such as feldspar. **2.** A fragment of such a mineral. **3.** An ornament made of spar. [Low German, from Middle Low German; akin to Old English *spǣr*†, gypsum.]

sparable. Variant of **sparrowbill.**

spa·rax·is (spə-ráksiss, spa-) *n.* Any plant of the South African genus *Sparaxis,* related to the iris and having colourful flowers.

spar deck *n.* A light upper deck of a ship. **—spar-decked** *adj.*

spare (spair) *v.* **spared, sparing, spares.** *—tr.* **1. a.** To treat mercifully; deal with leniently. **b.** To refrain from harming or destroying. **2.** To save or relieve (a person) from enduring (something unpleasant): *Spare us the gory details.* **3.** To refrain from using or applying; use with restraint. **4.** To give or grant out of one's resources; afford: *Can you spare ten minutes?* *—intr.* **1.** To be frugal. Usually used in the negative: *Don't spare on the cream.* **2.** *Literary.* **a.** To be merciful or lenient. **b.** To refrain or forbear. **—and to spare.** In abundance. **—with (something) to spare.** Leaving (something) left over unused or as a margin.
~*adj.* **sparer, sparest.** **1. a.** Not in immediate or regular use but ready when needed. **b.** In excess of what is needed; extra: *spare cash.* **c.** Unoccupied; leisure: *spare time.* **2. a.** Economical; meagre. **b.** Thin or lean. **—go spare.** *Informal.* To become frantic; panic: *The boss is going spare over the schedule again.* —See Synonyms at **lean, meagre.**
~*n.* **1.** A replacement, such as a spare tyre, reserved for future use. **2.** A spare part. **3.** In tenpin bowling: **a.** The act of knocking down all ten pins with two successive rolls of the ball by a single player. **b.** The score so made. [Middle English *sparen,* to leave unharmed, show mercy, Old English *sparian,* from Germanic *sparōjan* (unattested).] **—spare·ly** *adv.* **—spare·ness** *n.* **—spar·er** *n.*

spare part *n.* *Chiefly British.* An exact duplicate, as of a machine part, used to replace a worn or faulty part. Also called "spare".

spare part surgery *n.* *Informal.* Surgery involving the transplantation of body organs.

spare rib *n.* Also **spare ribs** (for sense 1). **1.** A cut of pork consisting of the ribs with most of the meat trimmed off. **2.** Any of these ribs. [Probably transposed variant of Low German *ribbespēr,* from Middle Low German : *ribbe,* rib + *spēr,* spit (influenced by SPARE).]

spare tyre *n.* **1.** An extra tyre carried for emergencies with a motor vehicle. **2.** *Informal.* A roll of flab around the middle of the body.

sparge (sparj) *tr.v.* **sparged, sparging, sparges.** To spray or sprinkle with moisture. [Probably from Latin *spargere,* to sprinkle.] **—sparg·er** *n.*

spar·id (spárrid) *adj.* Also **spar·oid** (spárroyd). Of or belonging to the family Sparidae, which includes the bream and similar fishes.
~*n.* Also **sparoid.** A member of the Sparidae. [New Latin *sparidae* : *Sparus* (genus), from Latin, gilthead, from Greek *sparos*† + -ID.]

spar·ing (spáir-ing) *adj.* **1.** Economical; frugal: *Sparing in her use of words.* **2.** Scanty; not profuse: *a sparing application.* **3.** Forbearing; lenient. **—spar·ing·ly** *adv.* **—spar·ing·ness** *n.*
Synonyms: *sparing, frugal, thrifty, economical.*

spark¹ (spark) *n.* **1.** An incandescent particle, especially: **a.** One thrown off from a burning substance. **b.** One resulting from friction. **c.** One remaining in an otherwise extinguished fire; an ember. **2.** A glistening particle of something, such as metal. **3. a.** A flash of light; especially, a flash produced by electric discharge. **b.** A short pulse or discharge of electric current. **4.** A trace or suggestion, as: **a.** A quality or feeling with latent potential; a seed: *the spark of genius.* **b.** An animating or activating factor: *the spark of revolt.* **5.** *Electricity.* **a.** The luminous phenomenon resulting from a disruptive discharge through an insulating material. **b.** The discharge itself, especially as occurring in an internal-combustion engine. **6.** A small diamond or other gem.
~*v.* **sparked, sparking, sparks.** *—intr.* **1.** To give off sparks. **2.** To operate correctly by producing a spark. Used of the ignition system of an internal-combustion engine. *—tr.* **1.** To set in motion; activate; provoke. Usually used with *off*: *sparked off a strike.* **2.** *U.S.* To rouse to action. —See Synonyms at **flash.** [Middle English *sparke,* Old English *spearca, spǣrca;* akin to Middle Dutch *sparke*†.] **—spark·er** *n.*

spark² *n.* **1.** A clever person. Used ironically in the phrase *bright spark.* **2.** *Rare.* A lover; a suitor.
~*v.* **sparked, sparking, sparks.** *Rare.* *—tr.* To court or woo. *—intr.* To play the suitor. [Perhaps figurative use of SPARK (burning particle).]

Spark, Muriel (Sarah) (1918–). British novelist, poet, and critic. Among her works, noted for their black humour, are *The Ballad of Peckham Rye* (1960), *The Prime of Miss Jean Brodie* (1961), and *Territorial Rights* (1979).

spark arrester *n.* **1.** A device to keep sparks from escaping, as at a chimney opening. **2.** A device to control electric sparking at a point where a circuit is made or broken.

spark chamber *n.* A device consisting of electrically charged parallel metal plates in a chamber filled with inert gas, used to detect and measure charged elementary particles as they pass from one plate to another, leaving a trail of sparks.

spark coil *n.* An induction coil used to produce a spark, as in an internal-combustion engine.

spark gap *n.* A gap in an otherwise complete electric circuit across which a discharge occurs at some prescribed voltage.

spar·kle (spárk'l) *intr.v.* **-kled, -kling, -kles.** **1.** To give off sparks. **2.** To give off or reflect flashes of light; glitter. **3.** To be witty and animated. **4.** To perform brilliantly; shine. **5.** To effervesce. —See Synonyms at **flash.**
~*n.* **1.** A small spark or gleaming particle. **2.** A glittering appearance. **3.** Animation; vivacity. **4.** Effervescence. [Middle English *sparklen,* frequentative of *sparken,* to SPARK.]

spar·kler (spárklər) *n.* **1.** One that sparkles. **2.** A firework on a piece of wire held in the hand that burns down gradually and gives off a shower of sparks. **3.** *Informal.* A diamond.

spar·kling wine *n.* Any of various effervescent, usually white, wines, produced by a process that involves fermentation in the bottle.

spark-plug (spárk-plug) *n.* Also *British* **spark·ing plug.** A device inserted in the head of an internal-combustion-engine cylinder that ignites the fuel mixture by means of an electric spark.

spark-plug *The electrical terminal which produces the spark to ignite the petrol-air mixture in an internal combustion engine.*

sparks (sparks) *n.* *Informal.* *Used with a singular verb.* **1.** A ship's radio operator. **2.** An electrician, especially in the building trade. [From SPARK (electrical discharge).]

spark transmitter *n.* *Electronics.* A now obsolete radio transmitter using a discharge across a spark gap to create a signal.

spar·ling (spárling) *n.* **1.** A fish, the European **smelt** *(see).* **2.** *U.S.* A young herring. [Middle English *sperlinge,* from Old French *esperlinge,* from Germanic.]

sparoid. Variant of **sparid.**

spar·ring partner (spáaring) *n.* **1.** A boxer who fights with another in training bouts. **2.** Any partner in a friendly contest or dispute.

spar·row (spárrō) *n.* **1.** Any of various small Old World birds of the genus *Passer,* especially the **house sparrow** *(see),* having greyish or brownish plumage. **2.** Any of various American finches resembling Old World sparrows. [Middle English *sparowe,* Old English *spearwa,* from Germanic.]

spar·row-bill (spárrō-bil, spárrə-) *n.* Also **spar·a·ble** (spárrə-bil). A small headless wedge-shaped iron nail used in fixing shoe soles.

spar·row·grass (spárrō-graass || spárrə-, -grass) *n.* Also **spar·ry·grass** (spárri-). *Regional.* Asparagus. [By folk etymology from ASPARAGUS.]

spar·row·hawk (spárrō-hawk) *n.* **1.** Any of various small hawks of the genus *Accipiter,* which prey on small birds and mammals; especially, *A. nisus,* of Europe and Asia. **2.** A small North American falcon, *Falco sparverius,* that hunts small birds and mammals.

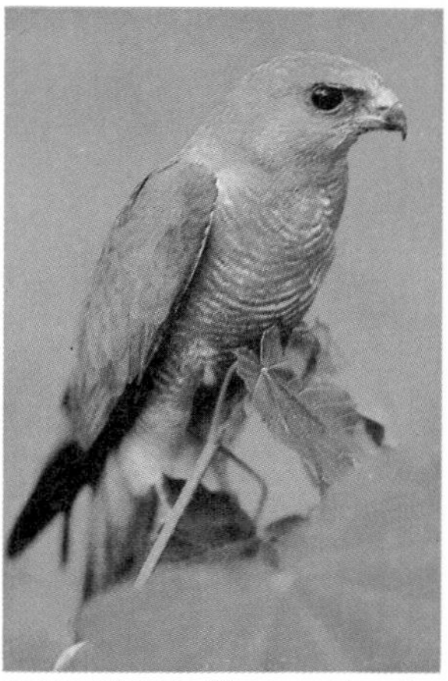
sparrowhawk *There are 23 species of sparrowhawk, and sparrows are only one of the small birds that these swift-flying predators hunt. The Levant sparrowhawk (above), however, feeds mainly on lizards and grasshoppers.*

sparse (sparss) *adj.* **sparser, sparsest.** Growing or distributed at widely spaced intervals; not dense: *a sparse crop.* See Synonyms at **meagre.** [Latin *sparsus,* past participle of *spargere,* to strew, scatter.] **—sparse·ly** *adv.* **—sparse·ness, spar·si·ty** (-əti) *n.*

Spar·ta (spártə). City-state of ancient Greece. Founded in *c.*1000 B.C., it became one of the most powerful city-states, renowned for its dedication to military discipline. The Spartans defeated the Athenians in the Peloponnesian Wars (431–404 B.C.), but finally fell to the Macedonians in the fourth century B.C. The modern settlement of Sparta was founded close by in the mid-19th century.

Spar·ta·cus (spártəkəss) (died 71 B.C.). Thracian gladiator. He raised an army of slaves that terrorised Roman Italy for two years (73-71 B.C.). He was finally defeated and killed by Crassus.

spar·tan (spárt'n) *adj.* **1.** *Capital* **S.** Of or pertaining to Sparta or its people. **2.** Resembling the Spartans in fortitude or self-discipline; rigorous; austere. **3.** Frugal: *a spartan existence.*
~*n.* **1.** *Capital* **S.** A citizen of Sparta. **2.** Someone of spartan character. **—Spar·tan·ism** *n.*

spasm (spáz'm) *n.* **1.** A sudden, involuntary contraction of a muscle or group of muscles. **2.** Any sudden burst of energy, activity, or emotion. [Middle English *spasme,* from Old French, from Latin *spasmus,* from Greek *spasmos,* from *span*†, to draw, pull.]

spas·mod·ic (spaz-móddik) *adj.* **1.** Pertaining to, affected by, or having the character of a spasm; convulsive. **2.** Happening intermittently; fitful: *spasmodic rifle fire.* **3.** Jerky; disjointed: *spasmodic*

prose. **4.** Occurring suddenly and violently: *spasmodic fury.* [New Latin *spasmodicus,* from Greek *spasmodikos,* from *spasmos,* SPASM.] —**spas·mod·i·cal·ly** *adv.*

Spass·ky (spáski ‖ spáaski), **Boris (Vasilievich)** (1937–). Russian chess player. He was U.S.S.R. Grand Master, International Grand Master, and World Chess Student champion, and U.S.S.R. and World Chess Champion (1969–72).

spas·tic (spástik) *adj.* **1.** Pertaining to or characterised by spasms; continuously convulsing or contracting. **2.** Caused by spasms or spastic paralysis. **3.** *Slang.* **a.** Awkward or ungainly. **b.** Poor in quality: *a spastic football match.* In both senses, usually considered offensive. —*n.* **1.** A person suffering from muscular spasms. **2.** A person suffering from spastic paralysis. [Latin *spasticus,* from Greek *spastikos,* from *span,* to pull, draw. See spasm.] —**spas·ti·cal·ly** *adv.* —**spas·tic·i·ty** (spass-tíssəti) *n.*

spastic paralysis *n.* A chronic pathological condition involving weakness of the limbs with exaggerated tendon reflexes and muscular spasms. It is a common result of cerebral palsy.

spat¹. Past tense and past participle of **spit** (eject saliva).

spat² (spat) *n., pl.* **spat** or **spats.** An oyster or similar bivalve mollusc in the larval stage, especially when it settles to the bottom and begins to develop a shell. —*intr.v.* **spatted, spatting, spats.** To spawn. Used of oysters and similar molluscs. [Anglo-French *spat†.*]

spat³ *n.* A cloth or leather gaiter covering the shoe upper and the ankle and fastening under the shoe with a strap. [Short for earlier SPATTERDASH.]

spat⁴ *n.* **1.** A brief, petty quarrel. **2.** *Informal.* A slap or smack. **3.** A spattering sound, as of raindrops. —*v.* **spatted, spatting, spats.** —*intr.* **1.** To engage in a brief, petty quarrel. **2.** To strike with a light spattering sound; slap. —*tr. Informal.* To slap. [Probably imitative.]

spatch·cock (spách-kok) *n.* A freshly killed fowl, split and cooked immediately. —*tr.v.* **1.** To cook like a spatchcock. **2.** *British Informal.* To interpolate or sandwich, especially in an inappropriate context. [18th century (Irish) : said to be shortened from *dispatch-cock,* but perhaps variant of earlier SPITCHCOCK.]

spate (spayt) *n.* **1.** A flash flood resulting from a downpour of rain or melting of snow: *The river was in full spate.* **2.** A sudden flood, rush, or outbreak. [Middle English *spate†.*]

spathe (spayth) *n. Botany.* A leaflike organ that encloses or spreads from the base of the spadix of certain plants, such as the cuckoopint or the calla. [Latin *spatha,* broad flat instrument, from Greek *spathē,* broad blade.] —**spa·tha·ceous** (spə-tháyshəss), **spa·those** (spáyth-ōz, spáth-, -ōss) *adj.*

spath·ic (spáthik) *adj.* Having good cleavage. Said of minerals. [From obsolete *spath,* spar, from German *Spat(h),* from Middle High German *spat.*]

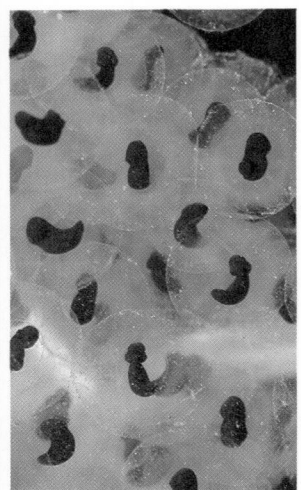

spawn *Fish and amphibians which disperse eggs and sperm into the water to be fertilised are said to spawn; the fertilised eggs are then called spawn. Here embryos of the common frog* (Rana temporaria) *can be seen developing.*

spa·tial, spa·cial (spáysh'l) *adj.* Of, pertaining to, involving, or having the nature of space. [Latin *spatium,* SPACE.] —**spa·ti·al·i·ty** (spáyshi-ál-əti) *n.* —**spa·tial·ly** *adv.*

spa·ti·o·tem·po·ral (spáyshi-ō-témpərəl) *adj.* **1.** Of, pertaining to, or existing in both space and time. **2.** Of or relating to space-time. [Latin *spatium,* SPACE + TEMPORAL.] —**spa·ti·o·tem·po·ral·ly** *adv.*

spat·ter (spáttər) *v.* **-tered, -tering, -ters.** —*tr.* **1.** To scatter (a liquid substance) in drops or small splashes. **2.** To spot, splash, or soil. **3.** To strike like a shower: *a handful of pebbles spattered the window.* **4.** To sully the reputation of; defame. —*intr.* **1.** To throw off drops or small splashes; splatter. **2.** To fall with a splash. —*n.* **1.** The act of spattering. **2.** A spattering sound. **3.** A drop or splash of something spattered; a spot or stain. [Perhaps a frequentative of Dutch *spatten,* from Middle Dutch (perhaps imitative).]

spat·ter·dash (spáttər-dash) *n.* A legging worn to protect the lower leg from splashes of mud or dirt.

spat·ter·work (spáttər-wurk) *n.* The reproduction of designs by spattering colour over a stencil.

spat·u·la (spáttewlə ‖ spáchələ) *n.* **1.** A small implement having a broad, flat, flexible blade that is used to spread or mix a semisolid substance such as icing, plaster, or paint. **2.** *Medicine.* An implement with a flat, blunt blade used to press down the tongue, to spread ointments, or to transfer powders. [Latin *spat(h)ula,* diminutive of *spatha,* blade, broad sword, from Greek *spathē.*] —**spat·u·lar, spat·u·lous** *adj.*

spat·u·late (spáttew-lət, -lit, -layt ‖ spáchə-) *adj.* Shaped like a spatula; having a broad tip and narrow base: *spatulate leaves.*

spaud·ler (spawdlər) *n.* A piece of armour worn to protect the shoulder.

spav·in (spávvin) *n.* Either of two diseases affecting the hock joint of horses: *bog spavin,* an infusion of lymph that enlarges the joint, and *bone spavin,* a bony deposit that stiffens the joint. [Middle English *spaveyne,* from Old French *espavin†.*] —**spav·ined** *adj.*

spawn (spawn) *n.* **1.** The eggs of aquatic animals such as bivalve molluscs, fishes, and amphibians. **2.** Offspring occurring in numbers; brood. Usually used derogatorily. **3.** A person regarded as the issue of some usually undesirable parent or family: *the spawn of the devil.* **4.** The product or outcome of something. **5.** Fragments of mycelia used to start a mushroom culture. —*v.* **spawned, spawning, spawns.** —*intr.* **1.** To deposit eggs; produce spawn. **2.** To produce offspring in numbers like spawn. —*tr.* **1.** To produce (spawn). **2.** To give birth to. Usually used derogatorily of human beings. **3.** To give rise to; engender. **4.** To plant with mycelia. [Middle English *spawne,* from *spawnen,* to spawn, from Anglo-French *espaundre,* from Old French *espandre,* to shed roe, from *espandre,* to shed, spread, from Latin *expandere,* to spread out, EXPAND.]

spawn·er (spáwnər) *n.* A female fish, especially at spawning time.

spawn·ing bed (spáwning) *n.* A nest made on the bed of a stream by fish such as salmon or trout for depositing spawn and milt.

spay (spay) *tr.v.* **spayed, spaying, spays.** To excise the ovaries of (a female animal). [Middle English *spayen,* from Old French *espeer,* to cut with a sword, from *espee,* sword, from Latin *spatha,* broad sword, from Greek *spathē.*]

speak (speek) *v.* **spoke** (spōk) or *archaic* **spake** (spayk), **spoken** (spókən) or *archaic* **spoke, speaking, speaks.** —*intr.* **1.** To utter words as ordinary speech; talk. **2. a.** To engage in discussion; converse; talk. Also used with an adverb to convey the speaker's attitude towards the message in such phrases as *strictly speaking, to speak frankly.* **b.** To acknowledge another; be on friendly social terms: *They are no longer speaking.* **3.** To deliver an address or lecture; make a speech. **4.** To convey a message: *Actions speak louder than words.* **5.** To be expressive. **6.** To emit a report on firing: *"Our cannons speak and the enemy's now open in full chorus"* (Ambrose Bierce). **7. a.** To make communicative sounds. **b.** To give an impression of speaking: *teach a dog to speak for a bone.* **8.** To be relevant or comprehensible: *Modern art does not always speak to modern man.* —*tr.* **1.** To articulate in a speaking voice. **2.** To converse in or be able to converse in (a language). **3. a.** To express aloud; declare; tell. **b.** To express without words: *His eyes spoke love.* **c.** To communicate in print or writing. **4.** To reveal; show to be. **5.** *Nautical.* To hail and communicate with (another vessel) at sea. —**so to speak.** That is to say; as it were. —**speak for.** **1.** To speak on behalf of; represent. **2.** To claim: *This ticket is spoken for.* —**speak for itself.** To be self-evident. —**speak of.** To refer to. —**speak out** or **up.** **1.** To speak more clearly or louder. **2.** To speak without hesitation or fear: *spoke up for human rights.* —**speak well for.** To express or indicate something favourable about. —**to speak of.** Worthy of mention or discussion. [Speak, spake, spoken; Middle English *speken, spake, spoken,* Old English *specan, spēc, gespecen.* Past tense *spoke* was formed on analogy with BREAK, BROKE, BROKEN.] —**speak·a·ble** *adj.*

Synonyms: speak, talk, converse, discourse, chatter, gossip.

-speak *n. comb. form.* Indicates a jargon associated with a specified group or field of activity; for example, *teenspeak, newspeak.* [From George Orwell's novel *1984* (1949), in which faceless technocrats develop *Duckspeak,* a language intended to prevent original thought.]

speak·eas·y (spéek-eezi) *n., pl.* **-ies.** A bar selling alcoholic drinks illegally, especially one in the United States during the period of Prohibition.

speak·er (spéekər) *n.* **1.** One who speaks. Often used in combination: *English-speakers.* **2.** One who delivers a public speech. **3.** *Often capital* **S.** The presiding officer of a legislative assembly,

THE WEAPON OF THE HUNTER
Primitive man invented the spear

The spear is one of the earliest man-made weapons, developed from primitive man's use of the stick. With a point hardened by fire, it could be thrust or thrown to bring down animals in the hunt. Stone tips were being fitted to spears 47,000 years ago in the Dordogne, France, but it was in the Bronze Age (from 3000 B.C.) and the Iron Age (from 1200 B.C.) that the spear became a prime weapon. Metalworkers shaped spearheads that were not only ornate, but efficient killing weapons. The medieval bill had a hooked blade and spearhead combined, and was the forerunner of the pike, which could be set into the ground to repel cavalry.

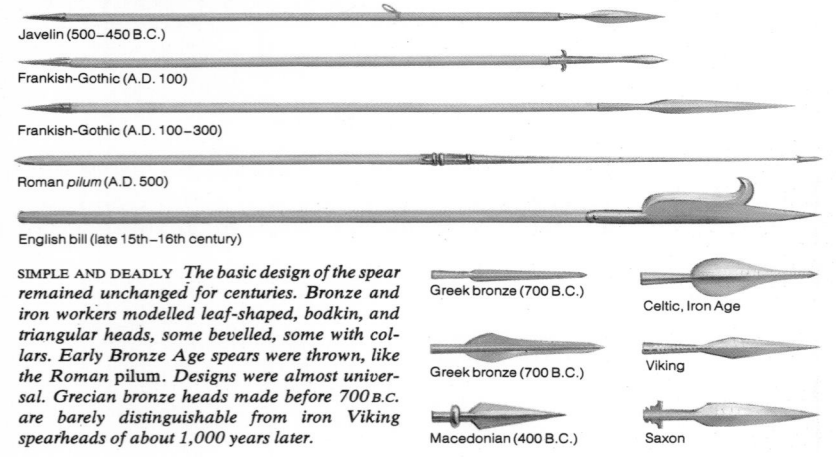

Bronze Age spear (700–500 B.C.)

Javelin (500–450 B.C.)

Frankish-Gothic (A.D. 100)

Frankish-Gothic (A.D. 100–300)

Roman *pilum* (A.D. 500)

English bill (late 15th–16th century)

SIMPLE AND DEADLY *The basic design of the spear remained unchanged for centuries. Bronze and iron workers modelled leaf-shaped, bodkin, and triangular heads, some bevelled, some with collars. Early Bronze Age spears were thrown, like the Roman pilum. Designs were almost universal. Grecian bronze heads made before 700 B.C. are barely distinguishable from iron Viking spearheads of about 1,000 years later.*

Greek bronze (700 B.C.)

Celtic, Iron Age

Greek bronze (700 B.C.)

Viking

Macedonian (400 B.C.)

Saxon

especially the British Parliament or U.S. House of Representatives. **4.** A **loudspeaker** (see).

Speaker's Corner. An area at the Marble Arch corner of Hyde Park, London, where, by tradition, anyone is free to make speeches to the public.

speak·ing (spéeking) adj. **1.** Of, pertaining to, or involving speech: within speaking distance. **2.** Inhabited largely by speakers of a specified language. Used in combination: English-speaking countries. **3.** Expressive or telling; eloquent. —**on speaking terms.** Sufficiently acquainted or friendly to allow conversation.

speaking clock n. British. A telephone service allowing callers to dial a recording giving the exact time. Formerly called "Tim".

speaking tube n. A tube or pipe formerly used for speaking from a room or building to another place.

spear (speer) n. **1.** A weapon consisting of a long shaft with a sharply pointed head. **2.** A shaft with a sharp point and barbs for spearing fish. **3.** A spearman. **4.** A slender stalk, as of asparagus. ~v. **speared, spearing, spears.** —tr. To pierce with or as with a spear. —intr. **1.** To stab with or as with a spear. **2.** To sprout like a spear. [Middle English spere, Old English spere.] —**spear·er** n.

spear·fish (spéer-fish) n., pl. **-fishes** or collectively **spearfish.** A **marlin** (see).

spear·head (spéer-hed) n. **1.** The sharpened head of a spear. **2. a.** The vanguard in a military thrust. **b.** A person or group seen as the driving force in a given action or endeavour. ~tr.v. **spearheaded, -heading, -heads.** To be the leader or leaders of (a drive or an attack).

spear·man (spéer-mən) n., pl. **-men** (-mən, -men). A soldier armed with a spear.

spear·mint (spéer-mint) n. An aromatic plant, Mentha spicata, native to Europe, having clusters of small purplish flowers and yielding an oil widely used as flavouring. [Perhaps so called from the sharpness of the leaf.]

spear side n. The male side of a family. Used humorously. Compare **distaff side.**

spear·wort (spéer-wurt ‖ -wawrt) n. Any of several plants related to the buttercup; especially, Ranunculus flammula, native to Eurasia, having lance-shaped leaves and yellow flowers.

spec¹ (spek) n. Informal. A speculative purchase or enterprise. —**on spec.** Taking a chance: in the hope of success or profit.

spec² n. Informal. A specification.

spec. 1. special. **2.** specification. **3.** speculation.

spe·cial (spésh'l) adj. Abbr. **sp., spec. 1.** Surpassing what is common or usual; exceptional. **2. a.** Distinct among others of a kind; singular. **b.** Primary: their special concern. **3.** Peculiar to a specific person or thing; particular. **4.** Having a limited or specific function, application, or scope. **5.** Esteemed; close: special friends. **6.** Additional; extra: a special holiday flight. **7.** Informal. Exceptionally fine: she's pretty special. ~n. Abbr. **sp., spec. 1.** Something arranged, issued, or made for a particular purpose or occasion, as: **a.** A dish specially featured on a menu. **b.** A television programme not forming part of a regular series and normally longer and more spectacular than an ordinary programme. **2.** A special constable. [Middle English, from Old French especial, from Latin speciālis, special, of a particular kind, from speciēs, kind, SPECIES.] —**spe·cial·ly** adv.

Usage: Special and specially have a wider application than especial and especially. Special and specially mean "particular, specific, as opposed to what is general or ordinary": I have a special interest in such problems. People have been specially trained. Especial and especially are the forms to use when the sense is that of "pre-eminence, exceptional degree": an especial talent; Especially in Britain.

Special Branch n. In Britain, the police department responsible for political security.

special clinic n. In Britain, a clinic, often attached to a hospital, for the detection and treatment of a particular medical condition, such as diabetes or venereal diseases.

special constable n. In Britain, an unpaid member of an auxiliary police force, assisting the regular force in such duties as traffic or crowd control. Also called "special".

special delivery n. A delivery service for important postal items, providing for delivery by a special messenger rather than by ordinary services. —**spe·cial-de·liv·er·y** adj.

special drawing rights pl.n. Abbr. **S.D.R., S.D.R.s** Rights accorded to certain member countries of the International Monetary Fund to draw on the Fund's reserves.

special effects pl.n. Illusory effects used in films and created by various techniques, such as animation or 3-D photography.

special hospital n. In Britain, a hospital for the care of mentally ill patients who are considered a danger to society.

spe·cial·i·sa·tion (spésh'l-ī-záysh'n ‖ U.S.-i-) n. **1.** The action of specialising or the process of becoming specialised. **2.** An area in which one specialises.

specialise, spe·cial·ize (spésh'l-īz) v. **-ised, -ising, -ises.** —intr. **1.** To train or employ oneself in a special study, field, or activity. **2.** Biology. To develop so as to become adapted to a specific environment or function. —tr. **1.** To make more specific or particular. **2.** To give a particular character or function to. **3.** Biology. To adapt by specialisation.

spe·cial·ism (spésh'l-iz'm) n. **1.** Confinement or limitation to some field of study or occupation. **2.** A field of specialisation.

spe·cial·ist (spésh'l-ist) n. Abbr. **sp. 1.** One who has devoted himself

to a particular branch of study or research. **2.** A doctor specialising in a particular field of medicine. —**spe·cial·is·tic** (-ístik) adj.

spe·ci·al·i·ty (spéshi-ál-əti) n., pl. **-ties. 1.** A distinguishing mark or feature; a special characteristic; a peculiarity. **2.** Plural. Special points of consideration; details; particulars. **3.** Chiefly British. Something at which one is particularly adept or for which one makes special provision, such as a pursuit, subject, product, or service.

special licence n. In the Church of England, a licence permitting a marriage to take place without publication of banns, outside the hours prescribed for marriages, or in a church other than a parish of one of the partners.

special plea n. **1.** Law. A plea asserting new or special matter to offset the opposing party's allegations, as an alternative to direct denial. **2.** A presentation of an argument that emphasises only a favourable or a single aspect of the question at issue. In this sense, also called "special pleading".

Special relativity n. Physics. The early part of the theory of **relativity** (see), dealing with uniform motion.

special session n. **1.** An extraordinary session of a court or of a legislative body. **2.** Plural. Sittings held by two or more British magistrates or justices for some special purpose, such as the granting of licences to sell alcoholic drinks.

special sort n. A special printing character not normally forming part of a particular font. Also called "peculiar".

spe·cial·ty (spésh'l-ti) n., pl. **-ties. 1.** Law. A special contract or agreement, especially a deed, kept under seal. **2.** U.S. A speciality (sense 3).

spe·ci·a·tion (spée-si-áysh'n, -shi-) n. Biology. The evolutionary process by which new species are formed. [SPECI(ES) + -ATION.]

spe·cie (spée-shee, -shi ‖ -see) n. Minted money; coin. —**in specie. 1.** In coin. **2.** Law. In kind; in the same kind or shape. [Latin (in) specie, (in) kind, from the ablative of speciēs, kind, SPECIES.]

specie point n. Finance. The **gold point** (see).

spe·cies (spée-sheez, -shiz ‖ -seez) n., pl. **species** (Note. Some distinguish in pronunciation between singular -shiz and plural -sheez). Abbr. **sp. 1.** Biology. **a.** A fundamental category of taxonomic classification, ranking after a genus, and consisting of organisms capable of interbreeding. **b.** A group of organisms belonging to such a category, represented in taxonomic nomenclature by a Latin adjective or epithet following a genus name. **2.** The human race. Preceded by the. **3.** Logic. A class of individuals or objects grouped by virtue of their common attributes and assigned a common name; a division subordinate to a genus. **4.** A kind, variety, or type. **5.** Roman Catholic Church. **a.** The outward appearance or form of the Eucharistic elements that is retained after their consecration. **b.** Either of the consecrated elements of the Eucharist. [Latin speciēs, appearance, likeness, a particular kind, from specere, to look at.]

specif. specifically.

spec·i·fi·a·ble (spéssi-fī-əb'l ‖ -fī-) adj. Capable of being specified.

spe·cif·ic (spi-síffik, spə-) adj. Abbr. **sp. 1.** Explicitly designated; particular; definite. **2.** Pertaining to, characterising, or distinguishing a species. **3.** Precise, distinctive, or unique, as a quality or attribute may be. **4.** Intended for, applying to, or acting upon a particular thing. **5.** Designating a disease produced by a particular microorganism or condition. **6. a.** Designating a customs charge levied upon goods by unit or weight rather than according to value. **b.** Designating a commodity rate applicable to the transport of a single commodity between named points. **7.** Physics. **a.** Designating an extensive physical quality per unit mass: specific heat capacity. **b.** Designating a property of a substance per unit mass, length, area, or volume. **c.** Designating a property of a substance divided by the same property of a standard reference substance: specific gravity. ~n. **1.** Often plural. A specific factor, such as a quality, statement, requirement, or attribute: discussing specifics. **2.** Medicine. A remedy intended for some particular ailment or disorder. [Medieval Latin specificus, from Latin speciēs, kind, SPECIES.] —**spe·cif·i·cal·ly** adv. —**spec·i·fic·i·ty** (spéssi-físəti) n.

-specific adj. comb. form. Confined in effect, relevance, or scope to the specified sphere; for example, **job-specific, sex-specific.**

spec·i·fi·ca·tion (spéssifi-káysh'n) n. Abbr. **spec. 1. a.** An act of specifying. **b.** A precisely stated requirement. **2. a.** Usually plural. A detailed and exact statement of particulars; especially, a statement prescribing materials, dimensions, and instructions for something to be built, installed, or manufactured. **b.** A single item or article that has been specified. **3.** An exact written description of an invention by an applicant for a patent.

specific gravity n. Abbr. **sp gr** Relative density (see).

specific heat capacity n. The amount of heat required to raise the temperature of unit mass of substance by unit interval of temperature under prescribed conditions, usually either at constant volume or constant temperature. It is measured in joules per kilogram per kelvin (SI units) or calories per gram per degree Celsius (c.g.s. units). Formerly called "specific heat".

specific impulse n. A performance measure for rocket propellants, equal to units of thrust per unit weight of propellant consumed per unit time. Also called "specific thrust".

specific performance n. Law. A remedy awarded by a court requiring the terms of a contract to be fulfilled where damages are insufficient.

specific resistance n. Electricity. Resistivity (see). Not in current technical usage.

spearwort This member of the buttercup family flourishes in damp soil, throwing up large, yellow flowers on long stems.

specific volume *n.* The volume of unit mass of a substance; the reciprocal of density.

spec·i·fy (spéssi-fī) *tr.v.* **-fied, -fying, -fies. 1.** To state explicitly, especially as a definite requirement. **2.** To include in a specification. [Middle English *specifien,* from Old French *specifier,* from Medieval Latin *specificāre,* from *specificus,* SPECIFIC.]

spec·i·men (spéssi-min, -mən) *n.* **1.** An individual, item, or part seen as representative of a class, genus, or whole; an example. Also used adjectivally: *a specimen copy.* **2.** A sample, as of tissue, blood, or urine, used for medical or scientific analysis and diagnosis. **3.** An object or organism selected and presented as part of a collection or series: *showed me his finest specimen.* **4.** *Informal.* A person of a specified, usually unpleasant, type: *an unsavoury specimen.* —See Synonyms at **example.** [Latin *specimen,* mark, token, example, from *specere,* to look at.]

spe·ci·os·i·ty (spe͞eshi-óssəti) *n., pl.* **-ities. 1.** The state or quality of being specious. **2.** A specious person or thing.

spe·cious (spe͞eshəss) *adj.* **1.** Seemingly fair, attractive, sound, or true, but actually not so; deceptive: *a specious resemblance.* **2.** Having the ring of truth or plausibility but actually fallacious: *a specious argument.* [Middle English, attractive, fair, from Latin *speciōsus,* good-looking, from *speciēs,* outward appearance, from *specere,* to look at.] —**spe·cious·ly** *adv.* —**spe·cious·ness** *n.*

speck (spek) *n.* **1.** A small spot, mark, or discoloration. **2.** A very small bit of something; a particle.
~*tr.v.* **specked, specking, specks.** To mark with specks; spot; speckle. [Middle English *specke,* Old English *speccat†.*]

speck·le (spéck'l) *n.* A speck or small spot; especially, a natural dot of colour occurring in large numbers on skin, plumage, or foliage.
~*tr.v.* **speckled, -ling, -les.** To mark with or as if with speckles. [Middle Dutch *spekkel;* akin to Old English *specca,* SPECK.]

speck·led trout (spéck'ld) *n.* The **brook trout** *(see).*

specs (speks) *pl.n. Informal.* Glasses; spectacles.

spec·ta·cle (spéktək'l) *n.* **1.** A public performance or display, especially a lavish visual entertainment. **2. a.** An object of interest; a marvel or curiosity. **b.** An object or scene considered regrettable: *made a spectacle of himself.* **3. a.** Something seen or able to be seen. **b.** The sight of something: *"We pleased ourselves with the spectacle of Dublin's commerce"* (James Joyce). **4.** *Plural.* **a.** A pair of glasses. **b.** Something resembling glasses in shape or function. —**through rose-tinted** or **rose-coloured spectacles.** Wtih naive optimism. [Middle English, from Old French, from Latin *spectāculum,* from *spectāre,* to look at, frequentative of *specere.*]

spec·ta·cled (spéktək'ld) *adj.* **1.** Wearing spectacles. **2.** Having markings suggesting spectacles. Said of animals.

spec·tac·u·lar (spek-táckew-lər) *adj.* **1.** Of the nature of a spectacle; visually impressive. **2.** Striking or remarkable; dramatic: *a spectacular resignation.*
~*n.* An entertainment, such as a film or television programme, with lavish visual presentation and usually featuring famous performers. —**spec·tac·u·lar·ly** *adv.* —**spec·tac·u·lar·i·ty** (-lárrəti) *n.*

spec·tate (spek-táyt || spék-tayt) *intr.v.* **-tated, -tating, -tates.** *Informal.* To be present as a spectator.

spec·ta·tor (spek-táytər || spék-taytər) *n.* **1.** One who attends and views a show, sports match, or other event. **2.** An observer of any event; an eyewitness; an onlooker. [Latin *spectātor,* from *spectāre,* look at. See **spectacle.**]

spectator sport *n.* A sport which attracts large numbers of people to come and watch it, as opposed to participate in it.

spectra. Plural of **spectrum.**

spec·tral (spéktrəl) *adj.* **1.** Of or resembling a spectre; ghostly. **2.** Of, pertaining to, or produced by a spectrum. —**spec·tral·i·ty** (spek-trál-əti), **spec·tral·ness** *n.* —**spec·tral·ly** *adv.*

spectral line *n. Physics.* A discrete peak of intensity in a spectrum; especially, one of the visible dispersed images of the slit through which light enters the collimator of a spectroscope, produced by light of a single wavelength.

spectral type *n.* Any of several methods of classifying stars according to their observed spectra. See **Harvard classification.**

spec·tre, *U.S.* **spec·ter** (spéktər) *n.* **1.** A ghost; a phantom; an apparition. **2.** Something fearful that has no reality. **3.** A mental image of something unpleasant: *the spectre of examinations.* [French, from Latin *spectrum,* appearance, image. See **spectrum.**]

spectro- *comb. form.* Indicates spectrum; for example, **spectrograph, spectroscope.** [From SPECTRUM.]

spec·tro·bo·lom·e·ter (spék-trō-bə-lómmitər, -trə-, -bō-) *n. Physics.* A bolometer combined with a spectroscope for investigating how the intensity of a source of radiant energy varies over the range of wavelengths emitted.

spec·tro·gram (spék-trə-gram, -trō-) *n. Physics.* Also **spectrograph.** A graph or photograph of a spectrum. [SPECTRO- + -GRAM.]

spec·tro·graph (spék-trə-graaf, -trō-, -graf) *n. Physics.* **1.** A spectroscope equipped to photograph spectra. **2.** Variant of **spectrogram.** [SPECTRO- + -GRAPH.] —**spec·tro·graph·ic** (-gráffik) *adj.* —**spec·tro·graph·i·cal·ly** *adv.* —**spec·trog·ra·phy** (spek-tróggrəfi) *n.*

spec·tro·he·li·o·gram (spék-trō-he͞eli-ə-gram, -trə-, -ō-) *n. Physics.* A photograph of the sun taken in a narrow wavelength band centred on a selected wavelength.

spec·tro·he·li·o·graph (spék-trō-he͞eli-ə-graaf, -trə-, -ō-, -graf) *n. Physics.* An instrument used to make spectroheliograms. —**spec·tro·he·li·o·graph·ic** (-gráffik) *adj.*

spec·tro·he·li·o·scope (spék-trō-he͞eli-ə-skōp, -trə-, -ō-) *n. Physics.* An instrument used to observe solar radiation. —**spec·tro·he·li·o·scop·ic** (-skóppik) *adj.*

spec·trol·o·gy (spek-trólləji) *n.* The study of spectres.

spec·trom·e·ter (spek-trómmitər) *n. Physics.* A spectroscope equipped with calibrated scales for measuring the positions of spectral lines. [SPECTRO(SCOPE) + -METER.] —**spec·tro·met·ric** (spék-trə-méttrik, -trō-) *adj.* —**spec·trom·e·try** (spek-trómmətri) *n.*

spec·tro·pho·tom·e·ter (spék-trō-fō-tómmitər, -trə-) *n. Physics.* An instrument used to determine the distribution of energy in a spectrum of luminous radiation. —**spec·tro·pho·to·met·ric** (-fō-tō-méttrik, -tə-) *adj.* —**spec·tro·pho·tom·e·try** (-tómmətri) *n.*

spec·tro·scope (spék-trə-skōp, -trō-) *n. Physics.* Any of various instruments for resolving and observing or recording spectra. [SPECTRO- + -SCOPE.] —**spec·tro·scop·ic** (-skóppik), **spec·tro·scop·i·cal** *adj.* —**spec·tro·scop·i·cal·ly** *adv.*

spectroscopic analysis *n. Physics.* The analysis of a spectrum to determine characteristics of its source, such as the analysis of the optical spectrum of an incandescent body to determine its composition or motion.

spec·tros·co·py (spek-tróskəpi) *n. Physics.* The study of spectra, especially the experimental observation of spectra. [SPECTRO- + -SCOPY.] —**spec·tros·co·pist** *n.*

spec·trum (spék-trəm) *n., pl.* **-tra** (-trə) or **-trums. 1.** *Physics.* The distribution of a characteristic of a physical system or phenomenon, especially: **a.** The distribution of energy emitted by a radiant source, as by an incandescent body, arranged in order of wavelengths. **b.** The distribution of atomic or subatomic particles in a system, as in a magnetically resolved molecular beam, arranged in order of masses. Also called "mass spectrum". **c.** A graphic or photographic representation of any such distribution. **2. a.** The complete range of electromagnetic radiation arranged in order of frequency or wavelength. Also called "electromagnetic spectrum". **b.** The complete range of colours as dispersed from light. **3. a.** A range of values of a quantity or set of related quantities. **b.** A broad sequence or range of related qualities, ideas, or activities: *the whole spectrum of 20th-century thought.* [Latin, appearance, image, form, from *specere,* to look at.]

spec·u·lar (spéckewlər) *adj.* Of, resembling, produced, or aided by a mirror or speculum. —**spec·u·lar·ly** *adv.*

spec·u·late (spéckew-layt) *intr.v.* **-lated, -lating, -lates. 1.** To conjecture on a given subject or situation, without knowing all the facts. **2.** To engage in the buying or selling of a commodity with an element of risk on the chance of large profit. —See Synonyms at **conjecture.** [Latin *speculārī,* to spy out, watch, observe, from *specula,* watchtower, from *specere,* to look at.] —**spec·u·lat·or** *n.*

spec·u·la·tion (spéckew-láysh'n) *n. Abbr.* **spec. 1. a.** The act of speculating; consideration of or conjecture about some subject or idea. **b.** A conclusion, opinion, or theory reached by speculating. **2. a.** Engagement in risky business transactions on the chance of quick or considerable profit. **b.** An instance of commercial speculating. **3.** A card game in which players buy trumps from each other on a chance of getting the highest trump dealt.

spec·u·la·tive (spéckew-lətiv, -laytiv) *adj.* **1.** Of, characterised by, or based upon contemplative speculation; conjectural or theoretical in nature rather than pragmatic or realistic. **2. a.** Given to or spent in speculation or conjecture. **b.** Seeming to speculate: *a speculative gaze.* **3. a.** Engaging in, given to, or involving financial speculation. **b.** Involving chance; risky. —**spec·u·la·tive·ly** *adv.* —**spec·u·la·tive·ness** *n.*

speculative philosophy *n.* Philosophy that is theoretical or transcendent, rather than demonstrative or empirical.

spec·u·lum (spéckew-ləm) *n., pl.* **-la** (-lə) or **-lums. 1.** A mirror or polished metal plate, used as a reflector in optical instruments. **2.** An instrument for dilating the opening of a body cavity, especially the vagina, for medical examination. **3.** *Biology.* **a.** A bright patch of colour on the wings of certain birds, especially ducks. Also called "mirror". **b.** A transparent spot on the wings of some butterflies or moths. [Latin, mirror, from *specere,* to look at.]

speculum metal *n.* An alloy of copper, tin, and other metals that takes a high polish and is used in mirrors and reflectors.

sped. Past tense and past participle of **speed.**

speech (speech) *n.* **1. a.** The faculty or act of speaking; utterance of articulate sounds. **b.** The faculty or act of expressing or describing thoughts, feelings, or perceptions in words. **2. a.** That which is spoken; an utterance. **b.** A line or set of lines spoken by a character in a dramatic work. **3.** Conversation; vocal communication. **4. a.** A talk or public address. **b.** A printed copy of an address. **5.** A person's habitual manner or style of speaking. **6.** The language or dialect of a nation or region. **7.** The sounding of a musical instrument. **8.** The study of oral communication, speech sounds, especially for elocution or dramatic effect, and vocal physiology. **9.** *Linguistics.* **Parole** *(see).* **10.** *Archaic.* Rumour. [Middle English *speche,* Old English *spēc, sprǣc.*]

speech community *n.* All the speakers of a particular language or dialect, whether located in one area or scattered.

speech day *n.* An annual occasion in schools in Britain and elsewhere when prizes are awarded for academic performance and speeches are made by the headmaster and others.

speech defect *n.* A defect in speaking, such as a lisp or stammer, having a physiological or psychological cause.

Speech from the throne *n.* A speech read by the sovereign or his or her representative at the opening of Parliament in Britain and certain Commonwealth countries outlining the government's legis-

PRONUNCIATION KEY

a, trap; aa, father; ai, fair; ar, star; aw, lawn; ay, play; b, bb, stab; rubber; ch, church; ck, ticket; d, dd, dead; ladder; e, dress; ee, bee; er, defer; ew, few; ewr, pure; ə, about; ər, letter; f, ff, fife; differ; g, gg, giggle; h, hat; i, kit; ī, price; īr, fire; j, judge; k, kick; l, ll, let; 'l, needle; m, mm, man; n, nn, no; 'n, sudden; ng, thing; o, lot; ō, no; o͝o, foot; o͞o, shoe; oor, poor; ow, cow; owr, hour; oy, boy; p, pp, pepper; r, rr, red; s, ss, sauce; sh, ship; t, tt, totter; th, thick; th, this; smooth; u, cut; ur, turn; v, vv, valve; w, wet; y, yes; z, zz, zebra; zh, vision; pleasure

IN FOREIGN WORDS:

aN, oN, Saint-Saëns; hl, Llanelli; Hluhluwe; kh, loch; lough; Khaled

STRESS MARK:

ín-sīt, insight; in-sít, incite

lative programme. Also called "gracious speech", "King's speech", "Queen's speech".

speech·i·fy (spéechi-fī) *intr.v.* **-fied, -fying, -fies.** To make a speech, especially a pompous one; orate. **—speech·i·fi·ca·tion** (-fi-káysh'n) **—speech·i·fi·er** *n.*

speech·less (spéech-ləss, -liss) *adj.* **1.** Lacking the faculty of speech; dumb. **2.** Temporarily unable to speak, as through astonishment. **3.** Refraining from speech; silent. **4.** Unexpressed or inexpressible in words: *speechless admiration.* —See Synonyms at **dumb.** **—speech·less·ly** *adv.* **—speech·less·ness** *n.*

speech-reading *n.* **Lip-reading** *(see).*

speech pathology *n.* **1.** The study of speech defects and disabilities and methods of correcting them. **2.** *Chiefly U.S.* Speech therapy. **—speech pathologist** *n.*

speech therapy *n.* The practice or profession of dealing with speech defects and disabilities. Also called "logopaedics", *chiefly U.S.* "speech pathology". **—speech therapist** *n.*

speed (speed) *n.* **1.** *Mathematics & Physics.* The rate or a measure of the rate of motion, especially: **a.** *Average speed,* or the distance travelled divided by the time of travel. **b.** *Instantaneous speed,* the limit of this quotient as the time of travel becomes vanishingly small; the first derivative of distance with respect to time. **c.** The magnitude of a **velocity** *(see).* **2.** A rate of performance; swiftness of action. **3.** The act or state of moving rapidly; rapidity; swiftness. **4.** A transmission gear or set of gears in a motor vehicle or bicycle. **5.** A rate of rotation, especially that of a record turntable, usually expressed in revolutions per minute or other unit time. **6.** *Photography.* **a.** A numerical expression of the sensitivity of a film, plate, or paper to light. **b.** The capacity of a lens to accumulate light at an appropriate aperture. See **f-stop.** **c.** The length of time required or permitted for a camera shutter to open and admit light. **7.** *Slang.* Any amphetamine taken to increase energy, reduce tiredness, and produce euphoria. **8.** *Archaic.* Prosperity; success; luck. **—at speed.** Rapidly.
~*v.* **sped** (sped) or **speeded, speeding, speeds.** *—tr.* **1. a.** To hasten. **b.** To send or dispatch with speed or haste. **2. a.** To increase the speed or rate of; accelerate. Often used with *up.* **b.** To set the speed of (a machine). **3. a.** *Archaic.* To wish Godspeed to. **b.** *Archaic.* To help to succeed or prosper; aid. **c.** To further, promote, or expedite (a matter or legal action). Often used with *along.* *—intr.* **1. a.** To go or move rapidly. **b.** To drive fast; exceed a traffic speed limit. **2.** To pass quickly. Used of time. **3.** To move, perform, or happen at a faster rate; accelerate. Usually used with *up.* **4.** *Slang.* To take or be under the influence of amphetamines. [Middle English *sped(e),* success, prosperity, speed, Old English *spǣd, spēd.*]
Synonyms: *speed, hurry, hasten, quicken, accelerate, precipitate, expedite.*

speed·ball (spéed-bawl) *n. Slang.* An intravenous dose of cocaine and heroin or morphine.

speed·boat (spéed-bōt) *n.* A fast motorboat.

speed·er (spéedər) *n.* One that speeds; especially, a driver who exceeds a legal or safe speed.

speed limit *n.* The maximum speed legally permitted on a given stretch of road.

speed mer·chant *n.* One who habitually drives a motor vehicle excessively fast.

speed·om·e·ter (spee-dómmitər) *n.* An instrument for measuring and indicating speed. Also informally called "speedo".

speed·ster (spéed-stər) *n.* **1.** A speeder. **2.** A fast vehicle, usually a sports car.

speed trap *n.* A stretch of road on which the speed of vehicles is secretly checked by police using electronic or other devices.

speed·way (spéed-way) *n.* **1. a.** A course for motorcycle racing. **b.** The sport of motorcycle racing. **2.** *U.S.* **a.** A car racetrack. **b.** A road designed for fast-moving traffic.

speed·well (spéed-wel) *n.* Any of various plants of the genus *Veronica,* having clusters of small, usually blue flowers.

Speed·writ·ing (spéed-rīting) *n.* A trademark for a shorthand technique involving modified alphabetic symbols which represent phonetic combinations.

speed·y (spéedi) *adj.* **-ier, -iest.** **1.** Characterised by rapid motion; swift. **2.** Accomplished or arrived at without delay; prompt; quick. —See Synonyms at **fast.** **—speed·i·ly** *adv.* **—speed·i·ness** *n.*

speer, speir (speer) *v.* **speered** or **speired, speering** or **speiring, speers** or **speirs.** *Scottish.* *—intr.* To ask questions. *—tr.* To ask; enquire. [Middle English, from Old English *spyrian,* to seek; akin to SPOOR.]

spe·le·ol·o·gy (spéeli-óllәji, spélli-) *n.* **1.** The study of the physical, geological, and biological aspects of caves. **2.** The exploration of caves. [Latin *spēleum,* cave, from Greek *spēlaion*† + -LOGY.] **—spe·le·o·log·i·cal** (-ə-lójik'l) *adj.* **—spe·le·ol·o·gist** (-óllәjist) *n.*

spell¹ (spel) *v.* **spelt** (spelt) or *chiefly U.S.* **spelled, spelling, spells.** *—tr.* **1.** To name or write in order the letters constituting (a word or part of a word). **2.** To be the ordered letters of; form (a word). **3.** To mean; be a sign of: *that tone of voice spells trouble.* *—intr.* To form a word or words correctly by naming the letters. **—spell out.** **1.** *Informal.* To make explicit and understandable: *He didn't need to spell out his threat.* **2.** To spell slowly, letter by letter, especially when trying to read or decipher. [Middle English *spellen,* read out, from Old French *espelir, espeller,* from Germanic.] **—spell·a·ble** *adj.*
Usage: Both *spelled* and *spelt* are used as past tenses and participles, the former being standard in American English, the latter being the usual form in British English.

spell² *n.* **1.** A word or formula used to work magic. **2.** Compelling attraction; fascination. **3.** A bewitched state; a trance. [Middle English *spell,* discourse, Old English *spel(l),* story, fable.]

spell³ *n.* **1.** A short, indefinite period of time. **2.** *Informal.* A period characterised by some specified condition, such as weather, activity, or illness: *a dry spell; a dizzy spell.* **3.** A short turn of work; a turn; a shift: *a spell at the helm.* **4.** *Australian.* A period or interval of rest. **5.** *Informal.* A short distance.
~*v.* **spelled, spelling, spells.** *—tr. Chiefly U.S.* **1.** To relieve (a person) from work temporarily by taking a turn. **2.** To allow to rest a while. [Perhaps from Middle English *spelen,* relieve at work, Old English *spelian*†, to substitute.]

spell·bind (spél-bīnd) *tr.v.* **-bound** (-bownd), **-binding, -binds.** To put or hold under or as if under a spell; enthral; enchant.

spell·bind·er (spél-bīndər) *n.* One that holds others spellbound.

spell·bound (spél-bownd) *adj.* Entranced; fascinated.

spell·er (spéllər) *n.* **1.** One who spells words, usually in a specified way. **2.** An elementary textbook to teach spelling.

spellican. Variant of **spillikin.**

spell·ing (spélling) *n. Abbr.* **sp.** **1. a.** The forming of words with letters in an accepted order; orthography. **b.** The art or study of orthography. **c.** A person's ability to spell. **2.** The way in which a word is spelt.

spelling bee *n.* A contest in which competitors are eliminated as they fail to spell a given word correctly. [Special (originally U.S.) use of BEE (insect, representing industrious and communal activity).]

spelling pronunciation *n.* A pronunciation of a word that is influenced by the way in which it is spelt and that often comes to replace earlier forms. The word "forehead" (fórrid), for example, is sometimes pronounced nowadays as (fór-hed).

spelt¹ (spelt) *n.* A hardy wheat, *Triticum spelta,* from which many cultivated wheats are derived. [Probably from Middle Dutch *spelte.*]

spelt². Past tense and past participle of **spell** (to form words).

spel·ter (spéltər) *n.* Impure zinc, especially in the form of ingots, slabs, or plates. [Obscurely akin to Middle Dutch *speauter*†; akin to Old French *peautre,* PEWTER.]

spe·lun·ker (spi-lúngkər, spée-lungkər) *n. U.S.* One who explores and studies caves. [From obsolete *spelunk,* cave, from Middle English, from Latin *spelunca,* from Greek *spēlunx;* akin to Greek *spēlaion.* See **speleology.**] **—spe·lunk·ing** *n.*

Spence (spenss), **Sir Basil** (1907–76). English architect. He designed the new cathedral for Coventry (finished 1962) and was consultant architect to many British universities.

spen·cer¹ (spén-sər) *n. Nautical.* A **trysail** *(see).* [Perhaps from the surname *Spencer.*]

spencer² *n.* **1.** A short double-breasted overcoat worn by men in the early 19th century. **2.** A close-fitting waist-length jacket formerly worn by women. **3.** A short-sleeved woman's vest. [After George *Spencer,* Earl Spencer (1758–1834).]

Spencer, Sir Stanley (1891–1959). English painter. He is best known for his religious paintings which interpret the Scriptures in terms of everyday life. He was knighted in 1959.

Spencer Gulf. Inlet of the Indian Ocean, on the southern coast of Australia between Eyre Peninsula to the west and Yorke Peninsula to the east.

Spen·ce·ri·an·ism (spen-séer-i-ən-iz'm) *n.* The system of logical positivism developed by Herbert Spencer (1820–1903), setting forth the idea that evolution is the mechanistic passage from the simple, indefinite, and incoherent to the complex, definite, and coherent. Also called "synthetic philosophy".

spend (spend) *v.* **spent** (spent), **spending, spends.** *—tr.* **1.** To pay out (money). **2.** To use, concentrate, or devote. Often used with *on: spending his energy on pleasures.* **3.** To use up, consume, or expend: *The gale spent its force.* **4.** To pass (time) in a specified manner or place. **5. a.** To throw away; waste; squander. **b.** To sacrifice. *—intr.* **1.** To pay out money. **2.** *Obsolete.* To be exhausted or consumed. [Spend, spent, spent; Middle English *spenden, spente, spent,* partly from Old English *spendan,* from Latin *expendere,* to EXPEND, and partly from Old French *despendre,* to dispend, squander.] **—spend·a·ble** *adj.*
Usage: In its main sense of "purchase", *spend* may be followed by *on (I've spent a fortune on a new bike),* and especially in American English by *for.* In the sense of "pass the time", it may be followed by *in: He spent the last part of his life (in) doing good.*

spend·er (spéndər) *n.* One that spends money in a specified way: *a big spender.*

Spend·er (spéndər), **Stephen** (1909–). English poet and critic. He was a leading member of the group of socialist poets in the 1930s, and fought with the Republicans in the Spanish Civil war. Much of his work is characterised by imagery of an industrialised society.

spend·ing money (spénding) *n.* **Pocket money** *(see).*

spend·thrift (spénd-thrift) *n.* One who squanders money; a prodigal spender.
~*adj.* Wasteful or extravagant. [SPEND + THRIFT (accumulated wealth).]

Speng·ler (spéng-glər, -lər; *German* shpéng-lər), **Oswald** (1880–1936). German philosopher. He argued that civilisations and cultures are subject to the same cycle of growth and decay as human beings. His chief work, *The Decline of the West* (1918–22),

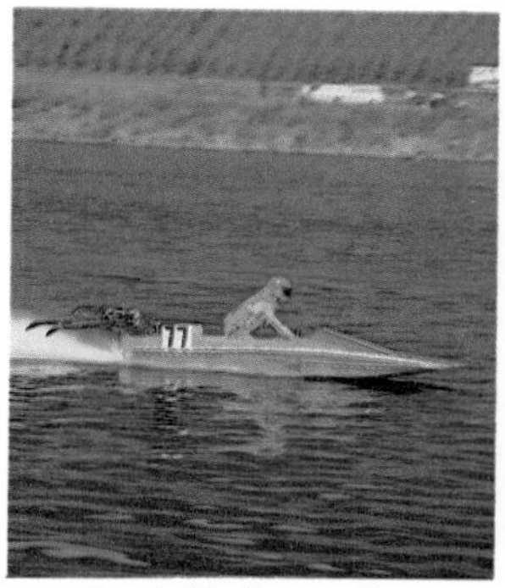

speedboat *The first speedboats were designed in France in about 1900, and used specially adapted car engines. Speedboat racing became popular internationally and speeds rose from about 30 kilometres per hour (20 miles per hour) in 1903 to the present-day speeds of around 160 kilometres per hour (100 miles per hour).*

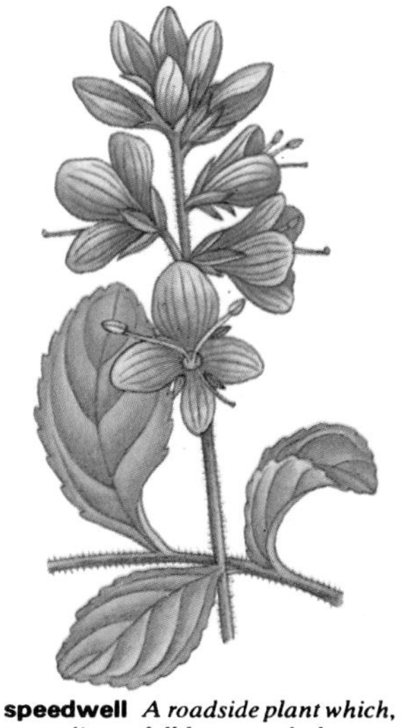

speedwell *A roadside plant which, according to folklore, speeds the traveller well. It has many local names and superstitions, including the belief in Germany and some parts of England that picking the flower will cause a storm – hence one of its local names, strike-fire. This is the common speedwell,* **Veronica officinalis.**

reflects the pessimistic atmosphere in Germany after World War I.

Spen·ser (spén-sər), **Edmund** (c.1552–99). English poet. He is known chiefly for his allegorical, epic romance *The Faerie Queen* (1590–96). His other works include the pastoral *Shepherd's Calendar* (1579) and the lyrical marriage poem, *Epithalamion* (1595).

Spen·se·ri·an sonnet (spen-séer-i-ən) *n.* A sonnet comprising three interlocking quatrains and a couplet with the rhyme pattern *abab bcbc cdcd ee.* [After Edmund SPENSER.]

Spenserian stanza *n.* A stanza consisting of eight lines of iambic pentameter and a final alexandrine, rhymed *ababbcbcc,* used by Edmund Spenser in *The Faerie Queene.*

spent (spent). Past tense and past participle of **spend.**
~*adj.* **1.** Consumed; used up; expended: *a spent bullet.* **2.** Depleted of energy, force, or strength; exhausted; worn out.

sperm¹ (sperm) *n.* **1.** A male gamete or reproductive cell, a **spermatozoon** (see). **2.** The male fluid of fertilisation, **semen** (see). [Middle English *sperme,* from Old French *esperme,* from Late Latin *sperma,* seed, sperm, from Greek *sperma.*]

sperm² *n.* The sperm whale or a substance associated with it, such as spermaceti or sperm oil. [Short for SPERMACETI.]

sperm–, spermi–, spermo– *comb. form.* Indicates: **1.** Sperm; for example, **spermicidal. 2.** Seed; for example, **spermophile.** [Greek *sperma,* seed.]

–sperm *n. comb. form. Botany.* Indicates a seed; for example, **gymnosperm.** [From SPERM (semen).] —**spermous** *adj. comb. form.*

sper·ma·ce·ti (spérmə-sétti, -séeti) *n.* A white, waxy substance consisting of various esters of fatty acids, obtained from the head of the sperm whale and used for making candles, ointments, and cosmetics. [Middle English, from Medieval Latin *spermacētī,* "sperm of the whale" : Late Latin *sperma,* SPERM + Latin *cētī,* genitive of *cētus,* whale (see **cetacean**).]

sper·ma·ry (spérmərí) *n., pl.* **-ries.** An organ in which male gametes are formed, especially in invertebrate animals. [New Latin *spermarium,* from Late Latin *sperma,* SPERM.]

sper·ma·the·ca (spérmə-théekə) *n.* A receptacle in certain female invertebrates, especially insects, in which spermatozoa are stored before fertilisation takes place. [New Latin : Late Latin *sperma,* SPERM + THECA.] —**sper·ma·the·cal** *adj.*

sper·mat·ic (sper-máttik) *adj.* **1. a.** Pertaining to, or resembling spermatozoa; spermous. **b.** Carrying or containing spermatozoa. **2.** Pertaining to a spermary or to a testis. [Late Latin *spermaticus,* from Greek *spermatikos,* from *sperma* (stem *spermat-*), SPERM.]

spermatic cord *n.* A cordlike structure consisting of the vas deferens and its accompanying arteries, veins, nerves, and lymphatic vessels. It passes from the abdominal cavity through the inguinal canal, and down into the scrotum to the back of the testicle, which is suspended in the scrotum by this structure.

spermatic fluid *n.* The male fluid of fertilisation, **semen** (see).

sper·ma·tid (spérmə-tid) *n.* Any of four haploid cells formed from a spermatocyte during meiosis in the male that develop into spermatozoa without further division. [SPERMAT(O)- + -ID.]

sper·ma·ti·um (sper-máyti-əm ‖ *chiefly U.S.* -máyshi-, -máysh-) *n., pl.* **-tia** (-ə). *Botany.* A nonmotile, sporelike structure in red algae and certain fungi, generally acting as a male gamete. [New Latin, from Greek *spermation,* diminutive of *sperma* (stem *spermat-*), SPERM.] —**sper·ma·tial** *adj.*

spermato–, spermat– *comb. form.* Indicates: **1.** Sperm; for example, **spermatogonium, spermatid. 2.** Seed; for example, **spermatophyte.** [Late Latin *sperma* (stem *spermat-*), SPERM.]

sper·ma·to·cyte (spérmət-ō-sīt, sper-mát-, -ə-) *n.* A diploid cell that is converted by meiotic division into four spermatids during spermatogenesis. [SPERMATO- + -CYTE.]

sper·ma·to·gen·e·sis (spérmətə-ō-jénnə-siss, sper-mát-, -ə-) *n.* The generation of spermatozoa from spermatogonia in the testis by meiosis and spermiogenesis. [New Latin : SPERMATO- + -GENESIS.] —**sper·ma·to·ge·net·ic** (-jə-néttik) *adj.*

sper·ma·to·go·ni·um (spérmət-ō-nium-əm, sper-mát-, -ə-) *n., pl.* **-nia** (-ə). Any of the cells of the gonads in male animals that are the progenitors of spermatocytes. [New Latin : SPERMATO- + -GONIUM.] —**sper·ma·to·go·ni·al** *adj.*

sper·ma·toid (spérmə-toyd) *adj.* Resembling sperm. [SPERMAT(O)- + -OID.]

sper·ma·to·phore (spérmət-ō-fawr, sper-mát-, -ə- ‖ -fōr) *n.* An extruded mass or capsule of spermatozoa in certain animals, such as some molluscs, insects, and amphibians. [SPERMATO- + -PHORE.] —**sper·ma·toph·or·al** *adj.*

sper·ma·to·phyte (spérmət-ō-fīt, sper-mát-, -ə-) *n. Botany.* Any plant of the division Spermatophyta, which includes all seed-bearing plants and is divided into angiosperms and gymnosperms. [New Latin *Spermatophyta* : SPERMATO- + -PHYTE.] —**sper·ma·to·phyt·ic** (-fíttik) *adj.*

sper·ma·tor·rhoe·a (spérmət-ō-rée-ə, sper-mát-, -ə-) *n.* Involuntary seminal discharge without orgasm. [New Latin : SPERMATO- + -RRHOEA.]

sper·ma·to·zo·id (spérmət-ō-zoyd, sper-mát-, -ə-) *n. Botany.* A ciliated male gamete produced in an antheridium; an antherozoid. [SPERMATOZO(ON) + -ID.]

sper·ma·to·zo·on (spérmət-ō-zó-on, sper-mát-, -ə-, -ən) *n., pl.* **-zoa** (-ə). A fertilising gamete of a male animal, usually a long nucleated cell with a thin, motile tail. It is produced in the testis by spermatogenesis. Also called "sperm", "sperm cell", "zoosperm". [New Latin : SPERMATO- + -ZOON.] —**sper·ma·to·zo·al, sper·ma·to·zo·an, sper·ma·to·zo·ic** *adj.*

sperm bank *n.* A place where sperm is stored for use in artificial insemination.

sperm count *n.* An estimation of the number of spermatozoa in a specimen of semen, used as an indication of male fertility.

spermi–, spermo– Variants of **sperm–.**

sper·mi·cide (spérmi-sīd) *n.* A usually chemical agent that kills spermatozoa. [SPERMI- + -CIDE.] —**sper·mi·cid·al** (-síd'l) *adj.*

sper·mine (spér-meen) *n.* A crystalline compound, $C_{10}H_{26}N_4$, found as a phosphate in semen, yeast, and certain body tissues.

sper·mi·o·gen·e·sis (spérmi-ə-jénnə-siss, -ō-) *n.* The transformation of a spermatid into a spermatozoon. [New Latin : *spermium,* spermatozoon, probably from SPERM + -GENESIS.]

sper·mo·go·ni·um (spérm-ə-gŏni-əm, -ō-) *n., pl.* **-nia** (-ə). *Botany.* A hollow structure in which spermatia are formed, as in certain fungi. [SPERMO- + -GONIUM.]

sperm oil *n.* A yellow, waxy oil, obtained chiefly from the head of the sperm whale and used as an industrial lubricant.

sperm·o·phile (spérm-ə-fīl, -ō-) *n.* Any of various North American ground squirrels of the genus *Citellus.* [New Latin *spermophilus,* "fond of seed" : SPERMO- + -PHILE.]

sper·mous (spérməss) *adj.* Spermatic.

sperm whale *n.* A toothed whale, *Physeter catodon,* having a very large head, with cavities containing sperm oil and spermaceti, and a long, narrow, toothed lower jaw. Also called "cachalot".

sper·ry·lite (spérri-līt) *n.* A white platinum mineral, essentially $PtAs_2$, occurring in the form of cube-shaped crystals. [After F.L. *Sperry,* 19th-century Canadian mineralogist.]

spes·sar·tite (spéssər-tīt) *n.* A brownish type of garnet used as a gemstone, consisting of a silicate of aluminium and manganese, usually with small amounts of iron. [French, from *Spessart,* mountain range in Germany.]

speug (spyug) *n. Scottish.* A sparrow.

spew (spew) *v.* **spewed, spewing, spews.** Also *archaic* **spue, spued, spuing, spues.** —*tr.* **1.** To vomit or spit out through the mouth. **2.** To throw out or send forth with force or vigour. Often used with *forth* or *out*: *spewing out insults.* —*intr.* **1.** To vomit. **2.** To be thrown out or sent forth with force or vigour. Often used with *forth* or *out*: *Lava spewed forth from the crater.*
~*n.* Also *archaic* **spue.** Something that is spewed; vomit. [Middle English *spewen,* Old English *spīwan* and *spīowan.*]

Spey (spay). River in northeastern Scotland, rising in the Mondhliath mountains and flowing for about 170 kilometres (105 miles) into the North Sea. Its rapid, unnavigable waters are noted for salmon, and are used in the renowned Speyside whiskies.

Spey·er (shpí-ər). *English* **Spires** (spīrz). City and port in Rheinland-Pfalz, West Germany, lying on the river Rhine south of Mannheim. Its products include ships, chemicals, paper, and textiles. The Imperial Cathedral (11th century) is one of Germany's finest Romanesque buildings.

sp gr specific gravity.

sphag·num (sfág-nəm) *n.* **1.** Any of various mosses of the genus *Sphagnum,* that decompose to form peat. **2.** A mass of these plants, used for potting plants and for surgical dressings. Also called "bog moss", "peat moss". [New Latin, from Latin *sphagnos,* a kind of moss, from Greek *sphagnos†.*] —**sphag·nous** *adj.*

sphal·er·ite (sfál-ə-rīt, sfáyl-) *n.* A yellow, brown, black, or white zinc ore, essentially ZnS with some cadmium and iron. Also called "blende", "zinc blende". [German *Sphalerit* : Greek *sphaleros,* slippery, from *sphallein†,* to trip + -ITE.]

sphene (sfeen, speen) *n.* A titanium ore, chiefly $CaTiSiO_5$. Also called "titanite". [French *sphène,* from Greek *sphēn,* wedge.]

sphe·nic (sféenik, sfénnik) *adj.* Wedge-shaped. [SPHEN(O)- + -IC.]

spheno–, sphen– *comb. form.* Indicates wedge-shaped; for example, **sphenogram, sphenodon.** [Greek *sphēn,* wedge.]

sphe·no·don (sféenə-don, sfénnə-) *n.* A reptile, the **tuatara** (see). [SPHEN(O)- + -ODON.]

sphe·no·gram (sféenə-gram, sfénnə-) *n.* A cuneiform character. [SPHENO- + -GRAM.]

sphe·noid (sfée-noyd) *n.* The sphenoid bone.
~*adj.* Also **sphe·noid·al** (see-nóyd'l). **1.** Wedge-shaped. **2.** Of or pertaining to the sphenoid bone. [New Latin *sphenoides,* from Greek *sphēnoeidēs* : SPHEN(O)- + -OID.]

sphenoid bone *n.* A compound bone with winglike projections, situated at the base of the skull. Also called "sphenoid".

spher·al (sféer-əl) *adj.* **1.** Of, pertaining to, or having the shape of a sphere; spherical. **2.** Symmetrical.

sphere (sfeer) *n.* **1.** *Geometry.* **a.** A three-dimensional surface, all points of which are equidistant from a fixed point. **b.** A figure or solid bounded by such a surface. **2.** Any object or figure resembling a sphere; a globe; a ball. **3.** *Literary.* A planet, star, or other heavenly body. **4.** *Literary.* The sky, appearing as a hemisphere to an observer: *the sphere of the heavens.* **5.** In ancient astronomy, any of a series of concentric, transparent, revolving globes on whose transparent surfaces the Moon, Sun, planets, and stars were thought to be fixed. **6. a.** The environment in which one exists, acts, or has influence; range; domain. **b.** Any area of activity or interest; a field. **7.** One's social stratum, rank, or position.
~*tr.v.* **sphered, sphering, spheres.** *Literary.* **1.** To form into a sphere. **2.** To put in or as in a sphere. **3.** To surround or encompass. [Middle English *spere, sphere,* from Old French *espere,* from Latin *sphaera, sphēra,* ball, globe, from Greek *sphaira†.*]

–sphere *n. comb. form.* Indicates: **1.** The shape of a sphere; for example, **bathysphere. 2.** A globular surrounding mass; for example, **atmosphere.** [From SPHERE.]

sphere of influence *n.* An area of the world dominated politically or economically by one country.

spher·i·cal (sférrik'l ‖ *U.S. also* sféer-ik'l) *adj.* Also **spher·ic** (sférrik ‖ sféer-ik). **1. a.** Having the shape of a sphere; globular. **b.** Having a shape approximating to that of a sphere. **2.** Of or pertaining to a sphere or spheres. **3.** *Literary.* Of or pertaining to heavenly bodies; celestial. **—spher·i·cal·i·ty** (sférri-kál-əti ‖ sféer-i-), **spher·i·cal·ness** *n.* **—spher·i·cal·ly** *adv.*

spherical aberration *n.* An optical defect of refracting and reflecting spherical surfaces in which light rays from one axial point, falling on the surface at different distances from the optical axis, do not come to a common focus.

spherical angle *n.* An angle formed at the intersection of the arcs of two great circles of a sphere.

spherical astronomy *n.* The branch of astronomy dealing with positions on the celestial sphere.

spher·i·cal-co·or·di·nate system (sférrik'l-kō-órdin-ət, -it, -ayt ‖ sféer-ik'l-) *n.* A three-dimensional system for locating points in space by means of a radius vector and two angles measured from the centre of a sphere with respect to two arbitrary, fixed, perpendicular directions.

spherical excess *n.* The difference between the sum of the angles of a spherical triangle and the sum of the angles of a plane triangle.

spherical geometry *n.* The geometry of circles, angles, and figures on the surface of a sphere. Also called "spherics".

spherical polygon *n.* Any part of a spherical surface that is bounded by arcs of three or more great circles.

spherical triangle *n.* A triangle on the surface of a sphere, having sides which are arcs of intersecting great circles.

spherical trigonometry *n.* The modified form of trigonometry applied to spherical triangles. Also called "spherics".

sphe·ric·i·ty (sfe-ríssəti, sfeer-) *n.* **1.** The state of being spherical. **2.** A measure of the extent to which a surface is spherical.

spher·ics (sférriks ‖ sféer-iks) *n. Used with a singular verb.* **1.** Spherical geometry or trigonometry. **2.** Atmospherics *(see).*

sphe·roid (sféer-oyd ‖ sférroyd) *n.* A spherelike body that is generated by revolving an ellipse around one of its axes. [Late Latin *sphaeroīdēs,* from Greek *sphaeroeidēs* : SPHERE + -OID.] **—sphe·roi·dal** (sfeer-róyd'l, sfe-), **sphe·roi·di·cal** *adj.* **—sphe·roi·dal·ly** *adv.* **—sphe·roi·dic·i·ty** (-issəti) *n.*

sphe·rom·e·ter (sfeer-rómmitər, sfe-) *n.* An instrument for measuring the curvature of a surface, such as that of a sphere or cylinder. [SPHER(E) + -METER.]

spher·ule (sfé-rewl, -rōōl ‖ sféer-) *n.* A miniature sphere or spherical body. [Late Latin *sphaerula,* diminutive of Latin *sphaera,* SPHERE.] **—spher·u·lar** *adj.*

spher·u·lite (sfé-rew-līt, -rōō- ‖ sféer-ə-) *n.* A small, usually spheroidal, crystalline body having a radiating structure and found in obsidian and other silicic lava flows. [SPHERUL(E) + -ITE.] **—spher·u·lit·ic** (-littik) *adj.*

sphinc·ter (sfíngktər) *n.* A ringlike muscle that normally maintains constriction of a bodily passage or orifice and that relaxes as required by normal physiological functioning. [Late Latin, from Greek *sphinktēr,* that which binds tight, from *sphingein†,* to bind tight.] **—sphinc·ter·al** *adj.*

sphin·go·my·e·lin (sfíng-gō-mī-ə-lin) *n.* A compound that contains sphingosine, phosphoric acid, choline, and a fatty acid group, found in the myelin sheath of nerves. [Greek *sphingein,* to draw tight + MYELIN.]

sphin·go·sine (sfíng-gə-seen, -sin) *n.* A long-chain organic compound occurring as a constituent of certain phospholipids in the brain. [Greek *sphingos-,* from *sphingein†,* hold fast, bind, draw tight + -INE.]

sphinx (sfingks) *n., pl.* **sphinxes** *or* **sphinges** (sfín-jeez). **1.** *Greek Mythology.* Usually *capital* **S.** A winged monster having the head of a woman and the body of a lion that destroyed all who could not answer its riddle. **2. a.** *Usually capital* **S.** The huge stone statue having a lion's body and a man's head, at Al Giza in Egypt. **b.** Any Egyptian figure having a lion's body and the head of a man, ram, or hawk. **3.** Any enigmatic person. [Middle English *spynx,* from Latin *Sphinx,* from Greek, perhaps from *sphingein†,* to draw tight, but dialectal variants, *Phix* and *Bix,* suggest perhaps a deity from Mount *Phikion* in Boeotia.]

sphinx moth *n.* The hawk moth *(see).*

sphra·gis·tics (sfrə-jístiks) *n. Used with a singular verb.* The study of engraved seals and signets. [French *sphragistique,* from Late Greek *sphragistikos,* from Greek *sphragis†,* seal, signet.]

sphyg·mic (sfig-mik) *adj. Physiology.* Pertaining to the pulse. [Greek *sphugmikos,* from *sphugmos,* pulsation, from *sphuzein†,* to throb.]

sphygmo-, sphygm- *comb. form.* Indicates the pulse; for example, **sphygmograph, sphygmoid.** [Greek *sphugmos,* pulsation. See **sphygmic.**

sphyg·mo·gram (sfíg-mə-gram, -mō-) *n.* A record or tracing produced by a sphygmograph. [SPHYGMO- + -GRAM.]

sphyg·mo·graph (sfíg-mə-graaf, -mō-, -graf) *n.* An instrument for recording the character and variations of the arterial pulse. [SPHYGMO- + -GRAPH.]

sphyg·moid (sfíg-moyd) *adj. Physiology.* Resembling a pulse; pulselike. [SPHYGM(O)- + -OID.]

sphyg·mo·ma·nom·e·ter (sfíg-mō-mə-nómmitər, -ma-) *n.* Also

sphyg·mom·e·ter (sfig-mómmitər). An instrument for measuring blood pressure in the arteries. [SPHYGMO- + MANOMETER.]

spi·ca (spíkə) *n.* A bandage applied in overlapping opposite spirals to immobilise a digit or limb. [Latin *spīca,* "point", ear of grain (from the resemblance of the V-shaped bandage to the V-shaped spikelets on an ear of grain).]

Spica *n.* The brightest star in the constellation Virgo, 210 light-years distant from Earth. [Latin *spīca,* "point", ear of grain. See **spica.**]

spi·cate (spíkayt) *adj. Botany.* Having or forming a spike. [Latin *spīcātus,* from the past participle of *spīcāre,* provide with spikes, from *spīca,* ear of grain, SPIKE.]

spic·ca·to (spi-ka'atō) *adj. Music.* Played with, designating, or pertaining to a bowing technique in which the bow is made to bounce slightly off the string.
~*adv. Music.* Employing such a technique.
~*n., pl.* **spiccatos.** *Music.* A spiccato technique or passage. [Italian, from the past participle of *spiccare†,* to separate.]

spice (spīss) *n.* **1.** Any of various aromatic and pungent vegetable substances, such as cinnamon or nutmeg, used to flavour foods or beverages. **2.** These substances collectively. **3.** Something that adds zest, flavour, or excitement. **4.** *Rare.* A pungent aroma; a perfume. ~*tr.v.* **spiced, spicing, spices. 1.** To season with spices. **2.** To add zest or excitement to. Often used with *up.* [Middle English, from Old French *espice,* from Late Latin *speciēs,* goods, spices, from Latin, appearance, kind, SPECIES.]

spice·ber·ry (spíss-bəri, -berri) *n., pl.* **-ries.** Any of various plants or shrubs having spicy berries, such as the wintergreen.

spice·bush (spíss-bōōsh) *n.* An aromatic shrub, *Lindera benzoin,* of eastern North America, having clusters of small, early-blooming yellow flowers. Also called "benjamin bush".

Spice Islands. See **Moluccas.**

spic·er·y (spí-səri) *n., pl.* **-ies. 1.** Spices collectively. **2.** The aromatic quality of spices. **3.** *Archaic.* A place where spices are stored.

spick-and-span, spic-and-span (spíkən-spánn) *adj. Informal.* **1.** Neat and clean; spotless. **2.** Brand-new; fresh. [Short for obsolete *spick and spannew* : *spick,* variant of SPIKE (nail) (influenced by Dutch *spiksplinter niew* "spike-splinter-new") + *span-new.*]

spic·ule (spíckewl) *n.* Also **spic·u·la** (spíckew-lə) *pl.* **-lae** (-lee). **1.** A small needle-like structure or part; especially, any of the silicate or calcium carbonate growths supporting the soft tissue of certain invertebrates, especially sponges. **2.** *Astronomy.* Any of the innumerable hairlike eruptions of hot gas from the Sun's chromosphere. [Latin *spīculum,* SPICULUM.] **—spic·u·lar, spic·u·late** (-layt, -lət) *adj.*

spic·u·lum (spíckew-ləm) *n., pl.* **-la** (-lə). A spicule or similar needle-like structure. [Latin *spīculum,* diminutive of *spīca,* point.]

spic·y (spí-si) *adj.* **-ier, -iest. 1. a.** Containing or flavoured with spice. **b.** Having the characteristics of spice, such as flavour and aroma. **2. a.** Piquant; pungent. **b.** Lively, keen, or spirited. **3.** Slightly scandalous; risqué. **—spic·i·ly** *adv.* **—spic·i·ness** *n.*

spi·der (spídər) *n.* **1. a.** Any of numerous arachnids of the order Araneae, having eight legs, a body divided into a cephalothorax and an abdomen, and several spinnerets that produce silk used to make nests, cocoons, or webs for trapping insects. **b.** Any of various similar arachnids. **2.** One that is similar to a spider, as in appearance, character, or movement. **3.** *Chiefly British.* A group of elastic cords radiating out from a central point and used to strap down loads, as on to a car. **4.** In snooker, a rest on high legs used when access to the cue ball is hampered by another ball. **5.** Any of various machines or devices with limbs radiating from a central point. **6.** *Australian.* An ice-cream soda. **7.** A lightly built, high cart or phaeton. [Middle English *spither, spithre,* Old English *spīthra.*] See feature, next page.

spider crab *n.* Any of various crabs, especially of the family Majidae, having long legs and a relatively small body.

spi·der·flow·er (spídər-flowr, -flow-ər) *n.* The **cleome** *(see).*

spider-hunting wasp *n.* Any of various wasps of the family Pompilidae, which catch spiders by paralysing them with their poisonous sting.

spi·der·man (spídər-man, -mən) *n., pl.* **-men** (-men). *British.* A building worker who erects the steel framework of tall buildings.

spider mite *n.* Any of various mites of the family Tetranychidae, such as *Tetranychus urticae,* which feed on plants and are serious pests of fruit trees and other crop plants. Also called "red spider", "red spider mite".

spider monkey *n.* Any of several tropical American monkeys of the genus *Ateles,* having long legs and a long, prehensile tail.

spider orchid *n.* Any of several European orchids of the genus *Ophrys,* having broad-lipped flowers. [Referring to the velvety spider-like lip of the flowers.]

spider plant *n.* Any of several plants of the genus *Chlorophytum;* especially, the South African species *C. elatum,* which has narrow, green and white leaves and is commonly grown as a house plant. [From the fancied resemblance of the leaves to a spider's legs.]

spi·der·wort (spídər-wurt ‖ -wawrt) *n.* Any of various New World plants of the genus *Tradescantia;* especially, *T. virginiana,* which has blue or purple flowers and is grown as a house plant.

spi·der·y (spídəri) *adj.* **1.** Resembling or suggesting a spider. **2. a.** Resembling a spider's legs; long and slender: *spidery pen-strokes.* **b.** Resembling a spider's web; especially, very fine and meshlike. **3.** Infested with spiders.

spie·gel·ei·sen (speeg'l-ī'z'n) *n.* An alloy of iron with approximately

spider crab *Like spiders, spider crabs have long legs in proportion to their bodies. Some species of this marine scavenger are a mere 10 millimetres across (less than half an inch). But some have a spread of up to 4 metres (13 feet).*

spider

SPINNERS OF GOSSAMER THREADS
Spiders are found throughout the world

Spiders are found all over the world, from mountaintops to dark caves – there are 30,000 different species. All hatch from eggs and most live for about a year.

All spiders – both male and female – produce silk from a group of spinnerets at the end of the body, but not all spin webs. The silk – about 0.005 millimetre (1/5,000 inch) in diameter – can be sticky or dry, and is used in various ways by the spider. Some spin webs with it, wanderers leave a silk trail behind them like an anchor line, some make their homes of silk, and young spiders migrate on the gossamer threads, which act like parachutes to disperse them over long distances. Spiders that make sticky webs to catch their prey spin dry cross threads on which to approach the prey so that they do not get stuck themselves.

All spiders feed on insects, although the tropical bird-eating spiders also prey on humming birds. The bird-eaters include the giant tarantula, which grows up to 90 millimetres (3½ inches) across the body. The European aquatic species feed mainly on fish and lizards and other small creatures.

Some, such as the wolf spider, capture their prey by running and pouncing on them, and the spitting spider spits two lines of sticky thread to enwrap them. But however the victims are caught, they are all stabbed by the spider's fangs which inject a poison. Although the poison is quickly fatal to the spider's prey, only a few species, such as the North American black widow, are dangerous to man. British species are not dangerous. The courtship of spiders typically consists of elaborate displays, with the male dancing frantically, touching the female, or vibrating her web in a special way. But contrary to popular belief, very few females devour their mates. If a male dies soon after mating it is usually from exhaustion or starvation.

DIVING FOR PREY *The European fisher-spider begins to eat a minnow after catching it under water. Tiny hairs covering the spider trap enough air to allow it to make a 45-minute dive.*

15 to 30 per cent manganese and small quantities of carbon and silicon, used in the Bessemer process. Also called "spiegel". [German *Spiegeleisen*, "mirror-iron" : *Spiegel*, mirror, from Old High German *spiagal*, from Medieval Latin *spēglum*, from Latin *speculum*, SPECULUM + *Eisen*, iron, from Old High German *īsan, īsarn*.]

spiel (speel) *n. Slang.* **1.** A voluble story or speech usually intended to persuade. **2.** Any talk that is considered glib or tedious: *gave us his usual spiel about morale.*
~*v.* **spieled, spieling, spiels.** *Slang.* —*intr.* To talk at length or extravagantly. —*tr.* To recite (a story, for example) at length or extravagantly. Often used with *off.* [German *Spiel*, "play", from Old High German *spil*, from Germanic *spillōn* (unattested), to play.] —**spiel·er** *n.*

spif·fing (spíffing) *adj. British Slang.* Excellent; very good. Not in current usage. [19th century: probably from dialect *spifft*, smartly dressed.]

spif·li·cate, spif·fli·cate (spíffli-kayt) *tr.v.* **-cated, -cating, -cates.** *British Slang.* To overcome or destroy; annihilate. Used by schoolchildren. [18th century : jocular coinage based on *-ate* as in *castigate, annihilate*, and so on.]

spig·ot (spíggət) *n.* **1.** The vent plug of a cask. **2.** A wooden tap placed in the bunghole of a cask. **3.** A short projection on a component, such as a pipe, designed to fit into a hole or slot in a mating part. [Middle English, perhaps from Latin *spiculum*, diminutive of *spicum*, variant of *spīca*, SPICA.]

spike¹ (spīk) *n.* **1. a.** A long, thick, sharp-pointed piece of wood or metal. **b.** A heavy nail. **2. a.** A sharp point. **b.** Any object with a sharp metal point; especially, such a point set upright in a base and used to hold papers, such as bills. **3.** *Plural. Informal.* A pair of track shoes with small projections on the soles to provide a better grip. **4.** *Slang.* A hypodermic syringe. **5. a.** A peak on a graph, especially one showing a maximum, as of voltage or current usage. **b.** An occurrence producing a peak shown on a graph. **6.** An unbranched antler of a young deer. **7.** A small young mackerel.
~*tr.v.* **spiked, spiking, spikes.** **1.** To secure or provide with a spike. **2.** To impale, pierce, or injure with or on a spike. **3.** To injure (another runner or player) with the spikes of one's shoes. **4.** To put an end to; thwart; block: *spike a plot.* **5.** *Slang.* To add alcohol to (a drink) without the knowledge of the drinker. **6.** *Slang.* To decide not to publish (an article or report) in a newspaper or magazine, originally by placing it on a spike. **7.** To drive (a volleyball) into the opposing court at a steep downward angle. [Middle English *spyk*, probably from Middle Dutch *spiker*; akin to SPOKE.]

spike² *n.* **1.** An ear of grain. **2.** *Botany.* A usually elongated, racemose inflorescence with stalkless or nearly stalkless flowers arranged along an axis, as in the foxglove. [Middle English *spik*, from Latin *spīca*, point, ear of grain.]

spike lavender *n.* A lavender plant, *Lavandula latifolia*, of southern Europe, yielding an oil used in perfumes and paints. [From SPIKE (inflorescence).]

spike·let (spík-lət, -lit) *n. Botany.* A small or secondary spike; especially, one of those forming the inflorescence of grasses or similar plants.

spike·nard (spík-naard) *n.* **1.** An aromatic plant, *Nardostachys jatamansi*, of India, having rose-purple flowers. Also called "nard". **2.** A costly ointment of the ancient world, probably prepared from this plant. Also called "nard". **3.** A North American plant, *Aralia racemosa*, having small, greenish flowers and an aromatic root. See **ploughman's spikenard.** [Middle English, from Medieval Latin *spīca nardi*, spike of a nard (translation of Greek *nardostakhus*) : Latin *spīca*, SPIKE + *nardus*, NARD.]

spik·y (spíki) *adj.* **-ier, -iest. 1.** Having a projecting sharp point or points. **2.** Resembling a spike, especially in shape. **3.** Irritable; ill-tempered. **4.** *British Informal.* Strongly favouring High Church practices and views. Used derogatorily. —**spik·i·ly** *adv.* —**spik·i·ness** *n.*

spile (spīl) *n.* **1.** A post used as a foundation; a pile. **2.** A wooden plug; a bung. **3.** *U.S.* A spout used in taking sap from a tree.
~*tr.v.* **spiled, spiling, spiles.** To support, plug, or tap with a spile. [Perhaps from Middle Dutch or Middle Low German *spile*, bar.]

spill¹ (spil) *v.* **spilt** (spilt) or **spilled, spilling, spills.** —*tr.* **1.** To cause or allow (a substance) to run or fall out of a container, especially accidentally. **2.** To shed (blood). **3. a.** To let the wind out of (a sail). **b.** To let the (wind) out of a sail. **4.** To eject or cause to fall: *The horse spilled his rider.* **5.** *Informal.* To divulge. —*intr.* **1.** To run or fall out of a container, especially accidentally. **2.** To spread out or flow as if spilt: *The audience started to spill out of the cinema.* **3.** To escape from a sail. Used of the wind.
~*n.* **1.** An act of spilling. **2.** That which is spilt. **3.** A fall, as from a horse. **4.** A spillway. [Middle English *spillen*, destroy, kill, shed (blood), spill, Old English *spillan*.] —**spill·er** *n.*

Usage: Both *spilled* and *spilt* are used as past tenses and past participles, the former being preferred in American English, the latter in British English.

spill² *n.* **1.** A piece of wood or rolled paper used to light a fire, for example. **2.** A small peg used as a plug; a spile. **3.** A spillway. [Probably from Middle Low German or Middle Dutch *spile*.]

spill·age (spíllij) *n.* **1.** An act or the process of spilling. **2.** That which is spilt; the amount spilt.

spil·li·kin, spil·i·kin (spíllikin) *n.* Also **spel·li·can** (spéllikən). A draw or stick used in the game of spillikins. Also called "jackstraw". [Diminutive of SPILL (strip of wood).]

spil·li·kins, spil·i·kins (spíllikinz) *n. Used with a singular verb.* A game played with a pile of straws or thin sticks, each player in turn trying to remove one from the pile without disturbing the others. Also called "jackstraws".

spill·way (spíl-way) *n.* A channel for water overflow, as from a reservoir. Also called "spill".

spilth (spilth) *n.* Spillage. [From SPILL.]

spin (spin) *v.* **spun** (spun) or *archaic* **span** (span), **spinning, spins.** —*tr.* **1.** To draw out and twist (fibres) into thread. **2.** To form (thread or yarn) in this manner. **3. a.** To form (a thread, web, or cocoon, for example) by extruding viscous filaments. Used chiefly of spiders and caterpillars. **b.** To produce (synthetic yarn) by extruding chemical substances. **4.** To draw out and twist in a manufacturing process: *spin glass into threads.* **5.** To narrate from memory or invent from one's imagination. Used chiefly in the

phrase *spin a yarn.* **6.** To cause to rotate; turn round or twirl. **7.** To turn on a lathe, usually into a round shape. **8.** To propel (a ball, especially a cricket ball) so as to revolve on an axis and change speed or direction on bouncing. **9.** To cause (an aircraft) to dive in a spin. **10.** To fish (a river, for example) using a spinner. —*intr.* **1.** To make thread or yarn by the drawing out and twisting of fibres. **2.** To form a thread, web, or cocoon, by extruding viscous filaments. **3.** To rotate rapidly; whirl. **4.** To seem to be whirling, as from dizziness; reel: *The news set my head spinning.* **5.** To ride or drive rapidly. Usually used with *along.* **6.** To fish with a spinner. **7.** To be spun by a bowler. Used of a ball, especially a cricket ball. **8.** To dive in a spin. Used of an aircraft. —**spin out. 1.** To prolong or draw out (a story or task, for example). **2.** To pass (time): *spun out the rest of the afternoon.* **3.** To cause (a sum of money) to last a long time. **4.** In cricket, to dismiss (a batsman) with spin bowling. —See Synonyms at **turn.**
~*n.* **1.** The act of spinning. **2.** A swift whirling motion. **3.** *Informal.* A state of mental confusion. **4.** *Informal.* A short excursion in or on a vehicle. **5. a.** The flight condition of an aircraft in a nosedown, spiralling, stalled descent. **b.** Any sudden, swift, or steep descending movement. **6.** A rotating motion imparted to a ball by a bowler or other sports player. **7.** *Physics.* **a.** The intrinsic angular momentum of an elementary particle. **b.** The total angular momentum of an atomic nucleus. **c.** A non-negative integral or half-integral quantum number that specifies the value of such momenta in units of Planck's constant divided by 2π. **8.** *Australian Informal.* A stroke of fortune of a specified kind: *a bad spin.* [Spin, spun, spun; Middle English *spinnen, spon* (plural), *spunne,* Old English *spinnan, spunnon* (plural), *gespunnen.*]
spi·na bi·fi·da (spī́nə bíffídə) *n.* A condition, present at birth, in which part of the spinal cord protrudes through a gap in the backbone. It may result in paralysis and incontinence and be associated with **hydrocephalus** *(see).* [New Latin, bifid spine.]
spin·ach (spín-ij, -ich) *n.* **1.** A widely cultivated plant, *Spinacia oleracea,* native to Asia, having succulent, edible leaves. **2.** The leaves of this plant, eaten as a vegetable. [Probably from Middle Dutch *spinaetse,* from Old French *espinache,* from Medieval Latin *spinachia,* from Arabic *'isfānāk,* from Persian *ispānāk.*]
spi·nal (spī́n'l) *adj.* **1.** Of, pertaining to, or situated near the spine or spinal cord; vertebral. **2.** Resembling a spine or spinous part.
~*n.* A spinal anaesthetic. —**spi·nal·ly** *adv.*
spinal anaesthesia *n.* **1.** Anaesthesia in part of the body produced by injecting an anaesthetic substance (*spinal anaesthetic*) into the spinal canal. **2.** *Pathology.* Loss of sensation in part of the body because of injury to or disease of the spinal cord.
spinal canal *n.* The canal formed by the successive openings in the vertebrae through which the spinal cord and its membranes pass. Also called "vertebral canal".
spinal column *n.* The series of articulated vertebrae extending from the base of the skull to the base of the trunk or the end of the tail, encasing the spinal cord and forming the supporting axis of the body; the backbone. Also called "spine", "vertebral column".
spinal cord *n.* The part of the central nervous system contained within the spinal canal and continuous at its cranial end with the medulla oblongata of the brain.
spinal meningitis *n. Pathology.* **Cerebrospinal fever** *(see).*
spin bowler *n.* In cricket, a bowler expert at spinning the ball. Also called "spinner". —**spin bowling** *n.*
spin·dle (spínd'l) *n.* **1. a.** A notched stick for spinning fibres into thread by hand. **b.** A pin or rod holding a bobbin or spool upon which thread is wound on a spinning wheel or spinning machine. **2.** Any of various slender mechanical parts that revolve or serve as axes for larger revolving parts, as in a lock or an axle. **3.** *Biology.* A group of fibres extending from one end of a cell to the other, formed during mitosis and meiosis and along which the chromosomes are distributed. **4.** Any slender, tapering rod or rodlike piece. **5.** A measure or yarn of varying length. **6.** A turned, usually decorative vertical support of a handrail.
~*intr.v.* **spindled, -dling, -dles.** To grow into a thin, elongated, or weakly form. Used especially of a plant. [Middle English *spindel,* rod of a spinning wheel, Old English *spinel.*]
spin·dle·legs (spínd'l-legz) *pl.n.* Also **spin·dle·shanks** (-shangks). **1.** Long, thin legs. **2.** *Used with a singular verb.* A tall, lanky person with long, thin legs. —**spin·dle·legged** *adj.*
spindle side *n.* The **distaff side** *(see).*
spindle tree *n.* Any of various shrubs or trees of the genus *Euonymus,* many species of which have pink or orange fruits. [So called because the wood is often used to make spindles.]
spin·dling (spíndling) *adj.* Spindly.
~*n.* A spindly plant or animal.
spin·dly (spíndli) *adj.* **-dlier, -dliest.** Slender, long, and usually weak-looking.
spin·drift (spín-drift) *n.* Wind-blown sea spray. Also called "spoondrift". [Variant of SPOONDRIFT.]
spin-dry·er, spin-dri·er (spín-drī́-ər) *n.* A machine that extracts moisture from wet laundry by spinning it round rapidly. Also called "spinner". —**spin-dry** *tr.v.*
spine (spīn) *n.* **1.** The spinal column of a vertebrate. **2.** Any of various pointed projections or appendages of animals, such as a quill on a porcupine. **3.** *Botany.* A sharp-pointed projection arising from the stem of a plant. **4.** *Anatomy.* A sharp projection arising from a bone. **5.** The vertical back of a book to which the pages are attached and which normally bears the title on the outside.

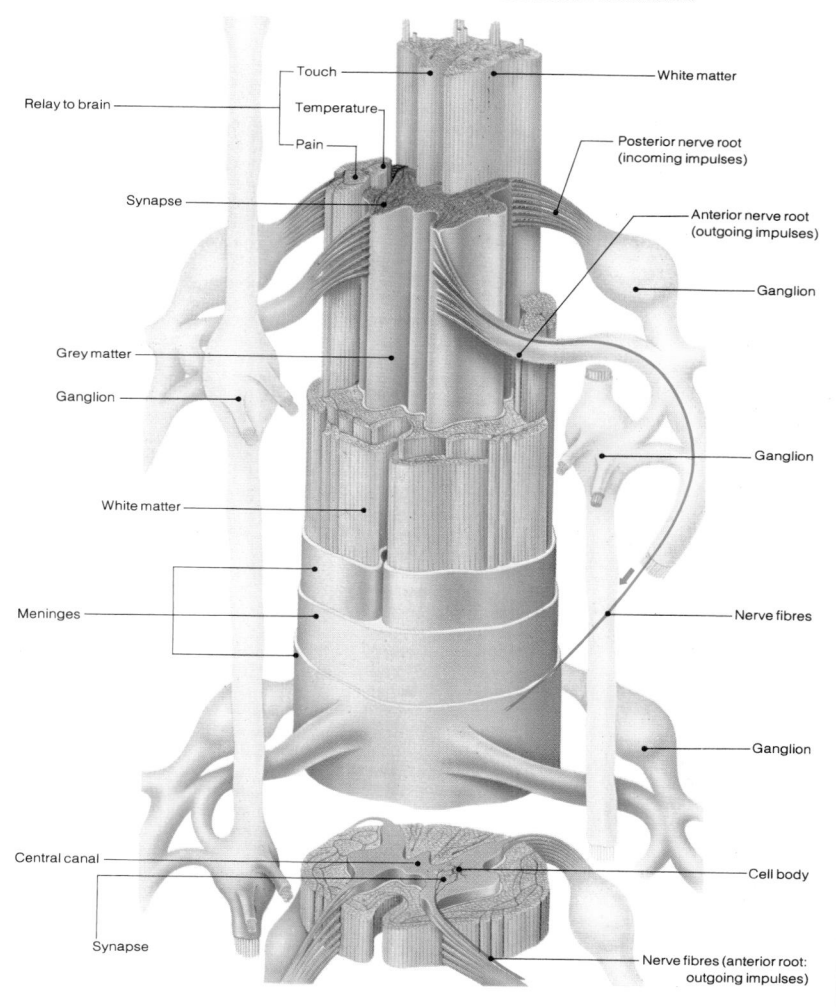

MAN'S INTERNAL TELEGRAPH SYSTEM
The spinal cord carries messages to and from the brain

The central nervous system, man's internal communications network, consists of the brain and spinal cord (shown below). The brain stem is the connecting link. The nerve fibres that make up the spinal cord transmit to the brain information about touch, position, pain, and temperature, and carry back instructions to muscles to react.

The spinal cord consists of grey cells and white nerve fibres that float in a protective cerebrospinal fluid, held in by tough membranes called meninges and surrounded by the bony structure of the spinal column. The grey matter surrounding the central canal consists of nerve cell bodies from which axons, the nerve fibres, relay impulses outward. Bundles of axons, forming the white matter, conduct these impulses to the brain. Synapses are the points of contact between axons and branching dendrites, which transmit incoming impulses to the cell bodies.

Nerve fibres radiate from the spinal cord to the muscles and skin. Sensory fibres enter the back of the cord bringing messages from body tissues; motor fibres leaving the front of the cord take instructions to the tissues. The muscle receptors, which can detect tension and pressure from regions as distant as the toes, fingertips, and tongue, all send messages to the brain via the spinal cord. The messages travel in a series of electrical impulses. The ganglion sorts them out and sends them up the right channel to the brain for analysis and decision. Impulses in motor nerves then instruct the muscles.

Labels: Relay to brain; Touch; Temperature; Pain; Synapse; Grey matter; Ganglion; White matter; Meninges; Central canal; Synapse; White matter; Posterior nerve root (incoming impulses); Anterior nerve root (outgoing impulses); Ganglion; Ganglion; Ganglion; Nerve fibres; Ganglion; Cell body; Nerve fibres (anterior root: outgoing impulses)

6. a. Strength of character. **b.** A main support or prop. **7.** A sharp-backed hill, mountain, or ridge. [Middle English, from Old French *espine,* from Latin *spīna,* thorn, prickle, spine.] —**spined** *adj.*
spine-chill·er (spín-chillər) *n.* A book, film, or other work that arouses a pleasurably terrifying thrill. —**spine-chill·ing** *adj.*
spi·nel (spi-nél) *n.* A mineral, magnesium aluminium oxide $MgAl_2O_4$. Spinels show a range of colours, depending on any additional elements present, and some are used as gemstones. [Italian *spinella,* diminutive of *spina,* thorn (from its sharply pointed crystals), from Latin *spīna.*]
spine·less (spín-ləss, -liss) *adj.* **1.** Lacking a vertebral column. **2.** Having no spiny projections. **3.** Lacking in courage, strength of character, or will-power. —**spine·less·ly** *adv.* —**spine·less·ness** *n.*
spi·nes·cent (spī-néss'nt) *adj. Biology.* **1.** Having a spine or spines.

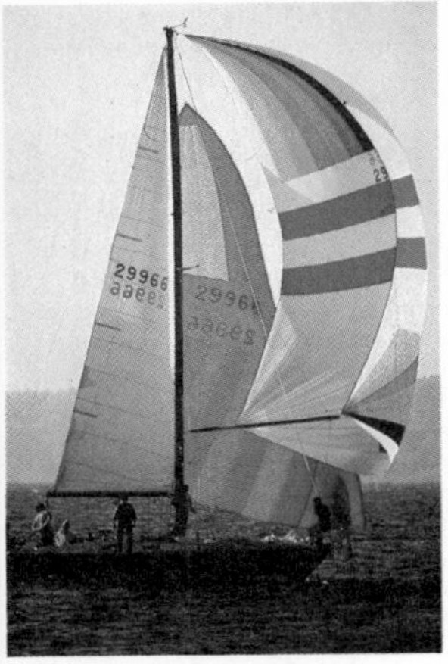

spinnaker *A yacht with two brightly coloured spinnakers running before the wind.*

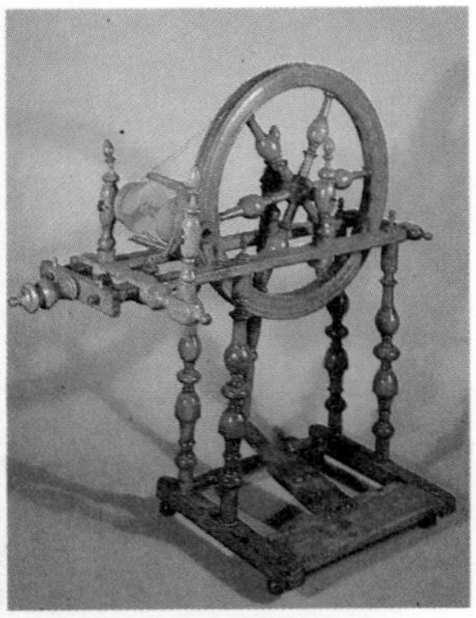

spinning wheel *The spinning wheel, which was probably invented in India, was introduced to Europe during the Middle Ages. The wheel, operated by a treadle, turns the spindle which twists the loose fibres into thread.*

PRONUNCIATION KEY

a, trap; aa, father; ai, **fair**; ar, **star**; aw, **lawn**; ay, **play**; b, bb, stab; **rubber**; ch, **church**; ck, ticket; d, dd, **dead**; **ladder**; e, dress; ee, **bee**; er, **defer**; ew, **few**; ewr, **pure**; ə, about; ər, letter; f, ff, **fife**; **differ**; g, gg, **giggle**; h, **hat**; i, kit; ī, price; īr, fire; j, **judge**; k, **kick**; l, ll, let; 'l, needle; m, mm, **man**; n, nn, **no**; 'n, sudden; ng, **thing**; o, **lot**; ō, **no**; o͝o, **foot**; o͞o, **shoe**; oor, **poor**; ow, **cow**; owr, **hour**; oy, **boy**; p, pp, **pepper**; r, rr, red; s, ss, **sauce**; sh, **ship**; t, tt, **totter**; th, **thick**; th, **this**; **smooth**; u, cut; ur, **turn**; v, vv, **valve**; w, **wet**; y, **yes**; z, zz, **zebra**; zh, vision; pleasure

IN FOREIGN WORDS:

aɴ, oɴ, Saint-Saëns; hl, **Llanelli**; **Hluhluwe**; kh, loch; lough; **Khaled**

STRESS MARK:

ín-sīt, insight; in-sī́t, incite

2. Having or tending towards the form of a spine. [Late Latin *spīnescēns* (stem *spīnescent-*), present participle of *spīnescere,* to grow thorny, from Latin *spīna,* thorn, SPINE.] **—spi·nes·cence** *n.*

spin·et (spín-it, -et, spi-nét) *n.* **1.** A small harpsichord with a single keyboard. **2.** *U.S.* A small, compact upright piano. [French *espinette,* from Italian *spinetta,* virginal, spinet, diminutive of *spina,* thorn, SPINE (referring to the plucking of the strings).]

spi·nif·er·ous (spī-nifførəss) *adj.* Also **spi·nig·er·ous** (-níjərəss). Spine-bearing; spiny. Said especially of plants. [Latin *spīnifer* : Latin *spīna,* thorn, SPINE + -FEROUS.]

spin·i·fex (spín-i-feks, -ə- || *chiefly U.S.* spī́n-) *n.* **1.** Any of various chiefly Australian grasses of the genus *Spinifex,* growing in arid regions and having spiny leaves or seeds. **2.** Any of various Australian grasses of the genus *Triodia,* having spiny leaves. Also called "porcupine grass". [New Latin : SPIN(E) + Latin *-fex,* "maker".]

spin·na·ker (spínnəkər; *nautical* spángkər) *n.* A large triangular sail set on a spar that swings out opposite the mainsail, used on racing yachts when running before the wind. [Probably from *Sphinx,* name of the first yacht to carry a spinnaker sail, in about 1866; perhaps influenced by *spanker.*]

spin·ner (spínnər) *n.* **1.** One that spins. **2.** An angler's lure that spins rapidly. **3.** In cricket: **a.** A ball bowled with a spin. **b.** A **spin bowler** *(see).* **4.** A spin-dryer. **5.** A fairing fitted over the hub of the propeller in some aircraft. **6.** A device consisting of a dial and an arrow that is spun to indicate the next move in certain board games.

spin·ner·et (spínnə-rét, -ret) *n.* **1.** A structure in spiders and certain insect larvae, containing passages through which silky filaments are secreted. **2.** A device for making rayon, nylon, and other synthetic fibres, consisting of a plate pierced with holes through which plastic material is extruded in filaments. [SPINNER + -ET.]

spin·ney (spínni) *n., pl.* **-neys.** *Chiefly British.* A small grove; a thicket; a copse. [Old French *espinei,* thicket, from Vulgar Latin *spīnēta* (unattested), from Latin *spīnētum,* thorn hedge, from *spīna,* thorn.]

spin·ning (spínning) *n.* **1.** The process of making fibrous or viscous material into yarn or thread. **2.** The act or technique of angling with a light rod and line, drawing a rotating lure through the water to imitate the movement of a small fish or insect.

spinning frame *n.* A machine that draws and twists fibres into yarn and winds it onto spindles.

spinning jenny *n.* An early spinning machine having several spindles. [18th century : from pet form of Jane or *Janet,* applied to machines that performed some of women's traditional tasks.]

spinning mule *n.* A type of spinning machine, a **mule** *(see).*

spinning wheel *n.* A domestic apparatus for making yarn or thread, comprising a foot- or hand-driven wheel and single spindle.

spi·node (spínnōd) *n. Mathematics.* A **cusp** *(see).*

spin off *tr.v.* To throw off while rotating at speed.

spin-off (spín-off, -awf) *n.* A usually useful object or result obtained incidentally through pursuing a different object or result.

spi·nose (spī́-nōz, -nōss) *adj.* Bearing spines; spiny. Said especially of plants. [Latin *spīnōsus,* from *spīna,* thorn, SPINE.] **—spi·nose·ly** *adv.* **—spi·nos·i·ty** (spī-nóssəti) *n.*

spi·nous (spī́nəss) *adj.* **1.** Resembling a spine or thorn. **2.** Having spines or similar projections; spiny.

spinous process *n.* The rearward projection from the arch of a vertebra.

Spi·no·za (spi-nṓzə), **Benedict de,** born Baruch de Spinoza (1632–77). Dutch philosopher. His controversial pantheistic doctrine advocated an intellectual love of God. His best-known work is his *Ethics* (1677). **—Spi·no·zism** (-nṓz-iz'm) *n.*

spin·ster (spínstər) *n.* **1.** A woman who is unmarried. **2.** A woman who is traditionally thought to be fussy and prim, and as being unlikely to get married. **3.** Formerly, a woman whose occupation is spinning. [Middle English *spinnester* : *spinnen,* SPIN + -STER.] **—spin·ster·hood** *n.* **—spin·ster·ish** *adj.*

spin·thar·i·scope (spin-thárri-skōp) *n.* A device for observing individual scintillations produced by ionising radiation, with the aid of a tube with a magnifying lens at one end and a phosphorescent screen and a speck of a radioactive salt at the other. [Greek *spintharis*†, spark + -SCOPE.] **—spin·thar·i·scop·ic** (-skóppik) *adj.*

spi·nule (spī́newl) *n.* A small spine or thorn. [Latin *spīnula,* diminutive of *spīna,* thorn, SPINE.]

spin·u·lose (spínnew-lōz, -lōss) *adj.* Also **spin·u·lous** (-ləss). **1.** Having spinules. **2.** Shaped like a spinule.

spin·y (spī́ni) *adj.* **-ier, -iest.** **1.** Bearing or covered with spines, thorns, or similar stiff projections. **2.** Shaped like a spine. **3.** Difficult; troublesome. **—spin·i·ness** *n.*

spiny anteater *n.* A mammal, the **echidna** *(see).*

spin·y-finned (spī́ni-find) *adj.* Having fins supported by sharp, spiny, inflexible rays. Said of some fishes. Compare **soft-finned.**

spiny lobster *n.* Any of various edible marine decapod crustaceans of the family Palinuridae, having a spiny carapace and lacking the large pincers characteristic of true lobsters. Also called "langouste", "rock lobster", and sometimes "crayfish".

spir·a·cle (spī́r-ək'l || spír-) *n.* **1.** *Zoology.* A respiratory aperture, such as: **a.** Any of several tracheal openings in the exoskeleton of an insect or spider. **b.** A small respiratory opening behind the eye of cartilaginous fishes, such as sharks, rays, and skates. **c.** The blowhole of a cetacean. **2.** *Geology.* A small volcanic vent formed by gases in a lava flow. **3.** Any opening through which air is admitted and expelled. [Latin *spīrāculum,* a breathing hole, from *spīrāre,* to breathe.] **—spi·rac·u·lar** (spīr-áckew-lər), **spi·rac·u·late** (-lət, -lit, -layt) *adj.*

spi·rae·a, *U.S.* **spi·re·a** (spīr-reé-ə, spī-) *n.* Any of various plants or shrubs of the genus *Spiraea,* having clusters of small white or pink flowers, and often cultivated as garden ornamentals. [Latin *spīraea,* meadowsweet, from Greek *spieraia,* from *speira,* coil, SPIRE.]

spi·ral (spī́r-əl) *n.* **1. a.** The locus in a plane of a point moving around a fixed centre at a monotonically increasing or decreasing distance from the centre. **b.** The three-dimensional locus of a point moving parallel to and about a central axis at a constant or continuously varying distance; a helix. **2.** Something having the form of such a curve: *spirals of smoke.* **3.** A continuously accelerating increase or decrease, often of related factors: *the wage-price spiral.* ~*adj.* Of or resembling a spiral; coiled or helical: *a spiral staircase.* ~*v.* **spiralled** or *U.S.* **spiraled, -ralling** or *U.S.* **-raling, -rals.** *—intr.* **1.** To take a spiral form or course. **2.** To rise or fall at a steady rate. *—tr.* To cause to spiral. [Medieval Latin *spīrālis,* from Latin *spīra,* coil, SPIRE (spiral).] **—spi·ral·ly** *adv.*

spiral binding *n.* A binding for notebooks and booklets in which a cylindrical spiral of wire or plastic is passed through a row of punched holes at the edge of each sheet.

spiral galaxy *n.* A galaxy having a nucleus and spiral arms consisting mainly of gas, dust, and stars. Formerly called "spiral nebula".

spiral of Archimedes *n.* The locus of a point moving towards or away from a central point at a constant speed along a line rotating around that central point at a constant speed. Its spiral has the equation $r = a\theta$, where a is a constant.

spi·rant (spī́r-ənt) *n. Phonetics.* A **fricative** *(see).* [Latin *spīrāns* (stem *spīrant-*), present participle of Latin *spīrāre,* to breathe.] **—spi·rant** *adj.*

spire[1] (spīr) *n.* **1.** A structure that tapers upwards to a point; especially a steeple. **2.** The top part or point of something that tapers upwards; a pinnacle. **3.** A slender, tapering shoot or stem, such as a newly sprouting blade of grass. **4.** Any slender, tapering object. ~*v.* **spired, spiring, spires.** *—tr.* To provide with a spire or spires. *—intr.* To rise taperingly, like a spire. [Middle English *spir(e),* slender stalk, Old English *spīr.*]

spire[2] *n.* **1. a.** A spiral. **b.** A single turn of a spiral; a whorl. **2.** *Zoology.* The area farthest from the aperture and nearest the apex on a coiled gastropod shell. [French, from Latin *spīra,* a coil, twist, spire, from Greek *speira.*]

spire·let (spī́r-lət, -lit) *n. Architecture.* A **flèche** *(see).*

spi·reme (spī́r-eem) *n. Biology.* **1.** The tangle of filaments that appears at the beginning of the prophase stage of meiosis or mitosis. **2.** Any of these filaments. [German *Spirem,* from Greek *speirēma,* coil, from *speira,* coil, SPIRE.]

Spires. See **Speyer.**

spi·rif·er·ous (spīr-riffərəss, spī-) *adj.* Having a spire, spiral structure, or spiral parts. [SPIR(E) + -FEROUS.]

spi·ril·lum (spīr-rílləm, spī-) *n., pl.* **-rilla** (-rillə). **1.** Any of various flagellated aerobic bacteria of the genus *Spirillum,* having an elongated spiral form. *S. minus* causes ratbite fever. **2.** Any spiral-shaped bacterium. Compare **bacillus, coccus.** [New Latin, diminutive of Latin *spīra,* SPIRE (spiral).]

spir·it (spírrit) *n.* **1.** That which is traditionally believed to be the vital principle or animating force within living beings, often contrasted with nonliving matter. **2.** *Capital* **S.** In Christian Science, God. **3.** Any supernatural being or power, such as: **a.** A ghost. **b.** One regarded as able to enter and take control of a person. **4.** That which is traditionally regarded as the nonmaterial essence or true nature of an individual, especially: **a.** The intangible, spiritual core of a person; the soul. **b.** The essential and activating principle of a person; the will. **5.** A person as characterised by a specified quality: *a free spirit.* **6.** An inclination or tendency of a specified kind: *a remark made in a spirit of friendliness.* **7. a.** *Often plural.* One's mood or emotional state: *in high spirits.* **b.** One's mood or disposition: *great in spirit.* **8.** An attitude or frame of mind: *take a remark in the spirit in which it was intended.* **9.** Liveliness; vigour; mettle. **10.** Strong loyalty or dedication: *team spirit.* **11.** The predominant mood or quality of an occasion or period: *the spirit of the age.* **12.** The real sense or significance of something: *the spirit of the law, rather than the letter.* **13.** *Often plural.* An alcohol solution of an essential or volatile substance. **14.** *Often plural.* A distilled alcoholic liquor, such as gin, whisky, or rum. **—in (the) spirit.** In the mind or the imagination. **—in** (or **out of**) **spirits.** In a cheerful (or gloomy) state of mind. **—the Spirit.** The Holy Ghost. ~*tr.v.* **spirited, -iting, -its.** **1.** To carry off mysteriously or secretly. Used with *away* or *off.* **2.** To impart courage, animation, or determination to; stimulate; encourage. Usually used with *up* or *on.* [Middle English, from Anglo-French, from Latin *spīritus,* breath, breath of a god, inspiration, from *spīrāre,* to breathe.]

spir·it·ed (spírritid) *adj.* **1.** Full of or characterised by animation, vigour, or courage: *a spirited debate.* **2.** Having a specified mood or nature. Used in combination: *high-spirited.* **—spir·it·ed·ly** *adv.* **—spir·it·ed·ness** *n.*

spirit gum *n.* A glue used to attach false beards and moustaches to the face. It consists of a gum dissolved in ether or alcohol.

spir·it·ism (spírrit-iz'm) *n.* Spiritualism. **—spir·it·ist** *n.* **—spir·it·is·tic** (-ístik) *adj.*

spirit lamp *n.* A lamp burning methylated spirits or some other alcohol-based fuel.

spir·it·less (spírrit-ləss, -liss) *adj.* Lacking energy, courage, or enthusiasm. **—spir·it·less·ly** *adv.* **—spir·it·less·ness** *n.*

spirit level *n.* An instrument for ascertaining whether a surface is horizontal, consisting essentially of an encased, liquid-filled tube containing an air bubble that moves to a central window when the instrument is set on a horizontal plane. Also called "level".

spir·i·to·so (spírri-tṓ-sō) *adv. Music.* In a spirited or lively manner. Used as a direction. [Italian, spirited.] **—spir·i·to·so** *adj.*

spir·it·ous (spírritəss) *adj.* **1.** Spirituous. **2.** *Archaic.* Refined; pure.

spir·it-rap·ping (spírrit-rapping) *n.* Supposed communication from the dead through messages rapped out on a table or a similar surface. **—spir·it-rap·per** *n.*

spirits of ammonia *n. Used with a singular verb.* **Sal volatile** *(see).*

spirits of salt *n. Used with a singular verb.* **Hydrochloric acid** *(see).* No longer in technical usage.

spirits of turpentine *n. Used with a singular verb.* Refined turpentine.

spirits of wine *n. Used with a singular verb.* Also **spirit of wine.** Rectified ethanol.

spir·i·tu·al (spírri-tew-əl, -choo-) *adj.* **1.** Of, pertaining to, consisting of, or having the nature of spirit or a spirit; not tangible or material. **2.** Of, concerned with, or affecting the soul. **3.** Of, from, or pertaining to God; divine. **4.** Of or belonging to a church or religious organisation; ecclesiastical. **5.** Of, pertaining to, or having highly developed or refined qualities of mind or sensibility. **6.** Linked by or sharing a deep intellectual or emotional affinity: *his spiritual heir.* **7.** Pertaining to or having the nature of spirits; supernatural.
~*n.* **1. a.** A religious folk song of black American origin. **b.** Any work composed in imitation of a black spiritual. **2.** *Usually plural.* Religious, spiritual, or ecclesiastical matters. **3.** The realm of the spirit. [Middle English, from Old French *spirituel,* from Latin *spīrituālis.* See **spirit, -al.**] **—spir·i·tu·al·ly** *adv.* **—spir·i·tu·al·ness** *n.*

spir·i·tu·al·ise, spir·i·tu·al·ize (spírri-tew-ə-līz, -tew-līz, -choo-) *tr.v.* **-ised, -ising, -ises.** **1.** To impart a spiritual nature to; refine. **2.** To invest with or treat as having a spiritual sense. **—spir·i·tu·al·i·sa·tion** (-lī-záysh'n ‖ *U.S.* -li-) *n.* **—spir·i·tu·al·is·er** *n.*

spir·i·tu·al·ism (spírri-tew-ə-liz'm, -tew-liz'm, -choo-) *n.* **1. a.** The belief that the dead communicate with the living, usually through a medium. **b.** The practices or doctrines of those holding such a belief. **2.** Any philosophy, doctrine, or religion emphasising the spiritual rather than the material; especially, any doctrine holding that spirit is the prime or only aspect of reality. Compare **materialism.** **—spir·i·tu·al·ist** *n.* **—spir·i·tu·al·is·tic** (-ístik) *adj.*

spir·i·tu·al·i·ty (spírri-tew-ál-əti, -choo-) *n., pl.* **-ties.** **1. a.** The state, quality, or fact of being spiritual. **b.** Attachment to or involvement in religious matters. **2.** Ecclesiastics collectively; the clergy. **3.** *Often plural.* Something belonging to the church or to an ecclesiastic, such as property or revenue. [Middle English, from Old French *spiritualité,* from Late Latin *spīrituālitās.* See **spiritual, -ity.**]

spir·i·tu·al·ty (spírri-tew-əl-ti, -chool-) *n., pl.* **-ties.** Spirituality.

spir·i·tu·el (spírri-tew-él, -choo-) *adj. Feminine* **spir·i·tu·elle.** Having or showing a refined mind and wit. [French, "spiritual".]

spir·i·tu·ous (spírri-tew-əss, -choo-) *adj.* **1.** Having the nature of or containing alcohol; alcoholic. **2.** Distilled, as contrasted with fermented. **—spir·it·u·os·i·ty** (-óssəti), **spir·i·tu·ous·ness** *n.*

spirit varnish *n.* **Varnish** *(see).*

spir·ket·ting, *U.S.* **spir·ket·ing** (spúrkiting) *n. Nautical.* **1.** Deck planking near the sides of a ship. **2.** The inside planking fitted above the waterways in a wooden ship. [From obsolete *spirket*†, the space between the side or floor timbers of a ship.]

spiro–¹ *comb. form.* Indicates spiral or coiled form; for example, **spirochaete.** [Latin *spīra,* coil, SPIRE.]

spiro–² *comb. form.* Indicates respiration or breathing; for example, **spirograph.** [Latin *spīrāre,* to breathe.]

spi·ro·chaete, *U.S.* **spi·ro·chete** (spī́r-ə-keet, -ō-) *n.* Any of various slender, nonflagellated, twisted bacteria of the order Spirochaetales, many of which are pathogenic, causing syphilis, relapsing fever, yaws, and other diseases. [New Latin *Spirochaeta* (genus) : SPIRO- (coil) + CHAETA.] **—spi·ro·chae·tal** (-kéet'l) *adj.*

spi·ro·chae·to·sis (spī́r-ə-kee-tṓ-siss) *n.* Any of various diseases, such as syphilis, caused by a spirochaete. [New Latin : SPIROCHAET(E) + -OSIS.]

spi·ro·graph (spī́r-ə-graaf, -graf) *n.* An instrument for registering the depth and rapidity of respiratory movements. [SPIRO- (breathing) + -GRAPH.] **—spi·ro·graph·ic** (-gráffik) *adj.* **—spi·rog·ra·phy** (spīr-róggrəfi, spī-) *n.*

spi·ro·gy·ra (spī́r-ə-jī́r-ə) *n.* Any of various green, filamentous freshwater algae of the genus *Spirogyra,* having chloroplasts in spirally twisted bands. [New Latin : SPIRO- (coil) + Greek *guros,* ring.]

spi·roid (spī́r-oyd) *adj.* Resembling a spiral. [New Latin *spiroides,* from Greek *speiroeidēs* : *speira,* SPIRE + -OID.]

spi·rom·e·ter (spīr-rómmitər, spī-) *n.* An instrument for measuring the volume of air entering and leaving the lungs. [SPIRO- (breathing) + -METER.] **—spi·ro·met·ric** (spī́r-ə-méttrik) *adj.* **—spi·rom·e·try** (-rómmətri) *n.*

spi·ro·no·lac·tone (spī́r-ənō-láktōn) *n.* A synthetic steroid drug that inhibits the action of the hormone aldosterone and is used mainly as a diuretic. [SPIRO- + *-no-* (infix) + LACTONE.]

spirt. Variant of **spurt.**

spir·u·la (spī́r-ōō-lə, -yōō- ‖ *U.S.* spírrə-) *n., pl.* **-lae** (-lee). Any small cephalopod mollusc of the genus *Spirula;* especially, *S. peronii,* having a coiled internal shell. [Late Latin *spīrula,* small twisted cake or cracknel, diminutive of Latin *spīra,* coil, SPIRE.]

spir·y (spī́r-i) *adj.* **-ier, -iest.** Resembling a spire in shape.

spit¹ (spit) *n.* **1.** Saliva, especially when spat; spittle. **2.** The act or an instance of spitting. **3.** Something resembling saliva, such as the frothy secretion of certain insects. **4.** A brief, scattered fall of rain or snow. **5.** *Chiefly British Informal.* A spitting image.
~*v.* **spat** (spat) or **spit, spitting, spits.** *—tr.* **1.** To eject from the mouth. Often used with *out.* **2. a.** To eject as if by spitting. **b.** To utter in a violent, contemptuous, or angry manner. Often used with *out: spit out an insult.* *—intr.* **1.** To eject saliva from the mouth. **2.** To express contempt or hostility by or as if by spitting. **3.** To make a hissing or sputtering noise. **4.** To rain or snow in light, scattered drops or flakes. **—spit it out.** *Informal.* To say what one is thinking without further delay; speak up. [*Spit, spat,* Middle English *spitten,* Old English *spittan.*]

spit² *n.* **1. a.** A slender, pointed rod on which meat is impaled for roasting in front of or over a fire. **b.** A similar device in a gas or electric oven, a **rotisserie** *(see).* **2.** A narrow ridge of sand or shingle extending into a body of water or across a bay.
~*tr.v.* **spitted, spitting, spits.** To impale on or as if on a spit. [Middle English *spit(e),* Old English *spitu.*]

spit·al (spítt'l) *n. Archaic.* **1.** A hospital; especially, one for the poor or for those suffering from contagious diseases. **2.** A wayside shelter. [Variant of obsolete *spittle,* shortened variant of HOSPITAL.]

Spit·al·fields (spítt'l-feeldz). District in the London borough of Tower Hamlets, belonging originally to the spital or rest house of St. Mary's Priory. It was formerly a silk-weaving centre, and today has a famous wholesale market for flowers, fruit, and vegetables.

spit and polish *n. Used with a singular verb.* Close attention paid to cleanliness, smart appearance, and ceremonial, especially in the armed forces.

spitch·cock (spích-kok) *n.* An eel split, cut up, and grilled or fried. [16th century : origin obscure. Compare **spatchcock.**]

spite (spīt) *n.* **1.** Malicious ill-will prompting an urge to hurt, annoy, or humiliate another. **2.** An instance of such feeling. **—in spite of.** Regardless of; despite.
~*tr.v.* **spited, spiting, spites.** **1.** To show spite towards. **2.** To thwart out of spite. [Middle English, insult, ill will, short for Old French *despit.* See **despite.**]

spite·ful (spī́tf'l) *adj.* Filled with, prompted by, or showing spite. See Synonyms at **vindictive.** **—spite·ful·ly** *adv.* **—spite·ful·ness** *n.*

spit·fire (spít-fīr) *n.* A quick-tempered or highly excitable person, especially a girl or woman.

Spit·head (spít-héd). Anchorage at the entrance to Portsmouth Harbour, forming a deep channel between the Isle of Wight and the southern coast of England. It was here that the Channel fleet mutinied in 1797. Spithead is the site of an annual naval review.

Spitsbergen. See **Svalbard.**

spitting cobra *n.* The **ringhals** *(see).*

spitting image *n.* A perfect, usually physical, likeness or counterpart. [Perhaps from the phrase *the very spit of,* an exact likeness, as if the image has been "spat out".]

spitting snake *n.* The **ringhals** *(see).*

spit·tle (spítt'l) *n.* **1.** Spit; saliva. **2.** The frothy liquid secreted by froghoppers; cuckoo spit; frog spit. [Middle English *spetil,* Old English *spātl.*]

spit·tle·bug (spítt'l-bug) *n.* The **froghopper** *(see).* Also called "spittle insect".

spit·toon (spi-tōōn) *n.* A bowl-shaped, usually metal vessel for spitting into. Also called "cuspidor". [SPIT + *-oon,* in such words as BALLOON and DOUBLOON.]

spitz (spits) *n.* A dog of a breed originating in Germany, having a long, thick, usually white coat and a tail curled over the back. [German *Spitz,* from *spitz,* "pointed" (from its pointed muzzle), from Old High German *spizzi.*]

Spitz (spits), **Mark (Andrew)** (1950–). U.S. swimmer. He won four individual gold medals in the Olympic Games at Munich (1972).

spiv (spiv) *n. British Slang.* **1.** A petty swindler or black marketeer. **2.** A flashily dressed and disreputable-looking man. [From dialectal *spiff*†, dandy.] **—spiv·vy** *adj.*

splanch·nic (splángk-nik) *adj.* Of or pertaining to the viscera. [Greek *splankhnikos,* of the bowels, from *splankhna,* inward parts.]

splash (splash) *v.* **splashed, splashing, splashes.** *—tr.* **1.** To dash or scatter (a liquid or semiliquid substance) about in flying masses. **2.** To dash a liquid or semiliquid substance upon; wet or soil with flying masses of such substance. **3.** To cause to dash such substance about: *He splashed his oar in the water.* **4.** To make (one's way) through such substance so as to dash or scatter it. **5.** To display (a story, poster or photograph) prominently. *—intr.* **1.** To dash or scatter a liquid or semiliquid substance about in flying masses. **2.** To fall into or move through such substance with this effect. Often used with *about* or *around.* **3.** To move, spill, or fly about in scattered masses. **—splash out.** *Chiefly British Informal.* To spend money ostentatiously or extravagantly. Often used with *on: splash out on a new car.*
~*n.* **1.** The act, an instance, or a sound of splashing. **2.** A flying mass of liquid or semiliquid substance. **3.** A mark or patch produced by or as if by scattered liquid or semiliquid substance: *a splash of light.* **4.** A striking though often short-lived impression; a stir. Used chiefly in the phrase *make a splash.* **5.** *British Informal.* A small amount, as of water or soda, added to a drink.
~*adv.* With a splash. [Variant of PLASH (splash).] **—splash·er** *n.*

splash·back (splásh-bak) *n.* A wall panel immediately above a basin, bath, sink, or cooker to protect the wall against splashes.

splash·board (splásh-bawrd ‖ -bōrd) *n.* **1.** A structure that protects

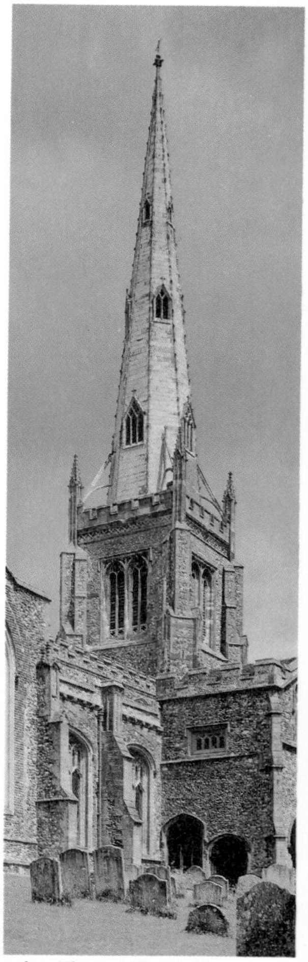

spire *Thaxted Church, Essex, England. A spire in the Perpendicular style.*

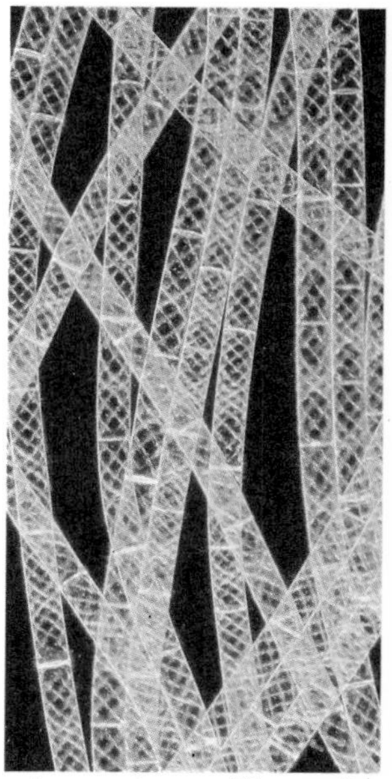

spirogyra *A genus of filament-like green algae (here magnified 22 times) which carry chlorophyll in spirals. Up to 60 centimetres (2 feet) long, clusters of the filaments are sometimes called mermaid's tresses.*

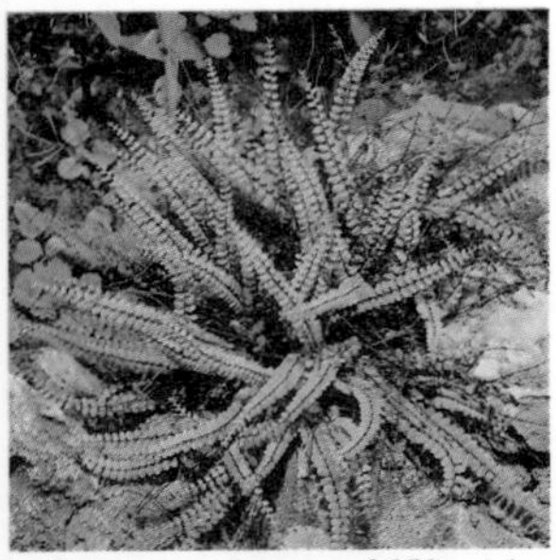

spleenwort *A genus of 650 species of evergreen ferns. This is the maidenhair spleenwort,* Asplenium trichomanes.

a vehicle from splashes of mud or water. **2.** A screen on a boat to keep water from splashing on the deck; a washboard.
splash down *intr.v.* To make a splashdown. Used of a missile or spacecraft.
splash·down (splásh-down) *n.* The landing of a missile or spacecraft in a body of water.
splash·er (spláshər) *n.* **1.** One that splashes. **2.** Anything that protects against splashes.
splash·y (spláshi) *adj.* **-ier, -iest. 1.** Making or liable to make splashes. **2.** Covered with splashes of colour. **3.** *Informal.* Showy; ostentatious. **—splash·i·ly** *adv.* **—splash·i·ness** *n.*
splat[1] (splat) *n.* A slat of wood, such as one in the middle of a chair back. [From obsolete *splat,* to split up; akin to SPLIT.]
splat[2] *n.* A slapping noise.
~adv. With a splat. [Imitative.]
splat·ter (spláttər) *v.* **-tered, -tering, -ters.** *—tr.* To spatter or splash. *—intr.* To spatter or splash. Used especially of a liquid. *~n.* A splash of liquid. [Perhaps a blend of SPLASH and SPATTER.]
splay (splay) *adj.* **1.** Spread out; broad. **2.** Turned outwards. **3.** Clumsy; awkward.
~n. **1.** An expansion; a spread. **2.** *Architecture.* Either of two side walls of a window or other opening that forms an oblique rather than right angle to the main wall.
~v. **splayed, splaying, splays.** *—tr.* **1.** To spread (the limbs, for example) out or apart, especially clumsily. Usually used with *out.* **2.** To make the edges of (a window or other aperture) slant or slope out; bevel. **3.** To dislocate (a bone). Used of an animal. *—intr.* **1.** To be spread out or apart. **2.** To slant or slope. Usually used with *out.* [Middle English *splayen,* to spread out, short for *displayen,* to DISPLAY.]
splay·foot (splay-fŏŏt) *n., pl.* **-feet** (-feet). **1.** A physical deformity characterised by abnormally flat and turned-out feet. **2.** A foot of this kind. **—splay·foot·ed** (-fŏŏtid) *adj.*
spleen (spleen) *n.* **1.** A large, dark red organ situated below and behind the stomach and containing lymphoid tissue. It forms lymphocytes and antibodies and helps to remove worn-out red blood cells and foreign particles from the blood stream. **2.** A homologous organ or tissue in other vertebrates. Also called "milt". **3.** *Obsolete.* **a.** This organ considered as the seat of mirth. **b.** Merriment. **c.** Caprice; whim. **4. a.** *Obsolete.* This organ considered as the seat of melancholy. **b.** Melancholy. **5.** Ill temper and malice. Used chiefly in the phrase *vent one's spleen.* [Middle English *splen(e),* from Old French *esplen,* from Latin *splēn,* from Greek.] **—spleen·y** *adj.*
spleen·ful (spléenf'l) *adj.* Ill-tempered, irritable, or spiteful. [The spleen was once thought of as the seat of negative emotions.] **—spleen·ful·ly** *adv.*
spleen·wort (spléen-wurt || -wawrt) *n.* Any of various ferns of the genus *Asplenium,* having feather-like, often evergreen fronds. [So called because it was thought to cure spleen disorders.]
splen·dent (spléndənt) *adj. Archaic.* **1.** Shining or lustrous; brilliant. **2.** Celebrated; illustrious. [Middle English, from Latin *splendēns* (stem *splendent-*) , present participle of *splendēre,* to shine.]
splen·did (spléndid) *adj.* **1.** Magnificent; grand. **2.** Imposing by reason of showiness. **3.** Glorious; illustrious. **4.** Gleaming with light or colour; radiant. **5.** Very good or satisfying: *had a splendid evening.* [French *splendide,* from Latin *splendidus,* from *splendēre,* to shine.] **—splen·did·ly** *adv.* **—splen·did·ness** *n.*
splen·dif·er·ous (splen-dífərəss) *adj.* Splendid. Usually used humorously or ironically. [Middle English, from Medieval Latin *splendiferus* : SPLENDOUR + -FEROUS.] **—splen·dif·er·ous·ly** *adv.* **—splen·dif·er·ous·ness** *n.*
splendour, *U.S.* **splen·dor** (spléndər) *n.* **1.** The state or quality of being splendid. **2.** Something splendid. **3.** *Heraldry.* The sun depicted with rays and a human face. [Middle English *splendure,* from Old French *splendeur,* from Latin *splendour,* from *splendēre,* to shine.] **—splen·dor·ous, splen·drous** (spléndrəss) *adj.*
sple·nec·to·my (spli-néktəmi) *n., pl.* **-mies.** A surgical removal of the spleen. [Latin *splēn,* SPLEEN + -ECTOMY.]
sple·net·ic (spli-néttik) *adj.* Also **sple·net·i·cal** (-'l). **1.** Of or pertaining to the spleen. **2.** Ill-tempered, irritable, or spiteful. **3.** *Archaic.* Melancholy.
~n. An ill-humoured person. [Late Latin *splēnēticus,* from Latin *splēn,* SPLEEN.] **—sple·net·i·cal·ly** *adv.*
splen·ic (splénnik, spléenik) *adj.* Of, in, near, or pertaining to the spleen. [Latin *splēnicus,* from Greek *splēnikos,* from *splēn,* SPLEEN.]
sple·ni·tis (spli-nītiss) *n.* Inflammation of the spleen. [Greek *splēnitis* : *splēn,* SPLEEN + -ITIS.]
sple·ni·us (spléeni-əss) *n., pl.* **-nii** (-ī). Either of two muscles of the back of the neck, extending from the backbone to the skull, that rotate and extend the head and neck. [New Latin, from Latin *splēnium,* patch, plaster, spleenwort, from Greek *splēnion,* from *splēn,* SPLEEN.] **—sple·ni·al** *adj.*
sple·no·meg·a·ly (spléenō-méggəli) *n.* Enlargement of the spleen. [Latin *splēn,* SPLEEN + MEGAL(O)- + -Y.]
splice (splīss) *tr.v.* **spliced, splicing, splices. 1. a.** To join (film or wire, for example) at the ends, usually with an adhesive. Often used with *to* or *together.* **b.** To join (ropes) by interweaving strands. **2.** To join (pieces of wood) by overlapping and binding or bolting. **3.** *Informal.* To unite in marriage. Usually used in the passive.
~n. **1.** A joint made by splicing. **2.** The place where parts have been spliced. [Probably from Middle Dutch *splissen.*] **—splic·er** *n.*
spline (splīn) *n.* **1. a.** Any of a series of projections on a shaft that fit into slots on a mating part, enabling one to drive the other. **b.** A slot or groove receiving such a projection. **2.** A wooden or metal strip; especially, one that fits into a groove at the edge of one board to join it to another.
~tr.v. **splined, splining, splines.** To cut splines into. [Of dialect (East Anglian) origin, perhaps akin to SPLINTER.]
splint (splint) *n.* **1.** A thin piece, as of wood, split off from a larger piece; a splinter. **2.** Any rigid device used to prevent motion of a joint or the ends of a fractured bone. **3.** A thin, flexible wooden strip, such as one used in weaving baskets and chair bottoms. **4.** A plate or strip of metal, such as one used in making armour. **5.** A bony enlargement of the cannon bone or splint bone of a horse.
~tr.v. **splinted, splinting, splints.** To support or restrict with or as if with a splint. [Middle English *splent, splint,* small strip of metal, splint, from Middle Low German or Middle Dutch *splinte.*]
splint bone *n.* Either of two small metacarpal or metatarsal bones in horses or related animals, on each side of the cannon bone.
splin·ter (splíntər) *n.* A sharp, slender piece, as of wood, bone, glass, or metal, split or broken off from a main body.
~v. **splintered, -tering, -ters.** *—intr.* **1.** To split or break into sharp, slender pieces. **2.** To split into parts; shatter. **3.** To break away from a parent group. Used with *off.* *—tr.* To cause to splinter. —See Synonyms at **break. —splin·ter·y** *adj.*
splinter group *n.* An independent group that has broken away from a parent group such as a church or political party.
split (split) *v.* **split, splitting, splits.** *—tr.* **1. a.** To divide sharply or cleanly, especially into lengthways sections or into two parts of approximately equal size. **b.** To separate from a whole. Often used with *off.* **2.** To break, burst, or rip apart with force; rend. **3.** To separate (persons or groups); disunite. Often used with *up.* **4.** To divide and share among people. **5.** To separate into layers, components, or parts. Often used with *up.* **6.** *Slang.* To depart from; leave. **7.** *U.S.* To mark (a vote or ballot) in favour of candidates from different parties. *—intr.* **1. a.** To become separated into parts; especially, to divide lengthways. **b.** To be separated from a whole. Often used with *off.* **2.** To become broken or ripped apart, especially as a result of internal pressure. **3. a.** To become divided or part company as a result of discord or disagreement. **b.** To end a relationship, especially to separate or divorce. Used with *up.* **4.** To divide or share something with others. **5.** *British Slang.* To betray information to the authorities; inform. Usually used with *on.* **6.** *Slang.* To depart. —See Synonyms at **break, tear.**
~n. **1.** The act or result of splitting. **2.** A gap, rift, or cleft. **3.** A piece split off from a larger whole; a splinter. **4.** A breach or rupture in a group; a schism. **5.** A split strip of flexible wood or other material used in basketmaking. **6.** *Informal.* **a.** A half-bottle of a carbonated beverage. **b.** An alcoholic drink of half the usual quantity. **7. a.** A dessert of sliced fruit, ice cream, and toppings: *banana split.* **b.** Something made up of two or more different constituents or ingredients. **8.** *Usually plural.* The act of stretching out the legs in opposite directions at right angles to the trunk while in the air or on the ground, performed in dancing, acrobatics or the like. Preceded by *the.* **9.** A single thickness of a hide split into layers. **10.** In ten-pin bowling, an arrangement of pins left standing after the first bowl with one or more intermediate pins knocked down.
~adj. **1.** Divided or separated; *split loyalties.* **2.** Fissured longitudinally; cleft. [Dutch *splitten,* from Middle Dutch.] **—split·ter** *n.*
Split (split). *Italian* **Spa·la·to** (spa-láatō). City on the Dalmatian coast, in Croatia, Yugoslavia. It has been a major Adriatic port since the early Middle Ages, and is a cultural, market, tourist, and manufacturing centre. It was held by Venice (1420–1797), and by Austria until 1918.
split ends *pl.n.* A condition of damaged hair in which the ends of individual hairs have a tendency to split.
split infinitive *n. Grammar.* An infinitive verb form with an element, usually an adverb, interposed between *to* and the verb form.
Usage: An example of a split infinitive is *to officially propose.* Although this construction is widely used in speech, and is often found in literature, it attracts strong criticism, perhaps because the word *to* and the following verb are felt to form a unit and should therefore not be separated. However, it is often difficult to avoid this construction without either causing a highly unnatural style of speech—in *I want to really help them,* placing *really* before *to* or after *help* is undesirable—or producing a different meaning —in *I really want to help them* it is the "wanting" rather than the "helping" that is now emphasised.
split-lev·el (split-lévv'l, -levv'l) *adj.* Of, within, or designating a building in which the floor levels of adjoining parts are separated by about half a storey.
~n. A split-level house.
split pea *n.* A pea dried and split, and used for cooking in soups and stews or as a vegetable.
split personality *n.* **1.** A condition in which an individual or group manifests two or more relatively distinct personalities. **2.** Such an individual or group. **3.** Loosely, **schizophrenia** *(see).*
split pin *n.* A strong, metal pin with two arms that can be bent outwards, used for holding wheels on axles and the like.
split ring *n.* A usually metal ring consisting of two spiral turns pressed flat together, between which keys or other objects may be slid on or off.
split-screen (split-skréen) *adj.* Of or designating a cinematic technique in which two or more images are projected simultaneously onto different parts of the same screen. **—split screen** *n.*
split second *n.* An instant; a flash.

split-second (splít-séckənd) *adj.* **1.** Performed in a very short space of time. **2.** Requiring or showing great precision and accuracy.

split shift *n.* A working shift split into two periods by an interval considerably longer than a lunch break.

split·ting (splítting) *adj.* **1.** Acute; piercing. **2.** Extremely painful.

splodge (sploj) *n.* Also *chiefly U.S.* **splotch** (sploch). An irregularly shaped stain, spot, or discoloured area.
~*tr.v.* **splodged, sploding, splodes.** Also *chiefly U.S.* **splotch, splotched, splotching, splotches.** To mark with a splodge or splodges. [*Splodge,* variant of *splotch,* perhaps blend of SPOT + BLOTCH.] —**splodg·y** *adj.*

splosh (splosh) *n.* A splash. [Imitative.] —**splosh** *v.*

splurge (splurj) *v.* **splurged, splurging, splurges.** *Informal.* —*intr.* **1.** To indulge in extravagant expense or luxury. **2.** To be showy or ostentatious. —*tr.* To spend extravagantly or wastefully. Often used with *on: splurged £150 on a new radio.*
~*n. Informal.* **1.** An extravagant display. **2.** An extravagant spending spree. [19th century (U.S.) : probably imitative.]

splut·ter (splúttər) *v.* **-tered, -tering, -ters.** —*intr.* **1.** To make a spitting sound. **2.** To speak incoherently, as when confused or angry. —*tr.* To utter or express hastily and incoherently.
~*n.* A spluttering noise or spluttering talk. [Perhaps alteration (influenced by SPLASH) of SPUTTER.] —**splut·ter·er** *n.*

Spock (spok), **Benjamin (McLane)** (1903–). U.S. paediatrician. He had a great influence on childcare in the West through his book *Baby and Child Care* (1946), which he drastically revised in 1979.

spode (spōd) *n. Often capital* **S.** A porcelain or chinaware of fine quality. [After Josiah *Spode* (1754–1827), British potter.]

spod·u·mene (spóddew-meen) *n.* A greenish to pinkish or lilac mineral, essentially $LiAlSi_2O_6$, used as a source of lithium and in transparent varieties as a gemstone. [French *spodumène,* from Greek *spodoumenos,* present participle of *spodousthai,* to be burned to ashes (because the mineral becomes ash-grey when exposed to flame), from *spodos†,* wood ashes.]

spoil (spoyl) *v.* **spoilt** (spoylt) or **spoiled, spoiling, spoils.** —*tr.* **1.** To impair the value or quality of; damage or ruin. **2. a.** To harm the character of (a child, for example) by overindulgence. **b.** To pamper; coddle. **3.** To make dissatisfied. Used with *for: spoiled him for the old life.* **4.** *Archaic.* **a.** To plunder; despoil. **b.** To take by force. —*intr.* **1.** To become tainted, rotten, or otherwise unfit for use; decay. Used especially of food. **2.** *Archaic.* To pillage. —See Synonyms at **decay, injure, pamper.** —**spoil for.** To be eager for; crave. Used chiefly in the phrase *be spoiling for a fight.*
~*n.* **1.** *Usually plural.* Goods or property seized from a victim after a conflict, especially after a military victory. **2.** *Plural.* Incidental benefits reaped by a winner. **3.** *Archaic.* The act of plundering; spoliation. **4.** Refuse material removed from an excavation. [Middle English *spoilen,* to despoil, plunder, from Old French *espoillier,* from Latin *spoliāre,* from *spolium,* hide torn from an animal, booty.]
Usage: Spoiled and *spoilt* are both used as past tense and past participle forms, the former being preferred in American English and the latter in British English.

spoil·age (spóylij) *n.* **1.** The condition or process of becoming spoiled; damage or decomposition. **2.** Material that has been spoiled. **3.** Waste caused by spoiling.

spoil·er (spóylər) *n.* **1.** One who seizes spoils or booty. **2.** One that causes spoilage; a corrupting agent. **3.** A long, narrow hinged plate on the upper surface of an aircraft wing, raised to reduce lift or speed. **4.** An air deflector on either end of a motor vehicle used to prevent the wheels from lifting off the road at high speeds.

spoil·sport (spóyl-spawrt ‖ -spōrt) *n.* One who mars the pleasures of others, often by inappropriate prudence or sobriety.

spoke¹ (spōk) *n.* **1.** Any of the rods or braces that connect the hub and the rim of a wheel. **2.** Any of the handles that project from the rim of a ship's steering wheel. **3.** A rung of a ladder. —**put a spoke in (someone's) wheel.** To thwart or foil (someone's) plans.
~*tr.v.* **spoked, spoking, spokes. 1.** To equip with spokes. **2.** To impede (a wheel) by inserting a rod. [Middle English *spake, spoke,* Old English *spāca.*]

spoke² Past tense and *archaic* past participle of **speak.**

spo·ken (spókən) Past participle of **speak.**
~*adj.* **1.** Uttered; expressed orally. **2.** Speaking or using speech in a specified manner or voice. Used in combination: *soft-spoken.* —**spoken for.** Reserved or engaged.

spoke·shave (spók-shayv) *n.* A drawknife (*see*).

spokes·man (spóks-mən) *n., pl.* **-men** (-mən). A person chosen or authorised to speak on behalf of another or others. [*Spokes,* possessive case of *spoke,* "speaking," from *spoke,* archaic past participle of SPEAK + MAN.]

spokes·per·son (spóks-perss'n) *n.* A spokesman or spokeswoman. [SPOKES(MAN) + PERSON.]

spokes·wom·an (spóks-wŏŏmən) *n., pl.* **-women** (-wimmin). A female spokesman. [SPOKES(MAN) + WOMAN.]

spo·li·a·tion (spōli-áysh'n) *n. Formal.* **1.** The act of despoiling or plundering; especially, the seizure of neutral vessels at sea by a belligerent power in time of war. **2.** *Law.* The intentional alteration or destruction of a document so as to invalidate it as evidence. [Middle English *spoliacioun,* from Latin *spoliātiō* (stem *spoliātiōn-*), from *spoliāre,* to despoil. See **spoil.**] —**spo·li·a·tor** (-aytər) *n.*

spon·da·ic (spon-dáy-ik) *adj.* Of, pertaining to, or consisting of spondees. [French *spondaïque,* from Late Latin *spondaicus, spondiācus,* from Greek *spondeiakos,* from *spondeios,* SPONDEE.]

spon·dee (spón-dee, *rarely* -di) *n.* A metrical foot in poetry consisting of two long or stressed syllables. [Middle English *sponde,* from Old French *spondee,* from Latin *spondeum,* from Greek *spondeios (pous),* "(meter) used at a libation", from *spondē,* libation.]

spon·du·licks, spon·du·lix (spon-déw-liks ‖ -dŏŏ-) *n. Slang.* Money. [19th century : origin obscure.]

spon·dy·li·tis (spóndi-lítiss) *n.* Inflammation of the joints of the vertebrae. [New Latin : Greek *spondulos, sphondulos†,* vertebra + -ITIS.]

sponge (spunj) *n.* **1.** Any of numerous primitive, chiefly marine invertebrate animals of the phylum Porifera, characteristically having a porous body supported by a skeleton composed of fibrous material or siliceous or calcareous spicules, and often forming colonies. **2. a.** The light, fibrous, absorbent skeleton of certain of these organisms. **b.** A piece of such a skeleton, used for bathing, cleaning, and other purposes. **3.** Any of various substances having spongelike qualities, such as certain forms of plastics, rubber, or cellulose. **4.** A porous metal used to absorb gases: *a platinum sponge.* **5.** A gauze pad used to absorb blood and other fluids, as in surgery and wound dressing. **6.** Dough that is leavened or in the process of being leavened. **7. a.** Any of various light cakes, such as sponge cake. **b.** *British.* A sponge pudding. **8. a.** A wash or rub with a sponge. **b.** A sponge bath. **9.** *Informal.* A sponger. —**throw in** or **up the sponge.** *Informal.* To give up; admit defeat.
~*v.* **sponged, sponging, sponges.** —*tr.* **1.** To moisten, wipe, or clean with a sponge. Often used with *down* or *off.* **2.** To wipe out; erase. **3.** To absorb or soak up. Often used with *up.* **4.** *Informal.* To obtain free by imposing on another's generosity: *sponge a meal.* —*intr.* **1.** To fish for sponges. **2.** *Informal.* To live by imposing on the generosity of others. Often used with *off* or *on.* [Middle English *spo(u)ng(e),* Old English *sponge,* from Latin *spongia,* from Greek *sphongos,* sponge, from the same Mediterranean origin as FUNGUS.]

sponge bag *n.* A waterproof bag for holding toilet articles.

sponge bath *n.* A washing of the body with a sponge or cloth, without immersion.

sponge cake *n.* A very light, porous cake made of flour, sugar, beaten eggs, and flavouring, sometimes containing no shortening. Also called "sponge".

sponge cloth *n.* A loosely woven cloth, usually of cotton.

sponge finger *n.* A sponge cake resembling a finger in shape.

sponge pudding *n.* A light steamed or baked pudding of sponge-like texture.

spong·er (spúnjər) *n.* **1.** A person or boat that gathers sponges. **2.** *Informal.* A person who sponges on others; a parasite.

sponge rubber *n.* A soft, porous rubber used in toys, cushions, gaskets, and weather stripping, and as a vibration dampener.

spon·gin (spúnjin) *n.* A fibrous protein that forms the skeletal structure of some sponges. [German *Spongin* : Latin *spongia,* SPONGE + -IN.]

spon·gi·o·blast (spúnji-ō-blaast, -blast) *n.* Any of the embryonic epithelial cells that give rise to the neuroglia cells. [Latin *spongia,* SPONGE + -BLAST.] —**spon·gi·o·blast·ic** (-blástik) *adj.*

spon·gy (spúnji) *adj.* **-gier, -giest. 1.** Like a sponge, especially in elasticity, absorbency, or porousness. **2.** Full of small holes. **3.** Soft and wet. —**spon·gi·ness** *n.*

spon·son (spón-s'n) *n.* **1.** Any of several structures that project from the side of a ship or tank; especially, a gun platform. **2.** An air-filled projection on the hull of a seaplane, canoe, or other vessel, giving greater stability. [19th century : origin obscure.]

spon·sor (spón-sər) *n.* **1.** A person or group that assumes responsibility for another person or group. **2.** A person or group that pledges financial support to or promotes an activity or organisation, for example. **3.** A legislator who proposes and urges the adoption of a bill. **4.** One who presents a candidate for baptism or confirmation; a godparent. **5.** A business enterprise that pays for or subsidises a broadcast, concert, sports event, or the like, usually in return for advertising time or space.
~*tr.v.* **sponsored, -soring, -sors.** To act as a sponsor for. [Latin, from *spondēre,* to make a solemn pledge.] —**spon·so·ri·al** (spon-sáwri-əl ‖ -sóri-) *adj.* —**spon·sor·ship** *n.*

spon·ta·ne·i·ty (spóntə-náy-əti, -née-) *n., pl.* **-ties. 1.** The condition or quality of being spontaneous. **2.** Spontaneous behaviour, impulses, or movements.

spon·ta·ne·ous (spon-táyni-əss) *adj.* **1.** Happening, arising, or performed without apparent external cause; self-generated. **2.** Voluntary and impulsive; unpremeditated: *spontaneous applause.* **3.** Unconstrained and unstudied in manner or characteristic behaviour. **4.** Growing without cultivation or human labour; indigenous. Said of plants. —See Synonyms below and at **voluntary.** [Late Latin *spontāneus,* from Latin *sponte,* of one's own accord, out of free will.] —**spon·ta·ne·ous·ly** *adv.* —**spon·ta·ne·ous·ness** *n.*
Synonyms: spontaneous, impulsive, instinctive, involuntary, automatic.

spontaneous abortion *n.* A miscarriage (*see*).

spontaneous combustion *n.* Ignition of a material, such as powdered coal or hay, without an external source of heat, caused by slow oxidation of the material producing a rise in temperature.

spontaneous generation *n. Biology.* The origination of live organisms from nonliving matter, once thought to explain the appearance of maggots in rotting meat. Compare **primordial soup.** See **abiogenisis.**

spon·toon (spon-tŏŏn) *n.* A short pike carried by subordinate infantry officers in the 18th and early 19th centuries. [French *sponton,* from Italian *spuntone,* from *spuntare,* to blunt, remove the point : *s-*, from Latin *ex-* (removal) + *punto,* point, from Latin *punctum,* from *pungere,* to pierce.]

spoof (spōōf) *n.* **1.** A good-humoured hoax. **2.** A gentle satirical imitation; a light parody. —See Synonyms at **caricature.**
~*v.* **spoofed, spoofing, spoofs.** —*tr.* **1.** To deceive. **2.** To do a spoof of; satirise gently. —*intr.* To do a spoof. [Originally a card game characterised by nonsense and hoaxing, invented by Arthur Roberts (1852–1933), British comedian.] —**spoof·er** *n.*

spook (spōōk) *n. Informal.* **1.** A ghost; a spectre. **2.** *U.S.* A spy.
~*v.* **spooked, spooking, spooks.** *U.S. & South African Informal.* —*tr.* **1.** To haunt. **2.** To frighten; especially, to startle and cause sudden or violent activity among (cattle, for example). —*intr.* To become frightened. [Dutch, from Middle Dutch *spoocke,* akin to Middle Low German *spōk*†.] —**spook·ish** *adj.*

spook·y (spóōki) *adj.* **-ier, -iest.** *Informal.* **1.** Ghostly; eerie; unnatural. **2.** *U.S.* Easily startled; skittish; nervous. —**spook·i·ly** *adv.* —**spook·i·ness** *n.*

spool (spōōl) *n.* **1.** A small wood, metal, plastic, or cardboard cylinder upon which wire, thread, film, magnetic tape, or string is wound. It usually has raised ends and a hole through the centre. **2.** The amount of thread or other material on a particular spool. **3.** Anything similar to a spool in shape or function.
~*v.* **spooled, spooling, spools.** —*tr.* To wind on a spool. Often used with *up.* —*intr.* To be wound on a spool. Often used with *up.* [Middle English *spole, spule,* from Old French *espole,* from Middle Dutch *spoele,* akin to Old High German *spuolo*†.]

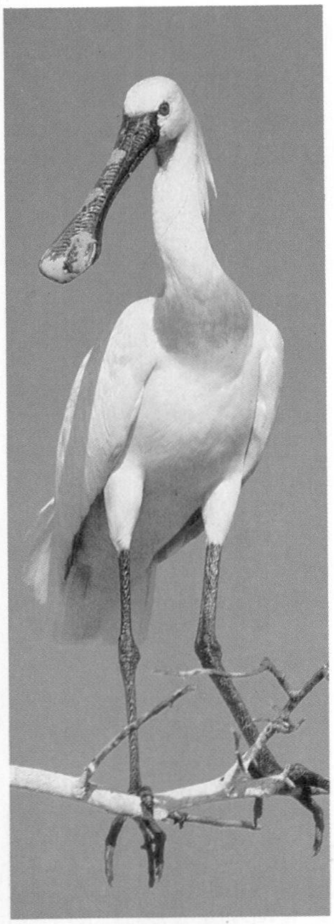
spoonbill *The long-legged spoonbill uses its wide flat bill to fish for crustaceans on the muddy bottoms of lakes and lagoons. Spoonbills are found worldwide in tropical and subtropical regions.*

spoon (spōōn) *n.* **1. a.** A utensil consisting of a small, shallow bowl on a handle, used in preparing, serving, or eating food. **b.** A spoonful. **2.** Something similar to a spoon or its bowl; especially: **a.** A shiny, curved metallic fishing lure. Also called "spoon bait". **b.** A paddle or oar with a curved blade. **3.** A golf club with more loft than a brassie. —**born with a silver spoon in (one's) mouth.** Born into wealthy or privileged circumstances.
~*v.* **spooned, spooning, spoons.** —*tr.* **1.** To lift, scoop up, or carry (food, for example) with or as if with a spoon. Often used with *out* or *up.* **2.** To shove or scoop (a ball) feebly into the air, as in golf. —*intr.* **1.** To fish with a spoon lure. **2.** To give the ball an upward scoop, as in golf. **3.** *Informal.* To show affection by kissing, caressing, or talking amorously. In this sense, not in current usage. [Middle English *spo(o)n,* Old English *spōn,* chip of wood.]

spoon·bill (spóōn-bil) *n.* **1.** Any of several long-legged wading birds mainly of the genus *Platalea,* of tropical and subtropical regions, having a long, flat bill with a broad, spatulate tip. **2.** Any of various broad-billed ducks, such as the shoveler.

spoon·drift (spóōn-drift) *n.* **Spindrift** *(see).* [Obsolete *spoon*†, to drive back and forth (said of a boat) + DRIFT.]

spoon·er·ism (spóōnər-iz'm) *n.* A usually unintentional transposition of the initial sounds of two or more words in spoken language, as in *Let me sew you to your sheet* for *Let me show you to your seat.* [After the Rev. William A. *Spooner* (1844–1930), English scholar and Warden of New College, Oxford, noted for such slips.]

spoon·feed (spóōn-feed) *tr.v.* **-fed** (-fed), **-feeding, -feeds. 1.** To feed (a baby, for example) with a spoon. **2. a.** To present (information, lessons, or the like) in such a thoroughgoing manner as to make any independent thought or effort on the part of the recipient unnecessary. **b.** To present with information in such a manner. **3.** To mollycoddle; pamper.

spoon·ful (spóōn-fōōl) *n., pl.* **-fuls.** The amount a spoon will hold.

spoor (spoor, spor) *n.* The track, trail, or footprint of an animal, especially a wild animal. See Synonyms at **trace.**
~*v.* **spoored, spooring, spoors.** —*tr.* To track by following a spoor. —*intr.* To track an animal by its spoor. [Afrikaans, from Middle Dutch *spo(o)r.*]

Spor·a·des or **Sporádhes** (spórrə-deez). Two groups of Greek islands in the southeast Aegean Sea. The southern group includes the **Dodecanese** (which see).

spo·rad·ic (spə-ráddik, spo- || spō-) *adj.* **1.** Occurring at irregular intervals in time; occasional. **2.** Appearing singly or at widely scattered localities; isolated in occurrence: *a sporadic disease.* —See Synonyms at **periodic.** [Medieval Latin *sporadicus,* from Greek *sporadikos,* isolated, scattered, from *sporas,* scattered, dispersed.] —**spo·rad·i·cal·ly** *adv.* —**spo·rad·i·cal·ness** *n.*

spo·ran·gi·um (spə-ránji-əm) *n., pl.* **-gia** (-ə). An asexual spore-bearing structure in certain plants, such as fungi, mosses, and ferns. [New Latin : SPOR(O)- + Greek *angeion,* vessel, container (see **angiology**).] —**spo·ran·gi·al** *adj.*

spore (spor || spōr) *n.* **1.** An asexual, usually single-celled reproductive organ characteristic of nonflowering plants such as fungi, mosses, or ferns. **2.** A similar structure formed by or involved in sexual reproduction in some other organisms. **3.** A microorganism, such as a bacterium, in a dormant or resting state.
~*intr.v.* **spored, sporing, spores.** To produce or carry spores. [New Latin *spora,* from Greek, a sowing, seed.] —**spo·ra·ceous** (spə-ráyshəss, sp) *adj.*

spore case *n.* A sporangium or other structure containing spores.

spo·ri·cide (spáw-ri-sīd, spó- || spō-) *n.* An agent that kills spores. —**spo·ri·ci·dal** (-sīd'l) *adj.*

sporo–, spori–, spor– *comb. form.* Indicates spore; for example, **sporocarp, sporangium.** [New Latin *spora,* spore, from Greek, a sowing, seed.]

spo·ro·carp (spáw-rə-kaarp, spó-, -rō- || spō-) *n. Botany.* **1.** A multicellular structure in which spores are formed in aquatic ferns. **2.** An **ascocarp** *(see).* [SPORO- + -CARP.]

spo·ro·cyst (spáw-rə-sist, spó-, -rə- || spō-) *n. Biology.* **1.** A protective case containing the spores of sporozoan protozoans. **2.** A saclike larval stage in many trematode worms, from which redia larvae are produced. [SPORO- + -CYST.]

spo·ro·cyte (spáw-rə-sīt, spó-, -rō- || spō-) *n. Biology.* A cell that produces haploid spores during meiosis. [SPORO- + -CYTE.]

spo·ro·gen·e·sis (spáw-rō-jénnə-siss, spó-, -rə- || spō-) *n.* The production or formation of spores. [SPORO- + -GENESIS.] —**spo·rog·e·nous** (spaw-rójənəss, spo-, spə- || spō-) *adj.*

spo·ro·go·ni·um (spáw-rə-gōni-əm, spó-, -rō- || spō-) *n., pl.* **-nia** (-ə). A stalked structure in mosses and liverworts that produces asexual spores. [New Latin : SPORO- + -GONIUM.]

spo·rog·o·ny (spaw-róggəni, spə-, spo- || spō-) *n.* The production of sporozoites by multiple fission of the zygote, characteristic of sporozoan protozoans. [SPORO- + -GONY.]

spo·ro·phore (spáw-rə-fawr, spó-, -rō- || spō-, -fōr) *n.* A spore-bearing structure, especially in fungi. [SPORO- + -PHORE.]

spo·ro·phyll (spáw-rə-fil, spó-, -rō- || spō-) *n.* A leaf or leaflike organ in mosses, ferns, and the like, that bears sporangia. [SPORO- + -PHYLL.]

spo·ro·phyte (spáw-rə-fīt, spó-, -rō- || spō-) *n.* **1.** The spore-producing phase in plants that reproduce by alternation of generations. **2.** An individual plant in this phase. Compare **gametophyte.** [SPORO- + -PHYTE.] —**spo·ro·phyt·ic** (-fíttik) *adj.*

-sporous *adj. comb. form.* Indicates having spores, especially a specified number or kind; for example, **homosporous.**

spo·ro·zo·an (spáw-rə-zō-ən, spó- || spō-) *n.* Any of numerous parasitic protozoans of the class Sporozoa, such as the malaria parasite, many of which have complex reproductive processes. [New Latin *Sporozoa* : SPORO- + -ZOA.] —**spo·ro·zo·an** *adj.*

spo·ro·zo·ite (spáw-rə-zō-īt, spó- || spō-) *n.* A sporozoan that has been formed by sporogony and is ready to penetrate a new host cell. [SPOROZO(AN) + -ITE.]

spor·ran (spórrən) *n.* A leather or fur pouch worn hanging on the belt at the front of the kilt in Highland dress. [Scottish Gaelic *sporan,* from Late Latin *bursa,* bag, from Greek, leather, hide.]

sport (sport || spōrt) *n.* **1.** A game or other activity, usually providing exercise and pleasure and involving competition. **2.** Sports collectively. **3. a.** Any pleasurable pastime; a diversion; a recreation. **b.** The pleasure provided by such a pastime. Used chiefly in the phrase *have good sport.* **4. a.** Light mockery; raillery; jest: *a remark made in sport.* **b.** An object of mockery. **5.** One at the mercy of or controlled by external forces: *a sport of fate.* **6.** *Informal.* A cheerful or good-natured person. **7.** *Informal.* A person who shows sportsmanlike qualities to a specified extent: *a bad sport.* **8.** *Informal.* A person who lives a merry, extravagant life. **9.** *Australian.* Used as an informal term of address. **10.** *Genetics.* An organism that shows a marked change from the parent stock; a mutation. **11.** *Archaic.* Amorous dalliance; flirting. —**in sport.** In jest; jokingly.
~*v.* **sported, sporting, sports.** —*intr.* **1.** To play happily; frolic. **2.** To joke or trifle. Often used with *with.* **3.** To mutate. —*tr.* To display or show off: *His shoes sported pink laces.*
~*adj. U.S.* Variant of **sports.** [Middle English *sporten,* to amuse, divert, short for *disporten,* DISPORT.] —**sport·ful** *adj.* —**sport·ful·ly** *adv.* —**sport·ful·ness** *n.*

sport·ing (spórt-ing || spōrt-) *adj.* **1.** Used in, appropriate for, or pertaining to hunting, racing, and other sports. **2.** Showing sportsmanship. **3.** Of or associated with gambling. —**sport·ing·ly** *adv.*

sporting chance *n. Informal.* A fair chance of success.

spor·tive (spórt-iv || spōrt-) *adj.* **1.** Playful; frolicsome. **2.** Pertaining to or interested in sports. **3.** *Archaic.* Amorous; wanton. —**spor·tive·ly** *adv.* —**spor·tive·ness** *n.*

sports (sports || spōrts) *adj.* Also *U.S.* **sport. 1.** Of, pertaining to, or used in sports. **2.** Suitable for casual or informal use. Said especially of clothes.

sports car *n.* A mass-produced car usually with two seats, having a low centre of gravity and, often, a folding or removable roof. Its steering and suspension are designed for precise control at high speeds on curving roads.

sports day *n. British.* A day at which athletic competitions take place in a school, college, or similar institution.

sports jacket *n.* A man's casual jacket, usually made of tweed or patterned wool fibre.

sports·man (spórts-mən || spōrts-) *n., pl.* **-men** (-mən). **1. a.** One who participates actively in sports, especially outdoor sports. **b.** One who participates in hunting, angling, or similar outdoor pursuits. **2.** One who abides by the rules of a contest, plays fair, and accepts victory or defeat graciously.

sports·man·like (spórts-mən-līk || spōrts-) *adj.* Also **sports·man·ly** (-li). Of, like, or befitting a good sportsman.

sports·man·ship (spórts-mən-ship || spōrts-) *n.* The qualities and conduct of a good sportsman; fair play and abidance by the rules.

sports·wear (spórts-wair || spōrts-) *n.* **1.** Clothes designed to be worn for sporting activities. **2.** Clothes designed for comfort and casual wear.

sports·wom·an (spórts-wōōmən || spōrts-) *n., pl.* **-women** (-wimmin). A woman who is active in sports.

sport·y (spórti || spōrti) *adj.* **-ier, -iest.** *Informal.* **1.** Of or appropriate to sportsman or sports. **2.** Interested or taking part in sports. **3.** Smart; natty. **4.** Dashing; flashy.

spor·u·late (spórrew-layt || spōrə-, spáwrə-) *intr.v.* **-lated, -lating, -lates.** To produce or release spores, especially by multiple cell fission. [New Latin *sporula,* diminutive of *spora,* SPORE.] **—spor·u·la·tion** (-láysh'n) *n.*

spot (spot) *n.* **1. a.** A particular place of relatively small and definite limits: *a holiday spot.* **b.** A place noted for a specified feature or activity: *a trouble spot; a favourite night spot.* **2.** A mark on a surface differing in colour from the surroundings and usually of round or irregular shape; especially, a stain or blot. **3.** A position; a location: *X marks the spot.* **4.** *Informal.* A situation, especially a difficult or embarrassing one; a predicament: *in a tight spot.* **5.** A brief amount of advertising time on a radio or television programme. **6.** An amount of time allocated to a performer or entertainer. **7.** A personal defect or blemish, often affecting one's reputation. **8.** A pimple or similar blemish on the skin. **9.** *Chiefly British Informal.* A small amount; a bit: *a spot of tea.* **10.** *Informal.* A spotlight. **11.** A coloured dot or other shape, such as a heart, on a playing card, domino, or dice used to distinguish suit, value, or the like. **12.** In billiards: **a.** The white ball that is distinguished by a black spot. Also called "spot ball". **b.** The player using this ball. **—change (one's) spots.** To change (one's) character, usually for the better. Usually used in the negative. **—knock spots off.** *British Informal.* To defeat or beat with ease. **—on the spot. 1.** Without delay; at once. **2.** At the scene of action. **3.** In a responsible or delicate position. **4.** Without moving forwards: *running on the spot.*
~*v.* **spotted, spotting, spots.** —*tr.* **1.** To cause a spot or spots to appear upon; especially: **a.** To soil with spots. **b.** To decorate with spots; dot. **2.** To place in a particular location; situate precisely. **3.** To locate or identify; discern. —*intr.* **1.** To become marked or be susceptible to marking with spots. **2.** To cause a discoloration; make a stain. **3.** *British.* To fall in intermittent droplets: *It's spotting with rain.*
~*adj.* **1.** Paid for or delivered immediately: *spot sales.* **2.** Paid immediately on delivery: *spot cash.* [Middle English *spot(te),* perhaps of Low German origin; akin to Middle Dutch *spotte,* from Common Germanic *sput-* (unattested).] **—spot·ta·ble** *adj.*

spot check *n.* A random or immediate inspection or investigation.

spot-check (spót-chék) *tr.v.* **-checked, -checking, -checks.** To subject to a spot check; inspect at random.

spot height *n.* A precise point, the height of which above sea level has been accurately measured and indicated on a map.

spot·less (spót-ləss, -liss) *adj.* **1.** Perfectly clean. **2.** Free from blemish; impeccable. **—spot·less·ly** *adv.* **—spot·less·ness** *n.*

spot·light (spót-līt) *n.* **1.** A strong beam of light that illuminates only a small area, used especially to centre attention on a stage actor. **2.** A lamp that produces such a light. Also called "spot". **3.** Public notoriety or prominence. **4.** Any artificial source of light with a strongly focussed beam, as on a motor vehicle.
~*tr.v.* **-lighted** or **-lit** (-lit), **-lighting, -lights. 1.** To illuminate with a spotlight. **2.** To focus attention on.

spot-on (spót-ón) *adj. Informal.* Exactly right or accurate.

spot·ted (spóttid) *adj.* **1.** Marked or stained with spots. **2.** Patterned with spots. **3.** Blemished; stained.

spotted dick *n. British.* A steamed or boiled suet pudding containing currants or other dried fruit. Also called "spotted dog". [From its resemblance to a Dalmatian *(spotted dog* or *dick).*]

spotted fever *n.* An epidemic form of **cerebrospinal meningitis** *(see).*

spotted hyena *n.* An African hyena, *Crocuta crocuta,* with a spotted coat. Also called "laughing hyena".

spot·ter (spóttər) *n.* One that looks for, locates, and usually reports something; especially: **1.** One that watches for enemy aircraft. **2.** One that locates enemy targets, especially in order to direct artillery fire. **3.** One who looks for and notes the type or number of trains, aircraft, and the like, as a hobby: *a train spotter.*

spot·ty (spótti) *adj.* **-tier, -tiest. 1.** Having or marked with spots; spotted. **2.** *British Informal.* Having many pimples. **3.** Lacking consistency of quality; uneven. **—spot·ti·ly** *adv.* **—spot·ti·ness** *n.*

spot-weld (spót-wéld, -weld) *tr.v.* **-welded, -welding, -welds.** To join (two metal sheets, wires, or the like) by one or more small welds created by electrically generated heat and pressure.
~*n.* A weld so formed.

spous·al (spów-z'l, -s'l) *adj. Archaic.* Of or pertaining to marriage.
~*n. Usually plural. Archaic.* Marriage. [Variant of ESPOUSAL.]

spouse (spowss, spowz) *n.* One's marriage partner; a husband or wife.
~*tr.v.* **spoused, spousing, spouses.** *Archaic.* To marry; wed. [Middle English *sp(o)use,* from Old French *(e)spous,* from Latin *spōnsus,* betrothed (person), betrothal, from *spondēre,* to make a solemn pledge, betroth.]

spout (spowt) *v.* **spouted, spouting, spouts.** —*intr.* **1.** To gush forth in a rapid stream or in spurts. Often used with *out.* **2.** To discharge a liquid or other substance continuously or in spurts. **3.** *Informal.* To speak volubly and tediously. —*tr.* **1.** To cause to flow or spurt out. **2.** *Informal.* To utter pompously and volubly.
~*n.* **1.** A tube, mouth, funnel, or pipe through which liquid or material such as grain is released or discharged, such as the mouth of a teapot or roof drainpipe. **2.** A continuous stream of liquid or material such as grain. **—up the spout.** *Slang.* **1.** Ruined, lost, or hopeless. **2.** *British.* Pregnant. [Middle English *spouten,* perhaps from Middle Dutch *spouten, spoiten.*] **—spout·er** *n.*

spp. species (plural).

S.P.Q.R. The Senate and the People of Rome. [Latin *Senatus Populusque Romanus*].

S.P.R. Society for Psychical Research.

Sprach·ge·fühl (shpraákh-gə-fewl, -fül) *n. German.* A feeling for language; an ear for the idiomatically correct or appropriate. [Literally, "language feeling".]

sprag (sprag) *n.* **1. a.** A piece of wood or metal wedged beneath a wheel or between spokes to keep a vehicle from rolling down a slope. **b.** A pointed stake lowered at an angle into the ground from a vehicle to prevent movement. **2.** A prop to support a mine roof.

sprain (sprayn) *n.* **1.** A painful wrenching or laceration of the ligaments of a joint. **2.** The condition resulting from such an injury.
~*tr.v.* **sprained, spraining, sprains.** To cause a sprain in (a joint). [17th century : perhaps from Old French *espraindre,* to squeeze out, strain, from Vulgar Latin *expremere* (unattested), variant of Latin *exprimere,* to press out : *ex-,* out + *premere,* to press.]

spraints (spraynts) *pl.n.* Otters' dung.

sprang. Past tense of **spring.**

sprat (sprat) *n.* **1.** A small marine food fish, *Clupea sprattus,* of northeastern Atlantic waters. Also called "brisling". **2.** Broadly, any of various similar fish, such as a young herring. [Earlier *sprot,* Middle English *sprotte,* Old English *sprott,* akin to Middle Low German or Middle Dutch *sprot*†.]

sprawl (sprawl) *v.* **sprawled, sprawling, sprawls.** —*intr.* **1.** To sit or lie with the body and limbs spread out awkwardly. Often used with *out.* **2.** To spread out in a straggling or disordered fashion, as handwriting, a town, or a crowd might. —*tr.* To spread out in a straggling or disordered fashion. Usually used in the passive.
~*n.* **1.** A sprawling position or posture. **2.** Haphazard growth or extension outwards, especially that resulting from new housing on the outskirts of a town: *urban sprawl.* [Middle English *sprewlen, spraulen,* Old English *sprēawlian.*] **—sprawl·er** *n.*

spray[1] (spray) *n.* **1. a.** Water or other liquid moving in a mass of dispersed droplets, as from a wave. **b.** Something resembling this, such as a cluster of small flying objects. **2.** A fine jet of liquid discharged from an atomiser or a pressurised container. **3.** Such a container. **4.** Any of numerous commercial products, including paints, cosmetics, and insecticides, dispensed in this way.
~*v.* **sprayed, spraying, sprays.** —*tr.* **1.** To disperse (a liquid) in a mass or jet of droplets. **2.** To apply (a liquid) in the form of a spray. **3.** To apply a spray to (a surface). **4.** To shoot out small projectiles at: *sprayed them with machine-gun fire.* —*intr.* **1.** To discharge sprays of liquid. **2.** To move in the form of a spray. [Originally, "to sprinkle", from Middle Dutch *spraeyen*†.] **—spray·er** *n.*

spray[2] *n.* **1.** A small branch bearing buds, flowers, or berries. **2.** An ornament or other object resembling this in shape or design. [Middle English, Old English *spræg*† (unattested).]

spray-dry (spráy-drī) *tr.v.* **-dried, -drying, -dreis.** To dehydrate (milk, for example) into a powder form by spraying into hot air.

spray gun *n.* A gunlike device that forces liquid through a nozzle so that it emerges as a spray.

spray-on (spráy-on) *adj.* Applied as a spray from a pressurised container: *spray-on deodorant.*

spread (spred) *v.* **spread, spreading, spreads.** —*tr.* **1.** To broaden or open to a fuller extent or width; stretch. Often used with *out: He spread out the map; spread sail.* **2.** To make wider the gap between; move farther apart. **3. a.** To distribute over a surface in a layer; apply: *spread jam.* **b.** To cover with a thin layer. **4.** To extend over a considerable area or period of time; distribute widely. **5.** To cause to become widely known; disseminate. **6. a.** To prepare (a table) for eating; set. **b.** To arrange (food or a meal) on a table. —*intr.* **1.** To be extended or enlarged. **2.** To become distributed or widely dispersed; increase in range of occurrence. **3.** To become known over a wider area; be disseminated. **4.** To become distributed in a thin layer: *margarine spreads easily.* **5.** To become separated; be forced farther apart. **6.** To be displayed or revealed. Often used with *out: The valley spread out before us.* **—spread (oneself).** *British Informal.* To expend money or energy lavishly to impress others or produce an effect. Often used with *around* or *about.*
~*n.* **1. a.** The act of spreading; extension; dispersion. **b.** Diffusion; dissemination, as of news. **2.** *Chiefly U.S.* **a.** An open area of land; an expanse. **b.** A ranch or farm. **3.** The extent or limit to which something is or can be spread over time or space; the range. **4.** A cloth covering for a bed, table, or the like. **5.** *Informal.* An abundant meal laid out on a table. **6.** A pastelike food to be spread on bread or biscuits. **7. a.** The facing pages of a book, magazine, or newspaper with related matter extending across the fold. **b.** An article or advertisement running across two or more columns. **8.** The increase in size of the hips and waist: *middle-age spread.* **9.** A gap between two points. **10.** A difference, as between a buying and selling price. **11.** The wingspan of an aircraft.
~*adj.* **1.** Extended; expanded. **2.** Flat and shallow. Said of a gem. **3.** *Phonetics.* **a.** Extended to form a long, narrow opening. Said of the lips. **b.** Articulated with spread lips. Said of a vowel. [Middle English *spred(d)en,* Old English *sprǣdan* (only in compounds, such as *tō-sprǣdan*).] **—spread·a·ble** *adj.*

spread eagle *n.* **1.** A figure of an eagle with wings and legs spread, used as an emblem. **2.** A posture or design resembling this.

spread-ea·gle (spréd-éeg'l, spred- || -eeg'l) *adj.* Also **spread-eagled** (-d). With the arms and legs stretched out.
~*v.* **spread-eagled, -gling, -gles.** —*tr.* **1.** To place in a spread-eagle position, especially as a means of punishment. **2.** To defeat or knock out. —*intr.* To perform a spread eagle in ice skating.

spread·er (spréddər) *n.* One that spreads; specifically: **1.** An implement for scattering fertiliser or seed. **2.** A device, such as a bar, for keeping wires or stays apart.

PRONUNCIATION KEY

a, **trap**; aa, **father**; ai, **fair**;
ar, **star**; aw, **lawn**; ay, **play**;
b, bb, **stab**; **rubber**;
ch, **church**; ck, **ticket**;
d, dd, **dead**; **ladder**; e, **dress**;
ee, **bee**; er, **defer**; ew, **few**;
ewr, **pure**; ə, **about**;
ər, **letter**; f, ff, **fife**; **differ**;
g, gg, **giggle**; h, **hat**; i, **kit**;
ī, **price**; īr, **fire**; j, **judge**;
k, **kick**; l, ll, **let**; 'l, **needle**;
m, mm, **man**; n, nn, **no**;
'n, **sudden**; ng, **thing**; o, **lot**;
ō, **no**; ŏŏ, **foot**; ōō, **shoe**;
oor, **poor**; ow, **cow**;
owr, **hour**; oy, **boy**;
p, pp, **pepper**; r, rr, **red**;
s, ss, **sauce**; sh, **ship**;
t, tt, **totter**; th, **thick**; th, **this**;
smooth; u, **cut**; ur, **turn**;
v, vv, **valve**; w, **wet**; y, **yes**;
z, zz, **zebra**; zh, **vision**;
pleasure

IN FOREIGN WORDS:

aN, oN, **Saint-Saëns**;
hl, **Llanelli**; **Hluhluwe**;
kh, **loch**; **lough**; **Khaled**

STRESS MARK:

ín-sīt, insight; in-sīt, incite

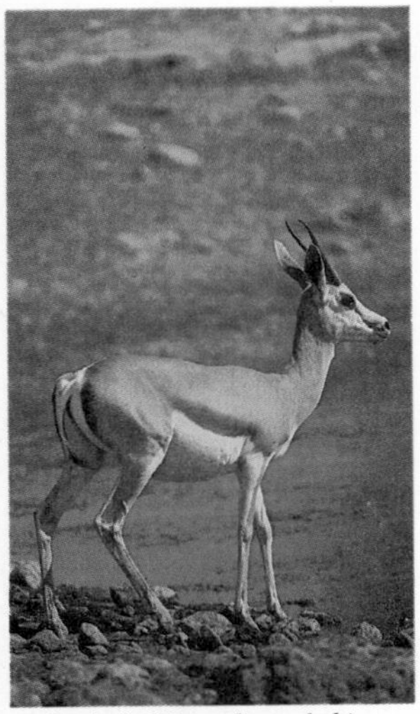

springbok *When alarmed, this southern African antelope flees in bounding leaps up to 3 metres high (10 feet) – a habit from which it gets its name. The national emblem of South Africa, the springbok once roamed the region in herds of up to a million animals; but it is now rare.*

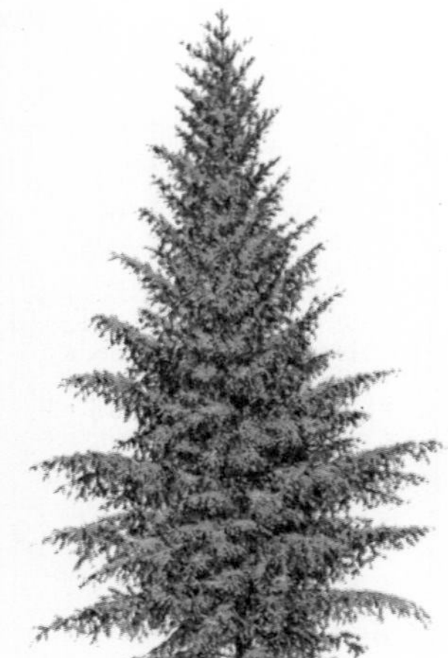

spruce *This group of fast-growing conifers is widely cultivated commercially for making paper.*

spread-on-impact bullet *n.* A **dum-dum bullet** *(see).*

Sprech·ge·sang (shprĕkh-gə-zang) *n. German.* A technique of vocal production halfway between speaking and singing. [Literally, "speaking song".] **—Sprech·ge·sing·er** (-zing-ger) *n.*

spree (spree) *n.* **1.** A gay, lively outing. **2.** A period or bout of unrestrained overindulgence in some activity: *a buying spree.* [19th century : earlier *spray,* perhaps alteration of Scottish *spreath,* cattle taken as booty, raid, plunder, from Gaelic *sprēidh,* from Latin *praeda,* spoil, booty.]

sprig (sprig) *n.* **1. a.** A small shoot or twig together with its leaves and flowers. **b.** An ornament or motif resembling this. **2.** A small brad without a head. **3.** *Informal.* A young person.
~tr.v. **sprigged, sprigging, sprigs. 1.** To decorate with a design of sprigs. **2.** To remove a sprig or sprigs from (a bush or tree). **3.** To fasten with a small headless brad. [Middle English *sprigg(e)*†.] **—sprig·ger** *n.*

sprigged (sprigd) *adj.* Designating a fabric or material decorated with a design of sprigs: *sprigged muslin.*

spright·ly (sprīt-li) *adj.* **-lier, -liest.** Buoyant or animated; full of life. See Synonyms at **nimble.**
~adv. Archaic. With briskness; gaily. [*Spright,* variant of SPRITE + -LY.] **—spright·li·ness** *n.*

spring (spring) *v.* **sprang** (sprang) or **sprung** (sprung), **sprung, springing, springs.** *—intr.* **1.** To move upwards, forwards, or in a specified manner in a single quick motion; leap: *He sprang over the fence.* **2.** To appear or emerge suddenly. Often used with *up.* **3.** To move suddenly on or as if on a spring: *The door sprang shut.* **4.** To arise from a source; develop; issue. Often used with *from.* **5.** To become warped, bent, or cracked. Used of wood. **6.** To move out of place; come loose, as a machine part may. **7.** To explode. Used of a mine. *—tr.* **1.** To cause to leap, dart, or come forth suddenly. **2.** To jump over; vault. **3.** To actuate or cause to move on or as if on a spring: *spring a bolt.* **4.** To explode (a mine). **5.** To cause to warp, bend, or crack, as by force. **6.** To develop or present unexpectedly: *spring a surprise; sprang a leak.* **7.** To provide with a spring or springs. **8.** *Slang.* To cause to escape from prison.
~n. **1.** An elastic device, such as a coil of wire, that regains its original shape after being compressed or extended. **2.** An actuating force or factor; a motive. **3. a.** The quality of elasticity; resilience. **b.** Energy; healthy bounce: *a spring in one's step.* **4.** The act or an instance of springing; especially, a jump or leap. **5.** A flock of teal. **6.** The return to normal shape after removal of stress; recoil. **7.** A natural fountain or flow of water from the earth's surface. **8.** A source, origin, or beginning. **9. a.** The season of the year, occurring between winter and summer, during which the weather becomes warmer and plants revive, extending from the vernal equinox to the summer solstice, and popularly considered to comprise March, April, and May in the Northern Hemisphere, and September, October, and November in the Southern Hemisphere. **b.** Any time of growth or youth. **10.** *Architecture.* The point where an arch or vault rises up from its support. Also called "springing". **11.** A warping, bending, or cracking, such as that caused by excessive force.
~adj. **1.** Of or acting like a spring. **2.** Having or supported by springs. **3.** Coming from a spring: *spring water.* **4.** Of, occurring in, or characteristic of the season of spring. **5.** Sown in the spring. Said of a crop. [Spring, sprang, sprung; Middle English *springen, sprang, sprungen,* Old English *springan, sprang* (past singular), *sprungen.*]

spring balance *n.* A device for weighing relatively small objects, consisting of a coiled spring, to the free end of which the object to be weighed is attached so that the spring extends. The amount of the extension is read off on a scale calibrated in units of weight.

spring·board (spríng-bawrd || -bōrd) *n.* **1.** A flexible board mounted on a fulcrum and having one end secured, used by gymnasts to gain momentum. **2.** A **diving board** *(see).* **3.** Anything that lends impetus to or helps to launch an activity, career, or the like.

spring·bok (spríng-bok) *n., pl.* **-boks** or collectively (for sense 1) **springbok.** Also **spring·buck** (-buk) (for sense 1) *pl.* **-bucks** or collectively **springbuck. 1.** A small brown and white antelope, *Antidorcas marsupialis,* of southern Africa, able to leap high into the air. **2.** *Capital* **S.** A member of a South African international sports team, especially the Rugby Union team. [Afrikaans : *spring,* to SPRING, from Middle Dutch *springen* + *bok,* male deer, BUCK.]

spring chicken *n.* **1.** A young chicken, slightly older than a poussin, weighing about 2½ pounds. **2.** *Informal.* A young or naive person. Usually used in the negative: *At her age, she's no spring chicken.*

spring-clean (spríng-klēen) *v.* **-cleaned, -cleaning, -cleans.** *—tr.* To clean (a house, for example) thoroughly and comprehensively, especially at the end of the winter. *—intr.* To spring-clean a room or house. **—spring-clean** *n.*

springe (sprinj) *n.* A device for snaring small game, made by attaching a noose to a branch under tension.
~v. **springed, springeing** or **springing, springes.** *—tr.* To trap with a springe; ensnare. *—intr.* To prepare a springe. [Middle English *sprenge, springe,* Old English *sprencg* (unattested).]

spring·er (spríng-ər) *n.* **1.** One that springs. **2.** A springer spaniel. **3.** A cow about to give birth. **4.** *Architecture.* **a.** The point where an arch is supported by a wall or column. **b.** The bottom stone of an arch resting on this point.

springer spaniel *n.* A dog of either of two breeds, the English and the Welsh springer spaniels, having drooping ears and a silky brown and white coat, and originally used for flushing game.

spring fever *n.* The feelings of languor, rejuvenation, or yearning that may affect people at the advent of spring.

Springfield rifle *n.* A magazine-fed, breech-loading, bolt-action .30-calibre rifle. Also called "Springfield". [First made at the former U.S. Armoury at *Springfield,* Massachusetts.]

spring-form mould (spríng-fawrm) *n.* A round baking tin with a high rim that can be expanded and removed from the base by releasing a clip. Also called "spring form".

spring greens *pl.n.* Young green cabbages picked before their hearts have developed.

spring·haas (spríng-haass) *n.* A nocturnal African rodent, *Pedetes capensis,* resembling a small kangaroo. [Afrikaans, "spring hare".]

spring·halt (spríng-hawlt || -holt) *n.* A **stringhalt** *(see).* [Alteration of STRINGHALT.]

spring·head (spríng-hed) *n.* A source, as of a stream.

spring·house (spríng-howss) *n. Chiefly U.S.* A small room or building constructed over a spring and used to keep food cool.

spring·ing (spríng-ing) *n. Architecture.* A **spring** *(see).*

spring·let (spríng-lət, -lit) *n.* A small spring of water; a rill.

spring-load·ed (spríng-lōdid) *adj.* Secured or returned to position by means of a spring.

spring lock *n.* A lock in which the bolt shoots automatically by means of a spring.

spring onion *n. Chiefly British.* A small, immature onion with a small bulb and long green leaves, usually eaten raw in salads.

spring roll *n. Chiefly British.* A Chinese dish consisting of a savoury filling rolled in thin egg pastry and deep fried. Also *U.S.* "egg roll".

spring·tail (spríng-tayl) *n.* Any of various small wingless insects of the order Collembola, having abdominal appendages that act as springs to catapult them through the air.

spring tide *n.* **1.** The tide generally having the greatest rise and fall, occurring at or shortly after the new moon and full moon of each month, when the Sun, Moon, and Earth are approximately aligned. Compare **neap tide. 2.** Any flood or rush, as of emotion.

spring·time (spríng-tīm) *n.* **1.** The season of spring. Also called "springtide". **2.** The earliest or most enthusiastic period.

spring·wood (spríng-wŏŏd) *n.* Young, usually soft wood that lies directly beneath the bark and develops in early spring. Compare **summerwood.**

spring·y (spríng-i) *adj.* **-ier, -iest.** Resilient; elastic. **—spring·i·ly** *adv.* **—spring·i·ness** *n.*

sprin·kle (spríngk'l) *v.* **-kled, -kling, -kles.** *—tr.* **1.** To scatter or release (water or sand, for example) in drops or small amounts. **2.** To scatter drops or small amounts upon. **3.** To distribute or intersperse in random fashion. *—intr.* **1.** To scatter small drops or particles of something. **2.** To fall or rain in small or infrequent drops.
~n. **1.** The act or an instance of sprinkling. **2.** A light, sparse rainfall. **3.** A small amount; a sprinkling. [Middle English *sprenklen,* probably from Middle Dutch *sprenkelen.*]

sprin·kler (spríngklər) *n.* One that sprinkles; specifically: **1.** An outlet on a sprinkler system. **2.** A device, attached to a hose or watering can, for sprinkling water onto grass and other plants.

sprinkler system *n.* A fire-extinguishing system consisting of a network of water pipes equipped to release water, usually automatically, at temperatures above a predetermined limit.

sprin·kling (spríngkling) *n.* A small amount or quantity, especially when tossed or sparsely distributed.

sprint (sprint) *n.* **1.** A short race run, swum, or the like at top speed. **2.** A short burst of great activity.
~v. **sprinted, sprinting, sprints.** *—intr.* To run at top speed. *—tr.* To cover (a specified distance) by sprinting. [Of Scandinavian origin, akin to Swedish dialectal *sprinta,* to jump, akin to Old Norse *spretta,* from Germanic *sprintan* (unattested).] **—sprint·er** *n.*

sprit (sprit) *n.* **1.** A pole extending diagonally across a fore-and-aft sail from the lower part of the mast to the peak of the sail. **2.** A **bowsprit** *(see).* [Middle English *spret(te), spryt(t),* Old English *sprēot,* pole.]

sprite (sprīt) *n.* **1.** A small or elusive supernatural being; an elf or pixie. **2.** Someone resembling a sprite in smallness or delicacy. [Middle English *spr(e)it,* from Old French *esp(i)rit,* from Latin *spīritus,* SPIRIT.]

sprit·sail (sprít-s'l, -sayl) *n.* A sail extended by a sprit.

sprock·et (sprókkit) *n.* **1.** A wheel rimmed with toothlike projections to engage the links of a chain in a drive system. Also called "sprocket wheel". **2.** Any one of these projections. **3.** A cylinder with a toothed rim that engages in the perforations in a film to pull it through a camera or projector. [16th century : origin obscure.]

sprog (sprog) *n. British Slang.* **1.** A small child. **2.** A military recruit. [20th century : origin obscure.]

sprout (sprowt) *v.* **sprouted, sprouting, sprouts.** *—intr.* **1.** To begin to grow; give off shoots or buds. **2.** To grow or develop quickly. Often used with *up.* *—tr.* To cause to grow or sprout.
~n. **1.** A young plant growth, such as a bud or shoot. **2.** Something resembling or suggestive of a sprout. **3.** *Plural.* A vegetable, **Brussels sprouts** *(see).* **4.** *Informal.* A young person. [Middle English *spruten,* Old English *sprūtan.*]

sprouting broccoli *n.* See **broccoli.**

spruce¹ (sprŏŏss || sprewss) *n.* **1.** Any of various coniferous evergreen trees of the genus *Picea,* such as the **Norway spruce** *(see),* having needle-like foliage, drooping cones, and soft wood often used for paper pulp. **2.** Any of various similar or related trees. **3.** The wood of any of these trees. [Short for *Spruce fir,* "Prussian fir", from Middle English *Spruce,* alteration of *Pruce,* from Old French, from Medieval Latin *Prussia,* PRUSSIA.]

spruce² *adj.* **sprucer, sprucest.** Neat or dapper in appearance. ∼*v.* **spruced, sprucing, spruces.** —*tr.* To make spruce; dress neatly. Usually used with *up.* —*intr.* To make oneself spruce. Used with *up.* [Perhaps from *Spruce,* Prussia, Prussian leather (from the fineness of the leather).] **—spruce·ly** *adv.* **—spruce·ness** *n.*

spruce beer *n.* A slightly fermented beverage made with an extract of spruce needles and twigs with sugar or treacle.

spruce pine *n.* A tree, the **black spruce** *(see).*

sprue¹ (sproo || sprew) *n.* A chronic, chiefly tropical disease characterised by diarrhoea, emaciation, and anaemia, due to deficient absorption of food from the small intestine. [Dutch *spruw,* from Middle Dutch *sprouwe,* akin to Middle Low German *sprūwe*†.]

sprue² *n.* **1.** A channel leading to or from a mould. **2.** Metal or plastic that solidifies in a sprue. [19th century : origin obscure.]

spruik (sprŏŏk) *intr.v. Australian Slang.* To address prospective customers, for example, fluently and enticingly. Used especially of salesmen and showmen. [20th century : perhaps akin to Dutch *spreken,* to speak.] **—spruik·er** *n.*

sprung. Past participle and alternative past tense of **spring.** ∼*adj.* Supported by springs: *a sprung mattress.*

sprung rhythm *n.* A forcefully accented verse rhythm in which each foot has a stressed syllable followed by an irregular number of unstressed syllables. [Coined by Gerard Manley HOPKINS.]

spry (sprī) *adj.* **sprier** or **spryer, spriest** or **spryest.** Active, vigorous, and healthy: *a spry octogenarian.* See Synonyms at **nimble.** [18th century (dialect and U.S.) : perhaps from Scandinavian, akin to Swedish dialectal *sprygg,* active.] **—spry·ly** *adv.* **—spry·ness** *n.*

spud (spud) *n.* **1.** A sharp tool resembling a spade for rooting or digging out weeds. **2.** *Informal.* A potato. ∼*tr.v.* **spudded, spudding, spuds. 1.** To remove (weeds, for example) with a spud. **2.** To begin drilling (an oil well). [Middle English *spudde*†, short knife.]

spud-bash·ing (spúd-bashing) *n. British Military Slang.* Peeling potatoes, especially as a chore or punishment.

spue. *Archaic.* Variant of **spew.**

spume (spewm) *n.* Foam or froth, especially on the sea. ∼*intr.v.* **spumed, spuming, spumes.** To froth or foam. [Middle English, from Old French *(e)spume,* from Latin *spūma.*] **—spu·mous, spum·y** *adj.*

spu·mo·ne, spu·mo·ni (spoo-mṓ-ni, spoo-) *n., pl.* **-ni** (-nee). An Italian ice cream with layers of different colours or flavours, containing candied fruit or nuts. [Italian, from *spuma,* foam, from Latin *spūma,* SPUME.]

spun. Past tense and past participle of **spin.**

spun glass *n.* **1. Glass fibre** *(see).* **2.** Fine blown glass having delicate, often spiral threading or filigree.

spunk (spungk) *n.* **1.** Touchwood or other tinder. **2.** *Informal.* Spirit; pluck. **3.** *British Vulgar Slang.* Semen. [16th century.]

spunk·y (spúngki) *adj.* **-ier, -iest.** *Informal.* Spirited. **—spunk·i·ly** *adv.* **—spunk·i·ness** *n.*

spun protein *n.* Textured vegetable protein *(see).*

spun silk *n.* A yarn made from short-fibred silk and silk waste, often mixed with cotton.

spun sugar *n. U.S.* **Candy floss** *(see).*

spun yarn *n.* A lightweight line made of several rope yarns loosely wound together, used for seizings on board ship.

spur (spur) *n.* **1.** Either of a pair of spikes or spiked wheels attached to a rider's heels and used to urge the horse forward. **2.** An incentive or goad; a stimulus. **3.** A spurlike attachment or projection, such as: **a.** A spinelike projection on the leg of some birds. **b.** A climbing iron; a crampon. **c.** A gaff attached to the leg of a gamecock. **d.** A short or stunted branch of a tree. **4.** A lateral ridge projecting from a mountain or mountain range. **5.** An oblique reinforcing prop or stay of timber or masonry. **6.** A branch railway line. Also called "spur track". **7.** *Botany.* A tubular extension of the corolla or calyx of a flower, as in a larkspur. **—on the spur of the moment.** On impulse or without preparation. **—win (one's) spurs.** To gain distinction, especially for the first time. ∼*v.* **spurred, spurring, spurs.** —*tr.* **1.** To urge (a horse) on by the use of spurs. **2.** To incite; prompt; stimulate. Often used with *on.* **3.** To put spurs on. —*intr.* To ride quickly, as by spurring a horse. [Middle English *spore, spure,* Old English *spora, spura.*]

spurge (spurj) *n.* Any of various plants of the genus *Euphorbia,* characteristically having milky juice and small flowers that in some species are surrounded by showy bracts. [Middle English, from Old French *(e)spurge,* "purge" (certain species were formerly used as purgatives), from *espurgier,* to purge, from Latin *expurgāre* : *ex-,* away + *purgāre,* to purge, purify.]

spur gear *n.* A gear with teeth radially arrayed on the rim parallel to its axis. Also called "spur wheel".

spurge laurel *n.* A low-growing shrub, *Daphne laureola,* native to southern Europe but widely cultivated for ornament, having glossy evergreen leaves and small yellowish-green flowers.

spu·ri·ous (spéwr-i-əss) *adj.* **1.** Lacking authenticity or validity, especially in essence or origin; not genuine; counterfeit; false. **2.** *Rare.* Illegitimate; bastard. **3.** *Botany.* Similar in appearance but unlike in structure or function. Said of plant parts that superficially resemble other parts. [Late Latin *spurius,* false, from Latin, illegitimate, perhaps from Etruscan; akin to *spurcus,* dirty, impure.] **—spu·ri·ous·ly** *adv.* **—spu·ri·ous·ness** *n.*

spurn (spurn) *v.* **spurned, spurning, spurns.** —*tr.* **1.** To reject or refuse disdainfully; scorn. **2.** *Archaic.* **a.** To kick at disdainfully. **b.** To tread on; trample. —*intr. Archaic.* To refuse something contemptuously. —See Synonyms at **refuse.** ∼*n.* **1.** A contemptuous rejection. **2.** *Archaic.* A kick or shove. [Middle English *spurnen, spornen,* Old English *spurnan, spornan.*] **—spurn·er** *n.*

spur-of-the-mo·ment (spúr-əv-thə-mṓmənt) *adj.* Made or occurring without planning or forethought.

spurred (spurd) *adj.* **1.** Wearing spurs. **2.** *Biology.* Having a spur or spurs: *spurred flowers.*

spur·rey (spúrri) *n., pl.* **-reys.** Also **spur·ry** *pl.* **-ies.** Any of several weedy, low-growing plants of the genera *Spergula* or *Spergularia;* especially, *Spergula arvensis,* native to Europe, having whorled leaves and small white flowers. [Dutch *spurrie,* from Middle Dutch *sporie, speurie,* probably from Medieval Latin *spergula.*]

spur·ri·er (spúrri-ər) *n.* A maker of spurs. [Middle English *sporior,* from *spore,* SPUR.]

spurt (spurt) *n.* Also **spirt** (for sense 1). **1.** A sudden and forcible gush or outburst, as of water or emotion. **2.** Any sudden outbreak or short burst of energy or activity. ∼*v.* **spurted, spurting, spurts.** Also **spirt, spirted, spirting, spirts** (for sense 1). —*intr.* **1.** To flow suddenly; gush. Often used with *out.* **2.** To make a short burst of effort. —*tr.* To force out in a burst; squirt. [Earlier *spirt, sprit,* to sprout, Middle English *sprutten,* Old English *spryttan.*]

spur track *n.* A railway **spur** *(see).*

sput·nik (spŏŏt-nik, spút-) *n.* Any of the artificial Earth satellites launched by the U.S.S.R., especially *Sputnik 1,* the first artificial satellite to orbit the Earth, launched October 4, 1957. [Russian *sputnik (zemlyi),* "fellow traveller (of Earth)" : *s-,* for *so,* with + *put',* path, way + *-nik,* agent noun suffix.]

sput·ter (spúttər) *v.* **-tered, -tering, -ters.** —*intr.* **1.** To throw out small particles in short bursts, often with spitting sounds. **2.** To make sporadic spitting sounds. **3.** To speak in a hasty or confused fashion; stammer. **4.** *Physics.* To cause the atoms of a solid to be removed from its surface by bombardment with ions in a discharge tube. —*tr.* **1.** To throw out (food particles, for example) in short bursts, often with spitting sounds. **2.** To utter in a hasty or confused fashion. **3.** *Physics.* **a.** To coat (a solid surface) with metal atoms by sputtering. **b.** To coat a solid surface by sputtering. ∼*n.* **1.** The act of sputtering. **2.** The sound of sputtering. **3.** The particles that are emitted during sputtering. **4.** Hasty or confused utterances. [Dutch *sputteren* (imitative).] **—sput·ter·er** *n.*

spu·tum (spéw-təm) *n., pl.* **-ta** (-tə). **1.** Saliva spat from the mouth. **2.** Matter, including saliva, mucus from the respiratory tract, and foreign material, coughed up and spat out. [Latin *spūtum,* from *spūtus,* past participle of *spuere,* to spit.]

spy (spī) *n., pl.* **spies. 1. a.** An agent employed by a state to obtain secretly intelligence relating to its potential or actual enemies at home or abroad. **b.** An agent employed by a business organisation to obtain secretly information relating to its competitors. **2.** One who secretly watches another or others. **3.** The act of watching covertly or secretly. ∼*v.* **spied, spying, spies.** —*tr.* **1. a.** To observe (a place or situation) carefully and secretly and gain information. Used with *out: spy out the land.* **b.** To discover by careful and secret observation. Used with *out.* **2.** To catch sight of; see. —*intr.* **1. a.** To observe secretly and closely. Often used with *on, into,* or *upon.* **b.** To engage in espionage. **2.** To investigate; pry. Used with *into: spying into their activities.* [Middle English *spie,* from Old French *espie,* from *espier,* to spy, watch, from Frankish *spehōn* (unattested).]

spy·glass (spī-glaass || -glass) *n.* A small telescope.

spy·hole (spī-hōl) *n.* A peephole; especially, one set in a front door to permit scrutiny of any callers.

sq. 1. sequence. **2.** square. **3.** the following.

Sq. 1. Squadron. **2.** Square. Used in street names.

Sqn. Ldr. squadron leader.

squab (skwob) *n.* **1.** A young, unfledged pigeon. **2.** A short, fat person. **3.** A soft cushion. **4.** A couch; a sofa. ∼*adj.* **1.** Newly hatched or unfledged. **2.** Short and fat; squat. [17th century : perhaps from Scandinavian, akin to Swedish dialectal *sqvabb*†, fat flesh, soft mass.] **—squab·by** *adj.*

squab·ble (skwóbb'l) *intr.v.* **-bled, -bling, -bles.** To engage in a minor but noisy quarrel; bicker. See Synonyms at **argue.** ∼*n.* A trivial but noisy quarrel. [Imitative, probably from Scandinavian; akin to Swedish dialectal *sqvabbel,* to quarrel (imitative).] **—squab·bler** *n.*

squad (skwod) *n.* **1.** A small group of persons working or acting together. **2.** *Military.* The smallest unit of personnel, used especially as a drill formation. **3.** A group of sportsmen from whom a team is selected. [French *escouade,* variant of *escadre,* from Italian *squadra,* SQUARE.]

squad car *n. U.S.* A **patrol car** *(see).*

squad·dy, squad·die (skwóddi) *n., pl.* **-dies.** *British Slang.* A soldier of the lowest rank. [Alteration (perhaps influenced by SQUAD) of *swaddy,* diminutive of dialect *swad;* soldier, bumpkin, perhaps from Scandinavian; compare Norwegian dialect *svadde,* fellow.]

squad·ron (skwóddrən) *n. Abbr.* **Sq. 1. a.** A group of naval vessels assigned to a particular task. **b.** A basic subdivision of a fleet. **2.** An armoured or cavalry unit consisting of two to four troops, a headquarters, and certain auxiliary units. **3.** An air force unit, subordinate to a wing and consisting of two or more flights. It is the

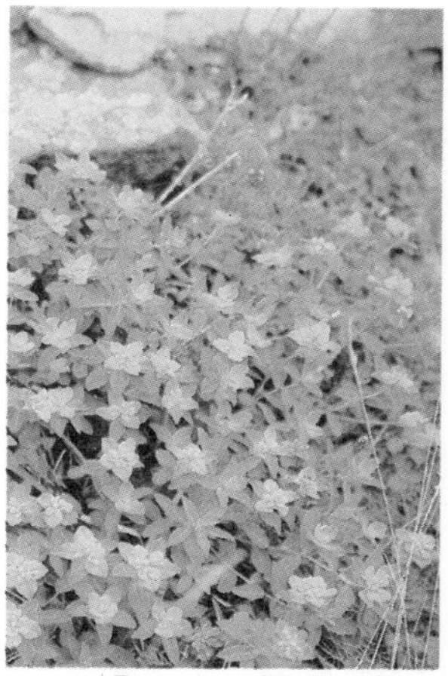

spurge *Petty spurge* (Euphorbia peplus) *has a milky-white juice in its stems and leaves which can make horses and cows ill or even kill them. The oily juice from the seeds was once used medicinally as a purgative; hence the name "spurge". In Africa, a member of the spurge family was used to make poison for the tips of arrows.*

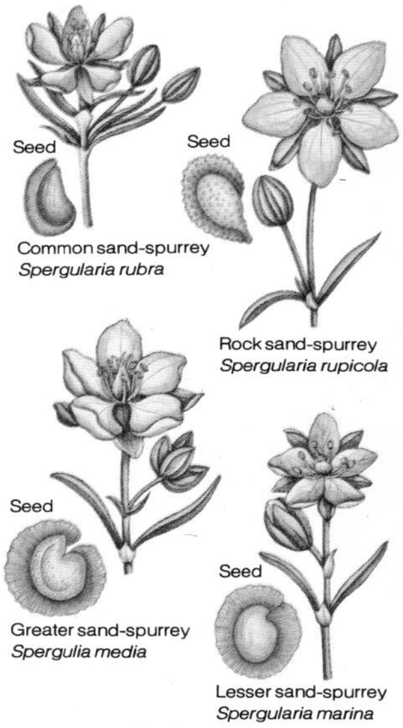
Seed
Seed
Common sand-spurrey
Spergularia rubra
Rock sand-spurrey
Spergularia rupicola
Seed
Seed
Greater sand-spurrey
Spergulia media
Lesser sand-spurrey
Spergularia marina

spurrey *A herb with thin, succulent leaves. It grows well in sandy or rocky soil.*

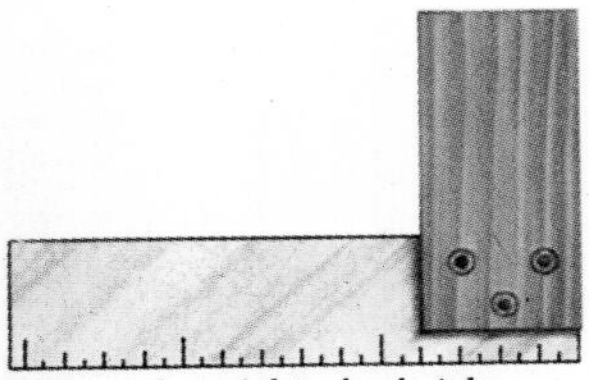

square *A straight-edged, right-angled instrument used by carpenters and metal workers to check that joints and surfaces are true.*

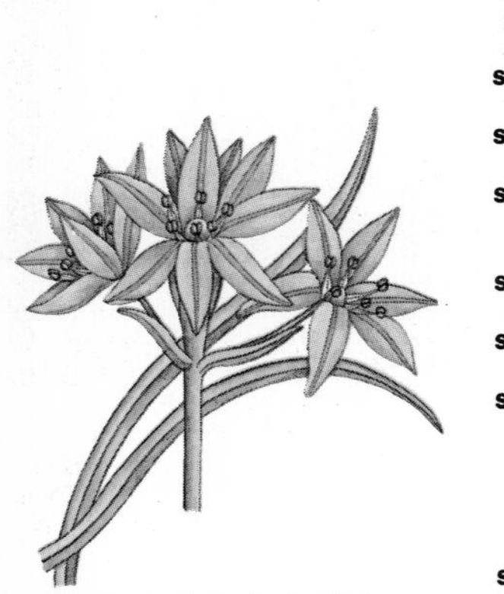

squill *A wiry little plant with long leaves that grows on cliffsides. This is the spring squill,* Scilla verna.

PRONUNCIATION KEY

a, trap; aa, father; ai, fair; ar, star; aw, lawn; ay, play; b, bb, stab; rubber; ch, church; ck, ticket; d, dd, dead; ladder; e, dress; ee, bee; er, defer; ew, few; ewr, pure; ə, about; ər, letter; f, ff, fife; differ; g, gg, giggle; h, hat; i, kit; ī, price; īr, fire; j, judge; k, kick; l, ll, let; 'l, needle; m, mm, man; n, nn, no; 'n, sudden; ng, thing; o, lot; ō, no; ŏŏ, foot; ōō, shoe; oor, poor; ow, cow; owr, hour; oy, boy; p, pp, pepper; r, rr, red; s, ss, sauce; sh, ship; t, tt, totter; th, thick; th, this; smooth; u, cut; ur, turn; v, vv, valve; w, wet; y, yes; z, zz, zebra; zh, vision; pleasure

IN FOREIGN WORDS:

aɴ, ᴏɴ, Saint-Saëns; hl, Llanelli; Hluhluwe; kh, loch; lough; Khaled

STRESS MARK:

ín-sīt, insight; in-sī́t, incite

basic tactical unit. [Italian *squadrone,* "square formation (of troops)", from *squadra,* SQUAD.]

squadron leader *n. Abbr.* **Sq. Ldr.** An officer of the Royal Air Force and certain other air forces ranking below a wing commander and above a flight lieutenant.

squa·lene (skwáy-leen) *n.* A natural unsaturated aliphatic hydrocarbon, $C_{30}H_{50}$, found in human sebum and other fatty deposits, that is an intermediate in the biosynthesis of cholesterol. [New Latin *Squalus,* genus of sharks (squalene is found in the liver oil of sharks), from Latin *squalus,* a sea fish + -ENE.]

squal·id (skwóllid) *adj.* **1.** Dirty or wretched in appearance. **2.** Morally repulsive; sordid. —See Synonyms at **dirty.** [Latin *squālidus,* from *squālēre,* to be filthy, from *squālus*†, scabby, filthy.] —**squa·lid·i·ty** (skwo-líddəti), **squal·id·ness** *n.* —**squa·lid·ly** *adv.*

squall (skwawl) *n.* **1. a.** A sudden, brief burst of wind, lasting longer than a gust, and often accompanied by rain. **b.** A sudden increase in wind speed by 8 metres per second (16 knots) or more to at least 11 metres per second (22 knots) and lasting for at least one minute. **2.** *Informal.* A disturbance or commotion. **3.** A loud yell.
~*intr.v.* **squalled, squalling, squalls.** To scream or cry harshly and loudly. [Probably from Scandinavian, akin to Swedish and Norwegian *skval,* splash, akin to Old Norse *skvala,* SQUEAL.] —**squall·er** *n.* —**squal·ly** *adj.*

squall line *n.* A zone of squalls and other violent changes in weather, marking the replacement of a warm air current by cold air.

squal·or (skwóllər) *n.* The state or quality of being squalid. [Latin, from *squālēre,* to be filthy. See **squalid.**]

squa·ma (skwáy-mə) *n., pl.* **-mae** (-mee). **1.** *Biology.* A scale or scalelike structure. **2.** A thin plate of bone. [Latin *squāma*†, scale.] —**squa·mate** (-mayt) *adj.*

squa·ma·tion (skway-máysh'n, skwə-) *n.* **1.** The condition of being scaly or of forming scales. **2.** An arrangement of scales, as on a fish.

squa·mo·sal (skwə-mṓ-z'l, -s'l) *n.* The squamous part of the temporal bone. [Latin *squāmōsus,* SQUAMOUS.] —**squa·mo·sal** *adj.*

squa·mous (skwáy-məss) *adj.* Also **squa·mose** (-mōz, -mōss). **1.** Covered with, formed of, or resembling scales; scaly. **2.** Of or designating epithelium consisting of flat, scalelike cells. **3.** Of or designating the portion of the temporal bone that forms part of the side of the cranium. [Latin *squāmōsus,* from *squāma*†, scale.] —**squa·mous·ly** *adv.* —**squa·mous·ness** *n.*

squa·mu·lose (skwáymew-lōz, -lōss) *adj.* Having or consisting of minute scales; minutely scaly. Said especially of plants. [New Latin *squāmula,* diminutive of Latin *squāma*†, scale.]

squan·der (skwóndər) *tr.v.* **-dered, -dering, -ders. 1.** To spend wastefully or extravagantly. **2.** *Archaic.* To scatter; disperse.
~*n. Rare.* Extravagant expenditure; prodigality. [16th century : origin obscure.] —**squan·der·er** *n.* —**squan·der·ing·ly** *adv.*

square (skwair) *n. Abbr.* **sq. 1.** A rectangle having four equal sides and four right angles. **2.** Any object, shape, arrangement, design, or the like having this form, such as: **a.** A square scarf. **b.** Any of the small square spaces constituting the surface of a chessboard. **c.** A military drill area within a barracks. **d.** An open, usually four-sided public area in a town, often having a central garden or grass and trees, sometimes including the surrounding buildings. **e.** The central area of a cricket field, used for the pitches or wickets. **f.** A **mortarboard** *(see).* **3. a.** A T-shaped or L-shaped instrument for drawing or testing right angles. **b.** A **try square** *(see).* **4.** The product of a number or quantity multiplied by itself. **5.** *Archaic.* A standard, rule, or pattern. **6.** *Informal.* One characterised by conventional or old-fashioned attitudes, appearance, or the like. —**back to square one.** *British.* Back to the very beginning, having made no progress. —**on the square. 1.** At right angles. **2.** Honestly and openly. —**out of square.** Not at a precise right angle.
~*adj.* **squarer, squarest.** *Abbr.* **sq. 1.** Having four equal sides and four right angles. **2.** Forming a right angle. **3. a.** Designating an area equal to a square whose edge is of a specified length: *a square foot.* **b.** Designating a square having edges of a specified length. Used after the noun: *a foot square.* **4.** Being at right angles to something, as: **a.** In cricket, at right angles to the wicket. **b.** Set at right angles to the mast and keel. Said of the yards of a square-rigged ship. **5.** Approximately square or rectangular in cross-section: *a square house.* **6.** Characterised by blocklike solidity or sturdiness. **7.** Honest; direct: *a square answer.* **8.** Just; equitable: *a square deal.* **9.** Orderly; neat. **10.** Paid-up; settled. **11.** *Sports.* Even; tied. **12.** *Informal.* Rigidly conventional or old-fashioned.
~*v.* **squared, squaring, squares.** —*tr.* **1.** To make square or rectangular in shape. **2.** To test for conformity to a desired plane, straight line, or right angle. **3.** To divide into squares. Often used with *off.* **4.** To bring into conformity or agreement. **5.** To set straight or at right angles: *square one's cap.* **6.** To pay or settle: *square a debt.* **7.** *Sports.* **a.** To even the score of; tie with. **b.** To level (the score, for example). **8.** To multiply (a number or quantity) by itself. **9.** *Informal.* **a.** To bribe. **b.** To secure the assent of or otherwise come to an arrangement with, usually corruptly. **c.** To arrange, usually corruptly; fix. —*intr.* **1.** To be at right angles. **2.** To agree or conform; balance. **3.** To settle a bill or debt. Often used with *up.* —**square away.** To square the yards of a sailing vessel. —**square up** or *chiefly U.S.* **off.** To assume a fighting stance. —**square up to.** To face or confront resolutely.
~*adv.* **1.** At right angles. **2.** In a square shape. **3.** *Informal.* Solidly. **4.** *Informal.* Directly; straight. **5.** *Informal.* In an honest manner; straightforwardly. [Middle English, from Old French *esquare,* from Vulgar Latin *exquadra* (unattested), from *exquadrāre* (unattested), to square : Latin *ex-* (intensive) + *quadrāre,* to square, from *quadrus,* a square.] —**square·ly** *adv.* —**square·ness** *n.* —**squar·er** *n.* —**squar·ish** *adj.*

square-bash·ing (skwáir-bashing) *n. British Military Slang.* Drill on a barrack square.

square bracket *n.* Either of two symbols, [or]. See **bracket.**

square dance *n.* **1.** A dance in which sets of four couples form squares. **2.** Any of various similar group dances of rural origin. —**square-dance** (skwáir-daanss || -danss) *intr.v.* —**square-danc·er** *n.*

square knot *n. U.S.* A **reef knot** *(see).*

square leg *n.* In cricket: **1.** A fielding position at right angles to the batsman, on the leg side. **2.** A player in this position.

square matrix *n. Mathematics.* A matrix in which there are equal numbers of rows and columns.

square meal *n.* A substantial, satisfying, and nourishing meal.

square measure *n.* A system of units used in measuring area.

square number *n.* A number that is the square of an integer: *1, 4, 9, and 16 are square numbers.*

square rig *n.* A sailing-ship rig with sails of rectangular cut set approximately at right angles to the keel line from horizontal yards. —**square-rigged** (skwáir-rígd) *adj.*

square-rig·ger (skwáir-ríggər) *n.* A square-rigged vessel.

square root *n.* A number that when squared gives a specified quantity: *4 is the square root of 16.*

square sail *n.* A four-sided sail bent to a yard set athwart the mast.

square wave *n.* A rectangular-shaped wave form that alternates between two fixed values for equal periods of time.

squar·rose (skwá-rōz, skwó-, -rōss) *adj.* **1.** *Biology.* Having rough or spreading hairs or scalelike projections. **2.** *Botany.* Spreading or curved backwards at the tip: *squarrose bracts.* [Latin *squarrōsus,* alteration (influenced by Latin *squāma,* scale) of *escharōsus* (unattested), scabby, from Greek *eskhara,* hearth, scab, SCAR.]

squash[1] (skwosh || *U.S. also* skwawsh) *v.* **squashed, squashing, squashes.** —*tr.* **1. a.** To beat, squeeze, or flatten to a compressed shape or a pulp; crush. **b.** To press or squeeze in tightly. Often used with *in* or *into.* **2.** To put down or suppress; quash. **3.** To silence (a person), as with crushing words. —*intr.* **1. a.** To be crushed or flattened. **b.** To squeeze in. Used with *in* or *into.* **2.** To move with a squelching sound.
~*n.* **1.** An act or sound of squashing or the state of being squashed. **2.** A crush; a crowded condition; a press. **3.** *Chiefly British.* A citrus-based soft drink. **4.** A racket game played with a soft rubber ball in a closed wall court between two players. [Alteration of QUASH.] —**squash·er** *n.*

squash[2] *n. U.S.* **1.** Any of various plants of the genus *Cucurbita,* having a marrow-like, fleshy, edible fruit with a hard rind. **2.** The fruit of such a plant, used as a vegetable. [Short for *isquoutersquash,* from Massachuset *askōōtasquash* : *askōt-* (unidentified root) + Proto-Algonquian *as̆kw-,* plant + *-ash,* inanimate plural ending.]

squash·y (skwóshi || skwáwshi) *adj.* **-ier, -iest. 1.** Easily squashed. **2.** Marshy; boggy. —**squash·i·ly** *adv.* —**squash·i·ness** *n.*

squat (skwot) *v.* **squatted, squatting, squats.** —*intr.* **1.** To crouch close to the ground, with the weight of one's body resting on one's heels or feet, with the knees bent. **2.** To live in an unoccupied dwelling or settle on unoccupied land without legal claim. **3.** *British Informal.* To sit. —*tr.* To put (oneself) in a crouching or squatting posture.
~*adj.* **squatter, squattest. 1.** Seated in a squatting position. **2.** Short and thick; low and broad.
~*n.* **1.** A squatting or crouching posture. **2.** The act of squatting or crouching. **3.** The place occupied by a squatter. [Middle English *squatten,* to crush, flatten, hence to squat, from Old French *esquatir* : *es-,* from Latin *ex-* (intensive) + *quatir,* to press flat, from Vulgar Latin *coactīre* (unattested), to press together, from Latin *cogere* (past participle *coāctus*), to drive together : *com-,* together + *agere,* to drive.]

squat·ter (skwóttər) *n.* **1.** One who lives in an unoccupied dwelling or settles on unoccupied land without legal claim. **2.** *Australian.* A prosperous farmer, especially a sheep farmer.

squaw (skwaw) *n.* **1.** A North American Indian woman. **2.** *U.S. Slang.* A woman or wife. Often used humorously, and considered offensive. [Massachuset *squa, eshqua,* from Proto-Algonquian *ethkwēwa* (unattested), "woman".]

squawk (skwawk) *v.* **squawked, squawking, squawks.** —*intr.* **1.** To utter a harsh scream; screech. **2.** *Informal.* To make a loud or angry protest. —*tr.* To utter with or as if with a squawk.
~*n.* **1.** A loud screech; a squall. **2.** *Informal.* A loud or insistent protest. [Imitative.] —**squawk·er** *n.*

squeak (skweek) *n.* **1.** A brief, thin, shrill cry or sound, such as that made by a mouse or an unoiled metal hinge. **2.** *Informal.* An escape. Used chiefly in the phrases *a close squeak* or *a narrow squeak.*
~*v.* **squeaked, squeaking, squeaks.** —*intr.* **1.** To utter or make a squeak. **2.** To pass or win by a slight margin. Used with *through* or *by.* **3.** *Informal.* To turn informer. —*tr.* To utter in a squeaky voice. [Middle English *squeken* (imitative); akin to Old Norse *skvakka,* to croak.] —**squeak·er** *n.*

squeak·y (skwéeki) *adj.* **-ier, -iest. 1.** Characterised by squeaking tones: *a squeaky voice.* **2.** Tending to squeak: *squeaky shoes.* —**squeak·i·ly** *adv.* —**squeak·i·ness** *n.*

squeal (skweel) *n.* **1.** A shrill, high-pitched cry, as of fear or surprise. **2.** A similar high-pitched sound, such as that made by tyres against a road surface when a car brakes suddenly.

~*v.* **squealed, squealing, squeals.** —*intr.* **1.** To utter or produce a squeal. **2.** *Slang.* To betray a friend or a secret; turn informer. **3.** *Informal.* To complain or protest shrilly. —*tr.* To utter or produce with a squeal. [Middle English *squelen* (imitative); akin to Old Norse *skvala,* to shriek.] **—squeal·er** *n.*

squeam·ish (skwéemish) *adj.* **1. a.** Easily nauseated or sickened. **b.** Nauseated: *felt squeamish at the sight of blood.* **2.** Easily shocked or disgusted. **3.** Excessively fastidious or scrupulous. [Middle English *squaymisch,* variant of *squaymous,* from Anglo-French *escoymos*†.] **—squeam·ish·ly** *adv.* **—squeam·ish·ness** *n.*

squee·gee (skwée-jée, -jee) *n.* **1.** A T-shaped implement having a crosspiece edged with rubber or leather, used to remove water from a surface such as a window. **2.** A similar implement or a rubber roller used in printing and photography.

~*tr.v.* **squeegeed, -geeing, -gees.** To wipe or smooth with a squeegee. [Probably from *squeege,* perhaps intensive variant of SQUEEZE.]

squeeze (skweez) *v.* **squeezed, squeezing, squeezes.** —*tr.* **1. a.** To press hard upon or together; compress. **b.** To press (someone's hand or arm) gently, as in affection: *squeezed her hand.* **2.** To exert pressure on, as by way of extracting liquid: *squeeze an orange.* **3. a.** To extract by applying pressure: *squeeze juice from a lemon.* **b.** To extract or produce under pressure or with difficulty. Often used with *out*: *squeezed a confession out of the suspects.* **4.** To extract by dishonest means; extort. **5.** To obtain room or passage for as by pushing or exerting pressure; cram; force: *squeezed himself into the crowded lift.* **6.** To oppress with exacting or exorbitant demands. **7.** To find time or space for; manage to fit in. Often used with *in*: *squeezed in two clients before lunch.* **8.** *Bridge.* To force (an opponent) to use a potentially winning card in a trick he cannot take. —*intr.* **1.** To give way under pressure. **2.** To exert pressure. **3.** To force one's way, as through a crowd.

~*n.* **1.** An act or instance of squeezing. **2. a.** A handclasp. **b.** A brief embrace. **3.** A crowded situation; a crush: *a tight squeeze.* **4.** A small amount squeezed out of something: *a squeeze of lemon juice.* **5.** Pressure exerted to obtain some concession or goal. **6.** Financial or economic pressure, as imposed by a government, resulting in a restriction on credit, pay awards, dividends, or the like. **7.** *Informal.* An act of blackmailing: *put the squeeze on his old employer.* **8.** A forced discard of a potentially winning card in bridge. [Earlier *squease,* intensive form of *quease,* to press, Middle English *queysen,* Old English *cwȳsan.*] **—squeez·er** *n.*

squeeze·box (skwéez-boks) *n. Informal.* An accordion.

squelch (skwelch) *v.* **squelched, squelching, squelches.** —*intr.* To make or move with a splashing, squashing, or sucking sound. —*tr.* **1.** To crush by or as if by trampling; suppress; squash. **2.** *Informal.* To put down or silence, as with a crushing remark.

~*n.* **1.** An act of squelching. **2.** A sound made by squelching. **3.** An electric circuit that cuts off a radio receiver when the signal is too weak for reception of anything but noise. [Imitative.] **—squelch·er** *n.* **—squelch·y** *adj.*

squib (skwib) *n.* **1.** A small firework that hisses when lit, and eventually goes off with a bang. **2.** A brief, satirical piece of writing such as a lampoon. **3.** *Chiefly Australian Informal.* A coward.

~*v.* **squibbed, squibbing, squibs.** —*intr.* **1.** To write or publish a squib. **2.** To let off a squib. —*tr.* **1.** To attack or lampoon with squibs. **2.** *Chiefly Australian Informal.* To act like a coward. [Probably imitative.]

squid (skwid) *n., pl.* **squids** or collectively **squid.** Any of various marine cephalopod molluscs of the genera *Loligo, Rossia,* and related genera, having a usually elongated body, ten arms surrounding the mouth, a vestigial internal shell, and a pair of triangular or rounded fins. Compare **octopus.**

~*intr.v.* **squidded, squidding, squids.** To fish with squid as bait. [17th century : origin obscure.]

squif·fy (skwiffi) *adj. British Informal.* Slightly drunk or intoxicated. [19th century : origin obscure.]

squig·gle (skwigg'l) *n.* A small wiggly mark or scrawl.

~*intr.v.* **squiggled, -gling, -gles.** **1.** To form a squiggle or squiggles. **2.** To squirm and wriggle. [Imitative.] **—squig·gly** *adj.*

squill (skwil) *n.* **1.** Any of several bulbous plants of the genus *Scilla,* native to Eurasia, having narrow leaves and bell-shaped blue, white, or pink flowers. Also called "scilla". Compare **sea onion. 2.** The dried inner scales of the bulbs of the sea onion, used as rat poison and formerly as a cardiac stimulant and expectorant. [Middle English, from Latin *squilla, scilla,* from Greek *skilla*†.]

squil·la (skwíl-ə) *n., pl.* **-las** or **-lae** (-ee). Any of various burrowing marine crustaceans of the order Stomatopoda, and especially of the genus *Squilla,* having a pair of jointed grasping appendages. Also called "mantis shrimp". [New Latin *Squilla,* type genus, from Latin *squilla*†, shrimp, prawn.]

squinch (skwinch) *n.* A quarter-spherical segment of masonry vaulting or corbelling thrown across the upper inside corners of a square tower as the transition to a circular or octagonal superstructure. [Variant of obsolete *scunch,* short for SCUNCHEON.]

squint (skwint) *v.* **squinted, squinting, squints.** —*intr.* **1.** To look with the eyes screwed up or almost closed, as from concentrating, close observation, or very bright light. **2.** To look or glance sideways or obliquely. Usually used with *towards* or *at.* **3.** To cross one's eyes or make them turn from looking in a parallel direction, as when attempting to look at one's nose. **4.** To suffer from **strabismus** *(see).* —*tr.* To cause (one's eyes) to squint.

~*n.* **1.** An instance of squinting. **2.** An inclination; a tendency. **3. Strabismus** *(see).* **4.** *British Informal.* A glance, view, or look: *Take a squint at it.* **5.** A **hagioscope** *(see).*

~*adj.* **1.** Not straight; oblique; askew. **2.** Affected with strabismus. [Short for ASQUINT.] **—squint·er** *n.*

squint-eyed (skwínt-īd) *adj.* **1.** Having strabismus. **2.** With squinting eyes. **3.** Looking askance.

squire (skwīr) *n.* **1.** An English country gentleman, especially one who is the chief landowner in a particular district. **2.** Formerly, a young nobleman attendant upon and ranked next below a knight in the feudal hierarchy. **3.** *U.S.* A judge or other local dignitary. **4.** A man who attends or escorts a woman. **5.** *British.* Used as an informal or familiar term of address for a man.

~*tr.v.* **squired, squiring, squires.** To attend as a squire or escort. [Middle English *squier, esquier,* from Old French *esquier, escuier,* "shield-bearer", from Late Latin *scūtārius,* from Latin *scūtum,* a shield.]

squire·ar·chy, squir·ar·chy (skwír-aarki) *n., pl.* **-chies.** Squires collectively; especially, the section of society made up of landed proprietors having considerable political power. **—squire·arch** *n.* **—squire·arch·al** (-árk'l), **squire·arch·i·cal** (-árkik'l) *adj.*

squireen (skwīréen) *n.* A minor member of the Irish landed gentry.

squirm (skwurm) *intr.v.* **squirmed, squirming, squirms.** **1.** To twist about in a wriggling motion; writhe. **2.** To feel or show signs of humiliation or embarrassment.

~*n.* An act of squirming or a squirming movement; a wriggle. [Perhaps imitative (associated with WORM.] **—squirm·er** *n.* **—squirm·y** *adj.*

squir·rel (skwírrəl || *U.S.* skwúrrəl, skwurl) *n.* **1.** Any of various arboreal rodents of the genus *Sciurus* and related genera, usually with grey or reddish-brown fur and a long, flexible, bushy tail. See **grey squirrel, red squirrel. 2.** Any of various related animals of the family Sciuridae, such as the **ground squirrel** or the **flying squirrel** *(both of which see).* **3.** The fur of a squirrel. Also used adjectivally: *a squirrel coat.* **4.** A coat, jacket, or wrap made from the fur of a squirrel. [Middle English *squyrel,* from Anglo-French *esquirel,* from Vulgar Latin *scūriōlus* (unattested), diminutive of *scūrius* (unattested), variant of Latin *sciūrus,* squirrel, from Greek *skiouros,* "shadow-tail" : *skia,* shadow + *oura,* tail.]

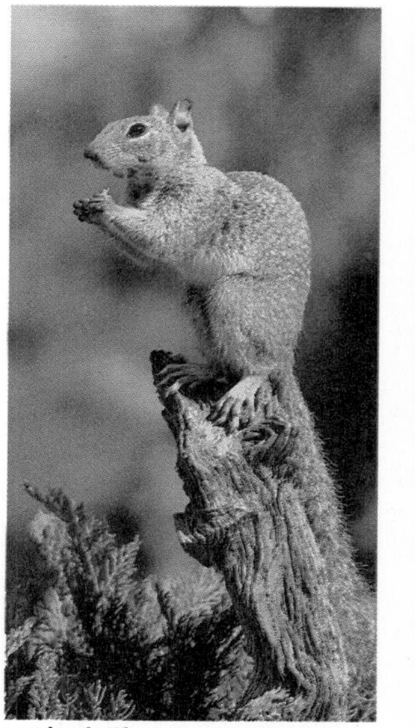

squirrel *There are about 250 species of squirrel, found almost worldwide. Most feed by day, living on a diet of nuts and seeds. This is the California ground squirrel,* Citellus beecheyi.

squirrel cage *n.* **1.** A cage consisting of a number of bars fitted to the circumference of circular end plates. The cage can be mounted to enable it to rotate as a small animal inside the cage runs in a direction perpendicular to its axis. **2.** The rotor of an induction motor *(a squirrel-cage motor)* having copper bars arranged in the shape of a squirrel cage. **3.** An electric fan with long narrow blades arranged like the bars in a squirrel cage.

squir·rel·fish (skwírrəl-fish || *U.S.* skwúrrəl-, skwúrl-) *n., pl.* **-fishes** or collectively **squirrelfish.** Any of various fishes of the genus *Holocentrus* and related genera, of warm marine waters, having large eyes and a usually reddish body.

squirrel monkey *n.* Either of two tropical American monkeys, *Saimiri sciureus* or *S. örstedii,* having short, thick fur and a long, nonprehensile tail.

squir·rel-tail grass (skwírrəl-tayl || *U.S.* skwúrrəl-, skwúrl-) *n.* A European grass, *Hordeum marinum,* that grows in salt marshes and has bushy spikelets.

squirt (skwurt) *v.* **squirted, squirting, squirts.** —*intr.* **1.** To be ejected in a thin swift stream. Used of a liquid. **2.** To eject liquid in a thin swift stream. —*tr.* **1.** To eject (liquid) in a thin swift stream. **2.** To soak or wet with liquid so ejected.

~*n.* **1.** The act of squirting. **2.** A device, such as a syringe, used to squirt. **3.** A squirted stream of liquid. **4.** *Informal.* **a.** An insignificant but arrogant or bumptious person. **b.** A short or puny person. [Middle English *squirten, swirten,* of Low German origin; akin to Low German *swirtjen* (imitative).] **—squirt·er** *n.*

squirt·ing cucumber (skwúrting) *n.* A hairy vine, *Ecballium elaterium,* of the Mediterranean region, having fruit that discharges its seeds and juice explosively when ripe.

squish (skwish) *v.* **squished, squishing, squishes.** *Informal.* —*tr.* To squash or compress with a squish. —*intr.* To emit or move with a squish.

~*n.* A squashy sound, as of mud being compressed. [Variant of SQUASH.] **—squish·y** *adj.*

squit (skwit) *n. British Slang.* A small insignificant person; a squirt. **—the squits** or **squitters.** *British Slang.* Diarrhoea. [Dialectal variant of SQUIRT (noun and verb).]

sr steradian.

Sr The symbol for the element strontium.

sr. senior.

Sr. **1.** senior (after a surname). **2.** señor. **3.** sister (religious).

Sra. señora.

S.R.C. Science Research Council (in Britain).

Sri Lan·ka (sréé lángkə, sri), **Democratic Socialist Republic of.** Formerly **Cey·lon** (si-lón, sə-). Island republic in the Indian Ocean, lying off southeastern India. Its central highlands are surrounded by coastal lowlands and swamps. With few natural resources apart from its fertile land, Sri Lanka is heavily dependent on the export of tropical products, especially tea, rubber, and coconuts. Rice is the chief import. Tourism is expanding rapidly. Some 72 per cent of the inhabitants are Buddhist Sinhalese and 21 per cent Hindu Tamils southern Indian stock, and conflict between them has recurred in recent years (notably 1977 and 1981). The island's spices attracted the Arabs (12th and 13th centuries), and Portuguese, Dutch (1658) and British, who conquered the island (1796–1815) and made it a

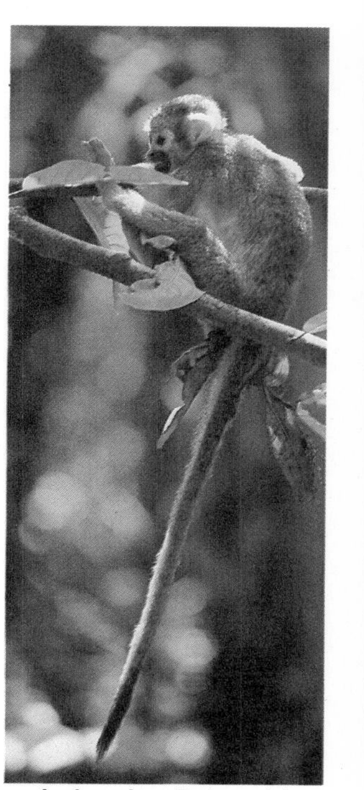

squirrel monkey *Eating mainly fruit and insects, the small squirrel monkey is found in the rain forests of Central and South America in groups of up to 500 animals.*

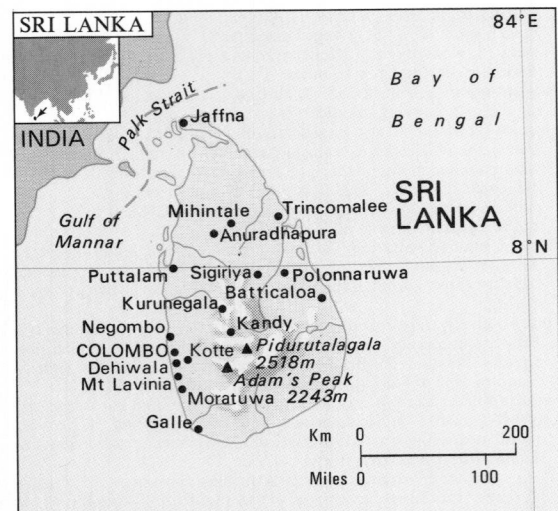

stack *In geological terms, a stack is a pillar of rock shaped by the eroding power of waves. This red sandstone stack is at Ladram Bay, Devon, England.*

stadium *The ancient Greek stadium at Delphi, used for athletics competitions and chariot races. The stadium was built in the second century* A.D.

colony (1802). Ceylon gained independence (1948) and became the Republic of Sri Lanka (1972). A new constitution was adopted in 1978. Area 65 610 square kilometres (25,325 square miles). Population, 15,200,000. Capital, Colombo.

Sri·na·gar (sri-núggər, sírri-). Also **Ser·i·na·gar** (səri-). Capital of Jammu and Kashmir, northwest India. The city lies on the river Jhelum, and is noted for its mosques, gardens, palaces, fort, and its many canals.

SRN. State Registered Nurse (in Britain).

sRNA *n.* **Transfer RNA** *(see).*

S.R.O. **1.** *British.* Statutory Rules and Orders. **2.** *U.S.* standing room only.

Srta. señorita.

ss scilicet.

SS **1.** Schutzstaffel: an elite military section of the Nazi party whose functions included the policing of the rest of the German army and the protecting of Hitler's person. **2.** steamship. **3.** saints. **4.** social security.

S.S. **1.** steamship. **2.** social security. **3.** Sunday school.

S.S.C. Solicitor to the Supreme Court (in Scotland).

SSE south-southeast.

SSM surface-to-surface missile.

ssp. subspecies.

S.S.R. Soviet Socialist Republic.

S.S.R.C. Social Science Research Council (in Britain).

SSSI Site of Special Scientific Interest.

SST supersonic transport.

SSW south-southwest.

st. **1.** stanza. **2.** statute. **3.** stet. **4.** stitch. **5.** stone. **6.** street. **7.** stumped; stumped by (in cricket).

-st. Variant of **-est** (verb inflection).

St. **1.** saint. **2.** statute. **3.** strait. **4.** street.

stab (stab) *v.* **stabbed, stabbing, stabs.** —*tr.* **1.** To pierce or wound with or as if with a pointed weapon. **2.** To plunge (a weapon or instrument) into something. —*intr.* **1.** To lunge with or as if with a pointed weapon. Often used with *at.* **2.** To inflict a wound in this way.
~*n.* **1.** A thrust made with a pointed instrument or weapon. **2. a.** A wound inflicted by stabbing. **b.** A sharp, localised pain; a pang. **3.** *Informal.* An attempt; a try; an effort: *had a stab at skating.* —**a stab in the back.** A treacherous attack; a betrayal. [Middle English *stabbe,* wound by stabbing, obscurely related to dialectal *stob,* to stab, perhaps from Middle English *stob,* stake, stick, variant of STUB.] —**stab·ber** *n.*

Sta·bat Ma·ter (staá-bat maátər, -bət) *n.* **1.** A medieval Latin hymn on the sorrows of the Virgin Mary at the Crucifixion. **2.** A musical setting for this hymn. [Latin, "the mother was standing" (opening words of the hymn).]

sta·bile (stáy-bīl ‖ -b'l, -beel) *adj.* Immobile; stable; unchangeable.
~*n.* An abstract sculpture, usually of sheet metal, with no moving parts. [Latin *stabilis,* STABLE.]

sta·bi·lise, sta·bi·lize (stáy-bi-līz, stá-, -bə-) *v.* **-lised, -lising, -lises.** —*tr.* **1.** To make stable. **2.** To maintain the stability of. —*intr.* To become stable. —**sta·bi·li·sa·tion** (-lī-záysh'n ‖ U.S. -li-) *n.*

sta·bi·lis·er (stáy-bi-līzzər, stá-, -bə-) *n.* **1.** One that stabilises. **2.** *Nautical.* A device in a ship or boat, such as a gyroscopically controlled fin, used to prevent excessive rolling. **3.** *Aeronautics.* Any aerofoil used to stabilise an aircraft in flight. **4.** *Chemistry.* A substance that renders or maintains a solution, mixture, suspension, or state resistant to chemical change.

sta·bil·i·ty (stə-bílləti) *n., pl.* **-ties.** **1.** The condition or quality of being stable, as: **a.** Resistance to sudden change, dislodgment, or overthrow. **b.** Constancy of character, emotional state, or purpose; steadfastness. **c.** Reliability; dependability. **2.** The ability of an object, such as a ship or an aircraft, to maintain equilibrium or resume

its original position after displacement by, for example, the sea or strong winds. **3.** A vow committing a Benedictine monk to one monastery for life.

stab kick *n.* In Australian Rules football, a short, low kick aimed at passing the ball to a team-mate or covering ground quickly.

sta·ble¹ (stáyb'l) *adj.* **-bler, -blest.** **1. a.** Resistant to sudden change of position or condition; not liable to change or fluctuation: *a stable personality; a stable economy.* **b.** Maintaining equilibrium; self-restoring. **2.** *Physics.* Having no known mode of decay; indefinitely long-lived. Said of certain elementary particles. **3.** Lasting or likely to last for a long time. **4.** *Chemistry.* Not easily decomposed or otherwise modified chemically. **5.** Consistently dependable or reliable. [Middle English, from Old French *estable,* from Latin *stabilis,* standing firm.] —**sta·ble·ness** *n.* —**sta·bly** *adv.*

stable² *n.* **1. a.** A building for the shelter and feeding of domestic animals, especially horses and cattle. **b.** The animals lodged in such a building, collectively. **2. a.** All of the racehorses belonging to a single owner or racing establishment. **b.** The personnel employed to look after and train such a collection of racehorses. **3.** Any source of common ownership, production, training, management, or the like: *boxers from the same stable.*
~*v.* **stabled, stabling, stables.** —*tr.* To put or keep (an animal) in a stable. —*intr.* To live or be kept in a stable. [Middle English, from Old French *estable,* from Latin *stabulum,* "standing place", enclosure, stable.]

sta·ble·boy (stáyb'l-boy) *n.* A man or boy who is employed in a stable to look after horses. Also called "stableman", "stablelad".

stable door *n.* A door divided in half horizontally so that either part may be left open or closed. Also *U.S.* "Dutch door".

stable fly *n.* A fly, *Stomoxys calcitrans,* that sucks the blood of humans and domestic animals.

sta·ble·mate (stáyb'l-mayt) *n.* **1.** Any of a number of horses belonging to the same stable. **2.** *Informal.* Any of a group of people who share a common experience, such as residence in a school or college.

sta·bling (stáybling) *n.* **1.** Stables collectively. **2.** Accommodation in a stable for animals.

stablish. *Archaic.* Variant of **establish.**

stac·ca·to (stə-kaá-tō) *adj.* **1.** *Abbr.* **stacc.** Designating music performed with a crisp, sharp attack to simulate rests between successive notes. Often used as a direction. **2.** Composed of abrupt, distinct, emphatic parts or sounds: *staccato machine-gun fire.*
~*n., pl.* **staccatos** or **-ti** (-tee). **1.** A staccato passage or movement. **2.** An abrupt, staccato manner or sound. [Italian, past participle of *(di)staccare,* to detach, from Old French *destach(i)er.* See **detach.**] —**stac·ca·to** *adv.*

stack (stak) *n.* **1.** A large, usually conical pile of straw or fodder arranged for outdoor storage. **2.** Any orderly pile, especially one arranged in layers. **3.** A group of three or more unslung rifles, supporting each other with their butts on the ground and forming a cone. **4.** See **chimney-stack, smokestack.** **5.** A vertical exhaust pipe, as on a ship or locomotive. **6.** Several rows of bookshelves forming one structure; a bookcase. **7.** *Usually plural.* The area of a library, usually inaccessible to the public, in which books are stored on shelves. **8.** An English measure of coal or cut wood, equal to 3.06 cubic metres (108 cubic feet). **9.** An arrangement of aircraft circling an airport at prescribed levels, awaiting instructions to land. **10.** A free-standing column of rock in the sea that has been separated from the coast by erosion. **11.** *Computing.* A temporary storage area in a computer memory. **12.** *Often plural. Informal.* A large amount or quantity: *stacks of work to get through.*
~*v.* **stacked, stacking, stacks.** —*tr.* **1.** To arrange in a stack; pile. **2.** To load with stacks of some material. **3.** To cheat by prearranging the order of (playing cards); rig. **4.** To direct (two or more aircraft) to circle at different heights above an airport while waiting to land. —*intr.* To circle an airport in a stack. Used of aircraft. [Middle English *stak, sta(ke),* from Old Norse *stakkr,* haystack, from Germanic.] —**stack·er** *n.*

stac·te (sták-tee) *n.* A spice used by the ancient Jews in making incense. Exodus 30:34. [Latin *stactē,* from Greek *staktē,* from the feminine of *staktos,* oozing, distilling, from *stazein,* to ooze.]

stad·dle (stádd'l) *n.* A foundation or supporting framework; especially, a stone platform upon which hay or straw is stacked to protect it from vermin. [Middle English *stathel,* Old English *stathol.*]

stad·hold·er (stád-hōldər, stát-) *n.* Also **stadt·hold·er** (stát-). **1.** Formerly, a governor or viceroy in a province of the Netherlands. **2.** Formerly, the chief magistrate of the United Provinces of the Netherlands. [Partial translation of Dutch *stadhouder,* translation of Latin *locum tenens,* "(one) holding the place (of another)," lieutenant : *stad,* place, from Middle Dutch *stad, stat* + *houder,* holder.] —**stad·hold·er·ate** (-ət, -it, -ayt) *n.*

stad·i·a system (stáydi-ə) *n.* A method of surveying in which distances are determined at one pointing only of the telescopic instrument, this having two parallel lines, *stadia hairs,* used to intercept intervals on a calibrated rod with bold graduation marks, a *stadia rod.* Also called "stadia tacheometry". [Italian, probably from Latin, plural of STADIUM (measure of length) + SYSTEM.]

sta·di·um (stáydi-əm) *n., pl.* **-dia** (-ə) or **-diums** (for sense 3). **1.** In ancient Greece, a course on which races were held, usually semicircular and having tiers of seats for spectators. **2.** An ancient Greek measure of distance, based on the length of such a course and probably equal to about 185 metres (607 feet). **3.** A large, often unroofed structure in which sporting events are held. **4.** A stage in the progress of something, such as a disease. [Middle English, measure of distance, from Latin, from Greek *stadion,* alteration of *spadion,* racetrack (particularly the racetrack of this length at Olympia), from *span,* to draw, pull. See **spasm.**]

staff[1] (staaf || staf) *n., pl.* **staffs** (except sense 4) or **staves** (stayvz) (except sense 3). **1. a.** A stick or cane carried as an aid or support in walking or climbing. **b.** A thick stick used as a weapon; a cudgel. **c.** A pole upon which a flag is displayed. **d.** A rod, baton, or the like carried as a symbol of authority. **2.** A rule or similar graduated stick used for testing or measuring, as in surveying. **3. a.** A group of assistants responsible to a manager or other person of authority. **b.** A group of military officers who serve a commanding officer but do not participate in combat and have no authority to command. **c.** The personnel who are employed to perform a specified job or task: *the nursing staff of a hospital.* **d.** The employees of a company, institution, or the like. **4.** *Music.* The set of horizontal lines and their intermediate spaces upon which notes are written or printed. In this sense, also called "stave". **5.** Figuratively, anything that is a staple or support: *the staff of my old age.*
~*tr.v.* **staffed, staffing, staffs.** To provide with a staff of employees. [Middle English *staf,* Old English *stæf,* stick, rod.]

staff[2] *n.* A building material that resembles stucco, composed of plaster of Paris and fibre and used especially as a wall covering over the skeleton of temporary buildings. [Probably from German *staffieren,* to dress, trim, adorn, from Middle Low German *stafferen, stofferen,* from Old French *estoffer,* to STUFF.]

Staf·fa (stáffə). Uninhabited island in the Inner Hebrides group, Strathclyde Region, Scotland. It has numerous sea caves, including the celebrated Fingal's Cave.

staff college *n.* In Britain, a college for training staff, especially one used for training military officers.

staff nurse *n.* A trained nurse in a hospital who ranks immediately below a ward sister.

staff officer *n.* A commissioned military officer who holds a position on the staff of a commander.

Staf·ford (stáffərd). County town of Staffordshire, in central England, lying on the river Sow above its confluence with the Trent. It has long been a shoemaking centre, but today electrical goods and engineering are more important industries.

Staf·ford·shire (stáffərd-shər, -sheer). County in central England. The county town is Stafford and the largest city, Stoke-on-Trent. The county has important industrial areas, with the famous Potteries district in the north.

Staffordshire bull terrier *n.* A dog of a breed developed in England, having a short, variously coloured coat, a stocky body, and widely set forelegs. Also called "Staffordshire terrier".

staff sergeant *n.* **1.** In Britain, a noncommissioned officer of the army who is the highest-ranking sergeant. **2.** In the United States, a noncommissioned officer of the rank above a sergeant and below a sergeant first class.

stag (stag) *n.* **1.** The adult male of various deer, especially the red deer. **2.** An animal, especially a pig, castrated after reaching sexual maturity. **3.** *U.S.* A man who attends a social affair without escorting a woman. **4.** *Finance.* In Britain, one who buys shares of new issue so as to make a quick profit by an immediate resale.
~*adj.* **1.** For or attended by men only: *a stag night.* **2.** *Informal.* Pornographic: *stag films.* [Middle English *stag(ge),* Old English *stagga.*]

stag beetle *n.* Any of numerous large beetles of the family Lucanidae, having long, powerful, antler-like mandibles.

stage (stayj) *n.* **1.** Any raised and level floor or platform. **2. a.** The raised platform upon which theatrical performances are presented. **b.** Any area in which actors perform. **c.** The acting profession or the world of theatre. Preceded by *the.* **3.** The scene or setting of an event or series of events: *Marston Moor was the stage for a famous Royalist victory.* **4.** A platform on a microscope on which slides to be viewed are mounted. **5.** A workmen's scaffold. **6.** *British.* A stopping place on a bus route that marks a division of the route for which a fixed fare is charged. Also called "fare stage". **7.** The distance between stopping places on a journey; a leg of a journey: *proceeded by easy stages.* **8.** A stagecoach. **9.** *Chiefly U.S.* A level or storey of a building; a floor. **10.** *U.S.* The height of the surface of a river or other fluctuating body of water in relation to some datum: *at flood stage.* **11. a.** A level, degree, or period of time in the course of a process; a step in development: *a larval stage.* **b.** A moment or point in the course of an action or series of events: *At this early stage it is hard to see who will win.* **c.** *N.Z.* Each year of study in a particular university subject. **12.** *Aerospace.* One of two or more successive propulsion units of a rocket vehicle that fires after the preceding one has been jettisoned. See **multistage rocket. 13.** *Geology.* A subdivision of a series representing rock formed during an age. **14.** *Electronics.* An element or group of elements in a complex arrangement of parts; especially, a single tube or transistor and its accessory components in an amplifier. **—hold the stage.** To dominate a social occasion or gathering. **—set the stage for.** To prepare or pave the way for.
~*v.* **staged, staging, stages.** *—tr.* **1. a.** To exhibit, present, or perform on or as if on a stage: *stage a boxing match.* **b.** To produce or direct (a theatrical performance). **2.** To arrange and carry out: *stage an invasion.* *—intr.* To be adaptable to or suitable for theatrical presentation. [Middle English, from Old French *estage,* from Vulgar Latin *staticum* (unattested), "standing place", position, from Latin *stāre,* to stand.]

stage business *n.* In the theatre, **business** *(see).*

stage·coach (stáyj-kōch) *n.* A four-wheeled horse-drawn vehicle formerly used to transport mail, parcels, and passengers.

stage·craft (stáyj-kraaft || -kraft) *n.* The practice of or skill in theatrical techniques such as directing, writing, or producing.

stage direction *n.* An instruction in the text of a play that prescribes how a certain part of the play should be acted or presented.

stage door *n.* A door at the back or side of a theatre admitting the actors, technicians, and other staff.

stage effect *n.* A special effect used on stage to simulate, by means of taped sounds and lighting, conditions such as thunder or wind.

stage fright *n.* Acute fear or nervousness felt by a person at the prospect of or while performing before an audience.

stage·hand (stáyj-hand) *n.* A person employed in a theatre to shift scenery, adjust lighting, or the like.

stage left *n.* The area of the stage to the left of a centrally placed actor facing the audience.

stage-man·age (stáyj-mánnij || -mannij) *tr.v.* **-aged, -aging, -ages. 1.** To serve as overall supervisor of the stage and actors for (a theatrical production). **2.** To manipulate or contrive from behind the scenes. **—stage manager** *n.* **—stage management** *n.*

stag·er (stáyjər) *n.* One who possesses the wisdom of long experience: *an old stager.* [STAGE (of theatre) + -ER.]

stage right *n.* The area of the stage to the right of a centrally placed actor facing the audience.

stage-struck (stáyj-struk) *adj.* Enthralled with the stage or with hopes of becoming an actor.

stage whisper *n.* **1.** The conventional whisper of an actor, intended to be heard by the audience. **2.** Any whisper intended to be overheard.

stagey. Variant of **stagy.**

stag·fla·tion (stág-fláysh'n) *n. Economics.* A condition in which a high rate of price and wage inflation is coupled with stagnant consumer demand and high unemployment. [*Stag*nation + in*flation.*] **—stag·fla·tion·ar·y** (-ri, -əri || -erri) *adj.*

stag·ger (stággər) *v.* **-gered, -gering, -gers.** *—intr.* **1.** To move or stand unsteadily, as if under a great weight; totter. **2.** To lose strength or confidence; waver. *—tr.* **1.** To cause to totter, sway, or reel. **2. a.** To cause to lose confidence, have doubts, or hesitate. **b.** To overwhelm with emotion or surprise. **3.** To place regularly, in oblique lines, on or as if on alternating sides of a middle line; set in a zigzag row or rows: *theatre seats staggered for clear viewing.* **4.** To arrange in alternating or overlapping time periods: *Examinations were staggered to prevent congestion of the hall.*
~*n.* **1.** The act of staggering; a tottering, swaying, or reeling motion. **2.** A staggered pattern, arrangement, or order. [Earlier (now dialect) *stacker,* Middle English *stakeren,* from Old Norse *stakra,* frequentative of *staka,* to push, cause to stumble.] **—stag·ger·er** *n.*

stag·ger·ing (stággəring) *adj.* Astonishing; amazing: *got through a staggering amount of work.* **—stag·ger·ing·ly** *adv.*

stag·gers (stággərz) *n. Usually used with a singular verb.* **1.** Any of various diseases marked by vertigo, confusion, and weakness. **2.** Any of various diseases of the nervous system in animals; especially, a cerebrospinal disease in horses, in which the animal loses coordination, staggers, and often falls. In this sense, also called "blind staggers".

stag·horn fern (stág-hawrn) *n.* Any of several tropical epiphytic ferns of the genus *Platycerium,* having large divided fronds that resemble antlers.

stag·hound (stág-hownd) *n.* A large hound used to hunt deer.

stag·ing (stáyjing) *n.* **1.** A temporary platform; a scaffold. **2. a.** The business of running stagecoaches as an enterprise. **b.** Travel by stagecoach. **3. a.** The process of producing and directing a dramatic work. **b.** A particular production of a dramatic work. **4.** The act of jettisoning a stage of a multistage rocket.

staging area *n.* A place where troops and equipment are assembled before moving out on a mission or other military operation.

staging post *n.* A place used to rest or refuel on a long journey such as an aeroplane flight.

stag·nant (stág-nənt) *adj.* **1.** Not moving or flowing; without a current; motionless. **2.** Foul from standing still; polluted; stale. **3. a.** Lacking liveliness or briskness; inactive; sluggish. **b.** Lacking growth; not developing. [Latin *stagnāns* (stem *stagnant-*), present participle of *stagnāre,* to be stagnant, from *stagnum,* pond, swamp.] **—stag·nan·cy** *n.* **—stag·nant·ly** *adv.*

stag·nate (stag-náyt || stág-nayt) *intr.v.* **-nated, -nating, -nates.** To be or become stagnant. [Latin *stagnāre.* See **stagnant.**] **—stag·na·tion** (-náysh'n) *n.*

stag party *n.* A party for men only, held especially by a prospective bridegroom a short time before his wedding. Compare **hen party.**

stag·y, stage·y (stáyji) *adj.* **-ier, -iest.** Having a theatrical character or quality; especially, artificial and affected. **—stag·i·ly** *adv.* **—stag·i·ness** *n.*

staid (stayd) *adj.* **1.** Steady and reserved in style, manner, or behaviour; sober. **2.** *Rare.* Fixed; permanent. —See Synonyms at **serious.** [From *staid,* obsolete past participle of STAY.] **—staid·ly** *adv.* **—staid·ness** *n.*

stain (stayn) *v.* **stained, staining, stains.** *—tr.* **1.** To discolour, soil, or spot. **2.** To bring into disrepute; taint; tarnish. **3.** To colour (glass, for example) with a coat of penetrating liquid dye or tint. **4.** To colour (specimens for the microscope) with a dye in order to heighten contrast between different structures, as of tissue. *—intr.* To produce or receive discolorations.
~*n.* **1.** A stained spot or smudge, as from foreign matter like blood

PRONUNCIATION KEY

a, **trap**; aa, **father**; ai, **fair**;
ar, **star**; aw, **lawn**; ay, **play**;
b, bb, **stab**; **rubber**;
ch, **church**; ck, **ticket**;
d, dd, **dead**; **ladder**; e, **dress**;
ee, **bee**; er, **defer**; ew, **few**;
ewr, **pure**; ə, **about**;
ər, **letter**; f, ff, **fife**; **differ**;
g, gg, **giggle**; h, **hat**; i, **kit**;
ī, **price**; īr, **fire**; j, **judge**;
k, **kick**; l, ll, **let**; 'l, **needle**;
m, mm, **man**; n, nn, **no**;
'n, **sudden**; ng, **thing**; o, **lot**;
ō, **no**; o͝o, **foot**; o͞o, **shoe**;
oor, **poor**; ow, **cow**;
owr, **hour**; oy, **boy**;
p, pp, **pepper**; r, rr, **red**;
s, ss, **sauce**; sh, **ship**;
t, tt, **totter**; th, **thick**; th, **this**;
smooth; u, **cut**; ur, **turn**;
v, vv, **valve**; w, **wet**; y, **yes**;
z, zz, **zebra**; zh, **vision**;
pleasure

IN FOREIGN WORDS:

aN, oN, **Saint-Saëns**;
hl, **Llanelli**; **Hluhluwe**;
kh, **loch**; **lough**; **Khaled**

STRESS MARK:

ín-sīt, **insight**; in-sī́t, **incite**

or gravy. **2.** A blemish upon one's moral character, personality, or reputation; a blot. **3.** A liquid substance applied especially to wood that penetrates the surface and imparts a rich colour. **4.** A coloured solution used for staining microscopic specimens. [Middle English *steynen,* short for *disteynen,* to deprive of colour, stain, from Old French *desteindre,* from Vulgar Latin *distingere* (unattested) : Latin *dis-* (reversal) + *tingere,* to dye.] —**stain·a·bil·i·ty** (-ə-bílləti) *n.* —**stain·a·ble** *adj.* —**stain·er** *n.*

stained glass *n.* Glass coloured by mixing pigments inherently in the glass, by fusing coloured metallic oxides onto the glass, or by painting and baking transparent colours on the glass surface. It is widely used in church windows. —**stained-glass** *adj.*

stain·less (stáyn-ləss, -liss) *adj.* **1.** Without stain or blemish. **2.** Resistant to stain or corrosion. —**stain·less·ly** *adv.*

stainless steel *n.* Any of various steels alloyed with sufficient chromium to resist corrosion or rusting associated with exposure of ordinary steel to water and moist air. —**stain·less-steel** *adj.*

stair (stair) *n.* **1.** *Usually plural.* A series or flight of steps; a staircase. **2.** One of a flight of steps. —**below stairs.** *British.* In the basement of a house formerly used by the servants. [Middle English *steir(e), stair(e),* Old English *stæger.*]

WINDOWS GLAZED WITH COLOUR
The modern revival of a medieval art form

From the beginning of the second millennium, while the massiveness of Romanesque architecture gave way to the airiness of Gothic, the craft of making stained-glass windows blossomed into an art form. Biblical scenes and figures were portrayed in windows created to open men's minds to an appreciation of God's light. Pictures were formed from coloured glass pieces of various shapes held in grooved lead strips, with iron frames (armatures) as dividing panels to give the window rigidity.

Medieval glass-making techniques were largely haphazard. Colour, produced by the beechwood ash added as a catalyst, depended for its shade on the composition of the mix and the conditions in which it was melted. Accurate control was impossible in the crude medieval

furnace. Yet the blue and red 13th-century glass of cathedrals such as Chartres in France and York in England, irregular in thickness and full of impurities, has a jewel-like luminosity never since reproduced . The red was in fact flashed – a thin red strip was fused onto clear glass, because colouring it while molten made it too dark.

In the 14th century, techniques improved to give finer glass and a wider variety of colours and shades. Yellow was produced by staining clear glass with silver salts. Developments in the 15th century included techniques for producing two or three colours on one piece of glass. In later centuries, stained glass gave way to enamel-painted pictures on clear glass, and the art of making stained-glass pictures declined, not to be revived until the 20th century.

ROMANESQUE WINDOW *The oldest complete stained-glass window, in Augsburg Cathedral in Germany, dates from the 11th century. It portrays five Old Testament figures, Hosea, David, and Daniel (above), Moses, and Jonas. Brown, gold, green, and white are predominant in medieval German glass.*

ABSTRACT ART *Twentieth-century artists have revived the glory of stained-glass windows. This window (right), by Georg Meistermann, is in the south aisle of St. Mary's Church, Cologne-Kalk.*

stair·case (stáir-kayss) *n.* A flight or series of flights of steps connecting separate levels, and its supporting structure.

stair rod *n.* Any of a number of thin metal bars used to keep a stair carpet in place on a flight of stairs.

stair·way (stáir-way) *n.* A flight of stairs; a staircase.

stair·well (stáir-wel) *n.* A vertical shaft around which a staircase has been built.

stake¹ (stayk) *n.* **1.** A piece of wood or metal sharpened at one end for driving into the ground, or used as a marker, a fence pole, or a tent peg. **2. a.** A vertical post to which an offender was formerly bound for execution by burning. **b.** Execution by burning at the stake. Preceded by *the.* **3.** A vertical post secured at the edge of a platform, as on a lorry, to stop the load from sliding off. —**pull up stakes.** *Chiefly U.S.* To conclude one's affairs and move on. ~*tr.v.* **staked, staking, stakes. 1.** To indicate the location or limits of with or as if with stakes. Often used with *out: stake out a claim.* **2. a.** To fasten or secure with a stake or stakes. **b.** To support with a stake or stakes. **3.** To tether or tie to a stake. [Middle English *stake,* Old English *staca.*]

stake² *n.* **1.** *Often plural.* **a.** Money or property risked in a wager or gambling game. **b.** The reward or prize, such as money, awarded to the winner of a contest or race, especially a horse race. **c.** A race offering a reward or prize to the winner; especially, a horse race in which money is contributed by the horse owners equally to make up the prize. **2.** A share or interest in any enterprise, especially a financial share. **4.** *U.S. Informal.* A **grubstake** *(see).* —**at stake.** In question; at risk; involved. ~*tr.v.* **staked, staking, stakes. 1.** To gamble or risk; hazard; bet. **2.** *Chiefly U.S.* To provide working capital for; finance. —**stake out.** *Chiefly U.S. Slang.* To keep watch on (a place) secretly. [Perhaps originally "something placed on a post as a wager in a game", from STAKE (post).]

Sta·kha·nov·ite (sta-kánnə-vīt, stə-, -ka'ano-) *n.* Especially in the U.S.S.R., a worker whose exceptional diligence and zeal earn him high government esteem. [After Alexei *Stakhanov,* Russian miner who set a productivity record in 1935 which was taken as a model.] —**Sta·kha·nov·ism** *n.*

sta·lac·tite (stál-ək-tīt || *chiefly U.S.* stə-lák-) *n.* A cylindrical or conical deposit, usually of calcite or aragonite, projecting downwards from the roof of a cavern as a result of the dripping of mineral-rich water. Compare **stalagmite.** [New Latin *stalactites,* from Greek *stalaktos,* dripping, verbal adjective from *stalassein†,* to drip.] —**sta·lac·ti·form** (stə-lákti-fawrm, sta-) *adj.* —**stal·ac·tit·ic** (stál-ək-títtik), **stal·ac·tit·i·cal** *adj.*

sta·lag (stál-ag; *German* shtál-) *n.* A German prisoner-of-war camp; especially, one for noncommissioned officers and privates. [German *Stalag,* short for *Stammlager,* "base camp" : *Stamm,* a base, stem + *Lager,* a camp, sleeping place.]

sta·lag·mite (stál-əg-mīt || *chiefly U.S.* stə-lág-) *n.* A cylindrical or conical deposit, usually of calcite or aragonite, projecting upwards from the floor of a cavern as a result of the dripping of mineral-rich water. Compare **stalactite.** [New Latin *stalagmites,* from Greek *stalagmos,* a dropping, from *stalassein†,* to drip. See **stalactite.**] —**stal·ag·mit·ic** (stál-əg-míttik) **stal·ag·mit·i·cal** *adj.*

St. Al·bans (áwl-bənz || ól-). City of Hertfordshire, southeast England. The site of the Roman town of Verulamium, it has many Roman remains including an amphitheatre, a mosaic pavement, and a hypocaust. St. Alban was martyred here (*c.* 303).

stale¹ (stayl) *adj.* **staler, stalest. 1.** Having lost freshness, effervescence, or palatability; flat or dry. **2.** Lacking in originality or spontaneity; trite: *a stale joke.* **3.** Impaired in efficacy, strength, or motivation, as from constant repetition of an activity. **4.** *Law.* Having lost legal efficacy or force through lack of exercise or action: *a stale claim.* —See Synonyms at **trite.** ~*v.* **staled, staling, stales.** —*tr.* To make stale. —*intr.* To become stale. [Middle English, old enough to clear, well-aged (said of alcoholic drink), from Old French *estale,* not moving, from *estaler,* to halt, from *estal,* a fixed place, from Frankish *stal* (unattested), position.] —**stale·ly** *adv.* —**stale·ness** *n.*

stale² *intr.v.* **staled, staling, stales.** To urinate. Used of horses and camels. ~*n.* Urine of horses or camels. [Middle English *stalen,* from Germanic; akin to Middle Low German *stallen.*]

stale·mate (stáyl-mayt) *n.* **1.** *Chess.* A position in which a player cannot make a legal move. **2.** A situation in which further action by either of two opponents is impossible; a deadlock. ~*tr.v.* **stalemated, -mating, -mates.** To bring into a stalemate. [Obsolete *stale,* stalemate, from Middle English, from Old French *estal* (see **stale**) + MATE (checkmate).]

Sta·lin (staʹal-in, *rarely* stál- || -een), **Joseph Vissarionovich,** born Joseph Vissarionovich Dzhugashvili (1879–1953). Soviet statesman. He was one of the main architects of the U.S.S.R., becoming leader (1927) and premier (1941). In his search for supreme power, he exiled Trotsky (1929), purged the government and army, forced the collectivisation of agriculture, and embarked on a policy of industrialisation. He triumphed as a leader during World War II, and attended the conferences at Tehran (1943), Yalta (1945), and Potsdam (1945). His rule was officially denounced in the U.S.S.R. in 1956.

Stalingrad. See **Volgograd.**

Sta·lin·ism (stáa-lin-iz'm, stá-) *n.* The bureaucratic and authoritarian exercise of state power and mechanistic application of Marxist-Leninist principles associated with Stalin's leadership, especially in the U.S.S.R. and other Communist states. **—Sta·lin·ist** *n.* & *adj.*

stalk¹ (stawk) *n.* **1. a.** The main stem of a herbaceous plant. **b.** A stem or similar structure that supports a plant part such as a flower, flower cluster, or leaf. **2.** Any slender or elongated support or structure. [Middle English *stalk(e),* probably diminutive of *stale,* ladder rung, handle, from Old English *stalu.*] **—stalk·y** *adj.*

stalk² *v.* **stalked, stalking, stalks.** *—intr.* **1.** To walk with a stiff, haughty, or angry gait: *stalked off in a huff.* **2.** To move threateningly or menacingly: *Pestilence stalked through the land.* **3.** To track game. *—tr.* **1.** To pursue or track stealthily. **2.** To traverse (a place or area) threateningly or menacingly. [Middle English *stalken,* Old English *(be)stealcian,* to walk cautiously, from Germanic; akin to STEAL.] **—stalk·er** *n.*

stalk·ing-horse (stáwking-hawrss) *n.* **1. a.** A horse trained to conceal the hunter while stalking. **b.** A canvas screen made in the figure of a horse, used for similar concealment. **2.** Anything used to cover one's true feelings, plans, or purpose; a decoy. **3.** *U.S.* Any sham candidate put forward to conceal the candidacy of another or to divide the opposition.

stall (stawl) *n.* **1.** A compartment for one domestic animal in a barn or shed. **2. a.** Any small compartment, booth, or cubicle. **b.** A booth from which a trader can sell his goods. **3.** An enclosed seat in the chancel or choir of a church, especially one reserved for a clergyman. **b.** A pew in a church. **4.** *Chiefly British.* **a.** A seat in the front part of a theatre. **b.** *Plural.* The area on the bottom level of a theatre towards the front. **5.** Any of the compartments in which a racehorse is kept immediately preceding the start of a race. **6.** A protective sheath, a **fingerstall** *(see).* **7.** An instance of stalling by an engine. **8.** The condition in which a decrease in an aircraft's speed, or increase in the angle of the aerofoil to the forward direction of the aircraft, causes a sudden fall in lift and may cause loss of control and a sharp decrease in altitude. **9.** *U.S. Informal.* A ruse or delaying tactic.
~v. **stalled, stalling, stalls.** *—tr.* **1.** To put or lodge (an animal) in a stall. **2.** To maintain (an animal) in a stall for fattening. **3.** To check the motion or progress of; bring to a standstill. **4.** To evade or put off by employing delaying tactics. Often used with *off*: *stall off creditors.* **5.** Accidentally to cause (an engine) to stop running. **6.** To cause (an aircraft) to go into a stall. *—intr.* **1.** To live or be lodged in a stall. Used of an animal. **2.** To stick fast in mud or snow. **3.** To come to a standstill. **4.** To employ delaying tactics to postpone action or to evade pressing circumstances. **5.** To stop running from mechanical failure. Used of an engine. **6.** To lose forward speed causing a stall. Used of an aircraft. [Middle English *stal(l),* Old English *steall,* standing place, stable.]

stall-feed (stáwl-feed) *tr.v.* **-fed** (-fed), **-feeding, -feeds.** To lodge and feed (an animal) in a stall for the purpose of fattening.

stall·ing angle (stáwling) *n.* The angle between the chord of an aerofoil and the undisturbed air flow at which a stall occurs. Also called "critical angle", "stall angle".

stal·lion (stál-yən) *n.* An adult male horse that has not been castrated. [Middle English *stalo(u)n,* from Old French *estalon,* from Germanic.]

stal·wart (stáwl-wərt, -wurt ‖ stól-, stál-) *adj.* **1.** Having physical strength; sturdy; robust. **2.** Resolute; uncompromisingly supportive. —See Synonyms at **strong.**
~n. One who is stalwart; especially, one who actively supports a cause or organisation, such as a political party. [Middle English (Scottish dialect) variant of *stalworth, stalwurth,* Old English *stælwierthe,* serviceable : *stæl,* place + *wierthe, weorth,* worth.] **—stal·wart·ly** *adv.* **—stal·wart·ness** *n.*

sta·men (stáy-men, -mən) *n., pl.* **-mens** or *rare* **stamina** (stámminə). The pollen-producing reproductive organ of a flower, usually consisting of a filament supporting an anther. [Latin *stāmen,* thread of the warp, stamen.]

stam·i·na (stámminə) *n.* **1.** The physical or mental strength required to resist or withstand disease, fatigue, or other hardship; endurance. **2.** *Rare.* Plural of stamen. [Latin, plural of *stāmen,* thread of the warp, thread of human life.]

stam·i·nal (stámmin'l) *adj.* **1.** Pertaining to, showing, or producing stamina. **2.** Pertaining to a stamen or stamens.

stam·i·nate (stámmi-nət, -nit, -nayt) *adj. Botany.* **1.** Having a stamen or stamens. **2.** Bearing stamens but lacking pistils.

stam·i·node (stámmi-nōd) *n.* Also **stam·i·no·di·um** (-nōdi-əm) *pl.* **-dia** (-ə). *Botany.* A sterile functionless stamen. [New Latin *staminodium,* from Latin *stāmen,* STAMEN.]

stam·i·no·dy (stámmi-nōdi) *n.* The transformation of a plant part, such as a petal or sepal, into a stamen. [New Latin *stamen* (stem *stamin-*) + -ODE + -Y.]

stam·mel (stámm'l) *n.* **1.** A coarse, red woollen cloth formerly used for undergarments. **2.** *Archaic.* The red colour of this cloth.
~adj. Obsolete. Red. [Probably variant of *stamin,* Middle English *stamyn,* from Latin *stāminea,* feminine of *stāmineus,* made of threads, from *stāmen,* thread of the warp.]

stam·mer (stámmər) *v.* **-mered, -mering, -mers.** *—intr.* To intrude involuntary pauses or repetitions, especially of initial consonants, into one's speaking, either because of a speech disorder or through tension, fear, or the like. *—tr.* To utter with a stammer.
~n. An instance or habit of stammering. [Middle English *stameren,* Old English *stamerian,* from Germanic.] **—stam·mer·er** *n.* **—stam·mer·ing·ly** *adv.*

stamp (stamp) *v.* **stamped, stamping, stamps.** *—tr.* **1.** To bring down (the foot) forcibly upon a hard surface. **2.** To bring the foot down upon (an object or surface) forcibly. **3.** To bring into a specified condition by or as if by thrusting downwards forcibly with the foot: *stamped the sand smooth.* **4.** To form or cut out by application of a mould, form, or die. **5.** To imprint or impress with a mark, design, or seal. **6.** To impress forcibly or permanently: *Her face was stamped on his mind.* **7.** To affix an adhesive stamp to (an envelope, for example). **8.** To identify, characterise, or reveal: *stamps the painting as being fake.* *—intr.* **1.** To thrust the foot forcibly downwards. **2.** To walk with forcible, heavy steps. **—stamp out.** To eradicate; destroy. —See Usage note at **stomp.**
~n. **1.** The act of stamping. **2. a.** An implement or device used to impress, cut out, or shape something to which it is applied. **b.** The impression or shape thus formed. **3.** A mark, design, or seal, the impression of which on a piece of paper indicates payment of a fee, ownership, approval, completion, or the like. **4. a.** A small piece of gummed paper sold by a government for attachment to an article that is to be posted; a postage stamp. **b.** Any similar piece of gummed paper issued for a specified purpose, as indicating, for example, that tax has been paid by an individual. **5.** Any identifying or characterising mark or impression: *bears the stamp of originality.* **6.** Characteristic nature or quality; class; kind: *Women of her stamp are one in a hundred.* **7.** *British Informal.* A contribution for National Insurance. [Middle English *stampen,* Old English *stampian* (unattested), to pound, stamp; noun partly from verb and from Old French *estampe*; both from Germanic.]

stamp duty *n.* A tax put on certain legal documents, such as deeds or conveyances, and certified by a piece of paper that bears an authorised stamp.

stam·pede (stám-peéd, stam-) *n.* **1.** A sudden headlong rush of startled animals, especially cattle or horses. **2.** A sudden headlong rush of a crowd of people. **3.** Any precipitous mass movement.
~v. **stampeded, -peding, -pedes.** *—intr.* To participate in a stampede. *—tr.* To cause to stampede. [Mexican Spanish *estampida,* from Spanish, uproar, crash, "a stamping or pounding", from *estampar,* to pound, stamp, from Germanic.] **—stam·ped·er** *n.*

stamp·ing ground (stámping) *n.* One's customary resort.

stamp mill *n.* **1.** A machine that crushes ore. **2.** A building in which ore is crushed.

stance (stanss, staanss) *n.* **1.** The posture or position of a standing person or animal; especially, the position assumed by a sportsman, such as a cricketer or golfer, when preparing to make a stroke. **2.** An emotional or intellectual attitude or position. [French, from Italian *stanza,* STANZA.]

stanch (staanch ‖ stanch) *tr.v.* **stanched, stanching, stanches.** Also **staunch** (staanch, stawnch). **1. a.** To stop or check (flow of a bodily fluid, especially blood). **b.** To stop or check the flow of (a bodily fluid, especially blood). **c.** To check the flow of blood from (a wound). **2.** To stop or check (an outflow or loss); stem: *stanched the flow of foreign investment out of the country.*
~adj. Variant of **staunch.** [Middle English *staunchen,* to stop from flowing, from Old French *estanch(i)er,* from Vulgar Latin *stancāre* (unattested), from *stancus*† (unattested), dried.] **—stanch·er** *n.*

stan·chion (staán-sh'n ‖ stán-) *n.* **1.** An upright pole, post, or support. **2.** A framework consisting usually of two vertical bars, used to secure cattle in a stall.
~tr.v. **stanchioned, -chioning, -chions. 1.** To build stanchions for; equip with stanchions. **2.** To confine (cattle) by means of stanchions. [Middle English *stanchon,* from Anglo-French, from Old French *estanchon,* from *estanc(h)e,* a stay, prop, from Latin *stāre.*]

stand (stand) *v.* **stood** (stŏŏd ‖ stōōd), **standing, stands.** *—intr.* **1. a.** To maintain an upright position on the feet. **b.** To be placed in or maintain an erect position upon a base, support, or bottom. **2. a.** To rise to a standing position. Often used with *up.* **b.** To assume a standing position in a manner specified: *stand straight; stand to one side.* **3.** To point or set. Used of a gun dog. **4.** To measure a specified height when in a standing position: *stands five feet tall.* **5. a.** To remain stable, upright, or intact: *hardly a house left standing after the earthquake.* **b.** To remain valid, effective, or unaltered: *The agreement still stands.* **6.** To maintain a position, attitude, or course: *stand firm.* **7. a.** To be expressed as or show a specified figure or amount. Used with *at*: *Your balance stands at £150.* **b.** To occupy a specified position or level on or as if on a scale; rank: *her reputation stands high.* **8.** To be in a position offering the likelihood or expectation of loss or gain: *stood to lose a fortune.* **9.** To be in a particular or specified state, condition, or situation: *stands corrected; stands in awe of him.* **10.** To act in the specified capacity or perform the specified function: *stand surety; stand guard.* **11.** To be situated or placed: *The castle stood in the woods.* **12. a.** To remain in a stationary position: *the train now standing at platform 9.* **b.** To remain in a state of inactivity: *machinery standing idle.* **13.** To remain without flowing or being disturbed; be stagnant. **14.** To be a candidate for public office: *will stand in the next election.* **15.** To take or hold a particular course or direction; steer: *a ship standing to windward.* *—tr.* **1.** To cause to stand; place upright. **2. a.** To resist or endure without yielding or without sustaining damage; withstand: *stand siege; can't stand the strain.* **b.** To tolerate; put up with; bear: *can't stand the sight of him.* **4. a.** To be subjected to; undergo: *stand trial.* **b.** To submit to and emerge successfully from: *an argument that will not stand close examination.* **5.** *Informal.* To pay the cost for; treat: *stand someone to a drink.* —See Synonyms at **bear.** **—stand down. 1.** *Law.* To leave the witness box, as after giving testimony. **2.** To withdraw, retire, or resign, as from a position of office or authority. **3. a.** To go off

stalagmites and stalactites *Limestone-rich water dripping into a cave forms stalactites on the cave's roof and stalagmites on its floor. Pillars are formed when the two meet. The large stalagmite shown here is in Wookey Hole, Somerset, England. It is called the Witch of Wookey after a local legend that a witch was turned to stone in the cave.*

stallion *A male horse. This is a shire stallion, an English draught breed formerly called the Great Horse of England.*

duty. Used of a member of the armed forces. **b.** To be taken off duty. **—stand for. 1. a.** To signify; indicate: *What does R.A.C. stand for?* **b.** To represent; symbolise: *the Royal Family and all it stands for.* **2.** To put oneself forward as a candidate for (a public office). **3.** To be a supporter or advocate of: *stands for freedom of the press.* **4.** *Informal.* To tolerate; endure; put up with. **—stand on. 1.** To be strict in the observance of; insist on: *Don't stand on ceremony.* **2.** In navigation, to maintain the same course or tack. **—stand over. 1.** To keep close surveillance on or watch closely, especially in a threatening manner. **2.** To hold over or be held over; postpone. **—stand to.** *British.* **1.** To take up positions in readiness for action. Used of soldiers. **2.** To cause (soldiers) to stand to.

~n. **1.** The act of standing. **2.** A ceasing of work or activity; a standstill; a halt. **3.** In cricket, a usually prolonged stay at the wicket by two batsmen; a partnership: *a record stand for the last wicket.* **4.** A stop on a theatrical, concert, or other performance tour: *a one-night stand.* **5.** The place or spot where a person stands. **6.** A booth, stall, or counter for the display of goods for sale. **7.** A parking space reserved for taxis. **8.** An act of or position for defence or resistance, especially when desperate or decisive in a campaign: *made a final stand at the river.* **9.** A stance or opinion one is prepared to uphold: *take a stand.* **10.** A large, raised structure for spectators at a sporting ground. **11.** A small rack, prop, or table for holding any of various articles: *a music stand.* **12.** A group or growth of tall plants or trees: *a stand of pine.* **13.** *U.S.* A **witness box** *(see).* [Stand, stood (past tense); Middle English *standen, sto(o)d,* Old English *standan, stōd* (past singular).] **—stand·er** *n.*

stan·dard (stándərd) *n. Abbr.* **std. 1.** A flag, banner, or ensign, especially: **a.** The ensign of a chief of state, nation, or city: *the Royal standard.* **b.** A pole topped with an emblem or flag of an army, especially one raised formerly in battle to indicate the rallying point for the soldiers of one side. **c.** The flag of a mounted military regiment. **2. a.** An acknowledged measure of comparison for quantitative or qualitative value; a criterion; a norm. **b.** An object that under stated conditions defines, represents, or records the magnitude of a **unit** *(see).* **3.** The set proportion by weight of gold or silver to alloy metal prescribed for use in coinage. **4.** The commodity or commodities used to back a monetary system. **5. a.** A degree or level of requirement, excellence, or attainment. **b.** *Usually plural.* A requirement of moral conduct. **6.** *Chiefly British.* A class or level in a primary school. **7.** A pedestal, stand, or base. **8.** *Botany.* **a.** The large upper petal of the flower of a sweet pea or related plant. **b.** Any of the narrow, upright petals of an iris. **9.** A shrub or small tree that through grafting or training has a single stem of limited height with a crown of leaves and flowers at its apex. —See Synonyms at **ideal.**

~adj. **1. a.** Serving as or conforming to a standard of measurement or value. **b.** Of a normal, familiar, and commonly used kind: *a standard type of plug.* **c.** Well known and widely accepted as an authority: *a standard atlas.* **d.** Of average but not exceptional quality: *The acting and production were pretty standard.* **e.** Supplied automatically as an ordinary part or feature of a product: *Its standard equipment includes a heated rear windscreen.* **2.** *Linguistics. Often capital* **S.** Conforming to usage, as in pronunciation, vocabulary, and grammatical construction, that is widely regarded as acceptable and typically associated with educated speakers of a language: *standard English.* —See Synonyms at **normal.** [Middle English, from Anglo-French *estaundart,* Old French *estendart,* flag marking a place for rallying, from *estendre,* to EXTEND.]

stan·dard-bear·er (stándərd-bair-ər) *n.* **1.** One who bears the colours of a military unit. **2.** One who is in the vanguard, as of a political or religious movement.

stan·dard-bred (stándərd-bred) *n.* One of an American breed of horses developed for harness racing.

standard candle *n.* In optics, a **candela** *(see).*

standard cell *n.* A voltaic cell that produces a constant known electromotive force, enabling it to be used as a method of calibrating electrical measuring instruments.

standard deviation *n. Abbr.* **s.d., S.D.** *Symbol* **σ, s** *Statistics.* **1.** The square root of the **variance** *(see).* **2.** A statistic used as a measure of dispersion in a distribution, the square root of the arithmetic average of the squares of the deviations from the mean. In this sense, also called "root mean square deviation".

standard gauge *n.* A railway track having a width of 56½ inches. **—stan·dard-gauge** (stándərd-gáyj) *adj.*

stan·dard·ise, stan·dard·ize (stándərd-īz) *tr.v.* **-ised, -ising, -ises. 1.** To cause to conform to a standard. **2.** To evaluate by comparison with a standard. **—stan·dard·i·sa·tion** (-ī-záysh'n || *U.S.* -i-) *n.*

standard lamp *n. British.* A lamp set on a tall polelike support resting on a base on the ground.

standard of living *n.* The quality of material comfort as enjoyed by a country, an individual, or a section of society; especially, this quality as gauged by statistical surveys of the number and type of consumer goods per household. Compare **quality of life.**

standard time *n.* The mean (solar) time of a meridian centrally located over a country or time zone and used for the whole area, that changes with longitude. Standard times are exact numbers of hours or half-hours ahead or behind Greenwich Mean Time.

stand by *intr.v.* **1.** To be available and ready for action if needed. **2.** To remain inactive; refrain from intervening: *couldn't just stand by and see him swindled.* *—tr.v.* **1.** To aid; support. **2.** To keep or maintain (one's word, policy, or promise).

stand·by (stánd-bī) *n., pl.* **-bys. 1.** One that can always be depended upon. **2.** That which is kept in readiness to fill a need: *Baked beans are a good standby to feed hungry mouths.* **—on standby.** Ready and waiting.

~adj. **1.** Kept in reserve for use when needed: *a standby generator.* **2.** Issued or available only immediately prior to a journey: *a standby air ticket.* **3.** Of, pertaining to, or waiting for an aircraft on which one can travel with a standby ticket: *standby passengers.*

~adv. Using a standby ticket: *flew standby to New York.*

stand·first (stánd-furst) *n.* The sentence or paragraph of copy that prefaces an article in a newspaper or magazine, designed to catch the reader's attention and to give some idea of the contents of the text. **—stand·first** *adj.*

stand in *intr.v.* To act as a stand-in.

stand-in (stánd-in) *n.* **1.** One who substitutes for an actor during lights and camera adjustments or in hazardous stunts. **2.** Any person who acts as a substitute: *He's the stand-in for the sick teacher.*

stand·ing (stánding) *n.* **1. a.** Status with respect to credit, rank, or reputation. **b.** High reputation; esteem. **2.** Length of time; duration: *a friendship of long standing.*

~adj. **1.** Remaining upright; erect. **2.** Made or performed from a standing or stationary position: *a standing jump.* **3. a.** Remaining valid or unchanged: *a standing arrangement.* **b.** Well-established and familiar: *a standing joke.* **4.** Not flowing; stagnant.

standing army *n.* A permanent army of paid soldiers.

standing crop *n. Ecology.* The total amount of living organisms in a particular area or at a particular level of a food chain at a given time, usually expressed in terms of **biomass** *(see).*

standing order *n.* **1.** An order or instruction given to a bank by a customer, requesting that a stated sum of money should be paid at regular intervals to a stated party. Also called "banker's order". **2.** Any of a series of rules stating or recommending the way in which a society or other body should conduct its business.

standing ovation *n.* An ovation in which those applauding stand.

standing room *n.* Space in which to stand, as in a public place or vehicle where all seats are filled.

standing stone *n.* A large, upright stone or slab of stone, usually found in ancient henge monuments.

standing wave *n.* A wave in which the amplitude of the resultant of a transmitted and a reflected wave is stationary in time and in which some of the energy of the transmitted wave is absorbed by the reflecting boundary. Also called "stationary wave".

stand off *intr.v.* **1.** To keep apart; remain aloof. **2.** *Nautical.* To take or maintain a course away from shore. *—tr.v. British.* To dispense with or dismiss (an employee) temporarily.

stand-off (stánd-off, -awf) *n.* **1.** *U.S.* A tie, as in a contest; a draw. **2.** *U.S.* An effect that neutralises or counterbalances. **3.** A stand-off half.

stand-off half *n.* **1.** In Rugby football, a player, especially one skilled in kicking, who provides the link between the scrum half and the rest of the backs. **2.** The position of such a player. Also called "stand-off", "fly half", *British* "outside half".

stand-off·ish (stánd-óffish, -áwfish) *adj.* Coldly reserved; aloof.

stand oil *n.* A drying oil, such as linseed, tung, or soya, heated with minimum oxidation until thickened and used in oil enamel paints.

stand out *intr.v.* **1.** To protrude; stick out. **2.** To be conspicuous, distinctive, or prominent. **3.** To hold out; maintain support or opposition. Used with *for* or *against*: *stand out against a verdict.* **4.** *Nautical.* To take or maintain a course away from shore.

stand·out (stánd-owt) *n. U.S.* One that is outstanding or excellent.

stand·pipe (stánd-pīp) *n.* **1.** A large vertical pipe into which water is pumped in order to produce a desired pressure. **2.** A vertical pipe with a tap erected outdoors, for use when a domestic supply is interrupted, for example.

stand·point (stánd-poynt) *n.* A position from which things are considered or judged; a point of view. [Translation of German *Standpunkt.*]

St. An·drews (ándrōōz). Coastal resort of Fife Region, east Scotland. It was once the ecclesiastical capital of Scotland and has the country's oldest university (1411). It is a renowned golfing centre with its Royal and Ancient Club (1754).

stand·still (stánd-stil, stán-) *n.* A condition in which activity or progress has ceased; a halt: *came to a standstill.*

stand up *intr.v.* To remain unimpaired or prove valid or satisfactory when subjected to testing conditions: *stood up to long wear.* *—tr.v. Informal.* To fail to keep an appointment with (a person). **—stand up for.** To side with; defend. **—stand up to.** To face up to; confront fearlessly.

stand-up (stánd-up) *adj.* **1.** Erect; upright: *a stand-up collar.* **2.** Taken or performed while standing: *a stand-up supper.* **3.** Designating a boxing or fist fight confined largely to heavy blows with little manoeuvring. **4.** Designating or practising a style of comic performance done solo and without stage properties.

Stan·ford-Bi·net scale (stánfərd-bi-náy) *n.* A revision of the **Binet-Simon scale** *(see)* used in one form or another since 1916. Also called "Stanford-Binet test", "Stanford Revision of the Binet scale". [Prepared at *Stanford* University, California.]

stang. *Obsolete.* Past tense of **sting.**

stan·hope (stánnəp || stán-hōp) *n.* A light open horse-drawn vehicle with one seat and two wheels. [Designed by the Reverend Fitzroy *Stanhope* (1787–1864), English clergyman.]

Stan·i·slav·sky (stánni-sláv-ski), **Konstantin Sergeyevitch Alexeyev** (1863–1938). Russian actor-producer. He cofounded (1898) the

PRONUNCIATION KEY

a, trap; aa, father; ai, fair; ar, star; aw, lawn; ay, play; b, bb, stab; rubber; ch, church; ck, ticket; d, dd, dead; ladder; e, dress; ee, bee; er, defer; ew, few; ewr, pure; ə, about; ər, letter; f, ff, fife; differ; g, gg, giggle; h, hat; i, kit; ī, price; īr, fire; j, judge; k, kick; l, ll, let; 'l, needle; m, mm, man; n, nn, no; 'n, sudden; ng, thing; o, lot; ō, no; ŏŏ, foot; ōō, shoe; oor, poor; ow, cow; owr, hour; oy, boy; p, pp, pepper; r, rr, red; s, ss, sauce; sh, ship; t, tt, totter; th, thick; th, this; smooth; u, cut; ur, turn; v, vv, valve; w, wet; y, yes; z, zz, zebra; zh, vision; pleasure

IN FOREIGN WORDS:

aN, oN, Saint-Saëns; hl, Llanelli; Hluhluwe; kh, loch; lough; Khaled

STRESS MARK:

ín-sīt, insight; in-sít, incite

star

THE LIFE AND DEATH OF A STAR
Starlight – the nuclear fusion of hydrogen atoms

Stars form when gigantic clouds of gas and dust that are scattered through the galaxies collapse under the inward pull of their own gravity. At the star's core, hydrogen atoms are crushed together to form helium in a process of nuclear fusion which releases energy and keeps the star burning for most of its life. This burning state is known as the main sequence, and most stars remain on the main sequence for a period which may be as long as 10,000 million years. The Sun is in this state now.

When the hydrogen is exhausted, stars of similar mass to the Sun expand into luminous red giants, which eventually decay into faint white dwarfs that cool, shrink, and fade into balls of ash that are often known as black dwarfs.

More massive stars remain on the main sequence for a shorter period of time and instead of becoming white dwarfs they explode as supernovae, eventually collapsing to become extremely dense neutron stars. A thimbleful of matter from a neutron star weighs hundreds of millions of tonnes. Astronomers believe that the biggest stars continue to collapse under their own gravity until they become black holes from which not even light can escape.

Because of their high temperature, stars give off their own light, whereas planets can be seen only by the Sun's light reflected from them. All stars – with the exception of the Sun – are such immense distances from the Earth that they appear as minute points of light, which seem to twinkle when seen through the Earth's atmosphere.

Stars are classified according to colour, temperature, and brightness, and so far about 250,000 have been catalogued. Only about 3,000 stars are visible to the naked eye, but about 1,500 million can be seen with the aid of instruments.

PROGRESSION FROM BIRTH TO DEATH OF A STAR THE SIZE OF THE SUN

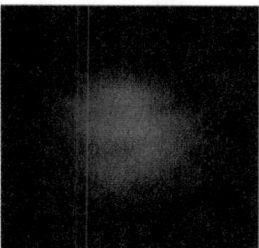    

The star forms out of clouds of gas and dust.

It then joins the main sequence for up to 10,000 million years.

Then it becomes a red giant and gets brighter and bigger.

It becomes unstable and begins to eject its outer layers.

Eventually it collapses into a white dwarf and its glow fades.

Moscow Art Theatre, where he devised a system of acting in which actors develop their own conception of their roles.

stank. Past tense of **stink.**

Stan·ley (stánli). See **Port Stanley.**

Stanley, Sir Henry Morton (1841–1904). British journalist and explorer. He found (1871) the lost explorer David Livingstone at Lake Tanganyika, and explored (1874–77) equatorial Africa. He founded (1879) the Congo Free State for Leopold II of the Belgians.

stan·na·ry (stánnəri) *n., pl.* **-ries.** A place or region where tin is mined. [Medieval Latin *stannāria,* neuter plural of Late Latin *stannum,* tin. See **stannic.**]

stan·nic (stánnik) *adj.* Of or containing tin, especially with valency 4. [Probably from French *stannique,* from Late Latin *stannum,* tin, from Latin *stannum†,* an alloy of silver and lead.]

stannic chloride *n.* A colourless caustic liquid, $Na_2SnCl_6 \cdot H_2O$, made from tin treated with chlorine and used in the manufacture of textiles, sensitised papers, and perfumes.

stan·nif·er·ous (sta-nífferəs) *adj.* Containing tin. [Late Latin *stannum,* tin + -FEROUS.]

stan·nite (stán-īt) *n.* A grey to black mineral, chiefly Cu_2FeSnS_4, having a metallic lustre. Also called "tin pyrites". [German *Stannit* : Late Latin *stannum,* tin (see **stannic**) + -ITE.]

stan·nous (stánnəss) *adj.* Of or containing tin, especially with valency 2. [Late Latin *stannum,* tin. See **stannic.**]

St. An·tho·ny's fire *n. Pathology.* **1.** Erysipelas *(see).* **2.** Ergotism *(see).* Not in technical usage. [From the belief that the intercession of St. Anthony helped to relieve these diseases.]

stan·za (stánzə) *n. Abbr.* **st.** Any of a number of distinct and separate units that divide up a poem, and that is composed of two or more lines usually characterised by a common pattern of metre, rhyme, and number of lines. [Italian, "a stopping or standing", from Vulgar Latin *stantia* (unattested), from Latin *stāns,* present participle of *stāre,* to stand.] —**stan·za·ic** (stan-záy-ik) *adj.*

sta·pe·li·a (stə-péeli-ə) *n.* Any plant of the African genus *Stapelia,* having fleshy stems, no leaves, and large, unpleasant-smelling flowers. Also called "carrion flower". [New Latin, after J. B. van Stapel (died 1636), Dutch botanist.]

sta·pes (stáy-peez) *n., pl.* **stapes** or **stapedes** (sta-pée-deez, stə-, stápi-deez). A small, sound-conducting bone of the inner ear, shaped somewhat like a stirrup. Also called "stirrup bone". Compare **anvil, malleus.** [New Latin, from Medieval Latin *stapēs,* perhaps variant of *staffa, stapha, stapeda,* stirrup : Latin *stāre,* to stand + *pēs* (stem *ped-*), foot.] —**sta·pe·di·al** (sta-péedi-əl, stə-) *adj.*

staphylo– *comb. form.* Indicates: **1.** *Anatomy.* The uvula; for example, **staphylorrhaphy.** **2.** *Microbiology.* Resembling a bunch of grapes; clustered; for example, **staphylococcus.** [New Latin, from Greek *staphulē,* bunch of grapes, grapevine, uvula.]

staph·y·lo·coc·cus (stáffil-ə-kóckəss, -ō-) *n., pl.* **-cocci** (-kóksī, -kók-ī, -ee). Any of various Gram-positive, spherical bacteria of the genus *Staphylococcus,* occurring in grapelike clusters. Also called "staph". [New Latin : STAPHYLO- + -COCCUS.] —**staph·y·lo·coc·cal** (-kóck'l), **staph·y·lo·coc·cic** (-kóksik) *adj.*

staph·y·lo·plas·ty (stáffil-ō-plásti, -ə-) *n.* Corrective surgery of the uvula and the soft palate. [STAPHYLO- + -PLASTY.] —**staph·y·lo·plas·tic** *adj.*

staph·y·lor·rha·phy, staph·y·lor·a·phy (stáffil-órrəfi) *n.* The correction of a cleft palate or divided uvula by plastic surgery. [STAPHYLO- + Greek *-rrhaphia,* sewing, suture, from *rhaptein,* to sew.]

sta·ple[1] (stáyp'l) *n.* **1.** A major commodity grown or produced in a region. **2.** A commodity in steady or constant demand, such as salt, flour, or coffee. **3.** A major part, element, or feature. **4.** Raw material. **5.** The graded fibre of cotton, wool, or flax.

~*adj.* **1.** In constant supply and demand. **2.** Important as an article of trade, production, or consumption in a particular region: *staple exports.* **3.** Principal; main: *a staple topic of conversation.*

~*tr.v.* **stapled, -pling, -ples.** To grade (fibres) according to length and fineness. [Middle English *staple* market town, from Old French *estaple,* from Middle Dutch *stapel,* pillar, emporium.]

sta·ple[2] *n.* **1.** A U-shaped metal loop with pointed ends, driven into a surface to hold a bolt, hook, or hasp, or to hold wiring in place. **2.** A thin piece of wire having the shape of a square bracket, used, by being forced through and flattened, as a fastening for papers, cloth, and similar materials.

~*tr.v.* **stapled, -pling, -ples.** To fasten by means of a staple or staples. [Middle English *stapel, stapul,* Old English *stapol,* post, pillar, from Germanic.]

sta·pler[1] (stáyplər) *n.* One who deals in staple goods or fibres.

stapler[2] *n.* A machine or hand-operated device used to bind material together by means of staples.

star (star) *n.* **1.** *Astronomy.* A light-emitting mass of gas in which the energy generated by nuclear reactions in the interior is balanced by the outflow of energy to the surface, and the inward-directed gravitational forces are balanced by the outward-directed gas and radiation pressures. **2.** Any of the celestial bodies visible at night from Earth as relatively stationary, usually twinkling points of light. **3.** Anything regarded as resembling such a body. **4. a.** A graphic design or emblem conventionally representing a star, having five or more radiating points, and often used as a symbol, as of rank or excellence. **b.** Any of a number of such symbols used to indicate relative position on a recognised scale of quality: *a three-star hotel.* **5. a.** An artistic performer or athlete whose superior talent or ability is acknowledged. **b.** *British Slang.* An excellent person: *Be a star, and make some coffee, will you?* **6.** An asterisk (*). **7.** A white spot on the forehead of a horse. **8.** In astrology: **a.** A heavenly body considered to influence a person's character or destiny. **b.** *Plural.* A horoscope: *Buy a magazine so I can read my stars.* —**see stars.** To experience bright, flashing sensations, as from a blow on the head. —**thank (one's) lucky stars.** To be thankful for one's good fortune. ~*v.* **starred, starring, stars.** —*tr.* **1.** To ornament or set with stars. **2. a.** To award or mark with or as with a star for excellence. **b.** To mark with an asterisk. **3.** To present or feature (a performer) in a leading role. —*intr.* **1.** To play the leading role in a film or theatrical production. **2.** To do an outstanding job; perform excellently. ~*adj.* **1.** Of or pertaining to a star: *star quality.* **2.** Pre-eminent; brilliant. [Middle English *ste(o)rre,* Old English *steorra.*]

star anise *n.* **1.** An aromatic tree, *Illicium verum,* of eastern Asia,

starfish *Rows of sucker-like tube-feet enable the starfish to creep along the ocean floor. Its mouth is on the underside of the central part, and it devours small seabed creatures as it crawls over them. Many of the 1,800 different species can regenerate lost arms.*

starling *Adult starlings of both sexes have an iridescent summer plumage of black, purple, and green (above). In winter the bills darken and the plumage changes to black with white spots, which are more pronounced in the female.*

star-of-Bethlehem *Star-like flowers and its abundance in Palestine have given* Ornithogalum umbellatum *its common name. The plant blooms in late spring, and the flowers close at night and do not open again until mid-morning, which has given it another name – ten o' clock lady.*

having purple-red flowers and anise-scented fruit. **2.** The fruit of this tree, used in Oriental cooking. Also called "Chinese anise".

star apple *n.* **1.** A tropical American tree, *Chrysophyllum cainito,* bearing smooth-skinned greenish-purple fruit. **2.** The edible fruit of this tree, having a star-shaped core.

star·board (stár-bərd, *also* -bawrd || -bōrd) *n.* The right-hand side of a ship or aircraft as one faces forwards. Compare **port.**
~*adj.* On the right-hand side.
~*tr.v.* **starboarded, -boarding, -boards.** To turn or shift (the helm of a vessel) to the right. [Middle English *sterbord,* Old English *stēorbord,* "rudder side" (early Teutonic ships had rudders on the right sides) : *stēor,* rudder + *bord,* ship's side, board.]

starch (starch) *n.* **1.** A naturally abundant nutrient carbohydrate, consisting of linked units of D-glucose, found chiefly in the seeds, fruits, tubers, roots, and stem pith of plants, notably in potatoes, wheat, and rice, varying widely in appearance according to source but commonly prepared as a white, amorphous, tasteless powder. **2.** Any of various substances, including natural starch, used to stiffen fabrics after washing them. **3.** Foods having a high content of starch. **4.** Stiffness or formality in manner or behaviour.
~*tr.v.* **starched, starching, starches.** To stiffen with starch. [Middle English *sterche, starche,* from *sterchen,* to stiffen (with starch), Old English *stercan* (attested only by past participle *sterced-*).]

Star Chamber *n.* **1.** A former English court (abolished in 1641) consisting of judges who were appointed by the Crown and sat in closed session on cases involving the security of the state. **2.** *Small* **s,** *small* **c.** Any court or tribunal that resembles the Star Chamber, especially in the manner of its secrecy and the severity of its judgments. [So called because the ceiling of the original courtroom was decorated with gilded stars.]

starch·y (stárchi) *adj.* **-ier, -iest. 1.** Of, of the nature of, or containing starch. **2.** Stiffened with starch. **3.** *Informal.* Stiff; formal. **—starch·i·ly** *adv.* **—starch·i·ness** *n.*

star connection *n. Electricity.* A connection of three or more phase supplies that joins one end of each branch at a common point. Compare **delta connection.**

star-crossed (stár-krost || -krawst) *adj.* Beset or dogged with bad luck: *star-crossed lovers.*

star·dom (stárdəm) *n.* **1.** The status of an actor or other performer acknowledged as a star. **2.** Stars collectively, as of the cinema.

star·dust (stár-dust) *n.* **1.** Distant stars seen as a mass of tiny glittering lights. **2.** A dreamy, misty, romantic quality.

stare (stair) *v.* **stared, staring, stares.** *—intr.* **1.** To look with a steady, often wide-eyed gaze, as from interest, astonishment, or hostility. **2.** *Chiefly British.* To stand out; be conspicuous or glaring. **3.** To stand on end or bristle, as animal hair or feathers. *—tr.* To affect by staring at: *He stared the boy into submission.* —See Synonyms at **gaze.** **—stare down** or **out.** To cause (a person) to avert his gaze by staring fixedly.
~*n.* The act of staring; an intent or fixed gaze. [Middle English *staren,* Old English *starian.*] **—star·er** *n.*

star facet *n.* Any of the eight small triangular facets in the crown of a brilliant-cut gem.

star·fish (stár-fish) *n., pl.* **starfishes** or collectively **starfish.** Any of various marine echinoderms of the class Asteroidea, characteristically having five arms extending from a central disc.

star·flow·er (stár-flowr, -flow-ər) *n.* Any of several plants having starlike flowers.

star·gaze (stár-gayz) *intr.v.* **-gazed, -gazing, -gazes. 1.** To gaze at or study the stars. **2.** To daydream.

star·gaz·er (stár-gayzər) *n.* **1. a.** One who stargazes. **b.** An astronomer or astrologer. Used humorously. **2.** Any of various marine bottom-dwelling fishes of the families Uranoscopidae and Dactyloscopidae, having eyes on the top of the head.

star grass *n.* Any of various plants of the genus *Hypoxis,* having grasslike leaves and star-shaped flowers.

stark (stark) *adj.* **starker, starkest. 1.** Without elaboration; bare; blunt: *stark truth.* **2.** Complete or utter; extreme: *stark poverty.* **3.** Harsh in appearance; bleak; grim: *stark cliffs.* **4.** Clearly defined; sharp: *in stark contrast.*
~*adv.* Utterly; entirely; absolutely: *stark raving mad; stark naked.* [Middle English *stark(e), sterk(e),* Old English *stearc,* hard, stern, severe, cruel.] **—stark·ly** *adv.* **—stark·ness** *n.*

Stark, Dame Freya (1893–). British travel writer. Her books include *The Valley of the Assassins* (1934) and *The Lycian Shore* (1956).

stark·ers (stárkərz) *adj. British Slang.* Completely naked.

star·let (stár-lət, -lit) *n.* **1.** A small star. **2.** A young film actress publicised as a future star.

star·light (stár-līt) *n.* The light given by the stars.
~*adj.* Starlit.

star·ling[1] (stárling) *n.* Any of various Old World birds of the family Sturnidae, characteristically having dark, often iridescent plumage; especially, *Sturnus vulgaris.* [Middle English *sterling, starling,* Old English *stærlinc* : *stær,* starling + -LING.]

starling[2] *n.* A protective structure of pilings surrounding a pier of a bridge. [Probably alteration of Middle English (now dialect) *staddling,* from *stadel, stathel,* foundation, Old English *stathol.*]

star·lit (stárlit) *adj.* Illuminated by starlight.

star-nosed mole (stár-nōzd) *n.* A mole, *Condylura cristata,* of eastern North America, having 22 small fleshy tentacles encircling the end of its nose.

star-of-Beth·le·hem (staar-əv-béthli-hem, -əm) *n.* **1.** A plant, *Ornithogalum umbellatum,* native to Europe, having narrow leaves and star-shaped white flowers. **2.** Any of several similar or related plants. [Probably from a fancied resemblance to the star that guided the Magi to the infant Jesus in Bethlehem (Matthew 2:2).]

Star of David *n.* A six-pointed star, or hexagram, formed by placing two triangles together, one upon the other or interlaced. It is a symbol of Judaism and appears on the Israeli flag. Also called "Magen David", "Shield of David".

Starr (star), **Ringo,** born Richard Starkey (1940–). British rock musician. He was drummer with the rock group, the Beatles, (1962–70). When the group disbanded (1970) he pursued a separate career as a musician and actor.

star·ry (staari) *adj.* **-rier, -riest. 1.** Of or resembling a star, especially in shape or brilliance. **2.** Set or filled with stars or with, or as if with, their light: *a starry night; starry eyes.* **—star·ri·ness** *n.*

star·ry-eyed (staari-īd) *adj.* Naively enthusiastic or romantic.

Stars and Stripes *n.* The flag of the United States. Preceded by *the.*

star sapphire *n.* A sapphire with a polished convex surface exhibiting a star-shaped figure.

star shell *n.* An artillery shell that explodes in midair with a shower of lights, used for illumination and signalling.

Star-Span·gled Banner (stár-spang-g'ld) *n.* **1.** The flag of the United States. Preceded by *the.* **2.** The national anthem of the United States.

start (start) *v.* **started, starting, starts.** *—intr.* **1. a.** To begin a journey or movement; move from a position of rest; set out: *started on her travels.* **b.** To begin a process, course of action, or undertaking: *Let's start at once. The show started with a dance routine.* **2. a.** To come into being or operation: *School starts at nine. The car won't start.* **b.** To have a beginning, origin, or lower limit: *Prices start at £4,000.* **3. a.** To move involuntarily: *started with fright.* **b.** To move suddenly; spring forth. **4.** To issue suddenly and forcefully; gush. **5.** To be in the line-up at the beginning of a race. **6.** To protrude or bulge: *eyes starting out of their sockets.* **7.** To become loosened or displaced, as from shrinkage. *—tr.* **1.** To set into motion, operation, or activity: *start the show.* Sometimes used with *off* or *up*: *Start up the engine. This started him off on one of his boring explanations.* **2. a.** To bring into being; initiate: *start a rumour; start a family.* **b.** To found; establish: *start a business.* **3. a.** To indicate the beginning of (a race). **b.** *Chiefly U.S.* To enter in a race. **4.** To cause or enable to begin an activity or venture, often with encouragement or instruction: *started her on painting at an early age.* **5.** To rouse (game) from its hiding place or lair; flush. **6.** To cause to work loose. **7.** *Chiefly British.* To conceive (a child). —See Synonyms at **begin.** **—start in.** To begin work or an activity. **—start out.** To set out on a journey, a course of action, or a career. **—start something.** *British Informal.* To pick a fight. **—to start with.** First of all; as a first consideration.
~*n.* **1.** A beginning; a commencement. **2.** A startled reaction or movement. **3.** *Plural.* Quick, brief spurts of effort or activity. Used chiefly in the phrase *by fits and starts.* **4.** A part that has become displaced or loosened. **5. a.** A place of beginning; a starting line. **b.** A time of beginning; a starting point. **6.** A signal to begin a race. **7.** A position of advantage over others, as in a race or endeavour; a lead: *got a start over the others; She got an hour's start before he began the chase.* **8.** An opportunity granted to pursue a career or course of action: *a good start in life.* **—for a start.** To start with. [Middle English *sterten,* Old English *styrtan* (attested only in the present participle *sturtende*), to leap up.]

START Strategic Arms Reduction Talks.

start·er (stártər) *n.* **1.** One that starts. **2.** An attachment for starting an internal-combustion engine without hand cranking. Also called "starter motor". **3.** One who signals the start of a race. **4.** A person or animal that starts in a race. **5.** *Chiefly British.* The first course of a meal. **6.** A chemical agent or bacterial culture used to start a reaction, as in the formation of acid in making yogurt, cheese, or vinegar. **—for starters.** *Informal.* To start with.

star thistle *n.* Any of several plants of the genus *Centaurea*; especially, *C. calcitrapa,* native to Eurasia, having spiny purplish flower heads.

start·ing block (stárting) *n.* Either of a pair of fixed supports on an athletics track, against which a runner pushes to gain initial momentum at the start of a race. Also called "block".

starting gate *n.* Any of a set of gates that are simultaneously raised to release the competitors in a horse or dog race.

starting grid *n.* In motor racing, an area where cars are staggered according to their relative practice times, before the start of a race.

starting handle *n. Chiefly British.* A **crank** *(see).*

starting pistol *n.* A pistol that is fired to signal the start of a race.

starting price *n.* The last odds given by bookmakers before the start of a horse or dog race.

star·tle (stárt'l) *v.* **-tled, -tling, -tles.** *—tr.* **1.** To cause to make a quick involuntary movement or start; rouse suddenly. **2.** To alarm, frighten, or surprise. *—intr.* To become startled.
~*n.* A sudden mild shock; a start. [Middle English *stertlen,* Old English *steartlian,* to kick, struggle, frequentative of *styrtan* (unattested), to leap up, START.] **—start·ling·ly** *adv.*

star·va·tion (staar-váysh'n) *n.* **1.** The act or process of starving. **2.** The condition of being starved.

starve (starv) *v.* **starved, starving, starves.** *—intr.* **1.** To suffer or die from extreme or prolonged lack of food. **2.** To suffer from deprivation; be in need. **3.** *Informal.* To be very hungry. **4.** *Archaic.* To suffer or die from cold. *—tr.* **1.** To cause to starve. **2.** To bring or force to a specified state by starving: *starved into surrender*. [Middle English *ste(o)rven*, Old English *steorfan*, to die.]

starve·ling (stárv-ling) *n.* One that is starving or ill-nourished.
~*adj.* **1.** Hungry or ill-nourished. **2.** Poor in quality; inadequate.

star·wort (stár-wurt ‖ -wawrt) *n.* **1.** Any of various plants having star-shaped flowers. **2.** Any of various aquatic plants of the genus *Callitriche*, having a rosette of floating leaves.

stash (stash) *tr.v.* **stashed, stashing, stashes.** *Informal.* To hide or store away in a secret place.
~*n.* *Chiefly U.S.* A secret store or cache, as of money, drugs, or valuables. [18th century : origin obscure.]

sta·sis (stáy-siss) *n., pl.* **-ses** (-seez). **1.** *Pathology.* Stagnation of a bodily fluid, especially of blood. **2.** A condition of balance among various forces. [New Latin, from Greek, a standing.]

-stasis *n. comb. form.* Indicates: **1.** Slowing or stoppage; for example, **bacteriostasis.** **2.** A stable state or a balance; for example, **homeostasis.** [New Latin, from Greek *stasis*, a standing.]

-stat *comb. form.* Indicates stationary or making stationary; for example, **rheostat, thermostat.** [New Latin *-stata*, from Greek *-statēs*, one that causes to stand.]

stat. **1.** immediately. [Latin *statim*.] **2.** stationary. **3.** statistics. **4.** statuary. **5.** statute.

stat·ant *adj. Heraldry.* In profile and having all four feet on the ground: *a lion statant.*

state (stayt) *n.* **1.** A condition or mode of being with regard to a set of circumstances; a position: *the state of play; a state of disrepair.* **2.** A condition of being in a stage or form, as of structure, growth, or development: *the foetal state.* **3.** A mental or emotional condition or disposition: *a state of shock.* **4.** *Informal.* A condition of excitement or distress: *got himself into a state.* **5.** *Physics.* The condition of a physical system as specified by a set of appropriate macroscopic or quantum variables: *the proton state of the nucleon.* **6.** A social position or rank: *lived in a way appropriate to her state.* **7.** Ceremony; pomp; formality: *robes of state.* **8.** *Sometimes capital* **S. a.** The supreme public power within a sovereign political entity. Often preceded by *the*: *has been taken over by the state.* **b.** The sphere of supreme civil power within a given polity, often contrasted with the religious authority of the church: *matters of state.* **9.** A mode of government marked by a specified characteristic: *a welfare state; a police state.* **10.** A body politic; specifically, one constituting a nation: *the member states of the European Economic Community.* **11.** *Sometimes capital* **S.** Any of the more or less internally autonomous territorial and political units composing a federation under a sovereign government: *the United States of America.*
—See Usage note at **nation.** —**lie in state.** To be placed in public view for honours prior to burial.
~*tr.v.* **stated, stating, states.** **1.** To set forth in words; declare. **2.** To present in speech or writing in a formal and deliberate manner: *stated the argument with cool precision.* **3.** To fix or settle; specify: *stated their conditions; at the stated time.*
~*adj. Sometimes capital* **S. 1. a.** Of, pertaining to, or maintained by a national government: *a state school; state control.* **b.** Of, pertaining to, or maintained by the government of an internally autonomous state: *the state legislature of Queensland; the State University of New York.* **2. a.** Of or involving pomp and ceremony. **b.** Reserved or used for or done on ceremonial occasions: *a state banquet.* [Middle English *stat(e)*, from Old French *estat*, from Latin *status*, manner of standing, condition, position, attitude.] —**state·hood** *n.*
Synonyms: state, condition, situation, status.

state capitalism *n.* A form of capitalism in which state control of capital, as through ownership of industries, plays a major part in a country's economic direction.

state·craft (stáyt-kraaft ‖ -kraft) *n.* The art of managing the affairs or business of a nation state.

State Department *n.* The foreign affairs department of the U.S. government.

State House *n.* **1.** *U.S.* A building in which a state legislature holds sessions. **2.** *Small* **s,** *small* **h.** *N.Z.* A private house built and owned by the state.

state·less (stáyt-ləss, -liss) *adj.* Having no national status. —**state·less·ness** *n.*

state·ly (stáyt-li) *adj.* **-lier, -liest. 1.** Marked by a graceful, dignified formality: *the stately progress of the royal party.* **2.** Majestic; grand.
—See Synonyms at **grand.**
~*adv.* In a grand, imposing manner. [Middle English *statly*, suitable to a person of rank, from *stat*, person of rank, STATE.] —**state·li·ness** *n.*

stately home *n.* In Britain, a large, imposing mansion, especially one that has historical, cultural, or architectural value and is open to public viewing.

state·ment (stáyt-mənt) *n.* **1.** The act of stating or declaring. **2.** Something stated; an assertion or formal declaration: *issued no statement.* **3.** An account showing an amount due, received, or paid, such as a bank sends regularly to one of its customers. **4.** The presentation of a phrase, tune, or theme in a musical composition.

Stat·en Island (státt'n). Island in New York Bay, southwest of Manhattan Island. It forms Staten Island borough, one of the five boroughs of New York city and Richmond County, New York State.

state of emergency *n.* A situation, as caused by a natural disaster or political collapse, officially recognised by a ruling body as warranting special action and measures. Also called "emergency".

state of the art *n.* The level or stage of development reached in a particular area, such as technology or industry.

state-of-the-art (stáyt-əv-thi-árt) *adj.* Of, pertaining to, or using the most advanced technology.

state of war *n.* The condition of being at war; especially, this condition as recognised by a formal declaration of war and as officially acknowledged by the two parties in conflict.

state·room (stáyt-rŏom, -rŏom) *n.* **1.** A large, sumptuous room used for state occasions. **2.** A private cabin or compartment on a ship or, in the United States, a train.

state's evidence *n. Sometimes capital* **S.** In the United States: **1.** Evidence for the prosecution in state or Federal trials. **2.** A person who gives evidence for the state in criminal proceedings.

States-Gen·er·al (státs-jén-rəl, -jénnə-) *n.* **1.** The legislative assembly in France before the Revolution. Also called "Estates-General". **2.** The two-chamber parliament of the Netherlands.

state·side (stáyt-sīd) *adj. U.S. Informal.* Of or in the United States.
~*adv. Chiefly U.S. Informal.* To, towards, or in the United States.

states·man (stáyts-mən) *n., pl.* **-men** (-mən). One who takes a prominent part in national or international political affairs; especially, a political leader respected for his outstanding wisdom, ability, and integrity. —**states·man·like, states·man·ly** *adj.* —**states·man·ship** *n.*

state socialism *n.* A form of socialism in which the state has considerable control over key areas of finance and industry.

States of the Church *pl.n.* The **Papal States** (see).

States' rights *n.* In the United States: **1.** All rights not delegated to the Federal Government by the Constitution nor denied by it to the states. **2.** A political stance advocating strict interpretation of the Constitution with regard to the limitation of Federal powers. —**States' righter** *n.*

states·wom·an (stáyts-wŏomən) *n., pl.* **-women** (-wimmin). A female statesman.

stat·ic (státtik) *adj.* Also **stat·i·cal** (-'l). **1.** *Physics.* **a.** Acting but causing no motion. Said of a force. **b.** Pertaining to or involving statics. **2.** *Electricity.* Of, pertaining to, or producing stationary charges; electrostatic. **3.** Of, pertaining to, or produced by random radio noise. **4.** Not changing or developing; fixed.
~*n.* Random noise produced in a receiver, such as hissing or crackling in a radio or specks on a television screen. [New Latin *staticus*, from Greek *statikos*, causing to stand, from *statos*, placed, standing.] —**stat·i·cal·ly** *adv.*

static electricity *n.* **1.** An accumulation of electric charge on an insulated body. **2.** Electric discharge resulting from this.

static line *n.* A line attached to a parachute and to an aircraft, such that the parachute is opened automatically when the wearer has jumped from the aircraft and fallen a certain distance.

stat·ics (státtiks) *n. Used with a singular verb.* A branch of mechanics dealing with the study of the forces acting on system of bodies in equilibrium. Compare **dynamics, kinetics.** [New Latin *statica*, from Greek *statikē* (*tekhnē*), (science) of weighing, from *statikos*, causing to stand, skilled in weighing. See **static.**]

sta·tion (stáysh'n) *n.* **1.** The place or position where a person or thing stands or is assigned to stand; a post: *a sentry station.* **2.** The place, building, or establishment from which a service is provided or operations are directed: *a police station; a petrol station; a polling station.* **3. a.** A stopping place along a route, especially one on a railway line where passengers and goods may be taken onto a train. **b.** The buildings of such a station. **4.** Social position; status; rank. **5.** An establishment equipped for observation and study: *a radar station.* **6.** An establishment equipped for radio or television transmission. **7. a.** The wavelength on which a particular television or radio programme is broadcast. **b.** The organisation broadcasting on this wavelength. **8.** In surveying, a point along an observation may be taken. **9.** In Australia: **a.** A large farm for raising cattle or sheep. **b.** A sheep-run or cattle-run. **10.** A military post, especially one in which British officers and administrative officials formerly resided in India. **11.** Any of the stations of the cross.
~*tr.v.* **stationed, -tioning, -tions.** To assign to a position or station; post. [Middle English *stacioun*, a standing still, from Latin *statiō* (stem *statiōn-*), from *stāre*, to stand.]

sta·tion·ar·y (stáysh'n-ri, -əri ‖ -erri) *adj. Abbr.* **sta., stat. 1. a.** Fixed in a position; not moving. **b.** Not able to be moved; not portable: *a stationary engine.* **2.** Remaining in a fixed condition or state, or at a fixed level: *Her temperature was stationary.* [Middle English *stationarye*, from Latin *statiōnārius*, from *statiō*, a standstill, STATION.]

stationary front *n.* A transition zone between two nearly stationary air masses of different density.

stationary orbit *n. Aerospace.* **Synchronous orbit** (see).

stationary point *n. Mathematics.* A point on a graph at which the tangent is either horizontal or vertical, indicating either a point of inflection or a maximum or minimum.

stationary satellite *n.* An artificial satellite in a synchronous orbit.

stationary wave *n.* A **standing wave** (see).

sta·tion·er (stáysh'n-ər) *n.* **1.** One who sells stationery. **2.** *Archaic.* A publisher or bookseller. [Middle English *staciouner*, from Medieval Latin *stationārius*, shopkeeper, from *statiō*, shop, from Latin, STATION.]

sta·tion·er·y (stáysh'n-ri, -əri ‖ -erri) *n.* **1.** Writing paper and envelopes. **2.** Writing materials such as paper, pens, and inks.

station house *n. Chiefly U.S.* A building used as a station, especially a police station.

steam *The Industrial Revolution was built on steam power, and by the 19th century engineers were using it to drive almost every mechanical device, including clocks such as this one in Vancouver, British Columbia, Canada.*

PRONUNCIATION KEY

a, trap; aa, father; ai, fair; ar, star; aw, lawn; ay, play; b, bb, stab; rubber; ch, church; ck, ticket; d, dd, dead; ladder; e, dress; ee, bee; er, defer; ew, few; ewr, pure; ə, about; ər, letter; f, ff, fife; differ; g, gg, giggle; h, hat; i, kit; ī, price; īr, fire; j, judge; k, kick; l, ll, let; 'l, needle; m, mm, man; n, nn, no; 'n, sudden; ng, thing; o, lot; ō, no; ŏŏ, foot; ōō, shoe; oor, poor; ow, cow; owr, hour; oy, boy; p, pp, pepper; r, rr, red; s, ss, sauce; sh, ship; t, tt, totter; th, thick; th, this; smooth; u, cut; ur, turn; v, vv, valve; w, wet; y, yes; z, zz, zebra; zh, vision; pleasure

IN FOREIGN WORDS:

aN, oN, Saint-Saëns; hl, Llanelli; Hluhluwe; kh, loch; lough; Khaled

STRESS MARK:

ín-sīt, insight; in-sít, incite

sta·tion·mas·ter (stáysh'n-maaster || -mastər) *n.* An official in charge of a railway station.
stations of the cross *pl.n. Sometimes capital* **S**, *capital* **C**. **1.** A series of usually 14 crosses, often accompanied by images, set up in a church or along a path commemorating 14 events in the Passion of Jesus. **2.** The devotional meditations performed before these crosses and images.
station wagon *n. Chiefly U.S.* An **estate car** *(see).*
stat·ism (stáytiz'm) *n.* The act or policy of strengthening the economic and political power of the state, as by increasing its control over industries and the mass media. [STATE + -ISM.]
stat·ist (stáytist *for sense 1,* státtist *for sense 2) n.* **1.** An advocate of statism. **2.** A statistician. **—stat·ist** *adj.*
sta·tis·tic (stə-tístik) *n.* **1.** Any numerical datum. **2.** An estimate of a parameter, as of the population mean or variance, obtained from a sample. [Back-formation from STATISTICS.] **—sta·tis·ti·cal** (-'l) *adj.* **—sta·tis·ti·cal·ly** *adv.*
statistical mechanics *n.* The study of the theory in which the properties of a physical system are predicted by the statistical behaviour of their constituent particles.
stat·is·ti·cian (státti-stísh'n) *n.* **1.** A mathematician specialising in statistics. **2.** A compiler of statistical data.
sta·tis·tics (stə-tístiks) *n. Abbr.* **stat.** **1.** *Used with a singular verb.* The mathematics of the collection, organisation, and interpretation of numerical data; especially, the analysis of population characteristics of social phenomena by inference from sampling. **2.** *Used with a plural verb.* A collection of numerical data. [German *Statistik,* originally "political science dealing with state affairs", from New Latin *statisticus,* of state affairs, from Latin *status,* state.]
sta·tive (stáytiv) *adj.* Belonging to or designating a class of verbs that express a state or condition; for example, *know, like,* and *doubt* are stative verbs.
~n. A verb of this class.
stato- *comb. form.* Indicates: **1.** Position; for example, **statocyst.** **2.** Resting, remaining, or surviving; for example, **statoblast.** [Greek *statos,* placed, standing.]
stat·o·blast (stát-ō-blast, -ə-, -blaast) *n.* An asexually produced, encapsulated bud of a freshwater bryozoan, from which new individuals develop after the parent colony has disintegrated. [STATO- + -BLAST.]
stat·o·cyst (stát-ō-sist, -ə-) *n.* A small organ of balance in many invertebrates, consisting of a fluid-filled sac containing statoliths that help indicate position when the animal moves. Also called "otocyst". [STATO- + CYST.]
stat·o·lith (stát-ō-lith, -ə-) *n.* **1.** A small, movable concretion of calcium carbonate, found in statocysts. **2.** Any of various starch grains found in some plant cells and thought to function in the plant's response to gravity. [STATO- + -LITH.]
sta·tor (stáytər) *n.* The stationary part of a motor, dynamo, turbine, or other rotary machine. [New Latin, from Latin, one that stands, from *stāre* (past participle *status*), to stand.]
stat·o·scope (státtə-skōp) *n.* A sensitive form of aneroid barometer used in aircraft to indicate small changes of height but not the absolute altitude. [Greek *statos,* stationary + -SCOPE.]
stat·u·ar·y (státtew-əri, stáchoo- || -erri) *n., pl.* **-ies.** *Abbr.* **stat.** **1.** Statues collectively. **2.** A sculptor. **3.** The art of making statues.
~adj. Of, pertaining to, or suitable for a statue or statues. [Latin *statuāria,* the art of making statues, and *statuārius,* sculptor, from *statuārius,* of a statue, from *statua,* STATUE.]
stat·ue (stáchōō, státtew) *n.* A three-dimensional figure or image, as of a famous person, sculpted, modelled, carved, or cast in material such as stone, clay, wood, or bronze. [Middle English, from Old French, from Latin *statua,* from *statuere,* to set up, erect.]
Statue of Liberty *n.* A colossal statue located in New York harbour, representing liberty as a woman with a torch raised in one hand and a book in the other arm.
stat·u·esque (státtew-ésk, stáchoo-) *adj.* Suggestive of a statue, as in proportion, grace, or dignity; stately. **—stat·u·esque·ly** *adv.*
stat·u·ette (státtew-ét, stáchoo-) *n.* A small statue.
stat·ure (stáchər) *n.* **1.** The natural height of a human or animal body in an upright position. **2. a.** A level, status, or degree, as of achievement or recognition; calibre. **b.** A high degree of worth or eminence. [Middle English *statur(e),* from Old French *(e)stature,* from Latin *statūra.*]
sta·tus (stáytəss || *chiefly U.S.* státtəss) *n.* **1.** The legal character or condition of a person or thing: *What is your marital status?* **2.** A relative position; especially, relative social or professional position. **3.** High standing; prestige. **4.** A state of affairs; a situation. —See Synonyms at **state.** [Latin *status,* state.]
status quo (kwō) *n.* The existing condition or state of affairs. [Latin, "state in which".]
status symbol *n.* That which is desirable because of the social prestige it confers upon its possessor: *He bought a sports car purely as a status symbol.*
stat·u·ta·ble (státtew-təb'l, stáchōō-) *adj.* Enacted, regulated, recognised, or authorised by statute; statutory.
stat·ute (státtewt, stáchōōt) *n. Abbr.* **st., St., stat.** **1.** A law enacted by a legislative body and formally recorded in writing; often distinguished from **common law** *(see).* **2.** An established law or rule, as of a body or an institution: *club statutes.* [Middle English *statut(e),* from Old French *(e)statut,* from Late Latin *statūtum,* from the neuter of *statūtus,* past participle of *statuere,* to set up, decree.]
statute book *n.* A written record of enacted legislation: *put a law on the statute book.*
statute law *n.* A law or rule established by legislative enactment. Compare **common law.**
statute mile *n.* See **mile.**
statute of limitations *n. Law.* A statute setting a time limit on enforcement of a right in certain cases.
stat·u·to·ry (státtew-tri, stáchoo-, -təri || stə-téwtəri) *adj.* **1.** Of or pertaining to a statute. **2.** Enacted, regulated, or authorised by statute. **3.** *Informal.* Designating an object, action, or behaviour that has become typical through its frequency: *got up and had her statutory cup of coffee.* [STATUTE + -ORY.]
statutory rape *n. U.S.* Sexual intercourse with a girl who is below the age of consent, treated as a criminal offence.
staunch (stawnch, staanch) *adj.* **stauncher, staunchest.** Also *rare* **stanch** (staanch || stanch). **1.** Firm and steadfast; true; loyal. **2. a.** Having a strong or substantial construction or constitution. **b.** Watertight. —See Synonyms at **faithful.**
~tr.v. Variant of **stanch.** [Middle English *staunche, stanch,* watertight, firm, strong, from Old French *estanche,* feminine of *estanc,* from *estanch(i)er,* STANCH.] **—staunch·ly** *adv.* **—staunch·ness** *n.*
stau·ro·lite (stáw-rə-līt, -rō-) *n.* A brownish-black mineral, $FeAl_4Si_2O_{10}(OH)_2$, often having crossed intergrown crystals and sometimes used as a gem. [French : Greek *stauros,* cross + -LITE.] **—staur·o·lit·ic** (-líttik) *adj.*
stau·ro·scope (stáwrə-skōp) *n.* An optical instrument used to study the crystal structure of minerals with polarised light. [Greek *stauros,* cross + -SCOPE.]
Sta·vang·er (sta-váng-ər, stə-). City in southwestern Norway, lying on the Stavangerfjord. A port and market centre, its industries include shipbuilding and fish-processing.
stave (stayv) *n.* **1.** A narrow strip of wood forming part of the sides of a barrel, tub, or the like. **2. a.** A rung of a ladder. **b.** A crosspiece on a chair. **3.** A long, thick stick, especially one used as a weapon; a staff. **4.** A musical **staff** *(see).* **5.** A set of verses; a stanza.
~v. **staved** or **stove** (stōv), **staving, staves.** *—tr.* **1.** To break in or puncture the staves of. **2.** To break or smash a hole in: *staved in a boat.* **3.** To crush or smash inwards. *—intr.* To be or become crushed or broken in. **—stave off.** To ward off; avert. [Back-formation from *staves,* plural of STAFF.]
Usage: The normal past tense and past participle forms of this verb are *staved: I think we've staved off her visit for another month. Stove* is restricted to nautical contexts: *The ship's side was stove in.*
staves. Alternative plural of **staff.**
staves·a·cre (stáyvz-aykər) *n.* **1.** A larkspur, *Delphinium staphisagria,* of southern Europe, having deep blue flowers. **2.** The poisonous seeds of this plant, formerly used externally as a parasiticide. [Middle English *staphisagre, stafisagre,* from Latin *staphis agria,* from Greek, "wild raisin" : *staphis, astaphis*†, raisin + *agria,* feminine of *agrios,* wild, "of the field", from *agros,* field.]
stay¹ (stay) *v.* **stayed, staying, stays.** *—intr.* **1.** To remain or continue in a specified place or condition: *stayed behind; stayed in bed; stay out of trouble.* **2. a.** To remain or sojourn as a guest or lodger. **b.** *Scottish.* To reside permanently; live. **c.** To wait; pause. **3.** To hold on; endure. **4.** In poker, to meet a bet without raising it. **5.** *Archaic.* **a.** To stop moving; cease. **b.** To keep up in a race or contest: *stayed with the rest of the runners till the last lap.* *—tr.* **1.** To stop or halt; check. **2.** To postpone; delay; especially, to delay or stop the effect or course of by intervening measures: *stayed legal proceedings.* **3.** To satisfy or appease (hunger, for example) temporarily. **4.** To remain for (a specified period of time): *She stayed the week.* **5.** To endure to the end; last out: *couldn't stay the course.* **6.** *Archaic.* To wait for; await. **—stay put.** To remain in the place or position that one is occupying.
~n. **1.** The action of stopping or coming to a stop. **2.** A sojourn or visit. **3.** A suspension or postponement of a legal action or execution. [Middle English *steyen,* to halt, from Old French *ester* (present stem *estei-*), to stand, stop, from Latin *stāre.*] **—stay·er** *n.*
Synonyms: stay, remain, wait, abide, tarry, linger.
stay² *tr.v.* **stayed, staying, stays.** **1.** To brace, support, or prop up. Often used with *up.* **2.** To strengthen or sustain mentally or spiritually; comfort.
~n. **1.** A support or prop: *She was a stay during the crisis.* **2.** A strip of bone, plastic, or metal, used to stiffen a garment or part such as a corset or shirt collar. **3.** *Plural.* A corset stiffened with stays, now rarely worn. [Old French *estayer,* to support, from *estaie,* support, from Germanic; see **stay** (rope).]
stay³ *n.* **1.** A heavy rope or cable, usually of wire, used as a brace or support for a mast or spar. **2.** Any rope used for a similar purpose; a guy line. **—in stays.** In the process of coming about to the opposite tack. Said of a ship.
~v. **stayed, staying, stays.** *—tr.* **1.** To brace or support with a stay or stays. **2.** To put (a ship) on the opposite tack. *—intr.* To come about to the opposite tack. Used of a ship. [Middle English *stey, stay,* Old English *stæg,* from Germanic *staga-* (unattested).]
stay-at-home (stáy-ət-hōm) *n.* One who habitually stays at home; especially, one who leads a sheltered, unadventurous life. **—stay-at-home** *adj.*
stay·ing power (stáy-ing) *n.* The ability to endure or last.
stay·sail (stáy-sayl; *nautical* stáyss'l) *n.* A triangular sail hoisted on a stay.
St. Bernard Passes. Two Alpine passes. The Great St. Bernard

Pass, height 2 472 metres (8,110 feet) links Piedmont, Italy, with Valais, Switzerland, and was the route by which Napoleon I crossed into Italy (1800). At its summit there is a hospice (11th century) founded by St. Bernard of Menthon, which formerly bred St. Bernard dogs to search for travellers trapped by snow. Beneath it is a road tunnel (1964). The Little St. Bernard Pass, height 2 187 metres (7,178 feet), which links Piedmont with Savoie, France, also has a hospice (11th century) founded by St. Bernard, and was the route by which Hannibal is believed to have invaded Italy.

St. Chris·to·pher. See **St. Kitts-Nevis.**

St. Cloud (saɴ kloͦo). Suburb of Paris, France, situated on the river Seine in the Hauts-de-Seine département. Formerly the site of a royal palace, it is also the site of the Sèvres porcelain factory and a racecourse.

STD sexually transmitted disease.

std. standard.

S.T.D. **1.** Doctor of Sacred Theology. **2.** Suscriber trunk dialling: a system in Britain enabling people to make long-distance telephone calls without the aid of an operator.

St. Da·vid's (dáyvidz). *Welsh* **Ty·dde·wi** (tee-thé-wi). Village of Dyfed, southwest Wales. Once a major place of pilgrimage, it has a cathedral (12th to 14th centuries).

St. De·nis (saɴ də-neé). Suburb of Paris, France, situated in the Seine-St. Denis département. Its abbey church (cathedral) (12th century) was the first in Gothic style. Several French monarchs are buried there.

stead (sted) *n.* **1.** The place, position, or function properly or customarily occupied by another. **2.** Advantage; avail. Used chiefly in the phrase *stand someone in good stead.*
~*tr.v.* **steaded, steading, steads.** *Archaic.* To be of advantage or service to; benefit; help. [Middle English, Old English *stede.*]

stead·fast, sted·fast (stéd-fəst, -faast || -fast) *adj.* **1.** Fixed or unchanging; steady: *a steadfast gaze.* **2.** Firmly loyal or constant; unswerving. —See Synonyms at **faithful.** [Middle English *stedefast,* Old English *stedefæst,* fixed in one place : *stede,* place, STEAD + *fæst,* fixed, FAST.] **—stead·fast·ly** *adv.* **—stead·fast·ness** *n.*

stead·ing (stédding) *n. Chiefly Scottish.* The outbuildings of a farmhouse.

stead·y (stéddi) *adj.* **-ier, -iest.** **1.** Firm in position or place; fixed. **2.** Direct and unfaltering; sure: *a steady aim.* **3.** Regular, even, and continuous in action, movement, quality, or pace: *slow but steady progress.* **4.** Not easily excited or upset; controlled: *steady nerves.* **5. a.** Regular; habitual: *a steady boyfriend.* **b.** Reliable; dependable. **c.** Temperate; sober.
~*v.* **steadied, -ying, -ies.** —*tr.* To make steady; stabilise. —*intr.* To become steady.
~*interj.* **1.** Used to urge care and self-control. **2.** *Nautical.* Used to direct the helmsman to keep the ship's head in the same direction.
~*n., pl.* **steadies.** *U.S. Slang.* A regular boyfriend or girlfriend.
~*adv.* In a steady manner. **—go steady.** *Informal.* To go out socially on a regular basis, as with a member of the opposite sex. [From STEAD, place (after Middle Low German *stēdig,* stable).] **—stead·i·er** *n.* **—stead·i·ly** *adv.* **—stead·i·ness** *n.*
Synonyms: *steady, even, equable, uniform, constant.*

stead·y-state theory (stéddi-stáyt) *n.* A cosmological theory that assumes that the large-scale view of the universe is independent of the position of the observer in space and time and that the expansion of the universe, required on other grounds, is compensated for by the continuous creation of matter. Compare **big-bang theory.**

steak (stayk) *n.* **1.** A slice of meat, beef unless otherwise specified, typically cut thick and usually grilled or fried. **2.** A thick slice of a large fish cut across the body. **3.** A cut of beef of any of various qualities, used for the specified purpose: *stewing steak.* [Middle English *ste(y)ke, styke,* from Old Norse *steik,* piece of meat roasted on a spit, from *steikja,* to roast on a spit.]

steak·house (stáyk-howss) *n.* A restaurant that serves steaks as a speciality.

steak tar·tare (taar-tár, tártər) *n.* Raw minced beef mixed with onion, seasoning, and raw egg. Also called "tartar steak".

steal (steel) *v.* **stole** (stōl), **stolen** (stṓlən), **stealing, steals.** —*tr.* **1. a.** To take (an object) without right or permission, often in a surreptitious way. **b.** To take or appropriate (an idea, for example) without permission or acknowledging the source. **2.** To get, take, gain, or effect secretly or artfully: *steal a kiss; steal a glance.* **3.** *Chiefly U.S.* To move, carry, or place surreptitiously: *He carefully stole the gin back into the cupboard.* —*intr.* **1.** To commit theft. **2. a.** To move stealthily or unobtrusively: *stole away from the party.* **b.** To happen, pass, or elapse gently and imperceptibly: *The days stole past.* —See Synonyms at **rob.**
~*n.* **1.** The act or an instance of stealing. **2.** *U.S. Informal.* A bargain. [Steal, stolen; Middle English *stelen, stole(n),* Old English *stelan, stolen.* Stole, Middle English *stole,* adopted from the past participle *stole(n)* and superseding the more regular form *stal,* Old English *stæl* (plural *stælon*).] **—steal·er** *n.*

stealth (stelth) *n.* **1.** The act of moving, proceeding, or acting in a covert way. **2.** Furtiveness; covertness. **3.** *Archaic.* The act of stealing. [Middle English *stalth, stelth,* probably from Old English *stǣlth* (unattested) : STEAL (move stealthily) + -TH.]

stealth·y (stélthi) *adj.* **-ier, -iest.** Characterised by stealth; cautiously unobtrusive and secretive. See Synonyms at **secret.** **—stealth·i·ly** *adv.* **—stealth·i·ness** *n.*

steam (steem) *n.* **1.** The hot gaseous phase of water formed when water boils. **2.** The white visible mist of water vapour containing small droplets of water, seen when hot water boils or evaporates. **3.** The use of steam as a source of power; especially, the use of steam-powered locomotives: *the age of steam.* Also used adjectivally: *a steam railway.* **4. a.** The power generated by the use of steam: *get up steam.* **b.** *Informal.* Energy, driving force, or means of progress: *running out of steam; got here under my own steam.* **5.** Pent-up emotions or nervous energy: *letting off steam.*
~*v.* **steamed, steaming, steams.** —*intr.* **1.** To produce or emit steam. **2.** To become or rise up as steam. **3.** To become misted or covered with steam. Used with *up.* **4.** To move by means of steam power. **5.** *Informal.* To be extremely angry or emotional. **6.** *Informal.* To move energetically and rapidly. —*tr.* **1.** To cook (food) by exposing to steam. **2.** To expose or subject to steam: *steamed a stamp off an envelope.* **3.** *Informal.* To cause to become bad tempered or irritated. Often used in the passive with *up*: *no need to get all steamed up.* [Middle English *steme,* vapour, exhalation, Old English *stēam,* from West Germanic *stauma* (unattested).]

steam bath *n.* **1.** A bath in which bodily impurities are sweated out by the action and heat of steam. **2.** A place where one takes such a bath.

steam·boat (steém-bōt) *n.* A small **steamship** *(see)*

steam boiler *n.* A closed tank in which water is converted into steam under pressure.

steam chest *n.* A compartment in a steam engine which encloses the slide valve and through which steam is delivered from the boiler to a cylinder.

steam engine *n.* An engine that converts the heat energy of pressurised steam into mechanical energy, especially one in which steam drives a piston in a closed cylinder.

steam·er (steémər) *n. Abbr.* **str.** **1.** A steamship. **2.** A container in which something, such as food, is steamed.

steamer trunk *n.* A small trunk originally designed to fit under the bunk of a steamship cabin.

steam heating *n.* A heating system by which steam is generated in a boiler and piped to radiators.

steam·ie (steémi) *n. Scottish Informal.* Especially formerly, a wash house open to the public.

steam iron *n.* A pressing iron that holds and heats water to be emitted as steam on the cloth being pressed.

steam organ *n.* A musical instrument fitted with steam whistles, played from a keyboard. Also *U.S.* "calliope".

steam point *n.* The temperature at which the vapour phase of water is in equilibrium with the liquid phase. At standard pressure, the steam point is 100°C. Compare **ice point.**

steam radio *n. British Informal.* Radio broadcasting considered as being old-fashioned by comparison with television.

steam·rol·ler (steém-rōl-ər) *n.* **1. a.** A steam-driven machine used chiefly for rolling road surfaces flat. **b.** Loosely, any heavy rolling machine similarly used. **2.** A ruthless or irresistible force or power.
~*v.* **steamrollered, -lering, -lers.** —*tr.* **1.** To work or roll (a surface) with a steamroller. **2. a.** To overwhelm or suppress ruthlessly; crush. **b.** To bring or impel by means of an irresistible force. —*intr.* To move or proceed with overwhelming or crushing force.

steam room *n.* A room filled with steam, in which one can take a steam bath.

steam·ship (steém-ship) *n. Abbr.* **SS, S.S.** A large vessel propelled by one or more steam-driven propellers. Also called "steamer".

steam shovel *n.* A steam-driven excavating machine.

steam table *n.* **1.** A table giving the properties of steam under different conditions of pressure. **2.** A table equipped to hold containers of cooked food kept warm by hot water or steam.

steam turbine *n.* A turbine operated by highly pressurised steam directed against or through vanes on a rotor.

steam·y (steémi) *adj.* **-ier, -iest.** **1.** Filled with, covered with, or emitting steam. **2.** *Informal.* Full of sexual passion; erotic. **—steam·i·ly** *adv.* **—steam·i·ness** *n.*

ste·ap·sin (sti-ápsin) *n.* An enzyme of pancreatic juice that catalyses the hydrolysis of fats to fatty acids and glycerol. [Greek *stear,* solid fat, suet, tallow (see **stearic**) + (PE)PSIN.]

ste·a·rate (steér-ayt || steé-ər-) *n.* A salt or ester of stearic acid. [STEAR(IC) + -ATE.]

ste·ar·ic (sti-árrik) *adj.* Of, pertaining to, or similar to stearin or fat. [French *stéarique,* from Greek *stear*†, solid fat, suet, tallow.]

stearic acid *n.* A colourless, odourless, waxlike fatty acid, $CH_3(CH_2)_{16}COOH$, occurring in natural animal and vegetable fats.

ste·a·rin (steér-in || steé-ər-) *n.* **1.** A colourless, odourless, tasteless ester of glycerol and stearic acid, $C_3H_5(C_{18}H_{35}O_2)_3$, used in the manufacture of soap and candles and for textile sizing. Also called "tristearin". **2.** Stearic acid, especially as used commercially. **3.** The solid form of fat. [French *stéarine* : Greek *stear,* solid fat, suet, tallow (see **stearic**) + -INE.]

ste·a·rop·tene (steér-róp-teen || steé-ə-) *n.* The part of a natural essential oil that separates out as a white, crystalline solid on cooling or standing. [STEAR(IC) + Greek *ptēnos,* winged, "volatile".]

ste·a·tite (steér-tīt, steé-ə-) *n.* A massive, white-to-green talc used in paints, ceramics, and insulation. Also called "soapstone". [Latin *steatītis, steatītēs,* from Greek *steatitis, steatitēs,* "tallow stone" : STEAT(O)- + -ITE.] **—ste·a·tit·ic** (-títtik) *adj.*

steato- *comb. form.* Indicates fat; for example, **steatopygia.** [Greek, from *stear* (stem *steat-*), solid fat, tallow. See **stearic.**]

ste·a·tol·y·sis (steér-tóllə-siss, steé-ə-) *n.* The digestive emulsification of fats prior to assimilation. [New Latin : STEATO- + -LYSIS.]

ste·a·to·py·gi·a (steér-tō-pījі-ə, steé-ə-) *n.* An excessive accumula-

steam engine *An Italian steam locomotive. The first practical steam engines were stationary; they were used in 18th-century Britain to pump water from mines.*

steamroller *Road-building machines are no longer powered by steam, but the steamroller has entered the language as an image of unstoppable power. Steam-powered machines, like the one shown here, were first used on English roads in the 1860s.*

steinbok *Most antelopes instinctively bound away from danger. But the steinbok, which spends most of each year alone, may react by lying flat on the ground and relying on its natural camouflage. Steinboks make their homes in dry scrubland in southern and eastern Africa as far north as Kenya.*

stele *This stone stele depicts the storm god Baal holding his spear-pointed thunderbolt in his left hand. It was carved by Syrian craftsmen in about 1800 B.C.*

tion of fat on the buttocks. [New Latin : STEATO- + Greek *pugē,* rump (see **pygidium**).] **—ste•a•to•pyg•ic** (-pījik), **ste•a•to•py•gous** (-pīgəss) *adj.*

ste•a•tor•rhoe•a (stée̍r-tə-rée̍r, stée̍-ə-, -tō-, -rée̍-ə) *n.* **1.** Excessive discharge of fat in the faeces. **2.** Overaction of the sebaceous glands; seborrhoea. [New Latin : STEATO- + -RRHOEA.]

stedfast. Variant of **steadfast.**

steed (steed) *n. Archaic & Poetic.* A horse, especially one that is spirited. [Middle English *stede,* Old English *stēda,* stallion.]

steel (steel) *n.* **1.** Any of various generally hard, strong, durable, malleable alloys of iron and carbon, usually containing between 0.02 to 1.5 per cent carbon, often with other constituents such as manganese, chromium, nickel, molybdenum, copper, tungsten, cobalt, or silicon, depending on the desired alloy properties, and widely used as a structural material. **2.** A quality suggestive of steel; especially, a hard, unflinching character. **3.** Something made of steel, especially: **a.** A weapon such as a sword, knife, or the like. **b.** A knife sharpener consisting of a handled steel rod. **c.** A slender strip or band of steel used for stiffening corsets or dresses. **6.** *Finance.* **a.** The steel industry. **b.** *Plural.* The market quotation for shares in the steel industry. **7. a.** Dark grey to purplish grey. Also called "steel grey". **b.** Dark greyish blue. Also called "steel blue". *~adj.* **1.** Made of or with steel. **2. a.** Resembling the properties of steel. **b.** Of the colour steel. **3.** Of or pertaining to the production of steel.
~tr.v. **steeled, steeling, steels. 1.** To cover, plate, edge, or point with steel. **2.** To make strong, resolute, or resistant; strengthen. [Middle English *stel(le), stiel,* Old English *stēli, stȳle.*]

Steel (steel), **David (Martin Scott)** (1939–). British politician. As leader of the Liberal Party he created the Alliance movement with the newly formed Social Democratic Party (1981).

steel band *n.* A musical band of a type originating in the West Indies, composed chiefly of percussion instruments fashioned from oil drums.

Steele (steel), **Sir Richard** (1672–1729). Irish-born playwright and essayist. He founded (1709) *The Tatler,* and was a leading contributor (1711–12) to the *Spectator,* for which he invented the character of the jovial English squire, Sir Roger de Coverley.

steel engraving *n.* **1.** The art or process of engraving on a steel plate. **2.** An impression produced with an engraved steel plate.

steel•head (stée̍l-hed) *n.* The rainbow trout of North America, when occurring in marine waters or large inland lakes.

steel wool *n.* **1.** Fine fibres of steel woven or matted together to form an abrasive for cleaning, smoothing, or polishing. **2.** A **wire wheel** *(see).*

steel•works (stée̍l-wurk) *n., pl.* **steelworks.** A plant where steel is made. **—steel•work•er** *n.*

steel•y (stée̍li) *adj.* **-ier, -iest. 1.** Made of steel. **2.** Like steel, as in coldness or hardness: *steely eyes.* **—steel•i•ness** *n.*

steel•yard (stíl-yərd, stée̍l-, -yaard) *n.* A balance consisting of a scaled arm suspended off centre, a hook at the shorter end on which to hang the object being weighed, and a counterbalance at the longer end. [STEEL + YARD (rod).]

Steen (stayn), **Jan** (*c.* 1626–79). Dutch painter. He specialised in domestic and tavern scenes, among them *The Music Lesson, The Skittle Alley,* and *The Lute Player.*

steenbok. Variant of **steinbok.**

steep[1] (steep) *adj.* **steeper, steepest. 1.** Having a sharp inclination; nearly perpendicular; precipitous. **2.** Rising or falling rapidly or precipitously. **3.** *Informal.* **a.** Excessive; unreasonable; exorbitant: *a steep price.* **b.** Difficult to believe; exaggerated.
~n. Literary. A precipitous slope; a steep place. [Middle English *stepe,* Old English *stēap,* lofty, deep, projecting.] **—steep•ly** *adv.* **—steep•ness** *n.*

steep[2] *v.* **steeped, steeping, steeps.** *—tr.* **1.** To soak in liquid in order to cleanse, soften, or extract some property. **2.** To infuse or subject thoroughly; immerse: *steeped in misery.* **3.** To make thoroughly wet. *—intr.* To undergo a soaking in liquid.
~n. **1. a.** The process of steeping. **b.** The state of being steeped. **2.** A liquid, bath, or solution in which something is steeped. [Middle English *stepen,* from Old English *stiepan* (unattested), from Germanic.] **—steep•er** *n.*

steep•en (stée̍pən) *v.* **-ened, -ening, -ens.** *—tr.* To make steeper. *—intr.* To become steeper.

stee•ple (stée̍p'l) *n.* **1.** A tall tower forming the superstructure of a building, especially a church, and usually surmounted by a spire. **2.** A spire. [Middle English *stepel, stepyl,* Old English *stīpel, stȳpel.*]

stee•ple•chase (stée̍p'l-chayss) *n.* **1. a.** A horse race over a course provided with artificial obstacles. **b.** A horse race across open country. **2.** A long-distance running race, usually of 3000 metres, over a course provided with hurdles and other obstacles.
~intr.v. **steeplechased, -chasing, -chases.** To take part in a steeplechase. [Church steeples were originally used as goals in such horse races.] **—stee•ple•chas•er** *n.*

stee•ple•jack (stée̍p'l-jak) *n.* A worker on steeples or other very high structures. [STEEPLE + JACK (labourer).]

steer[1] (steer) *v.* **steered, steering, steers.** *—tr.* **1.** To guide (a vessel or vehicle) by means of a device such as a rudder, paddle, or wheel. **2. a.** To direct the course of (a discussion or conversation, for example). **b.** To manoeuvre (a person) into a place or course of action. **3.** To set and follow (a particular course): *steered a course through the straits; tried to steer a middle course.* *—intr.* **1.** To guide a vessel or vehicle. **2.** To follow or move in a set course. **3.** To allow of being steered or guided in a specified fashion: *a boat that steers easily.* **—steer clear of.** To avoid; keep away from. [Middle English *steren,* Old English *stīeran.*] **—steer•a•ble** *adj.* **—steer•er** *n.*

steer[2] *n.* A young ox, especially one castrated and raised for beef. [Middle English *stere, steer,* Old English *stēor.*]

steer•age (stée̍r-ij) *n.* **1.** The action or practice of steering. **2.** The steering apparatus of a ship. **3.** The section of a passenger ship, originally near the rudder, providing the cheapest accommodation for passengers.

steer•age•way (stée̍r-ij-way) *n.* The minimum rate of motion required for the helm of a ship or boat to have effect.

steer•ing committee (stée̍r-ing) *n.* A committee whose function it is to suggest issues to be considered and to arrange the order of business, as for a legislative body or other assembly.

steering gear *n.* The mechanism by which a vehicle, ship, or aircraft is steered.

steering wheel *n.* A wheel that is turned to control the steering gear, as on a motor vehicle or motorboat.

steers•man (stée̍rz-mən) *n., pl.* **-men** (-mən). A helmsman.

steeve[1] (steev) *n.* A spar or derrick with a block at one end, used for stowing cargo.
~tr.v. **steeved, steeving, steeves.** To stow or pack (cargo) in the hold of a ship. [Middle English *steven,* to stow, from Spanish *estibar,* to cram, from Latin *stīpāre,* to stuff fully.]

steeve[2] *n. Nautical.* The angle formed by the bowsprit and the horizon or the keel.
~v. **steeved, steeving, steeves.** *Nautical.* *—tr.* To incline (a bowsprit) upwards at an angle with the horizon or the keel. *—intr.* To have an upward inclination. Used of a bowsprit. [17th century : origin obscure.]

Stefan-Boltzmann law (stéffən-bólts-man; *German* shtéffan-) *n.* A physical law stating that the total energy radiated from a black body is equal to the fourth power of its absolute temperature. [After Josef *Stefan* (1835–83), Austrian physicist, and Ludwig BOLTZMANN.]

Ste•fan Du•šan (stéffan dóo-shan) (*c.* 1308–55). King of Serbia (1331–55). He created a Serbian empire by subjugating Albania, Epirus, Macedonia, and Thessaly.

steg•o•don (stéggə-don, -dən) *n.* Also **steg•o•dont** (-dont). Any of various extinct elephant-like mammals of the genus *Stegodon* and related genera, of the Pliocene to Pleistocene epoch. [New Latin *Stegodon,* "ridge-toothed" (from the distinctive ridges on its molars) : Greek *stegos,* roof, "ridge", from *stegein,* to cover + -ODONT.]

steg•o•saur (stéggə-sawr) *n.* Also **steg•o•sau•rus** (-sáwrəss). Any of several herbivorous dinosaurs of the genus *Stegosaurus* and related genera, of the Triassic to the Cretaceous period, having a double row of upright bony plates along the back. [New Latin *Stegosaurus* : Greek *stegos,* roof, "ridge of plates" (see **stegodon**) + -SAUR.]

Steiermark. See **Styria.**

stein (stīn) *n.* An earthenware mug, especially one for beer, usually holding about a pint. [German *Stein,* probably short for *Steingut,* stoneware, earthenware : *Stein,* stone + *Gut,* goods, ware.]

Stein (stīn), **Gertrude** (1874–1946). U.S. author and poet. Her unique style, which experimented with syntax, was influenced by her study of psychology. Her best-known work is *The Autobiography of Alice B. Toklas* (1933).

Steinbeck (stín-beck), **John** (1902–68). U.S. novelist. His novels deal with social and economic conditions in California. They include *The Grapes of Wrath* (1939) and *East of Eden* (1952). He won the Nobel prize for literature in 1962.

stein•bok (stín-bok, -buk) *n.* Also **steen•bok** (stée̍rn-, stáyn-). **1.** An African antelope, *Raphicerus campestris neumanni,* having a brownish coat and short pointed horns in the male. **2.** An **ibex** *(see).* [Afrikaans, "stone buck".]

Stei•ner (stínər; *German* shtínər), **Rudolf** (1861–1925). Austrian teacher and philosopher. He developed **anthroposophy** *(see).*

ste•le (stée̍-lee, -li) *n., pl.* **-les** or **-lae** (-lee). Also **ste•la** (-lə) (for sense 1) *pl.* **-lae. 1.** An upright stone or slab with an inscribed or sculptured surface, used, especially in ancient times, to mark a grave, as a monument, or as a commemorative tablet. **2.** *Botany.* The central core of vascular tissue in a plant stem or root. [Latin *stēla,* from Greek *stēlē,* pillar.] **—ste•lar** (-lər) *adj.*

stel•lar (stéllər) *adj.* **1.** Of, relating to, or consisting of stars. **2.** Of, relating to, or worthy of a star performer. [Late Latin *stellāris,* from *stella,* star.]

stel•lar•a•tor (stéllə-raytər) *n.* An apparatus used in thermonuclear research to contain a plasma in a toroidal vessel by means of a magnetic field. [STELLAR + *-ator,* as in *generator*; the temperature used to heat the plasma approximates that in some stars.]

stel•late (stél-ət, -it, -ayt) *adj.* Also **stel•lat•ed** (ste-láytid ‖ stél-aytid). *Biology.* Arranged or shaped like a star; radiating from a centre. [Latin *stellātus,* from *stella,* star.] **—stel•late•ly** *adv.*

Stel•len•bosch (stéllen-boss; *Afrikaans* stéllem-bóss). City in western Cape Province, South Africa, lying on the river Eerste. Founded in 1679 by Governor Simon Van der Stel, it is the second-oldest settlement in South Africa. It is a cultural and marketing centre.

stel•li•form (stélli-fawrm) *adj.* Star-shaped. [New Latin *stelliformis* : Latin *stella,* star (see **stellate**) + -FORM.]

stel•li•fy (stélli-fī) *tr.v.* **-fied, -fying, -fies.** To transform into a star. [Middle English *stellifien,* from Old French *stellifier,* from Medieval Latin *stellificāre* : Latin *stella,* star + *facere,* to do, make.]

stel•lu•lar (stéllewlər) *adj.* **1.** Having the form of a small star or stars. **2.** Adorned with small stars. [Late Latin *stellula,* diminutive of Latin *stella,* star.]

St. El·mo's fire (élmōz) *n.* A bluish electrical glow caused by corona discharge on masts and other high parts of a ship at sea before and during electrical storms. Also called "corposant". [After *St. Elmo,* patron saint of sailors.]

stem[1] (stem) *n.* **1. a.** The main ascending axis of a plant, which bears the leaves, flowers, and axillary buds. **b.** The corresponding part in nonflowering plants. **c.** A slender stalk supporting or connecting another plant part, such as a leaf or flower; a stalk. **2.** A banana stalk bearing several bunches of bananas. **3.** Something analogous to a plant stem, especially: **a.** The tube of a tobacco pipe. **b.** The slender upright support of a wine glass or goblet. **c.** The small projecting shaft bearing the knob with which a watch is wound. **d.** The rounded rod in the centre of certain locks about which the key fits and is turned. **e.** The shaft of a feather or hair. **f.** The main line of descent of a family as distinguished from a branch. **g.** The upright stroke of a typeface or letter. **h.** The vertical line extending from the head of a musical note. **i.** The main part of a word to which inflectional affixes are added. **j.** The curved upright beam at the bow of a vessel into which the hull timbers are scarfed to form the prow. **k.** In an incandescent bulb or vacuum tube, the tubular glass structure mounting the filament or electrodes. **—from stem to stern.** From one end to the other of a ship.
~*v.* **stemmed, stemming, stems.** —*tr.* **1.** To remove the stem or stems of. **2.** To make headway against (a tide, current, or comparable force); breast. —*intr.* To have as a point of origin; derive or develop. Usually used with *from.* [Middle English *stem,* Old English *stemn, stefn,* stem, tree trunk, (timber used to build the) prow or stern of a ship.] **—stem·less** *adj.*

stem[2] *v.* **stemmed, stemming, stems.** —*tr.* **1.** To hold back (a flow, onrush, or movement) by or as if by damming. **2.** To plug or stop up (a blast hole, for example). **3.** To force the heel of (a ski or both skis) outwards, as in performing a stem turn. —*intr.* To force the heel of one ski or both skis outwards by shifting one's weight, in order to check one's speed, stop, or make a turn.
~*n.* In skiing, a stem turn. [Middle English *stemmen,* from Old Norse *stemma.*]

stem cell *n.* An unspecialised cell that gives rise to a certain type of specialised cell, such as a blood cell.

stem·ma (stémmə) *n., pl.* **stemmata** (-tə) or **-mas.** **1.** In ancient Rome, a scroll recording the genealogy of a family. **2.** Any family tree or pedigree. [Latin, garland, wreath, from Greek, from *stephein,* to encircle, crown, wreathe.]

stemmed (stemd) *adj.* **1.** Having the stem or stems removed. **2.** Provided with a stem or stems. Often used in combination: *thick-stemmed.*

stem·son (stém-s'n) *n. Nautical.* A piece of supporting timber bolted to the stem and keelson at their junction near the bow of a wooden vessel. [STEM (prow) + (KEEL)SON.]

stem turn *n.* In skiing, a turn made by stemming the downhill ski and placing one's weight upon it while bringing the other ski into a parallel position. Also called "stem", "stem christie".

stem·ware (stém-wair) *n.* Glassware mounted on a stem.

stem-wind·er (stém-wīndər) *n.* A stem-winding watch.

stem-wind·ing (stém-wīnding) *adj.* Designating a watch that is wound by turning a knob mounted on the end of the stem.

stench (stench) *n.* A strong and foul odour; a stink. See Synonyms at **smell.** [Middle English *stench,* Old English *stenc,* from Germanic *stenkw-* (unattested); akin to *stinkwan* (unattested), to STINK.]

sten·cil (stén-s'l, -sil) *n.* **1.** A sheet of celluloid, cardboard, or other material in which a desired lettering or design has been cut so that when ink or paint is passed over the sheet the pattern will be reproduced on the surface placed below. **2.** The lettering or design so produced. **3.** A sheet of thin waxed paper that can be typed or drawn on to produce a stencil suitable for use in a duplicator.
~*tr.v.* **stencilled** or *U.S.* **-ciled, -cilling** or *U.S.* **-ciling, -cils.** **1.** To mark (a surface) with a stencil. **2.** To produce by stencil. [Middle English *stencel,* to adorn with brilliant colours, from Old French *estenceler,* "to cause to sparkle", from *estencele,* spark, from Latin *scintilla,* spark.] **—sten·cil·ler** *n.*

Sten·dhal (staN-dál, stoN-, -daál), pen name of Henri Beyle (1783–1842). French writer. His work, which shows searching psychological insight, was an important influence on the development of the French novel. His novels include *Le Rouge et le noir* (1830), and *La Chartreuse de Parme* (1839).

Sten gun (sten) *n.* A type of lightweight machine gun. [*St-* from the initials of the inventors' names, *S*hepherd and *T*urpin + *-en* as in BRENGUN.]

sten·o (sténnō) *n., pl.* **-os.** *U.S. Informal.* A stenographer.

steno- *comb. form.* Indicates narrowness; for example, **stenophagous.** [Greek *stenos,* narrow.]

sten·o·graph (sténnə-graaf, -graf) *tr.v.* **-graphed, -graphing, -graphs.** To record in shorthand. [Back-formation from STENOGRAPHY.]

ste·nog·ra·pher (stə-nóggrəfər, ste-) *n. U.S.* A **shorthand typist** *(see).*

ste·nog·ra·phy (stə-nóggrəfi, ste-) *n.* **1.** The art or process of writing in shorthand. **2.** Material written down in shorthand. [STENO- + -GRAPHY.] **—sten·o·graph·ic** (sténnə-gráffik) *adj.* **—sten·o·graph·i·cal·ly** *adv.*

sten·o·ha·line (sténnō-háy-līn, -há-) *adj.* Able to live only within a narrow range of salt concentration. Said of certain aquatic organisms. Compare **euryhaline.** [STENO- + Greek *hals* (stem *hal-*), salt + -INE.]

ste·noph·a·gous (sti-nóffəgəss, ste-) *adj.* Feeding on a single kind or limited range of food. [STENO- + -PHAGOUS.]

ste·no·sis (sti-nṓ-siss, ste-) *n., pl.* **-ses** (-seez). *Pathology.* An abnormal narrowing of a passage or canal in the body. [New Latin, from Greek *stenōsis,* from *stenoun,* to constrict, from *stenos,* narrow.] **—ste·not·ic** (-nóttik) *adj.*

sten·o·ther·mal (sténnō-thérm'l) *adj. Biology.* Of or designating organisms adapted to living only within a limited range of temperature. [German *stenotherm* : STENO- + *thermē,* heat, THERM.]

sten·o·trop·ic (sténnō-tróppik) *adj.* Also **sten·o·top·ic** (-tóppik). *Biology.* Having narrow limits of adaptation to environmental conditions. Compare **eurytropic.** [STENO- + -TROPE + -IC.]

Sten·o·type (stén-ō-tīp, -ə-) *n.* **1.** A trademark for a keyboard machine used to record dictation by a phonetic system. **2.** *Small* **s.** A symbol or combination of symbols on a Stenotype representing a sound, word, or phrase. [STENO(GRAPHY) + TYPE.]

sten·o·ty·py (sténnə-tīpi) *n.* A form of shorthand using the letters of the alphabet to represent certain sounds or words. [STENOTYPE + -Y.] **—sten·o·ty·pist** *n.*

sten·tor (stén-tawr, -tər) *n.* **1.** Any of several trumpet-shaped aquatic microorganisms of the genus *Stentor,* having cilia around the oral cavity. **2.** *Often capital* **S.** A person with an extremely loud voice. [New Latin *Stentor,* from Greek *Stentōr.* See **stentorian.**]

sten·to·ri·an (sten-táw-ri-ən || -tṓ-) *adj.* Extremely loud. Said of the voice. [Greek *Stentōr,* name of a loud-voiced herald in the *Iliad,* from *stenein,* to groan, moan.]

step (step) *n.* **1. a.** The single complete movement of raising one foot and putting it down in another spot in the act of walking, running, or dancing. **b.** A manner of walking; a gait. **c.** The rhythm or pace of another or others, as in a march or dance: *break step; keep step.* **d.** The sound of a tread; a footstep. **e.** A footprint. **2. a.** The distance traversed by moving one foot ahead of the other. **b.** A very short distance: *just a step away.* **c.** *Plural.* Course; path: *followed in his father's steps.* **3. a.** A rest for the foot in ascending or descending. **b.** *Plural.* Stairs. **c.** *Plural.* A stepladder. **4. a.** Any of a series of actions or measures taken towards some end: *take steps to remedy the situation.* **b.** A stage in a process. **5.** A degree in progress or a grade or rank in a scale: *a step ahead of the others.* **6.** *Nautical.* The block in which the heel of a mast is fixed. **7.** A series of foot and body movements making up part of a dance: *hasn't learnt the polka step.* **8.** Any change in the level of a surface, as on a hillside or on the sea bed, that resembles a step on a set of stairs. **9.** *Music. Chiefly U.S.* **a.** A degree in a scale. **b.** The interval between two adjacent degrees in a scale. **—in step. 1.** Moving in rhythm or time. **2.** *Informal.* In conformity or harmony. **—out of step.** Not in step. **—step by step.** By degrees; gradually. **—watch (one's) step. a.** To be careful and sensible. **b.** To behave as is demanded or required.
~*v.* **stepped, stepping, steps.** —*intr.* **1.** To put or press the foot; tread: *stepped on my toe.* **2.** To move or go, especially a short distance, by taking a step or steps: *step aside; step into my office.* **3.** To move using the feet, in a particular manner: *step lively.* **4.** To move into a new situation as if by taking a single step: *stepping into a life of ease.* —*tr.* **1.** To move by taking (a number of steps or paces): *step five paces.* **2.** To measure by pacing. Usually used with *off* or *out*: *step off ten yards.* **3.** To furnish with steps; make steps in. **4.** *Chiefly U.S.* To set (the foot) down: *step foot on land.* **5.** *Nautical.* To place (a mast) in its step. **—step on.** To treat harshly or with arrogant indifference. **—step on it.** *Informal.* To hurry up; speed up. **—step out.** To walk with brisk strides. [Middle English *step(pe), stap(p)e,* Old English *stæpe, stepe.*]

step- *comb. form.* Indicates relationship through the previous marriage of a spouse or through the remarriage of a parent, rather than by blood; for example, **stepbrother.** [Middle English *step-, stip-,* Old English *stēop-.*]

step·broth·er (stép-bruthər) *n.* The son of one's step-parent by a former marriage.

step·child (stép-chīld) *n., pl.* **-children** (-childrən). The child of one's spouse by a former marriage.

step·daugh·ter (stép-dawtər) *n.* The daughter of one's spouse by a former marriage.

step down *intr.v.* **1.** To take a lesser position. **2.** To abdicate; resign. —*tr.v.* To reduce (power, for example) by stages.

step-down (stép-down) *adj.* Decreasing in stages.
~*n.* A reduction in amount or size.

step-down transformer *n.* A transformer that has a greater number of turns in the primary winding than in the secondary, used to transform high voltage to low voltage.

step·father (stép-faathər) *n.* The husband of one's mother by a later marriage.

step fault *n. Geology.* A series of parallel faults along which relative displacement downwards has occurred on the same side.

steph·a·no·tis (stéffə-nṓtiss) *n.* Any climbing plant of the tropical genus *Stephanotis*; especially *S. floribunda,* native to Madagascar, and widely cultivated as a house plant for its white waxy flowers. [New Latin, from Greek (adjective), fit for a wreath, from *stephanos,* wreath, crown.]

Ste·phen (steév'n) (*c.* 1097–1154). King of England. He was elected king (1135) on the death of Henry I, despite an oath of fealty to Henry's daughter Matilda. He was a weak king and most of his

PRONUNCIATION KEY

a, trap; aa, father; ai, **fair**;
ar, **star**; aw, **lawn**; ay, **play**;
b, bb, stab; **rubber**;
ch, **church**; ck, **ticket**;
d, dd, **dead**; **ladder**; e, **dress**;
ee, **bee**; er, **defer**; ew, **few**;
ewr, **pure**; ə, **about**;
ər, letter; f, ff, **fife**; **differ**;
g, gg, **giggle**; h, **hat**; i, **kit**;
ī, price; īr, **fire**; j, **judge**;
k, **kick**; l, ll, **let**; 'l, **needle**;
m, mm, **man**; n, nn, **no**;
'n, **sudden**; ng, **thing**; o, **lot**;
ō, no; o͝o, **foot**; o͞o, **shoe**;
oor, **poor**; ow, **cow**;
owr, **hour**; oy, **boy**;
p, pp, **pepper**; r, rr, **red**;
s, ss, **sauce**; sh, **ship**;
t, tt, **totter**; th, **thick**; th, **this**;
smooth; u, **cut**; ur, **turn**;
v, vv, **valve**; w, **wet**; y, **yes**;
z, zz, **zebra**; zh, **vision**;
pleasure

IN FOREIGN WORDS:

aN, oN, **Saint-Saëns**;
hl, **Llanelli**; **Hluhluwe**;
kh, **loch**; **lough**; **Khaled**

STRESS MARK:

ín-sīt, insight; in-sī́t, incite

reign was marked by civil war. After the death of his son (1153) he acknowledged Matilda's son (Henry II) as his heir.

Stephen, Sir Leslie (1832–1904). English man of letters. He was editor of the *Dictionary of National Biography* and his books include *Essays on Free Thinking and Plain Speaking* (1873). He was the father of Virginia Woolf.

Ste·phen·son (stéev'n-s'n), **George** (1781–1848). British engineer. He built (1815) the first successful steam locomotive, and (1825) the world's first passenger railway, between Stockton and Darlington. His engine, *The Rocket*, won (1829) a prize for maintaining an average speed of 29 miles per hour.

Stephenson, Robert (1803–59). British engineer. Son of George Stephenson. He collaborated with his father in building many of the railways in Britain and abroad. He also built the Menai Strait bridge and the high-level bridge over the Tyne at Newcastle.

step in *intr.v.* To intervene or interfere, as to provide help or take charge of a situation.

step-in (stép-in) *adj.* Put on by stepping into: *a step-in ski binding.* ~*n. Often plural.* A step-in garment, especially an undergarment.

step·lad·der (stép-laddər) *n.* A portable ladder with a hinged supporting frame and usually topped with a small platform. Also called "steps".

step·moth·er (stép-muthər) *n.* The wife of one's father by a later marriage.

step·par·ent (stép-pair-ənt) *n.* A stepfather or a stepmother.

steppe (step) *n.* A vast semiarid grass-covered plain, such as that found in southeastern Europe and Siberia. [Russian *step'*, from Old Russian *step'†*, lowland.]

step·ping·stone (stépping-stōn) *n.* **1.** A stone that provides a place to stand on, as in crossing a stream. **2.** An advantageous position for advancement towards some goal.

step pyramid *n.* A pyramid with outer faces made up of stone blocks rising in steps.

step rocket *n. Aerospace.* A **multistage rocket** (*see*).

step·sis·ter (stép-sistər) *n.* The daughter of one's step-parent by a former marriage.

step·son (stép-sun) *n.* The son of one's spouse by a former marriage.

step up *tr.v.* To increase, especially by stages: *step up production.*

step-up (stép-up) *adj.* Increasing in steps or by stages. ~*n.* An increase in size, amount, or activity.

step-up transformer *n.* A transformer that has fewer turns in the primary winding than in the secondary, used to transform low voltage to high voltage.

step·wise (stép-wīz) *adj.* **1.** Marked by a gradual progression as if step by step. **2.** *Music. U.S.* Moving one degree on a scale. —**step·wise** *adv.*

-ster *n. suffix.* Indicates: **1.** One who takes part in or is associated with; for example, **gangster, youngster**. **2.** One who makes or is given to making; for example, **pollster, prankster**. [Middle English *-ster(e), -estere,* Old English *-estre, -ister,* from West Germanic *-strjōn* (unattested), agent-noun suffix (primarily feminine).]

ster. sterling.

ste·ra·di·an (stə-ráydi-ən, ste-) *n. Abbr.* **sr** A unit of measure equal to the solid angle subtended at the centre of a sphere by an area on the surface equal to the square of the radius: *The total solid angle of a sphere is 4π steradians.* [STE(REO)- + RADIAN.]

ster·co·ra·ceous (stérkə-ráyshəss) *adj.* Also **ster·co·rous** (-rəss). Consisting of or pertaining to excrement. [Latin *stercus* (stem *stercor-*), dung + -ACEOUS.]

stere (steer) *n. Abbr.* **s** A unit of volume equal to one cubic metre. [French *stère*, from Greek *stereos*, solid, hard.]

ste·re·o (stérri-ō, stéer-i-ō) *n., pl.* **-os. 1. a.** A stereophonic high-fidelity sound system. **b.** Stereophonic sound. **2.** *Printing.* A stereotype. **3.** A stereoscopic system or photograph. ~*adj.* **1.** Stereophonic. **2.** Stereoscopic.

stereo-, stere- *comb. form.* Indicates solid, firm, or three-dimensional; for example, **stereophonic, stereoscope**. [Greek *stereos*, solid, hard.]

ster·e·o·bate (stérri-ō-bayt, stéer-i-) *n. Architecture.* **1.** A stylobate. **2.** The foundation of a stone building, its top course sometimes being a stylobate. [Latin *stereobata*, from Greek *stereobatēs*, "solid base" : *stereos*, solid, STEREO- + -*batēs*, "one that is based".]

ster·e·o·chem·is·try (stérri-ō-kémmistri, stéer-i-) *n.* The chemical study of spatial arrangements of atoms in molecules and of the effects of these arrangements on the molecule's properties.

ster·e·o·chro·my (stérri-ō-krōmi, stéer-i-) *n.* The art or process of painting murals using pigments mixed with water glass. [STEREO- + -CHROME + -Y.] —**ster·e·o·chrome** *n. & tr.v.* —**ster·e·o·chro·mic** (-krōmik) *adj.* —**ster·e·o·chro·mi·cal·ly** *adv.*

ster·e·o·gram (stérri-ō-gram, stéer-i-) *n.* **1.** A stereo record player consisting of a single unit. **2.** A picture or diagram designed to give the impression of solidity. **3.** A stereograph. [STEREO- + -GRAM.]

ster·e·o·graph (stérri-ō-graaf, stéer-i-, -graf) *n.* Two stereoscopic pictures, or one picture with two superposed stereoscopic images, designed to give a three-dimensional effect when viewed through a stereoscope or special glasses. ~*tr.v.* **stereographed, -graphing, -graphs.** To make (a stereographic picture). [STEREO- + -GRAPH.]

stereographic projection *n.* An azimuthal map projection in which a point is projected onto the tangent plane from a point on the opposite end of the diameter. It is an orthomorphic projection.

ster·e·og·ra·phy (stérri-óggrəfi, stéer-i-) *n.* The art or technique of

stereoscope *A viewing device using pairs of pictures taken by a camera with two lenses, for a three-dimensional effect.*

depicting solid bodies on a plane surface. [STEREO- + -GRAPHY.] —**ster·e·o·graph·ic** (-ə-gráffik), **ster·e·o·graph·i·cal** *adj.* —**ster·e·o·graph·i·cal·ly** *adv.*

ster·e·o·i·so·mer (stérri-ō-í-səmər, stéer-i-) *n. Chemistry.* Any of the structural molecular forms of a compound that exhibits stereoisomerism. See **isomer.**

ster·e·o·i·som·er·ism (stérri-ō-í-sómmə-ríz'm, stéer-i-) *n.* Isomerism created by differences in the spatial arrangement of atoms in a molecule. —**ster·e·o·i·so·mer·ic** (-sə-mérrik) *adj.*

ste·re·om·e·try (stérri-ómmətri, stéer-i-) *n.* The science of measuring volume. [STEREO- + -METRY.] —**ste·re·o·met·ric** (-ō-méttrik, -ə-), **ste·re·o·me·tri·cal** *adj.*

ster·e·o·mi·cro·scope (stérri-ō-míkrə-skōp, stéer-i-) *n.* A microscope optically equipped for stereoscopic viewing.

ster·e·o·phon·ic (stérri-ə-fónnik, stéer-i-, -ō-) *adj.* Of or pertaining to a high-fidelity sound system in which two channels are used to give an illusion of a more natural distribution of sources of sound. Compare **binaural, quadraphonic.** [STEREO- + PHONIC.] —**ster·e·o·phon·i·cal·ly** *adv.* —**ster·e·oph·on·y** (-óffəni) *n.*

ster·e·op·sis (stérri-ópsiss, stéer-i-) *n.* Stereoscopic vision. [New Latin : STEREO- + -OPSIS.]

ster·e·op·ti·con (stérri-ópti-kən, stéer-i- ‖ -kon) *n.* A **magic lantern** (*see*), especially one consisting of two separate units arranged so as to produce dissolving views. [New Latin : STEREO- + Greek *optikon,* neuter of *optikos,* OPTIC.]

ster·e·o·scope (stérri-ə-skōp, stéer-i-) *n.* An optical instrument used to impart a three-dimensional effect to two photographs of the same scene taken at slightly different angles and viewed through two eyepieces. [STEREO- + -SCOPE.]

ster·e·o·scop·ic (stérri-ə-skóppik, stéer-i-) *adj.* **1.** Of or pertaining to stereoscopy; especially, three-dimensional. **2.** Of or pertaining to a stereoscope. —**ster·e·o·scop·i·cal·ly** *adv.*

ster·e·os·co·py (stérri-óskəpi, stéer-i-) *n.* **1.** The viewing of objects as three-dimensional. **2.** The technique of making or using stereoscopes. [STEREO- + -SCOPY.] —**ster·e·os·co·pist** *n.*

ste·re·o·spe·cif·ic (stérri-ō-spə-síffik, stéer-i-) *adj. Chemistry.* Pertaining to, involving, or producing a regular arrangement of atoms in a molecule. Said especially of polymers with a regular arrangement of atoms or of reactions or catalysts producing such compounds.

ster·e·o·tax·is (stérri-ō-táksiss, stéer-i-, -ə-) *n. Biology.* Thigmotaxis (*see*). —**ster·e·o·tac·tic** (-táktik), **ster·e·o·tac·ti·cal** *adj.* —**ster·e·o·tac·ti·cal·ly** *adv.*

ster·e·o·type (stérri-ə-tīp, stéer-i-, -ō-) *n.* **1.** A conventional, formulaic, and usually oversimplified conception, opinion, or belief. **2.** A person, group, event, or issue considered to typify or conform to an unvarying standard pattern or manner: *the stereotype of a banker.* Also used adjectivally: *a stereotype male chauvinist.* **3. a.** A metal printing plate cast from a mould made out of papier-mâché, plastic, or rubber, taken from a raised printing surface, such as type. **b.** The method or process of making such a plate. ~*tr.v.* **stereotyped, -typing, -types. 1.** To make a stereotype of. **2.** To print from a stereotype. **3.** To give a fixed, unvarying form to. [French *stéréotype* : STEREO- + TYPE.] —**ster·e·o·typ·er** *n.* —**ster·e·o·typ·ic** (-típpik), **ster·e·o·typ·i·cal** *adj.*

ster·e·o·typed (stérri-ə-tīpt, stéer-i-, -ō-) *adj.* **1.** Not individualised; unoriginal; conventional. **2.** Printed or reproduced from stereotype plates. —See Synonyms at **trite.**

ster·e·o·typ·y (stérri-ə-tīpi, stéer-i-, -ō-) *n.* **1.** The process or art of making stereotype plates. **2.** Excessive repetition or lack of variation in movements, ideas, or patterns of speech.

ster·e·o·vi·sion (stérri-ō-vizh'n, stéer-i-) *n.* Visual perception of or exhibition in three dimensions.

ster·ic (stérrik, stéer-ik) *n.* Of or pertaining to the spatial arrangement of atoms in a molecule. [STER(EO)- + -IC.] —**ster·i·cal·ly** *adv.*

ste·rig·ma (stə-ríg-mə, ste-) *n.* A slender spore-bearing structure formed by certain fungi. [New Latin, from Greek *stērigma,* support, from *stērizein,* to support.]

ster·i·lant (stérri-lənt, stérrə-) *n.* A sterilising agent.

ster·ile (stérrīl ‖ *U.S.* stérrəl) *adj.* **1. a.** Incapable of reproducing sexually; barren; infertile. **b.** Incapable of producing seed, fruit spores, or other reproductive structures. Said of plants or their parts. **2.** Capable of producing little or no vegetation: *sterile land.* **3.** Free from bacteria or other microorganisms. **4.** Lacking in imagination or vitality; not stimulating; dry. **5.** Failing to produce any useful result; fruitless: *a sterile discussion.* **6.** Containing no archaeological remains: *a sterile stratum.* [French *stérile,* from Latin *sterilis,* unfruitful.] —**ster·ile·ly** *adv.* —**ste·ril·i·ty** (ste-rílləti, stə-), **ster·ile·ness** *n.*

Synonyms: sterile, infertile, barren, unfruitful, impotent.

ster·i·li·sa·tion (stérrə-lí-záysh'n, stérri- ‖ *U.S.* -li-) *n.* **1.** The procedure or act of making infertile. **2.** The removal of living microorganisms from materials.

ster·i·lise, ster·il·ize (stérrə-līz, stérri-) *tr.v.* **-ised, -ising, -ises.** To render sterile. —**ster·i·lis·er** *n.*

ster·let (stérlit) *n.* A sturgeon, *Acipenser ruthenus,* of the Caspian Sea and adjacent waters. [Russian *sterlyad',* perhaps akin to Germanic *sturjōn* (unattested), STURGEON.]

ster·ling (stérling) *n. Abbr.* **ster., stg. 1.** British money; especially, the pound as the basic monetary unit of the United Kingdom. **2.** British coinage of silver or gold, having as a standard of fineness 0.500 for silver and 0.91666 for gold. **3. a.** Sterling silver. **b.** Articles made of sterling silver, such as tableware. ~*adj. Abbr.* **ster., stg. 1.** Consisting of or relating to sterling or

British money. 2. Made of sterling silver. 3. Of the highest quality; of genuine worth. [Middle English *sterling, starling,* "small star" (from the small star stamped on the silver pennies), probably from Old English *steorling* (unattested) : *steorra,* STAR + -LING.]

sterling area n. The **scheduled territories** (*see*).

sterling silver n. 1. An alloy of 92.5 per cent silver with copper or another metal. 2. Collectively, objects made of this alloy.

stern[1] (stern) *adj.* **sterner, sternest.** 1. Not inclined to leniency; strict. 2. Expressing disapproval or displeasure: *a stern rebuke.* 3. Grave or severe in manner or appearance; grim; austere: *a silent, stern, rather forbidding manner.* 4. Resolute; inflexible; unyielding: *made of sterner stuff.* 5. Inexorable; relentless: *stern necessity.* —See Synonyms at **severe.** [Middle English *sterne, stierne,* Old English *styrne, stierne.*] —**stern·ly** *adv.* —**stern·ness** n.

stern[2] n. 1. The rear part of a ship or boat. 2. The rear part of anything. [Middle English *sterne,* probably from Old Norse *stjórn,* steering, rudder, from *stýra,* STEER.]

ster·nal (stérn'l) *adj. Anatomy.* Of, near, or pertaining to the sternum. [New Latin *sternalis,* from STERNUM.]

Stern·berg (shtáirn-bairk), **Josef von** (1894–1969). Austrian film director. He is best known for his series of films starring Marlene Dietrich, which include *The Blue Angel* (1930), *Blonde Venus* (1932), *Shanghai Express* (1932), and *The Scarlet Empress* (1934).

stern chaser n. A gun or cannon mounted on the stern of a ship for firing at a pursuing vessel.

Sterne (stern), **Laurence** (1713–68). English novelist and clergyman. He won fame with his witty, ribald novel *The Life and Opinions of Tristram Shandy, Gentleman* (1759–67). His other works include *A Sentimental Journey.*

stern·fore·most (stérn-fór-mōst, -məst ‖ -fór-) *adv. Nautical.* With the stern foremost; backwards.

stern·most (stérn-mōst) *adj. Nautical.* Farthest astern.

stern·post (stérn-pōst) n. The principal upright post at the stern of a vessel, usually serving to support the rudder.

stern sheets *pl.n.* The stern area of an open boat.

stern·son (stérn-s'n) n. A bar of metal or wood set between the keelson and the sternpost to fortify the joint. Also called "stern knee". [STERN + (KEEL)SON.]

ster·num (stér-nəm) n., *pl.* **-na** (-nə) or **-nums.** 1. A long flat bone articulating with the cartilages of and forming the midventral support of most of the ribs in tetrapod vertebrates, and also of the collarbone in humans and certain other vertebrates. Also called "breastbone". 2. The chitinous plate that forms a protective covering on the ventral surface of the body segment of an arthropod. [New Latin, from Greek *sternon,* breast, breastbone.]

ster·nu·ta·tion (stérnew-táysh'n) n. 1. The act of sneezing. 2. A sneeze. [Latin *sternūtātiō* (stem *sternūtātiōn*-), from *sternūtāre,* frequentative of *sternuere,* to sneeze.]

ster·nu·ta·tor (stérnew-taytər) n. A substance that irritates the nasal and respiratory passages and causes sneezing.

ster·nu·ta·to·ry (ster-néwtə-tri, -təri, stérnew-táytəri ‖ -nóotə-) *adj.* Causing or tending to cause sneezing.
~n., *pl.* **sternutatories.** A sternutatory substance, such as pepper.

stern·ward (stérn-wərd) *adj.* In or at the stern.
~adv. *Chiefly U.S.* Variant of **sternwards.**

stern·wards (stérn-wərdz) *adv.* Also *chiefly U.S.* **stern·ward** (-wərd). Towards the stern; astern.

stern·way (stérn-way) n. The backward movement of a vessel.

stern·wheel·er (stérn-wéelər, -hwéelər) n. A steamboat propelled by a paddle wheel at the stern.

ster·oid (stéer-oyd, stérroyd) n. Any of numerous naturally occurring, fat-soluble organic compounds having a 17-carbon-atom ring as a basis, and including the sterols and bile acids, many hormones, certain natural drugs such as digitalis compounds, and the precursors of certain vitamins. [STER(OL) + -OID.]

ster·ol (stéer-ol, stérrol ‖ -ōl, stérról) n. Any of a group of predominantly unsaturated solid alcohols of the steroid group, such as cholesterol and ergosterol, occurring in the fatty tissues of plants and animals. [Short for CHOLESTEROL.]

Ster·o·pe[1] (stérrəpi). Also **As·ter·o·pe** (ə-). *Greek Mythology.* One of the **Pleiades** (*see*). [Greek *(A)steropē,* from *(a)steropē, astrapē,* lightning, "twinkling".]

Sterope[2] n. One of the stars in the constellation **Pleiades** (*see*).

ster·tor (stér-tər, -tawr) n. A heavy snoring sound in deep sleep or a coma, caused by obstruction of the air passages. [New Latin, from Latin *stertere,* to snore.] —**ster·tor·ous** (-tərəss) *adj.* —**ster·tor·ous·ly** *adv.*

stet (stet) n. *Abbr.* **st.** A printer's term directing that a letter, word, or other matter marked for omission or correction is to be retained.
~tr.v. **stetted, stetting, stets.** To cancel a correction or omission previously made to (a letter, word, or section of printed matter) by marking with the word *stet* and with a row of dots. Compare **dele.** [Latin, let it stand, from *stāre,* to stand.]

steth·o·scope (stétha-skōp) n. An instrument consisting of a hollow disc connected by a tube to an earpiece used for listening to sounds produced within the body. [French *stéthoscope* : Greek *stēthos†,* chest, breast + -SCOPE.] —**steth·o·scop·ic** (-skóppik) *adj.* —**steth·o·scop·i·cal·ly** *adv.* —**ste·thos·co·py** (ste-thóskəpi) n.

Stet·son (stéts'n) n. A trademark for a hat having a high crown and wide brim, popular in the western United States. [Designed by John *Stetson* (1830–1906), U.S. hat-maker.]

Stettin. See **Szczecin.**

ste·ve·dore (stéev-ə-dawr, -i- ‖ -dōr) n. A person employed in the loading or unloading of ships.
~v. **stevedored, -doring, -dores.** —tr. To load or unload the cargo of (a ship). —intr. To work as a stevedore. [Spanish *estibador,* from *estivar,* to pack, from Latin *stīpāre,* to stuff.]

stevedore's knot n. A knot used to prevent a line from coming out of a pulley.

ste·ven·graph (stéev'n-graaf, -graf) n. A colourful, usually small, picture woven in silk. [After Thomas *Stevens,* 19th-century British weaver.]

Ste·vens (stéev'nz), **Wallace** (1879–1955). U.S. poet. His poetry is distinguished by its tight construction and its intellectual but lucid content, as in the collection *The Man with the Blue Guitar and Other Poems* (1937).

Ste·ven·son (stéev'n-s'n), **Adlai (Ewing)** (1900–65). U.S. politician. He held various offices in Roosevelt's wartime administrations, and was governor (1949–53) of Illinois. He was Democratic presidential candidate (1952, 1956) for the presidency, but was beaten by Eisenhower.

Stevenson, Robert Louis (1850–94). Scottish novelist, essayist, and poet. His works include *Travels with a Donkey in the Cévennes* (1879), *Virginibus Puerisque* (1881), *Treasure Island* (1883), and *The Strange Case of Dr. Jekyll and Mr. Hyde* (1886).

stew (stew ‖ stoo) v. **stewed, stewing, stews.** —tr. 1. To cook (food) by simmering or boiling slowly. 2. To leave (tea) for a long time before drinking, thus allowing the tannin to infuse and giving it an acrid taste. —intr. 1. To undergo cooking by boiling slowly or simmering. 2. *Informal.* To suffer under oppressive heat or stuffy confinement; swelter. 3. *Informal.* To worry; fret. 4. To become stewed. Used of tea.
~n. 1. A dish cooked by stewing; especially, a mixture of meat or fish and vegetables with stock. 2. *Informal.* A state of mental agitation or difficulty: *in a stew over her lost keys.* 3. *Usually plural. Archaic.* A brothel. [Middle English *stewen,* originally to bathe in hot water or steam, from Old French *estuver,* from Vulgar Latin *extūfāre* (unattested) : probably *ex-,* out of + *tufus* (unattested), hot vapour, from Greek *tuphos,* smoke, vapour, from *tuphein,* to smoke.]

stew·ard (stéw-ərd ‖ stoo-) n. 1. One who manages another's property, finances, or other affairs. 2. One in charge of domestic arrangements, as in an institution, club, or hotel. 3. An officer on a ship in charge of provisions and dining arrangements. 4. Any male member of the staff of a ship or aeroplane, who waits on the passengers. 5. An official who supervises or helps to manage an event such as a ball or race-meeting. 6. A **shop steward** (*see*).
~v. **stewarded, -arding, -ards.** —tr. To serve as steward of; manage; administer. —intr. To serve as a steward. [Middle English *stuarde, stywarde,* Old English *stīgweard,* "keeper of the hall" : *stig,* hall (see **sty**) + *weard,* keeper, ward.]

stew·ard·ess (stéw-ərd-iss, -éss ‖ stoo-) n. A female steward, especially one who waits on passengers on an aeroplane.

Stewart. See **Stuart.**

Stew·art (stéw-ərt ‖ stoo-), **Jackie,** born John Young Stewart (1939–). British motor-racing driver. In his racing career (1961–73) he won a record number of 27 Grand Prix races. He was world champion in 1969, 1971, and 1973.

Stewart, James (Maitland) (1908–). U.S. film actor. He is best known for his portrayals of the incorruptible hero in films such as *Destry Rides Again* (1939) and *The Philadelphia Story.*

stewed (stewd ‖ stood) *adj.* 1. Cooked by stewing: *stewed prunes.* 2. Having an acid taste through having been left a long time before drinking. Said of tea. 3. *Slang.* Drunk; intoxicated.

St. Ex. stock exchange.

St. George's. Capital and port of Grenada, West Indies. Situated on the southwest coast, it was founded by the French (1705) and was the capital of the British Windward Isles (1885–1958).

St. George's Channel. Strait between southern Ireland and southwest Wales. Linking the Atlantic Ocean with the Irish Sea, it is some 160 kilometres (100 miles) long and 75–145 kilometres (46–90 miles) wide.

St. Gott·hard Pass (gót-ərd, -aard). Alpine pass, south Switzerland. Rising to a height of 2 114 metres (6,935 feet), it has long been part of a trade route linking Switzerland with Italy. Beneath the pass there is a railway tunnel (1872–80) 15 kilometres (9.25 miles) long and a road tunnel (1970–80) 16 kilometres (10 miles) long.

Sth. South.

St. Helens, Mount. Volcano in Washington state, northwest United States. It erupted in April 1980, shearing some 450 metres (about 1,500 feet) from its crest, and covering a vast area with dust. Its height before the eruption was 2 948 metres (9,671 feet).

St. Hel·i·er (hélli-ər). Capital of Jersey, the Channel Islands. A port and resort, it is a market for cattle and early vegetables.

sthenic (sthénnik) *adj.* Characterised by excessive energy; vigorous. [Greek *sthenos,* strength + -IC, by analogy with *asthenic.*]

Sthe·no (sthéenō). *Greek Mythology.* One of the three Gorgons.

stib·ine (stíb-īn, -een) n. 1. A colourless, flammable, poisonous gas, SbH_3, often used as a fumigant. 2. A derivative of this formed by replacing one or more hydrogen atoms by hydrocarbon groups. [Latin *stibium,* variant of *stibi, stimmi,* antimony, from Greek, from Egyptian *stm* + -INE.]

stib·nite (stíb-nīt) n. A lead-grey mineral, Sb_2S_3, that is the chief source of antimony. Also called "antimony glance". [French *stibine,* stibnite, from Latin *stibium,* antimony (see **stibine**) + -ITE.]

stich (stik) n. A line of verse. [Greek *stikhos,* row, line, verse.]

sti·chom·e·try (sti-kómmətri) *n.* The division of a prose piece into lines of fixed length or, occasionally, into lines whose lengths correspond to the natural divisions of sense, as in manuscripts written before the adoption of punctuation. [Greek *stikhos,* STICH + -METRY.] **—stich·o·met·ric** (stíckə-méttrik) *adj.*

stich·o·myth·i·a (stík-ə-míthi-ə, -ō-) *n.* Also **sti·chom·y·thy** (sti-kómməthi). An ancient Greek arrangement of dialogue in drama, poetry, and disputation in which single lines of verse are spoken by alternate speakers. [Greek *stikhomuthia,* from *stikhomuthein,* to speak in alternating lines : *stikhos,* STICH + *muthos,* speech, tale, MYTH.] **—stich·o·myth·ic** (-míthik) *adj.*

-stichous *adj. comb. form.* Indicates rows; for example, **polystichous.** [Greek *-stikhos,* from *stikhos,* row, line, verse.]

stick[1] (stik) *n.* **1.** A long, slender piece of wood, especially: **a.** A branch or stem cut from a tree or shrub. **b.** A tree branch or other piece of wood used for fuel, cut for timber, or shaped for a specific purpose. **c.** A wand, staff, baton, or rod. **d.** Any of various sticklike implements used in games or sports: *a hockey stick.* **e.** A cane or walking stick. **2.** Something cut into or having the shape of a stick: *a stick of dynamite; a stick of rock.* **3. a.** The **control stick** *(see)* of an aeroplane. **b.** *Informal.* The lever or rod in a motor vehicle used for changing gear. **4.** *Nautical.* A mast or a part of a mast. **5.** *Printing.* **a.** A composing stick. **b.** The type contents of a composing stick. Also called "stickful". **6. a.** *Military.* A group of bombs released to fall across a target in a straight row. **b.** A group of paratroopers jumping in succession. **7.** *Informal.* An item of furniture. **8.** *Plural. Informal.* An area far from a city or town; backwoods: *They live way out in the sticks.* **9.** *Informal.* A person, especially one who is spiritless or boring: *a dry old stick.* **10.** *Informal.* **a.** Adverse criticism: *came in for a lot of stick.* **b.** Punishment or the threat of punishment: *He'll give us stick for being so late.* **11.** A long loaf of bread. **—get the wrong end of the stick.** To completely misunderstand or misconstrue something.
~tr.v. **sticked, sticking, sticks. 1.** To prop up (a vine or other plant) with sticks or brush on which to grow. **2.** *Printing.* To set (type) in a composing stick.
~interj. Plural. Used in hockey by the umpire to indicate that players have raised their sticks improperly above their shoulders. [Middle English, Old English, *sticca,* from West Germanic *stikka* (unattested).]

stick[2] *v.* **stuck** (stuk), **sticking, sticks.** *—tr.* **1.** To pierce, puncture, or penetrate with a pointed instrument, such as a knife or pin. **2.** To kill by piercing. **3.** To thrust or push (a knife, pin, or other pointed instrument) into or through another object. **4.** To fasten into place by forcing an end or point into something: *stick a hook into the wall.* **5.** To fasten or attach with or as if with pins, nails, or similar instruments. **6.** To fasten or attach with an adhesive material, glue, or tape: *stick a poster to the wall.* **7.** To cover or decorate with objects piercing the surface. **8.** To fix, impale, or transfix on a pointed object: *stick an olive on a toothpick.* **9.** To put, place, or thrust, or poke into a specified place or position: *stick your hands up; stuck a cigarette in his mouth.* **10.** *Informal.* To detain or delay. Usually used in the passive: *was stuck at the dentist all morning.* **11.** *Chiefly British Slang.* To bear; abide: *can't stick his silly jokes.* **12.** To make incapable of movement or progress; bring to a standstill or impasse. Usually used in the passive: *can't shift it—it's completely stuck; stuck on question three.* **13.** *Informal.* To confuse, baffle, or puzzle. Usually used in the passive: *never stuck for an answer.* **14.** To burden or encumber with something unpleasant or unwanted; saddle: *stuck with paying the bill.* **15.** *Informal.* To write: *Stick your address at the top of the page.* *—intr.* **1.** To be or become fixed or embedded in place by having the point thrust in. **2.** To become or remain attached or in close association by or as if by adhesion; cling: *"I'm all for us English sticking together when we're abroad"* (Somerset Maugham). **3.** To remain firm, determined, or resolute: *stick to a resolution.* **4.** To persist, endure, or persevere. Used with *at, to,* or *with*: *must stick at it in order to succeed.* **5. a.** *Informal.* To remain in the vicinity; linger. Usually used with *about* or *around*: *Stick around here until I get back.* **b.** To remain for a period of time: *Her face really stuck in my mind.* **6.** To scruple or hesitate. Used with *at* or *to*: *She sticks at nothing.* **7.** To be at or come to a standstill; become fixed, jammed, checked, or obstructed. **8.** To extend, project, or protrude. Used with *out, up, down,* or *through.* **—be stuck on.** *Informal.* To be in love with or infatuated by. **—get stuck in** or **into.** *Informal.* To begin or perform (a job) with a serious and determined attitude. **—stick by.** To remain loyal or faithful to. **—stick it out.** *Informal.* To persist or persevere to the end. **—stick out for.** To withhold consent, agreement, or compliance until something is done or granted. **—stick up for.** To defend or support. [Middle English, Old English *stician.*]

stick·er (stíckər) *n.* **1.** A person or thing that sticks. **2.** A gummed or adhesive label or patch. **3.** A tenacious, diligent, or persistent person. **4.** A thorn, prickle, or barb.

stick·ing plaster (stíking) *n.* A piece of adhesive material used to protect a wound or hold a dressing in position. Also called "plaster".

stick insect *n.* Any of several mainly tropical insects of the family Phasmidae, resembling sticks or twigs. Also *U.S.* "walking stick".

stick-in-the-mud (stíckin-th̲ə-mud) *n. Informal.* A very staid person who lacks initiative, imagination, or enthusiasm.

stick·le (stíck'l) *intr.v.* **-led, -ling, -les. 1.** To argue or contend stubbornly, especially about trivial or petty points. **2.** To have or raise objections; scruple. [Earlier *stightle,* to arbitrate, intervene, Middle English *stightlen,* Old English *stihtan, stihtian.*]

stick·le·back (stíck'l-bak) *n.* Any of various small freshwater and marine fishes of the family Gasterosteidae, having erectile spines along the back. [Middle English *stykylbak,* "prickly back" : *stykyl-,* from Old English *sticel,* prick, sting + *bak,* BACK.]

stick·ler (stícklər) *n.* **1.** A person who insists on something: *a stickler for neatness.* **2.** Anything puzzling or difficult.

stick·pin (stík-pin) *n. U.S.* A **tiepin** *(see).*

stick up *tr.v. Slang.* To rob, especially at gunpoint.

stick·up (stík-up) *n. Slang.* A robbery, especially at gunpoint.

stick·weed (stík-weed) *n.* Broadly, any of various plants having clinging seeds or fruit, especially ragweed.

stick·y (stícki) *adj.* **-ier, -iest. 1.** Having the property of adhering or sticking to a surface; adhesive. **2.** Covered with an adhesive agent: *a sticky floor.* **3.** Warm and humid; muggy. **4.** *Informal.* Painful or difficult: *a sticky problem.* **5.** *Economics.* Tending to remain the same despite other changes in the economy. Said of prices or wages.
~n. Australian Informal. An inquisitive look at something: *Let's have a sticky.* **—stick·i·ly** *adv.* **—stick·i·ness** *n.*

stick·y·beak (stícki-beek) *n. Australian & N.Z.* An interfering or inquisitive person.
~intr.v. Australian & N.Z. **-beaked, -beaking, -beaks.** To interfere or pry.

sticky end *n. Informal.* **1.** A wretched or unhappy finish: *will come to a sticky end.* **2.** A violent or unpleasant death.

sticky tape *n.* Cellulose adhesive tape.

sticky wicket *n.* **1.** A cricket pitch drying quickly in the sun after rain thus providing highly favourable conditions for spin bowling. **2.** *Informal.* A problematical or tricky position or situation. Used especially in the phrase *on a sticky wicket.*

Stieg·litz (stéeglits), **Alfred** (1864–1946). American photographer, a pioneer of colour photography and advocate of photography as an art form.

stiff (stif) *adj.* **stiffer, stiffest. 1.** Difficult to bend or stretch; not flexible, pliant, or limp; rigid. **2. a.** Not moving or operating easily or freely; resistant: *a stiff hinge.* **b.** Aching and lacking ease of movement, as from exertion or old age: *a stiff neck; stiff all over.* **3.** Drawn tightly; taut. **4.** Rigidly or excessively formal, awkward, or constrained; without ease or grace. **5.** Not liquid, loose, or fluid; firm; thick: *stiff batter.* **6.** Firm in purpose or resistance; stubborn; unyielding. **7.** Having a strong, swift, steady force or movement: *a stiff breeze.* **8.** Potent or strong: *a stiff drink.* **9.** Difficult to perform or deal with; demanding; arduous: *a stiff hike; a stiff examination.* **10.** Difficult to accept; harsh or severe: *a stiff penalty.* **11.** Excessively high: *stiff prices.* **12.** *Nautical.* Not heeling over much, in spite of great wind or the press of the sail. **13.** *Slang.* Well supplied; full: *The area was stiff with security men.*
~adv. **1.** To the point of being rigid: *frozen stiff.* **2.** Completely; totally: *bored stiff.*
~n. Slang. **1.** A corpse. **2.** An overformal, constrained, or priggish person: *a big stiff.* [Middle English *stif(fe),* Old English *stīf.*] **—stiff·ly** *adv.* **—stiff·ness** *n.*
Synonyms: *stiff, rigid, inflexible, inelastic, tense, taut.*

stiff·en (stíff'n) *v.* **-ened, -ening, -ens.** *—tr.* To make stiff or stiffer. *—intr.* **1.** To become stiff or stiffer. **2.** To become suddenly rigid or tense, as with indignation or fear. **—stiff·en·er** *n.*

stiff-necked (stíf-nékt) *adj.* Stubborn; unyielding. See Synonyms at **obstinate.**

stiff upper lip *n.* Great restraint and composure; concealment of emotions or feelings, as of sadness or fear.

sti·fle[1] (stīf'l) *v.* **-fled, -fling, -fles.** *—tr.* **1.** To kill by preventing respiration; smother or suffocate. **2.** To interrupt or cut off (the voice or breath). **3.** To keep or hold back; suppress; repress: *stifle his opinions.* *—intr.* **1.** To die of suffocation. **2.** To feel smothered or suffocated by or as if by close confinement in a stuffy room. [Middle English *stufflen,* probably formed as a frequentative from Old French *estouffer,* to choke, smother.] **—sti·fler** *n.*

stifle[2] *n.* The joint of the hind leg corresponding to the human knee in certain quadrupeds, such as the horse. Also called "stifle joint". [Middle English *stifle*†.]

sti·fling (stīfling) *adj.* Hot or stuffy almost to the point of being suffocating. **—sti·fling·ly** *adv.*

stig·ma (stíg-mə) *n., pl.* **stigmata** (-tə, *also* stig-máatə) or **-mas** (especially for sense 6). **1.** A mark or token of shame, disgrace, or reproach: *a certain stigma attached to being a divorcee.* **2.** *Archaic.* A mark burnt into the skin of a criminal or slave; a brand. **3.** Any small mark; a scar or birthmark. **4.** *Medicine.* **a.** A mark or rash that occurs as a symptom of hysteria. **b.** A mark indicative of a history of a disease or abnormality. **5.** *Biology.* A small mark, spot, or pore, such as the respiratory spiracle of an insect or an eyespot in certain algae. **6.** *Botany.* The apex of the pistil of a flower, upon which pollen is deposited at pollination. **7.** *Plural.* Marks or sores corresponding to and resembling the crucifixion wounds of Jesus, sometimes appearing on the bodies of certain persons in a state of religious ecstasy or hysteria. [Latin *stigma* (plural *stigmata*), from Greek, tattoo mark, from *stizein,* to prick, tattoo.]

stig·mas·ter·ol (stig-mástə-rol || -rōl) *n.* A sterol, $C_{29}H_{48}O$, obtained from soya beans or Calabar beans. [New Latin *(Physo)stigma,* genus of the Calabar bean (see **physostigmine**) + STEROL.]

stig·mat·ic (stig-máttik) *adj.* **1.** Pertaining to, resembling, or having a stigma or stigmata. **2. Anastigmatic** *(see).*

PRONUNCIATION KEY

a, trap; aa, father; ai, fair; ar, star; aw, lawn; ay, play; b, bb, stab; rubber; ch, church; ck, ticket; d, dd, dead; ladder; e, dress; ee, bee; er, defer; ew, few; ewr, pure; ə, about; ər, letter; f, ff, fife; differ; g, gg, giggle; h, hat; i, kit; ī, price; īr, fire; j, judge; k, kick; l, ll, let; 'l, needle; m, mm, man; n, nn, no; 'n, sudden; ng, thing; o, lot; ō, no; ŏŏ, foot; ōō, shoe; oor, poor; ow, cow; owr, hour; oy, boy; p, pp, pepper; r, rr, red; s, ss, sauce; sh, ship; t, tt, totter; th, thick; th̲, this; smooth; u, cut; ur, turn; v, vv, valve; w, wet; y, yes; z, zz, zebra; zh̲, vision; pleasure

IN FOREIGN WORDS:

aN, oN, Saint-Saëns; h̲l, Llanelli; Hluhluwe; k̲h, loch; lough; Khaled

STRESS MARK:

ín-sīt, insight; in-sīt, incite

~*n.* Also **stig·ma·tist** (stígmətist). A person marked with religious stigmata.

stig·ma·tise, stig·ma·tize (stíg-mə-tīz) *tr.v.* **-tised, -tising, -tises. 1.** To characterise or brand as disgraceful or ignominious. **2.** To brand or mark with a stigma or stigmata. **3.** To cause stigmata to appear on. [Medieval Latin *stigmatizāre,* to brand, from Greek *stigmatizein,* to mark, tattoo, from *stigma,* tattoo mark, STIGMA.] **—stig·ma·ti·sa·tion** (-tī-záysh'n || *U.S.* -i-) *n.* **—stig·ma·tis·er** *n.*

stig·ma·tism (stíg-mə-tiz'm) *n.* **1.** The state or condition of being affected by stigmata. **2.** *Optics.* The state of a refracting or reflecting system, especially the eye, that focuses light rays at a point, from an off-axis point. **3.** Normal eyesight.

stil·bene (stíl-been) *n.* A colourless or yellowish crystalline compound, $C_{14}H_{12}$, used in the manufacture of dyes and optical bleaches and as a phosphor. [Greek *stilbos,* shining, shimmering, from *stilbein*†, to shimmer + -ENE.]

stil·bite (stíl-bīt) *n.* A white or yellow lustrous zeolite mineral, essentially $(Na_2Ca)(Al_2Si_7O_{18})\cdot 7H_2O$. [French : Greek *stilbos,* shining, shimmering (see **stilbene**) + -ITE.]

stil·boes·trol (stil-beéss-trəl, -trol || -trōl) *n. Chemistry.* Also *U.S.* **stil·bes·trol** (-béss-) **Diethylstilboestrol** *(see).* [STILB(ENE) + OESTR(US) + -OL.]

stile¹ (stīl) *n.* **1.** A set or series of steps for getting over a fence or wall. **2.** A turnstile. [Middle English *stile,* Old English *stigel.*]

stile² *n.* A vertical member of a panel or frame, as in a door or window sash. [Probably from Dutch *stijl,* doorpost, from Middle Dutch, probably from Latin *stilus,* pole, post. See **style.**]

sti·let·to (sti-léttō) *n., pl.* **-tos** or **-toes. 1.** A small dagger with a slender, tapering blade. **2.** A small, sharp-pointed instrument used for making eyelet holes in needlework. **3.** A high heel on a woman's shoe that tapers to a sharp point at the bottom. Also called "stiletto heel". **4.** *Plural.* A pair of shoes with such heels. [Italian, diminutive of *stilo,* dagger, from Latin *stilus,* sharp-pointed post, pole, stake. See **style.**]

still¹ (stil) *adj.* **stiller, stillest. 1.** Free from sound; silent; quiet. **2.** Low in sound; hushed; subdued. **3.** Without movement; at rest. **4.** Free from disturbance, commotion, or agitation; tranquil; serene. **5.** Free from noticeable current, as water might be. **6.** Not carbonated; lacking effervescence: *still wine.* **7.** *Photography.* Of, designating, or pertaining to a single or static photograph as opposed to a cinematic film. —See Synonyms at **calm.**

~*n.* **1.** Silence; quiet; calm: *the still of the night.* **2.** A still photograph, especially one taken from a scene of a cinematic film and used for promotional purposes.

~*adv.* **1.** Without movement; motionlessly: *stand still.* **2.** Up to now or the time specified; now or in the future as before; yet: *still be here tomorrow; has still not finished.* **3.** In increasing amount or degree: *has become still worse.* **4.** Nevertheless; all the same: *I understand the difficulty but I still think he should go.* **5.** Even; besides: *still further complaints.* **6.** *Archaic & Regional.* Always; constantly. —See Synonyms at **but.**

~*v.* **stilled, stilling, stills.** —*tr.* **1.** To make still, quiet, or tranquil. **2.** To make motionless. **3.** To allay; calm. —*intr.* To become still. [Middle English *still(e),* Old English *stille.*] **—still·ness** *n.*

Synonyms: *still, quiet, silent, noiseless, hushed, tranquil.*

still² *n.* **1.** An apparatus for distilling liquids, particularly alcohols, consisting of a vessel in which the substance is vaporised by heat and a cooling device in which the vapour is condensed. **2.** A distillery. [From *still,* to distil, Middle English *stillen,* short for *distillen,* DISTIL.]

stil·lage (stíllij) *n.* A bench or frame, as in a factory, used to keep objects from touching the floor, as while they are draining or drying. [Probably from Dutch *stellagie,* frame, scaffold, from *stellen,* to stand.]

still·birth (stíl-burth) *n.* **1.** The birth of a dead child, usually when gestation has continued for over 28 weeks. **2.** A child dead at birth.

still·born (stíl-bawrn) *adj.* **1.** Dead at birth. **2.** Failing right at the beginning; abortive.

still hunt *n. Chiefly U.S.* The hunting of game by stalking or ambushing. **—still-hunt** (stíl-hunt) *v.*

stil·li·cide (stílli-sīd) *n. Law.* A right or duty connected with the spilling of water from one person's roof onto another's land. [Latin *stillicidium* : *stilla,* drop (of water) + *-cidium,* from *cadere,* to fall.

stil·li·form (stílli-fawrm) *adj.* Shaped like a drop or globule. [Latin *stillis,* a drop (see **distil**) + -FORM.]

still life *n., pl.* **still lifes. 1.** The representation of inanimate objects, such as flowers or fruit, in painting or photography. **2.** A picture of inanimate objects. **—still-life** *adj.*

still room *n. British.* **1.** A room used for distilling. **2.** A room in a large house used for storing preserves, provisions, or the like.

Still·son wrench (stíl-s'n) *n.* A trademark for a monkey wrench with serrated jaws, one of which has slight angular movement to facilitate gripping pipes and other round objects. Compare **pipe wrench.**

still·y (stílli) *adj. Poetic.* Quiet; calm. **—stil·ly** *adv.*

stilt (stilt) *n., pl.* **stilts** or **stilt** (for sense 3). **1.** Either of a pair of long, slender poles, each equipped with a raised footrest enabling the wearer to walk elevated above the ground. **2.** Any of various tall posts or pillars used as support, as for a dock or building. **3. a.** A long-legged wading bird, *Himantopus mexicanus* (or *H. himantopus*), having black and white plumage and a long slender bill. **b.** A related bird, *Cladorhyncus leucocephala,* of Australia.

~*tr.v.* **stilted, stilting, stilts.** To place or raise on or as if on stilts. [Middle English *stilte,* stilt, crutch, perhaps of Low German origin, akin to Low German and Flemish *stilte.*]

stilt·ed (stíltid) *adj.* **1.** Stiffly or artificially dignified or formal; pompous: *a very stilted manner.* **2.** *Architecture.* Having some vertical length between the impost and the beginning of the curve. Said of an arch. **—stilt·ed·ly** *adv.* **—stilt·ed·ness** *n.*

Stil·ton (stílltən) *n.* A rich, blue-veined cheese made from whole milk with added cream and having a wrinkled rind. [Originally sold at *Stilton,* Cambridgeshire.]

stim·u·lant (stímmewlənt) *n.* **1.** Anything that temporarily arouses or accelerates physiological activity, especially of a particular organ. **2.** A stimulus or incentive: *Social unrest often provides a stimulant to literature.* **3.** A drug, food, or drink that stimulates.

~*adj.* Serving as a stimulant. [Latin *stimulāns* (stem *stimulant-*), present participle of *stimulāre,* to STIMULATE.]

stim·u·late (stímmew-layt) *v.* **-lated, -lating, -lates.** —*tr.* To rouse to activity or heightened action, as by spurring or goading; animate. —*intr.* To act or serve as a stimulant or stimulus. —See Synonyms at **provoke.** [Latin *stimulāre,* to goad on, from *stimulus,* a STIMULUS.] **—stim·u·la·tive** (-lətiv, -laytiv) *adj.* **—stim·u·la·tor** (-laytər) *n.* **—stim·u·la·tion** (-láysh'n) *n.*

stim·u·lus (stímmew-ləss) *n., pl.* **-li** (-lī, -lee). **1.** Anything causing or regarded as causing a response. **2.** An agent, action, or condition that elicits or accelerates a physiological or psychological activity. **3.** Something that incites or rouses to action: *a stimulus to the imagination.* [Latin *stimulus*†, a goad.]

sting (sting) *v.* **stung** (stung) or *obsolete* **stang** (stang), **stung, stinging, stings.** —*tr.* **1.** To pierce or wound painfully with or as if with a sharp-pointed structure or organ, such as that of certain insects. **2.** To cause to feel a sharp, smarting pain: *stinging rain; Smoke stung our eyes.* **3.** To cause to suffer keenly in the mind or feelings: *Her words stung him bitterly.* **4.** To spur on by or as if by sharp irritation. **5.** *Slang.* To cheat or overcharge. —*intr.* **1.** To have, use, or wound with a sting. **2.** To feel a sharp, smarting pain. **3.** To cause a sharp, smarting pain or keen mental distress.

~*n.* **1.** The act of stinging. **2.** The wound or pain caused by or as if by stinging. **3.** A sharp, piercing organ or part, often ejecting a venomous secretion, such as the modified ovipositor of a bee or wasp or the spine of certain fishes. **4. a.** Something that causes a sharp pain, either physical or mental. **b.** Ability to cause pain or suffering; stinging power, quality, or capacity: *"The sting of fear is anxiety"* (Paul Tillich). **5.** A keen stimulus or incitement; a goad or spur. [Sting, stung (or stang), stung; Middle English *stingen, stang* (past plural *stungen*), *stungen,* Old English *stingan, stang* (past plural *stungon*), *stungen.*] **—sting·ing·ly** *adv.*

sting·a·ree (stíng-ə-ree; *Australian also* -reé) *n. U.S. & Australian.* A fish, the stingray. [Variant of STINGRAY.]

sting·er (stíng-ər) *n.* **1.** One that stings, as: **a.** A stinging organ or part. **b.** A sharp blow. **c.** Something that wounds mentally, such as an insult. **2.** *U.S.* A cocktail of crème de menthe and brandy.

sting·ing hair (stínging) *n.* A glandular plant hair that if touched expels an irritant fluid to deter animal predators.

stinging nettle *n.* A nettle with stinging hairs on the stem and leaves; especially, *Urtica dioica.*

sting·ray (stíng-ray) *n.* Any of various rays of the family Dasyatidae, having a whiplike tail armed with a venomous spine capable of inflicting severe injury. Also *U.S. & Australian* "stingaree".

stin·gy¹ (stínji) *adj.* **-gier, -giest. 1.** Giving or spending reluctantly or unwillingly; mean. **2.** Scanty or meagre. [Perhaps originally "sharp", "bad-tempered", from dialectal *stinge,* act of stinging, Middle English *sting,* Old English *sting, styng,* from *stingan,* to STING.] **—stin·gi·ly** *adv.* **—stin·gi·ness** *n.*

Synonyms: *stingy, mean, close, tight-fisted, niggardly, miserly, parsimonious.*

sting·y² (stíng-i) *adj. Informal.* Stinging or able to sting; piercing.

stink (stingk) *v.* **stank** (stangk) or **stunk** (stungk), **stunk, stinking, stinks.** —*intr.* **1.** To emit a strong foul odour. **2. a.** To be highly offensive or abhorrent. **b.** To be in extremely bad repute. **3.** *Slang.* To have or embody something to an extreme or offensive degree. Usually used with *of* or *with*: *He stinks of success.* **4.** *Slang.* To be of an extremely low or bad quality: *This film stinks.* —*tr.* **1.** To cause to stink; fill with stink. Usually used with *out* or *up*: *The smell of garlic stank the kitchen out.* **2.** To drive or force by a strong, foul, or suffocating smell. Used with *out.*

~*n.* **1.** A strong offensive odour; a stench. **2.** *Informal.* A great fuss or outcry: *to raise a stink.* —See Synonyms at **smell.** [Stink, stank (or stunk), stunk; Middle English *stinken, stank* (past plural *stunken*), *stunken,* Old English *stincan, stanc* (past plural *stuncon*), *stuncen,* from Germanic *stinkwan* (unattested).]

stink ball *n.* A container containing materials that emit a suffocating smoke or offensive vapours, formerly used in naval warfare. Also called "stinkpot".

stink bomb *n.* A small bomb, often in the form of a capsule, that emits a foul odour on explosion.

stink·er (stíngkər) *n.* **1.** One that stinks. **2.** *Slang.* A contemptible, disgusting, or irritating person. **3.** *Slang.* Something very difficult or very offensive: *The exam was a real stinker.*

stink·horn (stíngk-hawrn) *n.* Any of several foul-smelling fungi of the order Phallales, such as *Phallus impudicus,* having a thick, cylindrical stalk and a narrow cap.

stink·ing (stíngking) *adj.* **1.** Having a foul smell; fetid; rank. **2.** *Slang.* Very unpleasant or repulsive. **3.** *Slang.* Very drunk.

stilt *The black-winged stilt (above) is one of nine species of this long-legged bird. Stilts live in temperate and tropical regions, on the shores of lakes, marshes, and pools where their long legs and bills enable them to probe deep for small animals.*

~*adv. Slang.* To an offensive or extreme degree: *got stinking drunk; stinking rich.* —**stink·ing·ly** *adv.* —**stink·ing·ness** *n.*

stinking badger *n.* The **teledu** *(see).*

stinking iris *n.* A greyish-purple flowered iris, *Iris foetidissima,* the leaves of which emit a sickly sweet smell when crushed.

stinking mayweed A plant, the **mayweed** *(see).*

stinking smut *n.* A disease of wheat caused by the fungus *Tilletia caries* (or *T. foetida*), in which the centres of the grains are replaced by a mass of black fungal spores. Also called "bunt", "covered smut".

stink·pot (stíngk-pot) *n.* **1.** A stink ball. **2.** *Slang.* An unpleasant or comtemptible person.

stink·stone (stíngk-stōn) *n.* A variety of limestone that emits a disagreeable smell when struck or rubbed.

stink·weed (stíngk-weed) *n.* **1.** A yellow-flowered plant, *Diplotaxis muralis,* that emits an unpleasant smell if bruised. Also called "wall mustard". **2.** Any of various other plants having flowers or foliage with an unpleasant smell.

stink·wood (stingk-wŏŏd) *n.* **1. a.** A tree, *Ocotea bullata,* of southern Africa, having wood with an unpleasant smell. **b.** The hard, heavy wood of this tree, used in cabinetwork. **2.** Broadly, any of several other trees having wood with an unpleasant smell.

stint¹ (stint) *v.* **stinted, stinting, stints.** —*tr.* **1. a.** To restrict or limit, as in amount or number; be sparing with: *stinting the rations to make them last.* **b.** To restrict or limit (oneself or another): *stinted himself in order to buy a car.* **2.** *Archaic.* To stop; desist. —*intr.* **1.** To be frugal or sparing. **2.** *Archaic.* To stop or desist.
~*n.* **1.** A fixed amount or share of work or duty to be performed within a given period of time. **2.** A limitation or restriction: *working without stint.* [Middle English *stinten,* to stop, cut short, Old English *styntan,* to blunt, dull.] —**stint·er** *n.*

stint² *n.* **1.** Any of several small sandpipers of the genus *Calidris,* of northern regions. **2.** *Archaic.* A **dunlin** *(see).* [Middle English *stynt*†.]

stipe (stīp) *n. Biology.* A stalk or stalklike structure, such as the stemlike support of the cap of a mushroom or the stalk of a seaweed frond. [French, from Latin *stīpes,* post, tree trunk.]

sti·pel (stīp'l) *n. Botany.* A minute or secondary stipule at the base of a leaflet. [New Latin *stipella,* diminutive of *stipula,* STIPULE.] —**sti·pel·late** (-ət, it, -ayt, *also* stī-pél-) *adj.*

sti·pend (stī́-pend, -pənd) *n.* A fixed or regular payment, such as a salary for services rendered or an allowance; especially, the salary paid to a clergyman. [Middle English *stipendie,* from Old French, from Latin *stīpendium,* tax, tribute; akin to *stipulārī,* to STIPULATE.]

sti·pen·di·ar·y (stī-péndi-əri, sti- || -erri) *adj.* **1.** Receiving a stipend. **2.** Compensated by stipend: *stipendiary services.*
~*n., pl.* **stipendiaries. 1.** A person, such as a clergyman, who receives a stipend. **2.** A stipendiary magistrate. [Latin *stīpendiārius,* from *stīpendium,* tribute, STIPEND.]

stipendiary magistrate *n.* In England and Wales, a solicitor or barrister who is salaried and presides in a magistrates' court.

sti·pes (stī́-peez) *n., pl.* **stipites** (stíppi-teez). *Zoology.* **1.** A segment of the maxilla of an insect. **2.** Any stalklike support or structure. [New Latin, from Latin *stīpes,* post, tree trunk.] —**sti·pi·form** (stíp-pi-fawrm), **stip·i·ti·form** (stī-pítti-, stíppiti-) *adj.*

stip·i·tate (stíppi-tayt) *adj.* Having or supported on a stipe. [Latin *stīpes* (stem *stīpit-*), post, tree trunk. See **stipes.**]

stip·ple (stípp'l) *tr.v.* **-pled, -pling, -ples. 1.** To draw, engrave, or paint in dots or short strokes. **2.** To apply (paint, for example) in dots or short strokes. **3.** To dot, fleck, or speckle.
~*n.* **1.** The method of painting, drawing, or engraving by stippling. **2.** The effect produced by stippling or a work produced in this manner. [Dutch *stippelen,* frequentative of *stippen,* to speckle, dot, from *stip,* dot, point, from Middle Dutch.] —**stip·pler** *n.*

stip·u·lar (stíppewlər) *adj. Botany.* Of, pertaining to, or resembling a stipule or stipules.

stip·u·late¹ (stíppew-layt) *v.* **-lated, -lating, -lates.** —*tr.* **1. a.** To lay down as a condition of an agreement; require by contract. **b.** To specify or arrange in an agreement: *stipulate the date and price.* **2.** To guarantee or promise in an agreement. —*intr.* **1.** To make an express demand or provision in an agreement. Used with *for.* **2.** To form an agreement. [Latin *stipulārī*†, to bargain, demand.] —**stip·u·la·tor** (-laytər) *n.*

stip·u·late² (stíppew-lət, -lit, -layt) *adj. Botany.* Having stipules.

stip·u·la·tion (stíppew-láysh'n) *n.* **1.** The act of stipulating. **2.** Something stipulated; a term or condition in an agreement. —**stip·u·la·to·ry** (-lə-tri, -təri, láytəri) *adj.*

stip·ule (stíppewl) *n. Botany.* Any of the usually small, paired leaflike appendages at the base of a leaf or leafstalk in certain plants. [New Latin *stipula,* from Latin, stalk, stem; akin to *stipulārī,* to STIPULATE.]

stir¹ (stur) *v.* **stirred, stirring, stirs.** —*tr.* **1. a.** To pass an implement through (a liquid) in circular motions, so as to mix or cool the contents. **b.** To introduce (an ingredient) into a liquid or mixture in this way: *stirred sugar into his tea.* **c.** To mix together the ingredients of (a cake, for example) prior to cooking or use. **2.** To cause a slight movement in or alter the placement of slightly. **3.** To move (oneself) briskly or vigorously; bestir. **4.** To rouse (a person), as from sleep or indifference. **5.** To incite, provoke, or instigate. Often used with *up*: *stir up trouble: stir up old memories.* **6.** To excite the emotions of; move or affect strongly. —*intr.* **1.** To change position slightly: *stirred in her sleep.* **2. a.** To move about actively; bestir oneself. **b.** To move away from a customary place or position; venture. **3.** To provoke trouble between others, as by spreading rumours or teasing. —See Synonyms at **provoke.**
~*n.* **1.** An act of stirring; a mixing or poking movement. **2.** A very slight movement. **3.** A disturbance or commotion. **4.** An excited reaction; a ferment. [Middle English *stiren,* Old English *styrian,* to move, agitate, excite.] —**stir·rer** *n.*

stir² *n. Slang.* Prison. [19th century : origin obscure.]

stir·a·bout (stúr-ə-bowt) *n.* **1.** A kind of porridge made from boiling water or milk with oatmeal stirred into it. **2. a.** A busy, active person. **b.** A state of bustling activity or confusion.

stir crazy *adj. U.S. Slang.* Distraught or restless from long confinement in or as if in prison.

stirk (sturk) *n.* A yearling heifer or, sometimes, a bullock. [Middle English *stirk,* Old English *stirc.*]

Stir·ling (stúrling). Burgh in Central Region, Scotland, lying on the river Forth. It is dominated by its 11th-century castle, the birthplace of several Scottish kings. The town overlooks the battlefields of Stirling Bridge and Bannockburn, where the Scots won famous victories over the English (1297 and 1314).

Stir·ling's formula (stúrlingz) *n. Mathematics.* A formula for the approximate value of the factorial of a large number: $\log n! = n \log n - n$. [After James *Stirling* (died 1770), Scottish mathematician.]

Stir·ling·shire (stúrling-shər, -sheer, -shīr). Former county in central Scotland, lying south of the river Forth, and now divided between the Central and Strathclyde Regions.

stirps (sturps, steerps) *n., pl.* **stirpes** (stúr-peez, steér-payz). **1.** A line of descendants of common ancestry; a stock. **2. a.** A group of animals, equivalent to a superfamily. **b.** A variety of plants with stable characteristics which are retained under cultivation. **3.** *Law.* One from whom a family is descended. [Latin *stirps*†, stem, root, lineage.]

stir·ring (stúr-ing) *adj.* **1.** Rousing; thrilling: *a stirring call to arms.* **2.** Active; lively. —See Synonyms at **moving.** —**stir·ring·ly** *adv.*

stir·rup (stírrəp || *also* stúr-əp) *n.* **1.** A flat-based loop or ring hung from either side of a horse's saddle to support the rider's foot in mounting and riding. Also called "stirrup iron". **2.** Any of various parts or devices shaped like an inverted U, used to support, hold, or fix something. **3.** *Nautical.* A rope on a ship hanging from a yard and having an eye at the end through which a footrope is passed for support. [Middle English *stirope,* Old English *stigrāp.*]

stirrup bone *n. Anatomy.* The **stapes** *(see).*

stir·rup-cup (stírrəp-kup || stúr-əp-) *n.* **1.** A farewell drink given to a rider who is mounted ready to depart. **2.** Any farewell drink.

stirrup leather *n.* The strap used to fasten a stirrup to a saddle. Also called "stirrup strap".

stirrup pump *n.* A type of small hand water pump that is used for fighting fires or in gardening.

stish·ov·ite (stíshəv-īt) *n.* A dense tetragonal form of silicon dioxide formed under great pressure. [After S. M. *Stishov,* 20th-century Russian mineralogist.]

stitch (stich) *n. Abbr.* **st. 1.** A single complete movement of a threaded needle in sewing or surgical suturing. **2.** A single loop of yarn around a knitting needle or similar implement. **3.** The link, loop, or knot made in this way. **4.** A particular method of arranging the threads in sewing, knitting, or crocheting: *a purl stitch.* **5.** A sudden sharp pain in one's side, often resulting from physical exertion, such as running. **6.** *Informal.* An article of clothing: *not a stitch on.* —**in stitches.** *Informal.* Laughing uncontrollably.
~*v.* **stitched, stitching, stitches.** —*tr.* **1. a.** To fasten or join with stitches. **b.** To mend or repair with stitches. Used with *up.* **2.** To decorate or ornament with stitches. **3.** To fasten together (sheets of a book, for example) with staples or thread. —*intr.* To make stitches; sew. [Middle English *stiche,* Old English *stice,* a sting, prick.] —**stitch·er** *n.*

stitch·wort (stích-wurt || -wawrt) *n.* Any of several low-growing plants of the genus *Stellaria,* having small, white flowers. [Middle English *stichewort,* Old English *sticwyrt,* agrimony : STITCH + WORT (from its alleged ability to cure sharp pains in the side).]

stith·y (stíthi) *n., pl.* **-ies.** *Archaic.* **1.** An anvil. **2.** A forge or smithy. [Middle English *stethy,* from Old Norse *stedhi.*]

sti·ver (stī́vər) *n.* **1.** An obsolete Dutch coin worth $^1/_{20}$ of a guilder. **2.** Anything of small value; the smallest amount. [Dutch *stuiver,* from Middle Dutch *stuyver.*]

St. John's (jonz). The capital of Newfoundland, eastern Canada. An Atlantic port, it is the most easterly city in North America.

St. John's bread *n.* The long blackish, sugary, edible pod of the **carob** *(see).* [After St. JOHN the Baptist, who lived on honey and locusts while preaching (through confusion of the locusts with the carob, known also as locust bean). Matthew 3:4.]

St. Johns·wort (s'nt-jónz-wurt, s'n- || saynt-, -wawrt) *n.* Any of various plants or shrubs of the genus *Hypericum,* having yellow flowers with prominent stamens. [So called because it was gathered on *St. John's* Eve to ward off evil spirits.]

St. Kil·da (kíldə). The largest of a group of three islands in the Atlantic ocean, the most westerly of the Outer Hebrides, northwest Scotland. Its small population of Gaelic-speaking inhabitants was evacuated in 1930, and it is now a nature reserve.

St. Kitts-Ne·vis (s'nt-kíts-neéviss, s'n- || saynt-). Formerly **St. Kitts-Nevis-Anguilla** (-ang-gwíllə). Island state of the Caribbean. The two islands, St. Kitts (St. Christopher) and Nevis, five kilometres (three miles) apart, were the first Caribbean islands to be settled by the British (1623–28), but were disputed with France until 1783. In 1967 the self-governing British Associated State of St.

PRONUNCIATION KEY

a, trap; aa, father; ai, fair; ar, star; aw, lawn; ay, play; b, bb, stab; rubber; ch, church; ck, ticket; d, dd, dead; ladder; e, dress; ee, bee; er, defer; ew, few; ewr, pure; ə, about; ər, letter; f, ff, fife; differ; g, gg, giggle; h, hat; i, kit; ī, price; īr, fire; j, judge; k, kick; l, ll, let; 'l, needle; m, mm, man; n, nn, no; 'n, sudden; ng, thing; o, lot; ō, no; ŏŏ, foot; ōō, shoe; oor, poor; ow, cow; owr, hour; oy, boy; p, pp, pepper; r, rr, red; s, ss, sauce; sh, ship; t, tt, totter; th, thick; th, this; smooth; u, cut; ur, turn; v, vv, valve; w, wet; y, yes; z, zz, zebra; zh, vision; pleasure

IN FOREIGN WORDS:

aɴ, ᴏɴ, Saint-Saëns; hl, Llanelli; Hluhluwe; kh, loch; lough; Khaled

STRESS MARK:

ín-sīt, insight; in-sī́t, incite

Kitts-Nevis-Anguilla was created. However, the Anguillans resented the link, and finally became a separate United Kingdom dependency in 1980. St. Kitts-Nevis gained independence within the Commonwealth in 1983. Sugar is the mainstay of the economy, but tourism is becoming a major source of income. Area, 262 square kilometres (101 square miles). Capital, Basseterre (on St. Kitts). Population, 44,400 (1980). See map at **Latin America**.

St. Lau·rent (sán-law-róN), **Louis Stephen** (1882–1973). Canadian prime minister from 1948–57. The St. Lawrence Seaway (opened 1959) was built during his premiership.

St. Law·rence (lórrǝnss ‖ láwrǝnss). One of the principal rivers of North America. It issues from Lake Ontario and flows northeast to form part of the border between Canada and the United States, and enters the Gulf of St. Lawrence. Though partially icebound in winter, it remains a major artery for shipping between the Atlantic and the Great Lakes, and was improved by the opening of the St. Lawrence Seaway. From Lake Ontario to Anticosti Island, the river is some 1 200 kilometres (750) miles long.

St. Lawrence, Gulf of. A gulf of the Atlantic Ocean, eastern Canada, into which the St. Lawrence river flows. It lies between New-

---

stitch

THE ART OF DECORATIVE STITCHING
Embroidery goes back to the days of the ancient Egyptians

The art of decorative stitching, or embroidery, goes back to the ancient Egyptians, whose wall paintings show colourful examples of needlework. One of the earliest embroidered linen strips in existence is the 11th-century Bayeux Tapestry depicting the Norman conquest of England, which now hangs in the museum at Bayeux in Normandy.

Embroidery, as opposed to plain sewing, has been enjoyed by both royalty and commoners. In 1502 Catherine of Aragon, the first wife of Henry VIII, brought with her from Spain samples of her own needlework in her trousseau. And in 1588 Elizabeth I, another keen needlewoman, refounded the ancient Company of Broderers (Embroiderers) in London.

During the late 18th century there was a vogue in Europe for "needlepainting", in which scenes and portraits were stitched with wool on cloth to resemble oil paintings. Today there is a worldwide interest in needlework, ranging from canvaswork, or tapestry as it is often known, to blackwork – in which black silk threads are worked on a white or natural linen background; blackwork is particularly popular in New Zealand. Six groups of stitches used in needlework are shown below.

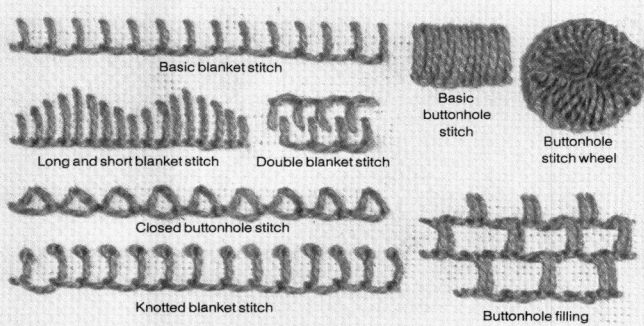

BLANKET STITCH *A broad stitch used for oversewing edges in plain needlework and also to embroider decorative outlines and borders.*

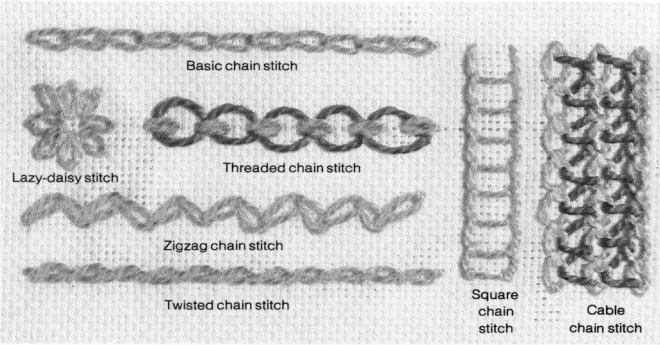

CHAIN STITCH *The basic chain stitch is a series of interlocking loops. When worked in close rows, it can be used to cover an area.*

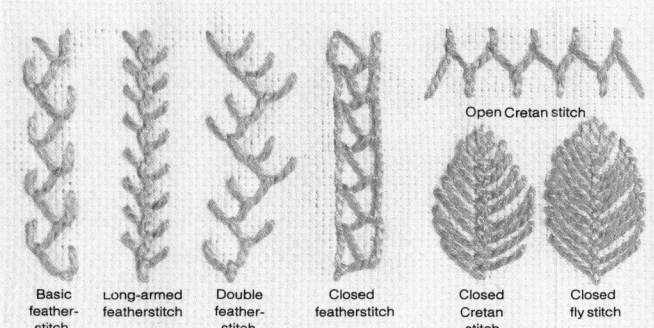

FEATHERSTITCH *The basic stitch and its variants are used mainly for borders. In 19th-century England they were used on smocks.*

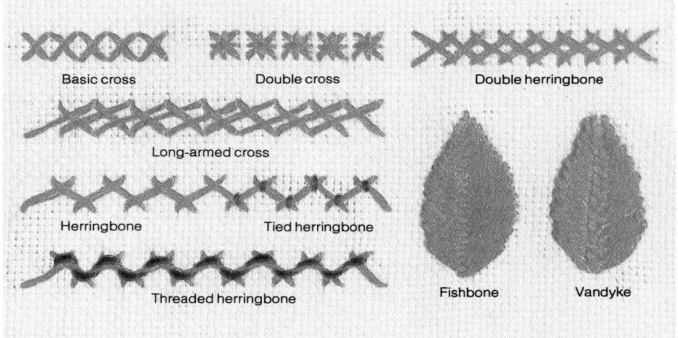

CROSS-STITCH *All types of cross-stitch are formed by two crossing arms. They can be used as outlines, borders, or to fill an area.*

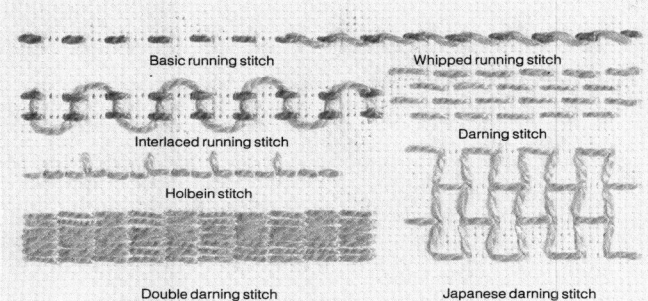

RUNNING STITCH *The basic running stitch is the main stitch in quilting. Variations are also used to decorate borders and bands.*

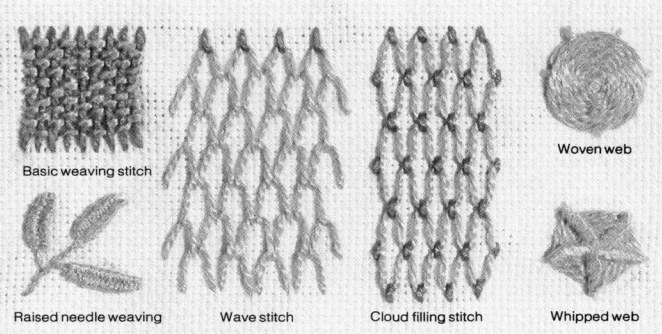

WEAVING STITCH *The basic weaving stitch, with its basket-like texture, is used to fill in an area with different coloured threads.*

stoa *A colonnaded promenade which the ancient Greeks used as a meeting place. This is the Stoa of Attalos in Athens.*

stoat Mustela erminea, *the stoat, normally has brown fur on its back and white fur on its undersides, as shown here. But in winter the coat turns completely white except for a black tip on the tail, and the animal is then known as an ermine.*

foundland and mainland Canada. Though closed to navigation by ice in the winter months, it has important fishing grounds.

St. Lawrence Seaway. A major waterway system connecting the Gulf of St. Lawrence and the Great Lakes. A joint U.S.-Canadian project, it was opened in 1959 and provides navigation channels between Montreal and Lake Ontario, and between Lake Ontario and Lake Erie. The seaway for the first time gave large ocean-going vessels access to the heart of North America.

St. Lou·is (lo͞o-iss). The largest city in Missouri, central United States. Founded in 1764 by the French, on the Mississippi just downstream from the confluence with the Missouri, it became an important centre for fur traders and explorers opening up the West. It was ceded to the United States in 1804, and is now a communications, commercial, industrial, and cultural centre.

St. Lu·cia, State of (lo͞o-shə, *rarely* -si-ə ‖ léw-). Volcanic island in the Windward group of the West Indies. Discovered by Columbus (1502), it changed hands repeatedly between England and France, before becoming an English colony in 1814. It won full independence within the Commonwealth (1979). The economy is primarily agricultural, but tourism is increasingly important. Area, 616 square kilometres (238 square miles). Population, 100,000 (estimated). Capital, Castries. See map at **Latin America.**

St. Ma·lo (maá-lō; *French* saɴ ma-lṓ). A port and popular resort in Ille-et-Vilaine département, northwestern France. A tidal power station, one of the first in the world, opened in 1966.

St. Mo·ritz (mə-ríts, mórrits). Alpine resort in Graubünden canton, southeastern Switzerland, situated in the upper Engadine (Inn valley). A famous winter sports centre, St. Moritz is the site of the Cresta Run for bobsleighs.

sto·a (stṓ-ə) *n., pl.* **-as** or **stoae** (-ee). An ancient Greek covered walk or colonnade, usually having columns on one side and a wall on the other. [Greek, porch.]

stoat (stōt) *n.* A small carnivorous mammal, *Mustela erminea,* similar to but larger than the weasel and having a black-tipped tail. In northern regions the brown coat turns white in winter and is called ermine. [Middle English : origin obscure.]

sto·chas·tic (sto-kástik, stə- ‖ stō-) *adj.* **1.** Of, designating, or characterised by conjecture; conjectural. **2.** *Statistics.* **a.** Random. **b.** Statistical. [Greek *stokhastikos,* capable of aiming, conjectural, from *stokhazesthai,* to aim at, guess at, from *stokhos,* target, aim.] **—sto·chas·tic·al·ly** *adv.*

stochastic process *n.* In statistics, a process consisting of a number of steps having a random variable, the successive values of which are not independent.

stochastic variable *n. Statistics.* A **random variable** *(see).*

stock (stok) *n. Abbr.* **stk. 1.** A supply accumulated for future use; a store or supply that may be drawn upon. **2.** The total merchandise kept on hand by a trader, commercial establishment, or manufacturer. **3.** All the animals kept or reared on a farm; livestock. **4.** *Finance.* **a.** The capital or fund that a company raises through the sale of shares entitling the holder to dividends and to other rights of ownership, such as voting rights. **b.** The number of shares that each stockholder possesses. **c.** The shares of a specified company or business enterprise. **d.** Formerly, the part of a tally or record of account given to a creditor. **e.** A debt symbolised by such a tally or tallies. **5.** The trunk or main stem of a tree or other plant as distinguished from the branches and roots. **6. a.** A plant or stem onto which a graft is made. **b.** A plant or tree from which cuttings and slips are taken. **7. a.** The original progenitor of a family line. **b.** The descendents of a common ancestor; a family line, especially one of a specified character: *comes from farming stock.* **c.** The type from which a group of animals or plants has descended. **d.** A race, family, or other related group of animals or plants. **e.** An ethnic group or other major division of mankind. **f.** A group of related languages. **g.** A group of related families of languages. **8.** The raw material out of which something is made. **9.** A broth in which meat, fish, bones, or vegetables have been simmered for a period of time, used as a base in preparing soup, gravy, or sauces. **10. a.** The chief upright part of something, particularly a supporting structure or block. **b.** *Plural.* The timber frame that supports a ship during construction. **c.** *Often plural.* A frame in which a horse or other animal is held for shoeing or for veterinary treatment. **11.** *Plural.* Formerly, an instrument of punishment, consisting of a heavy timber frame with holes for confining the ankles and, sometimes, the wrists. **12.** *Nautical.* The crosspiece at the end of an anchor's shank. **13.** The wooden block from which a bell is suspended. **14. a.** The rear wooden or metal handle or steadying support of a rifle, pistol, or automatic weapon, to which the barrel and mechanism are attached. Also called "gunstock". **b.** The long beam of field-gun carriages that trails along the ground to provide stability and support. **15.** Any handle, as of a whip, fishing rod, or various carpenter's tools. **16.** The frame of a plough, to which the share, handles, coulter, and other parts are fastened. **17.** *U.S.* The theatrical repertoire of a stock company. **18.** Any of several plants of the genus *Matthiola,* native to the Old World; especially, *M. incana,* widely cultivated for its clusters of showy, fragrant, variously coloured flowers, and *M. bicornis,* night-scented stock. **19.** That portion of a pack of cards or group of dominoes that is not dealt out but is drawn from during a game. **20.** *Geology.* An irregularly shaped intrusive body of igneous rock in the earth's crust, with an exposed surface of less than 100 square kilometres (40 square miles). **21.** Personal reputation or standing: *His stock with the students is falling.* **22.** Unexposed film. **23. a.** A stiff, long neckcloth, wound around the neck as a part of male dress in the 18th century. **b.** A long white cloth worn around the neck as a part of formal riding dress. **c.** A piece of black, or sometimes purple, silk attached to a clerical collar and worn by a clergyman over the chest. **24.** A brick of the kind most commonly used in building. **25.** See **rolling stock. 26.** See **diestock. 27.** *Archaic.* A stocking. **—in stock.** Available for sale or use. **—on the stocks.** In the process of being constructed or prepared. **—out of stock. 1.** Not immediately available for sale or use. **2.** Not having any immediately available for sale or use. **—take stock. 1.** To take an inventory. **2.** To make an estimate or reappraisal, as of resources, prospects, or a prevailing situation. **—take stock in.** *Informal.* To be interested in or attach importance to.

~v. **stocked, stocking, stocks.** *—tr.* **1.** To provide or furnish with a stock of something, especially: **a.** To supply (a shop) with merchandise. **b.** To supply (a farm) with livestock. **c.** To fill (a river) with fish. **2.** To keep in stock for future sale. **3.** To provide (a rifle, for example) with a stock. **4.** *Obsolete.* To put (someone) in the stocks as a punishment. *—intr.* **1.** To gather and lay in a supply of something. Used with *up* or *up on.* **2.** To put forth or sprout new shoots. Used of a plant.

~adj. **1.** Kept regularly in stock. **2.** Repeated regularly without any thought or originality; trite: *a stock answer.* **3. a.** Of or pertaining to the raising of livestock: *stock farming.* **b.** Used for breeding: *a stock mare.* **4.** Designating a conventional or traditional character of a particular dramatic genre, such as farce or pantomime. [Middle English *stok(ke),* Old English *stocc,* tree trunk.]

stock·ade (sto-káyd) *n.* **1.** A defensive barrier made of strong posts or timbers driven upright into the ground, side by side. **2.** *Chiefly U.S.* Any similarly fenced or enclosed area, especially one used for protection or imprisonment.

~tr.v. **stockaded, -ading, -ades.** To fortify, protect, or surround with a stockade. [Obsolete French *estocade,* from Spanish *estacada,* from *estaca,* stake, from Germanic.]

stock·breed·ing (stók-breeding) *n.* The rearing of livestock. **—stock·breed·er** *n.*

stock·bro·ker (stók-brōk-ər) *n.* A person who acts, for a commission, as an agent in the buying and selling of stocks or other securities. **—stock·bro·ker·age, stock·bro·king** *n.*

stockbroker belt *n. British Informal.* An area just outside a city, especially just outside London, that is mainly inhabited by wealthy commuters to the city.

stock car *n.* **1.** A car of a standard make, modified for a particular type of racing *(stock car racing)* in which deliberately contrived collisions are allowed. **2.** *U.S.* A railway truck for livestock.

stock certificate *n. U.S.* A share certificate.

stock company *n. U.S.* **1.** A **joint-stock company** *(see).* **2.** A repertory company.

stock cube *n.* A piece of compressed, dehydrated stock for use in cooking, commercially produced in the form of a cube.

stock dove *n.* A common Old World bird, *Columba oenas,* having greyish plumage. [Probably because it lives in hollow tree trunks.]

stock exchange *n. Abbr.* **St. Ex. 1.** A place where stocks and shares or other securities are bought and sold. **2.** An association of stockjobbers and stockbrokers who meet to buy and sell stocks and shares according to fixed regulations. **3.** The trend of prices or the business transacted at a stock exchange: *The stock exchange fell today.* Also called "stock market".

stock·fish (stók-fish) *n.* A fish, such as cod or haddock, cured by being split and air-dried without salt.

stock·hold·er (stók-hōldər) *n.* **1.** One who owns a share or shares of stock in a company. **2.** *Australian & N.Z.* A farmer who raises livestock. **—stock·hold·ing** *adj. & n.*

Stock·hau·sen (shtók-howz'n), **Karlheinz** (1928–). German composer. He is one of the leading exponents of electronic music. His works include *Gruppen* (1955–57) and *Stimmung* (1968).

Stock·holm (stók-hōm ‖ -hōlm). Capital city of Sweden, occupying several peninsulas and islands on the Baltic Sea at the eastern tip of Lake Mälaren. It has been the capital since 1634, and is also an important port and shipbuilding centre.

Stockholm syndrome *n.* The tendency of a hostage, under certain circumstances, to try to cooperate and occasionally even to aid his captors. [Referring to the cooperative behaviour of hostages held in a bank robbery in STOCKHOLM (1973).]

stock·i·nette, stock·i·net (stóki-nét) *n.* An elastic knitted fabric used, especially formerly, in making undergarments, bandages, or the like. [Perhaps variant of earlier *stocking-net* : STOCKING + NET.]

stock·ing (stócking) *n.* **1. a.** A close-fitting, usually knitted, covering for the foot and leg. **b.** *British Regional.* A sock. **2.** Something resembling such a covering. **—in one's stocking feet.** Wearing socks or stockings but no shoes. [From dialectal *stock,* stocking, Middle English *stokke(s),* stocking(s), probably humorous use of *stokkes,* the stocks (instrument of punishment), from *stokke,* STOCK (tree trunk).]

stocking cap *n.* A close-fitting, knitted, conical hat, often having a long tapering tassel, that resembles a stocking.

stocking filler *n. Chiefly British.* A small article, such as a toy or something to eat, for putting in a Christmas stocking.

stocking frame *n.* A knitting-machine. Also called "stocking loom", "stocking machine".

stocking stitch *n.* Alternate rows of plain and purl stitches, used in knitting. Also *U.S.* "stockinette stitch".

stock in trade *n.* **1.** All the merchandise and equipment kept on hand and used in carrying on a business. **2.** The resources available

to and habitually called upon by a person in a given situation.
stock·ish (stóckish) *adj.* Slow-witted; stupid. [Apparently STOCK (trunk, stump) + -ISH.] **—stock·ish·ly** *adv.* **—stock·ish·ness** *n.*
stock·ist (stóckist) *n. British.* A person who keeps a stock of certain goods for retail sale.
stock·job·ber (stók-jobbər) *n.* **1.** *British.* A person on the stock exchange who acts as an intermediary between brokers and does not deal with the public. **2.** *U.S.* A stockbroker. Often used derogatorily. **—stock·job·ber·y, stock·job·bing** *n.*
stock·man (stók-mən) *n., pl.* **-men** (-mən). **1.** A farmer who raises livestock. **2.** A worker employed to look after livestock. **3.** *U.S.* One employed in a stockroom or warehouse.
stock market *n.* The **stock exchange** *(see).*
stock·pile (stók-pīl) *n.* A supply of material stored for future use; especially, a carefully accrued reserve of essential or strategically important commodities.
~v. **stockpiled, -piling, -piles.** *—tr.* To accumulate a stockpile of. *—intr.* To accumulate a stockpile of a given material.
Stock·port (stók-pawrt || -pōrt). Town in Greater Manchester, England, lying at the head of the river Mersey. It rose to prominence during the Industrial Revolution as a cotton spinning centre.
stock·pot (stók-pot) *n.* A large pot used for simmering meat in order to make stock.
stock·room (stók-rōōm, -rōōm) *n.* A room in which a store of goods or materials is kept.
stock saddle *n.* A large, heavy, often ornamented, saddle with a raised, curved pommel used especially by stockmen.
stock-still (stók-stíl) *adv.* Completely motionless.
stock-tak·ing (stók-tayking) *n.* **1.** The process of taking an inventory of goods or stocks, as in a shop or factory. **2.** A reappraisal of a situation or of one's own position or prospects.
stock whip *n.* A whip with a short handle and a long lash, used for herding cattle.
Stock·wood (stók-wōōd), **(Arthur) Mervyn, the Right Reverend** (1913–). English church dignitary. He was Bishop of Southwark (1959–80). He is an advocate of church involvement in industrial and political issues and his publications include *Christianity and Marxism* (1949) and *The Cross and the Sickle* (1978).
stock·y (stócki) *adj.* **-ier, -iest.** Solidly built; sturdy; thickset. **—stock·i·ly** *adv.* **—stock·i·ness** *n.*
stock·yard (stók-yaard) *n.* A large enclosed yard, usually with pens or stables, in which livestock is temporarily kept until slaughtered, sold, or shipped elsewhere.
stodge (stoj) *n. Informal.* **1.** Starchy food that is heavy and filling. **2.** Someone or something that is dull and unimaginative.
~v. **stodged, stodging, stodges.** *—intr.* To eat greedily. *—tr.* To fill with food. [Probably blend of STUFF + *podge* (short fat person; see **podgy**), imitative.]
stodg·y (stóji) *adj.* **-ier, -iest. 1. a.** Dull, unimaginative, and commonplace. **b.** Prim or pompous; stuffy. **2.** Heavy; indigestible and starchy. [From *stodge,* thick food or mud, anything dull, from *stodge*†, to cram, gorge.] **—stodg·i·ly** *adv.* **—stodg·i·ness** *n.*
stoep (stōōp) *n. South African.* A porch, a **stoop** *(see).*
sto·gy (stōgi) *n., pl.* **-gies.** *U.S.* **1.** A long, thin, inexpensive cigar. **2.** A roughly made heavy shoe or boot. [After *Conestoga,* town in Pennsylvania.]
sto·ic (stō-ik) *n.* **1.** A person seemingly indifferent to or unaffected by joy, grief, pleasure, or pain. **2.** *Capital* **S.** A member of a Greek school of philosophy, founded by Zeno about 308 B.C. and later forming an important feature of Roman culture, holding that one should be free from passion and calmly accept all occurrences in submission to divine will or the natural order.
~adj. Also **sto·i·cal** (-'l) (for sense 1). **1.** Indifferent to pleasure and steadfast in the endurance of pain or grief; impassive: *stoic resignation.* **2.** *Capital* **S.** Of or pertaining to the Stoics or their beliefs. [Latin *Stōicus,* a Stoic, from Greek *Stōikos,* from *stoa,* portico, the porch where Zeno taught.] **—sto·i·cal·ly** *adv.*
stoi·chi·o·met·ric, stoi·chei·o·met·ric (stóyki-ō-méttrik, -ə-) *adj.* **1.** Having exact proportions for chemical combination: *a stoichiometric reaction.* **2.** Of or pertaining to stoichiometry. [Greek *stoikheio(n),* element + -METRIC.] **—stoi·chi·o·met·ri·cal·ly** *adv.*
stoi·chi·om·e·try, stoi·chei·om·e·try (stóyki-ómmətri) *n.* The methodology and technology by which the quantities of reactants and products in chemical reactions are determined. [Greek *stoikheion,* element + -METRY.]
sto·i·cism (stō-i-siz'm) *n.* **1.** Indifference to pleasure or pain; impassivity; an attitude of endurance or bravery. **2.** *Capital* **S.** The philosophy or doctrines of the Stoics.
stoke (stōk) *v.* **stoked, stoking, stokes.** *—tr.* **1.** To stir up and feed (a fire or furnace). Often used with *up.* **2.** To tend the fire of (a furnace). *—intr.* **1.** To feed or tend a furnace fire. **2.** *Informal.* To eat steadily and in large quantities. Used with *up.* [Back-formation from STOKER.]
stoke·hold (stōk-hōld) *n.* The area or compartment into which a ship's furnaces or boilers open. Also called "stokehole".
stoke·hole (stōk-hōl) *n.* **1.** The space about the opening in a furnace or boiler or the opening itself. **2.** A stokehold. [Translation of Dutch *stookgat.*]
Stoke-on-Trent (stōk-on-trént). City in Staffordshire, in central England. It lies on the river Trent and the Trent to Mersey canal, which was an important factor in its growth during the Industrial Revolution as a centre of the pottery industry.
stok·er (stōkər) *n.* **1.** One who is employed to feed fuel to and tend a furnace, as on a steamship or steam locomotive. **2.** A mechanical device for feeding coal to a furnace. [Dutch, from *stoken,* to poke, thrust, from Middle Dutch.]
stokes (stōks) *n. Symbol* **St** The centimetre-gram-second unit of kinematic viscosity equal to viscosity in poise divided by density in grams per cubic centimetre. [After Sir George *Stokes* (1819–1903), British physicist.]
Sto·kow·ski (stə-kóf-ski), **Leopold** (1882–1977). British-born U.S. conductor. He was associated with many U.S. orchestras and noted for his lavish orchestral arrangements.
STOL (stol || stōl) short takeoff and landing. Said of aircraft.
stole[1] (stōl) *n.* **1.** A woman's long scarflike garment of fur, feathers, or other fine material, worn about the shoulders. **2.** A long scarf, usually of embroidered silk or linen, worn over the left shoulder by deacons and over both shoulders by priests and bishops while officiating. [Middle English *stole,* long robe, Old English *stol,* from Latin *stola,* from Greek *stolē,* garment, array, equipment.]
stole[2]. Past tense of **steal.**
sto·len. Past participle of **steal.**
stol·id (stóllid) *adj.* Having or showing little emotion or sensibility; impassive: *stolid patience.* [Latin *stolidus.*] **—sto·lid·i·ty** (sto-líddəti, stə-), **stol·id·ness** *n.* **—stol·id·ly** *adv.*
stol·len (stō-lən, shtō-, stú-; *German* shtó-) *n.* A rich yeast bread, originally from Germany, often containing raisins, citron, and chopped nuts. [German *Stollen,* loaf-shaped Christmas cake (symbolising the Christ child in swaddling clothes), from Middle High German *stolle,* from Old High German *stollo,* post, support.]
sto·lon (stō-lon, -lən) *n.* **1.** *Botany.* A stem growing along the ground and taking root at the nodes to form new plants. **2.** *Zoology.* A stemlike structure of certain colonial organisms, from which new individuals develop by budding. [Latin *stolō* (stem *stolōn-*), branch, shoot.]
sto·lon·i·fer·ous (stō-lə-níffərəss, -lo-) *adj.* Bearing or forming stolons. **—sto·lon·if·er·ous·ly** *adv.*
sto·ma (stōmə) *n., pl.* **-mata** (-tə, stómmətə, *also* stō-maátə) or **-mas. 1.** *Botany.* One of the minute pores in the epidermis of a leaf or stem, through which gases and water vapour pass. **2.** *Anatomy.* **a.** An opening leading into the intestine, or from one part of the intestine to another. **b.** A hypothetical opening in the surface of the peritoneum, thought to be for the passage of fluid into the lymphatic vessels. **3.** *Zoology.* A mouthlike opening, such as the oral cavity of a nematode. [New Latin, from Greek, mouth.]
stom·ach (stúm-ək || -ik) *n.* **1. a.** The enlarged, saclike portion of the alimentary canal, one of the principal organs of digestion, located in vertebrates between the oesophagus and the small intestine. **b.** A similar digestive structure of many invertebrates. **2.** *Informal.* The abdomen or belly. **3.** An appetite for food. **4.** Any desire or inclination, especially for something difficult or unpleasant: *has no stomach for violence.* **5.** *Obsolete.* Courage or spirit. **6.** *Obsolete.* Pride or haughtiness.
~tr.v. **stomached, -aching, -achs. 1.** To bear; tolerate; endure. **2.** To take into or hold in the stomach; digest. [Middle English *stomak,* from Old French *stomaque,* from Latin *stomachus,* from Greek *stomakhos,* throat, mouth, gullet, from *stoma,* mouth.]
stom·ach·ache (stúm-ək-ayk || -ik-) *n.* Pain in the abdomen.
stom·ach·er (stúm-ə-kər, *rarely* -chər, -jər || -i-) *n.* A decorative, heavily embroidered or jewelled garment formerly worn, especially by women, over the chest and ending in a point over the stomach.
sto·mach·ic (stō-máckik, stə-, sto-) *adj.* Also **stom·ach·al** (stúm-ə-k'l || -i-). **1.** Of or pertaining to the stomach; gastric. **2.** Beneficial to or stimulating digestion in the stomach.
~n. Any medicine or agent that strengthens or stimulates the stomach.
stomach pump *n.* A suction pump with a flexible tube inserted into the stomach through the mouth and oesophagus to empty the stomach in an emergency, as in a case of poisoning.
stomach worm *n.* Any of various parasitic nematode worms that infest the stomachs of animals; especially, *Haemonchus megastoma,* a parasite of sheep and other ruminants.
sto·ma·ta. Plural of **stoma.**
sto·ma·tal (stō-mə-t'l, stó-) *adj.* Also **sto·ma·tous** (-təss). Of or having a stoma or stomata.
sto·mat·ic (stō-máttik, stə-) *adj.* **1.** Of or relating to the mouth. **2.** Stomatal.
sto·ma·ti·tis (stōmə-tītiss, stómmə-) *n.* Inflammation of the mucous tissue of the mouth. [New Latin : STOMAT(O)- + -ITIS.]
stomato-, stomat- *comb. form.* Indicates the mouth or a mouthlike part; for example, **stomatopod, stomatitis.** [Greek *stoma* (stem *stomat-*), mouth.]
sto·ma·tol·o·gy (stōmə-tólləji, stómmə-) *n.* The medical study of the physiology and pathology of the mouth. [STOMATO- + -LOGY.]
sto·ma·to·pod (stómmə-tə-pod, stōmə-, -tō-, stō-máttə-) *n.* Any of various marine crustaceans of the order Stomatopoda, which includes the squilla. [New Latin *stomatopoda* : STOMATO- + -POD.]
-stome *n. comb. form.* Indicates the mouth or a mouthlike opening; for example, **cyclostome.** [Greek *stoma,* opening, mouth.]
sto·mo·dae·um, sto·mo·de·um (stōmə-dée-əm) *n., pl.* **-dea** (-dée-ə). *Embryology.* The primitive oral cavity of an embryo. [New Latin : Greek *stoma,* mouth (see **stoma**) + *hodaios,* on the way, from *hodos,* way.] **—sto·mo·dae·al** *adj.*
stomp (stomp || stawmp) *intr.v.* **stomped, stomping, stomps. 1.** To tread or trample heavily or violently. **2.** To dance the stomp.

stock dove *Columba oenas, the stock dove, is a bird of open woods, farmland, and parkland in Europe and Asia. It is smaller than its close relative, the wood pigeon, and lacks the pigeon's white neck and wing markings.*

PRONUNCIATION KEY

a, trap; aa, father; ai, **fair**; ar, **star**; aw, **lawn**; ay, **play**; b, bb, **stab**; **rubber**; ch, **church**; ck, **ticket**; d, dd, **dead**; **ladder**; e, **dress**; ee, **bee**; er, **defer**; ew, **few**; ewr, **pure**; ə, **about**; ər, **letter**; f, ff, **fife**; **differ**; g, gg, **giggle**; h, **hat**; i, **kit**; ī, **price**; īr, **fire**; j, **judge**; k, **kick**; l, ll, **let**; 'l, **needle**; m, mm, **man**; n, nn, **no**; 'n, **sudden**; ng, **thing**; o, **lot**; ō, **no**; ōō, **foot**; ōō, **shoe**; oor, **poor**; ow, **cow**; owr, **hour**; oy, **boy**; p, pp, **pepper**; r, rr, **red**; s, ss, **sauce**; sh, **ship**; t, tt, **totter**; th, **thick**; th, **this**; **smooth**; u, **cut**; ur, **turn**; v, vv, **valve**; w, **wet**; y, **yes**; z, zz, **zebra**; zh, **vision**; **pleasure**

IN FOREIGN WORDS:

aN, ON, **Saint-Saëns**; hl, **Llanelli**; **Hluhluwe**; kh, **loch**; **lough**; **Khaled**

STRESS MARK:

ín-sīt, **insight**; in-sít, **incite**

Stone Age

ANCIENT AND MODERN STONE AGE
The simultaneous evolution of man and his tools

The ability to make and use tools is one of the features that most clearly distinguish man from ape. *Homo,* presumed to be the ancestor of Modern Man, emerged about 2 million years ago at the same time as the first stone tools, and is believed to have used crudely split small rocks and rock flakes for butchering and other purposes such as chopping and scraping.

The beginning of the Palaeolithic period, or Old Stone Age, is dated from the appearance of early stone tools. It embraces the millennia during which *Homo* evolved into Modern Man, and the art of stone tool-making advanced from the crude flaking of stones to the accurate shaping, by controlled hammer-blows, of a core of flint into finely flaked spears, axeheads, or scrapers.

Such tools may have been used for the killing and butchering of prehistoric animals.

As man evolved, his stone-working became more refined and productive, so that by the Mesolithic period, or Middle Stone Age, which began about 9000 B.C., he had among his tools numerous small, sharp blades less than 2 millimetres (one twelfth of an inch) thick. These could be set into shafts of wood or bone to be used as arrows or spears.

Agriculture began to spread outwards from the Middle East from about 6000 B.C., initiating the Neolithic period, or New Stone Age. An astonishing variety of both chipped and ground tools, some of the latter perforated for hafting, were used for cultivation and butchering.

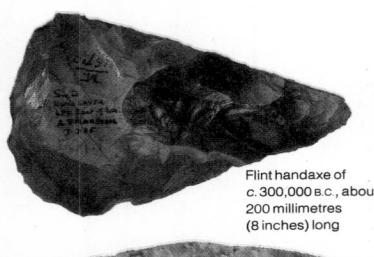

Flint handaxe of c. 300,000 B.C., about 200 millimetres (8 inches) long

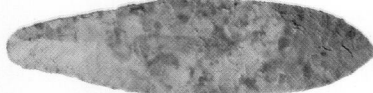

Farmer's flint dagger of c. 2000 B.C., about 200 millimetres (8 inches) long

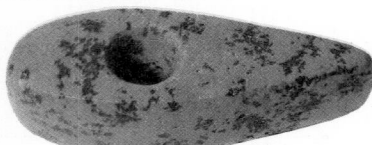

Polished stone battle-axe of c. 2000 B.C., about 200 millimetres (8 inches) long

Flint arrowhead of c. 1800 B.C., about 30 millimetres (1⅛ inches) long

TECHNOLOGY IN STONE *Tools are valuable clues to prehistoric development. By the New Stone Age, crudely flaked stones had been superseded by finely ground axes, farm tools, and weapons. They were significant aids in making permanent settlements.*

MODERN STONE AGE

A Nambicuara Indian (top) living near the Galera Caves in the Rondonia area of Brazil has little contact with the outside world. His people still use Stone-Age tools which they find in the caves, or which they make themselves from flints. The ancient stone axeheads need only the addition of modern wooden handles to make them into useful tools once again (bottom).

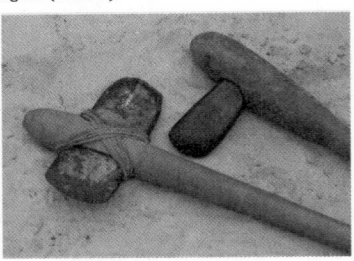

~*n.* 1. A dance involving a rhythmical and heavy step. 2. The jazz music for this dance. [Variant of STAMP (to pound).]

-stomy *n. comb. form.* Indicates a surgical operation in which a usually permanent opening is made into (a specified organ or part); for example, **colostomy.** [From -STOME.]

stone (stōn) *n., pl.* **stones** or **stone** (for sense 9). *Abbr.* **st.** 1. Solid and compact earthy or mineral matter; rock. 2. Such material of a particular type. Used in combination: *sandstone; soapstone.* 3. A small piece of rock. 4. Rock or a piece of rock shaped or finished for a particular purpose, especially: **a.** A stone used in construction work: *a coping stone; a paving stone.* **b.** A gravestone or tombstone. **c.** A grindstone, millstone, or whetstone. **d.** A milestone or boundary. 5. A gem or precious stone. 6. Something like a stone in shape or hardness, such as a hailstone. 7. *Botany.* The hard covering enclosing the kernel in certain fruits, such as the cherry or plum. 8. *Pathology.* A mineral concretion in a hollow organ, as in the kidney. See **calculus.** 9. A unit of weight in Britain and some other English-speaking countries, 14 pounds avoirdupois, used especially to express human body weight. 10. *Printing.* A table with a smooth surface on which page forms are composed, originally made of stone. 11. The oblate piece of stone or iron, with a gooseneck handle, used in the game of curling. 12. *Plural. Archaic.* The testicles. 13. Dull light to dark grey. —**cast the first stone.** To be the first to criticise or accuse. [Biblical allusion to Jesus' saying, "He that is without sin among you, let him cast a stone at her . . ." (John 8:7)]. ~*adj.* 1. Pertaining to or made of stone: *a stone wall.* 2. Made of stoneware or earthenware. ~*adv.* Utterly; completely: *stone cold.* ~*tr.v.* **stoned, stoning, stones.** 1. To hurl or throw stones at; pelt or kill with stones. 2. To remove the stones from (fruit, for example). 3. To furnish, fit, pave, or line with stones. 4. To rub on or with a stone in order to polish or sharpen. 5. *Obsolete.* To make hard like stone; make pitiless or indifferent. [Middle English *stane, stone,* Old English *stān.*] —**ston·er** *n.*

Stone Age *n.* The earliest known period of human culture, characterised by the use of stone tools.

stone axe *n.* An axe with two blunt edges used for hewing stone.

stone bass *n.* A large sea perch, *Polyprion americanus,* of Mediterranean and Atlantic waters. Also called "wreckfish".

stone-blind (stōn-blīnd) *adj.* Completely blind.

stone boiling *n.* A primitive way of boiling water by putting heated stones into it.

stone bramble *n.* A bramble, *Rubus saxatilis,* with small white flowers and red fruit.

stone-chat (stōn-chat) *n.* A small Old World bird, *Saxicola torquata,* having dark plumage. [From the bird's cry resembling the sound of falling pebbles.]

stone-crop (stōn-krop) *n.* 1. Any of various plants of the genus *Sedum,* having fleshy leaves and variously coloured flowers. 2. Any of various related plants. [Middle English *stoncrop,* Old English *stāncropp : stān,* STONE + *cropp,* cluster, CROP.]

stone curlew *n.* A wading bird, *Burhinus oedicnemus,* with a large round head and staring yellow eyes. Also called "thick-knee", *South African* "dikkop".

stone-cut·ter (stōn-kuttər) *n.* One that cuts or carves stone; especially, a machine that dresses stone. —**stone-cut·ting** *n.*

stoned (stōnd) *adj. Slang.* 1. Intoxicated; drunk. 2. Under the influence of a mind-altering drug.

stone-deaf (stōn-déf) *adj.* Completely deaf.

stone-fish (stōn-fish) *n., pl.* **-fishes** or collectively **stonefish.** Any of several tropical marine fishes of the family Scorpaenidae, having spines that eject a deadly venom. [From their resemblance to encrusted stones.]

stone-fly (stōn-flī) *n., pl.* **-flies.** Any of numerous winged insects of the order Plecoptera, occurring on banks of streams and used as fishing bait. [From their aquatic larvae, found under stones.]

stone fruit *n.* A drupe *(see).*

Stone-henge (stōn-hénj) *n.* A megalithic circle on Salisbury Plain, Wiltshire, England. Its surrounding bank and ditch date from *c.* 2800 B.C. The stone circle itself dates from *c.* 2200–1800 B.C., and was probably used as a religious centre. The mathematical accuracy of the stones' positioning suggests that it was also an observatory, used as a calendar of the seasons and to predict eclipses.

stone lily *n.* A fossil crinoid.

stone marten *n.* 1. A Eurasian mammal, *Martes foina,* having brown fur with lighter underfur. 2. The fur of this animal. Also called "beech marten".

stone-ma·son (stōn-mayss'n) *n.* One who prepares and lays stones in building. —**stone-ma·son·ry** *n.*

stone parsley *n.* A hedgerow plant, *Sison amomum,* with small white flowers and a fetid smell.

stone pit *n.* A quarry.

stone's throw *n.* A short distance.

stone-wall (stōn-wáwl) *v.* **-walled, -walling, -walls.** —*intr.* 1. In cricket, to bat defensively rather than trying to score. 2. *Informal.* To engage in delaying or obstructionist tactics. —*tr. Informal.* To delay or obstruct; especially, to hinder (parliamentary proceedings), as by making long speeches. —**stone-wall·er** *n.*

stone-ware (stōn-wair) *n.* A heavy, nonporous pottery, fired at a high temperature and often glazed with salt.

stone-work (stōn-wurk) *n.* 1. The technique or process of preparing, dressing, or working in stone. 2. Work made of stone; stone masonry. —**stone-work·er** *n.*

stone-wort (stōn-wurt ‖ -wawrt) *n.* Any of various green algae of the family Characae, that grow submerged in fresh or brackish water and are frequently encrusted with calcium carbonate deposits.

stonk (stongk) *n.* Heavy shelling by artillery. [Imitative.] —**stonk** *tr.v.*

stonk·ered (stóngkərd) *adj. Australian & N.Z. Informal.* 1. Utterly exhausted or defeated. 2. Puzzled; baffled. [20th century : from *stonker*†, to tire, etc.]

ston·y (stóni) *adj.* **-ier, -iest.** 1. Covered with or full of stones. 2. Hard as a stone. 3. Hard and unfeeling. 4. Impassive; showing no feeling or warmth: *a stony face.* 5. Emotionally numbing or paralysing: *a stony fear.* —**ston·i·ly** *adv.* —**ston·i·ness** *n.*

ston·y-broke (stóni-brók) *adj. British Slang.* Penniless; having no money at all.

stood. Past tense and past participle of **stand.**

stooge (stōōj) *n.* 1. A person who acts as the butt or foil for a comedian's jokes, often by asking questions. 2. Anyone who allows himself to be used for another's advantage.

~*intr.v.* **stooged, stooging, stooges.** To be or behave as a stooge. [20th century : origin obscure.]

stook (stŏŏk, stōōk) *n.* A shock of sheaves of corn.

~*tr.v.* **stooked, stooking, stooks.** To pile (sheaves of corn) into a shock. [Middle English *stouk,* probably from Middle Low German *stuke,* shock.]

stool (stōōl) *n.* **1.** A backless and armless single seat supported on legs or a pedestal. **2.** A low bench or support for the feet or knees in sitting or kneeling, such as a footrest or hassock. **3.** A seat enclosing a chamber pot; a commode. **4.** A piece of faecal matter. **5.** *Horticulture.* **a.** A stump or rootstock that produces shoots or suckers. **b.** A shoot or growth from such a stump or rootstock. **6.** In West Africa: **a.** The throne of a chief. **b.** The kingdom or sphere of sovereignty of a chief. **—fall between two stools.** To fail completely through being unable to reconcile or choose between two alternatives.

~*intr.v.* **stooled, stooling, stools.** **1.** To send up shoots or suckers. **2.** *Archaic.* To evacuate the bowels; defecate. **3.** *Slang.* To act as a stool pigeon. [Middle English *stol,* Old English *stōl.*]

stool·ball (stōōl-bawl) *n.* An old English country game very similar to cricket, formerly widespread and still played, though in a modified form, by women in some areas, especially in Sussex. [STOOL (the term for the wicket) + BALL.]

stool·ie (stōōli) *n. Chiefly U.S. Slang.* A stool pigeon for the police.

stool pigeon *n.* **1.** A pigeon used as a decoy. **2.** *Slang.* A person acting as a decoy or informer; especially, a spy for the police. [Decoy pigeons were originally tied to a stool.]

stoop[1] (stōōp) *v.* **stooped, stooping, stoops.** —*intr.* **1.** To bend forwards and downwards from the waist or middle of the back. **2.** To walk or stand, especially habitually, with the head and upper back bent forwards. **3.** To bend or slope downwards. **4.** To lower or debase oneself. Used with *to.* **5.** To descend from a superior position; condescend. Used with *to.* **6.** To swoop down. Used especially of a bird of prey. —*tr.* **1.** To bend (one's head or body) forwards and downwards. **2.** *Archaic.* To debase or subdue; humble.

~*n.* **1.** The act of stooping. **2.** A forward bending of the head and upper back, especially when habitual. **3.** An act of self-abasement or condescension. **4.** A swooping down, as of a bird of prey. [Middle English *stupen,* Old English *stūpian.*]

stoop[2] *n.* A small porch, platform, or staircase leading to the entrance of a house or building. Also *South African* "stoep". [Dutch *stoep,* front verandah, from Middle Dutch.]

stoop[3] *n. Archaic or Regional.* A pillar or upright post. [Middle English, variant of dialect *stulpe,* probably from Old Norse *stolpe.*]

stoop[4]. Variant of **stoup.**

stop (stop) *v.* **stopped, stopping, stops.** —*tr.* **1.** To close (an opening) by covering, filling in, or plugging up. Often used with *up.* **2.** To stop the flow of something from; stanch: *stop a wound.* **3.** To constrict (an opening or orifice). **4.** To obstruct or block the passage of (traffic, for example). **5.** To prevent the flow or passage of: *tried to stop the blood.* **6. a.** To arrest the movement or progress of; cause to halt: *A man stopped me and asked the time.* **b.** To prevent from continuing an action; cause to cease or desist: *stopped their chatter by banging on the table.* **c.** To restrain or prevent from an intended action: *couldn't stop him from calling the police.* **7.** To desist from; cease doing. Often used with a gerund: *stop running.* **8.** To cause (a machine, for example) to cease operating, functioning, or moving; halt. **9.** To give instructions to one's banker to not honour (a cheque). **10.** To withold; keep back: *stop his allowance.* **11.** In boxing, to defeat (an opponent) by rendering him unable to continue the fight. **12.** *Slang.* To be given or receive (a blow, bullet, or the like). **13.** *Music.* **a.** To close (a hole on a wind instrument) with the finger in order to sound a desired note. **b.** To press down (a string on a stringed instrument) in order to produce a desired note. **c.** To put one's hand inside (the bell of a French horn) in order to alter the pitch or tone quality. **d.** To produce (a particular note) by any of these methods. **14.** To close (an organ pipe) at one end, in order to make it sound an octave lower. **15.** In bridge, to hold a card or cards in (a particular suit) that will prevent one's opponents from winning all the tricks in that suit. —*intr.* **1.** To cease moving, progressing, acting, or operating; come to a halt or pause. **2.** To put an end to what one is doing; cease. **3.** To interrupt one's course or journey, as to make a quick visit or do an errand. Often used with *in* or *off*: *stop in at the supermarket for a minute.* **4.** *Informal.* To stay: *stopped at a friend's for a few nights.* **—stop at nothing.** To act with absolute determination or lack of scruples. **—stop down.** To reduce the effective aperture of (a camera lens). **—stop out.** To cover (part of an area of cloth, a printing plate, or the like) in order to prevent it being printed or etched.

~*n.* **1.** The act of stopping or the condition of being stopped; a cessation; a halt. **2.** A finish; an end. **3.** A stay or visit, as during a journey. **4. a.** An official stopping place: *a bus stop.* **b.** Any place stopped at. **5. a.** An act or instance of obstructing, blocking, or plugging up. **b.** A device or means that obstructs, blocks, or plugs up. **6. a.** See **stop payment. b.** See **stop order. 7.** A part in a machine that stops or regulates movement. **8.** A perforated screen or diaphragm that limits the effective aperture of a lens, producing an image of improved definition but lowered intensity. **9.** A punctuation mark, especially a full stop. Used in full in telegrams and cables instead of a full stop. **10.** *Music.* **a.** The act of stopping a string or hole on a musical instrument. **b.** A device such as a key for closing the hole on a wind instrument. **11.** *Music.* **a.** A tuned set of pipes, as in an organ. **b.** A knob, key, or pull that regulates such a set of pipes. **12.** *Nautical.* A line used for securing something temporarily: *a sail stop.* **13.** *Phonetics.* A consonant articulated with a complete obstruction of the passage of breath; specifically, (p), (b), (t), (d), (k), or (g) in English. Compare **continuant. 14.** The depression between the muzzle and top of the skull of a dog or cat. **15.** In bridge, a **stopper** *(see).* **16.** *Architecture.* A projecting stone, often carved, at the end of a moulding. **—pull out all the stops.** To exert oneself to the utmost. [Middle English *stoppen,* Old English *-stoppian,* from West Germanic *stoppōn* (unattested), to plug up, from Late Latin *stuppāre,* to stop up with a tow, from Latin *stuppa,* tow, from Greek *stuppē.*]

Usage: In British English, one usually stops something *happening*: in American English, one usually stops something *from happening.*

stop bath *n.* In photography, an acid solution used to check the developing process.

stop·cock (stóp-kok) *n.* A valve that regulates the flow of liquid through a pipe; a tap.

stope (stōp) *n.* A tunnel driven parallel to the strike of a vertical or near vertical vein so that ore can be excavated from the vein.

~*v.* **stoped, stoping, stopes.** —*tr.* To remove (ore) from a stope. —*intr.* To mine by means of a stope. [Perhaps from Low German *stope,* a step, from Middle Low German *stōpe.*]

Stopes (stōps), **Marie (Charlotte) Carmichael** (1880–1958). British scientist and pioneer advocate of birth control. With her husband she founded Britain's first birth control clinic (1921). Her books include *Married Love* (1918), and *Enduring Passion* (1928).

stop·gap (stóp-gap) *n.* An improvised substitute for something lacking; a temporary expedient.

stop-go (stóp-gō) *adj. British.* Of, designating, or tending to produce an economic cycle in which deflation and inflation alternate.

stop·ing (stōping) *n.* **1.** *Geology.* The breaking-up of country rock by advancing intrusive magma. **2.** *Mining.* The mining of ore by means of stopes, often by a series of stopes.

stop·light (stóp-līt) *n. U.S.* **1.** A red traffic light. **2.** A **brake light** *(see).*

stop order *n.* An order to a broker to buy or sell a stock when it reaches a stipulated level of decline or gain.

stop over *intr.v.* To make a stopover on a journey.

stop·o·ver (stóp-ōvər) *n.* **1.** An interruption in the course of a journey for stopping at or visiting a certain place; especially, a stop made in the course of a long-distance airline flight. **2.** A place visited briefly in the course of a journey.

stop·page (stóppij) *n.* **1.** The act of stopping or the condition of being stopped; a halt. **2.** Something that stops, obstructs, or blocks. **3.** An amount withheld, as from a person's wages; a deduction. **4.** The act of stopping work, as during industrial action.

Stop·pard (stóppaard), **Tom** (1937–). Czech-born English playwright. He first achieved success with *Rosencrantz and Guildenstern are Dead* (1967); later works include *Jumpers* (1972), and *The Real Thing* (1982). His plays are characterised by their witty dialogue and often deal with philosophical or ethical themes.

stop payment *n.* An order to one's bank not to honour a cheque.

stop·per (stóppər) *n.* **1.** Any device, such as a cork or plug, inserted to close an opening. **2.** One that causes something to stop. **3.** In bridge, a card or cards enabling one to prevent one's opponents from winning all the tricks. Also called "stop".

~*tr.v.* **stoppered, -pering, -pers.** To close with a stopper.

stop·ping (stópping) *n. British.* A filling in a tooth.

~*adj.* Halting at many stations. Said of a train.

stop·ple (stópp'l) *n.* A stopper; a plug.

~*tr.v.* **stoppled, -pling, -ples.** To close with a stopple. [Middle English *stoppell,* from *stoppen,* to STOP.]

stop press *n. British.* **1.** Late news that is added to a newspaper after the printing has started. **2.** A space in a newspaper that is set aside for such news.

stop·watch (stóp-woch) *n.* A timepiece that can be started and stopped by a trigger to measure duration of time.

stor·age (stáw-rij || stō-) *n. Abbr.* **stge., stor. 1. a.** The act of storing goods, as in a warehouse for safekeeping. **b.** The state of being stored. **2.** Space for storing goods. **3.** The price charged for keeping goods stored. **4.** *Computing.* process of storing information on a storage device. Also used adjectivally: *storage capacity.*

storage battery *n.* A group of reversible or rechargeable **secondary cells** *(see)* acting as a unit. Also called "accumulator", "secondary battery".

storage cell *n.* A **secondary cell** *(see).*

storage device *n. Computing.* A piece of equipment or medium on which computer data can be stored and from which it can be retrieved. Storage devices include magnetic tapes and tape cassettes, hard and floppy disks, and magnetic drums.

storage heater *n.* A type of electric heater that accumulates heat during off-peak electricity hours.

sto·rax (stáw-raks || stō-) *n.* **1.** Any of various trees of the genus *Styrax,* some of which yield an aromatic resin. **2.** An aromatic resin obtained from any of these trees. **3.** A brownish, aromatic resin used in perfume and medicine and obtained from any of several trees of the genus *Liquidambar;* especially, *L. orientalis,* of Asia Minor. In this sense, also called "styrax". [Middle English, from Latin, from Greek, variant of *sturax,* probably from Semitic; akin to Hebrew *tzōrī.*]

store (stor || stōr) *n.* **1.** A stock or supply reserved for future use. **2.** *Plural.* Supplies, especially of food, clothing, or arms. **3.** A place

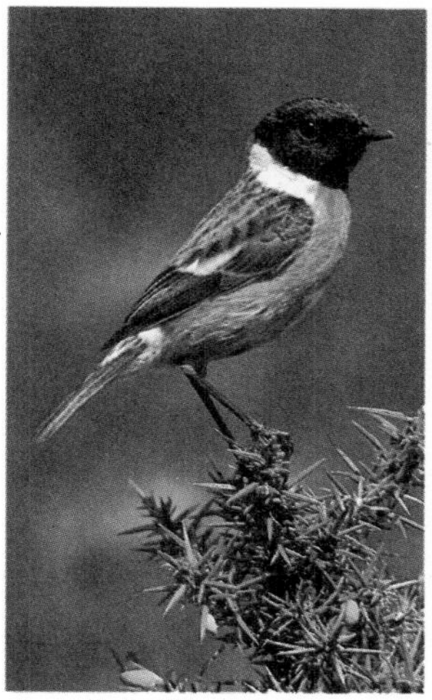

stonechat *This small, insect-eating heathland bird gets its name from its call – similar to the sound of two stones being clapped together. The male (above) is distinguished from the female by its white collar.*

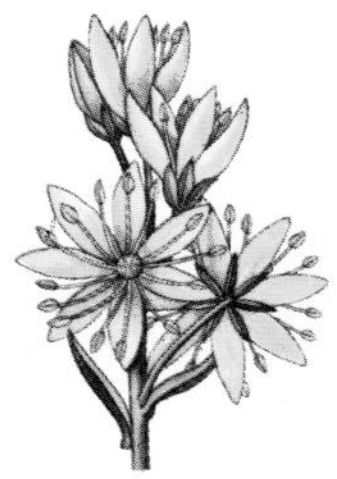

stonecrop *This creeping plant of rocks and walls stores water in its fleshy leaves. The leaves of the reflexed stonecrop, shown nere, were once eaten as a salad.*

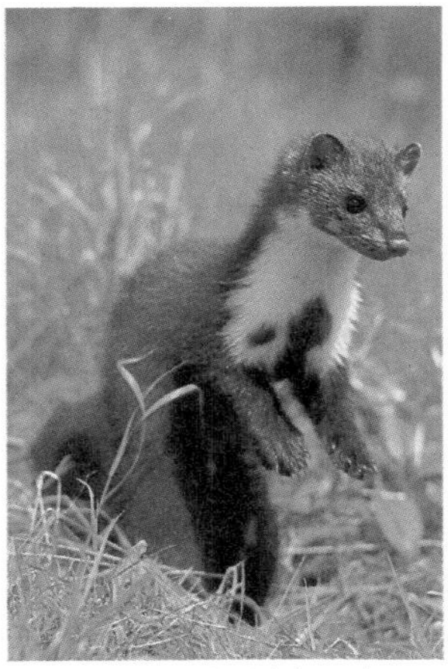

stone marten *Found throughout Europe and western Asia, the stone marten is a member of the weasel family and feeds chiefly on squirrels and birds. It often nests in hollow trees.*

where commodities are kept; a warehouse or storehouse. Also used in combination: *a storeman.* **4.** A great quantity or number; an abundance. **5.** *Computing.* A **memory** *(see).* **6. a.** A department store. **b.** *U.S.* Any shop. **—in store.** Set aside or reserved for the future; forthcoming. **—lay, put,** or **set store by.** To regard as important or valuable.

~tr.v. **stored, storing, stores. 1.** To reserve or put away for future use. **2.** To fill, supply, or stock with something. **3.** To deposit or receive in a storehouse or warehouse for safekeeping. **4.** *Computing.* To place (data) in a storage device for retention. [Middle English *stor,* from Old French *estor,* from *estorer,* to build, restore, from Latin *instaurāre.*] **—stor·a·ble** *adj.*

store·front (stór-frunt || stṓr-) *n.* **1.** The side of a shop facing a street. **2.** A room or set of rooms in a storefront. **—store·front** *adj.*

store·house (stór-howss || stṓr-) *n.* **1.** A place or building in which goods are stored; a warehouse. **2.** An abundant source or supply.

store·keep·er (stór-keepər || stṓr-) *n.* **1.** A person in charge of receiving or distributing stores or supplies, especially military or naval supplies. **2.** *U.S.* A shopkeeper.

store·room (stór-rŏŏm, -rōōm || stṓr-) *n.* A room in which things are stored.

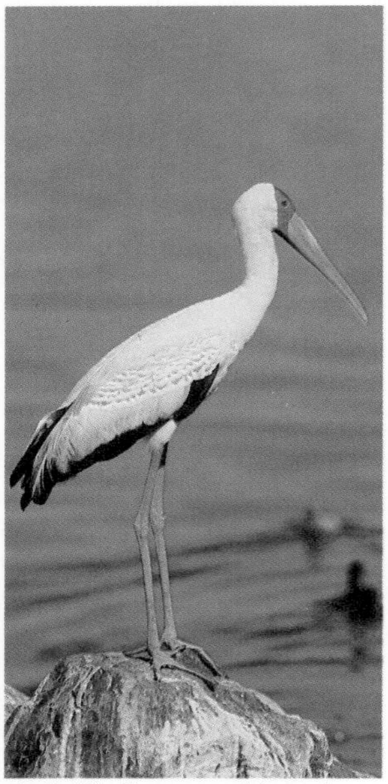

stork *The European white stork (above) is one of 17 species of the family* Ciconiidae. *Storks live near shores and marshes and feed on fish and small animals. They return to the same nest every year, rebuilding and enlarging it each time.*

sto·rey (stáwri || stṓri) *n., pl.* **-reys.** Also *chiefly U.S.* **sto·ry** *pl.* **-ies. 1.** A complete horizontal division of a building comprising the area between two adjacent levels. **2.** The set of rooms on the same level of a building. [Middle English, from Anglo-Latin *historia,* HISTORY (perhaps originally referring to a row of painted windows or of sculptures).]

Sto·rey (stáwri || stṓri), **David** (1933–). British novelist and dramatist. His works include the novels *This Sporting Life* (1960), and *Saville* (1976), and the play *In Celebration* (1969).

storey building *n. West African.* A house that consists of more than one storey. Also called "storey house".

sto·reyed (stáw-rid || stṓ-, -reed) *adj.* Also *chiefly U.S.* **sto·ried.** Having or consisting of a specified number of storeys. Used in combination: *a three-storeyed house.*

sto·ried (stáw-rid || stṓ-, -reed) *adj.* **1.** *Literary.* Celebrated or famous in history or legend. **2.** Ornamented with designs representing scenes from history or legend: *storied tapestry.*

stork (stork) *n.* **1.** Any of various large wading birds of the family Ciconiidae, having long red legs, a long, red, stout bill, and black and white plumage. **2.** Such a bird conventionally considered as the bringer of babies. Preceded by *the.* [Middle English *stork,* Old English *storc.*]

stork's-bill (stórks-bil) *n.* Any of various plants of the genus *Erodium,* having fruit with a narrow, beaklike point.

storm (storm) *n.* **1.** An atmospheric disturbance manifested in strong winds accompanied by rain, snow, or other precipitation, and often by thunder and lightning. **2.** *Meteorology.* A wind whose speed is 28.5 to 32.6 metres per second (64–75 miles per hour), force 11 on the Beaufort scale. **3.** A heavy shower of objects, such as bullets or missiles. **4.** A strong or violent outburst, as of emotion or protest. **5.** A violent disturbance or upheaval, as in political, social, or domestic affairs. **6.** *Military.* A violent, sudden attack on a fortified place. **—take by storm.** To have overwhelming and captivating effect on (an audience, for example).

~v. **stormed, storming, storms.** *—intr.* **1.** To blow forcefully; rain, snow, hail, or otherwise precipitate violently. Used with *it: It stormed last night.* **2.** To be extremely angry; rant and rage. **3.** To move or rush tumultuously, violently, or angrily: *She stormed into the room.* *—tr. Military.* To capture or try to capture by a violent, sudden attack. —See Synonyms at **attack.** [Middle English, Old English *storm.*]

storm belt *n.* A tract of the earth's surface in which storms are frequent.

storm·bound (stórm-bownd) *adj.* Delayed, confined, or cut off from communication by a storm.

storm centre *n.* **1.** *Meteorology.* The central area covered by a storm; especially, the point of lowest barometric pressure within a storm. **2.** The centre or source of trouble, disturbance, or argument.

storm cloud *n.* **1.** A heavy, dark rain-cloud that threatens stormy weather. **2.** Anything that presages violence, disturbance, or war.

storm collar *n.* A high coat-collar, often one that buttons up.

storm cone *n. British.* A tarred cone, hoisted to provide a warning of high winds.

storm door *n.* An outer or additional door added for protection against inclement weather.

storm glass *n.* A glass tube containing a liquid solution that forms crystals as an indication of bad weather.

storm in a teacup *n.* Great excitement or fuss over something trivial or unimportant.

Stor·mont (stáwr-mont). The former parliament of Northern Ireland or any subsequent administrative body for the Province. [From *Stormont* Castle, where it sat.]

storm petrel *n.* A small sea bird of the family Hydrobatidae; especially, *Hydrobates pelagicus,* of the North Atlantic and the Mediterranean. Also called "stormy petrel", "Mother Carey's chicken".

storm surge *n.* A rapid rise of sea level above predicted tidal levels when water is piled up against a coast by powerful onshore winds, sometimes breaching coastal defences. Also in nontechinical usage "tidal wave".

storm trooper *n.* **1.** A member of the **Sturmabteilung** *(see).* **2.** A member of a force of shock troops.

storm warning *n.* A pattern of lights or flags displayed along a coastline or at a port, to warn of an approaching storm.

storm window *n.* A secondary window attached over the usual window to protect against the wind and cold.

storm·y (stórmi) *adj.* **-ier, -iest. 1.** Subject to, characterised by, or affected by storms; tempestuous. **2.** Characterised by violent emotions, passions, speech, or actions: *a stormy argument.* **—storm·i·ly** *adv.* **—storm·i·ness** *n.*

stormy petrel *n.* **1.** A storm petrel. **2.** A person who brings discord or appears at the onset of trouble.

Stor·no·way (stáwrnə-way). Seaport and burgh on the east coast of the Isle of Lewis in the Outer Hebrides, Scotland. It is the administrative centre of the Western Isles Region.

Stor·ting, Stor·thing (stór-ting || stṓr-) *n.* The parliament of Norway. [Norwegian : *stor,* great + *thing,* assembly.]

sto·ry[1] (stáwri || stṓri) *n., pl.* **-ries. 1.** An account or recital of an event or series of events, either true or fictitious. **2.** A prose or verse narrative, usually fictional, intended to interest or amuse the hearer or reader; a tale. **3.** A type of fictional literary composition, a **short story** *(see).* **4.** An incident or experience that would be good material for a narrative. **5.** A plot, as of a novel or play. **6.** A report, statement, or allegation of facts. **7. a.** A news article. **b.** The event, situation, or other material for such an article. **8.** An anecdote. **9.** A lie. **10.** Romantic legend or tradition. **—quite another story.** An entirely different state of affairs. **—the old** or **same old story.** The well-known or very familiar course of events.

~tr.v. **storied, -rying, -ries. 1.** To decorate with scenes representing historical or legendary events. **2.** *Archaic.* To tell as a story. [Middle English *storie,* from Anglo-French *estorie,* from Latin *historia,* HISTORY.]

story[2]. *Chiefly U.S.* Variant of **storey.**

sto·ry·book (stáw-ri-bŏŏk || stṓ-, -bŏŏk) *n.* A book containing a collection of stories, usually for children.

~adj. Of the kind that occurs in a storybook; romantic; fairytale.

story line *n.* The plot of a book, film, or a dramatic work.

sto·ry·tell·er (stáw-ri-tellər || stṓ-) *n.* **1.** A person who tells or writes stories. **2.** *Informal.* A person who tells lies; a fibber. **—sto·ry·tell·ing** *n.*

stoss (stoss; *German* shtōss) *adj.* Facing the direction from which a glacier or ice sheet moves. Said of a rock or slope in its path. [From German *stossen,* to push, thrust, from Old High German *stōzan.*]

stot (stōt, stot) *v.* **stotted, stotting, stots.** *Scottish.* *—intr.* **1.** To rebound; bounce. **2.** To lurch; stagger. *—tr.* To cause to bounce. [Middle English (Scots), of obscure origin.]

sto·tin·ka (sto-tíng-kə || stō-) *n., pl.* **-ki** (-kee). A monetary unit equal to $^1/_{100}$ of the lev of Bulgaria. [Bulgarian : *sto-,* from *suto,* hundred + suffixes *-tin, -ka.*]

sto·tious (stṓshəss) *adj. Scottish & Irish Slang.* Drunk. [Probably from STOT in the sense "to lurch, stagger".]

stot·ter (stṓtər) *n. Scottish Slang.* An extremely attractive woman. [From STOT.]

stound (stownd) *n.* **1.** *Obsolete.* A short time; a while. **2.** *Chiefly Scottish.* A sudden tremor, as of pain or excitement. [Middle English *sto(u)nd,* Old English *stund.*]

stoup, stoop (stŏŏp) *n.* **1.** *Ecclesiastical.* A basin or font for holy water at the entrance of a church. **2.** *Northern British.* **a.** A bucket or pail. **b.** A cup, tankard, or other drinking vessel. [Middle English *stowp,* vessel, pail, from Old Norse *staup.*]

stour (stowr) *n. Chiefly Scottish.* **1.** Tumult; conflict. **2. a.** A driving storm. **b.** A sudden cloud of dust or spray. [Middle English, from Old French *estour,* armed combat, from Germanic; akin to Old High German *sturm,* STORM.]

stoush (stowsh) *n. Australian Informal.* A fight, conflict, or war. **—the big stoush.** *Australian Informal.* World War I.

~tr.v. **stoushed, stoushing, stoushes.** To fight or hit. [19th century : origin obscure.]

stout (stowt) *adj.* **stouter, stoutest. 1.** Determined, bold, or brave; resolute; staunch: *a stout heart.* **2.** Strong in body; sturdy. **3.** Strong in structure or substance; substantial; solid. **4.** Bulky in figure; thickset; inclined towards fatness. **5.** Powerful; forceful. —See Synonyms at **strong, fat.**

~n. A strong, very dark beer or ale brewed with malt or barley. [Middle English, from Old French *estout,* from Germanic.] **—stout·ly** *adv.* **—stout·ness** *n.*

stout-heart·ed (stówt-hártid) *adj.* Brave; courageous; dauntless. **—stout·heart·ed·ly** *adv.* **—stout·heart·ed·ness** *n.*

stove[1] (stōv) *n.* **1.** An apparatus in which electricity or a fuel is used to provide heat, as for cooking or comfort. **2.** A heated room or box used for a particular purpose, such as a kiln or hothouse.

~tr.v. **stoved, stoving, stoves.** To heat, treat, or keep in a stove. [Middle English, heated chamber, from Middle Low German or Middle Dutch.]

stove[2]. Alternative past tense and past participle of **stave.**

stove enamel *n.* A type of heat-resistant enamel paint.

stove·pipe (stṓv-pīp) *n.* **1.** A pipe, usually iron, used to conduct smoke or fumes from a stove into a chimney flue. **2.** A man's tall silk hat. Also called "stovepipe hat".

sto·ver (stṓvər) *n.* Any of various kinds of animal feed made from clover, stubble, or the like. [Middle English, food, provisions, short for Anglo-French *estovers,* supplies, from Old French *estovier,* to be necessary, from Latin *est opus,* it is necessary : *est* (it) is, from *esse,* to be + *opus,* need, necessity.]

stow (stō) *tr.v.* **stowed, stowing, stows. 1. a.** To place, arrange, or store away, especially in a neat, compact way. **b.** *Nautical.* To load or store (cargo, gear, or provisions) in the proper place. **2.** To fill by packing tightly. **3.** *Slang.* To cease; stop. Usually used in the imperative: *Stow it!* **4.** *Slang.* To consume (food) greedily. Often used with *away.* **5.** *Archaic.* To provide lodging for; quarter. [Middle English *stowen,* to place, put, from *stowe,* a place, Old English *stōw.*]

stow·age (stṓ-ij) *n.* **1. a.** The act, manner, or process of stowing. **b.** The state of being stowed. **2.** Space or room for storage. **3.** Goods in storage. **4.** A charge for storing goods.

stow away *intr.v.* To be a stowaway.

stow·a·way (stṓ-ə-way) *n.* One who hides aboard a ship or other form of transport in order to obtain free passage.

Stowe (stō), **Harriet Beecher** (1811–96). U.S. author. Her antislavery novel, *Uncle Tom's Cabin* (1852), had great political influence and did much to advance the cause of abolition.

STP¹ *n.* A synthetic hallucinogenic drug chemically related to amphetamine and mescaline. [Humorous allusion to the additional power ascribed to the oil substitute *S.T.P.* (*s*cientifically *t*reated *p*etroleum).]

STP² **1.** Professor of Sacred Theology [Latin *Sanctae Theologiae Professor*]. **2.** standard temperature and pressure.

St. Paul. The state capital of Minnesota, northern United States, situated at the head of navigation of the river Mississippi.

St. Peter Port. The capital of Guernsey in the Channel Islands. It is a busy port, and is also a tourist resort and yachting centre.

St. Petersburg. See **Leningrad.**

St. Pierre et Mique·lon (saN pi-áir ay meek-lóN). Two small island groups making up a French overseas département situated in the Atlantic Ocean south of Newfoundland. Frequently contested between England and France, they finally became French in 1814, and are the last French territory in North America.

str. **1.** steamer. **2.** strait. **3.** stringed (instruments).

stra·bis·mus (strə-bízməss, stra-) *n.* Also **stra·bil·is·mus** (strábbi-lízməss), **stra·bism** (stráybiz'm). A visual defect in which one eye cannot focus with the other on an objective because of imbalance of the eye muscles. Also called "squint". See **walleye.** [New Latin, from Greek *strabismos,* from *strabizein,* to squint, from *strabos,* squinting.] **—stra·bis·mal, stra·bis·mic** *adj.*

stra·bot·o·my (strə-bóttəmi, stra-) *n., pl.* **-mies.** The cutting of an ocular muscle or tendon to correct strabismus. [Greek *strabos,* squinting + -TOMY.]

Stra·chey (stráychi), **(Giles) Lytton** (1880–1932). British biographer and historian. He is known chiefly for his revolutionary biographies in which he debunked the grandeur of Victorian society. His works include *Eminent Victorians* (1918), *Queen Victoria* (1921), and *Elizabeth and Essex* (1928). He was a member of the Bloomsbury Group of writers and artists.

strad·dle (stràdd'l) *v.* **-dled, -dling, -dles.** *—tr.* **1.** To sit, stand, or be in a position astride of; bestride. **2.** To fire shots behind and in front of (a target) in order to determine the range. **3. a.** To fall on or take in parts of (two periods or areas, for example): *Her constituency straddles two counties.* **b.** To fall or lie on either side of (a dividing line). **4.** *U.S.* To vacillate between or seem to favour both sides of (an issue). *—intr.* **1.** To sit or stand with the legs apart. **2.** To be or be spread wide apart; sprawl. **3.** *U.S.* To appear to favour both sides of an issue.

~n. **1.** The act or posture of sitting astride. **2.** *U.S. Finance.* The privileged option of either delivering or buying securities at a stated price within a stated period of time. Compare **call, put.** **3.** *U.S.* An equivocal or noncommittal position. [Frequentative of *strad-,* obsolete past stem of STRIDE.] **—strad·dler** *n.*

Strad·i·var·i (stràddi-vaàri || *U.S. also* -várri), **Antonio** (1644–1737). Italian violin maker. At his workshop in Cremona he brought violin-making to its highest point of craftsmanship. He produced over 1,000 instruments, some of which still survive.

Strad·i·var·i·us (stràddi-vàir-i-əss) *n., pl.* **-varii.** Any of the famous violins made in the workshop of Antonio Stradivari. Also informally called "Strad".

strafe (strayf, straaf) *tr.v.* **strafed, strafing, strafes.** To attack (ground troops, for example) with bombs or machine-gun fire from low-flying aircraft.

~n. An act of strafing. [Humorous use from German slogan (1914) *(Gott) strafe (England),* "(God) punish (England)", from *strafen,* to punish, from Middle High German *strāfen*†, to rebuke.]

Straf·ford (stràffərd), **Thomas Wentworth, 1st Earl of** (1593–1641). English statesman. As a chief minister of Charles I and a leading agent of his absolutist rule, he became deeply unpopular. He was impeached by the Long Parliament and executed with the King's consent.

strag·gle (strágg'l) *intr.v.* **-gled, -gling, -gles.** **1.** To stray or fall behind. **2.** To grow, proceed, or spread out in a scattered or irregular manner or pattern. [Middle English *straglen,* perhaps frequentative of *straken,* to go, move, perhaps related to Old English *streccan,* to STRETCH.] **—strag·gler** *n.*

strag·gly (strággli) *adj.* **-glier, -gliest.** Spread out or proceeding irregularly.

straight (strayt) *adj.* **straighter, straightest.** **1.** Extending continuously in the same direction. **2.** Free from curves, angles or irregularities, as: **a.** Not wavy or curly: *straight hair.* **b.** Not bent or stooping: *a straight back.* **c.** Exactly vertical or horizontal; level or upright. **3.** Characterised by honesty and fairness; scrupulous. **4. a.** Logical; reasonable: *straight thinking.* **b.** Accurate; correct; in accordance with the truth: *set the record straight.* **5.** Direct and candid; not evasive: *a straight answer.* **6.** Uninterrupted; consecutive. **7.** Unmodified; unembellished: *gave us the straight facts.* **8.** Undiluted or unmixed: *straight whisky.* **9.** Involving no additional or extraneous elements: *a straight swap; a straight fight between Labour and Conservative.* **10.** Neatly arranged; orderly. **11.** Of, designating, or involved in serious drama as opposed to comedy, musicals, or the like: *a straight actor; a straight play.* **12.** Normal or conventional; conforming to established norms, as in one's opinions, lifestyle, or sexual preferences; especially: **a.** Heterosexual. **b.** Not being a drug-user.

~adv. **1.** In a straight line. **2.** In an erect posture; upright. **3.** Directly; without detour or delay. **4.** Without circumlocution; candidly. Often used with *out.* **5.** Honestly or virtuously. **6.** Continuously. **—go straight.** *Informal.* To reform after having been a criminal.

~n. **1.** A straight line, part, piece, or condition. **2.** A straight part on a racecourse, especially between the last turn and the winning post. **3.** A poker hand containing a numerical sequence of five cards of various suits. **4.** *Slang.* A normal or conventional person, especially: **a.** A heterosexual person. **b.** A person who is not a drug-user. [Middle English *streit, streight,* from the past participle of *strecchen,* to STRETCH.] **—straight·ly** *adv.* **—straight·ness** *n.*

straight and narrow *n.* The path of honest, moral, and law-abiding behaviour.

straight·a·way, straight away (stráyt-ə-wáy) *adv.* At once; immediately.

~adj. Extending or proceeding in a straight line or course.

~n. (-way). *U.S.* A straight course, stretch, or track.

straight chain *n. Chemistry.* An open linear molecular structure with no side chains. Compare **branched chain.**

straight·edge (stráyt-ej) *n.* A rigid flat rectangular bar, as of wood or metal, with a straight edge for testing or drawing straight lines. **—straight·edged** *adj.*

straight·en (stráyt'n) *v.* **-ened, -ening, -ens.** *—tr.* **1.** To make straight. **2.** To tidy. *—intr.* To become straight. **—straighten out.** **1.** To put to rights or restore order to; rectify. **2.** To reform or improve. **—straight·en·er** *n.*

straight face *n.* A face that betrays no sign of emotion, especially of amusement. **—straight-faced** (stráyt-fáyst) *adj.*

straight flush *n.* In poker, a run of five consecutive cards of the same suit.

straight·for·ward (stráyt-fór-wərd) *adj.* **1.** Proceeding in a straight course; direct. **2.** Honest; frank; candid. **3.** Simple; uncomplicated. **4.** Unambiguous; cut-and-dried. —See Synonyms at **fair.**

~adv. In a straightforward course. **—straight·for·ward·ly** *adv.* **—straight·for·ward·ness** *n.*

straight jacket. Variant of **strait jacket.**

straight-line (stráyt-lìn) *adj.* **1.** Of, pertaining to, or designating a type of machinery whose linkage produces or copies motion in straight lines. **2.** Designating the most usual method of amortisation of a loan or of providing for the depreciation of an asset, based on a series of equal payments or equal allowable amounts over a given period of time.

straight man *n.* One of two comedians who acts a "normal" role as a foil to his partner's obvious comedy.

straight off *adv.* Without delay or hesitation; at once.

straight ticket *n. U.S.* A vote cast for all the candidates of one party. Compare **split ticket.**

straight·way (stráyt-wáy, -way) *adv. Archaic.* Immediately.

strain¹ (strayn) *v.* **strained, straining, strains.** *—tr.* **1.** To pull, draw, or stretch tight. **2.** To exert or tax to the utmost. Often used reflexively. **3.** To injure or impair by overuse or overexertion; especially, to wrench: *strain a muscle.* **4. a.** To place too great a load on: *strained the lifting mechanism.* **b.** To stretch or force beyond the proper, reasonable, or legitimate limits: *strain a point.* **5.** To alter the relations between the parts of a structure or shape by applying an external force; deform. **6.** To pass (a substance) through a strainer or other filtering agent. **7.** To draw off or remove by filtration. **8.** To embrace or clasp tightly; hug. *—intr.* **1.** To make forceful and continuous efforts; exert oneself physically or mentally; strive hard. **2.** To be overexerted; especially, to be wrenched or twisted. **3.** To be subjected to great stress. **4.** To pull forcibly or violently: *straining at the leash.* **5.** To hesitate, as through scruple; baulk. Used with *at.* **6.** To filter, trickle, or ooze.

~n. **1. a.** The act of straining. **b.** The state of being strained. **2.** A great or extreme effort, exertion, or tension. **3.** Something that makes great or excessive demands on one's mental, emotional, or physical resources. **4.** A wrench or other injury resulting from excessive effort or use. **5.** *Physics.* A deformation produced by stress, measured by the change in dimension divided by the original dimension (length, area, or volume), or by the angular shear. —See Synonyms at **effort.** [Middle English *streynen,* from Old French *estreindere,* from Latin *stringere,* to draw tight, tie.]

strain² *n.* **1.** The collective descendants of a common ancestor; a race, stock, line, or breed. **2.** Any of the various lines of ancestry united in an individual or family; ancestry; lineage. **3.** *Biology.* A group of organisms of the same species, having distinctive characteristics but not usually considered a separate breed or variety. **4.** *Archaic.* A kind; a sort. **5. a.** An inborn or inherited tendency or character. **b.** A streak; a trace. **6.** The tone or tenor of a piece of speech or writing. **7.** *Often plural.* A passage of musical expression; an air; a tune. **8.** A passage of poetic expression. [Middle English *stren(e),* Old English *strēon,* acquisition, generation, offspring.]

PRONUNCIATION KEY

a, trap; aa, father; ai, fair; ar, star; aw, lawn; ay, play; b, bb, stab; rubber; ch, church; ck, ticket; d, dd, dead; ladder; e, dress; ee, bee; er, defer; ew, few; ewr, pure; ə, about; ər, letter; f, ff, fife; differ; g, gg, giggle; h, hat; i, kit; ī, price; īr, fire; j, judge; k, kick; l, ll, let; 'l, needle; m, mm, man; n, nn, no; 'n, sudden; ng, thing; o, lot; ō, no; ŏŏ, foot; ōō, shoe; oor, poor; ow, cow; owr, hour; oy, boy; p, pp, pepper; r, rr, red; s, ss, sauce; sh, ship; t, tt, totter; th, thick; th, this; smooth; u, cut; ur, turn; v, vv, valve; w, wet; y, yes; z, zz, zebra; zh, vision; pleasure

IN FOREIGN WORDS:

aN, oN, Saint-Saëns; hl, Llanelli; Hluhluwe; kh, loch; lough; Khaled

STRESS MARK:

ín-sīt, insight; in-sīt, incite

strained (straynd) *adj.* **1.** Forced; unnatural: *a strained smile.* **2.** Tense and uncomfortable, especially because of latent hostility: *a strained atmosphere.*

strain·er (stráynər) *n.* One that strains, especially: **1.** A filter, sieve, or the like used to separate liquids from solids. **2.** An apparatus for tightening, stretching, or strengthening.

strain gauge *n.* A device for detecting or measuring strain using the change in electrical resistance of a distorted thin wire or a piezoelectric crystal.

strain hardening *n.* The process of hardening metal by straining it so as to increase the number of internal crystal dislocations.

straining beam *n. Architecture.* A horizontal tie beam connecting two queen posts in a roof truss. Also called "straining piece".

strait (strayt) *n. Abbr.* **St., str. 1.** *Often plural.* A narrow passage of water joining two larger bodies of water. **2.** *Usually plural.* A position of difficulty, perplexity, distress, or need: *in desperate straits.* ~*adj. Archaic.* **1.** Narrow, constricting, or confined. **2.** Stringent or rigorous, as in moral conduct or religious observance. [Middle English *streit,* from Old French *estreit,* tight, narrow, from Latin *strictus,* from the past participle of *stringere,* to draw tight.]

strait·en (stráyt'n) *tr.v.* **-ened, -ening, -ens. 1.** *Archaic.* To limit, confine, or make narrow. **2.** To cause to experience difficulties or distress, particularly financial hardship. Used chiefly in the phrase *in straitened circumstances.*

strait·jack·et, straight jacket (stráyt-jackit) *n.* **1.** A long-sleeved jacket-like garment used to bind the arms tightly against the body as a means of restraining a violent patient or prisoner. Also called "strait waistcoat". **2.** Anything that restricts or restrains like a straitjacket, such as a rule or institution. ~*tr.v.* **straitjacketed, -eting, -ets.** To restrict or restrain by or as if by confining in a straitjacket.

strait-laced (stráyt-láyst) *adj.* Excessively strict in behaviour, morality, or opinions; puritanical; prudish. [Originally referring to tightly laced dress, hence, strict, exacting.]

Straits Settlements. See Malaya, Federation of.

strake (strayk) *n.* **1.** *Nautical.* A single continuous line of planking or metal plating extending on a vessel's hull from stem to stern. **2.** Any of the curved sections making up the metal rim of a wooden wheel. [Middle English *strake,* perhaps "thing stretched", related to Old English *streccan,* to STRETCH.]

stra·mash (strə-másh) *n. Scottish.* A state of uproar or confusion. [Probably imitative.]

stra·mo·ni·um (strə-mōni-əm) *n.* **1.** A plant, the **thorn apple** *(see).* **2.** The dried poisonous leaves of the thorn apple, used as the source of the alkaloid, hyoscyamine. [New Latin, perhaps an alteration of Tatar *turman,* horse medicine.]

strand[1] (strand) *n.* **1.** Land bordering a body of water; especially, the area between tide marks. **2.** *Poetic.* A country or region. ~*v.* **stranded, stranding, strands.** —*tr.* **1.** To drive or force aground; beach. **2.** To bring into or leave in a difficult or helpless position: *The collapse of the airline left us stranded in New York.* —*intr.* To become stranded. [Middle English *strand,* Old English *strand,* shore, akin to Old Norse *strönd†.*]

strand[2] *n.* **1.** Any of the long stringlike pieces of material that are twisted together to form a rope, cable, or the like. **2.** Any single fibre, thread, or other filament: *a strand of hair.* **3. a.** A string of beads. **b.** The material on which they are strung. **4.** Anything that is plaited or twisted, such as a rope or a plait of hair. **5.** A single element forming part of an interwoven whole: *one of the strands in his complex narrative.* ~*tr.v.* **stranded, stranding, strands. 1.** To make or form (a rope or cable, for example) by twisting strands together. **2.** To break one or more of the strands in (a rope, cable, or the like). [Middle English *strond†.*]

strand line *n.* A shore line; especially, one marking an earlier and higher water level.

strange (straynj) *adj.* **stranger, strangest. 1.** Previously unknown; unfamiliar. **2.** Strikingly unusual; queer, unaccountable, or extraordinary. **3.** Not of one's own or a particular locality, environment, or kind; exotic. **4.** Inexperienced in or unacquainted with something: *still strange to the job.* **5.** Unwell or dizzy: *feeling strange.* **6.** *Literary.* Alien or foreign. **7.** *Physics.* **a.** Designating a type of quark with unit quantum number strangeness. **b.** Of or designating an elementary particle that contains one or more charmed quarks and no charmed antiquarks. ~*adv.* In a strange manner: *acting strange.* [Middle English *straunge,* from Old French *estrange,* from Latin *extrāneus,* foreign, strange, from *extrā,* outside, beyond.] —**strange·ly** *adv.*

Synonyms: strange, peculiar, odd, queer, quaint, outlandish, singular, eccentric.

strange·ness (stráynj-nəss, -niss) *n.* **1.** The quality of being strange. **2.** *Symbol* **S** *Physics.* A quantum number, a property of certain types of elementary particle, originally postulated to account for the long lifetime of kaons, sigma particles, and lambda particles. [Sense 2, from the original lack of understanding of the nature of the particles which it describes.]

stran·ger (stráynjər) *n.* **1.** A person whom one does not know, or does not know well. **2.** A foreigner, newcomer, or outsider. **3.** One who is unaccustomed to or unacquainted with something specified. Used with *to: no stranger to the bar.* **4.** A visitor or guest. **5.** A newborn baby. Used in the phrase *a little stranger.* **6.** *Law.* One who is neither privy nor party to an act, proceeding, or other form of business. [Middle English *straunger,* from Old French *estrangier,*

from Vulgar Latin *extrāneārius* (unattested), from Latin *extrāneus,* STRANGE.]

stran·gle (stráng-g'l) *v.* **-gled, -gling, -gles.** —*tr.* **1. a.** To kill by choking or suffocating; throttle. **b.** To kill by cutting off the oxygen supply of. **2.** To suppress, repress, or stifle. **3.** To inhibit the growth or action of; restrict: *strangled by convention.* —*intr.* To die or suffer from suffocation or strangulation; choke. [Middle English *stranglen,* from Old French *estrangler,* from Latin *strangulāre,* to STRANGULATE.] —**stran·gler** *n.*

stran·gle·hold (stráng-g'l-hōld) *n.* **1.** Powerful control that restricts or prevents freedom of thought or action. **2.** An illegal wrestling hold used to choke an opponent.

stran·gles (stráng-g'lz) *n.* Used with a singular verb. An infectious disease of horses and related animals, caused by the bacterium *Streptococcus equi* and characterised by nasal inflammation and abscesses in the mouth. [From Middle English *strangle* (singular), strangulation, from *stranglen,* to STRANGLE.]

stran·gu·late (stráng-gew-layt) *v.* **-lated, -lating, -lates.** —*tr.* **1.** *Pathology.* To compress, constrict, or obstruct (a tube, duct, intestine, or other part) so as to cut off the flow of blood, air, or other fluid. **2.** *Rare.* To strangle. —*intr.* To be or become strangled or constricted. [Latin *strangulāre,* from Greek *strangalan,* from *strangalē,* halter.] —**stran·gu·la·tion** (-láysh'n) *n.*

stran·gu·ry (stráng-gewr-i) *n.* Also **stran·gur·i·a** (-gèwr-i-ə). Slow, painful urination with spasms of the urethra and bladder. [Middle English, from Latin *strangūria,* from Greek *strangouria : stranx* (stem *strang-*), drop + -URIA.]

strap (strap) *n.* **1.** A flat, narrow strip of leather, canvas, or other material, usually fitted with a buckle or other adjustable fastener, and used for binding, securing, or supporting objects. **2.** A flat, metal band used for fastening or clamping objects together or into position. **3.** A narrow band formed into a loop for grasping with the hand. **4.** A strip of leather used for beating, especially as a punishment in schools. ~*tr.v.* **strapped, strapping, straps. 1.** To fasten or secure with a strap. **2.** To beat with a strap. **3.** To bind (a wound or injured limb, for example) with bandages. Often used with *up.* [Variant of STROP.]

strap·hang·er (stráp-hang-ər) *n.* A standing passenger, as on a bus or underground train, who grips a hanging strap for support. —**strap·hang·ing** *n.*

strap·less (stráp-ləss, -liss) *adj.* Without a strap or straps. Said especially of a dress or undergarment designed to leave the shoulders bare.

strap·pa·do (strə-paʹa-dō, stra-, -páy-) *n., pl.* **-does. 1.** A torture in which the victim's hands are tied behind his back and attached to a pulley by means of which he is pulled up off the ground and then dropped halfway down with a jerk. **2.** The apparatus so employed. [French *(e)strapade,* from Italian *strappata,* from *strappare,* to drag, from Old French *estraper,* variant of *estreper,* from Latin *extirpāre,* to pluck up by the stem: *ex-,* out + *stirps,* stem (see **stirps**).]

strapped (strapt) *adj. Informal.* Suffering from a shortage, especially of money: *strapped for cash.* [From STRAP (rare sense "to make penniless").]

strap·per (stráppər) *n.* A tall, sturdy person.

strap·ping (strápping) *adj. Informal.* Tall and sturdy.

Stras·bourg (stráz-burg, -boorg; *French* strass-bóor.) City in northeast France, lying close to the Franco-German border, and formerly part of Germany (1871–1919). Since 1949 it has been the seat of the Council of Europe. Its cathedral, built between the 11th and 15th centuries, is a notable example of Rhenish architecture.

strass (strass) *n.* A type of lead glass, **paste** *(see).* [German, invented by Josef *Strasser,* 18th-century German jeweller.]

stra·ta. Plural of **stratum.** See Usage note at **stratum.**

strat·a·gem (strátta-jəm, -jim, -jem) *n.* **1. a.** A military manoeuvre designed to deceive or surprise an enemy. **b.** Any trick or scheme used to gain an advantage. **2.** Deception; trickery. —See Synonyms at **artifice.** [French *stratagème,* from Latin *stratēgēma,* from Greek, "act of a general", from *stratēgein,* to be a general, from *stratēgos,* general : *stratos,* army + *agein,* to lead.]

stra·te·gic (strə-téejik, stra-) *adj.* Also **stra·te·gi·cal** (-'l). **1.** Of or pertaining to strategy. **2. a.** Dictated by or essential for the furtherance of a military or other strategy: *a strategic withdrawal.* **b.** Essential to the effective conduct of war. **c.** Designed to destroy at source the military and economic potential of an enemy: *strategic nuclear weapons.* —**stra·te·gi·cal·ly** *adv.*

stra·te·gics (strə-téejiks, stra-) *n.* Used with a singular verb. The art of strategy.

strat·e·gist (stráttəjist) *n.* One who is skilled in strategy.

strat·e·gy (stráttəji) *n., pl.* **-gies. 1.** The science or art of military command as applied to the overall planning and conduct of large-scale combat operations. Compare **tactics. 2.** A plan of action resulting from the practice of this science. **3.** The use of skilful planning to secure one's own advantage, as in politics, business, or personal relations. **4.** A plan or design for achieving one's aims. [French *stratégie,* from Greek *stratēgia,* office of a general, from *stratēgos,* general. See **stratagem.**]

Strat·ford-up·on-A·von (strátfərd-əp-on-áyv'n ‖ -awn-). Town in Warwickshire, central England, famous for its associations with William Shakespeare, who was born and died there. The Royal Shakespeare Theatre stages annual seasons of plays there from April to October.

strath (strath) *n. Scottish.* A steep-sided, flat-floored valley wider than a glen. [Scottish Gaelic *srath,* (mountain) valley.]

Strath·clyde Region (stráth-klī́d, strath-). An administrative region of west Scotland, formed in 1975 and comprising the former counties of Ayr, Bute, Dunbarton, Lanark, and Renfrew, with parts of Stirling and Argyll. Industries, including shipbuilding, mining, textiles, and distilling, are concentrated in the lower Clyde valley. Glasgow is the administrative centre.

strath·spey (strath-spáy, stráth-) *n., pl.* **-speys.** A type of Scottish reel, or the music that accompanies it. [After *Strathspey,* valley of the river SPEY.]

strati- *comb. form.* Indicates stratum or strata; for example, **stratigraphy.** [From STRATUM.]

stra·tic·u·late (strə-tíckew-lət, -lit, -layt) *adj.* Having thin strata. [New Latin *straticulus* (unattested), diminutive of STRATUM.] **—stra·tic·u·la·tion** (-láysh'n) *n.*

strat·i·fi·ca·tion (stráttifi-káysh'n) *n.* **1. a.** The act or process of stratifying. **b.** The state of being stratified. **2.** A stratified configuration.

strat·i·fi·ca·tion·al grammar (stráttifi-káysh'n'l) *n. Linguistics.* A theory of grammar that conceives of language in terms of a hierarchical system of related levels, ranging from the conceptual to the phonemic, each of which has its own rules.

strat·i·form (strátti-fawrm) *adj.* Having the form of strata.

strat·i·fy (strátti-fī) *v.* **-fied, -fying, -fies.** *—tr.* **1.** To form, arrange, or deposit in strata. **2.** To arrange or divide according to different levels of caste, class, or status: *a stratified society.* **3.** To preserve (seeds) by placing them between layers of moist sand or similar material. *—intr.* To become layered; develop physical or social strata. [French *stratifier,* from New Latin *stratificare* : STRATUM + Latin *facere,* to make, do.]

stra·tig·ra·phy (strə-tíggrəfi) *n.* The study of rock strata, especially of their distribution, deposition, and chronological succession. [STRATI- + -GRAPHY.] **—strat·i·graph·i·cal** (strátti-gráffik'l), **strat·i·graph·ic** *adj.* **—strat·i·graph·i·cal·ly** *adv.*

stra·toc·ra·cy (strə-tóckrə-si) *n., pl.* **-cies.** Government by the army. [Greek *stratos,* army + -CRACY.]

stra·to·cu·mu·lus (stráytō-kéwmew-ləss, stráttō-) *n., pl.* **-li** (-lī). A low-lying heavy cloud occurring at about 450 to 1 800 metres (1,500 to 6,000 feet) as rounded grey masses, often covering the sky, but sometimes with small breaks. [STRAT(US) + CUMULUS.]

strat·o·pause (strát-ō-pawz, -ə-) *n.* The boundary between the stratosphere and the mesosphere in the Earth's atmosphere, at a height where the air becomes so thin that there are not enough oxygen molecules to form ozone.

strat·o·sphere (stráttə-sfeer) *n.* The part of the atmosphere between the troposphere and the mesosphere, extending from a height of about 15 to 50 kilometres (about 9 to 30 miles), and having a temperature that increases with height to a maximum of about 0°C. [French *stratosphère* : STRAT(UM) + (ATM)OSPHERE.] **—strat·o·spher·ic** (-sférrik || -sféer-ik) *adj.*

stra·tum (stráa-təm, stráy- || *U.S. also* strá-) *n., pl.* **-ta** (-tə) or *rare* **-tums. 1.** *Geology.* **a.** A bed or layer of rock having the same composition throughout. **b.** A number of beds or layers of rock of the same kind of material. **2.** A horizontal layer of any material, especially one of several parallel layers arranged one on top of the other, such as: **a.** A layer of tissue or cells. **b.** Any of the layers making up the Earth's atmosphere. **c.** A layer in which the archaeological remains of a particular stage or period are deposited. **3.** A class or category regarded as occupying a level in a hierarchy: *the middle strata of society.* [New Latin, from Latin *strātum,* neuter of *strātus,* stretched out. See **stratus.**] **—stra·tal** *adj.*

Usage: The standard plural form is *strata*: *All strata of society have been affected. Stratums* and *stratas* are both occasionally heard, used by people who are unaware of the irregular status of this noun, but they have no standing in educated English. Likewise, the use of *strata* as a singular is not standard, though it is often heard: *One particular strata has been affected more than others.*

stra·tus (stráy-təss, stráa- || *U.S. also* strá-) *n., pl.* **-ti** (-tī). A low-altitude cloud usually occurring below 600 metres (about 2,000 feet), and typically resembling a layer of fog. [Latin *strātus,* past participle of *sternere,* to stretch out, extend.]

Strauss (strowss; *German* shtrowss), **Johann**[1], known as Johann Strauss the Elder (1804–49). Austrian violinist and composer. He composed many dances, especially waltzes, and is best known for his *Radetzky March*

Strauss, Johann[2], known as Johann Strauss the Younger (1825–99). Austrian composer and conductor. He is best known for his dance music, especially the waltzes which include *The Blue Danube* (1867), and his operettas, such as *Die Fledermaus* (1874).

Strauss, Richard (1864–1949). German composer and conductor. He is known chiefly for his symphonic poems which include *Till Eulenspiegel* (1895) and *Don Quixote* (1897), and his operas, among them *Salome* (1905) and *Der Rosenkavalier* (1911).

Stra·vin·sky (strə-vínski, stra-), **Igor Feodorovich** (1882–1971). Russian composer. His early ballet, *The Rite of Spring* (1913), caused a scandal at the time, but like many of his works has been recognised as one of the musical landmarks of the 20th century. His later pioneering works include the *Symphony of Psalms* (1930) and *The Rake's Progress* (1951).

straw (straw) *n.* **1. a.** Stalks of threshed grain used for thatching or as bedding for animals, or woven into hats, baskets, or other articles. Also used adjectivally: *a straw hat.* **b.** Any one such stalk. **2.** A slender tube used for sucking up a liquid. **3.** Something of minimal value or importance. **4.** A usually worthless expedient resorted to in desperation: *clutching at straws.* **—draw the short straw.** To be unluckily chosen to do something unpleasant. **—straw in the wind.** A slight hint of something to come.

~tr.v. **strawed, strawing, straws.** *Archaic.* To scatter; strew. [Middle English *strawe,* Old English *strēaw.*]

straw·ber·ry (stráw-bri, -bəri || -berri) *n., pl.* **-ries. 1.** Any of various low-growing plants of the genus *Fragaria,* having white flowers and red, fleshy, edible fruit. **2.** The fruit of any of these plants. **3.** A related plant, the barren strawberry, *Potentilla sterilis,* having strawberry-like flowers but dry fruit. [Middle English *strawberry,* Old English *strēawberige* : STRAW (possibly from the strawlike slender runners trailing on the ground) + BERRY.]

straw·ber·ry-blonde (stráw-bri-blónd, -bəri- || -berri-) *adj.* Reddish-blonde. Said of hair.

~n. A woman with strawberry-blonde hair.

strawberry mark *n.* A small, soft, reddish birthmark.

strawberry roan *n.* A horse having reddish hair mixed with white.

strawberry tree *n.* A tree, *Arbutus unedo,* native to southern Europe, having evergreen leaves and strawberry-like fruit.

straw·board (stráw-bawrd || -bōrd) *n.* A coarse yellow cardboard made of straw pulp.

straw boss *n. U.S. Informal.* A worker who acts as a boss or assistant foreman in addition to his regular duties.

straw man *n. U.S.* A **man of straw** *(see).*

straw poll *n.* An unofficial or impromptu poll taken to assess the trend of opinion on a candidate or issue. Also *chiefly U.S.* "straw vote".

Straw·son (stráwss'n), **Sir Peter (Frederick)** (1919–). British philosopher. In *Introduction to Logical Theory* (1952), he examines the general nature of formal logic. Other works include *Philosophical Logic* (1967) and *Freedom and Resentment* (1974).

straw wine *n.* A dessert wine made from grapes that have been dried on straw.

straw·worm (stráw-wurm) *n.* A **caddis worm** *(see).*

stray (stray) *intr.v.* **strayed, straying, strays. 1. a.** To wander from a given place or group or beyond established limits; roam. **b.** To become lost. **2.** To rove, wander about, or meander. **3.** To deviate from a course that is regarded as right or moral; go astray; err. **4.** To digress or wander from a given subject or line of thought. —See Synonyms at **wander.**

~n. One that has strayed; especially, a domestic animal at large or that has been lost.

~adj. **1.** Straying or having strayed; lost or at large. **2. a.** Scattered, random, or isolated: *a few stray cars.* **b.** Not in its proper place or context: *brushed back some stray hairs.* [Middle English *straien,* from Old French *estraier,* from Vulgar Latin *estragāre* (unattested) : Latin *extrā-,* outside of + *vagārī,* to wander, roam, from *vagus,* wandering, VAGUE.] **—stray·er** *n.*

streak (streek) *n.* **1.** An irregular line, mark, or band differentiated by colour or texture from its surroundings. **2.** A trace or element of a particular quality or characteristic; a strain: *a mosochistic streak.* **3.** *Informal.* A brief stretch or run: *a losing streak.* **4.** *Geology & Chemistry.* The colour of the powder of a mineral, used as a distinguishing characteristic. **5.** A single discharge of atmospheric lightning. Also used adjectivally: *streak lightning.* **6.** An act of streaking. **7.** *Biology.* A growth of microorganisms produced by streaking.

~v. **streaked, streaking, streaks.** *—tr.* To mark with a streak or streaks; stripe; striate. *—intr.* **1.** To form streaks or become streaked. **2.** To move at high speed; rush. **3.** To run naked or partly naked through or across a public place as a way of attracting attention or amusing the crowd. **4.** *Biology.* To inoculate a culture medium with microorganisms by drawing a contaminated wire along the surface. [Middle English *strick(e),* Old English *strica.*] **—streak·er** *n.*

streak·y (stréeki) *adj.* **-ier, -iest. 1.** Marked with, characterised by, or occurring in streaks; streaked. **2.** Consisting of alternate streaks of meat and fat. Said of bacon. **3.** Variable or uneven in character or quality. **—streak·i·ly** *adv.* **—streak·i·ness** *n.*

stream (streem) *n.* **1.** A body of running water; especially, such a body moving over the earth's surface in a channel or bed, as a small natural watercourse. **2.** A steady current in such a body of water. **3.** A steady current of any fluid. **4. a.** A steady flow or procession, as of people or traffic, moving in the same direction. **b.** An uninterrupted succession or outpouring: *a stream of invective.* **5.** A prevailing trend or general drift, as of opinion, thought, or history. **6.** In many schools, any of the sets into which children of a given age-group are divided, usually according to ability. In this sense, compare **band. —on stream.** In or into production.

~v. **streamed, streaming, streams.** *—intr.* **1.** To flow in or as if in a stream. **2.** To pour forth or give off a stream; flow. Often used with *with*: *eyes streaming with tears.* **3.** To move or proceed in large numbers. **4.** To extend, wave, or float outwards in the air: *The banner streamed in the breeze.* **5.** To leave a continuous trail of light. *—tr.* **1.** To emit, discharge, or exude. **2.** *Chiefly British.* To group (schoolchildren) into streams. [Middle English *streme,* Old English *strēam.*] **—stream·y** *adj.*

stream·er (stréemər) *n.* **1.** A long, narrow flag, banner, or pennant. **2. a.** Any long, narrow pendant strip of ribbon, coloured paper, or other material. **b.** Such a strip that is wound into a tight roll that unwinds when thrown, used for fun by children and as party decorations. **3.** A shaft or ray of light extending upwards from the hori-

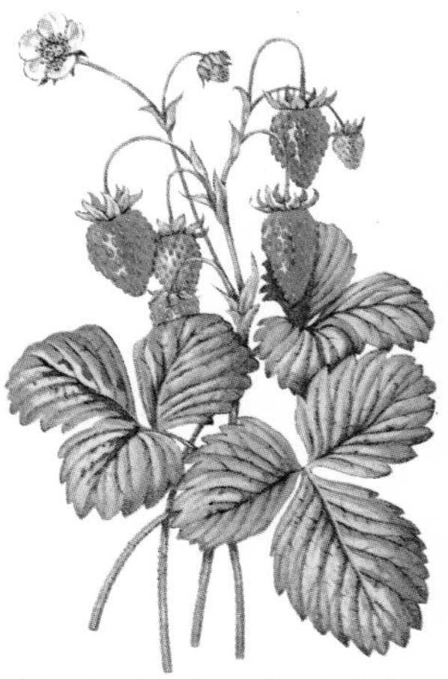

strawberries *The edible fruit of a ground-creeping plant of the genus* Fragaria. *Most cultivated varieties are said to have been developed from 18th-century hybrids between two American species.*

zon. **4.** A newspaper headline that runs across a full page; a banner. **5.** A long, narrow, luminous electrical discharge, as in the aurora.

stream·line (stréem-līn) *n.* **1.** A line in a fluid such that the tangent at every point on the line is aligned with the fluid's local velocity. **2.** The path of any one particle in a flowing fluid. **3.** Any contour of a body constructed so as to offer minimum resistance to a fluid flow.

~*tr.v.* **streamlined, -lining, -lines.** To make streamlined.

stream·lined (stréem-līnd) *adj.* **1.** Designed, constructed, or shaped so as to offer the least resistance to fluid flow. **2.** Simplified, modernised, or reorganised so as to improve efficiency. **3.** Having simple, smooth, or elegant contours.

streamline flow *n.* A flow characterised by lack of turbulence or interruption. Compare **laminar flow, turbulent flow.**

stream of consciousness *n.* **1.** *Psychology.* The conscious experience of an individual regarded as a continuous rather than a discrete series of events. **2.** A literary technique in which the thoughts and feelings of a character in a novel are recorded as they develop, by means of first-person narration. Compare **interior monologue.**

street (stréet) *n. Abbr.* **st., St. 1.** A public way or thoroughfare in a city, town, or village, usually including the pavements and the buildings lining either or both sides. **2.** Such a roadway for vehicles apart from the buildings and pavements. **3.** The people living, working, or habitually gathering in or along such a roadway: *The whole street knew about it.* **—streets ahead of.** *Informal.* Far superior to. **—the Street.** *U.S.* The financial area around the Stock Exchange in Wall Street, New York. **—up (one's) street.** *Informal.* Compatible with one's interests, tastes, or abilities. **—walk the streets. 1.** To wander through the streets of a town, especially in search of work or accommodation. **2.** To seek or solicit clients in the street. Used of a prostitute.

~*adj.* Pertaining to, taking place in, or found on a street or the streets of a town: *street life; a street party.* [Middle English *strete,* Old English *strǣt,* from West Germanic *strāta* (unattested), from Late Latin *strāta,* from Latin *strātus,* past participle of *sternere,* to extend, stretch out.]

Usage: *Streets* are usually in towns, and *roads* in the country, but in British English in particular there are many exceptions, and it is not possible to state simple rules which explain why *road, avenue, way,* and the like are used. American English often omits the term in speech: *I live at 360 Parker* (that is, Parker Street). British English also uses *in* while American English uses *on*: *I live in Parker Street.*

street Arab *n.* A homeless child who lives in the street of a city; an urchin. Also called "Arab".

street·car (stréet-kaar) *n. U.S.* A **tram** *(see).*

street·light (stréet-līt) *n.* Any of a series of lights that are attached to tall poles spaced at intervals along a public thoroughfare, and are illuminated automatically from dusk to dawn.

street value *n.* The retail value of an illegal commodity, calculated on the basis of the price at which it is sold to the consumer (its *street price*): *cocaine with a street value of £200,000.*

street·walk·er (stréet-wawkər) *n.* A prostitute who solicits in the streets. **—street·walk·ing** *n.*

street·wise (stréet-wīz) *adj.* Experienced in the ways of rough urban areas; capable of surviving or being successful on the streets.

Strei·sand (strī́-sand), **Barbra** (1942–). American singer and actress. Her stage and film performances include *Funny Girl* (1968), *Hello Dolly* (1969), and *A Star is Born* (1976).

stre·lit·zi·a (stre-lítsi-ə, stri-) *n.* Any plant of the South African genus *Strelitzia,* which includes the bird-of-paradise flower. [Named in honour of Charlotte of Mecklenburg-*Strelitz* (1744–1818), queen of England.]

strength (streng-th, strengk-th || strenth) *n.* **1.** The state, quality, or property of being strong; physical power. **2. a.** The power of resisting force, attack, strain, or stress; durability, solidity, or impregnability. **b.** The ability to maintain a moral or intellectual position firmly, especially in the face of opposition or temptation: *strength of character.* **3.** Capacity or potential for effective action: *a show of strength.* **4.** Military capability in terms of manpower and material resources: *the strength of the fleet.* **5.** The number of personnel constituting the normal or ideal complement of an organisation: *The police force is below strength.* **6.** The degree of intensity, force, effectiveness, or potency in terms of some particular property; for example: **a.** The degree of concentration, distillation, or saturation. **b.** Operative effectiveness or potency. **c.** Intensity, as of sound or light. **d.** The degree of ardour or vehemence, as of feelings or language: *tried to gauge the strength of support for his idea.* **7. a.** A source of power or force; that which makes strong. **b.** An attribute or quality of particular worth or utility; an asset. **8.** Effective or binding force; efficacy: *the strength of an argument.* **9.** Firmness of or a continuous rising tendency in prices, as on the stock market. **—go from strength to strength.** To become ever more powerful or successful. **—on the strength of.** Relying or depending on; based on. [Middle English *strengthe,* Old English *strengthu.*]

Synonyms: *strength, power, might, force, energy, potency.*

strength·en (stréng-thən, stréngk- || strén-) *v.* **-ened, -ening, -ens.** *—tr.* To make strong or stronger. *—intr.* To become strong or stronger. **—strength·en·er** *n.*

stren·u·ous (strénnew-əss) *adj.* **1.** Requiring or characterised by great effort or exertion: *a strenuous task.* **2.** Vigorously active; energetic, persistent, or unremitting: *strenuous opposition.* [Latin *strēnuus*†, brisk, nimble, quick.] **—stren·u·os·i·ty** (-óssəti), **stren·u·ous·ness** *n.* **—stren·u·ous·ly** *adv.*

strep (strep) *n.* **1.** Sore throat caused by infection with bacteria of the genus *Streptococcus.* **2.** A streptococcus. [Shortened form.]

strepto- *comb. form.* Indicates: **1.** A twisted chain; for example, **streptococcus. 2.** Streptococcus; for example, **streptokinase.** [Greek *streptos,* twisted, from *strephein,* to turn.]

strep·to·coc·cal (strépt-ə-kóck'l, -ō-) *adj.* Also **strep·to·coc·cic** (-kóksik). Of, pertaining to, or caused by a streptococcus.

strep·to·coc·cus (strépt-ə-kók-əss, -ō-) *n., pl.* **-cocci** (-sī, -ī, -ee). Any of various round to ovoid, often pathogenic bacteria of the genus *Streptococcus,* occurring in pairs or chains. [New Latin : STREPTO- + -COCCUS.]

strep·to·ki·nase (strépt-ə-kī́n-ayz, -ō-, -ayss) *n.* A proteolytic enzyme derived from haemolytic streptococci, capable of dissolving fibrin and used to dissolve blood clots. [STREPTO- + KINASE.]

strep·to·ly·sin (strépt-ə-lī́-sin, -ō-) *n.* An antigenic haemolysin derived from strains of *Streptococcus pyogenes.* [STREPTO- + -LYS(IS) + -IN.]

strep·to·my·cin (strépt-ə-mī́-sin, -ō-) *n.* An antibiotic, $C_{21}H_{39}N_7O_{12}$, produced from the bacterium *Streptomyces griseus* and used medicinally to combat various bacteria, especially tuberculosis. [New Latin *Streptomyces* : STREPTO- + Greek *mukēs,* fungus + -IN.]

strep·to·thri·cin (strépt-ə-thrī́-sin, -ō-, -thríssin) *n.* An antibiotic, $C_{19}H_{34}N_8O_8$, isolated from the bacterium *Streptomyces lavendulae* (or *Actinomyces lavendulae*) and active against both Gram-positive and Gram-negative bacteria. [New Latin *Streptothrix,* a genus of bacteria : STREPTO- + Greek *thrix,* hair + -IN.]

Stre·se·mann (shtráyzə-man), **Gustav** (1878–1929). German statesman. As minister of foreign affairs (1923–29), he negotiated the Locarno Pact (1925) of mutual security with France and Belgium, and secured Germany's entry (1926) into the League of Nations. He shared the Nobel peace prize with Aristide Briand (1926).

stress (stress) *n.* **1.** Importance, significance, or emphasis placed upon something: *laid great stress on the need for economy.* **2. a.** The degree of force with which a sound or syllable is spoken. **b.** The emphasis placed upon the sound or syllable spoken loudest in a given word or phrase. **3. a.** The relative emphasis given a syllable or word in verse in accordance with a metrical pattern. **b.** A syllable receiving a strong relative emphasis. **4.** *Music.* An accent. **5.** *Physics.* An applied force or system of forces that tends to strain or deform a body, measured by the force acting per unit area. **6. a.** A mentally or emotionally disruptive or disquieting influence. **b.** A state of tension or distress caused by such an influence.

~*tr.v.* **stressed, stressing, stresses. 1.** To place phonetic emphasis on; accent. **2.** To attribute particular importance to; emphasise. **3.** To subject to mental, physical, or mechanical stress. [Middle English *stresse,* hardship, distress, from Old French *estresse,* narrowness, from Vulgar Latin *strictia* (unattested), from Latin *strictus,* STRICT.] **—stress·ful** *adj.*

-stress *n. suffix.* Indicates a feminine agent; for example, **seamstress.** [-ST(ER) + -ESS.]

stretch (strech) *v.* **stretched, stretching, stretches.** *—tr.* **1.** To lengthen, widen, or distend by pulling: *stretch a woollen sweater.* **2.** To cause to extend from one place to another or across a given space. **3.** To make taut; tighten. **4.** To reach or put forth; extend. Often used with *out*: *stretched out his hand.* **5.** To extend (oneself) at full length, usually in a prone position. Often used with *out.* **6.** To straighten (oneself) by extending the limbs or flexing the muscles. **7.** To make do with or eke out: *stretch the budget by careful spending.* **8.** To extend or enlarge (the scope of a law or meaning of a word, for example) beyond the usual or proper limits. **9. a.** To make the fullest possible use of or demands upon (one's intellectual or material resources): *felt that he wasn't being stretched in the job.* **b.** To subject to unreasonable or intolerable strain: *stretch one's patience.* **10.** To wrench or strain (a muscle or ligament, for example); sprain. **11.** To prolong: *stretch out an argument.* *—intr.* **1. a.** To become lengthened, widened, or distended. **b.** To admit of being stretched; be elastic. **2.** To extend or reach over a particular distance or area or in a particular direction: *Ahead of us stretched the plain.* **3.** To lie down at full length. Usually used with *out.* **4.** To straighten oneself out by extending the limbs or flexing the muscles. **5.** To reach, usually with one's hand. Often used with *out.* **6.** To allow for or include something specified. Used with *to*: *My salary won't stretch to luxuries.* **7.** To extend over a given period of time: *This story stretches over two centuries.* **—stretch (one's) legs.** To stroll about after sitting for a long time.

~*n.* **1.** The act of stretching or the state of being stretched. **2.** The extent or scope to which something can be stretched; elasticity. **3.** A continuous or unbroken length, area, or expanse: *a stretch of motorway.* **4.** A straight section of a racecourse or track, especially that section leading to the finishing line. **5. a.** A continuous period of time, especially considered as occupied by a particular activity or marked by a particular state: *would work for three days at a stretch.* **b.** *Slang.* A term of imprisonment: *a two-year stretch.* **—by no stretch of the imagination.** By no means; not at all.

~*adj.* Capable of being stretched; elastic: *a stretch sock.* [Middle English *strecchen,* Old English *streccan,* to extend, from Germanic *strakkjan* (unattested).] **—stretch·a·ble** *adj.* **—stretch·y** *adj.*

stretch·er (stréchər) *n.* **1.** A kind of portable bed, usually consisting of canvas stretched over a frame, used to transport the sick, wounded, or dead. **2.** Any of various devices used for stretching and shaping, such as the wooden framework upon which canvas is

PRONUNCIATION KEY

a, trap; aa, father; ai, fair;
ar, star; aw, lawn; ay, play;
b, bb, stab; rubber;
ch, church; ck, ticket;
d, dd, dead; ladder; e, dress;
ee, bee; er, defer; ew, few;
ewr, pure; ə, about;
ər, letter; f, ff, fife; differ;
g, gg, giggle; h, hat; i, kit;
ī, price; īr, fire; j, judge;
k, kick; l, ll, let; 'l, needle;
m, mm, man; n, nn, no;
'n, sudden; ng, thing; o, lot;
ō, no; ŏŏ, foot; ōō, shoe;
oor, poor; ow, cow;
owr, hour; oy, boy;
p, pp, pepper; r, rr, red;
s, ss, sauce; sh, ship;
t, tt, totter; th, thick; th, this;
smooth; u, cut; ur, turn;
v, vv, valve; w, wet; y, yes;
z, zz, zebra; zh, vision;
pleasure

IN FOREIGN WORDS:

aN, oN, Saint-Saëns;
hl, Llanelli; Hluhluwe;
kh, loch; lough; Khaled

STRESS MARK:

ín-sīt, insight; in-sī́t, incite

stretched for an oil painting. **3.** A usually horizontal tie beam or brace serving to support or extend a framework. **4.** A brick or stone laid parallel to the face of a wall. Compare **header**. **5.** *Australian, N.Z., & South African.* A camp bed.

stretch·er-bear·er (stréchər-bair-ər) *n.* One who helps carry a stretcher or litter.

stretch marks *pl.n.* Whitish lines on the skin of the thighs, abdomen, or breasts, appearing especially as the result of stretching during pregnancy.

stret·to (strét-ō) *n., pl.* **-ti** (-ee) or **-tos**. *Music.* **1.** A close succession or overlapping of voices in a fugue, especially in the final section. **2.** A final section, as of an oratorio, performed with an acceleration in tempo to produce a climax. Also called "stretta".
~*adv. Music.* In a quicker time. Used as a direction. [Italian, "tight", from Latin *strictus,* STRICT.]

strew (strōō || strew) *tr.v.* **strewn** (strōōn || strewn) or **strewed, strewing, strews.** **1.** To spread here and there; scatter; sprinkle. **2.** To cover (a surface) with things scattered or sprinkled. **3.** To be or become dispersed over (a surface). [Middle English *strewen,* Old English *strēowian.*]

strewth. Variant of **struth**.

stri·a (strī-ə) *n., pl.* **striae** (-ee). **1.** A thin, narrow groove or channel. **2.** *Architecture.* A thin band between the grooves on a column. **3.** A thin line or band, especially any one of several that are parallel or close together, and share some distinctive feature such as colour or composition. [Latin, furrow, channel.]

stri·ate (strī-ət, -it, -ayt) *adj.* Also **stri·at·ed** (strī-áytid || strī-aytid). Marked with striae; striped, grooved, or ridged.
~*tr.v.* **striated, -ating, -ates.** To mark with striae. [Latin *striātus,* past participle of *striāre,* to make furrows, from *stria,* furrow, STRIA.]

striated muscle *n.* Muscle consisting of elongated, transversely striated fibres, often operating under voluntary control. Also called "skeletal muscle", "striped muscle".

stri·a·tion (strī-áysh'n) *n.* **1.** The state of being striated or having striae. **2.** An arrangement of striae. **3.** A stria.

strick·en (strícken) *adj.* **1.** Struck or wounded, as by a projectile. **2.** Afflicted with something overwhelming, such as strong emotion, disease, or trouble. Often used in combination: *conscience-stricken; grief-stricken.* **3.** Having the contents made even with the top of a measuring device or container; level. [Past participle of STRIKE.]

strick·le (strick'l) *n.* **1.** An instrument used to level off grain or other material in a measure; a strike. **2.** A foundry tool used to shape a mould in sand or loam. **3.** A tool for sharpening scythes.
~*tr.v.* **strickled, -ling, -les.** To apply a strickle to (sand in a mould, for example). [Middle English *strikelle,* Old English *stricel.*]

strict (strikt) *adj.* **stricter, strictest.** **1.** Precise; accurate; exact. **2.** Complete; absolute; maintained without exception or deviation: *strict hygiene.* **3.** Imposing an exacting discipline; allowing no indulgence or relaxation; not permissive: *strict standards.* **4.** Rigidly conforming to a particular code or norm: *a strict Muslim.* **5.** *Botany.* Stiff, narrow, and upright. —See Synonyms at **severe**. [Latin *strictus,* tight, narrow, from the past participle of *stringere,* to draw tight, tighten.] —**strict·ly** *adv.* —**strict·ness** *n.*

stric·ture (stríkchər) *n.* **1.** Something that restrains, limits, or restricts. **2.** An adverse remark or criticism; censure. **3.** *Pathology.* An abnormal narrowing of a duct or passage. [Middle English, from Latin *strictūra,* contraction, from *strictus,* STRICT.]

stride (strīd) *v.* **strode** (strōd) or *obsolete* **strid** (strid), **stridden** (strídd'n) or *obsolete* **strid, striding, strides.** —*intr.* **1.** To walk with long steps, especially in a hasty or purposeful manner. **2.** To take a single long step, as in passing over an obstruction. —*tr.* **1.** To stride over, along, or through. **2.** To straddle; bestride.
~*n.* **1.** The act of striding. **2. a.** A single long step. **b.** The distance travelled in such a step. **3. a.** A single coordinated movement of the four legs of a horse or other animal, completed when the legs are returned to their initial relative position. **b.** The distance travelled in such a cycle of movements. **4.** A progressive development; an advance: *making great strides.* **5.** *Plural. Australian Informal.* Trousers. —**take in (one's) stride.** To cope with (an unfamiliar situation, for example) without effort or difficulty. [Stride, strode (or strid), stridden; Middle English *striden, strode* (or *stride*), *stridden,* Old English *strīdan, strād* (singular, only in *bestrād*), *stridon* (plural, unattested), *striden* (unattested), from Germanic *strīdan* (unattested).] —**strid·er** *n.*

stri·dent (strīd'nt) *adj.* **1.** Loud, harsh, and grating; shrill. **2.** Having a disagreeably assertive or insistent quality. [Latin *strīdēns* (stem *strīdent-*), present participle of *strīdēre,* to make a harsh sound.] —**stri·dence, stri·den·cy** *n.* —**stri·dent·ly** *adv.*

stri·dor (strīd-ər, -awr) *n.* **1.** A strident sound. **2.** *Pathology.* A harsh, high-pitched sound in inhalation or exhalation. [Latin *strīdor,* from *strīdēre,* to make a harsh sound.]

strid·u·late (striddew-layt) *intr.v.* **-lated, -lating, -lates.** To produce a shrill grating or creaking sound; chirp. Used especially of insects such as crickets. [Latin *strīdulus,* creaking, STRIDULOUS.] —**strid·u·la·tion** (-láysh'n) *n.* —**strid·u·la·to·ry** (-laytəri, -lə-tri) *adj.*

strid·u·lous (stríddewləss) *adj.* **1.** Making or characterised by a strident sound or chirp. **2.** Of or affected with stridor. [Latin *strīdulus,* creaking, from *strīdēre,* to make a harsh sound.]

strife (strīf) *n.* **1.** Heated, often violent dissension; a state of bitter conflict. **2.** A struggle between rivals; a dispute or conflict. **3.** *Rare.* Earnest endeavour or striving. —See Synonyms at **discord**. [Middle English *strif,* from Old French *estrif.*]

strig·il (stríjil) *n.* **1.** An instrument used in ancient Greece and Rome for scraping the skin after a bath. **2.** A structure on the first leg of certain insects, such as bees, used for cleaning the antennae. [Latin *strigilis,* from *stringere,* to draw tight.]

stri·gose (strī-gōz, -gōss) *adj.* **1.** *Zoology.* Marked with fine, close-set grooves or streaks. **2.** *Botany.* Having stiff, closely pressed hairs or bristles. [New Latin *strigosus,* from Latin *striga,* swath, furrow.]

Strij·dom (stráydəm), **Johannes Gerhardus** (1893–1958). National Party prime minister of South Africa (1954–58), noted for his determined maintenance of the policy of apartheid.

strike (strīk) *v.* **struck** (struk), **struck** or **stricken** (strícken), **striking, strikes.** —*tr.* **1. a.** To hit sharply or forcefully, as with the hand or fist, or with a weapon or implement. **b.** To inflict (a blow). **c.** To send by means of a forceful blow: *struck the ball to the boundary.* **2. a.** To collide with or crash into: *struck the rocks and quickly sank.* **b.** To cause to hit sharply or forcefully; dash. **3.** To bring into a specified condition by or as if by a blow: *struck him dead.* **4. a.** To launch a military attack upon; assault. **b.** *Archaic.* To do (battle). **5.** To afflict suddenly, as with disease or impairment. **6.** To wound with the fangs. Used of a snake. **7.** To hook (a fish) that has taken the bait. **8.** To produce or impress by stamping, printing, or punching: *strike a medallion.* **9.** To play or produce by hitting a key on a musical instrument: *strike a B flat.* **10.** To indicate (the time) by a percussive sound: *The clock struck nine.* **11. a.** To produce (a flame, light, or spark) by friction. **b.** To cause to ignite by friction: *strike a match.* **12.** To delete, expunge, or remove by or as if by the stroke of a pen. Usually used with *off, out,* or *through.* **13.** To come upon, usually as the result of a search; discover: *struck gold.* **14.** To reach; fall upon: *A bright light struck her face.* **15.** To come suddenly to the mind of; occur to: *It struck me that the whole thing was a hoax.* **16. a.** To make a particular impression upon; seem to be to: *How do the new arrangements strike you? struck me as odd.* **b.** To make a powerful impression upon: *We were struck by his obvious sincerity.* **17.** To cause (an emotion) to penetrate deeply: *struck terror into their hearts.* **18. a.** To make or conclude (a bargain). **b.** To achieve or produce, as by careful calculation or contrivance: *strike a balance.* **19.** To fall into or assume (a pose, for example). **20.** *Nautical.* **a.** To haul down (a mast or sail). **b.** To lower (a flag or sail) in salute or surrender. **c.** To lower (cargo) into a hold. **21.** To remove (theatrical properties or scenery, for example) from the stage or other playing area. **22.** To take down and pack up the tents of (a camp). **23.** To level or smooth (a measure, as of grain); strickle. **24.** To put forth or send down (roots). **25.** To constitute (a jury) using a procedure whereby each party may eliminate an equal number of nominees. —*intr.* **1. a.** To deal a blow or blows with or as if with the fist or a weapon; hit. **b.** To occur or appear with devastating effect, as if dealing a blow: *All was going well when tragedy struck.* **2.** To aim a stroke or blow. **3.** To make contact suddenly or violently; collide. **4.** To begin or deliver an attack: *struck at daybreak; strikes at the roots of our democratic institutions.* **5.** To pierce; penetrate. Used chiefly of wind, cold, or damp. **6.** To jerk the line in order to hook a fish that has taken the bait. **7. a.** To make a percussive sound. **b.** To be indicated by sounds: *The hour has struck.* **8.** To become ignited. **9.** To discover something suddenly or unexpectedly. Used with *on* or *upon.* **10.** To proceed, especially in a new direction; set out; head. Often used with *off* or *out.* **11.** To engage in a strike as a form of protest or to support a demand. —See Synonyms at **affect**. —**strike it rich.** To gain sudden wealth. —**strike off. 1.** To remove the name of (a doctor or solicitor, for example) from a professional register, as for misconduct. **2.** To print. —**strike up. 1.** To start to play or sound vigorously: *The band struck up a waltz.* **2.** To initiate (a friendship, for example).
~*n.* **1.** An act or gesture of striking; a hit or thrust. **2.** An attack; especially, a military air attack upon a single group of targets. **3. a.** A cessation of work by employees in support of demands made upon their employer, as for higher pay or improved conditions. **b.** Any cessation of normal activity undertaken as a form of protest: *a hunger strike.* **4. a.** A sudden discovery, as of a precious mineral. **b.** Any sudden or unexpected piece of good luck. **5.** A pull on a fishing line by which the fish is hooked. **6.** In cricket, the position of being the batsman who is to face the bowling: *kept the strike by scoring off the last ball of the over.* **7.** In baseball, a pitched ball that is counted against the batter, especially one swung at and missed. **8.** In tenpin bowling, the knocking down of all the pins with the first bowl of a frame. **9.** *Geology.* The direction of a horizontal line in the plane of an inclined structural feature such as a rock bed or vein. **10.** A strickle. [Strike, struck (earlier stroke), stricken (or struck); Middle English *striken, strok* (or *strak*), *striken,* Old English *strīcan,* to stroke, rub, *strāc, stricen.*]

strike·bound (strīk-bownd) *adj.* Closed, immobilised, or slowed down by a strike.

strike·break·er (strīk-braykər) *n.* One who works or provides an employer with workers during a strike. —**strike·break·ing** *n.*

strike fault *n. Geology.* A fault in the Earth's crust parallel to the strike of the rock strata.

strike out *intr.v.* **1.** To proceed or begin with vigorous effort: *struck out on his own.* **2.** In baseball, to be retired after failing to hit three pitched balls. —*tr.v.* In baseball, to retire (a batter) by the recording of three strikes.

strike·out (strīk-owt) *n.* An act of striking out in baseball.

strik·er (strīkər) *n.* **1.** An employee who is on strike against his employer. **2.** Any device for striking, such as the clapper in a bell or the firing pin in a gun. **3.** In soccer, an attacking player who re-

mains close to his opponents' goal in order to capitalise on any scoring opportunity. **4.** In cricket, the batsman who has the strike.
strike-slip fault (strĭk-slĭp) *n. Geology.* A fault in which the dominant movement on the fault plane is horizontal. Also called a "transcurrent fault", "tear fault".
strik·ing (strīkĭng) *adj.* Making a powerful impression upon the mind or senses, especially because unusually attractive or prominent. **—strik·ing·ly** *adv.* **—strik·ing·ness** *n.*
striking circle *n.* In hockey, the semicircle area in front of the goal from which all scoring shots must be made. Also called "circle".
striking distance *n.* **1.** A distance over which it is possible to deliver an attack. **2.** A distance which is easily travelled over: *within striking distance of the coast.*
Strind·berg (strĭnd-bĕrg), **(Johan) August** (1849–1912). Swedish dramatist and novelist. He was a leading exponent of psychological realism in drama. His plays include *The Father* (1887), *Miss Julie* (1888), and *The Dance of Death* (1901). His best known novels are *The Red Room* (1879) and *The Ghost Sonata* (1907).
Strine (strīn) *n.* English in a form used in Australia, characterised

by a broad accent and picturesque vocabulary. Used humorously. *~adj. Informal.* Australian. [Exaggerated rendering of the Australian pronunciation of *Australian.*]
string (strĭng) *n.* **1.** A cord, thicker than thread and usually made of twisted fibres, used for fastening, tying, or lacing. **2.** Anything shaped into a long, thin line. **3.** A tough plant fibre, such as one running along the side of a pod. **4.** A set of objects threaded together: *a string of beads.* **5.** A continuous series of related acts, events, or items: *a string of excuses.* **6. a.** A set of animals, especially racehorses, belonging to a single owner; a stable. **b.** A group of businesses belonging to a single owner. **7.** A player or group of players having a specified ranking according to ability: *plays in goal for the second string.* **8.** *Music.* **a.** A cord stretched across the sounding board of an instrument, that is struck, plucked, or bowed to produce notes. **b.** *Plural.* Instruments collectively that have such strings; especially, the instruments of the violin family. **c.** *Plural.* Members of an orchestra who play these instruments. **9.** Any of the cords arranged in a crisscross pattern in a sports racquet. **10.** *Architecture.* **a.** A stringboard. **b.** A stringcourse. **11.** *Informal.* A limit-

MUSIC PRODUCED BY THE VIBRATION OF STRINGS

One simple principle is used in a large family of musical instruments

Stringed instruments produce their sound by the vibrations of strings made of gut, wire, silk, or nylon. The strings may be vibrated by bowing (violin), plucking with the fingers (guitar), or striking with hammers (dulcimer). Pitch is most frequently altered by shortening the length of a vibrating string, which then produces a higher note. Stringed instruments differ widely in size, and methods of construction, and their range of sounds is therefore enormous. Modern instruments have been developed over several centuries, and many early types are no longer played.

In an orchestra, the four main stringed instruments –

the violin, the viola, the violoncello (generally called the cello), and the double bass – are all members of the violin family. Each consists of a soundbox to which is attached a projecting neck. Four strings of different thicknesses are stretched from a tailpiece, over a wooden bridge on the lower part of the soundbox to the far end of the neck. The strings are stopped along the neck by the player's left hand to produce different notes. The strings are tuned by pegs at the end of the neck which tighten or slacken the tension and so raise or lower the note. A bow is drawn across the strings to produce vibrations which are transmitted by the bridge to the

soundbox where they are amplified to produce sound. The modern bow is a tapered, inward-curving stick with horsehair stretched across it.

The viol is not commonly played today but the harp is often found in orchestras. The harp has the largest range of all orchestral instruments and is constructed with the soundbox forming one side of a triangle across which the strings are stretched. The strings are plucked with the fingers. The piano is a development of the harp, but is normally classed as a keyboard instrument. Because of their size, the harp, cello, and double bass are played resting on the ground.

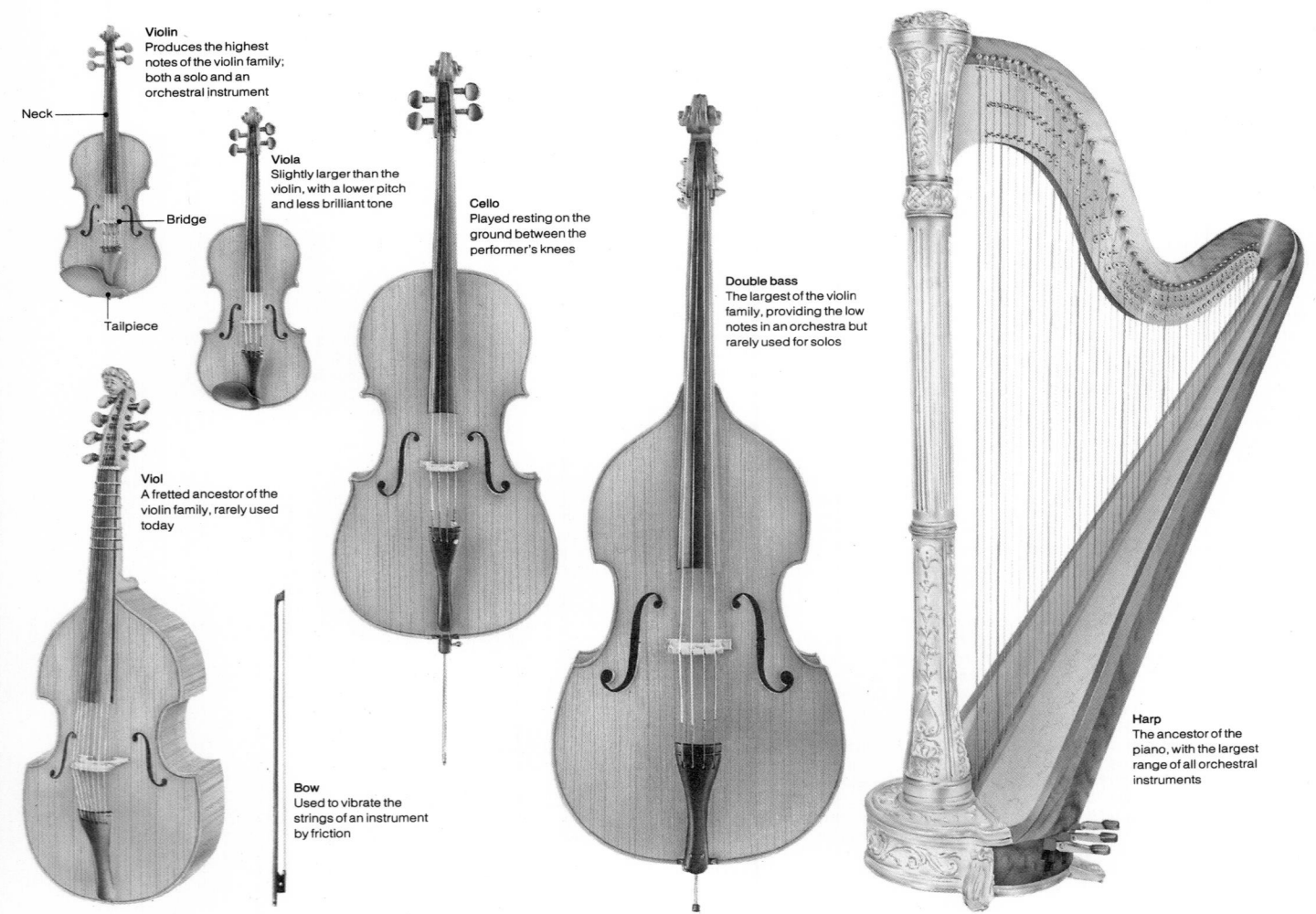

Violin
Produces the highest notes of the violin family; both a solo and an orchestral instrument

Neck

Viola
Slightly larger than the violin, with a lower pitch and less brilliant tone

Bridge

Tailpiece

Cello
Played resting on the ground between the performer's knees

Double bass
The largest of the violin family, providing the low notes in an orchestra but rarely used for solos

Viol
A fretted ancestor of the violin family, rarely used today

Bow
Used to vibrate the strings of an instrument by friction

Harp
The ancestor of the piano, with the largest range of all orchestral instruments

ing or hidden condition: *a gift with no strings attached.* —See Synonyms at **series.** —**on a string.** Totally under someone's control. —**pull strings.** To use one's influence or influential connections, often in secret, to gain an advantage.

~*adj.* Made of string or having a string or a mesh of strings: *a string bag.*

~*v.* **strung** (strung), **stringing, strings.** —*tr.* **1.** To fit or furnish with a string or strings. **2.** To thread on a string. **3.** To arrange or bring together so as to form a string: *managed to string together a few clichés.* **4.** To fasten, tie, or hang with a string or strings. **5.** To extend; stretch out: *string a wire across a room.* **6.** To remove the strings from (a vegetable). **7.** *Informal.* To hang (a person). Usually used with *up.* —*intr.* **1.** To form strings or become stringlike. **2.** To extend or progress in a string, line, or succession. **3.** In billiards and similar games, to determine the order of play by hitting the cue ball to the end cushion with the aim of bringing it back as close as possible to the head rail. —**string along. 1.** To follow another's lead. **2.** To deceive, or keep waiting with deceitful promises. [Middle English *stringe,* Old English *streng.*]

string bass *n.* A double bass *(see).*

string bean *n.* **1.** The green pod of any bean prepared for cooking by breaking into sections that retain the beans. Also called "green bean", "snap bean". **2.** *Chiefly U.S.* A **French bean** *(see).* [From the stringy fibres on the pod.]

string·board (string-bawrd || -bōrd) *n.* A board that runs along the side of a staircase to support or cover the ends of the steps.

string·course (string-kawrss || -kōrss) *n.* A distinctive horizontal band or moulding set in the face of a building as a design element. Also called "cordon", "table".

stringed instrument *n.* A musical instrument played by plucking, striking, or bowing taut strings.

strin·gen·do (strin-jéndō) *adv. Music.* With an accelerating tempo. Used as a direction. [Italian, "tightening", from *stringere,* to press together, to tighten, from Latin.] —**strin·gen·do** *adj.*

strin·gent (strínjənt) *adj.* **1.** Imposing rigorous and exacting standards or demands; severe. **2.** Constricted; tight. **3.** Characterised by scarcity of money or by financial restrictions: *stringent market*

The majority of non-orchestral stringed instruments also work on the principle of a strung neck attached to a soundbox. Unlike the violin family these instruments are normally plucked and frequently have frets – narrow, slightly raised metal bars across the width of the neck which facilitate the precise stopping of the strings with the left hand.

The lute was popular throughout Renaissance Europe and had a varying number of strings. It was gradually superseded by the guitar in the 17th century. The guitar was probably introduced into Spain by the Arabs and grew in popularity throughout Europe from the 14th century. The classical guitar of today has six gut or nylon strings which are plucked rather than strummed, and is a popular portable instrument. The folk guitar is generally larger than the classical guitar and has metal strings which give it greater volume. The electric guitar is unlike other stringed instruments in having no soundbox. The metal strings vibrate above a magnet wrapped in a metal coil. The vibrations alter the magnetic field and induce a small electrical charge in the coil which is then amplified and emitted through loudspeakers as sound. Electronic modification of the impulse makes the range of sounds almost limitless. The ukulele is a small four-string guitar which was developed in the 19th century in Hawaii and was popular with jazz bands until the mid-20th century. The banjo, which is also used in traditional jazz, was taken to America by African slaves and is a derivative of the lute. The mandolin is also derived from the lute and is most popular in Italy.

Throughout the world there is a great variety of stringed instruments. Other examples include the zither which is popular in Africa, and the Indian sitar, which has become more popular in the West since the 1960s.

Lute
Popular from 1400–1700, its strings, which varied in number, were often tuned in pairs

Ukulele
Used in early jazz music, as it was cheap and easy to play

Mandolin
Normally has eight strings which are tuned in pairs

Classical guitar
Not generally used with an orchestra; mainly a solo instrument

Banjo
It has five or more strings and a soundbox covered with skin, like a drum

Electric guitar
The mainstay of modern "pop" music, often amplified to high volume

---

PRONUNCIATION KEY

a, trap; aa, father; ai, fair; ar, star; aw, lawn; ay, play; b, bb, stab; rubber; ch, church; ck, ticket; d, dd, dead; ladder; e, dress; ee, bee; er, defer; ew, few; ewr, pure; ə, about; ər, letter; f, ff, fife; differ; g, gg, giggle; h, hat; i, kit; ī, price; īr, fire; j, judge; k, kick; l, ll, let; 'l, needle; m, mm, man; n, nn, no; 'n, sudden; ng, thing; o, lot; ō, no; ŏŏ, foot; ōō, shoe; oor, poor; ow, cow; owr, hour; oy, boy; p, pp, pepper; r, rr, red; s, ss, sauce; sh, ship; t, tt, totter; th, thick; <u>th</u>, this; smooth; u, cut; ur, turn; v, vv, valve; w, wet; y, yes; z, zz, zebra; <u>zh</u>, vision; pleasure

IN FOREIGN WORDS:

aN, oN, Saint-Saëns; <u>hl</u>, Llanelli; Hluhluwe; <u>kh</u>, loch; lough; Khaled

STRESS MARK:

ín-sīt, insight; in-sít, incite

conditions. [Latin *stringēns* (stem *stringent-*), present participle of *stringere,* to tighten.] **—strin·gen·cy** *n.* **—strin·gent·ly** *adv.*

string·er (stríng-ər) *n.* **1.** A person or thing that strings. **2.** *Architecture.* **a.** A long, horizontal structural timber used for any of several connective or supportive purposes. **b.** A stringboard. **3.** A heavy longitudinal member serving to strengthen the hull of a ship or fuselage of a plane. **4.** A part-time news correspondent who covers the news stories of his own local area.

string·halt (stríng-hawlt || -holt) *n.* Lameness accompanied by spasmodic movements in the hind legs of a horse. Also called "springhalt". [Perhaps STRING + HALT.]

string-pull·ing (stríng-pŏŏlling) *n. Informal.* The secret or unofficial use of influence to gain an advantage.

string quartet *n.* **1.** A quartet of musicians playing stringed instruments, traditionally a first and second violin, a viola, and a cello. **2.** A composition for such a quartet of performers.

string tie *n.* A narrow tie, usually tied in a bow.

string·y (stríng-i) *adj.* **-ier, -iest. 1.** Resembling, forming, or consisting of a string or strings. **2.** Slender and wiry. **3.** Fibrous or sinewy; tough: *stringy meat.* **—string·i·ly** *adv.* **—string·i·ness** *n.*

string·y·bark (stríng-i-baark) *n. Australian.* Any eucalyptus with tough, fibrous bark.

strip[1] (strip) *v.* **stripped** or *rare* **stript** (stript), **stripping, strips.** *—tr.* **1. a.** To remove the clothing or other covering from. **b.** To remove (clothing or other covering). **2. a.** To remove the furnishings from. **b.** To remove (furnishings) from. **3. a.** To deprive of honours, rank, or the like; divest. **b.** To deprive of possessions; dispossess. **4.** To reduce to essentials; remove all excess detail or extraneous matter from. **5. a.** To remove the foliage or bark from. **b.** To remove the leaves from the stalks of (tobacco). **6. a.** To remove (paint, wallpaper, or varnish, for example), as from walls or furniture, either manually or by chemical or mechanical means. **b.** To remove paint or other coverings from in this way. **7.** To dismantle (a mechanical apparatus) piece by piece. **8.** To damage or break the threads or teeth of (a nut, bolt, screw, or gear). **9.** To finish milking (a cow or other milk-giving creature). **10.** To rob; plunder; despoil. *—intr.* **1. a.** To undress completely. **b.** To perform a striptease. **2.** To fall away or be removed; peel.

~n. A striptease. Also used adjectivally: *a strip club.* [Middle English *stripen,* Old English *(be)strīepan,* to plunder, from Germanic *straupjan* (unattested).]

Synonyms: *strip, divest, denude, bare.*

strip[2] *n.* **1.** A long, narrow piece or tract, usually of uniform width. **2.** *British.* The clothes worn by a particular football team. **3.** An **airstrip** *(see).* **—tear a strip off.** *Informal.* To rebuke sharply.

~tr.v. **stripped, stripping, strips.** To cut or tear into strips. [Perhaps variant of STRIPE (line).]

strip cartoon *n. Chiefly British.* A **comic strip** *(see).*

strip-crop·ping (stríp-kropping) *n.* A technique of growing cultivated and sod-forming crops in alternating strips following the contour of the land, in order to minimise erosion.

stripe[1] (strīp) *n.* **1.** A long, narrow band distinguished, as by colour or texture, from the surrounding material or surface. **2.** A fabric having such a band or bands. **3.** A strip of cloth or braid worn on a uniform to indicate rank or length of service; a chevron. **4.** *Chiefly U.S.* Sort; kind: *men of a vicious stripe.*

~tr.v. **striped, striping, stripes.** To mark with a stripe or stripes. [Middle English *strype* (unattested), from Middle Dutch *strīpe,* akin to Middle High German *strīfe*†.]

stripe[2] *n. Archaic.* A stroke or blow, as with a whip. [Middle English *strype,* perhaps from Middle Low German *strippe,* a lash, strap, from Germanic *strip-* (unattested).]

striped (strīpt || strīpid) *adj.* Having a stripe or stripes.

striped muscle *n. Anatomy.* **Striated muscle** *(see).*

strip light *n.* A long electric fluorescent light. **—strip lighting** *n.*

strip·ling (strípplíng) *n.* An adolescent youth. [Middle English, probably STRIP + -LING, that is "slender as a strip".]

strip mining *n. U.S.* **Open-cast mining** *(see).*

strip·per (stríppər) *n.* **1.** One that strips; especially, a tool or chemical that strips wallpaper, paint, or some other coating. **2.** One who performs a striptease.

strip poker *n.* A poker game in which the player with the lowest hand forfeits an article of clothing.

strip·tease (stríp-teez, -téez) *n.* A form of entertainment featuring a performer, usually a woman, who slowly removes clothing to a musical accompaniment.

strip·y (strīpi) *adj.* **-ier, -iest.** Suggestive of or marked with stripes.

strive (strīv) *intr.v.* **strove** (strōv) or *rare* **strived, striven** (strívv'n) or **strived, striving, strives. 1.** To exert much effort or energy. **2.** To struggle against another or one another; contend. Often used with *with.* [Middle English *striven,* from Old French *estriver,* perhaps from *estrif,* STRIFE. Strove, striven; Middle English *stroof, streven,* analogous formations, from *striven.*] **—striv·er** *n.*

Usage: The usual past tense and part participle forms of this verb in standard English are *strove* and *striven. Strived* is sometimes heard as an alternative to *strove,* and rather more frequently as an alternative to *striven.*

strobe (strōb) *n.* **1.** A strobe light. **2.** A stroboscope.

strobe light *n.* An electric light that produces a series of repeated intense flashes, used in stroboscopes and also in light displays. Also called "strobe". **—strobe lighting** *n.*

stro·bi·la (strə-bī́-lə) *n., pl.* **-lae** (-lee). **1.** The body of an adult tapeworm, consisting of a series of segments or proglottides. **2.** The segmented polyp stage of certain jellyfish. [New Latin, from Greek *strobilē,* plug of lint resembling a pine cone, from *strobilos,* pine cone, STROBILUS.]

stro·bi·la·ceous (strōbi-láyshəss) *adj. Botany.* Of or resembling a strobilus; conelike.

stro·bi·la·tion (strōbi-láysh'n) *n.* Segmentation of the type found in tapeworms and certain jellyfish.

stro·bi·lus (strṓ-bi-ləss) *n., pl.* **-li** (-lī). Also **stro·bile** (-bīl). *Botany.* A fruiting structure characterised by rows of overlapping scales, such as a pine cone or the fruit of the hop. [New Latin *strobilus,* from Late Latin, a pine cone, from Greek *strobilos,* "round ball", from *strobos,* a whirling around, whirlwind.]

strob·o·scope (strṓbə-skōp, stróbbə-) *n.* Any of various instruments used to view, calibrate, balance, or otherwise adjust moving, rotating, or vibrating objects by making them appear stationary, using pulsed illumination or mechanical devices that intermittently interrupt observation. [Greek *strobos,* a whirling round + -SCOPE.] **—strob·o·scop·ic** (-skóppik) *adj.* **—strob·o·scop·i·cal·ly** *adv.*

strode. Past tense of **stride.**

Stro·heim (strṓ-hīm, *German* shtrṓ-), **Erich von** (1885–1957). Austrian-born U.S. film director and actor. As a director he was noted for uncompromising realistic detail as in *Greed* (1923). As an actor he is remembered for his portrayal of sadistic Prussian officers, particularly in *La Grande Illusion* (1937).

stroke (strōk) *n.* **1. a.** The act or an action of striking; an impact; a blow. **b.** A blow, as from a cane or whip, imposed as a punishment: *sentenced to six strokes.* **2. a.** The striking of a bell, gong, or similar instrument. **b.** The sound so produced. **c.** The time so indicated: *the stroke of midnight.* **3.** An unexpected event having a powerful immediate effect for good or ill: *a stroke of luck.* **4. a.** The sudden severe onset of a malady such as apoplexy or sunstroke. **b.** An attack of apoplexy; a cerebral haemorrhage. Not in technical usage. **5.** An inspired or effective idea or act: *a stroke of genius.* **6. a.** A single completed movement of the limbs and body, as in swimming or rowing. **b.** The rate or manner of executing such a movement. **7. a.** The member of a rowing crew who sits nearest the coxswain or the stern and sets the tempo of the other oarsmen. **b.** The position he occupies. **8. a.** A movement of the upper torso and arms for the purpose of striking a ball, as in cricket or tennis. **b.** The manner of executing such a movement. **9.** In golf, a single act of striking the ball, used as a unit of scoring. **10.** Any single act or movement: *has never done a stroke of work; cut interest rates at a stroke.* **11.** Any of a series of movements of a piston from one end of the limit of its motion to the other. **12.** A single mark made by a pen, brush, or other marking implement. **13.** A single deft touch, as in literary composition. **14.** A single flash of lightning. **15.** A light caressing movement, as of the hand. **16.** In transactional analysis, a momentary sense of well-being resulting from a positive gesture, expression, or action received from another person.

~tr.v. **stroked, stroking, strokes. 1.** To give or apply a stroke to. **2.** To rub lightly, as with the hand or something held in the hand; caress. **3.** To set the pace for (a rowing crew). **4.** In transactional analysis, to hearten or reassure by means of some positive gesture, expression, or action. [Middle English *stroke,* Old English *strāc.*]

stroke play *n.* A method of scoring in golf, **medal play** *(see).*

stroll (strōl) *v.* **strolled, strolling, strolls.** *—intr.* **1.** To go for a leisurely walk. **2.** To travel from place to place giving performances: *strolling players.* *—tr.* To walk through at a leisurely pace.

~n. A leisurely walk. [Perhaps from German dialectal *strollen*†.]

stroll·er (strṓl-ər) *n.* **1.** One who strolls. **2.** A strolling player. **3.** A vagabond. **4.** A **baby buggy** *(see).*

stro·ma (strṓmə) *n., pl.* **-mata** (-tə). *Biology.* Any tissue that serves as a framework; especially: **1.** The colourless dense material occurring around the grana in a chloroplast. **2.** A compact mass of fungal hyphae in which fruiting bodies are produced. **3.** The fibrous connective tissue forming the framework of the ovary and testis. [New Latin, from Late Latin, from Greek *strōma,* bedspread, mattress.] **—stro·mat·ic** (strō-máttik) *adj.*

Strom·bo·li (strómbəli). One of the volcanic Lipari islands in the Tyrrhenian Sea north of Sicily. Its crater contains molten lava, and continuously emits gases, and small-scale eruptions occur frequently. Occasionally it has exploded with violence (1930, 1966).

strong (strong || strawng, *and in compounds*) *adj.* **stronger, strongest. 1.** Physically powerful; capable of exerting great physical force; muscular. **2. a.** In sound health; robust. **b.** Economically or financially sound or thriving. **3.** Characterised by power, fortitude, or resolution with regard to character, will, morality, or intelligence. **4.** Having or showing impressive ability, talent, or resources in a specified field: *a strong batting line-up.* **5.** Capable of the effective exercise of authority: *strong leadership.* **6.** Capable of enduring; solid. **7.** Capable of being defended: *a strong flank.* **8.** Having force of conviction or feeling; well-grounded: *a strong faith.* **9.** *Finance.* Marked by or showing firmness and a rising tendency in prices or value: *The pound remained strong.* **10.** Not easily upset; resistant to harmful or unpleasant influences: *strong nerves.* **11.** Having a specified number: *an army 15,000 strong.* **12.** Having force of motion or action: *a strong current.* **13. a.** Persuasive, effective, and cogent: *a strong argument.* **b.** Forceful and pointed; emphatic: *a strong statement.* **c.** Immoderate or profane: *strong language.* **14.** Extreme; drastic: *strong measures.* **15.** Intense in degree or quality: *a strong emotion.* **16.** Having an intense effect on the senses: *a strong smell.* **17.** Having a high concentration of an active or essential ingredient: *strong coffee.* **18.** Powerfully efficacious with respect to its appro-

PRONUNCIATION KEY

a, trap; aa, father; ai, fair; ar, star; aw, lawn; ay, play; b, bb, stab; rubber; ch, church; ck, ticket; d, dd, dead; ladder; e, dress; ee, bee; er, defer; ew, few; ewr, pure; ə, about; ər, letter; f, ff, fife; differ; g, gg, giggle; h, hat; i, kit; ī, price; īr, fire; j, judge; k, kick; l, ll, let; 'l, needle; m, mm, man; n, nn, no; 'n, sudden; ng, thing; o, lot; ō, no; ŏŏ, foot; ōō, shoe; oor, poor; ow, cow; owr, hour; oy, boy; p, pp, pepper; r, rr, red; s, ss, sauce; sh, ship; t, tt, totter; th, thick; th, this; smooth; u, cut; ur, turn; v, vv, valve; w, wet; y, yes; z, zz, zebra; zh, vision; pleasure

IN FOREIGN WORDS:

aN, oN, Saint-Saëns; hl, Llanelli; Hluhluwe; kh, loch; lough; Khaled

STRESS MARK:

ín-sīt, insight; in-sī́t, incite

priate function: *a strong painkiller.* **19.** Existing to a considerable or striking degree: *a strong resemblance; a strong possibility.* **20.** Characterised by a high degree of saturation. Said of a colour. **21.** *Linguistics.* Designating those verbs in English or other Germanic languages that form a past tense other than by means of a dental suffix such as *-ed;* for example, *fly, flew; sing, sang.* In this sense, compare **weak.**
~*adv.* In a strong, powerful, or vigorous manner; forcibly; forcefully. **—going strong.** Still vigorous or effective. [Middle English *strong,* Old English *strang.*] **—strong·ly** *adv.*
 Synonyms: strong, stout, sturdy, tough, stalwart, tenacious.
strong-arm (stróng-árm) *adj. Informal.* Using physical force or coercion: *strong-arm tactics.*
strong·box (stróng-boks) *n.* A stoutly made box or safe in which valuables are deposited.
strong breeze *n.* A wind whose speed is 10.8 to 13.8 metres per second, force 6 on the Beaufort scale.
strong gale *n.* A wind whose speed is 20.8 to 24.4 metres per second, force 9 on the Beaufort scale.
strong·hold (stróng-hōld) *n.* **1.** A fortress. **2.** A place of security; a refuge. **3.** An area of predominance: *a Tory stronghold.*
strong interaction *n. Physics.* A force that acts between certain elementary particles, hadrons, and is about 100 times stronger than the electromagnetic interaction but acts over only very short distances (10^{-15} metre). Compare **electromagnetic interaction, gravitational interaction, weak interaction.**
strong man *n.* **1.** One who performs feats of strength at a circus, fair, or other show. **2.** A leader, especially a military dictator, who retains power by the use or threat of force.
strong meat *n.* Something unattractive or too difficult for the inexperienced: *Isn't Schopenhauer rather strong meat for sixth-formers?*
strong-mind·ed (stróng-míndid) *adj.* **1.** Having a determined will. **2.** Having a vigorous mentality. **—strong-mind·ed·ly** *adv.* **—strong-mind·ed·ness** *n.*
strong point *n.* A skill or quality in which one excels.
strong room *n.* A strongly built, secure, and fireproof room designed for the safekeeping of money or valuables.
strong suit *n.* A **long suit** (see).
stron·gyle, stron·gyl (strón-jil, -jīl) *n.* Any of various nematode worms of the family Strongylidae, often parasitic in the gastrointestinal tract of mammals, especially horses. [New Latin *Strongylus* (genus), from Greek *strongulos†,* round, compactly formed.]
stron·gyl·o·sis (strónji-lō-siss) *n.* Infestation with strongyles.
stron·ti·a (strón-ti-ə, -shə ‖ -chə) *n.* Strontium hydroxide. [From *strontian,* variant of STRONTIUM.]
stron·ti·an·ite (strón-ti-ə-nīt, -shi- ‖ -chə-nīt) *n.* A grey to yellowish-green strontium ore, essentially $SrCO_3$. [*Strontian,* variant of STRONTIUM + -ITE.]
stron·ti·um (strón-ti-əm, -shəm ‖ -chəm) *n. Symbol* **Sr** A soft, silvery, easily oxidised metallic element that ignites spontaneously in air when finely divided. It is used in pyrotechnic compounds and various alloys. Atomic number 38, atomic weight 87.62, melting point 769°C, boiling point 1,384°C, relative density 2.54, valency 2. [Earlier *strontian,* after *Strontian,* area in the Highland Region of Scotland where it was discovered.] **—stron·tic** (-tik) *adj.*
strontium hydroxide *n.* A white deliquescent powder that normally occurs as the octahydrate, Sr $(OH)_2$.8 H_2O, and is used in sugar refining. Also called "strontia".
strontium-90 *n.* The strontium isotope with mass 90, having a half-life of 28 years, used for its high-energy beta emission in certain nuclear electric power sources and constituting a radiation hazard in fallout.
strontium unit *n. Abbr.* **SU** A measure of the concentration of strontium-90 in an organic medium, such as soil, milk, or bone, relative to the calcium concentration in the same medium; 10^{-12} curie of strontium-90 per gram of calcium.
strop (strop) *n.* A flexible strip of leather or canvas used for sharpening a razor.
~*tr.v.* **stropped, stropping, strops.** To sharpen (a razor) on a strop. [Middle English *stroppe,* band of leather, from Middle Low German or Middle Dutch *strop,* from West Germanic *strupa* (unattested), from Latin *stroppus,* from Greek *strophos,* twisted cord, from *strephein,* to turn.]
stro·phan·thin (strō-fánthin) *n.* A toxic glycoside or mixture of glycosides extracted from seeds of *Strophanthus Kombé* and used medicinally as a cardiac tonic. [New Latin *Strophanthus* (genus) : Greek *strophos,* twisted cord (see **strop**) + *anthos,* flower + -IN.]
stro·phe (strófi) *n.* **1. a.** A stanza, especially the first of a pair of stanzas of alternating form on which the structure of a given poem is based. **b.** A rhythmic system constituting a section of a poem, typically consisting of a series of asymmetric lines. **2.** The first division of the triad (strophe, antistrophe, and epode) constituting a section of a Pindaric ode. **3. a.** The movement of the chorus in classical Greek drama while turning from one side of the orchestra to the other. **b.** The part of a choral ode sung while this movement is executed. [Greek *strophē,* a turning, from *strephein,* to turn.] **—stroph·ic** (stróffik, strófik) *adj.*
stroph·u·lus (stróffewlǝss) *n.* Formerly, any of various diseases causing a skin rash; especially a disease common among children, sometimes associated with intestinal disturbances, characterised by a papular eruption of the skin. Also called "red gum". [New Latin, from Greek *strophos,* twisted cord, from *strephein,* to turn.]
strop·py (stróppi) *adj.* **-pier, -piest.** *British Informal.* Bad-tempered,

insolent, or uncooperative. [20th century : perhaps alteration of OBSTREPEROUS.]
strove. Past tense of **strive.**
struck (struk). Past tense and past participle of **strike.**
struck measure *n.* A dry measure having the contents levelled off and not heaped.
struc·tur·al (strúk-chǝr-ǝl, -choor-) *adj.* **1.** Of, pertaining to, having, or characterised by structure. **2.** Used in or necessary to construction. **3.** *Geology.* Pertaining to the structure of rocks and other aspects of the Earth's crust. **4.** *Biology.* Of or pertaining to organic structure; morphological. **5.** Pertaining to or caused by the existing economic or political structure of a community or country: *Structural unemployment.* **—struc·tur·al·ly** *adv.*
structural formula *n.* A chemical formula that represents the configuration of atoms and bonds in a molecule. Compare **empirical formula, molecular formula.**
structural gene *n.* A gene that forms part of an **operon** *(see)* and that determines a particular amino acid sequence in a protein.
struc·tur·al·ise, struc·tur·al·ize (strúk-chǝrǝ-līz) *tr.v.* **-ised, -ising, -ises.** To incorporate or arrange into a structure. **—struc·tur·al·i·sa·tion** (-lī-záysh'n ‖ *U.S.* -li-) *n.*
struc·tur·al·ism (strúkchǝrǝl-iz'm) *n.* **1.** An approach to linguistics characterised by the description of language in terms of irreducible structural features. **2.** An approach to the understanding of phenomena, as in the fields of anthropology, sociology, or literature, chiefly characterised by analysis or interpretation in terms of the underlying structures and principles that are felt to generate the phenomena in question. **—struc·tur·al·ist** *n.*
structural isomer. See **isomer.**
structural steel *n.* Steel shaped for use in construction.
struc·ture (strúkchǝr) *n.* **1.** Something constructed by the bringing together of material parts, especially a building. **2.** Any complex entity made up of mutually connected elements. **3.** The manner in which something is constructed; the configuration or organisation of constituent elements. **4.** Constitution; make-up. **5.** The interrelation of parts or the principle of organisation in a complex entity. —See Synonyms at **building.**
~*tr.v.* **structured, -turing, -tures.** To provide with or form into a well-defined structure. [Middle English, from Old French, from Latin *structūra,* from *struere* (past participle *structus*), to construct.]
stru·del (strōod'l) *n.* A kind of pastry made with fruit or cheese rolled up in a thin sheet of dough and baked. [German *Strudel,* from Middle High German *strudel,* whirlpool.]
strug·gle (strúgg'l) *intr.v.* **-gled, -gling, -gles.** **1.** To make violent or strenuous physical effort, as in opposing a material force or trying to escape confinement. **2.** To contend, compete, or fight. **3.** To be strenuously engaged with a problem, task, or anything presenting a difficulty; grapple. **4. a.** To make any strenuous effort; strive: *struggling to be polite.* **b.** To strive to achieve recognition: *a struggling writer.* **5.** To progress or penetrate with difficulty.
~*n.* **1.** A strenuous physical effort. **2.** A determined effort to achieve a goal in spite of obstacles. **3.** Combat; strife. [Middle English *struglen†.*] **—strug·gler** *n.* **—strug·gling·ly** *adv.*
strum (strum) *v.* **strummed, strumming, strums.** **—***tr.* To play (a stringed musical instrument) by running the fingers lightly over the strings. **—***intr.* To play an instrument in this manner.
~*n.* The act or sound of strumming. **—strum·mer** *n.*
stru·ma (strōo-mǝ ‖ strēw-) *n., pl.* **-mae** (-mee) or **-mas.** **1.** *Pathology.* Goitre *(see).* **2.** *Botany.* A cushion-like swelling, especially at the base of a moss capsule; tumour.² [Latin *strūma†,* tumour.] **—stru·mat·ic** (-máttik), **stru·mose** (-mōz, -mōss), **stru·mous** (-mǝss) *adj.*
strum·pet (strúmpit) *n. Literary.* A prostitute. [Middle English *strompett†.*]
strung. Past tense and past participle of **string.**
strung out *adj. Slang.* **1.** Addicted to a drug. **2.** Physically debilitated or emotionally distressed, as from long-term drug addiction or because of the lack of a drug.
strut (strut) *v.* **strutted, strutting, struts.** **—***intr.* To walk with pompous bearing; swagger. **—***tr.* To brace with a strut or struts.
~*n.* **1.** A stiff, self-important gait. **2.** A bar or rod used to strengthen a framework by resisting longitudinal thrust. [Middle English *strouten,* to swell, stand out, protrude, Old English *strūtian,* to stand out stiffly.] **—strut·ter** *n.* **—strut·ting·ly** *adv.*
struth, strewth (strōoth ‖ strewth) *interj.* Used to express surprise or annoyance. [From *God's truth.*]
stru·thi·ous (strōo-thi-ǝss, -thi- ‖ strēw-) *adj.* **1.** Of, pertaining to, or resembling the ostrich or other flightless bird. **2.** Deliberately ignoring the truth. [Latin *strūthiō,* ostrich, from Greek *strouthion,* from *strouthos†,* sparrow, ostrich.]
strych·nine (strík-neen ‖ *chiefly U.S.* -nīn, -nin) *n.* An extremely poisonous white crystalline alkaloid, $C_{21}H_{22}N_2O_2$, derived from nux vomica and related plants, and used as a poison for moles and formerly medicinally as a stimulant for the central nervous system. [French, from New Latin *Strychnos,* genus of plants including nux vomica, from Latin *strychnos,* nightshade, from Greek *strukhnos†.*]
strych·nin·ism (strik-nin-iz'm, -neen-) *n.* Poisoning from excessive or prolonged ingestion of strychnine, resulting in painful muscular spasms. [STRYCHNINE + -ISM.]
Stu·art, Stew·art (stéw-ǝrt ‖ stōo-). The family name of the royal family of Scotland (1371–1707), England (1603–1707), and Great Britain (1707–14).
Stuart, Charles Edward, also known as the Young Pretender or Bonnie Prince Charlie (1720–88). Grandson of James II of England

and son of James Edward Stuart. In 1745 he led the last Jacobite rising, claiming the British throne for his father. He was defeated at the battle of Culloden (1746), and escaped to France.

Stuart, James Francis Edward, also known as the Old Pretender. (1688–1766). Pretender to the British throne; son of James II. He made two unsuccessful attempts (1708, 1715) to take the British throne. The Jacobite rising of 1745, led on James's behalf by his son Charles Edward Stuart, also failed.

stub (stub) *n.* **1. a.** The short blunt end remaining after something has been cut, broken off, or worn down, such as the stump of a tree, tooth, or pencil. **b.** A cigar or cigarette butt. **c.** Anything that has been shortened, blunted, or worn down. **2.** A counterfoil, such as that of a cheque or receipt.
~tr.v. **stubbed, stubbing, stubs. 1.** To pull up by the roots. **2.** To clear (a field) of stubs. **3.** To strike (one's toe or foot) against something. **4.** To extinguish (a cigarette butt) by crushing. [Middle English *stubbe,* Old English *stybb, stubb.*]

stub axle *n.* A short axle that supports a front wheel of a motor vehicle.

stub·ble (stúbb'l) *n.* **1.** The short, stiff stalks of a grain or hay crop remaining on a field after harvesting. **2.** Anything resembling stubble, especially the short, bristly hairs on a man's unshaven face. [Middle English *stuble,* from Old French, from Latin *stup(u)la,* variant of *stipula,* straw. See **stipule.**] **—stub·bly** *adj.*

stub·born (stúbbərn) *adj.* **1.** Doggedly and unreasonably asserting one's will or refusing to comply; refractory; obstinate. **2.** Characterised by perseverance; resolute or persistent: *stubborn resistance.* **3.** Difficult to treat or deal with; resistant to treatment or effort: *stubborn stains.* —See Synonyms at **contrary, obstinate.** [Middle English *stoborne*†.] **—stub·born·ly** *adv.* **—stub·born·ness** *n.*

Stubbs (stubz), **George** (1724–1806). English painter and engraver. He published *Anatomy of the Horse* (1766), a collection of engravings made from drawings of horses he had dissected.

stub·by (stúbbi) *adj.* **-bier, -biest. 1.** Resembling a stub; short and thick or thickset. **2.** Covered with or consisting of stubs; bristly. **—stub·bi·ly** *adv.* **—stub·bi·ness** *n.*

stub nail *n.* A short, thick nail.

stuc·co (stúckō) *n., pl.* **-coes** or **-cos. 1.** A durable finish for exterior walls, applied wet and usually composed of cement, sand, and lime. **2.** A fine plaster for interior wall ornamentation, such as mouldings. **3.** Ornamental work done using stucco.
~tr.v. **stuccoed, -coing, -coes** or **-cos.** To finish or decorate with stucco. [Italian, from Old High German *stukki,* fragment, crust.]

stuck. Past tense and past participle of **stick.**

stuck-up (stúk-úp) *adj. Informal.* Snobbish; conceited.

stud¹ (stud) *n.* **1. a.** A boss, nail head, rivet, or the like slightly projecting from a surface, used chiefly for decorative purposes. **b.** An almost flat, usually square metal object projecting slightly from the surface of a road, usually used to mark off lanes. **c.** Any of several small cylindrical projections, as on the sole of a football boot, designed to give extra grip. **2.** An upright post in the framework of a wall for supporting sheets of lath, wallboard, or the like. **3.** A headless bolt threaded at both ends so that one end can be screwed into a metal part and the other end inserted through a hole in a mating part, the assembly being secured by a second bolt screwed onto the other end. **4.** A small ornamental button mounted on a short pin for insertion through an eyelet, as on a dress shirt. **5.** Any of various protruding pins or pegs in machinery. **6.** A metal crosspiece used as a brace in a link, as in a chain cable.
~tr.v. **studded, studding, studs. 1.** To provide with or construct with a stud or studs. **2.** To set or adorn with studs or other prominent objects. **3.** To be dotted about on, especially ornamentally. [Middle English *stode,* post, prop, Old English *studu, stuthu.*]

stud² *n.* **1. a.** A group of animals, especially horses, kept for breeding. **b.** A stable or farm where they are kept. Also called a "stud farm". **2.** A stallion or other male animal kept for breeding. **3.** The condition of being available for breeding purposes: *at stud.* **4.** *Slang.* A man considered as being sexually active. **5.** Stud poker. [Middle English *stod,* Old English *stōd,* stable for breeding.]

stud·book (stúd-bo͝ok || -bo͝ok) *n.* A book registering the pedigrees of thoroughbred animals, especially of horses.

stud·ding (stúdding) *n.* **1.** The wood framework of a wall or partition. **2.** That with which a surface is studded.

stud·ding·sail (stúdding-sayl; *nautical* stún-s'l) *n. Nautical.* A narrow rectangular sail set from extensions of the yards of square-rigged ships. [Perhaps from Middle Low German and Middle Dutch *stōtinge,* a thrusting, from *stōten,* to force.]

stu·dent (stéwd'nt || sto͞od'nt) *n.* **1.** A person following a course of study; especially: **a.** One studying at a university or other place of tertiary education. Also used adjectivally: *a student nurse.* **b.** *Chiefly U.S.* Any person in full time education. **2.** One who makes a study of something. [Middle English, from Latin *studēns* (stem *student-*), present participle of *studēre,* to study, be diligent.]

stu·dent·ship (stéw-d'nt-ship || sto͞o-) *n.* **1.** The state of being a student. **2.** *British.* A type of scholarship, usually for postgraduate study.

students' union *n.* **1.** An organisation of the students in an establishment of higher education, providing social and recreational facilities and usually representing student interests. **2.** Its premises.

stud·ied (stúd-id || -eed) *adj.* **1.** Carefully contrived; affected or calculated: *a studied effect; a studied smile.* **2.** *Archaic.* Learned. **—stud·ied·ly** *adv.* **—stud·ied·ness** *n.*

stu·di·o (stéw-di-ō || sto͞o-) *n., pl.* **-os. 1.** The workroom of an artist or photographer. **2.** An establishment where an art is taught or studied: *a dance studio.* **3.** A room or place where cinema or video films are made. **4.** A room used for the recording or live transmission of television or radio productions. **5.** A place where music is recorded for commercial distribution; a recording studio. **6.** A studio flat. [Italian, from Latin *studium,* STUDY.]

studio couch *n.* A couch that can serve as a bed.

studio flat *n.* A small flat usually consisting of a single main room together with a kitchen and bathroom. Also called "studio".

stu·di·ous (stéw-di-əss || sto͞o-) *adj.* **1.** Devoted to study. **2.** Earnest; diligent. **3.** Giving or suggestive of careful attention; heedful: *studious of his appearance.* **4.** *Rare.* Deliberate; studied. **5.** Conducive to study. [Middle English, from Latin *studiōsus,* from *studium,* STUDY.] **—stu·di·ous·ly** *adv.* **—stu·di·ous·ness** *n.*

stud poker *n.* Poker in which the first round of cards (and often the last) is dealt face down and the others face up. Also called "stud". [Shortened from *stud horse poker,* perhaps alluding to the cards being "at stud", that is, available to the player as long as he bets and stays in the game.]

stud·y (stúddi) *n., pl.* **-ies. 1. a.** The act or process of studying; the pursuit of knowledge, as by reading, observation, or research. **b.** *Plural.* The work of one engaged in this act or process. **2. a.** Attentive scrutiny or careful investigation. **b.** An enquiry or examination, especially of an academic or scientific nature. **3. a.** A subject to be investigated or studied: *Human behaviour proves a fascinating study.* **b.** *Often plural.* A branch or department of learning; an academic or scientific subject: *environmental studies.* **4.** Something that deserves notice or requires careful attention: *Her attitude was a study in polite condescension.* **5.** *Formal.* An aim or endeavour: *made it my study to serve them.* **6. a.** A work resulting from academic endeavour, such as a monograph or thesis. **b.** A literary work on a particular subject. **c.** A preliminary sketch, as for a work of art. **7.** A musical composition designed as a technical exercise; an étude. **8.** A state of mental absorption, a **brown study** *(see).* **9.** A room intended or equipped for studying in. **10. a.** An actor who is memorising a part. **b.** The memorising of a part in a play.
~v. **studied, -ying, -ies.** *—tr.* **1. a.** To apply one's mind purposefully to the acquisition of knowledge or understanding of (any subject): *study a language.* **b.** To be engaged in the study of (a particular subject) as part of an educational course. **2.** To read, scrutinise, or investigate with close attention: *study a report; study a map.* **3.** To memorise (a part in a play). **4.** To give careful thought to; contemplate: *study the next move.* **5.** *Formal.* To endeavour; make it one's purpose. *—intr.* **1.** To apply oneself to learning, especially by reading. **2.** To pursue a course of study. **3.** To ponder; reflect; meditate. [Middle English *studie,* from Old French *estudie,* from Latin *studium,* from *studēre,* to be eager, study.]

stuff (stuf) *n.* **1.** The material out of which something is made or formed; substance. **2.** The basic substance or essential elements of anything; essence: *the stuff heroes are made of.* **3.** Any material not specifically identified. **4.** *Informal.* Household or personal articles collectively; belongings. **5.** Worthless objects; refuse or junk. **6.** Foolish or empty words or ideas. Used chiefly in the interjection *stuff and nonsense.* **7.** Woven material; especially, woollen fabric. **8.** *Informal.* A person's field of knowledge or competence: *knows her stuff.* **9.** *Slang.* **a.** Money; cash. **b.** An illegal drug, especially cannabis. **c.** Women collectively considered as sexual objects. Used chiefly in the phrase *a bit of stuff.* Considered offensive. **—do (one's) stuff.** *Informal.* To do what is expected of one; show one's particular skill.
~v. **stuffed, stuffing, stuffs.** *—tr.* **1. a.** To pack tightly; fill up; cram. **b.** To block (a passage or opening). **c.** To push roughly into a place: *stuffed the letter into my pocket.* **2. a.** To fill with an appropriate stuffing: *stuff a cabbage.* **b.** To fill the skin of (a dead animal) so as to restore its natural form. **3.** To fill to repletion with food. **4.** To apply a preservative and softening agent to (leather). **5.** *U.S.* To put fraudulent votes into (a ballot box). **6.** *Slang.* To take back and dispose of (something offered and rejected): *They offered me a four per cent rise, but I told them to stuff it.* **7.** *Vulgar Slang.* To have sex with (a woman). **—get stuffed.** *Vulgar Slang.* Used to express contempt for or anger with another. *—intr.* To overeat; gorge oneself. [Middle English *stuff(e),* from Old French *estoffe,* provisions, from *estoffer,* to cram, pad, from Germanic *stopfōn* (unattested), from Late Latin *stuppāre,* to plug up, from Latin *stuppa,* plug, cork, from Greek *stuppē.*] **—stuff·er** *n.*

stuffed derma *n.* **Derma** *(see).*

stuffed shirt *n. Informal.* A pompous, complacently self-important person.

stuff·ing (stúffing) *n.* **1.** Material used to stuff or fill, especially: **a.** Padding put in cushions, pillows, and upholstered furniture. **b.** Food put in the cavity of meat or vegetables. **2.** *Informal.* Strength, vigour, or self-confidence: *His illness knocked the stuffing out of him.*

stuffing box *n.* An enclosure containing packing to prevent leakage around a moving machine part. Also called "packing box".

stuff·y (stúffi) *adj.* **-ier, -iest. 1.** Lacking sufficient ventilation; airless; close. **2.** Having the respiratory passages blocked. **3.** *Informal.* Primly formal or boringly conventional; dull; stodgy: *a stuffy dinner party.* **—stuff·i·ly** *adv.* **—stuff·i·ness** *n.*

stull (stul) *n.* **1.** A timber or other prop supporting the roof of a mine opening. **2.** A platform braced against the sides of a working area in a mine.

stul·ti·fy (stúlti-fī) *tr.v.* **-fied, -fying, -fies. 1.** To reduce to a state of

PRONUNCIATION KEY

a, **trap**; aa, **father**; ai, **fair**; ar, **star**; aw, **lawn**; ay, **play**; b, bb, **stab**; **rubber**; ch, **church**; ck, **ticket**; d, dd, **dead**; **ladder**; e, **dress**; ee, **bee**; er, **defer**; ew, **few**; ewr, **pure**; ə, **about**; ər, **letter**; f, ff, **fife**; **differ**; g, gg, **giggle**; h, **hat**; i, **kit**; ī, **price**; īr, **fire**; j, **judge**; k, **kick**; l, ll, **let**; 'l, **needle**; m, mm, **man**; n, nn, **no**; 'n, **sudden**; ng, **thing**; o, **lot**; ō, **no**; o͝o, **foot**; o͞o, **shoe**; oor, **poor**; ow, **cow**; owr, **hour**; oy, **boy**; p, pp, **pepper**; r, rr, **red**; s, ss, **sauce**; sh, **ship**; t, tt, **totter**; th, **thick**; th, **this**; **smooth**; u, **cut**; ur, **turn**; v, vv, **valve**; w, **wet**; y, **yes**; z, zz, **zebra**; zh, **vision**; **pleasure**

IN FOREIGN WORDS:

aN, oN, **Saint-Saëns**; hl, **Llanelli**; **Hluhluwe**; kh, **loch**; **lough**; **Khaled**

STRESS MARK:

ín-sīt, **insight**; in-sít, **incite**

uselessness, futility, or enfeeblement. **2.** To cause to appear stupid, inconsistent, or ridiculous. **3.** *Law.* To allege or prove insane and so not legally responsible. Often used reflexively. [Late Latin *stultificāre* : Latin *stultus,* foolish + *facere,* to make.] **—stul·ti·fi·ca·tion** (-fi-káysh'n) *n.* **—stul·ti·fi·er** *n.*

stum (stum) *n.* **1.** Unfermented or partly fermented grape juice; must. **2.** Vapid wine renewed by an admixture of stum.
~tr.v. **stummed, stumming, stums. 1.** To revitalise (vapid wine) by adding stum so as to restart fermentation. **2.** To prevent further fermentation of (wine). [Dutch, from *stom,* unfermented, dumb, mute, translation of French *(vin) muet,* "mute (wine)".]

stum·ble (stúmb'l) *v.* **-bled, -bling, -bles.** *—intr.* **1. a.** To miss one's step in walking or running; trip and almost fall. **b.** To proceed unsteadily or falteringly; flounder. **c.** To act or speak falteringly or clumsily. **2.** To make a mistake; blunder. **3.** To fall into evil ways; err. **4.** To find accidentally or unexpectedly. Used with *on* or *upon.* *—tr.* To puzzle, embarrass, or disconcert.
~n. The act or an instance of stumbling. [Middle English *stumblen,* perhaps from Old Norse *stumla* (unattested).] **—stum·bler** *n.* **—stum·bling·ly** *adv.*

stum·ble·bum (stúmb'l-bum) *n. U.S. Slang.* A blundering or inept person. [STUMBLE + BUM (vagabond).]

stumbling block *n.* An obstacle or impediment.

stu·mer (stéw-mər || stóo-) *n. British Slang.* Anything worthless or fraudulent, especially a counterfeit banknote or forged cheque. [19th century : origin obscure.]

stump (stump) *n.* **1.** The part of a tree trunk left protruding from the ground after the tree has been felled. **2.** Any part, as of a branch, limb, or tooth, remaining after the main part has been cut away, broken off, or worn down. **3.** *Plural. Informal.* The legs. **4.** A short, thickset person. **5.** A heavy tread or footstep. **6.** A platform or other place used for making speeches in a political or other campaign. **7.** A short, pointed roll of leather or paper or a wad of rubber for rubbing on a charcoal or pencil drawing to shade or soften it. **8.** In cricket: **a.** Any one of the three upright sticks in a wicket. **b.** *Plural. Informal.* The end of the day's play: *At stumps, England were 180 behind.*
~v. **stumped, stumping, stumps.** *—tr.* **1.** To reduce to a stump; lop; truncate. **2.** To clear stumps from: *stump a field.* **3.** In cricket, to dismiss (a batsman who has just faced a delivery) by breaking his wicket while he is out of his crease. **4.** *Chiefly U.S.* To go through (a district) making political speeches. **5.** To shade (a drawing) with a stump. **6.** *Informal.* To baffle completely; confront with an insoluble problem. *—intr.* To walk clumsily or heavily. **—stump up.** *British Informal.* To pay (money owed or required). [Middle English *stumpe,* from Middle Low German *stump.*] **—stump·er** *n.* **—stump·i·ness** *n.* **—stump·y** *adj.*

stun (stun) *tr.v.* **stunned, stunning, stuns. 1.** To daze or render unconscious, as by a blow. **2.** To overwhelm or daze with a loud noise. **3.** To stupefy or overwhelm with shock or astonishment; astound.
~n. **1.** Something that stupefies. **2.** A state of stupefaction. [Middle English *stonen,* from Old French *estoner,* from Vulgar Latin *extonāre* (unattested) : Latin *ex-* (intensive) + *tonāre,* to thunder.]

stung. Past tense and past participle of **sting.**

stun grenade *n.* A grenade designed to detonate with a loud explosion and release smoke or disabling gas but without causing physical harm, used particularly in antiterrorist operations.

stunk. Past participle and alternative past tense of **stink.**

stun·ner (stúnnər) *n.* **1.** One that stuns. **2.** *Informal.* An exceptionally attractive person or thing.

stun·ning (stúnning) *adj.* **1.** Causing or capable of causing loss of consciousness or emotional shock. **2.** *Informal.* **a.** Of a strikingly attractive appearance. **b.** Extremely impressive or well-performed. **—stun·ning·ly** *adv.*

stunt[1] (stunt) *tr.v.* **stunted, stunting, stunts. 1.** To check the growth or development of. **2.** To check (growth or development).
~n. **1.** A state of retarded growth, or something causing such a state. **2.** One that is stunted. [Perhaps from Middle English *stont,* short in duration (but influenced in sense by Old Norse cognate *stuttr,* short, dwarfish), Old English *stunt,* dull, half-witted.] **—stunt·ed·ness** *n.*

stunt[2] *n.* **1.** A feat displaying unusual strength, skill, or daring. **2.** Any unusual act or display intended to attract attention.
~intr.v. **stunted, stunting, stunts.** To perform a stunt or stunts.

stunt man *n.* A person who substitutes for a film actor in scenes requiring physical prowess or involving physical risk.

stu·pa (stóopə) *n.* A Buddhist shrine usually consisting of a large domed structure. Also called a "tope". [Sanskrit *stūpa,* "tuft of hair", "crown of head".]

stupe (stewp || stoop) *n.* A hot compress, often treated with a counterirritant and applied to relieve pain. [Middle English, from Latin *stuppa,* tow, plug, from Greek *stuppē.*]

stu·pe·fa·cient (stéwpi-fáyshi-ənt || stóopi-) *adj.* Inducing stupor.
~n. A stupefacient drug, such as a narcotic. [Latin *stupefaciēns* (stem *stupefacient-*), present participle of *stupefacere,* STUPEFY.]

stu·pe·fac·tion (stéwpi-fáksh'n, styóopi- || stóopi-) *n.* **1.** The act of stupefying or the state of being stupefied. **2.** Great astonishment or consternation.

stu·pe·fy (stéwpi-fī, styóopi- || stóopi-) *tr.v.* **-fied, -fying, -fies. 1.** To dull the senses of; put into a stupor. **2.** To stun with amazement; astonish. [French *stupéfier,* from Latin *stupefacere* : *stupēre,* to be stunned + *facere,* to make.] **—stu·pe·fi·er** *n.*

stu·pen·dous (stew-péndəss, styóo- || stóo-) *adj.* **1.** Of awesome size, degree, force, or quality; astounding; prodigious. **2.** *Informal.* Extremely impressive or enjoyable. —See Synonyms at **enormous.** [Latin *stupendus,* from *stupēre,* to be stunned.] **—stu·pen·dous·ly** *adv.* **—stu·pen·dous·ness** *n.*

stu·pid (stéwpid, styóopid || stóopid) *adj.* **-pider, -pidest. 1.** In a stupor; stupefied. **2.** Slow to apprehend; dull; obtuse. **3.** Showing a lack of sense or intelligence. **4.** Uninteresting, boring, or trivial: *a stupid job.* **5.** *Informal.* Infuriating or intractable: *couldn't get the stupid car to start.*
~n. Informal. A stupid person. [French *stupide,* from Latin *stupidus,* from *stupēre,* to be stunned.] **—stu·pid·ly** *adv.* **—stu·pid·ness, stu·pid·i·ty** (stew-píddəti, styóo- || stóo-) *n.*
Synonyms: *stupid, slow, obtuse, dense, crass.*

stu·por (stéwpər || stóopər) *n.* **1.** A state of near unconsciousness; lethargy; torpor. **2.** A state of mental confusion; a daze. [Middle English, from Latin, from *stupēre,* to be stunned. See **stupid.**] **—stu·por·ous** *adj.*

stur·dy[1] (stúrdi) *adj.* **-dier, -diest. 1.** Substantially built; durable; strong. **2.** Physically strong and healthy; robust. **3.** Vigorous, lusty, or resolute: *a sturdy English sense of humour.* —See Synonyms at **strong.** [Middle English, giddy, rash, impetuous, from Old French *estourdi,* past participle of *estourir,* to stun, daze, from Vulgar Latin *exturdīre* (unattested), probably "to be stunned like a thrush drunk with grapes" : perhaps Latin *ex-,* completely + *turdus,* thrush.] **—stur·di·ly** *adv.* **—stur·di·ness** *n.*

sturdy[2] *n.* A disease of sheep, **gid** *(see).* [From STURDY (in earlier sense "giddy").] **—stur·died** *adj.*

stur·geon (stúrjən) *n.* Any of various large, edible freshwater and marine fishes of the family Acipenseridae, of the Northern Hemisphere, valued as a source of caviar and isinglass. [Middle English, from Anglo-French, from Vulgar Latin *sturiō* (unattested), from Germanic *sturjōn* (unattested). See also **sterlet.**]

Sturluson, Snorri. See **Snorri Sturluson.**

Sturm·ab·teil·ung (shtóorm-ap-tīloong) *n., pl.* **-teilungen** (-ən). *Abbr.* **S.A.** A Nazi German militia organised about 1924 and notorious for its violent and terroristic methods. Also called "Brown Shirts", "storm troopers". [German, "storm division".]

Sturm und Drang (shtóorm óont dráng) *n.* A German romantic literary movement of the late 18th century, the works of which typically depicted the impulsive man struggling against conventional society. [German, "storm and stress", originally the title of a romantic play (1776) by Friedrich Maximilian von Klinger (1752–1831), German poet and dramatist.]

stut·ter (stúttər) *v.* **-tered, -tering, -ters.** *—intr.* To speak with a spasmodic hesitation, prolongation, or repetition of sounds. *—tr.* To say with or as if with a stutter.
~n. The act or habit of stuttering. [Frequentative of obsolete *stut,* from Middle English *stutten,* perhaps of Low German origin, akin to Middle Low German *stōtern,* to stutter.] **—stut·ter·er** *n.* **—stut·ter·ing·ly** *adv.*

Stutt·gart (stóot-gaart; *German* shtóot-). The capital of Baden-Württemberg, on the river Neckar in southwestern West Germany. It is a major industrial centre producing electrical and photographic equipment, textiles, printed materials, and motor vehicles. It is also a tourist centre, and venue for industrial fairs.

St. Vin·cent and the Gren·a·dines (vínss'nt; grénnə-déenz). Island state in the West Indies, lying in the eastern Caribbean Sea. St. Vincent, the most populous of the Windward Islands, is a major tourist area. However, its volcano, Soufrière, is still active, and erupted violently in 1979. Hundreds of small islands make up the Grenadines group. The main exports are bananas, sweet potatoes, arrowroot, and spices. Formerly a French colony, the islands finally became British in 1805, and fully independent within the Commonwealth in 1979. Area, 388 square kilometres (150 square miles). Population, 100,000. Capital, Kingstown (on St. Vincent). See map at **Latin America.**

St. Vi·tus' dance (vītəss, -iz) *n. Pathology* A nervous disease, **chorea** *(see).* Not in technical usage. [After St. *Vitus,* third-century Christian child martyr, invoked by sufferers of the disease.]

sty[1] (stī) *n., pl.* **sties. 1.** An enclosure for pigs. **2.** Any filthy place.
~v. **stied, stying, sties.** *—tr.* To shut up in a sty. *—intr.* To live in a sty. [Middle English *sty,* Old English *stī, stig,* from Germanic *stijam* (unattested).]

sty[2]**, stye** (stī) *n., pl.* **sties** or **styes.** Inflammation of one or more sebaceous glands of an eyelid. [Obsolete *styany* (taken as *sty-on-eye*), Middle English *styanye* : *styan* (unattested), sty, "swelling", from Old English *stīgend,* present participle of *stīgan,* to rise + EYE.]

styg·i·an (stíji-ən) *adj. Sometimes capital* **S. 1.** Of or pertaining to the river Styx. **2. a.** Gloomy and dark. **b.** Infernal; hellish. [Latin *Stygius,* from Greek *Stugios,* from *Stux,* Styx.]

sty·lar (stīlər) *adj.* **1.** Of, pertaining to, or resembling a stylus. **2.** *Biology.* Of or pertaining to a style.

sty·late (stīlayt) *n. Biology.* Having a style or styles.

style (stīl) *n.* **1.** The way in which something is written, said, shown, or done, as distinguished from its substance. **2.** The combination of distinctive features of literary or artistic expression, execution, or performance characterising a particular person, people, school, or era. **3.** A sort; a kind; a type: *a style of furniture.* **4.** A quality of imagination and individuality expressed in one's actions and tastes and personal appearance: *She's got style; dresses with style.* **5. a.** A comfortable and elegant way of living or behaving: *dined in style.* **b.** A particular mode of living: *the style of a gentleman.* **6. a.** The

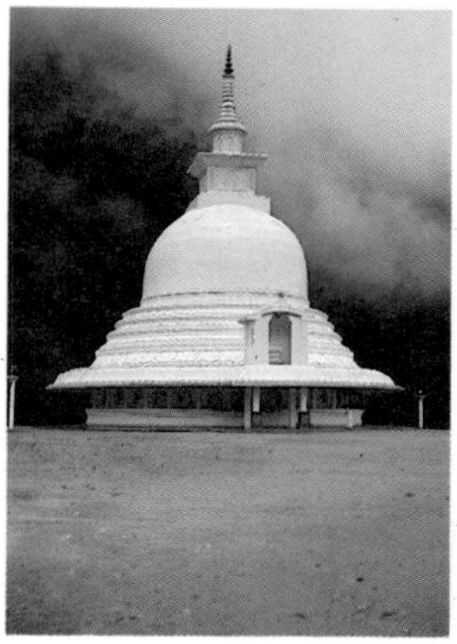

stupa *Buddhist shrines vary slightly in style in different countries, but almost all are built around a central dome – a shape derived from burial mounds that were common in India in pre-Buddhist times. Many – as on this Sri Lankan stupa – are topped by a stylised parasol, one of the traditional possessions of a Buddhist monk.*

fashion of the moment, especially of dress; a vogue. Used chiefly in the phrases *out of style* or *in style*. **b.** A particular fashion. **7.** A particular set of conventions favoured by a publisher or publication in presenting printed material, including usage, punctuation, spelling, typography, and arrangement. **8.** *Formal.* A name, title, or descriptive term: *has the style of Prince William of Wales.* **9.** A slender, pointed instrument used to write on wax tablets in ancient times. **10.** An implement used for etching or engraving. **11.** The shadow-casting projection on a sundial; a gnomon. **12.** *Botany.* The usually slender part of a pistil, rising from the ovary and tipped by the stigma. **13.** *Zoology.* Any slender, tubular, or bristle-like process. **14.** *Obsolete.* A pen. **15.** A surgical probing instrument; a stylet. —See Synonyms at **fashion.** —**cramp (someone's) style.** *Informal.* To inhibit (someone's) freedom of action or expression: *You rather cramped my style with Sarah at the party.*
~*v.* **styled, styling, styles.** —*tr.* **1.** To design; give style to: *style hair.* **2.** To make consistent with the rules of style. **3.** *Formal.* To call or name; designate: *styled themselves expert.* —*intr.* **1.** To admit of styling. Used of hair. [Middle English, from Old French, from Latin *stilus*†, writing instrument, style.] —**styl·er** *n.*

–style *adv. & adj. comb. form.* In or imitating the manner of the thing specified: *a thirties-style dress.*

style book *n.* A book giving rules and examples of usage, punctuation, and typography, used in the preparation of copy for publication. Also called "style guide".

sty·let (stílit) *n.* **1.** A slender, pointed instrument or weapon, such as a stiletto. **2.** A surgical probe; a style. **3.** A wire inserted into a catheter to maintain its shape or remove an obstruction. **4.** *Zoology.* A small, stiff, needle-like process in some invertebrates, such as the mouth parts of an aphid. [French, from Italian *stiletto*, STILETTO.]

sty·li·form (stíli-fawrm) *adj.* Having the shape of a style (sense 13); bristle-like. [STYLO- + -FORM.]

styl·ise, styl·ize (stíl-īz) *tr.v.* **-ised, -ising, -ises. 1.** To subordinate verisimilitude to principles of design in the representation of. **2.** To represent conventionally; conventionalise. —**styl·i·sa·tion** (-ī-záysh'n ‖ *U.S.* -i-) *n.* —**styl·is·er** *n.*

styl·ish (stílish) *adj.* **1.** In step with current fashion. **2.** Showing or having natural elegance. —**styl·ish·ly** *adv.* —**styl·ish·ness** *n.*

styl·ist (stílist) *n.* **1.** A writer or performer who cultivates an approved or distinctive artistic style. **2.** A designer of or consultant on styles in decorating, dress, cosmetics, or hairdressing.

sty·lis·tic (stī-lístik) *adj.* Of or pertaining to style, especially to artistic or literary style. —**sty·lis·ti·cal·ly** *adv.*

sty·lis·tics (stī-lístiks) *n. Used with a singular verb.* A branch of linguistics which studies the use of language styles in particular contexts.

sty·lite (stíl-īt) *n.* Any early Christian ascetic who lived unsheltered on the top of a high pillar. [Late Greek *stulitēs* : Greek *stulos*, pillar + -ITE.] —**sty·lit·ic** (stī-líttik) *adj.* —**sty·lit·ism** (-ī-iz'm) *n.*

stylo–, styl– *comb. form.* Indicates: **1.** *Biology.* A style; for example, **stylopodium. 2.** A point, pillar, or styloid process; for example, **stylograph.** [Latin *stilus*, stalk, STYLE.]

sty·lo·bate (stíl-ō-bayt, -ə-) *n. Architecture.* The immediate foundation of a row of classical columns. See **stereobate.** [Latin *stylobata*, from Greek *stulobatēs*, column base : *stulos*, column + -*bates*, "one that is based".]

sty·lo·graph (stíl-ə-graaf, -ō-, -graf) *n.* A fountain pen having a tubular writing point instead of a nib. Also called "stylographic pen". [STYLO- + -GRAPH.]

sty·log·ra·phy (stī-lóggrəfi) *n.* The art or a method of etching, engraving, or writing with a style. [STYLO- + -GRAPHY.] —**sty·lo·graph·ic** (stíla-gráffik), **sty·lo·graph·i·cal** *adj.*

sty·loid (stíl-oyd) *adj.* Slender and pointed. [New Latin *styloides*, resembling a style (after Greek *styloeidēs*, pillar-like) : STYL(O)- + -OID.]

sty·lo·lite (stíla-līt) *n.* A small columnar rock development in limestone and other calcareous rocks that is usually at right angles to the bedding planes, and is of irregular cross-section with striated sides. [STYLO- + -LITE.] —**sty·lo·lit·ic** (-líttik) *adj.*

sty·lo·po·di·um (stíla-pódi-əm) *n., pl.* **-di·a** (-ə). *Botany.* An enlargement at the base of the style of certain flowers. [New Latin : STYLO- + -PODIUM.]

sty·lops (stí-lops) *n.* Any of various minute parasitic insects of the order Strepsiptera, which live inside other insects. [New Latin, from Greek : *stulos*, pillar, column + *ōps*, eye (referring to the stalked eye of the male).]

sty·lo·stix·is (stí-lō-stíksiss, -lə-) *n.* **Acupuncture** (see). [New Latin, from Greek *stulos*, stylus, needle + *stixis*, spot, mark.]

sty·lus (stí-ləss) *n., pl.* **-luses** or **-li** (-lī). **1.** A sharp, pointed instrument used for writing, marking, or engraving. **2.** A needle or jewel in the cartridge of a gramophone pickup that senses the undulations in the record grooves. **3.** The sharp, pointed tool used for cutting record grooves. [Latin *stilus*, STYLE.]

sty·mie, sty·my (stími) *n.* **1.** A situation in golf in which one ball obstructs the line of play of another on the putting green. **2.** An impasse; a quandary.
~*tr.v.* **stymied, -mieing** or **-mying, -mies.** Also **sty·my, -mied, -mying, -mies.** To block, thwart, or baffle. [19th century : origin obscure.]

styp·sis (stipsiss) *n.* The action or application of a styptic. [Late Latin *stypsis*, from Greek *stupsis*, contraction, astringency, from *stuphein*, to contract. See **styptic.**]

styp·tic (stíptik) *adj.* Also **styp·ti·cal** (-'l). Arresting bleeding; haemostatic; astringent.
~*n.* A styptic drug or substance. [Middle English *stiptik*, from Late Latin *stypticus*, from Greek *stuptikos*, from *stuphein*, to contract.] —**styp·tic·i·ty** (stip-tíssəti) *n.*

styptic pencil *n.* A small cosmetic applicator used to stanch shaving and similar small cuts.

sty·rax (stír-aks) *n.* **1.** A resin, storax (see). **2.** Any tree of the genus *Styrax.* —**sty·ra·ceous** (-ə-káyshəss) *adj.*

sty·rene (stír-een) *n.* A colourless oily liquid, C_8H_8, the monomer for **polystyrene** (see). [Latin *styrax, storax,* STORAX (from which styrene is obtained by distillation) + -ENE.]

Styr·i·a (steér-i-ə). German **Stei·er·mark** (shtī-ər-maark). State and ancient province in southeast Austria. It is mountainous, and is a mining area, with deposits of lignite, iron ore, and magnesite. Graz is the capital.

Styx (stiks) *n. Greek Mythology.* A river of Hades, across which Charon ferried the souls of the dead. [Latin, from Greek *stux.*]

SU Strontium unit.

su·a·ble (séw-əb'l, sóō-) *adj.* Legally subject to a court suit; capable of or liable to being sued. —**su·a·bil·i·ty** (-ə-bílləti) *n.*

sua·sion (swáyzh'n) *n. Rare.* Persuasion. Used chiefly in the phrase *moral suasion.* [Middle English, from Latin *suāsiō* (stem *suāsiōn-*), from *suādēre* (past participle *suāsus*), to persuade.] —**sua·sive** (swáy-siv ‖ -ziv) *adj.*

suave (swaav, swayv) *adj.* Smoothly gracious, as in social manner; urbane. [French, from Latin *suāvis,* delightful.] —**suave·ly** *adv.* —**suav·i·ty, suave·ness** *n.*
    Synonyms: suave, smooth, urbane, diplomatic.

sub (sub) *n. Informal.* **1.** A submarine. **2.** A substitute. **3.** A subeditor. **4.** A subscription. **5.** *British.* An advance payment of wages. **6.** A subaltern.
~*v.* **subbed, subbing, subs.** —*intr. Informal.* To act as a substitute. —*tr.* **1.** *Informal.* **a.** To give or receive (an advance payment of wages). **b.** To request a loan from. **2.** To subedit. **3.** To apply a substratum to (a photographic film or plate base).

sub– *prefix.* Indicates: **1.** Under or beneath; for example, **submarine. 2.** Inferior or secondary in rank; for example, **sublieutenant. 3.** Somewhat short of or less than; for example, **subhuman, subtropical. 4.** Forming a subordinate or constituent part of a whole; for example, **subdivision, subset.** *Note:* Many compounds other than those entered here may be formed with *sub-.* In this dictionary in forming compounds, *sub-* is normally joined with the following element without space or hyphen: *subgroup.* However, many users prefer the hyphenated form, especially in less standardised compounds: *sub-foreman.* [In borrowed Latin compounds, *sub-* indicates: **1.** Under, as in **suppose. 2.** Below, beneath, as in **subaltern. 3.** Down, as in **supplicate. 4.** Up from under, from below, as in **supplant. 5.** Up, towards, as in **support. 6.** Subordinate, as in **subdeacon. 7.** Secretly, as in **suborn. 8.** In place of, as in **substitute.** Before *c, f, g, m, p,* and *r, sub-* becomes, respectively, *suc-, suf-, sug-, sum-, sup-,* and *sur-.* Sometimes it also becomes *sus-* before *c, p,* and *t.* Latin *sub-,* from *sub,* under, from below.]

sub. 1. *Logic.* subaltern. **2.** *Music.* subito. **3.** subscription. **4.** substitute. **5.** suburb; suburban.

sub·ac·id (súb-ássid) *adj.* Moderately acid or tart. —**sub·a·cid·i·ty** (súb-ə-síddəti, -a-) *n.*

sub·a·cute (súb-ə-kéwt) *adj.* Between acute and chronic. Said of a disease. —**sub·a·cute·ly** *adv.*

sub·aer·i·al (súb-aír-i-əl) *adj.* Located or occurring on or near the surface of the earth.

sub·al·pine (súb-ál-pīn) *adj.* **1.** Of or pertaining to regions at or near the foot of the Alps. **2.** Of, designating, or growing or living in mountainous regions just below the treeline.

sub·al·tern (súbb'l-tərn ‖ *U.S.* sə-báwl-) *adj.* **1.** *Chiefly British.* Holding a military rank just below that of captain. **2.** Lower in position or rank; secondary. **3.** *Logic.* **a.** Designating a particular proposition in relation to a universal with the same subject, predicate, and quality. **b.** Designating such a relationship.
~*n.* **1.** *Chiefly British.* A subaltern officer. **2.** A subordinate. **3.** *Abbr.* **sub.** *Logic.* A subaltern proposition or relation. [Late Latin *subalternus* : Latin *sub-,* below + *alternus,* ALTERNATE.]

sub·al·ter·nate (sub-áwl-tər-nət, -nit, -nayt ‖ -ól-) *adj.* **1.** Subordinate. **2.** Arranged alternately but tending to become opposite. Said of leaves. **3.** Following in turn. —**sub·al·ter·na·tion** *n.*

sub·ant·arc·tic (súb-ant-árktik ‖ -ártik) *adj.* Of or resembling regions just north of the Antarctic Circle.

sub·ap·i·cal (súb-áypik'l, -áppik'l) *adj.* Located below or near an apex. —**sub·ap·i·cal·ly** *adv.*

sub·a·po·stol·ic (súb-áppə-stóllik) *adj.* Of, pertaining to, or designating the era after that of the Apostles of Jesus.

sub·aq·ua (súb-ákwə ‖ *U.S. also* -áakwə) *adj.* Of or pertaining to underwater sport: *a subaqua club.* [SUB- + Latin *aqua,* water.]

sub·a·quat·ic (súb-ə-kwáttik, -kwóttik) *adj.* **1.** Living or growing partly on land and partly in water. **2.** Underwater.

sub·a·que·ous (súb-áykwi-əss, -ákwi-) *adj.* **1.** Formed or adapted for underwater use. **2.** Found or occurring under water.

sub·arc·tic (súb-árktik ‖ -ártik) *adj.* Of or like regions just south of the Arctic Circle.

sub·ar·id (súb-árrid) *adj.* Semiarid.

sub·a·tom·ic (súb-ə-tómmik) *adj.* **1.** Of or pertaining to the constituents of the atom. **2.** Having dimensions or participating in reactions characteristic of these constituents.

sub·au·di·tion (súb-aw-dísh'n) *n.* **1.** The act of understanding and mentally supplying a word or thought that has been implied but not expressed. **2.** A word or thought thus supplied. [Late Latin *subaudītiō*, from *subaudīre*, to supply an omitted word : *sub-*, secretly + *audīre*, to hear.]

sub·base (súb-bayss) *n. Architecture.* The lowermost front strip or moulding of a pedestal or wainscot.

sub·base·ment (súb-bayssmənt) *n.* Any storey or floor beneath the main basement of a building.

sub·bass (súb-bayss) *n. Music.* A pedal stop on an organ that produces the lowest notes, having 16 or 32 feet; a bourdon.

sub·cal·i·bre (súb-kál-ibər) *adj.* **1.** Smaller in calibre than the barrel of the gun from which it is fired. Said of projectiles. **2.** Of or pertaining to such projectiles.

sub·cat·e·go·ry (súb-kátti-gri, -gəri) *n.* A subdivision of a category.

sub·ce·les·tial (súb-si-lésti-əl || -léss-chəl) *adj.* **1.** Lower than celestial; terrestrial. **2.** Mundane.
~*n.* A subcelestial object.

sub·cep·tion (sub-sépsh'n, səb-) *n. Psychology.* Subliminal perception. [Subliminal per*ception*.]

sub·chas·er (súb-chayssər) *n. Nautical.* A submarine chaser.

sub·class (súb-klaass || -klass) *n.* **1.** A subdivision of a class. **2.** A taxonomic category ranking between a class and an order. **3.** *Mathematics.* A subset.
~*tr.v.* **subclassed, -classing, -classes.** To assign to a subclass.

sub·cla·vi·an (súb-kláyvi-ən) *adj. Anatomy.* **1.** Situated beneath the clavicle. **2.** Of or pertaining to a subclavian part.
~*n.* A subclavian structure, such as a vein, nerve, or muscle. [New Latin *subclavius* : SUB- + Latin *clāvis*, key (see **clavicle**).]

subclavian artery *n.* A short part of a major artery originating under the clavicle and continuous with the axillary artery extending to the upper extremities or forelimbs.

subclavian vein *n.* A part of a major vein of the upper extremities or forelimbs that is continuous with the axillary vein and is situated beneath the clavicle.

sub·cli·max (súb-klí-maks) *n.* **1.** A stage in the ecological succession of a plant or animal community immediately preceding a climax, and often persisting because of the effects of fire, flood, or other conditions. **2.** A plant or animal community at this stage. —**sub·cli·mac·tic** (-klī-máktik) *adj.*

sub·clin·i·cal (súb-klínnik'l) *adj.* Of or pertaining to a disease or the stage of a disease in which signs and symptoms are not yet apparent. —**sub·clin·i·cal·ly** *adv.*

sub·com·mit·tee (súb-kə-mitti) *n.* A subordinate committee composed of members appointed from or by the main committee, to deal with matters in more detail.

sub·con·scious (súb-kónshəss) *adj.* **1.** Not wholly conscious but capable of being made conscious. **2.** Acting or existing without being consciously recognised: *subconscious desires.*
~*n.* The subconscious mind; the unperceived source of conscious emotions, fantasies, and dreams. See Usage note at **conscious.** —**sub·con·scious·ly** *adv.* —**sub·con·scious·ness** *n.*

sub·con·ti·nent (súb-kónti-nənt) *n.* A large land mass on a continent, but in some geographical or political respect independent of it, such as India. —**sub·con·ti·nent·al** (-nént'l) *adj.*

sub·con·tract (súb-kón-trakt) *n.* A contract that assigns some of the obligations of a prior contract to another party.
~*v.* (-kən-trákt || -kon-, -kón-trakt) **subcontracted, -tracting, -tracts.** —*tr.* To make a subcontract for. Used of the original contractor. —*intr.* To make a subcontract.

sub·con·trac·tor (súb-kən-tráktər || -kón-traktər) *n.* A person or company that enters into a subcontract and assumes some of the obligations of the primary contractor; specifically, one who undertakes a particular part of the work in the construction of a building.

sub·con·tra·oc·tave (súb-kóntrə-ók-tiv, -tayv) *n. Music.* The octave that begins on the fourth C below middle C.

sub·con·tra·ry (súb-kóntrəri || -kón-trerri) —*adj. Logic.* **1.** Being or designating either or both of a pair of propositions related in such a way that they cannot both be false at once, although they may be true together.
~*n., pl.* **subcontraries.** *Logic.* Either of the two propositions of this type. —**sub·con·tra·ri·e·ty** *n.*

sub·cor·tex (súb-kór-teks) *n., pl.* **-tices** (-ti-seez). The portion of the brain immediately below the cerebral cortex. —**sub·cor·ti·cal** (-tik'l) *adj.* —**sub·cor·ti·cal·ly** *adv.*

sub·crit·i·cal (súb-krittik'l) *n.* Not having or involving a self-sustaining chain reaction. Said of nuclear reactions and reactors.

sub·cul·ture (súb-kulchər) *n.* **1.** One culture of microorganisms derived from another. **2.** A cultural subgroup, especially of a nation, differentiated by ethnic background, religion, beliefs, lifestyle, or other factors that functionally unify the group and act collectively on each member.
~*tr.v.* **subcultured, -turing, -tures.** To transfer (bacteria from a culture) on to a new culture medium. —**sub·cul·tur·al** *adj.*

sub·cu·ta·ne·ous (súb-kew-táyni-əss) *adj.* Located or introduced just beneath the skin. —**sub·cu·ta·ne·ous·ly** *adv.*

sub·dea·con (súb-déekən) *n.* **1. a.** Formerly in the Roman Catholic Church, a candidate ordained to the lowest of the major orders. **b.** In certain other churches, a minister with rank just below that of deacon. **2.** A minister who acts as assistant to the deacon at High Mass. [Middle English *subde(a)con*, from Late Latin *subdiaconus*, partial translation of Late Greek *hupodiakonos* : Greek *hupo-*, below, subordinate + *diakonos*, DEACON.]

sub·di·ac·o·nate (súb-dī-áckə-nət, -nit, -nayt) *n.* The office, order, or rank of subdeacon. [Late Latin *subdiaconātus*, from *subdiaconus*, SUBDEACON.] —**sub·di·ac·o·nal** *adj.*

sub·di·vide (súb-di-vĩd) *v.* **-vided, -viding, -vides.** —*tr.* **1.** To divide (a part or parts resulting from earlier division) into smaller parts. **2. a.** To divide into a number of parts. **b.** *U.S.* To divide (land) into lots for sale. —*intr.* To form into subdivisions. [Middle English *subdividen*, from Late Latin *subdīvidere* : Latin *sub-*, secondary, smaller + *dīvidere*, to DIVIDE.] —**sub·di·vid·er** *n.*

sub·di·vi·sion (súb-di-vízh'n, -vízh'n) *n.* **1.** The act or process of subdividing. **2.** Any of the subdivided parts. **3.** *Botany.* A taxonomic category ranking between a division and a class. **4.** *U.S.* An area composed of subdivided lots. —**sub·di·vi·sion·al** *adj.*

sub·dom·i·nant (súb-dómminənt) *n. Music.* **1.** The fourth note of a diatonic scale, coming below the dominant. **2.** A key or chord based on this note.
~*adj.* **1.** Influential but not quite dominant. **2.** *Music.* Of or pertaining to a subdominant.

sub·duc·tion zone (súb-dúksh'n) *n.* A long narrow zone along which oceanic lithosphere moves down into, and is assimilated by, the Earth's interior. Also called a "Benioff zone".

sub·due (səb-déw || sub-, -dóo) *tr.v.* **-dued, -duing, -dues. 1.** To conquer and subjugate; put down; vanquish. **2.** To quieten or bring under control by physical force or persuasion; make tractable. **3.** To make less intense or prominent; suppress; tone down: *A vote of approval subdued his anger.* **4.** To bring (land) under cultivation. —See Synonyms at **defeat.** [Middle English *subduen*, from Latin *subdūcere*, to lead away, withdraw (but influenced in sense by Latin *subdere*, to put under, subdue) : *sub-*, from under, away + *dūcere*, to lead.] —**sub·du·a·ble** *adj.* —**sub·du·al** *n.* —**sub·du·er** *n.*

sub·dued (səb-déwd || sub-, -dóod) *adj.* **1.** Uncharacteristically quiet, as through tiredness or shyness. **2.** Gentle; of only moderate strength or intensity: *subdued lighting.* **3.** Expressed only in an inhibited way: *subdued laughter.*

sub·dur·al (súb-déwr-əl || -dóor-) *adj. Anatomy.* Situated or occurring below the dura mater. [SUB + *dural*, from DURA (MATER).] —**sub·dur·al·ly** *adv.*

sub·ed·it (súb-éddit) *tr.v.* **-ited, -iting, -its.** To re-edit and correct (written or printed material). —**sub·ed·i·tor** (-ər) *n.* —**sub·ed·i·to·ri·al** (-éddi-táw-ri-əl || -tõ) *adj.*

sub·e·qua·to·ri·al (súb-ékwə-táwri-əl || -éekwə-, -tõri-) *adj.* Belonging to a region adjacent to the equatorial area.

su·ber·ic acid (sew-bérrik, soo-) *n.* A colourless crystalline dibasic acid, HOOC(CH$_2$)$_6$CO$_2$H, used in drug synthesis and plastics manufacture. Also called "octanedioic acid". [French *subérique*, from Latin *sūber*, cork (from which the acid is obtained).]

su·ber·in (séwbə-rin, sóobə-) *n.* A waxy waterproof substance present in the cell walls of cork tissue in plants. [French *subérine* : Latin *sūber*, cork (see **suberic acid**) + -IN.]

su·ber·ise, su·ber·ize (séwbə-rīz, sóobə-) *tr.v.* **-ised, -ising, -ises.** To cause (plant cell walls) to become impregnated with suberin during the formation of cork. [Latin *sūber*, cork. See **suberic acid**.] —**su·ber·i·sa·tion** (-rī-záysh'n || *U.S.* -ri-) *n.*

su·ber·ose (séwbə-rōz, sóobə-, -rõss) *adj.* Also **su·ber·ous** (-rəss). Of, pertaining to, or resembling cork or cork tissue; corky. [New Latin *suberosus*, from Latin *sūber*, cork. See **suberic acid**.]

sub·fam·i·ly (súb-fám-li, -fámmili) *n., pl.* **-lies. 1.** *Biology.* A taxonomic category ranking between a family and a genus. **2.** *Linguistics.* A division of languages below a family and above a branch.

sub·fix (súb-fiks) *n.* A subscript letter or sign.

sub·fusc (súb-fusk, -fúsk) *adj.* Dusky; dull-coloured.
~*n.* **1.** Dark, usually black, clothing worn with academic dress on formal occasions at Oxford University. **2.** Loosely, formal academic dress. [Latin *subfuscus*, dusky, from *fuscus*, dark brown.]

sub·ge·nus (súb-jéenəss) *n., pl.* **-genera** (-jénnərə). *Biology.* An occasionally used taxonomic category ranking below a genus and above a species. —**sub·ge·ner·ic** (-jə-nérrik) *adj.*

sub·gla·ci·al (súb-gláy-si-əl) *adj.* Formed or deposited beneath a glacier. —**sub·gla·cial·ly** *adv.*

sub·group (súb-grõop) *n.* **1.** A distinct group within a group. **2.** In algebra, a nonempty subset of a group. **3.** A subordinate group.

sub·head (súb-hed) *n.* Also **sub·head·ing** (-ing) (for sense 1). **1.** The heading or title of a subdivision of a printed subject. **2.** A subordinate heading or title.

sub·hu·man (súb-héwmən || -yóomən) *adj.* **1.** Below the human race in evolutionary development. **2.** Not fully human.

sub·i·ma·go (sub-i-máygō, -maágō) *n.* An insect, especially the mayfly, in a stage between the pupa and the imago. —**sub·im·ag·i·nal** (-imájin'l) *adj.*

sub·in·dex (súb-ín-deks) *n., pl.* **-dices** (-di-seez) or **-dexes. 1.** *Mathematics.* A distinguishing character or symbol directly beneath or next to and slightly below a number or letter; a subscript. **2.** An index to a section of a work.

sub·in·feu·date (súb-in-féwdayt) *tr.v.* **-dated, -dating, -dates.** Also **sub·in·feud** (-féwd), **-feuded, -feuding, -feuds.** To lease (lands) by subinfeudation.

sub·in·feu·da·tion (súb-in-few-dáysh'n) *n.* **1.** The sublease of a portion of a feudal estate by a vassal to a subtenant who pays fealty to the vassal. **2.** The tenure established. **3.** The lands so leased.

sub·in·feu·da·to·ry (súb-in-féwdə-tri, -təri) *adj.* Of or pertaining to subinfeudation.
~*n., pl.* **subinfeudatories.** A person who held his fief by subinfeudation.

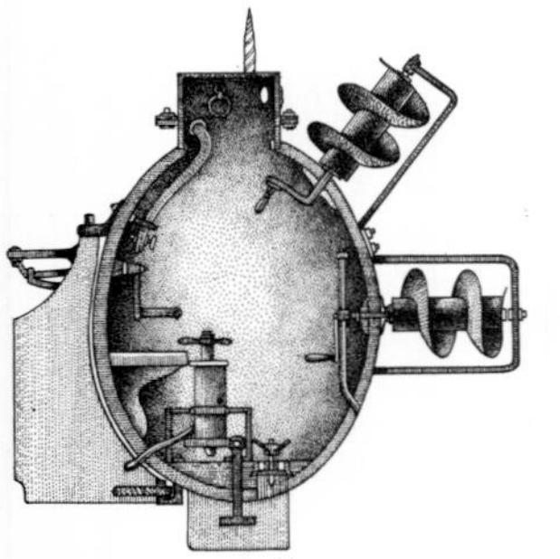

submarine *The earliest authenticated submarines, dating from the 1620s, were built of greased leather over a wooden frame and were propelled by oars. In use, however, they leaked badly under the pressure of water. The more reliable model shown here was a one-man craft known as the* Turtle. *Designed in 1776 by an American engineer, David Bushnell, it was the first to make use of buoyancy tanks – which could be flooded to submerge and pumped out to surface. The* Turtle *was moved underwater by cranking the propellers by hand.*

sub·ir·ri·gate (súb-írri-gayt) *tr.v.* **-gated, -gating, -gates.** To irrigate from beneath, as by means of underground pipes. **—sub·ir·ri·ga·tion** (-gáysh'n) *n.*

su·bi·to (sŏŏbi-tō) *adv. Music. Abbr.* **sub.** Quickly; suddenly. Used as a direction. [Italian, from Latin *subitō,* suddenly, from *subire,* to come secretly, steal upon : *sub-,* secretly + *īre,* to go.]

subj. 1. subject. **2.** subjective. **3.** subjunctive.

sub·ja·cent (súb-jáyss'nt) *adj.* **1.** Located beneath or below; underlying. **2.** Lying at a lower level but not directly beneath. [Latin *subjacēns* (stem *subjacent-*), present participle of *subjacēre,* to lie under : *sub-,* under + *jacēre,* to lie, from *jacere,* to throw.] **—sub·ja·cen·cy** *n.* **—sub·ja·cently** *adv.*

sub·ject (súb-jikt, -jekt) *adj.* **1.** Under the power or authority of another; owing obedience or allegiance to another. **2.** Prone; disposed. Used with *to.* **3.** Liable to incur or receive; exposed. Used with *to.* **4.** Contingent, conditional, or dependent. Used with *to.*
~n. Abbr. **subj. 1.** A person under the rule of another; especially, one who owes allegiance to a government or ruler: *a subject of the Crown.* **2. a.** A person or thing concerning which something is said or done; a topic. **b.** That which is treated or indicated in a work of art. **c.** *Music.* A **theme** *(see);* a melodic phrase which is subsequently developed. **3.** A course or area of study. **4.** A basis for action; a cause. Often used with *for: a subject for concern.* **5. a.** One that experiences or is subjected to something. **b.** One that is the object of clinical study, analysis, or treatment. **c.** A corpse intended for study and dissection. **6.** *Grammar.* A noun phrase in a sentence that denotes the doer of the action, the receiver of the action in passive constructions, or that which is described or identified. **7.** *Logic.* The term of a proposition about which something is affirmed or denied. **8.** *Philosophy.* **a.** The essential nature or substance of something as distinguished from its attributes. **b.** The mind or thinking part as distinguished from the object of thought.
~tr.v. (səb-jékt, súb-, *rarely* súb-jikt, -jekt) **subjected, -jecting, -jects. 1.** To submit to some discipline or authority; bring under control. **2.** To render liable to something. Often used in the passive. **3.** To cause to experience or undergo something. **4.** *Rare.* To subjugate. **5.** *Rare.* To submit for consideration. [Middle English *su(b)get, subject,* from Old French *su(b)get,* from Latin *subicere* (past participle *subjectus*), to bring under : *sub-,* under + *jacere,* to throw.] **—sub·jec·ta·ble** *adj.* **—sub·jec·tion** (səb-jéksh'n ‖ sub-) *n.*

sub·jec·ti·fy (səb-jékti-fī, sub-) *tr.v.* **-fied, -fying, -fies.** To render subjective; interpret subjectively.

sub·jec·tive (səb-jéktiv, súb-) *adj. Abbr.* **subj. 1. a.** Proceeding from, pertaining to, or taking place within an individual's mind in a manner unrelated to external reality; unfounded: *subjective fears.* **b.** Affected by or arising from one's personality or experience rather than rational thought or observation: *a subjective view.* **c.** Particular to a given individual; personal. **2.** Pertaining to the real nature of something; essential. **3.** Moodily introspective. **4.** *Psychology.* Existing only within the mind and incapable of external verification. **5.** *Medicine.* Designating a symptom or condition perceived by the patient and not by the examiner. **6.** Expressing or bringing into prominence the individuality of the artist or author. **7.** *Grammar.* Designating or being in the nominative case. **—sub·jec·tive·ly** *adv.* **—sub·jec·tive·ness, sub·jec·tiv·i·ty** (súb-jek-tívvəti) *n.*

subjective complement *n. Grammar.* A noun, noun phrase, or adjective serving as a complement to a verb and qualifying its subject. In *He made her a good husband, husband* is a subjective complement.

subjective genitive *n. Grammar.* **1.** The genitive case as indicating the subject of a specified action. Thus in the phrase *my love for her,* meaning "the love I bear her", the subject *(I)* is transferred to the genitive case *(my).* Compare **objective genitive. 2.** A noun or pronoun in this case.

subjective idealism *n. Philosophy.* The theory that all experience is of ideas in the mind.

sub·jec·tiv·ism (səb-jéktiv-iz'm, sub-) *n.* **1. a.** The doctrine that all knowledge is restricted to the conscious self and its sensory states. **b.** Any theory or doctrine, especially theological, that emphasises the subjective elements in experience. **2.** The theory that individual conscience is the only valid standard of moral judgment. **3.** The quality of being subjective. **—sub·jec·tiv·ist** *n.* **—sub·jec·tiv·is·tic** (-ístik) *adj.*

subject matter *n.* The matter under consideration in a written work, speech, or discussion; the theme. [Translation of Latin *subjecta materia,* translation of Greek *hupokeimenē hulē,* "underlying matter".]

sub·join (súb-jóyn) *tr.v.* **-joined, -joining, -joins.** To add at the end; append; annex. [From obsolete French *subjoindre,* from Latin *subjungere* : *sub-,* in addition + *jungere,* to join.]

sub·join·der (súb-jóyndər) *n.* Something subjoined. [From SUBJOIN.]

sub ju·di·ce (súb jŏŏdi-si, sŏŏb yŏŏdi-ki) *adj. Law.* **1.** Under judicial deliberation; before a judge or court of law, and thus outside the scope of public comment. **2.** Not yet decided; still subject to confidential discussion. [Latin, "under a judge".] **—sub ju·di·ce** *adv.*

sub·ju·gate (súb-jŏŏ-gayt, -jə-) *tr.v.* **-gated, -gating, -gates. 1.** To bring under dominion; conquer; subdue. **2.** To make subservient; subdue. —See Synonyms at **defeat.** [Middle English *subjugaten,* from Latin *subjugāre,* to place under a yoke : *sub-,* under + *jugum,* yoke.] **—sub·ju·ga·tion** (-gáysh'n) *n.* **—sub·ju·ga·tor** (-gaytər) *n.*

sub·junc·tion (səb-júngksh'n, súb-) *n.* **1.** The act of subjoining or the condition of being subjoined. **2.** Something that is subjoined. [Late Latin *subjunctiō* (stem *subjunctiōn-*), from *subjungere* (past participle *subjunctus*), SUBJOIN.]

sub·junc·tive (səb-júngktiv ‖ sub-) *adj. Abbr.* **subj.** *Grammar.* Designating a verb form or set of forms used to express a contingent or hypothetical action or state, for example one that is feared, desired, or doubted. Compare **indicative.**
~n. Abbr. **subj. 1.** The subjunctive mood. **2.** A subjunctive verb or construction. [Late Latin *(mōdus) subjunctīvus,* translation of Greek *hupotaktikē enklisis,* "mood of subordination" (originally regarded as proper to subordinate clauses), from Latin *subjungere,* SUBJOIN.] **—sub·junc·tive·ly** *adv.*

sub·king·dom (súb-king-dəm, -kíng-) *n. Biology.* A former taxonomic category constituting a major division of a kingdom.

sub·lap·sar·i·an·ism (súb-lap-sáir-i-ən-iz'm) *n. Theology.* **Infralapsarianism** *(see).* [New Latin *sublapsarius* : SUB- + LAPSE.] **—sub·lap·sar·i·an** *adj.* & *n.*

sub·lease (súb-léess) *tr.v.* **-leased, -leasing, -leases. 1.** To sublet (property). **2.** To rent (property) under a sublease.
~n. (súb-leess). A lease of property granted in turn by a lessee.

sub·les·see (súb-le-sée) *n.* One to whom a sublease is granted.

sub·les·sor (súb-le-sór) *n.* One granting a sublease.

sub·let (súb-let) *tr.v.* **-let, -letting, -lets. 1.** To rent (property one holds by lease) to another. **2.** To subcontract (work).
~n. **1.** An instance of subletting. **2.** *Chiefly U.S. Informal.* Property, especially a flat, rented by a tenant to another party.

sub·lieu·ten·ant (súb-lə-ténnənt, -le-, -lŏŏ-, *also* -lef-) *n.* An officer in the Royal Navy and certain other navies, ranking below a lieutenant, equivalent in rank to a lieutenant in the army and a flying officer in the Royal Air Force. **—sub·lieu·ten·an·cy** *n.*

sub·li·mate (súbbli-mayt) *v.* **-mated, -mating, -mates.** *—tr.* **1.** *Psychology.* To transform (an instinctual impulse, especially a sexual urge, which cannot be immediately fulfilled) into more socially acceptable forms of expression, behaviour, or activity. **2.** To cause (a solid or a gas) to change state without becoming a liquid. *—intr.* To change directly from the solid to the gaseous state or from the gaseous to the solid state without becoming a liquid.
~n. (*also* -mət, -mit). The material formed by sublimation.
~adj. Exalted or purified. [Latin *sublīmāre,* to raise, from *sublīmis,* uplifted, SUBLIME.] **—sub·li·ma·tion** *n.*

sub·lime (sə-blím) *adj.* **1.** Characterised by nobility; grand; majestic. **2. a.** Of high spiritual, moral, or intellectual worth. **b.** Not to be excelled; supreme. Sometimes used ironically: *sublime ignorance.* **3.** Inspiring awe; impressive; moving. **4.** *Poetic.* Of lofty appearance or bearing; proud. **5.** *Archaic.* Raised aloft; set high.
~n. **1.** That which is sublime. Preceded by *the.* **2.** *Rare.* The ultimate example of something. Preceded by *the.*
~v. **sublimed, -liming, -limes.** *—tr.* **1.** To render sublime; elevate; ennoble. **2.** *Chemistry.* To cause to sublimate. *—intr. Chemistry.* To sublimate. [Latin *sublīmis.* See **limen.**] **—sub·lime·ly** *adv.* **—sub·lim·er** *n.* **—sub·lim·i·ty** (sə-blímməti), **sub·lime·ness** *n.*

sub·lim·i·nal (súb-límmin'l, səb-) *adj. Psychology.* **1.** Being or acting below the threshold of conscious perception. Said of stimuli. **2.** Inadequate to produce conscious awareness. [SUB- + Latin *līmen* (stem *līmin-*), threshold (see **limen**).] **—sub·lim·i·nal·ly** *adv.*

subliminal advertising *n.* A now illegal advertising technique of interspersing straightforward film with persuasive, split-second images held to influence the viewer subliminally.

sub·lin·gual (súb-líng-gwəl) *adj.* Situated beneath or on the underside of the tongue: *sublingual salivary glands.*

sub·lit·to·ral (súb-líttərəl) *adj.* **1.** Near the seashore. **2.** Shallow and lying between the shoreline and the edge of the continental shelf.

sub·lu·nar·y (súb-lŏŏ-nəri ‖ -léw-) *adj.* Also **sub·lu·nar** (-nər). **1.** Situated beneath the moon. **2.** *Literary.* Of this world; earthly. [Late Latin *sublūnāris* : Latin *sub-,* beneath + *lūna,* moon.]

sub·lux·a·tion (súb-luk-sáysh'n) *n.* Incomplete dislocation of a joint.

sub·ma·chine gun (súb-mə-shéen) *n.* A lightweight automatic or semiautomatic gun fired from the shoulder or hip. Compare **machine gun.**

sub·man·dib·u·lar (súb-man-díbbewlər) *adj.* Submaxillary.

sub·mar·gin·al (súb-márjin'l) *adj.* **1.** Beneath a margin. **2.** Below the minimum requirements. **3.** Of low productivity; infertile.

sub·ma·rine (súb-mə-reen, -réen) *adj.* **1.** Located, occurring, or functioning beneath the surface of the water; undersea. **2.** Of or pertaining to a submarine.
~n. **1.** A vessel capable of operating submerged. **2.** *U.S. Informal.* A sandwich, a **hero** *(see).*

sub·mar·i·ner (súb-márrinər ‖ -mə-réenər) *n.* A member of the crew of a submarine.

sub·max·il·lar·y (súb-mak-síllәri ‖ *U.S.* -máksə-lerri) *adj.* Of or relating to the lower jaw or the region adjacent to it; submandibular.
~n., pl. **submaxillaries.** An anatomical part situated beneath the maxilla, such as the submaxillary salivary gland.

sub·me·di·ant (súb-méedi-ənt) *n. Music.* **1.** The sixth note of a diatonic scale. **2.** A key or chord based on this.
~adj. Of or pertaining to the submediant. [SUB- + MEDIANT.]

sub·merge (səb-mérj, sub-) *v.* **-merged, -merging, -merges.** *—tr.* **1.** To place or plunge under water or other liquid. **2.** To cover with water; inundate. **3.** To hide from view; obscure. **4.** To overwhelm. *—intr.* To go under or as if under water. [Latin *submergere* : *sub-,* under + *mergere,* to immerse, plunge.] **—sub·mer·gence** *n.*

sub·merged (səb-mérjd, sub-) *adj.* Also **sub·mersed** (-mérst) (for sense 1). **1.** *Botany.* Growing or remaining under water: *submerged* *leaves.* **2.** Growing permanently under water. Said of certain aquatic plants. **3.** Hidden.

sub·mer·gi·ble (səb-mérj-əb'l, sub-) *adj.* Submersible. **—sub·mer·gi·bil·i·ty** (-ə-bílləti) *n.*

sub·merse (səb-mérss, sub-) *tr.v.* **-mersed, -mersing, -merses.** To submerge. [Latin *submergere* (past participle *submersus*), SUBMERGE.] **—sub·mer·sion** (-mérsh'n || -mérzh'n) *n.*

sub·mers·i·ble (səb-mér-sib'l, sub-, -səb'l) *adj.* Able to be plunged into or to remain under water.

~*n.* **1.** A vessel capable of operating or remaining under water, such as a bathysphere. **2.** *Archaic.* A submarine.

sub·mi·cro·scop·ic (súb-mīkrə-skóppik) *adj.* Too small to be seen through an optical microscope. **—sub·mi·cro·scop·ical·ly** *adv.*

sub·min·i·a·ture (súb-mínnə-chər, -mínni-ə-, -tewr) *adj.* Smaller than miniature; exceedingly small.

sub·min·i·a·tur·ise, sub·min·i·a·tur·ize (súb-mínnə-chə-rīz, -mínni-ə-) *tr.v.* **-ised, -ising, -ises.** To make subminiature; especially, to manufacture or design (electronic equipment) in subminiature size. **—sub·min·i·a·tur·i·sa·tion** (-rī-záysh'n || *U.S.* -ri-) *n.*

sub·miss (səb-míss || sub-) *adj. Archaic.* **1.** Submissive. **2.** Soft in tone. [Latin *submissus,* past participle of *submittere,* SUBMIT.]

sub·mis·sion (səb-mísh'n || sub-) *n.* **1. a.** The act of submitting to the power of another. **b.** The state of having submitted. **2.** The state of being submissive or compliant; meekness. **3. a.** The act of submitting something, such as a document, for consideration. **b.** Something thus submitted. —See Synonyms at **surrender.**

sub·mis·sive (səb-míssiv || sub-) *adj.* **1.** Disposed to submit; docile. **2.** Indicating or marked by submission. —See Synonyms at **obedient.** **—sub·mis·sive·ly** *adv.* **—sub·mis·sive·ness** *n.*

sub·mit (səb-mít || sub-) *v.* **-mitted, -mitting, -mits.** —*tr.* **1.** To yield or surrender (oneself) to the will or authority of another or others. **2.** To subject to some condition or process. **3.** To refer (something) to the consideration or judgment of another. **4.** To offer as a proposition or contention: *I submit that they lied.* —*intr.* To yield or give way, especially to one considered physically, intellectually, or morally superior. —See Synonyms at **yield.** [Middle English *submitten,* from Latin *submittere,* to place under : *sub-,* under + *mittere,* to throw.] **—sub·mit·tal** *n.* **—sub·mit·ter** *n.*

sub·mon·tane (súb-móntayn || -mon-táyn) *adj.* Located under or at the base of a mountain or mountain range. [Late Latin *submontānus* : Latin *sub-,* under + *montānus,* mountainous, from *mōns,* mountain.] **—sub·mon·tane·ly** *adv.*

sub·mu·co·sa (súb-mew-kṓ-sə, -zə) *n.* The layer of connective tissue that lies beneath a mucous membrane. **—sub·mu·co·sal** *adj.*

sub·mul·ti·ple (súb-múltip'l) *n.* A number that is an exact divisor of another number: *2 is a submultiple of 10.* **—sub·mul·ti·ple** *adj.*

sub·nor·mal (súb-nórməl) *adj.* **1.** Less than normal; below the average. **2.** Mentally deficient. See **mental deficiency.**

~*n.* A person who is subnormal in some respect, as in intelligence or coordination. **—sub·nor·mal·ly** *adv.*

sub·nor·mal·it·y (súb-nawr-mál-əti) *n.* **1.** The state or condition of being subnormal. **2. Mental deficiency** *(see).*

sub·nu·cle·ar (sub-néw-kli-ər || -nōō-) *adj.* **1.** Of or pertaining to the constituents of the nucleus of an atom. **2.** Having dimensions or participating in reactions characteristic of such constituents.

sub·o·ce·an·ic (súb-ṓ-shi-ánnik, -si-) *adj.* Formed, situated, or occurring beneath the ocean or the ocean bed.

sub·or·der (súb-awrdər) *n.* **1.** *Biology.* A taxonomic category ranking after an order and before a family. **2.** A subdivision of any category termed an order. **—sub·or·di·nal** (-órdi-nəl) *adj.*

sub·or·di·nar·y (sub-órd'n-ri, -in-, -əri) *n.* Any of various heraldic bearings that are less important that the ordinaries.

sub·or·di·nate (sə-bórdi-nət, -bórd-, -nit || -nayt) *adj.* **1.** Belonging to a lower or inferior class or rank; minor; secondary. **2.** Occupying a secondary position; of relatively little importance. **3.** Subject to the authority or control of another.

~*n.* One that is subordinate.

~*tr.v.* (-nayt) **subordinated, -nating, -nates. 1.** To put in a lower or inferior rank or class. **2.** To treat as having little or less importance. **3.** To make subservient; subdue. [Medieval Latin *subōrdīnātus,* past participle of *subōrdīnāre,* to put in a lower rank : Latin *sub-,* below + *ōrdīnāre,* to arrange in order, from *ōrdō,* order.] **—sub·or·di·nate·ly** *adv.* **—sub·or·di·nate·ness, sub·or·di·na·tion** (-náysh'n) *n.* **—sub·or·di·na·tive** (-nətiv || -naytiv) *adj.*

subordinate clause *n. Grammar.* A clause that cannot stand alone as a full sentence and that functions within a sentence as an adjectival, adverbial, or noun phrase. Also called "dependent clause".

subordinate conjunction *n. Grammar.* A conjunction that introduces a subordinate clause, such as *that, who, because,* or *if.* Compare **coordinate conjunction.**

sub·or·di·na·tion·ism (sə-bórdi-náysh'n-iz'm || su-) *n. Theology.* The doctrine, often considered heretical, that the second and third persons of the Trinity are subordinate to the first person. **—sub·or·di·na·tion·ist** *n.*

sub·orn (sə-bórn) *tr.v.* **-orned, -orning, -orns. 1. a.** To induce (a person) to commit a wrong or unlawful act. **b.** To induce (a person) to commit perjury. **2.** To procure (perjured testimony). [Latin *subōrnāre* : *sub-,* secretly + *ōrnāre,* to equip.] **—sub·or·na·tion** (súb-awr-náysh'n) *n.* **—sub·orn·er** *n.*

sub·ox·ide (súb-óksīd) *n.* An oxide containing a lower proportion of oxygen than is present in the normal or most common oxide of the element.

sub·phy·lum (súb-fī-ləm, -fī-) *n., pl.* **-la** (-lə). *Biology.* A taxonomic category ranking between a phylum and a class.

sub·plot (súb-plot) *n.* A plot, as in a novel or play, that is secondary and incidental to the main plot.

sub·poe·na (səb-péenə, súb-, sə-) *n.* A legal writ requiring appearance or production in court to give or provide evidence.

~*tr.v.* **subpoenaed, -naing, -nas.** To serve or summon with such a writ. [Latin *sub poenā,* under penalty (first words in the writ) : *sub-,* under + *poenā,* penalty, from Greek *poine.*]

sub·po·lar (súb-pṓlər) *adj.* Near the polar regions.

sub-post office *n.* In Britain, a small, branch post office, normally within an ordinary shop.

sub·prin·ci·pal (súb-prín-sip'l) *n.* **1.** *Chiefly U.S.* An assistant principal. **2.** An auxiliary or bracing rafter in a frame. **3.** *Music.* An open diapason sub-bass in an organ.

sub·rep·tion (sub-répsh'n, səb-) *n.* **1.** A calculated misrepresentation through concealment of the facts. **2.** An inference drawn from such a misrepresentation. [Latin *subreptiō* (stem *subreptiōn-*), theft, from *subrepere* (past participle *subreptus*), to creep under, steal upon : *sub-,* under + *repere,* to creep.] **—sub·rep·ti·tious** (súb-rep-tíshəss) *adj.*

sub·ro·gate (súb-rə-gayt, -rō-) *tr.v.* **-gated, -gating, -gates. 1.** *Law.* To substitute (one person) for another. **2.** *Rare.* To substitute (one thing) for another. [Latin *subrogāre,* "to nominate an alternative candidate" : *sub-,* instead of + *rogāre,* to ask, propose.]

sub·ro·ga·tion (súb-rə-gáysh'n, -rō-) *n. Law.* The substitution of one person for another, especially of one creditor for another.

sub ro·sa (súb rṓzə) *adv.* In secret; privately; confidentially. [Latin, "under the rose", from the practice of hanging a rose over a meeting as a symbol of secrecy, from the legend that Cupid once gave Harpocrates, the god of silence, a rose to make him keep the secrets of Venus.] **—sub rosa** *adj.*

sub·rou·tine (súb-rōō-teen) *n. Computing.* A self-contained section of a computer program that can be identified and used more than once during the running of the program.

subs. subscription.

sub·scap·u·lar (súb-skáppewlər) *adj. Anatomy.* Situated below or on the underside of the scapula.

~*n.* A subscapular part, such as an artery or nerve.

sub·scribe (səb-skrīb || sub-) *v.* **-scribed, -scribing, -scribes.** —*tr.* **1.** To sign (one's name) at the end of a document. **2.** To sign one's name to in attestation, testimony, or consent: *subscribe a will.* **3.** To pledge or contribute (a sum of money). —*intr.* **1.** To contract to receive and pay for regular receipt of a newspaper or periodical or a public service, such as a telephone. **2.** To promise to pay or contribute money. **3.** To express agrement or approval; assent. Used with *to*: *subscribe to that view.* **4.** To sign one's name. **5.** To affix one's signature to a document as a witness or to show consent. **6.** To apply for shares offered on the stock exchange in a limited company. **7.** To undertake to purchase a book prior to publication. —See Synonyms at **assent.** [Middle English *subscriben,* from Latin *subscrībere* : *sub-,* under + *scrībere,* to write.] **—sub·scrib·er** *n.*

subscriber trunk dialling *n. Abbr.* **S.T.D..** A telephone service enabling subscribers to dial trunk calls and international calls without help from the operator.

sub·script (súb-skript) *adj.* Written beneath.

~*n.* A distinguishing character or symbol written directly beneath or next to and slightly below a letter or number. Compare **superscript.** [Latin *subscriptus,* past participle of *subscrībere,* SUBSCRIBE.]

sub·scrip·tion (səb-skrípsh'n || sub-) *n. Abbr.* **sub., subs. 1.** An order for an advance purchase, as of the issues of a periodical over a certain period of time or of tickets for a series of concerts, plays, or other cultural events. **2.** *Chiefly British.* A sum of money paid at fixed intervals for membership of a society, association, or similar body. **3.** An application for newly issued shares on the stock exchange. **4.** The act of subscribing, especially: **a.** The act of setting one's signature on a document. **b.** The acceptance of a position or belief, especially an article of faith. **c.** The act of contributing money, as to a charitable cause or to finance a future publication. **5.** That which is subscribed, especially: **a.** An inscription. **b.** A charitable donation. **—sub·scrip·tive** *adj.* **—sub·scrip·tive·ly** *adv.*

sub·sec·tion (súb-seksh'n) *n.* A division of a section.

sub·se·quence (súb-si-kwənss || -kwenss) *n.* **1.** That which is subsequent; a sequel. **2.** The fact or quality of being subsequent.

sub·se·quent (súb-si-kwənt || -kwent) *adj.* **1.** Following in time or order; succeeding. **2.** Designating a river that is a tributary to a consequent river. In this sense, compare **obsequent.** —See Usage Note at **consequent.** **—subsequent to.** Following; coming after. [Middle English, from Old French, from Latin *subsequēns,* present participle of *subsequī,* to follow close after : *sub-,* close to, after + *sequī,* to follow.] **—sub·se·quent·ly** *adv.* **—sub·se·quent·ness** *n.*

sub·serve (səb-sérv, sub-) *tr.v.* **-served, -serving, -serves.** To serve to promote (some end); be useful to; further. [Latin *subservīre,* to serve, be subject to : *sub-,* under + *servīre,* SERVE.]

sub·ser·vi·ent (səb-sérvi-ənt, sub-) *adj.* **1.** Subordinate in capacity or function. **2.** Obsequious; servile. **3.** Useful only to further some other purpose; purely instrumental. [Latin *subserviēns* (stem *subservient-*), present participle of *subservīre,* SUBSERVE.] **—sub·ser·vi·ence, sub·ser·vi·en·cy** *n.* **—sub·ser·vi·ent·ly** *adv.*

sub·set (súb-set) *n.* A set, as in mathematics, contained within a set.

sub·shrub (súb-shrub) *n.* **1.** A herbaceous plant having a woody lower stem. **2.** A low shrub; an undershrub.

sub·side (səb-sīd || sub-) *intr.v.* **-sided, -siding, -sides. 1.** To sink to

PRONUNCIATION KEY

a, trap; aa, father; ai, **fair;** ar, **star;** aw, **lawn;** ay, **play;** b, bb, stab; **rubber;** ch, **church;** ck, **ticket;** d, dd, **dead; ladder;** e, **dress;** ee, **bee;** er, **defer;** ew, **few;** ewr, **pure;** ə, about; ər, **letter;** f, ff, **fife; differ;** g, gg, **giggle;** h, **hat;** i, **kit;** ī, **price;** īr, **fire;** j, **judge;** k, **kick;** l, ll, **let;** 'l, **needle;** m, mm, **man;** n, nn, **no;** 'n, **sudden;** ng, **thing;** o, **lot;** ō, **no;** ōō, **foot;** ōō, **shoe;** oor, **poor;** ow, **cow;** owr, **hour;** oy, **boy;** p, pp, **pepper;** r, rr, **red;** s, ss, **sauce;** sh, **ship;** t, tt, **totter;** th, **thick;** th, **this;** **smooth;** u, **cut;** ur, **turn;** v, vv, **valve;** w, **wet;** y, **yes;** z, zz, **zebra;** zh, **vision;** **pleasure**

IN FOREIGN WORDS:

aN, ON, **Saint-Saëns;** hl, **Llanelli; Hluhluwe;** kh, **loch; lough; Khaled**

STRESS MARK:

ín-sīt, insight; in-sīt, incite

a lower or normal level. **2.** To sink or settle down, as into a sofa. **3.** To sink to the bottom; settle, as sediment does. **4.** To become less agitated or active; abate. —See Synonyms at **decrease.** [Latin *subsīdere,* to sink down : *sub-,* down + *sīdere,* to settle.]

sub·sid·ence (səb-sīd'nss, súb-sidənss) *n.* The act or process of subsiding; especially, the sinking or settlement of ground or of buildings erected on it.

sub·sid·i·ar·y (səb-síddi-əri, -síd-yəri || sub-, -erri) *adj.* **1.** Serving to assist or supplement; auxiliary. **2.** Secondary in importance; subordinate. **3.** *U.S.* Of, pertaining to, or of the nature of a subsidy.
~n., pl. **subsidiaries. 1.** One that is subsidiary. **2.** A subsidiary company. **3.** *Music.* A theme subordinate to a main theme or subject. [Latin *subsīdiārius,* in reserve, supporting, from *subsidium,* support, SUBSIDY.] **—sub·sid·i·ar·i·ly** *adv.*

subsidiary company *n.* A company having more than half of its shares owned by another company. Also called "subsidiary".

sub·si·dise, sub·si·dize (súb-si-dīz, -sə-) *tr.v.* **-dised, -dising, -dises. 1.** To assist or support with a subsidy. **2.** To secure the assistance of by granting a subsidy. **—sub·si·di·sa·tion** (-dī-záysh'n || *U.S.* -di-) *n.* **—sub·si·dis·er** *n.*

sub·si·dy (súb-si-di, -sə-) *n., pl.* **-dies. 1.** A sum of money provided to assist a person, enterprise, or nation, usually one unable to be self-financing; especially, government funds for such purposes as financing research, maintaining employment, encouraging development, or stabilising price levels. **2.** Formerly, money granted to the British Crown by Parliament. —See Synonyms at **bonus.** [Middle English *subsidie,* aid, assistance, from Anglo-French, from Latin *subsidium,* reserve troops, hence support, help, from *subsidēre,* to sit down, remain, be placed in reserve : *sub-,* down + *sedēre,* to sit.]

sub·sist (səb-síst || sub-) *v.* **-sisted, -sisting, -sists.** *—intr.* **1.** To be sustained; manage to live. Used with *on* or *by*: *subsisting on a meagre pension.* **2.** To reside in or consist of something specified: *The difference subsists in the quality of their work.* **3. a.** To exist; be. **b.** To remain or continue in existence. **4.** To be logically conceivable. *—tr. Archaic.* To maintain or support with provisions. [Latin *subsistere,* to stand still, stand up, remain standing : *sub-,* from below, up + *sistere,* to cause to stand.] **—sub·sist·er** *n.*

sub·sis·tence (səb-sístənss || sub-) *n.* **1.** The act or state of subsisting, especially in a very basic state. **2.** A means of subsisting; sustenance. —See Synonyms at **livelihood.**
~adj. Of, involving, or designating an agricultural system in which the farmer and his family consume the produce, leaving little or nothing to sell. **2.** Of or being money paid to an employee as an advance or to cover incidental expenses. **3.** Of or designating a level of income that is barely sufficient to meet the necessities of life. **—sub·sis·tent** *adj.*

sub·soil (súb-soyl) *n.* The partially decomposed layer of rock underlying the topsoil and overlying the solid rock beneath.
~tr.v. **subsoiled, -soiling, -soils.** To plough or turn up the subsoil of. **—sub·soil·er** *n.*

sub·so·lar (súb-sōlər) *adj.* Situated on the Earth apparently directly beneath the Sun.

sub·son·ic (súb-sónnik) *adj.* **1.** Infrasonic. **2.** Having a speed less than that of sound in a designated medium.

sub·spe·cies (súb-spée-sheez, -shiz || -seez) *n., pl.* **subspecies.** *Abbr.* **ssp** *Biology.* A subdivision of a taxonomic species, usually based on geographical distribution. **—sub·spe·cif·ic** (-spə-síffik) *adj.*

subst. 1. substantive. **2.** substitute.

sub·stance (súb-stənss) *n.* **1.** *Philosophy.* The essential nature of anything, as considered apart from its form or attributes; the primary or basic element that receives modifications. **2.** Any kind of matter; a material of which something is composed. **3.** The essence of what is said or written; the gist. **4. a.** That which is solid or real; reality as opposed to appearance. **b.** A solid or substantial quality or character. **5.** Density; body: *Air has little substance.* **6.** Material possessions; wealth: *a man of substance.* [Middle English, essence, from Old French, from Latin *substantia,* from *substāns,* present participle of *substāre,* to be present : *sub-,* up + *stāre,* to stand.]

sub·stan·dard (súb-stándərd) *adj.* **1.** Failing to meet a standard; below standard. **2.** Considered unacceptable usage by the educated members of a speech community.

sub·stan·tial (səb-stánsh'l, -staánsh'l || sub-) *adj.* **1.** Of, pertaining to, or having substance; material. **2.** Not imaginary; true; real. **3.** Solidly built; strong. **4.** Ample; sustaining: *a substantial breakfast.* **5.** Considerable in importance, value, degree, amount, or extent: *won by a substantial margin.* **6.** Practical; virtual: *in substantial agreement.* **7.** Possessing wealth or property; well-to-do. **8.** *Informal.* Fat; stout. Used humorously: *"Running did not come easily to a middle-aged woman of her substantial proportions"* (Ivy St. David).
~n. Plural. **1.** The essentials. **2.** Solid things. [Middle English *substancial,* from Late Latin *substantiālis,* from Latin *substantia,* SUBSTANCE.] **—sub·stan·ti·al·i·ty** (-stánshi-ál-əti), **sub·stan·tial·ness** *n.* **—sub·stan·tial·ly** *adv.*

sub·stan·ti·ate (səb-stán-shi-ayt, -staán-, -si- || sub-) *tr.v.* **-ated, -ating, -ates. 1.** To support with proof or evidence; verify. **2. a.** To give material form to; embody. **b.** To make firm or solid. **3.** To give substance to; make real or actual. —See Synonyms at **confirm.** [New Latin *substantiare,* from Latin *substantia,* SUBSTANCE.] **—sub·stan·ti·a·tion** (-áysh'n) *n.*

sub·stan·ti·val (súb-stən-tīv'l) *adj. Grammar.* Of, pertaining to, or of the nature of a substantive. **—sub·stan·ti·val·ly** *adv.*

sub·stan·tive (súb-stən-tiv; *for sense 6, usually* səb-stán-) *adj. Abbr.* **s., sb., subst. 1.** Independent in existence or function; not subordinate. **2.** Not imaginary; genuine; real. **3.** Of or pertaining to the essence or substance of something; essential. **4.** Of substantial amount. **5.** Having a solid basis; firm. **6.** Effective and permanent. **7.** Expressing or denoting existence, as does the verb *to be.* **8.** Being or functioning as a noun or noun phrase. **9.** Pertaining to or designating that part of law concerned with legal rights and duties, rather than with procedure. Compare **adjective.**
~n. Abbr. **s., subst.** A word or group of words acting as a noun. [Middle English *substantif,* from Old French, from Late Latin *substantīvus,* self-existent, from Latin *substantia,* "thing that exists", SUBSTANCE.] **—sub·stan·tive·ly** *adv.* **—sub·stan·tive·ness** *n.*

sub·sta·tion (súb-stayh'n) *n.* **1.** An electrical installation in which power from the generating station is converted or transformed for distribution. **2.** A subsidiary or branch station.

sub·stit·u·ent (səb-stíttew-ənt || sub-) *n. Chemistry.* An atom, radical, or group substituted for another in a compound as a result of a chemical reaction.
~adj. Of such an atom or group. [Latin *substituēns* (stem *substituent-*), present participle of *substituere,* to SUBSTITUTE.]

sub·sti·tute (súb-sti-tewt || -to͞ot) *n. Abbr.* **sub., subst. 1.** One that takes the place of another; a replacement, as: **a.** A substance, especially an artificial or inferior one, used in place of another. **b.** In sports such as cricket and soccer, a reserve player who may be called on to replace a member of a team for reasons of injury or tactics, for example. **2.** *Grammar.* A word or construction used in place of another word, phrase, or clause.
~v. **substituted, -tuting, -tutes.** *—tr.* **1.** To put or use (a person or thing) in place of another, especially: **a.** To replace (a member of a sports team) with a reserve player. **b.** To put (a reserve player) in the place of an existing member of a team. **2.** *Nonstandard.* To replace: *substitute olive oil by sunflower oil.* *—intr.* To take the place of another: *substituting for the sick player.* [Latin *substitūtus,* a replacement, from the past participle of *substituere,* to substitute : *sub-,* in place of + *statuere,* to cause to stand.] **—sub·sti·tut·a·bil·it·y** (-ə-bílləti) *n.* **—sub·sti·tut·a·ble** *adj.* **—sub·sti·tute** *adj.*

sub·sti·tu·tion (súb-sti-téwsh'n || -to͞osh'n) *n.* **1. a.** The act of substituting. **b.** The state of being substituted. **2.** That which is substituted. **—sub·sti·tu·tion·al** *adj.* **—sub·sti·tu·tion·al·ly** *adv.*

sub·sti·tu·tive (súb-sti-tew-tiv || -to͞o-) *adj.* Serving or capable of serving as a substitute.

sub·strate (súb-strayt) *n.* **1.** A chemical substance or substances that undergo change as a result of being acted on by an enzyme. **2.** *Biology.* A surface on which a plant or animal grows or is attached. **3.** *Electronics.* The material upon which the elements of a semiconducting component or integrated circuit are deposited. **4.** A substratum. [From SUBSTRATUM.]

sub·stra·tum (súb-straa-təm, -stray-, -straá-, -stráy- || *U.S. also* -strá-) *n., pl.* **-ta** (-tə) or **-tums. 1.** An underlying layer. **2.** The foundation or groundwork for something. **3.** *Philosophy.* The characterless substance that supports attributes of reality. **4.** *Biology.* A substrate. **5.** A thin coating of hardened gelatine used to hold the emulsion on a photographic plate or film. **6.** *Linguistics.* An indigenous language which is replaced by that of an incoming population, but which may affect the development of the new language. In this sense, compare **superstratum.** [Medieval Latin *substrātum,* from Latin, neuter past participle of *substernere,* to lie under : *sub-,* under + *sternere,* to spread out flat.] **—sub·stra·tive** *adj.*

sub·struc·tion (súb-strúksh'n) *n.* A foundation; the substructure, as of a building. [Latin *substructiō* (stem *substructiōn-*), from *substruere* (past participle *substructus*), to build beneath : *sub-,* beneath + *struere,* to build.] **—sub·struc·tion·al** *adj.*

sub·struc·ture (súb-strukchər) *n.* **1.** The supporting part of a structure; a foundation. **2.** *U.S.* The earth bank or bed supporting railway tracks. **—sub·struc·tur·al** *adj.*

sub·sume (səb-séwm, -so͝om || sub-, -sho͝om) *tr.v.* **-sumed, -suming, -sumes.** To place or include in a more comprehensive category or under a general principle. [New Latin *subsumere* : Latin *sub-,* under + *sūmere,* to take up.] **—sub·sum·a·ble** *adj.*

sub·sump·tion (səb-súmpsh'n || sub-) *n.* **1. a.** The act or an instance of subsuming. **b.** Something that is subsumed. **2.** *Logic.* The minor premise of a syllogism. [New Latin *subsumptio* (stem *subsumptiōn-*), from *subsumere,* SUBSUME.] **—sub·sump·tive** *adj.*

sub·teen (súb-téen) *n.* A child approaching teenage years. **—sub·teen** *adj.*

sub·ten·ant (súb-ténnənt) *n.* One who rents land, a house, or other property from a tenant. **—sub·ten·an·cy** *n.*

sub·tend (səb-ténd || sub-) *tr.v.* **-tended, -tending, -tends. 1.** *Geometry.* To be opposite to and delimit: *The side of a triangle subtends the opposite angle.* **2.** To underlie so as to enclose or surround. [Latin *subtendere,* to extend beneath : *sub-,* beneath + *tendere,* to extend.]

sub·ter·fuge (súb-tər-fewj) *n.* An evasive or deceitful tactic used to avoid an unwanted situation or to gain one's ends. See Synonyms at **artifice.** [French, from Late Latin *subterfugium,* from Latin *subterfugere,* to flee secretly : *subter,* secretly + *fugere,* to flee.]

sub·ter·min·al (súb-términ'l) *adj.* Coming nearly at the end.

sub·ter·ra·ne·an (súb-tə-ráyni-ən) *adj.* **1.** Situated or operating beneath the Earth's surface; underground. **2.** Hidden; existing or working in secret. [Latin *subterrāneus* : *sub-,* under + *terra,* earth.] **—sub·ter·ra·ne·an·ly** *adv.*

sub·ter·res·tri·al (súb-tə-réstri-əl, -te-) *adj.* Subterranean.
~n. An animal that lives underground.

sub·text (súb-tekst) *n.* A message which is not made explicit but which may be inferred from a statement or work of art or literature;

PRONUNCIATION KEY

a, trap; aa, father; ai, fair; ar, star; aw, lawn; ay, play; b, bb, stab; rubber; ch, church; ck, ticket; d, dd, dead; ladder; e, dress; ee, bee; er, defer; ew, few; ewr, pure; ə, about; ər, letter; f, ff, fife; differ; g, gg, giggle; h, hat; i, kit; ī, price; īr, fire; j, judge; k, kick; l, ll, let; 'l, needle; m, mm, man; n, nn, no; 'n, sudden; ng, thing; o, lot; ō, no; o͝o, foot; o͞o, shoe; oor, poor; ow, cow; owr, hour; oy, boy; p, pp, pepper; r, rr, red; s, ss, sauce; sh, ship; t, tt, totter; th, thick; th, this; smooth; u, cut; ur, turn; v, vv, valve; w, wet; y, yes; z, zz, zebra; zh, vision; pleasure

IN FOREIGN WORDS:

aN, oN, Saint-Saëns; hl, Llanelli; Hluhluwe; kh, loch; lough; Khaled

STRESS MARK:

ín-sīt, insight; in-sīt, incite

an underlying meaning: *a political speech with a sinister subtext.*
sub·tile (sútt'l) *adj. Archaic.* Subtle. **—sub·tile·ly** *adv.* **—sub·til·i·ty** (-ti-, sub-tílləti), **sub·tile·ness, sub·til·ty** *n.*
sub·til·ise, sub·til·ize (sútt'l-īz) *v.* **-ised, -ising, -ises.** *—tr.* To make subtle. *—intr.* To argue or discuss with subtlety; make fine distinctions. [Medieval Latin *subtīlizāre,* from Latin *subtīlis,* SUBTLE.] **—sub·til·i·sa·tion** (-ī-záysh'n || *U.S.* -i-) *n.*
sub·ti·tle (súb-tīt'l) *n.* **1.** A secondary and usually explanatory title, as of a literary work. **2. a.** A printed narration or portion of dialogue shown on the screen between the scenes of a silent film. **b.** A printed translation of the dialogue of a foreign-language film or television broadcast, shown at the bottom of the screen.
sub·tle (sútt'l) *adj.* **-tler, -tlest. 1. a.** So slight as to be difficult to detect or analyse; elusive. **b.** Not immediately obvious; abstruse. **2.** Fine or delicate: *a subtle flavour.* **3.** Able to make fine distinctions; keen. **4. a.** Characterised by skill or ingenuity; clever. **b.** Characterised by deftness or sensitivity: *the subtle approach.* **5. a.** Characterised by craft or slyness; devious. **b.** Operating in a hidden and usually injurious way; insidious. [Middle English *sutil, subtil,* thin, fine, clever, ingenious, from Old French, from Latin *subtīlis,* thin, fine.] **—sub·tle·ness** *n.* **—sub·tly** *adv.*
sub·tle·ty (sútt'lti) *n., pl.* **-ties. 1.** The quality or state of being subtle. **2.** Something subtle; especially, a nicety of thought or a fine distinction. —See Synonyms at **tact.**
sub·ton·ic (súb-tónnik) *n. Music.* The seventh tone of a diatonic scale, immediately below the tonic.
sub·top·i·a (súb-tōpi-ə) *n. British.* A suburban area, especially one that has been developed in an unattractive way. Used derogatorily. [*Sub*urban + u*topia.*] **—sub·top·i·an** *adj.*
sub·tor·rid (súb-tórrid || -táwrid) *adj.* Subtropical.
sub·to·tal (súb-tōt'l) *adj.* Less than total; incomplete.
~n. The total of part of a series of numbers.
~tr.v. **subtotalled** or *U.S.* **-taled, -talling** or *U.S.* **-taling, -tals.** To add up part of (a series of numbers).
sub·tract (səb-trákt || sub-) *v.* **-tracted, -tracting, -tracts.** *—tr.* To take away; deduct. *—intr.* To perform the arithmetical operation of subtraction. [Latin *substrahere* (past participle *substractus*), to draw away : *sub-,* away + *trahere,* to draw.] **—sub·tract·er** *n.*
sub·trac·tion (səb-tráksh'n || sub-) *n.* **1.** The act or process of subtracting; deduction. **2.** The arithmetical process or operation of finding a number or quantity that when added to one of two quantities produces the other.
sub·trac·tive (səb-tráktiv || sub-) *adj.* **1.** Producing or involving subtraction. **2.** Designating a colour produced by light passing through more than one colorant, each of which inhibits certain wavelengths, as in mixtures of pigments. Compare **additive.** See **primary colour. 3.** Designating a photographic process that produces a positive image by superposition or mixing of substances that selectively absorb coloured light.
sub·tra·hend (súb-trə-hend) *n.* A quantity or number to be subtracted from another. [Latin *subtrahendum,* gerundive of *subtrahere,* SUBTRACT.]
sub·trop·ics (súb-tróppiks) *pl.n.* The geographical areas bordering the tropics; roughly the areas 23 to 40° N and S, having no cold season. **—sub·trop·ic·cal** *adj.*
su·bu·late (súbbew-lət, -lit, -layt) *adj. Biology.* Awl-shaped; tapering to a point. [New Latin *subulatus,* from Latin *sūbula,* awl.]
sub·urb (súb-urb, *rarely* -ərb) *n. Abbr.* **sub. 1.** A usually residential area or community on the edge of a city or large town. **2.** *Plural.* The perimeter of country around a major city; environs. Preceded by *the.* [Middle English, from Old French *suburbe,* from Latin *suburbium* : *sub-,* near + *urbs,* city (see **urban**).]
sub·ur·ban (sə-búrbən || su-) *adj. Abbr.* **sub. 1.** Of, pertaining to, or characteristic of a suburb or life in a suburb, especially in being unsophisticated, narrow-minded, or conventional. **2.** Located or residing in a suburb. **3.** Typical of life in the suburbs.
~n. A suburbanite. **—sub·ur·ban·i·ty** (súb-ur-bánnəti, -ər-) *n.*
sub·ur·ban·ite (sə-búrbən-īt || su-) *n.* One who lives in a suburb.
sub·ur·bi·a (sə-búrbi-ə || su-) *n.* **1.** Suburbs or suburbanites collectively. **2.** The typical values and lifestyle of suburbanites.
sub·ur·bi·car·i·an (sə-búrbi-káir-i-ən, su-) *adj.* Designating any of the six dioceses surrounding Rome of which the pope is the metropolitan bishop. [Late Latin *suburbicārius,* situated near Rome : *sub-,* near + *urbicārius,* of the city (especially Rome), from Latin *urbicus,* from *urbs,* city (see **urban**).]
sub·ven·tion (səb-vénsh'n, sub-) *n.* **1.** The provision of help, aid, or support. **2.** A grant of financial aid; an endowment or subsidy, as that given by a government to an institution for research. [Middle English *subvencioun,* from Old French *subvention,* from Late Latin *subventiō* (stem *subventiōn-*), from Latin *subvenīre* (past participle *subventus*), to come to help : *sub-,* from below, up + *venīre,* to come.] **—sub·ven·tion·ar·y** (-ri, -əri || -erri) *adj.*
sub·ver·sion (səb-vérsh'n, sub- || -vérzh'n) *n.* **1.** The act of subverting, especially of subverting an established government or other institution. **2.** The condition of being subverted. **3.** Anything that subverts. [Middle English *subversioun,* from Old French *subversion,* from Late Latin *subversiō* (stem *subversiōn-*), from Latin *subvertere* (past participle *subversus*), SUBVERT.] **—sub·ver·sion·ar·y** *adj.*
sub·ver·sive (səb-vér-siv, sub- || -ziv) *adj.* Intended or serving to subvert; especially, intended to overthrow or undermine an established government or other institution.
~n. One who advocates or is regarded as advocating subversive means or policies. **—sub·ver·sive·ly** *adv.* **—sub·ver·sive·ness** *n.*
sub·vert (səb-vért, sub-) *tr.v.* **-verted, -verting, -verts. 1.** To destroy completely; ruin: *subvert those schemes.* **2.** To undermine the character, morals, or allegiance of; corrupt. **3.** To overthrow or tend to overthrow completely: *subvert the democratic system.* [Middle English *subverten,* from Old French *subvertir,* from Latin *subvertere,* to turn upside down : *sub-,* from below, up + *vertere,* to turn.] **—sub·vert·er** *n.*
sub·way (súb-way) *n.* **1.** An underground tunnel or passage, as for pedestrians under a busy road or for a water main. **2.** *Chiefly U.S.* An underground railway.
sub·zero (súb-zéer-ō) *adj.* **1.** Less than zero, especially on a temperature scale. **2.** Of, characterised by, or for use in temperatures below zero: *subzero nights.*
suc·ce·da·ne·um (súksi-dáyni-əm) *n., pl.* **-nea** (-ə). *Formal.* A substitute. [New Latin, from Latin *succēdāneus,* substituted, "following", from *succēdere,* SUCCEED.]
suc·ceed (sək-séed || suk-) *v.* **-ceeded, -ceeding, -ceeds.** *—intr.* **1.** To come next in time, order, or sequence; follow after; especially, to replace another in an office or position. Often used with *to*: *succeed to the throne.* **2.** To accomplish something desired or intended. **3.** To do well; end favourably; prosper: *He'll succeed in New Zealand.* *—tr.* **1.** To follow in time or order; come after. **2.** To replace; follow in office: *succeeded his father as chairman.* —See Synonyms at **follow.** [Middle English *succeden,* from Old French *succeder,* from Latin *succēdere,* to follow closely, go after : *sub-,* towards, next to + *cēdere,* to go.] **—suc·ce·dent** *adj.* **—suc·ceed·er** *n.*
suc·cès de scan·dale (sŏŏk-sáy də skoN-dáal; *French* sük-) *n.* Acclaim or success accorded something, such as a work of art, purely on the basis of its shocking nature or the scandal surrounding it. [French, "success of scandal".]
suc·cès d'es·time (dess-téem) *n.* **1.** A critical but not popular success or achievement. **2.** A work that is admired without necessarily being read, seen, or heard. [French, "success of respect".]
suc·cess (sək-séss || suk-) *n.* **1.** The achievement of something desired, planned, or attempted. **2. a.** The gaining of fame, prosperity, or status. **b.** The extent of such gain. **3.** One that is successful. **4.** *Archaic.* Any result or outcome. [Latin *successus,* from the past participle of *succēdere,* SUCCEED.]
suc·cess·ful (sək-séssf'l || suk-) *adj.* **1.** Having a favourable outcome. **2.** Having obtained something desired or intended. **3.** Having achieved fame, prosperity, or status. **—suc·cess·ful·ly** *adv.*
suc·ces·sion (sək-sésh'n || suk-) *n.* **1.** The act or process of following in order or sequence. **2.** A group of persons or things arranged or following in order; a sequence. **3. a.** The sequence in which one person after another succeeds to a title, throne, dignity, or estate. **b.** The right of a person or line of persons to so succeed. **c.** The person or line vested with such a right. **4. a.** The act or process of succeeding to the rights or duties of another. **b.** The act or process of becoming entitled as a legal beneficiary to the property of a deceased person. **5.** *Ecology.* The series of changes that take place in a community from its initial colonisation of the habitat to formation of a stable **climax community** *(see).* **—in succession.** Following one after another, without interruption. —See Synonyms at **series. —suc·ces·sion·al** *adj.* **—suc·ces·sion·al·ly** *adv.*
suc·ces·sive (sək-séssiv || suk-) *adj.* **1.** Following in uninterrupted order or sequence. **2.** Of, characterised by, or involving succession. **—suc·ces·sive·ly** *adv.* **—suc·ces·sive·ness** *n.*
suc·ces·sor (sək-séssər || suk-) *n.* One that succeeds another.
success story *n.* A case involving a person or thing that proves remarkably successful: *Penicillin was a great medical success story.*
suc·cin·ate (súksi-nayt) *n.* A salt of succinic acid.
suc·cinct (sək-síngkt, suk-) *adj.* **1.** Clearly expressed in few words; concise. **2.** Characterised by brevity and clarity in speech or writing: *a succinct style.* **3.** *Archaic.* Encircled as if by a girdle; girded. —See Synonyms at **concise.** [Latin *succinctus,* girded, concise, from the past participle of *succingere,* to gird below : *sub-,* below + *cingere,* to gird.] **—suc·cinct·ly** *adv.* **—suc·cinct·ness** *n.*
suc·cin·ic (suk-sínnik, sək-) *adj.* **1.** Of or relating to amber. **2.** Containing or derived from succinic acid. [French *succinique,* from Latin *succinum,* amber.]
succinic acid *n.* A colourless crystalline compound, $CO_2H(CH_2)_2CO_2H$, occurring naturally in amber and synthesised for use in pharmaceuticals and perfumes; 1, 4-butanedioic acid.
suc·co·ry (súckəri) *n., pl.* **-ries.** A plant, **chicory** *(see).* [Alteration (influenced by Middle Dutch *sūkerie,* succory) of Middle English *cicoree,* CHICORY.]
Suc·coth, Suk·koth (sŏŏk-ōt, -ōth) *n.* A Jewish harvest festival celebrated for nine days beginning on the eve of the 15th of Tishri. [Hebrew *sukkōth,* "(feast of) booths" (commemorating the temporary shelter of the Jews in the wilderness), from *sukkāh,* booth.]
suc·cour, *U.S.* **suc·cor** (súckər) *n.* **1.** Assistance or help in time distress; relief. **2.** One that affords assistance or relief.
~tr.v. **succoured** or *U.S.* **-cored, -couring** or *U.S.* **-coring -cours** or *U.S.* **-cors.** To render assistance to in time of distress. See Synonyms at **help.** [Middle English *sucurs* (taken as plural), from Old French, from Medieval Latin *succursus,* from Latin, past participle of *succurrere,* to turn to the aid of, run under : *sub-,* under + *currere,* to run.] **—su·cour·a·ble** *adj.* **—suc·cour·er** *n.*
suc·cu·bus (súckew-bəss) *n., pl.* **-buses** or **-bi** (-bī). Also **suc·cu·ba** (-bə) *pl.* **-bae** (-bee). **1.** A female demon supposed to descend upon and have sexual intercourse with a man while he sleeps. Compare **incubus. 2.** Any evil spirit; a demon. [Medieval Latin, from Late

Latin *succuba,* prostitute, from Latin *succubāre,* to lie under : Latin *sub-,* under + *cubāre,* to lie.]

suc·cu·lent (súckewlənt) *adj.* **1.** Full of juice or sap; juicy. **2.** *Botany.* Having thick, fleshy leaves or stems that conserve moisture. **3.** Desirable or attractive.
~*n.* A succulent plant, such as a sedum or a cactus. [Latin *succulentus,* from *succus,* juice.] —**suc·cu·lence, suc·cu·len·cy** *n.* —**suc·cu·lent·ly** *adv.*

suc·cumb (sə-kúm ‖ su-) *intr.v.* **-cumbed, -cumbing, -cumbs. 1.** To yield or submit to an overpowering force or overwhelming desire; give in or give up. Often used with *to: succumb to temptation.* **2.** To die. Used with *to: succumbed to smallpox.* [Middle English *succomben,* from Old French *succomber,* from Latin *succumbere,* to lie down under : *sub-,* under + *-cumbere,* to lie.]

suc·cus·sion (sə-kúsh'n ‖ su-) *n.* **1.** The act or process of shaking violently. **2.** The condition of being so shaken. **3.** *Medicine.* The shaking of a patient in order to detect a splashing sound, which indicates the presence of fluid in a body cavity, especially the pleural cavity. [Latin *succussiō* (stem *succussiōn-*), from *succutere* (past participle *succussus*), to shake from beneath : *sub-,* beneath + *quatere,* to shake.] —**suc·cus·sa·to·ry** (sə-kússə-tri, -təri ‖ su-) *adj.*

such (such; *occasional weak form* səch) *adj.* **1.** Of this or that kind: *We haven't had such fun as this for years!* **2.** Being the same or the same kind as that which is specified or implied. Sometimes used as a pronoun: *The weather was such that we could not go out.* **3.** Being the same in quality or kind: *pins, needles, and other such sewing aids.* **4.** Being the same as something implied but left undefined or unsaid: *Such people are never satisfied.* **5.** Of so extreme or great a degree or quality: *He's such a fool!* —**as such. 1.** As being the person or thing implied or previously mentioned; by one's or its very nature: *A diplomat as such must negotiate.* **2.** In itself or by itself: *Money as such will seldom bring happiness.* —**such as. 1.** For example. **2.** Of the stated or implied kind or degree; like. Sometimes followed by a clause: *language such as I had never heard.*
~*pron.* **1.** Such a person or persons or thing or things. **2.** A person or persons or thing or things implied or indicated: *Such were the results of that war.* **3.** One of such kind: *papers and such.*
~*adv.* **1.** To such an extent or degree; so very: *such long hair.* **2.** Very: *has not been in such good health lately.* **3.** In such a manner or way. [Middle English *su(c)ch, swulc,* Old English *swylc, swelc.*]

> *Usage:* Following *such as,* traditional grammars recommend the use of the subject form of personal pronouns, and this is normal in formal English: *Have you ever seen a man such as he?* Informal English usually uses the object form of the pronoun (for example, *him*) in such cases, and when the pronoun occurs at the end of a sentence this is quite common even in formal contexts.

such-and-such, such and such (súch-ənd-such) *adj.* Not yet named or known: *They agreed to meet at such and such an hour.*
~*n.* An as yet unknown or unnamed person or thing.

such·like (súch-līk) *adj.* Of a similar kind; like.
~*pron. Informal.* Persons or things of such a kind.

Su·chou. See Suzhou.

suck (suk) *v.* **sucked, sucking, sucks.** —*tr.* **1.** To draw (liquid) into the mouth by tensing muscles in the mouth and drawing in breath. **2. a.** To draw in by establishing a partial vacuum. **b.** To draw in by or as if by a current in a fluid. **c.** To absorb. Often used with *up* or *in.* **3.** To draw liquid or nourishment through or from. **4.** To hold, moisten, or manoeuvre (a sweet, for example) in the mouth, often by making sucking motions. —*intr.* **1.** To draw in by or as if by suction. **2.** To draw nourishment; suckle. **3.** To make a sucking sound or motion. —**suck in. 1.** *Chiefly U.S. Slang.* To take advantage of; cheat; swindle. **2.** To attract forcefully; engulf. —**suck up.** *Informal.* To flatter in order to gain favour. Used with *to.*
~*n.* **1.** The act of sucking. **2.** Suction. **3.** Something drawn in by sucking. [Middle English *s(o)uken,* Old English *sūcan.*]

suck·er (súckər) *n.* **1.** One that sucks; specifically, a young mammal before weaning. **2.** *Slang.* One who is easily deceived; a gullible person; a dupe. **3.** *Informal.* One unable to resist the appeal of something specified. Used with for: *a sucker for kittens.* **4. a.** A piston or piston valve, as in a suction pump or syringe. **b.** A tube or pipe, such as a siphon, through which anything is sucked. **5.** A flat or cup-shaped device, usually made of rubber, that can adhere to a surface by suction. **6.** *U.S.* A lollipop. **7.** Any of various fishes with sucking discs; especially, the **clingfish** *(see).* **8.** A structure or part adapted for clinging by suction, as found in certain animals. **9.** *Botany.* A secondary shoot arising from the base of a tree trunk or from the lower part of some shrubs, which gives rise to a new plant.
~*v.* **suckered, -ering, -ers.** —*tr.* **1.** To strip suckers or shoots from. **2.** *Chiefly U.S. Slang.* To take advantage of the gullibility of; fool. —*intr.* To send out suckers or shoots.

suck·er·fish (súckər-fish) *n., pl.* **-fishes** or collectively **suckerfish.** Also **suck·fish.** The **remora** *(see).*

suck·ing (súcking) *adj.* Too young to be weaned.

sucking louse *n.* Any insect of the order Anoplura. See **louse.**

suck·le (súck'l) *v.* **-led, -ling, -les.** —*tr.* **1.** To cause or allow to take milk at the breast or udder; nurse. **2.** To take in as sustenance; have as nourishment. **3.** *Literary.* To bring up; rear; nourish; foster: *suckled in poverty.* —*intr.* To suck at the breast. [Probably back-formation from SUCKLING.] —**suck·ler** *n.*

suck·ling (súckling) *n.* A young mammal or child that has not been weaned. [Middle English : SUCK + -LING.]

Suck·ling (súckling), **Sir John** (1609–42). English poet, courtier,

and wit. His works included *Aglaura* (1637), *Session of the Poets* (1637), and *Brennoralt, or The Discontented Colonel* (1640).

sucks (suks) *interj.* **1.** Used to express derision or open disobedience. **2.** Used to express disappointment.

su·crase (sóo-krayz, -krayss) *n. Chemistry.* **Invertase** *(see).* [French *sucre,* SUGAR + -ASE.]

su·cre (sóo-kray) *n.* **1.** The basic monetary unit of Ecuador, equal to 100 centavos. **2.** A coin worth one sucre. [Spanish, after Antonio José de *Sucre* (1795–1830), South American revolutionary.]

Sucre (sóo-kray). City in Bolivia, situated in a mountain valley on the eastern slope of the Andes at an altitude of 2 590 metres (8,500 feet). It is the legal capital of Bolivia, though the seat of government is La Paz. Sucre has oil refineries and is an agricultural centre.

su·crose (sóo-krōz, séw-, -krōss) *n.* A crystalline disaccharide carbohydrate, $C_{12}H_{22}O_{11}$, found in many plants, mainly sugar cane, sugar beet, and maple, and used widely as a sweetener, preservative, and in the manufacture of plastics and cellulose. Also called "sugar", "saccharose". [French *sucre,* SUGAR + -OSE.]

suc·tion (súksh'n) *n.* **1.** The act or process of sucking. **2.** The force that causes a fluid or solid to be drawn into an interior space or to adhere to a surface because of the difference between the external and internal pressures.
~*adj.* Creating or operating by suction. [Late Latin *sūctiō* (stem *sūctiōn-*), from Latin *sūgere* (past participle *sūctus*), to suck.]

suction pump *n.* A pump for drawing up a liquid by means of suction produced by a piston being drawn through a cylinder.

suction stop *n. Phonetics.* A **click** *(see).*

suc·to·ri·al (suk-táw-ree-əl ‖ -tó-) *adj. Biology.* **1.** Adapted for sucking or clinging by suction. **2.** Having suctorial organs or parts. [New Latin *sūctōrius,* from Latin *sūgere,* to suck. See **suction.**]

Su·dan, the (sóo-daʹan, -dán). Vast region of Africa lying between the Sahara and the tropical forest lands to the south. It stretches from the Atlantic to Ethiopia and Cameroon, including the south of the Democratic Republic of the Sudan, and the Sahel region.

Sudan, Democratic Republic of the. Formerly **Anglo-Egyptian Sudan.** The largest country in Africa, lying in the northeast of the continent. The north is desert or scrubland, and south mostly savannah, a vast area suitable only for livestock herding. About 77 per cent of the labour force are in agriculture, mostly at subsistence level, and cotton, groundnuts, sesame seed, and hides and skins are the chief exports. Sudan is one of the world's poorest countries, with massive foreign debts. However, its rivers have great potential for irrigation, and the Jonglei Canal will conserve water, draining much of the Sudd to provide good farmland. The country's mineral resources include extensive oil and gas reserves. The area was ruled jointly by Britain and Egypt from 1898 until independence (1956). A military coup (1969) brought to power General Nemery, and the civil war (1955–72) between the predominantly Arab north and the black south was ended. Area, 2 503 813 square kilometres (967,500 square miles). Population, 19,900,000. Capital, Khartoum. —**Su·dan·ese** *adj. & n.*

Su·dan·ic (sóo-dánnik ‖ sew-) *adj.* **1.** Of or pertaining to the Sudan

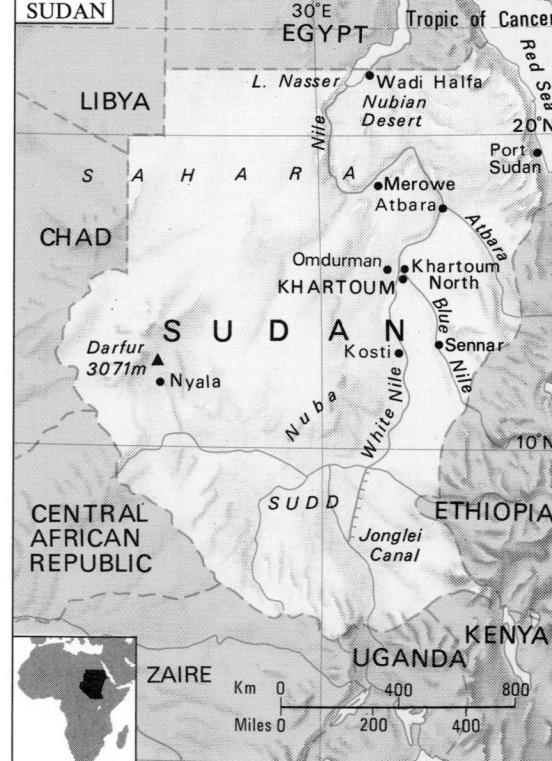

region. **2.** Of or pertaining to the languages of the region, chiefly Niger-Congo and Chari-Nile. **—Su·dan·ic** *n.*

su·da·to·ri·um (sōō-də-táw-ri-əm, séw- || -tṓ-) Also **su·da·ri·um** (-dáir-i-əm) *n., pl.* **-ia** (-ə). A hot-air room used, especially in ancient Rome, for sweat baths. [Latin *sūdātōrium,* from *sūdāre,* to sweat.]

su·da·to·ry (sōō-də-tri, séw-, -təri) *adj.* Sudorific. ~*n., pl.* **sudatories. 1.** A sudatorium. **2.** A sudorific.

sudd (sud) *n.* A floating mass of vegetation that often obstructs navigation on the White Nile. [Arabic, obstruction, from *sadda,* to obstruct.]

Sudd (sud). The vast swamp in southern Sudan caused by sudd obstruction of the White Nile and its tributaries.

sud·den (súdd'n) *adj.* **1.** Happening without warning; unforeseen. **2.** Characterised by hastiness; abrupt; rash: *That decision was a bit sudden.* **3.** Characterised by rapidity; quick; swift. **—all of a sudden.** Very quickly and unexpectedly; suddenly. [Middle English *sodan(e),* from Anglo-French *sodein, sudein,* from Late Latin *subitānus,* variant of Latin *subitāneus,* from *subitus,* sudden, past participle of *subīre,* to approach secretly, steal upon : *sub-,* secretly + *īre,* to go.] **—sud·den·ly** *adv.* **—sud·den·ness** *n.*

sudden death *n.* **1.** *Sports.* An extra game point, hole, or the like played to break a tie. **2.** Extra minutes of play added to a tied game, the winning team being the first team to score. Also used adjectivally: *a sudden-death playoff.*

sudden infant death syndrome *n.* **Cot death** *(see).*

Su·de·ten·land. (sōō-dáyt'n-land; *German* zōō-, -lant). Border region of northern Czechoslovakia, lying along the Sudeten Mountains. It was transferred from Austria-Hungary to Czechoslovakia (1919), and had a significant proportion of German-speaking inhabitants. The area was granted to Nazi Germany by the Munich agreement (1938), but together with similar areas of northwest and southwest Czechoslovakia (then also termed "Sudetenland"), was returned to Czechoslovakia in 1945. The area's German-speaking populations were subsequently expelled.

su·dor·if·er·ous (sōōdə-ríffərəss, séwdə-) *adj.* Producing or secreting sweat. [Late Latin *sūdōrifer* : Latin *sūdor,* sweat + -FEROUS.]

su·dor·if·ic (sōōdə-ríffik, séwdə-) *adj.* Causing or increasing sweat. ~*n.* A sudorific medicine. [New Latin *sūdōrificus* : Latin *sūdor,* sweat + -FIC.]

Su·dra (sōōdrə) *n.* **1.** The lowest of the major Hindu castes, originally composed of menials but later largely of artisans and labourers. **2.** A member of this caste. [Sanskrit *śūdra.*]

suds (sudz) *pl.n.* **1.** Soapy water containing soap bubbles. **2.** Foam; lather. [Originally, dregs, muddy water, probably from Middle Dutch *sudde, sudse,* marsh, swamp.] **—sud·sy** *adj.*

sue (sew, sōō) *v.* **sued, suing, sues.** *—tr.* **1.** To make a petition to; appeal to; beseech. **2.** To institute legal proceedings against by bringing a civil aciton, usually for redress of grievances. **3.** *Archaic.* To court; woo. *—intr.* **1.** To institute legal proceedings. **2.** To make an appeal or entreaty. Usually used with *for: sue for mercy.* **3.** *Archaic.* To woo. [Middle English *sewen,* to pursue, prosecute, from Anglo-French *suer, suire,* from Vulgar Latin *sequere* (unattested), to follow, from Latin *sequī.*] **—su·er** *n.*

suede, suède (swayd) *n.* **1.** Leather with a soft napped surface, usually produced by rubbing the flesh side. **2.** Fabric made to resemble this leather. In this sense, also called "suede cloth". [From *suède gloves,* partial translation of French *gants de suède,* "gloves of Sweden", from *Suède,* Sweden.]

su·et (sōō-it, séw-) *n.* The hard fat around the kidneys of cattle and sheep, used in cooking and making tallow. [Middle English *sewet,* from Anglo-French *sewet* (unattested), diminutive of *sue, seu,* from Latin *sēbum,* tallow, suet. See **sebum.**]

suet pudding *n.* A steamed, usually sweet, pudding containing or enclosed in a casing of suet and flour.

Su·e·to·ni·us (sōō-i-tōni-əss, séw-, swee-), born Gaius Suetonius Tranquillus (*c.*69–*c.*140 A.D.). Roman historian and biographer. His *De Vita Caesarum,* lives of the first 12 Caesars from Julius Caesar to Domitian, survives almost complete.

Su·ez (sōō-iz, séw- || -ez, *U.S. also* sōō-éz). *Arabic* **As-Suways.** Port in northeastern Egypt, situated at the northern end of the Gulf of Suez at the entrance to the Suez Canal.

Suez, Isthmus of. The strip of land in northeastern Egypt connecting Asia and Africa and traversed by the Suez Canal.

Suez Canal. A major shipping canal in northeastern Egypt, connecting the Mediterranean Sea with the Red Sea, via the Gulf of Suez. It is 165 kilometres (103 miles) long, and extends from Port Said in the north to Suez in the south. The canal was planned by the French engineer Ferdinand de Lesseps, who also supervised its construction (1859–69). Britain became the largest shareholder in the Suez Canal Company in 1875. In 1888 an international convention proclaimed the free right of transit to all shipping, to be guaranteed by Britain. An agreement of 1954 provided for British evacuation of the zone. In 1956 Nasser nationalised the canal company, provoking the Suez Crisis, in which Britain, France, and Israel attacked Egypt but were quickly forced to withdraw due to hostile world opinion. Restored to Egyptian control, the canal was subsequently closed (1967–75) because of Arab-Israeli hostilities.

suf. suffix.

suff. 1. sufficient. **2.** suffix.

Suff. 1. Suffolk. **2.** suffragan.

suf·fer (súffər) *v.* **-fered, -fering, -fers.** *—intr.* **1. a.** To feel pain or distress, as after sustaining loss, injury, or punishment. **b.** To be prone to a specified medical condition: *suffers from gout.* **2.** To tolerate or endure evil, injury, harm, pain, or death. **3.** To appear at a disadvantage: *suffer by comparison.* *—tr.* **1.** To undergo or sustain (something painful, injurious, or unpleasant): *suffer a nasty wound.* **2.** To experience: *suffer a change of heart.* **3.** To endure or bear; stand: *He cannot suffer boredom.* **4.** *Formal.* To permit; allow: *Rulers suffered us to speak.* —See Synonyms at **bear.** [Middle English *suff(e)ren,* to undergo, endure, allow, from Anglo-French *suffrir,* from Vulgar Latin *sufferīre* (unattested), from Latin *sufferre,* to sustain, "to bear up" : *sub-,* up from under + *ferre,* to bear.] **—suf·fer·er** *n.* **—suf·fer·ing·ly** *adv.*

suf·fer·a·ble (súffrəb'l, súffərəb'l) *adj.* Capable of being suffered, endured, or permitted; tolerable. **—suf·fer·a·bly** *adv.*

suf·fer·ance (súffrənss, súffərənss) *n.* **1.** The capacity to tolerate pain or distress. **2.** Sanction or permission implied or given by failure to prohibit; tacit assent; tolerance. **3.** *Archaic.* Suffering; misery. **4.** *Archaic.* Patient endurance. **—on sufferance.** Out of a reluctant sense of tolerance. [Middle English *suffrance,* from Old French, from Late Latin *sufferentia,* from Latin *sufferre,* SUFFER.]

suf·fer·ing (súffring, súffəring) *n.* **1.** The condition of one who suffers. **2.** The enduring of pain or distress.

suf·fice (sə-físs) *v.* **-ficed, -ficing, -fices.** *—intr.* **1.** To meet present needs or requirements; be sufficient: *These will suffice until next week.* **2.** To be capable or competent; be equal to a specified task: *No words will suffice to convey his grief.* *—tr.* To be enough or sufficient for; satisfy the needs or requirements of. **—suffice it.** Let it be enough; it is sufficient. Used chiefly in the phrase *suffice it to say.* [Middle English *suffisen,* from Old French *suffire* (present stem *suffis-*), from Latin *sufficere,* to put under, substitute, suffice : *sub-,* under + *facere,* to do, make.] **—suf·fic·er** *n.*

suf·fi·cien·cy (sə-físh'n-si) *n.* **1.** The state or quality of being sufficient. **2.** Adequate supplies, ability, numbers, or resources; especially, an adequate but not luxurious standard of living.

suf·fi·cient (sə-físh'nt) *adj.* **1.** *Abbr.* **suff.** As much as is needed; enough; adequate: *I haven't sufficient information to make a reasonable decision.* **2.** *Archaic.* Capable; competent; efficient. ~*n.* A sufficient quality. [Middle English, from Old French, from Latin *sufficiēns* (stem *sufficient-*), present participle of *sufficere,* SUFFICE.] **—suf·fi·cient·ly** *adv.*

sufficient condition *n. Logic.* A condition whose truth guarantees the truth of a proposition or state of affairs; for example, that it has just rained is a sufficient condition of the grass being wet; it is not a **necessary condition** *(see),* since any number of things might have made the grass wet.

suf·fix (súffiks) *n. Abbr.* **suf., suff.** An affix added to the end of a word or stem, serving to form a new word or to form an inflectional ending, as *-ness* in *gentleness, -ing* in *walking,* or *-s* in *sits.* ~*tr.v* (*also* su-fíks, sə-) **suffixed, -fixing, -fixes. 1.** To fix or add at the end; append. **2.** To add as a suffix. [New Latin *suffixum,* from Latin *suffīxus,* neuter past participle of *suffīgere,* to affix, fasten beneath : *sub-,* beneath + *fīgere,* to fix.] **—suf·fix·al** (súffiks'l, sə-fíks'l) *adj.* **—suf·fix·ion** (su-fíksh'n, sə-) *n.*

suf·fo·cate (súffə-kayt) *v.* **-cated, -cating, -cates.** *—tr.* **1. a.** To kill by preventing access of oxygen to (a person or animal). **b.** To extinguish (a fire, for example) by cutting off a supply of oxygen. **2.** To impair the respiration of; cause a choking sensation in. **3.** To cause discomfort to by or as if by cutting off the supply of air. **4.** To suppress the development, imagination, or creativity of; stifle. *—intr.* **1.** To die through lack of oxygen. **2.** To be stifled; smother. [Latin *suffocāre* : *sub-,* under, down + *faucēs,* throat, FAUCES.] **—suf·fo·ca·tion** (-káysh'n) *n.* **—suf·fo·ca·tive** (-kaytiv) *adj.*

Suf·folk[1] (súffək). County in East Anglia, England. Low and undulating, it is primarily agricultural. Lowestoft is a fishing port, and Ipswich, the county town, is the chief industrial centre.

Suffolk[2] *n.* Any of an English breed of hornless sheep producing high-quality mutton. [Originated in SUFFOLK.]

Suffolk Punch *n.* Any of a breed of draught horses originating in Suffolk, having a thickset, heavy body, short legs, and a chestnut coat. [*Punch,* after *Punch,* as in *Punch and Judy.*]

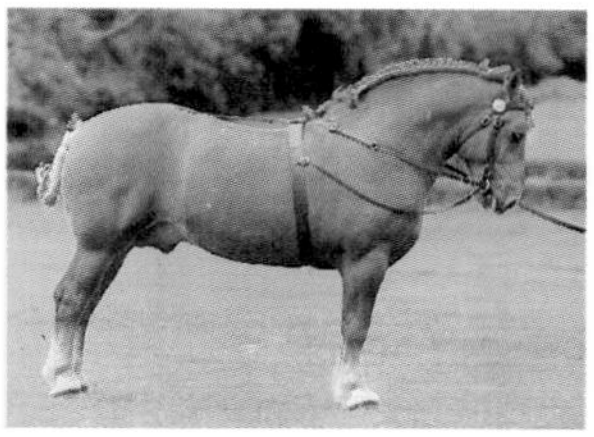

Suffolk Punch *The Suffolk Punch is a draught horse about 16 hands high and always chestnut in colour. Every horse of the breed can be traced back to a stallion foaled in 1768.*

suf·fra·gan (súffrəgən) *n. Abbr.* **Suff., Suffr. 1.** A bishop elected or appointed as an assistant to the bishop or ordinary of a diocese, having administrative and episcopal responsibilities but no jurisdictional functions. **2.** Any bishop regarded in his position as subordinate to his archbishop or metropolitan. Also called "suffragan bishop". [Middle English, from Old French, from Medieval Latin *suffrāgāneus,* from *suffrāgium,* SUFFRAGE.] **—suf·fra·gan** *adj.* **—suf·fra·gan·ship** *n.*

suf·frage (súffrij) *n.* **1.** The right or privilege of voting; franchise. **2.** The exercise of such a right. **3.** A vote cast in deciding a disputed question or in electing a person to office. **4.** *Usually plural. Archaic.* A short intercessory prayer. [Middle English, intercessory prayer, from Old French *suffrage, suffragies,* from Medieval Latin *suffrāgium,* vote, support, prayer, from Latin, ballot, right of voting.]

suf·fra·gette (súffrə-jét) *n.* In the early 20th century, a female advocate of suffrage for women; especially, a supporter of the the militant Woman's Social and Political Union, led by Emmeline and Christabel Pankhurst. **—suf·fra·get·tism** *n.*

suf·fra·gist (súffrəjist) *n.* An advocate of the extension of political voting rights, especially to women.

suf·fru·tes·cent (súf-rōō-téss'nt || -rew-) *adj.* Also **suf·fru·ti·cose** (su-frōōti-koz, sə-, -kōss || -fréwti-). *Botany.* Having a woody stem or base and herbaceous branches; somewhat shrubby. [New Latin *suffrutescens* : SUB- + FRUTESCENT.]

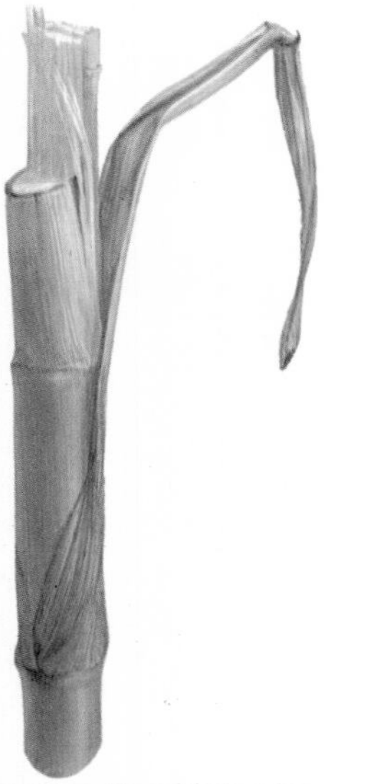

sugar cane *One of the bamboo family grown in tropical and subtropical regions around the world. Juice from the cane is boiled to remove the water and produce grains of sugar.*

suf·fuse (sə-féwz, su-) *tr.v.* **-fused, -fusing, -fuses.** To spread through or over: *"The sky above the roof is suffused with deep colours"* (Eugene O'Neill). [Latin *suffundere* (past participle *suffūsus*), to pour underneath or into : *sub-*, underneath + *fundere*, to pour.] **—suf·fu·sion** (-féwzh'n) *n.* **—suf·fu·sive** (-féw-siv || -ziv) *adj.*

Su·fi (sóofi) *n.* A member of a Muslim mystic sect that dates from the eighth century A.D. and developed chiefly in Iran. [Arabic *ṣūfīy*, "(man) of wool", from *ṣūf*, wool (probably from their woollen garments).] **—Su·fic, Su·fis·tic** (soo-fístik) *adj.*

Su·fism (sóof-iz'm) *n.* The beliefs and practices of the Sufis.

sug·ar (shóoggər) *n.* **1.** A sweet crystalline carbohydrate, **sucrose** *(see).* **2.** Any of a class of water-soluble crystalline carbohydrates, including sucrose and lactose, having a characteristically sweet taste. **3.** A particular amount of sugar, as a spoonful or cube: *takes two sugars in her tea.* **4.** *Chiefly U.S.* A sweetheart. Used as a term of endearment.

~v. **sugared, -aring, -ars.** *—tr.* **1.** To coat, cover, or sweeten with sugar. **2.** To make less distasteful or more appealing. *—intr.* To form sugar; granulate. [Middle English *suker, sugre*, from Old French *sukere, zuchre*, from Italian *zucchero*, from Medieval Latin *zuccarum, succarum*, from Arabic *sukkar*, from Persian *shakar*, from Prakrit *sakkara*, from Sanskrit *śarkarā†*, pebble, gravel, sugar.] **—sug·ar·less** *adj.*

sugar apple *n.* A tree, the **sweetsop** *(see)*, or its fruit.

sugar beet *n.* A form of the common beet, *Beta vulgaris*, having white roots from which sugar is obtained.

sugar bird *n.* A long-tailed South African bird, *Promerops cafer*, with a long curved bill used for extracting nectar from flowers.

sugar cane *n.* A tall grass, *Saccharum officinarum*, native to the East Indies, having thick, tough stems that are one of the chief commercial sources of sugar.

sug·ar·coat (shóoggər-kōt) *tr.v.* **-coated, -coating, -coats. 1.** To coat with sugar. **2.** To cause to seem more appealing or pleasant.

sugar daddy *n. Informal.* A wealthy, usually older man who gives expensive gifts to a young woman or man in return for sexual favours or companionship.

sug·ared (shóoggərd) *adj.* **1.** Sweetened with sugar. **2.** Made more appealing or pleasant.

sugar glider *n.* An Australian marsupial (a phalanger), *Petaurus breviceps*, that glides between trees and feeds on nectar.

sugar gum *n.* An Australian eucalyptus tree, *Eucalyptus cladocalyx*, yielding heavy, yellow-brown timber.

sugar loaf *n.* **1.** A large conical mass of pure concentrated sugar. **2.** Something resembling the shape of this. **—sug·ar-loaf** (shóoggər-lōf) *adj.*

sugar maple *n.* A maple tree, *Acer saccharum*, of eastern North America, having sap that is the source of maple syrup and maple sugar and hard, variously grained wood used in cabinetmaking.

sugar of lead *n.* **Lead acetate** *(see).*

sugar of milk *n.* **Lactose** *(see).*

sugar pea *n.* A variety of pea, the **mange-tout** *(see).*

sug·ar·plum (shóoggər-plum) *n. Archaic.* A small piece of sugary confectionery.

sugar soap *n.* An alkaline substance resembling sugar granules, used for smoothing surfaces and cleaning paintwork.

sug·ar·y (shóoggəri) *adj.* **-ier, -iest. 1.** Composed of, tasting like, resembling, or containing sugar. **2.** Deceitfully or cloyingly sweet or attractive. **—sug·ar·i·ness** *n.*

sug·gest (sə-jést || *U.S.* səg-) *tr.v.* **-gested, -gesting, -gests. 1.** To offer for consideration or action; propose. **2.** To bring or call to mind by logic or association; evoke. **3.** To make evident indirectly; intimate; imply. **4.** To serve as or provide a motive for; prompt: *Such a crime suggests apt punishment.* [Latin *suggerere* (past participle *suggestus*), to carry or put underneath, furnish, suggest : *sub-*, underneath + *gerere*, to carry.] **—sug·gest·er** *n.*

Synonyms: *suggest, imply, hint, intimate, insinuate.*

sug·gest·i·ble (sə-jéstəb'l || *U.S.* səg-) *adj.* Readily influenced by suggestion. **—sug·gest·i·bil·i·ty** (-ə-billəti) *n.*

sug·ges·tion (sə-jéss-chən, -jésh- || *U.S.* səg-) *n.* **1.** The act of suggesting. **2.** Something suggested; an idea or proposal. **3.** A trace or slight indication. **4. a.** The psychological process by which an idea is induced in or adopted by an individual without argument, command, or coercion. **b.** Any idea or response so induced. **5.** The thought process by which one idea or concept leads to another.

sug·ges·tive (sə-jéstiv || *U.S.* səg-) *adj.* **1. a.** Tending to suggest thoughts or ideas. **b.** Conveying a hint or suggestion; indicative. Sometimes used with *of: suggestive of his guilt, but not conclusive.* **2.** Tending to suggest something sexually improper or indecent. **—sug·ges·tive·ly** *adv.* **—sug·ges·tive·ness** *n.*

Su·har·to (soo-hártō) (1921–). Indonesian general and statesman. He assumed power (1967) after the downfall of Sukarno and was confirmed president (1968). He adopted a peaceful policy towards Malaysia and suppressed all opposition.

su·i·ci·dal (sóo-i-sīd'l, séw-) *adj.* **1. a.** Pertaining to, involving, or related to suicide. **b.** Feeling or showing a disposition to commit suicide. **2.** Dangerous to oneself or to one's interests; self-destructive; ruinous. **—su·i·ci·dal·ly** *adv.*

su·i·cide (sóo-i-sīd, séw-) *n.* **1.** The act or an instance of intentionally killing oneself. **2.** The destruction or ruin of one's own interests. **3.** One who commits suicide.

~adj. Involving suicide or extreme danger: *a suicide mission.*

~intr.v. **suicided, -ciding, -cides.** *Informal.* To commit suicide. [New Latin *suicida* (person), *suicidium* (act) : Latin *suī*, of oneself + -CIDE.]

su·i gen·e·ris (sóo-ī jénnəriss, séw-, -ee génnəriss) *adj.* Unique; individual. [Latin, "of its own kind".]

su·i ju·ris (sóo-ī jóor-iss, séw-, -ee yóor-) *adj. Law.* Capable of managing one's own affairs. [Latin, "of one's own right".]

su·int (sóo-int, séw-, swint) *n.* A natural grease formed from dried perspiration, found in the fleece of sheep and used as a source of potash. [French, from Old French *suer*, to sweat, from Latin *sūdāre*.]

Suisse. See **Switzerland.**

suit (soot, sewt) *n.* **1. a.** A set of outer garments consisting of a coat and trousers or skirt, and sometimes a waistcoat, that match in colour or fabric or that have been designed to be worn together. **b.** A garment or set of clothes designed to be worn for a specified purpose or as a fashionable outfit. Often used in combination: *a playsuit; a flying suit.* **2.** Any group of things united into a set or series by having a common form or function. **3.** Any of the four sets of 13 playing cards, spades, hearts, diamonds, and clubs, each with similar spots or pips, that constitute a pack. **4. a.** *Law.* An act or instance of suing in court, usually to recover a right or claim; a lawsuit. **b.** An act of pleading; a request. **5.** The act or an instance of courting. **—follow suit. 1.** To play a card of the same suit as the one led. **2.** To do as another has done; follow an example.

~v. **suited, suiting, suits.** *—tr.* **1.** To meet the requirements of; accommodate: *This candidate does not suit our needs.* **2. a.** To make appropriate or suitable; adapt: *We can suit the building to your specifications.* **b.** To be appropriate or suitable for; go well with: *Does the climate suit you?* **3.** To please; satisfy. **4.** *Archaic.* To dress. *—intr.* To be suitable or acceptable. **—suit (oneself).** To do as one pleases in a given circumstance. [Middle English *su(i)te*, attendance at a sheriff's court, litigation, uniform, garb, from Old French *siute, suite*, from Vulgar Latin *sequita* (unattested), pursuit, from *sequere* (unattested), to follow. See **sue.**]

suit·a·ble (sóot-əb'l, séwt-) *adj.* Appropriate to a given purpose or occasion; fitting; conventient. See Synonyms at **fit. —suit·a·bil·ity** (-ə-billəti), **suit·a·ble·ness** *n.* **—suit·a·bly** *adv.*

suit·case (sóot-kayss, séwt-) *n.* A usually rectangular and flat or boxlike piece of luggage having a handle and used for carrying personal belongings and clothing.

suite (sweet || *U.S. also* soot *for sense 4*) *n.* **1.** Any succession of related things intended to be used together. **2.** A series of connected rooms used as a living unit. **3.** A set of matched furniture pieces intended for use in the same room. **4.** *Music.* **a.** An instrumental composition consisting of a succession of movements, originally dances, having the same theme or in the same or (after 1750) related keys. **b.** An instrumental composition based on a selection from a larger musical work, such as a ballet or opera. **5.** A staff of attendants or a train of followers; a retinue. [French, from Old French *sieute*, following, retinue, from Vulgar Latin *sequita* (unattested). See **suit.**]

suit·ing (sóot-ing, séwt-) *n.* Fabric from which suits are made.

suit·or (sóot-ər, séwt-) *n.* **1.** A person who makes a petition or request. **2.** A person who sues in a court of law; a plaintiff; a petitioner. **3.** A man who is in the process of courting a woman. [Middle English *suitor*, from Anglo-French, follower, from Latin *secūtor*, from *sequī* (past participle *secūtus*), to follow.]

Su·kar·no (soo-kárnō), **Achmed** (1901–70). Indonesian statesman and first president of Indonesia (1945–67). He assumed dictatorial powers (1960) but was forced to relinquish power (1967) by the army, and General Suharto took control.

Sukarno, Mount. See **Jaya, Mount.**

su·ki·ya·ki (soo-ki-yaáki, soo-) *n.* A Japanese dish of sliced meat, vegetables, and seasoning fried together. [Japanese.]

Sukkoth. Variant of **Succoth.**

sul·cate (súl-kayt) *adj. Biology.* Having narrow longitudinal indentations; grooved. [Latin *sulcātus*, past participle of *sulcāre*, to furrow, from *sulcus*, furrow, SULCUS.]

sul·cus (súl-kəss) *n., pl.* **-ci** (-sī, -kī). **1.** A narrow, deep furrow or groove. **2.** *Anatomy.* Any of the narrow fissures separating adjacent cerebral convolutions. [Latin *sulcus*, furrow, groove.]

Su·lei·man I (sóo-lay-maán, -maan) (*c.*1494–1566). Turkish sultan, known as Suleiman the Magnifcent. He brought the Ottoman empire to its peak, improved the administration of the country and encouraged the arts and sciences.

sulf– *U.S.* Variant of **sulph-.**

sulfur. *U.S.* Variant of **sulphur.**

sulk (sulk) *intr.v.* **sulked, sulking, sulks.** To be sullenly aloof, bad-tempered, or withdrawn, as in silent protest.

~n. Usually plural. A mood or display of sulking: *had a fit of the sulks.* [Back-formation from SULKY.]

sulk·y[1] (súlki) *adj.* **-ier, -iest. 1.** Sullenly aloof, bad tempered, or withdrawn. **2.** Characteristic of or showing sullen bad-temper: *a sulky face.* [Perhaps from obsolete *sulke*, sluggish, perhaps ultimately from Old English *asolcen*, past participle of *āseolcan*, to be lazy, become slack.] **—sulk·i·ly** *adv.* **—sulk·i·ness** *n.*

sulky[2] *n., pl.* **-ies.** A light two-wheeled vehicle accommodating one person and drawn by one horse. [From SULKY (because it has only one seat for the driver).] **—sulk·y** *adj.*

Sul·la (súllə, sóollə), **Lucius Cornelius** (138–78 B.C.). Roman general. After a successful military career, he made himself dicatator (82–79 B.C.). He tried to reorganise Roman politics, but his influence did not long survive his retirement.

sul·lage (súllij) n. 1. Silt deposited by a current of water. 2. Sewage. [Probably from Old French *souiller,* to SOIL.]

sul·len (súllən) adj. 1. Showing brooding ill humour or having a tendency to silent or passive gloom and resentment; glumly bad-tempered; morose. 2. Gloomy or sombre in tone, colour, or portent: *a sullen sky.* [Middle English *solein, solain,* from Anglo-French *solein* (unattested), alone, sullen, from Old French *seul, sol,* alone, single, from Latin *sōlus.*] —**sul·len·ly** adv. —**sul·len·ness** n.

Sul·li·van (súllivən), **Sir Arthur (Seymour)** (1842–1900). British composer. He is best known for his collaboration with W.S. Gilbert in their light operas which include *H.M.S. Pinafore* (1878), *The Mikado* (1885), and *The Gondoliers* (1889).

Sullivan, John Lawrence (1858–1918). U.S. boxer. He won (1882) the heavyweight championship by defeating Paddy Ryan at Mississippi City, fighting with bare knuckles and on the turf.

Sullivan, Louis Henri (1856–1924). U.S. architect. His experimental use of steel frames for the construction of skyscrapers earned him the title "Father of Modernism". His famous dictum, "Form follows function", influenced many architects, notably his student Frank Lloyd Wright.

sul·ly (súlli) tr.v. **-lied, -lying, -lies.** 1. To mar the cleanness or lustre of; soil; stain. 2. To defile; tarnish. ~n., pl. **sullies.** Archaic. Something that sullies; a stain or spot. [Probably from Old French *souiller,* to SOIL.]

Sul·ly (sül-lée), **Maximilien de Béthune, Duc de** (1560–1641). French statesman. As finance minister (1598–1610) to Henry IV, he replenished the treasury and encouraged agriculture and industry.

Sul·ly-Pru·dhomme (sül-lee-prü-dóm), **René François Armand** (1839–1907). French poet. His early works were melancholic, while his later poems are concerned with scientific and philosophic theories. He won the Nobel prize in literature (1901).

sulph– comb. form. Indicates sulphur; for example, **sulphide, sulone.** [From SULPHUR.]

sul·pha·di·a·zine (súlfə-dĩ-ə-zeen) n. A sulpha drug, $C_{10}H_{10}N_4O_2S$, used in the treatment of various bacterial infections.

sul·pha drug (súlfə) n. Any of a group of sulphonamide compounds such as sulphathiazole and sulphadiazine, capable of inhibiting bacterial growth and activity and used to treat a wide variety of infections. [*Sulpha*nilamide + DRUG.]

sul·pha·nil·a·mide (súlfə-níllə-mĩd) n. A white odourless crystalline sulphonamide, $H_2N.C_6H_4.SO_2NH_2$, formerly used in the treatment of various bacterial infections. [SULPH- + ANIL(INE) + AMIDE.]

sul·phate (súl-fayt) n. A chemical compound containing the bivalent group SO_4. ~v. **sulphated, -phating, -phates.** —tr. 1. To treat or react with sulphuric acid or a sulphate. 2. *Electricity.* To cause lead sulphate to form on (the plates of a lead-acid accumulator). —intr. To become sulphated. [French : SULPH- + -ATE.]

sul·pha·thi·a·zole (súlfə-thĩ-ə-zōl) n. A sulpha drug, $C_9H_9N_3O_2S_2$, used to treat a variety of bacterial infections.

sul·phide (súl-fĩd) n. A compound of bivalent sulphur with an electropositive element or group, usually a metal. [SULPH- + -IDE.]

sul·phite (súl-fĩt) n. A salt or ester of sulphurous acid. [French, variant of SULPHATE.] —**sul·phit·ic** (sul-fíttik) adj.

sulphon– comb. form. Indicates: 1. Sulphonic; for example, **sulphonamide.** 2. Sulphonyl; for example, **sulphonmethane.** [From SULPHONE.]

sul·phon·a·mide (sul-fónnə-mĩd ‖ U.S. also -fŏnə-, -mid) n. Any of a group of organic sulphur compounds having the general formula RSO_2NH_2. The group includes the sulpha drugs.

sul·pho·nate (súlfə-nayt) n. A compound in which a hydrogen atom is replaced by the sulphonic acid group SO_2OH. ~tr.v. **sulphonated, -nating, -nates.** 1. To introduce one or more sulphonic-acid groups into (an organic compound), as by treating with concentrated sulphuric acid. 2. To treat with sulphonic acid. [SULPHON- + -ATE.] —**sul·pho·na·tion** (-náysh'n) n.

sul·phone (súl-fōn) n. Any of various organic sulphur compounds having a sulphonyl group, $-SO_2$, attached to two carbon atoms; especially, such a compound used to treat leprosy or tuberculosis. [SULPH- + ONE.]

sul·phon·ic acid (sul-fónnik) n. Any of several organic acids containing one or more sulphonic groups, $-SO_2OH$.

sul·phon·meth·ane (súl-fon-mée-thayn, -mé-) n. A colourless crystaline or powdered compound, $C_7H_{16}S_2O_4$, used as a hypnotic.

sul·pho·nyl (súlfənil) n. The bivalent radical SO_2. Also called "sulphuryl". [SULPHON- + -YL.]

sul·phur, U.S. **sul·fur** (súlfər) n. Symbol **S** 1. A pale yellow nonmetallic element occurring widely in nature both free and combined in several allotropic forms. It is used in black gunpowder, rubber vulcanisation, the manufacture of insecticides and pharmaceuticals, and in the preparation of important sulphur compounds, such as sulphuric acid. Atomic number 16, atomic weight 32.064, melting point (rhombic) 112.8°C, (monoclinic) 119.0°C, boiling point 444.6°C, relative density, (rhombic) 2.07, (monoclinic)1.957, valencies 2,4,6. 2. Any of various yellow or orange-yellow butterflies of the family Pieridae. [Middle English *sulphur, sulphur(e),* from Anglo-French *sulf(e)re,* from Latin *sulphur,* sulphur†.]

sul·phu·rate (súlfə-rayt) tr.v. **-rated, -rating, -rates.** To treat or combine with sulphur. [Late Latin *sulfurāre,* from Latin *sulphur,* SULPHUR.] —**sul·phu·ra·tion** (-ráysh'n) n.

sulphur bacteria pl.n. Bacteria of the order Beggiatoales, which derive their energy from the oxidation of sulphides.

sul·phur-bot·tom (súlfər-bottəm) n. The **blue whale** *(see).*

sulphur dioxide n. A colourless, extremely irritating gas or liquid, SO_2, used in many industrial processes, especially the manufacture of sulphuric acid. When dissolved in water it forms sulphurous acid.

sul·phu·re·ous (sul-fewr-i-əss) adj. Sulphurous.

sul·phu·ret (súl-fewr-et, -fər-) tr.v. **-retted** or U.S. **-reted, -retting** or U.S. **-reting, -rets.** To sulphurise. ~n. A sulphide. [New Latin *sulfuretum,* sulphide, from Latin *sulphur,* SULPHUR.]

sul·phu·ric (sul-féwr-ik) adj. Of, relating to, or containing sulphur, especially with valency 6.

sulphuric acid n. A highly corrosive, dense oily liquid, H_2SO_4, colourless to dark brown depending on purity, used to manufacture a variety of chemicals and materials including fertilisers, dyestuffs, paints, detergents, and explosives. Also called "oil of vitriol".

sul·phur·ise, sul·phur·ize (súl-fewr-ĩz, -fər-) tr.v. **-ised, -ising, -ises.** 1. To treat or impregnate with sulphur; sulphuret. 2. To bleach or fumigate with sulphur or sulphur dioxide. —**sul·phur·i·sa·tion** (-ĩ-záysh'n ‖ U.S. -i-) n.

sul·phur·ous (súl-fər-əss, -fewr-) adj. 1. Of, relating to, derived from, or containing sulphur, especially in its lower valency, 4. 2. Characteristic of or emanating from burning sulphur. 3. Fiery.

sulphurous acid n. A colourless solution of sulphur dioxide in water, H_2SO_3, characterised by a suffocating sulphurous odour, used as a bleaching agent, preservative, and disinfectant.

sulphur trioxide n. A corrosive compound SO_3, having three solid forms that may coexist in a given sample, used in the sulphonation of organic compounds.

sul·phur·yl (súl-fewr-il, -fər-) n. **Sulphonyl** *(see).*

sulphuryl chloride n. A colourless liquid, SO_2Cl_2, having a pungent odour, used as a chlorinating and dehydrating agent and solvent and in the manufacture of pharmaceuticals and dyestuffs.

sul·tan (súltən) n. The ruler of a Muslim country, especially of the former Ottoman Empire. [French, from Medieval Latin *sultānus,* from Arabic *sulṭān,* ruler, from Aramaic *shulṭānā,* "power", from *shəlēṭ,* to have power.]

sul·ta·na (sul-táanə; *for sense 3, usually* səl- ‖ U.S. *also* -tánnə) n. 1. The wife, mother, sister, or daughter of a sultan. Also called "sultaness". 2. The mistress of a sultan, king, or prince. 3. **a.** A small, sweet, seedless raisin of a kind originally produced in Asia Minor. **b.** The grape from which the sultana comes. [Italian, feminine of *sultano,* sultan, from Arabic *sulṭān,* SULTAN.]

sul·tan·ate (súltən-ət, -it, -ayt) n. 1. The office, power, or reign of a sultan. 2. The domain of a sultan.

sul·try (súltri) adj. **-trier, -triest.** 1. Very hot and humid. 2. Sensual; voluptuous: *a sultry Spanish dance.* [From obsolete *sulter,* variant of SWELTER.] —**sul·tri·ly** adv. —**sul·tri·ness** n.

sum (sum) n. 1. The amount obtained as a result of adding. 2. The whole amount, quantity, or number: *the sum of our knowledge.* In both senses, also called "sum total". 3. The highest point or degree; summit. 4. An amount of money: *They paid an enormous sum.* 5. An arithmetical problem: *good at sums.* 6. A summary; the gist. —**in sum.** Essentially and briefly; in short. ~v. **summed, summing, sums.** —tr. 1. To summarise; sum up. 2. To add. Often used with *up.* —intr. To add up; amount. Used with *to: The total summed to 739.* —**sum up.** 1. To summarise; recapitulate briefly. 2. To form a judgment about; appraise: *summed up his character.* [Middle English *summe, somme,* from Old French, from Latin *(res) summa,* the highest thing, sum, total (from the Greek and Roman habit of counting upwards and writing the total at the top), from *summus,* highest, topmost.]

su·mach (shŏŏ-mak, sŏŏ-, séw-) n. Also chiefly U.S. **su·mac.** 1. Any of various shrubs or small trees of the genus Rhus. Some species, such as **poison ivy** *(see),* cause an acute itching rash on contact. 2. The dried and powdered leaves of some Rhus species, especially R. coraria, used in tanning and dyeing. [Middle English, from Old French, from Arabic *summaq,* sumach tree, probably from Aramaic, "red".]

Su·ma·tra (sŏŏ-máatrə, sŏŏ-, sew-). The westernmost, and second largest island of Indonesia. A volcanic range, which rises to 3 805 metres (12,483 feet), extends along the west coast, and the east is swampland, with dense main forests in the interior. Sumatra has reserves of oil, natural gas, coal, and silver. Rubber, coffee, tea, and pepper are among the chief farm products. A Dutch colony from 1816, Sumatra was included in the new republic of Indonesia after World War II. —**Su·ma·tran** adj. & n.

Su·mer (sŏŏ-mər, séw-). The southern part of ancient Mesopotamia, the site of one of the world's oldest known civilisations dating back to the fifth millennium B.C. The Sumerians, who spoke a non–Semitic language, are credited with the invention of the cuneiform system of writing, wheeled vehicles, and the plough. By the third millennium a number of city-states had grown up on the alluvial plains of the lower Tigris and Euphrates, among them Kish, Uruk, and Ur. Sumer was overrun by Akkad (c. 2300 B.C.), and briefly revived by the third dynasty at Ur (c. 2100 B.C.). The civilisation declined after Amorite invasions (c. 2000 B.C.), and was later absorbed into the empires of Babylon and Assyria.

Su·me·ri·an (sŏŏ-méer-i-ən, sew-, sŏŏ-) adj. Of or pertaining to ancient Sumer, its people, culture, or language. ~n. 1. A member of an ancient Babylonian people, who established civilisation in Sumer. 2. The unclassified language used by these people, preserved in cuneiform on clay tablets. See **Japhetic.**

sum·ma cum lau·de (sŏŏm-aa kŏŏm lów-day, súm-, -mə, kum,

Sun

A THERMONUCLEAR FURNACE IN THE SKY
The closest star is our lifeline to the Universe

Our Sun is a vast globe of incandescent gas that provides the light and heat upon which all life on Earth depends. In the Universe, however, it is merely an average star and it seems so large and bright compared with other stars simply because it is so much closer.

Although the Sun has a mass 330,000 times greater than that of the Earth, it would have burned out millions of years ago if it blazed in the same way as wood or coal. In fact the Sun generates its power by the fusion process in which energy is created as the 15,000,000°C (27,000,000°F) heat at its core turns hydrogen gas into helium. It will continue radiating more energy per second than man has ever used for many aeons yet.

THE STRUCTURE OF THE SUN

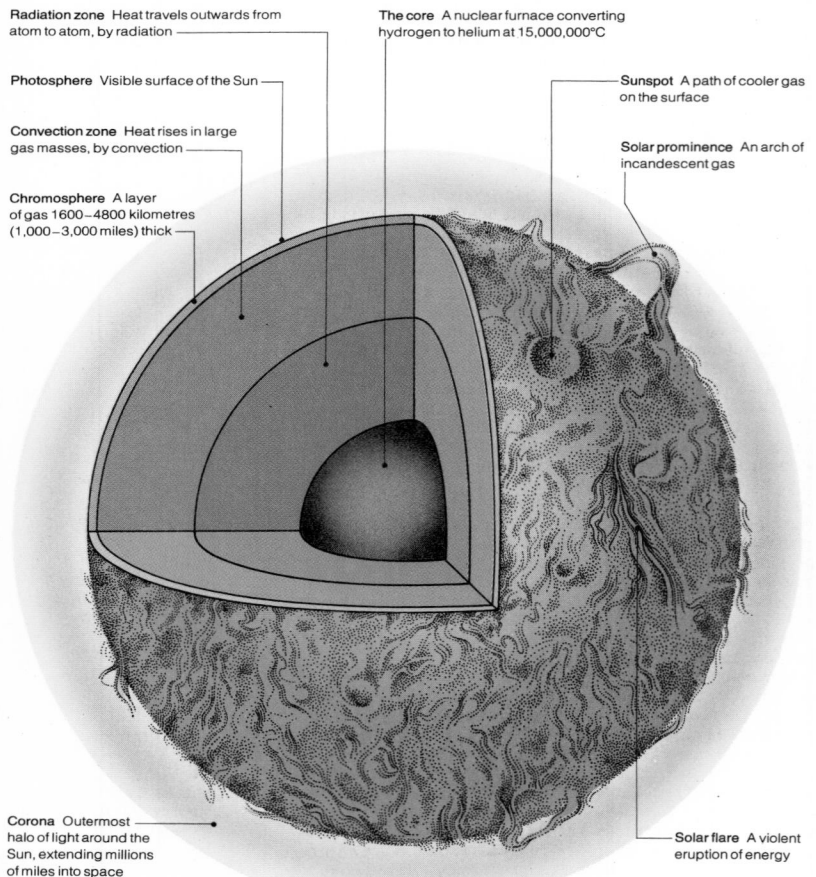

Radiation zone Heat travels outwards from atom to atom, by radiation

Photosphere Visible surface of the Sun

Convection zone Heat rises in large gas masses, by convection

Chromosphere A layer of gas 1600–4800 kilometres (1,000–3,000 miles) thick

The core A nuclear furnace converting hydrogen to helium at 15,000,000°C

Sunspot A path of cooler gas on the surface

Solar prominence An arch of incandescent gas

Corona Outermost halo of light around the Sun, extending millions of miles into space

Solar flare A violent eruption of energy

The Sun is a nuclear reactor with a dense, intensely hot core that gives out most of its energy in the form of X-rays, which seep out to heat the surrounding material. By the time it reaches the surface the radiation has given way to convection. It takes about 30 million years for light generated in the core to reach the Earth.

Escaping energy makes the outer region of the Sun seethe and gyrate. Some of the gigantic flares that shoot out in this dramatic boiling-off process can dwarf the planet Earth.

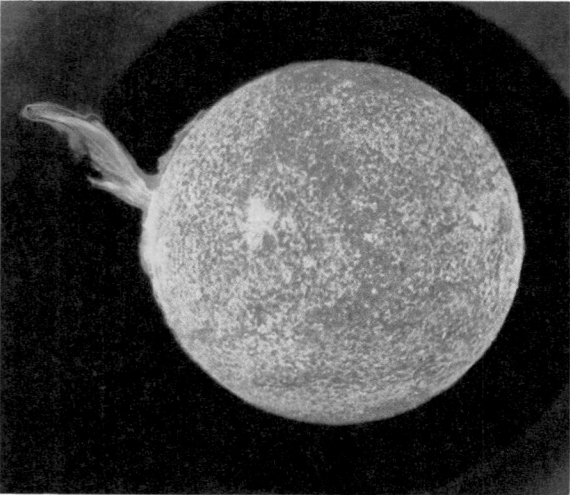

---

láw-, -di) *adv. Latin.* With the greatest praise. Used on university and college diplomas to designate the highest degree of academic distinction. Compare **cum laude, magna cum laude.** [New Latin.]

sum·ma·rise, sum·ma·rize (súmmə-rīz) *tr.v.* **-rised, -rising, -rises.** To make a summary of; abstract. —**sum·ma·ri·sa·tion** (-rī-záysh'n ‖ *U.S.* -ri-) *n.* —**sum·ma·rist** (-rist), **sum·ma·ri·ser** *n.*

sum·ma·ry (súmməri) *adj.* **1.** Presenting the substance in a condensed form; concise. **2.** Performed speedily and without ceremony: *summary justice.* **3.** *Law.* Of, pertaining to or designating the right of a court to try or judge a case without a jury: *summary jurisdiction.* —See Synonyms at **concise.**
~*n., pl.* **summaries.** A condensation of the substance of a larger work; an abstract or abridgment containing the main or important points. [Middle English, from Medieval Latin *summārius,* comprising the principal parts, from Latin *summa,* SUM.] —**sum·ma·ri·ly** (-li; *also, chiefly U.S.,* su-mérrəli) *adv.* —**sum·ma·ri·ness** *n.*

sum·ma·tion (su-máysh'n) *n.* **1.** The act or process of adding or totalling; addition. **2.** A sum or aggregate. **3.** A summing-up; a recapitulation. **4.** The interaction of two substances, such as drugs or hormones, with similar effects such that their combined effect is greater than their separate effects. [Medieval Latin *summātiō* (stem *summātiōn-*), from *summāre,* to sum up, from Latin *summa,* SUM.]

sum·mer¹ (súmmər) *n.* **1.** The usually warmest season of the year occurring between spring and autumn. In the Northern Hemisphere it extends from the summer solstice to the autumnal equinox and is popularly considered to comprise June, July, and August, while in the Southern Hemisphere it falls between the winter solstice and the vernal equinox or, popularly, December, January, and February. **2.** Any period regarded as a time of warmth, fruition, fulfilment, happiness, or beauty.
~*adj.* Pertaining to, characteristic of, or occurring in summer.
~*v.* **summered, -mering, -mers.** —*tr.* To lodge or keep during the summer. —*intr.* To pass the summer. [Middle English *somer, sumer,* Old English *sumor.*] —**sum·mer·ly** *adj. & adv.*

summer² *n. Architecture.* **1.** A heavy horizontal timber that serves as a supporting beam, especially for the floor above. **2.** A lintel. **3.** A large, heavy stone usually set on the top of a column or pilaster to support an arch or lintel. [Middle English *summer, somer,* from Anglo-French *sumer, somer,* "pack animal", from Vulgar Latin *saumārius* (unattested), variant of Late Latin *sagmārius,* from *sagma,* packsaddle, from Greek. See **sumpter.**]

summer cypress *n.* A plant, *Kochia scoparia,* native to Eurasia, having dense foliage that turns bright red in autumn. Also called "burning bush".

sum·mer·house (súmmər-howss) *n.* A small, roofed structure in a park or garden affording shade and rest; a gazebo.

summer pudding *n.* A pudding made from stewed soft fruits, such as raspberries and blackcurrants, enclosed in a bread casing.

summersault, summerset. Variants of **somersault.**

summer savory *n.* See **savory** (plant).

summer school *n.* An academic course held during the summer, outside university, college, or school terms.

summer solstice *n. Astronomy.* A **solstice** (see).

sum·mer·time (súmmər-tīm) *n.* **1.** The summer season. **2.** A daylight-saving time, such as British Summer Time.

sum·mer·wood (súmmər-wŏod) *n.* Wood that develops during the latter part of the growing season and is harder and less porous than springwood. Compare **springwood.**

sum·mer·y (súmməri) *adj.* Pertaining to or suggesting summer.

sum·ming-up (súmming-úp) *n.* A summary of the evidence in a trial by a judge, directed to a jury, together with guidance on what form the jury's decision should take in the light of their view of the evidence.

sum·mit (súmmit) *n.* **1.** The highest point or part; the top, especially of a mountain. **2.** The highest degree of achievement or status, especially of government. **3.** A conference involving heads of government and sometimes leading government ministers. Also used adjectivally: *summit talks.* [Middle English *somette,* from Old French *sommette, sumet,* diminutive of *som, sum,* top, from Latin *summum,* neuter of *summus,* highest, topmost.] —**sum·mit·al** *adj.*
    Synonyms: summit, peak, pinnacle, acme, apex, zenith, climax.

sum·mi·teer (súmmi-téer) *n.* One taking part in a summit conference.

sum·mon (súmmən) *tr.v.* **-moned, -moning, -mons. 1.** To call together; convene. **2.** To send for; request to appear. **3.** To order (a person) to appear in court by the issue of a summons. **4.** To order to do a specified act: *summon the captain to surrender.* **5.** To call forth; rouse; muster. Often used with *up: He summoned up a smile.* [Middle English *somo(u)nen,* from Old French *somondre,* from Vulgar Latin *summonere* (unattested), from Latin *summonēre,* to remind secretly : *sub-,* secretly + *monēre,* to remind, warn.]

sum·mon·er (súmmənər) *n.* **1.** A person who summons. **2.** Formerly, a court official who served summonses.

sum·mons (súmmənz) *n., pl.* **-monses. 1.** A call or order to appear or to do something. **2.** *Law.* An official order summoning a defendant or witness to report to a court.
~*tr.v.* **summonsed, -monsing, -monses.** To serve a court summons to. [Middle English *somo(u)ns,* from Old French *som(o)unse,* from Gallo-Roman *summonsa* (unattested), from Latin *summonita,* from the feminine past participle of *summonēre,* to remind secretly, SUMMON.]

sum·mum bo·num (sŏŏm-əm bŏnəm, súm-) *n. Latin.* The greatest or supreme good.

Su·mo (sóō-mō, séw-) *n.* The main Japanese form of wrestling, in which the object is to make one's opponent touch the ground with his body or to force him out of the ring. [Japanese.]

sump (sump) *n.* **1.** The crankcase or oil reservoir of an internal-combustion engine. **2. a.** Any low area that receives drainage. **b.** A cesspool. **3.** A hole at the lowest point of a mine shaft into which water is drained in order to be pumped out. [Middle English *sompe,* a swamp, morass, from Middle Low German or Middle Dutch *sump.*]

sump·ter (súmptər) *n. Archaic.* A pack animal. [Middle English *sum(p)ter, sometour,* driver of a pack animal, from Old French *som(-m)etier,* from Vulgar Latin *saumatārius* (unattested), from Late Latin *sagma,* packsaddle, from Greek, from *sattein*†, to pack.]

sump·tu·ar·y (súmp-tew-əri, -choo- || -erri) *adj.* **1.** Pertaining to expenditure; especially, regulating or limiting expenses. **2.** Regulating personal behaviour on moral or religious grounds: *sumptuary laws.* [Latin *sumptuārius,* from *sumptus,* expense, from the past participle of *sūmere,* to consume, spend, take.]

sump·tu·ous (súmp-tew-əss, -choo-) *adj.* Of a size or splendour suggesting great expense; lavish. [Middle English, from Old French *sumptueux,* from Latin *sumptuōsus,* from *sumptus,* expense. See **sumptuary.**] **—sump·tu·ous·ly** *adv.* **—sump·tu·ous·ness** *n.*

sun (sun) *n.* **1. a.** *Sometimes capital* **S.** A star that is the basis of the Solar System and that sustains life on Earth, being the source of heat and light. It has a mean distance from Earth of about 150 million kilometres (93 million miles) and a diameter of approximately 1.39 million kilometres (865,000 miles). Also called "Sol". **b.** The sun in a particular aspect or at a particular time or place: *the midnight sun.* **2.** Any star that is the centre of a planetary system. **3.** The radiant energy, especially heat and visible light, emitted by the sun; sunshine. **4.** *Archaic.* **a.** A day. **b.** A year. **—catch the sun.** To be tanned or sunburnt.
~*v.* **sunned, sunning, suns.** *—tr.* **1.** To expose to the sun's rays. **2.** To warm, dry, or tan in the sun. *—intr.* To bask in the sun. [Middle English *sonne, sunne,* Old English *sunne.*]

Sun. Sunday.

sun·baked (sún-baykt) *adj.* Hardened by the heat of the sun.

sun·bathe (sún-bayth) *intr.v.* **-bathed, -bathing, -bathes.** To expose the body to the direct rays of the sun. **—sun·bath·er** *n.*

sun·beam (sún-beem) *n.* A ray of sunlight.

sun bear *n.* A small, tropical Asian bear, *Helarctos malayanus,* that feeds chiefly on honey and insects.

sun·bed (sún-bed) *n.* An apparatus consisting of a couch with an overhead sun lamp, used to acquire an artificial suntan.

sun·bird (sún-burd) *n.* Any of various small, tropical Old World birds of the family Nectariniidae, having a slender, downward-curving bill and often brightly coloured plumage in the male.

sun bittern *n.* A cranelike tropical American bird, *Eurypyga helias,* having mottled brownish plumage.

sunblind *n. British.* An awning over the outside of a window.

sun·bon·net (sún-bonnit) *n.* A child's wide-brimmed bonnet with a projecting flap at the back for protecting the neck from the sun.

sun·bow (sún-bō) *n.* A rainbow-like display of colours resulting from the refraction of sunlight through a spray of water.

sun·burn (sún-burn) *n.* **1.** Inflammation or blistering of the skin caused by overexposure to direct sunlight or a sunlamp. **2.** Suntan.
~*v.* **sunburnt** (-burnt) or **-burned, -burning, -burns.** *—tr.* To affect with sunburn. *—intr.* To be affected with sunburn.

sun·burst (sún-burst) *n.* **1.** A sudden burst of sunlight, as through broken clouds. **2.** A pattern or design consisting of a central disc with radiating spires projecting in the manner of sunbeams. **3.** A jewelled brooch with such a design.

sun·dae (sún-day || -di) *n.* A dish of ice cream with toppings such as syrup, fruits, nuts, and whipped cream. [Perhaps from SUNDAY, referring to ice cream served on weekdays, left-over from Sunday.]

Sun·da Islands (sún-də, sóōn-, sóōn-). *Dutch* **Soenda.** Group of islands lying between the Indian Ocean and South China Sea. The group comprises the Greater Sunda Islands, which include Java, Sumatra, Borneo, and Sulawesi, and the Lesser Sunda Islands, now known as Nūsa Tenggara, which include Bali, Sumbawa, Sumba, and Timor. The territory is Indonesian, with the exception of Brunei, and the Malaysian states of Sabah and Sarawak.

sun dance *n.* A ritual dance performed by the North American Plains Indians at the summer solstice.

Sun·day (sún-di, -day) *n.* Abbr. **Sun., S.** The day of the week following Saturday and the second day of the weekend, observed as the Sabbath by Christians. See **Sabbath.** [Middle English *sone(n)-day, sun(en)day,* Old English *sunnandæg,* "day of the sun".]

Sunday best *n. Informal.* One's best or smartest clothes. [Traditionally clothes for wearing only in church on Sundays.]

Sunday driver *n. Informal.* A slow and exaggeratedly careful motorist, such as one who drives mainly for recreation.

Sunday painter *n.* One who paints pictures purely as a hobby.

Sunday school *n. Abbr.* **S.S. 1.** A school, generally affiliated with a church, that offers religious instruction for children on Sundays. **2.** The teachers and pupils of a Sunday school.

sun deck *n.* **1.** An upper, exposed, deck on a passenger ship. **2.** *U.S.* A roof, balcony, or terrace used for sun-bathing.

sun·der (súndər) *v.* **-dered, -dering, -ders.** *—tr.* To break apart; divide; sever. *—intr.* To break into parts. —See Synonyms at **separate.**
~*n. Rare.* A division or separation. [Middle English *sund(e)ren,* Old English *syndrian, sundrian.*] **—sun·der·ance** *n.*

Sun·der·land (súndərlənd). Port and industrial town in Tyne and Wear, northeastern England, situated at the mouth of the river Wear. In Monkwearmouth, the area north of the river, there stands a seventh-century abbey, house of the Venerable Bede. Coal has been shipped from the port since 1396.

sun·dew (sún-dew || -dōō) *n.* Any of several insectivorous plants of the genus *Drosera* having leaves covered with sticky hairs, which trap insects. [Translation of Latin *rōs sōlis.*]

sun·di·al (sún-dī-əl, -dīl) *n.* An instrument that indicates local apparent solar time by measuring the hour angle of the sun with a style (a projecting piece) that casts a shadow on a calibrated dial.

sun disc *n.* A symbol in Egyptian art consisting of a disc set between outspread wings, representing the sun god.

sun·dog (sún-dog || -dawg) *n. Meteorology.* **1.** A **parhelion** *(see).* **2.** A small halo or rainbow near the horizon just off the parhelic circle.

sun·down (sún-down) *n.* Sunset.

sun·down·er (sún-downər) *n.* **1.** *Informal.* In Australia, a tramp who looks for a place to sleep at sunset. **2.** An alcoholic drink taken at sunset.

sun·dress (sún-dress) *n.* A light, woman's or child's dress that exposes the back, shoulders, top of the chest, and arms to the sun.

sun·dries (sún-driz || -dreez) *pl.n.* Articles too small or numerous to be itemised; miscellaneous items. [From SUNDRY.]

sun·dry (súndri) *adj.* Various; several; miscellaneous. [Middle English *sundri, sondri,* Old English *syndrig,* apart, separate.]

sun·fish (sún-fish) *n., pl.* **-fishes** or collectively **sunfish. 1.** Any of various large marine fishes of the family Molidae; especially, *Mola mola,* having a round, laterally flattened body. **2.** Any of various North American freshwater fishes of the family Centrarchidae, having a laterally flattened, often brightly coloured body. [Referring to its shape and brilliant colour.]

sun·flow·er (sún-flow-ər, -flowr) *n.* **1.** Any of several plants of the genus *Helianthus;* especially, *H. annuus,* having tall, coarse stems and large yellow-rayed flowers that produce edible seeds rich in oil. **2.** Brilliant yellow to strong or vivid orange yellow.

sung. Past participle of **sing.**

Sung, Song (sóōng). Chinese dynasty (960–1279). Under their rule China achieved one of its highest levels of culture and prosperity.

sun·glass (sún-glaass || -glass) *n.* A **burning-glass** *(see).*

sun·glass·es (sún-glaassiz || -glassiz) *pl.n.* Glasses with tinted or polarising lenses to protect the eyes from the sun's glare.

sun·glow (sún-glō) *n.* A rose or yellow glow in the sky preceding sunrise or following sunset.

sun-god *n.* A god that personifies the sun.

sun·grebe (sún-greeb) *n.* A bird, the **finfoot** *(see).*

sun·hat (sún-hat) *n.* A hat with a wide brim, worn to protect the head, face, and neck from the sun.

sunk. Past participle and alternative past tense of **sink.**

sunk·en (súngkən). Alternative past participle of **sink.**
~*adj.* **1.** Depressed, fallen in, or hollowed: *sunken cheeks.* **2.** Situated beneath the surface of the water or ground; submerged. **3.** Below the surrounding level: *a sunken meadow.*

sunk fence *n.* A **ha-ha** *(see).*

sun lamp *n.* **1.** A lamp that radiates over a wide range of the spectrum from ultraviolet to infrared and is used in therapeutic and cosmetic treatments. **2.** A high-intensity lamp with parabolic mirrors, used in cinema photography.

sun·less (sún-ləss, -liss) *adj.* **1.** Without sunlight; dark or overcast. **2.** Gloomy; cheerless. **—sun·less·ness** *n.*

sun·light (sún-līt) *n.* The light of the sun; sunshine.

sun·lit (sún-lit) *adj.* Illuminated by the sun.

sun lounge *n. Chiefly British.* A room with a glass roof and walls or very large windows, designed to receive maximum sunlight.

sunn (sun) *n.* **1.** A plant, *Crotalaria juncea,* of tropical Asia and Australia, having clusters of yellow flowers. **2.** A tough fibre from the stems of this plant, used for cordage. Also called "Madras hemp", "sunn hemp". [Hindi *san,* from Sanskrit *śaṇa*†, hempen.]

Sun·na, Sun·nah (súnnə, sóōnnə) *n.* The body of traditional Muslim law, observed by the orthodox Muslims and based on the words and acts of Muḥammad. [Arabic *sunnah,* form, course, rule.]

Sun·ni (súnni, sóōnni) *n.* The great branch of Islam following orthodox tradition and accepting the first four caliphs as rightful successors of Muhammad. Compare **Shiah.** [Arabic *sunnīy,* "adherent of the Sunna", from *sunnah,* SUNNA.]

Sun·nite (sún-īt, sóōn-) *n.* A Muslim of the Sunni. [From SUNNI.]

sun·ny (súnni) *adj.* **-nier, -niest. 1.** Exposed to or filled with sunshine: *a sunny room.* **2.** Cheerful; light-hearted: *a sunny smile; a sunny soul.* **—sun·ni·ly** *adv.* **—sun·ni·ness** *n.*

sunny side *n.* **1.** The sunlit side, as of a street. **2.** The positive or encouraging aspect of a situation. **—on the sunny side of.** *Informal.* Younger than the age specified.

sun·ny-side up (súnni-sīd) *adv. Chiefly U.S.* Served with the fried side down and the yolk on top. Said of eggs. **—sunny-side up** *adj.*

sun·ray (sún-ray) *n.* **1.** A sunbeam. **2.** An ultraviolet ray from a sun lamp.

sun·rise (sún-rīz) *n.* **1. a.** The event or time of the daily first appearance of the sun above the eastern horizon. **b.** The time when the centre of the rising sun is on the horizon. **2.** The atmospheric effects of sunrise. **3.** An outset or emergence, as of civilisation.

sun roof *n.* **1.** A flat roof on a building used for sunbathing. **2.** A sliding panel in the roof of a car. In this sense, also called "sunshine roof".

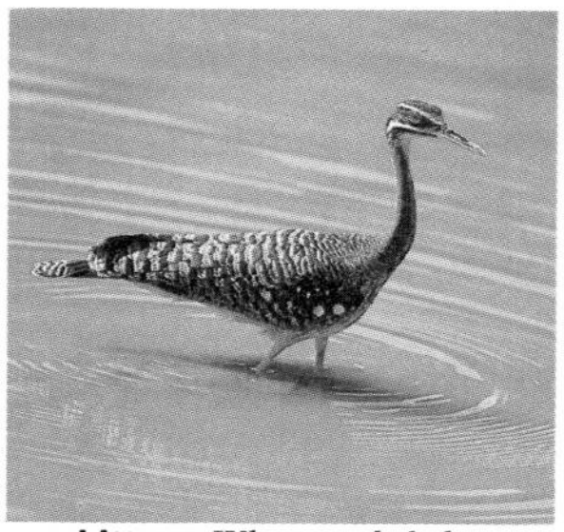

sun bittern *When startled, the sun bittern spreads its wings, displaying eye-shaped marks to deter its attacker. The birds live along the banks of forested rivers in South America and feed largely on insects.*

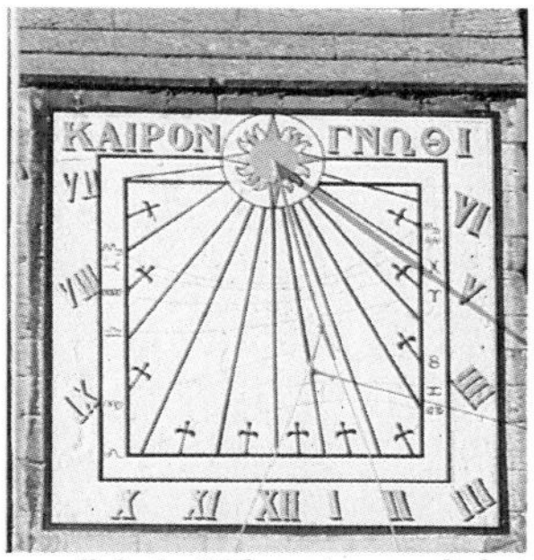

sundial *An 18th-century sundial at Ely Cathedral, Cambridgeshire, England. The shadow cast by the central gnomon gives the time at about 4.55 p.m.*

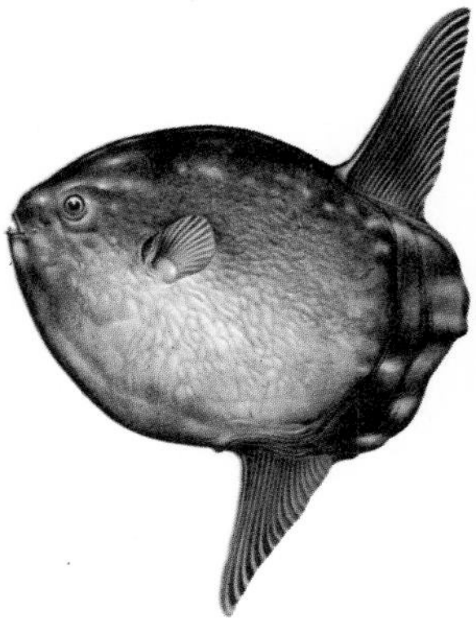

sunfish Mola mola, *the sunfish, gets its name because it resembles the sun with its rounded shape and radiating fins. Sunfish are the world's heaviest bony fish. One – captured off Sydney, Australia, in 1908 – weighed 2.28 tonnes (2.24 tons).*

sun screen *n.* A substance or preparation that protects the skin by blocking harmful ultraviolet rays.

sun·seek·er (sún-seekər) *n.* **1.** A holidaymaker who seeks sunny climates. **2.** A photoelectric device in spacecraft that keeps instruments constantly orientated towards the sun.

sun·set (sún-set) *n.* **1. a.** The event or time of the daily disappearance of the sun below the western horizon. **b.** The time when the centre of the setting sun is on the horizon. **2.** The atmospheric effects of sunset. **3.** The decline or final phase, as of life.

sun·shade (sún-shayd) *n.* Anything used as a protection from the sun's rays, such as an awning or a parasol.

sun·shine (sún-shīn) *n.* **1. a.** The light or warmth of the sun; the direct rays from the sun. **b.** An area lit up by the sun. **2. a.** Happiness or cheerfulness. **b.** A source of happiness or cheerfulness: *You are my sunshine.* **3.** Used as an affectionate or ironic form of address. —**sun·shin·y** *adj.*

sun·spot (sún-spot) *n.* **1.** Any of the relatively dark spots that appear briefly in groups on the surface of the Sun during an approximate 11-year cycle and are associated with strong magnetic fields. **2.** *British Informal.* A sunny place; especially, a holiday resort.

sun·star (sún-staar) *n.* Any starfish of the genus *Solaster,* having up to 13 arms.

sun·stone (sún-stōn) *n.* A type of feldspar, **aventurine** *(see).*

sun·stroke (sún-strōk) *n.* **Heat stroke** *(see)* caused by overexposure to the sun. Also called "insolation". [Translation of French *coup de soleil.*]

sun·tan (sún-tan) *n.* A brownish skin colour resulting from exposure to the ultraviolet rays of the sun or a sun lamp.
~*adj.* Designating a lotion, cream, or oil used to protect the skin from damage by the sun's rays, and sometimes accelerating their tanning effects. —**sun·tanned** *adj.*

sun trap *n.* An area which is sheltered and exposed to the sun.

sun·up (sún-up) *n. Chiefly U.S.* The time of sunrise.

sun·ward (sún-wərd) *adj.* Facing or directed towards the sun.
~*adv. U.S.* Variant of **sunwards**.

sun·wards (sún-wərdz) *adv.* Also *U.S.* **sunward**. Towards the sun.

sun·wise (sún-wīz) *adv.* From left to right, like the sun's course as viewed in the Northern Hemisphere.

Sun Zhong·shan (soon-jóng-shán), also known as Sun Yat-sen (1866–1925). Chinese revolutionary politician. He played a large part in the revolution against the Manchus. He united all the revolutionary parties under the Guomindang (1911) and was appointed provisional president of the Republic after the fall of the Manchus. He resigned (1912) in favour of Yüan Shih-kay.

su·o ju·re (soo-ō jóor-i, séw-, yóor-, -ay) *adv. Law.* In one's own right. [Latin.]

su·o lo·co (soo-ō lóckō, séw-, lóko) *adv. Law.* In a person or thing's rightful place. [Latin, in its (his, her) own place.]

Suomi. See **Finland.**

sup[1] (sup) *v.* **supped, supping, sups.** —*tr.* **1.** To take (a liquid) into the mouth by sips. **2.** *Northern English Regional.* To drink. —*intr.* To take liquid into the mouth in small amounts.
~*n.* A mouthful or taste of liquid. [Middle English *s(o)upen,* Old English *sūpan.*]

sup[2] *intr.v.* **supped, supping, sups.** *Archaic.* To eat the evening meal; have supper. [Middle English *soupen, suppen,* from Old French *s(o)uper,* from *soup,* piece of bread dipped in broth, soup, from Germanic.]

sup. **1.** above [Latin *supra.*] **2.** superior. **3.** *Grammar.* superlative. **4.** supine (noun). **5.** supplement; supplementary. **6.** supply.

su·per (soo-pər, séw-) *n.* **1.** *Informal.* A police superintendent. **2.** *Informal.* An extra person, especially a **supernumerary** *(see).* **3.** An article or product of a superior size, quality, or grade. **4.** *U.S.* A partner or caretaker in a building.
~*adj. Slang.* Ideal; first-rate. Sometimes used as an interjection. [By shortening.]

super– *comb. form.* Indicates: **1.** Placement above, over, or outside; for example, **supercolumnar, superimpose**. **2.** Superiority in size, quality, number, or degree; for example, **superfine, supermarket**. **3. a.** A degree exceeding a specified level; for example, **supersonic**. **b.** An extraordinary degree; for example, **superhero**. **4.** Addition; for example, **superadd**. **5.** *Chemistry.* The presence of a specified ingredient in a high proportion; for example, **superphosphate**. *Note:* Many compounds other than those entered here may be formed with *super-*. In this dictionary in forming compounds, *super-* is normally joined with the following element without space or hyphen: *superrefined.* However, many users prefer the hyphenated form, especially in less standardised compounds, for example **super-tight**. [Latin *super,* above, over.]

super. **1.** superintendent. **2.** superior. **3.** supernumerary.

su·per·a·ble (soo-pərəb'l, séw-) *adj.* Capable of being overcome or surmounted. [Latin *superābilis,* from *superāre,* to go over, overcome, from *super,* above, over.] —**su·per·a·bil·i·ty** (-pərə-bílləti), **su·per·a·ble·ness** *n.* —**su·per·a·bly** *adv.*

su·per·a·bound (soo-pərə-bównd, séw-) *intr.v.* **-bounded, -bounding, -bounds.** To be unusually or excessively abundant. [Middle English *superabounden,* from Late Latin *superabundāre* : Latin *super-,* excessively + *abundāre,* ABOUND.]

su·per·a·bun·dant (soo-pərə-búndənt, séw-) *adj.* Abundant to excess; more than ample. [Middle English, from Late Latin *superabundāns* (stem *superabundant-*), present participle of *superabundāre,* SUPERABOUND.] —**su·per·a·bun·dance** *n.* —**su·per·a·bun·dant·ly** *adv.*

su·per·add (soo-pər-ád, séw-) *tr.v.* **-added, -adding, -adds.** To add to something that has already been added to.

su·per·al·tern (soo-pər-áwl-tern, séw-) *n. Logic.* A universal proposition that is a ground for the immediate inference of a corresponding subalternate. [SUPER- + *altern,* as in SUBALTERN.]

su·per·an·nu·ate (soo-pər-ánnew-ayt, séw-) *tr.v.* **-ated, -ating, -ates. 1.** To allow to retire on a pension because of age or infirmity. **2.** To set aside or discard as old-fashioned or obsolete. [Back-formation from SUPERANNUATED.] —**su·per·an·nu·a·tion** (-áysh'n) *n.*

su·per·an·nu·at·ed (soo-pər-ánnew-aytid, séw-) *adj.* **1.** Retired or discharged because of age or infirmity. **2.** Too old or out of date to be worth preserving. **3.** Obsolete. —See Synonyms at **old.** [Medieval Latin *superannuātus,* past participle of *superannuārī,* to be too old : Latin *super,* above + *annus,* year, time of life.]

su·perb (soo-pérb, sew-, soo- ‖ sə-) *adj.* **1.** Of unusually high quality. **2.** Majestic; imposing. **3.** Rich; luxurious. [French *superbe,* from Latin *superbus,* superior, proud, arrogant.] —**su·perb·ly** *adv.* —**su·perb·ness** *n.*

su·per·cal·en·der (soo-pər-kál-indər, séw-, -kal-) *n.* A calender with a number of rollers for giving a high finish or gloss to paper. —**su·per·cal·en·der** *tr.v.*

su·per·car·go (soo-pər-kárgō, séw-) *n., pl.* **-goes** or **-gos.** An officer on board a merchant ship who has charge of the cargo and its sale and purchase. [Variant of earlier *supracargo,* from Spanish *sobrecargo* : *sobre,* over, from Latin *super-* + CARGO.]

su·per·charge (soo-pər-chaarj, séw-) *tr.v.* **-charged, -charging, -charges. 1.** To increase the power of (an engine) by fitting a supercharger. **2.** To charge excessively, as with emotion or tension. **3.** To pressurise (a fluid).
~*n.* An excess or extra charge.

su·per·charg·er (soo-pər-chaarjər, séw-) *n.* A blower or compressor for supplying air under high pressure to the cylinders of an internal-combustion engine. Also called "booster".

su·per·cil·i·ar·y (soo-pər-sílli-əri, séw- ‖ -erri) *adj.* **1.** Of or pertaining to the eyebrow. **2.** Located over the eyebrow or a corresponding region in animals. [New Latin *superciliaris,* from Latin *supercilium,* eyebrow. See **supercilious**.]

su·per·cil·i·ous (soo-pər-sílli-əss, séw-, soo-) *adj.* Showing or characterised by haughty scorn or indifference; disdainful. See Synonyms at **proud.** [Latin *superciliōsus,* from Latin *supercilium,* "upper eyelid", eyebrow, pride : *super-,* above + *cilium,* (lower) eyelid.] —**su·per·cil·i·ous·ly** *adv.* —**su·per·cil·i·ous·ness** *n.*

su·per·class (soo-pər-klaass, séw- ‖ -klass) *n. Biology.* A taxonomic category ranking below a phylum and above a class.

su·per·co·lum·nar (soo-pər-kə-lúm-nər, séw-) *adj. Architecture.* **1.** Having one order of columns above another. **2.** Situated above a colonnade or column.

su·per·con·duc·tiv·i·ty (soo-pər-kón-duk-tívvəti, séw-) *n.* A property of certain metals and alloys whereby they exhibit virtually no electrical resistance at temperatures close to absolute zero. —**su·per·con·duc·tive** (-kən-dúktiv ‖ -kon-) *adj.* —**su·per·con·duc·tor** (-kən-dúktər ‖ -kon-) *n.*

su·per·cool (soo-pər-kool, séw-) *v.* **-cooled, -cooling, -cools.** —*tr.* To cool (a liquid) below a transition temperature without the transition occurring; especially, to cool below the freezing point without solidification. —*intr.* To become supercooled. Used of a liquid.

su·per·crit·i·cal (soo-pər-kríttik'l, séw-) *n. Physics.* Having or involving a chain reaction that is self-sustaining and uncontrolled. Said of nuclear reactions, reactors, weapons, and the like.

su·per·dense theory (soo-pər-dénss, séw-) *n. Astronomy.* A theory of the origin of the universe, the **big-bang theory** *(see).*

su·per·dom·i·nant (soo-pər-dómminənt, séw-) *n. U.S.* The **submediant** *(see).*

su·per·du·per (soo-pər-doopər, séw-) *adj. Informal.* Great; marvellous. [Reduplication of SUPER (superior).]

su·per·e·go (soo-pər-éegō, séw-, -éggō) *n., pl.* **-egos.** *Psychology.* The division of the psyche that develops by the incorporation of the perceived moral standards of the community as they are transferred from parent to child, is mainly unconscious, and includes the conscience. See **ego, id.**

su·per·el·e·va·tion (soo-pər-élli-váysh'n, séw-) *n.* The difference in height between the outer and inner edges of a curve in a railway track or road.

su·per·em·i·nent (soo-pər-émminənt, séw-) *adj.* Pre-eminent. [Late Latin *superēminēns* (stem *superēminent-*), from Latin, present participle of *superēminēre,* to rise above : *super-,* above + *ēminēre,* to stand out (see **eminent**).] —**su·per·em·i·nence** *n.* —**su·per·em·i·nent·ly** *adv.*

su·per·er·o·gate (soo-pər-érrə-gayt, séw-, -érrō-) *intr.v.* **-gated, -gating, -gates.** *Rare.* To do more than is required, ordered, or expected. [Late Latin *superērogāre,* to spend more : Latin *super-,* excessively + *ērogāre,* to spend, pay out money from the public treasury (after asking the people's consent) : *ex-,* out of + *rogāre,* to ask.] —**su·per·er·o·ga·tor** *n.*

su·per·er·o·ga·tion (soo-pər-érrə-gáysh'n, séw-, -érrō-) *n.* The performance of more than is required, ordered, or expected.

su·per·e·rog·a·to·ry (soo-pər-e-róggə-tri, séw-, -i-, -təri) *adj.* Also **su·per·e·rog·a·tive** (-tiv). **1.** Performed or observed beyond the degree required or expected. **2.** Superfluous; unnecessary.

su·per·fam·i·ly (soo-pər-fám-li, séw-, -əli) *n., pl.* **-lies.** *Biology.* A taxonomic category ranking below an order or its subdivisions and above a family.

su·per·fat·ted (soō-pər-fáttid, séw-) *adj.* Containing extra fat. Said of soap.

su·per·fe·cun·da·tion (soō-pər-féekən-dáysh'n, séw-, -féckən-) *n.* The fertilisation of more than one ovum within a single menstrual cycle by separate acts of coitus, especially by different males.

su·per·fe·tate (soō-pər-fee-táyt, séw-, -fée-tayt) *intr.v.* -tated, -tating, -tates. To conceive when a foetus is already present in the uterus. [Latin *superfētāre* : *super-*, over, in addition to + *fētāre*, to breed, impregnate, from *fētus*, young, foetus.]

su·per·fe·ta·tion (soō-pər-fee-táysh'n, séw-) *n.* The presence in the uterus of foetuses of different ages resulting from the fertilisation of a second ovum some time after the start of pregnancy.

su·per·fi·cial (soō-pər-físh'l, séw-) *adj.* 1. Of, affecting, or being on or near the surface: *a superficial wound.* 2. a. Concerned with or comprehending only what is apparent, obvious, or insubstantial. b. Shallow; not thorough or searching. 3. a. Apparent rather than actual or substantial: *a superficial likeness.* b. Trivial; insignificant. 4. Involving only the surface area. Said of measurements. 5. *Geology.* Lying on the surface; not derived from the rocks below. Said of a deposit. [Middle English, from Late Latin *superficiālis*, from Latin *superficiēs*, surface, SUPERFICIES.] —**su·per·fi·ci·al·i·ty**, (-físhi-ál-əti), **su·per·fi·cial·ness** *n.* —**su·per·fi·cial·ly** *adv.*
Synonyms: superficial, shallow, cursory, perfunctory.

su·per·fi·ci·es (soō-pər-físh-eez, séw-, soō-, -i-eez) *n., pl.* **superficies.** *Rare.* 1. The surface of an area or body. 2. The external appearance or aspect of a thing. [Latin *superficiēs*, surface : *super-*, above, over + *faciēs*, FACE.]

su·per·fine (soō-pər-fín, séw-, -fín) *adj.* 1. Of exceptional quality or refinement. 2. Of extra fine texture. 3. Overdelicate or refined. —**su·per·fine·ness** *n.*

su·per·fix (soō-pər-fiks, séw-) *n. Linguistics.* A suprasegmental feature distinguishing the meaning or grammatical function of one word or phrase from that of another.

su·per·flu·id (soō-pər-floó-id, séw- ‖ -fléw-) *n.* A fluid, such as a form of helium, exhibiting frictionless flow at temperatures close to absolute zero. —**su·per·flu·id·i·ty** (-floo-iddəti) *n.*

su·per·flu·i·ty (soō-pər-floó-əti, séw- ‖ -fléw-) *n., pl.* -ties. 1. The quality or condition of being superfluous. 2. Something that is superfluous. 3. Overabundance; excess.

su·per·flu·ous (soō-pérfloo-əss, sew-, soō- ‖ -pérflew-) *adj.* 1. Beyond what is required or sufficient; extra. 2. Excessive; unnecessary or redundant. [Middle English, from Latin *superfluus*, overflowing, from *superfluere*, to overflow : *super-*, over + *fluere*, to flow.] —**su·per·flu·ous·ly** *adv.* —**su·per·flu·ous·ness** *n.*

su·per·gene (soō-pər-jeen, séw-) *n.* A group of genes closely linked on a chromosome so that they are rarely separated by crossing over and therefore tend to function as a single gene.

su·per·gi·ant (soō-pər-jī-ənt, séw-) *n.* Any of a class of bright low-density stars with diameters and luminosities thousands of times greater than that of the Sun.

su·per·gla·cial (soō-pər-gláy-si-əl, séw-, -shi-, -sh'l) *adj.* Formed or originating on the surface of a glacier.

Su·per·glue (soō-pər-gloó, séw- ‖ -glew) *n.* The trademark for a very strong type of glue which forms a tight bond in a few seconds. —**su·per·glue** *tr.v.*

su·per·grass (soō-pər-graass, séw- ‖ -grass) *n. Informal.* A criminal who gives information to the police.

su·per·heat (soō-pər-héet, séw-) *tr.v.* -heated, -heating, -heats. 1. To heat excessively; overheat. 2. To heat (steam or other vapour not in contact with its own liquid) beyond its saturation point at a given pressure. 3. To heat (a liquid) above its boiling point at a given pressure without causing vaporisation.
~*n.* (-heet). 1. The amount that a vapour is superheated. 2. The heat imparted in the process. —**su·per·heat·er** *n.*

su·per·he·ro (soō-pər-heer-ō, séw-) *n., pl.* -heroes. An imaginary or mythical personage, especially a cartoon character, endowed with superhuman strength or powers.

su·per·her·o·ine (soō-pər-herrō-in, séw-) *n.* A female superhero.

su·per·het·er·o·dyne (soṓopər-héttə-rə-dīn, séw-, -rō-) *adj.* Designating or pertaining to a form of radio reception in which the frequency of an incoming radio signal is converted to an intermediate frequency, by mixing with a locally generated signal, to facilitate amplification and the rejection of unwanted signals.
~*n.* A superheterodyne radio receiver. Also called "superhet". [*supersonic* + *heterodyne.*]

su·per·high frequency (soō-pər-hī, séw-) *n. Abbr.* shf, SHF Any radio frequency between 3,000 and 30,000 megahertz.

su·per·high·way (soō-pər-hī-way, séw-) *n. U.S.* A broad motorway for high-speed traffic, usually with six or more traffic lanes.

su·per·hu·man (soō-pər-héwmən, séw- ‖ -yóomən) *adj.* 1. Above or beyond the human; divine. 2. Beyond ordinary or normal human ability, power, or experience: *a superhuman effort.* —**su·per·hu·man·i·ty** (-hew-mánnəti ‖ -yoō-) *n.* —**su·per·hu·man·ly** *adv.*

su·per·im·pose (soō-pər-im-póz, séw-) *tr.v.* -posed, -posing, -poses. To lay or place upon or over something else. —**su·per·im·po·si·tion** (-ímpə-zísh'n) *n.*

su·per·in·cum·bent (soō-pər-in-kúmbənt, séw-) *adj.* Lying, resting, or suspended on or above something else. [Latin *superincumbēns* (stem *superincumbent-*), present participle of *superincumbere*, to lie down on or above : *super-*, above + *incumbere*, to lie down (see incumbent).] —**su·per·in·cum·bence, su·per·in·cum·ben·cy** *n.* —**su·per·in·cum·bent·ly** *adv.*

su·per·in·duce (soō-pər-in-déwss, séw- ‖ -dóss) *tr.v.* -duced,

-ducing, -duces. To introduce as an addition. [Latin *superindūcere*, to bring upon : *super-*, on, over, in addition + *indūcere*, to lead in, INDUCE.] —**su·per·in·duce·ment, su·per·in·duc·tion** (-dúksh'n) *n.*

su·per·in·fec·tion (soō-pər-in-feksh'n, séw-, -féksh'n) *n.* An infection that develops during the course of another infection, caused by microorganisms not susceptible to the drugs used to treat the first infection.

su·per·in·tend (soō-pər-in-ténd, séw-) *tr.v.* -tended, -tending, -tends. To have charge of; exercise supervision over; manage. [Late Latin *superintendere*, to oversee : *super-*, over + *intendere*, to direct one's attention to, INTEND.] —**su·per·in·ten·dence** *n.*

su·per·in·ten·dent (soō-pər-in-téndənt, séw-) *n. Abbr.* super., supt., Supt. 1. A person who supervises or directs some enterprise or institution. 2. a. In Britain, a police officer ranking between an inspector and a chief superintendent. b. In the United States, the head of a police department. 3. *U.S.* A porter or caretaker in a building —**su·per·in·ten·dent** *adj.* —**su·per·in·ten·den·cy** *n.*

su·pe·ri·or (soō-péer-i-ər, sew-, soō-, sə-) *adj. Abbr.* sup., super. 1. Higher in rank, station, or authority: *a superior officer.* 2. Of a higher nature or kind; above average in comparison: *superior in tone to the modern instrument.* 3. a. Of great value or excellence; extraordinary. b. Of high quality. 4. Greater in number or amount. 5. Affecting an attitude of disdain or conceit. 6. Above being affected or influenced; indifferent or immune: *superior to envy.* 7. Located higher; upper. 8. *Anatomy.* Designating a part or organ situated higher in the body in relation to another part. 9. *Astronomy.* Having an orbit further from the Sun than the orbit of the Earth. 10. *Botany.* Located above and not in contact with the calyx and corolla. Said of an ovary. 11. *Printing.* Set above the main line of type. 12. *Logic.* Of wider or more comprehensive application; generic. Said of a term or proposition.
~*n. Abbr.* sup., super. 1. One who surpasses another in rank or quality. 2. The head of a monastery, abbey, convent, or other ecclesiastical order or house. 3. *Printing.* A superior character or letter. [Middle English, from Old French, from Latin, comparative of *superus*, situated above, upper, from *super*, above, over.] —**su·pe·ri·or·i·ty** (-órrəti ‖ -áwrəti) *n.* —**su·pe·ri·or·ly** *adv.*

Superior, Lake. The largest freshwater lake in the world, and the largest of the Great Lakes of North America. The Canadian-United States border passes through it.

superior conjunction *n.* The position of a celestial body when it is on the opposite side of the Sun from Earth.

superior court *n.* 1. In Britain, a higher court not subject to control by any other court except by way of appeal. 2. In several U.S. states, a court of general jurisdiction, above the inferior courts and below those of final appeal.

superiority complex *n.* 1. An unfounded conviction that one is superior to others. 2. A psychological defence mechanism in which such a conviction counters feelings of inferiority.

superior planet *n.* Any planet of this Solar System whose mean distance from the Sun is greater than that of Earth.

su·per·ja·cent (soō-pər-jáyss'nt, séw-) *adj.* Resting immediately above or upon something else. Used with *to.* [Latin *superjacēns* (stem *superjacent-*), present participle of *superjacēre*, to lie above or upon : *super-*, over + *jacēre*, to lie, from *jacere*, to throw, lay.]

su·per·la·tive (soō-pérlətiv, sew-, soō-) *adj.* 1. Of the highest order, quality, or degree; surpassing or superior to all other or others. 2. Excessive or exaggerated. 3. *Grammar. Abbr.* sup., superl. Expressing or involving the extreme degree of comparison of adjectives and adverbs. Compare **comparative, positive.**
~*n.* 1. Something of the highest possible excellence. 2. The highest degree; the acme. 3. *Grammar. Abbr.* sup., superl. a. The superlative degree. b. An adjective or adverb expressing the superlative degree; for example, *brightest* is the superlative of *bright; most slowly* is the superlative of *slowly.* [Middle English *superlatyf,* from Old French *superlative,* from Late Latin *superlātīvus,* from *superlātus* (past participle of *superferre,* to carry over) : *super-*, over + *-lātus,* "carried".] —**su·per·la·tive·ly** *adv.*

su·per·lu·nar (soō-pər-loó-nər, séw-, -léw-) *adj.* Also **su·per·lu·na·ry** (-nəri). 1. Situated beyond the Moon. 2. *Literary.* Celestial.

su·per·man (soō-pər-man, séw-) *n., pl.* -men (-men). 1. A man with more than human powers. 2. In the philosophy of Nietzsche, an ideal superior man who, through the exercise of creative power and his ability to forgo transient pleasure, would live at a level of experience beyond standards of good and evil and would represent the goal of human evolution. [Translation of German *Übermensch.*]

Su·per·man (soō-pər, -man, séw-). A U.S. comic-strip and film hero who fights for truth and justice with his superhuman powers.

su·per·mar·ket (soō-pər-maarkit, séw-) *n.* A large self-service store selling food and household goods.

su·per·nal (soō-pérn'l, sew-, soō-) *adj.* 1. Celestial; heavenly. 2. Of, coming from, or being in the sky or high above. [Middle English, from Old French, from Latin *supernus.*] —**su·per·nal·ly** *adv.*

su·per·na·tant (soō-pər-náyt'nt, séw-) *adj.* Floating on the surface. [Latin *supernatāns* (stem *supernatant-*), present participle of *supernatāre,* to swim above, float : *super-*, above + *natāre,* to swim.] —**su·per·na·tant** *n.* —**su·per·na·ta·tion** (-nay-táysh'n) *n.*

su·per·nat·u·ral (soō-pər-nách-rəl, séw-, -náchə-) *adj.* 1. Of or pertaining to existence outside the natural world; especially not attributable to natural forces. 2. Attributed to the immediate exercise of divine power; miraculous. 3. Of or pertaining to the miraculous.
~*n.* That which is supernatural. Usually preceded by *the.* —**su·per·nat·u·ral·ly** *adv.* —**su·per·nat·u·ral·ness** *n.*

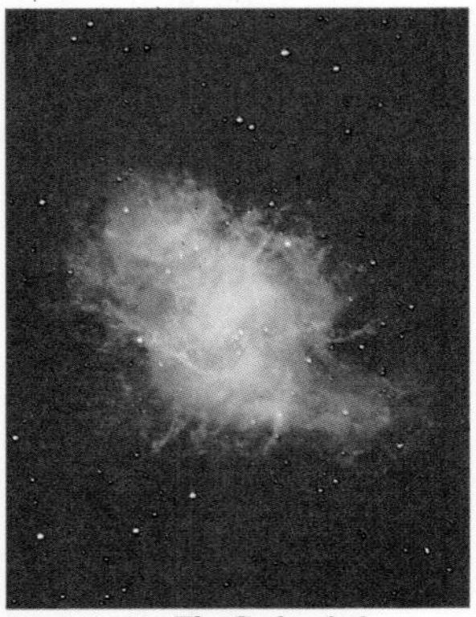

supernova *The Crab nebula (above) – which lies 6,000 light years away in the constellation Taurus – is the glowing debris of a star that exploded into a supernova in about 5000 BC. The glare of the explosion was seen on Earth and recorded by Chinese astronomers in A.D. 1054. At the centre of the nebula is a small, faint star – all that survives of the original shattered star. In 1968, astronomers discovered that this remnant star was a pulsar, a tiny and extremely dense star, which was spinning 30 times a second. Pulsars are so called because they send out flashes, or "pulses", of radiation on each rotation like the beam of a lighthouse.*

su·per·nat·u·ral·ism (sóō-pər-nách-rəliz'm, séw-, -náchə-) *n.* **1.** The quality of being supernatural. **2.** Belief in a supernatural agency that intervenes in the course of natural laws. **—su·per·nat·u·ral·ist** *adj.* & *n.* **—su·per·nat·u·ral·is·tic** (-rə-lístik) *adj.*

su·per·nor·mal (sóō-pər-nórməl, séw-) *adj.* Greatly exceeding the normal or average but still obeying natural laws. **—su·per·nor·mal·i·ty** (-nawr-mál-əti) *n.* **—su·per·nor·mal·ly** *adv.*

su·per·no·va (sóō-pər-nṓ-və, séw-) *n., pl.* **-vae** (-vee) or **-vas.** A rare celestial phenomenon involving the explosion of most of the material in a star, resulting in an extremely bright, short-lived object that emits vast amounts of energy. Compare **nova.**

su·per·nu·mer·ar·y (sóō-pər-néwmə-rəri, séw- || -nóōmə-, -rerri) *adj.* **1.** Exceeding a fixed, prescribed, or standard number; extra: *a supernumerary nipple.* **2.** Beyond the required or desired number. *~n., pl.* **supernumeraries.** *Abbr.* **super. 1.** Someone or something in excess of the regular, necessary, or usual number. **2.** An actor without a speaking part, such as one who appears in a crowd scene. [Late Latin *supernumerārius,* (a soldier) added to a legion in excess of its fixed number, from Latin *super numerum,* over the number : *super,* over + *numerus,* number, division of an army.]

su·per·or·der (sóō-pər-awrdər, séw-) *n. Biology.* A taxonomic category ranking above an order or one of its subdivisions and below a class.

su·per·or·di·nate (sóō-pər-órdi-nət, séw-, -nit, -nayt) *adj.* **1.** Of higher status or value. **2.** *Logic.* Bearing the relation of a universal proposition to a particular proposition in which the terms are the same. **—su·per·or·di·nate** *n.*

su·per·ox·ide (sóō-pər-ók-sīd, séw-) *n.* An oxide of an alkali or an alkaline-earth metal containing the ion O_2, such as NaO_2.

su·per·phos·phate (sóō-pər-fóss-fayt, séw-) *n.* **1.** An acid phosphate. **2.** A fertiliser made by sulphuric acid acting on phosphate rock consisting chiefly of tribasic calcium phosphate, to form a mixture of gypsum and monobasic calcium phosphate.

su·per·phys·i·cal (sóō-pər-fízzik'l, séw-) *adj.* **1.** Exceeding or beyond the purely physical. **2.** Not explained by known physical laws; supernatural.

su·per·pose (sóō-pər-pṓz, séw-) *tr.v.* **-posed, -posing, -poses. 1.** To place (one geometric figure) over another so that all like parts coincide. **2.** To set or place over or above something else. **—su·per·po·sa·ble** *adj.*

su·per·po·si·tion (sóō-pər-pə-zísh'n, séw-) *n.* **1.** The act of superposing or the state of being superposed. **2.** *Geology.* The principle that in a group of stratified sedimentary rocks the lowest were the earliest to be deposited.

su·per·pow·er (sóō-pər-pow-ər, -powr) *n.* A powerful and influential nation; especially, a nuclear power that dominates its satellites and allies in an international power bloc.

super rat *n.* A breed of rat which has developed an immunity, now passed on in its genes, to most rodent poisons.

su·per·sat·u·rate (sóō-pər-sáchər-ayt, séw-, -sáchoor-, -sáttewr-) *tr.v.* **-rated, -rating, -rates. 1.** To cause (a chemical solution) to be more highly concentrated than is normally possible under given conditions of temperature and pressure. **2.** To cause (a vapour) to exceed the normal saturation vapour pressure at a given temperature. **—su·per·sat·u·ra·tion** (-áysh'n) *n.*

su·per·scribe (sóō-pər-skrīb, séw-) *tr.v.* **-scribed, -scribing, -scribes. 1.** To write on the outside or upper part of (a letter, for example). **2.** To write (a name or address, for example) on the top or outside. [Latin *superscrībere,* to write over : *super-,* over + *scrībere,* to write.]

su·per·script (sóō-pər-skript, séw-) *adj.* Written or printed above a character or line of print.
~n. A character set, printed, or written above and immediately to one side of another. For example, *2* is the superscript in x^2. Compare **subscript.** [Latin *superscriptus,* past participle of *superscrībere,* SUPERSCRIBE.]

su·per·scrip·tion (sóō-pər-skrípsh'n, séw-) *n.* **1.** Something written above or outside something; specifically, the address on a letter or parcel. **2.** The part of a prescription that bears the Latin word *recipe* represented by the symbol ℞ in a prescription.

su·per·sede (sóō-pər-seéd, séw-) *tr.v.* **-seded, -seding, -sedes. 1.** To replace or succeed. **2.** To cause (something outdated or inferior) to be set aside or displaced. —See Synonyms at **replace.** [Middle English *superceden,* to postpone, from Old French *superseder,* from Latin *supersedēre,* to sit above, desist from : *super-,* above + *sedēre,* to sit.] **—su·per·sed·ence** *n.* **—su·per·sed·er** *n.* **—su·per·se·dure** (-seéjər, -seédewr) *n.*

su·per·se·de·as (sóō-pər-seédi-ass, séw-, -əss) *n. Law.* A writ containing a command to stay legal proceedings, as in the halting or delaying of the execution of a sentence. [Medieval Latin, from Latin (first word in the writ), "you shall desist", from *supersedēre,* to desist from, SUPERSEDE.]

su·per·sen·si·ble (sóō-pər-sénss-əb'l, séw-, -ib'l) *adj.* Also **su·per·sen·so·ry** (-əri). Beyond or above perception by the senses. **—su·per·sen·si·bly** *adv.*

su·per·sen·si·tive (sóō-pər-sén-sə-tiv, séw-, -si-) *adj.* Hypersensitive.

supersession (sóō-pər-sésh'n, séw-) *n.* The act of superseding or the state of being superseded.

su·per·son·ic (sóō-pər-sónnik, séw-) *adj.* Having, caused by, or related to a speed greater than the speed of sound in a specific medium. **—su·per·son·ic** *n.* **—su·per·son·i·cal·ly** *adv.*

su·per·son·ics (sóō-pər-sónniks, séw-) *n. Used with a singular verb.* The study of phenomena produced by the motion of a body through a medium at velocities greater than that of sound.

supersonic transport *n. Abbr.* **SST** An aircraft capable of flight at speeds exceeding the speed of sound.

su·per·star (sóō-pər-staar, séw-) *n.* A very famous figure in public entertainment, such as a film or sports star, who receives exaggerated publicity. **—su·per·star·dom** (-stárdəm) *n.*

su·per·sti·tion (sóō-pər-stísh'n, séw-) *n.* **1. a.** An unfounded belief that some action or circumstance completely unrelated to a course of events can influence its outcome. **b.** Fear of the mysterious or unknown. **2.** Any belief, practice, or rite unreasoningly upheld by faith in magic, chance, or dogma. **3. a.** Fearful or abject dependence upon such beliefs. **b.** Idolatry. [Middle English *supersticion,* from Old French *superstition,* from Latin *superstitiō* (stem *superstitiōn-*), probably "a standing over something (in amazement and awe)", excessive fear, superstition, from *superstāre,* to stand over : *super-,* over + *stāre,* to stand.]

su·per·sti·tious (sóō-pər-stíshəss, séw-) *adj.* **1.** Inclined to believe in superstitions. **2.** Of, characterised by, or proceeding from superstition. **—su·per·sti·tious·ly** *adv.* **—su·per·sti·tious·ness** *n.*

su·per·store (sóō-pər-stawr, séw- || -stōr) *n. Chiefly British.* A large, comprehensively stocked department store.

su·per·stra·tum (sóō-pər-stráa-təm, séw-, -stráy-, -straa-, -stray- || *U.S. also* -stra-) *n., pl.* **-ta** (-tə). A layer superimposed upon another, especially: **1.** *Geology.* A layer or stratum overlying another. **2.** *Linguistics.* The language of an invading population imposed on and supplanting the indigenous tongue. Compare **substratum.**

su·per·struc·ture (sóō-pər-strukchər, séw-) *n.* **1.** Any structure, whether physical or conceptual, that extends or develops from a basic form. **2.** That part of a building or other structure above the foundations. **3.** The parts of a ship's structure above the main deck. **4.** In Marxist theory, the institutions or ideology of a society as distinct from the basic relations of economy and material production. **—su·per·struc·tur·al** (-strúkchərəl) *adj.*

su·per·sub·stan·tial (sóō-pər-səb-stánsh'l, séw-, -sub-, -stáansh'l) *adj.* Transcending material substance or all substance.

su·per·tanker (sóō-pər-tangkər, séw-) *n.* A large tanker, especially one that carries more than 75,000 tons of oil products at sea.

su·per·tax (sóō-pər-taks, séw-) *n.* In Britain, income tax paid at higher rates on incomes above a certain level.

su·per·ton·ic (sóō-pər-tónnik, séw-) *n.* **1.** The second note of the diatonic scale. **2.** A key or chord based on this.

su·per·vene (sóō-pər-veén, séw-) *intr.v.* **-vened, -vening, -venes. 1.** To come or occur as something extraneous, additional, or unexpected. **2.** To follow immediately after; ensue. —See Synonyms at **follow, happen.** [Latin *supervenīre* : *super-,* in addition + *venīre,* to come.] **—su·per·ven·i·ence** *n.* **—su·per·ven·i·ent** (-i-ənt) *adj.* **—su·per·ven·tion** (-vénsh'n) *n.*

su·per·vise (sóō-pər-vīz, séw-) *tr.v.* **-vised, -vising, -vises. 1.** To direct and inspect the performance of (workers or work); oversee; superintend. **2.** To watch over (pupils in an examination, for example) to maintain order. —See Synonyms at **conduct.** [Medieval Latin *supervidēre* (past participle *supervīsus*), to look over : Latin *super-,* over + *vidēre,* to see.] **—su·per·vi·sion** (-vízh'n) *n.* **—su·per·vi·so·ry** (-vīzəri, -vīzəri) *adj.*

su·per·vi·sor (sóō-pər-vīzər, séw-) *n.* **1.** A person who supervises. **2.** A tutor in some British universities.

su·pi·nate (sóō-pi-nayt, séw-) *v.* **-nated, -nating, -nates.** *—tr.* **1.** To turn or place (the hand and forearm) so that the palm is upwards. **2.** To turn (the foot and lower leg) in a similar manner. *—intr.* To turn the palm and forearm upwards. [Latin *supīnāre,* to bend backwards, from *supīnus,* SUPINE.] **—su·pi·na·tion** (-náysh'n) *n.*

su·pi·na·tor (sóō-pi-naytər, séw-) *n.* A muscle in the forearm that makes supination possible.

su·pine[1] (sóō-pīn, séw-pīn) *adj.* **1.** Lying on the back and facing upwards. **2.** Having the palm upwards. Said of the hand. **3.** Indisposed to act or object; lethargic; passive. **4.** Inclined; sloping. —See Usage note at **prone.** [Latin *supīnus.*] **—su·pine·ly** *adv.* **—su·pine·ness** *n.*

su·pine[2] (sóō-pīn, séw-) *n. Abbr.* **sup.** A verbal noun found in some Indo-European languages, used usually after verbs to denote purpose; especially, the Latin supine, having an accusative in *-um* and an ablative in *-ū,* cited as the fourth of the principal parts. [Latin *(verbum) supīnum,* from *supīnus,* SUPINE. The reason for naming is uncertain.]

su·plex (sóō-pleks, séw-) *n.* A wrestling hold in which the victim is grasped round the waist from behind and carried backwards. [20th century : origin obscure.]

supp. supplement; supplementary.

sup·per (súppər) *n.* **1.** An evening meal, especially when light. **2.** A social gathering at which supper is served. **3.** A snack eaten before going to bed. **—sing for (one's) supper.** To perform a service to repay a favour. [Middle English *suppere,* from Old French *so(u)per,* from *so(u)per,* SUP.]

suppl. supplement; supplementary.

sup·plant (sə-pláant || -plánt) *tr.v.* **-planted, -planting, -plants.** To take the place of, as by force; oust. —See Synonyms at **replace.** [Middle English *supplanten,* from Old French *supplanter,* from Latin *supplantāre,* to trip up one's heel : *sub-,* up from under + *planta,* sole of the foot.] **—sup·plan·ta·tion** (sú-plaan-táysh'n, -plan-) *n.* **—sup·plant·er** *n.*

sup·ple (súpp'l) *adj.* **-pler, -plest. 1.** Readily bent; pliant. **2.** Moving and bending with agility; lithe. **3.** Mentally flexible. **4.** Yielding or changing readily; compliant. —See Synonyms at **flexible**. [Middle English *souple*, from Old French, from Latin *supplex*, beseeching, submissive.] —**sup·ple** v. —**sup·ple·ness** n.

sup·ple·jack (súpp'l-jak) n. A walking stick made from a strong tropical American twining plant, *Paullinia curassavica*.

sup·ple·ment (súppli-mənt ‖ -ment) n. *Abbr.* **sup., supp., suppl.** 1. Something added to complete a thing, make up for a deficiency, or extend or strengthen the whole. 2. A section, sometimes published separately, added to a book or document to give further information or to correct errors. 3. **a.** A separate section devoted to a special subject inserted into a newspaper or other periodical; especially, a colour magazine. **b.** A periodical devoted to a particular subject, associated with another publication but published separately. 4. In geometry: **a.** An angle which with an adjacent angle forms an angle of 180°. **b.** An arc which with an adjacent arc forms a semicircle. 5. A preparation, as of iron or yeast, taken to balance a diet or remedy a dietary deficiency.
~*tr.v.* (-ment, -mént ‖ -mənt) **supplemented, -menting, -ments.** To provide or form a supplement to. [Middle English, from Latin *supplēmentum*, from *supplēre*, to complete, SUPPLY.] —**sup·ple·men·tal** (-mént'l) *adj* & *n.* —**sup·ple·men·ta·tion** (-men-táysh'n) *n.* —**sup·ple·men·ter** (-mentər, -méntər) *n.*

sup·ple·men·ta·ry (súppli-mént-əri, -ri) *adj.* 1. Additional. 2. Provided to make up a deficiency. 3. Designating an angle that is a supplement.
~*n., pl.* **supplementaries.** Something that is supplementary; specifically, an additional question a member may put to a minister at question time in the British Parliament.

supplementary benefit n. *Abbr.* **S.B.** In Britain, payments made weekly or fortnightly by the Department of Health and Social Security to individuals or families without any or on a very low income, but not eligible for unemployment benefit. Formerly called "national assistance".

sup·ple·tion (sə-pléesh'n) n. The use of an etymologically unrelated word to complete an otherwise consistent paradigm; for example, the presence of *went* in *go, went, going, goes.* [Middle English, from Old French, from Medieval Latin *supplētiō* (stem *supplētiōn-*), a completing, from Latin *supplēre*, to fill up, SUPPLY.] —**sup·ple·tive** (sə-pléetiv) *adj. & n.*

sup·pli·ant (súppli-ənt) *adj.* Asking humbly and earnestly.
~*n.* One who supplicates. [Middle English, from Old French, present participle of *supplier*, to entreat, from Latin *supplicāre*, to SUPPLICATE.] —**sup·pli·ance** n. —**sup·pli·ant·ly** *adv.*

sup·pli·cant (súpplikənt) n. One who entreats or supplicates.
~*adj.* Supplicating.

sup·pli·cate (súppli-kayt) v. **-cated, -cating, -cates.** —*tr.* 1. To ask for humbly or earnestly. 2. To make a humble entreaty to; beseech. —*intr.* To make a humble and earnest petition, especially to a deity. [Middle English *supplicaten*, from Latin *supplicāre*, to kneel down, beg humbly : *sub-*, down, underneath + *plicāre*, to fold up.] —**sup·pli·ca·tion** (-káysh'n) n. —**sup·pli·ca·to·ry** (-kə-tri, -təri, -kaytəri, -káytəri) *adj.*

sup·ply¹ (sə-plī́) v. **-plied, -plying, -plies.** —*tr.* 1. To make (something needed, desired, or lacking) available for use; provide. 2. **a.** To furnish or equip with what is needed or lacking. **b.** *Anatomy.* To provide (a body part) with nerve impulses or a vital fluid, such as blood. 3. To fill sufficiently; satisfy: *supply a need.* 4. To make up for (a deficiency, for example); compensate for. 5. To serve temporarily in (the position or office of another); occupy as a substitute. —*intr.* To fill a position as a substitute.
~*n., pl.* **supplies.** *Abbr.* **sup.** 1. The act of supplying. 2. Something that is or can be supplied, especially a basic facility such as water or electricity. 3. An amount available or sufficient for a given use; a store; a stock. 4. *Usually plural.* Materials or provisions stored and dispensed when needed. 5. *Plural.* The grant made the British Parliament for the cost of government. 6. *Economics.* The amount of a commodity available for meeting a demand or for purchase at a given price. 7. One, especially a clergyman, serving as a temporary substitute. Also used adjectivally: *a supply teacher.* [Middle English *suppl(y)en*, from Old French *so(u)pleer, soup(p)leier*, from Latin *supplēre*, to fill up, complete : *sub-*, from below, up + *plēre*, to fill.] —**sup·pli·er** n.

sup·ply² (súppli) *adv.* In a supple way.

supply and demand (sə-plī́) n. The availability of and willingness of consumers to purchase goods or services, considered as the economic forces governing prices in the absence of administrative control, and, through prices, output and the distribution of income.

sup·port (sə-pórt ‖ -pórt) *tr.v.* **-ported, -porting, -ports.** 1. To bear the whole or partial weight of, especially from below. 2. To hold in position; prevent from falling, sinking, or slipping. 3. To encourage or lend strength to, especially in difficulties. 4. To provide for or maintain by supplying with money or other necessities. 5. To furnish evidence for; corroborate or substantiate. 6. **a.** To aid the cause of by approving, favouring, or advocating. **b.** To be an adherent of; give one's loyalty to. 7. To bear or endure; tolerate. 8. **a.** To act in a secondary or subordinate role to (a leading actor). **b.** To accompany (the main act, showing, or performance).
~*n.* 1. **a.** The act of supporting. **b.** The state of being supported. 2. One that supports. 3. Maintenance or subsistence. 4. A medical appliance worn to support and ease an injured part. 5. The solid material on which a painting is executed. [Middle English *suppor-*

ten, from Old French *supporter*, from Latin *supportāre*, to carry, convey : *sub-*, up, towards + *portāre*, to carry.]
　　Synonyms: support, uphold, maintain, advocate, champion.

sup·port·a·ble (sə-pórt-b'l ‖ -pórt-) *adj.* Bearable; endurable. —**sup·port·a·bil·i·ty** (-ə-bíllǝti) n. —**sup·port·a·bly** *adv.*

sup·port·er (sə-pórt-ər ‖ -pórt-) n. 1. A person or thing that supports. 2. One who promotes or advocates; a partisan; an adherent. 3. A sports fan loyal to a particular team or player. 4. A support or binding for some part of the body; especially, a jockstrap. 5. *Heraldry.* An animal or figure that supports a shield in a coat of arms.

sup·por·tive (sə-pórt-iv ‖ -pórt-) *adj.* 1. Furnishing support or assistance. 2. Inclined to provide emotional or psychological support. 3. Designating any system of medical treatment designed to maintain the patient's physiological well-being, rather than to treat a specific disorder.

support price n. A price level at which the European Economic Community or other international agency will intervene and buy agricultural produce in order to maintain price stability.

support system n. A network of personal or professional contacts available to a person or organisation to give practical or moral support when required.

support tights n. Thick, strong, nylon tights designed to reduce stress on the blood vessels in the legs of dancers or people with varicose veins, for example.

sup·pos·a·ble (sə-pózəb'l) *adj.* That can be supposed or conjectured. —**sup·pos·a·bly** *adv.*

sup·pose (sə-pōź ‖ spōz) v. **-posed, -posing, -poses.** —*tr.* 1. To assume (something) to be true or real for the sake of an argument or explanation. 2. To believe, especially on uncertain or tentative grounds; be inclined to think. 3. To imply as an antecedent condition; presuppose. 4. To consider as a suggestion. Often used to introduce a proposal: *Suppose we dine together.* 5. To expect or require. Used in the passive: *I was not supposed to be home.* —*intr.* To make an assumption; conjecture. —See Synonyms at **presume.** [Middle English *supposen*, to believe, assume, from Old French *supposer*, from Latin *suppōnere* (past participle *suppositus*), to put under, substitute, forge : *sub-*, under + *ponere*, to place.]
　　Usage: Supposing is generally used to express clauses of condition or reason (*Supposing nothing happens, we'll get there on time*). It may also be used to express wholly hypothetical states of affairs (*Supposing you won the pools . . .*) although many people prefer to use *suppose* in such contexts.

sup·posed (sə-pózd, -pózid) *adj.* Presumed to be true or genuine, especially on dubious grounds. —**sup·pos·ed·ly** (sə-pózidli) *adv.*

sup·po·sing (sə-pózing, spózing) *conj.* In the event that. Sometimes used without a main clause to convey anxiety: *Supposing they catch us!* See Usage note at **suppose.**

sup·po·si·tion (súppǝ-zísh'n) n. 1. The act of supposing. 2. An unproven statement or assumption, especially one tentatively accepted. —**sup·po·si·tion·al** *adj.* —**sup·po·si·tion·al·ly** *adv.*

sup·po·si·tious (súppǝ-zíshǝss) *adj.* 1. Hypothetical; supposed. 2. Fraudulent; supposititious.

sup·pos·i·ti·tious (sǝ-pózzi-tíshǝss) *adj.* 1. Substituted with fraudulent intent; spurious; counterfeit. 2. Hypothetical; supposed. [Latin *supposītīcius*, substituted, from *suppōnere* (past participle *supposítus*), to place under, substitute, SUPPOSE.] —**sup·pos·i·ti·tious·ly** *adv.* —**sup·pos·i·ti·tious·ness** n.

sup·pos·i·tive (sǝ-póz-i-tiv, -ǝ-) *adj.* Of the nature of, including, or involving supposition.
~*n.* *Grammar.* A conjunction introducing a supposition, such as *if* or *providing.* —**sup·pos·i·tive·ly** *adv.*

sup·pos·i·to·ry (sǝ-pózzi-tri, -tǝri) n., *pl.* **-ries.** A solid medication designed to melt within a body cavity other than the mouth, especially the rectum or vagina. [Medieval Latin *suppositōrium*, "something placed underneath", from Latin *suppositōrius*, "placed under", from Latin *suppōnere*, to place under, SUPPOSE.]

sup·press (sǝ-préss) *tr.v.* **-pressed, -pressing, -presses.** 1. To put an end to forcibly; subdue; crush. 2. To curtail or prohibit the activities of (a political party, for example). 3. To keep from being revealed, published, or circulated; withhold from the public. 4. To hold back (an impulse, for example); check: *suppress a smile.* 5. To reduce the incidence or severity of (a haemorrhage, for example); arrest. 6. To reduce or eliminate (noise or a specified frequency range) from an electronic signal or device. 7. *Psychology.* To exclude (desires or thoughts) consciously from one's awareness. [Middle English *suppressen*, from Latin *supprimere* (past participle *suppressus*), to press down : *sub-*, down + *premere*, to press.] —**sup·press·i·ble** *adj.* —**sup·pres·sive** *adj.*

sup·pres·sion (sǝ-présh'n) n. 1. The act of suppressing. 2. The state of being suppressed. 3. The act or process of suppressing an electronic frequency. 4. *Psychology.* The conscious exclusion of painful desires or thoughts from awareness. 5. *Botany.* The failure of an organ or part to develop.

sup·pres·sor, sup·pres·ser (sǝ-préssǝr) n. 1. One that suppresses. 2. A gene that reduces the phenotypic expression of a mutant gene. 3. A device that reduces or eliminates electrical noise from the ignition system of an internal-combustion engine to prevent interference with an electronic device, such as a radio. 4. An electrode placed between the screen grid and anode of an electronic vacuum tube to prevent secondary electrons from the anode reaching the screen. In this sense, also called "suppressor grid".

sup·pu·rate (súppewr-ayt) *intr.v.* **-rated, -rating, -rates.** To form or

discharge pus, as a wound may; fester or maturate. [Latin *suppūrāre* : *sub-*, under + *pūs* (stem *pūr-*), pus.]
sup·pu·ra·tion (súppewr-áysh'n) *n.* **1.** The formation or discharge of pus. Also called "maturation". **2.** Pus.
sup·pur·a·tive (súppewr-ətiv, -aytiv || súpprətiv) *adj.* Causing suppuration. **—sup·pur·a·tive** *n.*
supr. supreme.
su·pra (sŏŏ-prə, séw- || -praa) *adv. Latin.* Above; in the text that precedes. Compare **infra.**
supra– *prefix.* Indicates above, specifically: **1.** Higher than or over; for example, **suprarenal. 2.** Greater than; for example, **supramolecular. 3.** Preceding; for example, **supralapsarian.** [Latin, from *suprā*, above, beyond, earlier.]
su·pra·glot·tal (sŏŏ-prə-glótt'l, séw-) *adj.* **1.** *Anatomy.* Above or anterior to the glottis. **2.** *Linguistics.* Designating a phone or phoneme produced by the speech organs anterior to the glottis.
su·pra·lap·sar·i·an (sŏŏ-prə-lap-sáir-i-ən, séw-) *n.* Any of the Calvinists who believe that God's determination of the elect preceded the Fall and that the Fall itself had been predestined. [SUPRA- + Latin *lapsus*, fall, from the past participle of *lābī*, to slide.] **—su·pra·lap·sar·i·an** *adj.* **—su·pra·lap·sar·i·an·ism** *n.*
su·pra·lim·i·nal (sŏŏ-prə-límmin'l, séw-) *adj.* Above the threshold of conscious perception. Said of stimuli.
su·pra·mo·lec·u·lar (sŏŏ-prə-mə-léckewlər, séw-, -mō-, -mo-) *adj.* **1.** Consisting of more than one molecule. **2.** Of greater complexity than a molecule.
sup·ra·na·tion·al (sŏŏ-prə-násh'n-'l, séw-, -násh-n'l) *adj.* Going beyond national boundaries or concerns.
su·pra·or·bi·tal (sŏŏ-prə-órbit'l, séw-) *adj.* Located above the orbit of the eye.
su·pra·re·nal (sŏŏ-prə-réen'l, séw-) *adj.* Located on or above the kidney.
~n. A suprarenal gland. [New Latin *suprarenalis* : SUPRA- + Latin *rēnēs*, the kidneys (see **renal**).]
suprarenal gland *n.* An **adrenal gland** *(see).*
su·pra·seg·men·tal (sŏŏ-prə-seg-mént'l, séw-, -sig-) *adj. Linguistics.* Designating those phonetic features that form the background rather than the individual segments of a word or sentence, such as stress or intonation, for example.
su·prem·a·cist (sŏŏ-prémmə-sist, sŏŏ-, sew- || sə-) *n.* One who believes that a certain group is or should be supreme.
su·prem·a·cy (sŏŏ-prémmə-si, sŏŏ-, sew- || sə-) *n., pl.* **-cies. 1.** The condition or quality of being supreme. **2.** Supreme power.
su·prem·a·tism (sŏŏ-prémmə-tiz'm, sew-, sŏŏ- || sə-) *n.* A school of geometric abstract art cultivated by Russian artists such as Malevich in the early 20th century, revived in the 1960s, and influencing constructivists. [From *suprematist*, a member of this school, from French *suprémacie*, SUPREMACY.] **—su·prem·a·tist** *n. & adj.*
su·preme (sŏŏ-préem, sŏŏ-, sew- || sə-) *adj. Abbr.* **supr. 1.** Greatest in power, authority, or rank; paramount; dominant. **2.** Greatest in degree, significance, character, or achievement; utmost; extreme. **3.** Ultimate; final: *the supreme sacrifice.* [Latin *suprēmus*, superlative of *superus*, situated above, upper, from *super*, above.] **—su·preme·ly** *adv.* **—su·preme·ness** *n.*
su·prême (sŏŏ-préem, sew-, sŏŏ-, -prém || sə-) *adj.* Served with a rich sauce usually made with cream and egg yolks. Used after the noun. [French, SUPREME.]
Supreme Court *n. Abbr.* **S.C.** The highest Federal court in the United States, consisting of nine justices and having jurisdiction over all other courts in the nation.
Supreme Court of Judicature *n. Law.* In Britain, a court formed in 1873 to amalgamate most of the superior courts at the time. It now comprises the **High Court of Justice,** the **Court of Appeal,** and the **Crown Court** *(all of which see).*
Supreme Soviet *n.* The legislature of the Soviet Union, consisting of two equal houses, the *Soviet of the Union*, whose members are elected on the basis of population, and the *Soviet of the Nationalities*, whose members are elected by the various national groups.
su·pre·mo (sŏŏ-préemō, sew-) *n., pl.* **mos.** *British Informal.* A chief or leader having overall authority. [Spanish, SUPREME.]
supt., Supt. superintendent.
Su·qua·mish (sə-kwaámish) *n., pl.* **-mishes** or collectively **Suquamish. 1.** A member of a Salish-speaking people of North American Indians of the northwestern Pacific coast, west of Puget Sound. **2.** The language of this people.
sur– *prefix.* Indicates: **1.** Over, beyond, or above; for example, **surtax. 2.** Excessively; extremely; for example, **surbased.** [Middle English, from Old French *s(o)ur-*, from Latin *super-*, from *super*, above, over.]
sur. 1. surface. **2.** surplus.
su·ra (sŏŏr-ə) *n.* Any of the 114 chapters or sections of the Koran. [Arabic *sūrah*, "a step", from Hebrew *shūrāh*, row, line.]
Su·ra·ba·ya (sŏŏr-ə-bī-ə). *Dutch* **Soerabaja.** Port in Indonesia, situated in northeastern Java at the mouth of the Mas River. It is the country's second largest city and its major naval base.
su·rah (sŏŏr-ə, séwr-ə) *n.* A soft twilled fabric of silk or of a blend of silk and rayon. [French *surat*, originally made at SURAT.]
su·ral (sŏŏr-əl, séwr-əl) *adj.* Of or relating to the calf of the leg. [New Latin *suralis*, from Latin *sūra*†, calf of the leg.]
Su·rat (sŏŏr-ət, sŏŏ-raát, -rát). City in Gujarat state, India, situated on the river Tapti near its mouth on the Gulf of Khambat. It is an administrative and commercial centre, a small port, and a railway junction. In the 17th century British and Dutch trading posts were established here.
sur·base (súr-bayss) *n. Architecture.* A moulding or border above the base of a structure, such as a pedestal. [SUR- + BASE.]
sur·based (súr-bayst) *adj. Architecture.* **1.** Having a surbase. **2.** Pertaining to or designating an arch with a rise less than half its span. [French *surbaissé*, flattened (said of an arch), from the past participle of *surbaisser*, to depress, flatten : *sur-*, extremely + *baisser*, to lower, from *bas*, low, from Old French, low, BASE.]
sur·cease (sur-séess || *U.S. also* súr-seess) *v.* **-ceased, -ceasing, -ceases.** *Archaic. —tr.* To put an end to. *—intr.* To cease; stop.
~n. Archaic. A cessation; an end. [Middle English *sursesen*, from Old French *surseoir* (past participle *sursis*), to refrain, delay, from Latin *supersedēre*, to desist from, SUPERSEDE.]
sur·charge (súr-chaarj) *n.* **1.** An additional sum added to the usual amount or cost. **2.** An overcharge, especially when unlawful. **3.** An additional or excessive burden; an overload. **4. a.** A new value or denomination overprinted on a postage or revenue stamp. **b.** The stamp to which it has been applied. **5.** *Law.* The act of surcharging.
~tr.v. (*also* sur-chárj) **surcharged, -charging, -charges. 1.** To charge (a person) an additional sum. **2.** To overcharge (a person). **3. a.** To place an excessive burden upon; overload. **b.** To fill beyond usual capacity; overfill. **4.** To print a surcharge on (a postage or revenue stamp). **5.** *Law.* To show an omission of a credit in (an account). **6.** To require (a person) to reimburse funds spent without authorisation. [Middle English *surchargen*, from Old French *surcharger* : *sur-*, excessively + *charg(i)er*, CHARGE.]
sur·cin·gle (súr-sing-g'l) *n.* A girth that binds a saddle, pack, or blanket to the body of a horse. [Middle English *sursengle*, from Old French *so(u)rcengle* : *sur-*, over + *cengle*, belt, from Latin *cingula*, from *cingere*, to gird.]
sur·coat (súr-kōt) *n.* **1.** Formerly, a loose outer coat or gown. **2.** A tunic worn in the Middle Ages by a knight over his armour. [Middle English *surcote*, "overcoat", from Old French : SUR- + COAT.]
sur·cu·lose (súrkew-lōz, -lōss) *adj. Botany.* Producing suckers: *a surculose shrub.* [Latin *surculōsus*, woody, ligneous, from *surculus*, diminutive of *surus*, branch.]
surd (surd) *n.* **1.** A sum, such as $\sqrt{2} + \sqrt{3}$, containing one or more irrational roots of numbers. **2.** *Phonetics.* A voiceless consonant. No longer in technical usage.
~adj. Phonetics. Voiceless. No longer in technical usage. [Latin *surdus*, deaf, mute (used in mathematics to translate Arabic *jadhr aṣạmm*, "deaf root", translation of Greek *alogos*, "speechless", "irrational").]
sure (shoor, shor || shewr, shur) *adj.* **surer, surest. 1.** Incapable of being doubted or disputed; completely true; certain. **2.** Not hesitating or wavering; stable; steady; firm: *sure convictions.* **3.** Confident of some established fact or future outcome; certain in one's knowledge or expectation. Used with a clause or *of*: *sure that I'm right.* **4. a.** Bound to come about or to happen; inevitable. **b.** Having one's course directed; destined; bound. **5.** Certain not to miss or err; steady. **6. a.** Worthy of being trusted or depended upon; reliable. **b.** Of which one may be confident; safe. **7.** *Obsolete.* Free from harm or danger; safe; secure. **—for sure.** Certainly; unquestionably: *We'll win for sure.* **—make sure. 1.** To establish something without doubt. **2.** To ensure something: *made sure you were told.* **—sure of (oneself).** Rather too confident of one's abilities or worth. **—to be sure.** Indeed; of course.
~adv. Chiefly U.S. Informal. Certainly; indeed: *sure was easy.* **—sure enough.** As was to be expected.
~interj. Certainly; willingly. [Middle English *s(e)ure*, from Old French *sur*, from Latin *sēcūrus*, "free from care", safe : *sē*, without + *cūra*, care.] **—sure·ness** *n.*
Synonyms: *sure, certain, confident, assured.*
sure-fire (shŏŏr-fīr, shór- || shéwr-, shúr-) *adj. Informal.* Bound to be successful or perform as expected: *a sure-fire plan.*
sure-foot·ed (shŏŏr-fŏŏtid, shór- || shéwr-, shúr-) *adj.* Not liable to stumble or fall; agile. **—sure-foot·ed·ness** *n.*
sure·ly (shŏŏrli, shórli || shéwrli, shúrli) *adv.* **1.** Firmly and with confidence; unhesitatingly. **2.** Undoubtedly; certainly. Often used: **a.** As an intensive: *You surely can't be serious.* **b.** In incredulous questions: *Surely it's not Monday already?* **3.** Without fail: *Slowly but surely spring returns.*
~interj. Of course; willingly.
sure thing *n. Informal.* A guaranteed success.
~interj. U.S. Certainly; of course.
su·re·ty (shŏŏr-əti, shór-, *also* -ti || shéwr-, shúr-) *n., pl.* **-ties. 1.** A person who has contracted to be responsible for another; especially, a person who assumes any responsibilities, debts, or obligations in the event of the default of another. **2.** A pledge or formal promise made to secure against loss, damage, or default; a guarantee or security. **3.** Something beyond doubt; a certainty. **4.** The condition of being sure, especially of oneself. **—su·re·ty·ship** *n.*
surf (surf) *n.* **1.** The foaming white spray produced by waves as they break. **2.** The sound or effect of breaking waves.
~intr.v. **surfed, surfing, surfs.** To engage in surfing. [Probably variant of obsolete *suff*†.] **—surf·y** *adj.*
sur·face (súrf-iss, -əss) *n. Abbr.* **sur. 1. a.** The outer or the topmost boundary or boundaries of an object. **b.** A material layer constituting such a boundary. **c.** Such a layer with regard to its texture. **2.** The uppermost level of the land or sea. **3.** *Geometry.* **a.** The boundary of any three-dimensional figure. **b.** The two-dimensional locus of points located in three-dimensional space. **3.** The superfi-

PRONUNCIATION KEY

a, trap; aa, father; ai, fair; ar, star; aw, lawn; ay, play; b, bb, stab; rubber; ch, church; ck, ticket; d, dd, dead; ladder; e, dress; ee, bee; er, defer; ew, few; ewr, pure; ə, about; ər, letter; f, ff, fife; differ; g, gg, giggle; h, hat; i, kit; ī, price; īr, fire; j, judge; k, kick; l, ll, let; 'l, needle; m, mm, man; n, nn, no; 'n, sudden; ng, thing; o, lot; ō, no; ŏŏ, foot; ŏŏ, shoe; oor, poor; ow, cow; owr, hour; oy, boy; p, pp, pepper; r, rr, red; s, ss, sauce; sh, ship; t, tt, totter; th, thick; th, this; smooth; u, cut; ur, turn; v, vv, valve; w, wet; y, yes; z, zz, zebra; zh, vision; pleasure

IN FOREIGN WORDS:

aɴ, ᴏɴ, Saint-Saëns; hl, Llanelli; Hluhluwe; kh, loch; lough; Khaled

STRESS MARK:

in-sīt, insight; in-sīt, incite

cial or outward appearance of anything as distinguished from inner substance or matter. **4.** *Aeronautics.* An aerofoil. **—on the surface.** To all appearances. **—scratch the surface.** To make only a slight impression; achieve no deep effect.
~adj. **1.** Pertaining to, on, or at a surface: *surface algae in the water.* **2.** Superficial; apparent as opposed to real.
~v. **surfaced, -facing, -faces.** *—tr.* **1.** To form the surface of, as by smoothing or levelling; give a surface to. **2.** To provide with a particular surface. *—intr.* **1.** To rise to the surface. **2.** To emerge after concealment. **3.** To mine at or near the ground surface. [French (formed after Latin *superficiēs,* surface) : *sur-,* above + FACE.]
sur·face-ac·tive (súr-fiss-aktiv, -fəss-) *adj.* Designating a substance capable of reducing the surface tension of a liquid in which it is dissolved. Said especially of detergents.
surface mail *n.* **1.** Mail transported over land and sea, rather than by air. **2.** Such transportation of mail.
surface noise *n.* Noise, largely of a high frequency, produced by a gramophone stylus as it follows the groove of a rotating record.
surface of revolution *n. Geometry.* A surface generated by revolving a plane curve about an axis in its plane.
surface plate *n.* A **face plate** *(see).*
surface structure *n.* In the standard theory of transformational-generative grammar, the string of words and sounds as they occur in a sentence, or a diagrammatic representation of these, which can then be analysed according to **transformational rules** *(see)* to reveal an underlying sense or **deep structure** *(see)* not necessarily accessible to **constituent analysis** *(see).*
surface tension *n. Abbr.* **T** **1.** A property of liquids arising from molecular cohesive forces at or near the surface, as a result of which the surface tends to contract to a minimum area and has properties resembling those of a stretched elastic membrane. **2.** A measure of this property.
sur·face-to-air missile (súr-fiss-too-áir, -fəss- || -tə-) *n. Abbr.* **SAM** A missile launched from land or sea at an airborne target.
sur·face-to-sur·face missile (súr-fiss-tə-súr-fiss, -fəss(-), -tōō-) *n. Abbr.* **SSM.** A missile launched from land or sea at a target that is also on the earth's surface.
surface wave *n.* A wave created by an earthquake which travels along the surface of the earth.
sur·fac·tant (sur-fáktant, sər-, súr-faktənt) *n.* A surface-active agent. [*Surf*ace *act*ive + -ANT.]
surf·bird (súrf-burd) *n.* A shore bird, *Aphriza virgata,* of the Pacific coast of North and South America, having dark, spotted plumage.
surf·board (súrf-bawrd || -bōrd) *n.* A long, narrow, round-ended board used by surfers for riding on waves to the shore.
~intr.v. **surfboarded, -boarding, boards.** To engage in surfing.
surf·boat (súrf-bōt) *n.* A strong seaworthy boat that can be launched or landed in heavy surf.
surf·cast·ing (súrf-kaast-ing || -kast-) *n.* The sport of fishing from shore, casting one's line into the surf. **—surf·cast·er** *n.*
sur·feit (súr-fit || -feet) *v.* **-feited, -feiting, -feits.** *—tr.* To feed or supply to fullness or excess; satiate. *—intr. Archaic.* To overindulge. —See Synonyms at **satiate.**
~n. **1.** The act or an instance of overindulging in food or drink. **2.** The result of such overindulgence; satiety; disgust. **3.** An excessive amount. [Middle English, from Old French, from Vulgar Latin *superfactum* (unattested), from the neuter past participle of *superficere* (unattested), to overdo : Latin *super-,* excessively + *facere,* to do.] **—sur·feit·er** *n.*
surf·er (súrfər) *n.* One who engages in surfing.
sur·fi·cial (sur-físh'l, sər-) *adj.* Of, pertaining to, or occurring on the earth's geological surface. [*sur*face + super*ficial.*] **—sur·fi·cial·ly** *adv.*
surf·ing (súrfing) *n.* The sport of riding towards the shore on the crest or along the tunnel of a wave while lying or standing on a surfboard.
surf·perch (súrf-perch) *n., pl.* **-perches** or collectively **surfperch.** Any of various viviparous fishes of the family Embiotocidae, of North American Pacific coastal waters. Also called "sea perch".
surg. surgeon; surgery; surgical.
surge (surj) *v.* **surged, surging, surges.** *—intr.* **1.** To move in a billowing or swelling manner; rise and heave over violently, as waves do. **2.** *Rare.* To roll or be tossed about on waves, as a boat. **3.** To move like advancing waves: *The fans surged forward to see her.* **4.** To well or rise up suddenly and strongly: *anger surging up within us.* **5.** To increase suddenly. Used of an electric current or voltage. **6.** To slip around a windlass. Used of a rope. *—tr.* To loosen or slacken (a cable) gradually.
~n. **1.** A heavy, billowing, or swelling motion like that of great waves: *surge and flow.* **2. a.** A wave, ground swell, or billow. **b.** Such waves collectively. **c.** An undulating surface, such as one formed by hills. **3.** A sudden powerful onset, as of emotion. **4.** A sudden, transient increase in electric current. **5.** An instability in the power output of an engine. **6.** *Astronomy.* A short-lived, violent disturbance occurring during the eruption of a solar flare. **7.** *Nautical.* **a.** A temporary release or slackening of a cable. **b.** The part of a windlass into which the cable surges. [Old French *sourgir,* from Old Spanish *surgir,* from Latin *surgere,* "to lead straight up", rise : *sub-,* up from below + *regere,* to lead, rule.]
sur·geon (súrjən) *n. Abbr.* **surg.** **1.** A medical practitioner specialising in surgery. **2.** A medical officer in the Royal Navy. [Middle English *surg(i)en,* from Anglo-French, short for Old French *serurgien,* from *serurgie,* SURGERY.]
sur·geon·cy (súrjən-si) *n., pl.* **-cies.** *Chiefly British.* The position, office, rank, or duties of a surgeon.
sur·geon·fish (súrjən-fish) *n., pl.* **-fishes** or **surgeonfish.** Any of various bright-coloured tropical marine fishes of the family Acanthuridae, having a sharp, erectile spine near the base of the tail. [From its lance-like spines, which resemble surgeons' instruments.]
Surgeon General *n., pl.* **Surgeons General.** *Abbr.* **Surg. Gen.** **1.** The chief general officer in the medical departments of the U.S. Army or Navy. **2.** The chief medical officer in the U.S. Public Health Service.
surgeon's knot *n.* Any of several knots used in surgery for tying ligatures or stitching incisions.
sur·ger·y (súrjəri) *n., pl.* **-ies.** *Abbr.* **surg.** **1.** The branch of medicine concerned with the treatment of injury, deformity, and disease by operations. **2.** The skill or work of a surgeon. **3.** *Chiefly British.* **a.** A place where general practitioners or dentists advise and treat patients. **b.** The period during which a doctor or other specialist is present in the surgery. **c.** *Informal.* A place where a specialist, such as an M.P. or legal expert, will give advice to members of the public. **4.** *U.S.* An operating theatre. [Middle English *surgerie,* from Old French, short for *serurgerie, cerurgerie,* from *serurgie, cerurgie,* from Latin *chirurgia,* from Greek *kheirurgia,* from *kheirurgos,* working by hand : *kheir,* hand + *ergon,* work.]
sur·gi·cal (súrjik'l) *adj. Abbr.* **surg.** **1.** Pertaining to or characteristic of surgeons or surgery. **2.** Used in surgery. **3.** Resulting from or occurring after surgery. [From SURGEON.]
surgical boot *n.* A boot or shoe designed to compensate for deformities of the leg or foot.
surgical spirit *n.* Methylated spirit with small amounts of castor oil and oil of wintergreen, used especially for sterilising the skin before surgery.
su·ri·cate (séwr-i-kayt, sóor-) *n.* A small, greyish, gregarious burrowing mongoose, *Suricata suricatta,* of southern Africa, having a long tail. [French *suricate,* native name in South Africa.]
Su·ri·nam, Republic of (sóor-i-nám, -naám). *Formerly* **Dutch Guiana** or **Netherlands Guiana.** *Dutch* **Su·ri·na·me** (súr-i-naámə). A country in northeastern South America. It has a low-lying, marshy, coastal strip, a belt of grassland, and the densely forested Guiana Highlands in the south. The major part of all cultivated land is used for rice growing. Other crops include sugar-cane, bananas, citrus fruits, and coconuts. Surinam is one of the world's largest producers of bauxite, and its products which account for most of its foreign income. The population is mixed, with Creoles, Asian Indians, and Indonesians forming the largest groups. The first Europeans to reach the area were the Spanish (1499), but it was the British who established the first colony there (1650). In 1667 the territory was ceded to the Dutch. Known as Dutch Guiana, it was renamed Surinam (1949) and became an internally autonomous part of the Netherlands (1954). It has been fully independent since 1975. Area, 163 265 square kilometres (63,037 square miles). Population, 400,000. Capital, Paramaribo. See map at **Guyana.**
Surinam toad *n.* A South American toad, the **pipa** *(see).*
sur·ly (súrli) *adj.* **-lier, -liest.** Grumpy or habitually uncivil; gruff. [Variant of obsolete *sirly,* originally "lordly", masterful, imperious, from SIR.] **—sur·li·ly** *adv.* **—sur·li·ness** *n.*
sur·mise (sur-míz, sər-, súr-mīz) *v.* **-mised, -mising, -mises.** *—tr.* To infer reasonably, though without conclusive evidence. *—intr.* To make a guess or conjecture. —See Synonyms at **conjecture.**
~n. An idea or opinion based upon insufficiently conclusive evidence; a guess; a conjecture. [Middle English *surmysen,* to charge on or against, accuse, from Old French *surmettre* (past participle *surmis*), from Medieval Latin *supermittere,* from Late Latin, to throw upon : Latin *super-,* upon + *mittere,* to send off, throw.]
sur·mount (sər-mównt, sur-) *tr.v.* **-mounted, -mounting, -mounts.** **1.** To overcome (an obstacle, for example); conquer. **2.** To ascend to the top and cross to the other side of; get above and over. **3.** To place something above; top. **4.** To be above or on top of. [Middle English *surmonten,* from Old French *surmonter* : *sur-,* above + *monter,* to MOUNT.] **—sur·mount·a·ble** *adj.* **—sur·mount·a·ble·ness** *n.* **—sur·mount·er** *n.*
sur·mul·let (súr-múllit, -mullit) *n., pl.* **-lets** or collectively **surmullet.** *U.S.* The red mullet. [French *surmulet,* from Old French *sormulet* : probably *sor,* reddish brown, from Germanic + *mulet,* MULLET.]
sur·name (súr-naym) *n.* **1.** A family name as distinguished from a forename; in the West, a patrilineal name. **2.** Formerly, a nickname or epithet added to a person's name.
~tr.v. **surnamed, -naming, -names.** To give a surname to. [Middle English : SUR- + NAME.] **—sur·nom·i·nal** (sur-nómmin'l) *adj.*
sur·pass (sər-paáss, sur- || -páss) *tr.v.* **-passed, -passing, -passes.** **1.** To go beyond the limit, powers, or extent of; transcend. **2.** To be or go beyond, as in quantity, degree, or amount; exceed. —See Synonyms at **excel.** [Old French *surpasser* : *sur-,* over + *passer,* PASS.]
sur·pass·ing (sər-paáss-ing, sur- || -páss-) *adj.* Exceptional; exceeding: *monuments of surpassing splendour.*
~adv. Archaic & Poetic. Extremely. **—sur·pass·ing·ly** *adv.*
sur·plice (súr-pliss, -pləss) *n.* A loose-fitting white gown reaching down to the thighs or knees, having full flowing sleeves, worn over a cassock by certain clergymen and choristers. [Middle English *surplis,* from Old French *sourpeliz,* from Medieval Latin *superpellicium* (originally worn by clergymen of northern countries over their fur coats) : *super-,* over + *pellicium,* fur coat, from Latin *pellicius,* made of skin, from *pellis,* skin.] **—sur·pliced** *adj.*

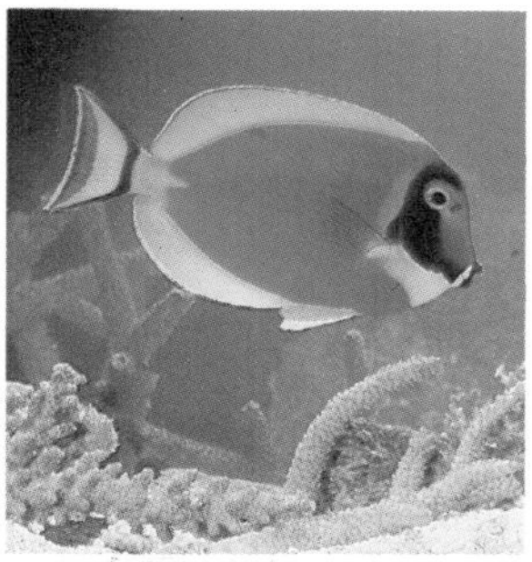

surgeonfish *Razor-sharp spines at the base of the tail give this fish its name. The species shown here is* Acanthurus leucosternon, *which is found in most warm seas, but particularly in the waters off Indonesia.*

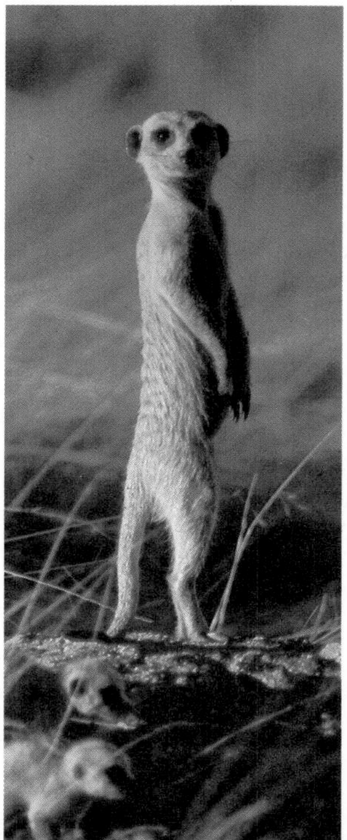

suricate *These small mongooses live in colonies of burrows in southern Africa. They are sometimes kept as pets, and used to catch rats and mice.*

IMAGES OF THE UNCONSCIOUS

A movement conceived by writers and realised by artists

The surrealist movement in literature and art asserted that the dream world of the unconscious has a reality superior to the world of the senses. The aim of the surrealist – according to the movement's leader, the French poet André Breton (1896–1966) in his *Surrealist Manifesto* of 1924 – should be to integrate the two worlds into a super-reality.

At first the surrealist movement was dominated by French writers such as Louis Aragon (1897–1982) and Jean Cocteau (1889–1963), who, under Breton's severe guidance, sought to release the unconscious with illogical but startling associations of words and images. The founders' attempts to ally surrealism with the socialist movement foundered with the rise of Stalinism during the 1930s.

Surrealist painting had its roots in the Dada movement, whose adherents, deeply affected by World War I and influenced by Freud's emphasis on the significance of the unconscious mind, explored the value of absurdity and rejected conventional notions of art.

The first surrealist artist was a German, Max Ernst (1891–1976), whose collages of incongruous objects appealed directly to the unconscious. René Magritte (1898–1967), a Belgian artist, demonstrated that precise realism in technique accentuated the incongruity of oddly juxtaposed objects.

The Spanish artist Salvador Dalí (1904–) attempted to portray the unconscious in disturbing, hallucinatory images. His distortions of objects such as the human body, or the limp watches in *The Persistence of Memory* (1931), have become surrealist clichés. The paintings of his compatriot Joan Miró (1893–) and the French artist André Masson (1896–) are still further removed from images of reality.

Surrealist art achieved lasting influence during the 1930s, partly due to its adherents' wild and humorous exhibitions, a far remove from the seriousness with which Breton propounded his original concept.

Surrealism was expressed in photography by the American painter, Man Ray (1890–1976) and in film by Man Ray, Cocteau, and by Dalí and Luis Buñuel (1900–), his fellow countryman, who jointly directed *Un Chien Andalou* (1929) and *L'Age D'Or* (1930).

THE HUMAN CONDITION I (1933) *René Magritte's painting is an example of naturalistic surrealism, based on images of reality. A landscape painting resting on an easel in front of a window through which can be glimpsed the landscape in the painting, temporarily confuses the viewer's perceptions. This picture within a picture seems to question our perception of the world, and also the convention of admiring a painting as an artificial representation of a scene or object.*

sur·plus (súr-pləss ‖ -pluss) *adj. Abbr.* **sur.** Being more than or in excess of what is needed or required: *surplus grain.* —*n.* **1.** An amount or quantity in excess of what is needed; something remaining or left over. **2.** The total of assets minus the sum of all liabilities. **3.** The excess of a company's net assets over the face value of its capital stock. **4.** The excess of receipts over expenditures. [Middle English, from Old French, from Medieval Latin *superplūs* : Latin *super-*, in addition + *plūs*, more.]

sur·plus·age (súr-pləss-ij ‖ -pluss-) *n.* **1.** A surplus. **2.** An excess of words. **3.** *Law.* Irrelevant matter in a pleading.

surplus value *n.* In the Marxian analysis of capitalism, the difference between the value of the product produced by labour and the actual price of labour as paid out in wages.

sur·print (súr-print) *tr.v.* **-printed, -printing, -prints.** In photoengraving: **1.** To overprint. **2.** To superimpose (a second negative) upon a previously printed image of the first negative. —*n.* That which is surprinted.

sur·pris·al (sər-príz'l) *n.* The act of surprising or the condition of being surprised.

sur·prise (sər-príz, sə-) *tr.v.* **-prised, -prising, -prises.** Also *rare* **sur·prize. 1.** To cause to feel wonder or astonishment. **2.** To attack or capture suddenly and without warning. **3.** To take or catch (a person) unawares. **4. a.** To cause (a person) to do or say something unintended. Used with *into.* **b.** To elicit by these means. Used with *out of* or *from.* —*n.* **1.** The act of surprising; an unexpected occurrence, encounter, or attack. **2.** The condition of being surprised; a feeling of amazement or wonder. **3.** Something that surprises, such as an unexpected encounter, event, or gift. —**surprised at.** Shocked by. —**take by surprise. 1.** To come upon suddenly and unexpectedly. **2.** To capture without warning. **3.** To astonish or astound. [Middle English *surprysen,* to be seized with, from Old French *surprendre* (past participle *surpris*), "to overtake" : *sur-*, over + *prendre*, to take, from Latin *prehendere*, to seize.] —**sur·pris·ed·ly** *adv.* —**sur·pris·er** *n.* —**sur·pris·ing·ly** *adv.*

　　Synonyms: *surprise, astonish, amaze, astound, dumbfound.*

surr. surrender.

sur·ra (soór-ə) *n.* A dangerous infectious disease of horses and other domesticated animals occurring in Asian countries. [Marathi.]

sur·re·al (sə-réerl, -rée-əl, súrri-əl ‖ -ráy-əl) *adj.* **1.** Having qualities attributed to surrealism. **2.** Dreamlike, distorted; bizarre. [Backformation from SURREALISM.] —**sur·real·ly** *adv.*

sur·re·al·ism (sə-réerl-iz'm, -rée-əl-, súrri-əl- ‖ -ráy-əl-) *n. Often capital* **S.** A literary and artistic movement evolving from Dada and launched in 1924 by the French poet André Breton (1896–1966), proclaiming the radical transformation of social, scientific, and philosophical values through the total liberation of the unconscious. Its exponents include writers such as **Artaud** and **Beckett** and artists such as **Magritte** and **Dali** *(all of whom see),* whose work is characterised by strange juxtapositions of mundane objects and the incongruous mingling of the banal with the bizarre. [French *surréalisme* : *sur-*, beyond + *réalisme*, realism, from *réel*, real, from Old French, from Late Latin *reālis*, REAL.] —**sur·re·al·ist** *adj. & n.* —**sur·re·al·is·tic** (-ístik) *adj.* —**sur·re·al·is·ti·cal·ly** *adv.*

sur·re·but·ter (súr-ri-búttər) *n.* Also **sur·re·but·tal** (-bútt'l). *Law. Rare.* The plaintiff's reply to the defendant's rebutter.

sur·re·join·der (súr-ri-jóyndər, -rə-) *n. Law. Rare.* The plaintiff's reply to the defendant's rejoinder.

sur·ren·der (sə-réndər) *v.* **-dered, -dering, -ders.** —*tr.* **1.** To relinquish possession or control of to another because of demand or compulsion. **2.** To give up in favour of another. **3.** To give up or give back (that which has been granted): *surrender a contractual right.* **4.** To give up or abandon: *surrender all hope.* **5.** To give over or resign (oneself) to something, as to capture or to an influence or an emotion. **6.** *Law.* To restore (an estate, for example); especially, to give up (a lease) before expiration of the term. —*intr.* To give oneself up, as to an enemy. —See Synonyms at **relinquish.** —*n. Abbr.* **surr. 1.** The act of surrendering. **2.** *Law.* **a.** The delivery of a prisoner, fugitive from justice, or other principal in a suit into custody. **b.** The restoring of an estate. **c.** The act of surrendering or being surrendered to bail. **3.** The voluntary discontinuation of a life insurance policy by its holder in return for a proportion of its value on maturity, its *surrender value.* [Middle English *sorendren,* from Old French *surrendre* : *sur-*, over + *rendre*, to deliver, RENDER.]

　　Synonyms: *surrender, submission, capitulation.*

sur·rep·ti·tious (súrrəp-tíshəss, súrrep-, súrrip-) *adj.* Performed, made, or acquired by secret or clandestine means or in a stealthy manner. See Synonyms at **secret.** [Latin *surreptícius,* from *surripere* (past participle *surreptus*), to seize or take away secretly : *sub-*, under, secretly + *rapere*, to seize.] —**sur·rep·ti·tious·ly** *adv.* —**sur·rep·ti·tious·ness** *n.*

sur·rey (súrri) *n., pl.* **-reys.** A 19th-century American horse-drawn four-wheeled pleasure vehicle having two or four seats. [Short for *Surrey cart,* first built in SURREY.]

Sur·rey (súrri). County in southeastern England. The North Downs cross it from east to west, their course broken by the valleys of the rivers Wey and Mole. The county has many dormitory towns from which workers commute into London, (including Guildford the county town), Reigate, Woking, and Weybridge.

Surrey, Henry Howard, Earl of (*c.* 1517–47). English poet. He and Sir Thomas Wyatt introduced Italian Renaissance verse forms, particularly the sonnet, into English literature. He also introduced blank verse with his translation of part of Virgil's *Aeneid.*

sur·ro·gate (súrrə-gət, -git, -gayt) n. **1.** A person or thing that is substituted for another; a substitute. **2.** Psychology. A person or thing that functions as a substitute for another individual in the life of a person or animal, such as a substitute parent. Also used adjectivally: a surrogate mother. **3.** In some U.S. states, a judge having jurisdiction over the probate of wills and the settlement of estates. ~tr.v. (-gayt) **surrogated, -gating, -gates. 1.** To put in the place of another, especially as a successor; replace. **2.** To appoint (another) as a replacement for oneself. [Latin surrogāre, subrogāre, to substitute, SUBROGATE.] **—sur·ro·gate·ship** n. **—sur·ro·ga·tion** (-gáysh'n) n.

sur·round (sə-równd ‖ West Indies also -rúngd) tr.v. **-rounded, -rounding, -rounds. 1.** To extend on all sides of simultaneously; encircle; exist round. **2.** To enclose or confine on all sides so as to bar escape or outside communication. ~n. **1.** Usually plural. The grounds of a country mansion or estate. **2.** Chiefly British. A border; especially, the area of uncovered floor between a carpet and the walls of a room. [Middle English sourrounden, to submerge, overflow, from Old French s(o)uronder, from Late Latin superundāre : Latin super-, over + undāre, to rise in waves, from unda, wave.]

sur·round·ings (sə-równ-dingz ‖ West Indies also -rúng-) n. The external circumstances, conditions, and objects that affect the existence and development of something; an environment.

sur·round-sound (sə-równd-sownd) n. High-fidelity sound reproduction which gives the impression of surrounding the listener.

sur·tax (súr-taks) n. **1.** An additional tax. **2.** Formerly, a graduated British income tax added to the normal income tax, levied on the amount by which a person's net income exceeded a certain sum. See **unified tax. —sur·tax** tr.v.

Sur·tees (súr-teez) **John** (1934–). British motorcycling and motor racing driver. He held many motorcycling championships and in 1964 was World motor racing Champion.

Surtees, Robert Smith (1803–64). British novelist. His humorous novels about Mr Jorrocks, the hunting grocer, portray the spirit of Victorian sporting life and manners. His books include Jorrocks' Jaunts and Jollities (1838) and Mr Sponge's Sporting Tour (1853).

sur·tout (súr-tŏŏ, -tōō) n. Formerly, a type of single-breasted man's frock coat with diagonal front pockets. [French, "over everything".]

Surt·sey (súrtsi). Island off the south coast of Iceland. It was formed (1963) by the eruption of an underwater volcano which continued to erupt sporadically for four years.

sur·veil·lance (sər-váylənss, sur-) n. **1.** Close observation of a person or group, especially of one under suspicion. **2.** The act of observing or the condition of being observed. [French, from surveiller, to watch over. See **surveillant**.]

sur·veil·lant (sər-váylənt, sur-) adj. Exercising surveillance. ~n. One who keeps close watch. [French, present participle of surveiller, to watch over : sur-, over + veiller, to watch, from Latin vigilāre, from vigil, awake, watchful.]

sur·vey (sər-váy, sur- ‖ súr-vay) v. **-veyed, -veying, -veys. —tr. 1.** To examine or look at in a comprehensive way. **2.** To inspect carefully; scrutinise. **3.** To range one's gaze at leisure over: From the hilltop she could survey the valley below. **4.** To determine the boundaries, the area, or the elevations of (land or structures on the earth's surface) by means of measuring angles and distances on the ground or of aerial photography, and then using the techniques of geometry and trigonometry. **5.** British. To inspect and determine the structural condition of (a building). **6.** To conduct a statistical survey on. —intr. To make a survey. —See Synonyms at **see**. ~n. (súr-vay ‖ sər-váy, sur-). **1.** A detailed inspection or investigation. **2.** A general or comprehensive view. **3. a.** The process of surveying. **b.** A report on or map of that which is surveyed. **c.** An area surveyed. **d.** A body of surveyors. **4. a.** A statistical enquiry, as into population characteristics or political trends, conducted through questionnaires, interviews, or general observation. **b.** A compilation of the results of such an enquiry. **c.** A random statistical sample. **5.** British. An inspection of a building to determine its structural condition. [Middle English surveyen, from Old French survee(i)r, from Medieval Latin supervidēre, to look over : Latin super-, over + vidēre, to look, see.]

sur·vey·ing (sər-váy-ing, sur- ‖ súr-vay-) n. The business or occupation of a surveyor.

sur·vey·or (sər-váy-ər ‖ súr-vay-ər) n. **1.** A person trained in the surveying and valuation of land or buildings. **2.** A **quantity surveyor** (see). **3.** A **marine surveyor** (see). **4.** A person qualified to inspect something to assess its value or to confirm that it has the qualities attributed to it.

surveyor's level n. A level having a telescope and attached spirit level mounted on a tripod and rotating round a vertical axis.

surveyor's measure n. A system of measurement used by surveyors, based on the chain as a unit.

sur·viv·al (sər-vív'l) n. **1.** The act of surviving or the fact of having survived. **2.** Something that survives, such as an ancient custom.

survival kit n. A compact package of necessities designed to sustain a person in an emergency, such as a natural disaster.

survival of the fittest n. **Natural selection** (see), conceived of as a struggle in which only those organisms best adapted to existing conditions survive.

survival value n. Usefulness in a species' struggle for survival.

sur·vive (sər-vív) v. **-vived, -viving, -vives. —intr.** To remain alive or in existence. —tr. To live, exist, or remain active beyond the extent of; outlive. [Middle English surviven, from Old French

so(u)rvivre, from Late Latin supervīvere : super-, over + vīvere, to live.] **—sur·viv·a·ble** (-vív-əb'l) adj. **—sur·vi·vor** (-ər) n.

sur·vi·vor·ship (sər-vív-ər-ship) n. Law. The right of a person who survives a partner or joint owner to the entire ownership of that which was previously owned jointly.

survivor syndrome n. A range of symptoms any or all of which may be exhibited by the survivors of traumatic ordeals, such as earthquakes or concentration camps.

sus (suss) n. Slang. Suspicion that one has committed a crime. ~tr.v. **sussed, sussing, susses.** Slang. **1.** To understand after examination or thought. Used with out: sussed out the situation. **2.** To suspect. Used chiefly in the phrase sus it.

Su·san·na¹ (sŏŏ-zánnə, sŏŏ-). In the Apocrypha, a captive in Babylon falsely accused of adultery and saved from death by Daniel.

Susanna² n. The book of the Apocrypha containing the story of Susanna.

sus·cep·tance (sə-séptənss) n. Electricity. The imaginary part of the complex representation of **admittance** (see). [susceptibility + conductance.]

sus·cep·ti·bil·i·ty (sə-séptə-bílləti) n., pl. **-ties. 1.** The condition or quality of being susceptible. **2.** The capacity to be affected by deep emotions or strong feelings; sensitivity. **3.** Plural. Sensibilities; sensitive feelings. **4. Magnetic susceptibility** (see).

sus·cep·ti·ble (sə-séptəb'l) adj. **1.** Readily subject to an influence, agency, or force; unresistant; yielding. Usually used with of or to. **2.** Liable to be stricken with or by something: susceptible to colds. **3.** Formal. Capable of admitting of something. Used with of: susceptible of misinterpretation. **4.** Highly impressionable. [Late Latin susceptibilis, capable of receiving, from Latin suscipere (past participle susceptus), to take up, receive : sub-, up from under + capere, to take.] **—sus·cep·ti·ble·ness** n. **—sus·cep·ti·bly** adv.

Usage: Susceptible is usually followed by to when it means "easily affected": very susceptible to flattery/diseases. It is usually followed by of, occasionally by to, when it means "admitting, permitting": a theory susceptible of several interpretations. The use of susceptible to, in the sense of "often displays", has attracted purist criticism: very susceptible to fits of pique.

sus·cep·tive (sə-séptiv) adj. **1.** Receptive. **2.** Susceptible. **—sus·cep·tive·ness, sus·cep·tiv·i·ty** (sə-sép-tívvəti, sússep-) n.

su·shi (sŏŏshi) n. A type of cold food eaten in Japan, consisting of raw or cooked fish, served in a sweet or sour sauce with rice. [Japanese.]

Su·si·an (sŏŏzi-ən) n. An unclassified language, **Elamite** (see). [Latin Susiānī, from Greek Sousianē, ancient province equivalent to Elam, after Sousa, its capital.]

sus laws pl.n. Slang. Formerly in Britain, a number of laws allowing the police to arrest a person considered to be about to commit an offence, especially a street crime, without providing formal evidence for their suspicion.

sus·lik, souslik (sŏŏss-lik, súss-, sŏŏss-) n. A ground squirrel, Citellus citellus, of central Eurasia, with a yellowish-brown coat, large eyes, and small ears. [Russian.]

sus·pect (sə-spékt) v. **-pected, -pecting, -pects. —tr. 1.** To surmise to be true or probable; imagine. **2.** To distrust; have doubt about. **3.** To think (a person) guilty without proof. —intr. To have or feel suspicion. ~n. (sús-pekt). One who is suspected, especially of committing a crime. ~adj. (sús-pekt). Open to or viewed with suspicion. [Middle English, from Latin suspectāre, intensive of suspicere (past participle suspectus), to look up at, watch : sub-, up from under + specere, to look at.]

sus·pend (sə-spénd) v. **-pended, -pending, -pends. —tr. 1.** To bar for a period from a privilege, office, or position, usually as a punishment: suspend a pupil from school. **2.** To cause to stop for a period; interrupt. **3. a.** To maintain in an undecided state; hold in abeyance: suspend judgment. **b.** To render temporarily ineffective or inoperative under certain conditions: suspend parking regulations. **4.** To hang so as to allow free movement. **5.** To support or keep from falling without apparent attachment, as by buoyancy. —intr. **1.** To cease for a period; delay. **2.** To fail to make payments or meet obligations. [Middle English suspenden, from Old French suspendre, from Latin suspendēre, to hang up : sub-, up from under + pendere, to hang.] **—sus·pend·i·ble** adj.

sus·pend·ed animation (sə-spéndid) n. A dormant condition resembling death, induced by reversible cessation of the vital functions.

suspended sentence n. A prison sentence imposed on a convicted person but not to be served unless a further crime is committed.

sus·pend·er (sə-spéndər) n. **1.** British. An elasticated strap or garter with such a strap used to hold up a sock or stocking. **2.** Plural. U.S. **Braces** (see).

suspender belt n. An undergarment, consisting of a belt with elasticated straps attached to hold up stockings.

sus·pense (sə-spénss) n. **1.** The state or quality of being undecided, uncertain, or doubtful. **2. a.** Anxiety or apprehension resulting from an uncertain, undecided, or mysterious situation. **b.** Excitement arising from uncertainty over an outcome. Also used adjectivally: a suspense novel. [Middle English, from Old French, from the feminine of suspens, suspended, from Latin suspensus, past participle of suspendēre, SUSPEND.] **—sus·pense·ful** adj.

suspense account n. A temporary account in which entries of credits or charges are made until their correct place of entry is determined.

sus·pen·sion (sə-spénsh'n) n. **1.** The act of suspending or the condition of being suspended, especially: **a.** A temporary abrogation or deferment. **b.** A debarment, as from office or privilege. **c.** A postponement of judgment, opinion, or decision. **2.** *Music.* **a.** The prolonging of one or more notes of a chord into a following chord to create a temporary dissonance. **b.** The note so prolonged. **3.** A device from which a part is suspended. **4.** The system of springs and other devices that insulates the body of a vehicle from shocks transmitted through the wheels. **5.** *Chemistry.* A relatively coarse, noncolloidal dispersion of solid particles in a liquid. See **colloid.** [French, or Latin *suspensio* (stem *suspensiōn-*). See **suspense.**]

suspension bridge n. A bridge having the roadway suspended from cables that are supported by two or more towers and are firmly anchored at both ends.

suspension points pl.n. *Chiefly U.S.* A series of dots, usually three, used to indicate the omission of a word or words; an ellipsis.

sus·pen·sive (sə-spén-siv) adj. **1.** Serving or tending to suspend or temporarily stop something. **2.** Characterised by or causing suspense. **—sus·pen·sive·ly** adv. **—sus·pen·sive·ness** n.

sus·pen·soid (sə-spén-soyd) n. A suspension of solid particles in a liquid. Also called "suspensoid sol". [SUSPENS(ION) + -OID.]

sus·pen·sor (sə-spén-sər) n. **1.** *Botany.* A stalklike cellular structure that forms in the zygote in flowering plants and pushes the embryo into the endosperm. **2.** Variant of **suspensory.** [New Latin, from Medieval Latin, one that suspends, from Latin *suspendēre* (past participle *suspensus*), SUSPEND.]

sus·pen·so·ry (sə-spén-səri) adj. **1.** Supporting or suspending: *a suspensory bandage.* **2.** Delaying the completion of something. ~n., pl. **suspensories.** Also **sus·pen·sor** (-sər). **1.** A support or truss. **2.** *U.S.* An **athletic support.**

suspensory ligament n. A ligament that supports an organ or bodily part, such as the structure that supports the lens of the eye.

sus·pi·cion (sə-spísh'n) n. **1. a.** The act or an instance of suspecting the existence of something, especially of something wrong, without sufficient evidence or proof. **b.** The state of being suspected. **2.** A minute amount; a hint; a trace. [Middle English *suspicio(u)n,* from Old French *suspicion,* from Latin *suspīciō* (stem *suspīciōn-*), from Latin *suspicere* (past participle *suspectus*), to look at secretly, SUSPECT.] **—sus·pi·cion·al** adj.

sus·pi·cious (sə-spíshəss) adj. **1.** Arousing or apt to arouse suspicion; questionable: *suspicious behaviour.* **2.** Tending to suspect; distrustful: *a suspicious nature.* **—sus·pi·cious·ly** adv. **—sus·pi·cious·ness** n.

sus·pire (sə-spīr) intr.v. **-pired, -piring, -pires.** *Poetic.* **1.** To breathe. **2.** To sigh. [Middle English *suspiren,* from Latin *suspīrāre,* to draw a deep breath : *sub-,* up from below + *spīrāre,* to breathe.] **—sus·pi·ra·tion** n.

Sus·que·han·na (súskwi-hánnə). River in the eastern United States, 715 kilometres (444 miles) long. It rises in Otsego Lake, New York State, and flows chiefly south to Chesapeake Bay.

Sus·sex (súss-iks ‖ -eks). Former English county. In 1974 it was divided into East Sussex and West Sussex.

Sussex cattle pl.n. Beef cattle of a reddish-brown breed developed in Sussex.

Sussex fowl n. A domestic fowl of a breed with white and black plumage, originally from Sussex.

Sussex spaniel n. A dog of a breed developed in Sussex, having long ears, short legs, and a silky golden-brown coat.

Sussex trug n. A trug (see).

sus·tain (sə-stáyn) tr.v. **-tained, -taining, -tains. 1.** To keep in existence; maintain; prolong. **2.** To supply with necessities or nourishment; provide for. **3.** To support from below; keep from falling or sinking; prop. **4.** To support the spirits, vitality, or resolution of; encourage. **5.** To keep up (a joke or an assumed role, for example) competently. **6.** To endure or withstand; bear up under: *sustain hardships.* **7.** To experience or suffer (loss or injury). **8.** To affirm the validity or justice of. **9.** To prove or corroborate; confirm. [Middle English *suste(y)nen,* from Old French *sustenir,* from Latin *sustinēre,* to hold up : *sub-,* up from under + *tenēre,* to hold.] **—sus·tain·a·ble** adj. **—sus·tain·ment** n.

sus·tain·er (sə-stáynər) n. **1.** One that or that which sustains. **2.** A small rocket motor that sustains the velocity of a spacecraft after the booster has been jettisoned.

sustaining pedal n. The right pedal of a piano, which stops the action of the dampers, allowing the strings to vibrate freely. Also called "reverberation pedal", informally "loud pedal."

sustaining program n. *U.S.* A radio or television programme that has no commercial announcements.

sus·te·nance (sústinənss) n. **1.** The act of sustaining or the condition of being sustained. **2.** The supporting of life or health; maintenance: *"victuals for my sustenance"* (Jonathan Swift). **3.** One that or that which sustains life or health; especially, food. **4.** Means of livelihood. [Middle English *sustena(u)nce,* from Old French *so(u)stenance,* from *so(u)stenir, sustenir,* SUSTAIN.]

sus·ten·tac·u·lar (súss-ten-táckewlər, -tən-) adj. *Anatomy.* Supporting. Said of fibres, ligaments, and the like. [Latin *sustentāculum,* a support, from *sustentāre,* frequentative of *sustinēre,* SUSTAIN.]

sus·ten·ta·tion (súss-ten-táysh'n, -tən-) n. *Rare.* Sustenance; food. [Middle English *sustentacion,* from Old French, from Latin *sustentātiō* (stem *sustentātiōn-*), from *sustentāre,* frequentative of *sustinēre,* SUSTAIN.] **—sus·ten·ta·tive** (sə-sténtətiv, súss-ten-taytiv, -tən-) adj.

Su·su (sōō-sōō) n., pl. **-sus** or collectively **Susu. 1.** A member of a West African people living in Guinea, the Sudan, and along the northern border of Sierra Leone. **2.** The Mande language spoken by the Susu.

su·sur·ra·tion (séw-sə-ráysh'n, sōō-) n. Also **su·sur·rus** (sew-súrrəss, sōō-). A soft, whispering or rustling sound; a murmur; a whisper. [Middle English, from Late Latin *susurātiō* (stem *susurātiōn-*) from Latin *susurāre,* to whisper, from *susurrus,* whisper.] **—su·sur·rant** (sew-súrrənt, sōō-), **su·sur·rous** (-súrrəss) adj. **—su·sur·rate** (séw-sə-rayt, sōō-) intr.v.

Sut·cliffe (sút-klif), **Herbert** (1894–1978). British cricketer. He was an opening batsman and played for Yorkshire and England. During his career (1919–45) he totalled 50,135 runs and made 149 centuries, including 16 Test centuries.

Suth·er·land (súthərlənd). Former county of northern Scotland. In 1975 it was incorporated into Highland Region.

Sutherland, Graham (Vivian) (1903–80). British painter. He was an official war artist (1941–45), and is best known for his portraits and religious paintings. His works include *Somerset Maugham* (1949) and his tapestry, *Christ in Majesty.*

Sutherland, Joan (1926–). Australian coloratura soprano. She has done much to revive the popularity of the bel canto operas of Bellini and Donizetti.

Sut·lej (sútlej). One of the "Five Rivers" of Punjab. It flows some 1 350 kilometres (about 850 miles) from southwest Tibet, through the Himalayas to join the Panjnad.

sut·ler (súttlər) n. Formerly, a camp follower who sold provisions to the soldiers. [Middle Dutch *soeteler,* bad cook, camp cook, probably from Middle High German *sudelen,* to do sloppy work.]

su·tra (sōō-trə ‖ séw-) n. Also **sut·ta** (-tə). **1.** Any of various aphoristic doctrinal summaries produced generally between 500 and 200 B.C. and later incorporated into Hindu and Buddhist literature. **2.** *Buddhism.* Any scriptural narrative; especially, any text traditionally regarded as a discourse of the Buddha. [Sanskrit *sūtra,* thread, string, collection of aphorisms or rules.]

sut·tee (súttee, su-tée) n. **1.** The act or practice, now forbidden by law, of a Hindu widow cremating herself on her husband's funeral pyre. **2.** A widow so cremated. [Sanskrit *satī,* good woman, faithful wife, from *sat,* "existing", virtuous.]

Sut·ton (sútt'n). Borough of Greater London, situated to the southwest of the capital. It was formed (1965) by the merger of the boroughs of Sutton and Cheam and of Beddington and Wallington, with the urban district of Carshalton.

Sutton Hoo (hōō). An archaeological site in eastern England, situated near Woodbridge in Suffolk. In 1939, a Saxon ship measuring 27 metres (89 feet) long was excavated here with a hoard of richly ornamented weapons, jewellery, and utensils. The ship may have been buried as a memorial to King Rædwald (died 624).

su·ture (sōō-chər, sōōt-yər ‖ séw-) n. **1.** *Surgery.* **a.** The process of joining two surfaces or edges of tissue together along a line by stitching. **b.** The material used in this procedure, as thread, gut, or wire. **c.** The line so formed. **2.** Any similar join or seam. **3.** *Anatomy.* The line of junction or an immovable joint between two bones, particularly of the skull. **4.** *Biology.* A seamlike joint or line of articulation, such as the line of dehiscence in a seed or fruit or the spiral seam marking the junction of whorls of a gastropod shell. ~tr.v. **sutured, -turing, -tures.** *Surgery.* To join by means of sutures; sew up. [French, from Latin *sūtūra,* a sewing together, seam, suture, from *suere* (past participle *sūtus*), to sew.] **—su·tur·al** adj. **—su·tur·al·ly** adv.

Su·va (sōōvə). The capital of Fiji, situated on the island of Viti Levu. It is a marketing centre and port for sugar, cotton, and pineapples grown on the island. Tourism is also important.

Su·wan·nee (sə-wónni) or **Swa·nee** (swónni). River in the southern United States. It rises in the Okefenokee swamp of southeast Georgia and flows south through Florida to the Gulf of Mexico. The river is about 400 kilometres (250 miles) long.

su·ze·rain (sōō-zə-rayn, séw- ‖ -rən) n. **1.** Formerly, a feudal lord to whom fealty was due. **2.** A nation that controls another nation in international affairs but allows it domestic sovereignty. ~adj. Characteristic of a suzerain; sovereign. [French *suzerain* : *sus,* up, above, from Latin *sūsum, sursum,* (turned) upwards, up : *sub-,* up + *versum,* neuter past participle of *vertere,* to turn + *(souv)erain,* from Old French *so(u)verein,* SOVEREIGN.]

su·ze·rain·ty (sōō-zə-rayn-ti, séw-, -rən-) n., pl. **-ties.** The power or domain of a suzerain.

Su·zhou, Su·chou or **Soo·chow** (sōō-jō). Also **Wu·xian** or **Wuhsien** (wōō-syén). City in Jiangsu province, eastern China, situated on the Grand Canal to the West of Shanghai. Founded in the fifth century B.C. it became a walled city and was noted for its pagodas and silk manufacture. Silk and cotton industries remain important.

Suz·man (sōōz-mən), **Helen,** born Helen Gavronsky (1917–). South African politician, for a long time the sole representative of the Progressive Party in the South African Parliament.

Su·zu·ki method (sōō-zōōki) n. A method of teaching the violin to very young children, by imitation and repetition. [After S. *Suzuki* (1898–), Japanese music teacher who devised it.]

s.v. 1. sailing vessel. **2.** side value.

Sval·bard (svál-baard; *Norwegian* svaál-baar). A Norwegian archipelago situated in the Arctic Ocean. It includes the Spitsbergen island group, and is mountainous and mostly covered by ice fields and glaciers. The treaty of Spitzbergen (1920), while recognising

Norwegian sovereignty, granted mineral and other rights to all 40 signatories, and both Norway and the U.S.S.R. maintain coal-mining settlements on the island. Svalbard commands the shipping lanes to Murmansk, the only major ice-free port in the U.S.S.R., and the two countries are in dispute over their common boundary across the Barents Sea, which has potentially valuable oil deposits.

SVD swine vesicular disease.

svelte (svelt) *adj.* **svelter, sveltest.** Slender or graceful in figure or outline; slim. [French, from Italian *svelto,* "stretched", slender, from *svellere,* to pull out, stretch out, from Vulgar Latin *exvellere* (unattested), from Latin *evellere* : *ex-,* out + *vellere,* to pull.]

Sven·ga·li (sveng-gaáli, sven-) *n.* A person with an uncanny power to compel another to do his will. [After the villain in *Trilby* (1894), a novel by George DU MAURIER.]

Sverd·lovsk (sveerd-lófsk). Formerly **Ekaterinburg** or **Yekaterinburg.** A city in the R.S.F.S.R., U.S.S.R., situated in the eastern foothills of the Ural mountains. It is an industrial and cultural centre, and a railway junction on the Trans-Siberian Railway.

Sverige. See **Sweden.**

Sve·vo (sváyvō), **Italo,** pen name of Ettore Schmitz (1861–1928). Italian novelist. He is best known for his psychological novel, *La Coscienza di Zeno* (*The Confessions of Zeno,* 1923).

Svizzera. See **Switzerland.**

sw short wave; short-wave.

SW southwest.

Sw. Sweden; Swedish.

S.W.A. South-West Africa.

swab, swob (swob) *n.* **1.** A small piece of cotton or other absorbent material, usually attached to the end of a stick or wire, and used for cleansing or applying medicine. **2.** A specimen of mucus or other material removed with such an instrument. **3.** A mop for cleaning decks, floors, or other large areas. **4.** A person who uses such a mop, especially on a ship. Also called "swabby". **5.** A lout.
~*tr.v.* **swabbed, swabbing, swabs.** To use a swab on; clean or treat with a swab. [Probably from Middle Dutch *swabbe,* mop.]

Swa·bi·a (swáybi-ə). *German* **Schwa·ben** (shvaábən). A medieval duchy in southwestern West Germany, which originally included parts of present-day France and Switzerland. The towns of Swabia formed a series of leagues, starting in 1331, the most important being that of 1488–1534, a powerful association of cities, princes, churchmen, and knights, whose army became a bastion of Habsburg authority under Maximilian I. In the reign of Charles V, its members became divided over the Reformation, and the league collapsed. **—Swa·bi·an** *adj. & n.*

swad·dle (swódd'l) *tr.v.* **-dled, -dling, -dles. 1.** To wrap or bind in bandages; swathe. **2.** To wrap (a baby) in swaddling clothes. **3.** To restrain or restrict; smother.
~*n. U.S.* A band or cloth used for swaddling. [Middle English *swadlen, swethelen,* from *swethel,* swaddling clothes, Old English *swæthel,* probably from *swathian,* to SWATHE.]

swaddling clothes *pl.n.* **1.** Formerly, strips of linen or other cloth wound about a newborn infant. **2.** Any restrictions imposed upon the immature. Also called "swaddling bands".

swag (swag) *n.* **1. a.** Goods or property obtained by forcible or illicit means. **b.** Loosely, any goods or valuables, especially when improperly gained. **2. a.** A length of drapery, especially a curtain, bunched and secured at two points so that it hangs in a curve. **b.** An ornamental festoon of flowers or fruit. **c.** A carving or moulding representing this. **3.** *Australian.* The pack of a swagman.
~*intr.v.* **swagged, swagging, swags. 1.** *Chiefly British.* To lurch or sway. **2.** *Australian.* To travel around with a pack or swag. [Probably from Scandinavian, akin to Norwegian *swagga,* to sway.]

swage (swayj) *n.* **1.** A tool used in bending or shaping cold metal. **2.** A stamp or die for marking or shaping metal with a hammer. **3.** A swage block.
~*tr.v.* **swaged, swaging, swages.** To bend or shape by using a swage. [19th century : from French *s(o)uage*†.]

swage block *n.* A metal block having holes or grooves for shaping metal objects.

swag·ger (swággər) *v.* **-gered, -gering, -gers.** —*intr.* **1.** To walk or conduct oneself with an over-confident or insolent air; strut. **2.** To brag; bluster. —*tr.* To influence or affect by swaggering.
~*n.* **1.** A swaggering movement or gait. **2.** Boastful or conceited expression; braggadocio. **3.** A dashing, confident air. [Probably from SWAG.] **—swag·ger·er** *n.* **—swag·ger·ing·ly** *adv.*

swagger stick *n.* A short metal-tipped cane typically carried by military officers.

swag·man (swág-mən, -man) *n., pl.* **-men** (-mən, -men). *Australian.* A man who seeks casual work while travelling about carrying his pack or swag; an itinerant worker.

Swa·hi·li (swə-héeli, swaa-) *n., pl.* **Swahili** or **-lis. 1.** A Bantu language of eastern and central Africa, widely used as a lingua franca. **2.** A member of a Bantu people of Zanzibar and the neighbouring mainland who were original speakers of this language. [Swahili, "(people) belonging to the coasts" : Arabic *sawāḥil,* plural of *sāḥil,* coast + *-īy,* belonging to.] **—Swa·hi·li·an** *adj.*

swain (swayn) *n.* **1.** *Archaic.* A country youth, especially a shepherd. **2.** A lover. Usually used humorously. [Middle English *swein, swayne,* from Old Norse *sveinn,* a boy, herdsman.]

swale *U.S.* **swail** (swayl) *n.* **1.** A low tract of land, especially moist or marshy ground. **2.** Shade. [Middle English, a shade, shady place, perhaps from Scandinavian, akin to Old Norse *svalr,* cool.]

swal·low[1] (swóllō) *v.* **-lowed, -lowing, -lows.** —*tr.* **1.** To cause (food, for example) to pass from the mouth via the throat and the oesophagus into the stomach by muscular action; ingest. **2.** To consume or destroy as if by ingestion; devour. Often used with *up*: *swallow up smaller businesses.* **3.** To ingest (something unpleasant) reluctantly. Often used with *down.* **4. a.** To bear humbly; tolerate: *swallow an insult.* **b.** To refrain from expressing; suppress: *swallow one's feelings.* **c.** To take back; retract: *swallow one's words.* **5.** To believe without question. **6.** To utter (words) indistinctly. —*intr.* To perform the act of swallowing.
~*n.* **1.** The act of swallowing; a gulp. **2.** The amount that is swallowed at any one time. **3.** *Nautical.* The channel through which a rope runs in a block or a mooring chock. [Middle English *swalowen, swolwen,* Old English *swelgan.*] **—swal·low·er** *n.*

swallow[2] *n.* **1.** Any of various birds of the family Hirundinidae; especially, *Hirundo rustica,* having long, pointed wings and a usually notched or forked tail. **2.** Broadly, any of various similar birds, such as a swift. [Middle English *swal(o)we, swalu,* Old English *sweal(e)we,* from Germanic *swalwi* (unattested).]

swallow dive *n.* A dive performed with the legs together and straight, the back arched, and the arms at first stretched out from the sides. Also *U.S.* "swan dive".

swallow hole *n.* A **sink hole** (sense 2) *(see).*

swal·low·tail (swóllō-tayl) *n.* **1. a.** The deeply forked tail of a swallow. **b.** Anything resembling such a tail. **2.** *Informal.* A swallow-tailed coat. **3.** Any of various butterflies of the family Papilionidae having a tail-like extension at the end of each hind wing.

swal·low-tailed (swóllō-tayld) *adj.* **1.** Having a deeply forked tail. Said of various birds. **2.** Resembling the tail of a swallow: *a swallow-tailed kite.*

swallow-tailed coat *n.* A **tail coat** *(see).*

swam. Past tense of **swim.**

swa·mi (swaámi) *n., pl.* **-mis. 1.** Lord; master. A Hindu title of respect. **2.** A Hindu religious teacher. **3.** Loosely, a mystic; a yogi. [Hindi *svāmī,* master, from Sanskrit *svāmin,* owner, prince, "one's own master".]

swamp (swomp ‖ *U.S. also* swawmp) *n.* **1.** A lowland region permanently saturated with water. **2.** Loosely, a stretch of marsh ground.
~*v.* **swamped, swamping, swamps.** —*tr.* **1.** To drench in or cover with water or other liquid. **2.** To inundate or burden; overwhelm: *swamped with work.* **3.** To fill or sink (a ship) with water.
~*intr.* To become swamped, as a ship may. [Perhaps of Low German origin, akin to Low German *zwamp,* swamp.] **—swamp·y** *adj.*

swamp boat *n.* A flat-bottomed boat, powered by an aircraft propeller projecting above the stern, and used in swamps or shallow waters. Also called "airboat".

swamp·er (swómp-pər) *n. U.S.* **1.** One who lives in or close to a swamp. **2.** One who clears a swamp or forest. **3. a.** A menial helper, as in a restaurant. **b.** A handyman; an assistant.

swamp fever *n.* **1.** A viral disease in horses, marked by progressive anaemia, a staggering gait, and fever. **2.** *U.S.* Malaria.

swamp·land (swómp-land) *n.* Land of swampy consistency; land having many swamps on it.

swan (swon) *n.* **1.** Any of various large aquatic birds, chiefly of the genus *Cygnus,* having webbed feet, a long slender neck, and usually white plumage. **2.** *Capital* **S.** The constellation, **Cygnus** *(see).* Preceded by *the.* **3.** A poet; a bard.
~*intr.v.* **swanned, swanning, swans. 1.** To pass with an air of blithe superiority: *She swanned by in her new mink coat.* **2. a.** To wander along without apparent worry or care. Used with *around* or *about.* **b.** To deal or proceed with the greatest of ease. Used with *through*: *swanned through her final exams.* [Middle English *swan(ne), suan,* Old English *swan, suan.*]

Swan (swon), **Sir Joseph Wilson** (1828–1914). British physicist and inventor. He invented the photographic dry plate (1871) and bromide paper (1879). He also devised a carbon-filament electric lamp (1860), which he improved for commercial production (1881).

swan dive *n. U.S.* A **swallow dive** *(see).*

Swanee. See **Suwannee.**

swank (swangk) *intr.v.* **swanked, swanking, swanks.** To act in an ostentatious or pretentious way.
~*n. Informal.* Ostentatious or pretentious behaviour; swagger. **2.** Showy elegance; style. **3.** *Chiefly British.* A conceited or swaggering person.
~*adj. Informal.* Variant of **swanky.** [19th century (Midlands dialect) : origin obscure.]

swank·y (swángki) *adj. Informal.* **1.** Conceited; showing swank. **2.** Ostentatious; showy. **—swank·i·ly** *adv.* **—swank·i·ness** *n.*

swan neck *n.* A bend in a handrail, tubing, or the like that is double-curved in the shape of a swan's neck.

swan·ner·y (swónnəri) *n., pl.* **-ies.** A place where swans are bred and kept.

Swan River daisy *n.* An Australian plant, *Brachycome iberidifolia,* cultivated for its showy blue or white flower heads.

swan's-down (swónz-down) *n.* **1.** The soft down of a swan. **2.** A soft woollen fabric used especially for baby clothes.

Swan·sea (swón-zi). *Welsh* **A·ber·ta·we** (ábbər-tów-i). Second largest city in Wales, the administrative centre of West Glamorgan. It is an industrial port situated on Swansea Bay at the mouth of the river Tawe, and coal and coke are major exports.

swan·skin (swón-skin) *n.* **1.** The skin of a swan with the feathers attached. **2.** Any of several flannel or cotton fabrics with a soft nap.

swan song *n.* **1.** According to legend, the beautiful music uttered only once in a swan's life, just as it is dying. **2.** A farewell appear-

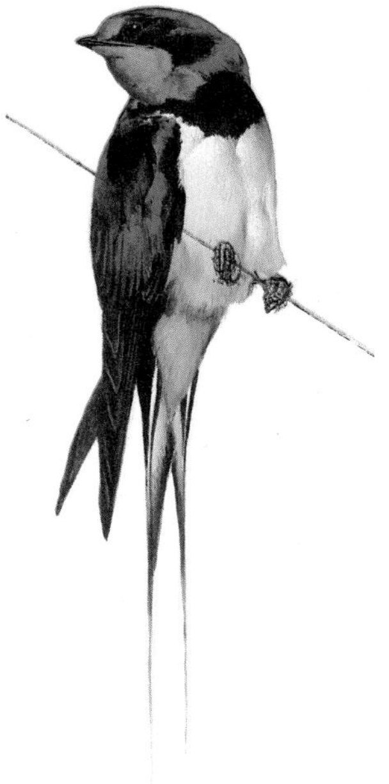

swallow *Flying fast and low, the swallow scoops up insects such as gnats and midges as they swarm on summer evenings. It is a close relative of the house martin and swift, but has a longer forked tail and a distinctive red chin.*

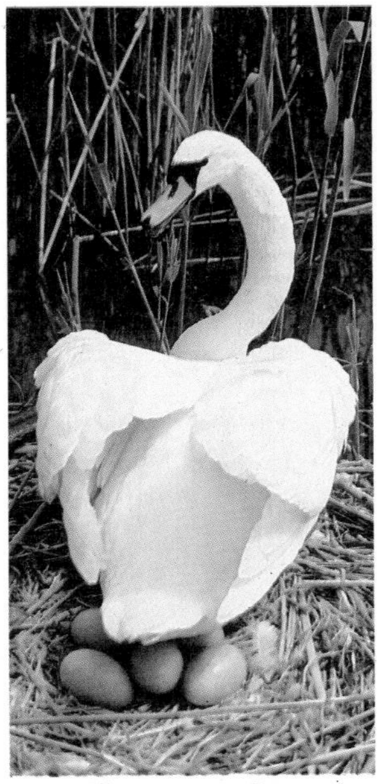

swan *The mute swan,* Cygnus olor *(above), is one of the heaviest flying birds, weighing up to about 23 kilograms (50 pounds).*

ance, declaration, or work. [Translation of German *Schwanenlied*.]

swan-up-per (swón-úppər) *n. British.* An official employed to catch and mark cygnets.

swan-up-ping (swón-úpping) *n. British.* The practice of catching cygnets and marking their beaks as an indication of ownership; especially, the annual marking of cygnets on the river Thames. [Referring to taking the swans up from the water to be marked.]

swap, swop (swop) *v.* **swapped** or **swopped, swapping** or **swopping, swaps** or **swops.** *Informal.* —*intr.* To exchange one thing for another. —*tr.* To exchange.
~*n. Informal.* An exchange of one thing for another. [Literally, "to strike hands in closing a bargain", Middle English *swappen*, to strike, hit, from Germanic (probably imitative); akin to German *schwappen*, to splash, whack.] —**swap-per** *n.*

SWA-PO, Swa-po (swaápō, swóppō) *n. The South-West Africa People's Organisation:* a Namibian independence movement.

sward (swawrd) *n.* Land covered with grassy turf; a lawn or meadow. [Old English *sweard, swearth*, skin of the body, rind of bacon; akin to Old Norse *svörthr*, skin.]

swarf (swawrf) *n.* Fine metallic filings or shavings removed by a cutting tool. [Probably from Scandinavian, akin to Old Norse *svarf*, filings.]

swarm¹ (swawrm) *n.* **1.** A large number of insects or other small organisms, especially when in motion. **2.** A group of bees, led by a queen bee, in migration to establish a new colony. **3.** A dense throng of persons or animals, especially when moving in mass.
~*v.* **swarmed, swarming, swarms.** —*intr.* **1. a.** To move or emerge in a swarm. **b.** To leave a hive as a swarm to start a new colony. Used of bees. **2.** To move as a large group or mass of creatures; congregate. **3.** To be overrun or filled. —*tr.* To fill with a crowd; throng. [Old English *swearm.*] —**swarm-er** *n.*

swarm² *v.* **swarmed, swarming, swarms.** —*tr.* To climb quickly by gripping with the arms and legs. —*intr.* To climb something in this way. Usually used with *up.* [16th century : origin obscure.]

swart (swawrt) *adj. Archaic.* Swarthy. [Middle English *swarte, swe(o)rt*, Old English *sweart*, from Germanic *swartaz* (unattested).]

swarth-y (swáwr-thi, -thi) *adj.* **-ier, -iest.** Having a dark or sunburnt complexion. [Earlier *swarty*, from SWART.] —**swarth-i-ly** *adv.* —**swarth-i-ness** *n.*

swash (swosh ‖ *U.S. also* swawsh) *n.* **1.** The splashing of water or other liquid as it hits a solid surface: *the swash of the sea against the rocks.* **2.** The sound of such a splashing.
~*v.* **swashed, swashing, swashes.** —*intr.* **1.** To strike, move, or wash with a splashing sound, as of water. **2.** *Archaic.* To swagger. —*tr.* **1.** To splash (a liquid). **2.** To splash a liquid against. [16th century : imitative.]

swash-buck-ler (swósh-bucklər) *n.* **1.** A flamboyant swordsman or adventurer. **2.** Any sword-wielding bully or ruffian. Also called "swasher". [From the striking of bucklers in fighting.]

swash-buck-ling (swósh-buckling) *adj.* Of or characteristic of a swashbuckler; flamboyant; full of bravado.

swash letter *n.* An ornamental italic letter formed with fancy flourishes and tails. [17th century : swash†, oblique, obliquely inclined.]

swas-ti-ka (swóstikə ‖ *U.S. also* swaa-steékə) *n.* **1.** An ancient cosmic or religious symbol, formed by a Greek cross with the ends of the arms bent at right angles either clockwise or anticlockwise. **2.** The emblem of Nazi Germany, officially adopted in 1935, and still used as a symbol by fascist groups. [Sanskrit *svastíka*, a sign of good luck, from *svastí*, well-being, good luck : *su-*, well + *asti*, "is", being.]

swat, swot (swot) *tr.v.* **swatted** or **swotted, swatting** or **swotting, swats** or **swots.** To deal a sharp blow to, usually with an instrument; slap: *swat flies.*
~*n.* A quick, sharp, or violent blow. [Variant of SQUAT (obsolete sense to "lay flat with a blow").]

swatch (swoch) *n.* **1.** A sample strip cut from a piece of cloth or other material. **2.** A small sample square of knitted or woven work, made in order to gauge tension. [17th century : origin obscure.]

swath (swawth, swoth). *n.* Also **swathe** (swayth ‖ swawth, swoth). **1.** The width of a scythe stroke or a mowing-machine blade. **2. a.** A path of this width made by mowing. **b.** The mown grass or grain lying on such a path. **3.** Something likened to a swath; a strip or belt. **4.** A devastating effect caused as if by a scythe: *cut swaths through her opponents.* —**cut a (wide) swath.** To create a great stir, impression, or display. [Middle English *swathe*, Old English *swæth, swathu*, track, trace, from Germanic *swath-* (unattested).]

swathe¹ (swayth ‖ *U.S. also* swawth, swoth) *tr.v.* **swathed, swathing, swathes.** **1.** To wrap or bind with bindings or bandages. **2.** To enfold or envelop: *swathed in furs.*
~*n.* A wrapping, binding, or bandage. [Middle English *swathen*, Old English *swathian†*, to wrap up.] —**swath-er** *n.*

swathe². Variant of **swath.**

swat-ter (swóttər) *n.* **1.** One that swats. **2.** A small meshed or flexible flap attached to a handle, used for killing insects. Also called "fly-swatter".

sway (sway) *v.* **swayed, swaying, sways.** —*intr.* **1.** To move back and forth with a swinging motion; oscillate. **2.** To incline or bend to one side; veer. **3.** To incline towards change, as in opinion or feeling; vacillate. **b.** To tend towards in outlook. —*tr.* **1.** To cause to swing from side to side. **2.** To cause to incline or bend towards one side. **3.** *Nautical.* To hoist (a mast or yard) into position. **4. a.** To deter or cause to swerve; dissuade. **b.** To exert influence on

or control over. **5.** *Archaic.* **a.** To rule or govern. **b.** To wield as a weapon or sceptre. —See Synonyms at **swing.**
~*n.* **1.** The act of moving from side to side with a swinging motion. **2.** Power; influence. **3.** *Archaic.* Dominion or rule. [Middle English *sweyen*, to move, go down, swing, probably from Old Norse *sveigja*, to bend, yield.] —**sway-ing-ly** *adv.*

sway-back (swáy-bak) *n.* An excessive inward or downward curvature of the spine, as in horses. —**sway-backed** *adj.*

Swa-zi (swaázi) *n., pl.* **-zis** or collectively **Swazi. 1.** A member of the Bantu people of Swaziland. **2.** The language of this people, closely related to Zulu. In this sense, also called "siSwati". —**Swa-zi** *adj.*

Swa-zi-land, Kingdom of (swaázi-land). Small, landlocked African country. In the 1970s, foreign investment made it one of the most prosperous of the small African states, and forestry, mining, and manufacturing are expanding. Even so, about 70 per cent of workers are in farming, and many others work in South Africa. A British protectorate from 1903, Swaziland became independent within the Commonwealth in 1968. In 1973 Sobhuza II (reigned 1921–82) assumed supreme power and abolished the constitution. Area, 17 363 square kilometres (6,704 square miles). Capital, Mbabane. Population, 600,000 (mid-1982 estimate). See map at **South Africa.**

Swazi Territory. In South Africa, the tribal homeland for the Swazi.

SWbS southwest by south.

SWbW southwest by west.

swear (swair) *v.* **swore** (swor ‖ swōr), **sworn** (sworn ‖ swōrn), **swearing, swears.** —*intr.* **1.** To make a solemn declaration, invoking a deity or some person or thing held sacred, in confirmation of the honesty or truth of such a declaration: *I swear to God I spoke the truth.* **2.** To make a solemn promise; vow. **3.** To use swearwords; blaspheme or curse: *He swears at everyone when he is drunk.* **4.** *Law.* To give evidence or testimony under oath. —*tr.* **1.** To declare solemnly by invoking a sacred personage or thing. **2.** To promise or pledge with a solemn oath; vow. **3.** To utter or bind oneself to (an oath). **4.** To administer a legal oath to. **5.** To say or affirm earnestly and with great conviction. —**swear by. 1.** To name (a sacred personage or thing) as invocation in taking an oath. **2.** To have great reliance upon or confidence in. —**swear in.** To administer a legal or official oath to: *swear in the mayor.* —**swear off.** *Informal.* To pledge to renounce or give up. —**swear out.** *U.S.* To obtain (a warrant for someone's arrest) by making a charge, under oath. [Middle English *swer(i)en, swor, swor(n)*, Old English *swerian, swōr* (past singular), *sworen.*] —**swear-er** *n.*

swear-word (swaír-wurd) *n.* A word used in an obscene, insulting, or blasphemous way.

sweat (swet) *v.* **sweated** or **sweat, sweating, sweats.** —*intr.* **1.** To excrete the secretion of the sweat glands through the pores in the skin; perspire. **2.** To exude in droplets, as does moisture from certain cheeses or sap from a tree. **3.** To condense atmospheric moisture. **4. a.** To release moisture, as does hay or plants left to dry out. **b.** To ferment, as tobacco does during curing. **5.** *Informal.* To work long and hard. **6.** *Informal.* To suffer much, as for a misdeed. **7.** *Informal.* To fret or worry. —*tr.* **1.** To excrete (moisture) through a porous surface, such as the skin. **2.** To exude (moisture) in droplets on a surface. **3.** To cause to perspire, as by drugs, heat, or strenuous exercise. **4.** To make damp or wet with perspiration. **5.** To cause to work excessively; overwork. **6.** To overwork and underpay (employees). **7.** To heat (metal parts) in order to make a soldered joint. **8.** To cook (vegetables or other food) very slowly with butter in a closed saucepan. —**sweat it out.** *Informal.* **1.** To endure anxiously. **2.** To await (something) anxiously. —**sweat out.** To attempt to cure by sweating: *sweat out a cold.*
~*n.* **1.** The product of the sweat glands of the skin. **2.** Any condensation of moisture in the form of droplets on a surface. **3.** The process of sweating or condition of being sweated. **4.** Strenuous, exhausting labour; drudgery. **5.** An exercise run given to a horse before a race. **6.** *Informal.* An anxious condition; impatience: *in a sweat.* —**no sweat.** *Slang.* Easily done or handled. Often used as an interjection. [Middle English *sweten, swaten*, Old English *swǣtan.*] —**sweat-i-ly** *adv.* —**sweat-i-ness** *n.* —**sweat-y** *adj.*

sweat-band (swét-band) *n.* **1.** A band of fabric or leather sewn inside the crown of a hat as protection against sweat. **2.** A headband tied around the forehead to absorb sweat, worn especially while playing a strenuous game such as tennis.

sweat-box (swét-boks) *n.* A box in which something, such as animal hides or fruit, is fermented by sweating.

sweat-ed (swéttid) *n.* **1.** Hard and underpaid: *sweated labour.* **2.** Produced by exploited and underpaid workers.

sweat-er (swéttər) *n.* **1.** One that sweats, especially profusely. **2.** That which induces sweating; especially, a sudorific. **3.** A long-sleeved garment made of wool or synthetic yarns and worn on the upper part of the body. Also called "jersey", "jumper".

sweat gland *n.* Any of the numerous small, tubular glands that in humans are found nearly everywhere in the skin and that secrete a watery fluid containing sodium chloride and urea externally through the pores.

sweat-ing sickness (swétting) *n.* **1.** An acute infectious disease that was epidemic in Europe during the 15th and 16th centuries, characterised by profuse sweating and fever. **2.** A disease of cattle that is transmitted by ticks and is widespread in southern Africa.

sweat-rag (swét-rag) *n. Slang.* **1.** A handkerchief. **2.** A sweatband.

sweat-shirt (swét-shurt) *n.* A long-sleeved cotton jumper worn especially as casual wear or for sport.

sweat·shop (swét-shop) *n.* A workplace or factory where employees work long hours for low wages under bad conditions.

sweat·suit (swét-sōōt, -sewt) *n. U.S.* A **warm-up suit** or **tracksuit** (*both of which see*).

Swed. Sweden; Swedish.

swede (sweed) *n.* **1.** A plant, *Brassica napobrassica,* cultivated for its root. **2.** The large, fleshy, edible root of this plant, usually white or yellow in colour, which is used as a vegetable and as fodder for livestock. Also *U.S.* "rutabaga", "Swedish turnip", *chiefly Scottish* "turnip". [So named after its introduction into Scotland from Sweden in the 18th century.]

Swede (sweed) *n.* **1.** A native or inhabitant of Sweden. **2.** A person of Swedish descent.

Swe·den (swéd'n). *Swedish* **Sve·rige** (sváir-ye). Kingdom of northern Europe, occupying the east of the mountainous Scandinavian peninsula. It has one of the world's highest living standards, and also one of its most extensive welfare programmes, taxes absorbing more than a third of the national income. Prosperity derives chiefly from manufacturing. The country has large forest and mineral resources, including iron, copper, lead, and uranium. It relies heavily on hydroelectric power, and increasingly on nuclear power, having few fossil fuel deposits. Sweden emerged as a unified nation in the 11th century. It became a great power in the 17th century, but lost its empire early in the next century. Area, 449 964 square kilometres (173,732 square miles). Population, 8,300,000. Capital, Stockholm.

Swe·den·borg (swéd'n-bawrg), **Emanuel** (1688–1772). Swedish scientist, philosopher, and religious writer. He began having visions (*c.*1743) and afterwards devoted himself to physical and spiritual research. Although he did not preach or found a religious sect, his writings inspired his followers to set up the New Jerusalem Church.

Swe·den·borg·i·an·ism (swéd'n-bórji-an-iz'm, -bórgi-) *n.* Also **Swe·den·borg·ism** (-bawrgiz'm). The theological philosophy of Emanuel Swedenborg that forms the basis for the New Jerusalem

Church, claiming direct mystical communication between the world and the spiritual realm and affirming Christ as the true God.

Swed·ish (swéedish) *adj.* Of or pertaining to Sweden, the Swedes, or their culture or language.
~*n.* **1.** The North Germanic language of Sweden. **2.** *Used with a plural verb.* The people of Sweden. Preceded by *the.*

Swedish massage *n.* A European style of therapeutic massage and exercises for muscles and joints, developed in the 19th century.

Swedish turnip *n. U.S.* A vegetable, the swede.

Swee·ney (swéeni) *n. British Slang.* The **Flying Squad** (*see*). [Rhyming slang, from *Sweeney Todd.*]

sweep (sweep) *v.* **swept** (swept), **sweeping, sweeps.** —*tr.* **1.** To clean or clear the surface or interior of with or as if with a broom or brush: *sweep a chimney.* **2.** To clean or clear away (dust or dirt, for example) with or as if with a broom or brush: *sweep snow from the steps.* **3. a.** To clear (a space) with or as if with a broom. **b.** To clear (objects) away with or as if with a broom: *swept the papers off her desk.* **4.** To touch or brush lightly: *Willow branches swept the ground.* **5. a.** To move, remove, or convey with a flowing motion, as by water: *The wind swept tiles from the roof.* **b.** To move or unbalance emotionally: *Love swept him off his feet.* **6.** To cause to depart; remove or destroy. **7.** To traverse with speed or intensity; range throughout: *Plague swept Europe.* **8.** To traverse, as when searching: *Her gaze swept the horizon.* **9.** To drag the bottom of (a body of water). **10.** To win all the stages of (a game or contest). **11.** To hit (a cricket ball) with a sweep. —*intr.* **1.** To clear or clean a surface with or as if with a broom or brush. **2. a.** To move, surge, or flow with smooth and steady force: *A cool wind swept over the plain.* **b.** To move swiftly or majestically: *She swept by in silence.* **3.** To trail, as a long garment does: *Her veil swept to the floor.* **4.** To extend gracefully or majestically: *The hills sweep down to the sea.* ~*n.* **1.** The act of sweeping; removal with or as if with a broom or brush. **2.** The motion of sweeping: *a sweep of the arm.* **3.** The range or scope encompassed by sweeping: *the sweep of a machine gun.* **4. a.** A reach or extent: *a sweep of green lawn.* **b.** A curving driveway. **5.** Any curve or contour: *the sweep of his hair.* **6.** One who sweeps; especially, a chimney sweep. **7.** *Usually plural.* Sweepings. **8. a.** The winning of all stages of a game or contest. **b.** A total victory or success. **9.** A long oar used to propel a boat. **10.** A long pole attached to a pivot and with a bucket at one end, used to raise water from a well. **11.** *Informal.* A sweepstake. **12.** *Electronics.* The steady motion of an electron beam across a cathode-ray tube. **13.** A cricketing shot in which the ball is hit near the ground on the leg side with a sweeping movement. —**make a clean sweep.** To get rid of all unwanted objects, people, obligations, or other obstacles. [Middle English swe(e)pen, probably from Old English *swēop,* past singular of *swāpan,* to sweep.]

sweep·back (swéep-bak) *n. Aeronautics.* **1.** The backward slant of the leading edge of an aerofoil. **2.** The degree of this slant.

sweep·er (swéepər) *n.* **1.** A person who sweeps. **2.** A **carpet sweeper** (*see*). **3.** In soccer, a player who defends from between the goal and the main defending players. **4.** A **minesweeper** (*see*).

sweep·ing (swéeping) *adj.* **1.** Removing with or as if with a broom or brushing movement. **2.** Influencing or affecting a great area; wide-ranging: *a sweeping definition.* **3.** Very general; without discrimination or reservation: *sweeping generalisations.* **4.** Overwhelming: *a sweeping victory.*
~*n.* **1.** The action or occupation of one who sweeps. **2.** *Plural.* That which is swept up; debris; litter. —**sweep·ing·ly** *adv.*

sweep-second hand (swéep-seckənd) *n.* A long hand on a clock or watch that measures seconds by moving the space of a minute for each second. Also called "sweep hand".

sweep·stake (swéep-stayk) *n.* Also *chiefly U.S.* **sweep·stakes** (-stayks). **1.** A lottery in which the participants' contributions form a fund to be awarded as a prize to the winner or winners. **2.** Any event or contest, especially a horse race, the result of which determines the winner of such a lottery. **3.** The lottery prize won.

sweet (sweet) *adj.* **sweeter, sweetest. 1. a.** Having a sugary taste. **b.** Containing or derived from a sugar. **2.** Pleasing to the senses, feelings, or the mind; gratifying: *sweet music; Revenge is sweet.* **3. a.** Adorable; charming; lovable: *a sweet child.* **b.** Good-natured, sweet-tempered. **c.** Kind; nice; pleasant and helpful: *It's sweet of you to give me a lift.* **4.** Not saline; fresh: *sweet water.* **b.** *U.S.* Not saline; unsalted: *sweet butter.* **5.** Not spoilt, sour, or decaying; fresh: *This milk is still sweet.* **6.** Free of acid. **7.** *Music.* **a.** Designating jazz characterised by adherence to a melodic line and to a time signature. **b.** Performing jazz in this way. **8.** Designating wine that is not dry or cider or sherry that is neither dry nor medium. —**sweet on.** *Informal.* Fond of (a person); infatuated with.
~*n.* **1.** The quality of being sweet; sweetness. **2.** Something that is sweet or contains sugar. **3.** *Chiefly British.* A piece of confectionery. **4.** *British.* Anything relatively sweet served as a pudding. **5.** A dear or beloved person. [Middle English swe(e)te, Old English *swēte.*] —**sweet·ish** *adj.* —**sweet·ly** *adv.* —**sweet·ness** *n.*

sweet alyssum *n.* A widely cultivated plant, *Lobularia maritima,* native to the Mediterranean region, having clusters of small, fragrant white or purplish flowers.

sweet-and-sour (swéet'n-sówr) *adj.* Made or cooked with vinegar and sugar, as in Chinese cooking: *sweet-and-sour sauce.*

sweet basil *n.* A species of **basil** (*see*).

sweet bay *n.* **1.** A tree, the **bay** (*see*). **2.** A small tree, *Magnolia virginiana,* of the southern United States, having large, fragrant white flowers.

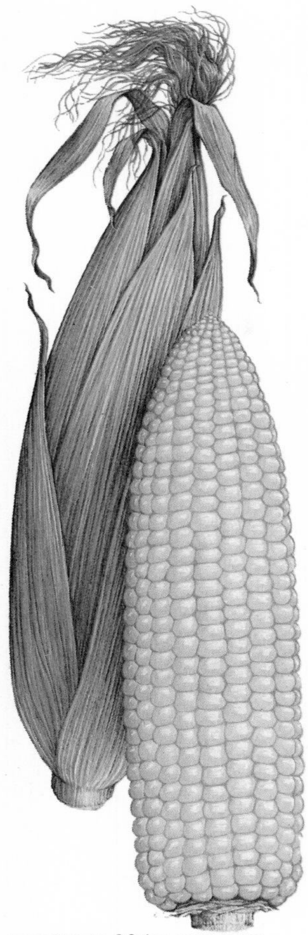

sweet corn *Maize, now grown around the world for the edible grains on its cob, is native to North and Central America. As well as being eaten as a vegetable, the grains are also ground into flour and crushed to extract cooking oil.*

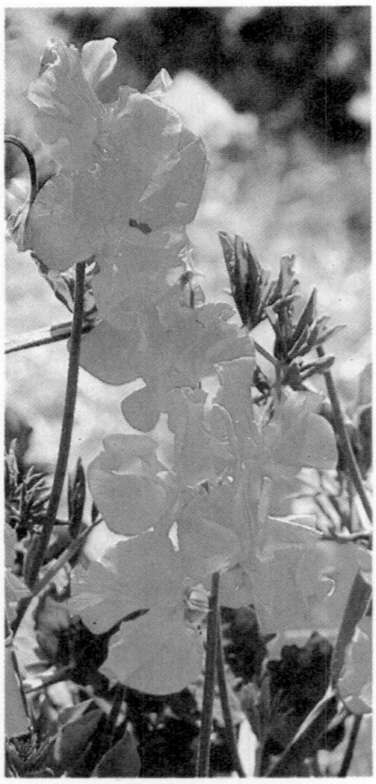

sweet pea *There are many garden varieties of this scented annual,* Lathyrus odoratus, *which is native to southern Italy. The blooms are prized by gardeners as cut flowers and for showing.*

sweet·bread (swéet-bred) *n.* The pancreas or thymus gland of a calf or lamb, used for food. [SWEET + BREAD (euphemism).]

sweet·bri·ar, sweet·bri·er (swéet-brī-ər, -brīr) *n.* A rose, *Rosa rubiginosa* (or *R. eglanteria*), native to Europe, having prickly stems, fragrant leaves, and pink flowers. Also called "eglantine".

sweet cherry *n.* **1.** A widely cultivated tree originating from the wild cherry *Prunus avium,* native to Eurasia, having white flowers and sweet, edible fruit. The sweet cherry group has two subdivisions, the **bigarreau** and the **gean** *(both of which see).* **2.** The fruit of this tree. See **cherry.**

sweet chestnut *n.* See **chestnut** (sense 1).

sweet cicely *n.* **1.** Any of various North American plants of the genus *Osmorhiza,* having aromatic roots, compound leaves, and clusters of small white flowers. **2.** An aromatic European plant, *Myrrhis odorata,* having compound leaves and clusters of small white flowers. In this sense, also called "myrrh".

sweet cider *n.* **1.** Sweet-tasting cider. **2.** *U.S.* Unfermented apple juice. Compare **hard cider.**

sweet clover *n.* A plant, the **melilot** *(see).*

sweet·corn, sweet corn (swéet-kawrn) *n.* A variety of maize, *Zea mayssaccharata,* having kernels that are sweet to eat when young.

sweet·en (swéet'n) *v.* **-ened, -ening, -ens.** *—tr.* **1.** To make sweet or sweeter by or as if by the addition of sugar. **2.** To make pleasurable or gratifying. **3.** To make bearable; alleviate; lighten. **4.** *U.S. Informal.* To increase the value of (collateral for a loan) by adding more securities. **5.** In poker, to increase the value of (an unwon pot) by adding stakes before reopening. *—intr.* To become sweet.

sweet·en·er (swéet'n-ər) *n.* **1.** That which is added to something to make it sweet; specifically, a sugar substitute such as saccharine. **2.** *Slang.* A bribe.

sweet·en·ing (swéet'n-ing) *n.* **1.** The act or process of making sweet. **2.** Something used to sweeten.

sweet fennel *n.* A variety of fennel, **finochio** *(see).*

sweet fern *n.* An aromatic shrub, *Comptonia peregrina,* of eastern North America, having shallowly lobed, fernlike, aromatic foliage.

sweet flag *n.* A plant, *Acorus calamus,* growing in moist places and having bladelike leaves, minute greenish flowers, and aromatic roots. Also called "calamus".

sweet gale *n.* A plant, the **bog myrtle** *(see).*

sweet gum *n.* **1.** A New World tree, *Liquidambar styraciflua,* having sharply lobed leaves, prickly, ball-like fruit clusters, and wood used to make furniture. Also called "bilsted". **2.** The wood or aromatic resin obtained from this tree.

sweet·heart (swéet-haart) *n.* **1.** One who loves and is loved by another. Often used as a term of affectionate address. **2.** A lovable, friendly, or generous person.

swee·tie (swéeti) *n.* **1.** *Informal.* A sweetheart; a dear. **2.** *British Informal & Regional.* A sweet (piece of confectionery).

sweet·ie-pie (swéeti-pī) *n. British Informal.* A dear; a sweetheart. Used as a term of address.

sweet·ing (swéeting) *n.* **1.** A sweet apple. **2.** *Archaic.* A sweetheart.

sweet marjoram *n.* A species of **marjoram** *(see).*

sweet·meal (swéet-meel) *adj.* Sweetened and made with wholemeal flour. Said of a biscuit.

sweet·meat (swéet-meet) *n.* Any delicacy made with a sweetening agent; specifically, a piece of crystallised fruit. [SWEET + MEAT (food).]

sweet pea *n.* A climbing plant, *Lathyrus odoratus,* native to southern Italy, cultivated for its variously coloured, fragrant flowers.

sweet pepper *n.* **1.** Any of several plants of the genus *Capsicum,* especially *C. frutescens* or *C. annuum,* cultivated for their large, mild-tasting fruits, which are eaten raw in salads or cooked as a vegetable. **2.** The fruit of such a plant. See **green pepper, red pepper.** Also called "capsicum", "pimiento".

sweet potato *n.* **1.** A tropical American vine, *Ipomoea batatas,* cultivated for its thick, orange-coloured, edible root. **2.** The root of this plant, eaten cooked as a vegetable.

sweet·shop (swéet-shop) *n. British.* A small shop selling confectionery, and sometimes tobacco and other items.

sweet·sop (swéet-sop) *n.* **1.** A tropical American tree, *Annona squamosa,* having yellowish-green fruit with sweet, edible pulp. **2.** The fruit of this tree. Also called "sugar apple".

sweet-tempered (swéet-témpərd) *adj.* Docile; by nature gentle and kind. **—sweet-tem·pered·ly** *adv.*

sweet tooth *n.* A fondness for sugar or sweet things.

sweet william *n.* A widely cultivated plant, *Dianthus barbatus,* native to Eurasia, having flat, clusters of red or pink flowers.

swell (swel) *v.* **swelled, swollen** (swṓlən) or **swelled, swelling, swells.** *—intr.* **1.** To increase in size or volume as a result of internal pressure; expand. **2. a.** To increase in force, size, number, or degree. **b.** To grow in loudness or intensity: *the sound swelled to a tremendous din.* **3.** To bulge out; protrude, as a sail may. Often used with *out.* **4.** To rise in or like billows above the surrounding level, as waves or clouds may. **5.** To rise up in level or overflow, as a river may. **6.** To be or become filled or puffed up with an emotion, such as pride. *—tr.* To cause to swell: *swelled the chorus of protest.*
~n. **1. a.** The act or process of swelling. **b.** The condition of being swollen. **2.** A swollen part; a bulge or protuberance. **3.** A regular undulating movement of waves out in the open sea, with no breaking, and considerable distance between successive crests. **4. a.** A rise in the land; a rounded hill. **b.** A long, gently sloping elevation, which rises from the sea bed, but which is far from the surface. **5.** *Informal & Archaic.* One who is fashionably dressed or prominent in fashionable society. **6.** *Music.* **a.** A crescendo followed by a gradual diminuendo. **b.** A sign in a score indicating this. **c.** A device on some instruments, such as the organ or harpsichord, for regulating volume.
~adj. **sweller, swellest. 1.** *Archaic.* Fashionably elegant; smart; stylish. **2.** *U.S. Informal* Fine; excellent: *a swell guy.* Often used interjectionally. [Middle English *swellen, swollen,* Old English *swellan, geswollen,* from Germanic *swellan* (unattested).]
Usage: The usual past participial form of this verb is *swollen* (*The river/Her neck/The sail was swollen*), but *swelled* is often used when increases in size or amount are being expressed (*The crowd was swelled by a large number of young people*). A contrast in meaning is sometimes possible, with *swollen* expressing a pejorative sense: compare *Their numbers have swelled to nearly a thousand* (statement of fact) and *Their numbers have swollen to nearly a thousand* (an undesirable development).

swell box *n.* A chamber housing one or more sets of organ pipes and having shutters that can be opened or shut to regulate the volume of tone.

swelled-headed. *U.S.* Variant of **swollen-headed.**

swell·fish (swél-fish) *n., pl.* **-fishes** or **swellfish.** The **puffer** *(see).*

swell·ing (swélling) *n.* **1.** The act of expanding. **2.** The state of being swollen or expanded. **3.** Something that is swollen; especially, an abnormally swollen or protuberant area on the body.

swel·ter (swéltər) *v.* **-tered, -tering, -ters.** *—intr.* To be affected by oppressive heat; sweat or feel faint from heat. *—tr.* **1.** To affect with oppressive heat. **2.** *Archaic.* To exude.
~n. Oppressive heat and humidity: *"All the swelter of that urban summer"* (Cyril Connolly). [Middle English *swelt(e)ren,* frequentative of *swelten,* to die, faint from heat, Old English *sweltan,* to die.]

swel·ter·ing (swéltəring) *adj.* Also *rare* **swel·try** (swéltri), **-trier, -triest. 1.** Oppressively hot and humid. **2.** Suffering from oppressive heat. **—swel·ter·ing·ly** *adv.*

swept. Past tense and past participle of **sweep.**

swept·back (swépt-bák) *adj.* Angled rearwards from the points of attachment. Said especially of aircraft wings.

swept·wing (swépt-wing) *adj.* Having sweptback wings.
~n. A sweptback wing.

swerve (swerv) *v.* **swerved, swerving, swerves.** *—intr.* To turn aside suddenly and swiftly from a straight or planned course; veer. *—tr.* To cause to swerve; deflect; turn aside.
~n. A deflection or deviation; a swerving movement. [Middle English *swerven,* perhaps originally "to make a circular motion in polishing", Old English *sweorfan,* to file away, scour, polish.]

S.W.G. Standard wire gauge.

swift (swift) *adj.* **swifter, swiftest. 1.** Moving or able to move with great speed; fast; fleet. **2.** Coming, occurring, or accomplished quickly; instant: *a swift retort.* **3.** Ready in acting or reacting; prompt: *swift to take steps.* —See Synonyms at **fast.**
~adv. Quickly; swiftly. Often used in combination: *swift-running.*
~n. **1.** A cylinder on a carding machine. **2.** A reel used to hold yarn as it is being wound off. **3.** Any of various dark birds of the family Apodidae, characteristically having long, narrow wings and a relatively short tail. **4.** Any of various small, fast-moving North American lizards of the genera *Sceloporus* and *Uta.* [Middle English *swift(e),* Old English *swift.*] **—swift·ly** *adv.* **—swift·ness** *n.*

Swift (swift), **Jonathan** (1667–1745). Irish-born satirist and poet. His works include *A Tale of a Tub* (1704), which attacked religious extremism, and his masterpiece, *Gulliver's Travels* (1726), a satirical attack on the politics, philosophy, and science of his time.

swift·let (swíft-lət, -lit) *n.* Any small cave-dwelling swift of the genus *Collocalia,* of southeast Asia and Australia, whose nests, constructed chiefly of solidified saliva, are used to make birds'-nest soup. [Diminutive of SWIFT. See **-let.**]

swift moth *n.* **1.** The **ghost moth** *(see).* **2.** Any of various moths of the family Hepialidae.

swig (swig) *n. Informal.* A large swallow or drink of liquid; a gulp.
~v. **swigged, swigging, swigs.** *—tr. Informal.* To drink eagerly and with great gulps. *—intr. Informal.* To take a large swallow; gulp. Ofted used with *at.* [16th century : origin obscure.]

swill (swil) *v.* **swilled, swilling, swills.** *—tr.* **1.** To drink eagerly, greedily, or to excess. **2.** To flood with water, as for cleaning or washing. Often used with *out.* **3.** To feed (animals) with slops. *—intr.* To drink greedily.
~n. **1.** The act or an instance of swilling. **2.** A mixture of liquid and solid food, such as table scraps, fed to animals, especially pigs; slops. **2.** Kitchen waste or rubbish; refuse. [Middle English *swilen,* Old English *swilian,* to wash out.] **—swill·er** *n.*

swim (swim) *v.* **swam** (swam) or *archaic* **swum** (swum), **swum, swimming, swims.** *—intr.* **1.** To propel oneself through water by means of movements of the body or parts of the body such as limbs or fins. **2.** To move as though gliding through water. **3.** To float on water or other liquid. **4.** To be covered or flooded with water or other liquid; be immersed. Usually used with *in* or *with.* **5.** *Informal.* To have a large amount of. Used with *in.* **6.** To experience a floating or dizzy sensation: *Her mind swam on hearing the terrible news.* **7.** To appear to spin or reel lazily: *The nurse's face swam before her eyes as she slowly came to.* *—tr.* **1.** To propel oneself through or across (a body of water) by swimming. **2.** To complete in (a race) by swimming. **3.** To perform (a particular stroke) in swimming. **4.** To cause to swim or float on a body of water.
~n. **1.** The act or movements of one that swims. **2.** A period or instance of swimming. **3.** A deep part in a river, containing a lot of

fish. **4.** A state of dizziness; a swoon. **—in the swim.** *Informal.* In the current trend of affairs; participating in what is fashionable. [Middle English *swimmen, swam(me), swummen,* Old English *swimman, swamm* (or *swom*), *swummen.*] **—swim·mer** *n.*
swim bladder *n.* An organ in fishes, the **air bladder** *(see).*
swim·mer·et (swímmər-ét) *n.* Any of the paired abdominal appendages of certain aquatic crustaceans, such as shrimps and lobsters, that function primarily as organs of respiration or locomotion. Also called "pleopod". [Diminutive of *swimmer,* from SWIM.]
swim·ming baths (swímming) *pl.n. Sometimes singular.* An indoor, usually public, swimming pool or set of swimming pools.
swimming costume *n.* An item of clothing worn for swimming or sunbathing; typically, trunks for a man, or a woman's one-piece garment that usually leaves the arms, legs, and most of the back bare. Also called "bathing costume", "bathing suit", "swimsuit".
swim·ming·ly (swímming-li) *adv.* With great ease and a high degree of success: *The campaign is proceeding swimmingly.*
swimming pool *n.* A pool built for swimming. Also called "pool".
swim·suit (swím-so͞ot, -sewt) *n.* A swimming costume.
Swin·burne (swín-burn, -bərn), **Algernon Charles** (1837–1909). British poet and critic. He is best known for his magnificently rich, often erotic verse, in which he attacked the conventions of Victorian morality.
swin·dle (swínd'l) *v.* **-dled, -dling, -dles.** *—tr.* **1.** To cheat or defraud (a person or group) of money or property. **2.** To obtain (money or property, for example) by fraudulent means. *—intr.* To practise fraud as a habitual means of obtaining money.
∼n. The act or an instance of swindling; a fraud. [Back-formation from *swindler,* from German *Schwindler,* from *schwindeln,* to be dizzy, swindle, cheat, from Old High German *swintilōn,* frequentative of *swintan,* to vanish, languish, become unconscious, from Germanic *swindan* (unattested).] **—swin·dler** *n.*
Swin·don (swíndən). Town in Wiltshire, southern England. It grew with the opening of workshops of the Great Western Railway (1841), and expanded under the Town Development Act (1952).
swine (swīn) *n., pl.* **swines** (for sense 2) or **swine** (for senses 1 and 2a). **1.** *Usually plural.* A pig. **2. a.** A contemptible, vicious, or coarse person. **b.** An extremely unpleasant or difficult task, problem, or the like. [Middle English *swin(e),* Old English *swīn.*]
swine fever *n.* An infectious, often fatal, viral disease of pigs characterised by fever, lethargy, and distressed breathing. Also *U.S.* "hog cholera".
swine·herd (swīn-herd) *n.* A person who looks after pigs.
swine·pox (swīn-poks) *n.* A disease of domesticated pigs caused by a virus similar to that causing cowpox and smallpox and characterised by skin lesions.
swine vesicular disease *n. Abbr.* **SVD** A highly infectious viral disease of pigs, similar to foot-and-mouth disease, characterised by fever and painful blisters on the feet and snout.
swing (swing) *v.* **swung** (swung), **swung, swinging, swings.** *—intr.* **1. a.** To move rhythmically back and forth, suspended from above or as if suspended from above; oscillate; sway: *a rope swinging from the mast.* **b.** To move back and forth while attached to a fixed point or thing: *Don't swing on that gate.* **c.** To ride on or propel a swing. **2. a.** To move, walk, run, or the like with a free-swaying motion: *shire horses swinging out of the yard.* **b.** To move from one fixed position to another with a free-swaying motion: *swinging from tree to tree.* **3. a.** To turn in place, as on a hinge or other pivot. **b.** To turn suddenly: *swung round.* **4.** To move in a curve; move from a straight path: *The car swung off the road; The ball swung in towards the wicket.* **5.** To change one's attitudes, emotions, habits, or the like; vacillate. **6.** *Slang.* To be executed by hanging: *You'll swing for this.* **7. a.** To have a compulsive rhythm. Used of popular music. **b.** To play with a compulsive rhythm. Used of popular music performers. **8.** To hit or attempt to hit with a curving, swaying motion of the arm: *She swung at him.* **9.** *Chiefly U.S. Slang.* **a.** To participate actively in youthful fads. **b.** To be a lively success in terms of enjoyment: *the swinging sixties.* **c.** To exchange sexual partners temporarily. *—tr.* **1.** To cause to swing. **2.** To move (a person on a swing) backwards and forwards by pulling or pushing. **3.** To move with a sweeping motion; brandish. **4.** To hang or suspend (something) so that it can sway or move freely. **5.** *Slang.* To manipulate or manage successfully: *Can you swing this deal?* **6.** To arrange or perform (popular music) in the style of swing. **7.** In cricket, to bowl (a ball) in a curving path.
∼n. **1.** The act or an instance of swinging, especially: **a.** A rhythmic back-and-forth movement. **b.** A single movement or series of movements in one particular direction. **c.** A punch or blow: *took a swing at him.* **d.** A movement from one attitude or opinion to another, such as a change of allegiance or voting: *the swing to Labour.* **2.** The distance traversed while swinging: *The pendulum's swing is 12 inches.* **3.** The manner in which a person or thing swings something, such as a bat or golf club. **4.** Freedom and scope of movement or action. **5. a.** A swaying, graceful motion. **b.** A sweep or swoop: *the swing of a bird across the sky.* **6.** A seat suspended from above for the enjoyment of those who sit on it and make it move back and forth. **7.** Lively or enjoyable activity or pace: *The party went with a swing.* **8.** *Informal.* The normal rhythm or pace of life; the ordinary flow of activities: *back into the swing of things.* **9.** A compulsive rhythm, as found in many types of popular music. **10. a.** An innovation in popular dance music developed about 1935, based on jazz but employing a larger band and simpler harmonic and rhythmic patterns. **b.** The rhythmic quality of this music. **—in full swing.** In action to the maximum speed, capacity, or ability. **—swings and roundabouts.** A situation in which something is gained and lost equally, or in which a gain is balanced by a loss. *∼adj.* Pertaining to or performing swing. [Middle English *swingen, swang* (past singular), *swungen* (past plural), *swungen,* Old English *swingan,* to whip, strike, fling oneself, *swang, swungon, geswungen.*]
Synonyms: *swing, oscillate, sway, rock, vibrate, fluctuate, undulate, waver.*
swing bridge *n.* A river or canal bridge that can be pivoted on a vertical central axis to allow ships to pass. Also called "turn bridge".
swing door *n.* Also **swing·ing door** (swíng-ing). A door, often either of a pair, that is hung on double-sided hinges enabling it to be opened in either direction.
swinge (swinj) *tr.v.* **swinged, swinges.** *Archaic.* To strike or beat. [Middle English *swengen,* to shake, dash, beat up, Old English *swengan,* to swing, shake.] **—swing·er** (swínjər) *n.*
swinge·ing (swínjing) *adj. British.* **1.** Powerful or brutal: *dealt a swingeing blow.* **2. a.** Harsh; drastic; punitive: *swingeing fines.* **b.** So large as to cause severe damage or distress: *swingeing cuts.*
swing·er (swíng-ər) *n.* **1.** One that swings. **2.** *Slang.* A person who actively seeks excitement and moves with the latest trends. **3.** *Slang.* A person who is sexually uninhibited; especially, one who engages in swapping sexual partners.
swin·gle·tree (swíng-g'l-tree) *n.* A pivoted horizontal crossbar to which the harness traces of a draught animal are attached and which is in turn attached to a vehicle or implement. Also called "singletree", "whiffletree", "whippletree". [From *swingle,* wooden instrument for beating hemp, Middle English *swingle,* from Middle Dutch *swinghel.*]
swing·om·e·ter (swíng-ómmitər) *n.* An indicator of the swing in voting, used especially on television during general elections.
swing-wing (swíng-wing) *adj.* Being or pertaining to an aircraft with movable wings that can be swept back for fast flight and brought forward for lower speeds, as on takeoff and landing.
∼n. **1.** A swing-wing aircraft. Also called "variable sweep". **2.** Either of the wings of such an aircraft.
swin·ish (swīnish) *adj.* Resembling or befitting swine; bestial; brutish. **—swin·ish·ly** *adv.* **—swin·ish·ness** *n.*
swipe (swīp) *n.* **1.** A heavy, sweeping blow. **2.** A lever; especially, one that raises the bucket in a well.
∼v. **swiped, swiping, swipes.** *—tr.* **1.** To hit with a sweeping blow. **2.** *Slang.* To steal; filch. *—intr.* To make a sweeping blow. [Perhaps variant of SWEEP.]
swipes (swīps) *pl.n. British.* Beer that is weak or inferior. [From SWIPE (verb), in earliest sense, to drink hurriedly, drink a lot.]
swirl (swurl) *v.* **swirled, swirling, swirls.** *—intr.* **1.** To rotate or spin in or as if in a whirlpool or eddy. **2.** To be dizzy or faint; reel. *—tr.* To cause to move with a whirling motion. **—**See Synonyms at **turn.**
∼n. **1.** The motion or act of whirling or spinning. **2.** Something that swirls; a whirlpool or eddy. **3.** Something that is or has been swirled. **4.** Confusion; turbulence; disorder. [Middle English (Scottish dialect) *swyrl,* eddy, whirlpool, probably of Low German origin, akin to Dutch *zwirrelen,* to whirl.] **—swirl·y** *adj.*
swish (swish) *v.* **swished, swishing, swishes.** *—intr.* **1.** To move or cut with a sibilant whistle or hiss. **2.** To rustle, as certain fabrics do. *—tr.* **1.** To cause to make a swishing movement or sound. **2.** To cut off with a swishing sound. **3.** To whip with a swish or rod.
∼n. **1. a.** A sharp sibilant or rustling sound: *the swish of scythes.* **b.** A movement making such a sound. **2. a.** A rod used for whipping. **b.** A stroke made with such a rod. **3.** *U.S. Slang.* A highly effeminate male.
∼adj. Slang. **1.** *Chiefly British.* Fashionable; posh; luxurious. **2.** *U.S.* Highly effeminate. [Imitative.]
swiss (swiss) *n. Sometimes capital* **S.** A crisp, sheer cotton cloth used for curtains, light garments, or the like. [From SWISS (because it was first manufactured in Switzerland).]
Swiss (swiss) *adj.* Of, pertaining to, or characteristic of Switzerland, its inhabitants, its various dialects, or its culture.
∼n., pl. **Swiss. 1.** A native or inhabitant of Switzerland. **2.** One of Swiss descent.
Swiss chard *n.* A vegetable, **chard** *(see).*
Swiss cheese *n.* A firm white or pale yellow cheese with holes, such as Gruyère.
Swiss cheese plant *n.* See **monstera.**
Swiss Guard *n.* **1.** The group of bodyguards in the Vatican, made up of mercenaries from Switzerland. **2.** Any of these bodyguards.
swiss roll *n.* A cake made of a layer of sponge spread with a filling such as jam or cream and rolled into a cylindrical shape. [SWISS, from Switzerland, where it probably originated.]
switch (swich) *n. Abbr.* **sw. 1.** A slender flexible rod, stick, twig, or the like; especially, such a rod used for whipping. **2.** The bushy tip of the tail of certain animals: *a cow's switch.* **3.** A thick bunch of real or synthetic hair used by women as part of a hairstyle. **4.** A flailing or lashing, as with a slender rod. **5.** *Electricity.* A device used to break or open an electrical circuit or to divert current from one conductor to another. **6.** *U.S.* A railway **point** *(see).* **7.** An exchange or swap, especially one done surreptitiously. **8.** Any sudden transference or shift, as of opinion or attention.
∼v. **switched, switching, switches.** *—tr.* **1.** To whip with or as if with a switch. **2.** To jerk or swish abruptly or sharply. **3.** To shift, transfer, change, or divert: *switch the conversation.* **4.** To exchange: *switch sides.* **5.** To connect, disconnect, or divert (an electric cur-

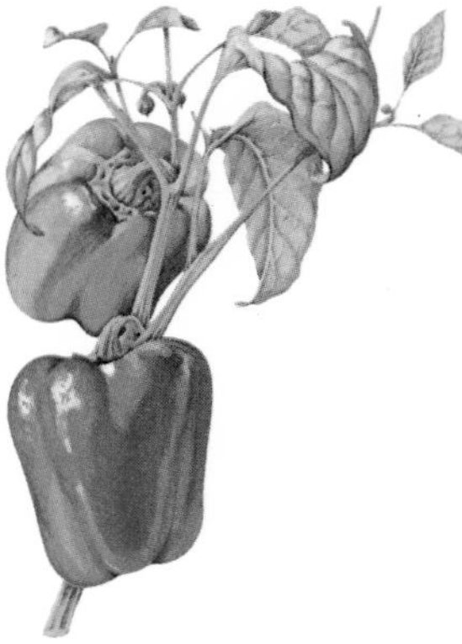

sweet pepper *A fruit of tropical origin, which can be grown under glass in temperate zones. Peppers turn red as they ripen, but are often eaten as a vegetable while still green.*

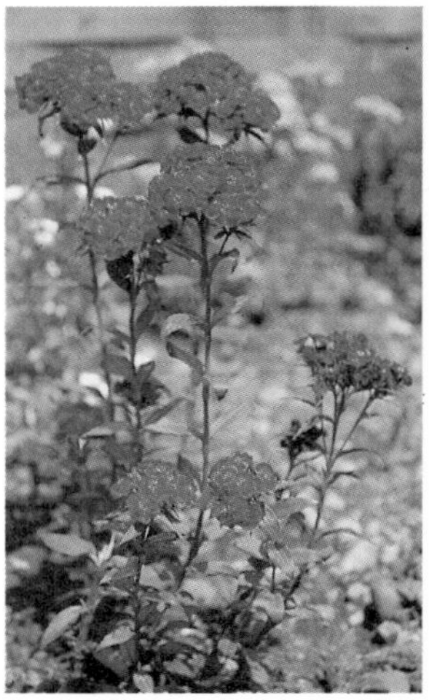

sweet william Dianthus barbatus, *a perennial flower which is a common garden plant, can grow to about 75 centimetres (2½ feet).*

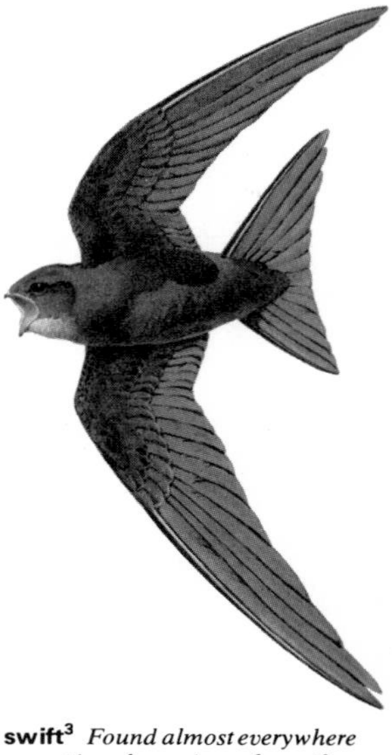

swift[3] *Found almost everywhere except in polar regions, the swift spends most of its waking hours in flight. It can reach speeds of 110 kilometres per hour (70 miles per hour) and catches insects on the wing with its wide-open mouth. This is the common swift,* Apus apus.

rent) by operating a switch. **6.** To cause (an electric current or appliance) to begin or cease operation. Used with *on* or *off*: *switch the radio off.* **7.** *U.S.* To move (rolling stock) from one track to another; shunt. **8.** *Informal.* To provide or produce quickly and effortlessly. Used with *on: switch on the charm.* —*intr.* **1.** To shift or change: *switch from coal to oil.* **2.** To be shifted or changed. —**switch off.** *Informal.* To lose interest; cease paying attention: *The lecturer's voice was so dull that I switched off after five minutes.* [Perhaps from Middle Dutch *swijch*, bough, twig.] —**switch·er** *n.*

switch·back (swĭch-bak) *n.* **1.** A road or trail that ascends a steep incline in a winding course. **2.** *Chiefly British.* A roller coaster.

switch·blade (swĭch-blayd) *n. U.S.* A flick knife *(see).*

switch·board (swĭch-bawrd ‖ -bŏrd) *n.* **1.** An installation that controls the interconnection of telephone lines, as in a telephone exchange or office. **2.** A panel or set of panels with switches, indicators, and other apparatus for operating electric circuits.

switch·gear (swĭch-geer) *n.* Electrical equipment whose function is to open and close high-current circuits.

switch·man (swĭch-mən) *n., pl.* **-men.** *U.S.* A pointsman *(see).*

swith·er (swĭthər) *intr.v.* **-ered, -ering, -ers.** *British Regional.* To be undecided or in a state of uncertainty; dither.
~*n.* Uncertainty; dither. [16th century : origin obscure.]

Swith·in or **Swith·un** (swĭth-in, -'n, *rarely* swĭth-), **Saint** (died 862). English prelate. He was Bishop of Winchester (852–62). According to tradition, if it rains on St. Swithin's day (July 15) it will rain for 40 days following: on that day in 971 the saint's body was to be transferred from churchyard to cathedral, contrary to his wishes, and heavy rain delayed the proceedings.

Switz. Switzerland.

Swit·zer (swĭtsər) *n. Rare.* **1.** A Swiss. **2.** A member of the Swiss Guard. [Middle High German *Swīzer,* from *Swīz,* SWITZERLAND.]

Swit·zer·land, Confederation of (swĭtsər-lənd). *French* **Suisse** (sweess); *German* **Schweiz** (shvīts); *Italian* **Sviz·ze·ra** (svítsera). Latin name **Hel·ve·tia.** Landlocked country in western Europe. It consists of three regions: the Alps in the south are divided from the Jura mountains of the northwest by the Mitteland plateau. The population includes German, French, and Italian speakers, with a small Romansch minority. Switzerland is a world centre of finance and tourism. Its main exports are watches, clocks, jewellery, instruments, and textiles. It became part of the Holy Roman Empire (10th century), but by 1499 had achieved independence as a loose confederation of cantons. A federal constitution was adopted in 1848. Resolute neutrality kept Switzerland out of both World Wars, and it is not a U.N. member. However, it has become the base of many international groups, including the Red Cross and World Health Organisation. Area, 41 288 square kilometres (15,937 square miles). Population, 6,300,000 (mid-1982 estimate). Capital, Bern.

swiv·el (swĭvv'l) *n.* **1.** A link, pivot, or other fastening so designed that it permits free turning of attached parts. **2.** A pivoted support that allows an attached object, such as a chair or gun, to turn in a horizontal plane. **3.** A cannon that turns on a pivot. Also called "swivel gun."
~*v.* **swivelled** or *U.S.* **swiveled, -elling** or *U.S.* **-eling, -els.** —*tr.* **1.** To turn or rotate on or as if on a swivel. **2.** To secure, fit, or support with a swivel. —*intr.* To turn on or as if on a swivel. —See Synonyms at **turn.** [Middle English *swyvel, swevill,* related to or from Old English *swīfan,* to revolve.]

swivel chair *n.* A chair that swivels on its base.

swivel pin *n.* A kingpin *(see).*

swizz (swiz) *n.* Also **swizzle.** *British Informal.* **1.** A shame; a disappointment. **2.** A trick; a swindle. [20th century : origin obscure.]

swiz·zle (swĭzz'l) *n.* **1.** Any of various mixed drinks, usually made with rum. **2.** A swizz.

swizzle stick *n.* A rod for stirring mixed drinks or for removing the effervescence from drinks by making them froth up.

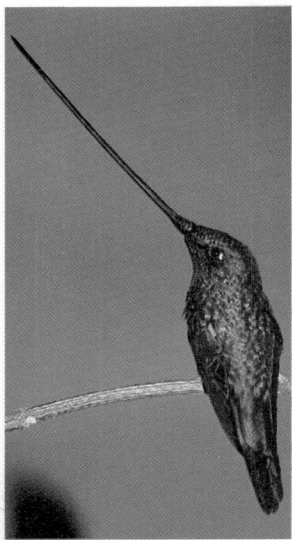

swordbill *One of about 320 species of hummingbird, found mostly in South America. All hummingbirds have long, slender bills, but the swordbill's is the longest – it is almost the length of the bird's body.*

swob. Variant of **swab.**

swol·len (swōlən). Past participle of **swell.**
~*adj.* Enlarged; distended.

swol·len-head·ed (swōlən-héddid) *adj.* Also *U.S.* **swelled-head·ed** (swéld-). Having an excessively high opinion of oneself; conceited.

swoon (swoon) *intr.v.* **swooned, swooning, swoons. 1.** To faint. **2.** To become rapturous or ecstatic.
~*n.* A fainting spell. [Middle English *swowenen, swounen,* probably back-formation from *swowening, swouning,* a gerund formed from *iswowen,* in a swoon, from Old English *geswōgen,* past participle of *swōgan†* (attested only in compounds), to suffocate, choke.]

swoop (swoop) *v.* **swooped, swooping, swoops.** —*intr.* To make a sudden sweeping, pouncing movement, like a bird descending upon its prey. —*tr.* To take or snatch suddenly. Often used with *up.* —*n.* A swift, sudden descent. —**at** or **in one fell swoop.** With one sudden action; all in one go. [Middle English *swopen,* to sweep along, Old English *swāpan,* to swing, sweep, drive.]

swoosh (swoosh, swōōsh) *n.* A low, swishing, hissing sound.
~*v.* **swooshed, swooshing, swooshes.** —*intr.* To make such a sound, especially by moving. —*tr.* To cause to make or move with such a sound. [Imitative.]

swop. Variant of **swap.**

sword (sord ‖ sôrd) *n.* **1.** A weapon having a handle and a long blade for cutting or thrusting, often worn ceremonially as a symbol of power or authority. **2.** Any instrument of death, combat, or destruction. **3.** Something that resembles a sword. **4. a.** The use of force, as in war. **b.** Military power or jurisdiction. Preceded by *the.* —**cross swords. 1.** To fight. **2.** To quarrel violently. —**put to the sword.** To kill, especially with a sword. [Middle English *sw(e)ord, swerd,* Old English *sw(e)ord.*]

sword arm *n.* **1.** The arm used to hold a sword. **2.** The right arm.

sword bayonet *n.* A long bayonet resembling and capable of functioning as a sword.

sword·bear·er (sórd-bair-ər ‖ sôrd-) *n.* A person who carries the sword of a monarch or dignitary on ceremonial occasions.

sword·bill (sórd-bil ‖ sôrd-) *n.* A hummingbird, *Ensifera ensifera,* of tropical South America, having a very long, slender bill.

sword cane *n.* A swordstick.

sword dance *n.* A dance performed with swords, especially one performed around swords laid on the ground.

sword·fish (sórd-fish ‖ sôrd-) *n., pl.* **-fishes** or collectively **sword·fish.** A large marine game and food fish, *Xiphias gladius,* having a long, swordlike extension of the upper jaw. Also called "broadbill".

sword grass *n.* Any of various grasses or grasslike plants having bladelike, pointed leaves.

sword·knot (sórd-not ‖ sôrd-) *n.* A decorative loop or tassel attached to the hilt of a sword.

sword lily *n.* A plant, the **gladiolus** *(see).* [Part translation of Latin *gladiolus,* small sword (referring to the sword-shaped leaves).]

Sword of Damocles *n.* An impending disaster or the permanent threat of it. See **Damocles.**

sword·play (sórd-play ‖ sôrd-) *n.* The action or art of using a sword; fencing. —**sword·play·er** *n.*

swords·man (sórdz-mən ‖ sôrdz-) *n., pl.* **-men** (-mən). **1.** A person skilled in the use of the sword. **2.** A person armed with a sword. —**swords·man·ship** *n.*

sword·stick (sórd-stik ‖ sôrd-) *n.* A cane or light walking stick designed to conceal a sword in its hollow shaft. Also called "swordcane".

sword·tail (sórd-tayl ‖ sôrd-) *n.* A small, brightly coloured freshwater fish, *Xiphophorus helleri,* of Central America, that has a long, tapering extension of the tail fin in the male.

swore. Past tense of **swear.**

sworn. Past participle of **swear.**

swot¹ (swot) *v.* **swotted, swotting, swots.** *British.* —*intr.* To study very hard and diligently; cram. —*tr.* To study (a subject) diligently; work hard at. Usually used with *up.*
~*n.* **1.** A person who studies diligently or too diligently. **2.** A difficult academic subject; a subject that needs hard work. **3.** Diligent study. [Dialect variant of SWEAT.]

swot². Variant of **swat.**

swounds, swouns. Variants of **zounds.**

swum. Past participle and *archaic* past tense of **swim.**

swung. Past tense and past participle of **swing.**

swung dash *n.* A curved dash (~) used, for example, to indicate the omission of a word or part of a word, or, in symbolic logic, as the sign for negation. In this dictionary it is used to represent a headword before a second or subsequent part of speech label.

Sy. Surrey.

Syb·a·ris (sĭbbəriss). Ancient Greek colony. It lay near the site of the modern town of Terranova di Sibari in northern Calabria. In the sixth century Sybaris controlled trade with the Etruscans. Its consequent wealth earned the Sybarites a reputation for pleasure-seeking luxury.

syb·a·rite (sĭbbə-rīt) *n.* Also *capital* **S.** A person devoted to pleasure and luxury; a voluptuary. [Latin *Sybarita,* native of Sybaris, from Greek *Subarités,* from *Subaris,* SYBARIS.] —**syb·a·rit·ic** (-rĭttik), **syb·a·rit·i·cal** *adj.* —**syb·a·rit·i·cal·ly** *adv.*

syc·a·mine (sĭckə-mīn, -min) *n.* A tree mentioned in the New Testament, thought to be a species of mulberry. Luke 17:6. [Latin *sȳcamīnus,* from Greek *sukaminos,* from Phoenician or Aramaic *shiqmīn* (plural), akin to Hebrew *shiqmīn,* plural of *shiqmāh,* mulberry tree. See also **sycamore.**]

SWITZERLAND

8°E • GERMAN FEDERAL REPUBLIC • 10°E

Schaffhausen • Bodensee (L. Constance) • Rhine • Winterthur • St Gallen • Basel (Basle) • Zürich • L. Zürich • Aare • LIECHTENSTEIN VADUZ A U S T R I A • Zug • SCHWYZ • Naaf-Kopf 2574m • FRANCE • J U R A • M T S • Reuss • Luzern (Lucerne) • UNTER-WALDEN URI • L. Lucerne • Chur • Neuchâtel BERN (Berne) • Mitteland • S W I T Z E R L A N D • G R A U B Ü N D E N • Inn • L. Neuchâtel Fribourg • Interlaken • L.Thun • Bernese Oberland • Grindelwald • St. Gotthard Pass • P • Lepontine Alps • Albula • Alps • St Moritz • VAUD • Jungfrau 4158m • Aletsch Glacier • V A L A I S • Lausanne • Montreux • Simplon Pass • T I C I N O • L. Léman (L. Geneva) • Rhone • Locarno • Geneva • Dent du Midi • Martigny • Pennine Alps • Zermatt • Ticino • I T A L Y • 46°N • Matterhorn 4477m • Monte Rosa 4634m. • Km 0 20 40 60 80 • Miles 0 20 40 60

sword

DEADLY CUT AND THRUST

Empires were built by the sword

The sword developed as a weapon from the spear, and for centuries it was the major instrument of warfare. It added a cutting action to the deadly thrust of the spear. From the Bronze Age (*c.* 3000 B.C.) onwards, the skill of the metal-worker reached its peak in the making of sword blades, which had to be flexible, strong, and able to take an edge. Precise combinations of copper and tin repeatedly doubled over and hammered together could meet these requirements and so, later, could iron when heated then plunged into cold water to become an even harder metal – steel.

From its discovery in the Middle East about 1000 B.C. until the 19th century, steel was used almost exclusively for making swords or knives, and empires depended on it. Some swords, such as the curved Greek falchion and the sword used by the Japanese Samurai, were purely slashing weapons of steel, strong enough to kill a man in one blow. The Roman Empire was built on the *gladius*, the short, double-edged cutting and thrusting weapon of the legions. Medieval Europe preferred a long, straight, double-edged weapon. From about the 16th century, as the use of armour declined, the lighter, pointed rapier, intended mainly for thrusting, was developed.

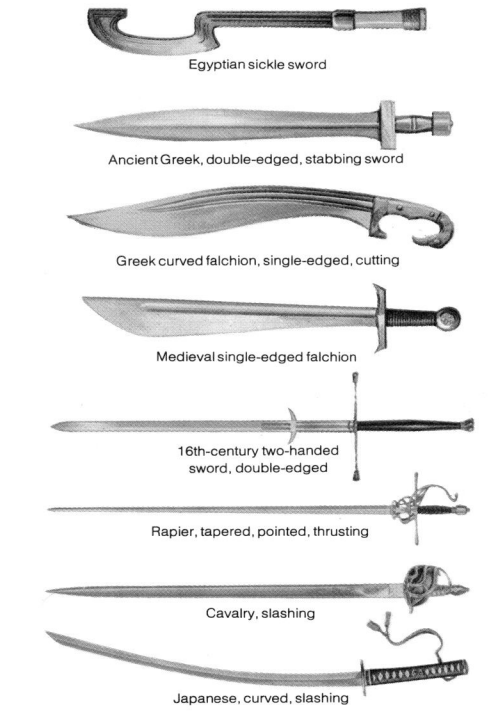

Egyptian sickle sword

Ancient Greek, double-edged, stabbing sword

Greek curved falchion, single-edged, cutting

Medieval single-edged falchion

16th-century two-handed sword, double-edged

Rapier, tapered, pointed, thrusting

Cavalry, slashing

Japanese, curved, slashing

syc·a·more (sícka-mawr ‖ -mōr) *n.* **1.** A Eurasian maple tree, *Acer pseudoplatanus,* having five-lobed leaves and winged fruits. **2.** A plane tree, *Platanus occidentalis,* of eastern North America. **3.** A tree, *Ficus sycomorus,* of northeastern Africa and adjacent Asia, related to the fig. This species is the sycamore of the Bible. [Middle English *sicamour,* from Old French *sicamor,* from Latin *sycomorus,* from Greek *sukamoros* : *suka-,* probably from Hebrew *shiqmāh,* mulberry tree (see **sycamine**) + *moron,* mulberry tree.]

syce, **sice** (sīss) *n.* A stableman or groom, especially formerly in India. [Hindi *sā'is,* from Arabic *sā'is,* from *sāsa,* to administer.]

sy·cee (sī-sée, -see) *n.* Lumps of pure silver bearing the stamp of a banker or assayer and formerly used in China as money. Also called "sycee silver". [Cantonese *sai si,* "fine silk" (so called because the pure silver can be spun into fine threads), corresponding to Mandarin Chinese *xi sī* : *xi,* thin, fine + *sī,* silk, thread.]

sy·co·ni·um (sī-kṓni-əm) *n., pl.* **-nia** (-ə). Also **sy·co·nus** (-kṓnəss). The fleshy multiple fruit of the fig, consisting primarily of the enlarged floral receptacle. [New Latin, from Greek *sukon,* the fig, probably from the same Mediterranean source as Latin *ficus,* FIG.]

syc·o·phan·cy (sícka-fən-si, *also* sī́kə-, -fan-) *n., pl.* **-cies.** The act, practice, or behaviour of a sycophant; servile flattery.

syc·o·phant (sícka-fənt, *also* sī́kə-, -fant) *n.* One who attempts to

win favour or advancement by flattering persons of influence; a servile self-seeker. [Latin *sycophanta,* from Greek *sukophantēs,* "fig-shower", "accuser" (from the use of the gesture of the fig in denouncing a criminal), hence an informer, flatterer : *sukon,* fig (see **syconium**) + *-phantēs,* shower, from *phainein,* to show.] —**syc·o·phan·tic** (-fántik), **syc·o·phan·ti·cal** *adj.* —**syc·o·phan·ti·cal·ly** *adv.*
　　Synonyms: *sycophant, toady, crawler, flatterer.*

sy·co·sis (sī-kṓ-siss) *n.* A chronic inflammation of the hair follicles, especially of the beard and scalp, caused by bacterial infection. [New Latin, from Greek *sukōsis,* eruption resembling a fig : *sukon,* fig (see **syconium**) + -OSIS.]

Syd·ney (síd-ni). The largest city in Australia, and capital of New South Wales. It surrounds Port Jackson or Sydney Harbour, an inlet on the southeast coast. Sydney is the centre of the nation's trade and finance. Its many beaches are popular tourist resorts. Other attractions include the Sydney Harbour Bridge (1932) and Sydney Opera House (1973). Sydney was developed by convict labour, and rapidly expanded in the late 19th century. Today it is one of the leading cultural centres in the southern hemisphere.

Syene. See **Aswan.**

sy·e·nite (sī́-ə-nīt) *n.* An igneous rock composed primarily of alkali feldspar together with other minerals, such as hornblende. [Latin *Syēnītēs (lapis),* "(stone) of Syene" (where it was first quarried), from Greek *Syēnē,* Syene, from Greek *Suēnē.*] —**sy·e·nit·ic** (-níttik) *adj.*

syl., syll. 1. syllable. **2.** syllabus.

syl·la·bar·y (sílla-bəri ‖ -berri) *n., pl.* **-ies.** A list of syllables; especially, a list or set of written characters, each one representing a syllable. [New Latin *syllabārium,* from Latin *syllaba,* SYLLABLE.]

syl·lab·ic (si-lábbik) *adj.* **1.** Of, pertaining to, or consisting of a syllable or syllables. **2.** Designating a consonant that forms a syllable without a vowel, as does the *l* in *riddle* (ríddl). **3.** Pronouncing every syllable distinctly: *a syllabic reading of a line of poetry.* **4.** Designating a form of verse based on the number of syllables per line rather than on the arrangement of accents or quantities. ~*n.* A syllabic sound. [Medieval Latin *syllabicus,* from Greek *sullabikos,* from *sullabē,* SYLLABLE.] —**syl·lab·i·cal·ly** *adv.*

syl·lab·i·fy (si-lábbi-fī) *tr.v.* **-fied, -fying, -fies.** Also *U.S.* **syl·lab·i·cate** (-kayt), **-cated, -cating, -cates.** To form or divide into syllables. —**syl·lab·i·fi·ca·tion** (-fi-káysh'n), **syl·lab·i·ca·tion** *n.*

syl·la·bise, syl·la·bize (sílla-bīz) *tr.v.* **-bised, -bising, -bises.** To syllabify. [Greek *sullabizein,* from *sullabē,* SYLLABLE.]

syl·la·bism (sílləbiz'm) *n.* **1.** The use of written characters that represent syllables. **2.** Division into syllables. [See **syllabise.**]

syl·la·ble (sílləb'l) *n. Abbr.* **syl., syll. 1.** A unit of spoken language consisting of a vowel or diphthong alone, of a syllabic consonant alone, or of either with one or more consonants. *Of, spoken,* and *consisting* have, respectively, one, two, and three syllables. **2.** One or more letters or phonetic symbols written or printed to approximate a spoken syllable. **3.** The slightest bit or expression. ~*tr.v.* **syllabled, -bling, -bles.** To pronounce (a line of verse, for example) in syllables. [Middle English *sillable,* from Old French *sillabe,* from Latin *syllaba,* from Greek *sullabē,* "a gathering (of letters)", from *sullambanein,* to gather together, spell together : *sun-,* together + *lambanein,* to take, grasp.]

syl·la·bub, sil·la·bub (sílla-bub) *n.* **1.** A cold dessert made with sweetened, thickened cream and wine, spirits, or fruit juice. **2.** A drink consisting of wine or spirits mixed with sweetened milk or cream. [16th Century : origin obscure.]

syl·la·bus (sílla-bəss) *n., pl.* **-buses** or **-bi** (-bī). *Abbr.* **syl., syll. 1.** An outline or brief statement of the main points of a text, lecture, or course of study. **2.** *British.* **a.** The topics or subjects to be studied for a particular course, which usually leads to examination. **b.** A list of these, detailing the course requirements. [Medieval Latin, list, from Greek *sullabus,* a misreading (in Cicero's *Letters to Atticus*) of *silluba,* earlier *sittuba†,* book title, label, table of contents.]

syl·lep·sis (si-léep-siss, -lép-) *n., pl.* **-ses** (-seez). *Grammar.* A construction in which one word seems to be in the same semantic relation to two or more other words but in fact is not; a zeugma. An example is: *She lost her coat and her temper.* [Latin, from Greek *sullēpsis,* "a taking together" : *sun-,* together + *lēpsis,* a taking, from *lambanein* (past participle *lēptos*), to take.] —**syl·lep·tic** (-léptik) *adj.*

syl·lo·gise, syl·lo·gize (sílla-jīz) *v.* **-gised, -gising, -gises.** —*intr.* To reason or argue by means of syllogisms. —*tr.* To deduce by syllogism. —**syl·lo·gi·sa·tion** (-jī-záysh'n) *n.* —**syl·lo·gis·er** *n.*

syl·lo·gism (sílla-jíz'm) *n.* **1.** *Logic.* A form of deductive reasoning consisting of a major premise, a minor premise, and a conclusion; for example, *All men are foolish* (major premise); *Smith is a man* (minor premise); *therefore, Smith is foolish* (conclusion). **2.** Reasoning from the general to the specific; deduction. **3.** A subtle or specious piece of reasoning. [Middle English *silogisme,* from Old French *syllogismus,* from Greek *sullogismos,* from *sullogizesthai,* to reckon together, infer : *sun-,* together + *logizesthai,* to reckon, reason, from *logos,* word, computation.]

syl·lo·gist (sílla-jist) *n.* A person who uses or is skilled in syllogistic reasoning.

syl·lo·gis·tic (sílla-jístik) *adj.* Also **syl·lo·gis·ti·cal** (-'l). Of, pertaining to, resembling, or consisting of a syllogism or syllogisms. ~*n.* Also **syl·lo·gis·tics** (-jístiks) (*used with a singular verb*). **1.** The branch of logic dealing with syllogisms. **2.** The art of reasoning by syllogism. —**syl·lo·gis·ti·cal·ly** *adv.*

sylph (silf) *n.* **1.** Any of a class of fairy-like beings without souls that were believed to inhabit the air. **2.** A slim, graceful woman or girl.

sycamore *Each seed of the European sycamore,* Acer pseudoplatanus *(above), is attached to a propeller-like vane, enabling it to whirl some distance from its parent tree before it falls to the ground.*

[New Latin *sylphus,* probably coined by Paracelsus by contracting Latin *sylvestris nympha,* nymph of the woods : *sylvestris,* from *sylva,* forest (see **sylvan**) + *nympha,* NYMPH.]

sylph·id (sílfid) *n.* A young or diminutive sylph.
~*adj.* Pertaining to or resembling a sylph. [French *sylphide,* from *sylphe,* sylph, from New Latin *sylphus,* SYLPH.]

syl·va, sil·va (sílvə) *n.* **1.** The trees or forests of a region. **2.** A written work on such trees or forests. [Latin, forest. See **sylvan.**]

syl·van, sil·van (sílvən) *adj.* **1.** Pertaining to or characteristic of woods or forest regions. **2.** Situated in or inhabiting a wood or forest. **3.** Abounding in trees; wooded. —See Synonyms at **rural.**
~*n.* One that lives in or frequents the woods. [Medieval Latin *silvānus,* from Latin *silva, sylva*†, forest.]

syl·van·ite (sílvə-nīt) *n.* A pale brass-yellow to silver-white gold and silver ore, chiefly (Au, Ag)Te_2. [French; found in TRANSYLVANIA.]

syl·va·tic (sil-váttik) *adj.* Growing or occurring in a wood. [Latin *silva,* forest + -ATIC.]

sylviculture. Variant of **silviculture.**

syl·vite (síl-vīt) *n.* Also **syl·vin** (-vin), **syl·vine** (-vīn, -vin), **syl·vin·ite** (-vin-īt). A colourless vitreous potassium chloride mineral, a major source of potassium compounds. [French, from *sylvine,* from New Latin *(sal digestivus) Sylvii,* "(digestive salt) of Sylvius", probably after Franz de la Boë *Sylvius* (1614–72), Dutch physician.]

sym–. Variant of **syn-,** used before the letters *b, m,* and *p.*

sym. 1. symbol. **2.** symphony.

sym·bi·ont (sím-bi-ont, -bī-) *n.* Also **sym·bi·ote** (-ōt). Any of the organisms in a symbiotic relationship. [Greek *sumbiōn,* present participle of *sumbioun,* to live together. See **symbiosis.**]

sym·bi·ō·sis (sím-bi-ṓ-siss, -bī-) *n. Biology.* Any relationship between two or more different organisms in close association, especially one that is of benefit to all the organisms involved. See **mutualism.** [New Latin, from Greek *sumbiōsis,* a living together, from *sumbioun,* to live together : *sun-,* together + *bios,* life.] **—sym·bi·ot·ic** (-óttik), **sym·bi·ot·i·cal** *adj.* **—sym·bi·ot·i·cal·ly** *adv.*

sym·bol (símb'l) *n. Abbr.* **sym. 1.** Something that represents or stands for, or is thought to typify, something else by association, resemblance, or convention; especially, a material object used to represent something invisible such as an idea: *the dove is a symbol of peace.* **2.** A printed or written sign used to represent an operation, element, quantity, quality, or relation, as in mathematics or music: *"Au" is the symbol for gold; "+" is the symbol for addition.*
~*tr.v.* **symbolled** or *U.S.* **symboled, -bolling** or *U.S.* **-boling, -bols.** To symbolise. [Latin *symbolum,* sign, token, from Greek *sumbolon,* token for identification (by comparing with its counterpart), from *sumballein,* to compare : *sun-,* together + *ballein,* to throw.]

sym·bol·ic (sim-bóllik) *adj.* Also **sym·bol·i·cal** (-'l). **1.** Of, pertaining to, or expressed by means of a symbol or symbols. **2.** Serving as a symbol. **3.** Characterised by the use of symbolism, as a work of art may be. **—sym·bol·i·cal·ly** *adv.* **—sym·bol·i·cal·ness** *n.*

symbolic logic *n.* A treatment of formal logic in which a calculus or rule-governed system of symbols is used to represent terms, propositons, and relationships. Also called "mathematical logic".

sym·bol·ise, sym·bol·ize (símb'l-īz) *v.* **-ised, ising, ises.** —*tr.* **1.** To be or serve as a symbol of. **2.** To represent or identify by a symbol or symbols. —*intr.* To use symbols. **—sym·bol·i·sa·tion** (-ī-záysh'n || *U.S.* -i-) *n.*

sym·bol·ism (símb'l-iz'm) *n.* **1.** The practice of representing things by means of symbols or of attributing symbolic meanings or significance to objects, events, or relationships. **2.** A system of symbols or representations. **3.** A symbolic meaning or representation. **4.** *Capital* **S.** The theory or the practice of the Symbolists.

sym·bol·ist (símb'l-ist) *n.* **1.** A person who uses symbols or symbolism. **2. a.** One who interprets or represents conditions or truths by the use of symbolism. **b.** *Capital* **S.** Any of a group of artists and poets, chiefly French, of the late 19th century who expressed their ideas and emotions indirectly through symbols. **—sym·bo·list, sym·bol·is·tic** (-ístik), **sym·bol·is·ti·cal** *adj.*

sym·bol·o·gy (sim-bólləji) *n.* **1.** The study or interpretation of symbols or symbolism. **2.** The use of symbols. **—sym·bo·log·i·cal** (símbə-lójik'l) *adj.* **—sym·bol·o·gist** (sim-bólləjist) *n.*

sym·met·al·lism (sím-métt'l-iz'm, si-) *n.* Also *chiefly U.S.* **sym·met·al·ism.** A system of coinage in which a unit of currency consists of a combination of two or more metals in fixed proportions. [SYM- + METAL + -ISM.]

sym·met·ri·cal *adj.* **1.** Of, pertaining to, or showing symmetry. **2.** *Botany.* Actinomorphic. **3.** *Logic & Mathematics.* Of, pertaining to, or designating something, such as a function or proposition, that remains unchanged for all permutations of its constituent parts. **4.** *Chemistry.* Having repetitive, similar faces. Said of a crystal. **—sym·met·ri·cal·ly** *adv.* **—sym·met·ri·cal·ness** *n.*

sym·me·trise, sym·me·trize (símmə-trīz, símme-, símmi-) *tr.v.* **-trised, -trising, -trises.** To make symmetrical; impart perfect balance to. **—sym·me·tri·sa·tion** (-trī-záysh'n || U.S. -tri-) *n.*

sym·me·try (símmətri, símmitri) *n., pl.* **-tries. 1.** A relationship of characteristic correspondence, equivalence, or identity among constituents of a system or between different systems: *symmetry in political and religious activism.* **2.** Exact correspondence of form and constituent configuration on opposite sides of a dividing line or plane or about a centre or axis. **3.** Structural or functional independence of direction; isotropy. **4.** Beauty as a result of balance or harmonious arrangement. —See Synonyms at **proportion.** [Obsolete French *symmetrie,* from Latin *symmetria,* from Greek *summetria,* from *summetros,* "of like measure".]

sym·pa·thec·to·my (símpə-théktəmi) *n., pl.* **-mies.** The removal of a part of a sympathetic nerve or a number of sympathetic ganglia. [SYMPATH(ETIC) + -ECTOMY.]

sym·pa·thet·ic (símpə-théttik) *adj.* Also **sym·pa·thet·i·cal** (-'l). **1.** Of, expressing, feeling, or resulting from sympathy. **2.** In agreement; favourable; inclined. Used with *to* or *towards.* **3.** Agreeable; congenial: *sympathetic surroundings.* **4.** Pertaining to or acting on the sympathetic nervous system. **5.** Pertaining to or involving oscillation produced by a nearby oscillating system at the same frequency. Said, for example, of vibrations of strings in certain musical instruments. [New Latin *sympatheticus,* from Greek *sumpathētikos,* from *sumpatheia,* SYMPATHY.] **—sym·pa·thet·i·cal·ly** *adv.*

sympathetic ink *n.* **Invisible ink** *(see).*

sympathetic magic *n.* Magic that seeks to achieve an effect at a distance as by means of an associated or symbolic object, such as a doll that is supposed to represent a person.

sympathetic nervous system *n.* A portion of the **autonomic nervous system** *(see).*

sym·pa·thin (símpəthin) *n.* A substance released at sympathetic nerve endings and involved in the transmission of impulses, now known to be adrenaline or noradrenaline. [SYMPATH(ETIC) + -IN.]

sym·pa·thise, sym·pa·thize (símpə-thīz) *intr.v.* **-thised, -thising, -thises. 1.** To feel or express compassion; commiserate. Used with *with.* **2.** To share or understand another's feelings or ideas. Used with *with.* **—sym·pa·this·er** *n.* **—sym·pa·this·ing·ly** *adv.*

sym·pa·tho·lyt·ic (símpə-thō-líttik) *adj.* Of or pertaining to an agent that opposes the activity of the sympathetic nervous system.
~*n.* A sympatholytic agent. [SYMPATH(ETIC) + -LYTIC.]

sym·pa·tho·mi·met·ic (símpə-thō-mī-méttik) *adj. Medicine.* Of or pertaining to an agent that stimulates the sympathetic nervous system.
~*n.* A sympathomimetic agent. [SYMPATH(ETIC) + MIMETIC.]

sym·pa·thy (símpəthi) *n., pl.* **-thies. 1. a.** The act of or capacity for sharing or understanding the feelings of another person. **b.** A feeling or expression of pity or sorrow for the distress of another; commiseration. **2. a.** A relationship or affinity between persons or things in which whatever affects one correspondingly affects the other. **b.** Mutual understanding or affection arising from this. **3.** Favour; agreement; accord: *She is in sympathy with my beliefs.* **4.** A feeling of loyalty; allegiance. **5.** *Physiology.* The mutual influence of different parts of the body on each other. —See Synonyms at **pity.** [Latin *sympathīa,* from Greek *sumpatheia,* from *sumpathēs,* affected by like feelings : *sun-,* like + *pathos,* emotion, feelings.]

sympathy strike *n.* A strike by a body of workers for the purpose of supporting a cause or another group of strikers.

sym·pat·ric (sim-páttrik) *adj. Ecology.* Occupying or occurring in the same or overlapping geographical areas. Said of populations of closely related species. Compare **allopatric.** [SYN- + Greek *patra, patrē,* fatherland, from *patēr,* father.] **—sym·pat·ri·cal·ly** *adv.*

sym·pet·al·ous (sim-pétt'l-əss) *adj. Botany.* **Gamopetalous** *(see).*

sym·phon·ic (sim-fónnik) *adj.* **1.** Pertaining to or having the character or form of a symphony. **2.** Harmonious in sound.

symphonic poem *n.* A musical composition for symphony orchestra, based on an extramusical theme such as a folk tale, usually consisting of a single, extended movement and typical chiefly of the late 19th century. Also called "tone poem".

sym·pho·ni·ous (sim-fṓni-əss) *adj.* In accord; harmonious. **—sym·pho·ni·ous·ly** *adv.*

sym·pho·nist (símfə-nist) *n.* One who composes symphonies.

sym·pho·ny (símfəni) *n., pl.* **-nies. 1.** *Abbr.* **sym.** *Music.* A usually long sonata for orchestra, typically consisting of four related movements. **2. a.** An instrumental passage in a vocal or choral composition. **b.** An instrumental overture or interlude, as in early opera. **3.** Harmony, especially of sound or colour. **4.** Anything characterised by a harmonious combination of elements. [Middle English *symphonie,* harmony of sound, from Old French, from Latin *symphōnia,* from Greek *sumphōnia,* from *sumphōnos,* harmonious : *sun-,* together + *phōnē,* voice, sound.]

symphony orchestra *n.* A large orchestra composed of string, woodwind, brass, and percussion sections, designed for playing symphonic works.

sym·phy·sis (símfi-siss) *n., pl.* **-ses** (-seez). **1.** *Anatomy.* **a.** A type of joint in which the bones are united by fibrocartilage, as between the vertebrae of the backbone. **b.** The line marking such a joint. **2.** The coalescence of similar parts or organs. [New Latin, from Greek *sumphusis,* a growing together (especially of bones), from *sumphuein,* to cause to unite : *sun-,* together + *phuein,* to make grow.] **—sym·phy·se·al, sym·phy·si·al** (-sée-əl, sim-fízzi-əl) *adj.*

sym·po·di·um (sim-pṓdi-əm) *n., pl.* **-dia** (-ə). *Botany.* A primary axis that develops from a series of short lateral branches and has a zigzag or irregular form, as in a cymose inflorescence. Also called "pseudaxis". Compare **monopodium.** [New Latin : SYN- + Greek *podion,* small foot, base, from *pous* (stem *pod-*), foot.] **—sym·po·di·al** *adj.* **—sym·po·di·al·ly** *adv.*

sym·po·si·ac (sim-pṓzi-ak, -pózzi-) *adj.* Of, of the nature of, appropriate to, or occurring at a symposium.
~*n. Archaic.* A meeting or conference; a symposium.

sym·po·si·arch (sim-pṓzi-aark, -pózzi-) *n.* **1.** The master or director of an ancient Greek symposium. **2.** A toastmaster. [Greek *sumposiarkhos, sumposiarkhēs* : *sumposion,* SYMPOSIUM + -ARCH.]

sym·po·si·um (sim-pṓzi-əm, -pózzi-) *n., pl.* **-siums** or **-sia** (-ə). **1.** A meeting or conference for discussion of some topic. **2.** A collection of writings on a particular topic, as in a magazine or other periodi-

PRONUNCIATION KEY

a, trap; aa, father; ai, fair; ar, star; aw, lawn; ay, play; b, bb, stab; rubber; ch, church; ck, ticket; d, dd, dead; ladder; e, dress; ee, bee; er, defer; ew, few; ewr, pure; ə, about; ər, letter; f, ff, fife; differ; g, gg, giggle; h, hat; i, kit; ī, price; īr, fire; j, judge; k, kick; l, ll, let; 'l, needle; m, mm, man; n, nn, no; 'n, sudden; ng, thing; o, lot; ō, no; ŏŏ, foot; ōō, shoe; oor, poor; ow, cow; owr, hour; oy, boy; p, pp, pepper; r, rr, red; s, ss, sauce; sh, ship; t, tt, totter; th, thick; th, this; smooth; u, cut; ur, turn; v, vv, valve; w, wet; y, yes; z, zz, zebra; zh, vision; pleasure

IN FOREIGN WORDS:

aN, oN, Saint-Saëns; hl, Llanelli; Hluhluwe; kh, loch; lough; Khaled

STRESS MARK:

ín-sīt, insight; in-sī́t, incite

cal. **3.** A convivial meeting among the ancient Greeks for drinking, music, and intellectual discussion. [Latin, from Greek *symposion*, drinking party : *sun-*, together + *posis*, drink.]

symp·tom (símp-təm, sím-) *n.* **1.** Any circumstance or phenomenon regarded as an indication or characteristic of a condition or event. **2.** *Medicine.* Any phenomenon experienced by an individual as a departure from normal function, sensation, or appearance, generally indicating disorder or disease. —See Synonyms at **sign.** [Greek *symptōma*, occurrence, phenomenon, from *sumpiptein*, to fall together, fall upon, happen : *sun-*, together + *piptein*, to fall.] —**symp·to·mat·ic** (-áttik) *adj.* —**symp·to·mat·i·cal·ly** *adv.*

symp·tom·a·tol·o·gy (símp-təmə-tólləji, sím-) *n.* **1.** The medical science of disease symptoms. Also called "semiology". **2.** The complex of symptoms of a disease. [New Latin *symptomatologia* : Greek *sumptōma* (stem *sumptōmat-*), SYMPTOM + -LOGY.]

syn-, sym- *prefix.* Indicates: **1.** Together or with; for example, **syndactyl, symmetalism. 2.** Same, alike, similar, or at the same time; for example, **sympatric. 3.** Union or fusion; for example, **sympetalous, syncarp.** [Greek *sun-*, from *sun*, together, with. In Greek compounds, *sun-* becomes *sum-* before *b, m, p; sul-* before *l; su-* before *s* and *z*; borrowed as *sym-, syl-*, and *sy-* respectively.]

syn. synonym; synonymous; synonymy.

syn·ae·re·sis (si-néer-ə-siss, -i- ‖ *U.S. also* -nérrə-) *n., pl.* **-ses** (-seez). Also *U.S.* **syn·er·e·sis** (for sense 1). **1.** The drawing together of two consecutive vowels, ordinarily pronounced separately, into a diphthong or simple vowel, as when *doest* (dōō-ist) contracts to *dost* (dust). Compare **diaeresis, synizesis. 2. Syneresis** *(see).* [Late Latin, from Greek *sunairesis*, a drawing together, from *sunairein* : *sun-*, SYN- + *hairein*, to take.]

syn·aes·the·sia, *U.S.* **syn·es·the·sia** (sín-eess-théez-yə, -théezh-yə, -théezhə ‖ -iss-) *n.* **1.** The experiencing of a sensation in one part of the body resulting from the stimulation of a different part. **2.** The sensation of a sense other than the sense being stimulated, as when a sound invokes a sensation of colour. [New Latin : SYN- + (AN)-AESTHESIA.] —**syn·aes·thet·ic** (-théttik) *adj.*

syn·a·gogue (sínnə-gog) *n.* **1.** A building or place of meeting for Jewish worship and religious instruction. **2.** A congregation of Jews for worship or religious study. **3.** The Jewish religion as organised or typified in such local congregations. Preceded by *the.* [Middle English *synagoge*, from Old French, from Latin *synagōga*, from Greek *sunagōgē*, assembly, from *sunagein*, to bring together : *sun-*, together + *agein*, to lead, drive.] —**syn·a·gog·al** (-gŏg'l, -gógg'l), **syn·a·gog·i·cal** (-gójik'l) *adj.*

syn·a·loe·pha, syn·a·le·pha (sínnə-léefə) *n.* The blending of two adjacent syllables into one syllable, especially of two successive vowels of adjacent syllables; for example, *th' elite* for *the elite.* [New Latin, from Greek *sunal(o)iphē*, from *sunaleiphein*, to smear or melt together, unite two syllables : *sun-*, together + *aleiphein*, to anoint.]

syn·apse (sín-aps ‖ *U.S.* sín-, si-náps) *n.* Also **synapsis.** The point at which a nerve impulse passes from an axon of one neurone to the dendrite of another. [New Latin *synapsis*, from Greek *sunapsis*, point of contact, from *sunaptein*, to join together : *sun-*, together + *haptein†*, to fasten, connect.]

syn·ap·sid (sin-ápsid) *n.* A reptile of the subclass Synapsida which existed during the Upper Carboniferous Permian and Triassic periods, having a single pair of lateral temporal openings in the skull.

syn·ap·sis (si-náp-siss) *n., pl.* **-ses** (-seez). **1.** *Biology.* The fusion of homologous chromosome pairs during meiosis. **2.** Variant of **synapse.** [New Latin. See **synapse.**]

syn·ap·tic (sin-áptik) *adj.* Pertaining to a synapse or synapsis.

syn·ar·thro·sis (sínnaar-thrő-siss) *n., pl.* **-ses** (-seez). Also **syn·ar·thro·di·a** (-di-ə) *pl.* **-diae** (-di-ee). *Anatomy.* Any of several forms of bone articulation in which the bones are rigidly joined without an intervening cavity. [New Latin, from Greek *sunarthrōsis* : *sun-*, together + *arthrōsis*, articulation, from *arthron*, a joint.]

sync (singk) *n. Informal.* Synchronisation: *The sound is out of sync.* ~*v.* **synced** (singkt), **syncing** (síngking), **syncs.** *Informal.* —*intr.* To synchronise. —*tr.* To synchronise (something) with another.

syn·carp (síng-kaarp ‖ sín-) *n. Botany.* A fleshy fruit composed of the fruits of several flowers or several carpels of a single flower. [SYN- + -CARP.]

syn·car·pous (sin-kárpəss, sing-) *adj. Botany.* Having or consisting of united carpels. [SYN- + -CARPOUS.] —**syn·car·py** (síng-kaarpi, sín-) *n.*

syn·chon·dro·sis (síng-kon-drő-siss, sín-) *n.* A slightly movable joint in which the ends of the bones are separated by hyaline cartilage, such as occurs between the ribs and the breastbone in humans. [SYN- + Greek *khondros*, cartilage + -OSIS.]

syn·chro[1] (síng-krő ‖ sín-) *n., pl.* **-chros.** *Machinery.* A **Selsyn** *(see).* [Short for SYNCHRONOUS.]

synchro[2] *n. Informal.* Synchronised swimming.

synchro- *comb. form.* Indicates synchronisation; for example, **syn·chromesh.** [Shortened from SYNCHRONISE.]

syn·chro·cy·clo·tron (síng-krő-síklə-tron ‖ sín-) *n.* A proton and positive ion accelerator, the chief components and configuration of which are similar to those of a **cyclotron** *(see)* and in which the phase of the accelerating potential is synchronised with the frequency of the accelerated particles by frequency modulation to compensate for relativistic increases in particle mass at high speeds.

syn·chro·flash (síng-krő-flash, -krə- ‖ sín-) *n.* A device on a camera that synchronises the peak of a flash created by a flash bulb with the widest opening of the shutter. —**syn·chro·flash** *adj.*

syn·chro·mesh (síng-krő-mesh, -krə- ‖ sín-) *adj.* Designating a

HOUSE OF ASSEMBLY, PRAYER, AND STUDY
The focal point of Jewish religious and cultural life

The first synagogues – the Jewish houses of assembly, prayer, and study – seem to have come into being as early as the 6th century B.C., during the exile of the Jews in Babylon, as substitutes for the Temple in Jerusalem. The word synagogue is from the Greek *sunagoge*, "assembly". The synagogue became the focal point of Jewish religious and cultural life, and it has remained so ever since.

Although a synagogue is usually rectangular, with seats downstairs for men and a gallery for women, it can be built on any plan. It normally contains a screened niche for the *aron hakodesh*, the Holy Ark, or chest which holds the scroll of Jewish law; *ner tamid*, a light which is symbolic of the Eternal Light, is placed directly above the Ark. Most synagogues also have a *bema* – a raised platform or pulpit.

The religious life of a synagogue and its congregation is led by a lay rabbi (Hebrew for "my master"), who operates as a full-time minister. He is elected by a board of fellow laymen, his necessary qualification being his knowledge of Jewish law, faith, and practice. The synagogue is thus a democratic institution – and any group of Jews is free to establish one.

Three main synagogue associations now exist – the Orthodox, the Reform, and the Liberal.

ANCIENT SYMBOL *In the Book of Exodus, the Lord tells Moses to make a six-branched candlestick for the Tabernacle – the portable place of worship used on the journey to the Promised Land. Today there are such candlesticks in synagogues throughout the world.*

SET FOR A WEDDING *The red velvet canopy has been erected in this North London synagogue for a wedding. Behind the canopy is the niche containing the Ark, with the Eternal Light hanging above it.*

gearbox in a motor vehicle in which the gears are synchronised at the same speeds before engaging to effect a smooth change. ~*n.* A system of gears using this principle.

syn·chron·ic (sing-krónnik, sin-) *adj.* Also **syn·chron·i·cal** (-'l). **1.** Synchronous. **2. a.** Studying the events of a particular time or era without consideration of historical data. **b.** Pertaining to or designating the study of language and linguistic phenomena without reference to any historical perspective. Compare **diachronic.** —**syn·chron·i·cal·ly** *adv.*

syn·chro·nic·i·ty (síng-krə-níssəti, sín-, -kro-) *n.* Coincidence that is felt to be significant or meaningful; especially, in the philosophy of

C.G. Jung, the simultaneous occurrence of two or more events that seem to be linked in a meaningful or significant way without apparently being causally related, for example, the sudden stopping of a clock at the moment of a person's death in the same vicinity.

syn·chro·nise, syn·chro·nize (síng-krə-nīz || sín-) *v.* **-nised, -nising, -nises.** —*intr.* **1.** To occur at the same time; be or become simultaneous. **2.** To operate in unison. —*tr.* **1.** To cause to operate with exact coincidence in time or rate. **2.** To arrange (historical events) so as to indicate parallel existence or occurrence. **3. a.** To cause (sound effects or dialogue) to coincide with an action, in film-making. **b.** To make sounds and actions coincide in (a film). [From SYNCHRONOUS.] **—syn·chro·ni·sa·tion** (-nī-záysh'n) *n.*

synchronised swimming *n.* A rhythmic, dancelike form of swimming, synchronised to music. Also informally called "synchro".

syn·chro·nism (síng-krə-niz'm || sín-) *n.* **1.** The condition of being synchronised or synchronous. **2.** A chronological listing of historical personages or events so as to indicate parallel existence or occurrence. **3.** The representation in the same art work of two or more events that occurred at different times. **—syn·chro·nis·tic** (-nístik), **syn·chro·nis·ti·cal** *adj.* **—syn·chro·nis·ti·cal·ly** *adv.*

syn·chro·nous (síng-krənəss || sín-) *adj.* **1.** Occurring at the same time. **2.** Moving or operating at the same rate. **3. a.** Having identical periods. **b.** Having identical period and phase. —See Synonyms at **contemporary.** [Late Latin *synchronos,* from Greek *sunkhronos* : *sun-,* same + *khronos,* time (see **chronic**).] **—syn·chro·nous·ly** *adv.* **—syn·chro·nous·ness** *n.*

synchronous converter *n.* An electrical machine in which a double-wound armature is used to convert alternating current into direct current, or vice versa.

synchronous motor *n.* A motor having a speed directly proportional to the frequency of the electric current that operates it.

synchronous orbit *n.* An orbit having a period the same as the period of axial rotation of the Earth and so oriented that any body in it maintains a position over one point on the Earth's surface. Also called "stationary orbit".

synchronous rotation *n.* **Captured rotation** *(see).*

syn·chro·ny (síng-krəni || sín-) *n., pl.* **-nies.** A synchronous occurrence, movement, or arrangement. [From SYNCHRONOUS.]

syn·chro·scope (síng-krə-skōp) *n.* Also **syn·chron·o·scope** (sing-krónnə-, sin-). An instrument that indicates whether or not two periodic motions are synchronous. [SYNCHRO- + -SCOPE.]

syn·chro·tron (síng-krə-tron || sín-) *n.* An accelerator in which charged particles are accelerated around a fixed circular path by a radio-frequency potential and held to the path by a time-varying magnetic field. [SYNCHRO- + (ELEC)TRON.]

synchrotron radiation *n.* Electromagnetic radiation emitted by high-energy charged particles, such as electrons, spiralling along the lines of force produced by a strong magnetic field. The radiation is emitted at a tangent to the orbit of the particles and occurs in synchrotrons and in some astronomical systems, such as supernova remnants.

syn·clas·tic (sing-klástik, sin-) *adj.* Designating a surface whose curvature at a particular point in a particular direction has the same sign as the curvature, at that point, in a perpendicular direction; that is, it is convex or concave in both directions, as a sphere or rugby ball is. Compare **anticlastic.** [SYN- (alike) + Greek *klastos,* bent, from *klan,* to bend.]

syn·cli·nal (sing-klín'l, sin-) *adj.* **1.** Sloping downwards from opposite directions to meet in a common point or line. **2.** *Geology.* Pertaining to, formed by, or forming a syncline.
~*n.* A syncline. [SYN- + Greek *klinein,* to lean.]

syn·cline (síng-klīn || sín-) *n.* A low, troughlike area in bedrock, in which rocks incline together from opposite sides. [Back-formation from SYNCLINAL.]

syn·cli·nor·um (sing-klī-náwrəm) *n.* A large syncline, with minor upfolds and downfolds in its limbs.

syn·com (síng-kom || sín-) *n.* A communications satellite in a synchronous orbit. [*Syn*chronous + *com*munication.]

syn·co·pate (síng-kə-payt) *tr.v.* **-pated, -pating, -pates. 1.** *Grammar.* **a.** To shorten (a word) by means of syncope. **b.** To drop (a letter or sound) from the spelling or pronunciation of a word. **2.** To modify (musical rhythm) by syncopation. [Medieval Latin *syncopāre,* from Late Latin *syncopē,* SYNCOPE.] **—syn·co·pa·tor** (-ər) *n.*

syn·co·pa·tion (síng-kə-páysh'n, -kō- || sín-) *n.* **1.** The act of syncopating or the condition of being syncopated. **2.** Something syncopated. **3.** *Music.* The displacement of an accent or accents in a bar to parts that are not normally accented, as when a normally weak beat is stressed. **4.** *Grammar.* Syncope.

syn·co·pe (síng-kəpi || sín-) *n.* **1.** *Grammar.* The shortening of a word by the omission of a sound, letter, or syllable from the middle of the word; for example, *bo's'n* for *boatswain.* **2.** *Pathology.* A brief loss of consciousness caused by a transient reduction of blood supply to the brain; a faint. [Late Latin, from Greek *sunkopē,* from *sunkoptein,* to chop up : *sun-,* together, thoroughly + *koptein,* to cut off.] **—syn·co·pal** (-kəp'l), **syn·cop·ic** (sing-kóppik, sin-) *adj.*

syn·cre·tise, syn·cre·tize (síng-kri-tīz, -krə- || sín-) *v.* **-tised, -tising, -tises.** —*tr.* To reconcile or attempt to reconcile (differing religious beliefs, for example). —*intr.* To combine differing beliefs. [New Latin *syncretizare,* from Greek *sunkrētizein.* See **syncretism.**]

syn·cre·tism (síng-kri-tiz'm, -krə- || sín-) *n.* **1.** The attempt or tendency to combine or reconcile differing beliefs, as in philosophy or religion. **2.** *Linguistics.* The diachronic fusion of two or more originally different inflectional forms into one. [New Latin *syncretismus,* from Greek *sunkrētismos,* union, from *sunkrētizein,* to unite (in the manner of the Cretan cities) against a common enemy : *sun-,* together + *Krēs* (stem *Krēt-*), CRETAN.] **—syn·cre·tist** *n.* **—syn·cret·ic** (-kréetik, -kréttik), **syn·cre·tis·tic** (-tístik) *adj.*

syn·cy·ti·um (sin-sítti-əm || *U.S.* -síshi-) *n., pl.* **-cytia** (-ə). *Biology.* A mass of protoplasm with many nuclei but no clear cell boundaries. [New Latin : SYN- + CYT(O)- + -IUM.] **—syn·cy·ti·al** *adj.*

synd. syndicate.

syn·dac·tyl, syn·dac·tyle (sin-dák-til, -tīl) *adj.* Also **syn·dac·ty·lous.** *Biology.* Having two or more wholly or partially fused digits.
~*n.* A syndactyl animal. [French *syndactyle* : SYN- + Greek *daktulos,* finger, DACTYL.] **—syn·dac·tyl·ism, syn·dac·ty·ly** (-dáktili) *n.*

syn·des·mo·sis (sín-dez-mṓ-siss) *n.* The articulation of bones by ligaments. [New Latin, from Greek *sundesmos,* ligament, from *sundein,* to bind. See **syndetic.**] **—syn·des·mot·ic** (-móttik) *adj.*

syn·det·ic (sin-déttik) *adj.* Also **syn·det·i·cal** (-'l). **1.** Serving to connect, as a conjunction does; copulative; conjunctive. **2.** Connected by a conjunction. [Greek *sundetikos,* from *sundetos,* bound together, from *sundein,* to bind together : *sun-,* together + *dein,* to bind.] **—syn·det·i·cal·ly** *adv.*

syn·dic (síndik) *n.* **1.** One appointed to represent a company, university, or other organisation in business transactions; a business agent. **2.** In various European countries, a civil magistrate or similar government official. [French, from Late Latin *syndicus,* from Greek *sundikos,* assistant in a court of justice, public advocate : *sun-,* with + *dikē,* judgment.] **—syn·di·cal** *adj.*

syn·di·cal·ism (síndik'l-iz'm) *n.* A radical political movement that advocates bringing industry and government under the control of trade unions, especially by the use of direct action such as general strikes and sabotage. [French *syndicalisme,* from *(chambre) syndicale,* trade union : *chambre,* chamber + *syndical,* of a trade union, from *syndic,* SYNDIC.] **—syn·di·cal·ist** *adj. & n.*

syn·di·cate (síndi-kət, -kit || -kayt) *n. Abbr.* **synd. 1. a.** An association of people or commercial firms organised to promote some common interest. **b.** An association of people formed to carry out a usually specified enterprise or activity: *a crime syndicate.* **2.** An agency that sells news articles and photographs for publication in a number of newspapers or periodicals simultaneously. **3.** The office, position, or jurisdiction of a syndic or body of syndics.
~*v.* (-kayt) **syndicated, -cating, -cates.** —*tr.* **1.** To organise into a syndicate. **2.** To sell (an article, for example) through a syndicate for publication. —*intr.* To organise a syndicate. [French *syndicat,* from *syndic,* SYNDIC.]

syn·di·o·tac·tic (síndi-ō-táktik, -ə-) *adj.* Designating a stereospecific polymer having alternating stereochemical configurations of the groups on successive carbon atoms in the chain. Compare **isotactic.** [Greek *sunduo,* two together + -TACTIC.]

syn·drome (sín-drōm, -drəm) *n.* **1.** A group of signs and symptoms that collectively indicate or characterise a disease, psychological disorder, or other abnormal condition. **2. a.** A set of signs or symptoms indicating the existence of an undesirable condition, problem, or quality. **b.** Loosely, such a condition, problem, or quality. [New Latin, from Greek *sundromē,* a running together, concurrence (of symptoms) : *sun-,* together + *dromos,* race, racecourse.] **—syn·drom·ic** (sin-drómmik) *adj.*

syne (sīn) *adv. Scottish.* Since. **—syne** *conj. & prep.*

syn·ec·do·che (si-nék-dəki) *n.* A figure of speech by which a more inclusive term is used for a less inclusive term or vice versa; for example, *the law* for *a policeman,* or *head* for *cattle.* [Latin, from Greek *sunekdokhē,* from *sunekdekhesthai,* "to take up (or understand) with another" : *sun-,* with + *ekdekhesthai,* to take from, take or understand in a certain sense : *ex,* out of + *dekhesthai,* to take, receive.] **—syn·ec·doch·ic** (sínnek-dóckik) *adj.*

synecious. Variant of **synoecious.**

syn·e·col·o·gy (sín-i-kólləji, -ee-) *n.* The study of the environmental interrelationships among communities of organisms. Compare **autecology.** [SYN- + ECOLOGY.] **—syn·e·co·log·ic** (-kə-lojik), **syn·e·co·log·i·cal** *adj.*

syn·er·e·sis (si-néer-ə-siss, -i-) *n., pl.* **-ses** (-seez). Also **syn·aer·e·sis** (for sense 1). **1.** *Chemistry.* Exudation of the liquid component of a gel. **2.** *U.S.* **Synaeresis** *(see).* [Late Latin *synaeresis,* from Greek *sunairesis,* from *sunairein,* to take or draw together, contract : *sun-,* together + *hairein,* to seize, take.]

syn·er·get·ic (sín-ər-jéttik, -er-) *adj.* Also **syn·er·gic** (si-nérjik). *Biology.* Of or pertaining to synergism.

syn·er·gid cell (si-nérjid) *n.* Either of two haploid cells situated close to the egg cell in the embryo sac of flowering plants. [Greek *sunergos,* working together (see **synergism**) + -ID.]

syn·er·gism (sín-ər-jiz'm, -er-, si-nér-) *n.* Also **syn·er·gy** (-ji) (for sense 1). **1.** *Biology.* The action of two or more substances, organs, or organisms to achieve an effect greater than the sum of their individual effects. **2.** *Theology.* The doctrine that individual salvation is effected by a combination of human will and divine grace. [New Latin *synergismus,* from Greek *sunergos,* working together : *sun-,* together + *ergon,* work.]

syn·er·gist (sín-ər-jist, -er-, si-nér-) *n.* **1.** *Biology.* A synergetic organ, drug, or substance. **2.** *Theology.* An adherent of synergism. **—syn·er·gis·tic** (-jístik), **syn·er·gis·ti·cal** *adj.*

syn·e·sis (sínni-siss) *n. Grammar.* A construction in which a form differs in number but agrees in meaning with the word governing it; for example, *If anyone arrives, tell them to wait.* [New Latin, from Greek *sunesis,* union, quick apprehension, intelligence, from

PRONUNCIATION KEY

a, trap; aa, father; ai, fair; ar, star; aw, lawn; ay, play; b, bb, stab; rubber; ch, church; ck, ticket; d, dd, dead; ladder; e, dress; ee, bee; er, defer; ew, few; ewr, pure; ə, about; ər, letter; f, ff, fife; differ; g, gg, giggle; h, hat; i, kit; ī, price; īr, fire; j, judge; k, kick; l, ll, let; 'l, needle; m, mm, man; n, nn, no; 'n, sudden; ng, thing; o, lot; ō, no; o͝o, foot; o͞o, shoe; oor, poor; ow, cow; owr, hour; oy, boy; p, pp, pepper; r, rr, red; s, ss, sauce; sh, ship; t, tt, totter; th, thick; th, this; smooth; u, cut; ur, turn; v, vv, valve; w, wet; y, yes; z, zz, zebra; zh, vision; pleasure

IN FOREIGN WORDS:

aN, oN, Saint-Saëns; hl, Llanelli; Hluhluwe; kh, loch; lough; Khaled

STRESS MARK:

ín-sīt, insight; in-sī́t, incite

sunienai, to bring together, understand : *sun-,* together + *hienai,* to send.]

synesthesia. *U.S.* Variant of **synaesthesia.**

syn·ga·my (sing-gəmi) *n. Biology.* The fusion of two gametes; fertilisation. [SYN- + -GAMY.] **—syn·gam·ic** (sing-gámmik, sin-), **syn·gam·ous** (sing-gəməss) *adj.*

Synge (sing), **John Millington** (1871–1909). Irish playwright. His plays, which draw on the speech and culture of Irish peasants and fishermen, include *The Playboy of the Western World* (1907).

syn·gen·e·sis (sin-jénnə-siss) *n. Biology.* Sexual reproduction. [New Latin : SYN- + -GENESIS.] **—syn·ge·net·ic** (sinjə-néttik) *adj.*

syn·graft (sing-graaft, sin- || -graft) *n.* An **isograft** *(see).*

syn·i·ze·sis, syn·e·ze·sis (sinni-zéé-siss) *n., pl.* **-ses** (-seez). **1.** The contraction of two syllables into one by joining in pronunciation two adjacent vowels, without forming a recognised diphthong, as when *tower* (tów-ər) is pronounced (taáər). Compare **synaeresis. 2.** *Biology.* The phase of meiosis in which the chromatin contracts into a mass at one side of the nucleus. [Late Latin *synizēsis,* from Greek *sunizēsis,* "collapse", from *sunizein,* to collapse : *sun-,* together + *hizein,* to sit down.]

syn·kar·y·on (sing-kárri-ən, sin-, -on) *n.* The nucleus of a fertilised egg immediately after the male and female nuclei have fused. [New Latin : SYN- + Greek *karuon,* nut.] **—syn·kar·y·on·ic** (-ónnik) *adj.*

syn·od (sinnəd, *also* sin-od) *n.* **1.** A council or assembly of churches or church officials; an ecclesiastical council. **2.** Any council or assembly. [Middle English, from Late Latin *synodus,* from Greek *sunodos,* meeting : *sun-,* together + *hodos,* road, way, journey.] **—syn·od·al** (-'l), **sy·nod·i·cal** (si-nóddik'l) *adj.*

sy·nod·ic (si-nóddik) *adj.* **1.** Pertaining to the conjunction of celestial bodies, especially the interval between two successive conjunctions of a planet or the moon with the sun. **2.** Of or pertaining to a synod. **—sy·nod·i·cal·ly** *adv.*

sy·noe·cious, sy·ne·cious (si-néeshəss) *adj. Botany.* Having male and female organs in the same flower or corresponding structure. [SYN- + (MON)OECIOUS.]

syn·o·nym (sinnə-nim, *also* sinno-) *n. Abbr.* **syn. 1.** A word having the same meaning as, or a meaning very similar to, that of another word in the same language; for example, *mix, blend,* and *mingle* are synonyms. Compare **antonym. 2.** A word or expression accepted as a figurative or symbolic substitute for another word or expression; as by word: *Her name has become a synonym for bravery.* **3.** *Biology.* A taxonomic name of an organism that is equivalent to or has been superseded by another designation. [Middle English *sinonyme,* from Latin *synonymum,* from Greek *sunōnumon,* from *sunōnumos,* SYNONYMOUS.] **—syn·o·nym·ic** (-nímmik), **syn·o·nym·i·cal** *adj.* **—syn·o·nym·i·ty** (-nímməti) *n.*

syn·on·y·mise, syn·on·y·mize (si-nónni-mīz) *tr.v.* **-mised, -mising, -mises.** To provide or analyse the synonyms of (a word). **—syn·on·y·mist** (si-nónnimist) *n.*

syn·on·y·mous (si-nónniməss) *adj. Abbr.* **syn. 1.** Expressing the same or a similar meaning; being a synonym or synonyms. **2.** Having a particular connotation through association with something specified: *Nazism is synonymous with evil.* [Medieval Latin *synonymus,* from Greek *sunōnumos* : *sun-,* same + *onoma, onuma,* name.] **—syn·on·y·mous·ly** *adv.*

syn·on·y·my (si-nónnəmi) *n., pl.* **-mies.** *Abbr.* **syn. 1.** The quality of being synonymous; equivalence of meaning. **2.** The study and classification of synonyms. **3.** A list, book, or system of synonyms. **4.** The use of synonyms for rhetorical emphasis or effect. **5.** A chronological list or record of the scientific names that have been applied to a species and its subdivisions.

syn·op·sis (si-nóp-siss) *n., pl.* **-ses** (-seez). A brief statement or outline of a subject; a summary; an abstract. [Late Latin, from Greek *sunopsis,* a viewing all together : *sun-,* together + *opsis,* view.]

syn·op·sise, syn·op·size (si-nóp-sīz) *tr.v.* **-sised, -sising, -sises.** To present or write a synopsis of. [Late Greek *sunopsizein,* from Greek *sunopsis,* SYNOPSIS.]

sy·nop·tic (si-nóptik) *adj.* Also **sy·nop·ti·cal** (-'l). **1.** Of or constituting a synopsis or summary. **2.** Presenting an account from the same point of view. **3.** *Often capital* **S.** Of or designating the first three Gospels of the New Testament (Matthew, Mark, and Luke), which correspond closely. **4.** Of or concerning the meteorological conditions at a given time: *a synoptic chart.* **—sy·nop·ti·cal·ly** *adv.*

syn·os·to·sis (sínnoss-tṓ-siss) *n.* The fusion of two skeletal bones. [New Latin : SYN- + Greek *osteon,* bone + -OSIS.] **—syn·os·tot·ic** (-tóttik) *adj.*

syn·o·vi·a (si-nṓvi-ə) *n.* A clear, viscid lubricating fluid secreted by the *synovial membranes* lining joint cavities, sheaths of tendons, and bursae. Also called "synovial fluid". [New Latin *synovia, sinovia* (coined by Paracelsus).] **—syn·o·vi·al** *adj.*

sy·no·vi·tis (sīn-ō-vī-tiss, sín-, -ə-) *n.* Inflammation of the synovial membrane lining a joint cavity, resulting in pain and swelling. [SYNOVIA + -ITIS.]

syn·sep·al·ous (sin-séppələss, sín-) *adj. Botany.* Gamosepalous.

syn·tac·tics (sin-táktiks) *n. Used with a singular or plural verb.* The branch of semiotics that deals with the formal properties of words and expressions, or, more generally, signs and symbols and their interrelations, without reference to their meaning. [From *syntactic,* of syntax, from New Latin *syntacticus,* from Greek *suntaktikos,* putting together, from *suntassein,* to put together. See **syntax.**]

syn·tax (sín-taks) *n.* **1. a.** The way in which words are put together grammatically to form phrases and sentences. **b.** The branch of grammar dealing with this. **c.** The rules for determining grammaticality. **2.** The system of rules governing the construction of well-formed formulas in a system of symbolic logic. **3.** The system of rules in operation in a computer program. [French *syntaxe,* from Late Latin *syntaxis,* from Greek *suntaxis,* from *suntassein,* to put together, arrange in order : *sun-,* together + *tassein,* to arrange.] **—syn·tac·tic** (sin-táktik), **syn·tac·ti·cal** *adj.* **—syn·tac·ti·cal·ly** *adv.*

syn·the·sis (sín-thə-siss, -thi-) *n., pl.* **-ses** (-seez). **1.** The combining of separate elements or substances to form a coherent whole. Compare **analysis. 2.** The whole so formed. **3.** *Chemistry.* Formation of a compound from its constituents. **4.** *Philosophy.* **a.** Reasoning from the general to the particular; logical deduction. **b.** In the philosophy of Hegel, the combination of thesis and antithesis in the dialectical process. [Latin, from Greek, a putting together, from *suntithenai,* to put together.] **—syn·the·sist** *n.*

syn·the·sise, syn·the·size (sín-thə-sīz, -thi-) *v.* **-sised, -sising, -sises.** Also **syn·the·tise** (-tīz). *—tr.* **1.** To combine so as to form a new, complex product, especially by artificial process. **2.** To produce by combining separate elements. *—intr.* To form a synthesis.

syn·the·sis·er (sín-thə-sīzər, -thi-) *n.* **1.** One that synthesises. **2.** A machine having a keyboard and using solid-state circuitry to produce a wide range of electronic sounds. See **Moog sythesiser.**

syn·thet·ic (sin-théttik) *adj.* Also **syn·thet·i·cal** (-'l). **1.** Pertaining to, involving, or of the nature of a synthesis. **2.** Produced by chemical synthesis; especially, not of natural origin; man-made. **3.** Not genuine; artificial; devised. **4.** *Linguistics.* Designating a language such as Latin or Russian that uses inflectional affixes to express syntactic relationships. In this sense, compare **polysynthetic. 5.** *Philosophy.* Designating a statement or proposition whose truth depends on some fact about the world, rather than depending entirely on the meanings of the words from which it is composed. In this sense compare **analytic.** —See Synonyms at **artificial.**
~n. A synthetic chemical compound or material. [Greek *sunthetikos,* skilled in putting together, component, from *sunthetos,* put together, compounded, composite, from *suntithenai,* to put together. See **synthesis.**] **—syn·thet·i·cal·ly** *adv.*

synthetic philosophy *n.* **Spencerism** *(see).*

sy·pher (sīfər) *tr.v.* **-phered, -phering, -phers.** To overlap and even (chamfered or bevelled plank edges) so that they form a flush surface. [Variant of CIPHER.]

syph·i·lis (síf-ə-liss, -i-) *n.* A chronic infectious venereal disease caused by a spirochaete, *Treponema pallidum,* transmitted by direct contact, usually in sexual intercourse, or passed from the mother to the foetus, and progressing through three stages characterised respectively by (*primary syphilis*) local formation of chancres, (*secondary syphilis*) ulcerous skin eruptions, and (*tertiary syphilis*) systemic infection leading to **general paralysis of the insane.** [New Latin, after the supposed first victim of the disease *Syphilus,* title character of a Latin poem *Syphilis, sive Morbus Gallicus* (1530) by Girolamo Fracastoro, Veronese doctor.] **—syph·i·lit·ic** (-líttik) *n. & adj.*

syph·i·loid (síf-ə-loyd, -i-) *adj.* Characteristic of syphilis. [SYPHIL(IS) + -OID.]

syph·i·lol·o·gy (síf-ə-lólləji, -i-) *n.* The sum of knowledge concerning the origin, nature, course, complications, and treatment of syphilis. [SYPHIL(IS) + -LOGY.] **—syph·i·lol·o·gist** *n.*

syph·i·lo·ma (síf-ə-lṓmə) *n., pl.* **-mas** or **-mata** (-tə). A lesion formed in an advanced stage of syphilis; a gumma. [New Latin : SYPHIL(IS) + -OMA.] **—syph·i·lom·a·tous** *adj.*

syphon. Variant of **siphon.**

Syr. Syria; Syriac; Syrian.

Syr·a·cuse (sīrə-kewz, *U.S.* sírrə-). *Italian* **Si·ra·cu·sa** (sirra-kṓōza). Seaport on the east coast of Sicily, Italy. It was founded by colonists from Corinth in the eighth century B.C., and became a brilliant centre of Greek culture. However, the city sided with Carthage in the Second Punic War, and fell to the Romans in 212 B.C. Archimedes, a native, directed the city's defence, and was killed during its subsequent sacking.

Syr Dar·ya (séer daar-yaá). River in the southern U.S.S.R. Some 2 250 kilometres (1,400 miles) long, it rises in the Tien Shan range near the border with China, and flows northwest to the Aral Sea.

Syr·i·a (sírri-ə). Official name **Syrian Arab Republic.** Country in the Middle East. Much of it is mountain, steppe, or desert, with fertile lowlands along the coast and in the valleys of the Euphrates and Orontes. Most Syrians are of Arab descent, but there are significant minorities of Kurds, Armenians, and Turkomans. Manufacturing and mining have replaced agriculture as the chief source of national income, though about 30 per cent of workers remain in farming. The main exports are crude oil, cotton, and cotton goods. Tourism is a major industry. Syria was a province of the Ottoman Empire (1516–1918). From 1920 it was a French League of Nations mandate. It became an independent republic (1946) and joined Egypt in the short-lived United Arab Republic (1958–61). The country took part in Arab-Israeli wars after 1948, being firmly aligned against Israel. Syrian troops intervened in the Lebanese civil war (1976), and remained in the country as a peace-keeping force. Area, 185 180 square kilometres (71,498 square miles). Population, 9,700,000. Capital, Damascus. See map, next page.

Syr·i·ac (sírri-ak) *n. Abbr.* **Syr.** An ancient Aramaic language spoken in Syria (3rd–13th century A.D.), surviving as the liturgical language of certain eastern Christian churches. **—Syr·i·ac** *adj.*

Syr·i·an (sírri-ən) *adj. Abbr.* **Syr.** Of or pertaining to Syria, its culture, or inhabitants.
~n. **1.** A native or inhabitant of Syria. **2.** A member of a Christian church using the Syriac language.

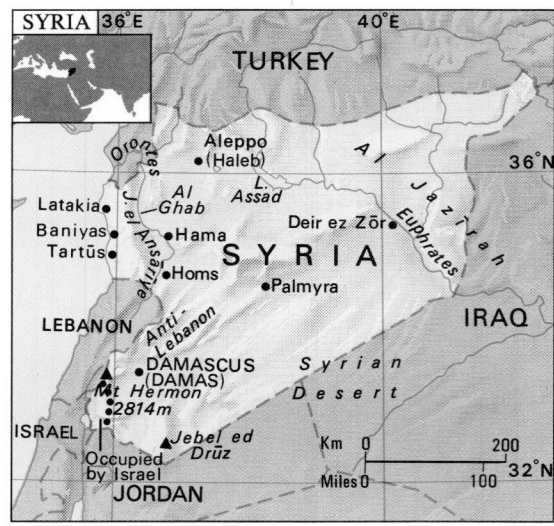

sy·rin·ga (si-ríng-gə) n. Either of two shrubs, the **mock orange** or **lilac** *(both of which see).* [New Latin *syringa,* "pipe" (from the use of its hollow stems to make pipes), from Greek *surinx,* SYRINX.]

syr·inge (sírrinj, si-rínj) n. **1.** A thin tube with a nozzle and a piston, rubber bulb, or other device that can draw in fluid by suction and expel it by force. **2.** A **hypodermic syringe** *(see).*
~*tr.v.* **syringed, -inging, -inges.** To clean, spray, or inject with a syringe. [Middle English *syring,* from Medieval Latin *syringa,* from Greek *surinx* (stem *suring-*), SYRINX.]

sy·rin·go·my·e·li·a (si-ríng-gō-mī-éeli-ə) n. A chronic disease of the spinal cord characterised by the presence of liquid-filled cavities and leading to spasticity and loss of awareness of pain and temperature. [New Latin : Greek *surinx,* pipe, cavity (see **syrinx**) + *muelos,* marrow, from *mus,* mouse, muscle.]

syr·inx (sírringks) n., pl. **syringes** (si-rín-jeez, sírrin-) or **syrinxes.** **1.** A **panpipe** *(see).* **2.** *Zoology.* The vocal organ of a bird, consisting of thin, vibrating muscles at or close to the division of the trachea. [Latin, from Greek *surinx†,* shepherd's pipe, panpipe, pipe.] —**sy·rin·ge·al** (si-rínji-əl) *adj.*

syr·phid (súrfid) n. Any fly of the family Syrphidae, many of which have a form or coloration mimicking that of bees or wasps. [New Latin *Syrphidae,* from Greek *surphos†,* gnat.] —**syr·phid** *adj.*

syr·up, *U.S.* **sir·up** (sírrəp ‖ súrrəp) n. **1.** A thick, sweet, sticky liquid, consisting of a sugar base, natural or artificial flavouring, and water. **2.** A highly concentrated solution of sugar in water. **3.** The juice of a fruit or plant boiled with sugar until thick and sticky. **4.** A medicine in a sweet-tasting liquid. **5.** Cloying sentimentality. [Middle English *sirop,* from Old French, from Medieval Latin *siropus,* from Arabic *sharāb,* beverage.] —**syr·up·y** *adj.*

sys·sar·co·sis (síssaar-kṓ-siss) n. The union of bones, such as the hyoid bone and lower jaw, by muscle. [New Latin, from Greek *sussarkōsis,* a growing together with flesh, from *sussarkousthai,* to be grown together with flesh : *sun-,* together + *sarkousthai,* passive of *sarkoun,* to grow fleshy, from *sarx,* flesh.]

sys·tal·tic (si-stál-tik, -stáwl- ‖ -stól-) *adj.* Alternately contracting and expanding, as the heart does; pulsating. [Late Latin *systalticus,* from Greek *sustaltikos,* from *sustellein,* to draw together, contract : *sun-,* together + *stellein,* to send, bind, repress, make compact.]

sys·tem (síst-əm, -im) n. **1.** A group of interacting, interrelated, or interdependent elements forming or regarded as forming a collective entity. **2.** A functionally related group of elements, as: **a.** The human body regarded as a functional physiological unit. **b.** A group of physiologically complementary organs or parts. **c.** A group of interacting mechanical or electrical components. **d.** A network of structures and channels, as for communications, travel, or distribution. **3.** A structurally or anatomically related group of elements or parts. **4.** A set of interrelated members, as of ideas, principles, rules, procedures, or laws: *metric system.* **5.** A social, economic, or political organisational form. **6.** A naturally occurring group of objects or phenomena. **7.** A set of objects or phenomena grouped together for classification or analysis, as in: **a.** A **crystal system** *(see).* **b.** *Geology.* The succession of rocks formed during a geological period. **c.** *Astronomy.* A group of associated stars, planets, or other bodies. **8.** A method; an orderly way of doing something. **9.** Orderliness: *bring some system into this chaos.* See Synonyms at **method.** —**get (something) out of (one's) system.** *Informal.* To free oneself from a desire to do or express something by fulfilling it. —**the system.** The established political social, and economic order or power structure. [Late Latin *systēma,* from Greek *sustēma,* a composite whole, from *sunistanai,* to bring together, combine : *sun-,* together + *histanai,* to cause to stand.]

sys·tem·at·ic (síst-ə-máttik, -i-) *adj.* Also **sys·tem·at·i·cal** (-'l). **1.** Of, characterised by, based upon, or constituting a system. **2.** Carried on in a step-by-step procedure. **3.** Characterised by purposeful regularity; methodical. **4.** Of or pertaining to classification or taxonomy. —See Synonyms at **orderly.** —**sys·tem·at·i·cal·ly** *adv.*

systematic name n. A name given to a chemical compound that describes the elements and groups it contains using a set of formal rules. Compare **trivial name.**

sys·tem·at·ics (síst-ə-máttiks, -i-) n. *Used with a singular verb. Biology.* The classification of organisms in an ordered system designed to indicate natural relationships.

sys·tem·a·tise, sys·tem·a·tize (síst-ə-mə-tīz, -i-) *tr.v.* **-tised, -tising, -tises.** Also **sys·tem·ise** (-mīz). To formulate as or reduce to a system: *systematising research data.* —**sys·tem·a·ti·sa·tion** (-tī-záysh'n ‖ -ti-) n. —**sys·tem·a·tis·er** n.

sys·tem·a·tism (síst-ə-mə-tiz'm, -i- ‖ si-stémmə-) n. **1.** The practice of classifying or systematising. **2.** Adherence to a system.

sys·tem·a·tist (síst-ə-mə-tist, -i- ‖ si-stémmə-) n. **1.** A person who adheres to or formulates a system. **2.** A taxonomist.

Sys·tème in·ter·na·tio·nal d'u·ni·tés (seess-tém án-tair-náss-yo-naʾal dew-nee-táy, dü-) n. *French.* International System of Units. See **SI units.**

sys·tem·ic (si-stémmik, -stéemik) *adj.* **1.** Of or pertaining to a system or systems. **2.** Of, pertaining to, or affecting the entire body. ~n. A systemic poison or agent. —**sys·tem·i·cal·ly** *adv.*

systems analysis n. An analysis by computer of the methods used in a scientific or technological operation, with a view to making them more efficient. —**systems analyst** n.

systems engineering n. The branch of engineering concerned with the application of systems analysis, information theory, and ergonomics to practical technological operations.

sys·to·le (sístəli) n. The rhythmic contraction of the heart, especially of the ventricles, by which blood is driven through the aorta and pulmonary artery after each dilation or **diastole** *(see).* [Greek *sustolē,* contraction, from *sustellein,* to contract. See **systaltic.**] —**sys·tol·ic** (si-stóllik) *adj.*

syz·y·gy (sízziji) n., pl. **-gies.** **1.** *Astronomy.* **a.** Either of two points in the orbit of a celestial body at which the body is in opposition to or in conjunction with the Sun. **b.** Either of two points in the orbit of the Moon at which the Moon lies in a straight line with the Sun and the Earth. **c.** The configuration of the Sun, the Moon, and the Earth lying in a straight line. **2.** In classical prosody, the combining of two feet into a single metrical unit. [Late Latin *syzygia,* from Greek *suzugia,* union, coupling, yoke, from *suzugos,* yoked, paired : *sun-,* together + *zugon,* a yoke.] —**sy·zyg·i·al** (si-zíji-əl) *adj.*

Szcze·cin (shchéch-een). *German* **Stet·tin** (shte-téen). Port in northwestern Poland, situated at the mouth of the river Oder on the Baltic Sea. It is a major outlet for Polish coal and has important shipbuilding, chemical, textile and engineering industries.

Szechwan. See **Sichuan.**

Szi·lard (síl-aard), **Leo** (1898–1964). Hungarian-born physicist. He emigrated to the United States in 1937 and during World War II worked on the construction of the atom bomb. He later regretted its construction and urged the abolition of all nuclear weapons.

t, T (tee) *n., pl.* **t's** or *rare* **ts, Ts** or **T's.** **1.** The 20th letter of the modern English alphabet. **2.** Any of the speech sounds represented by this letter. **3.** Anything shaped like the letter **T.** **—to a T.** Perfectly; precisely: *She fits the role to a T.* [*To a T*, perhaps from *to a tittle*, to the smallest detail, perfectly. See **tittle.**]

t, T, t., T. *Note:* As an abbreviation or symbol, *t* may be a small or a capital letter, with or without a full stop. Established forms or those generally preferred precede the definition. When no form is given, all four forms are in general use in that sense. **1. t.** in the time of. [Latin *tempore.*] **2. T** *Physics.* surface tension. **3. T.** tablespoon; tablespoonful. **4. t.** *Commerce.* tare. **5. t.** teaspoon; teaspoonful. **6. T** temperature. **7. t.** tempo. **8. t., T.** *Music.* tenor. **9. t.** *Grammar.* tense. **10. T** *Physics.* tera-. **11. t., T.** territory. **12. T** tesla. **13. T.** Testament. **14. t., T.** time. **15. T** *Mathematics.* time reversal. **16. t** ton; tons. **17. t** tonne; tonnes. **18. t** *Physics.* top. **19. t.** *Grammar.* transitive. **20. t** troy (weights). **21. T.** Tuesday (unofficial). **22.** The 20th in a series; 19th when *J* is omitted.

't (t). **1.** Contraction of *it.* **2.** *Northern English.* Contraction of *the.*

ta (taa) *interj. Chiefly British Informal.* Used to express thanks.

Ta The symbol for the element tantalum.

TA Territorial Army (formerly, in Britain).

T.A. transactional analysis.

Taal (taal) *n. South African.* **Afrikaans** *(see).* Preceded by *the.* [Dutch *taal*, language, speech, from Middle Dutch *tāle.*]

tab (tab) *n.* **1.** A projection, flap, or short strip attached to an object to facilitate opening, handling, or identification. **2.** A small, usually decorative, flap or tongue on a garment. **3.** A small auxiliary control surface attached to a larger one to stabilise an aeroplane. **4.** *Military. British.* A coloured insignia worn by a staff officer. **5.** *U.S.* A bill, as for a meal in a restaurant. **6.** A tabulator, as on a typewriter. **7.** A metal ring that is pulled off the top of a can of drink in order to make an opening. Also called "pull-tab", "ring-pull". **8.** *Northern British Slang.* A cigarette. **—keep tabs** or **a tab on.** To keep account of or watch carefully.

~*v.* **tabbed, tabbing, tabs.** To supply with a tab or tabs. [17th century : origin obscure; sense 6, shortening of TABULATOR.]

TAB¹ *n.* A combined vaccine against typhoid, paratyphoid A, and paratyphoid B. [*T*yphoid, paratyphoid *A*, paratyphoid *B*.]

TAB² Totalisator Agency Board (in Australia and New Zealand).

tab. table.

ta·ba·nid (tábbənid ‖ *U.S.* tə-báynid, -bánnid) *n.* Any of various blood-sucking flies of the family Tabanidae, which includes the horseflies. [New Latin *Tabanidae* : Latin *tabānus†*, horsefly + -IDAE.] **—ta·ba·nid** *adj.*

tab·ard (táb-ərd, -aard) *n.* **1.** A short tunic or capelike garment worn by a knight over his armour and emblazoned with his coat of arms. **2.** A similar garment worn by a herald and bearing his lord's coat of arms. [Middle English, from Old French *tabart†*.]

tab·a·ret (tábbə-rət, -rit) *n.* A strong upholstery fabric having alternating stripes of satin and moiré. [Originally a trademark.]

Ta·bas·co (tə-báskō) *n.* A trademark for a hot, pungent sauce made from the fruit of a species of pepper plant.

tab·by (tábbi) *n., pl.* **-bies.** Also **tab·bis** (tábbiss) (for sense 1). **1. a.** A striped or brindled domestic cat. **b.** A female domestic cat. **2.** A rich silk cloth, with a watered or wavy pattern. **3.** A plain weave fabric. **4.** *Chiefly U.S. Informal.* A prying woman; a gossip. ~*adj.* **1.** Striped or brindled. Said of domestic cats. **2.** Made of or resembling the cloth, tabby. [(Cloth) from French *tabis*, from Old French *atabis*, from Arabic *'attābī*, originally made at *Al-'attābīya*, a suburb of Baghdad, after Prince *Attāb*, who resided there; (cat) by comparison of cat to cloth; (woman) see **cat.**]

tab·er·na·cle (tábbər-nack'l) *n.* **1.** *Often capital* **T. a.** The portable sanctuary in which the Jews carried the Ark of the Covenant through the desert. **b.** The Jewish temple. **c.** A temporary or portable dwelling, as used by the Jews during the Exodus. **2.** *Often capital* **T.** A case or box on a church altar containing the consecrated host and wine of the Eucharist. **3.** A place of worship distinguished from a church; especially, one used by various denominations in Wales or by the Mormon Temple in the United States. **4.** A cano-

pied niche used as a shrine. **5.** The body considered as the temporary residence of the soul. **6.** *Nautical.* A boxlike support in which the heel of a mast is stepped.

~*v.* **tabernacled, -cling, -cles.** *—tr.* To enshrine. *—intr.* To dwell temporarily. [Middle English, from Old French, from Latin *tabernaculum*, tent, diminutive of *taberna*, hut, perhaps from Etruscan. See also **tavern.**] **—tab·er·nac·u·lar** (-náckewlər) *adj.*

ta·bes (táy-beez) *n., pl.* **tabes. 1.** Progressive bodily wasting or emaciation. **2.** Tabes dorsalis. [Latin *tābēs*, "a melting".] **—ta·bet·ic** (tə-béttik) *adj.*

tabes dor·sa·lis (dawr-sáy-liss, -sáa- ‖ -sá-) *n.* A form of syphilis resulting in a hardening of the dorsal columns of the spinal cord, and in shooting pains, unsteadiness, and loss of ability to coordinate voluntary movements. Also called "locomotor ataxia".

tab·la (túbblə; *also* táablə) *n.* A pair of small Indian hand drums. [Hindi, from Arabic *ṭablə*, drum.]

tab·la·ture (tábblə-chər, -tewr, -choor) *n.* **1.** *Music.* An early system of notation, used especially for lute music, using letters and symbols to indicate playing directions. **2.** An engraved tablet or surface. [French, from Medieval Latin *tabulātūra*, from *tabulātus*, tablet, from Latin, boarded, floored, from *tabula*, board. See **table.**]

ta·ble (táyb'l) *n. Abbr.* **tab. 1.** An article of furniture supported by one or more vertical legs and having a flat horizontal surface on which objects can be placed; especially: **a.** One at which meals are eaten: *a dinner table.* **b.** One having another specified use: *a bird table.* **c.** *Often plural.* One used in gambling games. **2.** The objects laid out for a meal upon a table: *lay the table.* **3.** The food and drink served at meals; fare: *kept an excellent table.* **4.** The company of people assembled around a table, as for a meal. **5.** The horizontal part of a machine tool where a piece is worked. **6.** Either of the leaves of a backgammon board. **7.** A plateau or tableland. **8. a.** A flat facet cut across the top of a gemstone. **b.** A stone cut in this fashion. **9.** *Music.* The front part of a stringed instrument, the **belly** *(see).* **10.** *Architecture.* **a.** A raised or sunken rectangular panel on a wall. **b.** A **stringcourse** *(see).* **11.** *Geology.* A horizontal rock stratum. **12.** In palmistry, a part of the palm framed by four lines. **13. a.** An orderly written, typed, or printed display of data, especially a rectangular array exhibiting one or more characteristics of designated entities or categories. **b.** *Plural.* A set of such tables listing basic arithmetical calculations to be learnt by heart. **14.** An abbreviated list, as of the contents of a book. **15.** A slab or tablet, as of stone, bearing an inscription or device. **16.** *Plural.* A system of laws or decrees; a code: *the tables of Moses.* **—drink (someone) under the table.** *Informal.* To succeed in remaining relatively sober for longer than (someone with whom one is drinking). **—on the table. 1.** *Chiefly British.* Submitted for consideration or acceptance. **2.** Postponed or put aside for consideration at a later date. **—turn the tables.** To reverse a situation and gain the upper hand. **—under the table.** *Informal.* **1.** Extremely drunk. **2.** Secretly or stealthily, especially as a bribe.

~*tr.v.* **tabled, -bling, -bles. 1.** To put or place on a table. **2.** *Chiefly British.* To submit (a proposal, for example) for consideration. **3.** To postpone consideration of (a piece of legislation, for example); shelve. **4.** *Rare.* To tabulate. [Middle English, tablet, board, table, from Old French, from Latin *tabula†*, board, list.]

tab·leau (tábblō ‖ *U.S. also* ta-blō) *n., pl.* **-leaux** (-z) or **-leaus. 1.** A vivid or graphic description. **2.** A striking incidental scene, as of a picturesque group of people. **3.** A moment during a scene of a play when all the actors on stage freeze in position and then resume action as before. **4.** A tableau vivant. [French, from Old French *tablel*, diminutive of *table*, TABLE.]

tableau vi·vant (vee-vón) *n., pl.* **tableaux vivants** (*pronounced as singular*). A scene presented on stage by costumed actors who remain silent and motionless as if in a picture. [French, "living picture".]

ta·ble·cloth (táyb'l-kloth ‖ -klawth) *n., pl.* **-cloths** (-kloths ‖ -klawthz, -klawths, -klothz). A cloth to cover a table, especially in preparation for a meal.

ta·ble-cut (táyb'l-kut) *adj.* Cut with a flat facet across the top. Said of a gemstone.

ta·ble d'hôte (taab'l dōt) *n., pl.* **tables d'hôte** (*pronounced as singular*). **1.** A communal table for all guests at a hotel or restaurant. **2.** A meal consisting of several courses and offering a limited number of choices, served at a fixed price in a restaurant or hotel. In this sense, also called "prix fixe". Compare **à la carte.** [French, "table of (the) host".] **—ta·ble d'hôte** *adv.*

ta·ble·land (táyb'l-land) *n.* A flat, elevated region, especially one with steep sides; a plateau; a mesa.

table licence *n.* A licence allowing alcoholic drinks to be served only with meals.

table linen *n.* Tablecloths and napkins.

table money *n.* An allowance made, especially to senior officers in the armed services, for the official entertaining of visitors.

Table Mountain. *Afrikaans* **Ta·fel·berg** (taaf'l-bairkh). The distinctive flat-topped mountain that rises steeply behind Cape Town, South Africa, to a height of 1 087 metres (3,567 feet).

table salt *n.* **1.** A refined mixture of salts, chiefly sodium chloride, used in cooking and as a seasoning. Also called "common salt". **2. Sodium chloride** *(see).*

ta·ble·spoon (táyb'l-spoon) *n.* **1.** A large spoon used for serving food. **2.** *Abbr.* **T., tbs., tbsp.** A household cooking measure, equivalent to four teaspoons or 15 millilitres.

ta·ble·spoon·ful (táyb'l-spoon-fool) *n., pl.* **-fuls.** *Abbr.* **T., tbs., tbsp.** The amount a tablespoon will hold.

tab·let (táb-lit, -lət) *n.* **1.** A small, flat pellet of compressed powdered medication to be taken orally. **2.** A slab or plaque, as of stone or ivory, with a surface intended for or bearing an inscription. **3.** A thin sheet or leaf, as of clay or ivory, used as a writing surface. **4.** A set of such leaves fastened together, as in a book. **5.** A pad of writing paper secured along one edge. **6.** A small, flat cake of a prepared substance, such as soap. [Middle English *tablette,* from Old French *tablete,* diminutive of *table,* TABLE.]

table talk *n.* Casual mealtime conversation; cultured chat.

table tennis *n.* A game that is like a scaled-down version of lawn tennis, played on a table with a net across it, using wooden bats faced with rubber and a small celluloid ball. See **Ping-Pong.** **—ta·ble-ten·nis** (táyb'l-tenniss) *adj.*

ta·ble-turn·ing (táyb'l-túrning) *n.* **1.** The movement of a table supposedly caused by the spirits of the dead operating through a human medium. **2.** Loosely, spiritualism. Often used derogatorily.

ta·ble·ware (táyb'l-wair) *n.* The dishes, glassware, and cutlery used in setting a table for a meal.

table wine *n.* A wine considered suitable to be served with a meal.

tab·loid (tábbloyd) *n.* A newspaper of small format giving the news in condensed form, usually with illustrated, often sensational material. Compare **broadsheet.** [From *Tabloid,* trademark for a tablet of condensed medicine : TABL(ET) + -OID.]

ta·boo, ta·bu (tə-bóo ‖ ta-) *n., pl.* **-boos, -bus.** **1.** A ban or inhibition attached to something by social custom or emotional aversion. **2.** A prohibition, especially in Polynesia and other South Pacific Islands, excluding something from use, approach, or mention because of its sacred and inviolable nature. **3.** An object, word, or act protected by such a prohibition.

~adj. Excluded or forbidden from use, approach, or mention.

~tr.v. **tabooed** or **tabued, -booing** or **-buing, -boos** or **-bus.** To exclude from use, approach, or mention; place under taboo. [Tongan *tabu,* perhaps "exceedingly marked", marked as sacred.]

Usage: When this word is used in a specialised discussion (for example, in anthropology), the spelling *tabu* is usual.

ta·bor, ta·bour (táy-bər, -bawr) *n.* A small drum played by a fifer to accompany the fife. [Middle English *tabo(u)r,* from Old French, perhaps from Persian *ṭabīr,* drum. See also **tambour.**]

tab·ou·ret, tab·o·ret (tábbə-rit, -ret ‖ -ray) *n.* **1.** A low stool without a back or arms. **2.** A low stand or cabinet. **3.** An embroidery frame. [French *tabouret,* diminutive of Old French *tabour,* TABOR.]

Ta·briz (ta-bréez). City in northwest Iran close to the borders with Turkey and the U.S.S.R. It is a commercial, industrial, and communications centre.

tab·u·lar (tábbewlər) *adj.* **1.** Having a plane surface; flat. **2.** Organised or arranged in table form. **3.** Calculated by means of a table. [Latin *tabulāris,* from *tabula,* TABLE.] **—tab·u·lar·ly** *adv.*

tab·u·la ra·sa (tábbewlə raa-zə, -sə) *n.* **1.** A need or opportunity to start from the beginning; a clean slate. **2.** The mind before it receives the impressions gained from experience; especially, in the philosophy of Locke, the unformed, featureless mind. [Latin, "erased tablet".]

tab·u·lar·ise, tab·u·lar·ize (tábbewlə-rīz) *tr.v.* **-ised, -ising, -ises.** To tabulate. **—tab·u·lar·i·sa·tion** (-rī-záysh'n ‖ *U.S.* -ri-) *n.*

tab·u·late (tábbew-layt) *tr.v.* **-lated, -lating, -lates.** **1.** To arrange, set out, record, or write in tabular form; condense and list. **2.** To cut or form with a plane surface.

~adj. (-lət, -lit, -layt). Having a plane surface. [Latin *tabula,* TABLE.] **—tab·u·la·tion** (-láysh'n) *n.*

tab·u·la·tor (tábbew-laytər) *n.* **1.** A person who tabulates. **2.** A machine into which data can be fed for tabulation. **3.** A mechanism on a typewriter for setting automatic stops or margins for columns. Also called "tab". **4.** *Computing.* A device for reading data from punched cards and producing printed lists or totals of the result.

tac·a·ma·hac (táckəmə-hak) *n.* **1.** Any of several aromatic resinous substances used in ointments and incenses. **2.** The **balsam poplar** *(see).* [Spanish *tacamahaca, tacamaca,* from Nahuatl *tecamaca.*]

ta·cet (táy-set, tá-, -ket). *Music.* Be silent. Used as a direction. [Latin, it is silent, from *tacēre,* to be silent.]

tach·e·om·e·ter (tácki-ómmitər) *n.* Also **ta·chym·e·ter** (ta-kímmitər, tə-). A theodolite adapted to measure distances, so that distances, elevations, and bearings may be determined rapidly during surveying. [TACHY- + METER.] **—tach·e·o·met·ric** (tácki-ō-méttrik), **tach·e·o·met·ri·cal** *adj.* **—tach·e·o·met·ri·cal·ly** *adv.* **—ta·che·om·e·try** (tacki-ómmətri) *n.*

tach·i·na fly (táckinə) *n.* Any of several bristly, usually greyish flies of the family Tachinidae, the larvae of which live as parasites within the bodies of other insects. [New Latin *Tachina,* type genus, from Greek *takhinos,* swift, from *takhos,* speed, akin to *takhus,* swift.]

tach·isme (tásh-iz'm, taash-) *n.* A French school of art, originating in the 1950s and very similar to the American school, **action painting** *(see),* characterised by irregular dabs and splotches of colour thrown haphazardly onto the canvas in a spontaneous fashion. [French, from *tache,* spot, stain.] **—tach·iste** (-ist, -éest) *n. & adj.*

ta·chis·to·scope (tə-kístə-skōp) *n.* An apparatus that projects a series of images onto a screen at rapid speed, used in experiments on visual perception or memory, for example. [Greek *takhistos,* most swift, very swift, from *takhus,* swift + -SCOPE.]

tacho– *comb. form.* Indicates speed; for example, **tachograph.**

tach·o·graph (táckə-graaf, -graf) *n.* A machine that records the measurements of a tachometer, especially one in a vehicle recording its speed and the times at which it was being driven. [Greek *takhos,* speed + -GRAPH.]

ta·chom·e·ter (ta-kómmitər, tə-) *n.* An instrument used to determine speed, especially the rotational speed of a shaft. [Greek *takhos,* speed, akin to *takhus,* swift + -METER.] **—tach·o·met·ric** (táckə-méttrik) *adj.* **—ta·chom·e·try** (-kómmətri) *n.*

tachy–, tacheo– *comb. form.* Indicates swift or accelerated; for example, **tachymeter, tachycardia.** [Greek *takhus*†, swift.]

tach·y·car·di·a (tácki-kárdi-ə) *n.* Excessively rapid heartbeat. [New Latin : TACHY- + Greek *kardia,* heart.]

ta·chyg·ra·phy (ta-kíggrəfi) *n.* The art or practice of rapid writing or shorthand; especially, the stenography of the ancient Greeks and Romans. [Greek *takhugraphos,* "swift writer" : TACHY- + -GRAPH.] **—ta·chyg·ra·pher, ta·chyg·ra·phist** *n.* **—tach·y·graph·ic** (tácki-gráffik), **tach·y·graph·i·cal** *adj.* **—tach·y·graph·i·cal·ly** *adv.*

tach·y·lyte, tach·y·lite (tácki-līt) *n.* A black, glassy basaltic rock. [German *Tachylyt,* "that which decomposes quickly (in acids)" : TACHY- + Greek *lutos,* soluble, from *luein,* to dissolve.] **—tach·y·lyt·ic** (-líttik) *adj.*

tachymeter. Variant of **tacheometer.**

tach·y·on (tácki-on) *n. Physics.* A hypothetical elementary particle that travels faster than the speed of light, mathematically equivalent to a normal particle moving backwards in time. [TACHY- + -ON.]

tach·y·pnoe·a, *U.S.* **tach·y·pne·a** (táckip-née-ə) *n.* Abnormally rapid breathing. [New Latin, from TACHY- + Greek *pnoea,* breathing.]

tac·it (tássit) *adj.* **1.** Not spoken; implied or understood: *Her glare was a tacit accusation.* **2. a.** Implied by or inferred from actions or statements. **b.** *Law.* Arising by operation of the law, rather than through direct expression. **3.** *Archaic.* Silent; not speaking. [Latin *tacitus,* silent, from the past participle of *tacēre,* to be silent.] **—tac·it·ly** *adv.* **—tac·it·ness** *n.*

tac·i·turn (tássi-turn) *adj.* Habitually untalkative; laconic; uncommunicative. [French *taciturne,* from Latin *taciturnus,* from *tacitus,* silent, TACIT.] **—tac·i·tur·ni·ty** (-túrnəti) *n.* **—tac·i·turn·ly** *adv.*

tack¹ (tak) *n.* **1.** A short, light nail with a sharp point and a flat head. **2.** *Nautical.* **a.** A rope for holding down the weather clew of a course. **b.** A rope for hauling the outer lower corner of a studdingsail to the boom. **c.** The part of a sail to which a tack is fastened, such as the weather clew of a course. **d.** The lower forward corner of a fore-and-aft sail. **3.** *Nautical.* **a.** The position of a vessel sailing to windward, relative to the trim of its sails. **b.** The act of changing from one tack to another. **c.** The distance or leg sailed between changes of tack. **d.** A sailing course that involves continual changes of tack. **4. a.** A course of action meant to minimise opposition to the attainment of a goal. **b.** An approach, especially one of a series. **5.** A large, loose stitch made as a temporary binding or as a mark. **6.** Stickiness, as of a newly painted surface.

~v. **tacked, tacking, tacks.** *—tr.* **1.** To fasten or attach with or as if with a tack or tacks. **2.** To fasten or mark (cloth or a seam, for example) with a loose, temporary stitch. **3.** To put together loosely and arbitrarily: *tacked some stories together.* **4.** To append; add. Used with *on.* **5.** *Nautical.* To bring (a vessel) into the wind in order to change tack. *—intr.* **1.** *Nautical.* **a.** To change the tack of a vessel. **b.** To change tack. Used of a vessel. **2.** To change one's course of action. [Middle English *tak(ke),* from Old North French *taque,* variant of Old French *tache,* nail, fastening, from Germanic.]

tack² *n. Informal.* Food; especially inferior food. [Origin unknown.]

tack³ *n.* The harness for a horse, including the bridle and saddle. Also used adjectivally: *tack room.* [Shortened from TACKLE.]

tack·et (táckit) *n. Chiefly Scottish.* A hobnail. [Middle English, from TACK (nail).]

tack hammer *n.* A light hammer used to drive tacks.

tack·le (táck'l; *also* táyk'l *for noun sense 2*) *n.* **1.** The equipment used in a sport or occupation, especially in fishing. **2. a.** A system of ropes and pulleys for raising and lowering weights. **b.** A rope and its pulley. **3.** *Sports.* In various ball games, an attempt by a player to impede the progress of, or remove the ball from the possession of, an opposing player, by interception or obstruction, or by seizing the player, depending on the rules of the game.

~v. **tackled, -ling, -les.** *—tr.* **1.** To take on and wrestle with (an

PRONUNCIATION KEY

a, trap; aa, father; ai, fair; ar, star; aw, lawn; ay, play; b, bb, stab; rubber; ch, church; ck, ticket; d, dd, dead; ladder; e, dress; ee, bee; er, defer; ew, few; ewr, pure; ə, about; ər, letter; f, ff, fife; differ; g, gg, giggle; h, hat; i, kit; ī, price; īr, fire; j, judge; k, kick; l, ll, let; 'l, needle; m, mm, man; n, nn, no; 'n, sudden; ng, thing; o, lot; ō, no; ŏŏ, foot; ōō, shoe; oor, poor; ow, cow; owr, hour; oy, boy; p, pp, pepper; r, rr, red; s, ss, sauce; sh, ship; t, tt, totter; th, thick; th, this; smooth; u, cut; ur, turn; v, vv, valve; w, wet; y, yes; z, zz, zebra; zh, vision; pleasure

IN FOREIGN WORDS:

aN, oN, Saint-Saëns; hl, Llanelli; Hluhluwe; kh, loch; lough; Khaled

STRESS MARK:

ín-sīt, insight; in-sít, incite

opponent or problem, for example) in order to overcome permanently; come to grips with. **2.** *Sports.* In various ball games, to attempt a tackle on (an opposing player). —*intr. Sports.* To tackle an opponent. [Middle English *takel,* probably from Middle Low German *takel,* from *taken,* to seize.] **—tack·ler** *n.*

tack·y[1], tack·ey (tácki) *adj.* **-ier, -iest.** Slightly adhesive or gummy to the touch; sticky. [From TACK (to attach).] **—tack·i·ness** *n.*

tacky[2] *adj.* **-ier, -iest.** *Slang.* **1.** Distasteful or offensive; tastless. **2.** Shabby; shoddy; cheapskate. [19th century : origin obscure.] **—tack·i·ly** *adv.* **—tack·i·ness** *n.*

tacky[3] *n., pl.* **-ies.** *South African Informal.* A plimsoll. [20th century : origin obscure.]

tac·node (ták-nōd) *n.* In geometry, a point at which two branches of a curve touch and continue without crossing, so as to have a common tangent at this point. Also called "osculation".

ta·co (taákō) *n., pl.* **-cos.** A tortilla folded around a filling, as of minced meat or cheese. [Mexican Spanish, from Spanish, wad, roll, plug, probably from Germanic.]

tac·o·nite (táckə-nīt) *n.* A type of chert, containing magnetite and haematite, mined as a low-grade iron ore. [After the *Taconic* Mountains in New England, United States, where it is found.]

tact (takt) *n.* **1.** The ability to appreciate the delicacy of a situation and to do or say the kindest or most fitting thing; diplomacy. **2.** Skill or ability in dealing with others, especially skill in not giving offence. **3.** *Archaic.* The sense of touch. [French, from Latin *tactus,* sense of touch, from the past participle of *tangere,* to touch.]

Synonyms: *tact, diplomacy, savoir-faire, finesse, subtlety.*

tact·ful (táktf'l) *adj.* Possessing or showing tact; considerate; discreet. **—tact·ful·ly** *adv.* **—tact·ful·ness** *n.*

tac·tic (táktik) *n.* An expedient for achieving a goal; a manoeuvre.

-tactic *adj. comb. form.* Indicates **1.** Pattern, orientation, or position in space; for example, **isotactic, atactic. 2.** Movement; for example, **geotactic, phototactic.**

tac·ti·cal (táktik'l) *adj.* **1.** Of, pertaining to, or using tactics. **2.** Characterised by adroitness, ingenuity, or skill. **3.** *Military.* **a.** Of, pertaining to, used in, or involving operations that are smaller, closer to base, or of less long-term significance than strategic operations: *a tactical unit.* **b.** Carried out in support of military or naval operations: *tactical bombing.*

tactical voting *n.* The practice of voting for a candidate or party one does not positively favour so as to prevent the election of another.

tac·ti·cian (tak-tísh'n, ták-) *n.* **1.** A person skilled in the planning and execution of military tactics. **2.** A clever manoeuvrer.

tac·tics (táktiks) *n.* **1. a.** *Used with a singular verb.* The technique or science of securing the objectives set by strategy; specifically, the art of deploying and directing troops, ships, and aircraft in efficient manoeuvres against the enemy. **b.** The manoeuvres so used. Compare **strategy. 2.** *Used with a plural verb.* Any procedure or set of manoeuvres engaged in to achieve some end or aim. [New Latin *tactica,* from Greek *(ta) taktika,* "(the) matters of arrangement", from the neuter plural of *taktikos,* of order or arrangement, of tactics, from *taktos,* arranged, in order, from *tassein, tattein,* to arrange (in battle formation).]

tac·tile (ták-tīl || *chiefly U.S.* -t'l) *adj.* **1.** Perceptible to the sense of touch; tangible. **2.** Used for feeling: *a tactile organ.* **3.** Of, pertaining to, or proceeding from the sense of touch: *a tactile reflex.* [Latin *tactilis,* from *tactus,* sense of touch.] **—tac·til·i·ty** (-tílləti) *n.*

tac·tion (táksh'n) *n. Rare.* The act of touching; contact. [Latin *tactiō* (stem *tactiōn-*), from *tangere* (past participle *tactus*), to touch.]

tact·less (tákt-ləss, -liss) *adj.* Lacking in delicacy; bluntly inconsiderate or indiscreet. **—tact·less·ly** *adv.* **—tact·less·ness** *n.*

tac·tu·al (ták-tew-əl, -choo-) *adj.* Of, producing, derived from, or pertaining to the sense of touch; tactile. [Latin *tactus,* sense of touch.] **—tac·tu·al·ly** *adv.*

tad (tad) *n. Chiefly U.S. Informal.* A small boy. [Probably from English dialectal *tad,* toad, from Middle English *tadde, tode,* TOAD.]

Tadmor. See **Palmyra.**

tad·pole (tád-pōl) *n.* The aquatic larval stage of a frog or toad, having a tail and external gills that disappear as the limbs develop and the adult stage is reached. [Middle English *taddepol,* "toad head" : *tadde, tode,* TOAD + *pol,* POLL (head).]

Ta·dzhik, Ta·jik (taá-jik, tá-, taa-jéek) *n., pl.* **Tadzhik, Tajik.** A member of a people of Iranian descent inhabiting the Tadzhik S.S.R. and regions of Afghanistan and China. **—Ta·dzhik** *adj.*

Tadzhik Soviet Socialist Republic. Also **Ta·dzhik·i·stan** (ta-jéek-i-staán). Constituent republic of the U.S.S.R. Predominantly mountainous, with parts of the Pamir systems it contains Communism Peak, at 7 495 metres (24,589 feet) the highest mountain in the Soviet Union. The Amu Darya, Syr Darya, and Zeravshan are the principal rivers. Tadzhiks make up just over 50 per cent of the population which is primarily engaged in agriculture. Tadzhikistan became a constituent republic of the U.S.S.R. in 1929. Dushanbe is the capital.

tae·di·um vi·tae (téedi-əm ví-tee, tídi-əm vée-tī) *n.* A feeling of great weariness and boredom with life. [Latin, weariness of life.]

tael (tayl, táy-əl) *n.* **1.** Any of varying units of weight used in eastern Asia, the most common being equivalent to $1\frac{1}{3}$ ounces. **2.** A former Chinese monetary unit, equivalent in value to a tael of standard silver. [Portuguese *tael,* from Malay *tahil, tail,* probably from Hindi *tolā,* a weight, from Sanskrit *tulā,* balance, weight.]

ta'en (tayn). *Archaic & Poetic.* Contraction of **taken.**

tae·ni·a, te·ni·a (téeni-ə) *n., pl.* **-niae** (-ee). **1.** A narrow band or ribbon for the hair worn in ancient Greece. **2.** *Architecture.* The band or fillet separating a Doric frieze from the architrave. **3.** Any ribbon-like anatomical structure. **4.** Any flatworm of the genus *Taenia,* which includes many tapeworms. [Latin, band, ribbon, from Greek *tainia.*]

tae·ni·a·cide (téeni-ə-sīd) *n.* An agent that kills tapeworms. [TAENIA (flatworm) + -CIDE.]

tae·ni·a·sis (tee-nī-ə-siss) *n.* **1.** Infestation with tapeworms. **2.** The symptoms resulting from tapeworm infestation. [TAENI(A) + -ASIS.]

taf·fe·ta (táffitə) *n.* A glossy, stiff, plain-woven fabric of silk, rayon, or nylon, used especially for women's garments.

~*adj.* **1.** Made of or resembling taffeta. **2.** Reminiscent of shot taffeta in being changeable; inconsistent or fickle. [Middle English *taffeta,* from Old French *taffetas,* from Old Italian *taffettà,* from Turkish *tafta,* from Persian *tāftah,* "woven", from *tāftan,* to weave.]

taffeta weave *n.* **Plain weave** *(see).*

taff·rail (táf-rayl, -ril, -rəl) *n. Nautical.* **1.** The rail around the stern of a vessel. **2.** The flat upper part of the stern of a vessel, made of wood and often richly carved. [Alteration of earlier *taff(e)rel,* "carved panel", from Dutch *taffereel,* variant of *tafeleel* (unattested), diminutive of *tafel,* panel, table, from Middle Dutch *tāvele,* from Latin *tabula,* TABLE.]

taf·fy (táffi) *n. U.S.* **1.** A chewy sweet of molasses or brown sugar boiled until very thick and then pulled with the hands or by machine until it is glossy and holds its shape. **2.** *Informal.* Wheedling flattery. [Perhaps from TOFFEE or TAFIA.]

Taf·fy (táffi) *n., pl.* **-fies.** A Welshman. Also used as a term of address. Often considered offensive. [Imitative of the name *Dafydd,* the Welsh version of *David,* patron saint of Wales.]

taf·i·a, taf·fi·a (táffi-ə) *n.* A cheap rum distilled from molasses and refuse sugar in the West Indies. [West Indian Creole, probably alteration of RATAFIA.]

tag[1] (tag) *n.* **1.** A strip of leather, paper, metal, or plastic attached to something or hung from a wearer's neck for the purpose of identification, classification, or labelling: *a price tag.* **2. a.** The plastic or metal tip with which shoelaces and some kinds of string are finished for ease in passing them through eyelets and to prevent them from fraying. **b.** A loop or other attachment by which something may be gripped or hung up. **3.** The contrastingly coloured tip of an animal's tail. **4.** A bright piece of feather, floss, or tinsel surrounding the shank of the hook on a fishing fly. **5. a.** A dirty, matted lock of wool. **b.** A loose lock of hair. **6.** A rag; a tatter. **7.** A small, loose fragment: *tags and snippets.* **8.** An ornamental flourish, as at the end of a signature. **9. a.** A brief quotation, as from the English or Latin classics or the Bible, inserted into a discourse to give it an air of erudition and authority: *Shakespearean tags.* **b.** A cliché, saw, or similar short, conventional idea used to embellish a discourse. **10. a.** The refrain or last lines of a song or poem. **b.** The closing lines of a speech in a play; a cue. **11.** A designation or epithet, especially when unwelcome. **12.** *Computing.* A label assigned to identify data in a computer store.

~*v.* **tagged, tagging, tags.** —*tr.* **1.** To label, identify, or recognise with or as if with a tag. **2.** To fix or attach something else, especially at the end: *tagged an extra paragraph on to the letter.* **3.** To add a literary tag or tags to (a speech, for example). **4.** *Informal.* To follow closely. **5.** To cut the tags from (a sheep). —*intr.* To follow along after; trail after. Usually used with *along.* [Middle English *tagge*†.]

tag[2] *n.* **1.** A children's game in which one player pursues the others until he is able to touch one of them, who then in turn becomes the pursuer. Also called "he", "tig", "tip", "touch". **2.** The act of touching one's partner in tag wrestling.

~*tr.v.* **tagged, tagging, tags. 1.** To touch (another player) in the game of tag. **2. a.** To touch the hand of (one's partner) in tag wrestling. **b.** In baseball, to touch (a runner) with the ball or the glove holding the ball in order to retire him. [Variant of *tig,* perhaps from TICK (tapping sound, originally "a light touch").]

Ta·ga·log (tə-gaá-log, -gá-) *n., pl.* **-logs** or collectively **Tagalog. 1.** A member of a people native to the Philippines and inhabiting Manila and its adjacent provinces. **2.** The Austronesian language spoken by this people. [Tagalog, "(people) from the (Pasig) river" : *taga,* coming from + *ilog,* river.] **—Ta·ga·log** *adj.*

tag·gers (tággərz) *pl.n.* Very thin sheet iron, usually plated with tin.

ta·glia·tel·le (tál-yə-télli || *U.S.* taál-) *n.* A type of pasta cut in flat, narrow strips. [Italian, from *tagliare,* to cut.]

tag·meme (tág-meem) *n.* The smallest syntactic unit that can be shown to have a grammatical function in terms of tagmemics. [Greek *tagma,* order, from *tassein,* to put in order + -EME.]

tag·mem·ics (tag-méemiks) *n. Used with a singular verb. Linguistics.* A theory of grammatical analysis that attempts to show both the formal status of a linguistic unit, such as a noun or morpheme, and its grammatical function in a larger linguistic unit. **—tag·mem·ic** *adj.*

Tagore (tə-gór || -gōr; *Bengali* ta-kóor), **Sir (Raban) Rabindranath** (1861–1941). Indian author, poet, and philosopher. He won the Nobel prize for literature in 1913 for his collection of poetry, *Gitanjali,* drawing on traditional Hindu themes.

tag question *n.* A question, such as *isn't it?* or *don't you think?,* appended to the end of a remark.

Ta·gus (táygəss). *Portuguese* **Te·jo** (túzhoo); *Spanish* **Ta·jo** (taákhō). River of Spain and Portugal. It is 940 kilometres (585 miles) and enters the Atlantic Ocean at Lisbon.

tag wrestling *n.* A wrestling contest between two teams of two

tahr *The tahr is a wild cousin of both the sheep and the goat – hence its scientific name,* Hemitragus *(semi-goat)* jemlahicus. *It lives on wooded hillsides in the Himalayas, India, and Arabia.*

wrestlers each, only one member of each team being allowed in the ring at any one time, the other being permitted to enter when he touches his partner on the hand.

ta·hi·na (tə-hée-nə, ta-) *n.* Also **ta·hi·ni** (-ni). A thick paste made from ground sesame seeds. [Arabic.]

Ta·hi·ti (tə-héeti, taa-, ta-). The largest of the Society Islands in French Polynesia. The first European to discover it was the English navigator, Captain Wallis (1767). The chief products are tropical fruits, copra, vanilla, and sugar cane. Papeete, the capital and chief port, is also the capital of French Polynesia.

Ta·hi·tian (tə-héesh'n, taa-, -héeti-ən) *n.* **1.** A native or inhabitant of Tahiti. **2.** The Polynesian language of Tahiti. **—Ta·hi·tian** *adj.*

tahr (tar) *n.* Any of several goatlike mammals of the genus *Hemitragus,* of mountainous regions of Asia. [Nepalese *thar.*]

tah·sil (tə-séel) *n.* An administrative subdivision of a district in India. [Hindi, from Arabic, "collection".]

tah·sil·dar, tah·seel·dar (tə-séel-daar) *n.* An official in India in charge of revenues and taxation in a tahsil. [Urdu *taḥsīldār,* from Persian : Arabic *taḥsīl,* collection + Persian *-dār,* holder.]

Tai (tī) *n.* A family of languages spoken in southeast Asia and south China, including Thai, Lao, and Shan. **—Tai** *adj.*

tai·a·ha (tī́-ə-haa) *n.* A long, spearlike Maori weapon. [Maori.]

Tai chi, Tai Chi, Tai Ji (tī jée || tī́ chée) *n.* A Chinese form of callisthenics consisting of a series of movements performed slowly and deliberately, for training both the body and the mind in balance, control, and coordination. Also called "Tai chi chuan". [Chinese *taì jí qúan,* great ultimate boxing.]

tai·ga (tī́gə; *also* tī-gaa) *n.* The subarctic coniferous forest of Siberia and of similar regions elsewhere in Eurasia and North America. [Russian *taïga,* from Turkic *taiga,* rocky mountain.]

taiglach. Variant of **teiglach.**

tail[1] (tayl) *n.* **1.** The posterior part of an animal, especially when elongated and extending beyond the trunk or main part of the body. **2.** The bottom, rear, or hindmost part of anything: *the tail of a shirt.* **3.** The rear end of a wagon or other vehicle. **4.** *Aeronautics.* **a.** The rear portion of a fuselage. **b.** An assembly of stabilising planes and control surfaces in this region. Also called "empennage". **5.** The vaned rear portion of any bomb or missile. **6.** Any appendage to the rear or bottom of a thing: *the tail of a kite.* **7.** The long, luminous stream of gas and dust forced from the head of a comet when it is close to the Sun. **8.** Something that follows or takes the last place: *the tail of the journey.* **9.** A retinue or train of followers. **10.** The end of a line or series of persons or things. **11.** The short closing line of certain stanzas of verse. **12.** The refuse or dross remaining from such processes as distilling or milling. **13.** *Printing.* The bottom of a page; the bottom margin. **14.** *Informal.* The trail of a person or animal in flight. **15.** *Informal.* A person assigned to watch and report on someone's movements and actions. **16.** *Slang.* **a.** The buttocks. **b.** The penis. **17.** *Slang.* Women collectively, seen as sexual objects. Considered offensive. **—turn tail.** To run away. **—with (one's) tail between (one's) legs.** In an utterly dejected or defeated state.
~*v.* **tailed, tailing, tails.** *—tr.* **1.** To provide with a tail: *tail a kite.* **2. a.** To deprive of a tail; dock. **b.** To cut the stalks off (fruit). **3.** To wash the bottom of (a baby, for example). Used chiefly in the phrase *top and tail.* **4.** To come towards the end of: *tailing the list.* **5.** To serve as the tail of: *The winning float tailed the parade.* **6.** To connect (objects often dissimilar or incongruous) by or as if by the tail or end: *tail two ideas together.* **7.** *Architecture.* To set one end of (a beam, board, or brick) into a wall. Used with *in* or *on.* **8.** *Informal.* To follow and keep under surveillance. **9.** *Australian.* To tend or herd (sheep or cattle). *—intr.* **1.** *Architecture.* To be inserted at one end, as a floor timber or beam. **2.** *Informal.* To follow. Usually used with *after.* **3.** *Nautical.* **a.** To go aground with the stern foremost. **b.** To be pointed in some direction with the stern when riding at anchor or on a mooring. **—tail off** or **away.** To dwindle.
~*adj.* **1.** Posterior; hindmost. **2.** Coming from behind: *a tail wind.* [Middle English *tayle,* Old English *tæg(e)l.*]

tail[2] *n. Law.* The limitation of the inheritance of an estate to a particular person or his direct descendants.
~*adj. Law.* In tail. Used after the noun and often in combination: *estate tail; fee-tail.* [Middle English *taille, tayle,* from Old French *taille,* cut, division, partition, from *taillier,* to cut, from Vulgar Latin *tāl(l)iāre* (unattested). See **tailor.**]

tail·back (táyl-bak) *n.* A long queue of traffic, especially one stretching back from roadworks or an accident, for example.

tail beam *n. Architecture.* A **tailpiece** *(see).*

tail·board (táyl-bawrd || -bōrd) *n.* A hinged board forming the rear wall of a wagon or truck that can be removed or let down to serve as a ramp in loading or unloading.

tail·coat (táyl-kōt, -kōt) *n.* A man's black coat that is cut away at the front and has a tapering tail at the back which is split into two up to the waist, worn as part of very formal evening dress or as part of a morning suit. Also called "swallow-tailed coat", "tails".

tail end *n.* **1.** The rear or hindmost part of anything. **2.** The very end; the conclusion.

tail·gate (táyl-gayt) *n.* **1.** Either of the pair of gates downstream in a canal lock. Compare **headgate. 2. a.** The tailboard of a vehicle. **b.** The sloping door that forms the back of a hatchback car.
~*v.* **tailgated, -gating, -gates.** *U.S. —tr.* To drive so closely behind (another vehicle) that one cannot stop or swerve in an emergency. *—intr.* To follow another vehicle at too short a distance.

tail-heav·y (táyl-hévvi, -hevvi) *adj.* Having too much weight at the rear either by overloading or from poor design and construction. Said especially of aircraft.

tail·ing (táyling) *n.* **1.** *Plural.* Refuse or dross remaining after such processes as milling, distilling, or mining. **2.** *Architecture.* The part of a tailed beam, brick, or board inside a wall.

taille (tī, taá-yə) *n.* A form of direct royal taxation levied in France before 1789 on nonprivileged subjects and lands, and tending to weigh most heavily on the peasants. [French, a cut, division, from *tailler,* to cut, from Vulgar Latin *tāl(l)iāre* (unattested). See **tailor.**]

tail·light (táyl-līt) *n. Chiefly U.S.* A **rear light** *(see).* Also called "tail lamp".

tai·lor (táylər) *n.* A person who makes, repairs, and alters garments such as suits, coats, and dresses.
~*v.* **tailored, -loring, -lors.** *—tr.* **1.** To make (a garment), especially to satisfy specific requirements or measurements. **2.** To fit or provide (a person) with clothes made to his measurements. **3.** To make, alter, or adapt for a particular end: *a speech tailored to a special audience.* *—intr.* To pursue the trade of a tailor. [Middle English *taillour,* from Anglo-French, variant of Old French *tailleur,* from Vulgar Latin *tāliātor* (unattested), "cutter", from *tāl(l)iāre* (unattested), to cut, from Latin *tālea*†, twig, cutting.]

tai·lor·bird (táylər-burd) *n.* Any of several Old World tropical birds of the genus *Orthotomus,* characteristically using plant fibres to stitch leaves together in making its nest.

tai·lored (táylərd) *adj.* Simple, trim, or severe in line or design: *a highly tailored suit.*

tai·lor-made (táylər-máyd, -mayd) *adj.* **1.** Made by a tailor. **2.** Perfectly fitted to a condition, preference, or purpose; made or as if made to order: *a job tailor-made for me.*
~*n.* **1.** A garment made by a tailor. **2.** *Informal.* A commercially manufactured cigarette, as opposed to one rolled by hand.

tailor's chalk *n.* A thin piece of hard chalk used in dressmaking for making temporary marks on clothing, as for seams or darts.

tail·piece (táyl-peess) *n.* **1.** Any piece forming an end to something; an appendage. **2.** *Printing.* An engraving or design placed as an ornament at the end of a chapter or at the bottom of a page. **3.** *Architecture.* A beam tailed into a wall. Also called "tail beam". **4.** *Music.* A triangular piece of ebony to which the lower ends of the strings of a violin, cello, or some other stringed instruments are attached.

tail·pipe (táyl-pīp) *n.* The pipe through which exhaust gases from an engine are discharged; the final section of a vehicle's exhaust.

tail·plane (táyl-playn) *n.* A horizontal aerofoil fitted to the tail of an aircraft.

tail·race (táyl-rayss) *n.* **1.** The part of a millrace below the water wheel through which the spent water flows. Compare **headrace. 2.** A channel for floating away mine tailings and refuse.

tail rotor *n.* A small rotor fitted at the back of a helicopter to produce a sideways thrust, used to counteract the tendency of the body to rotate in the opposite direction to the main rotor.

tails (taylz) *pl.n.* **1.** *Used with a singular verb.* The reverse side of a coin. Compare **heads. 2. White tie** *(see).* **3.** A **tailcoat** *(see).*

tail·skid (táyl-skid) *n.* A skid attached to the rear underside of certain aircraft to act as a runner.

tail·spin (táyl-spin) *n.* **1.** The descent of an aircraft in a **spin** *(see),* characterised by the rapid spiral movement of the tail section. **2.** *Informal.* A state of emotional collapse; panic.

tail·stock (táyl-stok) *n.* The adjustable stock of a lathe supporting the spindle containing the dead centre.

tail wind *n.* A wind blowing in the same direction as that of the course of a vehicle.

tain (tayn) *n.* **1.** A type of paper-thin tin plate. **2.** Tinfoil used as a backing for mirrors. [French, tinfoil, shortened from *étain,* tin, from Old French *estain,* from Latin *stagnum, stannum,* an alloy of silver and lead.]

Tai·no (tī́nō) *n., pl.* **-nos** or collectively **Taino. 1.** A member of an extinct aboriginal Arawakan Indian people of the West Indies. **2.** The language of this people. [Spanish, from a native name in the West Indies.] **—Tai·no** *adj.*

taint (taynt) *v.* **tainted, tainting, taints.** *—tr.* **1.** To stain or spoil (a person's honour or reputation). **2.** To make poisonous or rotten; infect or spoil. **3.** To affect with some unpleasant or harmful influence; corrupt. *—intr.* To become tainted or contaminated.
~*n.* **1.** A moral defect considered as a stain or spot. **2.** An infecting touch, influence, or tinge. [Middle English *taynten,* from Anglo-French *teinter,* from Old French *teint,* colour, from Latin *tinctus,* past participle of *tingere,* to dip in liquid, dye.]

tai·pan (tī́-pan) *n.* A large venomous Australian snake, *Oxyuranus scutellatus.* [Native Australian name.]

Tai·pei (tī́-páy). *Chinese* **Tai·bei** (-báy). Capital city of Taiwan. Situated in the north of the island, it is a major industrial centre.

Tai·ping (tī́-píng) *n.* Any of those who took part in the largest uprising in Chinese history (1850–64) against the Manchu dynasty, spreading from southwest China almost to Beijing. The movement was suppressed with the help of British and American troops. [Chinese, "Great Peace" (name of the movement).] **—Tai·ping** *adj.*

Tai·wan (tī́-waán, -wán), Official name **Republic of China.** *Portuguese* **For·mo·sa** (fawr-mṓ-sə). Mountainous island off the southeast coast of mainland China. The first Europeans to reach it were the Portuguese (1590) and it became an important centre for trade in the 19th century. China was forced to cede the island to Japan in 1895 but regained it after World War II in 1945. Following defeats by the Communists, the Chinese Nationalists, led by Jiang Jie-shi,

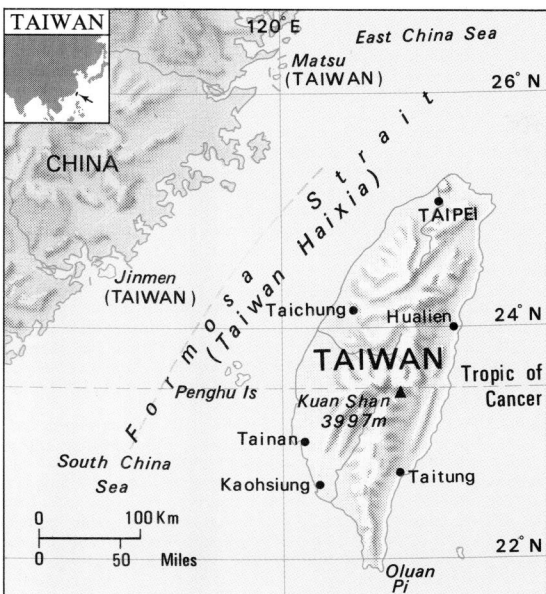

TAIWAN

East China Sea
Matsu (TAIWAN)
120° E
26° N
CHINA
Formosa Strait (Taiwan Haixia)
TAIPEI
Jinmen (TAIWAN)
Taichung
Hualien
24° N
TAIWAN
Tropic of Cancer
Penghu Is
Kuan Shan 3997m
Tainan
Kaohsiung
Taitung
22° N
South China Sea
0   100 Km
0   50   Miles
Oluan Pi

retreated to Taiwan and its neighbouring islands (1949). Under U.S. sponsorship, rapid industrialisation took place, and trade links between the two countries remain strong. Taiwan lost its United Nations seat to the People's Republic of China (1971), which regards Taiwan as one of its provinces. The United States broke off diplomatic relations and recognised the People's Republic in 1979. Electrical goods, clothing, and textiles are its main exports. Area, 35 989 square kilometres (13,895 square miles). Population, 18,500,-000 (mid-1982 estimate). Capital, Taipei.

taj (taaj, taa<u>zh</u>) *n.* A tall conical cap worn by certain Muslims as a headdress of distinction. [Arabic *tāj*, from Persian *tāj*, "crown".]

Tajik. Variant of **Tadzhik.**

Taj Ma·hal (mə-haál, -húl). A mausoleum in Agra, north India. It took almost 20 years (1630–48) to build from white marble carved and inlaid with other stones. It was constructed for Mumtaz-i-Mahal, wife of the Emperor Shah Jahan (who is also buried there).

Tajo. See **Tagus.**

ta·ka (túcka) *n.* The standard monetary unit of Bangladesh, equal to 100 paise. [Bengali.]

ta·ka·he (taá-kaa-hee, -kə-) *n.* An almost extinct flightless bird, *Notornis mantelli*, of New Zealand, having a large bill and brightly coloured plumage. [Maori *takahe* (imitative).]

take (tayk. *Note: the pronunciation* (tek) *is not considered standard*) *v.* **took** (took ‖ took), **taken** (táykən), **taking, takes.** —*tr.* **1.** To get into one's possession by force, skill, or artifice, especially: **a.** To capture physically; seize: *take an enemy fortress.* **b.** To kill, snare, or trap (fish or game, for example). **c.** To go away with; remove, often without proper permission: *Someone's taken my pen.* **d.** To capture in the course of a sport or game: *took two wickets; took my queen.* **e.** To obtain as a result of a victory; win: *took the seat at a by-election.* **f.** To seize authoritatively; confiscate. **2.** To grasp with the hands; grip: *take your partner's hand.* **3.** To carry along or cause to go with one to another place: *always takes his umbrella.* **4.** To encounter or catch in a particular situation; come upon; discover: *They'll never take me unawares.* **5.** To aim; *take a shot at.* **6.** To affect favourably; charm; captivate. Usually used in the passive: *completely taken by the puppy.* **7. a.** To put (food or drink, for example) into the body; eat, drink, inhale, or draw in: *take snuff.* **b.** To eat or drink habitually: *Do you take sugar?* **c.** To eat or drink as part of a course of medical treatment: *take tranquillisers.* **8.** To indulge or engage in (healthful or pleasurable treatment, for example): *take a holiday.* **9. a.** To bring or receive into a particular relation, association, or other connection: *take a new partner into the firm.* **b.** To marry: *take a wife.* **10.** To have sexual intercourse with. Used of a man, as in romantic fiction. **11.** To accept and place under one's care or keeping: *take the children for the weekend.* **12. a.** To appropriate for one's own or another's use or benefit; obtain by purchase; buy. **b.** To buy regularly; especially, to subscribe to: *takes the Times.* **c.** To rent: *take a cottage for the summer.* **13. a.** To assume for or upon oneself: *take the blame.* **b.** To charge or oblige oneself with the fulfilment of (a task or duty, for example); deal with in the appropriate way: *The chaplain took prayers.* **c.** To pledge one's obedience to or adopt as a symbol of one's obedience; impose (a vow or promise) upon oneself: *take the veil.* **d.** To use (time) for a particular end. **e.** To accept or adopt for one's own: *took my side in the argument.* **f.** To require for a correct fitting: *takes size 14.* **g.** To require or have as a fitting or proper accompaniment: *Intransitive verbs take no direct object.* **14.** To obtain through competition: *took the lead.* **15.** To have or come to have: *took the form of a dialogue; taking shape.* **16. a.** To select; pick out;

choose: *take any card.* **b.** To follow (a route or course of action): *took a wrong turning.* **c.** To use as a tool or instrument for doing something: *I'm going to take scissors to that hair of yours.* **d.** To use as a means of conveyance or transportation: *take a steamer to Europe.* **e.** To obtain or find: *take shelter.* **17.** To assume occupancy of: *take a seat.* **18.** To have as a requirement or necessity for something; require: *This job takes brains; It took three hours to get there.* **19.** To derive through conscious or subconscious influence: *She took her domineering tone from her mother.* **20.** To obtain or derive from a source or sources: *took the figures from an opinion poll.* **b.** To note or record: *took particulars of the case.* **21. a.** To put down in writing; write from dictation: *take a letter.* **b.** To put down an image, likeness, or representation of by or as if by drawing, painting, or photography: *take a photo.* **22. a.** To accept (something owed, offered, or given) either reluctantly or willingly: *took the bait.* **b.** To submit to (something inflicted); endure: *He can't take criticism.* **c.** To withstand or contain successfully: *The dam took the heavy flood waters.* **d.** To accept or believe (something put forth) as true or valid: *I'll take your word for it.* **e.** To follow (advice, a suggestion, or a lead, for example). **f.** To accept, handle, or deal with in a specified way: *takes things in his stride.* **g.** To consider in a particular relation or from a particular viewpoint: *Taken as a whole, it was a success.* **23. a.** To do, perform, or accomplish: *take a bath.* **b.** To perform or execute: *The horse took the jump.* **c.** To engage in or adopt, especially with an end in view: *taking precautions.* **24. a.** To allow to come in; admit; give access or admission to: *takes members only.* **b.** To provide room for; accommodate: *We can't take more than 300 guests.* **c.** To absorb or become saturated or impregnated with (dye, for example). **25. a.** To understand or interpret: *He took my criticism as an insult.* **b.** To consider; assume: *took her to be a policewoman.* Also used with *it: I take it you're coming.* **c.** To understand or appreciate: *I take your point.* **d.** To consider as a case in point: *Take children, for example.* **e.** To perceive or feel; experience: *took pride in her work; Don't take offence.* **26. a.** To convey or transport to a place: *This bus takes you to the station.* **b.** To conduct or lead: *That road takes us past the museum.* **c.** To cause to reach (a condition or state): *Her dedication took her to the top of her profession.* **27.** To go with, especially as a chaperone or as the person who pays: *take the children home; took him to the theatre.* **28.** To remove; do away with: *takes all the joy out of life.* **29.** To cause to die; kill; destroy: *The war took both our sons.* **30.** To subtract: *Two take one is one.* **31.** To commit oneself to the study of; enrol in: *take a course in physics.* **32.** *Slang.* To swindle; defraud; cheat: *taken for 40 quid.* —*intr.* **1.** To acquire possession. **2.** To engage or mesh; catch, as gears or other mechanical parts do. **3.** To start growing; root; germinate: *Have the seeds taken?* **4.** To have the intended effect; operate; work: *Glue won't take on that surface.* **5.** To become. Used especially in the phrase *take ill.* —**take aback.** To bewilder; astonish; nonplus. —**take after. 1.** To follow as an example. **2.** To resemble in appearance, temperament, or character: *He takes after his father.* —**take amiss.** To be offended by through misunderstanding. —**take apart. 1.** To divide or analyse (an object or theory, for example) into component parts; disassemble. **2.** *Informal.* To criticise or scold harshly or severely. **3.** *Slang.* **a.** To beat up; thrash. **b.** To defeat overwhelmingly, as in an argument; crush. —**take back. 1.** To retract something stated or written. **2.** To return (an article), especially for an exchange or refund. **3.** To cause to recollect an earlier time: *takes you back.* **4.** To regain. **5.** *Printing.* To move (a part of a printed line) to the preceding line. —**take five** or **ten.** *Chiefly U.S. Informal.* To take a short rest or break, as of five to ten minutes. —**take for. 1.** To consider or suppose to be; regard as: *I take him for a fool.* **2.** To consider mistakenly: *We took you for dead.* —**take it.** *Informal.* To endure abuse, criticism, or other harsh treatment: *You've got to learn to take it in the army.* —**take it lying down.** *Informal.* To submit to unfair or harsh or unjust treatment with no resistance. —**take it out on.** *Informal.* To abuse (another person or thing) in venting one's own anger or frustration. —**take on. 1.** To begin to employ. **2.** To undertake or begin to handle (a task, for example). **3.** To oppose in competition. **4.** To begin to have or acquire: *take on a new image.* **5.** *Informal.* To display emotion; fuss: *Don't take on so!* —**take (someone) out of (himself).** To make less withdrawn or introverted. —**take that.** Used to accompany the delivering of a blow or insult. —**take to. 1.** To have recourse to; go to, as for safety: *took to the woods.* **2.** To set out on: *take to the open road.* **3.** To develop as a habit or steady practice: *take to drink.* **4.** To become adept at: *took to it like a duck to water.* **5.** To become fond of or attracted to: *They took to each other.* —**take upon (oneself). 1.** To accept or assume the responsibility or trouble of. **2.** To assume the right of doing. —**take up with.** *Informal.* To develop a friendship or association with. —See Usage note at **have.**

~*n.* **1.** The act or process of taking. **2.** The number of fish, game birds, or other animals killed or captured at one time. **3.** *Informal.* **a.** A quantity of anything collected at one time; especially, the amount of money stolen by a thief, profit or receipts taken by a business, or tickets sold by a theatre or cinema. **b.** A share of money stolen or profits or receipts taken. **4. a.** The uninterrupted running of a film or television camera or set of recording equipment in making a film or television programme or cutting a record. **b.** Any of a series of films or recordings of the same scene or sound, the best of which will be picked for final use. **5.** A scene filmed or televised without interrupting the run of the camera. **6. a.** Any physical reaction, such as a rash, indicating a successful vaccination. **b.** A successful skin graft. **7.** An amount of copy set in type at one time. **—on the take.** *Slang.* Receiving or appropriating money illegally. [Middle English *taken, took, taken,* Old English *tacan, tōc, tacen* (unattested), from Old Norse *taka, tōk, tekinn.*]

take•a•way (táyk-ə-way) *adj. Chiefly British.* **1.** Selling cooked food to be eaten off the premises: *a takeaway Chinese restaurant.* **2.** A portion or portions of cooked food taken away from the place of sale to be eaten.
~*n.* A shop or restaurant selling takeaway food.

take down *tr.v.* **1.** To bring to a lower position from a higher. **2.** To dismantle; take apart: *take down the scaffolding.* **3.** To lower the arrogance or self-esteem of (a person). **4.** To put down in writing.

take•down (táyk-down) *adj.* Capable of being taken down or apart. Said chiefly of certain rifles.

take-home pay (táyk-hōm) *n.* The amount of one's salary remaining after income tax has been paid and various other deductions have been made.

take in *tr.v.* **1.** To grant admittance to; receive as a guest or lodger. **2.** To reduce in size; make smaller or shorter: *take in a skirt.* **3.** To include or comprise. **4.** To understand; absorb mentally. **5.** *Informal.* To deceive; swindle. **6.** To look at thoroughly; survey: *take in the sight.*

take-in (táyk-in) *n. Informal.* An act or instance of taking in or being taken in.

take off *tr.v.* **1.** To remove (clothing). **2.** To carry off or away. **3.** *Informal.* To imitate or copy, especially in a mocking or humorous manner. **4.** To leave off working for (a period of time): *take the afternoon off.* *—intr.v.* **1.** *Informal.* To go off; start. **2.** To rise up in flight. Used of an aircraft or rocket.

take•off (táyk-off, -awf) *n.* **1.** The act of rising in flight as an aircraft or rocket might do. **2.** *Informal.* An amusing or mocking imitation or caricature of another person. **—See Synonyms at caricature.**

take out *tr.v.* **1.** To extract; remove. **2.** To secure (a licence, for example) by application to an authority. **3.** *Informal.* To escort, as on a date. **4.** In bridge, to cancel (a partner's bid) by bidding a different suit. **5.** *Slang.* **a.** To destroy or eliminate (enemy aircraft, for example). **b.** To kill. **c.** *Sports Informal.* To render (an opponent) ineffective, as by close marking or harsh tackling.

take over *tr.v.* **1.** To undertake (a responsibility or task, for example) in succession to another. **2.** To assume control or management of; especially, to buy the majority of the shares of (a company). **3.** To move (part of a printed line) to the following line. *—intr.v.* To assume the management of or responsibility for something.

take•o•ver, take-o•ver (táyk-ōvər) *n.* The act or an instance of assuming control or management of or responsibility for something; especially: **1.** The forcible seizure of power, as in a state or political organisation. **2.** The acquisition of the majority of the shares of a company. **—take•o•ver** *adj.*

tak•er (táykər) *n.* A person who takes or takes up something, such as a wager or purchase.

take up *tr.v.* **1.** To raise up; lift. **2.** To reduce in size or length; shorten or tighten: *take up the slack.* **3.** To accept the offer, challenge, or bet of. Used with *on*: *I might take you up on that offer.* **4.** To accept (an offer, option, bet, challenge, or other proposal). **5.** To challenge or question. Used with *on*: *I'd like to take you up on that.* **6.** To use up or occupy (space or time, for example). **7.** To develop an interest in or devotion to: *take up astronomy.* **8.** To become the patron of. **9.** To pursue or raise (a matter). Used with *with*: *better take this up with the boss himself.* **10.** To absorb (a liquid or gas). *—intr.v.* To begin again; resume.

take-up (táyk-up) *n.* **1.** A device for reducing slack or taking up lost motion, as in a loom. **2.** The act of taking or tightening up.

ta•kin (taá-keen) *n.* A large buffalo-like ruminant, *Budorcas taxicolor,* of the mountains of central Asia, having backward-pointing horns and a shaggy coat. [Tibeto-Burman (Mishmi).]

tak•ing (táyking) *adj.* **1.** Captivating; winning: *a taking smile.* **2.** *Informal.* Contagious; catching. Said of an infectious disease.
~*n.* **1.** The act of a person or thing that takes. **2.** That which is taken, as a catch of fish. **3.** *Plural.* Receipts, especially of money. **—tak•ing•ly** *adv.* **—tak•ing•ness** *n.*

Takla Makan. See **Tarim Basin.**

tal•a•poin (tál-ə-poyn) *n.* A small African monkey, *Miopithecus talapoin* (or *Cercopithecus talapoin*), having a long tail and greenish fur. [French, "Buddhist monk" (from a fancied resemblance), from Portuguese *talapões,* plural of *talapão,* monk, from Mon *tala pōi,* "our lord" (polite address to a monk).]

talapoin *The talapoin monkey lives in troops of up to 100 in the mangrove swamps and forests of central and West Africa.*

tal•bot (táwl-bət || tól-, tál-) *n.* A large, white hunting dog of a breed now extinct.

talc (tal-k) *n.* **1.** A fine-grained white, greenish, or grey mineral, essentially $Mg_3Si_4O_{10}(OH)_2$, having a soft, soapy texture and used in talcum and face powder, as a paper coating, and as a filler for paint and plastics. Also called "talcum". **2.** Talcum powder.
~*tr.v.* **talcked** or **talced, talcking** or **talcing, talcs.** To apply talc to (a photographic plate, for example). [French *talc,* from Medieval Latin *talcum,* from Arabic *ṭalq,* from Persian *talk*†.]

talc•ose (tál-kōz, -kōss) *adj.* Also **talc•ous** (-kəss), **talck•y** (-ki). Made of, containing, or resembling talc.

tal•cum (tál-kəm) *n.* **1.** Soapstone or talc. **2.** Talcum powder. [Medieval Latin, TALC.]

talcum powder *n.* A fine, often perfumed powder made from purified talc, for use on the skin.

tale (tayl) *n.* **1.** A report or revelation; a recital of facts or happenings: *told her tale of woe.* **2.** A malicious story, piece of gossip, or petty complaint. **3.** A deliberate lie; a falsehood. **4.** A diverting or edifying narrative of real or imaginary events; a story. **5.** *Usually plural.* Anything, whether true or false, told or revealed in breach of confidence, especially to one in authority: *tell tales.* **6.** *Archaic.* A reckoning; a total: *the earthquake's tale of thousands dead.* [Middle English *tale,* Old English *talu,* discourse, narrative.]

tale•bear•er (táyl-bair-ər) *n.* One who spreads malicious stories or gossip; a telltale. **—tale•bear•ing** *adj.* & *n.*

tal•ent (tál-ənt) *n.* **1.** Natural endowment or ability of a superior quality. **2.** A specific mental or physical aptitude; an innate ability to perform successfully in a particular field. **3.** Gifted people collectively: *local talent.* **4.** *Informal.* Sexually attractive people: *not a lot of talent at this party.* **5.** A variable unit of weight and money used in ancient Greece, Rome, and the Middle East. **—See Synonyms at ability.** [Middle English *talent(e),* from Old English *talente,* unit of weight or money, and Old French *talent,* aptitude, both from Latin *talentum,* unit of weight or money (in Medieval Latin, also "mental aptitude", extended sense from the parable of the talents in Matthew 25:14–30), from Greek *talanton.*]

talent scout *n.* An agent who goes in search of talented people for entertaining, sports, business, or the like.

ta•ler, tha•ler (taálər) *n., pl.* **taler** or **-lers.** Any of numerous silver coins serving as a unit of currency in certain Germanic countries from the 15th to 19th centuries. [German *Taler.* See **dollar.**]

ta•les (táy-leez) *n., pl.* **tales.** *Law.* **1.** A group of persons summoned to fill vacancies on a jury that has become deficient in number. **2.** The writ allowing for such a summons of jurors. [Middle English, from the Medieval Latin phrase *tales de circumstantibus,* "such (persons) from those standing about" (used in the writ), from Latin *tālēs,* plural of *tālis,* such.]

ta•les•man (táy-leez-mən, táylz-, -man) *n., pl.* **-men** (-mən, -men). *Law.* A person summoned under a writ of tales.

tale•tell•er (táyl-tellər) *n.* **1.** An oral narrator. **2.** A person who tells tales; a talebearer. **—tale•tell•ing** *adj.* & *n.*

ta•li. Plural of **talus.**

Ta-lien. See **Lüda.**

Talin. See **Tallinn.**

tal•i•on (táli-ən) *n.* **1.** A punishment identical to the offence, such as the death penalty for murder. **2.** The principle of exacting compensation in this way. [Middle English *talioun,* from Old French *talion,* from Latin *tāliō* (stem *tāliōn-*), reciprocal punishment in kind.]

tal•i•ped (tál-i-ped) *adj.* Afflicted with talipes; clubfooted.
~*n.* A person with a clubfoot. [See **talipes.**]

tal•i•pes (tál-i-peez) *n.* A deformity of the human foot; especially, **clubfoot** *(see).* [New Latin *talipes* (stem *taliped-*), "walking on the ankles": Latin *tālus,* ankle, TALUS + -PED.]

tal•i•pot (tál-i-pot) *n.* A tall palm tree, *Corypha umbraculifera,* of tropical Asia. [Bengali *tālipōt,* palm leaf : Sanskrit *tālī,* fan palm, probably akin to *tāla* (see **toddy**) + *pattra,* feather, leaf.]

tal•is•man (tál-iz-mən, -iss-) *n., pl.* **-mans. 1.** A small object, such as a stone or amulet, usually marked with magical signs, that is believed to confer on its bearer supernatural powers or protection. **2.** Anything having apparently magical power. [French and Spanish *talisman,* from Arabic *ṭilsām* (plural *ṭilsamān*), from Late Greek *telesma,* completion, consecrated object, from *telein,* to fulfil, consecrate, from *telos,* aim, result.] **—tal•is•man•ic** (-mánnik) *adj.*

talk (tawk) *v.* **talked, talking, talks.** *—tr.* **1.** To articulate (something, such as thoughts and emotions) in words; express by means of speech: *talk treason.* **2.** To speak of or discuss (something): *talk music.* **3.** To speak or know how to speak in (an idiom or language). **4.** To gain, influence, or bring into a specified state by talking: *talked her into coming; talk his way out of trouble.* **5.** To spend (a period of time) by or as if by talking. Used with *away*: *talk the evening away.* *—intr.* **1. a.** To converse by means of spoken language. Often used with *to* or *with*: *talked to each other for hours.* **b.** To express thoughts, desires, hopes, or the like in words. Used with *about* or *of.* **2.** To articulate words: *The baby can talk.* **3.** To imitate the sounds of human speech: *The parrot talks.* **4.** To communicate one's thoughts in a way other than by spoken words: *talk with the hands.* **5.** To express one's thoughts in writing: *Voltaire talks about London in this text.* **6.** To parley or negotiate with someone: *Let's talk before fighting.* **7.** To gossip; spread rumours: *People will talk.* **8.** To allude to something: *What are you talking about?* **9.** To consult or confer with someone: *I'll have to talk to the others first.* **10.** To reveal information concerning oneself or others, especially under pressure: *Has the prisoner talked?* **11.** To be efficacious: *Nothing talks to them but money.* **—See Synonyms at speak. —talk about.** *Informal.* **1.** Used to express the opinion that the word or words immediately following are an understatement of the actual case: *Talk about stupid, he's a total idiot.* **2.** To imply as a result of what one is saying or doing: *If we decide to buy, we're talking about six years' savings gone.* **—talk at.** To address (someone) without regard to a response: *She talks at people, never to them.* **—talk big.** *Informal.* To brag. **—talk down. 1.** To address someone patronisingly or as if one were very superior. Used with *to.* **2.** To silence (a person), especially by speaking in a loud and domineering manner. **3.** To assist (an aircraft) to land by giving radio instructions. **—talk out. 1.** To discuss (a matter) exhaustively. **2.** To resolve or settle by discussion. **3.** *British.* To block (proposed legislation) by making prolonged speeches, introducing irrelevant material, or the like. **—talk over.** To consider thoroughly in conversation; discuss: *Let's talk it over.* **—talk round. 1.** To persuade: *I talked her round to my position.* **2.** To speak indirectly about

PRONUNCIATION KEY

a, trap; aa, father; ai, fair; ar, star; aw, lawn; ay, play; b, bb, stab; rubber; ch, church; ck, ticket; d, dd, dead; ladder; e, dress; ee, bee; er, defer; ew, few; ewr, pure; ə, about; ər, letter; f, ff, fife; differ; g, gg, giggle; h, hat; i, kit; ī, price; īr, fire; j, judge; k, kick; l, ll, let; 'l, needle; m, mm, man; n, nn, no; 'n, sudden; ng, thing; o, lot; ō, no; o͝o, foot; o͞o, shoe; oor, poor; ow, cow; owr, hour; oy, boy; p, pp, pepper; r, rr, red; s, ss, sauce; sh, ship; t, tt, totter; th, thick; th, this; smooth; u, cut; ur, turn; v, vv, valve; w, wet; y, yes; z, zz, zebra; zh, vision; pleasure

IN FOREIGN WORDS:

aN, oN, Saint-Saëns; hl, Llanelli; Hluhluwe; kh, loch; lough; Khaled

STRESS MARK:

ín-sīt, insight; in-sī́t, incite

(something): *talked round the subject without coming to the point.* **—talk through.** To show (someone) how to do something by going through it giving step-by-step instructions or explanations. **—talk to.** To give a reprimand to; confer with in an attempt to reform.
~n. **1.** An exchange of ideas or opinions; a conversation. **2.** A speech or lecture. **3.** Any hearsay, rumour, or speculation concerning something: *talk of war.* **4.** Any subject of conversation: *the talk of the town.* **5.** *Usually plural.* A conference or negotiation: *peace talks.* **6. a.** A particular manner of speech: *baby talk.* **b.** Any jargon or slang: *street talk.* **7.** Any empty speech or unnecessary discussion: *too much talk and not enough action.* [Middle English *talkien, talken,* probably frequentative formation (with *k*) from Old English *talian,* to reckon, tell, relate.]

Usage: In British English, one talks *to* someone; in American English one often talks *with* someone (*I talked with her briefly yesterday*) though *to* is also possible. *Talk with* in British English can be used only in the sense of "consult": *We talked with the senior officer.*

talk·a·tive (táwkətiv) *adj.* Liking to talk a lot; loquacious. **—talk·a·tive·ly** *adv.* **—talk·a·tive·ness** *n.*

Synonyms: *talkative, loquacious, wordy, garrulous, voluble, effusive, verbose.*

talk back *intr.v.* **1.** To make an impertinent reply: *His father slaps him when he talks back.* **2.** To make a belligerent response: *Our guns will talk back.*

talk·back (táwk-bak) *n.* A system of communication links in a television or radio studio enabling directions to be given while a programme is actually being produced.

talk·er (táwkər) *n.* A person who talks, especially a loquacious or garrulous person.

talk·ie (táwki) *n. Informal.* A cinema film with a sound track.

talk·ing book (táwking) *n.* A tape recording or record of a reading of a book, designed for use by the blind.

talking head *n.* The image of a person on a television documentary or interview who talks at length directly to the camera and is usually seated, with only the head and upper part of the body visible.

talking picture *n.* A talkie. Used especially when such films were first introduced.

talking shop *n. British Informal.* **1.** A meeting or discussion in which views are aired and policy is discussed. **2.** Any place, such as a legislative assembly, where there is much argument and discussion but little positive action.

talk·ing-to (táwking-tōō, -tōō) *n., pl.* **-tos.** *Informal.* A scolding, especially one given by a person in authority to a subordinate.

talk show *n. U.S.* A **chat show** *(see).*

talk·y (táwki) *adj.* **-ier, -iest.** Talkative or full of talk.

tall (tawl) *adj.* **taller, tallest. 1. a.** Having greater than average height: *a tall woman.* **b.** Having considerable height, especially in relation to width; lofty: *tall trees.* **2.** Having a specified height: *three feet tall.* **3.** *Informal.* Fanciful or exaggerated: *tall tales.* **4.** *Informal.* Exorbitant or difficult to fulfil or accomplish: *a tall order.* **5. a.** *Archaic.* Brave; courageous. **b.** *Obsolete.* Excellent; comely; fine. —See Synonyms at **high.**
~adv. Straight; with proud bearing: *stand tall.* [Middle English *tall,* seemly, handsome, valiant, probably from Old English *getæl,* swift, ready.]

tal·lage (tál-ij) *n.* **1.** An occasional tax levied by the Anglo-Norman kings on crown lands and royal towns. **2.** A tax levied by a feudal lord on his dependants.
~tr.v. **tallaged, -laging, -lages.** To levy a tax on. [Middle English *ta(i)llage,* from Old French *taillage,* "a cutting", from *taillier,* to cut, from Vulgar Latin *tāl(l)iāre* (unattested). See **tailor.**]

tall·boy (táwl-boy) *n. British.* A tall chest of drawers, often constructed in separate sections that are mounted vertically together. Compare **highboy.** [TALL + BOY; for this use of *boy,* compare **jack** (fellow, chap) in names of various tools and so on.]

Tal·linn (tál-in). *Russian* **Ta·lin.** *Formerly* **Re·vel** (ráy-vəl). Baltic seaport in the U.S.S.R. Once a Hanseatic town, it is a naval and military base. It was the capital of the independent republic of Estonia (1918–40), and is now the capital of the Estonian S.S.R.

tal·lith (tál-ith || taál-; *Hebrew* taa-léet) *n., pl.* **tallithim** (-im || taál-i-théem) or **talliths.** A fringed prayer shawl with bands of black or blue, worn especially by Orthodox Jewish men at prayer and on certain solemn occasions. [Hebrew (Mishnaic) *ṭallīth,* "cover", from Hebrew *ṭillēl,* he covered.]

tall oil (taal, tawl) *n.* An oily resinous liquid composed of a mixture of rosin acids and fatty acids obtained as a by-product in the treatment of pine pulp and used in soaps, emulsions, and lubricants. [Partial translation of German *Tallöl,* from Swedish *tallolja* : *tall,* pine, from Old Norse *thöll*†, young pine tree + *Öl,* oil.]

tal·low (tál-ō) *n.* **1.** A mixture of the whitish, tasteless, solid or hard fat obtained from parts of the bodies of cattle, sheep, or horses, and used in foodstuffs or to make candles, leather dressing, soap, and lubricants. **2.** Any of various similar fats, as from plants.
~tr.v. **tallowed, -lowing, -lows.** To smear or cover with tallow. [Middle English *talg, talgh, talow,* from Middle Low German *talg, talch.*] **—tal·low, tal·low·y** *adj.*

tal·low-drop (tál-ō-drop) *n.* A style of cutting a gemstone so that it is smooth and convex on one or both sides.

tal·low-wood (tál-ō-wŏŏd) *n.* **1.** A large Australian eucalyptus tree, *Eucalyptus microcorys.* **2.** The hard, greasy wood of this tree.

tal·ly (tál-i) *n., pl.* **-lies. 1.** A stick on which notches are made, used, especially formerly, to keep a count or record, as of amounts paid or owing. **2. a.** The reckoning or score kept on such a stick. **b.** Any reckoning or score kept of a game, account, or the like. **3.** A mark or number of marks used in recording a number of acts or objects. **4.** A label, ticket, piece of metal, or the like used for identification or classification. **5.** Anything that is very similar or corresponds to something else; a double or counterpart. **6.** A metal plate attached to a ship's machinery and bearing instructions for its use.
~v. **tallied, -lying, -lies.** *—tr.* **1.** To record on a tally. **2.** To reckon or count. **3.** To label with a tally. **4.** To cause to correspond or agree. *—intr.* **1.** To be alike; agree; correspond. **2.** To keep the score or reckoning of a thing. [Middle English *taly, talye,* from Norman French *tallie,* from Medieval Latin *tal(l)ia,* from Latin *tālea,* twig, cutting, stick. See **tailor.**]

tal·ly·ho (tál-i-hṓ) *interj.* Used to urge hounds in fox hunting.
~v. **tallyhoed, -hoing, -hos.** *—tr.* To urge on (hounds) or indicate the sighting of (a fox) by shouting "tallyho". *—intr.* To shout "tallyho".
~n., pl. **tallyhos. 1.** The cry of "tallyho". **2.** A kind of fast coach drawn by four horses. [Probably from French *taïaut,* from Old French *thialau, taho,* cry used to urge on hounds.]

tal·ly·man (tál-i-mən) *n., pl.* **-men** (-mən, -men). **1.** A recorder or scorekeeper. **2.** *British.* A travelling salesman who sells goods on credit and collects weekly or monthly payments for them.

Tal·mi gold (tál-mi, taál-) *n.* An alloy of gold and brass, used in making jewellery. [German *Talmigold,* partial translation of French *Talmi-or,* contraction of *Tallois-demi-or,* "half gold (made by) Tallois (a Parisian)".]

Tal·mud (tál-mŏŏd, -mud || taál-) *n.* The collection of ancient Rabbinic writings consisting of the Mishnah and the Gemara, constituting the basis of religious authority for traditional Judaism. It exists in two versions, the *Palestinian Talmud* and the longer *Babylonian Talmud.* [Hebrew (Mishnaic) *talmūd,* learning, instruction, from *lāmadh,* he learnt.] **—Tal·mu·dic** (tal-mŏŏd-ik, -múd-, -méwd- || taal-), **Tal·mu·di·cal** *adj.* **—Tal·mud·ist** (-mŏŏd-ist, -mud-) *n.*

tal·on (tál-ən) *n.* **1. a.** The claw of a bird of prey. **b.** The similar claw of a predatory animal. **2.** Anything similar to or suggestive of a claw. **3.** The part of a lock which the key presses in order to shoot the bolt. **4.** The part of the pack of cards in certain card games left on the table after the deal. **5.** *Architecture.* An ogee moulding. [Middle English, originally "heel", "hinder claw", from Old French, heel, spur, from (unattested) Vulgar Latin *tālō* (stem *tālōn-*), variant of Latin *tālus,* ankle, TALUS.]

ta·luk (taá-lŏŏk, taa-lŏŏk) *n.* In India: **1.** A subdivision of a tax district, consisting of several villages. **2.** Formerly, the hereditary estate of a family. [Urdu, estate, from Arabic.]

ta·lus[1] (táy-ləss) *n., pl.* **-li** (-lī). **1.** A tarsal bone that articulates with the tibia and fibula to form the anklebone. Also called "anklebone", "astragalus". **2.** The ankle. [New Latin, from Latin *tālus,* ankle, probably from Celtic, akin to Irish *sal*†, talon.]

talus[2] *n., pl.* **-luses. 1. a.** A sloping mass of debris at the base of a cliff. **b.** A **scree** *(see).* **2.** A sloping side of a rampart, fortification, or the like. [French, from Old French, probably from Latin *talūtium,* a technical term in mining in Spain, "outcrop indicating the presence of gold-bearing topsoil", from Celtic.]

tam (tam) *n.* **1.** A hat, the **tam-o'-shanter** *(see).* **2.** Variant of **tom** (a Rastafarian's hat).

TAM television audience measurement.

ta·ma·le (tə-maáli) *n.* A Mexican dish made of fried chopped meat and crushed peppers, highly seasoned, wrapped in maize husks, and steamed. [Mexican Spanish *tamal,* from Nahuatl *tamalli.*]

tam·an·du·a (támmən-dóo-ə, -déw-, tə-mándoo-aá) *n.* A chiefly arboreal anteater, *Tamandua tetradactyla,* of tropical America, having a dense, furry coat and a prehensile tail. [Portuguese *tamanduá,* from Tupi, "ant-catcher" : *tacy,* ant + *monduar,* to catch.]

tamandua *Largely nocturnal, this South American anteater is a tree-climber with a prehensile tail that it uses to grip branches. It has a long tongue and no teeth.*

tam·a·rack (támmə-rak) *n.* A North American larch tree, *Larix laricina,* having very small cones. [Algonquian.]

tam·a·rau, ta·ma·rao (támmə-rów, -row) *n.* A small, short-horned buffalo, *Anoa mindorensis,* of the island of Mindoro in the Philippines. [Tagalog *tamaráw, timaraw.*]

tam·a·rin (támmə-rin, -raN) *n.* Any of various small, long-tailed monkeys of the family Callithricidae of tropical South America. [French, from Galibi.]

tam·a·rind (támmə-rind) *n.* **1.** A tropical Old World tree, *Tamarindus indica,* with compound leaves and red-striped yellow flowers. **2.** The fruit of this tree, consisting of a long pod with seeds embedded in an edible pulp. [Medieval Latin *tamarindus,* from Arabic *tamr hindī,* "date of India" : *tamr,* date + *hindī,* of India, from Persian *Hind,* India.] **—tam·a·rind** *adj.*

tam·a·risk (támmə-risk) *n.* Any of numerous shrubs or small trees of the genus *Tamarix,* native to Eurasia, having small, scalelike leaves and spikelike clusters of flowers; especially *T. tetrandra,* which is often grown as an ornamental for its feathery foliage. [Middle English *tamarisc, thamarike,* from Late Latin *tamariscus,* variant of Latin *tamarīx*†.]

tamarisk *A native of the Middle East, the tamarisk was introduced into Britain in the 16th century. It thrives in coastal areas, where it is often grown as a windbreak.*

ta·ma·sha (tə-maáshə) *n.* In India, a public display or entertainment. [Urdu, from Arabic, "a stroll".]

tam·ba·la (támbələ) *n.* A monetary unit of Malawi equal to $^{1}/_{100}$ of a kwacha. [Bantu, "cockerel".]

tam·bour (tám-boor, -bawr, -bər) *n.* **1.** A drum. **2. a.** A small wooden embroidery frame consisting of two concentric hoops over which the fabric is stretched. **b.** Embroidery made on such a frame. **3.** A rolling front or top for a desk, consisting of narrow strips of wood glued side by side onto canvas. **4.** *Architecture.* Any of various types of circular structure, especially: **a.** The wall of a circular

tanager *There are over 200 species of tanager, all native to the Americas. They live chiefly in forests and feed on nectar, fruit, and insects. The blue-necked tanager (above) lives in the tropical forests of South America.*

building that is surrounded with columns. **b.** The vertical part of a cupola. **5.** The sloping buttress or projection on the side of a court designed for playing real tennis or fives.

~*v.* **tamboured, -bouring, -bours.** —*tr.* To do (embroidery) on a tambour. —*intr.* To use a tambour in doing embroidery. [Middle English, from Old French, from Arabic *ṭanbūr,* alteration (by confusion with *ṭanbūr,* lute, TAMBOURA) of Persian *ṭabīr,* drum, TABOR.]

tam·bou·ra, tam·bu·ra (tum-bo͝or-ə, tam-) *n.* An unfretted, four-stringed Indian musical instrument resembling a lute, used to provide a harmonic drone. [Hindi, from Persian *ṭanbūr,* from Arabic. See also **tambour.**]

tam·bou·rin (tám-bo͞o-rin, -ráɴ) *n.* **1.** A long, narrow drum used in Provence. **2.** A Provençal dance in lively two-beat rhythm, accompanied by the tambourin. **3.** A piece of music composed for such a dance. [Provençal *tamborin,* diminutive of *tambor,* TAMBOUR.]

tam·bou·rine (támbə-réen) *n.* A musical instrument consisting of a small drumhead with jingling discs fitted into the rim, carried and shaken with one hand and struck with the other. [French *tambourin,* diminutive of TAMBOUR.]

tame (taym) *adj.* **tamer, tamest. 1.** Brought from natural wildness into a domesticated, tractable, or cultivated state. **2.** Naturally unafraid; not timid. Said of animals. **3.** Submissive; servile: *tame obedience.* **4.** Without spirit or excitement; insipid; flat: *a tame Christmas party.* **5.** Sluggish; languid; inactive: *a tame river.*

~*tr.v.* **tamed, taming, tames. 1.** To make tractable; domesticate. **2.** To subdue or curb. **3.** To soften; tone down. [Middle English *tame,* Old English *tam.*] **—tam·a·ble, tame·a·ble** *adj.* **—tame·ly** *adv.* **—tame·ness** *n.* **—tam·er** *n.*

Tam·er·lane (támmər-layn) (1336–1405). Also **Tam·bur·laine** (támbər-layn) or **Ti·mur** (ti-mo͝or). Mongol conqueror. He led his nomadic hordes from his capital at Samarkand in Central Asia to overrun vast areas of Persia, Turkey, Russia, and India.

Tam·il (tám-il, -'l) *n., pl.* **-ils** or collectively **Tamil. 1.** A member of a Dravidian people of south India and Sri Lanka. **2.** The language spoken by this people. **—Tam·il** *adj.*

Tamil Na·du (naa-do͞o). *Formerly* **Ma·dras.** State in southeast India. After Indian independence the area of the Madras Presidency was divided into new Indian states (1953–56). The Tamil-speaking area became Tamil Nadu with its capital at Madras. It is one of the most highly urbanised and industrial areas of India.

Tam·ma·ny (támməni) *n.* An organisation of the U.S. Democratic Party in New York City, founded as a fraternal society in 1789 and notorious in the 19th century for its political corruption. Also called "Tammany Hall". [From *Tammany* Hall, its meeting place, after *Tamanend,* "the affable", 17th-century Delaware chief noted for his friendliness to whites.] **—Tam·ma·ny·ism** *n.* **—Tam·ma·ny·ite** *n.*

Tammerfors. See **Tampere.**

Tam·muz, Tham·muz (tám-o͞oz, -o͞oz, taa-mo͞oz) *n.* The tenth month in the Hebrew calendar, corresponding to part of June and part of July. [Hebrew *Tammūz,* from Babylonian *Du'uzu, Duzu* (name of a god), contractions of *Dumu-zi,* "the son who rises".]

tam·my[1] (támmi) *n.* A fine, glazed, woollen cloth formerly used for linings or undergarments. [17th century : origin obscure.]

tammy[2] *n., pl.* **-mies.** A tam-o'-shanter.

tam-o'-shan·ter (támmə-shántər) *n.* A brimless Scottish cap, usually woollen, often having a pompom in the centre, and usually pulled down to one side. Also called "tam", "tammy". [After the hero of Robert Burns's poem *Tam o'Shanter.*]

tamp (tamp) *tr.v.* **tamped, tamping, tamps. 1.** To pack down tightly by a succession of blows. **2.** To pack clay, sand, or dirt into (a drill hole) above an explosive. [Back-formation from TAMPION.]

Tam·pax (tám-paks) *n.* A trademark for a menstrual tampon having a cardboard applicator tube.

tam·per[1] (támpər) *intr.v.* **-pered, -pering, -pers. 1.** To interfere in a harmful manner. Used with *with*: *tampering with a mechanism.* **2.** To meddle rashly or foolishly. Used with *with*: *tamper with her feelings.* **3.** To interfere or exert influence surreptitiously so as to bring about an improper state of affairs. Used with *with*: *tamper with a contract.* —See Synonyms at **interfere.** [Originally "to prepare (clay) by mixing", variant of TEMPER.] **—tam·per·er** *n.*

tamper[2] *n.* **1.** One that tamps; especially, a small instrument for packing down tobacco into a pipe bowl. **2.** A neutron reflector in a nuclear bomb that also delays the expansion of the exploding material, making possible a longer-lasting, more energetic, and more destructive explosion.

Tam·pe·re (támpəri; *Finnish* támpe-re). *Swedish* **Tam·mer·fors** (támmər-fawrss). The second largest city in Finland. It is a major industrial centre and has a cathedral and university.

tam·pi·on (tám-pi-ən) *n.* Also **tom·pi·on** (tóm-). A plug or cover for the muzzle of a cannon or gun to keep out dust and moisture. [Middle English *tamp(y)on,* from Old French *tampon,* cotton plug, TAMPON.]

tam·pon (tám-pon, -pən) *n.* **1.** A plug of absorbent material inserted into the vagina to absorb menstrual blood. **2.** *Medicine.* An absorbent wad inserted into a bodily cavity or wound to check a flow of blood or absorb secretions.

~*tr.v.* **tamponed, -poning, -pons.** To plug or fill with a tampon. [French, from Old French, nasalised variant of *tapon,* from Frankish *tappo* (unattested), plug.]

tam-tam (tám-tam, túm-tum) *n.* Any of a set of musical instruments resembling the gong but made of thinner metal and having a shallower rim. [Hindi *ṭamṭam* (imitative).]

tan (tan) *v.* **tanned, tanning, tans.** —*tr.* **1.** To convert (hide) into leather, by treating it with a tanning agent, especially one containing tannin. **2.** To make brown by exposure to ultraviolet rays, especially those of the sun. **3.** *Informal.* To thrash; beat. —*intr.* To become brown from exposure to ultraviolet rays.

~*n.* **1.** Light or moderate yellowish brown to brownish orange. **2.** The brown colour imparted to the skin by ultraviolet rays, especially those of the sun. **3. Tanbark** *(see).* **4. Tannin** *(see),* or a solution derived from it.

~*adj.* **1.** Of the colour tan. **2.** Used in or pertaining to tanning. [Middle English *tannen,* from Old English *tannian* and Old French *tanner,* both from Medieval Latin *tannāre,* from *tannum,* oak bark (used in tanning), probably from Gaulish *tanno-,* oak, from Common Celtic *tann-* (unattested).]

tan tangent.

Ta·na (taánə). Also **Tsa·na** (tsaánə). Lake in Ethiopia. It has a surface area of approximately 3 100 square kilometres (1,197 square miles) and is 1 830 metres (6,000 feet) above sea level. It is the source of the Blue Nile.

tan·a·ger (tánnijər) *n.* Any of various small New World birds of the family Thraupidae, often having brightly coloured plumage. [New Latin *tanagra,* from Portuguese *tangará,* from Tupi : *atá,* to walk + *carâ,* around.]

Tananarive. See **Antavavarivo.**

tan·bark (tán-baark) *n.* **1.** The bark of various trees, especially the oak and hemlock, used as a source of tannin. **2.** Shredded bark from which the tannin has been extracted, used to cover circus arenas, racetracks, and other surfaces. Also called "tan".

tan·dem (tándəm) *n.* **1.** A two-wheeled carriage drawn by two horses harnessed one behind the other. **2.** A team of carriage horses harnessed in single file. **3.** A bicycle with two or more saddles, for two or more riders seated one behind the other. **4.** Any arrangement in which two or more persons or objects are placed one behind the other or operate in conjunction with one another: *working in tandem.*

~*adv.* One behind the other.

~*adj.* **1.** Positioned one behind the other. **2.** Working in conjunction with another or one another; cooperative. **3.** *British.* Designating, using, or pertaining to an intermediate automatic telephone exchange: *tandem dialling.* [Latin *tandem,* "exactly then", at length, finally (but jocularly taken to mean "lengthways", "one after another") : *tam,* so, so much + *-dem,* demonstrative suffix.]

Tan·doo·ri (tán-do͝or-i, tun-) *n.* A north Indian method of cooking in a charcoal-fired clay oven (a *tandoor*). [Urdu *tandoor,* oven.] **—Tan·doo·ri** *adj.*

tang[1] (tang) *n.* **1.** A sharp, often acrid taste, flavour, or smell, such as that of lemon juice or onions or sea air. **2.** A distinctive quality that adds piquancy. **3.** A trace, hint, or suggestion of something. **4. a.** A sharp point, shank, tongue, or prong. **b.** A projection by which a tool, such as a chisel, sword blade, or knife, is attached to its handle or stock. In this sense, also called "shank".

~*tr.v.* **tanged, tanging, tangs.** To furnish with a tang or give a tang to. [Middle English *tange,* serpent's tongue, insect's sting, probably from Old Norse *tangi,* a sting, point.] **—tang·y** *adj.*

tang[2] *n.* A loud ringing or vibrating sound; a twang.

~*v.* **tanged, tanging, tangs.** —*tr.* To cause to twang or clang. —*intr.* To twang or clang. [Imitative.]

Tang (tang) *n.* Chinese dynasty (618–907 A.D.). A high cultural period, it is regarded as the golden age of Chinese poetry. Buddhism and its art forms flourished. Expansionist policies and increased trade made the capital Changan (now Xi'an) a famous cosmopolitan centre. **—Tang** *adj.*

Tan·ga·nyi·ka, (táng-gən-yeékə, -gan-). Lake in east central Africa. It is situated in the Great Rift Valley, on the borders of Zaire, Burundi, Tanzania, and Zambia. Its surface area is about 33 000 square kilometres (12,738 square miles).

Tanganyika. See **Tanzania, United Republic of.**

tan·ge·lo (tánjə-lō) *n., pl.* **-los. 1.** A hybrid citrus tree that is a cross between certain varieties of grapefruit and tangerine. **2.** The fruit of this tree, having an acid, orange pulp. [*Tange*rine + pom*elo.*]

tan·gen·cy (tán-jən-si) *n.* Also **tan·gence** (-jənss). The condition of being tangent.

tan·gent (tánjənt) *adj.* **1.** Making contact at a single point or along a line; touching but not intersecting. **2.** Diverging from the main point; irrelevant.

~*n.* **1.** A line, curve, or surface touching but not intersecting another line, curve, or surface. **2.** *Abbr.* **tan a.** The ratio of the ordinate to the abscissa of the endpoint of an arc of a unit circle centred at the origin of a Cartesian coordinate system, the arc being of length *x* and measured anticlockwise from the point (1,0) if *x* is positive or clockwise if *x* is negative. **b.** The function of an acute angle in a right-angled triangle that is the ratio of the length of the side opposite the angle to the length of the side adjacent to the angle. **3.** A sudden change of course, as in thought or speech; a digression. Used chiefly in the phrase *at a tangent.* **4.** In a clavichord, a small upright brass pin at the back of a key, that strikes the string when the key is depressed and produces the sound. [New Latin *linea tangēns,* "touching line", from Latin *tangēns* (stem *tangent-*), present participle of *tangere,* to touch.]

tangent galvanometer *n. Physics.* A simple galvanometer having a small magnetic needle free to rotate in a horizontal plane and mounted at the centre on a flat vertical coil through which the current is passed.

tan·gen·tial (tan-jénsh'l) *adj.* Also **tan·gen·tal** (-jent'l). **1.** Of, per-

PRONUNCIATION KEY

a, trap; aa, father; ai, fair; ar, star; aw, lawn; ay, play; b, bb, stab; rubber; ch, church; ck, ticket; d, dd, dead; ladder; e, dress; ee, bee; er, defer; ew, few; ewr, pure; ə, about; ər, letter; f, ff, fife; differ; g, gg, giggle; h, hat; i, kit; ī, price; īr, fire; j, judge; k, kick; l, ll, let; 'l, needle; m, mm, man; n, nn, no; 'n, sudden; ng, thing; o, lot; ō, no; o͝o, foot; o͞o, shoe; oor, poor; ow, cow; owr, hour; oy, boy; p, pp, pepper; r, rr, red; s, ss, sauce; sh, ship; t, tt, totter; th, thick; th, this; smooth; u, cut; ur, turn; v, vv, valve; w, wet; y, yes; z, zz, zebra; zh, vision; pleasure

IN FOREIGN WORDS:

aɴ, oɴ, Saint-Saëns; hl, Llanelli; Hluhluwe; kh, loch; lough; Khaled

STRESS MARK:

ín-sīt, insight; in-sít, incite

taining to, or moving along or in the direction of a tangent. **2.** Only slightly connected; peripheral. **3.** Going off at a tangent; divergent. **—tan·gen·ti·al·i·ty** (tan-jénshi-ál-əti) *n.* **—tan·gen·tial·ly** *adv.*

tangent plane *n.* The plane containing all the lines tangent to a specified point on a surface.

Tan·ger (toN-zháy). *English* **Tan·gier** (tan-jéer, tán-, tán-jeer) or **Tan·giers** (-z). Port on the Moroccan side of the Strait of Gibraltar. An ancient Phoenician city, it was held by the Portuguese (1471–1662) and British (1662–84). From 1923–24 it was administered as the International Zone by Britain, France, and Spain, and from 1928 also by Italy. The international status was restored after World War II, but the city was returned to Morocco in 1956.

tan·ger·ine (tánjə-réen) *n.* **1.** A variety of the widely cultivated citrus tree, *Citrus reticulata,* bearing edible fruit having an easily peeled deep-orange skin and sweet, juicy pulp. **2.** The fruit of this tree. **3.** Strong reddish orange to strong or vivid orange. [Short for *tangerine orange,* "orange of Tangier", from TANGER (from where such oranges were first imported).] **—tan·ger·ine** *adj.*

tan·gi·ble (tán-jə-b'l, -ji-) *adj.* **1. a.** Discernible by the touch; capable of being touched; palpable. **b.** Visible and capable of being valued; material; corporeal: *tangible property.* **2.** Capable of being clearly and exactly comprehended; having real substance; concrete: *tangible evidence.* —See Synonyms at **real.**
~*n.* **1.** Something palpable or concrete. **2.** *Plural. Chiefly U.S.* Material assets. [Old French *tangible,* from Late Latin *tangibilis,* from Latin *tangere,* to touch.] **—tan·gi·bil·i·ty** (-bílləti), **tan·gi·ble·ness** *n.* **—tan·gi·bly** *adv.*

tan·gle[1] (táng-g'l) *v.* **-gled, -gling, -gles.** —*tr.* **1.** To mix together or intertwine in a confused mass; snarl. **2.** To involve in hampering or awkward complications; entangle. **3.** To trap; ensnare. —*intr.* **1.** To be or become entangled. **2.** To enter into argument, dispute, or conflict. Used with *with*: *tangled with the law.*
~*n.* **1.** A confused, intertwined mass. **2.** A jumbled or confused state or condition. **3.** A state of bewilderment. **4.** *Informal.* An argument; an altercation. [Middle English *tangilen,* nasalised variant of *tagilen,* probably from Scandinavian, akin to Swedish dialectal *taggla*†, to entangle.] **—tang·ly** *adj.*

tangle[2] *n. Chiefly Scottish.* **1.** A large brown seaweed, *Laminaria digitata,* found on the lower areas of a shore. **2.** Any large brown seaweed; oarweed. [Scottish, probably from Old Norse *thöngull.*]

tan·gled (táng-g'ld) *adj.* Complicated in a random or confused way.

tan·go (táng-gō) *n., pl.* **-gos.** **1.** A Latin-American ballroom dance in duple time, characterised by long gliding steps and sudden dramatic poses. **2.** The music for this dance.
~*intr.v.* **tangoed, -going, -gos.** To dance the tango. [American Spanish, originally an Afro-American drum dance, possibly of Niger-Congo origin.]

tan·gram (táng-gram || tán-, -grəm) *n.* A Chinese puzzle consisting of a square cut into five triangles, a square, and a rhomboid, to be reassembled into different figures. [Possibly Chinese *táng,* TANG (Chinese dynasty, hence "the Chinese") + -GRAM.]

tanh (than, tansh). hyperbolic tangent.

tan·ist (tán-ist, tháwn-) *n.* Among the ancient Celts, the heir apparent to the chief, elected during the chief's lifetime. [Irish Gaelic *tānaiste,* "second person", from Old Irish *tānaise*†, second, next.]

tan·ist·ry (tán-istri, tháwn-) *n.* The system of electing a tanist.

tank (tangk) *n.* **1.** A large, often metallic container for liquids or gases. **2.** A large, usually manmade, reservoir or cistern, as for drinking water or irrigation; especially, any of a kind common in India. **3.** *Military.* A powerful, turreted, heavily armoured combat vehicle that is mounted with cannon and guns and has caterpillar treads to traverse rough terrain. **4.** *U.S. Slang.* A jail or jail cell.
~*tr.v.* **tanked, tanking, tanks.** To place, store, or process in a tank. **—tank up.** *Informal.* **1.** To fill up a vehicle with petrol. **2.** *Slang.* **a.** To drink to the point of drunkenness. **b.** To cause to tank up. [Perhaps from Gujarati *tānkh,* pond, cistern, from Sanskrit *taḍāga,* pond, from Dravidian. *Tank* (military vehicle) was originally a British code name, from its resemblance to a benzene tank.]

tan·ka[1], **thang·ka** (tángkə, táangkə) *n.* A Tibetan religious painting, usually, on silk, mounted on a piece of rich material in the form of a hanging scroll. [Tibetan *thaṅka.*]

tanka[2] *n.* A Japanese verse form in five lines, the first and third composed of five syllables and the rest of seven. [Japanese, "short poem", from Chinese : *duǎn,* short + *ge,* song, poem.]

Tan·ka (tángkə, táangkə) *n., pl.* **-kas** or collectively **Tanka.** *Often small* **t.** A member of a people in southern China who live on small boats, clustered in colonies. [Cantonese *tan ka* : *tan,* tribal name represented by the character *dan,* "egg" + *ka,* variant of Mandarin Chinese *jia,* family, people.]

tank·age (tángkij) *n.* **1.** The capacity or contents of a tank or tanks. **2.** The act or process of putting or storing in a tank. **3.** The fee for such storage. **4.** Animal residues left after rendering fat in a slaughterhouse and used for fertiliser or feed.

tank·ard (tángkərd) *n.* **1.** A large drinking cup having a single handle and often a hinged cover; especially, a tall pewter or silver mug. **2.** The amount of liquid contained in a tankard. [Middle English *tankard,* probably related to Middle Dutch *tanckaert*†.]

tank destroyer *n.* A high-speed armoured vehicle equipped with antitank guns.

tanked (tangkt) *adj.* Also **tanked up.** *Slang.* Drunk.

tank engine *n.* A steam locomotive in which the water is carried in tanks mounted on the boiler. It has two rectangular tanks mounted each side *(side tank)* or a single tank around the boiler *(saddle tank).* Also called "tanker", "tank locomotive".

tank·er (tángkər) *n.* **1.** A ship, aeroplane, goods vehicle, railway wagon or other means of transport used to carry liquids, such as oil, in bulk. **2.** A tank engine.

tank farming *n.* The cultivation of plants in tanks of water without soil.

tank top *n.* A sleeveless, tightfitting, usually knitted upper garment with a low neck, worn by women or men over a blouse or shirt.

tank wagon *n.* A railway wagon with a tank for carrying liquids in bulk. Also called "tanker".

tan·nage (tánnij) *n.* **1.** The act, process, or skill of tanning. **2.** Something tanned.

tan·ner[1] (tánnər) *n.* A person who tans hides.

tanner[2] *n. British Slang.* A sixpenny piece (half a shilling). Not in current usage. [19th century : origin obscure.]

tan·ner·y (tánnəri) *n., pl.* **-ies.** A place where hides are tanned.

Tann·häu·ser (tán-hoyzər). In German legend, a minstrel knight who after having spent a time of revelry with Venus, the goddess of love, sought absolution from the Pope but was refused.

tan·nic (tánnik) *adj.* Pertaining to or obtained from tannin.

tannic acid *n.* A lustrous yellowish to light brown amorphous, powdered, flaked, or spongy mass having the approximate composition $C_{76}H_{52}O_{46}$, derived from the bark and fruit of many plants and used in tanning, as a mordant to fix dyes, to clarify wine and beer, and as an astringent and styptic. Also called "tannin".

tan·nin (tánnin) *n.* **1.** Tannic acid. **2.** Any of various chemically different substances capable of promoting tanning. Also called "tan". [French *tanin,* from *tanner,* to TAN.]

Tan·noy (tánnoy) *n.* A trademark for a public-address system.

Ta·no·an (taánō-ən) *n.* A language family of several American Indian peoples of New Mexico and Arizona. **—Ta·no·an** *adj.*

tanrec. Variant of **tenrec.**

tan·sy (tánzi) *n., pl.* **-sies.** Any of several plants of the genus *Tanacetum*; especially, *T. vulgare,* native to the Old World, having clusters of button-like yellow flowers and pungent, aromatic juice sometimes used medicinally and as a flavouring. [Middle English, from Old French *tanesie,* perhaps from Medieval Latin *athanasia,* an elixir of life, from Greek *athanasia,* immortality : *a-,* not, without + *thanatos,* death.]

tan·tal·ic (tan-tál-ik) *adj.* Of, pertaining to, or containing tantalum.

tan·ta·lise, tan·ta·lize (tántə-līz) *tr.v.* **-lised, -lising, -lises.** To tease or torment by or as if by exposing to view but keeping out of reach something that is much desired. [From TANTALUS.] **—tan·ta·li·sa·tion** (-lī-záysh'n) *n.* **—tan·ta·lis·er** *n.* **—tan·ta·lis·ing·ly** *adv.*

tan·ta·lite (tántə-līt) *n.* A black to red-brown mineral, essentially $(Fe,Mn)(Ta,Nb)_2O_6$, distinguished from columbite by the predominance of tantalum over niobium and used as an ore of both elements. [Swedish *tantalit,* from New Latin TANTALUM.]

tan·ta·lous (tántələss) *adj. Chemistry.* Of or containing trivalent tantalum. [TANTAL(UM) + -OUS.]

tan·ta·lum (tántələm) *n. Symbol* **Ta** A very hard, heavy grey metallic element that is exceptionally resistant to chemical attack below 150°C. It is used to make light-bulb filaments, electrolytic capacitors, lightning conductors, nuclear reactor parts, and some surgical instruments. Atomic number 73, atomic weight 180.948, melting point 2 996°C, boiling point 5 425°C, relative density 16.6, valencies 2, 3, 4, 5. [New Latin, after TANTALUS; when immersed in acid it is unaltered, like Tantalus standing in the water.]

tan·ta·lus (tántələss) *n.* A stand in which decanters are displayed locked up. [After TANTALUS.]

Tan·ta·lus (tántələss). *Greek Mythology.* A king who for his crimes was condemned in Hades to stand in water that receded when he tried to drink it, and with fruit hanging above him that receded when he reached for it. [Greek *Tantalos,* "bearer", "sufferer".]

tan·ta·mount (tántə-mownt || *West Indies also* -múngt) *adj.* Equivalent in effect or value. Used after the noun with *to.* [Originally a verb, to "be equal to", from Anglo-French *tant amunter,* to amount to so much : Old French *tant,* so much, from Latin *tantus,* from *tam,* so + *amo(u)nter,* to AMOUNT.]

tan·ta·ra (tántə-rə, -raá, tan-taárə || *U.S. also* -tárrə) *n.* **1.** A fanfare of a trumpet or horn. **2.** A sound resembling such a fanfare. [Latin *taratantara* (imitative).]

tan·tiv·y (tan-tívvi) *adv.* At full gallop or at top speed.
~*n., pl.* **tantivies.** **1.** A blast on a horn. **2.** A fast and furious gallop; top speed. [Perhaps imitative of galloping horses.]

tant mieux (tóN m-yér, -yö) *adv. French.* So much the better.

tan·to (táŋ-tō || taán-) *adv. Music.* Too much; to an excess. Used as part of a direction: *allegro non tanto.* [Italian.]

tant pis (tóN pée) *adv. French.* So much the worse.

tan·tra (tán-trə, tún-) *n. Sometimes capital* **T.** Any of a comparatively recent class of Hindu or Buddhist religious writings, in Sanskrit, concerned with mysticism and magic. [Sanskrit, loom, warp, hence principle, doctrine, from *tanōti,* he stretches or weaves.]

tan·trum (tántrəm) *n.* A fit of bad temper, especially when childish or petulant. [18th century : origin obscure.]

Tantung. See **Dandong.**

tan·yard (tán-yaard) *n.* A tannery.

Tan·za·ni·a, United Republic of (tánzə-néer, -née-ə). Commonwealth country in East Africa formed by the union of Tanganyika and Zanzibar in 1964. The mainland formed part of German East Africa until World War I, after which it was administered by the British until its independence in 1961. The sultanate of Zanzibar

tankard *An ivory tankard mounted in silver gilt by the Swedish craftsman Didrik Hysing (1676–1702).*

tanker *Modern oil tankers are the largest ships ever built. This one, the* Haql Episkopi, *was the largest of all when she was launched in Japan in 1968 – 345 metres long (1,132 feet) and 326 000 tonnes deadweight.*

tapestry *Detail from a Flemish tapestry,* The Hunt of the Unicorn, *made in about 1500.*

(and Pemba), a British protectorate from 1890, gained its independence in 1963. Tanzania is mostly plateau, broken by the Great Rift Valley, and mountain areas, including Mount Kilimanjaro. More than 85 per cent of the people living as subsistence cultivators or herders of cattle. Cotton, coffee, cloves, sisal, and diamonds dominate its exports. However, under Dr. Julius Nyrere, president since 1962, off-shore natural gas has been found, manufacturing and tourism are expanding, and the TanZam railway (opened 1975) to Dar es Salaam, is opening up the south's coal and iron deposits. Area, 945 087 square kilometres (364,804 square miles). Population, 19,900,000 (mid-1982 estimate). Capital Dodoma.

tan·zan·ite (tánzə-nīt) *n.* A hydrated calcium aluminium silicate mineral, exhibiting blue, violet, or greenish coloration, used as a gem. [Tanzan(ia) + -ite.]

Tao, Dao (tow, dow, tа́a-ō, dа́a-ō) *n.* In the philosophy of Taoism: **1.** The universal force that produces harmony in nature. **2.** The way or course in all aspects of life that is the most effective and least conspicuous, and is in harmony with the spirit of nature and the universe. [Chinese *dào,* way.]

Taoi·seach (tée-shə, thée-, -shək, -shəkh) *n.* The prime minister of the Republic of Ireland. [Irish, leader.]

Tao·ism, Dao·ism (tów-iz'm, dów-, *also* tа́a-ō-, dа́a-ō-) *n.* **1.** A principal philosophy and system of religion of China founded upon the teachings of Lao-tse, thought to have lived in the sixth century B.C., and based upon the concept of Tao, seeking to achieve practical and spiritual harmony with the universe. **2.** A more recent, popular version of Taoism, incorporating the use of charms and magic. **—Tao·ist** *adj. & n.* **—Tao·is·tic** (-ístik) *adj.*

tap¹ (tap) *v.* **tapped, tapping, taps.** *—tr.* **1.** To strike gently but audibly, and usually repeatedly. **2.** To give a light rap with: *tap a pencil.* **3.** To produce with a succession of light blows. **4.** *Chiefly U.S.* To reinforce or repair (shoe heels or toes) by attaching metal taps or a layer of leather or rubber. *—intr.* **1.** To deliver a gentle, light blow or blows. **2.** To walk making light clicks. *—n.* **1. a.** A gentle but audible blow. **b.** The sound made by it. **2.** A metal plate attached to the toe or heel of a shoe, as for tap-dancing. [Middle English, from Old French *taper,* from Germanic.]

tap² *n.* **1.** A device consisting of a valve and spout used to regulate delivery of a fluid at the end of a pipe. **2.** A plug for a bunghole, as in a cask; a spigot. **3. a.** Alcoholic drink drawn from a tap. **b.** Alcoholic drink of a particular brew, cask, or quality. **4.** *Surgery.* The removal of bodily fluid: *a spinal tap.* **5.** A tool for cutting an internal screw thread. Compare **die.** **6.** A connection made between two points of an electric circuit, used, for example, to provide an intermediate potential. **7.** A concealed listening or recording device fitted to a telephone line or other communications system. Also called "wiretap". **8.** *British.* A **taproom** (see). **—on tap. 1.** On draught; tapped from the cask or keg. Said especially of beer. **2.** *Informal.* Available for immediate use; ready.

~tr.v. **tapped, tapping, taps. 1.** To furnish (a cask, for example) with a spigot or tap. **2.** To pierce in order to draw off liquid: *tap a rubber tree.* **3. a.** To draw off (liquid) by tapping. **b.** To extract or exploit as if by tapping: *tapped every possible source of energy.* **4.** *Surgery.* To withdraw fluid from (a bodily cavity). **5.** To make a connection with or open outlets from: *tap a water main.* **6. a.** To fit an electronic tap to (a telephone line, for example). **b.** To listen to or record (a telephone conversation, for example) by means of a tap. **7.** To make a connection in (an electric circuit) so as to draw off an intermediate potential or current. **8.** To cut screw threads in (a collar, socket, or other fitting). **9.** *Slang.* To ask (a person) for money. [Middle English *tappe,* Old English *tæppa.*] **—tap·per** *n.*

ta·pa (tа́apə) *n.* **1.** The inner bark of the **paper mulberry** (see). **2.** A paper-like cloth made in the Pacific islands by pounding this or similar bark. [Marquesan and Tahitian.]

tap dance *n.* A dance in which the rhythm is tapped out by the heels and toes in rapid, often intricate steps, the sound emphasised by taps on the dancer's shoes. **—tap-dance** (tа́p-daanss ‖ -danss) *intr.v.* **—tap dancer** *n.*

tape (tayp) *n.* **1.** A narrow strip of strong woven fabric, such as that used in sewing or bookbinding. **2.** Any continuous narrow, flexible strip of cloth, metal, paper, or plastic, such as adhesive tape, magnetic tape, or ticker tape. **3.** A string stretched across the finishing line of a racetrack to be broken by the winner. **4.** A tape recording. **5.** A tape cartridge.

~v. **taped, taping, tapes.** *—tr.* **1. a.** To fasten, secure, strengthen, or wrap with tape. **b.** To bind together (the sections of a book) by applying strips of tape to. **2.** To measure with a tape measure. **3.** To record (sounds or pictures) on magnetic tape. **—get** or **have (someone** or **something) taped.** *Chiefly British Informal.* To understand thoroughly the mind or workings of; have fully summed up. *—intr.* To make a recording on magnetic tape. [Middle English *tap(p)e,* Old English *tæppa, tæppe.*]

tape cartridge *n.* **1.** A cartridge containing an endless loop of magnetic tape and designed for automatic use on insertion into a compatible sound or video recorder, or a computer system. Also called "tape". **2.** A similar but usually smaller cartridge containing unlooped tape. Also called "cassette", "tape".

tape deck *n.* **1.** A tape recorder and player having no built-in amplifiers or speakers, used as a component in a high-fidelity sound system. **2.** A system of spools, magnetic tape, and a read-write head, used as a computer storage system.

tape grass *n.* An aquatic plant, *Vallisneria spiralis,* having long, grasslike, submerged leaves. Also called "eelgrass".

tape-loop (tа́yp-loōp) *n.* A magnetic tape recording joined in an endless loop so that it constantly replays itself. Also called "loop".

tape machine *n. Chiefly British.* A telegraphic instrument that receives and records stock-market quotations on a paper tape. Also *U.S.* "ticker".

tape measure *n.* A tape of cloth, paper, or steel marked off in a linear scale, as in inches or centimetres, used for taking measurements. Also *U.S.* "tapeline".

ta·per (tа́ypər) *n.* **1.** A small or very slender candle. **2.** A long waxcoated wick used to light candles or gas lamps. **3.** Something that gives off a feeble light. **4.** A gradual decrease in thickness or width of an elongated object.

~v. **tapered, -pering, -pers.** *—intr.* **1.** To become gradually narrower or thinner towards one end. **2.** To lessen gradually, as in intensity or significance; diminish; slacken and finally stop. Used with *off.* *—tr.* To cause to taper.

~adj. Gradually decreasing in size towards a point; tapering. [Middle English, from Old English *tapor, tapur,* probably altered from *papur,* from *papur,* from Latin *papȳrus,* papyrus, wick made of papyrus.] **—ta·per·ing·ly** *adv.*

tape-re·cord (tа́yp-ri-kawrd, -rə-) *tr.v.* **-corded, -cording, -cords.** To record on magnetic tape.

tape recorder *n.* An apparatus used to record sound on magnetic tape and, usually, to play back sound so recorded.

tape recording *n.* **1. a.** Magnetised tape on which sound has been recorded. **b.** The sound recorded on a magnetic tape. Also called "tape". **2.** The act of recording on magnetic tape.

tap·es·try (tа́ppistri) *n., pl.* **-tries. 1.** A heavy textile fabric having a varicoloured, often pictorial, design woven across the warp, used for wall hangings or furniture coverings, for example. **2.** A textile imitating this. **3.** Anything suggestive of tapestry in its complexity, richness, or variety: *"the fair tapestry of human life"* (Thomas Carlyle). [Middle English *tapstery,* altered from *tapissery, tapecery,* from Old French *tapisserie,* from *tapisser,* to cover with carpet, from *tapis, tapiz,* carpet, from Medieval Greek *tapition,* variant of Greek *tapētion,* diminutive of *tapēs,* carpet.] **—tap·es·tried** *adj.*

ta·pe·tum (tə-pée-təm) *n., pl.* **-ta** (-tə). **1.** *Botany.* A layer of nutritive cells within the sporangium of ferns and related plants or within the anther of flowering plants. **2.** *Anatomy.* A membranous reflecting layer or region in the choroid coat of the eye of certain, notably nocturnal, animals. **3.** A stratum of fibres of the corpus callosum. [New Latin, from Medieval Latin, carpet, from Latin *tapēte,* from Greek *tapēs.* See **tapestry.**] **—ta·pe·tal** *adj.*

tape·worm (tа́yp-wurm) *n.* Any of various ribbon-like, often very long, segmented flatworms of the class Cestoda, that are parasitic in the intestines of vertebrates, including humans.

tap house *n. Archaic.* A tavern or bar.

tap·i·o·ca (tа́ppi-ōkə) *n.* A beady starch obtained from the root of the cassava, used for puddings and as a thickening agent in cooking. [Portuguese and Spanish, from Tupi *tipioca,* "residue".]

ta·pir (tа́y-pər, -peer ‖ tə-péer) *n.* Any ungulate mammal of the genus *Tapirus,* of tropical America or southern Asia, having a heavy body, short legs, and a fleshy proboscis. [Guarani *tapiira.*]

tap·is (tа́p-ee, -i) *n. Archaic.* A tapestry or similar cloth used as a wall hanging, table cover, or rug. **—on the tapis.** Being discussed or considered. [Middle English, a type of cloth, from Old French *tapiz,* from Vulgar Latin *tappetium* (unattested), from Late Latin, from Greek *tapētion,* diminutive of *tapēs* (stem *tapēt-*), tapestry.]

tap·pet (tа́ppit) *n.* A lever or projecting arm that moves or is moved by contact with another part, usually to communicate a certain motion, as between a driving mechanism and a valve. [From TAP (to strike lightly).]

taoism

TAOISM, PHILOSOPHY OF NATURE

Chinese sect believes in a natural path through life

There is a simple message in the Chinese philosophy of Taoism: follow the natural path of life. It declares that man can overcome all his difficulties by spontaneously following his nature – in much the same way that water effortlessly finds its own course. Taoism was founded in the 4th or 3rd century B.C. and was based on the teachings of the sage Lao Zi, who is reputed to have lived two centuries earlier. It takes its name from the book *Tao-te-Ching* (literally, Path of China) and was in sharp conflict with the earlier, bureaucratic teaching of the philosopher Kong Zi, or Confucius. He urged a belief in loyalty, respect for authority, the justice of the state, and the right of talent to be recognised.

Taoists turned to a belief that there is a mystical harmony of man with his surroundings and that truth is to be found in a love of nature. Taoism became a formal religion in the 1st century B.C., with a pantheon of gods and a priesthood. It was practised until recently, but it has declined since the People's Republic of China was formed in 1949.

MEETING OF MINDS *This painting by Wang Shu Ku shows a smiling encounter between Lao Zi (left) and Confucius, two philosophers whose beliefs were in sharp conflict.*

tap·pit-hen (táppit-hen) *n. Scottish.* **1.** A crested hen. **2.** A large mug with a knobbed lid. [Scottish *tappit,* tufted, crested, from *tap,* dialectal variant of TOP.]

tap·room (táp-room, -room) *n.* A bar, as in a hotel or pub.

tap·root (táp-root ‖ -root) *n. Botany.* The main root of certain plants, usually stouter than the lateral roots and growing straight downwards from the stem.

taps (taps) *n. Used with a singular verb.* In the U.S. armed forces, a bugle call or a drum signal sounded at night as an order to put out lights, and also sounded at military funerals and memorial services. [From TAP (light blow, drumbeat).]

ta·pu (taá-poo) *adj. N.Z.* Taboo. [Maori.] —**ta·pu** *n.*

Ta·pu·ya (tə-poo-yə, taa-) *n., pl.* **-yas** or collectively **Tapuya.** A Tapuyan-speaking Indian. —**Ta·pu·ya** *adj.*

Ta·pu·yan (tə-poo-yən, taa-) *n.* A South American Indian family of languages, now spoken only in remote regions of Brazil.

~*adj.* Of or pertaining to this family of languages or its speakers.

tap water *n.* Water containing dissolved salts as obtained from the normal domestic supply, as distinguished from distilled or deionised water.

tar[1] (tar) *n.* **1.** A dark, oily, viscid mixture, consisting mainly of hydrocarbons, produced by the destructive distillation of organic substances such as wood, coal, or peat. **2. Coal tar** (*see*). ~*tr.v.* **tarred, tarring, tars.** To coat with tar. —**tar and feather.** To punish a person by covering first with tar and then with feathers. [Middle English *taar, terr,* Old English *te(o)ru.*] —**tar·ry** (taári) *adj.*

tar[2] *n. Informal.* A sailor. [Short for TARPAULIN.]

Tarabalus al-Gharb. See Tripoli.

Tar·a·ca·hi·tian (tárrəkə-héesh'n) *adj.* Of or pertaining to a language family of the Uto-Aztecan group. [From *Tarahumara* and *Cahita,* names of two peoples in Mexico.]

taradiddle. Variant of **tarradiddle.**

ta·ra·ma·sa·la·ta (tə-ráamə-sə-láatə, -rámmə-, tárrəmə-) *n.* A pale pink, creamy paste made from the dried, salted, and pressed roe of mullet or cod, seasoned with lemon juice, and served as an hors-d'oeuvre. [Modern Greek : *taramas,* cod's roe + *salata,* SALAD.]

tar·an·tel·la (tárrən-téllə) *n.* **1.** A lively, whirling southern Italian dance once thought to be a remedy for tarantism. **2.** The music for this dance, in $^6/_8$ time. [Italian, diminutive formed from *Taranto,* seaport in south Italy, where tarantism was common.]

tar·an·tism (tárrənt-iz'm) *n.* A malady characterised by an uncontrollable urge to dance, epidemic in southern Italy from the 15th to the 17th century and believed to result from the bite of the tarantula. [New Latin *tarantismus,* after *Taranto.* See **tarantella.**]

ta·ran·tu·la (tə-rántew-lə) *n., pl.* **-las** or **-lae** (-lee). **1.** Any of various large, hairy, chiefly tropical spiders of the family Theraphosidae, capable of inflicting a painful but not seriously poisonous bite. **2.** A wolf spider, *Lycosa tarentula,* of southern Europe, once thought to cause tarantism. [Medieval Latin *tarantula,* from Italian *tarantola,* from *Taranto* (see **tarantella**), where it is common.]

ta·rax·a·cum (tə-ráksəkəm) *n.* **1.** Any plant of the genus *Taraxacum,* which includes the common dandelion, *T. officinale.* **2.** The root of any of these plants, the latex of which is used as a tonic and mild laxative. [Medieval Latin, from Arabic *tarakhshaqūq,* from Persian *talkh,* bitter + *chaqūq,* purslane.]

tar·boosh, tar·bush (taar-boosh) *n.* A brimless, usually red, felt cap with a silk tassel, worn by Muslim men, either by itself or as the base of a turban. [Egyptian Arabic *ṭarbush,* "sweating cap" : Turkish *ter,* sweat + Persian *pūshidān†,* to cover.]

Tar·de·noi·si·an (tárdə-nóyzi-ən) *adj.* Of, pertaining to, or designating a mesolithic culture characterised by the use of small flint tools. [After *Tardenois,* France, where the tools were found.]

tar·di·grade (tárdi-grayd) *n.* Any of various minute, slow-moving arthropods of the class Tardigrada, having eight legs and living in water or damp moss. Also called "water bear". ~*adj.* **1.** Of or belonging to the Tardigrada. **2.** Slow in thought or action; sluggish. [New Latin *Tardigrada,* from Latin *tardigradus,* slow-moving : *tardus,* slow (see **tardy**) + -GRADE.]

tar·dy (tárdi) *adj.* **-dier, -diest. 1. a.** Occurring or arriving later than expected or scheduled; late. **b.** Acting more slowly than expected, as through reluctance; dilatory. **2.** Moving or progressing slowly; sluggish. [Middle English *tardif, tardive,* slow, from Old French, from Common Romance *tardīvus* (unattested), from Latin *tardus†,* slow.] —**tar·di·ly** *adv.* —**tar·di·ness** *n.*

Synonyms: tardy, late, overdue, dilatory, lagging.

tar·dy·on (tárdi-on) *n.* An elementary particle that travels more slowly than the speed of light; a normal particle, as opposed to a tachyon. [Latin *tardus,* slow + -ON, after TACHYON.]

tare[1] (tair) *n.* **1.** Any of various small vetches of the genus *Vicia,* such as *V. hirsuta.* **2.** Any of several other weedy plants that grow in cornfields. **3.** The seed of any of these weeds. **4.** *Plural.* Noxious elements, likened to weeds growing among wheat. By allusion to Matthew 13:25: *"his enemy came and sowed tares among the wheat."* [Middle English *tare†,* seed of the vetch.]

tare[2] *n.* **1.** *Abbr.* **t.** The weight of a container or wrapper that is deducted from the gross weight to obtain net weight. **2.** A deduction from gross weight made to allow for the weight of a container. **3.** *Chemistry.* A counterbalance, especially an empty vessel used to counterbalance the weight of a similar container. **4.** The weight of a motor vehicle, especially a lorry, without a load, passengers, or fuel. ~*tr.v.* **tared, taring, tares.** To determine, allow for, or indicate the tare of (a container). [Middle English, from Old French, waste, deficiency, from Medieval Latin *tara,* from Arabic *ṭarḥah,* thing thrown away, from *ṭaraḥa,* to reject, throw.]

targe (tarj) *n. Archaic.* A light shield or buckler. [Middle English, from Old French. See **target.**]

tar·get (tárgit) *n.* **1.** An object with a marked surface that is shot at to test accuracy, such as a padded disc with coloured concentric circles for use in rifle or archery practice. Also used adjectivally: *target practice.* **2.** Anything aimed or fired at. **3. a.** An object of criticism or attack. **b.** Something viewed as an object to be acted on with the aim of transforming it. **4.** A desired end; a goal: *a target of £50.* Also used adjectivally: *a target figure.* **5.** A joint consisting of the neck and breast of a lamb. **6.** The sliding sight on a surveyor's levelling rod. **7.** A small, round shield, especially one worn on the arm in medieval times. **8. a.** A structure in a camera tube with a storage surface that is scanned by an electron beam to generate a signal output current similar to the charge-density pattern stored on

tapir *A hoofed mammal found in tropical forests near water, in Central and South America and in Malaysia. Tapirs feed mostly on leaves.*

the surface. **b.** A usually metal part in an X-ray tube on which a beam of electrons is focused and from which X rays are emitted. ~*tr.v.* **targeted, -geting, -gets. 1.** To have as a target. **2.** To make a target of. [Middle English, from Old French *targette*, diminutive of *targe*, light shield, from Frankish *targa* (unattested).]

target language *n.* The language into which something such as a text or document is translated. Also called "object language". Compare **source language.**

Tar·gum (tár-gəm, -gŏm, -gŏom, taar-gŏom) *n., pl.* **-gums** or **Targumim** (tár-gŏo-méem). Any of several Aramaic translations or paraphrasings of the Old Testament. [Mishnaic Hebrew *targūm*, translation, interpretation, from Hebrew *tirgēm*, he interpreted.] —**Tar·gum·ic** (-gŏomik), **Tar·gum·i·cal** *adj.* —**Tar·gum·ist** *n.*

tar·iff (tárrif) *n.* **1.** A list or system of duties or taxes imposed by a government on imported, or sometimes exported, goods, levied in order to raise revenue and, often, to protect indigenous producers. **2.** A duty or tax in such a system. **3.** Any schedule of prices, fares, or fees, especially in a bar, hotel, or restaurant. ~*tr.v.* **tariffed, -iffing, -iffs. 1.** To fix a duty or price on, according to a tariff. **2.** To fix a tariff on or draw up a tariff for. [French *tarif*, from Italian *tariffa* and Spanish *tarifa*, from Turkish *ta'rifa*, from Arabic *ta'rīf*, "information", "notification", from *'arafa*, to notify.]

tar·la·tan (tárlətən) *n.* A thin, stiffly starched open-weave muslin. [French *tarlatane*, perhaps from Portuguese *tarlatana*, irregular variant of *tiritana*, from French *tiretaine*, linsey-woolsey, TARTAN.]

tar·mac (tár-mak) *n.* **1.** *Capital* **T.** A trademark for a bituminous substance used as a binder in paving. **2.** An area paved with this substance, especially the area of an airport where the aircraft land and take off. **3.** A tarmacadam road or pavement. [Shortening of TARMACADAM.] —**tar·mac** *adj.*

tar·mac·ad·am (tármə-káddəm) *n.* A hard flat surface, as for a road or pavement, consisting of layers of crushed stone with a tar binder that is rolled until smooth. [TAR + MACADAM.]

tarn (tarn) *n.* A small mountain lake, especially one in a cirque. [Middle English *terne, tarne*, from Old Norse *tjörn, tjarn*†.]

tar·na·tion (taar-náysh'n) *interj. U.S.* Damnation. Used euphemistically.

tar·nish (tárnish) *v.* **-nished, -nishing, -nishes.** —*tr.* **1.** To dull the lustre of; discolour, especially by exposure to air or dirt. **2.** To detract from or spoil; taint. —*intr.* **1.** To lose lustre; become dull or discoloured. **2.** To become spoiled or tainted. ~*n.* **1.** The condition of being tarnished or tainted. **2.** Something that tarnishes; a stain or film that dulls or discolours. [French *ternir* (present stem *terniss*-), from Germanic *tarnjan* (unattested).] —**tar·nish·a·ble** *adj.*

ta·ro (taárō ‖ *U.S. also* tárrō) *n., pl.* **-ros. 1.** A widely cultivated tropical plant, *Colocasia esculenta*, having broad leaves and a large, starchy, edible rootstock. **2.** The rootstock of this plant. Also called "cocoyam", "dasheen", "eddoe". [Tahitian and Maori.]

tar·ok, tar·oc (tárrək) *n.* A card game developed in Italy in the 14th century, originally played with the full pack of 78 tarot cards. Also called "tarot", "tarots". [Italian *tarocchi*, plural of *tarocco*, TAROT.]

tar·ot (tárrō) *n.* **1.** Any of a set of 78 playing cards consisting of the major and the minor **arcana** (*see*), the former consisting of a joker plus 21 cards depicting vices, virtues, and elemental forces, and the latter consisting of 56 ordinary cards split into 4 suits. The major arcana is used as trumps in the game of tarok and by itself or with some or all of the minor arcana in fortunetelling. **2.** *Usually plural.* Tarok. [French, from Italian *tarocco*†.]

tar·pan (tár-pan) *n.* An extinct wild horse, *Equus caballus*, once common in Europe. [Kirghiz.]

tar·pa·per (tár-paypər) *n.* Heavy paper impregnated or coated with tar, used as a waterproof protective material in building.

tar·pau·lin (tár-páwlin, taar- ‖ *chiefly U.S.* tárpəlin) *n.* **1.** Waterproof canvas used to cover and protect things from moisture. **2.** A sheet of this material. **3. a.** A sailor's hat made of this fabric. **b.** *Archaic.* A sailor. [Earlier *tarpawling* : perhaps TAR + *-pawling*, covering, from PALL (cover).]

tar·pon (tárpən) *n., pl.* **tarpon** or **-pons.** Either of two fish of the genus *Megalops*, especially a large, silvery game fish, *Megalops atlantica*, of Atlantic coastal waters. [Dutch *tarpoen*†.]

tar·ra·did·dle, tar·a·did·dle (tárrə-didd'l ‖ -didd'l) *n. Informal.* **1.** A petty falsehood; a fib. **2.** Absurd or pretentious twaddle; nonsense. [18th century: perhaps akin to DIDDLE.]

tar·ra·gon (tárrə-gən ‖ *chiefly U.S.* -gon) *n.* **1.** An aromatic herb, *Artemisia dracunculus*, native to Eurasia. **2.** The leaves of this plant, used as seasoning. [Medieval Latin *tragonia, tarchon*, from Medieval Greek *tarkhōn*, from Arabic *ṭarkhūn*, perhaps "dragon wort", from Greek *drakontion*, adderwort, from *drakōn*, DRAGON.]

tar·ri·ance (tárri-ənss) *n. Archaic.* The act or an instance of tarrying; a delay or sojourn.

tar·ry (tárri) *v.* **-ried, -rying, -ries.** —*intr.* **1.** To delay or be late in going, coming, or acting. **2.** To wait; linger. **3.** To remain or stay temporarily; sojourn. —*tr. Archaic.* To await. —See Synonyms at **stay.** [Middle English *tarien*†.] —**tar·ri·er** *n.*

tar·sal (társs'l) *adj.* **1.** Of, pertaining to, or situated near the tarsus of the foot. **2.** Of or pertaining to the tarsus of the eyelid. ~*n.* Any of the seven small bones forming the posterior part of the skeleton of the foot. Also called "tarsale". [New Latin *tarsālis*, from TARSUS.]

tarsal gland *n.* Any of the small sebaceous glands situated below the conjunctiva of the eyelids.

tarot

TRUMPS FOR TELLING THE FUTURE
Dual-purpose playing cards devised 800 years ago

No one knows where the tarot came from. An 18th-century French scholar, Comte de Gébelin, tried to trace the cards back to ancient Egypt, on the premise that the Egyptians had put all their wisdom and science into their hieroglyphic alphabet, and that the tarot was related to this. Occult tradition has it that the town of Fez, in Morocco, became the world centre of scholarship after the destruction of the Library at Alexandria in the 3rd century A.D., and that the tarot was invented there in about 1200 as a means of communication among the multilingual community. What is certain is that the 22 picture cards of the tarot were added to 56 number cards of Oriental origin, probably in Italy in the 14th century.

Modern tarot games mostly use 54 cards: 32 suit cards and the 22 tarot cards, of which all but the fool are permanent trumps. The tarots are used for simple games and for fortune-telling, but the full pack is also used for more elaborate divination, when the tarot cards are called the major arcana; the suit cards are the minor arcana.

The identities of the trumps vary, but usually they are:

0.	The Fool	11.	Strength
1.	The Juggler	12.	The Hanged Man
2.	The Female Pope	13.	Death
3.	The Empress	14.	Temperance
4.	The Emperor	15.	The Devil
5.	The Pope	16.	The Tower (or Hospital)
6.	The Lovers	17.	The Star (or Stars)
7.	The Chariot	18.	The Moon
8.	Justice	19.	The Sun
9.	The Hermit	20.	The Day of Judgment
10.	The Wheel of Fortune	21.	The World

SIXTEENTH TRUMP *This hand-coloured engraving of The Tower is from a 19th-century Italian tarot pack.*

tar·seal (tár-seel) *tr.v.* **-sealed, -sealing, -seals.** *Australian & N.Z.* To surface (a road) with asphalt.
~*n. N.Z.* The surface of a tarsealed road. [TAR + SEAL.]

tar·si·er (tár-si-ər, -ay) *n.* Any of several small nocturnal primates of the genus *Tarsius,* of the Philippines and Indonesia, having large, round eyes and a long tail. [French, from *tarse,* ankle (from its elongated ankles), from New Latin *tarsus,* TARSUS.]

tar·so·met·a·tar·sus (tár-sō-méttə-tár-səss) *n., pl.* **-si** (-sī). A compound bone between the tibia and the toes of a bird's leg, formed by fusion of the tarsal and metatarsal bones. Also called "tarsus". [TARS(US) + METATARSUS.]

tar·sus (tár-səss) *n., pl.* **-si** (-sī). **1. a.** The section of the vertebrate foot between the leg and the metatarsus. **b.** The seven bones making up this section. **2.** A fibrous plate that supports and shapes the edge of the eyelid. **3.** *Zoology.* **a.** The tarsometatarsus. **b.** The distal segmented structure on the leg of an insect or an arachnid. [New Latin, from Greek *tarsos,* frame of wickerwork, (hence) flat surface, sole of the foot, ankle.]

tart[1] (tart) *adj.* **tarter, tartest. 1.** Having a sharp, pungent taste; sour. **2.** Sharp or bitter in tone or meaning; cutting. [Middle English *tart,* Old English *teart,* sharp, severe.] **—tart·ly** *adv.* **—tart·ness** *n.*

tart[2] *n.* **1.** *Chiefly British.* **a.** A pastry case having no top crust, with a usually sweet filling, such as fruit, jam, or custard. **b.** A covered pastry case with a fruit filling; a fruit pie. **2.** *Chiefly U.S.* A small pie for an individual serving, usually without a top crust, having a sweet filling. **3.** *Informal.* A promiscuous woman or prostitute, especially one dressed in a flashy, gaudy, or provocative manner. **—tart up. 1.** To improve the appearance of or redecorate, especially in a cheap, flashy, or gaudy manner. **2.** To dress (oneself) up and put on make-up, especially so as to look sexy and provocative. [Middle English *tarte,* from Old French, variant (influenced by Medieval Latin *tartarum,* TARTAR) of *torte,* from Latin *torta,* round bread, "twisted", from *torquēre,* to turn, twist.]

tar·tan[1] (tárt'n) *n.* **1.** Any of numerous textile patterns consisting of stripes of varying widths and colours crossing at right angles against a solid background, each forming a distinctive design worn by the members of a particular Scottish clan. **2.** A twilled woollen fabric or garment having such a pattern. **3.** Any fabric having a similar pattern. [Probably from Old French *tertaine, tiretaine,* linsey-woolsey, from Old Spanish *tiritaña,* a thin silk stuff, from *tiritar,* to rustle (imitative).] **—tar·tan** *adj.*

tartan[2] *n.* A small, single-masted Mediterranean ship with a large lateen sail. [French *tartane,* from Italian *tartana,* probably from Old Provençal *tartana*†, buzzard.]

tar·tan·ry (tártn'h-ri) *n.* A tendency to overemphasise supposedly typical Scottish mannerisms, dress, or idiom, when writing about or otherwise representing Scotland or the Scottish.

tar·tar[1] (tártər) *n.* **1.** A reddish acid compound, chiefly potassium bitartrate, found in the juice of grapes and deposited on the sides of casks during wine-making. **2.** A hard, yellowish deposit on the teeth, consisting of organic secretions and food particles deposited in various salts, such as calcium carbonate. [Middle English *tartre, tartar,* from Old French *tartre,* from Medieval Latin *tartarum,* from Medieval Greek *tartaron*†.]

tartar[2] *n.* *Sometimes capital* **T.** A ferocious, formidable, or violent-tempered person. [*Tartar,* variant of TATAR.]

Tartar. Variant of **Tatar.**

Tar·tar·e·an (taar-táir-i-ən, -táar-) *adj.* Of or pertaining to Tartarus.

tartar emetic *n.* A poisonous crystalline salt, potassium antimony tartrate, K(560)$C_4H_4O_6$, used as a mordant and formerly as an emetic.

Tar·tar·i·an (taar-táir-i-ən) *adj.* Of or pertaining to the Tatars or Tartary.

tar·tar·ic (taar-tárrik) *adj.* Of, pertaining to, or derived from tartar or tartaric acid.

tartaric acid *n.* Any of four isomeric crystalline organic compounds, $C_4H_6O_6$, used to make cream of tartar, as a sequestrant, in tanning, and in effervescent drinks, baking powders, and photographic chemicals.

tar·tar·ise, tar·tar·ize (tártə-rīz) *tr.v.* **-ised, -ising, -ises.** To treat, impregnate, or combine with tartar, tartar emetic, or cream of tartar. **—tar·tar·i·sa·tion** (-rī-záysh'n || *U.S.* -ri-) *n.*

tar·tar·ous (tártərəss) *adj.* Consisting of, derived from, or containing tartar.

tartar sauce (taar-tár) *n.* Mayonnaise with chopped onion, olives, pickles, and capers, and served as a sauce with fish. Also called "tartare sauce".

tartar steak *n.* **Steak tartare** *(see).*

Tar·ta·rus (tártərəss) *n.* **1.** *Greek Mythology.* **a.** The abysmal regions below Hades where the Titans were confined. **b.** A region of Hades reserved for the most wicked sinners. **2.** Any infernal or hellish region. [Latin, from Greek *Tartaros*†.]

Tar·ta·ry (tártəri). Also **Ta·ta·ry** (táatəri). A historical region comprising the areas of eastern Europe and Asia overrun by Tatars in the 13th and 14th centuries and extending as far east as the Pacific under Genghis Khan.

tart·let (tárt-lət, -lit) *n.* A small tart for an individual serving, with a sweet or savoury filling, such as fruit or cheese.

tar·trate (tártrayt) *n.* A salt or ester of tartaric acid.

tar·trat·ed (taar-tráytid) *adj.* Containing, combined with, or derived from tartaric acid.

Tar·tu (tártōō). *Swedish & German* **Dor·pat** (dór-pat). City in the western U.S.S.R., in Estonia, lying on the river Ema. It is an important industrial and commercial centre.

Tar·tuffe (taar-tŏŏf, -tŏŏf) *n.* A hypocrite; especially, one who affects religious piety. [After *Tartuffe,* title character and hypocrite in Molière's comedy (1664).] **—Tar·tuff·i·an** *adj.* **—Tar·tuff·ism** *n.*

tart·y (tárti) *adj.* Designating clothes, appearance, or behaviour, especially of women, that are sexually provocative in an obvious and vulgar way.

Tar·zan (tár-z'n, -zan) *n.* *Sometimes small* **t.** *Informal.* A man with a muscular physique, who possesses great physical strength and virility. Often used humorously. [After *Tarzan,* the hero of a number of stories by E. R. BURROUGHS.]

Tash·kent (tásh-ként). City in the central Asian U.S.S.R., lying in the foothills of the Tien Shan mountains. It is the capital of the Uzbek Soviet Socialist Republic. The city lies in a broad oasis along the river Chirchik, which produces cotton and fruit, and is one of the largest producers of finished textile goods in Asia.

ta·sim·e·ter (tə-símmitər, ta-) *n.* A device for measuring small temperature changes by the expansion or contraction of a solid. [Greek *tasis,* tension + -METER.]

task (taask || task) *n.* **1.** A specific piece of work assigned by a superior or done as part of one's duties. **2.** Anything that has to be done, especially when difficult or unpleasant. **3.** The function, duty, or purpose of a working person, unit, or thing: *My task is to see fair play.* **—take to task.** To reprimand or censure.
~*tr.v.* **tasked, tasking, tasks. 1.** To assign a task to or impose a task upon. **2.** To overburden with labour; tax. [Middle English *taske, tasque,* tax, work imposed, task, from Anglo-French *tasque,* variant of Old French *tasche,* from Medieval Latin *tasca, taxa,* from *taxāre,* to TAX.]
Synonyms: *task, job, chore, assignment.*

task force *n.* A temporary grouping of forces and resources, especially of military or police units, for the accomplishment of a specific objective.

task·mas·ter (táask-maastər || tásk-mastər) *n.* One who imposes work, especially heavy or exacting work.

Tas·ma·ni·a (taz-máyni-ə). Island and state of Australia, lying off the southeast of Australia, separated from the mainland by Bass Strait. The state also includes a number of small off-shore islands. The capital is Hobart. The island was discovered by the Dutch explorer, Abel Tasman, in 1642 and named Van Dieman's Land. It was taken by Britain (1803), and its name changed to Tasmania (1853). In 1901 the island became a state of the Commonwealth of Australia. It is mountainous, and much forested, and there are several large hydroelectric schemes. It exports iron, cooper, zinc, tungsten, metal products, timber and wood products, textiles, and wool.

Tasmanian devil *n.* A burrowing carnivorous marsupial, *Sarcophilus harrisii,* of Tasmania, having a predominantly blackish coat, powerful jaws, and a long tail.

Tasmanian wolf *n.* A marsupial, the **thylacine** *(see).*

Tas·man Sea (tázmən). Arm of the southern Pacific Ocean, lying between Australia and New Zealand.

tass (tass) *n.* *Chiefly Scottish.* **1.** A small cup or goblet. **2.** A small draught, especially of spirits. [Middle English, from Old French *tasse,* cup, from Arabic *tassah,* basin, from Persian *tast.*]

Tass (tass || *U.S. also* taass) *n.* The chief news agency of the Soviet Union. [Russian, from *T(elegrafnoe) A(gentstvo) S(ovetskovo) S(oyuza),* Telegraphic Agency of the Soviet Union.]

tasse (tass) *n.* Also **tas·set** (tássit). Any of a series of jointed overlapping metal plates hanging from the corselet, used as armour for the lower trunk and thighs. [Perhaps from Old French *tasse,* pouch, purse, from Middle High German *tasche,* from Old High German *tasca,* from Medieval Latin *tasca,* task, payment. See **task.**]

tas·sel (táss'l) *n.* **1.** An ornament consisting of a bunch of loose threads or cords bound at one end, hung from curtains, clothing, cushions, or the like. **2.** Something that resembles a tassel, such as the pollen-bearing inflorescence of a maize plant.
~*v.* **tasselled** or *U.S.* **-seled, -selling** or *U.S.* **-seling, -sels.** —*tr.* To fringe or decorate with tassels. —*intr.* To put forth a tassel-like inflorescence. Used especially of corn. [Middle English, clasp, fibula, tassel, from Old French *tassel*†.]

taste (tayst) *v.* **tasted, tasting, tastes.** —*tr.* **1.** To distinguish, experience, or judge the flavour or quality of by taking into the mouth. **2.** To eat or drink a small quantity of. **3.** To experience or partake of, especially for the first time: *tasted power.* **4.** *Archaic.* To like or appreciate. **5.** *Obsolete.* To test by touching. —*intr.* **1.** To distinguish, experience, or judge flavours or qualities in the mouth. **2.** To eat or drink a small amount. **3.** To have an experience; partake. Often used with *of.* **4.** To have a distinctive flavour, as specified. Often used with *of: The stew tastes salty; tastes of garlic.*
~*n.* **1. a.** The sense that distinguishes the sweet, sour, salty, and bitter qualities of dissolved substances in contact with the taste buds on the tongue. **b.** This sense in combination with the senses of smell and touch, which together receive a sensation of a substance in the mouth. **2. a.** The sensation of sweet, sour, salty, or bitter qualities produced by a substance in solution in the mouth. **b.** The sensation produced by any of these qualities together with a distinct smell and texture; a flavour. **3.** A small quantity eaten or tasted. **4.** A brief spell of participating in or experiencing something, often for the first time; a sample: *a taste of fear.* **5.** A distinctive impression left by an event or experience. **6.** A personal preference or liking for something; an inclination. **7. a.** The faculty of discerning what is aesthetically excellent, pleasing, or appropriate; discrimina-

tarsier *This small nocturnal primate has large toe pads which enable it to grip even smooth-barked trees in the Southeast Asian forests where it lives.*

tion. **b.** A manner indicative of the quality of such discernment: *dressed with taste.* **8. a.** The sense of what is proper, seemly, or least likely to give offence in a given social situation; discretion. **b.** A manner indicative of the quality of this sense: *a remark in poor taste.* **9.** *Obsolete.* The act of testing; a trial. —See Synonyms at **culture.** [Middle English *tasten,* to examine by touch, taste, from Old French *taster,* from Vulgar Latin *tastāre, taxitāre* (unattested), frequentative of Latin *taxāre,* to touch, frequentative of *tangere.*] —**tast·a·ble** *adj.*

taste bud *n.* Any of numerous spherical or ovoid nests of cells distributed over the tongue. The cells are embedded in the epithelium, consist of gustatory cells and supporting cells, and constitute the organs of taste.

taste·ful (táyst-f'l) *adj.* **1.** Exhibiting good taste. **2.** *Archaic.* Tasty. —**taste·ful·ly** *adv.* —**taste·ful·ness** *n.*

taste·less (táyst-less, -liss) *adj.* **1.** Lacking flavour; insipid. **2.** Exhibiting poor taste. **3.** *Archaic.* Unable to taste. —**taste·less·ly** *adv.* —**taste·less·ness** *n.*

tast·er (táystər) *n.* **1.** One who tastes, specifically: **a.** One who samples a food or drink for quality. **b.** One employed to sample food and drink prepared for a master, as a precaution against poisoning. **2.** Any of several devices or implements used in tasting.

tast·y (táysti) *adj.* **-ier, -iest. 1.** Having a pleasing flavour; savoury. **2.** *Slang.* Sexually attractive or appealing. **3.** *Archaic.* Having good taste; tasteful. —**tast·i·ly** *adv.* —**tast·i·ness** *n.*

tat¹ (tat) *v.* **tatted, tatting, tats.** —*intr.* To make tatting. —*tr.* To produce by tatting. [Probably back-formation from TATTING.] —**tat·ter** *n.*

tat² *n. Chiefly British Informal.* Worthless or shabby goods. [Back-formation from TATTY.]

tat³ *n.* See **tit for tat.**

ta-ta (tá-tá, tə-) *interj. British Informal.* Goodbye. [19th century: origin obscure.]

ta·ta·mi (tə-táami, -támmi) *n., pl* **-mis** or **-mi.** A straw mat used as a floor covering in Japan. [Japanese.]

Ta·tar (táatər) *n.* Also **Tar·tar** (tártər). **1. a.** A member of one of the Turkic-speaking tribes that originated in east central Asia or Siberia, and which, with the Mongolian peoples led by Genghis Khan, overran much of central and western Asia and eastern Europe in the 13th century. **b.** After the death of Genghis Khan (1227), a member of any of these groups, Tatar or Mongol. **2.** A descendant of these peoples, now living chiefly in parts of the Russian S.F.S.R. and Soviet Central Asia. **3.** Any of the Turkic languages of the Tatars. [Middle English *Tartre, Tatar,* from Old French *Tartare,* from Medieval Latin *Tartarus* (probably influenced by Latin (TARTARUS), from Persian *Tātār,* from *Tata,* Turkic ethnic name.] —**Ta·tar, Tar·tar** *adj.*

Tatar Autonomous Soviet Socialist Republic. Constituent republic of the U.S.S.R. occupying the valleys of the middle Volga and lower Kama rivers. The capital is Kazan. It is a leading producer of natural gas and petroleum in the U.S.S.R.

Tatary. Variant of **Tartary.**

ta·ter (táytər) *n. Regional.* A potato.

ta·ters (táytərz) *adj. British Slang.* Cold. [Perhaps alluding to the phrase *cold potatoes.*]

Ta·tra Mountains (táatrə, táttrə). Highest chain of mountains in the Carpathian range of east central Europe, lying in Poland and Czechoslovakia. The highest peak is Mount Gerlachovka, which rises to 2 655 metres (8,710 feet).

tat·ter (táttər) *n.* **1.** A torn and hanging piece of cloth; a shred. **2.** *Plural.* **a.** Torn and ragged clothing; rags. **b.** A condition of being reduced as if to shreds or rags: *left her nerves in tatters.* —*tr.v.* **tattered, -tering, -ters.** To make ragged; reduce to shreds. [Middle English *tatter, tatar,* from Old Norse *taturr* (unattested), *töturr,* from Germanic *tath-* (unattested).]

tat·ter·de·mal·ion (táttər-də-máyli-ən, -di- ‖ -mál-i-) *n. Rare.* A person wearing ragged or tattered clothing; a ragamuffin. —*adj.* Ragged; tattered. [TATTER + obscure second element.]

tat·tered (táttərd) *adj.* **1.** Torn into shreds or tatters; ragged. **2.** Having ragged clothes; dressed in tatters.

tat·ter·sall (táttər-sawl, -s'l) *n. Sometimes capital* T. **1.** A pattern of variously coloured lines forming squares on a plain, usually light background. **2.** Cloth woven with this pattern. Also used adjectivally: *tattersall check.* [Originally the pattern on blankets used at *Tattersall's* horse market in London, founded by Richard *Tattersall* (died 1795), English horseman.]

tat·ting (tátting) *n.* **1.** Handmade lace fashioned by looping and knotting a single strand of strong thread on a small hand shuttle. **2.** The act or art of making tatting. [Perhaps related to Scottish *tatet,* tuft.]

tat·tle (tátt'l) *v.* **-tled, -tling, -tles.** —*intr.* **1.** To reveal the plans or activities of another by chattering; blab; gossip. **2.** To chatter aimlessly; prate. —*tr.* To reveal through gossiping. —*n.* **1.** Aimless chatter; prattle. **2.** Gossip. [Middle Flemish *tatelen,* to babble (imitative).] —**tat·tling·ly** *adv.*

tat·tler (táttlər) *n.* **1.** A person who tattles. **2.** Any of several shore birds related to and resembling the sandpipers, and characteristically having a loud call.

tat·tle·tale (tátt'l-tayl) *n.* A person who tattles on others; a telltale.

tat·too¹ (tə-tóō, ta-) *n., pl.* **-toos. 1.** A signal sounded on a drum or bugle to summon soldiers to quarters at night. **2.** A display of military exercises performed as entertainment especially in the evening: *the Edinburgh tattoo.* **3.** A continuous even drumming or rapping.

—*v.* **tattooed, -tooing, -toos.** —*intr.* To beat out an even rhythm, as with the fingers. —*tr.* To beat or tap rhythmically on; rap or drum on. [Originally *tap-too, tap-tow,* from Dutch *taptoe,* "the shutting off of the taps (at taverns at the end of the day)" : *tap,* tap + *toe,* short for *doe toe,* "do to", shut.]

tattoo² *n., pl.* **-toos.** A permanent mark or design made on the skin by a process of pricking and ingraining an indelible pigment or by raising scars.

—*tr.v.* **tattooed, -tooing, -toos. 1.** To mark (the skin) with a tattoo or tattoos. **2.** To form (a mark or design) on the skin by this process. [Of Polynesian origin, akin to Tahitian *tatau,* Marquesan *tatu.*] —**tat·too·er, tat·too·ist** *n.*

tat·ty¹ (tátti) *adj.* Shabby, untidy, or ragged, especially in dress or appearance. [16th century (Scottish) : ultimately akin to Old English *tættec,* TATTER.] —**tat·ti·ly** *adv.* —**tat·ti·ness** *n.*

tatty² *n., pl.* **-ties.** *Scottish Informal.* A potato.

tau (taw, tow) *n.* The 19th letter of the Greek alphabet, written T, τ. Transliterated in English as *T, t.* [Greek, from Semitic, akin to Hebrew *tāw,* TAV.]

tau cross *n.* A Saint Anthony's cross *(see).*

taught. Past tense and past participle of **teach.**

taunt¹ (tawnt) *v.* **taunted, taunting, taunts. 1.** To deride or reproach with contempt; mock; jeer at. **2.** To provoke or incite by taunting: *taunted into action.* —See Synonyms at **ridicule.** —*n.* A scornful remark or jibe; a jeer. [Perhaps from Old French *tanter, tenter,* to test, tempt, from Latin *temptāre,* TEMPT.] —**taunt·er** *n.* —**taunt·ing·ly** *adv.*

taunt² *adj. Nautical.* Unusually tall. Said of a mast. [Probably from *ataunt,* as much as possible, fully rigged, from Old French *autant,* as much : *al,* other, one more + *tant,* so much, from Latin *tantum,* from *tam,* so.]

Taun·ton (táwn-tən; *locally* táan-). Town in Somerset, England, lying on the river Trove. It is the county town of Somerset.

tau particle *n.* A short-lived elementary particle which, together with its associated neutrino, is a member of the lepton family.

taupe (tōp) *n.* Brownish grey to dark yellowish brown. [French, "mole", from Latin *talpa†.*] —**taupe** *adj.*

Tau·po (tówpō). Largest lake in New Zealand, in the centre of North Island, in the district known as Hot Springs. Set among volcanic mountains, the lake is the centre of a popular holiday resort area.

tau·rine¹ (táw-rīn ‖ -rin) *adj.* Of or resembling a bull. [Latin *taurīnus,* from *taurus,* bull.]

tau·rine² (táw-reen, -rin) *n.* A derivative of the amino acid cysteine, 2-aminoethane sulphonic acid, $C_2H_7NO_3S$, found in bile. [TAUR(O)- + -INE (so called because first obtained from ox bile).]

tauro-, taur– *comb. form.* Indicates bull or bovine; for example, **taurocholic, taurine.** [Latin *taurus* and Greek *tauros,* bull.]

tau·ro·cho·lic acid (táwr-ō-kól-ik, -ə-, -kól-) *n.* A crystalline acid, $C_{26}H_{45}NO_7S$, occurring as a constituent of bile. [TAURO- + CHOLIC ACID (because first obtained from ox bile).]

tau·rom·a·chy (taw-rómməki) *n., pl.* **-chies.** Bullfighting or a bullfight. [Spanish *tauromaquia,* from Greek *tauromakhia :* TAURO- + *makhē,* battle, from *makhesthai,* to fight.]

Tau·rus (táwrəss) *n.* **1.** A constellation in the Northern Hemisphere near Orion and Aries. **2. a.** The second sign of the **zodiac** *(see).* Also called the "Bull". **b.** One born under this sign. [Middle English, from Latin, bull.] —**tau·re·an** (táwri-ən, taw-rée-ən) *n. & adj.*

taut (tawt) *adj.* **tauter, tautest. 1.** Pulled or drawn tight; not slack. **2.** Strained; tense. **3.** Kept in good order and condition neat; tidy: *a taut ship.* **4.** Strict in form; polished and well-organised: *a taut piece of writing.* —See Synonyms at **stiff.** [Earlier *taught, tought,* Middle English *toght, toht,* probably variant past participle of *togen, towen,* to pull, Old English *togian.*] —**taut·ly** *adv.* —**taut·ness** *n.*

taut·en (táwt'n) *v.* **-ened, -ening, -ens.** —*tr.* To make taut; stretch tight. —*intr.* To become taut.

tauto-, taut– *comb. form.* Indicates same or identical; for example, **tautomerism, tautonym.** [Greek *tautos,* identical, from *to auto,* the same (neuter) : *to,* the + *autos,* same.]

tau·tol·o·gise, tau·tol·o·gize (taw-tóllə-jīz) *intr.v.* **-gised, -gising, -gises.** To use tautology.

tau·tol·o·gy (taw-tólləji) *n., pl.* **-gies. 1. a.** Needless repetition of the same sense in different words; redundancy; for example, the statement *Pair off in twos* shows tautology. **b.** An instance of such repetition. **2.** *Logic.* A statement composed of simpler statements in a fashion that makes it true whether the simpler statements are true or false; for example, *Either it will rain tomorrow or it will not rain tomorrow.* [Late Latin *tautologia,* from Greek, from *tautologos,* repeating the same ideas : TAUTO- + *logos,* saying, word (see -LOGY).] —**tau·to·log·i·cal** (táwtə-lójik'l), **tau·to·log·ous** (taw-tóllə-gəss, *also* -jəss) *adj.* —**tau·to·log·i·cal·ly** *adv.*

tau·tom·er·ism (taw-tómmə-riz'm) *n.* Chemical isomerism characterised by relatively easy interconversion of isomeric forms in equilibrium. [TAUTO- + (ISO)MERISM.] —**tau·to·mer** (táwtəmər) *n.* —**tau·to·mer·ic** (táwtə-mérrik) *adj.*

tau·to·nym (táwtə-nim) *n.* A taxonomic designation, such as *Gorilla gorilla,* in which the genus and species names are the same. Now only used in zoology. [TAUT(O)- + -ONYM.] —**tau·to·nym·ic** (-nímmik), **tau·ton·y·mous** (taw-tónniməss) *adj.* —**tau·ton·y·my** *n.*

tav, taw (taav, taaf) *n.* The 23rd letter of the Hebrew alphabet, corresponding phonetically to *t* or *th* in English. [Hebrew *tāw,* probably "mark", "cross".]

tav·ern (távvərn) *n.* **1.** *Literary.* A pub or inn. **2.** Broadly, an establishment licensed to sell alcoholic drinks to be drunk on the premises; a bar. [Middle English *taverne*, from Old French, from Latin *taberna*, hut, inn, perhaps from Etruscan. See also **tabernacle**.]

ta·ver·na (tə-vérnə) *n.* A restaurant in Greece that sometimes also provides accommodation and live entertainment.

TAVR Territorial and Army Volunteer Reserve (in Britain).

taw[1] (taw) *tr.v.* **tawed, tawing, taws.** To convert (hide) into white leather by mineral tanning, as by soaking in alum and salt. [Middle English *tawen*, Old English *tawian*.] —**taw·er** *n.*

taw[2] *n.* **1.** A large, often fancy marble used for shooting. **2.** The line from which a player shoots in marbles. **3.** A game played with taws. [18th century : origin obscure.]

taw[3]. Variant of **tav**.

taw·dry (táwdri) *adj.* **-drier, -driest.** Gaudy and cheap-looking; vulgarly ornamental. [From *tawdry lace*, short for *Seynt Audries lace*, cheap and gaudy lace sold at fairs in honour of St. Audrey or Etheldrida (died A.D. 679), queen of Northumbria and patron saint of Ely who died of a throat tumour regarded as punishment for her fondness for laces.] —**taw·dri·ly** *adv.* —**taw·dri·ness** *n.*

taw·ny (táwni) *n.* Light brown to brownish orange, as is the colour of a lion's body. [Middle English *taune, tawny,* from Anglo-French *taune,* variant of Old French *tane,* tanned, from *taner, tanner,* to TAN.] —**taw·ny** *adj.*

tawny owl *n.* A large common European owl, *Strix aluco,* ranging in colour from tawny chestnut brown to greyish white.

tawse (tawz) *n.* Also **taws.** *Scottish.* A leather strap divided at one end into thin strips, used as an instrument of punishment in schools. [Probably originally the plural of obsolete *taw,* leather strip. See **taw** (verb).]

tax (taks) *n.* **1.** A compulsory financial contribution levied by a government to raise revenue, on the income, profits, or property of persons, groups, or businesses, or on the cost of goods and services. **2.** A burdensome or excessive demand; a strain: *a tax on his patience.*
~ *tr.v.* **taxed, taxing, taxes. 1.** To place a tax on (income, property, or goods). **2.** To exact a tax from (a person or organisation). **3.** *Law.* To examine and assess (court costs, for example). **4.** To make exacting or excessive demands upon. **5.** To make a charge against; accuse: *He was taxed with hypocrisy.* [Middle English *taxen,* to assess, tax, from Old French *taxer,* from Medieval Latin *taxāre,* from Latin, frequentative of *tangere,* to touch.] —**tax·a·ble** *adj.* —**tax·a·bil·i·ty** (táksə-bílləti), **tax·a·ble·ness** *n.* —**tax·er** *n.*

tax·a·tion (tak-sáysh'n) *n.* **1. a.** The act or practice of imposing taxes. **b.** The fact of being taxed. **2.** An amount of money levied by a tax.

tax avoidance *n.* The taking of legal measures to reduce one's tax liability. Also called "avoidance". Compare **tax evasion.**

tax-de·duct·i·ble (táks-di-dúktəb'l) *adj.* That may be set against one's income so that one's tax liability is reduced. Said especially of an expense incurred in the course of one's business.

tax·eme (táks-eem) *n.* A minimal linguistic feature of grammatical arrangement, such as the order or stress of words in a compound or phrase. [TAX(O)- + (PHON)EME.]

tax evasion *n.* The taking of illegal measures to reduce one's tax liability. Also called "evasion". Compare **tax avoidance.**

tax exile *n.* A person who settles in a country other than his own in order to avoid paying high rates of income tax.

tax-free (táks-frée) *adj.* Not subject to taxation. —**tax-free** *adv.*

tax haven *n.* A place that is attractive to companies or individuals because of its relatively low rates of taxation.

tax·i (táksi) *n., pl.* **-is** or **-ies.** A car that carries passengers for a fare, usually calculated by a taximeter. Also called "taxicab", "cab".
~ *v.* **taxied, taxiing** or **taxying, taxies** or **taxis. 1.** To be transported by taxi. **2.** To move slowly on the ground or on the surface of the water before takeoff or after landing. Used of an aircraft. —*tr.* **1.** To transport or convey in a taxi. **2.** To cause (an aircraft) to taxi. [Short for *taximeter cab*.]

taxi dancer *n.* A person, usually a woman, employed by a dance hall or nightclub to dance with the patrons for a fee.

tax·i·der·mist (táksi-dermist, -dérmist, tak-síddərmist) *n.* One whose profession is taxidermy.

tax·i·der·my (táksi-dermi) *n.* The art or operation of preparing, stuffing, and mounting the skins of dead animals for exhibition in a lifelike state. [*Taxi-,* variant of TAXO- + -DERM + -Y.] —**tax·i·der·mal** (-dérm'l), **tax·i·der·mic** (-dérmik) *adj.*

tax·i·me·ter (táksi-meetər) *n.* An instrument installed in a taxi to calculate and show the fare for a particular journey. [French *taximètre : taxe,* tax, charge, from Old French *taxer,* to TAX + -METER.]

tax·ing (táksing) *adj.* Burdensome; wearing. —**tax·ing·ly** *adv.*

tax·i·plane (táksi-playn) *n.* An aeroplane commercially available for short charter flights.

taxi rank *n.* *British.* An area reserved for taxis waiting for customers. Also called "taxistand".

tax·is (ták-siss) *n., pl.* **taxes** (-seez). **1.** *Biology.* The responsive movement of an entire organism towards or away from an external stimulus. It is not a chance movement. **2.** The moving of an organ, as in a dislocation or hernia, into the normal position by manipulation. [Greek, arrangement, order, from *tattein,* to arrange.]

-taxis, -taxy *comb. form.* Indicates: **1.** Order or arrangement; for example, **phyllotaxy. 2.** Movement towards or away from a specified stimulus; for example, **phototaxis.** [New Latin from Greek *taxis,* arrangement, order.]

taxo-, tax-, taxi- *comb. form.* Indicates arrangement or order; for example, **taxonomy.** [Greek *taxis,* arrangement, order. See **taxis.**]

tax·on (ták-son) *n., pl.* **taxa** (-sə). *Biology.* A category or formal unit in taxonomic classification, such as a phylum, order, family, genus, or species, characterised by common characteristics in varying degrees of distinction. [Back-formation from TAXONOMY.]

tax·on·o·my (tak-sónnəmi) *n. Abbr.* **taxon. 1.** The science, laws, or principles of classification. **2.** *Biology.* The theory, principles, and process of classifying organisms in established categories according to observed similarities or supposed evolutionary relationships. [French *taxonomie : * TAXO- + -NOMY.] —**tax·o·nom·ic** (táksə-nómmik), **tax·o·nom·i·cal** *adj.* —**tax·o·nom·i·cal·ly** *adv.* —**tax·on·o·mist** (tak-sónnəmist) *n.* See feature, next page.

tax·pay·er (táks-pay-ər) *n.* A person who pays or is legally liable to pay taxes.

tax return *n.* A declaration to the tax officials of one's personal income during a given period, so that the appropriate rate of taxation can be calculated.

tax shelter *n.* Any financial operation, such as the acquisition of loss-making assets or the use of special depreciation allowances, used as a means to reduce taxes on current earnings.

tax year *n.* A specific annual period used by a government in calculating taxes, running in Britain from April 6 to April 5 of the following year.

Tay (tay). Longest river in Scotland, rising on Ben Lui in the Grampian mountains and flowing for about 190 kilometres (118 miles) through lochs Dochart and Tay, and into the North Sea through the Firth of Tay. Before entering Loch Dochart it is known as the Fillan, and from there to Loch Tay as the Dochart.

Ta·yg·e·ta[1] (tay-íjitə). *Greek Mythology.* One of the **Pleiades** *(see).*

Tay-Sachs disease (táy-sáks) *n.* An inherited disorder in which excessive amounts of lipid accumulate in the brain, leading to mental subnormality, blindness, and early death. [After Warren *Tay* (died 1927), British physician, and B.P. *Sachs* (died 1944), U.S. neurologist.]

Tay·side (táy-sīd). Region of eastern Scotland. It was formed in 1975, and includes the former counties of Angus, Perthshire, and Kinross. Dundee is the administrative centre.

taz·za (tátsə) *n.* A shallow vessel, such as a bowl or vase, shaped like a saucer and often mounted on a pedestal. [Italian, probably from Arabic *tassah,* basin. See **tass.**]

Tb The symbol for the element terbium.

TB tuberculosis.

Tb. tubercle bacillus.

T.B. 1. torpedo-boat. **2.** tuberculosis.

T-bar lift (tée-baar) *n.* A ski lift consisting of a bar suspended like an inverted T against which skiers lean while being towed uphill.

Tbi·li·si (t-bi-lée-si, d-), or **Tif·lis** (tífflis). City in the southwestern U.S.S.R., the capital of the Georgian S.S.R., lying in the basin of the river Kura. It was a Muslim stronghold in the early Middle Ages, and after the 13th century was ruled by Mongols, Iranians, and the Ottoman Turks until it passed under Russian control in 1800. It is now by far the most important commercial, administrative, and cultural centre in Transcaucasia.

T-bone (tée-bōn) *n.* A tender steak taken from the thin end of the loin and containing a T-shaped bone. Also called "T-bone steak".

tbs., tbsp. tablespoon; tablespoonful.

Tc The symbol for the element technetium.

TCA cycle *n.* The **Krebs cycle** *(see).*

TCDD *n.* Tetrachlorobenzo-p-dioxin; **dioxin** *(see).*

Tchad. See **Chad.**

Tchai·kov·ski (chī-kóffski), **Piotr Ilyich** (1840–94). Russian composer. His music, marked by romantic melodies and its freedom of form, includes many orchestral and stage works, such as the *Pathétique* symphony (1893) and the opera *Eugene Onegin* (1879).

Tchekhov. See **Chekhov.**

td, TD, td. touchdown.

te (tee) *n.* Also **ti.** In tonic sol-fa, a syllable representing the seventh note of a diatonic scale. [Alteration of earlier *si,* from French, from Italian, probably representing Latin *Sancte Iohannes;* see **gamut.**]

Te The symbol for the element tellurium.

tea (tee) *n.* **1.** A shrub, *Camellia sinensis,* of eastern Asia, having fragrant white flowers and evergreen leaves. **2.** The dried leaves of this plant, prepared by various processes and in various stages of growth. **3. a.** An aromatic, slightly bitter drink made by steeping tea leaves in boiling water, often served with milk or lemon, and sugar. **b.** A cup of this drink. **4.** Any of various beverages made by steeping the leaves of certain other plants, or made from beef or other extracts. **5.** Any of various plants having leaves used to make a tealike infusion. **6. a.** *Chiefly British.* An afternoon refreshment usually of biscuits, sandwiches, or light cakes served with tea. **b.** A social occasion, such as a tea party, at which tea is served. **7.** *Chiefly British.* An evening meal; high tea. **8.** *Slang.* Cannabis. [Earlier *tay, tee* (probably via Dutch *thee* and Malay *teh*), from Chinese (Amoy) *te,* equivalent of Mandarin *chá.*]

tea bag *n.* A small porous bag holding tea leaves, dipped into a cup or teapot full of boiling water to make tea.

tea ball *n.* *Chiefly U.S.* A small perforated metal ball used for immersing tea leaves in hot water. Also called "tea infuser".

tea biscuit *n.* Any of various plain biscuits often served with tea.

tea cake *n.* *British.* A light, flat, bunlike cake, often with currants, usually toasted and served with butter.

teach (teech) *v.* **taught** (tawt), **teaching, teaches.** —*tr.* **1.** To impart

HOW ALL LIVING THINGS ARE CLASSIFIED

A system designed to cope with a myriad different species

The system of classifying living things, called taxonomy, was developed by Carolus Linnaeus, Professor of Medicine at the University of Uppsala, Sweden, from 1741 until 1778. Linnaeus was working at a time when many species were being discovered all over the world by explorers. He divided all living creatures into two kingdoms – Animals and Plants – each with many subdivisions, including phylums, classes, orders, and families.

The name given to a species consists of two words. The first is the generic name: it always starts with a capital letter and is printed in italics (or underlined in handwriting). The second is the specific name, which is italicised but not capitalised. The two together are called the scientific name. The specific name may be an ad-jective describing some characteristic of the species, such as the dark thrush, *Turdus obscurus*. Or it may be a place name or the name of a person, such as Naumann's thrush, *Turdus naumanni*, named after its discoverer. Common names will not suffice for classifying plants and animals, as an overwhelming number of species have no common names at all.

Since the time of Linnaeus, a great many creatures have been discovered that do not fit into either of the two kingdoms. A third kingdom of Protista is now used to classify viruses, protozoa (which have very small bodies), and other organisms not obviously plants or animals.

Below are examples of classifications for two species, animal and plant – the Siberian tiger and cos lettuce.

SIBERIAN TIGER

COS LETTUCE

KINGDOM: Animalia

PHYLUM: Chordata
The chordates are complex, multicellular animals that at some stage in their development have a supporting skeletal rod, or notochord, and gills (human beings have gills in their embryonic stage). In most chordates, a backbone replaces the notochord as they grow.

CLASS: Mammalia
Mammals suckle their young, and all have some hair. Most are born fully developed, and some can walk within minutes of birth.

ORDER: Carnivora
Carnivores eat meat – although some also eat large amounts of vegetable matter – and have teeth adapted for tearing flesh and crushing bones. The collarbone is small, embedded in muscle, and not rigidly fixed, so will not break when the animal leaps on its prey.

FAMILY: Felidae
Cats of all sizes.

GENUS: *Panthera*
The big cats (lion, tiger, panther, jaguar). Linnaeus gave all the cats the same generic name, *Felis*. A refinement of his system has been the addition of more generic names as anatomical differences are better understood; *Panthera* is one of these.

SPECIES: *Panthera tigris*
The tiger. The best simple definition of "species" is that any male could mate with any female of the same species and produce fertile offspring.

SUBSPECIES: *Panthera tigris longipilis*
The Siberian tiger. It has longer hair *(longipilis)* because it lives in a cold climate.

KINGDOM: Plantae

DIVISION: Tracheophyta
Vascular plants, having clearly defined supporting and conductive tissues that carry water and sap. Includes ferns, which reproduce by means of spores, gymnosperms, and flowering plants.

CLASS: Angiospermae
Flowering plants that have seeds contained in an ovary or fruit, compared to Gymnospermae, such as conifers, which have their seeds more exposed.

SUBCLASS: Dicotyledonae
Having two embryonic seed leaves that function at germination. Monocotyledons have only one.

ORDER: Asteridae
Plants with complex flowers and usually fused petals. Includes bellflowers, foxgloves, mints, and composites.

FAMILY: Compositae
The composites have a head, or inflorescence, of flowers that looks like a single flower. This may contain flat-petalled ray flowers or small, tubular disc flowers, or both – as in the daisy. In all flowers the petals are fused into a tube.

GENUS: *Lactuca*
Having a flowerhead of ray flowers and milky juice in the stem.

SPECIES: *Lactuca sativa*
Cultivated lettuce

VARIETY: *Lactuca sativa longifolia*
Cultivated lettuce with long leaves (cos lettuce).

---

knowledge or skill to; give instruction to: *taught foreign students on Saturdays.* **2.** To provide knowledge of or instruction in, as by giving formal lessons: *taught Latin at a local school.* **3. a.** To cause to learn by example or experience. **b.** To cause to appreciate the inadvisability of a particular course of action: *I'll teach him to go against my orders!* **4.** To advocate; preach: *a religion that teaches forgiveness.* —*intr.* To give instruction, especially as an occupation. [Teach, taught; Middle English *techen, tahte,* Old English *tǣcan, tǣhte* (past tense), *tǣht* (unattested past participle).]
   Synonyms: *teach, instruct, educate, tutor, coach, train, school, discipline, drill.*

teach·a·ble (tēech-ə·b'l) *adj.* Capable of or receptive to being taught. —**teach·a·bil·i·ty** (-ə-billəti), **teach·a·ble·ness** *n.* —**teach·a·bly** *adv.*

teach·er (tēechər) *n.* One that teaches; especially, a person who is employed to teach.

tea chest *n.* A large, lined box made of a light wood, used for transporting tea.

teach-in (tēech-in) *n.* An extended critical discussion of an important topical issue, typically one held in a college or university with the participation of students, lecturers, and guest speakers.

teach·ing (tēeching) *n.* **1.** The work or occupation of teachers. **2.** A precept or doctrine.

teaching aid *n.* Something, such as a film strip, tape recorder, or wall chart, that helps a teacher to convey information.

teaching fellow *n.* A postgraduate student who holds a fellowship that provides financial aid, in exchange for some teaching duties. —**teaching fellowship** *n.*

teaching hospital *n.* A hospital associated with a medical school and providing medical students with practical experience.

teaching machine *n.* Any of various devices designed to teach by presenting the student with a planned sequence of statements and questions and providing an immediate response to the answers.

tea cloth *n.* **1.** A small, usually white tablecloth. **2.** A **tea towel** *(see).*

tea cosy *n.* A **cosy** *(see).*

tea-cup (tēe-kup) *n.* **1.** A small cup, typically for serving tea or other hot beverages. **2.** The amount that a teacup will hold. In this sense, also called "teacupful".

tea dance *n.* A **thé dansant** *(see).*

tea garden *n.* **1.** An outdoor area, such as a garden adjoining a restaurant or café, in which tea may be served to customers. **2.** A large area where tea is grown; a tea plantation.

teague (tayg) *n.* **1.** *Northern Irish Slang.* A Catholic. Used derogatorily by non-Catholics. **2.** *Archaic.* An Irishman. [Anglicised spelling of the Irish name *Tadhg.*]

tea·house (tēe-howss) *n.* A public establishment, especially in the Far East, serving tea and other refreshments.

teak (teek) *n.* **1.** A tall evergreen tree, *Tectona grandis,* of southeastern Asia, having hard, heavy, durable wood. **2.** The yellowish-brown hard wood of this tree, used for furniture and in shipbuilding. **3.** Yellowish brown or greyish to moderate brown. [Portuguese *teca,* from Malayalam *tēkka.*] —**teak** *adj.*

tea·ket·tle (tēe-kett'l) *n.* See **kettle.**

teal (teel) *n., pl.* **teals** or collectively **teal. 1.** Any of several small, widely distributed ducks of the genus *Anas,* many of which have brightly marked plumage; especially *A. crecca,* the male of which has a chestnut-coloured head with a distinctive green eye-stripe. **2.** Moderate or dark bluish green to greenish blue. In this sense, also called "teal blue". [Middle English *tele,* akin to Middle Dutch *talinc,* Middle Low German *telink*†.] —**teal** *adj.*

tea leaf *n.* **1.** Any leaf of the tea shrub. **2.** *Plural.* **a.** The small, shredded pieces of this leaf that remain at the bottom of a teapot or teacup after the tea has been drunk. **b. Tea** (sense 2). **3.** *British Slang.* A thief. [Sense 3, rhyming slang.]

team (teem) *n.* **1.** A group of players making up one of the sides in a game or contest. **2.** Any group organised to work together: *a team of medical experts.* **3.** Two or more draught animals harnessed to a vehicle or farm implement. **b.** The vehicle along with the animal or animals harnessed to it. **4.** *Regional.* A brood or flock. **5.** *Obsolete.* Offspring; lineage.
   ~*v.* **teamed, teaming, teams.** —*tr.* **1.** To harness or join together (horses, for example) so as to form a team. **2.** To bring together with another so as to form a team. Often used with *up: Bill was teamed up with Ben.* **3.** *U.S.* To transport or haul with a draught team. —*intr.* To form a team. Often used with *up.* [Middle English *tem(e),* Old English *tēam,* offspring, brood, team of animals.]

team·mate (tēem-mayt) *n.* A fellow member of a team.

team spirit *n.* The morale of a team of people as engendered by a willingness for mutual cooperation.

team·ster (tēem-stər) *n.* **1.** A person who drives a team. **2.** *U.S.* A lorry driver.

team·work (tēem-wurk) *n.* Cooperative effort by the members of a team to achieve a common goal.

tea party *n.* An informal social gathering, usually in the afternoon, at which tea is served.

tea·pot (tēe-pot) *n.* A covered pot with a spout in which tea infuses and from which it is served.

tea·poy (tēe-poy) *n.* A small, usually three-legged, table, especially one on which tea is served. [Alteration (influenced by TEA) of Hindi *tipāī* : Hindi *tīn,* three, from Sanskrit *tri* + Middle Persian *pāī,* foot.]

tear¹ (tair) *v.* **tore** (tor ‖ tōr), **torn** (torn ‖ tōrn), **tearing, tears.** —*tr.* **1.** To pull apart or into pieces, especially so as to leave jagged or

irregular edges; rend. **2.** To make (an opening) by ripping. **3.** To lacerate (one's skin, for example). **4.** To extract or separate forcefully; wrench. Usually used with *away* or *from.* —*intr.* **1.** To become torn. **2.** To move with heedless speed; rush headlong. Often used with *off* or *along.* **—tear down.** To demolish or destroy: *tear down slums.* **—tear into.** To attack with great violence or vigour: *tore into his arguments.* **—tear off.** *Chiefly British.* To produce hurriedly and casually. **—tear up. 1.** To rip or tear into tiny pieces. **2.** To cancel or annul by or as if by tearing: *tore up an agreement.*
~*n.* **1.** An act of tearing. **2.** The result of tearing; a rip or rent. **3.** *Chiefly British.* A great rush; a hurry. [Tear, tore, torn; Middle English *teren, tore* (earlier *taar*), *toren,* Old English *teran, tær, toren.*]
Synonyms: *tear, rip, rend, split, cleave, sever, slit, slash.*

tear² (teer) *n.* **1.** A drop of the clear saline liquid that is secreted by the lachrymal gland of the eye, often as a result of some strong emotion such as grief or joy, and that lubricates the surface between the eyeball and the eyelid. **2.** A drop of any liquid or hardened fluid. **3.** *Plural.* The act of weeping. Often used with *in, into,* or *to: bored to tears; The farewell party left her in tears.* **—without tears.** Presented so as to be easily absorbed or learned: *French without tears.* [Middle English *tere, tear,* Old English *tēar, tehher.*]

tear away (tair) *tr.v.* To bring (especially oneself) to leave, despite reluctance: *could hardly tear myself away.*

tear·a·way (táir-ə-way) *n.* *British.* A rash, impetuous, youth; a hooligan.
~*adj. British.* Of the nature of a tearaway; reckless; impetuous.

tear·drop (téer-drop) *n.* **1.** A single tear. **2.** Something in the shape of a tear.

tear duct (teer) *n.* The **lachrymal duct** *(see).*

tear fault (tair) *n.* A **strike-slip fault** *(see).*

tear·ful (téerf'l) *adj.* **1.** Inclined to or about to cry. **2.** Accompanied by tears: *gave us a tearful account of her marriage.* **3.** Causing tears; pathetic; sad. **—tear·ful·ly** *adv.* **—tear·ful·ness** *n.*

tear gas (teer) *n.* Any of various vapours that on dispersal, usually from grenades or projectiles, irritate the eyes and cause blinding tears. Also called "lachrymator".

tear·ing (táir-ing) *adj. Chiefly British.* Reckless, rash, or impetuous in movement or action: *in a tearing hurry.*

tear-jerk·er (téer-jerkər) *n.* *Informal.* A grossly pathetic story, drama, performance or song liable to provoke sentimental tears. **—tear-jerk·ing** *adj.*

tear-out (táir-owt) *adj.* Designed to be detached by pulling or tearing, as from a folder: *tear-out matches.*

tea·rooms (tée-rōōmz, -rōōmz) *pl.n.* **1.** A restaurant or shop serving tea and other refreshments. Also called "teashop". **2.** *South African.* A small grocery or confectionery store, often open outside normal shopping hours.

tea rose *n.* **1.** Any of several cultivated roses derived from *Rosa odorata,* having fragrant, tea-scented yellowish or pink flowers. **2.** Pale to strong yellowish pink. **—tea-rose** *adj.*

tear sheet (tair) *n.* A page, often perforated, that is designed to be detached easily from a newspaper or periodical.

tease (teez) *v.* **teased, teasing, teases.** —*tr.* **1.** To annoy; pester; bother. **2.** To make fun of; playfully mock. **3.** To arouse hope, curiosity, or desire, especially sexual desire, in without affording satisfaction: *teased him with her sultry looks and skimpy dress.* **4.** To pull apart or loosen (body tissue, for example) for examination. **5.** To disentangle and dress the fibres of (wool, for example). **6.** To raise the nap of (cloth) by dressing, as with a fuller's teasel. **7.** *U.S.* To coax; importune. **8.** *Chiefly U.S.* To backcomb (the hair). —*intr.* To annoy or make fun of someone persistently.
~*n.* **1.** The act of teasing. **2.** A person or thing that teases; especially, one given to playful mocking. [Middle English *tesen, teesen,* to card (wool), tear apart, Old English *tǣsan,* from West Germanic *taisjan* (unattested).] **—teas·ing·ly** *adv.*

tea·sel, tea·zel, tea·zle (téez'l) *n.* **1.** Any of several plants of the genus *Dipsacus,* native to the Old World, having thistle-like flowers surrounded by prickly bracts. **2. a.** The bristly flower head of *D. fullonum,* used to produce a napped surface on fabrics. **b.** A similar object used for the same purpose.
~*tr.v.* **teaselled** or *U.S.* **-eled, -elling** or *U.S.* **-eling, -els.** To produce a napped surface on (a piece of cloth). [Middle English *tesel, tasel,* Old English *tǣsel,* from West Germanic *taisilā* (unattested), from *taisjan* (unattested), to card, TEASE.] **—tea·sel·ler** *n.*

teas·er (téezər) *n.* **1.** A person who teases. **2.** *Informal.* A problem or puzzle: *a brain teaser.*

tea service *n.* A set of articles, such as matching cups, saucers, and teapot, used in serving tea. Also called "tea set".

Teas·made (téez-mayd) *n.* A trademark for an automatic tea-making apparatus that can be preset to boil and pour water into a teapot and sound an alarm at a fixed time.

tea·spoon (téespōōn) *n.* **1.** A small, usually metal, spoon used especially with tea, coffee, and desserts. **2.** *Abbr.* **t., tsp. a.** The amount a teaspoon will hold. Also called "teaspoonful". **b.** A household cooking measure, $^1/_3$ tablespoon or $1^1/_3$ drams.

teat (teet) *n.* **1.** A mammary gland or nipple. **2.** Anything resembling a teat, especially a rubber device on a bottle enabling a liquid to be sucked out. [Middle English *tet(t)e,* from Old French, from West Germanic *titta* (unattested), TIT.]

tea towel *n.* **1.** A light, absorbent cloth, usually of linen or cotton, used to dry washed dishes and cutlery. Also called "tea cloth", *U.S.* "dish towel".

tea tree *n. Australian.* Any of various trees of the genus *Leptospermum,* the leaves of which were used as a tea substitute.

tea trolley *n. British.* A small table on wheels for serving tea or holding dishes. Also *U.S.* "tea wagon".

Tebet, Tebeth. Variants of **Tevet.**

Tebriz. See **Tabriz.**

tech (tek) *n. British Informal.* A technical college.

tech. 1. technical. **2.** technology.

tech·ne·ti·um (tek-née-ti-əm, -shi- || -shəm) *n. Symbol* **Tc** A silvery-grey metal, the first synthetically produced element, having 14 isotopes with masses ranging from 92 to 105 and half-lives up to 2.6×10^6 years. It is used as a tracer and to eliminate corrosion in steel. Atomic number 43, melting point 2,200°C, relative density 11.50, valencies 3, 4, 6, 7. [New Latin, from Greek *tekhnētos,* artificial, from *tekhnē,* art, skill. See **technical.**]

tech·nic (ték-nik) *n.* **1.** *Plural.* The theory, principles, or study of an art or process, especially an industrial or mechanical one. **2.** *Plural.* Technical details, rules, methods, or the like. **3.** *Rare.* Variant of **technique.**
~*adj.* Technical.

tech·ni·cal (ték-nik'l) *adj. Abbr.* **tech. 1. a.** Of or pertaining to that aspect of an art or science requiring practical, applied, mechanical, or scientific skills or knowledge. **b.** Qualified or skilled in the practical mechanical, or applied aspect of an art or science: *a technical expert.* **2. a.** Of, pertaining to, or characteristic of any specialised field or activity: *technical vocabulary.* **b.** Loosely, complicated: *Don't get technical.* **3.** Of, pertaining to, or providing knowledge of any of various subjects that involve practical, applied, mechanical, or industrial skills or knowledge: *a technical college.* **4.** Of, pertaining to, or derived from technique: *showed technical mastery but no feel or imagination.* **5.** Characterised by or based on a rigorously strict interpretation of the appropriate rules: *a technical victory.* **6.** *Finance.* Of or designating a market condition in which prices are determined or affected by internal manipulation and speculation, rather than by any external factors. [Latin *technicus,* from Greek *tekhnikos,* of art or skill, from *tekhnē,* art, skill.] **—tech·ni·cal·ly** *adv.* **—tech·ni·cal·ness** *n.*

technical college *n.* A state educational establishment, especially designed for school leavers and mature students, providing courses in any of various arts and science subjects.

tech·ni·cal·i·ty (ték-ni-kál-əti) *n., pl.* **-ties. 1.** Something meaningful or revelant only according to a strict point of view or ruling. **2.** The condition or quality of being technical.

technical knockout *n. Abbr.* **TKO** In boxing, a victory, with immediate termination of the match, awarded by the referee when it appears that one fighter is in too bad a condition to continue.

tech·ni·cian (tek-nísh'n, ték-) *n.* An expert in a particular skill or technique, as: **1.** A person whose occupation requires training in specific technical skills and processes: *a lighting technician in a television studio.* **2.** One considered from the point of view of his technical skill as opposed to his originality or imagination: *a boring poet although a fine technician.* [TECHN(IC) + -ICIAN.]

tech·ni·col·our (ték-ni-kullər) *adj.* In many vivid, bright colours. [From *Technicolor* (trademark), from TECHNICAL + COLOR.]

technicolour yawn *n. Australian Slang.* An act of vomiting.

tech·nique (tek-néek, ték-) *n.* Also *rare* **tech·nic** (ték-nik) (for sense 2). **1.** The systematic procedure by which a complex or specialised task is accomplished. **2.** The degree of skill or command of fundamentals exhibited, especially in artistic or sporting pursuits. [French, "technical", from Greek *tekhnikos.* See **technical.**]

tech·noc·ra·cy (tek-nóckrə-si) *n., pl.* **-cies. 1.** A system of organisation in which government and industry are controlled by scientific experts or technicians. **2.** A state or country under such a system. [Greek *tekhnē,* art, skill (see **technology**) + -CRACY.] **—tech·no·crat** (ték-nə-krat, -nō-) *n.* **—tech·no·crat·ic** (-kráttik) *adj.*

technol. technology.

tech·no·log·i·cal (ték-nə-lójik'l) *adj.* **1.** Pertaining to or involving technology, especially scientific technology. **2.** Resulting from scientific and industrial progress. **—tech·no·log·i·cal·ly** *adv.*

tech·nol·o·gy (tek-nólləji) *n., pl.* **-gies.** *Abbr.* **tech., technol. 1. a.** The application of science, especially to industrial or commercial objectives. **b.** The entire body of methods and materials used to achieve such objectives. **2.** Broadly, the body of knowledge available to a civilisation that is of use in fashioning implements, practising manual arts and skills, and extracting or collecting materials: *Iron Age technology.* [Greek *tekhnē,* skill, art + -LOGY.] **—tech·nol·o·gist, tech·no·lo·gi·an** (ték-nə-lṓj-i-ən, -lṓj'n) *n.*

techy. Variant of **tetchy.**

tec·ton·ic (tek-tónnik, ték-) *adj.* **1. a.** Pertaining to construction or building. **b.** Architectural. **2.** *Geology.* Pertaining to, causing, or resulting from structural deformation in the earth's crust. [Late Latin *tectonicus,* from Greek *tektonikos,* from *tektōn,* carpenter, builder.]

tec·ton·ics (tek-tónniks, ték-) *n. Used with a singular verb.* **1.** The art or science of construction, especially of large buildings. **2.** The geology of the earth's structural deformation. See **plate tectonics.**

tec·tor·i·al membrane (tek-táw-ri-əl || -tṓ-) *n.* The membrane covering the organ of Corti in the inner ear.

tec·trix (ték-triks) *n., pl.* **-trices** (-tri-seez). Any of the coverts of a bird's wing. [New Latin, feminine of Latin *tector,* coverer, from *tegere* (past participle *tectus*), to cover.]

tec·tum (téktəm) *n.* The roof of the midbrain.

ted¹ (ted) *tr.v.* **tedded, tedding, teds.** To strew or spread (newly mown grass, for example) for drying. [Middle English *tedden* (at-

teal *Found throughout the Northern Hemisphere, the teal is a dabbling duck which lives on moorland and marshes, rarely venturing into open water. It feeds on invertebrates and water plants.*

teasel *A tall plant with a prickly flower head. The spiky green bracts around the flower head are still used to tease, or raise, the nap of new woven cloth such as velour and cashmere.*

PRONUNCIATION KEY

a, trap; aa, father; ai, **fair**; ar, **star**; aw, **lawn**; ay, **play**; b, bb, stab; **rubber**; ch, **church**; ck, **ticket**; d, dd, **dead**; ladder; e, dress; ee, **bee**; er, **defer**; ew, **few**; ewr, **pure**; ə, about; ər, letter; f, ff, **fife**; differ; g, gg, **giggle**; h, **hat**; i, **kit**; ī, price; īr, **fire**; j, **judge**; k, **kick**; l, ll, **let**; 'l, **needle**; m, mm, **man**; n, nn, **no**; 'n, sudden; ng, **thing**; o, **lot**; ō, **no**; ōō, **foot**; ōō, **shoe**; oor, **poor**; ow, **cow**; owr, **hour**; oy, **boy**; p, pp, **pepper**; r, rr, **red**; s, ss, **sauce**; sh, **ship**; t, tt, **totter**; th, **thick**; th, **this**; smooth; u, **cut**; ur, **turn**; v, vv, **valve**; w, **wet**; y, **yes**; z, zz, zebra; zh, vision; pleasure

IN FOREIGN WORDS:

aN, oN, **Saint-Saëns**; hl, **Llanelli**; **Hluhluwe**; kh, loch; **lough**; **Khaled**

STRESS MARK:

ín-sīt, insight; in-sīt, incite

tested only in the gerund *teddyng*), from Old Norse *tedhja,* to spread dung, from *tadh,* spread dung.] **—ted·der** *n.*

ted[2] *n.* A Teddy boy.

teddy bear (téddi-bair) *n.* A child's toy bear, usually stuffed with soft material and covered with a soft, furlike material. Also called "teddy". [After President *Theodore* Roosevelt, once depicted in a cartoon as having spared the life of a bear cub on a hunting trip.]

Teddy boy *n.* In Britain, especially during the 1950s, one of a group of youths affecting a modified style of Edwardian dress and appearance, such as swept-back hair, long sideboards, and straight, tight trousers. Also informally called "ted".

Te De·um (tée dée-əm, táy dáy-əm, -o͞om) *n.* **1.** A Latin hymn, probably written in the early fifth century A.D., beginning with the words *Te Deum laudamus,* "We praise Thee, O God", sung especially at matins or on special occasions, as at a thanksgiving service. **2.** A musical setting of this text.

te·di·ous (téedi-əss) *adj.* Tiresome or uninteresting, especially by reason of extreme length or slowness; wearisome; boring; monotonous: *a tedious music lesson.* —See Synonyms at **boring.** [Middle English, from Old French *tedieus,* from Late Latin *taediōsus,* from Latin *taedium,* TEDIUM.] **—te·di·ous·ly** *adv.* **—te·di·ous·ness** *n.*

te·di·um (téedi-əm) *n.* **1.** The quality of being wearisome or monotonous; tediousness. **2.** The state of being bored; boredom; ennui. [Latin *taedium,* from *taedēre*†, to bore, weary.]

tee[1] (tee) *n.* Something shaped like a letter T, as: **1.** A T-shaped pipe connection. **2.** A joint or girder with a T-shaped cross section.

tee[2] *n.* **1.** A small mound, or a small peg with a concave top, on which a golf ball is placed for an initial drive. **2.** The area at the beginning of each hole from which a golfer makes his first stroke. ~*tr.v.* **teed, teeing, tees.** To place (a golf ball) on a tee. **—tee off. 1.** To drive a golf ball from the tee. **2.** To start; begin: *They teed off the sponsored walk with a toast.* **—tee up.** To place or set up a golf ball for driving. [Earlier *teaz*†.]

tee[3] *n.* A mark aimed at in certain games, such as curling or quoits. **—to a tee.** Perfectly; exactly. [Perhaps such marks were originally T-shaped.]

teehee. Variant of **tehee.**

teem[1] (teem) *v.* **teemed, teeming, teems.** *—intr.* **1. a.** To be full and, usually, in motion; abound or swarm. Used with *with: A drop of water teems with microorganisms; a mind teeming with ideas.* **b.** To exist in great quantity; be abundant: *teeming multitudes.* **2.** *Obsolete.* To produce young. *—tr. Archaic.* To give birth to; bear; produce. [Middle English *temen, teamen,* to give birth to, breed, Old English *tīeman, tȳman.*] **—teem·er** *n.*

teem[2] *v.* **teemed, teeming, teems.** *—intr.* To flow or pour in great quantity. Used chiefly of rain. *—tr. Archaic.* To pour out or empty. [Middle English *temen,* from Old Norse *tōma,* to empty, from Germanic *tōm-,* empty (unattested).]

teen[1] (teen) *adj. Chiefly U.S.* Teenage. **—teen** *n.*

teen[2] *n. Obsolete.* Injury; grief. [Middle English *tene, teone,* Old English *tēona.*]

-teen *n. suffix.* Used in the names of cardinal numbers **thirteen** to **nineteen.** [Middle English *-tene,* Old English *-tēne, -tȳne.*]

teen·age (téen-ayj) *adj.* Also **teen·aged** (-ayjd). Of, pertaining to, or designating a teenager or teenagers.

teen·ag·er (téen-ayjər) *n.* A person between the ages of thirteen and nineteen inclusive. See Synonyms at **young.**

teens (teenz) *pl.n.* **1.** The numbers that end in *-teen.* **2.** The years of one's age between thirteen and nineteen inclusive.

tee·ny (téeni) *adj.* **-nier, -niest.** Also **teen·sy** (téenzi), **-sier, -siest.** Tiny. [Alteration of TINY.]

teen·sy-ween·sy (téenzi-wéenzi) *adj.* Also **teeny-weeny** (téeni-wéeni). *Informal.* Tiny.

teen·y·bop·per (téeni-boppər) *n. Informal.* A girl in early adolescence who is an avid follower of contemporary fashions and tastes, especially in matters of pop music and clothes. Also called "bopper". [TEEN(-AGE) + BOP (music).]

tee·pee. Variant of **tepee.**

tee shirt. Variant of **T-shirt.**

Tees (teez). River in northeastern England, rising in the northern Pennines and flowing for about 110 kilometres (70 miles) into the North Sea. Its estuary lies near Middlesbrough. Teesside, a former county borough, included the industrial complex of which Middlesbrough, Stockton-on-Tees, and Redcar formed part.

tee·ter (téetər) *intr.v.* **-tered, -tering, -ters. 1.** To walk or move unsteadily or unsurely; totter. **2.** To be in a precarious position or condition: *teetering on the brink of disaster.* **3.** *U.S.* To vacillate. ~*n. U.S.* A **seesaw** *(see).* [Earlier *titter,* from Middle English *titeren,* probably from Old Norse *titra,* to tremble.]

tee·ter-tot·ter (téetər-tottər) *n. U.S.* A **seesaw** *(see).*

teeth (teeth) *pl.n.* **1.** Plural of **tooth. 2.** Power; force: *the law lacks teeth.* **—cut (one's) teeth.** To gain one's first experience; practise for the first time. Usually used with *in* or *on.* **—get (one's) teeth into.** To become actively involved in or get a firm grasp of. **—in the teeth of. 1.** Directly and forcefully against. **2.** In defiance of. **—kick in the teeth.** To treat with utter disrespect and callousness. **—lie in (one's) teeth.** To lie directly to or as if to someone's face. **—set (someone's) teeth on edge.** To grate or jar against the sensibilities of; produce an acutely unpleasant sensation in. **—show (one's) teeth.** To show a readiness to fight; threaten defiantly. **—to the teeth.** Completely; lacking nothing: *armed to the teeth.*

teethe (tee<u>th</u>) *intr.v.* **teethed, teething, teethes.** To grow teeth; cut one's teeth in infancy. [Middle English *tethen,* from *tethe.* See **tooth.**]

teeth·ing ring (tée<u>th</u>ing) *n.* A ring of hard rubber or plastic upon which a baby can bite while teething.

teething troubles *pl.n.* Difficulties arising in the initial stages of of a new enterprise, or faults occurring in a newly developed product or system.

tee·to·tal (tee-tṓt'l, tée-) *adj.* **1.** Of, practising, or advocating total abstinence from alcoholic drinks. **2.** *U.S. Informal.* Complete; entire.

tee·to·tal·ler, *U.S.* **tee·to·tal·er** (tee-tṓt'l-ər, tée-) *n.* A person who abstains completely from alcoholic drink. [*Tee,* first letter in TOTAL + TOTAL (ABSTINENCE).]

tee·to·tum (tée-tōtəm, -tō-túm) *n.* **1.** A kind of top spun with the fingers, usually having four lettered sides and used in games of chance. **2.** Broadly, any type of top spun with the fingers. [Earlier *T-totum,* from the letter *T* inscribed on one of the four sides, standing for Latin *tōtum,* all, and signifying "take all".]

teff, tef, t'ef (tef) *n.* A cereal, *Eragrostis abyssinica,* widely grown in Ethiopia for grain and in certain other countries for fodder. [Amharic *têf.*]

TEFL (teff'l). Teaching English as a foreign language.

Tef·lon (téf-lon) *n.* A trademark for a waxy, opaque material, polytetrafluoroethylene, used as a coating on cooking utensils and in industrial applications to prevent sticking.

teg (teg) *n.* A sheep in its second year.

teg·men (tég-mən, -men) *n., pl.* **-mina** (-minə). *Biology.* A covering or integument, such as the tough, leathery forewing of certain insects or the inner coat of a seed. [New Latin, from Latin, covering, from *tegere,* to cover.]

Te·gu·ci·gal·pa (te-go͞o-si-gál-pə). Capital and largest city of Honduras, lying in the mountain region of southern central Honduras on the river Choluteca.

teg·u·lar (téggew-lər) *adj.* Also **teg·u·lat·ed** (-laytid). **1.** Pertaining to, arranged like, or resembling a tile or tiles. **2.** Overlapping; imbricate: *tegular scales.* [From Latin *tēgula,* tile, from *tegere,* to cover.] **—teg·u·lar·ly** *adv.*

teg·u·ment (téggew-mənt) *n.* An outer covering; an integument. [Middle English, from Latin *tegumentum,* from *tegere,* to cover.] **—teg·u·men·ta·ry** (-méntəri), **teg·u·men·tal** (-mént'l) *adj.*

te·hee, tee·hee (tée-hée) *interj.* Used to express giggling, often mocking, laughter. ~*intr.v.* **teheed, -heeing, -hees.** To utter a giggling, often mocking, laugh.

Teh·ran or **Te·he·ran** (taír-raán, té-hə-, -rán). Capital city of Iran, lying in the northern part of the country near Mount Damavand. It is Iran's largest city and most important industrial and commercial centre. It became the capital of Persia in 1788.

Teil·hard de Char·din (tay-yár də shaar-dáɴ), **Pierre** (1881–1955). French Jesuit theologian. He maintained that the universe and mankind are in constant evolution towards a perfect state. He also made valuable contributions in the field of palaeontology.

tek·tite (ték-tīt) *n.* A dark brown to green glassy mass, about 20 millimetres (3/4 inch) in diameter and composed largely of silica, found in various parts of the world and on the Moon, and thought to have formed when a meteorite hit the ground.

tel. 1. telegram; telegraph; telegraphic. **2.** telephone.

te·la (tée-lə) *n., pl.* **-lae** (-lee). A weblike membrane that covers some portion of a bodily organ. [New Latin, from Latin *tēla,* web.]

tel·aes·the·sia, *U.S.* **tel·es·the·sia** (tél-eess-thée-zi-ə, -iss-, -<u>zh</u>i- || -ess-, -<u>zh</u>ə) *n.* Perception of or response to distant objects or stimuli without using normal sensory contact, that is, by extrasensory means. [New Latin : TELE- + Greek *aisthēsis,* perception + -IA.] **—tel·aes·thet·ic** (-théttik) *adj.*

tel·a·mon (téllə-mən, -mon) *n., pl.* **telamons, telamones** (-mṓ-neez). *Architecture.* A figure of a man used as a supporting pillar. Compare **caryatid.** [Latin, from Greek *telamōn,* bearer.]

tel·an·gi·ec·ta·sia (tel-ánji-ek-táy-zi-ə, til-, -<u>zh</u>i- || -<u>zh</u>ə) *n.* Also **tel·an·gi·ec·ta·sis** (-éktə-siss). A chronic dilation of groups of capillaries of the blood vascular system causing dark-red blotches on the skin. [New Latin : TEL(O)- (end) + Greek *angos,* vessel (see **angiology**) + *ectasis,* dilation, from Greek *ektasis,* expansion, stretching, from *ekteinein,* to stretch out : *ek-,* from *ex,* out + *teinein,* to stretch.] **—tel·an·gi·ec·tat·ic** (-táttik) *adj.*

Tel A·viv–Jaf·fa (tél ə-véev; jáffə). Largest city in Israel, lying in the central part of the country on the Mediterranean coast. It is both a leading resort and the most important industrial and commercial city in the country. Jaffa is an ancient Phoenician city; Tel Aviv was founded in 1909 by Jews who wished to escape from Arab-dominated Jaffa. The two cities were merged in 1950.

tele-, tel- *comb. form.* Indicates: **1.** Distance; for example, **telecommunication, telesthesia. 2.** Television; for example, **telecast.** [Greek *tēle,* at a distance, far off.]

tel·e·cast (télli-kaast || -kast) *v.* **-cast** or **-casted, -casting, -casts.** *—intr.* To broadcast by television. *—tr.* To broadcast (a programme) by television. ~*n.* A television broadcast. [TELE (television) + (BROAD)CAST.] **—tel·e·cast·er** *n.*

tel·e·com·mu·ni·ca·tions (télli-kə-méwni-káysh'nz) *n.* **1.** *Used with a singular verb.* The science and technology of communication by electronic transmission of impulses, as by telegraphy, cable, telephony, radio, or television. **2.** *Singular.* Communication over long distances.

PRONUNCIATION KEY

a, trap; aa, father; ai, fair; ar, star; aw, lawn; ay, play; b, bb, stab; rubber; ch, church; ck, ticket; d, dd, dead; ladder; e, dress; ee, bee; er, defer; ew, few; ewr, pure; ə, about; ər, letter; f, ff, fife; differ; g, gg, giggle; h, hat; i, kit; ī, price; īr, fire; j, judge; k, kick; l, ll, let; 'l, needle; m, mm, man; n, nn, no; 'n, sudden; ng, thing; o, lot; ō, no; o͝o, foot; o͞o, shoe; oor, poor; ow, cow; owr, hour; oy, boy; p, pp, pepper; r, rr, red; s, ss, sauce; sh, ship; t, tt, totter; th, thick; <u>th</u>, this; smooth; u, cut; ur, turn; v, vv, valve; w, wet; y, yes; z, zz, zebra; <u>zh</u>, vision; pleasure

IN FOREIGN WORDS:

aɴ, oɴ, Saint-Saëns; <u>hl</u>, Llanelli; Hluhluwe; <u>kh</u>, loch; lough; Khaled

STRESS MARK:

ín-sīt, insight; in-sī́t, incite

tel•e•du (télli-dōō) *n.* A brownish-black carnivorous mammal, *Mydaus javanensis,* of southeast Asia, that is capable of emitting an offensive odour. Also called "stinking badger". [Malay *tĕledu.*]

teleg. telegram; telegraph; telegraphic; telegraphy.

tel•e•ge•nic (télli-jénnik, -jéenik) *adj.* Presenting a pleasing appearance on television. [TELE- + (PHOTO)GENIC.]

te•leg•o•ny (ti-léggəni, te-, tə-) *n.* The supposed influence of one sire on offspring sired by subsequent males, of the same female. [TELE- (distance) + -GONY.] **—tel•e•gon•ic** (télli-gónnik), **te•leg•o•nous** (-léggənəss) *adj.*

tel•e•gram (télli-gram) *n. Abbr.* **tel., teleg. 1.** A communication transmitted by telegraph. **2.** The piece of paper that bears the message of a telegram. [TELE- + -GRAM.]

tel•e•graph (télli-graaf, -graf) *n. Abbr.* **tel., teleg. 1.** Any communications system that transmits and receives simple unmodulated electric impulses, especially one in which the transmission and reception stations are directly connected by wires. **2.** A message transmitted by such a system. **3.** *Capital* **T.** Used as part of the title of certain newspapers: *the Belfast Telegraph.*

~v. **telegraphed, -graphing, -graphs.** *—tr.* **1. a.** To transmit (a message) by telegraph. **b.** To send by means of a telegraphic message: *asked his bank to telegraph some money.* **2.** To send or convey a message to (a person) by telegraph. **3.** To make known unintentionally, as by a sign; especially, in sports, to make (an intended action, such as a pass) obvious to an opponent. *—intr.* To send or transmit a telegram or telegrams. [TELE- + -GRAPH.] **—te•leg•ra•pher** (ti-léggrəfər, te-, tə-), **te•leg•ra•phist** (-léggrəfist) *n.*

tel•e•graph•ese (télli-graaf-éez, -graf-) *n. Informal.* A style of writing that excludes all but the essential words to convey its meaning.

tel•e•graph•ic (télli-gráffik) *adj.* **1.** *Abbr.* **tel., teleg.** Pertaining to or transmitted by telegraph. **2.** Brief or concise, as the wording of a telegram typically is. **—tel•e•graph•i•cal•ly** *adv.*

telegraph plant *n.* A tropical Asiatic plant, *Desmodium gyrans,* having trifoliolate compound leaves, of which the lateral leaflets move or rotate.

telegraph pole *n.* A tall, sturdy pole used to support telegraph or telephone wires.

te•leg•ra•phy (ti-léggrəfi, te-, tə-) *n. Abbr.* **teleg.** The process or act of operating or making telegraphs.

Telegu. Variant of **Telugu.**

tel•e•ki•ne•sis (télli-kī-née-siss, -ki-) *n.* **1.** The movement of objects by scientifically unknown or inexplicable means, as by the exercise of mystical powers. **2.** The ability to produce such movement. [New Latin : TELE- + -KINESIS.] **—tel•e•ki•net•ic** (-néttik) *adj.*

Te•lem•a•chus (ti-lémməkəss, te-, tə-). In Homer, the son of Odysseus and Penelope who helped his father kill Penelope's suitors.

tel•e•mark (télli-maark, téllə-) *n. Often capital* **T.** A turn or stop in skiing executed by shifting the weight forward on the ski that will be on the outside of the turn and pulling its tip gradually inward. [Norwegian, after *Telemark,* region in southern Norway.]

te•lem•e•ter (télli-meetər, ti-lémmitər) *n.* Any of various devices used in telemetry.

~tr.v. **telemetered, -tering, -ters.** To measure and transmit (data) automatically from a distant source, as from a spacecraft or electric power grid, to a receiving station for recording or display. [TELE- + -METER.] **—tel•e•met•ric** (-méttrik), **tel•e•met•ri•cal** *adj.* **—tel•e•met•ri•cal•ly** *adv.*

te•lem•e•try (ti-lémmətri) *n.* The science and technology of automatic measurement and transmission of data by wire, radio, or other means from remote sources, as from space vehicles, to a receiving station for recording and analysis. [TELE- + -METRY.]

tel•en•ceph•a•lon (tél-en-kéffə-lon, -séffə-, -lən) *n.* The anterior portion of the forebrain, including the cerebral cortex, olfactory lobes, and related parts. Also called "endbrain". [TEL(O)- + ENCEPHALON.] **—tel•en•ce•phal•ic** (-si-fál-ik, -sə-, -se-) *adj.*

tel•e•ol•o•gy (télli-óllәji, téeli-) *n., pl.* **-gies. 1.** The philosophical study of manifestations of design or purpose in natural processes or occurrences. Compare **dysteleology. 2.** Such overall purpose or design as exhibited in natural phenomena. **3.** The doctrine that such overall purpose or design underlies and determines natural processes. [New Latin *teleologia* : Greek *teleos,* complete, from *telos,* completion, end + -LOGY.] **—tel•e•o•log•i•cal** (-ə-lójik'l), **tel•e•o•log•ic** *adj.* **—tel•e•o•log•i•cal•ly** *adv.* **—tel•e•ol•o•gist** (-óllәjist) *n.*

tel•e•ost (télli-ost, téeli-) *n.* Also **tel•e•os•te•an** (-ósti-ən). A member of the Teleostei (or Teleostomi), a group consisting of fishes having bony skeletons and including the majority of living species. [New Latin *Teleostei,* "ones having complete bony skeletons", and *Teleostomi,* "ones having complete mouths" : Greek *teleos,* complete (see **teleology**) + Greek *osteon,* bone and *stoma,* mouth (see **stomach**).] **—tel•e•ost, tel•e•os•te•an** *adj.*

te•lep•a•thy (ti-léppəthi, te-, tə-) *n.* **1.** Transference of thoughts between people by scientifically unknown or inexplicable means. **2.** The ability to produce or engage in such communication. Also called "thought transference". [TELE- + -PATHY.] **—tel•e•path•ic** (télli-páthik) *adj.* **—tel•e•path•i•cal•ly** *adv.* **—te•lep•a•thise, te•lep•a•thize** (ti-léppə-thīz, te-, tə-) *intr.v.* **—te•lep•a•thist** (-thist) *n.*

tel•e•phone (télli-fōn) *n. Abbr.* **tel. 1.** An instrument that directly modulates carrier waves with voice or other acoustic source signals to be transmitted to distant locations and that directly reconverts received waves into audible signals; especially, such an instrument connected to others by wire. **2.** A system of such instruments together with connecting and supporting equipment.

~v. **telephoned, -phoning, -phones.** *—tr.* **1.** To call or communicate with (a person) by telephone. **2.** To transmit (a recorded message, television picture, or document) by telephone, using special receiving and sending equipment. *—intr.* To communicate by telephone. [TELE- + -PHONE.] **—tel•e•phon•er** *n.* **—tel•e•phon•ic** (télli-fónnik) *adj.* **—tel•e•phon•i•cal•ly** *adv.*

telephone book *n.* **1.** A book in which one writes useful telephone numbers. **2.** A telephone directory.

telephone box *n.* A small enclosure containing a public telephone. Also called "telephone booth", "call box".

telephone directory *n.* A book listing alphabetically all the telephone subscribers in a particular area, together with their addresses and telephone numbers. Also called "telephone book".

telephone exchange *n.* Any of numerous central systems of switches and other equipment that establish connections between individual telephones. Also called "exchange".

telephone number *n.* A set of digits used to identify and call individual subscribers to a telephone system.

telephone receiver *n.* The part of a telephone in which incoming electrical impulses are converted into sound.

te•leph•o•nist (ti-léffənist, te-, tə-) *n.* One who works as an operator at a telephone switchboard.

te•leph•o•ny (ti-léffəni, te-, tə-) *n.* The electrical transmission of sound between distant points, especially by radio or telephone.

tel•e•pho•to (télli-fō-tō, -fō-) *adj.* Of, pertaining to, or designating a photographic lens or lens system used to produce a large image of a distant object.

tel•e•pho•tog•ra•phy (télli-fə-tóggrəfi) *n.* **1.** The process or technique of photographing distant objects, using a telephoto lens or telescope on a camera. **2.** The technique or process of transmitting charts, pictures, and photographs over a distance. **—tel•e•pho•to•graph•ic** (-fōtə-gráffik) *adj.*

tel•e•play (télli-play) *n. Chiefly U.S.* A play written or adapted for television.

tel•e•print•er (télli-printər) *n.* An electromechanical typewriter that transmits and receives messages coded in electrical signals by telegraph or telephone wires. Also *U.S.* "teletypewriter". See **telex.**

Tel•e•promp•ter (télli-promptər) *n.* A trademark for a type of **autocue** *(see).*

Tel•e•ran (télli-ran) *n.* A trademark for a system used in air traffic control in which the image of a ground-based radar unit is televised to aircraft in the vicinity so that a pilot may see his position in relation to other aircraft.

tel•e•scope (télli-skōp) *n.* An instrument for collecting and examining electromagnetic radiation, especially: **1.** An arrangement of lenses or mirrors or both that gathers visible light, permitting direct observation or photographic recording of distant objects. **2.** Any of various devices, such as a radio telescope, used to detect and observe distant objects by their emission, transmission, reflection, or other interaction with invisible radiation.

~v. **telescoped, -scoping, -scopes.** *—tr.* **1.** To cause to slide inwards or outwards in overlapping sections, as the cylindrical sections of a small hand telescope. **2.** To crush or compress inwards or together, especially as the result of a collision. **3.** To make shorter or more precise; condense: *He telescoped his speech into a few dramatic phrases.* *—intr.* To slide inwards or outwards in or as if in overlapping cylindrical sections; become telescoped. [New Latin *telescopium* or Italian *telescopio,* from Greek *teleskopos,* farseeing : TELE- + *skopos,* watcher.] See feature, next page.

tel•e•scop•ic (télli-skóppik) *adj.* **1.** Of or pertaining to a telescope. **2.** Seen through or obtained by means of a telescope. **3.** Visible only by means of a telescope. **4.** Incorporating a telescope: *a telescopic sight.* **5.** Able to discern distant objects; farseeing. **6.** Extensible or compressible by or as if by the successive sliding of overlapping concentric tubular sections: *a telescopic umbrella.* **—tel•e•scop•i•cal•ly** *adv.*

Tel•e•sco•pi•um (télli-skōpi-əm) *n.* A constellation in the Southern Hemisphere near Scorpius and Sagittarius. [New Latin, from *telescopium,* TELESCOPE.]

te•les•co•py (ti-léskəpi, te-, tə-) *n.* The art or study of making and operating telescopes. **—te•les•co•pist** *n.*

tel•e•spec•tro•scope (télli-spéktrə-skōp) *n.* A spectroscope used in conjunction with an astronomical telescope to enable a spectroscopic analysis to be made of radiation from distant stars or other celestial bodies.

tel•e•ster•e•o•scope (télli-stérri-ə-skōp, -stéer-i-) *n.* A binocular telescope for stereoscopic viewing of distant objects.

telesthesia. *U.S.* Variant of **telaesthesia.**

tel•e•tex (télli-teks) *n.* A system enabling typescript messages, especially those produced by word processors, to be electronically transmitted directly over the telephone system. [TELE- + TEX(T).]

tel•e•text (télli-tekst) *n.* **1.** Any of various systems for broadcasting viewdata. **2. Viewdata** *(see).*

tel•e•ther•mo•scope (télli-thérmə-skōp) *n.* An apparatus for indicating or recording the temperatures of remote locations.

tel•e•thon (télli-thon) *n.* A long, continuous television programme, usually to raise funds for charity. [TELE- + (MARA)THON.]

Tel•e•type (télli-tīp) *n.* A trademark for a brand of teleprinter.

~v. **Teletyped, -typing, -types.** *—intr.* To operate a Teletype. *—tr.* To send a message by Teletype.

tel•e•type•writ•er (télli-tīp-rītər) *n. U.S.* A **teleprinter** *(see).*

te•leu•to•so•rus (ti-lōō-tə-sáw-rəss, te-, tə-, -léw- || -sō-) *n.* A telium. [Greek *teleutē,* end (see **teleutospore**) + SORUS.]

te•leu•to•spore (ti-lōō-tə-spawr, tə-, -léw-, -tō- || -spōr) *n.* A telio-

telegraph *The first electrical telegraphic receiver (above) had a wooden disc which swung round to expose, letter by letter, the transmitted message. Invented by an Englishman, Francis Ronalds, the device was turned down by the British government in 1816. But the invention of faster equipment in 1837, and of the Morse code a year later, established the electric telegraph as a revolutionary means of communication.*

spore. [Greek *teleutē*, end, from *telos*, end, completion + SPORE.] —**te·leu·to·spor·ic** (-spórrik, -spáwrik) *adj.*

tel·e·vise (télli-vīz) *v.* **-vised, -vising, -vises.** —*tr.* **1.** To broadcast (a programme) by television. **2.** To film (an event) for a television broadcast. —*intr.* To broadcast by television. [Back-formation from TELEVISION.]

tel·e·vi·sion (télli-vizh'n, téllə-, -vízh'n) *n. Abbr.* **TV 1.** The transmission of visual images of moving and stationary objects, generally with accompanying sound, as electromagnetic waves and the reconversion of received waves into visual images. **2.** An electronic apparatus that receives such waves and displays the reconverted images on a screen. **3.** The integrated audible and visible content of the electromagnetic waves received and converted by such an apparatus; that which is shown by means of television. **4.** The industry of broadcasting television programmes. [French *télévision* : TELE- + VISION.] —**tel·e·vi·sion·al, tel·e·vi·sion·a·ry** (-əri ‖ -erri) *adj.*

television tube *n.* A form of cathode-ray tube designed for use in a television receiver. Also called "picture tube", "tube".

tel·ex (tél-eks) *n.* **1.** A communication system consisting of teleprinters connected to a telephonic network to send and receive signals. **2.** A message sent or received by such a system. **3.** A teleprinter used in such a system.
~*tr.v.* **telexed, -exing, -exes.** To send (a message) or communicate with (a person) by telex. [TEL(ETYPEWRITER) + EX(CHANGE).]

telfer. Variant of **telpher.**

tel·ic (téllik, téelik) *adj.* Directed or tending towards a definite goal or purpose; purposeful. [Greek *telikos*, final, from *telos*, end.]

te·li·o·spore (téeli-ə-spawr, -ō- ‖ -spōr) *n.* A dark, thick-walled spore produced at the end of the summer by rust fungi. It remains dormant through the winter and germinates in the spring to quit the basidium. Also called "telentospore". [TELIUM + SPORE.]

te·li·um (téeli-əm) *n., pl.* **-lia** (-ə). A dark, pustule-like structure formed on plant tissue infected by a rust fungus, and giving rise to teliospores. [New Latin, from Greek *teleios*, complete (formed in the final stage of the cycle of rust fungi), from *telos*, end, completion.] —**te·li·al** *adj.*

tell¹ (tel) *v.* **told** (tōld), **telling, tells.** —*tr.* **1.** To give a detailed account of; narrate; recount: *tell a story.* **2.** To communicate by speech or writing; express with words: *tell a lie; told us the news.* **3.** To make something known to; notify; inform: *told the authorities.* **4.** To show, explain, or make clear: *His face told us he wasn't joking; Will you tell me how to work the copier?* **5.** To make known; reveal; disclose: *tell a secret.* **6. a.** To command; order: *Do what I tell you.* **b.** To warn; advise: *I told you that would happen.* **7.** *Informal.* To assure: *I tell you, he's an honest man.* Often used for emphasis. **8.** To know or come to know, as through observation or experience; discern: *I can always tell when he's lying.* **9.** To distinguish or recognise; discriminate: *can't tell the difference between margarine and butter.* **10.** *Informal.* To make clear one's low or contemptuous opinion of (someone): *Well, that's certainly telling him!* —*intr.* **1.** To give an account, enumeration, or description. **2.** To give evidence or indication: *Silence told of their unease.* **3. a.** To have an effect or impact: *In this game every move tells.* **b.** To have an exhausting or detrimental effect: *Pressure began to tell on her.* **4.** To reveal the secrets of another: *Promise not to tell!* —**tell off. 1.** To count and set apart, especially aloud. **2.** *Informal.* To rebuke severely; scold. —**tell on.** *Informal.* To inform against; tattle on. —**tell (someone) where to get off.** *Slang.* To rebuff or correct in an aggressive manner. —**you're telling me.** I know that only too well. Used for emphasis. [Tell, told (past tense), told (past participle); Middle English *tellen, told* (or *tald*), *ytold* (or *ytald*), Old English *tellan, tealde, geteald.*] —**tell·a·ble** *adj.*

tell² or **tel** *n.* An artificial hillock, found especially in the Middle

---

---

telescope

EXTENDING THE EYE'S VIEW OF THE UNIVERSE
Lenses, mirrors, and electronics focused on the stars

The first telescope about which there is any definite knowledge was made by the Dutch optician Hans Lippershey in 1608. The following year the Italian astronomer Galileo made his own telescope and used it to make a series of spectacular discoveries, including the four main satellites of Jupiter, the phases of Venus, and the numerous stars in the Milky Way.

Telescopes are of two main types: refractors and reflectors. With a refractor, the light is collected by a glass lens, or objective, and brought to focus. There are various drawbacks; to avoid the "false colour" caused by the fact that light rays of different wavelengths are brought to different focal points, an objective has to be compound – made up of two parts made of different kinds of glass whose errors counteract each other. Moreover an objective has to be supported round its edge, and if too large will distort under its own weight. The world's largest refractor telescope, at the Yerkes Observatory, Wisconsin, in the United States, has an objective 1 metre (40 inches) across.

With a reflector, the light is collected by a curved mirror, and there is no false colour problem. Various optical arrangements are in use, and very large mirrors have been made; the largest of all is the 6 metre (236 inch) reflector at Zelenchukskaya in the Caucasus. The largest reflector in full use is at Palomar in California and is 5 metres (200 inches) across. There is also the MMT, or Multi-Mirror Telescope at Mount Hopkins in Arizona, where six 1.8 metre (72 inch) mirrors are used to bring light to a common focus.

Modern telescopes transfer the signals they receive to film or, in recent years, to electronic devices which are much more sensitive than film. They are also computer-controlled, and a modern observer need not be anywhere near the telescope, or even near the observatory, when carrying out an observational programme. Yet the Earth's atmosphere blurs images from space and limits the size of telescope which can be used efficiently. The next breakthrough will come with the Space Telescope, a 2.4 metre (94 inch) reflector due to be launched in 1985 from the Space Shuttle.

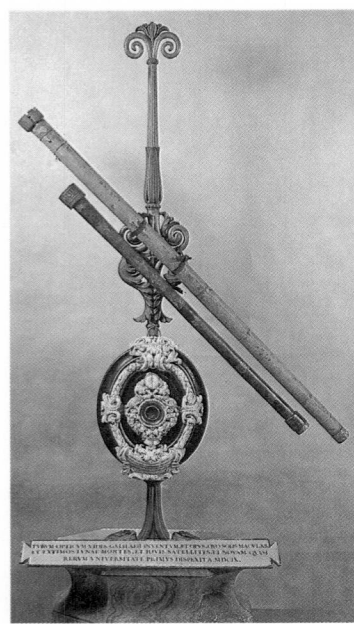

RADIO TELESCOPE *This radio telescope at Cambridge collects the long wavelength electromagnetic radiations from space and records them in the form of a chart marked with an automatic pencil on moving paper.*

EARLY TELESCOPE *Two of Galileo's telescopes are now in the Science Museum in Florence. Small and imperfect though they were (magnifying only 30 times) they enabled Galileo to make observations supporting the theory that the Earth moves round the Sun. The Church was violently hostile to such a view; Galileo was condemned by the Inquisition, and kept a virtual prisoner in his villa until his death in 1642.*

East, formed from the accumulation of debris, earth, or other material, on the site of an ancient settlement. [Arabic *tall,* hillock.]

Tell (tel), **(William).** Swiss hero. According to legend he was sentenced to shoot an apple off his son's head with a crossbow for an act of disrespect to the Austrian bailiff Gessler. He did so, then shot Gessler. The events supposedly took place *c.*1300.

tell·er (téllər) *n.* **1.** One who tells. **2.** A person appointed to count votes in a legislative assembly, such as the House of Commons. **3.** *Chiefly U.S. & Scottish.* A bank employee who deals directly with the public, receiving and paying out money. —**tell·er·ship** *n.*

tell·ing (télling) *adj.* **1.** Having force or effect; striking. **2.** Full of underlying meaning; revealing: *gave a short, telling cough.* —See Synonyms at **valid.** —**tell·ing·ly** *adv.*

tell·tale (tél-tayl) *n.* **1.** One who informs on another person; a tattler; a talebearer. **2.** Anything that provides evidence of something secret or hidden, as of a person's feelings or conduct; a revealing sign. Also used adjectivally: *a telltale blush; the telltale pile of empty wine bottles.* **3.** Any of various devices that indicate or register information, especially: **a.** A time clock for recording an employee's attendance. **b.** A device indicating the position of a ship's rudder. **c.** A compass used by the captain of a ship to check the course.

tel·lu·rate (téllewr-ayt) *n.* A salt or ester of telluric acid.

tel·lu·ri·an (te-léwr-i-ən, -loor-) *adj.* Of, pertaining to, or inhabiting the earth.
~*n.* **1.** An inhabitant of the earth; a terrestrial. **2.** Variant of **tellurion.** [Latin *tellūs* (stem *tellūr-*), earth.]

tel·lu·ric (te-léwr-ik, -toor-) *adj.* **1.** Of or relating to the earth; earthly; terrestrial. **2.** Derived from or containing tellurium, especially with valency 6. [From Latin *tellūs* (stem *tellūr-*), earth.]

telluric acid *n.* A white, crystalline inorganic acid, H_6TeO_6, that is used as a chemical reagent.

tel·lu·ride (téllewr-īd) *n.* A binary compound of tellurium. [TELLUR(IUM) + -IDE.]

tel·lu·ri·on (te-léwr-i-ən, -loor-, -on) *n.* Also **tel·lu·ri·an** (-ən). An instrument that shows how the movement of the earth on its axis and around the sun causes day and night and the seasons. [Latin *tellūs* (stem *tellūr-*), earth + -ION.]

tel·lu·ri·um (te-léwr-i-əm, -loor-) *n.* *Symbol* **Te** A brittle, silvery-white metallic element, occurring naturally combined with gold and other metals, produced commercially as a by-product of the electrolytic refining of copper, and used to alloy stainless steel and lead, in ceramics, and, in the form of bismuth telluride, in thermoelectric devices. Atomic number 52, atomic weight 127.60, melting point 449.8°C, boiling point 989.8°C, relative density range 6.11-6.27, valencies 2, 4, 6. [New Latin, from Latin *tellūs* (stem *tellūr-*), earth (by analogy with URANIUM, after the planet *Uranus*).]

tel·lu·ro·me·ter (téllewr-ómmitər) *n.* An electronic surveying device used to measure distances of up to 64 kilometres (40 miles) by the transmission of radio waves between two stations set up at the ends of the unknown distance, and measurement of the time the waves take to travel between the stations. [Latin *tellūs* (stem *tellūr-*), earth + -METER.]

tel·lu·rous (téllewr-əss, te-léwr-əss, -loor-) *adj.* Of, relating to, or derived from tellurium, especially with valency 4. [TELLURIUM + -OUS.]

tel·ly (télli) *n., pl.* **-lies.** *Chiefly British Informal.* Television.

telo-, tel- *comb. form.* Indicates: **1.** Completion, perfection, or finality; for example, **telophase.** **2.** End or situated at the end; for example, **telencephalon.** [From Greek *telos,* end, completion.]

te·lom·er·i·sa·tion (tee-lómmər-ī-záysh'n, ti-, te- ‖ *U.S.* -i-) *n.* The polymerisation of a chemical substance in the presence of a chain transfer agent to give products of relatively low molecular weight. [TELO- + (POLY)MERISATION.]

te·lo·phase (téel-ō-fayz, tél-, -ə-) *n.* The last phase of mitosis and meiosis, in which the daughter chromosomes are grouped either in two diploid daughter cells (mitosis) or four haploid gametes (meiosis). [TELO- + PHASE.]

tel·pher, tel·fer (télfər) *n.* Also **tel·pher·age** (-ij) (for sense 2). **1.** A device for transporting loads consisting of a light car suspended from overhead wire cables and usually driven by electricity. **2.** A transport system using these cars.
~*tr.v.* **telphered, -phering, -phers.** To transport by telpher. [From TEL(E)- + Greek *pherein,* to carry.]

tel·son (télss'n) *n.* A terminal structure of the posterior section of certain arthropods, such as the sting of a scorpion. [New Latin, from Greek, headland, limit, from *telos,* end.]

Tel·u·gu, Tel·e·gu (tél-ə-goo, -oo-, -goo) *n., pl.* **-gus** or collectively **Telugo. 1.** A Dravidian language spoken chiefly in Andhra Pradesh, India. **2.** A member of a Dravidian people who speak this language. —**Tel·u·gu** *adj.*

tem·blor (tém-blər, -blawr ‖ -blōr) *n.* *U.S. Regional.* An earthquake. [Spanish, from *temblar,* to shake, from Vulgar Latin *tremulāre* (unattested), TREMBLE.]

tem·er·ar·i·ous (témmə-raír-i-əss) *adj.* *Formal.* Presumptuously or recklessly daring; rash. [Latin *temerārius,* rash, from *temere,* rashly. See **temerity.**] —**tem·e·rar·i·ous·ly** *adv.* —**tem·e·rar·i·ous·ness** *n.*

te·mer·i·ty (ti-mérrəti, te-, tə-) *n.* Foolhardy or heedless disregard of danger; foolish boldness; recklessness; rashness. [Middle English *temeryte,* from Latin *temeritās,* from *temere,* blindly, rashly.]
Synonyms: temerity, audacity, impetuosity, effrontery, nerve, cheek, gall.

temp (temp) *n.* *Informal.* A person, such as a typist or secretary, who is employed or usually works on a temporary basis.

---

television

IMAGES THAT SPAN THE WORLD
Transmitting live pictures in a series of coloured lines

Scientists dreamed of "seeing by telegraph" as early as the 1870s, but the first public demonstration of television was by John Logie Baird in London in 1926.

Since 1945, television has proved as significant an invention as printing. Within a generation it has linked every nation with instant worldwide news coverage. It has shown live pictures of moon landings, sports events, and Presidential elections. With the rapid advance in satellite transmission, and in video and computer technology, its role continues to grow.

Television works by scanning a scene in lines and transmitting them in sequence as radio signals. The lines flash on the receiving screen so fast that the eye sees them as one picture.

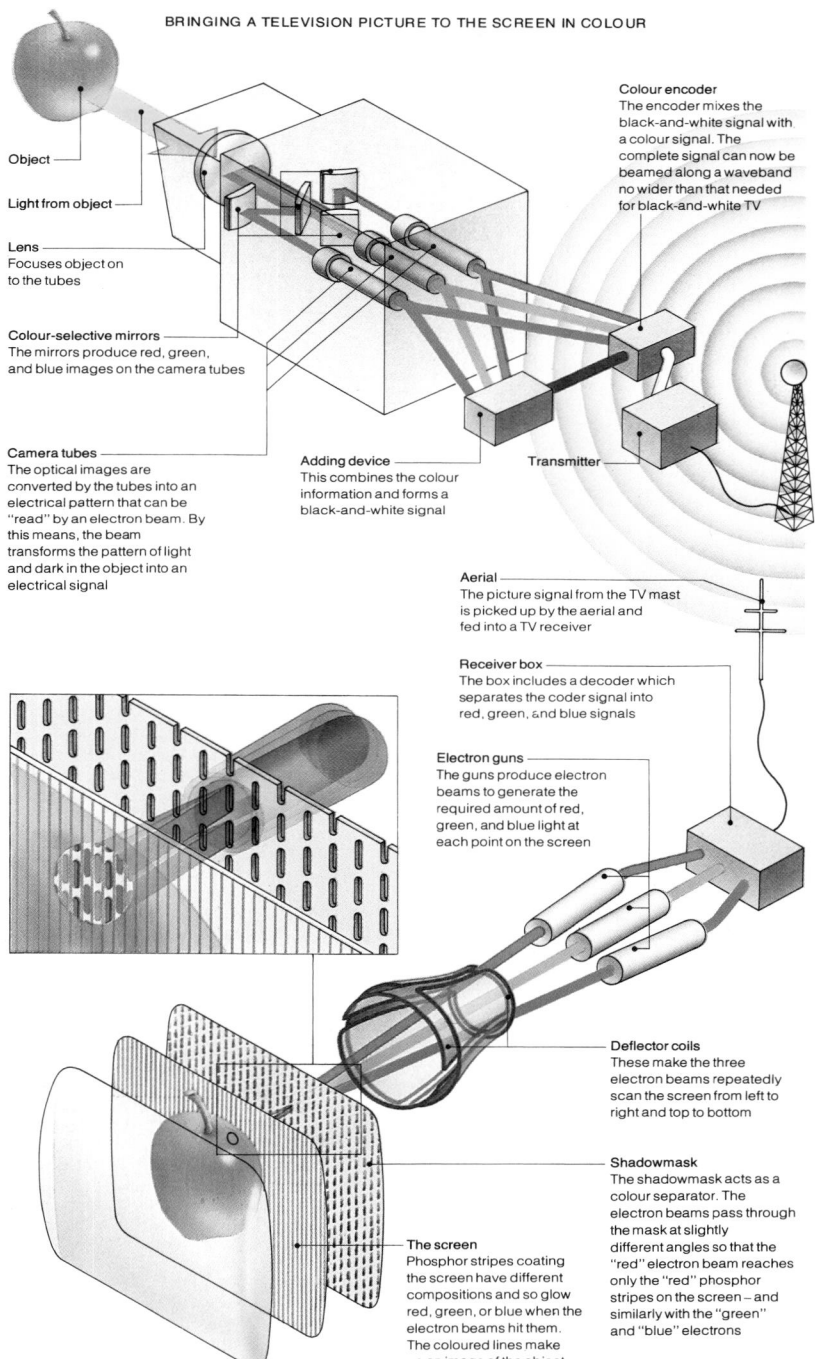

BRINGING A TELEVISION PICTURE TO THE SCREEN IN COLOUR

Object

Light from object

Lens
Focuses object on to the tubes

Colour-selective mirrors
The mirrors produce red, green, and blue images on the camera tubes

Camera tubes
The optical images are converted by the tubes into an electrical pattern that can be "read" by an electron beam. By this means, the beam transforms the pattern of light and dark in the object into an electrical signal

Adding device
This combines the colour information and forms a black-and-white signal

Colour encoder
The encoder mixes the black-and-white signal with a colour signal. The complete signal can now be beamed along a waveband no wider than that needed for black-and-white TV

Transmitter

Aerial
The picture signal from the TV mast is picked up by the aerial and fed into a TV receiver

Receiver box
The box includes a decoder which separates the coder signal into red, green, and blue signals

Electron guns
The guns produce electron beams to generate the required amount of red, green, and blue light at each point on the screen

Deflector coils
These make the three electron beams repeatedly scan the screen from left to right and top to bottom

Shadowmask
The shadowmask acts as a colour separator. The electron beams pass through the mask at slightly different angles so that the "red" electron beam reaches only the "red" phosphor stripes on the screen - and similarly with the "green" and "blue" electrons

The screen
Phosphor stripes coating the screen have different compositions and so glow red, green, or blue when the electron beams hit them. The coloured lines make up an image of the object

COLOUR SIGNALS *Light from the scene is broken into its constituent wavelengths (colours); which are coded into radio signals. These are received and reconstituted as separate beams of colour. They combine on the screen to reproduce the original scene in a series of lines and dots.*

temple *This Buddhist temple stands on the island of Penang in Malaysia.*

~*intr.v.* **temped, temping, temps.** *Informal.* To work as a temp.

temp. **1.** in the time of. [Latin *tempore*]. **2.** temperature.

tem·per (témpər) *v.* **-pered, -pering, -pers.** —*tr.* **1.** To modify by the addition of some moderating agent or quality; moderate: *tempered severity with kindness.* **2.** To bring to a suitable or desired consistency, texture, hardness, or other physical condition by or as by blending, admixture, kneading, or a similar process. **3.** To harden, strengthen, or toughen (a metal) by application of heat or by alternate heating and cooling. **4.** *Music.* To adjust or tune (a keyboard instrument) by temperament. —*intr.* To be or become tempered; especially, to reach a suitable degree of hardness or strength. Used of a metal.
~*n.* **1. a.** A person's habitual cast of mind or emotions; a disposition; a temperament: *a sweet temper.* **b.** A temporary state of mind or emotions having a particular character; a mood; a humour: *in a foul temper.* **2.** Calmness of mind or emotions; equanimity; composure: *lost my temper; keep one's temper.* **3. a.** A tendency to become easily angry or irritable: *Control your temper.* **b.** An outburst of rage: *a fit of temper.* **4. a.** The condition of being tempered. **b.** The degree of hardness and elasticity of a metal, usually steel, as a result of tempering. **5.** A substance or agent added to something to alter or modify it. **6.** *Archaic.* A middle course; a compromise between extremes. —See Synonyms at **mood.** [Middle English *temp(e)ren,* Old English *temprian,* to mingle, moderate, from Latin *temperāre,* "to mingle in due proportion", probably from *tempus* (stem *tempor-*), time, due season.] **—tem·per·a·bil·i·ty** (-ə-bílləti) *n.* **—tem·per·a·ble** *adj.* **—tem·per·er** *n.*

tem·per·a (témpərə) *n.* **1.** A painting medium in which pigment is mixed with water-soluble glutinous materials such as egg yolk or white. **2.** Painting done with this medium. [Italian, from *temperare,* to mingle, temper, from Latin *temperāre.* See **temper.**]

tem·per·a·ment (témprə-mənt, -pərə-) *n.* **1. a.** The manner of thinking, behaving, or reacting characteristic of a particular individual; a disposition: *a nervous temperament.* **b.** The distinguishing mental and physical characteristics that established the constitution of a person according to medieval physiology, caused by the dominance of one of the four humours. See **humour. 2.** A tendency to become irritable or to be too sensitive; a temper. **3.** *Music.* A method of selecting the intervals between the notes of a scale, such as **equal temperament** *(see),* the system used on modern keyboard instruments. —See Synonyms at **disposition.** [Middle English *temperament,* from Latin *temperāmentum,* "a mixing (of the humours)", from *temperāre,* to mingle, TEMPER.]

tem·per·a·men·tal (tém-prə-mént'l, -pərə-) *adj.* **1.** Of, pertaining to, or arising from temperament or temper. **2.** Excessively sensitive or irritable; easily excited or angered; moody. **3.** *Informal.* Tending to behave or perform in an erratic or unpredictable manner: *a temperamental old car.* **—tem·per·a·men·tal·ly** *adv.*

tem·per·ance (témpərənss, témprənss) *n.* **1.** The condition or quality of being temperate; moderation or self-restraint. **2. a.** Moderation in the consumption of alcoholic drinks. **b.** Total abstinence from alcoholic drinks. —See Synonyms at **abstinence.**

tem·per·ate (témpə-rət, témp-, -rit) *adj.* **1.** Exercising moderation and self-restraint, especially with regard to bodily and emotional indulgence: *a temperate drinker.* **2.** Moderate in degree or quality; tempered. **3. a.** Neither hot nor cold in climate; free from climatic extremes; mild. **b.** Occurring in or characteristic of the temperate zone: *temperate vegetation.* [Middle English, from Latin *temperātus,* from the past participle of *temperāre,* to moderate, TEMPER.]

temperate zone *n. Often capital* **T,** *capital* **Z.** Either of two middle latitude zones of the Earth, the *North Temperate Zone* and the *South Temperate Zone,* lying between about 23°30′ and 66°30′ north and south.

tem·per·a·ture (tém-pri-chər, -pəri-, -rə-, -pərə-) *n. Abbr.* **temp.** *Symbol* **T 1. a.** The degree of hotness or coldness of a body or environment. **b.** A specific degree of hotness or coldness as indicated on or referred to a standard scale; a scalar quantity that is independent of the size of the system and that determines the direction of heat flow between any two systems in thermal contact. **2.** A temperature above normal body temperature, caused by illness. [Originally "a tempering", moderate condition (of weather), from Latin *temperātūra,* from *temperāre,* to mix, TEMPER.]

temperature gradient *n.* The rate of change of temperature with displacement in a given direction from a given reference point.

tem·pered (témpərd) *adj.* **1.** Having a specified type of temper or disposition. Used in combination: *sweet-tempered.* **2.** *Music.* Tuned to temperament; specifically, tuned to equal temperament. Said of a scale, interval, semitone, or intonation. **3.** Having the requisite degree of hardness or elasticity. Said of a metal.

tem·pest (témpist) *n. Literary.* **1.** A violent onrush or storm of wind, frequently accompanied by rain, snow, or hail. **2.** An agitated or tumultuous condition: *battered by the political tempest.*
~*tr.v.* **tempested, -pesting, -pests.** *Poetic.* To disturb or agitate violently. [Middle English *tempeste,* from Old French, from Vulgar Latin *tempesta* (unattested), variant of Latin *tempestās,* storm, weather, season, from *tempus,* time, season. See **temporal.**]

tem·pes·tu·ous (tem-péstew-əss, təm-) *adj.* **1.** Pertaining to, characterised by, or resembling a tempest: *tempestuous weather.* **2.** Tumultuous; stormy; turbulent: *years of tempestuous marriage.* **—tem·pes·tu·ous·ly** *adv.* **—tem·pes·tu·ous·ness** *n.*

Tem·plar (témplər) *n.* **1.** A **Knight Templar** *(see).* **2.** *Small* **t.** *British.* A barrister having chambers in the Middle or Lower Temple in London. [Middle English *templer,* from Anglo-French, variant of Old French *templier,* from Medieval Latin *(mīles) templāri(u)s,* "(soldier) of the temple", from Latin *templum,* TEMPLE.]

tem·plate (tém-plət, -plit, *also* -playt) *n.* Also **tem·plet. 1.** A pattern or gauge, such as a thin metal plate with a cut pattern, used as a guide in making something accurately, as in woodworking, or in replication of a standard object. **2.** A piece of stone or timber used to distribute weight or pressure, as over a door frame. **3.** A macromolecule, such as DNA, RNA, or messenger RNA, the structure of which serves as a guide for the assembly of nucleic acids and polypeptides. [Earlier *templet* (influenced by PLATE), from French, diminutive of Old French *temple,* TEMPLE (device in a loom).]

tem·ple[1] (témp'l) *n.* **1.** A building or place dedicated to religious worship or the presence of a deity. Used chiefly with reference to the sacred buildings of the ancient world, and to those of eastern religions such as Hinduism, Buddhism, or Shintoism. **2.** *Capital* **T.** Any of three successive buildings in ancient Jerusalem dedicated to the worship of God. **3.** A Christian church; especially, a Mormon or French Protestant church. **4.** Anything considered to contain a divine presence: *The body is the temple of the soul.* **5.** Any place or building serving as the focus of a special activity or of something especially valued: *a temple of learning.* **6.** *Capital* **T.** Either of two Inns of Court in London, the **Inner Temple** and **Middle Temple** *(both of which see),* on the site formerly occupied by the Knights Templar. **7.** *U.S.* A synagogue. [Middle English *temple,* from Old English *tempel* and Old French *temple,* from Latin *templum,* sanctuary, space marked for observation by an augur.]

temple[2] *n.* The flat region on either side of the forehead above the cheek bone. [Middle English, from Old French, from Vulgar Latin *tempula* (unattested), variant of Latin *tempora,* plural of *tempus,* temple of the head.]

temple[3] *n.* A device in a loom that keeps the cloth stretched to the correct width during weaving. [Middle English *tempylle,* from Old French *temple,* from Latin *templum,* small piece of wood.]

tem·po (tém-pō) *n., pl.* **-pos** or **-pi** (-pee). **1.** *Abbr.* **t.** *Music.* The relative speed at which a composition is to be played, as indicated by a descriptive or metronomic direction to the performer. **2.** A characteristic rate or rhythm of activity; pace: *the quick tempo of modern life.* [Italian, "time", from Latin *tempus.* See **temporal.**]

tem·po·ral[1] (témp-ərəl, -rəl) *adj.* **1.** Pertaining to, concerned with, or limited by time. **2.** Pertaining to or concerned with earthly life or existence. **3.** Civil, secular, or lay, as distinguished from ecclesiastical: *the Lords temporal.* **4. a.** *Grammar.* Expressing time: *a temporal conjunction.* **b.** Of or pertaining to a verbal tense. [Middle English *temporal,* from Latin *temporālis,* from *tempus*† (stem *tempor-*), time.] **—tem·po·ral·ly** *adv.*

temporal[2] *adj.* Of, pertaining to, or near the temples of the skull. [Late Latin *temporālis,* from Latin *tempus* (stem *tempor-*), TEMPLE (of the head).]

temporal bone *n.* Either of two complex bones forming the sides and base of the skull and housing the middle and inner ear. Also called "temporal fossa".

tem·po·ral·i·ty (témpə-rál-əti) *n., pl.* **-ties. 1.** The condition of being temporal or temporary. **2. a.** Something that is temporal. **b.** *Usually plural.* Temporal possessions, especially of the church or clergy.

temporal lobe *n.* The part of each cerebral hemisphere associated with the perception and interpretation of sound and possibly with memory.

tem·po·rar·y (témpə-rəri, témp-, *also* -ri || -rerri) *adj.* Lasting, used, or enjoyed for a limited time; impermanent; transient: *a temporary job; temporary relief.* See Synonyms at **transient.**
~*n.* One that is employed only for a limited time. [Latin *temporārius,* from *tempus* (stem *tempor-*), time. See **temporal.**] **—tem·po·rar·i·ly** (-rərəli, *also* -rəli, -rérrəli) *adv.* **—tem·po·rar·i·ness** *n.*

tem·po·rise, tem·po·rize (témpə-rīz) *intr.v.* **-rised, -rising, -rises. 1.** To compromise or act evasively in order to gain time, avoid argument, or postpone a decision. **2. a.** To act or behave in a way appropriate to particular circumstances. **b.** To yield ostensibly or temporarily to what current conditions demand. [French *temporiser,* from Medieval Latin *temporizāre,* to wait one's time, from Latin *tempus* (stem *tempor-*), time. See **temporal.**] **—tem·po·ri·sa·tion** (-rī-záysh'n || *U.S.* -ri-) *n.*

tempt (tempt) *tr.v.* **tempted, tempting, tempts. 1.** To entice (a person) to commit a usually unwise or immoral act, especially by a promise of reward. **2.** To attract or invite: *I must say I'm tempted by the offer.* **3.** To provoke or to risk provoking: *They tempted fate rashly.* **4.** To incline or dispose strongly: *I was tempted just to give the whole thing up.* **5.** *Archaic.* To put to the test: *God tempted Abraham.* —See Synonyms at **lure.** [Middle English *tempten,* from Old French *tempter,* from Latin *temptāre*†, to try, test, tempt.] **—tempt·a·ble** *adj.* **—tempt·er** *n.*

temp·ta·tion (témp-táysh'n, tem-) *n.* **1.** The act of tempting or the condition of being tempted. **2.** Something that tempts or entices.

tempt·ing (témpting) *adj.* Alluring, enticing, or seductive. **—tempt·ing·ly** *adv.* **—tempt·ing·ness** *n.*

temp·tress (témp-trəss, -triss) *n.* A woman who seeks to seduce a man.

tem·pu·ra (tem-pŏŏr-ə, témpə-rə, -raa) *n.* A Japanese dish of vegetables and seafood dipped in batter and fried in deep fat. [Japanese, "fried food".]

ten (ten) *n.* **1. a.** The cardinal number that is one more than nine. **b.** A symbol representing this, such as 10, X, or x. **2.** A set made up of ten persons or things. **3. a.** The tenth in a series. **b.** A playing card marked with ten pips. **4.** Ten parts: *cut in ten.* **5.** A size, as in clothing, designated as ten. **6.** A bank note or coin having a denomination of ten: *I'll have the money in tens.* **7.** Ten hours after midnight or midday. [Middle English *ten,* Old English *tīen, tēne, tȳn.*] **—ten** *adj.* **—ten·fold** (-fōld, -fōld) *adj. & adv.*

ten. *Music.* **1.** tenor. **2.** tenuto.

ten·a·ble (ténnəb'l) *adj.* Capable of being defended or sustained, as against critical argument or military attack: *a tenable position.* [French *tenable,* from *tenir,* to hold, from Latin *tenēre.*] **—ten·a·bil·i·ty** (ténnə-bílləti), **ten·a·ble·ness** *n.* **—ten·a·bly** *adv.*

ten·ace (tén-ayss, -əss, -iss, te-náyss) *n.* In card games such as bridge and whist, the holding of a combination of two nonconsecutive high cards of a suit, such as the king and the jack. [French, TENACIOUS.]

te·na·cious (ti-náyshəss, te-, tə-) *adj.* **1. a.** Holding or tending to hold or maintain firmly. **b.** Persistent; resolute; stubborn. **2.** Holding together firmly; cohesive. **3.** Clinging to another object or surface; adhesive. **4.** Tending to retain; retentive. —See Synonyms at **strong.** [Latin *tenāx* (stem *tenāc-*), from *tenēre,* to hold.] **—te·na·cious·ly** *adv.* **—te·na·cious·ness** *n.*

te·nac·i·ty (ti-nássəti, te-, tə-) *n.* The condition or quality of being tenacious. See Synonyms at **courage, perseverance.**

te·nac·u·lum (ti-náckew-ləm, te-, tə-) *n., pl.* **-la** (-lə). A long-handled, slender, hooked instrument for lifting and holding parts, such as blood vessels, during surgery. [New Latin, from Late Latin, holder, from Latin *tenēre,* to hold.]

ten·an·cy (ténnən-si) *n., pl.* **-cies. 1.** The possession or occupancy of lands or buildings by title, under a lease, or on payment of rent. **2.** The period of a tenant's occupancy or possession. **3.** The occupation or period of occupation of an office or position; tenure.

ten·ant (ténnənt) *n.* **1.** One who temporarily holds or occupies land, a building, or other property owned by another. **2.** *Law.* One who holds or possesses lands, tenements, and sometimes personal property by any kind of title. **3.** An occupant, inhabitant, or dweller in any place.
~*tr.v.* **tenanted, -anting, -ants.** To hold as a tenant; occupy; inhabit. [Middle English *tena(u)nt,* from Old French *tenant,* from the present participle of *tenir,* to hold, from Latin *tenēre,* to hold.]

tenant farmer *n.* One who farms land owned by another and pays rent in cash or as a proportion of his produce.

ten·ant·ry (ténnəntri) *n., pl.* **-ries. 1.** Tenants collectively, especially tenant farmers. **2.** The state or condition of being a tenant; tenancy.

tench (tench) *n., pl.* **tenches** or collectively **tench.** An edible Eurasian freshwater fish, *Tinca tinca,* having small scales and two barbels near the mouth. [Middle English *tenche,* from Old French, from Late Latin *tinca,* perhaps from Gaulish.]

Ten Commandments *pl.n.* The ten injunctions given by God to Moses on Mount Sinai, the basis of Mosaic Law. Exodus 20:1–17. Preceded by *the.* Also called "Decalogue".

tend[1] (tend) *intr.v.* **tended, tending, tends. 1.** To move or extend in a particular direction: *Our course tended towards the north.* **2.** To show a natural likelihood or inclination to act in a particular way or produce a particular effect; be apt: *War tends to defeat its purposes.* **3.** To be disposed or inclined: *He tends towards sarcasm.* [Middle English *tenden,* from Old French *tendre,* from Latin *tendere,* to stretch, direct one's course, be inclined.]

tend[2] *v.* **tended, tending, tends.** *—tr.* **1.** To minister to the needs of; look after: *tend a child.* **2.** To be in charge of; mind: *tend a shop.* *—intr.* **1.** To serve or wait. Used with *on* or *upon.* **2.** *Chiefly U.S. Informal.* To apply one's attention. Used with *to.* [Middle English *tenden,* short for *attenden,* ATTEND.]

Usage: *Tend* and *attend* are distinguished in formal English: one may *tend the sick people of the town* or *attend to the sick people of the town.* The use of *to* with *tend,* in the sense of "apply one's attention", is not standard, especially in British English.

ten·den·cy (téndən-si) *n., pl.* **-cies.** A demonstrated inclination to think, act, develop, or behave in a certain way; a propensity: *a tendency to panic; a tendency to lie.* [Medieval Latin *tendentia,* from Latin *tendēns,* present participle of *tendere,* to stretch, TEND.]

Synonyms: *tendency, trend, current, drift, inclination.*

ten·den·tious, ten·den·cious (ten-dénshəss) *adj.* Written or said with the aim of promoting a particular point of view; not impartial; biased. Used derogatorily. [From TENDENCY.] **—ten·den·tious·ly** *adv.* **—ten·den·tious·ness** *n.*

ten·der[1] (téndər) *adj.* **-derer, -derest. 1. a.** Easily damaged, bruised, or broken; delicate; fragile: *tender skin.* **b.** Easily chewed or cut: *tender beef.* **2.** Young and vulnerable: *of tender age.* **3.** Needing to be handled with tact and sensitivity: *a tender subject.* **4.** Sensitive to frost or severe cold; not hardy. Said of a plant. **5. a.** Easily hurt; sensitive: *a tender conscience.* **b.** Painful; sore. **6. a.** Gentle and solicitous: *a tender mother.* **b.** Expressing gentle emotions; loving: *a tender glance.* **c.** Given to sympathy or kindness; soft: *a tender heart.* **7.** Considerate and protective; careful to ward off harmful influences or avoid harmful action. Often used with *of: tender of her reputation.* **8.** *Nautical.* Apt to lean under sail; crank.
~*tr.v.* **tendered, -dering, -ders.** *Archaic.* **1.** To make tender. **2.** To treat with tender regard. [Middle English *tender, tendre,* from Old French *tendre,* from Latin *tener,* tender, delicate. **—ten·der·ly** *adv.* **—ten·der·ness** *n.*

tender[2] *n.* **1.** The act of tendering. **2.** A formal offer, as: **a.** *Law.* An offer of money or goods in payment of an obligation. **b.** A written offer to supply goods or perform work at a stated cost or rate; a bid. **3.** Anything that may be tendered as payment, especially money: *legal tender.*
~*v.* **tendered, -dering, -ders.** *—tr.* **1.** To offer formally; present: *tendered my resignation.* **2.** To offer (money or goods) in payment: *tendered the correct fare.* *—intr.* To make a tender; bid: *tender for a contract.* —See Synonyms at **offer.** [From Old French *tendre,* to offer, stretch out: see **tend** (move towards).] **—ten·der·er** *n.*

tender[3] *n.* **1.** One who tends something. **2.** *Nautical.* A vessel attendant on another vessel or vessels, especially one that ferries supplies between ship and shore. **3.** A railway wagon attached to the rear of a steam locomotive and designed to carry fuel and water.

ten·der·foot (téndər-fo͝ot) *n., pl.* **-foots** or **-feet** (-feet). **1.** An inexperienced person or novice, especially one unaccustomed to rough conditions. **2.** A beginner in the ranks of the Scouts.

ten·der·heart·ed (téndər-hártid) *adj.* Easily moved by another's distress; compassionate. **—ten·der·heart·ed·ly** *adv.* **—ten·der·heart·ed·ness** *n.*

ten·der·ise, ten·der·ize (téndə-rīz) *tr.v.* **-ised, -ising, -ises.** To make (meat) tender, as by marinating, pounding, or applying a tenderiser. **—ten·der·i·sa·tion** (-rī-záysh'n || *U.S.* -ri-) *n.*

ten·der·is·er (téndə-rīzər) *n.* Any substance that tenderises meat by breaking down the meat fibres.

ten·der·loin (téndər-loyn) *n.* A cut of meat from under the short ribs that is the tenderest part of a loin of beef, pork, or the like.

ten·di·ni·tis (téndi-nītiss) *n.* Inflammation of a tendon and its muscle attachments. [New Latin *tendo* (stem *tendin-*), TENDON + -ITIS.]

ten·di·nous (téndinəss) *adj.* **1.** Of, having, or resembling a tendon or tendons. **2.** Sinewy. [New Latin *tendinosus,* from *tendo* (stem *tendin-*), from Medieval Latin *tendō,* TENDON.]

ten·don (téndən) *n.* A band of tough, inelastic fibrous tissue that connects a muscle with its bony attachment; a sinew. [From Medieval Latin *tendō* (stem *tendin-*), from Latin *tendere,* to stretch.]

ten·dril (tén-dril, -drəl) *n.* **1.** A long, slender, coiling extension, as of a stem, serving as an organ of attachment for certain climbing plants, such as the grape. **2.** Something resembling this: *wispy tendrils of hair.* [Probably from obsolete French *tendrillon,* diminutive of Old French *tendron,* cartilage, young shoot, from Vulgar Latin *tenerūmen* (unattested), from Latin *tener,* tender, delicate.

Ten·e·brae (ténni-bree, -bray) *n. Used with a singular or plural verb. Roman Catholic Church.* The office of matins and lauds sung on the last three days of Holy Week, with a ceremony of candles. [Medieval Latin, from Latin, darkness.]

ten·e·brif·ic (ténni-bríffik) *adj. Archaic & Literary.* Serving to obscure or darken. [Latin *tenebrae,* darkness (see **Tenebrae**) + -FIC.]

ten·e·brous (ténnibrəss) *adj.* Also **te·neb·ri·ous** (tə-nébbri-əss, te-). *Literary.* Dark and gloomy. [From Latin *tenebrae,* darkness. See **Tenebrae.**] **—ten·e·bros·i·ty** (ténni-bróssəti) *n.*

ten·e·ment (tén-i-mənt, -ə-) *n.* **1.** A building to live in; a dwelling-house; a residence. **2.** A large building divided into separate flats for rent, typically meeting only minimal standards of facilities and maintenance and usually found in deprived urban areas. Also called "tenement house". **3.** *Chiefly British.* A room or set of rooms leased to a tenant, especially one that is part of a large house or building. **4.** *Law.* Any kind of real property held by one person from another; a holding. [Middle English *tenement,* from Old French, from Medieval Latin *tenementum,* feudal holding, house, from Latin *tenēre,* to hold.] **—ten·e·men·tal** (-mént'l), **ten·e·men·ta·ry** (-méntəri) *adj.*

Te·ne·ri·fe or **Ten·e·riffe** (ténnə-réef; *Spanish* -réefay). Largest and most populated of the Canary Islands, the site of the capital city of Santa Cruz. It is admired for its scenic beauty.

te·nes·mus (ti-néz-məss, ti-, tə-, -néss-) *n.* **1.** A painful attempt to urinate or defaecate. **2.** Pain associated with urination or defaecation. [Medieval Latin, variant of Latin *tenesmos,* from Greek *teinesmos,* "a straining", from *teinein,* to stretch, strain.]

ten·et (tée-net, té-, -nit) *n.* A belief, doctrine, or principle, especially one held by a group of people. [Latin, he holds, from *tenēre,* to hold.]

Ten-Four (tén-fór || -fór) *interj. Slang.* Yes. Used by users of Citizens' Band Radio.

ten-gal·lon hat (tén-gal-ən) *n.* A felt hat having an exceptionally tall crown and wide brim, popular in the American West.

tenia. Variant of **taenia.**

ten·ner (ténnər) *n. Informal.* A ten-pound note or a ten-dollar note.

Ten·nes·see[1] (ténnə-sée, ténni-). State in the south central United States on the east bank of the Mississippi. The capital is Nashville; the largest city is Memphis. It is an agricultural state, a leading producer of the plantation crops, tobacco and cotton. Tennessee is the nation's leading producer of zinc, and its industries are expanding. It entered the Union in 1796.

Tennessee[2]. River in the south central United States, formed by the confluence of the rivers Holston and French Broad near Knoxville, in Tennessee. It flows for about 1 050 kilometres (650 miles) into the river Ohio at Paducah, in Kentucky. The Tennessee Valley Authority (TVA), formed in 1933, implemented a development plan for the river basin by constructing dams, providing navigable waterways, flood and erosion control, and hydroelectric power.

ten·nis (ténniss) *n.* **1.** A game played with rackets and a light ball by two players *(singles)* or two pairs of players *(doubles)* on a court divided by a net. Also used adjectivally: *a tennis shoe; a tennis ball.* **2. Lawn tennis** *(see).* **3. Real tennis** *(see).* [Middle English *tenetz, tennys,* probably from Old French *tenez,* imperative of *tenir,* to hold

PRONUNCIATION KEY

a, trap; aa, father; ai, **fair;** ar, star; aw, **lawn;** ay, **play;** b, bb, **stab; rubber;** ch, **church;** ck, **ticket;** d, dd, **dead; ladder;** e, **dress;** ee, **bee;** er, **defer;** ew, **few;** ewr, **pure;** ə, about; ər, letter; f, ff, **fife; differ;** g, gg, **giggle;** h, **hat;** i, **kit;** ī, price; īr, **fire;** j, **judge;** k, **kick;** l, ll, **let;** 'l, needle; m, mm, **man;** n, nn, **no;** 'n, **sudden;** ng, **thing;** o, **lot;** ō, **no;** o͝o, **foot;** o͞o, **shoe;** oor, **poor;** ow, **cow;** owr, **hour;** oy, **boy;** p, pp, **pepper;** r, rr, **red;** s, ss, **sauce;** sh, **ship;** t, tt, **totter;** th, **thick;** th, **this;** smooth; u, **cut;** ur, **turn;** v, vv, **valve;** w, **wet;** y, **yes;** z, zz, **zebra;** zh, vision; pleasure

IN FOREIGN WORDS:

aɴ, oɴ, **Saint-Saëns;** hl, **Llanelli; Hluhluwe;** kh, **loch; lough; Khaled**

STRESS MARK:

ín-sīt, insight; in-sít, incite

tennis

INDOOR AND OUTDOOR SPORT PLAYED AT ALL LEVELS

A gentle summer pastime that became a big-money sport

Tennis, once a gentle, summer afternoon pastime, is now not only an energetic game played among friends and in local clubs, but also an international big-money sport played at high speed and with great skill.

The game is for two or four competitors and is played with rackets and a ball on a court marked out either on grass, or on a hard, flat surface indoors or out. The object of the game is to win points by playing the ball within the marked-out area in a way that makes it as difficult as possible for the opponent to return it.

The name of the game probably comes from the French, *tenez*, "attention", once called by the server before commencing play. Players must serve from behind the baseline, first from the right-hand side, so that the ball clears the 915 millimetre (3 foot) net and bounces in the service court diagonally opposite. Thereafter players may strike the ball on the volley before it bounces or after it bounces once. A player loses the point if he fails to return the ball into his opponent's court. The outer sidelines are used only in doubles. The doubles court is nearly 11 metres (36 feet) wide, and the court is nearly 24 metres (78 feet) long.

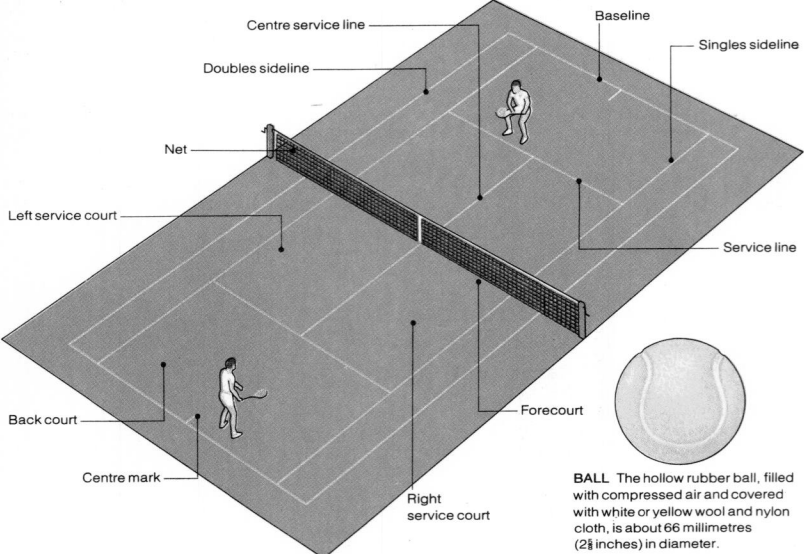

Centre service line — Doubles sideline — Net — Left service court — Back court — Centre mark — Right service court — Baseline — Singles sideline — Service line — Forecourt

BALL The hollow rubber ball, filled with compressed air and covered with white or yellow wool and nylon cloth, is about 66 millimetres (2⅝ inches) in diameter.

SCORING *A player must have four points and a lead of two points to take a game. The scores are called love (= 0), 15 (= 1), 30 (= 2), 40 (= 3), and game. If the score reaches 40 each (called deuce), the game continues until one player has a lead of two points. A player must win at least six games and have a lead of two to take a set. If the score reaches five all, the set continues until one player has a two-game lead. In some tournaments a tie-break game with special scoring is played if a set reaches six games all. Matches consist of the best of three sets when women are among the players, but may be the best of five when all the players are men.*

(probably from the call of the server to his opponent in the game), from Latin *tenēre*, to hold.

tennis elbow *n.* A painful inflammation of the outer elbow resulting from excessive use of the muscles of the forearm.

Ten·no (ténnō) *n., pl.* **Tenno** or **-nos.** *Sometimes small* **t.** The emperor of Japan considered as a religious leader and a divine being. [Japanese *tennō* "celestial emperor" : *ten,* from Chinese *tiān,* heaven + *no,* from Chinese *huang,* emperor.]

teno– *comb. form.* Indicates tendon; for example, **tenotomy.** [From Greek *tenōn,* tendon.]

Te·noch·ti·tlán (ti-nóchti-tlán, -tlaʼan). The ancient capital of the Aztec empire, on the site now occupied by Mexico City.

ten·on (ténnən) *n.* A projection on the end of a piece of wood shaped for insertion into a mortise.
  ~*tr.v.* **tenoned, -oning, -ons.** **1.** To provide with a tenon. **2.** To join with a tenon. [Middle English, from Old French, from *tenir,* to hold, from Latin *tenēre.*]

tenon saw *n.* A short saw with fine teeth and a reinforced blade back, used for cutting tenons.

ten·or (ténnər) *n.* **1. a.** The general sense, meaning, or drift apparent in something written or spoken. **b.** A steady prevailing course or direction: *couldn't change the dramatic tenor of his life.* **2. a.** *Law.* The exact meaning or actual wording of a document as distinct from its effect. **b.** An exact copy or transcript of a document. **3.** *Abbr.* **ten., T., t.** *Music.* **a.** The highest natural adult male voice. **b.** A part for this voice. **c.** One who sings this part. **d.** The largest and lowest-pitched bell of a set. Also called "tenor bell".
  ~*adj.* Of, pertaining to, or having the range of a tenor: *a tenor sax.* [Middle English, general meaning, from Old French, from Latin *tenor,* uninterrupted course, a holding on, from *tenēre,* to hold.]

ten·o·rite (ténnə-rīt) *n.* A black copper ore consisting predominantly of copper oxide, CuO, occurring in the oxidised zone of weathered copper lodes.

te·nor·rha·phy (ti-nórrə-fi, te- ‖ -náwrə-) *n., pl.* **-phies.** The surgical uniting of divided tendons with sutures. [TENO- + Greek *-rrhaphia,* from *rhaptein,* to sew.]

te·no·sy·no·vi·tis (tēenō-sī-nə-vítiss, ténnō-, -nō-) *n.* Inflammation of a tendon sheath. [TENO- + SYNOV(IA) + -ITIS.]

te·not·o·my (ti-nóttəmi, te-) *n., pl.* **-mies.** The surgical cutting of a tendon for the relief of deformities caused by shortening of a muscle. [TENO- + -TOMY.]

ten·pin bowling (tén-pin) *n.* A game played by rolling a ball down a wooden alley to knock down a triangular group of ten pins. Also called "bowling".

ten·rec (tén-rek) *n.* Also **tan·rec** (tán-, tón-). Any of various insectivorous, often hedgehog-like mammals of the family Tenrecidae, of Madagascar and adjacent islands. [French, from Malagasy *tàndraka.*]

tense¹ (tenss) *adj.* **tenser, tensest.** **1.** Tightly stretched; taut; strained: *tense muscles.* **2.** In a state of mental or nervous tension. **3.** Nerve-racking; full of suspense: *a tense situation.* **4.** *Phonetics.* Enunciated with taut vocal muscles, as the consonant *t.* Compare **lax.** —See Synonyms at **stiff.**
  ~*v.* **tensed, tensing, tenses.** —*tr.* To make tense. —*intr.* To become tense. Often used with *up.* [Latin *tensus,* past participle of *tendere,* to stretch out.] —**tense·ly** *adv.* —**tense·ness** *n.*

tense² *n. Abbr.* **t.** **1.** Any of the inflected forms in the conjugation of a verb that indicate the time (past, present, or future) as well as the continuance (imperfect) or completion (perfect) of the action or state. **2.** A set of such forms indicating a particular time: *the future tense.* [Middle English *tens,* tense, time, from Old French, from Latin *tempus,* time. See **temporal.**]

ten·sile (tén-sīl ‖ *chiefly U.S.* -s'l) *adj.* **1.** Of or pertaining to tension. **2.** Capable of being stretched or extended; ductile. [New Latin *tensilis,* from Latin *tensus,* "stretched", TENSE.] —**ten·sil·i·ty** (ten-sílləti) *n.*

tensile strength *n.* The resistance of a material to a force tending to tear it apart, expressed as the maximum longitudinal stress it can withstand.

ten·sim·e·ter (ten-símmitər) *n.* An apparatus used to measure differences in vapour pressure. [TENSI(ON) + -METER.]

ten·si·om·e·ter (tén-si-ómmitər) *n.* **1.** An instrument for measuring tensile strength. **2.** A torsion-balance apparatus used to measure the surface tension of a liquid. **3.** An instrument used to measure the moisture content of soil. [TENSIO(N) + -METER.]

ten·sion (ténsh'n) *n.* **1.** The act of stretching or the condition of being stretched. **2.** A force tending to produce elongation or extension. **3. a.** Mental, emotional, or nervous strain. **b.** An uneasy and potentially explosive condition of latent hostility and mistrust between persons or groups: *tension in the Middle East.* **c.** An atmosphere of suspense or suppressed excitement: *Tension mounts as the big match approaches.* **4.** The density of knitted fabrics determined by the size of needles and thickness of yarn, or the number of rows and stitches needed to complete a given sample of fabric. Also *U.S.* "gauge". **5.** A device for regulating tautness; especially, a device regulating the tautness of thread on a sewing machine. **6.** *Electricity.* Voltage or potential; electromotive force.
  ~*tr.v.* **tensioned, -sioning, -sions.** To subject to tension; make taut. [Old French, from Latin *tensiō* (stem *tensiōn-*), from *tensus,* TENSE.] —**ten·sion·al** *adj.*

ten·si·ty (ténssəti) *n. Rare.* The state of being tense; tenseness.

ten·sive (tén-siv) *adj.* Of or causing tension.

ten·sor (tén-sər, -sawr) *n.* **1.** *Anatomy.* Any muscle that tenses a part, making it firm. **2.** *Mathematics.* A set of components of a system in *n* dimensions, used to denote position determined within the context of more than one coordinate system, that may be linearly transformed between coordinate systems. —**ten·so·ri·al** (ten-sáw-ri-əl ‖ -sō-) *adj.*

ten-strike (tén-strīk) *n. U.S. Informal.* **1.** A strike in the game of tenpin bowling. **2.** A remarkably successful stroke or action.

tent¹ (tent) *n.* **1.** A portable shelter of canvas or other waterproof material stretched over a supporting framework of poles, ropes, and pegs. **2.** Something resembling this in construction or outline; especially, a medical tent placed over a patient's head so that his air supply may be regulated.
  ~*v.* **tented, tenting, tents.** —*intr.* To encamp in a tent. —*tr.* **1.** To form a tent over. **2.** To accomodate in tents. [Middle English *tente,* from Old French, from Vulgar Latin *tenta* (unattested), from the feminine past participle of *tendere,* to stretch.]

tent² *n.* In surgery, a small roll or plug, usually of lint or gauze, for placing in a wound or orifice to keep it open or for probing.
  ~*tr.v.* **tented, tenting, tents.** To keep (a wound or cut) open with a tent. [Middle English, a probe, from Old French *tente,* from *tenter,* to probe, test, from Latin *tentāre,* variant of *temptāre,* to feel, try, TEMPT.]

tent³ *n. Scottish.* Attention; heed. Used chiefly in the phrase *take tent.* [Middle English *tenten,* from *tent,* attention, short for *attent,* from Old French *attente,* from Latin *attenta,* feminine past participle of *attendere,* ATTEND.]

ten·ta·cle (téntək'l) *n.* **1.** *Zoology.* An elongated, flexible, unsegmented protrusion, such as one of those surrounding the mouth or oral cavity of the hydra, sea anemone, or squid. **2.** *Botany.* One of the hairs on the leaves of insectivorous plants, such as the sundew. **3.** Something resembling a tentacle, especially in ability to grasp or hold. [New Latin *tentaculum,* from Latin *tentāre,* variant of *temptāre,* to touch, feel, TEMPT.] **—ten·tac·u·lar** (ten-táckew-lər), **ten·tac·u·late** (-lət, -lit, -layt), **ten·ta·cled** *adj.*

tent·age (téntij) *n.* A supply of tents or tent equipment.

ten·ta·tive (téntətiv) *adj.* **1.** Of an experimental nature; provisional. **2.** Uncertain; hesitant: *a tentative smile.*
~*n.* Something tentative, such as a plan or proposal. [Medieval Latin *tentātīvus,* from Latin *tentātus,* past participle of *tentāre,* variant of *temptāre,* to feel, try, TEMPT.] **—ten·ta·tive·ly** *adv.* **—ten·ta·tive·ness** *n.*

tent caterpillar *n.* Any of several widely distributed destructive caterpillars of the genus *Malacosoma* that live in colonies in tentlike webs constructed in deciduous trees.

tent dress *n.* A full dress that flares out towards the bottom and is not taken in at the waist.

tent·ed (téntid) *adj.* **1.** Covered with tents: *a tented shoreline.* **2.** Sheltered in tents. **3.** Resembling a tent in shape.

ten·ter (téntər) *n.* **1.** A framework upon which milled cloth is stretched for drying without shrinkage. **2.** *Archaic.* A tenterhook. [Middle English *teyntur,* from Anglo-French *tentur* (unattested), from Medieval Latin *tentōrium,* from Latin *tentus,* past participle of *tendere,* to stretch.]

ten·ter·hook (téntər-ho͝ok || -ho͞ok) *n.* A hooked nail for securing cloth on a tenter. **—on tenterhooks.** In a state of uneasiness, suspense, or anxiety.

tenth (tenth) *n.* **1.** The ordinal number ten in a series. **2.** One of ten equal parts. [Middle English *tenthe,* variant of earlier *tethe,* Old English *tēotha, teogetha.*] **—tenth** *adj.* & *adv.*

tent stitch *n.* A short diagonal embroidery stitch that forms close even, parallel rows to fill in a pattern or a background.

ten·u·is (ténnew-iss) *n., pl.* **-ues** (-eez). *Phonetics.* A voiceless stop; for example, the English consonants *p, t* and *k* are tenues. [New Latin (translation of Greek *psilos,* plain), from Latin, TENUOUS.]

ten·u·ous (ténnew-əss) *adj.* **1.** Lacking substance and strength; weak; flimsy: *a tenuous argument.* **2.** Having a thin consistency; diluted; rarefied. **3.** Having a thin or slender form. [Earlier *tenuious,* from Latin *tenuis,* thin, rare, fine. **—ten·u·ous·ly** *adv.* **—ten·u·ous·ness** *n.*

ten·ure (tén-yər, -yoor) *n.* **1. a.** The holding of something; especially, the holding or occupying of property for services rendered, the holding of an office. **b.** The terms or condition for such a holding. **c.** The period or duration of such a holding. **2.** *Chiefly U.S.* Permanence of position, as granted to employees in certain fields after a fixed number of years. [Middle English, from Old French, earlier *teneüre,* from *tenir,* to hold, from Latin *tenēre,* to hold.] **—ten·u·ri·al** (te-néwr-i-əl || -no͝or-) *adj.* **—ten·u·ri·al·ly** *adv.*

ten·ured (tén-yərd, -yoord) *adj. Chiefly U.S.* Having tenure.

te·nu·to (ti-néw-tō, te-, -no͞o-) *adj. Abbr.* **ten.** *Music.* Held for the full time value; sustained. Said of a chord or note. **—te·nu·to** *adv.* [Italian, past participle of *tenere,* to hold, from Latin *tenēre.*]

te·o·cal·li (tée-ō-kál-i, -ə-; *Spanish* tày-ō-kaá-yee) *n., pl.* **-lis.** Also **te·o·pan** (-pan, -paan). **1.** A temple of ancient Mexico and Central America, usually built upon a mound of a truncated pyramidal shape. **2.** The mound itself. [Nahuatl : *teotl,* god + *calli,* house.]

te·o·sin·te (tée-ō-sín-ti, táy-, -ə-, -tay) *n.* A tall Central American grass, *Euchlaena mexicana* (or *Zea mexicana*), closely related to maize and sometimes cultivated for fodder. [Mexican Spanish, from Nahuatl *teocentli* : *teotl,* god + *centli,* dried ear of corn.]

Te·o·ti·hua·cán (táy-ō-tee-wə-kán, -waa-, -kaán). Ancient city of Mexico, one of the oldest urban settlements in ancient America.

te·pal (teép'l, tépp'l) *n. Botany.* A division of the perianth of a flower having petals and sepals that are indistinguishable. [French *tépale,* perhaps a blend of PETAL and SEPAL.]

te·pee, tee·pee, ti·pi (teé-pee) *n.* A cone-shaped tent of skins or bark, supported by poles, used by North American Indians. Compare **wigwam.** [Dakota *tipi,* dwelling.]

tep·id (téppid) *adj.* **1.** Moderately warm; lukewarm. **2.** Lacking wholehearted interest, support, or enthusiasm: *a tepid reception.* [Latin *tepidus,* from *tepēre,* to be lukewarm.] **—te·pid·i·ty** (te-píddəti), **tep·id·ness** *n.* **—tep·id·ly** *adv.*

te·qui·la (ti-kéelə, te-, tə-) *n.* **1.** An alcoholic liquor distilled from a Central American plant, *Agave tequilana.* **2.** The plant itself. [Mexican Spanish, from *Tequila,* district in Mexico.]

ter– *comb. form.* Indicates three, third, or threefold; for example, **tercentenary.** [Latin *ter,* thrice.]

tera– *comb. form.* Symbol **T** Indicates a million million (10^{12}); for example, **terahertz.** [Greek *teras,* monster. See **teratoid.**]

ter·a·hertz (térrə-herts) *n. Abbr.* **THz** One million million (10^{12}) hertz.

Te·rai (tə-rí) *n.* A belt of marshy, jungly land between the foothills of the Himalayas and the plains of northern India.

ter·aph (térrəf) *n., pl.* **-aphim** (-im). A small domestic image or idol revered by ancient Semitic peoples. [Hebrew *tərāphīm,* a pejorative appellation of these idols, perhaps from *rəpha'im,* "shades".]

terato– *comb. form.* Indicates: **1.** Abnormality; for example, **teratoma. 2.** A monstrous beast; for example, **teratoid.** [Greek *teras,* (stem *terat-*), monster, marvel.]

ter·a·to·gen (térrə-tō-jen, -tə-, te-ráttə-, te-) *n.* Any agent, such as the drug thalidomide or X-radiation, that induces abnormalities in a developing foetus. [TERATO- + -GEN.] **—ter·a·to·gen·ic** (-jénnik) *adj.* **—ter·a·tog·e·ny** (-tójəni) *n.*

ter·a·toid (térrə-toyd) *adj.* Like a monster; monstrous. [TERATO- + -OID.]

ter·a·tol·o·gy (térrə-tólləji) *n.* **1.** The biological study of the development, anatomy, or abnormalities of monsters. **2.** A story or stories about mythical creatures or beasts. [TERATO- + -LOGY.] **—ter·a·to·log·i·cal** (-tə-lójik'l) *adj.*

ter·a·to·ma (térrə-tṓmə) *n., pl.* **-mas** or **-mata** (-tə). A tumour consisting of different types of tissue, occurring frequently in the testes or ovaries. [TERATO- + -OMA.] **—ter·a·tom·a·tous** (-təss) *adj.*

ter·a·torn·is (terra-tórniss) *n.* A prehistoric bird as tall as a man, with a wing span of 5 metres, believed to have been the world's largest flying bird. [TERATO- + Greek *ornis,* bird.]

ter·bi·um (térbi-əm) *n. Symbol* **Tb** A soft, silvery-grey metallic rare-earth element, used as a solid-state dopant and as a laser material. Atomic number 65, atomic weight 158.924, melting point 1,356°C, boiling point 2,800°C, relative density 8.272, valencies 3, 4. [Discovered in *Ytterby,* a village in Sweden.]

terbium metal *n.* Any of several rare-earth metals separable from other metals as a group and including europium, terbium, and gadolinium.

terbium oxide *n.* An insoluble dark brown powder Tb_2O_3. Also called "terbia".

terce (terss) *n.* Also **tierce** (teerss). **1.** The third of the seven **canonical hours** *(see).* **2.** The time of day set aside for this prayer, usually the third after sunrise. [Middle English *tierce,* from Old French, from Latin *tertia* (noun), from *tertius,* third.]

ter·cel, tier·cel (térss'l) *n.* A male hawk, especially one used in falconry. [Middle English, from Old French, from Vulgar Latin *tertiōlus* (unattested), from Latin *tertius,* third (from the belief that the third egg of a brood was a male).]

ter·cen·te·nar·y (tér-sen-teén-əri, -tén-, ter-séntin- || -erri) *n., pl.* **-ies.** A 300th anniversary or its celebration. Also called "tricentenary", "tricentennial". **—ter·cen·te·nar·y** *adj.*

ter·cen·ten·ni·al (tér-sen-ténni-əl) *adj.* **1.** Of or lasting for 300 years. **2.** Occurring or happening every 300 years.
~*n.* A tercentenary.

ter·cet (tér-sit, -set) *n.* In prosody, a unit of three lines, often rhyming with each other or with other tercets. Also called "triplet". [Italian *terzetto,* diminutive of *terzo,* third, from Latin *tertius.*]

ter·e·bene (térrə-been) *n.* A mixture of terpenes prepared from oil of turpentine, used as an expectorant and antiseptic. [French *térébène,* from *térébinthe,* from Old French *terebinte,* TEREBINTH.]

te·reb·ic acid (tə-rébbik, tə-, -reébik) *n.* A white crystalline compound, $C_7H_{10}O_4$, resulting from the action of nitric acid on turpentine. [*Terebic,* from TEREBINTH.]

ter·e·binth (térrə-binth) *n.* A small tree, *Pistacia terebinthus,* of the Mediterranean region, that yields turpentine. [Middle English *therebinthe,* from Old French *t(h)erebinte,* from Latin *terebinthus,* from Greek *terebinthos, terminthos,* of Aegean origin.]

ter·e·bin·thine (térrə-bín-thīn || -thin) *adj.* Also **ter·e·bin·thic** (-thik). **1.** Of or pertaining to the terebinth. **2.** Pertaining to, consisting of, or resembling turpentine.

te·re·do (tə-reé-dō, te-, -ráy-) *n., pl.* **-dos.** Any marine mollusc of the genus *Teredo,* such as the shipworm. [New Latin *Teredo,* from Latin *terēdō,* a kind of worm, from Greek *terēdōn.*]

ter·e·phthal·ic acid (térref-thál-ik) *n.* A white insoluble carboxylic acid, $C_6H_4(COOH)_2$, used to manufacture such polyester resins as Terylene; 1,4-benzenedicarboxylic acid.

ter·ete (térreet, tə-reét, te-) *adj.* Nearly cylindrical in cross-section, as are certain plant stems. [Latin *teres* (stem *teret-*), rounded.]

ter·gi·ver·sate (térji-ver-sayt) *intr.v.* **-sated, -sating, -sates.** *Formal.* **1.** To use evasions or ambiguities; equivocate. **2.** To change sides; defect; apostatise. [Latin *tergiversārī,* "to turn the back", shift : *tergum,* back, TERGUM + *versus,* past participle of *vertere,* to turn.] **—ter·gi·ver·sa·tion** (-sáysh'n) *n.* **—ter·gi·ver·sa·tor** (-saytər) *n.*

ter·gum (tér-gəm) *n., pl.* **-ga** (-gə). *Zoology.* The upper or dorsal surface, especially of a body segment of an insect or other arthropod. [Latin *tergum*†, the back.] **—ter·gal** *adj.*

ter·i·ya·ki (térri-yaáki) *n.* A Japanese dish consisting of skewered and grilled slices of marinated meat or shellfish. [Japanese : *teri,* sunshine, "flame" + *yaki,* to broil.]

term (term) *n.* **1.** A period of time, usually having clearly defined limits, for which something lasts or is intended to last, especially: **a.** A limited period of time that a person serves: *a term of office; a 15-year prison term.* **b.** A period when an educational institution or court of law is in session. **c.** An approximately specified period with regard to which plans or predictions are made: *in the short term.* **2.** A point of time marking the end of a period, as: **a.** A fixed time by which a payment must be made. **b.** The end of a normal period of pregnancy. **3.** *Law.* **a.** A fixed period of time during which an estate may be held. **b.** The estate to be granted for a term. **c.** A period of time allowed a debtor to meet an obligation. **4. a.** A word or phrase that expresses a particular idea or has a particular function: *a term of abuse.* **b.** A word or expression that is part of the jargon of a particular group or activity. **c.** *Plural.* Language or manner of expression employed: *told us in no uncertain terms.* **5.** *Plural.* **a.** Conditions or stipulations that define the nature and limits of an agreement: *peace terms.* **b.** Conditions of payment, as for a service or purchase: *easy credit terms.* **c.** The relation between two persons or groups; footing. Preceded by *on*: *on speaking terms.* **6.** *Mathematics.* **a.** Each of the quantities composing a ratio or a fraction or forming a series. **b.** Each of the quantities connected by addition or subtraction signs in an equation. **7.** *Logic.* **a.** The word or phrase constituting the subject or the predicate of a proposition. **b.** Any of the three parts of a syllogism. **8.** *Archaic.* A limit or

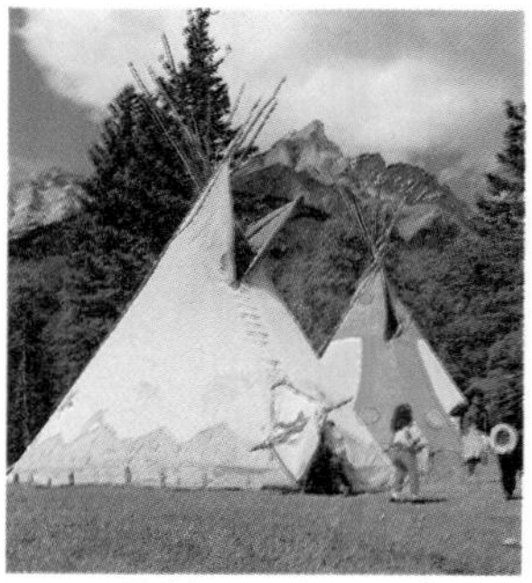

tepee *Children at play outside a tepee, the traditional and movable home of many North American Indian peoples.*

PRONUNCIATION KEY

a, trap; aa, father; ai, fair; ar, star; aw, lawn; ay, play; b, bb, stab; rubber; ch, church; ck, ticket; d, dd, dead; ladder; e, dress; ee, bee; er, defer; ew, few; ewr, pure; ə, about; ər, letter; f, ff, fife; differ; g, gg, giggle; h, hat; i, kit; ī, price; īr, fire; j, judge; k, kick; l, ll, let; 'l, needle; m, mm, man; n, nn, no; 'n, sudden; ng, thing; o, lot; ō, no; o͝o, foot; o͞o, shoe; oor, poor; ow, cow; owr, hour; oy, boy; p, pp, pepper; r, rr, red; s, ss, sauce; sh, ship; t, tt, totter; th, thick; th, this; smooth; u, cut; ur, turn; v, vv, valve; w, wet; y, yes; z, zz, zebra; zh, vision; pleasure

IN FOREIGN WORDS:

aN, oN, Saint-Saëns; hl, Llanelli; Hluhluwe; kh, loch; lough; Khaled

STRESS MARK:

ín-sīt, insight; in-sít, incite

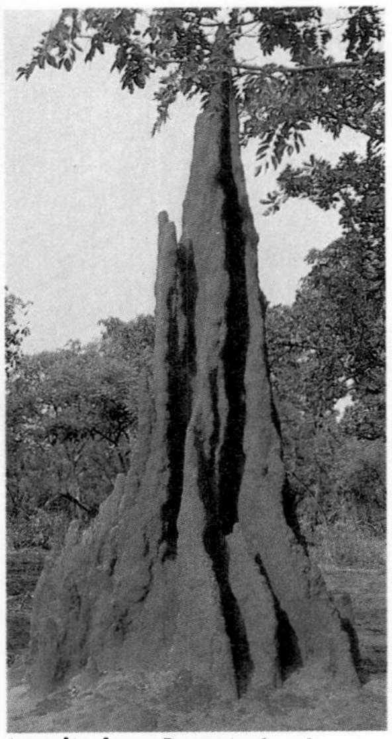

termitarium *In tropical and subtropical countries, termites build mounds as high as 7 or 8 metres (about 25 feet), using mud which is brought from a similar depth. The mounds harden in the sun to a rock-like consistency.*

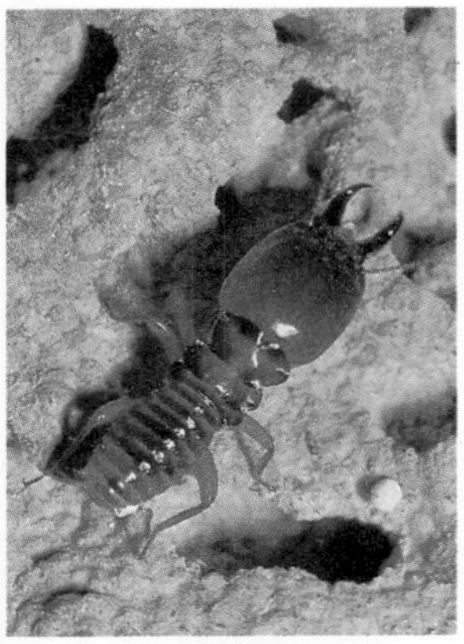

termite *Termites belong to a large family of social insects of the order* Isoptera. *This is a soldier termite from East Africa, a species which lives in giant colonies in large, pinnacled mounds.*

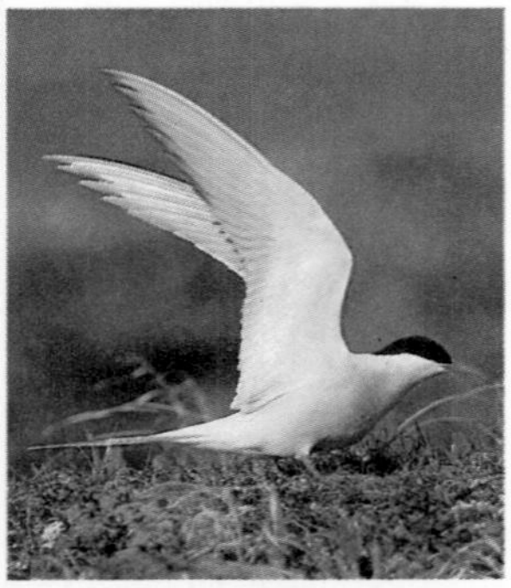

tern *The tern family holds the world record among birds for long-distance migration. Every year the Arctic tern (above) flies nearly 39 000 kilometres (24,000 miles) – from the Arctic to the Antarctic and back.*

boundary. **9.** A statue of a human head, or head and torso, rising from a square tapering pillar, originally marking a boundary. In this sense also called "terminus". **—bring to terms.** To force (a person) to submit or agree. **—come to terms. 1.** To reach an agreement. **2.** To face up to or accept a fact or condition. Used with *with.* **—in terms of.** With regard to; in relation to.

~tr.v. **termed, terming, terms.** To designate; call. [Middle English *terme,* from Old French, from Latin *terminus,* boundary line, boundary, limit.] **—term·less** *adj.* **—term·ly** *adv.*

term. 1. terminal. **2.** termination.

ter·ma·gant (tέrməgənt) *n.* A quarrelsome, brawling, or scolding woman; a shrew.

~adj. Overbearing, abusive, or shrewish. [Middle English *Termagaunt, Tervagaunt,* vicious Muslim deity in medieval mystery plays, from Old French *Tervagan(t),* from Italian *Trivigante*†.]

term·er (tέrmər) *n. Informal.* A person holding a position or confined to a place for a specified time. Usually used in combination: *These patients are long-termers.*

ter·mi·na·ble (tέrmin-əb'l) *adj.* **1.** Capable of being terminated. **2.** Terminating after a designated date: *a terminable annuity.* **—ter·mi·na·bil·i·ty** (-ə-bílləti), **ter·mi·na·ble·ness** *n.* **—ter·mi·na·bly** *adv.*

ter·mi·nal (tέrmin'l) *adj. Abbr.* **term. 1.** Pertaining to, situated at, or forming the end or boundary of something: *a terminal post.* **2.** *Botany.* Growing or appearing at the end of a stem, branch, stalk, or similar part. **3.** Pertaining to or occurring at the end of a section or series; final. **4.** Pertaining to or occurring in or at the end of a term or each term: *terminal exams.* **5.** Ending in death; fatal. **6.** Very serious; especially, resulting in ruin or collapse. Often used humorously: *terminal laziness.* —See Synonyms at **last.**

~n. Abbr. **term. 1.** A terminating point, limit, or part; an end; an extremity. **2.** Any ornamental figure or object situated at the end of something. **3.** *Electricity.* **a.** A position in an electric circuit or device at which an electric connection is normally established or broken. **b.** A passive conductor at such a position used to facilitate the connection. **4. a.** A terminus on a railway or bus line. **b.** A building providing services for departing or incoming air travellers, either at an airport or in the city which the airport serves. **5.** An important input/output device forming part of a computer system, especially one that is remote from the computer itself. [Latin *terminālis,* from *terminus,* boundary, TERMINUS.] **—ter·mi·nal·ly** *adv.*

terminal velocity *n.* **1.** The maximum velocity attained by a body falling through a fluid in the Earth's gravitational field. **2.** The maximum velocity attained by a projectile during its parabolic flight. **3.** The velocity of a projectile at the end of its flight. **4.** The maximum velocity that an aircraft can attain, as determined by its drag.

ter·mi·nate (tέrmi-nayt) *v.* **-nated, -nating, -nates.** *—tr.* **1.** To bring to an end or halt: *Terrorist action terminated the truce.* **2.** To occur at or form the end of; conclude; finish. **3.** To end (a pregnancy) prematurely by inducing an abortion. *—intr.* **1.** To come to an end: *Negotiations terminated yesterday.* **2.** To have as an end or result. Often used with *in*: *The war terminated in victory for the Allies.* **3.** To induce an abortion. —See Synonyms at **complete.** [Latin *termināre,* to limit, to terminate, from *terminus,* TERMINUS.] **—ter·mi·na·tive** (-nətiv, -naytiv) *adj.* **—ter·mi·na·tive·ly** *adv.*

ter·mi·na·tion (tέrmi-náysh'n) *n. Abbr.* **term. 1.** The act of terminating or the condition of being terminated. **2.** The spatial or temporal end of something; a limit or boundary; conclusion or cessation. **3.** A result or outcome of something. **4.** The end of a word, as an inflectional ending, suffix, or final morpheme. **5.** An abortion. **—ter·mi·na·tion·al** *adj.*

ter·mi·na·tor (tέrmi-naytər) *n.* **1.** One that terminates. **2.** The dividing line between the bright and shaded regions of the disc of the moon or an inner planet.

ter·mi·nol·o·gy (tέrmi-nólləji) *n., pl.* **-gies. 1.** The vocabulary of technical terms and usages appropriate to a particular trade, science, or art; nomenclature. **2.** The study of nomenclature. [Medieval Latin *terminus,* expression, from Latin, limit, TERMINUS + -LOGY.] **—ter·mi·no·log·i·cal** (-nə-lójik'l) *adj.* **—ter·mi·no·log·i·cal·ly** *adv.* **—ter·mi·nol·o·gist** (-nólləjist) *n.*

term insurance *n.* A type of life insurance contract for a fixed period, whereby the insured sum is payable only if the insured dies within that period.

ter·mi·nus (tέrmi-nəss) *n., pl.* **-nuses** or **-ni** (-nī). **1.** The end of something; a final point, extremity, or goal. **2.** A point, station, or town at either end of a railway line or bus route. **3. a.** A boundary or border. **b.** A stone or post marking such a border; especially, a **term** *(see).* [Latin, boundary line, boundary, limit.]

ter·mi·tar·i·um (tέrmi-táir-i-əm) *n., pl.* **-ria** (-i-ə). The moundlike nest of a termite colony. [TERMITE + -ARIUM.]

ter·mite (tέr-mīt) *n.* Any of numerous superficially antlike social insects of the order Isoptera, many species of which feed on wood and are highly destructive to living trees and wooden structures. Also called "white ant". [Latin *termes* (stem *termit-*), variant of *tarmes*†, wood-eating worm.]

term·or (tέrmər) *n. Law.* A person who holds an estate for a certain term or for life. [Middle English, from Anglo-French *termer,* from TERM.]

terms of reference *pl.n.* **1.** The points an individual or committee is charged to decide or report on. **2.** The factors defining the scope of an inquiry.

tern[1] (tern) *n.* Any of various sea birds of the family Sterninae, related to and resembling the gulls but characteristically smaller, and having black and white plumage and a forked tail. [Scandinavian, akin to Old Norse *therna*†.]

tern[2] *n.* A set of three; especially, a combination of three numbers that wins a lottery prize. [Latin *ternī,* three each, from *ter,* thrice.]

ter·na·ry (térnəri) *adj.* **1.** Composed of three or arranged in threes. **2.** *Mathematics.* **a.** Of, pertaining, or designating a number system that has three as its base. **b.** Involving three variables. **3.** *Chemistry.* Containing three different components or elements.

~n., pl. **ternaries.** A set or group of three. [Middle English, from Latin *ternārius,* from *ternī,* three each. See **tern.**]

ternary form *n.* A musical structure in three parts, in which the first section is followed by a contrasting section and then repeated. Also called "song form".

ter·nate (tér-nayt, -nət, -nit) *adj.* Consisting of three parts, or arranged in groups of three, as, for example, a compound leaf. [New Latin *ternatus,* from Medieval Latin *ternātus,* past participle of *ternāre,* multiply by three, from *ternī,* three each.] **—ter·nate·ly** *adv.*

terne (tern) *n.* **1.** An alloy of three or four parts lead to one part tin, with a tiny percentage of antimony. **2.** Terneplate. [French *terne,* dull, from Old French, from *ternir,* to tarnish + PLATE.]

terne·plate (térn-playt) *n.* Sheet iron or steel plated with terne, used as a roofing material. Also called "terne".

te·ro·tech·nol·o·gy (téer-ō-tek-nólləji) *n.* The management and maintenance of the plant of a business or industry; maintenance engineering. [Greek *terein,* to take care of + TECHNOLOGY.]

ter·pene (tér-peen) *n.* Any of various unsaturated hydrocarbons, $C_{10}H_{16}$, found in essential oils and oleoresins of plants, such as conifers, and used in organic syntheses. [*Terp(entine),* obsolete form of TURPENTINE + -ENE.] **—ter·pe·nic** (ter-péenik), **ter·pe·noid** (térpi-noyd, ter-pée-) *adj.*

ter·pin·e·ol (tər-pínni-ol || -ōl) *n.* Any of three isomeric alcohols, $C_{10}H_{17}OH$, occurring naturally in the essential oils of certain plants and used as a solvent, in perfumes, soaps, and medicine. [TERP(ENE) + -INE + -OL.]

Terp·sich·o·re (terp-síckəri). *Greek mythology.* The Muse of dancing and choral singing. [Greek *Terpsikhorē* : *terpein,* to delight, cheer + *khoros,* dance.]

terp·si·cho·re·an (térpsi-kə-rée-ən, -ko- || -káw-ri-ən, -kṓ-) *adj.* Of or pertaining to dancing. [From TERPSICHORE.]

terr. 1. terrace. **2.** territorial; territory.

Terra Adelie. See **Adelie Land.**

ter·ra al·ba (térrə ál-bə || áwl-) *n.* **1.** Finely pulverised gypsum used in making paper, paints, and plastics. **2.** A clay, **kaolin** *(see).* [New Latin, "white earth".]

ter·race (térrəss, térriss) *n.* **1. a.** An open, level, often paved area adjacent to a house, serving as an outdoor living area; a patio. **b.** The flat roof of a house serving a similar purpose, as in warmer climates. **2.** A relatively narrow horizontal shelf of land on the side of a slope, typically one of a landscaped series, having vertical or sloping sides and used for cultivation. **3.** *Geology.* A horizontal or gently inclined shelf or bench, as along the side of a river valley. **4.** *Usually plural.* The unroofed tiers around a football pitch where spectators stand. **5. a.** A row of houses, usually identical in design, built with connecting walls. **b.** A row of houses built on raised ground or on a sloping site. **6.** *Abbr.* **Terr, Trce.** A street, especially one having terraced houses. Used in street names: *Eaton Terrace.*

~tr.v. **terraced, -racing, -races.** To make into or supply with a terrace: *a terraced hillside.* [Old French *terrasse,* terrace, pile of earth, from Old Provençal *terrassa,* from *terra,* earth, from Latin.]

terraced house *n.* A house that forms one of a row of, usually identical, buildings linked by connecting walls.

ter·ra·cot·ta, ter·ra-cot·ta (térrə-kóttə) *n.* **1.** A hard, brownish red to yellow material composed of clay, fine sand, and sometimes pulverised pottery waste, usually unglazed, used in pottery and building construction. **2.** Ceramic ware made of this material. **3.** Brownish orange. [Italian, "baked earth".] **—ter·ra·cot·ta** *adj.*

ter·ra fir·ma (térrə fúrmə) *n.* Solid ground; dry land. [Latin.]

ter·rain (térrayn, te-ráyn, tə-) *n.* **1.** The relief or physical character of an area; its configuration. **2.** *U.S.* A particular geographical area; a region. [French, from Latin *terrēnum,* from *terrēnus,* TERRENE.]

ter·ra in·cog·ni·ta (térrə in-kóg-ni-tə) *n., pl.* **terrae incognitae** (térree-tee). Unknown or unmapped territory. [Latin.]

ter·ra·pin (térrə-pin) *n.* Any chelonian reptile of the family Enrydidae that is equally at home on land and in fresh water, such as the European pond tortoise, *Emys orbicularis.* [Algonquian (Virginia), from Eastern Algonquian *toolepeiwa* (unattested).]

ter·ra·que·ous (te-ráykwi-əss, ti-, tə-, -rákwi-) *adj.* Composed of both land and water. [Medieval Latin *terraqueus* : *terra,* earth, from Latin + *aqueus,* AQUEOUS.]

ter·rar·i·um (te-ráir-i-əm, ti-, tə-) *n., pl.* **-ums** or **-ria** (-i-ə). A small enclosure or closed container in which small plants are grown or small animals, such as turtles or lizards, are kept. [New Latin : Latin *terra, earth* + -ARIUM.]

ter·raz·zo (te-rát-sō, ti-, tə- || -rát-) *n.* A flooring material of marble or other stone chips set in concrete and polished smooth when dry. [Italian, TERRACE.]

ter·rene (térreen, te-réen, ti-, tə-) *adj.* Of or pertaining to the earth; earthly. [Middle English, from Latin *terrēnus,* from *terra,* earth.]

terre·plein (táir-playn, térrə-) *n.* The level ground on an embankment or the platform behind a parapet where heavy guns are mounted. [French *terre-plein,* from Italian *terrapieno,* from *terrapienare,* to fill with earth, terrace : *terra,* earth + *pieno,* full.]

ter·res·tri·al (ti-réstri-əl, te-, tə-) *adj.* **1.** Of or pertaining to the Earth, especially as distinct from the Moon, the stars, and the planets. **2.** Having a worldly, mundane character or quality. **3.** Of, pertaining to, or composed of land as distinct from water or air. **4.** *Biology.* Living or growing on land; not aquatic.
~n. An inhabitant of the earth, especially, a human being. [Middle English, from Latin *terrestris,* from *terra,* earth.] **—ter·res·tri·al·ly** *adv.* **—ter·res·tri·al·ness** *n.*
terrestrial planet *n.* Any of the four planets nearest the sun, resembling Earth in density and composition: Mercury, Venus, Earth, or Mars.
terrestrial space *n.* The region of space surrounding the earth (up to about 2 500 kilometres; 4,000 miles).
terrestrial telescope *n.* An optical telescope, usually containing a separate lens or prism to give an erect image, that is used to view objects on land or water rather than for making astronomical observations. Compare **astronomical telescope.**
ter·ret, ter·rit (térrit) *n.* **1.** Either of the metal rings on a horse's harness through which the reins pass. **2.** A similar ring on an animal's collar, used for attaching a leash. [Middle English *tyret, toret,* from Old French *to(u)ret,* diminutive of *tour,* "circular movement", from *tourner,* to TURN.]
terre-verte (táir-váirt, tér-vért) *n.* An olive-green pigment used by artists and commonly made from **glauconite** *(see).* [French, "green earth".] **—terre-verte** *adj.*
ter·ri·ble (térrəb'l, térrib'l) *adj.* **1.** Causing terror or fear; dreadful. **2.** Eliciting awe. **3.** Extreme in extent or degree; intense; severe: *a terrible storm.* **4.** Unpleasant; disagreeable: *a terrible time.* **5.** Extremely bad: *a terrible actor.* [Middle English, from Old French, from Latin *terribilis,* from *terrēre,* to frighten.] **—ter·ri·ble·ness** *n.*
ter·ri·bly (térrəbli, térribli) *adv.* **1.** In a terrible manner: *terribly wounded.* **2.** To a great extent; very much: *Would you mind terribly if I opened the window?* **3.** Very. Used as an intensive: *terribly nice.*
ter·ric·o·lous (te-ríckələss, ti-) *adj. Biology.* Living on or in the ground. [Latin *terricola,* land dweller : *terra,* earth + -COLOUS.]
ter·ri·er¹ (térri-ər) *n.* Any of various usually small, active dogs originally bred for hunting animals that live in burrows. [French *(chien) terrier,* from *terrier,* burrow, from *terre,* earth, from Latin *terra.*]
terrier² *n. Law.* A document or book enumerating boundaries, acreage, and the conditions of their tenure. [Old French *terrier,* from *terre,* land. See **terrier** (dog).]
Ter·ri·er (térri-ər) *n. British Informal.* A member of the Territorial and Army Volunteer Reserve.
ter·ri·fic (tə-ríffik, ti-) *adj.* **1.** Very good or fine; splendid; magnificent: *a terrific chef.* **4.** Awesome; astounding: *a terrific speed.* **3.** Causing terror or great fear; dreadful; terrifying: *a terrific wail.* **4.** Very bad or unpleasant; frightful: *a terrific headache.* [Latin *terrificus* : *terrēre,* to frighten + -FIC.] **—ter·rif·i·cal·ly** *adv.*
ter·ri·fy (térri-fī) *tr.v.* **-fied, -fying, -fies. 1.** To fill with terror; make deeply afraid. **2.** To force or drive by causing terror; scare; intimidate: *terrified him into signing the contract.* —See Synonyms at **frighten.** [Latin *terrificāre,* from *terrificus,* TERRIFIC.]
ter·rig·e·nous (te-ríjənəss, ti-) *adj.* Derived from the land, especially by erosive action. Said chiefly of sediments. [From Latin *terrigena,* born of the earth : *terra,* earth + -GENOUS.]
ter·rine (te-réen) *n.* **1.** A small earthenware dish with a tightly fitting lid used for cooking and serving patés or other delicacies. **2.** Food cooked in a terrine, especially a type of paté. [French.]
ter·ri·to·ri·al (térri-táw-ri-əl || -tṓ-) *adj. Abbr.* **terr. 1.** Of or pertaining to a territory or to its powers of jurisdiction. **2.** Pertaining or restricted to a particular territory; regional; local. **3.** Marked by or exhibiting a tendency to guard one's territory: *territorial instincts.* **4.** *Often capital* **T.** Of or designating a volunteer force maintained to provide a reserve.
~n. Often capital **T.** A member of a territorial army; especially, a member of the Territorial and Army Volunteer Reserve. **—ter·ri·to·ri·al·ly** *adv.*
Territorial and Army Volunteer Reserve *n. Abbr.* **TAVR.** In Britain, a standing volunteer reserve army originally formed in 1908. Also called "Territorial Army".
ter·ri·to·ri·al·ise, ter·ri·to·ri·al·ize (térri-táw-ri-əl-īz || -tṓ-) *tr.v.* **-ised, -ising, -ises. 1.** To make territorial, especially: **a.** To reduce to the status of a territory. **b.** To extend or restrict to a particular territory or territories. **2.** To make one's own territory. **—ter·ri·to·ri·al·i·sa·tion** (-ī-záysh'n || *U.S.* -i-) *n.*
ter·ri·to·ri·al·ism (térri-táw-ri-əl-iz'm || -tṓ-) *n.* **1.** A social system that gives authority and influence in a state to the landowners; landlordism. **2.** A former system of Protestant church government based on the primacy of civil power. In this sense, also called "territorial system". **—ter·ri·to·ri·al·ist** *n.*
ter·ri·to·ri·al·i·ty (térri-táw-ri-ál-əti || -tṓ-) *n.* **1.** The status of a territory. **2.** The behaviour of one who stays close to or jealously guards his territory.
territorial waters *pl.n.* Inland and coastal waters under the jurisdiction of a state; especially, the ocean waters within three miles of the shoreline.
ter·ri·to·ry (térri-tri, -təri) *n., pl.* **-ries.** *Abbr.* **t., T., terr. 1.** An area of land; a district; a region. **2.** The land and waters under the jurisdiction of a state, nation, or sovereign. **3.** *Capital* **T. a.** A part of Canada or Australia not accorded statehood or provincial status. **b.** A part of the United States not admitted as a state, which has a governor and other officers appointed by the president, and its own legislature. **4. a.** An area inhabited by an individual animal, a mating pair, or a group of animals and often vigorously defended against intruders. **b.** A comparable concrete or psychological area regarded by a person as his own inviolable domain. **5.** The area for which a person is responsible as representative or agent: *a salesman's territory.* **6.** The area of a sports field defended by a team. **7.** Any sphere of action or interest; a province. [Middle English, from Latin *territōrium,* from *terra,* land.]
ter·ror (térrər) *n.* **1.** Intense, overpowering fear. **2.** Anything that instils such fear; a terrifying person, thing, or occurrence. **3.** The ability to instil such fear; terribleness: *the terror of the haunted house.* **4.** Systematic violence carried out against private citizens, public property, and political enemies with the aim of enforcing demands or maintaining supremacy: *a reign of terror.* **5.** *Informal.* An annoying or intolerable pest; a nuisance. [Middle English *terrour,* from Old French, from Latin *terror,* from *terrēre,* to frighten.]
ter·ror·ise, ter·ror·ize (térrər-īz) *tr.v.* **-ised, -ising, -ises. 1.** To fill or overpower with terror; terrify. **2.** To coerce or maintain control over by intimidation or fear: *The vandals terrorised their neighbourhood.* **—ter·ror·i·sa·tion** (-ī-záysh'n || *U.S.* -i-) *n.* **—ter·ror·is·er** *n.*
ter·ror·ism (térrər-iz'm) *n.* The use of terror, violence, and intimidation, usually by an underground or revolutionary group but sometimes to achieve a political end. **—ter·ror·ist** *adj. & n.* **—ter·ror·is·tic** (-ístik) *adj.*
terror stricken *adj.* Also **terror struck.** Overcome by terror.
ter·ry (térri) *n., pl.* **-ries. 1.** Any of the uncut loops that form the pile of a fabric. **2.** A pile fabric, usually woven of cotton, with uncut loops on both sides, used for such articles as bath towels and nappies. In this sense, also called "terry cloth". [18th century : origin obscure.]
terse (terss) *adj.* **terser, tersest. 1.** Effectively concise; free of superfluity. **2.** Curt; brusque. —See Synonyms at **concise.** [Originally "polished", "refined", from Latin *tersus,* past participle of *tergēre,* to wipe off, polish. See **deterge.**] **—terse·ly** *adv.* **—terse·ness** *n.*
tertian fever *n.* A form of malaria caused by the invasion of *Plasmodium vivax* into new red blood cells, characterised by a 48-hour life cycle in the human body with a recurrence of fever paroxysms at the end of each such period. Also called "tertian malaria". [*Tertian,* from Latin *tertiānus,* of the third, from *tertius,* third.]
ter·ti·ar·y (tér-shəri, -shi-əri || -shi-erri) *adj.* **1.** Third in place, order, degree, or rank. **2.** Of, designating, or providing education above the secondary level, as in a college or university: *an examination at tertiary level; a tertiary course.* **3.** *Chemistry.* **a.** Pertaining to salts of acids containing three replaceable hydrogen atoms. **b.** Pertaining to organic compounds in which a group, such as an alcohol or amine, is bound to three non-elementary radicals. **4.** Of or pertaining to a **Third Order** *(see)* in a Roman Catholic monastic system. **5.** Involving the provision of services rather than the extraction or production of goods: *tertiary industry; tertiary occupation.* **6.** Of, pertaining to, or designating the short flight feathers nearest the body on the inner edge of a bird's wing.
~n., pl. **tertiaries. 1.** A tertiary feather. **2.** A member of a Roman Catholic tertiary order. [Latin *tertiārius,* from *tertius,* third.]
Ter·ti·a·ry (tér-shəri, -shi-əri, || -shi-erri) *adj.* Of, belonging to, or designating the geological time, and system of rocks of the first period of the Cenozoic era, extending from the Cretaceous period of the Mesozoic era to the Quarternary period of the Cenozoic era, characterised by the appearance of modern flora and fauna.
~n. The Tertiary period or system of deposits. Preceded by *the.*
tertiary accent *n. Linguistics.* A stress weaker than primary and secondary stress in phonetic systems recognising three or more degrees of stress. Also called "tertiary stress". Compare **primary accent, secondary accent.**
tertiary colour *n.* A colour resulting from the mixture of two secondary colours.
ter·ti·um quid (tér-shi-əm kwíd, -ti-) *n.* Something that cannot be classified into either of two groups, themselves considered to be exhaustive; an intermediate thing or factor. [Late Latin, "third something" (translation of Greek *triton ti*).]
tervalent. Variant of **trivalent.**
Ter·y·lene (térrə-leen, térri-) *n.* A trademark for a synthetic polyester fibre based on terephthalic acid that is used in making crease-resistant clothing, sheets, and the like.
ter·za ri·ma (táirt-sə rée-mə, térts-) *n., pl.* **terze rime** (-say, -may). A verse form consisting of a series of tercets having 10- or 11-syllable lines of which the middle line of one tercet rhymes with the first and third lines of the following tercet. [Italian, "third rhyme".]
TESL (téss'l). teaching English as a second language.
tes·la (tésslə) *n. Abbr.* **T** The unit of magnetic flux density in SI units, equal to one weber per square metre. [After Nikola TESLA.]
Tesla, Nikola (1856–1943). Croatian-born U.S. electrical engineer and inventor. His many inventions include the first practical system for distributing alternating current.
tesla coil *n.* A transformer with an air-core primary and a capacitor-tuned secondary, used as a source of high-frequency high voltage, as for X-ray tubes.
TESOL (tée-sol). teaching English to speakers of other languages.
tes·sel·late (téssi-i-layt, -ə-) *tr.v.* **-lated, -lating, -lates.** To form into or inlay with a mosaic pattern, as by using small squares of stone or glass. [Latin *tessellātus,* from *tessella,* a small cube, diminutive of *tessera,* TESSERA.] **—tes·sel·la·tion** (-láysh'n) *n.*
tes·ser·a (téssə-rə) *n., pl.* **-serae** (-ree). One of the small squares of stone or glass used in making mosaic patterns. [Latin, "a square", from Greek *tesseres, tessares,* four.] **—tes·ser·al** *adj.*

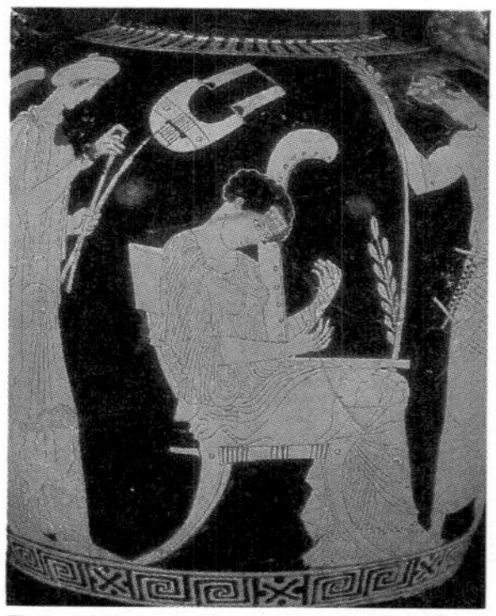

Terpsichore *According to Greek mythology, the muses would sing, dance, and play music at the feasts of the gods. Terpsichore, the muse of dance and song, is shown playing a harp on this Greek vase made in about 440* B.C.

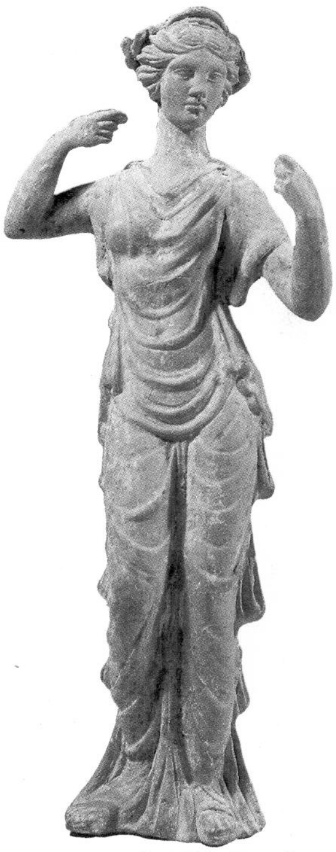

terracotta *In the 1880s, French archaeologists discovered hundreds of terracotta figurines buried in tombs at Myrina, an ancient Greek settlement on the coast of modern-day Turkey. This fired-clay figure of Aphrodite – the goddess of love and beauty in Greek mythology – was made there in about* A.D. *20.*

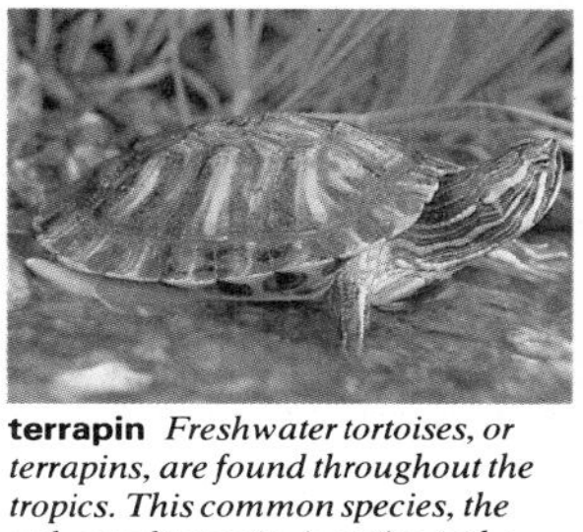

terrapin *Freshwater tortoises, or terrapins, are found throughout the tropics. This common species, the red-eared terrapin, is native to the Americas.*

tes·se·ract (téssə-rakt) n. Mathematics. The four-dimensional extension of a cube. [Greek tesseres, four + aktis, ray.]

tes·si·tu·ra (tessi-toor-ə, -téwr-ə) n. Music. The range within which most notes of a voice-part fall. [Italian, TEXTURE.]

test[1] (test) n. **1.** Any of various procedures by which a person or thing may be examined for certain properties or qualities as: **a.** A series of questions or problems designed to assess knowledge, skill, or aptitude. **b.** A series of operations or functions designed to assess effectiveness or conformity to an appropriate standard: nuclear weapons tests; an MOT test. **c.** A diagnostic medical examination: a pregnancy test. Also used adjectivally: test conditions; a test drive. **2.** Any means or circumstance by which something is examined or evaluated: put his theories to the test. **3.** A criterion; a standard. **4. a.** A physical or chemical reaction by which a substance may be detected or its properties ascertained. **b.** The reagent used in such determination. **c.** A positive result obtained. **5.** A cupel.
~v. tested, testing, tests. —tr. **1.** To subject to a test; examine. **2. a.** To determine the presence or properties of (a substance). **b.** To assay (metal) in a cupel. **3.** To try; tax: tested his patience. —intr. **1.** To exhibit certain properties under test conditions. **2.** To administer a test in order to analyse or diagnose. Used with for: test for acid content. [Middle English, cupel for treating ores, from Old French, pot, from Latin testum†, earthen vessel.]

test[2] n. A hard external covering, such as that of certain insects and other invertebrates. [Latin testa, shell. See testa.]

tes·ta (téstə-) n., pl. -tae (-tee). The often thick or hard outer coat of a seed. [Latin testa†, clay, brick, tile, shell.]

tes·ta·ceous (tess-táyshəss) adj. **1.** Biology. Of, pertaining to, or having a shell or shell-like outer covering. **2.** Having the characteristic reddish-brown or brownish-yellow colour of bricks. [Latin testāceus, from testa, shell. See test (shell).]

tes·ta·cy (téstə-si) n. Law. The condition of being testate.

tes·ta·ment (téstə-mənt) n. **1.** Law. A written document providing for the disposition of one's personal property after death; a will. Used chiefly in the phrase last will and testament. **2. a.** Any proof or tribute that testifies to or serves as evidence of something. **b.** A statement of belief or conviction; a credo. **3. a.** Archaic. A covenant between humanity and God. **b.** Capital T. Either of the two main divisions of the Bible, the Old Testament and the New Testament. **c.** Capital T. The New Testament. [Middle English, from Late Latin testāmentum (translation of Greek diathēkē, scripture), from Latin, will, from testārī, to be a witness, assert, make a will, from testis, witness.] —**tes·ta·men·ta·ry** (-méntəri) adj.

tes·tate (téss-tayt, -tət, -tit) adj. Having made a legally valid will before death. [Middle English, from Latin testātus, past participle of testārī, to make a will. See **testament**.]

tes·ta·tor (tess-táytər ‖ téss-taytər) n. A person who has made a legally valid will before death. [Middle English testatour, from Anglo-French, from Latin testātor, from testārī, to make a will. See **testament**.]

tes·ta·trix (tess-táytriks) n. A female testator. [Latin testātrix, feminine of testātor, TESTATOR.]

test ban n. An agreement between nations to forgo tests on certain types of nuclear weaponry.

test bed n. An arrangement of measuring instruments used to test engines and other pieces of machinery under load.

test case n. **1.** A legal action whose outcome is likely to set a precedent. **2.** Any issue whose outcome is likely to be treated as a precedent.

test cross n. Genetics. The crossing of a hybrid exhibiting the dominant phenotype of a particular gene back to a parent homozygous for the recessive allele of this gene, to determine whether the hybrid is homozygous or heterozygous.

test·ed (téstid) adj. Having been subjected to a test; certified through testing. Also used in combination to indicate: **1.** Tested by the specified means: tuberculin-tested; heat-tested. **2.** Tested for the specified quality or substance: toxin-tested.

tes·ter[1] (téstər) n. A canopy over a bed, cot, or the like. [Middle English, from Medieval Latin testerium, headpiece, from Late Latin testa, skull, head, from Latin, shell. See **testa**.]

tes·ter[2] n. A former English coin, the teston (see).

test·er[3] n. One that tests.

tes·tes. Plural of **testis**.

tes·ti·cle (téstik'l) n. Either of the male reproductive organs, situated in an external scrotum behind the penis in humans and most mammals, that produce spermatozoa and secrete androgens. Also called "testis". [Middle English testicule, from Latin testiculus, diminutive of testis, TESTIS.]

tes·tic·u·late (tess-tíckew-lət, -lit, -layt) adj. Also **tes·tic·u·lar** (-lər). **1.** Having the shape of a testicle; ovoid. **2.** Having testicles.

tes·ti·fy (tésti-fī) v. -fied, -fying, -fies. —intr. **1.** To make a declaration of truth or fact under oath; submit testimony. **2.** To make a serious or solemn statement in support of an argument, position, or asserted fact; affirm. **3.** To serve as witness or evidence. Used with to. **4.** To make an open profession of religious faith. —tr. **1.** To bear witness to; provide evidence for; prove. **2.** To state or affirm under oath. **3.** To declare publicly; make known. [Middle English testifien, from Latin testificārī : testis, witness + facere, to make.] —**tes·ti·fi·ca·tion** (-fi-káysh'n) n. —**tes·ti·fi·er** n.

tes·ti·mo·ni·al (tésti-mṓni-əl) n. **1.** A written statement providing evidence of a person's character or ability; a letter of recommendation. **2.** Something given as a tribute for a person's service or achievement.

~adj. Relating to or constituting a testimony or testimonial. [Middle English, noun and adjective, from Old French, from Late Latin testimōniālis, from Latin testimōnium, TESTIMONY.]

tes·ti·mo·ny (tésti-məni ‖ U.S. -mōni) n., pl. -nies. Abbr. test. **1.** A declaration or affirmation of fact or truth, such as that given before a court of law. **2.** Any evidence in support of a fact or assertion; a demonstration or proof. **3.** The collective written and spoken testimony offered in a legal case. **4.** A public declaration regarding a religious experience. **5. a.** The law of Moses, inscribed on the tablets of stone. Exodus 25:16. **b.** Often capital T. The ark containing these tablets. Exodus 16:34. [Middle English, from Latin testimōnium, from testis, witness.]

test·ing ground (tésting) n. An area or environment where something is subjected to a critical trial: a nuclear testing ground.

tes·tis (téss-tiss) n., pl. -tes (-teez). A testicle. [Latin, "witness" (to masculinity).]

test match n. Any of a series of international sports matches, especially in cricket or Rugby football. Also called "test".

tes·ton (téss-tən ‖ -ton) n. Also **tes·toon** (tess-tṓn). Any of various coins with the image of a head on one side, specifically: **1.** A 16th-century silver coin of France. **2.** An English coin stamped with the head of Henry VIII, originally worth a shilling and later sixpence. In this sense, also called "tester". [Middle English, from Old French teste and Italian testa, head, both from Late Latin testa, skull, from Latin, shell. See **testa**.]

tes·tos·ter·one (tess-tóstə-rōn) n. A male sex hormone, $C_{19}H_{28}O_2$, produced in the testicles and functioning to control secondary sexual characteristics. [TEST(IS) + STER(OL) + -ONE.]

test paper n. **1.** A paper saturated with a reagent, such as litmus, used in making chemical tests. **2. a.** A paper or booklet bearing examination questions. **b.** A paper or booklet bearing a student's work for an examination.

test pilot n. A pilot who flies aircraft of new or experimental design to test them for conformity to planned standards.

test tube n. A cylindrical clear glass tube usually open at one end and rounded at the other, used in laboratory experiments.

test-tube baby n. A baby conceived by fertilisation of an ovum outside the body and implanted in the womb at the blastocyst stage.

tes·tu·di·nal (tess-tū·din'l) adj. Also **tes·tu·di·nar·y** (-téwdi-nəri ‖ -nerri). **1.** Of, resembling, or relating to a tortoise or turtle. **2.** Of or pertaining to the shell of either of these.

tes·tu·do (tess-téw-dō ‖ -tṓo-) n., pl. -dines (-di-neez). An ancient Roman siege device consisting either of a movable arched screen or of shields held up to interlock over their bearers' heads, protecting the besiegers' approach to a wall. Also called "tortoise". [Latin testūdō, "tortoise", a covering, from testa, shell. See **testa**.]

tes·ty (tésti) adj. -tier, -tiest. **1.** Irritable; touchy; peevish: a testy old codger. **2.** Characterised by irritability, impatience, or exasperation: a testy remark. [Middle English testif, headstrong, from Anglo-French, from Old French teste, head. See **teston**.] —**tes·ti·ly** adv. —**tes·ti·ness** n.

Tet (tet) n. The lunar New Year as celebrated during January or February in Southeast Asia. [Vietnamese tét, from Ancient Chinese tsiet, "festival" (Mandarin Chinese jié).]

te·tan·ic (tə-tánnik, ti-, tə-) adj. Of or pertaining to tetanus.
~n. Any poison producing symptoms similar to those of tetanus. —**te·tan·i·cal·ly** adv.

tet·a·nise (tétt'n-īz) tr.v. -nised, -nising, -nises. To affect with tetanic convulsions; produce or induce tetanus in. —**tet·a·ni·sa·tion** (-ī-záysh'n ‖ U.S. -i-) n.

tet·a·nus (tétt'n-əss) n. **1.** An acute, often fatal infectious disease caused by a bacillus, Clostridium tetani, that generally enters the body through wounds, and is characterised by rigidity and spasmodic contraction of the voluntary muscles. Also called "lockjaw". **2.** A state of continuous muscular contraction caused by reaction to rapidly repeated stimuli, such as electric shocks. [Learned respelling of Middle English tetane, from Latin tetanus, from Greek tetanos, from adjective, "stretched", from teinein, to stretch.] —**tet·a·nal** (-'l), **tet·a·noid** (-oyd) adj.

tet·a·ny (tétt'n-i) n. An abnormal condition, occurring chiefly in young people, characterised by periodic painful muscular spasms caused by faulty calcium metabolism. [From TETANUS.]

tetch·y, tech·y (téchi) adj. -ier, -iest. Peevish; irritable. [Probably from obsolete tecche, tache, blemish, fault (of character), from Old French tache, teche, blemish, from Late Latin tacca (unattested), from Gothic taikns, sign.] —**tetch·i·ly** adv. —**tetch·i·ness** n.

tête-à-tête (tét-aa-tét, táyt-aa-táyt, -ə-) adv. Together without the intrusion of others; in intimate privacy: talk tête-à-tête.
~adj. For or between two only; private; intimate.
~n. **1.** A private conversation between two people. **2.** A sofa for two, especially an S-shaped one allowing the occupants to face each other. [French, "head to head".]

tête-bêche (tét-bésh) adj. Of, pertaining to, or designating a pair of postage stamps printed upside-down in relation to one another. [French : tête, head + bechevet, "double-headed" : bes, twice, from Latin bis (see bi-) + chevet, head (of a bed), from Latin capitium, head covering, from caput, head.]

teth (teth, tess, tet) n. The ninth letter in the Hebrew alphabet. [Hebrew ṭēth.]

teth·er (téthər) n. **1.** A rope, chain, or halter for an animal, tied fast at one end to allow only a limited range of movement. **2.** The range of one's resources; especially, the limits of one's endurance.

~*tr.v.* **tethered, -ering, -ers.** To restrict or bind with or as if with a tether. [Middle English *tethir,* from Old Norse *tjǒthr†.*]

Te·thys (téth-iss, teéth-). **1.** *Greek Mythology.* A Titaness and sea goddess who was both sister and consort of Oceanus. **2.** The sea which lay between the ancient continents of Laurasia and Gondwanaland. **3.** One of the satellites of Saturn.

tet·ra (téttrə) *n., pl.* **-ras** or collectively **-ra.** Any of various small, colourful tropical freshwater fishes of the family Characidae, popular in home aquariums. [Short for New Latin *Tetragonopterus* (former classification of tetras) : TETRAGON (from their squared-off dorsal fins) + -PTER.]

tetra–, tetr– *comb. form.* Indicates four; for example, **tetrachloride, tetracid.** [Greek.]

tet·ra·ba·sic (téttrə-báy-sik) *adj.* **1.** Containing four replaceable hydrogen atoms in a molecule. Said of an acid. **2.** Containing four univalent basic atoms or radicals. Said of a base or salt. —**tet·ra·ba·sic·i·ty** (-bay-síssəti) *n.*

tet·ra·chlo·ride (téttrə-kláw-rīd ‖ -klǒ-) *n.* A chemical compound containing four chlorine atoms per molecule.

tet·ra·chord (téttrə-kawrd) *n.* Especially in ancient music, a series of four diatonic notes encompassing the interval of a perfect fourth. [Greek *tetrakhordon,* from *tetrakhordos* : TETRA- + *khordē,* string.] —**tet·ra·chor·dal** (-kórd'l) *adj.*

te·trac·id (te-trássid) *adj.* **1.** Able to react with four molecules of a monobasic acid. Said of a base. **2.** Containing four replaceable hydrogen atoms. Said of an acid or acid salt.
~*n.* An acid containing four replaceable hydrogen atoms.

tet·ra·cy·clic (téttrə-síklik, *rarely* -sícklik) *adj.* Designating a molecule containing four rings in its structure.

tet·ra·cy·cline (téttrə-sī-klin, -klīn, -kleen) *n.* A yellow crystalline compound, $C_{22}H_{24}N_2O_8$, synthesised from chlortetracycline or derived from bacteria of the genus *Streptomyces* and used as an antibiotic. [TETRA- + CYCL(IC) + -INE.]

tet·rad (tét-rad, -rəd) *n.* **1.** A group or series of four. **2.** A tetravalent atom, radical, or element. **3. a.** A group of four chromatids formed during meiosis by the pairing of two homologous chromosomes that have each divided into two chromatids. **b.** A body formed of four cells, as, for example, pollen grains from one mother cell. [Greek *tetras* (stem *tetrad-*).] —**te·trad·ic** (te-tráddik) *adj.*

te·trad·y·mite (te-tráddi-mīt) *n.* A steel-grey bismuth ore, chiefly bismuth telluride. [Late Greek *tetradumos,* fourfold (since it occurs in compound twin crystals) : TETRA- + Greek *didumos,* double.]

tet·ra·dy·na·mous (téttrə-dínə-məss, -dínnə-) *adj. Botany.* Having six stamens, of which two are shorter than the others. [TETRA- + Greek *dynamis,* power (see **dynamic**) + -OUS.]

tet·ra·eth·yl lead (téttrə-ée-thīl ‖ -éth'l) *n.* A colourless, poisonous, oily liquid, $Pb(C_2H_5)_4$, used in petrol for internal-combustion engines as an antiknock agent. Also called "lead tetraethyl".

tet·ra·gon (téttrə-gən ‖ *chiefly U.S.* -gon) *n.* A polygon having four sides and four angles; a quadrilateral. [Late Latin *tetragōnum,* from Greek *tetragōnon* : TETRA- + -GON.]

te·trag·o·nal (te-trággən'l) *n.* **1.** Pertaining to or shaped like a quadrilateral. **2.** In crystallography, having a crystal system in which there are three axes at right angles of which only two are equal.

Tet·ra·gram·ma·ton (téttrə-grámmə-t'n, -ton) *n.* The four Hebrew letters usually transliterated as YHWH or JHVH (Yahweh or Jehovah) and used as a symbol or substitute for the ineffable name of God. [Middle English *Tetragramaton,* from Greek *tetragrammaton,* four-letter word : TETRA- + *gramma* (stem *grammat-*), letter.]

tet·ra·he·dral (téttrə-heédrəl) *adj.* **1.** Having four plane faces. **2.** Of, pertaining to, or formed in tetrahedrons. —**tet·ra·he·dral·ly** *adv.*

tet·ra·he·drite (téttrə-heé-drīt) *n.* A greyish-black copper ore, essentially $(CuFe)_{12}Sb_4S_{13}$, often containing other elements. [German *Tetraëdrit,* from Greek *tetraedros,* four-faced (it occurs in tetrahedral crystals). See **tetrahedron**.]

tet·ra·he·dron (téttrə-heé-drən, -hé-) *n., pl.* **-drons** or **-dra** (-drə). A polyhedron with four plane faces. [New Latin, from Late Greek *tetraedron,* from Greek *tetraedros,* four-faced : TETRA- + *hedra,* face.]

tet·ra·hy·dro·can·nab·i·nol (téttrə-hī-drō-kə-nábbi-nol, -drə- ‖ -nōl) *n.* A crystalline compound, the active principle of cannabis.

te·tral·o·gy (te-trál-əji) *n., pl.* **-gies.** **1.** In ancient Athens, a series of four dramas, three tragedies and one satyr play, performed at the festivals dedicated to Dionysus. **2.** Any series of four related theatrical or literary works. [Greek *tetralogia* : TETRA- + -LOGY.]

tetralogy of Fal·lot (fálō) *n.* A congenital deformity, giving rise to a "blue baby", involving four particular defects of the heart. [After E.-L. A. *Fallot* (1850–1911), French physician.]

te·tram·er·ous (te-trámmərəss) *adj.* **1.** Having or consisting of four similar parts. **2.** *Botany.* Having flower parts, such as sepals, petals, and stamens, in sets of four. [New Latin *tetramerus,* from Greek *tetrameres* : TETRA- + -MEROUS.] —**te·tram·er·ism** *n.*

te·tram·e·ter (te-trámmitər) *n.* A line of verse consisting of four metrical feet. [Late Latin *tetrametrus,* from Greek *tetrametros,* having four measures : TETRA- + -METER.] —**te·tram·e·ter** *adj.*

tet·ra·ple·gi·a (téttrə-pleé-ji-ə, -jə) *n.* **Quadriplegia** (see). [New Latin : TETRA- + -*plegia,* "stroke". Greek *plēssein,* to strike.] —**tet·ra·ple·gic** *n. & adj.*

tet·ra·ploid (téttrə-ployd) *adj. Genetics.* Having four times the haploid number of chromosomes.
~*n. Genetics.* A tetraploid individual, cell or nucleus. [TETRA- + -PLOID.]

tet·ra·pod (téttrə-pod) *adj.* Having four feet, legs, or leglike append-

ages. [Greek *tetrapous* (stem *tetrapod-*) : TETRA- + -POD.] —**tet·ra·pod** *n.*

te·trap·ter·ous (te-tráptərəss) *adj.* Having four wings. Said of certain insects. [Greek *tetrapteros* : TETRA- + -PTEROUS.]

tet·rarch (tét-raark, teét-) *n.* **1.** The ruler of any of the four divisions of a country or province. **2.** Any of four joint rulers. **3. a.** A subordinate ruler. **b.** In the Roman Empire, especially in Syria, a petty prince enjoying limited power under Roman hegemony. [Middle English *tetrarche,* from Latin *tetrarcha,* from Greek *tetrarchēs* : TETRA- + -ARCH.] —**tet·rarch·y, tet·rarch·ate** (-ayt, -ət, -it) *n.* —**te·trar·chic** (te-trárkik, tee-) *adj.*

tet·ra·spore (téttrə-spawr ‖ -spōr) *n. Botany.* Any of four spores produced in a group from a sporangium, as in certain algae. —**tet·ra·spor·ic, tet·ra·spor·ous** (-spáw-rəss ‖ -spǒ-) *adj.*

tet·ra·stich (téttrə-stik) *n.* A poem or stanza that consists of four lines. —**tet·ra·stich·al** (-stíck'l), **tet·ra·stich·ic** (-stíckik) *adj.*

te·tras·ti·chous (te-trástikəss) *adj. Botany.* Arranged in four vertical rows. Said of leaves or flowers on a stalk. [Late Latin *tetrastichus,* having four lines, from Greek *tetrastikhos* : TETRA- + -STICHOUS.]

tet·ra·va·lent (téttrə-váylənt) *adj.* Having a valency of 4.

tet·rode (téttrōd) *n.* **1.** An electronic vacuum tube with four electrodes, a cathode, a control grid, a screen grid, and an anode. **2.** A transistor with two connections to the base or gate to improve high-frequency performance. [TETR(A)- + -ODE (path).]

te·trox·ide (te-tróksīd) *n.* A chemical compound containing four oxygen atoms per molecule. [TETR(A)- + OXIDE.]

tet·ryl (téttrīl, téttril) *n.* A yellow crystalline explosive consisting of $(NO_2)_3C_6H_2N(NO_2)CH_3$, used chiefly as a primer or detonator. Also called "nitramine". [TETR(A)- + -YL.]

tet·ter (téttər) *n. Archaic.* **1.** Any of various skin diseases such as psoriasis, herpes, and, especially, eczema, characterised by eruptions and itching. **2.** A pimple, blister, or pustule. [Middle English *teter,* Old English *tet(e)r.*]

teuch·ter (téwkhtər) *n. Scottish.* **1.** A person from northwest Scotland. **2.** An unsophisticated, rustic person. [Perhaps from Scots Gaelic, "north-country man".]

Teu·ton (téwt'n ‖ tōōt'n) *n.* **1.** A member of an ancient people, probably of Germanic or Celtic origin, who lived in Jutland until the late second century B.C., when they migrated southwards. **2.** A member of a people speaking a Germanic language; especially, a German. [Latin *Teutonī.*]

Teu·ton·ic (tew-tónnik ‖ tew-) *adj.* **1.** Of, relating to, or characteristic of the Germanic people or the Teutons. **2.** Of or relating to the Germanic languages.
~*n.* The subfamily of Germanic languages.

Teutonic Knights. German military religious order founded (1190–91) at Acre. In 1211 they moved from Palestine to eastern Europe and after 50 years of campaigning subdued Prussia and many of the East Baltic States. The Order went into decline in the 15th century.

Teu·ton·ism (téwt'n-iz'm ‖ tōōt'n-) *n.* **1.** A German practice or idiom. **2.** The German character or civilisation.

Tevere. See **Tiber.**

Te·vet (táy-vet, -váyt) *n.* Also **Te·bet, Te·beth.** The fourth month of the Hebrew year. [Hebrew *tēbhēth,* from Akkadian *ṭebētu,* perhaps "month of sinking in", "muddy month", from *ṭebū,* to sink in.]

Tex·as (ték-səss ‖ *locally also* -siz). State in the south central United States, bordering on Mexico. The capital is Austin; the largest cities are Houston, Dallas, and San Antonio. It is the second-largest state in the Union, after Alaska. Its chief agricultural products are cotton, rice, and cattle, and the chief industry is the manufacture of chemicals. However, the great wealth of Texas is its vast oil resources. Texas was owned by Spain until it gained independence in 1836. It was annexed to the United States in 1845 and admitted as a state of the Union.

Texas fever *n.* An infectious disease of cattle and related animals, caused by a parasitic microorganism, *Babesia bigemina,* and transmitted by ticks.

text (tekst) *n.* **1. a.** The exact and original wording or words of something written or printed. **b.** The words of anything delivered orally, such as a speech or song, appearing in print. **2. a.** The body of a printed work as distinct from a preface, footnote, or appendix; the formal content. **b.** The words in a book as distinct from pictures or illustrations. **3.** A Scriptural passage to be read and expounded in a sermon. **4. a.** A reference used as the starting point of a discussion. **b.** The subject matter of a discourse. **5.** A textbook. **6.** *Printing.* Any of several styles of letters or types. [Middle English *texte,* from Old French, from Medieval Latin *textus* (Scriptural) text, from Latin, literary composition, "woven thing", from the past participle of *texere,* to weave.]

text·book (tékst-bŏŏk ‖ -bōŏk) *n.* A book used as a standard reference work for the formal study of a particular subject.
~*adj.* Typical; conforming to a stereotype: *a textbook example.*

tex·tile (téks-tīl ‖ *U.S. also* -t'l) *n.* **1.** Cloth; a fabric, especially one that is woven or knitted. **2.** Fibre or yarn for weaving or making into fabric. Also used adjectivally: *the textile industry.* [French, from Latin *textilis,* from *textus,* "woven thing". See **text**.]

tex·tu·al (tékstew-əl) *adj.* **1.** Of, pertaining to, or contained in a text. **2.** Based on or conforming to a text. [Middle English, from Old French *textuel.* See **text,** **-al.**] —**tex·tu·al·ly** *adv.*

textual criticism *n.* **1.** Study of a written work that seeks to establish the original text. **2.** Literary criticism stressing scholarly study and analysis of the text. In this sense, also called "criticism".

tex·tu·al·ism (tékstew-əl-iz'm) *n.* **1.** Strict adherence to a text, especially of the Scriptures. **2.** Textual criticism, especially of the Scriptures. —**tex·tu·al·ist** *n.*

tex·tu·ar·y (tékstew-əri ‖ -erri) *adj.* Textual.
~*n., pl.* **textuaries.** A specialist in the study of the Scriptures.

tex·ture (téks-chər, -tewr) *n.* **1.** The degree of roughness or smoothness of a surface; its feel: *the smooth texture of ivory.* **2. a.** The appearance of a fabric resulting from the woven arrangement of its yarns or fibres. **b.** A surface appearance suggesting the weave of a fabric. **c.** Consistency, as of a liquid. **3.** A grainy, fibrous, woven, or dimensional quality as opposed to a uniformly flat, smooth aspect; surface interest: *Brick walls give a room texture.* **4.** Distinctive or identifying qualities: *the texture of suburban life.* **5.** The representation of the structure of a surface as distinct from colour or form. **6.** In New Criticism, the particular aspect of a poem as distinct from its abstract or universal aspect. **7.** *Music.* A sound pattern created by melody, harmony, and rhythm.
~*tr.v.* **textured, -turing, -tures.** To give a distinctive texture to. [Originally, "weaving", from Latin *textūra,* from *textus,* woven thing. See text.] —**tex·tur·al** *adj.* —**tex·tur·al·ly** *adv.*

tex·tured (téks-chərd, *pedantically* -tewrd) *adj.* **1.** Having a specified kind of texture. Used in combination: *a rough-textured tweed.* **2.** Having marked texture: *a textured wall of stucco.*

textured vegetable protein *n. Abbr.* **TVP** A type of protein derived from soya beans. It is processed so as to have a meatlike texture, sometimes flavoured, and used chiefly as a meat substitute. Also called "textured soya protein", "spun protein".

tex·tus re·cep·tus (tékstəss ri-séptəss) *n.* Received text; specifically, the received text of the Greek New Testament. [Latin.]

tfr. transfer.

T.G. transformational (generative) grammar.

T.G.W.U. Transport and General Workers' Union.

–th¹ *n. suffix.* Indicates: **1.** The act or result of the act expressed in the verb root; for example, **spilth.** **2.** The quality suggested by the adjective root; for example, **width.** [Middle English *-th(e),* Old English *-thu, -tho,* from Common Germanic *-ithō* (unattested).]

–th², -eth *adj. & n. suffix.* Indicates ordinal numbers; for example, **millionth, fortieth.** [Middle English *-the, -te,* Old English *-(o)tha, -(o)the.*]

–th³. See **-eth.**

Th *Chemistry.* The symbol for the element thorium.

Th. Thursday.

Tha·ba·na Ntlen·ya·na (taa-báanə ntláyn-jənə). Mountain in the Drakensberg range of eastern Lesotho, at 3 482 metres (11,424 feet) the highest peak in southern Africa.

Thai (tī) *n., pl.* **Thais** or collectively **Thai. 1. a.** A native or inhabitant of Thailand. **b.** A member of the predominant ethnic group of Thailand, a people with both Mongoloid and Indonesian characteristics. **2.** The official language of Thailand, a member of the Tai family. Also called "Siamese". —**Thai** *adj.*

Thai·land (tī-land, -lənd). Formerly **Si·am** (sī-ám). Kingdom in Southeast Asia. Its heartland is the great plain of the Chao Phraya, a major rice-growing area. Nearly 75 per cent of the workforce are in farming, but manufacturing is expanding rapidly, and fishing and tourism are also important. The present dynasty, founded in 1782, kept Thailand the only Southeast Asian country that was never occupied by a European power (except in war). Absolute

monarchy was abandoned in 1932. Area, 514 000 square kilometres (198,250 square miles). Population, 49,800,000. Capital, Krung Thep (Bangkok).

thal·a·men·ceph·a·lon (thál-əm-en-kéffə-lon, -séffə-) *n. Anatomy.* **1.** The hindmost part of the forebrain. **2.** The **diencephalon** *(see).* [THALAM(US) + ENCEPHALON.] —**thal·a·men·ceph·a·lic** (-si-fál-ik, -ki-, -se-, -ke-) *adj.*

thal·a·mus (thál-ə-məss) *n., pl.* **-mi** (-mī). **1.** *Anatomy.* Either of two large ovoid masses of grey matter that relay sensory stimuli to the cerebral cortex. **2.** *Botany.* The receptacle of a flower. [New Latin, from Greek *thalamos,* inner chamber; perhaps akin to THOLOS.] —**tha·lam·ic** (thə-lámmik) *adj.* —**tha·lam·i·cal·ly** *adv.*

thal·as·saem·i·a, *U.S.* **thal·as·sem·i·a** (thál-ə-séemi-ə) *n.* An inherited blood disease in which there is an abnormality in the protein portion of the haemoglobin molecule, leading to severe anaemia. Also called "Cooley's anaemia". [Greek *thalassa†,* sea (that is, the Mediterranean) + -AEMIA.]

tha·las·sic (thə-lássik) *adj.* **1.** Of or pertaining to seas or oceans; pelagic. **2.** Of or pertaining to seas and gulfs as distinguished from the oceans. [French *thalassique,* from Greek *thalassa†,* sea.]

thal·as·soc·ra·cy (thál-ə-sóckrə-si) *n., pl.* **-cies.** Supremacy on the seas. [From Greek *thalassokratia :* *thalassa†,* sea + -CRACY.] —**thal·as·so·crat** (thə-lássə-krat) *n.*

thaler. Variant of **taler.**

Tha·li·a (thə-lī-ī-ə, -also tháyli-ə). *Greek Mythology.* **1.** The Muse of comedy and pastoral poetry. **2.** One of the three **Graces** *(see).* [Greek *Thaleia,* "the blooming one", from *thallein,* to flourish.]

tha·lid·o·mide (thə-líddə-mīd) *n.* A sedative and hypnotic drug, $C_{13}H_{10}N_2O_4$, withdrawn from sale in 1961 following the discovery that its use during early pregnancy could lead to foetal abnormalities, most notably the malformation of limbs. [(PH)THAL(IC ACID) + (IM)ID(E) + (I)MIDE.]

thal·lic (thál-ik) *adj.* Of, pertaining to, or containing thallium, especially with valency 3. [THALL(IUM) + -IC.]

thal·li·um (thál-i-əm) *n. Symbol* **Tl** A soft, malleable, highly toxic metallic element, used in rodent and ant poisons, in photocells, infrared detectors, and low-melting glass. Atomic number 81, atomic weight 204.37, melting point 303.5°C, boiling point 1,457°C, relative density 11.85, valencies 1, 3. [New Latin : Latin *thallus,* green shoot, THALLUS (from its green spectral line) + -IUM.]

thal·loid (thál-oyd) *adj.* Also **thal·loi·dal** (tha-lóyd'l, thə-). Of, resembling, or constituting a thallus. [THALL(US) + -OID.]

thal·lo·phyte (thál-ə-fīt) *n.* Any plant or plantlike organism of the now obsolete division Thallophyta, which included the algae, fungi, and bacteria. These are all now considered to be separate divisions. [New Latin *Thallophyta :* THALL(US) + -PHYTE.] —**thal·lo·phy·tic** (-fíttik) *adj.*

thal·lous (thál-əss) *adj.* Also **thal·li·ous** (-i-əss). Of, pertaining to, or containing thallium, especially with valency 1. [THALL(IUM) + -OUS.]

thal·lus (thál-əss) *n., pl.* **thalli** (-ī, -ee) or **-luses.** *Botany.* An undifferentiated stemless, rootless, leafless plant body. [New Latin, from Latin, young shoot, from Greek *thallos,* from *thallein,* to sprout.] [temz.]

Thames (temz). River in southeast England. It rises in the Cotswolds, Gloucestershire, and flows some 340 kilometres (210 miles) generally eastwards to the North Sea via a great estuary. In Oxford it is also known as the Isis. London lies at the head of navigation, and is protected against storm surges by a gated flood barrier, completed in 1982.

than (than, *weak form* thən) *conj.* **1.** Used in comparative statements to introduce the second element or clause of a comparison of inequality: *Gateau is richer than cake.* **2.** Used in statements of preference to introduce the less acceptable alternative: *I would rather dance than eat.* **3.** Used in statements expressing difference, especially after *else, other,* and compounds in which they appear: *elsewhere than in Britain; turned out to be none other than Mick Jagger.*
~*prep.* **1.** In comparison with: *She is much cleverer than me.* **2.** Used with expressions of degree or quantity: *more than twice the speed of sound; fewer than 100 people.* —**other than.** Apart from; except for. [Middle English *than(ne),* Old English *thanne, thænne.*]
Usage: In formal usage, sentences such as *She is bigger than I* are preferred to *She is bigger than me,* on the grounds that the sentence is short for *She is bigger than I am.* Similarly, *They liked him more than her* is said to be short for *They liked him more than they liked her,* and therefore different from *They liked him more than she,* which is short for *They liked him more than she liked him.* In informal usage, the objective form of pronouns *(me)* is generally used, and with third-person forms *(him, her),* this usage will often be encountered in relatively formal contexts: *John is much taller than him,* where *John is much taller than he* is felt to be stilted. The use of *what* (more characteristic of British than of American usage) is generally considered to be very informal, and many people avoid it altogether: *He looks much happier today than (what) he did yesterday.* See also **different.**

than·age (tháynij) *n.* **1.** The rank, jurisdiction, or office of a thane; thaneship. **2.** The land held by a thane. [Middle English, from Anglo-French : THANE + -AGE.]

Than·a·tos (thánnə-toss) *n.* **1.** Death as a personification or as a philosophical notion. **2.** *Psychology.* An alleged instinct to self-destruction; the death wish. Compare **Eros.** [Greek, "death".] —**than·a·tot·ic** (-tóttik) *adj.*

thane (thayn) *n.* Also **thegn** (for sense 1). **1.** In Anglo-Saxon England: **a.** A freeman granted land by the king in return for military service. **b.** A man ranking above an ordinary freeman and below a nobleman or ealdorman. **2.** In medieval Scotland, a feudal lord holding land granted by the king, and having the same rank as an earl's son. [Middle English *thayn, theyn,* Old English *theg(e)n,* from Germanic *thegnaz* (unattested); akin to Greek *teknon,* child.]

thane·ship (tháyn-ship) *n.* The position or office of a thane, especially in Scotland.

Than·et, Isle of (thánnit). Northeastern extremity of the county of Kent in southeastern England, formerly an island, now joined to the mainland by silting and the reclamation of land.

thangka. Variant of **tanka.**

thank (thangk) *tr.v.* **thanked, thanking, thanks. 1.** To express gratitude to; give thanks to: *thanked him for his help.* Often used in interjections: *thank God! thank goodness.* **2.** To hold responsible; blame. **—I'll thank you to.** Please. Used to intensify an indignant request. [Middle English *thanken,* Old English *thancian.*]

thank·ful (thángkf'l) *adj.* **1.** Grateful. **2.** Expressive of thanks. **—thank·ful·ness** *n.*

thank·ful·ly (thángkf'l-i) *adv.* **1.** In a thankful manner. **2.** *Informal.* Fortunately: *Thankfully, her injuries were only minor.*

thank·less (thángk-ləss, -liss) *adj.* **1.** Not feeling or showing gratitude; ungrateful. **2.** Unappreciated; unlikely to be appreciated: *a thankless task.* **—thank·less·ly** *adv.* **—thank·less·ness** *n.*

thanks (thangks) *pl.n.* **1.** An acknowledgment of a favour, gift, or benefit; gratitude. **2.** An expression of gratitude: *to give thanks.* **—no thanks to.** Without any help from; despite. **—thanks to.** On account of; because of.

~*interj.* Used to express thanks. **—thanks for nothing** or **thanks a bunch.** Used ironically in response to ill-treatment or disappointment. [Plural of obsolete *thank,* Old English *thanc,* from Germanic *thankaz* (unattested).]

thanks·giv·ing (thángks-givving, -gívving) *n.* An act of giving thanks; an expression of gratitude, especially to God.

Thanksgiving Day *n.* A national holiday set apart for giving thanks to God, celebrated in the United States on the fourth Thursday of November and in Canada on the second Monday of October. Also called "Thanksgiving".

thank·wor·thy (thángk-wurthi) *adj.* Worthy of thanks.

thank you *interj.* **1.** Used to express gratitude. **2.** Used in reply to an offer, typically accepting it, but in some varieties of English (such as South African) declining it. [Short for *I thank you.*]

thank·you (thángkew) *n.* An act or expression of thanks.

~*adj.* Expressing thanks: *a thankyou letter.*

Thá·sos (thássoss). Greek island, lying in the Aegean Sea off the northeast coast of Greece. In ancient times the Phoenicians worked its gold mines, now exhausted; lead-zinc ores are still exploited.

that (that; *weak form for relative pronoun and conjunction* thət) *adj., pl.* **those** (thōz). **1.** Being the one indicated, mentioned, implied, or understood. **2.** Being the one further removed or less obvious: *this card or that card.*

~*pron., pl.* **those. 1.** Used as a demonstrative pronoun with the sense of: **a.** The one indicated, mentioned, implied, or understood. **b.** The further or less immediate one. **c.** The one belonging to the kind or category specified: *The best whisky is that from Scotland.* **2.** Used as a demonstrative pronoun to indicate: **a.** The period, point of time, or incident already mentioned or implied: *felt for my key, and that was when I noticed it was missing; tore up the contract and with that left the room; joined the army after that.* **b.** The place already mentioned or implied: *spent years in the Greek Islands, and that was where he learned to paint.* **c.** The manner, means, or process indicated or already mentioned or implied: *did a computing course, and that's how she got her present job; You open it like that; Don't look at me like that!* **3.** Used as a relative pronoun: **a.** To introduce a restrictive clause: *never got the letter that I sent him.* **b.** To indicate at, in, to, or on which: *the day that we met; every time that I tried; everywhere that we went.* **4. a.** Something: *There is that about him which mystifies me.* **b.** *Plural.* Some people: *There are those who feel it is already too late.* **—and all that.** Also *British informal* **and that.** And so on; and everything related to that. **—at that.** Furthermore; as well: *scored a goal and a good one at that.* **—like that. 1.** Without effort or delay: *solved the problem just like that.* **2.** Of such a kind or character: *She just did what he told her—she's like that.* **—that's that.** That is final; there is an end to it.

~*adv.* **1.** To such an extent or degree; to that extent; so: *If it cost that much it ought to be good.* **2.** *Informal.* To a great extent; very. Used chiefly in negative statements, except in nonstandard usage: *I wasn't that worried. She was that narked!*

~*conj.* **1.** Used to introduce a subordinate clause stating a fact, wish, consequence, purpose, or reason: *We supposed that you were lost; she wishes that you would come; so tired that he fell asleep in his chair.* **2.** Used to introduce an elliptical exclamation of desire: *Oh, that I were rich!* [Middle English *that,* Old English *thæt.*]

that·a·way (thát-ə-way) *adv. Informal.* That way; in that direction.

thatch (thach) *n.* **1.** Plant stalks or foliage, such as reeds or palm fronds, used for roofing. **2.** A roof made of this material. **3.** Something resembling a thatched roof, especially the hair of the head.

~*tr.v.* **thatched, thatching, thatches.** To cover with or as if with thatch. [Middle English *thacche,* from *thacchen,* to thatch, cover, Old English *theccan.*] **—thatch·er** *n.* **—thatch·y** *adj.*

Thatch·er (tháchər), **Margaret (Hilda)** born Roberts (1925–). British politician. Prime Minister (1979–).

that'll. Contraction of *that will.*

that's. Contraction of *that has* or *that is.*

thau·ma·trope (tháwmə-trōp) *n.* A device, such as a card, with partial pictures on each side, which appear to merge when it is swung round. [Greek *thauma,* wonder, marvel + *-tropos,* turning.]

thau·ma·turge (tháwmə-turj) *n.* Also **thau·ma·tur·gist** (-ist). A performer of miracles or magic feats. [Medieval Latin *thaumaturgus,* from Greek *thaumatourgos* : *thauma* (stem *thaumat-*), wonder + *-ergos,* "working", from *ergon,* work.]

thau·ma·tur·gy (tháwmə-turji) *n.* The working of miracles or wonders; magic. **—thau·ma·tur·gic** (-túrjik), **thau·ma·tur·gi·cal** *adj.*

thaw (thaw) *v.* **thawed, thawing, thaws.** —*intr.* **1.** To change from a frozen solid to a liquid by gradual warming. **2.** To lose stiffness, numbness, or impermeability by being warmed. **3.** To become warm enough for snow and ice to melt. Used with *it.* **4.** To become less restrained or tense; relax. —*tr.* To melt or soften (a frozen solid) by gradual warming. —See Synonyms at **melt.**

~*n.* **1.** The process of thawing. **2.** A period of relatively warm weather during which ice and snow melt. **3.** A relaxation of reserve, restraints, hostilities, or tensions: *a thaw in East-West relations.* [Middle English *thawen,* Old English *thāwian,* from Germanic *thawōjan*† (unattested).]

THC tetrahydrocannabinol.

the[1] (thee; *weak forms* thə *before a consonant sound,* thi *or* thee *before a vowel sound* || *The weak forms* thi *or* thee *before a consonant and* thə *before a vowel are also to be heard*). The definite article, functioning as an adjective. It is used: **1.** Before singular or plural nouns and noun phrases that denote particular or previously specified persons or things. **2.** Before a singular noun, making it generic: *the human arm; plays the violin.* **3. a.** Before a noun, and generally stressed, emphasising its uniqueness or prominence: *That's* THE *show to see this year; Is she really* THE *Elizabeth Taylor?* **b.** Before a noun denoting one that is the best, most notable, or most desirable of its kind: *gave the performance of his life as Othello; This is the place to be!* **4. a.** Before a proper noun denoting something that is the only one of its kind: *the British Museum; the Bible; the Old Kent Road.* **b.** Before a noun denoting any of various natural phenomena that are, or are considered as being, unique: *flew through the air; the wind and the rain; always snows in the winter.* **5. a.** Before a title of rank or office, designating its holder: *the Queen; the prime minister.* **b.** Before a qualifying adjective or noun in certain epithets or titles: *Ivan the Terrible; Edward the Confessor.* **c.** Before the name of certain Scottish or Irish clans, designating the chieftain: *the O'Donoghue.* **6.** Before certain nouns referring to familiar features or adjuncts of daily life, typically indicating the most accessible individual example: *ought to see the doctor; listening to the radio; has gone to the lavatory.* **7. a.** Before nouns denoting parts of the body, instead of the possessive pronoun: *slapped him in the face.* **b.** Before nouns denoting personal possessions or pets, instead of the possessive pronoun: *I've got the car with me; took the dog for a walk.* This use may be considered offensive in phrases such as *the wife.* **8.** Before a noun, indicating the degree or amount of it required for a stated purpose or operation: *haven't the time to see her.* **9. a.** Before an adjective or participle, extending it to signify a class or group and giving it the function of a noun: *the British; a school for the blind; the sick, the wounded, and the dying.* **b.** Before certain passive past participles, indicating an individual in the specified condition: *The accused took the stand.* **c.** Before certain adjectives, indicating an abstract concept: *a taste for the bizarre.* **10.** Before an adjective used absolutely: *the finest we have to offer.* **11.** Before a present participle, signifying the action in the abstract: *the weaving of rugs.* **12.** Before a noun, with the force of *per*: *at a pound the box.* [Middle English *the,* Old English *thē̆* (originally a demonstrative adjective, later superseding *sē,* masculine singular).]

the[2] (thee, *weak forms as at* **the**[1]) *adv.* To that extent; by that much: *the sooner the better.* [middle English *the, thi,* Old English *thȳ, thē,* instrumental case of *thē̆,* THE, and *thæt,* THAT.]

the·an·thro·pism (thee-ánthrə-piz'm) *n. Theology.* The doctrine of the union of human and divine natures in Christ. [Late Greek *theanthrōpos,* god-man (*theos,* god + *anthrōpos,* man) + -IC.] **—the·an·throp·ic** (thée-an-thróppik) *adj.* **—the·an·thro·pist** (thee-ánthrəpist) *n.*

the·ar·chy (thée-aarki) *n., pl.* **-chies. 1.** Government or rule by God or a god; theocracy. **2.** A hierarchy or order of gods. [Late Greek *thearkhia* : THE(O)- + -ARCHY.]

the·a·tre, *U.S.* **the·a·ter** (théertər || thée-ətər, *South of England also* thee-éttər) *n.* **1.** A building, room, or, formerly, an outdoor structure such as an amphitheatre for the presentation of plays, films, or other dramatic performances. **2.** Any room with tiers of seats used for lectures or demonstrations; an auditorium. **3.** A room in a hospital or clinic in which surgical operations are performed. Also called "operating theatre". **4. a.** Dramatic literature or performance considered as a branch of art; drama. **b.** A school of dramatic theory. **c.** The milieu or world of actors and playwrights. Preceded by *the.* **d.** The quality or effectiveness of a theatrical production: *This play is good theatre.* **4.** The audience in a theatre. **5.** A place that is the setting for remarkable events; a scene: *a theatre of war.* **6.** *Australian.* A cinema.

~*adj.* **1.** Of or pertaining to the theatre: *theatre tickets.* **2.** Intended for use in a theatre of war: *theatre nuclear weapons.* [Middle English *theatre,* from Old French, from Latin *theātrum,* from Greek *theatron,* from *theasthai,* to watch, look at, from *thea*†, a viewing.]

the·a·tre·go·er (théertər-gō-ər || thée-ətər-, thee-éttər-) *n.* A person who goes to the theatre, especially habitually.

the·a·tre-in-the-round (théertər-in-thə-równd || thée-ətər-,

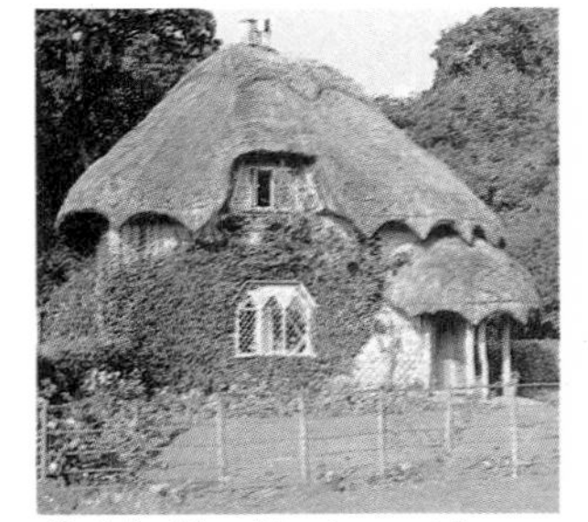

thatch *Thatching is one of the oldest and most effective methods of roofing a building and is still in use in many parts of the world. This English cottage is near Wimborne Minster in Dorset.*

PRONUNCIATION KEY

a, trap; aa, father; ai, fair;
ar, star; aw, lawn; ay, play;
b, bb, stab; rubber;
ch, church; ck, ticket;
d, dd, dead; ladder; e, dress;
ee, bee; er, defer; ew, few;
ewr, pure; ə, about;
ər, letter; f, ff, fife; differ;
g, gg, giggle; h, hat; i, kit;
ī, price; īr, fire; j, judge;
k, kick; l, ll, let; 'l, needle;
m, mm, man; n, nn, no;
'n, sudden; ng, thing; o, lot;
ō, no; ŏŏ, foot; ōō, shoe;
oor, poor; ow, cow;
owr, hour; oy, boy;
p, pp, pepper; r, rr, red;
s, ss, sauce; sh, ship;
t, tt, totter; th, thick; th, this;
smooth; u, cut; ur, turn;
v, vv, valve; w, wet; y, yes;
z, zz, zebra; zh, vision;
pleasure

IN FOREIGN WORDS:

aN, oN, Saint-Saëns;
hl, Llanelli; Hluhluwe;
kh, loch; lough; Khaled

STRESS MARK:

ín-sīt, insight; in-sít, incite

thee-éttər-) *n., pl.* **theatres-in-the-round** **1.** A theatre in which the stage is at the centre of the auditorium, surrounded by seats, and without a proscenium. **2.** Drama written or designed for such a theatre. Also called "arena theatre".

Theatre of Cruelty *n.* A form of theatre, initiated in the 1930s by Antonin Artaud, which aims to depict pain, suffering, and the presence of evil, especially by nonverbal means.

Theatre of the Absurd *n.* A form of theatre which rejects naturalism in order to present the absurdity of the human condition. It is considered to have been founded by Alfred Jarry, but is more readily associated with the work of writers such as Eugène Ionesco.

the•at•ri•cal (thi-áttrik'l) *adj.* **1.** Of, relating to, or suitable for the theatre or dramatic performance. **2.** Marked by the self-display or the exaggerated manner associated with actors; histrionic.
~*n.* **1.** *Informal.* An actor. **2.** *Usually plural.* A dramatic performance, especially by amateurs. **—the•at•ri•cal•ly** *adv.* **—the•at•ri•cal•ism** (-izm), **the•at•ri•cal•i•ty** (thi-áttri-kál-əti), **the•at•ri•cal•ness** *n.*

the•at•rics (thi-áttriks) *pl.n.* **1.** *Used with a singular verb.* The art of the theatre. **2.** Theatrical effects or mannerisms; histrionics.

the•ba•ine (thée-bi-een, -bay-, thi-báy- || -bə-) *n.* A poisonous alkaloid, $C_{19}H_{21}NO_3$, obtained from opium and having a slight narcotic action. [New Latin *thebaia,* (herb of) Thebes + -INE.]

Thebes[1] (theebz). City of ancient Egypt, occupying the site now partially occupied by Al Uqsur and Al Karnak, on both sides of the river Nile. It flourished from the mid-22nd to the 18th century B.C., both as a royal residence and as the centre of the worship of the god Amon. Excavations have unearthed ruins of great archaeological and historical importance, among them the nearby Valley of the Tombs of the Kings, and the temples of Karnak and Luxor.

Thebes[2]. City of ancient Greece, lying in eastern Boeotia northwest of Athens, on the site of present-day Thebes, or Thívai. Settlement of the site dates from the early Bronze Age, and it is the scene of the legends of Oedipus and Antigone. Following the Peloponnesian War, Thebes gained military ascendancy in Greece by twice defeating Sparta (375 B.C. and 371 B.C.). Its heyday was short-lived. In 336 B.C. the city was almost completely destroyed by Alexander.

the•ca (thée-kə) *n., pl.* **-cae** (-see, -kee). *Biology.* A case, covering, or sheath, such as the spore case of a moss capsule. [New Latin, from Latin *thēca,* a case, sheath, from Greek *thēkē.*] **—the•cal** (-k'l) *adj.*

the•cate (thée-kayt) *adj.* Also **the•cal** (-k'l). Having a theca; encased or sheathed. [THEC(A) + -ATE.]

thé dan•sant (táy DON-SÓN) *n., pl.* **thés dansants** (*pronounced as singular, or* táyz). A dance held while afternoon tea is served. Also called "tea dance". [French.]

thee (thee) *pron. Archaic, Poetic, & Regional.* **1.** The objective case of the second person singular pronoun *thou,* used as the direct or indirect object of a verb, as the object of a preposition, or after *than* or *as* in comparisons in which the first term is in the objective case. **2.** *Nonstandard.* Used in the nominative as well as the objective case in certain religious communities, especially in the Society of Friends in the 19th century. [Middle English, Old English, accusative and dative of *thū,* THOU.]

thee•lin (théelin) *n.* **Oestrone** *(see).* [Irregularly from Greek *thēlus,* female + -IN.]

theft (theft) *n.* **1.** The act or an instance of stealing; the dishonest taking and removing of another's personal property with the intent of permanently depriving the owner. **2.** *Archaic.* That which is stolen. [Middle English *theft(he),* Old English *thēofth,* from Common Germanic *thiufith* (unattested), from *thiuf* (unattested), THIEF.]

thegn. Variant of **thane.**

the•ine (thée-een, -in) *n.* **Caffeine** *(see).* [New Latin *thea,* tea + -INE; originally believed to be peculiar to tea.]

their (thair || tháy-ər). The possessive form of the pronoun *they.* Used attributively to indicate possession, agency, or reception of an action by the speaker: *their house; suffered their first defeat.* [Middle English, from Old Norse *their(r)a* (genitive plural).]

theirs (thairz || tháy-ərz) *pron.* Absolute form of *their. Used with a singular or plural verb.* Belonging to them; the one or ones belonging to them: *The blue boots are theirs. Mine is here, and theirs is the one on the stairs.* **—of theirs.** Belonging or pertaining to them: *a friend of theirs.* [Middle English, from THEIR.]

the•ism (thée-iz'm) *n.* Belief in the existence of a god or gods; especially, belief in a personal God as creator and ruler of the world, known to humankind through supernatural revelation. Compare **deism, pantheism.** [THE(O)- + -ISM.] **—the•ist** *n.* **—the•is•tic** (thee-ístik), **the•is•ti•cal** *adj.* **—the•is•ti•cal•ly** *adv.*

them (them, *weak form* thəm) *pron.* The objective case of the third person plural pronoun *they.* It is used: **1.** As the direct object of a verb: *She assisted them.* **2.** As the indirect object of a verb: *He offered them a new contract.* **3.** As the object of a preposition: *This letter is addressed to them.* **4.** After *than* or *as* in comparisons in which the first term is in the objective case: *The judges praised us more than them.* **5.** *Chiefly U.S. Informal.* In place of the reflexive pronoun *themselves,* as the indirect object of a verb: *They went to buy them a car.* **6.** In various elliptical, absolute, or interjectional phrases in which it is neither subject nor object: *Them and their big ideas!* **7.** *Nonstandard.* Those. [Middle English *the(i)m,* partly from Old Norse *theim,* partly from Old English *thǣm.*]

the•mat•ic (thi-máttik, thee-) *adj.* **1.** Of, based on, constituting, or relating to a theme or themes. **2.** *Linguistics.* Constituting part of the theme or stem of a word.
~*n.* A thematic vowel or sound sequence. [Greek *thematikos,* from *thema* (stem *themat-*), proposition, THEME.] **—the•mat•i•cal•ly** *adv.*

theme (theem) *n.* **1.** A topic of discourse, discussion, contemplation, or composition, often expressible as a phrase, proposition, or question. **2.** An idea, point of view, or perception embodied and expanded upon in a work of art; an underlying or essential subject of artistic representation; a motif: *the theme of the noble savage in literature.* **3.** *Chiefly U.S.* A short composition assigned to a student as a writing exercise. **4.** *Music.* A melody forming the basis of variations or other development in a composition. Also called "subject". **5.** *Linguistics.* **a.** A stem. **b.** A root. [Middle English *t(h)eme,* theme (of a discussion), from Old French *teme,* from Latin *thema,* from Greek, "thing placed", proposition.]

theme song *n.* **1.** A melody or song recurring throughout a dramatic performance and often intended to convey a mood. **2.** *U.S.* A **signature tune** *(see).*

Them•is (thémmiss, *also* théemiss). *Greek Mythology.* A daughter of Uranus and Gaea, and the goddess who personifies justice.

them•selves (thəm-sélvz || them-) *pron.* A specialised form of the third person plural pronoun. It is used: **1.** As a reflexive pronoun forming the direct or indirect object of a verb or the object of a preposition: *hurt themselves; give themselves time; talk to themselves.* **2.** For emphasis, after *they: They themselves weren't certain.* **3.** As an emphasising substitute: *Themselves in debt, they couldn't help us.* Sometimes nonstandard: *The Smiths and themselves are in trouble.* **4.** As an indication of (their) real, normal, or healthy condition or identity: *They haven't been themselves lately.*

then (then) *adv.* **1.** At that time: *I was a lot fitter then; If you're still in London then, come and visit us.* **2.** Next in time, space, or order; immediately afterwards. **3.** In that case; accordingly: *If you want to do it, then tell him.* **4.** In consequence; with the result that: *Leave by the back door, then nobody will notice.* **5.** In addition; moreover; besides. **6. a.** So it appears; so it may be deduced from what has gone before: *I take it, then, that you're interested.* **b.** By way of summing up or concluding what has gone before: *The allies, then, had suffered badly.* **7. a.** By way of qualifying what has just been stated: *didn't get the job, but then he never really wanted it.* **b.** In contrast; on the other hand: *Then again, we could go to the pub.*
~*pron.* A particular time or moment: *Until then let's stay here.*
~*adj.* Being so at that time: *the then headmistress.* [Middle English *thenne, thann,* Old English *thanne, thænne.*]

Usage: Careful speakers sometimes object to the use of *then* as an adjective, as in *the then prime minister,* preferring such phrases as *the prime minister of the time,* but it is widely used.

the•nar (thée-naar) *n.* **1.** The fleshy mound on the palm of the hand at the base of the thumb. **2.** The sole of the foot. [New Latin, from Greek *thenar,* palm of the hand.] **—the•nar** *adj.*

thence (thenss || *Scottish and U.S. also* thenss) *adv.* **1.** From that place; from there. **2.** From that time; thenceforth. **3.** From that circumstance or source; therefrom. [Middle English *thannes,* from *thanne,* from there, Old English *thanon.*]

thence•forth (thénss-fórth || thénss-, -fōrth) *adv.* From that time forwards; thereafter.

thence•for•wards (thénss-fór-wərdz || thénss-, -fōr-) *adv.* Also **thence•for•ward** (-wərd). From that time or place onwards.

theo-, the- *comb. form.* Indicates a god or gods; for example, **theism, theobromine.** [From Greek *theos,* god.]

the•o•bro•mine (thée-ō-brō-meen, -min) *n.* A bitter, colourless alkaloid, $C_7H_8N_4O_2$, derived principally from the cocoa bean, and used as a diuretic and a cardiac stimulant. [New Latin *Theobroma,* "food of the gods", genus including the cacao tree : THEO- + Greek *brōma,* food + -INE.]

the•o•cen•tric (théer-séntrik, thée-ō-, -ə-) *adj.* Centring on God as the prime concern: *a theocentric cosmology.* [THEO- + CENTR(E) + -IC.] **—the•o•cen•tric•i•ty** (-sen-tríssəti), **the•o•cen•trism** *n.*

the•oc•ra•cy (thi-óckrə-si) *n., pl.* **-cies. 1.** A form of government in which a god is regarded as the supreme ruler, and temporal power is in the hands of a priestly order claiming divine sanction. **2.** A state so governed. [Greek *theokratia* : THEO- + -CRACY.]

the•o•crat (théer-krat, thée-ō-, -ə-) *n.* **1.** One who rules in a theocracy. **2.** A believer in theocracy. [THEO- + -CRAT.] **—the•o•crat•ic** (-kráttik), **the•o•crat•i•cal** *adj.* **—the•o•crat•i•cal•ly** *adv.*

the•od•i•cy (thi-óddə-si, -óddi-) *n., pl.* **-cies.** A vindication of divine justice in the face of the paradox that God is both omnipotent and benevolent, and yet permits evil to exist among men. [French *Théodicée,* title of a work (1710) by Leibnitz : THEO- + Greek *dykē,* judgment.]

the•od•o•lite (thi-óddə-līt) *n.* A surveying instrument used to measure horizontal and vertical angles with a small telescope that can move in horizontal and vertical planes. [New Latin *theodelitus*†.]

The•od•o•ric (thi-óddorik) known as Theodoric the Great (A.D. *c.*454–526). King of the Ostrogoths, who established the Ostrogothic Kingdom that dominated Italy from the late fifth to the sixth century.

the•og•o•ny (thi-óggəni) *n., pl.* **-nies.** The origin and genealogy of the gods, especially as recounted in ancient epic poetry. [Greek *theogonia* : THEO- + -GONY.] **—the•o•gon•ic** (theer-gónnik, thée-ə-) *adj.* **—the•og•o•nist** (thi-óggənist) *n.*

the•o•lo•gi•an (theer-lō-ji-ən, thée-ə-, -jən) *n.* One versed in or studying theology.

the•o•log•i•cal (theer-lójik'l, thée-ə-) *adj.* Of or pertaining to a theology or religious philosophy. **—the•o•log•i•cal•ly** *adv.*

theological virtues *pl.n.* The virtues bestowed on man by a special grace of God; faith, hope, and charity.

the•ol•o•gise (thi-óllə-jīz) *v.* **-gised, -gising, -gises.** —*tr.* To make

PRONUNCIATION KEY

a, trap; aa, father; ai, fair; ar, star; aw, lawn; ay, play; b, bb, stab; rubber; ch, church; ck, ticket; d, dd, dead; ladder; e, dress; ee, bee; er, defer; ew, few; ewr, pure; ə, about; ər, letter; f, ff, fife; differ; g, gg, giggle; h, hat; i, kit; ī, price; īr, fire; j, judge; k, kick; l, ll, let; 'l, needle; m, mm, man; n, nn, no; 'n, sudden; ng, thing; o, lot; ō, no; ŏŏ, foot; ōō, shoe; oor, poor; ow, cow; owr, hour; oy, boy; p, pp, pepper; r, rr, red; s, ss, sauce; sh, ship; t, tt, totter; th, thick; th, this; smooth; u, cut; ur, turn; v, vv, valve; w, wet; y, yes; z, zz, zebra; zh, vision; pleasure

IN FOREIGN WORDS:

aN, ON, Saint-Saëns; hl, Llanelli; Hluhluwe; kh, loch; lough; Khaled

STRESS MARK:

ín-sīt, insight; in-sít, incite

theological in form or significance. —*intr.* To speculate about theology. **—the·ol·o·gis·er** *n.*

the·ol·o·gy (thi-óllәji) *n., pl.* **-gies.** **1.** The study of the nature of God and religious truth; rational inquiry into religious questions, especially those posed by Christianity. **2.** An organised, often formalised body of opinions concerning divinity and humanity's relationship to God. **3.** Loosely, any body of opinions considered, often humorously or disparagingly, as having a religious character: *monetarist theology.* [Middle English *theologie,* from Old French, from Latin *theologia,* from Greek : THEO- + -LOGY.]

the·o·ma·ni·a (thée-ō-máyni-ә, -ә-) *n.* Religious insanity; especially, a belief that one is God.

the·o·mor·phism (theer-mórf-iz'm, thée-ә-, -ō-) *n.* The depiction or conception of man as having the form of a god or of God. [THEO- + MORPH(O)- + -ISM.] **—the·o·mor·phic** *adj.*

the·oph·a·ny (thi-óffәni) *n., pl.* **-nies.** An appearance of God or of a god to a human being; a divine manifestation. [Medieval Latin *theophania,* from Late Greek *theophaneia* : THEO- + Greek *phainein,* to show.]

the·o·phyl·line (theer-fíl-een, thée-ә-, -in, *also* thi-óffil-) *n.* A colourless crystalline alkaloid, $C_7H_8N_4O_2$, derived from tea leaves and also made synthetically. It is an isomer of and has effects similar to theobromine. [THEO(BROMINE) + PHYLL(O)- + -INE.]

the·or·bo (thi-órbō) *n., pl.* **-bos.** A 17th-century lute having two necks and two sets of strings and pegs, one set above and somewhat to the side of the other. [Italian *tiorba*†.]

the·o·rem (théer-әm, -em, -im || thée-әr-) *n.* **1.** *Mathematics & Logic.* A statement or proposition that can be or has been proved on the basis of reasoning from explicit assumptions. **2.** A rule or statement of relations, usually expressed as a formula or equation: *binomial theorem.* [Late Latin *theōrēma,* from Greek, spectacle, intuition, theorem, from *theōrein,* to observe, look at, from *theōros,* spectator, from *thea,* a looking at.]

the·o·ret·i·cal (theer-réttik'l, théer- || thée-ә-) *adj.* Also **the·o·ret·ic** (-réttik). **1.** Pertaining to or based on theory. **2.** Restricted to theory, as: **a.** Lacking verification from experience or experiment. **b.** Lacking practical application. Compare **applied.** **3.** Existing only in theory; hypothetical or speculative. [Late Latin *theōrēticus,* from Greek *theōrētikos,* able to perceive, from *theōrein,* to observe. See **theorem.**] **—the·o·ret·i·cal·ly** *adv.*

the·o·re·ti·cian (théer-ә-tísh'n, -e- || thée-әr-) *n.* A student of theory in a science or other field of study.

the·o·ret·ics (theer-réttiks, théer- || thée-ә-) *n. Used with a singular verb.* The theoretical part of a science or other subject; principles.

the·o·rise, the·o·rize (théer-īz || thée-әr-) *intr.v.* **-rised, -rising, -rises.** **1.** To develop or formulate a theory or theories. **2.** To think in terms of theory; speculate. **—the·o·ri·sa·tion** (-ī-záysh'n || *U.S.* -i-) *n.* **—the·o·ris·er** *n.*

the·o·rist (théer-ist || thée-әr-) *n.* One skilled in the theoretical rather than practical aspects of a subject.

the·o·ry (théer-i || thée-әri) *n., pl.* **-ries.** **1. a.** Systematically organised knowledge applicable in a relatively wide variety of circumstances; especially, a system of assumptions, accepted principles, and rules of procedure devised to analyse, predict, or otherwise explain the nature or behaviour of a given set of phenomena: *the theory of evolution; Marxist economic theory.* **b.** Broadly, any set of beliefs or suppositions serving as a basis for action. **2. a.** That part of a subject dealing with its underlying rules and principles; abstract principles as distinct from practice or experiment: *musical theory.* **b.** The realm of abstract speculation or ideal circumstances: *In theory it should only take a week.* **3.** Broadly, a hypothesis or supposition; an opinion. [Late Latin *theōria,* from Greek, contemplation, theory, from *theōros,* spectator, from *theasthai,* to observe, from *thea,* a viewing.]

theory of games *n. Mathematics.* **Game theory** *(see).*

the·os·o·phy (thi-óssәfi) *n., pl.* **-phies.** **1.** Any of various philosophical or religious systems concerned with a direct intuitive or mystical apprehension of God. **2.** *Capital* **T.** The doctrines and beliefs of a modern religious sect, the Theosophical Society, incorporating aspects of Buddhism and Brahmanism. [Medieval Latin *theosophia,* from Late Greek *theosophia* : THEO- + -SOPHY.] **—the·o·soph·ic the·o·soph·i·cal** *adj.* **—the·o·soph·i·cal·ly** *adv.* **—the·os·o·phist** (thi-óssәfist) *n.*

ther·a·peu·tic (thérrә-péwtik) *adj.* **1.** Having healing or curative powers. **2.** Performed or serving to maintain health. **3.** Of or pertaining to therapeutics. [Greek *therapeutikos,* from *therapeutēs,* one who administers, from *therapeuein,* to administer to (medically). See **therapy.**] **—ther·a·peu·ti·cal·ly** *adv.*

ther·a·peu·tics (thérrә-péwtiks) *n. Usually used with a singular verb.* The branch of medicine concerned with the treatment of disease or disorders by remedial means. **—ther·a·peu·tist** *n.*

ther·a·pist (thérrәpist) *n.* A specialist in practising a certain form of therapy, such as physical therapy or psychotherapy.

the·rap·sid (thә-rápsid, thi-, the-) *n.* Any of the large, extinct reptiles of the order *Therapsida,* widespread in Permian and Triassic times, and thought to be the ancestors of the mammals. [New Latin *Therapsida,* from Greek *theraps,* attendant.]

ther·a·py (thérrәpi) *n., pl.* **-pies.** **1. a.** The remedial treatment of illness or disability. **b.** A course of such treatment. Often used in combination: *hydrotherapy; speech therapy.* **2. Psychotherapy** *(see).* [New Latin *therapīa,* from Greek *therapeia,* service, from *therapeuein,* to be an attendant, from *theraps,* attendant.]

Ther·a·va·da (thérrә-vaádә) *n.* A branch of Buddhism, predominating in Sri Lanka and Southeast Asia, based on a somewhat literal interpretation of the Pali scripture, and emphasising monastic life. Also called "Hinayana". [Pali *theravāda,* "doctrine of the elders" : *thera,* old, elder, from Sanskrit *sthavira,* thick, stout, old + *vāda,* speech, doctrine, from Sanskrit, sound, statement.]

there (thair) *adv.* **1.** At or in that place. **2.** To, into, or towards that place; thither: *run there.* **3.** At that point or position: *Hold it right there.* **4.** In that matter or respect: *There we must agree to differ.* **5.** Used to draw attention to someone or something: *There goes the bus!* **—there and then.** Immediately; right at that point. **—there it is.** That is the situation, whether one likes it or not.

~*pron.* (*weak form* thәr). **1.** Used, especially with the verb *be,* to introduce a sentence or clause whose real subject follows the verb: *There is someone at the door. There appears to be some disagreement.* **2.** That place: *There is where I should like to live.*

~*adj.* **1.** *Informal.* Existing in that place. Used for emphasis after a noun or demonstrative pronoun: *Take that one there. John there will help you.* **2.** *Nonstandard.* Used for emphasis between a demonstrative pronoun and a noun: *that there dog.*

~*interj.* Used to express emotion, such as relief, satisfaction, or consolation: *There, now I can have some peace!* [Middle English *ther(e),* Old English *thǣr, thēr.*]

Usage: When *there* appears before a linking verb, such as *be* or *seem,* the verb agrees in number with the following noun: *There is a man; There are several men.* When more than one noun follows the verb, the verb is usually singular if the first noun is singular *(There is a man and three girls in the car),* and plural if the first noun is plural *(There are three girls and a man in the car).* However, a quantity or circumstance perceived as singular or unified may take a singular verb: *There is only £4 in my account; There was laughter and dancing at the party.* Informally, there is a strong tendency to use the contraction *there's* even in sentences where the following noun is plural: *There's three men in the garden.*

there·a·bouts (tháir-ә-bówts) *adv.* Also *chiefly U.S.* **there·a·bout** (-bowt). Near that place, time, quantity, or degree; approximately.

there·af·ter (tháir-aáftәr || -áftәr) *adv. Formal.* From then on; after that: *an apprentice for three years, an assistant thereafter.*

there·at (tháir-át) *adv. Archaic.* **1.** At that place or point. **2.** By reason of that; as a result of that.

there·by (tháir-bī́, -bī) *adv.* **1.** By that means; as a result. **2.** In connection with that: *and thereby hangs a tale.*

there·for (tháir-fór) *adv. Archaic.* For that, this, or it.

there·fore (tháir-fawr || -fōr) *adv.* For that reason; consequently; hence: *The rumour's false and your judgment therefore wrong.* Also used to indicate a logical connection with a preceding clause: *I lost my money; therefore, I could not buy a ticket.*

there·from (tháir-fróm || -frúm) *adv. Archaic.* From that time, place, circumstance, or thing.

there·in (tháir-ín, -in) *adv.* **1.** *Law.* In that place or context. **2.** In that matter or particular.

there·in·af·ter (tháir-in-aáftәr || -áftәr) *adv. Law.* In a later or subsequent portion, as of a statute or book.

there·of (tháir-óv || -úv) *adv. Formal & Law.* **1.** Of or concerning this, that, or it. **2.** From that cause or origin; therefrom.

there·on (tháir-ón || -áwn) *adv. Formal & Archaic.* **1.** On or upon this, that, or it. **2.** Following that immediately; thereupon.

there·to (tháir-tóo) *adv.* **1.** *Formal.* To that, this, or it; thereunto. **2.** *Archaic.* In addition.

there·to·fore (tháir-tōo-fór, -tōo-, -tә- || -fōr) *adv. Formal & Law.* Until or prior to that time; before that.

there·un·der (tháir-úndәr) *adv. Formal & Law.* Under this or that.

there·up·on (tháir-ә-pón, -pon || -páwn, -pawn) *adv.* **1.** Directly following that. **2.** *Archaic.* **a.** On this or that. **b.** On that account. **c.** On that matter.

there·with (tháir-wíth, -wíth) *adv.* Also **there·with·al** (-with-áwl). *Archaic.* **1.** With that, this, or it. **2.** Immediately thereafter.

the·ri·an·throp·ic (théer-i-an-thróppik) *adj.* Partly human, partly animal. Said of such mythological creatures as the Minotaur. [Greek *thērion,* wild beast + ANTHROPO- + -IC.]

the·ri·o·mor·phic (théer-i-ō-mórfik, -ә-) *adj.* Having the form of a beast: *theriomorphic gods.* [Greek *thērion,* wild beast + -MORPHIC.]

therm (therm) *n.* A unit of heat equal to one hundred thousand British thermal units or 1.055 056 × 10^8 joules. [From Greek *thermē,* heat, from *thermos,* hot.]

therm-. Variant of **thermo-.**

-therm *n. comb. form.* Indicates heat; for example, **poikilotherm.** [From Greek *thermē,* heat. See **therm.**]

ther·mae (thérmee) *pl.n.* Public baths in the ancient Greek or Roman world. [Latin, from Greek *thermai,* from *thermē,* heat.]

ther·mal (thérm'l) *adj.* Also **ther·mic** (thérmik) (for sense 1). **1.** Of, pertaining to, using, producing, or caused by heat. **2.** Naturally hot or warm: *thermal springs.* **3.** Specially designed to minimise loss of body heat: *thermal underwear.*

~*n.* A rising current of warm air. [French, from Greek *thermē,* heat. See **therm.**] **—ther·mal·ly** *adv.*

thermal barrier *n.* A barrier to flight above a certain speed as a result of the heat produced by air friction. Also called "heat barrier".

thermal conductivity *n.* A measure of a substance's ability to transfer heat, expressed as the rate of conduction of heat between opposite faces of a hypothetical unit cube of the substance when there is unit temperature difference between the faces. It is measured in joules per second per metre per kelvin.

thermal efficiency *n.* The **efficiency** *(see)* of a machine.

thermal equator *n.* An imaginary line round the earth that links the point on each meridian that has the highest average temperatures.

thermal equilibrium *n.* A state of a system in which there is no net flow of heat among its components.

thermal spring *n.* A **hot spring** *(see)*.

ther·mal·ise, ther·mal·ize (thérm'l-īz) *v.* **-ised, -sing, -ises.** —*tr.* To cause (neutrons) in a moderator to become thermal neutrons. —*intr.* To become thermal neutrons. —**ther·mal·is·a·tion** (-ī-záysh'n ‖ *U.S.* -i-) *n.*

thermal neutron *n.* A neutron that is approximately in thermal equilibrium with the surrounding medium; especially, one produced by fission, slowed by a moderator, and having a mean velocity of about 2200 metres per second. Also called "slow neutron".

thermal reactor *n.* A nuclear reactor in which most of the fissions are caused by thermal neutrons.

thermal shock *n.* Stress in a material caused by a sharp change of temperature.

thermal unit *n.* See **British thermal unit.**

therm·i·on (thér-mi-ən, -mī- ‖ -on) *n.* An electrically charged particle or ion emitted by a conducting material at high temperatures. [THERM(O)- + ION.] —**therm·i·on·ic** (-ónnik) *adj.*

thermionic current *n.* A flow of thermions.

thermionic emission *n.* The emission of thermions from a conducting material at high temperatures.

therm·i·on·ics (thér-mi-ónniks, -mī-) *n. Used with a singular verb.* The physics of thermionic phenomena; especially, the study and design of thermionic valves.

thermionic valve *n.* An electronic vacuum tube in which the source of electrons is a heated electrode. Also *U.S.* "thermionic tube".

therm·is·tor (ther-místər) *n.* A resistor made of semiconductors having resistance that varies rapidly and predictably with temperature. [THERM(AL) + (RES)ISTOR.]

Ther·mit (thér-mit, -mīt). Also **Thermite** (-mīt). *n.* A trademark for a welding and incendiary mixture of fine aluminium powder with a metallic oxide which when ignited produces an intense heat.

thermo-, therm- *comb. form.* **1.** Indicates heat; for example, **thermogram.** **2.** Indicates thermoelectricity; for example, **thermionics.** [From Greek *thermē*, heat, from *thermos,* hot.]

ther·mo·bar·o·graph (thérmō-bárrə-graaf, -graf) *n.* A device that records both the pressure and temperature of a gas. [THERMO- + BARO- + -GRAPH.]

ther·mo·chem·is·try (thérmō-kémmistri) *n.* The branch of chemistry concerned with the heat produced or absorbed during reactions and other heat-associated chemical phenomena. —**ther·mo·chem·i·cal** (-kémmik'l) *adj.* —**ther·mo·chem·ist** *n.*

ther·mo·cline (thérm-ō-klīn, -ə-) *n.* A temperature gradient in a body of water, such as a lake, in which there is a marked variation of temperature with depth. [THERMO- -CLINE.]

ther·mo·cou·ple (thérm-ō-kupp'l, -ə-) *n.* **1.** A pair of wires of different metals joined at one end, used to measure temperature by the voltage produced at the junction. **2.** A circuit formed by two different wires joined at both ends, with one junction kept at a constant low temperature and the other at the temperature to be measured. The temperature is proportional to the current in the circuit.

ther·mo·dy·nam·ics (thérm-ō-dī-námmiks, -ə-) *n. Used with a singular verb.* The physics of the relationships between heat and other forms of energy, especially when used to study the properties of matter. —**ther·mo·dy·nam·ic** *adj.*

thermodynamic scale *n.* A temperature scale based on thermodynamic properties, such that zero on the scale is absolute zero.

thermodynamic temperature *n.* A physical quantity based on the average thermal energy of the random motion of the particles of a system in thermal equilibrium. The unit of thermodynamic temperature is the kelvin.

ther·mo·e·lec·tric·i·ty (thérmō-él-ek-tríssəti, -ilék- ‖ -trízzəti) *n.* **1.** Electricity generated by a flow of heat, as in a thermocouple. **2.** The branch of physics concerned with such electricity and related phenomena. —**ther·mo·e·lec·tric** *adj.* —**ther·mo·e·lec·tri·cal·ly** *adv.*

ther·mo·e·lec·tron (thérmō-i-lék-tron, -lek-) *n.* An electron produced as a result of thermionic emission.

ther·mo·gen·e·sis (thérm-ō-jénnə-siss, -ə-) *n.* The production of heat by physiological processes in the body.

ther·mo·gram (thérm-ō-gram, -ə-) *n.* A record made by a thermograph. [THERMO- + -GRAM.]

ther·mo·graph (thérm-ō-graaf, -ə-, -graf) *n.* A thermometer that records temperatures automatically. [THERMO- + -GRAPH.]

ther·mog·ra·phy (ther-móggrəfi) *n.* Any printing or writing process involving heat; especially, a letterpress technique that produces a raised effect by heating printed matter that has been dusted with special powder. [THERMO- + -GRAPHY.]

ther·mo·junc·tion (thérmō-júngksh'n) *n.* A point of contact between two dissimilar metals at which a thermoelectric current is produced.

ther·mo·la·bile (thérmō-láy-bīl ‖ -bil, -b'l) *adj.* Subject to destruction, decomposition, or great change by moderate heating. Said especially of certain biochemical compounds. Compare **thermostable.** [THERMO- + LABILE.]

ther·mo·lu·mi·nes·cence (thérmō-lŏŏ-mi-néss'nss, -léw-) *n.* Phosphorescence produced by gentle heating of some minerals which have previously absorbed radiation. —**ther·mo·lu·mi·nes·cent** *adj.*

ther·mol·y·sis (ther-móllə-siss) *n.* **1.** *Physiology.* The loss of heat from the body. **2.** *Chemistry.* The dissociation or decomposition of compounds by heat. [THERMO- + -LYSIS.] —**ther·mo·lyt·ic** (thérm-ō-líttik, -ə-) *adj.*

ther·mo·mag·net·ic (thérm-ō-mag-néttik, -ə-) *adj.* Of or pertaining to a change in the temperature of a body as a result of magnetisation or demagnetisation.

ther·mom·e·ter (thər-mómmitər) *n.* An instrument for measuring temperature; especially, one consisting of a graduated, sealed, glass tube with a bulb containing a liquid, typically mercury, that expands and rises in the tube as the temperature increases. [French *thermomètre* : THERMO- + -METER.] —**ther·mo·met·ric** (thérm-ə-méttrik, -ō-) *adj.* —**ther·mo·met·ri·cal·ly** *adv.*

ther·mom·e·try (thər-mómmətri, ther-) *n.* **1.** The measurement of temperature. **2.** The science and technology of temperature measurement. [THERMO- + -METRY.]

ther·mo·mo·tor (thérm-ō-mōtər, -ə-, -mōtər) *n.* An engine operated by heat, especially by the expansion of heated air.

ther·mo·nu·cle·ar (thérmō-néw-kli-ər ‖ -nŏŏ-) *adj.* **1.** Of, pertaining to, or derived from the fusion of atomic nuclei at high temperatures. **2.** Involving or designating nuclear weapons based on fusion, especially as distinguished from those based on fission.

ther·mo·pe·ri·od·ism (thérmō-péer-i-ədiz'm) *n.* Also **ther·mo·pe·ri·o·dic·i·ty** (-ə-díssəti). The response of certain plants to alternating low and high temperatures over a period, as of days and nights or successive seasons.

ther·mo·phil·ic (thérm-ō-fíllik, -ə-) *n. Biology.* Requiring high temperatures for normal development, as certain bacteria do. Compare **mesophilic, psychrophilic.** [THERMO- + -PHIL(E) + -IC.] —**ther·mo·phile** (-fīl), **ther·mo·phil** (-fil) *n.*

ther·mo·pile (thérm-ō-pīl, -ə-) *n.* A device to measure temperature or generate current, consisting of a number of thermocouples connected in series. [THERMO- + PILE (a heap, "series").]

ther·mo·plas·tic (thérm-ō-plástik, -ə-, -plaastik) *adj.* Becoming soft when heated and hardening when cooled, without change in inherent qualities. ~*n.* A thermoplastic resin, such as polystyrene.

Ther·mop·y·lae (thər-móppi-li, ther-, -lee). A locality in eastern Greece, south of Lamia. A pass between the sea and Mount Oeta to the south, it is the site of a heroic but unsuccessful defence by the Spartans against the Persians (480 B.C.).

ther·mo·set·ting (thérmō-setting) *adj.* Permanently hardening or solidifying on being heated. Said of certain synthetic resins.

Ther·mos flask (thér-moss) *n.* A trademark for a type of vacuum flask. Also called "Thermos".

ther·mo·si·phon (thérmō-sīf-n, -sīf'n) *n.* A cooling system in which the circulation of the coolant relies on differences in density between hot and cold parts of the fluid.

ther·mo·sphere (thérm-ō-sfeer, -ə-) *n.* The outermost shell of the atmosphere, between the mesosphere and outer space, within which temperatures increase steadily with altitude.

ther·mo·sta·ble (thérmō-stáy-b'l) *adj.* Unaffected by relatively high temperatures. Said especially of biochemical compounds. Compare **thermolabile.** —**ther·mo·sta·bil·i·ty** (-stə-bílləti) *n.*

ther·mo·stat (thérm-ə-stat, -ō-) *n.* A device that automatically responds to temperature changes to maintain a fixed temperature or activate control switches, as in refrigerators and air conditioners. [THERMO- + -STAT.] —**ther·mo·stat·ic** (-státtik) *adj.*

ther·mo·tax·is (thérm-ō-táksiss, -ə-) *n.* **1.** The directional movement of an entire cell or organism in response to heat. **2.** The normal regulation or adjustment of body temperature. [New Latin THERMO- + -TAXIS.] —**ther·mo·tac·tic** (-táktik), **ther·mo·tax·ic** *adj.*

ther·mo·ther·a·py (thérmō-thérrəpi) *n.* Therapy by application of heat.

ther·mo·tro·pism (thérm-ō-trôp-iz'm, -ə-, ther-móttrəp-) *n. Biology.* Directional growth of plants in response to heat. [THERMO- + -TROPISM.] —**ther·mo·trop·ic** (-trôpik, -tróppik) *adj.*

-thermy *n. comb. form.* Indicates heat; for example, **diathermy.** [New Latin *-thermia,* from Greek *thermē,* heat, from *thermos,* hot.]

the·ro·phyte (théer-ə-fīt, -ō-) *n.* A plant that overwinters as a seed; an annual. [Greek *theros,* summer + -PHYTE.]

the·ro·pod (théer-ə-pod, -ō-) *n.* Any of various bipedal carnivorous dinosaurs of the suborder Theropoda, of the Jurassic and Cretaceous periods, characteristically having small, grasping forelimbs. [New Latin *Theropoda* : Greek *thēr,* beast + -POD.] —**the·rop·o·dan** (theer-róppəd'n, thi-) *adj. & n.*

the·sau·rus (thi-sáw-rəss, thee-, thi-) *n., pl.* **-sauri** (-rī) or **-ruses.** **1.** A book of selected words or concepts, such as a specialised vocabulary for music, medicine, or the like. **2.** A book of systematically classified synonyms and antonyms. [Latin *thēsaurus,* TREASURE.]

these. Plural of **this.**

The·seus (thée-sewss, *also* -si-əss). *Greek Mythology.* A hero of Athens, who united Attica, slew the Minotaur, and married Phaedra.

the·sis (thée-siss; *for sense 5 also* thé-) *n., pl.* **-ses** (-seez). **1.** A dissertation advancing an original point of view as a result of research, especially as a requirement for an academic degree. **2.** Any proposition or theory that is maintained by argument. **3.** A hypothetical proposition, especially one put forth for the sake of argument; a premise. **4.** The first stage of **dialectic** *(see).* **5. a.** The unstressed part of a foot in verse **b.** The accented section of a musical measure. Compare **arsis.** [Late Latin, from Greek, a placing, a laying down, position, affirmation, from *tithenai,* to put, place.]

---

thes·pi·an (théspi-ən) *adj.* Of or pertaining to drama; dramatic. *~n.* An actor or actress.

Thess. Thessalonians (New Testament).

Thes·sa·lo·ni·an (théssə-lṓni-ən) *n.* A native or inhabitant of ancient Thessalonica. **—Thes·sa·lo·ni·an** *adj.*

Thes·sa·lo·ni·ans (théssə-lṓni-ənz) *n. Used with a singular verb. Abbr.* **Thess.** Either of two books of the New Testament consisting of Epistles from the Apostle Paul to the Christians of Thessalonica.

Thes·sa·lo·ni·ki (*Greek* théssa-lo-néekee). *English* **Sa·lon·i·ka** (sə-lónnikə). Port and second-largest city of Greece, situated in the northeast of the country. It was founded in *c.*315 B.C. and later became the capital of the ancient Roman province of Macedonia, where it was known as Thessalonica. It was there that Paul delivered his two epistles to the Thessalonians.

Thes·sa·ly (théssəli). *Greek* **Thes·sa·lía** (théssa-lée-ə). Region of central Greece, consisting of a flat, fertile plain between upland Epirus and the Aegean Sea.

the·ta (théetə || *chiefly U.S.* tháytə) *n.* The eighth letter in the Greek alphabet, written Θ, θ. Transliterated in English as *th.* [Greek *thēta,* from a Phoenician cognate of Hebrew *ṭēth,* TETH.]

The·tis (théttiss, théetiss). *Greek Mythology.* One of the Nereids, the wife of Peleus and mother of Achilles.

the·ur·gy (thée-urji) *n., pl.* **-gies.** **1.** Divine or supernatural intervention in human affairs. **2.** Magic performed supposedly with aid of beneficent spirits, as practised by Neo-Platonists. [Late Latin *theurgia,* from Greek *theourgia,* sacramental rite, "mystery" : THEO- + -URGY.] **—the·ur·gic** (thee-úrjik) *adj.* **—the·ur·gist** (thée-urjist) *n.*

thew (thew || thōō) *n. Usually plural.* Muscular power or strength; vigour. [Middle English, habit, characteristic, good physical quality, Old English *thēaw,* usage, custom, characteristic.] **—thew·y** *adj.*

they (thay) *pron.* The third person plural pronoun in the nominative case. **1.** Used to represent the persons or things last mentioned or implied: *There are three parts and they fit perfectly.* **2. a.** Used to represent unspecified persons or people in general: *They say he's having an affair. He's as tough as they come.* **b.** Used to represent those in positions of power; the authorities: *They're pulling down the old town hall.* **3.** *Archaic.* Used of persons as a demonstrative pronoun in the sense of *those*: *"Blessed are they which are persecuted"* (Matthew 5:10). **4.** *Nonstandard.* Used in referring to an indefinite singular antecedent: *If anyone wants a drink, they can get it themselves.* —See Usage note at **me.** [Middle English *thei,* partly from Old Norse *their,* partly from Old English *thā.*]

they'd (thayd). Contraction of *they had* or *they would.*

they'll (thayl). Contraction of *they will* or *they shall.*

they're (thair). Contraction of *they are.*

they've (thayv). Contraction of *they have.*

thi-. Variant of **thio-.**

thi·a·mine (thī́-ə-meen, -min) *n.* Also **thi·a·min** (-min). A B-complex vitamin, $C_{12}H_{17}ClN_4OS$, produced synthetically and occurring naturally in the bran coat of grains, in yeast, and in meat, that is necessary for carbohydrate metabolism, maintenance of normal neural activity, and the prevention of beriberi. Also called "vitamin B_1". [THI(O)- + (VIT)AMIN.]

thi·a·zine (thī́-ə-zeen, -zīn) *n.* Any of a class of organic chemical compounds containing a ring composed of one sulphur atom, one nitrogen atom, and four carbon atoms. [THI(O)- + AZINE.]

thi·a·zole (thī́-ə-zōl) *n.* **1.** A colourless or pale-yellow liquid, C_3H_3NS, containing a five-member ring composed of a nitrogen atom, a sulphur atom, and three carbon atoms, used in making dyes and fungicides. **2.** Any of various derivatives of this compound. [THI(O)- + AZOLE.]

thick (thik) *adj.* **thicker, thickest. 1. a.** Relatively great in depth or in extent from one surface to the opposite; not thin: *a thick board.* **b.** Relatively great in diameter or cross-section; wide in relation to length: *a piece of thick string.* **2.** Having a specified extent from one surface to the opposite; in thickness: *two inches thick.* **3.** Having constituent parts in a close, compact arrangement; dense; concentrated: *a thick forest.* **4.** Having a viscous consistency; not watery or fluid: *thick treacle.* **5. a.** Existing in great numbers; numerous. Often used in the phrase *thick on the ground.* **b.** Having a great amount or number; abounding: *The area was thick with security men.* **6.** Impenetrable by the eyes; deep: *a thick, gloomy blackness.* **7.** Not easy to hear or understand; indistinct; inarticulate: *the thick slurrings of a drunkard.* **8.** Very noticeable; pronounced: *a thick Birmingham accent.* **9.** Foggy, misty, or hazy: *thick weather.* **10.** *Informal.* Lacking mental agility; stupid: *Get that through your thick head.* **11.** *Informal.* Very friendly; intimate. **12.** *Informal.* Going beyond what is tolerable; excessive. Used chiefly in the phrase *a bit thick.*
~adv. So as to be thick; thickly: *Slice it thick.* **—lay it on thick.** *Informal.* **1.** To overstate or give an exaggerated account of something. **2.** To flatter excessively. **—thick and fast.** In rapid succession and great profusion.
~n. **1.** The thickest part of something. **2.** The most active, intense, or dense part: *in the thick of the fighting.* **—through thick and thin.** In both good and bad times; faithfully; unwaveringly. [Middle English *thikke,* Old English *thicce.*] **—thick·ish** *adj.* **—thick·ly** *adv.*

thick ear *n. British Informal.* A heavy blow to the ear, given in a fight or as a punishment.

thick·en (thíckən) *v.* **-ened, -ening, -ens.** *—tr.* To make thick or thicker. *—intr.* **1.** To become thickened. **2.** To become more intense, intricate, or complex: *the plot thickens.* **—thick·en·er** *n.*

thick·en·ing (thík-əning, -ning) *n.* **1.** Any material used to thicken a liquid. **2.** A thickened part of something.

thick·et (thíckit) *n.* **1.** A dense growth of shrubs or underbrush; a copse. **2.** Something suggestive of a thicket in impenetrability or thickness: *a thicket of unreality.* [Middle English *thikket* (unattested), Old English *thiccet,* from *thicce,* THICK.]

thick·head (thík-hed) *n.* A stupid person; a blockhead; a numbskull. **—thick·head·ed** (-héddid) *adj.*

thick-knee (thík-nee) *n.* A **stone curlew** *(see).* [From the bird's enlarged tibio-tarsal joint.]

thick·ness (thínk-nəss, -niss) *n.* **1.** The state or condition of being thick. **2.** The dimension between two of an object's surfaces, usually taken to be the dimension of least measure. **3.** A layer, sheet, stratum, or ply. **4.** The thick part or main body of something.

thick·set (thík-sét) *adj.* **1.** Heavily or stockily built; stout and compact. **2.** Positioned or placed closely together: *thickset rose bushes.*

thick-skinned (thík-skínd) *adj.* **1.** Having a thick skin. **2. a.** Insensitive. **b.** Not easily offended.

thick-wit·ted (thík-wíttid) *adj.* Stupid; dull.

thief (theef) *n., pl.* **thieves** (theevz). One who commits theft; especially, a person who steals using surreptitious rather than violent means. [Middle English *thefe,* Old English *thīof, thēof,* from Germanic *theubhaz* (unattested).]

thieve (theev) *v.* **thieved, thieving, thieves.** *—tr.* To take by theft; steal. *—intr.* To act as or be a thief; commit theft. —See Synonyms at **rob.** [Old English *thēofian,* from *thēof,* THIEF.]

thiev·er·y (théevəri) *n., pl.* **-ies.** The act or an instance of thieving.

thiev·ish (théevish) *adj.* **1.** Given to thieving or stealing. **2.** Of, similar to, or characteristic of a thief; stealthy; furtive. **—thiev·ish·ly** *adv.* **—thiev·ish·ness** *n.*

thigh (thī) *n.* **1.** The portion of the human leg between the hip and the knee. **2.** A corresponding structure in other animals. [Middle English *thih,* Old English *thēoh.*]

thigh·bone (thī́-bōn) *n.* The **femur** *(see).*

thig·mo·tax·is (thíg-mō-ták-siss, -mə-) *n.* Movement of an entire cell or organism in response to a direct tactile stimulus. Also called "stereotaxis". [New Latin : Greek *thigma,* touch, from *thinganein,* to touch + -TAXIS.] **—thig·mo·tac·tic** (-tik) *adj.* **—thig·mo·tac·ti·cal·ly** *adv.*

thig·mot·ro·pism (thíg-mō-trŏp-iz'm, -mə-, thig-móttrəp-) *n.* Directional growth of plants in response to contact with a surface or object. Also called "haptotropism". [Greek *thigma,* touch (see **thigmotaxis**) + -TROPISM.] **—thig·mo·tro·pic** (-trŏpik, -tróppik) *adj.*

thill (thil) *n.* Either of the two long shafts between which an animal is fastened when pulling a vehicle. [Middle English *thille*†.]

thim·ble (thímb'l) *n.* **1. a.** A small metal or plastic cup worn to protect the finger that pushes the needle in sewing. **b.** A thimbleful. **2.** Any of various tubular sockets or sleeves in machinery. **3.** *Nautical.* **a.** A metal ring fitted in an eye of a sail to prevent chafing. **b.** A metal ring around which a rope splice is passed. [Middle English *thymbyl,* Old English *thȳmel,* from *thūma,* THUMB.]

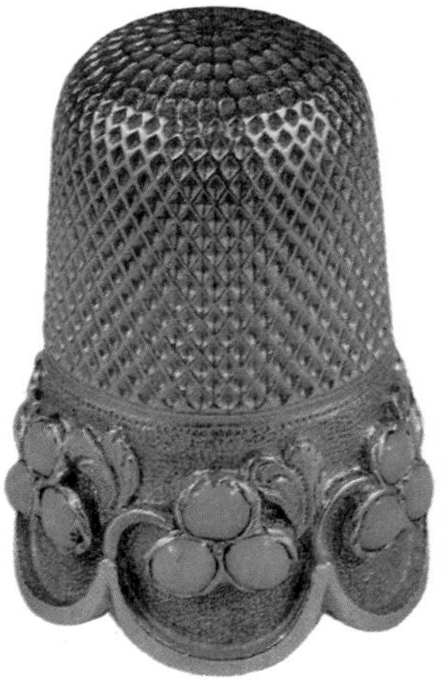

thimble *This seamstress's finger cap – of white and yellow gold inlaid with turquoise – is thought to have been made in England in the early 19th century.*

thim·ble·ful (thímb'l-fōōl) *n.* A very small quantity, as of a liquid.

thim·ble·rig (thímb'l-rig) *n.* **1.** A gambling game, usually a swindle, in which the operator shuffles three inverted thimble-shaped caps, under one of which he has placed a marker, such as a pea, and spectators bet on the location of the marker. **2.** A person who operates such a game.
~tr.v. **thimblerigged, -rigging, -rigs.** To swindle with or as if with the thimblerig. **—thim·ble·rig·ger** *n.*

Thim·phu (thím-foo). Also **Thim·bu** (thím-boo). Capital of Bhutan, lying high in the Chinchu valley in the west of the country.

thin (thin) *adj.* **thinner, thinnest. 1. a.** Relatively small in depth or in extent from one surface to the opposite; not thick. **b.** Not great in diameter or cross-section; narrow in relation to length; fine: *a thin strand.* **2.** Lean or slender; not fat. **3.** Having constituent parts widely separated; sparse; not dense or closely packed: *a thin rain; The crowd grew thinner.* **4.** Lacking force, substance, or body: *a thin brew.* **5.** Unconvincing, feeble, or flimsy: *That excuse is wearing a bit thin.* **6.** Difficult, uncomfortable, or disappointing: *having rather a thin time.* **7.** Lacking resonance or fullness; tinny. Said of sound or tone. **8.** Lacking radiance or intensity. Said of light or colour. **9.** *Photography.* Not having enough contrast to make satisfactory prints. Said of a negative.
~adv. So as to be thin; thinly.
~v. **thinned, thinning, thins.** *—intr.* **1.** To become thin or thinner. **2.** To become less dense. Often used with *out*: *The crowd began to thin out.* *—tr.* **1.** To make thin or thinner. **2. a.** To make less dense or crowded: *Plague thinned the enemy's ranks.* **b.** To remove so as to make less dense: *thin out seedlings.* [Middle English *thinne,* Old English *thynne.*] **—thin·ly** *adv.* **—thin·ness** *n.*

thin air *n.* A state of being invisible: *vanished into thin air.*

thine (thīn) *pron.* Absolute form of *thy. Archaic & Poetic.* **1.** Belonging to thee; the one or ones belonging to thee: *Thine is the kingdom.* **2.** Used instead of *thy* before an initial vowel or *h*: *thine enemy.* [Middle English *thin,* Old English *thīn.*]

thin-film *adj.* Designating or pertaining to an electronic device based on thin layers of metal or semiconductor deposited on a substrate.

thing (thing) *n.* **1.** Anything that can be perceived, known, or thought to have a separate existence; an entity. **2.** The real substance of that which is indicated as distinguished from its appearances or from the name, word, or symbol denoting it. **3.** An entity actually existing in space or time, in constrast to one merely postulated; an object or fact. **4.** An inanimate object as distinct from a living being: *seems more interested in things than in people.* **5.** A living being. Used to emphasise an attitude of pity, affection, contempt, or reproach: *the poor thing.* **6. a.** *Law.* That which can be possessed or owned as distinguished from a person. **b.** *Plural.* Possessions; belongings. **7.** An article of clothing; garment. **8.** *Plural.* The equipment needed for an activity or purpose: *Where are my sewing things?* **9.** An object or entity that cannot or need not be named specifically: *What's this thing for?* **10. a.** An act, deed, or achievement: *expects great things of us; I hope I've done the right thing.* **b.** A product of work: *likes making things with his hands.* **11.** A thought, notion, or statement: *What a funny thing to say!* **12.** A piece of information. **13.** An example or representative of a class: *the latest thing in home computers.* **14. a.** A matter to be dealt with; a concern: *a lot of things on her mind.* **b.** A point, factor, or reason: *and for another thing, it's far too expensive.* **15.** *Plural.* **a.** The general state of affairs; conditions: *How are things?* **b.** A particular or prevailing situation: *helped me to see things differently.* **16.** A characteristic; a particular feature: *one of the things I like about her.* **17.** A turn of events; a circumstance: *the nicest thing that's happened all day.* **18. a.** An illogical feeling or preoccupation; an obsession: *has a thing about cats.* **b.** Something to which undue importance is given: *no need to make such a thing of it.* **19.** *Slang.* An activity uniquely suitable and satisfying to one: *doing his thing.* **—be on to a good thing.** *Informal.* To be in a favourable position to exploit an opportunity. **—know a thing or two.** To have considerable knowledge or skill, especially as a result of long experience. **—see** or **hear things.** To have hallucinations. **—the thing.** **1.** What is conventionally regarded as proper or correct: *His behaviour wasn't quite the thing.* **2.** What is most important or most necessary: *The great thing is to keep on trying.* **3.** What is most fashionable; the rage: *streaked hair was the thing last year.* **4.** The point at issue: *The thing is, do you think he'll believe it?* [Middle English *thing,* Old English *thing,* creature, thing, deed, assembly, from Germanic *thingam* (unattested).]

thing·a·ma·bob, thing·um·a·bob (thíng-ə-mi-bob, -mə-) *n. Informal.* Something for which the exact name has been forgotten or is not known. Also called "thingamajig", "thingumajig", "thingummy". [Whimsical formation from THING.]

thing-in-it·self (thíng-in-it-sélf) *n., pl.* **things-in-themselves** (thíngz-in-t͟həm-sélvz). An ultimate metaphysical reality conceived by Kant as beyond the perception of human senses and thought; a noumenon.

think (thingk) *v.* **thought** (thawt), **thinking, thinks.** *—tr.* **1.** To have as a thought; formulate in the mind: *think great thoughts.* **2. a.** To reason about or reflect on; ponder: *Think how complex language is.* Often used with *through* or *over*: *Think the matter through.* **b.** To consider carefully: *Think what you need to bring.* Often used with *out.* **3.** To judge or regard; look upon: *I think it only fair.* **4.** To believe; suppose: *I think it is true.* **5. a.** To have in mind; plan or intend: *I think I'll go to bed. We thought to arrive early but couldn't.* **b.** To expect; anticipate: *I don't think you'll have any trouble.* **6.** To remember; call to mind: *I can't think now what his name was.* **7. a.** To visualise; imagine: *Think what a difference it would make.* **b.** To fathom; understand: *can't think why he did it.* **8.** To bring into a specified condition by mental activity: *She thought herself into a terror of going.* **9.** To be sufficiently thoughtful or attentive: *didn't think to say goodbye.* **10.** To have one's thoughts centred on; think largely or exclusively in terms of. *—intr.* **1. a.** To exercise the power of reason; conceive of ideas, draw inferences, and use judgment. **b.** To turn over ideas; ponder; reflect. **2.** To weigh the idea; consider the matter: *Think before you answer.* Often used with *about* or *of*: *They are thinking of moving.* **3.** To recall a thought or image to mind: *can't think of his name; think back to last summer.* **4.** To believe; suppose: *Do you think so?* **5.** To dispose the mind in a specified way: *Think rich.* **—think aloud.** To say what one is thinking. **—think better of.** To decide against after reconsidering. **—think nothing of.** To regard as routine or usual. **—think of.** **1.** To regard in the specified way; have as one's opinion of: *always thought of him as reasonable; What do you think of the latest offer?* **2.** To value or approve to the specified extent: *don't think much of that idea.* **3.** To have care or consideration for; be mindful of: *Think of your future.* **4.** To hit on the idea: *never thought of phoning the police.* **—think twice.** To weigh something carefully. **—think up.** To devise or invent.
~n. An act of thinking. [Think, thought, thought; Middle English *thenken, thoughte, thought,* Old English *thencan, thōhte, gethōht.*]

think·a·ble (thíngkəb'l) *adj.* Fit to be considered; conceivable; possible. **—think·a·bly** *adv.*

think·er (thíngkər) *n.* **1.** A person who devotes his time to thinking or is especially capable at thinking. **2.** A person who thinks or reasons in a specified way: *a careful thinker.*

think·ing (thíngking) *n.* **1.** Mental activity; thought. **2.** A way of reasoning or regarding a subject; judgment: *not to my thinking a good idea; the government's thinking on inflation.*
~adj. Characterised by thoughtfulness; rational: *a thinking animal.*

think tank, think-tank (thíngk-tangk) *n.* An institution or group of people established by a government, business, or other organisation to undertake detailed study of particular issues or problems.

thin·ner (thínnər) *n.* A liquid, such as turpentine, mixed with paint to reduce viscosity for ease in application.

thin-skinned (thín-skínd) *adj.* **1.** Having a thin rind or skin. **2.** Oversensitive, especially to reproach or insult.

thio–, thi– *comb. form. Chemistry.* Indicates a compound containing a divalent sulphur atom, especially one in which sulphur has replaced oxygen; for example, **thiophene, thiol.** [From Greek *theion,* sulphur.]

thi·o·car·bam·ide (thī́-ō-kárbə-mīd) *n.* **Thiourea** *(see).*

thi·o·cy·an·ic acid (thī́-ō-sī-ánnik) *n.* An unstable weak acid, HSCN, existing as a colourless gas or white solid.

thi·o·e·ther (thī́-ō-éethər) *n.* Any of various organic compounds containing sulphur and having the general formula RSR′, where R and R′ are organic groups. [THIO- + ETHER.]

Thi·o·kol (thī́-ō-kol, -ə- || -kōl) *n.* A trademark for any of various polysulphide polymers in the form of liquids, water dispersions, and rubbers used in seals and sealants.

thi·ol (thī́-ol || -ōl) *n.* Any of various organic compounds containing sulphur and having the general formula RSH, where R is an organic group. Also called "mercaptan". [THI(O)- + -OL.]

thion– *comb. form.* Indicates sulphur; for example, **thionine.** [From Greek *theion,* sulphur.]

thi·o·nine (thī́-ə-nīn, -ō-) *n.* Also **thi·o·nin** (-nin). A crystalline thiazene derivative used as a violet dye in microscopy. [THION- + -INE.]

thi·o·nyl (thī́-ənil) *adj.* Of, pertaining to, or containing the divalent group SO. [THION- + -YL.]

thi·o·pen·tone sodium (thī́-ō-pén-tōn) *n.* Also **thi·o·pen·tal sodium** (-pent'l). A hygroscopic powder, $C_{11}H_{17}N_2O_2SNa$, injected intravenously as a general anaesthetic. Also called "sodium pentothal", and "Pentothal Sodium", a trademark. [From THIO- + PENTA-.]

thi·o·phen (thī́-ō-fen, -ə-) *n.* Also **thi·o·phene** (-feen). A colourless liquid, C_4H_4S, used as a solvent. [THIO- + PHEN(O)- + -ENE.]

thi·o·sin·a·mine (thī́-ō-sínnə-meen, -ə-, -sin-ámmin) *n.* A white crystalline substance occurring in mustard oil, $CH_2{:}CHCH_2NH\ CSNH_2$, used in organic synthesis. Also called "1-allyl-2-thiourea". [THIO- + *sin-,* from Latin *sinapis,* mustard + AMINE.]

thi·o·sul·phate (thī́-ō-súlfayt, -ə-) *n.* A salt of thiosulphuric acid.

thi·o·sul·phu·ric acid (thī́-ō-sul-féwr-ik, -ə-) *n.* An acid, $H_2S_2O_3$, formed by the replacement of an oxygen atom by a sulphur atom in sulphuric acid, known only in solution or by its salts and esters.

thi·o·u·ra·cil (thī́-ō-yo͝or-ə-sil) *n.* A white crystalline substance, $C_4H_4N_2OS$, used in the treatment of hyperthyroidism. [THIO- + URACIL.]

thi·o·u·re·a (thī́-ō-yo͝or-i-ə, -yo͞o-réer, -rée-ə) *n.* A white, lustrous crystalline compound, $(NH_2)_2CS$, used in photography, photocopying paper, and various organic syntheses. Also called "thiocarbamide". [THIO- + UREA.]

Thí·ra (théerə). Also **San·to·ri·ni** (sántə-réeni). Southernmost of the Cyclades islands in the Aegean Sea, Greece. It is the remains of an ancient volcano. Excavations in the 1960s revealed remains of Thēra, a rich Minoan settlement.

third (thurd) *n.* **1.** The ordinal number three in a series. Also written 3rd. **2.** One of three equal parts. **3.** *Music.* **a.** In a diatonic scale, a note three degrees above or below any given note; especially, the third note of a scale. **b.** The interval between two such notes. **c.** The harmonic combination of these notes. **4.** *British.* An honours degree of the third and usually lowest class. **5.** The gear immediately above second in a motor vehicle transmission.
~adv. Also **third·ly** (thúrdli) (for sense 2). **1.** In the third place, rank, or order. **2.** Used to precede the third topic in a list. [Middle English *thride, thirde,* Old English *third(d)a, thridda.*] **—third** *adj.*

third class *n.* **1.** The group or class that is next below the second in quality, value, or the like. **2.** The class of accommodation on a train or other means of transport ranking next below second class and usually of the lowest level of luxury and price. **3.** A class of mail in Canada and the United States comprising unsealed printed matter other than newspapers and magazines. **—third-class** (thúrd-klaass || -klåss) *adj. & adv.*

third degree *n.* Rough treatment or torture of a prisoner, to obtain information or a confession.

third-de·gree burn (thúrd-di-grée) *n.* A severe burn in which the epidermis and dermis are destroyed and the tissues below are also damaged. No longer in technical usage.

third dimension *n.* The dimension of depth or thickness distinguishing an object or representation from an object or representation that exists just in one plane.

Third Estate *n. Sometimes small* **t,** *small* **e.** The third-highest social order in a country; specifically, the commons in contrast to the nobility and clergy. See **First Estate, Fourth Estate, Second Estate.**

third eyelid *n.* The **nictitating membrane** *(see).*

Third International *n.* See **International.**

third man *n.* In cricket: **1.** A deep fielding position behind and to the off side of the batsman's wicket. **2.** A player in this position.

Third Order *n.* A confraternity of lay people associated with any of various religious orders of the Roman Catholic Church.

third party *n.* **1.** *Law.* A person or party other than the two principals in a transaction, agreement, or case. **2.** A political party organised as opposition to the existing parties in a two-party system.

third-par·ty (thúrd-párti) *adj.* Providing insurance cover against liability arising from accident to other persons or their property.

third person *n. Grammar.* The form of a pronoun or verb used in referring to a person or thing other than the speaker or the one spoken to.

third rail *n.* An extra rail through which the current runs to power the train on some electric railways. **—third-rail** *adj.*

third-rate (thúrd-ráyt, -rayt) *adj.* Of very poor quality; distinctly inferior.

PRONUNCIATION KEY

a, trap; aa, father; ai, fair; ar, star; aw, lawn; ay, play; b, bb, stab; rubber; ch, church; ck, ticket; d, dd, dead; ladder; e, dress; ee, bee; er, defer; ew, few; ewr, pure; ə, about; ər, letter; f, ff, fife; differ; g, gg, giggle; h, hat; i, kit; ī, price; īr, fire; j, judge; k, kick; l, ll, let; 'l, needle; m, mm, man; n, nn, no; 'n, sudden; ng, thing; o, lot; ō, no; o͝o, foot; o͞o, shoe; oor, poor; ow, cow; owr, hour; oy, boy; p, pp, pepper; r, rr, red; s, ss, sauce; sh, ship; t, tt, totter; th, thick; t͟h, this; smooth; u, cut; ur, turn; v, vv, valve; w, wet; y, yes; z, zz, zebra; zh, vision; pleasure

IN FOREIGN WORDS:

aN, oN, Saint-Saëns; hl, Llanelli; Hluhluwe; kh, loch; lough; Khaled

STRESS MARK:

ín-sīt, insight; in-sī́t, incite

third reading *n.* In passing a law in a legislative body: **1.** In Britain, the final stage of discussion of a bill, following the report stage, during its passage through either House of Parliament. **2.** In the United States, the final reading of a bill before voting.
Third Reich. See **Reich.**
Third Republic *n.* **1.** The French republic and government from the fall of the Commune (1871) until the German occupation (1940). **2.** The period of this republic's existence.
third sex *n.* Homosexuals collectively. Preceded by *the.*
Third World *n.* **1.** The economically underdeveloped or developing countries of Africa, Asia, and Latin America. **2.** These countries when considered as politically non-aligned with the Communist or non-Communist blocs. Preceded by *the.*
thirst (thurst) *n.* **1. a.** The sensation of dryness in the mouth related to a need or desire to drink. **b.** A need or desire to drink. **c.** The physical condition of dehydration produced by a lack of water: *died of thirst.* **2.** An insistent desire; a craving.
~*intr.v.* **thirsted, thirsting, thirsts. 1.** To feel a need to drink. **2.** To have a strong craving; yearn. Used with *for.* —See Synonyms at **yearn.** [Middle English *thurst, thirst,* Old English *thurst.*]
thirst·y (thúrsti) *adj.* **-ier, -iest. 1.** Desiring or needing to drink. **2.** Arid; parched. **3.** Craving; feeling a strong desire: *thirsty for news.* **4.** Causing thirst: *thirsty work.* **5.** *Informal.* Using or needing a lot of petrol: *a thirsty engine.* **—thirst·i·ly** *adv.* **—thirst·i·ness** *n.*
thir·teen (thúr-téen) *n.* **1. a.** The cardinal number that is one more than twelve. **b.** A symbol representing this, such as 13 or XIII. **2.** A set made up of thirteen persons or things. **3.** The thirteenth in a series. **4.** A size, as in clothing, designated as thirteen. [Middle English *thrittene,* Old English *thrēotīne* : THREE + -TEEN.] **—thir·teen** *adj.* & *pron.*
thir·teenth (thúr-téenth) *n.* **1.** The ordinal number 13 in a series. Also written 13th. **2.** One of 13 equal parts. **—thir·teenth** *adj.* & *adv.*
thir·ti·eth (thúrti-əth, -ith) *n.* **1.** The ordinal number 30 in a series. Also written 30th. **2.** One of 30 equal parts. **—thir·ti·eth** *adj.* & *adv.*
thir·ty (thúrti) *n., pl.* **-ties. 1. a.** The cardinal number that is 10 more than 20. **b.** A symbol representing this, such as 30 or XXX. **2.** A set made up of 30 persons or things. **3.** The thirtieth in a series. **4.** A size, as in clothing, designated as 30. **5.** *Plural.* **a.** The range of numbers from 30 to 39, considered as a range of age, price, temperature, or the like. **b.** The years numbered 30 to 39 in a century. Also used adjectivally: *a thirties film.* [Middle English *thritty,* Old English *thrītig* : THREE + -TY.] **—thir·ty** *adj.* & *pron.*
Thir·ty-nine Articles (thúrti-nīn) *pl.n.* A set of points representing the traditional doctrinal position of the Church of England, to which all clergymen formally subscribe.
thir·ty-two·mo (thúrti-tōō-mō) *n., pl.* **-mos. 1.** The page size ($3^1/_2$ by $5^1/_2$ inches) that results when a printers' sheet is folded into 32 equal sections. **2.** A book composed of pages of this size. Also written 32mo.
Thirty Years' War *n.* A series of wars fought mainly in central and western Europe (1618–48), originally for religious reasons but increasingly involving political issues.
this (thiss; *weak form in certain fixed phrases* thəss) *adj., pl.* **these** (theez). **1.** Being the one just mentioned or present in space, time, or thought. **2.** Being the one nearer or more obvious than another, or compared with another. **3.** Being about to be stated or described: *began with these words.* **4.** *Informal.* A certain. Used for emphasis or vividness in describing one not previously mentioned: *This old tramp came up and asked me for some money.*
~*pron., pl.* **these** (theez). **1.** The person or thing present or nearby in space, time, or thought. **2.** The person, thing, or idea just mentioned or understood. **3.** What is about to be stated. **4.** The one that is nearer than another or the one compared with the other: *this one and that.* **5.** This period, point of time, or incident: *died soon after this; with this, he stormed out.*
~*adv. Informal.* To this extent; so: *a book about this thick.* [This, these; Middle English *this, thes,* Old English *thes* or *thēs, thēos, this* (masculine, feminine, neuter singular).] **—this·ness** *n.*
Usage: Some people argue that *this* should be used only when the reference is forwards (*I would like to say this*), and *that* should be used when the reference is backwards (*That was the reason I was late*); but while there is a genuine restriction on the use of *that,* which has backward reference only (you cannot say *I would like to ask that,* referring to something which is about to be asked), there is no basis in usage for a restriction on *this,* which is frequently used for reference backwards as well as forwards (as in *This has always been a problem*).
this·tle (thíss'l) *n.* **1.** Any of numerous weedy plants, chiefly of the genera *Cirsium, Carduus,* or *Onopordum,* having prickly leaves and usually purplish flowers surrounded by prickly bracts. **2.** Any of various similar or related plants. [Middle English *thistel,* Old English *thistel,* from Germanic *thistilaz* (unattested).]
this·tle·down (thíss'l-down) *n.* The silky down attached to the seeds of a thistle.
thith·er (thíthər || *Scottish and U.S.* thíthər) *adv. Archaic & Literary.* To or towards that place; in that direction; there: *hither and thither.*
~*adj. Archaic & Literary.* Located or being on the more distant side; farther. [Middle English *thither, thider,* Old English *thider, thæder.*]
thith·er·wards (thíthər-wərdz || thíthər-, -wawrdz) *adv.* Also **thith·er·ward** (-wərd). *Archaic & Literary.* In that direction; thither.
thix·o·tro·py (thíks-ə-trōpi, -ō-, thik-sóttrəpi) *n.* The property exhibited by certain gels, such as emulsion paints, of liquefying when stirred or shaken and returning to the semisolid state upon standing. [Greek *thixis,* "touching", from *thinganein,* to touch + -TROPY.] **—thix·o·trop·ic** (-tróppik, -trṓpik) *adj.*
tho, tho' (thō) *conj. Chiefly U.S.* Though.
thole¹ (thōl) *tr.v.* **tholed, tholing, tholes.** *Scottish & Archaic.* To endure; bear. [Middle English *tholen,* Old English *tholian,* to endure.]
thole² *n.* Also **thole·pin** (thṓl-pin). **1.** Either of a pair of wooden pegs set in the gunwale of a boat to serve as an oarlock. **2.** A peg or pin used to hold something in place. [Middle English *tholle,* Old English *thol(l).*]
thol·os (thól-oss, thṓl-) *n., pl.* **tholoi** (-oy). A dome-shaped tomb of the type associated with the Mycenaean culture of ancient Greece. [Greek *tholos*†.]
Tho·mism (tṓm-iz'm) *n.* The theological and philosophical system of St. Thomas Aquinas, which became the basis of scholasticism. **—Tho·mist** (-ist) *n.* & *adj.* **—Tho·mis·tic** (tō-místik) *adj.*
Thomp·son submachine gun (tomps'n) *n.* A type of .45-calibre submachine gun. Also informally called "Tommy gun". [After its co-inventor, John *Thompson* (1860–1940), U.S. army officer.]
Thom·son effect (tóm-s'n) *n.* A thermoelectric effect in which a temperature gradient within a solid material is caused by an electrical potential gradient. [After W. *Thomson,* Lord KELVIN.]
thong (thong || *U.S. also* thawng) *n.* **1.** A narrow strip of leather or other material used for binding or lashing. **2.** *U.S. & Australian.* A **flip-flop** *(see).* [Middle English *thong,* Old English *thwong, thwang.*]
Thor (thor). *Norse Mythology.* The god of thunder. [Old Norse *thōrr,* thunder.]
tho·rac·ic (thaw-rássik, tho-, thə- || thō-) *adj.* Of, relating to, or situated in or near the thorax. [Medieval Latin *thoracicus,* from Greek. See **thorax, -ic.**]
thoracic duct *n.* The main duct of the lymphatic system, ascending along the spinal cord and discharging into veins in the neck.
tho·ra·cot·o·my (tháw-rə-kóttəmi || thō-) *n., pl.* **-mies.** Surgical incision of the chest wall. [Latin *thōrāx* (stem *thōrāc-*), THORAX + -TOMY.]
tho·rax (tháw-raks || thṓ-) *n., pl.* **thoraces** (-rə-seez, -ráy-) or **-raxes. 1.** *Anatomy.* The part of the human body between the neck and the diaphragm, partially encased by the ribs; the chest. **2.** A corresponding part in other animals. **3.** The second or middle region of the body of an arthropod, in insects bearing the legs and wings. [Latin *thōrāx,* from Greek *thōrax*† (stem *thōrak-*), breastplate, coat of mail, chest covering.]
tho·rite (tháw-rīt || thṓ-) *n.* A vitreous brownish-yellow or black thorium ore, essentially $ThSiO_4$. [THOR(IUM) + -ITE.]
tho·ri·um (tháw-ri-əm || thṓ-) *n. Symbol* **Th** A silvery-white metallic element with 13 radioactive isotopes only one of which, thorium 232, occurs naturally. It is used in magnesium alloys and isotope 232 is a potential source of nuclear energy. Atomic number 90, atomic weight 232.038, approximate melting point 1,700°C, approximate boiling point 4,000°C, approximate relative density 11.66, valency 4. [New Latin, after THOR.]
thorium dioxide *n.* A heavy white powder, ThO_2, used mainly in ceramics, gas mantles, and nuclear fuels. Also called "thoria".
thorium series *n. Physics.* A radioactive series by which thorium-232 decays through intermediate nuclides to lead-208.
thorn (thorn) *n.* **1.** *Botany.* A modified branch in the form of a sharp, woody structure. **2.** Any of various shrubs, trees, or woody plants bearing such structures, such as the hawthorn. **3.** Loosely, any of various sharp, spiny protuberances; a prickle or spine. **4.** A source of continual annoyance or distress: *a thorn in one's flesh.* **5.** A runic letter originally representing the sounds (th) and (th) and used in writing early Germanic languages, including Old English. It now survives only in Icelandic, representing the sound (th). [Middle English *thorn,* Old English *thorn,* thorn, thornbush.]
thorn apple *n.* Any of various plants of the genus *Datura,* especially, *D. stramonium,* having white flowers and spiny fruits.
thorn·back (thórn-bak) *n.* Either of two rays, *Raja clavata,* of European waters, or *Platyrhinoidis triseriata,* of Pacific waters, having spines along the back.
thorn·bill (thórn-bil) *n.* **1.** Any of various South American hummingbirds of the genus *Chalcostigma* and related genera, having a thornlike bill. **2.** Any of various Australian songbirds of the genus *Acanthiza* and related genera, having short sharp bills.
thorn·y (thórni) *adj.* **-ier, -iest. 1.** Full of or covered with thorns or thorny plants. **2.** Thornlike; spiny. **3.** Painfully controversial or difficult to resolve; vexatious: *a thorny problem.* **—thorn·i·ness** *n.*
tho·ron (tháw-ron || thṓ-) *n.* A radioactive isotope of radon having a half-life of 54.5 seconds and produced by the disintegration of thorium. [THOR(IUM) + -ON.]
thor·ough (thúrrə || *U.S.* thúrrō) *adj.* **1.** Fully done; completed in every respect or detail: *a thorough search.* **2.** Completely as described; absolute; utter: *a thorough rogue.* **3.** Painstakingly accurate or careful: *a thorough worker.* [Middle English *thorow,* from *thorugh* (adverb), through, Old English *thuruh,* from *thurh,* THROUGH.] **—thor·ough·ly** *adv.* **—thor·ough·ness** *n.*
thor·ough·bred (thúrrə-bred || *U.S.* thúrrō-) *adj.* **1.** Bred of pure stock; purebred; unmixed. **2.** *Capital* **T.** Pertaining or belonging to the Thoroughbred breed of horses. **3.** Thoroughly trained, accomplished, or educated; well-bred. **4.** Marked by characteristics associated with a thoroughbred animal; especially, elegant, high-spirited, or distinguished: *a thoroughbred sports car.*
~*n.* **1.** A purebred or pedigree animal. **2.** *Capital* **T.** A horse of a

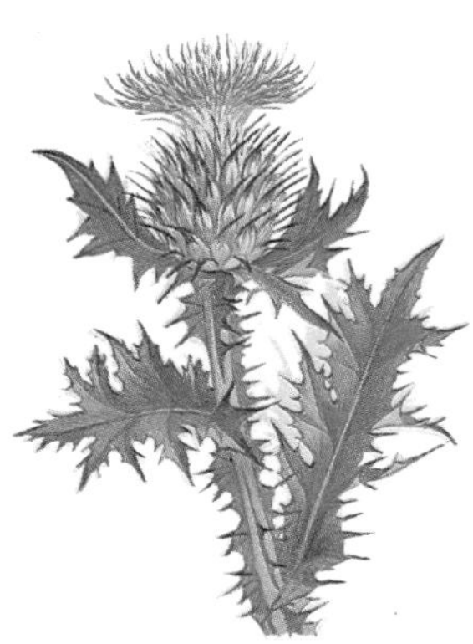

thistle *A prickly weed that seems to flourish in any habitat. The spear thistle, shown here, grows up to 1.8 metres (6 feet) tall.*

breed originating from a cross of Arab stallions with English mares and used widely in horseracing. **3.** A well-bred person.

thor·ough·fare (thúrrə-fair || *U.S.* thúrrō-) *n.* **1.** A public way or path from one place to another. **2.** Right of access or passage; public right of way: *no thoroughfare.* **3.** *Chiefly U.S.* A passage between two bodies of water, such as a canal or strait. [Middle English *thurghfare* : *thurgh,* THROUGH + FARE (passage).]

thor·ough·go·ing (thúrrə-gṓ-ing, -gō- || *U.S.* thúrrō-) *adj.* **1.** Very thorough; complete. **2.** Unmitigated; unqualified; out-and-out.

thor·ough·paced (thúrrə-payst || *U.S.* thúrrō-) *adj.* **1. a.** Trained in all paces or gaits. Said of a horse. **b.** Thoroughly trained. **2.** Thoroughgoing.

thor·ough·pin (thúrrə-pin || *U.S.* thúrrō-) *n.* An abnormal swelling on either side of the hock joint of horses and related animals. [From THOROUGH (passing through); it appears as if a pin were piercing the joint.]

thorp (thorp) *n. Archaic.* A hamlet or village. [Middle English *thorp,* Old English *throp, thorp.*]

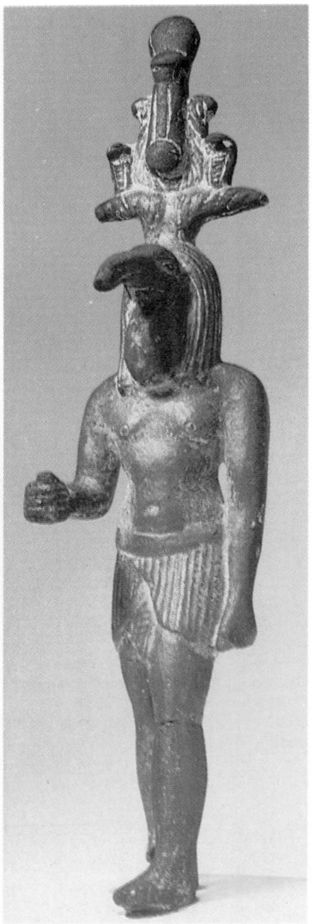

Thoth *In ancient Egypt, Thoth was the scribe of the gods, the inventor of numbers and measurer of time, from which he became the god of wisdom and magic. He was also the moon god and was usually, as here, represented with the head of an ibis.*

Thors·havn (tórs-ha-wən). Capital and chief town of the Faeroes, situated on the island of Strømø.

those. Plural of **that.**

Thoth (thōth, tōt). *Egyptian Mythology.* The god of the Moon and of wisdom and learning, whose sacred bird was the ibis. He is represented with the head and neck of an ibis, or as a baboon.

thou[1] (thow || *regional weak form* tha) *pron. Archaic, Poetic, & Regional.* The second person singular pronoun in the nominative case. **1.** Used to represent the person or personal being who is spoken to: *"Thou wilt never get thee a husband"* (Shakespeare). **2.** Used in apposition before a noun to indicate address: *"Thou drone, thou snail, thou slug, thou sot!"* (Shakespeare). [Thou, thee, thy or thine; Middle English *thu, the(e), thi* (before a consonant) and *thin* (before a vowel), Old English *thu* (or *thū*), *the* (or *thē*), *thīn.*]

thou[2] (thow) *n., pl.* **thous** or **thou. 1.** *Slang.* A thousand. **2.** One thousand of an inch (0.0254 millimetre).

though (thō || *Scottish* thō) *conj.* **1.** Despite the fact that; while; although: *Though I failed, I'm glad I tried.* **2.** Conceding or supposing that; even if: *Though I may fail, I will still try.* **3.** However; and yet: *He's the director, though you'd never think so to look at him.* ~*adv. Informal.* However; nevertheless. **—as though.** As if. [Middle English *thoh, though,* from Old Norse *thō.*]

Usage: The use of *though* as an adverb at the end of a sentence is very common in informal speech (*He did, though*); but formal speech and writing prefer the use of such words as *however* or *nevertheless.* See also **although.**

thought (thawt). Past tense and past participle of **think.** ~*n.* **1. a.** The act or process of thinking; cogitation. **b.** The faculty or power of reasoning. **2. a.** An object of thinking; what one is thinking about: *lofty thoughts.* **b.** A product of thinking; an idea, opinion, or judgment. **3.** The intellectual activity or output of a particular time, place, or group. **4.** Serious consideration: *give the matter some thought.* **5.** Heed; regard: *with no thought for his life.* **6.** Intention; purpose. **7.** Expectation; hope; anticipation. **8.** A trifle; a bit: *a thought more considerate.* —See Synonyms at **idea.** [Middle English *thought,* a thought, Old English *(ge)thōht.*]

thought·ful (tháwtf'l) *adj.* **1.** Given to thought; contemplative; reflective. **2.** Well thought-out: *a thoughtful essay.* **3.** Careful; heedful. **4.** Showing regard for others; considerate. **—thought·ful·ly** *adv.* **—thought·ful·ness** *n.*

Synonyms: *thoughtful, considerate, indulgent, solicitous.*

thought·less (tháwt-ləss, -liss) *adj.* **1.** Showing lack of thought, as: **a.** Careless; unthinking. **b.** Reckless; rash. **c.** Inconsiderate; inattentive. **2.** Unable to think. —See Synonyms at **careless. —thought·less·ly** *adv.* **—thought·less·ness** *n.*

thought-out (tháwt-ówt) *adj.* Produced or developed through the application of thought: *a well thought-out plan.*

thought-pro·vok·ing (tháwt-prə-vōking) *adj.* Stimulating serious or deep thinking: *a thought-provoking lecture.*

thought reading *n.* **Mind reading** *(see).*

thought transference *n.* **Telepathy** *(see).*

thou·sand (thówz'nd) *n., pl.* **thousand** (for senses 1, 2) or **-sands** (for sense 3). **1.** The cardinal number written 1,000, 1000, 10^3, or in Roman numerals M. **2. a.** A thousand monetary units, as of pounds: *He won a thousand at the races.* **b.** A banknote or coin having a denomination of a thousand. **3.** *Often plural.* An indefinitely large number: *thousands of people.* [Middle English *thousande,* Old English *thūsend.*] **—thou·sand** *adj. & pron.*

Thousand and One Nights *pl.n.* The **Arabian Nights** *(see).*

thousand island dressing *n.* A salad dressing made of mayonnaise with chilli sauce or ketchup and various seasonings. [Probably after THOUSAND ISLANDS.]

Thousand Islands. A group of more than 1,800 islands and 3,000 shoals in the St. Lawrence river, stretching for about 80 kilometres (50 miles) east of Lake Ontario. The largest is Wolfe Island.

thou·sandth (thówz'nth) *n.* **1.** The ordinal number thousand in a series. Also written 1,000th. **2.** One of a thousand equal parts. **—thou·sandth** *adj. & adv.*

thp thrust horsepower.

Thrace (thrayss). Region of southeastern Europe, now mostly in northeastern Greece, but also occupying parts of southern Bulgaria and European Turkey. It was colonised by Greeks in the seventh century B.C., and later passed successively to the Roman, Byzantine, and Ottoman Empires.

Thra·cian (thráy-sh'n, -shi-ən) *n.* **1.** A native or inhabitant of Thrace. **2.** The extinct Indo-European language related to Phrygian spoken by the ancient inhabitants of Thrace. **—Thra·cian** *adj.*

Thrale (thrayl), **Hester Lynch** (1741–1821). British literary figure, known for her friendship with Samuel Johnson which she accounted in her *Anecdotes of the Late Samuel Johnson* (1786).

thrall (thrawl) *n.* Also **thral·dom** (-dəm), *U.S.* **thrall·dom** (for sense 3). **1.** One who is in bondage or servitude; a slave or serf. **2.** One who is a slave to some craving or other powerful influence. **3.** Servitude; bondage. **4.** A state of being enthralled or transfixed. [Middle English *thral(l),* Old English *thrǣl,* from Old Norse *thræll,* from Germanic *thrah-* (unattested), to run.]

thrash (thrash) *v.* **thrashed, thrashing, thrashes.** —*tr.* **1.** To beat or flog with or as with a whip. **2.** To swing or strike wildly in a manner suggestive of the action of a flail: *thrashing her arms about.* **3.** To defeat utterly; vanquish. **4.** To thresh. **5.** *Nautical.* To sail (a boat) against opposing winds or tides. —*intr.* **1.** To move the body or a bodily part wildly or violently; lash out. Usually used with *about.* **2.** To strike or flail; strike out. **3.** To thresh. **4.** *Nautical.* To make one's way against opposing tides or winds. **—thrash out. 1.** To discuss fully and bring to a conclusion. **2.** To produce (a plan or agreement, for example) by thorough discussion. ~*n.* **1.** The act of thrashing. **2.** *Informal.* An occasion of thrashing something out; a meeting. [Originally a variant of THRESH.] **—thrash·er** *n.*

thrash·er[1] (thráshər) *n.* Any of various New World thrushlike songbirds of the genus *Toxostoma,* having a long tail, a long, curved beak, and, in several species, a spotted breast. [Perhaps a variant of dialectal *thrusher,* from THRUSH (songbird).]

thrasher[2]. Variant of **thresher** (shark).

thrash·ing (thráshing) *n.* A severe beating; a whipping.

thra·son·i·cal (thrə-sónnik'l, thray-) *adj.* Boastful. [Latin *Thrasō* (stem *Thrasōn-*), a bragging character in Terence's comedy *Eunuchus,* from Greek *Thrasōn,* from *thrasus,* bold, brave.] **—thra·son·i·cal·ly** *adv.*

thrawn (thrawn) *adj. Northern British.* **1.** Crooked; twisted; out of true. **2.** Cross; bad-tempered; perverse. [Middle English *thrawin,* twisted, from past participle of *thrawen,* to twist, turn, form Old English *thrāwan;* akin to THWART.]

thread (thred) *n.* **1. a.** A fine cord of a fibrous material, such as cotton or flax, made of two or more filaments twisted together, and used in needlework and the weaving of cloth. **b.** A piece of this material. **2.** A strand, or long thin piece of natural or manufactured material. **3.** Anything suggestive of the fineness or thinness of thread. **4.** Anything suggestive of the continuousness and sequence of thread: *the thread of an argument.* **5.** A helical or spiral ridge on a screw, nut, or bolt. **6.** *Plural. U.S. Slang.* Clothes. ~*v.* **threaded, threading, threads.** —*tr.* **1.** To pass one end of a thread through the eye of (a needle or similar device). **2.** To string (beads or similar objects) onto a thread. **3. a.** To pass or feed (thread or tape, for example) through or into something. **b.** To pass or feed tape, film, or similar material through or into (a machine or camera, for example). **4. a.** to pass cautiously through. **b.** To make (one's way) cautiously, as through a crowded or narrow place. **5.** To occur throughout; pervade. **6.** To machine a thread on (a screw, nut, or bolt). —*intr.* **1.** To wind cautiously through obstacles or along a narrow path. **2.** To proceed by a winding course. **3.** To form a thread when dropped from a spoon, as boiling sugar syrup. [Middle English *thre(e)d,* Old English *thrǣd.*] **—thread·er** *n.* **—thread·like** *adj.*

thread·bare (thréd-bair) *adj.* **1.** Having the nap worn down so that the filling or warp threads show through; frayed or shabby. Said of cloth. **2.** Wearing old, shabby clothing. **3.** Hackneyed; stale. —See Synonyms at **trite. —thread·bare·ness** *n.*

thread·fin (thréd-fin) *n.* Any of various chiefly tropical marine fishes of the subfamily Polynemidae, having threadlike rays extending from the lower part of the pectoral fin.

thread mark *n.* A marking made in paper currency by a threading of coloured silk fibres to make counterfeiting difficult.

thread·worm (thréd-wurm) *n.* Any of various threadlike nematode worms, especially the **pinworm** *(see).*

thread·y (thréddi) *adj.* **-ier, -iest. 1.** Consisting of or resembling thread; fibrous. **2.** Tending to form threads, as a syrupy liquid does; viscid. **3.** *Medicine.* Weak and shallow. Said especially of a pulse. **4.** Lacking fullness of tone; thin; weak. **—thread·i·ness** *n.*

threat (thret) *n.* **1.** An expression of an intention to inflict pain, injury, evil, or punishment on a person or thing. **2.** An indication of the impending arrival or occurrence of something harmful or undesirable: *the threat of rain.* **3.** A person, thing, or idea regarded as a possible danger; a menace. ~*tr.v.* **threated, threating, threats.** *Archaic.* To threaten. [Middle English *thret,* Old English *thrēat,* oppression, use of force, threat.]

threat·en (thrétt'n) *v.* **-ened, -ening, -ens.** —*tr.* **1.** To express a threat against: *threatened him with dismissal.* **2.** To serve as a threat to; endanger; menace. **3.** To give signs or warning of; portend. **4.** To express as a threat. —*intr.* **1.** To express or use threats. **2.** To indicate danger or other harm. [Middle English, Old English *thrēatnian.*] **—threat·en·er** *n.* **—threat·en·ing·ly** *adv.*

Synonyms: *threaten, menace, intimidate.*

three (three) *n.* **1. a.** The cardinal number that is one more than two. **b.** A symbol representing this, such as 3, III, or iii. **2.** A set made up of three persons or things. **3. a.** The third in a series. **b.** A playing card marked with three pips. **4.** Three parts: *cut in three:* **5.** A size, as in clothing, designated as three. **6.** Three hours after midnight or midday. [Middle English *three*, Old English *thrī(e)*, *thrēo*.] —**three** *adj & pron.* —**three·fold** (-fōld) *adj. & adv.*

three-card trick (thrée-kárd) *n.* A trick or game in which participants try to guess which of three cards lying face downwards is the queen.

three-col·our (thrée-kúllər) *adj.* Designating a colour printing or photographic process in which three primary colours are transferred by three different plates or filters to a surface, reproducing all the colours of the subject matter.

three-cor·nered (thrée-kórnərd) *adj.* **1.** Triangular; tricorne: *a three-cornered hat.* **2.** Involving three contestants or parties. Said especially of an election: *a three-cornered fight.*

three-D (thrée-deé) *adj.* Three-dimensional. Also written *3-D.* ~*n.* A three-dimensional medium, display, or performance, especially a cinematic or graphic display. Also written *3-D.*

three-day event (thrée-dáy) *n.* An equestrian competition lasting three days, in which riders do a dressage test, ride over a cross-country course, and do a showjumping round.

three-day measles *n. Informal.* German measles.

three-deck·er (thrée-déckər) *n.* **1.** A ship having three decks; especially, one of a class of sail-powered warships with guns on three decks. **2.** Anything with three layers; especially, a sandwich having three slices of bread.

three-decker pulpit *n.* A form of pulpit found in English parish churches consisting of the pulpit proper surmounting a reading desk and the clerk's stall.

three-di·men·sion·al (thrée-dī-ménsh'n'l, -di-) *adj.* **1.** Of, pertaining to, having, or existing in three dimensions. **2.** Having or appearing to have extension in depth; three-D.

Three Graces *pl.n.* The **Graces** *(see).*

three-lane road (thrée-láyn) *n.* A road with three carriageways, one for vehicles going in each direction and one for overtaking vehicles going in either direction.

three-leafed (thrée-leéft) *adj.* Also **three-leaved** (-leévd). *Botany.* Divided into three leaflets: *a three-leafed clover.*

three-leg·ged race (thrée-légd, -léggid) *n.* A race in which pairs of people run side by side with their adjacent legs tied together.

three-line whip (thrée-līn) *n.* In the British Parliament, the strongest form of notice issued by the leaders of a political party, requiring its members to vote on a forthcoming issue. [From the three underlinings on the written notice, indicating the greatest urgency.]

three-mast·er (thrée-maástər ‖ -mástər) *n.* A ship, usually a schooner, with three masts.

three-mile limit (thrée-mīl) *n. International Law.* The outer limit of the area extending three miles out to sea from the coast of a country that constitutes that country's **territorial waters** *(see).*

three-pence (thréppənss, thríppənss, thrúppənss; *for sense 2* thré-pénss) *n., pl.* **threepence** or **-pences. 1.** A pre-decimal British coin worth three pennies. **2.** The sum of three pence.

three-pen·ny bit (thrép-ni, thrip-, thrúp-, -əni) *n.* A pre-decimal British coin, a threepence.

three-phase (thrée-fáyz) *adj. Electricity.* Designating or pertaining to an electrical supply with three different equal voltages that have the same frequency and differ in phase by 120°.

three-piece (thrée-peéss) *adj.* Made in or consisting of three parts or pieces: *a three-piece suit.*

three-ply (thrée-plī, -plī) *adj.* **1.** Consisting of three layers. **2.** Having three strands. Said of knitting wool.

three-point landing (thrée-poynt) *n.* An aeroplane landing in which the tailskid or tail wheel and the two forward wheels all touch the ground simultaneously; a perfect landing.

three-point turn *n.* A way of turning a vehicle in a confined space so that by moving first forwards then backwards then forwards, the vehicle ends up facing in the opposite direction.

three-quar·ter¹ (thrée-kwór-tər, kwáw-, -kór-, -káw-) *adj.* Pertaining to, consisting of, or showing three-fourths of something or extending to three-quarters of the full or normal length.

three-quarter² *n.* **1.** In Rugby football, any of four players who play in the three-quarter line. **2.** The position of such a player.

three-quarter binding *n.* A type of bookbinding in which the leather or fabric covering the spine extends onto the covers for one third of their width.

three-quarter line *n.* In Rugby football: **1.** The positions of right wing, left wing, inside centre, and outside centre. **2.** The players occupying these positions.

three-ring circus (thrée-ring) *n. Chiefly U.S.* **1.** A circus having simultaneous performances in three separate rings. **2.** A situation characterised by bewildering and varied activity.

three Rs *pl.n.* Reading, writing, and arithmetic, considered as the fundamentals of elementary education. [From the facetious spelling *reading, 'riting,* and *'rithmetic.*]

three·score (thrée-skór ‖ -skór) *adj.* Sixty; three times twenty. —**three·score** *n.*

three·some (thréss'm) *adj.* Consisting of or performed by three. ~*n.* **1.** A group of three persons. **2.** Any activity involving three persons; especially, a golf match in which one player competes against two others who alternate their play.

three-square (thrée-skwáir) *adj.* Having an equilateral triangular cross-section: *a three-square file.*

three-wheel·er (thrée-weél-ər, -hweél-) *n.* A vehicle such as a motor car or a tricycle, with three wheels.

threm·ma·tol·o·gy (thrémmə-tólləji) *n.* The scientific breeding of

domestic plants and animals. [Greek *thremma* (stem *thremmat-*), creature, nursling + -LOGY.]

thren·o·dy (thrénnədi) *n., pl.* **-dies.** A song of mourning or lamentation. [Greek *thrēnōidia : thrēnos,* dirge, lament + *ōidē,* song, ODE.] —**thre·no·di·al** (thri-nódi-əl, thre-), **thre·nod·ic** (-nóddik) *adj.* —**thren·o·dist** (thrénnədist) *n.*

thre·o·nine (thrée-ə-nīn, -ō-, -nin) *n.* A colourless crystalline amino acid, $C_4H_9NO_3$, derived from the hydrolysis of protein, and an essential component of the human diet. [Irregularly from *threo-,* probably an anagram of ERYTHRO- + -INE.]

thresh (thresh) *v.* **threshed, threshing, threshes.** —*tr.* **1. a.** To beat the stems and husks of (grain or cereal plants) with a machine or flail to separate the grain or seeds from the straw. **b.** To separate (grain or seed) in this manner. **2.** *Rare.* To beat severely; thrash. —*intr.* **1.** To thresh grain. **2.** To thrash about; toss. [Middle English *thresshen,* Old English *therscan.*]

thresh·er (thréshər) *n.* Also **thrash·er** (thráshər) (for sense 3). **1.** One who threshes. **2.** A threshing machine. **3.** Any of various large sharks of the genus *Alopias,* especially *A. vulpinus,* having a tail with a long, whiplike upper lobe.

thresh·ing machine (thréshing) *n.* A farm machine used in threshing grain or seed plants. Also called "thresher".

thresh·old (thrésh-hōld, -ōld) *n.* **1.** The piece of wood or stone placed beneath a door; a doorsill. **2.** An entrance or doorway. **3.** The outset; the verge; the beginning: *on the threshold of his career.* **4.** A point or level above which a specified phenomenon occurs and below which it does not: *a tax threshold.* **5.** The intensity below which a mental or physical stimulus cannot be perceived and can produce no response: *a low threshold of pain.* **6.** The value or intensity of a physical quantity that produces a specific effect in some system or device, and below which no effect occurs. Used adjectivally: *a threshold voltage.* ~*adj.* Of, pertaining to, or designating an agreement according to which wage increases are tied to the cost of living. [Middle English *thresshold,* Old English *therscold, threscold.*]

threw. Past tense of **throw.**

thrice (thrīss) *adv.* **1.** Three times. **2.** In a threefold quantity or degree. **3.** *Archaic.* Extremely; greatly. [Middle English *thries,* adverbial genitive of *thrie,* Old English *thriga, thriwa.*]

thrift (thrift) *n.* **1.** Wise economy in the management of money and other resources; frugality. **2.** Any of several densely tufted, chiefly European plants of the genus *Armeria;* especially, *A. maritima,* having rounded clusters of pink flowers. In this sense, also called "sea pink". [Middle English, prosperity, a flourishing, savings, from Old Norse, prosperity, from *thrīfask,* to THRIVE.]

thrift·y (thrifti) *adj.* **-ier, -iest. 1.** Wisely economical; frugal. **2.** Industrious and thriving; prosperous. **3.** *Archaic.* Growing vigorously. —See Synonyms at **sparing.** —**thrift·i·ly** *adv.* —**thrift·i·ness** *n.* —**thrift·less** *adj.*

thrill (thril) *v.* **thrilled, thrilling, thrills.** —*tr.* **1.** To cause to feel a sudden intense sensation; excite greatly. **2.** To give great pleasure to; delight. **3.** To cause to quiver or vibrate. —*intr.* **1.** To feel a sudden tingle of emotion. **2.** To quiver, tremble, or vibrate. ~*n.* **1.** A sensation of great excitement. **2.** A tingling or trembling passing through the body as a result of sudden emotion. **3.** An exciting quality or situation. **4.** *Pathology.* A slight vibration that accompanies a heart or vascular murmur, felt when the hand is placed on the chest wall. [Middle English *thrillen,* variant of *thirlen,* to pierce, Old English *thyrlian,* from *thyr(e)l,* hole.]

thrill·er (thríllər) *n.* **1.** One that thrills. **2.** A book, film, or play that is full of mystery and suspense.

thrill·ing (thrilling) *adj.* **1.** Extremely exciting. **2.** Vibrating or pulsating.

thrips (thrips) *n., pl.* **thrips.** Any of various small, often wingless insects of the order Thysanoptera, many of which are destructive to plants. [Latin, woodworm, from Greek *thrips†.*]

thrive (thrīv) *intr.v.* **thrived, throve** (thrōv) or **thrived** or **thriven** (thrívv'n), **thriving, thrives. 1.** To grow vigorously; flourish. **2.** To improve steadily, as in wealth or position; prosper. [Thrive, throve, thriven; Middle English *thrīven, throfe, thriven,* to increase, flourish, from Old Norse *thrīfask,* "to grasp for oneself", reflexive of *thrīfa†,* to seize.] —**thriv·er** *n.* —**thriv·ing·ly** *adv.*

thro', thro. Variant of **through.**

throat (thrōt) *n.* **1.** *Anatomy.* **a.** The part of the digestive tract that lies between the rear of the mouth and the oesophagus and includes the pharynx. **b.** The front part of the neck. **2.** *Botany.* The outer, expanded part of a tubular corolla. **3.** Any narrow passage or part shaped like the human throat: *the throat of a tennis racket.* —**jump down (someone's) throat.** To speak sharply and critically to. —**stick in (one's) throat.** *Informal.* To be difficult to express or accept. [Middle English *throte,* Old English *throte, throtu,* from Germanic *thrut-* (unattested).]

throat·lash (thrōt-lash) *n.* Also **throat·latch** (-lach). A strap passing under the neck of a horse or other animal for holding a bridle or halter in place.

throat microphone *n.* A small microphone that when held or fastened next to the throat is activated by vibrations of the larynx.

throat·y (thrōti) *adj.* **-ier, -iest.** Uttered or sounding as if uttered deep in the throat; guttural, hoarse, or husky. —**throat·i·ly** *adv.* —**throat·i·ness** *n.*

throb (throb) *intr.v.* **throbbed, throbbing, throbs. 1.** To beat rapidly or violently; pound. **2.** To vibrate, pulsate, or sound with a steady, pronounced rhythm. —See Synonyms at **pulsate.**

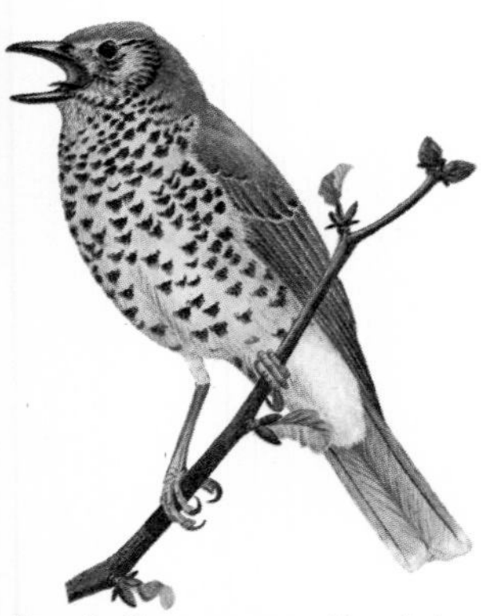

thrush *Common across Eurasia but found worldwide, thrushes are songbirds which live in woods and gardens. They feed chiefly on snails, often smashing open the shells on stones, but they also eat insects and fruit. This is a European species – the mistle, or missel, thrush.*

~n. The act of throbbing; a beat, palpitation, or vibration. [Middle English *throbben* (attested only in the present participle); imitative.] **—throb·bing·ly** *adv.*

throes (thrōz) *pl.n. Singular* **throe. 1.** Physical pain or anguish, as at the approach of death. **2.** A condition of agonising struggle or effort. **3.** *Singular.* A violent pang or spasm of pain. [Middle English *throwe,* Old English *thrawe*†, paroxysm.]

throm·bin (thrómbin) *n.* An enzyme in blood that facilitates clotting by reacting with fibrinogen to form fibrin. [THROMB(O)- + -IN.]

thrombo–, thromb– *comb. form.* Indicates a blood clot; for example, **thromboplastin, thrombin.** [From Greek *thrombos,* THROMBUS.]

throm·bo·cyte (thróm-bō-sīt, -bə-) *n.* A blood **platelet** *(see).*

throm·bo·cy·to·pe·ni·a (thrómbō-sītō-péeni-ə) *n.* A decrease in the number of platelets in the blood, resulting in reduced ability of the blood to clot. [THROMBOCYTE + Greek *penia,* poverty, want.]

throm·bo·em·bo·lism (thrómbō-émbəliz'm) *n.* The blocking of a blood vessel by a thrombus dislodged from the vein in which it originated.

throm·bo·phle·bi·tis (thrómbō-fle-bītiss, -fli-) *n.* Inflammation of a vein associated with the formation of a blood clot in it.

throm·bo·plas·tic (thróm-bō-plástik, -bə-, -plaástik) *adj.* **1.** Causing or promoting blood clotting. **2.** Of or pertaining to thromboplastin.

throm·bo·plas·tin (thróm-bō-plástin, -bə-) *n.* A protein complex essential for thrombin formation and blood clotting. Also called "thrombokinase". [THROMB(O)- + -PLAST + -IN.]

throm·bose (thróm-bōz, throm-bṓz) *v.* **-bosed, -bosing, -boses.** *—tr.* To affect with thrombosis. *—intr.* To become affected with thrombosis. [Back-formation from THROMBOSIS.]

throm·bo·sis (throm-bṓ-siss) *n., pl.* **-ses** (-seez). The formation, presence, or development of a thrombus. See **coronary thrombosis.** [New Latin, from Greek *thrombōsis,* a clotting, from *thrombousthai,* to clot, from *thrombos,* THROMBUS.] **—throm·bot·ic** (-bóttik) *adj.*

throm·bus (thróm-bəss) *n., pl.* **-bi** (-bī). A blood clot that forms in and blocks a blood vessel or that is formed in a heart cavity. [New Latin, from Greek *thrombos*†, lump, clot.]

throne (thrōn) *n.* **1.** The chair occupied by a sovereign, bishop, or other exalted personage on state or ceremonial occasions. **2.** The power, dignity, or rank of one who occupies a throne: *come to the throne.* **3.** *Plural. Theology.* One of the nine orders of angels. See **angel. 4.** *British Slang.* A lavatory. Used humorously.

~v. **throned, throning, thrones.** *—tr.* To enthrone. *—intr.* To occupy a throne; reign. [Middle English, learned respelling of earlier *trone,* from Old French, from Latin *thronus,* from Greek *thronos.*]

throng (throng) *n.* **1.** A large group of people gathered or crowded closely together. **2.** Any large group of things; a host.

~v. **thronged, thronging, throngs.** *—tr.* **1.** To crowd into; fill completely. **2.** To press in upon; surround in large numbers. *—intr.* To gather, press, or move in a throng. [Middle English *throng, thrang,* Old English *thrang,* probably from Germanic *thring-* (unattested), to press, crowd.]

thros·tle (thróss'l) *n.* **1.** *Poetic.* Any of various Old World thrushes; especially, the **song thrush** *(see).* **2.** A machine formerly used for spinning cotton, wool, or other fibre. [Middle English *throstle,* Old English *throstle.*]

throt·tle (thrótt'l) *n.* **1. a.** A valve in an internal-combustion engine that regulates the amount of vaporised fuel entering the cylinders. **b.** A similar valve in a steam engine regulating the amount of steam. Also called "throttle valve". **2.** A lever or pedal controlling this valve. **3.** *Regional.* The throat or windpipe.

~tr.v. **throttled, -tling, -tles. 1. a.** To regulate the flow of (fuel) in an engine. **b.** To regulate the speed of (an engine) with a throttle. **2.** To strangle; choke. **3.** To suppress. [Noun sense 1, perhaps diminutive of THROAT; verb senses 2 and 3, Middle English *throtelen,* to throttle, perhaps from *throte,* THROAT.] **—throt·tler** *n.*

through (throō) *prep.* Also *rare* **thro, thro',** *chiefly U.S.* **thru. 1.** In at one side and out at the opposite or another side of. **2.** Among or between; in the midst of: *a walk through the flowers.* **3.** By reason of. **4.** By the means or agency of. **5.** Here and there in; visiting various parts of: *a tour through France.* **6. a.** From the beginning to the end of: *stayed up through the night.* **b.** *Chiefly U.S.* Up to and including: *Monday through Friday.* **7.** At or to the end of; done or finished with, especially successfully: *We are through the initial testing period.* **8.** Without stopping for: *drove through a red light.* **9.** Because of: *He got the job through his father.*

~adv. Also *rare* **thro, thro',** *chiefly U.S.* **thru. 1.** From one end or side to another or opposite end or side. **2.** From beginning to end: *the whole night through.* **3.** Completely; thoroughly: *soaked through.* **4.** To a conclusion or accomplishment: *see the matter through.* **5.** Out into the open: *The sun broke through.* **—through and through. 1.** Throughout. **2.** In every respect; completely.

~adj. Also *chiefly U.S.* **thru. 1.** Passing or extending from one end, side, or surface to another: *a through lounge.* **2.** Allowing continuous passage; unobstructed: *a through road.* **3.** Conveying passengers directly to a destination without changes. Said of a train. **4.** *Informal.* Finished; done. **5.** *Informal.* At the end of one's effectiveness or resources: *He's through financially.* **6.** Connected to the person one wishes to speak to on a telephone line. **7.** *Informal.* No longer involved in an emotional relationship. [Middle English *thru(g)h, thurh,* Old English *thurh, thuruh.*]

Usage: The use of *through* as a preposition in the sense "up to and including" is American English *(Monday through Saturday).* The ambiguity of *to* or *till* in British English *(I shall stay from Monday to Saturday* - does this mean I shall leave on Saturday or Sunday?), and the awkwardness of the phrases *up to and including, Monday to Saturday inclusive,* has led to an increased use of the American construction in British in recent years, though not without attracting strong criticism from those who wish to keep British English as free as possible from American influence. A frequent compromise in British English is *through to (Monday through to Saturday).*

through·ly (thrṓoli) *adv. Archaic.* Thoroughly.

through·out (throo-ówt) *prep.* In, to, through, or during every part of; all through.

~adv. **1.** In or through all parts; everywhere. **2.** During the entire time or extent.

through·put (thrṓo-poŏt) *n.* **1.** *Computing.* The amount of material processed by a computer in a given period. **2.** Loosely, output.

through·way. Variant of **thruway.**

throve. Alternative past tense of **thrive.**

throw (thrō) *v.* **threw** (throō || threw), **thrown** (thrōn || thrṓ-ən), **throwing, throws.** *—tr.* **1.** To propel through the air with a swift motion of the arm; hurl. **2.** To discharge into the air by any means. **3.** To hurl with great force, suddenness, or carelessness: *She threw her clothes into a cupboard; He threw himself at his opponent.* **4.** To apply (oneself, for example) with energy: *threw herself into her new job.* **5.** To surrender (oneself) to something: *threw himself on the mercy of the court.* **6. a.** To put on or off hastily or carelessly: *throw on a cape.* **b.** To put quickly into use or place: *throw in extra troops.* **7.** To put abruptly or forcibly into a specified condition or place: *threw him into total confusion; threw the prisoner into jail.* **8.** To form on a potter's wheel: *throw a vase.* **9.** To twist (fibres) into thread. **10. a.** To roll (dice). **b.** To roll (a particular combination) with dice. **11.** To discard or play (a card). **12. a.** To cast (a shadow). **b.** To direct; send: *threw an anxious glance at him.* **13.** To bear (young). Used of cows or horses. Not in current usage. **14.** To deliver (a blow or punch). **15.** To move (a controlling lever or switch). **16.** To send (an opponent in wrestling) to the ground. **17.** To cause (a rider) to leave the saddle and fall to the ground. Used of a horse. **18. a.** To project (the voice). **b.** To cause (one's voice) to appear to be coming from elsewhere than one's mouth. **19.** To give way to (an emotional outburst): *throw a fit.* **20.** *Informal.* To disconcert; nonplus: *The news really threw her.* **21.** *Informal.* To arrange or give (a party, for example). *—intr.* To cast, fling, or hurl something. **—throw off. 1.** To cast out; reject. **2.** To give off; emit. **3.** To rid oneself of: *can't seem to throw off this cold.* **4.** To escape; evade: *managed to throw off his pursuers.* **—throw in the towel** or **sponge.** To give up; accept defeat. [Originally in boxing, a contestant acknowledged defeat by throwing his towel or sponge into the ring.] **—throw out. 1.** To give off; emit. **2.** To reject or discard. **3.** To dismiss or expel. **4.** To offer, as a suggestion or plan. —See Synonyms at **eject. —throw over. 1.** To overturn. **2.** To abandon (a lover, for example). **—throw up. 1.** To abandon; relinquish: *throw up a job.* **2.** To construct hurriedly. **3.** *Informal.* To vomit.

~n. **1.** An act of throwing; a cast; a fling. **2.** The distance, height, or direction of something thrown: *a low throw.* **3. a.** A roll or cast of dice. **b.** The combination of numbers so obtained. **4.** *Informal.* A chance; an attempt. **5.** The technique used to throw an opponent in wrestling. **6.** In dances such as jitterbug or rock'n'roll, a leaping movement in which one partner is apparently thrown into the air and supported by the other. **7.** *U.S.* **a.** A light coverlet. **b.** A scarf or shawl. **8.** *Machinery.* **a.** The length of the radius of a circle described by a crank, cam, or similar part. **b.** The maximum displacement of a part moved by a crank, cam, or the like. **9.** *Geology.* The vertical distance between a rock on one side of a fault and its continuation on the other side. **10.** *Physics.* A single movement of the indicator of a measuring instrument, as in a ballistic galvanometer. [Middle English *throwen, thrawen,* to turn, twist, hence to hurl, cast (presumably "to turn the body in the act of throwing"), Old English *thrāwan,* to turn, twist.] **—throw·er** *n.*

Synonyms: *throw, cast, hurl, fling, toss, sling, heave.*

throw away *tr.v.* **1.** To discard as useless. **2.** To fail to use (an opportunity, for example).

throw·a·way (thrṓ-ə-way) *adj.* **1.** Designed or intended to be discarded after use. **2.** Written or delivered in a low-key or offhand manner: *throwaway lines.*

~n. **1.** Anything designed to be discarded after use. **2.** *Chiefly U.S.* A handbill distributed on the street.

throw back *intr.v.* To revert to a type or stage in one's ancestral past. *—tr.v.* To cause or compel to be dependent: *Her husband's death threw her back on her own resources.*

throw·back (thrṓ-bak) *n.* **1.** A reversion to a former type or ancestral characteristic. **2.** Loosely, an **atavism** *(see).* **3.** Something that refers back to or results from a previous incident, period, or the like: *Her tidiness is a throwback to her days at boarding school.*

thrown. Past participle of **throw.**

throw in *tr.v.* **1.** To add (something extra) with no additional charge. **2.** To add or contribute (a remark) to a conversation.

throw-in (thrṓ-in) *n.* In soccer, a two-handed throw from behind the touchline, used to bring the ball back into play.

throw pillow *n. U.S.* A **scatter cushion** *(see).*

throw rug *n.* A **scatter rug** *(see).*

thru (throō). *Chiefly U.S.* Variant of **through.**

thrum[1] (thrum) *v.* **thrummed, thrumming, thrums.** *—tr.* **1.** To play (a stringed instrument) idly or monotonously. **2.** To repeat or recite

in a monotonous tone of voice. —*intr.* To strum idly on a stringed instrument.
~*n.* A thrumming sound. [Imitative.] —**thrum·mer** *n.*

thrum² *n.* **1. a.** The fringe of warp threads left on a loom after the cloth has been cut off. **b.** Any of these threads. **2.** Any loose end, fringe, or tuft of thread. **3.** *Plural. Nautical.* Short bits of rope yarn inserted into canvas to roughen the surface so that it can be used to prevent chafing.
~*tr.v.* **thrummed, thrumming, thrums. 1.** To cover or trim with thrums; fringe. **2.** *Nautical.* To sew thrums into (canvas). [Middle English *thrum*, Old English *thrum*.]

thrush¹ (thrush) *n.* **1.** Any of various songbirds of the family Turdidae, characteristically having brownish upper plumage and a spotted breast. **2.** Any of various similar or related birds. [Middle English *thrusch(e)*, Old English *thrysce*.]

thrush² *n.* **1.** An infection of the mouth or vagina with a fungus, *Candida albicans*, characterised by white eruptions. See **candidiasis**. **2.** A suppurative infection of a horse's foot caused by standing in a wet, unhygienic stall. [17th century : origin obscure.]

thrust (thrust) *v.* **thrust, thrusting, thrusts.** —*tr.* **1. a.** To push or drive quickly and forcibly. **b.** To cause to pierce or stab. **2.** To force (oneself or another) into a specified condition or situation. —*intr.* **1.** To shove against something; push. **2.** To pierce or stab at something with a pointed weapon. **3.** To force one's way. **4.** To push or project upwards.
~*n.* **1.** A forceful shove or push; a lunge. **2. a.** A driving force or pressure. **b.** The forward-directed force developed in a jet or rocket engine as a reaction to the backward ejection of fuel gases at high velocities. **3.** A stab. **4.** The general direction or tendency: *the thrust of an argument.* **5.** *Architecture.* Outward or lateral stress in a structure, such as an arch. **6.** *Geology.* A force of compression in the earth's crust producing folding. [Middle English *thrusten*, from Old Norse *thrȳsta*, to thrust, compress.]

thrust bearing *n. Machinery.* A type of bearing designed to transmit a force along a shaft as well as at right angles to it.

thrust·er (thrústər) *n.* A small rocket motor used to control a spacecraft.

thrust fault *n. Geology.* A reverse fault with a dip so low that the upthrow has moved far forward over the downthrow.

thrust·ing (thrúst-ing) *n.* **1.** Forceful. **2.** Aggressively ambitious. See Synonyms at **ambitious**. —**thrus·ting·ly** *adv.*

thru·way, through·way (thróo-way) *n. U.S.* An urban motorway.

Thu·cyd·i·des (thew-síddi-deez ‖ thōō-). Greek historian of the fifth century B.C.; author of *History of the Peloponnesian War.*

thud (thud) *n.* **1.** A dull sound, as that of a heavy object striking a solid surface. **2.** A blow or fall causing such a sound.
~*intr.v.* **thudded, thudding, thuds.** To make such a sound. [Middle English *thudden*, Old English *thyddan* (imitative).] —**thud** *adv.*

thug (thug) *n.* **1.** A brutal lout; a violent and criminally disposed man. **2.** Any of a former band of professional assassins in India. [Hindi *ṭhag*, cheat, thief, from Sanskrit *sthaga*, robber, from *sthagati*, to cover, hide.] —**thug·ger·y** *n.* —**thug·gish** *adj.*

thug·gee (thúggee, thu-gée) *n.* Formerly, the practices or methods of the thugs in India. [Hindi *ṭhagī*, robbery, from *ṭhag*, THUG.]

thu·ja, thu·ya (thōō-yə) *n.* Any coniferous tree of the genus *Thuja*, having scalelike leaves and small, scaly cones. Also called "arbor vitae". [New Latin, from Greek *thu(i)a†*, name of an African tree.]

Thu·le¹ (théw-lee, -li, thewl ‖ thōō-lee, -li, thōōl). The most northerly region of the ancient habitable world, conceived as an island north of Britain by ancient geographers. See **Ultima Thule**.

Thule². See **Dundas**.

thu·li·um (théw-li-əm ‖ thōō-) *n. Symbol* **Tm** A bright silvery rare-earth element having 18 known isotopes with mass numbers ranging from 153 to 176. The X-ray emitting isotope Tm 170 is used in small portable medical X-ray units. Atomic number 69, atomic weight 168.934, melting point 1,545°C, boiling point 1,727°C, relative density 9.332, valency 3. [From THULE.]

thumb (thum) *n.* **1.** The short first digit of the human hand, opposable to each of the other four digits. **2.** A corresponding digit in other animals, especially primates. **3.** The part of a glove or mitten that covers the thumb. **4.** *Architecture.* An **ovolo** *(see).* —**all thumbs.** Clumsy; awkward. —**hold thumbs.** *South African.* To cross (one's) fingers, by way of wishing someone well. —**twiddle (one's) thumbs.** To be underoccupied; be bored from having nothing to do. —**under the thumb of.** Under the influence, authority, or power of.
~*v.* **thumbed, thumbing, thumbs.** —*tr.* **1.** To handle or soil with the thumb. **2.** *Informal.* To solicit (a lift) from a passing vehicle by pointing one's thumb in the direction one is travelling; hitchhike. —**thumb (one's) nose.** To express scorn or derision by or as if by placing the thumb on the nose and wiggling the fingers. —**thumb through.** To browse rapidly through (the pages of a book or magazine). [Middle English *thom(b)e*, Old English *thūma*.]

thumb·hole (thúm-hōl) *n.* The hole on a wind instrument that is opened or closed with the thumb.

thumb index *n.* A series of rounded indentations cut into the front edge of a reference book, each labelled, as with a letter, to indicate a section of the book. —**thumb-in·dexed** (thúm-índext) *adj.*

thumb·nail (thúm-nayl) *n.* The nail of the thumb.
~*adj.* **1.** Of the size of a thumbnail. **2.** Brief: *a thumbnail sketch.*

thumb piano *n.* Any of various small African musical instruments played with the thumbs.

thumb·print (thúm-print) *n.* An impression of the ball of the thumb, especially when used as a means of identification.

thumb·screw (thúm-skrōō ‖ -skrew) *n.* **1.** A screw so designed that it can be turned with the thumb and fingers. **2.** An instrument of torture formerly used to compress the thumb.

thumbs down *n.* A mark of rejection, disapproval, or prohibition.

thumb·stall (thúm-stawl) *n.* A sheath or cap worn on the thumb in certain manual tasks or to protect it when injured.

thumbs up *n.* A mark of approval, acceptance, or encouragement.

thumb·tack (thúm-tak) *n. U.S.* A **drawing pin** *(see).*
~*tr.v.* **thumbtacked, -tacking, -tacks.** *U.S.* To affix with a thumbtack.

Thummim. See **Urim and Thummim**.

thump (thump) *n.* **1.** A blow with a blunt instrument or closed hand. **2.** The muffled sound produced by such a blow or a similarly muted noise; a thud.
~*v.* **thumped, thumping, thumps.** —*tr.* **1.** To beat with a blunt or dull instrument, or with the hand or foot, so as to produce a muffled sound or thud. **2.** *Informal.* To thrash soundly or thoroughly; drub. —*intr.* **1.** To hit or fall in such a way as to produce a thump. **2.** To walk with heavy steps; stomp. **3.** To throb audibly; pound. [16th century : imitative.] —**thump** *adv.* —**thump·er** *n.*

thump·ing (thúmping) *adj.* **1.** *Informal.* Large; enormous. **2.** Thoroughly enjoyable. —**thump·ing·ly** *adv.*

thun·ber·gi·a (thún-bérji-ə, -bérjə) *n.* Any climbing plant of the genus *Thunbergia*, native to Old World tropical regions. See **black-eyed Susan**. [After Carl *Thunberg* (died 1828), Swedish botanist.]

thun·der (thúndər) *n.* **1.** The rumbling or crashing sound emitted by rapidly expanding gases after the electrical discharge of lightning. **2.** Any similar sound. —**steal (someone's) thunder. 1.** To anticipate or adopt someone's idea or practice and get the credit oneself. **2.** To divert attention, praise, or recognition from another to oneself. [Phrase attributed to John Dennis (1657–1734), English dramatist, who had introduced a machine to simulate thunder in a play. After learning that a similar device had later been used in another play, he said that the playwright was stealing his thunder.]
~*v.* **thundered, -dering, -ders.** —*intr.* **1.** To produce thunder. **2.** To produce sounds like thunder. **3.** To utter loud, vociferous remarks or threats. —*tr.* To express violently, commandingly, or angrily; roar. [Middle English *thunder, thon(d)re*, Old English *thunor*.]

thun·der·bird (thúndər-burd) *n.* In the mythology of some North American Indians, thunder, lightning, and rain personified as a huge bird.

thun·der·bolt (thúndər-bōlt) *n.* **1.** The discharge of lightning that accompanies thunder. **2.** A flash of lightning imagined as a bolt or dart hurled from the heavens. **3.** Someone or something resembling a thunderbolt in suddenness, violence, destructive effect, or the like.

thun·der·box (thúndər-boks) *n. British Slang.* A lavatory, especially a portable one. [Referring to breaking wind.]

thun·der·clap (thúndər-klap) *n.* **1.** A single sharp crash of thunder. **2.** Anything of similar violence, loudness, or suddenness.

thun·der·cloud (thúndər-klowd) *n.* **1.** A large, dark cloud charged with electricity and producing lightning and thunder; a cumulonimbus cloud. **2.** Anything of dread or menacing aspect.

thun·der·er (thúndərər) *n.* One that thunders. —**The Thunderer.** A former nickname for *The Times* newspaper.

thun·der·head (thúndər-hed) *n. Chiefly U.S.* The swollen upper portion of a thundercloud, often associated with a thunderstorm.

thun·der·ing (thún-dring, -dəring) *adj. British Informal.* Used as an intensive: *a thundering bore.*
~*adv.* Used as an intensive: *a thundering good show.* —**thun·der·ing·ly** *adv.*

thun·der·ous (thúnd-rəss, -ərəss) *adj.* **1.** Of or pertaining to thunder or to a similar sound. **2.** Loud and unrestrained: *thunderous applause.* —**thun·der·ous·ly** *adv.*

thun·der·show·er (thúndər-showr, -show-ər) *n.* A brief rainstorm accompanied by thunder and lightning.

thun·der·stick (thúndər-stik) *n.* A **bullroarer** *(see).*

thun·der·stone (thúndər-stōn) *n.* **1.** Any of various mineral concretions formerly supposed to be thunderbolts, such as a **belemnite** *(see).* **2.** *Archaic.* A flash of lightning conceived as a stone.

thun·der·storm (thúndər-stawrm) *n.* A storm in which intense heating induces air to rise rapidly and form vast cumulonimbus clouds, with heavy rain, lightning, thunder, and sometimes hail.

thun·der·struck (thúndər-struk) *adj.* Also **thun·der·strick·en** (-strickən). Struck with sudden astonishment or amazement.

thun·der·y (thúndəri) *adj.* **1.** Indicating or characterised by thunder: *thundery weather.* **2.** Resembling thunder.

Thur., Thurs. Thursday.

Thur·ber (thúrbər), **James (Grover)** (1894–1961). U.S. humorist and cartoonist. His drawings and writings are collected in *My Life and Hard Times* (1933) and *The Thurber Carnival* (1945).

thu·ri·ble (théwr-ib'l ‖ thóor-) *n.* An incense vessel, a **censer** *(see).* [Middle English *thoryble*, from Old French *thurible*, from Latin *t(h)ūribulum*, from *t(h)ūs* (stem *t(h)ūr-*), incense, from Greek *thuos*, (sacrificial) incense, (burnt) offering.]

thu·ri·fer (théwr-ifər ‖ thóor-) *n.* An altar server or minister who carries a thurible. [New Latin, from Latin *thūrifer*, "incense bearing" : *thūs* (stem *thūr-*), incense (see **thurible**) + -FER.]

Thu·rin·gi·a (thewr-rínji-ə, -rínjə ‖ thoor-). German **Thü·ring·en** (tür-ing-ən). Former state of Germany, lying south of the Harz

Mountains. It was created in 1920 from a number of former duchies and principalities. After World War II it passed into the control of Soviet-occupied East Germany, and was abolished as an administrative unit in 1952. —**Thu·rin·gi·an** *adj. & n.*

Thurs·day (thúrz-di, -day) *n. Abbr.* **Thur., Thurs.** The day following Wednesday; the fourth day of the working week. [Middle English *thur(e)sday,* Old English *thūr(e)s dæg* (influenced by Old Norse *thōrsdagr,* "Thor's day"), from earlier *thunresdæg,* "Thor's day" (translation of Late Latin *Jovis diēs,* "Jupiter's day") : *thunres,* genitive of *thunor,* THUNDER + *dæg,* DAY.]

thus (thuss) *adv.* Also *nonstandard* **thus·ly** (thússli) (for sense 1). **1.** In a manner previously stated or to be stated; in this manner. **2.** To a stated degree or extent; so: *thus far.* **3.** Therefore; consequently. [Middle English, Old English *thus.*]

thuya. Variant of **thuja.**

thwack (thwak) *tr.v.* **thwacked, thwacking, thwacks.** To strike or hit with something flat; whack.
~*n.* A hard blow with something flat; a whack. [Imitative.]
—**thwack** *adv.* —**thwack·er** *n.*

thwart (thwort) *tr.v.* **thwarted, thwarting, thwarts. 1.** To prevent from taking place or being realised; frustrate; block. **2.** To challenge, oppose, or cross. —See Synonyms at **frustrate.**
~*n.* (*also* thort). A seat across a boat, on which the oarsman sits.
~*adj.* **1.** Extending, lying, or passing across something; transverse. **2.** *Archaic.* Perverse; stubborn. **3.** Adverse, unfavourable. Said of winds and currents.
~*adv. Archaic.* Athwart; across.
~*prep. Archaic.* Athwart; across. [Middle English *thwert,* athwart, across, perverse, from Old Norse *thvert,* neuter of *thverr,* transverse.]
—**thwart·ed·ly** *adv.* —**thwart·er** *n.*

thy (thī). The possessive form of the pronoun *thou. Archaic, Regional, & Poetic.* Used attributively to indicate possession, agency, or reception of an action by the one addressed by the speaker: *"He sees his brood about thy knee."* (Tennyson). [Middle English *thy, thin,* Old English *thīn,* thine.]

thy·la·cine (thílə-sīn, -seen) *n.* A wolflike marsupial, *Thylacinus cynocephalus,* of forest areas of Tasmania, having dark transverse bands across its back. Also called "Tasmanian wolf". [New Latin *thylacinus,* from Greek *thulakos†,* a sack.]

thyme (tīm) *n.* **1.** Any of several aromatic herbs or low shrubs of the genus *Thymus;* especially, *T. vulgaris,* of southern Europe, having small purplish flowers. **2.** The leaves of this plant, used as seasoning. [Middle English *t(h)yme,* from Old French *thym,* from Latin *thymum,* from Greek *thumon.*]

-thymia *n. comb. form.* Indicates state of mind or temperament; for example, **schizothymia.** [New Latin, from Greek *thumos,* soul, spirit, mind, temper.]

thy·mic (thímik) *adj.* Of or pertaining to the thymus.

thy·mi·dine (thími-deen) *n. Biochemistry.* A nucleoside consisting of thymine and the sugar ribose. [THYM(INE) + -ID(E) + -INE.]

thy·mine (thí-meen) *n. Biochemistry.* A pyrimidine base, $C_5H_6N_2O_2$, occurring in DNA. [THYM(IC) + -INE.]

thy·mol (thí-mol) *n.* A white, crystalline, aromatic compound, $(CH_3)_2CHC_6H_3(CH_3)OH$ derived from thyme oil and other oils and used as an antiseptic, in perfumery, and as a preservative. [THYM(E) + -OL.]

thy·mus (thí-məss) *n., pl.* **-muses** or **mi** (-mī). **1.** A ductless gland-like structure, situated just behind the top of the breastbone, that during early childhood plays some part in building resistance to disease by producing lymphocytes but in adults is usually vestigial. **2.** The corresponding structure in nonhuman vertebrates. [New Latin, from Greek *thumos†.*]

thy·ra·tron (thír-ə-tron) *n. Electronics.* A gas-filled tube having three electrodes, such that an electrical discharge and consequent current flow between the anode and cathode is initiated (but not controlled) by a potential applied to a grid. The device is used as a relay and particle counter. [Originally a trademark, from Greek *thura,* door, valve + -TRON.]

thy·ris·tor (thír-ristər) *n. Electronics.* A semiconductor rectifier, such as a silicon-controlled rectifier, in which passage of current is initiated by a voltage applied to a third electrode. It is the solid-state equivalent of a thyratron. [*thyratron* + tran*sistor.*]

thy·ro·cal·ci·to·nin (thír-ō-kál-si-tónin) *n.* A hormone, **calcitonin** (*see*). [THYRO(ID) + CALCITONIN.]

thy·roid (thí-royd) *adj.* Of or relating to the thyroid gland or the thyroid cartilage.
~*n.* **1.** The thyroid gland. **2.** The thyroid cartilage. **3.** A dried and powdered preparation of the thyroid gland of certain domestic animals, used in the treatment of hypothyroid conditions, such as cretinism. [Obsolete French *thyroide,* from Greek *thuroidēs, thureoeidēs,* shaped like a door or oblong shield, from *thureos,* door-shaped : *thura,* door + -OID.]

thyroid cartilage *n.* The largest cartilage of the larynx, having two broad processes that join in front to form the Adam's apple. Also called "thyroid".

thyroid colloid *n. Physiology.* **Colloid** (*see*).

thy·roid·ec·to·my (thír-oyd-éktəmi) *n., pl.* **-mies.** The surgical removal of all or part of the thyroid gland.

thyroid gland *n.* A two-lobed endocrine gland found in all vertebrates, located in front of and on either side of the trachea in humans, and producing the hormone thyroxine. Also called "thyroid".

thy·roid·i·tis (thír-oyd-ítiss) *n.* Inflammation of the thyroid gland.

thyroid-stim·u·lat·ing hormone (thír-oyd-stímmew-layting) *n.* Thyrotrophin.

thy·ro·tox·i·co·sis (thír-ō-tóksi-kó-siss, -ə-) *n.* The condition resulting from excessive production of thyroid hormone, characterised by weight loss, increased appetite, tremor, palpitations, anxiety, and intolerance of heat. [New Latin : THYRO(ID) + TOXICOSIS.]

thy·ro·tro·phin (thír-ə-trō-fin, -ō-, thír-róttrə-) *n.* Also **thy·rot·ro·pin** (-pin). A hormone secreted by the anterior pituitary that stimulates and regulates the development and secretion of the thyroid gland hormone. Also called "thyroid-stimulating hormone". [THYRO(ID) + -TROP(E) + -IN.]

thy·rox·ine (thír-rók-seen, -sin) *n.* Also **thy·rox·in** (-sin). An iodine-containing hormone, $C_{15}H_{11}I_4NO_4$, produced by the thyroid gland to regulate metabolism and made synthetically for treatment of underactivity of the thyroid gland. [THYR(OID) + OX(Y)- + -IN.]

thyrse (thurss) *n. Botany.* A branched flower cluster, as of the lilac, whose main axis does not terminate in a flower. Also called "thyrsus". [New Latin *thyrsus,* THYRSUS.] —**thyr·soid** (thúr-soyd) *adj.*

thyr·sus (thúr-səss) *n., pl.* **-si** (-sī). **1.** A staff tipped with a pine cone and twined with ivy, represented as carried by Dionysus, and his devotees. **2.** *Botany.* A thyrse. [New Latin, from Latin, from Greek *thursos†.*]

thy·self (thī-sélf ‖ *regional also* thi-, thə-, tha-) *pron. Archaic, Regional, & Poetic.* Yourself. Used as the reflexive or emphatic form of *thee* or *thou.*

THz terahertz.

ti¹. *Music.* Variant of **te.**

ti² (tee) *n, pl.* **tis.** Any of several trees or shrubs of the genus *Cordyline,* of tropical Asia and adjacent Pacific regions; especially, *C. australis,* of New Zealand, having a terminal tuft of long, palm-like narrow leaves. [Tahitian and Maori.]

Ti The symbol for the element titanium.

Ti·a·hua·na·co (tée-ə-wə-naákō). Ruins near the southeast end of Lake Titicaca, western Bolivia. The Tiahuanaco culture preceded that of the Incas, flourishing *c.* A.D. 1000 to 1300, and spread through Bolivia, northern Chile, and Peru.

Tian·jin or **Tien·tsin** (tyén-jín). Port in Hebei province, northeastern China, lying at the confluence of the Hai river and Grand Canal. It is an important industrial centre.

Tian Shan or **Tien Shan** (tyán shán). Mountain chain of central Asia, extending from the Pamirs in Tadzhik S.S.R., U.S.S.R. through northwestern China to the China-Mongolia border. The name means "heavenly mountains".

ti·ar·a (ti-áarə) *n.* **1.** An ornamental semicircular headpiece, made from a precious metal and jewels, worn by women on formal occasions. **2.** The triple crown formerly worn by the pope. [Latin *tiāra,* from Greek *tiara(s)†.*]

Ti·ber (tíbər). *Italian* **Te·ve·re.** River of central Italy. It rises in the Tuscan Apennines, and flows some 406 kilometres (252 miles) through Rome to the Tyrrhenian Sea at Ostia.

Tiberias, Sea of. See Sea of **Galilee.**

Ti·bet (ti-bét). *Chinese* **Xi·zang** or **Si·tsang.** Autonomous region of China, occupying a high plateau in the southwestern extremity of the country to the north and west of the Himalayas. Apart from the fertile valley of the Tsangpo, in southern Tibet, most of the land is suitable only for grazing. Tibet has rich reserves of salt, gold, radioactive ores, and copper. Tibet rose to prominence as an independent kingdom in the 7th century; from the 13th to the 18th century it was under the sway of the Mongols; in 1720 the Manchu dynasty of China took control of the region, and thereafter China exercised more or less effective suzerainty over it until 1951, when Tibet was formally made an autonomous region of China. It is a centre of Lamaist Buddhism, but the Dalai Lama and thousands of followers fled the country in 1954. Capital, Lhasa.

Ti·bet·an (ti-bétt'n) *adj.* Of or pertaining to Tibet, its people, or their language or culture.
~*n.* **1.** A member of the Mongoloid people of Tibet. **2.** The Tibeto-Burman language of Tibet.

Ti·bet·o·Bur·man (ti-béttō-búrmən) *n.* Also **Ti·bet·o·Bur·mese** (-búr-méez ‖ -méess). A language family including principally Tibetan, Burmese, Lolo, and Balti, sometimes classed as a subgroup of Sino-Tibetan. —**Ti·bet·o·Bur·man, Ti·bet·o·Bur·mese** *adj.*

tib·i·a (tíbbi-ə) *n., pl.* **-iae** (-ee) or **-ias. 1.** The inner and larger of the two bones of the lower human leg from the knee to the ankle. Also called "shin", "shinbone". **2.** A homologous bone in animals. **3.** The fourth division of an insect's leg, between the femur and the tarsi. **4.** A kind of ancient flute originally made from an animal's leg bone. [Latin *tībia†,* shinbone, pipe.] —**tib·i·al** *adj.*

tic (tik) *n.* **1.** A habitual spasmodic muscular contraction, usually in the face or extremities, and often of neurotic origin. **2.** Tic douloureux. [French, originally a veterinary term (perhaps imitative).]

tic dou·lou·reux (dŏŏlə-rúr, -rŏ ‖ -rŏō) *n.* **Trigeminal neuralgia** (*see*). [French, "painful tic".]

tick¹ (tik) *n.* **1.** The recurring sharp, clicking sound made by a machine, especially by a clock. **2.** *British Informal.* A moment. **3.** A mark used to indicate that an item has been approved, dealt with, or noted.
~*v.* **ticked, ticking, ticks.** —*intr.* **1.** To emit recurring clicking sounds, as a clock does. **2.** To function in a characteristic way, as if by means of a motivating mechanism: *What makes him tick?* —*tr.* **1.** To count or record by means of ticks: *The taximeter ticked off the fare; a clock ticking away the hours.* **2.** To mark (a sum, for exam-

ple) with a tick. [Middle English *tek* (noun; perhaps imitative); verb, 16th century, of Germanic origin.]
tick² *n.* **1.** Any of numerous bloodsucking parasitic arachnids of the families Ixodidae and Argasidae within the order Acarina, many of which transmit infectious diseases. **2.** Any of various usually wingless, louselike insects of the family Hippoboscidae, that are parasitic on sheep, goats, and other animals. [Middle English *tyke, teke,* Old English *ticca* (unattested).]
tick³ *n.* **1.** The cloth case of a mattress or pillow. **2.** Ticking. [Middle English *tikke,* perhaps from Middle Dutch *tēke,* from West Germanic *tēka* (unattested), from Latin *thēca,* cover, case, from Greek *thēkē.*]
tick⁴ *n. British Informal.* Credit; trust: *on tick.* [Short for TICKET.]
tick⁵ *n.* A children's game, **tag** *(see).* [From TICK (to mark, touch).]
tick bird *n.* The **oxpecker** *(see).*
tick-borne (tík-bawrn ‖ -bōrn) *adj.* Transmitted by ticks. Said of diseases such as typhus.
tick·er (tíckər) *n.* **1.** A **tape machine** *(see).* **2.** *Slang.* A watch. **3.** *Slang.* The heart.
ticker tape *n.* The paper strip on which a tape machine prints.
tick·er-tape parade (tíckər-tayp) *n.* A traditional hero's welcome, especially in New York City, in which ticker-tape or ribbons of paper are thrown from buildings as the celebrity parades by.
tick·et (tíckit) *n.* **1.** A paper slip or card indicating that its holder has paid for or is entitled to a service, right, or consideration, such as: **a.** One entitling its holder to use public transport: *a bus ticket.* **b.** One entitling its holder to admission to a place of entertainment, a lecture, or the like: *a theatre ticket.* **c.** One certifying its holder's discharge from the armed forces. **2.** A piece of card or paper enabling property, especially articles of clothing, to be identified and reclaimed by the owner: *a dry-cleaning ticket; a cloakroom ticket.* **3.** A certifying document; especially, a captain's or pilot's licence. **4.** A tag or label attached to goods for sale to indicate their price. **5.** *Chiefly U.S.* A list of candidates proposed or endorsed by a political party. **6.** A **parking ticket** *(see).* **7.** *Informal.* The proper thing: *A change of scene would be just the ticket for her.* **8.** *Plural. South African Informal.* Ruin; the end.
~*tr.v.* **ticketed, -eting, -ets. 1.** To attach a tag to; label. **2.** To designate for a specified use or end; destine. [Obsolete French *etiquet,* ticket, label, from Old French *estiquet(te),* from *estiquier,* to stick, from Middle Dutch *steken.*]
ticket agency *n.* An office that sells tickets for theatrical and other performances and usually charges a commission. **—ticket agent** *n.*
ticket office *n.* An office, as in a railway station, where transport tickets can be bought.
ticket tout *n. British Informal.* Someone who buys up tickets for popular events, such as Cup Finals, and sells them at inflated prices, typically outside the ground or venue.
tick·et·y-boo (tíckəti-bo͞o) *adj. British Slang.* Fine; perfect; just right. Not in current usage. [Perhaps from TICKET (the proper thing) + -Y (adjective suffix) + BOO.]
tick·ey (tícki) *n.* The former South African threepenny piece. [Afrikaans, possibly from Malay, *tiga,* three.]
tick fever *n.* Any febrile infectious disease transmitted by ticks.
tick·ing (ticking) *n.* A strong, tightly woven fabric of cotton or linen used to cover a mattress or pillow. Also called "tick".
tick·ing-off (tícking-off, -awf) *n. Chiefly British Informal.* A rebuke; a scolding.
tick·le (tíck'l) *v.* **-led, -ling, -les.** *—tr.* **1.** To touch (the body) lightly with a tingling sensation causing laughter or twitching movements. **2. a.** To tease or excite pleasurably; titillate. **b.** To fill with mirth or pleasure; delight. *—intr.* To feel or cause a tingling sensation on the skin. **—tickle pink.** *Informal.* To please; delight. Usually used in the passive: *She was tickled pink by the gift.*
~*n.* **1.** The act of tickling. **2.** A tickling sensation. [Middle English *tikelen,* probably from *tiken, ticken*†, to touch lightly.]
tick·ler (tícklər) *n.* **1.** One that tickles. **2.** *Chiefly British Informal.* A difficult problem. **3.** *U.S.* A memorandum book or file to aid the memory.
tick·lish (tíck'l-ish, tícklish) *adj.* **1.** Sensitive to tickling. **2.** Requiring skilful or tactful handling; delicate. **3.** Easily offended or upset; touchy. **—tick·lish·ly** *adv.* **—tick·lish·ness** *n.*
tick off *tr.v.* **1.** *Chiefly British Informal.* To scold or rebuke. **2.** *U.S. Informal.* To make angry; annoy.
tick over *intr.v.* **1.** To run at low speed with the clutch disengaged; idle. Used of an engine. **2.** To operate smoothly but uneventfully, at a normal or relatively low level of productivity. Used of companies, projects, and the like.
tick·o·ver (tík-ōvər) *n.* The speed of an engine while it is idling or ticking over. **—tick·o·ver** *adj.*
tick·seed (tík-seed) *n.* A plant, the **coreopsis** *(see).* [So called from its shape.]
tick·tack, tic-tac (tík-tak) *n.* **1.** *British.* A system of sign language by which bookmakers communicate odds to each other at race meetings. **2.** A steady ticking sound, as of a clock. [Imitative.]
tick·tack·toe, tick-tack-toe (tík-tak-tō) *n. U.S.* **Noughts and crosses** *(see).* [Probably TICKTACK (from the sounds made on slates on which the earlier form of the game was played) + TOE.]
tick·tock (tík-tok, -tók) *n.* The ticking sound made by a clock, especially a pendulum clock. [Imitative.] **—tick·tock** *intr.v.*
tick trefoil *n.* Any of various plants of the genus *Desmodium,* having compound leaves with three leaflets, clusters of small purplish or white flowers. [Its sticky seed pods adhere like ticks to animals.]
tick·y-tack·y (tícki-tácki) *n. Chiefly U.S. Informal.* Cheap, shoddy material. [Reduplication of TACKY (cheap, etc).]
t.i.d. *Medicine.* Three times a day [Latin *ter in die.*]
tid·al (tīd'l) *adj.* **1.** Pertaining to, affected by, or having tides: *a tidal river.* **2.** Dependent upon the state or times of the tide: *a tidal ship.* [TIDE + -AL.]
tidal basin *n.* A dock that is filled with water only at high tide.
tidal power *n.* See feature, next page.
tidal wave *n.* **1.** A **storm surge** *(see).* **2.** Loosely, a **tsunami** *(see).* **3.** Something resembling either of these in form or volume.
tidbit *n. U.S.* Variant of **titbit.**
tid·dler (tíddlər, tídd'l-ər) *n. British Informal.* **1.** A very small fish; especially, a stickleback. **2.** A young child, especially one small for its age. **3.** Any relatively small or unimportant object, organisation, or the like. [From TIDDLY (small).]
tid·dly¹ (tíddli, tídd'l-i) *adj. Chiefly British Slang.* Drunk. [19th century (meaning "a drink") : origin obscure.]
tiddly² *adj. British Informal.* Small; tiny. [From childish pronunciation of LITTLE.]
tid·dly·winks (tíddli-wingks, tídd'l-i-) *n.* Also **tid·dle·dy·winks** (tídd'l-di-). *Used with a singular verb.* A game in which players try to snap small counters into a cup by pressing them on the edge with a larger counter. [19th century : *tiddlywink*†.]
tide¹ (tīd) *n.* **1. a.** The twice-daily rise and fall in the surface level of the oceans, seas, and lower courses of rivers caused by the gravitational attraction of the Moon and, to a lesser extent, the Sun. **b.** A specific occurrence of such a variation. **c.** The waters in such a variation. See **flood tide, ebb tide, neap tide, spring tide. 2.** Any stress exerted on a body or part of a body by the gravitational attraction of another: *atmospheric tide; solar tide.* **3.** A tendency or movement regarded as alternating and inexorable: *The tide of public opinion has turned.* **4.** A time or season. Now archaic except in combination: *springtide; Christmastide.* **5.** *Archaic.* A favourable occasion; an opportunity. **6.** *Northern British.* A holiday or fair, usually occurring on a saint's day. **—swim with (or against) the tide.** To submit to (or oppose) majority views or trends.
~*v.* **tided, tiding, tides.** *—intr.* **1.** To rise and fall like the tide. **2.** To drift or ride with the tide. *—tr.* To carry along with or as if with the tide. **—tide over.** To support through a difficult period. *The five pounds tided him over until payday.* [Middle English *tid(e),* season, time, tide, Old English *tīd,* season, time.] **—tide·less** *adj.*
tide² *intr.v.* **tided, tiding, tides.** *Archaic.* To betide; befall. [Middle English *tiden,* Old English *tīdan,* "to fall as one's lot".] See feature, page 1731.
tide·mark (tīd-maark) *n.* **1.** A line or artificial indicator marking the high-water or low-water limit of the tides. **2.** *Chiefly British.* A mark showing the level a liquid has reached, such as that left when a bath has been emptied. **3.** *Chiefly British Informal.* A dirty mark on the skin showing the area which has been left unwashed.
tide table *n.* A list of the times of high and low tides on each day.
tide·wait·er (tīd-waytər) *n.* Formerly, a customs officer who boarded incoming ships at a harbour.
tide·wa·ter (tīd-wawtər ‖ *U.S. also* -wottər) *n.* **1.** Water that inundates land at high tide. **2.** Water affected by the tides; especially, tidal streams. **3.** *U.S.* Low coastal land drained by tidal streams.
tide·way (tīd-way) *n.* **1.** A channel in which a tidal current runs. **2.** The current itself.
tid·ings (tīdingz) *pl.n.* Information; news: *tidings of great joy.* [Plural of *tiding,* an event, Middle English *tiding,* Old English *tīdung,* perhaps from Old Norse *tidhendi,* events, from *tidhr,* occurring.]
ti·dy (tīdi) *adj.* **-dier, -diest. 1.** Orderly and neat in appearance or procedure. **2.** Orderly in habits; methodical. **3.** Substantial; considerable: *a tidy nest egg.* **4.** *U.S.* Adequate; satisfactory.
~*v.* **tidied, -dying, -dies.** *—tr.* To make tidy; put in order. *—intr.* To put things in order. Often used with *up.*
~*n., pl.* **tidies.** *n.* **1.** *British.* A small container for miscellaneous objects: *a desk tidy.* **2.** *U.S.* A fancy protective covering for the arms or headrest of a chair. [Middle English, timely, seasonable, fair, excellent, from *tid,* season, TIDE.] **—ti·di·ly** *adv.* **—ti·di·ness** *n.*
tie (tī) *v.* **tied, tying, ties.** *—tr.* **1.** To fasten or secure with a cord, rope, strap, or similar means. **2.** To fasten by drawing together the parts or sides with strings or laces and knotting them: *tie one's shoes.* **3. a.** To make (a knot or bow). **b.** To put a knot or bow in: *tie a ribbon.* **4.** To confine or restrict as if with cord. **5.** To bring together closely; unite. **6.** To end (a match or contest) with an equal score. **7.** To bind; commit. **8.** To restrict the freedom of action of. Often used with *down.* **9.** *Music.* To join (notes) by a tie. *—intr.* **1.** To be fastened with strings. **2.** To achieve equal scores in a contest.
~*n.* **1.** A cord, string, or other means by which something is tied. **2. a.** That which unites; a bond: *marital ties.* **b.** That which restricts one's freedom of action: *Pets can be a real tie.* **3.** A long, narrow band of fabric worn usually round the collar of a garment and tied in a knot or bow close to the throat, usually with the ends left hanging down the garment front. Also *U.S.* "necktie". **4.** A beam or rod that joins parts and gives support. **5.** *U.S.* A railway **sleeper** *(see).* **6. a.** A state of equality of scores, votes, or performance in a contest. **b.** A contest resulting in this; a draw. **7.** A match played between two teams; especially, one round in a knockout contest. **8.** *Music.* A curved line put either above or below two notes of the same pitch, indicating that the note is to be sustained for their combined duration. [Middle English *t(e)yen,* Old English *tīgan.*]
tie·back (tī-bak) *n. U.S.* **1.** A decorative loop of fabric, cord, or

PRONUNCIATION KEY

a, trap; aa, father; ai, fair; ar, star; aw, lawn; ay, play; b, bb, stab; rubber; ch, church; ck, ticket; d, dd, dead; ladder; e, dress; ee, bee; er, defer; ew, few; ewr, pure; ə, about; ər, letter; f, ff, fife; differ; g, gg, giggle; h, hat; i, kit; ī, price; īr, fire; j, judge; k, kick; l, ll, let; 'l, needle; m, mm, man; n, nn, no; 'n, sudden; ng, thing; o, lot; ō, no; o͝o, foot; o͞o, shoe; oor, poor; ow, cow; owr, hour; oy, boy; p, pp, pepper; r, rr, red; s, ss, sauce; sh, ship; t, tt, totter; th, thick; th, this; smooth; u, cut; ur, turn; v, vv, valve; w, wet; y, yes; z, zz, zebra; zh, vision; pleasure

IN FOREIGN WORDS:

aN, oN, Saint-Saëns; hl, Llanelli; Hluhluwe; kh, loch; lough; Khaled

STRESS MARK:

ín-sīt, insight; in-sī́t, incite

tidal power

TAPPING THE ENERGY OF THE OCEAN'S TIDES
A tidal power scheme with the capacity to generate enough electricity to light 24 small towns

The rise and fall of the world's tides represent a source of energy which could be used to generate huge supplies of electricity, but so far only limited attempts have been made to harness its potential. The first large-scale system to be put into operation, the generating station at La Rance in Brittany, France (below), was opened in 1966.

A barrage blocks the 750 metres (2,460 feet) across the estuary of the river Rance. When the tide comes in,

water is directed through tunnels leading to 24 giant turbines. Designed by Victor Kaplan, a German-born engineer, the turbines have blades that can be adjusted to present the correct angle to the oncoming water, whose force causes them to rotate. When the tide begins to ebb, the angle of the blades is changed so that the turbine is driven efficiently by water flowing out of the tunnels.

When a high tide is at its peak, the barrage is closed,

trapping the water in the tidal basin. Water can be released to drive the turbines when the tide is low but the demand for power is high.

Each of the 24 Rance turbines has a generating capacity of 10 megawatts, enough electrical power to light a town of 40,000 people. A difference of at least 6 metres (20 feet) depth between high and low water is necessary for a tidal power generator, so the number of suitable sites is limited.

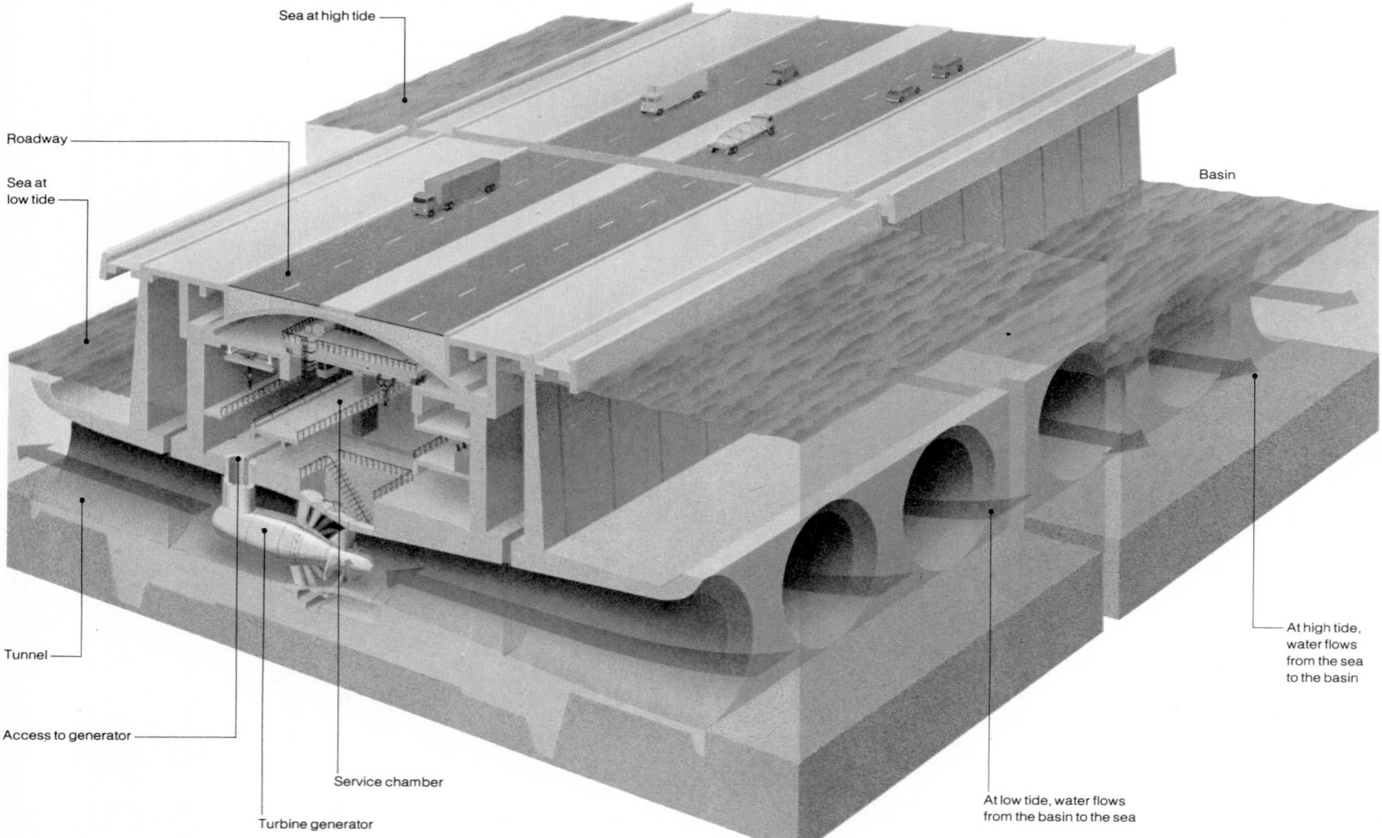

Sea at high tide

Roadway

Sea at low tide

Basin

Tunnel

Access to generator

Service chamber

Turbine generator

At high tide, water flows from the sea to the basin

At low tide, water flows from the basin to the sea

tiger *Found from Siberia to Sumatra, the tiger is a large cat which can weigh up to 250 kilograms (550 pounds) and reach a length of 4 metres (13 feet). It hunts at night, feeding chiefly on antelope.*

metal for parting and draping curtains to the sides. **2.** *Plural.* A pair of curtains meant to be tied back at about midlength.

tie beam *n.* A horizontal beam that connects the rafters in a roof.

tie-break (tī-brāyk) *n.* Also **tie-break·er** (-ər). In tennis, a means of deciding the winner of a set when neither competitor has won after a given number of games by playing a deciding number of points.

tie clip *n.* An ornamental clip that slides sideways onto the ends of a tie and into the shirtfront, thus holding the tie in place.

tied house (tīd) *n.* In Britain: **1.** A pub that is owned by a brewery and sells only the beers made by the brewery. Compare **free house**. **2.** A house or cottage that is owned by an employer and is assigned to the holder of a specific job. In this sense, also called "tied cottage".

tie-dye (tī-dī) *n.* **1.** A method of dyeing fabric in which parts of the fabric are tied so that they will not take the dye, giving the fabric a streaked or mottled look. **2.** A fabric dyed by this method.
~*tr.v.* **tie-dyed, -dyeing, -dyes.** To dye (fabric) by such a method.

tie in *tr.v.* **1.** To bring into conformity; coordinate. **2.** To use as a tie-in. —*intr.v.* To be in conformity; correspond or fit in.

tie-in (tī-in) *n.* **1.** A connection or relation. **2.** A book, record, souvenir, or other item designed to be sold after demand has been created by a film, television series, or the like. **3.** *U.S.* **a.** The sale of two (occasionally more) products or services so that a minor item is expected to be purchased with the major one. **b.** One of the products or services so offered, usually the minor one.

Tien Shan. See **Tian Shan**.

Tientsin. See **Tianjin**.

tie-pin (tī-pin) *n.* A kind of brooch or ornamental pin designed to

keep the long end of a tie attached to a shirt front. Also *U.S.* "stickpin".

tier¹ (teer) *n.* **1.** Any of a series of rows placed one above another, as in a theatre balcony. **2.** A level; a stratum: *tiers of local government.* ~*v.* **tiered, tiering, tiers.** —*tr.* To arrange in tiers. —*intr.* To rise in tiers. [Earlier *tire,* from French, sequence, rank, from *tirer,* to draw out, from Vulgar Latin *tīrāre*† (unattested).]

ti·er² (tī-ər) *n.* One that ties.

tierce (teers; *for sense 3, also* terss) *n.* **1.** Variant of **terce**. **2.** A former measure of liquid capacity, equal to a third of a pipe, or 42 wine gallons. **3.** In card games, a sequence of three cards of the same suit. **4.** The third position in fencing from which a parry or thrust can be made. **5.** *Music.* An interval of a third. [Middle English, one third, the third canonical hour, from Old French, from Latin *tertia* (noun), from Latin *tertius,* third.]

tiercel. Variant of **tercel**.

Ti·er·ra del Fue·go (ti-érrə del fwáy-gō, -áir-ə). Archipelago of islands off the extreme southeastern tip of South America, separated from the mainland by the Strait of Magellan. The eastern half belongs to Argentina, the western to Chile.

tier table (teer) *n.* A small table with two or more usually round tops.

tie up *tr.v.* **1. a.** To invest (money) in such a way that it is not available to be withdrawn and used: *Her money is all tied up in stocks and shares.* **b.** To subject (assets, for example) to such restrictions that they cannot be realised. **2.** To hinder, delay, or stop: *The strike tied up traffic for hours.* **3.** To connect; associate. Used with *with: The police tied up the murder with the robbery.* **4.** *Informal.* To bring to completion successfully: *tie up a contract.* **5.** *Informal.*

a. To be busy or very occupied: *I'm a bit tied up tonight.* **b.** To monopolise or pre-empt the use of: *He ties up the phone for hours.* —*intr.v.* To moor. Used of a ship.

tie-up (tī-up) *n.* **1.** *Informal.* **a.** A link or connection. **b.** An association or partnership; especially, a merger. **2.** *U.S.* A congested or immobilised condition, such as a traffic jam, work stoppage, or mechanical breakdown.

tiff (tif) *n.* **1.** A petty quarrel. **2.** A fit of irritation. —*intr.v.* **tiffed, tiffing, tiffs.** To quarrel. [18th century : origin obscure.]

tif·fa·ny (tiffəni) *n., pl.* **-nies.** A thin, transparent gauze of silk or cotton muslin. [Originally, dress for wearing on Twelfth Night (Epiphany), from Old French *tifanie,* Epiphany, from Medieval Latin *theophania,* THEOPHANY.]

Tiffany glass *n.* Favril glass *(see).* [After Louis *Tiffany* (died 1933), U.S. artist.]

tif·fin (tiffin) *n.* In India, a light lunch or snack. —*intr.v.* **tiffined, -fining, -fins.** To eat tiffin. [Short for obsolete *tiffing,* gerund of *tiff†,* to sip.]

Tiflis. See Tbilisi.

tig (tig) *n.* A children's game, **tag** *(see).* [Variant of TICK (ticking).]

ti·ger (tīgər) *n.* **1. a.** A large carnivorous feline mammal, *Panthera tigris,* of Asia, having a tawny coat with transverse black stripes. **b.** Broadly, any of various other similar felines. **2.** A fierce, aggressive, or audacious person. [Middle English *tigre,* from Old French, from Latin *tigris,* from Greek.] —**ti·ger·ish** *adj.*

Tiger balm *n.* A trademark for a mentholated ointment used as a decongestant inhalant and as a general panacea.

tiger beetle *n.* Any of numerous active, long-legged, predatory beetles of the family Cicindelidae, chiefly of warm, sandy regions.

tiger cat *n.* Broadly, any of various small felines resembling the tiger in either appearance or behaviour.

tiger lily *n.* A widely cultivated plant, *Lilium lancifolium,* native to Asia, having large, black-spotted reddish-orange flowers.

tiger moth *n.* Any of numerous moths of the family Arctiidae, characteristically having wings marked with spots or lines.

ti·ger's-eye (tīgərz-ī) *n.* Also **ti·ger·eye** (tīgər-ī). A yellow-brown semiprecious gemstone of quartz coloured by iron oxide. [From a fancied resemblance.]

tiger shark *n.* A large, chiefly tropical shark, *Galeocerdo cuvieri,* having a greyish-brown body marked with darker stripes.

tiger's milk *n.* A cold drink made from milk powder, orange juice, vegetable oil, and dried yeast.

tiger snake *n.* A venomous snake of the genus *Notechis,* of Australia and Tasmania, marked with brown and yellow stripes.

tight (tīt) *adj.* **tighter, tightest. 1.** Of such close construction, texture, or organisation as to be impermeable, especially by water or air. Often used in combination: *airtight; watertight.* **2.** Fastened, held, or closed securely. **3. a.** Compressed, leaving few or no intervening spaces; compact. **b.** Very full; leaving no spare time or room: *a tight schedule.* **4.** Drawn out to the fullest extent; taut. **5.** Cramped; constrained; rigid. **6.** Close-fitting, often uncomfortably so: *a tight fit.* **7.** Constricted: *a tight feeling in the chest.* **8.** *Informal.* Close-fisted; stingy. **9. a.** Difficult to obtain: *Money is tight.* **b.** Affected by scarcity: *a tight market.* **10.** Difficult to deal with or get out of: *a tight spot.* **11. a.** Strict in discipline or control. **b.** Characterised by such strict control: *runs a tight ship.* **12.** Closely contested: *a tight match.* **13.** *Regional.* Neat and trim. **14.** *Informal.* Drunk. —*adv.* **1.** Firmly; securely. **2.** Soundly: *sleep tight.* [Middle English *thyght,* probably variant of *thyght,* thickset, dense, from Old Norse *thēttr,* watertight, dense.] —**tight·ly** *adv.* —**tight·ness** *n.*

tight·en (tīt'n) *v.* **-ened, -ening, -ens.** —*tr.* To make tight or tighter. —*intr.* To become tight or tighter. —**tighten up.** To apply restrictions or constraints. Used with *on: The banks intend to tighten up on interest rates.* —**tight·en·er** *n.*

tight·fist·ed (tīt-fistid) *adj.* Stingy; mean. See Synonyms at **stingy.**

tight·knit (tīt-nit) *adj.* **1.** Closely connected or integrated: *a tight-knit community.* **2.** Carefully and closely organised.

tight·lipped (tīt-lipt) *adj.* **1.** Having the lips pressed together, as when tense or angry. **2.** Reticent.

tight·rope (tīt-rōp) *n.* **1.** A tightly stretched rope, usually of wire, on which acrobats perform high above the ground. **2.** A difficult or dangerous situation requiring a careful approach: *on a tightrope.*

tightrope walker *n.* An acrobat who performs on a tightrope.

tights (tīts) *pl.n.* **1.** A close-fitting, stretchable garment, elasticated at the waist and covering each leg and foot, worn by women and girls instead of stockings. Also *U.S.* "pantihose". **2.** Such a garment made from thicker fabric, worn by dancers, gymnasts, and the like of both sexes.

tight·wad (tīt-wod) *n.* *U.S. Slang.* One who hates to spend money; a miser. [TIGHT + WAD (money).]

tig·lic acid (tigglik) *n.* A thick, syrupy poisonous liquid, $CH_3CH:C(CH_3)CO_2H,$ derived from croton oil, having a spicy odour and used in making perfumes and flavouring agents. [From New Latin *(Croton) tiglium,* a seed of the (Croton) species, perhaps from Greek *tilos†,* liquid faeces (from the use of the seeds as a purgative).]

ti·gon (tī-gən, -gon) *n.* Also **ti·glon** (tīg-lən, tīg-, -lon). The hybrid offspring of a male tiger and a female lion. [Blend of TIGER and LION.]

Ti·gré (tée-grey ‖ *U.S.* tee-gráy) *n.* A Semitic language of northern Ethiopia.

ti·gress (tī-griss, -gress) *n.* **1.** A female tiger. **2.** A fiercely passionate woman.

Ti·gri·nya (tī-gréen-yə, tee-) *n.* A Semitic language of northern Ethiopia.

Ti·gris (tī-griss). River in southwestern Asia, rising in the Taurus Mountains of eastern Turkey and flowing for about 1 850 kilometres (1,150 miles) through Iraq to join the Euphrates and form the Shatt al Arab waterway, which passes through a delta and into the northern end of the Persian Gulf. Its flood-banks, along with those of the Euphrates, supported the agriculture on which the ancient civilisation of Mesopotamia was based.

tike. Variant of **tyke.**

tiger moth *The Jersey tiger moth is the largest of the six British species of tiger moth. It is found only in south Devon and the Channel Islands.*

---

tide

THE OCEAN'S EBB AND FLOW

The Earth's waters are subject to remote gravitational forces

The twice daily rise and fall of the oceans is caused by the gravitational effect on the Earth of the Moon and, less importantly, the Sun. Tidal ranges vary dramatically: the greatest is in the Bay of Fundy, Canada, where high and low water may differ by ˙5 metres (49 feet).

At any given time, there are two high tides on the Earth, the direct tide on the side facing the Moon and the indirect tide on the opposite side.

The direct tide is a bulge produced by the Moon pulling the Earth's water towards it more powerfully than it can pull the Earth itself.

The indirect tide occurs because the Moon's pull on the centre of the Earth is greater than on the water on the side of the Earth farthest from the Moon. So, as it were, the Earth is drawn away from the water most distant from the Moon, producing a second bulge.

As the Moon is in motion, circling the Earth once a month, the tides do not exactly coincide with the Earth's 24-hour cycle, but occur 50 minutes later each successive day.

The Sun has less effect than the Moon – just under half – because of its distance. Its influence is mostly masked by the Moon's, except at spring and neap tides, which occur every two weeks.

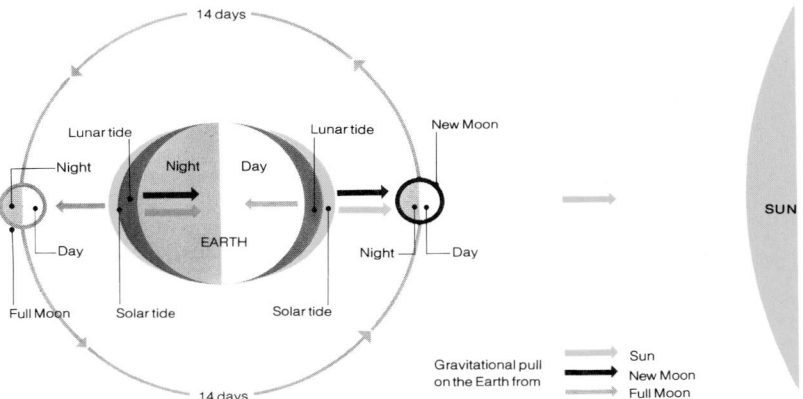

SPRING TIDES

SPRING TIDE *When the Moon, the Earth, and the Sun are in alignment, their gravitational pulls complement one another and produce an excep-tionally high tide called a spring tide. Spring tides occur every 14 days, at the time the Moon is full and also when it is new.*

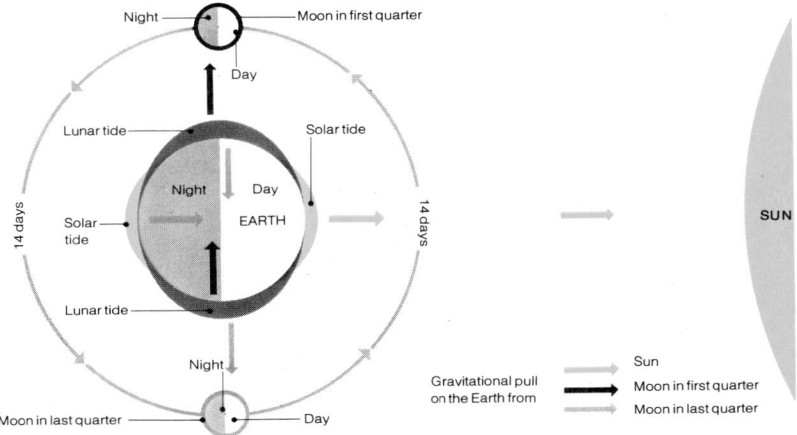

NEAP TIDES

NEAP TIDE *When the Moon, the Earth, and the Sun are at right angles, the Sun's pull partly neutralises the Moon's, so that high-water and low-water levels are less pronounced than at other times. These neap tides occur when the Moon is in its first quarter and its last quarter.*

tiki *New Zealand Maoris wore carved figurines like this jade tiki round their necks as good luck charms. Each tiki was believed to house the spirit of an ancestor.*

ti·ki (téeki) *n.* **1.** *Capital* **T.** A male figure in Polynesian mythology, sometimes identified as the first man. **2.** A wood or stone image of a Polynesian god. **3.** A Maori figurine representing an ancestor, often intricately carved from greenstone and worn about the neck as a talisman. [Maori.]

til (til, teel) *n.* The sesame plant, especially as used in India as a source of food and oil. [Hindi *til,* from Sanskrit *tila*†.]

ti·lap·i·a (ti-láppi-ə, -láypi-) *n.* Any African cichlid fish of the genus *Tilapia,* which broods eggs and young in the mouth and is used as a food fish. [New Latin, probably from an African name.]

til·bur·y (tíl-bri, -bəri || -berri) *n., pl.* **-ies.** A light open gig seating two persons, popular in the early 19th century. [Invented by *Tilbury,* a 19th-century London coach maker.]

Til·bur·y (tíl-bri, -bəri || -berri). Dockyard district in Essex on the north bank of the river Thames, opposite Gravesend, southeastern England. Tilbury serves as the chief container port of London. It was there in 1588 that Queen Elizabeth I spoke to the English navy on the eve of its engagement with the Spanish Armada.

til·de (tíld, -i, -ə) *n.* The diacritical mark (˜) placed over the letter *n* in Spanish to indicate the palatal nasal sound (ny) as in *cañon,* or over a vowel in Portuguese to indicate nasalisation as in *lã, pão.* [Spanish, from Latin *titulus,* superscription, TITLE.]

tile (tīl) *n.* **1.** A thin, flat, or convex slab of baked clay, plastic, concrete, cork, or other material, laid in rows to cover walls, floors, and roofs. **2.** A short length of pipe made of clay or concrete, used in sewers and drains. **3.** A hollow fired clay or concrete block used for building walls. **4.** Tiles collectively. **5.** Any of the marked playing pieces in games such as mah-jong. **—on the tiles.** *Informal.* Given over to debauchery: *a night on the tiles.*
~*tr.v.* **tiled, tiling, tiles.** To cover or provide with tiles. [Middle English *til(e), teyele,* Old English *tigele,* from West Germanic *tegala* (unattested), from Latin *tēgula,* from *tegere,* to cover.] **—til·er** *n.*

til·ing (tīling) *n.* **1.** Tiles collectively. **2.** A tiled surface.

till¹ (til) *tr.v.* **tilled, tilling, tills.** To prepare (land) for the growing of crops by ploughing, harrowing, and fertilising. [Middle English *tilien, til(l)en,* Old English *tilian,* to work at, labour, cultivate, from Germanic *tilōjan* (unattested), from *tilam* (unattested), aim, fixed point.] **—till·a·ble** *adj.*

till² *prep.* Until.
~*conj.* Until. [Middle English *till,* Old English *til,* probably from Germanic *tilam* (unattested), fixed point. See **till** (cultivate).]
Usage: *Till* and *until* are generally interchangeable, the choice between them being largely concerned with considerations of rhythm and balance. *Until* is the more commonly found at the beginning of a sentence. It also tends to stress the duration of time involved more than does *till,* which tends to be used more with reference to a point of time: *We shall have to stay here until he's finished working; Let's stay till ten o'clock and then we'll go.* Many people also find *till* less formal than *until,* as is reflected in the nonstandard use of an apostrophe with this word (*'till* or *'til).*

till³ *n.* A drawer, small box, or compartment for money, especially in a shop; for example, a **cash register** *(see).* [Middle English *tylle*†.]

till⁴ *n. Geology.* **Boulder clay** *(see).* [17th century (Scottish) : origin obscure.]

till·age (tíllij) *n.* **1.** The cultivation of land. **2.** The state of being tilled. **3.** Land that is tilled for crops.

til·land·si·a (ti-lándzi-ə) *n.* Any of various usually epiphytic plants of the genus *Tillandsia,* such as Spanish moss, of tropical and subtropical America. [New Latin, after Elias *Tillands* (died 1693), Swedish botanist.]

till·er¹ (tíllər) *n.* One that tills land.

tiller² *n.* A lever used to turn a rudder and steer a boat. [Middle English *tiler, telor,* beam of a crossbow, from Anglo-French *telier,* weaver's beam, from Medieval Latin *tēlārium,* from Latin *tēla,* web, warp of a fabric, weaver's beam.]

tiller³ *n.* **1.** A shoot, especially one that sprouts from the base of a grass. **2.** A sapling.
~*intr.v.* **tillered, -ering, -ers.** To send forth tillers. [Middle English *tiller* (unattested), Old English *telgor, telgra.*]

Til·ley lamp (tílli) *n.* A trademark for a portable lamp burning vaporised paraffin and having a special type of mantle designed to make it safe in the open air.

til·sit (tíl-sit; *German* -zit) *n.* A type of pale, firm, slightly pungent cheese with holes in it. [Originally made in TILSIT (Sovetsk).]

Tilsit. See **Sovetsk.**

tilt¹ (tilt) *v.* **tilted, tilting, tilts.** *—tr.* **1.** To cause to slope, as by raising one end; incline; tip. **2. a.** To aim or thrust (a lance) in a joust. **b.** To charge (an opponent). **3.** To forge with a tilt hammer. *—intr.* **1.** To slope; incline. **2.** To joust. Used with *at.* **3.** To quarrel. Used with *at.* **4.** To incline towards a specified view or position.
~*n.* **1. a.** An inclination from the horizontal or vertical; a slant. **b.** A sloping surface, as of the ground. **2.** The act of tilting. **3. a.** A medieval sport in which two mounted knights with lances charged together and attempted to unhorse one another. **b.** A thrust or blow with a lance. **4.** A dispute or other encounter between opponents. **5.** A tilt hammer. **6.** An inclination or bias towards a particular view or position. **—at full tilt.** At full speed. [Middle English *tylten, tilten,* perhaps from Old English *tyltan* (unattested; akin to *tealt,* unsteady), from Germanic.]

tilt² *n.* A canopy or awning for a boat, booth, or wagon.
~*tr.v.* **tilted, tilting, tilts.** To cover with a tilt. [Middle English *tild, teld,* Old English *teld,* a tent.]

tilth (tilth) *n.* **1.** The cultivation of land; tillage. **2.** The condition of land or soil with respect to encouraging plant growth. **3.** Tilled earth. [Middle English *tilth,* Old English *tilth,* from *tilian,* to TILL (cultivate).]

tilt hammer *n.* A heavy forge hammer having a pivoted lever by which it is tilted up and then allowed to drop.

tilt·yard (tílt-yaard) *n.* An enclosed area for tilting contests.

Tim. Timothy (New Testament).

Tim (tim) *n.* The **speaking clock** *(see).*

tim·bal, tym·bal (tímb'l) *n.* **1.** A kettledrum. **2.** A small cylindrical drum similar to a bongo or conga and used in Latin American music. [French *timbale,* variant (influenced by *cymbale,* cymbal) of obsolete *tamballe,* variant (influenced by *tambour,* tambour) of Spanish *atabal,* a kettledrum, from Arabic *aṭ-ṭabl,* the drum.]

tim·bale (tam-báal, tímb'l) *n.* **1.** A dish, usually of meat, fish, or vegetables in a sauce, or fruit with Chantilly, served in a bowl-shaped mould of pastry, rice, or pasta. **2.** A fireproof porcelain mould used for this dish. [French, "kettledrum", TIMBAL.]

tim·ber (tímbər) *n.* **1.** Trees or wooded land considered as a source of wood. **2. a.** Wood as a building material. **b.** A prepared piece of wood; especially, a beam in a structure. **c.** A rib in a ship's frame. **3.** Suitable or potential material: *He's executive timber.*
~*tr.v.* **timbered, -bering, -bers.** To support or shore up with timbers.
~*interj.* Used to warn of a falling tree. [Middle English *timber,* building, building material, Old English *timber.*]

tim·bered (tímbərd) *adj.* **1. a.** Constructed of or covered with timber. **b.** Built with exposed timbers. **2.** Wooded.

tim·ber-fram·ing (tímbər-fráyming) *n.* A method of building in which a frame of timber is erected and then filled in with plaster or bricks. **—tim·ber-frame** *adj.*

tim·ber·head (tímbər-hed) *n. Nautical.* A timber end that projects above the deck and is used as a bollard.

timber hitch *n. Nautical.* A knot used for fastening a rope around a spar or log to be hoisted or towed.

tim·ber·ing (tímbəring) *n.* Timber or work made of it.

tim·ber·land (tímbər-land) *n. U.S.* Forested land considered commercially.

timber line *n.* The limit of altitude or latitude limit beyond which trees do not grow. Also called "tree line".

timber wolf *n.* A greyish wolf, *Canis lupus,* of forested northern regions, especially of North America. Also called "grey wolf".

tim·ber·work (tímbər-wurk) *n.* The part of a structure made with timbers, such as the framework of a boat or house.

tim·bre (támbər, taɴbr, *also* tímbər) *n.* The quality of a sound that distinguishes it from other sounds of the same pitch and volume; especially, the distinctive tone of a musical instrument, a voice, or a voiced speech sound; tone colour. [French, from Old French, a bell struck with a hammer, timbrel, timbre, from Vulgar Latin *timbano* (unattested), a drum, from Medieval Greek *timbanon,* from Greek *tumpanon.* See **tympanum.**]

tim·brel (tímbrəl) *n.* An ancient percussion instrument similar to a tambourine. [Diminutive of Middle English *timbre,* from Old French, a drum, TIMBRE.]

Tim·buk·tu (tím-buk-tóo). *French* **Tom·bouc·tou** (toɴ-bŏŏk-tóo). City in central Mali, lying near the river Niger, to which it is connected by a series of canals. It was founded in the 11th century and rose to become one of the great trading centres (especially for gold) and a leading intellectual centre of Islam. It was sacked by Moroccans in 1593 and never regained its economic or cultural status.

time (tīm) *n.* **1. a.** A nonspatial continuum in which events occur in apparently irreversible succession from the past through the present to the future. **b.** Any point or period on this continuum, such as a day, month, or year. **2.** A quantity measuring duration by comparison with some periodic process, such as the Earth's rotation or the vibration of electromagnetic radiation, regarded in relativity theory as a fourth coordinate required to completely specify an event. See **space-time.** **3.** An indefinite but finite period on this continuum: *Time will tell; You'll recover in time.* **4.** A specific point on the continuum reckoned in hours and minutes: *Can you tell me the time?* **5.** A system by which such intervals are measured or such numbers are reckoned; solar time: *Greenwich mean time.* **6. a.** *Often plural.* An interval marked by similar events, conditions, or phenomena; especially, a span of years; an era: *Edwardian times; a time of troubles.* **b.** *Plural.* The present with respect to prevailing conditions and trends: *move with the times.* **7. a.** One's lifetime. **b.** One's heyday. **8.** A suitable or opportune moment or season. **9. a.** A moment or period designated, as by custom, for a specified activity: *harvest time; bedtime.* **b.** A moment or period designated for something to happen: *got to work on time.* **c.** A period allotted or given over to a specific activity: *Your time is up; I need time to think.* **d.** A period at one's disposal: *free time; Have you time for a chat?* **10.** An appointed or fated moment, especially of death or giving birth: *died before his time; Her time is near.* **11. a.** One of several instances: *We called on you twice but both times you were out.* **b.** *Plural.* Used to indicate the number of instances by which a quantity is or is to be multiplied: *It's at least three times as big.* **12.** An occasion or experience of a specified kind: *had a marvellous time; showed us a good time.* **13.** *Informal.* A prison sentence: *do time.* **14. a.** The customary period of work: *work full time.* **b.** The period spent working. **c.** A period of apprenticeship: *serve one's time.* **d.** The hourly pay rate: *earned double time on Sundays.* **15.** The rate of speed of a measured activity: *marching in double time.* **16.** The characteristic beat of musical rhythm: *three-four time.* **17.** *British.* The hour at which a bar in a pub closes; closing time: *Time, gentlemen, please!* **18.** *Plural. Capital T.* Used as the title of a newspaper: *The Oxford Times.* **—against time.** With a quickly approaching time limit. **—at one time. 1.** Simultaneously. **2.** At a period or moment in the past. **—at the same time.** However; nonetheless. **—at times.** On occasion; sometimes. **—behind the times.** Out-of-date; old-fashioned. **—bide (one's) time.** To wait for an opportune moment. **—for the time being.** Temporarily. **—from time to time.** Once in a while; at intervals. **—have no time for.** To dislike; be intolerant of: *I've no time for clock-watchers.* **—high time.** Past the time for; fully time. **—in good time. 1.** In a reasonable length of time. **2.** At or before the proper time. **—in no time.** Almost instantly; immediately. **—in time. 1.** Before the time limit expires. **2.** Within an indefinite amount of passing time. **3.** In tempo; keeping the rhythm. **—keep time. 1.** To indicate the correct time. **2.** To maintain the tempo or rhythm. **—kill time.** To occupy oneself in a desultory way while waiting for time to pass. **—make up time.** To compensate for lost time. **—mark time. 1.** To move the feet as though marching but without moving forward. **2.** To act or function in an unproductive or purposeless fashion. **3.** To stop doing something temporarily, usually with a view to restarting when conditions permit. **—once upon a time.** Long ago; once. Used especially to introduce fairy tales. **—on time. 1.** Promptly; according to schedule. **2.** *U.S.* By paying in instalments. **—pass the time of day.** To chat about general topics such as the weather. **—play for time.** To use delaying tactics in order to gain extra time. **—take (one's) time.** To do something in a careful or leisurely fashion. **—time after time.** Repeatedly. **—time and (time) again.** Often; frequently. **—the time of (one's) life.** A highly pleasurable experience. **—time of the month.** One's menstrual period. Used euphemistically. **—time out of mind.** Before recorded time.

~*adj.* **1.** Of or relating to time. **2.** Constructed so as to be able to be operated at or indicating a particular moment: *a time bomb.* **3.** Payable on a future date or dates: *a time loan.*

~*tr.v.* **timed, timing, times. 1.** To set the time for (an event or occasion). **2.** To adjust to keep accurate time. **3.** To regulate for the most appropiate sequence of movements or events. **4.** To record the speed or duration of. **5.** To set or maintain the tempo, speed, or duration of. [Middle English *time,* Old English *tīma.*]

time and a half *n.* A rate of pay that is one and a half times the regular rate, as for overtime work.

time and motion study *n.* An analysis of the working methods involved in an industrial operation with a view to improving efficiency. Also called "motion study".

time base *n. Electronics.* An electronic circuit that repeatedly produces a voltage increasing to a given value and falling abruptly to zero or a minimum value, used to deflect the electron beam horizontally in an oscilloscope or television.

time bill *n.* A bill of exchange payable at an indicated future time.

time bomb *n.* **1.** A bomb with a detonating mechanism that can be set for a particular time. **2.** A potentially dramatic or disastrous situation.

time capsule *n.* A sealed container preserving articles and records of contemporary culture for study in the distant future.

time·card (tīm-kaard) *n.* A card, either maintained by the employee or stamped by a time clock, recording an employee's arrival and departure time each day.

time clock *n.* A clock that records the arrival and departure times of employees, usually by punching timecards.

time constant *n. Physics.* A measure of the amount of damping in an oscillating system, such as a vibrating structure or a circuit carrying an alternating signal, measured by the time taken for the amplitude to fall to a value 1/e (about 0.368) of its initial value or to increase to (1 − 1/e) (0.632) of its final steady value.

time-con·sum·ing (tīm-kən-sew-ming, -so͞o- || -kon-, -sho͞o-) *adj.* Taking up a great deal of time or too much time.

time deposit *n.* A bank deposit that cannot be withdrawn before a date decided at the time of deposit.

time dilation *n.* Also **time dilatation.** The relativistic slowing of a clock that moves with respect to a stationary observer.

time exposure *n.* **1.** A photographic exposure made for a relatively long period of time. **2.** An image made by such an exposure.

time fuse *n.* A fuse designed to set off an explosive charge after a preset period of time, or to burn for a preset period.

time-hon·oured (tīm-onnərd) *adj.* Honoured because of age or age-old observance.

time immemorial *n.* **1.** Time long past, beyond memory or record. **2.** *Law.* Time antedating legal records.

time·keep·er (tīm-keepər) *n.* **1.** A timepiece. **2.** The person who keeps track of time, as in a sports event or in a place of employment. **—time·keep·ing** *n.*

time-lag, time lag (tīm-lag) *n.* The interval of time between two events, the second of which is usually a result of the first.

time-lapse (tīm-laps) *adj.* Of or using a cinematic technique for filming a naturally slow process, such as the unfolding of a leaf, by photographing it at intervals so that the continuous projection of the frames gives an accelerated view of it.

time·less (tīm-ləss, -liss) *adj.* **1.** Independent of time; unending; eternal. **2.** Unaffected by time; ageless. **—time·less·ly** *adv.* **—time·less·ness** *n.*

time lock *n.* A lock set to open at a specific time.

time·ly (tīm-li) *adj.* **-lier, -liest. 1.** Occurring at a suitable or opportune time; well-timed. **2.** *Archaic.* Early; premature.

~*adv.* **1.** Opportunely; in time. **2.** *Archaic.* Early; soon. [Middle English : TIME + -LY.] **—time·li·ness** *n.*

time machine *n.* An imaginary vehicle supposed to be capable of transporting people backwards and forwards in time.

time off *n.* A period of absence or rest from work as a result of illness, holidays, or the like.

time on *n. Sports. Australian.* Extra time.

time·ous (tīm-əss) *adj. Scottish.* Timely. [TIME + -OUS.] **—time·ous·ly** *adv.*

time-out (tīm-owt) *n.* Also **time out.** *Chiefly U.S.* **1.** A brief cessation of play at the request of a sports team for rest or consultation. **2.** Any short break from work or play.

time·piece (tīm-peess) *n.* An instrument, such as a clock or chronometer, that measures, registers, or records time.

tim·er (tīmər) *n.* **1.** A switch or regulator that controls or activates another mechanism at preset intervals. **2.** A timepiece, especially one used for measuring intervals of time. **3.** A person who keeps track of time; a timekeeper.

time reversal *n. Symbol* **T** A mathematical operation representing a transformation from a given physical system undergoing a given sequence of events (states) to a system in which the exact reverse sequence of states is undergone.

times (tīmz) *prep.* Multiplied by: *Five times two is ten.*

time's arrow *n. Physics.* The existence of a single direction for the passage of time such that time reversal does not occur in physical systems, as indicated by such phenomena as spontaneous increase in entropy, the spreading of waves from a source, or the expansion of the universe.

time·sav·ing (tīm-sayving) *adj.* Saving time through an efficient method or a shorter route. **—time·sav·er** *n.*

time scale *n.* A sequence of events used as a measure of duration or the passing of time.

time·serv·er (tīm-servər) *n.* A person who conforms to the prevailing ways and opinions of his time or condition for personal advantage; an opportunist. **—time·serv·ing** *adj.* & *n.*

time sharing *n.* **1.** *Computing.* A system in which two or more users communicate with a computer at the same time, data being processed successively for short periods in a way controlled by the computer so that each terminal appears to have sole use of the machine. Compare **batch processing. 2.** A system whereby a number of people each buy a share in a flat, villa, or other holiday accommodation, enabling them each to spend a given period there every year.

time sheet *n.* A sheet of paper recording the hours worked by an employee.

time signal *n.* An announcement, usually on the radio, of the correct time.

time signature *n. Music.* A symbol in the form of a numerical fraction, written at the beginning of a piece of music to indicate the number and length of notes in each bar. Thus 3/4 means there are three crotchets in each bar; 6/8 means six quavers. The lower number of the two indicates the time value of each note, regarded as a fraction of a semibreve. Also called "signature".

time span *n.* The length of time occupied by or allocated for a particular event or purpose: *the time span of a man's life.*

time·switch (tīm-swich) *n.* A switch whereby a mechanism can be preset to start or finish operating automatically.

time·ta·ble (tīm-tayb'l) *n.* **1.** A list of the times at which certain events, such as arrivals and departures at an airport or railway station, are expected to take place. **2.** A plan giving the times when classes or lectures will take place, as in a school or college. **3.** A schedule for any planned sequence of events. **—time·ta·ble** *tr.v.*

time-test·ed (tīm-testid) *adj.* Having been proved effective by prolonged testing.

time trial *n.* A competitive event, as in sports, that must be completed within a given time.

time value *n.* The length of a musical note in relation to the other notes in the score or in relation to the tempo.

time warp *n.* An imaginary distortion or interruption in the flow of time from past to future, featured typically in science fiction.

time·work (tīm-wurk) *n.* Work paid for in specific time units, as by the hour. Compare **placework. —time·work·er** *n.*

time·worn (tīm-wawrn || -wōrn) *adj.* **1.** Showing the effects of long use or wear. **2.** Used too often; trite.

time zone *n.* Any of the 24 equal longitudinal divisions of the Earth's surface in which a standard time, the mean time of a meridian near the centre, is kept, the primary division being that bisected by the Greenwich meridian. Each zone is 15 degrees of longitude in width, with local variations, and observes a clock time one hour earlier than the zone immediately to the east. Also called "international time zone". See feature, next page.

tim·id (timmid) *adj.* **-ider, -idest. 1.** Shrinking from dangerous or difficult circumstances; hesitant or fearful. **2.** Shrinking from public attention; shy. **3.** Characterised by hesitancy or lack of courage. —See Synonyms at **shy.** [Latin *timidus,* from *timēre*†, to fear.] **—ti·mid·i·ty** (ti-middəti), **tim·id·ness** *n.* **—tim·id·ly** *adv.*

tim·ing (tīming) *n.* **1.** The art or operation of regulating occurrence, pace, or coordination to achieve the most desirable effects, as in music, the theatre, athletics, or in a machine. **2.** The way in which the distribution of electricity to the plugs of an internal-combustion engine is synchronised with the speed of the engine.

PRONUNCIATION KEY

a, trap; aa, father; ai, fair;
ar, star; aw, lawn; ay, play;
b, bb, stab; rubber;
ch, church; ck, ticket;
d, dd, dead; ladder; e, dress;
ee, bee; er, defer; ew, few;
ewr, pure; ə, about;
ər, letter; f, ff, fife; differ;
g, gg, giggle; h, hat; i, kit;
ī, price; īr, fire; j, judge;
k, kick; l, ll, let; 'l, needle;
m, mm, man; n, nn, no;
'n, sudden; ng, thing; o, lot;
ō, no; o͝o, foot; o͞o, shoe;
oor, poor; ow, cow;
owr, hour; oy, boy;
p, pp, pepper; r, rr, red;
s, ss, sauce; sh, ship;
t, tt, totter; th, thick; th, this;
smooth; u, cut; ur, turn;
v, vv, valve; w, wet; y, yes;
z, zz, zebra; zh, vision;
pleasure

IN FOREIGN WORDS:

aN, oN, Saint-Saëns;
hl, Llanelli; Hluhluwe;
kh, loch; lough; Khaled

STRESS MARK:

in-sīt, insight; in-sīt, incite

ti·moc·ra·cy (tǐ-móckrə-si) *n., pl.* **-cies. 1.** A state described by Plato in which love of honour is the guiding principle. **2.** An Aristotelian state in which political power is proportional to property owned. [Old French *tymocracie,* from Medieval Latin *tīmocratia,* from Greek *timokratia : timē,* honour, worth + -CRACY.] **—ti·mo·crat·ic** (tǐm-ə-kráttik, -ō-) *adj.*

Ti·mor (tée-mawr, tǐ-). Mountainous Indonesian island, the largest and easternmost of the Lesser Sunda Islands. The western half of the island, formerly Netherlands Timor, became part of Indonesia in 1949. The eastern half was formerly Portuguese Timor, an overseas province of Portugal from 1914 until 1975.

tim·or·ous (tímmərəss) *adj.* Full of apprehensiveness; timid. [Middle English, from Old French *timoureus,* from Medieval Latin *timorōsus,* from Latin *timor,* fear, from *timēre†,* to fear.] **—tim·or·ous·ly** *adv.* **—tim·or·ous·ness** *n.*

Tim·o·thy (tímməthi) *n. Abbr.* **Tim.** Either of two books of the New Testament, each an epistle to St. Timothy attributed to St. Paul.

Timothy, Saint. Also **Ti·moth·e·us** (ti-mōthi-əss, tǐ- ‖ -móthi-). Christian leader of the first century A.D.; convert and companion of St. Paul; legendary martyr.

tim·o·thy grass (tímməthi) *n.* A grass, *Phleum pratense,* native to Eurasia, having narrow, cylindrical flower spikes, and widely cultivated for hay. Also called "timothy". [After *Timothy* Hanson, American farmer, who introduced it in the Carolinas about 1720.]

tim·pa·ni, tym·pa·ni (tímpəni) *pl.n.* A set of kettledrums. [Italian, plural of *timpano,* kettledrum, from Latin *tympanum,* TYMPANUM.] **—tim·pa·nist** *n.*

timpanum. Variant of **tympanum.**

tin (tin) *n.* **1.** *Symbol* **Sn** A malleable, silvery metallic element obtained chiefly from cassiterite. It is used to coat other metals to prevent corrosion, and forms part of numerous alloys, such as soft solder, pewter, type metal, and bronze. Atomic number 50, atomic weight 118.69, melting point 231.89°C, boiling point 2,507°C, relative density 7.31, valencies 2, 4. **2.** Tin plate. **3.** A tin container or box. **4. a.** An airtight container, usually made of tin-coated iron, in which meat, vegetables, or other foods are preserved; a can. **b.** The contents of such a container; a tinful. **5.** *British.* A type of loaf of bread baked in a long rectangular tin. **6.** *Slang.* Money. ~*tr.v.* **tinned, tinning, tins. 1.** To plate or coat with tin. **2.** To preserve by sealing in airtight tins; can. [Middle English *tin,* Old English *tin,* from Germanic *tinam* (unattested).]

tin·a·mou (tínnə-mōō) *n.* Any of various chicken-like or quail-like birds of the family Tinamidae, of Central and South America. [French, from Galibi *tinamu.*]

tin·cal (tíngk'l) *n.* Crude borax. [Malay *tingkal,* from Sanskrit *ṭankaṇa†.*]

tin can *n.* A container of tin-plated metal used especially for preserving food.

tinct (tingkt) *n. Archaic.* A colour or tint. ~*adj. Poetic.* Tinged or tinted. [Latin *tinctus,* past participle of *tingere,* to TINGE.]

tinct. tincture.

tinc·to·ri·al (tingk-táw-ri-əl ‖ -tô-) *adj.* Pertaining to the processes of dyeing or colouring. [Latin *tinctōrius,* from *tinctus,* past participle of *tingere,* to TINGE.]

tinc·ture (tíngkchər) *n. Abbr.* **tinct. 1.** *Archaic.* A dyeing substance; a pigment. **2.** An imparted colour; a tinge; a tint. **3.** A trace or hint. **4.** *Pharmacology.* An alcohol solution of a nonvolatile medicine: *tincture of iodine.* **5.** A particular heraldic metal, colour, or fur. **6.** *Informal.* An alcoholic drink. Used humorously. ~*tr.v.* **tinctured, -turing, -tures. 1.** To stain or tint with a colour. **2.** To infuse, as with a quality; impregnate. [Middle English, from

---

time zone

MAKING THE CLOCK CHASE THE SUN

What time it is depends on where you are

Midday is the time when the Sun is at its highest in the sky but, because the world rotates once every 24 hours, this occurs at different hours around the globe. Using the Sun's position as the arbiter of the clock, actual time varies minutely with every mile to east or west and it differs very significantly over more substantial distances. Noon in London, for example, would be 2 p.m. (14.00) in Turkey.

With the beginning of rapid travel by railway this variation began to pose timetable difficulties. In 1884 the International Meridian Conference adopted a plan for rationalising times proposed by Canadian railway planner, Sir Sandford Fleming. The 360 degrees of longitude were divided by 24 to give a 15-degree section or Time Zone for each hour of the day. As the line 0° longitude ran through the Royal Observatory at Greenwich, England, the time there became known as Greenwich Mean Time.

On the other side of the globe at 180° longitude, where time is always 12 hours different from Greenwich, the longitude line became the International Date Line. Those crossing it from east to west add 24 hours and lose a day. Those going the other way subtract 24 hours and repeat a day. Like all the dividing lines of the Time Zones, the IDL generally follows its longitude line but deviates to avoid land areas or island groups under one government.

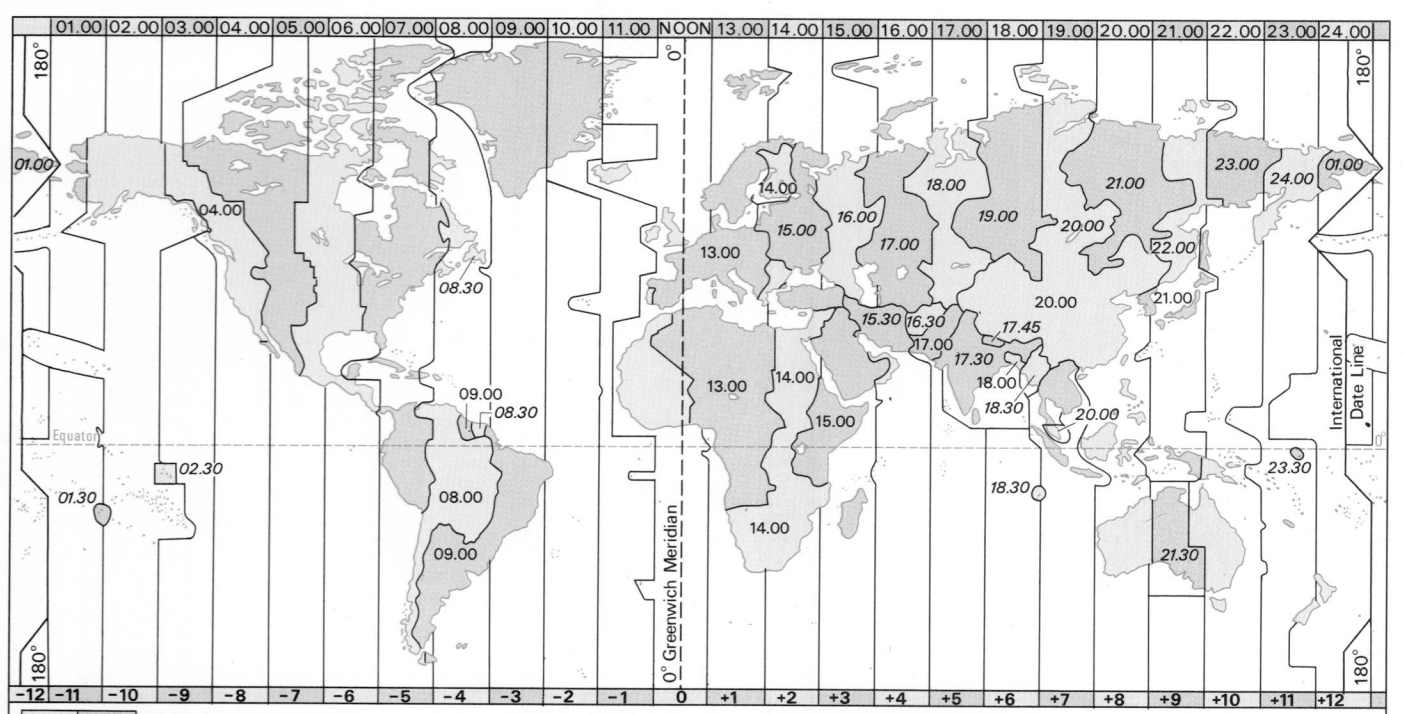

Standard Time Zones
Upright figures = Standard Time (e.g. 17.00)
Italic figures = variations from standard time (e.g. 15.30)
Figures with minus = hours behind GMT (e.g. – 4)
Figures with plus = hours ahead of GMT (e.g. + 4)

CHANGES FROM STANDARD TIME *Summer Time, or Daylight Saving Time, is adopted by some countries for part of the year. During Summer Time, these countries are one hour ahead of the time shown on the map. The United Kingdom uses Summer Time from late March to late October. Time zones in the U.S.S.R. are 1 hour ahead of Standard Time.*

Latin *tinctūra,* a dyeing, from *tinctus,* past participle of *tingere,* TINGE.]
tin·der (tíndər) *n.* Readily combustible material, such as dry twigs, used to kindle fires. [Middle English *tinder,* Old English *tynder,* from Germanic *tund-* (unattested), past participle form of *tend-* (unattested), to burn, kindle.]
tin·der·box (tíndər-boks) *n.* **1.** A metal box for holding tinder, and usually flint and steel. **2.** A potentially explosive place, person or situation.
tine (tīn) *n.* **1.** A branch of a deer's antlers. **2.** A prong on a fork, pitchfork, or similar implement. [Middle English *tind, tene,* Old English *tind,* from Germanic *tind-* (unattested), point.]
tin·e·a (tínni-ə) *n.* Any of several fungous skin diseases; especially, athlete's foot. [Latin *tinea*†, a gnawing worm, moth.]
tin ear *n. Informal.* An inability to reproduce accurately, or distinguish between, different sounds, especially different musical notes.
tin·foil (tín-foyl) *n.* **1.** A thin, pliable sheet of tin or of tin-lead alloy, formerly used as a protective wrapping. **2.** Any thin metal foil, such as aluminium foil.
ting (ting) *n.* A single high-pitched metallic sound, as of a small bell.
~intr.v. **tinged** (tingd), **tinging, tings.** To give forth such a sound. [Middle English *tyngen* (imitative).]
ting·a·ling (tíng-ə-líng) *n.* The high-pitched sound made by a small bell. [Imitative.] **—ting·a·ling** *adv.*
tinge (tinj) *tr.v.* **tinged** (tinjd), **tingeing** or **tinging, tinges. 1.** To impart a trace of colour to; tint. **2.** To modify, as by the admixture of a contrasting quality: *comedy tinged with tragedy.*
~n. **1.** A faint trace of a colour incorporated or added. **2.** A slight admixture of any modifying quality or property. [Middle English *tyngen,* from Latin *tingere,* to moisten, plunge, dye.]
tin·gle (tíng-g'l) *v.* **-gled, -gling, -gles.** *—intr.* **1.** To have a prickling, stinging sensation as from the cold, a sharp slap, or excitement: *tingle all over with joy.* **2.** To cause such a sensation or feeling. *—tr.* To cause to tingle.
~n. A tingling sensation. [Middle English *tinglen,* originally, to be affected with a ringing sound in the ears, perhaps variant of TINKLE.] **—tin·gler** *n.* **—tin·gly** *adj.*
tin god *n.* **1.** A person who is unjustifiably or mistakenly revered. **2.** A self-important person in a position of some authority.
tin hat *n. Informal.* A soldier's protective steel helmet.
tink·er (tíngkər) *n.* **1.** A travelling mender of metal household utensils. **2.** *Scottish & Irish.* A Gypsy. **3.** One who is clumsy at his work; a bungler. **4.** An act of tinkering with something.
~v. **tinkered, -ering, -ers.** *—intr.* **1.** To work as a tinker. **2.** To work at or fiddle with something, often clumsily or ineffectually, with the aim of effecting repairs or improvements. *—tr.* To mend, patch up, or experiment with. —See Synonyms at **interfere.** [Middle English *tyn(e)kere,* perhaps from *tynken,* to TINKLE (perhaps from the sounds made by a tinker at work).]
tinker's damn *n. Slang.* The slightest amount: *not worth a tinker's damn.* Also called "tinker's cuss". [From the tinker's reputed habit of cursing.]
tin·kle (tíngk'l) *v.* **-kled, -kling, -kles.** *—intr.* To make a series of light metallic sounds, such as those of a small bell. *—tr.* To cause to tinkle.
~n. **1.** A light, clear metallic sound or a sound suggestive of it. **2.** *British Informal.* A telephone call; a ring. **3.** *British Informal.* An act of urinating. [Middle English *tynclen,* frequentative of *tynken* (imitative).] **—tin·kly** *adj.*
tin liz·zie (lízzi) *n. Slang.* A dilapidated or cheap car. [TIN (by analogy with the common food tin) + *Lizzie,* pet form of *Elizabeth.*]
tin·ner (tínnər) *n.* **1.** A tin miner. **2.** A tinsmith. **3.** One who tins things; a canner.
tin·ni·tus (tínnitəss, ti-nītəss) *n.* A sound in the ears, such as buzzing, ringing, or whistling, caused by disease of the inner ear, certain drugs, or by a defect in the auditory nerve. [Latin *tinnītus,* from the past participle of *tinnīre,* to ring, tinkle (imitative).]
tin·ny (tínni) *adj.* **-nier, -niest. 1.** Of, containing, or yielding tin. **2.** Cheaply and badly made. **3.** Having a thin metallic sound. **4.** Tasting or smelling of tin, as food from a tin can.
~n., pl. **tinnies.** *Australian Slang.* A can of beer. **—tin·ni·ly** *adv.* **—tin·ni·ness** *n.*
tin-o·pen·er (tín-ōp-nər, -ənər) *n.* An instrument for piercing and opening tin cans.
Tin Pan Alley *n.* **1.** A district associated with players, composers, and publishers of popular music. **2.** The publishers, players, and composers of popular music considered as a group; the world of commercial popular music. [From slang *tin-pan,* noisy, tinny.]
tin plate *n.* Thin sheet iron or steel coated with tin.
tin-plate (tín-playt) *tr.v.* **-plated, -plating, -plates.** To coat with tin. **—tin-plat·er** *n.*
tin·pot (tín-pot) *adj.* Worthless; contemptible: *a tinpot dictator.*
tin pyrites *n.* A mineral, **stannite** *(see).*
tin·sel (tínss'l) *n.* **1.** Very thin sheets, strips, or threads of a glittering material used as a decoration. **2.** Anything superficially fine or attractive but basically valueless.
~adj. **1.** Made of or decorated or covered with tinsel. **2.** Gaudy and showy but basically valueless.
~tr.v. **tinselled** or *U.S.* **tinseled, -selling** or *U.S.* **-seling, -sels. 1.** To decorate with or as if with tinsel. **2.** To give a superficially fine or showy appearance to. [Earlier *tinselle,* adorned with metallic threads, probably from Old French *estincelle,* a spark, from Vulgar Latin *stincilla* (unattested), variant of Latin *scintilla,* spark.] **—tin·sel·ly** *adj.*
tin·smith (tín-smith) *n.* One who makes and repairs things made of light metal, such as tin.
tin·snips (tín-snips) *pl.n.* **Snips** *(see).*
tin·stone (tín-stōn) *n.* A mineral, **cassiterite** *(see).*
tint (tint) *n.* **1.** A shade of a colour, especially a pale or delicate variation; a tinge. **2.** A gradation of a colour made by adding white to it to lessen its saturation. **3.** A slight coloration; a hue. **4.** A barely detectable modifying quality; a trace. **5.** In engraving, a shaded effect produced by a series of fine parallel lines. **6.** *Printing.* A panel of usually pale colour on which matter in another colour, as an illustration, may be printed. **7.** A dye for the hair.
~tr.v. **tinted, tinting, tints.** To imbue with a tint; colour. [Variant (probably influenced by Italian *tinto,* tint) of earlier *tinct,* from Latin *tinctus,* a dipping or dyeing, from the past participle of *tingere,* to wet, dip]
tin·tack (tín-tak) *n.* A small, tin-covered nail with a broad flat head, usually made of iron.
Tin·tag·el (tin-táj'l). Village on the northern coast of Cornwall, southwestern England. It is the site of a ruined 12th-century castle, reputed to have been the birthplace of King Arthur.
tin·tin·nab·u·la·tion (tínti-nábbew-láysh'n) *n.* The ringing or tinkling of bells. [From TINTINNABULUM.]
tin·tin·nab·u·lum (tínti-nábbew-ləm) *n., pl.* **-la** (-lə). A small, tinkling bell or set of bells. [Latin, from *tintinnāre, tintinnīre,* to jingle, reduplication of *tinnīre,* to ring. See **tinnitus.**] **—tin·tin·nab·u·lar** (-lər), **tin·tin·nab·u·lar·y** (-ləri) *adj.*
tint·om·e·ter (tin-tómmitər) *n.* A **colorimeter** *(see)* for measuring concentration. [TINT + -METER.]
Tin·to·ret·to (tíntə-réttō) (1518–94). Venetian painter. Called "Il Tintoretto" because his father had been a dyer, he was a versatile painter, handling religious, mythological, and historical subjects, as well as portraits. Among his many surviving works are *St. George and the Dragon* (*c.* 1550), and the series of paintings illustrating the life of Christ and the Virgin in the Scuola di San Rocco, in Venice (1576–88).
tin·type (tín-tīp) *n.* A **ferrotype** *(see).*
tin whistle *n.* A **penny whistle** *(see).*
tin·works (tín-wurk) *pl.n. Used with a singular or plural verb.* A place where tin is smelted and rolled.
ti·ny (tīni) *adj.* **-nier, -niest.** Extremely small; minute. See Synonyms at **small.** [From Middle English *tine*† (adjective and noun, "a little") + -Y.]
-tion *n. suffix.* Indicates action, process, condition or result; for example, **adsorption.** [Middle English *-cioun,* from Old French *-tion,* from Latin *-tiō* (stem *-tiōn-*) : *-t-,* of the past participial stem + *-iōn-,* -ION.]
tip[1] (tip) *n.* **1.** The end or extremity of something, especially of something pointed or tapering. **2.** A piece or attachment fitted to the end of something, such as a ferrule, the end of a billiard cue, or the filter on a cigarette. **3.** The bud of a leaf on a tea plant. **—the tip of the iceberg.** A small perceptible part of something, such as a problem or task, that hides its true dimensions.
~tr.v. **tipped, tipping, tips. 1.** To furnish with a tip. **2.** To cover, decorate, or remove the tip of. **3.** To attach (an insert) in a book by gluing along the binding edge. Often used with *in.* [Middle English *tip(pe),* probably from Old Norse *typpi* (noun), *typpa* (verb), from Germanic *tupp-* (unattested), TOP.]
tip[2] *v.* **tipped, tipping, tips.** *—tr.* **1.** To knock over or upset. Usually used with *over.* **2.** To bring to a slanting position; tilt. **3.** *British.* **a.** To empty (the contents of a container), as by tilting it. **b.** To dump (rubbish). **4.** To touch or raise (one's hat) in greeting. *—intr.* **1.** To topple; overturn. Usually used with *over.* **2.** To become tilted; slant.
~n. **1.** An act of tipping; a tilt or slant. **2.** *British.* **a.** A place for dumping rubbish. **b.** *Informal.* A very dirty or untidy place. [Middle English *typen, tipen*†.]
tip[3] (tip) *tr.v.* **tipped, tipping, tips. 1.** To strike gently; tap. **2.** To hit (a ball), as in cricket or baseball, with a light glancing blow.
~n. **1.** A light blow; a tap. **2.** A game, **tag** *(see).* [Middle English *tippen,* perhaps from Low German.]
tip[4] *n.* **1.** A small sum of money given as an acknowledgment of services rendered; a gratuity. **2. a.** A piece of advance or inside information given as a guide, as to speculation on the stock market or betting on a race. **b.** Any piece of useful or helpful information.
~v. **tipped, tipping, tips.** *—tr.* **1.** To give a tip or gratuity to. **2.** To give advance or inside information to. **3.** To mention or regard as a likely winner: *widely tipped to get the top job.* *—intr.* To give a tip or tips. [Originally a slang word meaning "to give", "to pass to", from TIP (to tap).] **—tip·per** *n.*
tip-and-run (tip-ən-rún) *n.* A version of cricket in which the batsman must attempt a run if the ball hits his bat.
tipi. Variant of **tepee.**
tip off *tr.v.* To provide with a tip-off; warn.
tip-off (típ-off, -awf) *n.* An item of advance or inside information; a hint or warning.
Tip·pe·ra·ry (típpə-ráir-i). *Irish.* **Contae Tiobraid Árann.** County in south central Republic of Ireland. It includes the Golden Vale, one of Ireland's most fertile agricultural regions. The county town, Tipperary, has the ruins of a 13th-century Augustinian abbey.
tip·per truck (típpər) *n.* A type of lorry whose rear section can be

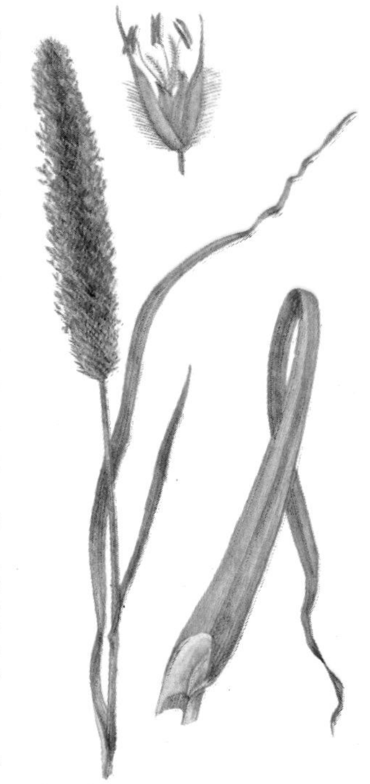

timothy grass Phleum pratense *was regarded as a weed until the middle of the 18th century, when an agriculturalist in the American colonies, Timothy Hanson, discovered its value as fodder. Now it is grown in most temperate countries.*

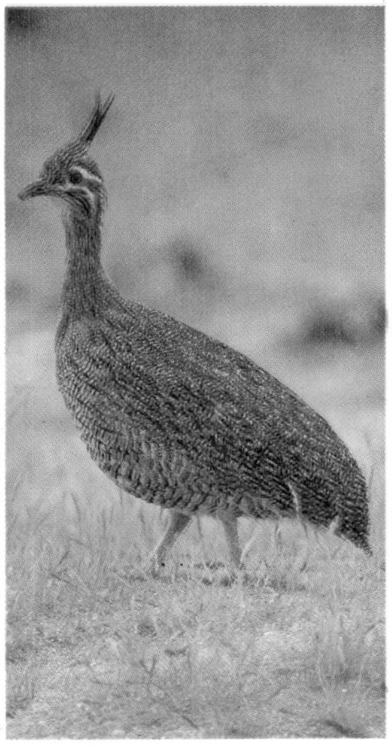

tinamou *The largely solitary tinamou of Central and South America spends most of its time on the ground and is a poor flier. This is the crested tinamou.*

tilted mechanically so that its load can be discharged. Also called "tipper lorry".

tip·pet (típpit) *n.* **1.** A covering for the shoulders, as of fur, with long ends that hang in front. **2.** A long stole worn by clergymen of the Anglican Church. **3.** A long, hanging part, as of a sleeve, hood, or cape. [Middle English *tipet*, probably a diminutive of TIP (end).]

Tip·pett, Sir Michael (Kemp) (típpit), (1905–). British composer. His works include the oratorio *A Child of Our Time* (1941), his first opera, *The Midsummer Marriage* (1955), and the cantata *The Vision of St. Augustine* (1966).

Tipp-Ex (típ-eks) *n.* A trademark for a quick-drying correction fluid used to obliterate marks made by writing or typing. —**Tipp-Ex** *tr.v.*

tip·ple (típp'l) *v.* **-pled, -pling, -ples.** —*intr.* To drink alcoholic liquor, especially habitually or intemperately. —*tr.* To drink (alcoholic liquor), especially habitually.
~*n.* An alcoholic drink, especially one taken habitually. [Back-formation from *tippler*, a tapster, bartender, from Middle English *tipler*†.] —**tip·pler** *n.*

tip·staff (típ-staaf ‖ -staf) *n., pl.* **-staves** (-stayvz ‖ -stavz) or **-staffs.** *Archaic.* A sheriff's officer or court official. [Short for *tipped staff*, a metal-tipped staff carried as a badge of the sheriff's office.]

tip·ster (típstər) *n. Informal.* A person who gives or sells tips to betters or speculators.

tip·sy (típsi) *adj.* **-sier, -siest. 1.** Slightly drunk. **2.** Likely to tip over; unsteady; crooked. [From TIP (to tilt, be unsteady).] —**tip·si·ly** *adv.* —**tip·si·ness** *n.*

tipsy cake *n. British.* Cake soaked with wine or sherry, decorated with almonds and served with custard.

tip·toe (típ-tō) *intr.v.* **-toed, -toeing, -toes. 1.** To walk or move with one's heels raised and only one's toes and the ball of the foot touching the ground. **2.** To walk stealthily or quietly.
~*n.* The tip of a toe. —**on tiptoe. 1.** Standing or walking with one's heels raised. **2.** Full of anticipation; eager. **3.** Silently; stealthily.
~*adj.* **1.** Standing or walking on tiptoe. **2.** Stealthy; wary.
~*adv.* On tiptoe.

tip·top (típ-tóp, -top) *n.* The highest point or degree.
~*adj.* Excellent; first-rate.
~*adv.* At the highest point of excellence.

tip-up (típ-up) *adj.* Having a horizontal part that may be tilted into an upright position, as in a cinema or theatre seat.

TIR International Road Transport [French *Transport International Routier*.]

ti·rade (tīr-ráyd, ti-, -ra'ad ‖ tír-ayd) *n.* A long vehement or blustering speech, especially of denunciation or censure; a diatribe. [French, "a stretching" (as in *tout d'une tirade*, all at one stretch), from Italian *tirata*, a volley, act of drawing, from *tirare*, to draw, from Vulgar Latin *tīrāre* (unattested). See **tier** (layer).]

Ti·ra·na or **Ti·ra·në** (ti-ra'anə). Capital city of Albania, lying on the river Ishm in Albania's central plain. It is the largest and industrially most important city in the country.

tire¹ (tīr) *v.* **tired, tiring, tires.** —*intr.* **1.** To become weak or fatigued as a result of exertion. **2.** To lose interest or grow impatient; weary. Often used with *of: He tired of reading.* —*tr.* **1.** To diminish the strength or energy of; weary; fatigue. Often used with *out.* **2.** To exhaust the interest or patience of; bore. [Middle English *tyren*, to stop, tire, Old English *tēorian*†.]

tire² *U.S.* Variant of **tyre.**

tire³ *tr.v.* **tired, tiring, tires.** *Archaic.* To adorn or attire.
~*n. Archaic.* **1.** Attire. **2.** A covering or ornament for the head or hair. [Middle English *tiren*, short for *attiren*, to ATTIRE.]

tired (tīrd) *adj.* **1. a.** Worn-out; fatigued. **b.** Impatient, fed up, or no longer interested. **2.** Overused; hackneyed.
Synonyms: *tired, weary, exhausted, fatigued, jaded.*

tire·less (tīr-ləss, -liss) *adj.* Untiring; indefatigable. —**tire·less·ly** *adv.* —**tire·less·ness** *n.*

Ti·re·si·as (tīr-rée-si-əss, -ré-, -ass ‖ -zi-). A blind prophet of Thebes prominent in many Greek myths and tragedies.

tire·some (tīr-səm) *adj.* Causing boredom or annoyance; tedious or irritating. See Synonyms at **boring.** —**tire·some·ly** *adv.* —**tire·some·ness** *n.*

tire·wom·an (tīrwōoman) *n., pl.* **-women** (-wimmin). *Archaic.* A lady's maid. [From TIRE (attire).]

Ti·rich Mir (téer-ich méer). Mountain peak in the Hindu Kush range, in northern Pakistan. It is the highest peak in the range and rises to 7 692 metres (25,236 feet).

tiro. Variant of **tyro.**

Ti·rol or **Ty·rol** (ti-rōl, tírrəl). Province in western Austria. The capital is Innsbruck. The province is almost entirely occupied by the Tirolean Alps and is a famous skiing centre. —**Ti·rol·ese** (-éez ‖ éess), **Ti·rol·e·an** (-ee-ən) *n. & adj.*

Ti·ru·chi·ra·pal·li (tírra-chírrə-púlli) or **Trich·i·nop·o·ly** (tríchi-nóp-pəli). City in southeastern India, lying on the river Cauvery. It is famous both for its gold and silver filigree crafts, and for the shrine of Srirangam, a monument to the god Siva, carved into the base of a huge rock.

'tis (tiz). *Archaic & Poetic.* Contraction of *it is.*

ti·sane, pti·san (ti-zán, tee- ‖ -za'an) *n.* A herbal infusion or similar preparation, drunk as a beverage or for its mildly medicinal effect. [French, from Latin *ptisana*, barley, PTISAN.]

Tish·ri (tíshri) *n.* The first month of the civil year in the Hebrew calendar. [Hebrew *Tishrī*, from Akkadian *Tashrītu*, from *shurrū*, to begin.]

Ti·siph·o·ne (tī-síffəni ‖ ti-). One of the three **Furies** *(see).*

tis·sue (tíshōo, tíssew) *n.* **1.** *Biology.* **a.** An aggregation of cells that are specialised to perform a certain function: *nervous tissue.* **b.** Cellular matter regarded as a collective entity. **2.** A soft, very absorbent piece of paper, generally made up of two thin layers, and used as a disposable handkerchief or towel. **3.** Unsized thin, translucent paper used for packing, wrapping, or protecting delicate articles. Also called "tissue paper". **4.** A woven fabric, usually of a fine, delicate texture. **5.** An interwoven or interrelated series; a web; a network: *His evidence was nothing but a tissue of lies.* [Middle English *tissu*, a rich cloth, fine gauze, from Old French, from the past participle of *tistre*, to weave, from Latin *texere*.]

tissue culture *n.* **1.** The growth in a suitable medium of specimens of tissue removed from a living organism. **2.** The tissue grown in this way.

tissue explant *n.* **Explant** *(see).*

tit¹ (tit) *n.* **1.** Any of various small Old World birds of the family Paridae, such as the **bluetit** *(see),* typically feeding on insects and seeds. Sometimes called "titmouse". **2.** Any of various similar or related birds. [Probably from Scandinavian, from a word referring to small objects; compare Icelandic *titlingr,* sparrow.]

tit² *n.* **1.** *Slang.* A woman's breast. **2.** A teat or nipple. **3.** *Vulgar Slang.* A stupid or contemptible person. [Middle English *titte,* Old English *titt,* from West Germanic *titta* (unattested).]

Tit. Titus (New Testament).

ti·tan (tít'n) *n.* A person of colossal size, strength, ability, or achievement; a giant. [From TITAN.]

Ti·tan¹ (tít'n). *Greek Mythology.* One of a family of primordial gods, the children of Uranus and Gaea, overthrown and succeeded by the Olympian gods. [Middle English, from Latin, from Greek *Titan,* from *titō*†, day, sun.]

Titan² *n. Astronomy.* The largest satellite of Saturn and probably the largest in the Solar System.

ti·tan·ate (tít'n-ayt) *n.* A salt of titanic acid. [TITAN(IUM) + -ATE (salt).]

Ti·tan·ess (tít'n-iss, -ess). *Greek Mythology.* A female Titan.

Ti·ta·ni·a¹ (ti-ta'an-yə, tī-, -táyn-, -i-ə). In medieval folklore, the queen of the fairies, wife of Oberon.

Titania² *n.* One of the satellites of the planet Uranus.

ti·tan·ic¹ (tī-tánnik) *adj.* **1. a.** Having great stature or enormous strength; huge; colossal. **b.** Of enormous scope, power, or influence. **2. Capital T.** Of or pertaining to the Titans. [After TITAN.] —**ti·tan·i·cal·ly** *adv.*

ti·tan·ic² (tī-tánnik, ti-, -táynik) *adj.* Pertaining to or containing titanium. Said especially of compounds containing titanium with a valency of 4. [TITAN(IUM) + -IC.]

titanic acid *n.* **1.** A white, powdered inorganic acid, H_2TiO_3, derived from an acid solution of titanates and used as a mordant. **2.** Titanium dioxide.

ti·tan·if·er·ous (tít'n-ífferəss) *adj.* Containing or yielding titanium. [TITANI(UM) + -FEROUS.]

Ti·tan·ism (tít'n-iz'm) *n.* The spirit of rebellion; defiance of and revolt against authority, convention, or the established order. [After TITAN.]

ti·tan·ite (tít'n-īt) *n.* A mineral, **sphene** *(see).* [German *Titanit* : TITAN(IUM) + -ITE.]

ti·ta·ni·um (tī-táyni-əm, ti- ‖ -tánni-) *n.* **Symbol Ti** A strong, low-density, highly corrosion-resistant, lustrous white metallic element that occurs widely in igneous rocks and is used to alloy aircraft metals for low weight, strength, and high-temperature stability. Atomic number 22, atomic weight 47.90, melting point 1,677°C, boiling point 3,277°C, relative density 4.54, valencies 2, 3, 4. [New Latin, from TITAN. So named by Martin Klaproth who had also named uranium after the planet Uranus. Uranus, in Greek mythology, is the father of the Titans.]

titanium dioxide *n.* A white powder, TiO_2, used as an opaque white pigment. Also called "titanic acid".

titanium white *n.* Titanium dioxide used as a paint pigment with great covering power and durability.

ti·tan·o·there (tī-tánnə-theer, -tánnō-) *n.* Any of various extinct herbivorous mammals of the genus *Brontotherium* and related genera, of the Eocene and Oligocene epochs, resembling the rhinoceros. [New Latin *Titanotherium,* "gigantic beast" : TITAN + -THERE.]

ti·tan·ous (tī-tánnoss, ti-, -táynəss) *adj.* Pertaining to or containing titanium. Said especially of compounds containing titanium with a valency of 3. [TITAN(IUM) + -OUS.]

tit·bit (tít-bit) *n.* Also *U.S.* **tid·bit** (tid-). A choice morsel, as of food or gossip.

titer. *U.S.* Variant of **titre.**

tit·fer (títfər) *n. British Slang.* A hat. [Rhyming slang, from *tit for tat.*]

tit for tat *n.* Repayment in kind, as for an injury; retaliation. [Variant of earlier *tip for tap.*]

tithe (tīth) *n.* **1.** A tenth part of one's annual income or produce, either in kind or money, contributed voluntarily for charitable purposes or due as a tax for the support of the clergy or church. **2.** Any tax or levy of one tenth. **3. a.** The tenth part of something. **b.** A very small part; a fraction.
~*tr.v.* **tithed, tithing, tithes. 1.** To contribute or pay a tenth part of (one's annual income). **2.** To levy a tithe upon. [Middle English *tithe,* Old English *tēotha, teogetha,* TENTH.] —**tith·a·ble** (títhəb'l) *adj.* —**tith·er** (títhər) *n.*

tith·ing (tī*th*ing) *n.* **1.** A tithe. **2.** In English history: **a.** A unit con-

Titian

sisting of ten householders in the system of **frankpledge** *(see).* **b.** A rural administrative division originally corresponding to the area occupied by such a unit.

ti·ti (tée-tee ‖ *U.S.* tee-tée) *n.* Any of various small, long-tailed South American monkeys of the genus *Callicebus,* having long, soft, often brightly coloured fur. [Spanish, perhaps of Tupian origin.]

ti·tian (tísh'n) *n.* Golden red or auburn. Said of hair. [Often used as a hair colour in paintings by TITIAN.] **—ti·tian** *adj.*

Ti·tian (tísh'n), born Tiziano Vecellio (tée·tsi-a'anō) *(c.* 1488–1576). Venetian painter. His greatest works include the altarpiece, *The Assumption of the Virgin* (1518), the *Pesaro Madonna (c.* 1520), and *Paul III and his·Grandsons* (1546). Titian's brilliant use of colour, and his use of backgrounds, landscapes, and sunsets as part of the composition, made him one of the greatest Renaissance artists.

Ti·ti·ca·ca (títti-ka'a-kaa). Lake of South America, lying high in the Andes mountains on the Peru-Bolivia border. It covers some 9 065 square kilometres (3,500 square miles) and is the largest freshwater lake in South America. It is plied by steamboats, and at a height of 3 810 metres (12,500 feet) above sea level, is the world's highest large lake.

tit·il·late (títti-layt) *tr.v.* **-lated, -lating, -lates. 1.** To stimulate by tickling or touching lightly. **2.** To arouse or excite agreeably. [From Latin *títillāre,* perhaps akin to *titta,* TEAT.] **—tit·il·lat·ing·ly** *adv.* **—tit·il·la·tion** (-láysh'n) *n.* **—tit·il·la·tive** (-laytiv) *adj.*

tit·i·vate, tit·ti·vate (títti-vayt) *tr.v.* **-vated, -vating, -vates.** To enhance the appearance of by means of decorative additions; smarten up. [Earlier *tidivate* : perhaps TIDY + (CULTI)VATE.] **—tit·i·va·tion** (-váysh'n) *n.*

tit·lark (tít-laark) *n.* A bird, the **pipit** *(see).* [TIT(MOUSE) + LARK.]

ti·tle (tí't'l) *n.* **1.** An identifying name given to a book, play, film, musical composition, work·of art, or the like. **2. a.** All the material that appears on the title page of a book. **b.** A general or descriptive heading, as of a book chapter. **c.** A particular book or other publication, rather than any one copy of it: *They publish mainly historical titles.* **3. a.** *Plural.* Written matter included in a film or television programme to give credits. **b.** A subtitle in a cinema film. **4. a.** The heading that names a legal document or statute. **b.** The heading given to any legal action or proceding, showing the name of the court, the name of the parties involved, and other relevant information. **5.** A division of a law book, declaration, or statute, generally larger than a section or article. **6.** *Law.* **a.** The sum of all the factors or events that constitute or justify a person's legal right to control and dispose of property or a claim. **b.** The legal instrument, such as a title deed, that provides evidence of such a right. **7. a.** Anything that provides ground for or justifies a claim. **b.** An acknowledged or alleged right. **8. a.** A formal appellation, such as *Mrs., Dr., Sir,* or *Professor,* prefixed to or substituted for a person's name, and used as a respectful term of address indicating office, rank, or attainment. **b.** Such an appellation as an indication of nobility. **9.** A descriptive appellation; an epithet. **10.** *Sports.* A championship. **11.** Proof that one has a source of income or area of work, as a prerequisite for ordination in the Church of England. **12.** *Roman Catholic Church.* A titular church. —See Synonyms at **right.** ~*tr.v.* **titled, -tling, -tles.** To give a title to; confer a name upon. [Middle English, from Old French, from Latin *titulus,* superscription, label, title.]

ti·tled (tí't'ld) *adj.* Having a title, especially of nobility.

title deed *n.* A deed that shows or provides evidence for a person's title to real property.

ti·tle·hold·er (tí't'l-hōldər) *n.* The unbeaten champion in a particular sporting competition.

title page *n. Abbr.* **t.p.** A page at the front of a book giving the complete title, the names of the author and publisher, and the place of publication.

title role *n.* The part of the character after whom a play or film is named. Also called "name part".

tit·mouse (tít-mowss) *n., pl.* **-mice** (-mīss). A bird, the **tit** *(see).* [Middle English *titmose* : TIT (bird) + Old English *māse,* titmouse, from West Germanic *maisō* (unattested); assimilated to MOUSE.]

Ti·to (tée'tō), **Marshal,** born Josip Broz (1892–1980). Communist leader of Yugoslavia. He led the Yugoslav resistance to Nazi occupation from 1941–45. After the war, the Yugoslav monarchy was abolished and Tito became prime minister (1945) and president (1953). In 1948 he broke with the U.S.S.R. and developed Yugoslavia's own brand of national communism, preserving a neutral position in foreign affairs and accepting aid from East and West.

Ti·to·grad (tée'tō-grad). Capital of Montenegro, southern Yugoslavia, known as Podgorica until 1946. It was almost completely rebuilt after being severely damaged in World War II.

Ti·to·ism (tée'tō-iz'm) *n.* The Communist policies and practices associated with Marshal Tito of Yugoslavia; especially, the assertion by a Communist state of its national interests independently of and often in opposition to Soviet policy. **—Ti·to·ist** *n. & adj.*

ti·trant (tí'trənt) *n. Chemistry.* The solution added in regulated amounts in a titration. [TITR(E) + -ANT.]

ti·trate (tí-tráyt ‖ *chiefly U.S.* tí-trayt) *v.* **-trated, -trating, -trates.** *—tr.* To determine the concentration of (a solution) by titration. *—intr.* To perform the operation of titration. [From French *titrer,* from *titre,* TITRE.]

ti·tra·tion (tī-tráysh'n) *n.* **1.** The process or method of determining the concentration of a substance in solution by adding to it a standard reagent of known concentration in carefully measured amounts until a reaction of definite and known proportion is completed, as shown by a colour change or by electrical measurement. **2.** An analogous technique applied to mixtures of gases.

ti·tre, *U.S.* **ti·ter** (tí'tər) *n.* **1.** The concentration of a substance in solution or the strength of such a substance determined by titration. **2.** The minimum volume needed to cause a particular result in titration. **3.** A measure of the amount of antibody present in blood serum. [French, qualification, TITLE (referring to the proportion of gold or silver in an alloy).]

tit·ter (títtər) *intr.v.* **-tered, -tering, -ters.** To utter a nervous, stifled giggle, as in ridicule or childish amusement. [Imitative.] **—tit·ter** *n.* **—tit·ter·er** *n.* **—tit·ter·ing·ly** *adv.*

tittivate. Variant of **titivate.**

tit·tle (títtl) *n.* **1.** A small diacritical mark, such as an accent, vowel point, or dot over an *i.* **2.** The tiniest bit; an iota. [Middle English

VIGOUR AND VIBRANCY IN AN ITALIAN MASTER
The 16th-century painter whose free style anticipated impressionism

Although Titian (Tiziano Vecellio, *c.* 1488–1576) trained under Gentile and Giovanni Bellini, he was greatly influenced by Giorgione. After the deaths of these masters, Titian was the most important painter of the Venetian school, and brought to it a vigour and colour it had not previously known. With his vibrant colours, especially reds and blues, he painted religious and mythological subjects and portraits.

In 1516, he succeeded Giovanni Bellini as official painter of Venice and in the same year began the large, dramatic *Assumption of the Virgin* (finished 1518) for the Frari church, which established his reputation. He painted other studies of the Madonna, including *The Madonna of the Cherries (c.* 1515), and *The Madonna with a Rabbit* (1530).

He also delighted in painting beautiful women with richly coloured auburn hair; among them were *Flora (c.* 1521), *Venus Anadyomene (c.* 1525), *La Bella (c.* 1536), *St. Mary Magdalen (c.* 1533), and *Venus of Urbino* (1538).

Titian was much sought after by Italian and European rulers, and in 1532 the Emperor Charles V became his patron. In 1548 he painted his famous equestrian portrait, *Charles V at the Battle of Muhlberg.* Earlier works, for the Duke of Ferrara, included *The Bacchanal of the Andrians, The Worship of Venus,* and *Bacchus and Ariadne.*

In his later years, Titian developed a very free style which almost anticipated impressionism, and is said to have applied paint with his fingers almost as much as with a brush so as to achieve the correct tonal effects. Among the works of his old age is a self-portrait.

A LANDMARK IN FORM *Titian achieved a remarkably lifelike quality in his* Young Englishman *(c. 1540), the eyes gazing directly from warm flesh tones offset by the deeper-toned background.*

titel, a diacritical mark, from Medieval Latin *titulus,* from Latin, TITLE.]

tit·tle-tat·tle (títt'l-tatt'l) *n.* Petty gossip; trivial talk.
~*intr.v.* **tittle-tattled, -tling, -tles.** To engage in idle talk or gossip; prattle. [Reduplication of TATTLE.]

tit·tup (títtəp) *intr.v.* **-tupped** or *U.S.* **-tuped, -tupping** or *U.S.* **-tuping, -tups.** To move in an affected, lively manner; prance.
~*n.* A lively, affected manner of moving or walking; a prance or caper. [Imitative of the sounds of a horse's hoofs.]

tit·u·ba·tion (títtew-báysh'n) *n.* A staggering or stumbling gait associated with a nodding movement of the head, characteristic of certain nervous disorders. [Latin *titubātiō* (stem *titubātiōn-*), from *titubātus,* past participle of *titubāre*†, to reel, stagger.]

tit·u·lar (tittew-lər) *adj.* **1.** Pertaining to, having the nature of, or constituting a title. **2.** Existing as such in name only; nominal: *the titular head of the company.* **3.** Bearing a title. **4.** Of or designating one of the ancient churches in or near Rome from which a cardinal takes his title.
~*n.* Also **tit·u·lar·y** (-ləri || -lerri) *pl.* **-ies.** A person who holds a title. [From Latin *titulus,* TITLE.] **—tit·u·lar·ly** *adv.*

titular bishop *n. Roman Catholic Church.* A bishop normally acting as an auxiliary bishop in a diocese, who is nominally appointed to a diocese in a remote part of the world.

Ti·tus (tītəss) *n. Abbr.* **Tit.** An epistle in the New Testament attributed to Saint Paul and addressed to Titus, his disciple.

Ti·u (tée-ōō). *Germanic Mythology.* The god of war and the sky, identified with the Norse god Tyr. [Old English *Tīw,* from Germanic *Tīwaz* (unattested), akin to Latin *deus,* god. See **Tuesday.**]

Ti·vo·li (tívvə-li; *Italian* téevo-). City in central Italy. It is the site of the Villa d'Este, with its famous Renaissance gardens, built in 1550, and it also has several Roman ruins, including the villa of Emperor Hadrian.

tiz·zy (tízzi) *n., pl.* **-zies.** *Slang.* A state of nervous confusion; a dither. [20th century : origin obscure.]

T-junction (tée-jungksh'n) *n.* A right-angled junction, as of two roads or pipes, forming a shape like the letter T.

TKO technical knockout.

Tl The symbol for the element thallium.

Tlax·ca·la (tlass-káalə). State in east central Mexico, formerly the territory of the Tlaxcaltec Indians. The state capital, also called Tlaxcala, is the site of the oldest Christian church in the New World, founded by Cortés in 1521.

TLC (tée-el-sée) *n. Informal.* Tender loving care.

Tlin·git (tlíng-git, -kit) *n., pl.* **-gits** or collectively **Tlingit. 1.** A member of any of a group of North American Indian seafaring peoples inhabiting the coastal areas of southern Alaska and northern British Columbia. **2.** A linguistic family of the Na-Dene phylum constituting only the language of the Tlingit.

Tm The symbol for the element thulium.

TM transcendental meditation.

tme·sis (tmée-siss, mée-) *n.* The separation of the parts of a compound word by one or more intervening words; for example, *where I go ever* instead of *wherever I go.* [Late Latin *tmēsis,* "a cutting", from Greek, from *temnein,* to cut.]

TMV tobacco mosaic virus.

TNT *n.* An explosive compound, **trinitrotoluene** *(see).*

to (tōō; *weak forms* tə *before a consonant sound,* tōō *or* tōō *before a vowel sound* || *The weak form* tə *is also to be heard before a vowel, particularly in U.S. speech; also* ti *in Scottish English.*) *prep.* **1.** In a direction towards; so as to approach or come near: *the road to Paris; bear to the right.* **2.** So as to reach or terminate in: *a trip to Paris.* **3.** Altogether and including: *drunk to the last man.* **4.** Through an intervening space or time; right up until: *a nine-to-five job; rotten to the core.* **5.** Through a standard intervening series or arrangement and terminating in: *from A to Z; strong to gale force winds.* **6.** To the extent of: *starved to death.* **7.** In contact with: *dancing cheek to cheek; apply polish to the shoes.* **8.** In front of: *face to face.* **9.** For the attention, benefit, or possession of: *Tell it to me.* **10.** For the purpose of; for: *She worked to that end.* **11.** For, of, or associated with: *the belt to this dress; secretary to the director.* **12.** Concerning or regarding; in response to: *deaf to her pleas.* **13.** In relation with: *parallel to the road.* **14.** Together with or as an accompaniment or addition for: *Sing to the music.* **15.** With regard to: *the way to his heart.* **16.** Composing or constituting; in: *two pints to the quart.* **17.** In correspondence or accordance with: *not to my liking; add sugar to taste.* **18.** So as to reach a specified total or result: *The bill came to £18; all adds up to a remarkable victory.* **19.** Before: *ten to five; only three weeks to Christmas.* **20.** In honour of: *a toast to his success.* **21.** Used in expressions of comparison or contrast: *bears no resemblance to the original plan; won by four goals to two; odds of 20 to 1.* **22.** Used to indicate: **a.** A progression towards a specified condition: *her rise to power.* **b.** An action resulting in a specified condition: *The flag was torn to shreds; To my amazement, he agreed.* **c.** A process of change resulting in a specified condition: *Their laughter soon turned to tears.*
~*adv.* **1.** Into a position or condition, especially shut or closed: *He slammed the door to.* **2.** Into consciousness: *He came to.* **3.** Into a state of application to the matter, action, or work at hand: *We sat down for lunch and fell to.* **4.** In proximity: *have never seen him close to.* **5.** *Nautical.* Turned into the wind. Used of a sailing vessel. [Middle English *to,* Old English *tō, te.*]

Usage: The use of *to* in place of an infinitive form of the verb is common at the ends of sentences in informal English: *You can go if you want to; Sing if you have to.* Formal English would either drop the *to* or use an alternative form *(Sing if you must).* Of course, the *to* must be retained in such constructions as *They work harder than they seem to* or *I'll go if you want me to.* See also Usage note at **try.**

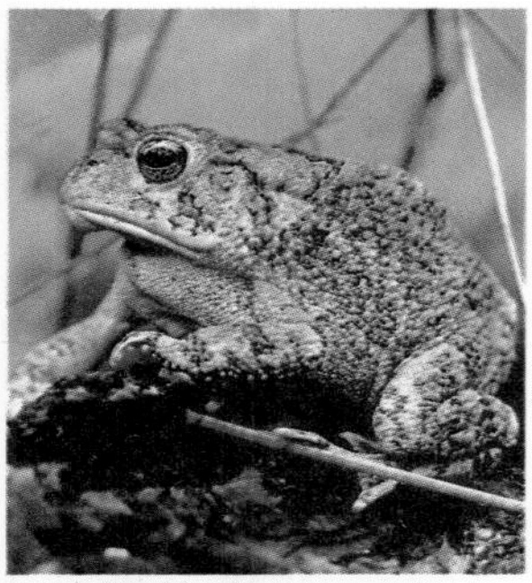

toad *Worldwide, there are about 250 species of toad, all members of the scientific family* Bufonidae. *The large glands behind their eyes contain a poison which makes them distasteful to predators.*

toad (tōd) *n.* **1.** Any of numerous tailless amphibians chiefly of the family Bufonidae, related to and resembling the frogs but characteristically more terrestrial and having rougher, drier skin. Compare **horned toad** *(see).* **2.** A repulsive person. [Middle English *tadde, tode,* Old English *tādi(g)e*†.]

toad·eat·er (tōd-eetər) *n.* A toady. [Originally, a charlatan's attendant who was hired to pretend to eat toads (thought to be poisonous) to prove that the charlatan could easily expel the poison.]

toad·fish (tōd-fish) *n., pl.* **toadfish** or **-fishes.** Any of various bottom-dwelling, chiefly marine fishes of the family Batrachoididae, having a broad, flattened head and a wide mouth.

toad·flax (tōd-flaks) *n.* Any of various plants of the genus *Linaria,* having narrow leaves and spurred, two-lipped flowers; especially, *L. vulgaris.* Also *chiefly U.S.* "butter and eggs". [TOAD + FLAX (from the flaxlike appearance of its foliage).]

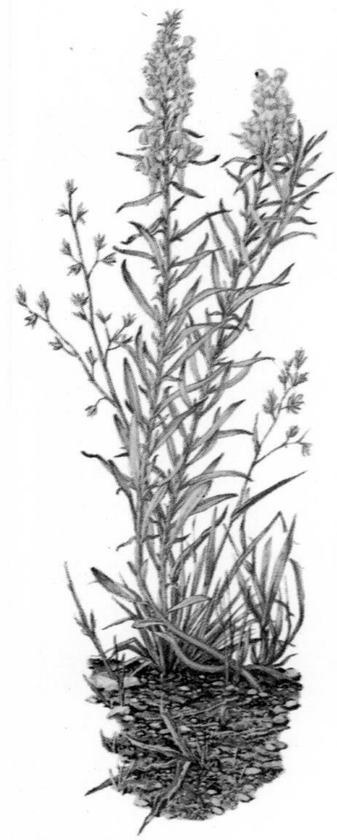

toadflax *Creeping roots spread this plant over uncultivated land.*

toad-in-the-hole (tōd-in-thə-hōl) *n. British.* A dish consisting of sausages baked in a batter.

toad spit *n.* An insect secretion, **cuckoo spit** *(see).*

toad·stone (tōd-stōn) *n.* Dark coloured basaltic or glassy volcanic rock. It is often associated with mineral veins, but contains no ore. [Probably from German, *Tödestein,* dead or worthless stone.]

toad·stool (tōd-stōōl) *n.* An inedible fungus with an umbrella-shaped fruiting body, as distinguished from an edible mushroom. [Middle English *todestool* : *tode,* TOAD + STOOL (from its stool-like shape and the popular association of it with toads, which were thought to be poisonous).]

toad·y (tōdi) *n., pl.* **-ies.** A servile flatterer; a sycophant. See Synonyms at **sycophant.**
~*v.* **toadied, -ying, -ies.** *—tr.* To be a toady to. *—intr.* To be a toady; fawn. [From TOADEATER.]

to and fro *adv.* In one direction and then the opposite; back and forth. [TO (adverb) + *fro,* Middle English, from Old Norse *frā,* FROM.] **—to-and-fro** (tōō-ən-frō) *adj.*

toast[1] (tōst) *v.* **toasted, toasting, toasts.** *—tr.* **1.** To heat and brown (bread, for example) by placing close to a fire, under a grill, or in a toaster. **2.** To warm thoroughly, as before a fire: *toast one's feet.* *—intr.* To become toasted.
~*n.* Sliced bread heated and browned. [Middle English *tosten,* from Old French *toster,* from Vulgar Latin *tostāre* (unattested), from Latin *torrēre* (past participle *tostus*), to dry, parch.]

toast[2] *n.* **1.** A person, institution, sentiment, or the like to whose health or in whose honour a group of people drink. **2.** The act of proposing the health or honour of a person or thing as a toast. **3.** One receiving much acclaim. **4.** *Archaic.* A lady to whose beauty or charms toasts are frequently proposed.
~*v.* **toasted, toasting, toasts.** *—tr.* To drink to the health or honour of. *—intr.* To propose or drink a toast. [From TOAST (from the notion that the name of the lady (sense 4) could flavour the drink like a piece of spiced toast).]

toast·er (tōstər) *n.* A device used to toast bread by exposure to electrically heated wire coils.

toast·ing fork (tōsting) *n.* A long-handled fork, on the prongs of which slices of bread, crumpets, or the like, may be placed and toasted in front of a fire.

toast·mas·ter (tōst-maastər || -mastər) *n.* One who proposes the toasts and introduces the guests or speakers at a banquet.

to·bac·co (tə-báckō) *n., pl.* **-cos** or **-coes. 1.** Any of various plants of the genus *Nicotiana;* especially, *N. tabacum,* native to tropical America, widely cultivated for its leaves, which are used primarily for smoking. **2.** The leaves of cultivated tobacco, dried and processed chiefly for use in cigarettes, snuff, or cigars, or for smoking in pipes. **3.** Products made from tobacco. [Earlier *tabac(c)o,* from Spanish *tabaco,* perhaps from a Taino word referring to leaves rolled for smoking (taken by the Spanish as referring to the plant itself).]

tobacco mosaic virus *n. Abbr.* **TMV** The virus that causes mosaic disease in tobacco plants and the first virus to be discovered (1892).

to·bac·co·nist (tə-báckənist) *n.* **1.** *Chiefly British.* A shopkeeper who sells tobacco, cigarettes, pipes, matches, and other equipment used by smokers. **2.** A dealer in tobacco. [Irregularly from TOBACCO + -IST.]

Tobago Island. See **Trinidad and Tobago.**

to-be (tə-bée, tōō-) *adj.* That is to be; future. Usually used in combination: *bride-to-be.*

To·bit (tōbit) *n.* A book of the Old Testament Apocrypha, named after its hero, a Hebrew captive in Nineveh. Also called "Tobias".

to·bog·gan (tə-bóggən) *n.* **1.** A long, light, runnerless vehicle made of thin boards curved upwards at the front, originally used by Canadian Indians and used for transporting goods over snow and ice. **2.** A similar vehicle, often equipped with runners used for coasting down slopes. In this sense, also called "sledge".
~*intr.v.* **tobogganed, -ganing, -gans.** To coast, ride, or travel on a toboggan. [Canadian French *tobagan,* from Algonquian; compare Micmac *tobākan.*] **—to·bog·gan·er, to·bog·gan·ist** *n.*

Toby jug (tōbi) *n.* A drinking mug usually in the shape of a stout man wearing a large three-cornered hat. Also called "Toby". [From *Toby,* pet form of *Tobias.*]

toc·ca·ta (tə-káatə, to-) *n.* A composition, for organ or other keyboard instrument, in a free style intended to show off the technical virtuosity of the performer. [Italian, "a touching" (originally a piece intended to show touch technique), from the feminine past participle of *toccare,* to touch, from Vulgar Latin *toccāre* (unattested), to strike, TOUCH.]

Toc H (tók áych) *n.* A Christian fellowship founded in 1915 and devoted to social service. [From obsolete telegraphic code for initials *T.H.,* for *Talbot House,* original headquarters of the fellowship in Poperinge, Belgium.]

To·char·i·an, To·khar·i·an (to-kaári-ən, tə-, -kaír-i) *n.* **1.** A member of a people of possible European origin, with an advanced culture, living in Asia until about the tenth century A.D. **2.** An Indo-European language with eastern and western dialects, *Tocharian A* and *Tocharian B* respectively, known chiefly from Buddhist scriptures written in the Brahmi script of Northern India. [French *Tocharien,* from Latin *Tochari,* from Greek *Tokharoi*†.]

to·col·o·gy, to·kol·o·gy (to-kólləji, tə- || tō-) *n.* Obstetrics. [Greek *tokos,* childbirth, from *tiktein,* to beget + -LOGY.]

to·coph·er·ol (to-kóffə-rol, tə- || tō-, -ōl) *n.* Any of a group of four chemically related compounds, differing slightly in structure, that together constitute **vitamin E** *(see).* Deficiency leads to sterility in rodents, and the vitamin is thought to be necessary for fertility in other vertebrates. [Greek *tokos,* childbirth (see **tocology**) + Greek *pherein,* to carry, bear + -OL.]

toc·sin (tóksin) *n.* **1.** An alarm sounded on a bell, or the bell on which it is sounded. **2.** Any warning sign; an omen. [French, from Old French *toquesain,* from Old Provençal *tocasenh* : *tocar,* to strike (a bell), touch, from Vulgar Latin *toccāre* (unattested), to ring a bell, TOUCH + *senh,* bell, from Latin *signum,* token, SIGN.]

tod[1] (tod) *n.* **1.** A unit of weight used in the wool trade, usually equivalent to 28 pounds. **2.** *British.* A bushy clump, especially of ivy. [Middle English *todd(e),* a unit of weight, probably from Low Dutch; akin to Middle Low German *toddelen,* to fall apart into bunches, and Old High German *zot(t)a,* a tuft, from Germanic *toddōn* (unattested).]

tod[2] *n. Northern British.* A fox. [Middle English : origin obscure.]

tod[3] *n.* **—on (one's) tod.** *British Slang.* Alone; on one's own. [Probably rhyming slang, from *Tod Sloan* (the name of a jockey), *alone.*]

to·day (tə-dáy, tōō-) *adv.* **1.** During or on this present day. **2.** During or at the present time.
~*n.* The present day, time, or age. [Middle English *to day,* Old English *tōdæg(e),* on this day : TO + *dæge,* dative of *dæg,* DAY.]

tod·dle (tódd'l) *intr.v.* **-dled, -dling, -dles. 1.** To walk with short, unsteady steps, as a small child does. **2.** *Informal.* **a.** To go; walk: *toddle down to the pub.* **b.** To depart: *must toddle off.* [16th century (Scottish and northern English) : origin obscure.] **—tod·dle** *n.*

tod·dler (tóddlər) *n.* A child who has learned to walk but not yet perfectly.

tod·dy (tóddi) *n., pl.* **-dies. 1.** A drink consisting of whisky or other spirits combined with hot water, sugar, spices, and lemon. Also called "hot toddy". **2. a.** The sweet sap of several tropical Asian palm trees, especially *Caryota urens,* used as a drink and as a leavening agent. **b.** An alcoholic drink fermented from this sap. [Earlier also *tarry,* from Hindi *tāṛī,* sap of a palm, from *tāṛ,* palm yielding toddy, from Sanskrit *tāla, tāra,* probably from Dravidian, akin to Kannada *taṛ,* Telegu *tāḍu.*]

to-do (tə-dóō, tōō-) *n., pl.* **-dos** (-z). *Informal.* A commotion or fuss. [From the infinitive *to do* (as in phrases *much to do, more to do*), but in sense influenced by ADO.]

to·dy (tṓdi) *n., pl.* **-dies.** Any of various small, colourful birds of the family Todidae, of the West Indies. [French *todier,* from Latin *todus*†, name of a small bird.]

toe (tō) *n.* **1. a.** One of the digits of the human foot. **b.** The corresponding digit in other vertebrate animals. **2.** The part of a shoe, sock, or the like that covers the toes. **3. a.** The base or lower tip of something, such as the end of the head on a golf club. **b.** Anything suggestive of a toe in form, function, or location. **—on (one's) toes.** Alert; ready to act. **—tread on (someone's) toes.** To offend or annoy someone, often accidentally, especially by interfering in his sphere of action or responsibility.
~*v.* **toed, toeing, toes.** *—tr.* **1.** To touch, kick, or trace with the toe. **?.** To drive (a golf ball) with the toe of the club. **3. a.** To drive (a nail or spike, for example) obliquely. **b.** To secure (beams, for example) with nails driven obliquely. *—intr.* To walk or move with the toes pointed in a specified direction: *He toes out.* [Middle English *ta, to,* Old English *tā.*]

to·e·a (tṓ-i-ə) *n.* A monetary unit of Papua, New Guinea, 1/100 of a kina. [From a Papuan language.]

toe·cap (tṓ-kap) *n.* A reinforced covering of leather or metal for the toe of a shoe or boot.

toe clip *n.* An attachment to a bicycle pedal that fits over the foot to prevent it from slipping.

toed (tōd) *adj.* Having a toe or toes, especially of the specified kind or number. Usually used in combination: *a two-toed sloth.*

toe·hold (tṓ-hōld) *n.* **1.** A small indentation or ledge on which the toe can find support in climbing; a small foothold. **2.** Any slight or initial advantage or means of access providing a basis for future progress: *Family connections gave him a toehold in politics.* **3.** A wrestling hold in which one competitor wrenches the other's foot.

toe-in (tṓ-in) *n.* The adjustment of the front wheels of a motor vehicle so that they turn slightly inwards, done to improve steering and minimise tyre wear.

toe·nail (tṓ-nayl) *n.* **1.** The nail on a toe. **2.** A nail driven obliquely, as to join vertical and horizontal beams.
~*tr.v.* **toenailed, -nailing, -nails.** To secure (beams) with obliquely driven nails.

toe rag *n. British Slang.* A person considered beneath contempt.

toff (tof) *n. British Slang.* **1.** A dandy; a swell. **2.** Any member of the upper classes. [Probably variant of TUFT, a titled undergraduate (from the gold tassel formerly worn on caps by titled students.]

tof·fee (tóffi || táwfi) *n., pl.* **-fies. 1.** A hard or chewy sweet substance made of sugar and butter boiled together. **2.** A small piece of this. **—for toffee.** In any way to any degree. Used to indicate a person's complete lack of competence in a specified field: *can't draw for toffee.* [Variant of TAFFY.]

tof·fee-ap·ple (tóffi-ápp'l) *n.* An apple coated with brittle toffee, usually fixed on the end of a thin stick.

tof·fee-nosed (tóffi-nōzd) *adj. Chiefly British Slang.* Snobbish; stuck-up.

toft (toft || tawft) *n. British Archaic.* **1.** A homestead. **2.** A hillock. [Middle English *toft,* Old English *toft,* site of a building, homestead, from Old Norse *topt.*]

to·fu (tṓ-fōō) *n.* **Bean curd** *(see).* [Japanese, from Chinese.]

tog (tog) *n. Informal.* **1.** A coat or cloak. **2.** *Plural.* Clothes.
~*tr.v.* **togged, togging, togs.** *Informal.* To dress or clothe. Often used with *up* or *out.* [Short for 16th-century cant *togeman(s), togman* : probably obsolete *toge,* cloak, from Middle English, from Old French *tog(u)e,* from Latin *toga,* TOGA + *-mans*†, a cant noun suffix.]

to·ga (tṓ-gə) *n., pl.* **-gas. 1.** A draped one-piece outer garment worn in public by citizens of ancient Rome. **2.** Any robe or gown characteristic of a particular office or profession. [Latin, from *tegere,* to cover.] **—to·gaed** (tṓ-gəd) *adj.*

to·geth·er (tə-géthər, tōō-) *adv.* **1.** In or into a single group, body, mass, or place: *We gather together; stick it together with glue.* **2.** Against or in contact with one another: *He rubbed his hands together.* **3.** One with another; mutually or reciprocally: *The shirt and tie go well together.* **4.** Regarded collectively; in total: *She is worth more than all of us together.* **5.** Simultaneously: *All the bells rang out together.* **6.** In uninterrupted sucession; at a stretch: *drunk for days together.* **7.** In harmony or accord: *We stand together on this issue.* **8.** *Informal.* **a.** In or into a coherent, compact, well-ordered aggregation: *Try to get your ideas together; got all my bits and pieces together.* **b.** In or into a state of self-possession or effective operation: *Pull yourself together; to get a show together at short notice.* **—get it together.** *Informal.* To manage to act effectively. **—together with.** As well as; and in addition.
~*adj. Slang.* **1.** Stable and well-organised; self-possessed. **2.** Unified and performing effectively. [Middle English *togeder(e),* Old English *tōgædere* : TO + *gad-* (unattested), as in *gæd,* fellowship; akin to GATHER.]
Usage: When *together with* is used following the subject of a sentence, it does not in formal English alter the relationship between the subject and the verb. Thus, in the sentence *The king, together with the two princes, is expected to arrive tonight,* the verb remains in the singular, agreeing with *king,* despite the plural noun following. A similar rule applies to such other phrases as *in addition to, as well as,* and *along with.* In informal speech, however, the proximity of the plural noun to the verb in such cases often prompts the use of a plural form of the verb.

to·geth·er·ness (tə-géthər-nəss, tōō-, -niss) *n.* The quality of being in close relationship or harmony; comradeship or intimacy.

tog·ger·y (tóggəri) *n., pl.* **-ies.** *Informal.* Clothing; togs.

tog·gle (tógg'l) *n.* **1.** A device used to secure or hold something, especially: **a.** A pin inserted in a nautical knot to keep it from slipping. **b.** A bar-shaped crosspiece, such as a button on a duffel coat, attached to the end of or inserted in a loop in a rope, chain, or strap to prevent slipping, to tighten, or to fasten. **2.** An apparatus having a toggle joint.
~*tr.v.* **toggled, -gling, -gles.** To furnish or fasten with a toggle or toggles. [18th century (nautical use) : origin obscure.]

toggle bolt *n.* A fastener consisting of a threaded bolt and a mated toggle.

toggle joint *n.* An elbow-like joint composed of two arms pivoted so that a force applied to their hinge to straighten them produces an outward force at the ends.

toggle switch *n.* A switch in which a projecting lever employing a toggle joint with a spring is used to open or close an electric circuit.

To·go, Republic of (tṓ-gō) *French.* **République Togolaise** (-layz, -lez). State of West Africa on the Gulf of Guinea. Coffee and cocoa are exported, but the economy is dominated by minerals, with phosphates accounting for 40 per cent of exports. Formerly the German protectorate of Togoland (1894–1914), the area was then divided between Britain and France. In 1956 the west voted to join Ghana on its independence (1957). French Togo became independent as the Republic of Togo in 1960. Since 1967 the country has been a one-party state under General Eyadema. Area, 56 785 square kilometres (21,919 square miles). Population, 2,800,000. Capital, Lomé. See map at **West African States. —To·go·lese** (-leez) *n. & adj.*

to·he·ro·a (tṓ-ə-rṓ-ə) *n.* **1.** A New Zealand bivalve mollusc, *Amphidesma ventricosum.* **2.** A soup made from this mollusc.

toil[1] (toyl) *intr.v.* **toiled, toiling, toils. 1.** To labour continuously and untiringly; work strenuously. **2.** To proceed or make one's way with difficulty, pain, or strenuous effort: *toiling over the mountains.*

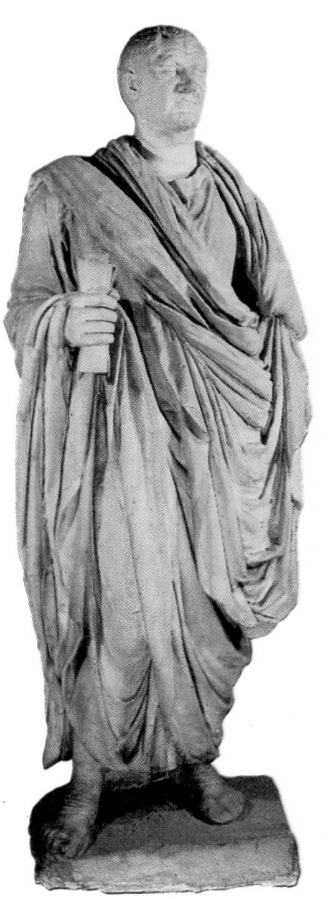

toga *This heavy outer garment made from fine white wool was difficult to drape – it was about 6 metres (20 feet) long and up to about 2 metres (7 feet) wide – hard to keep in place, and cumbersome to wear. Nevertheless, all men who were citizens of ancient Rome had to wear it on public occasions, by order of the emperor.*

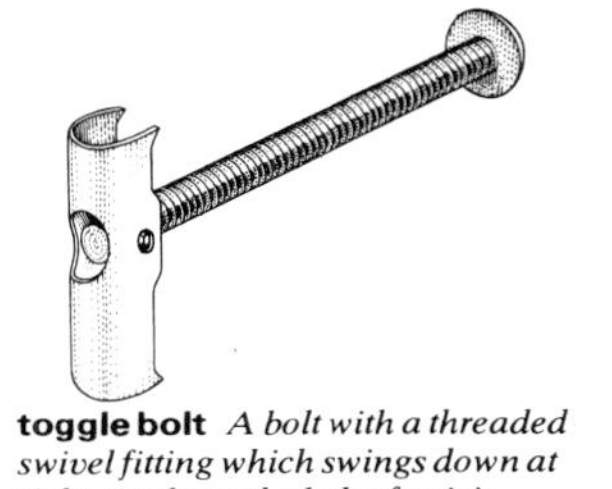

toggle bolt *A bolt with a threaded swivel fitting which swings down at right-angles to the bolt after it is pushed through a drilled hole. The bolt is then tightened, and the swivel grips the surface behind the hole.*

~*n.* **1.** Exhausting labour or effort. **2.** *Archaic.* Strife; contention. —See Synonyms at **work.** [Middle English *toilen,* to struggle, to battle, from Anglo-French *toiler,* Old French *tooilier,* to stir, agitate, from Latin *tudiculāre,* to stir about, from *tudicula,* a mill for crushing olives, diminutive of *tudes,* a hammer.]

toil² *n.* **1.** *Archaic.* A long net or a series of nets for trapping game. **2.** *Usually plural.* Anything in which one is trapped or caught up. [Old French *toile,* a net, from Latin *tēla;* akin to *texere,* to weave.]

toile (twaal) *n.* **1.** A sheer linen fabric. **2.** A copy of a garment made up using inexpensive material, so that alterations can be made to the design. [French, cloth, net. See **toil** (net).]

toi·let (tóy-lət, -lit) *n.* Also **toi·lette** (twaa-lét) (for senses 2, 4) **1.** A **lavatory** *(see).* **2.** The act or process of grooming and dressing oneself. **3. a.** The articles used in making one's toilet. **b.** A dressing table. **4.** *Archaic.* A person's style of dress. **5.** The cleansing of a bodily part, as after an operation. [French *toilette,* lavatory, dressing table, from Old French, cloth cover for a dressing table, a dressing table, diminutive of TOILE.]

toilet paper *n.* Thin, absorbent paper, usually in rolls, used for cleansing oneself after defecation or urination. Also called "toilet tissue"; "lavatory paper".

toilet roll *n.* **1.** A length of toilet paper rolled round a cylindrical cardboard tube. **2.** The cardboard tube.

toi·let·ry (tóylətri) *n., pl.* **-ries.** Any article or cosmetic used in dressing or grooming oneself.

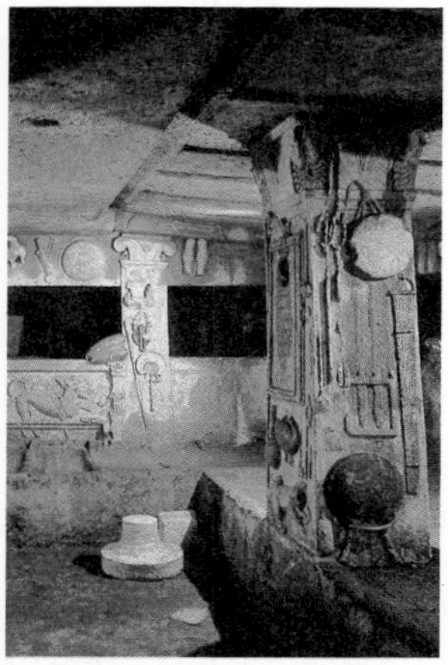

tomb *In many ancient cultures, tombs were furnished with goods for the use of the spirits of the dead. The Tomb of the Rilievi (above), at Cerveteri, Italy, dates from the second century* B.C.*; it contains household goods, and there are beds in the alcoves.*

toilet set *n.* A matching set of implements used in dressing and grooming, typically consisting of a hand mirror, a hairbrush, a comb, and a clothes brush.

toilet training *n.* The process of training a small child the voluntary control of bladder and bowel movements. **—toi·let-train** (tóy-lət-- trayn, -lit-) *tr.v.*

toilet water *n.* Cologne or mild perfume.

toil·some (tóyl-s'm) *adj.* Characterised by or requiring toil; done with difficulty. **—toil·some·ly** *adv.* **—toil·some·ness** *n.*

to-ing and fro-ing (tōō-ing ən frō-ing) *n., pl.* **to-ings and fro-ings.** Busy movement back and forth.

to·kay (tō-kay) *n.* A tropical Asian lizard, *Gekko gecko.* See **gecko.** [From Malay *toke* (imitative of its cry).]

To·kay (to-kī, tō-, -káy) *n.* **1.** A variety of grape originally grown near Tokay, Hungary. **2.** A sweet wine made from these grapes.

toke (tōk) *n. Slang.* A puff on a cigarette or, especially, a joint (a cannabis cigarette). [20th century : origin obscure.]

To·ke·lau Islands (tókəlow). Group of three atolls in the south central Pacific Ocean, formerly belonging to the Gilbert and Ellice Islands Colony, but since 1948 part of New Zealand. The islands' only product is copra.

to·ken (tōkən) *n.* **1.** Something that serves as an indication or representation, as of some fact, event, or emotion; a sign; a symbol. **2.** Something that tangibly signifies something, such as authority, validity, or identity: *The sceptre is a token of kingship.* **3.** A keepsake or souvenir. **4.** A piece of stamped metal or plastic used as a substitute for a coin, as in a public telephone, slot machine, or the like. **5.** A voucher exchangeable for a specified commodity of a stated value: *a record token.* —See Synonyms at **sign. —by the same token.** In the same manner; likewise.
~*tr.v.* **tokened, -kening, -kens.** To signify, betoken, or symbolise.
~*adj.* **1.** Done, made, or undertaken as a token, as of good faith or strength of feeling: *a token payment; a token strike.* **2. a.** Purely for the sake of form; nominal; perfunctory: *token resistance.* **b.** Indicative of minimal effort to comply with a statutory requirement or fulfil a moral obligation: *a token woman on the board.* [Middle English *taken, token,* Old English *tāc(e)n.*]

to·ken·ism (tōkən-iz'm) *n.* The practice or policy of making only a superficial effort or symbolic gesture towards the accomplishment of a goal, such as racial integration.

Tokharian. Variant of **Tocharian.**

tokology. Variant of **tocology.**

To·kyo (tōki-ō, tōk-yō). Capital of Japan, and one of the world's largest cities, situated in east central Honshu at the head of Tokyo Bay. It has extensive industrial complexes, and is the financial, administrative, educational, and cultural centre of Japan. Founded on the 12th-century village of Edo, it has been extensively rebuilt since World War II, and is now one of the most modern cities. Its seaport is Yokohama.

to·la (tōlə) *n.* A unit of weight used in India, equal to the weight of one silver rupee, or 180 troy grains. [Hindi *tolā,* from Sanskrit *tulā,* balance, weight.]

tol·booth, toll·booth (tól-bōōth, -bōōth || tōl-, -bəth) *n.* **1.** *Scottish.* A town hall. **2.** *Scottish.* A prison. **3.** *U.S.* A booth at a tollgate where the toll is collected. [Middle English *tolbothe,* toll station, tax-collection booth, town hall (beneath which there were prison cells) : TOLL + BOOTH.]

tol·bu·ta·mide (tol-béwtə-mīd || tōl-) *n.* A white powder, $C_{12}H_{18}N_2O_3S$, administered by mouth in the treatment of diabetes. [TOL(U) + BUT(YRIC ACID) + AMIDE.]

told. Past tense and past participle of **tell.**

tole, tôle (tōl) *n.* Lacquered or enamelled metalware, usually gilded, popular in the 18th century. [French *tôle,* sheet metal, sheet iron, from French dialect, a slab, table, variant of *table,* from Latin *tabula,* a board. See **table.**]

To·le·do (to-láydō, tə-). Capital of Toledo province, central Spain, situated on the river Tagus. It was an important Roman city, the capital of the Visigoth kingdom (534–712), and a Moorish provincial capital (712–1031), when it became famous as a centre of Arab and Hebrew learning. It was reconquered by El Cid and Alfonso VI of León and Castile (1085).

tol·er·a·ble (tól-rəb'l, tóllə-) *adj.* **1.** Able to be tolerated; endurable. **2.** Fair or adequate; passable. —See Synonyms at **average.** [Middle English, from Old French, from Latin *tolerābilis.* See **tolerate.**] **—tol·er·a·bil·i·ty** (-rə-billəti), **tol·er·a·ble·ness** *n.* **—tol·er·a·bly** *adv.*

tol·er·ance (tóllərənss) *n.* **1.** A disposition towards or capacity for allowing or respecting the beliefs or behaviour of others when these differ from one's own. **2. a.** Leeway for variation from a standard. **b.** The permissible deviation from a specified value of a structural dimension. **3.** The capacity to endure hardship or pain; endurance. **4. a.** Physiological resistance to poison. **b.** The capacity to absorb a drug continuously or in large doses without experiencing its pharmacological effects. [Middle English, from Old French, from Latin *tolerantia.* See **tolerate.**]

tol·er·ant (tóllərənt) *adj.* **1.** Inclined to tolerate the beliefs or behaviour of others; forbearing. **2.** Able to withstand or endure an adverse environmental condition. [From French *tolérant,* present participle of *tolérer,* to TOLERATE.] **—tol·er·ant·ly** *adv.*

tol·er·ate (tóllə-rayt) *tr.v.* **-ated, -ating, -ates. 1.** To show tolerance towards; especially, to allow (beliefs or practises that differ from one's own) to exist without interference or prohibition. **2.** To put up with; endure or countenance: *would not tolerate laziness.* **3.** *Medicine.* To have tolerance for (a drug or poison). —See Synonyms at **bear.** [From Latin *tolerāre,* to bear, tolerate.] **—tol·er·a·tive** (-rətiv, -raytiv) *adj.* **—tol·er·a·tor** (-raytər) *n.*

tol·er·a·tion (tóllə-ráysh'n) *n.* **1.** The act of tolerating or inclination to tolerate. **2.** Official recognition of the rights of individuals and groups to hold dissenting opinions, especially on religion. [From French, from Latin *tolerātio* (stem *tolerātiōn-*). See **tolerate.**]

tol·i·dine (tólli-deen) *n.* Any of several isomeric bases, $(H_2NC_6H_3CH_3)_2$, derived from toluene, used in the manufacture of dyes and synthetic resins. [TOL(UENE) + -ID(E) + -INE.]

toll¹ (tōl || tol) *n.* **1.** A fixed charge or tax for an access or privilege, especially for passage across a bridge or along a road. **2.** An amount or loss, as of lives, property, or health, incurred as a result of war, disaster, or other adverse condition: *took a heavy toll in lives.* **3.** *U.S.* A charge for a long-distance telephone call.
~*tr.v.* **tolled, tolling, tolls.** *Rare.* To exact as a toll. [Middle English *tol(le),* Old English *toll,* from Late Latin *tolonium, telōnium,* a tolbooth, customhouse, from Greek *telōnion,* from *telos,* tax.]

toll² *v.* **tolled, tolling, tolls.** —*tr.* **1.** To sound (a large bell) slowly at regular intervals. **2.** To announce or summon by tolling. —*intr.* To ring with slow and regular strokes. Used of a bell.
~*n.* **1.** The act of tolling. **2.** The sound of a tolling bell. [Middle English *tollen,* probably special use of *tollen, tullen,* to entice, lure, perhaps Old English *tollian* (unattested), perhaps from Germanic *tull* (unattested).]

tollbooth. Variant of **tolbooth.**

toll·bridge (tōl-brij || tól-) *n.* A bridge at which a toll is charged before crossing.

toll·gate (tōl-gayt || tól-) *n.* A gate barring passage to a road, tunnel, or bridge until a toll is collected.

toll·house (tōl-howss || tól-) *n.* A house occupied by the toll collector adjoining a tollgate.

Tol·tec (tól-tek || tōl-) *n, pl.* **-tecs** or collectively **Toltec.** A member of an ancient Nahuatl people of central and southern Mexico whose culture flourished in about A.D. 1000. **—Tol·tec, Tol·tec·an** (tol-téckən || tōl-) *adj.*

to·lu (tō-lōō, tə-, -léw) *n.* An aromatic resin, obtained from the tree *Myroxylon balsamum,* of South America. [Spanish *tolú,* from Santiago de *Tolú,* Colombia, its place of origin.]

tol·u·ene (tóllew-een) *n.* A colourless flammable liquid, $CH_3C_6H_5$, obtained from coal tar or petroleum and used in aviation and other high-octane fuels, in dyestuffs, explosives, and as a solvent for gums and lacquers. Also called "methylbenzene", "toluol". [TOLU (from which it was originally obtained) + -ENE.]

to·lu·i·dine (to-léw-i-deen, tə-, -lōō-) *n.* Any of three isomeric compounds, $H_2NC_6H_4CH_3$, used to make dyes. [TOLU(ENE) + -ID(E) + -INE.]

tol·u·ol (tóllew-ol || -ōl) *n.* Toluene. [TOLU + -OL.]

tol·yl (tóllil) *n.* The univalent organic radical $CH_3C_6H_4$. [TOL(U) + -YL.]

tom¹ (tom) *n.* The male of various animals; especially, a male cat that has not been neutered.
~*adj.* Male. [From the name *Tom.*]

tom² *n.* Also **tam** (tam). A hat, typically worn by Rastafarians to cover dreadlocks, with a large, baglike crown. [From TAM.]

tom·a·hawk (tómmə-hawk) *n.* **1.** A light axe used as a tool or weapon by North American Indians. **2.** Any similar implement or weapon. **3.** *Australian.* A hatchet.
~*tr.v.* **tomahawked, -hawking, -hawks. 1.** To attack or kill with or as if with a tomahawk. **2.** *Australian.* To shear (a sheep) roughly, as if using a hatchet. [Virginia Algonquian *tamahaac, tamohake* : Proto-Algonquian *temah-* (unattested), to cut off by tool + *-aakan* (unattested), noun suffix.]

tom·al·ley (tóm-al-i, tə-mál-i) *n., pl.* **-leys.** The liver of a lobster, esteemed as a culinary delicacy. [Of Cariban origin, akin to Carib *tumali,* sauce of lobster or crab liver.]

Tom and Jerry *n. U.S.* A hot drink consisting of rum, a beaten egg, milk or water, sugar, and spices. [From names of two characters,

Corinthian *Tom* and *Jerry* Hawthorn, in *Life in London* (1821), by Pierce Egan (1772–1849), English sportswriter.]

to·ma·to (tə-maá·tō ‖ *chiefly U.S.* -máytō) *n., pl.* **-toes. 1.** A plant, *Lycopersicon esculentum*, native to South America, widely cultivated for its edible, fleshy, usually red fruit. **2.** The fruit of this plant. [Variant of earlier *tomate*, from Spanish, from Nahuatl *tomatl*.]

tomb (to͞om) *n.* **1.** A vault or chamber serving as a repository for a dead body. **2.** Any grave or place of burial. **3.** A monument commemorating the dead. [Middle English *t(o)umbe*, from Anglo-French *tumbe*, Old French *tombe*, from Late Latin *tumba*, sepulchral mound, from Greek *tumbos*.]

tom·bac (tóm-bak) *n.* Any one of several alloys of copper and zinc, used in making inexpensive jewellery. [French, from Dutch *tombak*, from Malay *tambāga*, copper.]

tom·bo·la (tom-bōlə, tómbələ) *n. Chiefly British.* **1.** A lottery game in which winning tickets are drawn out of a revolving container. **2.** A simple form of the game of **bingo** *(see)*. [Probably from Italian, from *tombolare*, to tumble.]

Tombouctou. See **Timbuktu.**

tom·boy (tóm-boy) *n.* A high-spirited girl who prefers boys' games to those conventionally played by girls. [TOM (male) + BOY.] —**tom·boy·ish** *adj.*

tomb·stone (to͞om-stōn) *n.* A stone or monument, usually inscribed, marking a grave; a gravestone.

tom·cat (tóm-kat, -kát) *n.* A male cat, especially one that has not been neutered. [After *Tom*, hero of the anonymous work *The Life and Adventures of a Cat* (1760).]

Tom Col·lins (kóllinz) *n.* A cocktail of gin, lemon or lime juice, soda water, and sugar. [Said to be the name of the barman who invented it.]

Tom, Dick, and Harry *n.* Anyone at all; any man taken at random: *Every Tom, Dick, and Harry came to the party.*

tome (tōm) *n.* **1.** A book; especially, a weighty or scholarly book. Often used humorously. **2.** *Archaic.* One of the books in a work of several volumes. [French, from Latin *tomus*, cut, tome, roll of paper, from Greek *tomos*, from *temnein*, to cut, slice.]

-tome *n. comb. form.* Indicates a cutting instrument; for example, **microtome.** [From New Latin *-tomus*, from Greek *-tomos*, a cutting, from *temnein*, to cut.]

to·men·tose (tə-mént-ōz, tō-, -ōss, *also* tōmənt-) *adj. Biology.* Covered with dense, short, matted hairs. [New Latin *tomentosus*, from Latin *tōmentum*, cushion stuffing, TOMENTUM.]

to·men·tum (tə-mén-təm, tō-) *n., pl.* **-ta** (-tə). **1.** *Anatomy.* A network of extremely small blood vessels in the brain passing between the pia mater and cerebral cortex. **2.** *Biology.* A covering of closely matted woolly hairs. [New Latin, from Latin *tōmentum†*, cushion stuffing.]

tom·fool (tóm-fo͞ol) *n.* A stupid or foolish person; a blockhead. —*adj.* Extremely foolish. [Middle English : *Tom* (name) + FOOL.]

tom·fool·er·y (tóm-fo͞olǝri) *n., pl.* **-ies. 1.** Foolish behaviour. **2.** Something trivial or foolish; nonsense.

tom·my (tómmi) *n., pl.* **-mies.** *British Informal.* **1.** A British soldier, especially a private; a Tommy Atkins. **2.** *Archaic.* A workman's provisions. [From *Tommy*, pet form of *Tom* (name).]

Tommy At·kins (átkinz) *n.* A private of the regular British army. Also called "Tommy", "tommy". [Originally a name used in sample forms for privates in the British army.]

tommy bar *n.* A short metal bar used as a lever to turn a socket spanner or similar tool.

Tommy gun *n.* A **Thompson submachine gun** *(see)*.

tom·my·rot (tómmi-rot) *n. Informal.* Utter foolishness; nonsense. [*Tommy*, pet form of *Tom* + ROT.]

to·mog·ra·phy (tə-móggrəfi, to-, tō-) *n.* Any of several techniques for making X-ray pictures of a predetermined plane section of a solid object by blurring out the images of other planes. [Greek *tomos*, a cut, section *(see* **tome***)* + -GRAPHY.]

to·mor·row (tə-mórrō, to͞o- ‖ -máwrō) *n.* **1.** The day following today. **2.** The future, especially the near future. —*adv.* On the day following today. [Middle English *to morge, to mor(o)we*, Old English *tō morgen(ne)* : TO (at, on) + *morgenne*, dative of *morgen*, MORROW.]

tompion. Variant of **tampion.**

Tom Thumb *n.* **1.** A diminutive hero of English folklore. **2.** A tiny person; a midget.

tom·tit (tóm-tit, -tít) *n. British.* A tit or other small bird, especially a bluetit. [*Tom* (name) + TIT(MOUSE).]

tom-tom (tóm-tom) *n.* **1.** A small-headed, usually long and narrow, drum that is beaten with the hands. **2.** A monotonous rhythmical drumbeat or similar sound. [Hindi *ṭamṭam* See **tam-tam.**]

-tomy *n. comb. form.* Indicates a cutting of a specified part or tissue; for example, **craniotomy.** [From New Latin *-tomia*, from Greek *-tomos*, -TOME.]

ton¹ (tun) *n.* **1.** *Abbr.* **t. a.** An avoirdupois unit of weight used in Britain equal to 2,240 pounds (1016.046909 kilograms). Also called "long ton". **b.** An avoirdupois unit of weight used in the United States equal to 2,000 pounds (907.18 kilograms). Also called "short ton", "net ton". **2.** Any of various units of weight or capacity used in shipping: **a.** A unit of weight or volume used for measuring freight, and varying according to the material being shipped. Its most usual value is a weight of 1000 kilograms or a volume of either 40 cubic feet or 1 cubic metre. Also called "freight ton". **b.** A unit of volume for freight equal to 40 cubic feet. Also called "freight ton", "shipping ton", "measurement ton". **c.** A unit of capacity of

ships equal to 100 cubic feet. Also called "register ton". **d.** A unit of displacement of ships equal to a displacement of 35 cubic feet of sea water. Also called "displacement ton". **3.** A **metric ton** *(see)*. **4.** *Informal.* **a.** A very heavy weight: *It weighs a ton.* **b.** *Often plural.* A very large quantity of anything. **5.** *Chiefly British Slang.* An amount or score of a hundred, as for example in pounds, runs, or miles per hour. [Specialised (from 17th century) use of TUN.]

ton² (ton) *n.* Fashionable distinction; elegant style. [French, TONE.]

to·nal (tōn'l) *adj.* Of or pertaining to a tone, tones, or tonality. [Medieval Latin *tonālis*, from *tonus*, TONE.] —**to·nal·ly** *adv.*

to·nal·i·ty (tō-nál-ǝti, tǝ-) *n., pl.* **-ties. 1.** *Music.* **a.** A system or arrangement of seven notes built upon a tonic key. **b.** The arrangement of all the notes and chords of a musical composition in relation to a tonic. **2.** The scheme or interrelation of the tones in a painting.

ton·do (tón-dō) *n., pl.* **-di** (-dee) *or* **-dos.** A circular painting or sculpted relief. [Italian, from *rotondo*, from Latin *rotundus*, round.]

tone (tōn) *n.* **1. a.** A sound considered with reference to its quality in terms of volume, pitch, duration, or the like. **b.** *U.S.* A musical sound of distinct pitch, a **note** *(see)*. **2.** *Music.* **a.** The interval of a major second; a whole tone as distinguished from a semitone. **b.** The characteristic quality or timbre of a particular instrument or voice. **3.** The pitch of a word used to determine its meaning, as in Chinese. **4.** The particular or relative pitch of a word, phrase, or sentence. **5.** Manner of expression in speech or writing: *an angry tone of voice.* **6.** A general or prevailing character or atmosphere: *The tone of the debate was antagonistic.* **7. a.** A colour or shade of colour. **b.** The general effect produced, as in a picture, by light and colour. **8.** *Physiology.* **a.** The tension in resting muscles. Also called "tonus". **b.** Normal firmness of tissue. **9.** *Informal.* High quality; distinction; class: *A duke added tone to the occasion.* —*v.* **toned, toning, tones.** —*tr.* **1.** To give a particular tone or inflection to. **2.** To soften or change the colour of (a photographic negative, for example). **3.** *Archaic.* To utter with a musical tone; intone. —*intr.* **1.** To assume a particular colour quality. **2.** To harmonise in colour. —**tone down. 1.** To lessen or soften in tone. **2.** To make or become less pronounced or emphatic; moderate. —**tone up. 1.** To increase the tone of. **2.** To improve the tone of; strengthen. [Middle English *ton*, from Old French, from Latin *tonus*, a stretching, tone, sound, from Greek *tonos*.]

tone arm *n.* The pivoted arm of a record player that holds the cartridge and stylus.

tone colour *n.* The timbre of a singing voice or instrument. [Translation of German *Klangfarbe*.]

tone-deaf (tōn-déf) *adj.* Incapable of perceiving subtle distinctions of musical pitch.

tone language *n.* A language that distinguishes meanings among words of similar form by variations in pitch and tone.

tone·less (tōn-ləss, -liss) *adj.* **1.** Lacking tone. **2.** Lacking vitality; listless. —**tone·less·ly** *adv.* —**tone·less·ness** *n.*

to·neme (tōn-eem) *n. Phonetics.* A phoneme in a tone language distinguished from another only by its tone. [TON(E) + -EME.]

tone poem *n.* A **symphonic poem** *(see)*.

tone row *n.* A fixed sequence of notes, typically consisting of the 12 notes of the chromatic scale, used as a basis for musical composition. Also called "note row".

tong (tong ‖ *U.S. also* tawng) *n.* A secret society or fraternity of Chinese, especially one allegedly involved in organised crime. [Cantonese *tong*, a hall, auditorium, assembly hall, Mandarin Chinese, equivalent of *táng*.]

ton·ga (tóng-gə) *n.* A light two-wheeled horse-drawn cart or carriage used in India. [Hindi *tāngā*.]

Tong·a, Kingdom of (tóng-ǝ; *also*, -gǝ). Also **Friendly Islands.** State in the south Pacific, comprising some 169 tropical islands, 38 of which are inhabited. Most of the people live by growing fruit and vegetables, and fishing. Coconut products and bananas are the chief exports, and tourism is important. Offshore oil has been discovered. A British Protected State from 1900, Tonga became an independent member of the Commonwealth in 1970. Area, 699 square kilometres (270 square miles). Population 90,000 (1976). Capital, Nuku'alofa on Tongatapu island. See map at **Pacific Ocean.**

Ton·gan (tóng-ǝn, *also* -gǝn) *n.* **1.** A Polynesian language spoken in Tonga. **2.** A native or inhabitant of Tonga.

Tongking. See **Tonkin.**

tongs (tongz ‖ *U.S. also* tawngz) *pl.n.* A grasping device consisting of two arms joined at one end by a pivot or hinge. [Middle English *tang(e)s*, Old English *tangan*, plural of *tang(e)*.]

tongue (tung ‖ *Northern English also* tong) *n.* **1.** The fleshy muscular organ, attached in most vertebrates to the floor of the mouth, that is the principal organ of taste, an important organ of speech in humans, and moves to aid chewing and swallowing. **2.** A homologous invertebrate structure, as in insects or certain molluscs. **3.** The tongue of an animal, such as a cow, used as food. **4. a.** The faculty of speech. **b.** A particular spoken language or dialect. **5.** Style of utterance or manner of expression: *her sharp tongue.* **6.** Anything resembling a tongue in shape, especially in being long, often tapering, and attached at one end, such as: **a.** The flap of material under the laces or buckles of a shoe. **b.** A narrow spit of land; a promontory. **c.** A jet of flame. **d.** A bell clapper. **e.** The harnessing pole attached to the front axle of a horse-drawn vehicle. **7.** A protruding strip along the edge of a board that fits into a matching groove on the edge of another board. —**give tongue. 1.** To bay, as hounds do when pursuing their quarry. **2.** To voice; utter. —**hold (one's)**

tongue. To keep silent. —**on the tip of (one's) tongue.** On the verge of being remembered or expressed.
~*v.* **tongued, tonguing, tongues.** —*tr.* **1.** To separate or articulate (musical notes) by the technique of tonguing. **2.** To touch or lick with the tongue. **3. a.** To provide (a board) with a tongue. **b.** To join (boards) by means of a tongue and groove. **4.** *Archaic.* To scold. —*intr.* **1.** To separate notes on a wind instrument. **2.** To project, as a promontory. [Middle English *t(o)unge*, Old English *tunge*; akin to Latin *lingua*.]

tongue and groove *n.* A joint made by fitting a tongue on the edge of a board into a matching groove on another board.

tongue-in-cheek (túng-in-chéek ‖ tóng-) *adj.* Meant or expressed ironically or facetiously. —**tongue in cheek** *adv.*

tongue-lash-ing (túng-lashing ‖ tóng-) *n. Informal.* A severe scolding.

tongue-tie (túng-tī ‖ tóng-) *n.* Restricted mobility of the tongue resulting from abnormal shortness of the fold of tissue connecting the tongue to the floor of the mouth.
~*tr.v.* **tongue-tied, -tying, -ties.** To make tongue-tied.

tongue-tied (túng-tīd ‖ tóng-) *adj.* **1.** Speechless or confused in expression, as from shyness, embarrassment, or astonishment. **2.** Affected with tongue-tie.

tongue twister *n.* **1.** A word or phrase difficult to articulate rapidly, usually because of a succession of similar consonantal sounds; for example, *She sells seashells by the sea shore.* **2.** Anything difficult to pronounce.

tongu-ing (túng-ing ‖ tóng-) *n. Music.* An interruption of the wind stream through an instrument by a movement of the tongue.

–tonia *n. comb. form.* Indicates tonicity; for example, **myotonia.** [New Latin, from TONUS.]

ton-ic (tónnik) *n.* **1.** Anything that invigorates, refreshes, or restores. **2.** A medicine or other agent that restores or increases bodily well-being. **3.** *Music.* The primary note of a diatonic scale; a keynote. **4.** Tonic water. **5.** *Linguistics.* **a.** A tonic accent. **b.** A voiced sound.
~*adj.* **1.** Producing or stimulating physical, mental, or emotional vigour. **2.** *Music.* Pertaining to or based on the tonic. **3.** *Linguistics.* Carrying the principal stress; accented. Said of a syllable. **4.** *Physiology.* **a.** Of or pertaining to normal muscular tension. **b.** Characterised by continuous muscular contraction: *a tonic spasm.* [From New Latin *tonicus*, of tension or tone, from Greek *tonikos*, from *tonos*, a stretching, TONE.]

tonic accent *n.* A stress produced by rising pitch as distinguished from increased volume. Also called "pitch accent", "tonic".

to-nic-i-ty (tō-níssəti, tə-, to-) *n.* **1.** The property of having mental or physical tone, or of being tonic. **2.** Tonus (see).

tonic sol-fa (sól-fáa) *n. Music.* A system of teaching sight singing and ear-training in which notes of every major or minor scale, regardless of pitch, are identified in the same way by the use of the syllables *doh, ray, me, fah, soh, la,* and *te, doh* being the keynote or tonic of every major scale.

tonic water *n.* A non-alcoholic carbonated drink containing quinine, often used as a mixer with spirits. Also called "tonic".

to-night (tə-nít, tōō-) *adv.* In or during the present or coming night.
~*n.* This night or the night of this day. [Middle English *to night*, Old English *tōniht* : TO (at, on) + *niht*, NIGHT.]

ton-ka bean (tóngkə) *n.* **1.** Any of several South American trees of the genus *Dipteryx*, having seeds that yield coumarin. **2.** The seed of any of these trees. [Perhaps from Galibi *tonka*.]

Ton-kin (tón-kín) or **Tong-king** (tóng-). Region of northern Vietnam on the Gulf of Tonkin. It was part of French Indochina (1887–1946), and after the expulsion of the French, it formed the nucleus of North Vietnam (1954–75). Its chief city, Hanoi, is now the capital of the Socialist Republic of Vietnam.

Tonkin, Gulf of. *Chinese* **Beibu Wan** or **Pei-pu Wan.** Arm of the South China Sea lying between Vietnam and southern China, and bounded in the east by the island of Hainan.

ton-nage (túnnij) *n. Abbr.* **tonn. 1.** The number of tons of water a ship displaces afloat. See **displacement ton. 2.** The capacity of a merchant ship in units of 100 cubic feet. **3.** A duty or charge per ton on cargo, as at a port or canal. **4.** The total shipping of a country or port, expressed in tons, with reference to carrying capacity. **5.** Weight, measured in tons. [TON + -AGE.]

tonne (tun, *also* ton) *n. Abbr.* **t** A metric ton (see).

ton-neau (tón-ō, tún- ‖ tun-ṓ) *n., pl.* **-neaus** or **tonneaux** (-z). **1.** The rear seating compartment of an early type of motor car. **2.** A detachable waterproof cover used to protect the passenger seats of an open car. In this sense, also called "tonneau cover". [French, "barrel", "cask", from Old French *tonnel*. See **tunnel.**]

to-nom-e-ter (tō-nómmitər) *n.* **1.** Any of various instruments for measuring fluid or vapour pressure; especially, one for measuring fluid pressure within the eye. **2.** *Music.* An instrument or device, such as a graduated set of tuning forks, used to determine the pitch of a sound. [Greek *tonos*, tension, TONE + -METER.] —**to-no-met-ric** (tónə-méttrik) *adj.* —**to-nom-e-try** (tō-nómmətri) *n.*

to-no-plast (tō-nō-plast, -nə-, -plaast) *n.* The membrane surrounding the large central vacuole in plant cells. [From Greek *tonos*, a stretching, tension (referring to its regulation of the pressure exerted by cell sap) + -PLAST.]

ton-sil (tón-sil, -s'l) *n.* A mass of lymphoid tissue; especially, either of two such masses embedded in the lateral walls of the aperture between the mouth and the pharynx. See **adenoids.** [Latin *tonsillae* (plural), probably from *tōlēs†*, goitre.] —**ton-sil-ar** (-ər) *adj.*

ton-sil-lec-to-my (tón-sil-éktəmi, -s'l-) *n., pl.* **-mies.** The surgical removal of a tonsil. [Latin *tonsillae*, TONSIL(S) + -ECTOMY.]

ton-sil-li-tis (tón-sil-ítiss, -s'l-) *n.* Tonsil inflammation. [New Latin : Latin *tonsillae*, TONSIL(S) + -ITIS.] —**ton-sil-lit-ic** (-íttik) *adj.*

ton-sil-lot-o-my (tón-sil-óttəmi, -s'l-) *n., pl.* **-mies.** **1.** The surgical incision of a tonsil. **2.** The surgical removal of part of a tonsil. [Latin *tonsillae*, TONSIL(S) + -OTOMY.]

ton-so-ri-al (ton-sáw-ri-əl ‖ -sṓ-) *adj.* Of or pertaining to a barber or to hairdressing. Often used humorously. [From Latin *tonsōrius*, from *tonsor*, a barber, from *tonsus*, past participle of *tondēre*, to shear.]

ton-sure (tón-shər, -shoor, -sewr) *n.* **1.** The act of shaving the head or the top or crown of the head, especially as a preliminary to becoming a priest or a member of a monastic order. **2.** The part of a monk's or priest's head so shaven.
~*tr.v.* **tonsured, -suring, -sures.** To shave the head of. [Middle English, from Old French, from Medieval Latin *tonsūra*, from Latin, a shearing, from *tonsus*, past participle of *tondēre*, to shear, shave.]

ton-tine (tón-tīn, -teen, ton-téen) *n.* **1.** An insurance plan whereby a group of participants share an annuity, each share becoming larger as each participant dies, the final survivor receiving the whole. **2.** Each member's share of this. **3.** The subscriptions collectively; the total fund. **4.** The subscribers to such a plan, considered collectively. [French, after Lorenzo *Tonti*, Neapolitan banker, who introduced this scheme in France in about 1653.]

ton-up (tún-úp) *adj. British Informal.* Travelling or liking to travel at speeds of more than 100 miles per hour. Said especially of motorcyclists: *ton-up boys.*

to-nus (tōnəss) *n.* The normal condition of slight tension that occurs in a muscle even when at rest. Also called "tonicity". [New Latin, from Latin, tension, TONE.]

To-ny (tóni) *n., pl.* **-nies.** Any of several annual awards presented in the United States for outstanding achievement in the theatre. [After *Tony* (Antoinette) Perry, American actress (died 1946).]

too (tōō) *adv.* **1.** In addition; also; as well: *He's coming too.* **2.** To a greater degree than is necessary or desirable; excessively: *working too hard.* **3.** Very; extremely; immensely: *only too willing to be of service.* **4.** *Informal.* Indeed; so. Used for emphasis: *said she'd leave him, and she did too.* —See Synonyms at **also.** [Emphatic form of Middle English *to*, in addition to, TO.]
Usage: When preceded by *not, too* is often used as a form of understatement in such sentences as *She wasn't too pleased;* but the usage tends to be restricted to informal speech (more formal contexts preferring *none too* or *not very*). The use of the same construction to mean "not very" (*Her re-election is not now considered too likely*) is also mainly informal.

too-dle-oo (tōōd'l-ṓo) *interj.* Also **too-dle-pip** (-píp). *British Informal.* Goodbye. [Imitative, perhaps of a car horn.]

took. Past tense of **take.**

tool (tōōl) *n.* **1.** An instrument, such as a hammer or rake, used or worked by hand. **2. a.** A machine, such as a lathe, used to cut and shape machinery parts; a machine tool. **b.** The cutting part of such a machine. **3.** Anything used in the performance of an operation; an instrument: *the economic and intellectual tools to restore prosperity.* **4.** Anything regarded as necessary to the carrying out of one's occupation or profession: *Words are the tools of his trade.* **5.** A person used to carry out the designs of another; a dupe. **6. a.** A bookbinder's hand stamp. **b.** A design impressed on a book cover by this means. **7.** *British Slang.* A gun. **8.** *Vulgar Slang.* A penis. —**down tools.** To stop work or go on strike suddenly.
~*v.* **tooled, tooling, tools.** —*tr.* **1.** To form, work, or decorate with a tool or tools. **2.** To provide (a factory, industry, or shop) with the necessary tools, machinery, or equipment. Often used with *up.* **3.** To ornament (a book cover) with a bookbinder's tool. —*intr.* **1.** To work with a tool or tools. **2.** *Informal.* To travel in a vehicle. Often used with *along: tooling along the road.* [Middle English *to(o)l*, Old English *tōl.*] —**tool-er** *n.*
Synonyms: tool, instrument, implement, utensil, appliance, gadget.

tool-box (tṓol-boks) *n.* A case for carrying or storing hand tools.

tool-ing (tōōl-ing) *n.* Work or ornamentation done with tools; especially, stamped or gilded designs on books or leather.

tool-ma-ker (tṓol-maykər) *n.* A master machinist skilled in making tools and parts. —**tool-mak-ing** *n.*

tool pusher *n. Slang.* A person in charge of the entire drilling operation on an oil platform or at an oil well.

tool-shed (tṓol-shed) *n.* A small building in which tools are kept; especially, a shed or outhouse containing gardening tools.

toon (tōōn) *n.* **1.** A tall tree, *Cedrela toona* (or *Toona ciliata*), of tropical Asia and Australia, closely related to the mahoganies and having reddish, aromatic wood. **2.** The wood of this tree. [Hindi *tūn*, from Sanskrit *tunna†*.]

toot (tṓot) *v.* **tooted, tooting, toots.** —*intr.* **1.** To sound a horn, hooter, or whistle in short blasts. **2.** To make this sound or a sound resembling this. —*tr.* To blow or sound (a horn, hooter, or whistle).
~*n.* **1.** The act or sound of tooting. **2.** *Chiefly U.S. Slang.* A lively time; a spree, especially a drinking spree. Used chiefly in the phrase *go on the toot.* [Probably from Middle Low German *tūten* (imitative).] —**toot-er** *n.*

tooth (tōōth ‖ tōōth) *n., pl.* **teeth** (teeth). **1.** In most vertebrates, any of a set of hard, bonelike structures rooted in sockets in the jaws,

typically composed of a core of soft pulp surrounded by a layer of hard dentine that is coated with cement or enamel at the crown, and used to seize, hold, or masticate. **2.** A similar structure in invertebrates, such as any of the pointed denticles or ridges on the exoskeleton of an arthropod or the shell of a mollusc. **3.** Any usually small projection resembling a tooth in shape or function, as on a comb, gear, or saw. **4.** A small, notched projection along a margin, especially of a leaf. See also **teeth.** —**long in the tooth.** Old or elderly. —**tooth and nail.** With great ferocity; as hard as possible.
~*v.* (to͞oth, to͞oth) **toothed, toothing, tooths.** —*tr.* **1.** To furnish (a tool, for example) with teeth. **2.** To make a jagged edge on. —*intr.* To mesh; become interlocked. [Tooth, teeth; Middle English *to(o)th, te(e)th,* Old English *tōth, tēth.*]

tooth·ache (to͞oth-ayk ‖ to͞oth-) *n.* An aching pain in or near a tooth.

tooth·brush (to͞oth-brush ‖ to͞oth-) *n.* A small, long-handled brush used for cleaning teeth.

toothed (to͞otht, *rarely* to͞othd ‖ to͞otht) *adj.* **1.** Having teeth. **2.** Having a specified number or type of teeth. Used in combination: *saw-toothed.*

toothed whale *n.* Any whale of the suborder Odontoceti, characterised by having rudimentary teeth. Compare **whalebone whale.**

tooth·less (to͞oth-ləss, -liss ‖ to͞oth-) *adj.* **1.** Lacking teeth. **2.** Lacking force; ineffectual. —**tooth·less·ly** *adv.* —**tooth·less·ness** *n.*

tooth·mug (to͞oth-mug ‖ to͞oth-) *n.* A small mug, typically without a handle, often kept in a bathroom and used to hold water for rinsing the mouth out after brushing the teeth.

tooth·paste (to͞oth-payst ‖ to͞oth-) *n.* A paste used for cleaning the teeth, usually brushed on with a toothbrush.

tooth·pick (to͞oth-pik ‖ to͞oth-) *n.* A small piece of wood or other material, for removing food particles from between the teeth.

tooth·pow·der (to͞oth-powdər ‖ to͞oth-) *n.* A powder used for cleaning the teeth; a powdered dentifrice.

tooth shell *n.* A tusk shell (*see*).

tooth·some (to͞oth-s'm ‖ to͞oth-) *adj.* **1.** Delicious; savoury: *a toothsome morsel of pie.* **2.** Pleasant; attractive; tempting: *a toothsome offer.* —**tooth·some·ly** *adv.* —**tooth·some·ness** *n.*

tooth·wort (to͞oth-wurt ‖ to͞oth-, -wawrt) *n.* Any of various parasitic European plants of the genus *Lathraea;* especially *L. squamaria,* having pinkish flowers and a scaly rhizome resembling dentures.

tooth·y (to͞othi ‖ to͞othi) *adj.* **-ier, -iest.** Having or showing prominent teeth. —**tooth·i·ly** *adv.*

too·tle (to͞ot'l) *v.* **-tled, -tling, -tles.** —*tr.* To toot softly on (a flute, for example). —*intr.* **1.** To toot softly and repeatedly, as on a flute. **2.** To move or travel gently or pleasurably. Often used with *along.* [Frequentative of TOOT.] —**too·tle** *n.* —**too·tler** *n.*

toots (to͞ots) *n.* Also **toot·sy, toot·sie** (to͞otsi). *Chiefly U.S. Slang.* Dear; sweetheart. Used affectionately or humorously. [20th century : origin obscure.]

toot·sy, toot·sie (to͞otsi) *n., pl.* **-sies. 1.** A person's foot. Used humorously, especially by or to children. **2.** Variant of **toots.** [Variant of *footsy,* from FOOT.]

top¹ (top) *n.* **1.** The uppermost part, point, surface, or end of anything. **2.** The crown of the head. **3.** The part of a plant, such as a turnip or beetroot, that is above the ground. **4.** Something that covers or forms the uppermost part of something, such as a lid or cap. **5.** *Nautical.* **a.** A platform enclosing the head of each mast of a sailing ship, to which the topmast rigging is attached. **b.** A similar platform, used as a gunsight or for observation, in a warship. **6. a.** In various sports and games, a stroke that lands above the centre of the ball, giving it topspin. **b. Topspin** (*see*). **7.** The highest degree, pitch, or point; a peak; an acme; a zenith. **8. a.** The highest, most important, or most successful position or rank. **b.** A prominent position in this position. **9.** In various card games, the highest card or cards in a suit or a hand. **10.** The best part; the pick; the cream. **11.** A garment such as a blouse or T-shirt, that covers the upper part of the body. **12.** The upper part of something, especially when differentiated in some way, as by being of a different material, colour, or consistency: *stocking tops; top of the milk.* **13.** A drink consisting of a small amount of lemonade added to a specified alcoholic drink: *a beer top; a lager top.* **14.** *Chemistry.* The most volatile component of a distilled mixture; the component that distils first. **15.** *Abbr.* **t.** A quantum number, a property of certain postulated elementary particles. Also called "truth". —**blow (one's) top.** *Slang.* To lose one's temper. —**from top to toe. 1.** From head to foot. **2.** Completely. —**off the top of (one's) head.** Extemporaneously; impromptu. —**on top.** In a dominant, controlling, or successful position. —**on top of. 1.** *Informal.* **a.** In control of. **b.** Fully informed about. **2.** Besides; in addition to. **3.** In close proximity to. **4.** Following closely upon; coming immediately after. —**over the top. 1.** Over the front of a fortification, as an attack in trench warfare. **2.** Going beyond the acceptable; excessive. —**up top.** In terms of mental ability: *He hasn't got much up top.*
~*adj.* **1.** Of, pertaining to, situated on, or forming the top; uppermost. **2.** Utmost; highest. Often used in combination: *top-priority; top-quality; top-rank.* **3.** *Physics.* **a.** Designating a quark flavour required certain models of elementary particle theory to complement bottom. **b.** *Abbr.* **t.** Designating a particle that contains the top quark.
~*v.* **topped, topping, tops.** —*tr.* **1. a.** To remove the top from. **b.** To prune the upper branches from. **2.** To furnish, form, or serve as a top of. **3.** To reach the top of. **4.** To go over the top of. **5.** To exceed or surpass. **6.** To be at the head or top of; lead: *He topped*

the list of this season's goal-scorers. **7.** In various sports and games, to strike the upper part of (a ball), giving it forward spin. **8.** *Slang.* To kill, especially to execute by beheading or hanging. **9.** *Informal.* To wash the face of (a child or patient, for example). Used especially in the phrase *to top and tail.* **10.** *Chemistry.* To remove (the most volatile component) by distillation. —*intr.* To top a ball. —**top off.** To finish, usually in a satisfying way; complete. —**top out. 1.** To put the framework for the top storey on (a building). **2. a.** To lay the last or highest brick or stone of a building. **b.** To celebrate this event in a ceremony. [Middle English *top(pe),* Old English *topp,* from Germanic *toppaz* (unattested).]

top² *n.* A toy consisting of a symmetrical rigid body spun on a pointed end about the axis of symmetry. [Middle English *to(o)p,* Old English *topp†.*]

top–. Variant of **topo–.**

to·paz (tō-paz) *n.* **1.** A colourless, blue, yellow, brown, or pink aluminium silicate mineral, often in association with granitic rocks and valued as a gemstone, especially in the brown and pink varieties. **2.** Any of various yellow gemstones, especially a yellow variety of sapphire. **3.** A light-yellow variety of quartz. **4.** Either of two colourful South American hummingbirds, *Topaza pyra* or *T. pella.* [Middle English *topace,* from Old French *topace, topaze,* from Latin *topazus,* from Greek *topazos†.*]

top boot *n.* A high boot usually having its upper part trimmed with a contrasting colour or texture of leather.

top brass *n.* *Used with a singular or plural verb.* The most important people in a business, government, army, or the like.

top·coat (tóp-kōt) *n.* **1.** A lightweight overcoat. **2.** A final covering of paint.

top dog *n.* *Informal.* A person or group considered to have the highest status or authority, especially as a result of victory in some struggle or competition. —**top-dog** *adj.*

top-drawer (tóp-drór) *adj.* *Informal.* Of the highest social rank.

top-dress (tóp-dress, -dréss) *tr.v.* **-dressed, -dressing, -dresses.** To cover (land or a road surface) with loose material that is not worked in; especially, to cover (land that is to be cultivated) with fertiliser.

top dressing *n.* **1.** A covering of fertiliser spread on soil without

topaz *An aluminium and silicon-based mineral which is valued as a gemstone. This prized sherry-brown variety is found only in Brazil.*

---

tooth

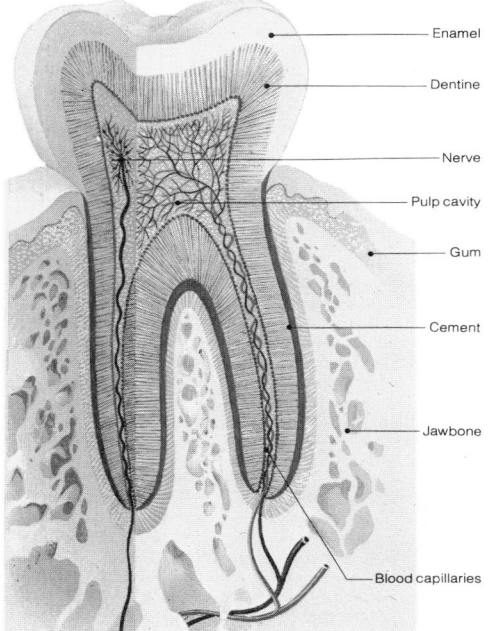

BITING, CUTTING, TEARING, AND GRINDING
Different types of teeth for different functions

Adult humans, who eat many varieties of food, have 32 teeth consisting of four types: 8 chisel-shaped incisors for biting, 4 canines for tearing, 8 premolars to cut food, and 12 molars (including the wisdom teeth) to grind food. Each tooth has a hard enamel surface covering a layer of dentine that is almost as hard. The part of the tooth in the jaw is covered with cement which anchors it in place. The only soft part of the tooth is its pulpy core of blood vessels and nerves.

HUMAN TOOTH *The enamel is the hardest part, but it is the most vulnerable because it cannot repair itself when it decays. Dentine is made up of cells that the body replaces.*

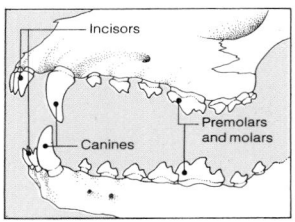

CARNIVORE *A wolf has large canines for tearing flesh. Premolars and molars cut and grind the food.*

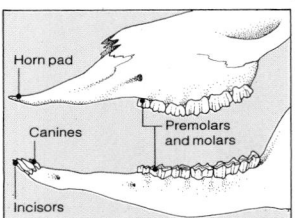

HERBIVORE *A cow has a horn pad in the upper jaw for incisors in the lower jaw to bite against.*

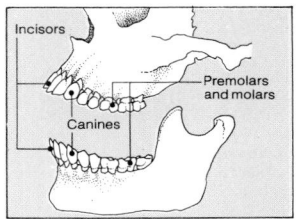

OMNIVORE *Man finds all four types of teeth necessary to deal efficiently with a meat and plant diet.*

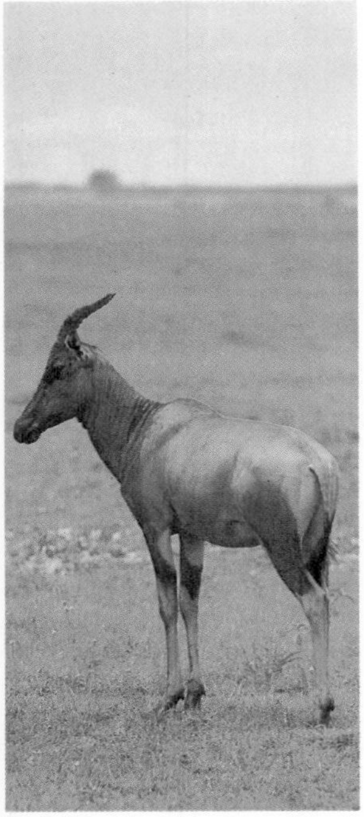

topi Damaliscus korrigum, *the topi, is a type of antelope which is native to the savannah lands of Africa. It is related to the sassaby and the blesbok.*

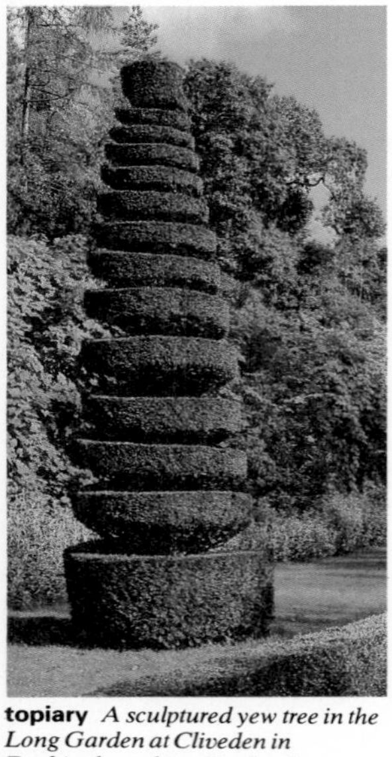

topiary *A sculptured yew tree in the Long Garden at Cliveden in Buckinghamshire, England.*

being ploughed under. **2.** A covering of loose gravel on a road.

tope¹ (tōp) *v.* **toped, toping, topes.** *Archaic.* —*tr.* To drink (alcoholic drinks) habitually and excessively. —*intr.* To drink to excess habitually. [Perhaps from obsolete *top,* drink, influenced by *tope,* an interjection used in proposing a toast, perhaps from French *tope!* agreed! from *toper,* to accept a bet, agree, from Spanish *topar* (perhaps imitative of the striking of hands of two adversaries as a sign of agreement to a bet).]

tope² *n.* Any of several small sharks, especially *Galeorhinus galeus.* [17th century : perhaps from Cornish.]

tope³ *n.* A Buddhist shrine, a **stupa** *(see).* [Hindi *tōp,* probably from Prakrit *thūpo,* from Sanskrit *stūpa,* tuft of hair, crown.]

topee. Variant of **topi.**

To·pe·ka (tə-péekə). State capital of Kansas, central United States. It is a major commercial centre for the state's livestock, wheat, and other farm products.

top·er (tṓpər) *n.* A chronic drinker; a drunkard. [From TOPE (to drink).]

top-flight (tóp-flīt) *adj.* First-rate; superior.

top fruit *pl.n.* Fruit, such as apples, peaches, and cherries, that is grown on trees rather than bushes.

top·full (tóp-fŏŏl) *adj.* Full to the brim.

top·gal·lant (tóp-gál-ənt; *nautical* tə-) *adj. Nautical.* Designating the mast above the topmast, its sails, or rigging. [Alluding to its superior position and to its making a gallant show.]

top-ham·per, top hamper (tóp-hámpər) *n.* **1.** *Nautical.* Any rigging, cables, spars, or other materials or weight not immediately necessary and stored either aloft or on the upper decks. **2.** Cumbersome and unnecessary or meaningless matter.

top hat *n.* A man's hat having a narrow brim and a tall cylindrical crown, usually made of silk and worn only on formal occasions.

top-heav·y (tóp-hévvi ‖ *U.S.* -hevvi) *adj.* **-ier, -iest. 1.** Likely to topple because overloaded at the top. **2.** Having too many executives in senior positions, and not enough actual workers. Said of a business enterprise. **3.** *Finance.* Overcapitalised. **—top-heav·i·ness** *n.*

To·phet (tṓ-fet, -fit) *n.* **1.** A place near Gehenna where human sacrifices were made. Jeremiah 19:4. **2.** Hell or a hellish place. [Middle English *Tophet(h),* from Hebrew *tōpheth,* (probably) "altar", place where children were burned, from the root *t-ph-th,* to burn.]

top-hole (tóp-hṓl) *adj. British Informal.* Very good; excellent.

to·phus (tṓ-fəss) *n., pl.* **-phi** (-fī). *Physiology.* A urate deposit found in tissue, such as cartilage, around the joints of people suffering from gout. Also called "chalkstone". [Latin *tōphus,* TUFA.] **—to·pha·ceous** (tō-fáyshəss) *adj.*

to·pi¹, to·pee (tṓ-pi, -pee ‖ *U.S. also* tō-pée) *n., pl.* **-pis.** A pith helmet worn for protection against sun and heat. [Hindi *topī*†, hat.]

to·pi² (tṓ-pi, tóppi) *n.* An African antelope, *Damaliscus Korrigum,* having a long muzzle and angular curved horns.

to·pi·ar·y (tṓpi-əri ‖ -erri) *adj.* Of, designating, or characterised by the clipping or trimming of shrubs or trees into decorative shapes, such as those of animals, birds, or geometric forms.
~*n., pl.* **topiaries. 1.** Topiary work or art. **2.** A topiary garden. [French *topiaire,* from Latin *topiārius,* of gardening, from *topia,* landscape gardening, from Greek *topia,* plural of *topion,* a field, small place, diminutive of *topos,* a place. See **topic.**] **—to·pi·a·rist** *n.*

top·ic (tóppik) *n.* **1.** A subject treated in a speech, essay, thesis, or portion of a discourse; a theme. **2.** A subject of discussion or conversation. **3.** A subdivision of a theme, thesis, or outline. [Originally from Aristotle's *Topics,* which contains commonplace arguments, from Latin *Topica,* from Greek *(Ta) Topika,* from *topikos,* of a place, commonplace, from *topos*†, a place.]

top·i·cal (tóppik'l) *adj.* **1.** Pertaining or belonging to a particular location or place; local. **2.** *Medicine.* Applied or pertaining to a local part of the body. **3.** Contemporary in reference or allusion; of current interest. **4.** Of or pertaining to a particular topic or topics. [Greek *topikos,* of a place. See **topic.**] **—top·i·cal·i·ty** (tóppi-kál-əti) *n.* **—top·i·cal·ly** *adv.*

topic sentence *n.* The sentence within a paragraph that states the main thought, and is usually placed at the beginning.

top·knot (tóp-not) *n.* **1.** A crest or knot of hair or feathers on the crown of the head. **2.** Any decorative ribbon, bow, or the like, worn as a headdress. **3.** Any of various spiny-scaled flatfish of the genera *Zeugopterus* and *Phrynorhombus;* especially *Z. punctatus.*

top·less (tóp-ləss, -liss) *adj.* **1. a.** Having no top. **b.** Having no part covering the breasts: *a topless bathing suit.* **c.** Not wearing a top: *a topless waitress.* **2.** *Archaic.* So high as to appear to extend out of sight: *the topless Alps.* **—top·less** *adv.*

top-lev·el (tóp-levv'l) *adj.* Occurring at the highest level of authority, management, diplomacy, or the like: *top-level negotiations.*

top·loft·y (tóp-lófti, -lofti ‖ -láwfti, -lawfti) *adj.* **-ier, -iest.** *Informal.* Haughty; pretentious. [Perhaps originally U.S., from TOP + LOFTY, or from *top loft,* topmost storey or gallery.] **—top·loft·i·ness** *n.*

top·mast (tóp-maast, -məst ‖ -mast) *n. Nautical.* The mast that is below the topgallant mast in a square-rigged ship and just above the lower mast in a fore-and-aft-rigged ship.

top·most (tóp-mōst) *adj.* Highest; uppermost.

top·notch (tóp-nóch) *adj. Informal.* First-rate; excellent.

topo–, top– *comb. form.* Indicates place or region; for example, **topology, toponymy.** [Greek *topos,* a place.]

to·pog·ra·phy (to-póggrə-fi, tə-) *n., pl.* **-phies.** *Abbr.* **topog. 1.** The detailed and accurate description of a place or region. **2.** The art of graphically representing on a map the exact physical configuration of a place or region. **3.** The features of a place or region. **4.** The surveying of the features of a place or region. [Middle English *topographie,* from Late Latin *topographia,* from Greek, from *topographein,* to describe a place : TOPO- + *graphein,* to write (see **-graphy**).] **—to·pog·ra·pher** (-fər) *n.* **—top·o·graph·ic** (tóppə-gráffik), **top·o·graph·i·cal** *adj.* **—top·o·graph·i·cal·ly** *adv.*

to·pol·o·gy (to-pólləji, tə-) *n.* **1.** The topographical study of a given place in relation to its history. **2.** The anatomy of specific areas of the body. **3.** The study of the properties of geometric configurations invariant under transformation by continuous mappings, that is, those properties of a figure or solid that are unaffected by continuous distortion, such as stretching without tearing or breaking. In this sense, also formerly called "analysis situs". [TOPO- + -LOGY.] **—top·o·log·i·cal** *adj.* **—to·pol·o·gist** (-pólləjist) *n.*

top·o·nym (tóppə-nim) *n.* **1.** Any name derived from a place or region. **2.** The name of a place; a place name. [Back-formation from TOPONYMY.] **—top·o·nym·ic** (-nímmik), **top·o·nym·i·cal** *adj.*

to·pon·y·my (to-pónnimi, tə-) *n., pl.* **-mies. 1.** The study of place names. **2.** *Anatomy.* Nomenclature with respect to a region of the body rather than to organs or structures. Not in current technical usage. [TOP(O)- + -ONYMY.]

top·os (tóp-oss) *n., pl.* **topoi** (-oy). A basic or stereotypical theme, idea, or the like, especially in literature. [Greek, stock topic, commonplace.]

top·o·type (tóppə-tīp) *n. Biology.* A specimen of an organism taken from the area typical for that species. [TOPO- + -TYPE.]

top·per (tóppər) *n.* **1.** One that takes off tops: *a carrot topper.* **2.** *Informal.* A top hat. **3.** *British Informal.* A good fellow; an excellent chap. **4.** *Informal.* Something that outdoes or caps what has gone before, especially a bantering remark.

top·ping (tópping) *n.* A sauce, icing, or garnish for food.
~*adj. Chiefly British Informal.* First-rate; excellent.

top·ple (tópp'l) *v.* **-pled, -pling, -ples.** —*tr.* **1.** To push over; overturn. **2.** To overthrow, as from an elevated or powerful position. —*intr.* **1.** To totter and fall. **2.** To lean over as if about to fall. [Frequentative of TOP (to remove the top of).]

tops (tops) *adj. Informal.* First-rate; excellent. **—the tops.** *Informal.* A first-rate or excellent thing or person.

top·sail (tóp-s'l, -sayl) *n.* **1.** A square sail set above the lowest sail on the mast of a square-rigged ship. **2.** A triangular or square sail set above the gaff of a lower sail on a fore-and-aft-rigged ship.

top-se·cret (tóp-séek-rət, -rit) *adj.* Designating materials or information of the highest level of security classification.

top shell *n.* Any primitive, winkle-like, marine mollusc of the family Trochidae.

top·side (tóp-sīd) *n.* **1.** A lean, boneless cut of beef from the top of the leg. **2.** *Often plural.* The upper parts of a ship that are above the main deck.
~*adv.* On or to the upper parts of a ship; on deck.

top·soil (tóp-soyl) *n.* The surface layer of soil.
~*tr.v.* **topsoiled, -soiling, -soils. 1.** To remove the topsoil from (land). **2.** To cover or spread with topsoil.

top·spin (tóp-spin) *n. Sports.* A forward spin given to a ball by hitting with a sharp, slightly forward-curved stroke.

top·stitch (tóp-stich) *tr.v.* **-stitched, -stitching, -stitches.** To sew a line of decorative stitching close to the seam or edge of (a garment) on the right side of the fabric.

top·sy-tur·vy (tópsi-túrvi) *adv.* **1.** Upside-down. **2.** In a confused manner or a state of utter disorder.
~*adj.* In a confused or disordered condition.
~*n.* Confusion; chaos. [Earlier *topsy-tervy, topsy-tirvy* : probably TOP + obsolete *tervy,* to overturn, Middle English *turven,* to wallow, probably from Old English *tierfan* (unattested), to roll.] **—top·sy-tur·vi·ly** *adv.* **—top·sy-tur·vi·ness** *n.*

top up *tr.v.* **1.** To fill (a container that already contains some liquid) to the top with liquid: *top the car up with petrol; top your drink up.* **2.** *Informal.* To fill up the glass of: *Can I top you up?*

top-up (tóp-up) *n. Informal.* A refill; especially, a replenishment of a glass that is not quite empty: *Can I give you a top-up?*

toque (tōk) *n.* **1.** A small brimless, close-fitting woman's hat. **2.** A plumed velvet cap with a full crown and small rolled brim, especially as worn by men and women in 16th-century France. [French, from Spanish *toca*†.]

tor (tor) *n.* **1.** A high rock or pile of rocks on the top of a hill. **2.** A rocky peak or hill. [Middle English *torre,* Old English *torr,* probably from Old Welsh *twrr,* bulge.]

to·rah (táw-rə, tṓ-, -raa; *Hebrew* taw-ráa) *n.* **1.** The body of Jewish literature and oral tradition as a whole, containing the laws and teachings of the religion. **2.** *Capital* **T. a.** The Pentateuch. **b.** The scroll of parchment or leather on which the Pentateuch is written, used in a synagogue during services. [Hebrew *tōrāh,* a law, instruction, from *yārāh,* to teach, instruct.]

Tor·bay (tór-báy). Coastal district of Devon, southwest England. It includes Torquay, Paignton, and Brixham, all lying on Tor Bay, and is one of Britain's major tourist areas.

tor·bern·ite (tórbər-nīt) *n.* A green hydrous crystalline phosphate of uranium and copper. [German *Torbernit,* after *Torbern* O. Bergman (1735–84), Swedish chemist.]

torch (torch) *n.* **1.** A small, portable light or lamp consisting of a bulb and dry batteries, encased usually in a metal or plastic cylinder. Also *U.S.* "flashlight". **2.** A portable light produced by the flame of an inflammable material wound about the end of a stick of wood and ignited; a flambeau. **3.** A portable apparatus that produces a very hot flame by the combustion of gases, used in welding and brazing. **4.** *U.S. Slang.* An arsonist. **5.** Anything that serves to illuminate, enlighten, or guide. **—carry a the torch for.** To love (someone who does not reciprocate). **—hand on the torch.** To keep a tradition or skill alive by teaching it to others. [Middle English *torche,* from Old French, a torch originally made of twisted straw dipped in wax, from Vulgar Latin *torca* (unattested), from *torquēre,* to twist.]

torch·bear·er (tórch-bair-ər) *n.* **1.** A person who carries a torch. **2.** A person who imparts knowledge, truth, or inspiration to others, as a leader of a movement.

tor·chère (tawr-sháir) *n.* A tall narrow table or stand, especially for supporting candlesticks. [French, from *torche,* TORCH.]

tor·chon lace (tór-sh'n, -shon) *n.* A lace made of coarse linen or cotton thread twisted in simple geometric patterns. [French *torchon,* duster, dishcloth, from Old French, twisted straw, from *torche,* TORCH.]

torch song *n.* A sentimental, often highly emotional popular song. [From the phrase *to carry a torch for.*]

tore[1]. Past tense of **tear.**

tore[2] (tor || tōr) *n. Mathematics & Architecture.* A **torus** *(see).* [French, from Latin TORUS.]

tor·e·a·dor (tórri-ə-dawr || táwri-) *n.* A bullfighter, especially one mounted on a horse. [Spanish, from *torear* (past participle *toreado*), to fight bulls, from *toro,* a bull, from Latin *taurus.*]

to·re·ro (tə-ráir-ō, to-) *n., pl.* **-ros.** A matador or one of his team. [Spanish, from Late Latin *taurārius,* from Latin *taurus,* a bull.]

to·reu·tics (to-ro͞o-tiks, tə-, -réw-) *n. Used with a singular verb.* The art of working metal or other materials by the use of embossing and chasing to form minute detailed reliefs. [From *toreutic,* from Greek *toreutikos,* from *toreutos,* worked in relief, from *toreuein,* to bore through, from *toreus,* a boring tool.] **—to·reu·tic** *adj.*

tor·goch (táwr-gōkh) *n.* A subspecies of the red-bellied char, *Salvelinus alpinus,* found in certain lakes in North Wales. [Welsh, "red belly" : *tor,* belly + *coch,* red.]

to·ri. Plural of **torus.**

tor·ic (tórrik || táw-rik, tō-) *adj.* Of, pertaining to, or shaped like a torus or a part of a torus.

toric lens *n.* A spectacle lens used to correct astigmatism that has one torus-shaped surface with different focal lengths in different directions.

to·ri·i (táw-ri-ee || tō-) *n., pl.* **torii.** The gateway of a Shinto temple, consisting of two uprights with a straight crosspiece at the top and a concave lintel above the crosspiece. [Japanese, "bird residence" : *tori,* bird + *i-,* from *iru,* to dwell.]

Torino. See **Turin.**

tor·ment (tór-ment) *n.* **1.** Great physical pain or mental anguish. **2.** A source of harassment, annoyance, or pain.
~*tr.v.* (tawr-mént || *U.S. also* tór-ment) **tormented, -menting, -ments. 1.** To cause to undergo great physical pain or mental anguish. **2.** To agitate or upset greatly. **3.** To annoy, pester, or harass. —See Synonyms at **harass.** [Middle English, instrument of torture, torment, from Old French, from Latin *tormentum, torquementum* (unattested), a twisted rope, (instrument of) torture, from *torquēre,* to twist.] **—tor·ment·ing·ly** *adv.*

tor·men·til (tórməntil) *n.* A Eurasian plant, *Potentilla erecta* (or *P. tormentilla*), having yellow flowers and leaves divided into five leaflets. [Middle English *tormentille,* from Medieval Latin *tormentilla*†.]

tor·men·tor, tor·ment·er (tawr-méntər || tór-mentər) *n.* **1.** One that torments. **2.** A hanging used at each side of the stage in a theatre directly behind the proscenium, to block the wing area and sidelights from the audience. **3.** A sound-absorbent screen used on a film set or in a film studio to prevent echo.

torn (torn || tōrn). Past participle of tear. **—that's torn it.** *British Slang.* Used to express alarm or distress when some unexpected complication ruins one's plans.
~*adj.* Undecided; struggling to make a choice.

tor·na·do (tawr-náydō) *n., pl.* **-does** or **-dos. 1.** A rotating column of air usually accompanied by a funnel-shaped downward extension of a cumulonimbus cloud and having a vortex several hundred yards in diameter whirling destructively at speeds of up to 480 kilometres (300 miles) per hour. Also called "cyclone". Compare **waterspout. 2.** A violent thunderstorm in West Africa and nearby Atlantic waters. **3.** Any whirlwind or hurricane. **4.** Anything resembling a tornado in vigour or destructiveness. —See Synonyms at **wind.** [Variant (influenced by Spanish *tornado,* turned) of Spanish *tronada,* thunderstorm, from the past participle of *tronar,* to thunder, from Latin *tonāre.*] **—tor·na·dic** (-náydik, -náddik) *adj.*

to·roid (táw-royd || tō-) *n.* **1.** In geometry: **a.** A surface generated by a closed curve rotating about, but not intersecting or containing, an axis in its own plane. **b.** A solid having such a surface. **2.** An object having the shape of such a figure. [TOR(US) + -OID.] **—to·roi·dal** (taw-róyd'l, to- || tō-) *adj.*

To·ron·to (tə-róntō). Capital of Ontario, eastern Canada, lying on Lake Ontario. It is the cultural centre of English-speaking Canada, a major port, financial and industrial centre, and an important transport nexus. It was founded in about 1787 and, as York, it became the capital of Upper Canada (1793), but was incorporated as the city of Toronto in 1834.

to·rose (táw-rōz, -rōss || tō-) *adj. Biology.* Cylindrical and having ridges or swellings. [Latin *torōsus,* from *torus,* a TORUS.]

tor·pe·do (tawr-péedō) *n., pl.* **-does. 1.** A cigar-shaped, self-propelled underwater projectile launched from an aircraft, ship, or submarine, and designed to detonate on contact with or in the vicinity of a target. **2.** Any of various submarine explosive devices, especially a submarine mine. **3.** An explosive fired in an oil or gas well to begin or increase the flow. **4.** Any of several cartilaginous fishes of the genus *Torpedo,* related to the skates and rays. See **electric ray.**
~*tr.v.* **torpedoed, -doing, -does. 1.** To attack, explode, or destroy with or as if with a torpedo or torpedoes. **2.** To immobilise or render ineffective (a scheme, policy, or the like). [New Latin *Torpedo,* genus of fish that give electric shocks, from Latin *torpēdō,* stiffness, numbness, the torpedo (fish), from *torpēre,* to be stiff.]

torpedo boat *n.* A fast, thinly plated boat equipped with heavy machine guns and torpedoes.

tor·pe·do-boat destroyer (tawr-pée-dō-bōt) *n.* A fast vessel, larger and more heavily armed than a torpedo boat, designed to destroy the latter, but often serving the same purpose.

tor·pe·fy (tórpi-fī) *tr.v.* **-fied, -fying, -fies.** To make torpid. [Latin *torpefacere* : *torpēre,* to be sluggish + *-facere,* -FY.]

tor·pid (tórpid) *adj.* **1.** Deprived of the power of motion or feeling; benumbed. **2.** Dormant; hibernating. **3.** Lethargic; apathetic. —See Synonyms at **inactive.** [Latin *torpidus,* from *torpēre,* to be stiff. See **torpedo.**] **—tor·pid·i·ty** (tawr-píddəti), **tor·pid·ness** *n.* **—tor·pid·ly** *adv.*

tor·por (tórpər) *n.* **1.** A condition of mental or physical inactivity or insensibility. **2.** Lethargy; apathy. —See Synonyms at **lethargy.** [Latin, from *torpēre,* to be stiff. See **torpedo.**]

torque[1] (tork) *n.* **1.** The moment of a force, a measure of its tendency to produce torsion and rotation about an axis, equal to the vector product of the radius vector from the axis of rotation to the point of application of the force by the force applied. **2.** Broadly, a turning or twisting force. [Latin *torquēre,* to twist.]

torque[2] *n.* A collar, necklace, or armband made of a strip of twisted metal, worn by the ancient Gauls, Germans, and Britons. [French, from Latin *torquēs,* twisted necklace, from *torquēre,* to twist.]

torque converter *n.* A mechanical or hydraulic device for changing the ratio of torque to speed between the input and output shafts of a mechanism.

tor·ques (tór-kweez) *n. Zoology.* A distinctive band of feathers, hair, skin, or coloration around the neck. [Latin *torquēs,* TORQUE (collar).]

torque wrench *n.* A wrench or spanner with a torque gauge built into it to enable nuts and bolts to be tightened to a given torque.

torr (tor) *n.* A unit of pressure equal to one millimetre of mercury (133.32 pascals). [After Evangelista *Torricelli;* see **Torricellian vacuum.**]

tor·re·fy, tor·ri·fy (tórri-fī || táwri-) *tr.v.* **-fied, -fying, -fies.** To scorch, roast, or dry (metallic ores or drugs, for example) by exposing to intense heat. [French *torréfier,* from Latin *torrefacere* : *torrēre,* to parch + *-facere,* -FY.] **—tor·re·fac·tion** (-fáksh'n), **tor·ri·fac·tion** *n.*

Tor·rens, Lake (tórrənz). Salt lake of South Australia. It has an area of 5 776 square kilometres (2,230 square miles) and is the continent's second largest lake. It partly dries out in summer.

tor·rent (tórrənt || táwrənt) *n.* **1.** A turbulent, swift-flowing stream. **2.** A raging flood; a deluge. **3.** Any turbulent or overwhelming flow: *a torrent of abuse.* [French, from Italian *torrente,* from Latin *torrēns* (stem *torrent-*), a burning, a torrent, from the present participle of *torrēre,* to dry, burn.]

tor·ren·tial (tə-rénsh'l, to- || taw-) *adj.* **1.** Of, pertaining to, or having the character of a torrent. **2.** Resembling a torrent; turbulent or unrestrained: *torrential applause.* **3.** Resulting from the action of a torrent or torrents: *torrential erosion.* **—tor·ren·tial·ly** *adv.*

Tor·res Strait (tórriss, tórriz, táwriz). Channel between New Guinea and Cape York, Australia, linking the Arafura and Coral seas. It is notorious for its reefs and shoals. The Spanish explorer Luis Torres discovered the strait in 1606.

Tor·ri·cel·li·an vacuum (tórri-sélli-ən, -chélli- || táwri-) *n.* The vacuum formed at the top of a vertical glass tube a *(Torricellian tube)* with one sealed end, which has been evacuated, partly filled with mercury, and inverted into a mercury reservoir so that its open end is submerged beneath the mercury. It functions as an indicator of atmospheric pressure. [After Evangelista *Torricelli* (1608–47), Italian physicist and mathematician.]

tor·rid (tórrid || táwrid) *adj.* **1.** Parched with the heat of the sun. **2.** Intensely hot; scorching; burning. **3.** Passionate; ardent. [Latin *torridus,* from *torrēre,* to dry, parch.] **—tor·rid·i·ty** (to-ríddəti, tə- || taw-), **tor·rid·ness** *n.* **—tor·rid·ly** *adv.*

Torrid Zone *n.* The region of the earth's surface between the Tropics of Cancer and Capricorn.

tor·sade (tawr-sáyd, -saád) *n.* A decorative trimming for hats, consisting of twisted ribbon or cord. [French, from (obsolete) *tors,* twisted, from Late Latin *torsus,* from the past participle of Latin *torquēre,* to twist.]

tor·sion (tórsh'n) *n.* **1. a.** The act of twisting or turning. **b.** The condition of being twisted or turned. **2.** The stress caused when one end of an object is twisted in one direction and the other end is held motionless or twisted in the opposite direction. [Middle English, from Old French, from Late Latin *torsiō* (stem *torsiōn-*), from *torsus,* "twisted". See **torsade.**] **—tor·sion·al** *adj.* **—tor·sion·al·ly** *adv.*

torsion balance *n.* An instrument with which small forces, such as those of gravity, electricity, or magnetism, are measured by means of the torsion they produce in a wire or slender rod.

torsion bar *n.* A part of a motor vehicle's suspension consisting of a bar that twists to maintain stability.

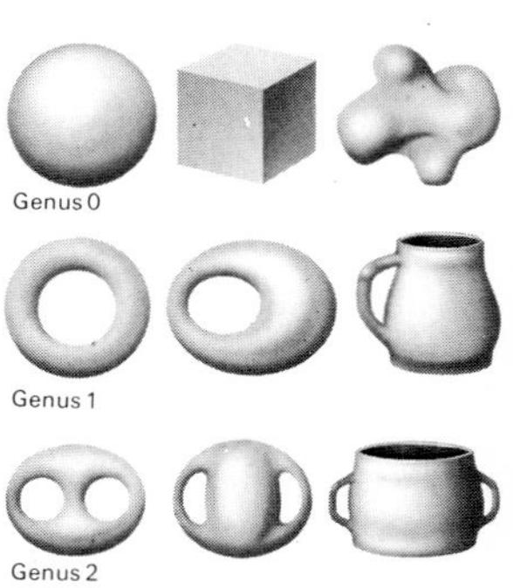

topology *In topological mathematics, the genus of an object is defined by the number of holes through it. If the shapes above were made of infinitely malleable Plasticine, those in each row could be changed into one another with no cutting, piercing, or joining. But they could not, under the same restrictions, be changed into the shapes of any other row.*

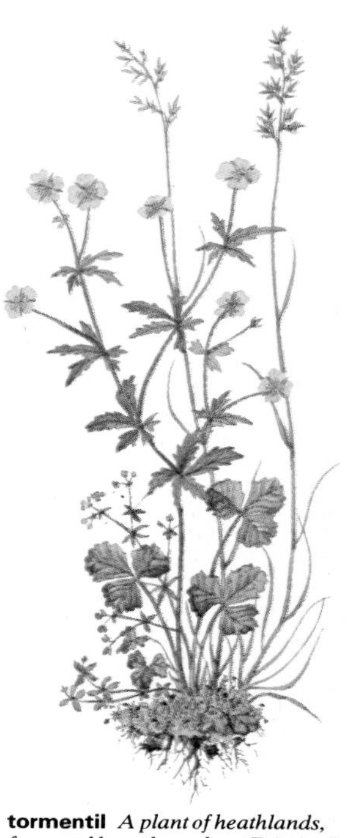
tormentil *A plant of heathlands, fens, and bogs throughout Britain. Its roots were once used to produce a red dye, and were also thought to cure the torment of stomachache – hence its name.*

torsk (torsk) *n., pl.* **torsks** or collectively **torsk.** A marine fish, *Brosme brosme,* of the family Gadidae found mainly in the north Atlantic. Also called "tusk", *U.S.* "cusk". [Norwegian, from Old Norse *thorskr.*]

tor·so (tór-sō) *n., pl.* **-sos** or **-si** (-see). **1.** The trunk of the human body. **2.** A statue of the trunk of the human body, especially with the head and limbs missing or truncated. **3.** Any truncated or unfinished thing. [Italian, a stalk, trunk (of a statue), from Latin *thyrsus,* THYRSUS.]

tort (tort) *n. Law.* Any wrongful act, damage, or injury done wilfully, negligently, or in circumstances involving strict liability, but not involving breach of contract, for which a civil lawsuit for damages can be brought. [Middle English, from Old French, from Medieval Latin *tortum,* from Latin, twisted, distorted, from the neuter past participle of *torquēre,* to twist.] **—tor·tious** (tórshəss) *adj.* **—tor·tious·ly** *adv.*

tor·te (tórtə, tort) *n.* A rich layer cake made with many eggs and little flour and usually containing chopped nuts, cream, fruit, or jam. [German *Torte,* perhaps from Italian *torta,* from Late Latin *tōrta*†, a kind of bread.]

tor·tel·li·ni (tórtə-lééni) *pl.n.* Small, round pieces of pasta folded over a filling. [Italian, diminutive of *tortelli,* another type of pasta, ultimately from Late Latin *torta.* See **tart** (pie).]

tort·fea·sor (tórt-féezər) *n. Law.* One who is guilty of tort. [French *tortfaiseur* : TORT + *faiseur,* doer, from *faire,* to do.]

tor·ti·col·lis (tórti-kólliss) *n.* A contracted state of the neck muscles producing an unnatural position of the head. Also called "wryneck". [New Latin : Latin *tortus,* past participle of *torquēre,* to twist (see **tort**) + *collum,* the neck.] **—tor·ti·col·lar** *adj.*

tor·til·la (tawr-tée-ə, -yə) *n.* A thin unleavened pancake made of corn meal, characteristic of Mexican cookery, usually served hot with various fillings. [American Spanish, diminutive of Spanish *torta,* a round cake, from Late Latin *torta,* TORTE.]

tor·toise (tór-təss; *also sometimes* -toyz) *n.* **1. a.** Any of various terrestrial reptiles of the order Chelonia, characteristically having thick, scaly limbs and a high, rounded shell. **b.** *Chiefly British.* A pond or water tortoise; a **terrapin** *(see).* **2.** One that moves slowly. **3.** A **testudo** *(see).* [Middle English *tortuce, tortu,* from Old French *tortue,* probably from Medieval Latin *tortūca*†.]

tor·toise·shell (tór-tə-shel, -təsh-, -təss-) *n.* **1.** The mottled, translucent brownish covering of the carapace of certain of the sea turtles, especially the hawksbill, used to make combs, jewellery, and other articles. **2.** Any of various similar synthetic substances used for the same purposes. **3.** A domestic cat having fur with brown, black, and yellowish markings. **4.** Any of several butterflies, chiefly of the family Nymphalidae, especially *Nymphalis polychloros,* the large tortoiseshell, and *Aglais urticae,* the small tortoiseshell, having wings with orange, black, and brown markings. **5.** Mottled yellowish-brown. **—tor·toise·shell** *adj.*

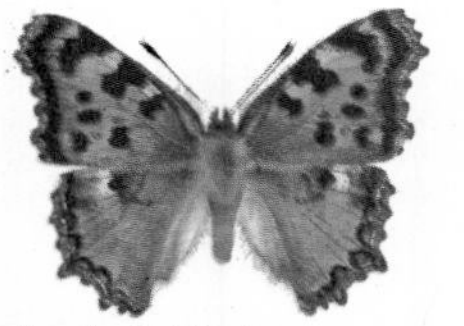

tortoiseshell *The large tortoiseshell butterfly,* Nymphalis polychloros, *has a wingspan of about 60 millimetres (2½ inches). In Britain, it is usually found only in parts of East Anglia.*

tor·tu·os·i·ty (tórtew-óssəti) *n., pl.* **-ties. 1.** The state of being tortuous; twistedness; crookedness. **2.** A bent or twisted part, passage, or thing; a twist; a turn; a winding.

tor·tu·ous (tórtew-əss, tórchoo-) *adj.* **1.** Having or marked by repeated turns or bends; winding; twisting. **2.** Not straightforward; deceitful; devious. **3.** Highly involved; circuitous; complex. [Middle English, from Old French, from Latin *tortuōsus,* from *tortus,* a twist, from the past participle of *torquēre,* to twist.] **—tor·tu·ous·ly** *adv.* **—tor·tu·ous·ness** *n.*

tor·ture (tórchər) *n.* **1.** The infliction of severe physical pain, especially as a means of punishment or coercion. **2.** The undergoing of such pain. **3.** Mental anguish. **4.** A cause of such pain or anguish. *~tr.v.* **tortured, -turing, -tures. 1.** To subject (a person or animal) to torture. **2.** To afflict with great physical or mental pain. **3.** To twist or turn abnormally; distort. [French, from Late Latin *tortūra,* a twisting, torment, from Latin *tortus,* "twisted". See **tortuous.**] **—tor·tur·er** *n.*

tor·tur·ous (tórchərəss) *adj.* **1.** Of or pertaining to torture. **2.** Causing or inflicting torture. **3.** Excruciatingly painful.

to·rus (táw-rəss ‖ tō-) *n., pl.* **tori** (-rī). **1.** *Architecture.* A large moulding of convex semicircular cross-section, usually found just above the plinth of the base of a classical column. Also called "tore". **2.** *Anatomy.* A bulging or rounded projection or swelling. **3.** *Biology.* A moundlike or rounded structure, such as the receptacle of a flower. **4.** In geometry, a toroid generated by a circle; a surface having the shape of a ring doughnut. In this sense, also called "anchor ring", "tore". [New Latin, from Latin *torus*†, a protuberance, round swelling.]

To·ry (táw-ri ‖ tō-) *n., pl.* **-ries. 1.** A member or supporter of the British Conservative Party. **2. a.** One who supported James II of England and opposed the Glorious Revolution of 1689. **b.** A member of a British political party, founded in 1689, that was the opposition party to the Whigs, became identified with conservative interests, and has been known as the Conservative Party since about 1832. **3.** Any American who during the War of American Independence favoured the English side. **4.** *Sometimes small* **t. a.** A member or supporter of any Conservative Party, as in Canada. **b.** A conservative or right-wing person. [Probably from Irish *tōraighe* (unattested), runaway, from Old Irish *tōir,* pursue. The name originally denoted an Irishman who, dispossessed by the English in the mid-17th century, became a bandit; it then became a term for any marauder, and was subsequently applied abusively to Irish Catholic royalists, then to supporters of James II, and after 1689 to the English party that initially opposed the Glorious Revolution.] **—To·ry** *adj.* **—To·ry·ism** *n.*

tosh (tosh) *n. British Informal.* Nonsense; rubbish; balderdash.

toss (toss ‖ tawss) *v.* **tossed, tossing, tosses.** *—tr.* **1.** To throw casually or lightly. Often used with *out, aside, down,* or other adverbs. **2.** To throw, fling, or heave continuously about; pitch to and fro. **3. a.** To throw lightly with or as if with the hand or hands; pitch gently or with a sudden slight jerk. **b.** To throw upwards. **4.** *Informal.* To discuss informally; bandy about. **5.** To move or lift (the head) with rapidity: " *'Idiot!' said the Queen, tossing her head impatiently*" (Lewis Carroll). **6.** To disturb or agitate; upset. **7. a.** To throw (a rider) to the ground. Used of a horse. **b.** To throw (a matador, for example) into the air, using the head or horns. Used of a bull. **8. a.** To throw up (a coin) in order to make a decision according to the side facing upwards when it lands. **b.** To throw up a coin in this way with (someone) in order to decide something. **9.** To mix (a salad) lightly so as to cover with dressing, oil, or the like. **10.** To throw (a pancake) up in the air and catch it again in the pan with the reverse side upwards. *—intr.* **1.** To be thrown here and there; be flung to and fro: *The boat tossed in the turbulent water.* **2.** To move oneself about vigorously; throw oneself from side to side: *toss in one's sleep.* **3.** To throw a coin to decide something. —See Synonyms at **throw. —toss off. 1.** To drink up in one swallow. **2.** To do, finish, accomplish, or perform in a casual, easy manner: *toss off a few jokes.* **3.** *British Vulgar Slang.* To masturbate. *~n.* **1.** The act of tossing or the condition of being tossed. **2.** The distance something can be tossed. **3.** A rapid movement or lift, as of the head. **4.** A fall from or the experience of being thrown from a horse. **—argue the toss.** To dispute an issue that has already been decided. **—not give a toss.** *Informal.* To not care at all about something. [16th century : origin obscure.] **—toss·er** *n.*

toss up *intr.v.* To toss a coin to settle an issue. *—tr.v.* To prepare (food or a meal) quickly or at short notice.

toss·up (tóss-up ‖ táwss-) *n. Informal.* **1.** The tossing of a coin to settle an issue. **2.** An even chance or choice.

tot[1] (tot) *n.* **1.** A small child. **2.** A small amount of something. **3.** A small measure of spirits. [18th century (dialect) : origin obscure.]

tot[2] *tr.v.* **totted, totting, tots.** *Informal.* To total or add. Usually used with *up.* [Shortening of TOTAL.]

tot[3] *n. British Slang.* Rags and bones; rubbish collected by a rag-and-bone man. [19th century : origin obscure.]

to·tal (tōt'l) *n.* **1.** The amount or quantity obtained by addition; a sum. **2.** A whole quantity; an entirety.
~adj. **1.** Constituting or pertaining to the whole; entire. **2.** Complete; utter; absolute.
~v. **totalled** or *U.S.* **totalled, -talling** or *U.S.* **-taling, -tals.** *—tr.* **1.** To determine the sum or total of. **2.** To equal a total of; amount to. **3.** *Chiefly U.S. Slang.* To demolish (a vehicle) completely in a road accident. *—intr.* To add up; amount. Often used with *to: It totals to three pounds.* [Middle English, of the whole, from Old French, from Medieval Latin *tōtālis,* from Latin *tōtus,* whole.]

total eclipse *n.* An eclipse in which the eclipsed body as seen from the earth is totally hidden. Compare **partial eclipse.**

to·tal·ise, to·tal·ize (tōt'l-īz) *tr.v.* **-ised, -ising, -ises.** To make or combine into a total. **—to·tal·i·sa·tion** (-ī-záysh'n ‖ *U.S.* -i-) *n.*

to·tal·is·er (tōt'l-īzər) *n.* **1.** Variant of **totalisator. 2.** *Chiefly U.S.* An adding machine.

to·tal·i·sa·tor (tōt'l-ī-zaytər) *n.* Also **to·tal·is·er** (for sense 1). **1.** A system of betting on races whereby the winners receive a share of the total amount bet, in proportion to the sums they have wagered individually, after management expenses and taxes have been deducted. Also informally called "tote", *chiefly U.S.* "pari-mutuel". **2.** The machine that records bets placed under this system.

to·tal·i·tar·i·an (tō-tál-i-táir-i-ən, tō-tal-, tə-) *adj.* Of or designating a government or political regime whose main characteristic is considered to be the imposition of monolithic unity in every sphere of the life of its subjects, upheld by authoritarian means. [TOTAL + (AUTHOR)ITARIAN.] **—to·tal·i·tar·i·an·ism** *n.*

to·tal·i·ty (tō-tál-əti, tə-) *n., pl.* **-ties. 1.** The state or condition of being total. **2.** The whole amount. **3.** The aggregate amount; a sum. **4. a.** The state of an eclipse when it is total. **b.** The length of time during which an eclipse is total.

to·tal·ly (tōt'l-i) *adv.* Entirely; wholly; completely.

to·ta·quine (tōtə-kween, -kwin ‖ -kwīn) *n.* A powdered yellowish, bitter mixture of quinine and alkaloids from cinchona bark, formerly used as an antimalarial. [New Latin *totaquina* : TOTA(L) + Spanish *quina,* cinchona bark (see **quinine**).]

to·ta·ra (tó-tərə) *n.* A conifer, *Podocarpus totara,* of New Zealand having hard reddish wood used in building and furniture-making.

tote[1] (tōt) *tr.v.* **toted, toting, totes.** *Informal.* **1.** To haul; lug. **2.** To have on one's person; pack: *toting guns.*
~n. Informal. A load; a burden. [18th century (U.S.) : of obscure (dialectal) origin.] **—tot·er** *n.*

tote[2] *n. Informal.* A totalisator. [Short for TOTALISATOR.]

tote bag *n. Informal.* A very large handbag or shopping bag.

to·tem (tōtəm) *n.* **1.** An animal, plant, or natural object serving among certain primitive peoples as the emblem of a clan or family by virtue of an asserted ancestral relationship. **2.** A representation of this being. **3.** A social group having a common totemic affiliation. **4.** Any venerated emblem or symbol. [Algonquian; compare Ojibwa *nintōtēm,* "my family mark", from a stem *ōtē-* (unattested), "to be from a local group".] **—to·tem·ic** (tō-témmik) *adj.*

to·tem·ism (tōtəm-iz'm) *n.* **1.** The belief in kinship through com-

PRONUNCIATION KEY

a, trap; aa, father; ai, fair; ar, star; aw, lawn; ay, play; b, bb, stab; rubber; ch, church; ck, ticket; d, dd, dead; ladder; e, dress; ee, bee; er, defer; ew, few; ewr, pure; ə, about; ər, letter; f, ff, fife; differ; g, gg, giggle; h, hat; i, kit; ī, price; īr, fire; j, judge; k, kick; l, ll, let; 'l, needle; m, mm, man; n, nn, no; 'n, sudden; ng, thing; o, lot; ō, no; ŏŏ, foot; ōō, shoe; oor, poor; ow, cow; owr, hour; oy, boy; p, pp, pepper; r, rr, red; s, ss, sauce; sh, ship; t, tt, totter; th, thick; th, this; smooth; u, cut; ur, turn; v, vv, valve; w, wet; y, yes; z, zz, zebra; zh, vision; pleasure

IN FOREIGN WORDS:

aN, oN, Saint-Saëns; hl, Llanelli; Hluhluwe; kh, loch; lough; Khaled

STRESS MARK:

ín-sīt, insight; in-sít, incite

mon totemic affiliation or the identification of an individual or group with a totem. **2.** The primitive kinship system of which this is a reflection. **—to·tem·ist** *n.* **—to·tem·is·tic** (-ístik) *adj.*

totem pole *n.* **1.** A post carved and painted with a series of totemic symbols and erected before a dwelling, as by certain Indian peoples of the northwestern coast of North America. **2.** *Chiefly U.S. Slang.* A hierarchy: *a low man on the totem pole.*

toth·er, t'oth·er (túthər) *pron. Archaic & Regional.* The other. [Middle English *the tother,* mistaken division of *thet other* : *thet,* the, Old English *thæt,* THAT + OTHER.]

to·ti·pal·mate (tṓti-pál-mayt, -mət, -mit) *adj.* Having webbing that connects each of the four toes, as water birds, such as pelicans and gannets, have. [Latin *tōtus,* whole (see **total**) + PALMATE.]

to·tip·o·ten·cy (tō-típpətən-si, tṓti-pṓtən-si) *n.* Also **to·tip·o·tence** (tō-tĭp'ə-təns, tō'tĭ-pōt'əns). **1.** The capacity of a blastomere to develop into a fully formed embryo. **2.** The ability of meristematic cells to specialise in response to hormones from growth centres. [Latin *tōtus,* whole (see **total**) + POTENCY.] **—to·tip·o·tent** *adj.*

tot·ter[1] (tóttər) *intr.v.* **-tered, -tering, -ters. 1. a.** To sway as if about to fall. **b.** To appear about to collapse: *a tottering empire.* **2.** To walk unsteadily or feebly. **3.** To waver; vacillate.
~*n.* The act or condition of tottering. [Middle English *tot(e)ren,* from Middle Dutch *touteren,* to stagger, from Old Saxon *taltron* (unattested).] **—tot·ter·er** *n.* **—tot·ter·y** *adj.*

tot·ter[2] *n. British Slang.* A rag-and-bone man. [TOT (rubbish) + -ER.] **—tot·ting** *n.*

tou·can (tóō-kən, -kan, -kaan) *n.* Any of various tropical American birds of the family Ramphastidae, having an extremely large, brightly coloured bill and variously coloured plumage. [French, from Portuguese *tucano,* from Tupi *tucana.*]

touch (tuch) *v.* **touched, touching, touches.** *—tr.* **1. a.** To cause or permit a part of the body to come into contact with. **b.** To cause or permit a part of the body, especially the hand, to come into contact with so as to feel. **2.** To bring something into contact with: *touch the plate with a spoon.* **3.** To bring (something) into contact with something else: *touch the match to the paper.* **4.** To tap or nudge very lightly. **5.** To strike or lay hands on in violence. Usually used in the negative: *Don't you dare touch her!* **6.** To use or partake of. Usually used in the negative: *She didn't touch her food.* **7.** To disturb or move by handling. **8. a.** To meet; adjoin; border. **b.** In geometry, to be tangential to. **9. a.** To reach; get to: *touched 90°.* **b.** To come up to; equal in quality: *His work couldn't touch his master's.* **10. a.** To handle or be involved in. Usually used in the negative: *I wouldn't touch that business.* **b.** To treat of; deal with as a subject. **11.** To be pertinent to; concern. **12.** To have an effect upon; act on; change. **13.** To injure or spoil slightly. **14.** To colour slightly; tinge. **15.** To affect the emotions of; move to tender response. **16.** To draw, mark, or shade with light strokes. Often used with *in.* **17.** *Rare.* To strike or pluck the keys or strings of (a musical instrument). **18.** *Rare.* To play (a musical piece). **19.** *Archaic.* To set fire to or kindle. **20.** *Archaic.* To stamp (tested metal). **21.** *Informal.* To borrow from; beg a loan from. Usually used with *for*: *I touched him for £50.* *—intr.* **1.** To touch someone or something. **2.** To be or come into contact. —See Synonyms at **affect.** **—touch at.** To stop briefly at (a port, for example). **—touch off. 1.** To cause to explode; fire. **2.** To initiate (a chain of events, for example); trigger. **3.** To make a portrait of in a sketchy or hasty manner. **—touch on** or **upon. 1.** To deal with (a topic) in passing. **2.** To pertain to; concern. **3.** To approach being; verge on.
~*n.* **1.** The act or an instance of touching. **2.** The physiological sense by which external objects or forces are perceived through contact with the body. **3.** A sensation experienced in touching something with a characteristic texture. **4.** A mild tap or shove. **5.** A discernible mark or effect left by contact with something. **6.** A subtle effect wrought by a small change or addition. **7.** A suggestion; a hint; a tinge. **8.** A mild attack: *a touch of flu.* **9.** A small amount; a trace; a dash: *a touch of paprika.* **10. a.** A manner or technique of striking the keys of a keyboard instrument, such as a piano or typewriter. **b.** The resistance to being struck by the fingers, characteristic of a keyboard. **11. a.** A person's characteristic manner or style of doing something. **b.** A characteristic manner in one's personal relationships. **12.** A facility; a knack: *lose one's touch.* **13.** The state of being in contact with a person or people, or a specified or unspecified reality: *getting out of touch.* **14.** *Rare.* A test or trial, as to establish quality. Used chiefly in the phrase *put to the touch.* **15.** *Archaic.* The official stamp indicating the quality of a metal product; the hallmark. **16.** *Slang.* **a.** The act of approaching someone to borrow or beg a loan. **b.** A sum of money borrowed. **c.** A person liable to be the victim of an approach for a loan. Often used in the phrases *soft touch, easy touch.* **17. a.** In soccer the area just outside the sidelines. **b.** In Rugby football, the area outside and including the sidelines. **18.** In fencing, a scoring hit. **19.** A children's game, **tag** *(see).* [Middle English *to(u)chen,* from Old French *tochier,* from Vulgar Latin *toccāre* (unattested), to strike, ring a bell, touch (probably imitative).] **—touch·a·ble** *adj.* **—touch·a·ble·ness** *n.* **—touch·er** *n.*

touch-and-go, touch and go (túch-ən-gṓ) *adj.* Of unclear outcome; critical; risky.

touch down *intr.v.* **1.** To land, especially briefly, as for repairs. Used of aircraft or spacecraft. **2.** In Rugby football, to touch the ground with the ball behind the goal line, as when scoring a try.

touch·down (túch-down) *n. Abbr.* **TD, td., td 1.** The contact, or moment of contact, of a landing aircraft or spacecraft with the landing surface. **2.** In Rugby football, an act or instance of touching down. **3.** In American football, a play worth six points, accomplished by being in possession of the ball when it is declared dead on or behind the opponent's goal line.

tou·ché (tóō-shay, tōō-sháy) *interj.* **1.** Used in fencing to acknowledge that one has been touched by one's opponent's foil. **2.** Used to express concession to an opponent for a point well made, as in an argument. [French, "touched".]

touched (tucht) *adj.* **1.** Emotionally affected or moved. **2.** Slightly demented or mentally unbalanced.

touch·hole (túch-hōl) *n.* The opening in early firearms and cannons through which the powder was ignited.

touch·ing (túching) *adj.* Eliciting a tender reaction; moving. See Synonyms at **moving.**
~*prep.* Concerning; about. **—touch·ing·ly** *adv.*

touch judge *n.* In Rugby football, either of the two linesmen who judge whether a ball has gone into touch and whether, in an attempted goal, the ball has passed between the two uprights, and who may inform the referee of instances of foul play.

touch·line (túch-līn) *n.* In various field sports such as soccer and Rugby football, either of the sidelines bordering the playing field.

touch-me-not (túch-mi-not, -mee-, -nót) *n.* Any of several plants of the genus *Impatiens.* See **balsam.** [Its seed pods burst open at the slightest touch when ripe.]

touch paper *n.* A type of paper impregnated with saltpetre so that it burns slowly and without a flame. [From TOUCH (archaic sense "to kindle").]

touch·stone (túch-stōn) *n.* **1.** A hard black stone, such as jasper or basalt, formerly used to test the quality of gold or silver by comparing the streak left on the stone by one of these metals with that of a standard alloy. **2.** A criterion; a standard.

touch-type (túch-tīp) *intr.v.* **-typed, -typing, -types.** To type without having to look at the keyboard, the fingers being trained to locate the keys by position. **—touch-typ·ist** *n.*

touch up *tr.v.* **1.** To make minor changes, additions, or improvements in (a work, photograph, or the like). **2.** *Informal.* To fondle or caress in a sexually stimulating manner.

touch-up (túch-up) *n.* The act or process of finishing or improving by small alterations and additions.

touch·wood (túch-wŏŏd) *n.* Decayed wood or similar material used as tinder; punk. [From TOUCH (archaic sense "to kindle").]

touch·y (túchi) *adj.* **-ier, -iest. 1.** Apt to take offence with very slight cause; oversensitive. **2.** Requiring tact or skill; precarious; risky: *a touchy situation.* **—touch·i·ly** *adv.* **—touch·i·ness** *n.*

tough (tuf) *adj.* **tougher, toughest. 1.** Strong and resilient; able to withstand great strain without tearing or breaking. **2.** Hard to cut or chew. **3.** Physically hardy; rugged. **4.** Severe; harsh. **5.** Aggressive; pugnacious. **6.** Demanding or troubling; difficult. **7.** Strong-minded; resolute. **8.** *Chiefly U.S.* Vicious; rough. **9.** *Informal.* Unfortunate; too bad. —See Synonyms at **strong.**
~*n. Chiefly U.S.* A hoodlum; a thug. [Middle English *togh,* Old English *tōh.*] **—tough·ly** *adv.* **—tough·ness** *n.*

tough·en (túff'n) *v.* **-ened, -ening, -ens.** *—tr.* To make tough or tougher. *—intr.* To become tough or tougher. **—tough·en·er** *n.*

toughened glass *n.* See **safety glass.**

tough·ie (túffi) *n. Informal.* **1.** A tough person or thing. **2.** A tough or tricky problem.

tough-mind·ed (túf-mīndid) *adj.* Not sentimental or timorous. **—tough-mind·ed·ly** *adv.* **—tough-mind·ed·ness** *n.*

Tou·lon (tōō-lóɴ). City in the Var département, southeastern France. It has been a major naval base since the 17th century.

Tou·louse (tōō-lóōz). Capital of the Haute-Garonne département, southern France. A major market, cultural centre, and canal port, it is also the centre of the French aviation industry.

Toulouse-Lautrec, Henri (Marie Raymond de) (1864–1901). French artist. He settled in Paris in 1881 and painted an unconventional side of life among the music halls and cafes of Montmartre.

tou·pee (tóō-pay || *chiefly U.S.* tōō-páy) *n.* **1.** A partial wig or hairpiece worn, usually by men, to cover a bald spot. **2.** A curl or lock of hair worn during the 18th century as a topknot on a periwig. [French *toupet,* a tuft of hair, forelock, diminutive of Old French *toup,* tuft; see **top** (summit).]

tour (toor, tor) *n.* **1.** A comprehensive trip or journey, usually taken for pleasure or education, with visits to places of interest. **2.** A group organised for such a trip or for a shorter sightseeing excursion. **3.** A brief trip to or through a place for the purpose of seeing it: *a tour of the house.* **4.** A journey to fulfil a round of engagements in several places: *a concert tour.* **5.** A period of duty at a single place or job. **—on tour.** Giving theatrical or concert performances, or the like, while touring.
~*v.* **toured, touring, tours.** *—intr.* To go on a tour. *—tr.* **1.** To make a tour of. **2.** To present (a theatrical performance) on a tour. [Middle English, one's turn, a turning, from Old French *tour,* *to(u)rn,* turn, circuit, from Latin *tornus,* lathe. See **turn.**]

tou·ra·co, tu·ra·co (tóor-ə-kō) *n., pl.* **-cos.** Any of various African birds of the family Musophagidae, many of which have brightly coloured plumage. [French, from a West African name.]

Tou·raine (tōō-ráyn; *French* tōō-rén). Former province of west central France. A rich agricultural area famous for its grain, fruit and wines, it is sometimes called the "Garden of France". It is also a major tourist area noted for its châteaux. Tours is the chief city.

tour·bil·lion (toor-bíl-yən, tur-, tóorbilən) *n.* **1.** A whirlwind. **2.** A

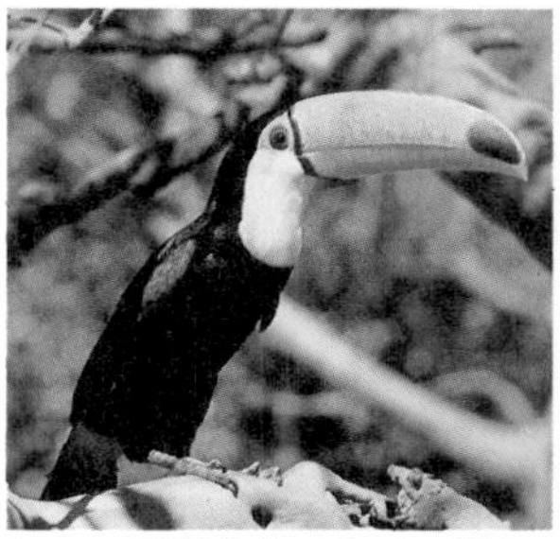

toucan *With its huge beak, which has a light honeycombed structure, the toucan is able to reach and pick fruit from trees. The birds are native to the tropical forests of the Americas.*

firework rocket that has a spiral flight. [French *tourbillon,* ultimately from Latin *turbō* (stem *turbin-*), whirlwind. See **turbine.**]

tour de force (to͝or də fórss, tór || fōrss) *n., pl.* **tours de force.** A feat of strength or virtuosity; a masterly achievement. [French.]

tour·er (to͝or-ər, tór-) *n.* A large open car for five or more persons, popular in the 1920s. Also called "touring car".

tour·ism (to͝or-iz'm, tór-) *n.* Also **tour·is·try** (-istri) (for sense 1). **1.** The practice of travelling for pleasure. **2.** The business of providing tours and services for tourists.

tour·ist (to͝or-ist, tór-) *n.* A person who is travelling for pleasure. *~adj.* Also **tour·is·tic** (toor-ístik, tawr-). Of or for tourists.

tourist class *n.* A grade of travel accommodation for passengers that is less luxurious than first class or cabin class.

tourist trap *n. Informal.* A place or event to which large numbers of tourists are attracted, and at which visitors are often exploited, as by overcharging.

tour·ist·y (to͝or-isti, tór-) *adj. Informal.* Like, suitable for, full of, or spoilt by tourists. Used derogatorily.

tour·ma·line (to͝or-mə-lin, túr-, -leen) *n.* A complex crystalline silicate containing aluminium, boron, and other elements, used in electronic instrumentation and as a gemstone. [French, from Sinhalese *toramalli,* cornelian.]

Tour·nai (toor-náy). Also **Tournay.** *Flemish* **Door·nik** or **Door·nijk** (dór-nik, do͝or-). Also **Tournay.** City of Hainaut province, western Belgium, lying on the river Scheldt. A market and industrial centre, it is noted for carpets, textiles, and hosiery.

tour·na·ment (to͝or-nəmənt, tór-, túr-) *n.* **1.** A contest involving a number of contestants who compete in a series of elimination games or trials. **2. a.** A medieval sport in which mounted contestants endeavoured to unseat one another with lances or swords; a jousting match. **b.** A meeting or festivity at which such matches and other chivalric displays took place. [Middle English *tornement,* from Old French *torneiement,* from *torneier,* to TOURNEY.]

tour·ne·dos (to͝or-nə-dō, túr-) *n., pl.* **-dos.** A small beef steak cut from the centre of the fillet, often bound in bacon or suet for cooking. [French : *tourner,* to TURN + *dos,* back.]

tour·ney (to͝or-ni, tór-, túr-) *intr.v.* **-neyed, -neying, -neys.** To compete in a medieval tournament.

~n., pl. **tourneys.** A medieval tournament. [Middle English *torneyen,* from Old French *torneier,* "to turn around" (from the combatants' turning around for each attack), from Vulgar Latin *tornidiāre* (unattested), to wheel, turn, from Latin *tornus,* a lathe, TURN.]

tour·ni·quet (tóor-ni-kay, tór-, túr- || *chiefly U.S.* -kit) *n.* Any device used to stop temporarily the flow of blood through a large artery in a limb; especially, a cloth band tightened around a limb, often over a pad placed to focus pressure on the artery. [French, "a turning instrument", swivel.]

Tours (toor). Capital of the Indre-et-Loire département, west central France. It is a tourist centre for the Loire valley, and a market and manufacturing centre.

tou·sle (tówz'l) *tr.v.* **-sled, -sling, -sles. 1.** To disarrange or rumple; dishevel. **2.** To handle roughly; mistreat.

~n. **1.** A dishevelled mass, as of hair. **2.** A dishevelled state. [Middle English *touselen,* frequentative of *-tusen*†, to pull about.]

tous-les-mois (to͞o-lay-mwaá) *n.* **1.** A West Indian plant, *Canna edulis,* with red flowers and purple stems, widely cultivated for its edible starchy rhizomes. **2.** The rhizome or starch obtained from this plant. [French, "every month", probably a phonetic approximation of West Indian *tolomane* (native name).]

Tous·saint l'Ou·ver·ture (toosáN lo͞ovairtűr), **Pierre Dominique** (*c.*1743–1803). Haitian revolutionary. With the help of the French he led a force which expelled the British and Spanish (1798). The French later seized him (1802) and he died in a French prison.

tout (towt) *v.* **touted, touting, touts.** *Informal. —intr.* **1.** To solicit customers, votes, or patronage, especially in a brazen way. **2. a.** To obtain horseracing information for use in betting, as by spying on the training of racehorses. **b.** To deal in such information. **3.** To buy sought-after tickets at the normal price and sell at inflated prices. *—tr.* **1.** To solicit or importune. **2.** To obtain or sell information on (a racing horse or stable) for the guidance of betters. **3.** To publicise as being of great worth; praise excessively: *highly touted by the press.* **4.** To sell (tickets that are hard to obtain), usually outside the relevant venue and at high prices.

~n. Informal. **1.** A person who obtains information on racehorses and their prospects and sells it to betters. **2.** A person who solicits customers persistently or brazenly. **3.** A person who touts tickets. [Middle English *tuten,* to peep, watch, Old English *tūtian* (unattested), from Germanic *tūt-* (unattested), to stick out, protrude.] **—tout·er** *n.*

tout court (to͞o ko͝or) *French.* Plainly and simply: *They're not Euro-communists—they're Communists tout court.*

to·va·risch, to·va·rish, to·va·rich (tə-vaárish, to-) *n. Russian.* Comrade. Used as a term of address.

tow¹ (tō) *tr.v.* **towed, towing, tows.** To draw, drag, or pull along usually by a chain or rope, or the like.

~n. **1.** An act of towing. **2.** The condition of being towed. Used chiefly in the phrases *on tow* or *in tow.* **3.** Something being towed, such as a barge or car. **4.** Something that tows, such as a tugboat. **5.** A rope or cable used in towing. **—in tow. 1.** Following or accompanying. **2.** Under one's sway or control; in one's charge. [Middle English *togen, towen,* Old English *togian;* akin to TUG.]

tow² *n.* **1.** Coarse broken flax or hemp fibre, either prepared for spinning or to be discarded. **2.** A bunch of synthetic fibres. [Middle English *towe,* probably Old English *tow-,* "spinning".]

tow·age (tō-ij) *n.* **1.** The act or service of towing. **2.** A charge for towing.

to·ward (tə-wáwrd, to͞o-, tord || tōrd) *prep. Chiefly U.S.* Towards. *~adj.* (tō-ərd || tord, tōrd). **1.** *Rare.* Favourable. **2. a.** *Archaic.* In progress. **b.** *Obsolete.* Imminent. [Middle English *toward,* Old English *tōweard,* coming, favourable, future : TO + -WARD.]

to·ward·ly (tō-ərd-li || tórd, tōrd-) *adj. Archaic.* **1.** Promising. **2.** Advantageous; favourable. **—to·ward·li·ness** *n.*

to·wards (tə-wáwrdz, to͞o-, tordz || tōrdz) *prep.* Also *chiefly U.S.* **toward. 1.** In the direction of. **2.** In a position facing: *The back of the chair was towards me.* **3.** Just before in time; approaching: *It began to rain towards morning.* **4.** With regard to; in relation to: *I can't understand his attitude towards us.* **5. a.** In furtherance of or partial fulfilment of: *£10 a month towards a new car.* **b.** By way of achieving; with a view to: *efforts towards peace.*

tow·bar (tō-baar) *n.* A rigid metal bar fixed to a vehicle, with suitable fittings enabling it to be attached to another vehicle, caravan, boat, or the like and used in towing.

tow·boat (tō-bōt) *n.* A **tugboat** *(see).*

tow·el (tów-əl, towl) *n.* A piece of absorbent cloth or paper used for wiping or drying. **—throw in the towel.** *Informal.* To give up; quit in defeat.

~v. **towelled** or *U.S.* **toweled, -elling** or *U.S.* **-eling, -els.** *—tr.* **1.** To wipe or rub dry with a towel. **2.** *Chiefly Australian Informal.* To beat or thrash. *—intr.* To dry oneself with a towel. [Middle English *towelle,* from Old French *toail(l)e,* from Frankish *thwahljō* (unattested), from Germanic *thwahan* (unattested), to bathe.]

tow·el·ling (tów-əl-ing, tówl-) *n.* **1.** Any of various absorbent fabrics, usually of cotton or linen, and having a nap, used for making towels, flannels, and the like. **2.** *Chiefly Australian Informal.* A beating or thrashing.

tow·er (tów-ər, towr) *n.* **1. a.** An exceptionally tall, usually equilateral, square or circular building. **b.** An exceptionally tall part of a building, usually having a particular function: *a church tower.* **2.** A tall framework or structure, the elevation of which is functional, as for observation, signalling, or pumping. **3.** A fortress or prison, often consisting of or incorporating a tower. **4.** A tall mobile wooden framework used in medieval warfare to help soldiers scale the walls of an enemy castle.

~intr.v. **towered, -ering, -ers. 1.** To rise to a conspicuous height; loom: *towering above our heads.* **2.** To be pre-eminent: *He towers above all others.* **3.** To soar or to fly directly upwards before swooping or falling. Used of certain birds. [Middle English *to(u)r,* from Old English *torr* and Old French *tor, tur,* both from Latin *turris,* from Greek, probably of Mediterranean origin.] **—tow·ered** *adj.*

tower block *n.* A high block of flats or offices with a large number of floors, occupying a relatively small ground area.

tower crane *n.* A crane consisting of a cantilever beam pivoted so that it can rotate at the top of a framework tower.

Tower Hamlets. Borough of Greater London created in 1965 from the boroughs of Stepney, Bethnal Green, and Poplar.

tow·er·ing (tów-ər-ing, tówr-) *adj.* **1.** Of imposing height. **2.** Outstanding; pre-eminent. **3.** Awesomely intense; furious: *a towering rage.* —See Synonyms at **high.**

tower of strength *n.* An extremely supportive or dependable person. [Popularised by use in Shakespeare's *Richard III* (1594); " . . .the King's name is a tower of strength" (Act V, scene 3).]

tow·head (tō-hed) *n.* **1.** A head of blonde hair. **2.** One having such hair. [From TOW (hemp).] **—tow·head·ed** (-hédded) *adj.*

tow·line (tō-līn) *n.* A **towrope** *(see).*

town (town || *West Indies also* tung) *n.* **1.** A large group of buildings and roads within a fixed boundary, where people live and work, larger than a village and, typically, smaller than most cities. **2.** The commercial district or centre of a town. **3.** The nearest town: *going to town.* **4.** Towns in general or urban life: *I prefer the country to the town.* **5.** The residents of a town. **6.** The ordinary, permanent inhabitants of a university town, as opposed to the academic community. Compare **gown. 7.** The dominant city or town of an area. **—go to town.** *Informal.* To do something energetically with no inhibitions or restrictions; go all out. **—on the town.** *Informal.* On a spree. **—paint the town red.** *Informal.* To go on an elaborate or wild spree. [Middle English *t(o)un, town,* Old English *tūn,* an enclosed place, homestead, village.]

town clerk *n.* **1.** Until 1974, the chief administrative officer, secretary, and legal adviser of a British town. **2.** *Chiefly U.S.* A public official in charge of keeping the records of a town.

town crier *n.* A person formerly employed by a town to walk the streets proclaiming announcements. Also called "bellman".

town·ee (town-eé) *n.* Also **town·ie** (tówni), **town·y** *pl.* **-ies.** *Informal.* **1.** A town-dweller as opposed to a country-dweller. **2.** A resident of a university town as opposed to a student. Usually used derogatorily.

town gas *n.* Coal gas supplied for domestic or industrial use.

town hall *n.* The building where many of the local government officials of a town are based, where municipal business is conducted, and where public meetings may be held.

town house *n.* **1.** A person's house or other residence in the city as distinguished from one in the country. **2.** A terraced house, especially a fashionable one. **3.** A town hall.

town meeting *n.* A legislative assembly of townspeople.

town planning *n.* The designing of a town or urban area such that houses, roads, and public amenities are planned as an integrated whole. **—town planner** *n.*

town•ship (tówn-ship || *West Indies also* túng-) **1.** In South Africa, an urban area specifically set aside for coloured or black people to live in. **2.** In Canada and the United States, a subdivision of a province or county having local government powers. **3.** In Australia and New Zealand, a small town. **4.** Formerly in England, a unit of local government such as a parish, part of a town, or a small town. **5.** The residents of a township.

towns•man (tównz-mən || *West Indies also* túngz-) *n., pl.* **-men** (-mən). **1.** A resident of a town. **2.** A fellow-resident of a town.

towns•peo•ple (tównz-peep'l || *West Indies also* túngz-) *pl.n.* The inhabitants or citizens of a town or city. Also called "townsfolk".

towns•wom•an (tównz-wŏŏmən || *West Indies also* túngz-) *n., pl.* **-women** (-wimmin). **1.** A woman resident of a town. **2.** A woman residing in the same town as oneself.

tow•path (tṓ-paath || -path) *n., pl.* **-paths** (-paath̲z || -paths, -path̲z). A path along a canal or river, still sometimes used by animals towing boats.

tow•rope (tṓ-rōp) *n.* A strong rope or cord used in towing a vehicle, especially a car. Also called "towline".

tox–, toxo–, toxico– *comb. form.* Indicates poison; for example, **toxaemia.** [From Latin *toxicum,* poison. See **toxic.**]

tox•ae•mi•a (tok-seémi-ə) *n.* **1.** A condition in which bacterial toxins produced at a local source of infection are contained in the blood. Also called "blood poisoning". **2.** The condition of pre-eclampsia or eclampsia in the later stages of pregnancy. [New Latin : TOX- + -AEMIA.] **—tox•ae•mic** *adj.*

tox•al•bu•min (tóks-ál-bew-min, -al-béw-) *n.* Any of various toxic albumin proteins.

tox•ic (tóksik) *adj.* **1.** Of or pertaining to a toxin. **2.** Harmful, destructive, or deadly; poisonous. [Late Latin *toxicus,* from Latin *toxicum,* poison for arrows, from Greek *toxikon,* from *toxikos,* of or for a bow, from *toxon,* a bow.] **—tox•i•cal•ly** *adv.*

tox•i•cant (tóksikənt) *n.* A poison or poisonous agent.
~adj. Poisonous; toxic. [Medieval Latin *toxicāns* (stem *toxicant-*), present participle of *toxicāre,* to poison, from Latin *toxicum,* poison. See **toxic.**]

tox•ic•i•ty (tok-síssəti) *n., pl.* **-ties. 1.** The quality or condition of being toxic. **2.** The degree to which a poison is toxic.

tox•i•co•gen•ic (tóksi-kō-jénnik) *adj.* Also **tox•i•gen•ic. 1.** Producing poison or toxic substances. **2.** Derived from toxic matter. [From TOXIC + -GENIC.]

tox•i•col•o•gy (tóksi-kólləji) *n.* The study of the nature, effects, and detection of poisons and the treatment of poisoning. [TOXIC + -LOGY.] **—tox•i•co•log•i•cal** (-kə-lójik'l) *adj.* **—tox•i•co•log•i•cal•ly** *adv.* **—tox•i•col•o•gist** (-kólləjist) *n.*

tox•i•co•sis (tóksi-kṓ-siss) *n., pl.* **-ses** (-seez). Any pathological condition resulting from poisoning. [New Latin : TOXIC + -OSIS.]

toxic shock syndrome *n.* A rare infection that is characterised by vomiting, fever, a rash, and a sharp drop in blood pressure. Most known cases have occured in women using vaginal tampons.

tox•in (tók-sin) *n.* Also **tox•ine** (-seen). A poisonous substance, secreted by certain organisms and capable of causing toxicosis when introduced into the body tissues but also capable of inducing a counteragent or an antitoxin. [TOX- + -IN.]

tox•in-an•ti•tox•in (tóksin-ánti-toksin) *n.* A mixture of a toxin, as from diphtheria, and its antitoxin with a slight excess of toxin, formerly used as an active (live) vaccine in the United States.

tox•oid (tóks-oyd) *n.* A toxin that has lost toxicity but has retained the capacity to stimulate the production of or combine with antitoxins, used in immunisation. [TOX- + -OID.]

tox•oph•i•lite (tok-sóffi-līt) *n. Formal.* A lover of archery; an archer.
~adj. Also **tox•o•phil•ic** (tóksə-fíllik). *Formal.* Of, pertaining to, or loving archery. [From *Toxophilus* (1545), a book by Roger Ascham, from Greek *toxon,* bow + *-philos,* -PHILE + -ITE.]

tox•o•plas•mo•sis (tóksō-plaz-mṓ-siss) *n.* A disease caused by infection with a microorganism, *Toxoplasma gondii,* usually producing only mild symptoms except if contracted by a pregnant woman, when it can cause blindness and mental retardation in the foetus. [New Latin : *toxoplasma,* from : Latin *toxicum,* poison (see **toxic**) + PLASMA + -OSIS.] **—tox•o•plas•mic** (-plázmik) *adj.*

toy (toy) *n.* **1.** An object designed to be played with, especially by children. Also used adjectivally: *toy soldiers.* **2.** Something of little importance; a trifle. **3.** A small ornament; a bauble; a trinket. **4.** A diminutive thing or person. **5.** A dog of a very small breed or one much smaller than is characteristic of its breed, usually kept as a pet. Also used adjectivally: *a toy poodle.*
~intr.v. **toyed, toying, toys.** To amuse oneself idly; trifle. Used with *with.* [Middle English *toye*†, dallying, amorous sport.]

t.p. title page.

tr. 1. *Grammar.* transitive. **2.** translated; translation; translator. **3.** transpose; transposition. **4.** treasurer. **5.** *Law.* trust; trustee.

tra•be•at•ed (tráybi-aytid) *adj.* Also **tra•be•ate** (-ət, -it, -ayt). *Architecture.* Having horizontal beams or lintels rather than arches. [Latin *trabs,* a beam, timber.] **—tra•be•a•tion** (-áysh'n) *n.*

tra•bec•u•la (trə-béckew-lə) *n., pl.* **-lae** (-lee). **1.** A small supporting beam or bar. **2.** *Anatomy.* Any of the supporting strands of connective tissue projecting into an organ and constituting part of the framework of that organ. **3.** *Botany.* A transverse rodlike or platelike structure, often extending across a cavity. [New Latin, from Latin, diminutive of *trabs,* a beam.] **—tra•bec•u•lar** (-lər) *adj.*

trace¹ (trayss) *n.* **1.** A visible mark or sign of the former presence or passage of some person, thing, or event. **2.** A barely perceptible indication of something; a touch. **3. a.** A minute quantity. **b.** A quantity of rainfall or other precipitation too small to be measured. **c.** A constituent, such as a chemical compound or element, present in quantities less than a standard limit. **4. a.** A footprint or track left by an animal or person. **b.** *U.S.* A path or trail through a wilderness that has been beaten out by the passage of animals or people. **5.** *Archaic.* A way or route followed. **6.** A line drawn by a recording instrument, such as a cardiograph.
~v. **traced, tracing, traces.** *—tr.* **1.** To follow the course or trail of. **2.** To ascertain the successive stages in the development or progress of. **3. a.** To search back in time to find the origin of. Often used with *back.* **b.** To locate or discover (a cause, for example) by searching or researching evidence. **4. a.** To delineate or sketch (a figure). **b.** To give an outline or rough idea of (a plan). Often used with *out.* **5.** To imprint (a design) on something. **6.** To form (letters) with special concentration or care. **7.** To copy by following lines seen through a sheet of transparent paper. **8.** To make a design or series of markings on (a surface). **9.** To cover or decorate with tracery. **10.** To record (a variable), as on a graph. *—intr.* **1.** To make one's way; follow a path. Used with *along* or *through.* **2.** To have origins; be traceable. Used with *back.* [Middle English, a path, a course, from Old French, from *tracier,* to make one's way, from Vulgar Latin *tractiāre* (unattested), to drag, from Latin *tractus,* a dragging. See **tract** (expanse).] **—trace•a•bil•i•ty** (-ə-bílləti), **trace•a•ble•ness** *n.* **—trace•a•ble** *adj.* **—trace•a•bly** *adv.* **—trace•less** *adj.* **—trace•less•ly** *adv.*
Synonyms: *trace, vestige, track, trail, spoor.*

trace² *n.* **1.** Either of two side straps or chains connecting a harnessed draught animal to the vehicle it is pulling. **2.** In fishing, a short connecting piece of line between the hook and the main line. **3.** A bar or rod, hinged at either end to another part, that transfers movement from one part of a machine to another. **—kick over the traces.** To free oneself from constraints; become unruly. [Middle English *trais,* a pair of traces, from Old French, plural of *trait,* a pulling, a strap, from Latin *tractus,* a dragging. See **tract** (expanse).]

trace element *n.* An element required in minute amounts by an organism to maintain certain essential physiological processes.

trac•er (tráyssər) *n.* **1.** One that traces. **2.** A person employed to locate missing goods or persons. **3.** An investigation or inquiry organised to trace missing goods or persons. **4.** Any of several instruments used in making tracings or other drawings. **5.** *Military.* A tracer bullet. **6.** An identifiable substance, such as a dye or radioactive isotope, that can be followed through the course of a mechanical or biological process, providing information on the process or on the redistribution of the parts or elements involved.

tracer bullet *n.* A bullet that leaves a luminous or smoky trail, and whose path can therefore be observed. Also called "tracer".

trac•er•y (tráyssəri) *n., pl.* **-ies.** Ornamental work or a pattern of interlaced and ramified lines; specifically, the lacy openwork in a Gothic window. [From TRACE (draw).] **—trac•er•ied** *adj.*

tra•che•a (trə-keé-ə || *U.S.* tráyki-ə) *n., pl.* **-as** or **-cheae** (-ee, -ī). **1.** *Anatomy.* A thin-walled tube of cartilaginous and membranous tissue descending from the larynx to the bronchi and carrying air to the lungs. Also called "windpipe". **2.** *Zoology.* Any of the internal respiratory tubes of insects and some other terrestrial arthropods. **3.** *Botany.* A **vessel** *(see).* [Middle English *trache,* from Medieval Latin *trāchēa,* from Late Latin *trāchīa,* from Greek *(artēria) trakheia,* "rough (artery)", from the feminine of *trakhus,* rough.] **—tra•che•al, tra•che•ate** *adj.*

tra•che•id (tráyki-id) *n.* Any of the elongated, tapering, supporting and conducting cells in woody tissue. [TRACHE(O)- + -ID.]

tra•che•i•tis (tráyki-ītiss) *n.* Inflammation of the trachea. [New Latin : TRACHE(O)- + -ITIS.]

tracheo–, trache– *comb. form.* Indicates the trachea; for example, **tracheotomy, tracheitis.** [New Latin, from Medieval Latin *trāchēa,* TRACHEA.]

tra•che•o•phyte (tráyki-ō-fīt, -ə-) *n.* Any plant with xylem- and phloem-conducting tissues; a vascular plant.

tra•che•ot•o•my (tráyki-óttəmi) *n., pl.* **-mies.** The act or procedure of cutting into the trachea through the neck, usually designed to facilitate breathing when the upper air passage is obstructed. Also called "tracheostomy". [TRACHEO- + -TOMY.]

tra•cho•ma (trə-kṓmə, tra-) *n.* A contagious viral disease of the conjunctiva of the eye characterised by inflammation, and scarring of the cornea, which may lead to blindness. [New Latin, from Greek *trakhōma* : *trakhus,* rough + -OMA.] **—tra•cho•ma•tous** *adj.*

tra•chyte (tráy-kīt, trá-) *n.* A light-coloured, fine-grained, igneous rock consisting essentially of alkali feldspar. [French, "rough stone" : Greek *trakhus,* rough (see **trachea**) + -ITE.] **—tra•chyt•ic** (trə-kíttik), **trach•y•toid** (-ki-toyd) *adj.*

trac•ing (tráyssing) *n.* **1.** A reproduction made by placing a transparent sheet on top of the original and copying the lines seen through it. **2.** A graphic record made by a recording instrument, such as a cardiograph.

track¹ (trak) *n.* **1. a.** A mark, such as a footprint, left by the passage of a person, animal, or thing; a trace. **b.** The path, route, or course indicated by such marks; a trail. **2.** A path or course travelled, such as a line of flight. **3.** A course of action; a method of inquiry or proceeding: *on the right track.* **4.** A rough path or road. **5.** A specially prepared road or course laid out for horse- or dog-racing or running events. **6.** *U.S.* Track events. **7.** A rail or set of parallel rails, such as those on which a train runs. **8.** An endless segmented

PRONUNCIATION KEY

a, trap; aa, father; ai, fair; ar, star; aw, lawn; ay, play; b, bb, stab; rubber; ch, church; ck, ticket; d, dd, dead; ladder; e, dress; ee, bee; er, defer; ew, few; ewr, pure; ə, about; ər, letter; f, ff, fife; differ; g, gg, giggle; h, hat; i, kit; ī, price; īr, fire; j, judge; k, kick; l, ll, let; 'l, needle; m, mm, man; n, nn, no; 'n, sudden; ng, thing; o, lot; ō, no; ŏŏ, foot; ōō, shoe; oor, poor; ow, cow; owr, hour; oy, boy; p, pp, pepper; r, rr, red; s, ss, sauce; sh, ship; t, tt, totter; th, thick; th̲, this; smooth; u, cut; ur, turn; v, vv, valve; w, wet; y, yes; z, zz, zebra; zh̲, vision; pleasure

IN FOREIGN WORDS:

aN, oN, Saint-Saëns; h̲l, Llanelli; Hluhluwe; k̲h, loch; lough; Khaled

STRESS MARK:

ín-sīt, insight; in-sī́t, incite

band of metal plates driven by the wheels of certain tractors and tanks to enable them to move across rough ground. **9.** The distance between each of a pair of wheels, such as the front wheels of a motor vehicle or the paired wheels of an aircraft undercarriage. **10.** The path of a particle as observed in a cloud chamber, bubble chamber, or photographic emulsion. **11.** A separate path on a magnetic recording tape: *nine-track tape.* **12.** A separate section of a gramophone record on which a particular composition, song, or movement is recorded. —See Synonyms at **trace.** **—cover (one's) tracks.** To keep what one has done secret or hidden. **—in (one's) tracks.** Exactly where one is at a given moment. **—keep track of.** To follow the course or progress of. **—lose track of.** To fail to follow the course or progress of. **—make tracks.** *Informal.* To move or go hurriedly. **—off the beaten track.** In a little-known or secluded place. **—on the track of. 1.** Following in pursuit. **2.** Coming near to an understanding of the character or intentions of.
~*v.* **tracked, tracking, tracks.** *—tr.* **1.** To follow the footprints or traces of; trail. **2.** To pursue successfully; seek and find. Often used with *down*: *tracked down the culprit.* **3.** To move over or along; traverse. **4.** To observe or monitor the course of (aircraft, for example), as by radar. **5.** To focus on and film (a moving person or object) by swivelling or changing position. Used of a camera or camera operator. *—intr.* **1.** To keep a constant distance apart. Used of a pair of wheels. **2.** To be in alignment. **3.** To pursue a track; trail. **4.** To move around, often in a set path, while focusing on and filming an object. Used of a camera. **5.** To move in the groove of a gramophone record. Used of a stylus or pickup. [Middle English *trak,* trace, trail, footprints, from Old French *trac,* perhaps Middle Dutch *trek,* a drawing, from *trekken,* to draw, pull. See **trek.**] **—track·a·ble** *adj.* **—track·er** *n.* **—track·less** *adj.*

track[2] *v.* **tracked, tracking, tracks.** *—tr.* To tow, or pull; especially, to tow (a boat) from a tow path. *—intr.* To be pulled along; travel by towing. [Probably from Dutch *trekken,* to pull, assimilated to TRACK (course, path, etc).] **—track·er** *n.*

track and field *n. U.S.* **Athletics** *(see).* **—track-and-field** *adj.*

track events *pl.n.* The running and racing events at an athletics meeting as distinguished from the field events.

tracking station *n.* An observing station for maintaining radar or radio contact with an object in the atmosphere or in space.

track-lay·ing vehicle (trák-lay-ing) *n.* A motor vehicle, such as a tank and certain tractors and excavators, in which the wheels drive an endless track to enable it to move across rough ground.

track record *n.* **1.** *Informal.* The past achievements and failures of an individual, group, or thing. **2.** The fastest run, highest jump, or the like achieved at a particular sports ground or racing track.

track rod *n.* A rod joining the front wheels of a motor vehicle to ensure that they can be steered together.

track shoe *n.* Either of a pair of light shoes worn by runners, often having steel spikes attached to the soles to give them a firm grip.

track suit *n.* A warm jacket and trousers that are tight-fitting around the ankles, wrists, and waist, and loose elsewhere, worn to keep warm, as during training or exercise.

tract[1] (trakt) *n.* **1.** An expanse of land; a region. **2.** *Anatomy.* **a.** A system of organs and tissues that together perform one specialised function: *the alimentary tract.* **b.** A bundle of nerve fibres having a common origin, termination, and function. **3.** *Archaic.* A stretch or lapse of time. [Latin *tractus,* "a drawing", course, tract, region, from *trahere* (past participle *tractus*), to draw.]

tract[2] *n.* A distributed paper or pamphlet containing a declaration or appeal, especially one put out by a religious or political group. [Middle English *tracte,* shortened from Latin *tractātus,* a discussion, treatise, from the past participle of *tractāre,* to pull violently, discuss. See **tractable.**]

tract[3] *n.* The verses from Scripture sung during Lent or on Ember days after the gradual in the Tridentine Mass. [Middle English *tracte,* from Medieval Latin *tractus,* from Latin, "a drawing out" (the verses are sung without a break by one voice). See **tract** (area).]

trac·ta·ble (trák-təb'l) *adj.* **1.** Easily managed or controlled; governable. **2.** Easily handled or worked; malleable. —See Synonyms at **obedient.** [Latin *tractābilis,* from *tractāre,* to pull violently, to take in hand, manage, frequentative of *trahere* (past participle *tractus*), to draw, pull.] **—trac·ta·bil·i·ty** (-tə-bílləti), **trac·ta·ble·ness** *n.* **—trac·ta·bly** *adv.*

Trac·tar·i·an·ism (trak-táir-i-ən-iz'm) *n.* The religious opinions and principles of the founders of the Oxford movement, put forth in a series of 90 pamphlets entitled *Tracts for the Times,* published in Oxford (1833–41). **—Trac·tar·i·an** *adj.* & *n.*

trac·tate (trák-tayt) *n.* A treatise; an essay. [Latin *tractātus,* TRACT.]

trac·tile (trák-tīl || *U.S. also* -t'l) *adj.* Capable of being drawn out in length, as certain metals; ductile. **—trac·til·i·ty** (trak-tílləti) *n.*

trac·tion (tráksh'n) *n.* **1.** The act of drawing or pulling a load, for example, especially by motive power. **2.** The condition of being drawn or pulled. **3.** Adhesive friction, as of a wheel on a road surface or rail. **4.** The pulling power of a locomotive. **5.** *Medicine.* The use of weights, straps, and the like to exert a continuous pull on a part of the body to assist the healing of injuries. [Medieval Latin *tractiō* (stem *tractiōn-*), from Latin *tractus,* past participle of *trahere,* to draw, pull.] **—trac·tion·al, trac·tive** *adj.*

traction engine *n.* A steam-powered vehicle formerly used on roads or over rough ground to pull heavy loads.

trac·tor (tráktər) *n.* **1.** A small vehicle, powered by an internal combustion engine, having large, heavily treaded tyres, or sometimes tracks, and used in farming for pulling machinery. **2.** A short, powerful motor vehicle having a cab and no body, used for pulling large trailers or transporting heavy containers, as in articulated lorries. **3.** An aircraft having a propeller mounted in front of the supporting surfaces. In this sense, also called "tractor aircraft". [New Latin, from Latin *tractus.* See **traction.**]

trade (trayd) *n.* **1.** An occupation, especially one requiring skilled labour; a craft. **2.** The business of buying and selling; commerce. **3. a.** A particular business, industry, or market. **b.** The persons working in or associated with a specific business or industry. **4. a.** The customers, collectively, of a specific business or industry. **b.** The amount of custom of a business or industry at a particular time or place: *the holiday trade.* **5.** An instance of buying or selling; a transaction. **6.** An exchange of one thing for another. **7.** *Plural.* The trade winds. —See Synonyms at **business.**
~*v.* **traded, trading, trades.** *—intr.* **1. a.** To engage in buying and selling for profit. **b.** To have business relations. Often used with *with*: *prepared to trade with Cuba.* **2.** To make an exchange of one thing for another. **3.** To shop or buy regularly at a given shop. *—tr.* **1.** To give in exchange for something else. **2.** To buy and sell (shares, for example). **3.** To pass back and forth: *We traded anecdotes.* **—trade on.** To put to advantage; exploit: *He traded on his war-wounds for sympathy.* [Middle English *tra(i)d, trade,* a course, way, track, from Middle Low German *trade,* a track, path.]

trade cycle *n.* A regular fluctuation in the trade or economic conditions of most capitalist countries consisting of a movement from a state of high activity (prosperity or boom) to a state of low activity (depression) and back again.

trade discount *n.* A discount on the list price granted by a manufacturer or wholesaler to buyers in the same trade.

trade gap *n. Economics.* **1.** An excess of a country's visible imports over its visible exports. **2.** The amount of this excess.

trade in *tr.v.* To give (an old item) to a dealer in part exchange or as partial payment for a new purchase.

trade-in (tráyd-in) *n.* **1.** A piece of merchandise accepted as partial payment for a new purchase. **2.** A transaction involving such an item. **3.** The amount allowed for such an item. Also used adjectivally: *trade-in value.*

trade·mark (tráyd-maark) *n.* **1.** A name, symbol, or other device identifying a product, officially registered and legally restricted to the use of the owner or manufacturer. **2.** A distinctive sign by which a person or thing comes to be known.
~*tr.v.* **trademarked, -marking, -marks. 1.** To label (a product) with a trademark. **2.** To register as a trademark.

trade name *n.* **1.** The name by which a commodity, service, process, or the like is known to the trade. **2.** A trademark consisting solely of a name. **3.** The name under which a business enterprise operates.

trade-off, trade-off (tráyd-off, -awf) *n.* An exchange of one thing in return for another; especially, a giving up of something desirable for something else regarded as more desirable. **—trade·off** *adj.*

trade paper *n.* A newspaper or periodical published regularly by or for a particular business or industry to give pertinent news and developments. Also called "trade journal", "trade magazine".

trade plate *n.* Either of a pair of number plates attached to a motor vehicle temporarily by a motor dealer or manufacturer before registration, after the road-fund licence has expired, or to transfer insurance liability, from the insured to a third party, usually to a garage.

trade price *n.* The price charged by a wholesaler to a retailer.

trad·er (tráydər) *n.* **1.** A person who trades; a dealer. **2.** A ship employed in foreign trade.

trade route *n.* A sea lane used by trading ships.

trad·es·can·tia (trád-iss-kánti-ə, -ess-) *n.* Any plant of the genus *Tradescantia,* characteristically having a jointed succulent stem and three-petalled flowers, such as the house plant, wandering Jew. [New Latin, after John *Tradescant* (1608–62), English botanist.]

trade secret *n.* **1.** A secret formula, method, or device that gives a manufacturer an advantage over competitors. **2.** A scheme, trick, or the like to which a person attributes his success and which he keeps secret.

trades·man (tráydz-mən) *n., pl.* **-men** (-mən). **1.** A person engaged in the retail trade, especially a shopkeeper. **2.** A skilled worker; a craftsman.

trades·peo·ple (tráydz-peep'l) *pl.n. British.* People engaged in the retail trade, especially shopkeepers.

trades·wom·an (tráydz-wŏŏmən) *n., pl.* **-women** (-wimmin). A female tradesman.

Trades Union Congress *n.* The umbrella organisation to which most British trade unions belong. Also called "T.U.C."

trade union *n.* Also **trades union.** *Abbr.* **T.U.** An association of workers in a particular trade or occupation or group of trades, formed to further and protect their common interests by concerted action, such as collective bargaining for improved wages, hours, and conditions. **—trade u·nion·ism** *n.* **—trade u·nion·ist** *n.*

trade wind *n.* An extremely consistent system of winds occupying most of the tropics, constituting the major component of the general circulation of the atmosphere, blowing northeasterly in the Northern Hemisphere and southeasterly in the Southern Hemisphere. [From the phrase *to blow trade,* to blow in a regular course, from TRADE (in the obsolete sense of a course).]

trad·ing estate (tráyding) *n. British.* An area in which numerous factories and business premises are situated, especially an area deliberately built or set aside for such a purpose.

trading post *n.* A station or general shop in a sparsely settled area established by traders to barter supplies for local products.

PRONUNCIATION KEY

a, trap; aa, father; ai, **fair**; ar, star; aw, **lawn**; ay, play; b, bb, stab; **rubber**; ch, **church**; ck, ticket; d, dd, **dead**; ladder; e, dress; ee, **bee**; er, defer; ew, **few**; ewr, **pure**; ə, about; ər, letter; f, ff, **fife**; differ; g, gg, **giggle**; h, **hat**; i, kit; ī, price; īr, fire; j, **judge**; k, **kick**; l, ll, let; 'l, needle; m, mm, **man**; n, nn, no; 'n, sudden; ng, **thing**; o, lot; ō, no; ŏŏ, foot; ōō, shoe; oor, **poor**; ow, **cow**; owr, **hour**; oy, **boy**; p, pp, **pepper**; r, rr, red; s, ss, **sauce**; sh, **ship**; t, tt, totter; th, **thick**; th, **this**; smooth; u, cut; ur, **turn**; v, vv, valve; w, **wet**; y, yes; z, zz, zebra; zh, vision; pleasure

IN FOREIGN WORDS:

aN, oN, **Saint-Saëns**; hl, **Llanelli**; **Hluhluwe**; kh, loch; **lough**; **Khaled**

STRESS MARK:

in-sīt, insight; in-sīt, incite

trading stamp *n.* A stamp given by a retailer to a buyer for each purchase of a specified amount and able to be redeemed in quantity, by the buyer, for merchandise.

tra·di·tion (trə-dísh'n) *n.* **1.** The passing down of elements of a culture from generation to generation, especially by oral communication. **2. a.** A mode of thought or behaviour followed by a people continuously from generation to generation; a cultural custom or usage. **b.** A set of such customs and usages viewed as a coherent body of precedents influencing the present. **c.** A set of such customs followed in a particular art. **3.** A body of unwritten religious precepts. **4.** Any time-honoured practice or a set of such practices. **5.** *Law.* The transfer of property to another. [Middle English *tradicion,* a handing down, a surrender, from Old French, from Latin *trāditiō* (stem *trāditiōn-),* from *trādere,* to hand over : *trāns-,* over + *dare,* to give.]

tra·di·tion·al (trə-dísh'n-'l) *adj.* Also **tra·di·tion·ar·y** (-əri || -erri). **1.** Pertaining to or in accord with tradition. **2.** Of or pertaining to trad jazz. **—tra·di·tion·al·ise** *tr.v.* **—tra·di·tion·al·ly** *adv.*

tra·di·tion·al·ism (trə-dísh'n'l-iz'm) *n.* **1.** Adherence to tradition; especially, excessive reverence for religious tradition. **2.** A religious doctrine holding that all knowledge is derived from original divine revelation and is transmitted by tradition. **—tra·di·tion·al·ist** *n.* & *adj.* **—tra·di·tion·al·is·tic** (-ístik) *adj.*

tra·di·tion-di·rect·ed (trə-dísh'n-dīr-rektid, -də-, -dī-) *adj.* Guided by tradition and the values of one's forebears, rather than by independent personal principles: *a tradition-directed personality.* Compare **inner-directed, other-directed.**

trad·i·tor (tráddi-tər) *n., pl.* **-tors** or **-tores** (-táw-reez || -tṓ-). Any of the early Christians who surrendered sacred objects or betrayed fellow Christians during the Roman persecutions. [Middle English *traditour,* from Latin *trāditor,* traitor, from *trādere,* to hand over, betray. See **tradition.**]

trad jazz (trad) *n.* Jazz of a traditional style based on the early jazz of New Orleans and Chicago in the 1920s. [*Trad*itional *jazz.*]

tra·duce (trə-déwss || -dṓoss) *tr.v.* **-duced, -ducing, -duces.** To speak falsely or maliciously of; slander; defame. See Synonyms at **malign.** [Latin *trādūcere,* to lead across, make public, expose to ridicule : *trāns-,* across + *dūcere,* to lead.] **—tra·duce·ment** *n.* **—tra·duc·er** *n.* **—tra·duc·i·ble** *adj.* **—tra·duc·ing·ly** *adv.*

tra·du·cian·ism (trə-déw-si-ən-iz'm, -shi-, -shən- || -dṓo-) *n. Theology.* The belief that the soul is inherited from the parents along with the body. Compare **creationism.** [Medieval Latin *trāduciānus,* believer in this doctrine, from *trādux,* inheritance, from Latin *trādūcere,* to lead across, TRADUCE.] **—tra·du·cian·ist** *n.* **—tra·du·cian·is·tic** (-ístik) *adj.*

Tra·fal·gar, Cape (trə-fál-gər; *Spanish* tra-fal-gár). Headland of southwest Spain, lying between the Strait of Gibraltar and Gulf of Cádiz. It gave its name to the naval battle of 1805, when the British, under Nelson, destroyed Napoleon's battlefleet.

traf·fic (tráffik) *n.* **1. a.** The commercial exchange of goods; trade. **b.** Illicit or blackmarket trade: *traffic in drugs.* **2. a.** The business of moving passengers and cargo by means of a system of transportation. **b.** The amount of cargo or number of passengers conveyed. **3. a.** The passage of persons, vehicles, or messages through routes of transportation or communication. **b.** The vehicles using a particular road or route: *heavy traffic.* **c.** The volume of messages passing through a system of communication. **4.** Connections; dealings: *have traffic with the devil.* —See Synonyms at **business.** ~*intr.v.* **trafficked, -ficking, -fics. 1.** To carry on trade, especially illegal trade. **2.** To have dealings. Usually used with *with.* [French *traffique,* from Old Italian *traffico,* from *trafficare*†, to trade.] **—traf·fick·er** *n.*

traf·fi·ca·tor (tráffi-kaytər) *n.* A metal and plastic illuminated arm formerly on motor vehicles that could be raised to indicate a left or right turn. Compare **indicator.** [Traffic + indic*ator.*]

traffic circle *n. U.S.* A **roundabout** *(see).*

traffic island *n.* A raised area over which cars may not pass, placed at a junction of thoroughfares or between opposing traffic lanes. Also called "island", "refuge".

traffic jam *n.* A situation in which a large number of motor vehicles on the road are brought to a standstill or can move only very slowly, caused by heavy traffic or an accident, for example.

traffic light *n.* A road signal that beams a red or green light or an amber warning light to direct traffic to stop or proceed. Also called "traffic signal".

traffic warden *n.* A person who is empowered to enforce parking rules and who assists the police in controlling road traffic.

trag·a·canth (trággə-kanth || *U.S. also* trájə-, -santh) *n.* **1.** Any of various thorny shrubs of the genus *Astragalus* of northern temperate regions, yielding a gum used in pharmacy, adhesives, and textile printing. **2.** The gum of such a shrub. [French, from Latin *tragacantha,* from Greek *tragakantha,* "goat's thorn" : *tragos,* goat (see **tragedy**) + *akantha,* thorn.]

tra·ge·di·an (trə-jéedi-ən) *n.* **1.** A writer of tragedies. **2.** An actor of tragic roles. [Middle English *tragedien,* from Old French, from *tragedie,* TRAGEDY.]

tra·ge·di·enne (trə-jéedi-én) *n.* A woman who plays tragic roles in the theatre. [French *tragédienne.*]

trag·e·dy (trájədi) *n., pl.* **-dies. 1.** A dramatic or literary work in which the principal character engages in a morally significant struggle ending in ruin or profound disappointment; specifically: **a.** A classical verse drama in which a noble principal character is brought to ruin essentially as a consequence of some extreme quality which is both his greatness and his downfall. **b.** A Renaissance or modern drama resembling the classical model in representing terrible struggle and calamity, but freer in style and choice of principal character. **c.** Any serious play or narrative that deals with sad or calamitous events and has an unhappy and usually morally significant ending. **2.** The branch of drama dealing with such plays. **3.** Any dramatic, disastrous event, especially one of some moral significance. **4.** The tragic aspect or element of something. [Middle English *tragedie,* from Old French, from Latin *tragoedia,* from Greek *tragōidia,* "goat-song" (probably the name of a form of choric ceremony associated with goat-satyr plays) : *tragos*†, goat + *ōidē,* song, from *aeidein,* to sing.]

trag·ic (trájik) *adj.* Also *rare* **trag·i·cal** (-'l). **1.** Pertaining to, in the style of, or having the character of tragedy. **2.** Writing or performing in tragedy: *a tragic poet.* **3.** Having the elements of tragedy; involving death, grief, or destruction: *a tragic accident.* **4.** Mournful or grave: *Don't look so tragic!* [French *tragique,* from Latin *tragicus,* from Greek *tragikos,* from *tragos,* goat. See **tragedy.**] **—trag·i·cal·ly** *adv.* **—trag·i·cal·ness** *n.*

trag·i·com·e·dy (tráji-kómmədi) *n., pl.* **-dies. 1.** A drama that combines elements of both tragedy and comedy. **2.** The branch of drama dealing with such plays. **3.** An incident or situation having both comic and tragic elements. [French *tragicomédie,* from Late Latin *tragicōmoedia,* from Latin *tragicocōmoedia* : TRAGIC + COMEDY.] **—trag·i·com·ic** *adj.* **—trag·i·com·i·cal·ly** *adv.*

trag·o·pan (trággə-pan) *n.* Any of several Asian pheasants of the genus *Tragopan,* of which the male has brightly coloured plumage and two hornlike appendages on the head. [Latin *tragopān,* fabulous bird in Ethiopia, from Greek *tragopan,* "goat of Pan" : *tragos,* goat (see **tragedy**) + *Pan,* PAN.]

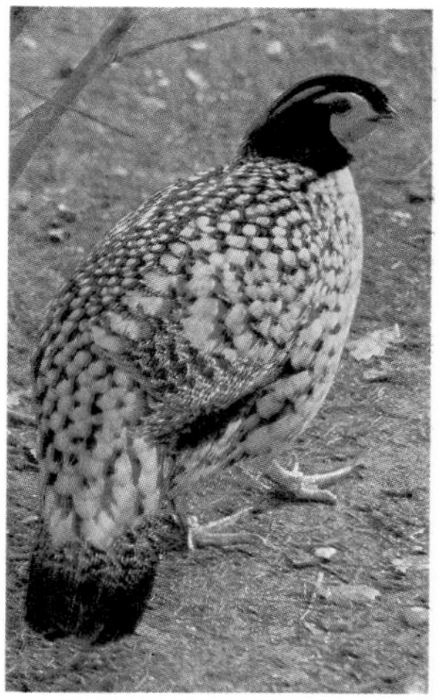

tragopan *The tragopan is a pheasant which lives in the high mountain forests of Asia. Unlike other pheasants, it nests in trees and the male is able to puff out two brightly coloured fleshy horns from its head during courtship. The species shown here is the Cabot's tragopan.*

tra·gus (tráy-gəss) *n., pl.* **-gi** (-jī, -gī). **1.** The projection of skin-covered cartilage in front of the opening of the external ear. **2.** Any of the hairs growing at the entrance of the external ear. [New Latin, from Greek *tragos,* goat (the hair resembles a goat's beard).]

tra·hi·son des clercs (trī-i-zoN day klairk) *n.* A betrayal of a cause or of standards by intellectuals. [French, from the title of a book (1927) by Julien Benda.]

trail (trayl) *v.* **trailed, trailing, trails.** —*tr.* **1.** To allow to drag or stream behind, as along the ground. **2.** To drag, pull, or tow. **3. a.** To form (a course, path, or track). **b.** To make a path or track through. **4.** To follow the traces or scent of, as in hunting; track. **5. a.** To follow slowly or wearily. **b.** To lag behind (an opponent). **6.** To advertise or pre-publicise (a film or television programme) by means of a trailer. **7.** To hint at the possibility of (a scheme or venture), as a subtle means of ascertaining other's attitudes to such a course. **8.** *Military.* To carry (a rifle) horizontally in the right hand with the arm extended straight downwards. —*intr.* **1.** To drag or be dragged along, brushing the ground. **2.** To extend, grow, or droop along the ground or over a surface, as a vine or plant might. **3.** To drift in a tenuous stream, as smoke from a cigarette. **4.** To become gradually fainter. Usually used with *away* or *off: Her voice trailed off sadly.* **5. a.** To walk slowly or wearily. **b.** To walk with dragging steps; trudge. **6.** To fall behind in competition; lag. ~*n.* **1.** Something that hangs down loosely or drags along the ground: *trails of ribbons.* **2.** That which is drawn along or follows behind; a train. **3.** The part of a gun carriage that rests or slides on the ground. **4. a.** A mark, trace, course, or path left by a moving body. **b.** The scent of a person or animal. **c.** A blazed path or beaten track, as through woods or wilderness. **5.** The act or an instance of trailing. —See Synonyms at **trace, way.** [Middle English *trailen,* probably from Old French *trailler* and Middle Low German *treilen,* to tow, both from Vulgar Latin *tragulāre* (unattested), to drag, from Latin *trāgula,* dragnet, from *trahere,* to pull.]

trail bike *n.* A light, strong motor bike with special suspension and ridged tyres, used for riding over rough ground.

trail·blaz·er (tráyl-blayzər) *n.* **1.** One who blazes a trail. **2.** A leader in any field; a pioneer. **—trail·blaz·ing** *n.* & *adj.*

trail boss *n. U.S.* The man in charge of a cattle drive in the West.

trail·er (tráylər) *n.* **1.** One that trails. **2.** A large transport vehicle designed to be hauled by a tractor, as in an articulated lorry. **3.** A two- or four-wheeled road vehicle used to carry a boat or other load to be towed behind a car. **4.** A short filmed advertisement for a film or television programme, containing extracts from the film or programme. **5.** *U.S.* A **caravan** *(see).*

trailing edge *n.* The rearmost edge of a structure, especially of an aerofoil.

trail rope *n.* A rope for guiding or dragging, as on a dirigible or gun carriage.

train (trayn) *n.* **1.** Something that follows or is drawn along behind, such as part of a dress or robe that trails behind the wearer. **2.** A body of persons following behind in attendance; a retinue: *a train of admirers.* **3.** A service unit of men, vehicles, and equipment following and attending an army. **4.** A long line of moving persons, animals, or vehicles. **5. a.** A string of connected railway carriages or goods wagons drawn by a locomotive. **b.** Transport or travel by railway. **6.** An orderly succession of related events or thoughts; a sequence. **7.** A set of linked mechanical parts: *a train of gears.* **8.** A string of gunpowder that acts as a fuse for exploding a charge. **—in train.** In preparation or under way. —See Synonyms at **series.** ~*v.* **trained, training, trains.** —*tr.* **1.** To coach in or accustom to some mode of behaviour or performance. **2.** To make proficient with specialised instruction and practice. **3.** To prepare physically, as with exercise or a regimen; make fit: *train a long-distance runner.*

train

THE VEHICLE THAT REPLACED THE HORSE
Development of the train over two centuries

The railway age made a hesitant start in 1804 when a steam locomotive, built by the Cornish engineer Richard Trevithick, ran between Merthyr Tydfil in South Wales and a canal a few miles away. Trevithick's engine could pull far more freight than a horse, at 8 kilometres (5 miles) an hour, but the weight soon damaged the rails and the scheme was abandoned.

In 1830 the world's first passenger railway was opened between Manchester and Liverpool by George Stephenson and his son Robert. Electric traction was pioneered in Germany in 1879; in the 1930s diesel trains came into use.

In 1982 the fastest train in the world was the French high-speed train. Its gas-turbine engine drives it at speeds up to 260 kilometres (160 miles) an hour, but special track had to be laid before it entered service in 1981. A tilting mechanism was devised to enable Britain's advanced passenger train to take bends at speed on existing track. Future trains may hover over a single rail and travel at speeds of 800 kilometres (500 miles) an hour.

WINNING DESIGN *In 1829 George and Robert Stephenson's Rocket won trials held by the Liverpool and Manchester Railway company. With a novel boiler design Rocket was able to pull a 14-ton train at 46 kilometres (29 miles) an hour – about twice as fast as its rivals. Trains soon replaced horse-drawn passenger coaches.*

MALLARD *In 1938 Britain's* Mallard, *a locomotive with steam technology similar to* Rocket's, *achieved a speed of 202 kilometres (126 miles) an hour while pulling a seven-coach train.*

FRENCH SPEED TEST *In March 1955 French Railways (SNCF) ran a Class CC 7107 electric locomotive, modified with a high gear ratio, at 331 kilometres (206 miles) an hour while pulling a light train.*

HIGH-SPEED SERVICE *The High Speed Train, introduced in 1976 by British Rail, has a top speed of 230 kilometres (143 miles) an hour, and normal service speeds of 200 kilometres (125 miles) an hour.*

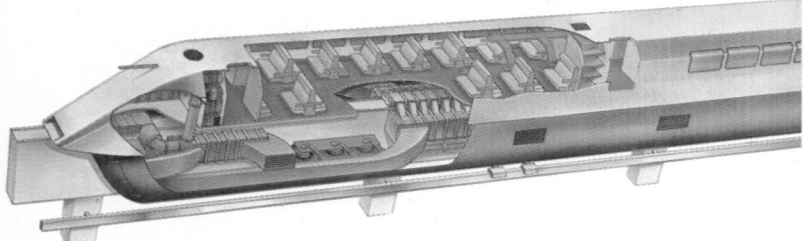

HOVER TRAINS *The linear electric induction motor has brought the possibility of trains without rotating parts, which hover over their rails either on an air cushion (above) or by magnetic levitation. Such machines might be capable of speeds as high as 800 kilometres (500 miles) an hour.*

4. To cause (a plant, for example) to take a desired course or shape, as by manipulating. **5.** To focus or direct; aim. Usually used with *on* or *upon: Train your sights on the hilltop.* **6.** *Rare.* To draw, drag, or trail. —*intr.* To give or undergo a course of instruction, coaching, or exercises. —See Synonyms at **teach.** [Middle English *trayne,* from Old French *train,* from *tra(h)iner,* to drag, from Vulgar Latin *trāgināre* (unattested), from *tragere* (unattested), variant of Latin *trahere.*] —**train·a·ble** *adj.*

train·band (trāyn-bǎnd) *n.* A militia trained as a supplement to the army in England from the 16th to the 18th century. [Originally *trained band.*]

train·bear·er (trāyn-bâir-ər) *n.* An attendant who holds up the train of a robe or dress, as in a procession.

train·ee (trā-née) *n.* A person who is being trained. Also used adjectivally: *a trainee salesman.* —**train·ee·ship** *n.*

train·er (trāynər) *n.* **1.** One who trains, especially one who coaches athletes, racehorses, or show animals. **2.** A contrivance or apparatus used in training. **3.** A type of running shoe.

train·ing (trāyning) *n.* **1.** The act, process, or routine of one who trains. **2.** The state of being trained. **3.** Good physical condition: *I'm out of training.*

train·load (trāyn-lōd) *n.* The full capacity of a freight or passenger train.

train spotter *n.* A person who engages in the pastime of collecting the numbers of railway locomotives.

traipse (trayps) *intr.v.* **traipsed, traipsing, traipses.** *Informal.* **1.** To walk about casually. **2.** To walk wearily or slowly; trudge. —*n.* A tiring walk. [16th century : origin obscure.]

trait (tray, trayt) *n.* **1.** A distinguishing feature, as of a person's character. **2.** *Rare.* A stroke; a touch. —See Synonyms at **quality.** [French, from Old French, pencil mark, stroke, from Latin *tractus,* a pulling, a drawing, from the past participle of *trahere,* to pull, drag.]

trai·tor (trāytər) *n.* A person who betrays his country, a cause, or a trust; especially, one who has committed treason. [Middle English *traitour,* from Old French, from Latin *trāditor.* See **traditor.**]

trai·tor·ous (trāytərəss) *adj.* **1.** Having the character of a traitor; disloyal. **2.** Constituting treason: *a traitorous act.* —See Synonyms at **faithless.** —**trai·tor·ous·ly** *adv.* —**trai·tor·ous·ness** *n.*

trai·tress (trāy-triss, -tress, -trəss) *n.* A female traitor.

tra·ject (trə-jékt) *tr.v.* **-jected, -jecting, -jects.** *Archaic.* To transmit (light or colour). [Latin *trājicere* (past participle *trājectus*), to throw across : *trāns-,* across + *jacere,* to throw.] —**tra·jec·tion** *n.*

tra·jec·to·ry (trájik-tri, -təri, trə-jéktəri) *n., pl.* **-ries. 1.** The path of a moving particle or body, especially such a path in three dimensions. **2.** In geometry, a curve that cuts all of a given family of curves or surfaces at the same angle. [Originally an adjective, from Medieval Latin *trājectōrius,* from Latin *trājectus.* See **traject.**]

tram¹ (tram) *n.* **1.** A vehicle used for public transport on the roads. It runs on rails and is electrically powered, usually by overhead wires. Also called "tramcar", *U.S.* "streetcar", "trolley car". **2.** A four-wheeled, open box-shaped wagon or iron car run on tracks in a mine. Also called "tram car". [Originally "shaft or frame of a truck", from Middle Low German, Middle Dutch *trame,* beam.]

tram² *n.* **1.** A machine gauge; a trammel. **2.** Accurate mechanical adjustment: *The device is in tram.* —*tr.v.* **trammed, tramming, trams.** To adjust or align (mechanical parts) with a trammel. [Shortened from TRAMMEL.]

tram³ *n.* A heavy silk thread used for the weft, or cross threads, in fine velvet or silk. [French *trame,* from Old French *traime,* woof, from Latin *trāma†.*]

tram·lines (trám-līnz) *pl.n.* **1.** The rails on which a tram runs. Also called "tramway". **2. a.** In tennis, either of the pairs of parallel lines that run down the sides of the court, or in badminton, any of the pairs that surround the court. **b.** The space between any of these pairs of lines. In this sense, also *U.S.* "alley".

tram·mel (trámm'l) *n.* **1.** *Often plural.* Something that restricts activity or free movement; a hindrance. **2.** *Chiefly U.S.* A shackle used to teach a horse to amble. **3.** A vertically set fishing net of three layers, consisting of a finely meshed net between two nets of coarse mesh. Also called "trammel net". **4. a.** An instrument for describing ellipses. **b.** A beam compass *(see).* **c.** The pivoted beam of a beam compass. **5.** An instrument for gauging and adjusting parts of a machine. Also called "tram". **6.** *Chiefly U.S.* An arrangement of links and a hook in a fireplace for raising or lowering a kettle. —*tr.v.* **trammelled** or *U.S.* **trammeled, -melling** or *U.S.* **-meling -mels. 1.** To confine or hinder. **2.** To entrap. Sometimes used with *up.* **3.** To adjust (a machine) by means of a trammel. [Middle English *tramale,* trammel net, from Old French *tramail,* from Late Latin *tremaculum : trēs,* three + *macula,* mesh, spot.] —**tram·mel·ler** *n.*

tra·mon·ta·na (tramən-táana) *n.* A cold north wind sweeping down from the mountains in Italy and the Mediterranean.

tra·mon·tane (trə-món-tayn, trámmən-) *adj.* **1. a.** Dwelling beyond or coming from the far side of the mountains, especially the Alps as viewed from Italy. **b.** Foreign. **c.** Barbarous. **2.** Sweeping down from the mountains. Said of a wind. —*n.* **1.** A person who lives beyond the mountains; an outsider; a foreigner. **2.** In Italy, a north or cold wind. [Middle English, from Italian *tramontana,* from Latin *trānsmontānus : trāns-,* beyond + *montānus,* mountainous (see **mountain**).]

tramp (tramp) *v.* **tramped, tramping, tramps.** —*intr.* **1.** To walk with a firm, heavy step; trudge. **2. a.** To go on foot; hike. **b.** To wander about aimlessly, as a tramp. —*tr.* **1.** To traverse on foot: *tramp the fields.* **2.** To tread down; trample: *tramp the snow down.* ~*n.* **1. a.** A heavy footfall; a stamp. **b.** A heavy rhythmic tread, as of a marching army. **c.** The sound produced by heavy walking or marching. **2. a.** A walking trip; a hike. **b.** An arduous walk. **3.** A person who travels aimlessly about on foot, doing odd jobs or begging for a living; a vagrant. **4.** *Chiefly U.S. Slang.* **a.** A prostitute. **b.** A promiscuous girl or woman. **5.** A cargo vessel that has no regular schedule but takes on freight wherever it may be found and discharges it wherever required. Also called "tramp steamer". **6. a.** A metal plate attached to the sole of a shoe for protection, as when using a spade to dig ground. **b.** The part of the spade on which the foot rests. [Middle English *trampen,* probably from Middle Low German.] **—tramp•er** *n.*

tram•ple (trámp'l) *v.* **-pled, -pling, -ples.** —*tr.* **1.** To beat down with the feet so as to crush, bruise, violate, or destroy; stamp upon. **2.** To treat harshly or ruthlessly, as if stepping or stamping upon. —*intr.* **1.** To tread heavily. **2.** To treat contemptuously or insensitively. Used with on: *He trampled on her felings whenever he could.* ~*n.* The action or sound of treading underfoot. [Middle English *tramp(e)len,* frequentative of *trampen,* to TRAMP.] **—tram•pler** *n.*

tram•po•line (trámpə-leen, -lin) *n.* A sheet of strong, taut canvas attached with springs to a metal frame and used for jumping on and performing acrobatic feats on, either as a competitive sport or for pleasure and exercise.

~*intr.v.* **trampolined, -lining, -lines.** To compete, perform, or exercise on a trampoline. [From Italian *trampolino,* "performance on stilts", from *trampoli,* stilts, from Germanic.] **—tram•po•lin•er, tram•po•lin•ist** *n.*

tram•way (trám-way) *n. British.* A set of tramlines.

trance (traanss || transs) *n.* **1.** A hypnotic, cataleptic, or ecstatic state. **2.** A state of detachment from one's physical surroundings, as in contemplation or daydreaming. **3.** A dazed state, as between sleeping and waking; a stupor.

~*tr.v.* **tranced, trancing, trances.** To put into a trance. [Middle English *traunce,* from Old French *transe,* from *transir,* "to pass (from life to death)", depart, from Latin *transīre,* to go across. See **transit.**]

trank (trangk) *n. Informal.* A tranquilliser.

tran•ny, tran•nie (tránni) *n., pl.* **-nies.** *Chiefly British Informal.* **1.** A transistor radio. **2.** In photography or graphics, a transparency; a slide. [*Tran-,* abstracted from *transistor,* etc. + -Y.]

tran•quil (trángkwil) *adj.* **1.** Free from agitation or other disturbance; calm; unruffled; serene: *a tranquil rural life.* **2.** Steady; even: *a tranquil flame.* —See Synonyms at **calm, still.** [Latin *tranquillus.*] **—tran•quil•li•ty** (trang-kwílləti) *n.* **—tran•quil•ly** *adv.* **—tran•quil•ness** *n.*

tran•quil•lise, tran•quil•lize, *U.S.* **tran•quil•ize** (trángkwil-īz) *v.* **-ised, -ising, -ises.** —*tr.* To make tranquil; quiet. —*intr.* To become tranquil. **—tran•quil•li•sa•tion** (-ī-záysh'n || *U.S.*-i-) *n.*

tran•quil•lis•er (trángkwil-īzər) *n.* **1.** Something that tranquillises, such as music. **2.** Any of various drugs used to calm or pacify.

trans- *comb. form.* Indicates: **1.** Across or over; for example, **transpolar. 2.** Beyond or above; for example, **transcend, transpontine. 3.** From one place to another; for example, **translocate. 4.** Moving, transferring, or transporting; for example, **transship. 5.** Changing; for example, **transliterate. 6.** Having a greater atomic number; for example, **transuranic. 7.** A chemical compound in which two identical atoms or groups are on opposite sides of the plane of a double bond; for example, **trans-butadiene.** Compare **cis-.** ***Note:*** Many compounds other than those entered here may be formed with *trans-.* In forming compounds, *trans-* is normally joined with the following element without space or hyphen: *transculturation.* If the second element begins with a capital letter, it is usually separated with a hyphen: *trans-Canadian.* Note, however, that certain compounds have become one word: *transatlantic, Transcaucasia.* [Latin *trāns,* across, over, beyond, through, through and through.]

trans. 1. transaction. **2.** *Grammar.* transitive. **3.** translated; translation; translator. **4.** transpose; transposition. **5.** transverse.

trans•act (tran-zákt, traan-, trən-, -sákt) *v.* **-acted, -acting, -acts.** —*tr.* To do, carry out, perform, manage, or conduct (business or affairs, for example). —*intr.* To do business; negotiate. [Latin *transigere* (past participle *transactus*), to drive or carry through, complete : *trāns-,* through + *agere,* to drive.] **—trans•ac•tor** *n.*

trans•ac•ti•nide (tránz-ákti-nīd, traanz- || tránss-) *n.* Any of the artificially produced chemical elements with an atomic number in excess of 103. [TRANS- + ACTINIDE.]

trans•ac•tion (tran-záksh'n, traan-, trən-, -sáksh'n) *n. Abbr.* **trans. 1.** The act of transacting or the fact of being transacted. **2.** Something transacted; especially, a piece of business. **3.** *Plural.* Published papers, discussions, or other proceedings, as of a conference, academic meeting, or the like. **—trans•ac•tion•al** *adj.*

transactional analysis *n.* A method of psychoanalysis concentrating on an individual's social exchanges or transactions in his relationships with others. Such exchanges are analysed in terms of roles (child, parent, or adult), goals, games, and the like.

trans•al•pine (tránz-ál-pīn, traanz-, tranz-, traanz- || transs-) *adj.* Pertaining to, living on, or coming from the other side of the Alps, especially as seen from Italy.

~*n.* One who lives beyond the Alps.

Transalpine Gaul. The section of Gaul northwest of the Alps.

trans•at•lan•tic (tránz-ət-lántik, traanz-, -at- || tránss-) *adj.* **1.** On or from the other side of the Atlantic. **2.** Spanning or crossing the Atlantic.

Trans•cau•ca•si•a (tránz-kaw-káyzi-ə, traanz-, -káyzhə || tránss-). Region of the southwestern central U.S.S.R., lying between the Black and Caspian seas. After the Russian Revolution, this oil-rich region was a short-lived Soviet republic (1917–23). It is now divided between the Soviet Socialist republics of Georgia, Armenia, and Azerbaijan S.S.Rs.

trans•ceiv•er (tran-séevər, traan-) *n.* A device consisting of a radio receiver and transmitter. [TRANS(MITTER) + (RE)CEIVER.]

tran•scend (tran-sénd, traan-) *v.* **-scended, -scending, -scends.** —*tr.* **1. a.** To pass beyond (a limit that humans can grasp): *an emotion that transcends understanding.* **b.** To exist above and independently of (material experience or the universe): *God transcends the world of phenomena.* **2.** To rise above or across; surpass; exceed: *Try to transcend your selfish desires* —*intr.* To be outstanding; excel. —See Synonyms at **excel.** [Middle English *transcenden,* from Old French *transcendre,* from Latin *transcendere,* "to climb over" : *trāns-,* over + *scandere,* to climb.]

tran•scen•dent (tran-séndənt, traan-) *adj.* **1.** Surpassing others of the same kind; pre-eminent. **2. a.** *Philosophy.* Transcending the Aristotelian categories. **b.** Especially in Kant's theory of knowledge, designating knowledge that is beyond the limits of experience. **3.** Above and independent of the material universe. Said of God. In this sense, compare **immanent. —tran•scen•dence, tran•scen•den•cy, tran•scen•dent•ness** *n.* **—tran•scen•dent•ly** *adv.*

tran•scen•den•tal (trán-sen-dént'l, traan-, -s'n-) *adj.* **1.** *Philosophy.* **a.** Concerned with the a priori or intuitive basis of knowledge. **b.** Asserting a fundamental irrationality or supernatural element in experience. **2.** Rising above common thought or ideas; exalted; mystical. **3.** *Mathematics.* **a.** Not capable of being determined by any combination of a finite number of equations with rational number coefficients. **b.** Not expressible as an integer or quotient of integers. Said of numbers, especially nonrepeating infinite decimals. **—tran•scen•den•tal•ly** *adv.*

tran•scen•den•tal•ism (trán-sen-dént'l-iz'm, traan-, -s'n-) *n.* **1.** *Philosophy.* **a.** The belief that knowledge of reality is dependent on a priori or intuitive knowledge rather than on objective experience. **b.** Any doctrine based on this belief, such as the philosophies of Kant and Emerson. **2.** The quality or condition of being transcendental. **3. a.** Any unrigorous philosophising or casual speculation. **b.** Exalted or irrational language. **—tran•scen•den•tal•ist** *n.*

transcendental meditation *n. Abbr.* **T.M.** A simple form of meditation derived from Hindu traditions and practised mainly in western countries, in which mental relaxation is promoted by the repeated silent utterance of a mantra.

trans•con•ti•nen•tal (tránz-kónti-nént'l, traanz- || tránss-) *adj.* Spanning or crossing a continent.

tran•scribe (tran-skrīb, traan-) *tr.v.* **-scribed, -scribing, -scribes. 1.** To write or type a copy of; write out fully, as from shorthand notes: *transcribe a letter.* **2.** *Computing.* To transfer (information) from one recording and storing system to another. **3.** To adapt or arrange (a musical composition) for a voice or instrument other than the original. **4.** To record, usually on tape, for broadcasting at a later date. **5.** To represent (speech sounds) by phonetic symbols. **6.** To represent in a different alphabet; transliterate. **7.** *Genetics.* To cause transcription of (DNA). [Latin *transcrībere,* to copy, "write over" : *trāns-,* from one place to another, across + *scrībere,* to write.] **—tran•scrib•a•ble** *adj.* **—tran•scrib•er** *n.*

tran•script (trán-skript, traan-) *n.* Something transcribed; especially, a written, typed, or printed copy, as of a legal record. [Middle English *transcri(p)t,* from Old French *transcrit,* from Latin *transcriptum,* from the past participle of *transcrībere,* TRANSCRIBE.]

tran•scrip•tion (tran-skrípsh'n, traan-) *n.* **1. a.** The act or process or an instance of transcribing. **b.** The state of being transcribed. **2.** Something that has been transcribed, especially: **a.** A representation of speech sounds in phonetic symbols. **b.** An adaptation of a musical composition. **c.** A recorded radio or television programme. **3.** *Genetics.* The transfer of genetic information in DNA to RNA, usually by the synthesis of messenger RNA in which DNA acts as a template. **—tran•scrip•tion•al, tran•scrip•tive** *adj.* **—tran•scrip•tion•al•ly, tran•scrip•tive•ly** *adv.*

trans•cul•tu•ra•tion (tránz-kúlchə-ráysh'n, traanz- || tránss-) *n.* Cultural change induced by the introduction of elements of a foreign culture. [TRANS- + CULTURE + -ATION.]

trans•cur•rent (transs-kúrrənt, traanss-) *adj.* Extending, passing, or running transversely.

transcurrent fault *n.* A **strike-slip fault (see).**

trans•duc•er (tranz-déw-sər, traanz-, transs-, traanss- || -dóo) *n.* *Physics.* Any of various substances or devices, such as a piezoelectric crystal or a photoelectric cell, that convert input energy of one form into output energy of another. [Latin *transdūcere,* to lead across, transfer : *trāns-,* across + *dūcere,* to lead.]

trans•duc•tion (tranz-dúksh'n, traanz-, transs-, traanss-) *n.* **1.** The transfer of genetic material from one bacterial cell to another by a bacteriophage. **2.** *Physics.* The process of converting energy from one form into another. [Latin *transductiō* (stem *transductiōn-*), a transfer, from *transdūcere,* to transfer. See **transducer.**]

tran•sect (tran-sékt, traan-) *tr.v.* **-sected, -secting, -sects.** To divide by cutting transversely. [TRANS- + Latin *secāre* (past participle *sectus*), to cut.] **—tran•sec•tion** *n.*

tran•sept (trán-sept, traan-) *n. Architecture.* **1.** The shorter portion of a cross-shaped church, consisting of two arms that run across

PRONUNCIATION KEY

a, trap; aa, father; ai, **fair;**
ar, **star;** aw, **lawn;** ay, **play;**
b, bb, **stab; rubber;**
ch, **church;** ck, **ticket;**
d, dd, **dead; ladder;** e, **dress;**
ee, **bee;** er, **defer;** ew, **few;**
ewr, **pure;** ə, **about;**
ər, **letter;** f, ff, **fife; differ;**
g, gg, **giggle;** h, **hat;** i, **kit;**
ī, **price;** īr, **fire;** j, **judge;**
k, **kick;** l, ll, **let;** 'l, **needle;**
m, mm, **man;** n, nn, **no;**
'n, **sudden;** ng, **thing;** o, **lot;**
ō, **no;** ŏŏ, **foot;** ōō, **shoe;**
oor, **poor;** ow, **cow;**
owr, **hour;** oy, **boy;**
p, pp, **pepper;** r, rr, **red;**
s, ss, **sauce;** sh, **ship;**
t, tt, **totter;** th, **thick;** th, **this;**
smooth; u, **cut;** ur, **turn;**
v, vv, **valve;** w, **wet;** y, **yes;**
z, zz, **zebra;** zh, **vision;**
pleasure

IN FOREIGN WORDS:

aN, oN, **Saint-Saëns;**
hl, **Llanelli; Hluhluwe;**
kh, **loch; lough; Khaled**

STRESS MARK:

ín-sīt, insight; in-sīt, incite

and at right-angles to the main body of the church. **2.** Either of the two arms. [New Latin *transeptum* : TRANS- + SEPTUM (partition).]

trans·e·unt (trán-zi-ənt, tráan-, -si-) *adj. Philosophy.* Productive of effects outside of the mind. Compare **immanent.** [Latin *transiēns* (oblique stem *transeunt-*), going over, TRANSIENT.]

trans·fer (transs-fér, traanss- || tránss-fer, tráanss-) *v.* **-ferred, -fer-ring, -fers.** *—tr.* **1.** To convey or shift from one person, thing, or place to another: *transferred to a new job.* **2.** To change or shift (the meaning of a word, phrase, or the like), especially by figurative use. **3.** To make over the possession or legal title of to another. **4.** To convey (a drawing, pattern, mural, or design) from one surface to another. **5.** To sell or move (a professional sportsman) from one club to another. *—intr.* **1.** To move oneself, as from one location, job, or school to another. **2.** To change from one train, aeroplane, or the like to another. —See Synonyms at **convey.**
∼*n.* (tránss-fer, tráanss- || -fər). Also **trans·fer·al** (transs-fér-əl, traanss-), **trans·fer·ral** (for senses 1, 2). *Abbr.* **tfr., transf. 1. a.** The act or process of transferring. **b.** The state of being transferred. **2.** Any person or object that has or has been transferred, especially: **a.** A sports player, especially a footballer, who has moved from one club to another. Also used adjectivally: *transfer list.* **b.** A design conveyed or to be conveyed from one surface, usually paper, to another. **3.** *Chiefly U.S.* A ticket entitling a passenger to change from one train, bus, or the like to another. **4.** *Law.* **a.** The conveyance of title, property, or shares from one owner to another. **b.** The document effecting such conveyance. [Middle English *transferren,* from Old French *transferer,* from Latin *trānsferre,* to bear across : *trāns-,* across + *ferre,* to bear.] **—trans·fer·a·bil·i·ty** (-ə-bílləti) *n.* **—trans·fer·a·ble** (transs-fér-əb'l, traanss-, tránss-fər-, tráanss-, -frəb'l) *adj.* **—trans·fer·rer** *n.*

transferable vote *n.* **1.** A vote that, although cast for one particular candidate, may be transferrred to another candidate specified by the voter, if for example, the voter's first choice is eliminated. **2.** The vote cast or indication made in favour of this second candidate. **3.** The system providing for such voting.

trans·fer·ase (tránss-fər-ayz, tráanss-, -ayss) *n.* Any of various enzymes that catalyse the transfer of radicals from one molecule to another.

transfer charge call *n.* A **reverse-charge call** *(see).*

trans·fer·ee (tránss-fer-eé, tráanss-) *n.* **1.** *Law.* One to whom a transfer of title or property is made. **2.** One who is transferred.

trans·fer·ence (tránss-fərənss, tráanss-, -frənss, transs-fér-ənss, traanss-) *n.* **1. a.** An act or process or an instance of transferring. **b.** The condition of being transferred. **2.** *Psychology.* The process in and by which an individual's feelings, thoughts, and wishes shift from one person to another; especially, this process in psychoanalysis where the analyst is made the object of the shift. **—trans·fer·en·tial** (tránss-fə-rénsh'l, tráanss-) *adj.*

transfer fee *n.* A sum of money paid for a transfer; especially, a fee paid for a footballer by one football club to another.

transfer income *n.* Income regarded as a simple transfer of funds from one part of the community to another, rather than as a return for goods and services. It includes government subsidies, unemployment benefits, pensions, and the like, and is not calculated as part of the national income. Also called "transfer payment".

trans·fer·or (transs-fér-ər, traanss-, tránss-fer-, tráanss-) *n. Law.* A person who makes a transfer of title or property.

transfer paper *n.* Any of various types of specially coated paper used for transferring designs from one surface to another.

trans·fer·rin (transs-férrin) *n.* A blood globulin that can combine reversibly with and transport iron ions in the body. [TRANS- + FERR(O)- + -IN.]

transfer RNA *n.* Any of various small RNA molecules, each specific for a particular amino acid, that during synthesis carry amino acids to the ribosomes and arrange them along the messenger RNA molecule, where they are joined by peptide bonds to form a protein. Also called "s RNA", "soluble RNA", "t RNA".

trans·fig·u·ra·tion (tránss-figgewr-áysh'n, tráanss-, -figgər-, tránss-figgewr-, traanss-, -figgər-) *n.* **1.** A radical transformation of figure or appearance; a metamorphosis. **2.** *Capital* **T. a.** The sudden emanation of radiance from Jesus's person that occurred on the mountain. Matthew 17:2; Mark 9:2. **b.** The Christian commemoration of this, observed on August 6. **3.** The act or an instance of transfiguring, or the state of being transfigured.

trans·fig·ure (transs-figgər, traaánss- || *chiefly U.S.* -figgewr) *tr.v.* **-ured, -uring, -ures. 1.** To transform the figure or appearance of; alter radically, especially so as to improve. **2.** To exalt; glorify. [Middle English, from Latin *trānsfigūrāre* : *trāns-,* change + *figūra,* FIGURE.] **—trans·fig·ure·ment** *n.*

trans·fi·nite (tránss-fī-nīt, tráanss-) *adj.* Beyond the finite.

transfinite number *n.* Any cardinal or ordinal number representing the size of a set of numbers too large to be counted.

trans·fix (transs-fiks, traanss-) *tr.v.* **-fixed, -fixing, -fixes. 1.** To pierce through with or as if with a pointed weapon. **2.** To fix fast; impale. **3.** To render motionless, as with terror, amazement, or awe. [Latin *transfīgere* (past participle *transfīxus*) : *trans-,* through + *fīgere,* to pierce, fix.] **—trans·fix·ion** (-fiksh'n) *adj.*

trans·form (transs-fórm, traanss-) *v.* **-formed, -forming, -forms.** *—tr.* **1.** To change markedly the form, character, or appearance of, especially for the better: *His new wife has transformed him!* **2.** To change the nature, function, or condition of; convert. **3.** *Mathematics.* To subject to a mathematical transformation. **4.** *Electricity.* To subject to the action of a transformer. *—intr.* To undergo a transformation. —See Synonyms at **change.**
∼*n.* (tránss-fawrm, tráanss-). The result, especially a mathematical quantity or linguistic construction, of a transformation. [Middle English, from Old French, from Latin *transformāre* : TRANS- + FORM.] **—trans·form·a·ble** (-fórməb'l) *adj.*

trans·for·ma·tion (tránss-fər-máysh'n, tráanss-, -fawr-) *n.* **1. a.** The act of transforming. **b.** The state or an instance of being transformed. **c.** Something that has been transformed. **2.** Any extreme or radical change, especially for the better. **3.** *Mathematics.* **a.** The replacement of the variables in an algebraic expression by their values in terms of another set of variables. **b.** A mapping of one space onto another or onto itself. **4.** *Physics.* A change of one nuclide into another as a result of an alpha decay or a beta decay. **5.** *Linguistics.* **a.** The process of converting a syntactic construction into a semantically equivalent construction according to the rules shown to generate the syntax of the language. **b.** A construction derived by such transformation. **5.** *Rare.* A woman's wig. [Middle English, from Late Latin *transformātio* (stem *transformātiōn-*). See **transform.**] **—trans·for·ma·tive** (transs-fórmətiv, traanss-) *adj.*

trans·for·ma·tion·al·gen·e·ra·tive grammar (transs-fər-máysh'n'l-jén-rətiv, tráanss-, -fawr-, -jénnə-) *n. Linguistics.* A grammar that accounts for the constructions of a language by linguistic transformations and phrase structures, on the assumption that languages have a **deep structure** and a **surface structure** *(both of which see).* Also called "transformational grammar".

trans·form·er (transs-fórmər, traanss-) *n.* **1.** One that transforms. **2.** A device used to transfer electric energy, usually that of an alternating current, from one circuit to another; especially, a pair of multiply wound, inductively coupled wire coils that effect such a transfer with a change in voltage, current, phase, or other electric characteristic. See **step-down transformer, step-up transformer.**

trans·fuse (trans-féwz, traanss-) *tr.v.* **-fused, -fusing, -fuses. 1.** To transfer (liquid) by pouring from one vessel into another. **2.** To permeate; infuse. **3.** *Medicine.* To administer a transfusion of or to. [Middle English *transfusen,* from Latin *trānsfundere* (past participle *trānsfūsus*) : *trāns-,* from one place to another + *fundere,* to pour.] **—trans·fus·er** *n.* **—trans·fus·i·ble** *adj.* **—trans·fu·sive** (-féw-siv, -ziv) *adj.*

trans·fu·sion (transs-féwzh'n, traanss-) *n.* **1.** The act or process or an instance of transfusing. **2.** *Medicine.* The injection of whole blood, plasma, or another solution into the bloodstream.

trans·gress (transs-gréss, traanss-, tranz-, traanz-) *v.* **-gressed, -gressing, -gresses.** *—tr.* **1.** To go beyond or over (a limit or boundary). **2.** To act in violation of (the law, for example). *—intr.* To trespass; sin. [Latin *trānsgredī* (past participle *trānsgressus*), to step across : *trāns-,* across + *gradī,* to step.] **—trans·gress·i·ble** *adj.* **—trans·gres·sive** *adj.* **—trans·gres·sive·ly** *adv.* **—trans·gres·sor** (-ər) *n.*

trans·gres·sion (transs-grésh'n, traanss-, tranz-, traanz-) *n.* **1.** The violation of a law, command, or duty; a crime or sin. **2.** The exceeding or overstepping of due bounds or limits. —See Synonyms at **breach.**

tran·ship. Variant of **transship.**

trans·hu·mance (transs-héwmənss, traanss-) *n.* The movement of livestock and herders to different grazing grounds with the changing of the seasons. [French, from *transhumer,* to make seasonal movement of livestock, from Spanish *transhumar* : Latin *trāns-,* from one place to another + *humus,* earth, ground.] **—trans·hu·mant** *adj.* & *n.*

tran·si·ent (trán-zi-ənt, tráan-, -si-, -zh-, -shi- || *chiefly U.S.* -shənt, -zhənt) *adj.* **1.** Passing away with time; transitory; fleeting. **2.** Passing through from one place to another; stopping only briefly: *transient labourers.* **3.** *Physics.* Decaying with time, especially as a simple exponential function of time. **4.** *Music.* Adopted only in passing, as a link; not essential to the harmony: *a transient chord.*
∼*n.* **1.** One that is transient. **2.** *Physics.* A transient phenomenon or property, especially a transient electric current. [Latin *transiēns* (stem *transient-*), present participle of *transīre,* to go over : *trāns-,* over, across + *īre,* to go.] **—tran·si·ence** (-ənss), **tran·si·en·cy** (-ən-si), **tran·si·ent·ness** *n.* **—tran·si·ent·ly** *adv.*
Synonyms: *transient, transitory, ephemeral, fleeting, fugitive, momentary, evanescent, temporary, provisional.*

trans·il·lu·mi·nate (tránz-i-lóomi-nayt, tráanz-, -léwmi- || tránss-) *tr.v.* **-nated, -nating, -nates.** *Medicine.* To place a strong light behind (a translucent body part) to show up fluid, lesions, cavities, or the like. **—trans·il·lu·mi·na·tion** (-náysh'n) *n.*

tran·sis·tor (tran-zístər, traan-, -sístər) *n.* **1.** A semiconductor device used for amplification, switching, and detection, typically containing two rectifying junctions, and usually having three terminals and characteristically operating so that the current between one pair of terminals controls the current between the other pair, one terminal being common to input and output. **2.** A radio equipped with transistors. In this sense, also called "transistor radio". [Originally a trademark : *trans*fer + *re*sistor.]

tran·sis·tor·ise, tran·sis·tor·ize (tran-zístər-īz, traan-, -sístər-) *tr.v.* **-ised, -ising, -ises. 1.** To equip (an electronic circuit or device) with transistors. **2.** To design or refit (a machine, factory, or the like) to use transistors.

tran·sit (trán-zit, tráan-, -sit) *n.* **1. a.** The act of passing over, across, or through; passage. **b.** The movement or conveyance of goods or persons from one place to another. **2.** A transition or change, especially from one life to another at death. **3.** *Astronomy.* **a.** The ap-

PRONUNCIATION KEY

a, trap; aa, father; ai, fair; ar, star; aw, lawn; ay, play; b, bb, stab; rubber; ch, church; ck, ticket; d, dd, dead; ladder; e, dress; ee, bee; er, defer; ew, few; ewr, pure; ə, about; ər, letter; f, ff, fife; differ; g, gg, giggle; h, hat; i, kit; ī, price; īr, fire; j, judge; k, kick; l, ll, let; 'l, needle; m, mm, man; n, nn, no; 'n, sudden; ng, thing; o, lot; ō, no; ŏŏ, foot; ōō, shoe; oor, poor; ow, cow; owr, hour; oy, boy; p, pp, pepper; r, rr, red; s, ss, sauce; sh, ship; t, tt, totter; th, thick; th, this; smooth; u, cut; ur, turn; v, vv, valve; w, wet; y, yes; z, zz, zebra; zh, vision; pleasure

IN FOREIGN WORDS:

aN, oN, Saint-Saëns; hl, Llanelli; Hluhluwe; kh, loch; lough; Khaled

STRESS MARK:

ín-sīt, insight; in-sī́t, incite

parent passage of a celestial body across the observer's meridian. **b.** The passage of a smaller celestial body across the disc of a larger celestial body. **4.** A surveying instrument similar to a theodolite that measures horizontal and vertical angles. **5.** A way, passage, or route. **—in transit. 1.** While being moved or conveyed. **2.** Only stopping temporarily; continuing one's journey. Said especially of airline passengers.
~v. **transited, -siting, -sits.** *—tr.* **1.** To pass over, across, or through. **2.** To revolve (the telescope of a surveying transit) about its horizontal transverse axis in order to reverse its direction. *—intr. Astronomy.* To make a transit. [Latin *transitus,* from the past participle of *transīre,* to go across. See **transient.**]

transit camp *n.* A temporary camp for the accommodation of people in transit such as emigrants, refugees, or soldiers.

transit instrument *n.* A telescope mounted on a horizontal east-west axis used to observe the passage of stars across the meridian.

tran·si·tion (tran-zísh'n, traan-, -sí<u>zh</u>'n || -sísh'n) *n.* **1. a.** The act or process or an instance of changing from one form, state, activity, or place to another. **b.** The length of time involved in such a change. **2.** Passage from one subject to another, as in discourse. **3.** *Music.* **a.** A modulation, especially a brief one. **b.** A passage connecting two themes. **4.** *Physics.* **a.** In quantum mechanics, the change of a system from one energy state to another. **b.** A change in a nuclide involving either a transformation to another nuclide or a change in energy level as a result of gamma-ray emission. **5.** In various arts, a change from one tradition or style to another, or a combination of elements of an older style and a newer style as in transitional architecture. **—tran·si·tion·al, tran·si·tion·ar·y** (-əri || -erri) *adj.* **—tran·si·tion·al·ly** *adv.*

transitional architecture *n.* Architecture of the period, around the year 1100, of transition from the Romanesque to the Gothic. In Britain it is marked by a combination of the Norman and early English styles.

transition element *n.* **1.** Any of the elements that serve as transitional links between the most and the least electropositive in a series of elements, and that are characterised by high melting points, densities, magnetic moments, multiple valencies, and the ability to form stable complex ions. **2.** Any of the elements in which an inner electron shell rather than an outer shell is only partially filled, generally taken to include elements 21–30, 39–48, and 57–80. Also called "transition metal".

transition temperature *n.* The temperature at which there is a sudden change in a particular physical property of a substance, such as its crystalline structure, conductivity, or magnetism. Also called "transition point".

tran·si·tive (trán-zə-tiv, traán-, -sə-, -zi-, -si-) *adj.* **1.** *Abbr.* **t., tr., trans.** *Grammar.* **a.** Expressing an action that is carried from the subject to the object. **b.** Designating a verb or verb construction that requires a direct object to complete its meaning; for example, the verb *vanquish* is always transitive, and the verb *win* is sometimes transitive. **2.** Characterised by or effecting transition. **3.** *Mathematics & Logic.* Designating a relationship such that if A and B have a particular relation, and B and C have the same relation, then so do A and C; for example, if A is a number which has a value less than that of B, and the value of B is less than that of C, then A is less than C: therefore "is less than" is a transitive relationship.
~n. Abbr. **t., tr., trans.** *Grammar.* A transitive verb. [Late Latin *transitīvus,* passing over (as from the subject to the object), from Latin *transitus,* TRANSIT.] **—tran·si·tive·ly** *adv.* **—tran·si·tive·ness, tran·si·tiv·i·ty** (-tívvəti) *n.*

tran·si·to·ry (trán-zi-tri, traán-, -si-, -zə-, -sə-, -təri) *adj.* Existing or occurring only briefly; short-lived; passing. See Synonyms at **transient.** [Middle English *transitorie,* from Anglo-French, from Late Latin *transitōrius,* from Latin, adapted for passing through, from *transitus,* TRANSIT.] **—tran·si·to·ri·ly** *adv.* **—tran·si·to·ri·ness** *n.*

transitory action *n.* A legal aciton or case that may be brought in any country, and not merely in the one in which it originated.

Transjordan. See **Jordan, Hashemite Kingdom of.**

Trans·kei (tránss-kī, traánss-, tránz-, traánz-), **Republic of.** An autonomous region of South Africa. Consisting of the homelands of the Xhosa tribe, it was established by the South African government in 1963 to implement their policy of apartheid. No other nation has recognised its sovereignty. Area, 43 077 square kilometres (16,632 square miles). Population (Xhosa), 1,900,000 (plus 1,000,000 in South Africa). Capital, Umtata. **—Trans·kei·an** *n. & adj.*

transl. translated; translation.

trans·late (tranz-láyt, traanz-, transs-, traanss-, trənz- || *U.S. also* tránss-layt, tránz-) *v.* **-lated, -lating, -lates.** *—tr.* **1.** To express in another language, systematically retaining the original sense. **2. a.** To put in simpler terms; explain. **b.** To see the significance of; infer; interpret. **3.** To convey from one form or style to another; convert. **4.** To transfer (a bishop) to another see. **5.** To move or transfer. **6. a.** *Theology.* To convey to heaven without natural death. **b.** To move or promote to a higher or more exalted position. Often used humorously: *He's been translated to the peerage.* **7.** *Physics.* To subject (a body) to translation. **8.** *Genetics.* To cause translation of (messenger RNA). **9.** *Archaic.* Tŏ transport; enrapture. *—intr.* **1. a.** To make a translation. **b.** To work as a translator. **2.** To admit of or be capable of translation. **3.** *Aerospace.* To move from one place to another in space by means of reaction power. [Middle English *translaten,* to transport, to translate, from Latin *translātus* (past participle of *transferre,* to carry across, transfer, translate) : *trāns-,* across + *-lātus,* "carried".] **—trans·lat·a·bil·i·ty** (-ə-bílləti), **trans·lat·a·ble·ness** *n.* **—trans·lat·a·ble** *adj.*

trans·la·tion (tranz-láysh'n, traanz-, transs-, traanss-, trənz-, trənss-) *n. Abbr.* **transl., trans., tr. 1. a.** The act or process or an instance of translating, especially from one language to another. **b.** The condition of being translated. **2.** A translated version of a text. **3.** *Physics.* Motion of a body in which every point of the body moves parallel to, and the same distance as, every other point of the body; nonrotational displacement. **4.** *Biochemistry.* The decoding of the genetic information in a messenger RNA molecule so that it may be used to synthesise protein molecules. **—trans·la·tion·al** *adj.*

trans·la·tor (tranz-láytər, traanz-, transs-, traanss-, trənz-, trənss- || *U.S. also* tránss-laytər, tránz-) *n. Abbr.* **tr., trans. 1.** One who translates; especially, one professionally employed to translate written works. **2.** An interpreter. **—trans·la·to·ri·al** (tráz-lay-táw-ri-əl, traanz-, tránss-, traánss- || -tṓ-) *adj.*

trans·lit·er·ate (tranz-líttə-rayt, traanz-, transs-, traanss-) *tr.v.* **-ated, -ating, -ates.** To represent (letters or words) in the corresponding characters of another alphabet. [TRANS- + Latin *littera,* LETTER + -ATE.] **—trans·lit·er·a·tion** (-ráysh'n) *n.*

trans·lo·cate (tránz-lō-káyt, traánz-, tránss-, -lə- || *U.S. also* -lṓ-kayt) *tr.v.* **-cated, -cating, -cates.** To cause to change from one position to another; displace; move.

trans·lo·ca·tion (tránz-lō-káysh'n, traánz- tránss-, traánss-, -lə-) *n.* **1.** A change in location. **2.** *Genetics.* A chromosomal aberration in which sections from different chromosomes are interchanged. **3.** The movement of mineral nutrients, food materials, and the like in plants.

trans·lu·cent (tranz-lṓō-s'nt, traanz-, transs-, traanss-, -léw-) *adj.* Transmitting light but causing sufficient diffusion to eliminate perception of distinct images. Compare **transparent, opaque.** [Latin *translūcēns* (stem *translūcent-*), present participle of *translūcēre,* to shine through : *trāns-,* through + *lūcēre,* to shine.] **—trans·lu·cence, trans·lu·cen·cy** *n.* **—trans·lu·cent·ly** *adv.*

trans·lun·ar (tránz-lṓō-nər, traánz-, tránss-, traánss-, -léw-) *adj.* Lying beyond the moon. Compare **cislunar.**

trans·lu·na·ry (tranz-lṓō-nəri, traanz-, transs-, traanss-, -léw-) *adj.* **1.** Translunar. **2.** Unearthly; visionary. [TRANS- + *-lunary.*]

trans·ma·rine (tránz-mə-réen, traánz-, tránss-, traánss-) *adj.* **1.** Crossing the sea. **2.** Being beyond or coming from across the sea. [Latin *transmarīnus* : *trāns-,* across, beyond + *mare,* sea.]

trans·mi·grant (tranz-mīgrənt, traanz-, transs-, traanss-) *n.* **1.** One who transmigrates; an immigrant. **2.** An immigrant in transit through a country on his way to the country in which he intends to settle.

trans·mi·grate (tránz-mī-gráyt, traánz-, tránss-, traánss- || *U.S.* -mī́-grayt, -mī-grayt) *intr.v.* **-grated, -grating, -grates. 1.** To migrate. **2.** To pass into another body after death. Used of the soul. **—trans·mi·gra·tor** (-ər) *n.* **—trans·mi·gra·to·ry** (-mī́-grə-tri, -təri, -mī-gráytəri) *adj.*

trans·mi·gra·tion (tránz-mī-gráysh'n, traánz-, tránss-, traánss-) *n.* **1.** The act or process of transmigrating. **2.** The passing of a soul into another body after death; metempsychosis. Also called "transmigration of souls". **—trans·mi·gra·tion·ism** *n.*

trans·mis·si·ble (tranz-míssə-b'l, traanz-, transs-, traanss-) *adj.* Capable of being transmitted. **—trans·mis·si·bil·i·ty** (-bílləti) *n.*

trans·mis·sion (tranz-mísh'n, traanz-, transs-, traanss-) *n.* **1. a.** The act or process of transmitting. **b.** The state of being transmitted. **2.** Something transmitted, such as a message. **3. a.** An assembly of gears and associated parts by which power is transmitted from the engine of a motor vehicle to a driving axle. **b.** A system of gears. **4.** The sending of modulated carrier waves from a transmitter; a broadcast. [Latin *transmissiō* (stem *transmissiōn-*), from *transmissus,* past participle of *transmittere,* TRANSMIT.] **—trans·mis·sive** (-míssiv) *adj.*

transmission line *n.* A coaxial cable, waveguide, or other system of conductors used to transfer information from one place to another.

trans·mis·siv·i·ty (tránz-mi-sívvəti, traánz-, tránss-, traánss-) *n. Physics.* A measure of the ability of a medium to transmit radiation given by the internal transmittance of unit length of a material.

trans·mit (tranz-mít, traanz-, transs-, traanss-) *v.* **-mitted, -mitting, -mits.** *—tr.* **1.** To send from one person, thing, or place to another; convey. **2.** To cause to spread; pass on: *transmit an infection.* **3.** To impart or convey to others by heredity; hand down. **4.** *Electronics.* **a.** To send (a signal), as by wire or radio. **b.** To broadcast (a television or radio programme). **5.** *Physics.* To cause (a disturbance) to propagate through a medium. **6.** To convey (force or energy) from one part of a mechanism to another. *—intr.* To send out a signal. **—**See Synonyms at **convey.** [Middle English *transmitten,* from Latin *transmittere,* to send across : *trāns-,* across + *mittere,* to send.] **—trans·mit·ta·ble, trans·mit·ti·ble** *adj.* **—trans·mit·tal** *n.*

trans·mit·tance (tranz-mítt'nss, traanz-, transs-, traanss-) *n.* **1.** The act or process of transmitting; a transmission. **2.** *Physics.* The ratio of the radiant energy transmitted to the total radiant energy incident on a given body. Compare **absorptance, reflectance.**

trans·mit·tan·cy (tranz-mítt'n-si, traanz-, transs-, traanss-) *n. Physics.* The transmittance of a solution divided by the transmittance of a pure solvent of identical dimensions.

trans·mit·ter (tranz-míttər, traanz-, transs-, traanss-) *n.* **1.** One that transmits. **2.** A telegraphic sending instrument. **3.** The portion of a telephone that converts the incident sounds into electrical impulses that are conveyed to a remote receiver. **4.** Electronic equipment that generates and amplifies a carrier wave, modulates it with a signal derived from speech or other sources, and radiates the resulting signal from an aerial. **5.** In physiology, a **neurotransmitter** *(see).*

trans·mog·ri·fy (tranz-móggri-fī, traanz-, transs-, traanss-) *tr.v.* **-fied, -fying, -fies.** To change into a different shape or form, especially one that is fantastic or bizarre. Often used humorously. [17th century : origin obscure.] **—trans·mog·ri·fi·ca·tion** (-fi-káysh'n) *n.*

trans·mon·tane (tranz-món-tayn, traanz-, transs-, traanss- || -mon-táyn) *adj.* Located beyond a mountain or mountain range; tramontane. [Latin *trānsmontānus,* TRAMONTANE.]

trans·mu·ta·tion (tránz-mew-táysh'n, tra̍anz-, tránss-, tra̍anss-) *n.* **1.** The act of transmuting. **2.** The state of being transmuted. **3.** In alchemy, the alleged conversion of base metals into gold or silver. **4.** *Physics.* The transformation of one element into another by one or a series of nuclear reactions. [Middle English, from Old French, from Late Latin *transmūtātiō* (stem *transmūtātiōn-*). See **transmute.**] **—trans·mu·ta·tion·al, trans·mut·a·tive** (-méwtətiv, -mew-táytiv) *adj.*

trans·mute (tranz-méwt, traanz-, transs-, traanss-) *tr.v.* **-muted, -muting, -mutes.** To change from one form, nature, substance, or state into another; transform. See Synonyms at **change.** [Middle English *transmuten,* from Latin *transmūtāre* : *trāns-,* from one to another + *mūtāre,* to change.] **—trans·mut·a·bil·i·ty** (-ə-bílləti), **trans·mut·a·ble·ness** *n.* **—trans·mut·a·ble** *adj.* **—trans·mut·a·bly** *adv.* **—trans·mut·er** *n.*

trans·na·tion·al (tránz-násh'n-'l, tra̍anz-, -náshn'l) *adj.* Not confined to a single nation; extending across national frontiers.

trans·o·ce·an·ic (tránz-ōshi-ánnik, tra̍anz-, -ṓ-si- || tránss-) *adj.* **1.** Situated beyond or on the other side of the ocean. **2.** Spanning or crossing the ocean.

tran·som (tránss'm) *n.* **1.** A horizontal bar that is situated between a door and a window above it. **2.** A horizontal dividing bar of wood or stone in a window. **3.** A window that has been divided with a transom. **4.** *Chiefly U.S.* A **fanlight** *(see).* **5.** *Nautical.* Any of several transverse beams affixed to the sternpost of a wooden ship and forming part of the stern. **6.** The horizontal beam on a cross or gallows, or the top piece of a trilith. [Middle English *traunson,* crossbeam, lintel, perhaps from Latin *transtrum* : *trāns-,* across + *-trum,* suffix denoting an instrument.] **—tran·somed** *adj.*

tran·son·ic (tran-sónnik, traan-) *adj.* Of or pertaining to aerodynamic flow or flight conditions at speeds close to the speed of sound. [TRANS- + (SUPER)SONIC.]

transp. transportation.

trans·pa·cif·ic (tránss-pə-síffik, tra̍anss-) *adj.* **1.** Crossing the Pacific Ocean. **2.** Situated across or beyond the Pacific Ocean.

trans·par·en·cy (transs-párrən-si, traanss-, tranz-, traanz-, trənss-, trənz-, -páir-ən-) *n., pl.* **-cies.** Also **trans·par·ence** (-párrənss, -páir-ənss) (for sense 1). **1.** The quality or state of being transparent. **2.** A transparent object; especially, a photographic slide whose image is made visible by light shining through from behind.

trans·par·ent (transs-párrənt, traanss-, tranz-, traanz-, trənss-, trənz-, -páir-ənt) *adj.* **1.** Capable of transmitting light so that objects or images can be seen clearly. Compare **translucent, opaque. 2.** Permeable to electromagnetic radiation of specified frequencies, as to visible light or radio waves. **3.** Of such fine or open texture that objects may be easily seen on the other side; diaphanous; sheer. **4.** Easily understood or detected; flimsy or obvious: *transparent lies.* **5.** Guileless; candid; open. [Middle English, from Old French, from Medieval Latin *trānspārēns* (stem *transpārent-*), present participle of *trānspārēre,* to be seen through : Latin *trāns-,* through + *pārēre,* to show (see **appear**).] **—trans·par·ent·ly** *adv.* **—trans·par·ent·ness** *n.*

tran·spi·ra·tion (trán-spi-ráysh'n, tra̍an-, -spə-) *n.* The act or process of transpiring, especially through the stomata of plant tissue or the pores of the skin.

tran·spire (tran-spír, traan-) *v.* **-spired, -spiring, -spires.** *—tr.* **1.** To secrete (water containing waste products) through the pores of the skin; perspire. **2.** To lose (water vapour) from the surface of a plant, mainly through open stomata. **3.** To become known; come to light. Used impersonally with a clause. **4.** *Informal.* **a.** To happen; occur. **b.** To come to pass; turn out. Used impersonally with a clause. *—intr.* **1.** To secrete water containing waste products through animal pores. **2.** To lose water vapour from a plant surface. **3.** To become known; come to light. **4.** *Informal.* **a.** To happen; occur. **b.** To come to pass; turn out. [French *transpirer,* from Old French : Latin *trāns-,* out + *spīrāre,* to breathe.]

Usage: *Transpire* is frequently used in the general sense of "happen, occur": *The accident transpired when the lights changed,* or "come to pass, turn out": *It transpired that the weather was awful,* but these uses attract purist criticism, which holds that the figurative sense of the word should be restricted to "come to light": *It transpired that he had been in prison once before.*

trans·plant (transs-pla̍ant, traanss- || -plánt) *v.* **-planted, -planting, -plants.** *—tr.* **1.** To uproot and replant (a growing plant). **2.** To transfer from one place or residence to another; resettle; relocate. **3.** In surgery, to transfer (tissue or an organ) from one body, or body part, to another. *—intr.* **1.** To admit or be capable of being transplanted. **2.** To survive transplanting.
~n. (tránss-plaant, tra̍anss- || -plant). **1.** Something transplanted. **2.** The act or process of transplanting: *a heart transplant.* [Middle English *transplaunten,* from Late Latin *transplantāre* : Latin *trans-,* across + *plantāre,* to plant (see **plant**).] **—trans·plan·ta·tion** (tránss-plaan-táysh'n, tra̍anss-, -plan-) *n.* **—trans·plant·er** *n.*

trans·po·lar (tránz-pṓlər, tra̍anz- || tránss-) *adj.* Extending across or crossing over either of the geographic polar regions.

tran·spond·er (tran-spóndər, traan-) *n.* A radio or radar receiver-transmitter activated for transmission by reception of a predetermined signal. [*trans*mitter + re*sponder.*]

trans·pon·tine (tránz-pón-tīn, tra̍anz- || tránss-) *adj.* **1.** Situated across or beyond a bridge. **2.** Of or pertaining to the part of London on the south side of the Thames or the melodramatic plays performed there in the 19th century. [TRANS- + Latin *pōns* (stem *pont-*), bridge + -INE.]

trans·port (tránss-pórt, tra̍anss- || -pṓrt, tránss-pawrt, tra̍anss-, -pōrt) *tr.v.* **-ported, -porting, -ports. 1.** To carry from one place to another; convey. **2.** To move to strong emotion; enrapture; carry away: *transported by the scene.* **3.** Especially formerly, to send abroad to a penal colony; deport. —See Synonyms at **convey.**
~n. (tránss-pawrt, tra̍anss-, -pōrt). **1.** The act of transporting; conveyance. **2.** The state or condition of being transported by emotion; rapture. **3.** A ship used to transport troops or military equipment. **4.** A vehicle, such as an aircraft, used to transport passengers, mail, or freight. **5. a.** The system of transporting passengers or goods in a particular country or area. **b.** The vehicles, such as buses and trains, used in such a system. **6.** Especially formerly, a deported convict. —See Synonyms at **ecstasy.** [Middle English *transporten,* from Old French *transporter,* from Latin *trānsportāre* : *trāns-,* from one place to another + *portāre,* to carry.] **—trans·port·a·bil·i·ty** (-ə-bílləti) *n.* **—trans·port·a·ble** (-pórt-əb'l || -pṓrt-) *adj.* **—trans·port·er** *n.* **—trans·port·ive** *adj.*

trans·por·ta·tion (tránss-pawr-táysh'n, tra̍anss- || -pōr-, -pər-) *n. Abbr.* **transp. 1.** The act of transporting. **2.** The state of being transported. **3.** *Chiefly U.S.* **a.** A means of transport; a conveyance. **b.** The business of transporting passengers, goods, materials, or the like. **4.** *U.S.* A charge for transporting; a fare.

transport café *n.* In Britain, a café serving cheap, simple food and situated on or near a main road, especially for the use of lorry drivers and other motorists.

transporter bridge *n.* A bridge that has a large moving platform supported by cables, used especially for carrying vehicles.

trans·pose (transs-pṓz, traanss-) *tr.v.* **-posed, -posing, -poses. 1.** To reverse or transfer the order or place of; interchange. **2.** To put into a different place or order: *transposed the words of a sentence.* **3.** *Mathematics.* To move (a term) from one side of an algebraic equation to the other side, reversing its sign to maintain equality. **4.** *Music.* To write or perform (a composition) in a key other than the original or given key. **5.** *Obsolete.* To transform.
~n. Mathematics. A matrix that is generated by interchanging the rows and columns of the original matrix. [Middle English *transposen,* from Old French *transposer* : Latin *trāns-,* from one place to another + French *poser,* to place, POSE.] **—trans·pos·a·ble** *adj.* **—trans·pos·er** *n.*

trans·po·si·tion (tránss-pə-zísh'n, tra̍anss-) *n.* Also **trans·pos·al** (transs-pṓz'l, traanss-). *Abbr.* **tr. 1.** The act of transposing. **2.** The state of being transposed. **3.** Something that has been transposed. [French. See **trans-, position.**] **—trans·po·si·tion·al** *adj.*

trans·sex·u·al (tránz-sék-sew-əl, tra̍anz-, trán-, tra̍an-, -shoo-, -shōōl) *n.* A person who is born belonging anatomically to one sex but who feels him- or herself to be, or desires to become, a member of the opposite sex; especially, one who has undergone a sex change, usually through surgery and hormone therapy. **—trans·sex·u·al** *adj.* **—trans·sex·u·al·ism** *n.*

trans·ship (transs-shíp, traanss-, tranz-, traanz-, tran-, traan-) *v.* **-shipped, -shipping, -ships.** Also **tran·ship.** *—tr.* To transfer from one vessel or vehicle to another for reshipment. *—intr.* To transfer cargo from one vessel or vehicle to another. **—trans·ship·ment** *n.*

tran·sub·stan·ti·ate (trán-səb-stán-shi-ayt, tra̍an-, -si- || -sub-) *tr.v.* **-ated, -ating, -ates. 1.** To change (one substance) into another; transmute; transform. **2.** *Theology.* To change the substance of (the Eucharistic bread and wine) into the body and blood of Christ. [Medieval Latin *transubstantiāre* : Latin *trāns-,* change + *substantia,* SUBSTANCE.]

tran·sub·stan·ti·a·tion (trán-səb-stán-shi-áysh'n, tra̍an-, -si- || -sub-) *n.* **1.** *Theology.* The doctrine that the bread and wine of the Eucharist are transformed into the body and blood of Christ, although their appearance remains the same. Compare **consubstantiation. 2.** The conversion of one substance into another; a transformation. **—tran·sub·stan·ti·a·tion·al·ist** *n.*

tran·su·date (trán-sew-dayt, tra̍an-, -zew-, tran-séw-, traan-, -zéw- || -sōō-, -zōō-) *n.* A substance that has undergone transudation.

trans·u·da·tion (trán-sew-dáysh'n, tra̍an-, -zew- || -sōō-, -zōō-) *n.* The passage of a fluid with some of its dissolved salts through a membrane or skin.

tran·sude (tran-séwd, traan-, -zéwd || -sṓōd, -zṓōd) *intr.v.* **-suded, -suding, -sudes.** To exude or pass through a membrane or skin, in the manner of perspiration. [New Latin *transudare* : Latin *trāns-,* through + *sūdāre,* to sweat.] **—tran·su·da·to·ry** (-ə-tri, -təri, trán-sew-dáytəri, tra̍an-, -zew-) *adj.*

trans·u·ran·ic (tránz-yoor-ánnik, tra̍anz- || tránss-) *adj.* Also **trans·u·ra·ni·an** (-ayni-ən), **trans·u·ra·ni·um** (-ayni-əm). Having an atomic number greater than 92. [TRANS- + URAN(IUM) + -IC.]

Trans·vaal (tránz-vaal, tra̍anz-, tránss-, tra̍anss-, -vaal || *locally also* -fa̍al). Province of northeast South Africa, lying between the Vaal and Limpopo rivers. It is the Republic's richest province, having enormous mineral wealth, especially gold and diamonds, and fertile veldt for crops and grazing. Pretoria is the capital and Johannesburg the largest city. Boer settlers set up the South African Republic (1857), which was annexed by Britain (1877). After enormous

PRONUNCIATION KEY

a, trap; aa, father; ai, fair; ar, star; aw, lawn; ay, play; b, bb, stab; rubber; ch, church; ck, ticket; d, dd, dead; ladder; e, dress; ee, bee; er, defer; ew, few; ewr, pure; ə, about; ər, letter; f, ff, fife; differ; g, gg, giggle; h, hat; i, kit; ī, price; īr, fire; j, judge; k, kick; l, ll, let; 'l, needle; m, mm, man; n, nn, no; 'n, sudden; ng, thing; o, lot; ō, no; ŏŏ, foot; ōō, shoe; oor, poor; ow, cow; owr, hour; oy, boy; p, pp, pepper; r, rr, red; s, ss, sauce; sh, ship; t, tt, totter; th, thick; th, this; smooth; u, cut; ur, turn; v, vv, valve; w, wet; y, yes; z, zz, zebra; zh, vision; pleasure

IN FOREIGN WORDS:

aN, oN, Saint-Saëns; hl, Llanelli; Hluhluwe; kh, loch; lough; Khaled

STRESS MARK:

ín-sīt, insight; in-sī́t, incite

gold finds on the Witwatersrand (1886) settlers, particularly Britons, flocked in. Tensions led to war between Britain and the Boers (1899), and as a result, Transvaal was made a crown colony (1902). It joined the Union of South Africa in 1910.

trans·val·ue (tranz-vál-yoo, traanz- || transs-) *tr.v.* **-ued, -uing, -ues.** To evaluate by a new standard or principle, especially one that varies from conventional standards. **—trans·val·u·a·tion** *n.*

trans·ver·sal (tranz-vérss'l, traanz- || transs-) *adj.* Transverse. ~*n.* In geometry, a line that intersects a system of lines. Also called "traverse".

trans·verse (tránz-verss, traánz-, tranz-vérss, traanz- || tránss-, transs-) *adj. Abbr.* **trans. 1.** Situated or lying across; athwart; crosswise. **2.** Designating a flute whose mouthpiece is on its side and is thus held horizontally and parallel to the players lips. Said of the modern flute as distinguished from the recorder.
~*n. Abbr.* **trans.** Something transverse, such as a part or beam. [Latin *trānsversus,* from the past participle of *trānsvertere,* to turn or direct across : *trāns-,* across + *vertere,* to turn.] **—trans·verse·ly** *adv.* **—trans·verse·ness** *n.*

transverse colon *n.* The part of the colon that lies across the upper part of the abdominal cavity.

transverse process *n.* A lateral projection from a vertebra.

transverse wave *n.* A wave in which the displacement of the transmitting field or medium is at right angles to the direction of propagation. Compare **longitudinal wave.**

trans·vest·ism (tranz-vést-iz'm, traanz- || transs-) Also **trans·ves·tit·ism** (-véstīt-) *n.* The practice or condition of being a transvestite. Also called "Eonism".

trans·ves·tite (tranz-vést-īt, traanz- || transs-) *n.* A person who wears clothes normally worn by the opposite sex, for sexual stimulation. Also called "cross-dresser". [From *transvest* : TRANS- + Latin *vestīre,* to dress, clothe.] **—trans·ves·tite** *adj.*

Tran·syl·va·ni·a (trán-sil-váyni-ə, traán-). *Romanian* **Ar·deal** (aard-yál) or **Transilvania;** *Hungarian* **Er·dély** (áir-day); *German* **Sie·ben·bürg·en** (zeéb'n-bürgən). Plateau region of central Romania, lying between the Carpathians and Transylvanian Alps. Rich in mineral, agricultural and forest resources, it has large iron and steel, chemical, and textile industries.

Transylvanian Alps. Also **the Southern Carpathians.** Mountain range of central Romania. It extends 360 kilometres (225 miles) eastwards from the Iron Gate gorge on the Danube. Mount Moldoveanu is its highest peak (2 543 metres; 8,343 feet).

trap¹ (trap) *n.* **1.** A device for catching and holding animals, such as a net, a concealed pit, or a sensitive clamplike apparatus that springs shut suddenly. **2. a.** Any stratagem or device for betraying, tricking, or exposing an unwary or unsuspecting person. **b.** Anything that serves to catch, catch out, or ensnare an unwary or unsuspecting person: *fell into the trap of underestimating amateur opposition.* **c.** Anything that attracts, catches, and holds. Also used in combination: *Our garden is a real suntrap.* **3.** A device for sealing a passage against the escape of gases; especially, a U-shaped or S-shaped bend in a drainpipe that prevents the return flow of gases by holding a quantity of water as a barrier. **4.** A device that hurls clay pigeons or discs into the air to be shot at. **5.** In golf, a **bunker** *(see).* **6.** A light two-wheeled vehicle with springs. **7.** A trap door. **8.** Any of the stall-like compartments in which a greyhound is held and which springs open to release the dog at the start of a race. **9.** *Usually plural. Informal.* In jazz, percussion instruments, such as snare drums, cymbals, or bells. **10.** *Slang.* The mouth.
~*v.* **trapped, trapping, traps.** *—tr.* **1.** To catch in or as if in a trap; ensnare. **2.** To seal off (gases) by a trap. **3.** To furnish or provide with a trap or traps. *—intr.* **1.** To set traps for game. **2.** To trap fur-bearing animals, especially as an occupation. [Middle English *trappe,* Old English *træppe*†.]

trap² *n. Usually plural. Obsolete.* Trappings; a caparison.
~*tr.v.* **trapped, trapping, traps.** To furnish with trappings. Often used with *out.* [Middle English *trappe,* probably from Old French *drap,* cloth, from Late Latin *drappus,* from Celtic.]

trap³ *n. Geology.* **1.** A fine-grained igneous rock with a characteristically steplike configuration. **2.** A structure in which oil or gas may collect. Also called "traprock". [Swedish *trapp,* from *trappa,* step, stair, from Middle Low German *trappe.*] **—trap·pe·an** (tráppi-ən), **trap·pous** (tráp-əss) *adj.*

trapan. Variant of **trepan** (to trick).

trap cut *n.* A method of cutting a gem so that it has a flat crown and an intricately shaped pavilion. [Probably from Dutch *trap,* stairs, flight of steps; akin to TRAP (steplike configuration).]

trap door *n.* **1.** A hinged or sliding door in a floor, roof, or ceiling. **2.** The opening covered by a trap door.

trap-door spider (tráp-dór || -dōr) *n.* Any of various spiders of the family Ctenizidae, that construct a silk-lined burrow concealed by a hinged lid.

tra·peze (trə-peéz) *n.* A short horizontal bar suspended from the ends of two parallel ropes, used for exercises or for acrobatic stunts. [French *trapèze,* from Late Latin *trapezium,* TRAPEZIUM.]

tra·pe·zi·form (trə-peézi-fawrm) *adj.* Formed in the shape of a trapezium. [TRAPEZI(UM) + -FORM.]

tra·pe·zi·um (trə-peézi-əm) *n., pl.* **-ums** or **-zia** (-ə). **1. a.** A quadrilateral having two parallel sides. **b.** *U.S.* A trapezoid. **2.** A bone in the wrist at the base of the thumb. [Late Latin, from Greek *trapezion,* small table, diminutive of *trapeza,* table, "four-footed" : *tra-,* four + *peza,* foot.]

tra·pe·zi·us (trə-peézi-əss) *n., pl.* **-uses.** Either of two large, flat, triangular muscles running from the base of the back of the head to the middle of the back and across to the shoulder blade. They support, and make it possible to raise, the head and shoulders. [New Latin *(musculus) trapezius,* "trapezium-shaped (muscle)".]

tra·pe·zo·he·dron (trə-peézō-heé-drən, tráppizō-, -hé-) *n., pl.* **-drons** or **-dra** (-drə). Any of several forms of crystal with trapeziums as faces. Also called "trisoctahedron". [TRAPEZ(IUM) + -HEDRON.]

trap·e·zoid (tráppi-zoyd) *n.* **1. a.** A quadrilateral having no parallel sides. **b.** *U.S.* A trapezium. **2.** A small bone in the wrist. [New Latin *trapezoides,* from Greek *trapezoeidēs,* trapezium-shaped : *trapeza,* table (see **trapezium**) + -OID.] **—trap·e·zoid, trap·e·zoi·dal** (-zóyd'l) *adj.*

trap·per (tráppər) *n.* One whose occupation is trapping animals for their furs.

trap·pings (tráppingz) *pl.n.* **1.** An ornamental covering or harness for a horse; a caparison. **2.** Articles of dress or adornment, especially those that are characteristic of or symbolise something, such as a particular position or office: *the trappings of a judge.* **3.** Objects, marks, or appearances that are characteristic of or symbolise something: *the trappings of power.*

Trap·pist (tráppist) *n.* A member of a branch of the Cistercian order of monks, known for austerity and absolute silence, established in 1664 in La Trappe, Normandy. **—Trap·pist** *adj.*

traprock *n.* A configuration in igneous rocks, **trap** *(see).*

trap·shoot·ing (tráp-shooting) *n.* The sport of shooting at clay pigeons or other objects hurled into the air from spring traps. **—trap·shoot·er** *n.*

tra·pun·to (trə-poontō) *n., pl.* **-tos.** Quilting having a raised effect made by outlining the design with running stitches and then filling it with padding such as cotton. [Italian, from the past participle of *trapungere,* to embroider : Latin *trans-,* through + *pungere,* to prick, pierce.]

trash (trash) *n.* **1. a.** Cheap or empty language, talk, or ideas. **b.** Worthless literary or artistic material. **2.** Something broken off or removed to be discarded; especially, plant trimmings. **3.** *Chiefly U.S.* Worthless or discarded material or objects; refuse. **4.** The bits of sugar cane that remain after the extraction of its juice. **5.** *Chiefly U.S.* A person or group of persons that is held in disdain.
~*tr.v.* **trashed, trashing, trashes. 1.** To cut off leaves or branches from; especially, to lop off the outer leaves from (growing sugar cane). **2.** *Slang.* **a.** To disprove or discredit (an argument). **b.** To beat (someone) up. **c.** *U.S.* To virtually destroy; reduce to trash. [16th century : origin obscure.] **—trash·i·ly** *adv.* **—trash·i·ness** *n.* **—trashy** *adj.*

trash can *n. U.S.* A **dustbin** *(see).*

trass (trass) *n.* A volcanic earth used in hydraulic cement. [Dutch *terras,* from French *terrasse,* pile of earth, from Old French *terrasse, terrace,* TERRACE.]

trat·to·ri·a (trát-ə-reé-ə; *Italian* -taw-; *also* tra-táwri-ə) *n.* An Italian restaurant. [Italian, from *trattore,* innkeeper, restaurateur, from French *traiteur,* from *traiter,* to entertain, TREAT.]

trau·ma (tráw-mə, trów-) *n., pl.* **-mas** or **-mata** (-tə). **1.** *Pathology.* A wound, especially one produced by sudden physical injury. **2.** *Psychiatry.* An emotional shock that creates substantial and lasting damage to the psychological development of the individual, generally leading to neurosis. [Greek, wound, hurt.]

trau·mat·ic (traw-máttik, trow-) *adj.* **1.** Of or causing a trauma: *a traumatic shock.* **2.** *Informal.* Awful; unpleasant. [Late Latin *traumăticus,* from Greek, from TRAUMA.] **—trau·mat·i·cal·ly** *adv.*

traumatise, trau·ma·tize (tráw-mə-tīz, trów-) *tr.v.* **-tised, -tising, -tises. 1.** To wound or injure. **2.** To cause (someone) to undergo a psychological trauma.

trau·ma·tism (tráw-mə-tiz'm, trów-) *n.* **1.** A trauma. **2.** Any condition arising from a trauma.

tra·vail (tráv-ayl || trə-váyl) *n.* **1.** *Literary.* **a.** Strenuous mental or physical exertion; labour; toil. **b.** Tribulation or agony; anguish. **2.** *Archaic.* The labour of childbirth.
~*intr.v.* **travailed, -vailing, -vails. 1.** *Literary.* To labour strenuously; toil. **2.** *Archaic.* To be in the labour of childbirth. [Middle English, from Old French, from *travailler,* to work hard, from Vulgar Latin *tripāliāre* (unattested), to torture, from *tripālium* (unattested), torture instrument (made of three stakes), from Latin *tripālis,* having three stakes : *tri-,* three + *pālus,* stake.]

trave (trayv) *n.* **1.** A wooden frame for confining a lively horse so that it can be shod. **2.** *Architecture.* **a.** A crossbeam. **b.** A section, as of a ceiling, formed by crossbeams. [Middle English, from Old French, stake, beam, from Latin *trabs.*]

trav·el (trávv'l) *v.* **-elled, -elling** or *U.S.* **-eled, -eling** or *U.S.* **-eling, -els.** *—intr.* **1.** To go from one place to another; journey: *travelled all over Europe.* **2.** To be transmitted; move, as sound or light moves. **3.** To move, advance, or proceed, especially in a specified way: *travelling faster than the speed of sound.* **4. a.** To be a travelling salesman: *He travels for a record company.* **b.** To be a travelling salesman selling specified merchandise. Used with *in*: *travels in cosmetics.* **5.** To admit of being transported without damage or loss of quality: *Some wines travel poorly.* **6.** *Informal.* To move swiftly. *—tr.* To pass or journey over or through; traverse.
~*n.* **1.** The act or process of travelling. **2.** The distance moved by a mechanical part. **3.** *Plural.* **a.** A series of journeys. **b.** *Chiefly U.S.* A written account of these. [Middle English *travailen,* to toil, make a (toilsome) journey, from Old French *travailler,* to TRAVAIL.]

travel agency *n.* A business that makes travel arrangements for customers, as by booking tickets for flights and other journeys,

trap-door spider *The burrow of the trap-door spider is concealed by a mud lid hinged with silk. The spider, which is found in tropical and subtropical regions around the world, lies in wait in the burrow, then flips open the door to pounce on passing prey.*

booking accommodation, arranging tours, or the like. **—travel agent** n.

trav·e·la·tor (trávv'l-aytər) n. A **moving pavement** (see).

trav·elled (trávv'ld) adj. **1.** Having travelled widely; experienced in travel. **2.** Much frequented by travellers. Usually used in combination: *a well-travelled route*.

trav·ell·er (tráv-lər, -'l-ər) n. **1. a.** A person who is travelling. **b.** One who has travelled or who customarily travels. **c.** *Chiefly British*. A gypsy. **2.** *Chiefly British*. A travelling salesman. **3.** *Nautical*. A metal ring that moves freely back and forth on a rope, rod, or spar. **b.** The rope, rod, or spar on which such a ring moves. **4.** A part of a mechanism that can move only in a fixed direction.

traveller's cheque n. A cheque purchasable, especially from a bank, in various denominations, which can be exchanged for money in banks or hotels of many countries, but only with the holder's own endorsement against his original signature.

trav·el·ler's-joy (tráv-lərz-jóy, -'l-ərz-) n. Any of several climbing vines of the genus *Clematis*; especially, *C. vitalba*, of the Old World, having clusters of greenish flowers and pale grey feathery fruit in dense clusters. Also called "old man's beard".

trav·el·ling salesman (tráv'ling) n. A salesman who solicits business orders or sells merchandise through personal dealings with potential customers met by travelling round a given territory. Also *British* "commercial traveller", *chiefly British* "traveller".

travelling wave n. A wave in which the peaks and troughs move continuously away from the source.

trav·e·logue, *U.S.* **trav·e·log** (trávv'l-og, *rarely* -ōg ‖ -awg) n. **1.** A lecture illustrated by travel slides or films. **2.** A narrated film about travels. [TRAVEL + -LOGUE.]

trav·el·sick·ness (trávv'l-sik-nəss, -niss) n. Nausea resulting from travelling in a moving vehicle. Also called "motion sickness". **—trav·el·sick** adj.

trav·erse (trávvərss, trávverss, trə-vérss) v. **-ersed, -ersing, -erses.**
—*tr.* **1.** To travel across, over, or through. **2.** To move to and fro over; cross and recross. **3. a.** To go up or down (a slope) diagonally, as when climbing or skiing. **b.** To go across (a slope) rather than down, as when skiing. **4.** To move (a gun, for example) laterally; cause to swivel. **5.** To extend across; cross. **6.** To look over carefully; examine. **7.** To go counter to; thwart. **8.** *Law*. To deny formally (an allegation of fact by the opposition) in a suit. **9.** *Nautical*. To brace (a yard) fore and aft. —*intr.* **1.** To move or go along, across, or back and forth. **2.** To turn laterally; swivel. **3.** To traverse a slope. **4.** In fencing, to slide one's blade down towards the hilt of an opponent's weapon, while exerting pressure against his blade.
~*n.* **1. a.** The act of traversing; a passing across, over, or through. **b.** A route or path across a slope or precipice, for example. **2.** Something across something else, especially: **a.** An intersecting line, a **transversal** (see). **b.** *Architecture*. A structural crosspiece; a transom. **c.** *Architecture*. A gallery, deck, or loft crossing from one side of a building, such as a church, to the other. **d.** A railing, curtain, screen, or other barrier. **e.** A defensive barrier across a rampart or trench, such as a bank of earth thrown up for protection from enfilade fire. **3.** Something that obstructs and thwarts; a hindrance; an obstacle. **4. a.** *Nautical*. The zigzag route of a vessel forced by contrary winds to sail on different courses. **b.** A diagonal or horizontal course made by a skier across a slope. **5.** The horizontal swivel of a mounted gun. **6. a.** A lateral movement, as of a lathe tool across a piece of work. **b.** A part of a mechanism that moves in this manner. **7.** In surveying, a line established by sighting in the measurement of a tract of land. **8.** *Law*. The formal denial of an allegation of fact in a suit.
~*adj.* Lying or extending across; transverse. [Middle English *traversen*, from Old French *traverser*, from Late Latin *trā(ns)versāre*, from Latin *transversus*, TRANSVERSE.] **—trav·ers·a·ble** adj. **—tra·vers·al** (trə-vérss'l) n. **—trav·ers·er** n.

trav·er·tine (trávvər-tin, -teen) n. **1.** A light-coloured, porous calcite, $CaCO_3$, deposited from solution in ground or surface waters. **2.** A compact type of calcium carbonate, used as a facing material in construction. [Italian *travertino*, earlier *tivertino*, from Latin *(lapis) Tīburtīnus*, "(stone) of Tibur".]

trav·es·ty (tráv-ə-sti, -i-) n., pl. **-ties. 1.** An exaggerated or grotesque imitation intended to ridicule; especially, a farcical and grotesque parody of a serious literary work or theme. **2.** Broadly, any event or situation that has become or been turned into a parody of itself: *The debate became a travesty.* **—See Synonyms at caricature.**
~*tr.v.* **travestied, -tying, -ties.** To make a travesty of; ridicule. [French *travesti*, past participle of *travestir*, to ridicule, from Italian *travestire*, "to disguise" : *tra-*, across, from Latin *trāns-*, indicates change + *vestire*, to dress, from Latin *vestīre*, from *vestis*, garment.]

tra·vois (trə-vóy, trávvoy) n., pl. **travois** (-z) or **travoises** (-ziz) or **tra·voise** (-z). A primitive sledge formerly used by the Plains Indians of North America, consisting of a platform or netting supported by two long trailing poles, the forward ends of which are fastened to a dog or horse. [Canadian French, variant of French *travail*, perhaps same as TRAVAIL.]

trawl (trawl) n. **1.** A large, tapered fishing net of flattened conical shape, towed along the sea bottom. Also called "trawl net". **2.** *U.S.* A multiple fishing line, a **setline** (see). Also called "trawl line".
~*v.* **trawled, trawling, trawls.** —*tr.* To catch (fish) by means of a trawl. —*intr.* **1.** To fish with a trawl net or line. **2.** To troll. [Perhaps from Dutch *tragel*, dragnet, from Middle Dutch *traghel*, from Latin *trāgula*, from *trahere*, to pull, draw.]

trawl·er (tráwlər) n. **1.** A vessel used for trawling. **2.** One who trawls.

tray (tray) n. **1.** A flat, shallow receptacle of wood, metal, or the like, with a raised edge or rim, used for carrying, holding, or displaying articles. **2.** A tray with food on it: *brought her up a tray*. **3.** A shallow, open, boxlike receptacle, often made of wire, and used to hold papers, letters, or the like. [Middle English *tray*, Old English *trīg*, *trēg*, from Germanic *traujam* (unattested); akin to TREE.]

treach·er·ous (tréchərəss) adj. **1.** Betraying a trust; traitorous; disloyal. **2. a.** Not to be relied upon; not dependable. **b.** Not to be trusted; deceptive; dangerous: *treacherous waters*. **—treach·er·ous·ly** adv. **—treach·er·ous·ness** n.

treach·er·y (tréchəri) n., pl. **-ies. 1.** Wilful betrayal of fidelity, confidence, or trust; perfidy; treason. **2.** An act or instance of this. [Middle English *trecherie*, *tricherie*, from Old French, from *trichier*, to TRICK.]

trea·cle (treek'l) n. **1.** *British*. **a. Golden syrup** (see). **b.** A type of thick dark syrup obtained in refining sugar. Also *U.S.* **molasses**. **2.** A medicinal compound formerly used as an antidote for poison. **3.** Cloying speech or sentiment. [Middle English *triacle*, antidote for poison, from Old French, from Latin *thēriaca*, from Greek *(antidotos) thēriakē*, from *thērion*, poisonous beast, diminutive of *thēr*, beast.] **—trea·cly** (treekli) adj.

tread (tred) v. **trod** (trod), or archaic **trode** (trōd), **trodden** (trŏd'n) or **trod, treading, treads.** —*tr.* **1.** To walk on, over, or along. **2.** To press down with the foot; trample: *treading grapes*. **3.** To make (a path, for example) by walking or trampling. **4.** To perform or execute by walking or dancing. Used chiefly in the phrase *tread a measure*. **5.** To deposit by walking or trampling: *Don't tread dirt onto my clean floor.* **6.** To copulate with. Used of male birds. —*intr.* **1.** To go on foot; walk; step. **2. a.** To tread so as to press, crush, or injure someone or something. Used with *on* or *upon*. **b.** To subdue

---

tree

THE LONG GROWING LIFE OF TREES
Annual renewal of tissue keeps trees functioning efficiently

Some trees grow for hundreds of years; new tissues formed each year by the cambium layers and by the tips of shoots and roots regularly renew a tree's ability to function efficiently.

Two layers of cambium tissue lying beneath the bark are responsible for the increase in girth of a tree's branches, trunk, and roots. The main cambium produces food-carrying cells and the outer cambium produces corky bark.

The main cambium manufactures microscopic cells that give rigid support, carry watery sap from the roots to the crown, store food, and carry food in solution both up and down the tree. Every spring this layer manufactures cells with thin walls and large spaces for carrying all the water and nutrients needed for growth; every

summer it produces denser wood composed of cells with thicker walls.

The spring and summer cells together form one annual growth ring. Often this is so clearly visible that the number of growth rings in a log can give a reliable indication of its age.

Below ground, the cambium cells in the roots increase the diameter of the roots each year and so help to anchor the tree in the ground. In the tree's crown, the cambium cells in the shoots increase the diameter of the twigs and branches.

Different cells are responsible for the onward extension of shoots and roots. The cells located in the tip of each twig and root divide frequently and enable the tree to grow upwards, outwards, and downwards.

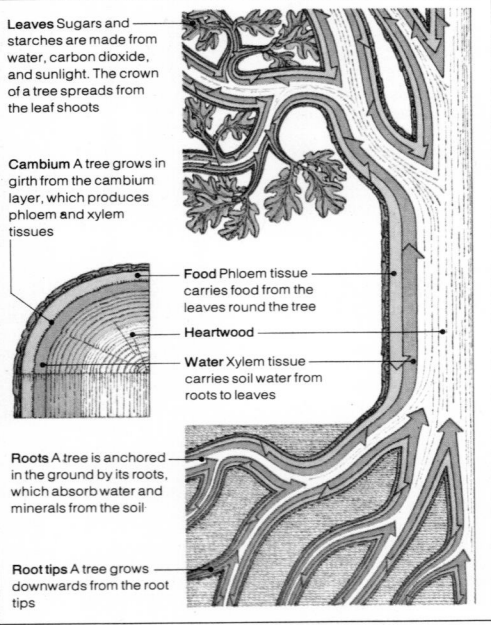

Leaves Sugars and starches are made from water, carbon dioxide, and sunlight. The crown of a tree spreads from the leaf shoots

Cambium A tree grows in girth from the cambium layer, which produces phloem and xylem tissues

Food Phloem tissue carries food from the leaves round the tree

Heartwood

Water Xylem tissue carries soil water from roots to leaves

Roots A tree is anchored in the ground by its roots, which absorb water and minerals from the soil

Root tips A tree grows downwards from the root tips

TRANSPORTING FOOD *A tree's food-carrying system lies beneath the bark. The main cambium tissue annually forms phloem cells on its outer side; these carry sugars made by the leaves down to the roots. On the inner side, the cambium produces xylem cells, which carry water and nutrients from roots to leaves. As the xylem, or wood, cells die, they may fill with resins and form the strong heartwood.*

or hurt. Used with *on* or *upon* : *trod on her feelings.* **—tread lightly.** To act or proceed tactfully and sensitively.

~n. **1. a.** The act, manner, or sound of treading. **b.** An instance of treading; a step. **2.** The horizontal part of a step in a staircase. Also called "treadboard". **3.** The part of a wheel that makes contact with the ground or rails. **4. a.** The grooved face of a motor-vehicle tyre. **b.** The thickness of the grooves and ridges on a tyre: *not much tread left.* **5.** The part of a sole of a shoe that touches the ground. [Tread, trod (or trode), trodden; Middle English *treden, trode, troden,* Old English *tredan, trœd* (plural *trǣdon*), *treden.*] **—tread·er** *n.*

tread·le (trédd'l) *n.* A pedal or lever operated by the foot for circular drive, as in a potter's wheel or sewing machine.

~intr.v. **treadled, -ling, -les.** To work a treadle. [Middle English *tredel,* Old English *tredel,* step of a stair, from *tredan,* TREAD.] **—tread·ler** (tréddlər) *n.*

tread·mill (tréd-mil) *n.* **1.** A mechanism used to produce rotary motion, operated by one or more persons or animals walking on moving steps inside a wheel, or treading an endless sloping belt, especially one used formerly as a prisoner's punishment. **2.** Any monotonous task or routine.

treas. treasurer; treasury.

trea·son (trééz'n) *n.* **1.** Violation of allegiance towards one's sovereign or country; especially, the betrayal of one's own country by waging war against it or by consciously and purposely acting to aid its enemies. **2.** Any betrayal of trust or confidence; treachery. [Middle English *treison,* from Anglo-French *tre(i)soun,* from Medieval Latin *trāditiō* (stem *trāditiōn-),* from Latin, a handing over. See **tradition.**] **—trea·son·ous** *adj.* **—trea·son·ous·ly** *adv.*

trea·son·a·ble (trééz'n-əb'l) *adj.* Pertaining to or involving treason. **—trea·son·a·ble·ness** *n.* **—trea·son·a·bly** *adv.*

treas·ure (trézhər) *n.* **1.** Accumulated, stored, or cached wealth in the form of valuables, such as money or jewels. **2.** A person or thing considered especially precious or valuable.

~tr.v. **treasured, -uring, -ures. 1.** To accumulate and save for future use; hoard. **2.** To value or prize highly: *treasured fond memories.* **—See Synonyms at appreciate.** [Middle English *tresor,* from Old French, from Vulgar Latin *tresaurus* (unattested), variant of Latin *thēsaurus,* from Greek *thēsauros*†.] **—treas·ure·a·ble** *adj.*

treasure house *n.* Any place that contains treasure or something considered to be treasure: *a treasure house of humour.*

treasure hunt *n.* A game in which players seek to be the first to find a hidden prize using a series of clues.

treas·ur·er (trézhərər) *n. Abbr.* **tr., treas. 1.** A person having charge of funds or revenues for a corporation, club, society, or the like. **2.** A financial officer or recorder of public funds for a government. [Middle English *tresourer,* from Old French *tresorier,* from *tresor,* TREASURE.] **—treas·ur·er·ship** *n.*

treasure trove (trōv) *n.* **1.** *Law.* Any treasure found hidden or buried and whose owner is unknown. In English law, treasure trove is money, bullion, or objects made of precious metal, and it belongs to the Crown. **2.** Any discovery of great value. [Anglo-French *tresor trove,* "discovered treasure" : Old French *tresor,* TREASURE + *trove,* past participle of *trover,* to find, compose (see **trouvère**).]

treas·ur·y (trézhəri) *n., pl.* **-ies.** *Abbr.* **treas. 1.** A place where treasure is kept or stored. **2.** A place where private or public funds are received, kept, managed, and disbursed. **3.** Such funds or revenues. **4. a.** Any collection of valuables or things considered to be valuable. **b.** A source of something valuable, such as wisdom. **5.** *Capital* **T.** The executive department of a government in charge of the collection, management, and expenditure of the public revenue. [Middle English *tresorie,* from Old French, from *tresor,* TREASURE.]

treasury bill *n.* In Britain, a bill similar to a bill of exchange, issued by the Bank of England, that bears no interest (but is purchased at a discount) and promises to pay the bearer a sum of money on a certain date, usually soon after purchase.

treasury note *n.* **1.** In Britain, a note that was issued as money during World War I. **2.** A note or bill issued by the U.S. Treasury as legal tender for all debts.

treat (treet) *v.* **treated, treating, treats.** *—tr.* **1.** To act or behave in a specified manner towards: *treated her horse well.* **2.** To regard or consider in a certain way. Usually used with *as: treated the affair as a joke.* **3. a.** To consider and deal with in a specified manner: *You haven't treated his case fairly.* **b.** To deal with in writing or speech, usually in a specified manner or style: *The book treats certain philosophical questions in detail.* **4.** To deal with or represent in a specified manner or style, as in art or literature: *treat a subject poetically.* **5. a.** To entertain or provide with a gift at one's own expense: *treated her to dinner and dancing.* **b.** To give (someone or oneself) something as a treat: *treated myself to a bottle of wine.* **6.** To subject to some process, action, or change, especially: **a.** To give medical aid to. **b.** To subject to a chemical or physical process or application. *—intr.* **1.** To deal with a subject or topic in writing, speaking, or thought. Usually used with *of: The essay treats of courtly love.* **2.** To pay for another's entertainment, food, or the like. **3.** *Rare.* To negotiate; bargain. Used with *with.*

~n. **1.** Something, such as food or entertainment, paid for by someone other than for whom the treat is primarily intended. **2.** The act of treating. **3.** Anything considered to be a special delight or pleasure. [Middle English *treten,* from Old French *traitier,* from Latin *tractāre,* to drag, handle, treat, frequentative of *trahere* (past participle *tractus*), to draw, drag.] **—treat·a·ble** *adj.* **—treat·er** *n.*

trea·tise (treé-tiz, -tiss) *n.* A formal account in writing treating systematically of some subject. [Middle English *tretis,* from Norman French, from Old French *traitier,* TREAT.]

treat·ment (treét-mənt) *n.* **1.** The act or manner of treating something, such as a person or a literary subject: *sensitive treatment of characters.* **2. a.** The application of remedies with the object of effecting a cure; therapy. **b.** The substance or remedy applied. **3.** A more detailed and full version of a film or television script. **—the (full) treatment. 1.** *Informal.* All that goes with or is usual to a particular person, thing, or event; especially, an elaborate way of treating something: *I want a haircut, shave, and the full treatment.* **2.** *Slang.* Aggressive, rough, or bad handling; brutal treatment: *gave the opposing team the treatment.*

trea·ty (treéti) *n., pl.* **-ties. 1. a.** A formal agreement between two or more states containing terms of trade, peace, alliance, or the like; a pact. **b.** A document embodying this. **2.** Any contract or agreement; especially, one between two persons concerning the buying of property. **3.** Negotiation for the purpose of reaching an agreement. [Middle English *tretee,* from Old French *traite,* from Medieval Latin *tractātus,* from Latin, past participle of *tractāre,* TREAT.]

treaty port *n.* A port kept open for trade according to the terms of a treaty; especially, formerly in the Far East, any of several such ports open to foreign commerce.

treb·le (trébb'l) *adj.* **1.** Triple; threefold. **2.** *Music.* Of, having, or performing the highest part, voice, or range. **3.** High-pitched; shrill.

~n. **1.** *Music.* **a.** The highest part, voice, instrument, or range; soprano. **b.** A player who performs the highest instrumental part. **c.** A singer who performs the highest voice part, especially a boy singer as opposed to a female soprano. **2.** A high, shrill sound or voice. **3.** A number or amount three times as much or as many as another. **4. a.** In darts, the narrow ring between the double and the bull's eye. **b.** A score obtained by hitting this ring.

~v. **trebled, -ling, -les.** *—tr.* To make triple. *—intr.* To become triple. [Middle English, from Old French, from Latin *triplus,* TRIPLE.] **—treb·le·ness** *n.* **—treb·ly** (trébbli) *adv.*

treble chance *n.* In Britain, a method of betting on the football pools in which points are awarded to correct guesses as to which matches will result in draws, home wins, or away wins. A guess that correctly predicts a draw is awarded more points than one guessing either of the other two types of result.

treble clef *n. Music.* A symbol, 𝄞, centred on the second line of a staff (the *treble staff*) to indicate the position of G above middle C. Also called "G clef".

treb·u·chet (trébbew-shet, -chét, -shét) *n.* Also **treb·uc·ket** (-ket, -két). A medieval catapult for hurling heavy stones. [Middle English, from Old French, pitfall, from *trebucher,* to stumble.]

tre·cen·to (tray-chéntō) *n.* The 14th century, with reference especially to Italian art and literature. [Italian, "three hundred", short for *(mil) trecento,* (one thousand) three hundred : *tre,* three, from Latin *trēs* + *cento,* hundred, from Latin *centum.*]

tree (tree) *n.* **1.** A usually tall woody plant, distinguished from a shrub by having comparatively greater height and, characteristically, a single trunk with branches arising at an appreciable distance from the ground, rather than several stems. **2.** Broadly, a plant or shrub resembling a tree but without a woody trunk, such as a palm. **3.** A wooden beam, post, stake, or bar used as a part of a framework or structure. **4.** *Archaic.* A gallows; a gibbet. **5.** *Often capital* **T.** *Archaic & Poetic.* The cross on which Jesus was crucified. **6.** A **saddletree** *(see).* **7.** Something suggestive of a tree: *a clothes tree.* **8.** A diagram showing a family lineage; a family tree. **9.** See **Christmas tree. —bark up the wrong tree.** *Informal.* To misdirect one's energies wastefully. **—grow on trees.** To be in abundant, free supply: *Money doesn't grow on trees.* **—up a tree.** *Informal.* In a situation of hopeless confusion or embarrassment.

~tr.v. **treed, treeing, trees. 1.** To force to climb a tree in evasion of pursuit. **2.** *Informal.* To force into a difficult position; corner. **3.** To stretch (shoes) on a shoetree. [Middle English *tree,* Old English *treo(w).*]

tree·creep·er (treé-kreepər) *n.* A small, brown-speckled bird, *Certhia familiaris,* having a downward-curved beak and habitually found creeping around tree trunks in search of food.

tree diagram *n.* A branching diagram especially suited to represent the analysis of a structure, such as a sentence, by subdividing it into component parts.

tree fern *n.* Any of various treelike tropical ferns, especially of the family Cyatheaceae, having a woody, trunklike stem and a terminal crown of large, divided fronds.

tree frog *n.* Any of various small, arboreal frogs of the family Polypedatidae, having long toes terminating in adhesive discs. Also called "tree toad".

tree heath *n.* A shrub or tree, the **briar** *(see).*

tree-hop·per (treé-hoppər) *n.* Any insect of the family Membracidae, that damages trees by sucking sap.

tree line *n.* The **timberline** *(see).*

tree mallow *n.* A tall biennial mallow plant, *Lavatera arborea,* of coastal regions and having purple-veined, dark pink flowers.

treen (treen) *pl.n.* Wooden dishes and utensils.

~adj. Made of wood: *treen ware.*

tree·nail (treé-nayl, trénn'l) *n.* Also **tre·nail** (trénn'l), **trun·nel** (trúnn'l). A wooden peg which swells when wet, used to fasten timbers, especially in shipbuilding.

tree of heaven *n.* A tree, the **ailanthus** *(see).*

tree of knowledge *n.* The tree in the Garden of Eden whose forbidden fruit was eaten by Adam and Eve, causing loss of innocence

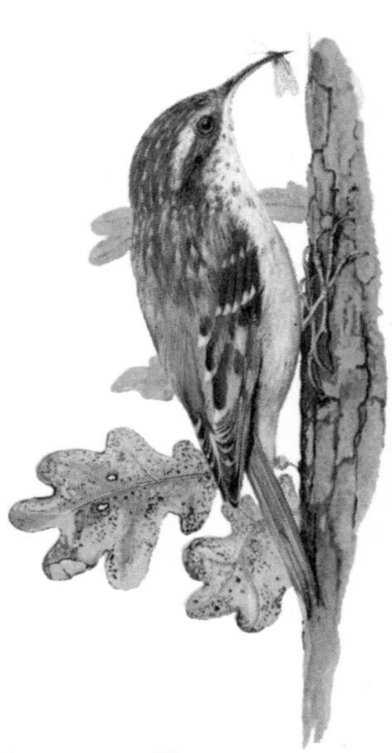

treecreeper *The treecreeper gets its name from its habit of walking on the trunks of trees in search of beetles, earwigs, and woodlice beneath the bark. It lives chiefly in coniferous forests and is found in North America, Europe, and Asia.*

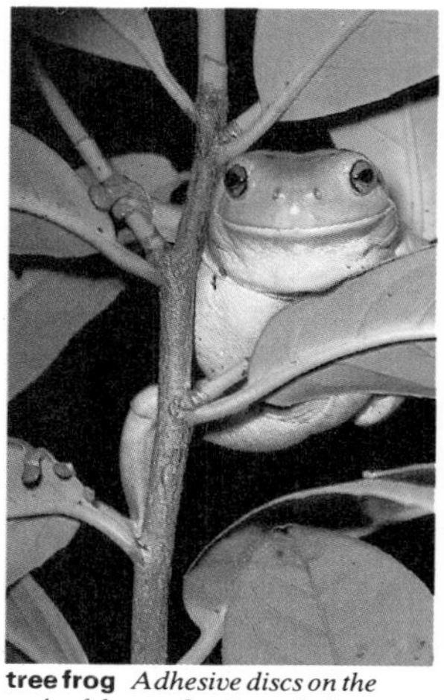

tree frog *Adhesive discs on the ends of the tree frog's toes help it to grip branches as it climbs through trees hunting for the insects on which it chiefly feeds. This is White's tree frog,* Litoria caerulea, *a species native to the tropical forests of New Guinea and parts of Australia.*

(the Fall). Genesis 2:9, 17; 3:6. Also called "tree of knowledge of good and evil".

tree of life *n.* 1. A tree, the **arborvitae** *(see).* 2. A tree in the Garden of Eden whose fruit, if eaten, gave man immortality. Genesis 3:22. 3. The tree in the new Jerusalem whose leaves were for the healing of the nations. Revelation 22:2.

tree-run·ner (trée-runnər) *n.* Any of various Australian birds. See **sittella.**

tree-shrew (trée-shrōō ‖ -shrew) *n.* Any squirrel-like, primitive primate of the family Tupaiidae, which retain many characteristics typical of the insectivores.

tree sparrow *n.* A woodland bird, *Passer montanus,* similar to the house sparrow but having a chestnut crown and white head markings.

tree surgery *n.* The treatment of diseased or damaged trees by filling cavities, pruning, and bracing branches. —**tree surgeon** *n.*

tree toad *n.* A tree frog *(see).*

tref (trayf) *adj.* Unclean and unfit for consumption according to Jewish dietary law, as pork, lobster, or horse meat are. Compare **kosher.** [Yiddish *treyf,* from Hebrew *terēphāh,* "torn", flesh of an animal torn by wild beasts, from *tāraf,* to tear.]

tre·foil (tréf-oyl, *rarely* trée-, tri-fóyl) *n.* 1. Any of various plants of the genera *Trifolium* and *Lotus,* having compound leaves with three leaflets. 2. Any ornament, symbol, or architectural form having the appearance of a trifoliate leaf. See **bird's-foot trefoil.** [Middle English, from Anglo-French *trifoil,* from Latin *trifolium,* three-leaved grass : *tri-,* three + *folium,* leaf.] —**tre·foiled** *adj.*

tre·ha·la (tri-háálə) *n.* A sugar-like, edible substance obtained from the pupal case of an Old World beetle, *Larinus maculatus.* [New Latin, from Turkish *tīgāla,* from Persian *tīghāl†.]*

tre·ha·lose (tri-háal-ōz, -ōss) *n.* A sweet-tasting, crystalline disaccharide, $C_{12}H_{22}O_{11}\cdot2H_2O$, found in trehala and in many fungi that store it instead of starch. [TREHAL(A) + -OSE.]

treil·lage (tráylij, tray-yáazh) *n.* Latticework; especially, a trellis for vines. [French, from Old French, from *treille,* arbour, from Latin *trichila†,* bower, arbour.]

trek (trek) *intr.v.* **trekked, trekking, treks.** 1. To make a slow or arduous journey. 2. Especially in South Africa: **a.** To draw or pull a wagon. Used of an ox. **b.** To travel by ox wagon. —*n.* 1. A journey or a part of a journey, especially when slow or difficult. 2. A migration; especially, one involving a slow journey with wagons, such as the migration of the Boers from 1835 to 1837. [Afrikaans, from Middle Dutch *trekken,* to pull, draw, travel, akin to Old High German *trechan†.]* —**trek·ker** *n.*

trel·lis (trélliss) *n.* 1. A structure of open latticework; especially, one used for supporting vines and other creeping plants. 2. An arbour or arch made with such a structure. —*tr.v.* **trellised, -lising, -lises.** 1. To provide with a trellis; especially, to support (a creeping plant) on a trellis. 2. To make into or in the form of a trellis. [Middle English *trelis,* from Old French *treliz,* a coarse fabric, later (influenced by *treillage,* TREILLAGE) trellis, from Vulgar Latin *trilícius* (unattested), from Latin *trilīx,* triple-twilled : *tri-,* three + *līcium†,* thread.]

trel·lis·work (trélliss-wurk) *n.* Latticework.

trem·a·tode (trémmə-tōd) *n.* Any of numerous parasitic flatworms of the class Trematoda, having a thick outer cuticle, and one or more suckers for attaching to host tissue. Also called "fluke". —*adj.* Of or belonging to the Trematoda. [New Latin *Trematoda,* from Greek *trēmatodēs,* having a vent to the intestinal canal (taken to mean "having holes", perhaps from the cavity of the suckers) : *trēma,* perforation + -ODE (like).]

trem·ble (trémb'l) *intr.v.* **-bled, -bling, -bles.** 1. To shake involuntarily, as from fear, cold, or sickness; quake or shiver; shake. 2. To feel or express fear or anxiety: *I tremble at the thought.* 3. To vibrate; quiver: *leaves trembling in the wind.* —See Synonyms at **shake.** —*n.* 1. The act or state of trembling. 2. *Sometimes plural.* A convulsive fit of trembling, especially as a result of a disease. [Middle English *trem(b)len,* from Old French *trembler,* from Vulgar Latin *tremulāre* (unattested), from Latin *tremulus,* TREMULOUS.] —**trem·bler** *n.* —**trem·bling·ly** *adv.* —**trem·bly** *adj.*

trem·bles (trémb'lz) *n.* *Usually used with a singular verb.* In veterinary medicine, **louping ill** *(see).*

trembling disease *n.* A disease, **kuru** *(see).*

tre·men·dous (tri-mén-dəss, trə- ‖ *chiefly Irish English* -jəss) *adj.* 1. Capable of making one tremble; terrible: *the tremendous tragedy of war.* 2. **a.** Extremely large in amount, extent, or degree; enormous: *a tremendous task.* **b.** *Informal.* Marvellous; wonderful; excellent: *We had a tremendous time.* —See Synonyms at **enormous.** [Latin *tremendus,* gerundive of *tremere,* to tremble.] —**tre·men·dous·ly** *adv.* —**tre·men·dous·ness** *n.*

trem·o·lite (trémmə-līt) *n.* A white to dark-grey calcium magnesium amphibole, $Ca_2Mg_5Si_8O_{22}(OH)_2$, usually occurring in aggregates, used as a substitute for asbestos. [French *trémolite,* first found in *Tremola,* valley in southern Switzerland.]

trem·o·lo (trémmə-lō) *n., pl.* **-los.** *Music.* 1. **a.** A tremulous effect produced by the rapid repetition of a single note, especially when playing a bowed instrument. **b.** A similar effect produced by the rapid alternation of two notes, usually a third or greater interval apart. Compare **trill.** 2. A device on an organ for producing this effect. Also called "tremolant", "tremulant". 3. A vibrato in singing, used for emotional effect or resulting from poor vocal control. Compare **vibrato.** [Italian, "tremulous".]

trem·or (trémmər; *in sense 2 also* tréemər) *n.* 1. A shaking or vibrating movement or short series of movements of the earth; a small earthquake: *an earth tremor.* 2. **a.** An involuntary trembling motion of the body, as from a state of nervous agitation or illness. **b.** A mental or emotional state characterised by such trembling. 3. A nervous quiver or shiver; a thrill. 4. Any trembling, shaking, or vibrating movement: *a tremor of aspen leaves.* 5. A tremulous sound; a quaver. [Middle English *tremour,* from Old French, from Latin *tremor,* from *tremere,* to tremble.]

trem·u·lous (trémmew-ləss) *adj.* Also **trem·u·lant** (-lənt). 1. **a.** Vibrating or quivering; trembling. **b.** Produced by or suggestive of someone tremulous: *tremulous handwriting.* 2. Timid; fearful; timorous. [Latin *tremulus,* from *tremere,* to tremble.] —**trem·u·lous·ly** *adv.* —**trem·u·lous·ness** *n.*

trenail. Variant of **treenail.**

trench (trench) *n.* 1. A deep furrow. 2. A ditch. 3. **a.** A long, narrow ditch embanked with its own soil and used for concealment and protection in warfare. **b.** *Plural.* A system of such ditches, used especially as a defensive position. 4. A long, deep, narrow depression in the sea bed. —*v.* **trenched, trenching, trenches.** —*tr.* 1. To cut or dig a trench or trenches in. 2. To fortify with a trench or trenches. 3. To carve or make a cut in. —*intr.* 1. To dig a trench or ditch. 2. To verge or encroach. Used with *on* or *upon.* [Middle English *trenche,* long narrow ditch, part cut through, from Old French, from *trenchier,* to cut, dig, probably from Vulgar Latin *trincāre* (unattested), from Latin *truncāre,* to mutilate, from *truncus,* torso.]

trench·ant (trénchənt) *adj.* 1. Keen; incisive; penetrating: *a trenchant comment.* 2. Forceful; effective; vigorous: *a trenchant argument.* 3. Distinct; sharply defined; clear-cut. 4. *Archaic & Poetic.* Sharp-edged. Said of a sword. —See Synonyms at **incisive.** [Middle English, cutting, from Old French, present participle of *trenchier,* to cut. See **trench.**] —**trench·an·cy** *n.* —**trench·ant·ly** *adv.*

trench coat *n.* A loose-fitting, belted, military style raincoat with pockets and straps on the shoulders.

trench·er¹ (trénchər) *n.* 1. A wooden board or plate, used especially in former times, for cutting or serving food on. 2. A stiff academic cap, a **mortarboard** *(see).* Also called "trencher cap". [Middle English *trenchour,* cutting board, from Anglo-French, from Old French *trenchier,* to cut. See **trench.**]

trencher² *n.* One that digs trenches.

trench·er·man (trénchər-mən) *n., pl.* **-men** (-mən). 1. A hearty, big eater. 2. *Archaic.* A sponger; a parasite; hanger-on.

trench fever *n.* An acute infectious relapsing fever caused by a microorganism, *Rickettsia quintana,* and transmitted by a louse, *Pediculus humanus.*

trench foot *n.* A form of frostbite of the feet, often afflicting soldiers obliged to stand in cold water for long periods of time.

trench knife *n.* A knife, used in warfare, having a long, double-edged blade.

trench mortar *n. Military.* A **mortar** *(see).*

trench mouth *n.* A form of gingivitis characterised by pain, foul odour, and the formation of a grey film over the diseased area. Also called "Vincent's disease".

trench warfare *n.* Warfare conducted between two armies who are facing each other in trenches.

trend (trend) *n.* 1. A direction of movement; a course; a flow: *a trend of thought.* 2. A general inclination or tendency: *a trend away from smoking.* 3. A fashion; a style. —Synonyms at **tendency.** —*intr.v.* **trended, trending, trends.** 1. To extend, bend, turn, or move in a specified direction: *The prevailing wind trends east-northeast.* 2. To have a general tendency; tend: *mood trending towards gloom.* [Middle English *trenden,* to turn, roll, revolve, Old English *trendan,* from Germanic *trand-* (unattested).]

trend-set·ter (trénd-sétting) *n.* One who initiates or popularises a fashion or trend. —**trend-set·ting** *adj.*

trend·y (tréndi) *adj.* **-ier, -iest.** *Informal.* 1. Of, in accordance with or consciously following the latest fad or fashion. Usually used derogatorily: *Fortunately, it is now considered trendy to be open-minded.* 2. Of or involving trendy people: *a trendy party.* —*n., pl.* **trendies.** *Informal.* A trendy person. Usually used derogatorily. —**trend·i·ly** *adv.* —**trend·i·ness** *n.*

Trent (trent). River of central England. Rising on Staffordshire's Biddulph Moor, it flows 270 kilometres (170 miles) to join the Ouse, forming the Humber estuary.

Trent, Council of *n.* A council of the Roman Catholic Church held periodically in Trento, Italy, between 1545 and 1563, which attempted to find a political solution to the Reformation, clarified Catholic doctrine, and initiated reform within the Church.

trente et qua·rante (trónt ay ka-rónt). **Rouge et noir** *(see).*

Tren·ti·no-Al·to A·di·ge (tren-téenō-ál-tō-áadi-jay). Formally **Ve·ne·zi·a Tri·den·ti·na** (ve-nétsi-ətree-den-téena) (1919–47) Autonomous Alpine region of northeast Italy. Agriculture, forestry, and tourism are the principal industries. Trento is the capital.

tre·pan¹ (tri-pán, trə-) *n.* 1. A rock-boring tool used in mining for sinking shafts. 2. An early type of trephine used in surgery. 3. A tool for making large circular holes or grooves. —*tr.v.* **trepanned, -panning, -pans.** 1. To bore (a shaft) with a trepan. 2. To cut a disc from with a trepan. 3. In surgery, to trephine. [Middle English *trepane,* from Medieval Latin *trepanum,* from Greek *trupanon,* auger, borer, from *trupan,* to pierce, from *trupē,* hole.] —**trep·a·na·tion** (tréppə-náysh'n) *n.*

trepan² *tr.v.* **-panned, -panning, -pans.** Also **tra•pan** (trə-). *Archaic.* To trap; ensnare; trick.
~*n. Archaic.* **1.** A prankster; a trickster. **2.** A trick; a stratagem. [17th century : originally *trapan,* probably thieves' slang for TRAP.]
tre•pang (tri-páng) *n.* **1.** Any of several sea cucumbers of the genus *Holothuria,* of the southern Pacific and Indian oceans. **2.** The eviscerated and dried or smoked body of any of these animals, used as food in China and the East Indies. Also called "bêche-de-mer". [Malay *tĕripang.*]
tre•phine (tri-féen, tre-, trə-, -fín) *n.* A surgical instrument having circular, sawlike edges, used to cut out discs of tissue, usually bone from the skull.
~*tr.v.* **trephined, -phining, -phines.** In surgery, to operate on with a trephine; trepan. [Earlier *trafine,* from Latin *trēs fīnes,* three ends; perhaps formed after TREPAN.] **—treph•i•na•tion** (tréffi-náysh'n) *n.*
trep•i•da•tion (trèppi-dáysh'n) *n.* **1.** A state of alarm or dread; nervous apprehension. **2.** Quivering or trembling, especially as a result of disease or illness. —See Synonyms at **fear.** [Latin *trepidātiō* (stem *trepidātiōn-*), from *trepidāre,* to hurry with alarm, tremble at, from *trepidus,* alarmed.]
trep•o•neme (tréppə-neem) *n.* Also **trep•o•ne•ma** (-néemə). Any of a group of spirochaetes of the genus *Treponema,* including those that cause syphilis and yaws. [New Latin *Treponema,* "twisted thread" (from its shape) : Greek *trepein,* to turn + *nēma,* thread.]
tres•pass (tréss-pəss || -paass, -pass) *intr.v.* **-passed, -passing, -passes. 1.** *Archaic.* To commit an offence or sin; err; transgress. **2.** To infringe upon the privacy, time, or attention of another. Used with *on* or *upon: "I must . . . not trespass too far on the patience of a good-natured critic"* (Henry Fielding). **3.** *Law.* To invade the property, rights, or person of another without his consent and with the intention, actual or implied, of committing violence; especially, to commit the tort of entering onto another's land without permission and causing damage.
~*n.* **1.** The transgression of a moral or social law, code, or duty. **2.** An intrusion or infringement upon another. **3.** *Law.* **a.** The tort of trespassing. **b.** A legal suit brought for this. —See Synonyms at **breach.** [Middle English *trespassen,* from Old French *trespasser,* from Medieval Latin *transpassāre* : Latin *trāns-,* across + Medieval Latin *passāre* to PASS.] **—tres•pass•er** *n.*
tress (tress) *n.* **1.** A lock, plait, or braid of hair, especially of a woman's hair. **2.** *Plural.* The long flowing hair or a woman. [Middle English *tresse,* from Old French *tresse, trece*†.]
tres•tle (tréss'l) *n.* **1.** A horizontal beam or bar held up by two pairs of divergent legs and used as a support. **2.** A framework consisting of vertical, slanted supports and horizontal crosspieces supporting a bridge. [Middle English *trestel,* from Old French, from Vulgar Latin *transtellum* (unattested), diminutive of Latin *transtrum,* crossbeam. See **transom.**]
trestle table *n.* A table consisting of a board or boards supported by a trestle.
tres•tle•tree (tréss'l-tree) *n. Nautical.* Either of two horizontal beams set into a masthead to support the crosstrees.
tres•tle•work (tréss'l-wurk) *n.* A trestle or system of trestles, such as that supporting a bridge.
tret (tret) *n.* Formerly, an allowance made to purchasers of goods sold by weight, so as to account for waste occurring during transport. [Middle English, from Anglo-French, Old French, a drawing, draught, variant of TRAIT; sense development obscure.]
Tretch•i•koff (tréchikof), **Vladimir** (1913–). Russian-born South African painter with immense popular appeal. He specialises in softly-lit, romanticised paintings of human figures and faces.
tre•val•ly (trə-vál-i) *n.* Any Australian food fish of the genus *Caranx.* [Probably alteration of CAVALLY.]
trews (trōōz || trewz) *pl.n.* Close-fitting, usually tartan trousers. [Irish *trius,* Gaelic *triubhas.*]
trey (tray) *n.* A card or dice, with three pips. [Middle English *treis, treye,* from Old French *treis,* from Latin *trēs,* three.]
tri– *comb. form.* Indicates: **1.** Three, as in number of parts or elements; for example, **trioxide. 2. a.** Appearance or occurrence in intervals of three; for example, **tricentennial. b.** Appearance or occurrence three times during; for example, **triweekly.** [Latin and Greek, three.]
tri•a•ble (trí-əb'l) *adj.* **1.** Capable of being tried. **2.** *Law.* Subject to judicial examination. **—tri•a•ble•ness** *n.*
tri•ac•id (trī-ássid, trí-) *adj.* Also **tri•a•cid•ic** (trí-a-síddik, -ə-). **1.** Able to react with three molecules of a monobasic acid. Said of a base. **2.** Containing three replaceable hydrogen atoms. Said of an acid or an acid salt.
~*n.* An acid containing three replaceable hydrogen atoms.
tri•ad (trí-əd, -ad) *n.* **1.** A group of three persons or things; a trio; a trinity. **2.** *Music.* A chord of three notes; especially, one built on a given root note plus a major or minor third and a perfect fifth. **3.** A literary form used in medieval Welsh and Irish literature, consisting of aphorisms grouped in threes. [Late Latin *trias* (stem *triad-*), the number three, from Greek.] **—tri•ad•ic** (trī-áddik) *adj.*
tri•age (trí-ij, trée-aazh || tree-áazh) *n.* **1.** The act of sorting according to quality. **2.** The act or process of assigning or allocating limited resources so as to achieve the greatest possible benefit; especially, the allocating of limited treatment facilities for battlefield casualties so as to maximise the number of survivors. [French, sorting : *trier,* pick out, sift (see **try**) + -AGE.]
tri•al (trí-əl) *n.* **1.** *Law.* The examination of evidence and applicable law by a competent tribunal, such as a judge and jury, to decide on a charge or claim: *a murder trial.* **2. a.** The act or process of testing, trying, or putting to the proof by actual or simulated use and experience: *a trial of one's faith.* **b.** A single complete instance of such testing, especially as part of a series of tests or experiments: *The new aircraft crashed during its third trial.* **3.** *Rare.* An effort or attempt: *He succeeded on his fourth trial.* **4.** A trouble, problem, or difficulty: *Life is full of little trials.* **5.** A test of patience or endurance: *He was a trial to his parents.* **6.** *Usually plural.* A series of competitions or tests designed to establish the individual ability and skill of the participants: *horse trials; held trials to pick the team.*
—on trial. 1. In the state or process of being tried, as before a court of law. **2.** In the state or process of being tested or tried out.
~*adj.* **1.** Of or pertaining to a trial or trials. **2.** Made, done, used, or performed during the course of a trial or trials: *gave his car a trial run.* [Anglo-French *trial, triel,* from Old French *trier,* TRY.]
trial and error *n.* **1.** An empirical method of attempting to solve a problem or achieve a certain result, consisting of repeating experiments until error is eliminated or the desired result is achieved. **2.** A method of learning or acquiring a skill by trying out various actions or processes until success is achieved. **—tri•al-and-er•ror** *adj.*
trial balance *n. Abbr.* **t.b.** In bookkeeping, a statement of all the open debit and credit items in a double-entry ledger made to make sure they are equal.
trial balloon *n. Chiefly U.S.* A preliminary statement or campaign tried out on a small scale to test public reaction. [Originally applied to a balloon for testing weather conditions.]
trial court *n. Law.* The court in which a case is first heard and where issues of fact are decided.
trial jury *n.* A **petit jury** *(see).*
trial marriage *n.* The living together of a couple for a trial period in order to ascertain their compatability with regard to marriage.
tri•am•cin•o•lone (trí-am-sínnə-lōn) *n.* A synthetic corticosteroid hormone applied as a cream or lotion to reduce inflammation. [*Tri-* + *amyl* + *cinene* (a terpine) + *prednisolone.*]
tri•an•gle (trí-ang-g'l) *n.* **1.** The plane figure formed by connecting three points not in a straight line by straight-line segments; a three-sided polygon. **2.** Something having the shape of this figure, such as the wooden frame in which snooker balls are placed at the start of a game. **3.** Any of various flat, three-sided drawing and drafting guides, used especially to draw straight lines at specific angles. **4.** *Music.* A percussion instrument consisting of a piece of metal in the shape of a triangle, open at one angle. **5.** See **eternal triangle.** [Middle English, from Old French, from Latin *triangulum,* from *triangulus,* three-angled : *tri-,* three + *angulus,* ANGLE.]
triangle of vectors *n. Mathematics.* A triangle formed by three lines representing the magnitudes and directions of three vectors, such as forces or velocities that are in equilibrium.
tri•an•gu•lar (trī-áng-gew-lər; *rarely* tri-) *adj.* **1.** Of, pertaining to, or shaped like a triangle; three-cornered; three-sided. **2.** Having a triangle for a base: *a triangular pyramid.* **3.** Pertaining to, involving, or consisting of three interrelated entities, such as three persons, objects, or ideas: *a triangular athletics match between Eire, Iran, and Spain.* **—tri•an•gu•lar•i•ty** (-lárrəti, trí-) *n.* **—tri•an•gu•lar•ly** *adv.*
tri•an•gu•late (trī-áng-gew-layt, *rarely* tri-) *tr.v.* **-lated, -lating, -lates. 1.** To divide into triangles. **2.** To survey by triangulation. **3.** To make triangular. **4.** To measure by using trigonometry.
~*adj.* (*also* -lət, -lit). **1.** Of or pertaining to triangles; triangular. **2.** Made up of or marked with triangles.
tri•an•gu•la•tion (trī-áng-gew-láysh'n, trí-, *rarely* tri-) *n.* **1.** A surveying technique in which a region is divided into a series of triangular elements based on a line of known length so that accurate measurements of distances and directions may be made by the application of trigonometry. **2.** The network of triangles so laid out. **3.** The location of an unknown point, as in navigation, by forming a triangle having the unknown point and two known points as the vertices.
Tri•an•gu•lum (trī-áng-gew-ləm) *n.* A constellation in the northern sky near Aries and Andromeda. [Latin, TRIANGLE.]
Triangulum Aus•tra•le (aw-stráyli, o-). A constellation in the southern sky near Apus and Norma. [Latin, "southern triangle".]
tri•ar•chy (trí-aarki) *n., pl.* **-chies. 1.** Government by three persons; a triumvirate. **2.** A country governed by three rulers. [Greek *triarkhia* : *tri-,* three + -ARCHY.]
Tri•as•sic (trī-ássik) *adj.* Of, belonging to, or designating the geological period, system of rocks, and sedimentary deposits of the first period of the Mesozoic era, after the Permian period of the Paleozoic era and before the Jurassic period of the Mesozoic era.
~*n. Geology.* The Triassic period or system of deposits. Preceded by *the.* [Late Latin *trias,* TRIAD (from the subdivision of the strata of this period into three groups in Germany).]
tri•a•tom•ic (trí-ə-tómmik) *adj. Chemistry.* Containing three atoms per molecule.
tri•ax•i•al (trí-áksi-əl) *adj.* Having three axes.
tri•a•zine (trí-əz-een, trī-áz-, -in) *n.* **1.** Any of three isomeric compounds, $C_3H_3N_3$, each having three carbon and three nitrogen atoms in a six-membered ring. **2.** Any compound derived from these isomers.
tri•a•zole (trí-əz-ōl, trī-áz-, -ol) *n.* **1.** Any of several compounds with composition $C_2H_3N_3$ having a five-membered ring of two carbon atoms and three nitrogen atoms. **2.** Any compound derived from one of these isomers.
trib•ade (tríbbəd) *n. Rare.* A lesbian. [French, from Latin *tribas,*

from Greek, "she who rubs", from *tribein*, to rub.] —**trib·a·dism** (-iz'm) *n.*

trib·al (trīb'l) *adj.* Pertaining to or of the nature of a tribe or tribes. ~*n.* A member of one of the indigenous tribal peoples of India. —**trib·al·ly** *adv.*

trib·al·ism (trīb'l-iz'm) *n.* **1.** The condition of being made up of or organised into tribes. **2.** The organisation, culture, or beliefs of a tribe. **3.** The sense of belonging to a tribe; tribal loyalty. —**trib·al·ist** *n.* —**trib·al·is·tic** (-ístik) *adj.*

tri·ba·sic (trī-báysik, trī-) *adj.* **1.** Containing three replaceable hydrogen atoms per molecule. Said of an acid. **2.** Containing three univalent basic atoms or radicals per molecule. Said of a base or salt.

tribe (trīb) *n.* **1.** A unit of social organisation, especially among primitive peoples but also surviving in some modern societies, consisting of a group of people claiming a common ancestry, usually sharing a common culture, and originally living together under a chief or headman. **2.** A political, ethnic, or ancestral division of ancient states and cultures, especially: **a.** Any of the three divisions of the ancient Romans, namely, the Latin, Sabine, and Etruscan. **b.** Any of the 12 divisions of ancient Israel. **c.** A phyle of ancient Greece. **3. a.** A group of persons with a common occupation, interest, or habit. Often used derogatorily: *a whole tribe of public school boys invaded the restaurant.* **b.** *Informal.* A large family. **4.** *Biology.* A taxonomic category sometimes placed between a family and a genus. [Middle English *tribu, tribe,* from Old French *tribu,* from Latin *tribus,* division of the Roman people, perhaps from *tri-* (unattested), three (referring to Latin, Sabine, and Etruscan).]

tribes·man (trībz-mən) *n., pl.* **-men** (-mən). A member of a tribe.

tribes·wom·an (trībz-wŏŏmən) *n., pl.* **-women** (-wimmin). A female member of a tribe.

tribo– *comb. form.* Indicates friction; for example, **triboelectricity, triboluminescence.** [From Greek *tribos,* rubbing.]

tri·bo·e·lec·tric·i·ty (trībō-éllek-tríssəti, -i-lék- ‖ -trízzəti) *n. Physics.* Electricity that is produced by friction. —**tri·bo·e·lec·tric** (-i-léktrik) *adj.*

tri·bol·o·gy (trī-bólləji) *n.* The study of friction and lubrication.

tri·bo·lu·mi·nes·cence (trībō-lŏŏ-mi-néss'nss, -léw-) *n. Physics.* Luminescence produced by certain crystals as a result of friction or crushing. —**tri·bo·lu·mi·nes·cent** *adj.*

tri·brach (trīb-rak, trīb-) *n.* A metrical foot of three short or unstressed syllables. [Latin *tribrachys,* from Greek *tribrakhus : tri-,* three + *brakhus,* short.] —**tri·brach·ic** (tri-bráckik, trī-) *adj.*

tri·bro·mo·eth·a·nol (trī-brómō-éthə-nol ‖ -nōl) *n.* Also **tri·brom·eth·a·nol** (-bróm-). A white crystalline compound, CBr₃CH₂OH, having a slight aromatic odour and taste, and used to produce complete unconsciousness.

trib·u·la·tion (tribbew-láysh'n) *n.* **1.** *Often plural.* Great affliction, trial, or distress; suffering: *the tribulations of the persecuted.* **2.** An experience or condition that causes such distress. [Middle English *tribulacioun,* from Old French *tribulation,* from Late Latin *tribulātiō* (stem *tribulātiōn-*), from *tribulāre,* to oppress, from Latin, to press, from *tribulum,* threshing sledge.]

tri·bu·nal (trī-béwn'l, trī-) *n.* **1.** A seat or court of justice. **2.** The platform or seat upon which a judge or other presiding officer sits in court. **3.** A committee or board set up to adjudicate or investigate a particular matter or dispute: *a rent tribunal.* **4.** Anything having the power of determining or judging: *the tribunal of public opinion.* [Latin *tribūnāl(e),* court of the tribunes, tribunal, from *tribūnālis,* of a tribune, from *tribūnus,* TRIBUNE (official).]

trib·une¹ (tríbbewn ‖ *U.S. also* tri-béwn) *n.* **1.** In ancient Rome, an official chosen by the plebs to protect their rights against the patricians. **2.** Any protector or champion of the common people. [Middle English, from Latin *tribūnus,* "head of the tribe", tribune, from *tribus,* tribe.] —**trib·u·nar·y** (-əri ‖ -erri) *adj.* —**trib·u·nate, trib·une·ship** *n.*

tribune² *n.* **1.** A raised platform or dais from which a speaker addresses an assembly. **2.** In a church: **a.** An apse. **b.** A bishop's throne within an apse. **c.** A raised area or gallery. [French, from Italian *tribuna,* from Medieval Latin *tribūna,* variant of Latin *tribūnāl(e),* TRIBUNAL.]

trib·u·tar·y (tríbbew-tri, -təri ‖ -terri) *adj.* **1.** Making additions or offering supplies; contributory; subsidiary. **2.** Having the nature of a tribute: *a tributary payment.* **3.** Paying or required to pay tribute. **4.** Flowing into a larger body of water. Said of a river or stream. ~*n., pl.* **tributaries. 1.** One that pays tribute. **2.** *Abbr.* **trib.** A stream or river flowing into a larger stream or river. In this sense, compare **distributary.** —**trib·u·tar·i·ly** *adv.* —**trib·u·tar·i·ness** *n.*

trib·ute (tríbbewt) *n.* **1. a.** A gift, payment, declaration, or other acknowledgement of gratitude, respect, or admiration: *"To love and grief tribute of verse belongs"* (John Donne). **b.** That which is a worthy or creditable reflection of the person or thing mentioned: *The new church was a tribute to their faith.* **2. a.** A sum of money or other valuables paid by one ruler or nation to another as acknowledgment of submission or as the price for protection by that nation. **b.** Any payment made for protection. **3. a.** In feudal times, any payment or tax given by a vassal to his overlord. **b.** The obligation to make such a payment. [Middle English *tribut,* from Latin *tribūtum,* from the neuter past participle of *tribuere,* to give, distribute (as among the Roman tribes), from *tribus,* TRIBE.]

tri·car·box·y·lic acid cycle (trī-kárb-ok-síllik) *n.* The **Krebs cycle** (see).

trice (trīss) *tr.v.* **triced, tricing, trices.** To hoist and secure (a sail, for example); lash. Usually used with *up.* ~*n.* A very short period of time; a moment; an instant. Used chiefly in the phrase *in a trice.* See Synonyms at **moment.** [Middle English *trisen,* from Middle Dutch, akin to Middle Dutch *triset†,* pulley; noun sense, Middle English *at a tryse,* "at a pull".]

tri·cen·ten·ni·al (trī-sen-ténni-əl) *adj.* Also **tri·cen·te·nar·y** (-téenəri, -ténnəri). Tercentenary. ~*n.* Also **tri·cen·te·nar·y.** A tercentenary event or celebration.

tri·ceps (trī-seps) *n., pl.* **triceps** or **-cepses** (-sepsiz). Any three-headed muscle, especially the large muscle running along the back of the upper arm and serving to extend the forearm. [Latin, three-headed : *tri-,* three + *caput,* head.]

tri·cer·a·tops (trī-sérrə-tops) *n.* A three-horned herbivorous dinosaur of the genus *Triceratops,* of the Cretaceous period, having a bony plate covering the neck. [New Latin *Triceratops : tri-* + Greek *keras* (stem *kerat-*), horn + *ōps,* eye, face.]

trich–. Variant of **tricho–.**

tri·chi·a·sis (tri-kí-ə-siss) *n.* **1.** A condition of ingrowing hairs about an orifice, especially of ingrowing eyelashes. **2.** The presence of hairlike bodies in the urine. [Late Latin, from Greek *trikhiasis :* TRICH(O)- + -IASIS.]

tri·chi·na (tri-kí-nə) *n., pl.* **-nae** (-nee) or **-nas.** A parasitic nematode worm, *Trichinella spiralis,* infesting the intestines of various mammals, and having larvae that move through the blood vessels and become encysted in the muscles. [New Latin, from Greek *trikhinos,* hairy, from *thrix,* hair.]

trich·i·nise, trich·i·nize (trícki-nīz') *tr.v.* **-nised, -nising, -nises.** To infect with trichinae. —**trich·i·ni·sa·tion** (-nī-záysh'n ‖ *U.S.* -ni-) *n.*

trich·i·no·sis (trícki-nō-siss) *n.* Also **trich·i·ni·a·sis** (-nī-ə-siss). A disease caused by eating inadequately cooked meat containing trichinae, and characterised by intestinal disorders, fever, muscular swelling, pain, and delirium. [New Latin : TRICHIN(A) + -OSIS.]

tri·chi·nous (trícki-nəss, tri-kí-) *adj.* **1.** Containing trichinae: *trichinous pork.* **2.** Of or relating to trichinae or trichinosis.

trich·ite (trik-īt) *n.* A small needle-shaped filament or crystal. [German *Trichit :* TRICH(O)- + -ITE.] —**tri·chit·ic** (trī-kíttik) *adj.*

tri·chlo·ride (trī-kláw-rīd ‖ -klō-) *n.* A compound containing three chlorine atoms per molecule.

tri·chlo·ro·a·ce·tic acid (trī-kláw-rō-ə-séetik, -séttik ‖ -klō-) *n.* A colourless, deliquescent, corrosive, crystalline compound, CCl₃COOH, used as a herbicide and applied locally as an astringent and antiseptic.

tri·chlo·ro·eth·yl·ene (trī-kláw-rō-éth'l-een ‖ -klō-) *n.* Also **tri·chlor·eth·yl·ene** (-kláwr- ‖ -klōr-), **tri·chlo·ro·eth·ene** (trī-kláw-rō-éeth-een). A colourless, toxic liquid, CHCl:CCl₂, used to degrease metals, as an extraction solvent for oils and waxes, as a refrigerant, in dry cleaning, and as a fumigant.

tri·chlo·ro·phe·nox·y·a·ce·tic acid (trī-kláw-rō-fen-óksi-ə-séetik, -séttik ‖ -klō-) *n.* A synthetic auxin, 2,4,5-trichlorophenoxyacetic acid, C₈H₅Cl₃O₃, that is used as a herbicide. Also called **"2, 4, 5-T".**

tricho–, trich– *comb. form.* Indicates hair or hairlike part; for example, **trichopteran, trichogyne.** [Greek *trikho-,* from *thrix* (stem *trikh-*), hair.]

trich·o·cyst (tríckə-sist) *n.* One of the minute capsule-like bodies in the outer cytoplasm of certain protozoans, capable of ejecting a threadlike or bristle-like extension. [TRICHO- + -CYST.] —**trich·o·cys·tic** (-sístik) *adj.*

trich·o·gyne (tríckə-jīn, -gīn) *n.* A receptive filament of the female reproductive structure of certain fungi or algae.

trich·oid (trík-oyd, trík-) *adj.* Resembling hair; hairlike. [Greek *trikhoeidēs :* TRICH(O)- + -OID.]

tri·chol·o·gy (tri-kólləji) *n.* The study of hair and its diseases.

trich·ome (trík-ōm, trík-) *n.* A hairlike or bristle-like outgrowth, as from the epidermis of a plant. [German *Trichom,* from Greek *trikhōma,* hair growth, from *trikhoun,* to furnish with hair, from *thrix* (stem *trikh-*), hair.] —**tri·chom·ic** (tri-kŏmik, trī-, -kómmik) *adj.*

trich·o·mon·ad (trík-ō-món-ad, -ə-, -mŏn-) *n.* Any of various flagellate protozoans of the genus *Trichomonas,* occurring in the digestive and urogenital tracts of vertebrates. [New Latin *Trichomonas* (stem *Trichomonad-*) : TRICHO- + MONAD.]

trich·o·mo·ni·a·sis (trík-ō-mə-ní-ə-siss, -ə-, -mo-, -mō-) *n.* **1.** A vaginal infection caused by a protozoan, *Trichomonas vaginalis,* and resulting in inflammation and discomfort. **2.** Any infection caused by trichomonads. [New Latin : *Trichomonas,* TRICHOMON(AD) + -IASIS.]

tri·chop·ter·an (trī-kóptərən, tri-) *n.* Any insect of the order Trichoptera, which comprises the caddis flies. [New Latin *Trichoptera,* "hairy winged" : TRICHO- + -PTER.]

tri·cho·sis (tri-kŏ-siss) *n.* Disease of the hair. [New Latin, from Greek *trikhōsis,* growth of hair, from *trikhoun,* to furnish with hair. See **trichome.**]

tri·chot·o·my (trī-kóttəmi, tri-) *n., pl.* **-mies.** A dividing into three parts. [Greek *trikha,* in three parts + -TOMY.] —**trich·o·tom·ic** (tríkə-tómmik, trícka-), **tri·chot·o·mous** (-kóttəməss) *adj.* —**tri·chot·o·mous·ly** *adv.*

–trichous *adj. comb. form.* Indicates specified kinds of hair; for example, **amphitrichous.** [Greek *-trikhos,* from *thrix* (stem *trikh-*), hair.]

tri·chro·ism (trí-krō-iz'm) *n.* The property possessed by certain minerals of exhibiting three different colours when illuminated by white light and viewed from three different directions. [Greek *tri-*

khroos, "tricoloured" : TRI- + -CHRO(OUS) + -ISM.] **—tri·chro·ic** (trī-krṓ-i) *adj.*

tri·chro·mat·ic (trī́-krō-máttik, -krə-) *adj.* Also **tri·chrome** (-krōm), **tri·chro·mic** (-krṓmik). **1.** Of, relating to, or having three colours, as in photography or printing. **2.** Having visual perception of the three primary colours, as in normal vision. **—tri·chro·ma·tism** (-krṓmətiz'm) *n.*

trick (trik) *n.* **1.** A device or action designed to achieve an end by deceptive or fraudulent means; a stratagem; a ruse. **2.** A mischievous action; a practical joke; a prank. **3.** A deceptive or delusive appearance; an illusion: *a trick of the sunlight.* **4.** A peculiar trait or characteristic, such as a mannerism: *had the trick of blinking as she spoke.* **5.** The best quality or method needed to accomplish something; a knack: *Patience is the trick here.* **6.** A feat of magic or legerdemain. **7.** A difficult, dexterous, or clever act, designed to amuse or entertain. **8.** In card games: **a.** All the cards played in a single round, one from each player. **b.** One such round. **9.** A period or turn of duty, as at the helm of a ship. **10.** *U.S. Slang.* **a.** A prostitute's client. **b.** A session with any one client, as carried out by a prostitute. —See Synonyms at **artifice. —do the trick.** *Informal.* To bring about the desired result. **—how's tricks.** *Informal.* Used to enquire how a person is or how things are going.
~v. **tricked, tricking, tricks.** *—tr.* **1.** To swindle or cheat; deceive; delude. **2.** To ornament, dress, or adorn. Used with *up* or *out.* *—intr.* To practise deception or trickery.
~adj. **1.** Of, pertaining to, or involving tricks. **2.** Designed or made for doing a trick or tricks: *a trick flower.* [Middle English *trik,* from Old French (dialect) *trique,* Old French *triche,* from *trichier,* to deceive, perhaps from Vulgar Latin *triccāre* (unattested), from Latin *trīcārī,* to start difficulties, dally, play tricks, from *trīcae*†, trifles, tricks. See also **intricate, extricate.**] **—trick·er** *n.*

trick·er·y (tríckəri) *n., pl.* **-ies.** The practice or use of tricks; deception by stratagem; artifice.

trick·ish (tríckish) *adj.* Characterised by or tending to use tricks or trickery. **—trick·ish·ly** *adv.* **—trick·ish·ness** *n.*

trick·le (tríck'l) *v.* **-led, -ling, -les.** *—intr.* **1.** To flow or fall in drops or in a thin, intermittent stream; drip gently but steadily. **2.** To move or proceed slowly or bit by bit: *The audience trickled in.* *—tr.* To cause to trickle: *trickle oil into the mayonnaise.*
~n. **1.** The act or condition of trickling. **2.** Any slow, small, or irregular quantity of something that moves, proceeds, or occurs intermittently. [Middle English *triklen* (perhaps imitative).]

trickle charger *n.* A mains-operated device for charging accumulators by passing a low current over a long period, used especially for charging car batteries.

trick or treat *n.* The custom practised, especially in the United States, by children on Hallowe'en, of going from door to door dressed in costume and saying "trick or treat", as a demand for sweets cakes, or the like.

trick·ster (trí kstər) *n.* One who plays tricks or deceives.

trick·sy (tríksi) *adj.* **1.** Playful; prankish; mischievous. **2.** Crafty or sly. **3.** *Archaic.* Smart; spruce; dapper. [From TRICK.]

trick·y (trícki) *adj.* **-ier, -iest. 1.** Given to or characterised by deception or trickery; crafty; sly; wily: *a tricky politician.* **2.** Requiring caution or skill; difficult: *a tricky question; a tricky situation.* —See Synonyms at **dishonest, sly. —trick·i·ly** *adv.* **—trick·i·ness** *n.*

tri·clin·ic (trī-klínnik) *adj.* Having three unequal axes intersecting at oblique angles. Said of certain crystals. [TRI- + -CLINIC.]

tri·clin·i·um (tri-klín-i-əm, trī-) *n., pl.* **-nia** (-ni-ə). **1.** A couch or set of couches surrounding three sides of a table, used by the ancient Romans for reclining at meals. **2.** A room containing such a couch or couches. [Latin *triclīnium,* from Greek *triklinion,* diminutive of *triklinos,* room with three couches : *tri-,* three + *klinē* couch.]

tri·col·our (trī́-kullər) *adj.* Also **tri·col·oured** (-d). Having three colours.
~n. (tríck'l-ər) **1.** A tricolour flag. **2.** *Sometimes capital* **T.** The French or Irish flag. Preceded by *the.*

tri·corn, tri·corne (trī́-kawrn) *n.* A hat having the brim turned up on three sides.
~adj. Having three projections, horns, or corners. [French *tricorne,* from Latin *tricornis,* three-horned : *tri-,* three + *cornū,* horn.]

tri·cor·nered (trī́-kawrnərd) *adj.* Having three corners.

tri·cos·tate (trī-kóstayt) *adj.* Having three costae or riblike ridges.

tri·cot (tréek-ō, trík-) *n.* **1.** A plain, warp-knitted cloth of any of various yarns. **2.** A soft ribbed cloth of wool or a wool blend, usually used for dresses. [French, from *tricoter*†, to knit.]

tric·o·tine (tríckə-téen, tréekə-) *n.* A sturdy worsted fabric with a double twill, used for dresses and suits. [French, from TRICOT.]

tri·crot·ic (trī-króttik) *adj. Medicine.* Having three waves or elevations to one beat of the pulse. [From Greek *trikrotos,* having a triple beat : *tri-,* three + *krotein,* to beat.] **—tri·cro·tism** (-krot-iz'm, trí-, -krət-) *n.*

tri·cus·pid (trī-kúspid, trī́-) *adj.* Also **tri·cus·pi·dal** (-'l), **tri·cus·pi·date** (-ayt). **1.** Having three points or cusps, as a molar tooth. **2.** *Anatomy.* Pertaining to the tricuspid valve of the heart.
~n. Anatomy. A tricuspid organ or part, especially a tooth. [Latin *tricuspis* (stem *tricuspid-*) : *tri-,* three + *cuspis,* point, CUSP.]

tricuspid valve *n.* The three-segmented valve of the heart that keeps the blood from flowing back from the right ventricle into the right atrium.

tri·cy·cle (trī́-sik'l) *n.* A vehicle, used especially by small children, that has three wheels, two at the back and one at the front and is usually propelled by pedals. Also informally called "trike". **—tri·cy·cle** *intr.v.*

tri·cy·clic (trī-sícklik, -síklik) *adj. Chemistry.* Having or pertaining to a molecular structure with three rings.

tri·dac·tyl (trī-dáktil, trī́-) *adj.* Also **tri·dac·ty·lous** (-əss). Having three toes, claws, or similar parts on each limb. [Greek *tridaktulos,* three-fingered : *tri-,* three + *daktulos,* finger (see **dactyl**).]

tri·dent (trī́d'nt) *n.* A long, three-pronged fork or weapon as used by one hunting fish or formerly by gladiators; especially, the three-pronged spear carried by Neptune or Poseidon.
~adj. Also **tri·den·tate** (trī-déntayt, trī́-). Having three teeth, prongs, or similar protrusions. [Latin *tridēns* (stem *trident-*), three-toothed : *tri-,* three + *dēns,* tooth.]

Tri·den·tine (tri-dén-tīn, trī-, -teen, -tin) *adj.* Of or relating to the Council of Trent or to the results or decrees of that Council.
~n. A Roman Catholic who conforms rigorously to the Tridentine Creed formulated at the Council of Trent. [Medieval Latin *Tridentīnus,* from *Tridentum,* ancient form of TRENT.]

Tridentine Mass *n.* The Mass in the rite laid down by Pius V in 1570 following the reforms of the Council of Trent, used throughout the Roman Catholic Church until replaced by the various revisions which followed the Second Vatican Council.

triecious. Variant of **trioecious.**

tried. Past tense and past participle of **try.**

tri·en·ni·al (trī-énni-əl, trī́-) *adj.* **1.** Occurring every third year. **2.** Lasting three years.
~n. **1.** A third anniversary. **2.** A triennial thing, event, or celebration. [From TRIENNIUM.] **—tri·en·ni·al·ly** *adv.*

tri·en·ni·um (trī-énni-əm, trī́-) *n., pl.* **-ums** or **-nia** (-ə). A period of three years. [Latin *triennium* : *tri-,* three + Latin *annus,* year.]

tri·er (trī́-ər) *n.* One that tries; especially, a person who continues to make repeated attempts at something, despite failure.

tri·er·arch (trī́-ə-raark) *n.* In ancient Greece: **1.** The captain of a trireme. **2.** An Athenian who had the responsibility of outfitting and maintaining a trireme as a part of his civic duties. [Latin *triērarchus,* from Greek *triērarkhos* : *triēres,* trireme + -ARCH.]

tri·er·ar·chy (trī́-ə-raarki) *n., pl.* **-chies.** In ancient Greece: **1.** The authority or office of the commander of a trierarch. **2.** The ancient Athenian system whereby individual citizens furnished and maintained triremes as a part of their public duty.

Tri·es·te (tree-ést; *Italian* -éstay). *Serbo-Croat* **Trst.** Seaport and capital of Friuli-Venezia Giulia region, northeast Italy. It is an important industrial and tourist centre. It was held by Austria from 1382 until 1919 and was the subject of a dispute with Yugoslavia after World War II.

tri·fa·cial (trī-fáysh'l) *adj. Anatomy.* Trigeminal.

tri·fid (trī́-fid) *adj.* Divided or cleft into three narrow parts or lobes. [Latin *trifidus* : *tri-,* three + -FID.]

tri·fle (trī́f'l) *n.* **1.** Something of slight importance or very little value. **2.** A small amount of something; a little: *The book only cost a trifle.* **3.** A dessert typically consisting of a layer of sponge cake covered with jam or fruit, soaked in wine, sprinkled with almonds, and topped with custard and whipped cream. **4. a.** A moderately hard variety of pewter. **b.** *Plural.* Utensils made from this. **—a trifle.** Slightly; somewhat: *a trifle stingy.*
~v. **trifled, -fling, -fles.** *—intr.* **1.** To deal with something as if it were of little significance or value. Usually used with *with: not a person to be trifled with.* **2.** To act, perform, or speak with little seriousness or purpose; jest. **3.** To play or toy with something; handle things idly. *—tr.* To waste (time or money, for example). Often used with *away.* [Middle English *trifle, truf(f)le,* from Old French *truf(f)le,* variant of *tru(f)fe*†, trickery, deceit.] **—tri·fler** *n.*

tri·fling (trífling) *adj.* **1.** Of slight importance; insignificant. **2.** Characterised by frivolity or idleness. —See Synonyms at **trivial. —tri·fling·ly** *adv.*

tri·fo·cal (trī-fṓk'l, trī́-) *adj.* Having three focal lengths.
~n. Plural. Glasses having trifocal lenses.

tri·fold (trī́-fōld) *adj.* Triple; having three parts. [TRI- + -FOLD.]

tri·fo·li·ate (trī-fṓli-ət, -it, -ayt) *adj.* Also **tri·fo·li·at·ed** (-aytid). Having three leaves, leaflets, or leaflike parts: *a trifoliate compound leaf.*

tri·fo·li·o·late (trī-fṓli-əl-ət, -it, -ayt) *adj.* Having three leaflets.

tri·fo·ri·um (trī-fáw-ri-əm || -fṓ-) *n., pl.* **-foria** (-ə). *Architecture.* A gallery of arches set in the wall above the arches of the nave choir, and sometimes the transept of a church. [Medieval Latin *triforium*†, special name (in Gervase of Canterbury, *c.* 1185) applied to the gallery in Canterbury Cathedral, but subsequently taken to mean "structure with three openings" (Latin *tri-,* three + *fores,* doors) and thus applied to the elevated gallery characteristic of Gothic architecture, sometimes having three arches or openings.]

tri·form (trī́-fawrm) *adj.* Having three different forms or parts.

tri·fur·cate (trī-fur-kət, -fúr-, -kit, -kayt) *adj.* Also **tri·fur·cat·ed** (-kaytid). Having three forks or branches. **—tri·fur·ca·tion** (-káysh'n) *n.*

trig[1] (trig) *adj. Archaic & Regional.* **1.** Trim; neat; tidy. **2.** In good condition; firm; strong.
~tr.v. **trigged, trigging, trigs.** *Archaic & Regional.* To make trim or neat, especially in dress. Often used with *up* or *out.* [Middle English, true, active, from Old Norse *tryggr;* akin to TRUE.] **—trig·ly** *adv.* **—trig·ness** *n.*

trig[2] *tr.v.* **trigged, trigging, trigs. 1.** To stop (a wheel) from rolling, as with a trig. **2.** To prop up; support.
~n. A wedge or other braking device. [Perhaps from Scandinavian, akin to Old Norse *tryggr,* true, firm. See **trig** (trim).]

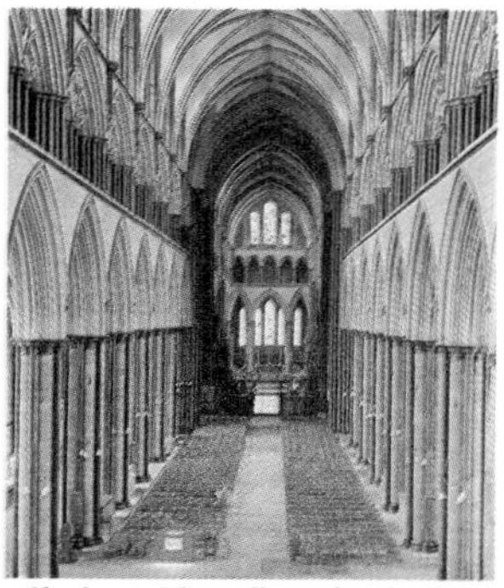

triforium *The gallery of arches at Salisbury Cathedral, England. The triforium is the middle of the three tiers of arches along the nave.*

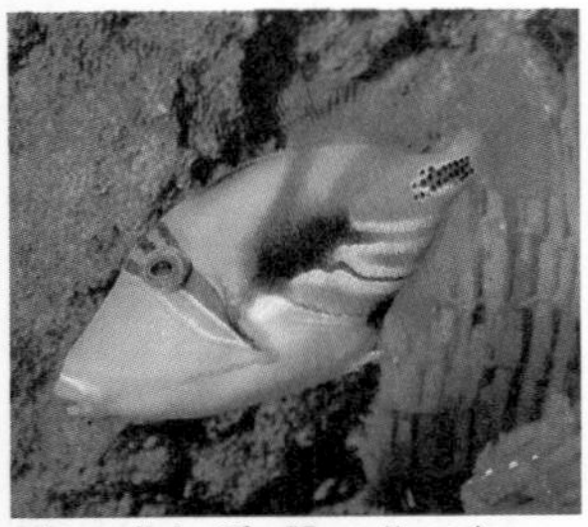

triggerfish *The Hawaiian trigger fish,* Rhineacanthus aculeatus *(above), is one of a family which derives its name from a triggering mechanism in the spines of the dorsal fin. The first spine can be locked erect, and, once in this position, can be released only by the second spine. The mechanism enables the fish to hold its position in protective crevices.*

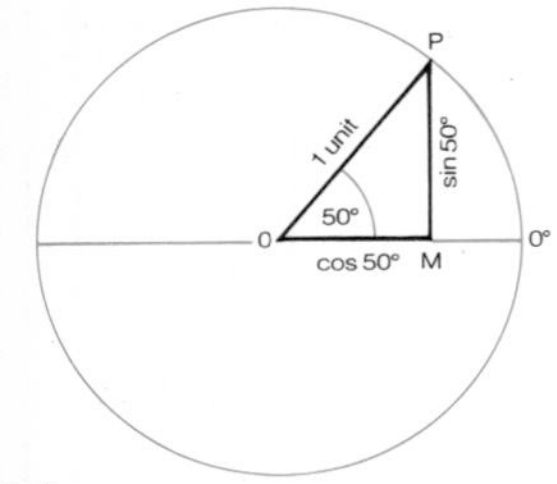

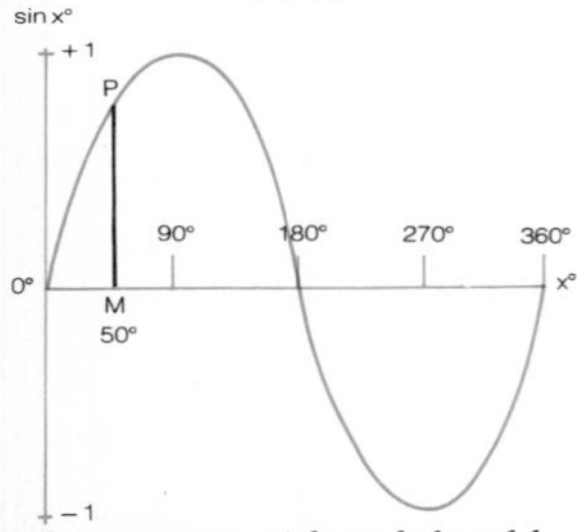

trigonometry *A knowledge of the relationships between the angles and sides of a right-angled triangle – the study called trigonometry – is useful in navigation, surveying, and other disciplines where distances have to be calculated from the measurement of angles. Three main ratios are used: sine, cosine, and tangent. In the triangle above (upper illustration), the sine of the 50° angle is the ratio of the height, PM, to the length of the longest side, or hypotenuse, OP. The cosine is the ratio of OM to OP. And the tangent is the ratio of PM to OM. If the hypotenuse is 1 unit long, the lengths of the other two sides are equal to the sine and cosine. If OP were 2 units long, PM would equal twice the sine, and so on. The graph (lower illustration) shows how the sine ratio changes as the angle increases from 0° to 360°. The graph of the cosine has a similar wavelike pattern.*

trig. trigonometric; trigonometry.

tri·gem·i·nal (trī-jémmin'l) *adj. Anatomy.* Pertaining to the trigeminal nerve; trifacial.

trigeminal nerve *n.* Either of the fifth pair of cranial nerves that divides into the ophthalmic, maxillary, and mandibular nerves. [New Latin, from Latin, three born at a birth, threefold (probably from its three branches) : *tri-,* three + *geminus,* twin-born, twin.]

trigeminal neuralgia *n.* Intensely painful paroxysms of the facial area around the trigeminal nerve. Also called "tic douloureux".

trig·ger (tríggər) *n.* **1.** The lever pressed by the finger to discharge a firearm. **2.** Any similar device used to release or activate a mechanism. **3.** Anything that activates or sets off an action or series of events: *Murder was the trigger for the uprising.* **4.** *Electronics.* A pulse or a circuit that initiates the action of another component. ~*tr.v.* **triggered, -gering, -gers. 1.** To initiate; activate; set off. Often used with *off: triggered off public outcry.* **2.** To fire or explode (a weapon). [Earlier *tricker,* from Dutch *trekker,* something pulled, from Middle Dutch *trecker,* from *trecken,* to pull, travel. See **trek.**]

trig·ger·fish (tríggər-fish) *n., pl.* **-fishes** or collectively **triggerfish.** Any of various brightly coloured fishes of the family Balistidae, of warm coastal seas, characteristically having sharp, erectile dorsal spines.

trigger flower *n.* Any of numerous plants of the genus *Stylidium,* confined mainly to Australia, that have a column of fused stamens which dusts the backs of insects with pollen.

trig·ger-hap·py (tríggər-happi) *adj. Informal.* Inclined to react in a violent, rash manner at the slightest provocation, as by firing a gun.

tri·glyc·er·ide (trī-glíssə-rīd, trī-) *n.* A natural fat or oil formed by combination of one molecule of glycerol with three molecules of fatty acids.

tri·glyph (trígglif, trī́-glif) *adj. Architecture.* An ornament in a Doric frieze, consisting of a projecting block having three parallel vertical channels on its face. [Latin *trīglyphus,* from Greek *trigluphos* : *tri-,* three + *gluphē,* carving, GLYPH.] **—tri·glyph·ic** (tri-glíffik, trī-) *adj.*

tri·gon (trī́-gən, -gon) *n.* **1.** A triangular lyre or harp of Roman and Greek antiquity. **2.** In astrology, a **triplicity** *(see).* **3.** *Archaic.* A triangle. [Latin *trigonum,* triangle, from Greek *trigōnon,* from *trigōnos,* triangular : *tri-,* three + -GON.]

trig·o·nal (tríggən'l) *adj.* **1.** Triangular. **2.** In crystallography, pertaining to or belonging to the crystal system with three unequal axes that are equally inclined to each other at an angle other than 90°.

trigonometric function *n.* **1.** A function of an angle expressed as the ratio of two of the sides of a right-angled triangle that contains the angle, named sine, cosine, tangent, or the like. In general, for any angle formed in a coordinate plane by the intersection of the abscissal axis with the radius vector from the origin to a point in the plane, the ratio of any two of the values abscissa, ordinate, and radius vector of that point. Also called "circular function". **2.** A function composed of a combination of trigonometric functions.

trig·o·nom·e·try (triggə-nómmətri) *n. Abbr.* **trig.** The study of the properties and applications of trigonometric functions. [New Latin *trigonometria* : Greek *trigōnon,* triangle, TRIGON + -METRY.] **—trig·o·no·met·ric** (-nə-méttrik), **trig·o·no·met·ri·cal** *adj.* **—trig·o·no·met·ri·cal·ly** *adv.*

trig·o·nous (tríggənəss, *also* trī́-gōnəss) *adj.* Three-sided, especially in cross section: *a trigonous stem.* Compare **triquetrous.** [From Greek *trigōnos,* three-cornered. See **tri-, -gon.**]

tri·graph (trī́-graaf, -graf) *n.* A conjunction of three letters representing a single speech sound; for example the letters *e, a,* and *u* in the word *beau* form a trigraph. Also called "triphthong". [TRI- + -GRAPH, after *digraph.*]

tri·he·dral (trī-héed-rəl, -héd-) *adj.* Formed by the plane surfaces of a trihedron.
~*n.* A trihedron.

tri·he·dron (trī-héed-rən, -héd-) *n., pl.* **-drons** or **-dra** (-rə). A figure formed by the intersection of three noncoplanar lines. Also called "trihedral". [New Latin : TRI- + -HEDRON.]

tri·hy·drate (trī-hī́-drayt) *n.* A compound containing three molecules of water of crystallisation per molecule in the compound.

tri·hy·dric (trī-hī́drik) *adj.* Also **tri·hy·drox·y** (trī-hī-dróksi). Containing three hydroxide groups per molecule. Said especially of alcohols.

trike (trīk) *n. Informal.* A **tricycle** *(see).*

tri·lat·er·al (trī-láttrəl, trī́-, -láttərəl) *adj.* Having three sides. [Latin *trilaterus* : *tri-,* three + *latus* (stem *later-*), side (see **lateral**).] **—tri·lat·er·al·ly** *adv.*

tri·lat·er·al·ism (trī́-láttrəl-iz'm, -láttərəl-) *n.* The political policy of encouraging friendly relations between three nations or regions, especially between North America, Japan, and Western Europe. **—tri·lat·er·al·ist** *n.*

tril·by (trílbi) *n., pl.* **-bies.** *British.* **1.** A felt hat with an indented crown and narrow brim, worn by a man. **2.** *Plural. Slang.* Feet. [19th century : after the heroine of *Trilby,* a novel by George du Maurier. The hat was popularised in the stage version.]

tri·lin·e·ar (trī-línni-ər, trī-) *adj.* Pertaining to, having, or bounded by three lines.

tri·lin·gual (trī-líng-gwəl) *adj.* Having or expressed in three languages.

tri·lit·er·al (trī-líttrəl, trī́-, -líttərəl) *adj.* Consisting of three letters. Used chiefly of consonantal roots in Semitic languages.
~*n.* A three-letter word or word element.

tri·lith (trī́-lith) *n.* A group of three large stones usually with two standing upright and supporting a third, often found in prehistoric henge monuments. [Greek *trilithon* : TRI- + -LITH.]

trill (tril) *n.* **1.** A fluttering or tremulous sound, such as that made by certain birds; a warble. **2.** *Music.* The rapid alternation of two notes either a whole tone or a semi-tone apart. Compare **tremolo. 3.** *Phonetics.* **a.** A rapid vibration of one speech organ against another, as of the tongue against the alveolar ridge in Spanish *rr.* **b.** A speech sound pronounced with such a vibration.
~*v.* **trilled, trilling, trills.** —*tr.* **1.** To sound, sing, or play with a trill. **2.** *Phonetics.* To articulate with a trill. —*intr.* To produce or give forth a trill. [Italian *trillo,* from *trillare*†, to trill.]

tril·lion (tríl-yən) *n., pl.* **trillion** (for senses 1, 2). **1.** The cardinal number represented by 1 followed by 18 zeros, usually written 10^{18}. **2.** *U.S.* A **billion** *(see).* **3.** *Plural.* An indefinitely large number; a great many. [French : TRI- + (M)ILLION, by analogy with *billion.*] **—tril·lion** *adj.*

tril·lionth (tríl-yənth) *n.* **1.** The ordinal number one trillion in a series. **2.** One of a trillion equal parts. **—tril·lionth** *adj. & adv.*

tril·li·um (trílli-əm) *n.* Any of various plants of the genus *Trillium,* of North America and eastern Asia, usually having a single whorl of three leaves, and a variously coloured, three-petalled flower. [New Latin : TRI- + *(vertic)illium* : Latin *(vertic)illus,* whorl, VERTICIL + -IUM.]

tri·lo·bate (trī́-lōb-ayt, -lōb-, -ləb-) *adj.* Also **tri·lo·bal** (-lṓb'l), **tri·lo·bat·ed** (-lō-baytid, -lṓ-), **tri·lobed** (-lōbd). Having three lobes, as certain leaves do.

tri·lo·bite (trī́-lō-bīt, -lə-) *n.* Any of numerous extinct marine arthropods of the class Trilobita, of the Palaeozoic era, having a segmented exoskeleton divided by furrows into three longitudinal lobes. [New Latin *Trilobites* (division), from Greek *trilobos,* "three-lobed" : *tri-,* three + *lobos,* LOBE.] **—tri·lo·bit·ic** (-bíttik) *adj.*

tri·loc·u·lar (trī́-lóckew-lər) *adj.* Having three chamber-like divisions or cavities. Said especially of plant reproductive structures.

tril·o·gy (trílləji) *n., pl.* **-gies.** A group of three dramatic or literary works by the same author that are related in subject or theme, such as three ancient Greek tragedies written to be performed in immediate succession. [Greek *trilogia* : TRI- + -LOGY.]

trim (trim) *v.* **trimmed, trimming, trims.** —*tr.* **1. a.** To make neat or tidy by clipping, smoothing, or pruning: *trimmed his beard.* **b.** To make tidy or put into order, especially in appearance. Often used with *up: trimmed himself up.* **2.** To remove (excess) by or as if by cutting: *trim off the rotten bark; trimmed the budget.* **3.** To ornament; decorate: *trim the dress with a band of lace.* **4.** *Informal.* **a.** To thrash. **b.** To defeat soundly. **c.** To cheat. **d.** To rebuke or scold. **5.** *Nautical.* **a.** To adjust (the sails and yards of a ship) so that they receive the wind properly. **b.** To balance (a ship) by shifting its cargo or contents. **6.** To balance (an aircraft) in flight by regulating the control surfaces and tabs. —*intr.* **1.** *Nautical.* **a.** To be in or retain equilibrium. Used of a ship. **b.** To make the sails and yards of a ship ready for sailing. **2. a.** To affect cautious neutrality between conflicting interests. **b.** To fashion one's views for momentary popularity or advantage.
~*n.* **1. a.** Order, arrangement, or appearance; condition: *in good trim.* **b.** A condition of good health, fitness or order: *got himself in trim.* **2. a.** Mouldings, framework, or other exterior ornamentation. **b.** Adornment or decoration, as for clothing. **3.** Dress or equipment. **4.** Excised or rejected material, such as film that has been cut in editing. **5.** A clipping or trimming to make neat: *The verge needs a trim; My fringe needs a trim.* **6.** *U.S.* A commercial window display. **7.** *Nautical.* **a.** The readiness of a vessel for sailing, with regard to ballast, sails, and yards. **b.** The balance of a ship. **c.** The difference between the draught at the bow and at the stern. **8.** The position of an aircraft relative to its horizontal axis.
~*adj.* **trimmer, trimmest. 1.** In good or neat order or condition. **2.** In good shape; slim. [Perhaps from Middle English *trimmen* (unattested), Old English *trymman, trymian,* to strengthen, arrange.] **—trim·ly** *adv.* **—trim·ness** *n.*

tri·ma·ran (trī́mə-ran, -rán) *n.* A sailing vessel with three hulls set side by side. [TRI- + (CATA)MARAN.]

tri·mer (trī́mər) *n. Chemistry.* A oligomeric compound consisting of three identical monomeric molecules or groups. [TRI- + -MER.]

trim·er·ous (trímmərəss) *adj.* **1.** Having three similar segments or parts. **2.** *Botany.* Having flower parts, such as petals, sepals, and stamens, in sets of three. Also written *3-merous.* [New Latin *trimerus,* from Greek *trimerēs* : TRI- + -MEROUS.] **—trim·er·ism** *n.*

tri·mes·ter (trī-méstər, tri-) *n.* **1.** A period or term of three months. **2.** *U.S.* In some universities, any of three equal academic terms into which the year is divided. Compare **semester.**
~*adj.* Also **tri·mes·tral** (-méstrəl), **tri·mes·tri·al** (-méstri-əl). Of or pertaining to periods of three months. [French *trimestre,* from Latin *trimestris,* "of three months" : *tri-,* three + *mēnsis,* month.]

trim·e·ter (trímmitər) *n.* A line of verse consisting of three metrical feet. [Latin *trimetrus,* from Greek *trimetros* : TRI- + METER.] **—tri·met·ric** (trī-méttrik), **tri·met·ri·cal** *adj.*

tri·meth·a·di·one (trī-méthə-dī́-ōn) *n.* A granular, crystalline substance, $C_6H_9NO_3$, used in treating petit mal epilepsy. Also called "troxidone".

trimetric projection *n.* A method of projection, used especially for mechanical drawings, in which the representation involves three axes with arbitrary angles and scales.

tri·met·ro·gon (trī-méttrə-gən, -gon) *n.* A system of aerial photography in which one vertical and two oblique photographs are simultaneously taken for use in topographic mapping. [TRI- + Greek *metron*, measure, METER + -GON.]

trim·mer (trímmər) *n.* **1.** A person or machine that trims, especially any of various devices used for trimming, such as a hedge trimmer. **2.** A person who changes his opinions to suit the needs of the moment; a timeserver. **3.** *Electronics.* A variable component used to make fine adjustments to capacity, resistance, or the like. **4.** *Architecture.* A beam across an opening, such as a hearth, into which the ends of joists can be fitted.

trim·ming (trímming) *n.* **1.** That which is added as decoration; especially, a band of lace, embroidery, or the like used to decorate clothing. **2.** *Plural.* Accessories; extras: *roast turkey with all the trimmings.* **3.** *Plural.* That which is removed when something is trimmed; excess. **4.** *Informal.* A sound defeat, beating, or punishment.

tri·mo·lec·u·lar (trī-mə-léckew-lər, -mo-, -mō-) *adj.* Pertaining to or formed from three molecules.

tri·month·ly (trī-múnthli) *adj.* Done, occurring, or appearing every three months. —**tri·month·ly** *adv.*

tri·morph (trī-mawrf) *n.* **1.** A substance that occurs in three distinct forms. **2.** One of the forms in which such a substance occurs. [Back-formation from TRIMORPHIC.]

tri·mor·phic (trī-mór-fik) *adj.* Also **tri·mor·phous** (-fəss). **1.** *Biology.* Having or occurring in three differing forms. **2.** *Chemistry.* Crystallising in three distinct forms. [TRI- + -MORPH(OUS) + -IC.] —**tri·mor·phi·cal·ly** *adv.* —**tri·mor·phism** *n.*

Tri·mur·ti (tri-moórti) *n. Hindu Mythology.* The Vedaic triad of Brahma, Vishnu, and Shiva. [Sanskrit *trimūrti : tri,* three + *mūrti†,* form.]

tri·nal (trín'l) *adj.* Having three parts; threefold; triple. [Latin *trīnālis,* from Latin *trīnus,* TRINE.]

tri·na·ry (trínəri) *adj.* Consisting of three parts or proceeding by threes; ternary. [From Late Latin *trīnārius,* from Latin *trīnus,* TRINE.]

trine (trīn) *adj.* **1.** Threefold; triple. **2.** In astrology, of or designating the trine aspect of two planets. ~*n.* **1.** A group of three. **2.** In astrology, the aspect of two planets when 120 degrees apart. [Middle English, from Old French, from Latin *trīnus,* from *trīnī,* three each.]

Trin·i·dad and To·ba·go, Republic of (trínni-dad, -dád; tə-báygō, tō-). A state of the southeastern Caribbean, an independent republic within the Commonwealth. Both islands are woody and hilly; oil and asphalt have replaced sugar as the chief product. Population, 1,100,000. The capital is Port-of-Spain.

Tri·nil man (tréenil) *n.* **Java man** (*see*). [After *Trinil,* village in Java, where remains were found.]

Trin·i·tar·i·an (trínni-taír-i-ən) *adj.* **1.** Describing or relating to the Trinity. **2.** Believing or professing belief in the Trinity or the doctrine of the Trinity. Compare **Unitarian. 3.** Pertaining to the Order of the Holy Trinity. ~*n.* **1.** A person who believes in the doctrine of the Trinity. **2.** A member of the Order of the Holy Trinity, founded in 1198 for the ransoming of Christian captives from the Muslims. —**Trin·i·tar·i·an·ism** *n.*

tri·ni·tro·ben·zene (trī-nítrō-bén-zeen, -ben-zéen) *n.* A yellow crystalline compound, C₆H₃(NO₂)₃, derived from trinitrotoluene and used as an explosive.

tri·ni·tro·cre·sol (trī-nítrō-krée-sol ‖ -sól) *n.* A yellow crystalline compound, CH₃C₆H(NO₂)₃OH, used in high explosives.

tri·ni·tro·glyc·er·in (trī-nítrō-glíssə-reen, -rin) *n. Chemistry.* **Nitroglycerin** (*see*).

tri·ni·tro·phe·nol (trī-nítrō-fée-nol ‖ -nōl) *n.* **Picric acid** (*see*).

tri·ni·tro·tol·u·ene (trī-nítrō-tóllew-een) *n.* A yellow crystalline compound, CH₃C₆H₂(NO₂)₃, used mainly as a high explosive. Also called "TNT", "trinitrotoluol".

trin·i·ty (trínnəti, trínniti) *n., pl.* **-ties. 1.** The state or condition of being three. **2.** A group of three; a triad. Also called "triunity". [Middle English *trinite,* from Old French, from Latin *trīnitās,* from *trīnus,* TRINE.]

Trinity *n.* **1.** *Theology.* The union of three divine figures, the Father, Son, and Holy Ghost, in one Godhead. **2.** Trinity Sunday.

Trinity Brethren *pl.n.* The members of Trinity House.

Trinity House *n.* A British association that takes measures to safeguard shipping around the coastline, as by providing and maintaining lighthouses and buoys.

Trinity Sunday *n.* The first Sunday after Pentecost, or Whitsunday, dedicated to the Trinity. Also called "Trinity".

Trinity term *n.* In some British universities and colleges, the summer term. [After TRINITY SUNDAY.]

trin·ket (tríngkit) *n.* **1.** Any small ornament, such as a piece of jewellery. **2.** A trivial thing; a trifle. [16th century : origin obscure.]

tri·noc·u·lar (trī-nóckew-lər) *adj.* Pertaining to or having a binocular eyepiece with an additional lens system for photographic recording. Said especially of microscopes. [TRI- + (BI)NOCULAR.]

tri·no·mi·al (trī-nōmi-əl, trí-) *adj.* **1.** Consisting of three names or terms, as a taxonomic designation may. **2.** *Mathematics.* Having three algebraic terms connected by plus or minus signs. ~*n.* **1.** A three-part taxonomic designation indicating genus, species, and subspecies or variety, such as *Brassica oleracea botrytis,* the cauliflower. **2.** *Mathematics.* A trinomial algebraic expression. [TRI- + (BI)NOMIAL.]

tri·o (trée-ō) *n., pl.* **-os. 1.** Any three people or things joined or associated. **2.** *Music.* **a.** A composition for three performers.

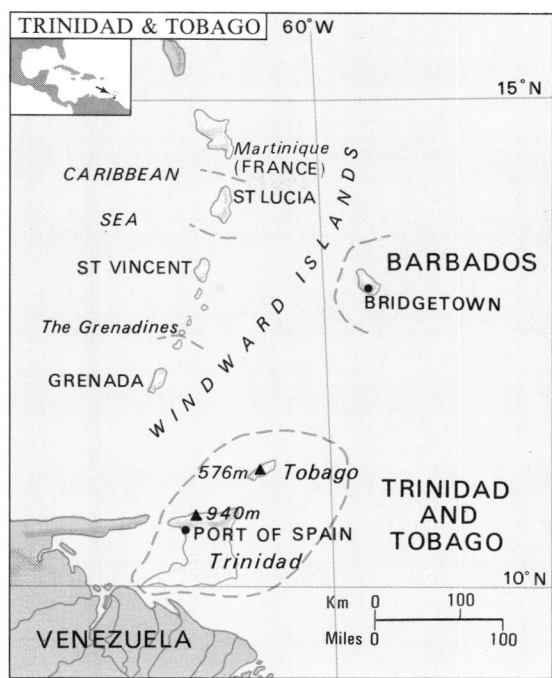

trillium *There are 30 species of trillium, all distinguished by having their leaves, sepals, and petals in groups of three. This is Trillium grandiflorum, a native of eastern North America.*

b. The people (collectively) who perform this composition. **c.** The middle section of a minuet or scherzo, a march, or of various dance forms. [Italian, variant (influenced by *duo*) of Latin *tria,* neuter of *trēs,* three.]

tri·ode (trī-ōd) *n.* A type of thermionic valve containing an anode, a cathode, and a control grid. [TRI- + -ODE (path).]

tri·oe·cious, tri·e·cious (trī-éeshəss, trī-) *adj. Botany.* Having male, female, and hermaphrodite flowers borne on separate plants. [New Latin *Trioecia,* former order of such plants : TRI- + Greek *oikia,* dwelling, from *oikos,* house.] —**tri·oe·cious·ly** *adv.*

tri·ol (trī-ol ‖ -ōl) *n. Chemistry.* Trihydric alcohol. [TRI- + -OL.]

tri·o·le·in (trī-óli-in) *n. Chemistry.* **Olein** (*see*).

tri·o·let (trée-ō-let, trī-, -ə-, -lət, -lit) *n.* A poem or stanza of eight lines constructed on two rhymes, the scheme being *abaaabab.* [French, diminutive of *trio,* trio, from Italian, TRIO.]

tri·ox·ide (trī-ók-sīd, trí-) *n.* Also **tri·ox·id** (-sid). A chemical compound containing three oxygen atoms per molecule.

trip (trip) *n.* **1. a.** A going from one place to another, especially by ship or aeroplane; a voyage; a journey: *a trip to America.* **b.** Any excursion or journey: *a trip to the shops.* **2.** *Slang.* **a.** The mental state or experience induced by a hallucinogen, such as LSD: *an acid trip.* **b.** A hallucinogenic drug: *drop a trip.* **c.** Any experience or state of mind that is considered similar to the effects of a hallucinogenic drug in being stimulating, exciting, or extremely subjective: *a power trip.* **3.** A light or nimble tread or step. **4.** A stumble or fall. **5.** A way of causing a stumble or fall, as by catching the foot of someone walking. **6.** A mistake, slip, or blunder. **7. a.** A catch for tripping a mechanism. **b.** The action of such a catch. ~*v.* **tripped, tripping, trips.** —*intr.* **1.** To stumble; fall: *tripped over.* **2.** To move nimbly with or as if with light, rapid steps: *trip along.* **3.** To make a mistake; go wrong: *tripped up on the last question.* **4.** To be released, as a tooth on an escapement wheel in a watch. **5.** *Rare.* To take a trip. **6.** *Slang.* To experience a hallucinogenic drug. —*tr.* **1.** To cause to stumble or fall. Often used with *up.* **2.** To trap or catch in an error or inconsistency. **3.** *Archaic.* To perform (a dance) nimbly. **4.** To release a catch, trigger, or switch that sets (a mechanism, for example) in operation. **5.** *Nautical.* **a.** To raise (an anchor) from the bottom. **b.** To tip or turn (a yardarm) into a position for lowering. **c.** To lift (an upper mast) in order to remove the pin or fid before lowering. [Middle English, short journey, light movement, from *trippen,* to move nimbly, cause to stumble, from Old French *trip(p)er,* from Middle Dutch *trippen,* to hop.]

tri·pal·mi·tin (trī-pál-mətin, trí-) *n. Chemistry.* **Palmitin** (*see*).

tri·par·tite (trī-pár-tīt, trí-) *adj.* **1.** Composed of or divided into three parts. **2.** Pertaining to or executed by three parties. **3.** *Botany.* Divided into three parts. Said especially of leaves.

tri·par·ti·tion (trī-paar-tish'n) *n.* Division into three parts or among three parties: *the tripartition of a defeated nation.*

tripe (trīp) *n.* **1.** The pale, rubbery lining of the stomach of cattle or other ruminants, used as food. **2.** *Informal.* Anything with no meaning or value; rubbish or nonsense. [Middle English, from Old French *tripe†.*]

tri·ped·al (trī-pédd'l) *adj.* Having three feet or legs; tripodal. [Latin *tripedālis : tri-,* three + *pēs* (stem *ped-*), foot.]

tri·pet·al·ous (trī-pétt'l-əss) *adj. Botany.* Having three petals.

trip·ham·mer (trip-hámmər) *n.* Also **trip hammer.** A heavy, power-

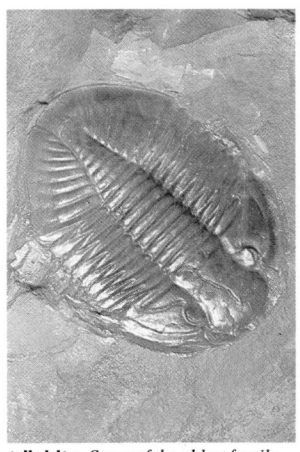

trilobite *Some of the oldest fossils on Earth show that these marine shellfish, now extinct, flourished for 350 million years and were in existence at least 600 million years ago. Trilobites had compound eyes, similar to those of a modern insect, and some deep-sea species developed a special double lens to help them see in the low light. The horseshoe crab is their only living relative.*

tripod *The device used by surveyors and cameramen is a very ancient invention. On this Greek vase, painted in the fifth century* B.C., *Hercules is shown holding a sacred tripod he has stolen from the Delphi oracle. On the right, the oracle's patron god Apollo pleads with him to return it.*

triptych *A triptych altarpiece, now in the Museum of Folklore in Basel, Switzerland.*

operated hammer that is lifted by a cam or lever and then dropped.

tri·phen·yl·me·thane (trī-fēen-īl-mēe-thayn, -fēn-) *n.* A colourless, crystalline hydrocarbon, $(C_6H_5)_3CH$, from which a large number of synthetic dyes are derived by substitution.

tri·phib·i·ous (trī-fíbbi-əss, trī́-) *adj.* Taking place on land, at sea, and in the air. Said of military operations. [TRI- + (AM)PHIBIOUS.]

triph·thong (tríf-thong, *also* tríp- || *U.S. also* -thawng) *n.* **1.** A compound vowel sound resulting from the combination of three simple ones and functioning as a unit. **2.** A **trigraph** *(see).* [TRI- + (DI)PHTHONG.] **—triph·thon·gal** (-thóng-g'l || -tháwng-) *adj.*

triph·y·lite (tríffi-līt) *n.* Also **triph·y·line** (-leen). A vitreous bluish-grey mineral $LiFePO_4$. [TRI- + Greek *phulon,* tribe (see **phyletic**) + -ITE (from its three bases).]

tri·pin·nate (trī-pínnayt, trī́-) *adj. Botany.* Divided into leaflets that are subdivided into smaller, further subdivided leaflets or lobes, as are the fronds of some ferns. **—tri·pin·nate·ly** *adv.*

tri·plane (trī́-playn) *n.* An aeroplane with wings placed above each other in three levels.

tri·ple (trípp'l) *adj.* **1.** Consisting of three parts; threefold. **2.** Three times as many or as much.

~n. **1.** A number or quantity three times as great as another. **2.** A group or set of three; a triad.

~v. **tripled, -ling, -les.** *—tr.* To make three times as great in number or amount. *—intr.* To be or become three times as great in number or amount. [Middle English, from Old French, from Latin *triplus* : *tri-,* three + *-plus,* "-fold".] **—tri·ply** *adv.*

Tri·ple Alliance (trípp'l) *n.* An alliance between three countries, especially: **1.** The alliance of England, Sweden, and the Netherlands against France in 1668. **2.** The alliance of England, France, and the Netherlands against Spain in 1717, called the Quadruple Alliance when joined by Austria in 1718. **3.** The Dreibund formed by Germany, Austria, and Italy in 1882.

Triple Entente *n.* The military alliance formed by Great Britain, France, and Russia prior to World War I as a means of counterbalancing the Dreibund.

triple jump *n.* An athletics field event in which the competitor, after a run-up, must cover in a continous movement the greatest distance possible with a hop, step, and a jump.

triple point *n. Physics.* The point at which the solid, liquid, and gas phases of a given substance are all in equilibrium with each other.

trip·let (tríp-lət, -lit) *n.* **1.** A group or set of three of one kind. **2.** Any of three children born at one birth. **3.** In prosody, a **tercet** *(see).* **4.** A group of three musical notes having the time value of two notes of the same kind. **5.** *Physics.* A **multiplet** *(see)* with three components. [*Triple* + double*t.*]

tri·ple·tail (trípp'l-tayl) *n.* Any of several chiefly marine fishes of the genus *Labotes*; especially, the North American *L. surinamensis,* having prominent dorsal and anal fins that resemble extra tails.

triple time *n.* A musical time or rhythm having three beats in each bar, with the accent on the first beat. Also called "triple measure". **—tri·ple-time** (trípp'l-tīm, -tīm) *adj.*

tri·ple-tongu·ing (trípp'l-túng-ing || *Northern England also* -tóng-) *n.* The playing of a wind instrument in a fast tempo, moving the tongue as if to pronounce repeatedly t, k, and t. Compare **double-tonguing, single-tonguing. —tri·ple-tongue** *v.*

tri·plex (tríp-leks || trī́p-) *adj.* Composed of three parts; threefold; triple. [Latin, threefold, triple.] **—tri·plex** *n.*

Tri·plex (tríp-leks) *n.* In Britain, a trademark for a type of safety glass consisting of two glass sheets sandwiching a transparent sheet of plastic, used especially in car windows.

trip·li·cate (tríppli-kət, -kit, -kayt) *adj.* Threefold; especially, made with three identical copies.

~n. **1.** Any of a set of three identical objects or copies. **2.** The state of being in three copies: *The contract was in triplicate.*

~tr.v. (-kayt) **triplicated, -cating, -cates. 1.** To increase threefold; triple. **2.** To make three identical copies of. [Latin *triplicātus,* past participle of *triplicāre,* to triple, from *triplex* (stem *triplic-*), TRIPLEX.] **—trip·li·cate·ly** *adv.* **—trip·li·ca·tion** (-káysh'n) *n.*

tri·plic·i·ty (tri-plíssəti, trī-) *n., pl.* **-ties. 1.** The condition or quality of being triple. **2.** A group or set of three. **3.** In astrology, any of four groups of the zodiac, each consisting of three signs. In this sense, also called "trigon". [Middle English *triplicite,* a trigon, from Late Latin *triplicitās,* quality of being triple, from TRIPLEX.]

trip·lo·blas·tic (trípplō-blástik) *adj.* Having a body made up from three embryonic germ layers. Said of all animals except protozoans, sponges, and coelenterates. Compare **diploblastic.** [*Triplo-,* threefold, from Greek *triploos* + -BLAST + -IC.]

trip·loid (tríppioyd) *adj.* Having three times the haploid number of chromosomes in each nucleus.

~n. An organism having such sets of chromosomes. [Greek *triploos,* triple + (HAPL)OID.]

tri·pod (trī́-pod) *n.* **1.** A three-legged stool, table, or the like. **2.** An adjustable three-legged stand, as for supporting a camera. [Latin *tripūs* (stem *tripod-*), from Greek *tripous,* three-footed : *tri-,* three + *-pous,* -POD.] **—trip·o·dal** (-'l, tríppəd'l) *adj.*

trip·o·li (tríppəli) *n.* A porous, lightweight, siliceous rock of various colours, used as an abrasive. [Found in TRIPOLI, Libya.]

Trip·o·li (tríppəli). *Arabic* **Tarabalus al-Gharb.** Ancient name **Oea.** Capital and chief port of Libya. Founded by the Phoenicians, probably in the 7th century B.C., it was held in turn by the Romans, Vandals, Byzantines, and Arabs. It fell to the Ottoman Turks (1551) and was a stronghold of Barbary Pirates (16th–19th centuries). The city was taken by the Italians (1910) and British (1943).

tri·pos (trī́-poss) *n., pl.* **-poses.** At Cambridge University, any of the courses or examinations for the B.A. degree with honours. [Variant of Latin *tripūs,* TRIPOD, referring to a stool on which formerly an appointed bachelor of arts sat at a graduation ceremony to deliver a humorous address; later, to verses written for this occasion, to a list of students qualified for honours in mathematics written on the back of the verses, and later to honours examinations in mathematics and in other subjects.]

trip·per (tríppər) *n.* **1.** *Chiefly British Informal.* A short-term holidaymaker. **2.** A tripping device on a mechanism.

trip·pet (tríppit) *n.* A cam or projection in a mechanism designed to strike another part at regular intervals. [Middle English *tripet,* piece of wood used in a game, from *trippen,* to TRIP.]

trip·ping (trípping) *adj.* Moving or stepping lightly and briskly; easy; nimble: *a tripping tongue.* **—trip·ping·ly** *adv.*

trip·tane (tríp-tayn) *n.* A liquid hydrocarbon, C_7H_{16}, used as an antiknock additive in aviation fuels. [Short for *trimethylbutane.*]

trip·tych (tríp-tik, *also* -tich) *n.* **1.** A tableau of three hinged or folding panels bearing a religious story in painting or carving, used as an altarpiece. **2.** A hinged writing tablet consisting of three leaves, used in ancient times. [Greek *triptukhos,* threefold : *tri-,* three + *ptukhē,* fold (see **diptych**).]

trip·tyque (trip-tēek) *n.* A customs permit for the passage of a motor vehicle. [French, TRIPTYCH (referring to its three sections).]

trip·wire (tríp-wīr) *n.* A wire that activates an alarm, trap, or the like when brushed in passing.

tri·que·trous (trī́-kwēe-trəss, -kwe-) *adj.* Triangular and acutely angled, especially in cross section: *a triquetrous stem.* Compare **trigonous.** [Latin *triquetrus,* three-cornered.]

tri·reme (trī́-reem, trīr-) *n.* An ancient Greek or Roman galley or warship, having three tiers of oars on each side. [Latin *trirēmis,* having three tiers of oars : *tri-,* three + *rēmus,* oar.]

tri·sac·cha·ride (trī-sáckə-rīd, trī́-) *n. Chemistry.* A carbohydrate that upon hydrolysis yields three monosaccharides.

tri·sect (trī-sékt, trī́-) *tr.v.* **-sected, -secting, -sects.** To divide into three, usually equal, parts. [TRI- + -SECT.] **—tri·sec·tion** (-séksh'n) *n.* **—tri·sec·tor** (-séktər) *n.*

tri·sep·al·ous (trī-sépp'l-əss) *adj.* Having three sepals.

tri·shaw (trī́-shaw) *n.* A light, pedalled rickshaw with three wheels. [TRI- + (RICK)SHAW.]

tri·skel·i·on (trī-skélli-ən, tri-, -on) *n., pl.* **-ia** (-ə). Also **tri·skele, tri·scele** (trī́ss-keel, tríss-). A figure consisting of three curved lines or branches, or three stylised human arms or legs, radiating from a common centre. [New Latin, from Greek *triskelēs,* three-legged : *tri-,* three + *skelos,* leg.]

tris·mus (trízməss) *n. Pathology.* **Lockjaw** *(see).* [Greek *trismos, trigmos,* a scream, a grating (of the teeth).] **—tris·mic** *adj.*

tris·oc·ta·he·dron (tríss-óktə-hēed-rən, -héd-) *n., pl.* **-drons** or **-dra** (-rə). **1.** In geometry, a solid figure having 24 congruent triangular faces and an octahedron as a base. **2.** In crystallography, a **trapezohedron** *(see).* [Greek *tris,* thrice + OCTAHEDRON.] **—tris·oc·ta·he·dral** *adj.*

tri·so·mic (trī-sṓmik, trī́-) *adj. Genetics.* Having one chromosome represented three times in an otherwise diploid set. [TRI- + (CHROMO)SOM(E) + -IC.] **—tri·some** (trī́-sōm) *n.*

Tris·tan (trístən). Also **Tris·tram** (tríss-trəm). A hero of medieval legend who fell in love with Iseult, the bride of King Mark of Cornwall, after they accidentally drank a love potion.

Tris·tan da Cu·nha (trístən də kōōn-ə, -yə). Group of volcanic islands in the South Atlantic. Only one of the four, Tristan, is inhabited, by fewer than 300 people, descendants of a British garrison placed there in 1816 when Napoleon was exiled to St. Helena, of which the group is a dependency. Edinburgh is the capital.

tri·ste·a·rin (trī-stēer-in, -stēe-ər-) *n. Chemistry.* **Stearin** *(see).*

trist·ful (trístf'l) *adj.* Also **triste** (trist, treest). *Archaic.* Sorrowful; gloomy. [Middle English *trist,* from Old French *triste,* from Latin *trīstis*†, gloomy.] **—trist·ful·ly** *adv.* **—trist·ful·ness** *n.*

tris·tich (trístik) *n.* A stanza or strophic unit of three lines. [TRI- + (DI)STICH.] **—tri·stich·ic** (tri-stíckik) *adj.*

tri·stim·u·lus (trī-stímmew-ləss) *adj.* Of or pertaining to the values of the three primary colours that when combined additively produce a colour to match the colour of an unknown sample.

tri·sul·phide (trī-súl-fīd, trī́-) *n.* A sulphide containing three sulphur atoms per molecule.

tri·syl·la·ble (trī́-síllәb'l, trí-, -sillәb'l) *n.* A word consisting of three syllables. **—tri·syl·lab·ic** (-si-lábbik) *adj.* **—tri·syl·lab·i·cal·ly** *adv.*

tri·tan·o·pi·a (trītə-nṓpi-ə, tríttə-) *n.* A rare visual defect involving an inability to distinguish the colour blue. [New Latin, "ability to see only one third (of the colours of the spectrum)" : Greek *tritos,* a third + *anopia,* blindness : AN- (not) + -OPIA.] **—tri·tan·op·ic** *adj.*

trite (trīt) *adj.* **triter, tritest. 1.** Overused and commonplace; lacking interest or originality. **2.** *Archaic.* Frayed or worn by use. [Latin *trītus,* past participle of *terere,* to rub (away), wear out.] **—trite·ly** *adv.* **—trite·ness** *n.*

Synonyms: *trite, hackneyed, shopsoiled, stereotyped, commonplace, threadbare, stale, banal.*

tri·the·ism (trī́-thee-iz'm) *n.* A belief in three gods; specifically, the belief that the Father, Son, and Holy Ghost are three separate and distinct gods. **—tri·the·ist** *n.* **—tri·the·is·tic** (-ístik) *adj.*

trit·i·ate (trítti-ayt || tríshi-) *tr.v.* **-ated, -ating, -ates.** To treat with tritium; especially, to replace the hydrogen atoms in (a molecule) by tritium atoms for labelling. [TRITIUM + -ATE.] **—trit·i·a·tion** *n.*

trit·i·ca·le (trítti-kaáli, -káyli) *n.* A fertile, hybrid cereal obtained by crossing wheat and rye. [Latin *triticum,* wheat + *secale,* rye.]

trit·i·um (trítti-əm || *U.S. also* tríshi-) *n.* A rare radioactive hydrogen isotope with atomic mass 3 and half-life 12.5 years, prepared artificially for use as a tracer and as a constituent of hydrogen bombs. [New Latin, from Greek *tritos,* third.]

tri·ton¹ (trít'n) *n.* Any of various chiefly tropical marine gastropod molluscs of the genus *Cymatium* and related genera, having a pointed, spirally twisted, often colourfully marked shell. [After TRITON, whose trumpet is a shell.]

tri·ton² (trī́-ton) *n.* The nucleus of a tritium atom consisting of two neutrons and one proton. [TRIT(IUM) + -ON.]

Tri·ton¹ (trít'n). *Greek Mythology.* **1.** A god of the sea, son of Poseidon and Amphitrite, portrayed as having the head and trunk of a man and the tail of a fish. **2.** Any of a race of lesser sea deities.

Triton² *n.* The larger satellite of the planet Neptune.

tri·tone (trī́-tōn) *n. Music.* An interval composed of three whole tones. [Greek *tritonos,* having three tones : TRI- + TONE.]

trit·u·rate (tríttewr-ayt, tríchər-) *tr.v.* **-rated, -rating, -rates.** To crush, grind, or pound into fine particles or a powder; pulverise.
~*n.* (-ət, -it, -ayt). A triturated substance, especially a powdered drug. Also called "trituration". [Late Latin *trītūrāre,* to pulverise corn, from Latin *trītūra,* a rubbing or chafing, from *trītus,* past participle of *terere,* to rub.] **—trit·u·ra·ble** (-əb'l) *adj.*

trit·u·ra·tion (tríttewr-áysh'n, tríchər-) *n.* **1.** The act or process of triturating something. **2.** A triturate. **3.** The composing of a dental amalgam by mortar and pestle.

tri·umph (trī́-əmf, -umf) *intr.v.* **-umphed, -umphing, -umphs. 1.** To be victorious or successful; win; prevail. **2.** To rejoice over a success or victory; exult. **3.** In ancient Rome, to receive honours upon return from a victory.
~*n.* **1.** The instance or fact of being victorious; success. **2.** A remarkable achievement or feat. **3.** Exultation or merriment derived from victory or success. **4.** A public celebration in ancient Rome to welcome a returning victorious commander and his army. [Middle English, from Old French *triumphe(r),* from Latin *triumphāre,* from *triumphus,* a triumph, variant of Old Latin *triumpus,* probably from Greek *thriambos,* hymn to Bacchus.] **—tri·umph·er** *n.*

tri·um·phal (trī-úmf'l) *adj.* **1.** Pertaining to or having the nature of a triumph. **2.** Celebrating or commemorating a victory: *a triumphal procession; a triumphal arch.* —See Usage note at **triumphant.**

tri·um·phant (trī-úmfənt) *adj.* **1.** Exulting in success or victory. **2.** Victorious; conquering; successful. **—tri·um·phant·ly** *adv.*
Usage: *Triumphant* and *triumphal* are not usually interchangeable. *Triumphant* now generally means exulting in success or victory: *The football team returned home triumphant. Triumphal* is a more specific term, describing the formal celebration of a triumph: *There was a triumphal procession to mark the navy's return.*

tri·um·vir (trī-úm-vər, tri-, trī́-əm-, -vur) *n., pl.* **-virs** or **-viri** (-vi-ree, -və-, -rī). Any of three men sharing public administration or civil authority, as in ancient Rome. [Latin, singular of *triumvirī,* from *trium virōrum,* "(one) of three men", genitive of *trēs virī,* three men.] **—tri·um·vi·ral** *adj.*

tri·um·vi·rate (trī-úmvər-ət, tri-, -it, -ayt) *n.* **1.** A group of three men jointly governing a realm. **2. a.** The office or term of a triumvir. **b.** Government by triumvirs. **3.** Any association or group of three. [Latin *triumvirātus,* from *triumvir,* TRIUMVIR.]

tri·une (trī́-yōōn) *adj.* Being three in one. Said especially of the single Godhead of the Trinity.
~*n. Rare.* **1.** A trinity. **2.** *Capital* **T.** The holy Trinity. [TRI- + Latin *ūnus,* one.]

tri·u·ni·ty (trī-yōōnəti) *n., pl.* **-ties.** A **trinity** *(see).*

tri·va·lent (trī-váylənt, trī́-) *adj.* Also **ter·va·lent** (ter-, tér-). *Chemistry.* **1.** Having a valency of 3. **2.** Having three valencies. **—tri·va·lence, tri·va·len·cy** *n.*

tri·valve (trī́-valv) *adj.* Having three valves.

triv·et (trívvit) *n.* **1.** A three-legged stand made of iron or a similar metal, used for supporting cooking vessels in a fireplace. **2.** A metal stand with short feet, used under a hot dish on a table. [Middle English *trevet,* probably Old English *trefet,* from Latin *tripēs,* "three-footed" : *tri-,* three + *pēs,* foot.]

triv·i·a¹ (trívvi-ə). Plural of **trivium.**
~*pl.n.* Insignificant or inessential matters; trivialities; trifles. [New Latin, plural of TRIVIUM (sense influenced by TRIVIAL).]

triv·i·al (trívvi-əl) *adj.* **1.** Of little importance or significance; trifling. **2.** Ordinary; commonplace. **3.** Concerned with or involving trivia. **4.** *Mathematics.* Having or pertaining to solutions with zero values. **5.** Of or pertaining to the trivium. [Latin *triviālis,* pertaining to the TRIVIUM (hence, commonplace, of little account; sense development perhaps influenced by later scorn for medieval learning).] **—triv·i·al·ly** *adv.*
Synonyms: *trivial, trifling, paltry, petty.*

triv·i·al·ise (trívvi-ə-līz) *tr.v.* **-ised, -ising, -ises.** To make trivial; devalue. **—triv·i·al·i·sa·tion** (-lī-záysh'n || *U.S.* -li-) *n.*

triv·i·al·i·ty (trívvi-ál-əti) *n., pl.* **-ties. 1.** The condition or quality of being trivial. **2.** A trivial matter, idea, or occurrence.

trivial name *n.* **1.** In taxonomic nomenclature, the term following the genus name and designating the species, as *troglodytes* in *Pan troglodytes,* the chimpanzee. **2.** A vernacular name as distinguished from a taxonomic designation. **3.** *Chemistry.* A name for a compound that is not systematic and gives no indication of the compound's molecular structure, such as *toluene* for *methylbenzene.*

triv·i·um (trívvi-əm) *n., pl.* **-ia** (-ə). The first division of the seven liberal arts in medieval schools, consisting of grammar, logic, and rhetoric. Compare **quadrivium.** [Medieval Latin, from Latin, place where three roads meet : *tri-,* three + *via,* road, way.]

tri·week·ly (trī-weékli, trī́-) *adj.* Happening, done, or appearing: **1.** Three times a week. **2.** Every three weeks.
~*adv.* **1.** Three times a week. **2.** Every three weeks.
~*n., pl.* **triweeklies.** A periodical published triweekly.

-trix *n. suffix, pl.* **-trices** or **-trixes.** Indicates: **1.** Feminine agency, corresponding to masculine or common nouns in *-tor;* for example, **testatrix. 2.** A geometric line, point, or surface; for example, **directrix.** [Latin *-trix* (stem *-tric-*).]

t RNA *n.* **Transfer RNA** *(see).*

Tro·bri·and Islands (trṓbri-and, -ənd). Archipelago lying off Papua New Guinea, by which the islands are administered. The chief island is Kirwana (or Trobriand).

tro·car (trṓ-kaar) *n.* A sharp-pointed surgical instrument within a cannula, used to puncture a body cavity and remove fluid. [French *trocart,* "three-sided instrument" (referring to its triangular shape) : *trois,* three, + *carre,* side.]

tro·cha·ic (trə-káy-ik, trō-) *adj.* Of, pertaining to, or consisting of trochees.
~*n.* A trochaic metrical foot, line of verse, or poem. [French *trochaïque,* from Latin *trochaicus,* from Greek *trokhaikos,* from *trokhaios.* See **trochee.**]

tro·chal (trṓk'l) *adj.* Shaped like a wheel: *the trochal disc of a rotifer.* [Greek *trokhos,* wheel, from *trekhein,* to run.]

tro·chan·ter (trō-kántər) *n.* **1.** Any of several bony processes on the upper part of the femur of many vertebrates. **2.** The second proximal segment of the leg of an insect. [Greek *trokhantēr,* from *trekhein,* to run. See **trochal.**]

troche (trōsh, *rarely* trōk, -i) *n.* A small circular medicinal lozenge; a pastille. [Earlier *trochies* (plural), from Middle English *trociske* (singular), from Late Latin *trochiscus,* from Greek *trokhiskos,* diminutive of *trokhos,* wheel. See **trochal.**]

tro·chee (trṓ-kee, -ki) *n.* A metrical foot consisting of a long syllable followed by a short (in quantitative verse), or a stressed syllable followed by an unstressed (in accentual verse). There are four trochees in the following line: *Peter, Peter, pumpkin eater.* Also called "trochaic". Compare **iamb.** [Latin, from Greek *trokhaios (pous),* running (foot), from *trekhein,* to run.]

troch·le·a (tróckli-ə) *n., pl.* **-leae** (-ee). An anatomical structure that resembles a pulley, such as the part of the distal end of the humerus that articulates with the ulna. [Latin, system of pulleys, from Greek *trokhileia.*]

troch·le·ar (tróckli-ər) *adj.* **1.** Of, resembling, or situated near a trochlea. **2.** Of or pertaining to the trochlear nerve. **3.** *Botany.* Shaped like a pulley.
~*n.* The trochlear nerve.

trochlear nerve *n.* Either of the fourth pair of cranial nerves that supplies the superior oblique muscle of the eyeballs. Also called "trochlear".

tro·choid (trṓk-oyd, trók-) *adj.* Also **tro·choi·dal** (trō-kóyd'l, tro-). **1.** Capable of or exhibiting rotation about a central axis. **2.** Permitting rotation, as does a pulley or pivot.
~*n.* In geometry, a plane curve formed by the locus of a point on the radius or on an extension of the radius of a circle, as the circle rolls along a fixed straight line. [Greek *trokhoeidēs,* resembling a wheel, wheel-like, circular : *trokhos,* wheel (see **troche**) + -OID.] **—tro·choi·dal·ly** *adv.*

troch·o·phore (trók-ō-fawr, -ə- || -fōr) *n.* The small aquatic larva of various invertebrates, including certain molluscs and annelids. [Greek *trokhos,* wheel (see **troche**) + -PHORE (from its spheroidal body and ring of cilia).]

trod. Past tense and alternative past participle of **tread.**

trod·den. Past participle of **tread.**

trode. *Archaic.* Past tense of **tread.**

trof·fer (tróffər) *n.* An inverted, usually metal trough suspended from a ceiling as a fixture for fluorescent lighting tubes. [From *troff-,* variant of TROUGH.]

trog (trog) *intr.v.* **trogged, trogging, trogs.** *British Informal.* To trudge; plod wearily. Often used with *along.* [TRUDGE + SLOG.]

trog·lo·dyte (tróg-lə-dīt, -lō-) *n.* **1.** A prehistoric cave dweller. **2.** A person likened to a caveman, as in reclusiveness or brutishness. **3.** An anthropoid ape, such as the gorilla. [Latin *Trōglodyta,* from Greek *Trōglodutēs,* singular of *Trōglodutai,* variant (influenced by *trōglos,* cave, and *-dutai,* those who enter) of *Trōgodutai*†, name of an Ethiopian people.] **—trog·lo·dyt·ic** (-díttik), **trog·lo·dyt·i·cal** *adj.*

tro·gon (trṓ-gon) *n.* Any of various colourful tropical birds of the family Trogonidae, which includes the quetzal. [New Latin, "gnawer", from Greek *trōgōn,* present participle of *trōgein,* gnaw.]

troi·ka (tróykə) *n.* **1. a.** A kind of small Russian carriage drawn by a team of three horses abreast. **b.** A team of three horses abreast. **2.** A triumvirate. [Russian *troyka,* from *troye,* three (collectively).]

troil·ism (tróyl-iz'm) *n.* Sexual intercourse engaged in by three people, usually two women and one man. [Probably from French *trois,* three (as in *ménage à trois*) + *-l-,* as in *dualism.*]

Troi·lus (trō-i-ləss, tróy-). *Greek Mythology.* A son of Priam of Troy, killed by Achilles. He is depicted as Cressida's lover in medieval romance.

Tro·jan (trṓjən) *n.* **1.** A native or inhabitant of ancient Troy. **2.** A person of courageous determination or energy.
~*adj.* Of or pertaining to ancient Troy or its residents. [Middle English, from Latin *Trōjānus,* from *Trōjā,* TROY.]

trogon *There are more than 30 species of trogon, an insect-eating bird mostly native to the tropical forests of the Americas, Africa, and Asia. The copper-tailed trogon (above) is the only species found in the United States.*

PRONUNCIATION KEY

a, trap; aa, father; ai, fair; ar, star; aw, lawn; ay, play; b, bb, stab; rubber; ch, church; ck, ticket; d, dd, dead; ladder; e, dress; ee, bee; er, defer; ew, few; ewr, pure; ə, about; ər, letter; f, ff, fife; differ; g, gg, giggle; h, hat; i, kit; ī, price; īr, fire; j, judge; k, kick; l, ll, let; 'l, needle; m, mm, man; n, nn, no; 'n, sudden; ng, thing; o, lot; ō, no; ŏŏ, foot; ōō, shoe; oor, poor; ow, cow; owr, hour; oy, boy; p, pp, pepper; r, rr, red; s, ss, sauce; sh, ship; t, tt, totter; th, thick; th, this; smooth; u, cut; ur, turn; v, vv, valve; w, wet; y, yes; z, zz, zebra; zh, vision; pleasure

IN FOREIGN WORDS:

aN, oN, Saint-Saëns; hl, Llanelli; Hluhluwe; kh, loch; lough; Khaled

STRESS MARK:

ín-sīt, insight; in-sī́t, incite

trompe l'oeil *A section of Peruzzi's painting* View of Rome *illustrates the artistic device called trompe l'oeil, a French phrase meaning literally "deceives the eye".*

Trojan horse *n.* **1.** *Greek Mythology.* The hollow wooden horse in which the Greeks hid and gained entrance to Troy, later opening the gates to their army. In this sense, also called "Wooden Horse". **2.** Any subversive group or device insinuated within enemy ranks.

Trojan War *n. Greek Mythology.* The prehistoric ten-year war waged against Troy by the confederated Greeks, ending in the burning of Troy. It is known chiefly through Homeric legend, which gives the cause as the abduction of the Spartan queen, Helen, by Paris, a Trojan prince.

troll[1] (trōl; *also, especially for senses 5, 6,* trol) *v.* **trolled, trolling, trolls.** *—tr.* **1.** To fish for by trailing a baited line from behind a slowly moving boat. **2.** To trail (a baited line) in fishing. **3.** To sing in succession the parts of (a round, for example). **4.** To sing heartily: *troll a carol.* **5.** To roll or revolve. *—intr.* **1.** To fish by trailing a line, as from a moving boat. **2.** To sing heartily or gaily. **3.** To be sung or uttered in a rolling, hearty manner: *The tune trolled on.* **4.** To roll or spin round. **5.** *British Informal.* To wander; stroll. Often used with *along.* **6.** *Chiefly British Slang.* To cruise looking for sexual partners. Used of a man.
~*n.* **1.** The act of trolling for fish. **2.** A lure used for trolling, such as a spoon or spinner. [Middle English *trollen*†, to ramble, roll.]

troll[2] (trōl, trol) *n.* **1.** A supernatural creature of Scandinavian folklore variously portrayed as a friendly or mischievous dwarf, or sometimes a dangerous giant, that lives in caves, in the hills, or under bridges. **2.** A tiny, hairy plastic monster, often put as decoration on the end of a pencil. [Old Norse *troll*†, monster, demon.]

trol·ley (trólli) *n., pl.* **-leys.** **1.** *Chiefly British.* Any of various low two- or four-wheeled carts, especially: **a.** A small, sometimes tiered, table on casters used for carrying food, dishes, and other household objects from room to room. **b.** A shopping cart used in supermarkets. **c.** A luggage cart used in stations, airports, or the like. **2.** *British.* A trolley bus. **3.** A wheeled carriage, cage, or basket that is suspended from and travels on an overhead track. **4.** A device that collects electric current from an underground conductor, an overhead wire, or a third rail, and transmits it to the motor of an electric vehicle. **5.** *Chiefly British.* A small truck or car operating on a track and used in a mine, quarry, or factory for conveying materials.
~*v.* **trolleyed, -leying, -leys.** *—tr.* To convey by trolley. *—intr.* To travel by trolley. [Originally dialect, from TROLL (to move about).]

trolley bus *n.* An electric bus that does not run on tracks and is powered by electricity from an overhead wire. Also *British* "trolley".

trolley car *n. U.S.* A **tram** *(see).*

trol·lop (tróllәp) *n.* **1.** A slovenly, untidy woman. **2.** A loose woman; a strumpet. [17th century : perhaps akin to TRULL.]

Trol·lope (tróllәp), **Anthony** (1815–82). British novelist. His ecclesiastical novels set in the imaginary county of Barsetshire include *The Warden* (1885), *Barchester Towers* (1857), and *The Last Chronicle of Barset* (1867). Among his novels dealing with political life are *Phineas Finn* (1869) and *The Eustace Diamonds* (1873).

trom·bic·u·li·a·sis (trom-bickew-lī-ә-siss) *n.* Also **trom·bic·u·lo·sis** (-lō-siss), **trom·bi·di·a·sis** (trómbi-dī-ә-siss). *Pathology.* Infestation with mites of the genus *Trombicula,* which if untreated results in severe dermatitis. [New Latin : *Trombicula,* genus of mites, diminutive of *Trombidium*† + -IASIS.]

trom·bone (trom-bōn ‖ trәm-, tróm-bōn) *n.* **1.** A brass musical instrument consisting of a long cylindrical tube bent upon itself twice, ending in a bell-shaped mouth, and varied in length to produce different notes by means of a U-shaped slide. **2.** The member of an orchestra who plays trombone. [French, from Italian, augmentative of *tromba,* trumpet, from Old High German *trumpa,* TRUMP.] **—trom·bon·ist** *n.*

trom·mel (trómm'l) *n.* A revolving cylindrical sieve used for sizing rock and ore. [German *Trommel,* barrel, drum, from Middle High German *trummel,* from *trumme,* drum, akin to Middle Dutch *tromme,* DRUM.]

tromp (tromp) *v.* **tromped, tromping, tromps.** *Informal. —intr.* To walk heavily and noisily; tramp. *—tr.* **1.** To trample underfoot. **2.** *U.S. Informal.* To defeat soundly; trounce. **—tromp on.** *U.S. Informal.* To abuse verbally. [Blend of TRAMP and STOMP.]

trompe (tromp) *n.* An apparatus in which water falling through a perforated pipe entrains air into and down the pipe to produce an air blast for a furnace or forge. [French, "trumpet", from Old French. See **trump** (trumpet).]

trompe l'oeil (trónp lő-i) *n.* **1.** A technique of depicting objects so realistically that the viewer is tricked into believing they really exist in three dimensions. **2.** A trick painting in this style, such as a window frame on a sheer brick wall. [French, "deceive the eye".]

tron (tron) *n. Scottish.* Also **trone** (trōn). A bulk weighing machine for merchandise. [Middle English, from Old French *trone,* from Latin *trutina,* from Greek *trutanē,* balance, pair of scales.]

-tron *n. comb. form.* Indicates: **1.** A vacuum tube; for example, **dynatron.** **2.** A device for manipulating subatomic particles; for example, **cyclotron.** [Greek, suffix denoting instrument.]

tro·na (trōnә) *n.* A natural vitreous grey or white mineral, $Na_2CO_3 \cdot NaHCO_3 \cdot 2H_2O$, used as a source of sodium compounds. [Swedish, probably from Arabic *trōn,* short for *naṭrūn,* natron.]

Trond·heim (trónd-hīm; *Norwegian* trón-yem). Formerly **Ni·da·ros** (needә-rooss). Seaport of central Norway. Founded (997) on the south side of Trondheim Fjord, it is an important fishing centre.

troop (troop) *n. Abbr.* **trp.** **1.** A group or company of people, animals, or things. **2.** *Military.* **a.** A division of a cavalry unit, commanded by a captain. **b.** A group of soldiers. **c.** *Informal.* A soldier: *40 troops died.* **3.** *Plural.* Military units; soldiers. **4.** A unit of two or more patrols of Scouts or Girl Guides. **5.** *Informal.* A great many; a lot. —See Synonyms at **flock.**
~*v.* **trooped, trooping, troops.** *—intr.* **1.** To move or go as a throng. **2.** To proceed; move along: *children trooping home.* **3.** *Archaic.* To consort; associate. Used with *with.* *—tr. Chiefly British Military.* To parade (a flag) ceremonially. Used chiefly in the phrases *troop the colour, trooping of the colour.* [French *troupe,* backformation from *troupeau,* herd, from Medieval Latin *troppus*†.]

troop carrier *n.* A vehicle, aircraft, or ship built to carry troops.

troop·er (troopәr) *n.* **1. a.** A cavalryman. **b.** A cavalry horse. **2.** *Australian & U.S.* A policeman mounted on a horse or motor cycle. **3.** *Chiefly British Informal.* A troopship. **—swear like a trooper.** To swear frequently and obscenely.

troop·ship (troop-ship) *n.* A ship, usually one that has been modified or converted, designed for carrying troops.

troost·ite (troost-īt) *n.* A reddish mineral, a variety of **willemite** *(see),* in which the zinc is partly replaced by manganese. [After Gerald *Troost* (1776–1850), U.S. geologist.]

trop. tropic; tropical.

tro·pae·o·lum (tro-peé-ә-lәm, trō-) *n., pl.* **-lums** or **-la** (-lә). Any trailing or climbing succulent plant of the South American genus *Tropaeolum;* especially, the garden nasturtium, *T. majus,* which has orange, yellow, or red spurred flowers and smooth leaves. [New Latin, from Latin *tropaeum,* TROPHY (referring to the leaves and flowers, which resemble shields and helmets).]

trope (trōp) *n.* **1.** The figurative use of a word or expression; a figure of speech. **2.** A word or phrase interpolated as an embellishment in the sung parts of certain medieval liturgies. [Latin *tropus,* from Greek *tropos,* a turn, way, manner, from *trepein,* to turn.]

-trope *n. comb. form.* Indicates: **1.** Orientation or development towards; for example, **heliotrope.** **2.** A version; for example, **allotrope.** [Greek *tropos,* turn, turning, from *trepein,* to turn.]

troph·al·lax·is (tróffә-láksiss ‖ trōfә-) *n.* The mutual exchange of food between adults and larvae that occurs among certain social insects such as ants and wasps. [New Latin, from TROPHO- + Greek *allaxis,* exchange, from *allassein,* to change.]

troph·ic (tróffik ‖ *chiefly U.S.* trōfik) *adj.* Of or pertaining to nutrition or to the nutritive processes. [Greek *trophikos,* nursing, from *trophē,* food, from *trephein,* to nourish.] **—troph·i·cal·ly** *adv.*

trophic level *n. Ecology.* A group of organisms that occupy the same position on a food chain in that they obtain their food, ultimately from plants, by the same number of steps.

tropho- *comb. form.* Indicates nutrition; for example, **trophoblast.** [Greek *trophē,* food, from *trephein,* to nourish.]

troph·o·blast (tróf-ә-blast, -ō-, -blaast ‖ trōf-) *n.* The outermost layer of cells of the morula that attaches the fertilised ovum to the wall of the mammalian uterus and acts as a nutritive pathway. Also called "trophoderm". [TROPHO- + -BLAST.] **—troph·o·blas·tic** (-blástik) *adj.*

troph·o·zo·ite (tróf-ә-zó-īt, -ō- ‖ trōf-) *n.* A protozoan of the class Sporozoa in the active feeding stage. [TROPHO- + ZO(O)- + -ITE.]

tro·phy (trōfi) *n., pl.* **-phies.** **1.** A prize or memento, such as a cup or plaque, received as a symbol of victory, especially in sports. **2.** An accumulation of captured arms or other spoils kept as a memorial of victory. **3.** A specimen or part, such as a lion's head, preserved as a token of a successful hunt. **4.** In ancient Greece and Rome, the captured arms and spoils of a defeated enemy set up as a memorial, often on the field of battle. **5.** *Architecture.* A marble carving or bronze cast depicting a group of weapons, armour, or the like placed upon a four-sided or circular base as an ornament. **6.** Any memento, as of one's personal achievements. [French *trophee,* from Latin *trophaeum,* from Greek *tropaion,* "monument of the enemy's defeat", from *tropaios,* of turning, of defeat, from *tropē,* a turn, repulse of the enemy. See **trope.**]

-trophy *n. comb. form.* Indicates a specified type of nutrition or growth; for example, **hypertrophy.** [New Latin *-trophia,* from Greek, from *trophē,* food. See **tropho-.**]

trop·ic (tróppik) *n. Abbr.* **trop.** **1.** *Astronomy.* Either of two circles on the celestial sphere parallel to and at an angular distance of 23° 27′ from the equator and forming the limits of the apparent northern and southern passages of the Sun. **2.** *Geography.* Either of the two corresponding parallels of latitude on the earth that constitute the boundaries of the Torrid Zone. See **tropic of Cancer, tropic of Capricorn.** **3.** *Plural.* The region of the earth's surface lying between these latitudes; the Torrid Zone. Usually preceded by *the.*
~*adj.* Of or pertaining to the tropics; tropical. [Middle English *tropik,* solstice point at which the Sun "turns" back and moves towards the Earth, from Late Latin *tropicus,* from Greek *tropikos,* of turning, from *tropē,* a turn. See **trope.**]

-tropic *adj. comb. form.* Indicates turning in response to a specified stimulus; for example, **phototropic.** [Greek *tropos,* a turn, TROPE.]

trop·i·cal[1] (tróppik'l) *adj. Abbr.* **trop.** **1.** Of, indigenous to, or characteristic of the tropics. **2.** Hot and humid; sultry; torrid. **—trop·i·cal·ly** *adv.*

trop·i·cal[2] (tróppik'l; *also* trōpik'l) *adj.* Of or pertaining to a rhetorical trope.

tropical cyclone *n.* A very low pressure area 80 to 160 kilometres (50 to 100 miles) in radius that originates in tropical regions and is frequently marked by winds of hurricane strength circulating around the calm eye in the centre of the region.

trop·i·cal·ise (tróppik'l-īz) *tr.v.* **-ised, -ising, -ises.** **1.** To make tropical. **2.** To make suitable for a tropical climate, as by adapting to tropical temperatures.

tropical storm *n.* A tropical cyclone having winds ranging from 48 kilometres (30 miles) to 160 kilometres (75 miles) per hour.

tropical year *n.* The time interval between two successive passages of the Sun through the vernal equinox; the calendar year, or 365.2422 mean solar days. Also called "solar year". See **year.**

trop·ic·bird (tróppik-burd) *n.* Any of several predominantly white sea birds of the genus *Phaëthon,* of warm regions, having a pair of long, slender, projecting tail feathers.

tropic of Cancer *n.* The parallel of latitude 23° 30′ north of the equator, the northern boundary of the Torrid Zone, and the most northerly latitude at which the Sun reaches an altitude of 90°.

tropic of Capricorn *n.* The parallel of latitude 23° 30′ south of the equator, the southern boundary of the Torrid Zone, and the most southerly latitude at which the Sun reaches an altitude of 90°.

tro·pine (trṓ-peen, -pin) *n.* Also *U.S.* **tro·pin** (-pin). A white, crystalline, poisonous alkaloid, $C_8H_{15}NO$, having an odour like that of tobacco and used to treat spasms. [Short for ATROPINE.]

tro·pism (trṓp-iz'm) *n. Biology.* The directional growth movement of a plant part in response to an external stimulus. Also called "tropic movement". [Greek *tropos,* turn (see **-trope**) + -ISM.] **—tro·pis·mat·ic** (-iz-máttik), **tro·pis·tic** (-ístik) *adj.*

-tropism *n. comb. form.* Indicates the growth of a plant part in response to a specified stimulus; for example, **phototropism.** [Greek *tropos,* turn. See **tropo-.**]

tropo– *comb. form.* Indicates turning or change, especially change of temperature or condition; for example, **troposphere.** [Greek *tropos,* a turn, change.]

tro·pol·o·gy (tro-póllәji, trō-) *n., pl.* **-gies. 1.** The use of tropes in speech or writing. **2.** A mode of Biblical scholarship insisting on the morally edifying interpretation of tropes in Scripture. [Late Latin *tropologia,* from Late Greek : Greek *tropos,* TROPE + -LOGY.] **—tro·po·log·ic** (tróppә-lójik, trṓpә-), **tro·po·log·i·cal** *adj.* **—tro·po·log·i·cal·ly** *adv.*

tro·po·pause (tróppә-pawz, trṓpә-) *n.* The boundary between the upper troposphere and the lower stratosphere that varies in altitude from 8 kilometres (5 miles) at the poles to 16 kilometres (10 miles) at the equator.

tro·po·phyte (tróppә-fīt, trṓpә-) *n.* A plant adapted to changeable climatic conditions. **—tro·po·phyt·ic** (-fíttik) *adj.*

tro·po·sphere (tróppә-sfeer, trṓpә-) *n.* The lowest region of the atmosphere between the earth's surface and the tropopause, characterised by decreasing temperature with increasing altitude. **—tro·po·sphe·ric** *adj.*

-tropous *adj. comb. form.* Indicates a turning away; for example, **amphitropous, anatropous.** [Greek *-tropos,* of turning, from *trepein,* to turn.]

trop·po (tróppō) *adv. Music.* Too much. Usually used with the negative in the cautionary phrase *ma non troppo,* as a direction: *allegro ma non troppo.* [Italian.]

-tropy *n. comb. form.* Indicates the condition of turning; for example, **allotropy, thixotropy.** [Greek *-tropia,* from *-tropos,* -TROPOUS.]

trot (trot) *n.* **1.** The gait of a horse or other four-footed animal, between a walk and a canter in speed, in which diagonal pairs of legs move forwards together. **2.** A ride on a horse at this pace. **3.** A human gait, faster than a walk; a brisk step. **4.** A race for trotters. **5.** An old woman; a crone. **6.** *Chiefly British Rare.* A toddler. **7.** *Australian Slang.* A run of luck. **8.** *U.S. Informal.* A translation used by a student; a crib. **—on the trot. 1.** In succession. **2.** Busy, bustling about. **—the trots.** *Slang.* Diarrhoea.
∼v. **trotted, trotting, trots.** *—intr.* **1.** To go or move at a trot. **2. a.** To proceed rapidly; hurry. **b.** To go; move. Often used with *along.* **3.** To fish in a fast-moving current using a weighted line. *—tr.* To cause to move at a trot. **—trot out.** *Informal.* To bring out and show for or as if for inspection or admiration. [Middle English, from Old French, from *troter,* to trot, from Vulgar Latin *trottāre* (unattested), from Frankish *trottōn* (unattested).]

Trot (trot) *n. British Slang.* **1.** A Trotskyist. **2.** Loosely, any Communist. Used derogatorily.

troth (trōth; *rarely* troth || trawth) *n. Archaic.* **1.** Good faith; fidelity. **2.** One's pledged fidelity; especially, a betrothal: *plight one's troth.*
∼tr.v. **trothed, trothing, troths.** *Archaic.* To pledge or betroth. [Middle English *trouth(e),* Old English *trēowth,* TRUTH.]

troth·plight (trṓth-plīt, tróth- || tráwth-) *n. Archaic.* A betrothal.
∼tr.v. **trothplighted, -plighting, -plights.** *Archaic.* To betroth. [Middle English *trouth plight* : TROTH + PLIGHT (pledge).]

Trot·sky (trótski), **Leon,** born Lev Davidovich Bronstein (1879–1940). Russian revolutionary. He was one of the leaders of the Bolshevik Revolution (1917). His policy for permanent revolution led to dismissal from the Politburo by Stalin (1926) and eventual exile from Russia (1929). He moved to Mexico (1937), where he was assassinated three years later.

Trot·sky·ism (trótski-iz'm) *n.* The theories of Communism advocated by Leon Trotsky and his followers, who argued for the permanent worldwide revolution of the proletariat and bitterly opposed the leadership of Stalin. **—Trot·sky·ist** *adj. & n.*

Trot·sky·ite (trótski-īt) *n.* A Trotskyist. Used derogatorily. **—Trot·sky·ite** *adj.*

trot·ter (tróttәr) *n.* **1.** A horse that trots; especially, one trained for harness racing. **2.** *Informal.* A foot; especially, the foot of a pig prepared as food.

trou·ba·dour (tro͞obә-door, -dawr || -dōr) *n.* **1.** Any of a class of lyric poets of the 12th and 13th centuries attached to the courts of Provence and northern Italy, who composed songs in complex metrical forms. Compare **trouvère. 2.** A strolling minstrel. [French, Old French, from Old Provençal *trobador,* from *trobar,* to invent, compose poetry, variant of Old French *trover.* See **trouvère.**]

troub·le (trúbb'l) *n.* **1.** A state of distress, affliction, danger, or need. **2.** Something that contributes to such a state; a difficulty or problem: *One trouble after another delayed the job.* **3.** Exertion; effort; pains: *went to a lot of trouble.* **4.** A condition of pain, disease, or malfunction: *heart trouble.* **5.** *Plural.* Political unrest or war. Usually used euphemistically: *the Troubles in Cyprus.* **—in trouble.** *Informal.* **1.** At a disadvantage. **2.** Due to be admonished or punished: *in big trouble with the boss.* **3.** *Chiefly British.* Pregnant. Said euphemistically of an unmarried woman.
∼v. **troubled, -ling, -les.** *—tr.* **1.** To agitate; stir up: *troubled waters.* **2.** To afflict with pain or discomfort. **3.** To cause distress or confusion in; vex; perturb. **4.** To inconvenience; bother: *May I trouble you to close the window?; Please don't trouble yourself.* **5.** *West Indian.* To interfere with. *—intr.* To take pains: *to trouble over every detail.* [Middle English, from Old French, from *troubler,* to trouble, from Vulgar Latin *turbulāre,* from *turbulus,* confused, from Latin *turbidus,* TURBID.] **—troub·ler** *n.* **—troub·ling·ly** *adv.*

troub·le·mak·er (trúbb'l-maykәr) *n.* A person who habitually stirs up trouble or strife. **—troub·le·mak·ing** *adj. & n.*

troub·le-shoot·er (trúbb'l-sho͞otәr) *n. Chiefly U.S.* A person who locates and eliminates sources of trouble, as in mechanical operations or diplomatic affairs. **—troub·le·shoot·ing** *n. & adj.*

troub·le·some (trúbb'l-s'm) *adj.* **1.** Causing trouble, especially repeatedly; worrisome. **2.** Difficult; trying. —See Synonyms at **hard. —troub·le·some·ly** *adv.* **—troub·le·some·ness** *n.*

trouble spot *n.* A place of recurring trouble or unrest, especially political unrest.

troub·lous (trúbblәss) *adj. Archaic & Poetic.* Attended with trouble; uneasy; troubled. **—troub·lous·ly** *adv.* **—troub·lous·ness** *n.*

trou-de-loup (tro͞o-dә-lo͞o) *n., pl.* **trous-de-loup** (*pronounced as singular*). *Military.* Any of a series of conical pits having pointed stakes set upright in their centres, formerly used to provide an obstacle to enemy cavalry. [French, "wolf's pit".]

trough (trof || trawf; *some bakers say* trow) *n.* **1.** A long, narrow, generally shallow receptacle, especially one for holding water or feed for animals. **2.** A gutter under the eaves of a roof. **3.** A long, narrow depression, as between waves or ridges. **4.** A low point in a business cycle or on a statistical graph. **5.** *Meteorology.* An elongated region of low atmospheric pressure, often associated with a front. **6.** *Physics.* A minimum point in a wave or alternating signal. [Middle English *trough,* Old English *trog.*]

trounce (trownss) *tr.v.* **trounced, trouncing, trounces. 1.** To thrash; beat. **2.** To defeat decisively. [16th century (meaning "harrass, afflict") : origin obscure.]

troupe (tro͞op) *n.* A company or group, especially of touring actors, singers, or dancers.
∼intr.v. **trouped, trouping, troupes.** To tour with a theatrical company. [French, TROOP.]

troup·er (tro͞opәr) *n.* **1.** A member of a theatrical company. **2.** A veteran actor or performer. **3.** *Informal.* A plucky and staunch colleague or worker.

troup·i·al (tro͞opi-әl) *n.* Any of several tropical American birds of the genus *Icterus,* related to the orioles and New World blackbirds; especially, *I. icterus,* having orange and black plumage. [French *troupiale,* from *troupe,* flock, TROOP (from its living in flocks).]

trou·ser (trówzәr) *adj.* Of, for, or being a part of, trousers: *a trouser pocket.* [Back-formation from TROUSERS.]

trou·sers (trówzәrz) *pl.n.* An outer garment for covering the body from the waist to the ankles, divided into two tubelike sections to fit each leg separately. **—wear the trousers.** *Chiefly British.* To be the dominant party: *Who wears the trousers in this house?* [Variant (influenced by DRAWERS) of earlier *trouse,* from Gaelic *triubhas* (singular), TREWS.]

trou·ser-suit (trówzәr-so͞ot, -sewt) *n. Chiefly British.* A woman's two-piece outfit consisting of trousers and a matching jacket or top.

trous·seau (tro͞o-sō || tro͞o-sṓ) *n., pl.* **-seaux** (-z) or **-seaus.** The special wardrobe assembled by a bride before her wedding, especially in former times. [French, from Old French, diminutive of *trusse,* a bundle. See **truss.**]

trout (trowt) *n., pl.* **trouts** (for all senses) or **trout** (for senses 1, 2). **1.** Any of various freshwater or anadromous food and game fishes of the genera *Salmo* and *Salvelinus,* usually having a speckled body. **2.** Broadly, any of various similar fishes. **3.** *British Slang.* A silly old person. [Old English *trūht,* from Late Latin *tructa*†.]

trou·vère (tro͞o-váir) *n.* Also **trou·veur** (-vúr, -vṓr). Any of a school of poets flourishing in northern France from the 11th to the 13th centuries, who chiefly wrote narrative works, such as the chansons de geste. Compare **troubadour.** [French, from Old French *trovere,* from *trover,* to invent, find, compose poetry, from Vulgar Latin *tropāre* (unattested), to use tropes, from Latin *tropus,* TROPE.]

tro·ver (trṓvәr) *n. Law.* A common-law action to recover damages for personal property illegally withheld or wrongfully converted to use by another. [Anglo-French, from Old French. See **trouvère.**]

trow (trō) *intr.v.* **trowed, trowing, trows.** *Archaic.* To think; suppose; trust. [Middle English *trowen, trewen,* Old English *trēowian.*]

trow·el (trów-әl) *n.* **1.** A flat-bladed hand tool for levelling, spreading, or shaping substances such as cement or mortar. **2.** A small

trotter *A trotter is a horse which has been trained to race competitively without breaking into a canter or a gallop and drawing a light chariot. The sport of trotting is especially popular in the United States.*

PRONUNCIATION KEY

a, trap; aa, father; ai, fair;
ar, star; aw, lawn; ay, play;
b, bb, stab; rubber;
ch, church; ck, ticket;
d, dd, dead; ladder; e, dress;
ee, bee; er, defer; ew, few;
ewr, pure; ә, about;
әr, letter; f, ff, fife; differ;
g, gg, giggle; h, hat; i, kit;
ī, price; īr, fire; j, judge;
k, kick; l, ll, let; 'l, needle;
m, mm, man; n, nn, no;
'n, sudden; ng, thing; o, lot;
ō, no; o͝o, foot; o͞o, shoe;
oor, poor; ow, cow;
owr, hour; oy, boy;
p, pp, pepper; r, rr, red;
s, ss, sauce; sh, ship;
t, tt, totter; th, thick; th, this;
smooth; u, cut; ur, turn;
v, vv, valve; w, wet; y, yes;
z, zz, zebra; zh, vision;
pleasure

IN FOREIGN WORDS:

aN, oN, Saint-Saëns;
hl, Llanelli; Hluhluwe;
kh, loch; lough; Khaled

STRESS MARK:

ín-sīt, insight; in-sīt, incite

implement with a pointed, scoop-shaped blade used in gardening for digging or lifting plants, and similar tasks.

~*tr.v.* **trowelled** or *U.S.* **troweled, -elling** or *U.S.* **-eling, -els.** To spread, smooth, dig, or scoop with or as if with a trowel. [Middle English *trowell,* from Old French *truelle,* from Late Latin *truella,* variant of Latin *trulla,* diminutive of *trua†,* stirring spoon, ladle.]

trox·i·done (trŏksi-dōn) *n.* **Trimethadione** *(see).*

troy (troy) *adj. Abbr.* **t** Of or expressed in troy weight. [Middle English *troye,* from Anglo-French, probably first used at a fair in *Troyes,* France.]

Troy (troy). Ancient city in northwestern Asia Minor near the Dardanelles, also called Ilion (Latin Ilium). Its remains were first excavated (1870–90) by Heinrich Schliemann. The site revealed ten major periods of occupation since the Early Bronze Age. The Troy of Homer's *Iliad* and *Odyssey* was probably a city destroyed by fire in the middle of the 13th century B.C. after a long siege.

Troyes (*French* trwaa). Capital of the Aube département, and formerly of the Champagne, northeastern France, on the river Seine.

troy weight *n. Abbr.* **t** A system of units used in weighing precious metals and gems, in which the grain is the same as in the avoirdupois system and the pound contains 12 ounces, 240 pennyweights, or 5,760 grains. [See **troy.**]

trp. troop.

trs. transpose.

Trst. See **Trieste.**

tru·an·cy (trŏo-ən-si ‖ trĕw-) *n., pl.* **-cies.** Also **tru·ant·ry** (-tri). 1. An act or instance of playing truant. 2. The condition of being truant.

tru·ant (trŏo-ənt ‖ trĕw-) *n.* 1. One who is absent without permission, especially from school. 2. A person who shirks work or duty. ~*adj.* 1. Absent without permission, especially from school. 2. Idle, lazy, or neglectful. —**play truant.** To absent oneself from school, especially habitually, without authorisation.

~*intr.v.* **truanted, -anting, -ants.** To play truant. [Middle English, beggar, idle rogue, from Old French, from Gaulish *trugant-.*]

truce (trŏoss ‖ trewss) *n.* A temporary cessation or suspension of hostilities by agreement of the contending forces; an armistice. [Middle English *trewes,* plural of *trewe,* truce, peace, Old English *trēow,* faith, pledge.]

Trucial States. See **United Arab Emirates.**

truck¹ (truk) *n.* 1. a. *Chiefly British.* A sturdy motor vehicle with an open back designed for transporting loads. b. *Chiefly U.S.* A **lorry** *(see).* 2. A two-wheeled barrow for moving heavy objects by hand. 3. A wheeled platform, sometimes equipped with a motor, for conveying loads in a warehouse or freight yard. 4. *British.* A railway freight wagon without a top. 5. One of the swivelling frames of wheels under each end of a railway carriage, tram, or the like. 6. The swivelling frame of wheels under a skateboard. 7. *Nautical.* A disc-shaped block at the head of a mast with holes used for hoisting or lowering flags or sails.

~*v.* **trucked, trucking, trucks.** —*tr.* To transport by truck. —*intr.* 1. To carry goods by truck. 2. *Chiefly U.S.* To drive a truck. 3. *Chiefly U.S. Slang.* To make one's way; saunter: *trucking on down the avenue.* [Perhaps short for TRUCKLE ("pulley").]

truck² *v.* **trucked, trucking, trucks.** —*tr.* 1. To exchange; barter. 2. *Rare.* To peddle. —*intr.* To have dealings or commerce; traffic. ~*n.* 1. Trade goods; articles of commerce. 2. Barter; exchange. 3. The payment of wages in goods or kind rather than money. 4. *U.S.* Garden produce grown for the market. 5. *Informal.* Dealings; business: *I'll have no truck with them.* 6. *Informal.* Worthless articles; rubbish. [Middle English *trukken,* from an Anglo-French, akin to Medieval Latin *trocāre,* to exchange, barter.]

truck·age (trúckij) *n. U.S.* 1. The transportation of goods by truck. 2. A charge for this.

truck·er (trúckər) *n. U.S.* 1. A truck driver. 2. A person or company engaged in trucking goods.

truck farm *n. U.S.* A **market garden** *(see).* Also called "truck garden". —**truck farmer** *n.* —**truck farming** *n.*

truck·le (trúck'l) *n.* A small wheel or roller; a caster.

~*intr.v.* **truckled, -ling, -les.** To be servile or submissive; yield weakly. Used with *to.* [Middle English *trocle,* pulley, from Anglo-French, from Latin *trochlea,* system of pulleys. See **trochlea.**]

truckle bed *n. British.* A low bed on casters that can be rolled under another bed when not in use. Also called "trundle bed".

truck·load (trúk-lōd) *n.* The quantity or weight that a truck carries.

truck·man (trúk-mən) *n., pl.* **-men** (-mən). *U.S.* 1. A truck driver. 2. A person engaged in the trucking business; a trucker.

truck system *n.* The system of paying wages in goods instead of money, especially as practised during the Industrial Revolution.

truc·u·lence (trúckew-lənss) *n.* Also **truc·u·len·cy** (-i). 1. Pugnacity; belligerence. 2. Savagery.

truc·u·lent (trúckew-lənt) *adj.* 1. Disposed to fight; defiant; recalcitrant. 2. Savage and cruel; fierce. 3. Vitriolic; scathing. [Latin *truculentus,* from *trux* (stem *truc-*), fierce.] —**truc·u·lent·ly** *adv.*

Tru·deau (trŏo-dō ‖ -dō; *French* trü-), **Pierre (Elliott)** (1919–). Canadian statesman. As prime minister (1968–79) he opposed French separatism and introduced (1970) a brief spell of martial law to counteract agitation in Quebec.

trudge (truj) *intr.v.* **trudged, trudging, trudges.** To walk in a laborious or weary way; plod.

~*n.* A long, tedious walk. [16th century : origin obscure.]

trudg·en, trudg·eon (trújən) *n.* A swimming stroke in which a double overarm movement is combined with a scissors kick. Also called

truffle *An edible fungus which grows underground, mostly in chalky soil near the roots of beech or evergreen oak trees. It is eaten as a delicacy, and dogs and pigs are trained to find them by smell.*

"trudgen stroke". [Introduced from Argentina by John *Trudgen,* 19th-century British swimmer.]

true (trŏo ‖ trew) *adj.* **truer, truest.** 1. Consistent with fact or reality; not false or erroneous. 2. a. Exactly conforming to a rule, standard, or pattern: *true to form.* b. Proper: *a true soufflé.* 3. Reliable; accurate: *a true prophecy.* 4. Real; genuine: *true suede.* 5. Faithful, as to a friend, vow, or cause; steadfast; loyal: *a true socialist.* 6. *Archaic.* Honourable; upright. 7. Sincerely felt or expressed; unfeigned: *true sorrow.* 8. Fundamental; essential: *her true motives.* 9. Rightful; legitimate: *the true heir.* 10. Accurately shaped or fitted. 11. Accurately placed, delivered, or thrown. 12. Determined with reference to the earth's axis, not the magnetic poles: *true north.* 13. Conforming to the requirements of the definiton; properly or accurately so called: *The horseshoe crab is not a true crab.* 14. Flat and horizontal: *a true level.* 15. *Physics.* Not apparent or relative. Said of a physical property. —See Synonyms at **real, faithful.** —**come true.** To become fact; conform to expectation or prediction. —**too true.** Correct; right. Often used as a rueful interjection. ~*adv.* 1. Rightly; truthfully. 2. Unswervingly; exactly: *aimed true.* 3. So as to conform to the ancestral type or stock: *breed true.* ~*tr.v.* **trued, truing** or **trueing, trues.** To adjust or fit so as to conform with a standard. Often used with *up.* ~*n.* 1. Truth. 2. Proper alignment or adjustment: *in or out of true.* [Middle English *trewe,* Old English *trēowe,* loyal, trustworthy.] —**true·ness** *n.*

true bearing *n.* The angular distance clockwise from a meridian of longitude.

true bill *n.* 1. *Law.* In the United States and formerly in Britain, a bill of indictment endorsed by a grand jury. 2. A true assertion.

true-blue, true blue (trŏo-blŏo ‖ trĕw-, -blew) *n.* 1. *Chiefly British.* A staunch conservative. 2. A person of unswerving loyalty. [Originally a 17th-century Scottish Presbyterian or Covenanter, from the colour blue adopted in opposition to the Royalists' red.] —**true-blue** *adj.*

true-born (trŏo-bawrn ‖ trĕw-) *adj.* Being authentically or genuinely as specified, by or as if by birth.

true-life (trŏo-līf ‖ trĕw-) *adj.* Based on fact; having happened in reality. Said of reports, stories, and works of literature.

true-love (trŏo-luv ‖ trĕw-) *n.* 1. One's beloved; a sweetheart. 2. A plant, **herb Paris** *(see).*

true lovers' knot *n.* A love knot *(see).*

true-pen·ny (trŏo-penni ‖ trĕw-) *n., pl.* **-nies.** *Archaic.* An honest fellow; a trusty person. [By association with a genuine coin.]

true rhyme *n.* Perfect rhyme *(see).*

true rib *n.* Any of the ribs, in humans any of the upper seven, that are attached to the sternum by a costal cartilage.

Truf·faut (trŏo-fō ‖ trŏo-fō; *French* trü-), **François** (1932–). French film director. His films include *Les Quatre-cents Coups* (a prize-winner at Cannes Film Festival, 1959), *Jules et Jim* (1961), and *Le Dernier Métro* (1980).

truf·fle (trúff'l) *n.* 1. Any of various fleshy subterranean fungi, chiefly of the genus *Tuber,* often valued as food. 2. A small, round, rich sweet made from chocolate, egg, and butter, and usually flavoured with a liqueur. [Obsolete French, variant of Old French *truffe,* from Old Provençal *trufa,* from Vulgar Latin *tūfera* (unattested), from Latin *tūber,* tuber, truffle.]

trug (trug) *n. British.* A shallow, usually oval, basket made from strips of wood and used for carrying flowers, vegetables, or fruit. Also called "Sussex trug". [16th century : dialect variant of TROUGH.]

tru·ism (trŏo-iz'm ‖ trĕw-) *n.* A statement of an obvious or self-evident truth. See Synonyms at **cliché.** —**tru·is·tic** (trŏo-ístik) *adj.*

Tru·jil·lo Mo·li·na (trŏo-khée-yō mo-léenə ‖ mō-), **Rafael Leonidas** (1891–1961). Dominican dictator, president (1930–38, 1942–52) of the Dominican Republic. His policies brought some social and economic progress, but his tyranny led to his assassination.

trull (trul) *n. Archaic.* A strumpet; a harlot. [Perhaps from German *Trulle,* from Middle High German *trolle,* clumsy person, akin to Old Norse *troll,* creature, TROLL.]

tru·ly (trŏo-li ‖ trĕw-) *adv.* 1. Sincerely; genuinely. 2. Truthfully; accurately. 3. Indeed; really: *truly ugly.*

Tru·man (trŏomən), **Harry S.** (1884–1972). U.S. statesman. He was the 33rd president (1945–53) of the United States, succeeding to office on the death of F.D. Roosevelt. He authorised (1945) the use of the nuclear bomb on Japan, which ended World War II. He initiated (1949) the establishment of NATO.

tru·meau (trŏomō, trŏo-mō) *n., pl.* **trumeaux** (-z). *Architecture.* A piece of wall, pillar, or other divider between two openings, such as a pair of windows or a twin archway. [French, panel between two windows, from Old French *trumel,* from Frankish *thrum* (unattested), piece, bit.]

trump¹ (trump) *n.* 1. In card games: a. *Often plural.* A suit whose cards are declared to outrank all other cards for the duration of a hand or game. b. Any card of such a suit. 2. A key resource to be used at the opportune moment. 3. *Informal.* A reliable or admirable person. —**come up trumps.** 1. To turn out well; end satisfactorily. 2. To be successful. ~*v.* **trumped, trumping, trumps.** —*tr.* 1. To take (a card or trick) with a trump. 2. To outdo (an opponent) with or as if with a trump. —*intr.* To play a trump card. —**trump up.** To devise fraudulently; concoct; counterfeit. [Variant of TRIUMPH.]

trump² *n. Archaic.* A trumpet or trumpet call: *the last trump.* [Middle English *trompe,* from Old French, from Old High German *trumpa,* akin to Old Norse *trumba*†.]

trump card *n.* **1.** A playing card cut or turned up to determine which suit shall be trumps. **2.** Any card of the agreed trump suit. **3.** A powerful resource or gambit used when all else has failed.

trumped-up (trúmpt-úp) *adj.* Devised in order to deceive; concocted: *trumped-up charges.*

trump·er·y (trúmpəri) *n., pl.* **-ies. 1.** Showy but worthless finery; bric-a-brac. **2.** Nonsense; rubbish.
~*adj.* Showy but valueless. [Middle English *trompery,* from Old French *tromperie,* from *tromper*†, to cheat.]

trum·pet (trúmpit) *n.* **1. a.** A soprano brass wind instrument consisting of a long metal tube looped once and ending in a flared bell, the modern type being equipped with three valves for producing variations in pitch. **b.** The member of an orchestra who plays the trumpet. **2.** Something shaped like or sounding like a trumpet. **3.** An organ stop that produces a tone like that of the trumpet. **4. a.** Music produced by a trumpet. **b.** A resounding call, such as that of the elephant. **5.** An ear trumpet. **—blow (one's) own trumpet.** *British.* To boast; show off.
~*v.* **trumpeted, -peting, -pets.** *—intr.* **1.** To play a trumpet. **2.** To give forth a resounding call. Used especially of an elephant. *—tr.* To sound or proclaim loudly. [Middle English *trompette,* from Old French, diminutive of *trompe,* TRUMP (trumpet).]

trum·pet·er (trúmpitər) *n.* **1.** A trumpet player, especially one in a cavalry regiment. **2.** A person who announces something, as on a trumpet; a herald. **3.** Any of several large birds of the genus *Psophia,* of tropical South America, having a loud, resonant call. **4.** The trumpeter swan. **5.** Any of several large Australian and New Zealand food fishes; especially, the species *Latris lineata,* which is silvery with yellow stripes. **6.** A breed of domestic pigeon.

trumpeter swan *n.* A large white swan, *Cygnus buccinator,* of western North America, having a black bill and a loud, bugle-like call. Also called "trumpeter".

trum·pet-ma·jor (trúmpit-máyjər) *n.* Formerly, the head trumpeter of a cavalry regiment.

trun·cal (trúngk'l) *adj.* Of or pertaining to a trunk, as of a body or tree. [Alteration of TRUNK + -AL.]

trun·cate (trung-káyt, trúng-kayt) *tr.v.* **-cated, -cating, -cates. 1. a.** To shorten by or as if by cutting off the end or top; lop. **b.** To cut short; abbreviate (a quoted passage, for example). **2.** To replace (the edge of a crystal) with a plane face.
~*adj.* (trúng-kayt). **1.** Appearing to terminate abruptly, as a leaf or a coiled gastropod shell that lacks a spire. **2.** Truncated. [Latin *truncāre,* to maim, from *truncus,* torso, TRUNK.] **—trun·cate·ly** *adv.* **—trun·ca·tion** (-káysh'n) *n.*

trun·ca·ted (trung-káytid || trúng-kaytid) *adj.* **1.** Having the apex cut off and replaced by a plane, especially one parallel to the base. Said of a solid geometric figure such as a cone or pyramid. **2.** Cut short or abbreviated, as a quoted passage may be. **3.** Truncate.

trun·cheon (trúnchən) *n.* **1.** A short cudgel carried by policemen. **2.** A staff carried as a symbol of office or authority; a baton. **3.** A thick cutting from a plant, as for grafting.
~*tr.v.* **truncheoned, -cheoning, -cheons. 1.** To beat with a truncheon. Used especially of a policeman. **2.** *Archaic.* To bludgeon. [Middle English *tronchon,* fragment, club, from Old French, from Vulgar Latin *trunciō,* from Latin *truncus,* torso, TRUNK.]

trun·dle (trúnd'l) *n.* **1.** The motion or noise of rolling. **2.** A small wheel or roller. **3. a.** The pinion of a lantern. **b.** Any of the bars on a lantern pinion.
~*v.* **trundled, -dling, -dles.** *—tr.* **1.** To push or propel on wheels or rollers. **2.** *Archaic.* To spin; twirl. *—intr.* To move along in a slow and cumbersome manner by or as if by rolling. [Variant of dialectal *trendle,* wheel, from Middle English *trendil,* Old English *trendel,* circle, from Germanic *trand-*; akin to TREND.] **—trun·dler** *n.*

trundle bed *n.* A **truckle bed** *(see).*

trunk (trungk) *n.* **1.** The main woody axis of a tree. **2. a.** The human body excluding the head and limbs; the torso. **b.** An analogous part of other organisms, such as the thorax of an insect. **3.** A main body, apart from tributaries or appendages. **4.** *Architecture.* The shaft of a column. **5.** A proboscis; specifically, the long, prehensile proboscis of an elephant. **6.** See **trunk line. 7.** A large packing case or box that is fastened with clasps, used as luggage or for storage. **8.** *U.S.* The **boot** *(see)* of a car. **9.** A chute or conduit. **10.** *Nautical.* **a.** A shaft connecting two or more decks. **b.** The housing for the centreboard of a vessel. **c.** A structure projecting above part of a main deck, such as a covering over a ship's hatches or a cabin. **11.** *Plural.* Men's shorts worn for swimming or athletics.
~*adj.* Of or designating the main body or line of a system: *a trunk road.* [Middle English *trunke,* from Old French *tronc,* a tree trunk, from Latin *truncus.*]

trunk call *n. Chiefly British.* A telephone call made on a trunk line.

trunk·fish (trúngk-fish) *n., pl.* **-fishes** or collectively **trunkfish.** Any of various tropical marine fishes of the family Ostraciidae, having boxlike armour enclosing the body. Also called "boxfish".

trunk hose *pl.n.* Short, ballooning breeches, extending from the waist to midthigh, worn by men in the 16th and 17th centuries. Also called "trunk breeches". [Probably from obsolete *trunk,* to cut short, from Latin *truncāre,* to TRUNCATE.]

trunk line *n.* **1.** A direct line between two distant telephone switchboards. **2.** The main line of a transport system, such as a railway or canal system.

trunnel. Variant of **treenail.**

trun·nion (trún-yən, -i-ən) *n.* A pin or gudgeon; especially, either of two small cylindrical projections on a cannon or movable container forming an axis on which it pivots. [French *trognon,* core of fruit, tree trunk, from Old French, perhaps from *estrongner,* to cut off the branches, variant of *estronchier* : *es-,* from Latin *ex-,* off + *tronchier,* to cut, from Latin *truncāre,* to TRUNCATE.] **—trun·nioned** *adj.*

Tru·ro (trŏŏr-ō || trέwr-ō). Administrative centre of Cornwall, southwest England. Lying at the confluence of the rivers Kenwyn and Allen, it is a small port and tourist centre.

truss (truss) *n.* **1.** *Medicine.* A supportive device or belt worn to prevent the protrusion of a hernia. **2.** *Engineering.* A framework of wooden beams or metal bars, often arranged in triangles, to support a roof, bridge, or similar structure. **3.** *Architecture.* A bracket; a corbel. **4.** Something gathered into a bundle; a pack. **5.** *British.* A bundle of a set weight of straw or hay, generally 60 pounds (27 kilograms) of new hay, 56 pounds (25 kilograms) of old hay, or 36 pounds (16 kilograms) of straw. **6.** *Nautical.* An iron fitting by which a lower yard is secured to a mast. **7.** A compact cluster of flowers or fruit at the end of a stalk.
~*tr.v.* **trussed, trussing, trusses. 1.** To tie up or bind. Often used with *up.* **2.** To bind or skewer the wings or legs of (a fowl) before cooking. **3.** To enclose or confine (the body) in tight-fitting clothes. Often used with *up.* **4.** To support or brace with a truss. [Middle English *trusse,* a bundle, from Old French *tr(o)usse,* from *tr(o)usser,* to tie in a bundle, perhaps from Vulgar Latin *torsāre* (unattested), from *torsus* (unattested), past participle of Latin *torquēre,* to twist.]

truss bridge *n.* A bridge supported by trusses.

truss·ing (trússing) *n.* **1.** The parts forming a truss. **2.** A system of trusses supporting a structure.

trust (trust) *n.* **1.** Firm reliance on the integrity, ability, or character of a person or thing; confident belief; faith. **2.** The person or thing in which confidence is placed. **3.** Custody; care. **4.** Something committed into the care of another; a charge. **5.** The condition and resulting obligation of having confidence placed in one: *a position of public trust.* **6.** Reliance on something in the future; hope. **7.** Reliance on the intention and ability of a purchaser to pay in the future; credit. **8.** *Abbr.* **tr.** *Law.* **a.** A legal title to property held by one party (the trustee) for the benefit of another (the beneficiary). **b.** The confidence reposed in a trustee when giving him legal title to property to administer for another, and his obligation with respect to the property and the beneficiary. **c.** The property so held. **d.** The right of the beneficiary to the property. **9.** A group of companies organised for the purpose of reducing competition and controlling prices throughout a business or industry. **10.** A **trust territory** *(see).* **—in trust.** In the charge of a trustee.
~*v.* **trusted, trusting, trusts.** *—intr.* **1.** To rely; depend. Used with *in* or *to.* **2.** To be confident; hope. **3.** To sell on credit. *—tr.* **1.** To have confidence in; feel sure of. **2.** To expect with assurance; assume. **3.** To believe. **4.** To place in the care of another; entrust. **5.** To grant discretion to confidently: *Shall I trust her with the boat?* **6.** To extend credit to. —See Synonyms at **rely.**
~*adj.* Maintained in trust. [Middle English *truste,* probably from Old Norse *traust,* confidence, firmness.] **—trust·a·bil·i·ty** (-ə-bílləti) *n.* **—trust·a·ble** *adj.* **—trust·er** *n.*

Synonyms: *trust, faith, confidence, reliance, dependence.*

trust account *n.* **1.** A savings account deposited in the name of a trustee, after whose death the balance is payable to a specified beneficiary. Also called "trustee account". **2.** Property under trustee control.

trust·bust·er (trúst-bustər) *n. U.S. Informal.* A government official who works to dissolve illegal business combinations (trusts).

trust company *n.* A commercial bank or other company that manages trusts.

trus·tee (trúss-tée, truss-) *n. Abbr.* **tr. 1.** A person or agent, such as a bank, holding legal title to property in order to administer it for a beneficiary. **2.** A member of a board elected or appointed to direct the funds and policy of an institution. **3.** A garnishee.
~*tr.v.* **trusteed, -teeing, -tees. 1.** To place (property) in the care of a trustee. **2.** To garnishee (property).

trustee process *n.* **Garnishment** *(see).*

trustee savings bank *n.* See **savings bank.**

trus·tee·ship (trúss-tée-ship, truss-) *n.* **1.** The position or function of a trustee. **2. a.** The administration of a territory by a country or countries, supervised by the United Nations. **b.** *Often capital* **T.** A region so administered; a trust territory. Compare **mandate.**

trust·ful (trústf'l) *adj.* Trusting. **—trust·ful·ly** *adv.*

trust fund *n.* An estate, especially money and securities, held or settled in trust.

trust·ing (trústing) *adj.* Inclined to believe or confide readily; full of trust. **—trust·ing·ly** *adv.* **—trust·ing·ness** *n.*

trust territory *n.* A colony or territory placed under the administration of a country or countries by commission of the United Nations. Also called "trust". Compare **mandate.**

Trust Territory of the Pacific Islands, U.S. See **Belau, Republic of; Guam; Marshall Islands; Micronesia, Federated States of; Northern Marianas.**

trust·wor·thy (trúst-wurthi) *adj.* Warranting trust; dependable; reliable. **—trust·wor·thi·ly** *adv.* **—trust·wor·thi·ness** *n.*

trust·y (trústi) *adj.* **-ier, -iest.** Dependable; faithful; reliable.
~*n., pl.* **trusties.** A trusted person; specifically, a convict granted privileges for good behaviour. **—trust·i·ly** *adv.* **—trust·i·ness** *n.*

truth (trōōth || trewth) *n., pl.* **truths** (trōōthz, trōōths || trewthz, trewths). **1.** Conformity to knowledge, fact, or logic. **2.** Fidelity to

trumpeter swan *The trumpeter of North America is the largest of the swan family. Fully grown, it can be 1.5 metres long (5 feet) and have a wingspan of nearly 2.5 metres (more than 8 feet). Once hunted to near extinction for its meat and feathers, it is now a protected species and the population has increased to about 5,000 birds, mostly in Alaska.*

an original or standard. **3. a.** Reality; actuality. **b.** *Often capital* **T.** That which is considered to be the supreme reality and to have the ultimate meaning and value of existence. **4.** A statement proven to be or accepted as true; the opposite of a falsehood. **5.** Sincerity; integrity; honesty. **6.** *Physics.* **Top** (see). —**truth to tell.** To tell the truth; speaking frankly. [Middle English *trewthe, treothe,* Old English *trēowth, trīewth.*]

    Synonyms: *truth, veracity, verity, verisimilitude, authenticity.*

truth drug *n. Informal.* Any drug that reduces inhibitions and promotes relaxation, as used by certain authorities during interrogation. Also called "truth serum".

truth·ful (trŏōth-f'l ‖ trēwth-) *adj.* **1.** Consistently telling the truth; honest. **2.** Corresponding to reality; true. —**truth·ful·ly** *adv.* —**truth·ful·ness** *n.*

truth-function (trŏōth-fŭngksh'n ‖ trēwth-) *n.* A compound proposition in logic, such as a conjunction or negation, the truth-value of which is always determined by the truth-values of the components.

truth set *n. Mathematics & Logic.* A set of values that satisfy a given equation or statement. Also called "solution set".

truth table *n. Logic.* A table listing the truth-values of a proposition that result from all the possible combinations of the truth-values of its components.

truth-val·ue (trŏōth-văl-yŏō ‖ trēwth-) *n. Logic.* Either the truth or the falsity of a proposition.

try (trī) *v.* **tried, trying, tries.** —*tr.* **1.** To taste, sample, or otherwise test in order to determine strength, effect, worth, or desirability. **2. a.** To examine or hear (evidence or a case) by judicial process. **b.** To put (an accused person) on trial. **3.** To subject to strain or hardship; tax: *The last steep ascent tried her every muscle.* **4.** To melt (lard, for example) in order to separate out impurities; render down. Often used with *out.* **5.** To make an effort (to do or accomplish something); attempt. Used chiefly with an infinitive or *and: Try to do it; try and find out.* **6.** To smooth, fit, or align accurately. —*intr.* To make an effort; strive.
    —*n., pl.* **tries. 1.** An attempt; an effort. **2.** A test; a trial. **3. a.** In Rugby football, the act of touching the ball down behind the opposing team's goal line, giving the team the right to kick for goal. In Rugby Union a try scores four points and in Rugby League three points. **b.** The score so gained. [Middle English *trien,* to separate, pick out, sift, from Old French *trier†.*]
    Usage: Try and is widely encountered in informal speech, especially in such established phrases as *try and stop, try and get* (*Try and get some rest*), *try and make* (*You try and make me do it!*). Formal usage prefers the use of *to* at all times: *tried to buy a car.*

try·ing (trī-ing) *adj.* Causing annoyance, strain, or distress. —**try·ing·ly** *adv.* —**try·ing·ness** *n.*

trying plane *n.* A long plane used to produce level surfaces on planks.

try·ma (trī-mə) *n., pl.* **-mata** (-mətə). A drupe, such as a walnut, having a tough epicarp that separates from the shell of the fruit. [New Latin, from Greek *truma, trumē,* a hole (from the hollow drupe).]

try on *tr.v.* **1.** To put on (an article of clothing) to see whether it fits or suits one. **2.** *Chiefly British Informal.* To attempt to fool or deceive somebody with (tricks or games): *Don't try on your tricks with me.* —**try it on.** *British Informal.* **1.** To attempt to fool or deceive somebody. **2.** To make sexual advances: *He tried it on with me, so I told him just where he could get off.*

try-on (trī-on) *n. Informal.* **1.** The act of trying on clothes. **2.** *British.* An attempt to fool or deceive.

try out *tr.v.* To put to experimental use in order to test. —*intr.v. Chiefly U.S.* To undergo a competitive qualifying test, as for a job. Used with *for.*

try·out (trī-owt) *n. Informal.* **1.** An experimental test or trial. **2.** *Chiefly U.S.* A test to ascertain the qualifications of applicants, as for an athletics team or for a theatrical part.

try·pan·o·some (trĭppənə-sōm, trĭ-pánnə-) *n.* Any of various parasitic protozoans of the genus *Trypanosoma,* transmitted to the vertebrate bloodstream by certain insects, and often causing diseases such as sleeping sickness. [New Latin *Trypanosoma,* "augerbodied" (from its shape) : Greek *trupanon,* an auger, borer, from *trupan,* to bore, from *trupa, trupē,* a hole + -SOME (body).] —**try·pan·o·som·ic** (-sŏmĭk) *adj.*

try·pan·o·so·mi·a·sis (trĭppən-ə-sō-mī-ə-siss, tri-pán-, -ō-, -sə-) *n.* Any disease caused by a trypanosome. [New Latin : TRYPANOSOM(E) + -IASIS.]

try·pars·am·ide (tri-pársə-mīd) *n.* A white crystalline powder, $C_8H_{10}AsN_2O_4Na·{}^1\!/_2H_2O$, used in the treatment of spirochaetal and trypanosomic diseases. [Originally a trade name : *tryp*anosome + *arsen*ic + *amide.*]

tryp·sin (trĭpsĭn) *n.* One of the proteolytic enzymes of the pancreatic juice, important in the digestive processes. [Greek *tripsis,* a rubbing (first obtained by rubbing the pancreas with glycerin), from *tribein,* to rub + -IN.] —**tryp·tic** (trĭptĭk) *adj.*

tryp·sin·o·gen (trip-sínnə-jən, -jen) *n.* The substance produced by the pancreas that is converted into trypsin when acted upon by certain enzymes. [From TRYPSIN + -GEN.]

tryp·to·phan (trĭptə-făn) *n.* Also **tryp·to·phane** (-fayn). An amino acid, $C_{11}H_{12}N_2O_2$, found in certain pulses, that is an essential element in human nutrition. [TRYP(SIN) + (PEP)T(IC) + -PHAN(E).]

try·sail (trī-s'l, -sayl) *n. Nautical.* A small fore-and-aft sail hoisted abaft the foremast and mainmast in a storm to keep a ship's bow to

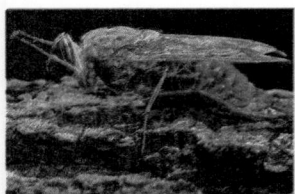
tsetse fly *The tsetse fly is exclusive to Africa where it transmits sleeping sickness to humans and a similar disease, nagana, to cattle.*

the wind. Also called "spencer". [From TRY (noun, in the obsolete nautical sense of "lying to in a storm").]

try square *n.* A carpenter's tool consisting of a ruled metal straightedge set at right angles to a wooden straight piece, used for measuring and marking square work. Also called "square".

tryst (trist, *rarely* trīst) *n. Archaic & Poetic.* **1.** An agreement between lovers to meet at a certain time and place. **2.** The meeting or meeting place so arranged.
    ~*intr.v.* **trysted, trysting, trysts.** *Archaic & Poetic or Scottish.* To arrange or keep a tryst. [Middle English, from Old French *triste,* an appointed station in hunting, perhaps from Scandinavian, akin to Old Norse *treysta,* to trust, make firm.] —**tryst·er** *n.*

tsade. Variant of **sade.**

Tsana. See **Tana, Lake.**

Tsangpo. See **Brahmaputra.**

tsar, tzar (zar, tsar) *n.* Also *chiefly U.S.* **czar. 1.** A king or emperor; specifically, one of the former monarchs of the Russian empire. **2.** Formerly, any of several south Slavonic monarchs, such as the kings of Bulgaria. **3.** See **czar.** [Russian *tsar',* from Gothic *kaisar,* emperor, ultimately from Latin *Caesar.*] —**tsar·dom** *n.*
    Usage: The spelling of *tsar* and its derivatives with the Latin transliteration *cz* dates from a German commentary of the 16th century; *ts,* as the more accurate phonetic transcription, is now the preferred spelling in British English. However, the older *czar* is still the accepted form in American English, and this is the usual spelling for the extended sense of "petty tyrant" or "supremo".

tsar·e·vitch (záar-vich, tsáarə-vich; *Russian* tsaryáyveech) *n.* The eldest son of a tsar. [Russian : TSAR + *-evich,* male patronymic suffix.]

tsa·rev·na (zaa-révnə, tsaa-; *Russian* tsaryénə) *n.* **1.** The daughter of a tsar. **2.** The wife of a tsarevitch. [Russian : TSAR + *-evna,* feminine patronymic suffix.]

tsar·ism (záar-iz'm, tsáar-) *n.* The system of government in Russia under the tsars; autocracy. —**tsar·ist** *n. & adj.*

tsa·rit·sa (zaa-rítsə, tsaa-) *n.* **1.** An empress of Russia. **2.** The wife of a tsar. Also called "tsarina". [Russian : TSAR + *-itsa,* feminine suffix.]
    Usage: The Russian word for "empress" is correctly *tsaritsa,* with the Slavonic feminine suffix. The form *tsarina* is a borrowing from German, with the Teutonic suffix *-in* influenced by Romance words such as *signorina.*

tsessebe. Variant of **sassaby.**

tset·se fly, tzet·ze fly (tsétsi, tétsi) *n.* Any of several bloodsucking African flies of the genus *Glossina,* often carrying and transmitting pathogenic trypanosomes to human beings and livestock. [Afrikaans, from Tswana.]

TSH. thyroid stimulating hormone.

Tshi. Variant of **Twi.**

Tshi·lu·ba (chi-lŏŏbə) *n.* The language of the Luba people, used as a trade language in Zaire. See **Luba.** —**Tshi·lu·ba** *adj.*

T-shirt, tee shirt (tée-shurt) *n.* A short-sleeved, collarless casual shirt worn by both sexes. [So called from its shape.]

Tshom·be (chómbi), **Moise (Kapenda)** (1919–69). Congolese statesman. He was president (1960–63) of the breakaway province of Katanga, and prime minister of the Congo (1964–65) until dismissed by President Kasavubu, and condemned to death in absentia in 1967.

Tsinan. See **Jinan.**

Tsinghai. See **Qinghai.**

tsk tsk *interj. Informal.* Used to express disapproval, especially ironically.

tsp. teaspoon; teaspoonful.

T-square (tée-skwair) *n.* A T-shaped ruler with a short, sometimes sliding, perpendicular crosspiece at one end, used by draughtsmen for establishing and drawing parallel lines.

tsu·na·mi (tsŏō-náami, sŏō-) *n.* A very large ocean wave caused by an underwater earthquake or volcanic eruption. Also in nontechnical usage "tidal wave". [Japanese : *tsu,* port + *nami,* wave.]

tsu·tsu·ga·mu·shi disease (tsŏōt-sŏō-gə-mŏōshi, sŏōt-, -sə-) *n.* Scrub typhus (see). [Japanese : *tsutsuga,* illness + *mushi,* an insect.]

Tsve·ta·ye·va (tsvi-tī-ivə), **Marina Ivanovna** (1892–1941). Russian poet. Her highly original verse is distinguished by its staccato rhythms and its directness.

Tswa·na (tswáanə, swáanə) *n.* **1.** A member of a Bantu people of southern Africa, living mainly in Botswana. **2.** The Sotho language of the Tswana people. —**Tswa·na** *adj.*

T.T. **1.** teetotal; teetotaller. **2.** Tourist Trophy. **3.** tuberculin-tested.

TTL **1.** through the lens; used to designate a type of camera light meter. **2.** transistor–transistor logic.

T.U. trade union.

Tu·a·mo·tu Archipelago (tŏōə-mó-too). *French* **Tou·a·mo·tou** (too-amō-tŏŏ). Group of 80 small islands in the southern Pacific Ocean, part of French Polynesia.

Tuan (tŏō-áan, twáan) *n.* A Malayan form of respectful address, equivalent to the English *Sir* or *Mr.* [Malay : master, lord.]

Tua·reg (twáareg) *n., pl.* **-regs** or collectively **Tuareg.** A member of one of the tall, nomadic, Hamitic-speaking peoples who occupy the western and central Sahara and an area along the Niger and have adopted the Muslim religion. [Arabic *Tawāriq.*] —**Tau·reg** *adj.*

tu·a·ta·ra (tŏō-ə-táarə) *n.* A lizard-like reptile, *Sphenodon punctatum,* of New Zealand, the only surviving representative of the order Rhynchocephalia that flourished during the Mesozoic era. [Maori.]

tub (tub) *n.* **1. a.** A large round, flat-bottomed vessel, usually wider than it is tall, originally made of wooden staves held together with

hoops, and used for packing, storing, or washing. **b.** A small container resembling such a vessel in shape and used for packaging ice cream or margarine, for example. **c.** The contents of a tub or the amount that a tub will hold. Also called "tubful". **2.** *Informal.* A bath or the act of taking a bath. **3.** *Informal.* **a.** A wide, clumsy, slow-moving boat. **b.** A strong broad boat used for rowing practice. **4. a.** A bucket used for conveying ore or coal up a mine shaft. **b.** A coal wagon used in a mine.
~*v.* **tubbed, tubbing, tubs.** —*tr.* **1.** To pack or store in a tub. **2.** *Informal.* To wash or bathe in a tub. —*intr. Informal.* To take a bath. [Middle English *tubbe, tobbe,* from Middle Dutch and Middle Low German *tubbe†.*] —**tub·ba·ble** *adj.* —**tub·ber** *n.*

tu·ba (téw-bə ‖ tōō-) *n., pl.* **-bas** or **-bae** (-bee) (for sense 3). **1.** A large, valved, brass musical wind instrument with a bass pitch. **2.** A reed stop in an organ, having eight-foot pitch. **3.** An ancient Roman war trumpet. [Italian, from Latin, a trumpet, akin to Latin *tubus,* TUBE.]

tu·bal (téw'l ‖ tōōb'l) *adj.* Of, pertaining to, or occurring in a tube, especially the Fallopian tube.

tu·bate (téw-bayt ‖ tōō-) *adj.* Forming or having a tube.

tub·by (túbbi) *adj.* **-bier -biest.** **1.** *Informal.* Short and fat. **2.** Having a dull sound; lacking resonance. —**tub·bi·ness** *n.*

tube (tewb ‖ tōōb) *n.* **1. a.** A hollow cylinder that conveys a fluid or functions as a passage; a duct. **b.** An organic structure so shaped or so functioning; a duct. **2.** A small, flexible cylindrical container sealed at one end and having a cap at the other, for pigments, toothpaste, or other pastelike substances. **3.** The cylindrical part of a wind instrument. **4. a.** A **vacuum tube** (*see*). **b.** A **cathode-ray tube** (*see*), especially in a television set. **c.** Any electronic **valve** (*see*). **5.** *Botany.* The lower, joined part of a gamopetalous corolla or a gamosepalous calyx. **6.** *British.* **a.** An underground railway tunnel. **b.** An underground railway system, especially the one in London. Preceded by *the.* Also used ajectively: *a tube train.* **7.** *Australian Informal.* A can of beer. **8.** *Chiefly U.S. Informal.* Television. Preceded by *the.* **9.** *Plural. Informal.* The Fallopian tubes.
~*tr.v.* **tubed, tubing, tubes.** **1.** To provide with a tube or tubes; insert a tube in: *tube a tyre.* **2.** To place in or enclose in a tube. [French, from Latin *tubus†.* See. also **tuba.**]

tube foot *n.* Any of the numerous external, fluid-filled muscular tubes of echinoderms, such as the starfish, serving primarily as organs of locomotion.

tube·less tyre (téwb-ləss, -liss ‖ tōōb-) *n.* A pneumatic vehicular tyre in which the air is held in the assembly of casing and rim without an inner tube.

tu·ber (téw-bər ‖ tōō-) *n.* **1.** *Botany.* A swollen, usually underground stem or root, such as the potato or dahlia, bearing buds from which new plant shoots arise. **2.** *Anatomy.* A swelling; a tubercle. [Latin *tūber,* a lump, swelling, tumour.]

tu·ber·cle (téw-bər-k'l, -ber- ‖ tōō-) *n.* **1.** A small, rounded prominence or growth, such as a wartlike excrescence on the roots of some leguminous plants or a knoblike projection in the skin or on a bone. **2.** *Pathology.* **a.** A nodule or swelling. **b.** The characteristic lesion of tuberculosis. [Latin *tūberculum,* diminutive of *tūber,* TUBER.]

tubercle bacillus *n. Abbr.* **Tb.** A rod-shaped bacterium, *Mycobacterium tuberculosis,* that causes tuberculosis.

tu·ber·cu·lar (tew-bérkew-lər ‖ tōō-, tōō-) *adj.* **1.** Of, pertaining to, or covered with tubercles; tuberculate. **2.** Of, pertaining to, or suffering from tuberculosis. **3.** Possessing or characterised by the presence of tubercles.
~*n.* A person suffering from tuberculosis.

tu·ber·cu·late (tew-bérkew-lət, -lit ‖ tōō-, tōō-) *adj.* Also **tu·ber·cu·la·ted** (-láytid). **1.** Having tubercles. **2.** Tubercular. —**tu·ber·cu·late·ly** *adv.* —**tu·ber·cu·la·tion** (-láysh'n) *n.*

tu·ber·cu·lin (tew-bérkew-lin ‖ tōō-, tōō-) *n.* A sterile liquid derived from cultures of tubercle bacilli, used in the diagnosis and treatment of tuberculosis. [Latin *tūberculum,* TUBERCLE + -IN.]

tuberculin test *n.* The **Mantoux test** (*see*). —**tu·ber·cu·lin·test·ed** (tew-bérkew-lin-téstid) *adj.*

tu·ber·cu·loid (tew-bérkew-loyd ‖ tōō-, tōō-) *adj.* **1.** Resembling tuberculosis. **2.** Resembling a tubercle.

tu·ber·cu·lo·sis (tew-bérkew-lṓ-siss ‖ tōō-, tōō-) *n. Abbr.* **TB, T.B.** **1.** An infectious disease of humans and animals, caused by a microorganism, *Mycobacterium tuberculosis,* and manifesting itself in lesions of the lung, bone, and other parts of the body. **2.** Tuberculosis of the lungs. In this sense, also called "consumption", "phthisis". [New Latin : Latin *tūberculum,* TUBERCLE + -OSIS.]

tu·ber·cu·lous (tew-bérkew-ləss ‖ tōō-, tōō-) *adj.* **1.** Of, pertaining to, or having tuberculosis. **2.** Of, affected with, or caused by tubercles. [New Latin *tuberculosus,* from Latin *tūberculum,* TUBERCLE.]

tube·rose (téwbə-rōz ‖ téwb-, tōōbə-, tōōb-, -rōss, -róz) *n.* A tuberous plant, *Polianthes tuberosa,* native to Mexico, cultivated for its fragrant white flowers, which yield an expensive perfume, *tuberose obsolute.* [New Latin (*Polianthes*) *tuberosa,* from the feminine of Latin *tūberōsus,* TUBEROUS.]

tu·ber·os·i·ty (téwbə-róssəti ‖ tōōbə-) *n., pl.* **-ties.** A projection or protuberance, especially one at the end of a bone for the attachment of a muscle or tendon.

tu·ber·ous (téwbə-rəss ‖ tōōbə-) *adj.* Also **tu·ber·ose** (-róz, -rōss). **1.** *Botany.* **a.** Producing or bearing tubers. **b.** Resembling a tuber: *a tuberous root.* **2.** *Rare.* Covered with small, rounded projections; knobby. [Latin *tūberōsus,* full of lumps, from *tūber,* TUBER.]

THE KILLER WAVES
Monstrous ripples that follow an earthquake under the sea

Essentially, tsunamis are no more than ripples. But they come on a monstrous scale.

Just as circular ripples spread from a pebble tossed into a pond, so tsunamis surge across the sea from an underwater earthquake or volcanic eruption. In deep water, the swells are so long and so slight that ships hardly notice them. But as tsunamis reach shallow water, they pile up into crests that can be as much as 60 metres (200 feet) high. Their speed is astonishing, too: many travel faster than 600 kilometres (375 miles) an hour; one, in April 1946, is known to have raced across 3620 kilometres (2,250 miles) of the Pacific to Hawaii in 4 hours and 34 minutes, an average speed of more than 790 kilometres (nearly 495 miles) an hour.

Almost all tsunamis are confined to the Pacific, the ocean whose basin is surrounded by a ring of volcanoes. The word itself comes from Japan; it was adopted by scientists of other countries to replace the misleading phrase "tidal wave" because tsunamis are triggered by geological, not tidal, movements.

Usually, just before a tsunami strikes a coast, the sea itself is sucked back, leaving ships in harbours beached. Then the vast wave smashes onto the land, often causing enormous destruction. In 1883, for example, 30,000 people died on Java in a tsunami triggered by the eruption of Krakatoa. In 1896, a tsunami killed more than 20,000 people and flattened 10,000 homes in Sanriku, a town on Tokyo Bay.

A MOUNTAIN OF WATER *A tsunami reaches out for the land in a print by the 19th-century Japanese artist, Hokusai. On a miniature scale in the background is the volcanic cone of Mount Fuji. The Japanese have long known the con-* *nection between the gigantic killer waves and movements of the Earth's crust; ancient monuments along the coast of Japan carry inscriptions that give the warning: "When you feel an earthquake, expect a tsunami."*

tube worm *n.* Any sedentary, tube-dwelling bristle worm, such as the lugworm or the ragworm.

tu·bi·fex (téwbi-feks ‖ tōōbi-) *n., pl.* **-fexes** or collectively **tubifex.** Any of various small, slender, reddish freshwater worms of the genus *Tubifex,* often used as food for tropical aquarium fish. [New Latin *Tubifex* : Latin *tubus,* TUBE (each one is partially enclosed in a tube) + *-fex,* "maker".]

tub·ing (téwb-ing ‖ tōōb-) *n.* **1.** A length of tube or material in the form of a tube. **2.** Tubes collectively. **3.** A system of tubes.

tub thumper *n. Informal.* A soapbox orator; a vehement public speaker. —**tub-thump·ing** (túb-thumping) *n. & adj.*

Tu·bua·i Islands (toobwá-ee). Formerly **Austral Islands.** Group of small volcanic islands in the southern Pacific Ocean, part of French Polynesia.

tu·bu·lar (téw-bewlər ‖ tōō-) *adj.* **1.** Having the form of a tube. **2.** Made or consisting of a tube or tubes. —**tu·bu·lar·i·ty** (-bew-lár-rəti) *n.*

tubular bells *pl.n.* A musical instrument consisting of a set of long metal tubes that are tuned to the musical scale and struck with a mallet to simulate the sound of bells. Compare **chimes.**

tu·bu·late (téw-bew-lət, -lit, -layt ‖ tōō-) *adj.* Also **tu·bu·lat·ed** (-láytid). **1.** Formed into or resembling a tube; tubular. **2.** Provided with a tube.
~*tr.v.* (-layt) **tubulated, -lating, -lates.** To provide with or form into a tube. [Latin *tubulātus,* from *tubulus,* diminutive of *tubus,* TUBE.] —**tu·bu·la·tion** (-láysh'n) *n.* —**tu·bu·la·tor** (-laytər) *n.*

tu·bule (téw-bewl ‖ tōō-) *n.* A very small tube or tubular structure. [Latin *tubulus,* diminutive of *tubus,* TUBE.]

tu·bu·lif·er·ous (téw-bew-lífferəss ‖ tōō-) *adj.* Having or consisting of tubules. [TUBULE + -FEROUS.]

tu·bu·li·flo·rous (téw-bewli-fláw-rəss ‖ tōō-, -flṓ-) *adj.* Having flowers or florets with tubular corollas. [From TUBUL(E) + -FLOROUS.]

tuatara *The lizard-like tuatara is the sole survivor of a group of reptiles that flourished 150 million years ago. It grows to about 700 millimetres (28 inches) long and is found only on a few islands off the coast of New Zealand.*

tufted duck *Found in Europe and parts of Asia, the tufted duck lives on lakes and ponds. It feeds mainly on freshwater mussels, fish, frogs, and insects and will dive down more than 3 metres (about 10 feet) to find food.*

tu·bu·lous (téw-bewləss || to͞o-) *adj.* **1.** Tubular. **2.** Composed of tubes or having tubular parts. [New Latin *tubulosus,* from Latin *tubulus,* TUBULE.] **—tu·bu·lous·ly** *adv.*

T.U.C. *n.* The **Trades Union Congress** *(see).*

Tu·ca·na (tew-káy-nə, to͞o-, -kaá-) *n.* A constellation in the polar region of the Southern Hemisphere near Indus and Hydrus, containing the smaller **Magellanic cloud** *(see).* [Tupi *tucana,* TOUCAN.]

tu·chun (to͞o-cho͞on, do͞o-jo͞on, -jūn) *n., pl.* **-chuns** or **tuchun.** Formerly, a Chinese military governor of a province. [Chinese *dū jūn* : *dū,* to supervise + *jūn,* army.] **—tu·chun·ate** *n.* **—tu·chun·ism** *n.*

tuck[1] (tuk) *v.* **tucked, tucking, tucks.** *—tr.* **1.** To make one or more folds in. **2.** To gather up the ends of (a garment, for example) and thrust into a space between two surfaces so as to secure or confine: *tuck one's shirt into one's trousers.* **3. a.** To put (something) into a place or space where it will be concealed, confined, or snug: *tuck the letter into your bag; a cabin tucked away in the woods.* **b.** To store in a safe spot; save. Used with *away*: *He's millions tucked away.* **4.** To cover (a child, for example) snugly in bed. Used with *in* or *up.* **5.** To draw in; contract. *—intr.* To make tucks. **—tuck in** or **away.** *Chiefly British Informal.* To eat (food) heartily or greedily.
∼n. **1.** A flattened pleat or fold in a garment, especially a very narrow one stitched in place. **2.** An act of tucking something in. **3.** *Nautical.* The part of a ship's hull under the stern where the ends of the bottom planks come together. **4.** *British Informal.* Food, especially sweets and cakes. [Middle English *tukken, tucken,* to pull or put up, put away (hence, consume), from Middle Low German and Middle Dutch *tucken*; akin to TUG.]

tuck[2] *n. British Regional.* A beat or tap, especially on a drum. [From obsolete *t(o)uk,* to beat the drum, sound the trumpet, from Middle English *tukken,* from Old North French *toquer,* to strike, touch, from Vulgar Latin *toccāre* (unattested), to TOUCH.]

tuck[3] *n. Archaic.* A slender sword; a rapier. [Earlier *to(c)ke,* from French (Normandy dialect) *étoc,* from Old French *estoc,* "a tree trunk", sword, sword point, from Frankish *stok* (unattested).]

tuck·er[1] (túckər) *n.* **1.** One that tucks. **2.** A piece of linen or frill of lace formerly worn by women around the neck and shoulders. **3.** *Australian Informal.* Food. [TUCK (fold, food) + -ER.]

tucker[2] *tr.v.* **-ered, -ering, -ers.** *Australian & U.S. Informal.* To weary; exhaust. Usually used in the passive and with *out*: *I'm all tuckered out.* [Frequentative of TUCK (to pull under).]

tuck·et (túckit) *n.* A trumpet fanfare. [From obsolete *t(o)uk,* to sound the trumpet. See **tuck** (drumbeat).]

tuck shop (túck-shop) *n. British.* A shop that sells sweets and cakes, especially one in a school. [From TUCK (food).]

-tude *n. suffix.* Indicates a condition or state of being; for example, **exactitude.** [Old French, from Latin *-tūdō.*]

Tu·dor (téw-dər || to͞o-). The family name of the English royal family from Henry VII (1485) to Elizabeth I (1603).
∼n. A member of this family, especially when a monarch: *the Tudors and Stuarts.*
∼adj. **1.** Of or pertaining to the Tudors. **2. a.** Of, pertaining to, or characteristic of the period of Tudors (1485–1603). **b.** Of, designating, or characteristic of the architectural style of the Tudor period, with exposed beams as a typical feature.

Tues·day (téwz-di, -day || to͞oz-) *n. Abbr.* **Tues.** The day of the week following Monday; the second day of the working week. [Middle English *tiwesday, tuesdai,* Old English *tīwesdæg,* "day of Tiu" : *Tīw,* TIU + *dæg,* DAY.]

tu·fa (téw-fə || to͞o-) *n.* **1.** The porous, spongy calcium carbonate deposited round a spring. **2.** *U.S.* **Tuff** *(see).* [Obsolete Italian *tufa, tufo,* from Latin *tōphus, tōfus*†.] **—tu·fa·ceous** (tew-fáyshəss) *adj.*

tuff (tuf) *n.* A rock composed of cemented or fused fragments less than 2 millimetres (1/12 inch) in diameter which have been ejected from a volcano. Also *U.S.* "tufa". [French *tuf, tuffe,* from obsolete Italian *tufo,* TUFA.] **—tuff·a·ceous** (tuf-áyshəss) *adj.*

tuf·fet (túffit) *n.* **1.** A clump or tuft of grass. **2.** A small mound or hillock. [Perhaps variant of TUFT.]

tuft (tuft) *n.* **1.** A short cluster of hair, feathers, grass, or the like, attached at the base or growing close together. **2.** A dense clump of trees or bushes.
∼v. **tufted, tufting, tufts.** *—tr.* **1.** To provide or ornament with a tuft or tufts. **2.** To pass threads through the layers of (a quilt, mattress, or upholstery), securing the thread ends with a knot or button in the depressions thus created. *—intr.* To separate or form into tufts; grow in a tuft. [Middle English *tuft, toft,* from Old French *tof(f)e,* from Germanic.] **—tuft·er** *n.* **—tuft·y** *adj.*

tuft·ed duck (tuftid) *n.* A diving duck, *Aythya fuligula,* with a drooping purple-black crest in the male.

tug (tug) *v.* **tugged, tugging, tugs.** *—tr.* **1.** To pull at vigorously; strain at. **2.** To move by pulling with great effort or exertion; haul; drag: *tugged her out of bed.* **3.** To tow by tugboat. *—intr.* **1.** To pull hard: *She tugged at my boots.* **2.** To toil or struggle; strain. **3.** *Archaic.* To vie; contend.
∼n. **1.** A strong pull or pulling force: *the tug of the sea.* **2.** A hard struggle between opposing forces or parties: *a tug between duty and desire.* **3.** A tugboat. **4.** A rope, chain, or strap used in hauling; especially, a harness trace. [Middle English *tuggen, toggen,* intensive form akin to Old English *tēon,* to draw, pull, tow.] **—tug·ger** *n.*

tug·boat (túg-bōt) *n.* A powerful small boat designed for towing larger vessels. Also called "towboat", "tug".

tug of love *n. Informal.* A struggle between a divorced or separated couple for the custody of their child or children.

tug of war *n.* **1.** A contest of strength and skill in which two teams tug on opposite ends of a rope, each trying to pull the other across a line marked out between them. **2.** A struggle for supremacy.

tug·rik (to͞og-reek, -rik) *n.* The basic monetary unit of the Mongolian People's Republic, equal to 100 möngö. Also called "tögrög". [Mongolian *dughurik,* "round object", wheel.]

tu·i (to͞o-i) *n.* A New Zealand honeyeater, *Prosthemadera novaeseelandiae,* having greenish-brown plumage and two patches of curly white feathers at the throat. Also called "parson bird". [Maori.]

tu·i·tion (tew-ísh'n || to͞o-) *n.* **1.** Teaching or instruction, especially of individuals or small groups, and often on a commercial basis. **2.** A fee for instruction. **3.** *Archaic.* Guardianship. [Middle English, protection, tutelage, from Old French, from Latin *tuitiō* (stem *tuitiōn-*), protection, a watching, from *tuērī,* to look at, watch, protect.] **—tu·i·tion·al, tu·i·tion·ar·y** (-əri || -erri) *adj.*

tu·la·rae·mi·a (to͞o-lə-réemi-ə, téw-) *n.* An infectious disease caused by the bacterium *Pasteurella tularensis,* transmitted from infected rodents to humans by insect vectors or by handling infected animals, and characterised by fever and swelling of the lymph nodes. Also called "rabbit fever". [New Latin : *Tulare,* a county in California where it was discovered + -AEMIA.]

tu·lip (téw-lip || to͞o-) *n.* **1.** Any of several bulbous plants of the genus *Tulipa,* native to Asia, widely cultivated for their showy, bell-shaped, variously coloured flowers. **2.** The flower or bulb of this plant. [New Latin *Tulipa,* from Turkish *tül(i)bend,* TURBAN (from its turban-shaped flower).]

tulip tree *n.* Either of two trees of the genus *Liriodendron*; *L. tulipifera* of North America and *L. chinensis* of China, both having tulip-shaped yellow flowers and soft, easily worked wood. Also called "tulip poplar".

tu·lip·wood (téw-lip-wo͝od || to͞o-) *n.* **1.** The wood of the tulip tree. **2.** The irregularly striped, ornamental wood of any of several other trees. **—tu·lip·wood** *adj.*

tulle (tewl || to͞ol; *French* tül) *n.* A fine starched net of silk, rayon, or nylon, used for veils, tutus, or evening dresses, for example. [French, originally produced in *Tulle,* southwestern France.]

tum (tum) *n. Informal.* The stomach. [See **tummy.**]

tum·ble (túmb'l) *v.* **-bled, -bling, -bles.** *—intr.* **1. a.** To fall or roll end over end: *kittens tumbling over each other.* **b.** To fall helplessly or precipitately; pitch headlong. **c.** To move in confusion or disorder; proceed haphazardly: *Children tumbled out of the bus.* **2.** To perform acrobatic feats, such as somersaults or twists. **3. a.** To fall or be toppled, as from a position of power or eminence. **b.** To collapse: *and the walls came tumbling down.* **c.** To drop suddenly and rapidly: *Prices tumbled.* **4.** To come accidentally; stumble. Used with *on* or *upon.* **5.** *Informal.* To come to a sudden understanding; catch on: *tumbled to what she was saying.* *—tr.* **1.** To cause to fall suddenly or violently; overturn or overthrow. **2.** To spill, throw, or mix together haphazardly. **3.** To disturb the order of; disarrange; rumple. **4.** To toss or whirl in a drum or tumbler, especially: **a.** To treat in a tumbling box. **b.** To dry in a tumble drier.
∼n. **1.** An act of tumbling; a fall. **2.** A condition of confusion or disorder. **3.** A disorderly heap or mass. [Middle English *tumblen,* from Middle Low German *tummelen,* Old High German *tumalōn,* frequentative of *tāmōn*; akin to Old English *tumbian,* to dance, and French *tomber,* to fall.]

tum·ble·bug (túmb'l-bug) *n.* Any of various beetles of the family Scarabaeidae, that roll up balls of dung to protect their eggs and serve as food for the newly hatched larvae.

tum·ble-down (túmb'l-down) *adj. Informal.* Dilapidated; rickety.

tumble drier *n.* A machine that dries clothes by tumbling them in a heated rotating drum. Also called "tumbler drier".

tum·ble-home (túmb'l-hōm) *n.* The inward curve of a ship's or boat's topsides above the point of greatest breadth.

tum·bler (túmblər) *n.* **1.** One that tumbles; specifically, an acrobat or gymnast. **2. a.** A drinking glass, originally with a rounded bottom. **b.** A flat-bottomed glass having no handle or stem. **c.** The contents of or the amount held by a drinking glass; a tumblerful. **3.** A toy made with a weighted, rounded base so that it can rock over and then right itself. **4.** Any of a breed of domestic pigeons characteristically tumbling or somersaulting in flight. **5.** A piece in a gunlock that forces the hammer forward by action of the mainspring. **6.** The part in a lock that releases the bolt when moved by a key. **7. a.** The drum of a tumble drier. **b.** A tumbling box. **8. a.** A projecting piece on a revolving or rocking part in a mechanism that transmits motion to the part it engages. **b.** The rocking frame that moves a gear into place in a selective transmission, as in a motor vehicle.

tumbler gear *n. Machinery.* A set of gears operated by a tumbler.

tum·ble·weed (túmb'l-weed) *n.* Any of various densely branched New World plants, chiefly of the genus *Amaranthus,* that when withered break off and are rolled about by the wind.

tumbling box *n.* A revolving drum in which objects, such as gemstones, are reduced in size, polished, or cleaned by tumbling with abrasives. Also called "rumble", "tumbler", "tumbling barrel".

tum·brel, tum·bril (túm-brəl, -bril) *n.* **1.** A two-wheeled covered cart formerly used to transport tools and ammunition. **2.** A farm cart that can be tilted to dump a load, as of dung. **3.** A crude cart used to carry condemned prisoners, as to the stake or to the guillotine during the French Revolution. [Middle English *tomberel,* from Old French, from *tomber,* fall, to leap, overturn, from Frankish *tūmon*, perhaps from Germanic *tumōjan-* (unattested), to leap. See **tumble**.]

tu·me·fa·cient (tèwmi-fáy-si-ənt, -shi-, -shənt ‖ tōomi-) *adj.* Producing or tending to produce swelling or tumefaction. [Latin *tumefaciēns* (stem *tumefacient-*), present participle of *tumefacere*, to cause to swell : *tumēre*, to swell + *facere*, to make.]

tu·me·fac·tion (tèwmi-fáksh'n ‖ tōomi-) *n.* **1. a.** The action or process of puffing or swelling. **b.** A swollen condition. **2.** A puffy or swollen part. [French, from Latin *tumefactus*, past participle of *tumefacere*, to cause to swell. See **tumefacient**.] —**tu·me·fac·tive** *adj.*

tu·me·fy (tèwmi-fī ‖ tōomi-) *v.* **-fied, -fying, -fies.** —*tr.* To cause to swell. —*intr.* To swell; become tumid. [Old French *tumefier* : Latin *tumēre*, to swell + -FY.]

tu·mes·cent (tew-méss'nt ‖ tōo-) *adj.* Swelling; somewhat tumid. [Latin *tumēscēns* (stem *tumēscent-*), present participle of *tumēscere*, to begin to swell, from *tumēre*, to swell.] —**tu·mes·cence** *n.*

tu·mid (tèw-mid ‖ tōo-) *adj.* **1.** Swollen; distended. Said of a bodily part or organ. **2.** Of a bulging shape; protuberant. **3.** Overblown; bombastic: *tumid prose.* [Latin *tumidus*, from *tumēre*, to swell.] —**tu·mid·i·ty** (tew-míddəti ‖ tōo-), **tu·mid·ness** *n.* —**tu·mid·ly** *adv.*

tum·my (túmmi) *n., pl.* **-mies.** *Informal.* The stomach. [Baby-talk variant of STOMACH.]

tu·mour, *U.S.* **tu·mor** (tèw-mər ‖ tōo-) *n.* **1.** A noninflammatory abnormal growth arising from existing tissue but growing independently of the normal rate or structural development of such tissue and serving no physiological function. **2.** Any swollen part. [Latin *tumour*, from *tumēre*, to swell.]

tu·mult (tèw-mult, -m'lt ‖ tōo-) *n.* **1.** The din and commotion of a great crowd: *the tumult of the marketplace.* **2.** A disorderly commotion or disturbance; especially, a riot or insurrection. **3.** Agitation of the mind or emotions. [Middle English *tumulte*, from Old French, from Latin *tumultus.*]

tu·mul·tu·ar·y (tew-múltew-əri ‖ tōo-) *adj.* Marked by haste, disorder, or confusion. [Latin *tumultuārius*, from *tumultus*, TUMULT.]

tu·mul·tu·ous (tew-múltew-əss ‖ tōo-) *adj.* **1.** Full of tumult and commotion; noisy; clamorous: *tumultuous applause.* **2.** Making a tumult; turbulent; riotous: *a tumultuous crowd.* **3.** Confusedly or violently agitated: *a tumultuous heart.* —**tu·mul·tu·ous·ly** *adv.* —**tu·mul·tu·ous·ness** *n.*

tu·mu·lus (tèw-mew-ləss ‖ tōo-) *n., pl.* **-li** (-lī). An ancient artificial mound; especially, a burial mound or a barrow. [Latin, a raised heap of earth, hillock, tumulus.] —**tu·mu·lar** (-mewlər) *adj.*

tun (tun) *n.* **1.** A large cask for liquids, especially beer or wine. **2.** A measure of capacity for wine and other liquids, usually equivalent to 252 wine gallons. [Middle English *tunne, tonne,* a measure of wine, Old English *tunne,* cask, vat, from Medieval Latin *tunna.*]

tu·na¹ (tèw-nə, tōo-) *n., pl.* **-nas** or collectively **tuna. 1. a.** Any of various, often large marine food fishes of the genus *Thunnus* and related genera, many of which, including *T. thynnus* and the albacore, are commercially important sources of tinned fish. Also called "tunny". **b.** Any of several related fishes, such as the bonito. **2.** The tinned or commercially processed flesh of any of these fishes. In this sense, also called "tuna fish". [American Spanish, ultimately from Latin *thunnus.* See **tunny.**]

tu·na² (tōo-nə, tèw-) *n.* **1.** Any of several tropical American cacti of the genus *Opuntia*, which includes the prickly pears; especially, *O. tuna*, bearing edible red fruit. **2.** The fruit of such a plant. [Spanish, from Taino.]

tu·na³ (tèw-nə ‖ tōo-) *n. N.Z.* A freshwater eel. [Maori.]

tun·a·ble, tune·a·ble (tèwn-əb'l ‖ tōon-) *adj.* **1.** *Archaic.* Tuneful or melodious. **2.** *Rare.* Able to be tuned. —**tun·a·ble·ness** *n.*

tun·dra (túndrə) *n.* An area between the perpetual snow and ice of Arctic regions and the tree line, having a permanently frozen subsoil and supporting low-growing vegetation such as lichens, mosses, dwarf shrubs, and stunted trees. [Russian, from Lapp *tundar*; akin to Finnish *tunturi,* an Arctic hill, a bare hill.]

tune (tewn ‖ tōon) *n.* **1.** A succession of musical notes forming a melody, especially one of simple and easily remembered character. **2. a.** Correct musical pitch. **b.** The state of being properly adjusted for pitch: *a piano out of tune.* **3. a.** Agreement in pitch: *play in tune with the piano.* **b.** Concord or agreement; harmony: *in tune with the times.* **c.** *Archaic.* Frame of mind; disposition. **4.** *Electronics.* The adjustment of a receiver or circuit for maximum response to a given signal or frequency. **5.** *Archaic.* A musical sound or note. —**call the tune.** To be in a position to control events. —**change (one's) tune.** To change one's approach or attitude. —**to the tune of.** To the sum or amount of.
—*v.* **tuned, tuning, tunes.** —*tr.* **1.** To put (a musical instrument) in the desired pitch with mechanical adjustments. **2.** To adjust so as to bring into harmony or accord; adapt; attune: *tune oneself to life in the tropics.* **3.** To adjust (an engine) for maximum performance. **4.** To adjust (a radio or television receiver) to receive signals at a particular frequency. **5.** *Archaic.* To utter musically; sing. —*intr.* To become attuned. —**tune in.** To tune a radio or television to receive a particular programme. [Middle English, variant of TONE.]

tune·ful (tèwn-f'l ‖ tōon-) *adj.* **1.** Full of tune; melodious; musical. **2.** Producing musical sounds. —**tune·ful·ly** *adv.* —**tune·ful·ness** *n.*

tune·less (tèwn-ləss, -liss ‖ tōon-) *adj.* **1.** Not melodious or tuneful; unmusical. **2.** Giving no music; silent. —**tune·less·ly** *adv.* —**tune·less·ness** *n.*

tun·er (tèwn-ər ‖ tōon-) *n.* **1.** One that tunes: *a piano tuner.* **2.** A device for tuning; especially, an electronic circuit or device used to

select signals at a specific radio frequency for amplification and conversion to sound.

tune up *tr.v.* **1.** To bring (a musical instrument) into proper pitch. **2.** To adjust (a motor or engine) to efficient working order. —*intr.v.* To bring an instrument or set of instruments, as in an orchestra, into proper pitch before a performance.

tune-up (tèwn-up ‖ tōon-) *n.* An adjustment of a motor or engine to put it in the most efficient working order.

tung oil (tung) *n.* A yellow oil extracted from the seeds of the tung tree and used as a drying agent in varnishes and paints and for waterproofing. Also called "Chinese wood oil".

tung·state (túng-stayt) *n.* A chemical compound derived from tungstic acid and containing tungsten with a valency of 6. [TUNGST(EN) + -ATE.]

tung·sten (túng-stən, *rarely* -sten, -stin) *n. Symbol* **W** A hard, brittle, corrosion-resistant, grey to white metallic element extracted from wolframite, scheelite, and other minerals, having the highest melting point and lowest vapour pressure of any metal. Tungsten and its alloys are used in high-temperature structural materials, electrical elements, notably lamp filaments, and instruments requiring thermally compatible glass-to-metal seals. Atomic number 74, atomic weight 183.85, melting point 3 410°C, boiling point 5 927°C, relative density 19.3 (20°C), valencies 2, 3, 4, 5, 6. Also *rare* "wolfram". [Swedish, "heavy stone" : *tung,* heavy, from Old Norse *thungr* + *sten,* from Old Norse *steinn.*] —**tung·sten·ic** (tung-sténnik) *adj.*

tungsten carbide *n.* An extremely hard, fine grey powder with composition WC, used in tools, wear-resistant machine parts, and abrasives.

tungsten lamp *n.* An incandescent electric lamp with a tungsten filament.

tungsten steel *n.* A hard, heat-resistant steel containing tungsten.

tung·stic (túng-stik) *adj.* Of, pertaining to, or containing tungsten, especially with a valency of 6. [From TUNGSTEN.]

tungstic acid *n.* Any of various acids containing tungstites; especially, a powder, H_2WO_4, used in making textiles and plastics.

tung·stite (túng-stīt) *n.* A yellow or yellowish-green mineral, essentially WO_3, resulting from the alteration of tungsten ores. [TUNGST(EN) + -ITE.]

tung tree *n.* Any of several Asian trees of the genus *Aleurites*; especially, *A. cordata,* cultivated for its seeds that yield a commercially valuable drying oil. Also called "tung-oil tree". [Mandarin Chinese *tóng* + TREE.]

Tun·gus (tōong-gōoss, túng-, -gōoz) *n., pl.* **-guses** or collectively **Tungus. 1.** A member of a Mongoloid people inhabiting eastern Siberia. **2.** The Tungusic language of this people. [Russian *Tunguz,* a Tungus, from Yakut *tungus,* from Turkic *tungus,* pig (probably because many Tungus were pig breeders).] —**Tun·gus** *adj.*

Tun·gus·ic (tōong-gōoss-ik, tung-, -gōoz-) *n.* A subfamily of the Altaic family of languages, including the Tungus and Manchu languages, spoken in eastern Siberia and northern Manchuria. —*adj.* Of or pertaining to the Tungus people or to Tungusic.

tu·nic (tèw-nik ‖ tōo-) *n.* **1. a.** A loose-fitting garment, sleeved or sleeveless, extending to the knees and worn by women and men especially in ancient Greece and Rome. **b.** A medieval surcoat. **2. a.** A long plain close-fitting jacket, usually with a high stiff collar, forming part of a military or police uniform. **b.** A long plain sleeved or sleeveless blouse worn over a skirt by women. **c.** A **gym-slip** (*see*). **3.** *Anatomy.* A coat or layer enveloping an organ or part. **4.** *Botany.* A membranous outer covering, as of a seed. **5.** A tunicle. [Latin *tunica,* a sheath, tunic, from a Phoenician source, from Aramaic *kittūnā,* akin to Hebrew *kəthōnet.* See also **chiton.**]

tu·ni·ca (tèw-ni-kə ‖ tōo-) *n., pl.* **-cae** (-kee, -see, -kī). *Anatomy.* An integument; a tunic. [New Latin, from Latin, TUNIC.]

tu·ni·cate (tèwni-kət, -kit, -kayt ‖ tōoni-) *n.* Any of various chordate marine animals of the subphylum Urochordata (or Tunicata), having a cylindrical or globular body enclosed in a tough outer covering, or tunic, and including the sea squirts and salps. —*adj.* **1.** Of or pertaining to the tunicates. **2.** *Anatomy.* Having a tunic. **3.** *Botany.* Having concentric layers, as does the bulb of an onion. [Latin *tunicātus,* past participle of *tunicāre,* to clothe with a tunic, from *tunica,* TUNIC.]

tu·ni·cle (tèw-nik'l ‖ tōo-) *n.* A short vestment worn over the alb by a subdeacon or with the dalmatic by a bishop or cardinal. Also called "tunic". [Middle English, from Latin *tunicula,* diminutive of *tunica,* TUNIC.]

tuning fork *n.* A small two-pronged instrument that when struck produces a sound of fixed pitch.

Tu·nis (tèw-niss ‖ tōo-). Capital of Tunisia. Lying in the northeast of the country on a lagoon inland from the Gulf of Tunis, it is southwest of the site of Carthage.

Tu·nis·i·a, Republic of (tew-nízzi-ə, -nissi- ‖ tōo-). Largely desert country of North Africa. The economy is dominated by oil, which accounts for more than a third of the country's exports. Despite little farmland, 40 per cent of workers are in agriculture, and olive oil is a major export. A French protectorate from 1881, Tunisia became independent in 1956. A year later, the Bey was deposed, and an Arab republic declared. Area, 163 610 square kilometres (63,170 square miles). Population, 6,700,000. Capital, Tunis. —**Tu·ni·si·an** *n. & adj.* See map, next page.

tun·nel (túnn'l) *n.* **1.** A passage excavated underground, through a hill or mountain, or under a river or sea, especially one for a road or railway. **2.** An underground gallery in a mine. **3.** An animal's burrow. **4.** *Archaic.* The flue of a chimney.

~*v.* **tunnelled** or *U.S.* **tunneled, -nelling** or *U.S.* **-neling, -nels.** —*tr.* **1.** To make a tunnel under or through. **2.** To make by or as if by excavating: *tunnel a passage; tunnel one's way out.* —*intr.* **1.** To make a tunnel. **2.** *Physics.* To pass through a barrier by the tunnel effect. Used of a particle. [Middle English *tonel,* a pipelike net for catching birds, from Old French *ton(n)el,* a cask, from *tonne,* a tun, from Medieval Latin *tunna, tonna,* TUN.] —**tun·nel·ler** *n.*

tunnel diode *n. Electronics.* A semiconductor diode with a very narrow, heavily doped, p-n junction across which electrons travel by the tunnel effect. Also called "Esaki diode".

tunnel disease *n. Medicine.* **Decompression sickness** *(see).*

tunnel effect *n. Physics.* An effect, explained by quantum mechanics, by which a particle can pass through a barrier even though it does not have enough energy to overcome the barrier according to classical mechanics.

tunnel vision *n.* **1.** A defect or restriction of lateral vision. **2.** *Informal.* An inability to take a broad or long-term view of a situation because of obsessive concentration on a single one of its problems or aspects.

tun·ny (túnni) *n., pl.* **-nies** or collectively **tunny.** A fish, the **tuna** *(see).* [French *thon,* from Provençal *ton,* from Latin *thunnus,* from Greek *thunnos,* akin to Hebrew *tannīn,* "great sea monster".]

tup (tup) *n.* **1.** *Chiefly British.* A male sheep; a ram. **2.** A heavy metal body; especially, the head of a power hammer.
~*tr.v.* **tupped, tupping, tups.** To copulate with (a ewe). Used of a ram. [Middle English *toupe, tup(pe)†,* a ram.]

Tu·pa·ma·ro (tŏŏpə-maárō) *n., pl.* **-ros.** A member of an extreme left-wing urban guerrilla organisation in Uruguay. [After *Tupac Amaru,* 18th-century Peruvian Indian leader of a rebellion against the Spanish.] —**Tu·pa·ma·ro** *adj.*

tu·pe·lo (téw-pi-lō, -pə- ‖ tŏŏ-) *n., pl.* **-los.** **1.** Any of several trees of the genus *Nyssa;* especially, *N. aquatica,* of the southeastern United States, having soft, light wood. **2.** The wood of any of these trees. [Creek *ito opilwa,* "swamp tree" : *ito,* tree + *opilwa,* swamp.]

Tu·pi (tŏŏ-pée, tŏŏpi) *n., pl.* **-pis** or collectively **Tupi.** **1.** A member of a group of South American Indian peoples living along the coast of Brazil, in the Amazon valley, and in Paraguay. **2.** The language of these peoples, a branch of Tupi-Guarani. —**Tu·pi, Tu·pi·an** (-ən) *adj.*

Tu·pi-Gua·ra·ni (tŏŏ-pée-gwaárə-née, tŏŏpi-) *n.* A family of languages spoken throughout large areas of coastal Brazil, the Amazon valley, and northeastern South America. —**Tu·pi-Gua·ra·ni, Tu·pi-Gua·ra·ni·an** *adj.*

turbine

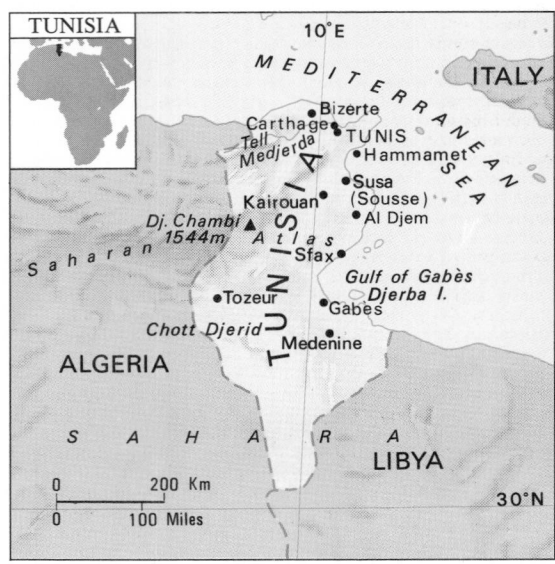

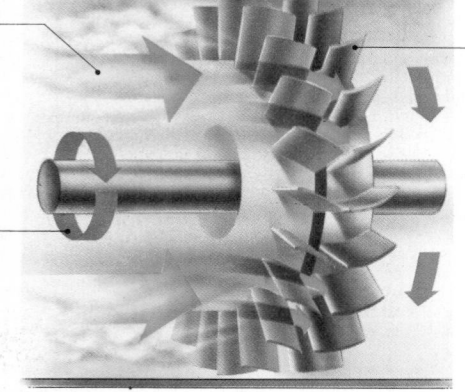

THE ENGINE WITH CONTINUOUS ROTARY MOTION

The turbine principle is found in power stations, and jet aircraft

A turbine, which moves with a spinning motion, is more efficient than a reciprocating engine, which has a to-and-fro movement. In the latter, the constant change of direction wastes energy, but the smooth continuous motion of the turbine allows it to attain very high speeds.

Running water was mankind's earliest power source and a Frenchman, Benoît Fourneyron, is generally credited with building the first practical water-driven turbine in 1827. Now about a quarter of the world's electricity is generated by water turbines. However, water sources suitable for driving hydroelectric generators are not available everywhere, and steam-driven turbines

were developed for other locations. The first working device was produced in 1883 by a Swiss, Carl Gustaf de Laval, but the British engineer Charles A. Parsons built a more practical model in 1884. Steam-turbine generators are now in worldwide use. Some produce enough power for a city of a million people.

Work on gas turbines started in this century. They are useful standby generators at power stations and have dramatically affected the field of aviation as jet engines – first built in the 1930s by two engineers working independently of each other, the German Hans Pabst von Ohain and the Briton Frank Whittle.

Steam at high pressure flows past a set of stationary vanes. The angle and shape of these guiding vanes ensure that the maximum energy of the steam will be exploited

The steam hits the next set of vanes, attached to a rotating shaft. In an actual turbine the steam would pass on through many more sets of stationary and rotating vanes

As the steam expands through the vanes, it causes them to rotate and turn the shaft, which can drive a generator to produce electricity

STEAM TURBINE *Modern turbines follow essentially the same pattern as that used by Parsons in 1884. Only two sets of vanes are shown above, but a typical turbine would have many sets, alternately guiding and rotating, to extract maximum energy from the steam.*

---

tuppence. *British Informal.* Variant of **twopence.**

tuppenny. *Chiefly British Informal.* Variant of **twopenny.**

tup·pen·ny ha'pen·ny (túp-ni háyp-ni, túppəni) *adj. Informal.* Of poor quality or of little value.

Tupperware (túppər-wair) *n.* A trademark for a range of polyethylene containers used especially in the home for storing food.

tu quo·que (téw kwŏkwi, tŏŏ, kwókwi) *n. Latin.* A retort accusing an accuser of a similar fault or offence. [Latin, "you also".]

turaco. Variant of **touraco.**

Tu·ra·ni·an (tewr-ráyni-ən, -raáni- ‖ tŏŏ-) *n.* **1.** A language group, **Ural-Altaic** *(see).* **2.** A member of any of the peoples who speak languages of this group. [Persian *Tūrān,* region north of the Oxus River.] —**Tu·ra·ni·an** *adj.*

tur·ban (túrbən) *n.* **1.** A man's headdress of Muslim origin but also worn by Sikhs and some Hindus, consisting of a long scarf of linen, cotton, or silk wound round the head or a cap. **2.** Any hat or headdress resembling a turban; especially, a type of brimless hat worn by women. [French *turbant, tolliban,* from Italian *turbante, tolipante,* from Turkish *tül(i)bend,* Persian *dulband†.*] —**tur·baned** *adj.*

tur·ba·ry (túrbəri) *n., pl.* **-ries.** **1.** A place where peat can be dug; a peat bog. **2.** *Law.* In England, the right to dig peat or turf on common land or someone else's ground. [Middle English *turbary(e),* turf land, peat bog, from Anglo-French, from Old French *t(o)urberie,* Medieval Latin *turbāria,* from *turba,* turf, from Germanic.]

tur·bel·la·ri·an (túr-bi-laír-i-ən, -bə-) *n.* Any of various chiefly aquatic ciliate flatworms of the class Turbellaria. [New Latin *Turbellaria,* from Latin *turbellae* (plural), bustle, stir (their cilia vibrate and produce little whirls in the water), from *turba,* turmoil, uproar. See **turbid.**] —**tur·bel·la·ri·an** *adj.*

tur·bid (túrbid) *adj.* **1.** Containing sediment or foreign particles stirred up or suspended; muddy; cloudy: *turbid water.* **2.** Heavy, dark, or dense, as smoke or fog. **3.** In turmoil; muddled: *the turbid life of Bombay.* [Latin *turbidus,* wild, confused, muddy, from *turba,* turmoil, uproar, probably from Greek *turbē,* disorder.] —**tur·bid·i·ty** (tur-bíddəti), **tur·bid·ness** *n.* —**tur·bid·ly** *adv.*

tur·bi·nal (túrbin'l) *adj.* Also **tur·bi·nate** (túrbi-nət, -nit, -nayt). **1.** Having the shape of a cone resting on its apex. **2.** Having the shape of a scroll.
~*n. Anatomy.* A turbinate bone. [Latin *turbō* (stem *turbin-*), a spinning thing, top. See **turbine.**]

tur·bi·nate (túrbi-nət, -nit, -nayt) *adj.* Also **tur·bi·nat·ed** (-ñaytid). **1.** Variant of **turbinal. 2.** *Zoology.* Spiral and decreasing sharply in diameter from base to apex. Said of a shell. **3.** *Anatomy.* Designating a small scroll-like bone that extends horizontally along the lateral wall of the nasal passage. [Latin *turbinātus,* from *turbō* (stem *turbin-*), a top. See **turbine.**]

tur·bine (túr-bīn, -bin) *n.* Any of various machines in which the kinetic energy of a moving fluid is converted to rotational energy by the impulse or reaction of the fluid with a series of buckets or blades arrayed about the circumference of a wheel or cylinder. See **gas turbine, impulse turbine, reaction turbine.** [French, from Latin *turbō* (stem *turbin-*), a spinning thing, top, whirlwind, perhaps from Greek *turbē,* disorder.]

tur·bit (túrbit) *n.* Any of a breed of domestic pigeons having a small crested head and a ruffled breast. [Perhaps from Latin *turbō,* top (see **turbine**), referring to its shape.]

tur·bo (túrbō) *n., pl.* **-os.** A car or other vehicle with an engine fitted with a turbocharger.

turbo– *comb. form.* Indicates turbine, or pertaining to or driven by a turbine; for example, **turbojet.** [From TURBINE.]

tur·bo·charg·er (túrbō-chaarjər) *n.* A device that uses the exhaust gas of an internal-combustion engine to drive a turbine that in turn drives a supercharger attached to the engine.

tur·bo·elec·tric (túrbō-i-léktrik, -ə-) adj. Designating, pertaining to, or using electricity produced by a turbine.

tur·bo·fan (túrbō-fán, -fan) n. 1. A turbojet engine in which a fan supplements the total thrust by forcing air diverted from the main engine directly into the hot turbine exhaust. 2. An aircraft in which such an engine is used.

tur·bo·gen·er·a·tor (túrbō-jénnə-raytər) n. A large electric generator in a power station driven by a turbine.

tur·bo·jet (túrbō-jét, -jet) n. 1. A jet engine having a turbine-driven compressor and developing thrust from the exhaust of hot gases. 2. An aircraft in which such an engine is used.

tur·bo·prop (túrbō-próp, -prop) n. 1. A turbojet engine used to drive an external propeller. Also called "prop-jet". 2. An aircraft in which such an engine is used. [Short for *turbopropeller*.]

tur·bo·ram·jet (túrbō-rám-jet) n. 1. A turbojet engine that at high speeds compresses air taken in as a ramjet and increases exhaust velocities with an afterburner. 2. An aircraft in which such an engine is used.

tur·bo·su·per·charg·er (túrbō-sŏŏ-pər-chaarjər, -séw-) n. A supercharger that uses an exhaust-driven turbine to maintain air-intake pressure in high-altitude aircraft.

tur·bot (túrbət) n., pl. **-bots** or collectively **turbot. 1.** A European flatfish, *Scophthalmus maximus,* prized as food. **2.** Any of various similar or related flatfishes. [Middle English, from Old French, probably from Old Swedish *törnbut,* turbot, "thorn-flatfish" (presumably referring to its shape) : *törn,* thorn + *but,* flat fish.]

tur·bu·la·tor (túrbew-laytər) n. Any device designed to cause turbulence in fluids. [From TURBULENT.]

tur·bu·lence (túrbewlənss) n. 1. The state or quality of being agitated, violently disturbed, or in commotion. 2. Turbulent flow. 3. Disturbances in the atmosphere, such as air pockets and currents.

tur·bu·lent (túrbewlənt) adj. 1. Violently agitated or disturbed: *turbulent rapids.* 2. Having a restless, uncertain, or chaotic character; stormy: *a turbulent period of history.* 3. Inclined to unrest or disorder; unruly; tumultuous. [Latin *turbulentus,* from *turba,* confusion. See turbid.] —**tur·bu·lent·ly** adv.

turbulent flow n. The motion of a fluid having local velocities and pressures that fluctuate randomly. Also called "turbulence". Compare **laminar flow, streamline flow.**

Turcoman. Variant of Turkoman.

turd (turd) n. 1. *Vulgar.* A piece of excrement. 2. *Vulgar Slang.* A worthless or contemptible person. [Old English *tord.*]

tu·reen (tə-réen, tewr-, tŏŏ-) n. A broad, deep, often oval, dish with a lid used for serving soups, stews, or the like. [Earlier *ter(r)ene,* from French *terrine,* "earthen vessel", from Old French, feminine of *terrin,* from Vulgar Latin *terrīnus,* from Latin *terra,* earth.]

turf (turf) n., pl. **turfs** or archaic **turves** (turvz). 1. A surface layer of earth containing a dense growth of grass and its matted roots; sod. 2. A piece cut from such a layer of earth or sod. 3. A piece of peat that is burned for use as fuel. —**the turf.** 1. A racecourse. 2. The sport or business of racing horses; the world of racing. —**turf out.** *British Informal.* To throw out; expel; eject. [Middle English *turf,* Old English *turf.*] —**turf·y** adj.

turf accountant n. British. A **bookmaker** (see).

Tur·ge·nev (toor-gyáyn-yef, tur-, -gáyn-, -yev), **Ivan Sergeyevich** (1818–83). Russian writer. His collection of stories, *A Sportsman's Sketches* (1852), contributed towards the emancipation of the serfs. His novels, such as *Fathers and Children* (1862), are eloquent portrayals of the ineffectual Russian gentry.

tur·ges·cence (tur-jéss'nss) n. 1. The process of swelling up, or the condition of being swollen. 2. Pomposity; self-importance. [Latin *turgēscens* (stem *turgēscent-*), present participle of *turgēscere,* inceptive of *turgēre,* to be swollen. See turgid.] —**tur·ges·cent** adj.

tur·gid (túrjid) adj. 1. Distended; swollen; bloated. 2. Excessively ornate in style or language; grandiloquent. 3. Fully expanded from water intake. Said of plants. [Latin *turgidus,* from *turgēre†,* to be swollen, swell.] —**tur·gid·i·ty** (tur-jíddəti), **tur·gid·ness** n. —**tur·gid·ly** adv.

tur·gor (túr-gər, -gawr) n. *Biology.* The normal fullness or tension produced by the fluid content of blood vessels, capillaries, and plant or animal cells. The maintenance of turgor is the primary method of support in herbaceous plants. [Late Latin, from Latin *turgēre,* to be swollen. See turgid.]

Tu·rin (téwr-rín, tew- ‖ tŏŏ-). *Italian* **Tor·i·no** (to-réenō). City of northwestern Italy. The capital of Piedmont and of Turin province, it was founded by the Romans at the confluence of the Po and Dora Riparia rivers. It is the former capital of the Kingdom of Sardinia (1720), and of Italy (1861–65). The 15th century cathedral has a chapel containing the "Shroud of Turin", considered by some to be the cloth in which the body of Christ was wrapped after the Crucifixion.

tur·i·on (téwr-i-ən, tóor-) n. A bud produced by many aquatic plants that is shed from the parent plant and remains dormant until the spring. [French, from Latin *turiō* (stem *turiōn-*), shoot.]

Turk (turk) n. 1. A native or inhabitant of Turkey. 2. A member of any of the Turkic-speaking peoples who originated in Turkestan. 3. *Informal.* A brutal or tyrannical person.

Turk. Turkey; Turkish.

Tur·ka·na, Lake (toor-ka'anə, tur-). Formerly **Lake Rudolf.** Lake of east Africa. The continent's fifth largest lake, approximately 250 kilometres (185 miles) long and up to 55 kilometres (34 miles) wide,

it lies in the Great Rift Valley on the borders of Kenya, Ethiopia, and Sudan.

Turkestan, Chinese. See **Xinjiang Uygur Zizhiqu.**

Tur·ki·stan or **Tur·ke·stan** (túrki-staán, -stán). Region of central Asia. A crossroads for trade and conquest, it has historically been the subject of dispute, and is now divided between China, Afghanistan, and the U.S.S.R. Soviet Turkistan is divided into the Kazakh, Kirgiz, Tadshik, Turkmen and Uzbek Soviet Socialist Republics.

tur·key (túrki) n., pl. **-keys** or collectively **turkey. 1. a.** A large North American bird, *Meleagris gallopavo,* that has brownish plumage and a bare, wattled head and neck and is widely domesticated for food. **b.** A related bird, *Agriocharis ocellata,* of Mexico and Central America. **2.** *U.S. Slang.* A film, play, or other production that fails; a flop. —**talk turkey.** *Chiefly U.S. Informal.* To discuss in a straightforward and direct manner. [Short for TURKEY COCK.]

Turkey, Republic of (túrki). State in southeastern Europe and western Asia, mostly covering the Anatolian plateau (Asia Minor). Farming is the main occupation, cotton, tobacco, and textile yarns and fabrics providing 66 per cent of exports. Turkey has reserves of coal, lignite, oil, and iron, and chrome is exported. Tourism and expatriate workers are important sources of foreign exchange. The country was the centre of the Ottoman Empire for almost 700 years, but became a republic in 1923. There have been several military governments since 1946, and Turkey pursues a course between East and West, joining NATO (1952), and signing a non-aggression and trade pact with the U.S.S.R. (1978). Relations with Greece are uneasy because of Cyprus and the disputed border. Istanbul is the largest city and chief port. Area, 780 756 square kilometres (301,382 square miles). Population, 47,700,000. Capital, Ankara. —**Tur·kish** adj.

turkey buzzard n. A New World vulture, *Cathartes aura,* having dark plumage and bare red head and neck similar to that of the turkey. Also called "turkey vulture".

turkey cock n. 1. A male turkey. 2. *Informal.* A strutting, conceited man. [Originally applied to the guinea fowl (with which the American bird was later mistakenly identified), first imported by the Portuguese from Africa by way of Turkey.]

Turkey red n. A brilliant red. [The colour was often used in cotton cloth manufactured in Turkey.] —**Tur·key-red** (túrki-réd, -red) adj.

turkey trot n. A ragtime dance of the early 20th century, characterised by a springy walk with the feet well apart and a swinging up-and-down movement of the shoulders.

Tur·ki (túr-kee) adj. 1. Of or pertaining to Turkic. 2. Of or pertaining to the Turkic-speaking peoples, especially those speaking an Eastern Turkic language.
~n. Any Turkic language or Turkic speaker.

Tur·kic (túrkik) n. A subdivision of the Altaic family of languages, including Turkish, Turkoman, Azerbaidzhani, Tatar, Uzbek, Uigur, Kirgiz, Karakalpak, Chuvash, Chagatai, and Yakut.
~adj. 1. Of or pertaining to the language or people of Turkey. 2. Of or pertaining to Turkic.

Turk·ish (túrkish) adj. Abbr. **Turk. 1.** Of or pertaining to Turkey or the Turks. **2.** Of or pertaining to the Turkic language of Turkey.
~n. The Turkic language of Turkey. When written in the Arabic script, as it was until 1930, it is generally referred to as "Ottoman Turkish" or "Osmanli".

Turkish bath n. 1. A steam bath inducing heavy perspiration, usually followed by a shower and often a massage. 2. *Often plural.* An establishment where such bathing facilities are available.

Turkish coffee n. Strong, sweet black coffee made from very finely ground beans and served in tiny cups.

Turkish delight n. A gelatinous sweet of Turkish origin, cut into cubes and dredged in icing sugar.

Turkish Empire. See **Ottoman Empire.**

Turkish Federated State of Cyprus. The northern part of Cyprus, occupied by Turkey in 1974, and proclaimed a federated state the following year.

Turkish towel n. A thick rough terry towel.

Turk·men Soviet Socialist Republic (túrk-mən, -men). Also **Turk·**

turkey *The wild turkey (above), which is native to the woodlands of North America, was introduced into Europe in the 16th century. It is the ancestor of modern farmyard breeds, reared for their meat, such as the English pied turkey (below).*

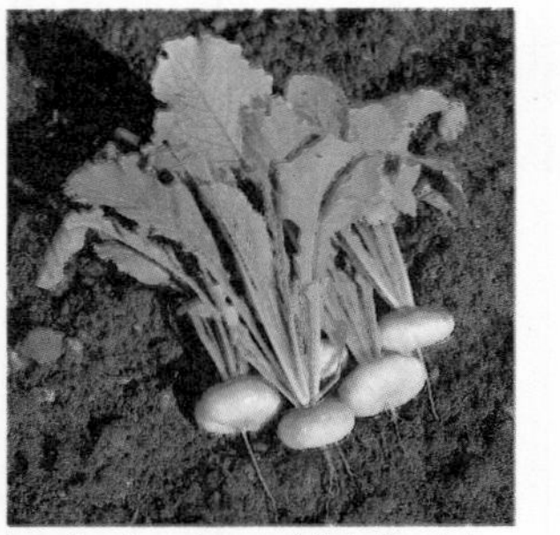

turnip *A root crop of Asiatic origin related to cabbages, cauliflowers, and broccoli. It is grown as a winter feed for sheep, and as a vegetable for human consumption.*

me·ni·a (-méeni-ə) or **Turk·men·i·stan** (túrk-ménni-staán, -stán). Constituent republic of the U.S.S.R, lying east of the Caspian Sea, and established as a republic in 1925. Largely consisting of the desert of the Kara Kum, it has a population concentrated around oases, where subsistence farming is the chief occupation. Ashkhabad is the capital. **—Turk·me·ni·an** *adj.*

Tur·ko·man, Tur·co·man (túrkə-mən, -man, -maan) *n., pl.* **-mans.** Also **Turk·man** (túrk-) (for sense 1), **Turk·men** (-men) (for sense 2). **1.** Any of a formerly nomadic people inhabiting the Turkmen, Uzbek, Kazakh, and Kara-Kalpak republics of the U.S.S.R. **2.** The Turkic language of this people. **—Tur·ko·man, Tur·co·man** *adj.*

Turks and Cai·cos Islands (káy-koss). Two groups of islands in the Bahamas, western Atlantic Ocean, forming a self-governing British colony. Grand Turk is the seat of government.

Turk's-cap lily (túrks-káp) *n.* Any of various cultivated lilies having colourful, turban-shaped flowers, such as the **martagon** *(see).*

Turk's-head (túrks-héd) *n. Nautical.* A turban-shaped knot made by winding a smaller rope around a larger one.

Tur·ku (toór-kōō). *Swedish* **Å·bo** (áw-bōō). Provincial capital of southwest Finland, the country's capital until 1812. An ice-free Baltic port, it exports timber and dairy products.

Turkut. See **Old Turkic.**

tur·mer·ic (túrmərik) *n.* **1.** A plant, *Curcuma longa,* of India, having yellow flowers and an aromatic rootstock. **2.** The powdered rootstock of this plant, used to flavour or colour food and as a yellow dye. **3.** Any of several other plants having similar roots. [Earlier *tarmaret,* from Old French *terre mérite,* from Medieval Latin *terra merita,* "meritorious earth", alteration of a native name.]

turmeric paper *n.* Paper saturated with turmeric and used as an indicator for the presence of alkalis, which turn the paper brown, or for boric acid, which turns it red-brown.

tur·moil (túr-moyl) *n.* A state of violent agitation or utter confusion; tumult. [16th century : origin obscure.]

turn (turn) *v.* **turned, turning, turns.** *—tr.* **1.** To cause to move around a central point; cause to rotate or revolve: *The wind turns the sails of the windmill.* **2.** To cause to move around in order to achieve a desired result: *turn the handle to open.* **3.** To alter or control the functioning of (a mechanical device, for example), especially by means of a rotating or similar movement: *turn the radio down.* **4.** To perform or accomplish by rotating or revolving: *turn a somersault.* **5. a.** To change the position of so that the underside becomes the upperside: *turn the steak.* **b.** To dig or plough (soil) to bring the undersoil to the surface. **c.** To reverse the material of (a collar or cuff, for example) so that the inner side becomes the outer. **d.** To reverse or fundamentally disturb the order, disposition, or character of: *turned the room upside down in her search; turned the argument completely on its head.* **6. a.** To produce a rounded shape in (wood or metal, for example) by applying a cutting tool while rotating on a lathe. **b.** To produce a rounded form in by any means: *turn a heel in knitting a sock.* **c.** To give shape or form to by rotating: *turn a vase on a potter's wheel.* **d.** To give distinctive, artistic, or elegant form to: *turn a phrase.* **7.** To weigh in the mind; think over; ponder. Often used with *over*: *turn an idea over.* **8. a.** To change the position of by moving through an arc of a circle: *turned her chair to face me.* **b.** To change the position of by folding, twisting, or bending: *turn the blankets down.* **c.** To change the position of so as to show another side: *turn the page.* **d.** To injure by twisting: *turn an ankle.* **e.** To upset or make nauseated: *That turns my stomach.* **9. a.** To change the direction or course of: *turn the car round.* **b.** To cause (a cricket ball) to change direction on pitching; spin. **10.** To divert or deflect: *turn aside a blow.* **11.** To reverse the course of; cause to retreat: *turn the enemy.* **12.** To make a course around or about: *turn the corner.* **13.** To change, affect, or influence the character or tendency of: *a speech that turned the election.* **14.** To disturb the emotional or mental balance of; unsettle: *"Sudden prosperity had turned Garrick's head."* (Lord Macaulay). **15.** To set or point in a specified way or direction: *turned her back on them.* **16.** To set going in a specified direction; direct: *turned our steps back home.* **17.** To aim or focus; train: *turn a spotlight on the intruders.* **18.** To direct (the attention, interest, or mind, for example) towards or away from something: *turn a deaf ear.* **19.** To devote or apply (oneself or one's efforts, for example) to something: *turned my hand to a bit of decorating.* **20.** To reach or surpass (a specified age, time, or amount): *only just turned thirty.* **21.** To cause to act or go against; make antagonistic. **22.** To send, drive, or let go: *threatened to turn us out; turn the dog loose.* **23.** To pour, let fall, or otherwise release (contents) from a receptacle: *turn the dough onto a floured board.* **24.** To make sour; curdle: *The milk has turned.* **25.** To affect or change the colour of: *Autumn turns the leaves.* **26.** To change or convert; transform. Often used with *into*: *turned the cinema into a bingo hall.* **27.** To cause to take on a specified character, nature, or appearance: *Worry turned her hair grey.* **28. a.** To make a bend or curve in: *turn a bar of steel.* **b.** To blunt or dull (the edge of a cutting instrument). **29.** To earn: *turn an honest penny.* *—intr.* **1.** To move round an axis or centre; rotate; revolve. **2.** To appear to revolve or whirl, as in dizziness or giddiness: *My head keeps turning.* **3.** To roll from side to side or back and forth: *tossed and turned all night.* **4.** To operate a lathe. **5.** To change one's position so as to face in a different or opposite direction: *turned away at the sight; Everyone turned round as I entered.* **6. a.** To move so as to follow a different or opposite course; take a new direction: *turned and ran; turned into a side street.* **b.** To change direction on pitching. Used of a cricket ball. **7.** To change in behaviour or attitude so as to become hostile or antagonistic: *turned against her former colleagues.* **8.** To attack suddenly and violently with no apparent motive: *The dog turned on me.* **9.** To direct one's attention, interest, or thought towards or away from something. **10.** To adopt a new religion; become converted. **11.** To switch one's loyalty from one side or party to another. **12.** To have recourse for help, support, or information: *didn't know who to turn to; turned to drugs.* **13.** To devote or apply oneself to something, as to a field of study. **14. a.** To depend for its outcome; rely: *Success turns on the effectiveness of our advertising.* **b.** To have a particular focal point or central feature; hinge: *The debate turned on the issue of subsidies.* **15. a.** To undergo a change: *Our luck finally turned.* **b.** To change by passing from one state into another; become transformed: *Our surprise turned to horror.* **c.** To change so as to assume the specified nature, role, or characteristics; become: *turned traitor; It suddenly turned cold; turn into a pumpkin.* **16.** To become sour; curdle or ferment. **17.** To change colour. **18.** To become dull or blunt after bending back. Used of the edge of a cutting instrument. **—turn down.** **1.** To reduce the speed, volume, intensity, or flow of. **2.** *Informal.* To reject or refuse (an offer or proposal, for example). **—turn in.** **1. a.** To deliver over, as to the police: *turned herself in.* **b.** *Chiefly U.S.* To hand in; give in: *turn in an income-tax return.* **2.** To register or produce: *turned in a creditable performance.* **3.** *Informal.* To go to bed. **—turn to.** To begin work; apply oneself to a task.

~n. **1.** An act of turning or being turned around an axis or centre; a rotation or revolution. **2.** The act or an action of turning to face or move in a different or opposite direction: *a right turn.* **3.** A point at which something turns or turns off; a bend or junction; a turning: *take the first turn on the left.* **4.** A point of change in time: *the turn of the century.* **5.** A deviation from an existing course or trend; a new departure or development: *took a turn for the worse.* **6.** A right, duty, or opportunity to do something allotted to an individual according to some roster or implicitly agreed order of succession: *My turn to do the washing up.* **7.** A period of participation in something: *a turn at creative writing.* **8.** A characteristic mood, style, or habit; a natural inclination: *a speculative turn of mind.* **9.** A propensity or adeptness: *a turn for carpentry.* **10.** A deed or action having a specified effect on another: *One good turn deserves another.* **11.** Advantage or purpose: *It served her turn.* **12.** A short walk or excursion: *a turn in the park.* **13.** A twist or other distortion in shape. **14.** The condition of being twisted or wound. **15. a.** A winding of one thing about another. **b.** A single wind or convolution, as of wire upon a spool. **16.** *Music.* A figure or ornament consisting of four notes in rapid succession, the second and fourth of which are identical, with the first a degree above, and the third a degree below. **17.** A distinctive form of style or expression: *a nice turn of phrase.* **18.** An attack of illness or severe nervousness; a fit; a spell. **19.** *Informal.* A momentary shock or scare: *I had quite a turn when I heard the news.* **20. a.** A brief performance, as in the theatre or circus; an act: *a music-hall turn.* **b.** A performer in such an act. **21. a.** A transaction on the stock market involving both a sale and a purchase. **b.** The profit made by a jobber on such a transaction, being the difference between the buying and selling prices of a stock or commodity. **22.** *Australian.* A party. **—at every turn.** At every point or moment; continually. **—by turns.** Alternately; one after another. **—in turn.** In the proper order or sequence. **—out of turn.** **1.** Not in the proper order or sequence. **2.** At an inappropriate time or in an inappropriate manner. **—take turns.** To take part or do something in order, one after another. **—to a turn.** To a precise degree; perfectly: *The roast was done to a turn.* [Middle English *turnen, tornen,* from Old English *tyrnan, turnian* and Old French *to(u)rner,* both from Latin *tornāre,* to turn in a lathe, round off, from *tornus,* a lathe, from Greek *tornos,* tool for drawing a circle, circle, lathe.]

Synonyms: *turn, rotate, revolve, gyrate, spin, whirl, circle, eddy, swirl, swivel, roll.*

turn·a·bout (túrn-ə-bowt) *n.* **1.** The act of turning round and facing or moving in the opposite direction. **2.** A shift or reversal in opinion, policy, or allegiance.

turn·a·round (túrn-ə-rownd) *n. Chiefly U.S.* **Turnround** *(see).*

turn bridge *n.* A **swing bridge** *(see).*

turn·buck·le (túrn-buck'l) *n.* A metal coupling device consisting of an oblong piece internally threaded at both ends, into each end of which a threaded rod is screwed. It is used for tightening a rod or wire rope.

turn·coat (túrn-kōt) *n.* One who traitorously switches allegiance.

turn·er (túrnər) *n.* One who or that which turns; specifically, a person who works a lathe.

Tur·ner (túrnər), **Joseph Mallord William** (1775–1851). British painter. Perhaps the most original of English painters, his abstract treatment of light, colour, and space was taken up by the French impressionists. His works include *The Fighting Téméraire* (1839), and *Rain, Steam, and Speed* (1844).

turn·er·y (túrnəri) *n., pl.* **-ies.** **1.** The work or workshop of a lathe operator. **2.** Objects made on a lathe.

turn·ing (túrning) *n.* **1. a.** A deviation or change of course. **b.** A point at which a road or path turns off from another: *missed our turning and got lost.* **2.** The shaping of metal or wood on a lathe.

turning circle *n.* The circle with the smallest circumference within which a motor vehicle can turn.

turning point *n.* **1.** A point at which significant changes occur or

Turner

"HE SEEMS TO PAINT WITH TINTED STEAM"

The artist who pursued the mystery of light and space

From his humble beginnings as a London barber's son, Joseph Mallord William Turner rose to fame and fortune faster than any other English landscape painter. He first had a watercolour accepted by the Royal Academy when he was 15, in 1790. By the time he was 24 he had more commissions for watercolours and drawings than he could handle; at 27 he was elected a member of the Royal Academy.

To discover subjects for his work, Turner spent his summers touring. In Britain he visited Yorkshire, the Lake District, Scotland, and Wales. In 1802 in Paris, Turner saw the Italian paintings Napoleon had seized, and made many copies. In 1819 he made the first of several visits to Italy, which led to a great development in his treatment of light and colour.

No artist has excelled Turner's originality in the use of colour, treatment of light, and creation of mood. He painted a wide range of subjects, and strove to treat significant themes. His early works include historical landscapes featuring human events such as the Roman legend of Dido and Aeneas. His later works include magnificent studies of nature's power, especially in sea and sky. In his quest to unravel the mysteries of light, Turner pushed beyond the understanding of his contemporaries. But Constable understood him: "He seems to paint with tinted steam, so evanescent, so airy." Although he was always harshly criticised for his lack of finish, Turner enjoyed success and recognition until he was 40, when he decided to paint only what suited him and to experiment with his ideas of light and space. His work fell out of favour and was not rediscovered until modern times.

Most of the 19,500 oils, watercolours, and drawings he left to the nation are in the Tate Gallery and the British Museum.

RADIANT SKY AND SEA Keelmen Heaving in Coals by Night *(1835) displays Turner's unsurpassed skill in giving a luminous quality and a mood of drama to a scene. His original and imaginative approach to landscape presaged the impressionist style.*

crucial decision must be made; a decisive moment. **2.** *Mathematics.* A maximum or minimum point on a curve.

tur·nip (túrnip) *n.* **1.** A widely cultivated plant, *Brassica rapa,* native to the Old World, having a large, edible yellow or white root. **2.** The root of this plant, eaten as a vegetable. **3.** Any of several similar or related plants. **4.** *Scottish & Northern English.* A **swede** *(see).* [Earlier *turnepe : tur-* (origin and meaning unknown) + *nepe,* turnip, from Middle English *nepe,* Old English *nǣp,* from Latin *nāpus* (see **napiform**).]

turnip cabbage *n.* A vegetable, **kohlrabi** *(see).*

turn-key (túrn-kee) *n., pl.* **-keys.** The keeper of the keys in a prison; a jailer.
~*adj. Chiefly U.S.* Supplied, or requiring the supply of something, in a fully equipped or operational state: *a turnkey apartment.*

turn off *tr.v.* **1.** To stop the operation, activity, or flow of; shut off or switch off. **2.** *British.* To discharge (an employee). **3.** *Informal.* **a.** To fail to interest sexually. **b.** To annoy, bore, or repel: *This continuous chatter turns me off.* —*intr.v.* To leave a path or road at a particular point and take another: *turn off at junction 14.*

turn-off (túrn-off, -awf) *n.* **1.** The point where a road or path branches off from the main thoroughfare. **2.** *Slang.* Something that is irritating or repellent, especially sexually.

turn on *tr.v.* **1. a.** To cause to operate or flow by turning a switch or control: *turn on the television.* **b.** *Informal.* To produce as if by turning a switch: *turn on the charm.* **2.** *Informal.* **a.** To excite sexually.

b. To produce a pleasurable response in; delight or stimulate. —*intr.v. Slang.* To take a hallucinogenic or narcotic drug.

turn-on (túrn-on ‖ -awn) *n. Slang.* Someone or something that excites, stimulates, or interests, especially sexually.

turn out *tr.v.* **1.** To switch off (a light, for example). **2.** To produce or manufacture. **3.** To empty the contents of: *turn out the attic.* **4.** To dress or equip. **5.** To put (a horse) out to pasture for rest or retirement. —*intr.v.* **1.** To come out or assemble, as for a public event or entertainment. **2. a.** To be found or proved, as after experience or trial: *It turned out that she had been lying all along.* **b.** To come to be in the end; end up: *turned out to be a fine day.* **3.** *Informal.* To get out of bed.

turn-out (túrn-owt) *n.* **1.** The number of people at a gathering; attendance. **2.** The proportion of registered voters actually voting in a given election. **3.** The amount of goods produced; output. **4.** The way in which a person or group is dressed or equipped. **5.** An outfit of a carriage with its horse or horses; an equipage.

turn over *tr.v.* **1.** To transfer or hand over, especially to the police. **2.** To cause (an internal-combustion engine) to go through at least one cycle. **3. a.** To buy and resell (stock) or invest and get back (capital) in the course of trade. **b.** To do business to the extent or amount of: *turn over millions every year.* —*intr.v.* To go through at least one cycle. Used of an internal-combustion engine.

turn·o·ver (túrn-ōvər) *n.* **1.** The act of turning over; an upset or overthrow. **2.** A small pastry made by covering one half of a circu-

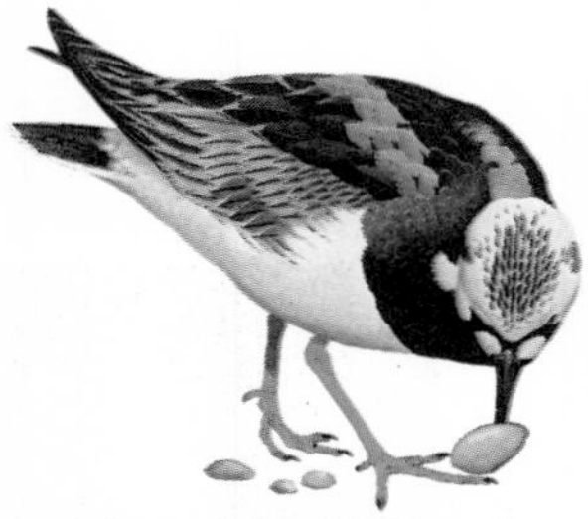

turnstone *At low tide this wader walks along sands and rocks lifting not only stones, but wood, shells, seaweed, and anything else that may hide the sandhoppers and mud-dwellers it eats. The turnstone breeds on the most northerly coasts of Europe, Asia, and America but it flies south in the winter, sometimes as far as South America and Australia.*

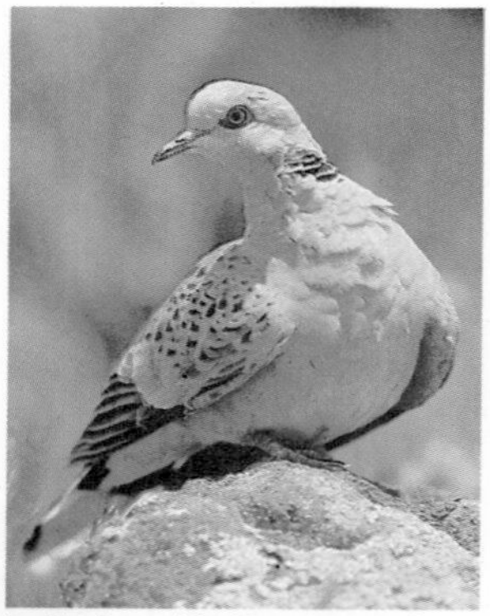

turtle dove *The European turtle dove,* Streptopelia turtur *(above), is noted for its soft, cooing call in summer. Turtle doves are referred to in the Bible's Song of Solomon as symbols of summer, when "The flowers appear on the earth, the time of the singing of birds is come, and the voice of the turtle is heard in our land".*

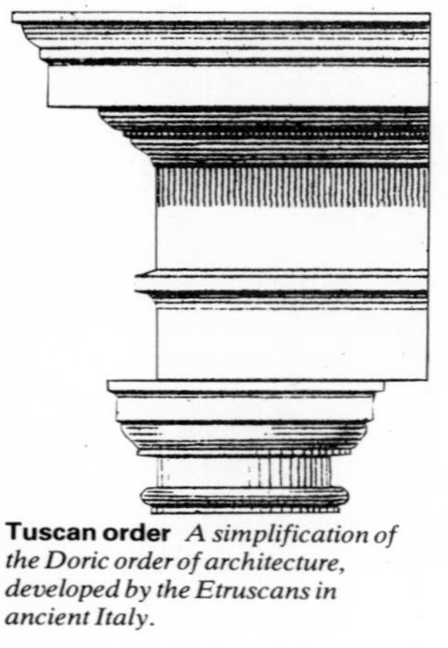

Tuscan order *A simplification of the Doric order of architecture, developed by the Etruscans in ancient Italy.*

lar piece of dough with fruit, preserves, or other filling, and sealing the other half over on top. **3. a.** The number of times a particular stock of goods is sold and restocked during a given period of time. **b.** The rate at which a stock of goods is turned over. **4. a.** The total amount or value of business transacted during a given period of time. **b.** The ratio of this amount to the value of a company's issued shares, showing the number of times the company's share-capital has been turned over in the given period. Also called "capital turnover". **5. a.** The number of workers taken on by an employer to replace those who have left. **b.** The ratio of this number to the number of employed workers.
~*adj.* Capable of being folded down or over: *a turnover collar.*

turn·pike (túrn-pīk) *n. Abbr.* **tpk. 1.** Formerly in Britain: **a.** A toll-gate. **b.** A road whose upkeep was paid for by tolls levied on its users. **2.** In the United States, a motorway whose users pay a toll. [Middle English *turnepike,* a revolving barrier furnished with spikes used to block a road : *turnen,* to TURN + PIKE.]

turn·round (túrn-rownd || *West Indies also* -rungd) *n.* Also *U.S.* **turnaround. 1.** A reversal or major change of direction: *a turnround in the economy.* **2. a.** The time needed to complete the process whereby a ship, aircraft, train, or the like arrives, unloads, takes on fuel, passengers, and cargo, and is ready to leave again. **6.** The time needed to complete any manufacturing or industrial process.

turn·sole (túrn-sōl) *n.* Any plant, such as the heliotrope, that moves or is believed to move in response to the Sun. [Middle English *turnesole,* from Old French *tournesol,* Italian *tornasole* : *tornare,* from Latin *tornāre,* to TURN + *sole,* the Sun, from Latin *sōl.*]

turn·spit (túrn-spit) *n.* One that turns a roasting spit; especially, a small dog formerly used in a treadmill to turn a roasting spit.

turn·stile (túrn-stīl) *n.* **1.** A mechanical device used to control passage from one public area to another, typically consisting of several horizontal arms supported by and radially projecting from a central vertical post. **2.** A similar structure that permits the passage of persons, but not of horses or cattle.

turn·stone (túrn-stōn) *n.* A wading bird, *Arenaria interpres,* having tortoiseshell-coloured plumage in summer, and dull brown in winter. [From its habit of turning over stones in search of food.]

turn·ta·ble (túrn-tayb'l) *n.* **1.** A circular horizontal rotating platform equipped with a railway track, used for turning locomotives. **2.** A similar device for turning road vehicles. **3. a.** The circular horizontal rotating platform of a record player on which the record is placed. **b.** The mechanical path of a record player excluding the amplifying circuitry and speakers. **4.** Any similar rotating platform or disc, as on a microscope.

turntable ladder *n.* A ladder, usually mounted on a fire engine, that can be mechanically rotated and extended.

turn up *tr.v.* **1.** To find; unearth. **2.** *British Informal.* To cause to vomit; nauseate. *—intr.v.* **1.** To be found; come to light: *turned up at last.* **2.** To make an appearance; arrive. **3.** *Informal.* To happen, especially unexpectedly.

turn·up (túrn-up) *n.* **1.** Something that is turned up or turns up; specifically, the turned-up fold at the bottom of a trouser leg. **2.** *British Informal.* An unexpected occurrence or turn of events. Often used in the phrase *a turnup for the books.*

tur·pen·tine (túrpən-tīn) *n. Abbr.* **turp. 1.** A thin volatile essential oil, consisting of a mixture of terpenes, obtained by steam distillation or other means from the wood or the exudate of certain pine trees, and used as a paint thinner, solvent, and medicinally as a liniment. Also called "oil of turpentine", "spirits of turpentine", "turps". **2.** The sticky mixture of resin and volatile oil from which this oil is distilled. **3.** A similar resinous liquid obtained from the terebinth. **4.** Any of several similar liquids obtained from petroleum and used as thinners for paints and varnishes. Also called "turpentine substitute", "white spirit".
~*tr.v.* **turpentined, -tining, -tines. 1.** To apply turpentine to or mix turpentine with. **2.** To extract turpentine from (a tree). [Middle English *turpentyne,* resin of the terebinth, from Old French *ter(e)bentine,* from Latin *terebinthina,* from *terebinthus,* TEREBINTH.]

tur·peth (túrpith) *n.* **1.** A vine of the genus *Ipomoea,* of tropical Asia and Australia, having roots that yield a resinous substance used medicinally as a purgative. **2.** The root of this plant. [Middle English *turbit,* from Old French, from Medieval Latin *turbit(h)um, turpetum,* from Arabic *turbiḍ, turbeḍ.*]

Tur·pin (túrpin), **Dick** (1706–39). British highwayman who was hanged on what is now York Racecourse.

tur·pi·tude (túrpi-tewd || -tōōd) *n.* **1.** Baseness; depravity. **2.** A base, immoral act. [Latin *turpitūdō,* from *turpis*†, ugly, vile.]

turps (turps) *n. Used with a singular verb. Informal.* Turpentine. [Colloquial shortening of TURPENTINE.]

tur·quoise (túr-kwoyz, -kwaaz, -kwawz, -koyz) *n.* **1.** A blue to blue-green mineral, a basic hydrous phosphate of aluminium and copper, mainly $CuAl_6(PO_4)_4(OH)_8{\cdot}4H_2O$. It is prized as a gemstone in its polished blue form. **2.** Light to brilliant bluish green. [Middle English *turkeis,* from Old French *(pierre) turqueise,* "Turkish (stone)", from *turqueis,* Turkish (it was first found in Turkestan), from *Turc,* TURK.] **—tur·quoise** *adj.*

tur·ret (túrrit, túrrət) *n.* **1.** A small ornamented tower or tower-shaped projection on a building. **2.** *Military.* A low, heavily armoured structure, usually rotating horizontally, containing mounted guns and their crew, as on a warship or tank. **3.** A dome-like gunner's enclosure projecting from the fuselage of a military aircraft. **4.** A tall wooden structure mounted on wheels, used in ancient warfare by besiegers to scale the walls of a fortress. **5.** An attachment for a lathe consisting of a rotating, cylindrical block holding various cutting tools. [Middle English *t(o)uret,* from Old French *t(o)urete,* diminutive of *t(o)ur,* a TOWER.]

tur·ret·ed (túrrit-id, túrrət-) *adj.* **1.** Furnished with a turret or turrets. **2.** Having the shape or form of a turret, as do certain long-spired gastropod shells.

tur·tle[1] (túrt'l) *n.* **1.** Any of various marine reptiles of the order Chelonia, having horny, toothless jaws and the body enclosed in a bony or leathery shell into which the head, limbs, and tail can be withdrawn in most species. **2.** *U.S.* Any chelonian reptile. **—turn turtle.** To turn upside-down; capsize.
~*intr.v.* **turtled, -tling, -tles.** To hunt for turtles, especially as an occupation. [Perhaps variant of French *tortue,* TORTOISE.]

turtle[2] *n. Archaic.* A turtledove: *"the voice of the turtle is heard in our land"* (Song of Solomon 2:12). [Middle English *turtle,* Old English *turtla, turtle,* from Latin *turtur*†.]

tur·tle·back (túrt'l-bak) *n.* A projection built so as to arch over the deck of a ship at the bow and sometimes also at the stern, as a protection against high seas.

tur·tle·dove (túrt'l-duv) *n.* A slender European dove, *Streptopelia turtur,* having a white-edged tail and a soft, cooing voice. [TURTLE (dove) + DOVE.]

tur·tle·neck (túrt'l-nek) *n.* **1.** A relatively high, round collar on a sweater, that fits closely about the neck. **2.** A sweater having such a collar.

turves. *Archaic.* Plural of **turf.**

Tus·can (túskən) *adj.* **1.** Of or pertaining to Tuscany, its people, or their dialect of Italian. **2.** Of or pertaining to the Tuscan order.
~*n.* **1.** A native or inhabitant of Tuscany. **2.** Any of the Italian dialects spoken in Tuscany, especially the dialect of Florence.

Tuscan order *n. Architecture.* A classical order similar to Roman Doric, but having an unfluted shaft with a simplified base, capital, and entablature.

Tus·ca·ny (túskəni). *Italian* **Tos·ca·na** (toskáanə). Region of western central Italy. It was inhabited in pre-Roman times by the Etruscans, and became, with the rise of the Medicis of Florence, a Grand Duchy (1569–1860). Its dialect was selected as textbook Italian on the country's unification. The chief cities are Florence (the capital), Leghorn, and Pisa.

tu·sche (tōōsh || *U.S.* tōōshə) *n.* A substance used for drawing in lithography and as a resist in etching and silk-screen printing. [German *Tusche,* from *tuschen,* to ink up, from French *toucher,* to TOUCH.]

tush[1] (tush) *interj.* Used to express mild reproof, disapproval, or admonition: *Tush, tush, my dear, it's nothing to fuss about.*

tush[2] *n. Rare.* A tusk. [Middle English *tusche,* Old English *tūsc.*]

tusk[1] (tusk) *n.* **1.** An elongated, pointed tooth, usually one of a pair, extending outside the mouth in certain animals, such as the walrus, elephant, or wild boar. **2.** Any long, projecting tooth or toothlike part.
~*tr.v.* **tusked, tusking, tusks.** To dig or gore with the tusks or a tusk. [Middle English *tux, tuske,* Old English *tūx, tūsc.*]

tusk[2] *n.* A fish, the **torsk** *(see).*

tusk·er (túskər) *n.* An animal bearing tusks, such as a wild boar.

tusk shell *n.* Any marine mollusc of the class Scaphopoda, having a tusk-shaped shell. Also called "tooth shell".

tus·sah (túss-ə, -aw) *n.* Also **tus·ser** (-ər), **tus·sore** (-ər, -awr, *also* tōō-sór || -ōr). **1.** An Asian silkworm, *Antheraea paphia,* that produces a coarse brownish or yellowish silk. **2.** The silk itself, or a fabric woven from it. [Hindi *tasar,* from Sanskrit *tasara,* a shuttle (probably from the shape of its cocoon).]

Tus·saud (tōō-sáwd, tə-, -sō), **Madame,** born Marie Groshoerz (1761–1850). French-born wax modeller. She was imprisoned during the French Revolution and modelled heads of the guillotined victims. She moved to England (1802) and eventually opened a museum which is still a tourist attraction in London.

tus·sis (tússiss) *n. Medicine.* A cough. [Latin.] **—tus·sal, tus·sive** *adj.*

tus·sle (túss'l) *intr.v.* **-sled, -sling, -sles.** To fight or struggle roughly.
~*n.* **1.** A rough-and-tumble struggle; a scuffle. **2.** Any disorderly struggle or conflict: *a tussle for power.* [Middle English *tussillen,* probably from *-t(o)usen,* to TOUSLE.]

tus·sock, tuss·uck (tússək) *n.* **1.** A clump or tuft of growing grass or a similar plant. **2.** A tuft, as of hair or feathers. [Probably variant of dialectal *tusk*†, a tuft of hair, rushes.] **—tus·sock·y** *adj.*

tussock grass *n.* Any of various grasses or sedges that typically grow in tussocks; especially, species in the genus *Poa.*

tussock moth *n.* Any of various moths of the family Lymantriidae, having hairy caterpillars that are often destructive to trees.

Tu·tan·kha·mun (tōō-təng-kaa-mōōn, -mōōn) or **Tu·tan·kha·men** (-káa-men, -tang-, -mən) (*c.* 1358–*c.* 1340 B.C.). Egyptian pharaoh of the 18th dynasty. His tomb and its magnificent contents was discovered almost intact (1922) by the British archaeologists Howard Carter and the Earl of Carnarvon.

tu·te·lage (téw-ti-lij, -tə- || tōō-) *n.* **1.** The function or capacity of a guardian; guardianship. **2.** The act or capacity of a tutor; instruction; teaching. **3.** The state of being under a guardian or tutor. [Latin *tūtēla,* a watching, from *tūtor,* TUTOR.]

tu·te·lar·y (téw-ti-ləri, -tə- || tōō-, -lerri) *adj.* Also **tu·te·lar** (-lər). **1.** Of or pertaining to a guardian or guardianship. **2.** Acting as a guardian or protector, especially over a particular place or person; protective.

~*n.* A tutelary saint, deity, or spirit. [Late Latin *tūtēlāris,* from Latin *tūtēla,* TUTELAGE.]
tu·tor (téw-tər || tōō-) *n.* **1. a.** A private teacher, often employed by a household. **b.** One who gives additional, special, or remedial instruction. **2.** In most British universities and colleges, a member of staff who is responsible for the welfare of a number of students and usually for supervising their studies. **3.** In Roman and Scottish law, the guardian of a minor and of the minor's property. **4.** *British.* A practical instruction book: *a guitar tutor.*
~*v.* **tutored, -toring, -tors.** —*tr.* **1.** To act as a tutor to; especially, to instruct or teach privately. **2.** To discipline or treat sternly, as a tutor might. **3.** To act as the guardian to; have the care of. —*intr.* To function as a tutor or private instructor. —See Synonyms at **teach.** [Middle English *tutour,* from Old French, from Latin *tūtor,* a guardian, from *tūtus,* past participle of *tuērī,* to watch, protect.]
tu·to·ri·al (tew-táw-ri-əl || tōō-, -tō-) *n.* A period of intensive tuition given, especially in a university, to an individual student or a small number of students.
~*adj.* Of or pertaining to a tutor. [Latin *tūtōrius.* See **tutor, -al.**]
tutorial system *n.* An instructional system in which college or university tutors are responsible for the special supervision of students individually or in small groups.
tu·tor·ship (téw-tər-ship || tōō-) *n.* **1.** The office or functions of a tutor. **2.** Tutelage.
tut·san (túts'n) *n.* **1.** A yellow-flowered evergreen undershrub, *Hypericum androsaemum,* having berries that turn purplish black when ripe. **2.** Either of two related plants, *H. hircinum* or *H. inodorum.* See **Saint John's wort.** [Middle English, from Anglo-French *tutsaine* (French, *toute-saine*), "all healthy" (the plants were believed to have various healing properties).]
tut·ti (tŏŏt-ee, -i || tōōt-) *adv. Music.* All together. Used as a direction to indicate that all performers are to take part.
~*n., pl.* **tuttis. 1.** A passage of ensemble music intended to be executed by all the performers simultaneously. **2.** The tonal effect thus produced. [Italian, all, from Latin *tōtus.*] —**tut·ti** *adj.*
tut·ti-frut·ti (tŏŏtti-frŏŏtti, tŏŏti-, -frŏŏti) *n.* **1.** A confection, especially ice cream, containing a variety of chopped candied fruits. **2.** A flavouring simulating the flavour of many fruits. **3.** A preserve of chopped, mixed fruits.
~*adj.* Having a combination of fruit flavours. [Italian, "all fruits".]
tut-tut (tút-tút; *as an interjection, usually a single or repeated voiceless alveolar click*) *interj.* Also **tut.** Used to express annoyance, impatience, or mild reproof.
~*intr.v.* **tut-tutted, -tutting, -tuts.** Also **tut.** To say *tut-tut* in annoyance, impatience or mild reproof.
~*n.* An exclamation of *tut-tut.*
tut·ty (tútti) *n.* An impure zinc oxide obtained as a sublimate from the flues of zinc-smelting furnaces and used as a polishing powder. [Middle English *tutie,* from Old French, from Arabic *tūtiyā.*]
tu·tu (tōō-tōō) *n.* A skirt worn for classical ballet consisting of many layers of gathered sheer fabric, which is either brief and encircles the waist or extends to below the knee. [French.]
Tu·tu (tōō-tōō), **Desmond Mpilo, Bishop** (1931–). Prominent black South African theologian and campaigner for black rights, General Secretary of the South African Council of Churches.
Tu·va·lu (tōōvə-lōō), **State of.** *Formerly* **Ellice Islands.** Country of the southwestern Pacific, consisting of nine islands. Established as a British protectorate in 1892, it became part of the Gilbert and Ellice Islands Colony in 1915, from which it broke away in 1975. Independence was granted in 1978. Area, 26 square kilometres (10 square miles). Population, 7,350. Capital, Fongafela on Funafuti. See map at **Pacific Ocean.**
tu-whit tu-whoo (tōō-wít tōō-wōō, tə-, -hwít, -hwōō) *n.* A conventional rendering of the call of an owl.
tux·e·do (tuk-séedō) *n., pl.* **-dos.** *Chiefly U.S. Sometimes capital* **T. 1.** A **dinner jacket** *(see).* **2.** *U.S.* **Black tie** *(see).* [From the name of a club in *Tuxedo* Park, New York, where it became popular.]
tu·yère (twee-yáir) *n.* The pipe, nozzle, or other opening through which air is forced into a blast furnace or forge to facilitate combustion. [French, from Old French *tuyere,* from *tuyau,* a pipe, probably from Frankish *thūta* (unattested), imitative.]
TV *n. Informal.* Television. —**TV** *adj.*
TV dinner *n.* A packaged ready-to-serve meal, usually frozen in an aluminium tray, that can be heated in an oven.
TVP textured vegetable protein.
Twad·dell scale (twóddʼl, two-dél) *n.* A scale for measuring relative density, especially of acids. [After William *Twaddell* (died *c.* 1840), Scottish inventor.]
twad·dle (twóddʼl) *intr.v.* **-dled, -dling, -dles.** Also **twat·tle** (twóttʼl). To talk foolishly.
~*n.* Also **twat·tle. 1.** Foolish, trivial, or idle talk or chatter. **2.** Silly pretentious speech or writing. [From earlier *twattle,* alteration of TATTLE.] —**twad·dler** *n.*
twain (twayn) *adj. Archaic.* Two.
~*n. Poetic.* A set of two: *"Oh, East is East, and West is West, and never the twain shall meet"* (Rudyard Kipling). [Middle English *tweien, tweyen,* Old English *twēgen* (nominative and accusative masculine), two.]
Twain (twayn), **Mark,** pen name of Samuel Langhorne Clemens (1835–1910). U.S. novelist. He is best known for his two masterpieces, *Tom Sawyer* (1876), and *Huckleberry Finn* (1884), based on his boyhood experiences.
twang (twang) *v.* **twanged, twanging, twangs.** —*intr.* **1.** To emit a sharp, vibrating sound, as the string of a musical instrument sounds when plucked. **2.** To be released or to resound with a sharp, vibrating sound. Used especially of an arrow. —*tr.* **1.** To cause to make a sharp, vibrating sound. **2.** To utter with a twang.
~*n.* **1.** A sharp, vibrating sound, such as that made by a plucked string. **2.** A notably nasal tone of voice, especially as a peculiarity of certain regional accents. **3.** Any sound resembling either of these. [Imitative.] —**twang·y** *adj.*
'twas (twoz, *weak form* twəz || twuz). *Regional and Poetic.* Contraction of *it was.*
twat (twot, twat) *n. Vulgar Slang.* **1.** The female genitalia. **2.** A woman or girl considered as a sexual object. This term is considered to be extremely offensive. **3.** A worthless or vile person. Used derogatorily. [17th century : origin obscure.]
tway·blade (twáy-blayd) *n.* **1.** Any of various small terrestrial orchids of the genus *Listera,* having two basal, unstalked leaves and a terminal cluster of greenish or reddish flowers. **2.** Any other orchid with only two leaves. [Translation of Medieval Latin *bifolium,* "two-leaved" : obsolete English *tway,* two, Middle English *twei,* Old English *twēge,* short for *twēgen,* TWAIN + BLADE.]
tweak (tweek) *tr.v.* **tweaked, tweaking, tweaks. 1.** To pinch, pluck, or twist sharply. **2.** *Slang.* In motor racing, to tune (a car or engine) finely for peak performance, as before a race.
~*n.* A sharp, twisting pinch. [Probably variant of dialectal *twick,* Middle English *twikken*; akin to TWITCH.] —**tweak·y** *adj.*
twee (twee) *adj. British Informal.* **1.** Excessively or affectedly pretty, sentimental or quaint. **2.** *Rare.* Sweet; cute. [From *tweet,* childish or affected pronunciation of SWEET.]
tweed (tweed) *n.* **1.** A coarse, rugged, often knobbly woollen cloth made in any of various twill weaves, and used chiefly for suits and coats. Also used adjectivally: *a tweed suit.* **2.** *Plural.* Clothing made of this cloth. [Originally a trademark, misspelling (influenced by the river TWEED) of *tweel, tweeled,* Scottish variants of TWILL.]
Tweed (tweed). River of northern Great Britain. Rising in the Tweedsmuir Hills in the Borders Region of Scotland, it flows some 156 kilometres (97 miles) to the North Sea at Berwick.
Tweeddale. See **Peeblesshire.**
twee·dle·dum and twee·dle·dee (twéedʼl-dúm; twéedʼl-dée) *n.* Two persons or groups resembling each other so closely that they are practically indistinguishable. [After *Tweedledum and Tweedledee,* proverbial rival violinists supposedly representative of Handel and G.B. Bononcini, who had a musical rivalry.]
tweed·y (twéedi) *adj.* **tweedier, tweediest. 1.** Of, made of, or resembling tweed. **2.** *Chiefly British Informal.* Given to the healthy, outdoor, country life, especially that led by members of the British gentry (who are reputed to wear a lot of tweed). —**tweed·i·ness** *n.*
'tween (tween). *Poetic.* Contraction of **between.**
tween-decks (twéen-deks) *n.* The space between two decks of a ship. —**tween-deck** (-dek) *adj.*
tween·y (twéeni) *n., pl.* **tweenies.** *British Informal.* A between maid, as one who helps two others, such as the cook and housemaid.
tweet (tweet) *intr.v.* **tweeted, tweeting, tweets.** To utter a weak, chirping sound, as a young or small bird does.
~*n.* A weak, chirping sound.
~*interj.* Also **tweet tweet.** Used to imitate the sound of a bird. [Imitative.]
tweet·er (twéetər) *n.* A loudspeaker designed to reproduce high-pitched sounds in a high-fidelity audiofrequency system. Compare **woofer.** [From TWEET.]
tweeze (tweez) *tr.v.* **tweezed, tweezing, tweezes.** *Chiefly U.S.* To handle or extract with tweezers. [Back-formation from TWEEZERS.]
tweez·ers (twéezərz) *pl.n.* Any small, usually metal, pincer-like tool used for plucking or handling small objects. [Originally "a set or case of small instruments", from obsolete *tweezes,* plural of *tweeze, etweese,* from the plural of *etwee,* from French *étui,* ÉTUI.]
twelfth (twelth, twelfth) *n.* **1.** The ordinal number 12 in a series. **2.** Any of 12 equal parts. **3.** *Music.* **a.** A 12-degree interval in a diatonic scale; an octave plus a fifth. **b.** A note 12 degrees below or above a given note. [Middle English *twelfthe,* Old English *twelfta.*] —**twelfth** *adj.* & *adv.*
Twelfth-day (twélth-day, twélfth-) *n.* The day of Epiphany, January 6, 12 days after Christmas and traditionally marking the end of the Christmas season.
twelfth man *n.* A reserve player for a cricket team.
Twelfth-night (twélth-nīt, twélfth-, -nīt) *n.* The evening of January 5, before Twelfth-day, formerly celebrated with various festivities. —**Twelfth-night** *adj.*
Twelfth·tide (twélth-tīd, twélfth-) *n.* The season of Epiphany.
twelve (twelv) *n.* **1. a.** The cardinal number that is one more than 11; a dozen. **b.** A symbol representing this, such as 12 or XII. **2.** A set made up of twelve persons or things. **3.** The twelfth in a series. **4.** A size, as in clothing, designated as 12. **5.** Midnight or midday. Also called "twelve o'clock". [Middle English *twelfe, twelve,* Old English *twelf.*] —**twelve** *adj.*
Twelve Apostles *pl.n.* The 12 disciples chosen by Jesus. Preceded by *the.* Also called the "Twelve".
twelve·mo (twélv-mō) *n., pl.* **-mos. Duodecimo** *(see).*
twelve·month (twélv-munth) *n.* A year or period of twelve months.
Twelve Tables *n.* The earliest code of Roman laws, written down 451–450 B.C. Preceded by *the.* [Translation of Latin *Duodecim Tabulae,* referring to the 12 original compilations (fifth century B.C.)

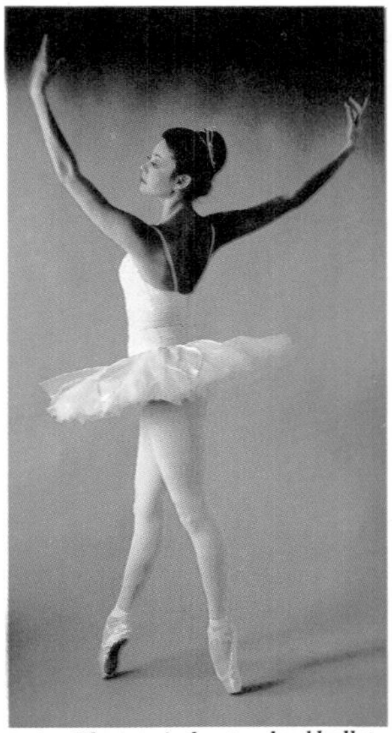

tutu *The tutu is the standard ballet dancer's skirt. There are two kinds, the brief tutu seen here and the Romantic tutu which extends below the knees to about 30 centimetres (12 inches) from the floor.*

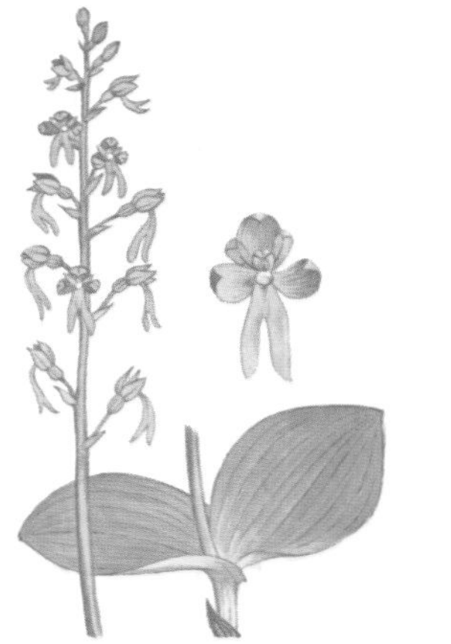

twayblade *One of the most common of British orchids, found in damp woods and meadows. It gets its name from its two, or "tway", leaves growing at the base of the stem.*

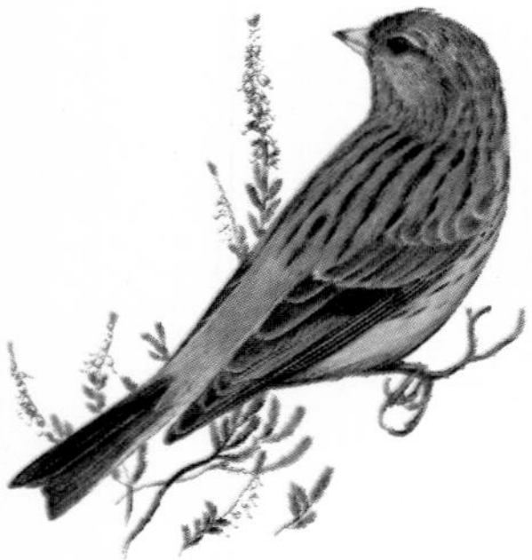

twite *Found throughout Europe and Asia, twites live in colonies on hill slopes and moorlands, often moving to coastal marshes in winter. They feed chiefly on plants and get their name from their nasal call which sounds rather like "twa-it".*

which, when complete, were incised on bronze plates and hung in the Forum.]

twelve•note (twélv-nōt) *adj. Music.* Pertaining to, consisting of, or based on an atonal arrangement of the traditional 12 chromatic notes, as invented and used by Arnold Schoenberg. Also *chiefly U.S.* "twelve-tone".

twen•ti•eth (twénti-əth, -ith) *n.* **1.** The ordinal number 20 in a series. **2.** Any of 20 equal parts. **—twen•ti•eth** *adj. & adv.*

twen•ty (twénti) *n. pl.* **-ties. 1. a.** The cardinal number that is 10 more than 10; a score. **b.** A symbol representing this such as 20 or XX. **2.** A set made up of 20 persons or things. **3.** The twentieth in a series. **4.** A size, as in clothing, designated as 20. **5.** A bank note or coin having a denomination of 20. **6.** *Plural.* **a.** The range of numbers from 20 to 29, considered as a range of age, price, or temperature, for example. **b.** *Capital* **T.** The years numbered 20 to 29 in a century. Also used adjectivally: *a Twenties hairstyle.* [Middle English *twenty,* Old English *twēntig.*] **—twen•ty** *adj.*

twen•ty-one (twénti-wún) *n. U.S.* **pontoon** *(see).*

twen•ty-twen•ty (twénti-twénti) *adj.* Having perfect vision. Usually written *20/20.*

'twere (twer, twair, *weak form* twər). *Poetic.* Contraction of *it were.*

twerp, twirp (twerp) *n. Slang.* A weak, stupid, or contemptible person; a fool. [20th century : origin obscure.]

Twi, Tshi (twee, chwee) *n.* A dialect of Akan spoken in western Africa, especially by the Ashanti. **—Twi, Tshi** *adj.*

twi•bil, twi•bill (twī-bil) *n.* **1.** A battle-axe with two cutting edges. **2.** A mattock with one arm like an axe and the other like an adze. [Middle English, Old English *twibil(l)* : *twi-,* two + BILL (instrument).]

twice (twīss) *adv.* **1.** In two cases or on two occasions; two times. **2.** In doubled degree or amount: *twice as many.* [Middle English *twice, twiges,* Old English *twiges,* from *twige, twiga,* twice.]

twice-laid (twīss-layd) *adj.* Made from strands of old or used rope.

Twick•en•ham (twíckənəm). District of west London. Situated in the borough of Richmond on the north bank of the Thames, it is a mainly residential area.

twid•dle (twídd'l) *v.* **-dled, -dling, -dles.** *—tr.* To turn over or around, especially idly or lightly; fiddle with: *twiddle the knobs on the radio.* *—intr.* **1.** To turn something over or around idly or lightly; fiddle. Used with *with.* **2.** To twirl or rotate aimlessly.
~n. The act of twiddling; an idle, twirling motion. [Probably a blend of TWIRL and FIDDLE.] **—twid•dler** *n.*

twig¹ (twig) *n.* A small branch or slender shoot, as of a tree or shrub. [Middle English *twig(ge),* Old English *twigge.*]

twig² *v.* **twigged, twigging, twigs.** *British Informal.* *—intr.* To suddenly comprehend a situation; catch on. *—tr.* **1.** To understand. **2.** *Rare.* To observe or watch; to notice. [18th century : origin obscure.]

twig•gy (twíggi) *adj.* **-gier, -giest. 1.** Resembling a twig or twigs; slender; fragile. **2.** Abounding in twigs.

twi•light (twī-līt) *n.* **1.** The time interval during which the Sun's centre is below the horizon at an angle less than 6° (*civil twilight*), 12° (*nautical twilight*), or 18° (*astronomical twilight*). **2.** The state of illumination of the atmosphere during this interval, especially after a sunset. **3.** Any dim or faint illumination. **4.** Any period or condition of decline, as after growth, glory, or success; a waning: *in the twilight of her life.*
~adj. Pertaining to or characteristic of twilight. [Middle English *twilight,* "light between (night and day)", half-light : *twi-,* half, two, Old English *twi-* + LIGHT.]

Twilight of the Gods *n.* **Götterdämmerung** *(see).*

twilight sleep *n.* An analgesic and amnaesic condition induced by an injection of morphine and scopolamine, characterised by the absence of sensibility to pain without loss of consciousness, and administered during labour in childbirth.

twilight zone *n.* **1.** An area or state that is not clearly defined or limited. **2.** A dilapidated or run-down area of a city.

twill (twil) *n.* **1.** A cloth with diagonal parallel ribs produced by passing the weft yarn alternately over one warp yarn and then under two or more. **2.** The weave used to produce such cloth.
~tr.v. **twilled, twilling, twills.** To weave (cloth) so as to produce the pattern of twill. [Middle English *twyl(l), twyle,* Old English *twilic,* "two-threaded" : *twi-,* two (see **twilight**) + Latin *(bi)līx,* "two-threaded" : BI- + *līcium,* a thread (see **trellis**).] **—twill** *adj.*

'twill (twil). *Regional and Poetic.* Contraction of *it will.*

twilled (twild) *adj.* Woven so as to have diagonal parallel ribs.

twin (twin) *n.* **1.** Either of two offspring born at the same birth. **2.** Either of two identical or similar persons, animals, or things; a counterpart. **3.** *Capital* **T.** *Plural.* The constellation and sign of the zodiac, **Gemini** *(see).* Preceded by *the.* **4.** A crystal composed of two parts which are orientated differently, but joined together so that a crystallographic direction or plane is common to both. Also called "macle".
~adj. **1.** Being two or either of two offspring born at the same birth. **2.** Being either of two identical or similar persons, animals, or things: *a twin bed.* **3.** Consisting of two identical or similar related or connected parts.
~v. **twinned, twinning, twins.** *—intr.* **1.** To give birth to twins. **2.** *Archaic.* To be either of twin offspring. **3.** To be paired or coupled. *—tr.* **1.** To give birth to, as twins. **2.** To provide a match or counterpart to; pair. [Middle English *twin, twyn* (adjective and noun), Old English *twinn* (adjective only), *getwinn.*]

twin•ber•ry (twín-bəri, -bri, -berri) *n., pl.* **-ries.** The **partridgeberry** *(see).* [From the single berry formed from a pair of flowers.]

twine (twīn) *v.* **twined, twining, twines.** *—tr.* **1.** To twist (threads, for example) together; intertwine. **2.** To form by twisting, intertwining, or interlacing. **3.** To encircle or coil about: *A vine twined the fence.* **4.** To wind, coil, or wrap around (something): *twined a rope around the post.* *—intr.* **1.** To become twisted, interlaced, or interwoven. **2.** To wind or coil. Usually used with *around.* **3.** To go in a winding course; twist about: *a stream twining through the forest.*
~n. **1.** A strong string or cord formed from two or more threads of hemp, cotton, or the like twisted together. **2.** Any thing or part formed by twining: *a twine of dough.* **3.** A tangle; a knot. **4.** The act or process of twining. [Middle English *twinen,* from *twin,* a rope of two strands, Old English *twīn,* from *twī-,* two.] **—twin•er** *n.*

twin•flow•er (twín-flow-ər, -flowr) *n.* A creeping evergreen plant, *Linnaea borealis,* of northern regions, having roundish leaves and paired, bell-shaped, pinkish flowers.

twinge (twinj) *n.* **1.** A sharp, sudden physical pain. **2.** A mental or emotional pang: *a twinge of conscience.*
~v. **twinged, twinging, twinges.** *—tr.* **1.** To cause to feel a sharp pain. **2.** *Obsolete.* To tweak; pinch. *—intr.* To feel a twinge or twinges. [Middle English *twengen, twynchen,* to pinch, wring, Old English *twengan.*]

twin•kle (twíngk'l) *v.* **-kled, -kling, -kles.** *—intr.* **1.** To shine with slight, intermittent gleams, as distant lights or stars do; flicker or glimmer. **2.** To be bright or sparkling, as with delight. Used of the eyes. **3.** *Archaic.* To blink or wink. *—tr.* To cause to twinkle. —See Synonyms at **flash.**
~n. **1.** A slight, intermittent gleam of light; a glimmer; a sparkle. **2.** A sparkle of merriment or delight in the eye. **3.** A brief interval; a twinkling. [Middle English *twynklen,* Old English *twinclian,* frequentative of *twincan* (unattested), to wink, from West Germanic *twink-* (unattested).] **—twin•kler** *n.*

twin•kling (twíngkling) *n.* The time it takes to blink once; an instant. Also called "twinkling of an eye".

twinned (twind) *adj.* **1.** Born at a single birth. **2.** Paired or coupled with something identical or similar. **3.** Formed from crystals by the process of twinning.

twin•ning (twínning) *n.* **1.** The bearing of twins. **2.** A pairing or union of two similar or identical things. **3.** The formation of twin crystals.

twin-screw (twín-skrōō || -skrew) *adj.* Having two propellers, one on either side of the keel, that usually revolve in opposite directions. Said of a ship.

twin-set (twín-set) *n. Chiefly British.* A matching cardigan and sweater worn by a woman.

twin town *n. British.* **1.** Either of two towns in different countries usually similar in some way, such as size or industrial make-up, that are formally associated, especially by having reciprocal cultural visits. **2.** Either of two towns facing each other across a river.

twirl (twurl) *v.* **twirled, twirling, twirls.** *—tr.* **1.** To rotate or revolve briskly; swing in a circle; spin. **2.** To twist or wind around: *twirl thread on a spindle.* *—intr.* **1.** To move or spin around rapidly, suddenly, or repeatedly. **2.** To whirl or turn suddenly; make an about-face. Usually used with *about* or *around.*
~n. **1.** A twirling or being twirled; a quick spinning or twisting. **2.** Something twirled; a curl or twist. [Perhaps alteration (influenced by WHIRL) of obsolete *tirl,* TRILL.]

twirp. Variant of **twerp.**

twist (twist) *v.* **twisted, twisting, twists.** *—tr.* **1. a.** To entwine (two or more threads) so as to produce a single strand. **b.** To form in this manner: *twist a length of rope.* **2.** To wind or coil (vines or rope, for example) around something. **3.** To interweave: *twist flowers in one's hair.* **4. a.** To impart a coiling or spiral shape to. **b.** To turn repeatedly while holding one end firm. **5. a.** To turn or open by turning. **b.** To pull, break, or snap by turning. Used with *off: twist off a dead branch.* **6.** To wrench or sprain: *twist one's wrist.* **7.** To alter the normal aspect of; contort: *twist one's mouth into a wry smile.* **8.** To alter or distort the intended meaning of. *—intr.* **1.** To be or become twisted. **2.** To move or progress in a winding course; meander. **3.** To squirm; writhe: *twist with pain.* **4. a.** To turn round, especially in an uneasy way. **b.** To rotate or revolve. **5.** To dance the twist. —See Synonyms at **distort.**
~n. **1.** Something twisted or formed by winding, especially: **a.** A length of yarn, cord, or thread, especially a strong silk thread used mainly to bind the edges of buttonholes. **b.** Tobacco leaves processed into the form of a rope or roll. **c.** *British.* A simple packet made by rolling a piece of paper round something and twisting the ends. **d.** Bread or other bakery products for which the dough was twisted before baking. **e.** A sliver of citrus peel twisted over or dropped into a drink to impart flavour. **2. a.** The act of twisting or the condition of being twisted; a spin or twirl; a rotation. **b.** A sharp bend or turn. **3.** A vigorous wrench or turn. **4. a.** The state of being twisted into a spiral; torsional stress or strain. **b.** The degree or angle of such stress. **5.** A sprain or wrench, as of a muscle. **6. a.** A sudden or unexpected change in a course of events or a surprising revelation, as in a novel, play, or the like: *Saki's stories always have a twist in the tail.* **b.** A sudden change or departure from a pattern, usually for the worse: *a twist of fate.* **7.** A contortion or distortion, as of the face. **8.** A personal inclination or eccentricity; a penchant or flaw: *a twist in her character.* **9.** A dance, popular especially in the 1960s, characterised by vigorous twisting of the waist from side to side with the knees bent. Preceded by *the.*

10. *British Informal.* A trick or swindle. [Middle English *twysten,* from Old English *-twist,* a rope.] —**twist·a·bil·i·ty** (-ə-bílləti) *n.* —**twist·a·ble** *adj.* —**twist·ing·ly** *adv.*

twist drill *n.* A drill having deep helical grooves along the shank from the point.

twist·ed (twístid) *adj.* Perverted; weird and evil: *a twisted mind.*

twist·er (twístər) *n.* **1.** One that twists; specifically, a mechanical device for spinning or twisting yarn or rope. **2.** *British Informal.* A dishonest person; a swindler. **3.** *U.S. Informal.* A cyclone or a tornado.

twist grip *n.* A ratchet-controlled, rotating device attached to the ends of some handlebars. On some bicycles and motorcycles it is used as a gear-changing control and on most motorcycles it is used as an accelerator.

twit[1] (twit) *tr.v.* **twitted, twitting, twits.** To taunt, ridicule, or tease, especially for embarrassing mistakes or faults. See Synonyms at **ridicule.**
~*n.* **1.** The act of twitting. **2.** A reproach, gibe, or taunt. [Earlier *(a)twite,* Middle English *atwiten,* Old English *ætwitan,* to reproach with : *æt-* (indicating opposition), from *æt,* from, AT + *witan,* to reproach, ascribe to.]

twit[2] *n. British Informal.* A stupid person; an idiot: *an upper-class twit.* [19th century (originally dialect) : perhaps from TWIT (a person who taunts).]

twitch (twich) *v.* **twitched, twitching, twitches.** —*tr.* To draw, pull, or move suddenly and sharply; jerk: *The fisherman twitched his line.* —*intr.* **1.** To move jerkily or spasmodically. **2.** To ache sharply from time to time; twinge.
~*n.* **1.** A sudden involuntary or spasmodic muscular movement: *a nervous twitch.* **2.** A sudden pulling; a jerk or tug. **3.** A looped cord used to restrain a horse by tightening it around the animal's upper lip. —**in a twitch.** *Informal.* In a state of nervousness or agitation. [Middle English *twicchen,* perhaps of Low German origin, akin to Low German *twikken.*] —**twitch·ing·ly** *adv.*

twitch grass *n.* **Couch grass** *(see).*

twitch·er (twíchər) *n. Informal.* A birdwatcher who relentlessly pursues the aim of spotting a particular bird, disregarding the sanctuary and well-being of the birds.

twitch·y (twíchi) *adj. Informal.* Agitated or nervous.

twite (twīt) *n.* A Eurasian finch, *Acanthis flavirostris,* resembling the linnet, but having no red plumage on the crown, and found in moorland regions. [Imitative of its call.]

twit·ter (twíttər) *v.* **-tered, -tering, -ters.** —*intr.* **1.** To utter a succession of light chirping or tremulous sounds, as a bird does; chirrup. **2.** To titter; giggle. **3.** To tremble or talk nervously, as with excitement. —*tr.* To utter or say with a twitter: *twittered his greeting.*
~*n.* **1.** The light chirping sounds made by certain birds. **2.** Light, tremulous speech or laughter. **3.** A state of agitation or excitement; a flutter. Used especially in the phrase *in a twitter.* [Middle English *twiteren,* akin to Old High German *zwizzirōn,* from West Germanic *twittwīrōjan* (imitative).] —**twit·ter·er** *n.* —**twit·ter·y** *adj.*

twixt, 'twixt (twikst) *prep. Archaic & Poetic.* Betwixt.

two (tōō) *n.* **1. a.** The cardinal number that is one more than one. **b.** A symbol representing this, such as 2, II, or ii. **2.** A set made up of two persons or things. **3. a.** The second in a series. **b.** A playing card marked with two pips. **4.** A size, as in clothing, designated as two. **5.** Two hours after midnight or midday. —**in two. 1.** So as to be in two separate units: *split in two.* **2.** So as to have two thicknesses or layer: *fold in two.* —**put two and two together.** To reach a correct, usually obvious conclusion after considering a given set of circumstances. —**that makes two of us.** That is true of or applies to myself as well. [Middle English *two,* Old English *twā, tū.*] —**two** *adj.*

two-bit (tōō-bit) *adj. U.S. Slang.* **1.** Worth very little; insignificant. **2.** Cheap; shoddy. [From TWO BITS.]

two bits *n. U.S. Informal.* **1.** Twenty-five cents. **2.** A petty sum.

two-by-four (tōō-bī-fôr, -bi- ‖ -fôr) *adj.* Measuring two by four inches, or in the same ratio in other units.
~*n.* Any length of timber measuring about 2 by 4 inches or trimmed to 1⅝ inches in thickness and 3⅜ inches in width.

two-di·men·sion·al (tōō-dī-ménsh'n'l, -di-) *adj.* **1.** Having only two dimensions, usually length and width; planar; flat. **2.** *Informal.* Lacking dimension or completion; limited in range or depth.

two-edged (tōō-éjd) *adj.* **1.** Having a cutting edge on both sides. Said of a razor or sword blade, for example. **2.** Having two contrasting effects, meanings, or interpretations.

two-faced (tōō-fáyst) *adj.* **1.** *Informal.* Hypocritical or double-dealing; deceitful. **2.** Having two faces or surfaces. —**two-fac·ed·ly** (-fáyssid-li, -fáyst-) *adv.* —**two-fac·ed·ness** *n.*

two-fold (tōō-fōld, -fōld) *adj.* **1.** Having two components. **2.** Having twice as much or twice as many; double.
~*adv.* Two times as much or as many; doubly.

2,4,5-T (tōō-fôr-fív-tée) *n.* **Trichlorophenoxyacetic acid** *(see).*

two-hand·ed (tōō-hándid) *adj.* **1.** Requiring the use of two hands at once: *a two-handed sledgehammer.* **2.** Made to be operated or engaged in by two people. **3.** Able to use both hands with equal facility; ambidextrous. **4.** Having two hands.

two-mast·er (tōō-maást-ər ‖ -mást-) *n.* A sailing vessel rigged with two masts.

two-name (tōō-náym) *adj. Finance. U.S.* Pertaining to or designating a commercial paper bearing the signatures of two persons liable to the obligation.

two-party system (tōō-párti) *n.* A political system, such as currently prevails in the United States and traditionally in Great Britain, in which two major political parties dominate.

two·pence (túppənss; *in sense 1 also* tōō-pénss, -penss) *n.* Also *informal* **tup·pence.** *British.* **1.** Two pennies regarded as a monetary unit. **2.** A silver coin worth two pennies, since 1662 minted only for distribution on Maundy Thursday. **3.** A copper coin of this value minted during the reign of George III. **4.** A very small amount; a whit: *didn't care twopence about politics.*

two·pen·ny (túppəni, túp-ni; *in sense 1 also* tōō-penni) *adj.* Also *British Informal.* **tup·pen·ny** (túp-ni). **1.** Worth or costing twopence. **2.** Cheap; worthless; tuppeny-ha'penny.

two-phase (tōō-fáyz) *adj.* Pertaining to two alternating electrical currents with phases at 90°; quarter-phase.

two-piece (tōō-péess) *adj.* Made in or consisting of two parts or pieces: *a two-piece suit.*
~*n.* A two-piece suit or swimming costume.

two-ply (tōō-plī, -plī) *adj.* **1.** Made of two interwoven layers. **2.** Consisting of two thicknesses or strands: *two-ply knitting yarn.*
~*n., pl.* **-plies.** Any two-ply material, such as wool or yarn.

two-seat·er (tōō-séetər) *n.* A motor vehicle, especially a sports car, or an aeroplane that has seating for two people.

Two Sic·i·lies, the (síss'l-iz ‖ -eez). The former kingdoms of Sicily and Naples, ruled jointly (1443–58; 1504–1713; 1759–1815), and united (1815–60).

two-sid·ed (tōō-sídid) *adj.* Having two sides or involving two positions: *a two-sided dispute.*

two·some (tōō-səm) *n.* **1.** Two people together; a pair or couple; a duo. **2.** A game played by two people, in golf.

two-step (tōō-step) *n.* **1.** A ballroom dance in 2/4 time and characterised by long, sliding steps. **2.** The music composed for such a dance. —**two-step** *adj.*

two-stroke (tōō-strōk) *adj.* Designating an internal-combustion engine in which the piston or pistons make two strokes for each explosion. Compare **four-stroke.**

two-time (tōō-tīm) *tr.v.* **-timed, -timing, -times.** *Informal.* **1.** To deceive or betray. **2.** To be unfaithful to (a spouse or lover). —**two-tim·er** (-tīmər) *n.* —**two-tim·ing** (-tīming) *adj.*

two-tone (tōō-tōn) *adj.* Of two shades or colours: *two-tone shoes.*

'twould (twōōd, *weak form* twəd). *Regional and Poetic.* Contraction of *it would.*

two-up (tōō-up) *n.* A gambling game, played especially in Australia, in which bets are made on whether two coins tossed up will both land with heads or tails facing upwards.

two-way (tōō-wáy) *adj.* **1.** Affording passage to vehicular traffic in two directions: *a two-way street.* **2.** Permitting communication in two directions: *two-way radio.* **3. a.** Expressive of or involving mutual action or responsibility. **b.** Involving two participants on a reciprocal basis. **4.** Permitting the flow in either of two directions: *a two-way valve.* **5.** Controlling an electric current at two places.

–ty[1] *n. suffix.* Indicates a condition or quality; for example, **royalty.** [Middle English *-te(e), -tie,* from Old French *-te, -tet,* from Latin *-tās* (stem *-tāt-*), akin to Greek *-tēs,* Sanskrit *-tat, -tati.*]

–ty[2] *suffix.* Indicates a multiple of ten; for example, **forty, fifty, sixty.** [Middle English *-ty, -ti,* Old English *-tig.*]

ty·coon (tī-kōōn, tī-) *n.* **1.** *Informal.* A wealthy and powerful businessman or industrialist; a magnate. **2.** A title formerly applied to the Japanese shogun. [Japanese *taikun,* title of a shogun, from Ancient Chinese *t'ai kiuən,* emperor : *tài,* great (Mandarin *dá*) + *kiuən,* prince, sovereign (Mandarin *jūn*).]

tyke, tike (tīk) *n.* **1.** *Informal.* A small child, especially a mischievous one. **2.** *Chiefly Scottish.* A mongrel or cur. **3.** *Chiefly Scottish.* A mean or uncouth fellow; a boor. **4.** A **Yorkshire tyke** *(see).* [Middle English, from Old Norse *tīk,* a bitch.]

Ty·ler (tílər), **Wat** (died 1381). English rebel. He led the peasants' revolt (1381) against Richard II's poll tax. He was killed by the Lord Mayor of London, Sir William Walworth, after making fresh demands of the King, who had already made concessions.

ty·lo·sis (tī-lō-sis) *n., pl.* **-loses** (-seez). Also **ty·lose** (tī-lōz, -lōss). *Botany.* An ingrowth from an adjoining cell into a water-conducting vessel, often found in old, damaged, or diseased wood, that may wholly block the vessel. [Greek *tulōsis : tulē,* callus + -OSIS.]

tymbal. Variant of **timbal.**

tym·pan (tímpən) *n.* **1.** *Printing.* A padding of paper or cloth placed over the platen of a printing press to provide support for the sheet being printed. **2.** *Architecture.* A tympanum. **3.** A tightly stretched sheet or membrane, as on the head of a drum. [Middle English *tympan, timpan,* a drum, Old English *timpana,* from Latin *tympanum.* See **tympanum.**]

tympani. Variant of **timpani.**

tym·pan·ic (tim-pánnik) *adj.* Also **tym·pa·nal** (tímpən'l) (for sense 2). **1.** Pertaining to or resembling a tympanum. **2.** *Anatomy.* Of or pertaining to the tympanum. [From TYMPANUM.]

tympanic bone *n.* The part of the temporal bone of the skull that partially encloses the auditory canal and supports the tympanic membrane.

tympanic cavity *n.* The **middle ear** *(see).*

tympanic membrane *n.* The thin, semitransparent, oval-shaped membrane separating the middle ear from the external ear. Also called "eardrum", "tympanum".

tym·pa·nist (tímpənist) *n.* The member of an orchestra who plays the kettledrums and other percussion instruments. [Latin *tympanista,* from Greek *tumpanistēs,* from *tumpanizein,* to beat a drum, from *tumpanon,* a drum. See **tympanum.**]

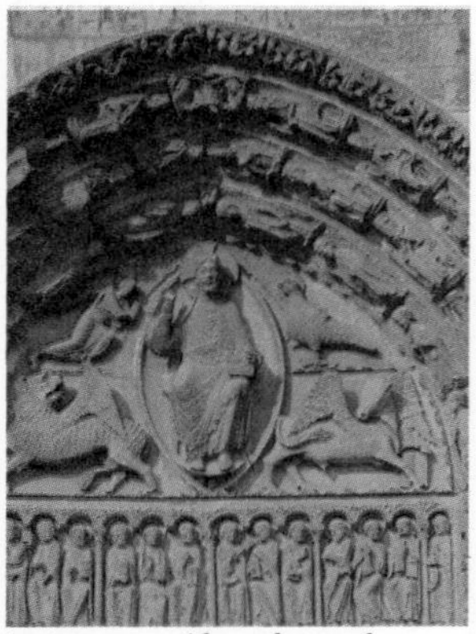

tympanum *Above the royal entrance to the 12th-century cathedral of Chartres in France, the tympanum is decorated with the figure of Christ triumphant, surrounded by symbols of the evangelists.*

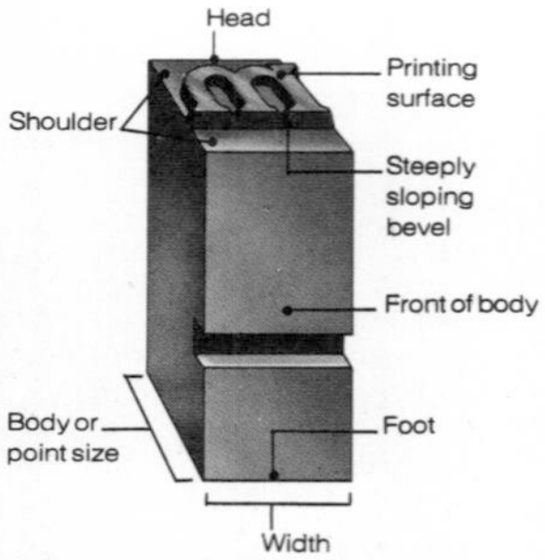

type *The use of movable type for printing, invented in Europe in the 15th century, is no different in principle from the woodblock printing of illustrations, practised for centuries before in China. A piece of metal type, such as the lower-case letter "m" (above), is cast in a mould of a chosen size and style. Modern printing is increasingly done on film, rendering the "hot metal" tradition obsolete.*

tym·pa·ni·tes (tímpə-nī́-teez) *n.* A distension of the abdomen resulting from the accumulation of gas or air in the abdomen. [Middle English, from Late Latin *tympanītēs,* from Greek *tumpanitēs,* from *tumpanon,* a drum. See **tympanum.**]

tym·pa·ni·tis (tímpə-nī́tiss) *n.* Inflammation of the middle ear. [TYMPANUM + -ITIS.]

tym·pa·num, tim·pa·num (tímpə-nəm) *n., pl.* **-na** (-nə) or **-nums.** **1. a.** The **middle ear** *(see).* **b.** The tympanic membrane; the eardrum. **c.** The middle ear and the tympanic membrane combined. **2.** *Zoology.* A membranous external auditory structure, as in certain insects. **3.** *Architecture.* **a.** The recessed, ornamental space or panel enclosed by the cornices of a triangular pediment. **b.** A similar space between an arch and the lintel of a portal. Also called "tympan". **4.** The diaphragm of a telephone. **5.** The tympan on a drum; a drumhead. [Medieval Latin, the eardrum, from Latin, a drum, from Greek *tumpanon.*]

tym·pa·ny (tímpəni) *n., pl.* **-nies. 1.** Tympanites. **2.** *Archaic.* An inflated manner or style; bombast. [Medieval Latin *tympanias,* "a drumlike swelling", from Greek *tumpanias,* from *tumpanon,* a drum. See **tympanum.**]

Tyn·dale (tínd'l), **William** (*c.* 1494–1536). English protestant reformer and biblical translator. His highly literary translation of the New Testament (begun at Cologne 1525) became the basis of the Authorised, or King James, Version of the Bible. He was strangled at the stake as a heretic, and his body afterwards burned.

Tyn·dall effect (tínd'l) *n.* The **Rayleigh scattering** of light by very small particles. [After John *Tyndall* (1820–93), Irish physicist.]

Tyne (tīn). River of northeastern England. Formed by the confluence of the North and South Tynes at Hexham, it flows 48 kilometres (30 miles) east to the North Sea.

Tyne and Wear (weer). Metropolitan county of northeastern England. Established in 1974, it includes areas formerly in Northumberland and Durham. Newcastle-upon-Tyne is the administrative centre.

Tyn·wald (tínwəld) *n.* The parliament of the Isle of Man.

typ·al (tī́p'l) *adj. Rare.* Pertaining to or serving as a type; typical.

type (tīp) *n.* **1. a.** A group of persons or things sharing common traits or characteristics that distinguish them as an identifiable group or class; a kind; a category. **b.** A subdivision of a kind or category: *three main types of error.* **2.** A person or thing having the features of a group or class; a standard example: *a type of the red-haired Celt.* **3.** An example or model; an embodiment: *"He was the perfect type of a military dandy"* (Joyce Cary). **4.** *Informal.* **a.** A person regarded as being typical of a specified class, such a profession, rank, or social group: *a bar full of rugby types.* **b.** One embodying the features or characteristics associated with a specified group or class: *She's not the ballet type.* **5.** A figure, representation, or symbol of something to come, such as an event in the Old Testament that foreshadows another in the New Testament. **6. a.** A taxonomic designation, such as the name of a species or genus, used as the basis of ascription to or characterisation of the next highest taxonomic category. **b.** A specimen or sample used as the basis of description of a species; a holotype. **7.** *Printing.* **a.** A small block of metal or wood bearing a raised letter or character on the upper end, that, when inked and pressed upon paper, leaves a printed impression. **b.** Such pieces collectively. **c.** Letters or characters photographically exposed onto light-sensitive material, such as film or bromide paper, subsequently used to prepare a printing image in photocomposition. **d.** A typeface: *in heavy type.* **e.** Letters and characters produced by traditional printing methods or by photocomposition; printing matter. **8.** A pattern, design, or image impressed or stamped upon the face of a coin. **—true to type.** Appearing or behaving in a characteristic way.
~*adj.* **1.** Standard; typical: *type examples.* **2.** Of or pertaining to printing or typesetting: *type size.*
~*v.* **typed, typing, types.** —*tr.* **1.** To write (something) with a typewriter; typewrite. **2.** To determine the type of (a blood sample or tissue). **3.** To classify according to a particular type: *typed her a heroine.* **4.** To represent or typify. **5.** To prefigure; foreshadow. —*intr.* To work at a typewriter; typewrite. [Middle English, from Late Latin *typus,* a form, type, from Latin, figure, image, from Greek *tupos,* a blow, impression, from *tuptein,* to strike.]
Synonyms: *type, kind, sort, nature, character, ilk.*
Usage: In standard English, *type* is followed by *of* in constructions such as *that type of leather,* though the *of* is sometimes omitted in regional speech. Many people prefer to restrict their use of *type* to those contexts where a specific, clearly definable category is involved, and to use *kind* or *sort* where the reference is more general *(that sort of thing; the kind of person I would trust).*

-type *n. comb. form.* Indicates: **1.** Type or representative form; for example, **monotype. 2.** Stamping or printing type, or photographic process; for example, **collotype. 3. a.** Belonging to a specified type or class: *reference-type works.* **b.** Resembling or related to something specified: *a Chablis-type wine.* [French, from Latin *-typus,* from Greek *-tupos,* from *tupos,* TYPE.]

type·bar (tī́p-baar) *n.* Any of the movable bars in a typewriter carrying letters or characters.

type·case (tī́p-kayss) *n.* A case divided into compartments for holding printing type.

type·cast (tī́p-kaast || -kast) *tr.v.* **-cast, -casting, -casts. 1.** To cast in an acting role akin or suited to one's own personality, background, or physical appearance. **2.** To assign repeatedly to the same kind of part or role: *typecast as a scarlet woman.*

type·face (tī́p-fayss) *n. Printing.* **1.** The surface of a body of type that makes the impression. **2.** The impression itself. **3.** The size, design, or style of the letter or character on the type. **4.** The full range of type of the same design. Also called "face".

type foundry *n.* A factory where metal printing type is cast. **—type founder** *n.* **—type founding** *n.*

type genus *n.* The name of a taxonomic genus that is designated as representative of the family to which it belongs; for example, the genus *Canis,* which includes dogs and wolves, is the type genus of the family Canidae.

type-high (tī́p-hī́) *adj.* As high as the standard height of type, 0.9175 of an inch in Britain, and 0.9186 of an inch in the United States.

type metal *n. Printing.* An alloy used for making metal types, consisting mainly of tin, lead, and antimony.

type·script (tī́p-skript) *n.* **1.** A typewritten copy, as of a book or document. **2.** Typewritten matter.

type·set (tī́p-set) *tr.v.* **-set, -setting, -sets.** To set (type) for printing.

type·set·ter (tī́p-settər) *n.* **1.** A person who sets type; a compositor. **2.** A machine used for setting type.

type species *n.* The name of a taxonomic species designated as representative of the genus to which it belongs; for example, *Panthera pardus,* the leopard, is the type species of the genus *Panthera.*

type specimen *n.* A **holotype** *(see).*

type·write (tī́p-rīt) *v.* **-wrote** (-rōt), **-written** (-ritt'n), **-writing, -writes.** —*tr.* To write (a letter, for example) with a typewriter; type. —*intr.* To write with a typewriter; type. [Back-formation from TYPEWRITER.]

type·writ·er (tī́p-rītər) *n. Abbr.* **typw. 1.** A keyboard machine, sometimes electrically powered, that prints characters and numerals, traditionally by means of a set of metal hammers bearing raised type that strike the paper through an inked ribbon or carbon tape, or using various other devices, such as a **daisywheel** or **golfball** *(both of which see),* when actuated by pressed keys. **2.** *Archaic.* A typist. **3.** *Printing.* A style of type that resembles typewritten copy.

type·writ·ing (tī́p-rīting) *n.* **1.** The act, process, or skill of using a typewriter. **2.** Copy produced by typewriting; typescript.

typh·li·tis (tif-lī́tiss) *n.* Inflammation of the caecum. [New Latin, from Greek *tuphlon,* caecum (from *tuphlos,* blind) + -ITIS.] **—typh·li·tic** (-líttik) *adj.*

ty·phoid (tī́-foyd) *n.* An acute, highly infectious disease caused by the typhoid bacillus, *Salmonella typhi,* transmitted by contaminated food or water and characterised by red rashes, high fever, and, in severe cases, intestinal haemorrhaging. Also called "enteric fever", "typhoid fever".
~*adj.* Also **ty·phoi·dal** (tī-fóyd'l). Of, pertaining to, or resembling typhoid. [TYPH(US) + -OID.]

Ty·phon (tī́-f'n, -fon). *Greek Mythology.* A monster called by Hesiod the son of Typhoeus.

ty·phoon (tī́-fōōn, tī-) *n.* A small, intense tropical cyclone occurring in the western Pacific or the China Sea. See Synonyms at **wind.** [Cantonese *daai fung,* "great wind", corresponding to Chinese (Mandarin) *dàfēng¹* : *dà,* great + *fēng,* wind (but in form influenced by Greek *Tuphōn,* TYPHON).] **—ty·phon·ic** (tī-fónnik) *adj.*

ty·phus (tī́-fəss) *n.* Any of several forms of an infectious disease caused by microorganisms of the genus *Rickettsia,* especially when flea-borne as in *endemic typhus,* louse-borne as in *epidemic typhus,* or mite-borne as in *scrub typhus,* and characterised generally by severe headache, sustained high fever, depression, delirium, and widespread rashes. Also called "ship fever", "typhus fever". [New Latin, from Greek *tuphos,* (fever causing) delusion, from *tuphein,* to make smoke.] **—ty·phous** (-fəss) *adj.*

typ·i·cal (típpik'l) *adj.* Also **typ·ic** (típpik). **1.** Exhibiting the traits or characteristics peculiar to a kind, class, group, or the like; representative of a whole group: *a typical suburban community.* **2. a.** Of or pertaining to a representative specimen; characteristic; distinctive. **b.** Characteristic of a particular individual: *That sort of behaviour is typical of her.* **3. a.** Conforming to a type. **b.** *Biology.* Having the characteristics of a particular taxonomic. **4.** Of the nature of, constituting, or serving as a type; emblematic. —See Synonyms at **characteristic, usual.** [Late Latin *typicālis,* from *typicus,* typical, from Greek *tupikos,* impressionable, from *tupos,* impression, TYPE.] **—typ·i·cal·i·ty** (típpi-kállәti), **typ·i·cal·ness** *n.*

typ·i·cal·ly (típpi-kli, -k'l-i) *adj.* **1.** In the respects usually associated with the specified category: *She is typically English.* **2.** In normal or typical circumstances; usually: *Roads are typically used by cars.*

typ·i·fy (típpi-fī) *tr.v.* **-fied, -fying, -fies. 1.** To serve as a typical example of; embody the essential characteristics of. **2.** To represent by an image, form, or model; symbolise. [From TYP(E) + -FY.] **—typ·i·fi·ca·tion** (-fi-káysh'n) *n.* **—typ·i·fi·er** *n.*

typ·ist (tī́pist) *n.* One who operates a typewriter, especially as a form of employment.

ty·po (tī́pō) *n., pl.* **-os.** *Informal.* A typographical error.

ty·pog·ra·pher (tī-póggrəfər) *n.* **1.** A printer or compositor. **2.** One skilled in the design or layout of printed matter.

typographical error *n.* A mistake in printing, typing, or writing.

ty·pog·ra·phy (tī-póggrəfi) *n., pl.* **-phies. 1. a.** The process of printing material using type. **b.** The art and technique of this. **2.** The arrangement or appearance of printing matter. [Medieval Latin *typographia* : Greek *tupos,* impression, TYPE + -GRAPHY.] **—ty·po·graph·ic** (tīp-ə-gráffik, -ō-), **ty·po·graph·i·cal** *adj.* **—ty·po·graph·i·cal·ly** *adv.*

ty·pol·o·gy (tī-póllәji) *n., pl.* **-gies. 1.** The study of types, especially according to a systematic classification. **2.** A theory or doctrine of types, as in scriptural studies. [Greek *tupos,* impression, TYPE + -LOGY.] —**ty·po·log·i·cal** (tĭpə-lójik'l) *adj.* —**ty·po·log·i·cal·ly** *adv.* —**ty·pol·o·gist** (tī-póllajist) *n.*

typw. typewriter; typewritten.

Tyr, Tyrr (teer, tewr, tür). *Norse Mythology.* A god of war, son of Odin. [Old Norse *Tȳr.*]

ty·ra·mine (tĭr-ə-meen, tírrə-) *n.* A colourless, crystalline amine, $C_8H_{11}NO$, found in mistletoe, putrefied animal tissue, certain cheeses, and ergot, and also produced synthetically, used in medicine. [TYR(OSINE) + AMINE.]

ty·ran·ni·cal (ti-ránnik'l, tī-, tĭr-) *adj.* Also **ty·ran·nic** (-ránnik). 1. Of, pertaining to, or characteristic of a tyrant. 2. Despotic; arbitrary; oppressive. —**ty·ran·ni·cal·ly** *adv.* —**ty·ran·ni·cal·ness** *n.*

ty·ran·ni·cide (ti-ránni-sīd, tī-, tĭr-) *n.* 1. The killing of a tyrant. 2. One who kills a tyrant. —**ty·ran·ni·ci·dal** (-sīd'l) *adj.*

tyr·an·nise, tyr·an·nize (tírrə-nīz) *v.* -nised, -nising, -nises. —*intr.* 1. To exercise absolute power, especially arbitrarily. 2. To rule as a tyrant. —*tr.* To treat tyrannically; crush; oppress. [French *tyranniser,* from Late Latin *tyrannizāre,* from Latin *tyrannus,* TYRANT.] —**tyr·an·nis·er** *n.* —**tyr·an·nis·ing·ly** *adv.*

ty·ran·no·saur (ti-ránnə-sawr, tī-, tĭr-) *n.* Also **ty·ran·no·saur·us** (-sáwrəss). Any large carnivorous dinosaur of the genus *Tyrannosaurus,* of the Cretaceous period; especially *T. rex,* which had small forelimbs and a large head. [New Latin : Greek *turannos,* TYRANT + -SAUR.]

tyr·an·nous (tírrənəss) *adj.* Characterised by tyranny; despotic; tyrannical. —**tyr·an·nous·ly** *adv.*

tyr·an·ny (tírrəni) *n., pl.* -nies. 1. A government in which a single ruler exercises absolute power, especially in an unjust, cruel, or arbitrary manner. 2. The office, authority, or jurisdiction of such a ruler. 3. Absolute power, especially when exercised unjustly or cruelly. 4. The arbitrary use of such power; a tyrannical act. 5. Excessively rigorous control: *the tyranny of etiquette.* [Middle English *tyrannye,* from Old French *tyrannie,* from Late Latin *tyrannia,* from Greek *turannia,* from *turannos,* TYRANT.]

ty·rant (tĭr-ənt) *n.* 1. An absolute ruler who governs arbitrarily without constitutional or other restrictions, especially one in ancient Greece. 2. A ruler who exercises power in a harsh, cruel manner; an oppressor. 3. Any tyrannical or despotic person. [Middle English *tyra(u)nt,* from Old French *tyran(t),* from Latin *tyrannus,* from Greek *turannos,* probably from a source in Asia Minor.]

tyrant flycatcher *n.* A bird of the family Tyrannidae, the **flycatcher** *(see).* [Referring to its habit of repelling all birds from the territory surrounding its nest.]

tyre, *U.S.* **tire** (tīr) *n.* 1. A solid or air-filled covering for a wheel, typically of rubber or a similar elastic synthetic material, fitted round the wheel's rim to absorb shock and provide traction. 2. A hoop of iron or heavy rubber fitted about the rim of a wheel. ~*tr.v.* **tyred, tyring, tyres.** To fit with a tyre or tyres.

Tyre (tīr). Port of northwestern Lebanon, present-day Sur. Founded by the Phoenicians, it became one of the great trade centres of the ancient world. Taken by the Crusaders in 1124, it was destroyed by Muslims in 1291, and was never completely rebuilt.

tyre chain *n.* A snow chain *(see).*

Tyr·i·an pur·ple (tírri-ən) *n.* A reddish dyestuff obtained from the bodies of certain molluscs of the genus *Murex,* and highly prized in ancient times. [After *Tyre,* source of the dye.]

ty·ro, ti·ro (tĭr-ō) *n., pl.* -ros. An inexperienced person; a beginner; a neophyte. [Medieval Latin *tȳrō,* from Latin *tīrō†,* a young soldier, recruit.]

ty·ro·li·enne (ti-rṓli-én) *n.* 1. A Tyrol peasant dance in ¾ time. 2. A song composed for this dance, featuring the yodel. [French, *(danse) tyrolienne,* Tyrolean (dance).]

Tyrol. See Tirol.

Ty·rone (ti-rṓn). County of west Northern Ireland. It is a hilly, predominantly agricultural county, and its traditional flax and brewing industries have declined. Omagh is the county town.

ty·ro·sin·ase (tĭr-ə-sin-ayz, -ō-, tírrō-, ti-róssin-, -ayss) *n.* A copper-containing enzyme of plant and animal tissues that catalyses the production of melanin from tyrosine. [TYROSIN(E) + -ASE.]

ty·ro·sine (tĭr-ə-seen, tírrə-, -sin) *n.* A white crystalline non-essential amino acid, $C_9H_{11}NO_3$, from the hydrolysis of protein, that is a precursor of adrenaline, thyroxine, and melanin. [Greek *turos,* cheese + -INE.]

ty·ro·thri·cin (tĭr-ō-thrī-sin) *n.* A greyish to brown mixture of antibiotics obtained from cultures of the soil bacteria *Bacillus brevis,* and applied locally for the treatment of infections caused by Gram-positive bacteria. [New Latin *Tyrothrix* (stem *Tyrothric-*), generic name for certain spore-forming bacteria, "cheese-haired" : Greek *turos,* cheese + *thrix,* hair + -IN.]

Tyrr. Variant of Tyr.

tzar, tzarevitch, tzarevna, tzaritsa. Variants of tsar, tsarevitch, tsarevna, tsaritsa.

tzetze fly. Variant of tsetse fly.

Tzi·gane (tsi-gáan, si-, tsee-, see-) *n.* A Gypsy, especially a Hungarian gypsy. ~*adj.* Of or pertaining to Tziganes or their music. [French, from Hungarian *czigány.*]

PRONUNCIATION KEY

a, trap; aa, father; ai, fair; ar, star; aw, lawn; ay, play; b, bb, stab; rubber; ch, church; ck, ticket; d, dd, dead; ladder; e, dress; ee, bee; er, defer; ew, few; ewr, pure; ə, about; ər, letter; f, ff, fife; differ; g, gg, giggle; h, hat; i, kit; ī, price; īr, fire; j, judge; k, kick; l, ll, let; 'l, needle; m, mm, man; n, nn, no; 'n, sudden; ng, thing; o, lot; ō, no; ŏŏ, foot; ōō, shoe; oor, poor; ow, cow; owr, hour; oy, boy; p, pp, pepper; r, rr, red; s, ss, sauce; sh, ship; t, tt, totter; th, thick; th, this; smooth; u, cut; ur, turn; v, vv, valve; w, wet; y, yes; z, zz, zebra; zh, vision; pleasure

IN FOREIGN WORDS:

aN, ON, Saint-Saëns; hl, Llanelli; Hluhluwe; kh, loch; lough; Khaled

STRESS MARK:

ín-sīt, insight; in-sīt, incite

U

u, U (yōō) *n., pl.* u's *or rare* us, Us *or* U's. 1. The 21st letter of the modern English alphabet. 2. Any of the speech sounds represented by this letter. 3. Anything shaped like the letter U. Often used in combination: *a U-turn.*

u, U, u., U. *Note:* As an abbreviation or symbol, *u* may be a capital or a small letter, with or without a full stop. Established forms or those generally preferred precede the definition. When no form is given, all four forms are in general use in that sense. 1. u., U. uncle. 2. U *Mathematics.* union. 3. u. unit. 4. U. university. 5. u., U. upper. 6. U The symbol for the element uranium. 7. The 21st in a series; 20th when *J* is omitted.

U¹ (yōō) *adj. British Informal.* Considered to be typical of or appropriate to the upper class, especially in language usage. Compare non-U. [Abbreviation of *upper class.*]

U² (yōō) *n., pl.* Us *or* U's. In Britain, a film designated as being suitable for a person of any age. Also used adjectively: *a U film.* [Abbreviation of *universal.*]

U³ (ōō) *n.* A Burmese title of respect used before the name of a man.

Uabh Failghe. See Offaly.

UAM underwater-to-air missile.

UAR, U.A.R. United Arab Republic.

UART *n.* Universal asynchronous receiver transmitter; a type of radio set.

UB40 *n.* An unemployed person claiming unemployment benefit. [From the number of the form filled in by claimants of unemployment benefit.]

Ubangi-Shari. See Central African Republic.

Ü·ber·mensch (yōō-bər-mensh; *German* ü̆-) *n., pl.* -menschen (-'n). *German.* A superman, as in the philosophy of Nietzsche. [German, "over-man".]

u·bi·e·ty (yōō-bī́-əti) *n.* The condition of being located in a particular place. [Medieval Latin *ubietās,* from *ubi,* where.]

u·biq·ui·tous (yōō-bíkwitəss) *adj.* Being or seeming to be everywhere at the same time; omnipresent: *their ubiquitous influence.* [From UBIQUITY.] —u·biq·ui·tous·ly *adv.* —u·biq·ui·tous·ness *n.*

u·biq·ui·ty (yōō-bíkwəti) *n.* Existence everywhere at the same time; omnipresence. [New Latin *ubiquitas,* from Latin *ubíque,* everywhere : *ubī,* where + *-que,* generalising particle.]

U-boat (yōō-bōt) *n.* A German submarine. [German *U-boot,* short for *Unterseeboot,* "undersea boat".]

U-bolt (yōō-bōlt ‖ -bolt) *n.* A bolt shaped like the letter U, fitted with a thread and nut at each end.

u.c. *Printing.* upper case.

U.C. University College.

UCCA (úckə) Universities Central Council on Admissions.

Uc·cel·lo (ōō-chéllō), Paolo, born Paolo di Dono (1397–1475). Florentine painter and craftsman, best known for his experiments with perspective and foreshortening. Among his works are three paintings of *The Rout of San Romano* (1456–60).

Uchee, Uchean. Variants of Yuchi.

U.D.A., UDA Ulster Defence Association.

u·dal (yōōd'l) *n.* A system of freehold possession of land that preceded the feudal system and is still used in Orkney and Shetland. [Orkney and Shetland dialect, from Old Norse *ōthal,* corresponding to Old English *ēthel, ōthel,* from Germanic *ōth-* (unattested); akin to ATHELING.] —u·dal *adj.*

ud·der (uddər) *n.* The baglike mammary organ characteristic of cows, sheep, and goats, having two or four teats. [Middle English *udder,* Old English *ūder.*]

UDI Unilateral Declaration of Independence.

u·do (ōō-dō) *n.* A Japanese plant, *Aralia cordata,* of which the young shoots are cooked and eaten as a vegetable. [Japanese.]

u·dom·e·ter (yōō-dómmitər) *n.* A rain gauge (see). [French *udomètre,* from Latin *ūdus,* damp + -METER.]

U.D.R., UDR Ulster Defence Regiment.

UFO, u·fo (*sometimes* yōōfō) *n., pl.* -FOs, -fos. An unidentified flying object (see).

u·fol·o·gy (yōō-fólləji) *n.* The study of UFOs or the practice of

trying to spot them. [UFO + -LOGY.] —u·fo·log·i·cal (yōōfə-lójik'l) *adj.* —u·fol·o·gist (yōō-fólləjist) *n.*

U·gan·da (yōō-gándə ‖ *U.S. also* -ga̅andə). Land-locked republic in east central Africa. Most of the country lies on a high plateau, more than 1 070 metres (3,500 feet) above sea level. Some 90 per cent of Ugandans live by subsistence farming, and coffee accounts for over 75 per cent of exports. There are reserves of copper and tin, and the Owen Falls hydroelectric scheme satisfies most energy needs. A British protectorate from 1894, Uganda became independent within the Commonwealth in 1962, with the kabaka (king) of Buganda as president. He was succeeded by Milton Obote (1966), who returned to power in 1980, following the overthrow of the dictatorship of Idi Amin (1971–78). Area, 236 036 square kilometres (91,134 square miles). Population, 13,700,000. Capital, Kampala.

U·ga·rit·ic (ōōgə-ríttik) *n.* The Semitic language of the ancient city-state of Ugarit (on the site of Ras Shamra in present-day Syria). —U·ga·rit·ic *adj.*

U.G.C. University Grants Committee.

ugh (ōōkh, ukh, *and various back unrounded vowel-sounds*) *interj.* Used to express horror, disgust, or repugnance.

ug·li (úggli) *n., pl.* -lis *or* -lies. A citrus fruit indigenous to Jamaica: a cross between a grapefruit and a tangerine. Also called "ugli fruit". [Perhaps from UGLY (from its ugly wrinkled rind).]

ug·li·fy (úggli-fī) *tr.v.* -fied, -fying, -fies. To make ugly; disfigure. [UGLY + -FY.] —ug·li·fi·ca·tion (-fi-káysh'n) *n.*

ug·ly (úggli) *adj.* -lier, -liest. 1. Displeasing to the eye; unsightly. 2. Repulsive or offensive in any way; objectionable. 3. Morally reprehensible. 4. Threatening; ominous: *ugly weather.* 5. Marked by or inclined towards anger or bad feelings: *An ugly scene developed.* [Middle English *ugli(c),* frightful, repulsive, from Old Norse *uggligr,* from *uggr†,* fear.] —ug·li·ly *adv.* —ug·li·ness *n.*

ugly duckling *n.* One considered ugly or unpromising at first but having the potential of becoming beautiful or admirable in maturity. [After the cygnet in the story by Hans Christian Andersen.]

U·gri·an (ōō-gri-ən, yōō-) *n.* 1. A member of a group of Finno-Ugric peoples of western Siberia and Hungary, including the Magyars. 2. Ugric. [Old Russian *Ugrin'* (plural *Ugre*), from Common Slavonic *Og'rin'* (unattested), from Turkic *Onogouroi.* See also Hungary.] —U·gri·an *adj.*

U·gric (ōō-grik, yōō-) *n.* A branch of the Finno-Ugric subfamily of languages consisting of Magyar (Hungarian), Ostyak, and Vogul. **—U·gric** *adj.*

ug·some (úg-s'm) *adj. Archaic.* Disgusting; loathsome. [Middle English *ugsom* : *uggen*, to inspire dread or disgust, from Old Norse *ugga*, to fear, UGLY + -SOME.]

uhf, UHF ultrahigh frequency.

uh-uh (ú'ú, ə'ə) *interj. Informal.* **1.** No. **2.** Used to express the realisation that trouble is near.

uh-huh (ú-hu, ə̄-hə, *often nasalised, also* m̄-hm) *interj. Informal.* Yes.

uh·lan, u·lan (o͞o-laan, yo͞o-, -lən, o͞o-laˊan) *n.* A member of a body of cavalry armed with lances that formed part of the former Polish army, and later, the former German army. [German *u(h)lan*, from Polish *ulan*, from Turkish *oğlan*, "youth", from *oğul*, son.]

u·hu·ru (o͞o-ho͝or-o͞o, -ho͞or-o͞o) *n. East African.* Liberty; freedom. Used chiefly as a slogan by African independence movements. [Swahili.]

Ui·gur, Ui·ghur (wēˊe-goor, yo͞o-i-) *n.* **1.** A member of a Turkic people dominant in Mongolia and eastern Turkestan from the 8th to the 12th centuries, now inhabiting northwestern China. **2.** The East Turkic language of this people. **—Ui·gu·ri·an** (-go͝or-i-ən) *adj.*

u·in·ta·there (yoo-intə-theer) *n.* Any of a number of extinct mammals resembling the rhinoceros, fossils of which have been found in North America. Also called "dinoceras". [After the *Uinta* Mountains, Utah, where fossil remains were discovered + -*there*, from Greek *thērion*, wild beast.]

u·in·ta·ite (yo͞o-íntə-īt) *n.* A bitumen, **gilsonite** *(see).* [After the *Uinta* basin (Utah and Wyoming), where it was discovered.]

U·ist (yo͞o-ist). Name of two islands in the Outer Hebrides, off the northwestern coast of Scotland, North Uist and South Uist. Most of the population are crofters.

uit·land·er (áyt-landər) *n. South African.* **1.** A foreigner. **2.** *Capital* **U.** A native of Great Britain who resided in either of the former republics of the Orange Free State and Transvaal. [Afrikaans, from Dutch.]

u·ja·maa (o͞ojə-maˊa) *n.* **1.** A plan for developing cooperation and communal ideals amongst different peoples in Tanzania. Also used adjectivally: *a ujamaa village.* **2.** A village practising this. [Swahili, family, brother : *u-*, prefix indicating state or condition + *jamaa*, family, from Arabic *jamāˊa*, community.]

Ujiji. See **Kigoma-Ujiji.**

Uj·jain (o͞o-jīn, o͞oj-, -jayn) *n.* City in the state of Madhya Pradesh, in central India, on the river Siprā. It is one of the seven sacred Hindu cities in India.

U.K., UK United Kingdom.

u·kase (yo͞o-káyz, -káyss ‖ yo͞o-kayss, o͞o-ka'az) *n.* **1.** A proclamation of the tsar having the force of law in imperial Russia. **2.** Any authoritative order or decree; an edict. [French, from Russian *ukaz*, decree, from *ukazat'*, to order, direct : *u-*, intensive prefix, "away" + *-kazat'*, to show.]

u·ki·yo·e (o͞o-kēˊe-yo͞o-áy, -yáy) *n.* A Japanese style of art in painting and printmaking, characterised by the simple depiction of scenes or objects from ordinary life. [Japanese : *ukiyo*, life + *e*, picture.]

U·krain·i·an (yo͞o-kráyni-ən, *rarely* -kríni-) *n.* **1.** An inhabitant or native of the Ukraine. **2.** A Slavonic language, similar to but distinct from Russian, that is spoken by most natives of the Ukraine. Also formerly called "Little Russian". [Ukrainian *Ukrayina*, from Old Russian *Ukraina*, "borderland" : *u-*, away from, at + *kraĭ*, edge, brink, end.] **—U·krain·i·an** *adj.*

Ukrainian Soviet Socialist Republic. Also **Ukraine** (yo͞o-kráyn). Formerly **Little Russia.** Constituent republic of the U.S.S.R., in the southwestern part of the country. The capital is Kiev. After the Russian Federative S.S.R. the Ukraine is the most heavily populated and economically important of the Soviet republics. Its steppe lands are one of the great wheat-producing regions of Europe and the republic as a whole provides nearly a quarter of the U.S.S.R.'s food supply. It is also a major producer of coal and iron ore.

u·ku·le·le (yo͞okə-láyli ‖ o͞okə-) *n.* A small four-stringed guitar originally from Hawaii. [Hawaiian *'ukulele*, "jumping little flea" (said to be nickname of Edward Putvis, 19th-century British officer, who popularised the instrument) : *'uku*, flea + *lele*, jumping.]

ulan. Variant of **uhlan.**

U·lan Ba·tor (o͞o-laan baˊa-tawr). Capital of the Mongolian People's Republic, lying on the river Tola. It is the chief commercial and industrial city of the country and, lying on the Trans-Siberian railway, is also the main transport junction.

U·la·no·va (o͞o-lán-əvə, -laˊan-), **Galina Sergeyevna** (1910–). Russian prima ballerina. She is noted for her roles in *Swan Lake* and *Giselle.* Since 1962 she has been ballet mistress to the Bolshoi.

-ular *adj. suffix.* Indicates a relationship or resemblance; for example, **tubular.** [Latin -*ulāris*, from -*ulus*, -ULE.]

Ul·bricht (o͞ol-brikht), **Walter** (1893–1973). East German statesman. He was general secretary of the Socialist Unity Party from 1950, and became chairman (1960) of the newly-established council of state. He erected the Berlin Wall (1961).

ul·cer (úl-sər) *n.* **1. a.** An inflammatory, often suppurating lesion on the skin or an internal mucous surface of the body, resulting in necrosis of the tissue and taking a long time to heal. **b.** A necrotic lesion of the stomach or duodenum. **2.** Any corrupting condition or influence. [Middle English, from Old French *ulcere*, from Latin *ulcus* (stem *ulcer-*), a sore, ulcer.]

ul·cer·ate (úl-sə-rayt) *v.* -ated, -ating, -ates. —*intr.* To become affected with or as if with an ulcer. —*tr.* To affect with ulcers. **—ul·cer·a·tive** (-rətiv, -raytiv) *adj.*

ul·cer·a·tion (úl-sə-ráysh'n) *n.* **1.** The development of an ulcer. **2.** An ulcer or ulcerous condition.

ul·cer·ous (úl-sərəss) *adj.* **1.** Pertaining to or exhibiting ulcers. **2.** Corrupting; having a bad influence. **—ul·cer·ous·ly** *adv.*

-ule *n. suffix.* Indicates smallness; for example, **granule**, **valvule.** [French -*ule*, from Latin -*ulus* (masculine), -*ula* (feminine), -*ulum* (neuter), diminutive suffixes.]

u·le·ma, u·la·ma (o͞ol-i-mə, -ə-, -maa) *n., pl.* **-mas** or **ulema.** **1.** The body of scholars or priests trained in traditional Muslim religion and law. **2.** A Muslim scholar or religious leader. [Turkish *'ulemā*, from Arabic *'ulamā*, "wise men", plural of *'ālim*, wise, learned, from *'alima*, to know.]

-ulent *adj. suffix.* Indicates abundance or fullness; for example, **flatulent.** [Old French, from Latin -*ulentus.*] **—ulence** *n. suffix.*

u·lex·ite (yo͞o-leks-īt, -liks-, yo͞o-léks-) *n.* A white mineral, $NaCaB_5O_9.8H_2O$, that forms round masses of very fine acicular crystals. [After George *Ulex* (died 1883), German chemist + -ITE.]

ul·lage (úllij) *n.* **1.** The amount of liquid, grain, or the like within a container that is lost during shipment or storage, as through leakage. **2.** The amount by which a container, such as a cask or bottle, falls short of being full. [Middle English, from Anglo-French *ulliage*, Old French *ouillage*, from *ouiller*, to fill up a cask to the bunghole, from *oeil*, eye, bunghole, from Latin *oculus.*]

Ulls·wa·ter (úlz-wawtər). Second-largest lake in England, lying in the Lake District, and about 12 kilometres (7.5 miles) long.

Ulm (o͞olm). Industrial city in southern West Germany, lying on the river Danube. Mentioned in records as early as the mid-9th century, it was a leading commercial centre during the Middle Ages.

ul·na (úl-nə) *n., pl.* **-nas** or **-nae** (-nee). *Anatomy.* **1.** The bone extending from the elbow to the wrist on the side opposite to the thumb. **2.** The corresponding bone in the forelimb of other vertebrates. [New Latin, from Latin, elbow, arm.] **—ul·nar** (-nər) *adj.*

u·lot·ri·chous (yo͞o-lóttri-kəss) *adj.* Having wiry or woolly hair. Said especially of negroid peoples. [New Latin, "woolly-haired", from Greek *oulothrix* (stem *oulotrikh-*) : *oulos*, woolly, curly + *thrix*, hair.] **—u·lot·ri·chy** (-ki) *n.*

ul·ster (úl-stər) *n.* A loose, long overcoat made of a heavy cloth and often belted. [After ULSTER, (the coat was first made in Belfast).]

Ul·ster (úl-stər). Northernmost of the four ancient provinces of Ireland, no longer of political or administrative meaning. It consisted of nine counties, six of which (Antrim, Armagh, Down, Fermanagh, Londonderry, and Tyrone) now constitute Northern Ireland, itself still popularly known as Ulster. The three other counties (Cavan, Donegal, and Monaghan) are in the Republic of Ireland.

Ulster Defence Association *n. Abbr.* **U.D.A., UDA** A Protestant paramilitary organisation in Northern Ireland.

Ul·ster·man (úl-stər-mən, -man) *n., pl.* **-men** (-mən, -men). A native or inhabitant of Ulster. **—Ul·ster·wo·man** *n.*

ult. **1.** ultimate; ultimately. **2.** ultimo. **—See** Usage note at **inst.**

ul·te·ri·or (ul-téer-i-ər) *adj.* **1.** Lying beyond what is evident, revealed, or avowed; especially, concealed intentionally so as to deceive: *an ulterior motive.* **2.** Lying beyond or outside the area of immediate interest. **3.** Occurring later; subsequent. [Latin, farther, comparative of *ulter* (unattested), on the other side.]

ul·ti·ma (últimə) *n.* The last syllable of a word. [Latin, feminine of *ultimus*, farthest, last. See **ultimate.**]

ul·ti·mate (últi-mət, -mit) *adj. Abbr.* **ult. 1.** Completing a series or process; final; conclusive. **2.** Representing the farthest possible extent of analysis or division into parts: *ultimate constituent.* **3.** Fundamental; elemental. **4.** Of the greatest possible size or significance; maximum. **5.** Farthest; most remote. **6.** Representing the greatest possible sophistication or development of something: *the ultimate bicycle.* **—See** Synonyms at **last.**

~*n.* **1.** The basic or fundamental element or principle. **2.** The final point; the conclusive result. **3.** The maximum; the greatest extreme. [Medieval Latin *ultimātus*, past participle of *ultimāre*, to come to an end, from Latin *ultimus*, farthest, last, superlative degree of *ulter* (unattested), on the other side.] **—ul·ti·mate·ness** *n.*

ul·ti·mate·ly (últi-mət-li, -mit-) *adv.* At last; in the end; eventually.

ultima Thu·le (théw-li, tho͞o-) *n.* **1.** The northernmost region of the habitable world as thought of by ancient geographers. **2.** Any distant territory or destination. **3.** A remote goal or ideal. [Latin, "farthest Thule".]

ul·ti·ma·tum (últi-máy-təm ‖ -maˊa-) *n., pl.* **-tums** or **-ta** (-tə). A final statement of terms made by one party to another; especially, in diplomatic negotiations, a statement that expresses or implies the threat of serious penalties if the terms are not accepted. [New Latin, from Medieval Latin, neuter of *ultimātus*, last, ULTIMATE.]

ul·ti·mo (últi-mō) *adv. Abbr.* **ult.** In or of the month before the present one. Compare **proximo.** [Latin *ultimo (mense)*, in last (month), from *ultimus*, last, ULTIMATE.]

ul·ti·mo·gen·i·ture (últi-mō-jénni-chər, -choor, -tewr) *n. Law.* A principle by which the youngest child inherits the estate of one or both of his parents. Compare **primogeniture.** [Latin *ultimus* + -*geniture*, as in PRIMOGENITURE.]

ul·tra (últrə) *adj.* Immoderately adhering to a belief, fashion, or course of action; extreme.

~*n.* An extremist. [Originally shortened from French *ultra-royaliste.* See **ultra-.**]

ultra- *prefix.* Indicates: **1.** Surpassing or beyond a specified limit, range, or scope; for example, **ultramicroscopic**, **ultrasonic.** **2.** Exceeding what is usual, moderate, or proper to an extreme degree; for example, **ultraconservative.** *Note:* Many compounds other than those entered here may be formed with *ultra-*. In forming compounds, *ultra-* is normally joined with the following element without a space or hyphen: *ultramodern; ultrafashionable.* However, if the second element begins with a capital letter or with the letter *a*, it is separated with a hyphen: *ultra-British, ultra-atomic.* [Latin, from *ultrā*, beyond, from *ulter* (unattested), on the other side.]

ul·tra·cen·tri·fuge (últrə-séntri-fewj) *n.* A convection-free high-velocity centrifuge used in the separation of colloidal or submicroscopic particles. —**ul·tra·cen·trif·u·gal** (-sen-triffewg'l, -séntri-féwg'l) *adj.* —**ul·tra·cen·trif·u·ga·tion** (-few-gáysh'n) *n.*

ul·tra·con·ser·va·tive (últrə-kən-sérvətiv ‖ -kon-) *adj.* Conservative to an extreme, especially in political beliefs; reactionary. ~*n.* One who is extremely conservative.

ul·tra·crep·i·da·ri·an (últrə-kréppi-daír-i-ən) *adj.* Acting or speaking outside one's experience, knowledge or ability. ~*n.* One who acts or speaks beyond the sphere of his experience or knowledge; especially, an ignorant critic. [Latin *ultrā crepidam*, "beyond the sole", alluding to a story about the Greek painter Apelles and a cobbler, who pointed out to Apelles that he had painted a slipper with the wrong number of ties. Having made this successful criticism, the cobbler criticised on the following day the leg of the figure in the painting, to which Apelles replied that he should confine himself to remarks about slippers and not judge "beyond the sole".]

ul·tra·fiche (últrə-feesh) *n.* A microfiche in which the reduction factor is 100 or more. [ULTRA- + (MICRO)FICHE.]

ul·tra·fil·tra·tion (últrə-fil-tráysh'n) *n.* Filtration of colloidal solution through a semipermeable membrane. —**ul·tra·fil·ter** (-filtər) *n.*

ul·tra·high frequency (últrə-hī) *n. Abbr.* **uhf, UHF** A band of radio frequencies from 300 to 3,000 megahertz.

ul·tra·ism (últrə-iz'm) *n.* Extremism, especially in politics; radicalism. [ULTRA + -ISM.] —**ul·tra·ist** *adj. & n.* —**ul·tra·is·tic** (-ístik) *adj.*

ul·tra·ma·rine (últrə-mə-réen) *n.* 1. A blue pigment made from powdered lapis lazuli. 2. Any similar pigment made synthetically by heating clay, sodium carbonate, and sulphur together. 3. Vivid or strong blue to purplish blue. ~*adj.* 1. Having a deep to purplish blue colour. 2. Of or from some place beyond the sea. [Medieval Latin *ultrāmarīnus*, "(coming from) beyond the sea" (because lapis lazuli was imported from Asia by sea) : Latin *ultrā-*, beyond + *mare*, sea.]

ul·tra·mi·crom·e·ter (últrə-mī-krómmitər) *n.* An extremely accurate micrometer.

ul·tra·mi·cro·scope (últrə-míkrə-skōp) *n.* A microscope with high-intensity illumination used to study very minute objects, such as colloidal particles, by means of their diffraction system, which appears as a bright spot against a black background. Also called "dark-field microscope". —**ul·tra·mi·cros·co·py** (-mī-króskəpi) *n.*

ul·tra·mi·cro·scop·ic (últrə-mīkrə-skóppik) *adj.* 1. Too small to be seen with an ordinary microscope. 2. Of or relating to an ultramicroscope.

ul·tra·mod·ern (últrə-móddərn, -módd'n) *adj.* Extremely modern; absolutely up-to-date. —**ul·tra·mod·ern·ism** *n.* —**ul·tra·mod·ern·ist** *n.* —**ul·tra·mod·ern·is·tic** (-ístik) *adj.*

ul·tra·mon·tane (últrə-món-tayn ‖ -mon-táyn) *adj.* 1. Of or designating peoples or regions lying on the other side of the mountains, especially, south of the Alps. 2. Strongly supporting the authority of the papal court over national or diocesan authority in the Roman Catholic Church. ~*n.* 1. A person living beyond the mountains, especially, south of the Alps. 2. *Often capital* U. A Roman Catholic who advocates support of papal policy in ecclesiastical and political matters. [Medieval Latin *ultrāmontānus*, beyond the mountain (applied by the French to the papal court at Rome) : Latin *ultrā-*, beyond + *mōns* (stem *mont-*), mountain.]

Ul·tra·mon·ta·nism (últrə-món-ti-niz'm, -tə-, -tay-) *n.* The policy that absolute authority in the Roman Catholic Church should be vested in the pope. Compare **Gallicanism.** —**Ul·tra·mon·ta·nist** *n.*

ul·tra·mun·dane (últrə-mun-dáyn, -mún-dayn) *adj.* Extending or being beyond the world or the limits of the universe. [Latin *ultrāmundānus* : *ultrā-*, beyond + *mundus*, the world.]

ul·tra·na·tion·al·ism (últrə-násh-n'l-iz'm, -násh'n-'l-) *n.* Extreme nationalism, especially when opposed to international cooperation. —**ul·tra·na·tion·al** *adj.* —**ul·tra·na·tion·al·ist** *n. & adj.* —**ul·tra·na·tion·al·is·tic** (-ístik) *adj.*

ul·tra·short (últrə-shórt) *adj.* Designating or pertaining to radio waves with a wavelength less than 10 metres.

ul·tra·son·ic (últrə-sónnik) *adj.* Pertaining to or designating acoustic frequencies above the range audible to the human ear, or above approximately 20 kilohertz.

ul·tra·son·ics (últrə-sónniks) *n. Used with a singular verb.* 1. The acoustics of ultrasonic sound. 2. A technology using ultrasonic sound, as for medical therapy.

ul·tra·sound (últrə-sownd) *n.* Ultrasonic sound.

ul·tra·struc·ture (últrə-strúkchər) *n.* The detailed structure of a cell, tissue, or organ that can be seen by electron microscopy but not by light microscopy. Also called "fine structure". —**ul·tra·struc·tur·al** (-strúkchərəl) *adj.*

ul·tra·vi·o·let (últrə-vĭ-ə-lət, -lit) *adj. Abbr.* **UV, U.V.** 1. Of, belonging, or designating the range of radiation wavelengths from about 0.4 micrometres, just beyond the violet in the visible spectrum, to about 4.0 nanometres, on the border of the X-ray region. 2. Generating, using, or sensitive to such radiation.

~*n.* Ultraviolet radiation or the ultraviolet region of the electromagnetic spectrum.

ultraviolet lamp *n.* A mercury-vapour lamp that produces ultraviolet light.

ul·tra vi·res (últrə vír-eez, ōoltraa véer-ayz) *adv. Law.* Beyond one's legal authority or rights. [Latin.] —**ul·tra vi·res** *adj.*

ul·tra·vi·rus (últrə-vír-əss) *n.* A virus small enough to pass through the finest filter.

ul·u·late (yóolew-layt ‖ *chiefly U.S.* úllew-) *intr.v.* **-lated, -lating, -lates.** To howl, hoot, wail, or lament loudly. [Latin *ululāre*, to howl (imitative).] —**ul·u·la·tion** (-láysh'n) *n.*

um (um, 'm, erm) *interj.* Used when hesitating in speech, or to express doubt or uncertainty.

u·man·gite (yōo-máng-gīt) *n.* A rare ore of selenium, Cu_3Se_2. [German *Umangit*, after Sierra de *Umango*, province in northwestern Argentina + -ITE.]

Ulysses. The Latin name for **Odysseus.**

U·may·yad (ōo-mí-ad, ōo-, -yad). Also **Om·mi·ad** (ə-, o-). A dynasty of rulers of the Muslim Empire (A.D. 661–750) and Muslim Spain (A.D. 756–1031). [After *Ummayah*, its founder.]

um·bel (úmb'l, úm-bel) *n. Botany.* A flat-topped or rounded flower cluster in which the individual flower stalks arise from about the same point as in the carrot and related plants. [New Latin *umbella*, from Latin, an umbrella, diminutive of *umbra*, shadow.]

um·bel·late (úm-bəl-ət, -bel-, -bil-, -it, -ayt, um-bél-) *adj.* Having, forming, or of the nature of an umbel.

um·bel·lif·er (um-béllifər) *n.* Any umbelliferous plant.

um·bel·lif·er·ous (úm-bə-líffərəss, -be-, -bi-) *adj. Botany.* 1. Bearing umbels. 2. Belonging to the plant family Umbelliferae. [New Latin *umbellifer* : *umbella*, UMBEL + -FEROUS.]

um·bel·lule (um-béllewl, úm-bə-lewl, -be-, -bi-) *n.* Also **um·bel·let** (úm-bə-lit, -be-, -bi-, -lét). *Botany.* Any of the smaller secondary umbels forming a compound umbel. [New Latin *umbellula*, diminutive of *umbella*, UMBEL.]

um·ber (úmbər) *n.* 1. A natural brown earth composed of ferric oxide, silica, alumina, lime, and manganese oxides and used as pigment. 2. Any of the shades of brown produced by umber in its various states. ~*tr.v.* **umbered, -bering, -bers.** To coat or colour with or as with umber. [Old French *umbre*, short for *terre d'Umbre*, "earth of Umbria".] —**um·ber** *adj.*

Um·ber·to I (ōom-baírtō) (1844–1900). King of Italy. He succeeded his father, Victor Emmanuel II, in 1878, and led Italy into the Triple Alliance with Austria and Germany (1882). He was assassinated by an anarchist at Monza.

Umberto II (1904–83). Last King of Italy. He became king (May 1946) on the abdication of his father, Victor Emmanuel III, but was forced to abdicate a month later when a national referendum voted for a republic.

um·bil·i·cal (um-bíllik'l, úmbi-lík'l) *adj.* 1. Of, pertaining to, or resembling an umbilicus. 2. Pertaining to or located near the central area of the abdomen. ~*n. Aerospace.* An umbilical cord.

umbilical cord *n.* 1. *Anatomy.* The flexible, cordlike structure connecting the foetus at the navel with the placenta and containing two umbilical arteries and one vein that nourish the foetus and remove its wastes. 2. *Aerospace.* **a.** Any of various external electrical lines or fluid tubes supplying a rocket before launch. **b.** The line that supplies an astronaut with oxygen and in some cases with communications while he is outside the spacecraft. In this sense, also called "umbilical".

um·bil·i·cate (um-bílli-kət, -kit, -kayt) *adj.* Also **um·bil·i·cat·ed** (-kaytid) 1. Having a central mark or depression resembling a navel. 2. Having an umbilicus. —**um·bil·i·ca·tion** (-káysh'n) *n.*

um·bil·i·cus (um-bílli-kəss, úmbi-lí-kəss) *n., pl.* **-ci** (-sī). 1. The navel. 2. *Biology.* Any similar small opening or depression, such as the hollow at the base of the shell of some gastropod molluscs or an opening in the shaft of a feather. [Latin *umbilīcus*; akin to Greek *omphalos*, navel, and UMBO.]

um·ble pie (úmb'l) *n.* A **humble pie** (see).

um·bles (úmb'lz) *Archaic.* Entrails, **numbles** (see).

um·bo (úmbō) *n., pl.* **umbones** (um-bō-neez). 1. A boss or knob at the centre of a shield. 2. *Biology.* A similar knoblike protuberance, such as the central hump on a mushroom cap. 3. *Anatomy.* A small projection at the centre of the outer surface of the tympanic membrane of the ear. [Latin *umbō* (stem *umbōn-*); akin to NAVEL.]

um·bo·nate (úmbə-nət, -nit, -nayt) *adj.* Also **um·bo·nal** (um-bōn'l), **um·bon·ic** (um-bónnik). Having or resembling a knob or knoblike protuberance. [Latin *umbō* (stem *umbōn-*), knob + -ATE.]

um·bra (úm-brə) *n., pl.* **-bras** or **-brae** (-brée). 1. A dark area; specifically, the blackest part of a shadow from which all light is cut off. 2. *Astronomy.* **a.** The shadow region over an area of the Earth where a solar eclipse is total. **b.** The darkest region of a sunspot. [Latin *umbra*, shadow.]

um·brage (úmbrij) *n.* 1. Offence; resentment: *took umbrage at their rudeness.* 2. *Archaic & Poetic.* **a.** Something that affords shade. **b.** Shadow or shade. 3. *Archaic.* A shadowy or indistinct indication; a hint. [Middle English, shade, from Old French, from Vulgar Latin *umbrāticum* (unattested), neuter of Latin *umbrāticus*, of a shadow, from *umbra*, shadow, UMBRA.]

um·bra·geous (um-bráyjəss) *adj.* 1. Affording or forming shade; shady or shading. 2. Inclined to take umbrage; touchy. —**um·bra·geous·ly** *adv.* —**um·bra·geous·ness** *n.*

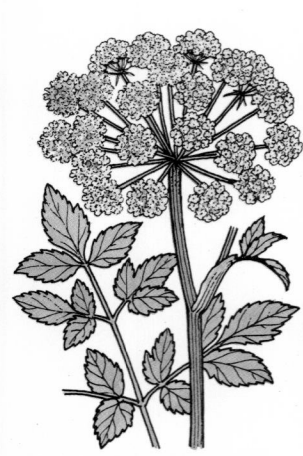

umbel *The flower heads of wild angelica* Angelica sylvestris *are arranged on spokes that spread from the central stem. The parsley family, of which angelica is a member, is known to botanists as the Umbelliferae or "umbel-bearers" because of this umbrella-like arrangement.*

um·brel·la (um-bréllə) *n.* **1.** A device for protection from the weather consisting of a collapsible canopy mounted on a central rod. **2.** Anything that covers or protects. **3.** *Military.* An air **cover** (see). **4.** An all-encompassing category, organisation, or authority by means of which many different things or groups are linked. **5.** *Zoology.* The contractile gelatinous, rounded mass constituting the major part of the body of most jellyfishes. ~*adj.* Covering or encompassing a wide variety of things: *an umbrella term.* [Italian *ombrella,* diminutive of *ombra,* shade, from Latin *umbra.*]

umbrella bird *n.* Any of several tropical American birds of the genus *Cephalopterus;* especially, *C. ornatus,* having a retractile black crest and a long, feathered wattle.

umbrella tree *n.* **1.** Any of several trees of the genus *Magnolia,* of the southeastern United States; especially, *M. tripetala,* having large leaves clustered in an umbrella-like form at the ends of the branches. **2.** Any of several other trees having leaves growing in an umbrella-like cluster.

Um·bri·a (úm-bri-ə; *Italian* ŏŏm-). Largely mountainous region of central Italy, comprising the provinces of Perugia and Terni. The principal town is Perugia. It gets its name from the tribe called the Umbri, who settled in the region in the 7th century B.C.

Um·bri·an (úmbri-ən) *adj.* **1.** Of or pertaining to Umbria or its people, culture, dialect, or ancient language. **2.** Designating a Renaissance school of painting which included Perugino and Raphael. ~*n.* **1.** An inhabitant or native of ancient or modern Umbria. **2.** The extinct Italic language of ancient Umbria.

u·mi·ak, oo·mi·ak (ŏŏmi-ak) *n.* A large open Eskimo boat made of skins stretched on a wooden frame, usually propelled by paddles. Compare **kayak.** [Eskimo.]

um·laut (ŏŏm-lowt) *n. Linguistics.* **1.** A change in a vowel sound caused by partial assimilation to a vowel or semivowel, originally occurring in the following syllable, now usually lost. An example in English *bed,* produced by umlaut from the earlier Germanic form in Gothic *badi.* Also called "vowel mutation". Compare **ablaut. 2.** A vowel sound changed in this manner, such as the German *ä, ö,* or *ü.* **3.** The diacritical mark (¨) placed over a vowel to indicate an umlaut, especially in German. —See **diaeresis.** ~*tr.v.* **umlauted, -lauting, -lauts. 1.** To modify (a vowel sound) by umlaut. 2 To write or print (a vowel) with an umlaut. [German *Umlaut : um-,* prefix indicating alteration, "around", from Middle High German *um(b)-,* from *umbe,* from Old High German *umbi + Laut,* sound, from Middle High German *lūt,* from Old High German *hlūt.*]

um·pire (úm-pīr) *n.* **1.** A person appointed to make rulings and control the progress of the game in various sports, especially tennis, cricket, and baseball. Compare **referee. 2.** A person selected or empowered to settle a dispute between other persons or groups. **3.** A judge; an arbiter. —See Synonyms at **judge.** ~*v.* **umpired, -piring, -pires.** —*tr.* To act as umpire in or of; referee; arbitrate. —*intr.* To be or act as an umpire. [Middle English *(an) oumpere,* originally *(a) noumpere,* (an) umpire, from Old French *nomper, nonper,* "non-peer" (that is, not a contestant but a third person called in to arbitrate) : *non-,* not + *per,* match, equal, PEER.] —**um·pir·age** (-ij), **um·pire·ship** (-ship) *n.*

ump·teen (úmp-téen, úm-) *adj. Informal.* Large but indefinite in number: *umpteen reasons; umpteen guests.* [Humorous term based on -TEEN; *umpty,* Morse code signaller's term for *dash,* also meaning a great number (through association with numerals in -TY.] —**ump·teen** *pron.* —**ump·teenth** *adj.*

Um·ta·li (ŏŏm-táali). City in eastern Zimbabwe, near the border with Mozambique. Its scenic mountain setting makes it a popular tourist town.

un-[1] *prefix.* Indicates not or contrary to; for example, **unhappy.** *Note:* Many compounds other than those entered here may be formed with *un-.* In forming compounds, *un-* is normally joined with the following element without space or a hyphen: *unnamed.* However, if the second element begins with a capital letter, it is separated with a hyphen: *un-American.* [Middle English *un-,* Old English *un-.*]

un-[2] *prefix.* Indicates: **1.** Reversal of an action; for example, **unlock, unmake. 2.** Deprivation; for example, **unman, unsex, unfrock. 3.** Release or removal from; for example, **unearth, unyoke, unhorse. 4.** Intensified action; for example, **unloose.** [Middle English *un-,* Old English *un-,* variant of *ond-, and-,* against.]

Usage: The prefixes *non-, un-,* and *in-* are all used in combination to indicate negation. It often happens that two of these prefixes can be applied to the same adjective, with a resulting difference of emphasis in each case. *Non-* tends to suggest simply the absence or irrelevance of the quality conveyed by the original adjective, and is therefore fairly neutral and literal in force. *Un-* and *in-* (including its assimilated forms *il-, im-,* and *ir-*) tend to suggest the contrary of the desired or expected qualities conveyed by the original adjective and has a more strongly negative and derogatory force. Thus *nonscientific* and *nonhuman* apply to matters unrelated to the realm of the scientific or the human, whereas *unscientific* and *inhuman* suggest the contrary of normal standards of scientific or human conduct. However, this distinction applies only when both negative forms of an adjective are in current usage.

'un, un (ən, 'n) *pron. Informal & Regional.* One; a person, animal, or thing of a specified kind: *She's a good 'un.* [Weak form of **one.**]

UN, U.N. United Nations.

UNA United Nations Association (in the United Kingdom).

un·a·bashed (ún-ə-básht) *adj.* Not disconcerted or embarrassed; poised. —**un·a·bash·ed·ly** (-báshid-li, -básht-) *adv.*

un·a·bat·ed (ún-ə-báytid) *adj.* With no loss of force or intensity: *They fought with unabated violence.* —**un·a·bat·ed·ly** *adv.*

un·a·ble (un-áyb'l, ún-) *adj.* **1.** Lacking the necessary power, authority, or means; not able. **2.** Lacking mental or physical capability or efficiency: *unable to walk.*

un·a·bridged (ún-ə-bríjd) *adj.* Having the original content; not condensed or shortened. Said of books, documents, or the like.

un·ac·cent·ed (ún-ak-séntid, -ək- || -ák-sentid) *adj.* **1.** Having no diacritical mark. Said of a word, syllable, or letter. **2.** Having weak stress or no stress, or lacking some other specific phonological feature. Said of a speech segment or syllable.

un·ac·com·pa·nied (ún-ə-kúmpə-nid, -kúmp- || -need) *adj.* **1.** Not accompanied: *unaccompanied luggage.* **2.** *Music.* Solo; without accompaniment.

un·ac·com·plished (ún-ə-kúm-plisht, -kóm-) *adj.* **1.** Not completed or done; unfinished. **2.** Lacking accomplishments.

un·ac·count·a·ble (ún-ə-kównt-əb'l) *adj.* **1.** Not able to be accounted for; inexplicable; mysterious. **2.** Not liable to be held to account; not accountable. —**un·ac·count·a·bil·i·ty** (-ə-bílləti), —**un·ac·count·a·ble·ness** *n.* —**un·ac·count·a·bly** *adv.*

un·ac·count·ed-for (ún-ə-kównt-id-fawr) *adj.* **1.** Not explained, understood, or taken into account; inexplicable or unexpected. **2.** Missing or absent without explanation, as from a roll call or after a military operation.

un·ac·cus·tomed (ún-ə-kústəmd) *adj.* **1.** Not used to; not accustomed. Used with *to.* **2.** Unfamiliar: *unaccustomed surroundings.*

u·na cor·da (ŏŏnə kórdə) *adv. Music.* With the soft pedal depressed. Used as a direction to a pianist. [Italian, "one string" (the action of the pedal causes one piano string to be struck instead of three.)]

un·a·dop·ted (ún-ə-dóptid) *adj.* **1.** Not adopted. Said of a child. **2.** *British.* Not maintained by a local authority. Said of a road.

un·a·dorned (ún-ə-dórnd) *adj.* Without embellishment or artificiality; simple; natural.

un·a·dul·ter·at·ed (ún-ə-dúltə-raytid) *adj.* **1.** Not mingled or diluted with extraneous matter; pure. **2.** Out-and-out; utter.

un·ad·vised (ún-əd-vízd || -ad-) *adj.* **1.** Having received no advice; not informed. **2.** Ill-advised; rash; imprudent. —**un·ad·vis·ed·ly** (-vízid-li) *adv.* —**un·ad·vis·ed·ness** *n.*

un·af·fect·ed[1] (ún-ə-féktid) *adj.* Not changed, modified, or affected.

unaffected[2] *adj.* Without pretension; sincere; genuine. —See Synonyms at **naive, sincere.** —**un·af·fect·ed·ly** *adv.* —**un·af·fect·ed·ness** *n.*

un·al·loyed (ún-ə-lóyd) *adj.* **1.** Not in mixture with other metals; pure. **2.** Complete; unqualified: *an unalloyed success.*

un·a·neled (ún-ə-néeld) *adj. Archaic.* Not having received extreme unction.

u·nan·i·mous (yŏŏ-nánnimӘss) *adj.* **1.** Sharing the same opinions or views; being in complete harmony or accord. **2.** Based on or characterised by complete assent or agreement. [Latin *ūnanimus,* "of one mind" : *ūnus,* one + *animus,* soul, mind.] —**u·na·nim·i·ty** (yŏŏ-nə-nímmԥti, -na-), **u·nan·i·mous·ness** *n.* —**u·nan·i·mous·ly** *adv.*

un·an·swer·a·ble (un-áan-sԥr-əb'l, ún- || -án-) *adj.* **1.** Impossible to answer. Said of a question. **2.** Irrefutable; incontrovertible.

un·ap·peal·a·ble (ún-ə-péeləb'l) *adj. Law.* Not subject to appeal.

un·ap·proach·a·ble (ún-ə-próch-əb'l) *adj.* **1.** Not friendly; aloof; distant. **2.** Not accessible; inapproachable. —**un·ap·proach·a·bil·i·ty** (-ə-bílləti), **un·ap·proach·a·ble·ness** *n.* —**un·ap·proach·a·bly** *adv.*

un·apt (ún-ápt) *adj.* **1.** Not suitable or appropriate; inapt. Often used with *for.* **2.** Not likely; not liable. Used with *to.* **3.** Slow-witted; stupid. —**un·apt·ly** *adv.* —**un·apt·ness** *n.*

un·arm (ún-árm) *tr.v.* **-armed, -arming, -arms.** *Archaic.* To divest of armour or arms; especially, to assist in taking off armour.

un·armed (ún-ármd) *adj.* **1.** Lacking weapons or armour; defenceless. **2.** *Biology.* Having no thorns or spines. **3.** Not fitted with a detonator. Said of a bomb, missile, or other explosive device.

un·a·shamed (ún-ə-sháymd) *adj.* **1.** Open and without restraint or embarrassment: *unashamed luxury.* **2.** Not feeling or revealing any remorse, shame, or need for apology. —**un·a·sham·ed·ly** (-sháy-mid-li) *adv.* —**un·a·sham·ed·ness** *n.*

un·asked (ún-áaskt || -áskt) *adj.* **1.** Uninvited. **2.** Not requested or demanded.

un·as·sail·a·ble (ún-ə-sáyl-əb'l) *adj.* **1.** Not capable of being disputed or disproven; undeniable; unquestionable. **2.** Not capable of being attacked or seized successfully; impregnable. —**un·as·sail·a·bil·i·ty** (-ə-bílləti), **un·as·sail·a·ble·ness** *n.* —**un·as·sail·a·bly** *adv.*

un·as·sum·ing (ún-ə-séwm-ing, -sŏŏm- || -shŏŏm-) *adj.* Not pretentious, boastful, or ostentatious; modest. —**un·as·sum·ing·ly** *adv.* —**un·as·sum·ing·ness** *n.*

un·at·tached (ún-ə-tácht) *adj.* **1.** Not attached or joined, especially to surrounding tissue. **2. a.** Not committed to or dependent upon a person, group, or organisation. **b.** Not engaged, married, or involved in a serious sexual or romantic relationship. **3.** *Law.* Not possessed or seized as security.

un·at·tend·ed (ún-ə-téndid) *adj.* **1.** Not being attended to, looked after, or watched. **2.** Without attendants; not in company; alone. **3.** Not being paid attention to or listened to.

un·at·test·ed (ún-ə-téstid) *adj.* Not attested. Used in linguistic descriptions, as in the etymologies of this dictionary, to designate a

---

form whose existence is not established by documentary evidence but is reliably inferred from comparative evidence.

u·nau (yōo-now, ōo-, -naw) *n.* A two-toed **sloth** (*see*).

un·a·vail·ing (ún-ə-váyling) *adj.* Having no effect; achieving nothing; futile. **—un·a·vail·ing·ly** *adv.*

u·na vo·ce (yōonə vōsi, ōo-naa vō-chay) *adv. Latin.* With one voice; unanimously.

un·a·void·a·ble (ún-ə-vóyd-əb'l) *adj.* 1. Not able to be avoided; inevitable. 2. *Law.* Not able to be voided or nullified. **—un·a·void·a·bil·i·ty** (-bílləti-ə), **un·a·void·a·ble·ness** *n.* **—un·a·void·a·bly** *adv.*

un·a·ware (ún-ə-waír) *adj.* Not aware or cognisant. *~adv.* Unawares.

un·a·wares (ún-ə-waírz) *adv.* 1. By surprise; unexpectedly. 2. Without knowledge or plan: *We came upon it unawares.* [Middle English *unwares,* variant of *unware* (adverb), Old English *unwær* : UN- + AWARE + -s (adverbial suffix).]

un·backed (ún-bákt) *adj.* 1. Lacking backing or support. 2. Designating a candidate, horse, or the like on which no bets are placed. 3. Not having a back, as a bench. 4. Never ridden. Said of a horse.

un·bal·ance (ún-bál-ənss, un-) *tr.v.* **-anced, -ancing, -ances.** 1. To upset the balance, stability, or equilibrium of. 2. To derange. *~n.* The condition of being unbalanced; lack of balance.

un·bal·anced (ún-bál-ənst, un-) *adj.* 1. Not balanced. 2. a. Mentally deranged. b. Not of sound judgment; erratic; irrational. 3. Not satisfactorily adjusted, so that debit and credit do not correspond. Said of an account.

un·bar (ún-bár) *tr.v.* **-barred, -barring, -bars.** To remove the bar or bars from; unlock; open.

un·bat·ed (ún-báytid) *adj.* 1. Unabated. 2. *Archaic.* Not blunted by a guard on the tip. Said of a fencing foil, sword, or the like.

un·bear·a·ble (un-baír-əb'l, ún-) *adj.* Not able to be endured; intolerable. **—un·bear·a·bly** *adv.*

un·beat·a·ble (un-béetəb'l, ún-) *adj.* 1. Unable to be surpassed or defeated. 2. First-rate; excellent. **—un·beat·a·bly** *adv.*

un·beat·en (ún-béet'n, ún-) *adj.* 1. a. Undefeated. b. Not broken. Said of a record, as in sports. 2. Untrodden.

un·be·com·ing (ún-bi-kúmming, -bə-) *adj.* 1. Not appropriate, attractive, or flattering: *an unbecoming dress.* 2. Not seemly; indecorous; improper: *an unbecoming remark.* —See Synonyms at **improper. —un·be·com·ing·ly** *adv.* **un·be·com·ing·ness** *n.*

un·be·got·ten (ún-bi-gótt'n, -bə-) *adj.* 1. Not yet begotten; as yet unborn. 2. Self-existent; eternal.

un·be·known (ún-bi-nṓn, -bə-) *adv.* Also **un·be·knownst** (-nṓnst). Without the knowledge of. Usually used with *to.* *~adj.* Not known. Usually used with *to.* [UN- + obsolete *beknown,* known, Middle English *beknowen,* past participle of *beknowen,* to get to know, Old English *becnāwan* : BE- + *cnāwan,* KNOW.]

un·be·lief (ún-bi-léef, -bə-) *n.* Lack of belief or faith, especially in religious matters.

un·be·liev·a·ble (ún-bi-léev-əb'l, -bə-) *adj.* Incapable of being believed; incredible. **—un·be·liev·a·bil·i·ty** (-ə-bílləti), **un·be·liev·a·ble·ness** *n.* **—un·be·liev·a·bly** *adv.*

un·be·liev·er (ún-bi-léevər) *n.* One who lacks belief or faith, especially in a particular religion.

un·be·liev·ing (ún-bi-léeving, -bə-) *adj.* Lacking belief; sceptical, especially in religious matters. **—un·be·liev·ing·ly** *adv.*

un·bend (ún-bénd) *v.* **-bent** (-bént), **-bending, -bends.** —*tr.* 1. To relax; release from mental tension, strain, or formality. 2. To release (a bow, for example) from flexure or tension. 3. *Nautical.* To untie or loosen (a rope or sail). 4. To straighten (something crooked or bent). —*intr.* 1. To become less tense; relax. 2. To become less strict or less formal. 3. To become straight.

un·bend·ing (ún-bénding) *adj.* 1. Unyielding or uncompromising. 2. Stern or severe. **—un·bend·ing·ly** *adv.* **—un·bend·ing·ness** *n.*

un·bi·ased (ún-bī́-əst) *adj.* Without bias or prejudice; impartial. See Synonyms at **fair. —un·bi·ased·ly** *adv.* **—un·bi·ased·ness** *n.*

un·bid·den (ún-bídd'n) *adj.* 1. Not commanded; voluntary. 2. Not invited; unasked: *unbidden company.*

un·bind (ún-bínd) *tr.v.* **-bound** (-bównd), **-binding, -binds.** 1. To untie or unfasten (wrappings or bindings, for example). 2. To release from restraints or bonds; free.

un·birth·day (ún-búrth-di, -day) *n. Informal.* Any day that is not one's birthday. Also used adjectively: *an unbirthday party.*

un·blessed (ún-blést) *adj.* 1. Deprived of a blessing. 2. Unholy; evil. **—un·bless·ed·ness** (-bléssid-) *n.*

un·blink·ing (ún-blíngking, un-) *adj.* 1. Without blinking. 2. Without visible emotion. 3. Fearless in facing reality. **—un·blink·ing·ly** *adv.*

un·blown (ún-blṓn) *adj.* Unopened. Said of a flower.

un·blush·ing (ún-blúshing, un-) *adj.* 1. Without shame or embarrassment. 2. Not blushing. —See Synonyms at **shameless. —un·blush·ing·ly** *adv.*

un·bolt (ún-bṓlt ‖ -bólt) *tr.v.* **-bolted, -bolting, -bolts.** To release the bolts of (a door or gate); unlock.

un·bolt·ed (ún-bṓlt-id ‖ -bólt-) *adj.* Not sifted. Said of flour, grain, or the like.

un·born (ún-bórn) *adj.* Not yet in existence; not yet born.

un·bos·om (ún-bōóz'm, un- ‖ -bōóz'm) *v.* **-omed, -oming, -oms.** —*tr.* 1. To confide (one's thoughts or feelings). 2. To relieve (oneself) of troublesome thoughts or feelings. —*intr.* To reveal one's thoughts or feelings.

un·bound (ún-bównd, un-) Past tense and past participle of **unbind.**

~adj. 1. Not bound. Said of a book. 2. Free from bonds or shackles; unconfined. 2. *Linguistics.* Designating a morpheme that is or can be a full and independent word when standing alone.

un·bound·ed (ún-bównd-id, un-) *adj.* 1. Having no boundaries or limits. 2. Not kept within bounds; unrestrained: *unbounded enthusiasm.* **—un·bound·ed·ly** *adv.* **—un·bound·ed·ness** *n.*

un·bowed (ún-bówd, un-) *adj.* 1. Not bowed; not bent. 2. Not subdued; unyielding: *The warriors returned bloody but unbowed.*

un·brace (ún-bráyss) *tr.v.* **-braced, -bracing, -braces.** 1. To set free by removing bands or braces. 2. To release from tension; relax. 3. To weaken; make slack.

un·bred (ún-bréd) *adj.* 1. Not taught or instructed; untaught. 2. *Archaic.* Ill-bred; impolite.

un·bri·dle (ún-brīd'l, un-) *tr.v.* **-dled, -dling, -dles.** 1. To take the bridle off (a horse). 2. To remove restraints from; free.

un·bri·dled (ún-brīd'ld, un-) *adj.* 1. Not wearing or fitted with a bridle. 2. Unrestrained; uncontrolled. **—un·bri·dled·ly** *adv.*

un·bro·ken (ún-brṓkən, un-) *adj.* 1. Not broken or tampered with; intact. 2. Not violated or breached. 3. Uninterrupted; continuous; even. 4. Not tamed; not trained to accept a harness. Said of a horse. 5. Not disordered or disturbed. 6. Not surpassed. Said of a record, as in sports. **—un·bro·ken·ly** *adv.* **—un·bro·ken·ness** *n.*

un·buck·le (ún-búck'l, un-) *tr.v.* **-led, -ling, -les.** 1. To loosen or undo the buckle or buckles of. 2. To remove by unbuckling.

un·bur·den (ún-búrd'n, un-) *tr.v.* **-dened, -dening, -dens.** To free from or relieve of a burden or trouble: *unburden one's mind.*

un·but·ton (ún-bútt'n, un-) *v.* **-toned, -toning, -tons.** —*tr.* 1. To unfasten the button or buttons of. 2. To free or remove (a button) from a buttonhole. 3. To make informal or relaxed. —*intr.* 1. To undo a button or buttons. 2. To relax.

un·called-for (ún-káwld-fawr, un-) *adj.* 1. Unwarranted; impertinent; unnecessary. 2. Not required or requested.

un·can·ny (un-kánni, ún-) *adj.* **-nier, -niest.** 1. So unexpected as to seem preternatural: *She bore an uncanny resemblance to my sister.* 2. Exciting wonder and fear; strange: *an uncanny laugh.* —See Synonyms at **weird. —un·can·ni·ly** *adv.* **—un·can·ni·ness** *n.*

un·cap (ún-káp, un-) *v.* **-capped, -capping, -caps.** —*tr.* To remove the cap or covering of (a container). —*intr.* To remove one's head covering as a sign of deference.

un·cared-for (ún-kaírd-fawr, un-) *adj.* Not looked after; neglected.

un·car·ing (ún-kaíring, un-) *adj.* Devoid of concern or sympathy.

un·ceas·ing (ún-séessing, un-) *adj.* Not ceasing or letting up; continuous. **—un·ceas·ing·ly** *adv.* **—un·ceas·ing·ness** *n.*

un·cer·e·mo·ni·ous (ún-sérri-mṓni-əss) *adj.* 1. Without the due formalities; abrupt; rude. 2. Not ceremonious; informal. **—un·cer·e·mo·ni·ous·ly** *adv.* **—un·cer·e·mo·ni·ous·ness** *n.*

un·cer·tain (un-sér·t'n, ún-, -tin) *adj.* 1. Not known or established; questionable; doubtful: *an uncertain outcome.* 2. Not determined; vague; undecided: *uncertain plans.* 3. Not having sure knowledge. 4. Subject to change; variable: *uncertain weather.* 5. Unsteady; fitful: *uncertain light.* **—un·cer·tain·ly** *adv.*

un·cer·tain·ty (un-sér·t'n-ti, ún-, -tin-) *n., pl.* **-ties.** Also **un·cer·tain·ness** (for sense 1). 1. The condition of being in doubt; lack of certainty. 2. Something that is uncertain.

  Synonyms: uncertainty, doubt, dubiety, scepticism.

uncertainty principle *n.* The principle in quantum mechanics that the product of the uncertainties in the values of certain related variables, as of the position and momentum of a particle, is greater than or equal to Planck's constant divided by 4π. Also called "Heisenberg uncertainty principle".

un·chain (ún-cháyn) *tr.v.* **-chained, -chaining, -chains.** To release from or as if from a chain or bond; set free.

un·chan·cy (un-cháan-si, ún- ‖ -chán-) *adj. Scottish.* 1. Unlucky; ill-fated. 2. Threatening; dangerous. [UN- (not) + CHANCY (in obsolete sense, "lucky").]

un·charged (ún-chárjd) *adj.* 1. Not loaded. Said of a weapon. 2. *Law.* a. Not subject to a charge. Said of land. b. Not formally accused. 3. Lacking electric charge.

un·char·i·ta·ble (ún-chárritəb'l, un-) *adj.* Not charitable or generous; unkind; judging harshly. **—un·char·i·ta·ble·ness** *n.* **—un·char·i·ta·bly** *adv.*

un·chart·ed (ún-chártid, un-) *adj.* Not charted or recorded on or as if on a map or plan; unexplored; unknown.

un·chaste (ún-cháyst, un-) *adj.* Not chaste or modest. **—un·chaste·ly** *adv.* **—un·chaste·ness, un·chas·ti·ty** (-chástəti) *n.*

un·chris·tian (ún-kríst-yən, un-, -kríss-chən) *adj.* 1. Not in accordance with the spirit or principles of Christianity; especially, lacking any consideration for one's fellow human beings. 2. Not Christian; heathen. 3. *Informal.* Uncivilised; barbarous.

un·church (ún-chúrch) *tr.v.* **-churched, -churching, -churches.** 1. To expel from a church or from church membership; excommunicate. 2. To deprive (a congregation, sect, or building) of the status of a church.

un·cial (ún-si-əl, -shi-, -sh'l) *adj. Sometimes capital* **U.** Of, pertaining to, or designating a style of writing characterised by fairly rounded capital letters and found especially in Greek and Latin manuscripts of the fourth to the ninth century A.D. It provided the model from which most of the capital letters in the modern Roman alphabet are derived. *~n. Sometimes capital* **U.** 1. The uncial style or hand. 2. An uncial letter or manuscript. [Late Latin *unciālēs (litterae),* "letters of an inch long" (applied loosely by St. Jerome to uncial letters), plural of

Latin *unciālis,* of an inch, from *uncia,* a twelfth part, ounce, inch, from *ūnus,* one.]

un·ci·form (ún-si-fawrm) *adj.* Hook-shaped.
~*n.* Any hook-shaped part or structure; especially, the **hamate bone** *(see).* In this sense, also called "uniform bone". [New Latin *unciformis* : Latin *uncus,* hook + -FORM.]

un·ci·nate (ún-si-nət, -nit, -nayt) *adj.* 1. Hooked at the tip. 2. Of or possessing uncini. [Latin *uncīnātus,* from *uncīnus,* hook, UNCINUS.]

un·ci·nus (un-sī-nəss) *n., pl.* **-ni** (-nī). A small hooklike structure, such as any of the setae of certain annelid worms. [New Latin, from Latin, hook, barb, from *uncus,* hook.]

un·cir·cum·cised (ún-súrkəm-sīzd) *adj.* 1. Not circumcised. 2. Not Jewish; Gentile. 3. Heathen. 4. Spiritually impure. —**un·cir·cum·ci·sion** (-sízh'n) *n.*

un·civ·il (ún-sívv'l, un-, -sívvil) *adj.* 1. Impolite; discourteous; rude. 2. *Archaic.* Uncivilised; barbarous. —**un·civ·il·ly** *adv.*

un·civ·i·lised (ún-sívv'l-īzd, un-, -sívvil-) *adj.* 1. Not civilised; barbarous. 2. Lacking education, manners, culture, or sophistication.

un·clad (ún-kládd) *adj.* Not wearing clothes; naked.

un·clasp (ún-klaásp ‖ -klásp) *v.* **-clasped, -clasping, -clasps.** —*tr.* 1. To release or loosen the clasp of. 2. To release or loosen from a grasp or embrace. —*intr.* To release or relax a clasp or grasp.

un·class·i·fied (ún-klássi-fīd, un-) *adj.* 1. Not placed or included in order or in a class or category. 2. Not classified for security purposes. Said of information.

un·cle (úngk'l) *n.* 1. *Abbr.* **u., U. a.** The brother of one's mother or father. **b.** The husband of one's aunt. **c.** Any close adult male friend of one's parents. In both senses often used with a Christian name as a title or form of address. —**my uncle.** *Slang.* The pawnbroker. [Middle English *uncle,* from Old French *oncle,* from Late Latin *aunculus,* variant of Latin *avunculus,* maternal uncle, diminutive of *avus,* grandfather.]

un·clean (ún-kléen, un-) *adj.* **-cleaner, -cleanest.** 1. Not clean; foul or dirty. 2. Morally defiled; unchaste. 3. Ceremonially impure. —**un·clean·ly** *adv.* —**un·clean·ness** *n.*

un·clear (ún-kléer) *adj.* **-clearer, -clearest.** Not clearly defined; confused or ambiguous.

un·clench (ún-klénch) *v.* **-clenched, -clenching, -clenches.** —*tr.* To loosen from a clenched position; relax; open: *unclench one's fists.* —*intr.* To become unclenched.

Uncle Sam *n. Abbr.* **U.S.** A personification of the U.S. Government, represented as a tall, thin man with a white beard and wearing a blue tailcoat, red-and-white-striped trousers, and a tall hat with a band of stars. [Extension from *U.S.* (for *United States*); said to be a jocular interpretation of this abbreviation (stamped on U.S. Army supply packages during the War of 1812).]

Uncle Tom *n. Chiefly U.S.* 1. A black person who is held to be humiliatingly subservient or deferential to whites. 2. Any person regarded as a traitor to his own group by excessive tolerance of or cooperation with the oppressors of that group. [After the black slave in *Uncle Tom's Cabin* (1851–52), novel by Harriet Beecher Stowe.]

un·clog (ún-klóg) *tr.v.* **-clogged, -clogging, -clogs.** To clear a blockage from (a drain, for example).

un·close (ún-klŏz) *v.* **-closed, -closing, -closes.** —*tr.* To open or disclose. —*intr.* To become opened or disclosed.

un·clothe (ún-klŏth) *tr.v.* **-clothed** or **-clad** (-kládd), **-clothing, -clothes.** To remove the clothing or cover from; strip.

un·co (úngkō) *adj. Scottish.* 1. Unusual; odd; striking. 2. Mysterious; uncanny.
~*n., pl.* **uncos.** *Scottish.* 1. An unusual or amazing person. 2. A stranger. 3. *Plural.* News.
~*adv. Scottish.* To an excessive degree; remarkably. [Middle English (Scottish) *unkow,* variant of UNCOUTH.]

un·coil (ún-kóyl) *v.* **-coiled, -coiling, -coils.** —*tr.* To unwind; untwist. —*intr.* To become unwound or untwisted.

un·com·fort·a·ble (un-kúmf-təb'l, -kúmfər-) *adj.* 1. Experiencing physical discomfort. 2. Uneasy; ill-at-ease. 3. Causing anxiety; disquieting. —**un·com·fort·a·ble·ness** *n.* —**un·com·fort·a·bly** *adv.*

un·com·mer·cial (ún-kə-mérsh'l) *adj.* 1. Not engaged in or involving trade or commerce. 2. Not in accordance with the spirit or methods of commerce; not businesslike. 3. Not commercially viable; uneconomical.

un·com·mit·ted (ún-kə-míttid) *adj.* Not pledged to a specific cause or course of action.

un·com·mon (un-kómmən, ún-) *adj.* **-moner, -monest.** 1. Not common; unusual; rare. 2. Wonderful; remarkable. 3. Unusually large or intense.
~*adv. Archaic & Regional.* Uncommonly. —**un·com·mon·ness** *n.*

un·com·mon·ly (un-kómmənli) *adv.* 1. In a manner or to a degree that is not common or usual. 2. Used as an intensive: *That chap was uncommonly polite.*

un·com·mu·ni·ca·tive (ún-kə-méwni-kətiv, -kaytiv) *adj.* Not disposed to be communicative; taciturn; reserved. —**un·com·mu·ni·ca·tive·ly** *adv.* —**un·com·mu·ni·ca·tive·ness** *n.*

un·com·pro·mis·ing (un-kómprə-mīzing, ún-) *adj.* Not making concessions; inflexible; rigid. —**un·com·pro·mis·ing·ly** *adv.*

un·con·cern (ún-kən-sérn ‖ -kon-) *n.* 1. Lack of interest; indifference; apathy. 2. Lack of concern or apprehensiveness.

un·con·cerned (ún-kən-sérnd ‖ -kon-) *adj.* 1. Not interested; indifferent. 2. Not anxious or apprehensive; unworried. —See Synonyms at **indifferent.** —**un·con·cern·ed·ly** (-sérnid-li) *adv.* —**un·con·cern·ed·ness** *n.*

un·con·di·tion·al (ún-kən-dísh'n'l ‖ -kon-) *adj.* Without conditions or limitations; absolute. —**un·con·di·tion·al·ly** *adv.*

un·con·di·tioned (ún-kən-dísh'nd ‖ -kon-) *adj.* 1. Unconditional; absolute; unrestricted. 2. *Psychology.* Not resulting from conditioning or learning; reflex or instinctive.

unconditioned response *n.* A response evoked by a stimulus independently of any learning or conditioning process. Formerly called "unconditioned reflex".

un·con·form·a·ble (ún-kən-fórm-əb'l ‖ -kon-) *adj.* 1. Not conforming or capable of conforming. 2. *Geology.* Showing unconformity. —**un·con·form·a·bil·i·ty** (-ə-bílləti), **un·con·form·a·ble·ness** *n.* —**un·con·form·a·bly** *adv.*

un·con·for·mi·ty (ún-kən-fórməti ‖ -kon-) *n., pl.* **-ties.** 1. Lack of conformity; nonconformity. 2. *Geology.* An eroded space, or space caused by lack of deposit, that separates younger strata from older rocks. Compare **disconformity.**

un·con·nect·ed (ún-kə-néktid) *adj.* 1. Not joined or connected. 2. Not coherent; disconnected. —**un·con·nect·ed·ly** *adv.* —**un·con·nect·ed·ness** *n.*

un·con·quer·a·ble (ún-kóngkərəb'l) *adj.* Incapable of being overcome or defeated.

un·con·scion·a·ble (ún-kónsh'n-əb'l) *adj.* 1. Not restrained by conscience; unscrupulous. 2. Beyond prudence or reason; immoderate; excessive. —**un·con·scion·a·ble·ness** *n.* —**un·con·scion·a·bly** *adv.*

un·con·scious (un-kónshəss, ún-) *adj.* 1. Completely lacking in awareness, as in a coma or deep sleep. 2. Without conscious awareness. 3. *Psychology.* Pertaining to or originating in the unconscious; unavailable for direct conscious scrutiny: *unconscious resentment.* 4. Not consciously intended; involuntary.
~*n. Psychology.* The division of the psyche not subject to direct conscious observation but inferred from its effects on conscious processes and behaviour. Preceded by *the.* —See Usage note at **conscious.** —**un·con·scious·ly** *adv.* —**un·con·scious·ness** *n.*

un·con·sid·ered (ún-kən-síddərd ‖ -kon-) *adj.* 1. Not reasoned or considered; rash: *an unconsidered remark.* 2. Not taken into account; disregarded.

un·con·sti·tu·tion·al (ún-kón-sti-téwsh'n-'l ‖ -tóosh'n-) *adj.* Not in accord with or not permitted by the principles set forth in a constitution. —**un·con·sti·tu·tion·al·i·ty** (-ál-əti) *n.* —**un·con·sti·tu·tion·al·ly** *adv.*

un·con·trol·la·ble (ún-kən-trŏl-əb'l ‖ -kon-) *adj.* Not able to be controlled or governed. —**un·con·trol·la·bil·i·ty** (-ə-bílləti), **un·con·trol·la·ble·ness** *n.* —**un·con·trol·la·bly** *adv.*

un·con·ven·tion·al (ún-kən-vénsh'n-'l ‖ -kon-) *adj.* Not adhering to or in accord with conventional standards, manners, or styles. —**un·con·ven·tion·al·i·ty** (-ál-əti) *n.* —**un·con·ven·tion·al·ly** *adv.*

un·co·or·di·na·ted (ún-kō-órdi-naytid) *adj.* 1. Lacking planning, method, or organisation. 2. Lacking physical or mental coordination. —**un·co·or·di·na·ted·ly** *adv.*

un·cork (ún-kórk) *tr.v.* **-corked, -corking, -corks.** 1. To draw the cork from. 2. To free from a sealed or constrained state: *uncork feelings of anger.*

un·count·a·ble (ún-kównt-əb'l) *adj.* Not able to be counted; innumerable.

un·count·ed (ún-kównt-id) *adj.* 1. Not counted. 2. Unable to be counted; innumerable: *uncounted hosts of angels.*

un·cou·ple (ún-kúpp'l, un-) *tr.v.* **-pled, -pling, -ples.** 1. To disconnect (something coupled). 2. To release; unleash.

un·couth (un-kóoth, ún-) *adj.* 1. Crude; unrefined; rude. 2. Awkward or clumsy; ungraceful: *an uncouth gait.* 3. *Archaic.* Foreign; unfamiliar. [Middle English *unc(o)uth,* unknown, strange, Old English *uncūth* : *un-,* not + *cūth,* known, past participle of *cunnan.*] —**un·couth·ly** *adv.* —**un·couth·ness** *n.*

un·cov·e·nant·ed (ún-kúvvənəntid) *adj.* 1. Not bound by a covenant. 2. Not promised or guaranteed by a covenant. 3. Not approved or permitted by a covenant.

un·cov·er (un-kúvvər, ún-) *v.* **-ered, -ering, -ers.** —*tr.* 1. To remove the cover from; unveil or uncap. 2. To bring to light or disclose; reveal. 3. To remove the hat from (one's head) in respect or reverence. —*intr.* 1. To remove a cover. 2. To bare the head in respect or reverence.

un·cov·ered (ún-kúvvərd, un-) *adj.* 1. Having no cover or protection. 2. Lacking insurance cover. 3. Bareheaded.

un·cross (ún-króss ‖ -kráwss) *tr.v.* **-crossed, -crossing, -crosses.** To move (one's legs, for example) from a crossed position.

un·crowned (ún-krównd) *adj.* 1. Not having yet been crowned. 2. Having the power or influence of a monarch or other prominent figure but not the title.

UNC·TAD (úngk-tad) *n.* United Nations Conference on Trade and Development.

unc·tion (úngksh'n) *n.* 1. The act of anointing as part of a religious, ceremonial, or healing ritual. See **Sacrament of the Sick.** 2. An ointment or oil; a salve. 3. Something that serves to soothe or restore; a balm. 4. Affected, insincere, or exaggerated charm or earnestness; unctuousness. [Middle English, from Latin *unctiō* (stem *unctiōn-*), from *unguere* (past participle *unctus*), to anoint.]

unc·tu·ous (úngk-tew-əss, -choo-) *adj.* 1. Having the quality or characteristics of oil or ointment; greasy; slippery. 2. Containing or composed of oil or fat. 3. Characterised by affected, exaggerated, or insincere charm or earnestness. 4. Abundant in organic materials; soft and rich: *unctuous soil.* [Middle English, from Medieval Latin *unctuōsus,* from Latin *unctum,* ointment, from *unctus,* past

participle of *unguere,* to anoint.] **—unc·tu·os·i·ty** (-óssəti), **unc·tu·ous·ness** *n.* **—unc·tu·ous·ly** *adv.*
un·cus (úngkəss) *n., pl.* **unci** (ún-sī). *Biology.* A hook-shaped part or process; especially, the projection from the lower surface of the cerebrum. [New Latin, from Latin, hook.]
un·cut (ún-kút) *adj.* **1.** Not cut. **2.** Having the page edge not slit or trimmed. Said of a book. **3.** Not ground to a specific shape. Said of a gemstone. **4.** Not condensed, abridged, or shortened, as by editing for the purposes of censorship.
un·damped (ún-dámpt) *adj.* **1.** *Physics.* Not tending towards a state of rest; not damped. Said of oscillations. **2.** Not stifled or discouraged; unchecked: *His ardour was undamped.*
un·daunt·ed (ún-dáwnt-id, un- || -da̋ant-) *adj.* Not discouraged or disheartened; resolute; fearless. See Synonyms at **brave.** **—un·daunt·ed·ly** *adv.* **—un·daunt·ed·ness** *n.*
un·dec·a·gon (un-déckə-gən, -gon) *n.* A polygon having eleven angles and eleven sides. [Latin *undecim,* eleven, after *decagon.*]
un·de·ceive (ún-di-se̋ev) *tr.v.* **-ceived, -ceiving, -ceives.** To free from illusion or deception. **—un·de·ceiv·able** *adj.* **—un·de·ceiv·er** *n.*
un·de·cid·ed (ún-di-sīdid) *adj.* **1.** Not yet determined or settled; open. **2.** Not having reached a decision; uncommitted. **—un·de·cid·ed·ly** *adv.* **—un·de·cid·ed·ness** *n.*
un·de·fend·ed (ún-di-féndid) *adj.* **1.** Not defended. **2.** Without having a defence entered. Said of a lawsuit.
un·de·mon·stra·tive (ún-di-mónstrətiv) *adj.* Not tending to outward expressions of feeling; reserved. **—un·de·mon·stra·tive·ly** *adv.* **—un·de·mon·stra·tive·ness** *n.*
un·de·ni·a·ble (ún-di-nī́-əb'l) *adj.* **1.** Not able to be denied; irrefutable; certain. **2.** Unquestionably good; outstanding; excellent. **—un·de·ni·a·bly** *adv.*
un·der (úndər) *prep.* **1.** In or to a lower position or place than: *a signature under a painting.* **2.** Beneath the surface of: *under the ground.* **3.** Beneath the assumed surface or guise of: *under a false name.* **4.** Less than; smaller than. **5.** Less than the required amount or degree of; less than the standard of: *under voting age.* **6.** Inferior to in quality, status, or rank. **7. a.** Subject to the authority, rule, instruction, or influence of: *under a dictatorship; under the impression that it was already finished.* **b.** During the reign, regime, or government of: *Under Stalin there was little free discussion.* **8.** During the time conventionally assigned to a specified sign of the zodiac: *born under Virgo.* **9.** Undergoing or receiving the effects of: *under intensive care.* **10.** Subject to the restraint or obligation of: *under contract.* **11.** Within the group or classification of: *listed under biology; under the heading of.* **12.** In the process of: *under discussion.* **13.** In view of; because of: *under these conditions.* **14.** With the authorisation of; attested by; by virtue of: *under the king's seal.* **15.** Sowed or planted with: *an acre under oats.* **16.** Powered or propelled by: *under steam.* —See Usage Note at **below.**
~*adv.* **1.** In or into a place below or beneath something. **2.** In or into a subordinate or inferior condition or position. **3.** So as to be submerged or enveloped by something. **4.** *Informal.* In or into a state of unconsciousness. **5.** So as to be less than the required amount or degree. **—go under. 1.** To sink or drown. **2.** To yield or surrender, as to an anaesthetic, for example. **3.** To fail or fall through. Used of a business.
~*adj.* **1.** Located or moving beneath or on the lower surface. **2.** Lower in rank, power, or authority; subordinate; inferior. **3.** Less than is required or customary; substandard. **4.** Lower in amount or degree. [Middle English *under,* Old English *under.*]
under- *prefix.* Indicates: **1.** Location below or under; for example, **underground, underclothes. 2.** Inferiority in rank or importance; for example, **undersecretary. 3.** Degree, rate, or quantity that is lower or less than normal, proper, or sufficient; for example, **underestimate, undernourished. 4.** Secrecy or treachery; for example, **undermine, underhand.** ***Note:*** Many compounds other than those entered here may be formed with *under-.* In forming compounds, *under-* is joined with the following element without space or a hyphen: *underrate; undergrow.* [Middle English *under-,* Old English *under-,* from UNDER.]
un·der·a·chieve (úndər-ə-che̋ev) *intr.v.* **-chieved, -chieving, -chieves.** To perform below an expected level, especially in schoolwork. **—un·der·a·chiev·er** *n.*
un·der·act (úndər-ákt) *v.* **-acted, -acting, -acts.** —*tr.* **1.** To perform (a dramatic role) weakly or feebly. **2.** To understate (a dramatic role) intentionally. —*intr.* To perform a dramatic role weakly or with intentional restraint.
un·der·age (úndər-áyj) *adj.* Below the customary or required age; especially, below the legal age, as for drinking or voting.
un·der·arm[1] (úndər-aarm) *adj.* **1.** Located, placed, or used under the arm. **2.** In or of the armpit.
~*n.* The armpit.
underarm[2] *adj. Sports.* Executed with the hand kept below the level of the shoulder, as when bowling in cricket, or serving in tennis.
~*adv.* With an underarm motion or delivery.
un·der·bel·ly (úndər-belli) *n., pl.* **-lies. 1.** The lowest part of an animal's body. **2.** Any vulnerable or weak part or aspect. Used chiefly in the phrase *soft underbelly.*
un·der·bid (úndər-bíd) *v.* **-bid, -bidding, -bids.** —*tr.* **1.** To bid lower than (a competitor). **2.** In bridge, to bid less than the full value of (one's hand). —*intr.* To make too low a bid. **—un·der·bid·der** *n.*
un·der·bod·y (úndər-boddi) *n.* The underside or lower part, as of an animal's body or a vehicle.

undercroft *The tomb of the Duc de Berry (1340–1416) lies in the undercroft beneath Bourges Cathedral in France.*

un·der·bred (úndər-bréd) *adj.* **1.** Not of pure stock; of mixed breeding. Said of an animal. **2.** Ill-bred; vulgar. Said of a person.
un·der·brush (úndər-brush) *n. Chiefly U.S.* **undergrowth** *(see).*
un·der·bush (úndər-bŏŏsh) *n. Chiefly U.S.* **undergrowth** *(see).*
un·der·buy (úndər-bī) *tr.v.* **-bought** (-báwt), **-buying, -buys. 1.** To buy something at a lower price than (someone else). **2.** To buy for less than the actual value. **3.** To buy an insufficient quantity of.
un·der·cap·i·tal·ise, un·der·cap·i·tal·ize (úndər-káppit'l-īz) *tr.v.* **-ised, -ising, -ises.** To provide (a commercial enterprise or other venture) with insufficient capital for efficiency or viability.
un·der·car·riage (úndər-karrij) *n.* **1.** The landing gear of an aircraft. **2.** The supporting framework of a carriage or other vehicle.
un·der·cart (úndər-kaart) *n. Informal.* The undercarriage of an aircraft.
un·der·charge (úndər-chárj) *v.* **-charged, -charging, -charges.** —*tr.* **1.** To charge (someone) less than is customary or required. **2.** To load (a firearm) with an insufficient charge. —*intr.* To make or levy charges lower than is customary or required.
~*n.* (*also* -chaarj). An insufficient or improper charge.
un·der·clay (úndər-klay) *n.* A grey clay, **fireclay** *(see),* occurring beneath coal seams.
un·der·clothes (úndər-klōthz, -klōz) *pl.n.* Also **un·der·cloth·ing** (-klōthing). **Underwear** *(see).*
un·der·coat (úndər-kōt) *n.* Also **un·der·coat·ing** (-ing) (for senses 3, 4). **1.** A coat worn beneath another coat. **2.** A covering of short hairs or fur concealed by the longer outer hairs of an animal's coat. **3. a.** A coat of paint or sealing material applied to a surface before the topcoat is applied. **b.** The paint or sealing material used for this. **4.** *U.S.* An **underseal** *(see).*
~*tr.v.* **undercoated, -coating, -coats.** To apply an undercoat to.
un·der·cool (úndər-kŏŏl) *tr.v.* **-cooled, -cooling, -cools.** To **supercool** *(see).*
un·der·cov·er (úndər-kúvvər, -kuvvər) *adj.* Performed or acting in secret; especially, concerned with or engaged in espionage or secret inquiries: *an undercover investigation.*
un·der·croft (úndər-kroft || -krawft) *n.* An underground chamber or vault; especially, a crypt. [Middle English *under croft* : UNDER + *croft(e),* vault, from Medieval Latin *crupta,* variant of Latin *crypta,* CRYPT.]
un·der·cur·rent (úndər-kurrənt) *n.* **1.** A current, as of air or water, below another current or beneath a surface. **2.** An underlying feeling, tendency, force, or influence often contrary to what is superficially evident: *quietly but with an undercurrent of passion.*
un·der·cut (úndər-kút) *v.* **-cut, -cutting, -cuts.** —*tr.* **1.** To make a cut under or below. **2.** To cut material away from, as in carving, in order to create an overhang. **3.** To charge less than (a competitor) for goods or services. **4.** To undermine or outmanoeuvre (a rival), as by swift or unexpected action. **5.** To strike (a ball) with backspin by hitting downwards as well as forwards, as in golf and tennis. —*intr.* To undercut someone or something.
~*n.* (-kut). **1.** A cut made in the under part to remove material. **2.** A part so removed. **3.** *Chiefly British.* The tender under part of a sirloin of beef. **4.** *Sports.* **a.** A spin given to a ball, a **backspin** *(see).* **b.** A cut or slice imparting such a spin. **5.** *Chiefly U.S.* A notch cut in a tree to direct its fall and ensure a clean break.
un·der·de·vel·oped (úndər-di-vélləpt) *adj.* **1.** Not adequately or normally developed; immature; deficient: *an underdeveloped mind in an underdeveloped body.* **2.** In photography, processed in too weak a developing solution, or for too short a time, or at too low a temperature to produce a normal degree of contrast. **3.** Poor and economically primitive, usually because of insufficient capital and an inadequate social infrastructure. **—un·der·de·vel·op·ment** *n.*
un·der·dog (úndər-dog || -dawg) *n.* **1.** One who loses or is expected to lose a contest or struggle, as in sport or politics. **2.** One who is at a disadvantage or is being oppressed.
un·der·done (úndər-dún) *adj.* Cooked lightly or insufficiently.
un·der·dressed (úndər-drést) *adj.* Dressed too informally for a given situation.
un·der·drive (úndər-drīv) *n.* A gearing device causing the output drive shaft to rotate at a slower rate than the engine input shaft.
un·der·em·ployed (úndər-im-plóyd) *adj.* Not adequately or fully employed.
un·der·es·ti·mate (úndər-ésti-mayt) *v.* **-mated, -mating, -mates.** —*tr.* **1.** To estimate at too low a quantity, degree, or size. **2.** To have too low a regard for the worth, strength, or character of. —*intr.* To make too low an estimate of a quantity, degree, or size.
~*n.* (-mət, -mit, -mayt). An estimate that is too low. **—un·der·es·ti·ma·tion** (-máysh'n) *n.*
un·der·ex·pose (úndər-ik-spṓz, -ek-) *tr.v.* **-posed, -posing, -poses.** To expose insufficiently; especially, to expose (film, for example) for too short a time or to insufficient light or radiation to produce normal image contrast. **—un·der·ex·po·sure** (-spṓzhər) *n.*
un·der·feed (úndər-fe̋ed) *tr.v.* **-fed** (-féd), **-feeding, -feeds. 1.** To feed insufficiently. **2.** To supply with fuel from below.
un·der·felt (úndər-felt) *n.* **1.** A thick felt fabric used for laying under carpets to increase their resilience or to give extra insulation. **2.** A piece of such felt laid under a carpet.
un·der·floor (úndər-flór || -flṓr) *adj.* Located beneath the floor: *underfloor heating.*
un·der·foot (úndər-fŏŏt) *adv.* **1.** Under the foot or feet, and often on the ground: *trampled the flowers underfoot.* **2.** Below one's feet; directly below. **3.** In the way. **4.** In a state of subjection.

un·der·fur (úndər-fur) *n*. The dense, soft, fine fur beneath the coarse outer hairs of certain mammals.

un·der·gar·ment (úndər-gaarmənt) *n*. A garment that is worn under outer garments; especially, one worn next to the skin.

un·der·gird (úndər-gúrd) *tr.v*. **-girded** or **-girt, -girding, -girds.** To gird, support, or strengthen from beneath, by or as if by passing a rope underneath.

un·der·glaze (úndər-gláyz) *adj*. Applied to pottery before it is glazed. Said of a pigment or decoration.
~ *n*. (-glayz). A pigment or decoration so applied.

un·der·go (úndər-gő) *tr.v*. **-went** (-wént), **-gone** (-gón ‖ -gáwn, -gáan) **-going, -goes** (-gőz). 1. To experience; be subjected to. 2. To endure; suffer; sustain. [Middle English *undergon*, to submit to, go through : *under*, UNDER + *gon*, to GO.]

un·der·grad·u·ate (úndər-gráddew-ət, -grájoo-, -it) *n*. A university student who has not yet received a first degree. Also informally called "undergrad". **—un·der·grad·u·ate** *adj*.

un·der·ground (úndər-grownd) *adj*. 1. Occurring, operating, or situated below the surface of the earth. 2. Hidden or concealed; clandestine. 3. Of, pertaining to, or designating an organisation involved in secret or illegal activity, such as the subversion of an established political or social order. 4. Of, pertaining to, or describing an avant-garde movement or its music, publications, and art, usually privately produced and often concerned with social or artistic experiment.
~ *n*. 1. A clandestine, often nationalist, organisation engaged in or encouraging the usually violent overthrow of a government in power, such as an occupying military government. 2. An underground railway; especially, the underground railway system in London. Usually preceded by *the*.
~ *adv*. (*also* -grównd). 1. Below the surface of the earth. 2. In or into secrecy or hiding: *They went underground*.

underground railway *n*. An urban railway system usually running in tunnels below the ground. Also *chiefly U.S*. "subway".

un·der·grown (úndər-grőn, -grōn) *adj*. Not fully grown; puny.

un·der·growth (úndər-grőth) *n*. Low-growing plants, saplings, and shrubs beneath taller trees. Also *chiefly U.S*. "underbrush", "underbush".

un·der·hand (úndər-hánd, -hand) *adj*. 1. Secret and deceitful; treacherous; sneaky; underhanded. 2. *Sports*. Underarm. **—See** Synonyms at **dishonest, secret.**
~ *adv*. 1. With an underhand movement. 2. Slyly and secretly.

un·der·hand·ed (úndər-hándid) *adj*. 1. Secret and deceitful. 2. Lacking the required number of workers or players; shorthanded. **—un·der·hand·ed·ly** *adv*. **—un·der·hand·ed·ness** *n*.

un·der·hung (úndər-húng) *adj*. 1. **a**. Protruding beyond the upper jaw. Said of a lower jaw. **b**. Having such a lower jaw. 2. Resting on or mounted along a supporting track. Said of a sliding door.

un·der·in·sure (úndər-in-shoőr, -shór ‖ -shéwr) *tr.v*. **-sured, -suring, -sures.** 1. To insure (possessions) below their full value. 2. To fail to protect (oneself) with adequate insurance.

un·der·laid (úndər-láyd) *adj*. 1. Placed or laid underneath. 2. Supported or raised by something from beneath; having an underlay.

un·der·lay (úndər-láy) *tr.v*. **-laid, -laying, -lays.** 1. To put (one thing) under another. 2. To provide with a base or sublining. 3. *Printing*. To raise or support by underlays.
~ *n*. (-lay). 1. Something laid underneath; especially, felt or foam rubber placed under a carpet for added insulation and resilience. 2. *Printing*. A piece of paper or other material used under type to raise the level of a printing bed.

un·der·let (úndər-lét) *tr.v*. **-let, -letting, -lets.** 1. To let (property) at less than the proper value. 2. To sublet.

un·der·lie (úndər-lĩ) *tr.v*. **-lay** (-láy), **-lain** (-láyn), **-lying, -lies.** 1. To lie or be located under or below. 2. To be the support or basis of; account for: *Many facts underlie my decision*. 3. *Finance*. To take precedence over (another claim, security, liability, or the like).

un·der·line (úndər-lĩn ‖ -lĩn) *tr.v*. **-lined, -lining, -lines.** 1. To draw a line under, especially to distinguish or emphasise (a written word or passage). 2. To emphasise or stress.
~ *n*. (-lĩn, -lĩn). A line drawn under writing to indicate emphasis or italic type.

un·der·ling (úndərling) *n*. A subordinate or lackey.

un·der·ly·ing (úndər-lĩ-ing) *adj*. 1. Basic; fundamental. 2. Implicit; hidden: *an underlying meaning*. 3. *Finance*. Taking precedence; prior: *an underlying claim*.

un·der·manned (úndər-mánd) *adj*. Without sufficient workers or troops; shorthanded.

un·der·men·tioned (úndər-ménsh'nd) *adj*. Mentioned or referred to later or below, in a written work.

un·der·mine (úndər-mĩn) *tr.v*. **-mined, -mining, -mines.** 1. To dig a mine or tunnel beneath. 2. To weaken by wearing away a base or foundation: *Water undermined the foundations*. 3. **a**. To weaken or impair by degrees or imperceptibly; sap: *Late hours undermine one's health*. **b**. To weaken, injure, or ruin insidiously or secretly: *His campaign undermined the chairman's authority*.

un·der·most (úndər-mŏst) *adj*. Lowest in position, rank, or place.
~ *adv*. In or to the lowest place.

un·der·neath (úndər-néeth) *adv*. In or to a place beneath; below.
~ *prep*. Under; below; beneath. See Usage note at **below.**
~ *adj*. Lower; under.
~ *n*. The lower part or side. [Middle English *undernethe*, from Old English *underneothan* : UNDER + *neothan*, below.]

un·der·nour·ish (úndər-núrrish) *tr.v*. **-ished, -ishing, -ishes.** To provide with insufficient quantity or quality of nourishment to sustain proper health and growth. **—un·der·nour·ish·ment** *n*.

un·der·paint·ing (úndər-paynting) *n*. A sketch of a painting, revealing the design, shading, and often colouring, over which the final painting is executed.

un·der·pants (úndər-pants) *pl.n*. An undergarment, chiefly for boys and men, worn over the lower abdomen, buttocks, hips, and sometimes thighs.

un·der·part (úndər-paart) *n*. 1. A part on the lower surface, especially of an animal or plant. 2. A subordinate role, as in a play.

un·der·pass (úndər-paass ‖ -pass) *n*. 1. A passage underneath something; especially, a section of road that passes under another road or a railway line. 2. An intersection formed in this way.

un·der·pay (úndər-páy) *tr.v*. **-paid, -paying, -pays.** To pay insufficiently or less than deserved. **—un·der·pay·ment** *n*.

un·der·pin (úndər-pín) *tr.v*. **-pinned, -pinning, -pins.** 1. To support from below, as with props, girders, masonry, or the like. 2. To corroborate or substantiate.

un·der·play (úndər-pláy, -play) *v*. **-played, -playing, -plays.** *—tr*. 1. To act (a role) subtly or with restraint. 2. To act (a role) weakly or sketchily. 3. To present or deal with subtly or with restraint; play down. *—intr*. 1. To underplay a·role. 2. In card games, to play a low card while holding a higher card of the same suit.

un·der·plot (úndər-plot) *n*. A subsidiary plot, as in a play or novel.

un·der·price (úndər-príss) *tr.v*. **-priced, -pricing, -prices.** To price below normal or appropriate value.

un·der·priv·i·leged (úndər-prívvə-lijd, -prívvi-) *adj*. Lacking the rights, opportunities, and economic or educational advantages enjoyed by other members of one's community; deprived.

un·der·pro·duc·tion (úndər-prə-dúksh'n ‖ -prō-) *n*. Production below full capacity or below demand.

un·der·proof (úndər-prőof ‖ -próof) *adj*. Having a smaller proportion of alcohol than **proof spirit** (*see*).

un·der·prop (úndər-próp) *tr.v*. **-propped, -propping, -props.** 1. To prop (something) from below. 2. To support or sustain.

un·der·quote (úndər-kwőt) *tr.v*. **-quoted, -quoting, -quotes.** 1. To offer (goods or services) for sale at a price lower than the official list or market price; undersell. 2. To quote a lower price than that quoted by (another).

un·der·rate (úndər-ráyt) *tr.v*. **-rated, -rating, -rates.** To regard (someone's abilities, for example) as having less value or quality than is due; undervalue; underestimate.

un·der·run (úndər-rún) *tr.v*. **-ran** (-rán), **-run, -running, -runs.** 1. To run or pass beneath. 2. *Nautical*. To haul (a line or cable) onto a boat for inspection or repair.

un·der·score (úndər-skőr, -skawr ‖ -skőr, -skōr) *tr.v*. **-scored, -scoring, -scores.** 1. To draw a line under. 2. To emphasise or stress.
~ *n*. A line drawn under writing to indicate emphasis or italic type.

un·der·sea (úndər-see) *adj*. Pertaining to, existing, occurring, or designed for use beneath the surface of the sea.
~ *adv*. (-sée). Beneath the surface of the sea.

un·der·seal (úndər-séel) *tr.v*. **-sealed, -sealing, -seals.** To place a protective coating on the underside of; especially, to apply a heavy tar or rubber-like substance on the underneath of a motor vehicle to prevent corrosion. Also *U.S*. "undercoat".

Underseal *n*. A trademark for a preparation used to protect the underside of vehicles.

Under Secretary *n*. 1. An officer in the British government service of the grade between Deputy Secretary and Assistant Secretary. Also called "Permanent Under Secretary". 2. In Britain, any of various junior ministers in certain government departments. Also called "Parliamentary Under Secretary".

un·der·sell (úndər-sél) *tr.v*. **-sold** (-sőld), **-selling, -sells.** 1. To sell goods at a lower price than (another seller). 2. To sell (goods) for less than the full or normal price. 3. To advertise or publicise moderately or inadequately. 4. To present or regard (oneself) as having less ability or worth than one actually has. **—un·der·sell·er** *n*.

un·der·set (úndər-set) *n*. An ocean undercurrent.

un·der·sexed (úndər-sékst) *adj*. Having less sexual potency or desire than normal.

un·der·shirt (úndər-shurt) *n*. *U.S*. A **vest** (*see*).

un·der·shoot (úndər-shőōt) *v*. **-shot, -shooting, -shoots.** *—tr*. 1. To shoot a projectile below or short of (a target). 2. *Aeronautics*. **a**. To start one's final approach to (a landing area) too low or too soon. **b**. To land an aircraft short of (a landing area). *—intr*. To shoot or land short of a target or a landing area.

un·der·shot (úndər-shot) *adj*. 1. Driven by water passing from below. Said of a waterwheel. 2. Projecting beyond the upper jaw. Said of a lower jaw.

un·der·shrub (úndər-shrub) *n*. A low-growing shrub.

un·der·side (úndər-sĩd, sĩd) *n*. The side or surface that is underneath; the bottom side.

un·der·signed (úndər-sĩnd, -sĩnd) *adj*. 1. Having placed one's signature at the bottom of a document. 2. Having a signature at the bottom or the end. Said of documents. 3. Signed at the bottom of a document: *the undersigned names*.
~ *n., pl*. **undersigned.** The person who has signed at the bottom of a document. Preceded by *the*.

un·der·sized (úndər-sĩzd) *adj*. Also **un·der·size** (-sĩz). Being of less than normal or sufficient size.

un·der·skirt (úndər-skurt) *n*. 1. A petticoat. 2. One skirt of a layered dress or skirt gown over which outer skirts are draped.

un·der·sleeve (úndər-sleev) *n*. A sleeve worn under an outer sleeve;

especially, an ornamental sleeve designed to extend below or show through slashes in the outer sleeve.

un·der·slung (úndər-slúng) *adj.* **1.** Having springs attached to the axles from below. Said of a vehicle. **2.** Supported from above. **3.** Having a low centre of gravity.

un·der·soil (úndər-soyl) *n.* Soil below the ground surface.

un·der·staffed (úndər-staaft ‖ -stáft) *adj.* Having too small a staff or fewer staff than usual: *an understaffed hospital.*

un·der·stand (úndər-stánd) *v.* **-stood** (-stŏŏd), **-standing**, **-stands.** —*tr.* **1.** To perceive and comprehend the nature and significance of: *"I don't pretend to understand the Universe—it's a great deal bigger than I am"* (Thomas Carlyle). **2.** To know thoroughly by close contact with or long experience of: *understood the customs of the Far East.* **3. a.** To grasp or comprehend the meaning intended or expressed by (another): *understand Shakespeare.* **b.** To comprehend the meaning, language, sounds, form, or symbols of: *Do you understand French?* **4.** To know and be tolerant or sympathetic towards (the needs, feelings, or views of another): *My wife doesn't understand me.* **5.** To learn indirectly, as by hearsay; gather; assume. **6.** To take something as meaning; conclude; infer: *Am I to understand that you are staying the night?* **7.** To accept as an agreed fact or condition; regard as definite: *It is understood that the fee will be five pounds.* **8.** To supply or add (a meaning or words, for example) mentally. —*intr.* **1.** To have understanding, knowledge, sympathy, or comprehension: *"Hear and understand."* (Matthew 15:10). **2.** To learn indirectly or at second-hand; gather: *They were just married, or so I understand.* **3.** To draw an inference. —**give (someone) to understand.** *Formal.* To cause (someone) to believe or think. —**make (oneself) understood.** To communicate (one's) meaning clearly. —See Synonyms at **apprehend.** [Middle English *understanden,* Old English *understandan* : UNDER- + STAND.] —**un·der·stand·a·ble** *adj.* —**un·der·stand·a·bly** *adv.*

un·der·stand·ing (úndər-stánding) *n.* **1.** The quality or condition of one who understands; comprehension. **2.** The faculty by which one understands; intelligence. **3.** Individual or specified judgment or outlook in a matter; opinion; interpretation. **4.** An agreement between two or more persons or groups, especially when informal and implicit. **5.** A reconciliation of differences; an agreement: *They finally reached an understanding.* **6.** A usually harmonious relationship between people. —**on the understanding that.** On condition that; provided that. —See Synonyms at **reason.** ~*adj.* **1.** Having or characterised by comprehension, good sense, or discernment. **2.** Intelligently sympathetic and compassionate. —**un·der·stand·ing·ly** *adv.*

un·der·state (úndər-stáyt) *v.* **-stated**, **-stating**, **-states.** —*tr.* **1.** To express with undue restraint and cause to seem less important than is the case. **2.** To express with restraint or lack of emphasis, especially ironically or for dramatic impact. **3.** To state (a number, quantity, or the like) lower than is warranted: *understate one's age.* —*intr.* To understate something. —**un·der·state·ment** (-stáytmənt, -stayt-) *adj.*

un·der·steer (úndər-stéer, -steer) *intr.v.* **-steered**, **-steering**, **-steers.** To turn or tend to turn less sharply than the driver intends. Used of a motor vehicle. ~*n.* (-steer). A tendency towards or instance of understeering.

un·der·stood (úndər-stŏŏd) *adj.* **1.** Agreed upon; assumed. **2.** Not expressed; implied.

un·der·strap·per (úndər-strappər) *n.* A subordinate; an underling.

un·der·stra·tum (úndər-stráa-təm, -stráy-, -straa-, -stray- ‖ -strá-, -stra-) *n., pl.* **-tums** or **-ta** (-tə). A substratum.

un·der·stud·y (úndər-studdi) *v.* **-ied**, **-ying**, **-ies.** —*tr.* **1.** To study or know (a role) so as to be able to replace the regular actor or actress when required. **2.** To act as an understudy to. —*intr.* To act as an understudy. ~*n., pl.* **understudies. 1.** An actor or actress who studies a role so as to be able to replace the regular actor or actress when required. **2.** Any person trained to do the work of another.

un·der·take (úndər-táyk) *v.* **-took** (-tŏŏk ‖ -tŏŏk), **-taken**, **-taking**, **-takes.** —*tr.* **1. a.** To decide or agree to do: *undertake a task.* **b.** To set about; begin. **2.** To take upon oneself; commit oneself to: *He undertook to pay all the costs.* **3.** To promise; guarantee. —*intr. Archaic.* To make oneself responsible. Used with *for.* [Middle English *undertaken,* to accept, take in hand : UNDER- + TAKE.]

un·der·tak·er (úndər-taykər) *n.* One whose business it is to arrange for the burial or cremation of the dead and to assist at funeral rites.

un·der·tak·ing (úndər-táyking *for sense 3*) *n.* **1. a.** A task or assignment undertaken. **b.** An enterprise or venture. **2.** A guaranty, engagement, or promise. **3.** The profession or duties of an undertaker.

un·der·the·count·er (úndər-thə-kówntər) *adj.* Transacted or sold illicitly. —**under the counter** *adv.* Compare **over-the-counter.**

un·der·the·ta·ble (úndər-thə-táyb'l) *adj.* Not straightforward; secret or underhand.

un·der·things (úndər-thingz) *pl.n.* Underwear.

un·der·thrust (úndər-thrust) *n. Geology.* A reverse geological fault in which the rocks on the under surface of a fault plane move below the static rocks on the upper surface.

un·der·tint (úndər-tint) *n.* A slight or subtle tint.

un·der·tone (úndər-tōn) *n.* **1.** A tone of low pitch or volume, especially of spoken sound. **2. a.** A pale or subdued colour. **b.** A colour applied under or seen through another colour. **3.** An underlying or implied tendency or meaning; an undercurrent.

un·der·tow (úndər-tō) *n.* **1.** The seaward pull of waves receding af-

ter they have broken on a shore. **2.** Any strong undercurrent moving in a direction other than that of the surface current.

un·der·trick (úndər-trik) *n.* A trick, especially in bridge, the loss of which prevents a declarer from making his contract.

un·der·trump (úndər-trúmp) *intr.v.* **-trumped**, **-trumping**, **-trumps.** In card games, to play a trump lower than one already played when a trump has not been led.

un·der·val·ue (úndər-vál-yōō) *tr.v.* **-ued**, **-uing**, **-ues. 1.** To assign too low a value to; underestimate. **2.** To have too little regard or esteem for. —**un·der·val·u·a·tion** (-áysh'n) *n.*

un·der·vest (úndər-vest) *n.* A vest.

un·der·wa·ter (úndər-wáwtər) *adj.* Being, occurring, used, or performed beneath the surface of the water. —**un·der·wa·ter** *adv.*

un·der·way (úndər-wáy) *adj.* Occurring or employed while in motion: *underway refuelling.*

un·der·wear (úndər-wair) *n.* Clothing worn under the outer clothes and next to the skin. Also called "underclothes", "underclothing".

un·der·weight (úndər-wáyt) *adj.* Weighing less than is normal, healthy, or required. ~*n.* Insufficiency of weight.

un·der·went. Past tense of **undergo.**

un·der·whelm (úndər-wélm, -hwélm) *tr.v.* **-whelmed**, **-whelming**, **-whelms.** To fail to excite or make enthusiastic. Often used humorously. [UNDER- + *-whelm,* as in OVERWHELM.]

un·der·wing (úndər-wing) *n.* **1.** Either of a pair of hind wings partially or wholly covered by the forewings, as in certain moths. **2.** Any of various moths of the genus *Calocala,* having brightly coloured underwings.

un·der·wood (úndər-wŏŏd) *n.* Shrubs and small trees growing beneath taller trees; underbrush; undergrowth.

un·der·world (úndər-wurld) *n.* **1.** Any region, realm, or dwelling place conceived to be below the surface of the earth; especially, the world of the dead in classical mythology; Hades. **2.** Those engaged in usually organised crime and vice, considered collectively. **3.** *Rare.* The opposite side of the earth; the antipodes. **4.** *Archaic.* The world beneath the heavens; the earth.

un·der·write (úndər-rīt, -rīt) *v.* **-wrote** (-rŏt, -rōt), **-written** (-rítt'n, -ritt'n), **-writing**, **-writes.** —*tr.* **1. a.** To write (one's signature, for example) at the bottom; subscribe. **b.** To sign or endorse (a document). **2.** To assume financial responsibility for; guarantee (an enterprise) against failure: *underwrite a theatrical production.* **3. a.** To sign (an insurance policy), thus assuming liability in case of certain losses. **b.** To insure. **c.** To insure against losses totalling (a given amount). **4.** *Finance.* To guarantee the purchase of (a full issue of shares or bonds); specifically, to agree to buy the unsold part of (a share issue) at a fixed time and price. **5.** To support or agree to (a decision, for example). —*intr.* To act as an underwriter; especially, to issue an insurance policy. [Middle English, translation of Latin *subscrībere.*]

un·der·writ·er (úndər-rītər) *n. Abbr.* **U/w 1.** A person or firm engaged in an insurance business; specifically, an insurance agent who assesses the risk of enrolling an applicant for coverage or a policy. **2.** A person or company that guarantees the purchase of a full issue of shares or bonds.

un·de·scend·ed testicle (ún-di-séndid) *n.* A testicle that has remained within the inguinal canal and has not descended to the scrotum.

un·de·serv·ed (ún-di-zérved) *adj.* Not merited; unjustifiable; unfair. —**un·de·serv·ed·ly** (-zérvid-li) *adv.*

un·de·sir·a·ble (ún-di-zīr-əb'l) *adj.* **1.** Not desirable; unwanted. **2.** Unpleasant; objectionable. ~*n.* An undesirable person. —**un·de·sir·a·bil·i·ty** (-ə-bílləti) *n.* —**un·de·sir·a·bly** *adv.*

un·de·vel·oped (ún-di-vélləpt) *adj.* **1.** Not developed or fully grown; immature. **2.** Not put to full use or not having reached full potential: *undeveloped talent.* **3.** Not yet economically exploited to the full.

un·dies (ún-diz ‖ -deez) *pl.n. Informal.* Underwear; especially, women's underwear.

un·dine (ún-deen, -dīn, un-déen, ŏŏn-) *n.* A female water spirit who, according to Paracelsus, could earn a soul by marrying a mortal and bearing his child. [New Latin *Undina,* from Latin *unda,* wave.]

un·di·rect·ed (ún-di-réktid, -dī-, -dīr-) *adj.* **1.** Without object or purpose. **2.** Having no prescribed destination. Said of mail.

un·dis·charged (ún-diss-chárjd) *adj.* **1.** Not unloaded. Said of a ship's cargo. **2. a.** Not fulfilled: *an undischarged obligation.* **b.** Not paid: *an undischarged debt.* **3.** Not released or freed from obligation: *an undischarged bankrupt.*

un·dis·tin·guished (úndi-stíng-gwisht) *adj.* **1.** Not set apart; without any distinction: *His appearance was undistinguished.* **2.** Having no particularly good features; mediocre.

un·dis·trib·u·ted (ún-di-stríbbewtid ‖ -dístri-bewtid) *adj. Logic.* Not referring or applying to all members of a class. Said of a term or proposition.

un·do (ún-dŏŏ, un-) *v.* **-did** (-díd), **-done** (-dún), **-doing**, **-does** (-dúz). —*tr.* **1.** To reverse or erase; cancel; annul. **2.** To untie, disassemble, or loosen: *undo a shoelace.* **3.** To open (a parcel, for example); unwrap. **4. a.** To ruin the reputation or prospects of. **b.** To throw into confusion; unsettle. —*intr.* To come open or undone. [Middle English *undon,* from Old English *undōn,* to unfasten, untie, annul, destroy : UN- + *dōn,* to DO.] —**un·do·er** *n.*

un·do·ing (ún-dŏŏ-ing, un-) *n.* **1.** The act of reversing or annulling something accomplished; cancellation. **2.** The act of unfastening or loosening. **3. a.** Ruin; destruction. **b.** The act of bringing to ruin. **c.** The cause of ruin; downfall.

un·do·mes·ti·cat·ed (ún-də-mésti-kaytid, -dō-) *adj.* **1 a.** Not tame. Said of an animal. **b.** Not being a type of animal typically kept and put to work by human beings. **2.** Uninterested in or unaccustomed to family life or basic household chores.

un·doubt·ed (un-dówtid) *adj.* Accepted as beyond question.

un·doubt·ed·ly (un-dówtid-li) *adv.* It is not to be doubted that. See Usage note at **doubtless.**

un·dreamt-of (un-drémt-ov, ún-, -drémpt- ‖ -uv) *adj.* Also **un·dreamed-of** (-drémt-, -drémpt-, -dreémd-). Barely or not entertained even in wishful fantasy: *undreamt-of success.*

un·dress (ún-dréss, un-) *v.* **-dressed, -dressing, -dresses.** —*tr.* **1.** To remove the clothing of; strip. **2.** To remove the bandages from (a wound or burn, for example). —*intr.* To take off one's clothing; strip. ~*n.* **1.** Informal as distinguished from formal dress or uniform. **2.** Nakedness or near nakedness.

un·dressed (ún-drést, un-) *adj.* **1. a.** Naked. **b.** Not fully dressed. **2.** Not specially prepared or processed: *undressed leather.* **3. a.** Not prepared for cooking or eating. Said of certain meats. **b.** Without dressing or sauce. Said of a salad. **4.** Not treated or bandaged: *an undressed wound.*

un·due (ún-déw, un- ‖ -dōo) *adj.* **1.** Exceeding what is appropriate or normal; excessive. **2.** Not just, proper, or legal: *undue use of power.* **3.** Not yet payable or due.

un·du·lant (úndewlənt ‖ úndələnt) *adj.* Resembling waves in occurrence, appearance, or motion. [UNDUL(ATE) + -ANT.]

undulant fever *n.* **Brucellosis** (*see*).

un·du·late (úndew-layt ‖ úndə-) *v.* **-lated, -lating, -lates.** —*tr.* **1.** To cause to move in a smooth wavelike motion. **2.** To give a wavelike appearance or form to. —*intr.* **1.** To move in waves or in a smooth wavelike motion; ripple. **2.** To have a wavelike appearance or form. —See Synonyms at **swing.** ~*adj.* (-lət, -lit, -layt). Also **un·du·la·ted** (-laytid). Having a wavy outline or appearance: *leaves with undulate margins.* [Late Latin *undulāre,* from *undula,* diminutive of Latin *unda,* wave.]

un·du·la·tion (úndew-láysh'n ‖ úndə-) *n.* **1.** A regular rising and falling or movement to alternating sides; a movement in waves. **2.** A wavelike form, outline, or appearance. **3.** Any of a series of waves or wavelike segments; a pulsation.

un·du·la·to·ry (úndew-lətri, -lətəri, -laytəri, -láytəri) *adj.* Of, pertaining to, or caused by undulation; undulating.

un·du·ly (ún-déw-li, un- ‖ -dōo) *adv.* **1.** Excessively; immoderately. **2.** In disregard of a legal or moral precept.

un·du·ti·ful (ún-déwti-f'l, un- ‖ -dōoti-) *adj.* **1.** Lacking a sense of duty. **2.** Unreliable or disobedient.

un·dy·ing (un-dī-ing, ún-) *adj.* Endless; everlasting; immortal.

un·earned (ún-érnd) *adj.* **1.** Not gained by work or service. **2.** Not deserved. **3.** Not yet earned: *unearned interest.*

unearned income *n.* An income coming from property, interests, or other investments as opposed to from wages and salaries.

unearned increment *n.* An increase in the value of a property resulting from factors independent of the owner's efforts, such as a general rise in demand for land.

un·earth (ún-érth, un-) *tr.v.* **-earthed, -earthing, -earths. 1.** To bring up out of the earth; dig up; uproot. **2.** To bring to light; discover.

un·earth·ly (un-érthli) *adj.* **-lier, -liest. 1.** Not of the earth; ideal or spiritual; supernatural. **2.** Ghostly; weird and unaccountable; unnatural. **3.** Ridiculously unreasonable or uncustomary; absurd: *out of bed at an unearthly hour.* —See Synonyms at **weird.** —**un·earth·li·ness** *n.*

un·ease (un-éez, ún-) *n.* A sense of discomfort, dissatisfaction, or apprehension.

un·eas·y (un-éezi, ún-) *adj.* **-ier, -iest. 1.** Lacking a sense of security; anxious or apprehensive: *The farmers were uneasy until the crop was in.* **2.** Causing constraint or awkwardness: *an uneasy silence.* **3.** Awkward or unsure in manner; constrained: *uneasy with strangers.* **4.** Not conducive to or causing rest: *an uneasy sleep.* —**un·eas·i·ly** *adv.* —**un·eas·i·ness** *n.*

un·em·ploy·a·ble (ún-im-plóy-əb'l, -em-) *adj.* Not able to find or keep a job. ~*n.* One who cannot be employed.

un·em·ployed (ún-im-plóyd, -em-) *adj.* **1.** Out of work; jobless. **2.** Not being used; idle.

un·em·ploy·ment (ún-im-plóymənt, -em-) *n.* **1.** The state of being out of work. **2.** The number or percentage of people in a community who are out of work.

unemployment benefit *n.* In Britain, regular payment made by the state to an unemployed person who has contributed to a state fund. See **supplementary benefit.**

un·en·light·ened (ún-in-lít'nd, -en-) *adj.* **1.** Not educated; ignorant. **2.** Not informed of something. **3.** Prejudiced, superstitious, and unreasoning.

un·e·qual (ún-éekwəl, un-) *adj.* **1.** Not the same in extent, quantity, rank, or social position. **2.** Consisting of or having ill-matched opponents: *an unequal running race.* **4.** Having unbalanced sides or parts; asymmetric. **5.** Not even or consistent; variable; irregular. **6.** Not having the required abilities; inadequate. Used with *to*: *"It was maddening to be unequal to many enterprises"* (D.H. Lawrence). ~*n.* One that is unequal. —**un·e·qual·ly** *adv.*

un·e·qualled (ún-éekwəld, un-) *adj.* Not matched or parallelled by others of its kind; unrivalled.

un·e·quiv·o·cal (ún-i-kwívvək'l) *adj.* Admitting of no doubt or misunderstanding; unambiguous; clear. —**un·e·quiv·o·cal·ly** *adv.*

un·err·ing (ún-ér-ing, un- ‖ -érring) *adj.* Committing no mistakes; consistently accurate. —**un·err·ing·ly** *adv.*

U·NES·CO (yōo-néskō) *n.* United Nations Educational, Scientific, and Cultural Organisation: an independent agency of the United Nations, established to promote international cooperation in science, art, and education.

un·es·sen·tial (ún-i-sénsh'l) *adj.* Not necessary; not of importance. ~*n.* A non-essential.

un·e·ven (ún-éev'n, un-) *adj.* **-vener, -venest. 1. a.** Not equal, as in size, length, or quality. **b.** Having ill-matched opponents. **2. a.** Not consistent or uniform: *an uneven colour.* **b.** Not consistent in quality: *an uneven performance.* **3.** Not smooth or level: *uneven surface of a cobblestone road.* **4.** Not straight or parallel: *uneven margins.* **5.** *Archaic.* Not fair or equitable. **6.** Designating an odd number. —See Synonyms at **rough.** —**un·e·ven·ly** *adv.* —**un·e·ven·ness** *n.*

un·e·vent·ful (ún-i-véntf'l) *adj.* Lacking in significant or disrupting incidents. —**un·e·vent·ful·ly** *adv.* —**un·e·vent·ful·ness** *n.*

un·ex·am·pled (ún-ig-záamp'ld, -eg- ‖ -ik-, -zámp'ld) *adj.* Without precedent; unparallelled: *a display of unexampled aggression.*

un·ex·cep·tion·a·ble (ún-ik-sépsh'n-əb'l, -ek-) *adj.* Beyond any reasonable objection; quite satisfactory. —**un·ex·cep·tion·a·ble·ness** *n.* —**un·ex·cep·tion·a·bly** *adv.*

un·ex·cep·tion·al (ún-ik-sépsh'n'l, -ek-) *adj.* **1.** Not varying from the normal; usual; ordinary. **2.** Not subject to exceptions; absolute. —**un·ex·cep·tion·al·ly** *adv.*

Usage: Unexceptional and *unexceptionable* are not interchangeable. *Unexceptional* means "usual, ordinary"; *unexceptionable* means "not open to objection", "to which one cannot take exception". Compare: *Her argument was unexceptional* (it was familiar), *Her argument was unexceptionable* (it was quite acceptable).

un·ex·pect·ed (ún-ik-spéktid, -ek-) *adj.* Coming without warning; unforeseen. —**un·ex·pect·ed·ly** *adv.* —**un·ex·pect·ed·ness** *n.*

un·fail·ing (ún-fáyling) *adj.* **1.** Constant; unflagging: *unfailing patience.* **2.** Inexhaustible; endless: *an unfailing supply.* **3.** Incapable of error; infallible. —**un·fail·ing·ly** *adv.*

un·fair (ún-fáir, un-) *adj.* **-fairer, -fairest. 1.** Not just or even-handed; biased: *an unfair decision.* **2.** Contrary to laws or conventions; unethical: *unfair trading.* —**un·fair·ly** *adv.* —**un·fair·ness** *n.*

un·faith·ful (ún-fáythf'l, un-) *adj.* **1.** Not adhering to a pledge or contract; disloyal. **2.** Having sexual relations with someone who is not one's spouse or long-term sexual partner; specifically, guilty of adultery. **3.** Not justly representing or reflecting the original; inaccurate: *an unfaithful translation.* **4.** *Archaic.* Without or deficient in religious faith; unbelieving. —See Synonyms at **faithless.** —**un·faith·ful·ly** *adv.* —**un·faith·ful·ness** *n.*

un·fal·ter·ing (un-fáwl-təring, ún- ‖ -fól-) *adj.* Not hesitating; steady; unwavering.

un·fa·mil·iar (ún-fə-míl-yər) *adj.* **1.** Not within one's knowledge; strange: *unfamiliar faces.* **2.** Not being acquainted; not conversant: *unfamiliar with flying.* —**un·fa·mil·i·ar·i·ty** (-i-árrəti) *n.* —**un·fa·mil·iar·ly** *adv.*

un·fas·ten (ún-fáass'n, un- ‖ -fáss'n) *v.* **-tened, -tening, -tens.** —*tr.* To separate the connecting parts of; unloosen or open. —*intr.* To become loosened or separated.

un·fa·thered (ún-fáathərd, un-) *adj.* **1. a.** Having no father; fatherless. **b.** Having no known father; illegitimate; bastard. **2.** Of uncertain or unknown origin or authenticity: *unfathered rumours.*

un·fath·om·a·ble (un-fáth'm-əb'l) *adj.* **1.** Too deep to be measured. **2.** Incomprehensible; inscrutable. —**un·fath·om·a·ble·ness** *n.* —**un·fath·om·a·bly** *adv.*

un·fa·vour·a·ble (ún-fáyv-rəb'l, un-, -ərəb'l) *adj.* **1.** Unpromising; not propitious. **2.** Adverse; opposed. **3.** Harmful. **4.** Unpleasing. —**un·fa·vour·a·ble·ness** *n.* —**un·fa·vour·a·bly** *adv.*

un·feed (ún-féed) *adj.* Not paid a fee.

un·feel·ing (un-féeling) *adj.* **1.** Not sensitive to others' feelings; unsympathetic; callous. **2.** Having no physical feeling or sensation; insentient. —**un·feel·ing·ly** *adv.* —**un·feel·ing·ness** *n.*

un·feigned (un-fáynd, ún-) *adj.* Not simulated; genuine. See Synonyms at **sincere.** —**un·feign·ed·ly** (un-fáynid-li) *adv.*

un·fet·tered (un-féttərd) *adj.* Unrestrained; free.

un·fin·ished (un-fínnisht, un-) *adj.* **1.** Not brought to an end; incomplete: *unfinished business.* **2.** Not having received special processing; natural: *unfinished wood.*

un·fit (ún-fít, un-) *adj.* **1.** Not meant or adapted for some usually specified purpose; inappropriate. Usually used with *for.* **2.** Below the required standard; unqualified. Usually used with *for.* **3.** Not in good health; in bad physical condition. ~*tr.v.* **unfitted, -fitting, -fits.** To cause to be unsuited or unqualified; disqualify. —**un·fit·ly** *adv.* —**un·fit·ness** *n.*

un·fix (ún-fíks) *tr.v.* **-fixed, -fixing, -fixes.** To unfasten.

un·flag·ging (un-flágging, un-) *adj.* Not weakening or stopping; untiring.

un·flap·pa·ble (ún-fláp-əb'l) *adj.* *Informal.* Not easily upset or excited, even in a crisis; calm. —**un·flap·pa·bil·i·ty** (-ə-bílləti) *n.*

un·fledged (ún-fléjd, un-) *adj.* **1.** Not yet sufficiently developed to fly. Said of a young bird lacking flight feathers. **2.** Inexperienced, immature, or untried.

un·flinch·ing (un-flínching, ún-) *adj.* Without fear or indecision; unshrinking; resolute. —**un·flinch·ing·ly** *adv.*

un·fold (ún-fóld, un- *Note:* un- *especially for senses tr. 3 and intr. 2, 3*) *v.* **-folded, -folding, -folds.** —*tr.* **1.** To open and spread out;

extend (something folded). **2.** To remove the coverings from; disclose to view. **3.** To reveal gradually by written or spoken explanation; make known. *—intr.* **1.** To become spread out; open out. **2.** To be revealed gradually to the understanding. **3.** To develop.

un·for·get·ta·ble (ún-fər-géttəb'l ‖ -fawr-) *adj.* Earning a permanent place in the memory; memorable. **—un·for·get·ta·bly** *adv.*

un·formed (ún-fórmd) *adj.* **1.** Having no definite shape or structure; shapeless and unorganised. **2.** Not yet developed to maturity. **3.** Not yet given a physical existence; uncreated.

un·for·tu·nate (ún-fórch-nət, -nit, -ənət, -ənit) *adj.* **1.** Characterised by undeserved lack of good fortune; unlucky. **2.** Causing misfortune; disastrous. **3.** Regrettable; deplorable: *an unfortunate lack of good manners.* *~n.* A victim of bad luck, disaster, poverty, or other misfortune. **—un·for·tu·nate·ly** *adv.* **—un·for·tu·nate·ness** *n.*

un·found·ed (ún-fówndid, un-) *adj.* **1.** Not yet established. **2.** Not based on fact or sound evidence; groundless: *unfounded accusations.* **—un·found·ed·ly** *adv.* **—un·found·ed·ness** *n.*

un·freeze (ún-fréez) *v.* **-froze** (-fróz), **-frozen** (-fróz'n), **-freezing, -freezes.** *—tr.* **1.** To thaw out. **2.** To ease or eliminate restrictions on (wages, prices, credit, or manufactured goods). *—intr.* To thaw.

un·fre·quent·ed (ún-fri-kwéntid ‖ -fréekwəntid) *adj.* Receiving few or no visitors.

un·friend·ly (ún-fréndli, un-) *adj.* **-lier, -liest. 1.** Not disposed to friendship; hostile; disagreeable. **2.** Indicating a bad prospect; unfavourable. **—un·friend·li·ness** *n.*

un·frock (ún-frók, un-) *tr.v.* **-frocked, -frocking, -frocks.** To strip of priestly privileges and functions.

un·fruit·ful (ún-fróot-f'l, un- ‖ -fréwt-) *adj.* **1.** Not bearing fruit or offspring; barren. **2.** Unprofitable or unsuccessful. **—See** Synonyms at **sterile. —un·fruit·ful·ly** *adv.* **—un·fruit·ful·ness** *n.*

un·furl (ún-fúrl) *v.* **-furled, -furling, -furls.** *—tr.* To spread or open out; unroll. *—intr.* To become spread or opened out.

un·gain·ly (un-gáynli, ún-) *adj.* **-lier, -liest. 1.** Without grace or ease of movement; clumsy. **2.** Difficult to move or use; unwieldy. **—See** Synonyms at **awkward.** *~adv.* In a clumsy manner. **—un·gain·li·ness** *n.*

un·gen·er·ous (ún-jénnərəss, un-) *adj.* **1.** Not generous; stingy. **2.** Harsh in judgment; unkind. **—un·gen·er·ous·ly** *adv.*

un·get·at·a·ble (ún-get-áttəb'l) *adj. Informal.* Inaccessible.

un·girt (ún-gúrt) *adj. Archaic.* **1.** Having the belt, girdle, or other restraining or supporting garment removed or loosened. **2.** Loose or free; slack.

un·god·ly (ún-gódli, un-) *adj.* **-lier, -liest. 1.** Not revering God; impious. **2.** Sinful; wicked. **3.** *Informal.* **a.** Outrageous; unreasonable: *He called at an ungodly hour.* **b.** Very unpleasant or annoying: *an ungodly din.* **—un·god·li·ness** *n.*

un·gov·ern·a·ble (ún-gúvvərnəb'l, un-, -gúv-nəb'l) *adj.* Not able to be controlled: *an ungovernable temper.* See Synonyms at **unruly. —un·gov·ern·a·ble·ness** *n.* **—un·gov·ern·a·bly** *adv.*

un·gra·cious (ún-gráyshəss, un-) *adj.* **1.** Lacking social manners; rude. **2.** Not welcome or acceptable; unattractive: *an ungracious task.* **—un·gra·cious·ly** *adv.* **—un·gra·cious·ness** *n.*

un·gram·mat·i·cal (ún-grə-máttik'l) *adj.* **1.** Not in accord with the rules of a prescriptive grammar. **2.** Not in accord with a language as used by a native speaker.

un·grate·ful (un-grayt·f'l, ún-) *adj.* **1.** Without due feeling or expression of gratitude, thanks, or appreciation. **2.** Not agreeable or pleasant; repellent: *an ungrateful task.* **3.** Not increasing yield when cultivated. Said of land. **—un·grate·ful·ly** *adv.* **—un·grate·ful·ness** *n.*

un·grudg·ing (ún-grújing, un-) *adj.* Generous; willing or freely given: *ungrudging praise.* **—un·grudg·ing·ly** *adv.*

un·gual (úng-gwəl ‖ ún-) *adj.* **1.** Of or pertaining to the fingernails or toenails. **2.** Of, resembling, or bearing a hoof, nail, or claw. [Latin *unguis*, UNGUIS.]

un·guard·ed (ún-gárdid, un-) *adj.* **1.** Without guard or protection; vulnerable. **2.** Unprepared or imprudent; incautious: *caught in an unguarded moment.* **3.** Free from guile; open. **—un·guard·ed·ly** *adv.* **—un·guard·ed·ness** *n.*

un·guent (úng-gwənt; *rarely* -gew-ənt ‖ ún-, -jənt) *n.* A salve for soothing or healing; an ointment. [Middle English, from Latin *unguentum*, from *unguere*, to anoint.]

un·guic·u·late (ung-gwíckew-lət, un-, -lit, -layt) *adj.* **1.** *Zoology.* Having nails or claws. Said of a mammal. **2.** *Botany.* Having a claw-shaped base: *unguiculate petals.* *~n.* A mammal having nails or claws. [New Latin *unguiculatus*, from Latin *unguiculus*, fingernail, diminutive of *unguis*, UNGUIS.]

un·guis (úng-gwiss ‖ ún-) *n., pl.* **-gues** (-gweez). **1.** A nail, claw, hoof, or clawlike structure. **2.** The clawlike base of some petals. [Latin *unguis*, claw, nail.]

un·gu·la (úng-gew-lə) *n., pl.* **-lae** (-lee). *Mathematics.* **1.** A cone or cylinder truncated by a plane not parallel to its base. **2.** *Rare.* A hoof. [Latin, "hoof" (from its shape), diminutive of UNGUIS.] **—un·gu·lar** (-lər) *adj.*

un·gu·late (úng-gew-lət, -lit, -layt ‖ ún-) *adj.* **1. a.** Having hoofs. **b.** Hooflike. **2.** Of or belonging to the former order Ungulata, now divided into the orders Perissodactyla and Artiodactyla, and including hoofed mammals such as horses, cattle, deer, and pigs. *~n.* An ungulate mammal. [Late Latin *ungulātus*, from Latin *ungula*, diminutive of *unguis*, UNGUIS.]

un·gu·li·grade (úng-gewli-grayd) *adj.* Walking on hooves. Said of

horses and similar animals. [Latin *ungula*, hoof (see **ungula**) + -GRADE.]

Unh. The symbol for the element unnilhexium.

un·hal·low (ún-hál-ō, un-) *tr.v.* **-lowed, -lowing, -lows.** *Archaic.* To profane; desecrate.

un·hal·lowed (ún-hál-ōd, un-) *adj.* **1.** Not hallowed or consecrated. **2.** *Literary.* Immoral; wicked.

un·hand (ún-hánd) *tr.v.* **-handed, -handing, -hands.** To remove one's hand or hands from; let go: *"Unhand me, you villain."*

un·hand·y (ún-hándi) *adj.* **-ier, -iest. 1.** Difficult to handle or manage; unwieldy; cumbersome: *an unhandy desk.* **2.** Lacking manual skill or dexterity. **—un·hand·i·ly** *adv.* **—un·hand·i·ness** *n.*

un·hap·py (un-háppi, ún-) *adj.* **-pier, -piest. 1.** Not happy or joyful; sad. **2.** Not bringing or enjoying good fortune; unlucky. **3.** Not suitable or tactful; inappropriate. **—un·hap·pi·ly** (*often* -háppəli) *adv.* **—un·hap·pi·ness** *n.*

un·har·ness (ún-hárniss) *tr.v.* **-nessed, -nessing, -nesses. 1.** To remove the harness from. **2.** To release or liberate (energy or emotions, for example). **3.** To take armour off (someone).

un·health·y (un-hélthi, ún-) *adj.* **-ier, -iest. 1.** In a state of ill health; sick. **2.** Characterising or symptomatic of ill health: *an unhealthy pallor.* **3.** Causing or conducive to poor health; unwholesome. **4. a.** Harmful to character or moral health; corrupting. **b.** Indicating a morbid or disturbed mental state: *an unhealthy interest in violence.* **5.** *Informal.* Of a risky nature; dangerous. **—un·health·i·ly** (*often* -hélthəli) *adv.* **—un·health·i·ness** *n.*

un·heard (ún-hérd) *adj.* **1.** Not sensed by the ear. **2.** Not given a hearing; not listened to. **3.** *Archaic.* Obscure; unknown.

un·heard-of (ún-hérd-ov, un- ‖ -uv) *adj.* **1.** Not previously known; unknown. **2.** Without precedent. **3.** Highly offensive or outrageous.

un·hes·i·tat·ing (un-hézzi-tayting, ún-) *adj.* **1.** Prompt; ready. **2.** Unfaltering; steadfast. **—un·hes·i·tat·ing·ly** *adv.*

un·hinge (ún-hinj, un-) *tr.v.* **-hinged, -hinging, -hinges. 1.** To remove (a door) from the hinges. **2.** To confuse; disrupt. **3.** To derange; unbalance: *He was unhinged by a traumatic shock.*

un·ho·ly (ún-hōli, un-) *adj.* **-lier, -liest. 1.** Not hallowed or consecrated. **2.** Wicked; immoral. **3.** *Informal.* Outrageous; unreasonable. **—un·ho·li·ly** *adv.* **—un·ho·li·ness** *n.*

un·hook (ún-hōōk, un- ‖ -hōók) *tr.v.* **-hooked, -hooking, -hooks. 1.** To release or remove from a hook. **2.** To unfasten the hooks of.

un·hoped-for (ún-hōpt-fawr, ún-) *adj.* Not expected but pleasant; beyond what was anticipated.

un·horse (ún-hórss, un-) *tr.v.* **-horsed, -horsing, -horses. 1.** To cause to fall from a horse. Usually used in the passive. **2.** To overthrow or dislodge; upset.

un·hou·seled (ún-hówz'ld) *adj. Archaic.* Not having received the Eucharist. Said of a dying or dead person. [UN- (not) + HOUSEL.]

uni– *comb. form.* Indicates the state of being single or one or consisting of only one; for example, unicameral, unicostate. [Latin, from *ūnus*, one.]

U·ni·at (yōōni-at) *n.* Also **U·ni·ate** (-ayt, -ət, -it). A member of a Uniat Church. *~adj.* Of or pertaining to a Uniat Church or its members, practices, or doctrines. [Russian *uniyat*, from Polish *uniat*, from *unja*, "church-union" (of the Greek and the Roman Catholic Churches), from Late Latin *ūniō*, UNION.]

Uniat Church *n.* Also **Uniate Church.** Any Eastern Orthodox Church that acknowledges the supremacy of the pope but retains its own distinctive liturgy.

u·ni·ax·i·al (yōōni-áksi-əl) *adj.* **1.** Having only one axis; monaxial. Said especially of plants having a single main stem. **2.** Having one direction along which double refraction of light does not take place. Said of a crystal.

u·ni·cam·er·al (yōōni-kám-rəl, kámmə-) *adj.* Having or consisting of a single legislative chamber. [UNI- + CAMERA (chamber).]

UNICEF (yōōni-sef) *n.* United Nations International Children's Emergency Fund.

u·ni·cel·lu·lar (yōōni-séllewlər) *adj. Biology.* Consisting of one cell; one-celled: *unicellular organisms.*

u·ni·col·our (yōōni-kullər) *adj.* Of a single colour; monochromatic.

u·ni·corn (yōōni-kawrn) *n.* **1.** An imaginary creature usually represented as a white horse with a spiralled horn projecting from its forehead. **2.** A representation of this creature, often used in heraldry. **3.** A two-horned animal, possibly the wild ox or rhinoceros, mentioned in the Old Testament. [Middle English, from Old French, from Latin *ūnicornis* : UNI- + *cornū*, horn.]

u·ni·cos·tate (yōōni-kóss-tayt ‖ -káwss-) *adj.* Having a single main costa, rib, or riblike part: *a unicostate leaf.* [UNI- + COSTA.]

u·ni·cy·cle (yōōni-sīk'l) *n.* A vehicle consisting of a frame mounted over a single wheel and usually propelled by pedals. Also called "monocycle". **—u·ni·cy·clist** (-sīklist) *n.*

un·i·den·ti·fied flying object (ún-ī-dénti-fīd) *n.* **1.** *Abbr.* **UFO** A flying or apparently flying object of an unknown nature. **2.** A **flying saucer** (*see*).

u·ni·di·men·sion·al (yōōni-dī-ménsh'n'l, -di-) *adj.* **1.** Existing in one dimension only. **2.** Lacking depth; superficial.

u·ni·di·rec·tion·al (yōōni-di-réksh'n'l, -dī-, -dīr-) *adj.* Having, operating, or moving in one direction only.

U·ni·fi·ca·tion Church (yōōni-fi-káysh'n) *n.* The church of the Moonies (*see*).

u·ni·fied field theory (yōōni-fīd) *n.* A physical theory that combines the treatment of two or more types of fields in order to deduce previously unrecognised interrelationships; especially, such a theory, as yet unidentified, unifying the theories of nuclear, electromagnetic, and gravitational forces.

unified tax *n.* A graduated income tax as operated in Britain.

u·ni·fi·lar (yōoni-fīlər) *adj.* Having or utilising only one thread, wire, fibre, or the like.

u·ni·fo·li·ate (yōoni-fōli-ət, -it, -ayt) *adj.* Having a single leaf.

u·ni·fo·li·o·late (yōoni-fōli-ə-layt, -lət, -lit) *adj.* Compound in structure, but having a single leaflet.

u·ni·form (yōoni-fawrm) *adj.* **1. a.** Always the same; unchanging; unvarying: *a uniform gait.* **b.** Without fluctuation or variation; consistent; regular: *a uniform flow.* **2.** Being the same as another or others; identical; consonant: *a uniform size.* **3.** Consistent in appearance; having an unvaried texture, colour, or design. **4.** Conforming to the same standard; consistent in application, judgment, or the like. —See Synonyms at **steady.** ~*n.* **1.** Distinctive dress intended to identify those who wear it as members of a specific group: *soldiers in uniform.* **2.** A single outfit of such dress. ~*tr.v.* **uniformed, -forming, -forms. 1.** To make uniform. **2.** To provide with or dress in a uniform. [Old French *uniforme,* from Latin *ūniformis,* of one form : UNI- + -FORM.] —**u·ni·for·mi·ty** (-fórməti), **u·ni·form·ness** *n.* —**u·ni·form·ly** *adv.*

u·ni·for·mi·tar·i·an·ism (yōoni-fórmi-taír-i-ən-iz'm) *n. Geology.* The theory that all geological phenomena may be explained as the result of existing forces having operated in the past. —**u·ni·for·mi·tar·i·an** *adj. & n.*

u·ni·fy (yōoni-fī) *v.* **-fied, -fying, -fies.** —*tr.* **1.** To make into a unit; consolidate. **2.** To make uniform. —*intr.* To be made into a unit. [French *unifier,* from Late Latin *ūnificāre* : UNI- + Latin *facere,* to make.] —**u·ni·fi·ca·tion** (-fi-káysh'n) *n.* —**u·ni·fi·er** *n.*

u·ni·lat·er·al (yōoni-láttrəl, -láttərəl) *adj.* **1. a.** Of, on, pertaining to, involving, or affecting only one side. **b.** Performed or undertaken by only one side: *unilateral disarmament.* **2.** Obligating only one of two or more parties, nations, or persons: *a unilateral contract.* **3.** Emphasising or recognising only one side of a subject. **4.** Having only one side. **5.** Tracing the lineage of one parent only: *a unilateral genealogy.* Compare **bilateral. 6.** *Botany.* Having leaves or other parts on one side of an axis only. —**u·ni·lat·er·al·ly** *adv.* —**u·ni·lat·er·al·ism** *n.* —**u·ni·lat·er·al·ist** *n. & adj.*

u·ni·lat·er·al·ist (yōoni-láttrəlist) *n.* One who favours unilateral action, especially unilateral disarmament. Compare **multilateralist.** —**u·ni·lat·er·al·ist** *adj.*

u·ni·loc·u·lar (yōoni-lóckewlər) *adj. Botany.* Having a single compartment or chamber: *a unilocular ovary.* [UNI- + LOCULUS.]

un·i·mag·in·a·ble (ún-i-májinəb'l) *adj.* Beyond one's comprehension; inconceivable. —**un·i·mag·in·a·bly** *adv.*

un·im·peach·a·ble (ún-im-péechəb'l) *adj.* **1.** Beyond doubt; unquestionable. **2.** Blameless; beyond reproach. —**un·im·peach·a·bil·i·ty** (-bílliti) *n.* —**un·im·peach·a·bly** *adv.*

un·im·proved (ún-im-prōovd) *adj.* **1.** Not improved; not bettered. **2.** Not made use of or put to advantage. **3.** Not built upon or cultivated so as to increase in value. Said of land.

un·in·cor·po·rat·ed (ún-in-kórpə-raytid) *adj. Law.* Not required to be registered. Said of a company.

un·in·hab·it·a·ble (ún-in-hábbitəb'l) *adj.* Not fit for habitation.

un·in·hib·i·ted (ún-in-híbbitid) *adj.* **1.** Not inhibited; open: *uninhibited laughter.* **2.** Free from normal social or moral constraints. —**un·in·hib·i·ted·ly** *adv.* —**un·in·hib·it·ed·ness** *n.*

un·in·spired (ún-in-spírd) *adj.* Not stimulating to the mind or imagination; mediocre; dull.

un·in·tel·li·gent (ún-in-téllijənt) *adj.* **1.** Not intelligent; stupid. **2.** Not endowed with intelligence. Said of nonsentient beings. —**un·in·tel·li·gence** *n.* —**un·in·tel·li·gent·ly** *adv.*

un·in·ten·tion·al (ún-in-ténsh'n'l) *adj.* Not deliberate or intended. —**un·in·ten·tion·al·ly** *adv.*

un·in·ter·est·ed (ún-in-trəst-id, un-, -trist-, -tərest-, -trest-) *adj.* **1.** Not paying attention; not interested; indifferent; concerned. See Usage note at **disinterested. 2.** Not having a financial interest. —**un·in·ter·est·ed·ly** *adv.* —**un·int·en·est·ed·ness** *n.*

un·in·ter·rup·ted (ún-íntər-rúptid, -intər-) *adj.* Without interruption; continuous. —**un·in·ter·rup·ted·ly** *adv.*

u·ni·nu·cle·ate (yōoni-néw-kli-ət, -it, -ayt ‖ -nōo-) *adj.* Having a single nucleus. Said of a cell.

un·ion (yōon-yən, -i-ən) *n.* **1.** The act of uniting or the state of being united. **2.** A combination so formed; especially, an alliance or confederation of persons, parties, or political entities for mutual interest or benefit. **3.** *Symbol* **U** *Mathematics.* A set consisting of all members of two or more given sets. Compare **intersection. 4.** Agreement, especially resulting from an alliance; concord; harmony. **5. a.** The state of matrimony. **b.** A marriage. **c.** Sexual intercourse. **6.** Formerly in Britain: **a.** A combination of parishes for joint administration of relief for the poor. **b.** A workhouse maintained by such a union. **7.** A **trade union** *(see).* **8.** A coupling device for connecting parts, as pipes or rods. **9.** A device on a flag or ensign, occupying the upper inner corner or the entire field, that signifies the union of two or more sovereignties. **10.** *Capital* **U. a.** An organisation or society at a college or university that deals with student administration and provides facilities for recreation. **b.** A building housing such facilities. **11.** A piece of fabric made from two different kinds of yarn. —**the Union. 1. a.** The union of the English and Scottish thrones (1603–1707) or parliaments (from 1707). **b.** The union of Great Britain and Ireland (1801–1920) or of Great Britain and Northern Ireland (since 1920). **2.** The United States of America, especially during the Civil War. **3.** The former Union of South Africa. ~*adj.* Of or pertaining to a trade union. [Middle English, from Late Latin *ūniō* (stem *ūniōn-*), unity, from Latin *ūnus,* one.]

union card *n.* A membership card in a trade union.

union catalogue *n.* A library catalogue combining the contents of a number of catalogues or the contents of more than one library.

un·ion·ise, un·ion·ize (yōon-yən-īz, -i-ən-) *v.* **-ised, -ising, -ises.** —*tr.* **1.** To organise (a work force) into a trade union. **2.** To recruit into a trade union. —*intr.* **1.** To organise or form a trade union. **2.** To join a trade union. —**un·ion·i·sa·tion** (-ī-záysh'n ‖ *U.S.* -i-) *n.*

un·ion·ism (yōon-yən-iz'm, -i-ən-) *n.* **1.** The principle or theory of forming a union. **2.** The principles, theory, or system of unions, especially trade unions. **3.** Loyalty to a union, especially to a trade union. **4.** *Capital* **U.** Loyalty to the Union of Great Britain and Ireland or Northern Ireland. —**un·ion·ist** *n.*

Unionist Party *n.* Formerly, the dominant political party of Northern Ireland, supported by the Protestant majority and identified with the Union with Britain.

Union Jack *n.* **1.** The flag of the United Kingdom. Also officially

---

unicorn

A MYTHICAL SYMBOL OF PURITY
A beast that looks as if it should exist

The unicorn has a long pedigree. It was portrayed on Assyrian reliefs, was firmly accepted by the Greeks and Romans, and was familiar in art and legend in medieval Europe, the Middle East, and China. Supposedly, it lived in India, and the myth may have originated in garbled descriptions of the one-horned Indian rhinoceros. In European art, the unicorn hunt was a favourite subject and the animal remains a common heraldic beast. Its true significance, however, is allegorical. The unicorn was portrayed as pure white – a symbol of purity, often of Christ himself. The horn was believed to have magical properties and "unicorn horn" – often from a rhinoceros or narwhal (a single-horned whale) – was much valued as a talisman.

MEDIEVAL MYTH *The unicorn in this Gothic tapestry shows in its body the attributes of a horse and in its beard and cloven hooves those of a goat.*

The common medieval motif of a lady with a unicorn recalls the myth that the animal could be caught only by a virgin.

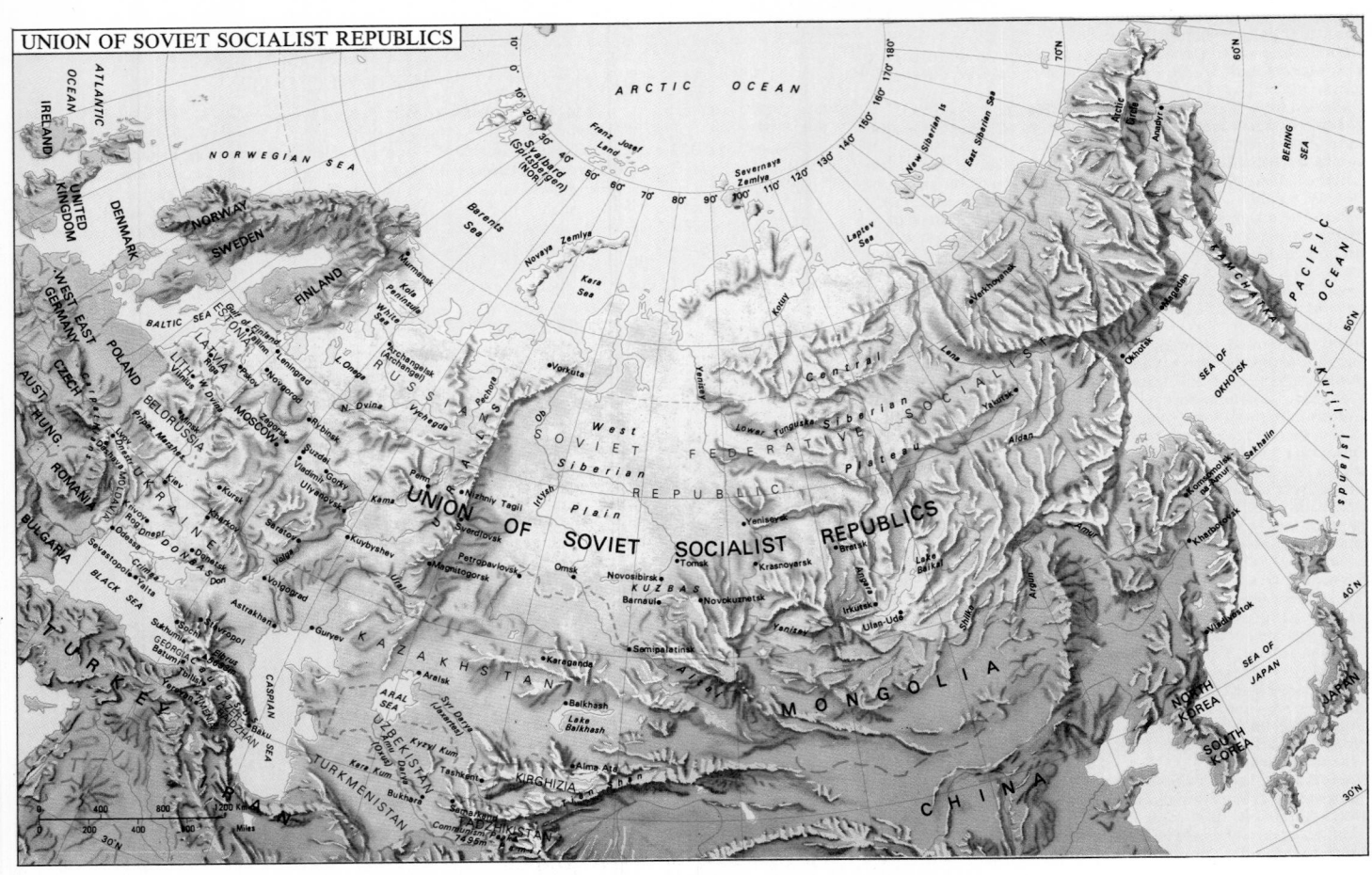

UNION OF SOVIET SOCIALIST REPUBLICS

called the "Union Flag". **2.** *Usually small* **u,** *small* **j.** *Chiefly U.S.* Any flag consisting entirely of a union. [UNION (device on a flag, specifically the combined crosses of St. George, St. Andrew, and St. Patrick) + JACK (flag).]

Union of Soviet Socialist Republics. Also **Soviet Union.** Formerly **Russia.** Federation of 15 national republics lying in eastern Europe and northern Asia, in extent the largest, and in population the third largest, country in the world. The population is concentrated west of the Urals, in the Volga-Baikal belt, and in central Asia; Moscow, Leningrad, and Kiev are the biggest cities. The largely industrial economy is centrally planned. The country is self-sufficient in most minerals and in energy, and its chief exports are crude oil, industrial plant, natural gas, iron and steel, timber, and coal, mostly to other Comecon countries. Cereals, potatoes, sugar beet, livestock, and cotton are the main farm products. A unified Russian state emerged when several principalities united under Moscow (15th century), and gradually expanded into Asia. The Russian empire became a great power in the 18th century, and by 1914, its boundaries were roughly those of today. The Revolution (1917) brought Lenin and the Communists to power, and the U.S.S.R. was set up (1922). Area, 22 402 200 square kilometres (8,649,539 square miles). Population, 270,000,000. Capital, Moscow.

union shop *n.* A business or other place of employment whose employees are required to join an often named trade union within a stated period after being hired. Compare **closed shop, open shop.**

u·nip·a·rous (yŏŏ-níppərəss) *adj.* **1.** Producing only one offspring at a time. **2.** Having produced only one offspring. Said of a woman. **3.** *Botany.* Forming a single axis at each branching. Said of some flower clusters. [UNI- + -PAROUS.]

u·ni·per·son·al (yŏŏni-pérss'n'l) *adj.* **1.** Being manifested as or existing in the form of only one person: *a unipersonal spirit.* **2.** *Grammar.* Used only in one person; specifically, used only in the third person singular. Said of certain verbs, for example *snows.*

u·ni·pla·nar (yŏŏni-pláy-nər ‖ -naar) *adj.* Situated or occurring in one plane.

u·ni·po·lar (yŏŏni-pólər) *n.* **1.** *Physics.* Having, acting by means of, or produced by a single pole. **2.** *Anatomy.* Of or designating a nerve cell having a single process extending from the cell body.

u·nique (yŏŏ-néek ‖ yŏŏ-) *adj.* **1.** Being the only one of its kind; solitary; sole. **2.** Being without an equal or equivalent; unparalleled. **3.** *Informal.* Outstanding; remarkable. **4.** *Mathematics.* Giving, having, or designating a single solution: *a unique solution to an equation.* —See Synonyms at **single.** [French, from Latin *ūnicus,* only, sole.] —**u·nique·ly** *adv.* —**u·nique·ness** *n.*

Usage: The absolute sense of the word *unique* precludes its being used in any comparative way. In careful usage, intensifying adverbs (such as *most, almost, rather, very,* or *somewhat*) are avoided. On the other hand, phrases such as *the most unique,* in the sense of "most unusual", will often be encountered in casual speech, and suggest that a less absolute sense has emerged in modern English, although this readily attracts criticism. *Almost* and *nearly* are not usually criticised when used with *unique* in informal contexts on the grounds that no sense of degree is involved. The intensifying use of *quite* (*It's quite unique!*) is also widely used in modern informal English.

u·ni·sex (yŏŏni-seks) *adj.* **1.** Designed to be worn or used by people of either sex: *a unisex sauna.* **2.** Selling or using unisex goods.

u·ni·sex·u·al (yŏŏni-sék-sew-əl, -shoo-, -shŏŏl, -sh'l) *adj.* **1.** Of only one sex. **2.** *Biology.* Having either male or female sexual organs but not both. —**u·ni·sex·u·al·i·ty** (-ál-əti) *n.* —**u·ni·sex·u·al·ly** *adv.*

u·ni·son (yŏŏ-ni-s'n, -z'n) *n.* **1. a.** Identity of musical pitch; the interval of a perfect prime. **b.** The agreement or coincidence in pitch of musical parts. **c.** The performance or combination of musical parts at the same pitch or in octaves. **2.** Any speaking of the same words simultaneously by two or more speakers. **3.** Any instance of agreement; concord; harmony. —**in unison. 1.** In harmony or agreement. **2.** Simultaneously. [Old French, from Late Latin *ūnisonus,* of the same sound : UNI- + Latin *sonus,* sound.]

u·nis·o·nous (yŏŏ-níss'n-əss) *adj.* Also **u·nis·o·nal** (-'l), **u·nis·o·nant** (-ənt). Sounding or composed to sound in unison.

u·nit (yŏŏnit) *n. Abbr.* **u. 1. a.** A single individual or entity. **b.** An individual, group, structure, or other entity regarded as an elementary structural or functional constituent of a whole. **2.** A group regarded as a distinct entity within a larger group. **3. a.** A mechanical part or module. **b.** An entire apparatus or the equipment that performs a specific function. **c.** A group of people performing a usually specified function: *an editorial unit.* **4.** A precise quantity in terms of which the magnitudes of other quantities of the same kind can be stated. **5. a.** The number immediately to the left of the decimal point in the Arabic numeral system. **b.** The least positive integer; one. **6.** A single share in a unit trust. **7.** A place in a building or complex set aside for a specified activity: *an intensive care unit.* **8.** A piece of furniture to be fitted and used with complementary pieces: *a kitchen unit.* **9.** *Military.* **a.** An organised tactical or administrative group that is a subdivision of a larger group. **b.** A large piece of equipment, such as a tank or ship. **10.** An amount of a drug required to produce a specific result.

~*adj.* Designating or having a value of one in some unitary system: *a line of unit length.* [16th century : from Latin *ūnus,* one, probably by analogy with *digit* (used to replace *unity* as a translation of Greek *monas*, MONAD, in Euclid).]

Unit. Unitarian; Unitarianism.

U·ni·tar·i·an (yōōni-taĭr-i-ən) *n.* **1.** A monotheist who rejects the doctrine of the Trinity. Compare **Trinitarian. 2.** *Abbr.* **Unit.** A member of a Christian denomination that rejects the doctrine of the Trinity and emphasises freedom and tolerance in religious belief and the autonomy of each congregation. See **Universalist. 3.** *Small* **u.** An advocate of unity or centralisation, especially in government. ~*adj. Abbr.* **Unit. 1.** Of, pertaining to, or supporting the Unitarians or their beliefs. **2.** *Small* **u.** Pertaining to or advocating unity or centralisation, especially in government. [New Latin *unitarius*, from Latin *ūnitās*, UNITY.] —**U·ni·tar·i·an·ism** *n.*

u·ni·tar·y (yōōni-tri, -təri ‖ -terri) *adj.* **1.** Of, pertaining to, or characteristic of a unit; whole. **2.** Having the nature of a unit. **3.** Based on or characterised by unity. **4.** Serving or used as a unit, especially of measurement. **5.** Pertaining to or designating a political system in which all governing power rests with a central government.

unitary symmetry *n.* An approximate symmetry law in which all hadrons comprise combinations, allowed by group theory, of any two or three quarks.

unit cell *n.* The smallest group of atoms, ions, or molecules having a spatial configuration characteristic of a particular crystal lattice.

unit character *n. Genetics.* A character inherited as a single unit and determined by a single gene.

u·nite (yōō-nīt, yōō- ‖ yōō-) *v.* **united, uniting, unites.** —*tr.* **1.** To bring together into a whole. **2.** To bring together or combine (people) in interest, purpose, or action, as in an association. **3.** To join (a couple) in marriage. **4.** To cause to adhere; bond. **5.** To have or demonstrate in combination: *He unites common sense with vision.* —*intr.* **1.** To become or seem to become joined, formed, or combined into a unit. **2.** To join and act together in a common purpose or endeavour. **3.** To be or become bound together by adhesion. —See Synonyms at **join.** [Middle English *uniten*, from Late Latin *ūnīre* (past participle *ūnītus*), from Latin *ūnus*, one.]

u·nit·ed (yōō-nīted, yōō- ‖ yōō-) *adj.* **1.** Joined; combined. **2.** Produced by two or more people acting jointly. **3.** Being in agreement. —**u·nit·ed·ly** *adv.*

United Arab Emirates. Formerly **Tru·cial States** (trōōsh'l). Federation of seven emirates (Abū Dhabi, Ajman, Dubai, Fujairah, Rās al Khaimah, Sharjah, and Umm al Qaiwain) on the southern coast of the Gulf. Most of the land is flat, sandy desert. The mainstay of the economy is petroleum production. The seven emirates, known as the "Pirate Coast", concluded a treaty with Britain (1853), and from 1892, Britain looked after their foreign affairs and defence. The present federation (formed 1971) has a friendship treaty with Britain. A single council of ministers replaced the emirate ministries in 1974. Area, 83 600 square kilometres (32,278 square miles). Population, 1,200,000. Capital, Abū Dhabi.

United Arab Republic. The union of the Arab Republic of Egypt and the Syrian Arab Republic (1958–61).

United Kingdom. Official name **United Kingdom of Great Britain and Northern Ireland.** Constitutional monarchy of northwest Europe, comprising England, Wales, Scotland, and Northern Ireland. Manufacturing is the largest sector of its economy, with some 30 per cent of the workforce, and the main exports are industrial plant, chemicals, crude oil (extracted from the North Sea since the mid-1970s), and motor vehicles. The country is self-sufficient in energy, fossil fuels catering for 95 per cent of its needs. Agriculture employs only 2 per cent of workers, yet provides 50 per cent of the nation's food. Some 30 per cent of workers are in the public sector. The country joined the European Economic Community in 1973. London, Birmingham, and Glasgow are the major cities. Wales became an English principality in 1284. Scotland and England were officially joined as Great Britain in 1707. The United Kingdom was formed by the union of Great Britain and Ireland in 1801, but southern Ireland broke away in 1921. Area, 244 046 square kilometres (94,201 square miles). Population, 56,100,000. Capital, London.

United Nations *n. Abbr.* **UN** An international organisation of independent countries, formed in 1945 to promote international security and cooperation. See feature, next page.

United Nations Trust Territory *n.* A trust territory (see).

United Party *n.* A former South African political party (1934–77), the official Opposition for most of the period after World War II.

United Provinces *n.* **1.** The Dutch republic that existed from the revolt of the Netherlands against Spain to its conquest by France (1579–1795). **2.** Former name of Uttar Pradesh State, India.

United Reformed Church *n.* A Protestant church formed by the merger of the Presbyterian Church of England and some Congregational Churches in England and Wales in 1972.

United States of America. Federal republic of 50 constituent states and the District of Columbia, smaller than Canada in extent, but in population the fourth largest country in the world. It is both the world's leading industrial nation and one of the world's major food suppliers. It is the world's leading producer of coal, natural gas, beef, maize, cheese, soya beans, copper, aluminium, and synthetic rubber. The country is largely self-sufficient, enjoying one of the world's highest living standards. However, crude oil accounts for nearly 25 per cent of its imports. Machinery, chemicals, motor vehicles, and cereals (maize and wheat) are the chief exports. The industrial centres of New York, Chicago, Los Angeles, Philadelphia, Houston, and Detroit are the largest cities. The union was formed in 1787, the original 13 states being the Thirteen Colonies along the Atlantic seaboard. The last two states to be admitted to the Union were Alaska and Hawaii. Area, 9 363 123 square kilometres (3,614,165 square miles). Population, 232,000,000. Capital, Washington (District of Columbia). See map, page 1801.

unit factor *n.* A gene that determines a unit character.

u·ni·tive (yōōnitiv ‖ yōō-nītiv) *adj.* Tending to promote unity.

unit magnetic pole *n.* The strength of a magnetic pole that will repel a similar magnetic pole with a force of one dyne when the poles are one centimetre apart.

unit of account *n.* **1.** A unit of money used for accounting purposes rather than as a means of payment, and not necessarily corresponding to actual currency denomination. Also *chiefly U.S.* "money of account". **2.** The standard currency unit of a country. **3.** An artificial currency unit used, for example, by the European Community for fixing farm prices.

unit price *n.* A price of goods calculated for each unit, such as a kilogram or litre.

unit process *n.* Any of several standard chemical engineering processes, such as distillation, used in industry.

UNITED KINGDOM

A PARLIAMENT FOR THE WORLD
The dream that inspired the founding of the United Nations

The United Nations came formally into being on October 24, 1945, succeeding the League of Nations. It was formed at the initiative of the countries that had fought Hitler's Germany.

Under the U.N. charter, member states bound themselves to "settle their international disputes by peaceful means" and to "refrain ... from the threat or use of force against ... any state". Although these promises have not always been realised, the organisation has created an international forum that embraces the vast majority of the world's nations.

From an original membership of 51 in 1945, the total rose to 156 in 1981 when Belize joined. There are still some states that are not members – among them North and South Korea, Taiwan, Switzerland, Monaco, Tonga, and the Vatican City.

The central body of the U.N. – its Parliament – is the General Assembly, based in New York, but its subsidiary agencies are located throughout the world. The International Court of Justice, for instance, is in The Hague; the World Health Organisation in Geneva; the Food and Agriculture Organisation in Rome; and the International Monetary Fund in Washington.

The most powerful arm of the U.N. is the Security Council, which, in theory, has the authority to impose decisions on member states. (The General Assembly has the right only to make recommendations to governments.) The council has 15 members: 10 of them are elected by the General Assembly for two years each, and five are permanent members. The five are the world's leading nuclear powers – the Soviet Union, the United States, China, Britain, and France; each has the right to veto any Security Council resolution.

The U.N., through the Security Council, helps to keep the peace throughout the world, and has sent observers and troops to such trouble spots as Lebanon, Cyprus, Korea, Kashmir, and the Congo (now Zaire). Through its Economic and Social Council, it also coordinates worldwide campaigns against poverty and disease. The U.N. civil service, the Secretariat, is headed by a Secretary-General elected by the General Assembly. It is funded by contributions from member states; the largest single contributor, the United States, provides a quarter of the U.N. budget.

GENERAL ASSEMBLY

SECURITY COUNCIL

SECRETARIAT

INTERNATIONAL COURT OF JUSTICE

MILITARY OBSERVERS AND PEACE-KEEPING FORCES

ECONOMIC AND SOCIAL COUNCIL

SPECIALIST AGENCIES, INCLUDING:

International Atomic Energy Agency

U.N. Conference on Trade and Development

U.N. Children's Fund

U.N. High Commission for Refugees

U.N. Development Programme

SPECIALIST AGENCIES, INCLUDING:

International Telecommunication Union

World Meteorological Organisation

U.N. Educational, Scientific and Cultural Organisation

World Health Organisation

International Labour Organisation

International Monetary Fund

International Bank for Reconstruction and Development (World Bank)

International Civil Aviation Organisation

Food and Agriculture Organisation

General Agreement on Tariffs and Trade

unit trust *n. British.* An investment company purchasing shares in numerous enterprises and issuing equal units for public sale from the combined portfolio. Also *U.S.* "mutual fund". Compare **investment trust.**

u·ni·ty (yōōnəti) *n., pl.* **-ties. 1.** The state of being one; singleness. **2.** The state, quality, or condition of harmony or agreement; concord. **3.** The state of being combined into a whole; unification. **4.** A combination or union of parts into a whole. **5. a.** An ordering of all elements in a work of art or literature so that each contributes to a unified aesthetic effect. **b.** The effect thus produced. **6.** Singleness or constancy of purpose or action; continuity. **7.** *Mathematics.* **a.** The number 1. **b.** An element *I* in a groupoid satisfying $x·I = x = I·x$ for each x in the groupoid. Also called "identity". **8.** *Plural.* Three principles of dramatic composition, derived from Aristotle's *Poetics.* They require that a drama should have only one plot, the action of which should be contained within one day and confined to one locality. [Middle English *unite,* from Old French, from Latin *ūnitās* (stem *ūnitāt-*) from *ūnus,* one.]

univ. 1. universal. **2.** university.

Univ. 1. Universalist. **2.** University.

u·ni·va·lent (yōōni-váylənt) *adj. Chemistry.* Monovalent.
~*n. Genetics.* A chromosome that is not paired with its homologue during meiosis.

u·ni·valve (yōōni-valv) *n.* **1.** A mollusc, especially a gastropod, having a shell consisting of single piece. **2.** The shell of such a mollusc. ~*adj.* Pertaining to or having such a shell.

u·ni·ver·sal (yōōni-vérss'l) *adj. Abbr.* **univ. 1.** Of, pertaining to, extending to, or affecting the entire world or all within the world; worldwide. **2.** Including, pertaining to, or affecting all members of the class or group under consideration: *the universal scepticism of philosophers.* **3.** Applicable or common to all purposes, conditions, or situations. **4.** Of or pertaining to the universe or cosmos; cosmic. **5.** Comprising all or many subjects; comprehensively broad: *universal interests.* **6.** *Mechanics.* Adapted or adjustable to many sizes or uses. **7.** *Logic.* Predicable of all the members of a class or genus denoted by the subject. Said of a proposition. Compare **particular.** ~*n.* **1.** *Philosophy.* **a.** A universal logical proposition. **b.** A general or abstract concept or term considered absolute or axiomatic, such as a Platonic idea. **2.** Any general or widely held principle, concept, or notion. **3.** A trait or pattern of behaviour characteristic of all the members of a particular culture or of all human beings. **4.** *Linguistics.* **a.** Any feature posited as an obligatory characteristic of all languages and therefore innate in every child before language is even acquired. **b.** A formal rule posited as essential for the analysis of any language. —**u·ni·ver·sal·ly** *adv.* —**u·ni·ver·sal·ness** *n.*

universal constant *n.* A fundamental constant *(see).*

universal donor *n.* A person of blood type O, whose blood is compatible with most other blood types and can therefore be safely used for most transfusions.

universal gas constant *n. Physics.* The gas constant *(see).*

u·ni·ver·sal·ise, u·ni·ver·sal·ize (yōōni-vérss'l-īz) *tr.v.* **-ised, -ising, -ises.** To make universal; generalise. —**u·ni·ver·sal·i·sa·tion** (-ĭ-záysh'n ‖ *U.S.* -ĭ-) *n.*

u·ni·ver·sal·ism (yōōni-vérss'l-iz'm) *n.* **1.** *Capital* **U.** *Theology.* The doctrine of universal salvation. Also called "apocatastasis". **2.** Universality. —**u·ni·ver·sal·is·tic** (-ístik) *adj.*

U·ni·ver·sal·ist (yōōni-vérss'l-ist) *n. Abbr.* **Univ.** One who believes that salvation is extended to all humankind; especially, a member of a Christian denomination that adheres to this doctrine. ~*adj.* Of or pertaining to Universalism or Universalists.

u·ni·ver·sal·i·ty (yōōni-ver-sál-əti) *n., pl.* **-ties. 1.** The quality, fact, or condition of being universal. **2.** Intellectual versatility.

universal joint *n.* A joint or coupling that allows parts of a machine not collinear with each other limited freedom of movement in any direction while transmitting rotary motion. Also called "universal coupling".

universal language *n.* An artificial language, such as Esperanto, designed for use by all nationalities.

universal motor *n.* An electric motor capable of running on either a direct-current or an alternating-current supply.

universal set *n.* A mathematical set containing all elements of the variety under consideration.

Universal Soul *n.* The Hindu concept of Brahman as the sacred syllable Om. Also called "Universal Spirit".

universal suffrage *n.* National suffrage extended to all adults above a certain age regardless of sex or race unless they are judged criminal or insane.

universal time *n. Abbr.* **U.T.** Greenwich Mean Time *(see).*

u·ni·verse (yōōni-verss) *n.* **1.** *Sometimes capital* **U.** All observed or postulated physical phenomena; the cosmos. **2. a.** The earth together with all its inhabitants and created things. **b.** All humankind. **3.** In science fiction: **a.** Another system of time, space, and matter coexisting with or corresponding to our own in an as yet undiscovered dimension, as, for example, in antimatter. **b.** Loosely, a vast and undiscovered star system or galaxy. **4.** The sphere or realm in which something exists or takes place. **5.** *Logic.* The universe of discourse. **6.** *Statistics.* A **population** *(see).* [Middle English *univers,* from Old French *univers,* from Latin *ūniversum,* the whole world (translation of Greek *to holon,* "the whole"), neuter of *ūniversus,* whole, entire, "turned into one" : UNI- + *versus,* past participle of *vertere,* to turn.] See feature, next page.

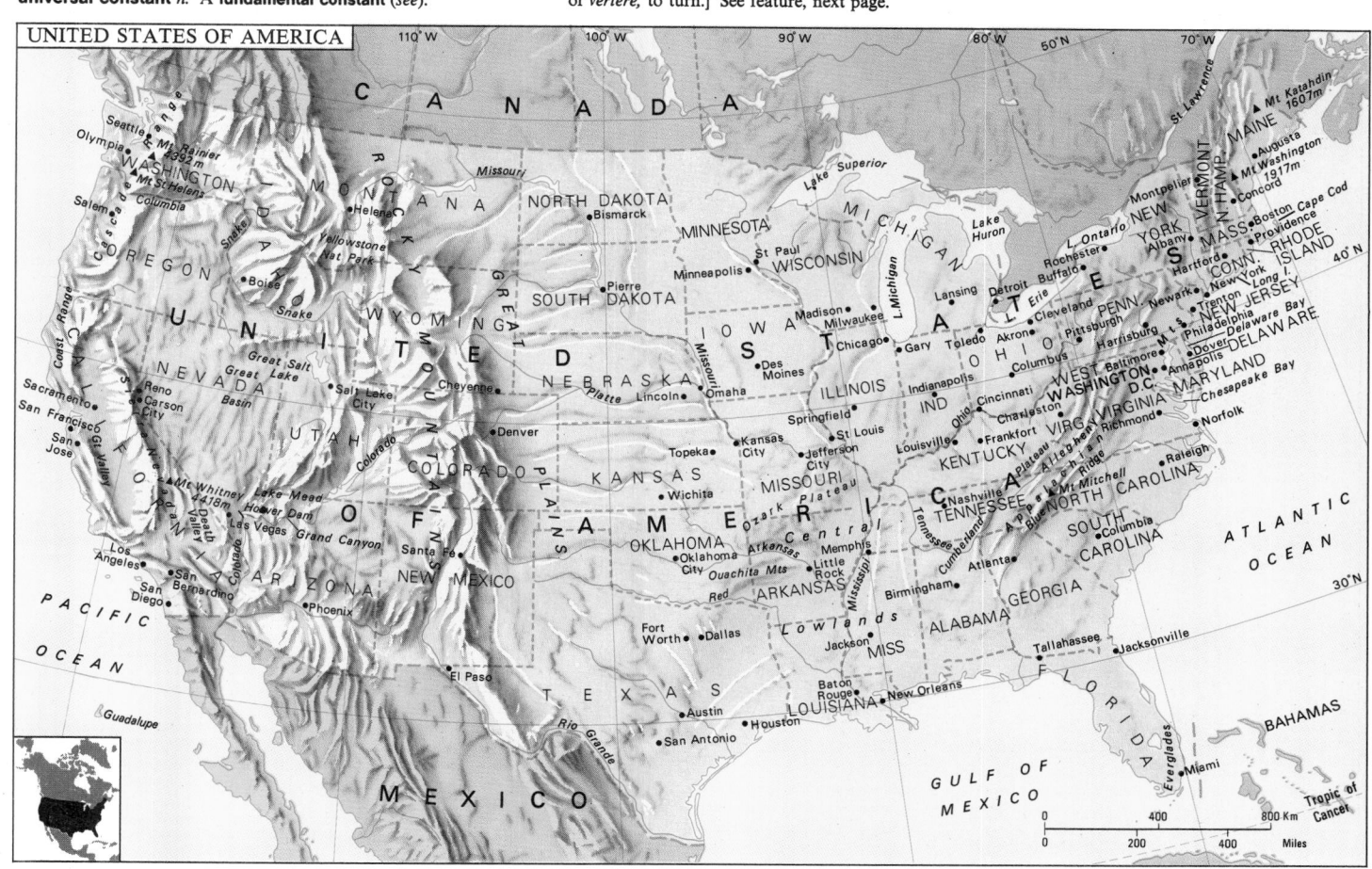

UNITED STATES OF AMERICA

universe

THE MIRACLE OF THE CREATION IS ALL AROUND US

The visible Universe is as astonishing as any science fiction

The study of the Universe, its origins, and its history is called cosmology. The prevailing scientific belief is that all the matter in the Universe came into existence when a "primeval atom" (or "cosmic egg") exploded at a definite moment more than 15,000 million years ago.

There is much evidence for this theory (generally known as the Big-Bang theory): wherever radio-astronomers point their instruments, they pick up background radiation – the aftermath of the "Big Bang". The change in the wavelength of the light from distant galaxies (it shifts towards the red end of the spectrum) indicates that they are moving away at immense speed.

The oscillating Universe theory predicts that the galaxies will eventually slow down, stop, and draw together again for a new Big Bang, so beginning a new cycle.

THE BIG-BANG THEORY

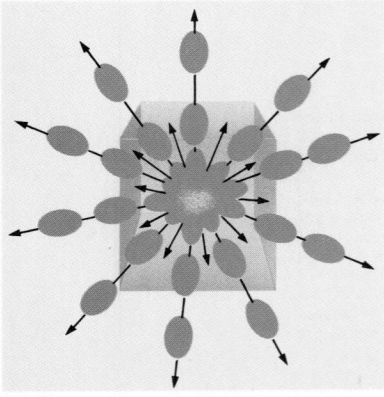 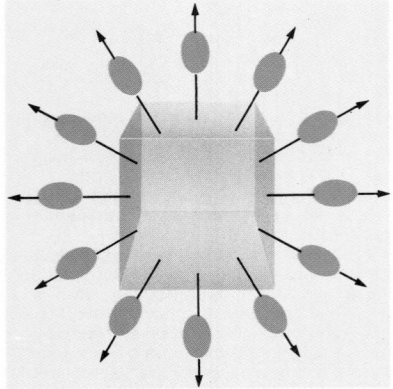

According to this theory, the Universe had its origin in an enormous explosion. The gas and dust flung out from the explosion condensed into

galaxies that are still moving outwards. Present knowledge fits this theory back to the instant of the Big Bang, about which nothing is known.

THE OSCILLATING UNIVERSE THEORY

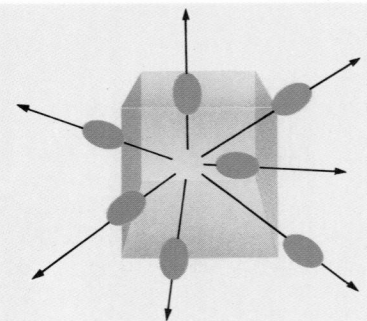 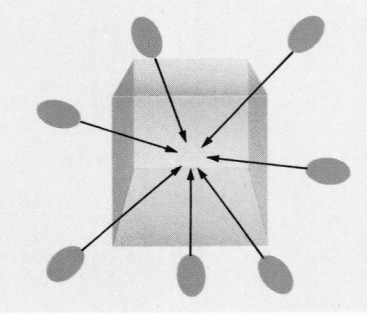

Every particle of matter exerts an attractive force on every other particle. Some scientists believe that the Universe expands and contracts in endless

cycles; the laws of physics may differ in each cycle. Some estimates of the critical amount of matter in the Universe suggest this cannot be so.

THE STEADY-STATE THEORY

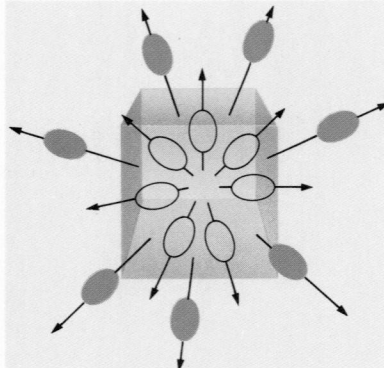 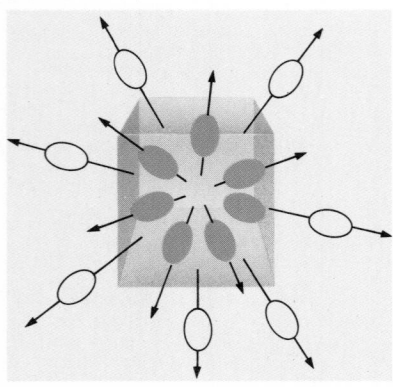

An alternative to the Big-Bang theory was proposed in the 1940s. The steady-state theory (now generally abandoned) holds that the Universe

was not created at any given time, nor will it ever die. Its appearance remains constant because, as it expands, new matter is created to fill the space.

universe of discourse *n. Logic.* A field containing all the entities referred to in a discourse or argument. Also called "universe".

u·ni·ver·si·ty (yōōni-vérssəti, -vérsti) *n., pl.* **-ties.** *Abbr.* **U., uni., univ., Univ. 1.** An institution for higher learning with teaching and research facilities that awards undergraduate and postgraduate degrees. **2.** The buildings and grounds of a university. **3.** The students, teaching staff, and governing body of a university, regarded collectively. [Middle English *universite,* from Old French, from Medieval Latin *ūniversitās (magistrorum et scholarium),* "society (of masters and students)", from Late Latin *ūniversitās* (stem *ūniversitāt-*), a society, guild, from Latin, the whole, from *ūniversus,* whole. See **universe.**]

u·niv·o·cal (yōō-nívvək'l) *adj.* Having only one meaning.
~*n.* A word or term having only one meaning. [Late Latin *ūnivōcus* : UNI- + Latin *vōx* (stem *vōc-*), voice.] —**u·niv·o·cal·ly** *adv.*

un·just (un-júst, un-) *adj.* **1.** Violating principles of justice; unfair. **2.** *Archaic.* Faithless; dishonest. —**un·just·ly** *adv.* —**un·just·ness** *n.*

un·kempt (ún-kémpt, un-) *adj.* **1. a.** Uncombed; dishevelled: *unkempt hair.* **b.** Lacking a neat or cared-for appearance; untidy: *an unkempt lawn.* **2.** *Archaic.* Unpolished; rude; rough. —See Synonyms at **sloppy.** [UN- (not) + *kempt,* past participle of archaic *kemb,* to comb, Middle English *kemben,* Old English *cemban.*] —**un·kempt·ly** *adv.* —**un·kempt·ness** *n.*

un·kind (un-kīnd, ún-) *adj.* **-kinder, -kindest. 1.** Unfeeling; unsympathetic. **2.** Cruel; harsh: *an unkind wind.* —**un·kind·ness** *n.*

un·kind·ly (un-kīndli, ún-) *adv.* In an unkind manner.
~*adj.* **-lier, -liest.** Unkind. —**un·kind·li·ness** *n.*

un·knit (ún-nít) *v.* **-knit** or **-knitted, -knitting, -knits.** —*tr.* **1.** To unravel or undo (something knitted or tied). **2.** To smooth out (something wrinkled, especially the brow). —*intr.* To become unknit or undone.

un·know·a·ble (ún-nṓ-əb'l, un-) *adj.* Impossible to know or comprehend; beyond the range of human experience or understanding.
~*n.* Something that cannot be known. —**the Unknowable.** The ultimate reality underlying all phenomena that is beyond human comprehension. —**un·know·a·ble·ness** *n.* —**un·know·a·bly** *adv.*

un·know·ing (ún-nṓ-ing, un-) *adj.* Not knowing; uninformed; unaware. —**un·know·ing·ly** *adv.*

un·known (ún-nṓn) *adj.* **1.** Not known; unfamiliar; strange. **2. a.** Not identified, discovered, or ascertained: *an unknown factor.* **b.** Not established or verified. **3.** Not famous: *an unknown author.* —**unknown to.** Without the knowledge of.
~*n.* **1.** One that is unknown. **2.** The world postulated as existing beyond sensory perception; the supernatural. Preceded by *the.* **3.** *Mathematics.* **a.** A quantity of unknown numerical value. **b.** The symbol for this quantity. —**unknown·ness** *n.*

unknown quantity *n.* A person, thing, or event whose outcome, behaviour, or effects cannot be predicted.

Unknown Soldier *n.* An anonymous soldier whose tomb is set up in public as a tribute to all the unidentified casualties of a national war. Preceded by *the.*

un·lace (ún-láyss) *tr.v.* **-laced, -lacing, -laces. 1. a.** To loosen or undo the lace or laces of. **b.** To remove or loosen the clothing of. **2.** *Obsolete.* To disgrace.

un·lade (ún-láyd) *v.* **-laded, -lading, -lades.** —*tr.* **1.** To unload (a cargo). **2.** To unload (a ship). —*intr.* To discharge a cargo.

un·lash (ún-lásh) *tr.v.* **-lashed, -lashing, -lashes.** To untie the lashing of; loosen.

un·latch (ún-lách) *v.* **-latched, -latching, -latches.** —*tr.* To unfasten or open by releasing the latch. —*intr.* To become or admit of being unfastened or opened.

un·law·ful (ún-láwf'l, un-) *adj.* **1.** Not lawful; in violation of law; illicit. **2.** *Archaic.* Illegitimate. Said of offspring. —**un·law·ful·ly** *adv.* —**un·law·ful·ness** *n.*

unlawful assembly *n.* An assembly of three or more people collaborating for any unlawful purpose.

un·lay (ún-láy) *v.* **-laid** (-láyd) **, -laying, -lays.** *Nautical.* —*tr.* To untwist the strands of (a cable or rope). —*intr.* To untwist.

un·lead·ed (ún-léddid) *adj.* **1.** Not surfaced or weighted with lead. **2.** Not mixed with lead. Said of fuels. **3.** *Printing.* Not spaced or separated with lead; set solid. Said of typeset matter.

un·learn (ún-lérn) *tr.v.* **-learnt** (-lérnt) or *U.S.* **-learned, -learning, -learns.** To put (something learnt) out of the mind; forget.

un·learn·ed (ún-lérnid *for senses 1, 2;* -lérnd, -lérnt *for sense 3*) *adj.* **1.** Not educated; ignorant or illiterate. **2.** Not skilled or versed in a specified discipline. **3.** *Chiefly U.S.* Unlearnt. —See Synonyms at **ignorant.** —**un·learn·ed·ly** (-lérnidli) *adv.*

un·learnt (ún-lérnt) *adj.* Also *chiefly U.S.* **unlearned.** Not acquired by training or studying: *an unlearnt response.*

un·leash (ún-léesh, un-) *tr.v.* **-leashed, -leashing, -leashes.** To release or loose from or as if from a leash: *unleash one's fury.*

un·leav·ened (ún-lévv'nd) *adj.* **1.** Made without leavening. Said especially of the bread of the Passover. **2.** Not lightened or alleviated: *A week of drudgery unleavened by amusement.*

un·less (ən-léss, un-, ún-) *conj.* Except on the condition that; except under the circumstances that.
~*prep. Rare.* Except; except for. [Middle English *unlesse,* alteration of *onlesse (than* or *that),* originally *(up)on less than,* "on a less condition than," hence except, if . . . not : ON + LESS.]

Usage: The expressions *unless and until* and *unless or until* are sometimes heard in emphatic speech and writing, but they attract criticism on the grounds that the senses of the two words overlap, and that one of the words is sufficient to express the meaning: *You will receive no further credit unless/until this sum is paid.*

un·let·tered (ún-léttərd) *adj.* **1. a.** Not educated. **b.** Illiterate. **2.** Without lettering. —See Synonyms at **ignorant**.

un·li·censed (ún-líss'nst, un-) *adj.* **1.** Having no licence. **2.** Unauthorised. **3.** Unrestrained.

un·like (ún-lík) *adj.* **1.** Not alike; different; dissimilar. **2.** Not equal. ~*prep.* **1.** Different from; not like. **2.** Not typical of: *It's unlike Emily to lose her cool that way.* —**un·like·ness** *n.*

un·like·li·hood (un-líkli-hŏod, ún-) *n.* The state of being unlikely or improbable; improbability.

un·like·ly (un-líkli, ún-) *adj.* **-lier, -liest. 1.** Not likely; improbable. **2.** Likely to fail: *a most unlikely candidate.* —**un·like·li·ness** *n.*

un·lim·ber (ún-límbər) *v.* **-bered, -bering, -bers. 1.** To detach (a gun or caisson) from its limber. **2.** To make ready for action. —*intr.* To prepare for action.

un·lim·it·ed (un-límmitid, ún-) *adj.* **1.** Having no limits, bounds, or qualifications. **2.** *Finance. British.* Unlimited in liability should business fail. —**un·lim·it·ed·ly** *adv.* —**un·lim·it·ed·ness** *n.*

un·lined (ún-límd) *adj.* **1.** Not marked with lines. **2.** Not wrinkled: *an unlined brow.* **3.** Not backed with a lining: *an unlined coat.*

un·link (ún-língk) *tr.v.* **-linked, -linking, -links.** To disconnect the links of; unfasten.

un·list·ed (un-lístid, ún-) *adj.* **1.** Not appearing on a list. **2.** Designating stock or securities not listed on a stock exchange. **3.** *U.S.* Ex-directory.

un·live (ún-lív) *tr.v.* **-lived, -living, -lives.** To live in such a manner as to undo or annul (earlier years or their consequences); reverse.

un·load (ún-lŏd, un-) *v.* **-loaded, -loading, -loads.** —*tr.* **1. a.** To remove the load or cargo from. **b.** To discharge (a cargo or load). **2. a.** To relieve (oneself, for example) of something oppressive; unburden. **b.** To relieve oneself of (a duty, for example) by giving it to another. **c.** To pour forth (one's troubles). **3.** To remove the charge from (a firearm). **4.** To dispose of, especially by selling in great quantity; dump. —*intr.* To discharge a cargo or other burden. —**un·load·er** *n.*

un·lock (ún-lók, un-) *v.* **-locked, -locking, -locks.** —*tr.* **1. a.** To undo (a lock) by turning a key or a corresponding part. **b.** To undo the lock of. **2. a.** To cause to open; unfasten. **b.** To give access to: *unlocked her heart.* **3.** To set free; release. **4.** To provide a solution to: *unlock a mystery.* —*intr.* To become or admit of being unlocked.

un·looked-for (un-lŏokt-fawr, ún- ‖ -lŏokt-) *adj.* Not looked for or expected; unforeseen.

un·loose (un-lŏoss, un-) *tr.v.* **-loosed, -loosing, -looses. 1.** To let loose or unfasten; release; set free. **2.** To relax; ease (one's grip, for example). [Middle English *unlo(o)sen* : UN- (intensive) + *lo(o)sen,* to loosen, from *lo(o)s,* LOOSE.]

un·loos·en (un-lŏoss'n, ún-) *tr.v.* **-ened, -ening, -ens.** To make less tight or firmly secured; unloose.

un·love·ly (ún-lúvli) *adj.* **-lier, -liest.** Not beautiful or pleasant; disagreeable; repugnant. —**un·love·li·ness** *n.*

un·luck·y (ún-lúcki, ún-) *adj.* **-ier, -iest. 1.** Subjected to or marked by misfortune. **2.** Forecasting bad luck; inauspicious. **3.** Not producing the desired outcome; disappointing; regrettable. —**un·luck·i·ly** *adv.* —**un·luck·i·ness** *n.*

un·made (ún-máyd) *adj.* Not made up tidily for sleeping in. Said of a bed.

un·make (ún-máyk) *tr.v.* **-made** (-máyd), **-making, -makes. 1.** To deprive of position, rank, or authority; depose. **2.** To ruin; destroy. **3.** To alter the characteristics of. —**un·mak·er** *n.*

un·man (ún-mán) *tr.v.* **-manned, -manning, -mans. 1.** To cause to lose courage. **2.** To deprive of virility; emasculate. **3.** To remove the men from.

un·man·age·able (un-mánnijəb'l, ún-) *adj.* Difficult to control.

un·man·ly (ún-mánli, un-) *adj.* **-lier, -liest. 1.** Not showing or marked by qualities conventionally associated with men, such as strength or self-control. Said typically of a man. **2. a.** Dishonourable; degrading. **b.** Cowardly. —**un·man·li·ness** *n.*

un·manned (ún-mánd) *adj.* **1.** Without a crew: *an unmanned ship.* **2.** *Obsolete.* Untrained. Said of a hawk.

un·man·nered (ún-mánnərd, un-) *adj.* **1.** Without manners; rude. **2.** Without mannerisms.

un·man·ner·ly (ún-mánnərli, un-) *adj.* Rude; ill-mannered. —**un·man·ner·li·ness** *n.*

un·marked (ún-márkt) *adj.* **1.** Not bearing a mark. **2.** Not observed or noticed. **3.** Not marked with corrections, a price, or the like. **4.** *Linguistics.* Of or pertaining to that one of a connected pair of words or linguistic units which is the more general or neutral; for example, in the pairs *dog* and *dogs* and *dog* and *bitch, dog* is the unmarked form.

un·mask (ún-máask ‖ -másk) *v.* **-masked, -masking, -masks.** —*tr.* **1.** To remove a mask from. **2.** To disclose the true character of; expose. **3.** *Military.* To expose the presence of (weapons), as by removing camouflage. —*intr.* To remove one's mask.

un·mean·ing (un-méening) *adj.* **1.** Meaningless. **2.** Expressionless; vacant. —**un·mean·ing·ly** *adv.* —**un·mean·ing·ness** *n.*

un·meas·ured (un-mézhərd) *adj.* **1.** Not yet measured. **2.** Measureless. **3.** *Music.* Without a fixed beat or bars.

un·men·tion·a·ble (un-ménsh'n-əb'l, ún-) *adj.* **1.** Not fit to be mentioned. **2.** Unspeakable. —**un·men·tion·a·ble·ness** *n.* —**un·men·tion·a·bly** *adv.*

un·men·tion·a·bles (un-ménsh'n-əb'lz) *pl.n.* Underwear. Now only in humorous usage.

un·mer·ci·ful (un-mérssif'l, ún-) *adj.* **1.** Having no mercy; merciless. **2.** Excessive: *unmerciful heat.* —**un·mer·ci·ful·ly** *adv.* —**un·mer·ci·ful·ness** *n.*

un·mind·ful (un-míndf'l, ún-) *adj.* Careless; forgetful; oblivious. Used with *of*: *unmindful of the time.* See Synonyms at **forgetful**. —**un·mind·ful·ly** *adv.* —**un·mind·ful·ness** *n.*

un·mis·tak·a·ble, un·mis·take·a·ble (ún-mi-stáykəb'l) *adj.* Obvious; evident; easily identifiable. —**un·mis·tak·a·ble·ness** *n.* —**un·mis·tak·a·bly** *adv.*

un·mit·i·gat·ed (un-mítti-gaytid) *adj.* **1.** Not diminished or moderated in intensity or severity; unrelieved. **2.** Absolute; unqualified. Used as an intensive: *an unmitigated lie.* —**un·mit·i·gat·ed·ly** *adv.*

un·moor (ún-mŏor, -mór) *v.* **-moored, -mooring, -moors.** —*tr.* **1.** To release from or as if from moorings. **2.** To release (a ship) from all but one anchor. —*intr.* To cast off moorings.

un·mor·al (ún-mórrəl ‖ -máwrəl) *adj.* Having no moral quality or sense; amoral. —**un·mo·ral·i·ty** (-mə-rál-əti, -mo- ‖ -maw-) *n.* —**un·mor·al·ly** *adv.*

un·mur·mur·ing (ún-múrmər-ing) *adj.* Not quibbling or complaining. —**un·mur·mur·ing·ly** *adv.*

un·muz·zle (ún-múzz'l) *tr.v.* **-zled, -zling, -zles. 1.** To remove the muzzle from. **2.** To free from censorship; allow to speak or write freely.

un·my·e·lin·a·ted (ún-mí-əlin-aytid) *adj.* Lacking a myelin sheath. Said of certain nerve fibres.

un·named (ún-náymd) *adj.* **1.** Having no name. **2.** Not referred to by name.

un·nat·u·ral (un-nách-rəl, ún-, -ərəl) *adj.* **1.** Violating natural law. **2.** Inconsistent with an individual pattern or custom. **3.** Deemed to deviate from a behavioural, ethical, or social norm: *unnatural practices.* **4.** Contrived or constrained; artificial: *an unnatural manner.* **5.** Outrageously violating natural or proper feelings; inhuman. —**un·nat·u·ral·ly** *adv.* —**un·nat·u·ral·ness** *n.*

un·nec·es·sar·y (un-néss-ə-sri, ún-, -i-, -səri, -serri) *adj.* Not necessary; needless or superfluous. —**un·nec·es·sar·i·ly** (-srəli, -sərəli, -serrəli, -sérrəli) *adv.* —**un·nec·es·sar·i·ness** *n.*

un·nerve (ún-nérv) *tr.v.* **-nerved, -nerving, -nerves.** To deprive of composure, confidence, or firmness of resolve.

unnil–. *comb. form.* Indicates a chemical element with an atomic number between 101 and 109.

un·nil·bi·um (oon-ílbi-əm) *n.* The chemical element **nobelium** *(see).*

un·nil·hex·i·um (oonnil-héksi-əm) *n.* Symbol **Unh** A synthetic radioactive chemical element with an atomic number of 106.

un·nil·pent·i·um (oonnil-pénti-əm) *n.* Symbol **Unp** A synthetic radioactive chemical element with an atomic number of 105.

un·nil·quad·i·um (oonnil-kwóddi-əm) *n.* Symbol **Unq** A synthetic radioactive chemical element with an atomic number of 104. Formerly called "kurchatovium", "rutherfordium".

un·nil·sept·i·um (oonnil-sépti-əm) *n.* Symbol **Uns** A synthetic radioactive chemical element with an atomic number of 107.

un·nil·tri·um (oonnil-trí-əm, un-íltri-əm) *n.* The chemical element **lawrencium** *(see).*

un·nil·un·i·um (oonnil-yóoni-əm) *n.* The chemical element **mendelevium** *(see).*

un·num·bered (ún-númbərd) *adj.* **1.** Not numbered; countless. **2.** Not marked with an identifying number.

U.N.O. (*sometimes* yŏo-nŏ). United Nations Organisation.

un·ob·tru·sive (ún-əb-trŏo-siv ‖ -ob-, tréw-, -ziv) *adj.* **1.** Not readily noticeable. **2.** Discreet. —**un·ob·tru·sive·ly** *adv.* —**un·ob·tru·sive·ness** *n.*

un·oc·cu·pied (ún-óckew-pīd, un-) *adj.* **1.** Not inhabited; vacant. **2.** Not occupied by foreign troops. **3.** Unemployed; idle.

un·of·fi·cial (ún-ə-físh'l ‖ -ŏ-) *adj.* **1.** Not official. **2.** Not acting officially. **3.** Not ratified by official trade union representatives: *unofficial strike action.* —**un·of·fi·cial·ly** *adv.*

un·or·gan·ised (ún-órgə-nīzd, un-) *adj.* **1.** Lacking order, system, or unity. **2.** Having no organic properties. **3.** Not unionised.

un·or·tho·dox (ún-órthə-doks, un-) *adj.* Not orthodox. —**un·or·tho·dox·ly** *adv.* —**un·or·tho·dox·y** (-i) *n.*

Unp The symbol for the element unnilpentium.

un·pack (ún-pák) *v.* **-packed, -packing, -packs.** —*tr.* **1.** To remove the contents of (a suitcase, for example). **2.** To remove from a container or from packaging. **3. a.** To remove a pack from (a pack animal). **b.** To unload the contents of (a motor vehicle). —*intr.* To unpack goods, a trunk, or the like. —**un·pack·er** *n.*

un·paid (ún-páyd) *adj.* **1.** Not yet paid: *an unpaid bill.* **2.** Serving without pay; unsalaried. **3.** Awaiting wages due.

un·pal·at·a·ble (un-pál-ətəb'l, ún-) *adj.* **1.** Unpleasant to the taste. **2.** Disagreeable; unpleasant: *unpalatable truths.*

un·par·al·leled (un-párrə-leld, ún-) *adj.* Without parallel; unmatched; unequalled.

un·par·lia·men·ta·ry (ún-párl-i-méntri, un-, -ə-, -méntəri, -yə-) *adj.* Not in accordance with parliamentary procedure.

un·peg (un-pég) *tr.v.* **-pegged, -pegging, -pegs. 1.** To remove the peg or pegs from. **2.** To allow (wages, prices, and the like) to fluctuate without restriction.

un·peo·ple (un-péep'l) *tr.v.* **-pled, -pling, -ples.** To depopulate.

un·per·fo·rat·ed (ún-pérfə-raytid) *adj.* **1.** Lacking perforations. **2.** *Philately.* Imperforate.

un·per·son (un-perss'n) *n., pl.* **unpersons. 1.** A person whose existence is denied or ignored by the authorities, especially in a totalitarian state. **2.** An insipid or unimpressive person. In both senses, also called "nonperson".

un·pick (ún-pík) *tr.v.* **-picked, -picking, -picks.** To undo (sewing) by removing stitches: *unpick a seam.*

un·pin (ún-pín) *tr.v.* **-pinned, -pinning, -pins. 1.** To remove a pin or pins from. **2.** In chess, to free (a piece).

un·pleas·ant (un-plézz'nt) *adj.* **-anter, -antest.** Not pleasing; offensive; disagreeable. **—un·pleas·ant·ly** *adv.*

un·pleas·ant·ness (un-plézz'nt-nəss, -niss) *n.* **1.** The condition or quality of being unpleasant. **2. a.** An unpleasant experience or situation. **b.** An argument or quarrel.

un·plug (ún-plúg, un-) *tr.v.* **-plugged, -plugging, -plugs. 1.** To remove a plug, stopper, or obstruction from. **2. a.** To remove (an electric plug) from a socket. **b.** To disconnect (an electric appliance) by removing its plug from a socket.

un·plumbed (ún-plúmd) *adj.* **1.** Not explored as to depth or meaning; not fathomed: *unplumbed waters; an unplumbed theory.* **2.** Having no plumbing. Said of a building, for example.

un·pop·u·lar (ún-póppew-lər, un-) *adj.* **1.** Lacking public approval or acceptance. **2.** Not approved of; out of favour: *You're unpopular with her these days.* **—un·pop·u·lar·i·ty** (-lárrəti) *n.*

un·prec·e·dent·ed (un-préssi-dentid, ún-, -prée-si-, -d'nt-id) *adj.* Without precedent; unheard of. **—un·prec·e·dent·ed·ly** *adv.*

un·pre·dict·a·ble (ún-pri-díkt-əb'l, -prə-) *adj.* Not predictable. **—un·pre·dict·a·bil·i·ty** (-ə-bílləti), **un·pre·dict·a·ble·ness** *n.* **—un·pre·dict·a·bly** *adv.*

un·prej·u·diced (ún-préjōōdist, un-) *adj.* Free from prejudice; impartial. See Synonyms at **fair.**

un·pre·med·i·tat·ed (ún-pri-méddi-taytid, -prée-) *adj.* Spontaneous; not planned: *"His one act of rebellion was quite unpremeditated"* (R. Prawer Jhabvala). See Synonyms at **extemporaneous.**

un·pre·pared (ún-pri-páird, -prə-) *adj.* **1.** Having made few or no preparations. **2.** Not equipped to meet a contingency. **3.** Not steeled, as to face a shock. **4.** Impromptu. **—un·pre·par·ed·ly** (-paír-id-li, -paírd-) *adv.* **—un·pre·par·ed·ness** *n.*

un·pre·pos·sess·ing (ún-préepə-zéssing, -zessing) *adj.* Failing to impress favourably; unattractive; nondescript. **—un·pre·pos·sess·ing·ly** *adv.*

un·pre·ten·tious (ún-pri-ténshəss, -prə-) *adj.* Lacking affectation or pretention; unostentatious; modest. **—un·pre·ten·tious·ness** *n.*

un·priced (ún-príst) *adj.* **1.** Having no fixed or attached price. **2.** *Archaic & Poetic.* Priceless.

un·prin·ci·pled (ún-prín-si-p'ld, un-, -sə-) *adj.* Lacking principles or moral scruples; unscrupulous: *unprincipled behaviour.*

un·print·a·ble (ún-príntəb'l, un-) *adj.* Not fit for publication, especially on grounds of infringing public taste or morality, libel laws, or the like.

un·pro·duc·tive (ún-prə-dúktiv ‖ -prō-) *adj.* **1.** Producing or yielding little or nothing. **2.** *Economics.* Adding nothing to exchangeable value. **—un·pro·duc·tive·ly** *adv.* **—un·pro·duc·tive·ness** *n.*

un·pro·fes·sion·al (ún-prə-fésh'n'l ‖ -prō-) *adj.* **1.** Not conforming to the standards of a profession. **2.** Amateurish. **3. a.** Not in a profession. **b.** Not a qualified member of a professional group. **—un·pro·fes·sion·al·ly** *adv.*

un·prof·it·a·ble (ún-próffit-əb'l, un-) *adj.* **1.** Not making a profit. **2.** Not profitable; serving no purpose; useless. **—un·prof·it·a·bil·i·ty** (-ə-bílləti) *n.* **—un·prof·it·a·bly** *adv.*

un·prompt·ed (ún-prómptid, un-) *adj.* Spontaneous; not asked for or suggested.

un·pro·nounce·a·ble (ún-prə-nówn-səb'l ‖ -prō-) *adj.* **1.** Difficult to pronounce correctly. **2.** Not fit to be mentioned. Said of obscenities.

un·pro·vid·ed (ún-prə-vídid ‖ -prō-) *adj.* Not supplied, furnished, or equipped. Used with *with.* **—unprovided for.** Not provided with an adequate means of support: *He left his children unprovided for.*

un·put·down·a·ble (ún-pŏot-dównəb'l, -pŏot-) *adj. Informal.* So interesting that the reader cannot put it aside. Said of a book.

Unq The symbol for the element unnilquadium.

un·qual·i·fied (ún-kwólli-fīd, un-. *Note: usually* ún- *for sense 1, un- for sense 2) adj.* **1.** Lacking the required qualifications. **2.** Without reservations; unconditional: *unqualified admiration.* Often used as an intensive: *an unqualified disaster.*

un·ques·tion·a·ble (un-kwéss-chən-əb'l, ún-, -kwésh-) *adj.* Beyond question or doubt; indisputable; certain. **—un·ques·tion·a·bil·i·ty** (-ə-bílləti), **un·ques·tion·a·ble·ness** *n.* **—un·ques·tion·a·bly** *adv.*

un·ques·tioned (un-kwéss-chənd, ún-, -kwésh-) *adj.* **1.** Not subjected to questioning. **2. a.** Unquestionable. **b.** Not called into question or examination; not doubted.

un·ques·tion·ing (un-kwéss-chən-ing, ún-, -kwésh-) *adj.* Asking no questions; not doubting or hesitating. **—un·ques·tion·ing·ly** *adv.*

un·qui·et (ún-kwí-ət, un-) *adj.* **-eter, -etest. 1.** Emotionally or mentally uneasy; agitated; disturbed. **2.** Characterised by unrest or uncertainty; turbulent: *unquiet times.* **—un·qui·et·ly** *adv.* **—un·qui·et·ness** *n.*

un·quote (ún-kwŏt, un-) *interj.* Used in speaking to indicate the end of a quotation.

un·rav·el (ún-rávv'l, un-) *v.* **-elled** or *U.S.* **-eled, -elling** or *U.S.* **-eling, -els. —tr. 1. a.** To undo or unpick the knitted or woven fabric of. **b.** To separate (entangled threads). **2.** To separate and clarify the elements of (something mysterious or baffling); solve. **—intr.** To become unravelled.

un·read (ún-réd) *adj.* **1.** Not read, studied, or perused. **2.** Having read little; ignorant: *unread in the classics.*

un·read·a·ble (ún-réed-əb'l, un-) *adj.* **1.** Illegible. **2.** Not interesting to read; dull. **3.** Incomprehensible; obscure. **—un·read·a·bil·i·ty** (-ə-bíllati), **un·read·a·ble·ness** *n.* **—un·read·a·bly** *adv.*

un·read·y[1] (ún-réddi, un-) *adj.* **-ier, -iest. 1.** Not ready or prepared. **2.** Slow in grasp or response; not prompt. **—un·read·i·ly** *adv.* **—un·read·i·ness** *n.*

unready[2] *adj. Archaic.* Unadvised; rash. Now used only in the title *Ethelred the Unready.* [UN- (lacking) + REDE + -Y, assimilated to *unready* (not ready).]

un·re·al (ún-réerl, un-, -rée-əl ‖ -réel) *adj.* **1.** Not real or substantial; imaginary; artificial. **2.** *Slang.* Amazing; out of this world: *Unreal, man!* **—un·re·al·i·ty** (-ri-ál-əti, -ree-) *n.*

un·re·al·is·tic (ún-reer-lístik, -réer-, -rée-ə- ‖ -reel-ístik, -réel-) *adj.* **1.** Lacking verisimilitude. **2.** Unlikely. **3. a.** Deluded; irrational. **b.** Not feasible or practicable. **—un·re·al·is·ti·cal·ly** *adv.*

un·rea·son (ún-réez'n) *n.* **1.** Absence or lack of reason; irrationality. **2.** Nonsense; absurdity.

un·rea·son·a·ble (un-réez'n-əb'l, ún-, -réeznəb'l) *adj.* **1.** Not governed by or based upon reason. **2.** Exceeding reasonable limits; exorbitant; immoderate. **—See Synonyms at excessive. —un·rea·son·a·ble·ness** *n.* **—un·rea·son·a·bly** *adv.*

unreasonable behaviour *n. Law.* Misconduct by a spouse given as grounds for divorce, especially when this demonstrates emotional or sexual incompatibility.

un·rea·son·ing (un-réez'n-ing, ún-, -réezning) *adj.* Not governed by reason; irrational. **—un·rea·son·ing·ly** *adv.*

un·re·con·struct·ed (ún-rée-kən-strúktid, -ree- ‖ -kon-) *adj.* **1.** Left unrepaired: *unreconstructed ruins.* **2.** Unreconciled to social and economic change: *an unreconstructed male chauvinist.*

un·reeve (ún-réev) *v.* **-reeved** or **-rove** (-rōv), **-reeved** or **-roven** (-rōv'n), **-reeving, -reeves.** *Nautical.* **—tr.** To withdraw (a rope, cable, or line) from a block, thimble, or other opening. **—intr. 1.** To become unreeved. **2.** To unreeve a rope.

UNREF. United Nations Refugee Emergency Fund.

un·re·fined (ún-ri-fínd, -rə-) *adj.* **1.** Not processed. Said of natural products such as oil or sugar. **2.** Coarse or brutish.

un·re·gen·er·ate (ún-ri-jénnə-rət, -rə-, -rit) *adj.* **1.** Not reformed or repentant. **2.** Obstinately prejudiced. **—un·re·gen·er·a·cy** (-rə-si) *n.* **—un·re·gen·er·ate·ly** *adv.*

un·re·hearsed (ún-ri-hérst, -rə-) *adj.* Not rehearsed. See Synonyms at **extemporaneous.**

un·re·lent·ing (ún-ri-lénting, -rə-) *adj.* **1.** Inexorable; merciless: *relenting fate.* **2.** Not diminishing in intensity, speed, or effort. **—un·re·lent·ing·ly** *adv.* **—un·re·lent·ing·ness** *n.*

un·re·li·a·ble (ún-ri-lí-əb'l, -rə-) *adj.* Not reliable. **—un·re·li·a·bil·i·ty** (-ə-bílləti), **un·re·li·a·ble·ness** *n.* **—un·re·li·a·bly** *adv.*

un·re·lieved (ún-ri-léevd, -rə-) *adj.* Not varied in any way; uniform: *unrelieved boredom.* **—un·re·liev·ed·ly** (-léevid-li) *adv.*

un·re·li·gious (ún-ri-líjəss, -rə-) *adj.* **1.** Irreligious. **2.** Having no connection with religion. **—un·re·li·gious·ly** *adv.*

un·re·mit·ting (ún-ri-mítting, -rə-) *adj.* Never slackening; incessant; persistent. **—un·re·mit·ting·ly** *adv.* **—un·re·mit·ting·ness** *n.*

un·re·quit·ed (ún-ri-kwítid, -rə-) *adj.* Not reciprocated. Said of feelings: *He pined away from unrequited love.*

un·re·served (ún-ri-zérvd, -rə-) *adj.* **1.** Not reserved for a particular use or person: *an unreserved seat.* **2.** Given without reservation; unqualified: *unreserved praise.* **3.** Not reserved in manner; frank. **—un·re·serv·ed·ly** (-zérvid-li) *adv.* **—un·re·serv·ed·ness** *n.*

un·re·spon·sive (ún-ri-spón-siv, -rə-) *adj.* Not responsive. **—un·re·spon·sive·ly** *adv.* **—un·re·spon·sive·ness** *n.*

un·rest (ún-rést, un-) *n.* **1.** Uneasiness; disquiet. **2.** Agitation; rebellion: *social unrest.*

un·re·strained (ún-ri-stráynd, -rə-) *adj.* **1. a.** Unchecked. **b.** Not given to restraint. **2.** Not constrained; natural. **—un·re·strain·ed·ly** (-stráynid-li) *adv.*

un·rid·dle (ún-rídd'l) *tr.v.* **-dled, -dling, -dles.** To solve or explain (a riddle or mystery).

un·ri·fled (ún-ríf'ld) *adj.* Having a smooth bore. Said of a gun.

un·rig (ún-ríg) *tr.v.* **-rigged, -rigging, -rigs.** *Nautical.* To strip (a vessel) of rigging.

un·right·eous (un-ríchəss, ún-, -rít-yəss) *adj.* **1.** Not righteous; wicked: *an unrighteous man.* **2.** Not right or fair; unjust: *unrighteous laws.* **—un·right·eous·ly** *adv.* **—un·right·eous·ness** *n.*

un·rip (ún-ríp) *tr.v.* **-ripped, -ripping, -rips.** To open, separate, or detach by ripping. [UN- (intensive) + RIP.]

un·ripe (ún-ríp) *adj.* **-riper, -ripest.** Also **un·rip·ened** (-rípənd) **1.** Not matured or ripe. **2.** Not fully developed; immature. **3.** Not ready or prepared. **—un·ripe·ness** *n.*

un·ri·valled (ún-rívv'ld, un-) *adj.* Unequalled; supreme.

un·roll (ún-rōl, un-) *v.* **-rolled, -rolling, -rolls. —tr. 1.** To unwind and open out (something rolled up). **2.** To unfold; reveal. **—intr.** To become unrolled.

un·root (ún-rŏot ‖ -rŏot) *tr.v.* **-rooted, -rooting, -roots.** *Archaic.* To uproot.

un·round (ún-równd, un- ‖ *West Indies also* -rúngd) *tr.v.* **-rounded, -rounding, -rounds.** *Phonetics.* To pronounce (a vowel sound) with the lips in a flattened or neutral position.

UNRRA United Nations Relief and Rehabilitation Administration.

un·ruf·fled (ún-rúff'ld, un-) *adj.* Not ruffled or agitated; calm. See Synonyms at **cool.**

un·ru·ly (un-rŏoli ‖ -réwli) *adj.* **-lier, -liest.** Difficult or impossible to govern; not amenable to control or discipline: *unruly locks of hair;*

the unruly mob. [Middle English *unruly* : UN- + *ruly,* easy to govern, from *rule,* RULE.] **—un·rul·i·ness** *n.*
Synonyms: *unruly, ungovernable, intractable, refractory, recalcitrant, wilful, headstrong, wayward.*
UNRWA United Nations Relief and Works Agency.
un·sad·dle (ún-sádd'l, un-) *v.* **-dled, -dling, -dles.** *—tr.* **1.** To remove the saddle from. **2.** To throw from the saddle; unhorse. *—intr.* To remove the saddle from a horse.
Uns The symbol for the element unnilseptium.
un·said (ún-séd, un-) *adj.* Not mentioned: *best left unsaid.*
un·sat·u·rate (un-sáchər-ət, ún-, -sáttewr-, -it, -ayt) *n.* An unsaturated chemical compound.
un·sat·u·rat·ed (ún-sáchər-aytid, un-, -sáttewr-) *adj.* **1.** Of or designating a compound, especially of carbon, containing atoms that share more than one valency bond. **2.** Capable of dissolving more of a solute at a given temperature. **—un·sat·u·ra·tion** (-áysh'n) *n.*
un·sa·vour·y (ún-sáyvəri, un-) *adj.* **1.** Distasteful or disagreeable. **2.** Morally offensive: *an unsavoury old lecher.* **—un·sa·vour·i·ly** *adv.* **—un·sa·vour·i·ness** *n.*
un·say (ún-sáy, -say) *tr.v.* **-said** (-séd, -sed), **-saying, -says** (-séz, -sez || -sáyz, -sayz). To retract (something said).
un·scathed (ún-skáyt͟hd, un-) *adj.* Unharmed; uninjured.
un·schooled (ún-skōōld) *adj.* **1.** Not schooled; uninstructed. **2.** Not the result of training; natural.
un·sci·en·tif·ic (ún-sī-ən-tíffik, -sī-) *adj.* **1.** Not in accordance with the principles of science; especially, deemed lacking in objectivity. **2.** Not familiar with science. **—un·sci·en·tif·i·cal·ly** *adv.*
un·scram·ble (ún-skrámb'l, un-) *tr.v.* **-bled, -bling, -bles.** **1.** To disentangle; straighten out; resolve. **2.** To restore (a scrambled message) to intelligible form. **—un·scram·bler** *n.*
un·screw (ún-skrōō, un- || -skréw) *v.* **-screwed, -screwing, -screws.** *—tr.* **1.** To take out the screw or screws from. **2.** To loosen, adjust, or detach by rotating. *—intr.* To become or admit of being unscrewed.
un·scru·pu·lous (un-skrōō-pewləss, ún- || -skréw-) *adj.* Without scruples; contemptuous of what is right or honourable. **—un·scru·pu·lous·ly** *adv.* **—un·scru·pu·lous·ness** *n.*
un·seam (ún-séem) *tr.v.* **-seamed, -seaming, -seams.** To undo the seam or seams of.
un·search·a·ble (ún-sérchəb'l, un-) *adj.* Beyond research; inscrutable; imponderable.
un·sea·son·a·ble (un-séez'n-əb'l, ún-, -séeznəb'l) *adj.* **1.** Not suitable to or appropriate for the season. **2.** Not characteristic of the time of year. **3.** Poorly timed; inopportune. **—un·sea·son·a·ble·ness** *n.* **—un·sea·son·a·bly** *adv.*
un·sea·soned (ún-séez'nd) *adj.* **1.** Not made savoury with seasoning. **2.** Inadequately aged or seasoned; not ripe or mature: *unseasoned wood.* **3.** Inexperienced. **—un·sea·soned·ness** *n.*
un·seat (ún-séet) *tr.v.* **-seated, -seating, -seats.** **1.** To remove from a seat, especially from a saddle. **2.** To dislodge from a position or office.
un·seem·ly (un-séemli) *adj.* **-lier, -liest.** Not in good taste; indecorous; unbecoming. See Synonyms at **improper.**
~adv. In an unseemly manner. **—un·seem·li·ness** *n.*
un·seen (ún-séen) *adj.* **1.** Not directly evident; invisible. **2.** Not previously read or studied: *We were set an unseen translation.*
~n. Chiefly British. An exercise involving translation of an unseen text, usually one that is to be translated into one's own language.
un·sel·fish (ún-sélfish, un-) *adj.* Not selfish; generous. **—un·sel·fish·ly** *adv.* **—un·sel·fish·ness** *n.*
un·set (ún-sét) *adj.* **1.** Not yet firm, stiff, or solidified, as jelly or concrete. **2.** Unmounted. Said especially of a precious stone. **3.** *Printing.* Not yet typeset.
un·set·tle (ún-sétt'l, un-) *v.* **-tled, -tling, -tles.** *—tr.* **1.** To displace from a settled condition; disrupt. **2.** To agitate mentally; make uneasy; disturb. *—intr.* To become unsettled.
un·set·tled (ún-sétt'ld, un-) *adj.* **1. a.** Disordered; disturbed: *unsettled times.* **b.** Worried; restless. **2.** Variable; uncertain: *unsettled weather.* **3.** Not determined or resolved: *an unsettled issue.* **4.** Not paid or adjusted: *an unsettled bill.* **5.** Not disposed of according to law: *an unsettled estate.* **6.** Unpopulated. **7.** Not fixed or established, as in a residence or routine. **—un·set·tled·ness** *n.*
un·sex (ún-séks, un-) *tr.v.* **-sexed, -sexing, -sexes.** To deprive of sexual capacity or sexual attributes.
un·shak·a·ble, un·shake·a·ble (un-sháykəb'l, ún-) *adj.* Incapable of being shaken or weakened; rigid; entrenched: *unshakeable convictions.* **—un·shak·a·bly** *adv.*
un·shap·en (ún-sháypən, un-) *adj.* Also **un·shaped** (-sháypt) (for sense 1). **1.** Not shaped or formed. **2.** Misshapen.
un·sheathe (ún-shéet͟h, un-) *tr.v.* **-sheathed, -sheathing, -sheathes.** To draw from or as if from a sheath or scabbard.
un·ship (ún-shíp) *v.* **-shipped, -shipping, -ships.** *—tr.* **1.** To unload from a ship; discharge. **2.** To remove (a tiller or other piece of nautical gear) from its proper place. *—intr.* To be removable or detachable.
un·sight·ed (ún-sītid) *adj.* **1.** Not sighted or examined. **2.** Not equipped with or assisted by a sight for aiming. **3.** Blind. **4.** Not having a clear view. **—un·sight·ed·ly** *adv.*
un·sight·ly (un-sīt-li) *adj.* **-lier, -liest.** Unpleasant or offensive to look at; unattractive. **—un·sight·li·ness** *n.*
un·sized (ún-sīzd) *adj.* Not coated or treated with size.
un·skil·ful (ún-skílf'l, un-) *adj.* Without skill or proficiency; not adroit; clumsy. **—un·skil·ful·ly** *adv.* **—un·skil·ful·ness** *n.*
un·skilled (ún-skíld) *adj.* **1.** Lacking skill or technical training. **2.** Requiring no training or skill. **3.** Showing no skill; crude.
un·slaked lime (ún-sláykt) *n.* **Calcium oxide** *(see).*
un·sling (ún-slíng) *tr.v.* **-slung** (-slúng), **-slinging, -slings.** **1.** To remove from a sling or a slung position. **2.** *Nautical.* To remove the slings of (a yard, for example).
un·snap (ún-snáp) *tr.v.* **-snapped, -snapping, -snaps.** To undo the snaps of; unfasten.
un·snarl (ún-snárl) *tr.v.* **-snarled, -snarling, -snarls.** To free of snarls; disentangle.
un·so·cia·ble (ún-sōsh-əb'l, un-) *adj.* **1.** Not disposed to seek the company of others; not companionable; reserved. **2.** Not conducive to social exchange: *an unsociable atmosphere.* **—un·so·cia·bil·i·ty** (-ə-bílləti), **un·so·cia·ble·ness** *n.* **—un·so·cia·bly** *adv.*
un·so·cial (ún-sōsh'l) *adj. Chiefly British.* **1.** Not compatible with or conducive to a full social life: *Because of the night shift duty she has to keep unsocial hours.* **2.** Unsociable. **—un·so·cial·ly** *adv.*
un·so·lic·it·ed (ún-sə-líssitid || -sō-) *adj.* Not solicited or asked for.
un·so·phis·ti·cat·ed (ún-sə-físti-kaytid || -sō-) *adj.* Not sophisticated. See Synonyms at **naive.** **—un·so·phis·ti·cat·ed·ly** *adv.*
un·sound (ún-sównd || *West Indies also* -súngd) *adj.* **-sounder, -soundest.** **1.** Not in strong or healthy condition; not sound or stable. **2.** Not soundly based in logic or fact; invalid. **3.** Not based on sound commercial or economic principles; not viable. **4.** Failing to conform to a given set of principles or dogmas: *an ideologically unsound policy.* **—un·sound·ly** *adv.* **—un·sound·ness** *n.*
un·spar·ing (un-spáir-ing) *adj.* **1.** Not frugal. **2.** Unmerciful; severe. **—un·spar·ing·ly** *adv.* **—un·spar·ing·ness** *n.*
un·speak·a·ble (un-spéekəb'l) *adj.* **1.** Beyond description; inexpressible: *unspeakable happiness.* **2.** Inexpressibly bad or objectionable. **—un·speak·a·ble·ness** *n.* **—un·speak·a·bly** *adv.*
un·sphere (ún-sféer) *tr.v.* **-sphered, -sphering, -spheres.** *Archaic.* To remove (a star, for example) from its sphere.
un·spoilt (ún-spóylt) *adj.* Also **un·spoiled** (-spóylt, -spóyld). Not marred in beauty or character by modernisation, industrialisation, or the like: *an unspoilt fishing village.*
un·spo·ken (ún-spōkən, un-) *adj.* **1.** Not uttered or expressed: *She bristled with unspoken resentment.* **2.** Understood without the need for words: *an unspoken pact between them.* **—un·spo·ken·ly** *adv.*
un·spot·ted (ún-spóttid) *adj.* **1.** Unnoticed; unseen. **2.** Not spotted or stained. **3.** Morally unblemished. **—un·spot·ted·ness** *n.*
un·sta·ble (ún-stáyb'l, un-) *adj.* **-bler, -blest.** **1. a.** Tending strongly to change. **b.** Not constant; fluctuating. **2. a.** Of fickle temperament; irresponsible. **b.** Psychologically maladjusted. **3.** Not firmly placed; unsteady. **4.** *Chemistry.* **a.** Decomposing readily. **b.** Highly or violently reactive. **5.** *Physics.* **a.** Decaying with relatively short lifetime. Said of subatomic particles. **b.** Radioactive. **—un·sta·ble·ness** *n.* **—un·sta·bly** *adv.*
un·stead·y (ún-stéddi, un-) *adj.* **-ier, -iest.** **1.** Not securely in place; unstable. **2.** Fluctuating; inconstant. **3.** Wavering; uneven: *an unsteady voice.* **4.** Unsure; precarious: *unsteady legs.*
~tr.v. **unsteadied, -ying, -ies.** To cause to become unsteady. **—un·stead·i·ly** *adv.* **—un·stead·i·ness** *n.*
un·step (ún-stép) *tr.v.* **-stepped, -stepping, -steps.** *Nautical.* To remove (a mast) from a step.
un·stick (ún-stík) *tr.v.* **-stuck** (-stúk), **-sticking, -sticks.** To free from being stuck.
un·stop (ún-stóp) *tr.v.* **-stopped, -stopping, -stops.** **1.** To remove a stopper or stop from. **2.** To remove an obstruction from; open.
un·stopped (ún-stópt) *adj.* **1.** Not stopped. **2.** *Phonetics.* Capable of being prolonged. Said of vowels, nasals, and fricative or liquid consonants. Not in current technical usage. **3.** Subject to enjambment. Said of line of poetry.
un·strat·i·fied (ún-strátti-fīd) *adj.* Lacking definite layers. Said of rocks.
un·streamed (ún-stréemd) *adj.* In British schools, not segregated or divided into streams according to ability.
un·stressed (ún-strést) *adj.* **1.** Not stressed or having the weakest stress. Said of a segment of speech. **2.** Not emphasised.
un·stri·at·ed (ún-strī-áytid || *chiefly U.S.* -strī-aytid) *adj.* **1.** Lacking striations; smooth-textured. **2.** Composed of spindle-shaped cells that lack striations; unstriped. Said of involuntary muscle.
un·string (ún-stríng) *tr.v.* **-strung** (-strúng), **-stringing, -strings.** **1.** To remove from a string. **2.** To unfasten the strings of. **3.** To weaken the nerves or resolve of; unnerve.
un·striped (ún-strīpt) *adj.* **1.** Not striped. **2.** Unstriated. Said of involuntary muscle.
un·struc·tured (ún-strúkchərd, un-) *adj.* **1.** Lacking a clear or formal structure or organisation. **2.** *Psychology.* Having no intrinsic or objective meaning; meaningful by subjective interpretation only. Said of items, such as inkblots or incomplete sentences, on projective tests. Compare **structured.**
un·strung (ún-strúng) *adj.* **1.** Having a string or strings loosened or removed. **2.** Emotionally upset; unnerved.
un·stuck (ún-stúk) *adj.* **1.** Freed from being stuck. **2.** Mentally unhinged. **—come unstuck.** *Informal.* To fail to achieve an intended result; go wrong: *All her plans came unstuck.*
un·stud·ied (ún-stúddid, un-) *adj.* **1.** Not contrived for effect; natural. **2.** Not having been instructed; unversed. Used with *in.*
un·sub·stan·tial (ún-səb-stánsh'l, -staánsh'l || -sub-) *adj.* **1.** Lacking material substance; insubstantial. **2.** Lacking firmness or strength; flimsy. **3.** Lacking basis in fact; insubstantial. **—un·sub·stan·ti·al·i·ty** (-stánshi-ál-əti) *n.* **—un·sub·stan·tial·ly** *adv.*

un·suc·cess·ful (ún-sək-sésf'l ‖ -suk-) *adj.* Not succeeding; without success. —**un·suc·cess·ful·ly** *adv.* —**un·suc·cess·ful·ness** *n.*

un·suit·a·ble (ún-sōot-əb'l, un-, -sēwt-) *adj.* Not suitable; inappropriate. —**un·suit·a·bil·i·ty** (-ə-bíllət i), **un·suit·a·ble·ness** *n.* —**un·suit·a·bly** *adv.*

un·sung (ún-súng) *adj.* 1. Not sung. 2. Not honoured or praised in song; uncelebrated: *unsung heroes.*

un·sure (ún-shōor, un-, -shór ‖ -shéwr) *adj.* 1. Lacking confidence. 2. Uncertain of the facts. 3. Precarious; unstable; unreliable. —**un·sure·ly** *adv.* —**un·sure·ness** *n.*

un·sus·pect·ed (ún-sə-spéktid) *adj.* 1. Not under suspicion. 2. Not known to exist. —**un·sus·pect·ed·ly** *adv.*

un·sus·pect·ing (ún-sə-spékting) *adj.* Not suspicious; trusting. —**un·sus·pect·ing·ly** *adv.*

un·swathe (ún-swáyth ‖ -swáwth, -swáath) *tr.v.* **-swathed, -swathing, -swathes.** *Archaic.* To remove the swathings from; unbind.

un·swear (ún-swáir) *v.* **-swore** (-swór ‖ -swór), **-sworn** (-swórn ‖ -swórn), **-swearing, -swears.** —*tr.* To retract (an oath). —*intr.* To recant or retract something sworn.

un·swerv·ing (un-swérving) *adj.* Unwavering; constant: *unswerving loyalty.* —**un·swerv·ing·ly** *adv.*

un·tan·gle (ún-táng-g'l, un-) *tr.v.* **-gled, -gling, -gles.** 1. To free from a tangle; disentangle. 2. To clarify; resolve.

un·taught (ún-táwt) *adj.* 1. Not instructed; ignorant. 2. Not acquired by instruction; natural; untutored. —See Synonyms at **ignorant.**

un·teach (ún-téech) *tr.v.* **-taught** (-táwt), **-teaching, -teaches.** 1. To cause to forget or unlearn something. 2. To negate (what has been taught) with contradictory information.

un·ten·a·ble (ún-tén-əb'l, un-, -téen-) *adj.* 1. Incapable of being maintained, defended, or vindicated: *an untenable proposition.* 2. Not suitable for occupation. —**un·ten·a·bil·i·ty** (-ə-bíllət i) *n.*

un·think (ún-thíngk) *tr.v.* **-thought** (-tháwt), **-thinking, -thinks.** To dismiss from the mind; disregard.

un·think·a·ble (un-thíngkəb'l) *adj.* 1. Not thinkable; inconceivable. 2. Not to be thought of or considered; out of the question. 3. Contrary to what is reasonable or probable. —**un·think·a·ble·ness** *n.* —**un·think·a·bly** *adv.*

un·think·ing (ún-thíngking, un-) *adj.* 1. Not thinking or mindful; inattentive; heedless. 2. Not deliberate; inadvertent. —**un·think·ing·ly** *adv.* —**un·think·ing·ness** *n.*

un·thought-of (un-tháwt-ov, ún- ‖ -uv) *adj.* Inconceivable; not imagined or considered.

un·thread (ún-thréd) *tr.v.* **-threaded, -threading, -threads.** 1. To draw out the thread from (a needle, for example). 2. To unravel. 3. To find one's way out of (a labyrinth, for example).

un·ti·dy (un-tíd i, ún-) *adj.* **-dier, -diest.** 1. Not neat and tidy; slovenly. 2. Lacking orderliness or organisation. —See Synonyms at **sloppy.**

~*tr.v.* **untided, -dying, -dies.** To make untidy. —**un·ti·di·ly** *adv.* —**un·ti·di·ness** *n.*

un·tie (ún-tí) *v.* **-tied, -tying, -ties.** —*tr.* 1. To undo or loosen (a knot or something knotted). 2. To free from something that binds or restrains. 3. To straighten out (difficulties or perplexities). —*intr.* To become untied.

un·til (ən-tíl, un-, ún-; *weak form* ən-til, -t'l) *prep.* 1. **a.** Up to the time of: *We danced until dawn.* **b.** As far as: *Keep going straight until the third set of traffic lights.* 2. Before a specific time. Used with a negative: *not until Friday.* 3. *Chiefly Scottish.* To; unto.

~*conj.* 1. Up to the time that. 2. Before. Used with a negative: *You can't have your pudding until you eat your greens.* 3. To the point or extent that. See Usage note at **till.** [Middle English *until(l),* to, towards, up to, till : *un-,* from Old Norse *und,* unto + *til,* TILL.]

un·time·ly (un-tímli, ún-) *adj.* **-lier, -liest.** 1. Occurring or done at an inappropriate time; inopportune. 2. Occurring too soon; premature: *untimely death.*

~*adv.* 1. Inopportunely. 2. Prematurely. —**un·time·li·ness** *n.*

un·tir·ing (un-tír ing, ún-) *adj.* 1. Not tiring. 2. Not ceasing despite fatigue or difficulties; persistent. —**un·tir·ing·ly** *adv.*

un·ti·tled (un-tít'ld) *adj.* 1. Having no right or claim. 2. Having no title: *an untitled novel; untitled nobility.*

un·to (ún-tōo, -tōo; *also, before consonant sounds only,* úntə) *prep.* *Poetic & Archaic.* To: *Unto us a child is born.* [Middle English *un-,* to (see until) + TO.]

un·told (ún-tóld) *adj.* 1. Not told or revealed: *untold secrets.* 2. Beyond description or enumeration: *untold suffering.*

un·touch·a·ble (un-túch-əb'l, ún-) *adj.* 1. Not to be touched. 2. Out of reach; unobtainable. 3. Beyond the reach of criticism, impeachment, or attack. 4. Loathsome, unpleasant, or defiling to the touch.

~*n.* A **harijan** *(see).* —**un·touch·a·bil·i·ty** (-ə-bíllət i) *n.*

un·touched (ún-túcht, ún-) *adj.* 1. Not used or touched: *untouched by human hand.* 2. Not discussed or referred to. 3. Not moved emotionally. 4. Not harmed or damaged: *killed her, but left the child untouched.* 5. Not modified or changed: *untouched photographs.*

un·to·ward (un-tə-wáwrd, -tōo-, -tō-ərd ‖ -tórd, -tórd) *adj.* 1. Unfavourable; unpropitious. 2. Characterised by disaster or misfortune. 3. Inappropriate; offensive: *untoward advances.* 4. *Archaic.* Hard to control; refractory. —**un·to·ward·ly** *adv.* —**un·to·ward·ness** *n.*

un·tram·melled (un-trámm'ld, ún-) *adj.* Unrestrained; not confined to rigid boundaries.

un·trav·elled (ún-trávv'ld, un-) *adj.* 1. Not traversed, as a road. 2. Not having travelled widely or far.

untouchable *The harijans, or "untouchables", form the lowest level in the Indian caste system. Traditionally, they are allowed only limited contact with other Hindu castes and are restricted to menial occupations. Officially, the Indian government has outlawed untouchability and given special privileges to former untouchables; but in practice discrimination lingers on.*

un·tread (ún-tréd) *tr.v.* **-trod** (-tród), **-trodden** (-tródd'n) or **-trod, -treading, -treads.** *Archaic.* To retrace (one's course).

un·tried (ún-tríd) *adj.* 1. Not attempted, tested, or proved. 2. Not tried in court.

un·true (ún-trōo, un- ‖ -tréw) *adj.* **-truer, -truest.** 1. Contrary to fact; false. 2. Deviating from a standard; not straight, even, or exact. 3. Disloyal; unfaithful. —**un·tru·ly** *adv.*

un·truss (ún-trúss) *v.* **-trussed, -trussing, -trusses.** —*tr.* 1. To unfasten; undo. 2. *Archaic.* To undress. —*intr.* *Archaic.* To remove one's clothes, especially one's breeches.

un·truth (ún-trōoth, un- ‖ -tréwth) *n.* 1. A lie. 2. The state or quality of being untrue; falsity.

un·truth·ful (ún-trōoth-f'l, un- ‖ -tréwth-) *adj.* 1. Given to falsehood; mendacious. 2. Contrary to truth. —See Synonyms at **dishonest.** —**un·truth·ful·ly** *adv.* —**un·truth·ful·ness** *n.*

un·tuck (ún-túk) *tr.v.* **-tucked, -tucking, -tucks.** To cause to hang out or not be tucked in: *Your shirt has become untucked.*

un·tu·tored (ún-téwtərd ‖ -tōotərd) *adj.* 1. Having had no formal education or instruction: *an untutored genius.* 2. Unsophisticated; unrefined: *an untutored palate.* —See Synonyms at **ignorant.**

un·twine (ún-twín) *v.* **-twined, -twining, -twines.** —*tr.* 1. To loosen or separate (strands of twisted fibre, for example). 2. To disentangle. —*intr.* To become untwined.

un·twist (ún-twíst, un-) *v.* **-twisted, -twisting, -twists.** —*tr.* To loosen or separate (that which is twisted together) by turning in the opposite direction; unwind. —*intr.* To become untwisted.

un·used (ún-yōozd, un- *for senses 1, 2;* -yōost *for sense 3) adj.* 1. Not in use or put to use. 2. Never having been used. 3. Not accustomed. Used with *to: unused to city traffic.*

un·u·su·al (un-yōozh-oo-əl, ún-, -yōozh-wəl, -'l, -yoo-əl) *adj.* Not usual or common. —**un·u·su·al·ly** *adv.* —**un·u·su·al·ness** *n.*

un·ut·ter·a·ble (un-úttrəb'l, -úttərəb'l) *adj.* 1. Not capable of being uttered or expressed; too profound to be expressed in words. 2. Not capable of being pronounced. 3. Utter; complete: *an unutterable idiot.* —**un·ut·ter·a·ble·ness** *n.* —**un·ut·ter·a·bly** *adv.*

un·var·nished (ún-várnisht, un-) *adj.* 1. Not varnished. 2. Stated or otherwise presented without any effort to soften, disguise, or obfuscate: *The unvarnished truth.*

un·veil (ún-váyl, un-) *v.* **-veiled, -veiling, -veils.** —*tr.* 1. To remove a veil or other covering from. 2. To disclose; reveal. —*intr.* To take off one's veil; reveal oneself.

un·veil·ing (un-váyling, ún-) *n.* A ceremony at which a portrait, monument, or other work of art is disclosed for the first time to public view.

un·voice (ún-vóyss) *tr.v.* **-voiced, -voicing, -voices.** *Phonetics.* To utter without vibrating the vocal cords; devoice.

un·voiced (ún-vóyst) *adj.* 1. Not expressed or uttered. 2. *Phonetics.* Voiceless.

un·waged (ún-wáyjd) *adj.* Not receiving a salary or wage. Said especially of a student or unemployed person.

un·war·rant·a·ble (un-wórrənt-əb'l ‖ -wáwrənt-) *adj.* Not justifiable; inexcusable. —**un·war·rant·a·bly** *adv.*

un·war·rant·ed (un-wórrənt-id ‖ -wáwrənt-) *adj.* Having no justification; groundless.

un·war·y (un-wáir-i, ún-) *adj.* **-ier, -iest.** Not alert to danger or deception; unguarded. —**un·war·i·ly** *adv.* —**un·war·i·ness** *n.*

un·washed (ún-wósht ‖ -wáwsht) *adj.* Not washed; unclean.

~*n.* The lower classes or the masses. Used derogatorily in the phrase *the great unwashed.*

un·watched (ún-wócht ‖ *U.S. also* -wáwcht) *adj.* Not manned. Said of an automatic device.

un·wa·ver·ing (un-wáyvəring) *adv.* Not wavering; constant: *unwavering accuracy; unwavering honesty.* —**un·wa·ver·ing·ly** *adv.*

un·wea·ried (un-wéer-id, un- ‖ -eed) *adj.* 1. Not tired; fresh. 2. Never wearying; tireless. —**un·wea·ried·ly** *adv.*

un·well (un-wél, un-) *adj.* Not well; ailing; ill. —See Synonyms at **sick.**

un·wept (ún-wépt) *adj.* 1. Not mourned or wept for: *the unwept dead.* 2. Not shed. Said of tears.

un·whole·some (ún-hōl-s'm, un-) *adj.* 1. Injurious to physical, mental, or moral health. 2. Suggestive of disease or degeneracy. 3. Offensive or loathsome. —**un·whole·some·ly** *adv.* —**un·whole·some·ness** *n.*

un·wield·y (un-wéeldi) *adj.* **-ier, -iest.** 1. Difficult to carry or manage because of bulk or shape. 2. Cumbersomely large or unmanageable: *an unwieldy bureaucracy.* 3. Clumsy; ungainly. —See Synonyms at **heavy.** —**un·wield·i·ly** *adv.* —**un·wield·i·ness** *n.*

un·willed (ún-wíld) *adj.* Involuntary; spontaneous.

un·will·ing (un-wílling, un-) *adj.* 1. Hesitant; loath. 2. Done, given, or said reluctantly: *unwilling consent.* —**un·will·ing·ly** *adv.* —**un·will·ing·ness** *n.*

un·wind (ún-wínd, un-) *v.* **-wound** (-wównd), **-winding, -winds.** —*tr.* 1. To reverse the winding or twisting direction of; unroll; uncoil. 2. To separate the tangled parts of; disentangle. —*intr.* 1. To become unwound. 2. *Informal.* To become less tense; relax. —**un·wind·a·ble** *adj.*

un·wink·ing (ún-wíngking, un-) *adj.* Vigilant; careful. —**un·wink·ing·ly** *adv.* —**un·wink·ing·ness** *n.*

un·wis·dom (ún-wízdəm) *n.* Lack of wisdom; foolishness.

un·wise (ún-wíz) *adj.* **-wiser, -wisest.** Lacking wisdom; foolish or imprudent. —**un·wise·ly** *adv.* —**un·wise·ness** *n.*

un·wish (ún-wísh) *tr.v.* **-wished, -wishing, -wishes.** 1. To cease to wish for. 2. To wish out of existence.

un·wished-for (un-wísht-fawr, ún-) *adj.* Not wished for or desired: *unwished-for criticism.*

un·wit·ting (un-wítting) *adj.* 1. Not knowing; unaware: *an unwitting victim of fraud.* 2. Not intended; unintentional. [Middle English *un-*, not + *witting*, present participle of *wit(t)en*, to know, Old English *witan.*] —**un·wit·ting·ly** *adv.* —**un·wit·ting·ness** *n.*

un·wont·ed (un-wŏnt-id ‖ -wónt-, *chiefly U.S.* -wáwnt-, -wúnt-) *adj.* Not habitual or ordinary; unusual. —**un·wont·ed·ly** *adv.* —**un·wont·ed·ness** *n.*

un·world·ly (ún-wúrldli, un-) *adj.* **-lier, -liest.** 1. Not of this world; extraterrestrial. 2. Concerned with matters of the spirit or soul. 3. Not worldly-wise; naive. —**un·world·li·ness** *n.*

un·wor·thy (un-wúrthi, ún-) *adj.* **-thier, -thiest.** 1. Insufficient in worth; undeserving. Usually used with *of.* 2. Not suiting or befitting. Usually used with *of.* 3. Lacking value or merit; worthless. 4. Vile; despicable. —**un·wor·thi·ly** *adv.* —**un·wor·thi·ness** *n.*

un·wrap (ún-ráp, un-) *v.* **-wrapped, -wrapping, -wraps.** —*tr.* To remove the wrappings from; open. —*intr.* To become or admit of being unwrapped.

un·writ·ten (ún-rítt'n, un-) *adj.* 1. Not written or recorded. 2. Forceful or effective through custom or tradition; not codified: *an unwritten rule.*

unwritten law *n.* A code, rule, or law of morality, conduct, procedure, or the like whose authority comes from custom, tradition, or general usage rather than formal legislation or regulation.

un·yield·ing (ún-yéelding, un-) *adj.* Inflexible; unwilling to move from a given position. See Synonyms at **inflexible.**

un·yoke (ún-yŏk, un-) *v.* **-yoked, -yoking, -yokes.** —*tr.* 1. To release (a draught animal) from a yoke. 2. To separate or disjoin. 3. To liberate. —*intr.* 1. To remove a yoke. 2. *Archaic.* To stop working.

un·zip (ún-zíp, un-) *v.* **-zipped, -zipping, -zips.** —*tr.* To open or unfasten (a zip or something held by a zip). —*intr.* To become unzipped.

up (up) *adv.* 1. From a lower towards a higher position. 2. In or at a higher position. 3. **a.** From a reclining to an upright position: *setting up the deckchairs.* **b.** Out of bed: *It's time you got up.* 4. **a.** Above a surface: *coming up for air.* **b.** From or off a surface: *pick it up.* **c.** Above the horizon: *The sun came up.* 5. **a.** Into view or consideration: *brought up the problem of redundancy pay.* **b.** Into existence or operation: *set up a committee.* 6. In or towards a position conventionally regarded as higher, as on a scale, chart, or map. 7. Towards the speaker or the place or person referred to: *She went right up to the policeman.* 8. **a.** In or towards a better position: *going up in the world.* **b.** *British.* In or towards a capital city or university, especially Oxford or Cambridge: *I'm going up to London; She's going up to Oxford to read maths.* 9. Before a court, magistrate, or an official board: *Your case is coming up for consideration.* 10. To or at a higher price. 11. So as to advance, increase, or improve: *Sales have gone up again.* 12. **a.** With or to a greater volume: *turn the music up.* **b.** To a higher pitch. 13. Into a state of excitement or turbulence: *He's quite wound up.* 14. **a.** So as to detach or unearth: *pull up weeds.* **b.** As an ejection from inside the body: *threw his meal up.* 15. To a stop: *She drew up at the kerb.* 16. Apart; into pieces: *tore it up.* 17. *Nautical.* To windward. 18. Completely; entirely: *Eat your meal up.* 19. Used as an intensive to suggest thoroughness or conclusiveness of an action: *cleaning up; typing up a list.* 20. **a.** All together: *add up; collect up.* **b.** From nothing: *cook up a plot; dreamed up from thin air.* 21. *U.S.* Each; apiece: *The score was eight up.* —**up** or **up with.** Used interjectionally as a cry of support: *Up United!*
~*adj.* 1. High or relatively high. 2. **a.** Standing; erect. **b.** Out of bed. 3. **a.** Moving or directed upwards: *an up escalator.* **b.** *British.* Towards a big city, especially London. Said of a train, railway line, platform, or the like. 4. Actively functioning; healthy: *up and about.* 5. Rising towards the flood level. 6. **a.** Marked by agitation or acceleration: *The winds are up.* **b.** Prepared to fight: *up in arms.* 7. *Informal.* Taking place; going on: *What's up?* 8. Being considered; under study: *a contract up for renewal.* 9. Charged; on trial. 10. Finished; over: *His time was up.* 11. Failed or lost hopelessly: *It's all up with me.* 12. *Informal.* Well-informed: *not up on sports.* 13. Being ahead of an opponent: *up two holes in a golf match.* 14. **a.** In tennis and similar games, not having bounced twice. Said of the ball. **b.** In the saddle. Said of a jockey. **c.** At bat. Said of a baseball player. 15. *Nautical.* Bound for a specified place. 16. In the process of being repaired. Said of a road. 17. *Physics.* Designating a quark with two-thirds the charge on the proton, and no strangeness, charm, or bottom. —**up against.** Confronted with; facing. —**up for.** 1. Free for: *up for sale; up for grabs.* 2. Running as a candidate for: *up for re-election.* —**up to.** 1. Occupied with; especially, devising or scheming: *idlers up to no good.* 2. Primed or prepared for: *Are you up to the challenge?* 3. Dependent upon: *It's up to us.* 4. As far as and including: *up to five of them.*
~*prep.* 1. From a lower to or towards a higher point on. 2. Towards or at a point farther along: *up the road.* 3. In a direction towards the source of: *up river.* 4. Against: *up the wind.* —**up yours.** *Slang.* Used interjectionally as an insult to express contempt or refusal.
~*n.* 1. An upward slope; a rise or ascent (of a ball, for example). 2. An upward movement or trend. —**on the up and up.** *Informal.* 1. *British.* Rising rapidly in status, achievement, or mood. 2. *U.S.* Open and honest.
~*v.* **upped, upping, ups.** —*tr.* 1. To increase or improve. 2. To

raise. —*intr.* 1. To get up; rise. 2. *Informal.* To act suddenly or unexpectedly. Usually used with *and*: *upped and left.* [Middle English *up*, upward, and *uppe*, on high, Old English *úp* and *uppe.*]

up– *prefix.* Indicates: 1. Up; for example, **uplift.** 2. Upper or better; for example, **upmost.** 3. Upwards; for example, **upsweep.** 4. Upside-down; for example, **upend, upturn.** 5. Resulting; for example, **upshot.** *Note:* Many compounds other than those entered here may be formed with *up-.* In this dictionary in forming compounds, *up-* is normally joined with the following element without space or hyphen: **upend.** However, the separate word **up** appears in a few phrases that are hyphenated. Among those entered here are: **up-and-coming, up-and-down, up-bow, up-market,** and **up-to-the-minute.** —See Usage note at **down.** [Middle English *up-*, Old English *úp-, upp-*, upwards, on high.]

up-and-com·ing (úp-ən-kúmming) *adj.* Likely to achieve success or improved status; promising or enterprising: *an up-and-coming young actress; an up-and-coming suburb.* —**up-and-com·er** *n.*

up and down *adv.* Backwards and forwards or in all directions: *pacing up and down.* —**up and down** *prep.*

up-and-down (úp-ən-dówn ‖ *West Indies also* -dúng) *adj.* 1. Characterised by alternating upward and downward movement; fluctuating. 2. *Chiefly U.S.* Vertical; perpendicular.

up-and-o·ver (úp-ən-ŏvər, -ənd-) *adj.* Opened by being raised and slipped over into a horizontal position: *an up-and-over door.*

U·pan·i·shad (ōō-púnni-shŏd, yōō-, -pánni-, -shad, -shaad) *n.* Any of a group of philosophical treatises contributing to the theology of Hinduism, elaborating upon the earlier Vedas. [Sanskrit *upaniṣad*, "a sitting down near to" : *úpa*, near to + *ni*, down + *sad-*, to sit.] —**U·pan·i·shad·ic** (-shúddik, -sháddik, -sháadik) *adj.*

u·pas (yōō-pəss ‖ -pass) *n.* 1. A tree, *Antiaris toxicaria*, of tropical Asia, once thought to be fatal to anyone who came near to or touched it, that yields a juice used as an arrow poison. Also called "upas-tree". 2. The poison obtained from this tree or similar trees or plants. [Javanese, poison, dart poison.]

up·beat (úp-beet) *n.* 1. *Music.* An unaccented beat, upon which the conductor's hand is raised; especially, the last beat of a bar. Compare **downbeat.** 2. An upward trend, as in one's fortune or career. Used chiefly in the phrase *on the upbeat.*
~*adj. Informal.* Optimistic; happy; cheerful.

up-bow (úp-bō) *n.* A stroke executed towards the heel of the bow on a violin or similar stringed instrument. Compare **down-bow.**

up·braid (up-bráyd, úp-) *tr.v.* **-braided, -braiding, -braids.** To reprove sharply; scold or chide vehemently; censure. See Synonyms at **scold.** [Middle English *upbreyden*, Old English *úpbrēdan*, "to throw up against", reproach : *úp-*, up + *bregdan*, to move quickly, throw, weave.] —**up·braid·er** *n.* —**up·braid·ing·ly** *adv.*

up·bring·ing (úp-bring-ing) *n.* The rearing and training received during childhood.

up·build (úp-bíld, up-) *tr.v.* **-built** (-bílt), **-building, -builds.** To build up; enlarge or enhance. —**up·build·er** *n.*

up·cast (úp-kaast ‖ -kast) *adj.* Directed or thrown upwards.
~*n.* 1. Something cast upwards. 2. A ventilating shaft, as in a mine.

up·com·ing (úp-kumming) *adj. U.S.* Anticipated; forthcoming.

up·coun·try (úp-kúntri ‖ *U.S.* -kuntri) *n.* The inland or interior region of a country.
~*adj.* (-kúntri). 1. Located in, originating from, or characteristic of the upcountry. 2. Countrified; unsophisticated.
~*adv.* (up-kúntri). In, to, or towards the upcountry.

up·date (úp-dáyt) *tr.v.* **-dated, -dating, -dates.** 1. To bring up to date: *update a textbook.* 2. *Computing.* To amend (data or programs, for example) so as to produce a new version, with a new address number.
~*n.* (úp-dayt). Current or updated information. 2. The act of updating something.

up·draught (úp-draaft ‖ -draft) *n.* An upward current of air.
~*adj.* Designating a carburettor in which the mixture is drawn upwards against gravity.

up·end (up-énd) *v.* **-ended; -ending, -ends.** —*tr.* To stand, set, or turn on one end. 2. To overturn or overthrow; upset. —*intr.* To be upended.

up-front, up front (úp-frúnt) *adj.* Frank; direct; forthright. —**up-front** *adv.*

up·grade (up-gráyd ‖ *chiefly U.S.* úp-grayd) *tr.v.* **-graded, -grading, -grades.** 1. To raise to a higher grade, standard, or position. 2. To improve the quality of (a manufactured product, for example).
~*n.* (úp-grayd). *U.S.* An incline leading uphill.
~*adj. U.S.* Uphill.
~*adv. U.S.* Uphill.

up·growth (úp-grōth) *n.* 1. Upward growth or development. 2. Something that has grown up.

up·heav·al (up-héev'l) *n.* 1. A sudden and violent disruption or upset. 2. *Geology.* A lifting up of the earth's crust by the movement of stratified or other rocks. [UP- + HEAVE + -AL.]

up·hill (up-híl) *adj.* 1. Going up a hill or slope. 2. Prolonged and laborious.
~*n.* (úp-hil). An upward slope or incline.
~*adv.* (-híl). 1. To or towards higher ground; upwards. 2. Against adversity; with difficulty.

up·hold (up-hŏld) *v.* **-held** (-héld), **-holding, -holds.** —*tr.* 1. **a.** To maintain or affirm in the face of a challenge. **b.** To support or stand by (a person or cause, for example). 2. To prevent from falling or sinking; support. 3. To hold aloft; raise. —*intr. Northern*

British. To declare; maintain. —See Synonyms at **support.** [Middle English *upholden* : UP- + HOLD.] —**up·hold·er** *n.*

up·hol·ster (up-hōl-stər, əp- ‖ -hŏl-) *tr.v.* **-stered, -stering, -sters.** **1.** To provide (chairs, sofas, or similar soft furniture) with stuffing, springs, cushions, and covering fabric. **2.** To furnish (rooms) with curtains, carpets, and similar accessories. [Back-formation from UPHOLSTERER.]

up·hol·ster·er (up-hōl-stərər, əp- ‖ -hŏl-) *n.* A person who upholsters furniture as an occupation. [Obsolete *upholster,* a dealer in or repairer of small wares, Middle English *upholdester,* one who upholds or repairs, from *upholden,* to UPHOLD.]

up·hol·ster·y (up-hōl-stəri, əp-, -stri ‖ -hŏl-) *n., pl.* **-ies.** **1.** The fabrics and other materials used in upholstering. **2.** The act, craft, or business of upholstering.

uphroe. Variant of **euphroe.**

UPI, U.P.I. United Press International.

up·keep (ŭp-kēp) *n.* **1.** The act or process of maintaining something in good condition and repair. **2.** The cost of such maintenance.

up·land (ŭp-lənd ‖ -land) *n. Often plural.* The higher parts of a region, country, or tract of land. —**up·land** *adj.*

upland cotton *n.* **1.** A cotton plant, *Gossypium hirsutum,* native to tropical America and widely cultivated for its fibre. **2.** The fibre of this plant.

up·lift (up-lĭft) *tr.v.* **-lifted, -lifting, -lifts.** **1.** To lift up or raise aloft. **2.** To raise to a higher spiritual, intellectual, or social level; exalt; elevate.
~*adj.* (ŭp-lĭft). Uplifting: *an uplift bra.*
~*n.* (ŭp-lĭft). **1.** The act, process, or result of raising or lifting up. **2.** Any agent or influence causing upward movement or lifting. **3.** A movement to improve social, moral, or intellectual standards. **4.** *Geology.* An upheaval.

up·mar·ket (ŭp-märkĭt) *adj. Chiefly British.* **1.** Of, designating, or intended for consumers belong to the higher socioeconomic groups. **2.** Superior in quality or style. Compare **down-market.**

upmost. Variant of **uppermost.**

up·on (ə-pŏn ‖ up-ón, ə-páwn, -pún) *prep.* On. [Middle English (formed after Old Norse *upp ā*) : UP + ON.]
    Usage: Upon is basically interchangeable with *on,* although it is slightly more formal. It is always used however, in fixed phrases such as the following: *Once upon a time; upon my word; (winter) is almost upon us; (row) upon (row) of (seats).* See Usage note at **on.**

up·per (ŭppər) *adj. Abbr.* **up, u., U. 1.** Higher in place, power, position, or rank. **2. a.** Situated on higher ground. **b.** Lying farther inland. **c.** Northern. **3.** *Capital* **U.** *Geology & Archaeology.* Being a later division of the period named. **4.** *Mathematics.* Designating or pertaining to the highest value in a set.
~*n.* **1.** That part of a shoe or boot above the sole. **2.** *Informal.* An upper berth. **3.** *Plural. Informal.* The upper teeth or a set of upper dentures. **4.** *Slang.* A drug, often an amphetamine, used as a stimulant. Compare **downer.** —**on (one's) uppers.** *Informal.* Impoverished. [Referring to someone whose shoe soles have worn away].

upper atmosphere *n.* That part of the atmosphere above 30 kilometres high and inaccessible to direct observation by balloon.

upper bound *n.* A number that is not exceeded by any number in a given set.

upper case *n. Abbr.* **u.c. 1.** Capital letters. **2.** The case of printing type containing the capital letters and special characters.

up·per-case (ŭppər-káyss) *adj. Abbr.* **u.c.** *Printing.* Pertaining to or designating capital letters; capital.
~*tr.v.* **upper-cased, -casing, -cases.** To print in upper-case letters.

upper class *n. Often plural.* The usually small class in a society considered to rank highest, socially or economically; especially, the aristocracy. —**up·per-class** (ŭppər-kláass ‖ -kláss) *adj.*

upper crust *n. Informal.* The upper class.

up·per·cut (ŭppər-kut) *n. Boxing.* A short swinging blow directed upwards, as to the opponent's chin. —**up·per·cut** *v.*

upper hand *n.* A position of control or advantage. Preceded by *the.*

Upper House *n.* The branch of a bicameral legislature such as the House of Lords in the British Parliament. Also called "Upper Chamber". Compare **Lower House.**

up·per·most (ŭppər-mōst) *adj. Also* **up·most** (ŭp-mōst). Highest in position, place, rank, or influence; topmost; foremost.
~*adv.* In the highest or most prominent rank, position, or place; first: *whatever else is uppermost in your mind.*

Upper Vol·ta (vŏl-tə ‖ vŏl-). *French* **Haute-Volta.** Landlocked state in the Sahel region of West Africa. It is one of the world's poorest countries, depending on aid, mostly from France. Over 90 per cent of its people are farmers, most at subsistence level. Some cattle and cotton are exported. A French colony from 1896, Upper Volta became independent in 1960. Area, 274 200 square kilometres (105,869 square miles). Population, 6,700,000. Capital Ouagadougou. See map at **West African States.**

up·pish (ŭppish) *adj.* **1.** *British Informal.* Tending to be snobbish or arrogant. **2.** Designating a stroke in cricket which sends the ball too high, so that it is liable to be easily caught. [UP + -ISH.] —**up·pish·ly** *adv.* —**up·pish·ness** *n.*

up·pi·ty (ŭppəti, ŭppiti) *adj. Informal.* **1.** Petulant or recalcitrant. **2.** Snobbish; uppish. [From UP.]

Upp·sa·la *or* **Up·sa·la** (ŭp-saalə, ŏŏp-, up-saálə, ŏŏp-; *Swedish* ŏŏp-saalə). City in eastern Sweden, lying on the river Fyrisån, just northwest of Stockholm. Its 13th century cathedral has traditionally been used for the coronation of Swedish monarchs.

up·raise (up-ráyz, ŭp-) *tr.v.* **-raised, -raising, -raises.** *Archaic & Poetic.* To raise or lift up; elevate.

up·rear (up-réer, ŭp-) *v.* **-reared, -rearing, -rears.** —*tr.* To raise or lift up. —*intr.* To be raised up; rise.

up·right (ŭp-rīt) *adj.* **1. a.** In a vertical position, direction, or stance. **b.** Erect in posture or carriage. **2.** Morally respectable; honourable; righteous. —See Synonyms at **vertical.**
~*adv.* In a vertical or erect position: *walk upright.*
~*n.* **1.** A perpendicular position; verticality. **2.** Something standing upright, such as a beam. **3.** An upright piano. [Middle English *upright,* Old English *ūpriht* : UP- + RIGHT.] —**up·right·ly** *adv.* —**up·right·ness** *n.*

upright piano *n.* A piano having the strings mounted vertically in a rectangular case with the keyboard at a right angle to the case. Also called "upright". Compare **grand piano.**

up·rise (ŭp-rīz, ŭp-) *intr.v.* **-rose** (-rōz), **-risen** (-rĭzz'n), **-rising, -rises. 1.** To get up or stand up; rise. **2.** To go, move, or incline upwards; ascend. **3.** To rise into view, especially from below the horizon.
~*n.* (ŭp-rīz). **1.** The act or process of rising up. **2.** Something that rises or slopes up.

up·ris·ing (ŭp-rīzing, -rīzing) *n.* **1.** A revolt; an insurrection. **2.** *Archaic.* An upward motion. —See Synonyms at **rebellion.**

up·riv·er (ŭp-rĭvvər) *adv.* Towards or near the source of a river; in the direction opposite to that of the flow of water.
~*n.* A region lying upriver. —**up·riv·er** *adj.*

up·roar (ŭp-rawr ‖ -rōr) *n.* **1.** A condition of noisy excitement and confusion; a tumult. **2.** A heated controversy. —See Synonyms at **noise.** [Alteration (influenced by ROAR) of Dutch *oproer,* from Middle Dutch : *op,* up + *roer,* confusion.]

up·roar·i·ous (ŭp-ráw-ri-əss, ŭp- ‖ -rō-) *adj.* **1.** Causing or accompanied by an uproar. **2.** Loud and full, as laughter; boisterous. **3.** Causing hearty laughter; hilarious. [UPROAR + -IOUS.] —**up·roar·i·ous·ly** *adv.* —**up·roar·i·ous·ness** *n.*

up·root (ŭp-rŏŏt ‖ -rŏŏt) *tr.v.* **-rooted, -rooting, -roots. 1.** To tear or remove (a plant and its roots) from the ground. **2.** To destroy or remove completely; eradicate. **3.** To force to leave an accustomed or native location. —**up·root·ed·ness** *n.* —**up·root·er** *n.*

up·rush (ŭp-rush) *n.* An upward rush, as of blood to the face or an emotion from the subconscious.

ups and downs *pl.n.* Alternating periods of good and bad fortune or high and low spirits.

up·set (up-sét) *v.* **-set, -setting, -sets.** —*tr.* **1.** To overturn or capsize; tip over. **2.** To disturb in usual or normal functioning, order, or course. **3.** To distress or perturb mentally or emotionally. **4.** To defeat unexpectedly. **5.** To cause illness or indigestion in (the stomach). **6.** To make shorter and thicker by hammering on the end; swage. —*intr.* **1.** To become overturned; tip over; capsize. **2.** To become disturbed.
~*n.* (ŭp-set). **1. a.** An act of upsetting. **b.** The condition of being upset. **2.** A disturbance, disorder, or agitation. **3.** A bodily disorder: *a stomach upset.* **4.** A game or contest in which the favourite is defeated. **5. a.** A tool used for upsetting; a swage. **b.** An upset part or piece.
~*adj.* (ŭp-sét). **1.** Overturned; capsized. **2.** Disordered; disturbed. **3.** Suffering from indigestion, nausea, or a similar condition: *an upset stomach.* **4.** Agitated; distraught. **5.** Overthrown; defeated. [Originally "to set up", "erect", later "to overset", Middle English *upsetten* : UP + *setten,* to SET.] —**up·set·ter** *n.* —**up·set·ting·ly** *adv.*

upset price *n. U.S. & Scottish.* The reserve price at an auction.

up·shot (ŭp-shot) *n.* The final result; the outcome. See Synonyms at **effect.** [Originally the last shot at an archery contest, hence an outcome or decision.]

up·side-down (ŭp-sīd-dówn ‖ *West Indies also* -dúng) *adj.* **1.** Overturned completely so that the upper side is down. **2.** In great disorder or confusion; topsy-turvy.
~*adv. Also* **upside down. 1.** With the upper side down. **2.** Topsy-turvy. —**turn upside-down.** To ransack. [Alteration (influenced by obsolete *upside*) of earlier *upsedown,* Middle English *up so doun,* "up as if down" : UP + SO + DOWN.] —**up·side-down·ness** *n.*

upside-down cake *n.* A single-layer cake or sponge pudding baked with sliced fruit at the bottom, then served with the fruit side up.

up·sides (ŭp-sīdz) *adv. British.* Equal, as by retaliation or revenge. Used with *with.*

up·si·lon (yŏŏp-sī-lən, ŏŏ-, -lon, *also* yŏŏpsi- ‖ upsi-) *n.* The 20th letter in the Greek alphabet, written Υ, υ. Transliterated in English as *U, u,* or *y,* and as *v* or *f* when it follows a vowel in Modern Greek. [Medieval Greek *u psilon,* "simple upsilon" (name adopted for graphic *u* as distinguished from graphic *oi,* both of which were pronounced identically as (ee) in Late Greek) : Greek *u,* upsilon + *psilon,* neuter of *psilos,* bare, simple, mere.]

up·spring (ŭp-spring) *intr.v.* **-sprang** (-spráng) *or* **-sprung** (-sprúng), **-sprung, -springing, -springs.** *Archaic & Poetic.* **1.** To spring up, as from the soil. **2.** To come into being; arise.

up·stage (ŭp-stáyj, up-) *adj.* **1.** At, pertaining to or involving the rear of a stage. **2.** *Informal.* Haughty; aloof.
~*adv.* Towards, to, on, or at the back part of the stage.
~*tr.v.* **upstaged, -staging, -stages. 1.** To distract the audience's attention from (another actor), as by standing behind him or forcing him to face upstage. **2.** *Informal.* To steal the show from; force out of the spotlight. **3.** *Informal.* To treat haughtily.

up·stairs (ŭp-stáirz) *adv.* **1.** In, on, or to an upper floor or storey; up the stairs. **2.** *Informal.* In or to a higher rank. **3.** *Informal.* Mentally: *not all there upstairs.* —**kick upstairs.** *Informal.* To dispose of by promoting to an ineffectual position.

~*adj.* Of or on an upper floor or floors: *an upstairs bathroom.* ~*n.* Used with a singular or plural verb. **1.** A floor or the floors above ground level or a given level. **2.** *British Informal.* Formerly, the masters of a house as opposed to their servants. Compare **downstairs.**

up·stand·ing (up-stánding, úp-) *adj.* **1.** Standing erect or upright. **2.** Morally upright; honest. —**be upstanding.** To stand up. Used in the imperative in courts of law when the judge enters or leaves. —**up·stand·ing·ness** *n.*

up·start (úp-staart) *n.* **1.** One that springs up suddenly; specifically, a person of humble origin who attains sudden wealth or consequence; a parvenu. **2.** A person having an exaggerated sense of his own importance or ability: *cocky little upstart.*
~*adj.* **1.** Suddenly raised to a position of consequence. **2.** Characteristic of an upstart; self-important; presumptuous.
~*intr.v.* (-stárt) **upstarted, -starting, -starts.** *Archaic.* To spring or start up suddenly.

up·state (úp-stayt) *adj. U.S.* Pertaining to or designating that part of a state lying inland or farther north of a large city.
~*n.* The upstate region. —**up·state** (-stáyt) *adv.* —**up·stat·er** *n.*

up·stream (úp-stréem, -streem) *adv.* In, at, or towards the source of a stream or current.
~*adj. Finance.* Closer to the point of production or manufacture than to the point of sale.

up·stroke (úp-strŏk) *n.* **1.** An upward stroke, as of a brush. **2.** The upward movement of a piston in a reciprocating engine or pump in which the cylinder is cleared of fluid.

up·surge (úp-surj) *n.* A rapid upward swell or rise.

up·sweep (úp-sweep) *n.* **1.** A curve or sweep upwards. **2.** *U.S.* A hairstyle that is smoothed upwards at the back and piled on top of the head.
~*tr.v.* (-sweep, -sweep) **upswept** (-swépt, -swept), **-sweeping, -sweeps.** To brush, curve, or sweep upwards.

up·swing (úp-swing) *n.* An upward swing or trend; an increase, as in movement or activity: *an upswing on the stock market.*

up·sy-dai·sy (úpsi-dáyzi, úpsa-) *interj.* Used when swinging a child into the air or expressing concern over its fall. [From earlier *up-a-daisy;* irregularly from UP; compare LACKADAISICAL.]

up·take (úp-tayk) *n.* **1.** Understanding; comprehension: *very quick on the uptake.* **2.** A passage for drawing up smoke or air; a flue or ventilating shaft. **3.** An act of taking in or absorbing, especially into a living organism.

up·throw (úp-thrŏ) *n.* **1.** A throwing upwards. **2.** *Geology.* An upward displacement of rock on one side of a fault.

up·thrust (úp-thrust) *n.* **1.** A thrusting or pushing upwards. **2.** *Geology.* An upheaval of the earth's surface.

up·tight (úp-tít) *adj. Slang.* **1.** Tense; nervous; repressed. **2.** Angry. —**up·tight·ness** *n.*

up-to-date, up to date (úp-tə-dáyt) *adj.* Informed of or reflecting the latest improvements, facts, or style; modern. —**up-to-date·ly** *adv.* —**up-to-date·ness** *n.*

up-to-the-min·ute, up to the minute (úp-tə-<u>th</u>ə-mínnit) *adj.* Being or having the most recent information, style, or fashion. —**up-to-the-min·ute·ness** *n.*

up·town (úp-tówn) *adv. Chiefly U.S.* In or towards the upper part of a town or city.
~*n.* (-town). *Chiefly U.S.* The upper part of a town or city. Compare **downtown.** —**up·town** *adj.*

up·turn (up-túrn, úp-turn) *v.* **-turned, -turning, -turns.** —*tr.* **1.** To turn (soil, for example) up or over. **2.** To upset; overturn. **3.** To direct upwards. —*intr.* To turn over or up.
~*n.* (úp-turn). An upward movement, curve, or trend.

UPU Universal Postal Union.

up·ward (úp-wərd) *adj.* Directed or moving towards a higher place or position.
~*adv. Chiefly U.S.* Variant of **upwards.** —**up·ward·ly** *adv.* —**up·ward·ness** *n.*

up·wards (úp-wərdz) *adv.* Also *chiefly U.S.* **upward. 1.** In, to, or towards a higher place, level, or position. **2.** To or towards the source, origin, or interior. **3.** Towards the head or upper parts. **4.** Towards a higher amount, degree, or rank: *Prices soared upwards.* **5.** Towards a later time or greater age. **6.** Towards something greater or better. —**upwards of.** More than; in excess of. [Middle English *upward,* Old English *úpweard* : UP- + -WARD.]

up·wind (úp-wínd) *adv.* In or towards the direction from which the wind blows.
~*adj.* **1.** Going against the wind. **2.** On the windward side.

Ur (ur, oor). Ancient city of Sumer, southern Mesopotamia, whose site was discovered in the 19th century. The great ziggurat of Ur, which still stands in crumbling condition, was built by King Ur-Nammu, who established the third dynasty of Ur in *c.* 2060 B.C.

ur-¹. Variant of **uro-¹, uro-².**

ur-² *n. prefix. Sometimes capital* **U.** Indicates: **1.** Primitive, basic; for example, *ur-legend.* **2.** The original version of; for example, *urtext.* [German.]

u·ra·cil (yóor-ə-sil, yór-) *n.* A pyrimidine, $C_4H_4N_2O_2$, a constituent of RNA. [UR(O)- + AC(ETIC) + -IL(E).]

u·rae·mi·a, *U.S.* **u·re·mi·a** (yoor-réemi-ə, yŏŏ-) *n.* The presence of excess urea and other waste products in the blood, which occurs in kidney disease and is characterised by headache, nausea, vomiting,

and lethargy. Also called "azotaemia". [New Latin : UR(O)- + -AEMIA.] —**u·rae·mic** *adj.*

u·rae·us (yoor-rée-əss, yŏŏ-) *n., pl.* **uraei** (-ī) or **uraeuses.** The figure of the sacred serpent, depicted on the headdress of ancient Egyptian rulers and deities as an emblem of sovereignty. [New Latin, from Late Greek *ouraios,* from Egyptian for "cobra".]

U·ral (yŏor-əl, yór-). River in the U.S.S.R., rising in the south Ural mountains and flowing south and west for about 2 540 kilometres (1,580 miles) until it empties into the Caspian Sea at Gurjev.

U·ral-Al·ta·ic (yŏor-əl-al-táy-ik, yór-) *n.* A hypothetical group of languages including the Uralic and Altaic families, characterised by agglutination and vowel harmony. Also called "Turanian". —**U·ral-Al·ta·ic** *adj.*

U·ral·ic (yoor-rál-ik, yŏŏ-) *n.* Also **U·ra·li·an** (-ráyli-ən). A family of languages including the Finno-Ugric and Samoyed subfamilies.
~*adj.* Of or designating this language family.

u·ral·ite (yŏor-əl-īt, yór-) *n.* An amphibole mineral that replaces pyroxene in some igneous and metamorphic rocks. [German *Uralit,* after the URAL MOUNTAINS + -ITE.]

Ural Mountains. Also **Urals.** Mountain range of the U.S.S.R., extending for about 2 400 kilometres (1,500 miles) southwards from the Arctic coast. It is generally considered to form, with the river Ural, the boundary between the European and the Asian U.S.S.R.

uran-. Variant of **urano-.**

u·ra·ni·a (yoor-ráyni-ə, yŏŏ-) *n.* Uranium dioxide *(see).* [New Latin : URANIUM + -a (oxide).]

U·ra·ni·a (yoor-ráyni-ən, -yŏŏ- ‖ yew-). *Greek Mythology.* The Muse of astronomy. [Latin, from Greek *Ourania,* "the heavenly one", from *ouranos,* heaven. See **Uranus.**]

U·ra·ni·an (yoor-ráyni-ən, yŏŏ-) *adj.* **1.** Of or pertaining to the planet Uranus. **2.** Celestial. **3.** Of or pertaining to astronomy or to the Muse Urania. **4.** Of or pertaining to homosexuality.
~*n.* **1.** A fictional inhabitant of the planet Uranus. **2.** *Rare.* A homosexual.

u·ran·ic (yoor-ránnik, yŏŏ-) *adj.* **1.** *Archaic.* Of or relating to the heavens; celestial. **2.** *Chemistry.* Of, pertaining to, or derived from uranium, especially with a valency higher than in comparable uranous compounds. [Sense 1, from Latin *ūranus,* heaven, from Greek *ouranos.* See **Uranus.** Sense 2, from URANIUM.]

u·ran·ide (yŏor-ən-īd, yór-) *n.* Any element having an atomic number in excess of 91. [URAN(IUM) + -IDE.]

u·ra·ni·nite (yoor-ráyni-nīt, yŏŏ-, -ránni-) *n.* A complex brownish-black mineral, chiefly UO_2 partially oxidised to U_3O_8 and containing variable amounts of radium, lead, thorium, rare-earth metals, helium, argon, and nitrogen. Also called "pitchblende". [German *Uranin,* uraninite : URAN(IUM) + -IN.]

u·ran·ism (yŏor-ən-iz'm, yór-) *n. Rare.* Homosexuality, especially of males. [19th century : from German *Uranismus,* from Greek *ouranios,* heavenly (taken as meaning "spiritual"), from *ouranos†,* sky, heaven.]

u·ran·ite (yŏor-ən-īt, yór-) *n.* Either of two uranium-bearing minerals, torbernite (copper uranite) or **autunite** (lime uranite). [URAN(IUM) + -ITE.]

u·ra·ni·um (yoor-ráyni-əm, yŏŏ-) *n. Symbol* **U** A heavy silvery-white metallic element, radioactive, easily oxidised, and having 14 known isotopes of which uranium-238 is the most abundant in nature. The element occurs in several minerals, including uraninite and carnotite, from which it is extracted and processed for use in research, nuclear fuels, and nuclear weapons. Atomic number 92, atomic weight 238.03, melting point 1,132°C, boiling point 3,818°C, relative density 18.95, valencies 3, 4, 5, 6. [New Latin, after the planet URANUS (to contrast with the recently named TELLURIUM).]

uranium-235 *n.* The uranium isotope with mass number 235 and half-life 7.13×10^8 years, fissionable with slow neutrons and capable in a critical mass of sustaining a chain reaction that can proceed explosively with appropriate mechanical arrangements.

uranium-238 *n.* The most common isotope of uranium, having mass number 238 and half-life 4.51×10^9 years, nonfissionable but producing when irradiated with neutrons fissionable plutonium-239.

uranium dioxide *n.* A black toxic crystalline powder, UO_2, formerly used in ceramic glazes, now used to pack nuclear fuel rods. Also called "urania".

uranium series *n.* A radioactive series of elements that starts with uranium-238 and ends with the stable element lead-206.

uranium trioxide *n.* A radioactive orange powder, UO_3, used in uranium refining and as a colouring agent in ceramics.

urano-, uran-. *comb. form.* Indicates: **1.** The heavens; for example, **uranography. 2.** Uranium; for example, **uranyl.** [Greek *ouranos†,* sky, heaven.]

u·ra·nog·ra·phy (yŏor-ə-nóggrə-fi, yór-) *n.* The branch of astronomy concerned with mapping the stars, galaxies, or other heavenly bodies. [URANO- + -GRAPHY.] —**u·ra·nog·ra·pher** (-fər), **u·ra·nog·ra·phist** *n.* —**u·ra·no·graph·ic** (-nə-gráffik), **u·ra·no·graph·i·cal** *adj.*

u·ra·nous (yŏor-ənəss, yór-, *also* yoor-ráynəss, yŏŏ-) *adj. Chemistry.* Of or pertaining to uranium, especially with a valency lower than in comparable uranic compounds.

U·ra·nus¹ (yŏor-ənəss, yór-; yoor-ráynəss, yŏŏ-). *Greek Mythology.* The earliest supreme god, a personification of the sky, who was the son and consort of Gaea and the father of the Cyclopes and Titans. [Latin *Ūranus,* from Greek *Ouranos,* personification of *ouranos†,* heaven.]

Uranus² *n.* The seventh planet from the Sun, revolving about it

Uraeus *The serpent emblem – the ancient Egyptian symbol of protection, sovereignty, and power – was put on the headdress of gods and kings, at whose enemies it was expected to spit venom. Here it is worn by a prince, a son of the pharaoh Ramses III.*

every 84.02 years at a distance of approximately 2 870 million kilometres (1,790,000,000 miles). It has an equatorial diameter of 48 300 kilometres (30,000 miles), a mass 14.6 times that of Earth, and five satellites. [After the god URANUS.]

u·ra·nyl (yŏŏr-ə-nil, yór-) *n.* The divalent radical UO₂. [URAN(IUM) + -YL.]

urase. Variant of **urease.**

u·rate (yŏŏr-ayt, yór-) *n.* A salt or ester of uric acid. [UR(IC ACID) + -ATE.] —**u·rat·ic** (yoor-ráttik, yŏŏ-) *adj.*

ur·ban (úrbən) *adj.* **1.** Pertaining to, located in, living in or constituting a town or city. **2.** Characteristic of the geography, life, or functions of a town or city. Compare **rural.** [Latin *urbānus*, from *urbs*†, city.]

urban district *n.* **1.** A former administrative district of England, Wales, and Northern Ireland, resembling a borough but lacking a borough charter. **2.** Any of 49 medium-sized towns in the Republic of Ireland possessing elected councils.

ur·bane (ur-báyn, úr-) *adj.* Having or showing the refined manners of polite society; elegant. See Synonyms at **suave.** [French *urbain, urbaine,* from Latin *urbānus,* characteristic of city life, URBAN.] —**ur·bane·ly** *adv.* —**ur·bane·ness** *n.*

ur·ban·ise, ur·ban·ize (úrbən-īz) *tr.v.* **-ised, -ising, -ises. 1.** To make urban in nature or character. **2.** To cause or increase the migration of (country people) into cities. —**ur·ban·i·sa·tion** (-ī-záysh'n ‖ *U.S.* -i-) *n.*

ur·ban·ism (úrbən-iz'm) *n.* **1.** The culture or lifestyle of city dwellers. **2.** *Chiefly U.S.* The study of this. **3.** *Chiefly U.S.* Urbanisation.

ur·ban·ite (úrbən-īt) *n.* A city dweller.

ur·ban·i·ty (ur-bánnəti, úr-) *n., pl.* **-ties. 1.** Refinement and elegance of manner; polished courtesy. **2.** *Plural.* Courtesies; civilities.

urban renewal *n.* The government-sponsored destruction of slum areas with a view to the construction of new housing.

urban sprawl *n.* The spread of urban areas into the countryside.

ur·bi et or·bi (úr-bee et ór-bee, ŏŏr-, -bi) *Latin.* To the city (of Rome) and to the world. Said of a solemn blessing by the pope.

U.R.C. United Reformed Church.

ur·ce·o·late (úr-si-ə-lət, ur-sée-, -lit, -layt) *adj.* Urn-shaped: *an urceolate corolla.* [New Latin *urceolatus,* from Latin *urceolus,* diminutive of *urceus,* jug, akin to *urna,* URN.]

ur·chin (úrchin) *n.* **1.** A poor, dirty, ragged child; a ragamuffin. **2.** A small, mischievous child; a scamp. **3.** A **sea urchin** *(see).* **4.** *Archaic & Regional.* A hedgehog. [Middle English variant of *(h)irchon,* hedgehog, from Old North French *herichon,* from Latin *(h)ērīcius,* from *(h)ēr,* hedgehog.]

ur·dé, ur·dée (úr-di, -day, -dee) *adj. Heraldry.* Having points; pointed. [16th century : probably a misreading of French *videé* in the phrase *crois aiquisseé et videé,* cross sharply pointed and reduced.]

Ur·du (ŏŏr-dŏŏ, úr-, -dŏŏ) *n.* A Hindustani language spoken in Pakistan, where it is the principal language, in Afghanistan, and by Muslims in India. [Hindi *urdū,* short for *zabān-i-urdū,* "language of the camp" : Persian *zabān,* language + *urdū,* army, camp, from Turkish *ordū,* HORDE.]

–ure *n. suffix.* Indicates: **1.** An act or process; for example, **erasure. 2.** A resulting condition; for example, **composure. 3.** A function or office or a body performing a function; for example, **legislature.** [Middle English, from Old French, from Latin *-ūra.*]

u·re·a (yŏŏr-i-ə, yór-; yoor-rée-ə, yŏŏ-, -réer) *n.* A white crystalline or powdery compound, CO(NH₂)₂, found as an excretion product of protein metabolism in mammalian urine and other body fluids. A synthesised form is used as fertiliser, in animal feed, and in resins. [New Latin, from French *urée,* formed from *urine,* URINE.] —**u·re·al, u·re·ic** (yoor-rée-ik, yŏŏ-) *adj.*

u·re·a-for·mal·de·hyde resin (-fawr-mál-di-hīd) *n.* Any of various thermosetting resins made by combining urea and formaldehyde and widely used to make moulded household and mechanical objects and in cavity wall insulation.

u·re·ase (yŏŏr-i-ayz, yór-, -ayss) *n.* Also **u·rase** (yŏŏr-ayz, yór-, -ayss). An enzyme occurring in urine, various plants, and as a secretion of certain microorganisms that catalyses the hydrolysis of urea to ammonia and carbon dioxide and is used to determine the urea content of blood and urine. [URE(A) + -ASE.]

u·re·di·um (yoor-rée-di-əm, yŏŏ-) *n., pl.* **-dia** (-di-ə). Also **u·re·din·i·um** (yŏŏr-i-dínni-əm, yór-) *pl.* **-ia** (-ə). A reddish, pustule-like structure formed on the tissue of a plant infected by a rust fungus, having hyphae that produce uredospores. Also called "uredosorus". [New Latin, from Latin *ūrēdo* (stem *ūrēdin-*), blight, burning itch, UREDO.] —**u·re·di·al** *adj.*

u·re·do (yoor-réedō, yŏŏ-) *n., pl.* **uredines** (-réedi-neez) *Pathology.* **Urticaria** *(see).* [Latin *ūrēdo,* blight, burning itch, from *ūrere,* to burn.]

u·re·do·spore (yoor-réed-ō-spawr, yŏŏ-, ə- ‖ -spōr) *n.* A reddish spore that is produced in the uredium of a rust fungus and that spreads to and infects other plants.

u·re·ide (yŏŏr-i-īd, yór-) *n. Chemistry.* Any of various derivatives of urea. [URE(A) + -IDE.]

uremia. *U.S.* Variant of **uraemia.**

u·re·o·te·lic (yoor-i-ō-téelik, yór-; yoor-rée-, yŏŏ-; -téllik) *adj.* Excreting most excess nitrogen in the form of urea. Said of such animals as amphibians and mammals. [UREA + Greek *telos,* end + -IC (referring to urea as the end-product).]

u·re·ter (yoor-réetər, yŏŏ-) *n.* The long, narrow duct that conveys urine from the kidney to the urinary bladder. [New Latin, from

Greek *ourētēr,* from *ourein,* to urinate, from *ouron,* urine.] —**u·re·ter·al, u·re·ter·ic** (yŏŏr-i-térrik, yór-) *adj.*

u·re·thane (yŏŏr-i-thayn, yór-) *n.* **1.** A colourless crystalline or white granular compound, C₃H₇NO₂, used as a treatment for leukaemia and as a solvent. Also called "ethyl carbamate". **2.** Any of several esters, other than the ethyl ester, of carbamic acid. **3.** **Polyurethane** *(see).* [French *uréthane* : UR(O)- (urine) + ETH(YL) + -AN(E).]

u·re·thra (yŏŏr-rée-thrə, yŏŏ-) *n., pl.* **-thras** or **-thrae** (-three). The canal through which urine is discharged in most mammals and which serves as the male genital duct. [Late Latin *ūrēthra,* from Greek *ourēthra,* from *ourein,* to urinate, from *ouron,* urine.] —**u·re·thral** *adj.*

u·re·thri·tis (yŏŏr-i-thrī-tiss, yór-) *n.* Inflammation of the urethra. [New Latin, URETHR(A) + -ITIS.] —**u·re·thrit·ic** (-thríttik) *adj.*

u·re·thro·scope (yoor-réethrə-skōp, yŏŏ-) *n.* An instrument for examining the interior of the urethra. [URETHR(A) + -SCOPE.] —**u·re·thros·co·py** (yŏŏr-i-thróskəpi, yór-) *n.*

u·ret·ic (yoor-réttik, yŏŏ-) *adj.* Of or relating to urine; urinary. [Late Latin *ūrēticus,* from Greek *ourētikos,* from *ourein,* to urinate, from *ouron,* urine.]

U·rey (yŏŏr-i), **Harold Clayton** (1893–). U.S. physicist. He is known chiefly for his discovery (1931) of deuterium, and his work on the separation of isotopes and the structure of atoms and molecules. He won (1934) the Nobel prize for chemistry.

urge (urj) *v.* **urged, urging, urges.** —*tr.* **1.** To drive forwards or onwards forcefully; impel; spur. **2.** To entreat earnestly and repeatedly; plead with; exhort: *The board was urged to approve the budget.* **3.** To advocate persistently; recommended emphatically: *urge passage of the bill.* **4.** To persuade, force, or otherwise move to some course of action. **5.** *Archaic & Literary.* To stimulate; excite. —*intr.* **1.** To present a forceful argument, claim, or case. **2.** To exert an impelling force; push vigorously.
~*n.* **1.** The act of urging. **2.** An irresistible or impelling force, influence, or instinct. [Latin *urgēre,* to push, press.] —**urg·ing·ly** *adv.*
Synonyms: urge, press, exhort, encourage, coax.

ur·gen·cy (úrjən-si) *n., pl.* **-cies. 1.** The quality or condition of being urgent; imperativeness; pressing importance: *the urgency of their appeal.* **2.** A pressing necessity.

ur·gent (úrjənt) *adj.* **1.** Compelling immediate action; imperative; pressing: *She's away on urgent business.* **2.** Insistent or importunate; earnest: *urgent pleas.* **3.** Conveying or relating a sense of urgency: *an urgent tone.* [Middle English, from Old French, from Latin *urgēns* (stem *urgent-*), present participle of *urgēre,* to push, press, URGE.] —**ur·gent·ly** *adv.*
Synonyms: urgent, pressing, imperative.

–urgy *n. comb. form.* Indicates a technique or technology; for example, **metallurgy, theurgy.** [New Latin *-urgia,* from Greek *-ourgos,* "worker", from *ergon,* work.]

–uria *n. comb. form. Pathology.* Indicates: **1.** A diseased condition of the urine; for example, **pyuria. 2.** A substance in the urine; for example, **albuminuria.** [New Latin, from Greek *-ouria,* from *ouron,* urine.]

u·ric (yŏŏr-ik, yór-) *adj.* Pertaining to, contained in, or obtained from urine. [UR(O)- + -IC.]

uric acid *n.* A white crystalline compound, C₅H₄N₄O₃, the end product of purine metabolism in man and other primates, birds, terrestrial reptiles, and most insects.

u·ri·co·su·ric (yŏŏr-i-kō-séwr-ik, yór-, -kə-, -sóor- ‖ -shóor-) *adj.* Promoting the excretion of uric acid in the urine. Said of certain drugs used to treat gout. [*Urico-,* combining form of URIC ACID + -s- (connective) + URIC.]

u·ri·co·te·lic (yŏŏr-i-kō-téelik, yór-, -kə-, -téllik) *adj.* Excreting most excess nitrogen in the form of uric acid. Said of birds. [*Urico-,* combining form of URIC ACID + Greek *telos,* end + -IC (referring to uric acid as the end-product).]

ur·i·dine (yŏŏr-i-deen, yór-) *n.* A white, odourless powder, C₉H₁₂N₂O₆, that is the nucleoside of uracil, important in carbohydrate metabolism and used in biochemical experiments. [UR(O)- + -ID(E) + -INE.]

U·ri·el (yŏŏr-i-əl, yór-). One of the four archangels in Hebrew tradition. [Hebrew *ūrī'ēl,* probably "God is my light".]

U·rim and Thum·mim (yŏŏr-im, yór-, ŏŏr-; thúmmim) *pl.n.* Objects carried by the chief priests of ancient Israel and probably used to divine the will of God. Exodus 28:30; Leviticus 8:8.

urin– Variant of **urino-.**

u·ri·nal (yŏŏr-ín'l, yŏŏr-in'l) *n.* **1. a.** An upright wall fixture used by men for urinating. **b.** A room or other place containing such a fixture or fixtures. **2.** A receptacle for urine, such as one used by a bedridden patient. Also called "urinary". [Middle English, chamber pot, from Old French *urinal,* from Late Latin *ūrīnal,* from *ūrīna,* URINE.]

u·ri·nal·y·sis (yŏŏr-i-nál-ə-siss, yór-) *n., pl.* **-ses** (-seez). The chemical analysis of urine. [New Latin : URIN(O)- + (AN)ALYSIS.]

u·ri·nant (yŏŏr-inənt, yór-) *adj. Heraldry.* With the head downwards. [Latin *ūrīnāns* (stem *ūrīnant-*), diving, present participle of *ūrīnārī,* to dive.]

u·ri·nar·y (yŏŏr-i-nəri, yór- ‖ -nerri) *adj.* Of or relating to urine, its production, function, or excretion.
~*n., pl.* **urinaries.** A urinal.

urinary bladder *n.* A muscular membrane-lined sac situated in the anterior part of the pelvic cavity and used as a urine reservoir prior to excretion.

urinary calculus *n.* A solid concretion of mineral and organic substances in the urinary system. Also called "urolith".

u·ri·nate (yoor-i-nayt, yór-) *intr.v.* **-nated, -nating, -nates.** To excrete urine. [Medieval Latin *ūrīnāre,* from Latin *ūrīna,* URINE.] **—u·ri·na·tion** (-náysh'n) *n.* **—u·ri·na·tive** (-nətiv, -naytiv) *adj.*

u·rine (yoor-in, yór- ‖ -īn) *n.* The fluid and dissolved substances, including urea, secreted by the kidneys, stored in the bladder, and excreted from the body through the urethra. [Middle English, from Old French, from Latin *ūrīna.*]

u·ri·nif·er·ous (yoor-i-niffərəss, yór-) *adj.* Conveying urine.

urino-, urin- *comb. form.* Indicates urine; for example, **urinalysis, urinogenital.** [Latin *ūrīna,* URINE.]

urinogenital. Variant of **urogenital.**

u·ri·nous (yoor-i-nəss, yór-) *adj.* Also **u·ri·nose** (-nōz, -nōss). Of, resembling, or containing urine.

urn (urn) *n.* **1.** A vase of varying size and shape, usually large with a pedestal, and used especially as a receptacle for the ashes of the cremated dead. **2.** A large vaselike vessel, often made of stone and planted with flowers, used as a garden ornament. **3.** A large closed metal vessel with a tap used for warming or serving tea or coffee; a samovar. **4.** *Botany.* The spore-bearing part of a moss capsule. [Middle English *urne,* a vessel containing the ashes of the dead, burial urn, from Latin *urna.*]

uro-¹, ur- *comb. form.* Indicates urine or the urinary tract; for example, **urogenital, uridine.** [New Latin, from Greek *ouro-,* from *ouron,* urine.]

uro-², ur- *comb. form.* Indicates a tail; for example, **uropod.** [New Latin, from Greek *oura,* tail.]

u·ro·chord (yoor-ō-kawrd, yór-, -ə-) *n. Zoology.* A notochord limited to the caudal region, as in larval tunicates. [URO- (tail) + CHORD.] **—u·ro·chor·dal** (-kórd'l) *adj.*

u·ro·chrome (yoor-ō-krōm, yór-, -ə-) *n.* The pigment responsible for the normal yellow colour of urine. [URO- + -CHROME.]

u·ro·dele (yoor-ō-deel, yór-, -ə-) *n.* Any amphibian of the order Urodela, characterised by a long body and tail and including the newts and salamanders. [French *urodèle* : URO- (tail) + Greek *dēlos,* evident.] **—u·ro·dele** *adj.*

u·ro·gen·i·tal (yoor-ō-jénnit'l, yór-, -ə-) *adj.* Also **u·ri·no·gen·i·tal** (-inō-). Of, pertaining to, or involving both the urinary and genital functions.

u·ro·lith (yoor-ō-lith, yór-, -ə-) *n. Pathology.* A **urinary calculus** *(see).* [URO- + -LITH.] **—u·ro·lith·ic** (-líthik) *adj.*

u·rol·o·gy (yoor-róllaji, yóō-) *n.* The medical study of the physiology and pathology of the urogenital tract. [URO- + -LOGY.] **—u·ro·log·i·cal** (yoor-ə-lójik'l, yór-, -ō-) *adj.* **—u·rol·o·gist** (-róllajist) *n.*

-uronic *adj. comb. form.* Indicates a connection with urine; for example, **hyaluronic.** [Greek *ouron,* urine.]

u·ro·pod (yoor-ə-pod, yór-, -ō-) *n.* Either of a pair of posterior abdominal appendages of certain crustaceans, such as the lobster or shrimp. [URO- (tail) + -POD.] **—u·rop·o·dal** (yoor-róppəd'l, yoō-), **u·rop·o·dous** (-róppədəss) *adj.*

uropygial gland *n.* An oil-secreting gland at the base of a bird's tail. Also called "oil gland".

u·ro·pyg·i·um (yoor-ə-píji-əm, yór-, -ō-) *n.* The posterior part of a bird's body, from which the tail feathers grow; the rump. [New Latin, from Greek *ouropugion* : URO- (tail) + *pugē,* rump.] **—u·ro·pyg·i·al** *adj.*

u·ros·co·py (yoor-róskəpi, yoō-) *n., pl.* **-pies.** *Medicine.* The examination of urine with a microscope. [URO- + -SCOPY.]

u·ro·style (yoor-ō-stīl, yór-, -ə-) *n.* A rod-shaped bone forming the terminal section of the backbone in frogs and toads. [URO- (tail) + Greek *stulos,* column.]

-urous *adj. comb. form.* Indicates a tail or type of tail; for example, **anurous.** [New Latin *-urus,* from Greek *-ouros,* from *oura,* tail.]

Ur·sa Major (úr-sə) *n.* A constellation in the region of the north celestial pole, near Draco and Leo, containing the seven stars that form the Plough. Also called the "Great Bear". [Latin *ursa,* feminine of *ursus,* bear. See **ursine.**]

Ursa Minor *n.* A constellation having the shape of a ladle with **Polaris** *(see)* at the tip of its handle. Also *U.S.* "Little Bear", "Little Dipper".

ur·sine (úr-sīn) *adj.* Of or characteristic of a bear. [Latin *ursīnus,* from *ursus,* bear.]

Ur·spra·che (oor-shpraakhə) *n.* A reconstructed language set up as the parent of groups of related languages, as, for example, Indo-European, the hypothetical ancestor of Latin, Greek, Slavic, Celtic, and Germanic. Compare **protolanguage.** [German, "protolanguage."]

Ur·su·line (úrss-yoo-līn, úrsh-, -lin ‖ -ə-, -leen) *n.* A member of an order of nuns of the Roman Catholic Church, founded in about 1537 and devoted to the education of girls. [After Saint *Ursula,* legendary British princess supposedly martyred with 11,000 handmaidens by Huns at Cologne in the 5th century.] **—Ur·su·line** *adj.*

Ur·text (oor-tekst) *n.* **1.** A reconstructed proto-text set up as the basis of variants in extant later texts. **2.** *Small* **u.** The original text of a work of art, especially of of musical composition. [German, "proto-text".]

ur·ti·cant (úrtik-ənt) *adj.* Causing itching or stinging. **~n.** A substance that causes itching or stinging.

ur·ti·car·i·a (úrti-káir-i-ə) *n.* A skin condition characterised by intensely itching red, raised patches and usually caused by allergic

reactions to internal or external agents. Also called "hives", "nettle rash", "uredo". [New Latin, from Latin *urtīca,* nettle. See **urticate.**]

ur·ti·cate (úrti-kayt) *—intr.v.* **-cated, -cating, -cates.** To produce urticaria or a stinging sensation. *—tr.* To practise urtication on. [Medieval Latin *urtīcāre,* from Latin *urtīca†,* nettle.]

ur·ti·ca·tion (úrti-káysh'n) *n.* **1.** The sensation of having been stung by nettles. **2.** *Medicine.* Formerly, a lashing with nettles as treatment of a paralysed part of the body. **3.** Urticaria.

U·ru·guay (yoor-ə-gwī, ŏórrə-, -ōō-, -gwī ‖ -gway). State on the east coast of South America. Its economy rests on cattle and sheep, with meat, hides, and wool accounting for 70 per cent of its exports. Disputed by Spain and Portugal from the 17th century, and by Brazil and Argentina in the 19th century, Uruguay emerged as an independent nation in 1828. Area, 176 215 square kilometres (68,019 square miles). Population, 3,000,000. Capital, Montevideo. **—U·ru·guay·an** (-gwī-ən) *n. & adj.*

Uruguay. River in South America. It flows for about 1 610 kilometres (1,000 miles) from southern Brazil into the Rio de la Plata.

Urum·qi or **Urum·ch'i** (ōō-rōōm-chi). Also **Wu-lu-mu-ch'i.** Capital of Xinjiang-Uigur Zizhiqu, northwest China, known as Tihwa before 1954. It is a major agricultural and industrial centre.

Urundi. See **Burundi.**

u·rus (yoor-əss, yór-) *n.* An extinct bovine mammal, the **aurochs** *(see).* [Latin *ūrus,* from Germanic.]

u·ru·shi·ol (yoor-rōōshi-ol, yōō-, -ə-, ōō- ‖ -ōl) *n.* A toxic substance present in the resin of plants of the genus *Rhus,* which includes poison ivy and the lacquer tree, *R. verniciflua,* from which a black Japanese lacquer is obtained. [Japanese *urushi,* lacquer + -OL.]

us (uss, *weak form* əss ‖ *North of England also* uz, əz) *pron.* The objective case of the first person plural pronoun *we.* It is used: **1.** As the direct object of a verb: *He assisted us.* **2.** As the indirect object of a verb: *They offered us a ride.* **3.** As the object of a preposition: *They came to us first.* **4.** After *than* or *as* in comparisons in which the first term is in the objective case: *They gave you more than us.* **5.** *Chiefly British Informal.* Me: *Go on, give us a smile.* **6.** *Chiefly U.S. Informal.* In place of the reflexive pronoun *ourselves,* as the indirect object of a verb: *We'll get us some dinner.* **7.** In various elliptical, absolute, or interjectional phrases in which it is neither subject nor object: *How, us? Lucky us!* See Usage notes at **me, we.** [Middle English *us,* Old English *ūs.*]

US, U.S. 1. United States. **2.** unserviceable. **3.** useless.

u.s. ubi supra.

USA, U.S.A. 1. Union of South Africa. **2.** United States Army. **3.** United States of America.

us·a·ble, use·a·ble (yōōz-əb'l) *adj.* **1.** Capable of being used. **2.** In a fit condition for use; intact or operative. **—us·a·bil·i·ty** (-ə-bílləti), **us·a·ble·ness** *n.* **—us·a·bly** *adv.*

USAF, U.S.A.F. United States Air Force.

us·age (yōō-sij, -zij) *n.* **1. a.** The act or manner of using or treating; use or employment. **b.** The act of using. **2.** Customary practice; habitual use. **3.** The actual or expressed way in which a language or its elements are used, interrelated, or pronounced in expression: *contemporary English usage.* **4.** An instance of this; a particular expression in speech or writing: *a nonce usage.* **—See** Synonyms at **habit.** [Middle English, from Old French, from *user,* to USE.]

Usage: Usage is a more specialised term than *use. Use* is preferable when the sense relates broadly to employment or usefulness: *Those materials have a wide use these days. Usage* is preferred when the sense relates to "customary use", as in the "Usage notes" throughout this dictionary.

us·ance (yōōz-nss) *n.* **1.** *Commerce.* The length of time, established by custom and varying between countries, that is allowed for payment of a foreign bill of exchange. **2.** *Archaic.* Interest accruing on a loan. [Middle English *usaunce,* custom, usage, from Old French *usance,* from Vulgar Latin *ūsantia* (unattested), from *ūsāre* (unattested), to USE.]

U.S.D.A.W. (úss-daw, úz-). Union of Shop, Distributive and Allied Trades.

use (yōōz) *v.* **used** (yōōzd), **using, uses.** *—tr.* **1.** To bring or put into service; employ, as for some purpose: *use soap for washing; use*

our telephone. **2.** To make a practice or a habit of employing: *uses margarine in her sandwiches; doesn't use his wits.* **b.** To employ or utter (words or phrases): *uses clichés all the time.* **3.** To conduct oneself towards in a specified manner: *used you unkindly.* **4.** To consume or expend the whole of; deplete or exhaust. Often used with *up.* **5.** *Informal.* To exploit for one's own advantage or gain: *He gave nothing to his friends; he merely used them.* **6.** To take (a habit-forming drug), especially habitually. **7.** To make a practice of calling or designating oneself by (a title, name, or the like): *He doesn't use "Sir" in his private life.* —*intr.* To do or be habitually. Now used only in the past tense to show a former habitual action or state: *This bathroom used to be a stable; I used to play football every Saturday.* —See Usage note at **utilise.**
~*n.* (yōōss). **1. a.** The act of using; the application or employment of something, as for some purpose: *the use of a pencil for writing.* **b.** The condition or fact of being used or occupied: *This toilet is no longer in use.* **c.** The fact of having been used: *This car has had a lot of use.* **2.** The manner of using; usage: *the proper use of power tools.* **3. a.** The permission, privilege, or benefit of using something: *have use of the car.* **b.** The power or ability to use something: *lose the use of one arm.* **4.** The need or occasion to use or employ: *Do you still have any use for this book?* **5.** The quality of being suitable or adaptable to an end; usefulness: *There's no use in discussing it.* **6.** The goal, object, or purpose for which something is used. **7.** *Archaic.* Accustomed or usual procedure; habitual practice; custom. **8.** *Law.* **a.** The enjoyment of property, as by occupying or exercising it. **b.** The benefit or profit of lands and tenements of which the legal title and possession are vested in another who holds them in trust for the beneficiary. **c.** The arrangement establishing the equitable right to such benefits and profits. **9.** The special or distinctive form of ritual, ceremony, or public worship practised in a particular church, ecclesiastical district, or community. **—have no use for.** To have no tolerance for or patience with; dislike. **—make use of. 1.** To find occasion to use. **2.** To exploit. [Middle English *usen,* from Old French *user,* from Vulgar Latin *ūsāre* (unattested), frequentative of Latin *ūtī*† (past participle *ūsus*), to use.]

Usage: As an auxiliary verb, *use* always occurs in the past tense, followed by *to*: *He used to play football.* In interrogative sentences, there is some variation in usage. *Used he to (play football)?* is an older construction, found especially in British English, and still sometimes used in formal speech; the more modern and widely used form in both British and American informal English is *did he use(d) to.* A similar set of distinctions applies to the negative forms: *He usedn't to go/used not to go* is the older construction, found especially in British English, and preferred by conservative speakers; the alternative form, *didn't use(d) to,* is the more common form nowadays. In all of these constructions the pronunciation is usually yōōst, yōōss; compare yōōzd, yōōz for other senses.

used (yōōzd) *adj.* Not new; secondhand: *a used car.* **—used to** (yōōst). Accustomed to or familiar with: *I'm not used to all this rich food.*

use·ful (yōōss-f'l) *adj.* **1.** Capable of being used advantageously or beneficially; serviceable. **2.** Commendably productive: *doing some useful work at school.* **—use·ful·ly** *adv.* **—use·ful·ness** *n.*

use·less (yōōss-ləss, -liss) *adj.* **1.** Having no beneficial purpose or use; of little or no worth; meaningless. **2.** Futile; pointless; to no avail. **—use·less·ly** *adv.* **—use·less·ness** *n.*

us·er (yōōzər) *n.* **1.** One that uses. **2.** *Law.* The exercise or enjoyment of any right or property. **3.** *Slang.* A drug addict.

ush·er (úshər) *n.* **1.** One who serves as official doorkeeper and usually keeps order, as in a law court or legislative chamber. See **serjeant at arms. 2.** A person employed to escort people to their seats, as in a cinema, theatre, or stadium. **3.** A male attendant at a wedding. **4.** An official who precedes persons of rank in a procession. ~*tr.v.* **ushered, -ering, -ers. 1.** To serve as an usher to; escort. **2.** To lead or conduct; cause to enter. Used with *through* or *into*: *ushered her through the door.* **3.** To precede and introduce; serve as the beginning of. Usually used with *in.* [Middle English, from Anglo-French *usser,* variant of Old French *ussier,* from Medieval Latin *ūstiārius,* variant of Latin *ōstiārius,* doorkeeper, from *ōstium,* entrance, river mouth, from *ōs,* mouth, orifice.]

ush·er·ette (úshə-rét) *n.* A woman who takes tickets and shows people to their seats in a cinema.

Üs·kü·dar (űskü-daar). Urban district of Turkey, incorporated in Istanbul and formerly known as Scutari. During the Crimean War (1854–56), it was a British base, and the site of the military hospital run by Florence Nightingale.

us·que·baugh (úskwi-baw || -baa) *n. Irish & Scottish.* Whisky. [Irish and Scots Gaelic *uisge beatha,* "water of life".]

U.S.S. 1. United States Senate. **2.** United States Ship.

U.S.S.R. Union of Soviet Socialist Republics.

Us·ti·nov (yōōsti-nof, -nov), **Peter (Alexander)** (1921–). British actor, director, and playwright. His films include *Spartacus* (1960), for which he got an Academy Award, and *Murder on the Nile* (1978).

u·su·al (yōōzh-oo-əl, yōōzh-wəl, -'l, -yoo-əl) *adj. Abbr.* **usu. 1.** Such as is commonly or frequently encountered, experienced, observed, or used; ordinary; normal. **2.** Habitual or customary; particular. **—the usual.** One's customary meal, drink, or the like. [Middle English, from Old French, from Late Latin *ūsuālis,* ordinary, from Latin *ūsus,* use, custom, from the past participle of *ūtī,* to USE.] **—u·su·al·ly** *adv.* **—u·su·al·ness** *n.*

Synonyms: *usual, typical, habitual, customary, accustomed.*

u·su·cap·tion (yōōss-yōō-kápsh'n, yōōz- || -ə-) *n. Law.* Formerly, ownership resulting from prolonged possession.

u·su·fruct (yōōss-yōō-frukt, yōōz- || -ə-) *n. Law.* The right to make use of and enjoy the profits and advantages of something belonging to another so long as the property is not damaged or altered in any way. [Latin *ūsusfrūctus,* "use (and) enjoyment" : *ūsus,* use (see **usual**) + *frūctus,* enjoyment, FRUIT.]

u·su·fruc·tu·ar·y (yōōss-yōō-frúk-tew-əri, yōōz-, -choo- || -ə-, -erri) *n., pl.* **-ies.** A person who holds property by usufruct. ~*adj.* Of or of the nature of a usufruct.

u·su·rer (yōōzh-ərər,-rər) *n.* **1.** A person who lends money at an exorbitant or unlawful rate of interest. **2.** *Obsolete.* A moneylender. [Middle English, from Anglo-French, from Medieval Latin *ūsūrārius,* from Latin *ūsūra,* interest, USURY.]

u·su·ri·ous (yōō-zéwr-i-əss, yōō-, -zóor-, -zhóor-) *adj.* **1.** Practising usury. **2.** Of, pertaining to, or constituting usury: *a usurious rate of interest.* **—u·su·ri·ous·ly** *adv.* **—u·su·ri·ous·ness** *n.*

u·surp (yōō-zúrp, yōō- || *chiefly U.S.* -súrp) *v.* **-surped, -surping, -surps.** —*tr.* **1.** To seize and hold (the power, position, or rights of another) by force and without legal right or authority. **2.** To take over or occupy physically and wrongfully (territory or possessions for example); appropriate. —*intr.* To commit such illegal seizure; encroach. [Middle English *usurpen,* from Old French *usurper,* from Latin *ūsūrpāre,* to take forcibly into use.] **—u·surp·er** *n.* **—u·sur·pa·tion** (yōō-zur-páysh'n) *n.*

u·su·ry (yōō-zhōō-ri, -zhə-, -zhri, -zhoor-i) *n., pl.* **-ries. 1.** The act or practice of lending money at an exorbitant or illegal rate of interest. **2.** Such an excessive rate of interest. **3.** *Archaic.* The act or practice of lending money at any rate of interest. [Middle English, from Anglo-French *usurie* (unattested), from Medieval Latin *ūsūria,* from Latin *ūsūra,* use of money lent, interest, from *ūsus,* use. See **usual.**]

ut (ut, ōōt) *n. Music.* A syllable representing the note *C,* otherwise represented by *do,* in the French system of tonic sol-fa. See **gamut.** [Latin *ut,* that (first word of a hymn to St. John the Baptist).]

U.T. universal time.

U·tah (yōō-taa || *locally* -taw). State in the western United States, one of the so-called Rocky Mountain states. The capital and largest city is Salt Lake City. It is an important mining state, and has valuable deposits of petroleum. The region was first settled permanently in 1847 by Mormons seeking refuge from persecution, and the state has ever since been the home of the American Mormons. It was admitted to the Union in 1896.

Ute (yōōt) *n., pl.* **Ute** or **Utes. 1.** A member of a Uto-Aztecan-speaking North American Indian people formerly inhabiting Utah, Colorado, and New Mexico and now living on reservations in Utah and Colorado. **2.** The language of this people.

u·ten·sil (yōō-tén-s'l, -sil) *n.* **1.** An instrument or container, especially one used domestically, as in a kitchen. **2.** Any instrument or tool; an implement. —See Synonyms at **tool.** [Middle English *utensele,* from Old French *utensile,* from Latin *ūtēnsilia,* "things for use", from the neuter plural of *ūtēnsilis,* fit for use, from *ūtī,* to USE.]

u·ter·ine (yōōtə-rīn || -rin) *adj.* **1.** Of or pertaining to the uterus. **2.** Having the same mother but different fathers. [Late Latin *uterīnus,* from *uterus,* UTERUS.]

u·ter·us (yōōtərəss) *n.* **1.** A pear-shaped muscular organ located in the pelvic cavity of female mammals that receives and holds the fertilised ovum during the development of the foetus and is the principal agent in its expulsion at birth. Also called "womb". **2.** A similar part of the female reproductive tract in many invertebrates, serving as a repository for the storage or development of eggs or embryos. [Latin *uterus.*]

Ut·gard (ŏŏt-gaard, ŏŏt-). *Norse Mythology.* The home of Utgard-Loki. Also called "Jotunheim".

Ut·gard-Lo·ki (ŏŏt-gaard-lōki). *Norse Mythology.* An invincible giant.

U·ther Pen·drag·on (yōōthər). A legendary king of Britain and father of King Arthur.

u·tile (yōō-tīl || -til) *adj. Rare.* Useful. [Middle English *utyle,* from Old French *utile,* from Latin *ūtilis.* See **utility.**]

u·til·ise, u·til·ize (yōōti-līz, yōōtə-) *tr.v.* **-ised, -ising, -ises. 1.** To put to use for a certain purpose. **2.** To make productive use of or to find a use for. [French *utiliser,* from Italian *utilizzare,* from *utile,* useful, from Latin *ūtilis.* See **utility.**] **—u·til·is·a·ble** *adj.* **—u·til·i·sa·tion** (-lī-záysh'n || *U.S.* -li-) *n.* **—u·til·is·er** *n.*

Usage: The tendency for *utilise* to replace *use* in business and official English is open to criticism as an example of needless jargon. Careful usage maintains a distinction between these verbs, *use* having a general sense of "put into service" (*The machinery should be used as little as possible*), *utilise* having a narrower sense of "make useful or productive" (*We shall utilise the spare parts to save money*).

u·til·i·tar·i·an (yōō-tílli-táir-i-ən, yōōtili-) *adj.* **1.** Of or pertaining to utilitarianism. **2.** Useful and practical rather than decorative. ~*n.* An advocate of utilitarianism. [UTILIT(Y) + -ARIAN.]

u·til·i·tar·i·an·ism (yōō-tílli-táir-i-ən-iz'm, yōōtili-) *n.* **1.** The ethical theory, originally proposed by Jeremy Bentham and John Stuart Mill, that all moral, social, or political action should be directed towards achieving the greatest good for the greatest number of people, where "good" is taken to be "happiness". **2.** The belief that what is useful is good.

u·til·i·ty (yōō-tílləti) *n., pl.* **-ties. 1.** The condition or quality of being useful; usefulness. **2.** A useful article or device. **3.** A public service, such as gas, electricity, water, or transport. **4.** In utilitarianism, the

PRONUNCIATION KEY

a, trap; aa, father; ai, fair;
ar, star; aw, lawn; ay, play;
b, bb, stab; rubber;
ch, church; ck, ticket;
d, dd, dead; ladder; e, dress;
ee, bee; er, defer; ew, few;
ewr, pure; ə, about;
ər, letter; f, ff, fife; differ;
g, gg, giggle; h, hat; i, kit;
ī, price; īr, fire; j, judge;
k, kick; l, ll, let; 'l, needle;
m, mm, man; n, nn, no;
'n, sudden; ng, thing; o, lot;
ō, no; ŏŏ, foot; ōō, shoe;
oor, poor; ow, cow;
owr, hour; oy, boy;
p, pp, pepper; r, rr, red;
s, ss, sauce; sh, ship;
t, tt, totter; th, thick; th, this;
smooth; u, cut; ur, turn;
v, vv, valve; w, wet; y, yes;
z, zz, zebra; zh, vision;
pleasure

IN FOREIGN WORDS:

aN, oN, Saint-Saëns;
hl, Llanelli; Hluhluwe;
kh, loch; lough; Khaled

STRESS MARK:

ín-sīt, insight; in-sít, incite

principle that the greatest good is the greatest happiness for the greatest number.
~*adj.* Useful or practical and, especially in wartime, standardised. [Middle English *utilite*, usefulness, from Old French, from Latin *ūtilitās* (stem *ūtilitāt-*), from *ūtilis*, useful, from *ūtī*, to USE.]

utility room *n.* A room in a house usually containing a boiler, washing-machine, dryer, or other domestic appliances, and often also used for storage.

ut in·fra (ŏŏt ín-fraa, ut, -frə). *Abbr.* **ut inf.** *Latin.* As below.

u·ti pos·si·de·tis (yŏŏtī póssi-déetiss) *n.* A principle of international law providing that a belligerent state is entitled to absolute possession and control of the territory occupied by it at the end of a war. [Latin, as you possess.]

ut·most (út-mōst, -məst) *adj.* 1. Being or situated at the farthest limit or point; most extreme. 2. Of the highest or greatest degree, amount, intensity, or the like: *a matter of the utmost secrecy.*
~*n.* The greatest possible amount, degree, or extent; the maximum. [Middle English *utmost, ut(te)mast*, Old English *ūt(e)mest*, outermost : *ūt(e)*, out + *-mest*, -MOST.]

U·to-Az·tec·an (yŏŏtō-áz-teckən) *n.* 1. A large language family of North and Central American Indians, including Ute, Pima, Hopi, Shoshone, Nahuatl, and other languages. 2. A member of a people speaking a Uto-Aztecan language. [UTE + AZTEC.] —**U·to-Az·tec·an** *adj.*

u·to·pi·a (yŏŏ-tōpi-ə) *n. Sometimes capital* **U.** 1. A condition, place, or situation of social or political perfection. 2. Any idealistic goal or concept for social and political reform. Compare **dystopia.** [After *Utopia*, an imaginary island and ideal commonwealth, the subject of Sir Thomas More's book of this title (1516) : New Latin, "no-place" : Greek *ou*†, not, no + *topos*, place (see **topic**).]

u·to·pi·an (yŏŏ-tōpi-ən) *adj.* Excellent or ideal but existing only in visionary or impractical thought or theory.
~*n.* A zealous but impractical reformer of human society.

u·to·pi·an·ism (yŏŏ-tōpi-ən-iz'm) *n.* The ideals or principles of a utopian; idealistic and impractical social theory.

U·trecht (yŏŏ-trekt, -trékt; *Dutch* ü-trekht). City in the central Netherlands, lying on a branch of the lower Rhine. It was a leading commercial town in the Middle Ages and is now an industrial and financial centre. The Peace of Utrecht brought the War of the Spanish Succession to an end in 1713–14.

u·tri·cle (yŏŏtrik'l) *n.* Also **u·tric·u·lus** (yŏŏ-tríckew-ləss) *pl.* **-li** (-lī). 1. A small, delicate membranous sac connecting with the semicircular canals of the inner ear and functioning in the maintenance of bodily equilibrium and coordination. 2. *Botany.* A small, bladderlike one-seeded fruit. [French *utricule*, from Latin *ūtriculus*, diminutive of *ūter*, leather bag or bottle, perhaps from Greek *hudria*, water pot, pitcher, from *hudōr*, water.] —**u·tric·u·lar** (-lər) *adj.*

U·tril·lo (yŏŏ-tríllō; *French* ü-tree-yŏ), **Maurice** (1883–1955). French painter, best known for his paintings of Paris street scenes.

ut su·pra (ŏŏt sŏŏ-praa, ut séw-, -prə). *Abbr.* **ut sup.** *Latin.* As above.

Ut·tar Pra·desh (ŏŏttər prə-désh, -dáysh). Formerly **United Provinces.** State in north central India. With more than 88 million people, it is the country's most populous state. The capital is Lucknow. Agriculture and food processing are the chief economic activities.

ut·ter[1] (úttər) *tr.v.* **-tered, -tering, -ters.** 1. To express audibly; emit (a sound): *uttered a sign of relief.* 2. To express in words; say or write: *uttered his name; uttered the truth.* 3. To put (counterfeit

money, for example) into circulation. —See Synonyms at **vent.** [Middle English *utt(e)ren, qutren*, from Middle Dutch *ūteren*, to drive away, announce, speak.] —**ut·ter·a·ble** *adj.* —**ut·ter·er** *n.*

utter[2] *adj.* Complete; absolute; entire. [Middle English *utter*, Old English *ūtera, ūttra*, outer, external, comparative of *ūt*, OUT.]

ut·ter·ance[1] (úttrənss, úttərənss) *n.* 1. **a.** The act of uttering or expressing vocally. **b.** The power of speaking. 2. Something that is uttered or expressed.

ut·ter·ance[2] (úttərənss) *n. Archaic.* The uttermost end or extremity; bitter end; death: *fight to the utterance.* [Middle English *utt(e)raunce*, from Old French *outrance*, from *outrer*, to go beyond limits, from Vulgar Latin *ultrāre* (unattested), from Latin *ultrā*, beyond, from *uls*, beyond.]

ut·ter·ly (úttərli) *adv.* Completely; absolutely; entirely.

ut·ter·most (úttər-mōst, -məst) *adj.* 1. Utmost. 2. Farthest.
~*n.* Utmost. [Middle English *uttermost, uttermest* : UTTER (outer, complete) + -MOST.]

U-turn (yŏŏ-turn) *n.* 1. A turn, as by a vehicle, completely reversing the direction of travel. 2. Any complete change or reversal, as of mind or policy: *Will the government make a U-turn on wages?*

UV, U.V. Ultraviolet.

u·va·rov·ite (yŏŏ-vaárə-vīt, ŏŏ-) *n.* An emerald-green garnet, $Ca_3Cr_2(SiO_4)_3$, found in chromium deposits. [German *Uvarovit;* discovered by Count Sergei *Uvarov* (1785–1855), Russian statesman.]

u·ve·a (yŏŏvi-ə) *n.* The pigmented vascular layer of the eye including the iris, ciliary body, and choroid. [Medieval Latin *ūvea*, from Latin *ūva*, grape (from its round shape).] —**u·ve·al** *adj.*

u·ve·i·tis (yŏŏvi-ítiss) *n.* Inflammation of the uvea. [New Latin : UVE(A) + -ITIS.]

u·vu·la (yŏŏvew-lə) *n.* The small, conical, fleshy mass of tissue suspended from the centre of the soft palate above the back of the tongue. [Middle English, from Late Latin, "small grape" (from the shape of the uvula), diminutive of Latin *ūva*, a grape.]

u·vu·lar (yŏŏvew-lər) *adj.* 1. Pertaining to or associated with the uvula. 2. *Phonetics.* Articulated by vibration of the uvula or with the back of the tongue near or touching the uvula.

u·vu·li·tis (yŏŏvew-lītiss) *n.* Inflammation of the uvula. [New Latin : UVUL(A) + -ITIS.]

U/w underwriter.

ux·o·ri·al (uk-sáw-ri-əl ‖ ug-, -záw-, -sŏ́-, -zŏ́-) *adj. Formal & Literary.* Pertaining to, characteristic of, or befitting a wife. [From Latin *uxōrius*, of a wife, UXORIOUS.]

ux·o·ri·cide (uk-sáw-ri-sīd ‖ ug-, -záw-, -sŏ́-, -zŏ́-) *n. Formal & Literary.* 1. The killing of one's wife by her husband. 2. A man who kills his wife. [Medieval Latin *uxōricīdium*, the murder of one's wife : Latin *uxor*, wife + -CIDE.] —**ux·o·ri·cid·al** (-sīd'l) *adj.*

ux·o·ri·ous (uk-sáw-ri-əss ‖ ug-, -záw-, -sŏ́-, -zŏ́-) *adj. Formal & Literary.* 1. Excessively or irrationally devoted to one's wife. 2. Indicative of or revealing such devotion. [Latin *uxōrius*, from *uxor*, wife.] —**ux·o·ri·ous·ly** *adv.* —**ux·o·ri·ous·ness** *n.*

Uz·bek (ŏŏz-bek, úz-) *n.* Also **Uz·beg** (-beg), **Us·bek** (ŏŏss-, úss-), **Us·beg** 1. A member of a group of Turkic people inhabiting the Uzbek S.S.R. 2. The Turkic language spoken by the Uzbeks.

Uzbek Soviet ·Socialist Republic. Also **Uz·bek·i·stan** (ŏŏz-becki-staán). Constituent republic of the U.S.S.R., lying in central Asia. The capital and largest city is Tashkent. It is the chief supplier of cotton and rice to the U.S.S.R. and it has also valuable reserves of petroleum and natural gas.

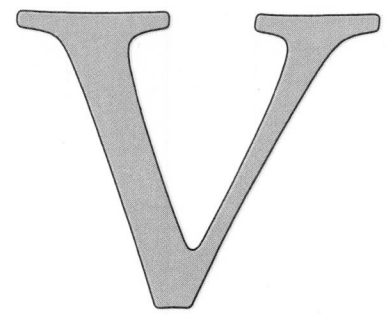

v, V (vee) *n., pl.* **v's** or *rare* **vs, Vs** or **V's. 1.** The 22nd letter of the modern English alphabet. **2.** Any of the speech sounds represented by this letter. **3.** Anything shaped like the letter V.

v, V, v., V. *Note:* As an abbreviation or symbol, *v* may be a small or a capital letter, with or without a full stop. Established forms or those generally preferred precede the definition. When no form is given, all four forms are in general use in that sense. **1. V** The symbol for the element vanadium. **2. V** *Physics.* velocity. **3. V.** venerable (in titles). **4. v.** verb. **5. v.** verse. **6. v.** version. **7. v.** verso. **8. v.** versus. **9. v., V.** very. **10. v., V.** vice (in titles). **11. V** victory (used by the Allies in World War II). **12. v.** vide. **13. v., V.** village. **14. v.** violin. **15. V.** viscount; viscountess. **16. v.** vocative. **17. v.** voice. **18. V** *Electricity.* volt. **19. V** volume. **20. v.** volume (book). **21. v.** von. **22. v.** vowel. **23. v, V** The Roman numeral for five. **24.** The 22nd in a series; 21st when *J* is omitted.

V-1 (vée-wún ‖ -wón) *n.* A **flying bomb** *(see).* [German *Vergeltungswaffe eins,* "retaliation weapon (number) one".]

V-2 (vée-tōō) *n.* A long-range liquid-fuelled rocket used by the Germans as a ballistic missile in World War II. [German *Vergeltungswaffe zwei,* "retaliation weapon (number) two".]

V.A. 1. vice admiral. **2.** vicar apostolic. **3.** *U.S.* Veterans' Administration. **4.** Royal Order of Victoria and Albert.

Vaal (vaal ‖ *locally* faal). River in northeastern South Africa, rising in the southeastern Transvaal and flowing for about 1 200 kilometres (750 miles) into the Orange river.

vac (vak) *n. Chiefly British Informal.* A **vacation** *(see).*

vac. vacuum.

va·can·cy (váykən-si) *n., pl.* **-cies. 1.** The state or condition of being vacant or unoccupied; emptiness. **2.** An empty or unoccupied space; a gap. **3.** A position, office, or place of accommodation that is unfilled or unoccupied. **4.** Emptiness of mind; inanity. **5.** A crystal defect caused by the absence of an atom, ion, or molecule in a crystal lattice. **6.** *Archaic.* A period of leisure; idleness. [VAC(ANT) + -ANCY or from Medieval and Late Latin *vacāntia.*]

va·cant (váykənt) *adj.* **1.** Containing nothing; empty; unfilled. **2.** Without an incumbent or occupant: *a vacant professorship.* **3.** Not occupied or put to use: *a vacant property.* **4.** *Law.* Not claimed, as by an heir: *a vacant estate.* **5. a.** Lacking intelligence or knowledge: *"Then gay ideas crowd the vacant brain"* (Alexander Pope). **b.** Expressionless; blank; unresponsive: *a vacant stare.* **6.** Unfilled by any activity: *vacant hours.* —See Synonyms at **empty.** [Middle English *vaca(u)nt,* from Old French *vacant,* from Latin *vacāns* (stem *vacānt-*), present participle of *vacāre,* to be empty.] —**va·cant·ly** *adv.* —**va·cant·ness** *n.*

vacant possession *n. Law.* Ownership of an unoccupied house or dwelling, and hence the right of immediate occupation.

va·cate (və-káyt, *rarely* vay- ‖ *U.S.* váy-kayt) *v.* **-cated, -cating, -cates.** —*tr.* **1. a.** To cease to occupy or hold; give up; leave. **b.** To empty of occupants or incumbents. **2.** *Law.* To make void; countermand; annul. —*intr.* To leave a job, office, lodging, or the like. [Latin *vacāre,* to be empty.]

va·ca·tion (və-káysh'n ‖ *U.S.* vay-) *n.* **1.** A fixed period of holidays; especially, one during which the law courts and universities suspend activities. **2.** *Chiefly U.S.* A holiday. **3.** *Archaic.* An act or instance of vacating.

—*intr.v.* **vacationed, -tioning, -tions.** *U.S.* To take or spend a holiday. [Middle English *vacacioun,* from Old French *vacation,* from Latin *vacātiō* (stem *vacātiōn-*), freedom, release from occupation, from *vacāre,* to be empty, be free. See **vacate.**] —**va·ca·tion·er, va·ca·tion·ist** *n.*

vac·ci·nal (váksin'l) *adj.* Caused by or pertaining to vaccine or vaccination.

vac·ci·nate (váksi-nayt) *v.* **-nated, -nating, -nates.** *Medicine.* —*tr.* To inoculate with a vaccine in order to produce immunity against smallpox, diphtheria, typhoid fever, poliomyelitis, cholera, typhus, and other infectious diseases. —*intr.* To perform a vaccination. [From VACCINE.] —**vac·ci·na·tor** (-naytər) *n.*

vac·ci·na·tion. (váksi-náysh'n) *n.* **1.** Inoculation with a vaccine in

order to protect against a given disease. **2.** A scar left on the skin by such an inoculation.

vac·cine (vák-seen, -sin ‖ *U.S. also* vak-séen) *n.* **1.** A suspension of attenuated or killed disease-causing microorganisms, as of viruses or bacteria, incapable of inducing severe infection but capable, when inoculated, of stimulating the production of antibodies (and therefore ·conferring immunity) against the virulent microorganisms. **2.** Such a suspension prepared from the cowpox virus and inoculated against smallpox.

~*adj.* **1.** Of or derived from cows, especially from cows infected with cowpox. **2.** Of or pertaining to cowpox. **3.** Of or pertaining to vaccination. [French *(virus) vaccine,* (virus) of cowpox, from Latin *vaccīnus,* pertaining to cows, from *vacca,* cow.]

vac·cin·i·a (vak-sínni-ə) *n.* **Cowpox** *(see).* [New Latin, from Latin *vaccīnus,* of cows. See **vaccine.**]

vache·rin (vásho-rán, vásh-) *n.* A French dessert consisting of a meringue shell filled with cream, fruit, or ice cream.

vac·il·late (vássi-layt) *intr.v.* **-lated, -lating, -lates. 1.** To swing indecisively from one course of action or opinion to another; be irresolute; waver. **2.** To sway from one side to the other; fluctuate; oscillate. —See Synonyms at **hesitate.** [Latin *vacillāre†,* to waver.] —**vac·il·la·tion** (-láysh'n) *n.* —**vac·il·la·tor** (-laytər) *n.*

vac·il·lat·ing (vássi-layting) *adj.* Also *rare* **vac·il·lant** (vássilənt), **vac·il·la·to·ry** (-lə-tri, -təri, -laytəri, -láytəri). Inclined to waver; irresolute. —**va·cil·lat·ing·ly** *adv.*

va·cu·i·ty (va-kéw-əti, və-) *n., pl.* **-ties. 1.** Total absence of matter; emptiness. **2.** An empty space; a vacuum. **3.** Lack of thought or intelligence; emptiness of mind. **4.** Absence of meaningful occupation; idleness: *"the crew, being patient people, much given to slumber and vacuity"* (Washington Irving). **5.** The quality or fact of being devoid of something specified: *a vacuity of taste.* **6.** Something, especially a remark, utterly without substance or point; an inanity. [Old French *vacuite,* from Latin *vacuitās* (stem *vacuitāt-*), from *vacuus,* empty. See **vacuum.**]

vac·u·o·lat·ed (váckew-ə-laytid, -ō-) *adj.* Also **vac·u·o·late** (-lət, -lit, -layt). Containing a vacuole or vacuoles.

vac·u·ole (váckew-ōl) *n.* Any small cavity in the cytoplasm of a cell, plant, or animal, that contains air, water, sap, partially digested food or other materials. [French, "little vacuum", from Latin *vacuum,* VACUUM.] —**vac·u·o·lar** (-ōlər) *adj.* —**vac·u·o·la·tion** (-ə-láysh'n, -ō-) *n.*

vac·u·ous (váckew-əss) *adj.* **1.** Devoid of matter; empty. **2. a.** Stupid; dull. **b.** Expressionless. **3.** Devoid of substance or meaning; inane. **4.** Purposeless; unoccupied; idle. —See Synonyms at **empty.** [Latin *vacuus,* empty. See **vacuum.**] —**vac·u·ous·ly** *adv.* —**vac·u·ous·ness** *n.*

vac·u·um (váckew-əm, vák-yōom, -yōom) *n., pl.* **-ums** or **vacua** (váckew-ə) (except for sense 4). *Abbr.* **vac. 1. a.** The absence of matter. **b.** A space empty of matter. **c.** A space in which the pressure is significantly lower than atmospheric pressure. **d.** A space relatively empty of matter. **2.** A state or feeling of emptiness; a void. **3.** A state of being sealed off from external or environmental influences; isolation. **4.** A vacuum cleaner.

~*adj.* **1.** Pertaining to or used to create a vacuum. **2.** Containing air or other gas at a reduced pressure. **3.** Working by means of suction or by maintaining of a partial vacuum.

~*v.* **vacuumed, -uming, -ums.** —*tr.* To clean with a vacuum cleaner. —*intr.* To use a vacuum cleaner. [Latin, neuter of *vacuus,* empty, from *vacāre,* to be empty.]

vacuum aspiration *n. Medicine.* A therapeutic method of abortion carried out under anaesthetic, before the twelfth week of pregnancy.

vacuum cleaner *n.* An electrical appliance that draws light dirt from surfaces by suction. —**vacuum-clean** *v.*

vacuum distillation *n.* A form of distillation in which the liquid to be distilled is maintained at a reduced pressure in order to lower its boiling point.

vacuum extractor *n. Medicine.* A suction cap that can be attached to the head of a foetus in order to aid delivery.

vacuum flask *n.* A bottle or flask having a partial vacuum between its inner and outer walls, designed to maintain the desired temperature of the contents. Also called "flask", "Thermos flask", "Dewar flask", *U.S.* "vacuum bottle".

vacuum gauge *n.* A device for determining the pressure in a partial vacuum.

vac·u·um-packed (váckew-əm-pákt, vák-yŏŏm, -yŏŏm-, -pakt) *adj.* 1. Packed in an airtight container with little or no air. 2. Sealed under low pressure or a partial vacuum.

vacuum pump 1. A pump used to evacuate an enclosure. 2. A **pulsometer** *(see).*

vacuum tube *n.* An electronic **valve** *(see).*

V.A.D. *n.* A member of Voluntary Aid Detachment, serving as nursing assistants during World War I.

va·de me·cum (váa-di-máy-kŏŏm, váy-, -mée-, -kum, -kəm) *n.,pl.* **vade mecums.** 1. A useful thing that a person constantly carries with him. 2. A guidebook or other ready reference book. [Latin, "go with me".]

va·dose (váy-dōz, -dŏss) *adj.* Of, pertaining to, or designating water that occurs below the earth's surface and above the water table. [Latin *vadōsus,* full of shallows, from *vadum,* ford.]

Va·duz (va-dŏŏts, -dŏŏts; *German* fa-). Capital of Liechtenstein. It is a tourist centre and the site of a castle, built in 16th-century style.

vag·a·bond (vágga-bond) *n.* 1. A person without a fixed home who moves from place to place and has no apparent means of support. 2. A vagrant; a tramp. 3. A wandering rogue; a rascal. ~*adj.* 1. Of, pertaining to, or characteristic of a wanderer; nomadic. 2. Aimless; drifting; straying. 3. Irregular in course or behaviour; unpredictable. ~*intr.v.* **vagabonded, -bonding, -bonds.** To lead a vagabond's life; roam about. [Middle English *vagabound,* from Old French *vagabond,* from Latin *vagābundus,* wandering, from *vagārī,* to wander, from *vagus,* wandering, undecided, VAGUE.] —**vag·a·bond·age** *n.* —**vag·a·bond·ism** *n.*

va·gar·y (váygəri, və-gaír-i) *n., pl.* **-ies.** An extravagant or erratic notion or action; a flight of fancy. See Synonyms at **caprice.** [Originally "a roaming tour", ramble, from Latin *vagārī,* to wander, from *vagus,* wandering, undecided, VAGUE.]

va·gi·na (və-jí-nə) *n., pl.* **-nas** or **-nae** (-nee) 1. *Anatomy.* **a.** The passage leading from the external genital orifice to the uterus in female mammals. **b.** A similar structure in some invertebrates. 2. *Biology.* A sheathlike structure or part, such as that formed by the base of a leaf enclosing a stem. [Latin *vāgīna,* sheath.] —**vag·i·nal** (-n'l, *also* vájin'l) *adj.*

vag·i·nate (váji-nayt, -nət, -nit) *adj.* Also **vag·i·nat·ed** (-naytid). Forming or enclosed in a sheath.

vag·i·nec·to·my (váji-néktəmi) *n., pl.* **-mies.** 1. Surgical excision of all or part of the vagina. 2. Surgical excision of the serous membrane covering the testis and epididymis. [VAGIN(O-) + -ECTOMY.]

vag·i·nis·mus (váji-níz-məss, -níss-) *n.* Sudden and painful contraction of the muscles surrounding the vagina. [New Latin : VAGIN(O-) + -ISM.]

vag·i·ni·tis (váji-nítiss) *n.* Inflammation of the vagina. Also called "colpitis". [New Latin : VAGIN(O-) + -ITIS.]

vagino-, vagin- *comb. form.* Indicates the vagina; for example, **vaginectomy.** [From Latin *vāgīna.*]

va·got·o·my (vay-góttəmi, va-) *n., pl.* **-mies.** Surgical cutting of any of the branches of the vagus nerve, used to diminish the secretion of acid and pepsin by the stomach and to control a peptic ulcer. [VAG(US) + -TOMY.]

va·go·to·ni·a (váyg-ə-tŏni-ə, -ō-) *n.* Pathological overactivity of the vagus nerve. [New Latin : VAG(US) + -TONIA.]

va·go·trop·ic (váyg-ə-tróppik, -ō-, -trŏpik) *adj.* Affecting or acting on the vagus nerve. Said chiefly of drugs. [VAG(US) + -TROPIC.]

va·gran·cy (váygrən-si) *n., pl.* **-cies.** 1. The state of being a vagrant. 2. The conduct or mode of existence of a vagrant. 3. *Rare.* A wandering in mind or thought.

va·grant (vágrənt) *n.* 1. A person who wanders from place to place without a fixed home or livelihood and ekes out a living by begging or stealing; a tramp; a vagabond. 2. A wanderer; a rover. ~*adj.* 1. Wandering from place to place; homeless and without work; roving. 2. Wayward; unrestrained. 3. Moving in a random fashion; not fixed in place. [Middle English *vag(a)raunt,* from Anglo-French, probably from Latin *vagārī,* to wander, from *vagus,* wandering, undecided, VAGUE.] —**va·grant·ly** *adv.*

vague (vayg) *adj.* **vaguer, vaguest.** 1. Not clearly expressed or outlined; inexplicit; indefinite: *vague instructions.* 2. **a.** Uncertain or indefinite in thought or expression: *She was vague about her future.* **b.** Mildly confused or muddled, as in one's thinking. 3. Lacking definite shape, form, or character; not clearly defined: *vague plans.* 4. Ambiguous in meaning or application: *"Right" and "wrong" seem vague to too many people.* 5. Indistinctly felt, perceived, understood, or recalled; hazy: *a vague uneasiness.* —See Synonyms at **ambiguous.** [Old French, from Latin *vagus†,* wandering, undecided, vague. See also **extravagant.**] —**vague·ly** *adv.* —**vague·ness** *n.*

va·gus (váy-gəss) *n., pl.* **-gi** (-jī, -gī). Either of the tenth and longest pair of cranial nerves, passing through the neck and thorax into the abdomen and supplying sensation to part of the ear, the larynx, and the pharynx, motor impulses to the vocal-cord muscles, and motor and secretory impulses to the abdominal and thoracic viscera. Also called "vagus nerve", "pneumogastric nerve". [New Latin *vagus (nervus),* "wandering (nerve)", from Latin *vagus,* wandering, VAGUE.] —**va·gal** (váyg'l) *adj.*

va·hi·ne (vaa-héeni) *n.* In Tahiti, a woman, especially one who is married. [Maori.]

vail (vayl) *v.* **vailed, vailing, vails.** *Archaic.* —*tr.* 1. To lower (a banner, for example). 2. To doff (a hat or headpiece) as a token of respect or submission. —*intr.* 1. To descend; to lower. 2. To doff one's hat. [Middle English *valen,* short for *avalen,* to let fall, from Old French *avaler,* to lower, from Vulgar Latin *advallāre* (unattested), from Latin *ad vallem,* "to the valley" : *ad,* to + *vallis, vallēs,* valley.]

vain (vayn) *adj.* **vainer, vainest.** 1. Not yielding the desired outcome; unsuccessful; futile; fruitless: *a vain attempt.* 2. Lacking substance or worth; hollow; idle: *vain talk.* 3. Showing undue preoccupation with or pride in one's appearance or accomplishments; conceited: *He wasn't just immodest, he was shamelessly vain.* 4. *Archaic.* Foolish. —**in vain.** 1. Without effect or avail; to no use or purpose: *Our labour was in vain.* 2. Without due respect or piety; profanely. Used chiefly in the phrase *take the name of God in vain.* [Middle English, from Old French, from Latin *vānus,* empty.] —**vain·ly** *adv.* —**vain·ness** *n.*

vain·glo·ri·ous (váyn-gláw-ri-əss ‖ -glŏ́-) *adj.* 1. Showing excessive vanity; boastful. 2. Characterised by or proceeding from vainglory. —**vain·glo·ri·ous·ly** *adv.* —**vain·glo·ri·ous·ness** *n.*

vain·glo·ry (váyn-gláw-ri ‖ -glŏ́-, -glaw-, -glŏ-) *n., pl.* **-ries.** 1. Boastful and unwarranted pride in one's accomplishments or qualities. 2. Vain and ostentatious display. [Middle English *vein glory, wayn-glori,* from Old French *vaine glorie,* from Latin *vānus glōria,* empty pride : *vānus,* VAIN + *glōria,* pride, GLORY.]

vair (vair) *n.* 1. A fur, probably squirrel, much used in medieval times to line and trim robes. 2. *Heraldry.* A heraldic representation of squirrel fur. [Middle English *veir, vaire,* variegated fur, from Old French *vair,* from Latin *varius,* variegated, VARIOUS.]

Vaish·na·va (víshnəvə) *n.* A Hindu sect that worships Vishnu. [Sanskrit *viṣṇava,* of Vishnu, from *Viṣṇu,* VISHNU.] —**Vaish·na·vism** *n.*

Vais·ya (vísh-yə, víss-) *n.* 1. The Hindu merchant and business caste, originally composed of farmers and herders. 2. A member of this caste. See **caste.** [Sanskrit *vaisya,* "settler".]

val. valuation; value.

val·ance (vál-ənss) *n.* 1. A short ornamental curtain or piece of drapery hung across the top of a window or along a shelf, canopy, or the like, or from the frame or mattress of a bed to the floor, often to conceal structural detail. 2. A decorative board or metal strip similar to this. ~*tr.v.* **valanced, -ancing, -ances.** To supply with a valance. [Middle English *valaunce,* perhaps from Anglo-French *valance* (unattested), equivalent to Old French *avaler,* to lower (see **vail**) + -ANCE.]

vale[1] (vayl) *n. Archaic & Poetic.* 1. A valley; a dale. 2. The world as a scene of sorrow: *this vale of dross and tears.* [Middle English *vale, vaal,* from Old French *val,* from Latin *vallēs, vallis.*]

va·le[2] (váy-li, vá-, váa-, -lay) *interj. Archaic.* Used to express leave-taking or farewell. ~*n. Archaic.* A farewell. [Latin *valē,* imperative of *valēre,* to be strong or well.]

val·e·dic·tion (vál-i-díksh'n) *n.* 1. An act or instance of saying goodbye; a farewell; a leave-taking. 2. A speech or statement made at a time of leaving. [From Latin *valedīcere,* to say farewell : *valē,* VALE (farewell) + *dīcere,* to say (by analogy with *benediction*).]

val·e·dic·to·ry (vál-i-díktəri) *adj.* Pertaining to or by way of a farewell. ~*n., pl.* **valedictories.** A farewell address.

Va·len·cia[1] (və-lén-shi-ə, -si-; *Spanish* ba-lénth-ya). Region of eastern Spain, lying on the Mediterranean coast and comprising the provinces of Alicante, Castellón de la Plana, and Valencia. Its fertile coastal plain has given won it the name of the "garden of Spain".

Valencia[2]. City in eastern Spain, with a port on the Mediterranean lying on the river Turia. It is the capital of the province of the same name and the third-largest city in Spain. It dates from at least the second century B.C. and was the headquarters of the Loyalist government (1936–37) during the Spanish Civil War.

Va·len·ci·ennes (vál-ən-si-én, -oN-, -énz) *n.* A fine type of lace with a floral pattern originally manufactured at Valenciennes, Nord département, France. Also called "Valenciennes lace".

va·len·cy (váylən-si) *n., pl.* **-cies.** Also *chiefly U.S.* **va·len·ce** (váylənss). 1. *Chemistry.* **a.** The capacity of an atom or group of atoms to combine in specific proportions with other atoms or groups of atoms. **b.** An integer, often one of several for any given element, used to represent this capacity in terms of an arbitrary assignment of 1 to an atom or group capable of forming a single bond with chlorine and of -1 to an atom or group capable of forming a single bond with hydrogen. 2. Broadly, the capacity of something to unite, react, or interact with something else. [Late Latin *valentia,* strength, capacity, from Latin *valēns* (stem *valent-*), present participle of *valēre,* to be strong.]

valency bond *n.* A covalent bond between atoms.

valency electron *n.* An electron in an outer or next to the outer shell of an atom that can participate in forming chemical bonds with other atoms.

valency shell *n.* A shell of an atom that contains the valency electrons.

val·en·tine (vál-ən-tīn) *n.* 1. **a.** A greetings card of a sentimental or humorous nature sent, usually, to one of the opposite sex on Saint

Valentine's Day (February 14). **b.** A card or gift sent as a token of love to one's sweetheart on Saint Valentine's Day. **2.** A person singled out as one's sweetheart on Saint Valentine's Day.

Valentine's Day, Valentines Day. Saint Valentine's Day *(see).*

Val·en·ti·no (vál-ən-tée̍nō), **Rudolf** born Rodolpho Gugliemi di Valentina d'Antonguolla (1895–1926). Italian film actor. His roles in *The Sheik* (1921), *Blood and Sand* (1922), and other romantic films of the silent cinema made him the leading idol of the 1920s.

Valéra, Eamon de. See **De Valéra, Eamon.**

va·le·ri·an (və-léer-i-ən) *n.* **1.** Any of various plants of the genera *Valeriana* or *Centranthus,* having dense clusters of small white or pinkish flowers; especially, *V. officinalis,* native to Eurasia and widely cultivated. **2.** The dried roots of *V. officinalis,* used medicinally as a sedative. [Middle English, from Old French *valeriane,* from Medieval Latin *valeriāna (herba),* apparently from Latin *Valeriānus,* of Valeria, Roman province, from *Valerius,* name of a Roman gens.]

va·le·ric acid (və-léer-ik, -lérrik) *n.* **Pentanoic acid** *(see).* [Obtained from the root of VALERIAN.]

Va·lé·ry (va-le-rée), **Paul (Ambroise)** (1871–1945). French poet, essayist, and critic. He is best remembered for his philosophic poems, *La jeune Parque* (1917) and *Charmes* (1922).

val·et (vál-it, -i, -ay || *U.S. also* va-láy) *n.* **1.** A man's male servant, who looks after his clothes and performs other personal services. **2.** An employee in a hotel or on a ship, for example, who performs personal services for guests or passengers.

~*v.* **valeted, -eting, -ets.** —*tr.* To act as a personal servant to; attend. —*intr.* To work as a valet. [French, from Old French *vaslet,* originally "young nobleman", "squire", from Medieval Latin *vassellitus* (unattested), diminutive of *vassus* (unattested), VASSAL.]

va·let de cham·bre (vál-ay də- shóNbr, va-láy, shóNbrə) *n., pl.* **valets de chambre** (*pronounced as singular*). *French.* A man's valet.

Valetta. See **Valletta.**

val·e·tu·di·nar·i·an (vál-i-téw-di-náir-i-ən || -tóō-) *n.* A chronic invalid; especially, one constantly and morbidly concerned with his health.

~*adj.* **1.** Chronically ailing; sickly; infirm. **2.** Endeavouring to recover health. **3.** Constantly and morbidly concerned with one's health. [Latin *valētūdinārius,* in poor health, from *valētūdō* (stem *valētūdin-*), state of health, from *valēre,* to be strong.] —**val·e·tu·di·nar·i·an·ism** *n.*

val·e·tu·di·nar·y (vál-i-téw-din-ri, -əri || -tóō-, -erri) *adj.* Valetudinarian.

~*n.* A valetudinarian.

val·gus (vál-gəss) *adj. Pathology.* Displaced outwards from the central line of the body.

~*n., pl.* **valguses. 1.** A deformity of the foot causing the sufferer to walk on the outer side of the foot. **2.** Any of various other deformities involving a turning or twisting from the midline of the body. [Latin *valgus*†, bowlegged.]

Val·hal·la (val-hál-ə) *n.* Also **Wal·hal·la** (val-, wal-, wol-). *Norse Mythology.* The great hall of immortality in which the souls of warriors slain heroically were received by Odin and enshrined. [Old Norse *Valhöll* : *valr,* those slain in battle + *höll,* hall.]

val·iant (vál-yənt) *adj.* Possessing, acting with, or showing valour; brave; courageous. See Synonyms at **brave.** [Middle English *valiaunt,* from Anglo-French, from Vulgar Latin *valiente* (unattested), from Latin *valēns,* present participle of *valēre,* to be strong.] —**val·ian·cy, val·iance, val·iant·ness** *n.* —**val·iant·ly** *adv.*

val·id (vál-id) *adj.* **1.** Well-grounded; sound; supportable: *a valid objection.* **2.** Producing the desired results; efficacious: *valid methods.* **3. a.** Legally sound and effective; incontestable; binding: *a valid title.* **b.** Current; in effect: *valid till the end of the month.* **4.** *Logic.* **a.** Containing premises from which the conclusion may logically be derived: *a valid argument.* **b.** Correctly inferred or deduced from a premise: *a valid conclusion.* **5.** *Archaic.* Of sound health; robust. [French *valide,* from Old French, from Latin *validus,* strong, effective, from *valēre,* to be strong.] —**va·lid·ly** *adv.* —**va·lid·i·ty** (və-líddəti, va-), **va·lid·ness** *n.*

Synonyms: *valid, sound, convincing, telling, conclusive.*

val·i·date (vál-i-dayt) *tr.v.* **-dated, -dating, -dates. 1.** To declare or make legally valid. **2.** To substantiate; verify. —See Synonyms at **confirm.** —**val·i·da·tion** (-dáysh'n) *n.*

va·line (váyl-een, vál-) *n.* A crystalline amino acid, $C_5H_{11}NO_2$, essential for normal growth and health. [VAL(ERIC ACID) + -INE.]

va·lise (və-léez, va-, -léess) *n. Chiefly U.S.* A piece of hand luggage such as a small suitcase or bag. [French, from Italian *valigia,* akin to Medieval Latin *valisia*†.]

Val·i·um (vál-i-əm) *n.* A trademark for a tranquilliser or sedative used to relieve tension and anxiety. Also called "diazepam".

Val·ky·rie (val-kéer-i, -kírri, vál-kirri || *U.S. also* -kīr-i) *n.* Also **Wal·ky·rie** (val-). *Norse Mythology.* Any of Odin's handmaidens who hover over battlefields, choosing warriors to be victorious and conducting the souls of slain heroes to Valhalla. [Old Norse *valkyrja,* "chooser of the slain".]

Va·lla·do·lid (vál-ə-dō-líd, -do-, -də-; *Spanish* bál-ya-do-lée̲th, -lée). City in northern Spain, the capital of the province of the same name, lying at the confluence of the rivers Pisuerga and Esgueva.

val·la·tion (va-láysh'n, və-) *n. Archaic.* An earthwork wall used for military defence; a rampart. [Late Latin *vallātiō* (stem *vallātiōn-*), from Latin *vallāre,* to surround with a rampart, from *vallum,* palisade, rampart, from *vallus,* stake.] —**val·la·to·ry** (-láytəri) *adj.*

val·lec·u·la (va-léckew-lə, və-) *n., pl.* **-lae** (-lee). *Biology.* A shallow groove, depression, or furrow. [Late Latin, variant of Latin *vallicula,* diminutive of *vallēs,* VALLEY.] —**val·lec·u·lar** (-lər), **val·lec·u·late** (-lət, -lit, -layt) *adj.*

Val·le d'A·os·ta (vál-lay da-óstə). Region of northwestern Italy, occupying the upper basin of the river Dora Baltea. It has a distinct French linguistic and cultural heritage and was made an autonomous region in 1945. Aosta is the cpaital.

Val·let·ta or **Va·let·ta** (və-léttə). Capital city of Malta, lying on a high promontory between two deep harbours on the northeastern coast. It contains numerous relics of the Knights of Malta as well as the 16th-century cathedral and governor's palace.

val·ley (vál-i) *n., pl.* **-leys. 1.** An elongated lowland between ranges of mountains or hills, or other uplands, often having a river or stream running along the bottom. **2.** An extensive land area drained or irrigated by a river system: *the Indus valley.* **3.** Any depression or hollow resembling or suggesting a valley, as where two slopes of a roof meet. [Middle English *valey,* from Anglo-French, from Vulgar Latin *vallāta* (unattested), from Latin *vallis, vallēs.*]

Valley of the Kings. Long, narrow valley in Egypt, the site of ancient Thebes and now occupied by Luxor and Karnak. It is the site of at least 60 tombs of Egyptian pharaohs of the 18th, 19th, and 20th dynasties, including the tomb of Tutankhamun.

Valley of the Ten Thousand Smokes. Valley in the Katmai National Monument, a national park in southern Alaska. Since the massive volcanic eruption of Mount Novarupta in 1912, the valley has emitted hot gases through its countless cracks.

val·lum (vál-əm) *n.* A large rampart erected as a means of defence, especially one built by the ancient Romans. [Latin, collective noun from *vallus,* stake.]

Va·lois[1] (vál-waa, val-wáa). French royal dynasty, from 1328–1589. They succeeded the Capetian line when Philip Count of Valois, was called to the throne as Philip VI (1328–50). They were succeeded by the Bourbons.

Valois[2]. A historic region and former duchy of northern France.

Valois, Dame Ninette de. See **de Valois, Dame Ninette.**

va·lo·ni·a (və-lṓni-ə) *n.* An extract from the dried acorn cups of an oak tree, *Quercus aegilops,* of eastern Europe and Asia Minor, used chiefly in tanning and dyeing. [Italian *vallonia,* from Modern Greek *balania,* plural of *balani,* acorn, from Greek *balanos.*]

val·or·ise, val·or·ize (vál-ə-rīz) *tr.v.* **-ised, -ising, -ises.** To establish and maintain the price of (a commodity) artificially, especially by government action. [Back-formation from French *valorisation,* from *valour,* VALOUR.] —**val·or·i·sa·tion** (-rī-záysh'n || *U.S.* -ri-) *n.*

val·or·ous (vál-ərəss) *adj.* Having or showing great personal bravery; valiant. See Synonyms at **brave.** —**val·or·ous·ly** *adv.* —**val·or·ous·ness** *n.*

val·our, *U.S.* **val·or** (vál-ər) *n.* Courage and boldness, especially as shown in battle; bravery in the face of great danger. See Synonyms at **courage.** [Middle English *valour,* value, worth, from Old French, from Latin *valour,* from *valēre,* to be strong, be of value.]

Val·pa·rai·so (vál-pə-rī-zō || -ráy-; *Spanish* bal-pa-ra-ée-sō). City in central Chile, lying on the Pacific coast just to the northwest of Santiago. It is Chile's chief port and second largest city. The city is built on a natural amphitheatre, and funicular railways connect the industrial docklands with the higher residential districts.

valse (vaalss, valss) *n.* A waltz. Used especially in titles of pieces of music. [French.]

val·u·a·ble (vál-yoo-əb'l, -yŏŏb'l || -yəb'l) *adj.* **1.** Having considerable monetary or material value for use or exchange: *a few moments of your valuable time.* **2.** Highly useful or serviceable for a particular purpose: *valuable advice.* **3.** Having admirable or esteemed qualities or characteristics. —See Synonyms at **costly.**

~*n. Plural.* Valuable personal possessions, such as jewellery. —**val·u·a·ble·ness** *n.* —**val·u·a·bly** *adv.*

val·u·a·tion (vál-yoo-áysh'n) *n. Abbr.* **val. 1.** The act or process of assessing the value or price of something; an appraisal. **2.** The assessed value or price of something. **3.** An estimation or appreciation of the worth, merit, or character of something: *set a high valuation on friendship.* —**val·u·a·tion·al** *adj.*

val·u·a·tor (vál-yoo-aytər) *n.* One who makes valuations; a valuer.

val·ue (vál-yŏŏ, -yōō) *n. Abbr.* **val. 1.** An amount, as of goods, services, or money, considered to be a fair and suitable equivalent for something else; a fair price or return: *The meal was expensive, but good value.* **2. a.** The amount of money for which something can be exchanged on the open market; monetary or material worth. **b.** Power to buy or exchange: *The value of the pound has fallen.* **3. a.** Relative worth in terms of utility, quality, desirability, or importance: *the value of a good education; a novel of little value.* **b.** The usefulness of something in producing a particular effect or furthering a particular end: *The gesture cost them nothing, but had great propaganda value.* **4.** *Plural.* Those qualities regarded by a person or group as important and desirable; a set of standards and principles: *rejected the materialistic values of western society.* **5.** Precise meaning or import, as of a carefully considered word. **6.** *Mathematics.* An assigned or calculated numerical quantity. **7.** *Music.* The relative duration of a note or rest. **8.** The relative darkness or lightness of a colour in a picture. **9.** *Phonetics.* The sound quality of a letter or diphthong. —**good value.** *Informal.* Interesting and entertaining company: *She's very good value.* —**value for money.** Well worth the money paid; fair exchange.

~*tr.v.* **valued, -uing, -ues. 1.** To determine or estimate the worth or value of; appraise. **2.** To regard highly; prize; esteem. **3.** To rate

PRONUNCIATION KEY

a, trap; aa, father; ai, fair; ar, star; aw, lawn; ay, play; b, bb, stab; rubber; ch, church; ck, ticket; d, dd, dead; ladder; e, dress; ee, bee; er, defer; ew, few; ewr, pure; ə, about; ər, letter; f, ff, fife; differ; g, gg, giggle; h, hat; i, kit; ī, price; īr, fire; j, judge; k, kick; l, ll, let; 'l, needle; m, mm, man; n, nn, no; 'n, sudden; ng, thing; o, lot; ō, no; ŏŏ, foot; ōō, shoe; oor, poor; ow, cow; owr, hour; oy, boy; p, pp, pepper; r, rr, red; s, ss, sauce; sh, ship; t, tt, totter; th, thick; th̲, this; smooth; u, cut; ur, turn; v, vv, valve; w, wet; y, yes; z, zz, zebra; zh̲, vision; pleasure

IN FOREIGN WORDS:

aN, oN, Saint-Saëns; h̲l, Llanelli; Hluhluwe; k̲h, loch; lough; Khaled

STRESS MARK:

ín-sīt, insight; in-sī́t, incite

according to relative estimate of worth or desirability; evaluate. **4.** To assign a value to (a unit of currency, for example). **—**See Synonyms at **appreciate.** [Middle English, from Old French, from the feminine past participle of *valoir,* to be worth, from Latin *valēre,* to be strong, be of value.]

val·ue-ad·ded tax (vál-yoo-áddid) *n. Abbr.* **VAT, V.A.T.** A tax on the estimated market value added to any product or service at each stage of its manufacture or distribution, ultimately passed on to the consumer.

val·ued (vál-yōōd, -yōōd) *adj.* Highly regarded; much esteemed.

valued policy *n.* An **agreed-value policy** *(see).*

value judgment *n.* A judgment based upon or reflecting one's personal moral and aesthetic values; a subjective evaluation.

val·ue·less (vál-yoo-ləss, -liss) *adj.* Having no value; worthless.

val·u·er (vál-yoo-ər) *n.* A person whose job is to assess the monetary value of real property, such as land, buildings, or works of art.

val·vate (vál-vayt) *adj.* **1.** Having valvelike parts. **2.** *Botany.* Meeting at the edges without overlapping, as petals may.

valve (valv) *n.* **1. a.** Any of various devices that regulate the flow of gases, liquids, or loose materials through structures, such as piping, or through apertures by opening, closing, or obstructing ports or passageways. **b.** The movable control element of such a device. **c.** *Music.* A device in a brass wind instrument that permits change in pitch by allowing a rapid varying of the length of the tube. **2.** *Anatomy.* A membranous structure in a hollow organ or passage, as in an artery or vein, that retards or prevents the return flow of a bodily fluid. **3.** *Biology.* **a.** Any of the paired, hinged shells of many molluscs and of brachiopods. **b.** A similar paired part, as of the cell wall of a diatom. **4.** *Botany.* **a.** Any of the sections into which a seed pod or other dehiscent fruit splits. **b.** A lidlike covering of an anther. **5.** A partially evacuated sealed glass tube containing a cathode and anode, usually with one or more intervening electrodes (grids) between which a current can be maintained. The device is used for rectification and, when there are one or more grids, for amplification and as the main component of an oscillator. Also called "electronic valve", *U.S.* "vacuum tube". **6.** *Archaic.* Any of the leaves of a double or folding door.
~*tr.v.* **valved, valving, valves.** To provide with or control by means of a valve or valves. [Middle English, leaf of a door, from Latin *valva.*]

valve gear *n. Machinery.* The system of rocker arms, pushrods, and the like operating the valves in an engine.

valve-in-head engine *n. U.S.* An **overhead-valve engine** *(see).*

val·vu·lar (vál-vew-lər) *adj.* Pertaining to, having, or operating by means of valves or valvelike parts.

val·vule (vál-vewl) *n.* Also **val·vu·la** (-vew-lə) *pl.* **-lae** (-lee). A small valve or valvelike structure. [New Latin *valvula,* diminutive of Latin *valva,* leaf of a door, VALVE.]

val·vu·li·tis (vál-vew-lītiss) *n.* Inflammation of a valve, especially of a cardiac valve. [New Latin : *valvula,* VALVUL(E) + -ITIS.]

vam·brace (vám-brayss) *n.* Armour used to protect the forearm. [Middle English *va(u)mbras,* from Anglo-French *vauntbras,* short for Old French *avauntbras,* "forearm" : *avant,* before (see **vanguard**) + *bras,* arm, from Latin *bracchium.*] **—vam·braced** *adj.*

va·moose (və-mōōss, va-) *intr.v.* **-moosed, -moosing, -mooses.** *Chiefly U.S. Slang.* To leave hurriedly. [Spanish *vamos,* "let's go", from Latin *vādāmus,* from *vādere,* to go.]

vamp¹ (vamp) *n.* **1.** The upper part of a boot or shoe covering the instep and extending over the toe. **2. a.** Something patched up or refurbished. **b.** Something rehashed, such as a book based on old material. **3.** An improvised musical accompaniment.
~*v.* **vamped, vamping, vamps.** —*tr.* **1.** To provide (a shoe) with a new vamp. **2.** To patch up; refurbish. **3.** To put together; fabricate; or improvise. Usually used with *up.* **4.** *Music.* To improvise (a simple accompaniment or tune). —*intr.* To improvise simple accompaniments, variations of tunes, or the like. [Middle English *vampe,* from Anglo-French *vaumpé* (unattested), Old French *avantpie* : *avant,* before + *pie(d),* foot, from Latin *pēs.*] **—vamp·er** *n.*

vamp² *n. Informal.* An unscrupulously seductive woman who uses her sex appeal to entrap and exploit men.
~*v.* **vamped, vamping, vamps.** *Informal.* —*tr.* To seduce or exploit (a man) in the manner of a vamp. —*intr.* To play the part of a vamp. [Shortening of VAMPIRE.]

vam·pire (vám-pīr) *n.* **1.** In folklore, a reanimated corpse that rises from the grave at night to bite and then suck the blood of sleeping persons. **2.** One who preys upon others, such as an extortionist or a vamp. **3. a.** Any of various tropical American bats of the family Desmodontidae, that feed on the blood of living mammals. **b.** Any of various other bats, such as those of the family Megadermatidae, erroneously believed to feed on blood. In senses 3a and 3b, also called "vampire bat". [French, from German *Vampir,* from Magyar *vampir,* probably from Russian *upyr',* from Kazan Tatar *ubyr,* witch.] **—vam·pir·ic** (vam-pírrik) *adj.*

vam·pir·ism (vám-pīr-iz'm) *n.* **1.** Belief in the vampires of folklore. **2.** The practice of a vampire; bloodsucking.

van¹ (van) *n.* **1.** A covered motor vehicle for transporting goods and, sometimes, people. **2.** *Chiefly British.* A covered railway carriage for carrying goods, mail, or luggage, especially a **guard's van** *(see).* **3.** *British.* A gypsy **caravan** *(see).* [Short for CARAVAN.]

van² *n.* The vanguard; the forefront. [Short for VANGUARD.]

van³ *n.* **1.** *Archaic.* Any winnowing device, such as a fan. **2.** *Poetic.* A wing. [Middle English *van(ne),* variant (western and southern) of FAN and partly from Old French *van,* both from Latin *vannus.*]

van⁴ *n. British Informal.* An **advantage** *(see)* in tennis. **—van in.** Advantage to the server. **—van out.** Advantage to the receiver.

van·a·date (vánnə-dayt) *n.* *n.* Any of three anions, VO_3, VO_4, or V_2O_7. [From VANADIUM.]

va·nad·ic (və-náddik, -náydik) *adj.* Of or containing trivalent or pentavalent vanadium. [VANADIUM + -IC.]

va·nad·ic acid *n.* **1.** An acid containing a vanadate group, especially HVO_3, H_3VO_4, or $H_4V_2O_7$, not existing in a pure state. **2.** Vanadium pentoxide. [VANADATE + -IC.]

va·nad·i·nite (və-náddi-nīt) *n.* A deep ruby-red or yellow to brown mineral of vanadium and lead sometimes with impurities of arsenic and phosphorus, essentially $(PbCl)Pb_4(VO_4)_3$. [VANAD(IUM) + -IN + -ITE.]

va·na·di·um (və-náydi-əm) *n. Symbol* **V** A bright white soft ductile metallic element found in several minerals, notably vanadinite and carnotite, having good structural strength and used in rust-resistant high-speed tools, as a carbon stabiliser in some steels, as a titanium-steel bonding agent, and as a catalyst. Atomic number 23, atomic weight 50.942, melting point 1,917°C, boiling point 3,000°C, relative density 6.11, valencies 2, 3, 4, 5. [New Latin, after Old Norse *Vanadīs,* name of the goddess Freya : *vana-,* akin to *Vanr,* fertility god + *dīs*†, woman, goddess.]

vanadium pentoxide *n.* A yellow to red crystalline powder, V_2O_5, used as a catalyst in various organic reactions and as a starting material for other vanadium salts. Also called "vanadic acid".

vanadium steel *n.* Steel alloyed with vanadium for added strength, hardness, and high-temperature stability.

van·ad·ous (vánnə-dəss, və-náy-) *adj.* Of or containing divalent vanadium. [VANAD(IUM) + -OUS.]

Van Allen belt *n.* Either of two zones of electrically charged particles, trapped by the Earth's magnetic field, which form two belts above the atmosphere over the equatorial regions. They lie at about 3 200 kilometres (2,000 miles) and 17 700 kilometres (11,000 miles) from the Earth. [After J.A. *Van Allen* (born 1914), U.S. physicist.]

va·nas·pa·ti (və-núspə-ti, -náspə-) *n.* A hydrogenated vegetable fat used in India as a cooking oil in place of ghee. [Hindi, from Sanskrit, name of a plant : *vana,* forest + *pati,* lord.]

Van·brugh (ván-brə, *sometimes* van-brōō), **Sir John** (1664–1726). English architect and playwright. He designed Castle Howard and Blenheim Palace. His plays include *The Provok'd Wife* (1697), and *The Relapse* (1696).

Vance (vanss), **Cyrus** (1917–). U.S. statesman. He represented President Johnson in Korea (1968), and was U.S. negotiator at the Paris peace talks on Vietnam (1968–69). He was secretary of state (1977–80).

Van·cou·ver (van-kōōvər). City in southwestern British Columbia, Canada, lying across the Strait of Georgia from Vancouver Island. It is Canada's chief Pacific port, and third-largest city.

Vancouver Island. Island off British Columbia, Canada. It is the largest offshore island on the west coast of North America, occupying 32 137 square kilometres (12,408 square miles).

V & A., V and A. Victoria and Albert Museum.

van·dal (vánd'l) *n.* **1.** A person who wilfully or maliciously defaces or destroys public or private property. **2.** One who spoils or destroys artistic or cultural achievement. [From VANDAL.]

Van·dal (vánd'l) *n.* A member of a Germanic people that overran Gaul, Spain, and northern Africa in the fourth and fifth centuries A.D. and sacked Rome in A.D. 455. [Latin *Vandalus,* "wanderer" from Germanic.] **—Van·dal·ic** (van-dál-ik) *adj.*

van·dal·ise, van·dal·ize (vándə-līz) *tr.v.* **-ised, -ising, -ises.** To commit an act of vandalism on. [From VANDAL.]

van·dal·ism (vándə-liz'm) *n.* **1.** The wilful or malicious destruction of public or private property, especially of anything beautiful or artistic. **2.** The spoiling or destruction of artistic or cultural achievement.

Van de Graaff generator (ván də graaf, graf) *n.* An electrostatic generator in which electric charge is either removed from or transferred to a large hollow spherical electrode by a rapidly moving belt, in some configurations producing potentials over a million volts, and used with an acceleration tube as an electron or ion accelerator. [After Robert *Vande Graaff* (1901–67), U.S. physicist.]

Van·der·bilt (vándər-bilt), **Cornelius** (1794–1877). American businessman. He was founder of the family fortune which he built up on railway and shipping interests.

Van der Post (van dər pōst, fan), **Sir Laurens (Jan)** (1906–). South African author. Among his best-known works are *The Lost World of the Kalahari* (1958) and *A Story like the Wind* (1972).

van der Rohe, Ludwig Mies. See **Mies van der Rohe.**

van der Waals force (ván dər waalz || wawlz) *n.* A weak interatomic or intermolecular attraction arising from the interaction of dipoles induced in neighbouring atoms or molecules. [After Johannes D. *van der Waals* (1837–1923), Dutch physicist.]

Van Diemen's Land. See **Tasmania.**

Van Dyck or **Vandyke** (ván dīk, van), **Sir Anthony** (1599–1641). Flemish painter. He was painter to Charles I, and is famous for his portraits of the English court. His style greatly influenced the development of British portraiture. His works include *Charles I on Horseback,* and *Thomas Killigrew and Lord Croft.*

Van·dyke (ván-dīk, van-) *n.* **1.** A painting by Sir Anthony Van Dyck. **2.** A Vandyke beard or collar.
~*tr.v.* **vandyked, -dyking, -dykes.** To cut or shape (cloth) with deeply indented or scalloped edges, as on a Vandyke collar.

vampire bat Desmodus rotundus, *the common vampire bat, which is native to Central and South America, is one of several species known as vampire bats. All are small – between 60 and 90 millimetres long (2⅓–3½ inches) and weighing up to only 50 grammes (1¾ ounces) – and all feed on the blood of living mammals, occasionally including man. The bats feed at night, biting their resting victims so lightly that the prey often remains undisturbed. The bites are not serious in themselves, but they can transmit rabies and other diseases.*

Vandyke beard n. A short, pointed beard. Also called "Vandyke". [A style worn by subjects in many Vandyke portraits.]

Vandyke brown n. Moderate to dark brown. [From its frequent use by VAN DYCK.] —**Van·dyke-brown** adj.

Vandyke collar n. A large collar of linen or lace having a deeply indented or scalloped edge. Also called "Vandyke". [A type of collar depicted in many Van Dyck portraits.]

vane (vayn) n. **1.** A thin plate of wood or metal, often shaped like a cock or an arrow, that pivots on an elevated vertical spindle to indicate the direction of the wind; a weather vane; a weathercock. **2.** Any of several usually relatively thin, rigid, flat, or sometimes curved surfaces radially mounted along an axis, that is turned by or used to turn a fluid, such as a blade in a turbine or a sail on a windmill. **3.** The flattened part of a feather, consisting of a series of barbs on either side of the shaft. **4. a.** The movable target on a levelling rod. **b.** A sight on a quadrant or compass. **5.** Any of the metal guidance or stabilising fins attached to the tail of a bomb or other missile. [Middle English vane, fane, Old English fana, banner, from Germanic fanon (unattested).]

Vä·nern (vénnərn, váirnərn). Lake in southwestern Sweden, drained by the river Götaälv into the Kattegatt. It is the largest lake in Sweden and the third largest in Europe.

va·nes·sa (və-néssə) n. Any butterfly of the genus Vanessa, such as the painted lady and red admiral. Also called "vanessid butterfly". [New Latin (reason for name obscure).]

van Eyck (ván ík, van), **Jan** (c. 1390–1441). Flemish painter. He is noted for his realistic paintings, brilliant colouring, and minute detail. His works include The Arnolfini Marriage, Man in a Red Turban, and The Adoration of the Lamb, begun by his brother Hubert.

vang (vang) n. Nautical. A guy rope running from the peak of a gaff or derrick to the deck. [Earlier fang, a device for gripping, Old English, from Old Norse fang, catch, grasp; akin to Dutch vang, from vangen, to catch, seize.]

Van Gogh (ván gókh, van, góf ‖ gó; Dutch khókh), **Vincent** (1853–90). Dutch painter. His early work portrayed Dutch peasant life in sombre, dark colours; his later work in Provence (1888) was painted in bold brilliant colours. His life was filled with suffering and despair, culminating in insanity and his suicide.

van·guard (ván-gaard) n. **1. a.** The foremost position in an army or fleet advancing into battle. **b.** The foremost or leading position, as in an artistic or intellectual trend or movement. **2.** Those occupying any such position. Also called "van". [Middle English vantgard, short for avaunt garde, from Old French. See **avant-garde**.]

va·nil·la (və-nílla) n. **1.** Any of various tropical American orchids of the genus Vanilla; especially, V. planifolia, cultivated for its long, narrow seed pods from which a flavouring agent is obtained. **2.** The aromatic seed pod of this plant. Also called "vanilla pod", chiefly U.S., "vanilla bean". **3.** A flavouring extract prepared from these seed pods or produced synthetically. Also used adjectivally: vanilla ice cream. [Spanish vainilla, "little sheath" (from its elongated fruit), from vaina, sheath, pod, from Latin vāgīna.]

va·nil·lic (və-níllik) adj. Of, pertaining to, or derived from vanilla or vanillin.

va·nil·lin (və-níllin, vánnilin) n. A white or yellowish crystalline compound, $C_8H_8O_3$, found in vanilla pods and certain balsams and resins and used in perfumes, flavourings, and pharmaceuticals.

Va·nir (váa-neer) pl.n. Norse Mythology. An early race of gods who dwelt with the Aesir in Asgard. [Old Norse Vanr, fertility god.]

van·ish (vánnish) v. **-ished, -ishing, -ishes.** —intr. **1.** To disappear or become invisible, especially quickly or in an unexplained or magical manner. **2.** To fade or decay to nothing; pass out of perceived existence: The choir's last notes vanished. **3.** Mathematics. To become zero. Used of a function or variable. —tr. To cause to disappear. [Middle English vanisshen, from Old French esvanir (present stem esvaniss-), from Vulgar Latin exvānīre (unattested), variant of Latin ēvānēscere : ex-, away from + vānēscere, to disappear, "become empty", from vānus, empty.] —**van·ish·er** n.

vanishing cream n. A cosmetic face cream containing less oil than cold cream, which becomes colourless when applied and is used as a powder base or skin cleanser.

vanishing point n. **1.** A point in a drawing at which parallel lines drawn in perspective converge or seem to converge. **2.** A point at which a thing disappears or ceases to exist.

van·i·ty (vánnəti) n., pl. **-ties. 1.** The quality or condition of being vain; preoccupation with or excessive pride in one's appearance or accomplishments; conceit. **2.** Lack of usefulness, worth, or effect; hollowness; futility; worthlessness. **3. a.** Something that is vain, futile, or worthless. **b.** Something about which one is vain or conceited. **4.** U.S. A dressing table. [Middle English vanite, from Old French, from Latin vānitās stem vānitāt-), from vānus, empty, vain.]

vanity case n. A small handbag or case used by women for carrying cosmetics or toiletries.

Vanity Fair n. Sometimes small v, small f. Any place or scene of empty, idle amusement and ostentation, especially the social world. [From the fair in Bunyan's Pilgrim's Progress.]

vanity unit n. A type of dressing-table for a bathroom or bedroom consisting of a small basin with a flat surround built into a free-standing cupboard unit.

van·quish (váng-kwish ‖ ván-) tr.v. **-quished, -quishing, -quishes. 1. a.** To defeat or conquer in battle; subjugate. **b.** To defeat in any contest, conflict, or competition. **2.** To overcome or subdue (an emotion, for example); suppress: His success vanquished his fears. —See Synonyms at **defeat**. [Middle English vencusen, vaynquys-

shen, from Old French vainquir (present stem vanquiss-), variant of vaintre, from Latin vincere.] —**van·quish·a·ble** adj. —**van·quish·er** n. —**van·quish·ment** n.

Van Rie·beeck (van rée-bek, fan), **Jan (Anthonisz)** (1619–77). Dutch commander of the first settlement at the Cape of Good Hope, established in 1652. He is now looked back on as the founding father of white South Africa.

van·tage (vaán-tij ‖ ván-) n. **1. a.** An advantage in a competition or conflict; superiority. **b.** A position, condition, or opportunity likely to provide superiority or advantage. Often used in the phrase vantage ground. **2.** A position that affords a broad overall view or perspective as of a place or situation. Often used in the phrase vantage point. **3.** In tennis, an **advantage** (see). [Middle English, from Anglo-French, short for Old French avantage, ADVANTAGE.]

van·ward (ván-wərd) adj. Rare. Located in the van or front; advanced.
—adv. Rare. Towards or to the van or front; forward.

Va·nu·a·tu (vaánōō-áatōō). Formerly **New Hebrides.** Group of 12 small islands and numerous islets in the southwest Pacific Ocean. The largest island is Espiritu Santo. The islands are largely volcanic and forested. The chief exports are copra, fish, and beef. From 1897 the islands were administered as a condominium by France and Great Britain, until 1980 when they became the 44th member of the Commonwealth. Area, 14 763 square kilometres (5,699 square miles). Population, 100,000. Capital, Vila, on Efate.

Van't Hoff (vont háwf, font, hóff), **Jacobus Henricus** (1852–1911). Dutch chemist, a pioneer in the field of stereochemistry. In 1901 he was awarded the first Nobel prize for chemistry.

vap·id (váppid) adj. **1.** Lacking life, spirit, or animation; dull; insipid: vapid conversation. **2.** Lacking taste, zest, or flavour; flat; stale: vapid beer. [Latin vapidus.] —**va·pid·i·ty** (va-píddəti, və-), **vap·id·ness** n. —**vap·id·ly** adv.

va·por·es·cence (váypə-réss'nss) n. The formation of vapour.

va·po·ret·to (váppə-rét-o, váypə-) n., pl. **-ti** (-tee) or **tos.** A steamboat carrying passengers along a regular route, especially one that operates like a bus along the canals of Venice. [Italian, diminutive of vapore, steamboat, ultimately from Latin vapor, steam.]

va·por·if·ic (váypə-riffik) adj. **1.** Producing or turning to vapour. **2.** Having the nature of vapour; vaporous. [VAPOUR + -FIC.]

va·por·ise, va·por·ize (váypə-rīz) v. **-ised, -ising, -ises.** —tr. To convert (a solid or liquid) to vapour, especially by heating. —intr. To be converted into vapour. —**va·por·is·a·ble** adj. —**va·por·i·sa·tion** n.

va·por·is·er (váypə-rīzər) n. One that vaporises; especially, a device used to vaporise medicine for inhalation.

va·por·ous (váypərəss) adj. **1.** Pertaining to or resembling vapour. **2. a.** Producing vapours; volatile. **b.** Giving off or full of vapours. **3.** Insubstantial, vague, or ethereal: "the imponderable mysterious and vaporous illusions of twilight" (John Cowper Powys). **4.** Extravagantly fanciful; high-flown: vaporous conjecture. —**va·por·os·i·ty** (váypə-róssəti), **va·por·ous·ness** n. —**va·por·ous·ly** adv.

va·pour, U.S. **va·por** (váypər) n. **1.** Any barely visible or cloudy diffused matter, such as mist, fumes, or smoke, suspended in the air. **2. a.** The state of a substance that exists below its critical temperature and that may be liquefied by application of sufficient pressure. **b.** Broadly, the gaseous state of any substance that is liquid or solid under ordinary conditions. **3. a.** The vaporised form of a substance for use in industrial, military, or medical processes. **b.** A mixture of a vapour and air, such as the explosive petrol-air mixture burnt in an internal-combustion engine. **4.** Archaic. **a.** Something unsubstantial, worthless, or fleeting. **b.** A fantastic or foolish idea. **5.** Plural. Archaic. **a.** Exhalations within a body organ, especially the stomach, supposed to affect the mental or physical condition. **b.** A nervous disorder such as depression or hysteria. Preceded by the. —v. **vapoured, -pouring, -pours.** —tr. To vaporise. —intr. **1.** To be emitted or dispersed as vapour. **2.** To engage in idle, boastful talk. **3.** Archaic. To rise as vapour. [Middle English vapour, from Old French vapeur, vapour, from Latin vapor, steam.]

vapour bath n. **1.** A closed compartment or bath with an apparatus for applying steam to the body. **2.** A bath taken in such a place.

vapour density n. The density of a gas or vapour divided by the density of hydrogen both at standard temperature and pressure.

va·pour·er moth (váypərər) n. A common moth, Orgyia antiqua, the tufted caterpillars of which are a serious pest of trees. [From VAPOUR (verb, in archaic sense, "to rise as vapour"), referring to the rapid flight of the male.]

va·pour·ing (váypəring) adj. Foolishly bombastic; boastful.
—n. Boastful or bombastic talk or behaviour. —**va·pour·ing·ly** adv.

va·pour·ish (váypərish) adj. **1.** Suggestive of or like vapour. **2.** Archaic. Affected by the vapours; inclined towards low spirits.

vapour lock n. A pocket of vaporised petrol in the fuel line of an internal-combustion engine that obstructs normal flow of fuel.

vapour pressure n. The pressure exerted by a vapour in equilibrium with its solid or liquid phase.

vapour trail n. A visible condensation trail in the sky caused by a high-flying aircraft passing through a region of supercooled air. Also called "condensation trail", "contrail".

va·que·ro (va-kaír-ō ‖ vaa-) n., pl. **-ros.** U.S. A cowboy; a herdsman. [Spanish, from vaca, cow, from Latin vacca.]

var. 1. variable. **2.** variant. **3.** variation. **4.** variety. **5.** various.

va·ra (váarə) n. A Spanish, Portuguese, and Latin American unit of linear measure, varying from 80 to 110 centimetres (32 to 43 inches). [Spanish and Portuguese, "rod", "yardstick", from Latin *vāra,* forked pole, from *vārus,* bent inward.]

va·rac·tor (váir-áktər, -aktər) *n.* A semiconductor device with a capacitance that varies with the voltage applied to it. [*Var*ying *reactor.*]

Va·ra·na·si (və-raánə-si). City in the state of Uttar Pradesh, in north central India, lying on the river Ganges. It was formerly called Benares. It is the holiest Hindu city, called Kasi by Hindus, and has more than 1,500 temples, shrines, and palaces.

Va·ran·gi·an (və-ránji-ən) *n.* Any of a group of Scandinavian seafarers who established a dynasty in Russia in the 9th century, and from whom Byzantine emperors in the 10th and 11th centuries recruited their bodyguards (the *Varangian Guard*). [Medieval Latin *Varangus,* from Medieval Greek *Barangos,* from Old Norse *Væringi,* probably "confederate", from *vār,* agreement, pledge.]

var·ec (várrek) *n.* The ash of **kelp** *(see).* [French, from Old Norse *wrek* (unattested), something driven ashore, WRECK.]

Va·rèse (va-ráyz), **Edgard** (1885–1965). French-born composer. He emigrated to the United States (1916). His compositions, characterised by dissonance, unpitched sounds, and complex rhythms, include *Ionisation* (1931), and *Poème Electronique* (1958).

Var·gas (vár-gəss), **Getúlio Dornelles** (1883–1954). Brazilian politician. He seized power (1930) and won an election in 1934. From 1937 he governed as dictator after forming a fascist New State, modelled on Portugal. He was ousted in 1945 and re-elected in 1950. A political crisis (1954) led to his resignation and suicide.

va·ri·a (váir-i-ə) *n.* A miscellany, especially of literary works. [Latin, neuter plural of *varius,* VARIOUS.]

va·ri·a·ble (váir-i-əb'l) *adj. Abbr.* **var.** **1. a.** Liable, likely, or able to change or vary; subject to variation; changeable. **b.** Inconstant; fickle. **c.** Of uneven quality. **2.** *Mathematics.* Having no fixed quantitative value. **3.** Changing, as in direction or intensity: *variable winds.* **4.** Designating an electrical component, the value of which can be varied: *a variable resistor.*
~*n. Abbr.* **var.** **1.** Anything that varies or is liable to variation. **2.** A variable star. **3.** *Mathematics.* **a.** A quantity capable of assuming any of a set of values. **b.** A symbol representing such a quantity. **4.** *Logic.* **a.** A symbol often *p, q,* or *r,* representing a proposition. **b.** A symbol, often *x, y,* or *z,* representing a class of objects or the name of an individual object in a function or a sentence. **—va·ri·a·bil·i·ty** (-ə-bílləti), **va·ri·a·ble·ness** *n.* **—va·ri·a·bly** *adv.*

variable cost *n.* Cost that fluctuates directly with output changes.

variable star *n.* A star whose brightness varies because of internal changes or periodic eclipsing of component stars.

va·ri·ance (váir-i-ənss) *n.* **1. a.** The act of varying; alteration or modification. **b.** The state or quality of being variant or variable; variation; difference. **c.** A difference between what is expected and what actually occurs. **2.** A difference of opinion; dissension; a dispute. **3.** *Law.* **a.** A discrepancy between two statements or documents in a legal proceeding. **b.** *U.S.* A licence to engage in an act contrary to a usual rule. **4.** *Statistics.* The dispersion of a set of data as measured by taking the mean of the squares of the variations from the mean of the frequency distribution. **5.** *Chemistry.* The number of thermodynamic variables required to specify a state of equilibrium of a system, given by the phase rule. —See Synonyms at **discord.** **—at variance. 1.** In a state of discrepancy; differing; conflicting. Said of things: *The facts are at variance.* **2.** In a state of dispute or dissension; quarrelling: *The factions are at variance.*

va·ri·ant (váir-i-ənt) *adj.* **1.** Having or exhibiting variation; differing. **2.** Tending or liable to vary; variable; changeable. **3. a.** Deviating from a standard or norm. **b.** Exhibiting slight difference.
~*n. Abbr.* **var.** Something that differs, usually only slightly, from another in form, such as a different spelling or pronunciation of the same word. [Middle English, from Old French, from Latin *variāns* (stem *variānt-*), present participle of *variāre,* VARY.]

va·ri·ate (váir-i-ət, -it, -ayt) *n.* **1.** *Statistics.* A random variable with a numerical value that is defined on a given sample space. **2.** *Rare.* A variable. [Latin *variāre,* VARY.]

va·ri·a·tion (váir-i-áysh'n) *n. Abbr.* **var.** **1. a.** The act, process, or result of varying; change or deviation. **b.** The state or fact of being varied. **2.** The extent or degree of such varying or deviation: *a variation of ten kilograms in weight.* **3.** A natural compass error, **magnetic declination** *(see).* **4.** Something that is slightly different from another of the same type. **5.** *Biology.* **a.** Marked difference or deviation from characteristic form, function, or structure. **b.** An organism or plant exhibiting such difference or deviation. **6.** *Mathematics.* A function that relates the values of one variable to those of other variables. **7.** A musical form that is an altered version of some given theme, diverging from it by melodic ornamentation and by changes in harmony, rhythm, or key. **b.** Any of a series of such forms based on a single theme. **8.** In classical ballet, a solo dance. —See Synonyms at **difference.** [Middle English, from Old French, from Latin *variātiō* (stem *variātiōn-*), from *variāre,* VARY.] **—va·ri·a·tion·al** *adj.*

var·i·cel·la (várri-séllə) *n.* **Chickenpox** *(see).* [New Latin, irregular diminutive of VARIOLA.] **—var·i·cel·loid** *adj.*

var·i·ces. Plural of **varix.**

varico-, varic- *comb. form.* Indicates varix or varicose veins; for example, **varicocele, varicosis.** [Latin *varix* (stem *varic-*), VARIX.]

var·i·co·cele (várri-kō-seel, -kə-) *n.* **1.** A varicose condition of the veins of the testicle, producing a swelling of the scrotum. **2.** Any of various other varicose conditions. [VARICO- + -CELE (tumour).]

va·ri·col·oured (váir-i-kullərd) *adj.* Having a variety of colours; variegated; motley.

var·i·cose (várri-kōz, -kōss) *adj.* **1.** Designating blood or lymph vessels that are abnormally dilated, knotted, and tortuous, as in the legs or less commonly in the rectum or testes. **2.** Causing unusual swelling. [Latin *varicōsus,* from VARIX.]

var·i·co·sis (várri-kṓ-siss) *n.* The state of being varicose. [VARIC(O)- + -OSIS.]

var·i·cos·i·ty (várri-kóssəti) *n., pl.* **-ties. 1.** Varicosis. **2. a.** A varicose distension or swelling. **b.** The state of having varicose veins.

var·i·cot·o·my (várri-kóttəmi) *n., pl.* **-mies.** Subcutaneous incision to remove varicose veins. [VARICO- + -TOMY.]

va·ried (váir-id || -eed) *adj.* **1.** Having various kinds or forms; marked by variety. **2.** Modified or altered. **3.** Varicoloured; variegated. —See Synonyms at **miscellaneous. —var·ied·ly** *adv.*

va·rie·gate (váir-i-gayt, -i-ə-) *tr.v.* **-gated, -gating, -gates. 1.** To change the appearance of, especially by marking with different colours; streak. **2.** To give variety to; make varied. [Late Latin *variē-gāre,* from Latin *varius,* VARIOUS.]

va·rie·gat·ed (váir-i-gaytid, -i-ə-) *adj.* **1.** Having streaks, marks, or patches of a different colour or colours. **2.** Having lighter or white areas due to mutation or infection, for example. Said of leaves and petals. **3.** Distinguished or characterised by variety; diversified.

va·rie·ga·tion (váir-i-gáysh'n, -i-ə-) *n.* The state of being variegated; diversified coloration.

va·ri·e·tal (və-rī́-ət'l) *adj.* Of, indicating, or named after a biological variety. [From VARIETY.] **—va·ri·e·tal·ly** *adv.*

va·ri·e·ty (və-rī́-əti) *n., pl.* **-ties.** *Abbr.* **var. 1. a.** The condition or quality of being various or varied; diversity. **b.** A lack of monotony or sameness that keeps something interesting. **2.** A number or collection of varied things, especially of a particular group; an assortment: *a great variety of races living in London.* **3. a.** A different kind, sort, or form of something of the same general classification. **b.** Something belonging to such a kind, form, or sort. **4.** *Biology.* **a.** A taxonomic group below the species. Used by specialists in different fields as a substitute for various taxonomic categories such as race, stock, strain, and breed. **b.** An organism, especially a plant, belonging to such a group. **5.** The type of theatrical entertainment or branch of the theatre consisting of variety shows. Also used adjectivally: a *variety act.* See Synonyms at **musical comedy.** [French *variete,* from Latin *varietās* (stem *varietāt-*), from *varius,* VARIOUS.]

variety meat *n. U.S.* Offal.

variety show *n.* A theatrical entertainment consisting of successive diverse acts, such as songs, dances, and comedy sketches.

variety store *n. U.S.* A retail store carrying a large variety of cheap goods. Also called "variety shop".

va·ri·form (váir-i-fawrm) *adj.* Having a variety of forms; diversiform. [VARI(O)- + -FORM.]

vario-, vari- *comb. form.* Indicates variety or difference; for example, **variometer, variform.** [Latin *varius,* VARIOUS.]

va·ri·o·la (və-rī́-ələ, váir-i-ṓlə) *n.* **Smallpox** *(see).* [New Latin, from Medieval Latin, pustule, from Latin *varius,* speckled, VARIOUS.]

va·ri·o·late (váir-i-ə-layt, -lət, -lit) *adj.* Having pustules or scars like those of smallpox.
~*tr.v.* **variolated, -lating, -lates.** To inoculate with smallpox. **—va·ri·o·la·tion** (-láysh'n) *n.*

va·ri·o·lite (váir-ə-līt) *n.* A basic rock, originally glassy, which has developed a variolitic texture. [Medieval Latin *variola,* smallpox, VARIOL(A) + -ITE.]

var·i·o·lit·ic (váir-i-ō-líttik) *adj.* Of or designating a structure or texture consisting of spherules of minute radiating fibres, generally of plagioclase, and having a pock-marked appearance.

va·ri·o·loid (váir-i-ə-loyd) *n.* A mild form of smallpox in persons who have previously been vaccinated or who have previously had the disease.
~*adj.* Resembling smallpox. [VARIOL(A) + -OID.]

va·ri·o·lous (váir-i-ōləss, və-rī́-ə-ləss) *adj.* Pertaining to, characteristic of, or resembling smallpox. [VARIOL(A) + -OUS.]

va·ri·om·e·ter (váir-i-ómmitər) *n.* A variable inductor used to measure variations in terrestrial magnetism. **2.** A form of variable inductor. **3.** An indicator in a glider or other aircraft showing the rate of climb or descent. [VARIO- + -METER.]

va·ri·o·rum (váir-i-áw-rəm, várri- || -ṓ-) *n.* **1.** An edition particularly of the complete works of a classical author, with notes by scholars or editors. **2.** An edition containing various versions of a text.
~*adj.* Designating or pertaining to a variorum. [Short for Latin *editiō cum notīs variōrum,* edition with the notes of various (commentators), from *variōrum,* genitive plural of *varius,* VARIOUS.]

va·ri·ous (váir-i-əss) *adj. Abbr.* **var. 1. a.** Of diverse kinds. **b.** Unlike; different. **2.** More than one; numerous; several. **3.** Many-sided; varying; versatile. **4.** Having a variegated nature or appearance. **5.** Being one of a class or group but individual and separate: *The various reports all agreed.* **6.** *Archaic.* Changeable; variable.
~*pron. Nonstandard.* Some; a certain amount: *spoke to various of the demonstrators.* [Latin *varius,* speckled, variegated, changeable.] **—var·i·ous·ly** *adv.* **—var·i·ous·ness** *n.*

Var·is·can (vərískən) *adj.* Hercynian.

var·is·cite (várri-sīt) *n.* A green mineral, a hydrated phosphate of aluminium, essentially $AlPO_4.2H_2O$, that occurs as modular masses. [German *Variscit,* from Medieval Latin *Variscia,* ancient name of the Vogtland district of Saxony + -ITE.]

va·ris·tor (váir-ístər) *n.* A semiconductor device with a variable,

vase *The Portland vase (above) is one of the finest surviving examples of Roman art. It is made of dark blue glass decorated with white figures and is thought to date from about the first century* AD. *It was named after the Duke of Portland, who acquired it in the 18th century. It is now in the British Museum, London.*

voltage-dependant resistance; especially, one with a negative voltage characteristic. [From *vary*ing tran*sistor.*]

va•ri•type (váir-i-tīp) *v.* **-typed, -typing, -typing.** *—tr.* To prepare and set (copy) on a Varityper. *—intr.* To use a Varityper. **—var•i•typ•ist** *n.*

Va•ri•typ•er (váir-i-tīpər) *n.* A trademark for a type of typewriter that can be used to prepare copy in a variety of typefaces.

va•rix (váir-iks) *n., pl.* **-ices** (várri-seez, váir-i-). **1.** A vein that is abnormally dilated and twisted. **2.** Any of the longitudinal ridges marking a resting stage in the development of the lip of a gastropod shell. [Latin, swollen vein.]

var•let (várlit) *n. Archaic.* **1.** An attendant or servant. **2.** A knight's page. **3.** A rascal; a knave. [Middle English, from Old French, variant of *vaslet, valet,* VALET.]

var•let•ry (várlitri) *n. Archaic.* **1.** A crowd of attendants or menials. **2.** A disorderly crowd; a rabble.

var•mint (vármint) *n. Regional.* A person or animal considered undesirable, obnoxious, or troublesome. [Variant of VERMIN.]

Var•na (várnə). City in eastern Bulgaria, lying on the Black Sea. It is the country's chief port and naval base, and a major industrial centre. It was called Stalin (1949–57).

var•nish (várnish) *n.* **1. a.** An oil-based preparation containing a solvent and an oxidising or an evaporating binder, used to coat a surface with a hard, glossy, thin film. Also called "oil varnish". **b.** A similar preparation consisting of shellac or a synthetic resin, which is dissolved in a solvent, such as alcohol. The solvent evaporates leaving a hard glossy film. Also called "spirit varnish". **c.** A naturally produced substance, such as the sap of certain trees, that dries forming a hard glossy surface. **2. a.** The smooth coating or gloss resulting from the application of varnish. **b.** Something resembling or likened to varnish. **3.** Any deceptively attractive external appearance; an outward show.
~tr.v. **varnished, -nishing, -nishes. 1.** To cover with varnish. **2.** To give a smooth and glossy finish to. **3.** To give a deceptively nice appearance to; gloss over. **4.** To cover (nails) with nail polish. [Middle English *vernisch,* from Old French *vernis,* from Medieval Latin *veronix,* sandarac, from Medieval Greek *berenikē,* perhaps from Greek *Berenikē,* Berenice, city in Cyrenaica, Libya, where varnishes were first used.] **—var•nish•er** *n.*

varnish tree *n.* Any of several trees having milky juice used to make varnish; especially, the **lacquer tree** *(see).*

var•si•ty (várssəti) *n., pl.* **-ties. 1.** *British Informal.* A university; especially, formerly, Oxford or Cambridge. Now chiefly used adjectivally to designate a sporting event between Oxford and Cambridge: *the varsity match.* **2.** *Australian, South African, & N.Z. Informal.* Any university. **3.** *U.S.* The principal team representing a university, college, or school in sports or other competitions. [Shortened and altered from UNIVERSITY.] **—var•si•ty** *adj.*

Var•u•na (vúrrŏŏ-nə, várrŏŏ-). *Hinduism.* The Vedic god of the skies and seas. [Sanskrit *Varuṇa.*]

va•rus (váir-əss) *n. pl.* **-uses. 1.** A deformity of the legs causing them to bend inwards; knock-knees. **2.** A deformity of the foot causing the person to walk on the inner edge of the sole. [Latin, "knock-kneed".]

varve (varv) *n. Geology.* **1.** A layer of sediment deposited in one year. **2.** A pair of distinct layers of sediment, indicating seasonal deposits. [Swedish *varv,* layer, turn, from *varva,* to bend, turn, from Old Norse *hverfa.*]

va•ry (váir-i) *v.* **-ied, -ying, -ies.** *—tr.* **1.** To make or cause changes in the characteristics or attributes of; modify or alter. **2.** To make diverse; give variety to: *vary one's diet.* **3.** To introduce under new aspects; express in a different manner. *—intr.* **1. a.** To undergo or show change: *a varying society.* **b.** To vary in direct relation to a specified variable. Used with *with: Her temper varies with the number of children at home.* **2.** To be different; deviate or depart. Used with *from.* **3.** To undergo successive or alternate changes in attributes or qualities. —See Synonyms at **change.** [Middle English *varien,* from Old French *varier,* from Latin *variāre,* from *varius,* speckled, changeable.] **—var•i•er** *n.*

vas (vass, vaass) *n., pl.* **vasa** (váy-zə, vaá- || -sə). An organic vessel or duct. [Latin *vās*†, vessel.]

Va•sa•ré•ly (va-za-re-leé; *Hungarian* vósho-ray), **Victor** (1908–). Hungarian-born painter. He moved to Paris (1930) where his abstract works showed the influence of constructivism. By the 1960s he was regarded as one of the leading exponents of op art.

Va•sa•ri (və-saá-ri, *Italian* va-zaá-), **Giorgio** (1511–74). Italian painter, architect, and art historian. His *Lives of the Most Eminent Italian Architects, Painters, and Sculptors,* traces the history of Renaissance art from Giotto to Michelangelo.

vas•cu•lar (váskew-lər) *adj. Biology.* Of, characterised by, or containing vessels for the transmission or circulation of plant or animal fluids such as blood, lymph, or sap. [Latin *vāsculum,* diminutive of *vās,* vessel, VAS.]

vascular bundle *n.* A strand of supportive and conductive plant tissue consisting essentially of xylem and phloem.

vas•cu•lar•i•sa•tion, vas•cu•lar•i•za•tion (váskewlə-rī-záysh'n || *U.S.* -ri-) *n.* The development of vessels, especially new blood capillaries, in an organ or part.

vascular plant *n.* Any plant of the division Tracheophyta, which includes the ferns and seed-bearing plants characterised by a system of specialised conductive and supportive tissue.

vascular tissue *n.* Plant tissue consisting of vascular bundles.

vas•cu•lum (váskew-ləm) *n., pl.* **-la** (-lə). A small box or case used for carrying newly collected plant specimens. [Latin *vāsculum,* small vessel. See **vascular.**]

vas def•er•ens (déffə-renz || -rənz) *n., pl.* **vasa deferentia** (-rénshi-ə). Either of a pair of vertebrate ducts that carry sperm from the epididymal duct to the ejaculatory duct. [New Latin, "carrying-off vessel".]

vase (vaaz, *old-fashioned* vawz || vayz, *chiefly U.S.* vayss) *n.* An open vessel, usually tall and often shaped like a cylinder, made of glass, crystal, earthenware, or the like, and used chiefly for holding flowers or as an ornament. [French, from Latin *vās,* vessel, VAS.]

va•sec•to•my (və-séktəmi, va-) *n., pl.* **-mies.** Surgical cutting of the vas deferens, used, when both are cut, as a means of male sterilisation. [VAS (DEFERENS) + -ECTOMY.]

Vas•e•line (vássə-leen, -leén, -lin) *n.* A trademark for a petroleum jelly used primarily as a vehicle for external applications of medicinal agents, as a soothing or lubricating covering for the skins, and as a protective coating for metal surfaces.

vaso–, vas– *comb. form.* Indicates a blood vessel; for example, **vasomotor.** [Latin *vās,* vessel, VAS.]

va•so•ac•tive (váy-zō-áktiv, -sō- || vá-) *adj.* Causing dilation or constriction of the blood vessels, especially the arteries.

va•so•con•stric•tion (váy-zō-kən-stríksh'n, -sō- || vá-, -kon-) *n.* Constriction of a blood vessel.

va•so•con•stric•tor (váy-zō-kən-stríktər, -sō- || vá-, -kon-) *n.* An agent, such as a nerve or a drug, that causes vasoconstriction. **—va•so•con•stric•tive** *adj.*

va•so•dil•a•ta•tion (váy-zō-dī́-lay-táysh'n, -sō-, -lə- || vá-, -dí-) *n.* Also **va•so•dil•a•tion** (-láysh'n). Dilation of a blood vessel.

va•so•di•la•tor (váy-zō-dī-láytər, -sō- || vá-, -di-) *n.* An agent, such as a nerve or drug, that causes vasodilatation. **—va•so•di•la•tive** *adj.*

va•so•mo•tor (váy-zō-mṓtər, -sō- || vá-) *adj.* Causing or regulating vasoconstriction or vasodilatation.

va•so•pres•sin (váy-zō-préssin, -sō- || vá-) *n.* A hormone secreted by the pituitary gland that increases the reabsorption of water by the kidneys and constricts the blood vessels. Also called "antidiuretic hormone". [From *Vasopressin* (a trademark).]

vas•sal (váss'l) *n.* **1.** A person who held land from a feudal lord and received protection in return for homage and allegiance. **2.** One that is subject or subservient to another; a subordinate or dependent. Also used adjectivally: *a vassal state.* **3.** Loosely, a minion or slave. [Middle English, from Old French, from Medieval Latin *vassallus,* from Vulgar Latin *vassus* (unattested), servant, valet, from Celtic *wasso-* (unattested), young man, squire.]

vas•sal•age (vássəlij) *n.* **1.** The condition of being a vassal. **2.** The service, homage, and fealty required of a vassal. **3.** *Literary.* A position of subordination or subjection; servitude. **4.** The land held by a vassal; a fief. **5.** Vassals collectively or the vassals of a particular lord.

vast (vaast || vast) *adj.* **vaster, vastest. 1.** Very great in size, number, amount, or quantity. **2.** Very great in area or extent; immense. **3.** Very great in degree or intensity: *made a vast difference.* —See Synonyms at **enormous.**
~n. **1.** *Archaic & Poetic.* An immense space. **2.** *Regional.* A great number, amount, or quality. [Latin *vastus,* immense, vast.] **—vast•ly** *adv.* **—vast•ness** *n.*

vas•ti•tude (vaáss-ti-tewd, váss- || -tŏŏd) *n. Rare.* Also **vas•ti•ty** (-təti). Immensity; vastness. [Latin *vastitās,* from *vastus,* VAST.]

vast•y (vaásti || vásti) *adj.* **-ier, -iest.** *Archaic.* Vast.

vat (vat) *n.* A large vessel, such as a tub, cistern, or barrel, used to store or hold liquids.
~tr.v. **vatted, vatting, vats.** To place into or treat in a vat. [Middle English *vat, fat,* Old English *fæt,* from Germanic *fatam* (unattested), vessel.]

VAT, V.A.T. (*often* vat). Value-added tax.

vat dye *n.* Any of a series of dyes that produce a fast colour by impregnating the fibre with a reduced soluble form that is then oxidised to an insoluble form.

vat•ic (váttik) *adj.* Also **vat•i•cal** (-'l). Of or characteristic of a prophet; oracular. [Latin *vātēs,* prophet.]

Vat•i•can (váttikən) *n. Abbr.* **Vat. 1.** The official residence of the pope in Vatican City, within the city of Rome, Italy. Preceded by *the.* **2.** The papal government; the papacy. Also used adjectivally: *a Vatican decree.* [French, from Latin *Vāticānus (mōns),* the Vatican (Hill), of Etruscan origin.]

Vatican City. *Italian* **Città del Vaticano.** Independent state, the smallest in the world, lying within Rome, in central Italy. Its independence was established by the Lateran Treaty (1929) between Pius XI and King Victor Emmanuel II. The state is ruled by the pope, and administered by a lay governor and council appointed by him. It is the supreme government of the Roman Catholic Church, which with tourism and sale of its postage stamps provides the state's income. St. Peter's basilica lies within the Vatican City, sometimes known as the Holy See. Area, 44 hectares (0.17 square miles). Population, 1,000.

Vatican Council *n.* Either of two Roman Catholic ecumenical councils: **1.** *First Vatican Council* (1869–70), which accepted the definition of papal infallibility. **2.** *Second Vatican Council* (1962–65), convened to discuss the position of the Church in the modern world and which led to wide-ranging reforms, in particular the replacement of Latin by vernacular languages in public worship.

Vat•i•can•ism (váttikən-iz'm) *n.* The policies and authority of the

Vatican, especially with regard to papal infallibility. Often used derogatorily.

va·tic·i·nal (va-tíssi-n'l, va-) *adj. Rare.* Prophetic.

va·tic·i·nate (va-tíssi-nayt, va-) *v.* **-nated, -nating, -nates.** *Rare.* —*tr.* To prophesy; foretell. —*intr.* To be a prophet. [Latin *vāticinārī,* from *vātēs,* prophet. See **vatic.**] —**va·tic·i·na·tor** (-naytar) *n.*

va·tic·i·na·tion (va-tíssi-náysh'n, va-) *n. Rare.* **1.** The act of prophesying. **2.** A prediction or prophecy.

vau. Variant of **vav.**

vau·de·ville (vṓ-da-vil, váw-, -veel ‖ *U.S. also* vŏd-vil, váwd-, vód-) *n.* **1.** *U.S.* **Music hall** (*see*). **2.** A light comic play that often includes songs, pantomime, and dances. **3.** A popular, often satirical, song. [French, from Old French *vaudevire,* short for *chanson du Vau de Vire,* type of satirical song, especially those of O. Basselin, 15th-century poet born in *Vau de Vire,* in the Valley of Vire, a region in Normandy, from *vau, val,* VALE.]

vau·de·vil·li·an (vō-da-víll-an, váw-, -víl-yan, -veél- ‖ vŏd-, váwd-, vód-) *n.* One who works in vaudeville, especially as a performer. ~*adj.* Of or pertaining to vaudeville.

Vau·dois (vō̄-dwaa, -dwaaz, vṓ-dwáa, -dwáaz) *pl.n.* The **Waldenses** (*see*).

Vaughan Wil·liams (váwn wíl-yamz), **Ralph** (1872–1958). British composer. He was greatly influenced by folk tunes and Tudor music, as is evident in his *Fantasia on a Theme by Thomas Tallis* (1910). His works include nine symphonies, the ballet *Job* (1931), and the opera *The Pilgrim's Progress* (1948–49).

vault¹ (vawlt ‖ volt) *n.* **1. a.** An arch, usually of stone, brick, or concrete, forming the supporting structure of a ceiling or roof. **b.** Any arched overhead covering resembling or thought to resemble a vault, such as the sky. **2.** A room or space with arched walls and ceiling, especially when underground, such as a cellar or storeroom. **3.** A room or compartment, often built of steel, for the safekeeping of valuables: *a bank vault.* **4.** A burial chamber, especially when underground. **5.** *Anatomy.* An arched cavity. ~*tr.v.* **vaulted, vaulting, vaults.** **1.** To construct or supply with an arched ceiling; cover with a vault. **2.** To build or make in the shape of a vault; arch. [Middle English *vaute, voute,* from Old French, from Vulgar Latin *vol(vi)ta* (unattested), a turn, vault, variant of Latin *volūta,* feminine past participle of *volvere,* to turn.]

vault² *v.* **vaulted, vaulting, vaults.** —*tr.* To jump or leap over, especially with the aid of a support, such as the hands or a pole. —*intr.* **1.** To jump or leap, especially with the use of the hands or a pole. **2.** To achieve or surmount something, as if by bounding vigorously: *vault into a position of wealth.* ~*n.* The act of vaulting; a jump. [Old French *volter,* from Italian *voltare,* to turn (a horse), leap, gambol, from Vulgar Latin *volvitāre* (unattested), frequentative of Latin *volvere,* to turn.] —**vault·er** *n.*

vault·ing¹ (váwlt-ing ‖ vólt-) *n.* **1.** The practice or craft of building vaults. **2.** Vaults collectively. **3.** A vault or vaulted construction.

vaulting² *adj.* **1.** Leaping upwards or over. **2.** Reaching too far; exaggerated: *vaulting ambition.* **3.** Used for leaping over: *a vaulting horse.*

vaunt (vawnt ‖ vaant) *v.* **vaunted, vaunting, vaunts.** —*tr.* To describe in boastful terms; brag about. —*intr.* To boast; brag. —See Synonyms at **boast.** ~*n.* A boastful remark or speech of extravagant self-praise. [Middle English *va(u)nten,* from Old French *vanter,* from Late Latin *vānitāre* (attested only in the present participle *vānitāns*), to be vain, from Latin *vānus,* empty, vain.] —**vaunt·er** *n.* —**vaunt·ing·ly** *adv.*

vaunt-cour·i·er (váwnt-kōórri-ar, -kúrri- ‖ váant-) *n. Archaic.* One sent in advance, especially a herald. [Old French *avant-cour(r)ier : avant,* in front of + COURIER.]

vav (vawv, vaav) *n.* Also **vau** (vow), **waw** (wow). The sixth letter of the Hebrew alphabet. [Hebrew.]

vav·a·sour, vav·a·sor, vav·as·sor (vávva-soor, -sawr ‖ -sōr) *n.* In the feudal system, a vassal who ranked directly below a baron or peer, with other vassals under him. [Middle English *vavasour,* from Old French, from Medieval Latin *vavassor,* perhaps contraction of *vassus vassōrum,* "vassal of vassals". See **vassal.**]

vb. verb; verbal.

V.C. **1.** vice chairman. **2.** vice chancellor. **3.** vice consul. **4.** Victoria Cross. **5.** Vietcong.

VCR video cassette recorder.

VD, V.D. venereal disease.

v.d. **1.** vapour density. **2.** various dates.

VDU *n., pl.* **VDUs** or **VDU's.** A **visual display unit** (*see*).

Ve·a·dar, Ve·a·dar (váy-a-daar, vée-) *n.* An extra month of the Hebrew year, having 29 days, added in leap years after the regular month of Adar. Also called "Adar Sheni". [Hebrew *va'adhar,* "and Adar".]

veal (veel) *n.* The meat of a calf. [Middle English *veel,* from Old French, from Latin *vitellus,* diminutive of *vitulus,* calf, "yearling".]

veal·y (veéli) *adj.* **-ier, -iest.** **1.** Of or like veal. **2.** Not fully developed; immature.

vec·tor (véktar) *n.* **1.** *Mathematics.* A quantity completely specified by a magnitude and a direction. Compare **scalar.** **2.** *Pathology.* An organism that carries pathogens from one host to another. **3.** Broadly, any force or influence. ~*tr.v.* **vectored, -toring, -tors.** To guide (a pilot, aircraft, or the like) by means of radio communication, according to vectors. [Latin *vector,* carrier, from *vehere* (past participle *vectus*), to carry.] —**vec·to·ri·al** (vek-táw-ri-al ‖ -tō̄-) *adj.*

vector field *n.* A region of space in which a vector quantity exerts a

field, at any point of which the field strength can be represented by a vector.

vector product *n.* A vector, **C,** that has magnitude equal to the product of the magnitudes of two vectors, **A** and **B,** and the sine of the angle between **A** and **B,** and having a direction perpendicular to the plane containing **A** and **B** and in a right-handed coordinate system directed so that a right-handed rotation about **C** carries **A** into **B** through an angle not greater than 180 degrees. It is usually written **A** × **B.** Also called "cross product". Compare **scalar product.**

vector sum *n.* A vector that is the resultant of two other vectors, as determined by the parallelogram rule.

Ve·da (váy-da, vée-) *n.* Any of the oldest sacred writings of Hinduism, including the psalms, incantations, hymns, and formulas of worship incorporated in four collections called the Rig-Veda, the Yajur-Veda, the Sama-Veda, and the Atharva-Veda. [Sanskrit *veda,* "knowledge".] —**Ve·dic** (-dik) *adj.*

ve·da·li·a (vi-dáyli-a, va-) *n.* An Australian beetle, *Rodolia cardinalis,* that is used in all citrus-growing regions to control the scale insect *Icerya purchasi.* [New Latin : origin obscure.]

Ve·dan·ta (vi-dánta, ve-, va-, -dáanta) *n.* The system of Hindu philosophy that further develops the implications in the Upanishads that all reality is a single principle, Brahman, and teaches that the believer's goal is to transcend the limitations of individual consciousness and realise his unity with Brahman. [Sanskrit *vedanta,* "complete knowledge of the Veda" : *veda,* VEDA + *anta,* end.] —**Ve·dan·tic** *adj.* —**Ve·dan·tism** *n.* —**Ve·dan·tist** *n.*

V-E Day (vée-ée) *n.* The day of victory for the Allied forces in Europe during World War II; officially, May 8, 1945. [Short for *Victory in Europe Day.*]

Ved·da, Ved·dah (védda) *n.* Any of a small, dark-skinned, wavy-haired aboriginal people of Sri Lanka. [Singhalese, "hunter", from Dravidian, akin to Tamil *vēṭṭam,* hunting.]

ve·dette, vi·dette (vi-dét, va-) *n.* **1.** A mounted sentry stationed in advance of an outpost. **2.** A small scouting boat used to observe and report on an opposing naval force. In this sense, also called "vedette boat". [French, from Italian *vedetta,* variant (influenced by *vedere,* to see) of *veletta,* from Spanish *vela,* a watch, from *velar,* to watch, from Latin *vigilāre,* from *vigil,* awake.]

Ve·dic (váy-dik, vée-) *adj.* Of or pertaining to the Veda or Vedas or to the Hindu culture that produced them. ~*n.* The early Sanskrit in which the Vedas are written.

veep (veep) *n. U.S. Slang.* **1.** A vice president. **2.** *Capital* **V.** The Vice President of the United States. [From the abbreviation V.P.]

veer¹ (veer) *v.* **veered, veering, veers.** —*intr.* **1.** To turn aside from a course, direction, or purpose; swerve; shift. **2.** To shift in direction by a clockwise motion. Used of the wind. Compare **back.** **3.** *Nautical.* To change the direction of a ship by turning the head away from the direction of the wind; wear ship. —*tr.* **1.** To alter the direction of; turn. **2.** *Nautical.* To change the course of (a ship) by turning away from the direction of the wind. ~*n.* A change in direction; a swerve. [French *virer,* from Vulgar Latin *vīrāre* (unattested), perhaps variant (influenced by Latin *vibrāre,* VIBRATE) of Latin *gȳrāre,* GYRATE.]

veer² *tr.v.* **veered, veering, veers.** *Nautical.* To let out or release (an anchor chain or line, for example). [Middle English *veren,* from Middle Dutch *vieren.*]

veg (vej) *n., pl.* **veg.** *British Informal.* A vegetable: *meat and two veg.*

Ve·ga (véega ‖ váyga) *n.* The brightest star in the constellation Lyra. [Medieval Latin, from Arabic (*al nasr*) *al wāqi',* the constellation Lyra, "the falling (vulture)".]

Ve·ga (Carpio) (váyga), **Lope Felix de** (1562–1635). Spanish poet and his country's first great dramatist. Most of his themes were drawn from history, and of almost 2,000 plays 500 still survive.

ve·gan (véegan) *n.* A strict vegetarian; one who consumes no animal products at all. [Shortened from VEGETARIAN.] —**ve·gan** *adj.*

veg·e·ta·ble (véj-tab'l, véja-, véji-) *n.* **1. a.** A plant cultivated for an edible part or parts, such as its roots, stems, leaves, or flowers. **b.** The edible part of such a plant. **2.** An organism classified as a plant; a member of the plant kingdom. **3.** A person who leads a monotonous, passive, or merely physical (that is, without a normal mental life) existence. ~*adj.* **1.** Of, pertaining to, or derived from a plant or plants. **2.** Suggesting or like a vegetable, as in passivity or dullness of existence; monotonous; inactive. [Middle English, living, growing, from Old French, from Medieval Latin *vegetābilis,* from Late Latin, enlivening, from Latin *vegetāre,* to enliven, from *vegetus,* lively, from *vegēre,* to be lively.]

vegetable butter *n.* Any of various edible fatty substances resembling butter and of plant origin.

vegetable ivory *n.* A hard, ivory-like material obtained from the **ivory nut** (*see*) and used in making small objects such as buttons.

vegetable marrow *n.* A **marrow** (*see*).

vegetable oil *n.* Any of various oils obtained from plants, used in food products and industrially.

vegetable oyster *n.* A plant, **salsify** (*see*).

vegetable silk *n.* Any of several silky fibres from the seed pods of certain plants.

vegetable sponge *n.* A **dishcloth gourd** (*see*).

vegetable tallow *n.* Any of various waxy fats obtained from certain plants used in making soap and candles.

vegetable wax *n.* A waxy substance of plant origin, usually secreted in thin flakes by the epidermal cells.

veg·e·tal (véjit'l) *adj.* **1.** Of, pertaining to, or characteristic of a plant or plants. **2.** Pertaining to growth rather than to sexual reproduction; vegetative. [French, from Old French *vegeter,* to grow, from Late Latin *vegetāre,* from Latin, to enliven. See **vegetable.**]

veg·e·ta·ri·an (véji-táir-i-ən) *n.* **1.** One who eats no meat or fish. **2.** One who practises or advocates vegetarianism.
~*adj.* **1.** Eating no meat or fish. **2.** Pertaining to, practising, or advocating vegetarianism. **3.** Consisting of vegetables or nonflesh foods: *a vegetarian diet.* **4.** Serving, presenting, or advocating no meat or fish: *a vegetarian cookbook; a vegetarian café.* [From VEGETABLE (coined in 1847 by the Vegetarian Society at Ramsgate.]

veg·e·ta·ri·an·ism (véji-táir-i-ən-iz'm) *n.* The practice of or belief in avoiding eating meat or fish or, more strictly, eating only vegetables and plant products, usually for health or moral reasons.

veg·e·tate (véji-tayt) *intr.v.* **-tated, -tating, -tates. 1.** To grow or sprout as a plant does. **2.** *Pathology.* To grow or spread abnormally. **3.** To lead an existence that is monotonous, passive, or lacks mental stimulation. [Late Latin *vegetāre,* to grow, from Latin, to enliven. See **vegetable.**]

veg·e·ta·tion (véji-táysh'n) *n.* **1.** The plants of an area or region; plant life collectively. **2.** The act or process of vegetating. **3.** *Pathology.* Any abnormal growth on the body.

veg·e·ta·tive (véji-tətiv, -taytiv) *adj.* Also **veg·e·tive** (-tiv). **1.** Of, pertaining to, or characteristic of plants or plant growth. **2.** *Biology.* **a.** Of, pertaining to, or capable of growth. **b.** Of, pertaining to, or functioning in processes such as growth or nutrition, rather than sexual reproduction. **c.** Of or pertaining to asexual reproduction, such as fission or budding. **3.** Monotonous, passive, or lacking mental stimulation.

ve·he·ment (vée-ə-mənt, -i- || -hə-, -hi-) *adj.* **1.** Characterised by forcefulness of expression or intensity of emotion, passion, or conviction; ardent; emphatic: *vehement denial.* **2.** Marked by or full of vigour or energy; strong; violent. [Old French, from Latin *vehemēns*† (stem *vehement-*).] **—ve·he·mence, ve·he·men·cy** *n.* **—ve·he·ment·ly** *adv.*

ve·hi·cle (vée-ik'l, -ək'l || -hick'l) *n.* **1.** Any conveyance for carrying passengers, goods, or equipment, moving along the ground or in the air or space, often one moving on wheels such as a car. **2.** Anything through or by which something, such as thought, power or information is conveyed, transmitted, expressed, or achieved: *the play was a vehicle for her political views.* **3.** A play, role, or piece of music used to display the special talents of one performer or company. **4.** In pharmacology, a substance of no therapeutic value used as the medium in which active medicines are administered. **5.** A substance, such as oil, in which paint pigments are mixed for application. [French *véhicule,* from Latin *vehiculum,* from *vehere,* to carry.] **—ve·hic·u·lar** (vi-híckew-lər, və- || vee-) *adj.*

veil (vayl) *n.* **1.** A piece of cloth, often wide-meshed and semi-transparent, worn by women over the head, shoulders, and often part of the face for concealment, protection, or as a token of modesty. **2.** A length of netting attached to a woman's hat or headdress for decoration, hanging before all or part of the face. **3.** The part of a nun's headdress that frames the face and falls over the shoulders. **4.** A piece of light fabric hung to separate or conceal what is behind it; a curtain. **5.** Anything that conceals, separates, or screens like a curtain: *a veil of secrecy.* **6.** *Biology.* A membranous covering, such as that partially or completely enveloping the developing fruiting body of certain mushrooms; a velum. **—beyond the veil.** In the afterlife; after death. **—draw a veil over.** To refrain from discussing or describing. **—take the veil.** To become a nun.
~*v.* **veiled, veiling, veils.** —*tr.* **1.** To cover with a veil. **2.** To conceal, mask, or disguise with or as if with a veil: *veiling kindness under apparent severity.* —*intr.* To wear a veil. [Middle English *veile,* from Anglo-French, from Latin *vēla,* neuter plural of *vēlum,* covering, veil.]

veiled (vayld) *adj.* **1.** Covered with a veil. **2.** Partially concealed, masked, or disguised: *veiled threats; veiled promises.*

veil·ing (váyling) *n.* **1.** A veil. **2.** Gauzy material used for veils.

vein (vayn) *n.* **1.** *Anatomy.* A vessel that transports blood towards the heart. **2.** Loosely, any blood vessel. **3.** *Botany.* Any of the vascular bundles that form the branching framework and support of a leaf. **4.** *Zoology.* Any of the chitinous, usually longitudinal ribs that stiffen and support the wing of an insect. **5.** *Geology.* A sheet of rock or mineral which infills a fissure or crevice in a pre-existing rock and is an economic source of ore; a lode. Compare **bed, mass. 6.** A long, wavy strip with a colour different from its surround, as in wood or marble, or as mould in cheese. **7.** Any fissure, crack, or cleft. **8.** A distinctive character, quality, or tendency; a strain or streak: *a vein of pessimism.* **9.** A transient or temporary attitude or mood; turn of mind: *a talk in a serious vein.*
~*tr.v.* **veined, veining, veins. 1.** To supply or fill in streaked patterns with or as if with veins. **2.** To mark or decorate with veins. [Middle English *veine,* from Old French, from Latin *vēna*†, vein.] **—vein·al, vein·y** *adj.*

veined (vaynd) *adj.* Exhibiting veins; having veinlike features or markings.

vein·let (váyn-lət, -lit) *n.* A small or secondary vein, as of an insect's wing.

vein·stone (váyn-stōn) *n.* Mineral matter in a vein exclusive of the ore; gangue.

Ve·la (véelə) *n.* A constellation of the Southern Hemisphere in the Milky Way, near Antlia and Carina. [Latin *vēla,* sail, VEIL (from the sail-like shape of the constellation).]

PRONUNCIATION KEY

a, trap; aa, father; ai, fair; ar, star; aw, lawn; ay, play; b, bb, stab; rubber; ch, church; ck, ticket; d, dd, dead; ladder; e, dress; ee, bee; er, defer; ew, few; ewr, pure; ə, about; ər, letter; f, ff, fife; differ; g, gg, giggle; h, hat; i, kit; ī, price; īr, fire; j, judge; k, kick; l, ll, let; 'l, needle; m, mm, man; n, nn, no; 'n, sudden; ng, thing; o, lot; ō, no; o͝o, foot; o͞o, shoe; oor, poor; ow, cow; owr, hour; oy, boy; p, pp, pepper; r, rr, red; s, ss, sauce; sh, ship; t, tt, totter; th, thick; th, this; smooth; u, cut; ur, turn; v, vv, valve; w, wet; y, yes; z, zz, zebra; zh, vision; pleasure

IN FOREIGN WORDS:

aN, oN, Saint-Saëns; hl, Llanelli; Hluhluwe; kh, loch; lough; Khaled

STRESS MARK:

ín-sīt, insight; in-sī́t, incite

ve·la·men (vi-láy-mən, və-, -mən) *n., pl.* **velamina** (-lámminə). **1.** *Anatomy.* Any membranous covering or integument; a velum. **2.** *Botany.* The spongy outer covering of the aerial roots of epiphytic orchids and certain other plants, capable of absorbing atmospheric moisture. [Latin *vēlamen,* covering, from *vēlāre,* to cover, from *vēlum,* covering. See **velum.**]

ve·lar (véelər) *adj.* **1. a.** Of or pertaining to a velum. **b.** Concerning or using the soft palate. **2.** *Phonetics.* Formed with the back of the tongue on or near the soft palate, as (g) in *good* and (k) in *cup.*
~*n.* A velar sound. Also called "guttural". [New Latin *velaris,* from Latin *vēlum,* VELUM.]

ve·lar·ise, ve·lar·ize (véelə-rīz) *tr.v.* **-ised, -ising, ises.** *Phonetics.* To articulate (a sound) by retracting the back of the tongue towards the soft palate. **—ve·lar·is·a·tion** (-rī-záysh'n || *U.S.* -ri-) *n.*

ve·late (véel-ayt, -ət, -it) *adj. Biology.* Having or covered by a velum or veil. [Latin *vēlātus,* past participle of *vēlāre,* to cover, from *vēlum,* veil, covering. See **velum.**]

Ve·láz·quez (vi-láss-kwiz, ve-, -kiz, -kez, -kwith; *Spanish* be-láth-keth), **Diego Rodriguez de Silva y** (1599–1660). Spanish painter. He was appointed (1623) court painter to Philip IV, and worked on many portraits of the royal family. Among his other works are *Pope Innocent X,* and the *Rokeby Venus.*

Vel·cro (vél-krō) *n.* A trademark for a material used as a fastener, usually consisting of a backing with a surface of minute nylon hooks and loops that fasten tightly with another piece of Velcro when pressed together. The two surfaces can be separated with a strong tug or abrupt pulling action.

veld, veldt (felt, velt) *n.* **1. a.** The open grassland area of South Africa; open country. **b.** Grazing or farming land. **2.** A particular tract of such land. [Afrikaans *veld,* from Middle Dutch *velt, veld,* field, open country.]

veld·skoen (félt-sko͞on) *n.* A **velskoen** *(see).* [Afrikaans, "field shoe", alteration of VELSKOEN.]

vel·i·ger (véllijər) *n.* The free-swimming larva of certain marine gastropods. [New Latin : *vel(um),* sail + *-ger,* -GEROUS.]

vel·le·i·ty (ve-lée-əti, və-, -láy-) *n., pl.* **-ties.** *Rare.* **1.** The lowest level of volition. **2.** A mere wish not accompanied by action or effort to obtain it. [Medieval Latin *velleitās,* from Latin *velle,* to wish.]

vel·lum (véllәm) *n.* **1.** A fine parchment made from the skins of calf, lamb, or kid and used for the pages and binding of fine books. **2.** A work written or printed on vellum. **3.** A heavy off-white fine-quality paper resembling vellum. [Middle English *velim,* from Old French *velin,* from *veel,* calf, VEAL.] **—vel·lum** *adj.*

ve·lo·ce (vi-lṓchi, ve-, və-) *adv. Music.* Rapidly. Used as a direction. [Italian, from Latin *vēlōx* (stem *vēlōc-*), fast. See **velocity.**]

vel·o·cim·e·ter (vél-ō-símmitər, véel-) *n.* A device for measuring velocity or speed. [Latin *vēlōx* (stem *vēlōc-*) + -METER.]

ve·loc·i·pede (vi-lóssi-peed, və-) *n.* **1.** An early bicycle propelled by pushing the feet along the ground while straddling the vehicle. **2.** Any of several early bicycles having pedals attached to the front wheel. [French *vélocipède,* "swift-footed" : Latin *vēlōx,* fast (see **velocity**) + -PED.]

ve·loc·i·ty (vi-lóssəti, və-) *n., pl.* **-ties. 1.** Broadly, rapidity or speed. **2.** *Abbr.* **v** *Physics.* A vector quantity, the rate of change of position in a given direction. **3.** Distance travelled in a given amount of time. [French *vélocité,* from Latin *vēlōcitās* (stem *vēlōcitāt-*), from *vēlōx* (stem *vēlōc-*), fast.]

velocity modulation *n.* The modulation of an electron beam by alternately accelerating and decelerating them by means of a radio-frequency field in a cavity resonator.

ve·lo·drome (véel-ə-drōm, vél-, -ō-) *n.* A sports arena specially built with a banked track for cycle and, often, motorcycle racing. [French *vélodrome,* from Latin *vēlōx,* swift + -DROME.]

ve·lours, ve·lour (və-lóor) *n., pl.* **-lours** (-lóor). **1.** Any of various closely napped, velvet-like fabrics, used chiefly for clothing and upholstery. **2.** A felt resembling velvet, used in making hats. [French, from Old French *velo(u)s,* from Latin *villōsus,* hairy, from *villus,* shaggy hair, wool.]

ve·lou·té (vi-lo͞o-tay, ve-, və- || *U.S.* véllo͞o-táy) *n.* A white sauce made with flour, butter, and a chicken or veal stock. [French, "velvety".]

vel·skoen (fél-sko͞on, vél-) *n. South African.* A shoe or ankle boot of rough suede. Also called "veldskoen". [Afrikaans, "hide shoe".]

ve·lum (vée-ləm) *n., pl.* **-la** (-lə). **1.** *Biology.* A covering or partition of thin membranous tissue, such as the veil of a mushroom. **2.** *Anatomy.* Any of various veil-like structures, such as the soft palate. [New Latin, from Latin *vēlum,* veil, covering, sail.]

ve·lure (və-léwr, -lóor) *n.* **1.** *Archaic.* Velvet or a velvet-like fabric. **2.** A soft pad used for smoothing silk hats. [Variant of French *velours,* VELOURS.]

ve·lu·ti·nous (vi-lo͞o-tinəss, və-, -léw-) *adj.* Covered with dense, soft, silky hairs; velvety. [New Latin *velutinus,* from Medieval Latin *velūtum,* velvet, from *villūtus,* velvety, shaggy. See **velvet.**]

vel·vet (vélvit) *n.* **1. a.** A fabric made usually of silk or a synthetic fibre such as rayon or nylon, and having a smooth, dense pile and a plain back. **b.** Anything likened to the surface of this fabric. **2.** Smoothness; softness. **3.** The soft covering on the newly developing antlers of deer and related animals. **—on velvet.** A position of prosperity or advantage.
~*adj.* **1.** Made of or covered with velvet. **2.** Resembling velvet. **3.** Soft and rich: *velvet tones.* [Middle English *veluet,* from Old French *veluotte,* from *velu,* shaggy, from Medieval Latin *villūtus,* from Latin *villus,* shaggy hair, wool.] **—vel·vet·y** *adj.*

vel·vet·een (vélvi-téen, -teen) n. A velvet-like fabric made of cotton.

Ven. venerable.

ve·na (vée-nə, váy-) n., pl. **-nae** (-nee, -nī). n. Anatomy. A vein. [Latin *vēna*, VEIN.]

ve·na ca·va (káy-və, káa-) pl. **venae cavae** (-vee, -vī). Either of the two large veins in air-breathing vertebrates that enter and return blood to the right atrium of the heart. [Latin, "hollow vein".]

ve·nal (véen'l) adj. **1. a.** Open or susceptible to bribery. **b.** Capable of betraying one's honour, duty, or scruples for a price; corruptible. **2.** Marked by corrupt or morally reprehensible dealings: *a venal era.* **3.** Obtainable by purchase or bribery rather than by merit. [Latin *vēnālis*, for sale, from *vēnum*, sale.] —**ve·nal·ly** adv.

ve·nal·i·ty (vee-nál-ǝti, vi-) n., pl. **-ties. 1.** The quality of being open to bribery or corruption. **2.** The use of a position of trust for dishonest gain.

ve·nat·ic (vee-náttik, vi-) adj. Also **ve·nat·i·cal** (-'l). **1.** Pertaining to or used in hunting. **2.** Devoted to or engaged in hunting for sport or livelihood. [Latin *vēnāticus*, from *vēnārī*, to hunt.]

ve·na·tion (vee-náysh'n, ve-) n. The distribution or arrangement of veins in a leaf or insect's wing. [From VENA.] —**ve·na·tion·al** adj.

vend (vend) v. **vended, vending, vends.** —tr. **1.** Law. To sell. **2.** To sell small goods, especially in the street; peddle. **3.** Rare. To offer (an idea, for example) for public consideration. —intr. **1.** To sell goods; be a vendor. **2.** To have a market. [French *vendre*, from Latin *vēndere* : *vēnum*, sale + *dare*, to give.]

Ven·da¹ (vén-də) n., pl. **-das** or collectively **Venda. 1.** A member of a black South African people living chiefly in Venda and northern Transvaal. **2.** The Bantu language of this people. —**Ven·da** adj.

Venda². One of the segregated Bantu homelands in South Africa, lying in eastern Transvaal. It officially became a republic in 1979, but only South Africa recognises its independence. Area, 6 500 square kilometres (2,509 square miles). Population (Venda), 350,000 (plus 112,000 in South Africa). Capital, Thohoyandou.

ven·dace (vén-dayss) n., pl. **-daces** or collectively **vendace.** A small whitefish, *Coregonus albula*, found in certain lakes in northern Europe. [New Latin *vandesius*, from Old French *vendese, vendoise*, from Gaulish *vindesia* (unattested); akin to Gaulish *vindos* (unattested), white.]

vend·ee (vén-dée) n. A buyer.

Ven·dée (von-dáy). Département in western France, lying on the Bay of Biscay. It is largely an agricultural region, with some forest land and fishing ports. The administrative centre is La Roche-sur-Yon. The Vendée Wars were a series of peasant revolts (1793–96).

ven·det·ta (ven-déttə, vén-) n. **1.** A hereditary blood feud between two families, perpetuated by retaliatory acts of revenge. **2.** A hostile and malicious campaign. **3.** Any act or attitude motivated by vengeance. [Italian, revenge, from Latin *vindicta*, from the feminine past participle of *vindicāre*, to revenge, VINDICATE.]

vend·i·ble (véndəb'l) adj. Capable of being sold; suitable for sale. ~n. Something that can be sold.

vending machine n. A machine that dispenses goods such as cigarettes or confectionery when money is inserted. Also called "automat", "vendor".

ven·dor, ven·der (vén-dər, *for sense 2 also* -dór) n. **1.** A person who sells or vends; a pedlar. **2.** Law. The party to a contract who sells something, especially a piece of property. **3.** A vending machine.

ven·due (vén-dew) || -doo, U.S. also -dóo) n. U.S. A public sale; an auction. [Dutch *vendu*, from Old French *vendue*, from *vendre*, VEND.]

ve·neer (və-néer) n. **1.** A thin finishing or surface layer, as of fine wood or laminated plastic, bonded to an inferior substratum, such as an inexpensive wood. **2.** Any of the thin layers glued together in making plywood. **3.** An outward show that enhances but misrepresents what lies beneath; a superficially impressive appearance: *a veneer of politeness.* ~tr.v. **veneered, -neering, -neers. 1.** To overlay (a surface) with a decorative or fine material. **2.** To glue together (layers of wood) in making plywood. **3.** To conceal (something common or crude) with an attractive but superficial appearance; gloss over. [Earlier *fineer*, from German *Furnier*, from *furniren*, to furnish, veneer, from French *fournir*, to FURNISH.] —**ve·neer·er** n.

ve·neer·ing (və-néer-ing) n. **1.** Material used as a veneer. **2.** A surface of veneer.

venepuncture. Variant of **venipuncture.**

ven·er·a·ble (vénnə-rəb'l) adj. **1.** Worthy of reverence or respect by virtue of dignity, character, position, or age. **2.** Commanding respect or reverence by association: *venerable relics.* **3.** Abbr. **V., Ven.** Honoured above others. Used as: **a.** A title of respect for an Anglican archdeacon. **b.** A title given to a Roman Catholic who has attained the first degree of sanctity. See Synonyms at **old.** [Middle English, from Old French, from Latin *venerābilis*, from *venerārī*, VENERATE.] —**ven·er·a·ble·ness, ven·er·a·bil·i·ty** (-rə-bílləti) n. —**ven·er·a·bly** adv.

ven·er·ate (vénnə-rayt) tr.v. **-ated, -ating, -ates.** To regard with respect, reverence, or heartfelt deference. See Synonyms at **revere.** [Latin *venerārī*, from *venus* (stem *vener-*), love.] —**ven·er·a·tor** n.

ven·er·a·tion (vénnə-ráysh'n) n. **1.** The act of venerating. **2.** Profound respect or reverence. **3.** The condition or status of one who is venerated. —See Synonyms at **honour.**

ve·ne·re·al (vi-néer-i-əl, və-) adj. **1.** Of or pertaining to sexual intercourse. **2. a.** Transmitted by sexual intercourse. **b.** Of or pertaining to venereal disease. **3.** Of or pertaining to the genitals. [Middle English *venerealle*, from Latin *venereus*, from *venus* (stem *vener-*), love, lust.]

venereal disease n. Abbr. **VD** Any of several contagious diseases, such as syphilis and gonorrhoea, contracted through sexual intercourse.

ve·ne·re·ol·o·gy (vi-néer-i-óllǝji, və-) n. The medical study of venereal disease. [VENERE(AL) + -LOGY.] —**ve·ne·re·ol·o·gist** n.

ven·er·y¹ (vénnəri) n. Archaic. Indulgence in or the pursuit of sexual activity. [Middle English *venerie*, from Medieval Latin *veneria*, from Latin *venus* (stem *vener-*), love.]

venery² n. Archaic. The act, art, or sport of hunting; the chase. [Middle English *venerie*, from Old French, from *vener*, to hunt, from Latin *vēnārī*.]

ven·e·sec·tion (vénni-séksh'n, véeni-, -seksh'n) n. Surgery. **Phlebotomy** (*see*). [Medieval Latin *vēnae sectiō*, cutting of a vein : Latin *vēnae*, genitive of *vēna*, vein + *sectiō*, SECTION.]

Ve·ne·tia (vi-née-shə, və-, ve-, -shi-ə). Italian **Veneto.** Region of northeastern Italy, on the Adriatic Sea. Venice is the capital.

Venetia Tridentina. See **Trentino-Alto Adige.**

Ve·ne·tian (vi-néesh'n, və-, -néeshi-ən) adj. Of or pertaining to Venice, its culture, or its inhabitants. ~n. **1.** A native or inhabitant of Venice. **2.** Usually small **v.** A venetian blind. [Middle English *Venecien*, from Old French, from Medieval Latin *Venetiānus*, from Latin *Venetia*, VENICE.]

venetian blind n. Sometimes capital **V.** Often plural. A window screen consisting of a number of thin horizontal slats that may be raised and lowered by means of one cord and all set at a desired angle by means of another cord, thus regulating the amount of light admitted.

venetian blue n. Strong blue to greenish blue.

Venetian glass n. Fine, delicate glassware originally made near Venice.

venetian red n. **1.** Deep to strong reddish brown. **2.** A pigment of this colour made from ferric oxide.

Venetian school n. A school of painting originating in Venice in the 15th century and flourishing in the 16th century, notable for its mastery of colour and perspective.

Venezia. See **Venice.**

Ven·e·zue·la (vénni-zwáylə, vénne-, vénnə- || -zwéelə; Spanish bén-ne-swélla), **Republic of.** Country on the north coast of South America. It is a major oil producer, and one of Latin America's richest countries. Oil and oil products account for 90 per cent of its exports, iron ore another 5 per cent. The economy is being restructured and new industries developed. Ruled by Spain from 1500, Venezuela was liberated by Simón Bolívar (1821), forming part of Gran Colombia until 1830. A series of dictators ended with the overthrow of Pérez Jimenéz (1958). Venezuela claims the Essequibo territory, some 73 per cent of neighbouring Guyana. Area, 912 050 square kilometres (352,145 square miles). Population, 18,400,000. Capital, Caracas. —**Ven·e·zue·lan** n. & adj.

venge (venj) tr.v. **venged, venging, venges.** Archaic. To avenge. [Middle English *vengen*, from Old French *venger.* See **vengeance.**]

venge·ance (vénjənss) n. The act or motive of punishing another in payment for a wrong or injury he has committed; retribution: *He had been betrayed, and now wanted vengeance.* —**with a vengeance. 1.** With great violence or fury. **2.** To a greater extent; excessively. Used as an intensive: *The weather has turned cold with a vengeance.* [Middle English, from Old French, from *venger*, to revenge, from Latin *vindicāre*, to revenge, VINDICATE.]

venge·ful (vénjf'l) adj. **1.** Desiring vengeance; vindictive: *a vengeful old man.* **2.** Indicating or proceeding from a desire for revenge: *a vengeful frown.* **3.** Inflicting or serving to inflict vengeance: *a vengeful blow.* —See Synonyms at **vindictive.**

ve·ni·al (véen-i-əl) adj. Easily excused or forgiven; pardonable: *a venial offence.* [Middle English, from Old French, from Late Latin *veniālis*, from *venia*, forgiveness.] —**ve·ni·al·i·ty** (-ál-əti), **ve·ni·al·ness** n. —**ve·ni·al·ly** adv.

venial sin n. Theology. A sin which, though evil, does not totally estrange the soul from God's grace. Compare **mortal sin.**

Ven·ice (vénniss). *Italian.* **Ve·ne·zia** (ve-néts-ya). Port in northeast Italy. The capital of Venetia, and of Venezia province, it lies in its lagoon, on 118 alluvial islands, mostly separated by narrow canals crossed by some 400 bridges. A road and rail causeway link it to the mainland. Founded in the fifth century A.D., Venice built a wealthy maritime‑empire around the northeast Mediterranean by the 13th century. As the Venetian Republic it gained extensive lands in north Italy (15th century); however, from 1600 eastern territories were lost to the Turks, and the republic fell to Austria (1797), and was ceded to Italy (1866). Venice is world famous for its art and architecture, including the Byzantine cathedral of St. Mark (begun 830). Tourism, textiles, and glass are its main industries. The city is sinking, but since severe flooding in 1966 its art treasures are being preserved following international appeals.

ven·i·punc·ture, ven·e·punc·ture (vénni-punkchər, vééni-) *n.* Puncture of a vein, as for drawing blood, intravenous feeding, or administration of medicine. [VENA + PUNCTURE.]

ve·ni·re (və-nír-i) *n. Chiefly U.S. Law.* **1.** A writ issued by a judge to a sheriff, ordering him to summon prospective jurors. Also called "venire facias". **2.** The panel of prospective jurors from which a jury is selected. [Medieval Latin *venīre (facias),* "(you are to cause) to come" (words used in the writ), from Latin *venīre,* to come.]

ve·ni·re·man (və-nír-i-mən) *n., pl.* **-men** (-mən). *Chiefly U.S.* A person summoned to jury duty under a venire.

ven·i·son (vénz'n, vénni-z'n, -s'n) *n.* **1.** The flesh of a deer, used for food. **2.** *Archaic.* The flesh of any game animal thus used. [Middle English *veneso(u)n,* from Old French, from Latin *vēnātiō* (stem *vēnā-tiōn-*), hunting, game, from *vēnārī,* to hunt.]

Venn diagram (ven) *n.* A diagram in which mathematical sets or the terms of a logical argument or syllogism are represented by circles, the position and overlap of which indicate the way in which the different sets or terms are related. [After John *Venn* (1834-1923), British logician.]

ven·o·gram (vénnə-gram, véenə-) *n.* An X-ray picture of a vein or veins. [Latin *vēna,* VEIN + -GRAM.]

ve·nog·ra·phy (ve-nóggrəfi, vi-) *n.* The study using X-rays of a vein or veins following the injection of a radio-opaque substance. [Latin *vēna,* VEIN + -GRAPHY.]

ven·om (vénnəm) *n.* **1.** A poisonous secretion of some animals, such as certain snakes, spiders, scorpions, or insects, usually transmitted by a bite or sting. **2.** *Rare.* Any poison. **3.** Malice; evil; spite. [Middle English *venim,* from Old French, from Vulgar Latin *venīmen* (unattested), variant of Latin *venēnum,* poison.]

ven·om·ous (vénnəməss) *adj.* **1.** Secreting and transmitting venom: *a venomous snake.* **2.** Full of or containing venom. **3.** Malicious; malignant; spiteful: *a venomous utterance.* —**ven·om·ous·ly** *adv.* —**ven·om·ous·ness** *n.*

ve·nose (vée-nōz, -nōss) *adj.* **1.** Having noticeable veins or veinlike markings. **2.** Venous. [Latin *vēnōsus,* VENOUS.]

ve·nos·i·ty (vi-nóssəti) *n.* **1.** The condition or quality of being venous or venose. **2.** An accumulation of blood in the venous system.

ve·nous (véenəss) *adj.* **1.** Of or pertaining to a vein or veins. **2.** Designating or pertaining to blood carried in the veins. [Latin *vēnōsus,* from *vēna,* vein.] —**ve·nous·ly** *adv.* —**ve·nous·ness** *n.*

vent¹ (vent) *n.* **1.** An opening permitting the passage or escape of liquids, gases, fumes, steam, or the like: *a vent above the kitchen stove.* **2.** A means of escaping or leaving a confined space; an exit. **3.** The small hole at the breech of an ancient gun through which the charge is ignited. **4.** *Geology.* A volcano shaft or an aperture in the Earth's crust through which lava and gases can escape. **5.** *Zoology.* The cloacal or anal excretory opening in animals such as birds, reptiles, amphibians, and fish. —**give vent to.** To give utterance to; express or release: *gave vent to their indignation.* ~*v.* **vented, venting, vents.** —*tr.* **1.** To give utterance to; express: *venting his sorrows.* **2.** To relieve through the expression of emotion. **3.** To discharge through a vent. **4.** To provide with a vent. —*intr.* To come to the surface to breathe. Used of an otter or beaver. [Middle English *venten,* to provide with an outlet, Old French *esventer,* to let out air, from Vulgar Latin *exventāre* (unattested) : Latin *ex-,* out + *ventus,* wind.] —**vent·less** *adj.*
   Synonyms: *vent, express, utter, voice, air, broach.*

vent² *n.* A narrow opening, often forming a flap, at the side or back of a garment such as a jacket. [Middle English *vent, fent,* from Old French *fente,* slip, from Vulgar Latin *findita* (unattested), from past participle of Latin *findere,* to cleave.]

vent·age (véntij) *n.* **1.** A small opening; a vent. **2.** Any of the small finger-holes in the tube of a wind instrument such as a recorder.

ven·tail (vén-tayl) *n.* The lower front part of a medieval helmet, fitting over the neck. [Middle English, from Old French *vantail,* leaf of a window, from *vent,* wind, air, from Latin *ventus.*]

ven·ter¹ (véntər) *n.* One that vents.

venter² *n.* **1. a.** *Biology.* The abdomen or belly. **b.** The wide swelling portion of a muscle. **2.** *Botany.* The swollen base of an archegonium containing the developing egg cell. **3.** *Law.* The womb as the source of offspring. [Anglo-French, from Latin, belly, womb.]

ven·ti·late (vénti-layt) *tr.v.* **-lated, -lating, -lates.** **1.** To admit fresh air into in order to replace stale air. **2.** To circulate within (a room or mine, for example) in order to freshen. Used of air. **3.** To provide with a vent or a similar means of airing. **4.** To expose (a substance) to the circulation of fresh air, as for the purpose of retarding spoilage. **5.** To expose to public discussion or examination: *The workers ventilated their grievances.* **6.** To aerate or oxygenate (blood). [Middle English *ventilaten,* to blow away, from Latin *ventilāre,* to fan, from *ventus,* wind.] —**ven·ti·la·tion** *n.*

ven·ti·la·tor (vénti-laytər) *n.* **1.** One that ventilates; especially, a device, such as an exhaust fan, that expels stale air and circulates fresh air. **2.** *Medicine.* A device used to ensure the passage of air into and out of the lungs in patients who cannot breathe normally. —**ven·ti·la·to·ry** (-lətri, -laytəri, -láytəri) *adj.*

ven·tral (véntrəl) *adj.* **1.** *Anatomy.* **a.** Pertaining to or situated on or close to the belly; abdominal. **b.** Pertaining to the anterior aspect or front of the human body or the lower surface of the body of an animal. **2.** *Botany.* Of or on the upper or inner surface of an organ such as a leaf facing the main axis; adaxial. [French, from Latin *ventrālis,* from *venter,* VENTER.] —**ven·tral·ly** *adv.*

Venus

OUR NEAREST NEIGHBOUR IN THE SKY
The atmosphere of the planet Venus is hot and poisonous

Venus is almost a twin of the Earth in size and mass, and as it is closer to us than any other planet it shines brightly in the night sky. Spacecraft from America and Russia have shown that the atmosphere is very dense, giving a pressure 90 times the pressure of the air on Earth. It is made up mainly of carbon dioxide, and the clouds that surround the planet contain large amounts of sulphuric acid. The surface of Venus has volcanoes that are probably active, a huge rolling plain, and two high areas of land. The temperature exceeds 475°C (887°F).

No life can exist on Venus now, but in the early days of the solar system, when the Sun was less luminous, Venus may have had oceans and life may have appeared. As the Sun grew brighter, the oceans boiled and evaporated, and Venus became a furnace-like world.

THE CLOUDS OF VENUS *Unmanned spacecraft have sent back photographs of Venus from space and from the surface. Photographs from space (above) show that the planet is covered by permanent cloud. Pictures from the surface show a gloomy, rock-strewn landscape. Winds are sluggish (a few kilometres per hour), but in the very dense atmosphere they have tremendous force.*

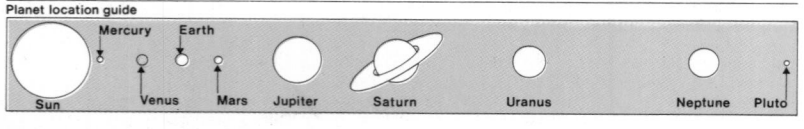

Planet location guide

Sun | Mercury | Earth | Venus | Mars | Jupiter | Saturn | Uranus | Neptune | Pluto

ventral fin *n. Zoology.* A **pelvic fin** *(see).*

ven·tri·cle (véntrik'l) *n.* A small anatomical cavity or chamber, as of the brain or heart, especially: **1.** The chamber on the left side of the heart that receives arterial blood from the left atrium and contracts to drive it into the aorta. **2.** The chamber on the right side of the heart that receives venous blood from the vena cava and drives it via the right atrium into the pulmonary artery. **3.** Any of the four fluid-filled cavities of the brain. Also called "ventriculus". [Middle English, from Old French, from Latin *ventriculus,* diminutive of *venter,* VENTER.] **—ven·tric·u·lar** (ven-tríckewlər) *adj.*

ven·tri·cose (véntri-kōz, -kōss) *adj.* Also **ven·tri·cous** (-kəss). *Biology.* Inflated or swollen, especially on one side. [New Latin *ventricosus,* from Latin *venter,* VENTER.] **—ven·tri·cos·i·ty** (-kóssəti) *n.*

ven·tric·u·lus (ven-tríckew-ləss) *n., pl.* **-li** (-lī). **1.** A hollow digestive organ; especially, the stomach of an insect or the gizzard of a bird. **2.** A ventricle. [Latin, VENTRICLE.]

ven·tril·o·quise, ven·tril·o·quize (ven-trílla-kwīz) *intr.v.* **-quised, -quising, -quises.** To engage in ventriloquism.

ven·tril·o·quism (ven-tríllə-kwiz'm) *n.* Also **ven·tril·o·quy** (-kwi). A method of producing vocal sounds so that they seem to originate in a source other than the speaker, as from a mechanical dummy. [Late Latin *ventriloquus,* "speaking from the belly" : Latin *venter,* VENTER + *loquī,* to speak.] **—ven·tri·lo·qui·al** (véntri-lṓkwi-əl) *adj.* **—ven·tri·lo·qui·al·ly** *adv.* **—ven·tril·o·quist** (ven-tríllə-kwist) *n.* **—ven·tril·o·quis·tic** (-kwístik) *adj.*

Ven·tris (véntriss), **Michael (George Francis)** (1922–56). British architect and scholar. He deciphered Linear B, a hieroglyphic script of late Minoan Crete.

ven·ture (vénchər) *n.* **1.** An undertaking that is dangerous, daring, or of doubtful outcome. **2.** Something at hazard in such an undertaking; a stake. **—at a venture.** By mere chance or fortune; at hazard; at random.
~*v.* **ventured, -turing, -tures.** —*tr.* **1.** To expose to danger or risk; stake: *ventured his entire fortune on the enterprise.* **2.** To brave the dangers of: *ventured the high seas in a light boat.* **3.** To express at the risk of denial, criticism, or censure; dare: *ventured a mild cough of protest.* —*intr.* **1.** To take a risk or dare; make a venture. **2.** To go somewhere by or as if by taking a risk: *ventured into the forest.* [Middle English *venturen, venteren,* short for *aventuren,* from *aventure,* ADVENTURE.] **—ven·tur·er** *n.*

Venture Scout *n.* A Scout, aged about 16 or more, who belongs to a senior branch of the Scouts.

ven·ture·some (vénchər-s'm) *adj.* **1.** Disposed to venture or to take risks; daring; bold. **2.** Involving risk or danger; hazardous. **—ven·ture·some·ly** *adv.* **—ven·ture·some·ness** *n.*

ven·tu·ri (ven-téwr-i, -tóor-) *n.* **1.** A short tube with a constricted throat that is used to determine fluid pressures and velocities by measurement of differential pressures generated at the throat as a fluid traverses the tube. Also called "venturi tube". **2.** A constricted throat in the air passage of a carburettor, causing a reduction in pressure by means of which fuel vapour is drawn out of the carburettor bowl. [After G.B. *Venturi* (1746–1822), Italian physicist, whose study inspired its invention.]

ven·tur·ous (vénchərəss) *adj.* **1.** Courageous and daring; adventurous; bold. **2.** Hazardous, dangerous, or risky. **—ven·tur·ous·ly** *adv.* **—ven·tur·ous·ness** *n.*

ven·ue (vénnew) *n.* **1.** A location designated for an event, such as a meeting, concert, or sports match. **2.** *Law.* **a.** The locality where a crime is committed or a cause of action occurs. **b.** Formerly, the locality or political division from which a jury must be called and in which a trial must be held. **c.** Formerly, the clause within a declaration naming the locality in which the trial is occurring or will occur. **3.** Formerly, the clause in an affidavit naming the locality where it was made and sworn to. [Middle English, arrival, assault, from Old French, from the feminine past participle of *venir,* to come, from Latin *venīre.*]

ven·ule (vénnewl) *n.* A minute vein, such as one joining with a capillary or branching from a vein in an insect's wing. [Latin *vēnula,* diminutive of *vēna,* VEIN.] **—ven·u·lar** (-ər) *adj.*

Ve·nus¹ (véenəss) *Roman Mythology.* The goddess of love and beauty, identified with the Greek Aphrodite. [Middle English *Venus,* Old English *Venus,* from Latin, personification of *venus,* love.]

Venus² *n.* The second planet from the sun, having an average radius of 6 100 kilometres (3,800 miles), a mass 0.815 times that of the earth, and a sidereal period of revolution about the sun of 224.7 days at a mean distance of approximately 108 million kilometres (67.2 million miles). [After the goddess VENUS.]

Ve·nu·sian (vi-néw-zi-ən, və-, -si- ‖ -nóo-, -zh'n) *adj.* Pertaining to or characteristic of the planet Venus.
~*n.* A hypothetical inhabitant of the planet Venus.

Venus's comb *n.* **Shepherd's needle** *(see).*

Venus's flower basket *n.* A sponge of the genus *Euplectella,* of deep marine waters, having a delicate, white, lattice-like, cylindrical skeleton.

Venus's-flytrap *n.* Also **Venus flytrap.** An insectivorous plant, *Dionaea muscipula,* of boggy areas of the southeastern United States, having hinged leaf blades that close and entrap insects.

Venus's girdle *n.* A ribbon-shaped marine animal, *Cestum veneris,* having a jelly-like iridescent body up to 1.5 metres (5 feet) in length.

Ve·nus's-hair (véenə-siz-hair) *n.* A maidenhair fern, *Adiantum capillus-veneris,* of subtropical and temperate areas.

Ve·nus's-look·ing-glass (véenə-siz-lóok-ing-glaass ‖ -lóok-, -glass) *n.* Any of various annual weedy plants of the genus *Legousia* (or *Specularia*); especially *L. hybrida,* which has purple flowers.

ver. **1.** verse. **2.** version.

ve·ra·cious (və-ráyshəss, vi-, ve-) *adj.* **1.** Honest; truthful. **2.** Accurate; precise. [Latin *vērāx* (stem *vērāc-*), truth.] **—ve·ra·cious·ly** *adv.* **—ve·ra·cious·ness** *n.*

ve·rac·i·ty (və-rássəti, vi-, ve-) *n., pl.* **-ties.** **1.** Habitual adherence to the truth. **2.** Conformity to truth or fact; accuracy; precision. **3.** Something that is true. —See Synonyms at **honesty, truth.** [Medieval Latin *vērācitās,* from Latin *vērāx,* truth. See **veracious.**]

Ve·ra·cruz (véer-ə króoz, vair-; *Spanish* bérra króoss). City and port in Veracruz state, Mexico, lying on the Gulf of Mexico. It is the industrial centre of one of Mexico's richest oil-producing regions.

ve·ran·dah, ve·ran·da (və-rándə) *n.* A porch or balcony, usually roofed and often partly enclosed, extending along the outside of a building; a gallery. [Hindi, from Portuguese, from *varare* (unattested), to surround with poles, from *vara,* pole, from Latin *vāra,* forked pole, from *vārus,* bent inward.] **—ver·ran·dahed** *adj.*

ve·rat·ri·dine (və-ráttri-deen, vi-, ve-, -din) *n.* A yellowish-white, amorphous powdered alkaloid, $C_{36}H_{51}NO_{11}$, obtained from sabadilla seeds. [VERATR(INE) + -ID + -INE.]

ver·a·trine (vérrə-treen, -trin) *n.* A poisonous mixture of colourless crystalline alkaloids extracted from sabadilla seeds and formerly used medicinally as a counterirritant. [French *vératrine,* from New Latin *Veratrum,* genus name of a hellebore, from Latin *vērātrum,* hellebore, perhaps from *veru,* spit.]

verb (verb) *n. Abbr.* **v., vb.** **1.** In most languages, that part of speech that expresses existence, action, or occurrence. **2.** Any of the words exemplifying this part of speech; for example, *be, run,* or *conceive.* **3.** Any phrase or other construction used as a verb.
~*adj. Grammar.* Verbal: *a verb phrase.* [Middle English *verbe,* from Old French, from Latin *verbum,* word.]

ver·bal (vérb'l) *adj. Abbr.* **vb.** **1.** Of, pertaining to, or associated with words: *a verbal symbol.* **2.** Concerned with words rather than with the facts or ideas they represent: *a merely verbal ceasefire.* **3.** Expressed or transmitted in speech; unwritten: *a verbal contract.* **4.** Literal; word for word: *a verbal translation.* **5.** *Grammar.* **a.** Pertaining to, having the nature or function of, or derived from a verb. **b.** Used to form verbs: *a verbal suffix.*
~*n. Grammar.* **1.** A verbal noun, adjective, or other word based on a verb and preserving some of the verb's characteristics. **2.** *Slang.* A spoken, as opposed to written, confession made by a suspect during police questioning and introduced as evidence at his trial. [Old French, from Late Latin *verbālis,* from Latin *verbum,* word, VERB.] **—ver·bal·ly** *adv.*

Usage: *Verbal* is used as well as *oral* to express the notion of "by word of mouth", but it can also refer to what is written *(He sent me a verbal account of what was said at the meeting). Oral* can refer only to what is spoken, and is thus often preferred when there is a possibility of ambiguity (in such phrases as *verbal agreement).*

ver·bal·ise, ver·bal·ize (vérb'l-īz) *v.* **-ised, -ising, -ises.** —*tr.* **1.** To express in words: *He couldn't verbalise what he was feeling.* **2.** To convert (a noun, for example) to verbal use. —*intr.* **1.** To express oneself in words. **2.** To be verbose. **—ver·bal·i·sa·tion** (-ī-záysh'n ‖ *U.S.* -i-) *n.* **—ver·bal·i·ser** *n.*

ver·bal·ism (vérb'l-iz'm) *n.* **1.** An expression in words; a word or phrase. **2.** A meaningless or clichéd phrase or sentence, especially one resulting from an emphasis on words over content or idea. **3.** A disposition towards or the habitual use of such merely declamatory, ornate, or empty constructions.

ver·bal·ist (vérb'l-ist) *n.* **1.** One skilled at using words. **2.** One who favours words over ideas or facts. **—ver·bal·is·tic** *adj.*

verbal noun *n.* A noun derived from a verb; in English, either a gerund or an infinitive; for example, the word *smoking* and the phrases *to think* and *to be* in the sentences *Smoking causes cancer* and *To think is to be.*

ver·ba·tim (ver-báy-tim, vər-, *also* -baa-) *adj.* Using exactly the same words; word for word. [Middle English, from Medieval Latin, from Latin *verbum,* word, VERB.] **—ver·ba·tim** *adv.*

ver·be·na (vər-béenə, ver-) *n.* **1.** Any of various chiefly New World plants of the genus *Verbena;* especially, any of several species cultivated for their showy, variously coloured flowers. See **vervain.** **2.** Any of several similar or related plants, such as the **lemon verbena** *(see).* [New Latin *Verbena,* from Latin *verbēna,* usually in plural *verbēnae,* sacred boughs of olive or myrtle. See **vervain.**]

ver·bi·age (vérbi-ij) *n.* **1.** Words in excess of those needed for clarity or precision; wordiness. **2.** The favouring or use of such an excess of words. **3.** *Rare.* The manner in which one expresses oneself in words; diction. [French, from Latin *verbum,* word, VERB.]

verb·i·fy (vérbi-fī) *v.* **-fied, -fying, -fies.** —*tr.* To use (a noun, for example) as a verb; form into a verb. —*intr.* To be verbose.

ver·bose (vər-bṓss) *adj.* Using or containing an excessive number of words; wordy; prolix. See Synonyms at **talkative.** [Latin *verbōsus,* from *verbum,* word, VERB.] **—ver·bose·ly** *adv.* **—ver·bose·ness, ver·bos·i·ty** (-bóssəti) *n.*

ver·bo·ten (fər-bṓt'n, fair-, vər-) *adj. Informal.* Rigorously forbidden. [German, from Old High German *farboten,* past participle of *farbiotan,* to forbid.]

verb. sap. (vérb sáp) *Latin.* Used to conclude a remark or clinch an argument by suggesting that no further explanation is needed. [Abbreviation of Latin phrase *verbum sapienti (sat est),* a word to the wise (suffices).]

ver·dant (vérd'nt) *adj.* **1.** Green with vegetation; covered with a

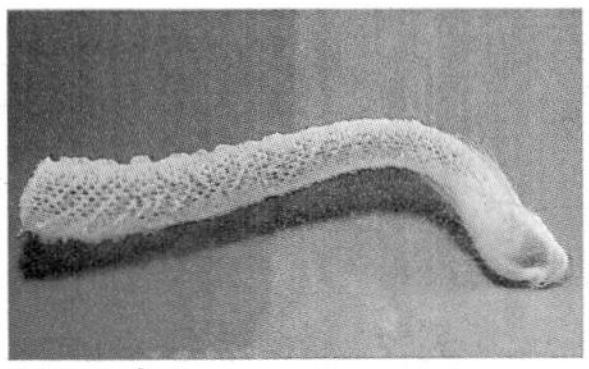

Venus's flower basket *The glassy, latticed skeleton of the Venus's flower basket sponge is traditionally given to newlyweds in Japan as a symbol of fidelity. The sponge often becomes the permanent home of pairs of small crustaceans which enter through the holes in its walls to feed in safety, and grow too large to escape.*

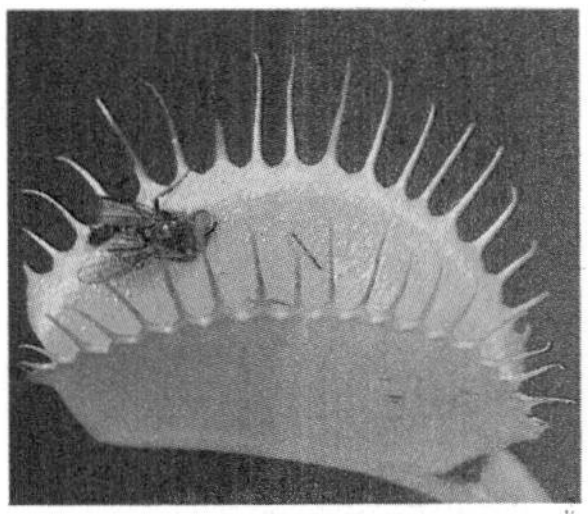

Venus's-flytrap *An insect-eating plant of the southeastern United States. Any insect landing on the trap touches trigger hairs that cause the trap – a modified leaf – to close tight. The insect is then dissolved by a digestive secretion.*

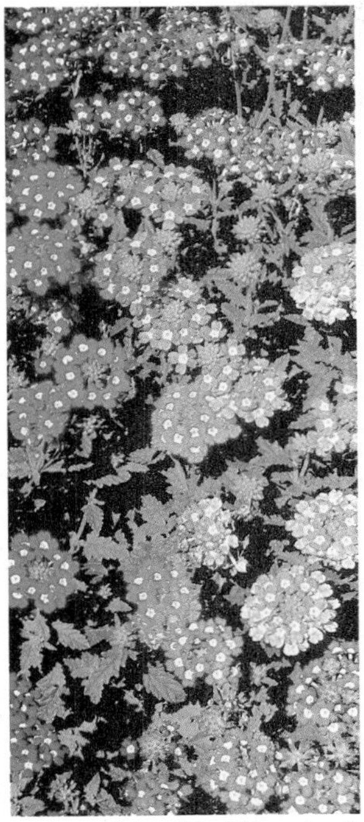

verbena *Most of the 250 species of verbena are native to the tropics, but cultivated varieties such as those shown here are now grown worldwide as garden plants. Only one species of verbena –* Verbena officinalis, *or vervain – is native to Britain. It was once used in medicines and love potions* green growth: *verdant, fertile land.* **2.** Green in colour. **3.** Inexperienced or unsophisticated. [Perhaps from Old French *verdeant,* present participle of *verdoier, verdier,* to become green, from *verd, vert,* green, from Latin *viridis,* from *virēre,* to be green.] **—ver·dan·cy** *n.* **—ver·dant·ly** *adv.*

verd antique, verde antique (verd) *n.* **1.** A dull-green mottled or veined serpentine marble used in interior decoration. **2.** Verdigris on ancient bronze, copper, and brass. **3.** A green porphyry. [French, "ancient green".]

Verde, Cape. Peninsula of Senegal, jutting into the Atlantic ocean. Its tip, Cape Almadies, is the westernmost extremity of Africa.

ver·der·er (vérdərər) *n.* Formerly, the official in charge of the royal forests of England. [Anglo-French, from Old French *verdier,* from *verde, verte,* green, "forest." See **verdant.**]

Ver·di (váir-di, -dee), **Giuseppe** (1813–1901). Italian composer. Among his works are the operas *Rigoletto* (1851), *Il Trovatore* (1853), *La Traviata* (1853), and *Aida* (1871). His work introduced the new status of music drama to Italian opera.

ver·dict (vérdikt) *n.* **1.** The decision reached by a jury at the conclusion of a legal proceeding: *a verdict of not guilty.* **2.** An expressed conclusion; a judgment: *the verdict of history.* [Middle English *verdit,* from Anglo-French, variant of Old French *veirdit, voirdit,* "true saying" : *veir,* true, from Latin *vērus* + *dit,* saying, from Latin *dictum,* from the neuter past participle of *dīcere,* to speak, say.]

ver·di·gris (vérdi-griss, -greess, -gree) *n.* **1.** A blue or green basic copper acetate, used as a paint pigment, fungicide, and insecticide. **2.** A green patina or crust of copper carbonate formed on copper, brass, and bronze exposed to air or sea water for long periods of time. In this sense, also called "aerugo", "verd antique". Compare **patina.** [Middle English *vertegres,* from Old French *vertegrez, vert-de-Grice,* "green of Greece".]

ver·di·ter (vérditər) *n.* Either of two basic carbonates of copper, azirite and malachite, used as a blue or green pigment. [Old French *verd de terre,* "green of earth".]

Ver·dun (ver-dún; *French* vair-dáN, -dőN). Town in northeastern France, lying on the river Meuse, in the Meuse département. In 1916 the battle of Verdun, which lasted from February to December was one of the longest and fiercest battles of World War I.

ver·dure (vér-jər, -dewr) *n.* **1.** The fresh, vibrant greenness of flourishing vegetation. **2.** Such vegetation itself: *lush verdure.* **3.** Any fresh or flourishing condition: *the verdure of childhood.* [Middle English, from Old French, from *verd,* green. See **verdant.**] **—ver·dur·ous** *adj.* **—ver·dur·ous·ness** *n.*

Ver·ee·nig·ing (fə-réeniking; *Afrikaans* -ráynəkhəng). City in northeastern South Africa, lying on the river Vaal in the southern part of the state of Transvaal. It was founded as the centre of the surrounding coal-mining area in 1892 and is now one of the chief manufacturing centres in South Africa.

verge[1] (verj) *n.* **1.** The extreme edge, rim, or margin of something; the brink: *the verge of a stream.* **2. a.** An enclosing boundary. **b.** The space enclosed by such a boundary. **3.** *British.* The stretch of grass bordering a road. **4.** The point beyond which an action, state, or condition is likely to begin or occur: *the verge of a nervous breakdown.* **5.** *Architecture.* **a.** The edge of the tiling that projects over a roof gable. **b.** The body of a classical column; a pillar. **6.** A rod, wand, or staff carried as an emblem of authority or office. **7.** In feudal times, the rod held by a tenant swearing fealty to his lord. **8.** Formerly, the area of jurisdiction of the Lord High Steward, especially the surroundings of the royal court. **9.** The spindle of a balance wheel in an early clock or watch; especially, such a spindle in a clock with vertical escapement. **10.** The male reproductive organ of an invertebrate. —See Synonyms at **border.**
~*intr.v.* **verged, verging, verges. 1.** To approach the verge or limit; come near. Usually used with *on* or *upon: Her idea verged on genius.* **2.** To constitute a verge or limit; be a border. Used with *on* or *upon: a housing estate verging on the slum area.* [Middle English, margin, from Old French, from Latin *virga*†, rod, strip.]

verge[2] *intr.v.* **verged, verging, verges.** To slope or incline. Used with *to* or *towards.* [Latin *vergere,* to tend towards.]

verg·er (vérjər) *n.* **1.** A person who takes care of the interior of a church and acts as an attendant during ceremonies. **2.** A person who carries the verge before a scholastic, legal, or religious dignitary in a procession.

Vergil. See **Virgil.**

ver·glas (váir-glaa) *n.* A thin coating of ice or sleet, as on a rock. [French, from Old French *verre-glaz,* "glass-ice" : *verre,* from Latin *vitrum,* glass + *glaz,* ultimately from Latin *glaciēs,* ice.]

ve·rid·i·cal (ve-ríddik'l, vi-, və-) *adj.* Also **ve·rid·ic** (-ríddik). **1.** Expressing the truth; accurate; veracious. **2.** *Psychology.* Designating dreams, visions; hallucinations, or the like that coincide accurately with future events or apparently unknowable present realities. [Latin *vēridicus* : *vērus,* true + *dīcere,* to say.] **—ve·rid·i·cal·i·ty** (-ríddi-kál-əti) *n.* **—ve·rid·i·cal·ly** *adv.*

ver·i·est (vérri-ist) *adj. Archaic.* Used as an intensive: *the veriest fop and fool.* [Superlative of VERY.]

ver·i·fi·ca·tion (vérrifi-káysh'n) *n.* **1.** The act of verifying or condition of being verified. **2. a.** A confirmation of the truth of a theory or fact. **b.** The evidence for such a confirmation. **c.** A formal statement of such a confirmation. **3.** *Law.* **a.** Formerly, a short formulaic oath concluding a pleading and affirming that the pleader is ready to prove his allegations. **b.** The evidence used in trying to prove such allegations. **—ver·i·fi·ca·tive** (-kaytiv) *adj.*

ver·i·fy (vérri-fī) *tr.v.* **-fied, -fying, -fies. 1.** To prove the truth of by the presentation of evidence or testimony; substantiate. **2.** To determine or test the truth or accuracy of, as by comparison, investigation, or reference: *Scientific claims are not accepted until verified.* **3.** *Law.* **a.** To affirm formally or under oath. **b.** To append a verification to (a pleading); conclude with a verification. —See Synonyms at **confirm.** [Middle English *verifien,* from Old French *verifier,* from Medieval Latin *vērificāre* : Latin *vērus,* true + *facere,* to make.] **—ver·i·fi·a·ble** (-fī-əb'l || -fī-əb'l) *adj.* **—ver·i·fi·er** *n.*

ver·i·ly (vérrəli, vérrili) *adv. Archaic.* **1.** In truth; in fact; of a certainty. **2.** With confidence; assuredly. [Middle English *verraily,* from *verray,* true, VERY.]

ver·i·sim·i·lar (vérri-símmilər) *adj.* Appearing to be true or real; probable; likely. [Latin *vērisimilis* : *vēri,* of truth, from *vērum,* truth, from *vērus,* true + *similis,* SIMILAR.] **—ver·i·sim·i·lar·ly** *adv.*

ver·i·si·mil·i·tude (vérri-si-mílli-tewd || -tood) *n.* **1.** The quality of appearing to be true or real; likelihood. **2.** Something that has the appearance of being true or real. —See Synonyms at **truth.** [Latin *vērisimilitūdō,* from *vērisimilis,* VERISIMILAR.]

ve·rism (véer-iz'm || vérriz'm) *n.* Realistic portrayal in art and literature. [Italian *verismo,* from *vero,* true, from Latin *vērus.*] **—ver·ist** *n.* & *adj.* **—ve·ris·tic** (vi-rístik, və-, ve-) *adj.*

ve·ris·mo (ve-ríz-mō, *Italian* -réez-) *n.* A late 19th-century artistic movement, originating in Italy and influential particularly in opera, which concentrated on realistic, everyday themes, and tended to treat them in a melodramatic way. [Italian, from *vero,* true.]

ver·i·ta·ble (vérritəb'l) *adj.* **1.** Unquestionably true; actual. **2.** Having the qualities of. Used as an intensive: *He's a veritable wolf.* —See Synonyms at **real.** [Middle English, from Old French, from *verite,* VERITY.] **—ver·i·ta·ble·ness** *n.* **—ver·i·ta·bly** *adv.*

ver·i·ty (vérrəti) *n., pl.* **-ties. 1.** The condition or quality of being real, accurate, or correct. **2.** A statement, principle, or belief considered to be of established and permanent truth. —See Synonyms at **truth.** [Middle English *verite,* from Old French, from Latin *vēritās* (stem *vēritāt-*), from *vērus,* true.]

ver·juice (vér-jooss || -jewss) *n.* **1.** The acidic juice of sour or unripe fruit, such as grapes or crab apples. **2.** Bitterness or sourness, as of temper. [Middle English *verjus,* from Old French *vertjus* : *vert,* green (see **verdant**) + *jus,* JUICE.]

ver·kramp·te (fər-krámp-tə, -krúmp-) *n.* **1.** In South Africa, a person of very conservative political views who opposes liberalisation of government policy, especially in respect of the race laws. **2.** *South African.* Any extremely conservative, bigoted, or narrow-minded person. Compare **verligte.** [Afrikaans, "restricted".] **—ver·kramp** (-krámp, -krúmp), **ver·kramp·te** *adj.*

Ver·laine (vair-láyn, vər-), **Paul** (1844–96). French poet. After associating with the Parnassian poets, whose influence is evident in his early poetry, he became a leader of the symbolists. His works include *Les Poètes maudits* (1884) and *Sagesse* (1881).

ver·lig·te (fər-líkh-tə) *n.* **1.** In South Africa, any of the more progressive National Party supporters who favour a slight liberalisation of government and party policy, especially in respect of the race laws. **2.** *South African.* Any relatively progressive and broad-minded person. Compare **verkrampte.** [Afrikaans, "enlightened".] **—ver·lig** (-líkh), **ver·lig·te** *adj.*

Ver·meer (vər-méer, ver-, vair-), **Jan** (1632–75). Dutch painter. He painted mostly interior scenes where he used to great effect his mastery of highlighting and colour. About 40 of his paintings are known, including *The Lady standing at the Virginals.*

ver·meil (vér-mayl, -mil) *n.* **1.** *Poetic.* Vermilion or bright-red. **2.** Gilded metal, such as silver, bronze, or copper.
~*adj.* Bright red in colour. [Middle English *vermayl,* from Old French *vermeil,* from Late Latin *vermiculus,* from Latin, small worm, cochineal (which yields a red dye), from *vermis,* worm.]

vermi– *comb. form.* Indicates a worm or worms; for example, **vermicide.** [Latin *vermis,* worm.]

ver·mi·cel·li (vérmi-chélli, -sélli) *n.* **1.** A food consisting of wheat flour paste made into long threads, thinner than spaghetti. **2.** An edible decoration for cakes or desserts, consisting of tiny strands of chocolate or chocolate-coloured sugar. [Italian, plural of *vermicello,* diminutive of *verme,* worm, from Latin *vermis.*]

ver·mi·cide (vérmi-sīd) *n.* A substance used to kill worms. [VERMI- + -CIDE.] **—ver·mi·cid·al** (-sīd'l) *adj.*

ver·mic·u·lar (ver-míckewlər, vər-) *adj.* **1.** Having the shape or motion of a worm. **2.** Having wormlike markings; vermiculate. **3.** Caused by or pertaining to worms. [Medieval Latin *vermiculāris,* from Latin *vermiculus,* diminutive of *vermis,* worm.] **—ver·mic·u·lar·ly** *adv.*

ver·mic·u·late (ver-míckew-layt, vər-) *tr.v.* **-lated, -lating, -lates.** To adorn or decorate with wavy or winding lines: *vermiculate a jar.*
~*adj.* (-lət, -lit, -layt). **1.** Bearing wormlike wavy lines. **2.** Having a wormlike motion; twisting or wriggling. **3.** Sinuous; tortuous; devious. **4.** Infested with worms; worm-eaten. [Latin *vermiculārī,* to be full of worms, from *vermiculus,* small worm. See **vermeil.**]

ver·mic·u·la·tion (ver-míckew-láysh'n, vər-, vér-mickew-) *n.* **1.** Motion resembling that of a worm; especially, the wavelike contractions of the intestine; peristalsis. **2.** Wormlike marks or carvings, as in a mosaic or masonry. **3.** The condition of being worm-eaten.

ver·mic·u·lite (ver-míckew-līt, vər-) *n.* Any of a group of micaceous hydrated silicates of varying composition, related to the chlorites and used as heat insulation and as a planting medium for starting plant seeds and cuttings. [Latin *vermiculus,* small worm (see **vermeil**) + -ITE (from the wormlike projections it forms when subjected to the blowpipe).]

PRONUNCIATION KEY

a, trap; aa, father; ai, fair; ar, star; aw, lawn; ay, play; b, bb, stab; rubber; ch, church; ck, ticket; d, dd, dead; ladder; e, dress; ee, bee; er, defer; ew, few; ewr, pure; ə, about; ər, letter; f, ff, fife; differ; g, gg, giggle; h, hat; i, kit; ī, price; īr, fire; j, judge; k, kick; l, ll, let; 'l, needle; m, mm, man; n, nn, no; 'n, sudden; ng, thing; o, lot; ō, no; oo, foot; oo, shoe; oor, poor; ow, cow; owr, hour; oy, boy; p, pp, pepper; r, rr, red; s, ss, sauce; sh, ship; t, tt, totter; th, thick; th, this; smooth; u, cut; ur, turn; v, vv, valve; w, wet; y, yes; z, zz, zebra; zh, vision; pleasure

IN FOREIGN WORDS:

aN, oN, Saint-Saëns; hl, Llanelli; Hluhluwe; kh, loch; lough; Khaled

STRESS MARK:

ín-sīt, insight; in-sīt, incite

ver·mi·form (vérmi-fawrm) *adj.* Resembling or having the shape of a worm. [New Latin *vermiformis* : VERMI- + -FORM.]

vermiform appendix *n.* The wormlike, closed, projection of the caecum found in certain mammals including humans, in whom it is vestigial. Also called "appendix," "vermiform process".

ver·mi·fuge (vérmi-fewj) *n.* Any agent that expels or destroys intestinal worms. Also called "anthelminthic". [VERMI- + -FUGE.] **—ver·mi·fug·al** (-féwg'l) *adj.*

ver·mil·ion, ver·mil·lion (vər-míl-yən, ver-) *n.* **1.** A bright red **mercuric sulphide** *(see),* used as a pigment. **2.** Vivid red to reddish orange. Also called "Chinese red", "cinnabar". ~*adj.* Also **ver·mil·lion.** Vivid red to reddish orange in colour. ~*tr.v.* **vermilioned, -ioning, -ions.** Also **ver·mil·lion.** To colour or dye vermilion. [Middle English *vermelyon,* from Old French *vermeillon,* from *vermeil,* VERMEIL.]

ver·min (vérmin) *n., pl.* **vermin. 1.** *Plural.* Collectively, various small animals or insects that are destructive, annoying, or injurious to health, such as cockroaches or rats. **2.** *Plural.* Collectively, various animals that prey on game, such as foxes or weasels. **3. a.** *Rare.* A vile, destructive, or worthless person. **b.** Such persons collectively: *"the most pernicious race of little odious vermin that nature ever suffered to crawl upon the surface of the earth"* (Jonathan Swift). [Middle English, from Old French, from Vulgar Latin *vermīnum* (unattested), from Latin *vermis* (stem *vermin-*), worm.]

ver·mi·na·tion (vérmi-náysh'n) *n.* **1.** Infestation with vermin or worms. **2.** The breeding of worms, larvae, or vermin.

ver·min·ous (vérminəss) *adj.* **1.** Of, pertaining to, or infested with vermin. **2.** Of the nature of vermin; repulsive; noxious. **—ver·mi·nous·ly** *adv.*

ver·miv·o·rous (ver-mívvərəss) *adj.* Feeding on worms. [VERMI- + -VOROUS.]

Ver·mont (vər-mónt, ver-). State in the northeastern United States, one of the New England states, lying to the east of upper New York state with a northern boundary with Canada. The capital is Montpelier; the largest city is Burlington. It was admitted to the Union in 1791.

ver·mouth (vér-məth, -mōōth, *chiefly U.S.* vər-mōōth, ver-) *n.* Any of several white wines, either sweet or dry, flavoured with aromatic herbs and spices, and often used chiefly as an ingredient in cocktails. [French *vermout,* from German *Wermut,* WORMWOOD.]

ver·nac·u·lar (vər-náckewlər) *n.* **1.** The standard native language of a country or locality. **2.** The informal everyday speech of a country or locality. **3.** The idiom of a particular trade or profession: *in the legal vernacular.* **4.** An idiomatic word, phrase, or expression. **5.** The commonly used name of a plant or animal as distinguished from the taxonomic designation. ~*adj.* **1.** Native to or commonly spoken by the members of a particular country or locality. Said of a language or dialect. **2.** Using the native language of a locality as distinct from literary language. Said of a writer. **3.** Pertaining to, spoken in, or written in the native language or dialect. **4.** Pertaining to the style of architecture and decoration peculiar to a specific culture or locality. **5.** *Rare.* Occurring or existing in a particular locality; endemic: *a vernacular disease.* **6.** Designating or pertaining to the commonly used nonscientific name of a plant or animal. [Latin *vernāculus,* domestic, from *verna,* native slave, probably from Etruscan.] **—ver·nac·u·lar·ly** *adv.*

ver·nac·u·lar·ism (vər-náckewlər-iz'm) *n.* **1.** The use of, or the doctrine favouring the use of, the vernacular. **2.** A vernacular word, phrase, or expression.

ver·nal (vérn'l) *adj.* **1.** Of, pertaining to, or occurring in the spring. **2.** Characteristic of or resembling spring. **3.** Fresh and young; youthful. [Latin *vernālis,* from *vernus,* of spring, from *vēr,* spring.] **—ver·nal·ly** *adv.*

vernal equinox *n.* **1.** *Astronomy.* The point in Aries at which the ecliptic intersects the celestial equator, the sun having a northerly motion. **2.** The time when the sun passes through this point, about March 21, when day and night are approximately equal all over the earth. Compare **autumnal equinox.**

vernal grass *n.* Any of various Eurasian grasses of the genus *Anthoxanthum,* such as the sweet-scented *A. odoratum.*

ver·nal·i·sa·tion, ver·nal·i·za·tion (vérn'l-ī-záysh'n || *U.S.* -i-) *n.* The exposure of certain plants or their seeds to a period of low temperature which is necessary for them to flower or flower earlier than usual. Used especially of winter varieties of cereals.

ver·na·tion (ver-náysh'n) *n. Botany.* The arrangement of the folded leaves in a bud. [New Latin *vernatio,* from Latin *vernāre,* to flourish, from *vernus,* VERNAL.]

Verne (vairn), **Jules** (1828–1905). French writer. The founder of modern science fiction, he foresaw submarines and space travel. The best known of his adventure stories are *Journey to the Centre of the Earth* (1864) and *Around the World in 80 Days* (1873).

Ver·ner's Law (vér-nərz, vaír-). *Linguistics.* A law stating essentially that Proto-Germanic non-initial voiceless fricatives in voiced environments became voiced when the previous syllable was unstressed in Proto-Indo-European. [After Karl Adolf *Verner* (1846–96), Danish philologist.]

ver·ni·er (vérni-ər) *n.* **1.** A small, movable auxiliary graduated scale attached parallel to a main graduated scale, calibrated to indicate fractional parts of the subdivisions of the larger scale, and used on certain precision instruments to increase accuracy in measurement. **2.** Any auxiliary device designed to facilitate fine adjustments or measurements on precision instruments. Also called "vernier scale".

~*adj.* Of or pertaining to a vernier. [After Pierre *Vernier* (1580–1637), French mathematician.]

vernier calliper *n.* A measuring instrument consisting of an L-shaped frame with a linear scale along its longer arm and an L-shaped sliding attachment with a vernier scale, used to read directly the dimension of an object represented by the separation between the inner or outer edges of the two shorter arms.

vernier rocket *n.* A small rocket engine used primarily to make fine adjustments in velocity and trajectory. Also called "thruster", "vernier engine".

Ve·ro·na (və-rốnə, vi-, ve-). City in northeastern Italy, lying on the river Adige in the Venetia region. A strategic pre-Roman city, it is now a major industrial and agricultural centre.

Ver·o·nal (vérrə-n'l || -nawl) *n.* A trademark for **barbitone** *(see).*

Ve·ro·ne·se (vérrō-náy-zay, *Italian* -say), **Paolo.** born Paolo Caliari. (1528–1588). Italian painter of the Venetian school. He is known particularly as a decorative artist. His works include *Marriage at Cana,* and the *Feast in the House of Levi.*

ve·ron·i·ca[1] (və-rónnikə) *n.* Any of various plants of the genus *Veronica,* which includes the speedwells. [Perhaps from the name *Veronica.*]

veronica[2] *n.* **1.** The representation or image of the face of Jesus, which, according to legend, was impressed upon the handkerchief offered to him by Saint Veronica on the road to Calvary. **2.** The handkerchief itself. **3.** Any similar representation of Jesus' face on a textile fabric. [Medieval Latin, from Late Latin *Veraiconica,* (Saint) Veronica : *vēra, vērus,* true + *iconica, iconicus,* pertaining to an image, from *icon,* image, ICON.]

veronica[3] *n.* In bullfighting, a manoeuvre in which the matador stands immobile and passes the cape slowly before the charging bull. [Spanish, from the name *Veronica.*]

Ver·roc·chio (və-rócki-ō, ve-, -rốki-), **Andrea del.** born Andrea di Michele de Francesco di Cioni. (1435–1488). Florentine sculptor, painter, and craftsman. He is best known for his magnificent equestrian statue of *Colleoni* at Venice.

ver·ru·ca (və-rōō-kə, vi-, ve-) *n., pl.* **-cas** or **-cae** (-see). **1.** *Medicine.* A wart especially one on the sole of the foot. **2.** *Biology.* A wartlike projection, as on some leaves. [Latin *verrūca.*]

ver·ru·cose (vérroo-kōz, -kōss, və-rōō-) *adj.* Also **ver·ru·cous** (-kəss). Covered with warts or wartlike projections. [Latin *verrucōsus,* from *verrūca,* VERRUCA.]

vers versed sine.

Ver·sailles (vair-sí, ver-). City in north central France, lying on the southwestern outskirts of Paris. It was a village until Louis XIV built his palace and transferred his court to it (1682). Both the German Empire and the Third French Republic were proclaimed at Versailles (1871) and the negotiations which ended World War I by the Treaty of Versailles (1919) were conducted there.

Versailles, Treaty of *n.* **1.** The treaty (1919) imposed on Germany after the end of World War I. **2.** The treaty (1783) ending the War of American Independence. See **Paris, Treaty of.**

ver·sant (vérss'nt) *n.* **1.** The slope of a side of a mountain or mountain range. **2.** The general slope of any region. [French, from Latin *versāns* (stem *versant-*), present participle of *versārī,* to turn frequently. See **versatile.**]

ver·sa·tile (vérssə-tīl || *chiefly U.S.* -t'l) *adj.* **1.** Capable of turning competently from one task, subject, or occupation to another; having a generalized aptitude. **2.** Having varied uses or serving many functions: *The potato is a most versatile vegetable.* **3.** Inconstant or variable; changeable. **4.** *Biology.* Capable of moving freely in all directions, as the antenna of an insect or the loosely attached anther of a flower may be. [French, from Latin *versātilis,* from *versārī,* frequentative of *vertere,* to turn.] **—ver·sa·tile·ly** *adv.* **—ver·sa·til·i·ty** (-tílləti), **ver·sa·tile·ness** *n.*

verse (verss) *n. Abbr.* **v., ver. 1. a.** A line of words arranged in accordance with the principles of prosody; one line of poetry. **b.** A subdivision of any metrical composition, such as a stanza of a hymn or of a long poem. **2.** Metrical or rhymed composition; poetry as distinct from prose. **3.** Light metrical composition as distinct from serious poetry. **4.** An instance of such composition; a light poem. **5.** A specified type of metrical composition, such as *elegiac verse, blank verse,* or *free verse.* **6.** A specified type of metrical structure: *iambic verse.* **7.** Any of the numbered subdivisions of a chapter in the Bible. ~*v.* **versed, versing, verses.** *Rare.* —*tr.* To versify (prose, for example). —*intr.* To versify; write poetry. [Middle English *vers,* from Old English *fers* and Old French *vers,* from Latin *versus,* "a turning of the plough," furrow, line, verse, from the past participle of *vertere,* to turn.]

versed (verst) *adj.* Knowledgeable, skilled, or trained. Used with *in: versed in canon law.* [French *versé* or Latin *versātus,* past participle of *versārī,* to be engaged in, frequentative of *vertere,* to turn.]

versed cosine *n. Abbr.* **covers** *Mathematics.* A trigonometric function of an angle equal to one minus the sine of that angle. Also called "coversine".

versed sine *n. Abbr.* **vers** *Mathematics.* A trigonometric function of an angle equal to one minus the cosine of that angle. Also called "versine". [New Latin *sinus versus,* "inverse-order sine", from Latin *versus,* turned. See **verse** (poetry).]

ver·si·cle (vérssik'l) *n.* **1.** A short verse. **2.** A short sentence spoken or chanted by a priest and followed by a response from the congregation. [Middle English, from Old French *versicule,* from Latin

versiculus, diminutive of *versus,* VERSE.] **—ver·si·cu·lar** (ver-síckewlər) *adj.*
ver·si·col·our (vérssi-kullər) *adj.* Also **ver·si·col·oured** (-kullərd). **1.** Having a variety of colours; variegated. **2.** Changing in colour; iridescent. [Latin : *versus,* turned, changed (see **verse**) + COLOUR.]
ver·si·fi·er (vérssi-fī-ər) *n.* One who versifies. See Synonyms at **poet.**
ver·si·fy (vérssi-fī) *v.* **-fied, -fying, -fies.** *—tr.* **1.** To change from prose into metrical form. **2.** To treat or tell in verse; write a poem about: *versify Bible stories.* *—intr.* To write verses; especially, to write light or worthless poetry. [Middle English *versifien,* from Old French *versifier,* from Latin *versificāre* : *versus,* VERSE + -FY.] **—ver·si·fi·ca·tion** (-fi-káysh'n) *n.*
ver·sine (vér-sīn) *n. Mathematics.* A versed sine.
ver·sion (vérsh'n, vérzh'n) *n. Abbr.* **v., ver. 1.** A description, narration, or account related from the specific or subjective viewpoint of the narrator: *Her version of the accident differed from his.* **2. a.** A translation. **b.** *Usually capital* **V.** A translation of the entire Bible or of a part of it: *the King James Version.* **3.** A variation of any prototype; a variant: *"At home we played soccer . . . and sometimes a version of hurling"* (Brendan Behan). **4.** An adaptation of a work of art or literature into another medium or style: *Lamb's version of Shakespeare; the film version.* **5.** *Medicine.* **a.** Manipulation of a foetus in the uterus to bring it into a favourable position for delivery. **b.** A deflection of an organ, such as the uterus, from its normal position. [From Medieval Latin *versiō* (stem *versiōn-*), conversion, translation, from Latin *vertere,* to turn, change.] **—ver·sion·al** *adj.*
vers li·bre (vaír léebr) *n. French.* **Free verse** *(see).*
ver·so (vér-sō) *n., pl.* **-sos.** *Abbr.* **v., vo. 1.** *Printing.* The left-hand page of a book or the reverse side of a sheet of paper as opposed to the **recto** *(see).* **2.** The back of a coin or medal. Compare **obverse.** [Latin *versō (folio),* "(the page) being turned", the page one sees when the leaf is turned over, ablative of *versus,* turned. See **versus.**]
verst (verst) *n.* A Russian measure of linear distance, equivalent to just over a kilometre (about two-thirds of a mile). [French *verste,* from Russian *versta,* "line".]
ver·sus (vér-səss || -səz) *prep. Abbr.* **v., vs. 1.** Against. Used in law and in sports: *the plaintiff versus the defendant; Spurs versus QPR at Wembley.* **2.** As an alternative to; in contrast with: *death versus dishonour.* [Medieval Latin, from Latin, turned towards, from the past participle of *vertere,* to turn.]
vert (vert) *n.* **1.** In former English forest law: **a.** Any green vegetation that can serve as cover for deer. **b.** The right to cut such vegetation. **2.** *Heraldy.* The colour green. [Middle English *verte,* from Old French *vert,* green. See **verdant.**]
vert. vertical.
ver·te·bra (vérti-brə) *n., pl.* **-brae** (-bree) or **-bras.** Any of the bones or cartilaginous segments forming the spinal column. [Latin, joint, vertebra, "something to turn on", from *vertere,* to turn.]
ver·te·bral (vértibrəl) *adj.* **1.** Relating to or of the nature of a vertebra. **2.** Having or consisting of vertebrae.
vertebral canal *n. Anatomy.* The **spinal canal** *(see).*
vertebral column *n. Anatomy.* The **spinal column** *(see).*
ver·te·brate (vérti-brət, -brit, -brayt) *n.* Any member of the subphylum Vertebrata, a primary division of the phylum Chordata that includes the fishes, amphibians, reptiles, birds, and mammals, all of which are characterised by a segmented bony or cartilaginous spinal column.
~adj. **1.** Having a backbone or spinal column. **2.** Of or characteristic of a vertebrate or vertebrates. [Latin *vertebrātus,* from *vertebra,* VERTEBRA.]
ver·te·bra·tion (vérti-bráysh'n) *n.* The process or result of division into vertebrae or similar segments.
ver·tex (vér-teks) *n., pl.* **-texes** or **-tices** (-ti-seez). **1.** The highest point of anything; the apex; the summit. **2.** *Anatomy.* **a.** The highest point of the skull. **b.** The top of the head. **3.** *Astronomy.* The highest point reached in the apparent motion of a celestial body. **4.** In geometry: **a.** The point at which two or more lines or edges intersect. **b.** The fixed point that is one of the three generating characteristics of a conic section. [Latin, whirl, crown of the head, highest point, from *vertere,* to turn.]
ver·ti·cal (vértik'l) *adj. Abbr.* **vert. 1.** At right angles to the horizon; extending perpendicularly from a plane; upright. Compare **horizontal. 2.** Pertaining to or situated at the vertex or highest point; directly overhead. **3.** *Anatomy.* Of or pertaining to the vertex of the head. **4.** *Economics.* Pertaining to, composed of, or controlling all the grades, stages, or levels in the manufacture and sale of a product. **5.** Moving straight up or down or up and down.
~n. Abbr. **vert. 1.** A vertical line, plane, circle, or the like. **2.** A vertical position. **3.** A vertical pillar, pole, or the like. [French, from Late Latin *verticālis,* from Latin *vertex* (stem *vertic-*), VERTEX.] **—ver·ti·cal·i·ty** (vérti-kál-əti), ver·ti·cal·ness *n.* **—ver·ti·cal·ly** *adv.*
Synonyms: *vertical, upright, perpendicular, plumb.*
vertical circle *n. Astronomy.* Any great circle on the celestial sphere, passing through the zenith and the nadir, and thus perpendicular to the horizon.
vertical file *n.* A collection of ephemeras, such as pamphlets, sheets of paper, and mounted photographs, arranged for ready reference, as in a library.
vertically opposite angles *pl.n.* Either pair of the two pairs of equal angles formed opposite each other by two intersecting lines.
vertical take-off *n.* The take-off of an aircraft in a perpendicularly upward direction.
vertical union *n. U.S.* An **industrial union** *(see).*

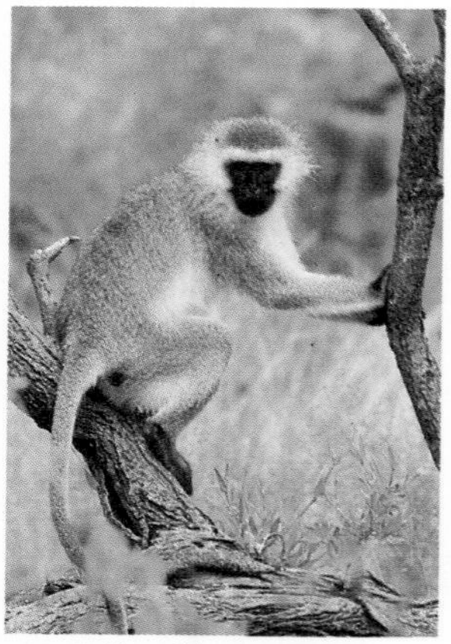

vervet *One of the commonest monkeys in East Africa, the vervet,* Cercopithecus aethiops, *is recognisable by its black face and often greenish fur.*

ver·ti·ces. Alternative plural of **vertex.**
ver·ti·cil (vérti-sil) *n. Biology.* A circular arrangement, as of flowers or leaves, about a point on an axis; a whorl. [Latin *verticillus,* the whirl of a spindle, diminutive of *vertex,* whirl, VERTEX.]
ver·ti·cil·las·ter (vérti-si-láss-tər) *n. Botany.* An inflorescence, such as that of the white dead-nettle, resembling a whorl but actually arising in axils of opposite leaves. [VERTICIL + -ASTER.] **—ver·ti·cil·las·trate** (-trət, -trit, -trayt) *adj.*
ver·ti·cil·late (ver-tíssil-ət, vérti-síl-ət, -it, -ayt) *adj.* Also **ver·ti·cil·lat·ed** (-aytid). Arranged in or forming a whorl or whorls. **—ver·ti·cil·late·ly** *adv.* **—ver·ti·cil·la·tion** (-áysh'n) *n.*
ver·tig·i·nous (ver-tíjinəss) *adj.* **1.** Revolving; whirling; rotary. **2.** Affected by vertigo; dizzy. **3.** Tending to produce vertigo: *vertiginous speed.* **4.** Liable to quick change; unstable; inconstant. [Latin *vertīginōsus,* from *vertīgō* (stem *vertīgin-*), VERTIGO.] **—ver·tig·i·nous·ly** *adv.* **—ver·tig·i·nous·ness** *n.*
ver·ti·go (vérti-gō, *rarely* ver-tī-) *n., pl.* **-goes** or **vertigines** (ver-tíji-neez). **1.** The sensation of dizziness and the feeling that oneself or one's environment is whirling about. **2.** A confused, disorientated state of mind. [Latin *vertīgō,* "a whirling", from *vertere,* to turn.]
ver·tu. Variant of **virtu.**
Verulamium. See **St. Albans.**
ver·vain (vér-vayn) *n.* A perennial plant, *Verbena officinalis,* native to Europe having clusters of tiny, purplish-blue flowers. [Middle English *verveine,* from Old French, from Latin *verbēna,* often in plural *verbēnae,* sacred leaves or twigs of olive, myrtle, or laurel.]
verve (verv) *n.* **1.** Energy and enthusiasm in the expression of ideas and especially in artistic endeavour: *The play lacks verve.* **2.** Vitality; liveliness; vigour. [French, from Old French, fancy, fanciful expression, from Latin *verba,* plural of *verbum,* word.]
ver·vet (vérvit) *n.* A small, long-tailed African monkey, *Cercopithecus aethiops,* having a yellowish-brown or greenish coat. [French, short for *vert grivet* : *vert,* green (see **verdant**) + GRIVET.]
Ver·woerd (fər-vóort), **Hendrik Frensch** (1901–1966). South African statesman. While prime minister (1958–66), he pursued a policy of apartheid, and took South Africa out of the Commonwealth (1961). He was assassinated in Cape Town.
ver·y (vérri || vúrri) *adv. Abbr.* **v., V. 1.** In a high degree; extremely; exceedingly: *very happy.* **2.** Truly. Used as an intensive with superlatives: *the very best way to proceed.* **3.** Precisely: *the very same one.* **—not very. 1.** Not at all: *not very satisfied with the service.* **2.** Only a little: *He's not very much better.*
~adj. **verier, -iest. 1.** Complete; absolute; utter: *at the very end of his career.* **2.** Identical; selfsame: *There goes the very man I met.* **3.** Used as an intensive to emphasise the importance of the thing described: *The very mountains crumbled.* **4.** Particular; precise: *the very centre of town.* **5.** Mere: *The very mention of the name was frightening.* **6.** Actual: *caught in the very act.* **7.** As if actual. Used to reinforce a metaphor: *His fists are very rocks.* **8.** *Archaic.* Genuine; real; true: *"Like very sanctity she did approach"* (Shakespeare). [Middle English *verray,* from Old French *ver(r)ai,* true, real, from Vulgar Latin *vērāius* (unattested), from Latin *vērus,* true.]
Usage: *Very* may be used to modify a past participle, as in *She was very tired; She seems very interested,* where the past participle clearly has an adjectival function. However, in such sentences as *she was delayed/disliked/inconvenienced,* where the participle still seems partly verbal in function, more formal usage prefers *much, very much,* or *greatly,* and *very* has often been criticised in this kind of context.
very high frequency *n. Abbr.* **VHF, vhf** A band of radio frequencies falling between 30 and 300 megahertz.
Ve·ry light (véer-i, vérri) *n.* A coloured flare fired from a pistol (a *Very pistol*) as a signal or for temporary illumination. [After Edward W. *Very* (died 1910), U.S. naval officer.]
very low frequency *n. Abbr.* **VLF, vlf** A band of radio frequencies falling between 3 and 30 kilohertz.
ve·si·ca (véssi-kə, vée-si-, vi-sī-) *n., pl.* **-cae** (-see, -kee, -kī). **1.** A bladder; especially, the urinary bladder or the gallbladder. **2.** A vesica piscis. [Latin *vēsīca,* bladder, blister.] **—ves·i·cal** (véssik'l) *adj.*
vesica pis·cis (véssikə píssiss) *n.* A pointed oval shape formed by or as if by the intersection of two circles and used in medieval art, often as an aureole, to surround a sacred figure. Also called "vesica". [Latin, "fish's bladder".]
ves·i·cant (véssikənt) *n.* A blistering agent; especially, such an agent, as mustard gas, used in chemical warfare. **—ves·i·cant** *adj.*
ves·i·cate (véssi-kayt) *v.* **-cated, -cating, -cates.** *—tr.* To blister. *—intr.* To be or become blistered. [Late Latin *vēsīcāre,* from Latin *vēsīca,* bladder, blister, VESICA.] **—ves·i·ca·tion** (-káysh'n) *n.*
ves·i·ca·to·ry (véssi-kətri, -kaytəri, -káytəri) *adj.* Vesicant.
~n., pl. **vesicatories.** A vesicant.
ves·i·cle (véssik'l) *n.* **1.** A small bladder-like vacuole, cell, or cavity. **2.** *Anatomy.* A small bladder or sac, especially one containing fluid. **3.** *Pathology.* A serum-filled blister formed in or beneath the skin. **4.** An air-filled cavity found in certain aquatic plants. **5.** A small cavity formed in volcanic rock during solidification. [French *vésicule,* from Latin *vēsīcula,* diminutive of *vēsīca,* VESICA.]
ve·sic·u·lar (vi-síckewlər) *adj.* **1.** Of or pertaining to vesicles. **2.** Composed of or containing vesicles. **3.** Having the form of a vesicle. **—ve·sic·u·lar·ly** *adv.*
ve·sic·u·late (vi-síckew-layt) *v.* **-lated, -lating, -lates.** *—tr.* To make vesicular; blister. *—intr.* To become blistered or vesicular.

~*adj.* (-lət, -lit, -layt) **1.** Of, pertaining to, or resembling vesicles. **2.** Full of or bearing vesicles; vesicular. **—ve·sic·u·la·tion** (-láysh'n) *n.*

Ves·pa·sian (ve-spáyzh-'n, -yən, -spáyzi-ən), Latin name Titus Flavius Vespasianus (A.D. 9–79). Roman emperor (69–79). He restored the empire's finances, reformed the army, patronised the arts, and began the building of the Coliseum.

ves·per (véspər) *n.* **1.** A bell used to summon persons to vespers. Also called "vesper bell". **2.** *Archaic.* Evening.

~*adj.* **1.** Of or pertaining to vespers. **2.** Pertaining to, appearing in, or appropriate to evening: *a vesper serenade.* [From VESPER.]

Vesper *n.* Formerly, the **evening star** *(see).* [Middle English, from Latin, evening, the evening star.]

ves·per·al (véspərəl) *n.* **1.** A book containing the words and hymns to be used at vespers. **2.** A covering used to protect the altar cloth between services.

ves·pers (véspərz) *pl.n. often capital* **V. 1. a.** The sixth of the seven **canonical hours** *(see).* **b.** The time of day set aside for this prayer, in the late afternoon or evening. **2.** Any service of worship held in the late afternoon or evening. **3.** *Roman Catholic Church.* A service held on Sundays or holy days which includes the office of vespers.

ves·per·tine (véss-pər-tīn, -per-) *adj.* Also **ves·per·ti·nal** (-tīn'l). **1.** Pertaining to or appearing in the evening. **2.** *Botany.* Opening or blooming in the evening. **3.** *Zoology.* Becoming active in the evening; crepuscular. **4.** *Astronomy.* Moving towards the horizon in the evening. [Latin *vespertīnus,* from *vesper,* evening, VESPER.]

ves·pi·ar·y (véspi-əri || -erri) *n., pl.* **-ies.** A nest or colony of wasps or hornets. [Latin *vespa,* wasp + (AP)IARY.]

ves·pid (véspid) *n.* Any of various insects of the family Vespidae, which includes the common wasp and hornet. [New Latin *Vespidae,* from Latin *vespa,* wasp. See **vespiary.**] **—ves·pid** *adj.*

ves·pine (véss-pīn) *adj.* Of, pertaining to, or resembling a wasp or wasps. [From Latin *vespa,* wasp. See **vespiary.**]

Ves·puc·ci (ve-spŏŏchi), **Amerigo** (1454–1512). Italian navigator. He made several voyages to the New World and discovered (1499) the mouths of the Amazon, and (1501) the mouth of the Rio de la Plata. America is named after him.

ves·sel (véss'l) *n.* **1.** A hollow utensil used as a container, especially for liquids. **2.** A boat, ship, barge, or the like designed to transport passengers or freight on water. **3.** An airship. **4.** *Anatomy.* A duct, canal, or other tube for containing or circulating a bodily fluid: *a blood vessel.* **5.** *Botany.* Any of the tubular conductive structures of plant vascular tissue, consisting of cylindrical cells that are attached end to end. **6.** A person considered as a receptacle or agent of some specified quality: *a vessel of mercy.* [Middle English, from Old French *vaissel, vessel,* from Late Latin *vascellum,* diminutive of Latin *vās,* vessel, VAS.]

vest (vest) *n.* **1.** A simple undergarment covering the upper part of the body. **2.** *Chiefly U.S. & Australian.* A waistcoat. **3.** *Rare.* A fabric trimming or decoration worn by women to cover the bosom. **4.** *Archaic.* Clothing; dress. **5.** *Archaic.* An ecclesiastical vestment.

~*v.* **vested, vesting, vests.** *—tr.* **1.** To clothe or dress, as with ecclesiastical vestments. **2.** To place (authority, property, or rights, for example) in the control of someone. Used with *in: He vested his estate in his son.* **3.** To place authority, power, or the like, in the control of. Used with *with: The council was vested with enormous power.* *—intr.* **1.** To dress oneself, especially in ecclesiastical vestments. **2.** To be or become legally vested in a person or persons; come into the possession of someone. [French *veste,* from Italian, from Latin *vestis,* garment.]

ves·ta (véstə) *n.* A short friction match made of wax or wood. [After the goddess VESTA.]

Vesta¹. *Roman Mythology.* The goddess of the hearth, identified with the Greek goddess Hestia and worshipped in a temple containing the sacred fire tended by the vestal virgins. [Latin.]

Vesta² *n.* The third-largest asteroid in the solar system, having a diameter of approximately 380 kilometres (240 miles). [After the goddess VESTA.]

ves·tal (vést'l) *adj.* **1.** Pertaining to or sacred to Vesta. **2.** Pertaining to or characteristic of the vestal virgins; chaste; pure.

~*n.* **1.** A vestal virgin. **2.** A virgin woman. **3.** *Rare.* A nun.

vestal virgin *n.* Any of the four or six virgin priestesses who tended the sacred fire in the temple of Vesta in ancient Rome.

vest·ed (véstid) *adj.* **1.** *Law.* **a.** Settled, complete, or absolute; without contingency. Said of property or a right. **b.** Having unqualified present or future possession of a property or right. Said of a person, persons, or an organisation. **2.** Dressed or clothed, especially in ecclesiastical vestments.

vested interest *n.* **1.** *Law.* A right or title to ownership of property that can be conveyed to another. **2.** A strong concern for something, such as a state of affairs or an institution, from which one expects private benefit. **3.** *Usually plural.* A group that has a vested interest.

ves·ti·ar·y (vésti-əri || -erri) *adj.* Of or pertaining to clothes.

~*n., pl.* **vestiaries.** A dressing room, cloakroom, or vestry. [Middle English *vestiarie,* from Old French, from Medieval Latin *vestiārium,* from Latin, wardrobe, from *vestiārius,* of clothes, from *vestis,* garment.]

vestibular nerve *n.* A division of the **acoustic nerve** *(see).*

ves·ti·bule (vésti-bewl) *n.* **1.** A small entrance hall or antechamber between two doors of a house or building. **2.** *Chiefly U.S.* An enclosed area at the end of a passenger car on a railway train. **3.** *Anatomy.* Any cavity, chamber, or channel that serves as an approach or entrance to another cavity or canal. [French, from Latin *vestibulum*†.] **—ves·tib·u·lar** (ve-stíbbewlər) *adj.*

ves·tib·u·lo·coch·le·ar nerve (ve-stibbew-lō-kóckli-ər) *n.* The **acoustic nerve** *(see).*

ves·tige (véstij) *n.* **1.** A visible trace, evidence, or sign of something that has once existed but now no longer exists or appears. **2.** A very small quantity; a hint: *a vestige of garlic; not a vestige of truth in his claim.* **3.** *Biology.* A small, degenerate, or rudimentary organ or part existing in an organism as a usually nonfunctioning remnant of an organ or part fully developed and functional in a preceding generation or earlier developmental stage. —See Synonyms at **trace.** [French, from Latin *vestīgium*†, footprint, trace.]

ves·tig·i·al (ve-stíji-əl, -stíjəl) *adj.* **1.** Of, pertaining to, or constituting a vestige. **2.** *Biology.* Occurring or persisting as a rudimentary or degenerate structure. **—ves·tig·i·al·ly** *adv.*

vest·ment (véss-mənt, vést-) *n.* **1.** A garment; especially, a robe or gown worn as an indication of office or state. **2.** *Ecclesiastical.* Any of the ritual robes worn by clergymen, altar boys, or other assistants at services or rites; especially, a garment worn at the celebration of the Eucharist. [Middle English *vestiment,* from Old French, from Latin *vestimentum,* from *vestīre,* to dress, from *vestis,* garment. See **vest.**] **—vest·ment·al** (vest-méntʹl) *adj.*

vest-pock·et (vést-pockit) *adj. Chiefly U.S.* **1.** Designed to fit into a waistcoat pocket. **2.** Relatively small; diminutive.

ves·try (véstri) *n., pl.* **-tries. 1.** A room in or adjoining a church where the clergy put on their vestments and where these robes and other sacred objects are stored; a sacristy. **2.** A meeting room in a church. **3.** In the Anglican and Episcopal churches, a committee of members of the parish or congregation that administers the affairs of the parish or congregation. **4.** In the Anglican Church, a meeting of this group or of the entire congregation or the place in which the meeting is held. [Middle English *vestrie,* variant of *vestiarie,* VESTIARY.]

ves·try·man (véstri-mən) *n., pl.* **-men** (-mən). A member of a vestry.

ves·ture (véss-chər, -tewr) *n. Archaic.* **1.** Clothing; apparel. **2.** Anything that covers or cloaks: *hills in a vesture of mist.*

~*tr.v.* **vestured, -turing, -tures.** *Archaic.* To cover with vesture; clothe. [Middle English, clothes, from Old French, from Late Latin *vestītūra,* from Latin *vestīre,* to clothe. See **vestment.**]

ve·su·vi·an (vi-séw-vi-ən, və-, -sōō-) *n.* A match formerly used for lighting cigars; a fusee. [From VESUVIUS.]

ve·su·vi·an·ite (vi-séw-vi-ə-nīt, və-, -sōō-) *n.* A mineral, **idocrase** *(see).* [*Vesuvian,* of VESUVIUS (because first found in the lava of the volcano) + -ITE.]

Ve·su·vi·us (vi-séw-vi-əss, və-, -sōō-). Active volcano in southern Italy. Rising some 1 280 metres (4,200 feet) from the Bay of Naples, it has a seismological station on its west slope. In A.D. 79 the first recorded eruption destroyed Pompeii, Stabiae, and Herculaneum.

vet¹ (vet) *n.* A person trained and authorised to treat animals medically. Also called "veterinary", formally "veterinary surgeon", *U.S.* "veterinarian".

~*tr.v.* **vetted, vetting, vets. 1.** *Informal.* To give medical treatment to (an animal). **2.** To examine or investigate and appraise for acceptability: *vet a manuscript; carefully vetted for the job.* [Shortening of VETERINARY.]

vet² (vet) *n. U.S. Informal.* An ex-serviceman; a military veteran.

vet. 1. veteran. **2.** veterinary. **3.** veterinary surgeon.

vetch (vech) *n.* **1.** Any of various climbing or twining plants of the genus *Vicia,* having pinnate leaves and small, usually purplish flowers. **2.** Any of various similar related plants such as the milk vetches and the kidney vetch. [Middle English *fecche,* from Old North French *veche,* from Latin *vicia.*]

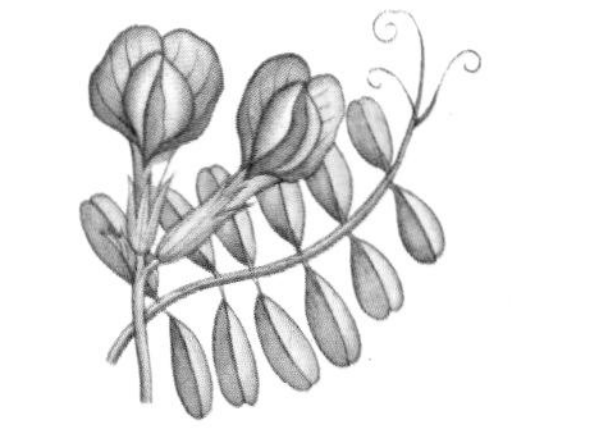

vetch *A clinging European wild plant that winds its way through bushes. Its flowers, similar to the pea, are purple or white.*

vetch·ling (véchling) *n.* Any of several plants of the genus *Lathyrus,* having pinnate leaves, slender tendrils, winged or angled stems, and variously coloured pealike flowers. [VETCH + -LING.]

veter. veterinary.

vet·er·an (véttrən, véttərən) *n. Abbr.* **vet. 1.** One who has a long record of service in a given activity or capacity or long experience, especially one who has seen much active service as a member of the armed forces. **2.** *U.S.* An ex-serviceman.

~*adj.* **1.** Experienced because of long service: *a veteran politician.* **2.** Pertaining to or suggestive of a veteran or veterans. [French *vétéran,* from Latin *veterānus,* from *vetus* (stem *veter-*), old.]

veteran car *n.* A motor car made before 1919. Compare **vintage car.**

Veterans Day *n.* November 11, observed as a national holiday in the United States, the U.S. equivalent of **Armistice Day** *(see).*

vet·er·i·na·ri·an (vèttrə-náir-i-ən, vèttərə-) *n. U.S.* A vet.

vet·er·i·nar·y (vétt'n-ri, véttrin-, vèttərin-, -əri || -erri) *adj. Abbr.* **vet., veter.** Of, pertaining to, or designating the science of the diagnosis and treatment of diseases and injuries of animals, especially domestic animals.

~*n., pl.* **veterinaries.** A vet. [Latin *veterīnārius,* from *veterīnae,* cattle.]

veterinary medicine *n.* The medical science of the prevention, diagnosis, and treatment of animal diseases and injuries. Also called "veterinary science".

veterinary surgeon *n. Abbr.* **vet. V.S.** *Formal.* A vet.

vet·i·ver (véttivər) *n.* **1.** A grass, *Vetiveria zizanioides,* of tropical Asia, cultivated for its aromatic roots that yield an oil used in perfumery. **2.** The root of this plant. [French *vetiver, vetyver,* from Tamil *veṭṭivēru* : *veṭṭi,* worthlessness + *vēru,* useless.]

ve·to (vée-tō) *n., pl.* **-toes. 1.** The vested power or constitutional

PRONUNCIATION KEY

a, **trap**; aa, **father**; ai, **fair**; ar, **star**; aw, **lawn**; ay, **play**; b, bb, **stab**; **rubber**; ch, **church**; ck, **ticket**; d, dd, **dead**; **ladder**; e, **dress**; ee, **bee**; er, **defer**; ew, **few**; ewr, **pure**; ə, **about**; ər, **letter**; f, ff, **fife**; **differ**; g, gg, **giggle**; h, **hat**; i, **kit**; ī, **price**; īr, **fire**; j, **judge**; k, **kick**; l, ll, **let**; 'l, **needle**; m, mm, **man**; n, nn, **no**; 'n, **sudden**; ng, **thing**; o, **lot**; ō, **no**; ŏŏ, **foot**; ōō, **shoe**; oor, **poor**; ow, **cow**; owr, **hour**; oy, **boy**; p, pp, **pepper**; r, rr, **red**; s, ss, **sauce**; sh, **ship**; t, tt, **totter**; th, **thick**; th, **this**; **smooth**; u, **cut**; ur, **turn**; v, vv, **valve**; w, **wet**; y, **yes**; z, zz, **zebra**; zh, **vision**; **pleasure**

IN FOREIGN WORDS:

aN, oN, **Saint-Saëns**; hl, **Llanelli**; **Hluhluwe**; kh, **loch**; **lough**; **Khaled**

STRESS MARK:

in-sīt, insight; in-sīt, incite

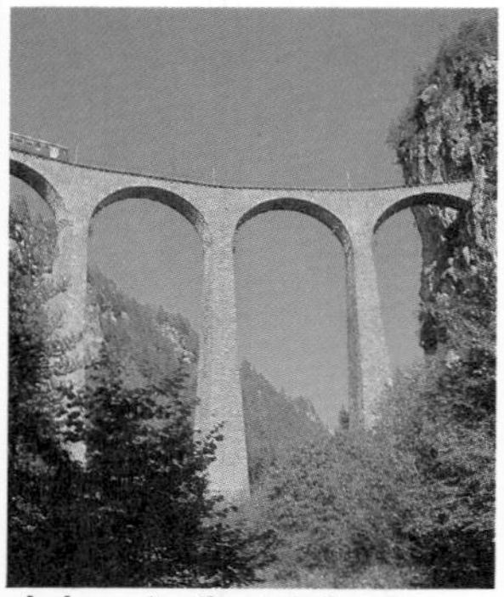

viaduct *A railway viaduct crosses a sheer-sided valley near Filisur, in Switzerland.*

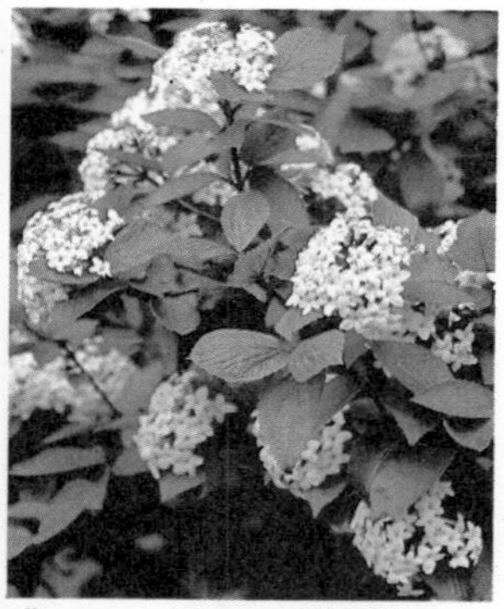

viburnum *There are 200 different species of viburnum – this is the hybrid shrub* Viburnum juddii. *The genus, which is common in temperate regions around the world, also includes the guelder rose and the wayfaring tree.*

right of a sovereign or a branch or department of government, especially the right of a chief executive or an upper legislative body, to reject a bill passed by a (lower) legislative body and thus prevent or delay its enactment into law. **2.** The exercise of this right. **3.** *U.S.* The official document communicating the rejection and the reasons for it. Also called "veto message". **4.** The right of any full or permanent member of various other policy-making bodies, such as the United Nations Security Council, to prevent the passage of a resolution. **5.** Any authoritative prohibition or rejection of a proposed or intended act.

~*tr.v.* **vetoed, -toing, -toes. 1.** To prevent (a legislative bill) from becoming law by exercising the power of veto. **2.** To forbid or prevent authoritatively; prohibit. [Latin *vetō,* I forbid, from *vetāre*†, to forbid.] **—ve·to·er** *n.*

vex (veks) *tr.v.* **vexed, vexing, vexes. 1.** To irritate or annoy, as with petty matters; bother; pester. **2.** To cause serious suffering to; plague or afflict. **3.** To confuse; baffle; puzzle. **4.** *Formal.* To debate (a problem) at length; bring up repeatedly for discussion. **5.** *Archaic.* To toss about or stir up; agitate. —See Synonyms at **annoy.** [Middle English *vexen,* from Old French *vexer,* from Latin *vexāre,* to shake, annoy.] **—vex·er** *n.* **—vex·ing·ly** *adv.*

vex·a·tion (vek-sáysh'n) *n.* **1.** The act of vexing. **2.** The state or condition of being vexed; annoyance. **3.** One that vexes; a source of irritation or annoyance.

vex·a·tious (vek-sáyshəss) *adj.* **1.** Causing or creating vexation; annoying; irksome. **2.** Full of vexation; disturbed; annoyed. **3.** *Law.* Instituted without sufficient grounds, to serve solely as an annoyance to a defendant. Said of legal actions. **—vex·a·tious·ly** *adv.* **—vex·a·tious·ness** *n.*

vexed (vekst) *adj.* **1.** Irritated; annoyed; troubled. **2.** Much debated; subject to controversy. Used chiefly in the phrase *a vexed question.* **—vex·ed·ly** (véksid-li) *adv.* **—vex·ed·ness** *n.*

vex·il·lar·y (vek-síllәri || *U.S.* véksə-lerri) *n., pl.* **-ies. 1.** A member of the oldest class of army veterans who served under a special standard in ancient Rome. **2.** A standard-bearer.

~*adj.* Also **vex·il·lar** (vek-síllər, véksilər). Of or pertaining to a banner or standard. [Latin *vexillārius,* from *vexillum,* flag. See **vexillum.**]

vex·il·late (vek-síll-ayt, véksil-, -ət, -it) *adj.* Having a vexillum.

vex·il·lol·o·gy (véksi-lólləji) *n.* The study of flags. [Latin *vexillum,* flag + -LOGY.] **—vex·il·lol·o·gist** *n.*

vex·il·lum (vek-síl-əm) *n., pl.* **vexilla** (-ə). **1.** *Botany.* A usually enlarged upper petal of certain flowers; a standard. **2.** *Zoology.* The weblike part of a feather; a vane. **3.** In Ancient Rome, a military flag or standard. **4.** The small division of troops serving under such a standard. **5.** A ceremonial flag of a bishop, used especially in processions. [Latin, flag, diminutive of *vēlum,* cloth, veil, sail.]

V.F. 1. vicar forane. **2.** video frequency. **3.** visual field.

v.g. very good.

V.G. vicar general.

vhf, VHF very high frequency.

v.i. vide infra.

V.I. 1. Virgin Islands. **2.** volume indicator.

vi·a (ví-ə, vír || vée-ə) *prep.* **1. a.** By way of; through: *the route to Cardiff via Reading and Oxford.* **b.** By way of and stopping at: *We can go home via the shops.* **2.** By means of: *I'll get the parcel to you via a friend of mine.* [Latin *viā,* ablative of *via,* road, way.]

vi·a·ble (ví-əb'l) *adj.* **1.** Capable of living. Said of a newborn infant, or a foetus that has reached the stage of development that will permit it to survive and develop under normal conditions. **2.** Capable of living, developing, or germinating under favourable conditions. Said of seeds, spores, or eggs. **3.** Capable of actualisation, as a project might be; practicable: *a viable method of reducing costs.* —See Synonyms at **possible.** [French, from Old French, from *vie,* life, from Latin *vīta.*] **—vi·a·bil·i·ty** (ví-ə-bílləti) *n.*

Vi·a Do·lo·ro·sa (vée-ə dóllə-rṓ-sə || dṓlə-) *n.* **1.** Jesus' route from Pilate's judgment hall to Calvary. **2.** A difficult or painful course or experience. [Latin, "sad road".]

vi·a·duct (ví-ə-dukt) *n.* A series of spans or arches used to carry a road or railway over a wide valley or over other roads or railways. [Latin *via,* road, way (see **via**) + (AQUA)DUCT.]

vi·al (ví-əl) *n.* A small container, usually glass, for liquids. Also called "phial".

~*tr.v.* **vialled** or *U.S.* **vialed, -alling** or *U.S.* **-aling, -als.** To put or keep in or as if in a vial. [Middle English *viole,* variant of *fiole,* PHIAL.]

vi·a me·di·a (ví-ə mée-di-ə, vée-ə máy-) *n.* A middle route, policy, or course avoiding extremes. [Latin.]

vi·and (ví-ənd) *n.* **1.** An article of food. **2.** *Plural.* Provisions; victuals. [Middle English *viaunde,* from Old French *viande,* from Vulgar Latin *vī(v)anda* (unattested), variant of Latin *vīvenda,* gerundive of *vīvere,* to live.]

Viang·chang, Vien·tiane (vyén-tyán, -tyaán). Capital and largest city of Laos. It lies on the north bank of the Mekong (the border with Thailand), and has many canals. It is the country's main trade outlet (via Bangkok), and has been its capital since 1899. Nearby is the ruined capital of a Lao kingdom (1707–1827).

vi·at·ic (vī-áttik) *adj.* Also **vi·at·i·cal** (-'l). *Formal.* Of or pertaining to travelling, a road, or a way. [Latin *viāticus.* See **viaticum.**]

vi·at·i·cum (vī-átti-kəm, vi-) *n., pl.* **-ca** (-kə) or **-cums. 1.** Holy communion as given to a dying person or one in danger of death. **2.** *Rare.* Supplies for a journey. [Latin *viāticum,* travelling provisions, from *viāticus,* of a road or journey, from *via,* way, road. See **via.**]

vibes (vībz) *pl.n.* **1.** *Slang.* An unspoken and often unconscious message given by one person or group to another, or the resulting emotional reaction; vibrations: *bad vibes.* **2.** *Informal.* A vibraphone. [Shortened from VIBRATIONS.] **—vib·ist** *n.*

vi·brac·u·lum (vī-bráckew-ləm) *n., pl.* **-la** (-lə). *Zoology.* Any of the long, whiplike filaments on the surface of certain bryozoan colonies. [New Latin, diminutive formation from Latin *vibrāre,* to shake, brandish, VIBRATE.] **—vi·brac·u·lar** (-lər) *adj.* **—vi·brac·u·loid** (-loyd) *adj.*

vi·brant (víbrənt) *adj.* **1.** Exhibiting, characterised by, or resulting from vibration; vibrating. **2.** Pulsing or throbbing with energy or activity: *vibrant verse.* [Latin *vibrāre* (see **vibrate**) + -ANT.] **—vi·bran·cy** *n.* **—vi·brant·ly** *adv.*

vi·bra·phone (víbrə-fōn) *n.* An electronic percussion instrument similar to a marimba but having metal bars and rotating discs in the resonators to produce a vibrato. Also called "vibra-harp", informally "vibes". [VIBRA(TE) + -PHONE.] **—vi·bra·phon·ist** (-fōnist) *n.*

vi·brate (vī-bráyt || *U.S.* ví-brayt) *v.* **-brated, -brating, -brates.** —*intr.* **1.** To move back and forth rapidly; oscillate. **2.** To produce a sound; resonate. **3.** To be moved emotionally; thrill: *vibrate with excitement.* **4.** To fluctuate or waver in making choices; vacillate. —*tr.* **1.** To cause to tremble or quiver. **2.** To cause to move back and forth rapidly. **3.** To produce (sound) by vibration. —See Synonyms at **swing.** [Latin *vibrāre.*]

vi·bra·tile (víbrə-tīl || *U.S. also* -t'l) *adj.* **1.** Characterised by vibration. **2.** Capable of or adapted to vibratory motion. [French, from Latin *vibrāre,* VIBRATE.] **—vi·bra·til·i·ty** (-tílləti) *n.*

vi·bra·tion (vī-bráysh'n) *n.* **1.** The act or an instance of vibrating. **2.** The condition of being vibrated. **3.** *Physics.* **a.** A rapid linear motion of a particle or of an elastic solid about an equilibrium position. **b.** Any periodic process. **4.** A single complete vibrating motion; a quiver; a tremor. **5.** *Usually plural. Slang.* **a.** A distinctive emotional reaction by a person to another person or thing, capable of being instinctively sensed or experienced. **b.** The atmosphere or subtle message producing such a reaction. **—vi·bra·tion·al** *adj.*

vi·bra·to (vi-braátō || vee-) *n., pl.* **-tos.** *Music.* A tremulous or pulsating effect produced in an instrumental or vocal tone by barely perceptible minute and rapid variations in pitch. Compare **tremolo.** [Italian, from Latin *vibrātus,* past participle of *vibrāre,* VIBRATE.]

vi·bra·tor (vī-bráytər || *U.S.* ví-braytər) *n.* **1.** Something that vibrates. **2.** An electrically or battery operated device used for massage. **3.** A dildo with a vibrating tip, used for sexual stimulation. **4.** An electrical device consisting basically of a vibrating conductor interrupting a current.

vi·bra·to·ry (víbrə-tri, -təri, vī-bráytəri) *adj.* Also **vi·bra·tive** (vībráytiv || víbrətiv). **1.** Of, characterised by, or consisting of vibration. **2.** Causing vibration. **3.** Vibrating or capable of vibration.

vib·ri·o (víbbri-ō) *n., pl.* **-os.** Any of various S-shaped or comma-shaped microorganisms of the genus *Vibrio,* especially *V. cholerae,* which causes cholera. [New Latin, arbitrarily from Latin *vibrāre,* VIBRATE (from their vibratory motion).] **—vib·ri·oid** (-oyd) *adj.*

vi·bris·sa (vī-bríss-ə) *n., pl.* **-brissae** (-bríssee). A stiff hair or hair-like projection, such as a nostril hair, any of the whiskers of a cat, or any of the modified feathers near the beak of an insectivorous bird. [Latin *vibrissae* (plural), from *vibrāre,* VIBRATE.]

vi·bur·num (vī-búrnəm) *n.* **1.** Any of various shrubs or trees of the genus *Viburnum,* characteristically having clusters of small white flowers and berry-like red or black fruit. **2.** The bark of certain of these trees containing substances used medicinally. [New Latin *Viburnum,* from Latin *vīburnum*†, wayfaring tree.]

vic. 1. vicar. **2.** vicinity.

vic·ar (víckər) *n. Abbr.* **vic. 1.** In the Church of England, the appointed priest of a parish. **2.** In the Episcopal Church of the United States, a clergyman in charge of a chapel. **3.** In the Anglican Communion generally, a clergyman acting in the place of a rector or bishop. **4.** *Roman Catholic Church.* A deputy or representative for an ecclesiastic. See **Vicar of Christ. 5.** One who fulfils the duties of another; a substitute; a deputy. [Middle English, from Old French *vicaire,* from Latin *vicārius,* a substitute, from *vicārius,* substituting, acting for, from *vicis,* change, turn, office.]

vic·ar·age (víckərij) *n.* **1.** The residence of a vicar. **2.** *Rare.* The benefice of a vicar.

vicar apostolic *n., pl.* **vicars apostolic.** *Abbr.* **V.A.** *Roman Catholic Church.* **1. a.** A titular bishop who, as a representative of the Holy See, administers a region that is not yet a diocese. **b.** A titular bishop appointed to administer to a vacant see in which the succession of bishops has been interrupted. **2.** Formerly, a bishop delegated by the pope to act in his stead in a particular region.

vicar fo·rane (fo-ráyn || faw-, fō-) *n., pl.* **vicars forane.** *Abbr.* **V.F.** *Roman Catholic Church.* A priest who by a bishop's appointment exercises limited jurisdiction over the clergy in a distant district of a diocese. [From Late Latin *forānus,* FOREIGN.]

vicar general *n., pl.* **vicars general.** *Abbr.* **V.G. 1.** *Roman Catholic Church.* A priest acting as deputy to a bishop to assist him in the administration of his diocese. **2.** An ecclesiastical official, usually a layman, who assists an Anglican archbishop or bishop in administrative and judicial duties.

vi·car·i·al (vi-kaír-i-əl, vī-) *adj.* **1.** Of or pertaining to a vicar or vicars. **2.** Acting as or having the position of a vicar. **3.** Vicarious or delegated, as powers of an ecclesiastical office might be.

vi·car·i·ate (vi-káir-i-ət, vī-, -it, -ayt) *n.* Also **vic·ar·ate** (víckər-). **1.** The office rank, or authority of a vicar. **2.** The district under a vicar's jurisdiction. [Medieval Latin *vicāriātus,* from Late Latin *vicārius,* vicar, VICARIOUS.]

vi·car·i·ous (vi-káir-i-əss, vī-) *adj.* **1.** Performed or endured by one person substituting for another; fulfilled by the substitution of the actual offender with some other person or thing: *vicarious punishment.* **2.** Acting in place of someone or something else; delegated; substituted: *a vicarious power of authority.* **3.** Experienced or enjoyed through sympathetic or imaginative participation in the experiences of another: *a vicarious thrill.* **4.** *Physiology.* Occurring in or performed by a part of the body not normally associated with a certain function. [Latin *vicārius,* substituting, from *vicis,* change, turn, office.] **—vi·car·i·ous·ly** *adv.* **—vi·car·i·ous·ness** *n.*

Vicar of Christ *n. Roman Catholic Church.* The pope considered as the earthly deputy of Christ.

vic·ar·ship (víckər-ship) *n.* The office or tenure of a vicar.

vice¹ (vīss) *n.* **1.** An evil, degrading, or immoral practice or habit; a serious moral failing. **2.** Wicked or evil conduct or habits; indulgence in degrading practices; depravity; corruption. **3. a.** Sexual immorality; especially, prostitution. **b.** Sexual perversion. **4.** A slight personal failing; a foible: *His only vice is partiality for practical jokes.* **5.** A flaw or imperfection; a defect; a fault: *the vices in his theory.* **6.** *Archaic.* A physical defect or weakness. **7.** An item of abnormal or perverse behaviour in a domestic animal such as a tendency in a horse to bite. **8.** *Capital* **V.** A character representing a particular or generalised vice, often represented in English morality plays as a or jester or buffoon. —See Synonyms at **fault.** [Middle English, from Old French, from Latin *vitium,* blemish, offence, vice.]

vice², *U.S.* **vise** *n.* A clamping device, especially one with a pair of adjustable jaws, used for holding a workpiece while it is hammered, filed, sawn, or the like.

~*tr.v.* **viced, vicing, vices.** To secure with or as if with a vice.

vice³ (vīss) *n. Abbr.* **v., V.** One who acts in the place of another; a deputy.

~*prep.* (vī-si) In place of; replacing. [Latin *vice,* ablative of *vicis,* change.]

vice– *prefix.* Indicates one representing or substituting or able to act or deputise for another; for example, **vice-chairman, vice-chamberlain, viceregal.** [Middle English *vis-,* from Old French, from Late Latin *vice-,* from Latin *vice,* in place of, VICE.]

vice-ad·mir·al (vīss-ádmərəl, vīss-) *n. Abbr.* **V.A., V. Adm.** A naval officer ranking between an admiral and a rear admiral, equivalent in rank to a lieutenant-general in the Army or an air marshall in the Air Force. **—vice-ad·mir·al·ty** (-ti) *n.*

vice-chan·cel·lor (vīss-chaán-slər, vīss-, -sələr || -chán-) *n. Abbr.* **V.C. 1.** In many universities, the principal or chief administrator, especially where the chancellorship is a purely honorary post. **2.** *U.S. Law.* A judge in equity courts ranking below a chancellor. **3.** *British Law.* Formerly, a judge in the court of chancery who assisted the Lord Chancellor. **4.** A deputy or substitute for a head of state or official bearing the title chancellor. **—vice-chan·cel·lor·ship** *n.*

vice-consul (vīss-kónss'l) *n. Abbr.* **V.C.** A consular officer who is subordinate to and a deputy of a consul or consul general. **—vice-con·su·lar** (-kón-sew-lər) *adj.* **—vice-con·su·late** (-kón-sew-lət, -lit, -layt) *n.* **—vice-con·sul·ship** *n.*

vice·ge·ren·cy (vīss-jérrən-si, -jéerən-) *n., pl.* **-cies. 1.** The position, function, or authority of a vicegerent. **2.** A district under a vicegerent's jurisdiction.

vice·ge·rent (vīss-jérrənt, -jéer-ənt) *n.* **1.** A person appointed by a ruler or head of state to act as an administrative deputy. **2.** *Roman Catholic Church.* **a.** The pope. **b.** Any other bishop or priest considered as the earthly deputy of God or Christ. [Medieval Latin *vicegerēns* : VICE- + GERENT.] **—vice·ge·ral, vice·ge·rent** *adj.*

vic·e·nar·y (víssi-nri, -nəri || -nerri) *adj.* **1.** Consisting of or pertaining to 20. **2.** Designating a notation system based on 20. [Latin *vīcēnārius,* from *vīcēnī,* 20 each, from *vīgintī,* 20.]

vi·cen·ni·al (vī-sénni-əl, vi-) *adj.* **1.** Happening once every 20 years. **2.** Existing or lasting for 20 years. [Late Latin *vīcennium,* period of 20 years : Latin *vīciēs,* 20 times, from *vīgintī,* 20 + *annus,* year.]

Vi·cen·za (vee-chéntsə). City in Venetia, northeastern Italy. The capital of Vicenza province, it is an industrial centre. A powerful medieval city, it has a Gothic cathedral and some fine examples of Palladian architecture.

vice-president (vīss-prézzi-d'nt, vīss- || -dent) *Abbr.* **V.P., V. Pres. 1.** An officer ranking immediately below a president, usually empowered to assume the president's duties under such conditions as absence, illness, or death. **2.** *U.S.* A deputy of a president, especially in a large business enterprise, in charge of a separate department or location: *vice-president in charge of marketing.* **—vice-pres·i·den·cy** *n.* **—vice-pres·i·den·tial** (-dénsh'l) *adj.*

vice·re·gal (vīss-réeg'l) *adj.* **1.** Of or pertaining to a viceroy. **2.** *Chiefly Australian.* Of or pertaining to a governor-general. [VICE- + REGAL.] **—vice·re·gal·ly** *adv.*

vice-regent (vīss-réejənt) *n.* One who acts as a regent's deputy. **—vice-re·gen·cy** *n.* **—vice-re·gent** *adj.*

vice·reine (vīss-ráyn, -rayn) *n.* **1.** The wife of a viceroy. **2.** *Rare.* A female viceroy. [French : VICE- + *reine,* queen, from Latin *rēgīna,* feminine of *rēx,* king.]

vice·roy (vīss-roy) *n., pl.* **-roys.** A governor of a country, province, or colony, ruling as the representative of a sovereign or king. [French : *vice-* + *roi,* king, from Latin *rēx.*]

vice·roy·al·ty (vīss-róy-əlti || -roy-) *n., pl.* **-ties. 1.** The office, rank, or authority of a viceroy. **2.** The term of service of a viceroy. **3.** A district or province governed by a viceroy. Also called "viceroyship".

vice squad *n.* A police division charged with the control of vice, especially prostitution and gambling.

vi·ce ver·sa (vī-si vér-sə || vīss) *Abbr.* **v.v.** The order or meaning being reversed; with principal items transposed; conversely. Said of a preceding statement: *He betrayed her, or vice versa.* [Latin, "the position being changed" : *vice,* ablative singular of *vicis,* change, office, position + *versā,* ablative feminine singular of *versus,* past participle of *vertere,* to turn, change.]

Vi·chy (véeshi, víshi; *French* vee-shee) *n.* A health resort of central France. Situated on the Allier river in the Allier département, it is world famous for its mineral springs. During World War II, it was the seat of the collaboratist Pétain government.

vi·chy·ssoise (véeshi-swaáz, víshi-) *n.* A thick, creamy leek and potato soup, usually served cold. [French, "of Vichy".]

Vichy water *n.* **1.** A naturally effervescent mineral water from the springs at Vichy, France, reputed to have medicinal benefits. **2.** Any sparkling mineral water resembling this. Also called "Vichy", "vichy".

vic·i·nage (víssinij) *n.* **1. a.** A limited region around a particular area; a neighbourhood; a vicinity. **b.** A number of places collectively that are situated near one another. **2.** The residents of a particular neighbourhood. **3.** The state of living in a neighbourhood; proximity; nearness. [Middle English *vesinage,* from Old French *visenage,* from Vulgar Latin *vīcīnāticum* (unattested), from *vīcīnus,* neighbour. See **vicinity.**]

vic·i·nal (víssin'l) *adj.* **1.** Of, belonging to, or restricted to a limited area or neighbourhood; nearby; adjacent. **2.** Designating a local road as opposed to a main road or highway. **3.** *Chemistry.* Approximating, resembling, or taking the place of a fundamental crystal form or face. **4.** *Chemistry.* Designating or pertaining to substituted atoms or groups on adjacent atoms in a molecule. Compare **gem.** [Latin *vīcīnālis,* from *vīcīnus,* neighbour. See **vicinity.**]

vi·cin·i·ty (vi-sínnəti, vī-) *n., pl.* **-ties.** *Abbr.* **vic. 1.** The state of being near in space or relationship; proximity; propinquity: *two restaurants in close vicinity.* **2.** A nearby, surrounding, or adjoining region; a neighbourhood; a locality. [Latin *vīcīnitās* (stem *vīcīnitāt-*), from *vīcīnus,* neighbour, from *vīcus,* village.]

vi·cious (víshəss) *adj.* **1.** Having the nature of vice, evil, or immorality; depraved; debased. **2.** Addicted to vice, immorality, or depravity; malicious; reprobate; evil. **3.** Characterised by spite or malice: *vicious gossip.* **4.** Failing to meet a standard or criterion; having a fault, flaw, or defect: *a vicious syllogism.* **5.** *Archaic.* Impure; foul; diseased. **6.** Disposed to or characterised by violence or destructive behaviour. **7.** Behaving in an unruly or potentially dangerous manner: *a vicious animal.* **8.** Being of an extreme or intense degree: *a vicious hurricane.* —See Synonyms at **cruel.** [Middle English, from Old French, from Latin *vitiōsus,* from *vitium,* VICE.] **—vi·cious·ly** *adv.* **—vi·cious·ness** *n.*

vicious circle *n.* **1.** A situation in which the solution of one problem in a chain of circumstances creates a new problem that leads back to the original problem and increases the difficulty of solving it. **2.** A condition in which a disorder or disease gives rise to another which subsequently affects the first. **3.** *Logic.* A **circle** *(see).*

vi·cis·si·tude (vī-síssi-tewd, vi- || -tōōd) *n.* **1.** *Usually plural.* Any change or variation in something; mutability. **2.** Natural change or variation; alterations manifested in nature and human affairs. **3.** An alteration or variation in fortune. **4.** An alternating change; a succession. [From French, from Latin *vicissitūdō,* from *vicissim,* in turn, from *vicis,* change, turn.]

vi·cis·si·tu·di·nar·y (vī-síssi-téw-din-əri, vi-, -d'n- || -tōō-, -erri) *adj.* Also **vi·cis·si·tu·di·nous** (-əss). Characterised by or subject to vicissitudes.

Vick·ers (víckərz), **Jon** (1926–). Canadian tenor. He is acclaimed for his performances in operas by Wagner and Verdi.

Vicks·burg (víks-burg). A river port of southeastern United States. Situated on the Mississippi at its confluence with the Yazoo river, it was the site of a siege in the American Civil War that culminated in the Confederate surrender (1863).

Vick·y (vícki), pen name of Victor Weisz (1913–66). German-born Hungarian cartoonist. He made his name as a political cartoonist with various London newspapers.

Vi·co (véekō), **Giambattista** also called Giovanni Battista Vico (1668–1744). Italian historical philosopher. He was the first philosopher to see history in terms of the rise and fall of human societies, and to make use of myths and legends as historical evidence.

vi·comte (vee-KÓNT) *n. Feminine* **vi·com·tesse** (-KON-téss). A French nobleman, equal in rank to a British viscount. [French, VISCOUNT.]

vic·tim (víktim) *n.* **1.** Someone who is put to death or subjected to torture or suffering by another. **2.** A living creature slain and offered as a sacrifice to a deity or as part of a religious rite. **3.** One who is harmed by or made to suffer from an act, circumstance, agency, or condition: *victims of war.* **4.** A person who suffers injury, loss, or death as a result of a voluntary undertaking: *a victim of his own scheming.* **5.** A person who is tricked, swindled, or taken advantage of; a dupe. [Latin *victima.*]

vic·tim·ise, vic·tim·ize (vikti-mīz) *tr.v.* **-ised, -ising, -ises. 1.** To single out unfairly for punishment, or abuse; discriminate against and

PRONUNCIATION KEY

a, trap; aa, father; ai, fair; ar, star; aw, lawn; ay, play; b, bb, stab; rubber; ch, church; ck, ticket; d, dd, dead; ladder; e, dress; ee, bee; er, defer; ew, few; ewr, pure; ə, about; ər, letter; f, ff, fife; differ; g, gg, giggle; h, hat; i, kit; ī, price; īr, fire; j, judge; k, kick; l, ll, let; 'l, needle; m, mm, man; n, nn, no; 'n, sudden; ng, thing; o, lot; ō, no; ŏŏ, foot; ōō, shoe; oor, poor; ow, cow; owr, hour; oy, boy; p, pp, pepper; r, rr, red; s, ss, sauce; sh, ship; t, tt, totter; th, thick; th, this; smooth; u, cut; ur, turn; v, vv, valve; w, wet; y, yes; z, zz, zebra; zh, vision; pleasure

IN FOREIGN WORDS:

aN, oN, Saint-Saëns; hl, Llanelli; Hluhluwe; kh, loch; lough; Khaled

STRESS MARK:

ín-sīt, insight; in-sít, incite

bully. **2.** To subject to a swindle or fraud. **3.** To make a victim of by or as if by slaying. —**vic·tim·i·sa·tion** (-mī-záysh'n ‖ *U.S.* -mi-) *n.* —**vic·tim·is·er** *n.*

vic·tim·less (víktim-ləss, -liss) *adj.* Designating a legal offence, such as possession of drugs, in which there is no victim involved, except perhaps the offender himself.

vic·tor (víktər) *n.* **1.** One who defeats or vanquishes an adversary; the winner in a fight, battle, or war. **2.** A winner of a contest or struggle. [Middle English, from Latin, from *vincere* (past participle *victus*), to conquer.]

Victor Emmanuel II (1820–78). The last king of Sardinia and first king of Italy. He became king of Sardinia (1849–61) on the abdication of his father, Charles Albert. After becoming king of Italy (1861) he completed its unification by acquiring Venice (1866), and Rome (which he made his capital) (1871).

vic·to·ri·a (vik-táw-ri-ə ‖ -tṓ-) *n.* **1.** A low, light, four-wheeled carriage for two with a folding top and an elevated driver's seat in front. **2.** A touring car with a folding top usually covering only the rear seat. **3.** A **victoria plum** (*see*). **4.** Any of various water lilies of the South American genus *Victoria,* having large, round, floating leaves. [After Queen VICTORIA.]

Victoria¹ (vik-táw-ri-ə ‖ -tṓ). State of southeastern Australia. The second smallest and most densely populated of the Australian states, it is, with irrigation, a leading farming state, producing cereals, fruit and vegetables, dairy produce, wine, meat and wool. It supplies some 70 per cent of Australia's petroleum, its other minerals including natural gas, brown coal, and gold. Victoria's industries, concentrated around the capital, Melbourne, include metals and machinery, textiles, clothing, footwear, and vehicles.

Victoria². The capital of British Columbia, Canada. Situated on the southeast tip of Vancouver Island, it was founded (1843) by the Hudson Bay Company.

Victoria³. Capital of Hong Kong. Lying on the northeast shore of Hong Kong Island, it is the colony's biggest city, and chief port, and is also known as Hong Kong.

Victoria, Lake. Also **Victoria Ny·an·za.** Africa's largest lake and the world's second-largest freshwater body. It covers 69 452 square kilometres (26,815 square miles), and lies in a shallow depression between the two arms of the Great Rift Valley. The Victoria Nile is its only outlet. The lake was originally named Lake Ukerewe.

Victoria, Queen (1819–1901). Queen of Great Britain and Empress of India. She was the daughter of George III's fourth son, Edward, Duke of Kent, and became Queen (1837) on the death of her uncle, William IV. In 1876 she was proclaimed Empress of India by Disraeli. Her great sense of duty and strict moral code set the pattern for 19th-century Britain. During her reign, constitutional government was fully developed, and the crown's prestige restored.

Victoria Cross *n. Abbr.* **V.C.** An award in the shape of a bronze Maltese cross, the highest military decoration awarded in the British and Commonwealth armed forces for conspicuous valour.

Victoria Falls. Falls on the Zambezi river, on the border between Zambia and Zimbabwe. There are three main sections: the Eastern Cataract, the Rainbow Falls, and the Main Falls. Forming the world's third-largest falls, their total width can span over a kilometre (just over half a mile). They were discovered (1855) by David Livingstone, and named in honour of Queen Victoria.

Vic·to·ri·an (vik-táw-ri-ən ‖ -tṓ-) *adj.* **1.** Of or pertaining to Queen Victoria or the period of her reign: *a Victorian novel.* **2.** Exhibiting qualities usually associated with the time of Queen Victoria, such as moral severity or hypocrisy, middle-class stuffiness, and pompous conservatism. **3.** Pertaining to, designating, or constructed in the highly ornamented, massive style of architecture, decor, and furnishings popular in 19th-century England. **4.** Of or pertaining to any of the various geographical units named Victoria.

~*n.* A person belonging to or exhibiting characteristics typical of the period of Queen Victoria.

Vic·to·ri·a·na (vik-táw-ri-a'anə ‖ -tṓ-, -ánnə, -áynə) *n. Used with a singular verb.* Assorted objects such as books, photographs, and ornaments, of the Victorian period. [VICTORIA + -ANA.]

Vic·to·ri·an·ism (vik-táw-ri-ən-iz'm ‖ -tṓ-) *n.* **1.** The state of having Victorian characteristics, as in attitude, style, or taste. **2.** Something exhibiting Victorian characteristics.

victoria plum *n.* A plum of a variety having large, red, sweet fruits. Also called "victoria". [After Queen VICTORIA.]

vic·to·ri·ous (vik-táw-ri-əss ‖ -tṓ-) *adj.* **1.** Having overcome an opponent or enemy; triumphant; conquering. **2.** Characteristic of or expressing a sense of victory or fulfilment: *a victorious smile.* [Middle English, from Latin *victōriōsus,* from *victōria,* VICTORY.] —**vic·to·ri·ous·ly** *adv.* —**vic·to·ri·ous·ness** *n.*

vic·to·ry (vík-tri, -təri) *n., pl.* **-ries.** *Abbr.* **V 1.** Final and complete defeat of the enemy in a military engagement. **2.** Any successful struggle against an opponent or obstacle. **3.** The state of having triumphed. [Middle English, from Old French *victorie,* from Latin *victōria,* from *victor,* VICTOR.]

vic·tress (vík-triss, -tress) *n.* A female victor.

vict·ual (vitt'l) *n.* Also *nonstandard* **vit·tle.** *Usually plural.* **1.** Food fit for human consumption. **2.** Provisions; food supplies.

~*v.* **victualled** or *U.S.* **victualed, -ualling** or *U.S.* **-ualing, -uals.** Also *nonstandard* **vit·tle, -tled, -tling, -tles.** —*tr.* To provide with food. —*intr.* **1.** To lay in food supplies. **2.** *Rare.* To eat. [Middle English *vitaille,* from Old French, from Late Latin *victuālia,* plural of *victuālis,* provision, from Latin *victus,* sustenance, from the past participle of *vīvere,* to live.]

vict·ual·ler (vitt'l-ər) *n.* Also *U.S.* **vict·ual·er.** **1.** A supplier of victuals; a sutler. **2.** A supply ship. **3.** *Chiefly British.* One who is allowed to sell alcohol, such as an innkeeper or publican; a licensed victualler.

vi·cu·ña (vi-kéwn-ə, vī-, -kṓ-, -kṓon-yə) *n.* Also **vi·cu·na.** **1.** A llama-like ruminant mammal, *Vicugna vicugna,* of the central Andes, having fine, silky fleece. **2. a.** The fleece of this animal. **b.** Fabric made from this fleece. [Spanish, from Quechua *wikúña.*]

Vi·dal (vi-dál, -daál), **Gore** (1925–). U.S. novelist and essayist. His works include *Burr* (1974), a historical study, and *Myra Breckinridge* (1968), a satirical novel.

vi·de (vī-dee, -di, vídday) *Latin. Abbr.* **v., vid.** See. Used to direct a reader's attention: *vide page 64.* [Imperative of *vidēre,* to see.]

vide an·te (ánti ‖ *U.S.* aánti) *Latin.* See before.

vide in·fra (infrə) *Abbr.* **v.i.** *Latin.* See below.

vi·de·li·cet (vi-déeli-set, vī-, -dáyli-ket) *adv. Abbr.* **viz.** (see note at **viz**). That is; namely. Used to introduce examples, lists, or items. [Latin *vidēlicet,* it is easy (literally, permissible) to see, plainly, namely : *vidēre,* to see (see **vide**) + *licet,* it is permitted, from *licēre,* to be permitted. See **leisure**.]

vid·e·o (víddi-ō) *adj.* Of or pertaining to television, especially to systems for recording and playing back television sound and images.

Victoria Cross

FOR VALOUR

"The Commonwealth's most esteemed military medal

The Victoria Cross was instituted by Queen Victoria in 1856. Its Maltese cross is of bronze (early crosses were cast from cannons captured from the Russians at Sebastopol in 1855). The medal is awarded for conspicuous bravery or devotion to duty in the face of the enemy, and has been won by all ranks and ages. It is the Commonwealth's highest military award for bravery.

The oldest V.C. was Lieutenant W. Raynor, aged 69, in the Indian Mutiny (1857), the youngest 15-year-old Andrew Fitzgibbon, for gallantry in China in 1860. Commonwealth troops of both sexes, nurses, and civilians if they are serving with troops, are all eligible.

A total of 1,350 men have won the award, including three people twice. Almost half of these were awarded during World War I. Since World War II there have been 11 awards – including four to Australians during action in Vietnam, and two to Britons during the Falklands War of 1982.

STRIKING SIMPLICITY *The Victoria Cross has the inscription "For Valour" beneath the royal crest. On the reverse side, is inscribed the recipient's name and the date of the action for which the award was made.*

Victoriana

POPULAR ART OF THE VICTORIAN AGE
Increased wealth created a new demand for household ornaments

The reign of Queen Victoria (1837–1901) was a period of industrial expansion in Britain when new techniques of mass production made household goods cheaper and more widely available. Increased prosperity also created a fresh demand for decorative art, but because the new middle class had no tradition of art appreciation its taste was largely for bright, gaudy, ornate goods. Victoriana – the everyday art of the Victorian period – varies greatly in style and quality of construction. Although much of it lacks sophistication by today's standards, there is some which modern taste finds highly desirable.

Throughout the period there was a demand for papier-mâché goods such as firescreens, trays, and small tables, which were varnished and sometimes inlaid with mother-of-pearl. Increased wealth, and travel by the newly developed railways, led to a demand for souvenirs from places people visited. Fairings – china figures with captions on the base – were popular souvenirs at fairs, and Goss and other potteries produced miniatures of Bronze Age vases, Roman ewers, and Celtic drinking cups.

Coloured glass bowls, vases, and candlestick holders were popular, as was painted tinware. In the 1860s, the advent of electroplating led to the demise of the Sheffield-plate industry and surviving examples of the silver-plated products are much sought after today. Other examples of Victoriana include statues made of brass or gun-metal, ornate clocks, and embroideries for wall hanging.

The movement to greater ornament and richness was exemplified by the Great Exhibition of 1851 at which many exhibits were grotesquely overelaborate. In contrast, however, many copies of Sheraton and Hepplewhite furniture designs were being made by the 1870s. In late Victorian times, the designer and craftsman William Morris helped lead a move to greater simplicity of design and better workmanship, and Japanese art was discovered in the 1890s. In modern times, Victoriana has become much sought after since it exists in sufficient quantities to be within the range of most collectors. Even where it lacks sophistication, it often has an innocent charm.

A VICTORIAN DRAWING ROOM *This drawing room demonstrates the Victorian love of decoration, with every available space filled with ornaments. On the high shelf along the wall there are vases and dishes, and beneath them are drawings, paintings, and early photographs. Other ornaments include a bronze nymph, copies of Etruscan vases, and gilt Venetian mirrors.*

~*n., pl.* **-os. 1.** A video cassette recorder or video player. **2.** A recording made for playing back on a television set. **3.** A short video film made as promotional material or, especially, to accompany the playing of a pop music record: *nice video, shame about the song.* **4.** The visual portion of a televised broadcast, as distinguished from **audio** *(see).* **5.** *Chiefly U.S.* Television: *a star of stage, screen, and video.* [From Latin *vidēre,* to see. See **vide.**]
video camera *n.* A small hand-held camera similar to a cine camera but recording on video cassettes for subsequent playback through a television set.
video cassette *n.* A video tape contained in a cassette.
video cassette recorder *n. Abbr.* **VCR** A device for receiving broadcast television signals and for recording and playing back television pictures and sound by means of magnetic tape cassettes. Also called "video".
video disc *n.* A flat disc on which moving pictures and sound are recorded for playing through a television set. A laser beam is used to sense variations in height on the surface of the disc, and convert them into electronic pulses for playback.

video frequency *n.* A frequency suitable for use in producing television images, lying in the range 50 hertz to 5 megahertz.
video game *n.* Any of various games, played either between two persons or between one person and the machine, in which electronic controls are manipulated to manoeuvre small images on a display screen such as a television screen.
vid·e·o·phone (víddi-ō-fōn) *n.* A communication device that incorporates both telephone and television, allowing two people to talk to each other and see each other at the same time. [VIDEO + (TELE)-PHONE.]
video player *n.* A device for playing video discs or tapes through a television set. Also called "video".
video recorder *n.* A device for recording and playing back television signals using magnetic tape, cassettes, or other media.
vid·e·o·scan (víddi-ō-skan) *n.* A technique of machine character recognition in which a video camera records the shapes of the characters and matches the signals with data held in machine storage.
vid·e·o·tape (víddi-ō-tayp) *n.* A relatively wide **magnetic tape** *(see)* used to record television images, usually together with the associ-

ated sound, for subsequent playback or broadcasting. —**vid·e·o·tape** v.

video terminal n. A **visual display unit** (see).

vide post (pŏst) Latin. See below; see after.

vide su·pra (sōō-prə, sèw-) Abbr. **v.s.** Latin. See above.

vi·dette. Variant of **vedette**.

vid·i·con (víddi-kon) n. A small television camera tube that forms a charge-density image on a photoconductive surface for subsequent electron-beam scanning, used especially for hand-held cameras and closed-circuit systems. [VID(EO) + ICON(OSCOPE).]

vie (vī) v. **vied, vying, vies.** —intr. To strive for victory or superiority; contend; compete, as in an athletic contest. Used with for or with. —tr. Archaic. **1.** To offer or display for the sake of competition; match. **2.** To wager; bet. —See Synonyms at **rival.** [Shortened from Middle English envien, from Old French envier, to challenge, bid, from Latin invītāre, INVITE.]

Vi·en·na (vi-énnə). German **Wien** (veen). The capital of Austria, situated on the river Danube. In 1918, with the collapse of the Austro-Hungarian empire, Vienna was reduced from being the capital of one of the world's largest empires to the capital of a small country. Hitler's march into Vienna (1938) temporarily united Austria and Germany, but at the end of World War II the Allies divided the city into occupied sectors; it was not until 1955 that it was again a free city. An important cultural centre, Vienna was the home of Haydn, Mozart, Beethoven, Schubert, Brahms, Mahler, and Strauss. —**Vi·en·nese** (-ə-néez, veer- || néess) n. & adj.

Vientiane. See **Viangchan.**

Vierwaldstättersee. See **Lucerne, Lake.**

Vi·et·cong (vi-ét-kóng, vée-et-) n., pl. **Vietcong.** Also **Vi·et Cong.** Abbr. **V.C. 1.** In the Vietnam war, the National Liberation Front of South Vietnam, a communist revolutionary movement. **2.** The guerrilla and armed forces of this movement. **3.** A member of this movement or these forces. [Short for Vietnamese Viet Nam Cong Sam, Vietnamese Communist.] —**Vi·et·cong** adj.

Vi·et·minh (vi-ét-mín, vée-et-) n., pl. **Vietminh.** Also **Vi·et Minh. 1.** The Vietnamese league for national independence formed by an alliance of patriotic and revolutionary forces under the leadership of Ho Chi Minh that defeated the Japanese and the French between 1941 and 1954. **2.** A member of this front, especially of its armed forces. [Vietnamese, short for Viet Nam Doc Lap Dong Minh Hoi, Vietnam Federation of Independence.] —**Vi·et·minh** adj.

Vi·et·nam, Socialist Republic or (vi-ét-nám, vée-et-, -náam) Also **Vi·et Nam.** State of southeast Asia. It has two fertile rice-growing areas, the Mekong and Red-Black river deltas, separated by the Annamese range. The Kinh (Han Chinese people) founded the province of Tonkin in North Vietnam (c. 100 B.C.). Independent (939), it expanded to control all Vietnam by 1802, but was incorporated into French Indochina in the late 19th century. Liberation movements arose, and the Vietminh, active during the Japanese occupation of World War II, defeated the French at Dien Bien (1954). The country was then divided at the 17th parallel into North Vietnam, a Soviet client state led by Ho Chi Minh, and South Vietnam. The French withdrew from the south (1956), and from 1960, the north attempted to destabilise it. This brought U.S. intervention to aid the south which ended in 1973. The south fell to the communists (1975), and the present state was set up (1976). Ethnic Chinese began fleeing the country (1978), and Vietnamese "boat people" became an international refugee problem. Vietnam occupied Kampuchea in late 1978. Some 70 per cent of Vietnamese are farmers, and since 1976 there have been government development schemes, and reallocation of land. The north's considerable mineral resources, including coal, lignite, iron ore, chrome, bauxite, oil and gas, have been used in rapid industrialisation. Vietnam is a member of Comecon. Area, 329 556 square kilometres (127,209 square miles). Population, 56,600,000. Capital, Hanoi.

Vi·et·nam·ese (vi-ét-nə-méez, vée-et-, -na- || -méess) n., pl. **Vietnamese. 1.** A native or inhabitant of Vietnam. **2.** The language of Vietnam, commonly considered as belonging to the Mon-Khmer subfamily of Austro-Asiatic languages. Formerly called "Annamese". —**Vi·et·nam·ese** adj.

view (vew) n. **1.** An examination or inspection. **2.** A systematic survey; coverage: a wide-ranging view of trends in philosophy. **3.** Often plural. A specific perception, observation, or interpretation; a thought: her views on the situation. **4.** Often plural. A personal opinion. **5.** The field of vision: The ship came into view. **6. a.** A prospect or vista: From here you get a fine view of the town. **b.** Visual access or vantage: a room with a view. **c.** A picture of a landscape. **d.** An aspect, as of something seen from a given vantage point. **7.** Consideration: have a plan in view. **8.** Expectation; chance: has no view of success. **9.** In hunting, especially fox-hunting, a sighting of the quarry. **10.** Law. A formal inspection by a judge or jury of a corpse, a disputed property, or the scene of an alleged crime. —See Synonyms at **opinion.** —**in view of.** Taking into account; in consideration of. —**on view.** Being exhibited; placed so as to be seen. —**take a dim** or **poor view of.** To regard disapprovingly or unfavourably. —**with a view to.** With the intention or hope of.

~v. **viewed, viewing, views.** —tr. **1.** To see; behold; be present at a showing of: view the exhibition. **2.** To examine; inspect: view the figures. **3.** To survey or study mentally; consider: We view the recent developments with alarm. **4.** In hunting, especially fox-hunting, to sight (the quarry). **5.** To watch (television). **6.** To visit and inspect (a house, for example) when considering a purchase. **7.** Law. To inspect formally (a corpse, a disputed property, or the scene of

an alleged crime). —intr. To watch television. —See Synonyms at **see.** [Middle English vewe, from Old French veue, from the feminine past participle of veoir, to see, from Latin vidēre.]

view·da·ta (véw-day-tə, -daa-, -da-) n. Information or other graphic material appearing on a television or other display screen.

Viewdata n. The former name for **Prestel** (see).

view·er (véw-ər) n. **1.** One who views; especially, one who views television. **2.** Any of various optical devices used to facilitate the viewing of photographic transparencies by illuminating or magnifying them.

view·find·er (véw-fīndər) n. A system of lenses in a camera enabling the operator to see the scene that is to be photographed. Also called "finder".

view hal·loo, view hal·loa (hə-lōō, ha- || hóllər) n. **1.** A strident call given during a fox hunt by a servant or a follower to inform the huntsman that a fox has been sighted. **2.** A loud cry or clarion call announcing a sudden appearance or advent.

~interj. Used in fox-hunting to announce the sighting of a fox.

view·ing (véw-ing) n. **1.** The act or habit of watching television. **2.** Television programmes collectively: peak-hour viewing.

view·less (véw-ləss, -liss) adj. **1.** Lacking a view. **2.** Poetic. Invisible.

view·point (véw-poynt) n. A point of view.

vi·ges·i·mal (vi-jéssim'l) adj. **1.** Twentieth. **2.** Proceeding or occurring in intervals of 20. **3.** Based on or pertaining to 20. [From Latin vīgēsimus, vīcēsimus, twentieth, from vīcēnī, twenty each, from vīgintī, twenty.]

vig·il (víjil) n. **1. a.** A watch kept during normal sleeping hours. **b.** The duration of such a watch. **2.** The eve of a religious festival as observed by devotional watching. **3.** Usually plural. Ritual devotions observed on the eve of a holy day. [Middle English vigile, from Old French, from Latin vigilia, from vigil, alert.]

vig·i·lance (víjilənss) n. **1.** The state or quality of being vigilant; watchfulness. **2.** A chronic inability to sleep.

vigilance committee n. **1.** In inadequately policed communities, especially in North America, an informal council exercising police power for the capture, speedy trial, and summary punishment of criminal offenders. **2.** Any similar body of citizens organised to protect members of the community.

vig·i·lant (víjilənt) adj. On the alert; watchful. See Synonyms at **aware.** [Middle English, from Old French, from Latin vigilāns

VIETNAM

(stem *vigilant-*), present participle of *vigilāre,* to be alert, from *vigil,* alert.] —**vig·i·lant·ly** *adv.*

vig·i·lan·te (vĭji-lánti) *n.* One belonging to a vigilance committee. [Spanish, from Latin *vigilāns,* VIGILANT.]

vigil light *n.* **1.** A small candle kept burning in the chancel of some Christian churches to symbolize the presence of the Blessed Sacrament; an altar light. **2.** A candle lit by a worshipper for a special devotional purpose.

vi·gnette (vĭn-yét, veen-, *rarely* -ét) *n.* **1. a.** An unenclosed decorative design placed at the beginning or end of a book or a chapter of a book. **b.** Decorative tracery along the border of a page. **2.** An unbordered portrait that shades off into the surrounding colour at the edges. **3.** A literary, dramatic, or cinematic sketch having the intimate charm and subtlety attributed to vignette portraits: *The film was just a series of vignettes of medieval life.*
~*tr.v.* **vignetted, -gnetting, -gnettes. 1.** To soften the edges of (a picture) in the style of a vignette. **2.** To illustrate or embellish with vignettes. **3.** To portray in a vignette. [French, from Old French, "young vine", diminutive of *vigne,* VINE.]

vi·gnet·ter (vĭn-yét-ər, veen-, *rarely* -ét-) *n.* Also **vi·gnet·tist** (-ist) (for sense 2). **1.** A device used to print borderless illustrations and photographs. **2.** A person who makes or specialises in vignettes.

Vi·gny (veen-yée), **Alfred Victor, comte de** (1797–1863). French poet, novelist, and dramatist. He was one of the leaders of the French Romantic movement. His works include the play *Chatterton* (1835), *Cinq Mars* (1826), a historical novel, and *Les Destinées* (1864), a collection of poems which reveal his stoical pessimism.

vi·go·ro·so (vĭggə-rŏ-sō, vée gə-, -zō) *adv. Music.* Vigorous; with emphasis and spirit. Used as a direction. [Italian, from Medieval Latin *vigōrōsus,* from Latin *vigour,* VIGOUR.] —**vi·go·ro·so** *adj.*

vig·or·ous (vĭggərəss) *adj.* **1.** Strong and healthy; robust; hardy. **2.** Energetic; lively. —See Synonyms at **active, healthy.** —**vig·or·ous·ly** *adv.* —**vig·or·ous·ness** *n.*

vig·our, *U.S.* **vig·or** (vĭggər) *n.* **1.** Active physical or mental strength. **2.** The capacity for natural growth and survival, as of plants or animals. **3.** Expressive power or forcefulness, as of language. **4.** The most flourishing or active stage; the prime; the high point: *in the vigour of manhood.* **5.** *Chiefly U.S.* Legal effectiveness or validity. **6.** Energetic and rigorous exercise of power: *effected with vigour and resolution.* [Middle English *vigour,* from Old French, from Latin *vigor,* from *vigēre,* to be lively or vigorous.]

Vi·king (vī́king) *n. Sometimes small* **v.** Any of the Scandinavian mariners whose pirate bands attacked and pillaged coastal settlements of northern and western Europe from the eighth to the eleventh centuries. [Old Norse *vīkingr†.*] —**Vi·king** *adj.*

vil. village.

vi·la·yet (vi-lä́a-yet, vée-laa-yét) *n.* An administrative division of Turkey. [Turkish *vilāyet,* from Arabic *wilāyah,* province, from *wāli,* governor.]

vile (vīl) *adj.* **viler, vilest. 1.** Loathsome to the mind or senses; disgusting: *vile language; a vile smell.* **2.** Unpleasant or objectionable: *a vile play.* **3.** Miserably poor; wretched: *a vile existence.* **4.** Depraved; ignoble. **5.** Degrading; menial. [Middle English *vyle,* from Old French *vil,* from Latin *vīlis†.*] —**vile·ly** *adv.* —**vile·ness** *n.*

vil·i·fy (vĭlli-fī) *tr.v.* **-fied, -fying, -fies.** To defame; denigrate. See Synonyms at **malign.** [Middle English *vilifien,* from Late Latin *vīlificāre* : Latin *vīlis,* VILE + *facere,* to make.] —**vil·i·fi·ca·tion** (-fi-káysh'n) *n.* —**vil·i·fi·er** *n.*

vil·i·pend (vĭlli-pend) *tr.v.* **-pended, -pending, -pends.** *Rare.* **1.** To view or treat with contempt; despise. **2.** To disparage or abuse. [Middle English *vilipenden,* from Old French *vilipender,* from Latin *vīlipendere* : *vīlis,* VILE + *pendere,* to weigh, consider.]

vil·la (vílla) *n.* **1.** A large, luxurious country residence. **2.** In ancient Rome, a country estate with a substantial house. **3.** *Chiefly Scottish.* A detached or semi-detached middle-class house in the suburbs. **4.** *Chiefly British.* A holiday home, as at a seaside resort or holiday camp. [Italian, from Latin *vīlla,* country house.]

Vi·lla (vée-ə; *Spanish* béel-ya), **Pancho,** born Doroteo Arango, also known as Francisco Villa (1877–1923). Mexican bandit and revolutionary. He was active in successive revolts against Mexican governments (1910–15). After coming to terms with the Mexican Government (1920) he disbanded his army. He was assassinated.

vil·lage (vĭllij) *n. Abbr.* **v., V., vil. 1.** A small group of dwellings in a rural area, usually ranking in size between a hamlet and a town. **2.** In some North American states, an incorporated community smaller in population than a town. **3.** An old and distinctive urban district having its own particular character, usually quainter and better preserved than its surroundings, and in some cases actually being a former rural village now absorbed into a metropolitan or suburban area. **4.** The inhabitants of a village; villagers.
~*adj.* **1.** Of or pertaining to a village. **2.** Characteristic of villages; rustic. [Middle English, from Old French, from *ville,* village, farm, from Latin *vīlla,* VILLA.]

vil·lag·er (vĭllijər) *n.* An inhabitant of a village.

vil·lain (vĭllən; *for senses 3 and 4 also* vĭl-in, -ayn) *n.* **1.** A depraved, base-minded person; a scoundrel. **2.** A dramatic or fictional character who is typically at odds with the hero. **3.** *British Slang.* A criminal. **4.** *Obsolete.* A vile, brutish peasant. **5.** Variant of **villein.** [Middle English *vilain,* from Old French, originally "feudal serf", from Medieval Latin *vīllānus,* from Latin *vīlla,* country house.]

vil·lain·ess (vĭllə-niss, -ness, -néss) *n.* A female villain.

vil·lain·ous (vĭllənəss) *adj.* **1.** Viciously wicked or criminal. **2.** Ex-

---

Viking

SEA-WARRIORS FROM SCANDINAVIA

Viking colonies ranged from North America to Russia

"From the fury of the Northmen deliver us, O Lord!" For more than two centuries this prayer was uttered by Christians throughout the British Isles and Europe as the Vikings – the fierce, Scandinavian sea-warriors – sailed out in their longships in search of new domains. The pagan Norsemen – from Norway, Sweden, and Denmark – sought new territories because of overpopulation at home. Their incursions were also encouraged by the comparative weakness of the European nations.

The Viking expansion began between 786 and 800, when they raided the coasts of Saxon England, sacking the Northumbrian monasteries of Lindisfarne (Holy Island) in 793 and Jarrow in 794. In the 850s their tactics changed from raids to sustained invasion. This Danish Viking influx was checked by Alfred the Great of Wessex and his successors. A second wave of raids in the late 960s culminated 50 years later in the English acceptance of Canute – a former raider and the son of a Danish king – as sole ruler (1015–34).

The Vikings used their longboats to navigate rivers as well as oceans, and in the 9th and 10th centuries they settled in Iceland, Ireland, Spain, Italy, and Normandy (Norman is a variant of Northmen). Eventually, their colonies extended from central Russia to North America – where, in the 980s, they landed at a place which they named "Vinland" after the wild grapes growing there. It may have been the Canadian island of Newfoundland, where the remains of a Viking settlement were discovered in 1963.

In the wake of the warriors came the Viking farmers and craftsmen. Trade routes were forged from the Baltic Sea to Byzantium, and Viking merchants brought to Europe furs and amber from the far North and silks and spices from the East. The Viking colonies had a system of law and social order, and the Vikings introduced their rich literary culture, including the stirring Norse sagas and legends.

By the end of the 11th century the Viking Age had ended. In the autumn of 1066 (shortly before the successful Norman invasion) King Harold of England defeated a force of Viking raiders at Stamford Bridge, near York. It was the Vikings' last major attack abroad and within a few decades most of the once all-conquering warriors had returned to their homes in Scandinavia. They lacked the wealth, manpower, political expertise, and endurance to stay where they were not wanted. Those who did remain eventually became part of the societies they had once overrun and ruled.

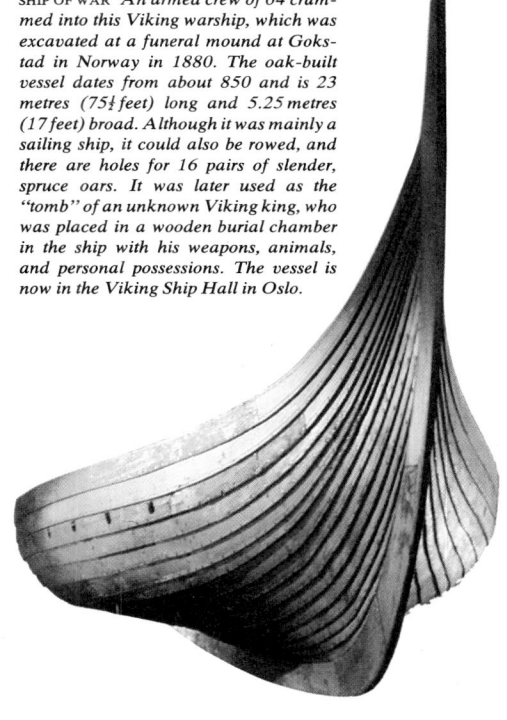

SHIP OF WAR *An armed crew of 64 crammed into this Viking warship, which was excavated at a funeral mound at Gokstad in Norway in 1880. The oak-built vessel dates from about 850 and is 23 metres (75¼ feet) long and 5.25 metres (17 feet) broad. Although it was mainly a sailing ship, it could also be rowed, and there are holes for 16 pairs of slender, spruce oars. It was later used as the "tomb" of an unknown Viking king, who was placed in a wooden burial chamber in the ship with his weapons, animals, and personal possessions. The vessel is now in the Viking Ship Hall in Oslo.*

vineyard *Part of the vineyard at Schloss Staufenberg, near Durbach in West Germany.*

tremely unpleasant; obnoxious. **—vil·lain·ous·ly** *adv.* **—vil·lain·ous·ness** *n.*

vil·lain·y (vílləni) *n., pl.* **-ies.** **1.** Viciousness of conduct or action. **2.** Baseness of mind or character. **3.** A treacherous or vicious act.

Vil·la-Lo·bos (víllə lṓ-boss, vée-lə, -laa; *Portuguese* vééla lṓ-bōōss), **Heitor** (1887–1959). Brazilian composer. He was mainly self-taught, and his many works are influenced by Brazilian folksong.

vil·la·nelle (víllə-nél) *n.* A 19-line poem of fixed form consisting of five tercets and a final quatrain based on two rhymes, with the first and third lines of the first tercet repeated alternately as a refrain closing the succeeding stanzas and joined as the final couplet of the quatrain. [French, from Italian *villanella,* an old rustic Italian song, from *villanello,* rustic, from *villano,* peasant, from Medieval Latin *vīllānus.* See **villain.**]

vil·lat·ic (vi-láttik) *adj. Rare.* Rustic; rural. [Latin *vīllāticus,* from *vīlla,* VILLA.]

-ville (vil) *n. comb. form. Chiefly U.S. Slang.* Indicates a place of a specified kind; for example, *Redneckville.*
~*n. & adj. comb. form.* Indicates a condition or state of a specified kind; for example, *dullsville; thrillsville.* [Abstracted from town names common in the United States (for example, *Charlottesville*), from French *ville,* town, ultimately from Latin *villa.*]

vil·lein (víl-ən, -in, -ayn) *n.* Also **vil·lain.** In feudal times, a member of a class of serfs who held the legal status of freemen in their dealings with all persons except their lord, to whom they owed certain services or rents in return for their land. [Middle English *villein,* variant of *vilain,* VILLAIN.]

vil·lein·age (víl-ən-ij, -in-, -ayn-) *n.* **1.** The legal status or condition of a villein. **2.** The legal tenure by which a villein held his land. Also called "bondage".

vil·li·form (vílli-fawrm) *adj.* Having the form of a villus or the appearance of villi.

Vil·lon (vee-yóN), **François** (*c.* 1431–*c.* 1463). French poet. He led a life of vagrancy after studying at the University of Paris. A sentence to hang was commuted to banishment in 1463 and nothing is known of him after that date. His only surviving works are the satirical *Testament* (*c.* 1461) and a few other poems.

vil·los·i·ty (vi-lóssəti) *n., pl.* **-ties.** **1.** The condition of being villous. **2.** A villous surface or coating. **3.** A villus or set of villi.

vil·lous (víl-əss) *adj.* Also **vil·lose** (-ōz, -ōss). **1.** Of, pertaining to, resembling, or covered with villi. **2.** *Botany.* Covered with fine, unmatted hairs. [Middle English, from Latin *villōsus,* from *villus,* shaggy hair, VILLUS.] **—vil·lous·ly** *adv.*

vil·lus (víl-əss) *n., pl.* **villi** (-ī). **1.** *Biology.* Any minute projection arising from a mucous membrane. **2.** *Botany.* A fine, hairlike epidermal outgrowth. [Latin, shaggy hair.]

Vil·ni·us (vílni-əss, -ōōss). Capital of the Lithuanian S.S.R. Founded in the tenth century on the river Vilija, it became the capital of the grand duchy of Lithuania in 1323. In 1569 it was severely damaged in the wars following the union between Poland and Lithuania, and became part of Russia on the partition of Poland (1795). Between 1920 and 1939 it again reverted to Poland.

vim (vim) *n. Informal.* Ebullient vitality and energy. [Latin *vim,* accusative of *vīs,* power.]

Vim·i·nal (vímmin'l) *n.* One of the seven hills of Rome. [Latin *Vīminālis (collis),* "(hill) of osiers" (from the willow copse on the hill), from *vīmen,* osier.]

vi·min·e·ous (vi-mínni-əss) *adj. Botany.* Having or pertaining to long, flexible shoots. [Latin *vimineus,* from *vīmen,* osier.]

vin-. Variant of **vini-.**

vi·na (véénə) *n.* A stringed musical instrument of India that has a long, fretted fingerboard with resonating gourds at each end. [Hindi *vīṇā,* from Sanskrit *vīṇā*†.]

vi·na·ceous (vī-náyshəss) *adj.* Having the colour of red wine; wine-red. [Latin *vīnāceus,* of wine, from *vīnum,* wine.]

vin·ai·grette (vín-ay-grét, -i-) *n.* **1.** A small decorative bottle or container with a perforated top, used for holding an aromatic restorative, such as smelling salts. **2.** Vinaigrette sauce.
~*adj.* Served or prepared with vinaigrette sauce. [French, from Old French *vinaigre,* VINEGAR.]

vinaigrette sauce *n.* A cold sauce or dressing made of vinegar and oil flavoured with herbs and other seasonings.

vi·nasse (vi-náss) *n.* The residue left in a still after the process of distillation. [French, from Latin *vīnācea,* feminine of *vīnāceus,* of wine, VINACEOUS.]

vin·blas·tine (vin-bláss-teen, -blaáss-) *n.* An alkaloid obtained from a periwinkle plant, *Vinca rosea,* that is used to treat cancer of the lymphatic system. [Shortened from *vincaleucoblastine* : New Latin *vinca,* periwinkle + *leucoblast* (LEUCO- + -BLAST) + -INE.]

vin·ca (víngkə) *n.* Any plant of the genus *Vinca;* especially, a **periwinkle** *(see).* [New Latin, from Latin *(per)vinca,* PERIWINKLE.]

Vin·cent's disease (vínss'nts) *n. Pathology.* **Trench mouth** *(see).* Also called "Vincent's angina". [After Hyacinthe *Vincent* (1862–1950), French physician.]

Vinci, Leonardo da. See **Leonardo da Vinci.**

vin·ci·ble (vínss-əb'l, -ib'l) *adj. Rare.* Capable of being overcome or defeated. [Latin *vincibilis,* from *vincere,* to conquer.] **—vin·ci·bil·i·ty** (-ə-bílləti, -i-) *n.*

vin·cu·lum (víngkew-ləm) *n., pl.* **-la** (-lə). **1.** *Mathematics.* A bar drawn over two or more algebraic terms to indicate that they are to be treated as a single term. **2.** *Anatomy.* **a.** A ligament. **b.** Any connecting band or fold, such as the umbilical cord or the membranes below the tongue. **3.** A bond or tie. [Latin, band, cord, from *vincīre*†, to tie.]

Vin·da·loo (víndə-lṓō) *adj.* Served with a hot, sour curry sauce: *chicken Vindaloo.* [Hindi.]

vin·di·ca·ble (víndikəb'l) *adj.* Justifiable. [VINDIC(ATE) + -ABLE.]

vin·di·cate (víndi-kayt) *tr.v.* **-cated, -cating, -cates.** **1.** To clear of accusation, blame, suspicion, or doubt with supporting arguments or proof. **2.** To justify or support: *vindicate one's claim.* **3.** To justify or prove the worth of, especially in the light of later developments. [Latin *vindicāre,* to claim, defend, revenge, from *vindex,* claimant, defender, avenger.] **—vin·di·ca·tor** (-kaytər) *n.*

vin·di·ca·tion (víndi-káysh'n) *n.* **1.** The act of vindicating or condition of being vindicated. **2.** The evidence, argument, event, or the like, that serves to justify a claim or deed.

vin·di·ca·to·ry (víndi-kə-tri, -təri, -kaytəri, -káytəri) *adj.* **1.** Vindicating; justifying. **2.** Exacting retribution; punitive.

vin·dic·tive (vin-díktiv) *adj.* **1.** Disposed to seek revenge; revengeful. **2.** Unforgiving; bitter; spiteful. **3.** *Law.* Designating damages awarded in excess of simple compensation in order to punish the defendant. [From Latin *vindicta,* vengeance, from *vindicāre,* to revenge, VINDICATE.] **—vin·dic·tive·ly** *adv.* **—vin·dic·tive·ness** *n.*
Synonyms: *vindictive, spiteful, vengeful, revengeful.*

vine (vīn) *n.* **1.** Any plant having a flexible stem supported by climbing, twining, or creeping along a surface. **2.** The stem of such a plant. **3. a.** A grapevine. **b.** Grapevines collectively: *products of the vine.* [Middle English, from Old French *vine, vigne,* from Latin *vīnea,* from the feminine of *vīneus,* of wine, from *vīnum,* wine.] **—vin·y** *adj.*

vine·dress·er (vī́n-dressər) *n.* A person who cultivates and tends grapevines.

vin·e·gar (vínnigər) *n.* **1.** A sour, impure dilute solution of acetic acid obtained by fermentation beyond the alcohol stage and used as a condiment and preservative. **2.** *Informal.* Sourness; ill temper. [Middle English *vinegre,* from Old French *vinaigre, vyn egre* : *vin,* wine, from Latin *vīnum* + *aigre,* sour, from Latin *acer,* sharp.]

vinegar eel *n.* A small nematode worm, *Turbatrix aceti,* that feeds on the organisms that cause fermentation in vinegar. Also called "eelworm", "vinegar worm".

vinegar fly *n.* Any of various flies of the genus *Drosophila* that often become pests by breeding in poorly sealed preserves and pickles.

vin·e·gar·roon (vínnigə-rṓōn) *n.* Also **vin·e·ga·rone** (-rṓn). A large, nonvenomous scorpion-like arachnid, *Mastigoproctus giganteus,* of the southern United States and Mexico, that emits a strong odour of vinegar when disturbed. [Mexican Spanish *vinagrón,* from Spanish *vinagre,* vinegar, from Old French *vinaigre.* See **vinegar.**]

vin·e·gar·y (vínnigər-i) *adj.* Also **vin·e·gar·ish** (-ish). **1.** Having the nature of vinegar; sour; acid: *a vinegary taste.* **2.** Sour in disposition or speech; ill-tempered.

vine maple *n.* A maple, *Acer circinatum,* of western North America, having red fruits and white and purple flowers.

vin·er·y (vī́nəri) *n., pl.* **-ies.** An area or greenhouse for growing vines.

vine·yard (vín-yərd; *also spelling pronunciations* vī́n-, -yaard) *n.* **1.** A plot of ground planted with cultivated grapevines. **2.** *Informal.* A sphere of spiritual, mental, or physical endeavour.

vingt-et-un (vánt-ay-úrn, váNt-, -ōōn, -ṓN) *n.* A card game, **pontoon** *(see).* [French, twenty-one (the maximum score of a hand).]

vini-, vino-, vin- *comb. form.* Indicates wine; for example, **viniculture, vinometer, vinyl.** [From Latin *vīnum,* wine.]

vi·nic (vī́nik) *adj.* Of, contained in, or derived from wine. [From Latin *vīnum,* wine. See **vine.**]

vin·i·cul·ture (vínni-kulchər, -kúlchər || vī́ni-) *n.* The cultivation of grapes and making of wine; viticulture. **—vin·i·cul·tur·al** *adj.* **—vin·i·cul·tur·ist** *n.*

Vin·land (vín-lənd, -land). Also **Vine·land** (vī́n-). An area of Newfoundland. Situated around the Hudson Straits and the Gulf of St. Lawrence according to the Vinland Map (1440), the area was supposedly explored by Leif Ericsson in the 11th century.

vi·no (véénō) *n., pl.* **-nos.** *Informal.* Wine. [Italian and Spanish, from Latin *vīnum,* wine. See **vine.**]

vi·nom·e·ter (vī-nómmitər, vi-) *n.* A hydrometer used to determine the percentage of alcohol in a wine.

vin or·di·naire (váN órdi-naír) *n., pl.* **vins ordinaires** (*pronounced as singular*). *French.* An ordinary inexpensive wine; a table wine.

vi·nous (vī́nəss) *adj.* **1.** Of or pertaining to wine or its consumption: *a vinous party.* **2.** Affected or caused by the consumption of wine: *a vinous nose; vinous laughter.* **3.** Having the colour of wine. [Latin *vinōsus,* from *vīnum,* wine. See **vine.**] **—vi·nos·i·ty** (vī-nóssəti) *n.*

Vin·son Massif (vínss'n). A mountain peak of Antarctica. One of the Ellsworth Mountains, it rises to 5 139 metres (16,860 feet), the continent's highest point.

vin·tage (víntij) *n.* **1.** The yield of wine or grapes from a particular vineyard or district during one season. **2.** Wine, usually of high quality, identified as to year and vineyard or district of origin. Also called "vintage wine". **3.** The year in which or place where a particular wine was bottled. **4.** The harvesting of a grape crop or the initial stages of winemaking. **5.** The season for such harvesting or winemaking. **6.** *Informal.* Any group or collection of persons or things sharing certain characteristics. **7.** *Informal.* A year or period of origin: *a dress of 1942 vintage.*
~*adj.* **1.** Designating wine of an outstandingly good year. **2.** Characterised by excellence, maturity, and enduring appeal; venerable; classic. **3.** Typical of the best work of a specified author or other

artist: *vintage Coward.* **4.** Old or outmoded. [Middle English *vyntage,* variant (influenced by *vineter,* VINTNER) of *vendage,* from Old French, from Latin *vindēmia,* grape gathering : *vīnum,* wine (see **vine**) + *dēmere,* to take off : *dē-,* off + *emere,* to take.]

vintage car *n.* A motor car made between 1919 and 1930. Compare **veteran car.**

vin·tag·er (vı́ntijər) *n.* A harvester of wine grapes.

vintage year *n.* **1.** The year in which a vintage wine is produced. **2.** Any year of outstanding achievement or success.

vint·ner (vı́ntnər) *n.* A wine merchant. [Middle English *vineter,* from Old French *vinetier,* from Medieval Latin *vīnātārius,* from Latin *vīnētum,* vineyard, from *vīnum,* wine. See **vine.**]

vi·nyl (vī́n'l, vı́nil) *n.* **1.** The univalent chemical radical CH_2:CH-, derived from ethene. **2.** Any of various compounds containing this group, typically highly reactive, easily polymerised, and used as basic materials for plastics. **3.** Any of various synthetic resins, typically tough, flexible, and shiny, used, for example, in coverings, clothing, and paints. **—on vinyl.** Commercially recorded. [VIN(I)- + -YL.] **—vi·nyl** *adj.*

vinyl chloride *n.* A flammable gas, CH_2:CHCl, used as a monomer for polyvinyl chloride (PVC). Also called "chloroethene".

Vi·ny·lite *n.* A trademark for a type of vinyl plastic.

vi·ol (vī́-əl) *n.* **1.** Any of a family of stringed instruments, chiefly of the 16th and 17th centuries, having a fretted fingerboard, usually six strings, a flat back, and played with a curved bow. **2.** A viola da gamba. [Old French *viole,* from Old Provençal *viola,* VIOLA (instrument).]

vi·o·la[1] (vi-ṓlə, vée-ə-lə) *n.* **1.** A four-stringed musical instrument of the violin family, slightly larger than a violin, tuned a fifth lower, and having a deeper, more sonorous tone; the alto or tenor violin. **2.** An organ stop usually of eight-foot or four-foot pitch yielding stringlike tones. [Italian, from Old Provençal *viola, viula,* perhaps from *violar,* to play the viola (imitative).]

vi·o·la[2] (vī́-ə-lə, vée-, -ō-, vī-ṓlə, vi-) *n.* Any plant of the genus *Viola,* which includes the violets and pansies. [New Latin *Viola,* from Latin *viola,* VIOLET.]

vi·o·la·ble (vī́-ə-ləb'l) *adj.* Capable of being violated or easily broken. **—vi·o·la·bil·i·ty** (-lə-bı́lləti), **vi·o·la·ble·ness** *n.* **—vi·o·la·bly** *adv.*

vi·o·la·ceous (vī́-ə-láyshəss, vée-) *adj.* **1.** Of or belonging to the family Violaceae, which comprises the violets and pansies. **2.** Having a violet colour. [Latin *violāceus* : *viola,* VIOLET + -ACEOUS.]

vi·o·la da brac·cio (vi-ṓlə də bráachō) *n.* A stringed instrument of the viol family with approximately the range of the viola. [Italian, "viola of the arm".]

vi·o·la da gam·ba (vi-ṓlə də gámbə || *U.S.* gáambə). **1.** A stringed instrument, the bass of the viol family, with approximately the range of the cello. Also called "viol", "bass viol", "gamba". **2.** An organ stop of eight-foot pitch yielding tones similar to those of the viola da gamba. [Italian, "viola of the leg".]

vi·o·la d'a·mo·re (vi-ṓlə da-máw-ray || daa-, -mṓ-) *n.* A stringed instrument, the tenor of the viol family, having 7 stopped strings and 7 or 14 sympathetic strings that produce a characteristic silvery tone. [Italian, "viola of love".]

vi·o·late (vī́-ə-layt || -ō-) *tr.v.* **-lated, -lating, -lates. 1.** To break (a law or regulation, for example) intentionally or unintentionally; fail to keep; transgress. **2.** To injure the person or property of; especially, to rape. **3.** To do harm to (property or qualities considered sacred); profane; desecrate. **4.** To disturb rudely or improperly; break in upon without right: *violate the peace.* [Middle English *violaten,* from Latin *violāre,* from *vīs,* force.] **—vi·o·la·tive** (-lətiv, -laytiv) *adj.* **—vi·o·la·tor** (-laytər) *n.*

vi·o·la·tion (vī́-ə-láysh'n || -ō-) *n.* **1.** The act of violating or the condition of being violated. **2.** An instance of violation; a transgression: *violations of the ceasefire.* —See Synonyms at **breach.**

vi·o·lence (vī́-ə-lənss || -ō-, vī́lənss) *n.* **1.** Physical force exerted for the purpose of violating, damaging, or abusing: *"The essence of war is violence"* (T.B. Macaulay). **2.** An act or instance of violent action or behaviour. **3.** Intensity or severity, as in natural phenomena; untamed force: *the violence of a hurricane.* **4.** The abusive or unjust exercise of power; an outrage; a wrong. **5.** Abuse or injury to meaning, content, or intent: *do violence to a text.* **6.** Vehemence of feeling or expression; fervour.

vi·o·lent (vī́ə-lənt || -ō-, vī́lənt) *adj.* **1.** Displaying or proceeding from extreme or uncontrolled physical force or rough action. **2.** Exhibiting intense force or effect; extreme: *violent contrast.* **3.** Caused by or displaying undue mental or emotional force: *a violent antipathy.* **4.** Characterised by the immoderate use of force; severe; harsh. **5.** Caused by unexpected force or injury rather than by natural causes: *a violent death.* [Middle English, from Old French, from Latin *violentus.*] **—vi·o·lent·ly** *adv.*

violent storm *n.* A wind whose speed is 28.5 to 32.6 metres per second (56 to 63 knots), force 11 on the Beaufort scale.

vi·o·let (vī́-ə-lət, -lit || -ō-, vī́-lət) *n.* **1.** Any of various low-growing plants of the genus *Viola,* having spurred, irregular flowers that are characteristically purplish-blue but sometimes yellow or white. **2.** Any of several similar but unrelated plants, such as the **African violet** *(see).* **3.** Any of a group of colours, reddish blue in hue, that may vary in lightness and saturation; the hue of that portion of the spectrum that may be evoked in the normal observer by radiant energy of wavelengths approximately 420 nanometres. **4.** A dye or pigment of this colour. **5. a.** Any object of this colour. **b.** Clothing of this colour. [Middle English, from Old French *violete,* diminutive of *viole,* from Latin *viola,* from the same Mediterranean origin as Greek *ion,* violet. See **iodine.**] **—vi·o·let** *adj.*

violet *The common violet,* Viola riviniana *(above), flowers in spring in woodlands, hedgerows, meadows, and on heaths throughout Europe and parts of North America.*

vi·o·lin (vī-ə-lı́n || -ō-, -lin) *n. Abbr.* **v. 1.** A stringed instrument played with a bow, having four strings tuned at intervals of a fifth, an unfretted fingerboard, and a shallower body than the viol, and capable of great flexibility in range, tone, and dynamics. Also informally called "fiddle". **2.** A violinist. [Italian *violino,* diminutive of *viola,* VIOLA (instrument).]

vi·o·lin·ist (vī-ə-lı́nnist, -linnist) *n.* A person who plays the violin.

vi·o·list *(For sense 1* vi-ṓlist, *for sense 2* vī́-əlist) *n.* **1.** *U.S.* A person who plays the viola. **2.** A person who plays a viol.

Viol·let-le-Duc (vi-ō-láy-lə-dúk, *French* -lel-), **Eugène Emmanuel.** (1814–79). French architect and author. He was a leader of the Gothic revival in France and designed the restoration of many medieval buildings including Notre Dame in Paris, and the city of Carcassonne.

vi·o·lon·cel·list (vī́-ə-lən-chéllist, vée-, -lin-) *n.* A **cellist** *(see).*

vi·o·lon·cel·lo (vī́-ə-lən-chéllō, vée-, -lin-) *n., pl.* **-los.** A **cello** *(see).* [Italian, diminutive of *violone,* VIOLONE.]

vi·o·lone (vī́-ə-lōn, vée-ə-lṓ-nay) *n.* **1.** A stringed instrument, the double bass of the viol family, with approximately the range of a modern double bass. **2.** A 16-foot organ stop yielding stringlike tones similar to a cello. [Italian, augmentative of *viola,* VIOLA (instrument).]

vi·o·my·cin (vī́-ō-mī́-sin, -ə-) *n.* An antibiotic obtained from various species of the bacterium *Streptomyces,* used to treat tuberculosis. [VIO(LET) (referring to the colour of the soil mould) + -MYCIN.]

VIP (vée-ī-pée) *n., pl.* **VIPs** or **VIP's.** A person regarded as being very important, and therefore accorded specially courteous or luxurious treatment; a dignitary or celebrity. [*V*ery *I*mportant *P*erson.]

vi·per (vī́pər) *n.* **1.** Any of various venomous Old World snakes of the family Viperidae; especially, a common Eurasian species, *Vipera berus,* which is also called "adder". **2.** A **pit viper** *(see).* **3.** Broadly, any venomous or supposedly venomous snake. **4.** A treacherous or malicious person. [Old French *viperc,* from Latin *vīpera,* snake, contracted from *vivipara* (unattested), "that which produces living young" (from the ancient belief that vipers were viviparous) : *vīvus,* alive + *parere,* to produce.]

vi·per·ine (vī́pə-rīn || -rin) *adj.* Of, resembling, or characteristic of a viper.

vi·per·ous (vī́pər-əss) *adj.* Also **vi·per·ish** (-ish). **1.** Suggestive of a viper or venomous snake. **2.** Venomous; spiteful; malicious.

viper's bugloss *n.* A bristly plant, *Echium vulgare,* native to Eurasia, having bright blue flowers. Also *U.S.* "blueweed".

vir·a·gin·i·ty (vı́rrə-jı́nnəti) *n.* Masculine mentality and psychology in a woman. [From Latin *virāgō* (stem *virāgin-*), manlike woman, VIRAGO.] **—vir·a·gin·ous** (vi-rájinəss) *adj.*

vi·ra·go (vi-ráa-gō, -ráy-) *n., pl.* **-goes** or **-gos. 1.** A noisy, domineering woman; a scold. **2.** *Archaic.* A large, strong, or courageous woman; an Amazon. [Latin *virāgō,* from *vir,* man.]

vi·ral (vī́r-əl) *adj.* Of, pertaining to, or caused by a virus. [From VIRUS.]

vir·e·lay (vı́rri-lay) *n.* Also *French* **vi·re·lai** (veer-láy). Any of several medieval French verse and song forms, especially one in which each stanza has two rhymes, the end rhyme recurring as the first rhyme of the following stanza. [Middle English *virelai,* from Old French, variant (influenced by *lai,* LAY) of *vireli,* perhaps originally a meaningless refrain.]

vir·e·o (vı́rri-ō) *n., pl.* **-os.** Any of various small New World birds of the genus *Vireo,* having greyish or greenish plumage. [Latin *vireo,* greenfinch, from *virēre,* to be green.]

vi·res·cence (vi-réss'nss) *n.* The state or process of becoming green; specifically, the abnormal development of green coloration in plant parts normally not green.

vi·res·cent (vi-réss'nt) *adj.* Becoming green; greenish. [Latin *virēscēns* (stem *virēscent-*), present participle of *virēscere,* to become green, from *virēre,* to be green.]

vir·ga (vúrgə) *n.* Wisps of precipitation streaming from a cloud but evaporating before reaching the earth. [Latin, twig, stripe.]

vir·gate[1] (vúr-gət, -git, -gayt) *adj.* Shaped like a wand or rod; straight, long, and slender. [Latin *virgātus,* made of twigs, from *virga,* twig. See **virga.**]

virgate[2] *n.* An early English measure of land area of varying extent but most often equivalent to about 30 acres. [Medieval Latin *virgāta,* from *virga,* a measure, yard, from Latin, twig. See **virga.**]

Vir·gil or **Ver·gil** (vérjil), born Publius Vergilius Maro (70-19 B.C.). Roman poet. His greatest work is his epic poem *Aeneid,* which tells of the wanderings of Aeneas after the sack of Troy, the founding of Rome, and the Julian dynasty. Among his other works are his *Eclogues,* and the *Georgics.*

vir·gin (vúrjin) *n.* **1.** A person who has not experienced sexual intercourse. **2.** A chaste or unmarried woman; a maiden. **3.** An unmarried woman who has taken religious vows of chastity. **4.** *Capital* **V.** Mary, the mother of Jesus. Preceded by *the.* Also called "Blessed Virgin". **5.** Any female animal that has not mated. **6.** *Capital* **V.** The constellation and the sign of the zodiac, **Virgo** *(see).*
~*adj.* **1.** Characteristic of or appropriate to a virgin; chaste; maidenly. **2.** In a pure or natural state; untouched; unsullied: *virgin snow.* **3.** Unused, uncultivated, or unexplored: *the virgin west of 19-century America.* **4.** Existing in native or raw form; not processed or refined. **5.** Happening for the first time; initial: *"guiding my virgin steps on the hard road of letters"* (Somerset Maugham). **6.** Obtained directly from the first pressing. Said of vegetable oils.

PRONUNCIATION KEY

a, trap; aa, father; ai, **fair**; ar, star; aw, **lawn**; ay, **play**; b, bb, stab; **rubber**; ch, **church**; ck, **ticket**; d, dd, **dead**; **ladder**; e, dress; ee, **bee**; er, defer; ew, **few**; ewr, **pure**; ə, about; ər, letter; f, ff, **fife**; **differ**; g, gg, **giggle**; h, **hat**; i, **kit**; ī, price; īr, **fire**; j, **judge**; k, **kick**; l, ll, **let**; 'l, needle; m, mm, **man**; n, nn, **no**; 'n, **sudden**; ng, **thing**; o, **lot**; ō, **no**; ŏŏ, **foot**; ōō, **shoe**; oor, **poor**; ow, **cow**; owr, **hour**; oy, **boy**; p, pp, **pepper**; r, rr, **red**; s, ss, **sauce**; sh, **ship**; t, tt, **totter**; th, **thick**; th, **this**; **smooth**; u, **cut**; ur, **turn**; v, vv, **valve**; w, **wet**; y, **yes**; z, zz, **zebra**; zh, **vision**; **pleasure**

IN FOREIGN WORDS:

aN, oN, **Saint-Saëns**; hl, **Llanelli**; **Hluhluwe**; kh, **loch**; **lough**; **Khaled**

STRESS MARK:

ı́n-sīt, insight; in-sī́t, incite

Virginia creeper Parthenocissus tricuspidata veitchii, *the small-leafed Virginia creeper (above), is a native of China and Japan. It has tendrils with adhesive tips, which allow it to climb walls and fences.*

viscacha *Mountain viscachas (above) shelter in rock crevices and burrows at night, emerging to feed on plants by day. They live in the mountains of South America at altitudes of up to 5000 metres (nearly 16,500 feet).*

7. Unprocessed. Said of wool. **8.** Obtained by smelting ore, rather than recycling scrap. Said of metals. **9.** *Physics.* Not having experienced any collisions. Said of neutrons. [Middle English, from Old French *virgine,* from Latin *virgō†* (stem *virgin-*).]

vir·gin·al[1] (vúrjin'l) *adj.* **1.** Pertaining to, characteristic of, or befitting a virgin; chaste; pure. **2.** Remaining in a state of virginity. **3.** Untouched or unsullied; fresh.

virginal[2] *n. Often plural.* A small, legless rectangular harpsichord popular in the 16th and 17th centuries. [From VIRGIN (because it was played by young girls).]

virgin birth *n. Sometimes capital* **V**, *Capital* **B**. *Theology.* The doctrine that Jesus was miraculously begotten by God and born of Mary, who was a virgin.

Vir·gin·ia[1] (vər-jínni-ə). State of the United States. Bordering the Mid-Atlantic, it has land borders with Maryland, West Virginia, Kentucky, Tenessee, and North Carolina. First settled by the English (1607), it was named after Queen Elizabeth, "the Virgin Queen". One of the original 13 states, it was re-admitted to the Union in 1870, following the American Civil War, during which it was part of the Confederacy. Richmond is the state capital.

Virginia[2] *n.* Cured tobacco of a kind originally grown in Virginia.

Virginia creeper *n.* **1.** A North American climbing vine, *Parthenocissus quinquefolia,* having compound leaves with five leaflets and bluish-black, berry-like fruit. Also called "woodbine". **2.** A similar vine from China and Japan, *P. tricuspidata* (or *Ampelopsis veitchii*). Also called "Japanese ivy".

Virginia fence *n. U.S.* A **worm fence** *(see).* Also *U.S.* "Virginia rail fence".

Virginia reel *n.* **1.** A country dance in which couples, initially facing each other from two parallel lines, perform various figures to the instructions of a caller. **2.** A piece of music for this dance.

virginia stock *n. Sometimes capital* **V**. An annual plant, *Malcolmia maritima,* from southern Europe, having four-pettalled lilac, red, or white flowers and often grown in gardens. [After *Virginia,* where it was cultivated.]

Virgin Islands. An archipelago in the Caribbean. A group of about one hundred islands east of Puerto Rico in the West Indies. About one-third of the islands are owned by Britain; the remaining two-thirds are the property of the United States.

vir·gin·i·ty (vər-jínnəti) *n., pl.* **-ties.** **1.** The condition of being a virgin; virginal chastity. **2.** The state of being pure, unsullied, or untouched.

Virgin Mary *n.* The mother of Jesus, **Mary** *(see).* Usually preceded by *the.*

Virgin Queen *n.* See **Elizabeth I of England.** Usually preceded by *the.*

Vir·go (vúrgō) *n.* **1.** A constellation in the region of the celestial equator near Leo and Libra. **2. a.** The sixth sign of the **zodiac. b.** One born under this sign. Also called the "Virgin". [Latin *virgō,* VIRGIN.]

virgo in·tac·ta (in-táktə, ín-) *n., pl.* **virgines intactae** (vúr-ji-neez in-ták-tee, -gi-nayz -tī). A virgin girl or woman with an intact hymen. [Latin, "untouched virgin".]

vir·gu·late (vúrgew-lət, -lit, -layt) *adj.* Shaped like a small rod. [From Latin *virgula,* small rod. See **virgule.**]

vir·gule (vúrgewl) *n.* A punctuation mark, a **solidus** *(see).* [French, comma, from Latin *virgula,* small rod, from *virga,* rod, twig.]

vir·id (vírrid) *adj.* Green with or as if with vegetation; verdant. [Latin *viridis,* green, from *virēre,* to be green.] **—vi·rid·i·ty** (vi-ríddəti) *n.*

vir·i·des·cent (virri-déss'nt) *adj.* **1.** Green or slightly green. **2.** Turning green. [Latin *viridis,* green, VIRID + -ESCENT.] **—vir·i·des·cence** *n.*

vi·rid·i·an (vi-ríddi-ən) *n.* A durable bluish-green pigment. [From Latin *viridis,* green, VIRID.]

vir·ile (vírrīl || *U.S. also* vírrəl) *adj.* **1.** Of or having the characteristics of an adult male. **2.** Having qualities traditionally associated with men, such as strength, vigour, or force. **3.** Of or pertaining to male sexual functions. [Middle English, from Old French *viril,* from Latin *virīlis,* from *vir,* man.]

vir·i·lism (vírriliz'm) *n.* The abnormal development of male characteristics in a woman. [VIRILE + -ISM.]

vi·ril·i·ty (vi-ríllәti, və-) *n., pl.* **-ties.** **1. a.** Masculine vigour; potency. **b.** Manhood. **2.** Qualities of strength or for forcefulness traditionally ascribed to men.

vi·ri·on (vīr-i-on, vírri-) *n.* The complete inert form of a virus as found outside a host cell, consisting of a protein coat surrounding a strand or strands of nucleic acid. [From *viri-,* combining form of VIRUS + -ON (particle).]

vi·rol·o·gy (vīr-óllәji) *n.* The study of viruses and viral diseases. [VIR(US) + -LOGY.] **—vi·ro·log·i·cal** (vīr-ə-lójik'l) **—vi·rolo·gist** (vīr-óllәjist) *n.*

vir·tu (vur-tōō, veer-) *n.* Also **ver·tu** (ver-). **1.** A knowledge of or taste for the fine arts. **2.** The quality of being beautiful, rare, or otherwise interesting to a collector. Used in the phrases *articles of virtu* and *objects of virtu.* **3.** Such articles or objects collectively. [Italian *virtu,* taste, virtue, from Latin *virtūs,* VIRTUE.]

vir·tu·al (vúr-choo-əl, -tew-, -chōōl) *adj.* Being as specified in essence or effect though not in actual fact, form, or name: *He resigned from his job, but it was a virtual dismissal.* [Middle English *virtuall,* effective, powerful, from Medieval Latin *virtuālis,* from Latin *virtūs,* capacity, VIRTUE.] **—vir·tu·al·i·ty** (-ál-əti) *n.*

virtual focus *n.* The point from which divergent rays of reflected or refracted light seem to have emanated, as from the image of a point in a plane mirror.

virtual image *n.* An image from which rays of reflected or refracted light appear to diverge, as from an image seen in a plane mirror.

vir·tu·al·ly (vúr-choo-əli, -chəli, -tew-) *adv.* In essence or in effect though not in actual fact; for all practical purposes; essentially; nearly but not absolutely.

virtual particle *n. Physics.* A particle that is not detected but is considered to exist for a very brief period of time, during which it is emitted by one real particle and absorbed by another, thereby transmitting a force between the two. Electromagnetic interaction, for example, is considered to result from exchange of *virtual photons* between charged particles.

virtual storage *n. Computing.* Memory in which the effective capacity is increased by the linking of the main memory to an external memory, such as a magnetic disk, so that they function together.

vir·tue (vúr-tew, -chōō) *n.* **1.** The quality of moral excellence, righteousness, and responsibility; probity; goodness. **2.** Conformity to standard morality or mores, as by abstention from vices; rectitude. **3. a.** A specific type of moral excellence or other exemplary quality considered meritorious; a worthy practice or ideal: *the virtue of integrity.* **b.** Any of the particular moral excellences considered exemplary in philosophy and theology. See **cardinal virtues. 4.** Chastity or virginity, especially that of a woman: *lost her virtue.* **5. a.** A particular efficacious or beneficial quality. **b.** A preferable quality; an advantage: *The plane has the virtue of speed.* **6.** Effective force or power; efficacy. **7.** *Plural. Theology.* One of the orders of angels. See **angel. —by** or **in virtue of.** On the grounds or basis of; by reason of. **—make a virtue of necessity.** To appear to do freely or by inclination what one is forced to do anyway. [Middle English *vertu,* from Old French, from Latin *virtūs,* manliness, strength, capacity, from *vir,* man.]

vir·tu·os·i·ty (vúr-tew-óssəti, -choo-) *n., pl.* **-ties.** The technical skill, fluency, or style exhibited by a virtuoso.

vir·tu·o·so (vúr-tew-ṓ-sō, -choo-, -zō) *n., pl.* **-sos** or **-si** (-see, -zee). **1.** A musician with masterly ability, technique, or personal style; a brilliant performer. **2.** One with masterly skill or technique in any field, especially in the arts. **3.** A connoisseur or dilettante.
~adj. Showing or requiring virtuosity: *a virtuoso performance.* [Italian, from Late Latin *virtuōsus,* virtuous, skilful, from Latin *virtūs,* VIRTUE.] **—vir·tu·os·ic** (-óssik) *adj.*

vir·tu·ous (vúr-choo-əss, -tew-) *adj.* **1.** Exhibiting virtue; righteous: *virtuous conduct.* **2.** Possessing or characterised by chastity; pure: *a virtuous woman.* —See Synonyms at **moral. —vir·tu·ous·ly** *adv.* **—vir·tu·ous·ness** *n.*

vir·u·lent (vírrew-lənt, vírrōō- || vírrə-) *adj.* **1.** Extremely harmful or pathogenic and taking rapid effect. Said of a disease, toxin, or microorganism. **2.** Bitterly hostile or antagonistic; venomously spiteful; full of hate. **3.** Intensely irritating, obnoxious, or harsh: *virulent prejudice.* [Middle English, from Latin *vīrulentus,* from *vīrus,* VIRUS.] **—vir·u·lence** (-lənss) *n.* **—vir·u·lent·ly** *adv.*

vi·rus (vīr-əss) *n., pl.* **-ruses.** **1.** Any of various submicroscopic pathogens consisting essentially of a core of a single nucleic acid surrounded by a protein coat, having the ability to replicate only inside a living cell. **2.** Any disease believed to be caused by a virus. **3.** Any malevolent and corrupting force: *the virus of racism.* —See Usage note at **germ.** [Latin *vīrus,* poison, slime.]

vis. 1. visibility. **2.** visual.

vi·sa (véezə || *U.S. also* -sə) *n.* **1.** An official authorisation appended to a passport or similar document, permitting entry into and travel within a particular country or region. **2.** Any authorisation or mark of authorisation.
~tr.v. **visaed** (-zəd), **-saing** (*often* -zəring), **-sas.** **1.** To make a visa in (a passport). **2.** To give a visa to. [French, from Latin *vīsa,* "things seen", neuter plural of *vīsus,* past participle of *vidēre,* to see.]

vis·age (vízzij) *n. Literary.* **1.** The face or facial expression of a person; a countenance. **2.** Appearance; aspect: *the visage of winter.* [Middle English, from Old French, from *vis,* face, from Latin *vīsus,* from the past participle of *vidēre,* to see.]

vis·aged (vízzijd) *adj. Literary* Having a specified kind of visage. Used in combination: *square-visaged.*

vis·ard. Variant of **vizard.**

vis-à-vis (véez-aa-vée, víz-, -ə-, -a-, -vee) *n., pl.* **vis-à-vis.** Either of two persons or things opposite, each other, such as partners in various dances. **2.** Either of two persons corresponding to each other in status, ability or position; a counterpart. **3.** A carriage carrying two passengers sitting opposite each other.
~adv. Face to face.
~prep. **1.** Compared with; in relation to. **2.** Opposite to; face to face with. [French, "face to face".] **—vis-·à-vis** *adj.*

Vi·sa·yan (vee-sī-ən, -saa-yən) *n., pl.* **-yans** or collectively **Visayan.** Also **Bi·sa·yan** (bee-). **1.** A member of the largest group of native people of the Philippines, found in the Visayan Islands. **2.** The Austronesian language spoken by these people. **—Vi·sa·yan** *adj.*

Visc. viscount; viscountess.

vis·ca·cha, viz·ca·cha (vi-skaacha, -skáchə) *n.* Any of several gregarious, burrowing South American rodents of the genera *Lagostomus* and *Lagidium,* related to and resembling the chinchilla. [Spanish, from Quechua *wiscacha.*]

vis·cer·a (víssərə) *pl.n. Singular* **viscus** (vískəss). **1.** The internal organs of the body, especially those contained within the abdominal and thoracic cavities. **2.** Loosely, the intestines. [Latin *vīscera,* plural of *vīscus†,* body organ.]

vis·cer·al (víssərəl) *adj.* **1.** Pertaining to, situated in, or affecting the viscera. **2.** Pertaining to or derived from emotions and intuition rather than the intellect: *a visceral senses of disaster.*

visceral leishmaniasis *n.* A tropical disease, **leishmaniasis** *(see).*

vis·cer·o·mo·tor (víssə-rō-mōtər) *adj. Physiology.* Producing or related to movements of the viscera. [VISCER(A) + MOTOR.]

vis·cid (víssid) *adj.* **1.** Thick and adhesive. Said of a fluid. **2.** Covered with a sticky or clammy coating, as certain leaves are. [Late Latin *viscidus,* from Latin *viscum,* mistletoe, birdlime. See **viscous.**] **—vis·cid·i·ty** (vi-síddəti), **vis·cid·ness** *n.* **—vis·cid·ly** *adv.*

vis·com·e·ter (vi-skómmitər) *n.* Also **vis·co·sim·e·ter** (viskə-símmitər). Any of various instruments or pieces of apparatus used to measure viscosity. Also called "viscosimeter". [VISCO(SITY) + -METER.] **—vis·co·met·ric** (vísk-ō-méttrik, -ə-) *adj.*

Vis·con·ti (veess-kón-tee, viss-), **Gian Galeazzo** (1351–1402). Duke of Milan (1378–1402). By conquest, intrigue, and purchase he united Milan with neighbouring cities into one powerful state.

Visconti, Luchino, born Luchino Visconti de Modrone (1906–76). Italian film director. His films, which are noted for their visual composition, include *The Leopard* (1963), *The Damned* (1969), and *Death in Venice* (1971).

vis·cose (vísk-ōss, -ōz) *n.* **1.** A thick, golden-brown viscous solution of cellulose xanthate, used in the manufacture of rayon and cellophane. **2.** Viscose rayon.
~*adj.* **1.** *Rare.* Viscous. **2.** Of, relating to, or made from viscose. [Middle English, sticky, viscid, from Late Latin *viscōsus,* VISCOUS.]

viscose rayon *n.* A rayon made by reconverting cellulose from a soluble xanthate form to tough fibres by washing in acid.

vis·cos·i·ty (vi-skóssəti) *n., pl.* **-ties. 1.** The condition or property of being viscous. **2.** *Physics. Symbol* **η.** The degree to which a fluid resists flow under an applied force, measured by the tangential stress on the fluid divided by the resulting velocity gradient under conditions of streamline flow. [Middle English, from Medieval Latin *viscōsitās* (stem *viscōsitāt-*), from *viscōsus,* VISCOUS.]

vis·count (vī-kownt) *n. Abbr.* **V., Visc., Visct.** A peer ranking below an earl and above a baron. [Middle English, from Old French *visconte,* from Medieval Latin *vicecomes* : VICE (substitute) + *comes,* COUNT.] **—vis·count·cy** (-si), **vis·count·y** (-i) *n.*

vis·count·ess (vī-kownt-iss || -ess, -éss) *n. Abbr.* **V., Vis., Visc., Visct. 1.** The wife or widow of a viscount. **2.** A female viscount.

vis·cous (vískəss) *adj.* **1.** Having relatively high resistance to flow. **2.** Viscid; sticky. [Middle English *viscouse,* from Anglo-French *viscous,* from Late Latin *viscōsus,* from Latin *viscum,* mistletoe, birdlime (made from mistletoe berries).] **—vis·cous·ly** *adv.* **—vis·cous·ness** *n.*

Visct. viscount; viscountess.

vis·cus. Singular of **viscera.**

vise. *U.S.* Variant of **vice** (tool).

Vish·nu (vísh-nōō) *n.* The Hindu deity worshipped as the preserver and second member of the trinity with Brahma and Shiva, and as the chief deity by the Vaishnava. [Sanskrit *Viṣṇuḥ.*]

vis·i·bil·i·ty (vízzi-bílləti) *n., pl.* **-ties. 1.** The fact, state, or degree of being visible. **2.** *Abbr.* **vis.** The greatest distance under given weather conditions to which it is possible to see without the aid of instruments. [French *visibilité,* from Latin *vīsibilis,* VISIBLE.]

vis·i·ble (vízzəb'l, vízzib'l) *adj.* **1.** Capable of being seen; perceptible to the eye: *a visible object.* **2.** Obvious to the eye: *a visible change of expression.* **3.** Manifest; apparent: *no visible solution.* **4.** Available; on hand: *the visible supply.* **5.** Publicly conspicuous; in the public eye: *a highly visible politician.* **6.** Prepared to receive visitors. **7.** Constructed or designed to keep important parts in easily accessible view: *a visible file.* **8.** Represented visually, as by symbols. **9.** *Economics.* Designating items of international trade consisting of goods rather than services. Compare **invisible.**
~*n. Plural. Economics.* Imports and exports of goods as opposed to those of services. Compare **invisible.** [Middle English, from Old French, from Latin *vīsibilis,* from *vīsus,* sight, VISION.] **—vis·i·ble·ness** *n.* **—vis·i·bly** *adv.*

visible balance *n. Economics.* The **balance of trade** *(see).*

visible radiation *n.* Electromagnetic radiation that can be detected by the normal human eye; light.

visible speech *n.* A system of phonetic notation used as an aid for teaching speech to the deaf and consisting of diagrams of the organs of speech in the positions required to articulate sounds.

Vis·i·goth (vízzi-goth) *n.* A member of the western group of Goths that invaded the Roman Empire in the fourth century A.D. and settled in France and Spain, establishing a monarchy that lasted until the early eighth century A.D. Compare **Ostrogoth.** [From Late Latin *Visigothi* (plural), probably "West Goths".] **—Vis·i·goth·ic** (-góthik) *adj.*

vi·sion (vízh'n) *n.* **1. a.** The faculty of sight: *poor vision.* **b.** That which can be, is, or has been seen. **2.** Unusual competence in discernment or perception; intelligent foresight: *a woman of vision.* **3.** The manner in which one sees or conceives of something. **4.** A mental image produced by the imagination: *He has visions of himself as a hero.* **5. a.** The mystical experience of seeing as if with the eyes the supernatural or a supernatural being. **b.** That which is thus experienced or seen. **6.** A person or thing of extraordinary beauty. **7.** The image on a television screen.
~*tr.v.* **visioned, -sioning, -sions.** To see in or as if in a vision. [Middle English, from Old French, from Latin *vīsiō* (stem *vīsiōn-*), from *vīsus,* sight, from the past participle of *vidēre,* to see.] **—vi·sion·al** *adj.* **—vi·sion·al·ly** *adv.*

vi·sion·ar·y (vízh'n-əri || -erri) *adj.* **1.** Characterised by vision or foresight: *a visionary statesman.* **2.** Having the nature of or seen in fantasies or dreams. **3.** Characterised by or given to mystical visions, prophecies, or revelations. **4.** Characterised by or given to impractical ideas; unrealistic: *a visionary fool* **5.** Not practicable at present; idealistic; utopian: *a visionary scheme.*
~*n., pl.* **visionaries. 1.** One who has visions; a seer; a prophet. **2.** One who is given to impractical or speculative ideas; a dreamer. **3.** One with great imagination or foresight.

vis·it (vízzit) *v.* **-ited, -iting, -its.** —*tr.* **1.** To go or come to see (a person), as by way of friendship or duty; call on: *visiting his sister.* **2.** To go or come to see (a place), as on a tour: *visit a museum.* **3.** To stay with as a guest. **4. a.** To go or come to see in a professional capacity: *The priest visited the condemned man.* **b.** To go or come to (an institution, for example) in an official capacity, as to inspect or examine. **5.** To go or come to for a particular purpose: *I visit the bank on Fridays.* **6.** To go or come to for medical or other treatment: *visit the dentist.* **7.** To afflict; assail: *A plague visited the village.* **8. a.** To inflict punishment upon or for: *"I shall visit their sin upon them".* (Exodus 32:34). **b.** To inflict (anger or retribution, for example) upon someone or something. **9.** *Archaic.* To come to in order to comfort or bless. Said of the Deity. —*intr.* **1.** To pay a call or calls. **2.** To inflict punishment; take revenge. **3.** *U.S. Informal.* To converse or chat: *Stay and visit with me for a while.*
~*n.* **1.** An act or instance of visiting a person, place, or thing. **2.** A stay or sojourn as a guest. **3. a.** An act of visiting in a professional capacity: *The doctor's visit was very brief.* **b.** An act of visiting in an official capacity, as for an inspection or examination. **4.** *Law.* The boarding of a foreign ship during wartime to establish its nationality, purpose, and cargo. Used especially in the phrase *right of visit and search.* [Middle English *visiten,* from Old French *visiter,* from Latin *visitāre,* to go to see, from *vīsāre,* to view, from *vīsus,* sight, VISION.] **—vis·it·a·ble** *adj.*

vis·i·tant (vízzitənt) *n.* **1.** A supernatural being; a ghost or spectre. **2.** A visitor; especially, a pilgrim or tourist. **3.** A migratory animal or bird that stops in a particular place for a limited period of time.
~*adj. Archaic.* Visiting. [Latin *visitāns* (stem *visitānt-*), present participle of *visitāre,* to VISIT.]

vis·i·ta·tion (vízzi-táysh'n) *n.* **1.** A visit for the purpose of making an official inspection or examination, such as one made by a bishop to a church in his diocese. **2. a.** A visit or social call. **b.** A visit or social call that is unwelcome or unduly long. Used humorously. **3.** *U.S.* A divorced or separated parent's right of access to the children of the marriage. **4. a.** A visit of punishment or affliction or of comfort and blessing, regarded as being ordained by God. **b.** A calamitous event or experience; a grave misfortune. **5.** The appearance or arrival of a supernatural being. **6.** *Capital* **V. a.** The visit of the Virgin Mary to her cousin Elizabeth. Luke 1:39–56. **b.** The Church festival held on July 2 in commemoration of this visit. **—vis·i·ta·tion·al** *adj.*

vis·i·ta·to·ri·al (vízzitə-táw-ri-əl || -tō-) *adj.* Also **vis·i·to·ri·al** (vízzi-). **1.** Of or pertaining to an official visitor or visit. **2.** Having the right or power of visitation.

visiting card *n. British.* A small card printed with one's name and address, presented as an introduction or left when the person one wishes to see is absent. Also called "card", *U.S.* "calling card".

visiting fireman *n. U.S. Informal.* **1.** An influential visitor who is entertained impressively. **2.** A visitor to a city who is welcomed because he is thought to be a free spender.

visiting professor *n.* A person, especially a lecturer or professor on sabbatical leave, holding a professorship at the invitation of a university or other institution, often in another country for an academic year.

vis·i·tor (vízzitər) *n.* **1.** One who pays a visit; a guest; a caller. **2.** A sightseer or tourist. **3.** A migratory animal, especially a bird, pausing in transit at a place; a visitant. **4.** An official, especially at a college, holding nominal powers of inspection or supervision.

vis ma·jor (víss máyjər) *n., pl.* **vires majores** (vīr-eez mə-jáw-reez || -jō-) *Law.* An overwhelming force of circumstance or nature having unavoidable consequences that can exempt one from the obligations of a contract. [Latin, "greater force".]

vi·sor, vi·zor (vīzər) *n.* **1.** A fixed or movable shield fitted at the top of a car windscreen to protect against glare. **2.** A protective shield held or worn in front of the face, used when welding or doing other dangerous tasks. **3.** *Chiefly U.S.* A peak on a cap. **4.** The front piece of the helmet of a suit of armour, capable of being raised and lowered and designed to protect the eyes, nose, and forehead. **5.** *Archaic.* Any means of concealment or disguise; a mask.
~*tr.v.* **visored** (vīzərd) **-soring, -sors.** Also **vi·zor.** To mask or protect with a visor. [Middle English *viser,* from Anglo-French, from Old French *vis,* face, from Latin *vīsus,* sight, VISION.]

vis·ta (vístə) *n.* **1.** A distant view seen through a passage, as between buildings or rows of trees; a scene; a prospect. **2.** The passage framing the approach to such a scene; an avenue. **3.** A comprehensive awareness of a series of remembered, present, or anticipated events: *"He opened a vista into a mean life."* (Rebecca West). [Italian, from *visto,* past participle of *vedere,* to see, from Latin *vidēre.*]

Vis·tu·la (vístewlə). *Polish* **Wis·ła** (veéss-waa). River in Poland. Rising in the Beskid mountains, it flows 1 094 kilometres (680 miles) north and northwest to enter the Baltic at Gdansk.

vis·u·al (vízzew-əl, vízhew-, vízhoo- || vízh'l) *adj. Abbr.* **vis. 1.** Serving, resulting from, or pertaining to the sense of sight. **2.** Capable of being seen by the eye; visible. **3.** *Physics.* Optical. **4.** Done,

PRONUNCIATION KEY

a, **trap**; aa, **father**; ai, **fair**;
ar, **star**; aw, **lawn**; ay, **play**;
b, bb, **stab**; **rubber**;
ch, **church**; ck, **ticket**;
d, dd, **dead**; **ladder**; e, **dress**;
ee, **bee**; er, **defer**; ew, **few**;
ewr, **pure**; ə, **about**;
ər, **letter**; f, ff, **fife**; **differ**;
g, gg, **giggle**; h, **hat**; i, **kit**;
ī, **price**; īr, **fire**; j, **judge**;
k, **kick**; l, ll, **let**; 'l, **needle**;
m, mm, **man**; n, nn, **no**;
'n, **sudden**; ng, **thing**; o, **lot**;
ō, **no**; ōō, **foot**; ōō, **shoe**;
oor, **poor**; ow, **cow**;
owr, **hour**; oy, **boy**;
p, pp, **pepper**; r, rr, **red**;
s, ss, **sauce**; sh, **ship**;
t, tt, **totter**; th, **thick**; th, **this**;
smooth; u, **cut**; ur, **turn**;
v, vv, **valve**; w, **wet**; y, **yes**;
z, zz, **zebra**; zh, **vision**;
pleasure

IN FOREIGN WORDS:

aN, oN, **Saint-Saëns**;
hl, **Llanelli**; **Hluhluwe**;
kh, **loch**; **lough**; **Khaled**

STRESS MARK:

in-sīt, **insight**; in-sīt, **incite**

maintained, or executed by the sight only: *visual navigation.* **5.** Having the nature of or producing an image in the mind. **6.** Involving sight: *visual instruction; visual humour.*
~*n. Usually plural.* Any form of graphic material, such as a film, display, or photograph, used for educational or publicity purposes. [Middle English, from Late Latin *vīsuālis,* from Latin *vīsus,* VISION.] **—vis·u·al·ly** *adv.*

visual aids *pl.n.* Graphic material and the devices for presenting it, such as posters and display boards, used in education to impart instruction by visual means.

visual arts *pl.n.* Arts such as painting and sculpture whose works exist in permanent and static form rather than requiring performance, as ballet does, and whose aesthetic appeal is primarily to the visual sense, as opposed to such arts as music and poetry.

visual display unit *n.* An electronic device for displaying computer-prompted words and diagrams on a cathode-ray screen. Also called "VDU", "video terminal".

visual field *n. Abbr.* **V.F.** The entire area visible to the immobile eye or eyes at a given moment; the field of vision.

vis·u·al·ise, vis·u·al·ize (vízzew-ə-līz, ví*zh*ew-, ví*zh*oo- || ví*zh*-) *v.* **-ised, -ising, -ises.** *—tr.* To form a mental image or vision of; envisage. *—intr.* To form a mental image or images. **—vis·u·al·i·sa·tion** (-lī-záysh'n || *U.S.* -li-) *n.* **—vis·u·al·is·er** *n.*

visual purple *n.* A pigment of the retina, **rhodopsin** *(see).*

vi·tal (vít'l) *adj.* **1.** Of, affecting, or characteristic of life: *vital processes.* **2.** Necessary to the continuation of life; life-sustaining: *vital functions.* **3.** Full of life; energetic; vigorous; animated: *Her dancing is vital yet controlled.* **4.** *Poetic.* Imparting life or animation; invigorating. **5. a.** Having immediate importance; essential; indispensable: *vital to our success.* **b.** Crucial; decisive: *a vital innings.* **6.** Concerned with or recording data pertinent to lives. **7.** *Archaic.* Destructive to life; fatal; deadly: *a vital wound.* —See Synonyms at **necessary.** [Middle English, from Old French, from Latin *vītālis,* from *vīta,* life.] **—vi·tal·ly** *adv.* **—vi·tal·ness** *n.*

vital capacity *n. Physiology.* The maximum amount of air that can be expelled from the lungs after breathing in as deeply as possible.

vital force *n.* A hypothetical life force suggested by early biologists as the driving force behind the evolution and development of organisms. [Translation of French *élan vital.*]

vi·tal·ise, vi·tal·ize (vít'l-īz) *tr.v.* **-ised, -ising, -ises. 1.** To endow with life. **2.** To invigorate or animate. **—vi·tal·i·sa·tion** (-ī-záysh'n || *U.S.* -i-) *n.* **—vi·tal·is·er** *n.*

vi·tal·ism (vít'l-iz'm) *n.* The philosophical doctrine that life processes possess a unique character radically different from physiochemical phenomena and therefore cannot be explained in empirical terms. **—vi·tal·ist** *n.* **—vi·tal·is·tic** (-ístik) *adj.*

vi·tal·i·ty (vī-tál-əti) *n., pl.* **-ties. 1.** Vigour; energy; exuberance. **2.** The power to survive or evolve: *impaired the firm's vitality.* **3.** That which distinguishes the living from the nonliving; an energy, force, or principle characteristic of life; vital force. **4.** The capacity to live, grow, or develop.

vi·tals (vít'lz) *pl.n.* **1.** Any bodily parts or organs regarded as the centre or source of life: *sensed disaster in his vitals.* **2.** Those bodily organs whose continued functioning is essential for life. **3.** The reproductive organs, especially those of the male. **4.** Those elements essential to continued functioning, as in a system.

vital stain *n.* Any biological stain that can be used to colour living material, as for examination under a microscope.

vital statistics *pl.n.* **1.** Data that record significant events and dates in human life, as the rate of births, deaths, and marriages. **2.** *Informal.* The measurements of a woman's bust, waist, and hips.

vi·ta·min (vítta-min, vítə-) *n.* Also *rare* **vi·ta·mine** (-min, -meen). Any of various relatively complex organic substances occurring naturally in plant and some animal tissue, and essential in small amounts for the control of metabolic processes. [German *Vitamine* : Latin *vīta,* life + AMINE (so called because it was once thought to contain an amino acid).] **—vi·ta·min·ic** (mínnik) *adj.*

vitamin A *n.* Vitamin A_1 or a mixture of vitamins A_1 and A_2, occurring principally in fish-liver oils and some yellow and dark-green vegetables, functioning in normal cell growth and development. A deficiency causes hardening and roughening of the skin, night blindness, and degeneration of mucous membranes. Also called "retinol".

vitamin A_1 *n.* A yellow crystalline compound, $C_{20}H_{30}O$, extracted from fish-liver oils. See **vitamin A.**

vitamin A_2 *n.* A golden-yellow oil, $C_{20}H_{28}O$, occurring in pike-liver oils and having approximately 40 per cent of the biological activity of vitamin A_1. See **vitamin A.**

vitamin B *n.* **1.** Vitamin B complex. **2.** A member of the vitamin B complex, especially thiamine.

vitamin B_1. **Thiamine** *(see).*

vitamin B_2 *n.* **Riboflavin** *(see).*

vitamin B_6 *n.* **Pyridoxine** *(see).*

vitamin B_{12}. A complex, cobalt-containing coordination compound produced in the normal growth of certain microorganisms, found in liver, and widely used to treat pernicious anaemia. Also called "cyanocobalamin".

vitamin B_c *n.* **Folic acid** *(see).*

vitamin B complex *n.* A group of vitamins originally thought to be a single substance, generally regarded as including thiamine, riboflavin, niacin, pantothenic acid, biotin, pyridoxine, folic acid, lipoic acid, inositol, and vitamin B_{12}, and occurring chiefly in yeast, liver, eggs, and some vegetables.

vitamin C *n.* **Ascorbic acid** *(see).*

vitamin D *n., pl.* **D vitamins.** Any of several chemically similar compounds produced in general by ultraviolet irradiation of sterols, obtained from milk, fish, and eggs, required for normal bone growth, and used to treat rickets in children and osteomalacia in adults. Also called "calciferol".

vitamin E *n.* Any of several chemically related viscous oils, especially $C_{29}H_{50}O_2$, found chiefly in grains and vegetable oils. A deficiency causes sterility in certain mammals, but the effects in humans are uncertain. Also called "tocopherol".

vitamin G *n. Chiefly U.S.* **Riboflavin** *(see).*

vitamin K *n., pl.* **K vitamins.** Any of several natural and synthetic substances essential for the promotion of blood clotting and prevention of haemorrhage; especially menaquinone *(vitamin K_2)* and phylloquinone *(vitamin K_1).*

vitamin P *n.* **Bioflavonoid** *(see).*

vi·tel·lin (vi-téllin, vī-) *n.* A protein found in egg yolk. [VITELL(US) + -IN.]

vi·tel·line (vi-tél-īn, vī-, -in) *adj.* **1.** Pertaining to or associated with the yolk of an egg: *the vitelline membrane.* **2.** Having the yellow colour of an egg yolk; dull yellow. [VITELL(US) + -INE.]

vitelline membrane *n. Zoology.* A membrane that forms around a fertilised egg to prevent other sperm from entering.

vi·tel·lus (vi-télləs, vī-) *n., pl.* **-luses** or **-li** (-téllī). *Rare.* The yolk of an egg. [Latin.]

vi·ti·ate (víshi-ayt) *tr.v.* **-ated, -ating, -ates. 1.** To impair the value or quality of; make faulty or impure; spoil. **2.** To corrupt morally; pervert. **3.** To invalidate or render (a contract, for example) legally ineffective. [Latin *vitiāre,* from *vitium,* defect, fault.] **—vi·ti·a·ble** (-əb'l) *adj.* **—vi·ti·a·tion** (-áysh'n) *n.* **—vi·ti·a·tor** (-aytər) *n.*

vit·i·cul·ture (vítti-kulchər, víti-) *n.* The cultivation of grapes, especially for wine-making. [Latin *vītis,* vine + CULTURE.] **—vit·i·cul·tur·al** (-kúlchərəl) *adj.* **—vit·i·cul·tur·ist** *n.*

vit·i·li·go (vítti-lígō) *n.* A skin disease, **leucoderma** *(see).* [Latin *vitilīgō,* cutaneous eruption.]

Vi·to·ria (vee-táwri-ə). A city in northern Spain. The capital of Álava province, it was founded (sixth century) by the Visigoths. Wellington defeated the French there in the Peninsular War (1813).

vit·re·ous (víttri-əss) *adj.* **1.** Pertaining to, resembling, or having the nature of glass; glassy. **2.** Obtained or made from glass. **3.** Of or pertaining to the vitreous body or vitreous humour. [Latin *vitreus,* from *vitrum*†, glass.] **—vit·re·os·i·ty** (-óssəti) **vit·re·ous·ness** *n.*

vitreous body *n.* A gelatinous body of matter composed mainly of vitreous humour that fills the part of the eyeball between the retina and the lens.

vitreous enamel *n.* **Porcelain enamel** *(see).*

vitreous humour *n.* A watery fluid that is a major component of the vitreous body.

vitreous silica *n.* Silica that has been fused to form a hard transparent heat-resistant glass, used especially for making scientific apparatus.

vi·tres·cence (vi-tréss'nss) *n.* **1.** Transformation into glass. **2.** The state of becoming vitreous or like glass.

vi·tres·cent (vi-tréss'nt) *adj.* **1.** Tending to become glass or like glass. **2.** Capable of being turned into glass. [Latin *vitrum,* glass (see **vitreous**) + -ESCENT.]

vit·ri·fi·ca·tion (víttrifi-káysh'n) *n.* **1.** The act or process of vitrifying or the state of being vitrified. **2.** Something vitrified.

vit·ri·form (víttri-fawrm) *adj.* Resembling glass in form or appearance. [Latin *vitrum,* glass + -FORM.]

vit·ri·fy (víttri-fī) *v.* **-fied, -fying, -fies.** *—tr.* To change or make into glass or a similar substance, especially through melting. *—intr.* To become vitreous. [French *vitrifier,* from Old French : Latin *vitrum,* glass (see **vitreous**) + -FY.] **—vit·ri·fi·a·bil·i·ty** (-fī-ə-billəti) *n.* **—vit·ri·fi·a·ble** (-fī-əb'l, -fī-) *adj.*

vit·ri·ol (víttri-əl, -ol || -ōl) *n.* **1.** *Chemistry.* **a.** Sulphuric acid. **b.** Any of various sulphates of metals, such as ferrous sulphate (green vitriol), zinc sulphate (white vitriol), or copper sulphate (blue vitriol). **2.** Vituperative statements or feelings.
~*tr.v.* **vitrioled** or **-olled, -oling** or **-olling, -ols. 1.** To expose or subject to vitriol. **2.** To attack or injure with vitriol. [Middle English, from Old French, from Medieval Latin *vitriolum,* from Latin *vitrum,* glass (from the appearance of its sulphates). See **vitreous.**]

vit·ri·ol·ic (víttri-óllik) *adj.* **1.** Of, similar to, or derived from a vitriol. **2.** Bitterly scathing; caustic: *a vitriolic review.*

vit·ri·ol·ise, vit·ri·ol·ize (víttri-əl-īz) *tr.v.* **-ised, -ising, -ises. 1.** To expose or subject to vitriol. **2.** To convert into vitriol. **3.** To attack or injure with vitriol. **—vit·ri·ol·i·sa·tion** (-ī-záysh'n || *U.S.* -i-) *n.*

Vi·tru·vi·us (vi-trōōvi-əss), (late 1st c. B.C. and early 1st c. A.D.). Roman architect and engineer. His treatise, *De architectura,* the only complete Roman architectural work to survive, influenced architects of the Classical revival, such as Palladio and Alberti, and others through to the 18th century.

vit·ta (vít-ə) *n., pl.* **-tae** (-ee). **1.** *Biology.* A streak or band of colour. **2.** *Botany.* An oil tube in the fruit of certain plants, such as the carrot or parsley. [Latin, headband.] **—vit·tate** (-ayt) *adj.*

vit·tle (vítt'l). *Nonstandard.* Variant of **victual.**

vi·tu·per·ate (vī-téw-pə-rayt, vi- || -tōō-) *tr.v.* **-ated, -ating, -ates.** To rail against severely or abusively; revile; berate. See Synonyms at **malign.** [Latin *vituperāre.*] **—vi·tu·per·a·tor** (-raytər) *n.*

vi·tu·per·a·tion (vī-téw-pə-ráysh'n, vi- || -tōō-) *n.* **1.** Abusive censure or blame. **2.** Invective; railing. **3.** The act of vituperating.

vi·tu·per·a·tive (vī-téw-pə-rətiv, vi-, -raytiv || -tōō-) *adj.* Harshly abusive; acrimonious: *a vituperative note.* —**vi·tu·per·a·tive·ly** *adv.*

vi·va¹ (vée-və) *interj.* Used to express acclamation, salute, or applause.
~*n.* A shout of "viva". [Italian, from *vivere,* to live, from Latin *vivere.*]

vi·va² (vívə) *n. British.* An examination consisting of an interview rather than of written papers; a viva voce examination.
~*v.* **vivaed** or **-va'd** (vívəd), **-vaing** (*often* vívəring), **-vas** or **va's.** —*tr.* To examine by means of a viva. —*intr.* To undergo a viva. [Shortened from VIVA VOCE.]

vi·va·ce (vi-váa-chi, -chay ‖ vee-) *adv. Music.* Lively; vivaciously; briskly. Used as a direction. [Italian, from Latin *vivāx,* VIVACIOUS.]

vi·va·cious (vi-váyshəss, vī-) *adj.* Animated; sprightly; spirited. [Latin *vivāx* (stem *vivāci-*), lively, from *vivere,* to live.] —**vi·va·cious·ly** *adv.* —**vi·va·cious·ness** *n.*

vi·vac·i·ty (vi-vássəti, vī-) *n.* The condition or quality of being vivacious; liveliness.

Vi·val·di (vi-vál-di), **Antonio** (1675–1741). Italian composer and violinist. He is chiefly remembered for his concertos, particularly *The Four Seasons,* a set of four violin concertos.

vi·van·diè·re (vée-voND-yaír) *n.* Formerly, especially in France, a woman who accompanied troops to sell them extra food, supplies, and drink. [French, feminine of *vivandier,* provisioner, from Old French, from *viande,* VIAND.]

vi·var·i·um (vi-vaír-i-əm, vī-) *n., pl.* **-ums** or **-varia** (-ə). A place or enclosure for keeping and breeding living animals for observation or research. [Latin : *vivus,* alive (see vivify) + -ARIUM.]

vi·va vo·ce (vívə vō-si, -chi) *adj.* By word of mouth; spoken; oral. ~*n.* A viva voce examination. [Middle Latin, "with the living voice".] —**vi·va vo·ce** *adv.*

vive (veev) *interj. French.* Used to acclaim, salute, or applaud a person or personification specified: *Vive la France!*

vi·ver·rine (vī-vérrīn, vi- ‖ -vérrin) *n.* A member of the family Viverridae, which includes carnivorous mammals such as the civets and mongooses. [From Latin *viverra,* ferret.] —**vi·ver·rine** *adj.*

viv·id (vívvid) *adj.* **1.** Perceived as bright and distinct; brilliant: *the vivid evening star.* **2. a.** Having intensely bright colours: *a vivid tapestry.* **b.** Very bright or strong. Said of colour. **3.** Full of the vigour and freshness of immediate experience: *vivid emotions.* **4. a.** Evoking lifelike images within the mind; heard, seen, or felt as if real: *a vivid description.* **b.** Active in forming or retaining lifelike images: *a vivid imagination.* [Latin *vividus,* full of life, lifelike, from *vivere,* to live.] —**viv·id·ly** *adv.* —**viv·id·ness** *n.*

viv·i·fy (vívvi-fī) *tr.v.* **-fied, -fying, -fies. 1.** To give or bring life to; animate. **2.** To make more lively, intense, or striking; enliven. [French *vivifier,* from Late Latin *vivificāre* : Latin *vivus,* alive + *facere,* to do.] —**viv·i·fi·ca·tion** (-fi-káysh'n) *n.* —**viv·i·fi·er** *n.*

vi·vip·a·rous (vi-víppərəss, vī-) *adj.* **1.** *Zoology.* Giving birth to living offspring that develop within the mother's body. Said of most mammals. Compare **oviparous, ovoviviparous. 2.** *Botany.* **a.** Germinating or producing seeds that germinate before becoming detached from the parent plant. **b.** Producing bulbils or new plants rather than seed. [Latin *viviparus* : *vivus,* alive (see vivify) + -PAROUS.] —**viv·i·par·i·ty** (vívvi-párrəti) *n.* —**vi·vip·a·rous·ly** *adv.*

viv·i·sect (vívvi-sékt, -sekt) *v.* **-sected, -secting, -sects.** —*tr.* To perform vivisection on (a live animal). —*intr.* To carry out vivisection. [Back-formation from VIVISECTION.] —**viv·i·sec·tor** (-ər) *n.*

viv·i·sec·tion (vívvi-séksh'n) *n.* **1.** The act of cutting into or dissecting the body of a living animal, especially for scientific research. **2.** Extremely detailed and often destructive criticism or analysis, as of a film or book. [Latin *vivus,* alive (see vivify) + -SECTION.] —**viv·i·sec·tion·al** *adj.*

viv·i·sec·tion·ist (vívvi-séksh'n-ist) *n.* **1.** A person who performs a vivisection. **2.** A person who favours the continued use of vivisection for scientific research, and opposes the movement to abolish it.

vix·en (víks'n) *n.* **1.** A female fox. **2.** A quarrelsome, shrewish, or malicious woman. [Middle English *fixene,* Old English *fyxe,* she-fox.] —**vix·en·ish** *adj.* —**vix·en·ly** *adj.* & *adv.*

Vi·yel·la (vī-éllə) *n.* A trademark for a soft fabric made of a mixture of wool and cotton, used especially for clothing. —**Vi·yel·la** *adj.*

viz. videlicet. *Note: Viz.* is never pronounced (viz) when formally reading something aloud: it is replaced by its gloss, "namely." In informal speech, however, it is often pronounced (viz). Though *viz* is an abbreviation of *videlicet,* it is rarely read out as "videlicet"—except in humorous or highly formal contexts.

viz·ard (vízzərd) *n.* Also **vis·ard.** *Archaic.* **1.** A visor on a helmet. **2.** A mask. [Earlier *vizar, viser,* variants of VISOR.]

viz·ca·cha. Variant of **viscacha.**

vi·zier (vi-zéer, víz-eer ‖ -yər) *n.* Also **vi·zir.** A high officer, such as a provincial governor or chief adviser, in various Muslim governments, especially in the Ottoman Empire. [French *vizir,* from Turkish *vezīr,* from Arabic *wazīr,* porter, from *wazara,* to bear, carry.] —**vi·zier·i·al** (vi-zéer-i-əl) *adj.*

vi·zier·ate (vi-zéer-ət, víz-eer-, -it, -ayt ‖ -yər-) *n.* The office, authority, or term of office of a vizier. Also called "vizieralty", "viziership".

vi·zor. Variant of **visor.**

vizs·la (vízhlə) *n.* A hunting dog of a Hungarian breed, having a smooth golden-red coat. [After *Vizsla,* Hungary, where the breed originated.]

V-J Day (vée-jáy) *n.* The day of victory for the Allied forces over Japan in World War II; in Britain, August 15, 1945, and in the United States, September 2, 1945. [Short for *Victory in Japan Day.*]

Vlaanderen. See **Flanders.**

Vlach (vlaakh) *n.* A member of a widely scattered people, speaking a Romanian dialect, living in southeastern Europe in early medieval times.
~*adj.* Of, pertaining to, or designating this people, their culture, or their Romanian dialect.

Vla·di·mir I, (vláddi-meer, *Russian* vla-dée-), **St.** also known as Vladimir the Great (*c.* 965–1015). The first Christian ruler of Russia. He extended Russia's dominions from the Ukraine to the Baltic Sea, making Kiev his capital.

Vla·di·vos·tok (vláddi-vóstok, *Russian* -vuss-tók). A Pacific seaport of the U.S.S.R. The capital of the Primorye Territory, R.S.F.S.R. between Amur Bay and the Golden Horn, it is a major Russian naval base.

Vla·minck (vla-máNK), **Maurice de** (1876–1958). French painter. With Derain and Matisse he was one of the leading exponents of fauvism. He is noted for his stormy, aggressive landscapes.

vlei (flay) *n. South African.* A low-lying stretch of soggy ground; a marsh. [Afrikaans, from Dutch *vallei,* akin to VALLEY.]

Vlissingen. See **Flushing.**

vlf, VLF very low frequency.

V neck (vée-nek) *n.* **1.** A neck or collar of a garment that has a V-shaped front, tapering to a point rather than being rounded. **2.** A garment, especially a sweater, having such a neck. —**V-neck, V-necked** (-nekt) *adj.*

vo. verso.

voc. vocative.

vocab. vocabulary.

vo·ca·ble (vōkəb'l) *n.* **1.** A word considered only as a sequence of sounds or letters rather than as a unit of meaning. **2.** A sound that can be voiced; a vowel.
~*adj.* Capable of being voiced or spoken. [French, from Old French, from Latin *vocābulum,* an appellation, from *vocāre,* to call.]

vo·cab·u·lar·y (və-kábbew-ləri, vō- ‖ -lerri) *n., pl.* **-ies.** *Abbr.* **vocab.** (*sometimes* vō-kab). **1.** A list of words and often phrases, usually arranged alphabetically and defined or translated; a lexicon or glossary. **2.** All the words of a language. **3.** The sum of words used by, understood by, or at the command of a particular person or group. **4.** A command or reserve of expressive techniques; repertoire: *a dancer's vocabulary of movement.* [Medieval Latin *vocābulārium,* from *vocābulārius,* of words, from Latin *vocābulum,* an appellation, name. See **vocable.**]

vo·cal (vōk'l) *adj.* **1. a.** Of or pertaining to the voice. **b.** For or rendered by the voice rather than an instrument: *a vocal line.* **2.** Uttered or produced by the voice: *a vocal prayer.* **3.** Having a voice; capable of emitting sound or speech. **4.** Full of voices; resounding with speech: *a vocal gathering.* **5.** Quick to speak or criticise; outspoken: *vocal dissidents.* **6.** *Phonetics.* **a.** Vocalic. **b.** Voiced.
~*n.* **1.** *Phonetics.* A vocal sound. **2.** *Plural.* The music sung by a vocalist, rather than the instrumental accompaniment. [Middle English, from Latin *vōcālis,* speaking, talking, from *vōx,* voice.] —**vo·cal·ly** *adv.* —**vo·cal·ness** *n.*

vocal cords *pl.n.* The lower of two pairs of bands or folds in the larynx that vibrate when pulled together and when air passes over them from the lungs, thereby producing vocal sounds. Also called "vocal folds".

Usage: Association of the voice with music and therefore with musical chords sometimes leads to the nonstandard spelling *vocal chords.* The form *vocal folds* is preferred by specialists.

vo·cal·ic (vō-kál-ik, və-) *adj.* **1.** Containing many vowel sounds. **2.** Pertaining to or having the nature of a vowel or vowels.

vo·cal·ise¹, vo·cal·ize (vōk'l-īz) *v.* **-ised, -ising, -ises.** —*tr.* **1.** To make vocal; produce with the voice. **2.** To give voice to; articulate. **3.** To mark (a vowelless Hebrew text, for example) with diacritical vowel points. **4.** *Phonetics.* **a.** To change (a consonant) into a vowel. **b.** To voice. —*intr.* **1.** To use the voice; especially, to sing. **2.** *Phonetics.* To be changed into a vowel. —**vo·cal·i·sa·tion** (-ī-záysh'n ‖ *U.S.* -i-záysh'n) *n.* —**vo·cal·is·er** *n.*

vo·cal·ise² (vō-kə-léez, -ka-) *n.* A wordless musical composition, especially for the voice. [French.]

vo·cal·ism (vōk'l-iz'm) *n.* **1.** The use of the voice in speaking or singing. **2.** The act, technique, or art of singing. **3.** A vowel or vocalic sound. **4.** A system of vowels, as within a specific language.

vo·cal·ist (vōk'l-ist) *n.* A singer, especially in a jazz or pop group.

vocal score *n.* A musical score transcribing the voice parts in full and the orchestral parts reduced to a piano accompaniment.

vo·ca·tion (və-káysh'n, vō-) *n.* **1.** A regular occupation or profession; especially, one for which one is specially suited or qualified. **2.** An urge or predisposition to undertake a certain kind of work, especially a religious career; a calling. [Middle English *vocacioun,* divine call to a religious life, from Old French *vocation,* from Latin *vōcātiō* (stem *vōcātiōn-*), a calling, summoning, from *vocāre,* to call.]

vo·ca·tion·al (və-káysh'n'l, vō-) *adj.* **1.** Of or pertaining to vocations or one's vocation. **2.** Pertaining to, providing, or undergoing training in a special skill to be pursued as a trade or profession. —**vo·ca·tion·al·ly** *adv.*

voc·a·tive (vóckətiv) *adj.* **1.** Pertaining to, characteristic of, or used in calling. **2.** *Abbr.* **v., voc.** Designating, pertaining to, or inflected in the grammatical case used in certain languages, such as Latin or Polish, to denote the person or thing being addressed.
~*n. Abbr.* **v., voc. 1.** The vocative case. **2.** A form or construction in this case. [Middle English *vocatif,* from Old French, from Latin *vocātīvus,* from *vocāre,* to call. See **vocation.**] —**voc·a·tive·ly** *adv.*

vole *The common field vole (above) builds its nest in meadowland and lives on grass, roots, and seeds. Voles, which are related to fieldmice, are native to North and Central America, Europe, and Asia.*

vo·cif·er·ate (vō-síffə-rayt, və-) *v.* **-ated, -ating, -ates.** —*intr.* To cry out vehemently, especially in protest; exclaim. —*tr.* To utter (a protest, for example) loudly and insistently. [Latin *vōciferārī* : *vōx* (stem *vōci-*), voice (see **vocal**) + *ferre,* to bear] —**vo·cif·er·a·tion** (-ráysh'n) *n.* —**vo·cif·er·a·tor** (-raytər) *n.*

vo·cif·er·ous (vō-síffərəss, və-) *adj.* **1.** Making an outcry, as in protest. **2.** Characterised by loudness and vehemence. [From VOCIFERATE.] —**vo·cif·er·ous·ly** *adv.* —**vo·cif·er·ous·ness** *n.*

vo·coid (vṓ-koyd) *n.* A speech sound articulated with air from the lungs flowing through the mouth over the centre of the tongue without friction; a vowel or semivowel. [Latin *vōx* (stem *vōc-*), voice (see **vowel**) + -OID.] —**vo·coid** *adj.*

vod·ka (vódkə) *n.* An alcoholic drink of Russian origin, formerly distilled from fermented wheat mash, now also made from a mash of rye, wheat, or potatoes. [Russian, diminutive of *voda,* water.]

voet·sek (fŏŏt-sek, -sak) *interj. South African Slang.* Used as a rough command to scare or chase away an animal or person. [Afrikaans, from Dutch *voort seg ik,* "away say I".]

voet·stoots (fŏŏt-stoorts) *adj. Law. South African.* Designating a sale of an item, especially a house, in which its condition, good or bad, is accepted by the buyer who cannot then claim redress if it proves unsatisfactory. [Afrikaans, from Dutch, from phrase *met de voet te stoten,* "to push (aside) with the foot", hence figuratively, (to sell) without assuming responsibility.] —**voet·stoots** *adv.*

vogue (vōg) *n.* **1.** The prevailing fashion, practice, or style: *in vogue.* **2.** Popular acceptance or favour; popularity.
~*adj.* Fashionable; in widespread current use; popular: *vogue words.* —See Synonyms at **fashion.** [French, fashion, "rowing", from *voguer,* to row, go along smoothly, from Old French, from Old Low German *wogon* (unattested).] —**vog·uish** *adj.*

Vo·gul (vṓg'l) *n.* **1.** A member of a people living in western Siberia. **2.** The language of this people, of the Finno-Ugric family of languages. [Russian, from Ostyak *Uogal', Uogat'.*]

voice (vóyss) *n. Abbr.* **v. 1. a.** The sound or sounds produced by the vocal organs of a vertebrate, especially by those of a human being. **b.** The natural and characteristic manner of speaking or sound of the speech of a specified person: *recognised your voice.* **2.** The ability to produce such sounds: *lost her voice.* **3.** Any sound resembling or reminiscent of vocal utterance: *the voice of the bugles.* **4.** The specified quality, condition, or timbre of vocal sound: *a hoarse voice.* **5. a.** Oral or verbal expression: *give voice to one's anger.* **b.** Any means of making something known: *the voice of the nation; the voice of experience.* **c.** The right or opportunity to express a choice or opinion: *had no voice in their own future.* **6.** *Obsolete.* **a.** Rumour or report. **b.** Reputation or fame. **7.** *Grammar.* A verb form indicating the relation between the subject and the action expressed by the verb. See **active, passive. 8.** *Phonetics.* The expiration of air through vibrating vocal folds, used in the production of the vowels and voiced consonants. Compare **breath. 9. a.** Musical tone produced by the vibration of vocal folds and resonated within the throat and head cavities. **b.** The quality or condition of a person's singing: *a bass voice; in excellent voice.* **c.** A singer: *a choir of fine voices.* **10.** Any of the melodic parts for a musical composition. In this sense, also called "voice part". —**throw (one's) voice.** To make one's voice seem to come from elsewhere, as a ventriloquist does. —**with one voice.** In unison; unanimously.
~*tr.v.* **voiced, voicing, voices. 1.** To express or utter; give voice to: *voice an objection.* **2.** *Phonetics.* To utter with voice. **3.** *Music.* To regulate the tone of (the pipes of an organ, for example). —See Synonyms at **vent.** [Middle English, from Old French *vois, voix,* from Latin *vōx.*]

voice box *n.* The larynx.

voiced (voyst) *adj.* **1.** Having a voice or having a specified kind of voice. Often used in combination: *harsh-voiced.* **2.** *Phonetics.* Uttered with vibration of the vocal folds, as the consonants *d* and *b* are in English. Compare **voiceless.**

voice·ful (vóyssf'l) *adj. Poetic.* Having a voice; especially, having a loud voice; resounding. —**voice·ful·ness** *n.*

voice·less (vóyss-ləss, -liss) *adj.* **1. a.** Having no voice; mute; silent. **b.** Not expressed by means of the voice. **2.** *Phonetics.* Uttered without vibration of the vocal cords, as the consonants *t* and *p* are in English. Compare **voiced. 3.** Unable to sing. **4.** Not having the right to speak or vote. —See Synonyms at **dumb.** —**voice·less·ly** *adv.* —**voice·less·ness** *n.*

voice-o·ver (vóyss-ṓvər, -ōvər) *n.* **1.** In cinematic films and television, the voice of a narrator or commentator who does not appear on camera. **2.** The script read by such a narrator.

voice part *n. Music.* A voice.

voice·print (vóyss-print) *n.* An electronically recorded graphic representation of voice, typically with time plotted on the horizontal axis, frequency on the vertical, and amplitude exhibited in a series of contour lines.

voice vote *n.* A vote that is decided on the relative volume of noise of those shouting "aye" and "no".

void (voyd) *adj.* **1.** Containing no matter; empty. **2.** Unoccupied; unfilled. Said of an office or position. **3.** Devoid; lacking. Used with *of: void of understanding.* **4.** Ineffective; useless. **5.** Having no legal force or validity; null. **6.** Having no cards in a suit: *Her hand was void in diamonds.* —See Synonyms at **empty.**
~*n.* **1.** Something that is void; an empty space; a vacuum. **2.** An open space or break in continuity; a gap. **3.** A feeling or state of emptiness, loneliness, or loss. **4.** In card games, the state of not having any cards in a particular suit. **5.** An empty space or gap, as in a wall for a window.
~*v.* **voided, voiding, voids.** —*tr.* **1.** To make void or of no effect; invalidate. **2. a.** To empty or take out (the contents of something). **b.** To evacuate (body wastes). **3.** *Archaic.* To leave; vacate. —*intr.* To evacuate body wastes. —See Synonyms at **nullify.** [Middle English, from Old French *voide, vuide,* from Vulgar Latin *vocitus* (unattested), from *vocāre,* to be empty.] —**void·er** *n.*

void·a·ble (vóydəb'l) *adj.* Capable of being voided; especially, capable of being annulled. —**void·a·ble·ness** *n.*

void·ance (vóydənss) *n.* **1. a.** The act of voiding, emptying, or evacuating. **b.** The act of making legally void; annulment. **2.** The condition of being vacant; emptiness.

void·ed (vóydid) *adj. Heraldry.* Having the central area cut out or left vacant, leaving a narrow border or outline.

voile (voyl; *French* vwaal) *n.* A light sheer fabric of cotton, rayon, silk, or wool used in dressmaking or for furnishings. [French, from Latin *vēla,* neuter of *vēlum,* cloth, veil.]

voir dire (vwár deér) *n. Law.* **1.** A preliminary examination concerning the competence of a prospective witness or juror. **2.** The oath administered in such an examination. [Old French, "to speak the truth" : *voir,* truth, from Latin *vērus* + *dire,* to say, from Latin *dīcere.*]

voix cé·leste (vwaá si-lést, say-) *n.* An organ stop that produces a gentle tremolo effect. Also called "vox angelica". [French, "celestial voice".]

vol. **1.** volcano. **2.** volume. **3.** volunteer.

vo·lant (vṓlənt) *adj.* **1.** Flying or capable of flying. **2.** *Poetic.* Moving quickly or nimbly; agile. **3.** *Heraldry.* Depicted with the wings extended as in flying. [Latin *volāns* (stem *volānt-*), present participle of *volāre,* to fly.]

Vo·la·pük (vóllə-pŏŏk, vṓlə-, -pŏŏk, -pük) *n.* An international language invented in 1879, based mainly on English, Latin, and German, and other European languages. [*Vol,* from English WORLD + *pük,* from English SPEECH: coined by its inventor Johann Schleyer (1831–1912), German linguist.] —**Vo·la·pük·ist** *n.*

vo·lar (vṓlər) *adj.* Of or pertaining to the sole of the foot or the palm of the hand. [From Latin *vola,* palm, sole.]

vol·a·tile (vóllə-tīl || *U.S.* -t'l) *adj.* **1.** Evaporating readily at normal temperatures and pressures. **2.** Capable of being readily vaporised. **3.** Changeable, as: **a.** Inconstant; fickle. **b.** Tending to violence; explosive. **c.** Lighthearted; flighty. **d.** Unstable; unpredictable. **e.** Ephemeral; fleeting. **4.** Designating a computer memory which loses stored information when power is cut off. **5.** *Obsolete.* Flying or capable of flying; volant.
~*n.* A volatile substance. [Middle English *volatil,* flying, fleeting, from Old French, from Latin *volātilis,* from *volāre,* to fly.]

volatile oil *n.* A rapidly evaporating oil, especially an essential oil, that does not leave a stain.

vol·a·til·ise, vol·a·til·ize (vo-látti-līz, vō-, və-, vóllәti-) *v.* **-ised, -ising, -ises.** —*intr.* **1.** To become volatile. **2.** To pass off in vapour; evaporate. —*tr.* **1.** To make volatile. **2.** To cause to evaporate. —**vol·a·til·is·a·ble** *adj.* —**vol·a·til·i·sa·tion** (-lī-záysh'n || *U.S.* -li-) *n.* —**vol·a·til·is·er** *n.*

vol·a·til·i·ty (vóllə-tílləti) *n.* The quality or state of being volatile.

vol-au-vent (vól-ə-von, -ō-, -vong, -VON, -vÓN) *n.* A light pastry shell filled with a savoury mixture such as meat or fish in a sauce. [French, "flight in the wind".]

vol·can·ic (vol-kánnik) *adj.* **1.** Of or resembling an erupting volcano. **2.** Produced by or discharged from a volcano. **3.** Powerfully explosive: *a volcanic temper.*

volcanic glass *n.* A volcanic igneous rock of vitreous or glassy texture, such as obsidian or pitchstone.

vol·can·ise, vol·can·ize (vólkə-nīz) *tr.v.* **-ised, -ising, -ises.** To subject to or change by the effects of volcanic heat. —**vol·can·i·sa·tion** (-nī-záysh'n || *U.S.* -ni-) *n.*

vol·can·ism (vólkən-iz'm) *n.* Also **vul·can·ism** (vúlkən-). Volcanic force or activity. [VOLCANO + -ISM.]

vol·ca·no (vol-káynō) *n., pl.* **-noes** or **-nos.** *Abbr.* **vol. 1.** A vent in the earth's crust through which molten lava and gases are ejected. **2.** A mountain formed by the materials so ejected. [Italian, from Latin *Volcānus,* VULCAN.]

Volcano Islands. See **Iwo Jima.**

vol·can·ol·o·gy (vól-kə-nólləji) *n.* Also **vul·can·ol·o·gy** (vúl-). The branch of earth science concerned with volcanic phenomena. —**vol·can·o·log·i·cal** (-nə-lójik'l) *adj.* —**vol·can·ol·o·gist** *n.*

vole¹ (vōl) *n.* Any of various rodents of the genus *Microtus* and related genera, resembling rats or mice but having a relatively short tail. [Earlier *volemouse,* "field mouse", from Norwegian *voll,* field, from Old Norse *vǫllr.*]

vole² *n.* The winning of all the tricks in a card game; a grand slam. [French, from *voler,* to fly, from Old French, from Latin *volāre.*]

Vol·ga (vólgə). River of European Russia. Europe's longest river, and the U.S.S.R's most important, it rises in the Valdai Hills and flows 3 690 kilometres (2,293 miles) east into the Caspian Sea at Astrakhan. Almost entirely navigable, it provides hydro-electric power and irrigation.

Vol·go·grad (vól-gə-grad, -gō-; *Russian* vəlgə-grát). Formerly **Sta·lin·grad** (staálin-grad). City in the U.S.S.R. on the river Volga. It is an important river port and trading centre. The Battle of Stalingrad (1942–43), in which the city was almost destroyed, was a turning point in World War II.

vol·i·tant (vóllitənt) *adj.* **1.** Flying or capable of flying. **2.** Moving

PRONUNCIATION KEY

a, trap; aa, father; ai, fair; ar, star; aw, lawn; ay, play; b, bb, stab; rubber; ch, church; ck, ticket; d, dd, dead; ladder; e, dress; ee, bee; er, defer; ew, few; ewr, pure; ə, about; ər, letter; f, ff, fife; differ; g, gg, giggle; h, hat; i, kit; ī, price; īr, fire; j, judge; k, kick; l, ll, let; 'l, needle; m, mm, man; n, nn, no; 'n, sudden; ng, thing; o, lot; ō, no; ŏŏ, foot; ōō, shoe; oor, poor; ow, cow; owr, hour; oy, boy; p, pp, pepper; r, rr, red; s, ss, sauce; sh, ship; t, tt, totter; th, thick; th, this; smooth; u, cut; ur, turn; v, vv, valve; w, wet; y, yes; z, zz, zebra; zh, vision; pleasure

IN FOREIGN WORDS:

aN, oN, Saint-Saëns; hl, Llanelli; Hluhluwe; kh, loch; lough; Khaled

STRESS MARK:

ín-sīt, insight; in-sīt, incite

about rapidly. [Latin *volitāns* (stem *volitānt-*), present participle of *volitāre,* frequentative of *volāre,* to fly.]

vol·i·ta·tion (vólli-táysh'n) *n.* The act of flying or the ability to fly; flight. **—vol·i·ta·tion·al** *adj.*

vo·li·tion (və-lísh'n, vō-) *n.* **1.** An act of willing, choosing, or deciding. **2.** A conscious choice; a decision. **3.** The power or capability of choosing; the will. [French, from Medieval Latin *volitiō* (stem *volitiōn-*), from Latin *velle* (present stem *vol-*), to wish.] **—vo·li·tion·al** *adj.* **—vo·li·tion·al·ly** *adv.*

vol·i·tive (vóllitiv) *adj.* **1.** Pertaining to or originating in the will. **2.** Expressing a wish or permission.

volk (folk) *n. South African. Often capital* **V.** The Afrikaner people. Preceded by *the.* [Afrikaans, from Dutch, people.]

Völk·er·wan·der·ung (főlkər-van-dər-ŏŏng, -vaan-) *n. German.* The migraton from the 2nd to the 11th century of Germanic and Slavic peoples into Southern and Western Europe.

vol·ley (vólli) *n., pl.* **-leys. 1. a.** The simultaneous discharge of a number of missiles. **b.** The missiles thus discharged. **2.** A bursting forth of a number of things simultaneously: *a volley of oaths.* **3.** *Sports.* A shot, stroke, hit, or kick made at a moving ball before it touches the ground. **4.** In cricket: **a.** A ball bowled so as to reach the batsman before bouncing. **b.** The flight of such a ball. ~*v.* **volleyed, -leying, -leys.** —*tr.* **1.** To discharge (missiles or abuse, for example) in or as if in a volley. **2.** *Sports.* To strike, hit, or kick (a moving ball) before it touches the ground. —*intr.* **1.** To be discharged in or as if in a volley. **2.** To sound loudly and continuously, as guns may. **3.** *Sports.* To make a volley. [French *volée,* from Vulgar Latin *volāta* (unattested), flight, from Latin *volātus,* past participle of *volāre,* to fly.] **—vol·ley·er** *n.*

vol·ley·ball (vólli-bawl) *n.* **1.** A court game in which two teams volley a ball by hand over a high net, each team attempting to ground it on the oppossing team's side. **2.** The ball used in this game.

vo·lost (vól-ost, vŏl-) *n.* **1.** In the Soviet Union, a local unit of the government; a rural soviet. **2.** In tsarist Russia, an administrative division consisting of several villages. [Russian.]

vol·plane (vól-playn) *intr.v.* **-planed, -planing, -planes.** To glide towards the ground with the engine cut off. Used of an aircraft or winged missile. ~*n.* The glide of an aircraft. [French *vol plané* : *vol,* flight, from *voler,* to fly, from Latin *volāre* (see **volant**) + *plané,* past participle of *planer,* to PLANE (to soar).]

Vol·sci (vól-skee, -sī) *pl.n.* A people of ancient Latium in Southwestern Italy whose territory was conquered by the Romans in the fourth century B.C.

Vol·scian (vól-ski-ən, -shi-, -si-) *n.* **1.** The Italic language of the Volsci, related to Umbrian. **2.** A member of the Volsci. **—Vol·scian** *adj.*

Vol·sun·ga Saga (vól-sŏŏng-gə) *n.* An Icelandic saga, recorded in the 13th century, dealing with the exploits of a family of warriors, in particular Sigurd, descended from the great heroic king Volsung. The saga is related to the German **Nibelungenlied** *(see).* [Old Norse, "Saga of the Volsungs".]

volt¹ (vōlt ‖ volt) *n. Abbr.* **V** The SI unit of electric potential and electromotive force, equal to the difference of electric potential between two points on a conducting wire carrying a constant current of one ampere when the power dissipated between the points is one watt. [After Count VOLTA.]

volt², volte (volt ‖ vōlt) *n.* **1.** A circular movement executed by a horse in dressage. **2.** In fencing, a sudden movement made in order to avoid a thrust. [French *volte,* a turn, from Italian *volta,* from Vulgar Latin *volvita* (unattested), from *volvitāre* (unattested), frequentative of Latin *volvere,* to turn.]

vol·ta (vól-tə) *n., pl.* **-te** (-tay). **1.** A brisk dance, in triple time, that was popular in the 16th century. **2.** A piece of music for such a dance. **3.** *Music.* A time, turn, or occasion of a specified ordinal number. Used as a direction: *prima volta.* [Italian, turn, from feminine past participle of *volgere,* to turn, from Latin *volvere,* to roll.]

Vol·ta (vól-tə), **Alessandro (Giuseppe Antonio Anastasio) Count** (1745–1827). Italian physicist. A pioneer in the sphere of electricity, he invented the *electrophorus* (1775), a device to accumulate electricity, and the voltaic pile (1800).

Vol·ta (vól-tə ‖ vŏl-). River of Ghana. West Africa's chief river, it is formed by the union of the Black Volta and the White Volta 64 kilometres (40 miles) northwest of Jenji. Its course carries it 1,125 kilometres (700 miles) southeast and south to the Gulf of Guinea. It has been dammed to produce hydro-electricity.

volt·age (vōl-tij ‖ vól-) *n.* Electromotive force or potential difference, usually expressed in volts.

voltage divider *n.* A resistor or series of resistors provided with taps at certain points to make available a fixed or variable fraction of the applied voltage.

vol·ta·ic (vol-táy-ik ‖ vŏl-) *adj.* **1.** Pertaining to or designating electricity or electric current produced by chemical action; galvanic. **2.** Producing electricity by chemical action. [After Count VOLTA.]

voltaic battery *n.* An electric battery composed of a primary cell or cells.

voltaic cell *n. Electricity.* A **primary cell** *(see).*

voltaic couple *n.* A pair of dissimilar conductors in contact or in the same electrolytic solution, resulting in a difference of potential between them. Also called "galvanic couple".

voltaic pile *n.* A source of direct current consisting of a number of alternating discs of two different metals separated by acid-

---

volcano

THE FIRE BENEATH THE CRUST OF THE EARTH
Molten rock from deep underground is still altering the land surface

Volcanoes exist because molten rock in the Earth's interior is held under pressure, like air in a car tyre. A volcano grows where this molten rock, or magma, erupts through a crack in the Earth's outer skin of solid rock.

The eruption can be slow and relatively steady, so that cooling magma builds up into a cone around the crack, or vent. It was this sort of eruption that gave birth in 1963 to the new Icelandic island of Surtsey. Or the outburst can be devastatingly explosive. The eruption in 1980 of Mount St. Helens in Washington State, U.S.A., for instance, blew off the top 400 metres (about 1,300 feet) of the peak with a force equivalent to 500 Hiroshima bombs.

There are more than 500 active volcanoes around the world. Most are on the Ring of Fire which circles the Pacific, and almost all lie along the edges of the shifting, continent-sized "plates" that make up the Earth's crust.

NEW VOLCANO *The steaming cone of a volcano that appeared on Heimaey island, Iceland, in 1973.*

HOW A VOLCANO GETS ITS SHAPE

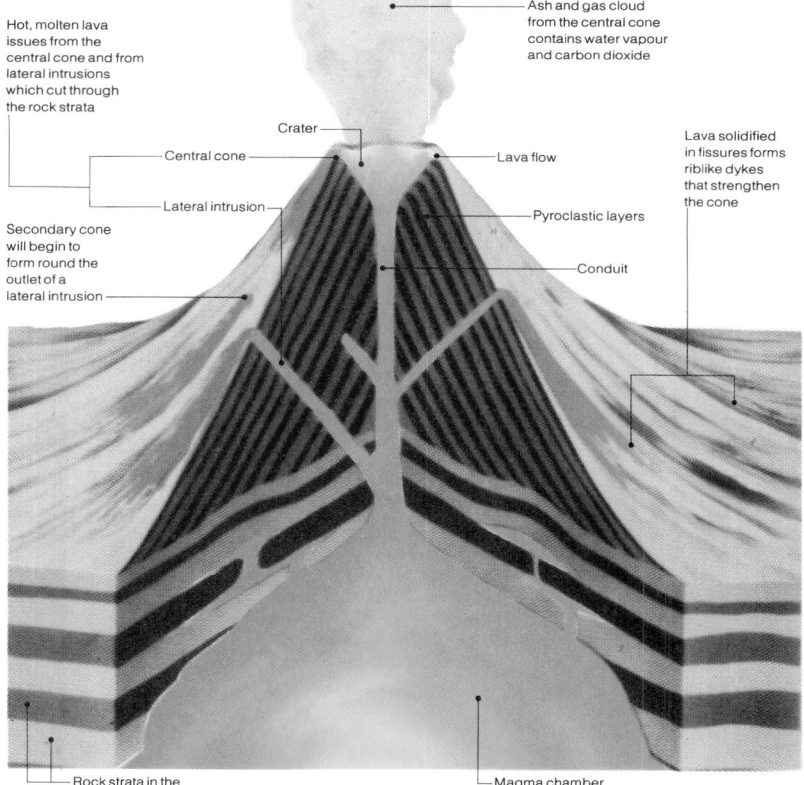

Hot, molten lava issues from the central cone and from lateral intrusions which cut through the rock strata

Ash and gas cloud from the central cone contains water vapour and carbon dioxide

Crater

Central cone

Lateral intrusion

Lava flow

Lava solidified in fissures forms riblike dykes that strengthen the cone

Secondary cone will begin to form round the outlet of a lateral intrusion

Pyroclastic layers

Conduit

Rock strata in the Earth's outer crust

Magma chamber contains molten rock

The classic cone shape of a volcano grows from the debris of its own eruptions. Each time fragments of rock or lava are hurled from the central conduit, some fall back around the crater to harden into a solid skin. Rocks in these layers are known as pyroclastic, from Greek words meaning "broken by fire".

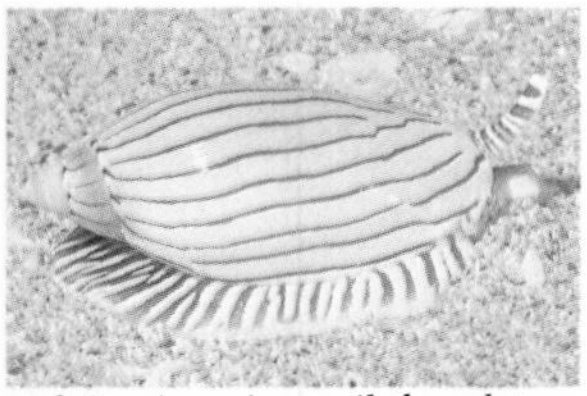

volute *A marine snail, the volute generally has a large colourful shell and is most commonly found in warm shallow waters. This is a Jamrack's volute, found off the west coast of Australia.*

moistened pads, forming primary cells connected in series. Also called "pile".

Voltaic Republic. See **Upper Volta, Republic of.**

Vol·taire (vol-táir), pen-name of François-Marie Arouet (1694–1778). French philosopher and writer. His writings epitomise the Age of Enlightenment, often attacking injustice and intolerance. His best-known works include *Candide* (1759) and the *Dictionnaire philosophique* (1764).

vol·ta·ism (vóltə-iz'm, *often* vóltər-) *n. Electricity.* **Galvanism** *(see).* [VOLTA(IC) + -ISM.]

vol·tam·e·ter (vol-támmitər || vōl-) *n.* A **coulombmeter** *(see).*

volt·am·me·ter (vólt-ám-meetər, -eetər) *n.* An instrument designed to measure current or potential. [VOLT-AM(PERE) + -METER.]

volt-am·pere (vólt-ám-pair || vólt-, -peer) *n.* A unit of electric power equal to the product of one volt and one ampere, equivalent to one watt.

volte. Variant of **volt** (movement).

volte-face (vólt-fáass, -fáss || vólt-) *n., pl.* **-faces** *(pronounced as singular)* or **volte-face.** An about-face; a reversal, as in policy.

volt·me·ter (vólt-meetər) *n.* An instrument, such as a galvanometer, for measuring potential differences in volts.

vol·u·ble (vóllew-b'l) *adj.* **1.** Characterised by a ready flow of words in speaking; fluent; loquacious. **2.** *Archaic.* Turning easily on an axis; rotating. **3.** Twining or twisting, as a plant. —See Synonyms at **talkative.** [French, from Latin *volūbilis,* from *volvere* (past participle *volūtus*), to turn.] **—vol·u·bil·i·ty** (-bílləti), **vol·u·ble·ness** *n.* **—vol·u·bly** *adv.*

vol·ume (vóllewm) *n.* **1.** *Abbr.* **v., vol.** A collection of written or printed sheets bound together; a book. **2.** *Abbr.* **v., vol.** A book that forms part of a series or set of books. Also used adjectivally and in combination: *a two-volume edition.* **3.** Any written material that has been assembled as an individual unit, such as a set of issues of a magazine in a library. **4.** A roll of parchment; a scroll. **5.** *Abbr.* **V a.** The size or extent of a three-dimensional object or region of space. **b.** Broadly, the capacity of such a region or of a specified container. **6.** *Often plural.* A large amount: *volumes of praise.* **7. a.** The amplitude or loudness of a sound. **b.** A control, as on a radio, for adjusting loudness. **8.** A quantity or total: *The volume of sales has increased.* **—speak volumes.** To be informative or deeply significant. [Middle English, roll of parchment, from Old French, from Latin *volūmen,* from *volvere,* to roll, turn.]

vol·umed (vóllewmd) *adj. Poetic.* Forming a rounded or dense mass: *volumed smoke.*

vo·lu·me·ter (vo-léw-mitər, və-, -lŏŏ-) *n.* Any of several instruments for measuring the volume of liquids, solids, and gases.

vol·u·met·ric (vóllew-méttrik) *adj.* Of or pertaining to measurement of volume. Compare **gravimetric. —vol·u·met·ri·cal·ly** *adv.*

volumetric analysis *n.* **1.** Quantitative analysis using accurately measured, especially titrated, volumes of standard chemical solutions. **2.** The analysis of a gas by volume.

vo·lu·mi·nous (və-léw-minəss, vo-, -lŏŏ-) *adj.* **1.** Having great volume, fullness, size, or number. **2. a.** Filling or capable of filling volumes. Said of writing. **b.** Prolific in speech or writing. **3.** *Archaic.* Having many coils; winding: *the voluminous labyrinth.* [Late Latin *volūminōsus,* having many folds, from Latin *volūmen,* roll of writing, VOLUME.] **—vo·lu·mi·nos·i·ty** (-mi-nóssəti), **vo·lu·mi·nous·ness** *n.* **—vo·lu·mi·nous·ly** *adv.*

vol·un·ta·rism (vólləntəriz'm) *n.* **1.** *Philosophy.* The doctrine that the will is primary or dominant over the intellect. **2.** The view that a project or course of action should be based on voluntary participation. **3.** Voluntaryism. **—vol·un·ta·rist** *n.* **—vol·un·ta·ris·tic** (-ístik) *adj.*

vol·un·tar·y (vóllən-tri, -təri || -terri) *adj.* **1.** Arising from one's own free will; acting on one's own initiative: *"Ignorance, when it is voluntary, is criminal"* (Samuel Johnson). **2.** Acting or serving in a specified capacity willingly and without constraint or guarantee of reward. **3.** Controlled by, consisting of, supported by, or done with the aid of contributions or volunteers: *voluntary organisations.* **4.** Capable of exercising will; volitional. **5.** Proceeding from impulse; spontaneous. **6.** *Law.* **a.** Acting or performed without external persuasion or compulsion. **b.** Without legal obligation. **c.** Without payment: *a voluntary conveyance.* **7.** Normally controlled by or subject to individual volition: *voluntary responses.*
~*n., pl.* **voluntaries. 1.** Any act or work not imposed or demanded by another. **2.** The section of a competitor's performance whose contents are chosen by the competitor himself, as in a music or skating competition. **a.** *Music.* A piece of solo organ music, occasionally improvised, that is played usually before and sometimes during or after a church service. **b.** A composition based on or intended for such a performance. **3.** *Obsolete.* A volunteer. [Middle English, from Latin *voluntārius,* from *voluntās,* will, free will, from *velle* (present stem *vol-*), to wish.] **—vol·un·tar·i·ly** (|| *also* -térrəli) *adv.* **—vol·un·tar·i·ness** *n.*

Synonyms: *voluntary, intentional, deliberate, wilful, willing, spontaneous.*

vol·un·tar·y·ism (vóllən-tri-iz'm, -təri- || -terri-) *n.* The principle of reliance on voluntary donations rather than state funds, as for churches or schools. Also called "voluntarism". **—vol·un·tar·y·ist** *n.*

voluntary muscle *n.* Muscle normally controlled by individual volition. See **striated muscle.**

vol·un·teer (vóllən-téer) *n. Abbr.* **vol. 1.** A person who performs or gives his services of his own free will. **2.** *Law.* **a.** A person who renders aid, performs a service, or assumes an obligation voluntarily. **b.** A person who holds property under a deed made without requiring anything in return, such as the heir in a will. **3.** A person who voluntarily does military service, especially when temporary. **4.** A cultivated plant growing from self-sown or accidentally dropped seed.
~*adj.* **1.** Pertaining to or consisting of volunteers: *a volunteer militia.* **2.** Enlisted or serving as a volunteer. **3.** Growing from self-sown or accidentally dropped seed. Said of a plant or crop.
~*v.* **volunteered, -teering, -teers.** —*tr.* To give or offer to give on one's own initiative. —*intr.* To enter into or offer to enter into any undertaking of one's own free will. [French *volontaire,* from Latin *voluntārius,* VOLUNTARY.]

vo·lup·tu·ar·y (və-lúp-tew-əri, -choo-, -chəri || -erri) *n., pl.* **-ies.** A person whose life is given over to luxury and sensual pleasures; a sensualist. [Latin *voluptuārius,* from *voluptārius,* from *voluptās,* pleasure. See **voluptuous.**] **—vo·lup·tu·ar·y** *adj.*

vo·lup·tu·ous (və-lúp-tew-əss, -choo-) *adj.* **1.** Consisting of or characterised by strong visual and tactile delights: *voluptuous forms.* **2.** Devoted to or frequently indulging in sensual gratifications. **3. a.** Full and appealing in form, especially in a sexually appealing way: *a voluptuous mouth.* **b.** Directed towards or anticipating sensuous gratification: *voluptuous thoughts.* **c.** Arising from the satisfying of luxurious or sensual desires. [Middle English, from Old French *voluptueux,* from Latin *voluptuōsus,* from *voluptās,* pleasure.] **—vo·lup·tu·ous·ly** *adv.* **—vo·lup·tu·ous·ness** *n.*

vo·lute (və-léwt, vo-, vō-, -lŏŏt) *n.* **1.** A spiral, scroll-like ornament such as that used on an Ionic capital. **2.** A twisted or spiral formation, such as any of the whorls of a gastropod shell. **3.** Any of various marine gastropod molluscs of the family Volutidae, having a spiral, often colourfully marked shell.
~*adj.* Also **vo·lut·ed** (-id). Having a spiral form; spirally twisted or rolled. [French, from Latin *volūta,* scroll, from the feminine past participle of *volvere,* to turn.]

vo·lu·tion (və-léwsh'n, vo-, vō-, -lŏŏsh'n) *n.* **1.** A turn or twist about a centre; a spiral. **2.** *Zoology.* Any of the whorls of a spiral shell. [From Latin *volvere* (past participle *volūtus*), to turn. See **volute.**]

vol·va (vól-və) *n., pl.* **-vae** (vee). A cuplike structure around the base of the stalk of certain fungi, a remnant of the veil. [Latin *volva, vulva,* covering.] **—vol·vate** (-vayt) *adj.*

vol·vox (vól-voks) *n.* Any of various flagellate green algae of the genus *Volvox,* that form hollow, spherical multicellular colonies. [New Latin, from Latin *volvere,* to turn, roll. See **volute.**]

vol·vu·lus (vólvewləss) *n., pl.* **-luses.** A partial or complete obstruction of the intestine caused by abnormal twisting. [New Latin, from Latin *volvere,* to turn. See **volute.**]

vo·mer (vṓmər) *n.* A flat thin bone that forms part of the nasal septum. [Latin *vōmer,* ploughshare.] **—vo·mer·ine** (-īn, vómmər-, -in) *adj.*

vom·i·ca (vómmi-kə) *n., pl.* **-cae** (-see). **1.** The profuse expectoration of putrid matter. **2. a.** An abnormal pus-containing cavity in a lung, caused by the deterioration of tissue. **b.** The purulent matter contained in such a cavity. [Latin, boil, ulcer, from *vomere,* to VOMIT.]

vom·it (vómmit) *v.* **-ited, -iting, -its.** —*intr.* **1.** To eject part or all of the contents of the stomach through the mouth, usually in a series of involuntary spasmodic movements. **2.** To be discharged forcefully and abundantly; spew forth. —*tr.* **1.** To eject from the stomach through the mouth. **2.** To eject or discharge in a gush; spew out.
~*n.* **1.** The act of ejecting matter from the stomach. **2.** Matter ejected from the stomach. **3.** An emetic. [Middle English *vomiten,* from Latin *vomere* (past participle *vomitus*).] **—vom·it·er** *n.*

vomiting gas *n. Chemistry.* **Chloropicrin** *(see).*

vom·i·tive (vómmitiv) *adj.* Pertaining to or causing vomiting.
~*n.* An emetic.

vom·i·to·ry (vómmi-tri, -təri) *adj.* Inducing vomiting; vomitive.
~*n., pl.* **vomitories. 1.** Something that induces vomiting. **2.** An aperture through which matter is discharged. **3.** Any of the passageways of a Roman amphitheatre leading from the outside wall to the foot of the banked seats.

vom·i·tu·ri·tion (vómmi-tewr-ísh'n) *n.* Forceful but ineffectual attempts at vomiting; retching. [VOMIT + (MICT)URITION.]

vom·i·tus (vómmitəss) *n.* **1.** Vomited matter. **2.** Vomiting. [Latin, past participle of *vomere,* to VOMIT.]

von Braun, Wernher. See von **Braun.**

von Neumann, John. See von **Neumann.**

von Richthofen, Baron Manfred. See von **Richthofen.**

von Sternberg, Josef. See von **Sternberg.**

von Stroheim, Erich. See von **Stroheim.**

voo·doo (vŏŏdoo) *n., pl.* **-doos. 1.** A religious cult of African origin practised in the Western Hemisphere mainly by the blacks of Haiti and characterised by a belief in sorcery and fetishes and by rituals in which participants communicate by trance with ancestors, saints, or animistic deities. **2.** A charm, fetish, spell, or curse believed by adherents of this cult to hold magic power. **3.** A person who practises voodoo. —See Synonyms at **magic.**
~*tr.v.* **voodooed, -dooing, -doos.** To place under the influence of a voodoo spell. [Dahomey *vodu.*] **—voo·doo** *adj.*

voo·doo·ism (vŏŏdoo-iz'm) *n.* **1.** The view of life and death embodied in the voodoo cult. **2.** The practice of voodoo. **—voo·doo·ist** *n.* **—voo·doo·is·tic** (-ístik) *adj.*

Voor·trek·ker (fóor-treckər, vóor-) *n. Often small* **v. 1.** Any of the original Boer pioneers who migrated inland from the Cape of Good

Hope in the 1830s; a participant in the **Great Trek** *(see).* **2.** In South Africa, a member of an Afrikaner youth organisation similar to the Scouts and Girl Guides. [Dutch : *voor,* forward, advance + TREK + -ER.]

vo·ra·cious (və-ráyshəss, vo-, vaw-) *adj.* **1.** Consuming or eager to consume great amounts of food; ravenous. **2.** Having an insatiable appetite for some activity or pursuit: *a varacious reader.* [Latin *vorax* (stem *vorāci-*), from *vorāre,* to devour.] **—vo·ra·cious·ly** *adv.* **—vo·ra·ci·ty** (-rássəti), **vo·ra·cious·ness** *n.*

vor·la·ge (fór-laagə || -fôr-) *n.* A posture assumed in skiing in which the skier leans forwards from the ankles, usually without lifting the heels. [German *Vorlage* : *vor,* before, from Old High German *fora* + *Lage,* stance, from Old High German *lāga.*]

-vorous *adj. comb. form.* Indicates eating or feeding on; for example, **herbivorous.** [Latin *-vorus,* from *vorāre,* to devour.]

Vor·ster (fórstər), **Balthazar Johannes** (1915–). South African politician, leader of the National Party and prime minister of South Africa (1966–78) and subsequently president of South Africa (1978–79). He is a leading advocate of apartheid.

vor·tex (vór-teks) *n., pl.* **-texes** or **-tices** (-ti-seez). **1.** Fluid flow involving rotation about an axis; a whirlwind; a whirlpool. **2.** Any activity or situation that is regarded as drawing into its centre and engulfing all that surrounds it: *swept up in the vortex of hippie culture.* [Latin *vortex, vertex,* from *vertere,* to turn.]

vor·ti·cal (vórti-k'l) *adj.* Also **vor·ti·cose** (-kōz, -kōss). Pertaining to or resembling a vortex; whirling. [From Latin *vortex* (stem *vortic-*), VORTEX.] **—vor·ti·cal·ly** *adv.*

vor·ti·cel·la (vórti-séllə) *n., pl.* **-lae** (-ee). Any of various bell-shaped, ciliated, stalked protozoans of the genus *Vorticella.* [New Latin *Vorticella,* from Latin *vortex* (stem *vortic-*), VORTEX.]

vor·ti·cism (vórti-siz'm) *n.* A short-lived English art movement that arose in 1914 as a result of the impact of futurist ideas on a small group of artists and writers led by Wyndam Lewis. **—vor·ti·cist** *n.*

vor·tig·i·nous (vawr-tíjinəss) *adj.* Whirling; vortical. [From Latin *vortīgō* (stem *vortīgin-*), variant of *vertīgō,* a whirling, from *vertere,* to turn. See **vortex.**]

Vosges Mountains (vōzh). Mountain range of eastern France. Extending 240 kilometres (150 miles) south-southwest to north-northeast, it is separated from Germany's Black Forest by the Rhine's rift valley. Before World War I, the mountains formed the border between Germany and France.

vo·tar·ess (vṓtə-riss, -ress). *n.* Also **vo·tress** (vṓt-). A female votary.

vo·ta·ry (vṓtə-ri) *n., pl.* **-ries.** Also **vo·ta·rist** (-rist). **1.** A person bound by vows to live the religious life; a monk or nun. **2.** Any person fervently devoted, as to a religion, leader, or ideal.
~adj. Archaic. **1.** Consecrated by a vow. **2.** Resembling or pertaining to a vow. [From Latin *vōtus,* past participle of *vovēre,* to vow.]

vote (vōt) *n.* **1.** A formal expression of preference, opinion, or will, as in favour of a candidate for office or a proposed resolution of an issue. **2.** That by which such a preference is made known, such as a raised hand or a ballot. **3.** The number of votes cast in an election or to resolve an issue: *a heavy vote in his favour.* **4.** A group of voters: *the Labour vote.* **5.** The result of an election, referendum, or the like. **6. a.** The right to participate as a voter; suffrage. **b.** A person who has such a right. **7.** Something that is to be or has been decided, expressed, or granted by voting. **—cast (one's) vote.** To make known, deposit, or give in one's vote.
~v. **voted, voting, votes.** *—intr.* **1.** To express one's preference, will, or opinion by a vote; cast one's vote. **2.** To cast one's vote in a specified manner: *vote Liberal.* *—tr.* **1.** To express one's preference for; endorse by a vote. **2.** To bring into existence or make available by vote: *vote new funds for a programme.* **3.** To bring to a specified condition by voting: *voted her out; voted the Tories into office.* **4.** To declare or pronounce by general consent: *voted the play a success.* **5.** *Informal.* To suggest; advocate: *I vote that we forget all about it.* **—vote down.** To defeat by casting a negative vote. [Latin *vōtum,* vow, from *vōtus,* past participle of *vovēre,* to vow.] **—vot·a·ble, vote·a·ble** *adj.* **—vote·less** *adj.* **—vot·er** *n.*

voting machine *n.* An apparatus used at a polling station that mechanically records and counts votes.

vo·tive (vṓtiv) *adj.* **1.** Given or dedicated in fulfilment of a vow or pledge: *a votive offering.* **2.** Expressing a wish, desire, or vow: *a votive prayer.* [Latin *vōtīvus,* from *vōtum,* vow, VOTE.]

votive mass *n. Roman Catholic Church.* A mass that may be celebrated at the priest's discretion, as for a special intention or in honour of a given saint, instead of the mass appointed for the day.

vouch (vowch) *v.* **vouched, vouching, vouches.** *—tr.* **1.** To substantiate by supplying evidence; verify. **2.** *Law.* Formerly, to summon (a landowner) as a witness to give proof of ownership. **3.** *Archaic.* To cite (an authority, doctrine, or principle, for example) as supporting evidence for one's statements, opinions, or actions. **4.** *Obsolete.* To assert; declare. *—intr.* **1.** To furnish a guarantee; give personal assurance. Used with *for.* **2.** To function or serve as a guarantee; furnish supporting evidence. Used with *for: a deed that vouched for his courage.*
~n. Obsolete. A declaration of opinion; an assertion. [Middle English *vouchen,* to summon (as a witness), from Old French *voucher,* from Latin *vōcāre,* to call.]

vouch·er (vówchər) *n.* **1.** A person who vouches; a supporter, sponsor, or witness. **2.** A signed or stamped document that serves as proof that the terms of a transaction have been met. **3.** *Chiefly British.* A document or card that can be exchanged for goods or services: *a gift voucher.*

vouch·safe (vówch-sáyf, vowch-) *tr.v.* **-safed, -safing, -safes.** *Literary.* To condescend to grant or bestow (a reply, favour, or privilege, for example); deign: *vouchsafed us no explanation.* [Middle English *vouchen sauf,* "to warrant as safe" : VOUCH (obsolete sense "to warrant") + SAFE.] **—vouch·safe·ment** *n.*

vous·soir (vōō-swaár) *n.* Any of the wedge-shaped stones that form the curved parts of an arch or vaulted ceiling. [French, from Old French *vossoir,* from Vulgar Latin *volsōrium* (unattested), from *volsus* (unattested), variant of Latin *volutus.* See **volution.**]

vow (vow) *n.* **1.** An earnest promise or pledge that binds one to perform a specified act or behave in a certain manner; especially, a solemn promise to live and act in accordance with the prescriptions of a religious body: *a nun's vows.* **2.** A formal declaration or assertion. **—take vows.** To enter a religious order.
~v. **vowed, vowing, vows.** *—tr.* **1.** To promise or pledge solemnly. **2.** To make a pledge or threat to undertake: *vowing revenge on their persecutors.* **3.** To declare or assert emphatically or formally: *"Well, I vow it is as fine a boy as ever was seen!"* (Henry Fielding). *—intr.* To express a promise or pledge; make a vow. [Middle English *vowe,* from Old French, from Latin *vōtum.* See **vote.**] **—vow·er** *n.*

vow·el (vów-əl, vowl) *n. Abbr.* **v.** **1.** *Phonetics.* A speech sound created by the relatively free passage of breath through the larynx and oral cavity, usually forming the most prominent and central sound of a syllable. Compare **consonant. 2.** A letter that represents such a sound, as, in the English alphabet, *a, e, i, o, u,* and sometimes *y.*
~adj. Of or constituting a vowel or vowels. [Middle English *vowelle,* from Old French *vouel,* from Latin *(littera) vōcālis,* "sounding (letter)", from *vōx* (stem *vōc-*), voice.] **—vowelless** *adj.*

vowel fracture *n. Linguistics.* **Breaking** *(see).*

vowel gradation *n. Linguistics.* **Ablaut** *(see).*

vow·el·ise, vow·el·ize (vów-ə-līz) *tr.v.* **-ised, -ising, -ises.** To provide with vowel points. **—vow·el·i·sa·tion** (-lī-záysh'n || *U.S.* -li-) *n.*

vowel mutation *n. Linguistics.* **Umlaut** *(see).*

vowel point *n.* Any of a number of diacritical marks written above or below consonants to indicate a preceding or following vowel, as in languages such as Hebrew and Arabic that are usually written without vowel letters.

vox an·gel·i·ca (vóks an-jéllikə) *n.* An organ stop, the **voix céleste** *(see).* [Latin, "angelic voice".]

vox hu·ma·na (vóks hew-maánə) *n.* An organ reed stop that produces tones supposedly imitative of the human voice. [Latin, "human voice".]

vox pop (vóks póp) *n., pl.* **vox pops.** *British Informal.* The opinion of a person who is interviewed informally in a public place by a radio or television reporter. **2.** The act of canvassing for such opinions, as by television reporters. [Abbreviation of VOX POPULI.]

vox po·pu·li (vóks póppew-lī, -lee) *n.* Popular opinion or sentiment. [Latin, "voice of the people".]

voy·age (vóy-ij) *n.* **1.** A long journey, usually to a foreign or distant land; especially, a journey across an open sea or ocean. **2.** A record or account of a journey of exploration or discovery. **3.** *Obsolete.* An ambitious project or undertaking.
~v. **voyaged, -aging, -ages.** *—intr.* To make a voyage. *—tr.* To travel or sail over in a journey. [Middle English, from Old French *veiyage,* from Latin *viāticum.* See **viaticum.**] **—voy·ag·er** *n.*

vo·ya·geur (vwī-aa-zhúr, vóy-ə-, -zhôr) *n., pl.* **-geurs** *(pronounced as singular).* A woodsman, boatman, or guide, especially one employed by fur companies to transport furs and supplies between remote stations. [French, "voyager".]

voy·eur (vwī-úr, vwī-, vwaa-yúr) *n.* One who derives sexual pleasure from watching other people undress or engage in sexual activity. [French, "watcher", from *voir,* to see.] **—voy·eur·ism** *n.* **—voy·eur·is·tic** (vwī-ur-ístik) *adj.* **—voy·eur·ist·i·cal·ly** *adv.*

V.P. vice president.

V-par·ti·cle (veé-paartik'l) *n.* Any of several neutral elementary particles with half-lives in the range of 10^{10} to 10^{6} second. [From the V-shaped tracks left by their decay products in a cloud chamber.]

V. Pres. vice president.

V.R. 1. Queen Victoria (Latin *Victoria Regina).* **2.** variant reading. **3.** Volunteer Reserve.

vrai·sem·blance (vráy-som-blónss, -SON-blÓNSS) *n.* The outward appearance of being true or true to life, especially in literature; verisimilitude. [French : *vrai,* true + SEMBLANCE.]

V. Rev. Very Reverend.

V.R.I. Victoria, Queen and Empress (Latin *Victoria Regina et Imperatrix).*

vroom (vrōōm) *interj.* Used to imitate the sound of a fast-moving motor vehicle.

vrot (frot) *adj South African Slang.* **1.** Rotten; putrid. **2.** Disappointing; unsuccessful: *a vrot performance.* [Afrikaans, from Dutch *verrotten,* to rot.]

vs. versus.

v.s. vide supra.

V.S. veterinary surgeon.

V-shaped (veé-shaypt) *adj.* Having the shape of the letter *V: geese flying in a V-shaped formation.*

V sign *n.* **1.** A symbol of victory formed by holding the raised index and middle fingers in the shape of a V, with the palm facing outwards. **2.** The same sign but with the palm facing inwards, used as an indication of hate, contempt, or defiance.

V.S.O. 1. very special old (applied to cognac, Armagnac or port). **2.** Voluntary Service Overseas; a British organisation that arranges

PRONUNCIATION KEY

a, trap; aa, father; ai, **fair**; ar, **star**; aw, **lawn**; ay, **play**; b, bb, stab; **rubber**; ch, **church**; ck, **ticket**; d, dd, **dead**; **ladder**; e, **dress**; ee, **bee**; er, defer; ew, **few**; ewr, **pure**; ə, about; ər, letter; f, ff, **fife**; **differ**; g, gg, **giggle**; h, **hat**; i, **kit**; ī, price; īr, fire; j, **judge**; k, **kick**; l, ll, **let**; 'l, needle; m, mm, **man**; n, nn, **no**; 'n, sudden; ng, **thing**; o, **lot**; ō, no; ōō, **foot**; ōō, **shoe**; oor, **poor**; ow, **cow**; owr, **hour**; oy, **boy**; p, pp, **pepper**; r, rr, **red**; s, ss, **sauce**; sh, **ship**; t, tt, **totter**; th, **thick**; th, **this**; **smooth**; u, **cut**; ur, **turn**; v, vv, **valve**; w, **wet**; y, **yes**; z, zz, **zebra**; zh, **vision**; pleasure

IN FOREIGN WORDS:

aN, ON, **Saint-Saëns**; hl, **Llanelli**; **Hluhluwe**; kh, loch; lough; **Khaled**

STRESS MARK:

ín-sīt, insight; in-sī́t, incite

for young people to do voluntary work and teaching in developing countries. .

V.S.O.P. very superior old pale (usually applied to cognac or Armagnac that is at least four years old).

VT fuse *n. Military.* A **proximity fuse** *(see).* [V(ARIABLE) T(IME) FUSE.]

VTOL vertical takeoff and landing.

VTR video tape recorder.

vug, vugh (vug) *n. Geology.* A small cavity in a rock or vein, especially one lined with crystals. [Cornish *vooga,* cave.]

Vul·can (vúlkən). *Roman Mythology.* The god of fire and craftsmanship, especially metalworking, identified with the Greek god Hephaestus. [Latin *Vulcānus, Volcānus,* perhaps obscurely related to Cretan *Welkhanoc,* from Hittite *Valhannasses*†.]

vul·ca·ni·an (vul-káyni-ən) *adj.* Also **Vul·ca·ni·an, Vul·can·ic** (-kánnik) (for sense 2). **1.** *Geology.* Pertaining to or coming from a volcano or volcanic eruption. **2. a.** Pertaining to the god Vulcan. **b.** Pertaining to craftsmanship or metalworking.

vul·can·ise, vul·can·ize (vúlkə-nīz) *tr.v.* **-ised, -ising, -ises. 1.** To improve the strength, resiliency, and freedom from stickiness and odour of (rubber) by combining with sulphur or other additives in the presence of heat and pressure. **2.** To treat (other substances) similarly. [From VULCAN.] **—vul·can·is·a·ble** *adj.* **—vul·can·i·sa·tion** (-nī-záysh'n ‖ *U.S.* -ni-) *n.* **—vul·can·iz·er** *n.*

vulcanism. Variant of **volcanism.**

vul·can·ite (vúlkən-īt) *n.* A hard material made by heavy vulcanisation of rubber, used for insulators and containers. Also called "ebonite". [VULCAN + -ITE.]

vul·can·ol·o·gy (vúlkə-nólləji) *n.* **Volcanology** *(see).*

vulg. vulgar.

Vulg. Vulgate.

vul·gar (vúlgər) *adj.* **1. a.** Deficient in taste, delicacy, or refinement. **b.** Ill-bred; boorish; crude. **c.** Tasteless in appearance or quality; garish: *a vulgar display of wealth.* **2.** *Abbr.* **vulg.** Obscene or indecent; offensive; coarse or bawdy: *a vulgar joke.* **3.** Of or associated with the masses as distinguished from the educated or cultivated classes; common. **4.** *Abbr.* **vulg.** Spoken by or expressed in a form of a language spoken by the common people; vernacular: *the vulgar tongue.* **—See Synonyms at coarse.**
~*n.* **1.** *Archaic.* The common people; especially, the ignorant and uncultivated: *"The vulgar thus through imitation err."* (Alexander Pope). **2.** *Obsolete.* The vernacular. [Middle English, from Latin *vulgāris,* from *vulgus*†, the common people.] **—vul·gar·ly** *adv.* **—vul·gar·ness** *n.*

vulgar fraction *n.* A **simple fraction** *(see).*

vul·gar·i·an (vul-gaír-i-ən) *n.* A vulgar person; especially, one who makes a conspicuous display of his money.

vulgarise, vul·gar·ize (vúlgə-rīz) *tr.v.* **-ised, -ising, -ises. 1.** To render vulgar; debase; cheapen. **2.** To popularise. **—vul·gar·i·sa·tion** (-rī-záysh'n ‖ *U.S.* -ri-) *n.* **—vul·gar·is·er** *n.*

vul·gar·ism (vúlgəriz'm) *n.* **1.** Vulgarity. **2.** A word, phrase, or manner of expression common in ordinary speech but considered incorrect. **3.** An obscene, indecent, or crude word or phrase.

vul·gar·i·ty (vul-gárrəti) *n., pl.* **-ties. 1.** The condition or quality of being vulgar; tastelessness; coarseness. **2.** Something, as an act or expression, that offends good taste or propriety.

vulture *Adapted for feeding on dead animals, vultures have feeble claws but powerful beaks. Some species can tear the toughest hides. The largest have wingspans of more than 2.5 metres (nearly 9 feet).*

Vulgar Latin *n.* The common speech of ancient Rome, differing from the literary or standard Latin used by the educated classes and forming the basis for the development of the Romance languages. Compare **Classical Latin.**

vul·gate (vúl-gayt, -gət, -git) *n.* **1.** The common speech of a people; the vernacular. **2.** A widely accepted text or version of a work. ~*adj.* Widely distributed and accepted; popular. [From Latin *vulgātus,* common, popular. See **Vulgate.**]

Vulgate *n. Abbr.* **Vulg.** The Latin translation of the Bible made by Saint Jerome at the end of the fourth century A.D., now used in a revised form as the Roman Catholic authorised version. See **Bible.** [Late Latin *vulgāta (ēditiō),* "the popular (edition)", from Latin *vulgātus,* common, popular, from *vulgāre,* to make commonly known, from *vulgus,* common people. See **vulgar.**]

vul·ner·a·ble (vúln-ərəb'l, -rəb'l, *also* vún-) *adj.* **1.** Susceptible to injury, either physical or emotional; unprotected from danger. **2.** Susceptible to physical attack; insufficiently defended. **3. a.** Liable to censure or criticism; assailable. **b.** Suffering from emotional or psychological insecurity. **c.** Liable to succumb to persuasion or temptation. **4.** *Bridge.* In a position to receive greater penalties or bonuses. Said of a team that has won one game of a rubber. [Late Latin *vulnerābilis,* from Latin *vulnerāre,* to wound, from *vulnus* (stem *vulner-*), wound.] **—vul·ner·a·bil·i·ty** (-ərə-bílləti), **vul·ner·a·ble·ness** *n.* **—vul·ner·a·bly** *adv.*

vul·ner·ar·y (vúlnə-rəri ‖ -rerri) *adj. Rare.* Used in the healing or treating of wounds.
~*n. Rare.* A remedy so used. [Latin *vulnerārius,* from *vulnus* (stem *vulner-*), wound. See **vulnerable.**]

Vul·pec·u·la (vul-péckewlə) *n.* A constellation in the Northern Hemisphere near Cygnus and Sagitta. [Latin *vulpēcula,* diminutive of *vulpēs,* fox. See **vulpine.**]

vul·pine (vúl-pīn ‖ -pin) *adj.* Also **vul·pec·u·lar** (-péckewlər). **1.** Of, resembling, or characteristic of a fox. **2.** Clever; devious; cunning. [Latin *vulpīnus,* from *vulpēs,* fox.]

vul·ture (vúlchər) *n.* **1.** Any of various large birds of the family Accipitridae, of the Old World, or the family Cathartidae, of the New World, characteristically having dark plumage, a naked head and neck, and feeding on carrion. **2.** A person of a rapacious or predatory nature. [Middle English, from Old French *voltour,* from Latin *vultur.*]

vul·tur·ine (vúl-chər-īn, -chŏŏr-, -tewr-) *adj.* Also **vul·tur·ous** (-əss). **1.** Pertaining to or characteristic of a vulture. **2.** Suggestive of a vulture; rapacious; predatory.

vul·va (vúl-və) *n., pl.* **-vae** (-vee). The external female genitalia including the labia majora, labia minora, clitoris, and vestibule of the vagina. [Latin *vulva, volva,* womb, covering.] **—vul·val, vul·var, vul·vate** (-vayt) *adj.* **—vul·vi·form** (-vi-fawrm) *adj.*

vul·vi·tis (vul-vītiss) *n. Pathology.* Inflammation of the vulva. [New Latin : VULV(A) + -ITIS.]

vul·vo·vag·i·ni·tis (vúlvō-váji-nītiss) *n. Pathology.* Inflammation of the vulva and vagina. [*Vulvo-,* combining form of VULVA + VAGIN(A) + -ITIS.]

vv. verses.

v.v. vice versa.

vy·ing (vī-ing) *adj.* Competing; contending. **—vy·ing·ly** *adv.*

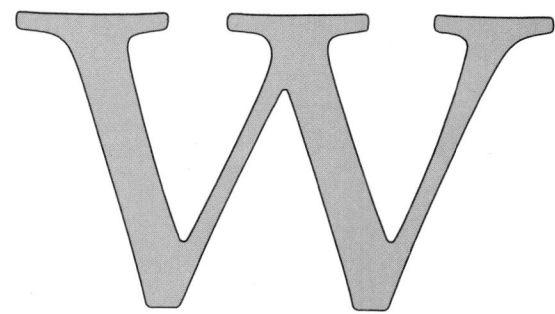

W

w, W (dŭbb'l-yōō, -yōō) *n., pl.* **w's** or *rare* **ws**, **W's** or **Ws**. **1.** The 23rd letter of the modern English alphabet. **2.** Any of the speech sounds represented by this letter.

w, W, w., W. *Note:* As an abbreviation or symbol, *w* may be a small or a capital letter, with or without a full stop. Established forms or those generally preferred precede the definition. When no form is given, all four forms are in general use in that sense. **1. W** The symbol for the element tungsten. [Formerly called WOLFRAM.] **2. W** *Electricity.* watt. **3. W.** Wednesday. **4. w.** week. **5. w.** weight. **6. W.** Welsh. **7.** west; western. **8. w.** wicket. **9. w.** wide (in cricket). **10. w.** width. **11. w.** wife. **12. w.** with. **13 W** women's (size in clothing). **14. w, W** *Physics.* work. **15.** The 23rd in a series.

W.A. Western Australia.

W.A.A.A.F. Women's Auxiliary Australian Air Force.

Waac (wak) *n.* A member of the Women's Army Auxiliary Corps.

WAAC Women's Army Auxiliary Corps (formerly in Britain and the United States).

Waaf (waf) *n.* A member of the Women's Auxiliary Air Force.

WAAF Women's Auxiliary Air Force (formerly in Britain).

wabble. Variant of **wobble.**

Wac (wak) *n. U.S.* A member of the Women's Army Corps.

WAC, W.A.C. Women's Army Corps (in the United States).

wack (wak) *n.* A friend. Usually used in direct address to a male Liverpudlian.

wack·er (wăckər) *n.* Also **whacker**. *Northern English Informal.* A Liverpudlian.

wack·y (wăcki) *adj.* **-ier, -iest.** Also **whack·y** (wăcki, hwăcki). *Informal.* Highly irrational or erratic; crazy; silly. [Probably variant of dialectal *whacky*, a fool, from *whack-head*, "one stunned by a heavy blow on the head", from WHACK.]

wad (wod) *n.* **1.** A small mass of soft material, often folded or rolled, used especially for padding, stuffing, packing, or stopping holes. **2.** A compressed ball, roll, or lump of something, as of tobacco. **3. a.** A plug, as of cloth or paper, used to hold in a powder charge in a muzzle-loading gun or cannon. **b.** A disc, as of felt or paper, to keep the powder and shot in place in a shotgun cartridge. **4.** *Informal.* A large bundle of something rolled up tightly; especially, a bundle of bank notes. **5.** *Often plural. Informal.* A large amount, especially of money. **6.** *Geology.* Hydrated manganese oxides, usually in a soft, black, earthy form, probably resulting from the decomposition of other manganese minerals.
~*v.* **wadded, wadding, wads.** —*tr.* **1.** To compress into a wad. **2.** To pad, pack, line, or plug with wadding. **3. a.** To hold (shot or powder) in place with a wad. **b.** To insert a wad in (a gun). —*intr.* To form into a wad. [Perhaps akin to Dutch *watten*, padding.]

wad·ding (wódding) *n.* **1.** A wad or wads collectively. **2.** A soft or fibrous substance used for padding or stuffing, especially layers of carded cotton or wool. **3.** Material for gun wads.

wad·dle (wódd'l) *intr.v.* **-dled, -dling, -dles. 1.** To walk with short steps that tilt the body from side to side, as a duck does. **2.** To walk heavily and clumsily with a pronounced sway.
~*n.* A waddling gait. [Probably frequentative of WADE.]

wad·dy (wóddi) *n., pl.* **-dies.** *Australian.* A heavy straight stick used as a club or thrown as a missile by Australian Aborigines.
~*tr.v.* **waddied, -dying, -dies.** To strike with a waddy. [An Australian native name, perhaps from English WOOD.]

wade (wayd) *v.* **waded, wading, wades.** —*intr.* **1.** To walk in or through water or something that similarly impedes normal movement. **2.** To make one's way arduously. Often used with *through*: *wade through a boring report.* **3.** To make a vigorous and determined start or attack. Used with *in* or *into.* —*tr.* To cross or pass through by wading.
~*n.* The act of wading. [Middle English *waden*, to go, walk through (water), Old English *wadan*, to go, wade.]

Wade, (Sarah) Virginia (1945–). British tennis player. She won the Wimbledon women's singles championship (1977). She also won the United States (1968), Italian (1971) and Australian (1972) titles.

wad·er (wáydər) *n.* **1.** One that wades. **2.** Any of numerous long-legged birds of the order Charadriiformes, such as cranes, that fre-quent shallow water. Also called "wading bird". **3.** *Plural.* Waterproof high boots or a waterproof garment that covers the legs and extends as far as the waist, worn especially by anglers.

wadge (woj) *n.* Also **wodge**. *British Informal.* A thick bundle; a wad. [Alteration of WEDGE (probably influenced by WAD).]

wa·di (wóddi, *rarely* wáddi, wáadi) *n., pl.* **-dis.** Also **wa·dy** *pl.* **-dies.** In north Africa and southwest Asia, a valley, gully, or riverbed that remains dry except during the rainy season. [Arabic *wādī*.]

wad·mal (wódm'l) *n.* A rough, thick, woollen cloth, formerly used for outer garments by country people in Northern Europe. [Middle English, from Old Norse *vathmal* : *vath*, cloth + *mal*, measure.]

wad·set (wód-set) *n.* An obsolete Scottish form of mortgage. [Middle English : *wad*, Scottish variant of obsolete *wed* ("covenant", "pledge") + SET; probably from Old English phrase *tō wedde settan* (unattested), to put to pledge.]

WAF, W.A.F. Women in the Air Force (in the United States).

wa·fer (wáyfər) *n.* **1.** A small, thin, crisp, sweetened biscuit, eaten especially with ice cream. **2.** A small, thin disc of unleavened bread used in the Eucharist. **3.** In pharmacology, a flat tablet of rice paper or dried flour paste encasing a powdered drug. **4.** A small disc of adhesive material used as a seal for papers. **5.** *Electronics.* A small, thin, flat circular disc of a semiconducting material, such as pure silicon, that is masked, oxide-coated, doped, and otherwise processed for ultimate separation into numerous individual electronic devices or for packaging as an integrated circuit.
~*tr.v.* **wafered, -fering, -fers.** To seal or fasten together with a wafer. [Middle English *wafre*, from Anglo-French, from Old North French *waufre*, from Middle Low German *wāfel*. Compare **waffle.**]

waff (waf, waaf) *v.* **waffed, waffing, waffs.** *Northern British.* —*intr.* To wave; flutter. —*tr.* To cause to wave or flutter.
~*n. Northern British.* **1.** A waving motion. **2.** A waft; a gust of air. **3.** A glimpse. [Middle English (northern) *waffen*, variant of *waven*, to WAVE.]

waf·fle¹ (wóff'l) *n.* A light, crisp batter cake baked in a waffle iron. [Dutch *wafel*, from earlier *waefel*, from Middle Low German *wāfel*. Compare **wafer.**]

waffle² *intr.v.* **-fled, -fling, -fles.** *Chiefly British Informal.* To speak or write in a verbose but aimless or meaningless manner.
~*n. Chiefly British Informal.* Evasive, vague, or verbose speech or writing. [Of dialect origin, frequentative of *waff*, to yelp.]

waffle iron *n.* An appliance having hinged, indented metal plates that impress a grid pattern into waffle batter as it bakes.

waft (woft, waaft ‖ wawft, waft) *v.* **wafted, wafting, wafts.** —*tr.* To carry, cause to go, or send floating gently through the air or over water: *a breeze wafting the odour of roses.* —*intr.* To float easily and gently on or as if on the air or water; drift.
~*n.* **1.** Something, such as a scent, carried through the air. **2.** A light breeze; a rush of air. **3.** The act of wafting or waving. **4.** *Nautical.* **a.** A flag used for signalling or indicating wind direction. **b.** A signal with such a flag. [Originally "to convoy (ships)", from obsolete *wafter*, a convoy, Middle English *waughter*, from Middle Dutch *wachter*, from *wachten*, to watch, guard.]

waft·age (wóft-ij, waaft- ‖ wáwft-, wáft-) *n.* Conveyance over water or passage through the air.

waf·ture (wóf-chər, waaf- ‖ wáwf-, wáf-) *n. Archaic.* **1.** The act or action of waving; a waving movement. **2.** The action of wafting.

wag¹ (wag) *v.* **wagged, wagging, wags.** —*intr.* **1.** To move briskly and repeatedly from side to side, to and fro, or up and down. **2.** To move rapidly in talking, especially in gossiping. Used of the tongue. —*tr.* To wag (a part of the body) as in playfulness, agreement, admonition, or chatter: *wagged his tail.*
~*n.* An act or motion of wagging. [Middle English *waggen*, ultimately from Old English *wagian*, to totter.] —**wag·ger** *n.*

wag² *n.* A humorous or facetious person.
~*tr.v.* **wagged, wagging, wags.** *Chiefly Australian & N.Z.* To play truant from (school). [Perhaps from obsolete *waghalter*, someone likely to be hanged : WAG (verb) + HALTER (hangman's noose).]

wage (wayj) *n.* **1.** *Sometimes plural.* Payment to a worker for labour or services; especially, remuneration on an hourly, daily, or weekly

wagtail *Like other wagtails, the yellow wagtail (above) likes water and is found in marshes and river meadows. It nests on the ground among grasses.*

basis or by the piece. Also used adjectivally: *wage packet.* Compare **salary. 2.** *Plural. Economics.* The portion of the national product that represents the aggregate paid for all contributing labour and services as distinguished from the portion retained by management or reinvested in capital goods.
~*tr.v.* **waged, waging, wages.** To engage in or carry on (something aggressive and sustained, such as a war or campaign). [Middle English, a pledge, wage, soldier's pay, from Old North French, from Germanic *wadhjam* (unattested).]

wage earner *n.* **1.** A person who works for wages. **2.** One whose earnings support a household.

wa·ger (wáyjər) *n.* **1.** An agreement under which each better pledges a certain amount to the other depending upon the outcome of an unsettled matter. **2.** The matter bet on; a gamble. **3.** Something staked on an uncertain outcome; a bet.
~*v.* **wagered, -gering, -gers.** —*tr.* To risk or stake (an amount or possession) on an uncertain outcome; bet. —*intr.* To make a wager; bet. [Middle English, a pledge, prize at a contest, from Anglo-French *wageure,* from Old North French *wagier,* to pledge, from *wage,* a pledge, WAGE.] **—wa·ger·er** *n.*

wager of battle *n.* A former method of trial in Britain, first introduced in Norman times, whereby a defendant's innocence was put to the test in single combat.

wager of law *n.* A former method of trying an accused person in Britain, in which the accused swore his innocence under oath and 11 people who knew him had to do likewise.

wa·ges (wájiz) *n. Used with a singular or plural verb. Literary.* A fitting return or recompense; a requital: *"For the wages of sin is death"* (Romans 6:23).

wage scale *n.* The scale of wages paid to employees for the various jobs within an industry or organisation.

wage·work·er (wáyj-wurkər) *n. U.S.* A wage earner.

wag·ga (wóggə) *n. Australian.* A blanket made from from sacks or hessian bags. [After WAGGA WAGGA.]

Wag·ga Wag·ga (wóggə wóggə). Town of New South Wales, southeastern Australia. Situated on the river Murrumbidgee, it is a trade and service centre for the Riverina and Western Slopes regions.

wag·ger·y (wággəri) *n., pl.* **-ies. 1.** Waggish behaviour or spirit; drollery. **2.** A droll remark or act. [From WAG (joker).]

wag·gish (wággish) *adj.* Characteristic of a wag; playfully humorous. See Synonyms at **playful. —wag·gish·ly** *adv.* **—wag·gish·ness** *n.*

wag·gle (wágg'l) *v.* **-gled, -gling, -gles.** —*tr.* To move (an attached part) with short, quick motions: *She waggled her foot impatiently.* —*intr.* To move shakily; wobble.
~*n.* A waggling motion. [Frequentative of WAG.] **—wag·gly** *adj.*

Wag·ner (vaág-nər), **(Wilhelm) Richard** (1813–83). German composer. He developed the use of leitmotifs to pioneer opera as music drama. His most famous work is his operatic cycle, *Der Ring des Nibelungen,* an epic treatment of German mythology.

Wag·ne·ri·an (vaag-néer-i-ən) *adj.* **1.** Of or pertaining to Richard Wagner, his music, or his theories. **2.** Characteristic or suggestive of the music dramas of Wagner, especially their grandness and emphasis on drama as well as music.
~*n.* Also **Wag·ner·ite** (vaág-nər-īt). An admirer or disciple of Richard Wagner.

wag·on (wággən) *n.* Also *chiefly British* **wag·gon. 1.** A four-wheeled, usually horse-drawn vehicle having a large rectangular body for transporting loads and often a detachable cover. **2.** *British.* A railway goods vehicle, especially an open goods car. **3.** *Chiefly U.S.* **a.** A light transport or delivery vehicle, such as a milk float. **b.** A **station wagon** *(see).* **c.** A police van used for transporting prisoners. **d.** A child's low four-wheeled cart. **e.** A trolley used when serving drinks or food. **4.** *Obsolete.* A chariot. **—off the wagon.** *Slang.* No longer abstaining from alcoholic drinks. **—on the wagon.** *Slang.* Abstaining from alcoholic drinks.
~*tr.v.* **wagoned, -oning, -ons.** Also *chiefly British* **wag·gon.** To transport by wagon. [Earlier *wagen, waghen,* from Dutch, from Middle Dutch; akin to Old English *wægn,* WAIN.]

wag·on·er (wággənər) *n.* **1.** A wagon driver. **2.** *Obsolete.* A driver of a chariot.

wag·on·ette (wággə-nét) *n.* A light horse-drawn wagon with two seats, facing lengthways, placed behind the driver's seat.

wa·gon-lit (vág-ON-lée, vaág-, -on-, -lee) *n., pl.* **wagons-lits** or **wagon-lits** (-z, *or pronounced as singular*). A sleeping car on a European railway train. [French : *wagon,* railway car + *lit,* bed.]

wag·on·load (wággən-lōd) *n.* The load held by one wagon.

wagon train *n.* A line or train of wagons travelling cross-country.

wag·tail (wág-tayl) *n.* Any of various birds of the genus *Motacilla* and related genera, having a long, wagging tail.

Wah·ha·bi, Wa·ha·bi (waa-haá-bi, wə-) *n.* Also **Wah·ha·bite** (-bīt). A member of a Muslim sect founded by Abd-al Wahhab in the 18th century, known for its strict observance of the original words of the Koran and flourishing mainly in Saudi Arabia. **—Wah·ha·bism, Wa·ha·bism** (-biz'm) *n.*

wa·hi·ne (waa-hée-ni, -nay) *n.* A woman or wife, especially a Polynesian or Maori woman. [Hawaiian and Maori.]

wah-wah, wa·wa (waá-waa) *n.* **1.** A wavering sound produced by alternately covering and uncovering the bell of a trumpet or trombone with a mute. **2.** A similar sound produced by an electric guitar by means of an electronic attachment (a *wah-wah pedal*).

waif[1] (wayf) *n.* **1. a.** A stray homeless person, especially a forsaken or orphaned child. **b.** An abandoned young animal. **2.** Something found and unclaimed, such as an object cast up by the sea. [Middle English *waife, wayf,* ownerless property, from Anglo-French *waif, weif,* variant of Old North French *gaif,* from Scandinavian.]

waif[2] *n.* A small flag for signalling; a waft. [Probably from Scandinavian, akin to Old Norse *veif,* a waving thing.]

Wai·ka·to (wī-káttō). Longest river of New Zealand. Rising in Lake Taupo on North Island it flows 425 kilometres (260 miles) through dairylands to enter the Tasman Sea south of Auckland.

wail (wayl) *v.* **wailed, wailing, wails.** —*intr.* **1.** To grieve or protest loudly and bitterly; lament. **2.** To make a prolonged, high-pitched sound suggestive of a cry: *wailing winds.* —*tr.* **1.** *Poetic.* To lament over; bewail. **2.** To express plaintively. —See Synonyms at **cry.**
~*n.* **1.** A long, loud, high-pitched cry as of grief or pain. **2.** Any similar sound. [Middle English *wailen, weilen,* probably from Old Norse *veila* (unattested), to moan, lament; akin to *vei,* WOE.] **—wail·er** *n.* **—wail·ing·ly** *adv.*

wail·ful (wáylf'l) *adj.* **1.** Resembling a wail; mournful; plaintive. **2.** Issuing a sound like a wail.

Wail·ing Wall (wáyling) *n.* A wall in the old city of Jerusalem believed to be a remnant of the Temple of Herod (the second temple of Jerusalem) and revered by Jews as a place of pilgrimage, lamentation, and prayer. Also called the "Western Wall".

wain (wayn) *n. Poetic & Regional.* A large, open farm wagon. [Middle English, Old English *wæg(e)n, wǣn.*]

wain·scot (wáyn-skət, wén-, -skot || -skōt) *n.* **1.** A facing or panelling, usually of wood, applied to the walls of a room. **2.** The lower part of an interior wall when finished in a material different from that of the upper part.
~*tr.v.* **wainscoted** or **-scotted, -scoting** or **-scotting, -scots.** To line or panel (a room or wall) with wainscot. [Middle English *waynscot(te), weynshet,* from Middle Low German *wagenschot,* perhaps "timber for wagons" : *wagen,* WAGON + *schot,* planking.]

wain·scot·ing (wáyn-skət-ing, wén-, -skot- || -skōt-) *n.* Also **wain·scot·ting. 1.** A wainscoted surface of a wall or walls; panelling. **2.** Wood or other material for such panelling.

wain·wright (wáyn-rīt) *n.* A builder and repairer of wagons.

waist (wayst) *n.* **1.** The part of the human trunk between the bottom of the rib cage and the pelvis. **2. a.** The part of a garment that encircles the waist of the body. **b.** Formerly, the upper part of a garment, extending from the shoulders to the waistline; especially, the bodice of a woman's dress. **3.** The middle section or part of an object, especially when narrower than the rest, as on a violin or hourglass. **4.** *Nautical.* The middle part of the deck of a ship between the forecastle and the quarter-deck. **5.** The centre portion of an aircraft; the fuselage. [Middle English *wa(a)st,* Old English *wæst* (unattested), growth, size of body; akin to WAX (to grow).]

waist·band (wáyst-band || -bənd) *n.* A band of material encircling and fitting the waist, as on a pair of trousers or a skirt.

waist·cloth (wáyst-kloth || -klawth) *n., pl.* **-cloths** (-kloths || -klawthz, klawths, -klothz). *Archaic.* A loincloth.

waist·coat (wáyss-kōt, wáyst-, *old-fashioned* wéss-kət, -kit) *n.* **1.** *Chiefly British.* A waistlength, close-fitting, sleeveless garment, usually buttoning up the front and typically worn by men over a shirt and under a suit jacket. Also *U.S.* "vest". **2.** A garment formerly worn by men under a doublet.

waist·ed (wáystid) *adj.* **1.** Having a waist or a part like a waist. **2.** Having a waist of a specified kind. Used in combination: *low-waisted.*

waist·line (wáyst-līn) *n.* **1. a.** The natural indentation of the body at the waist; the place at which the circumference of the waist is smallest. **b.** The measurement of this circumference. **2.** The point or line at which the skirt and bodice of a dress join.

wait (wayt) *v.* **waited, waiting, waits.** —*intr.* **1. a.** To remain inactive, defer action, or stay in one spot until something anticipated occurs or until a specified time: *Wait until I get home!* **b.** To tarry until another catches up: *Wait for me!* **2.** To be in a state of readiness or expectancy: *waiting for our results.* **3.** To be temporarily neglected, unattended to, or postponed: *The trip had to wait.* **4.** To work as a waiter or waitress. —*tr.* **1.** To remain or stay in expectation of; await: *wait one's turn.* **2.** *Informal.* To delay (a meal or event); postpone. —See Synonyms at **stay. —wait for it.** *Chiefly British Informal.* Used as an exclamation before saying something that is surprising, important, or newsworthy. **—wait on.** Also (for senses 1, 2, 3) **wait upon. 1. a.** To serve the needs of; be in attendance upon. **b.** To take orders from and serve food and drink to (customers in a restaurant). **c.** To be the waiter in attendance on (a table in a restaurant). **2.** To make a formal call upon; visit. **3.** *Literary.* To follow as a result. **4.** *Regional.* To wait for. **—wait out.** To wait until the termination of: *wait out a war.* **—wait up.** To postpone going to bed in anticipation of something or someone.
~*n.* **1.** The act of waiting or the time spent waiting. **2.** *Plural. British.* **a.** Formerly, a group of musicians employed by a town or city to play in parades, public ceremonies, or the like. **b.** A group of musicians who perform carols in the streets at Christmas time. **—lie in wait.** To be on the watch; especially, to wait in ambush. [Middle English *waiten, wayten,* to watch, lie in wait, wait, from Old North French *waitier,* from Germanic *wahtan* (unattested), to watch.]

Usage: *Wait* is generally used intransitively (*I'll wait*); *await* is generally transitive (*A car awaits her at the station*). When used with reference to persons and physical objects, *wait for* is normal (*We were waiting for a train*), *await* being extremely formal (*We were awaiting the train*). When used with reference to intangible things or

PRONUNCIATION KEY

a, trap; aa, father; ai, fair; ar, star; aw, lawn; ay, play; b, bb, stab; rubber; ch, church; ck, ticket; d, dd, dead; ladder; e, dress; ee, bee; er, defer; ew, few; ewr, pure; ə, about; ər, letter; f, ff, fife; differ; g, gg, giggle; h, hat; i, kit; ī, price; īr, fire; j, judge; k, kick; l, ll, let; 'l, needle; m, mm, man; n, nn, no; 'n, sudden; ng, thing; o, lot; ō, no; ŏŏ, foot; ōō, shoe; oor, poor; ow, cow; owr, hour; oy, boy; p, pp, pepper; r, rr, red; s, ss, sauce; sh, ship; t, tt, totter; th, thick; th, this; smooth; u, cut; ur, turn; v, vv, valve; w, wet; y, yes; z, zz, zebra; zh, vision; pleasure

IN FOREIGN WORDS:

aN, oN, Saint-Saëns; hl, Llanelli; Hluhluwe; kh, loch; lough; Khaled

STRESS MARK:

ín-sīt, insight; in-sít, incite

abstract notions, *await* is much less restricted (*We're awaiting the announcement*), and is only a little more formal than *wait for*.

wait-a-bit (wáytəbit) *n.* Any of several plants having sharp, often hooked thorns. [Translation of South African Dutch *wacht-en-bitje* (because the thorns catch hold of passers-by).]

wait·er (wáytər) *n.* **1.** A man who serves at a table, as in a restaurant. **2.** A tray or salver.

wait·ing (wáyting) *n.* The act of remaining stationary or inactive; especially, the act of parking a car by the roadside: *No waiting.* **—in waiting.** In attendance, especially at a royal court.

waiting game *n.* The stratagem of allowing time to pass before acting, in order to gain an advantage.

waiting list *n.* A list of persons waiting, as for an appointment, vacancy, or the like.

waiting room *n.* A room, as at a railway station or doctor's surgery, for the use of persons waiting.

wait·ress (wáy-triss, -trəss) *n.* A woman or girl who serves at a table, as in a restaurant.

waive (wayv) *tr.v.* **waived, waiving, waives. 1.** To relinquish or give up (a claim or right) voluntarily. **2.** To refrain from insisting upon or enforcing (a rule or penalty, for example); dispense with. **3.** To put aside temporarily; defer. —See Synonyms at **relinquish.** [Middle English *weiven,* to outlaw, abandon, relinquish, from Anglo-French *weyver,* variant of Old North French *gaiver,* from *gaif,* ownerless property. See **waif.**]

waiv·er (wáyvər) *n.* **1.** The intentional relinquishment of a right, claim, or privilege. **2.** A document that evidences such an act. [Anglo-French *weyver,* from *weyver,* to WAIVE.]

Waj·da (vī́-də, -daa), **Andrzej** (1926–). Polish film director. His trilogy, *A Generation* (1954), *Kanal* (1956), and *Ashes and Diamonds* (1958), depicts wartime and postwar Poland. Later films include *The Wedding* (1972) and *Man of Iron* (1981).

wake¹ (wayk) *v.* **woke** (wōk) or *rare* **waked** (waykt), **woken** (wṓkən) or *chiefly British & regional* **woke** or *archaic* **waked, waking, wakes.** *—intr.* **1. a.** To cease to sleep; become awake; awaken. Often used with *up.* **b.** To be brought into a state of awareness, attention, or alertness. Often used with *to, up,* or *up to: woke to the facts; wake up and listen.* **2.** *Archaic & Irish.* To keep watch or guard, especially over a corpse. **3.** To be or remain awake. Now used chiefly in the present participle: *during all his waking hours.* *—tr.* **1.** To rouse from sleep; awaken. Often used with *up.* **2.** To stir, as from a dormant or inactive condition; rouse: *wake old animosities.* **3.** To make aware; alert: *It woke him to the facts.* **4. a.** *Archaic.* To keep a vigil over. **b.** *Archaic & Irish.* To hold a wake over.

~n. **1. a.** *Archaic.* A watch; a vigil. **b.** A watch over the body of a deceased person before burial, sometimes accompanied by festivity. **2. a.** In Britain, a parish festival held annually, often in honour of the patron saint. **b.** *Usually plural.* In northern England, an annual holiday during which many factories close for a week or more. **3.** The condition of being awake: *between wake and sleep.* [Middle English *wakien* and *waken,* Old English *wacian,* to be awake and *wacan* (unattested), to rouse.]

Usage: The verbs *wake, waken, awake,* and *awaken* each have transitive and intransitive uses. *Awake* is largely used intransitively (*I awoke at six*), and *waken* transitively (*I wakened her at six*). In passive constructions, the verbs *awaken* and *waken* are more widely used than the verbs *awake* or *wake* (*I was awakened/wakened by the phone*). *Wake* is especially common with *up,* is the most frequently used of all these verbs, and may be transitive or intransitive. *Awake* and *awaken* are the more prevalent verbs in figurative usage: *She awoke to the danger; Her suspicions were awakened.*

wake² *n.* **1.** The visible track of turbulence left by something moving through water: *the wake of a ship.* **2.** The track or course left behind anything that has passed: *The war left nothing but destruction in its wake.* **—in the wake of. 1.** Following directly upon. **2.** In the aftermath of; as a consequence of. [Probably Middle Low German *wake,* from Old Norse *vǫk,* a hole or crack in ice.]

Wake·field (wáyk-feeld). City and administrative centre of West Yorkshire, northern England. Situated on the river Calder.

wake·ful (wáykf'l) *adj.* **1. a.** Not sleeping or not able to sleep. **b.** Without sleep; sleepless. **2.** Watchful; alert; vigilant. **—wake·ful·ly** *adv.* **—wake·ful·ness** *n.*

wake·less (wáyk-ləss, -liss) *adj.* Unbroken. Said of sleep.

wak·en (wáykən) *v.* **-ened, -ening, -ens.** *—tr.* **1.** To rouse from sleep; awake. **2.** To rouse from a quiescent or inactive state; stir. *—intr.* To become awake; wake up. See Usage note at **wake.** [Middle English *wak(e)nen,* Old English *wæcn(i)an.*] **—wak·en·er** *n.*

wake-rife (wáyk-rīf) *adj. Chiefly Scottish.* Wakeful; alert; vigilant. [Middle English : WAKE (noun) + RIFE.]

wake-rob·in (wáyk-robbin) *n.* Any of various plants of the family Araceae, especially the cuckoopint. [WAKE (rouse) + *Robin* (man's name).]

Waks·man (wáksmən), **Selman Abraham** (1888–1973). Russian-born U.S. biologist. He discovered the antibiotics actinomycin (1940), and streptomycin (1943). He won the Nobel prize for physiology or medicine (1952).

Wa·la·chi·a (wo-láyki-ə, wə-). Region of south Romania, southeast Europe. Situated between the Transylvanian Alps and the river Danube, it was founded as a principality (1290) and was ruled by Turkey from 1387 until united with Moldavia (1859) to form Romania. Its chief town is Bucharest.

Wal·den·ses (wawl-dén-seez, wol-) *pl.n.* A Christian sect of dissenters originating in southern France in the late 12th century under the leadership of Peter Waldo, a Lyons merchant. Also called "Vaudois". **—Wal·den·si·an** (-si-ən, -sh'n) *adj & n.*

wald·grave (wáwl-grayv, wáwld- || wól-, wóld-) *n.* In medieval Germany, a king's officer in charge of a royal forest. [German *Waldgraf*: *Wald,* forest + *Graf,* count, ruler.]

Wald·heim (vált-hīm), **Kurt.** (1918–). Austrian statesman. He was secretary general of the United Nations (1972–81).

Wal·dorf salad (wáwl-dawrf || wól-) *n.* A salad of diced raw apples, celery, and walnuts mixed with mayonnaise. [Originally served in the *Waldorf*-Astoria Hotel, New York City.]

wale¹ (wayl) *n.* **1.** A mark raised on the flesh, as by a whip; a weal. **2. a.** Any of the parallel ribs or ridges in the surface of a fabric such as corduroy. **b.** The texture or weave of such a fabric: *a wide wale.* **3.** A ridge woven round a basket to strengthen it. **4.** *Nautical.* **a.** The gunwale. **b.** Any of the heavy planks or strakes extending along the sides of a wooden ship. [Middle English *wale,* a ridge, gunwale, Old English *walu,* a ridge of earth or stone, weal.]

wale² (wayl) *n. Northern British.* **1.** A choice. **2.** Something that is chosen or picked out as the best.

~tr.v. **waled, waling, wales.** *Northern British.* To choose; select. [Middle English, from Old Norse *val,* choice.]

Wa·ler (wáylər) *n.* A horse exported from Australia, especially from New South Wales. [*(New South) Wal(es)* + -ER.]

Wales (waylz). *Welsh* **Cym·ru** (kṓomri). Principality of Great Britain. Bounded by the Irish channel to the north and west, the Bristol Channel to the south, and England to the east, it forms the western peninsula of Great Britain. It is crossed by many mountains, including the Cambrians which rise to 1 085 metres (3,560 feet) at Mount Snowdon, and is drained by the rivers Usk, Severn, Dee, and Wye. The north is an agricultural region where livestock are bred and cereals and vegetables are grown, while the extensive coalfield of the south has fuelled many industries including iron and steel, tinplate, and copper manufacture. Decreased demand during the 1970s and 1980s, however, has led to the closure of many plants and diversification into light industry. Incorporated with England since the Act of Union (1536) it has a distinctive culture and a language still widely spoken. Its capital is Cardiff.

Wa·le·sa (va-wén-sə), **Lech** (1943–). Polish trade union leader. He was an electrician at the Lenin shipyard in Gdansk between 1966–76 and from 1980. He became the chairman of the Strike Committee in 1980 and was chairman of Solidarity, an independent trade union banned in 1981.

Walhalla. Variant of **Valhalla.**

walk (wawk) *v.* **walked, walking, walks.** *—intr.* **1.** To advance at a walk; move by steps. **2.** To roam about in visible form; appear. Used of a ghost or other spirit. **3.** To travel or go on foot, especially for pleasure or exercise. **4.** To conduct oneself or behave in a particular manner; live. **5.** In cricket, to leave one's crease in acknowledgment that one is out. **6.** In basketball, to move illegally while holding the ball; travel. **7.** To disappear as a result of theft; be stolen: *My calculator's walked!* *—tr.* **1.** To go or pass over, on, or through by walking: *walk the streets.* **2.** To bring to a specified condition or state by walking: *walk someone to exhaustion.* **3.** To cause to walk or proceed at a walk: *walk a horse uphill.* **4.** To accompany in walking; escort on foot: *walk her home.* **5.** To assist or force to walk. **6.** To traverse on foot in order to survey or measure; pace off. **7.** To move (a heavy or cumbersome object) in a manner suggestive of walking. **—walk all over.** To treat contemptuously or inconsiderately. **—walk away from.** *Chiefly U.S. Informal.* **1.** To outdo, outrun, or defeat with little difficulty. **2.** To survive (an accident) with very little injury. **—walk away with.** *Informal.* To win very easily. **—walk into. 1.** To obtain (a job, for example) easily. **2.** To encounter or be caught by (a trap, for example), inadvertently or through carelessness. **—walk off. 1.** To leave abruptly or rudely. **2.** To purge or rid oneself of by walking: *walked off his anger.* **—walk off with.** *Informal.* **1.** To walk away with. **2.** To steal. **—walk out on.** *Informal.* To desert; abandon.

~n. **1. a.** The gait of a human being or other biped in which the feet are lifted alternately with one part of a foot always on the ground. **b.** The gait of a quadruped, slower than a trot, in which at least two feet are always touching the ground. **c.** The gait of a horse in which the feet touch the ground in the four-beat sequence of near hind foot, off forefoot, off hind foot, near forefoot. **d.** The self-controlled movement in space of an astronaut. **2.** The act or an instance of walking; especially, a stroll for pleasure or exercise. **3. a.** The rate at which one walks; a walking pace. **b.** The characteristic way in which one walks. **4.** The distance covered or to be covered by walking. **5.** A place designed for walking on or along, such as a pavement or promenade. **6.** A route or circuit particularly suitable for walking: *one of the prettiest walks in the area.* **7.** A race in which contestants must walk. **8.** An enclosed area for the exercise or pasture of livestock. **9. a.** An arrangement of trees or shrubs planted in widely spaced rows. **b.** The space between such rows. **10.** *Chiefly British.* The round of a postman, trader, or the like. [Middle English *walken* and *walkien,* respectively from Old English *wealcan,* to roll, toss, and *wealcian,* to roll up, muffle up.]

walk·a·bout (wáwk-ə-bowt) *n.* **1.** A period spent by an Australian Aborigine wandering in the bush. Often used in the phrase *go walkabout.* **2.** A stroll made by an important person, such as a monarch or foreign dignitary, among a crowd.

walk·a·way (wáwk-ə-way) *n. U.S.* A **walkover** *(see).*

walk·er (wáwkər) *n.* **1.** One that walks. **2.** A light, wheeled framework with a seat in the middle, used to support a baby learning to

Wailing Wall *The Wailing or Western Wall is a place of prayer and pilgrimage sacred to the Jews. Part of it, dating from the second century* B.C., *is all that remains of the Second Temple of Jerusalem, destroyed by the Romans in* A.D. *70. Fifty metres (160 feet) high, it is now part of a larger wall around a mosque.*

wallaby *Native to Australasia, wallabies resemble their larger cousins, the kangaroos.*

wall creeper *The ability of* Tichodroma muraria, *the wall creeper (above), to half-climb, half-flutter on rock faces looking for food has earned it the name butterfly bird among mountaineers. It inhabits alpine areas from southern Europe to the Chinese Himalayas.*

walk. **3.** A light framework with bars that can be leant on, used by a disabled person for support and balance when walking.

walk·ie-talk·ie (wáwki-táwki, -tawki) *n.* Also **walk·y-talk·y** *pl.* **-ies.** A battery-powered, portable sending and receiving radio set.

walk-in (wáwk-ín, -in) *adj.* **1.** Large enough to admit entrance: *a walk-in wardrobe.* **2.** *U.S.* Located so as to be entered directly from the street: *a walk-in apartment.* **—walk-in** (-in) *n.*

walk·ing (wáwking) *adj.* Regarded as having the capabilities or qualities of a specified inanimate object: *He's a walking bomb.*

walking bass *n.* In jazz, an accompaniment played on a bass instrument, especially a double bass, one note to each beat of the bar.

walking papers *pl.n. Chiefly U.S. Informal.* Notice of discharge or dismissal.

walking stick *n.* **1.** A cane or staff used as an aid in walking. **2.** *U.S.* A **stick insect** *(see).*

walk of life *n.* An occupation, profession, or social class: *People from all walks of life supported the cause.*

walk-on (wáwk-on || -awn) *n.* A minor role, usually non-speaking, in a theatrical production. Also called "walk-on part".

walk out *intr.v.* **1.** To go on strike. **2.** To leave or resign, especially abruptly, as a sign of disagreement or anger. **3.** *British Archaic.* To go out together as a courting couple.

walk·out (wáwk-owt) *n.* **1.** A strike by workers. **2.** The act of leaving a meeting, company, or organisation, especially as a sign of protest.

walk over *tr.v.* **1.** *Informal.* To treat inconsiderately or contemptuously. **2.** To gain an easy or uncontested victory over.

walk·o·ver (wáwk-ōvər) *n.* **1.** A horse race with only one horse entered, won by the formality of walking the course. **2.** A victory secured as a formality in a contest through the failure of one party to compete. **3.** *Informal.* An easily won contest or an easy achievement.

walk through *tr.v.* To perform (a play, acting role, or dance, for example) in a rudimentary fashion, as at a first rehearsal.

walk-through (wáwk-thrōō) *n.* A rehearsal at which the performers walk through their parts or steps.

walk·up, walk-up (wáwk-up) *n. U.S.* **1.** A block of flats or offices with no lift. **2.** A flat or office in such a building. **—walk·up** *adj.*

walk·way (wáwk-way) *n.* **1.** A passage or path for walking, such as one that connects parts of a building. **2.** A **moving pavement** *(see).*

Walkyrie. Variant of **Valkyrie.**

walky-talky. Variant of **walkie-talkie.**

wall (wawl) *n.* **1.** An upright structure of masonry, wood, plaster, or other building material serving to enclose, divide, or protect an area; specifically, a vertical construction forming an inner partition or exterior side of a building. Also used adjectivally and in combination: *wall hangings; wallpaper.* **2.** *Usually plural.* A continuous structure of masonry or other material forming a rampart and built for defensive purposes. **3.** A structure of stonework, cement, or other material built to retain a flow of water; a dam, levee, or dyke. **4.** Something resembling a wall in appearance, function, or construction, such as a very steep or vertical rock face on a mountain. **5.** *Anatomy.* The internal surface of a body cavity: *the abdominal wall.* **6.** In surfing, the vertical surface of a wave. **7.** Something resembling a wall in impenetrability or strength: *a wall of silence.* **8.** An extreme or desperate condition or position, such as defeat or ruin. Used in such phrases as *drive to the wall* and *go to the wall.* **9.** In soccer, a group of players forming a line in order to try to prevent the opposition from taking a direct shot at the goal. **10.** The physical and psychological barrier allegedly encountered by marathon runners, usually after about 20 miles (32 kilometres). Preceded by *the.* **—up the wall.** *Informal.* **1.** Crazy; mad. **2.** Very angry; furious.
~*tr.v.* **walled, walling, walls.** **1.** To enclose, surround, or fortify with or as if with a wall. **2.** To divide or separate with or as if with a wall: *wall off half a room.* **3.** To enclose within a wall; immure. **4.** To block or close (an opening or passage, for example) with or as if with a wall. [Middle English *wal(le),* Old English *weall,* from Latin *vallum,* palisade, wall, from *vallus,* stake.]

wal·la·by (wólləbi) *n., pl.* **-bies** or collectively **wallaby.** **1.** Any of various marsupials of the genus *Wallabia* and related genera, of Australia and adjacent islands, related to and resembling the kangaroos but smaller. **2.** *Capital* **W.** A member of Australia's international Rugby Union team. [Australian native name *wolabā.*]

wallaby grass *n.* Any of various tussock grasses of the genus *Danthonia,* abundant in Australasia and used as winter fodder.

Wallace (wólliss, wólləss), **Edgar,** born Horatio E.W. Richard (1875–1932). British novelist. His books include *The Four Just Men* (1905), and *Sanders of the River* (1911).

Wallace, Sir William (*c.* 1270–1305). Scottish patriot. He led the resistance to Edward I, and captured Stirling Castle (1297). He was proclaimed warden of Scotland, but was later routed at Falkirk (1298) and eventually captured and hanged.

Wallace's line *n.* The hypothetical dividing line between the Oriental and Australasian zoogeographical regions, running between the Indonesian islands Bali and Lombok. [After Alfred Russel *Wallace* (1823–1913), British naturalist.]

wal·lah, wal·la (wóllə) *n. British Informal.* **1.** One employed in a specified occupation or activity. Used in combination: *a kitchen wallah.* **2.** A man; a chap. [Hindi *-wālā,* adjectival suffix, mistaken by Europeans for a suffix indicating a man.]

wal·la·roo (wóllə-rōō) *n., pl.* **-roos.** A kangaroo, *Macropus robustus,* of hilly regions of Australia. [Australian native name *wolárū.*]

wall bars *pl.n.* A framework of horizontal bars attached to a wall, used for gymnastic exercises.

wall·board (wáwl-bawrd || -bōrd) *n.* Any of several structural boards or sheets of various materials, such as gypsum plaster encased in paper or compressed wood fibres and chips, used in construction as a substitute for plaster or wood panels.

wall creeper *n.* A long-billed crimson and greyish bird, *Tichodroma muraria,* of alpine regions of the Old World, characteristically seeking food on rocky cliffs or walls.

walled plain *n.* A very large, flat-bottomed, crater-like feature on the moon's surface, having a diameter up to about 240 kilometres (150 miles).

Wal·ler (wóllər), **Edmund** (1606–87). British poet. He is known chiefly for his harmonious love lyrics, which include *On a Girdle* and *Go, Lovely Rose* (from his *Poems* of 1645).

Waller, Thomas Wright, known as Fats, (1904–43). U.S. jazz musician and songwriter. His many compositions include *Honeysuckle Rose* and *Ain't Misbehavin'.*

wal·let (wóllit) *n.* **1.** A small, flat folding case, usually made of leather or vinyl material, for holding paper money, cards, photographs, or other articles. **2.** *Archaic & Regional.* A small bag for carrying personal necessities on a journey, especially as formerly used by a pilgrim. [Middle English *walet,* a pilgrim's knapsack or provisions bag, probably from Anglo-French *walet* (unattested), from Germanic.]

wall·eye (wáwl-ī) *n.* **1.** *Pathology.* **a.** An eye in which the cornea is white or opaque, as in leucoma of the eye. **b.** An eye in which the iris is white, partly coloured, or a different colour from the other eye. **c.** A squint in which the lines of sight of the eyes diverge. **2.** A freshwater food and game fish, *Stizostedion vitreum,* of North America, having large, conspicuous eyes. Also called "walleyed pike" or "pike perch". [Back-formation from WALLEYED.]

wall·eyed (wáwl-īd, -īd) *adj.* **1.** Having or affected by walleye. **2.** *U.S.* Having large bulging or staring eyes, as some fish do. [Variant (influenced by WALL) of Middle English *wawil-eghed,* from Old Norse *vagleygr* : *vagl* (unattested), perhaps film over the eye + *-eygr,* -eyed, from *auga,* an eye.]

wall fern *n.* A fern, the common **polypody** *(see).*

wall·flow·er (wáwl-flowr) *n.* **1.** A widely cultivated plant, *Cheiranthus cheiri,* native to Europe, having fragrant, variously coloured flowers and common on rocks and old walls. **2.** Any of various similar, related plants. **3.** *Informal.* A person who does not participate in the activity at a social event, especially a dance, because of shyness or unpopularity.

wal·lies (wálliz) *pl.n. Scottish.* False teeth. [From WALLY (made of china).]

Wal·lis (wólliss), **Sir Barnes (Neville)** (1887–1979). British aeronautical engineer. Among his many contributions to aircraft design were the airship R100 (first flew 1930), the Wellesley (1935) and the Wellington (1939) and the bouncing bombs (1943) which were used to destroy the Ruhr dams in Germany in World War II. He also designed (1945–71) swept wing supersonic aircraft.

wall knot *n. Nautical.* A knot made at the end of a rope by undoing the strands and weaving them together, to prevent unravelling. [18th century: probably from Scandinavian and akin to Norwegian and Swedish *valknut,* Danish *valknude,* double knot, secure knot.]

wall mustard *n.* A plant, **stinkweed** *(see).*

Wal·loon (wo-lōōn, wə-) *n.* **1.** A member of a French-speaking people of Celtic descent inhabiting southern and southeastern Belgium and adjacent regions of France. Compare **Fleming.** **2.** The French dialect of this people. [Old French *Wallon,* from Medieval Latin *Wallō* (stem *Wallōn-*), a foreigner, Welshman, from Germanic.] **—Wal·loon** *adj.*

wal·lop (wólləp) *v.* **-loped, -loping, -lops.** *Informal.* —*tr.* **1.** To beat soundly; thrash. **2.** To defeat thoroughly. —*intr.* **1.** *Informal.* To move in a rolling, clumsy manner; lumber. **2.** To boil noisily and vigorously.
~*n. Informal.* **1.** A hard or severe blow. **2. a.** The capacity or effect of striking such a blow: *a punch that packs a wallop.* **b.** The capacity to create a forceful effect; impact. **3.** *British Slang.* Beer. [Earlier "to make violent, heavy motions", from Middle English *walopen,* to gallop, from Old North French *waloper,* from Frankish *walahlaupan* (unattested), "to jump well" : *wala* (unattested), well + *hlaupan* (unattested), to jump, run.]

wal·lop·er (wólləpər) *n.* **1.** One that wallops. **2** *Australian Slang.* A policeman.

wal·lop·ing (wólləping) *adj. Informal.* Very large; huge; strapping: *a walloping fish.*
~*adv. Informal.* Used as an intensifier: *a walloping great fish.*
~*n. Informal.* A sound thrashing or defeat.

wal·low (wóllō) *intr.v.* **-lowed, -lowing, -lows.** **1.** To roll the body about indolently or clumsily in water, snow, mud, or the like. **2.** To luxuriate or indulge oneself unrestrainedly, as in sensual pleasure or emotions: *wallow in self-pity.* **3.** To move with difficulty in a clumsy or rolling manner; flounder. **4.** To swell or surge forth; billow.
~*n.* **1.** An act of wallowing. **2.** A pool of water, mud, or the like where animals go to wallow. **3.** The depression, pool, or pit produced by wallowing animals. [Middle English *walowen,* Old English *wealwian.*] **—wal·low·er** *n.*

wall·pa·per (wáwl-paypər) *n.* Paper, usually coloured and printed with designs, pasted to the wall as a decorative covering.
~*v.* **wallpapered, -pering, -pers.** —*tr.* To cover with wallpaper. —*intr.* To decorate a wall or room with wallpaper.

wall plate *n.* **1.** A horizontal timber situated along the top of a wall at eaves level for bearing the ends of joists or rafters. **2.** A plate used to attach a bracket or similar device to a wall.

wall rock *n.* The rock that forms the walls of a vein or lode.

wall rocket *n.* Any of various yellow-flowered plants of the genus *Diplotaxis* found growing on lime rocks and walls, especially *D. muralis.*

Wall Street *n.* The controlling financial interests of the United States. [From the name of the main street of the financial district of New York City.]

wall-to-wall (wáwl-tə-wáwl, -tōō-) *adj.* **1.** Covering a floor completely: *wall-to-wall carpeting.* **2.** Ubiquitous; pervasive: *wall-to-wall muzak.*

wal·ly[1] (wóli) *adj. Scottish.* **1.** Made of china. Said of an ornament. **2.** Fine; excellent.
~*n. Scottish.* An ornament; a trinket. [16th century (adjective, "excellent"), 18th century (noun, "toy, trinket") : origin obscure.]

wal·ly[2] *n., pl.* **-lies.** *British Slang.* An inept and foolish person. [From *Wally,* diminutive of *Walter.* Compare **charlie.**]

wal·nut (wáwl-nut, -nət ‖ wól-) *n.* **1.** Any of several trees of the genus *Juglans,* having round fruit enclosing an edible nut. **2.** The ridged or corrugated two-lobed nut of such a tree. **3.** The hard, dark-brown wood of such a tree, used for gunstocks and in cabinetwork. **4.** Moderate yellowish-brown.
~*adj.* **1.** Made of the wood of the walnut. **2.** Having the colour walnut. [Middle English *walnot,* Old English *walh-hnutu* (translation of Latin *nux gallia,* "Gaulish or foreign nut").]

Wal·pole (wáwl-pōl, wól-), **Horace,** 4th Earl of Orford (1717–97). British writer and wit, son of Sir Robert Walpole. His novel, *Castle of Otranto* (1765), set the fashion for gothic literature.

Walpole, Sir Hugh (Seymour) (1884–1941). New Zealand-born novelist. His books include *The Cathedral* (1922) and *The Herries Chronicle* (a tetralogy, 1930–35).

Walpole, Sir Robert, 1st Earl of Orford (1676–1745). British statesman. As First Lord of the Treasury and Chancellor of the Exchequer (1715–17, 1721–42) he led the Whig administration and was regarded as Britain's first prime minister (although the office was not officially recognised until 1905).

Wal·pur·gis Night (val-pŏŏr-giss, vaal-, -púr-). The eve of May Day which according to German legend was the occasion of a witches' Sabbath on the Brocken peak in the Harz mountains. [Partial translation of German *Walpurgisnacht* : *Walpurgis,* St. Walburga, seventh-century English nun and missionary, whose feast day falls on May Day + NIGHT.]

wal·rus (wáwl-rəss, -russ ‖ wól-) *n., pl.* **-ruses** or collectively **walrus.** A large marine mammal, *Odobenus rosmarus,* of Arctic regions, having tough, wrinkled skin and large tusks. [Probably from Dutch, perhaps a metathetic formation influenced by *walvisch,* "whale fish", from a Germanic source akin to Old English *horschwœl,* Old Norse *hrosshvalr,* "horse-whale".]

walrus moustache *n.* A bushy, drooping moustache. [From the resemblance to the tusks of a walrus.]

Wal·ter (vaáltər), **Bruno,** born B.W. Schlesinger (1876–1962). German conductor. His repertory was wide, but he is remembered especially for his interpretations of Mozart and Mahler.

Wal·ter Mit·ty (wáwl-tər mítti ‖ wól-) *n.* An ordinary, often inadequate, person who indulges in fantastic daydreams about his own triumphs. [After the hero of *The Secret Life of Walter Mitty,* a story by James Thurber.]

Wal·ton (wáwl-tən, wól-), **Ernest Thomas Sinton** (1903–). Irish physicist. With Sir John Cockcroft he was the first to succeed (1931) in splitting the atom. He shared the Nobel prize (1951) with Cockcroft for their work in nuclear physics.

Walton, Izaak (1593–1683). English author. He wrote biographies of John Donne and other churchmen, but is best known for the fishing classic *The Compleat Angler* (1653, enlarged frequently).

Walton, Sir William (Turner) (1902–83). British composer. He established his reputation (1923) with *Façade,* an extravaganza accompanying poems by Edith Sitwell, but his later work, such as the oratorio *Belshazzar's Feast* (1931), *Symphony No. 1* (1935), and his film music, is neo-Romantic in style.

waltz (wawlss, wawlts ‖ wolss, wolts) *n.* **1.** A smooth, flowing ballroom dance in which couples rotate and progress at the same time. **2.** A piece of music for this dance in triple time with a strong accent on the first beat.
~*v.* **waltzed, waltzing, waltzes.** —*intr.* **1.** To dance the waltz. **2.** To move effortlessly, confidently, or casually. **3.** To accomplish a task, chore, or assignment with little effort. Often used with *through*: *waltzed through her exams.* —*tr.* **1.** To dance the waltz with. **2.** To lead or force to move briskly and purposefully; march: *waltzed him into the headmaster's office.* [German *Walzer,* from Middle High German *walzen,* to roll, turn, dance, from Old High German *walzan,* to roll.] —**waltz·er** *n.*

Wal·vis Bay (wáwl-viss, -fish). Atlantic port of Namibia. An exclave of Cape Province, Republic of South Africa, with which it is connected by railway, it exports minerals, including uranium. Fishing is also important.

waly. *Scottish.* Variant of **wally.**

wam·ble (wómb'l) *intr.v.* **-bled, -bling, -bles.** *Chiefly British Regional.* **1.** To move in a weaving, wobbling, or rolling manner. **2.** To turn or roll. Used of the stomach.
~*n. Chiefly British Regional.* **1.** A wobble or roll. **2.** A feeling of nausea. [Middle English *wam(e)len,* to feel nausea, probably from Scandinavian; akin to Old Norse *vamla.*] —**wam·bling·ly** *adv.* —**wam·bly** *adj.*

Wam·pa·no·ag (wámpə-nṓ-ag) *n., pl.* **-ags** or collectively **Wampanoag. 1.** A member of an Algonquian-speaking North American Indian people, formerly inhabiting eastern Rhode Island and adjacent parts of Massachusetts. **2.** The language of this people. —**Wam·pa·no·ag** *adj.*

wam·pum (wómpəm) *n.* **1.** Small cylindrical beads made from polished shells, formerly used by North American Indians as currency and as jewellery. Also called "peag". **2.** *U.S. Informal.* Money. [Short for WAMPUMPEAG.]

wam·pum·peag (wómpəm-peeg) *n.* Wampum made from white shell beads. [From Algonquian (Southeastern New England) *wampumpeage,* "white strings".]

wan (won) *adj.* **wanner, wannest. 1.** Unnaturally pale, as from physical or emotional distress. **2.** Suggestive of or indicating weariness, illness, or unhappiness; melancholy: *a wan expression.*
~*intr.v.* **wanned, wanning, wans.** *Poetic.* To become pale. [Middle English *wan,* gloomy, wan, Old English *wann†,* dusky, dark, livid.] —**wan·ly** *adv.* —**wan·ness** *n.*

wand (wond) *n.* **1.** A supple, thin twig or stick. **2.** A stick or baton used by a magician, conjurer, or diviner. **3.** A slender rod carried as a symbol of office. **4.** A conductor's baton. [Middle English *wand(e), wond(e),* from Old Norse *vöndr.*]

wan·der (wóndər) *v.* **-dered, -dering, -ders.** —*intr.* **1.** To move about with no destination or purpose; roam aimlessly. **2.** To make one's way by an indirect route in a leisurely fashion; amble; stroll: *wander towards town.* **3.** To proceed in an irregular course; meander: *This path wanders over hill and dale.* **4.** To go astray: *wander from the path of righteousness.* **5.** To think or express oneself unclearly or incoherently: *His mind is beginning to wander.* **6.** To stray from a subject or issue; digress; become sidetracked: *wandering off the point.* —*tr.* To wander across or through: *wander the forests.*
~*n.* The act or an instance of wandering; a stroll; an amble. [Middle English *wand(e)ren,* Old English *wandrian.*] —**wan·der·er** *n.* —**wan·der·ing·ly** *adv.*

Synonyms: *wander, ramble, roam, rove, range, meander, stray.*

wandering albatross *n.* The largest of the albatrosses, *Diomedea exulans,* having a wingspan of over three metres (ten feet).

wandering Jew *n.* Either of two trailing plants, *Tradescantia fluminensis* or *Zebrina pendula,* native to tropical America, having usually striped variegated foliage and popular as house plants. [Fancifully named after the WANDERING JEW.]

Wandering Jew *n.* The subject of a medieval legend, condemned to wander until the Day of Judgment for having mocked Christ on the day of Crucifixion.

wan·der·lust (wóndər-lust, vaándər-lŏŏst) *n.* A strong or irresistible impulse to travel. [German *Wanderlust* : *wandern,* to wander + *Lust,* desire, delight.]

wan·der·oo (wóndə-rṓō) *n.* A monkey, *Macaca silenus,* of south-central Asia, having a glossy black coat and a ruff of grey hair about the face. [Singhalese *vanduru,* plural of *vandurā,* "forest-dweller", monkey, from Sanskrit *vānara,* from *vana,* a forest.]

wan·doo (won-dṓō) *n.* A white-barked eucalyptus tree, *Eucalyptus wandoo* (or *E. redunca*), having durable, reddish-brown wood. [From a native Australian language.]

wane (wayn) *intr.v.* **waned, waning, wanes. 1.** To decrease gradually in extent, intensity, or degree; dwindle; decline: *Their influence was waning.* **2.** To show a decreasing illuminated area from full moon to new moon. Used of the moon. Compare **wax. 3.** To approach an end.
~*n.* **1.** The act or process of waning; a gradual declining or diminishing. **2.** A period or phase of waning; specifically, the period of the decrease of the moon's visible surface. **3.** A defective edge of a plank where it has been imperfectly sawn. —**on the wane.** In a period of decline; waning. [Middle English *wan(i)en,* Old English *wanian,* to lessen. In the sense "defective edge of a log", from Middle English *wane,* defect, shortage, Old English *wana.*]

wan·gle (wáng-g'l) *v.* **-gled, -gling, -gles.** *Informal.* —*tr.* **1.** To make, achieve, or get by contrivance: *tried to wangle his way into the top job.* **2.** To manipulate or juggle (accounts, for example), especially fraudulently. **3.** To extricate (oneself) from difficulty. —*intr.* **1.** To use indirect, devious, or fraudulent methods. **2.** To extricate oneself by subtle or indirect means, as from difficulty.
~*n. Informal.* An act of wangling. [Originally a printer's term, "to manipulate or devise a substitute for", perhaps blend of WAGGLE and dialectal *wankle,* unsteady, wavering, Middle English *wankel,* Old English *wancol.*] —**wang·ler** *n.*

wan·i·gan, wan·ni·gan (wónnigən) *n. U.S.* **1.** A supply chest in a logging camp. **2.** A hut in a logging camp, either mounted on wheels or on a raft or boat. [Ojibwa *wanikkan,* "man-made hole".]

wank (wangk) —*intr.v.* **wanked, wanking, wanks.** *Chiefly British.* **1.** *Vulgar Slang.* To masturbate. **2.** *Vulgar Slang.* To behave or speak in a pretentious, silly, or ostentatious manner.
~*n. Chiefly British.* **1.** *Vulgar Slang.* An instance of masturbating. **2.** *Slang.* Pretentious, silly, or showy behaviour. [20th century : origin obscure.]

Wankel engine (vángk'l; *also* wángk'l ‖ *U.S.* vaángk'l, waángk'l) *n.* A rotary internal-combustion engine in which a triangular rotor turning in a specially shaped housing performs the functions allotted to the pistons of a conventional engine, thereby allowing great savings in weight and moving parts. [After Felix *Wankel* (1902–), German engineer.] See feature, next page.

walnut *The edible fruit of the walnut tree; the male flowers are carried in slender catkins.*

walrus *These Arctic mammals feed largely on shellfish raked up by their tusks, which can grow up to a metre (3.3 feet) long.*

PRONUNCIATION KEY

a, trap; aa, father; ai, fair;
ar, star; aw, lawn; ay, play;
b, bb, stab; rubber;
ch, church; ck, ticket;
d, dd, dead; ladder; e, dress;
ee, bee; er, defer; ew, few;
ewr, pure; ə, about;
ər, letter; f, ff, fife; differ;
g, gg, giggle; h, hat; i, kit;
ī, price; īr, fire; j, judge;
k, kick; l, ll, let; 'l, needle;
m, mm, man; n, nn, no;
'n, sudden; ng, thing; o, lot;
ō, no; ŏŏ, foot; ōō, shoe;
oor, poor; ow, cow;
owr, hour; oy, boy;
p, pp, pepper; r, rr, red;
s, ss, sauce; sh, ship;
t, tt, totter; th, thick; th, this;
smooth; u, cut; ur, turn;
v, vv, valve; w, wet; y, yes;
z, zz, zebra; zh, vision;
pleasure

IN FOREIGN WORDS:

aN, oN, Saint-Saëns;
hl, Llanelli; Hluhluwe;
kh, loch; lough; Khaled

STRESS MARK:

ín-sīt, insight; in-sī́t, incite

Wankel

THE SEARCH FOR EFFICIENCY: FELIX WANKEL'S SOLUTION

A masterpiece of ingenuity and design – but not yet practical enough

In all conventional gas, petrol, and diesel engines, the rotary motion needed to turn a crankshaft is produced not directly but at one remove, by reciprocating parts – pistons and connecting rods moving back and forth thousands of times a minute. Engineers have long looked for engines that dispense with reciprocating parts and rotate a shaft directly. The most successful of these is the jet engine, but the most successful on a smaller scale is the Wankel engine, designed by a German, Felix Wankel, and first brought into production in 1956.

In the Wankel engine, a triangular rotor geared to a drive shaft is driven round inside a cylinder. As it rotates, the rotor draws in fuel, compresses it so that a spark ignites it, and finally expels the burnt gases as in a conventional four-stroke cycle. The result is a simple, smooth-running, and powerful engine that has been used in several production-model cars. It has fewer moving parts and runs well at high speeds. But problems of high fuel consumption, wear at the rotor tips, and high exhaust emissions have so far limited its application.

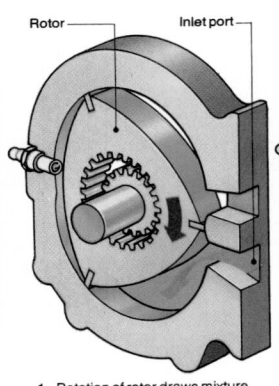 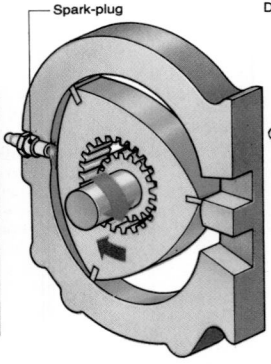 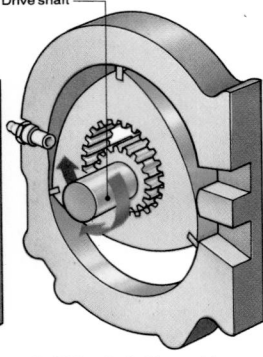 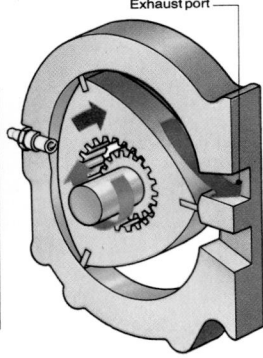

1. Rotation of rotor draws mixture through inlet port into space between rotor and cylinder wall

2. Mixture is compressed into a smaller space by the turning rotor; spark-plug sparks

3. Mixture, ignited by spark from spark-plug, explodes and drives rotor round

4. As rotor turns, exhaust outlet is exposed and burnt gases are expelled

WANKEL ENGINE *The central rotor is a triangle with bulging sides, which rotates inside a cylinder. There are holes in the side of the cylinder for fuel intake and exhaust outlet. The spaces between the rotor and the cylinder alter in size as the rotor turns. Where the spark occurs, the space is small, compressing the fuel. The spark explodes it, turning the rotor and with it the shaft.*

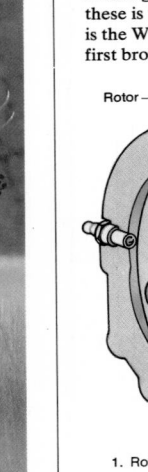

wapiti *Also called the American elk, the wapiti is the largest living deer after the moose, standing over 1.5 metres (5 feet) high at the shoulder and with antlers up to 1.2 metres (4 feet) long. It was once common throughout North America, but is now confined to mountainous regions.*

wank·er (wángkər) *n. Chiefly British. Slang.* A person who behaves in a silly, pretentious, or ostentatious manner. Used derogatorily. [WANK + -ER.] —**wank·y** *adj.*

Wan·li Chang·cheng. See **Great Wall of China.**

wan·na (wónnə ‖ wáwnə, wúnnə). *Informal.* Contraction of *want to.*

want (wont ‖ wawnt, wunt) *v.* **wanted, wanting, wants.** **1.** To desire; wish for. Often used with the infinitive: *He wants to leave; always wants the biggest piece.* **2.** To need or require: *" 'Your hair wants cutting,' said the Hatter."* (Lewis Carroll). **3. a.** To desire the presence or assistance of: *You're wanted by the boss.* **b.** To seek with intent to capture: *The fugitive is wanted by the police.* **4. a.** To lack or fall short in (something, especially a desirable quality): *She wants tact.* **b.** To fall short by (a specified amount): *"Wants a few minutes of five o'clock."* (Charles Dickens). **5.** *Informal.* Should or ought. Used with the infinitive: *You want to get your head examined.* —*intr.* **1.** To have need; be lacking. Used with *for: wants for nothing.* **2.** To be destitute or needy. **3.** To be disposed; like; wish: *Call her if you want.* —**want in** (or **out**). *Informal.* **1.** *Chiefly Scottish & U.S.* To wish to enter (or leave): *The dog wants out.* **2.** To wish to join (or leave) a project, business, or other undertaking.

~*n.* **1.** The condition or quality of lacking something usual or necessary; lack; absence: *stayed at home, for want of anything better to do.* **2.** Pressing need; destitution: *live in want.* **3.** Something needed or desired: *moderate wants.* [Middle English *wanten,* from Old Norse *vanta,* to be lacking.]

Usage: Want, in the sense of "need", is found chiefly in British English: *The car wants washing.* (*The car wants washed* is nonstandard British English). The use of *want* with *for* in the general sense of "wish, desire" is nonstandard American English (*She wants for you to travel by train*), though it is acceptable everywhere to say *what she wants is for you to travel by train.* Likewise, *She wants you should travel by train* is nonstandard American English.

want·ing (wónt-ing ‖ wáwnt-, wúnt-) *adj.* **1.** Absent, lacking, or deficient. **2.** Not up to standards or expectations.

~*prep.* **1.** Without. **2.** Minus; less: *an hour wanting fifteen minutes.*

wan·ton (wón-tən ‖ wáwn-) *adj.* **1.** Immoral or unchaste; lewd. **2.** Marked by or influenced by unprovoked, gratuitous maliciousness; capricious; arbitrary: *wanton destruction.* **3.** Pointlessly and unrestrainedly excessive: *wanton extravagance.* **4.** *Poetic.* Luxuriant; overabundant: *wanton tresses.* **5.** *Archaic & Poetic.* Frolicsome; playful. **6.** *Obsolete.* Rebellious; refractory.

~*v.* **wantoned, -toning, -tons.** —*intr.* To act, grow, or move in a wanton manner; be wanton. —*tr.* To waste or squander wantonly. ~*n.* An immoral, lewd, or licentious person, especially a woman. [Middle English *wantowen,* lacking discipline, lewd : *wan-, un-,* lacking, Old English *wan-* + *towen,* Old English *togen,* past participle of *tēon,* to draw, bring up.] —**wan·ton·ly** *adv.* —**wan·ton·ness** *n.*

wap·en·take (wáppən-tayk, wóppən-) *n.* A historical division of some northern counties in England, corresponding roughly to the hundred in other shires. [Middle English *wapentake,* subdivision, court of each division, Old English *wǽpengetæc,* from Old Norse *vápnatak,* "taking of weapons" (vote by an assembly by brandishing of weapons, hence assembly) : *vápna,* genitive plural of *vápn,* a weapon + *tak,* a taking, from *taka,* to take.]

wap·i·ti (wóppiti) *n., pl.* **-tis** or **wapiti.** A large North American deer, *Cervus canadensis.* Also called "elk". [Shawnee *wapiti,* "white rump" : Proto-Algonquian *wap-* (unattested), white + *-itwiy-* (unattested), rump.]

wap·pen·shaw, wap·pen·schaw (wáppən-shaw, wóppən-) *n.* Also **wappenshawing** (-ing). Formerly, in Scotland, a periodical muster of the fighting men of a district, for inspection purposes. [16th century (later revived by Sir Walter Scott) : northern and Scottish dialect *wapen,* from Old Norse *vapn,* WEAPON + *s(c)haw,* SHOW.]

war (wawr) *n.* **1. a.** A state of open, armed, often prolonged conflict carried on between nations, states, or parties. **b.** *Often capital* **W.** A particular instance of such conflict: *the Trojan War.* **c.** The period of such conflict. **d.** A formally declared state of war in which certain internationally recognised conventions are supposed to apply. **2. a.** Any condition of active antagonism or contention: *an advertising war.* **b.** A concerted effort or campaign to combat or put an end to something: *the continuing war against disease.* **3.** The techniques or procedures of war; military science; strategy. —**at war.** In an active state of conflict or contention: *"Life and death are at war within us"* (Thomas Merton). —**have been in the wars.** *Informal.* To be damaged or injured, as from fighting or rough treatment. ~*intr.v.* **warred, warring, wars.** **1.** To wage or carry on war. **2.** To be in a state of antagonism or rivalry; contend. ~*adj.* Of, resulting from, or used in war: *a war wound; a war cry.* [Middle English *werre, warre,* from Old North French *werre;* akin to Old High German *werra,* confusion, strife.]

War Warwickshire.

war. warrant.

war·a·tah (wórrə-taʼa, -taa) *n. Australian.* Any shrub of the genus *Telopea;* especially *T. speciosissima,* which has bright red flowers borne in terminal clusters. [From a native Australian language.]

war baby *n.* A child born during wartime.

War·beck (wáwr-bek), **Perkin** (c. 1474–99). Flemish-born impostor, and pretender to the English throne. In the Yorkist plot against Henry VII he claimed to be Richard, Duke of York (presumed murdered with his brother, Edward). After unsuccessful sieges he was captured by Henry's troops, tried, and executed.

war·ble¹ (wáwrb'l) *v.* **-bled, -bling, -bles.** —*tr.* To sing with trills, runs, or other melodic embellishments. —*intr.* **1.** To sing with trills, runs, or quavers. **2.** To produce a warbling sound.

~n. The act or an instance of warbling. [Middle English, from Old North French *werbler,* from *werble,* a warbling, melody, from Frankish *hwirbilōn* (unattested), to whirl, trill.]

war·ble² *n.* **1.** An abscessed swelling under the hide of the back of cattle or other animals, caused by the larva of a warble fly. **2.** The warble fly, especially in its larval stage. **3.** A hard lump of tissue on a horse's back caused by rubbing of the saddle. [16th century : perhaps from a Scandinavian compound corresponding to obsolete Swedish *varbulde.*] **—war·bled** *adj.*

warble fly *n.* Any of several flies of the family Oestridae, especially of the genus *Hypoderma,* whose larvae form warbles within the bodies of cattle and other animals.

war·bler (wáwrblər) *n.* **1.** Any of various small, brownish or greyish Old World birds of the family Sylviidae. **2.** Any of various small New World birds of the family Parulidae, many of which have yellowish plumage or markings. **3.** One that warbles.

war bonnet *n.* A ceremonial headdress used by some North American Plains Indians consisting of a cap or band and a trailing extension decorated with erect feathers.

war bride *n.* A woman who marries a serviceman during wartime, especially when she and her husband are of different nationalities.

war club *n.* A weapon consisting of a weight of iron or stone fixed to a handle, formerly used by American Indians.

war correspondent *n.* A journalist, reporter, or commentator assigned to report directly from a war or combat area.

war crime *n.* Any of various crimes committed during a war and considered to be in violation of the conventions of warfare, such as mistreatment of prisoners of war or genocide. **—war criminal** *n.*

war cry *n.* **1.** A cry uttered by combatants as they attack; a battle cry. **2.** A phrase or slogan used to rally people to a cause.

ward (wawrd) *n.* **1.** A division of a city or town for administrative and representative purposes; especially, an electoral district. **2.** A historical division of some northern English and Scottish counties corresponding roughly to the hundred or wapentake. **3.** A large room in a hospital, especially one set aside for the care of a particular group of patients. **4.** One of the divisions of a prison or other penal institution. **5.** An open court or area of a castle or fortification enclosed by walls. **6. a.** *Law.* A child or incompetent person placed under the care or protection of a guardian or court. Also called "ward of court". **b.** Any person under the protection or care of another. **7.** The state of being under guard; custody. **8.** The act of guarding or protecting; especially, guardianship of a minor or incompetent. **9.** A means of protection; a defence. **10.** A defensive movement or attitude, especially in fencing; a guard. **11. a.** The projecting ridge of a lock or keyhole that prevents the turning of any key other than the proper one. **b.** The notch cut into a key that corresponds to such a ridge.

~tr.v. **warded, warding, wards. 1.** To turn aside; parry; avert; deflect. Usually used with *off: ward off a blow.* **2.** *Archaic.* To guard, watch over, or protect. [Middle English *ward(e),* a guarding, place for guarding, person or thing in one's care, Old English *weard,* a watching over.]

-ward *adj. suffix.* Indicates direction towards; for example, **skyward, westward.**

~adv. suffix. Chiefly U.S. Variant of **-wards.** [Middle English *-ward,* Old English *-weard.*]

Usage: The suffixes *-ward* and *wards* are both used to express direction of movement: *backward(s), eastward(s), homeward(s).* As adverbs, the forms without *-s* are predominant in American English, while those with *-s* prevail in British English. Only the forms without *-s* are regularly used as adjectives: *a backward glance.*

Ward, Barbara, Baroness Jackson (1914–81). British economist and conservationist. Her books on ecology and political economy include *Spaceship Earth* (1966) and *Only One Earth* (1972).

Ward, Mrs Humphry, born Mary Augusta Arnold (1851–1920). Tasmanian-born novelist. Her books are concerned with religious and social issues, the best known being *Robert Elsmere* (1888).

Ward, Sir Joseph George (1856–1930). New Zealand statesman. He was Prime Minister (1906–12, 1928–30).

war dance *n.* A tribal dance performed before a battle or as a celebration after a victory.

ward·ed (wáwrdid) *adj.* Having notches or wards. Said of a key or lock.

war·den (wáwrd'n) *n.* **1.** A person who is in charge of or takes care of someone or something. **2.** An official charged with the enforcement of certain laws and regulations, such as an air-raid warden or traffic warden. **3.** *British.* The principal or governor of certain colleges, universities, schools, or hospitals. **4.** *British Archaic.* **a.** The chief executive official in charge of a port or market. **b.** Any of various crown officers having administrative duties. **5.** A churchwarden. **6.** *U.S.* The governor of a prison. [Middle English *wardein,* from Old North French, variant of Old French *guarden,* GUARDIAN.] **—war·den·ship** *n.*

ward·er¹ (wáwrdər) *n.* **1.** A prison guard. **2.** A guard, porter, or watchman of a gate or tower. [Middle English, from Anglo-French *wardere,* from Old North French *warder,* variant of Old French *garder,* to keep, GUARD.] **—war·der·ship** *n.*

warder² *n.* A baton formerly carried as a symbol of authority and used by a ruler or commander to signal orders. [Short for Middle English *warderer,* perhaps a jocular use of obsolete *warderere,* "look out behind" : Anglo-French *ware,* beware, from Germanic + *derere,* behind, from Vulgar Latin *dē retrō* (unattested) : Latin *dē,* from + *retrō,* behind.]

ward heeler *U.S. Slang.* A local worker for a professional politician. Usually used derogatorily.

ward·i·an case (wáwrdi-ən) *n.* A case with glass sides, designed for growing or transporting delicate ferns or similar plants. [After N. B. *Ward* (died 1868), British botanist.]

ward·mote (wáwrd-mōt) *n.* Formerly, a meeting of the citizens of a ward; especially, a meeting of the liverymen and the alderman of a ward in the City of London. [Middle English. See **ward, moot.**]

ward·ress (wáwrd-riss, -ress) *n.* A female prison guard.

ward·robe (wáwr-drōb) *n.* **1.** A tall cabinet or cupboard with a rail, hooks, or shelves, in which clothes are kept. **2.** Garments collectively; especially, all the articles of clothing belonging to one person. **3. a.** The costumes belonging to a theatre or theatrical company. **b.** The place in which they are kept. **4.** The department in charge of clothes, jewellery, and the like in a royal or noble household. [Middle English *warderobe,* from Old North French : *warder,* to guard, keep, from Germanic + *robe,* ROBE.]

wardrobe trunk *n.* A large trunk with drawers and a hanging rail, designed to stand on end and serve as a wardrobe.

ward·room (wáwrd-rōōm, -rŏŏm) *n.* **1.** The living area and dining room for the commissioned officers, excepting the captain, on a warship. **2.** These officers collectively.

-wards *adv. suffix.* Also *chiefly U.S.* **-ward.** Indicates in the direction towards; for example, **backwards, windwards.**

ward·ship (wáwrd-ship) *n.* **1.** The state of being a ward or in the charge of a guardian. **2.** Guardianship; custody.

ware¹ (wair) *n.* **1.** Manufactured articles of the same general kind. Often used in combination to indicate: **a.** Articles made of the specified material: *glassware.* **b.** Articles of the specified type: *ovenware; computer software.* **c.** Pottery or ceramics of a specified type or make: *earthenware; Delft ware.* **2.** *Plural.* **a.** Articles of commerce; goods. **b.** Any immaterial asset or benefit, such as a service or personal accomplishment, that is regarded as an article of commerce. [Middle English *ware,* Old English *waru.*]

ware² *tr.v.* **wared, waring, wares.** *Archaic.* To beware of. Used chiefly in the imperative: *Ware hounds!.*

~adj. Archaic & Poetic. **1.** Watchful; wary. **2.** Aware. [Middle English *waren,* Old English *warian.*]

ware³ *tr.v.* **wared, waring, wares.** *Chiefly Scottish.* To spend, waste, or squander (money, goods or time, for example). [Middle English, from Old Norse *verja,* to invest, spend money, literally, to clothe; akin to Old English *werian,* to clothe, WEAR.]

ware·house (wair-howss) *n.* **1.** A place in which goods or merchandise are stored; a storehouse. **2.** *British.* A large shop, usually selling goods wholesale.

~tr.v. **warehoused, -housing, -houses.** To place or store in a warehouse, especially in a bonded or government warehouse.

ware·house·man (wair-howss-mən) *n., pl.* **-men** (-mən). A person who owns, manages, or works in a warehouse.

war·fare (wáwr-fair) *n.* **1.** The waging of war; especially, military operations marked by a specified characteristic: *guerrilla warfare; chemical warfare.* **2.** Conflict of any kind; struggle; strife: *psychological warfare.* [Middle English *werrefare,* a going to war : *warre, werre,* WAR + *fare,* a journey, Old English *faru* and *fær.*]

war·fa·rin (wáwrfərin) *n.* A trademark for a colourless crystalline compound, $C_{19}H_{16}O_4$, used to kill rodents and medicinally as an anticoagulant. [Patented by *W*isconsin *A*lumni *R*esearch *F*oundation + (COUM)ARIN.]

war game *n.* **1.** *Sometimes plural.* A simulated battle in military training manoeuvres. **2.** A board game using models or blocks to represent troops and weapons, used to test tactical knowledge.

war·head (wáwr-hed) *n.* A part of the armament system in the forward part of a projectile, such as a guided missile, torpedo, or bomb, containing the explosive charge.

War·hol (wáwr-hol, -hōl), **Andy** born Andrew von Warhol (1931–). American pop artist and film producer. He became known in the 1960s with outsize paintings of everyday objects, such as soup tins, and silk-screen portraits of film stars. His films, which are usually erotic and controversial, include *The Chelsea Girls* (1966).

warhorse (wáwr-hawrss) *n.* **1.** A horse used in combat; a charger. **2.** *Informal.* A person who has been through many battles, struggles, or fights; an old campaigner.

war·i·son (wórri-s'n, wárri-) *n.* A bugle call giving the command to attack; a war cry. [Middle English, wealth, reward, from Old Northern French, variant of Old French *garison,* provision, store, defence, GARRISON; sense derives from misuse by Sir Walter Scott.]

war·like (wáwr-līk) *adj.* **1.** Belligerent; hostile. **2.** Of or pertaining to war; martial. **3.** Threatening or indicative of war.

war·lock (wáwr-lok) *n.* A male witch, sorcerer or wizard. [Middle English *warloghe,* Old English *wǣrloga,* "oath-breaker" : *wǣr,* faith, pledge + *-loga,* liar, from *lēogan,* to lie.]

war·lord (wáwr-lawrd) *n.* A military commander exercising civil power in a given region, whether in nominal allegiance to the national government or in defiance of it.

warm (wawrm) *adj.* **warmer, warmest. 1.** Somewhat hotter than temperate; having or producing a comfortable and agreeable degree of heat; moderately hot: *a warm climate.* **2.** Having the natural heat of living beings. **3.** Preserving or imparting heat: *a warm overcoat.* **4.** Having or causing a sensation of unusually high bodily heat, as from exercise or hard work. **5.** Marked by enthusiasm; fervent; ardent: *warm support.* **6.** Characterised by liveliness, excitement or disagreement; heated; animated: *a warm debate.* **7.** Marked by or revealing friendliness or sincerity; sympathetic; cordial: *a warm re-*

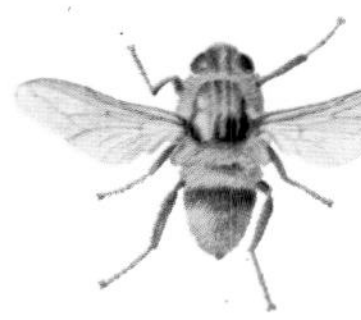

warble fly *A parasitic fly whose larvae burrow under the skin of cattle, ending up along the animal's back where they raise lumps, or warbles. The larvae make holes in the skin, through which they breathe, ruining the hide's value as leather.*

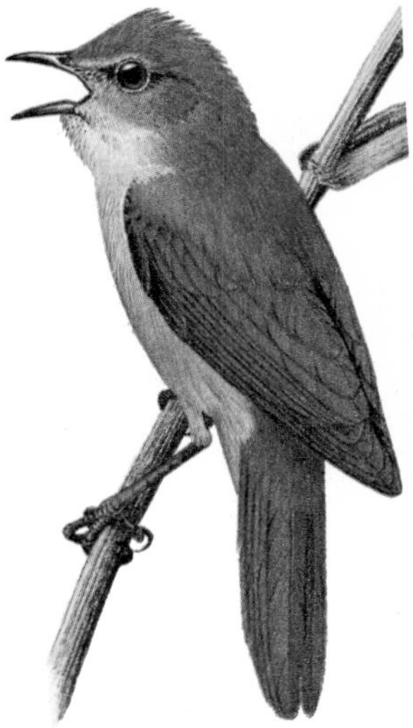

warbler *The reed warbler (above) lives on reed beds and is a favourite target of the cuckoo, which often lays its eggs in the reed warbler's nest. Warblers, which are found throughout Europe, Africa, and Asia, live on woodlice, insects, and berries.*

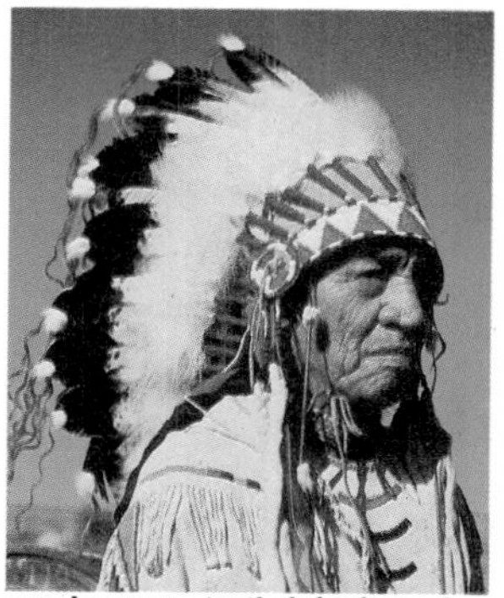

war bonnet *A tribal chieftain of the North American plains displays the ceremonial headdress, with its eagle feathers, which his ancestors wore into battle.*

ception. **8.** Loving; passionate; amorous: *a warm embrace.* **9.** Excitable, impetuous, or quick to be aroused: *a warm temper.* **10.** Predominantly red or yellow in tone; suggesting heat: *a warm brownish colour.* **11.** Recently made; fresh: *a warm trail.* **12.** Close to discovering, guessing, or finding something, as in certain games. **13.** *Informal.* Uncomfortable because of danger or annoyance. ~*v.* **warmed, warming, warms.** —*tr.* **1.** To make warm or warmer. Often used with *up.* **2.** To make zealous or ardent; inspire with life, zest, or colour; enliven. **3.** To fill with pleasant emotions: *warmed by the thought of her return.* —*intr.* **1.** To become warm or warmer. Often used with *up.* **2.** To become ardent, enthusiastic, or animated. Usually used with *to: began to warm to his subject.* **3.** To become kindly disposed or friendly. Usually used with *to* or *towards*: *felt the audience warming to her.* ~*n.* *Informal.* **1.** A warming or heating. **2.** A warm place. Preceded by *the.* [Middle English *warm,* Old English *wearm.*] —**warm·er** *n.* —**warm·ish** *adj.* —**warm·ly** *adv.* —**warm·ness** *n.*

warm-blood·ed (wáwrm-blúddid) *adj. Zoology.* Homoiothermic.

warmed-o·ver (wáwrmd-óvər) *adj. U.S. Informal.* **1.** Reheated; warmed up. Said of food. **2.** Not new, fresh, or spontaneous; stale.

warm-heart·ed (wáwrm-hártid) *adj.* Kind; friendly; sympathetic. —**warm·heart·ed·ly** *adv.* —**warm·heart·ed·ness** *n.*

warming pan *n.* A metal pan with a cover and a long handle, designed to hold hot liquids or coals and formerly used to warm a bed. Also called "bedpan".

war·mon·ger (wáwr-mung-gər ‖ -mong-) *n.* One who advocates or attempts to stir up war. —**war·mon·ger·ing** *adj. & n.*

warm sector *n.* A wedge of warm air between the warm front and the cold front of a depression.

warmth (wawrmth) *n.* **1.** The state, sensation, or quality of producing or having a moderate degree of heat. **2.** Excitement or intensity, as of love or passion; ardour; zeal. **3.** Friendliness, sincerity, or affection. **4.** The glowing effect produced by using predominantly red or yellow colours. [Middle English *warmth,* Old English *wiermthu* (unattested).]

warm up *intr.v.* **1.** To exercise or practice, as in preparation for an athletic event. **2.** To become ready for operation. Used of an engine, for example. **3.** To become more enthusiastic, exciting, or animated. —*tr.v.* **1.** To reheat (food). **2.** To make (a car, for example) ready for operation by raising to efficient working temperature. **3.** To exercise (a horse, for example), immediately prior to a competition. **4.** To make more enthusiastic, exciting, or animated: *warm up the conversation with some juicy gossip.*

warm-up (wáwrm-up) *n.* An act, process, or period of warming up.

warn (wawrn) *v.* **warned, warning, warns.** —*tr.* **1.** To make aware of potential or probable harm, danger, or evil; caution. **2.** To admonish as to action or behaviour. **3.** To notify (a person) to go or stay away. Usually used with *off* or *away.* **4.** To notify or apprise in advance: *He warned us that he might be late.* —*intr.* To give a warning. [Middle English *warnen,* Old English *w(e)arnian,* to take heed, warn.] —**warn·er** *n.*

Synonyms: warn, admonish, caution, forewarn.

warn·ing (wáwrning) *n.* **1.** An intimation, threat, or sign of impending danger or evil. **2. a.** Advice to beware, as of a person or thing. **b.** Counsel to desist from an undesirable course of action. **3.** A cautionary or deterrent example. ~*adj.* Acting or serving as a warning. —**warn·ing·ly** *adv.*

warning coloration *n.* The conspicious markings by which a poisonous or distasteful animal can be recognised by potential predators. Also called "aposematic coloration."

War of American Independence *n.* The war fought between Great Britain and her colonies in North America (1775–83) by which the colonies won independence. Also called "American Revolution", "Revolutionary War".

War of 1812 *n.* A war between the United States and Great Britain (1812–14), fought over the rights of neutrals on the high seas and issues related to American westward expansion.

war of nerves *n.* A conflict in which attempts are made to wear down or destroy the morale of one's opponent by psychological means, such as propaganda, delaying tactics, and intimidation.

War of Secession *n.* The **Civil War** *(see)* of the United States.

War of the Spanish Succession *n.* A war fought by Great Britain, the Netherlands, and the Holy Roman Empire against France and Spain (1701–14), over the succession in Spain after the death of Charles II. The Treaty of Utrecht placed Louis XIV's grandson Philip V on the Spanish throne.

warp (wawrp) *v.* **warped, warping, warps.** —*tr.* **1.** To turn or twist out of shape, especially lastingly. **2.** To turn from a correct, healthy, or true course; pervert; corrupt. **3.** In weaving, to arrange (yarn or thread) so as to form a warp. **4.** *Nautical.* To move (a vessel) by hauling on a line that is fastened to or around a piling, anchor, or pier. **5.** To flood (land) so as to deposit alluvial sediment for agriculture. —*intr.* **1.** To become warped, as through the action of heat or damp. **2.** To turn aside from a true, correct, or natural course; go astray; deviate. **3.** *Nautical.* To warp a vessel. —See Synonyms at **distort.** ~*n.* **1.** The state of being warped. **2.** A distortion or twist, especially in a piece of wood. **3.** A warped condition of the mind; a perversion or deviation. **4.** The threads that run lengthways in a fabric, crossed at right angles by the weft. **5.** *Nautical.* A towline used in warping a vessel. [Middle English *werpen,* to warp, throw, Old English *weorpan,* to throw (away).] —**warp·er** *n.*

war paint *n.* **1.** Pigments applied to the face or body by certain

tribes, such as the Indians of North America, preparatory to going to war. **2.** *Informal.* Cosmetics such as lipstick, rouge, or mascara. **3.** *Informal.* Official dress; regalia.

war·path (wáwr-paath ‖ -path) *n., pl.* **-paths** (-paathz ‖ -paths, -pathz). **1.** The route taken by a party of North American Indians on the attack. **2.** A hostile course or mood. Used in the phrase *on the warpath.*

war·plane (wáwr-playn) *n.* A combat aircraft.

war·rant (wórrənt ‖ wáwrənt) *n. Abbr.* **war., wrnt. 1.** Authorisation or certification; sanction, as given by a superior. **2.** Justification, as for an action or belief; grounds. **3.** Something that provides assurance or confirmation. **4.** A writing, writ, or other order that serves as authorisation for something, specifically: **a.** A voucher authorising payment or receipt of money. **b.** A warehouse receipt for goods received for storage. **c.** *Law.* A judicial writ authorising an officer to make a search, seizure, or arrest or to carry out a judicial sentence. **d.** *Military.* A warrant officer's certificate of appointment. ~*tr.v.* **warranted, -ranting, -rants. 1. a.** To guarantee the truth of (a statement); assert confidently. **b.** To assure (a person) of a fact. **2.** To attest to or make oneself answerable for the quality or authenticity of; especially, to guarantee (a product) to be as represented in terms of type, quality or quantity. **3.** To guarantee the immunity or security of. **4.** To provide adequate grounds for; justify. **5.** To grant authorisation or sanction to; authorise or empower. **6.** *Law.* To guarantee clear title to (real property, for example). [Middle English *war(r)ant,* protector, protection, authorisation, from Old North French *warant,* probably from Medieval Latin *warantus,* from Old High German *werenti,* "the one protecting", present participle of *werren,* to protect, guarantee.] —**war·rant·a·ble** *adj.* —**war·rant·a·ble·ness** *n.* —**war·rant·a·bly** *adv.* —**war·rant·er** *n.*

war·ran·tee (wórran-tée ‖ wáwran-) *n. Law.* A person to whom a warranty is made.

warrant officer *n. Abbr.* **WO, W.O.** *Military.* An officer intermediate in rank between a noncommissioned officer and a commissioned officer, having authority by virtue of a warrant.

war·ran·tor (wórran-tər, -tór ‖ wáwran-) *n. Law.* A person who makes a warrant or gives a warranty to another.

war·ran·ty (wórran-ti ‖ wáwran-) *n., pl.* **-ties. 1.** Official authorisation, sanction, or warrant. **2.** Justification or valid grounds for an act or course of action. **3.** *Law.* **a.** An assurance by the seller of property that the goods or property are as represented or will be as promised; especially, such as assurance accompanied by an explicit acceptance of responsibility for any repairs that become necessary during a stated period. **b.** A guarantee by the party being insured that the facts are as stated in reference to an insurance risk or that conditions will be fulfilled to keep the contract effective. **c.** A covenant by which the seller of land binds himself and his heirs to defend the security of the estate conveyed. **d.** A judicial writ; a warrant. [Middle English *warantie,* from Old North French, from the feminine past participle of *warantir,* to guarantee, from *warant,* protection, WARRANT.]

war·ren (wórran ‖ wáwran) *n.* **1. a.** An area where rabbits live in burrows. **b.** A colony of rabbits. **2.** Formerly, an enclosure for small game animals or birds. **3.** Any mazelike place in which one may easily get lost. [Middle English *warenne,* from Old North French, from Germanic.]

war·ren·er (wórranər ‖ wáwranər) *n.* One who keeps a warren.

war·ri·gal (wórrəg'l) *n. Australian.* A dingo. ~*adj.* Untamed; wild. [From a native Australian language.]

war·ri·or (wórri-ər ‖ wáwri-) *n.* One engaged or experienced in battle. Also used adjectively: *a warrior race.* [Middle English *werreour,* from Old North French *werreieor,* from *werreier,* to make war, from *werre,* WAR.]

War·rum·bun·gle Range (wórrəm-búng-g'l). Volcanic range of New South Wales, Australia. A national park since 1953, it rises to 1 228 metres (4,028 feet) at Mount Exmouth.

War·saw (wáwr-saw). *Polish* **War·sza·wa** (vaar-sháavə). Capital of Poland. Situated on the river Vistula, it was founded in the 13th century, first became the capital in 1596 and was ruled by Russia as an independent kingdom (1815–1917), becoming the capital again in 1918. It was badly damaged during the German occupation and its Jewish ghetto was destroyed. Some 400,000 of the Jewish population were moved to concentration camps and the remaining 60,000 or so were massacred after an attempted uprising (1943). Rebuilt according to its previous plan, it is a major cultural, commercial, industrial, and educational centre.

Warsaw Pact *n.* A treaty of mutual military alliance signed in Warsaw in 1955 by Albania, Bulgaria, Czechoslovakia, East Germany, Hungary, Poland, Romania, and the U.S.S.R. Also called "Eastern European Mutual Assistance Treaty".

war·ship (wáwr-ship) *n.* Any ship constructed or equipped for use in battle.

war·sle (wáwrss'l) *v.* **-sled, -sling, -sles.** *Northern British.* —*intr.* To wrestle or struggle. —*tr.* To wrestle with. [Middle English, metathetic variant of WRESTLE.] —**war·sler** *n.*

Wars of the Roses. *See* Roses, Wars of the.

wart (wawrt) *n.* **1.** A limited area of enlarged skin cells caused by a virus, covered with a keratinous layer, and occurring typically on the hands or feet. Also called "verruca". **2.** Any similar protuberance, as on a plant. —**warts and all.** Without attempting to disguise defects. [Middle English *werte, wart,* Old English *wearte.*]

wart hog *n.* A wild African pig, *Phacochoerus aethiopicus,* having tusks and wartlike protuberances on the face.

war·time (wáwr-tīm) *n.* A period in which a war is in progress. Often used adjectivally: *wartime austerities.*
wart·y (wáwrti) *adj.* **-ier, -iest. 1.** Having or covered with warts or wartlike protuberances. **2.** Of or resembling a wart or warts.
war whoop *n.* A war cry, especially of North American Indians.
War·wick (wórrik), **Richard Neville, Earl of** (1428–1471). English statesman, known as The Kingmaker. During the Wars of the Roses he fought for the Yorkists and secured the throne (1461) for Edward IV. He then changed sides and restored (1470) the Lancastrian Henry VI. He was killed at the battle of Barnet which regained the throne for Edward.
War·wick·shire (wórrik-shər, -sheer). County of central England. Having lost its industrial region around Coventry and Birmingham to the newly created West Midlands (1974), its economy is now mainly agricultural, including market gardening, wheat growing, and dairy farming.
war·y (wáir-i) *adj.* **-ier, -iest. 1.** On one's guard; alert to possible danger or deception; watchful. **2.** Characterised by caution: *a wary glance.* [From obsolete *ware,* wary, from Middle English *ware,* Old English *wær.*] **—war·i·ly** *adv.* **—war·i·ness** *n.*
was (woz, *weak form* wəz || wuz). First and third person singular past indicative mood of **be.**
wash (wosh || wawsh) *v.* **washed, washing, washes.** *—tr.* **1.** To cleanse, using water or other liquid, and often a cleansing agent such as soap or bleach, by immersing, flushing, rubbing, or scrubbing. **2.** To remove by, or as if by, washing: *wash a stain from one's hands.* Often used with *off, out,* or *away*: *wash away one's guilt; wash out a dirty mark.* **3.** To clean (itself) by licking. Used of an animal. **4.** To make moist or wet; dampen; drench: *Tears washed her cheeks.* **5.** To flow over, against, or past: *shores washed by ocean tides.* **6.** To carry along or sweep away through the action of flowing or moving water. Often used with *off, out,* or *away*: *His body was washed out to sea.* **7.** To erode, remove, damage, or destroy by moving water. Used with *out* or *away: The roads were washed out.* **8.** To serve as an effective cleaning agent for: *This soap washes wool.* **9.** To cover or coat with a watery layer of paint or other colouring substance. **10.** *Chemistry.* **a.** To purify (a gas) by passing through or over a liquid, as to remove soluble matter. **b.** To pass a solvent, such as distilled water, through (a precipitate). **11.** *Mining.* To remove particulate constituents from (an ore) by immersion in or agitation with water. *—intr.* **1.** To wash oneself: *wash for dinner.* **2.** To wash clothes, dishes, or the like in or by means of water or other liquid. **3.** To undergo washing without fading, shrinkage, or other damage: *This fabric will wash.* **4.** *British Informal.* To hold up under examination; be convincing: *Your excuse won't wash!* **5.** To be cleaned or removed by washing. Usually used with *out*: *The colours washed out.* **6.** To be carried away, removed, or drawn along by the action of flowing or moving water: *Bits of wreckage washed up on the shore.* Often used with *out* or *away*: *Some of the topsoil washed away in the storm.* **7.** To flow, sweep, or beat. Often used with *against, along,* or *over*: *The waves washed over the pilings.* **—wash down. 1.** To clean (a car, for example) by washing with water from top to bottom. **2.** To follow the ingestion of (food, for example) with a drink. **—wash (one's) hands of. 1.** To refuse to accept responsibility for. **2.** To abandon or renounce. **—wash up. 1.** *British.* To wash crockery, cutlery, and the like after use. **2.** *U.S.* To wash one's face and hands.
~n. **1.** The act or process of washing or being washed. **2.** A quantity of articles, especially clothing, washed or intended for washing. **3.** Kitchen refuse fed to pigs; swill. **4.** Malt or similar substances undergoing fermentation prior to distillation. **5.** Any preparation or product used in washing or coating, especially: **a.** A cosmetic or medicinal liquid, such as a mouthwash. **b.** A thin water-based paint or distemper. **6. a.** A thin layer of watercolour or Indian ink spread on a surface. **b.** Any light tint or hue: *a wash of red sunset.* **7. a.** The rush or surge of water or waves. **b.** The sound of this. **8. a.** The removal or erosion of soil, subsoil, or the like by the action of moving water. **b.** A deposit of recently eroded debris. **9. a.** An area of low or marshy ground washed by tidal waters. **b.** A stretch of shallow water. **10.** A turbulence in air or water caused by the motion or action of an oar, propeller, jet, or aerofoil. **11.** *Western U.S.* The dry bed of a stream. **—come out in the wash. 1.** To turn out well in the end. **2.** To come inevitably to light. Used of scandal.
~adj. U.S. Informal. **1.** Used for washing. **2.** Capable of being washed; washable. [Middle English *waschen, wasshen,* Old English *wæscan, wacsan,* from Germanic *wa(t)skan* (unattested).]
wash·a·ble (wósh-əb'l || wáwsh-) *adj.* Capable of being washed without fading or other damage. **—wash·a·bil·i·ty** (-ə-bílləti) *n.*
wash-and-wear (wósh-ən-wáir, -ənd- || wáwsh-) *adj.* Treated so as to be easily or quickly washed or rinsed clean and to require little or no ironing: *a wash-and-wear shirt.*
wash·ba·sin (wósh-bayss'n || wáwsh-) *n.* A basin that can be filled with water for washing the face and hands. Also *chiefly British* "wash-hand basin".
wash·board (wósh-bawrd || wáwsh-, -bōrd) *n.* **1. a.** A board having a corrugated surface of metal, wood, or the like, upon which clothes can be rubbed in the process of laundering. **b.** Such a board used as a percussion instrument. **2.** *U.S.* A **skirting board** *(see).* **3.** *Nautical.* A thin plank fastened to the side of a boat or to the sill of a port to keep out the sea and the spray.
wash·bowl (wósh-bōl || wáwsh-) *n. U.S.* A washbasin.
wash·cloth (wósh-kloth || wáwsh-, -klawth) *n., pl.* **-cloths** (-kloths || -klawthz, -klawths, -klothz). *U.S.* A **facecloth** *(see).*
wash·day (wósh-day || wáwsh-) *n.* A day, often the same day of every week, set aside for doing the household washing.
wash drawing *n.* **1.** The technique of producing drawings or paintings using washes of colour. **2.** A drawing or painting so produced.
washed-out (wósht-ówt || wáwsht-) *adj.* **1.** Lacking colour or intensity; pale; faded. **2.** *Informal.* Exhausted; tired-looking.
washed-up (wósht-úp || wáwsht-) *adj.* **1.** No longer successful or needed; finished. **2.** *Chiefly U.S.* Ready to give up; wearied.
wash·er (wósh-ər || wáwsh-) *n.* **1.** One that washes. **2.** *Machinery.* A small perforated disc, as of metal, rubber, leather, or plastic, placed beneath a nut or at an axle bearing or joint to relieve friction, prevent leakage, or distribute pressure. **3.** A machine or apparatus for washing; especially, a washing machine, a dishwasher, or an industrial plant for washing gases. **4.** *Australian.* A facecloth.
washer-up (wósh-ər-úp || wáwsh-) *n. British Informal.* A person who does the washing-up.
wash·er·wom·an (wósh-ər-wŏŏmən || wáwsh-) *n., pl.* **-women** (-wimmin) A woman who washes clothes for a living; a laundress.
wash·ing (wósh-ing || wáwsh-) *n.* **1.** The act or process of one that washes. **2.** A quantity of articles washed or intended to be washed at one time: *the week's washing.* **3.** The residue after an ore or other material has been washed. **4.** The liquid that is used to wash something. Sometimes used in the plural. **5.** A thin coat of paint or other liquid.
washing machine *n.* A domestic apparatus, usually powered by electricity and often plumbed into the domestic water supply and drains, used to wash clothes, household linen, and the like.
washing powder *n.* Detergent in the form of powder for washing clothes and other textiles.
washing soda *n.* A hydrated **sodium carbonate** *(see),* used as a general cleanser. Also called "sal soda".
Wash·ing·ton (wósh-ing-tən || wáwsh-). Coastal state of the northwest United States. Bordering Canada and the Pacific Ocean which indents the state at Puget sound, it is chiefly mountainous except for the basin of the river Columbia in the east. It is crossed by the Cascade and Coast mountain ranges. The capital is Olympia.
Washington, George (1732–1799). American statesman and general. He commanded the American forces during the War of Independence (1775–83), and became (1789) first president of the United States.
Washington D.C. Capital of the United States. Situated in the east of the country on the river Potomac, it is coterminous with the District of Columbia, and was built as a planned city (1790–1800) by a Frenchman, Pierre L'Enfant. The federal capital since 1800, it was burnt by the British (1814). Its many famous buildings include the White House, the Capitol, and the Lincoln Memorial.
washing-up (wósh-ing-úp || wáwsh-) *n.* **1.** The act of washing plates, dishes, glass, silver, saucepans, and the like, after a meal. **2.** The plates and dishes waiting to be washed.
wash leather *n.* **1.** Soft leather, such as chamois or split sheepskin. **2.** A piece of such leather, typically used for cleaning cars and windows or polishing metal.
wash out *tr.v.* **1.** To clean the inside of: *wash out a jam jar.* **2.** To cause the postponement or abandonment of (an outdoor event): *The match was washed out by a freak storm.*
wash·out (wósh-owt || wáwsh-) *n.* **1. a.** The erosion of a relatively soft geological surface by a transient stream of water. **b.** A channel produced by this. **2.** *Informal.* A total failure or disappointment.
wash·room (wósh-rŏŏm, -rōōm || wáwsh-) *n.* **1.** *British.* A room having communal washing facilities. **2.** *n. U.S.* A lavatory.
wash sale *n. U.S.* The illegal buying of stock by a seller's agents to give the impression of an active market.
wash·stand (wósh-stand || wáwsh-) *n.* A stand designed to hold a basin and jug of water for washing.
wash·tub (wósh-tub || wáwsh-) *n.* A tub or similar container used for washing clothes.
wash·y (wóshi || wáwshi) *adj.* **-ier, -iest. 1.** Watery; diluted: *washy tea.* **2.** Lacking intensity or vigour; wishy-washy. **—wash·i·ness** *n.*
was·n't (wózz'nt || wúzz'nt). Contraction of *was not.*
wasp (wosp || wasp, wawsp) *n.* Any of numerous social or solitary insects, chiefly of the superfamilies Vespoidea and Sphecoidea, commonly having a slender black and yellow striped abdomen, membranous wings, and in the females an ovipositor often modified as a sting. [Middle English *waspe,* Old English *wæsp, wæps.*]
Wasp, WASP, wasp (wosp || wasp, wawsp) *n.* In the United States, a person of Caucasoid, northern European, largely Protestant stock whose members are held by some to constitute the most privileged and influential group in American society. [*W*hite *A*nglo-*S*axon *P*rotestant.] **—Wasp, Wasp·ish, Wasp·y** *adj.*
wasp·ish (wósp-ish || wásp-, wáwsp-) *adj.* **1.** Pertaining to or suggestive of a wasp. **2.** Easily irritated or annoyed; irascible; snappish. **—wasp·ish·ly** *adv.* **—wasp·ish·ness** *n.*
wasp waist *n.* A very slender or tightly corseted waist. **—wasp·waist·ed** *adj.*
wasp·y (wóspi || wáspi, wáwspi) *adj.* **-ier, -iest.** Characteristic of a wasp; wasplike.
was·sail (wóss-ayl, wáss-, -'l || wáwss-) *n.* **1.** A salutation or toast formerly given in drinking someone's health or as an expression of good will at a festivity. **2.** The drink used in such toasting, commonly ale or wine spiced with roasted apples and sugar. **3.** A riotous festivity characterised by much drinking.
~intr.v. **wassailed, -sailing, -sails.** To engage in or drink a wassail. [Middle English *wassayl,* contraction of *wæs hæil,* from Old Norse

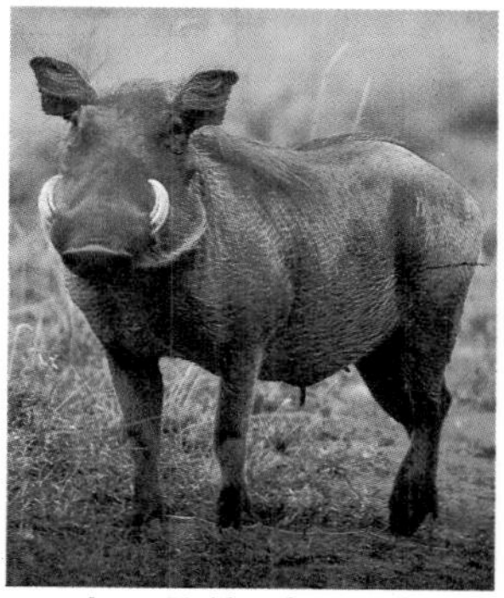

wart hog *Unlike other members of the pig family, the wart hog –* Phacochoerus aethiopicus *– goes down on bent forelimbs to dig for food. It inhabits much of Africa south of the Sahara.*

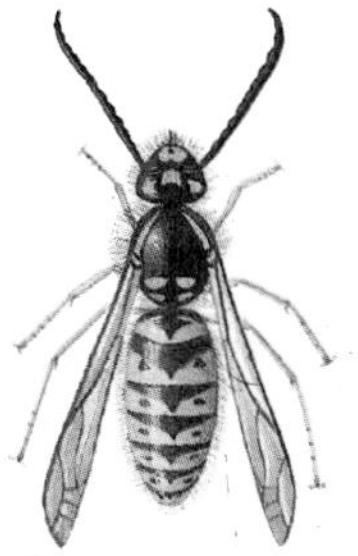

wasp *Rows of wasp pupae – insects in the dormant stage between larva and adult – fill the cells of a comb (below); the white grubs on the edge of the comb are wasp larvae. Most species of social wasp – including the common wasp of Britain (shown above 1½ times lifesize) – build a new colony each year. The queen builds the first cells out of wasp 'paper', made by chewing dry wood into a pulp. Later, new worker wasps enlarge the nest until, by late summer, the colony may contain 2,000 insects.*

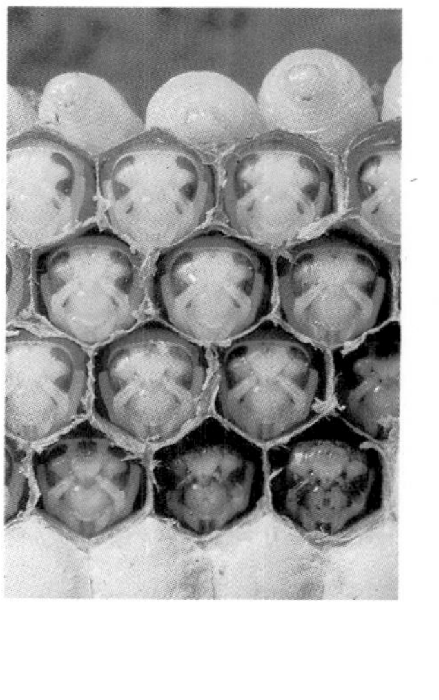

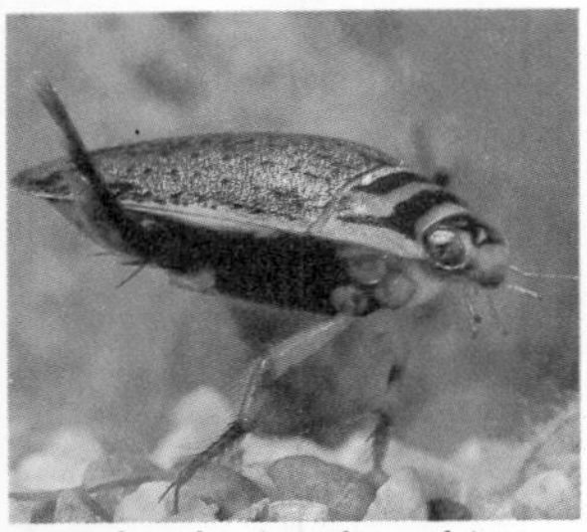

water beetle *A predator of rivers, lakes, and streams. The water beetle and its larvae will sometimes attack and eat small fish such as sticklebacks. The beetle lays its eggs in the stems of water plants.*

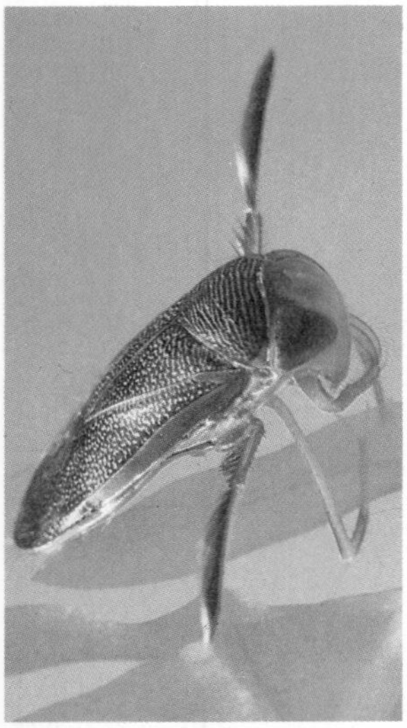

water boatman *This pond-dwelling insect propels itself underwater by using its powerful back legs as oars. Water boatmen feed on algae and diatoms which they draw from the ooze of the pond bed.*

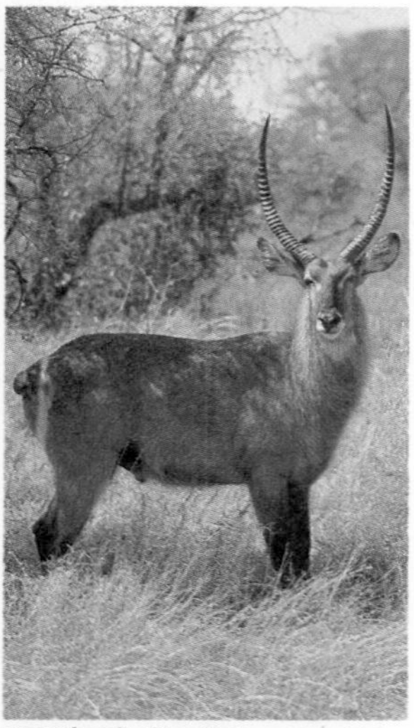

waterbuck *Despite its name, this large coarse-haired antelope from East Africa is found on plains and in woodland as well as beside lakes and rivers. It does, however, always graze within range of water.*

ves heill, be in good health : *ves,* imperative singular of *vesa, vera,* to be + *heill,* hale, healthy.] **—was·sail·er** *n.*

Was·ser·man reaction (wássər-mən, wóssər-; *German* vássər-man) *n.* A diagnostic test for syphilis involving the fixation or inactivation of a complement by antibodies to the causative organism, *Treponema pallidum,* in a blood serum sample. Also called "Wassermann test". See **complement fixation.** [After August von *Wassermann* (1866–1925), German bacteriologist.]

wast. *Archaic.* Second person singular past tense of **be.**

wast·age (wáystij) *n.* **1.** Loss by deterioration, wear, destruction, or the like. **2.** The gradual process of wasting. **3.** An amount that is wasted or lost by wear. **4.** See **natural wastage.**

waste (wayst) *v.* **wasted, wasting, wastes.** *—tr.* **1.** To use, consume, or expend thoughtlessly or carelessly; use to no avail; squander. **2.** To cause to lose energy, strength, or vigour; exhaust, tire, or enfeeble. **3.** To fail to take advantage or make profitable use of lose: *waste an opportunity.* **4. a.** To lay waste; devastate. **5.** *U.S. Slang.* To kill. *—intr.* **1.** To lose energy, strength, or vigour; become weak or enfeebled. Often used with *away.* **2.** To become wasted or consumed. **3.** *Archaic.* To pass: *Time is wasting.*

~n. **1.** The act of wasting or the condition of being wasted; thoughtless or careless expenditure, consumption, or use: *a waste of talent; gone to waste.* **2.** A place, region, or land that is uninhabited or uncultivated; a desert or wilderness. **3. a.** Any useless or worthless by-product of a manufacturing process; useless excess material. **b.** Something that escapes without being used, such as steam. **4.** Rubbish, refuse. **5. a.** The undigested residue of food eliminated from the body. **b.** The useless by-products of metabolism.

~adj. **1.** Regarded or discarded as worthless or useless: *waste paper.* **2.** Used as a conveyance or container for refuse: *a waste bin.* **3.** Not cultivated or inhabited. **4.** Excreted from the body as useless. [Middle English *wasten,* from Old North French *waster,* from Vulgar Latin *wāstāre* (unattested), from Latin *vāstāre,* to make empty, from *vāstus,* empty.]

wast·ed (wáystid) *adj.* **1.** Needless or superfluous: *wasted words; a wasted journey.* **2.** Physically haggard, as from disease or dissipation. —See Synonyms at **haggard.**

waste·ful (wáystf'l) *adj.* **1.** Characterised by heedless wasting; extravagant. **2.** *Archaic.* Causing waste or devastation; destructive. **—waste·ful·ly** *adv.* **—waste·ful·ness** *n.*

waste·land (wáyst-land) *n.* **1.** An uncultivated or desolate area; a barren or ravaged land. **2.** Any place, era, or aspect of life considered as lacking in spiritual, aesthetic, or other humanising qualities; a vacuum: *a cultural wasteland.*

waste·pap·er basket (wáyst-páypər) *n.* An open-topped container for paper and other dry rubbish, usually made of wickerwork. Also *U.S.* "wastebasket".

wastepaper bin *n.* An open-topped container for dry rubbish, usually made of metal.

waste pipe *n.* A pipe carrying off liquid waste from baths, washbasins, sinks, and the like. Compare **soil pipe.**

waste product *n.* **1.** Useless or worthless debris produced during or as a result of a manufacturing or other process. **2.** Organic waste matter such as urine, faeces, or dead cells.

wast·er (wáystər) *n.* A person who wastes; a spendthrift or ne'er-do-well; a wastrel.

wast·ing (wáysting) *adj.* **1.** Gradually deteriorating or being convinced. **2.** Sapping the strength, energy, or substance of the body; emaciating: *a wasting disease.*

wasting asset *n.* A fixed asset, such as a mine or oil well, or a property on a lease, that diminishes in value over the years.

wast·rel (wáystrəl) *n.* A profligate or loafer; a good-for-nothing. [WASTE + *-rel,* diminutive suffix (often derogatory), from Old French *-erel(le).*]

watch (woch || *U.S. also* wawch) *v.* **watched, watching, watches.** *—intr.* **1.** To look or observe attentively or carefully. **2.** To look and wait expectantly or in anticipation. Used with *for: watch for an opportunity.* **3.** To be on the lookout or alert; be constantly observant or vigilant. **4.** To stay awake at night while serving as a guard, sentinel, or watchman. **5.** To stay awake at night as a religious exercise; keep vigil. *—tr.* **1.** To look at steadily; observe carefully or continuously. **2.** To guard; keep a watchful eye on. **3.** To observe the course of mentally; keep informed about: *watching the opinion polls.* **—watch it.** *Informal.* To be careful. Usually used in the imperative. **—watch out.** To be careful or on the alert; take care.

~n. **1.** The act or process of keeping awake or mentally alert, especially for the purpose of guarding. **2.** Any of the periods into which the night was formerly divided; a part of the night. **3.** A period of close observation, often in order to discover something: *a watch during the child's illness.* **4.** A person or group of persons serving, especially at night, to guard or protect. **5.** The post or period of duty of a guard, sentinel, or watchman. **6.** A small, portable timepiece, driven by springs or powered by batteries; especially one worn on the wrist or carried in the pocket. **7. a.** A period of wakefulness, especially one observed as a religious vigil. **b.** A wake. **8.** *Nautical.* **a.** Any of the periods of time into which the day aboard ship is divided and during which a part of the crew is assigned to duty. **b.** The members of a ship's crew on duty during a specific watch. **c.** A chronometer on a ship. **—keep watch.** To be alert, looking or waiting (for someone). **—on the watch.** On the lookout; waiting for something or someone expectantly. [Middle English *wa(c)chen, wecchen,* Old English *wæccan,* to be or stay awake, keep vigil.]

watch·case (wóch-kayss) *n.* The casing for the mechanism of a watch.

watch·dog (wóch-dog) *n.* **1.** A dog trained to guard property. **2.** A person who serves as a guardian or protector against waste, loss, or illegal practices. Often used adjectivally: *a watchdog committee.*

watch·er (wóchər) *n.* **1.** One that watches or observes. **2.** One who observes the progress or development of something. Used in combination: *a China-watcher.* **3.** A person keeping vigil, as at a sick person's bedside.

watch·ful (wóchf'l) *adj.* **1.** Closely observant or alert; vigilant. **2.** *Archaic.* Awake; not sleeping. —See Synonyms at **aware.** **—watch·ful·ly** *adv.* **—watch·ful·ness** *n.*

watch glass *n.* **1.** A concavo-convex glass disc used to cover the face of a watch. **2.** A similarly shaped shallow glass dish used as a beaker cover or evaporating surface.

watch·mak·er (wóch-maykər) *n.* One whose occupation is making or repairing watches. **—watch·mak·ing** *n.*

watch·man (wóch-mən) *n., pl.* **-men** (-mən, -men). A man employed to stand guard or keep watch.

watch night *n.* A religious service held on New Year's Eve, especially by Methodists.

watch pocket *n.* A small pocket in a waistcoat, originally intended for holding a pocket watch.

watch·tow·er (wóch-towr, -tow-ər) *n.* An observation tower upon which a guard or lookout is stationed to keep watch, as for enemies or forest fires or over prisoners.

watch·word (wóch-wurd) *n.* **1.** A prearranged reply to a challenge, as from a guard or sentry; a password. **2.** A rallying cry; a slogan embodying the essential principles of a group.

wa·ter (wáwtər || *U.S. also* wóttər, *so also in compounds*) *n.* **1.** A clear, colourless, nearly odourless and tasteless liquid, H_2O, essential for most plant and animal life and the most widely used of all solvents. Melting point 0°C (32°F), boiling point 100°C (212°F), relative density (4°C) 1.0000. **2. a.** Any of various forms of water: *salt water; holy water.* **b.** *Usually plural.* Naturally occurring mineral water, as at a spa: *taking the waters at Bath.* **3. a.** Any body of water, such as a sea, lake, river, or stream. **b.** *Plural.* A particular stretch of sea or ocean; especially, the territorial waters of a state: *escorted out of British waters.* **4.** Water as supplied to consumers; the water supply: *turning off the water for repairs.* **5. a.** Depth of water considered in terms of its suitability for navigation. **b.** The level of the tide: *high water.* **6.** Any one of the liquids passed out of the body, such as urine, perspiration, or tears. **7.** *Often plural.* The fluid surrounding the foetus in the uterus; amniotic fluid. **8.** An aqueous solution of any substance, especially a gas: *ammonia water.* **9.** A wavy finish or sheen, as of a fabric. **10.** *Finance.* Shares in a company that has watered its share capital. Also called "watered stock". **11. a.** The transparency and lustre of a gem. **b.** Degree; quality: *of the first water.* **12.** In ancient thought, one of the four **elements** *(see).* **—above water.** Out of trouble. **—back water.** To cause a boat to slow, stop, or reverse its motion by placing the blade of an oar or paddle in the water and pushing it towards the boat. **—break water.** To release fluid when the amniotic sac is ruptured in childbirth. Used of a woman in labour. **—by water.** By boat. **—hold water.** To be logical or consistent: *His story holds water.* **—make** (or **pass**) **water.** To urinate. **—pour** or **throw cold water on.** *Informal.* To make discouraging remarks about (a plan, for example). **—water under the bridge.** Something that happened in the past and should be forgotten.

~v. **watered, -tering, -ters.** *—tr.* **1.** To pour or sprinkle water upon; make wet. **2. a.** To give drinking water to. **b.** To lead (an animal) to drinking water. **3.** To dilute or weaken by or as if by adding water. Often used with *down.* **4.** To give a sheen to the surface of (silk, linen, or metal). **5.** To increase (the share capital of a company) without any corresponding increase in the true value of the company's assets. **6.** To irrigate (land). *—intr.* **1.** To produce or discharge fluid; *eyes watering from the smoke.* **2.** To produce saliva in anticipation of food. Used of the mouth. **3.** To take on a supply of water. Used of a ship. **4.** To drink water. Used of an animal. **—make (one's) mouth water.** To cause to anticipate with relish. [Middle English *water,* Old English *wæter.*] **—wa·ter** *adj.* **—wa·ter·er** *n.* **—wa·ter·ish** *adj.*

wa·ter·age (wáwtər-ij) *n. British.* **1.** The movement of goods or merchandise by water. **2.** The fee paid for this.

water bailiff *n. British.* An official responsible for enforcing laws on fishing or shipping.

water ballet *n.* **1.** The art of dancelike movement in water; synchronised swimming. **2.** Any performance of this kind.

water bear *n.* A **tardigrade** *(see).*

wa·ter·bed (wáwtər-bed) *n.* An inflatable mattress designed to be filled with water and used as a bed.

water beetle *n.* Any of various aquatic beetles, especially of the family Dytiscidae, characteristically having a smooth, oval body and flattened hind legs specially adapted for swimming.

water bird *n.* Any swimming or wading bird.

water biscuit *n.* A plain unsweetened biscuit.

water blister *n.* A blister having a nonpurulent watery content.

water boatman *n.* Any of various aquatic insects of the families Corixidae and Notonectidae, having long, oarlike hind legs adapted for swimming.

wa·ter·borne (wáwtər-born || -bōrn) *adj.* **1.** Floating on or supported by water; afloat. **2.** Transported by water, as freight may be. **3.** Transmitted in water, as a disease germ may be.

wa·ter·brain (wáwtər-brayn) A disease of sheep, **gid** *(see).*

water brash *n.* Regurgitation of watery acid from the stomach; heartburn.

wa·ter·buck (wáwtər-buk) *n.* Any of several African antelopes of the genus *Kobus,* having curved, ridged horns and frequenting swamps or bodies of water.

water buffalo *n.* A large buffalo, *Bubalus bubalis,* of southern Eurasia having spreading backward-curving horns and often domesticated, especially as a draught animal. Also called "carabao".

water bug *n.* Any of various insects of wet places; especially, a large aquatic insect of the family Belostomatidae.

wa·ter·bus (wáwtər-buss) *n.* A large motorboat used for carrying fare-paying passengers on rivers or canals, as in Venice.

water cannon *n.* An apparatus capable of firing water at high pressure, used especially to disperse crowds or control riots.

Water Carrier. The constellation and sign of the zodiac **Aquarius** *(see).* [Translation of Latin *aquarius.*]

water chestnut *n.* **1.** A Chinese sedge, *Eleocharis tuberosa,* having an edible corm. **2.** The succulent corm of this plant, used in Oriental cookery. **3.** A floating aquatic plant, *Trapa natans,* native to Asia, bearing nutlike fruit. Also called "water caltrop".

water clock *n.* Any of various time-keeping or time-measuring devices, such as a **clepsydra** *(see),* based on the motion of running water. Also called "water glass".

water closet *n. Abbr.* **w.c.** A room or booth containing a lavatory.

wa·ter·col·our (wáwtər-kullər) *n.* **1.** A paint composed of a water-soluble pigment. **2.** A work done in watercolours. **3.** The art of using watercolours. **—wa·ter·col·our** *adj.* **—wa·ter·col·our·ist.**

wa·ter-cool (wáwtər-kōōl) *tr.v.* **-cooled, -cooling, -cools.** To cool (an engine) with water, especially with circulating water.

water cooler *n.* A vessel, device, or apparatus for cooling, storing, and dispensing drinking water.

wa·ter·course (wáwtər-kawrss || -kōrss) *n.* **1.** A **waterway** *(see).* **2.** The bed or channel of a waterway.

wa·ter·cress (wáwtər-kress) *n.* **1.** A plant, *Nasturtium officinale,* native to Eurasia, growing in freshwater ponds and streams and having pungent leaves used in salads, soups, and as a garnish. **2.** Any of several similar, related plants.

water cure *n. Medicine.* Hydropathy or hydrotherapy.

water cycle *n.* The cycle of evaporation and condensation that controls the distribution of the earth's water as it evaporates from the seas, rivers, and lakes into the atmosphere, condenses into a precipitated form as rain, sleet, or snow and flows back into the sea by way of rivers. Also called "hydrological cycle", "hydrologic cycle".

water diviner *n.* A person able to detect the existence of water under the ground by using a divining rod.

water dog *n.* **1.** A dog accustomed to water, especially one trained to retrieve waterfowl. **2.** One who is at home in or on the water.

watered-down (wáwtərd-dówn || *U.S. also* wóttərd-) *adj.* Reduced in effectiveness or impact.

watered stock *n. Finance.* **Water** *(see).*

wa·ter·fall (wáwtər-fawl) *n.* A steep descent of water from a height; a cascade.

water flea *n.* Any of various small aquatic crustaceans of the order Cladocera, characteristically swimming with a jerking motions.

Wa·ter·ford (wáwtər-fərd || wóttər). *Irish* **Contae Port Lairge.** County of Munster province, south Republic of Ireland. Bordering the Atlantic Ocean, it has the Comeragh and Monavullagh mountain ranges, and is crossed by the rivers Suir and Blackwater. Its chief industries are the raising of cattle, fishing, brewing, and distilling. Waterford is the county town.

Waterford glass *n.* A fine kind of bluish-tinted domestic glassware made in the town of Waterford in the Republic of Ireland.

wa·ter·fowl (wáwtər-fowl) *n., pl.* **-fowls** or collectively **waterfowl.** A swimming bird, such as a duck or goose.

wa·ter·front (wáwtər-frunt) *n.* An area of land, especially built-up land in a town, abutting on a body of water, such as a lake or harbour. Also used adjectivally: *A waterfront café.*

water gap *n.* A transverse cleft in a mountain ridge through which a stream flows.

water gas *n.* A fuel gas containing about 40 per cent carbon monoxide, 50 per cent hydrogen, and small amounts of carbon dioxide and nitrogen, made by passing steam and air over heated coke.

water gate *n.* **1.** A **floodgate** *(see).* **2.** A gate that provides access to a body of water.

water gauge *n.* An instrument indicating the level of water, as in a boiler, tank, reservoir, or stream. Also called "water glass".

water glass *n.* **1.** A drinking glass or goblet. **2.** A tube or similar structure having a glass bottom for making observations below the surface of the water. **3. Sodium silicate** *(see).* **4.** A water gauge. **5.** A **water clock** *(see).*

water hammer *n.* **1.** A banging noise heard in a water pipe following an abrupt alteration of the flow with resulting pressure surges. **2.** A similar noise in steam pipes, caused by steam bubbles entering a cold pipe partially filled with water.

water hen *n.* Any of various birds of the family Rallidae, especially the gallinule.

water hole *n.* A small natural depression in which water collects; especially, a pool used by animals as a watering place.

water hyacinth *n.* A floating aquatic plant, *Eichhornia crassipes,* native to tropical America, having bluish-purple flowers and often forming dense masses in ponds and streams.

water ice *n.* A dessert made from frozen puréed fruit or flavoured syrup. Also called "sorbet".

wa·ter·ing can (wáwtər-ing || *U.S. also* wóttər-) *n.* A vessel with a long spout and sometimes a perforated nozzle, used to water plants. Also *U.S.* "watering pot".

watering hole *n. Informal.* A place serving alcoholic drinks to the public. Used humorously. [After the watering places where wild animals congregate to drink.]

watering place *n.* **1.** A place where animals find water. **2.** A health resort with mineral springs; a spa.

water jacket *n.* A casing containing water circulated by a pump, used around a part to be cooled, especially in water-cooled internal-combustion engines.

water jump *n.* An obstacle consisting of a pond or ditch, usually preceded by a fence, over which riders or athletes must jump in a steeplechase or show jumping competition.

wa·ter·less (wáwtər-ləss, -liss || *U.S. also* wóttər-) *adj.* **1.** Without water; dry. **2.** Not requiring water. Said especially of a cooling system.

water level *n.* **1.** The height of the surface of a body of water. **2.** *Geology.* A **water table** *(see).* **3.** The water line of a ship.

water lily *n., pl.* **water lilies. 1.** Any of various aquatic plants of the genus *Nymphaea,* having floating leaves and showy, variously coloured flowers; especially, the common white water lily *N. alba.* **2.** Any of various similar or related plants.

water line *n.* **1.** *Nautical.* **a.** The line on the hull of a ship to which the water surface rises. **b.** Any of several lines parallel to this marked on the hull of a ship, indicating the depth to which the ship sinks under various loads. **2.** A line or stain, as that left on a sea wall, indicating the height to which water has risen or may rise.

wa·ter·logged (wáwtər-logd || *U.S. also* wóttər-, -lawgd) *adj.* **1.** Heavy and sluggish in the water because of flooding in the hold. Said of a ship. **2.** Soaked or saturated with water: *water-logged fields.* [WATER + *-logged,* probably "made (unmanageable) like a log in water", from LOG.]

Wa·ter·loo (wáwter-lōō || *U.S. also* wótter-) *n.* A disastrous or crushing defeat. Usually used in the phrase *meet one's Waterloo.* [After *Waterloo* in Belgium, where Napoleon met his defeat (1815).]

water main *n.* A principal pipe in a system of pipes for conveying water, especially one installed underground.

wa·ter·man (wáwtər-mən) *n., pl.* **-men** (-mən, -men). **1.** A boatman. **2.** A skilled oarsman. **—wa·ter·man·ship** *n.*

wa·ter·mark (wáwtər-maark) *n.* **1.** A mark showing the height to which water has risen; especially, a line indicating the levels of high and low tide. **2.** A translucent design impressed on paper during manufacture and visible when the finished paper is held to the light. **3.** The metal pattern that produces this design.
~*tr.v.* **watermarked, -marking, -marks. 1.** To mark (paper) with a watermark. **2.** To impress (a pattern or design) as a watermark.

water meadow *n.* A meadow irrigated and fertilised by the periodic flooding of a nearby river.

wa·ter·mel·on (wáwtər-mellən) *n.* **1.** A vine, *Citrullus vulgaris,* native to Africa, cultivated for its large, edible fruit. **2.** The fruit of this plant, having a hard green rind and sweet, watery, pink or reddish flesh.

water milfoil *n.* Any of various aquatic plants of the genus *Myriophyllum,* having feathery, finely dissected leaves.

water mill *n.* A mill with water-driven machinery. See feature, next page.

water moccasin *n.* A venomous snake, *Agkistrodon piscivorus,* of the southern United States. Also called "cottonmouth".

water mole *n. Australian.* The **duck-billed platypus** *(see).*

water nymph *n.* A nymph living in or near water, such as a **naiad,** a **nereid,** or an **oceanid,** *(all of which see).*

water of crystallisation *n.* Water in chemical combination with a crystal and necessary for the maintenance of crystalline properties but capable of being removed by sufficient heat.

water of hydration *n.* Water chemically combined with a substance so that it can be removed, as by heating, without substantially changing the chemical composition of the substance.

water ouzel *n.* A bird, the **dipper** *(see).*

water pepper *n.* **1.** A marsh plant, *Polygonum hydropiper* having reddish stems, greenish flowers, and acrid-tasting leaves. **2.** Any of various similar and related plants. Also called "smartweed".

water pimpernel *n.* A plant, the **brookweed** *(see).*

water pipe *n.* **1.** A pipe that carries water. **2.** A **hookah** *(see).*

water pistol *n.* A toy gun that squirts water.

water plantain *n.* Any of various aquatic plants of the family Alismataceae, having branching clusters of small white or pinkish flowers; especially, *Alisma plantago-aquatica.*

water polo *n.* A water sport with two teams of swimmers, each of which tries to pass a ball into the other's goal.

wa·ter·pow·er (wáwtər-powr, -pow-ər) *n.* **1.** The power of running or falling water as used for driving machinery, especially for generating electricity. **2.** A source of such power, such as a waterfall. **3.** A water right owned by a mill.

wa·ter·proof (wáwtər-prōōf || -prōōf) *adj.* **1.** Impenetrable to or unaffected by water. **2.** Made of or treated with rubber, plastic, or a sealing agent to resist water penetration.
~*n.* A waterproof material or garment.

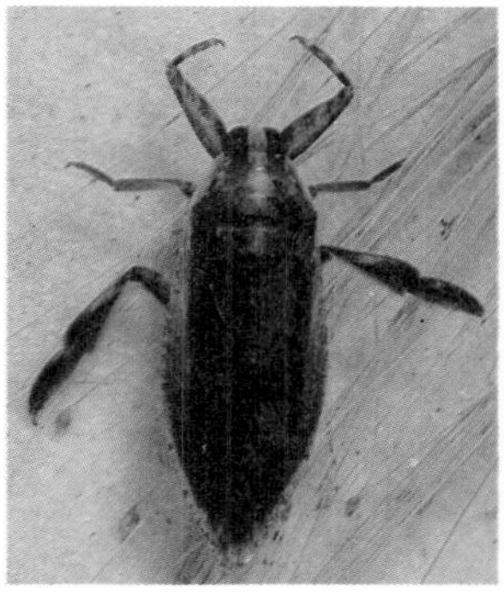

water bug *One of the most rapacious of insects, the giant water bug grows to a length of about 10 centimetres (4 inches) and can overpower fish twice its size. The female forces the unwilling male to carry its eggs by sticking them on its back.*

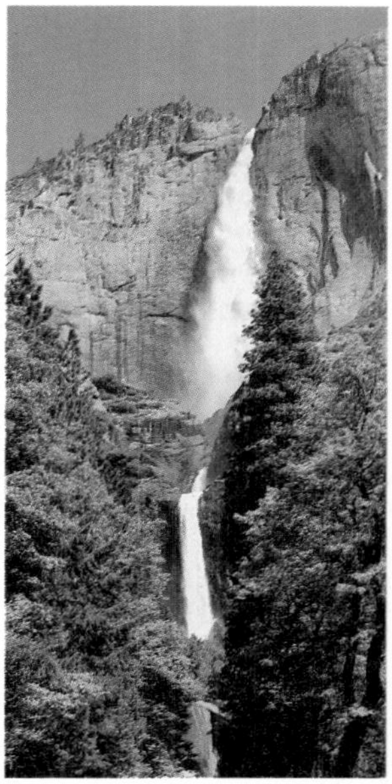

waterfall *Yosemite Falls in the Yosemite National Park, United States, have a total drop of 740 metres (2,400 feet).*

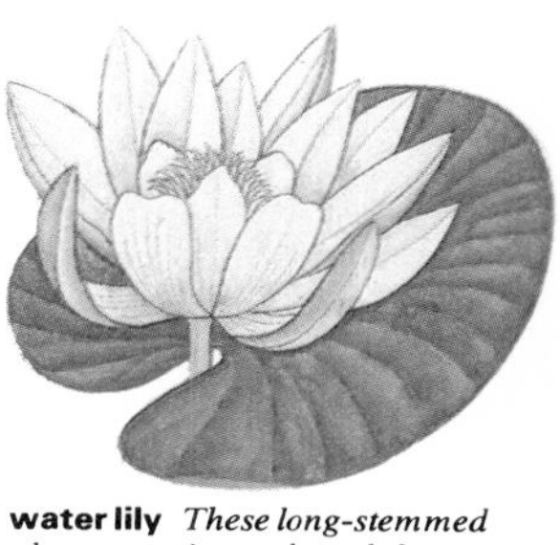

water lily *These long-stemmed plants grow in ponds and slow-flowing streams. The stems of the white water lily,* Nymphaea alba *(above), are sometimes eaten as a delicacy in parts of northern Europe.*

watermill

POWER FROM WATER WHEELS

The principal source of energy for 1,500 years

Simple watermills – half-horsepower paddle wheels set horizontally on an axle – were known to the ancient Greeks. The Romans devised vertical wheels that could generate about 3 horsepower. These remained the principal source of energy for 1,500 years. By the 18th century, Europe had some 500,000 watermills, the best of which generated 5–10 horsepower. Their uses included grinding corn, crushing ore, pounding iron, drilling gun barrels, and fulling cloth. Watermills began to become obsolete as the steam engine spread in the early 19th century.

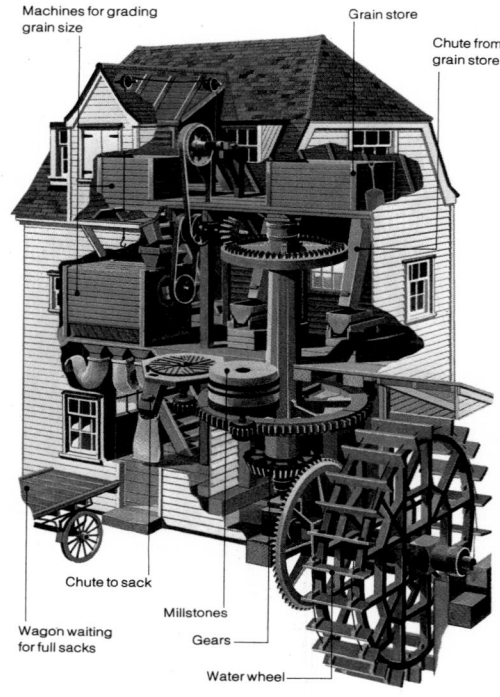

Machines for grading grain size

Grain store

Chute from grain store

Chute to sack

Millstones

Wagon waiting for full sacks

Gears

Water wheel

HOW A WATERMILL WORKS *A grain mill – shown with some sections cut away – used a vertical water wheel. The wheel's motion was accelerated and transferred to the horizontal millstones by gear-wheels. Early medieval wheels were set directly in a stream, and so were subject to little control.*

Later it was discovered that they could be controlled more easily by setting the wheel in a channel from the river; the water flow in the channel could be regulated with sluice gates. The grain to be ground into flour was stored on the top floor of the mill and dropped down a chute to the millstones, where another chute guided the ground meal into sacks, to be removed by wagons.

~*tr.v.* **waterproofed, -proofing, -proofs.** To make waterproof. [WATER + -PROOF.]

water purslane *n.* A trailing weed, **purslane** *(see).*

water-rail (wáwtər-rayl) *n.* A shy, marsh-dwelling bird of northern Europe, *Rallus aquaticus,* having a long, red bill.

water rat *n.* 1. Any of various semiaquatic rodents, such as the water vole or muskrat. 2. *Slang.* One who frequents a waterfront area, especially a loafer or petty thief.

water rate *n.* A charge levied on consumers for the use of a public water supply.

wa·ter·re·pel·lent (wáwtər-ri-péllənt, -rə-) *adj.* Resisting penetration by but not entirely impervious to water.

wa·ter·re·sis·tant (wáwtər-ri-zístənt, -rə-) *adj.* Resistant to wetting but not waterproof.

water right *n.* The right to draw or otherwise make use of water from a particular source, such as a lake, irrigation canal, or stream.

water sapphire *n.* A deep-blue cordierite from Sri Lanka often used as a gemstone.

wa·ter·scape (wáwtər-skayp) *n.* A seascape.

water scorpion *n.* Any of various aquatic insects of the family Nepidae, having a respiratory tube that resembles a scorpion's tail.

wa·ter·shed (wáwtər-shed) *n.* 1. A ridge of high land dividing two areas that are drained by different river systems. 2. The region

draining into a river, river system, or body of water. 3. A crucially important time or event; a turning point. [Probably translation of German *Wasserscheide.*]

wa·ter·side (wáwtər-sīd) *n.* Land bordering any body of water; a bank; a shore. —**wa·ter·side** *adj.*

wa·ter·ski (wáwtər-skee) *intr.v.* **-skied, -skiing, -skis.** To ski on water while being towed by a speedboat.
~*n.* A broad ski used in water-skiing. —**wa·ter·ski·er** *n.*

water snake *n.* Any of various aquatic or semiaquatic snakes of the genus *Natrix.*

water softener *n.* 1. Any substance that reduces the temporary or permanent hardness of water. 2. Any device or apparatus used to treat water in order to reduce its hardness.

water soldier *n.* A perennial aquatic plant, *Stratiotes aloides,* that remains submerged except at flowering time, when rosettes of long, narrow, serrated leaves, surrounding three-petalled white flowers, break the surface.

water spaniel *n.* A spaniel of a breed characterised by a curly, water-resistant coat, often used for retrieving waterfowl.

water spider *n.* A spider, *Argyroneta aquatica,* that constructs and lives in an underwater chamber, which it fills with air bubbles trapped in the hairs of its body.

wa·ter·spout (wáwtər-spowt) *n.* 1. A funnel-shaped tornado or lesser whirlwind occurring over water and resulting in a whirling column of spray and mist. Compare **tornado.** 2. A hole or pipe from which water is discharged.

water sprite *n.* A sprite or nymph living in or near the water.

water strider *n.* A **pondskater** *(see).*

water supply *n.* 1. The water available for a community or region. 2. The sources and delivery system of such water.

water table *n.* 1. The level under the ground in permeable or porous rock below which the ground is completely saturated with water. Also called "water level". 2. A projecting ledge, moulding, or stringcourse on a building, designed to throw off rainwater.

water tiger *n.* The predacious larva of a **diving beetle** *(see).*

wa·ter·tight (wáwtər-tīt) *adj.* 1. So assembled or constructed that water cannot enter or escape; waterproof. 2. Having no flaws or loopholes; incapable of being faulted or misconstrued: *a watertight argument; a watertight contract.*

water tower *n.* 1. A standpipe or tank mounted on a tower used as a reservoir or for maintaining equal pressure on a water system.

water vapour *n.* Water diffused as a vapour in the atmosphere, especially at a temperature below the boiling point.

water vole *n.* A large aquatic vole, *Arvicola terrestris.* Also called "water rat".

water wagtail *n.* The **pied wagtail** *(see).*

wa·ter·way (wáwtər-way) *n.* 1. A river, channel, canal, or other navigable body of water used for travel or transport. Also called "watercourse". 2. A channel at the edge of a ship's deck to drain away water.

wa·ter·weed (wáwtər-weed) *n.* 1. Any of various aquatic plants. 2. Pondweed.

water wheel *n.* 1. A wheel propelled by falling or running water, used as a source of power. 2. A wheel, with buckets attached to its rim, used for raising water.

water wings *pl.n.* A device consisting of a pair of joined inflatable waterproof bags placed under the arms of a person, especially a child, learning to swim.

wa·ter·works (wáwtər-wurks) *pl.n.* 1. a. The reservoirs, tanks, buildings, pumps, pipes, and other apparatus that constitute a public water supply system. b. A single unit, such as a pumping station, within such a system. Often used with a singular verb. 2. An exhibition of moving water, such as a fountain or waterfall. 3. *Informal.* a. Tears: *turned on the waterworks.* b. The urinary system.

wa·ter·y (wáwtəri ‖ *U.S. also* wóttəri) *adj.* **-ier, -iest.** 1. Filled with, consisting of, or containing water; moist; wet: *watery soil.* 2. Resembling or suggestive of water; liquid. 3. a. Containing too much water; diluted: *watery soup.* b. Sodden, as from overcooking in water. 4. Without force; insipid: *watery prose.* 5. Secreting or discharging water or watery fluid, especially as a symptom of disease. —**wa·ter·i·ness** *n.*

watery grave *n.* Death by drowning.

Wat·ling Street (wót-ling). Roman road in England. It ran from London via St. Albans and Leicester to Wroxeter near Shrewsbury.

Wat·son-Crick model (wóts'n-krík) *n.* The molecular model constructed by J.D. Watson and F.H.C. Crick to show the structure of DNA. See **double helix.**

Wat·son (wóts'n), **James Dewey** (1928–). American biologist. With Francis Crick he worked out the detailed structure of DNA (deoxyribonucleic acid), which led to the unravelling of the genetic code. He shared the Nobel prize for medicine (1962).

Watson, John Christian (1867–1941). Australian statesman. He was leader of the Labour Party (1901–1907), and became (1904) Australia's first Labour prime minister.

watt (wot) *n. Abbr.* **W** An SI unit of power equal to one joule per second. [After James WATT.]

Watt (wot), **James** (1736–1819). British engineer. He made fundamental improvements to the Newcomen steam engine, which resulted in the modern high-pressure steam engine (patented 1769).

wat·tage (wóttij) *n.* 1. An amount of power, especially electric power, expressed in watts. 2. The electric power required by an appliance or device.

Wat·teau (wótō, *French* va-tó), **(Jean) Antoine** (1684–1721).

French painter, the originator of the *fêtes galantes* (scenes of gallantry). Among his masterpieces is the *Embarcation for Cythera* (1717).

watt-hour (wót-ówr) *n. Abbr.* **W-hr, whr.** A unit of energy, especially electrical energy, equal to the energy of one watt acting for one hour and equivalent to 3,600 joules.

wat·tle (wótt'l) *n.* **1.** Poles intertwined with twigs, reeds, or branches for use in construction, as of walls or fences. **2.** Materials thus used. **3.** A fleshy, often brightly coloured fold of skin hanging from the neck or throat, characteristic of certain birds and some lizards. **4.** Any of various Australian trees or shrubs of the genus *Acacia.* ~*tr.v.* **wattled, -tling, -tles. 1.** To construct from wattle. **2.** To weave into wattle. **3.** To bind together by intertwining twigs or other material. [Middle English *wattel,* Old English *watel, watul*†.] **—wat·tle** *adj.* **—wat·tled** *adj.*

wattle and daub *n.* Wattle plastered with clay or mud, formerly used as a building material. **—wattle-and-daub** *adj.*

wat·tle·bird (wótt'l-burd) *n.* **1.** Any of several birds of the genus *Anthochaera,* of Australia and adjacent regions, having wattles on each side of the head. **2.** Any of various New Zealand birds of the family Callaeidae, having wattles on either side of the bill.

watt·me·ter (wót-meetər) *n.* An instrument for measuring in watts the power flowing in a circuit.

Wa·tu·si (wə-tóó-zi, waa-, -si) *n., pl.* **-sis** or collectively **Watusi.** A member of a pastoral people of Rwanda and Burundi in central equatorial Africa, distinguished by their tall stature.

Waugh, Evelyn (Arthur St. John) (1903–1966). British novelist. His satirical novels, such as *Decline and Fall* (1928) and *Vile Bodies* (1930), lampooned fashionable society. His later works, notably *Brideshead Revisited* (1945), revealed his interest in Roman Catholicism, to which he converted (1930).

wave (wayv) *v.* **waved, waving, waves.** *—intr.* **1.** To be moved back and forth or up and down by or as by a current of air; shake, sway, flutter, or undulate: *branches waving in the wind.* **2.** To make a signal with an up-and-down or back-and-forth movement with the hand or with an object in the hand: *waved at us from across the street.* **3.** To have an undulating, wavelike form or appearance; curve or curl: *Her hair waves naturally.* *—tr.* **1.** To move or sweep back and forth or up and down through the air, either once or repeatedly: *waved her fan; waved his magic wand.* **2. a.** To signal or express by waving the hand or something held in the hand: *He waved goodbye.* **b.** To signal to (a person) to move in a specified direction: *waved us on; waved him aside.* **3.** To arrange into curves, curls, or undulations: *wave one's hair.*
~*n.* **1. a.** A ridge or swell moving along the surface of a large body of water and generated by the action of gravity or the wind. **b.** A small ridge or swell moving across the interface of two fluids and dependent on the surface tension. **2.** *Often plural.* The sea or the surface of the sea: *vanished beneath the waves.* **3.** Something resembling a wave or waves, as **a.** A moving curve or a succession of curves in or upon a surface; an undulation: *waves of wheat in the wind.* **b.** A curve or a succession of curves, as in the hair. **c.** Any curved shape, outline, or pattern. **4.** A movement up and down or back and forth: *a wave of the hand.* **5.** A sudden surge or rise, as of an emotion or pattern of behaviour, sweeping irresistibly over an individual or through a group; a surge: *a wave of indignation; a wave of panic selling.* **6.** A widespread, persistent meteorological condition, especially of temperature: *a cold wave.* **7.** A group of people, animals, or instances that act, move, or exist together, especially one of a series or succession: *came with the first wave of settlers.* **8.** *Physics.* **a.** A disturbance or oscillation propagated from point to point in a medium or in space and described, in general, by mathematical specification of its amplitude, velocity, frequency, and phase. **b.** A graphic representation of the variation of such a disturbance with time. **9.** *Plural. Chiefly U.S. Slang.* A disturbance or upset. Used in the phrase *make waves.* [As verb, Middle English *waven,* Old English *wafian,* to move back and forth (especially with the hands). As a noun, perhaps variant (influenced by the verb WAVE) of Middle English *wawe, waghe,* probably Old English *wǣg,* motion, wave.] **—wavelike** *adj.* **—wav·er** *n.*

wave·band (wáyv-band) *n.* A range of frequencies, especially any of those assigned to radio transmissions.

wave equation *n.* **1.** A partial differential equation in one, two, or three dimensions, the solution of which represents the propagation of a wave with constant velocity. **2.** The fundamental equation of wave mechanics, the **Schrödinger wave equation** *(see).*

wave·form (wáyv-fawrm) *n.* The mathematical representation of a wave, especially a graph of amplitude at a fixed point against time.

wave front *n.* A surface of a propagating wave that is the locus of all points having identical phase, the surface being usually, but not always, perpendicular to the direction of propagation.

wave function *n.* A mathematical function used in wave mechanics to describe a given state of a quantum system, the square of the amplitude of the function at a given point being representative of the probability of the system in that state being found at that point.

wave·guide (wáyv-gīd) *n. Electronics.* A system of material boundaries in the form of a solid dielectric rod or dielectric-filled tubular conductor, usually of rectangular cross-section, capable of guiding high-frequency electromagnetic waves.

wave·length (wáyv-length, -lengkth || -lenth) *n.* **1.** *Physics.* In a periodic wave, the distance between two points of corresponding phase in consecutive cycles. **2.** *Informal.* A person's characteristic way of thinking and feeling: *We're not on the same wavelength.*

wave·let (wáyv-lit, -lət) *n.* A small wave or ripple.

wa·vell·ite (wáyvə-līt) *n.* A white, yellowish, or brownish hydrated aluminium phosphate, $Al_6(PO_4)_4(OH)_6{\cdot}9H_2O$, that occurs usually as small spheres with radiating internal structure. [After William *Wavell* (died 1829), British physician.]

wave mechanics *n.* The formulation of quantum mechanics, based on the wave equation of Schrödinger.

wave·me·ter (wáyv-meetər) *n.* A device for determining the wavelength or frequency of radio waves.

wave number *n.* The frequency of a wave divided by its velocity of propagation; the reciprocal of the wavelength.

wave-par·ti·cle duality (wáyv-pártik'l) *n. Physics.* The exhibition of both wavelike and particle-like properties by a single entity, such as a photon or an electron. See **quantum theory.**

wave power *n.* Energy obtained by using the momentum of waves to generate electricity. **—wave-pow·ered** *adj.* See feature, next page.

wa·ver (wáyvər) *intr.v.* **-vered, -vering, -vers. 1.** To swing or move back and forth; sway. **2.** To show irresolution or indecision; vacillate. **3.** To become uncertain or unsure; falter: *Her confidence never wavered.* **4.** To tremble, quaver, or shake. Used of a sound, such as a voice or a musical note. **5.** To flicker, flash, or glimmer. Used of light. —See Synonyms at **hesitate, swing.**
~*n.* An act of wavering. [Middle English *waveren,* to wander, stray, fluctuate, from Old Norse *vafra,* to move unsteadily, hover.] **—wa·ver·er** *n.* **—wa·ver·ing·ly** *adv.*

wave theory *n.* A theory put forward by Christian Huygens (1629–95) that light is transmitted in the form of waves. Compare **corpuscular theory.**

wave train *n. Physics.* A succession of similar wave pulses.

wave trap *n.* An electronic filtering device designed to exclude unwanted signals or interference from a receiver.

wa·vy (wáyvi) *adj.* **-vier, -viest. 1.** Moving or proceeding in a wavelike form or motion; sinuous. **2.** Having curls, curves, or undulations: *wavy hair.* **3.** Characteristic of, resembling, or suggestive of waves. **4.** Abounding in, having, or rising in waves: *a wavy sea.* **—wav·i·ly** *adv.* **—wav·i·ness** *n.*

waw. Variant of **vav.**

wax[1] (waks) *n.* **1. a.** Any of various natural or synthetic, viscous or solid heat-sensitive substances, consisting essentially of high molecular weight hydrocarbons or esters of fatty acids, characteristically insoluble in water but soluble in most organic solvents. **b.** A substance secreted by bees; beeswax. **c.** A waxy substance found in the ears; cerumen. **2.** A solid plastic or pliable liquid substance of mineral origin, primarily petroleum, such as ozocerite or paraffin, used in paper coating, as insulation, in crayons, and often in medicinal preparations. **3.** A resinous mixture used by shoemakers to wax their thread. **4.** Any person or thing resembling or suggestive of wax, especially in being readily moulded and impressionable.
~*tr.v.* **waxed, waxing, waxes.** To coat or treat with wax.
~*adj.* Made of or resembling to wax. [Middle English *wax, wexe,* Old English *weax, wæx,* beeswax.]

wax[2] *intr.v.* **waxed, waxing, waxes. 1.** To increase gradually in size, number, strength, or intensity. **2.** To show an increasing illuminated area; increase in illumination or progress towards being full. Used of the moon. Compare **wane. 3.** To grow or become as specified: *wax angry.* [Middle English *wexen,* Old English *weaxan.*]

wax[3] *n. British Informal.* A temper; a rage. Not in current usage.

wax bean *n.* The **butter bean** *(see).*

wax·ber·ry (wáks-bəri, -bri) *n., pl.* **-ries.** The waxy fruit of the wax myrtle or the snowberry.

wax·bill (wáks-bil) *n.* Any of various tropical Old World birds of the genus *Estrilda* and related genera, having a short, often brightly coloured waxy beak.

wax·en (wáks'n) *adj.* **1.** Consisting of or covered with wax. **2.** Suggestive of wax, as: **a.** Pale. **b.** Smooth and shiny. **c.** Pliable or impressionable.

wax insect *n.* Any insect that secretes wax, especially the Oriental species *Ericerus pe-la,* bred on a small scale for its wax.

wax myrtle *n.* A shrub, *Myrica cerifera,* of the southeastern United States, having evergreen leaves and small, berry-like fruit with a waxy coating. Also called "candleberry".

wax palm *n.* Any of several palm trees that yield wax, such as *Copernica cerifera,* the source of carnauba wax, or *Ceroxylon andicola,* of South America.

wax paper *n.* Also **waxed paper.** Paper that has been made moistureproof by treatment with wax.

wax·plant (wáks-plaant || -plant) *n.* A tropical Old World vine, *Hoya carnosa,* having waxy white or pinkish flowers.

wax·wing (wáks-wing) *n.* Any of several birds of the genus *Bombycilla,* having crested heads, predominantly brown plumage, and waxy red tips on the secondary wing feathers.

wax·work (wáks-wurk) *n.* **1.** The art of modelling in wax. **2. a.** Figures or ornaments made of wax; especially, life-size wax representations of famous persons. **b.** A single such representation. **3.** *Plural.* An exhibition of waxwork in a museum. **—wax·work·er** *n.*

wax·y[1] (wáksi) *adj.* **-ier, -iest. 1.** Resembling wax in colour or consistency, especially: **a.** Pale, smooth, and lustrous. **b.** Pliable or impressionable. **2.** Consisting of, abounding in, or covered with wax. **—wax·i·ness** *n.*

waxy[2] *adj. British Informal.* Bad-tempered; annoyed. Not in current usage.

way (way) *n.* Also *regional* **ways** (wayz) (for sense 9). **1. a.** A road,

waxbill *The small seed-eating waxbill is an African relative of the sparrow. Its nest is a frequent target of the whydah bird, which lays its eggs there and leaves the waxbill to raise its young.*

waxwing *Berries are the favourite food of the waxwing, which breeds in the far north of Europe, Asia, and North America, but can move as far south as Mediterranean latitudes during the winter. The bird gets its name from the red blobs at the ends of some of its wing feathers; the blobs look like red sealing wax.*

wave power

MAKING USE OF THE OCEANS' PERPETUAL MOTION

Wave power may be a reliable source of "free" energy

As the world's oil and fossil fuel resources are depleted, nations are searching for cheap energy from renewable supplies. In certain maritime countries, wave power seems to hold out real hope in an uncertain future.

In some parts of the oceans, waves generate power more continuously than in others. The size of the waves depends on the wind – not only on its strength but also on the distance of open sea over which it is frequently blowing. Where winds blow frequently in the same direction – as they do across the North Atlantic towards the coasts of Britain – their energy is stored and concentrated in powerful waves. In equatorial regions there is too little wind and in the polar regions there is too much ice for waves to build up. Only the areas between the latitudes 35° and 60° north and south can expect to benefit from wave power if it becomes a practical source of energy.

Wave power, where available, has some advantages over competing forms of renewable energy. The seas are rougher in winter, so more power is available when it is most needed, which is not the case with solar power. Wave power would also be more reliable than wind power, because the surface of the ocean is rarely motionless (less than 1 per cent of the time), but the air does have long periods of calm. Although wave power promises much and does not require complex technology, there are still difficulties to be faced before it is applied.

One of the most promising devices being investigated is the Salter Duck, which is efficient enough to use 35 per cent of the waves' energy; but it is estimated that a 2,000-megawatt-producing power unit of Ducks (which would supply about one-twelfth of Britain's present annual need) would stretch for 30 kilometres (19 miles). The cost of building such huge machines and the difficulties of keeping them securely anchored and working reliably in greatly varying seas have meant that the capital cost of installing wave power makes it uneconomic.

THE BRISTOL OSCILLATING CYLINDER

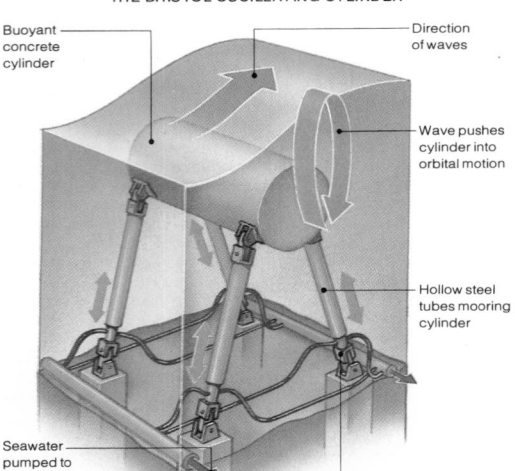

The Bristol Oscillating Cylinder bobs up and down on the waves; this motion is used by pumps on the seabed to suck in water and pump it at high pressure to a water turbine.

THE OSCILLATING WATER COLUMN

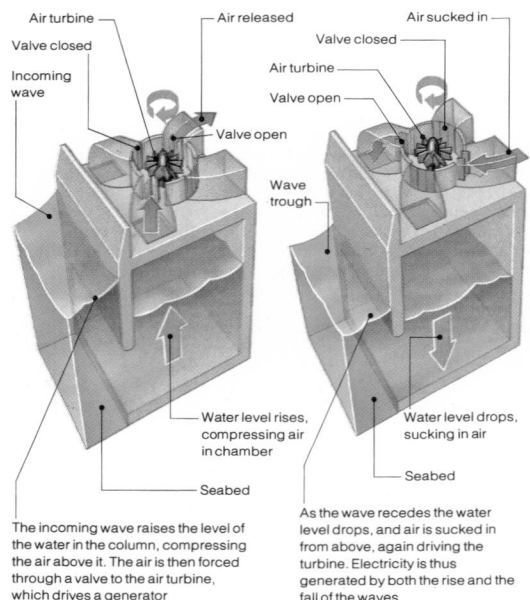

The incoming wave raises the level of the water in the column, compressing the air above it. The air is then forced through a valve to the air turbine, which drives a generator.

As the wave recedes the water level drops, and air is sucked in from above, again driving the turbine. Electricity is thus generated by both the rise and the fall of the waves

THE SALTER DUCK

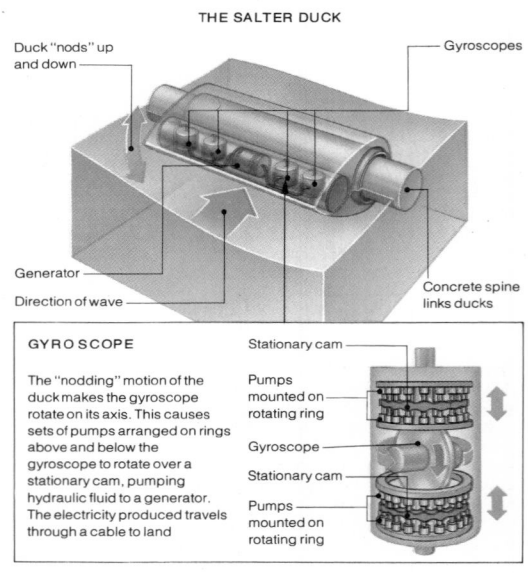

GYROSCOPE

The "nodding" motion of the duck makes the gyroscope rotate on its axis. This causes sets of pumps arranged on rings above and below the gyroscope to rotate over a stationary cam, pumping hydraulic fluid to a generator. The electricity produced travels through a cable to land

The nodding motion of the Salter Duck absorbs power from the waves more efficiently than most competitors, but it transfers that power through gyroscopes and pumps in a complex system whose reliability is so far unproved.

The principle of the Oscillating Water Column was applied by the Japanese in the 1960s to illuminate small navigational buoys. Larger devices are now producing electricity and aiding research in both Japan and Britain.

---

path, or track providing a route from one place to another. **b.** Such a road considered as a place where people live: *She lives over the way.* **c.** A specific street: *Landsdowne Way.* **d.** A right of way in law. **2. a.** Room or space free of obstacles and allowing forward movement: *clear the way for a parade; get out of my way.* **b.** An absence of factors impeding progress or action; opportunity for advance or activity: *an agreement that has opened the way for a lasting peace.* **3.** A course that is or may be used in going from one place to another: *Show me the way to go home.* **4. a.** Progress or travel along a particular route, in a particular direction, or towards a particular end: *on my way to work; leading the way in the fight against cancer.* **b.** Forward movement or progress towards a desired end, effected as specified: *elbowed his way to the front; fought her*

way to the top in a competitive business. **c.** Forward motion or rate of progress of a vessel through water: *The ship gathered way.* **5.** A path or course of experience, life, or conduct: *went our separate ways after the war.* **6. a.** A method or manner of performing an action or achieving an end: *There must be some way of mending it; Should I do it this way?* **b.** A means or expedient that may be employed to effect a result: *had no way of contacting you.* **7. a.** Often *plural.* A characteristic or habitual mode of living, behaving, or happening: *the American way of life; mend one's ways; these little debts have a way of mounting up.* **b.** A particularly effective or persuasive manner: *a way with words; has a way with women.* **8.** Freedom or scope to do as one wishes: *if I had my way; always gets her own way.* **9.** Distance in general, whether spatial, temporal, or con-

ceptual: *a good way off; have come some way towards an agreement.* **10. a.** Direction of motion or aspect: *come this way; glanced my way.* **b.** A district or region considered as lying in a specified direction: *call by if you're ever over our way; down Mexico way.* **11.** An aspect, particular, or feature: *I agree with you in some ways. The situation is in no way comparable.* **12.** The range or scope of one's observation or experience: *Wealth never came his way.* **13.** *Informal.* A state or condition, especially with regard to health or prosperity: *in a bad way financially.* **14.** Type, category, or description: *not much in the way of a plot.* **15.** *Plural.* A set of parallel longitudinal strips on a surface that serves to guide a moving part in a machine. **16.** *Plural. Nautical.* The timbered structure from which a ship slides when launched. —See Synonyms at **method.** **—by the way** or **by.** Incidentally; in passing. **—by way of. 1.** Through; by route of. **2.** As a means of; in order to serve as: *He made no comment by way of apology.* **—give way. 1.** To yield, submit, or agree. **2.** To fall or break down under pressure. **—go out of (one's** or **the) way.** To inconvenience oneself in doing something beyond that which is required. **—have** or **want it both ways.** To have or want the benefit or enjoyment of two states of affairs that are mutually incompatible. **—in a way.** To some extent. **—put (someone) in the way of.** To provide with (an opportunity of gaining an advantage). **—see (one's) way (clear) to.** To be willing or find it possible to do something. **—under way. 1.** In motion or operation; already initiated or started. **2.** Making progress or headway. **3.** *Nautical.* Not anchored and not moored to a fixed object.
~*adv. Informal.* **1.** At a great distance; far: *way off yonder.* **2.** By a great distance or to a great degree: *way over budget.* [Middle English *wey(e), wei(e),* way, Old English *weg,* a road, path. Adverbial use, from AWAY.]
  Synonyms: way, path, route, course, passage, pass, trail.
-way *adj. comb. form.* Indicates composition from a specified number of elements: *a two-way mirror; a three-way partnership.*
way·bill (wáy-bil) *n.* A document containing a list of goods and shipping instructions relative to a shipment.
way·far·er (wáy-fair-ər) *n.* One who travels; especially, one who travels by foot. [Middle English *weyfarere : wey,* WAY + *fare,* a journey, travelling, Old English *faru.*] **—way·far·ing** *adj.*
wayfaring tree *n.* A shrub, *Viburnum lantana,* having clusters of white flowers and berries that turn from red to black. [It frequently grows along roadsides.]
way·lay (way-láy ‖ wáy-lay) *tr.v.* **-laid, -laying, -lays. 1.** To lie in wait for and ambush. **2.** To stop and accost unexpectedly. **—way·lay·er** *n.*
way·leave (wáy-leev) *n.* A right of way over or through land, as for the transport of goods or the running of a pipeline that differs from an ordinary right of way in being granted to an applicant for a specific purpose. [WAY + LEAVE (permission).]
Wayne (wayn), **John,** born Marion Michael Morrison (1907–79). U.S. film actor. He is noted for his tough hero roles in classic westerns such as *Stagecoach* (1939), *Red River* (1948), and *True Grit* (1969), for which he won an Academy Award.
way-out (wáy-ówt) *adj. Informal.* Strange or unconventional.
-ways *adj. & adv. comb. form.* Indicates manner, direction, or position; for example, **sideways.** [Middle English *-ways, -weys,* from *way(e)s, wey(e)s,* in (such) a way, Old English *weges,* adverbial genitive of *weg,* WAY.]
ways and means *pl.n.* **1.** Methods or resources that may be used to achieve a particular end. **2.** The methods of raising the revenue needed to meet the expenditure of a state.
way·side (wáy-sīd) *n.* The side or edge of a road. **—fall by the wayside.** To fail to continue; give up.
~*adj.* Near or at the edge of a road: *a wayside inn.*
way·ward (wáy-wərd) *adj.* **1.** Wanting one's own way in spite of the advice or wishes of another; wilful; headstrong. **2.** Swayed by caprice; erratic; unpredictable. —See Synonyms at **contrary, unruly.** [Middle English *wayward,* short for *awayward,* turned away : AWAY + -WARD.] **—way·ward·ly** *adv.* **—way·ward·ness** *n.*
way·worn (wáy-wawrn ‖ -wōrn) *adj.* Wearied from travelling.
Wb *Physics.* weber.
WbN west by north.
WbS west by south.
W.C. water closet.
W.C.C. World Council of Churches.
W/Cdr. Wing Commander.
we (wee; *weak form* wi) *pron.* The first person plural pronoun in the nominative case. **1.** Used to represent the speaker or writer and one or more others that share in the action of a verb. **2.** Sometimes used instead of *I* by a monarch, or by an editor who purports to speak for a publication. **3.** *Informal.* Used in place of *you* in playful intimacy, especially with children, or in a patronising manner: *Are we going to eat our cereal?* **4.** Often used to represent people in general: *We cannot see beyond the grave.* —See Usage note at **me.** [Middle English *we,* Old English *wē.*]
W.E.A. Workers' Educational Association.
weak (week) *adj.* **weaker, weakest. 1.** Lacking physical strength, energy, or vigour; feeble: *He was weak after his illness.* **2.** Liable to fail under pressure, stress, or strain; lacking resistance: *a weak link in a chain.* **3.** Lacking firmness of character, strength of will, or force of conviction. **4. a.** Lacking effectiveness or force; inadequate: *a weak defence.* **b.** Not easily defended or sustained: *in a weak bargaining position.* **5. a.** Lacking strength or intensity: *a weak voice.* **b.** Having a low concentration of an active or essential ingre-

dient: *weak tea; a weak gin and tonic.* **6.** Lacking the capacity to function well or in a normal manner; unsound or easily upset: *a weak stomach; a weak heart.* **7.** Having or showing less than average ability, talent, or resources in a specified field: *a weak student; a weak batting line-up.* **8.** Based on or showing faulty logic, lack of coherence, or poor presentation; not persuasive or convincing: *a weak argument; a weak plot.* **9.** Incapable of the effective exercise of authority; lacking the power or political will to rule: *a weak government; weak leadership.* **10.** Lacking or deficient in a specified thing, as a quality or component. **11.** *Linguistics.* Of or designating those verbs in English or other Germanic languages that form a past tense by means of a dental suffix; for example, *start, started; have, had; bring, brought.* Compare **strong. 12.** *Phonetics.* Unstressed or unaccented. **13.** *Prosody.* Designating a verse ending having a final unstressed syllable. **14.** *Finance.* Marked by or showing lack of firmness and a falling tendency in prices or value: *a weak pound.* [Middle English *waike, we(i)ke,* from Old Norse *veikr,* pliant, flexible.] **—weak·ly** *adv.*
  Synonyms: weak, feeble, frail, infirm, decrepit, debilitated.
weak·en (wéekən) *v.* **-ened, -ening, -ens.** —*tr.* To make weak or weaker. —*intr.* To become weak or weaker. **—weak·en·er** *n.*
weaker sex *n.* The female sex. Usually used facetiously, preceded by *the.*
weak·fish (wéek-fish) *n., pl.* **-fishes** or collectively **weakfish.** Any of several marine food and game fishes of the genus *Cynoscion;* especially, *C. regalis,* of North American Atlantic waters. [Obsolete Dutch *weekvische, weekvis : week,* soft, WEAK (probably from its soft, fleshy mouth, which pulls very weakly on a line when caught) + Middle Dutch *visch, vis,* FISH.]
weak interaction *n.* An interaction between elementary particles that is some 10^{12} times weaker than the strong interaction and is responsible for some particle decays, the beta decay of a radioactive nucleus, and for the emission and absorption of neutrino. Also called "weak force". Compare **electromagnetic interaction, gravitational interaction, strong interaction.**
weak-kneed (wéek-néed) *adj.* Irresolute; timid.
weak·ling (wéekling) *n.* A person of weak constitution or character.
weak·ly (wéekli) *adj.* **-lier, -liest.** Sickly; delicate in health.
weak-mind·ed (wéek-míndid) *adj.* **1.** Irresolute; indecisive. **2.** Feeble-minded; foolish. **—weak-mind·ed·ness** *n.*
weak·ness (wéek-nəss, -niss) *n.* **1. a.** The state or quality of being weak. **b.** An instance or display of this. **2.** A defect or failing. **3. a.** A special fondness; a foible: *a weakness for chocolates.* **b.** Something for which one has an irresistible desire. —See Synonyms at **fault.**
weak sister *n. U.S. Informal.* A member of a group who is considered a weakling or an incompetent.
weal¹ (weel) *n. Archaic.* **1.** Prosperity; happiness: *in weal and woe.* **2.** The welfare of the community; the general good: *the public weal.* [Middle English *we(o)la,* Old English *we(o)la,* wealth, well-being.]
weal² *n.* **1.** A ridge on the flesh raised by a blow; a welt. **2.** A hard, raised, white patch on the skin caused by acute irritation, as from an insect bite or nettle sting. Also called "wheal". [Variant (influenced by WHEAL) of WALE (ridge).]
weald (weeld) *n. British. Archaic.* **1.** A woodland. **2.** An area of open rolling upland. [Middle English *weld(e), weeld,* Old English *weald,* variant of *wald,* WOLD.]
wealth (welth) *n.* **1.** A great quantity of valuable material possessions or resources; riches. **2.** The state of being rich; affluence. **3.** A profusion or abundance: *a wealth of advice.* **4.** *Economics.* All goods and resources having economic value. [Middle English *welthe,* well-being, riches, from *wele,* WEAL (welfare).]
wealth·y (wélthi) *adj.* **-ier, -iest. 1.** Prosperous; affluent. **2.** Possessing in abundance. **—wealth·i·ly** *adv.* **—wealth·i·ness** *n.*
wean¹ (ween) *tr.v.* **weaned, weaning, weans. 1.** To accustom (the young of a mammal) to solid food after a diet of mother's milk. **2.** To detach (a person) from that to which he is accustomed or devoted. [Middle English *wenen, wa(i)nen,* Old English *wenian,* to accustom, train, wean.]
wean² (ween ‖ wayn) *Northern British n.* A child. [Contraction of Scottish *wee ane,* wee one.]
wean·ling (wéenling) *n.* A recently weaned child or animal.
~*adj.* Recently weaned.
weap·on (wéppən) *n.* **1.** Any instrument or bodily part used as a means of attack or defence in combat. **2.** Any means employed to get the better of another.
~*tr.v.* **weaponed, -oning, -ons.** To supply with a weapon; arm. [Middle English *wepen, wepne,* Old English *wæp(e)n,* from Germanic *wæpnam†* (unattested).]
weap·on·eer (wéppə-néer) *n.* **1.** An individual who arms and otherwise prepares a nuclear weapon for release onto a target. **2.** An individual who designs or devises nuclear or other weapons. **—weap·on·eer·ing** *n.*
weap·on·ry (wéppənri) *n.* Weapons collectively.
wear¹ (wair) *v.* **wore** (wawr ‖ wōr), **worn** (wawrn ‖ wōrn), **wearing, wears.** —*tr.* **1.** To be dressed in or have on or about the body, as for clothing, adornment, or protection: *wearing a hat; must wear your seat belt; wore a delightful perfume.* **2.** To have or carry habitually on one's person: *wears glasses.* **3.** To affect or exhibit: *wear a smile.* **4.** To bear, carry, or maintain in a specified manner: *wears her hair long.* **5.** To fly or display (colours), as does a ship, jockey, or knight. **6.** To impair, consume, waste, efface, or erode by or as if by long or hard use, friction, or exposure to the elements: *worn by*

repeated child-bearing. Often used with *away, down,* or *off: shoes worn down at the heels.* **7. a.** To produce by constant use, rubbing, or exposure: *They eventually wore hollows in the steps.* **b.** To bring to the specified condition through attrition or prolonged use: *pebbles worn smooth.* **8. a.** To fatigue; weary: *worn by the effort.* **b.** To diminish; exhaust: *His incessant criticism wore her patience.* **9.** *British*

weather

UNDERSTANDING A METEOROLOGICAL PHOTOGRAPH
Satellite pictures help to predict the weather

Weather prediction, or meteorology, has become more precise in the past decade with the development of satellite photography and computer techniques. Weather conditions can now be seen on photographs taken at high level and on which meteorological symbols have been superimposed.

Isobars are lines drawn between points of equal atmospheric pressure, in the way that contour lines on a map show areas of equal height. At the centre of a high-pressure region, the weather is commonly warm and dry. At the centre of a low-pressure region it is generally cool and rainy.

In the Northern Hemisphere, winds in a high-pressure area circulate in a clockwise direction. Winds in a low-pressure area (or depression) circulate in an anticlockwise direction. The reverse applies in the Southern Hemisphere. Wind direction is marked on a weather map by arrows. The closer the isobars are together, the stronger will be the winds around the centres of pressure.

Boundaries between warm and cool air are called fronts. A warm front is where warm air is replacing cold air on the Earth's surface; it is represented on a map by shaded semicircles along a line pointing in the direction in which the front is moving. A cold front is where cold air is replacing warm air, and is represented by triangles on a line pointing in the direction of movement. A warm front brings a period of fairly steady rain; a cold front generally brings sharp showers with sunny intervals.

An occluded front is represented by alternating triangles and semicircles; it occurs where the temperature is fairly even at ground level, but varies considerably at higher altitudes. This gives rise to cloud and frequently to rain.

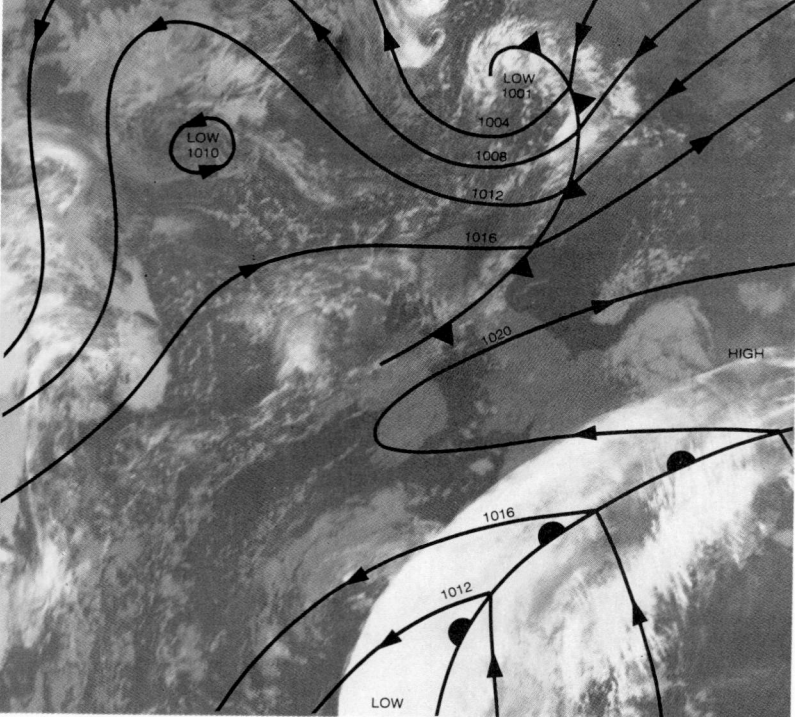

WEATHER SYMBOLS

━●━●●━ Warm front   ━▲━▲━▲ Cold front   ━▲━●▲━●▲ Occluded front   ━━━→ Isobar (arrow indicates direction of wind)

A COLD OCTOBER MORNING *This photograph was taken by a satellite at 9.09 a.m. (GMT) on October 16, 1981. The infrared process was used, so that the lighter images indicate lower temperatures. Thus the higher (therefore colder) clouds appear whiter than lower and warmer clouds. The ground temperature of the British Isles was close to freezing, the sea about 12°C (54°F), so the land appears paler than the sea.*

The brilliant white cloud mass in the bottom right of the picture is associated with a depression which had passed over southern Britain, causing *rain. The sharp edge of this cloud mass indicates a jet stream, or very strong winds, at about 9000 metres (30,000 feet), while the winds at ground level were very light. The spirals of cloud north of Shetland (top centre) and south of Iceland (top left) are small low-pressure centres.*

The band of cloud stretching from Norway to Northern Ireland is the remains of a decaying cold front. The cloud on the left edge of the picture is another depression, which brought gales and rain to northern Britain two days later. The numbers represent millibars of atmospheric pressure.

Informal. To accept or agree to; find acceptable: *asked for a day off, but her boss wouldn't wear it.* **—intr. 1. a.** To withstand the effects of use or activity in the specified way: *That suit will wear badly.* **b.** To withstand the effects of time and experience in the specified way: *Those friendships wear best that are based on mutual understanding.* **2.** To be brought to the specified condition through attrition or prolonged use: *This jersey has worn through; His excuses wore thinner over the years.* **3.** To pass gradually or tediously: *The hours wore on endlessly.* **—wear down.** To break down the resistance of by relentless pressure. **—wear off. 1.** To diminish gradually and vanish: *The pain wore off.* **2.** To become effaced; rub off: *The gilt soon wore off.* **—wear out. 1.** To make or become unusable through heavy use. **2.** To use up; consume: *She is wearing out her welcome.* **3.** To exhaust; tire completely. **—n. 1.** The act of wearing or state of being worn; use: *The coat has had heavy wear.* **2.** Clothing, especially of a specified kind or for a specified use. Often used in combination: *footwear; rainwear; menswear.* **3.** Gradual impairment, waste, or diminution from use or attrition: *signs of wear.* **4.** The capacity to withstand use; durability: *The tyre has plenty of wear left.* [Middle English *wer(i)en,* Old English *werian,* wear, carry.] **—wear·a·bil·i·ty** *n.* **—wear·a·ble** *adj.* **—wear·er** *n.*

wear² *v.* **wore, worn, wearing, wears.** *Nautical.* **—tr.** To make (a sailing ship) come about with the wind aft: *wear ship.* **—intr.** To come about with the stern to windward. [Earlier *weare†.*]

wear and tear *n.* Loss, damage, or depreciation resulting from ordinary use or exposure.

wea·ri·ful (wēer-i-f'l) *adj. Rare.* **1.** Wearisome; tedious. **2.** Full of weariness. **—wea·ri·ful·ly** *adv.* **—wea·ri·ful·ness·** *n.*

wea·ri·less (wēer-i-lioss, -liss) *adj.* Tireless. **—wea·ri·less·ly** *adv.*

wear·ing (wâir-ing) *adj.* Tiring; exhausting. **—wear·ing·ly** *adv.*

wea·ri·some (wēer-i-səm) *adj.* Causing exasperation or fatigue; tedious. **—wea·ri·some·ly** *adv.* **—wea·ri·some·ness** *n.*

wea·ry (wēer-i) *adj.* **-rier, -riest. 1.** Exhausted, especially from prolonged exertion; fatigued. **2.** Expressive of or prompted by fatigue or resignation: *a weary smile.* **3.** Exhausted in patience, tolerance, spirit, or interest: *weary of his jibes.* **4. a.** Causing fatigue; exhausting. **b.** Irksome; tedious; wearisome. —See Synonyms at **tired.** **—v.** **wearied, -rying, -ries. —tr.** To make weary; fatigue. **—intr.** To become weary; grow tired or exasperated. [Middle English *wery, weri(e),* Old English *wērig,* from Germanic *wōriga* (unattested).] **—wear·i·ly** *adv.* **—wear·i·ness** *n.*

wea·sand (wēez'nd, wizz'nd) *n. Archaic.* The gullet or throat. [Middle English *wesa(u)nt, wesand, wosen,* Old English *wāsend, wǣsend* (unattested), gullet, from West Germanic *wāsand-* (unattested).]

wea·sel (wēez'l) *n.* **1.** Any of various small carnivorous mammals of the genus *Mustela,* having a slender body, long tail, short legs, and brownish fur; especially, *M. nivalis.* **2.** *Chiefly U.S.* A treacherous or sneaky person. **—intr.v.** *U.S. Informal.* **weaseled, -seling, -sels.** To be evasive; equivocate. **—weasel out.** *U.S. Informal.* To back out of a situation or commitment in a sneaky or cowardly manner. [Middle English *wesele, wesill,* Old English *we(o)sule, wesle,* from West Germanic *wisulōn†* (unattested).] **—wea·sel·ly** *adj.*

weasel word *n.* A word of an equivocal nature used to deprive a statement of its force or to evade a direct commitment. [Alluding to the weasel's supposed ability to suck up the contents of an egg without doing obvious damage to the shell.]

weath·er (wéthər) *n.* **1.** The state of the atmosphere at a given time and place, described by specification of variables such as temperature, moisture, wind velocity, and pressure. **2.** The unpleasant or destructive effects of atmospheric conditions: *We must protect the houses from the weather.* **b.** Violent conditions, such as high winds and heavy rain, at sea and in the air: *We flew into weather over the Azores.* **—make heavy weather of.** To exaggerate the difficulty of something to be done. **—under the weather.** *Informal.* **1.** Slightly indisposed; unwell. **2. a.** Drunk. **b.** Suffering from a hangover. **—v.** **weathered, -ering, -ers. —tr. 1.** To expose to the action of the weather, as for drying, seasoning, or colouring. **2.** To discolour, disintegrate, wear, or otherwise affect by exposure. **3.** To pass through safely; survive: *weather a crisis.* **4.** To cause (a roof, for example) to slope so as to shed water. **5.** *Nautical.* To pass to windward of, despite bad weather. **—intr. 1.** To become discoloured, disintegrate, or otherwise show the effects of exposure to the weather: *The cottage walls had weathered and mellowed.* **2.** To resist or withstand the effects of weather or adverse conditions. **—adj. 1.** Of, pertaining to, or designating the side of a ship towards the wind; windward. **2.** Of, pertaining to, or used in weather forecasting. [Middle English *weder, wethyr,* Old English *weder.*]

weather balloon *n.* A balloon used to carry instruments aloft to gather meteorological data in the atmosphere.

weath·er-beat·en (wéthər-beet'n) *adj.* **1.** Worn by exposure to the weather. **2.** Tanned or coarsened from being outdoors.

weath·er·board (wéthər-bawrd ‖ -bōrd) *n.* Any of a series of boards having one edge thicker than the other, overlapped to clad the outer walls of buildings. Also *U.S.* "clapboard".

weath·er·board·ing (wéthər-bawrding ‖ -bōrding) *n.* **1.** Weatherboards collectively. **2.** A wall or other area made of weatherboards.

weath·er-bound (wéthər-bownd) *adj.* Delayed, halted, or kept indoors by bad weather.

weath·er·cock (wéthər-kok) *n.* **1.** A weather vane in the form of a cock. **2.** One that is fickle. **—intr.v.** **weathercocked, -cocking, -cocks.** To have a tendency to veer in the direction of the wind. Used of an aircraft or a missile.

weather deck *n.* The deck of a ship that is open to the sky.

weather eye *n.* An eye trained to recognise indications of weather changes. **—keep (one's) weather eye open.** To stay alert; keep on the lookout.

weather forecast *n.* A description of prevailing and expected weather conditions, as in a newspaper or a television broadcast. **—weather forecaster** *n.*

weath·er·glass (wéthər-glaass || -glass) *n.* A barometer or similar instrument used to indicate atmospheric conditions.

weath·er·ing (wéthəring) *n.* Any of the chemical or mechanical processes by which rocks exposed to the weather decay to soil.

weath·er·ly (wéthərli) *adj. Nautical.* Capable of sailing close to the wind with little drift to leeward. **—weath·er·li·ness** *n.*

weath·er·man (wéthər-man) *n., pl.* **-men** (-men). **1.** A person who makes weather forecasts, especially on radio or television. **2.** *Capital* **W.** A member of a U.S. anarchist group active in the late 1960s.

weather map *n.* A map or chart depicting the meteorological conditions over a specific geographical area at a specific time.

weath·er·proof (wéthər-proof || -proof) *adj.* Able to withstand exposure to weather without damage.
~tr.v. **weatherproofed, -proofing, -proofs.** To make weatherproof.

weather ship *n.* An oceangoing vessel equipped to make meteorological observations.

weather station *n.* A station at which meteorological observations are gathered, recorded, and released.

weath·er-strip (wéthər-strip) *tr.v.* **-stripped, -stripping, -strips.** To fit or equip with weather stripping.

weather stripping *n.* **1.** A narrow piece of material, such as rubber, felt, or metal, installed around doors and windows to protect an interior from external extremes of temperature. Also called "weather strip". **2.** Such pieces collectively.

weather vane *n.* A vane for indicating wind direction.

weath·er-wise (wéthər-wīz) *adj.* Skilled in predicting shifts in the weather, public opinion, or the like.

weath·er·worn (wéthər-wawrn || -wōrn) *adj.* Weather-beaten.

weave (weev) *v.* **wove** (wōv) or **weaved** (only form for transitive sense 6 and intransitive sense 2), **woven** (wṓv'n) or *rare* **wove, weaving, weaves.** *—tr.* **1. a.** To make (cloth) by interlacing the threads of the weft and the warp on a loom. **b.** To interlace (threads) into cloth. **2.** To construct by interlacing or interweaving strips or strands of material: *weave a basket.* **3. a.** To interweave or combine (elements) into a whole: *He wove the incidents into a story.* **b.** To fashion or contrive (something complex or elaborate) in this way. **4.** To introduce (something new or contrasting) into some material or composition: *wove folk tunes into the symphony.* **5.** To spin (a web or cocoon, for example). Used of a spider or insect. **6.** To make (a path or way) by winding in and out or from side to side: *weave one's way through traffic.* *—intr.* **1. a.** To engage in weaving an article. **b.** To work at a loom. **2.** To move in and out or from side to side: *The dancers wove in and out of the trees; He was so drunk that he wove from side to side.* **—get weaving.** *British Informal.* **1.** To get started; begin some activity. **2.** To hurry up.
~n. The pattern, method of weaving, or construction of a fabric: *a twill weave; a loose weave.* [Weave, wove, woven; Middle English *weven, wo(o)f, woven* or *weven,* Old English *wefan, wæf, wefen.*]

weav·er (wéevər) *n.* **1.** One who weaves, especially as an occupation. **2.** A weaverbird.

weav·er·bird (wéevər-burd) *n.* Any of various chiefly tropical Old World birds of the family Ploceidae, many of which build complex communal nests of intricately woven vegetation. Also called "weaver", "weaver finch".

weaver's hitch *n. Nautical.* A knot, the **sheet bend** *(see).* Also called "weaver's knot".

web (web) *n.* **1. a.** A textile fabric, especially one being woven on a loom or in the process of being removed from it. **b.** The structural part of cloth as distinguished from its pile or pattern. **2.** A latticed or woven structure; an interlacing of materials. **3.** A structure of threadlike filaments characteristically spun by spiders or certain insect larvae. **4.** Anything intricately constructed; a complex or elaborate network, especially one designed to ensnare or deceive: *a web of deceit.* **5.** A fold of skin or membranous tissue; especially, the membrane connecting the toes of certain water birds and mammals. **6.** The vane of a feather. **7.** *Architecture.* The surface between the ribs of a ribbed vault. **8.** A metal sheet or plate connecting the heavier sections, ribs, or flanges of any structural element. **9.** A thin metal plate or strip, as the bit of a key, the blade of a saw, or the like. **10.** A continuous roll of paper, such as newsprint, especially of the kind used in web printing presses.
~tr.v. **webbed, webbing, webs. 1.** To provide with a web. **2.** To cover or envelop with a web. **3.** To ensnare in a web. [Middle English *web(be),* Old English *web(b).*] **—webbed** *adj.* **—web·by** *adj.*

Webb (web), **Beatrice,** born Beatrice Potter (1858–1943). British socialist. See **Webb, Sidney James.**

Webb, Mary (Meredith) (1881–1927). British novelist. She wrote tragic novels, the best-known being *Precious Bane* (1924).

Webb, Sidney (James), 1st Baron Passfield (1859–1947). British economist and socialist. He was one of the founders of the London School of Economics (1895). He and his wife, Beatrice Webb, helped to found (1884) the Fabian Society. Together they wrote *History of Trade Unionism* (1894) and *English Local Government* (1906–29).

web·bing (wébbing) *n.* **1.** Sturdy cotton or nylon fabric woven in widths generally of from one to six inches, for use where strength is required, as for seat belts, brake lining, or upholstering. **2.** Anything forming a web.

we·ber (váybər, wébbər) *n. Abbr.* **Wb** The SI unit of magnetic flux equal to the magnetic flux that in linking a circuit of one turn produces in it an electromotive force of one volt as it is uniformly reduced to zero within one second. [After Wilhelm E. *Weber* (1804–91), German physicist.]

Web·er (váybər), **Carl Maria von** (1786–1826). German composer. He is best known for his opera, *Der Freischütz* (1821), which was the first in the German romantic tradition.

Weber, Max (1864–1920). German social scientist. He was one of the founders of the modern analytical method of sociology. His works include *The Protestant Ethic and the Spirit of Capitalism* (1904) and *Methodology of the Social Sciences* (1904).

Webern (váybərn), **Anton von** (1883–1945). Austrian composer. His works, which are characterised by brevity and tonal dissonance, include 2 symphonies and a concerto for nine instruments (1934).

web-foot·ed (wéb-fŏŏtid) *adj.* Having feet with webbed toes.

web member *n.* Any of the structural elements connecting the top and bottom flanges of a lattice girder or the outside members of a truss.

web offset *n.* An offset method of printing using a web press.

web press *n.* A rotary printing press that prints on a continuous roll of paper.

web·ster (wéb-stər) *n. Archaic.* A weaver. [Middle English *web(e)ster,* Old English *webbestre,* feminine of *webba,* a weaver, from *webb,* a WEB.]

Webster, John (*c.* 1580–*c.* 1634). English dramatist. His works include *The White Devil* (1612), and *The Duchess of Malfi* (*c.* 1613).

Webster, Noah (1758–1843). U.S. lexicographer and author. He is best known for his *American Dictionary of the English Language* (1828), which did much to standardise American spelling.

web·wheel (wéb-weel, -hweel) *n.* **1.** Any wheel in which the rim, spokes, and hub are cast or formed from one piece of metal. **2.** A spokeless wheel.

wed (wed) *v.* **wedded, wed** or **wedded, wedding, weds.** *—tr.* **1.** To take as husband or wife; marry. **2.** To perform the marriage ceremony for; join in matrimony. **3. a.** To join, unite, or associate. **b.** To cause to be indissolubly attached or devoted. Used chiefly in the passive: *wedded to socialism.* *—intr.* To take a husband or wife; marry. [Middle English *wedden,* Old English *weddian,* to engage (to do something), marry.]

we'd (weed, wid). Contraction of *we had, we should,* or *we would.*

Wed. Wednesday.

wed·ding (wédding) *n.* **1.** The act of marrying; the ceremony or celebration of a marriage. Also used adjectivally: *wedding guests.* **2.** The anniversary of a marriage: *a silver wedding.* **3.** A close association or union. —See Synonyms at **marriage.**

wedding breakfast *n.* A celebratory meal taken by the bride and groom and guests after a wedding.

wedding cake *n.* A large decorated cake, often arranged in tiers, pieces of which are given to wedding guests and kept for absent friends and relations.

wedding ring *n.* A ring, often a plain gold band, given by one spouse to the other during the wedding ceremony and typically worn throughout married life.

wedge (wej) *n.* **1.** A piece of metal or wood tapered into a solid V-shape for insertion in a narrow crevice and used for splitting, tightening, securing, or levering. **2. a.** Anything in the shape of a wedge: *a wedge of cheese.* **b.** A wedge-shaped formation, as in ground warfare. **3.** A wedge heel. **4.** Any tactic, event, policy, or idea that tends to divide or split associations of people. **5.** *Meteorology.* A region of relatively high atmospheric pressure in which the isobars are V-shaped. **6.** *Golf.* An iron with a very slanted face, used to lift the ball from sand, for example. **7.** Any of the triangular characters of cuneiform writing. **—the thin end of the wedge.** An apparently unimportant occurrence that seems likely to lead to more or more serious occurrences of a similar nature.
~v. **wedged, wedging, wedges.** *—tr.* **1.** To split or force apart with or as if with a wedge. **2.** To tighten or fix in place with a wedge. **3.** To crowd, push, or force into a limited space. *—intr.* To become lodged or jammed like a wedge. [Middle English *wegge,* Old English *wecg,* a wedge, ingot of metal.]

wedge heel *n.* **1.** A solid heel on a woman's shoe that forms a continuous wedge shape tapering from the back of the shoe to the front. **2.** A shoe with a wedge heel. Also called "wedge", *U.S.* "wedgie".

Wedg·wood (wéj-wŏŏd) *n.* A type of pottery or china made by Josiah Wedgwood (1730–95) and his successors; especially, jasperware, a fine ware with classical figures in white cameo relief on an unglazed blue or otherwise coloured background.

Wedgwood blue *n.* A clear, pale or greyish blue, characteristically found as an unglazed background on Wedgwood pottery.

Wedgwood, Dame C(icely) V(eronica) (1910–). British historian. Among her works are *The Thirty Years' War* (1938), *Oliver Cromwell* (1939), and *The Political Career of Rubens* (1975).

wed·lock (wéd-lok) *n.* The state of being married; matrimony. See Synonyms at **marriage. —out of wedlock.** Of, to, or by parents not married to one another: *born out of wedlock.* [Middle English *wedlo(c)ke,* Old English *wedlāc,* "pledge-giving", marriage vow : *wedd,* a pledge + *-lāc,* suffix denoting activity.]

Wednes·day (wénz-di, wédd'nz-, -day) *n. Abbr.* **Wed.** The day of

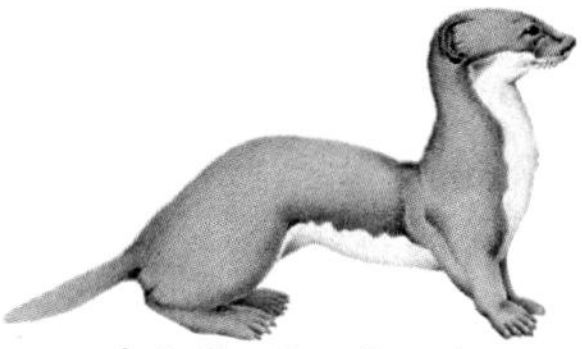

weasel *A slim, short-legged mammal that uses its acute hearing to hunt its prey of mice, frogs, and sometimes rabbits. Weasels, which are native to Eurasia and the Americas, are closely related to stoats. This is a European species,* Mustela nivalis.

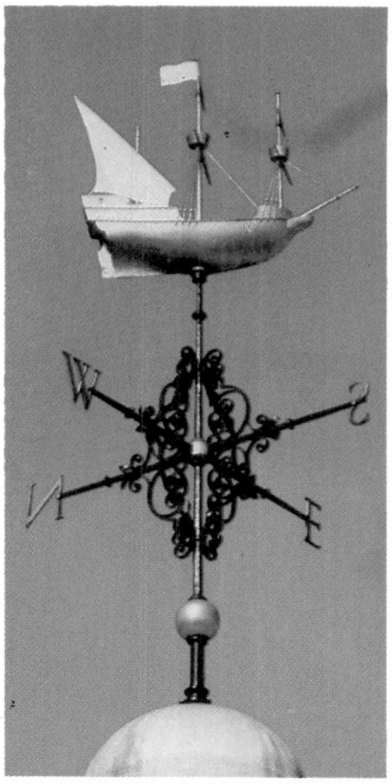

weather vane *A ship replaces the more usual cockerel on this weather vane on top of London's Trinity House – headquarters of the organisation responsible for navigational aids such as lighthouses in British waters.*

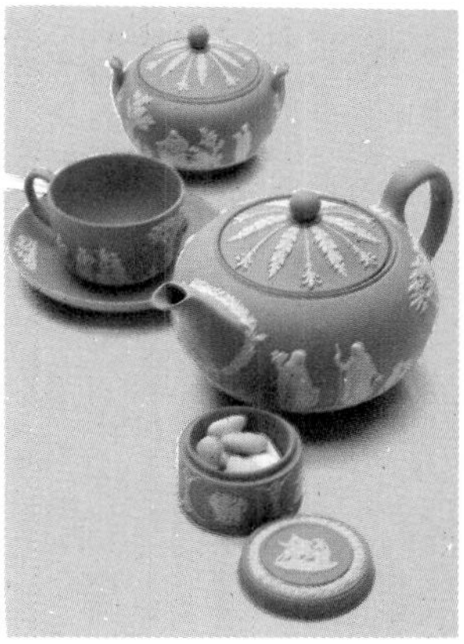

Wedgwood *Stoneware decorated with white classical figures is properly called Jasperware. It was developed in about 1774 by the British potter Josiah Wedgwood and all genuine Jasperware carries the name Wedgwood. Jasperware is made in blue, green, lavender, yellow, and black, but it is the blue stoneware that is best known and has given rise to the term "Wedgwood blue".*

the week following Tuesday; the third day of the working week. [Middle English *Wodnesday,* Old English *Wōdnesdæg,* "Woden's day" (translation of Latin *Mercurii diēs,* "day of Mercury").]

wee¹ (wee) *adj.* **weer** (wée-ər), **weest** (wée-ist). **1.** Very small; tiny. **2.** Very early: *the wee small hours.*
~*n. Scottish.* A short time; a little bit: *bide a wee.* [Middle English *we,* from *we(i),* a little, a small amount, Old English *wǣge,* a weight.]

wee²(wee) *n.* Also **wee-wee** (wée-wee). *British Informal.* **1.** Urine. **2.** An act of urinating. Used by and to children.
~*intr.v.* **weed, weeing, wees.** Also **wee-wee.** *British Informal.* To urinate. Used by and to children. [20th century : shortened from *wee-wee*†.]

weed (weed) *n.* **1.** A plant considered undesirable, unattractive, or troublesome; especially, one growing where it is not wanted in cultivated ground. **2.** Any of various usually common or abundantly growing plants. Usually used in combination: *seaweed; chickweed.* **3.** The leaves or stems of a plant as distinguished from the seeds: *dill weed.* **4. a.** *Informal.* Tobacco. Often preceded by *the.* **b.** *Informal.* A cigarette. **c.** *Chiefly U.S. Slang.* Marijuana. **5.** Something useless, detrimental, or worthless; especially, an animal unfit for breeding. **6.** *Informal.* A weak, slightly built, or cowardly person.
~*v.* **weeded, weeding, weeds.** —*tr.* **1.** To remove weeds from; clear of weeds: *weed a flowerbed.* **2. a.** To remove (weeds). Usually used with *out*: *weed out dandelions.* **b.** To eliminate as unsuitable or unwanted. Usually used with *out*: *weed out unqualified applicants.* —*intr.* To remove weeds from a plot. [Middle English *weed,* Old English *wēod*†.] **—weed·er** *n.*

weed·kill·er (wéed-killər) *n.* Any substance, such as a synthetic plant hormone, used to kill weeds.

weeds (weedz) *pl.n.* **1.** *Plural.* Mourning clothes: *widow's weeds.* **2.** *Singular. Archaic.* A token of mourning, as a black band worn usually on the sleeve. [Middle English *wede,* a garment, Old English *wǣd* and *wǣde,* a garment, from Germanic *wǣdhiz* (unattested).]

weed·y (wéedi) *adj.* **-ier, -iest. 1.** Full of or consisting of weeds. **2.** Resembling or characteristic of a weed. **3.** *Informal.* Timid; unassertive: *Don't be so weedy.* **4.** *Informal.* Of a thin, slight build. **—weed·i·ly** *adv.* **—weed·i·ness** *n.*

wee folk *pl.n.* Fairies; elves. Preceded by *the.*

week (week) *n. Abbr.* **w., wk. 1. a.** A period of seven days: *a week of rain.* **b.** A seven-day calendar period, especially one starting with Sunday and continuing to the next Saturday: *this week.* **2. a.** A week designated by an event or holiday occurring within it: *Christmas week.* **b.** A week set aside for the honouring of some specified cause or institution: *Gay Pride Week.* **3. a.** The part of a calendar week devoted to work; the working week: *doing a three-day week.* **4. a.** One week from a specified day: *I'll see you Friday week.* **b.** One week ago from a specified day: *It was Friday week that we last met.* [Middle English *wike, weke,* Old English *wice, wicu.*]

week·day (wéek-day) *n.* Any day of the week except Sunday and, usually, Saturday.

week·end (wéek-énd, -end) *n.* The end of the week; usually, Saturday and Sunday, and often the period from Friday evening to the end of Sunday evening.
~*adj.* **1.** Occurring or done at the weekend: *a weekend job.* **2.** For use at weekends: *a weekend cottage.*
~*intr.v.* **weekended, -ending, -ends.** To spend the weekend.

week·end·er (wéek-éndər || -endər) *n.* **1.** A person who takes a holiday or pays a visit, especially habitually, at weekends. **2.** *Australian.* A weekend or holiday cottage.

week·ly (wéekli) *adv.* **1.** Once a week. **2.** Every week. **3.** By the week.
~*adj.* **1.** Occurring or done once a week or each week. **2.** Computed by the week.
~*n., pl.* **weeklies.** A publication issued once a week.

week·night (wéek-nīt) *n.* The night or evening of a weekday.

ween (ween) *tr.v.* **weened, weening, weens.** *Archaic.* To think; suppose. [Middle English *wenen,* Old English *wēnan,* from Germanic *wǣniz* (unattested), opinion.]

wee·ny (wéeni) *adj.* **-nier, -niest.** *Informal.* Very small; tiny; wee. [Blend of WEE and TINY or TEENY.]

weep (weep) *v.* **wept** (wept), **weeping, weeps.** —*tr.* **1.** To mourn; lament or cry over. **2.** To shed (tears). **3.** To bring to a specified condition by weeping: *She wept herself into a state of exhaustion.* **4.** To ooze, exude, or let fall (drops of liquid), as a wound or sore might. —*intr.* **1.** To express intense, usually painful, emotion by shedding tears; shed tears. **2.** To mourn or grieve. Used with *for.* **3.** To emit or run with drops of moisture. —See Synonyms at **cry.**
~*n. Often plural. Informal.* A period or fit of weeping. [Middle English *we(o)pen,* Old English *wēpan.*]

weep·er (wéepər) *n.* **1.** One that weeps. **2.** A hired mourner. **3.** A token of mourning, such as a black hatband or veil.

weep·ing (wéeping) *adj.* Having slender, drooping branches: *a weeping fig.*

weeping willow *n.* A widely cultivated tree, *Salix babylonica,* native to China, having long, drooping branches and narrow leaves.

weep·y (wéepi) *adj.* **-ier, -iest.** Tearful; prone to crying.
~*n., pl.* **weepies.** *Informal.* A sentimental work of fiction, especially a film.

wee·ver (wéevər) *n.* Any of several marine fishes of the family Trachinidae, having venomous spines. [Perhaps from Old French *wivre,* a serpent, viper, from Latin *vīpera,* VIPER.]

wee·vil (wéevil, wéev'l) *n. Zoology.* Any of numerous beetles, chiefly of the family Curculionidae and characteristically having a downward-curving snout, that are destructive to plants and stored plant products. [Middle English *wevel,* Old English *wifel,* a beetle.] **—wee·vil·y, wee·vil·ly** *adj.*

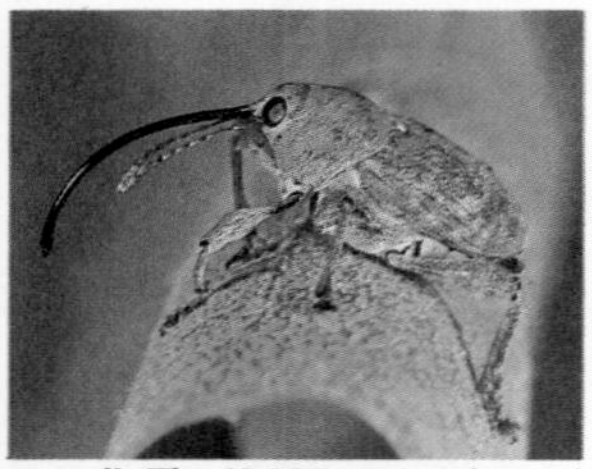

weevil *The 60,000 species of weevil make up the most widespread and numerous family of beetles. Many weevils feed on a single species or genus of plant, and most of their larvae feed on the internal tissues of roots, stems, or seeds, often causing considerable damage to crops.*

wee-wee. Variant of **wee.**

w.e.f. with effect from.

weft (weft) *n.* **1. a.** The horizontal threads interlaced through the warp in a woven fabric; filling; woof. **b.** Yarn to be used for the weft. **2.** Woven fabric. [Middle English *wefte, weft,* Old English *wefta, weft,* from Germanic *weft-* (unattested), from *webh-* (unattested), WEAVE.]

wei·ge·la (wī-gée-lə, wi-, -jée-, wīgilə, *often* wi-jéeli-ə) *n.* Any of various shrubs of the genus *Weigela*; especially, *W. florida,* widely cultivated for its pink, white, or red flowers. [New Latin, after Christian E. *Weigel* (1748–1831), German physician.]

weigh¹ (way) *v.* **weighed, weighing, weighs.** —*tr.* **1.** To determine the weight of by or as if by using scales or a balance. **2.** To measure off, especially by using scales, an amount equal in weight to. Usually used with *out*: *weigh out a pound of cheese.* **3. a.** To balance in one's mind to determine the worth of; evaluate; consider or compare. Often used with *up*: *weighed up the pros and cons.* **b.** To choose carefully; deliberate over: *weigh one's words.* **4.** To cause to sag by the addition of weights or burdens; oppress; force down. Used with *down.* **5.** *Nautical.* To raise (anchor). —*intr.* **1.** To have or be of a specified weight. **2.** To carry weight; be considered important; have influence; especially, to have the specified degree of importance or influence: *a fact that weighed heavily in his favour.* **3.** To be a burden or weight; bear down. Used with *on* or *upon*: *His troubles weighed down on him.* **—weigh into.** To attack. [Middle English *weghen, weien,* Old English *wegan,* to carry, balance in the scale, weigh.] **—weigh·er** *n.*

weigh² *n. Nautical.* Way. Used only in the phrase *under weigh.* [Variant (erroneously from the phrase *to weigh anchor*) of WAY.]

weigh·bridge (wáy-brij) *n.* A weighing machine having a metal platform at ground level, used for weighing heavy loads such as vehicles.

weigh in *intr.v.* **1.** To be weighed before or after a sporting contest. **2.** To have a specified weight measured at a weigh-in: *weighed in at 15 stone.* **3.** To have one's luggage weighed and checked before boarding an aeroplane. **4.** *Informal.* To enter an argument, discussion, or the like, especially to contribute a telling point: *She weighed in with a few pertinent facts.*

weigh-in (wáy-in) *n.* The act or occasion of checking the weight of a sports contestant, especially of a boxer before a fight or a jockey after a race.

weight (wayt) *n. Abbr.* **wt. 1.** A measure of the heaviness or mass of an object. **2.** The gravitational force exerted by the Earth or another celestial body on an object, equal to the product of the object's mass and the local value of the acceleration of free fall. **3. a.** A unit measure of this force. **b.** A system of such measures. **4.** The measured heaviness of a specific object. **5.** Any object used principally to exert a force by virtue of its gravitational attraction to the Earth, especially: **a.** A metallic solid used as a standard of comparison in weighing. **b.** An object used to hold something down. **c.** A counterbalance in a machine. **d.** A dumbbell or a solid metal disc balanced on a crossbar, lifted for exercise or in athletic competition. **6.** *Mathematics.* One of a set of numbers assigned as multipliers to quantities to be averaged to indicate the relative importance of each quantity's contribution to the average. **7. a.** Anything heavy; a load. **b.** Burden; oppressiveness; pressure: *the weight of responsibilities.* **8.** The greatest part or stress; preponderance: *the weight of evidence.* **9. a.** Influence; importance; authority: *His opinions carried little weight with her.* **b.** Ponderous quality; significance: *the weight of his words.* **10.** A classification according to comparative lightness or heaviness: *the best boxer in Britain at this weight.* Usually used in combination: *a heavyweight boxer; a lightweight suit.* —See Synonyms at **importance. —by weight.** According to weight rather than volume or other measure. **—pull (one's) weight.** To do one's fair share. **—throw (one's) weight about** or **around.** To make an aggressive show of one's importance.
~*tr.v.* **weighted, weighting, weights. 1.** To add heaviness to, by or as if by attaching a weight; make heavy or heavier. **2.** To load down; burden. **3.** To treat (fabric) with chemical substances in order to give it body or extra weight. **4.** *Mathematics.* To assign a weight or weights to. **5.** To cause to have a particular bias or confer a particular advantage: *The entry procedure tends to be weighted in favour of Oxbridge graduates.* **6.** To assign to (a horse) the weight it must carry as a handicap in a race. [Middle English *wighte, weit(e),* Old English *wiht, gewiht.*]

weighting (wáyting) *n.* A special consideration or allowance; especially, an extra payment added to an employee's salary to compensate for high living costs in a particular area: *London weighting.*

weight·less (wáyt-ləss, -liss) *adj.* **1.** Having little or no weight. **2.** Experiencing little or no gravitational force. **—weight·less·ly** *adv.* **—weight·less·ness** *n.*

weight·lift·ing (wáyt-lifting) *n.* The lifting of heavy weights in a prescribed manner as an exercise or in athletic competition. **—weight·lift·er** *n.*

weight·watch·er (wáyt-wochər) *n.* One who takes care to keep his body weight within certain limits, as by diet and exercise. **—weight·watching** *n.*

weight·y (wáyti) *adj.* **-ier, -iest. 1.** Heavy; ponderous. **2.** Burdensome; oppressive. **3.** Of great consequence; momentous: *weighty decisions.* **4.** Carrying weight, as: **a.** Forceful; efficacious: *a weighty* *argument.* **b.** Authoritative; influential. —See Synonyms at **heavy.** **—weight·i·ly** *adv.* **—weight·i·ness** *n.*

Weil (vīl) **Simone** (1909–43). French mystic and religious philosopher. Her writings include *Waiting on God* (1951), and *The Need for Roots* (1952).

Weill (vīl), **Kurt** (1900-1950). German composer. He collaborated with Brecht on *The Threepenny Opera* (1928), and *The Rise and Fall of the City of Mahagonny* (1927).

Wei·mar (vī-maar). City of Erfurt district, southwestern East Germany. Situated on the river Ilm, it was a cultural centre during the 18th and 19th centuries. It was the capital of Saxe-Weimar-Eisenach (1815–1918) and was where the constitution of the Weimar Republic (1918–1933), the name of the German Republic, was drawn up. The Republic was overthrown by Hitler.

Wei·mar·an·er (vī-mə-raanər, wī-, -raanər) *n.* A large dog of a breed originating in Germany, having a smooth greyish coat.

weir (weer) *n.* **1.** A dam placed across a river or canal to raise or divert the water, as for a millrace, or to regulate the flow. **2.** A fence or wattle placed in a stream to catch or retain fish. [Middle English *wer(r)e,* Old English *wer.*]

weird (weerd) *adj.* **weirder, weirdest. 1.** Suggestive of or concerned with the supernatural; unearthly; eerie; uncanny. **2.** Of an odd and inexplicable character; unusual; bizarre; fantastic. **3.** *Archaic.* Of or pertaining to fate or the Fates.
~n. Scottish & Archaic. **1.** Fate; destiny. **2.** One's assigned lot or fortune; kismet. **—dree (one's) weird.** To endure or submit to one's fate. [Middle English *werde, wirde,* having power to control fate, from *wird, werd,* fate, destiny, Old English *wyrd.*] **—weird·ly** *adv.* **—weird·ness** *n.*
Synonyms: *weird, eerie, uncanny, unearthly.*

weird·o (weérd-ō) *n., pl.* **-oes.** Also **weird·ie** (weérdi). *Slang.* An unusually strange or eccentric person.

Weiss (vīss), **Peter** (1916–82). Swedish author, born in Germany. His works include *The Persecution and Assassination of Marat* (1964) and *The Investigation* (1965).

Weiz·mann (vīts-man), **Chaim (Azriel)** (1874–1952). Israeli statesman and chemist. He was the first president of Israel (1949–1952).

we·ka (wéckə) *n.* A flightless bird, *Gallirallus australis,* of New Zealand, having brown, mottled plumage. [Maori.]

welch. Variant of **welsh.**

Welch. *Archaic.* Variant of **Welsh.**

wel·come (wélkəm) *adj.* **1.** Received with pleasure and hospitality into one's company or home: *a welcome guest.* **2.** Agreeable or gratifying: *a welcome respite.* **3.** Cordially permitted or invited: *You're welcome to join us.* **4.** Used as a polite acknowledgement of an expression of gratitude: *"Thank you!" "You're welcome!"* **—make (someone) welcome.** To receive someone hospitably.
~n. **1.** A cordial greeting to or reception of an arriving person. **2.** The state of being welcome: *to outstay one's welcome.* **3.** A greeting or reception of the specified kind: *an unfriendly welcome.*
~tr.v. **welcomed, -coming, -comes. 1.** To greet, receive, or entertain cordially or hospitably. **2.** To receive or accept gladly: *welcome a little privacy.* **3.** To greet or receive in a particular, usually unpleasant, way: *was welcomed with a hail of bullets.*
~interj. Used to greet cordially a visitor or recent arrival. [Middle English *welcume,* alteration (by influence of WELL) and of Old French *bien venu*) of Old English *wilcuma,* a welcome guest, and *wilcume,* the greeting of welcome : *wil-,* pleasure + *cuma,* corner.] **—wel·come·ly** *adv.* **—wel·come·ness** *n.* **—wel·com·er** *n.*

weld[1] (weld) *v.* **welded, welding, welds.** *—tr.* **1. a.** To join (metals) by applying heat, sometimes with pressure and sometimes with an intermediate or filler metal having a high melting point. **b.** To produce by welding. **2.** To bring into close association; bring together as a unit. *—intr.* To be or become capable of being welded.
~n. **1.** The union of two metal parts by welding. **2.** The joint so formed. [Variant (influenced by past tense and past participle *welled*) of WELL (to pour forth, in the obsolete sense of to weld).] **—weld·able** *adj.* **—weld·a·bil·i·ty —weld·er** *n.* **—weld·less** *adj.*

weld[2] (weld) *n.* **1.** A plant, the **dyer's rocket** *(see).* **2.** The yellow dye obtained from this plant. [Middle English *welde, wold,* Old English *wealde, walde* (unattested).]

wel·fare (wél-fair) *n.* **1. a.** Health, happiness, and general well-being. **b.** Prosperity. **2.** Welfare work. **3.** *U.S.* Social assistance. [Middle English *welfare,* well-being, from the phrase *wel faren,* to fare well, Old English *wel faran* : *wel,* WELL + *faran,* to go, FARE.]

welfare state *n.* **1.** A social system whereby the state assumes primary responsibility for the welfare of its citizens, as by means of government-run health and social security schemes. **2.** A nation characterised by its adoption of this system.

welfare work *n.* Organised work, especially done by government or charitable agencies, designed to improve the social and economic conditions of the poor and other disadvantaged members of society.

wel·far·ism (wélfair-iz'm) *n. U.S.* The set of policies, practices, and social attitudes associated with the welfare state. Used derogatorily.

wel·kin (wélkin) *n. Archaic.* **1.** The vault of heaven; the sky: *make the welkin ring.* **2.** The upper air. [Middle English *w(e)olcne, welken,* a cloud, the sky, firmament, Old English *wolc(e)n.*]

well[1] (wel) *n.* **1.** A deep hole or shaft dug or drilled to obtain water, oil, gas, or the like. **2.** A cavity or space resembling this in shape or function, such as an inkwell. **3.** An open space extending vertically through the floors of a building, as for stairs or ventilation. **4.** An enclosure in a ship's hold for the pumps. **5.** A cistern with a perforated bottom in the hold of a fishing vessel for keeping fish alive. **6.** *British.* The central space in a law court, directly in front of the judge's bench where the counsel or solicitor sits. **7. a.** A spring or fountain. **b.** A mineral spring. **c.** *Plural.* A watering place; a spa. **8.** A source to be drawn upon: *a well of information.*
~v. **welled, welling, wells.** *—intr.* **1.** To rise to the surface, ready to flow. **2.** To rise or surge from some inner source: *She felt anger welling up in her mind.* *—tr.* To pour forth. [Middle English *well(e), walle,* Old English *wælla, well, wiella.*]

well[2] *adv.* **better** (béttər), **best** (best). **1.** Satisfactorily: *The interview went quite well.* **2. a.** In a good or proper manner; with skill: *sing well.* **b.** With care or attention. **3.** In a comfortable or affluent manner: *live well.* **4.** Advantageously: *married well.* **5. a.** With reason or propriety; properly; reasonably: *I can't very well say no.* **b.** Probably; indeed: *You may well need your umbrella.* **6.** Prudently: *You would do well to say nothing.* **7.** Closely or familiarly; intimately: *I know him well.* **8.** In a kindly or approving manner; graciously; favourably: *speak well of him.* **9.** Thoroughly; completely: *well cooked.* **10.** Entirely; fully: *well worth seeing.* **11.** To a considerable or suitable extent or degree: *I'm well pleased.* **12.** Far: *well in advance.* ***Note:*** The adverb *well* combines with many adjectives, usually derived from the participles of verbs, to form attributive modifiers before nouns: *a well-regulated life; a well-read woman.* In such use the elements are joined with a hyphen. However, when *well* modifies an adjective used predicatively, the two words are usually written separately: *His life was well regulated. The woman is well read.* **—as well. 1.** In addition; also. **2.** With equal or better effect: *I might as well go.* **—as well as.** In addition to; moreover. **—pretty well.** Nearly. **—well and truly.** Completely; absolutely. **—well away. 1.** Having made considerable progress. **2.** *Informal.* Drunk. **—well in with.** In a position to influence or be favoured by: *well in with the management.*
~adj. **1.** In a satisfactory state or circumstances; right; proper. Usually used predicatively: *All is well.* **2. a.** In good health; not ailing or diseased. **b.** Cured or healed. Said chiefly of a wound. **3. a.** Advisable; prudent: *It would be well not to ask.* **b.** Fortunate; gratifying: *It is well that you stayed.* —See Synonyms at **healthy. —(just) as well. 1.** Advisable; prudent. **2.** Fortunate; good. **—leave well (enough) alone.** To refrain from meddling with what is satisfactory.
~interj. **1.** Used to express surprise. **2.** Used to introduce a remark, resume a narrative, or simply to gain time to collect one's thoughts. [Middle English *wel(e), well,* Old English *wel.*]
Usage: *As well as,* in the sense of "in addition to", does not have the force of *and,* and therefore a singular noun preceding *as well as* continues to govern a singular verb: *The London firm, as well as its Scottish subsidiary, is short of capital.* A plural verb is sometimes casually used, but not generally acceptable.

well-advised (wél-əd-vīzd || -ad-) *adj.* **1.** Sensible; prudent: *You'd be well-advised to stay.* **2.** Considered; showing careful thought: *a well-advised action.*

well-appointed (wél-ə-póyntid) *adj.* Properly furnished and equipped: *a well-appointed flat.*

we'll (weel). Contraction of *we will* and *we shall.*

well-a-way (wéllə-wáy) *interj.* Also **well·a·day** (-dáy). *Archaic.* Alas! Woe is me!
~n., pl. **wellaways.** Also **well·a·day.** A lamentation. [Middle English *weilawey, wellaway,* Old English *wei lā wei,* variant (influenced by Old Norse *vei,* woe) of *wā lā wā* : *wā,* woe + *lā,* LO + *wā,* woe.]

well-bal·anced (wél-bál-ənst) *adj.* **1.** Evenly proportioned, balanced, or regulated. **2.** Mentally stable; sensible; sane.

well-be·ing (wél-beé-ing, -bee-) *n.* The state of being healthy, happy, or prosperous; welfare.

well-born (wél-bórn) *adj.* Coming of good stock; especially, born of a noble family.

well-bred (wél-bréd) *adj.* **1.** Of good upbringing; well-mannered; refined. **2.** Of good breed or pedigree. Said of an animal.

well-built (wél-bílt) *adj.* **1.** Soundly built. **2.** Tall and muscular.

well-chosen (wél-chṓz'n) *n.* Carefully chosen for a deliberate effect: *well-chosen words.*

well-connected (wél-kə-néktid) *adj.* Related to or otherwise connected with upper-class or influential people.

well-dis·posed (wél-diss-pṓzd) *adj.* Disposed to be kindly, friendly, or sympathetic.

well-done (wél-dún) *adj.* **1.** Cooked all the way through: *a well-done steak.* **2.** Satisfactorily or properly accomplished.

well-earned (wél-érnd) *adj.* Fully deserved.

Welles (welz), **(George) Orson** (1915–). American actor and film director. He starred in and directed *Citizen Kane* (1940). His other films include *The Magnificent Ambersons* (1942), *The Third Man* (1949), *The Trial* (1962), and *Catch-22* (1970).

well-fa·voured (wél-fáyvərd) *adj.* Attractive; comely; handsome.

well-formed (wél-fórmd) *n.* **1.** Having a good shape or attractive form. **2.** Properly constituted according to a set of logical or grammatical rules: *a well-formed formula; a well-formed sentence.*

well-found (wél-fównd) *adj.* Properly furnished or equipped; well-appointed: *well-found premises.*

well-found·ed (wél-fówndid) *adj.* Well-substantiated; based on sound judgment, reasoning, or evidence.

well-groomed (wél-grŏŏmd || -grŏŏmd) *adj.* **1.** Showing attentive care to personal appearance; neat. **2.** Carefully tended or curried: *a well-groomed horse.* **3.** Trim and tidy: *well-groomed hair.*

well-ground·ed (wél-grówndid) *adj.* **1.** Adequately versed in a sub-

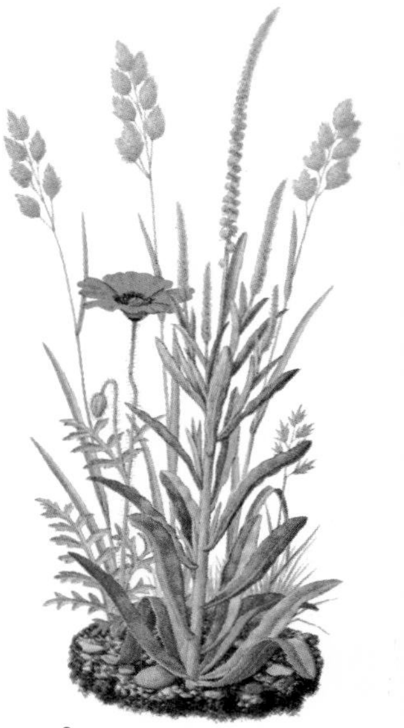

weld[2] *This wild flower was once cultivated for a deep, butter-coloured dye which was squeezed from its flowers and used in the woollen industry. It is shown here growing in front of a poppy and several grasses.*

PRONUNCIATION KEY

a, trap; aa, father; ai, fair;
ar, star; aw, lawn; ay, play;
b, bb, stab; rubber;
ch, church; ck, ticket;
d, dd, dead; ladder; e, dress;
ee, bee; er, defer; ew, few;
ewr, pure; ə, about;
ər, letter; f, ff, fife; differ;
g, gg, giggle; h, hat; i, kit;
ī, price; īr, fire; j, judge;
k, kick; l, ll, let; 'l, needle;
m, mm, man; n, nn, no;
'n, sudden; ng, thing; o, lot;
ō, no; ŏŏ, foot; ōō, shoe;
oor, poor; ow, cow;
owr, hour; oy, boy;
p, pp, pepper; r, rr, red;
s, ss, sauce; sh, ship;
t, tt, totter; th, thick; th, this;
smooth; u, cut; ur, turn;
v, vv, valve; w, wet; y, yes;
z, zz, zebra; zh, vision;
pleasure

IN FOREIGN WORDS:

aN, oN, Saint-Saëns;
hl, Llanelli; Hluhluwe;
kh, loch; lough; Khaled

STRESS MARK:

ín-sīt, insight; in-sīt, incite

ject; having a sound basic knowledge. **2.** Having a sound basis; well-founded.

well·head (wél-hed) *n.* **1.** The source of a well or stream. **2.** The top or head of a well, especially an oil well. **3.** A principal source or fountainhead.

well·heeled (wél-héeld) *adj. Slang.* Having plenty of money.

well·hung (wél-húng) *adj. Vulgar Slang.* Having a large penis or large genitalia. Said of a man. [WELL + *hung,* in obsolete sense, said especially of animals, "having pendent organs", past participle of HANG.]

wel·lies (wélliz) *pl.n. Informal.* Wellington boots.

Wel·ling·ton (wélling-tən). Capital of New Zealand, situated on Cook Strait on the south coast of North Island. It was founded in 1840 and has been the seat of government since 1865. Surrounded by mountains, it is a port exporting dairy produce, wool, and meat, and has engineering, textiles, soap and brick industries.

Wellington, Arthur Wellesley, 1st Duke of, also known as The Iron Duke (1769–1852). British soldier and statesman. He commanded the British army during the Peninsula War, defeating the Napoleonic forces in Spain in 1813, and invading France in 1814. He defeated Napoleon at the Battle of Waterloo (1815), which finally ended the Napoleonic wars. He became prime minister (1828–30). He passed the Catholic Relief Bill (1829), but opposed the Reform Bill (1831–32).

Wellington boot *n. Sometimes small* **w. 1.** A calf- or knee-length, waterproof, rubber, or rubberised boot. Also called "gumboot". **2.** A leather boot extending to the top of the knee in front but cut lower at the back. Also called "Wellington". [After the 1st Duke of WELLINGTON.]

wel·ling·ton·i·a (wélling-tóni-ə) *n.* A redwood tree, the **giant sequoia** *(see).* [After the 1st Duke of WELLINGTON.]

well·in·ten·tioned (wél-in-ténshənd) *adj.* **1.** Well-meant. **2.** Well-meaning.

well·knit (wél-nít) *n.* **1.** Well-built but compact. **2.** Tightly constructed or properly put together: *a well-knit story.*

well·known (wél-nṓn) *adj.* **1.** Widely known; familiar or famous. **2.** Fully known.

well·man·nered (wél-mánnərd) *adj.* Polite; courteous.

well·mean·ing (wél-méening) *adj.* Having or prompted by good intentions, though often with unhappy consequences.

well·meant (wél-mént) *adj.* Kindly or honestly intended.

well·nigh (wél-ní) *adv.* Nearly; almost.

well·off (wél-óff, -áwf) *adj.* **1.** In fortunate circumstances. **2.** Wealthy; prosperous. **3.** Adequately provided.

well·oiled (wél-óyld) *adj. Informal.* Drunk.

well·preserved (wél-pri-zérvd) *adj.* Not seeming or looking old.

well·read (wél-réd) *adj.* Knowledgeable through having read extensively: *clever, but not well-read.*

well·rounded (wél-równdid) *adj.* **1.** Apt and complete: *a well-rounded speech.* **2.** Plump and pleasantly curving; shapely: *a well-rounded figure.* **3. a.** Marked by breadth, fullness, and variety: *a well-rounded education.* **b.** Having a broad, full, and varied background and education.

Wells (welz). City of Somerset, southwest England, at the foot of the Mendips. It is known for its cathedral (12th-13th century) with its carved west front, and for its medieval city walls.

Wells (welz), **H(erbert) G(eorge)** (1866–1946). British novelist. He won success with science-fiction works such as *The Time Machine* (1895). His concern for social and political issues was expressed in comic novels such as *The History of Mr. Polly* (1910), and in later theoretical works such as *The Outline of History* (1920).

well·spo·ken (wél-spṓkən) *adj.* **1.** Having an educated, socially acceptable way of speaking. **2.** Chosen or expressed with aptness or propriety.

well·spring (wél-spring) *n.* **1.** The source of a stream or spring; a fountainhead. **2.** An abundant source or supply: *a wellspring of ideas.*

well·stacked (wél-stákt) *adj. Informal.* Having a full and shapely figure; especially, having large breasts. Said of a woman and often considered offensive.

well·tem·pered (wél-témpərd) *adj. Music.* Adjusted to or conforming to the system of equal temperament. Said of a musical instrument or a scale.

well·thought·of (wél-tháwt-ov ‖ -uv) *adj.* Respected; esteemed.

well·thought·out (wél-thawt-ówt) *adj.* Carefully considered or devised.

well·thumbed (wél-thúmd) *adj.* Showing signs of frequent use. Said of a book.

well·timed (wél-tímd) *adj.* Occurring or done at an opportune time.

well·to·do (wél-tə-dṓ) *adj.* Prosperous; affluent; well-off. [From the phrase *to do well.*]

well·tried (wél-tríd) *adj.* Thoroughly tested; of proven value.

well·turned (wél-túrnd) *adj.* **1.** Shapely: *a well-turned ankle.* **2.** Concisely or aptly expressed: *a well-turned phrase.*

well·up·hol·stered (wél-up-hṓl-stərd, -əp- ‖ -hṓl) *adj. Informal.* Fat; corpulent. Used humorously.

well·wish·er (wél-wishər) *n.* A person who wishes another well; one who extends good wishes. **—well·wish·ing** *adj.* & *n.*

well·worn (wél-wáwrn ‖ -wṓrn) *adj.* **1.** Showing signs of much wear or use. **2.** Repeated too often; trite; hackneyed.

Wels·bach burner (wélz-bak; *German* vélss-bakh) *n.* A trademark for a gauze mantle impregnated with cerium and thorium compounds and used with a gas burner that becomes incandescent

when heated, producing light. Also called "gas mantle". [After Baron Carl Auer von *Welsbach* (1858–1929), Austrian chemist.]

welsh, welch (welsh) *intr.v.* **welshed** or **welched, welshing** or **welching, welshes** or **welches.** *Slang.* **1.** To swindle a person by not paying a debt or wager. **2.** To fail to fulfil an obligation: *welsh on a promise.* [19th century : origin obscure.] **—welsh·er** *n.*

Welsh (welsh) *adj.* Also *archaic* **Welch.** *Abbr.* **W.** Of or pertaining to Wales, its people, its language, or its culture.

~*n.* **1.** *Used with a plural verb.* The people of Wales. Preceded by *the.* **2.** The Celtic language of Wales. [Middle English *Wal(i)sche,* Old English *Wælisc, Wel(i)sc,* from *W(e)alh,* a Welshman, from Germanic *walhaz* (unattested), foreign, from Latin *Volcae,* name of a Celtic people.]

Welsh corgi *n.* A corgi *(see).*

Welsh dresser *n.* A dresser consisting of a set of open shelves on top of a sideboard or set of cupboards. [Originally made and used in Wales.]

Welsh·man (wélsh-mən) *n., pl.* **-men** (-mən, -men). A male native of Wales.

Welsh onion *n.* A perennial plant, *Allium fistulosum,* originally from Siberia, bearing globose clusters of yellowish-white flowers on a swollen hollow stem.

Welsh poppy *n.* A poppy, *Meconopsis cambrica,* with large yellow flowers.

Welsh rabbit *n.* A dish made of melted or toasted cheese, and sometimes milk, seasonings, and beer, served hot on toast. Also called "Welsh rarebit". [A fanciful culinary term.]

Welsh springer spaniel *n.* See **springer spaniel.**

Welsh terrier *n.* A terrier of a breed originating in Wales, having a wiry black-and-tan coat and resembling a small Airedale.

welt (welt) *n.* **1.** A strip of leather or other material stitched into a shoe between the sole and the upper. **2.** A strip of material, such as tape or covered cord, sewn into a seam as reinforcement or trimming; welting. **3. a.** A ridge or bump raised on the skin by a lash or blow or sometimes by an allergic disorder; a weal. **b.** *Informal.* A lash or blow producing such a mark.

~*tr.v.* **welted, welting, welts. 1.** To reinforce or trim with a welt or welting. **2.** To beat severely; flog. **3.** To raise a welt or welts on. [Middle English *welte, walt,* perhaps Old English *wealt†, waelt* (both unattested).]

Welt·an·schau·ung (vél-tan-shṓw-ŏong) *n., pl.* **-ungs** or **-ungen** (-ŏongən). A comprehensive world view or philosophy of life, especially from a particular standpoint. [German, "world view".]

wel·ter (wéltər) *intr.v.* **-tered, -tering, -ters. 1.** To writhe, roll, or wallow. **2.** To lie soaked in blood. **3.** To be deeply immersed or involved in something. **4.** To roll and surge, as the sea does.

~*n.* **1.** Turbulence; tossing: *"bright welter of wave-cords"* (Ezra Pound). **2. a.** A state of upheaval or turmoil. **b.** A confused mass; a jumble: *a welter of papers and magazines.* [Middle English *welteren,* perhaps from Middle Dutch.]

wel·ter·weight (wéltər-wayt) *n.* **1. a.** An amateur boxer weighing between 63.5 and 67 kilograms (10 stone and 10 stone 8 pounds). **b.** A professional boxer weighing between 10 stone and 10 stone 7 pounds (63.5 and 66.5 kilograms). **2.** A wrestler weighing between 68 and 74 kilograms (10 stone 10 pounds and 11 stone 9 pounds). [19th century *welter†,* heavy-weight horseman or boxer + WEIGHT.]

welt·ing (wélting) *n.* Material, such as a cord or strip, used to welt a seam.

Welt·schmerz (vélt-shmairts) *n.* Sadness over the evils of the world, especially as an expression of romantic pessimism. [German, "world pain".]

wel·witsch·i·a (wel-wíchi-ə) *n.* A gymnosperm plant, *Welwitschia mirabilis,* found in desert regions of southwest Africa, having a short, upright, mainly underground stem, two straplike leaves, and conelike arrangements of its flowers. [After F.M.J. *Welwitsch* (1807–72), Austrian-born Portuguese botanist.]

Wem·bley (wémbli). Area of the Borough of Brent, Greater London. Its stadium is the scene of the annual Football Association Cup Final and similar sporting events.

wen¹ (wen) *n.* A cyst containing sebaceous matter, especially one on the scalp. **—the Great Wen.** London. [Middle English *wenne, wen,* Old English *wen(n), wæn(n).*]

wen² *n.* An Old English runic letter represented by the Modern English *w.* [Old English *wen,* variant of *wyn(n),* pleasure, joy (a word beginning with the letter chosen to represent the letter).]

wench (wench) *n.* **1.** A young woman or girl; especially, a peasant girl. Now used familiarly or humorously. **2.** *Archaic.* A female servant. **3.** *Archaic.* A wanton woman; a prostitute.

~*intr.v.* **wenched, wenching, wenches.** *Archaic.* To be promiscuous or consort with prostitutes. Used of a man. [Middle English *wenche,* short for *wenchel,* a girl, maid, Old English *wencel,* a child of either sex, maid.] **—wench·er** *n.*

wend (wend) *v.* **wended** or *archaic* **went** (went), **wending, wends.** —*tr.* To proceed on or along (one's way); go. —*intr. Archaic.* To go one's way; proceed. [Middle English *wenden,* Old English *wendan,* to turn around or away, direct, happen.]

Wend (wend) *n.* A member of a Slavonic people inhabiting Saxony and Brandenburg. Also called "Sorb", "Sorbian".

Wend·ish (wéndish) *adj.* Of or pertaining to the Wends or their language.

~*n.* The West Slavonic language of the Wends. Also called "Lusatian", "Sorbian".

Wendy house (wéndi) *n. British.* A small model house for children to play in. [After the house built for *Wendy,* a girl in J.M. Barrie's play *Peter Pan* (1904).]

Wens·ley·dale (wĕnzli-dāyl) *n.* **1.** A long-haired breed of sheep. **2.** A type of white, or sometimes blue, cheese with a crumbly texture. [After *Wensleydale,* North Yorkshire.]

went. 1. Past tense of **go. 2.** *Archaic.* Past tense and past participle of **wend.**

wen·tle·trap (wĕnt'l-trăp) *n.* Also **wen·del·trap** (wĕnd'l-). Any of various marine snails of the family Epitoniidae, having a tapering spiral shell with raised longitudinal ridges. [Dutch *wenteltrap,* from Middle Dutch *wendeltrappe,* "winding stair", spiral shell : *wendel,* winding, from *wenden,* to wind + *trappe,* a step, stairs.]

wept. Past tense and past participle of **weep.**

were (wer, wair; *weak form* wər). **1.** Plural and second person singular of the past indicative of **be. 2.** Past subjunctive of **be.**

Usage: In clauses expressing clearly hypothetical conditions, *were* is the standard form of the verb *be: if I were you; she spoke as if she were ill. Was* is often heard in such sentences, but generally only in informal speech. When the clause expresses a condition that is not purely hypothetical or contrary to fact, *was* is standard: *I looked to see if/whether the way was clear.* This is also the case in indirect speech: *She asked whether I was happy with the car.* There are, however, several occasions when the hypothetical status of the expression is unclear, and in such cases, usage is mixed *(she spoke as though everything were/was settled);* but *were* continues to be the predominant form in formal contexts, especially in American English. In formal conditional sentences *were* may be inverted: *Were she to study, she would learn* (= *If she were to study she would learn*).

we're (weer). Contraction of *we are.*

weren't (wernt). Contraction of *were not.*

were·wolf (wéer-wulf, waír-) *n., pl.* **-wolves** (-wŏŏlvz). In legend and folklore, a person transformed into a wolf or capable of assuming the form of a wolf; a lycanthrope. [Middle English *wer(e)wolf,* Old English *wer(e)wulf* : probably *wer,* a man + *wulf,* a WOLF.]

wer·geld (wúr-geld, waír-) *n.* Also **wer·gild** (-gild). In Anglo-Saxon and Germanic law, a price set upon a man's life on the basis of his rank and paid as compensation by the family of a slayer to the kindred or lord of a slain man to free the culprit of further punishment or obligation. [Middle English (Scottish) *weregehelde,* Old English *wergeld,* "man-payment" : *wer,* a man + *geld,* payment.]

wer·ner·ite (wúrnə-rīt) *n. Mineralogy.* **Scapolite** (*see*). [French, after A.G. Werner (1750–1817), German mineralogist.]

wert (wert). *Archaic.* Second person singular past indicative and past subjunctive of **be.**

Wes·ker (wéskər), **Arnold** (1932–). British playwright. His works include *Chips with Everything* (1962) and *Said the Old Man to the Young Man* (1978).

wes·kit (wéskit) *n. Informal.* A waistcoat. [Variant of WAISTCOAT.]

Wes·ley (wéss-li, wéz), **John** (1703–91). English religious leader and founder of Methodism. He and his brother Charles (1707–88), a writer of hymns, were ordained into the Church of England, but came under the influence of the more austere evangelical Christianity of the Moravians. Wesley travelled throughout the country preaching at open-air meetings, often to large working-class audiences. Although Methodism encountered the opposition of the Anglican Church, it was only formally founded after Wesley's death.

Wes·ley·an (wéz-li-ən, wéss-) *adj.* Of or pertaining to John or Charles Wesley or to Methodism.
~*n.* A Methodist, especially one belonging to the Wesleyan Methodist denomination based on the teachings of John and Charles Wesley. —**Wes·ley·an·ism** *n.*

Wes·sex (wéssiks). Former kingdom of the West Saxons, England. With varying boundaries it extended from the English Channel to the Thames and beyond, and from Devon to Sussex.

west (west) *n. Abbr.* **w, W, W., w. 1. a.** The direction opposite that of the earth's axial rotation; the general direction of the sunset. **b.** The cardinal point on the mariner's compass 270° clockwise from north and directly opposite east. **2.** Any area or region lying in this direction. **3.** *Often capital* **W. a.** The part of the earth west of Asia and Asia Minor, especially Europe and North America; the Occident. **b.** The Western Hemisphere. **c.** The western part of any country or region. **3. a.** One of four positions arranged like the four compass points. **b.** In card games such as bridge, a player considered to occupy this position. —**the West. 1.** The developed countries of the non-Communist world, especially Europe and North America. **2.** In the United States, the region west of the Mississippi.
~*adj.* **1.** To, towards, of, facing, or in the west. **2.** Coming from or originating in the west. Said of a wind. **3.** *Capital* **W.** Officially or conventionally designating the western part of a country, continent, or other geographical area: *West Bengal; West Germany.*
~*adv.* In, from, or towards the west. —**go west.** *Informal.* **1.** To die. **2.** To founder; collapse; end in disaster. [Middle English *west,* Old English *west.*]

West, Mae. (1892–1980). U.S. actress. She is remembered as the sex symbol of the 1930s in comedies such as *I'm No Angel* (1933), and *My Little Chickadee* (1939).

West, Dame Rebecca, born Cicely Isabel Fairfield. (1892–83). British novelist, journalist and critic. Among her books are *The Thinking Reed* (1936) and *The Birds Fall Down* (1966).

West African States. Region of Africa lying between the Sahara and the Gulf of Guinea. With the exception of Liberia, all eleven states are former colonies of European countries which gained their independence after World War II.

West Asia. See **Middle East, The.**

West Atlantic *n.* A branch of the Niger-Congo language family, including Fulani and Wolof.

West Bank. Territory on the west bank of the river Jordan. It was part of Palestine before passing to Jordan in 1949, and was captured by the Israelis (1967). Including part of Jerusalem, Nablus, Hebron, and the hills of Judaea and Samaria, it is considered to be strategically important by the Israelis, and to be the natural homeland for the Palestinians by the Palestine Liberation Organisation.

West Bengal. State of northeast India. Situated on the Bay of Bengal and bordered by Bangladesh in the east, it was part of the former province of Bengal partitioned in 1947 between India and Pakistan. It includes part of the Ganges delta and extends to the Himalayas in the far north. Its capital is Calcutta.

West Berlin. See **Berlin.**

west·bound (wést-bownd) *adj. Abbr.* **w.b.** Going towards the west.

west by north *n. Abbr.* **WbN** The direction or point on the mariner's compass halfway between due west and west-northwest; 78° 45′ west of due north. —**west by north** *adv. & adj.*

west by south *n. Abbr.* **WbS** The direction or point on the mariner's compass halfway between due west and west-southwest; 101° 15′ west of due north. —**west by south** *adv. & adj.*

West Country *n.* The southwestern counties of England, especially Somerset, Devon, and Cornwall.

West End *n.* The western part of central London, well-known for its fashionable shops and places of entertainment, and including Mayfair, Piccadilly Circus, Oxford Street, and Hyde Park.

west·er (wéstər) *intr.v.* **-ered, -ering, -ers. 1.** To move westwards. Used of the Sun, the Moon, or a star. **2.** To shift to the west. Used of the wind.
~*n.* A westerly. [Middle English *west(e)ren,* from WEST.]

west·er·ly (wéstərli) *adj.* **1.** Situated in or towards the west. **2.** Coming from the west. Said of a wind.
~*n., pl.* **westerlies.** A storm or wind from the west. [From obsolete *wester,* western, from Middle English *wester,* Old English *westra.*] —**west·er·ly** *adv.*

west·ern (wéstərn) *adj. Abbr.* **w, W, w., W. 1.** Situated towards, in, or facing the west. **2.** Coming from the west. Said of a wind. **3.** Growing in the west. **4.** *Often capital* **W.** Of, pertaining to, or characteristic of western regions or the West. **5.** *Capital* **W.** Of, pertaining to, or characteristic of the developed countries of the non-Communist world, especially Europe and North America: *Western technology.* **6.** *Often capital* **W.** Of, pertaining to, or characteristic of the American West. **7.** *Capital* **W.** Of or pertaining to the Western church.
~*n. Often capital* **W.** A novel or film dealing with frontier or cowboy life in the American West. [Middle English *west(e)ren,* Old English *westerne.*]

Western Australia. Largest state of Australia. Covering approximately a third of the country, it is bounded by the Indian Ocean on the north, west, and south and is mainly desert in the interior. Its mineral reserves include gold, iron, coal, oil, and bauxite. Its population is densest in the fertile southeast where wheat and fruit are grown and livestock are raised, while industries, chiefly situated around the capital, Perth, include oil refining and iron and steel.

Western Church *n.* **1.** The church of the Western Roman Empire, acknowledging the primacy of the see of Rome. **2.** Any of the churches that have developed from this, especially the Roman Catholic Church.

west·ern·er (wéstərnər) *n. Sometimes capital* **W. 1.** A native or in-

Wensleydale *The rams of this prolific English breed of sheep are often crossed with other breeds. Wensleydales grow into large animals with a heavy fleece of long, curly wool.*

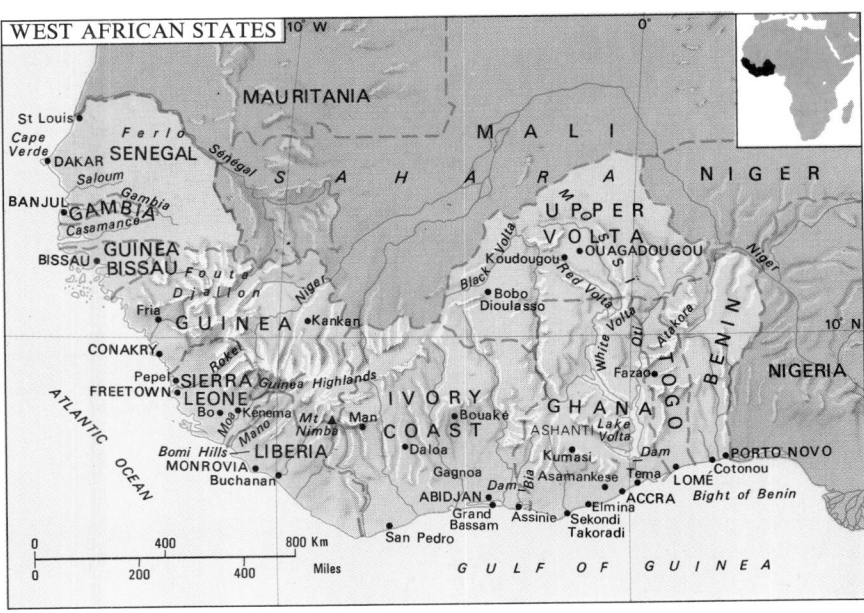

habitant of the west, particularly Europe and North America. **2.** A native or inhabitant of the western United States.

Western Europe. Political region of Europe. Most of the 24 independent states of Western Europe look to the United States for military alliance, while the countries of Eastern Europe fall into the Soviet sphere of influence. Switzerland and Austria maintain strict neutrality.

Western Hemisphere *n.* The half of the earth that includes all of North and South America, the surrounding waters, and all neighbouring islands.

western hemlock *n.* A sprucelike tree, *Tsuga heterophylla,* from North America, characteristically having drooping leaf shoots and branches in irregular whorls.

west·ern·ise, west·ern·ize (wéstər-nīz) *tr.v.* **-ised, -ising, -ises.** To influence with, or cause to adopt, customs and styles of living characteristic of the industrially developed countries of the West. —**west·ern·i·sa·tion** (-nī-záysh'n ‖ *U.S.* -ni-) *n.*

Western Isles. See **Hebrides.**

west·ern·most (wéstərn-mōst) *adj.* Farthest west.

western roll *n.* A method of performing the high jump in athletics, in which the whole body is flung upwards and rolls over the bar in

a position parallel to it. [Apparently so called to contrast this method with a different one, the *eastern roll.*]

Western Roman Empire *n.* The western part of the Roman Empire, especially after the division established by the emperor Theodosius in A.D. 395, and lasting until A.D. 475. Also called "Western Empire". See **Byzantine Empire.**

Western Sahara. Territory of northwest Africa. Bordering the Atlantic Ocean it is extremely arid and has reserves of phosphates. Formerly Spanish Sahara, it was divided (1976) between Morocco and Mauritania, although Mauritania later withdrew (1979). The Polisario Front, a guerrilla movement resisting Moroccan rule, proclaimed (1976) the Saharan Arab Democratic Republic, and was supported by Algeria and Libya.

Western Wall *n.* The **Wailing Wall** *(see).*

West Frisians. See **Frisian Islands.**

West Germanic *n.* A subdivision of the Germanic languages that includes High German, Low German, Dutch, Afrikaans, Flemish, Frisian, English, and Yiddish.

West Germany. The unofficial name for the German Federal Republic. See **Germany.**

West Gla·mor·gan (glə-mórgən). County of south Wales. It com-

WESTERN EUROPE

prises the Tawe and Neath valleys, Swansea Bay, and the Gower peninsula, and borders the Bristol channel. It was formed (1974) from the former county of Glamorganshire, and the county borough of Swansea, which is the administrative centre.

West Greek *n.* A principal dialectal division of Ancient Greek, comprising Doric and Northwest Greek.

West Highland terrier *n.* A dog of a small breed of terrier having short legs and tail and a white coat. Also called "West Highland white terrier".

West Indies. Archipelago of Central America. Extending between Florida and Venezuela, it separates the Atlantic Ocean from the Caribbean Sea and the Gulf of Mexico. It includes the Greater Antilles (Cuba, Hispaniola, Jamaica and Puerto Rico), the Lesser Antilles (Barbados, Trinidad, Tobago, and the Leeward and Windward Isles) and independent Bahamas, Cuba, Dominican Republic, Haiti, and the Virgin Islands.

west·ing (wésting) *n.* 1. *Nautical.* **a.** The distance sailed by a ship on a westerly course. **b.** The longitudinal distance from a given meridian on a westward course. 2. A westward direction or movement. [From WEST.]

West I·ri·an (irri-ən). *Indonesian* **Ir·i·an Ja·ya** (irrən, ée-i-, jĭ-ə). Province of Indonesia, Southeast Asia, the western half of New Guinea. Before its transfer to Indonesia (1963) it was known as Netherlands New Guinea. It is largely swampland.

West Lo·thi·an (lóthi-ən). Former county of eastern central Scotland, bordering the Firth of Forth. It was absorbed (1975) into Lothian Region, of which it is now a district.

West·meath (wést-méeth). *Irish* **Contae Na Hiarmhidhe.** Inland county of Leinster province, north central Republic of Ireland. It has many lakes, including loughs Ree and Ennell.

West Midlands. Metropolitan county of west central England. Covering most of the Black Country, and with Birmingham at its centre, it was created (1974) from northeast Worcestershire, southeast Staffordshire, and northwest Warwickshire.

West·min·ster (wést-min-stər, west-mín-. *Note: the pronunciation* -minni-, -mínni- *is nonstandard.*), **City of.** Borough of Greater London, southeast England. Situated on the north bank of the river Thames, it contains many famous buildings, including the Houses of Parliament, Westminster Abbey, and Buckingham Palace, as well as Hyde Park.

West·mor·land (wést-mər-lənd, wéss-). Former county of northwestern England. Incorporated (1974) into Cumbria, it included much of the Lake District. The county town was Appleby.

west-north·west (wést-north-wést *Nautical* -nor-) *n. Abbr.* **WNW** The direction or point on the mariner's compass halfway between west and northwest; 67° 30′ west of due north.
~*adj.* Situated towards, facing, or in this direction.
~*adv.* In, from, or towards this direction.

Wes·ton standard cell (wéstən) *n.* A standard cadmium primary cell that produces an electromotive force of 1.018,636 volts at 20°C. It consists of a mercury anode and a cadmium amalgam cathode immersed in an electrolyte of saturated cadmium sulphate. Also called "cadmium cell". [From a trademark.]

West·phal·i·a (wést-fáyli-ə, west-). *German* **West·fa·len** (vést-faalən). Former province of Prussia, part of North Rhine-Westphalia, western West Germany since 1946. It was created as a duchy (12th century), passing to Prussia through the Congress of Vienna (1815). Chiefly low-lying, it includes the industrial Ruhr valley in the west.

West Saxon *n.* 1. An Old English dialect spoken in Wessex, the chief literary dialect of England before the Norman Conquest. 2. A member of a Saxon people inhabiting Wessex during the centuries before the Norman Conquest.

West Slavonic *n.* The western division of the Slavonic languages, consisting of Czech, Polish, and Slovak.

west-south·west (wést-sowth-wést; *nautical* -sow-) *n. Abbr.* **WSW** The direction or point on the mariner's compass halfway between west and southwest; 112° 30′ west of due north.
~*adj.* Situated towards, facing, or in this direction.
~*adv.* In, from, or towards this direction.

West Sussex. County of south England. Extending northwards from the English Channel across the South Downs to the west end of the Weald, it is mainly agricultural, producing dairy goods, barley, and vegetables. The administrative centre is Chicester.

West Virginia. Mountain state of eastern central United States. Divided by the Allegheny mountains, 80 per cent of the state lies to the west on the hilly Appalachian plateau, while to the east lies the Great Appalachian Valley. The capital is Charleston.

West Yorkshire. County of northern central England, created (1974) from part of the former West Riding of Yorkshire and the industrial county boroughs of Bradford, Dewsbury, Halifax, Huddersfield, Leeds, and Wakefield. It has textile industries and coal fields. Wakefield is the administrative centre.

west·ward (wéstwərd) *adj.* Also **west·ward·ly** (-li). Towards, facing or in the west.
~*n.* A westward direction, point, or region.
~*adv. Chiefly U.S.* Variant of **westwards**.

west·wards (wést-wərdz) *adv.* Also *chiefly U.S.* **westward** (-wərd). Towards the west.

wet (wet) *adj.* **wetter, wettest.** 1. Covered or saturated with a liquid, especially water; moistened; damp. 2. Not yet dry or firm: *wet plaster.* 3. Stored or preserved in liquid. 4. Used or prepared with water or other liquids. 5. **a.** Rainy or humid: *wet weather.* **b.** Char-

acterised by frequent or heavy rainfall or snowfall: *a wet climate.* 6. Designating a process, system, or device in which liquids play a prominent part: *a wet photocopier.* 7. *British Informal.* Feeble; faint-hearted. [Perhaps shortened from *wet behind the ears* (immature, inexperienced).] 8. *British Informal.* Characteristic of, pertaining to, or composed of the liberal members of a group, especially of the liberal wing of the British Conservative party: *a wet rebellion in the Cabinet.* 9. *Informal.* **a.** Allowing the production and sale of alcoholic drinks: *a wet state.* **b.** *British.* Allowing the sale of alcoholic drinks on Sundays: *a wet county.* —**wet through.** Completely wet; sodden.
~*n.* 1. That which makes wet; moisture. 2. Rainy or snowy weather: *go out into the wet.* 3. *British Informal.* A feeble, timid, or stupid person. 4. *British Informal.* A relatively liberal member of a group; especially, a member of the British Conservative party, typically opposing hard-line economic policies: *Tory wets.* 5. *British Slang.* A drink. 6. *U.S. Informal.* One who supports the legal production and sale of alcoholic drinks.
~*v.* **wetted** or **wet, wetting, wets.** —*tr.* 1. To make wet; moisten or dampen: *wet a sponge.* 2. To make (a bed, one's clothes, or oneself) wet by urinating. —*intr.* To become wet. [Middle English *wet,* Old English *wǽt, wēt.*]
 Synonyms: *wet, damp, moist, dank, humid.*
 Usage: The past tense and past participle forms of this verb are *wet* in American English, and in British English when the action takes place without deliberation (*We got wet through; The baby wet the bed*). In other circumstances, *wetted* is used in British English (*They wetted the wall before applying the paste*), and this form has some use also in American English. See also **fit** and **quit**.

wet-and-dry-bulb thermometer (wét-and-drī-bulb) *n.* A **psychrometer** *(see).*

wet·back (wét-bak) *n.* A Mexican immigrant who crosses the U.S. border illegally, as by swimming or wading across the Rio Grande.

wet blanket *n. Informal.* One who discourages enjoyment, enthusiasm, or the like. [Originally a soaked blanket used in putting out fires.]

wet cell *n.* A primary cell having an electrolyte in the form of a liquid bath. Compare **dry cell.**

wet dream *n.* An erotic dream had by a man or boy accompanied by sexual climax and emission of semen.

wet fish *n.* Uncooked fish, usually fresh, smoked, or frozen, as sold in a fishmonger's shop as opposed to a fish-and-chip shop. Also used adjectivally: *a wet-fish merchant.*

wet fly *n.* An artificial fishing fly designed to be used under water. Compare **dry fly.**

weth·er (wéthər) *n.* A gelded male sheep. [Middle English *wether,* wether, a ram, Old English *wether.*]

wet·lands (wét-landz) *pl.n. Sometimes singular.* A lowland area, such as a marsh or swamp, that is saturated with moisture, especially when considered as the natural habitat of wildlife.

wet look *n.* A very shiny finish given to the surface of fabrics used to make clothes, shoes, and accessories. Also used adjectivally: *A wet-look handbag.*

wet monsoon *n. Meteorology.* A **monsoon** *(see).*

wet nurse *n.* A woman who breast-feeds another woman's child.

wet-nurse (wét-núrss) *tr.v.* **-nursed, -nursing, -nurses.** 1. To serve as a wet nurse for. 2. To treat with excessive care or solicitude.

wet pack *n.* The usual form of a therapeutic **pack** *(see),* having been immersed in hot or cold water and then wrung out.

wet rot *n.* 1. A disease of timber caused by various fungi of the genus *Coniophora.* 2. Any fungus causing wet rot.

wet suit *n.* A tight-fitting rubber suit worn for warmth by divers, wind-surfers, and the like.

wetting agent *n.* Any compound that causes a liquid to spread more easily across or penetrate into the surface of a solid by reducing the surface tension of the liquid.

we've (weev, wiv). Contraction of *we have.*

Wex·ford (wéks-fərd). County of Leinster province, southeast Republic of Ireland. Bordering the Irish sea, it was the first county colonised by the English (1169). The county town is Wexford.

Wey·den (vīd'n), **Rogier van der,** also known as Roger de la Pasture (*c.*1400–64). Flemish painter. He is best known for his altarpiece, the *Deposition* (*c.*1435).

wf *Printing.* wrong font.

WFTU World Federation of Trade Unions.

wh. white.

whack (wak, hwak) *v.* **whacked, whacking, whacks.** —*tr.* 1. To strike with a sharp blow; slap. 2. To score or get by hitting. Usually used with *up: whacked up a huge number of runs.* —*intr.* To deal a sharp, resounding blow.
~*n.* 1. **a.** A sharp, swift blow. **b.** The sound made by such a blow. 2. *Informal.* A fair share: *Give me my whack.* 3. *Informal.* An attempt; a try: *have a whack at it.* —**out of whack.** *U.S. Informal.* Improperly ordered or balanced; not functioning correctly. [Perhaps variant of THWACK.]

whacked (wakt, hwakt) *adj. British Informal.* Tired out; exhausted.

whack·er. Variant of **wacker.**

whack·ing (wáking, hwácking) *adj. Chiefly British Informal.* Superlative; very great.
~*adv. Chiefly British Informal.* Used as an intensive: *whacking great tusks.*

whacky. *U.S.* Variant of **wacky.**

whale¹ (wayl, hwayl) *n., pl.* **whales** or collectively **whale.** 1. Any of

various marine mammals of the order Cetacea, having a generally fishlike form with forelimbs modified to form flippers and a tail with horizontal flukes; especially, one of the very large species as distinguished from the smaller dolphins, porpoises, and others. **2.** *Informal.* A superlative example of the thing specified. Used with *of*: *a whale of a time.*
~intr.v. **whaled, whaling, whales.** To engage in the hunting of whales. [Middle English *whale,* Old English *hwæl.*]
whale² *v.* **whaled, whaling, whales.** *Chiefly U.S.* *—tr.* To strike repeatedly with a whip, stick, or the like; flog. *—intr.* To attack vehemently. Often used with *away.* [Variant of WALE.]
whale·back (wáyl-bak, hwáyl-) *n.* A steamship with the bow and upper deck rounded so as to shed water.
whale·boat (wáyl-bōt) *n.* **1.** A long rowing boat, pointed at both ends and designed to move and turn swiftly, formerly used in the pursuit and harpooning of whales. **2.** Any boat of similar size and shape. Also called "whaler".
whale·bone (wáyl-bōn, hwáyl-) *n.* **1.** The durable, elastic, hornlike material forming plates or strips in the upper jaw of whalebone whales. Also called "baleen". **2.** An object made of this material, such as a corset stay.
whalebone whale *n.* Any of various whales of the suborder Mysticeti, lacking teeth and characteristically filtering plankton through plates of whalebone. Also called "mysticete". Compare **toothed whale.**
whale oil *n.* A yellowish oil obtained from whale blubber, used in making soap and candles and as a lubricating oil.
whal·er (wáyl-ər, hwáyl-) *n.* **1.** One who hunts or processes whales. **2.** A whaling ship. **3.** A whaleboat.
whale shark *n.* A large shark, *Rhincodon typus,* of warm marine waters, having a spotted body and feeding chiefly on plankton.
whal·ing (wáyl-ing, hwáyl-) *n.* The business or practice of hunting, killing, and processing whales.
wham (wam, hwam) *n.* **1.** A forceful, resounding crash or blow. **2.** The sound of such a crack or blow; a thud.
~v. **whammed, whamming, whams.** *Informal.* *—tr.* To strike or smash into with resounding impact. *—intr.* To smash with great force. [Imitative.]
whang¹ (wang, hwang) *n. Informal.* **1.** A thong or whip of hide or leather. **2. a.** A lashing blow, as by a whip. **b.** The sound of such a blow.
~tr.v. **whanged, whanging, whangs.** *Informal.* **1.** To beat or whip with a thong. **2.** To beat with a sharp blow or blows. [Variant of Middle English *thwang,* THONG.]
whang² *v.* **whanged, whanging, whangs.** *Informal.* *—tr.* To strike so as to produce a loud, reverberant noise. *—intr.* To produce a loud, reverberant noise.
~n. Informal. A loud, reverberant noise. [Imitative.]
whang·ee (wang-ée, hwang-, -gée) *n.* **1.** Any of several bamboo-like Asian grasses of the genus *Phyllostachys.* **2.** A walking stick made from the woody stem of such a plant. [Chinese *huáng,* a type of bamboo, probably *Phyllostachys aurea.*]
wharf (wawrf, hwawrf) *n., pl.* **wharves** (wawrvz, hwawrvz) or **wharfs.** **1.** A specially made landing place, such as a concrete platform, at which vessels may tie up and load or unload. **2.** *Obsolete.* A shore or river bank.
~v. **wharfed, wharfing, wharfs.** *—tr.* **1.** To moor (a vessel) at a wharf. **2.** To take to or store on a wharf. **3.** To furnish, equip, or protect with a wharf or wharves. *—intr.* To berth at a wharf. [Middle English *wharfe, wherf,* Old English *hwearf.*]
wharf·age (wáwr-fij, hwáwr-) *n.* **1.** The use of a wharf or wharves. **2.** The charges for this. **3.** Wharves collectively.
wharf·in·ger (wáwr-finjər, hwáwr-) *n.* The owner or manager of a wharf. [WHARF + *-inger,* as in words like HARBINGER.]
Whar·ton (wáwrt'n, hwáwrt'n), **Edith (Newbold Jones)** (1862–1937). U.S. novelist. Her novels include *The House of Mirth* (1905) and *The Age of Innocence* (1920).
what (wot, hwot || *regional weak forms* wət, hwət) *pron.* **1.** Used as an interrogative pronoun in various types of question: **a.** Used in questions asking for a specification or identification: *What is your name? What does she do for a living? What are these papers on my desk?* **b.** Used in requests for repetition, clarification, or explanation: *He said what? What are these papers doing on my desk? What do you think she meant by that? What did you do that for?* **c.** Used when questioning the value or significance of a person or thing: *What are possessions to a dying man?* **d.** Used in rhetorical questions as the equivalent of a negative statement: *What's the point in arguing?* **2.** That or those which. Used as a relative pronoun: **a.** The thing or things that: *What I like about him is his honesty. Listen to what I tell you.* **b.** Anything or everything that; whichever thing that: *come what may; did what they could to save him.* **3. a.** *Nonstandard.* Which, who, or that: *It's the poor what gets the blame.* **b.** *Informal.* Something: *I'll tell you what.* **—and what not.** And other less prominent or unspecified things; and so on. **—what about.** **1.** What information is there on? **2.** What do you think about? have you considered? **—what have you.** That which remains and need not be mentioned; all the rest. **—what if.** What would occur if? suppose that? **—what of it.** How is it important? what does it matter? **—what's what.** *Informal.* The fundamentals and details of a situation or process; the true state or condition. **—what with.** Taking into consideration; in view of: *What with the heat and humidity, we really suffered.*
~adj. **1.** Which particular one or ones of many: *What university are you attending? What sort of car is that? You should know what musical that song is from.* **2.** Of what kind or nature: *What news is there of the Test Match?* **3.** Whatever; all that; as much or many as: *They soon repaired what damage had been done.* **4.** How astonishing or exceptional in good or bad qualities: *What weather! What a bore! I'd forgotten what a fool he was.* **5.** *Archaic.* How much; which degree of: *What love do you bear for her?*
~adv. **1.** How; how much; in what respect: *What does it matter?* **2.** To what an astonishing or exceptional degree: *What lovely weather!*
~interj. **1.** Used to express surprise, incredulity, or other strong and sudden excitement. **2.** *British Informal.* Used to request agreement: *A fine evening, what?* Now chiefly with humorously. [Middle English *what,* Old English *hwæt.*]
what·ev·er (wot-évvər, hwot- || wət-, hwət-) *pron.* Also *poetic* **what·e'er** (-áir), **what ever** (for sense 4). **1.** Everything or anything that: *Do whatever you please.* **2.** What amount that; the whole of what: *Whatever is left over is yours.* **3.** No matter what; regardless of what: *Whatever happens, we'll meet here tonight.* **4.** *Informal.* What. Used as an intensive: *Whatever does he mean?* **5.** An unspecified but similar thing: *write with pencils, pens, or whatever.*
~adj. **1.** Of any number or kind; any: *Whatever requests you make will be granted.* **2.** All of; the whole of: *He applied whatever strength he had left to the task.* **3.** No matter what: *I'll stand by her, whatever she's done.* **4.** Of any kind at all. Used for emphasis following the noun modified: *No campers whatever are allowed.*
what for *n. Informal.* Punishment; sharp retribution: *I'll give him what for!*
what·not (wót-not, hwót-) *n.* **1.** A minor or unspecified object or article; a trivial item. **2.** A set of light, open shelves for ornaments.
what's (wots, hwots) **1.** Contraction of *what is.* **2.** Contraction of *what has.*
what·so·ev·er (wót-sō-évvər, hwót-) *pron.* Also *poetic* **what·so·e'er** (-áir). Whatever.
~adj. Whatever. Used for emphasis: *no power whatsoever.*
wheal (weel, hweel) *n.* Variant of **weal** (a welt). [Variant (influenced by obsolete *wheal,* to suppurate) of WALE (ridge).]
wheat (weet, hweet) *n.* **1.** Any of various cereal grasses of the genus *Triticum;* especially, *T. aestivum,* widely cultivated in many varieties for its edible grain. **2.** The grain of such a plant, ground to produce flour used in cooking, especially for bread, cakes, and pasta products. [Middle English *whet(e),* Old English *hwǣte.*]

wheatear *A migratory bird, the wheatear spends the northern winter in tropical Africa and Asia and the spring and summer in Europe. It lives chiefly on uplands and heathlands and feeds on insects and spiders.*

wheat·ear (wéet-eer, hwéet-) *n.* A brown, black, and white bird, *Oenanthe oenanthe,* of northern regions. [Back-formation from *wheatears* (taken as plural), "white-rumped (bird)" : probably WHITE + Middle English *ers,* ARSE.]
wheat·en (wéet'n, hwéet'n) *adj.* Of, pertaining to, or derived from wheat.
wheat germ *n.* The vitamin-rich embryo of the wheat kernel, separated before milling for use as a cereal or food supplement.
wheat·meal (wéet-meel, hwéet-) *n.* Brown wheat flour.
~adj. Designating flour, or bread made from such flour, from which a proportion of the wheat kernel has been extracted.
Wheat·stone bridge (wéet-stōn, hwéet-) *n.* An instrument or circuit consisting of four resistors, or their equivalent, connected in a loop, with a galvanometer linking the junction between one pair and the other, used to determine the value of an unknown resistance when the other three resistances are known. [After Sir Charles *Wheatstone* (1802–75), British physicist.]
wheat·worm (wéet-wurm, hwéet-) *n.* A nematode worm, *Anguina tritici,* that is parasitic on and destructive to wheat.
whee·dle (wéed'l, hwéed'l) *v.* **-dled, -dling, -dles.** *—tr.* **1.** To persuade or attempt to persuade by flattery or guile; cajole: *wheedled us into agreeing.* **2.** To obtain through the use of flattery or guile. *—intr.* To use flattery or cajolery to achieve one's ends. [Perhaps from German *wedeln,* "to wag the tail", fawn, from Middle High German *wadelen,* from Old High German *wadal,* tail.] **—whee·dler** *n.* **—whee·dling·ly** *adv.*
wheel (weel, hweel) *n.* **1.** A solid disc or a rigid circular ring connected by spokes to a hub, designed to turn round an axle passed through the centre. **2.** Anything resembling such a device in appearance or movement or having such a device as its principal part or characteristic, as: **a.** In the Middle Ages, an instrument to which a victim was bound for torture. **b.** A type of firework that rotates while burning. **c.** A device for directing the course of a ship. **d.** The steering device on a vehicle. **e.** *U.S. Informal.* A bicycle. **f.** A spinning wheel. **g.** A water wheel. **h.** A potter's wheel. **i.** A device used in roulette and other games of chance. **3.** *Plural.* The procedures and processes involved in an enterprise: *the wheels of commerce.* **4. a.** The act or process of turning; a revolution or rotation. **b.** Circular motion. **5.** *Military.* A manoeuvre to change the direction of movement of a formation, as of troops or ships, in which the formation is maintained while the outer unit describes an arc and the inner unit remains in the same place as a pivot. **6.** *Plural. Slang.* A motor vehicle or access thereto. **7.** *Chiefly U.S. Slang.* One with a great deal of power or influence. Usually used in the phrase *a big wheel.* **—at** or **behind the wheel.** **1.** Operating the steering mechanism of a vehicle; driving. **2.** In charge; directing or controlling. **—oil the wheels.** To make things go smoothly. **—wheels within wheels.** A complex series of actions and interactions.
~v. **wheeled, wheeling, wheels.** *—tr.* **1.** To roll, move, or transport on a wheel or wheels, especially: **a.** To push (a container or vehicle equipped with wheels). **b.** To transport (a person or object)

in or on such a container or vehicle. **c.** To propel (oneself) in a wheelchair. **2.** To cause to turn round or as if round a central axis; revolve; rotate. —*intr.* **1.** To turn round or as if round a central axis; revolve; rotate. **2.** To roll, move, or transport oneself on or as if on a wheel or wheels. **3.** To fly or move in a curving or circular course. **4.** To turn or whirl round in place; pivot. Often used with *round.* **5.** To reverse one's opinion or practice. Often used with *about.* —**wheel and deal.** *Informal.* To conduct one's business in a complex, scheming way. [Middle English *wheel(e),* Old English *hwēol, hweogol.*]

wheel and axle *n.* A mechanical device, analogous to the lever, consisting of two coaxial wheels of different diameter conjoined so that the effort applied by a cord to the larger wheel in the form of a torque is transmitted as an action by a cord around the circumference of the smaller, yielding a mechanical advantage equal to the ratio of the diameters of the wheels.

wheel animalcule *n.* A microorganism, a **rotifer** *(see).*

wheel·back chair (wéel-bak, hwéel-) *n.* An upright wooden chair, having a back whose frame is made from a single strip of wood that is bent to fit into the seat at either side.

wheel balancing *n.* The process of checking that the wheels of a motor vehicle are perfectly balanced when rotating, in order to avoid unwanted vibrations at high speed.

wheel·bar·row (wéel-barrō, hwéel-) *n.* A one- or two-wheeled vehicle with handles, used to convey small, heavy, or unwieldy loads by hand, as in a garden or on a building site.

wheel·base (wéel-bayss, hwéel-) *n.* The distance from front to rear axle in a motor vehicle.

wheel·chair (wéel-chair, hwéel-) *n.* A chair mounted on large wheels for the use of the sick or disabled.

wheeled (weeld, hweeld) *adj.* Having a wheel or wheels. Often used in combination: *four-wheeled.*

wheel·er (wéel-ər, hwéel-) *n.* **1.** One that wheels. **2.** A thing that moves on or is equipped with a wheel or wheels. Often used in combination: *a three-wheeler.* **3.** A wheel horse.

wheel·er-deal·er (wéel-ər-déelər, hwéel-) *n. Informal.* A person who wheels and deals; a sharp operator.

wheel horse *n.* In a team, the horse that follows the leader and is harnessed nearest to the front wheels.

wheel·house (wéel-howss, hwéel-) *n.* An enclosed area on the deck or bridge of a vessel from which the vessel is controlled when under way. Also called "pilothouse".

wheel·ie (wéel-i, hwéel-) *n. Informal.* An act of riding a bicycle with the front wheel lifted off the ground: *do a wheelie.* [Diminutive of WHEEL.]

wheel lock *n.* **1.** A firing mechanism in certain obsolete small arms, in which a small wheel produces sparks by revolving against a flint. **2.** A locking mechanism attached to one wheelnut of the wheel of a car, preventing its removal.

wheel·man (wéel-mən, hwéel-, -man) *n., pl.* **-men** (-mən, -men). Also **wheels·man** (wéelz-, hwéelz-) (for sense 2). **1.** A bicyclist. **2.** *U.S.* One who steers a ship; a helmsman.

wheel·work (wéel-wurk, hwéel-) *n.* An arrangement of gears or wheels in a mechanical device.

wheel·wright (wéel-rīt, hwéel-) *n.* One whose trade is the building and repairing of wheels.

wheen (ween, hween) *n. Scottish.* A number; a few: *a wheen o'bairns.* [Middle English, Old English *hwēne,* instrumental of *hwōn,* (a few).]

wheeze (weez, hweez) *v.* **wheezed, wheezing, wheezes.** —*intr.* **1.** To breathe with difficulty, producing a hoarse whistling sound. **2.** To make a sound suggestive of laborious breathing. —*tr.* To produce or utter with a hoarse whistling sound.
—*n.* **1.** A wheezing sound. **2.** *Informal.* A clever idea or trick. **3.** *Informal.* An old joke. [Middle English *whesen,* probably from Old Norse *hvæsa,* to hiss.] —**wheez·ing·ly** *adv.*

wheez·y (wéezi, hwéezi) *adj.* **-ier, -iest. 1.** Given to wheezing. **2.** Marking a wheezing sound. —**wheez·i·ly** *adv.* —**wheez·i·ness** *n.*

whelk¹ (welk || *rarely* hwelk) *n.* **1.** Any of various large, sometimes edible marine snails of the family Buccinidae, having pointed, turreted shells. **2.** The flesh of an edible whelk, eaten as food. [Middle English *weoloc, wioloc†.*]

whelk² *n. Pathology.* A swelling, protuberance, or pustule. [Middle English *whelke,* Old English *hwylca†.*] —**whelk·y** *adj.*

whelm (welm, hwelm) *tr.v.* **whelmed, whelming, whelms.** *Archaic.* **1.** To overwhelm. **2.** To cover with water; submerge. [Middle English *whelmen,* to turn over, Old English *hwelman* (unattested).]

whelp (welp, hwelp) *n.* **1.** A young offspring of a dog, wolf, or similar animal. **2. a.** A mere child or youth. **b.** An impudent boy or young man. **3.** Any of the ridges on the barrel of a windlass or capstan.
—*v.* **whelped, whelping, whelps.** —*intr.* To give birth to a whelp or whelps. —*tr.* To give birth to (a whelp or whelps). [Middle English *w(h)elpe,* Old English *hwelp,* from Germanic.]

when (wen, hwen || *regional weak forms* wən, hwən) *adv.* **1.** At what time: *When does the show start? I'll tell you when you can leave.* **2.** During which time: *When was he at Oxford?* **3.** At, on, or during which. Used with expressions of time: *on the day when war was declared; one of those weeks when everything goes wrong.*
—*conj.* **1.** At the time that: *in the spring, when the snow melts.* **2.** At the moment at which; as soon as: *Switch off the pump when the pressure reaches 30 pounds.* **3.** At the times at which; whenever: *When the wind blows, the doors rattle.* **4.** During the time at which; while: *when I was younger.* **5.** Despite the fact that: *carried on talk-*

ing when he knew we were bored. **6.** Considering that; since; if: *Why bother when you know he'll refuse?* **7.** Whereupon; and then: *We were in a strong position, when suddenly rain stopped play.*
—*pron.* What or which time: *Since when has this been going on?*
—*n.* The time or date: *Have they decided the where and when?* [Middle English *when, wane,* Old English *hwanne, hwenne.*]

when·as (wen-áz, hwen-) *conj. Archaic.* **1.** When or whenever. **2.** Whereas. **3.** Considering that; inasmuch as.

whence (wenss, hwenss) *adv. Formal & Archaic.* **1.** From where; from what place, source, or cause. **2.** From or out of which: *returned to the land whence he came.*
—*conj. Formal & Archaic.* **1.** And from here; and thence: *The path led to a sundial, whence it continued to the end of the garden.* **2.** By reason of which; and from this: *He was not dead, whence we derived some comfort.* [Middle English *whennes,* from *whenne,* whence, Old English *hwanon.*]

whence·so·ev·er (wénss-sō-évvər, hwénss-) *adv. Archaic.* From whatever place or source.
—*conj.* From any place or source that.

when·ev·er (wen-évvər, hwen-) *adv.* Also **when ever** (for sense 2), *poetic* **when·e'er** (-áir). **1.** At whatever time: *Whenever you feel like leaving, just let me know.* **2.** When. Used as an intensive: *Whenever did you hear that?* **3.** *Informal.* At any unspecified time: *next Tuesday, Wednesday, or whenever.*
—*conj.* Also *poetic* **when·e'er.** **1.** At any time that: *Come whenever it suits you.* **2.** Every time that: *He smiles whenever he sees her.* —See Usage note at **ever.**

when·so·ev·er (wén-sō-évvər, hwén-) *adv.* At whatever time at all; whenever.
—*conj.* Whenever.

where (wair, hwair) *adv.* **1.** At or in what place: *Where is the telephone?* **2.** In what situation or position: *Where would we be without your help?* **3.** From what place or source: *Where did you get this idea?* **4.** To what place; towards what end: *Where is this argument leading?* **5.** At or in which. Used with expressions of place: *the house where I live; the point where his argument is least convincing.*
—*conj.* **1.** In the place in which: *Where she works, they have a staff canteen.* **2.** In or to a place in which: *lives where the weather is warm; We should go where it's quieter.* **3.** In or to any place in which; wherever: *has to go where the work is.* **4.** In a situation in which: *Where anyone else would have been furious, she just laughed.* **5.** In which place; and there: *walked outside, where I was waiting.*
—*pron.* Which place: *Where did they come from?*
—*n.* The place or occasion: *We know the when but not the where of it.* [Middle English *wher(e),* Old English *hwǣr.*]

where·a·bouts (waír-ə-bówts, hwaír-ə-) *adv.* About where; in, at, or near what place: *Whereabouts do you live?*
—*n.* (-bowtss). *Used with a singular or plural verb.* The approximate location of someone or something.

where·as (wair-áz, hwair-) *conj.* **1.** It being the fact that; inasmuch as. Often used to introduce a formal document. **2. a.** While on the one hand. **b.** On the other hand; by contrast with that.

where·at (wair-át, hwair-) *conj. Archaic.* **1.** At which place. **2.** At which point or event; whereupon.

where·by (wair-bī, hwair- || *U.S.* hwar-, hwer-, war-, wer-) *adv.* **1.** *Formal.* In accordance with or by means of which: *a new law, whereby some players may be banned.* **2.** *Archaic.* By what means; how: *"Whereby shall I know this?"* (Luke 1:18).

where·fore (waír-fawr, hwaír- || ōr) *adv. Archaic.* **1.** For what purpose or reason; why. **2.** On account of which.
—*conj. Archaic.* Why: *Wherefore did he come?*
—*n.* A purpose or cause. Now used chiefly in the phrase *whys and wherefores.* [Middle English *wherfor* : WHERE + FOR.]

where·from (wair-fróm, hwair-) *adv. Archaic.* From what or where; whence.

where·in (wair-ín, hwair-) *adv. Archaic.* **1.** In what; how: *Wherein did I sin?* **2.** In which thing, place, or situation: *the bed wherein I lay.*

where·in·to (wair-in-tōo, hwair-, -tōo) *adv. Archaic.* Into what or which.

where·of (wair-óv, hwair- || -úv) *adv. Archaic.* **1.** Of what or which. **2.** Of whom.

where·on (wair-ón, hwair- || -awn) *adv. Archaic.* On which or what.

where·so·ev·er (waír-sō-évvər, hwaír-) *conj.* Also *poetic* **where·so·e'er** (-áir). In, to, or from whatever place at all; wherever.

where·through (wair-thrōo, hwair-) *adv.* Through, because of, or during which.

where·to (wair-tōo, hwair-) *adv.* Also *archaic* **where·un·to** (-ún-tōo, -tōo). **1.** To what place; towards what end. **2.** To which.

where·up·on (waír-əp-ón, hwaír-, -áwn) *adv. Archaic.* On which or what: *a table whereupon a lavish feast was spread.*
—*conj.* **1.** At which point; after which. **2.** As a consequence of which.

wher·ev·er (wair-évvər, hwair-, wər-, hwər-) *adv.* Also **where ever** (for sense 2), *poetic* **wher·e'er** (-áir). **1.** In or to whatever place: *Whenever she goes, he goes too.* **2.** Where. Used as an intensive: *Wherever did you hear that?* **3.** *Informal.* At or in any unspecified place: *can be used in the home, the office, or wherever.*
—*conj.* Also *poetic* **where·e'er.** **1.** In or to whichever place or situation that: *sit wherever you like.* **2.** In every place or situation that: *followed wherever she went.* [Middle English *wherever* : WHERE + EVER.] —See Usage note at **ever.**

where·with (wair-with, hwair-, -with) *adv.* With what or which: *the pen wherewith I write.*

whelk *A marine snail that lives on the fringes of the sea and can grow up to 15 centimetres (6 inches) long. It feeds on other small marine animals or carrion, hunting by scent. Some species are edible.*

whimbrel *A shorter curved bill and a striped forehead distinguish the whimbrel from its close relative, the curlew. Its call – a series of high-pitched whistles, often in groups of seven cries – has given it the colloquial name of seven whistler.*

~*pron. Archaic.* The thing or things with which: *"Make ready wherewith I may sup"* (Luke 17:8).

where·with·al (wáir-wi<u>th</u>-awl, hwáir-, with-, -áwl) *adv. Archaic.* Wherewith.
~*pron. Archaic.* Wherewith.
~*n.* The necessary means, especially financial means: *to have the wherewithal for war.*

wher·ry (wérri, hwérri) *n., pl.* **-ries.** **1.** A light, swift rowing boat built for one person and often used in racing. **2.** A kind of sailing barge used in East Anglia. [Middle English *wheryt*†.]

whet (wet, hwet) *tr.v.* **whetted, whetting, whets.** **1.** To sharpen (a knife or other tool); hone. **2.** To make more keen; stimulate; heighten: *The noise whetted his curiosity.*
~*n.* **1.** Something that sharpens or stimulates. **2.** *Informal.* An appetiser or aperitif. [Middle English *whetten,* Old English *hwettan.*]

wheth·er (wé<u>th</u>ər, hwé<u>th</u>ər) *conj.* **1.** If it is so that; if the case is that. Used in indirect questions to introduce one alternative: *Ask whether the museum is open.* **2.** If it happens that; in case. Used to introduce the first of a set of possibilities and sometimes one or more other possibilities: *Whether he wins or (whether he) loses, this is his last fight; I'm seeing her, whether in Rome, London, or Paris.*
~*pron. Archaic.* Which of the two. Use in direct or indirect questions. **—whether or no.** Regardless of circumstances. [Middle English *whether,* Old English *hwæther, hwether.*]

whet·stone (wét-stōn, hwét-) *n.* A stone for honing tools.

whew (hwew, hwōō) *interj.* Used to express relief or amazement. Usually partially unvoiced in imitation of a whistle. [Middle English *whewe* (imitative).]

whey (way, hway) *n.* The watery part of milk that separates from the curds, as in the process of making cheese. Also called "serum". [Middle English *whey,* Old English *hwæg,* from Germanic *khwuja-* (unattested).] **—whey·ey** *adj.*

whey-face (wáy-fayss, hwáy-) *n.* A person with a pallid face. **—whey-faced** *adj.*

which (wich, hwich) *pron.* **1.** What particular one or ones: *Which of these is yours? One of these is yours, I'm not sure which.* **2.** The thing, animal, group of people, or event previously designated or implied, specifically: **a.** Used as a relative pronoun in a clause that provides additional information about the antecedent: *my house, which is small and old.* **b.** Used as a relative pronoun preceded by *that* or *those,* or by a preposition in a clause that defines or restricts the antecedent: *the subject on which he spoke; took those which belonged to him.* **c.** Used instead of *that* as a relative pronoun in a clause that defines or restricts the antecedent: *The film which was shown later was better.* **3.** *Archaic.* The person designated or implied. Used as a relative pronoun: *Our Father, which art in Heaven.* **4.** Any of the things, events, or persons designated or implied; whichever: *Choose which you like best.* **6.** A thing or circumstance that: *He left early, which was wise.*
~*adj.* **1.** What particular one or ones of a number of things or persons: *Which part of town? He asked me which colour I preferred.* **2.** Any one or any number of; whichever: *Use which door you please.* **3.** Being the one or ones previously designated: *It started to rain, at which point we ran.* Sometimes used to refer to a clause: *told us he was married, which surprised me.* [Middle English *which, wilke,* Old English *hwilc, hwelc.*]

which·ev·er (wich-évvər, hwich-) *pron.* **1.** Any one or ones. **2.** No matter which; regardless of what one or ones.
~*adj.* **1.** Any one or any number of a group of things or persons: *Read whichever books you please.* **2.** No matter what; regardless of which: *It's a long trip whichever road you take.*

which·so·ev·er (wích-sō-évvər, hwích-) *pron.* Whichever.
~*adj.* Whichever. Used for emphasis.

whick·er (wíck-ər, hwíck-) *intr.v.* **-ered, -ering, -ers.** To whinny or snigger.
~*n.* A whinny or snigger. [Imitative.]

whidah. Variant of **whydah.**

whiff (wif, hwif) *n.* **1.** A slight, gentle gust or breath of air; a waft: *a whiff of cool air.* **2.** A brief, passing odour carried in the air; a momentary smell: *"a whiff of lilac drifted across the room"* (Elizabeth Bowen). **3.** A slight trace or suggestion: *a whiff of scandal.* **4.** An inhalation, as of air, perfume or tobacco smoke: *Take a whiff of this pipe.* **5.** *British.* A small cigar.
~*v.* **whiffed, whiffing, whiffs.** —*intr.* **1.** To be carried in brief gusts; waft. **2.** To draw in or breathe out air, smoke, or some other vapour. **3.** *British Informal.* To have an unpleasant smell. —*tr.* **1.** To blow or convey in whiffs. **2.** To inhale through the nose; smell; sniff. **3.** To draw in or breathe out (air or tobacco smoke, for example). [Imitative.] **—whiff·er** *n.*

whif·fle (wiff'l, hwiff'l) *v.* **-fled, -fling, -fles.** —*intr.* **1.** To move or think erratically; vacillate. **2.** To blow in fitful gusts; puff. Used of the wind. **3.** To produce a light whistling sound, as of wind. **4.** To move as if blown by wind; flutter. —*tr.* To blow, displace, or scatter with gusts of air. [From WHIFF (to blow).]

whif·fle·tree (wiff'l-tree, hwiff'l-) *n. U.S.* A **swingletree** *(see).*

Whig (wig, hwig) *n.* **1.** In the 17th century, a supporter of the Presbyterian cause in Scotland. **2.** From the late 17th to the mid-19th century, a member or supporter of one of the two major British political parties, opposed to the Tories and eventually succeeded by the Liberals. Early Whigs chiefly represented the aristocracy and sought the limitation of the power of the monarchy, while in the late 18th and early 19th centuries the Whigs came increasingly to represent the new industrial interests and to become a party of reform. **3.** In modern politics, one who identifies strongly with the Whig tradition, typically (in Britain) a member of the Liberal party. **4.** In the United States, a member of a political party (1834–55) formed to oppose the Democratic Party, succeeded by the Republican Party, and favouring high tariffs and a loose interpretation of the Constitution. [Probably short for *Whiggamore,* one of a body of 17th-century Scottish insurgents : perhaps *whig*†, to drive + Middle English *mere,* horse, MARE.] **—Whig, Whig·gish** *adj.*

Whig·ger·y (wíg-əri, hwíg-) *n., pl.* **-ies.** Also **Whig·gism** (-iz'm). The principles or practices of Whigs.

while (wīl, hwīl) *n.* **1.** A period of time. Usually used in adverbial phrases: *stay for a while; sang (all) the while.* **2.** The time, effort, or trouble taken in doing something: *It is not worth my while to go yet.* **—once in a while.** Now and then; very occasionally.
~*conj.* **1.** As long as; during the time that: *It was lovely while it lasted.* **2.** Although: *While I respect your opinion, I can't agree with you.* **3.** Whereas: *While some of us are rushed off our feet, John never does a stroke of work.* **4.** And similarly; what is more: *Postal charges are rising by 20%, while telephone charges may go up even more.* **5.** *Northern British.* Until: *had to wait while he finished.*
~*prep. Northern British.* Until: *while next week.*
~*tr.v.* **whiled, whiling, whiles.** Also **wile, wiled, wiling, wiles.** To spend (time) idly or pleasantly. Usually used with *away*: *whiled the hours away.* [Middle English *while, qwile,* Old English *hwīl.*]

Usage: The use of *while* in sentences like *Jean is French, John is English, while Jan is Polish* tends to attract criticism from purists, who find it inelegant. Indeed, all senses of *while* other than the strictly temporal have received criticism, usually on the grounds of a potential ambiguity: *She spent her youth in Wales, while her mother grew up in England.* See also **whilst.**

whiles (wīlz, hwīlz) *conj. Archaic.* While. [Middle English, adverbial genitive of WHILE.]

whi·lom (wī-ləm, hwī-) *adj. Archaic.* Former; erstwhile.
~*adv. Archaic.* Formerly. [Middle English *whilom,* Old English *hwīlum,* dative plural of *hwīl,* WHILE.]

whilst (wīlst, hwīlst) *conj. Chiefly British.* While. [Middle English *whylst,* from WHILES.]

Usage: *Whilst* has now been generally replaced by *while* in standard English. It is still used in certain literary contexts, and may still be heard among older British speakers.

whim (wim, hwim) *n.* **1.** A sudden or capricious idea; a passing fancy. **2.** Arbitrary thought or impulse; caprice: *governed by whim.* **3.** *Mining.* A vertical horse-powered drum used as a hoist. —See Synonyms at **caprice.** [Short for earlier *whim-wham*†.]

whim·brel (wím-brəl, hwím-) *n.* A greyish-brown wading bird, *Numenius phaeopus,* having long legs and a long, downward-curving bill. [Imitative of its cry.]

whim·per (wím-pər, hwím-) *v.* **-pered, -pering, -pers.** —*intr.* **1.** To cry or sob with soft intermittent sounds; whine. **2.** To complain whiningly. —*tr.* To utter in a whimper. —See Synonyms at **cry.**
~*n.* A low, broken, whining sound; a whine. [Dialectal *whimp* (imitative).] **—whim·per·er** *n.* **—whim·per·ing·ly** *adv.*

whim·si·cal (wím-zik'l, hwím-) *adj.* **1.** Capricious; playful; arbitrary. **2.** Unusual; fantastic; odd. [From WHIMSY.] **—whim·si·cal·i·ty** (-zi-káləti) *n.* **—whim·si·cal·ly** *adv.*

whim·sy, whim·sey (wím-zi, hwím-) *n., pl.* **-sies, -seys.** **1.** A tendency to have or show a fanciful, often humorous approach to life; whimsicality: *loved whimsy and nonsense verse.* **2.** An odd or capricious idea; an idle fancy. **3.** Anything quaint, fanciful, or odd. —See Synonyms at **caprice.** [Probably from WHIM.]

whin[1] (win, hwin) *n.* A spiny shrub, **gorse** *(see).* [Middle English *whynne*†.]

whin[2] *n.* Whinstone. [Middle English *quin*†.]

whin·chat (wín-chat, hwín-) *n.* A brownish Old World bird, *Saxicola rubetra,* frequenting open country. [From WHIN (gorse) (the bird is often found around gorse bushes).]

whine (wīn, hwīn) *v.* **whined, whining, whines.** —*intr.* **1.** To utter a plaintive, high-pitched, protracted sound, as in pain, fear, supplication, or complaint. **2.** To complain or protest in a peevish, protracted fashion. **3.** To produce a sustained noise of relatively high pitch. Used of a machine. —*tr.* To utter with a whine.
~*n.* **1.** A whining sound. **2.** A peevish complaint. [Middle English *whinen,* Old English *hwīnan.*] **—whin·er** *n.* **—whin·ing·ly** *adv.* **—whin·y** *adj.*

whinge (winj, hwinj) —*intr.v.* **whinged, whinging, whinges.** *Informal.* To whine or complain.
~*n. Informal* A whine; a complaint. [Northern English dialect, from Late Old English *hwinsian* (imitative); akin to German *winseln,* to WHINE.]

whin·ny (wínni, hwínni) *v.* **-nied, -nying, -nies.** —*intr.* To neigh, especially in a gentle tone. Used chiefly of a horse. —*tr.* To express in a whinny.
~*n., pl.* **whinnies.** The sound made in whinnying; a neigh. [Probably from WHINE (imitative).]

whin·stone (wín-stōn, hwín-) *n.* Any of various hard, dark-coloured rocks, especially basalt and chert. Also called "whin".

whip (wip, hwip) *v.* **whipped, whipping, whips.** —*tr.* **1.** To strike with repeated strokes, as of a lash, strap, or rod; beat. **2. a.** To punish or chastise in this manner; flog; thrash. **b.** To afflict, castigate, or reprove severely. **3.** To drive, urge, force, or bring by or as if by means of a whip: *whipped his horse on; tried to whip the team into shape.* **4.** To strike or affect in a manner similar to whipping or lashing: *Icy winds whipped his face.* **5.** To beat (cream or eggs, for example) into a froth or foam. **6.** To move (something) with a sudden, rapid motion; take, put, or remove quickly: *whipped out a revolver; whipped off his cap.* **7.** To sew with a loose overcast or overhand stitch; whipstitch. **8.** To wrap or bind (a rope, for example) with twine to prevent unravelling or fraying. **9.** *Nautical.* To hoist by means of a rope passing through an overhead pulley. **10.** To fish (a stream or pool) by casting the line onto the water with a whipping motion. **11.** *Informal.* To defeat; outdo: *well and truly whipped by a superior team.* —*intr.* **1.** To move or proceed briskly: *just going to whip down to the shops; whipped through the report in 10 minutes.* **2.** To move in a manner similar to a whip; thrash or snap about: *Branches whipped against the windows.*

~*n.* **1.** An instrument, either a flexible rod or a flexible thong or lash attached to a handle, used for driving animals or administering corporal punishment. **2.** A whipping or lashing motion or stroke. **3.** Flexibility, as in the shaft of a golf club. **4.** A whipper-in. **5.** In the British Parliament and other legislative bodies: **a.** A member of a party responsible for enforcing party discipline, and especially for ensuring the attendance and supervising the voting behaviour of members at an important division. **b.** A written notice requiring party members to attend a particular session and vote according to the party line. See **three-line whip. c.** The condition of being subject to the discipline of a particular party: *resigned the Labour whip.* **6.** A sweet dish made with beaten egg whites or cream, often with fruit or fruit flavouring: *prune whip.* **7.** A windmill arm. **8.** *Nautical.* A hoist consisting of a single rope passing through an overhead pulley. **9.** A fairground ride, consisting of small cars that move in a rapid, whipping motion. —**whip in.** To keep (a pack of hounds) together by using a whip; act as a whipper-in. —**whip up. 1.** To arouse; excite: *whip up a crowd; whip up enthusiasm.* **2.** *Informal.* To prepare (a meal, for example) quickly. [Middle English *wippen*, perhaps from Middle Low German or Middle Dutch, to vacillate, swing.] —**whip·per** *n.*

whip bird *n.* Any of various Australian birds having a cry resembling the crack of a whip, such as *Psophodes olivaceus.*

whip·cord (wíp-kawrd, hwíp-) *n.* **1.** A worsted fabric with a distinct diagonal rib. **2.** A strong twisted or braided cord sometimes used in making whiplashes.

whip graft *n.* A horticultural graft in which a tongue cut on the sloping base of the scion is inserted into a slit made on the sloping top of the stock.

whip hand *n.* A dominating position; the upper hand. Preceded by *the.*

whip·lash (wíp-lash, hwíp-) *n.* **1.** The lash or thong of a whip. **2.** An injury to the spine in the neck region caused by an abrupt jerking motion of the head, either backwards or forwards. In this sense, also called "whiplash injury". —**whip·lash** *adj.*

whip·per-in (wíppər-ín, hwíppər-) *n., pl.* **whippers-in. 1.** In foxhunting, one who assists the huntsman in handling a pack of hounds. Also called "whip". **2.** *Archaic.* A parliamentary whip.

whip·per·snap·per (wíppər-snappər, hwíppər-) *n.* An impertinent but insignificant person. [Perhaps from *whipsnapper,* suggesting noisy but insignificant activity.]

whip·pet (wíppit, hwíppit) *n.* A short-haired, swift-running dog of a breed developed in England, resembling the greyhound but smaller. [Perhaps from obsolete *whippet,* to move quickly, from *whip it.*]

whip·ping (wipping, hwipping) *n.* **1.** A thrashing administered especially as punishment. **2.** Material, such as cord or thread, used to lash or bind parts.

whipping boy *n.* **1.** One who gets the blame for the faults of others, especially of his superiors; a scapegoat. **2.** A boy formerly educated with a prince or other young nobleman and whipped for the latter's misdeeds.

whip·ple·tree (wipp'l-tree, hwípp'l-) *n.* A swingletree (*see*).

whip·poor·will (wíppər-wil, hwíppər- ‖ *U.S. also* -wil) *n.* A brownish nocturnal North American bird, *Caprimulgus vociferus,* having a distinctive call of which its name is imitative.

whip·saw (wíp-saw, hwíp-) *n.* A narrow two-man crosscut saw.

~*tr.v.* **whipsawed** or **-sawn** (-sawn), **-sawing, -saws. 1.** To cut with a whipsaw. **2.** To defeat or get the better of in two ways at once or by the joint actio of two parties.

whip scorpion *n.* Any of various nonvenomous scorpionlike arachnids of the order Pedipalpi, such as the vinegarroon.

whip snake *n.* Any of various slender nonvenomous snakes, such as *Coluber gemonensis* of Eurasia and any of the genus *Masticophis,* of the New World.

whip·stall (wíp-stawl, hwíp-) *n.* A usually intentional stall in which a small aircraft enters a vertical climb, pauses, slips backwards momentarily, then drops nose downwards.

whip·stitch (wíp-stich, hwíp-) *tr.v.* **-stitched, -stitching, -stitches.** To sew with overcast stitches, as in finishing a fabric edge or binding two pieces of fabric together.

~*n.* A stitch or stitches made in this manner.

whip·stock (wíp-stok, hwíp) *n.* The handle of a whip.

whip·worm (wíp-wurm, hwíp-) *n.* A slender, parasitic roundworm, *Trichuris trichiura,* that infests the large intestine in humans.

whirl (wurl, hwurl) *v.* **whirled, whirling, whirls.** —*intr.* **1.** To revolve rapidly about a centre or axis. **2.** To rotate or spin rapidly. **3.** To turn aside or away rapidly; wheel. **4.** To have the sensation of spinning; reel. **5.** To move along rapidly in or as if in a wheeled vehicle. —*tr.* **1.** To cause to rotate or turn rapidly. **2.** To drive or carry along at great speed, in a circular or curving course. **3.** To hurl. —See Synonyms at **turn.**

~*n.* **1.** The act of rotating or revolving rapidly. **2.** Something that whirls or is whirled, as a cloud of dust. **3.** A state of confusion; a tumult; a turmoil. **4.** A hurried succession or round of events: *the social whirl.* **5.** A state of mental confusion or giddiness; dizziness: *My head is in a whirl.* **6.** *Informal.* A short trip; a spin. **7.** *Informal.* A brief try. Usually used in the phrase *give it a whirl.* [Middle English *whirlen,* from Old Norse *hvirfla.*] —**whirl·er** *n.*

whirl·i·gig (wúr-li-gig, hwúr-) *n.* **1.** Any of various spinning toys. **2.** A roundabout or merry-go-round. **3.** Something that is continuously whirling or in a state of constant movement or change. **4.** The whirligig beetle. [Middle English *whirlegigge* : *whirlen,* WHIRL + *gigg(e),* spinning top.]

whirligig beetle *n.* Any of various beetles of the family Gyrinidae that circle about rapidly on the surface of quiet water.

whirl·pool (wúrl-pool, hwúrl-) *n.* **1.** Water in rapid rotating movement, as from the converging of two tides, tending to draw any floating object into the centre and down; an eddy or vortex. **2.** Anything suggesting the rapid turbulence of whirling water.

whirl·wind (wúrl-wind, hwúrl-) *n.* **1.** A column of air centred on an area of low atmospheric pressure, rotating violently around a more or less vertical axis and moving forward; a tornado. **2.** A small, momentary current of such whirling air over dusty flat land; a dust devil. **3.** Anything rushing or whirling impetuously, confusedly, or destructively. —See Synonyms at **wind.**

~*adj.* Very rapid or impetuous: *a whirlwind courtship.*

whirl·y·bird (wúr-li-burd, hwúr-) *n.* Chiefly *U.S. Informal.* A helicopter. [From WHIRL + BIRD.]

whirr (wur, hwur) —*intr.v.* **whirred, whirring, whirrs.** Also *chiefly U.S.* **whir.** To move so as to produce a continuous vibrating or buzzing sound, as some machines or the wings of certain birds do.

~*n.* A sound of buzzing or vibration. [Middle English *whirren,* from Scandinavian, akin to Danish *hvirre.*]

whisht (wisht, hwisht) *interj. Scottish & Irish.* Hush.

~*tr.v.* **whisted, whishting, whishts.** To hush; silence. [Middle English (imitative).]

whisk (wisk, hwisk) *v.* **whisked, whisking, whisks.** —*tr.* **1.** To move or remove with quick light sweeping motions: *whisking away the flies with its tail.* **2.** To carry or convey quickly and unobtrusively: *was whisked off to the Palace in an official car.* **3.** To whip (eggs or cream). —*intr.* To move lightly, nimbly, and rapidly.

~*n.* **1.** A quick light sweeping motion. **2.** A small bundle, as of twigs or feathers, especially one used for brushing away dust or flies. **3.** A kitchen utensil, typically made of looped wire, for beating or whipping foodstuffs. [Middle English (Scottish) *quhisken,* from Scandinavian, akin to Swedish *viska†.*]

whisk·er (wísk-ər, hwisk-) *n.* **1.** *Plural.* **a.** The unshaven hair on a man's face; the beard, especially that part of it growing on the sides of the face. **b.** A moustache. **2.** A hair from the beard. **3.** Any of the long stiff bristles or hairs growing near the mouth of certain animals. **4.** *Informal.* A narrow margin; a hair's-breadth: *He lost by a whisker.* **5.** *Nautical.* One of two spars or booms projecting from the side of a bowsprit for spreading the jib or flying-jib guys. Also called "whisker boom". **6.** *Chemistry.* Any of the extremely fine filamentary crystals that can be grown from supersaturated solutions of certain minerals and metals and that possess extraordinary shear strength and unusual electrical or surface properties. [From WHISK.] —**whisk·ered, whisk·er·y** *adj.*

whis·key (wiski, hwíski) *n., pl.* **-keys. 1.** Whisky distilled in Ireland or in the United States. **2.** A drink of whiskey.

Usage: When made in Scotland (or Canada), the spelling is *whisky;* this is the dominant British form. *Whiskey* is the usual American English spelling, and it is also used of Irish whiskey.

whiskey sour *n.* A cocktail made with whiskey, lemon juice, and sugar.

whisky (wiski, hwíski) *n., pl.* **-kies. 1.** An alcoholic spirit distilled from fermented grain, typically from malted barley in Scotland and Ireland, and from maize or rye in the United States and Canada, and containing approximately 40 to 50 per cent ethanol by volume. **2.** A drink of whisky. [Shortened from obsolete *Whiskybae,* variant of USQUEBAUGH.]

whis·per (wíss-pər, hwíss-) *n.* **1.** Soft speech produced without vibration of the vocal cords. **2.** Something uttered in this manner. **3.** A secretly or surreptitiously expressed belief, rumour, or hint. **4.** A low rustling sound.

~*v.* **whispered, -pering, -pers.** —*intr.* **1.** To speak softly, without the resonance produced by vibration of the vocal cords. **2.** To speak quietly or secretively, as by way of gossip, slander, or intrigue. **3.** To make a soft rustling sound, as surf or leaves do. —*tr.* **1.** To utter very softly. **2.** To say or suggest secretly or confidentially. [Middle English *whisperen,* Old English *hwisprian* (imitative).] —**whis·per·er** *n.*

whispering campaign *n.* A concerted effort to discredit a person or group by disseminating unfavourable allegations and rumours by word of mouth.

whist (wist, hwist) *n.* A card game for two pairs of players, in which each pair tries to win as many as possible of the 13 available tricks. [Perhaps variant of WHISK, from the whisking up of the tricks.]

whis·tle (wiss'l, hwiss'l) *v.* **-tled, -tling, -tles.** —*intr.* **1.** To produce a clear musical sound or series of sounds by forcing air through an aperture formed by pursing the lips. **2.** To produce a clear, shrill, sharp musical sound or series of sounds by some other method, as by blowing on or through a device. **3.** To produce a high-pitched sound when moving swiftly through the air: *Bullets whistled past.*

white clover *A plant important to bee-keepers because of the abundant nectar its flowers contain. Its leaves usually grow in groups of three; the rarer four-leaved clover is said to bring good luck to the finder.*

white-eye *There are about 80 species of this warbler-like bird, living in Africa, Asia, and the Pacific regions. This is an Oriental white-eye which ranges from Afghanistan to the islands of Southeast Asia.*

4. To emit a sharp, high-pitched, often shrill note or cry, as some birds and animals do. **5.** To summon or signal by whistling: *whistled to his dog to follow him.* **6.** *Informal.* To request or expect something with no chance of success: *wants his money back, but he can whistle for it.* —*tr.* **1.** To produce by whistling: *whistle a tune.* **2.** To summon, signal, or direct by whistling.

~*n.* **1.** A device or instrument for making whistling sounds by means of the breath, air, or steam. **2.** A sound produced by such a device or by whistling through the lips. **3.** Any whistling sound, as of an animal, a projectile, or the wind. **4.** The act of whistling. **5.** A whistling sound used to summon or command, or to give a signal. **6.** *Informal.* The mouth and throat. Used chiefly in the phrase *wet one's whistle.* **—blow the whistle on.** *Informal.* To expose and so put a stop to (any shady or undesirable activity or those involved in it). [Middle English *whist(e)len,* Old English *hwistlian* (imitative).]

whis·tler (wíss-lər, hwíss-) *n.* **1.** One that whistles. **2.** Any of various birds that produce a whistling sound, such as certain Australian flycatchers and the goldeneye duck. **3.** A marmot, *Marmota caligata,* of the mountains of northwestern North America, having a greyish coat and a shrill, whistling cry. **4.** *Physics.* An electromagnetic wave of audio frequency produced by atmospheric disturbances such as lightning, having a characteristically decreasing frequency responsible for a whistling sound of descending pitch in detection equipment. **5.** A horse having a respiratory disease characterised by wheezing.

Whis·tler (wíss-lər, hwíss-), **James (Abbott) McNeill** (1834–1903). U.S. painter. His works concentrate more on tone and colour than draughtsmanship. They include a portrait of his mother (*Arrangement in Grey and Black,* 1872), and *Old Battersea Bridge.*

whistle stop *n.* **1.** One of a series of brief visits or appearances, especially by a candidate in an election. **2.** *U.S.* A small town at which a train stops only if signalled.

whis·tle-stop (wíss'l-stop, hwíss'l-) *intr.v.* **-stopped, -stopping, -stops.** *Chiefly U.S.* To conduct a political campaign by making brief appearances or speeches in a series of small towns.

~*adj.* Conducted in this way: *a whistlestop tour.*

whistling swan *n.* A North American swan, *Cygnus columbianus,* having a black beak marked with yellow at the base.

whit (wit, hwit) *n.* A particle; the least bit. Usually used with a negative. [Variant of Middle English *wi(g)ht,* creature, WIGHT.]

Whit (wit, hwit) *n.* **1. Pentecost** *(see).* **2. Whitsuntide** *(see).*

white (wīt, hwīt) *n. Abbr.* **wh.** **1.** An achromatic colour of maximum lightness, the complement of black, the other extreme of the neutral grey series. Although typically a response to maximum stimulation, white appears always to depend upon contrast. **2.** The white or nearly white part of something, as: **a.** The albumen of an egg. **b.** The white part of an eyeball. **c.** A blank area on a printed surface. **3.** Something white or nearly white, as: **a.** White clothes: *dressed all in white.* **b.** *Plural.* A white or cream outfit or item of clothing, as worn for some sports: *cricket whites.* **c.** A white wine. **d.** A white pigment: *titanium white.* **e.** A white breed of animal. **f.** The white ball in billiards or snooker. **g.** The white or light-coloured pieces in draughts or chess, or the player using them. **h.** The outermost ring of a target. **i.** A hit in this ring. **4.** *Sometimes capital* **W. a.** A person belonging to a race or group characterised by relatively light complexion. **b.** In South Africa, a member of the classified race group comprising such persons, usually of European descent. **5.** Any of various butterflies of the family Pieridae having white wings with some black markings, such as the **cabbage white** *(see).* **7.** *Plural. Medicine.* Leucorrhoea. **8.** A member of any of several reactionary or counterrevolutionary political groups active in Europe from the 18th to the early 20th centuries.

~*adj.* **whiter, whitest. 1.** Being of the colour white; devoid of hue, as new snow is. **2.** Approaching this colour, as: **a.** Translucent and having a pale yellow colour: *white wine.* **b.** Pale green. Said of certain grapes. **c.** Pale grey; silvery and lustrous, as silver or tin or objects made of such metals. **d.** Silvery or light grey with age: *white hair.* **e.** Bloodless as from illness or fear; blanched. **3.** Light or whitish in colour or having light or whitish parts. Used with animal and plant names: *white whale; white clover.* **4. a.** Having the comparatively pale complexion typical of Caucasoids. **b.** Of, pertaining to, characteristic of, or consisting of white people: *white opinion; a predominantly white neighbourhood.* **c.** Reserved for white people, as in a system of racial segregation: *a white beach.* **5.** Not written or printed upon; blank. **6. a.** Pure; untainted; innocent. **b.** *Informal.* Fair; decent; honourable. **7. a.** Wearing a white habit: *white nuns.* **b.** Marked by the wearing of white by the bride: *a white wedding.* **8.** Accompanied by or mantled with snow: *a white Christmas.* **9. a.** Incandescent: *white heat.* **b.** Intensely heated; impassioned: *white with fury.* **10.** Reactionary or counterrevolutionary. **11.** Whitish in colour as a result of some degree of processing. Said of some foodstuffs: *white bread; white rice.* Compare **brown. 12.** With milk or cream added. Said of coffee.

~*tr.v.* **whited, whiting, whites. 1. a.** *Printing.* To create or leave blank spaces in (printed or illustrated matter). **b.** To efface with correction fluid. In both senses, often used with *out*: *white out a line.* **2. a.** *Archaic.* To whiten; whitewash. **b.** *Obsolete.* To blanch. [Middle English *white,* Old English *hwīt,* white, white of an egg.] **—whit·ish** *adj.*

White, Patrick (1912–). Australian novelist. His works include *The Happy Valley* (1939), *Voss* (1957), and *A Fringe of Leaves* (1976). He was awarded the Nobel prize (1973).

white admiral *n.* A Eurasian butterfly, *Limenitis camilla,* having brown wings marked with white.

white alkali *n.* **1.** Any of several mineral salts, such as sodium sulphate or sodium chloride, that appear as a white deposit on certain alkaline soils. **2.** Refined sodium carbonate.

white ant *n.* A **termite** *(see).*

white asbestos, *n.* A variety of asbestos, **chrysotile** *(see).*

white·bait (wīt-bayt, hwīt-) *n.* **1.** The young of various fishes, such as the herring, considered a delicacy when fried. **2.** Any of various other small edible fishes.

white·beam (wīt-beem, hwīt-) *n.* A European tree, *Sorbus aria,* the leaves of which have a whitish down on the undersurface.

white bear *n.* The **polar bear** *(see).*

white blood cell *n.* A **leucocyte** *(see).*

white bryony *n.* A climbing European vine, *Bryonia dioica,* having lobed leaves, greenish-white flowers, and scarlet berries.

white·cap (wīt-kap, hwīt-) *n.* A wave with a crest of foam.

white cedar *n.* **1.** Any of several North American conferous trees having light-coloured wood, such as *Thuja occidentalis,* both having scalelike leaves. **2.** The wood of any of these trees.

white cell *n.* A **leucocyte** *(see).*

white cloud *n.* A small, brightly coloured freshwater fish, *Tanichthys albonubes,* native to China and popular in home aquariums.

white clover *n.* A common clover, *Trifolium repens,* native to Eurasia, having rounded white flower heads.

white coal *n.* Water regarded as a source of power.

white-col·lar (wīt-kóllər, hwīt-) *adj.* Of, pertaining to, or designating those workers, usually salaried, whose work usually does not involve manual labour and who maybe expected to dress with some degree of formality. Compare **blue-collar.**

white corpuscle *n.* A **leucocyte** *(see).*

white currant *n.* **1.** A shrub, *Ribes sativum,* cultivated for its edible berries. **2.** The small, round, white berry of this shrub.

white damp *n.* A poisonous gas, consisting primarily of carbon monoxide, that occurs in coal mines.

whited sepulchre *n.* A hypocrite; an evil person who pretends to be holy or good. Matthew 23:27.

white dwarf *n.* A faint highly dense star that is believed to represent the final stage in the evolution of a star of about the mass of the Sun.

white elephant *n.* **1.** A rare whitish or light-grey form of the Asian elephant, often regarded with special veneration in regions of south-eastern Asia. **2.** Something that is large, costly, and perhaps impressive, but expensive to maintain, unproductive, and consequently unwanted. **3.** An expensive project or venture which comes to nothing or turns out to be a failure. **4.** Any possession no longer wanted by its owner. [Referring to custom of the kings of Siam, who would express displeasure with a courtier by the gift of a white elephant, the upkeep of which was ruinously expensive.]

white-eye (wīt-ī, hwīt-) *n.* Any of various small greenish birds of the genus *Zosterops,* of Africa, southern Asia, and the Pacific islands, having a narrow ring of white feathers around each eye. Also *Australian* "silver-eye".

white·face (wīt-fayss, hwīt-) *n.* Completely white make-up, as worn by clowns.

white-faced (wīt-fáyst, hwīt-) *adj.* **1.** Pale; pallid. **2.** Having a white patch extending from the muzzle to the forehead.

white feather *n.* A sign of cowardice. [A gamecock with a white feather is regarded as a poor fighter.]

white·fish (wīt-fish, hwīt-) *n., pl.* **-fishes** or collectively **whitefish. 1.** Any of various freshwater food fishes of the genus *Coregonus,* occurring in the Northern Hemisphere and having a generally silvery colour. **2.** Any of various similar or related fishes.

white flag *n.* A white cloth or flag signalling surrender or truce.

white·fly (wīt-flī, hwīt-) *n., pl.* **-flies.** Any of various small whitish insects of the family Aleyrodidae, often injurious to plants.

white-foot·ed mouse (wīt-fŏŏtid, hwīt-) *n.* The **deer mouse** *(see).*

white fox *n.* The **arctic fox** *(see)* in its winter colour phase.

White Friar *n.* A **Carmelite** *(see).* [After the colour of his habit.]

white frost. Hoarfrost *(see).*

white gold *n.* An alloy of gold and nickel or palladium, and sometimes containing small amounts of silver, copper or zinc, having the colour of platinum.

white goods *pl.n.* Electrical household appliances such as refrigerators and washing machines, typically having a white exterior.

white gum *n.* Any of various Australian eucalyptus trees having pale-coloured bark.

White·hall (wīt-háwl, hwīt-, -háwl). The British government; especially, the government departments as distinguished from Parliament. [From *Whitehall,* a street in London where many departments of the government are located.]

White·head (wīt-hed, hwīt-), **A(lfred) N(orth)** (1861–1974). British philosopher and mathematician. One of the founders of mathematical logic, his *Principia Mathematica* (1910–13) was written in collaboration with Bertrand Russell.

white-head·ed (wīt-héddid, hwīt-) *adj.* **1.** Having white hair or plumage on the head. Said of a bird or animal. **2. a.** White-haired, as from old age. **b.** Fair-haired. **3.** *Chiefly Irish.* Favourite; darling: *the white-headed boy.*

white heat *n.* **1. a.** The temperature of a white-hot substance. **b.** The physical condition of a white-hot substance. **2.** A state of intense emotion or excitement.

white hole *n.* A hypothetical astrophysical object formed by the emergence of matter and energy from a space-time singularity through the event horizon.

white hope n. See **great white hope**.

white horehound n. A plant, the **horehound** (see).

white horses pl.n. Waves capped with foam; whitecaps.

white-hot (wĭt-hót, hwĭt-) adj. So hot as to glow with a bright white light; broadly, hotter than red-hot.

White House n. **1.** The official residence of the president of the United States in Washington, D.C. **2.** The supreme executive authority of the U.S. government.

white iron pyrites n. A mineral, **marcasite** (see).

white lead n. **1.** A heavy white poisonous compound of basic lead carbonate, lead silicate, or lead sulphate, used in paint pigments. Also called "ceruse". **2.** A form of putty consisting of white lead in boiled linseed oil.

white leather n. Also **whit·leath·er** (wĭt-lĕthər, hwĭt-). Leather that has been specially treated so as to make it white.

white leg n. A disease, **milk leg** (see).

white lie n. A diplomatic or well-intentioned untruth.

white light n. Light, such as sunlight, that contains the whole spectrum of visible radiation in approximately equal proportions.

white line n. A solid or broken line of white paint marked on a road surface to indicate traffic lanes.

white magic n. Magic used for good purposes or against evil.

white man's burden n. The gratuitously assumed duty of the white peoples to govern and bring white civilisation to the nonwhite peoples of the world. [From "The White Man's Burden" (1899), a poem by Rudyard Kipling.]

white matter n. White brain and spinal-cord tissue, consisting mostly of myelinated nerve fibres. Compare **grey matter**.

white meat n. Light-coloured meat, especially of poultry. Compare **red meat**.

white metal n. Any of various whitish alloys, having relatively low melting points, such as pewter, and containing high percentages of tin, lead or antimony.

white mica n. A mineral, **muscovite** (see).

white mulberry n. A tree, Morus alba, native to China, having whitish or purplish fruit. It leaves provide food for silworms.

white mustard n. A Eurasian plant, Brassica hirta (or Sinapis alba), from whose seeds the condiment mustard is prepared.

whit·en (wĭt'n, hwĭt'n) v. **-ened, -ening, -ens.** —tr. To make white, as by bleaching or the application of whitewash. —intr. To become white. —**whit·en·er** n.

white·ness (wĭt-nəss, hwĭt-, -niss) n. **1.** The condition or quality of being white. **2.** Paleness or pallor. **3.** Moral purity; innocence. **4.** A white substance or area.

white noise n. Acoustical or electrical noise in which the intensity is the same at all frequencies within a given band.

white oak n. A large oak, Quercus alba, of eastern North America, having heavy, hard, light-coloured wood.

white·out (wĭt-owt, hwĭt-) n. **1.** A polar weather condition caused by a heavy cloud cover over the snow, in which the light coming from above is approximately equal to the light reflected from below, and which is characterised by the absence of shadow, the invisibility of the horizon, and the discernibility of only very dark objects. **2.** Australian. **Correction fluid** (see).

white paper n. Often capital **W**, capital **P**. An official statement or report published by a government, providing information on a particular issue and presenting the government's own policy.

white pepper n. See **pepper**.

white pine n. **1.** A timber tree, Pinus strobus, of eastern North America, having needles in clusters of five and durable, easily worked wood. **2.** The wood of any of these trees.

white plague n. Informal. Tuberculosis of the lungs.

white pointer n. A white shark.

white poplar n. A tree, Populus alba, native to Eurasia, having leaves with whitish undersides. Also called "abele".

white rat n. A white variety of rat used as a laboratory animal in scientific research.

White Russian adj. Byelorussian (see).

white sapphire n. A pure form of corundum, used as a gem.

white sauce n. A sauce made with butter, flour, and milk, cream, or stock, sometimes used as a basis for other sauces.

White Sea Russian **Be·lo·ye Mo·re**. Gulf of the Barents Sea, northwestern U.S.S.R. Part of the Arctic Ocean, it lies between the Kola and Kanin peninsulas, and has the port of Archangel on its shore. It is linked by canal with the Baltic Sea.

white shark n. A large, whitish, man-eating shark, Carcharodon carcharias. Also called "great white shark", "white pointer".

white slave n. A woman held unwillingly for purposes of prostitution. —**white-slave** adj. —**white slavery** n.

white slaver n. A procurer of white slaves.

white spirit n. A distillate of petroleum, **turpentine** (see).

white squall n. A sudden squall occurring in tropical or subtropical waters, characterised by the absence of a dark cloud and the presence of white-capped waves or broken water.

white supremacy n. The theory that the white race is inherently superior to and therefore entitled to rule over all other races. —**white supremacist** n.

white·thorn (wĭt-thorn, hwĭt-) n. The **hawthorn** (see).

white·throat (wĭt-thrōt, hwĭt-) n. Either of two Old World songbirds, Sylvia communis or S. curruca, having brownish plumage and a white throat.

white tie n. **1.** A white bow tie worn as a part of men's formal evening dress. **2.** The most formal type of men's evening dress, which includes a tailcoat. Also called "tails". Compare **black tie**.

white trash n. Southern U.S. A poor white (see) or poor whites as a class. Used derogatorily.

white vitriol n. Chemistry. Zinc sulphate (see).

white-wall tyre (wĭt-wawl, hwĭt-) n. A tyre on a motor vehicle having a white band on the visible side. Also called "whitewall".

white-wash (wĭt-wosh, hwĭt- || -wawsh) n. **1.** A mixture of lime and water, often with whiting, size, or glue added, that is used to whiten walls, concrete, or the like. **2.** An attempt to conceal or gloss over mistakes or failures, especially so as to free those responsible from possible blame. **3.** Informal. A defeat in a game in which the loser scores no points. —tr.v. **whitewashed, -washing, -washes. 1.** To paint or coat with or as if with whitewash. **2.** To gloss over (a mistake, for example). **3.** Informal. To prevent (an opponent) from scoring any points in a game. —**white-wash·er** n.

white water n. Turbulent or frothy water, as in rapids.

white whale n. A small whale, Delphinapterus leucas, white when full-grown, chiefly of northern waters. Also called "beluga".

white-wood (wĭt-wŏŏd, hwĭt-) n. The soft, light-coloured wood of any of various trees such as the tulip tree, basswood, or cottonwood. —**white-wood** adj.

whit·ey (wĭt-i, hwĭt-) n., pl. **-eys.** Chiefly U.S. Slang. A white man or white people collectively. Used derogatorily, especially by blacks.

whith·er (with-ər, hwith-) adv. **1.** To what place, result, or condition: Whither are we wandering? **2.** To which: the shores whither the storm tossed them. —conj. **1.** To whatever place, result, or condition: "whither thou goest, I will go" (Ruth 1:16). **2.** To the place in or to which. [Middle English whider, whither, Old English hwider.]

whith·er·so·ev·er (with-ər-sō-évvər, hwith-) conj. To whatever place; to any place whatsoever.

whit·ing¹ (wĭt-ing, hwĭt-) n. A pure white grade of chalk that has been ground and washed for use in paints, ink, and putty. [Middle English whityng, from whiten, to white, from WHITE.]

whiting² n. **1.** A food fish, Gadus merlangus, of European Atlantic waters, related to the cod. **2.** Any of various Australian marine food fishes of the genus Sillago. **3.** Any of several marine fishes of the genera Menticirrhus and Merluccius, of North American coastal waters. [Middle English whitynge, from Middle Dutch wijting : apparently WHIT(E) + -ING (one having the quality of).]

whit·ish (wĭt-ish, hwĭt-) adj. Somewhat or almost white.

Whit·lam (wĭt-lăm, hwĭt-) **(Edward) Gough** (1916–). Australian politician. He was prime minister (1972–75).

whitleather. Variant of **white leather**.

whit·low (wĭt-lō, hwĭt-) n. An abscess of the area of a finger or toe around the nail. [Middle English whitflawe, whit(f)lowe : WHITE + flawe, fissure, FLAW.]

Whit·man (wĭt-mən, hwĭt-), **Walt(er)** (1819–92). U.S. poet. His Leaves of Grass (1855), which he later expanded, was written without regard to conventional metre and rhyme, and examines ideas which include freedom and comradeship.

Whit Monday n. The Monday following Whit Sunday.

Whit·sun (wĭts'n, hwĭts'n) adj. Of, pertaining to, or observed on Whit Sunday or at Whitsuntide. —n. Whitsuntide. [Middle English whitsone, short for whitsonday, WHIT SUNDAY.]

Whit Sunday n. Pentecost (see). [Middle English whitsonday, Old English hwīta sunnandæg, "white Sunday" (from a tradition of clothing the newly baptised in white robes on Whitsunday).]

Whit·sun·tide (wĭts'n-tīd, hwĭt-s'n) n. The week beginning with Pentecost, especially the first three days of this week. Also called "Whit".

whit·tle (wĭtt'l, hwĭtt'l) v. **-tled, -tling, -tles.** —tr. **1.** To cut small bits or pare shavings from (a piece of wood). **2.** To fashion or shape in this way. **3.** To reduce, wear down, or destroy gradually as if by whittling with a knife. Usually used with down, away, or off: He whittled down his expenses by 60 pounds. —intr. To whittle wood with a knife. [Middle English whyttel, knife, variant of thwitel, from thwiten, to whittle down, Old English thwītan.] —**whit·tler** n.

Whit·tle (wĭtt'l, hwĭtt'l), **Sir Frank** (1907–). British aeronautical inventor. While in the R.A.F. he designed and developed the jet engine for aircraft which first flew in 1941.

whit·tlings (wĭttlingz, hwĭttlingz) pl.n. The chips and shavings from a piece of wood being whittled.

whiz, whizz (wiz, hwiz) v. **whizzed, whizzing, whizzes.** —intr. **1.** To make a whirring, buzzing, or hissing sound, as of something rushing through the air. **2.** Informal. To move or fly at a high speed. —tr. Informal. To move or take rapidly: whizzed him off to hospital. —n., pl. **whizzes. 1.** A whizzing sound or a swift movement producing such a sound. **2.** Slang. One who has remarkable skill in a specified field: a whiz at tennis. [Imitative.]

whiz kid n. Informal. A person who achieves great success, especially in business, at a relatively early age, usually as a result of exceptional talent or acumen. Sometimes used derogatorily.

whizz-bang (wiz-băng, hwiz-) n. A small-calibre high-speed shell used during World War I. It was fired in a flat trajectory and so was heard only an instant before landing and exploding.

who (hŏŏ; weak forms hŏŏ, sometimes ŏŏ, ŏŏ) pron. **1.** What or which person or persons. Used as the nominative case of the interrogative pronoun in direct or indirect questions: Who left? Do you

whortleberry *The erect green stems, pendulous globular flowers, and, in autumn, the blue-black berries of the whortleberry are a familiar sight in hilly districts of Europe. In Britain, the plant is also known as bilberry, blaeberry, and huckleberry.*

PRONUNCIATION KEY

a, trap; aa, father; ai, fair; ar, star; aw, lawn; ay, play; b, bb, stab; rubber; ch, church; ck, ticket; d, dd, dead; ladder; e, dress; ee, bee; er, defer; ew, few; ewr, pure; ə, about; ər, letter; f, ff, fife; differ; g, gg, giggle; h, hat; i, kit; ī, price; īr, fire; j, judge; k, kick; l, ll, let; 'l, needle; m, mm, man; n, nn, no; 'n, sudden; ng, thing; o, lot; ō, no; o͝o, foot; o͞o, shoe; oor, poor; ow, cow; owr, hour; oy, boy; p, pp, pepper; r, rr, red; s, ss, sauce; sh, ship; t, tt, totter; th, thick; th, this; smooth; u, cut; ur, turn; v, vv, valve; w, wet; y, yes; z, zz, zebra; zh, vision; pleasure

IN FOREIGN WORDS:

aN, oN, Saint-Saëns; hl, Llanelli; Hluhluwe; kh, loch; lough; Khaled

STRESS MARK: ʹ

ín-sīt, insight; in-sít, incite

know who won? **2.** That. Used as a relative pronoun when the antecedent is human **a.** In a clause that defines or restricts the antecedent: *The boy who came yesterday.* **b.** In a clause that provides additional information about the antecedent: *My brother, who is a doctor, advised me to diet.* **3.** And he, she, or they in turn. Used as a relative pronoun: *I got the story from Iain, who had heard it from his friend Terry.* **4.** *Archaic.* Any person or persons that; whoever: *Who dares, wins.* [Who, whose, whom; Middle English *who* or *qwa, whoos, whom(e),* Old English *hwā̆, hwæs, hwǣm.*]

Usage: *Who* (and *whoever*) are the appropriate forms to use when the pronoun is subject of a clause, or follows the verb *to be* (*Who arrived?, That is the man who arrived*). *Whom* (and *whomever*) are the recommended forms when the pronoun is object of a verb or governed by a preposition *(That is the man whom I saw, To whom did you speak).* However, constructions with *whom* are generally felt to be formal, or appropriate to writing, and they are often avoided in general conversation *(Who did you speak to?),* though *whom* has to be used when governed by a preposition. Confusion sometimes occurs when the relative clause contains a parenthetic verb phrase, as in *He saw a man who he says was at the party*: *who* is appropriate to this construction, according to the above rules, because it is the subject of the verb *was,* the *he says* being parenthetic, but many people, doubtless aware of the strict grammatical rule concerning the use of *whom,* and sensing the use of a subject pronoun immediately following, in this example, opt mistakenly for the use of the object form *(He saw a man whom he says . . .).*

WHO World Health Organisation.

whoa (wō || hō, hwō) *interj.* Used in commanding a horse to stop. [Middle English *whoo,* variant of HO (halt).]

who·dun·it, who·dun·nit (ho͞o-dúnnit) *n. Informal.* A mystery story, typically one based on a search for the perpetrator of a crime, usually a murder. [WHO + DONE + IT.]

who·ev·er (ho͞o-évvər) *pron.* **1.** Anyone that; any person who. **2.** No matter who; regardless of which person or persons: *The culprit will be punished, whoever he is.* **3.** What person ever; who. Used as an intensive: *Whoever told you that?* —See Usage note at **who.**

whole (hōl) *adj.* **1.** Containing all the appropriate component parts; complete: *The archaeologists found a whole 12th-century chess set.* **2.** Not divided or disjoined; in one unit: *bake the apples whole.* **3. a.** Sound; healthy or intact: *a whole organism.* **b.** *Archaic.* Restored; healed. **4.** Constituting the full amount, extent, or duration; entire: *He cried the whole trip home.* **5.** Having the same parents: *a whole sister.* **6.** *Mathematics.* Integral; not fractional.
~adv. Completely; wholly: *gave us a whole new perspective.*
~n. **1.** All of the component parts or elements of a thing. **2.** A complete entity or system. **—as a whole.** Altogether; all things considered. **—on the whole.** Considering everything; in general. [Middle English *hool, (w)holle,* sound, unharmed, Old English *hāl.*]

whole blood *n.* Blood drawn from a living human being for use in transfusion, from which no constituent has been removed.

wholefood (hṓl-fo͞od) *n.* Food that is refined and processed as little as possible from its natural state, such as brown rice. Also used adjectivally *a wholefood shop.*

whole gale *n.* A wind of 24.5 to 28.4 metres per second (55 to 63 miles per hour), force 10 on the Beaufort Wind Scale.

whole-heart·ed (hṓl-ha̍rtid) *adj.* Marked by or undertaken with sincerity, enthusiasm, or complete commitment. See Synonyms at **sincere. —whole-heart·ed·ly** *adv.* **—whole-heart·ed·ness** *n.*

whole hog *n. Slang.* The whole way or the fullest extent. Used chiefly in the phrase *go the whole hog.* [Perhaps referring to buying a whole pig's carcass rather than individual joints.]

whole life insurance *n.* A type of life insurance policy whereby the insured pays premiums throughout his lifetime, and the sum insured is payable on his death, whenever it may be.

whole·meal (hṓl-meel) *adj.* **1.** Made from the entire grain of wheat, including the bran: *wholemeal flour.* **2.** Made with wholemeal flour: *wholemeal bread.*

whole milk *n.* Milk from which no constituent has been removed.

whole·ness (hṓl-nəss, -niss) *n.* The state or quality of being whole.

whole note *n. Music. U.S.* A **semibreve** *(see).*

whole number *n.* **1.** An integer. **2.** A natural number.

whole·sale (hṓl-sayl) *n. Abbr.* **whsle.** The sale of goods in large quantities, as for resale by a retailer.
~adj. **1.** Pertaining to or engaged in the sale of goods in this way. **2.** Sold in large bulk or quantity, usually at a lower cost. **3.** Made or accomplished extensively and indiscriminately; blanket: *the wholesale elimination of life by nuclear weapons.*
~adv. **1.** In large bulk or quantity; on wholesale terms. **2.** Extensively and indiscriminately.
~v. **wholesaled, -saling, -sales.** *—tr.* To sell wholesale. *—intr.* **1.** To engage in wholesale selling. **2.** To be sold wholesale. [From the phrase *by (the) whole sale.*] **—whole·sal·er** *n.*

whole·some (hṓls'm) *adj.* **1.** Conducive to sound health or well-being; salubrious. **2.** Conducive to moral or social well-being; salubrious. **3.** Physically, mentally, or morally sound; healthy. —See Synonyms at **healthy.** [Middle English *holsom,* Old English *hālsum* (unattested).] **—whole·some·ly** *adv.* **—whole·some·ness** *n.*

whole tone *n.* A musical interval equal to two semitones. Also *U.S.* "whole step".

whole·wheat (hṓl-weet, -hweet) *adj.* Wholemeal.

who'll (ho͞ol, ho͝ol, o͞ol, o͝ol). Contraction of *who will* or *who shall.*

whol·ly (hṓli, hṓl-li) *adv.* **1.** Entirely; totally: *wholly irrelevant.* **2.** Exclusively; without reservation or exception: *a life wholly devoted to the cause.*

whom (ho͞om, *occasional weak form* ho͝om) *pron.* The objective case of **who.** See Usage note at **who.**

whom·ev·er (ho͞om-évvər) *pron.* The objective case of **whoever.**

whom·so·ev·er (ho͞om-sō-évvər) *pron. Formal.* The objective case of **whosoever.**

whoop (ho͞op, wo͞op || ho͝op) *n.* **1.** A cry of exultation or excitement. **2.** A hooting cry, as of a bird. **3.** The paroxysmal gasp characteristic of whooping cough.
~v. **whooped, whooping, whoops.** *—intr.* **1.** To utter a loud shout or cry expressing exultation or excitement. **2.** To utter a hooting cry. **3.** To make the paroxysmal gasp characteristic of whooping cough. *—tr.* **1.** To utter with a whoop. **2.** To chase, call, urge on, or drive with a whoop or whoops: *whooping the horses on down the road.* **—whoop it up.** *Slang.* **1.** To have a wild, noisy celebration. **2.** To arouse interest or enthusiasm. [Middle English (imitative).]

whoop·ee (wo͝o-pée, wo͝oppee, wo͞o-, *or with* h-) *interj. Slang.* Used to express excitement and exuberance. **—make whoopee** (wo͞op-pee). To celebrate riotously. [From WHOOP.]

whoop·er (ho͞op-ər, wo͞op-) *n.* **1.** One that whoops. **2.** An Old World swan, *Cygnus cygnus* (or *Olor cygnus*), having a loud cry. Also called "whooper swan".

whoop·ing cough (ho͞op-ing || wo͞op-) *n.* An infectious disease caused by the bacterium *Haemophilus pertussis,* involving catarrh of the respiratory passages and characterised by spasms of coughing interspersed with deep, noisy inspiration. Also called "pertussis".

whooping crane *n.* A large, long-legged North American bird, *Grus americana,* now very rare, having black and white plumage and a shrill, trumpeting cry.

whoops (wo͞ops, hwo͞ops, wo͝ops, hwo͝ops) *interj.* Used to express mild surprise or apology, as in reaction to a fall or mistake.

whoosh (wo͞osh, wo͝osh, hwo͞osh, hwo͝osh) *intr.v.* **whooshed, whooshing, whooshes.** To hurtle or gush with a low hissing sound suggestive of great speed.
~n. A whooshing sound. [Imitative.]

whop (wop, hwop) *tr.v.* **whopped, whopping, whops.** **1.** To beat; thrash. **2.** To defeat utterly.
~n. A heavy blow or thud. [Middle English *whappen,* variant of dialect *wappen*†.]

whop·per (wóppər, hwóppər) *n.* **1.** Something exceptionally big or remarkable. **2.** A gross untruth. [WHOP + -ER.]

whop·ping (wóp-ing, hwóp-) *adj.* Exceptionally big or remarkable.
~adv. Thoroughly; resoundingly: *a whopping great lie.*

whore (hor || hōr) *n.* **1.** A prostitute. **2.** A promiscuous woman. Used derogatorily.
~intr.v. **whored, whoring, whores.** **1.** To have sexual intercourse or consort with whores. **2.** To be or act as a whore. [Middle English *ho(o)re,* Old English *hōre.*]

whore·dom (hór-dəm || hṓr-) *n.* **1.** Fornication or prostitution. **2.** In Biblical use, idolatry. [Middle English *hordom,* from Old Norse *hōrdōmr.*]

whore·house (hór-howss || hṓr-) *n.* A brothel.

whore·mas·ter (hór-maastər || hṓr-, -mastər) *n. Archaic.* One who consorts with whores; a fornicator.

whore·mong·er (hór-mung-gər || hṓr-, -múng-) *n.* A whoremaster.

whore·son (hór-s'n || hṓr-). *n. Archaic.* A bastard. Used derogatorily, sometimes in direct address.
~adj. Archaic. Abominable; bastardly.

whor·ish (hór-ish || hṓr-) *adj.* Characteristic of a whore; lewd. **—whor·ish·ly** *adv.* **—whor·ish·ness** *n.*

whorl (wurl, hwurl || wawrl, hwawrl) *n.* **1.** A small flywheel that regulates the speed of a spinning wheel. **2.** *Botany.* An arrangement of three or more parts, such as leaves or petals, radiating from a single organ or node. **3.** *Zoology.* A single turn or volution of a spiral shell. **4.** One of the three basic patterns by which fingerprints are classified, characterised by ridges forming complete circles. Compare **arch, loop. 5.** *Architecture.* An ornamental device consisting of stylised vine leaves and tendrils. **6.** A coil, curl, or convolution: *whorls of golden hair.* [Middle English *whorle,* perhaps variant of *whirle,* a whirl, from *whirlen,* to WHIRL.]

whorled (wurld, hwurld || wawrld, hwawrld) *adj.* Having, forming or arranged in a whorl or whorls.

whor·tle·ber·ry (wúrt'l-berri, hwúrt'l-, -bəri, -bri) *n., pl.* **-ries.** *Botany.* **1.** A small European shrub, *Vaccinium myrtillus,* having edible blackish berries. **2.** The fruit of this shrub. Also called "bilberry", "huckleberry", "blaeberry". [Dialect variant of Middle English *hurtleberry* : *hurt*†, + BERRY.]

whose (ho͞oz, *for sense 2 occasional weak form* o͞oz) *pron.* **1.** The one belonging to which person or persons. Used as the possessive form of *who* in direct or indirect questions: *Whose is that bike?* **2.** Of or belonging to which person or thing. Used as a relative pronoun: *a law whose provisions are not yet clear.*
~adj. Of or belonging to which person. Used in direct or indirect questions: *Whose bike is that?* [Middle English *whos, whas, hwas,* Old English *hwæs.*]

Usage: *Whose* can refer to both animate and inanimate entities — that is, it relates to nouns which in other circumstances would be referred to as *which.* There is an alternative possessive form, *of which,* but this is usually very cumbersome.

who·so (ho͞o-sō) *pron. Formal.* Who; whoever; whatever person.

who·so·ev·er (ho͞o-sō-évvər) *pron. Formal.* Whoever.

W-hr, whr. *Electricity.* watt-hour.

whsle. wholesale.
why (wī, hwī) *adv.* **1.** For what purpose, reason, or cause; with what intention, justification, or motive: *Why were you absent?.* **2.** On account of which: *the reason why he was so annoyed.*
~*conj.* The reason for which: *That's why I arrived so late; why I mention it is that I thought you'd be interested.*
~*n., pl.* **whys. 1.** The cause or intention underlying a given action or situation. **2.** A difficult problem or question; a mystery.
~*interj.* Used to express indignation, surprise, or impatience. [Middle English *why,* Old English *hwȳ.*]
Usage: In the construction *the reason why,* the repetition of the notion of "reason", which is part of the sense of *why,* often leads to criticism. Critics would prefer using *why* or *the reason* alone.
whyd·ah, whid·ah (wíddə, hwíddə) *n.* Any of several African weaverbirds of the genus *Vidua,* the breeding plumage of the male being predominantly black with long tail feathers. Also called "widow bird". [Variant of WIDOW (BIRD), altered by association with *Whidah* (Ouidah), Dahomey.]
W.I. 1. West Indian; West Indies. **2.** Women's Institute (in Britain).
Wich·i·ta (wíchi-taw) *n., pl.* **-tas** or collectively **Wichita. 1.** A member of a confederacy of Caddoan-speaking North American Indians, formerly living between the Arkansas river and central Texas. **2.** The language of these people.
wick¹ (wik) *n.* **1.** A cord or strand of loosely woven, twisted fibres, as on a candle or oil lamp, that draws up fuel to the flame by capillary action. **2.** Any similar device that conveys liquid by capillary action. **—get on (someone's) wick.** *British Informal.* To annoy intensely. [Middle English *wike,* Old English *wēoce,* akin to Middle Low German *wēke* and Old High German *wiohha*†.]
wick² *n. Obsolete.* A village or town. Now surviving only in place names such as *Warwick.* [Middle English *wik(e),* Old English *wīc,* from West Germanic *wīka* (unattested), from Latin *vīcus.*]
wick·ed (wíckid) *adj.* **-eder, -edest. 1. a.** Evil; depraved; bad; sinful: *wicked habits.* **b.** Vicious; savage: *a wicked murder.* **2.** Mischievous or playfully malicious: *a wicked joke.* **3.** Harmful; pernicious: *a wicked cough.* **4.** Obnoxious; offensive: *a wicked stench.* **5.** *Informal.* Formidable; excellent: *had a wicked, spinning tennis serve.* [Middle English, from *wicke,* wicked, Old English *wicca,* wizard.] **—wick·ed·ly** *adv.* **—wick·ed·ness** *n.*
wick·er (wíckər) *n.* **1.** A flexible shoot, as of a willow, used in weaving baskets or certain articles of furniture. **2.** Wickerwork.
~*adj.* Constructed, consisting of, or covered with wicker. [Middle English *wiker,* from Scandinavian, akin to Swedish *viker.*]
wick·er·work (wíckər-wurk) *n.* **1.** Woven wicker. **2.** Objects or articles made of this.
wick·et (wíckit) *n.* **1.** A small door or gate, especially one built into or near a larger one. **2.** A sluice gate for regulating the amount of water in a millrace or a canal or for emptying a lock **3.** *U.S.* A small window or opening, often fitted with glass or a grating. **4.** In cricket: **a.** Either of the two sets of three stumps, topped by bails, that forms the target of the bowler and is defended by the batsman. **b.** The area between these two sets of stumps, the **pitch** *(see).* **c.** The turn of a batsman or the termination of his innings: *India scored five runs for two wickets.* **d.** The period during which two batsmen are in together. **5.** *U.S.* In croquet, a **hoop** *(see).* **—keep wicket.** To play as a wicketkeeper. **—on a good wicket.** In a favourable situation. **—on a sticky wicket. 1.** On a soft, damp wicket, as in cricket. **2.** In an unfavourable situation. [Middle English, from Old North French *wiket,* from Germanic.]
wick·et·keep·er (wíckit-keepər) *n.* In cricket, the player positioned immediately behind the wicket guarded by the batsman who is facing the bowling.
wick·i·up, wik·i·up (wícki-up) *n.* Also **wik·i·up.** A frame hut covered with matting, bark, brush, or similar materials, used by the nomadic Indians of North America. [Fox *wikiyapi,* "house", from Proto-Algonquian *wikiwahmi* (unattested), WIGWAM.]
Wick·low (wík-lō). Coastal county of Leinster province, Republic of Ireland. Bordering the Irish Sea, it is largely pastureland with the Wicklow mountains at its centre, rising to 926 metres (3,039 feet) at Lugnaquilla. The county town and port is Wicklow.
Wi·dal reaction (vi-dál, vee-) *n.* A test for typhoid fever in which the presence or absence of antibodies against the causative bacteria is determined by agglutination techniques. [After Fernand *Widal* (died 1929), French physician.]
widdershins. Variant of **withershins.**
wide (wīd) *adj.* **wider, widest. 1.** Extending over a relatively large area from side to side; broad. **2.** Having a specified extent from side to side; in width: *a ribbon two inches wide.* **3. a.** Having great range or scope: *a wide selection; wide reading.* **b.** Including or extending to many different things: *a wide observation.* **4.** Full or ample, as clothing might be. **5.** Fully open or extended: *look with wide eyes.* **6.** Located or located away from or missing a given goal or point: *wide of the target.* **7.** Failing to realise or deal with a relevant point or issue: *wide of the mark.* **8.** *Phonetics.* Lax. —See Usage note at **broad.**
~*adv.* **1.** Over a large area; extensively: *journey far and wide.* **2.** To the full extent; completely: *the door was open wide.* **3.** So as to miss the target; astray. **4.** *Sports.* At or towards the sides of a pitch or court: *kept playing the ball wide to stretch the Italian defence.*
~*n.* A ball bowled outside of the batsman's reach in cricket, counting as a run for the batting team. [Middle English *wide,* Old English *wīd.*] **—wide·ly** *adv.* **—wide·ness** *n.*
wide-an·gle lens (wīd-ang-g'l) *n.* A lens that has a relatively short focal length and permits an angle of view wider than about 70°.
wide-a·wake (wīd-ə-wáyk) *adj.* **1.** Completely awake. **2.** Alert; watchful.
~*n.* A soft felt hat with a wide brim.
wide-bodied (wīd-bóddid) *adj.* Also **wide-body** (-bóddi). Designating a jet aircraft having a wide fuselage to accomodate a large number of passengers.
wide boy *n. British Informal.* A man who makes his living by underhand or shady means.
wide-eyed (wīd-īd) *adj.* **1.** With the eyes completely opened, as in wonder. **2.** Innocent; credulous.
wid·en (wīd'n) *v.* **-ened, -ening, -ens.** —*tr.* To make wider. —*intr.* To be or become wide or wider. **—wid·en·er** *n.*
wide-o·pen (wīd-ōpən) *adj.* **1.** Opened completely: *a wide-open door.* **2.** Vulnerable, as to attack: *left himself wide-open.* **3.** With the outcome uncertain: *a wide-open match.* **4.** Without laws or law enforcement: *a wide-open town.*
wide-screen (wīd-skréen) *adj.* Pertaining to or involving a screen whose width is greater than its height.
wide·spread (wīd-spréd, -spred) *adj.* **1.** Spread or scattered over a considerable extent. **2.** Occurring or accepted widely.
widgeon. Variant of **wigeon.**
wid·ow (wíddō) *n.* **1.** A woman whose husband has died and who has not remarried. **2.** In card games, an additional hand dealt to the table. **3.** An incomplete line of type, especially one ending a paragraph, carried over to the top of the next page or column.
~*tr.v.* **widowed, -owing, -ows. 1.** To make a widow of. Used chiefly in the past participle. [Middle English *wid(e)we,* Old English *widuwe.*] **—wid·ow·hood** *n.*
widow bird. The **whydah** *(see).* [From its black plumage.]
wid·ow·er (wíddō-ər) *n.* A man whose wife has died and who has not remarried. [Middle English *widewer,* from *widewe,* WIDOW.]
widow's cruse *n.* An unfailing or inexhaustible supply. [Biblical allusion (I Kings 17:10-16).]
widow's mite *n.* A small but relatively generous contribution made by one who has little. [Biblical allusion (Mark 12:42).]
widow's peak *n.* A hairline having a V-shaped point at the middle of the forehead. Also called "peak". [From the superstition that it is a sign of early widowhood.]
widow's walk *n. U.S.* A railed, rooftop gallery on a dwelling, designed to observe vessels at sea.
width (width, wit-th || with) *n. Abbr.* **w. 1.** The state, quality, or fact of being wide. **2.** The measurement of the extent of something from side to side; the size of something in terms of its wideness. **3.** Something that has a particular width; especially, in sewing, a piece of fabric measured from selvage to selvage: *a skirt having four widths.* **4.** The distance extending parallel with the shortest sides of a rectangular swimming pool. [From WIDE.]
width·wise (width-wīz, wit-th- || with-) *adv.* From side to side; in terms of width.
wield (weeld) *tr.v.* **wielded, wielding, wields. 1.** To handle (a weapon or tool, for example). **2.** To exercise or exert (power or influence). —See Synonyms at **handle.** [Middle English *welden,* Old English *wealdan* and *wieldan.*] **—wield·a·ble** *adj.* **—wield·er** *n.*
wield·y (wéeldi) *adj.* **-ier, -iest.** Easily wielded or managed.
Wien. See **Vienna.**
wie·ner (wéenər) *n.* A wienerwurst. [German, short for WIENERWURST.]
Wie·ner schnit·zel (véenər shníts'l). A breaded veal cutlet. [German, "Vienna cutlet".]
wie·ner·wurst (wéenər-wurst, -woorst, -wŏosht) *n. U.S.* A type of smoked pork or beef sausage, similar to a frankfurter. Also called "wiener". [German, "Vienna sausage".]
wife (wīf) *n., pl.* **wives** (wīvz). *Abbr.* **w. 1.** A woman married to a man. **2.** *Archaic.* A woman, especially one of peasant stock. Now used chiefly in certain phrases: *old wives' tales.* **—take to wife.** *Archaic.* To marry. [Middle English *wif(e),* Old English *wīf,* from Germanic *wīf* (unattested), woman.] **—wife·hood, wife·dom** *n.* **—wife·less** *adj.* **—wife·ly** *adj.*
wife-swapping (wīf-swopping) *n.* The act or practice of couples exchanging their wives or partners, usually for a night or short period of time, for sexual activity.
wig (wig) *n.* A headpiece of artificial or human hair worn as personal adornment, part of a costume, or to conceal baldness.
~*tr.v.* **wigged, wigging, wigs.** *British Informal.* To scold or censure. [Shortened from PERIWIG.] **—wigged** *adj.* **—wig·less** *adj.*
wig·an (wíggən) *n.* A stiff fabric used for stiffening. [First made in *Wigan,* northwest England.]
wi·geon, wid·geon (wíjən) *n. pl.* **-eons** or collectively **wigeon.** Any of various ducks, such as the Eurasian species *Anas penelope* such as having a brown and whitish plumage.
wig·ger·y (wíggəri) *n., pl.* **-ies. 1.** A wig or wigs collectively. **2.** The practice of wearing wigs.
wig·ging (wígging) *n. British Informal.* A telling off or scolding. [19th century : slang use of WIG (false hair).]
wig·gle (wígg'l) *v.* **-gled, -gling, -gles.** —*intr.* To move, twist, or proceed with short irregular movements from side to side or up and down. —*tr.* To cause to move in such a fashion: *wiggle one's toes.*
~*n.* The act of wiggling; a wiggling movement or course. **—get a wiggle on.** *U.S. Slang.* To hurry or hurry up. [Middle English *wiglen,* from Middle Dutch or Middle Low German *wiggelen.*] **—wig·gler** *n.* **—wig·gly** *adj.*

whydah *Like the cuckoo, some species of whydah use foster parents to rear their young. The female lays its eggs in the nest of the waxbill – then leaves the waxbill to hatch and feed the nestlings. Whydahs are native to the grasslands of Africa and feed on seeds and insects.*

wigeon *Flocks of wigeons make their homes along estuaries and mudflats in North America and Europe. They are sometimes mistaken for geese because they graze on grass.*

wight[1] (wīt) *n. Archaic.* A human being; a person. [Middle English *wight,* Old English *wiht.*]

wight[2] *adj. Archaic.* Courageous; brave. [Middle English *wiht,* from Old Norse *vīgt,* neuter of *vīgr,* able in battle.]

Wight (wīt), **Isle of.** County and island off the south of England. Separated from the mainland by the Solent and Spithead channels, it is a chiefly agricultural area.

Wig·ner (wíg-nər), **Eugene Paul** (1902–). U.S. physicist. Born in Hungary, he worked on the first atomic reactor, as well as on the atomic bomb. He shared the Nobel prize for physics (1963).

Wig·town (wíg-town). Former county of southwest Scotland. Merged (1975) with Dumfries and Galloway, it includes the Rhinns of Galloway double peninsula and the port of Stranraer.

wig·wag (wíg-wag) *v.* **-wagged, -wagging, -wags.** —*tr.* **1.** To move (a flag, for example) back and forth, especially as a means of signalling. **2.** To signal (a message) by such motions. —*intr.* **1.** To move back and forth; to wag. **2.** To signal by waving the hand or a device, such as a flag.
~*n.* **1.** The act or practice of giving signals by wigwagging. **2.** A message so relayed. [Dialectal *wig,* perhaps from WIGGLE + WAG.] **—wig·wag·ger** *n.*

wig·wam (wíg-wam || *chiefly U.S.* -wom) *n.* **1. a.** A North American Indian dwelling, commonly having an arched or domed framework overlaid with bark, hides, or mats. Compare **tepee. b.** Loosely, any tent used by North American Indians. **2.** A play tent used by children. [Eastern Abnaki *wikəwam,* from Proto-Algonquian *wikiwahmi* (unattested), perhaps from root *wik-* (unattested), to dwell.]

wikiup. Variant of **wickiup.**

Wil·ber·force (wílbər-fawrss || -fōrss), **William** (1759–1833). British politician and social reformer. He served as an M.P. (1780–1825) and campaigned for the abolition of the slave trade, achieved in 1807, and for the abolition of slavery, achieved in 1833.

wil·co (wílkō) *interj.* Used, especially in radio communications, to indicate that one will carry out an instruction. [Abbreviation of *I will comply.*]

wild boar *The ancestor of the domestic pig, the wild boar was hunted in England in medieval times but it is now found only in mainland Europe, northern Africa, and southern Asia. It can run at speeds of up to 50 kilometres per hour (30 miles per hour) and is ferocious if cornered.*

wild (wīld) *adj.* **wilder, wildest. 1.** Occurring, growing, or living in a natural state; not domesticated, cultivated, or tamed: *wild strawberries.* **2.** Not inhabited; desolate: *wild country.* **3.** Uncivilised or barbarous; savage: *wild natives.* **4. a.** Lacking discipline, restraint, or control; unruly. **b.** Excessive in noise and behaviour; lively and loud: *a wild party; the conference became wild.* **5.** Disorderly; disarranged: *Her hair was wild.* **6.** Boisterous; ungoverned; frenzied: *wild laughter.* **7.** Full of intense, irrepressible emotion: *wild with jealousy.* **8. a.** *Chiefly U.S.* Eccentric; notoriously odd or amusing: *a wild character.* **b.** Extravagant; fantastic: *a wild idea.* **9.** Furiously disturbed or turbulent; tempestuous: *a wild night at sea.* **10.** Reckless; risky: *a wild gamble.* **11.** Random or spontaneous; whimsical: *make a wild guess.* **12.** Deviating widely; erratic: *a wild shot.* **13.** In card games, having an arbitrary equivalence or value determined by the holder's needs or choice: *playing poker with jokers wild.* **—wild about.** *Informal.* Attracted to or excited by: *wild about her new boyfriend; not wild about rice pudding.*
~*adv.* In a wild manner. **—run wild.** To live, behave, or grow in an unrestrained manner.
~*n. Often plural.* An uninhabited or uncultivated region: *the wilds of Greenland.* **—the wild.** A natural, unrestrained life or state; nature. [Middle English *wilde,* Old English *wilde.*] **—wild·ly** *adv.* **—wild·ness** *n.*

wild and woolly *adj. Informal.* Marked by or characteristic of the rough, lawless atmosphere of former frontier America.

wild basil *n.* See **basil.**

wild boar *n.* A wild Eurasian pig, *Sus scrofa,* having a grey or black coat and prominent tusks. Also called "boar".

wild carrot *n.* A plant, **Queen Anne's lace** *(see).*

wild·cat (wīld-kat) *n.* **1.** A Eurasian wild cat, *Felis sylvestris,* with a thick coat and a bushy tail. **2.** Any of various wild felines of small to medium size; especially, one of the genus *Lynx.* **3.** A quick-tempered or fierce person, especially a woman. **4.** An oil well drilled in an area not known to yield oil.
~*adj.* **1.** Risky or unsound, especially financially. **2.** Accomplished or operating without official sanction or authority.
~*v.* **wildcatted, -catting, -cats.** —*tr.* To prospect for (oil, for example) in an area not known to be productive. —*intr.* To wildcat in an area not known to be productive. **—wild·cat·ter** *n.*

wildcat strike *n.* A strike not authorised by the appropriate union.

wild celery *n.* An aromatic plant, *Apium graveolens,* that is the ancestor of cultivated celery.

wild cherry *n.* A Eurasian cherry tree, *Prunus avium,* having white flowers and red round fruits. It is the ancestor of the cultivated sweet cherry. Also called "gean".

wild dog *n.* The **dingo** *(see).*

Wilde (wīld), **Oscar, (Fingal O'Flahertie Wills)** (1854–1900). Irish-born dramatist, poet, and humorist. Renowned as a wit in London literary circles, he achieved recognition with the novel *The Picture of Dorian Grey* (1891); other works include *Poems* (1881) and the plays *Lady Windermere's Fan* (1892) and *The Importance of Being Earnest* (1895). Convicted and sentenced (1895) to two years' imprisonment for a homosexual relationship with Lord Alfred Douglas (1870–1945), on his release he went into exile in France, where he wrote his most famous poem, *The Ballad of Reading Gaol* (1898).

wil·de·beest (wíl-di-beest, víl-, -də-) *n., pl.* **-beests** or collectively **wilde beest.** A mammal, the **gnu** *(see).* [Obsolete Afrikaans : Dutch *wild,* wild, from Middle Dutch *wilt, wilde* + *beest,* beast, from Middle Dutch *beeste,* from Old French *beste,* BEAST.]

wil·der (wíldər) *v.* **-dered, -dering, -ders.** *Archaic.* —*tr.* **1.** To lead astray; mislead. **2.** To bewilder; confuse; perplex. —*intr.* **1.** To lose one's way. **2.** To become bewildered. [Perhaps a back-formation from WILDERNESS.] **—wil·der·ment** *n.*

Wil·der (wīldər), **Billy (Samuel)** (1906–). Austrian-born U.S. film director. His films include *Double Indemnity* (1944), *Some Like It Hot* (1959) and *Fedora* (1978).

Wilder, Thornton (Niven) (1897–1975). U.S. playwright and novelist. His work includes the novel the *Bridge of San Luis Rey* (1927) and the plays *Our Town* (1938) and *The Skin of Our Teeth* (1942).

wil·der·ness (wíldər-nəss, -niss) *n.* **1.** Any unsettled, uncultivated region left in its natural condition, especially: **a.** A large wild tract of land covered with dense vegetation or forests. **b.** An extensive area that is barren or empty, such as a desert or ocean; a waste. **c.** A piece of land set aside to grow wild. **2.** Something likened to a wild region in bewildering vastness, confusion, or unchecked profusion: *a wilderness of industrial estates.* **3.** A period of being removed from a usually specified activity: *has come out of the political wilderness.* [Middle English *wildernesse,* Old English *wildēornes,* from *wildēor,* wild beast.]

wild-eyed (wīld-īd) *adj.* Glaring in or as if in anger, terror, stupor, or madness.

wild·fire (wīld-fīr) *n.* **1.** A highly flammable material formerly used in warfare. **2.** A raging fire that travels and spreads rapidly. **3.** Lightning occurring without thunder being heard. **4.** A luminosity that appears at night hovering over marshland; ignis fatuus.

wild flower *n.* **1.** A flowering plant that grows in a natural, uncultivated state. **2.** The flower of such a plant.

wild·fowl (wīld-fowl) *n., pl.* **-fowls** or collectively **wildfowl.** A wild bird, such as a duck, goose, or quail, hunted as game.
~*intr.v.* **wildfowled, -fowling, -fowls.** To hunt wildfowl. **—wild·fowl·er** *n.*

wild ginger *n.* A North American plant, *Asarum canadense,* having broad leaves, a single brownish flower, and an aromatic root.

wild-goose chase (wīld-gōōss). A hopeless or foolish pursuit of an unattainable or imaginary object. [Originally a race similar to the flight of geese, where the object was to follow accurately and at a definite interval.]

wild hyacinth *n.* Any of various wildflowers superficially resembling a hyacinth, such as the bluebell.

wild·ing (wīlding) *n.* **1.** A plant that grows wild or has escaped from cultivation; especially, a wild apple tree or its fruit. **2.** A wild animal. [From WILD.]

wild·life (wīld-līf) *n.* Wild animals and vegetation; especially, animals living in a natural, undomesticated state.

wild·ling (wīldling) *n.* A wild plant or animal; especially, a wild plant transplanted to a cultivated spot.

wild marjoram *n.* See **marjoram.**

wild mustard *n.* **Charlock** *(see).*

wild oat *n.* **1.** *Usually plural.* A grass, *Avena fatua,* native to Eurasia, related to the cultivated oat. **2.** *Plural.* The indiscretions of youth, especially sexually promiscuous behaviour. Used in the phrase *sow one's wild oats.*

wild olive *n.* Any of various trees resembling the olive; especially, the **oleaster** *(see).*

wild pansy *n.* Any of several pansy-like plants of the genus *Viola.*

wild rice *n.* **1.** A tall aquatic grass, *Zizania aquatica,* of northern North America, bearing edible grain. **2.** The grain of this plant.

wild rose *n.* Any of various uncultivated roses, having a single whorl of petals and including the dogrose.

wild rubber *n.* Rubber extracted from uncultivated rubber trees.

wild rye *n.* Any of various grasses of the genus *Elymus,* resembling cultivated rye in having bristly spikes.

wild type *n.* The typical form of an organism as it occurs in nature, as distinguished from mutant specimens that may result from selective breeding.

Wild West *n.* The western United States during the period of its settlement, especially with reference to its lawlessness.

wild·wood (wīld-wŏŏd) *n.* A forest or wooded area in its natural state.

wile[1] (wīl) *n.* **1.** *Usually plural.* **a.** A deceitful stratagem or trick. **b.** A disarming or seductive manner, device, or procedure. **2.** Trickery; cunning; deceit. —See Synonyms at **artifice.**
~*tr.v.* **wiled, wiling, wiles.** To influence or lead by means of wiles; entice; lure. [Middle English *wil,* perhaps from Old Norse *wihl-* (unattested).]

wile[2]. Variant of **while** (verb).

wil·ful, *U.S.* **will·ful** (wíl-f'l). **1.** Said or done in accordance with one's will; intended; deliberate. **2.** Inclined to impose one's will; obstinate; headstrong. —See Synonyms at **contrary, voluntary, unruly. —wil·fuly** *adv.* **—wil·full·ness** *n.*

Wilkes (wilks), **John** (1727–97). British politician and journalist. He worked for parliamentary reform, American independence, and religious toleration.

Wil·kins (wílkinz), **Maurice Hugh Frederick** (1916–). British biophysicist. Born in New Zealand, he worked, during World War II, on the atomic bomb in California. He shared the Nobel prize with Crick and Watson (1962) for work on the structure of DNA.

will[1] (wil) *n.* **1.** The mental faculty by which one deliberately chooses or decides upon a course of action. **2.** A disposition to exercise this faculty; determination: *a will to win.* **3.** That which is desired or decided upon, especially by a person in authority. **4.** Deliberate intention or wish: *against his will.* **5.** Free discretion; pleasure; inclination: *wandered about at will.* **6.** Bearing or attitude towards others; disposition: *full of good will.* **7.** The power to exert control over conflicting mental and emotional tendencies and arrive at one's own decision: *He's got enough will to resist temptation.* **8. a.** A legal declaration of how a person wishes his possessions to be disposed of after his death. **b.** The document containing this declaration. **—a will of (one's) own.** A tendency to behave in an erratic or unpredictable way. Used humorously. **—with a will.** With eagerness and energy.

~*v.* **willed, willing, wills.** *—tr.* **1.** To decide upon; choose: *Tell me what you have willed.* **2.** To desire; yearn for: *will one's own destruction.* **3.** To decree; dictate; order: *The queen willed that he should be exiled.* **4.** To resolve with a forceful will; determine: *God willed that we would question our existence.* **5.** To influence or induce by sheer force of will or by supernatural power: *We tried to will the sun to come out.* **6.** To bequeath; grant in a legal will. *—intr.* **1.** To exercise the will; use the power of the will. **2.** To decree or make a firm choice. [Middle English *will(e),* Old English *will, willa.*] **—will·a·ble** *adj.*

will² (wil; *weak forms* L, 'l, wəl) *v.* past **would** (wōōd; *weak forms* d, əd, wəd) also *archaic* **wouldest** (wōōddist) or **wouldst** (wōōdst) for second person singular, present **will** (also *archaic* **wilt** (wilt) for second person singular). Used as an auxiliary followed by an infinitive without *to* or, in reply to a question or suggestion, with the infinitive understood. It can indicate: **1.** Simple futurity: *They will appear later.* **2. a.** Likelihood or certainty: *You will regret this.* **b.** Inevitability: *Everyone will die.* **3.** Willingness: *Will you help me with this package?* **4.** Requirement or command: *You will report to me afterwards.* **5.** Customary or habitual action: *She would spend hours in the library.* **6.** Capacity or ability: *This metal will not crack under heavy pressure.* **7.** Probability or expectation: *That will be the postman ringing.* **8.** Determination; resolution: *I will do it if I have to burst a blood vessel!* —See Usage note at **shall.** *—intr.* To have a desire: *Sit here, if you will.* *—tr.* To desire; wish: *Do what you will.* [Will, would, wouldest; Middle English *willen, wolde, woldest,* Old English *wyllan, wolde, woldest.*]

willed (wild) *adj.* Having a will of a specified kind. Usually used in combination: *weak-willed.*

wil·lem·ite (wíllə-mīt) *n.* A vitreous to resinous silicate of zinc, Zn_2SiO_4, a minor ore of zinc. [Dutch *willemit,* from *Willem,* William, after *William* I (died 1843), king of the Netherlands.]

wil·let (wíllit) *n.* A long-billed American shore bird, *Catoptrophorus semipalmatus.* [Imitative of its cry.]

Wil·liam I¹ (wíl-yəm), known as William the Conqueror (*c.*1027–87). The first Norman king of England (1066–87) and Duke of Normandy (1035–87). He invaded England (1066) on the grounds that succession to the English throne had been promised to him by his cousin Edward the Confessor. He defeated Harold at Hastings and as king adopted a feudal constitution.

William I², Known as William the Silent (1533–84). Prince of Orange. Inheriting the principality in 1544, he was made governor of Holland, Zeeland, and Utrecht (1559) by Philip II of Spain, whom he opposed for his persecution of Protestants. He led the revolt against Spanish rule (1568) but succeeded only briefly in unifying the Protestant north with the Catholic south.

William II¹ (1859–1941). German emperor (1888–1918). The grandson of Queen Victoria, he pursued aggressive policies, supporting the Afrikaners in South Africa, and Austria's demands on Serbia (1914) although when war became apparent, he strove for peace. He was forced to abdicate after Germany's defeat in World War I.

William II², known as William Rufus (*c.* 1056–1100). King of England (1087–1100). He was the second son of William the Conqueror, on whose death he succeeded to the throne.

William III, known as William of Orange (1650–1702). King of England (1689–1702). Married to Mary, daughter of James II (1677), he was asked by the opposition to James to invade England, and landed at Torbay (1688). He was proclaimed joint monarch with Mary (1689) after James fled, and defeated him at the Boyne (1690).

William IV (1765–1837). King of Great Britain and Ireland (1830–37). The third son of George III and brother of George IV, he was known as the sailor king because of his naval career, rising to the office of Lord High Admiral (1827–28). He left no surviving legitimate children and was succeeded by his niece Victoria.

Williams, Shirley (Vivien Teresa Brittain) (1930–). British politician. She held office in two Labour governments (1974–79), but became a founder of the Social Democratic Party (1981) and was re-elected as an M.P. for that party in 1982.

Williams, Tennessee, born Thomas Lanier Williams (1911–83). U.S. playwright. His works examine family tensions and feelings of frustration, particularly in women. Frequently set in the Deep South, his plays include *The Glass Menagerie* (1944), *A Streetcar Named Desire* (1947), and *Cat on a Hot Tin Roof* (1955).

Williams, William Carlos (1883–1963). U.S. imagist poet. It was not until the 1940s that he established his reputation with the work in 5 volumes, *Paterson* (1946–58). His poetry is noted for its clarity, naturalism, and concern with American themes.

Williamson, Malcolm (Benjamin Graham Christopher) (1931–). Australian composer, a British resident since 1953. His works include symphonies, the opera *Our Man in Havana* (1963), and the *Mass of Christ the King* (1977). A pianist and organist, he was appointed Master of the Queen's Music (1975).

William Tell. See **Tell, William.**

William the Lion (1143–1214). King of Scotland (1165–1214). The brother of Malcolm IV and grandson of David I, he invaded Northumberland and was captured and taken to France. He was forced to perform homage for his kingdom as the price of freedom, but in 1189 Richard I of England abandoned all claims on payment of 10,000 marks.

wil·lies (wílliz) *pl.n. Slang.* Feelings of uneasiness. Preceded by *the*: *This place gives me the willies.* [19th century : origin obscure.]

will·ing (wílling) *adj.* **1.** Disposed to accept or tolerate; prepared: *willing to overlook your mistakes.* **2.** Acting or ready to act gladly; eagerly compliant: *very willing to help; willing helpers.* **3.** Done, given, accepted, or offered freely and heartily. —See Synonyms at **voluntary. —will·ing·ly** *adv.* **—will·ing·ness** *n.*

will-o'-the-wisp (wíl-əthə-wísp, -əth-) *n.* **1. Ignis fatuus** *(see).* **2.** One that is alluring, delusive, or misleading. [Originally *Will with the wisp,* from *Will,* pet form of *William* + WISP, in obsolete sense handful of hay (used as torch).]

wil·low (wíllō) *n.* **1.** Any of various deciduous trees or shrubs of the genus *Salix,* having usually narrow leaves, flowers borne in catkins, and strong, lightweight wood. **2.** The wood of any of these trees. **3.** Something made from willow, especially a cricket bat. **4.** A textile machine consisting of a spiked drum revolving inside a chamber fitted internally with spikes, used to open and clean unprocessed cotton or wool.

~*tr.v.* **willowed, -lowing, -lows.** To open and clean (textile fibres) with a willow. [Middle English *wilowe,* Old English *welig.*]

wil·low·herb (wíllō-herb) *n.* Any of various plants of the genus *Epilobium,* such as *E. angustifolium,* rosebay willowherb, having narrow leaves and terminal clusters of pink, purplish, or white flowers.

willow pattern *n.* A traditional, Chinese-style, blue-on-white design typically consisting of a willow tree, bridge, river, and figures, used on household china.

Willow South (wíllō). City near Anchorage in Alaska, that is scheduled to be the new state capital to replace Juneau.

willow warbler *n.* A Eurasian warbler, *Phylloscopus trochilis,* having a yellowish-brown plumage with pale underparts.

wil·low·y (wíllō-i) *adj.* **-ier, -iest. 1.** Planted with or abounding in willows. **2.** Resembling or suggestive of a willow tree, especially: **a.** Flexible; pliant. **b.** Slender and graceful.

will·pow·er (wíl-pow-ər, -powr) *n.* The ability to exercise control over one's actions and bring them into line with one's decisions or wishes; strength of mind and purpose.

wil·ly (wílli) *n., pl.* **-lies.** *Chiefly British Informal.* A penis. [From *willy,* pet form of *William.*]

wil·ly-nil·ly (wílli-nílli) *adv.* Whether desired or not.

~*adj.* Being or occurring whether desired or not. [Variant of *will I nill I,* "be I willing, be I unwilling".]

Wil·ming·ton (wílmingtən). Capital of Delaware, eastern United States. Situated on the Delaware river, it was founded by Swedes in 1638 and is an important port with extensive shipyards.

Wil·son (wíl-s'n), **Sir Angus (Frank Johnstone)** (1913–). British novelist and short-story writer. His satirical works include *Anglo-Saxon Attitudes* (1956), *The Old Men at the Zoo* (1961), *As If by Magic* (1973), and *Setting the World on Fire* (1980).

Wilson, Charles Thomson Rees (1869–1959). British physicist. He invented the Wilson cloud chamber, which permitted the observation and photography of the movement of charged particles (1911). He won the Nobel prize in physics (1927).

Wilson, Colin (Henry) (1931–). British author. His works cover a wide spectrum, including thrillers such as *Necessary Doubt* (1964), and studies of the paranormal, such as *The Occult* (1971).

Wilson, Edmund (1895–1972). U.S. author and critic. His works include *Axel's Castle* (1931), a study of the symbolists, *To The Finland Station* (1940), *The Scrolls from the Dead Sea* (1955), and *The American Earthquake* (1958).

Wilson, Sir (James) Harold (1916–). British Labour prime minister (1964–70; 1974–76). He succeeded Hugh Gaitskell as party leader (1963) and became prime minister with the Labour victory of 1964 and faced many problems which included those of Rhodesia and Northern Ireland, and resistance amongst his supporters to the introduction of a prices and incomes policy. He resigned without warning in 1976.

Wilson, (Thomas) Woodrow. (1856–1924). Twenty-eighth President of the United States (1913–21). His presidency saw the introduction of prohibition and resistance to U.S. involvement in World War I, although he reversed the latter policy after the German U-boat campaign (1917). He laid the basis for a peace settlement and at the Paris Peace Conference achieved the acceptance of the League of Nations in the Treaty of Versailles (1919). He was awarded the Nobel peace prize (1919), but the treaty was rejected by the U.S. Senate, and he suffered a physical breakdown.

Wilson cloud chamber (wíl-sən). See **cloud chamber.** [After C.T.R. WILSON.]

Wilson's disease *n.* A hereditary disorder of copper metabolism in which excess copper is deposited in tissues and organs, such as the liver (causing jaundice and cirrhosis) and brain (causing mental deterioration). [After S. *Wilson* (1878–1937), British neurologist.]

wilt¹ (wilt) *v.* **wilted, wilting, wilts.** *—intr.* **1.** To become limp or flaccid; droop: *Plants wilted in the heat.* **2.** To become less active, energetic, or spirited; weaken. *—tr.* To cause to wilt.

PRONUNCIATION KEY

a, **trap**; aa, **father**; ai, **fair**;
ar, **star**; aw, **lawn**; ay, **play**;
b, bb, **stab**; **rubber**;
ch, **church**; ck, **ticket**;
d, dd, **dead**; **ladder**; e, **dress**;
ee, **bee**; er, **defer**; ew, **few**;
ewr, **pure**; ə, about;
ər, letter; f, ff, **fife**; **differ**;
g, gg, **giggle**; h, **hat**; i, **kit**;
ī, **price**; īr, **fire**; j, **judge**;
k, **kick**; l, ll, let; 'l, **needle**;
m, mm, **man**; n, nn, **no**;
'n, sudden; ng, **thing**; o, **lot**;
ō, **no**; ōō, **foot**; ōō, **shoe**;
oor, **poor**; ow, **cow**;
owr, **hour**; oy, **boy**;
p, pp, **pepper**; r, rr, **red**;
s, ss, **sauce**; sh, **ship**;
t, tt, **totter**; th, **thick**; th, **this**;
smooth; u, **cut**; ur, **turn**;
v, vv, **valve**; w, **wet**; y, **yes**;
z, zz, **zebra**; zh, vision;
pleasure

IN FOREIGN WORDS:

aN, oN, **Saint-Saëns**;
hl, **Llanelli**; **Hluhluwe**;
kh, **loch**; **lough**; **Khaled**

STRESS MARK:

ín-sīt, insight; in-sít, incite

~n. **1.** The act of wilting or the state of being wilted. **2.** Any of various plant diseases characterised by slow or rapid collapse of terminal shoots, branches, or entire plants. [Variant of dialectal *wilk, welk,* from Middle English *welken,* from Middle Dutch.]

wilt². *Archaic.* Second person singular present tense of **will.**

Wil·ton (wílton) *n.* A kind of carpet having a velvety surface formed by the cut loops of a pile. [From *Wilton,* Wiltshire, England.]

Wilts. Wiltshire.

Wilt·shire¹ (wilt-sher, -sheer). County of south central England. With the Marlborough Downs in the north and Salisbury Plain in the south, it is chiefly agricultural with the growing of wheat and barley and the raising of pigs, sheep, and dairy cattle. Large areas of Salisbury Plain are used for military training. The town of Wilton is famous for its carpets. Inhabited since ancient times, the area has prehistoric remains at Stonehenge, Avebury, and Silbury Hill. The county town is Salisbury.

Wilt·shire² *n.* A sheep of a horned breed with very short fleece, reared for meat.

wi·ly (wílí) *adj.* **-lier, -liest.** Full of wiles; guileful; calculating. See Synonyms at **sly.** [WILE + -LY.] **—wil·i·ly** *adv.* **—wil·i·ness** *n.*

wim·ble (wimb'l) *n.* Any of numerous hand tools for the boring of holes, as a brace and bit or a gimlet.

~*tr.v.* **wimbled, -bling, -bles.** To bore with or as if with a wimble. [Middle English, from Anglo-French, perhaps from Middle Dutch *wimmel.*]

Wim·ble·don (wimb'ldən). District in the Greater London Borough of Merton. It is the location of the All-England Lawn Tennis Club, where international championships have been held since 1877.

wimp (wimp) *n.* British *Informal.* One who lacks strength of character or resolution; an insipidly ineffectual person. [Back-formation from W(H)IMPER.]

wim·ple (wimp'l) *n.* **1.** A cloth wound round the head, framing the face, and drawn into folds beneath the chin, worn by women in medieval times and as part of the habit of certain orders of nuns. **2.** *Archaic.* **a.** A fold or pleat in cloth. **b.** A ripple, as on the surface of water. **c.** A curve or bend. **d.** *Scottish.* A cunning twist.

~*v.* **wimpled, -pling, -ples.** —*tr.* **1.** To cover or furnish with a wimple. **2.** *Archaic.* **a.** To cause to form ripples. **b.** To cause to form or lie in folds. —*intr.* **1.** *Archaic.* To form or lie in folds. **2. a.** To ripple. **b.** To meander. [Middle English *wimpel,* Old English *wimpel.*]

Wim·py (wimpi) *n.* A trademark for a type of hamburger.

Wims·hurst machine (wimz-hurst) *n.* An electrostatic generator having mica or glass discs rotating in opposite directions with metal carriers on which charges are produced by induction, used chiefly as a demonstration apparatus. [After James *Wimshurst,* 19th century British engineer.]

win (win) *v.* **won** (wun ‖ won), **winning, wins.** —*intr.* **1.** To achieve victory over others in any kind of contest. **2.** To achieve success in an effort or venture. **3.** To struggle through to a desired place or condition: *We won through; She won home.* **4.** To finish first in a race: *won by a length.* —*tr.* **1.** To achieve victory in: *win a race; win an argument.* **2.** To be the successful party in predicting or guessing (an outcome, such as the result of a bet): *Willis won the toss for England.* **3.** To receive or gain through victory in a contest: *won the World Cup; won the seat from Labour at the last election.* **4.** To receive as a reward for performance: *won a medal in the Falklands conflict.* **5.** To achieve through effort or merit: *win an advantage; won recognition.* **6.** To take in battle; capture. **7.** To succeed in gaining the favour or support of; prevail upon. Sometimes used with *over* or *round: His eloquence won us over.* **8. a.** To gain the affection or loyalty of: *won a friend for life.* **b.** To appeal successfully to (someone's loyalty, sympathy, or other emotion). **c.** To persuade (a person) to marry one. **9.** In mining: **a.** To discover and open (a vein or deposit); render fit for mining. **b.** To extract from a mine. **10.** *Archaic.* To reach with effort or difficulty: *The ship won a safe port.* **—win out.** *Informal.* To succeed or prevail.

~*n.* **1.** A victory or success, especially in a competition. **2.** An amount won or earned: *a pools win.* [Win, won, won; Middle English *winnen,* to win, strive, Old English *winnan,* to strive.]

wince¹ (winss) *intr.v.* **winced, wincing, winces.** To shrink or start involuntarily, as in pain or distress; flinch.

~*n.* A wincing movement or gesture. [Middle English *wincen,* to kick, wince, from Anglo-French *wencir* (unattested), from Germanic.] **—winc·er** *n.*

wince² *n.* A roller on which cloth may be moved and lowered into a vat of dye. [Variant of WINCH.]

win·cey·ette (win-si-ét) *n.* A fairly light cotton fabric with a soft nap, used especially in making nightclothes.

winch (winch) *n.* **1.** A stationary motor-driven or hand-powered hoisting machine having a drum round which a rope or chain winds as the load is lifted. **2.** The crank used to give motion to a grindstone or similar device.

~*tr.v.* **winched, winching, winches.** To hoist or move with or as if with a winch. [Middle English *winche,* a pulley, Old English *wince.*] **—winch·er** *n.*

Win·ches·ter¹ (win-chistər ‖ -chestər). County town of Hampshire, southern England. Situated on the river Itchen, it was once the capital of Wessex and after the Norman Conquest and the rise of London, remained England's chief seat of learning. Its Norman cathedral, built on a Saxon church, is the longest in Britain and the burial place of many Saxon monarchs.

Winchester² *n.* A trademark for a breechloading repeating rifle with lever action and a magazine attached horizontally under the barrel. [After Oliver *Winchester* (1810–80), U.S. manufacturer.]

wind¹ (wind) *n.* **1.** A current of air moving at any speed; especially, a natural and perceptible movement of air parallel to or along the ground. **2. a.** A movement or current of air blowing from one of the four cardinal points of the compass: *the four winds.* **b.** The direction from which a strong or prevailing current of air comes: *The wind is northeast.* **3.** Moving air carrying an odour, scent, or sound. **4.** A current or stream of air generated by a fan, bellows, or other artificial means. **5. a.** A wind instrument, such as a flute or clarinet. **b.** The section of an orchestra or band that plays these instruments. **6.** Gas produced in the body during digestion; flatulence. **7.** Respiration; breath; especially, normal or adequate breathing. **8.** A pervasive or irresistible force or influence: *a wind of change.*

WHY THE WIND BLOWS

Air temperature differences cause winds and breezes

The world's winds are caused by unequal air temperatures in different parts of the globe. Air heated by the sun at the equator expands and rises, moving outwards at high levels. As it cools, most of it subsides around 30°N and 30°S – just beyond the tropics. Its weight creates regions of high pressure, which send winds blowing at low levels into the low-pressure areas near the equator. These north-south winds are deflected by the rotation of the Earth, so they blow from the northeast in the Northern Hemisphere and the southeast in the Southern Hemisphere; they are known as the trade winds because they were used by merchant sailing ships. Over the polar regions the cold ground causes the air to sink, and winds blow outwards.

Between the tropical and polar air movements in each hemisphere there is a variable zone where cold polar air meets warm tropical air. This creates cyclonic depressions ("lows"), but the general air movement is deflected eastwards as westerly winds.

If the Earth were a smooth ball covered entirely by either sea or flat land, these air movements would be uniform. It is the presence of large areas of land and sea that interferes with the major air currents. Land heats up and cools down more quickly than the sea, so the continents are hotter than the sea in summer and cooler than the sea in winter. This effect brings the monsoon winds to India and other tropical areas. As the land becomes intensely hot in summer, the air rises, forming a low-pressure area. Cool, moist air sweeps in from the ocean, bringing torrential rain. In winter, the air cools rapidly over the land and moves towards the low-pressure areas over the warmer seas.

This same phenomenon causes daily sea breezes in coastal areas in hot, sunny weather. In the late afternoon, breezes blow shorewards as cooler air from the sea moves in to replace the rising hot air above the land; in the morning, breezes blow seawards as air moves away from the cooler land to the warmer sea.

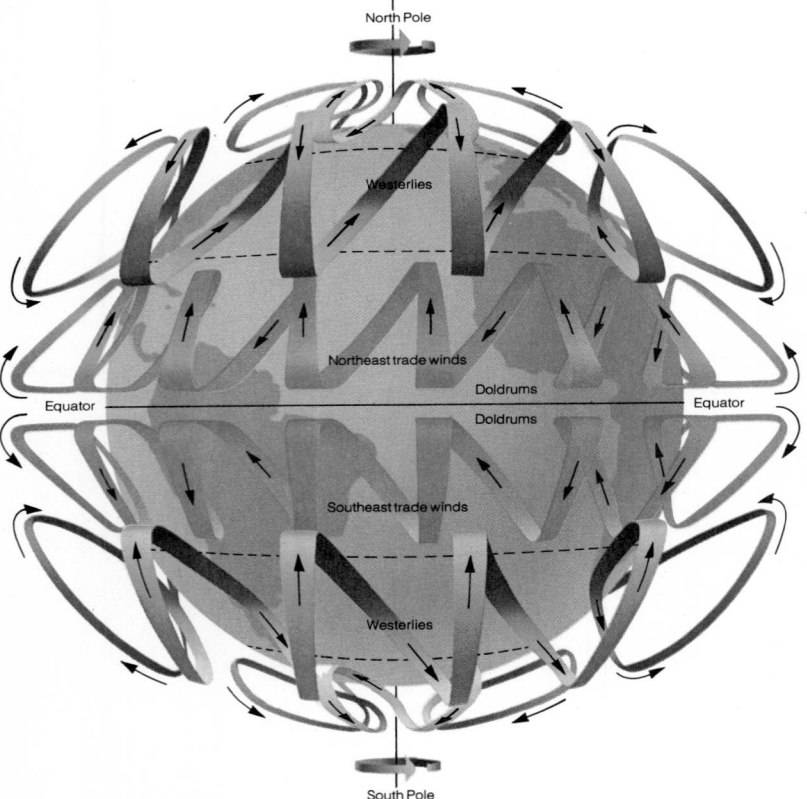

MAJOR WIND PATTERNS *Each hemisphere has three major wind systems – the trade winds, the westerlies, and the polar winds. Along the equator, windless regions known as the doldrums occur, where sailing ships can find themselves becalmed for long periods.*

9. Utterance empty of meaning; verbiage. **—before the wind.** Moving forward with the wind behind. **—between wind and water. 1.** The part of a ship near its waterline exposed to buffeting by waves. **2.** At or in a vulnerable point. **—break wind.** To eject intestinal gas from the anus or mouth. **—get wind of.** *Informal.* To receive a hint or intimation of. **—get the wind up.** *Informal.* To become frightened. **—how the wind blows** or **lies.** What developments arise or what the current trends are. **—in the wind.** Likely to occur; in the offing. **—put the wind up.** *Informal.* To frighten. **—raise the wind.** *Informal.* To obtain the requisite funds. **—sail close to the wind. 1.** To sail or travel as directly against the wind as possible. **2.** To live or manage frugally and economically. **3.** To approach near to the limits of what is acceptable; verge on impropriety, dishonesty, or danger. **—take the wind out of (someone's) sails.** To rob of an advantage; deflate.
~*tr.v.* **winded, winding, winds. 1.** To expose to the free movement of air; ventilate or dry. **2. a.** To catch a scent or trace of. **b.** To pursue by following a scent. **3.** To cause to be out of or short of breath, especially by a blow to the stomach. **4.** To afford a recovery of breath: *winded their horses after a gallop.* [Middle English *wind*, Old English *wind*.]

Synonyms: *wind, breeze, zephyr, blast, gust, gale, whirlwind, tornado, hurricane, typhoon.*
wind² (wīnd) *v.* **wound** (wownd) or *rare* **winded, winding, winds.**
~*tr.* **1.** To wrap (something) round an object or centre once or repeatedly: *wound thread round a reel; wound a scarf round his neck.* **2.** To wrap or encircle in a series of coils; entwine. **3.** To unwind or remove by unwinding. Used with *off.* **4.** To proceed on (one's way) with a curving or twisting course. **5.** To present or introduce in a disguised or devious manner: *He wound a plea for money into his letter.* **6.** To turn (a crank of handle, for example) in a series of circular motions. **7.** To coil the spring of (a clock or other mechanism) by turning a stem, cord, or the like. Often used with *up.* **8.** To lift or haul by means of a windlass or winch. —*intr.* **1.** To move in or as if in a bending or coiling course: *The road winds round up to the monastery.* **2. a.** To move in or have a spiral or circular course. **b.** To be or become coiled or spiralled about something. **3.** To be twisted or warped. Used of a board, for example. **4.** To proceed misleadingly or insidiously in speech or conduct. **5.** To become wound. **—wind down.** To decrease or diminish in activity, energy, intensity, or scope, especially so as to stop gradually: *winds down after work; winding down our South African operations.*
~*n.* **1.** The act of winding. **2.** A single turn, twist, or curve. [Wind, wound, wound; Middle English *winden, wond, wonden,* Old English *windan, wond, wunden.*]
wind³ (wīnd) *tr.v.* **winded** (wīndid) or **wound** (wownd), **winding, winds. 1.** To blow (a wind instrument). **2.** To sound by blowing. [From WIND (air).] **—wind·er** *n.*
wind·age (wīndij) *n.* **1. a.** The effect of wind on the course of a projectile. **b.** The point or degree at which the wind gauge or sight of a rifle or gun must be set to compensate for the effect of the wind. **2.** In ballistics, the difference, in a given firearm, between the diameter of the projectile fired and the diameter of the bore of the firearm. **3.** The disturbance of air caused by the passage of a fast-moving object, such as a railway train or missile. **4.** *Nautical.* The part of the surface of a ship that is left exposed to the wind.
wind·bag (wind-bag) *n. Informal.* A talkative person who communicates nothing of substance or interest.
wind·blast (wind-blaast ‖ -blast) *n.* **1.** A very strong gust of wind. **2.** Injury caused by air friction to the pilot of a high-speed aircraft who has used his ejection seat.
wind·blown (wind-blōn) *adj.* **1.** Blown or dispersed by the wind. **2.** Growing or shaped in a manner governed by the prevailing winds. **3.** Windswept. Said of a woman's hair style.
wind·borne (wind-born ‖ -bōrn) *adj.* Carried by the wind. Said especially of plant seeds and pollen.
wind·bound (wind-bownd) *adj.* Unable to sail because of high or contrary winds. Said of a sailing ship.
wind·break (wind-brayk) *n.* A hedge, row of trees, or fence serving to lessen or break the force of the wind.
wind·bro·ken (wind-brōkən) *adj.* Suffering from the heaves or some other impairment of respiration. Said of a horse.
wind·burn (wind-burn) *n.* Reddening and irritation of the skin caused by prolonged exposure to strong winds. **—wind·burnt** (wind-burnt) *adj.*
wind·cheat·er (wind-cheetər) *n.* A close-fitting jacket, often with elasticated cuffs and waistband, worn especially as protection from the cold and the wind. Also called "windjammer", *U.S.* "windbreaker".
wind-chill factor (wind-chil) *n. Meteorology.* A measure of the cooling power of the air in relation to wind speed and air temperature.
wind cone (wind) *n.* A wind indicator, a **windsock** (see).
wind·er (wīndər) *n.* **1.** A person, thing, or mechanism that winds, especially: **a.** A key or other device for winding up a spring-driven mechanism. **b.** An engine for raising and lowering cages in a mine shaft. **2.** A spool, barrel, or other object round which material is wound. **3.** Any of the steps of a winding staircase.
Win·der·mere (windər-meer), **Lake.** Lake in Cumbria, northwest England. Situated in the Lake District, it is the largest lake in England, being 17 kilometres (10.5 miles) long and 1.6 kilometres (1 mile) wide, and is drained by the river Leven into Morecambe Bay.
wind·fall (wind-fawl) *n.* **1.** Something that has been blown down by

the wind, such as a ripened fruit. **2.** A sudden and unexpected piece of good fortune or financial gain.
wind·flow·er (wind-flowr) *n.* The **wood anemone** (see).
wind·gall (wind-gawl) *n.* A soft tumour on a horse's leg just above the fetlock.
wind gauge *n.* **1.** An **anemometer** (see). **2.** A device attached to the sights of a gun, enabling allowance to be made for the effect of wind on the projectile.
wind gap (wind) *n.* A shallow gap or ravine on the side of a deep mountain ridge.
wind harp (wind) *n.* An **Aeolian harp** (see).
Wind·hoek (wind-hook, wint-, vint-). Capital of Namibia. Situated on a plateau in the centre of the country, it was capital of German South West Africa (1892) until taken by South African troops during World War I.
wind·hover (wind-hovvər ‖ -huvvər) *n. British Regional.* A **kestrel** (see). [WIND + HOVER, from its habit of hovering in one spot.]
wind·ing (wīnding) *n.* **1. a.** The act of one that winds. **b.** One complete turn of something wound. **2. a.** A thing in a wound condition; a spiral. **b.** A curve or bend, as in a road. **3.** *Electricity.* **a.** Wire wound into a coil. **b.** The manner in which such a coil is wound. **c.** A single loop of such a coil.
~*adj.* **1.** Twisting or turning; sinuous. **2.** Spiral: *a winding staircase.* **—wind·ing·ly** *adv.*
winding sheet (wīnding) *n.* A sheet for wrapping a dead body; a shroud.
wind instrument (wind) *n.* Any musical instrument sounded by wind, especially by the player's breath, such as a clarinet, trumpet, or harmonica.
wind·jam·mer (wind-jammər) *n.* **1.** A large sailing ship. **2.** A crew member of a windjammer. **3.** A windcheater. [From WIND + JAM (verb).]
wind·lass (windləss) *n.* Any of numerous hauling or lifting machines consisting essentially of a drum or cylinder wound with rope and turned by a crank.
~*tr.v.* **windlassed, -lassing, -lasses.** To raise with a windlass. [Middle English *wyndlas,* variant of *windas,* from Anglo-French, from Old Norse *vindáss* : *vinda,* to wind + *áss†,* pole.]
win·dle·straw (wind'l-straw) *n. British Regional.* A thin dried grass stalk. [Middle English *windlestraw* (unattested), Old English *windelstrēaw* : *windel,* basket, from *windan,* to WIND + *strēaw,* STRAW.]
wind·mill (wind-mil) *n.* **1.** A mill or other machine that runs on the energy generated by a wheel of adjustable blades, slats, or sails rotated by the wind. **2.** Anything similar to a windmill in appearance or operation. **3.** A toy consisting of vanes of coloured paper or plastic pinned to the end of a stick in such a way that they turn when blown on. Also *U.S.* "pinwheel". **4.** A person or thing imagined to be threatening or evil. Used chiefly in the phrase *tilting at windmills.* [Sense 4 is a reference to Cervantes' Don Quixote, who imagined windmills were evil giants.] See feature, next page.
win·dow (windō) *n.* **1.** An opening constructed in a wall or roof, as of a building or vehicle, that functions to admit light or air to an enclosure and is usually framed and spanned with glass mounted to permit opening and closing. **2. a.** A framework enclosing a pane of glass; a sash. **b.** A pane of glass, clear plastic, or the like; a windowpane. **3.** Any opening that resembles a window in function or appearance, such as the transparent space on an envelope that reveals the address printed on the enclosure. **4.** A code name for strips of foil dropped from aircraft as a radar countermeasure; chaff. **5.** The area or space immediately behind a window, especially at the front of a shop. **6.** A part of the electromagnetic spectrum in which radiation passes through a specified medium; for example, the radio window in the ionosphere lies between 50 gigahertz and 15 megahertz. **7.** A brief period during which a specified event can take place: *A launch window.*
~*tr.v.* **windowed, -dowing, -dows.** To provide with or as if with a window. [Middle English *window(e),* from Old Norse *vindauga* : *vindr,* wind, air + *auga,* eye.]
window box *n.* **1.** A usually long and narrow box for growing plants typically placed outdoors on a windowsill or ledge. **2.** Either of the vertical grooves on the inner sides of a window frame for the weights that counterbalance a sliding sash.
win·dow-dress·ing (windō-dressing) *n.* **1. a.** A decorative display of retail merchandise in shop windows. **b.** Goods and trimmings used in such displays. **2.** A superficially attractive presentation, as of statistics, ideas, or policies, intended to highlight what is favourable and to conceal what is unpalatable. **—win·dow-dress·er** *n.*
win·dow·pane (windō-payn) *n.* A plate of glass in a window.
window seat *n.* Any place for sitting next to a window, as in the recess of a bay window or on a public transport vehicle.
window shade *n. U.S.* A **blind** (see).
win·dow-shop (windō-shop) *intr.v.* **-shopped, -shopping, -shops.** To look at goods in shop windows without making purchases. **—win·dow-shop·per** *n.*
win·dow·sill (windō-sil) *n.* The horizontal ledge at the base of a window opening.
wind·pipe (wind-pīp) *n. Anatomy.* The **trachea** (see).
wind·pol·li·nat·ed (wind-pólli-naytid) *adj.* Pollinated by wind-borne pollen. Said of certain plants.
wind rose (wind) *n.* Any of a class of meteorological diagrams depicting the distribution of wind direction over a period of time. [German *Windrose,* "a rose of winds", compass card.]
wind·row (wind-rō) *n.* **1.** A long row of cut hay or grain left to dry

windmill

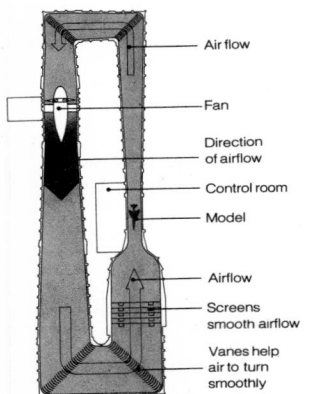

wind tunnel *The artificially created airflow in a wind tunnel is used to study the aerodynamic performance of cars and aircraft. The study is usually carried out on small-scale models.*

winepress *Juice was once extracted from grapes by treading them underfoot in large tubs, but today the grapes are more usually pressed by machine. Flowing through the slatted walls of the press, the juice is collected in vats and fermented into wine. This winepress is at the Château de la Chaise in France.*

ENERGY FROM THE AIR

A machine from the past with relevance for the future

The windmill first appeared in Persia in the 7th century and had reached Europe by the late 12th century. Thereafter its use spread rapidly. Improvements brought in over the centuries included the fantail to turn the sails automatically into the wind, and sails that could be regulated to control the amount of power delivered.

By the early 19th century, there were probably about 10,000 windmills in England and Wales, grinding grain, driving mechanical saws, raising coal, pumping water, and making paper. From that time their importance declined as steam-powered machinery became more widely used, but many windmills remained in use in remote areas – such as the American West and Australia – to raise water from underground.

A new interest in wind power arose during the 1970s world oil crisis, an interest strengthened by anxieties about the safety of nuclear energy. Several large wind-powered electricity generators are now on trial or in use.

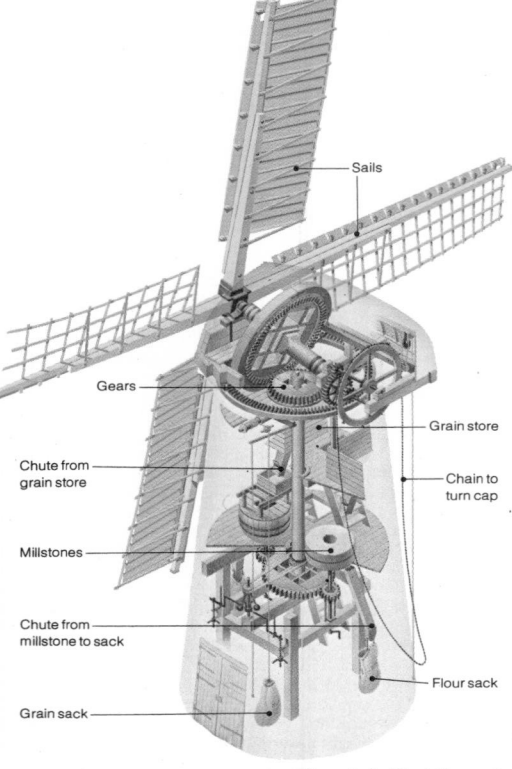

THE MECHANISM OF THE WINDMILL *The windmill at its most refined was a large and complex piece of machinery. The sails spanned up to 18 metres (60 feet) and weighed up to 5 tonnes. They made 10–15 revolutions a minute, and a gearing system turned the two millstones at 100 revolutions a minute.*

In the mill above, the miller had to turn the sails into the wind by pulling a looped chain that turned the cap on a cogged track, but in many mills a fantail did the task automatically. The miller could grind 270–320 kilograms (600–700 pounds) of grain an hour, but if the day was windless he would have to be prepared to work through the night.

in a field before being bundled. **2.** A row, as of leaves or snow, heaped up by the wind.
~*tr.v.* **windrowed, -rowing, -rows.** To shape or arrange into a windrow.

wind scale *n.* Any scale, such as the Beaufort scale, that gives a numerical value to the force or speed of wind.

wind-screen (wind-skreen, win-) *n.* A sheet of curved or flat toghened glass that forms the front window of a motor vehicle. Also called "screen", *U.S.* "windshield".

windscreen wiper *n.* An electrically operated rubber blade, usually

one of a pair, that clears the windscreen of a motor vehicle of rain, snow, or dirt.

wind-shake (wind-shayk) *n.* A crack or separation between growth rings in timber, attributed to the straining of tree trunks in high winds.

wind-shield (wind-sheeld) *n.* **1.** Something placed to protect a person or object from the wind. **2.** *U.S.* A windscreen.

wind-sock (wind-sok) *n.* A large, tapered, open-ended sleeve, pivotally attached to a standard, that indicates the direction of the wind blowing through it. Also called "air sock", "drogue", "wind cone", "wind sleeve".

Wind-sor¹ (winzər). The family name of the British royal family since 1917.

Windsor². Town in Berkshire, southern central England. Windsor Castle has been a royal residence since the time of William the Conqueror (11th century).

Windsor, Duke of. See **Edward VIII.**

Windsor chair *n.* A type of comfortable wooden chair typically having a high, curving, spoked back with arms, and outward-slanting legs connected by a crossbar.

Windsor knot *n.* A wide, triangular, tie knot.

wind-storm (wind-stawrm) *n.* A storm with high winds or violent gusts but little or no rain.

wind-suck-er (wind-suckər) *n.* A horse given to noisily swallowing quantities of air. —**wind-suck-ing** *adj. & n.*

wind-surf-ing (wind-surfing) *n.* The sport of sailing over water on a small, open vessel consisting of a large surfboard equipped with a sail. —**wind-surf** *intr.v.* —**wind-surf-er** *n.*

wind-swept (wind-swept) *adj.* **1.** Exposed to or moved by the force of the wind. **2.** Dishevelled by or as if by exposure to the wind: *a windswept appearance.*

wind tee (wind) *n.* A large weather vane with a horizontal T-shaped wind indicator, commonly found at airfields.

wind tunnel (wind) *n.* A chamber through which air is forced at controllable velocities in order to study the aerodynamic flow around and effects on aerofoils, scale models, or other objects mounted within.

wind up (wind). **1.** To bring to an end; conclude; settle. **2.** To make anxious, tense, or excited: *The children are getting wound up about their holidays.* **3.** To arrange for liquidation of (a company). ~*intr.v.* **1.** *Informal.* **a.** To bring something to a conclusion: *wound by by proposing a toast.* **b.** To come finally to a specified condition or situation: *wound up on the wrong side of the law.* **2.** To go into liquidation. Used of a company.

wind-up (wind-up) *n. Chiefly U.S. Informal.* **1.** The act of bringing something to a conclusion. **2.** The concluding part, as of an action, presentation, or speech.

wind-ward (windwərd) *n.* **1.** The direction from which the wind blows. **2.** The side exposed to the wind. —**to (the) windward of.** Favourably situated with respect to. ~*adj.* **1.** Of or moving towards the quarter from which the wind blows. **2.** Of or on the side exposed to the wind or to prevailing winds. ~*adv.* In a direction from which the wind blows; against the wind. Compare **leeward.**

Windward Islands. Archipelago of volcanic origin, southeast West Indies. The southern part of the Lesser Antilles, it extends southwards from the Leeward Islands, and includes Dominica, Grenada, St. Lucia, St. Vincent, and Martinique.

wind-y (windi) *adj.* **-ier, -iest. 1.** Characterised by the prevalence of strong winds: *a windy day.* **2.** Exposed to or swept by the wind. **3. a.** Characterised by lack of substance; empty; airy. **b.** Characterised by long-windedness, self-importance, or verbosity; full of talk. **4.** Affected by or causing flatulence. **5.** *Informal.* Nervous; frightened; shaky. —**wind-i-ly** *adv.* —**wind-i-ness** *n.*

wine (win) *n.* **1.** The fermented juice of any of various kinds of grapes making an alcoholic drink. **2.** The fermented juice of any of various other fruits or plants: *pear wine.* **3.** Something that intoxicates or exhilarates. **4.** The dark purplish colour of red wine. —**new wine in old bottles.** New thought or principles that cannot be integrated with old traditional ways. ~*v.* **wined, wining, wines.** —*tr.* To provide or entertain with wines: *The guests were wined and dined.* —*intr.* To drink wine. [Middle English *win(e),* Old English *wīn,* from West Germanic *wīna-* (unattested), from Latin *vīnum.*]

wine-bib-ber (win-bibbər) *n.* One who drinks excessive amounts of wine. [WINE + BIB, in archaic verbal sense, to drink.] —**wine-bib-bing** *adj. & n.*

wine cellar *n.* **1.** A place, especially a cellar, for storing wine. **2.** A stock of wines.

wine gallon *n.* A former unit of liquid measure used for wine, equivalent to the modern U.S. gallon (231 cubic inches or 3.79 litres).

wine-glass (win-glaass ‖ -glass) *n.* **1.** A glass from which wine is drunk; especially, a stemmed glass of a standard size having a capacity of approximately one sixth of a standard bottle of wine. **2.** The amount a wineglass will hold. In this sense, also called a "wineglassful".

wine-grow-er (win-grō-ər) *n.* One who owns a vineyard and produces wine. —**wine-grow-ing** *adj. & n.*

wine lake *n.* A large surplus of wine periodically occurring as a result of overproduction by growers within the European Economic Community. Compare **butter mountain.**

wine palm *n.* Any of various palm trees having sap or juice from which wine is prepared.

wine·press (wĭn-press) *n.* A vat in which the juice is pressed from grapes.

win·er·y (wĭnəri) *n., pl.* **-ies.** A winemaking establishment.

wine-skin (wĭn-skin) *n.* A bag for holding and dispensing wine, made from goatskin or other animal skin.

wine-tast·ing (wĭn-taysting) *n.* The act or occasion of evaluating the quality of wine by tasting it. —**wine-tast·er** *n.*

wing (wing) *n.* **1.** Either of a pair of specialised organs of flight, as: **a.** The feather-covered modified forelimb of a bat. **b.** The membranous tissue supported by the elongated digits of the forelimb of a bat. **c.** A veined, membranous structure extending from the thorax of an insect. **d.** The enlarged pectoral fin of a flying fish. **2.** Any organ or structure homologous to or resembling a wing. **3.** *Botany.* **a.** A thin or membranous extension, as of the fruit of the sycamore or ash or along a twig or stem. **b.** Any of the lateral petals of the flower of a pea or related plant. **4.** Either of two winglike appendages believed to be part of the bodies of supernatural or fabulous creatures, such as angels, demons, or dragons. **5.** *Aeronautics.* An aerofoil whose principal function is providing lift; especially, either of two such aerofoils symmetrically positioned on each side of the fuselage of an aircraft. **6.** Anything that resembles a wing in appearance, function, or position relative to a main body: *water wings.* **7.** *Literary.* A means of flight or of rapid movement: *Fear lent wings to his feet.* **8.** Something that is moved by or moves against the air, as a weather vane. **9.** The part of the body of a motor vehicle around the wheels. Also *U.S.* "fender". **10.** An aerofoil fitted to a racing car to improve road holding. **11.** A folding section, as of a double door or of a movable partition. **12.** In the theatre: **a.** A flat of scenery projecting onto the stage from the side. **b.** The unseen backstage area on either side of the stage. **13.** A section of a building or structure projecting from the main or central part. **14.** Either of the two side projections on the back of a wing chair. **15.** A group affiliated with or subordinate to an older or larger organisation: *the political wing of the I.R.A.* **16.** A section of a party or other group holding distinct, especially radical, political views: *the right wing; the left wing.* **17.** *Military.* Either the left or right flank of an army or a naval fleet lined up for battle. **18.** *Sports.* **a.** Either of the forward positions played near the sideline, as in soccer or hockey. **b.** One playing in such a position. **19. a.** In the Royal Air Force and some other air forces, a tactical unit usually consisting of three to five squadrons. **b.** In the U.S. air force, a unit larger than a group but smaller than a division. **20.** *Plural.* Emblematic wings worn on the jacket by one who has qualified as an air pilot. —**clip (someone's) wings.** To restrict the movement, activity, or freedom of. —**in the wings.** Ready to come forward when required. —**on the wing. 1.** In flight; flying. **2.** Moving; travelling. —**spread** or **stretch (one's) wings.** To develop or exploit one's talents to the full. —**take wing. 1.** To fly off; soar away. **2.** To leave in a rush. —**under (one's) wing.** Under one's protection; in one's care.
~*v.* **winged, winging, wings.** —*intr.* To move on or as if on wings; fly. —*tr.* **1.** To furnish with wings. **2.** To feather (an arrow). **3. a.** To send (an arrow, for example) in flight. **b.** To cause or enable to move quickly; speed. **4.** To make (one's) way swiftly by or as if by flying. **5.** To wound superficially, as in the wing or arm. **5.** To furnish (a building, for example) with side or subordinate extensions. —**wing it.** *Slang.* To improvise or ad-lib in a theatrical performance. [Middle English *wenge(n)*, from Old Norse *vængi,* accusative plural of *vængr,* bird's wing.]

wing and wing *adv. Nautical.* With sails extended on both sides.

Win·gate (wĭn-gayt), **Orde (Charles)** (1903–1944). British general. He worked with Jewish guerrillas in Palestine (1935–39), and during World War II defeated the Italians in Ethiopia (1941). In Burma he organised the specially trained Chindit forces.

wing·bow (wing-bō) *n.* A mark of colour on the bend of the wing in a domestic fowl.

wing-case (wing-kayss) *n.* Either of the two hard, leathery, modified forewings that cover and protect the delicate hindwings of certain insects at rest, especially beetles.

wing chair *n.* An armchair with a high back from which project large, enclosing sidepieces or wings.

wing collar *n.* A stiff, stand-up, shirt collar with the corners turned down, that is worn by men especially on formal occasions.

wing commander *n. Abbr.* **W/Cdr.** An officer of the Royal Air Force and certain other air forces, ranking between a group captain and a squadron leader.

wing-ding (wing-ding) *n. Chiefly Australian & N.Z. Slang.* A lavish or lively party or celebration. [20th century : origin obscure.]

winged (wingd; *also poetic* wing-id) *adj.* **1.** Having wings or winglike appendages. **2.** Moving on or as if on wings; flying. **3.** Soaring; elevated; sublime. **4.** Swift; fleet.

wing·er (wing-ər) *n.* **1.** *British.* A forward playing on the wing, as in soccer or hockey. **2.** One who belongs to the specified political wing of a party or other group. Used in combination: *left-wingers.*

wing·less (wing-ləss, -liss) *adj.* Having no wings or having only rudimentary wings. Said especially of primitive insects of the subclass Apterygota, which includes the springtails and bristletails.

wing·let (wing-lət, -lit) *n.* A small or rudimentary wing.

wing loading *n.* The gross weight of an aircraft divided by the wing area. Used in stress analysis.

---

wine

"READING" A WINE BOTTLE

The shape alone often reveals the place where the contents were made

Traditionally, different types of wine are associated with different-shaped bottles.

Bordeaux wines have tall, narrow bottles with squarish shoulders, and are coloured green for red wine (claret), green or clear for white.

Burgundy wines have wider bottles with sloping shoulders; they are dark green for red wine, lighter green for white.

German and Alsace wines have tall, slender bottles with no shoulders. Rhine (hock) bottles are reddish-brown, Moselle and Alsace bottles are green.

Port and sherry bottles are similar to Bordeaux bottles, but are squatter with squarer shoulders and longer necks; they are green, dark brown, or black.

Chianti may still sometimes be sold in green flasks in straw jackets, but Bordeaux-shaped bottles are more often used.

Champagnes and sparkling wines are in Burgundy-type bottles, but made of much thicker glass; they have tinfoil round the neck and a wired-on cork.

The standard wine bottle contains 70 or 75 centilitres of wine, but there are also larger versions with special names: magnum = 2 ordinary bottles; flagon = 3; double magnum or Jeroboam = 4; Rehoboam = 6; Champagne and Burgundy Impériale or Methuselah = 8 (Bordeaux 6); Salmanazar = 12; Balthazar = 16; Nebuchadnezzar = 20.

The label on the bottle should give the name of the country of origin, the region, château, or estate from which the wine comes, probably the vintage (the year in which it was made), and the name of the shipper or producer.

Within the large regions – such as Bordeaux, Burgundy, or the Rhine – are areas or villages famous for their wine (such as Médoc or Sauternes, Chablis or Beaujolais, Nierstein or Hochheim), and within them again are the individual vineyards. In France, Germany, and Italy strict laws govern the use of these names.

The words *Appellation Contrôlée* on French bottles mean that the wine comes from the place named and was made according to local custom. *Vins Délimités de Qualité Supérieure* are not generally of such high standard but are of better quality than *vins ordinaires.*

Mise au Château, Mise au domaine, or *Mise en bouteilles au château* means that the wine was bottled on the estate that produced it. *Cru* means growth, and some wines are classified by quality as *grand cru, premier cru,* and so on. Some labels name the grape – Cabernet Sauvignon, for instance, Riesling or Gewürztraminer.

On German labels, *Kellerabzug* and *Originalabzug* mean estate-bottled. German wine is divided into *Tafelwein* (table wine), which can be purely German or an EEC blend, *Qualitätswein* (quality wine) and *Qualitätswein mit Prädikat* (quality wine of distinction). With the last of these an indication will be given of the condition of the grapes: *Spätlese* (made from late-gathered grapes) is not as good as *Auslese* (made from selected, fully ripe grapes); even more expensive are *Beerenauslese* (made from individually selected overripe grapes) and *Trockenbeerenauslese* (made from grapes left on the vine until shrunken and highly enriched).

A characteristically shaped bottle of central Germany is the *Bocksbeutel,* or Franconian flagon, containing the white "stone wine" of Würzburg.

Bordeaux red   Burgundy   Burgundy pot   Chianti   Côte de Provence   Franconian flagon   Loire

Hock   Moselle   Alsace   Bordeaux white   Champagne   Vintage port   Port

THE COMMONEST SHAPES *Above are 14 of the commonest shapes of wine bottle. On the left are three of the traditional bottles of France, then Chianti of Italy in its old-style wicker basket – now fast disappearing. On the far right are the squat, long-necked port bottles.*

winter aconite *A woodland plant of the Northern Hemisphere which forms green seed pods (above) after its yellow flower has bloomed very early in spring.*

winter cherry *Sometimes called bladder cherry or Chinese lantern, this creeping perennial has small white flowers in summer and orange-red berries in winter. In autumn the berries are enclosed in a red, lantern-like casing.*

wing nut *n.* A nut with winglike projections for thumb and forefinger leverage in turning. Also called "butterfly nut".
wing·o·ver (wíng-ōvər) *n.* A flight manoeuvre or stunt in which an aircraft enters a climbing turn until almost stalled and is allowed to fall while the turn is continued until normal flight is attained in a direction opposite the original heading.
wing·span (wíng-span) *n.* The linear distance from wing tip to wing tip of an aircraft, bird, or insect. Also called "wingspread".
wing tip *n.* The extreme edge of a wing, as of a bird or aircraft.
wink[1] (wingk) *v.* **winked, winking, winks.** *—intr.* **1.** To close and open the eyelid of one eye deliberately, as to convey a message, signal, or suggestion. **2.** To close and open the eyelids of both eyes; blink. **3. a.** To shine fitfully; twinkle: *winking stars.* **b.** To flash intermittently, as the direction indicator on a car does. *—tr.* **1.** To close and open (an eye or the eyes) rapidly. **2.** To signal or express as by the winking of an eye or by flashing a light. **—wink at.** To pretend not to see: *winked at corruption in his ministry.*
∼n. **1.** An act of winking. **2.** The extremely brief time required for a wink. **3.** A signal or hint conveyed by winking. **4.** A gleam; a twinkle. **5.** *Informal.* A brief moment of sleep. **—tip (someone) the wink.** *British Informal.* To give a hint to. [Middle English *winken,* Old English *wincian,* to close one's eyes.]
wink[2] *n.* Any of the small, round discs used in the game of tiddlywinks. [Shortened from TIDDLYWINKS.]
wink·er (wíngkər) *n.* **1.** One that winks. **2.** A **blinker** *(see).*
win·kle (wíngk'l) *n.* Any of various snail-like marine gastropod molluscs of the genus *Littorina,* such as *L. littorea,* the flesh of which is edible. Also called "periwinkle".
∼tr.v. **winkled, -kling, -kles.** *Informal.* To prise out; extract. Usually used with *out.* [Shortened from PERIWINKLE.]
winkle-pickers (wíngk'l-pickərz) *pl.n. Informal.* Men's and women's shoes with very pointed toes, originally fashionable in the 1950s and 1960s.
win·ner (wínnər) *n.* **1.** One that wins, especially in a sporting contest. **2.** *Informal.* One that is assured of success: *His latest film is a winner.*
win·ning (wínning) *adj.* **1.** Successful; victorious. **2.** Charming; engaging: *a winning personality.*
∼n. **1.** The act of one that wins; victory. **2.** *Plural.* That which has been won; especially, money won by gambling. **3.** A section of a mine that has been recently prepared or opened for working. **—win·ning·ly** *adv.* **—win·ning·ness** *n.*
winning gallery *n.* In real tennis, an opening below the side penthouse. A ball played into this opening is counted as a win.
winning post *n.* The post at the end of a racecourse.
Win·ni·peg (wínni-peg). Capital of Manitoba province, south central Canada. Situated at the confluence of the Red and Assiniboine rivers, and south of Lake Winnipeg, it is the main wheat market and commercial centre for the Prairie Provinces.
win·now (wínnō) *v.* **-nowed, -nowing, -nows.** *—tr.* **1.** To separate the chaff from (grain) by means of a current of air. **2.** To blow (chaff) off or away. **3.** To scatter or disperse by blowing. **4.** To blow upon; cause to flutter or fly: *hair winnowed by the breeze.* **5.** To examine closely in order to separate the good from the bad; analyse; sift. **6.** To separate (a desirable or undesirable part); eliminate by sorting. Often used with *out.* **7.** *Archaic.* To beat or fan (the air) as with wings. *—intr.* **1.** To separate grain from chaff. **2.** To separate the good from the bad.
∼n. **1.** A device for winnowing grain. **2.** An act of winnowing. [Middle English *windowen, wynwen,* Old English *windwian,* from *wind,* WIND.] **—win·now·er** *n.*
win·o (wīnō) *n., pl.* **winos.** *Slang.* A person, especially a tramp or vagrant, who is habitually drunk on wine.
win·some (wín-səm) *adj.* Winning; charming; engaging. [Middle English *winsum,* Old English *wynsum* : *wyn,* joy + *-sum,* -SOME.] **—win·some·ly** *adv.* **—win·some·ness** *n.*
win·ter (wíntər) *n.* **1.** The usually coldest season of the year, occurring between autumn and spring. In the Northern Hemisphere it extends from the winter solstice to the vernal (or spring) equinox and is popularly considered to comprise December, January, and February; in the Southern Hemisphere it falls between the summer solstice and the autumnal equinox, or, popularly, June, July, and August. **2.** *Poetic.* A year as expressed through the recurrence of this season. **3.** Any period characterised by coldness, misery, barrenness, or death.
∼v. **wintered, -tering, -ters.** *—intr.* To pass or spend the winter. *—tr.* To lodge, keep, or care for during the winter: *wintering the sheep in the stable.*
∼adj. **1.** Pertaining to, characteristic of, suitable for, or occurring in winter: *a winter coat; winter weather.* **2. a.** Capable of being stored for use during the winter. Said of fruits or vegetables. **b.** Planted in the autumn and harvested in the spring or summer: *winter wheat.* [Middle English, Old English *winter,* from Germanic *wentrus* (unattested), probably akin to WET.] **—win·ter·er** *n.* **—win·ter·less** *adj.* **—win·ter·ly** *adj.*
winter aconite *n.* A frequently cultivated European plant, *Eranthis hyemalis,* having a solitary yellow flower that blooms in winter or early spring.
winter cherry *n.* The **Chinese lantern plant** *(see).*
win·ter-feed (wíntər-feed) *tr.v.* **-fed** (-fed), **-feeding, -feeds.** To feed (livestock) when grazing is not possible, as in the winter.
win·ter·green (wíntər-green) *n.* **1. a.** A low-growing plant, *Gaultheria procumbens,* of eastern North America, having white or pinkish flowers, aromatic evergreen leaves, and spicy, edible red berries. Also called "checkerberry". **b.** A medicinal oil or flavouring obtained from this plant. **2.** Any of several similar or related plants, such as: **a.** Any plant of the genus *Pyrola,* such as *P.minor,* having round pink flowers. [Translation of Dutch *wintergroen.*]
win·ter·ise, win·ter·ize (wíntə-rīz) *tr.v.* **-ised, -ising, -ises.** To prepare or equip (a house or car, for example) for winter weather.
winter jasmine *n.* A shrub, *Jasminum nudiflorum,* native to China but widely cultivated for its yellow, winter-blooming flowers.
win·ter·kill (wíntər-kil) *v.* **-killed, -killing, -kills.** *Chiefly U.S. —tr.* To kill (plants, for example) by exposing to extremely cold winter weather. *—intr.* To die from exposure to cold winter weather. Used especially of plants. **—winterkill** *n.*
Winter Olympic Games *pl.n.* An international sporting event in which representatives of different countries compete in winter sports, held in the same year as the **Olympic Games** *(see).* Also called "Winter Olympics".
winter rose *n.* A plant, the **Christmas rose** *(see).*
winter savory *n.* See **savory** (plant).
winter solstice *n. Astronomy.* A **solstice** *(see).*
winter sports *n.* Sports, such as skiing or bobsleighing, that take place on snow and ice.
win·ter·time (wíntər-tīm) *n.* The winter season.
win·try (wíntri) *adj.* **-trier, -triest.** Also **win·ter·y** (wín-təri, -tri) **-ier, -iest. 1.** Characteristic of winter; cold. **2.** Suggestive of winter; cheerless. [Old English *wintrig.*] **—win·tri·ly** *adv.* **—win·tri·ness** *n.*
win·y (wīni) *adj.* **-ier, -iest.** Having the qualities or taste of wine; intoxicating; heady.
winze (winz) *n.* In mining, an inclined or vertical shaft or passage between levels. [Variant of earlier *winds,* probably from Middle English *wynde,* windlass, perhaps from Middle Dutch or Middle Low German *winde.*]
wipe (wīp) *tr.v.* **wiped, wiping, wipes. 1.** To subject to light rubbing or friction, as with a cloth or paper, in order to clean or dry: *wipe the dishes; wipe the table.* **2.** To remove or get rid of by or as if by wiping. Usually used with *off* or *away*: *wiped away her tears; Wipe that smile off your face.* **3.** To rub, move, or spread over something: *wiped his shoes on the rug.* **4.** In plumbing, to form (a joint) by spreading solder with a piece of cloth or leather.
∼n. **1.** The act of wiping. **2.** Something used for wiping, as: **a.** A commercially produced treated tissue: *a box of baby wipes.* **b.** *Slang.* A handkerchief. **3.** *Informal.* **a.** A blow; a swipe. **b.** A sideswipe; a gibe. [Middle English *wipen,* Old English *wīpian.*]
wipe out *tr.v.* **1.** To destroy; annihilate: *wiped out a tribe.* **2.** To remove; eradicate: *wipe out a memory.* *—intr.v. Slang.* In surfing, to lose balance and fall or jump off a surfboard.
wipe-out (wīp-owt) *n.* **1.** The act or an instance of wiping out. **2.** *Slang.* A fall or jump off a surfboard. **3.** Total loss of radio reception as a result of interference by another signal.
wip·er (wīpər) *n.* **1.** One that wipes. **2.** A device designed for wiping, such as a windscreen wiper. **3.** In a machine, a cam that projects from a rotating horizontal shaft to activate another part. **4.** *Electricity.* A movable electrical contact, as in a rheostat.
wire (wīr) *n.* **1. a.** A usually pliable metallic strand or rod made in many lengths and diameters, sometimes clad and often electrically insulated, used chiefly for structural support or to conduct electricity. **b.** Such strands collectively, used as a fencing material, for example. **2.** A group of such strands bundled or twisted together as a functional unit; a cable. **3.** Something resembling a wire, as in slenderness or stiffness. **4.** *Chiefly U.S. Informal.* The telegraph service: *sent it by wire.* **5.** *Informal.* A telegram. **6.** The screen on which sheets of paper are formed in a papermaking machine. **7.** A metal snare, as for catching rabbits. **8.** *U.S.* The finishing line of a racetrack. **—get (one's) wires crossed.** *Informal.* To get confused or mixed up. **—pull wires** *Chiefly U.S.* To use secret or underhand means to accomplish something; pull strings.
∼adj. Made of or resembling a wire or wires: *a wire brush.*
∼v. **wired, wiring, wires.** *—tr.* **1.** To bind, connect, or attach with a wire or wires. **2.** To equip with a system of electrical wires. **3.** *Informal.* **a.** To send by telegraph: *wire congratulations.* **b.** To send a telegram to. **4.** To snare with a wire. **5.** In croquet, to hit (a ball) behind a hoop and block an opponent's shot. *—intr.* To send a telegram; telegraph. [Middle English *wir(e),* Old English *wīr.*]
wire cloth *n.* A mesh woven of fine wire.
wire-draw (wīr-draw) *tr.v.* **-drew** (-drōō || -drew), **-drawn** (-drawn), **-drawing, -draws. 1.** To draw (metal) into wire. **2.** To protract (a subject, for example) inordinately; spin out. **—wire·draw·er** *n.*
wire gauge *n.* **1.** A gauge for measuring the diameter of wire, usually in the form of a disc having variously sized slots in its periphery or a long graduated plate with similar slots along its edge. **2.** A standardised system of wire sizes.
wire gauze *n.* A material woven of very fine wires.
wire glass *n.* Sheet glass reinforced with wire-netting.
wire·grass (wīr-graass || -grass) *n.* Any of various grasses having tough, wiry roots or rootstocks, such as **Bermuda grass** *(see).*
wire-haired (wīr-haird) *adj.* Having a coat of stiff, wiry hair. Said of breeds of dogs: *a wire-haired terrier.*
wire·less (wīr-ləss, -liss) *adj.* **1.** Without wires. **2.** Radio.
∼n. **1.** Radio. **2.** A radio set.
∼v. **wirelessed, -lessing, -lesses.** *—tr.* To communicate with by wireless telegraphy or radiotelephone. *—intr.* To communicate in this way; radio.

wireless telegraphy *n.* Telegraphy by radio rather than by long-distance transmission lines. Also called "radio telegraphy".
wireless telephone *n.* **Radiotelephone** *(see).*
wire·net·ting (wír-nétting) *n.* Netting made of woven wire, as for fences.
wire recorder *n.* A forerunner of the tape recorder that recorded sound on a spool of wire rather than on magnetic tape.
wire·tap (wír-tap) **wiretapped, -tapping, -taps.** *tr.v.* To tap (a telephone line). **—wire·tap** *n.* **—wire·tap·per** *n.*
wire wheel *n.* **1.** A spoked wheel, especially one on a sports car. **2.** A rotary wire brush, especially one that is power operated. Also called "steel wool".
wire wool *n.* A tangled mass of fine wire used to rub metal surfaces to remove dirt or rust.
wire·work (wír-wurk) *n.* **1.** Wire fabric. **2.** Articles made of wire or wire fabric.
wire·worm (wír-wurm) *n.* The wirelike larva of various click beetles, that cause severe damage by boring into the roots of many plants.
wire-wove (wír-wōv) *adj.* **1.** Designating a high-grade writing paper with a smooth finish. **2.** Made of woven wire.
wir·ing (wír-ing) *n.* **1.** The act of attaching, connecting, or installing wires. **2.** A system of electric wires, as in a building.
wir·ra (wírrə) *interj. Irish.* Used to express sorrow or perplexity. [Short for Irish Gaelic *a Muire,* "Oh, Mary".]
Wir·ral (wírrəl),**The.** Peninsula in Merseyside, northwest England. Situated between the Mersey and Dee estuaries, it includes Wallasey, Birkenhead, Ellesmere Port, and Port Sunlight.
wir·y (wír-i) *adj.* **-ier, -iest. 1.** Made of or consisting of wire. **2.** Resembling wire, as in fineness and stiffness: *wiry hair.* **3.** Sinewy and lean; slender but tough. Said of people and animals. **—wir·i·ly** *adv.* **—wir·i·ness** *n.*
Wis·con·sin (wiss-kónsin). State in the northern central United States. Extending from the Mississippi river to lakes Superior and Michigan, it has over 8,500 lakes and is mainly low-lying with extensive forests. It is the chief dairy state of the United States. The capital is Madison.
wis·dom (wízdəm) *n.* **1.** Enlightened understanding of what is true or right, usually acquired through long experience, as distinguished from a partial or specialised knowledge: *"The only wisdom we can hope to acquire/ Is the wisdom of humility"* (T.S. Eliot). **2.** Common sense; sagacity; good judgment. **3.** Accumulated learning; erudition. **4.** Wise sayings or teaching: *the wisdom of the ancients.* —See Synonyms at **knowledge.** [Middle English *wisedom,* Old English *wīsdōm* : *wīs,* WISE + -DOM.]
Wisdom of Jesus, the Son of Si·rach (sír-ak) *n.* A book of the Apocrypha, **Ecclesiasticus** *(see).*
Wisdom of Solomon *n.* A book of the Apocrypha.
wisdom tooth *n.* Any of four molars, the last on each side of both jaws, usually erupting much later than the others. [Translation of New Latin *dentes sapientiae* (plural).]
wise[1] (wīz) *adj.* **wiser, wisest. 1.** Imbued with, based on, or suggestive of wisdom or discernment for what is true or right: *a wise decision.* **2.** Possessed of or showing common sense; prudent; sensible: *It would be wise not to mention this to anyone.* **3.** Shrewd; crafty: *a wise move.* **4.** *Informal.* Having knowledge or information; informed; aware: *came away none the wiser; soon got wise to his plan.* **5.** *Archaic.* Archaic. Having magical or occult powers. **6.** *Chiefly U.S.* Offensively self-assured; arrogant. **—wise up.** *Chiefly U.S. Slang.* To become aware or sophisticated. Often used with *to.* [Middle English *wis(e),* Old English *wīs.*] **—wise·ly** *adv.*
wise[2] *n. Archaic.* **1.** Method or manner of doing; fashion; way. **2.** Degree or respect: Used chiefly in the phrases *in no wise* and *in any wise.* [Middle English *wise,* Old English *wīse, wīs,* manner.]
-wise *adv. comb. form.* Indicates: **1.** Manner, direction, or position; for example, **clockwise. 2.** *Informal.* With reference to; for example, **taxwise.** [Middle English *-wise,* in a certain manner, Old English *-wīsan,* from *wīse* (manner).]
Usage: The indiscriminate use of *-wise,* as in *taxwise, timewise, moneywise,* is associated by many people with an unpleasant business jargon. In careful speech it is preferable to use a longer phrase instead, for example, *as far as tax is concerned.*
wise·a·cre (wīz-aykər) *n. Informal.* An offensively self-assured person who affects to be wise. [Middle Dutch *wijsseggher,* soothsayer, variant (influenced by *segghen,* to say) of Old High German *wīssago, wīzago,* seer.]
wise·crack (wīz-krak) *n. Informal.* A flippant, cleverly sardonic remark or retort; a joke or gibe. See Synonyms at **joke.**
~*intr.v.* **wisecracked, -cracking, -cracks.** *Informal.* To make a wisecrack. **—wise·crack·er** *n.*
wise guy *n. Informal.* A self-assured person who affects an air of superior knowledge; a know-all.
Wise·man (wīzmən), **Nicholas Patrick Stephen** (1802–65). British cardinal. He was the first Roman Catholic Archbishop of Westminster (1850), after the controversial restoration of the English Catholic hierarchy.
wi·sent (wéez'nt, véez'nt) *n.* The European bison, *Bison bonasus.* See **bison.** [German *Wisent,* from Old High German *wisunt.*]
wish (wish) *n.* **1.** A feeling of longing or desire for something. **2. a.** An expression, often unspoken, or confession of such a desire: *make a wish.* **b.** A known or expressed aspiration or request: *went against my wishes.* **3.** An object of desire; something wished for: *You've got your wish.* **4.** *Usually plural.* An expressed desire for the welfare, happiness, or health of someone: *Send her my best wishes.*
~*v.* **wished, wishing, wishes.** —*tr.* **1.** To have as a wish, as: **a.** To want: *I wish to leave now.* **b.** To desire (something unattainable): *I wish I'd never been born.* **c.** To desire or request (someone) to do something: *I wish you'd come to the point.* **d.** To desire or long for (someone or something) to be in a specified state: *wished him a thousand miles away; I wish this job were finished.* **2.** To entertain or express a hope that a specified state or quality will befall or be enjoyed by (someone): *wish you all a Happy New Year; wished him no harm.* **3.** To confer or impose; foist. Used with *on: wouldn't wish him on my worst enemy.* —*intr.* **1.** To have or feel a desire. Usually used with *for: wish for the moon.* **2.** To express a wish. [Middle English *wisshen,* Old English *wȳscan.*] **—wish·er** *n.*
wish·bone (wísh-bōn) *n.* **1.** The forked bone, or furcula, anterior to the breastbone of most birds, formed by the fusion of the clavicles. **2.** Anything of a similar shape; especially, a V-shaped member of the suspension of a motor vehicle. [So called from its use as a wish token. When it is snapped apart by two people, the person getting the longer piece will supposedly have his wish fulfilled.]
wish·ful (wíshf'l) *adj.* Having or expressing a wish or longing. **—wish·ful·ly** *adv.* **—wish·ful·ness** *n.*
wish fulfilment *n.* **1.** The gratification of a desire. **2.** In psychoanalysis, the mind's enactment of a suppressed or frustrated desire, as in dreaming or fantasy.
wishful thinking *n.* Belief based on what one wishes to be true, rather than on what is actually true. **—wishful thinker** *n.*
wish-wash (wísh-wosh || -wawsh) *n. Informal.* **1.** A thin, watery drink. **2.** Insipid talk or writing. [Reduplication of WASH.]
wish·y-wash·y (wíshi-woshi || -wawshi) *adj.* **-ier, -iest.** *Informal.* **1.** Watery; thin; weak. **2.** Lacking in substance, quality, or force; feeble; insipid. [Reduplication of *washy,* from WASH.]
wisp (wisp) *n.* **1.** A small bunch or bundle, as of straw, hair, or grass. **2. a.** Someone or something thin, frail, slight, or brief: *a wisp of a smile; a wisp of a girl.* **b.** A thin or faint streak or fragment, as of smoke or clouds. **3.** A flock of birds, especially of snipe.
~*v.* **wisped, wisping, wisps.** —*tr.* **1.** To twist into a wisp. **2.** To rub down (a horse) with a wisp of straw. —*intr.* To move or drift in the manner of a wisp of smoke. [Middle English *wisp, wips*†.] **—wisp·y** *adj.*
wist. *Archaic.* Past tense and past participle of **wit** (to know).
wis·ter·i·a (wi-stéer-i-ə) *n.* Any of several climbing woody vines of the genus *Wisteria,* having compound leaves and drooping clusters of showy purplish or white flowers. [New Latin *Wisteria,* after Caspar *Wistar* (1761–1818), U.S. anatomist.]
wist·ful (wístf'l) *adj.* Full of a melancholy yearning; longing pensively. [Originally "attentive", from obsolete *wistly*† (influenced by *wishful*).] **—wist·ful·ly** *adv.* **—wist·ful·ness** *n.*
wit[1] (wit) *n.* **1.** The natural ability to perceive or know; understanding; intelligence; good sense: *had the wit to wrap up in the cold weather.* **2.** *Usually plural.* **a.** Ingenuity; resourcefulness: *using one's wits; live by one's wits.* **b.** Sound mental faculties; mind; sanity: *scared out of one's wits.* **3. a.** The ability to perceive and express in an ingeniously humorous manner the relationship or similarity between seemingly incongruous or disparate things: *Shavian wit.* **b.** One noted for this ability; especially, one skilled in repartee. **c.** This quality of wit as manifested in speech or writing. —See Synonyms at **mind. —at (one's) wits' end.** At the limit of one's mental resources; utterly at a loss. **—have** or **keep (one's) wits about (one).** To remain alert or calm, especially in a crisis. [Middle English, Old English.]
Synonyms: *wit, humour, repartee, sarcasm, irony.*
wit[2] *v.* **wist** (wist), **witting,** present indicative **I wot** (wot), **thou wost** (wost), **he wot, we, you, they wite** (wīt) or **witen** (wīt'n). *Archaic.* —*tr.* To be or become aware of; know; learn. —*intr.* To know. **—to wit.** That is to say; namely. [Middle English *witen,* Old English *witan.*]
wit·an (witt'n, wíttan) *pl.n.* In Anglo-Saxon England, the **witenagemot** *(see).* [Old English *witan,* plural of *wita,* councillor.]
witch (wich) *n.* **1.** A woman who practises black magic and sorcery or is believed to have dealings with the devil. **2.** An ugly or vicious old woman; a hag. **3.** *Informal.* A bewitching young woman or girl.
~*tr.v.* **witched, witching, witches. 1.** To work or cast a spell upon; bewitch. **2.** To cause, bring, or effect by witchcraft. [Middle English *wicche,* Old English *wicce* (feminine), *wicca* (masculine).]
witch·craft (wích-kraaft || -kraft) *n.* **1.** The practices of a witch; black magic; sorcery. **2.** A fascinating or irresistible influence, attraction, or charm. —See Synonyms at **magic.**
witch doctor *n.* A medicine man or shaman, especially among African peoples, reputedly having powers both to heal and to harm through sorcery and herbalism.
witch elm. Variant of **wych elm.**
witch·er·y (wíchəri) *n., pl.* **-ies. 1.** Sorcery; witchcraft. **2.** Power to charm or fascinate.
witch·es'-broom (wíchiz-broom, -broom) *n.* An abnormal, brushlike growth of weak, closely clustered shoots or branches on a tree or woody plant, caused by fungi or viruses.
witches' Sabbath *n.* A midnight meeting of demons, witches, and sorcerers, supposely presided over by Satan and marked by orgies and demonic rites. Also called "sabbat".
witch·et·ty grub (wíchiti) *n.* Any of various long, edible, wood-boring grubs that are the larvae of certain Australian moths and beetles. [*Witcheety,* from an Aboriginal name.]
witch hazel, wych hazel *n.* **1.** Any of several shrubs of the genus *Hamamelis*; especially, *H. virginiana,* of eastern North America,

witch doctor *A Sumatran witch doctor, or medicine man, preparing a pig for sacrifice.*

witch hazel *Native to North America and the Far East, witch hazel is a genus of shrubs and small trees with sweet-smelling flowers which appear after the leaves have been shed. The bark of one species,* Hamamelis virginiana, *provides an astringent liquid used as an antiseptic and skin cleanser. The species shown here is the Chinese witch hazel,* Hamamelis mollis.

having yellow flowers that bloom in late autumn or winter. **2.** An alcoholic solution containing an extract of the bark and leaves of this shrub, applied externally as a mild astringent. [Middle English *wyche,* WYCH (ELM) + HAZEL.]

witch hunt *n.* **1.** A rigorous search to detect witches, especially in the Middle Ages. **2.** A campaign launched on the pretext of investigating subversive or dishonest activities but aimed at exposing and harassing political opponents or holders of dissenting views. **—witch-hunt·er** *n.* **—witch-hunt·ing** *adj.* & *n.*

witch·ing (wíching) *adj.* **1.** Pertaining to or appropriate for witchcraft: *the witching hour.* **2.** Having power to charm or enchant; bewitching.
~*n.* Witchcraft. **—witch·ing·ly** *adv.*

witch of Ag·nes·i (an-yáyzi || *chiefly U.S.* aan-) *n.* A plane mathematical curve with the equation $x^2y = 4a^2(2a-y)$. [After Maria Gaetana *Agnesi* (1718–99), Italian mathematician; probably referring to the resemblance of the curve to a witch's hat.]

wite[1] (wīt) *n. British Regional.* Blame; fault. [Middle English *wite,* Old English *wīte,* fine, penalty.]

wite[2]**.** *Archaic.* Also **wit·en.** First, second, and third person plural present indicative of **wit** (to know).

wit·e·na·ge·mot (wít'n-ə-gi-mōt) *n.* **1.** An Anglo-Saxon advisory council to the king, composed of about 100 nobles, prelates, and other officials, convened at intervals to discuss administrative and judicial affairs. **2.** The members of this council. In both senses, also called "witan". [Old English *witena gemōt* : *witena,* genitive plural of *wita,* councillor + *gemōt,* meeting, assembly; see **moot.**]

with (with || with) *prep. Abbr.* **w. 1. a.** As a companion of; accompanying: *Who went with him?* **b.** In the partnership of: *painted the house with a friend.* **2.** In the company or house of: *spent the weekend with a friend.* **3.** Having as a possession, attribute, or characteristic: *a man with a moustache; the girl with the stutter.* **4.** In a manner characterised by: *perform with skill; spoke with confidence.* **5.** In the charge or keeping of: *She left the letter with the doorman.* **6.** In the opinion or estimation of: *if it's all right with you.* **7. a.** In support of; on the side of: *voted with the opposition.* **b.** Of the same opinion or belief as: *He is with us on that.* **8.** In the same way as; like: *He believes, with Orwell, that some animals are more equal than others.* **9.** In the same group or mixture as; among: *Mix the flour with the eggs. Go and stand with the others.* **10.** In the membership or employment of: *He is with a publishing company.* **11. a.** Having or using as a means or agency: *spattered with mud; threatened him with the sack; eat with a fork.* **b.** Using as a material or ingredient: *filled his glass with beer; made it with fruit from the garden.* **12. a.** In spite of; notwithstanding: *With all his talent, he could not get a job.* **b.** Taking into account; in view of: *With all his talent, he ought to get a job. With our luck, it'll probably rain.* **13.** In the same direction as: *bend with the wind.* **14.** At the same time as: *rise with the sun.* **15.** In the matter of or in regard to: *satisfied with her progress.* **16.** In comparison or contrast to: *a dress identical with the one she has just bought.* **17.** In a harmonious relationship to: *The curtains don't really go with the carpet.* **18.** Having received: *With her permission, he left.* **19. a.** And; plus; added to: *beans with chips.* **b.** Inclusive of; counting: *That makes ten of us, with the children.* **20.** In opposition or antagonism to; against: *wrestling with an opponent; quarrelled with his neighbour.* **21.** To; onto: *Couple the first car with the second.* **22.** So as to be free of or separated from: *part with a friend.* **23.** In the course of: *We grow older with the hours.* **24.** In proportion to: *wines that improve with age.* **25.** *Informal.* Understanding; following the line of thought of: *Are you still with me?* **26.** As well as; in favourable comparison to: *She sings with the best of them.* **27. a.** Under the influence of; because of: *trembling with fear.* **b.** As a result of; thanks to: *With improved medical facilities, many of these patients now live longer.* **c.** Immediately following or attendant upon: *With the death of his brother, he inherited the title. He tore up the contract and, with that, stormed out.* **28.** In a situation in which there is or are: *He scored the winning goal with only seconds to go. With their best batting already gone, England are in trouble.* **29.** In the case of; as far as concerns: *With most people, voting is determined by economic factors.* **30.** In the care of: *leave it with me and I'll see to it.* **31.** Used to indicate the other party in any type of transaction or relationship: *chatting with his neighbour; works with handicapped children.* **32.** Used without a verb in expressions having the force of a wish or command: *On with the show! To hell with your stupid ideas!* **—in with.** In league or association with: *He is in with the wrong crowd.* **—with it.** *Informal.* **1.** Aware of modern trends; up-to-date. **2.** Alert and understanding: *I'm not with it this morning.* [Middle English *with,* with, against, by means of, Old English *with,* against or in opposition to, together with.]

Usage: When *with* introduces a phrase following a singular subject, it does not affect the relationship between that subject and the verb: *The king, with his two sons, has arrived.* In casual speech, the plural meaning of the whole sometimes causes speakers to make the verb plural, but this is better avoided. See also **together, well.**

with·al (with-áwl || with-) *adv.* **1.** *Literary.* Besides; in addition. **2.** *Literary.* Despite that; nevertheless. **3.** *Archaic.* Therewith: *a maid for him to marry withal.*
~*prep. Archaic.* With. [Middle English *with al(le)* : WITH + ALL.]

with·draw (with-dráw, with-) *v.* **-drew** (-drōō || -dréw), **-drawn** (-dráwn), **-drawing, -draws.** —*tr.* **1.** To take back or away; remove: *withdrew fifty pounds from his account.* **2.** To recall; retract: *withdrew the charges.* —*intr.* **1.** To move or draw back; retreat; retire. **2. a.** To remove oneself from activity or a social environment. **b.** To remove the centre of one's concern away from external activity; become detached. [Middle English *withdrawen* : *with,* away from, WITH + *drawen,* to pull, DRAW.]

with·draw·al (with-dráw-əl, with-, -dráwl, *often* -dráwrəl) *n.* Also **with·draw·ment** (-dráwmənt). **1.** The act or an instance of withdrawing, especially: **a.** A retreat, retirement, or disengagement. **b.** A detachment, as from emotional involvement. **c.** A removal of something that has been deposited: *made a large withdrawal from her account.* **2.** Termination of the administration of a habit-forming substance, which usually precipitates specific mental and physical *withdrawal symptoms.* **3.** The act of **coitus interruptus** *(see).*

withdrawn. Past participle of **withdraw.**
~*adj.* **1.** Remote; isolated. **2.** Socially retiring; introverted; shy. **3.** Detached; preoccupied.

withe (with, with, wīth) *n.* A tough, supple twig, especially a willow twig, used for binding things together; a withy.
~*tr.v.* **withed, withing, withes.** To bind with withes. [Middle English *withe, withe,* Old English *withthe.*]

with·er (wíthər) *v.* **-ered, -ering, -ers.** —*intr.* **1.** To dry up or shrivel from or as if from loss of moisture: *The flowers withered in the sun.* **2.** To lose freshness, vitality, or strength; fade: *Hope withered away; withered under his sarcasm.* —*tr.* **1.** To cause to shrivel or fade. **2.** To cause to feel belittled; cut down; abash: *withered her with a glance.* [Middle English *widderen,* perhaps variant of *wederen,* to weather, from *weder,* WEATHER.]

with·er·ite (wíthə-rīt) *n.* A white, yellow, or grey vitreous mineral, barium carbonate, $BaCO_3$. [After William *Withering* (1741–99), English physician.]

with·ers (witharz) *pl.n.* The high point of the back of a horse, or of a similar or related animal, at the base of the neck and between the shoulder blades. [Perhaps from obsolete *wither-,* denoting opposition (the withers resist or "oppose" a load), from Middle English *wither-,* Old English *wither-,* from *wither,* against.]

with·er·shins (wíthər-shin) *adv.* Also **wid·der·shins** (wíddər-). *Chiefly Scottish.* In a direction opposite to the course of the sun; anticlockwise. [Middle Low German *weddersin(ne)s,* from Middle High German *widersinnes,* "countercourse" : *wider,* against + *sinnes,* genitive of *sin,* journey, direction.]

with·hold (with-hōld, with-) *v.* **-held** (-héld), **-holding, -holds.** —*tr.* **1.** To keep in check; restrain. **2.** To refrain from giving, granting, or permitting: *withhold permission.* —*intr.* To refrain; forbear. **—**See Synonyms at **keep.** [Middle English *withholden* : *with,* back, away from, WITH + *holden,* to HOLD.] **—with·hold·er** *n.*

with·hold·ing tax (with-hōlding, with-) *n.* In the United States, a portion of an employee's pay withheld by his employer, who then pays it to the government as partial payment of the employee's income tax.

with·in (with-ín || with-) *adv. Formal.* **1.** In or into the inner part; inside. **2.** In or belonging to a community or group: *the enemy within.* **3.** Inside the body, mind, heart, or soul; inwardly: *Purify me within.*
~*prep.* **1.** In the inner part or parts of; inside: *The kingdom of heaven is within you.* **2.** Inside the limits or extent of in time, degree or distance: *within ten miles of home; separated within a year of their marriage.* **3.** Inside the fixed limits of; not exceeding or transgressing: *within the laws of the land.* **4.** In the scope, sphere, or range of: *within the medical profession; within sight but not within reach.*

with·in·doors (with-ín-dórz || with-, -dōrz) *adv. Archaic.* Indoors.

with-it (wíth-it || wíth-) *adj. Informal.* Up-to-date; trendy.

with·out (with-ówt, with-) *adv.* **1.** *Formal.* In or on the outside. **2.** *Formal.* Externally; outwardly. **3.** With something lacking or missing: *We can get along without.*
~*prep.* **1.** Not having; lacking: *a family without a car.* **2. a.** With no or none of; in the absence of: *without help.* **b.** Not accompanied by: *no smoke without fire.* **3.** *Archaic.* At, on, to, or towards the outside or exterior of: *without the walls.* **4.** With neglect or avoidance of: *went by without speaking to us.*
~*conj. Archaic & Regional.* Unless. [Middle English *withouten,* Old English *withūtan* : *with,* not together with, separated, WITH + *ūtan,* outside of, from *ūt,* OUT.]

with·out·doors (with-ówt-dórz || with-, -dōrz) *adv. Archaic.* Outside of a house or shelter; outdoors.

with·stand (with-stánd, with-) *v.* **-stood, -standing, -stands.** —*tr.* **1.** To oppose with effort or force; resist. **2.** To resist or endure successfully; stand up to: *withstood years of hard wear.* —*intr.* To offer resistance. **—**See Synonyms at **oppose.** [Middle English *withstanden,* Old English *withstandan* : *with,* against, WITH + *standan,* to STAND.] **—with·stand·er** *n.*

with·y (wíthi || wíthi) *adj.* Resembling a withe in wiriness or toughness: *a withy young boxer.*
~*n., pl.* **withies. 1.** A rope or band made of withes. **2.** A long, flexible twig, such as that of an osier. **3.** A tree or shrub having such twigs. [Middle English *wythy,* flexible twig, willow wand, Old English *wīthig.*]

wit·less (wít-ləss, -liss) *adj.* Lacking intelligence or wit; stupid. **—wit·less·ly** *adv.* **—wit·less·ness** *n.*

wit·ling (wít-ling) *n. Archaic.* One who thinks himself a wit.

wit·ness (wít-nəss, -niss) *n.* **1.** One who has perceived something and who can give evidence for its occurrence: *Were there any witnesses to the accident?* **2.** Anything that serves as evidence; a testimony. **3.** *Law.* **a.** One who is called upon to testify before a court. **b.** One who is called upon to be present at a transaction in order to

PRONUNCIATION KEY

a, trap; aa, father; ai, fair;
ar, star; aw, lawn; ay, play;
b, bb, stab; rubber;
ch, church; ck, ticket;
d, dd, dead; ladder; e, dress;
ee, bee; er, defer; ew, few;
ewr, pure; ə, about;
ər, letter; f, ff, fife; differ;
g, gg, giggle; h, hat; i, kit;
ī, price; īr, fire; j, judge;
k, kick; l, ll, let; 'l, needle;
m, mm, man; n, nn, no;
'n, sudden; ng, thing; o, lot;
ō, no; ōō, foot; ōō, shoe;
oor, poor; ow, cow;
owr, hour; oy, boy;
p, pp, pepper; r, rr, red;
s, ss, sauce; sh, ship;
t, tt, totter; th, thick; th, this;
smooth; u, cut; ur, turn;
v, vv, valve; w, wet; y, yes;
z, zz, zebra; zh, vision;
pleasure

IN FOREIGN WORDS:

aN, oN, Saint-Saëns;
hl, Llanelli; Hluhluwe;
kh, loch; lough; Khaled

STRESS MARK:

ín-sīt, insight; in-sít, incite

attest to what took place. **c.** One who signs his name to a document for the purpose of attesting to its authenticity. **4.** An attestation to a fact, statement, or event.
~*v.* **witnessed, -nessing, -nesses.** —*tr.* **1.** To be present at or have direct personal knowledge of (an event, for example). **2.** To provide or serve as evidence of. **3.** To be the setting or site of: *This auditorium witnesses many ceremonies.* **4.** To attest to the legality or authenticity of (a document) by signing one's name. **5.** To consider as evidence or proof. Used parenthetically in the imperative: *The C.B.I. (witness its recent report) is clearly losing patience with the government.* —*intr.* To furnish or serve as evidence; testify. [Middle English *witnes(se),* Old English *witnes,* witness, knowledge, from *wit,* knowledge, WIT.] —**wit·ness·er** *n.*

witness box *n.* The place in a courtroom from which a witness presents testimony. Also *U.S.* "witness stand", "stand".

wit·ted (wíttid) *adj.* Having wits or understanding as specified. Used in combination: *dim-witted; half-witted.*

Wit·ten·berg (wítt'n-berg; *German* vítt'n-bàirk). Town of Halle district, central East Germany. Situated on the river Elbe, it is where Martin Luther nailed his 95 theses to the door of the Schlosskirche (1517), so initiating the Protestant Reformation.

Witt·gen·stein (vít-gən-shtīn, -stīn), **Ludwig Johann Josef** (1889–1951). Austrian philosopher. A follower of Frege and Russell, he worked on theories of language and in his *Tractatus Logico-Philosophicus* (1921) he helped to develop logical positivism. His other important work, *Philosophical Investigations,* published (1953) after his death, examined linguistic ambiguities in philosophical statements.

wit·ti·cism (wítti-siz'm) *n.* A witty remark or saying. See Synonyms at **joke.** [From WITTY (influenced by CRITICISM).]

wit·ting (wítting). *Archaic.* Present participle of **wit** (to know).
~*adj.* **1.** Aware or conscious. **2.** Done intentionally or with premeditation; deliberate. —**wit·ting·ly** *adv.*

wit·tol (witt'l) *n. Archaic.* A man who tolerates his wife's infidelity. [Middle English *wetewold* : *weten, witen,* to WIT (know) + *(coke)wold,* CUCKOLD.]

wit·ty (wítti) *adj.* **-tier, -tiest. 1.** Possessing, characterised by, or demonstrating wit in speech or writing; ingenious and humorous. **2.** *Archaic.* Intelligent. —**wit·ti·ly** *adv.* —**wit·ti·ness** *n.*

Wit·wa·ters·rand (wit-wáwtərz-rand, wít-wawtərz-; *locally* -waatərz-, -raand, -rónt, -raant). Region of south Transvaal, Republic of South Africa, also informally known as the Rand or the Reef. Dominated by ridges forming the watershed of the Vaal and Olifant rivers, its gold reserves, exploited since 1886, account for almost one third of world output.

wive (wīv) *v.* **wived, wiving, wives.** *Archaic.* —*tr.* **1.** To marry (a woman); take as a wife. **2.** To provide a wife for. —*intr.* To marry a woman. [Middle English *wiven,* Old English *wīfian,* from *wīf,* WIFE.]

wivern. Variant of **wyvern.**

wives. Plural of **wife.**

wiz (wiz) *n. Informal.* A person considered exceptionally gifted or skilled; a wizard. [Short for WIZARD.]

wiz·ard (wízzərd) *n.* **1.** A male witch; a sorcerer or magician. **2.** A person who is skilful or clever at a particular activity: *a wizard at cooking.* **3.** *Archaic.* A wise man or sage.
~*adj.* **1.** Of or pertaining to wizards or wizardry. **2.** *Chiefly British Informal.* Excellent; wonderful. [Middle English *wysard* : *wys, wis,* WISE + -ARD.]

wiz·ard·ry (wízzədri) *n.* The art, skill, or practice of a wizard; witchcraft; sorcery.

wiz·en[1] (wízz'n) *v.* **-ened, -ening, -ens.** —*intr.* To wither or sear; dry up; shrivel. —*tr.* To cause to wither or dry up.
~*adj.* Variant of **wizened.** [Middle English *wisenen,* Old English *wisnian.*]

wiz·ened (wízz'nd) *adj.* Also **wizen.** Shrivelled or dried up, as through age; withered.

wk. 1. weak. **2.** week.

WL, w.l. waterline.

WLM Women's Liberation Movement.

W.M.O World Meteorological Organisation.

WNW west-northwest.

WO, W.O. 1. warrant officer. **2.** wireless operator.

woad (wōd) *n.* **1.** An Old World plant, *Isatis tinctoria,* formerly cultivated for its leaves that yield a blue dye. **2.** The dye obtained from this plant. [Middle English *wod(e),* Old English *wād*†.]

woad·wax·en (wōd-waks'n) *n.* A shrub, **dyer's greenweed** *(see).* [Variant (influenced by WOAD) of WOODWAXEN.]

wob·be·gong (wóbbi-gong) *n.* Any of various Australian sharks of the family Orectolobidae, having brown and white markings. [From a native Australian language.]

wob·ble, wab·ble (wóbb'l) *v.* **-bled, -bling, -bles.** —*intr.* **1.** To move or sway unsteadily from side to side. **2.** To tremble or quaver; shake: *Her voice wobbled with emotion.* **3.** To waver or vacillate in one's opinions, feelings, or the like. —*tr.* To cause to wobble.
~*n.* The act or an instance of wobbling, as in a movement or sound. —See Synonyms at **shake.** [Perhaps from Low German *wabbeln.*] —**wob·bler** *n.*

wobble board *n.* In Australia, a flexible, rectangular sheet, as of masonite, used as a musical instrument, that produces a low booming sound when bent back and forwards.

wob·bly (wóbbli) *adj.* **-blier, -bliest.** Tending to wobble; unsteady; shaky.

Wob·bly (wóbbli) *n., pl.* **-blies.** A member of the Industrial Workers of the World (I.W.W.). [20th century : origin obscure.]

Wode·house (wŏŏd-howss), **Sir P(elham) G(renville)** (1881–1975). British comic novelist. He introduced his most famous characters, the aristocratic Bertie Wooster and his manservant Jeeves in *The Inimitable Jeeves* (1923).

Wo·den, Wo·dan (wōd'n). The chief god in Anglo-Saxon mythology, often identified with the Norse god Odin. [Old English *Wōden.*]

wodge. Variant of **wadge.**

woe (wō) *n.* **1.** Deep sorrow; grief. **2.** *Literary.* Misfortune; calamity: *"Woe unto you that are full!"* (Luke 6:25). **3.** *Usually plural.* A difficulty; a trouble: *Life is full of woes.* —See Synonyms at **regret.**
~*interj. Literary.* Used to express sorrow or dismay: *Woe is me!* [Middle English *wo(e),* Old English *wā* (interjection).]

woe·be·gone (wō-bi-gon ‖ -gaan, -gawn) *adj.* **1.** Mournful, sorrowful, or pathetic in appearance. **2.** *Archaic.* Struck by disaster; afflicted. [Middle English *wo begon* : *wo(e),* WOE + *begon,* beset, from *begon,* to beset, go about : *be-,* about + *gon,* to GO.]

woe·ful (wōf'l) *adj.* **1.** Afflicted with woe; mournful. **2.** Pitiful, wretched, or deplorable: *a woeful attempt at a poem.* —**woe·ful·ly** *adv.* —**woe·ful·ness** *n.*

wog·gle (wógg'l) *n.* A leather ring used to secure the neckerchief of a Scout or Guide uniform.

wok (wok) *n.* A large bowl-shaped metal pan used, especially in Chinese cooking, for frying, steaming, and the like. [Cantonese.]

woke. Past tense and *chiefly British & regional* past participle of **wake.**

wok·en. *Chiefly British & Regional.* Past participle of **wake.**

wold (wōld) *n.* A stretch of open, unforested, rolling countryside or moorland. [Middle English *wold,* a forest, hill, Old English *weald, wald,* from Germanic *walthus* (unattested).]

wolf (wŏŏlf) *n., pl.* **wolves** (wŏŏlvz). **1. a.** A carnivorous mammal, *Canis lupus,* of northern regions, that hunts in packs and is related to and resembles the dogs. **b.** The fur of such an animal. **2.** Any of various similar or related mammals. **3.** The destructive larva of any of various moths, beetles, or flies. **4. a.** One who is rapacious, predatory, and fierce. **b.** *Informal.* A man given to avid amatory pursuit of women. **5.** *Music.* **a.** A harshness in some notes of a bowed stringed instrument produced by defective vibration. **b.** Dissonance in some intervals of a keyboard instrument tuned to a system of unequal temperament. —**cry wolf.** To raise a false alarm. —**have** or **hold a wolf by the ears.** To be in a dangerous or precarious situation. —**keep the wolf from the door.** To ward off or avert hunger or poverty. —**throw to the wolves.** To abandon to certain destruction. —**wolf in sheep's clothing.** A person who conceals his malicious nature or intentions under a friendly exterior.
~*tr.v.* **wolfed, wolfing, wolfs.** To eat voraciously. Often used with *down.* [Middle English *wolf(e),* Old English *wulf.*] —**wolf·ish** *adj.* —**wolf·ish·ly** *adv.*

wolf *Wolves, which were once common in Eurasia and North America, are now found only in remote forests. They live in packs within specific territories and feed chiefly on mice and carrion as well as large hoofed mammals such as deer.*

Wolf (volf), **Hugo** (1860–1903). Austrian composer. Chiefly a composer of songs, he set the poetry of Goethe and Italian and Spanish writers, and wrote the opera *Der Corregidor* (1895).

Wolf Cub *n. Chiefly British.* Formerly, a Cub Scout.

wolf dog *n.* **1.** A dog trained to hunt or ward off wolves. **2.** The offspring of a dog and a wolf.

Wolfe (wŏŏlf), **James** (1727–59). British army officer. He led the successful assault on the French stronghold of Louisbourg in Nova Scotia. He was killed at the battle of the Plains of Abraham (1759), which won the city of Quebec and New France for Britain.

Wolfe, Thomas (Clayton) (1900–38). U.S. novelist. His works include *Look Homeward Angel* (1929) and the posthumously published *You Can't Go Home Again* (1940).

Wolff·i·an body (wŏŏlfi-ən) *n.* The **mesonephros** *(see).* [After Kasper Friedrich *Wolff* (1733–94), German embryologist.]

wolf fish *n.* Any of several northern slender marine fishes of the genus *Anarhichas,* having sharp, powerful teeth and no pelvic fins.

wolf·hound (wŏŏlf-hownd) *n.* Any of various large dogs trained to hunt wolves or other large game. See **borzoi, Irish wolfhound.**

wolf pack *n.* Submarines or aircraft that attack as a group.

wolf·ram (wŏŏlfrəm) *n.* The element **tungsten** *(see).* [German *Wolfram* : perhaps Middle High German *wolf,* wolf, + *rām,* dirt, black, probably akin to Sanskrit *Rāma,* RAMA.]

wolf·ram·ite (wŏŏlfrə-mīt) *n.* Any of several red-brown to black minerals with the general formula $(Fe,Mn)WO_4$, a major source of tungsten. [German *Wolframit,* from WOLFRAM.]

wolfs·bane (wŏŏlfs-bayn) *n.* A plant, the **monkshood** *(see).*

wolf spider *n.* Any spider of the family Lycopsidae, having long stout legs and hunting their prey. Also called "hunting spider".

wolf spider Lycosa lugubris, *drawn here about 1½ times life size, is one of numerous species known as wolf spiders. Unlike most spiders, which wait beside their webs for their insect prey, wolf spiders usually hunt by chasing and then pouncing on their victims like wolves – hence their name.*

wolf whistle *n.* A short, distinctive whistle rising to a high note and then diminishing again to a low note, used by a man to express sexual admiration for a woman. —**wolf-whistle** (wŏŏlf-wiss'l) *v.*

wol·las·ton·ite (wŏŏlləstə-nīt) *n.* A mineral, calcium silicate, $CaSiO_3$, found in metamorphic rocks and used in various ceramics, paints, plastics, and cements. [After William *Wollaston* (1766–1828), British physicist.]

Wol·las·ton prism (wŏŏlləstən) *n.* A prism cut from quartz that separates the ordinary and extraordinary components of unpolarized light. [After W. H. *Wollaston*; see **wollastonite.**]

Wol·lon·gong (wŏŏlləng-gong). City in New South Wales, southeastern Australia. Situated on the Tasman Sea, it has coal, iron and steel, chemical, and textile industries.

Woll·stone·craft (wŏŏl-stən-kraaft ‖ -kraft), **Mary** (1759–97). Brit-

wombat *An Australian burrowing marsupial, the wombat has a rearward-facing pouch. A kangaroo's pouch, by contrast, opens forwards. Wombats have rodent-like teeth and feed mainly on grass and roots.*

woodchuck *Also known as a ground hog, the woodchuck is a type of marmot native to the woodlands of North America. Woodchucks live in colonies underground and hibernate each winter.*

woodcock Scolopax rusticola, *the woodcock (above), is a wading bird which is common in woods with wet or boggy ground in Europe and Asia. Its russet plumage provides excellent camouflage as it sits among the fallen leaves on the woodland floor.*

ish radical and feminist. As a publisher's adviser, she met various radicals including Tom Paine and her husband William Godwin. Her works include *A Vindication of the Rights of Women* (1792), and a reply to Burke in *View of the French Revolution* (1794). She died giving birth to her daughter, who became Mary Shelley.

Wo·lof (wóllof || *U.S.* wō-lawf) *n.* A West Atlantic language of Senegal. **—Wo·lof** *adj.*

Wolse·ley (wŏŏlzli), **Garnet Joseph, 1st Viscount** (1833–1913). British field-marshal. He won the battle of Tall al Kabir (1882), led the expedition to relieve General Gordon at Khartoum (1884–85), and became commander-in-chief of the Army (1895–1899).

Wolsey, Thomas (*c.* 1475–1530). English cardinal. He rose to become the Bishop of Lincoln and Archbishop of York (1514) and a cardinal and Lord Chancellor of England (1515). He controlled foreign policy and worked for the increase of England's power. He was indecisive over Henry VIII's wish to divorce Catherine of Aragon, was prosecuted (1529), and arrested for high treason (1530).

Wol·ver·hamp·ton (wŏŏlvər-hámptən). Town in the West Midlands, west central England. It has long been a centre for metal-working, particularly locks and keys. Other industries include motor vehicles, bicycles, chemicals, and aircraft.

wol·ver·ine (wŏŏlvə-reen) *n.* A carnivorous mammal, *Gulo gulo* (or *G. luscus*), of northern regions, having dark fur and a bushy tail. Also called "glutton", "carcajou". [Earlier *wolvering,* irregularly from WOLF.]

wolves. Plural of **wolf.**

wom·an (wŏŏmmən) *n., pl.* **women** (wímmin). **1. a.** An adult female human being, as distinguished from a man or a girl. **b.** A woman of a specified status or occupation, or concerned with a specified sphere of activity. Used in combination: *a noblewoman; a policewoman.* **2.** Women collectively; womankind: *Woman is more resistant than man.* **3.** Feminine quality or aspect; womanliness. Usually preceded by *the*: *brought out the woman in him.* **4.** A female employed to do household duties. **5.** *Informal.* A wife or female lover. —See Usage note at **lady.**
~*adj.* Female as opposed to male. [Middle English *wumman, wimman,* Old English *wīfmann* : *wīf,* WIFE + *man(n),* person, MAN.]

wom·an·hood (wŏŏmmən-hŏŏd) *n.* **1.** The state of being a woman. **2.** Feminine nature or qualities. **3.** Womankind.

wom·an·ise, wom·an·ize (wŏŏmmə-nīz) *v.* **-ised, -ising, -ises.** *—tr.* To give feminine characteristics to. *—intr.* To indulge in casual affairs with women habitually or excessively. Used of a man. **—wom·an·is·er** *n.*

wom·an·ish (wŏŏmmənish) *adj.* **1.** Characteristic of a woman; womanly. **2.** Considered more typical of or appropriate to the nature of a woman than of a man; effeminate; weak. **—wom·an·ish·ly** *adv.* **—wom·an·ish·ness** *n.*

wom·an·kind (wŏŏmmən-kīnd) *n.* Female human beings collectively; women.

wom·an·ly (wŏŏmmənli) *adj.* **-lier, -liest.** Having the qualities, such as warmth and compassion, thought of as being typical of or appropriate to a woman. **—wom·an·li·ness** *n.*

womb (wŏŏm) *n.* **1.** The **uterus** *(see).* **2. a.** A place where something is generated or developed. **b.** Any protective and confining organ, receptacle, or place. **3.** *Obsolete.* The belly. [Middle English *womb(e),* Old English *wamb,* from Germanic *wambō* (unattested).]

wom·bat (wóm-bat) *n.* Either of two Australian marsupials, *Phascolomis ursinus* or *Lasiorhinus latifrons,* somewhat resembling small bears. [Native Australian name.]

wom·en·folk (wímmin-fōk) *pl.n.* **1.** Women collectively. **2.** A particular group of women, as those belonging to one family.

Women's Institute *n.* In Britain and some Commonwealth countries, an organisation, especially in rural areas, that holds meetings and talks for women interested in social and domestic matters.

women's lib·ber (líbbər) *n. Informal.* An adherent of the Women's Movement. Usually used derogatorily.

Women's Liberation Movement *n. Abbr.* **WLM** The social and political movement that originated in Europe and the United States in the 19th century seeking to bring into effect the principles of **feminism** *(see).* Among the early exponents of the movement were emancipated black slaves in the United States and suffragettes in Britain. Also called "Women's movement", informally "Women's Lib". **—women's liberationist** *n.*

womera *n.* Variant of **woomera.**

won[1] (wun, won) *intr.v.* **wonned, wonning, wons.** *Archaic.* To dwell or abide. [Middle English *won(i)en,* Old English *wunian.*]

won[2] (won) *n., pl.* **won. 1.** The basic monetary unit of South Korea, equal to 100 jeon, jon or chon. **2.** The basic monetary unit of North Korea, equal to 100 jeon, jon or chon. [Korean.]

won[3]. Past tense and past participle of **win.**

won·der (wúndər) *n.* **1.** That which arouses awe, astonishment, or admiration; a marvel. Also used adjectivally: *a wonder cure; a wonder horse.* **2.** The feeling or emotion aroused by a wonder, characterised by admiration, awe, and sometimes bewilderment. **3.** A matter for surprise: *It's a wonder you weren't killed. No wonder it's not working —you haven't plugged it in.* **4.** *Plural. Informal.* Something miraculous or impressively successful in effect: *The advert did wonders for sales.* **5.** See **Seven Wonders of the World. —for a wonder.** Surprisingly. **—small wonder.** It is hardly surprising.
~*v.* **wondered, -dering, -ders.** *—intr.* **1. a.** To ponder with curiosity; speculate. **b.** To entertain doubts: *I often wonder about his honesty.* **2.** To have a feeling of awe or admiration; marvel. *—tr.* **1.** To feel curiosity about. **2.** *Chiefly British.* To feel surprise at: *I wonder that you're still awake.* **3.** Used to express a polite inquiry or request: *I wonder whether you would mind shutting the door.* [Middle English *wonder,* Old English *wundor.*] **—won·der·er** *n.*
Usage: The use of a double negative construction with this verb is commonly found in informal English, though it should be avoided in more formal contexts: *I shouldn't wonder if she doesn't arrive by ten* (in the sense "I expect her to arrive by ten").

won·der·ful (wúndərf'l) *adj.* **1.** Capable of exciting wonder; astonishing: *amazed at the scheme's wonderful simplicity.* **2.** Fine; excellent. **—won·der·ful·ly** *adv.* **—won·der·ful·ness** *n.*

won·der·land (wúndər-land) *n.* **1.** A marvellous imaginary realm. **2.** A marvellous place or scene that is real and not imaginary.

won·der·ment (wúndərmənt) *n.* **1.** Astonishment, awe, or surprise. **2.** Puzzlement or curiosity. **3.** Something that produces wonder; a marvel.

Wonders of the Ancient World. The **Seven Wonders of the World** *(see).*

won·der·worker (wúndər-wurkər) *n.* One who performs miracles or achieves exceptional success.

won·drous (wúndrəss) *adj. Literary.* Wonderful.
~*adv. Archaic.* To a wonderful or remarkable extent. **—won·drous·ly** *adv.*

won·ga-won·ga (wóngga-wóngga) *n.* **1.** A large pigeon, *Leucosarcia melanoleuca,* of Australia. **2.** Any of several Australian vines of the genus *Pandorea;* especially, *P. pandorea.* [From a native Australian language.]

won·ky (wóngki) *adj.* **-kier, -kiest.** *British Informal.* **1.** Shaky; unsteady. **2.** Not straight; askew. **3.** Wrong; faulty. [20th century : origin obscure.]

Won·san (wón-sán). Capital of Kangwon province, southeastern North Korea. Situated on the Sea of Japan, it is an industrial and communications centre, port, and naval base.

wont (wōnt || wont, *U.S. also* wawnt, wunt) *adj. Formal.* Accustomed or used to. Usually used with an infinitive: *He was wont to drink port after dinner.*
~*n. Formal.* Usage or custom: *rose early, as was her wont.*
~*v.* **wont, wont** or **wonted, wonting, wonts.** *Archaic. —tr.* To accustom. *—intr.* To be in the habit of doing something. [Middle English *wont,* from the past participle of *wonen,* to be accustomed, dwell, to WON.]

won't (wōnt). Contraction of *will not.*

wont·ed (wōnt-id || wónt-, *U.S. also* wáwnt-, wúnt-) *adj. Formal.* Accustomed; usual. Used before the noun: *at the wonted hour.*

woo (wōō) *v.* **wooed, wooing, woos.** *—tr.* **1.** To seek the affection of with intent to marry. **2. a.** To seek to achieve; try to gain; court: *wooed the favour of the public with tax cuts.* **b.** To make efforts to gain the favour or compliance of; tempt: *wooing the electorate.* **3.** To entreat, solicit, or importune. *—intr.* To court a woman. [Middle English *wowen,* Old English *wōgian*†.] **—woo·er** *n.*

wood[1] (wŏŏd) *n.* **1. a.** The tough, fibrous cellular substance constituting the xylem of trees and shrubs, lying beneath the bark and consisting largely of cellulose and lignin. **b.** Such a substance used for any of a wide variety of purposes, as for building material or fuel. **2.** *Often plural.* A dense growth of trees; a small forest. **3.** An object or part made of wood, especially: **a.** *Music.* A woodwind instrument. **b.** A golf club having a wooden head. **c.** A cask or barrel for storing wine or other alcoholic drinks: *a pint of beer from the wood.* **d.** The frame of a tennis racket, as opposed to its strings. **e.** A wooden ball used in the game of bowls. **—not see the wood for the trees.** To be unable to get an overall or general view because of a confusing mass of details. **—out of the wood** or **woods.** Free of difficulties or dangers. **—touch wood. 1.** To place the hand against a wooden object in an act of superstition to avert bad luck or misfortune, especially after having made a positive statement about someone or something. **2.** Used as an interjection in place of or as well as the act of touching wood.
~*adj.* **1.** Made or consisting of wood; wooden. **2.** Associated with, used on, or containing wood: *a wood screw; a wood box.* **3.** Growing or living in woods or forests.
~*v.* **wooded, wooding, woods.** *—tr.* **1.** To supply or fuel with wood. **2.** To cover with trees; forest. *—intr.* To gather or be supplied with wood. [Middle English *wode,* Old English *wudu.*]

wood[2] *adj. Archaic.* Violently insane. [Middle English *wo(o)d,* Old English *wōd.*]

Wood, Sir Henry (Joseph), born Paul Klenovsky (1869–1944). British conductor and organist. He introduced the Promenade Concerts in London at the Queen's Hall (1895), which he conducted until his death, and championed many contemporary composers.

Wood, John (1704–54). English architect. Known as Wood of Bath, from the 1720s he designed many of its buildings and streets in the Palladian style. His son John Wood (1728–81) designed the Assembly Rooms and the Royal Crescent.

wood alcohol *n.* **Methanol** *(see).*

wood anemone *n.* Either of two plants, *Anemone nemorosa,* of Europe, or *A. quinquefolia,* of eastern North America, having deeply divided leaves and a solitary white or pink flower. Also called "windflower".

wood ant *n.* A reddish European ant, *Formica rufa,* whose anthills are found in woodlands.

wood avens *n.* A plant, **herb bennet** *(see).*

wood·bine (wŏŏdbīn) *n.* Any of various climbing vines, especially: **1.** An Old World honeysuckle, *Lonicera periclymenum,* having yellowish flowers. **2.** *U.S.* The **Virginia creeper** *(see).* [Middle English

ACHIEVEMENTS OF ANTIQUITY

Seven marvels that astounded the ancient Greeks

In the 2nd century B.C., the Greek writer Antipater of Sidon was one of several writers who listed the greatest buildings and monuments of his day. Because seven was a magic number in Greek, Hebrew, and Chinese cultures, he selected seven of these wonders.

The Egyptian pyramids These are the only "wonders" still surviving and are now more than 4,000 years old.

The hanging gardens of Babylon Built by Nebuchadnezzar II in the 7th century B.C., they consisted of a series of terraces on which trees and flowers were grown. They stretched along the banks of the Euphrates, from which they were watered by irrigation channels.

The statue of Zeus at Olympia A colossal figure with an ivory body and gold cloak, created in the 5th century B.C. by the Athenian Pheidias. It burned down in A.D. 475.

The temple of Artemis at Ephesus, Asia Minor Built of marble in the 6th century B.C., it was rebuilt in the 4th century B.C. and finally destroyed in the 3rd century A.D. There are fragments in the British Museum, London.

The Mausoleum at Halicarnassus, Asia Minor The tomb of Mausolus, a ruler of the city in the 4th century B.C. It was destroyed by an earthquake before the 15th century.

The Colossus of Rhodes A huge statue of the sun-god, standing about 36 metres (120 feet) high at the mouth of Rhodes harbour. It was erected about 305 B.C. and destroyed by an earthquake in the 3rd century B.C.

The Pharos of Alexandria Thought to be the first lighthouse in the world, and to have stood 122 metres (400 feet) high, with a spiral ramp leading to the beacon. It was built in 270 B.C. on the island of Pharos at the entrance to the harbour of Alexandria in Egypt, and was destroyed in the 14th century.

THE GREAT PYRAMIDS *Standing on the west bank of the Nile near Cairo, they were built by slave labour between 3000 and 1800 B.C. as tombs for the Egyptian pharaohs. Inside, the mummified bodies were surrounded with treasure.*

wodebinde, Old English *wudubinde :* wudu, WOOD + *bindan,* to BIND.]

wood·block (wood-blok) *n.* **1.** A woodcut. **2.** *Music.* A partially hollowed out block of hard wood struck with a drumstick, used as a percussion instrument.

wood·bor·er (wood-bawror ‖ -bōror) *n.* Any of various insects, insect larvae, or molluscs that bore into wood.

wood·carv·ing (wood-kaarving) *n.* **1.** The art of carving in wood. **2.** An object carved from wood. **—wood·carv·er** *n.*

wood·chat (wood-chat) *n.* An Old World bird, *Lanius senator,* having black and white plumage with a reddish crown.

wood·chuck (wood-chuk) *n.* A common rodent, *Marmota monax,* of northern and eastern North America, having a short-legged, heavy-set body and grizzled brownish fur. Also called "ground hog". [Variant (by folk etymology) of Cree *oček,* from Proto-Algonquian *wečyeka* (unattested), "fisher".]

wood coal *n.* **1.** Charcoal. **2.** Lignite.

wood·cock (wood-kok) *n., pl.* **-cocks** or collectively **woodcock.** Either of two related game birds, *Scolopax rusticola,* of the Old World, or *Philohela minor,* of North America, having brownish plumage, short legs, and a long bill. [Middle English *wodecok,* Old English *wuducocc : wudu,* WOOD + *cocc,* COCK.]

wood·craft (wood-kraaft ‖ -kraft) *n.* **1.** The act, process, or art of working with wood. **2.** Skill and experience in matters pertaining to the woods, such as hunting, fishing, or camping.

wood·cut (wood-kut) *n.* **1.** A piece of wood upon which a design for printing is engraved, especially along the grain. Also called "wood block". **2.** A print made from such a piece of wood. Also called "woodblock", "woodprint".

wood·cut·ter (wood-kuttor) *n.* A person who cuts wood or trees. **—wood·cut·ting** *n.*

wood·ed (woodid) *adj.* Having or covered with trees or woods.

wood·en (woodd'n) *adj.* **1.** Made or consisting of wood. **2.** Stiff; inflexible. **3.** Lifeless; expressionless. **—wood·en·ly** *adv.* **—wood·en·ness** *n.*

wood engraving *n.* **1.** A piece of wood upon which a design for printing is engraved, usually across the grain. **2.** The art or process of making wood engravings. **3.** A print made from such a piece of wood.

wood·en·head (woodd'n-hed) *n. Informal.* A stupid person; a blockhead. **—wood·en·head·ed** (-heddid) *adj.*

Wooden Horse *n.* The **Trojan horse** *(see).*

wooden spoon *n.* A booby prize, especially awarded to one who comes last in a sports competition. [After the former custom at Cambridge of presenting a wooden spoon to the lowest-ranking of the students taking honours in the mathematical tripos.]

wood grouse *n.* A bird, the **capercaillie** *(see).*

wood ibis *n.* Any of several large wading birds of the family Ciconiiformes, related to and resembling the storks; especially, *Mycteria americana* of the New World.

wood·land (woodland) *n.* Land having a cover of trees and shrubs. *~adj.* Of or indigenous to such a wooded area. **—wood·land·er** *n.*

wood·lark (wood-laark) *n.* An Old World songbird, *Lullula arborea,* resembling but smaller than the skylark.

wood louse *n.* Any of various small terrestrial crustaceans having a flattened segmented body and found in damp, shady places, especially under logs and stones. Also called "slater", "pill bug".

wood·man (wood-mon) *n., pl.* **-men** (-mon). A woodcutter or woodsman.

wood·note (wood-nōt) *n.* **1.** A song or call characteristic of a woodland bird. **2.** A piece of music or poetry resembling a bird's song in its spontaneity.

wood nymph *n.* A nymph of the forest; a dryad.

wood·peck·er (wood-peckor) *n.* Any of various birds of the family Picidae, having strong claws and a stiff tail adapted for clinging to and climbing trees, and a chisel-like bill for drilling through bark and wood.

wood pigeon *n.* A large Eurasian pigeon, *Columba palumbus,* having a white band on each wing. Also called "ringdove".

wood·pile (wood-pīl) *n.* A pile of wood, especially when stacked for use as fuel.

wood·print (wood-print) *n.* A woodcut *(see).*

wood pulp *n.* Any of various cellulose pulps ground from wood, chemically processed, and used to make paper.

wood·ruff (wood-ruf) *n.* Any of various plants of the genera *Galium* and *Asperula* in the bedstraw family; especially, *G. odoratum,* which has fragrant white flowers and whorls of narrow leaves, formerly used, when dried, as bedding and stuffing. [Middle English *woderofe,* Old English *wudurofe : wudu,* WOOD *-rofe,* of uncertain origin; perhaps akin to Middle Low German *röve,* turnip.]

wood·rush (wood-rush) *n.* Any of various plants of the genus *Luzula,* resembling rushes but having long white hairs on the leaves and stems and generally found in drier habitats.

wood·screw (wood-skrōō ‖ -skrew) *n.* A tapered metal screw that is driven into wood, plaster, and the like with a screwdriver.

wood·shed (wood-shed) *n.* A shed in which firewood is stored.

woods·man (woodz-mon) *n., pl.* **-men** (-mon). One who works or lives in the woods or is versed in woodcraft; a forester.

wood sorrel *n.* Any of various plants of the genus *Oxalis,* having compound leaves with three leaflets; especially, *O. acetosella,* which has mauve-veined white flowers.

wood spirit *n.* **Methanol** *(see).*

Wood·stock[1] (wood-stok). Town of Oxfordshire, south central England. Situated north of Oxford, it was the site of a royal palace, where Elizabeth I was imprisoned by Mary I (1554). The nearby Blenheim palace (1724) was designed by Sir John Vanbrugh.

Woodstock[2]. Town in southeastern New York, United States. It was the site (1969) of a huge rock music festival.

wood sugar *n.* **Xylose** *(see).*

woods·y (woodzi) *adj.* **-ier, -iest.** *U.S. Informal.* Of, relating to, or suggestive of the woods.

wood tar *n.* A black, syrup-like viscous fluid that is a by-product of the destructive distillation of wood and is used in pitch, wood preserving oils, preservatives, and medicines.

wood·turn·ing (wood-turning) *n.* The art or process of shaping wood into various forms on a lathe. **—wood·turn·er** *n.*

wood vinegar *n. Chemistry.* **Pyroligneous acid** *(see).*

wood warbler *n.* A woodland bird, *Phylloscopus sibilatrix,* having a yellow breast and distinct yellow eyestripe.

Wood·ward (wood-word), **Robert Burns** (1917–79). U.S. chemist. The first scientist to synthesise various organic compounds includ-

woodlark *The woodlark, Lullula arborea, lives on bush-sprinkled heaths and at the edges of forests throughout Europe. It often sings from treetops.*

wood louse *A land-based relative of crabs and shrimps which lives in damp places. It avoids sunlight and dies within a few hours if its body becomes dry.*

woodpecker *Most woodpeckers hammer the bark off trees with their beaks to feed on larvae and grubs concealed beneath it, but the European green woodpecker (above) often feeds from ants' nests on the ground.*

ing quinine, cortisone, and chlorophyll, he was awarded the Nobel prize in chemistry (1965).

wood·wax·en (wŏŏd-waks'n) *n.* A shrub, the **dyer's greenweed** *(see).* [Middle English *wodewexen,* Old English *wudu weaxe : wudu,* WOOD + probably *weaxan,* to grow, WAX.]

wood·wind (wŏŏd-wind) *n.* **1.** A group of musical wind instruments formerly made of wood but nowadays often of metal or plastic, that includes the bassoons, clarinets, flutes, oboes, and sometimes the saxophones. **2.** *Used with a singular or plural verb.* The section of an orchestra composed of woodwind instruments. —**wood·wind** *adj.*

wood·work (wŏŏd-wurk) *n.* **1.** The art or skill of woodcarving or carpentry. **2.** Objects made of or work done in wood; especially, wooden interior fittings in a house, such as doors, staircases, or windowsills. —**wood·work·er** *n.* —**wood·work·ing** *n. & adj.*

wood·worm (wŏŏd-wurm) *n.* **1.** Any of various insect larvae that bore into wood, especially those of the furniture beetle and death-watch beetle. **2.** The riddled effect produced in wood by such larvae.

wood·y (wŏŏddi) *adj.* **-ier, -iest. 1.** Forming or consisting of wood; ligneous: *woody tissue.* **2.** Characterised by the presence of wood or xylem: *woody plants.* **3.** Characteristic or suggestive of wood: *a woody smell.* **4.** Covered with trees; wooded. —**wood·i·ness** *n.*

woody nightshade *n.* **Bittersweet** *(see).*

woof[1] (wŏŏf || wŏof) *n.* **1.** The threads that run crosswise in a woven fabric, at right angles to the warp threads; the weft. **2.** The texture of a woven fabric. [Variant (influenced by WARP) of Middle English *oof,* Old English *ōwef : ō-,* from *on,* ON + *wefan,* to weave.]

woof[2] (wŏŏf) *n.* **1.** The deep, gruff bark of a dog. **2.** A sound similar to this.
~*intr.v.* **woofed, woof·ing, woofs.** To utter a woof. [Imitative.]

woof·er (wŏŏfər || wŏoffər) *n.* A loudspeaker designed to reproduce bass frequencies. Compare **tweeter.** [From WOOF (sound).]

woof·ter (wŏŏftər) *n. Chiefly British Informal.* A male homosexual, especially if effeminate. Usually used derogatorily. [Variant of POOFTER, with *W-* as in *woman.*]

wool (wŏŏl) *n.* **1.** The dense, soft, often curly hair forming the coat of sheep and certain other mammals. **2. a.** Yarn carded, spun, and processed from this for use in woven, knitted, and embroidered textiles. **b.** Loosly, any yarn used for knitting, even when mixed with synthetic fibres. **3.** Any filamentous or fibrous covering or substance suggestive of the texture or appearance of wool: *steel wool.* —**pull the wool over (someone's) eyes.** To deceive; trick. ~*adj.* Of, pertaining to, or consisting of wool or woollen material. [Middle English *wolle, wull,* Old English *wull.*]

wooll·en, *U.S.* **wool·en** (wŏŏlən) *adj.* Of, pertaining to, or consisting of wool. ~*n. Plural.* Fabric or clothing made from wool, especially when knitted.

Woolf (wŏŏlf), **Leonard (Sidney).** (1880–1969). British writer, the husband of Virginia Woolf. A member of the Fabians and co-founder with his wife of the Hogarth Press (1917), his works include *After the Deluge* (1931–39) and an autobiography (1960–69).

Woolf, Virginia (Adeline), born Virginia Adeline Stephen (1882–1941). British novelist and member of the Bloomsbury group. Writing in an experimental stream-of-consciousness style, her work includes *Mrs. Dalloway* (1925), *To the Lighthouse* (1927), *The Waves* (1931), and the posthumous *The Moment* (1948). She also wrote essays and critical works. She committed suicide.

wool fat *n.* **Lanolin** *(see).*

wool·gath·er·ing (wŏŏl-gathəring) *n.* Absent-minded indulgence in fanciful daydreams. —**wool·gath·er·er** *n.*

wool·grow·er (wŏŏl-grō-ər) *n.* A person who breeds sheep or other animals for the production of wool. —**wool·grow·ing** *adj.*

wool in the grease *n.* **Grease** *(see).*

wool·ly (wŏŏlli) *adj.* **-lier, -liest. 1. a.** Pertaining to, consisting of, or covered with wool. **b.** Resembling wool. **2.** *Informal.* **a.** Lacking clarity; or definition; hazy; fuzzy: *woolly thinking.* **b.** Lacking decisiveness; resolution, or commitment: *a woolly liberal.* ~*n., pl.* **woollies. 1.** *Informal.* A garment made of wool; especially, a cardigan, sweater, or the like. **2.** *Usually plural. Chiefly U.S.* A sheep. —**wool·liy** *adv.* —**wool·li·ness** *n.*

woolly aphis *n.* Any aphid, such as those of the genera *Eriosoma* and *Prociphalus,* that secretes white, waxy strands around its body.

woolly bear *n.* The hairy caterpillar of any of various tiger moths, especially that of *Arctia caja.*

woolly mammoth *n.* See **mammoth.**

wool·pack (wŏŏl-pak) *n.* **1.** A large bag used for packing wool or fleeces for shipment. **2.** A cumulus cloud.

wool·sack (wŏŏl-sak) *n.* In Britain: **1.** The official seat of the Lord Chancellor in the House of Lords. **2.** The Lord Chancellorship. Preceded by *the.*

wool·shed (wŏŏl-shed) *n.* A building or complex of buildings in which sheep are sheared and wool is prepared for market.

wool·skin (wŏŏl-skin) *n.* A sheepskin with the wool still on it.

wool·sort·er's disease (wŏŏl-sawtərz) *n.* A type of pneumonia resulting from infection of the lungs with anthrax bacilli.

wool·sta·pler (wŏŏl-stayplər) *n.* A dealer in wool; especially, one who buys wool from the producer, grades it, and sells it to a manufacturer. —**wool·sta·pling** *adj. & n.*

woom·e·ra, wom·e·ra (wŏŏmmərə) *n. Australian.* A notched stick used by Australian Aborigines to hold a spear, giving increased leverage. [From an Australian native name (New South Wales).]

Woom·e·ra Mar·a·lin·ga (wŏŏmmərə márrə-líng-gə). Town in

woolly bear *Named because of its hairy appearance, this caterpillar is the juvenile form of a moth. Its adult form is better known as the garden tiger moth.*

---

woodwind

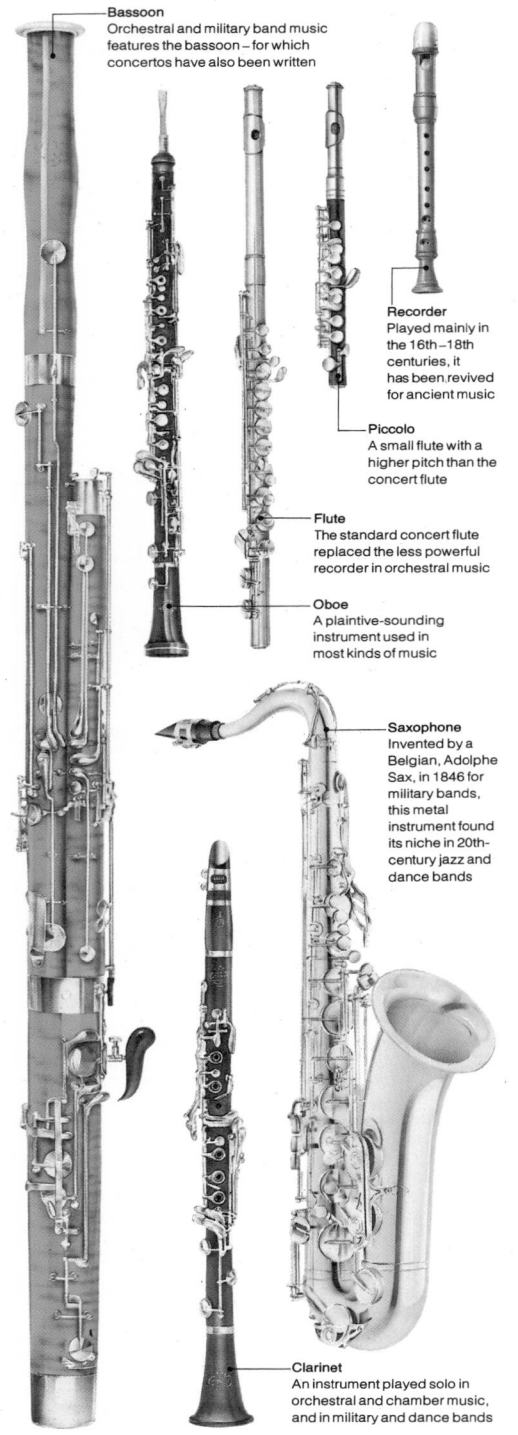

SOUND OF THE WOODWINDS

The instrument's length governs its musical range

Woodwind instruments, once made of wood (except for the saxophone), are now also made of metal or plastic. They are played either through a mouth-hole, as with the flute and recorder, or by means of a vibrating reed, as with the saxophone and clarinet. Oboes and bassoons have double reeds, which help to roughen the tone. Players vary the pitch by closing and opening holes in the instrument's body. The instrument's length dictates its range – a longer body produces lower notes.

Bassoon
Orchestral and military band music features the bassoon – for which concertos have also been written

Recorder
Played mainly in the 16th–18th centuries, it has been revived for ancient music

Piccolo
A small flute with a higher pitch than the concert flute

Flute
The standard concert flute replaced the less powerful recorder in orchestral music

Oboe
A plaintive-sounding instrument used in most kinds of music

Saxophone
Invented by a Belgian, Adolphe Sax, in 1846 for military bands, this metal instrument found its niche in 20th-century jazz and dance bands

Clarinet
An instrument played solo in orchestral and chamber music, and in military and dance bands

south central South Australia. Situated on an Aboriginal reserve near Lake Torrens, it is the site of the Long Range Weapons Establishment (since 1947), a space and missile rocket test centre. A U.S. tracking station is near by.

Woop Woop (wŏŏp-wŏŏp) *n. Australian Informal.* Any remote district or town. Used humorously. [20th century : origin obscure.]

Woot·ton (wŏŏtt'n), **of Ab·in·ger** (ábbinjər), **Barbara Frances, Baroness** (1897–). British social scientist. Her books include *Freedom under Planning* (1945), *Social Science and Social Pathology* (1959), and *Crime and Penal Policy* (1978).

woo·zy (wŏŏzi || wŏŏzzi) *adj.* **-ier, -iest.** *Informal.* **1.** Dazed; stunned; confused. **2.** Dizzy or queasy, as from drink. [Perhaps variant of OOZY.] **—woo·zi·ly** *adv.* **—woo·zi·ness** *n.*

wop-wops (wóp-wops) *n. N.Z. Informal.* A remote district or town: *He lives out in the wop-wops.* [20th century : origin obscure.]

Worces·ter[1] (wŏŏstər). County town of Hereford and Worcester, western central England. Situated on the river Severn, it has a 14th-century cathedral with a Norman crypt, and was the site of Cromwell's defeat of Charles II and the Scots (1541). Its industries include Royal Worcester porcelain, sauce, gloves, and machinery.

Worcester[2] *n.* A fine china or porcelain made in Worcester from 1751. Also called "Worcester porcelain", "Worcester china".

Worces·ter·shire (wŏŏstər-shər, -sheer). Former county of western central England. In 1974 it was included in the new county of Hereford and Worcester. The county town was Worcester.

Worcestershire sauce *n.* A piquant sauce made from soya sauce, vinegar, and spices, originally made in Worcester. Also called "Worcester sauce".

Worcs. Worcestershire.

word (wurd) *n.* **1. a.** A sound or a combination of sounds that symbolises and communicates a meaning and may consist of a single morpheme or of a combination of morphemes. **b.** A written or printed representation of this. **2. a.** Something that is said; a short conversation or discussion: *Could I have a quick word with you?* **3.** *Plural.* The text of a vocal musical composition; the lyrics. **4.** An assurance or promise; a declared intention: *said he'd do it and was as good as his word; I give you my word.* **5. a.** A command or direction; an order: *executed at the general's word.* **b.** A verbal signal; a password or watchword: *Mum's the word.* **6. a.** News or information: *the latest word.* **b.** Rumour: *Word has it he's married.* **7.** A sequence of 32, 36, 48, or 64 bits used to store or operate upon information in a computer system. **8. a.** *Plural.* A dispute or argument; a quarrel. **b.** A quarrelsome remark: *Words were exchanged between umpire and batsman.* **9.** *Capital* **W. a.** The **Logos** *(see).* **b.** The Scriptures or Gospel of the Christian Church: *the Word of God.* **—(upon) my word. 1.** Used to express surprise, shock, or admiration. **2.** *Australian.* Used to express agreement. **—put in a (good) word for.** To recommend; speak favourably of. **—take (someone) at (his) word.** To be convinced of another's sincerity and act in accordance with his statement. **—word for word. 1.** Repeated in the same words; verbatim. **2.** Finding an equivalent translation for each word in turn.

~tr.v. **worded, wording, words. 1.** To express in words. **2.** *Australian Informal.* To advise; infòrm. Often used with *up.* [Middle English *word,* Old English *word.*]

word·age (wúrdij) *n.* **1.** The use of an excessive number of words; verbiage. **2.** The number of words used, as in a novel or an article. **3.** Wording.

word association *n.* **1.** An early psychoanalytical technique in which the patient says the first word to come into his mind in response to a key word. **2.** A party game in which players in turn say a word connected with the previous one.

word blindness *n.* Either of two disorders causing difficulties with reading and writing, **alexia** or **dyslexia** *(both of which see).* **—word-blind** *adj.*

word·book (wúrd-bŏŏk || -bōōk) *n.* A vocabulary; a dictionary.

word·break (wúrd-brayk) *n. Printing.* The point of division of a word when it is run on from one line to the next.

word class *n. Linguistics.* A part of speech, such as a noun, verb, or adjective.

word deafness *n.* A form of aphasia in which information in the form of speech is incomprehensible. **—word-deaf** *adj.*

word·ing (wúrding) *n.* **1.** The act or style of expressing in words; phraseology; diction. **2.** The words themselves as they our deployed or arranged.

word·less (wúrd-ləss, -liss) *adj.* Without words; unspoken; inarticulate; silent. **—word·less·ly** *adv.* **—word·less·ness** *n.*

word order *n.* The syntactic arrangement of words in a sentence, clause, or phrase.

word-perfect (wúrd-pér-fikt || -fekt) *adj.* **1.** Memorised perfectly: *a word-perfect recitation.* **2.** Remembering or repeating one's words perfectly.

word play *n.* **1.** Verbal wit. **2.** A play on words; a pun.

word processor *n.* An electronic device consisting of a keyboard similar to a typewriter, a microprocessor, and a cathode-ray screen that together enable copy, as for letters or documents, to be stored on magnetic disk, corrected, and printed. **—word processing** *n.*

word square *n.* **1.** A group of words arranged in a square that read the same vertically and horizontally. **2.** A puzzle whose solution is a word square.

Words·worth (wúrds-wərth, -wurth), **William.** (1770–1850). British poet. He was influenced by his early life in the Lake District and by the optimism of the immediately post-revolutionary France. Conveying a mystical feeling of unity with nature, his works include *Poems in Two Volumes* (1807), containing "Ode to Immortality" and "The Daffodils", and his verse autobiography, *The Prelude* (written 1805, published 1850). He became Poet Laureate in 1843.

word·y (wúrdi) *adj.* **-ier, -iest. 1.** Expressed in or using more words than are necessary. **2.** Pertaining to, consisting of, or having the nature of words; verbal. —See Synonyms at **talkative. —word·i·ly** *adv.* **—word·i·ness** *n.*

wore. 1. Past tense of **wear** (to be clothed in). **2.** Past tense of **wear** (to turn. Used of a ship).

work (wurk) *n.* **1.** Physical or mental effort or activity directed towards the production or accomplishment of something; toil; labour. **2.** Employment; a job: *look for work; out of work.* **3.** The means by which one earns one's livelihood; a trade, craft, business, or profession. **4. a.** Something that is being, or must be, done, made, or performed, especially as a part of one's occupation; a duty or task: *begin the day's work.* **b.** The amount of this done or required. **5. a.** Something done, made, or performed through the agency, effort, or activity of a person or thing: *said the killings were the work of a vicious maniac; a work of genius.* **b.** A task or action occupying the specified amount of time: *It was the work of a few minutes.* **6. a.** *Often plural.* The output of an artist or artisan considered or collected as a whole: *the works of Verdi.* **b.** A piece of needlework or embroidery. **7.** Any material or piece being processed in a machine during manufacture; a workpiece. **8. a.** A place of employment: *Don't phone me at work.* **b.** The part of a day during which one works: *met her after work; late for work.* **9.** The manner or style of working or the quality of treatment; workmanship: *good work.* **10.** Action producing an intended or expected effect: *waited for the poison to do its work.* **11.** A froth produced during the process of fermentation, as on vinegar, cider, or other liquid. **12.** *Physics. Abbr.* **w, W** The transfer of energy from one physical system to another; especially, the transfer of energy to a body by the application of force, usually calculated as the product of the force and the distance moved by the point of application in the direction of the force. —See **works. —have one's work cut out.** Have a lot to do. **—out of work.** Unemployed. **—make short work of.** *Informal.* **1.** To deal with very quickly or easily. **2.** To overcome (an opponent). **—set to work.** To begin doing something.

~v. **worked** or *archaic* **wrought** (rawt), **working, works.** *—intr.* **1.** To exert one's efforts for the purpose of doing, making, or achieving something; labour or toil. **2. a.** To be employed; have a job. **b.** To have an influence, result, or effect, as on a person, the mind, or the like: *The plea for help worked on their compassion.* **3. a.** To operate; function. **b.** To operate effectively: *Is the phone working?* **c.** To arrive at or be brought to a specified state, especially gradually or by repeated movement: *The stitches worked loose.* **4.** To proceed or progress slowly and laboriously. **5.** To move or contort from emotion or pain: *His mouth worked with fear.* **6.** To behave or respond in a specified way when handled or processed: *Not all metals work easily.* **7.** To ferment. **8.** *Nautical.* **a.** To be under strain in heavy seas so that seams loosen and fastenings become slack. **b.** To sail against the wind. **9.** To undergo small motions that result in friction and wear: *The gears work against each other.* **10.** To attempt to influence or persuade. Used with *on* or *upon.* *—tr.* **1.** To cause or effect; bring about: *I can't work miracles.* **2.** To cause to operate or function; handle or use: *work a power mower.* **3.** To make or force to work or to do work: *Sue works her employees hard.* **4.** To excite, rouse, or provoke: *He worked me into a rage.* **5.** *Informal.* To arrange, especially by somewhat devious means; contrive: *Try to work it so we both get our holiday at the same time.* **6.** *Informal.* To use or employ for one's own ends or purposes; exploit: *You have to learn how to work the system.* **7.** *Informal.* To practise trickery or deception on; cheat. **8.** To carry on one's occupation in; cover: *This postman works our street.* **9.** To cause to ferment. **—work back.** *Australian Informal.* To work overtime. **—work off.** To get rid of by work or effort: *work off extra pounds; work off a debt.* **—work over.** *Slang.* To inflict severe physical damage upon; beat up. **—work up. 1.** To develop or proceed gradually towards a point: *The film works up to a thrilling climax.* **2.** To arouse the emotions of; excite; stir up: *worked up the crowd into a frenzy.* **3.** To produce by working: *work up an appetite.* [Middle English *werke, worke,* Old English *we(o)rc,* act, deed, work.]

Synonyms: *work, labour, toil, drudgery.*

-work *n. comb. form.* Indicates: **1.** Work done using the specified tools or materials; for example, **needlework, pokerwork. 2.** A product of work done in the specified medium; for example, **woodwork, paintwork. 3.** Work performed in a specified way or of a specified type; for example, **nightwork, piecework.**

work·a·ble (wúrkə-b'l) *adj.* **1.** Capable of being worked, dealt with, or handled. **2.** Capable of working effectively or successfully; practicable or feasible. —See Synonyms at **possible. —work·a·bil·i·ty** (-bíllәti), **work·a·ble·ness** *n.* **—work·a·bly** *adv.*

work·a·day (wúrkə-day) *adj.* **1.** Pertaining or appropriate to working days; everyday. **2.** Mundane; commonplace: *the workaday world.* [Middle English *werkeday,* a workday : *werke,* WORK + DAY.]

work·a·hol·ic (wúrkə-hóllik) *n.* A person who suffers from a compulsive need to work excessively hard. [WORK + *alcoholic.*] **—work·a·hol·ism** (-hol-iz'm) *n.*

work·bag (wúrk-bag) *n.* A bag to hold material, such as needlework, on which one is working, or implements needed for work.

PRONUNCIATION KEY

a, trap; aa, father; ai, fair; ar, star; aw, lawn; ay, play; b, bb, stab; rubber; ch, church; ck, ticket; d, dd, dead; ladder; e, dress; ee, bee; er, defer; ew, few; ewr, pure; ə, about; ər, letter; f, ff, fife; differ; g, gg, giggle; h, hat; i, kit; ī, price; īr, fire; j, judge; k, kick; l, ll, let; 'l, needle; m, mm, man; n, nn, no; 'n, sudden; ng, thing; o, lot; ō, no; ŏŏ, foot; ōō, shoe; oor, poor; ow, cow; owr, hour; oy, boy; p, pp, pepper; r, rr, red; s, ss, sauce; sh, ship; t, tt, totter; th, thick; th, this; smooth; u, cut; ur, turn; v, vv, valve; w, wet; y, yes; z, zz, zebra; zh, vision; pleasure

IN FOREIGN WORDS:

aN, oN, Saint-Saëns; hl, Llanelli; Hluhluwe; kh, loch; lough; Khaled

STRESS MARK:

ín-sīt, insight; in-sít, incite

work·bench (wúrk-bench) *n.* A sturdy table or bench at which a machinist, mechanic, or carpenter works.

work·book (wúrk-bŏŏk ‖ -bŏŏk) *n.* **1.** A booklet containing problems and exercises, typically one that is published in conjunction with a textbook and has spaces in which answers are to be written. **2.** A manual containing operating instructions, as for an appliance or a machine. **3.** A book in which a record is kept of work proposed or accomplished.

work·box (wúrk-boks) *n.* A box or basket for implements or materials used in sewing or other work. Also called "work basket".

work·day (wúrk-day) *n.* A working day. —*adj.* Workaday.

work·er (wúrkər) *n.* **1. a.** One that works. **b.** One who works in a specified way or at a specified occupation: *a fast worker; an office worker.* **2. a.** An employee, as opposed to an employer or manager. **b.** One who does manual or industrial labour. **3.** One who belongs to the working class. **4.** One of the sterile females of certain social insects, such as the ant or bee, that performs specialised work.

work·er-priest (wúrkər-prĕest) *n. Roman Catholic Church.* A priest, especially in France, who spends time in secular employment.

workers' cooperative *n.* An enterprise in which all workers share control over production, distribution, and exchange, often with equal profit-sharing, regardless of individual function.

work ethic *n.* A belief in the virtues of dutiful hard work and its moral superiority to leisure, play, or other activities that are considered unproductive.

work force *n.* **1.** Those workers employed in a specific project; a staff. **2.** All workers potentially available to a nation, project, industry, or the like.

work function *n.* The energy required to remove an electron from a solid; especially, the work exerted against coulomb forces in removing an electron from just inside to just outside the surface of a metal.

work hardening *n.* The increase in strength that sometimes accompanies plastic deformation of a solid, especially a metal. —**work-hard·en** *tr.v.*

work·horse (wúrk-hawrss) *n.* **1.** A horse that is used for labour rather than for racing or riding. **2.** *Informal.* A person who works tirelessly, especially at difficult or arduous tasks.

work·house (wúrk-howss) *n.* **1.** A former public institution in Britain in which the poor were fed and housed in return for labour. **2.** An American prison in which limited sentences are served by manual labour.

work in *tr.v.* To insert by adjustment, ingenious contrivance, or effort. —*intr.* To be thus inserted.

work-in *n.* A method of industrial action where workers prevent the closure of a plant or office by occupying and running it themselves. Compare **sit-in**.

work·ing (wúrking) *adj.* **1.** Pertaining to, used for, or spent in working: *a working breakfast; working clothes.* **2.** Adequate or appropriate for performing work or achieving effective results: *in working order; a working majority.* **3.** Capable of being used as the basis of further work: *a working hypothesis.* —*n.* **1.** *Usually plural.* The way in which something works. **2.** The excavations in a mine or quarry or the part of them being worked.

working capital *n.* **1.** The assets of a business enterprise that can be applied to its operation. **2.** The current assets of an individual or business enterprise as opposed to the current liabilities.

working class *n. Often plural.* The poorest, most underprivileged stratum of a society, whose members earn wages rather than salaries, typically by means of unskilled manual labour; the proletariat. —**working-class** (wúrking-kláass ‖ -kláss) *adj.*

working day *n.* **1.** That part of a day set aside for work: *a six-hour working day.* **2.** A day on which work is usually done, as opposed to a weekend or holiday.

working drawing *n.* An engineering drawing, architect's plan, or the like, that is used by a machinist, builder, or other worker to make or build the subject of the drawing.

working man *n.* A man who works for wages, especially at manual labour.

working papers *pl.n.* Legal documents necessary in certain countries to guarantee the right of an individual to employment.

working party *n.* **1.** A temporary committee set up to research and investigate a particular matter. **2.** A group of prisoners or soldiers sent out for manual labour.

working storage *n.* The part of a computer's data-storage disk that is reserved for data to be temporarily stored during the running of a program.

working substance *n.* **1.** A substance, especially a fluid, that undergoes changes of pressure, temperature, and volume in a heat engine. Also called "working fluid". **2.** The substance in a thermometer that expands and contracts.

working week *n.* Also *U.S.* **work week.** That part of a week set aside for work: *a three-day working week.*

work·less (wúrk-lŏss, -liss) *adj.* Unemployed.

work·load (wúrk-lōd) *n.* The amount of work assigned to or done by a machine, worker, or unit of workers in a given time period.

work·man (wúrk-mən) *n., pl.* **-men** (-mən). **1.** A man who performs some form of manual or industrial labour. **2.** A person who works in a specified way: *A bad workman blames his tools.*

work·man·like (wúrkmən-līk) *adj.* **1.** Characteristic of or befitting a skilled workman or craftsman: *workmanlike pottery.* **2.** Of satisfactory but not outstanding quality: *a workmanlike performance.*

work·man·ship (wúrkmən-ship) *n.* **1.** The art, skill, or technique of a workman. **2.** The quality of such art, skill, or technique: *silver of poor workmanship.* **3.** Something produced or achieved by work or effort; handiwork.

work of art *n.* **1.** A piece of artistic work deemed valuable or superior. **2.** Anything likened to this in beauty or workmanship.

work out *tr.v.* **1.** To find a solution for; solve. **2.** To formulate or develop: *work out a plan.* **3.** To exhaust (a mine, soil, or the like). **4.** To fulfil (an obligation or debt, for example) by working instead of paying money. **5.** To accomplish by work or effort. —*intr.v.* **1.** To come or make its way out: *a nail working out of a board.* **2.** To have a specified result: *work out badly.* **3.** To prove successful, effective, or satisfactory: *Did your job work out?* **4.** To perform a series of exercises or drills.

work·out (wúrk-owt) *n.* A period of exercise or practice, especially in athletics.

work·peo·ple (wúrk-peep'l) *pl.n.* Those who work for wages.

work·piece (wúrk-peess) *n.* Any piece or part in the process of manufacture by machine or by hand.

work·room (wúrk-rŏŏm, -rŏŏm) *n.* A room where work is done, especially manual work.

works *pl.n. Used with a singular or plural verb.* **1.** A factory, plant, or similar buildings or complex of buildings where a usually specified type of industry is carried on. Often used in combination: *a gasworks; a steelworks.* **2.** The internal mechanism of an object: *the works of a watch.* **3.** Engineering structures, such as bridges or dams. **4.** A structure for fortification or defence. —**in the works.** *Informal.* Being processed or prepared. —**the works.** *Informal.* **1.** Everything; the whole of a set: *He had the works, from the avocado to the port and cigars.* **2.** Extreme punitive treatment.

work-sharing (wúrk-sháiring) *n.* The practice of **job-sharing** (see).

work·shop (wúrk-shop) *n.* **1.** An area, room, or establishment in which manual or industrial work is done. **2. a.** A group of people who meet for a seminar in some specialised field: *a creative-writing workshop.* **b.** A meeting or seminar held by such a group.

work·shy (wúrk-shī) *adj.* Habitually avoiding work.

work·stud·y (wúrk-studdi) *n.* A management method of evaluating the job-performance of employees in terms of the time and effort expended.

work·ta·ble (wúrk-tayb'l) *n.* A table designed for a specific task or activity, such as needlework or graphic arts.

work·top (wúrk-top) *n.* A wide flat surface used for working on, especially one in a kitchen. Also called "work surface".

work-to-rule (wúrk-tə-rŏŏl, -tŏŏ- ‖ -réwl) *n. Chiefly British.* A type of industrial action in which employees deliberately follow all working rules, however trivial, so painstakingly that production is drastically cut. —**work to rule** *intr.v.*

work·week (wúrk-week) *n. Chiefly U.S.* A working week.

work·wom·an (wúrk-wŏŏmən) *n., pl.* **-women** (-wimmin). A women who performs some form of labour.

world (wurld) *n.* **1.** The earth. **2.** The universe. **3.** The earth and its inhabitants collectively. Also used adjectivally: *world champion; world English.* **4.** The human race. **5. a.** Humankind considered as social creatures; human society: *turned her back on the world.* **b.** People as a whole; the public: *The story burst upon the world.* **6.** *Often capital* **W.** A specified part of the earth: *the Western World.* **7.** A particular period in history, including its people, culture, and social order: *the Victorian world.* **8.** Any realm, domain, or kingdom: *the insect world.* **9.** A field or sphere of human activity: *the world of advertising.* **10.** Everything that concerns or contributes to the life of an individual: *felt his whole world collapsing around him.* **11.** A specified way of life or state of being: *the world of the rich.* **12.** Secular life and its morality as distinguished from the religious or spiritual life: *a man of the world.* **13. a.** Human existence; mortal life: *came into the world.* **b.** A supposed state of existence beyond death: *the next world.* **14.** *Often plural.* A large amount; much: *did him a world of good; worlds apart.* **15.** A planet or other celestial body: *the possibility of life on another world.* —**dead to the world.** Fast asleep or unconscious. —**for all the world.** *Informal.* To all intents and purposes; for all practical purposes: *He looked for all the world like a film star.* —**on top of the world.** *Informal.* Elated, exultant, or blissful. —**out of this world.** *Informal.* Excellent; fine. —**world without end.** Forever and ever. [Middle English *w(e)orld,* Old English *world, weorold,* from Germanic, from *weraz* (unattested), man + *aldh-* (unattested), age.] See maps, pages 1894–7.

World Bank *n.* An international bank founded in 1945 to assist the economic development of the Third World by means of loans from richer nations. Also officially called "International Bank for Reconstruction and Development".

world-class (wúrld-klaass ‖ -klass) *adj.* Being one of or worthy of the best in the world.

World Council of Churches *n. Abbr.* **W.C.C.** An ecumenical grouping of Christian Churches, excluding the Roman Catholics, founded in 1948 to further the aims of Christian unity.

World Court *n.* **1.** The Permanent Court of International Justice, established by the League of Nations (1920). **2.** The **International Court of Justice** (see).

World Cup *n.* **1.** A soccer championship competition, held every four years, between 24 national teams selected in a qualifying competition. **2.** The trophy awarded to the winners of this competition.

World Health Organisation *n. Abbr.* **W.H.O.** A United Nations agency, founded in 1948 and based in Geneva, that serves to coordinate and improve health activities worldwide.

---

world line n. Physics. The line representing the path of an object through the four-dimensional space-time continuim.

world·ling (wúrldling) n. A person absorbed in or devoted to this world; a worldly person.

world·ly (wúrldli) adj. **-lier, -liest. 1.** Of, pertaining to, or devoted to the temporal world; not spiritual or religious; secular. **2.** Sophisticated or cosmopolitan; worldly-wise. **—world·li·ness** n.

world·ly-wise (wúrldli-wīz) adj. Experienced in the ways of the world; sophisticated and shrewd, often to the point of cynicism.

world power n. A political entity whose actions consistently influence or change the course of international events.

world-shak·ing (wúrld-shayking) adj. Of great significance.

world soul n. A spiritual principle relating to the world as the human soul relates to a human being.

world view n. A particular way of viewing and interpreting the world; a philosophy of life.

World War I n. Abbr. **W.W.I** A war fought from 1914 to 1918, in which Great Britain, France, Russia, Belgium, Italy, Japan, the United States, and other allies defeated Germany, Austria-Hungary, Turkey, and Bulgaria. Also called "First World War", "Great War".

World War II n. Abbr. **W.W.II** A war fought from 1939 to 1945, in which Great Britain, France, the U.S.S.R., the United States, and other allies defeated Germany, Italy, and Japan. Also called "Second World War".

world-wea·ry (wúrld-weer-i) adj. **-rier, -riest.** Tired of the world and the pleasures afforded by it. **—world-wea·ri·ness** n.

world·wide (wúrld-wīd) adj. Reaching or extending throughout the world; universal. **—world·wide** adv.

World Wildlife Fund n. Abbr. **WWF.** An organisation founded in 1961 to raise money for the protection and conservation of wildlife throughout the world.

worm (wurm) n. **1.** Any of various invertebrates, such as those of the phyla Annelida, Nematoda, or Platyhelminthes, having a long, flexible rounded or flattened body, often without obvious appendages. **2.** Any of various insect larvae having a soft, elongated body. **3.** Any of various unrelated animals resembling a worm in habit or appearance, as the shipworm or the slow-worm. **4.** An object or device that is like a worm in appearance or action, such as a threaded screw, a spiral-shaped tube in a heat exchanger, or a condenser in a still. **5.** A shaft with a helical groove cut in it so that it can function as part of a worm gear. **6.** An insidiously tormenting or devouring force: *"The worm of conscience still begnaw thy soul"* (Shakespeare). **7.** Informal. **a.** A pitiable creature; a poor wretch. **b.** A contemptible despicable person; one of no moral worth. **8.** Plural. Pathology. Intestinal infestation with worms or wormlike parasites. In this sense, also called "helminthiasis".
~v. **wormed, worming, worms.** —tr. **1.** To make (one's way) with or as if with the sinuous crawling motion of a worm. **2.** To elicit by artful or devious means. Used with *out*. **3.** To cure of intestinal worms. **4.** Nautical. To wrap yarn or twine around (rope). —intr. **1.** To move in a sinuous manner suggestive of a worm. **2.** To make one's way by artful or devious means. Used with *into* or *out of*. [Middle English *worm*, Old English *wyrm*, worm, serpent.]

worm·cast (wúrm-kaast) n. A coil of evacuated earth or sand that has passed through the body of an earthworm or lugworm and been deposited on the ground's surface, especially along the sea shore.

worm-eat·en (wúrm-eet'n) adj. **1.** Bored through or gnawed by worms. **2.** Full of wormholes. **3.** Decayed; worn-out; decrepit.

worm gear n. **1.** A gear consisting of a threaded shaft and a wheel with teeth that mesh into it. **2.** A worm wheel.

worm·hole (wúrm-hōl) n. A hole made by a burrowing worm. **—worm-holed** adj.

worm screw n. The threaded shaft of a worm gear. Also called "worm".

worm·seed (wúrm-seed) n. The dried unopened flowers of the **sea wormwood** (see).

worm's-eye view (wúrmz-ī) n. A view from below or from a lowly or grass-roots level. Compare **bird's-eye view.**

worm wheel n. The toothed wheel of a worm gear. Also called "worm gear".

worm·wood (wúrm-wŏŏd) n. **1.** Any of several aromatic plants of the genus *Artemisia*; especially, *A. absinthium*, native to Europe, yielding a bitter extract used in making absinthe and in flavouring certain wines. Also called "absinthe". **2.** Something distressing or embittering. [Middle English *wormwode*, variant (influenced by WORM and WOOD) of *wermode*, Old English *wermōd*, from Germanic *wer-mōd-, wor-mōd-* (unattested). See also **vermouth.**]

worm·y (wúrmi) adj. **-ier, -iest. 1.** Infested with or damaged by worms. **2.** Suggestive of a worm; especially, grovelling or insinuating. **—worm·i·ness** n.

worn (wawrn ‖ wōrn). Past participle of **wear.**
~adj. **1.** Affected by wear or use. **2.** Impaired or damaged by wear or use: *worn elbows on a coat.* **3. a.** Exhausted; spent. **b.** Showing exhaustion; drawn. —See Synonyms at **haggard.** [Middle English, past participle of *weren*, to WEAR.]

worn-out (wáwrn-ówt ‖ wōrn-) adj. **1.** Worn or used until no longer usable: *a worn-out suit.* **2.** Thoroughly exhausted; spent.

wor·ri·ment (wúrrimənt) n. Chiefly U.S. Informal. **1.** The act of worrying or state of being worried. **2.** A source of anxiety; a worry.

wor·ri·some (wúrri-səm) adj. **1.** Causing worry or anxiety. **2.** Tending to worry; anxious. **—wor·ri·some·ly** adv.

wor·rit (wúrrit) v. **worried, -riting, -rits.** Archaic & Regional. —intr.

To fret; worry. —tr. To pester; annoy. [Probably alteration of WORRY, perhaps influenced by WHERRIT.]

wor·ry (wúrri ‖ wórri) v. **-ried, -rying, -ries.** —intr. **1.** To feel uneasy about some uncertain or threatening matter; be troubled or agitated. **2.** To pull, bite, or tear at something: *The dog worried at the bone.* **3.** To work or proceed doggedly in the face of difficulty or hardship; struggle: *worried away at a problem.* —tr. **1.** To cause to feel anxious, distressed, or troubled. **2.** To bother; annoy: *Don't worry me with your complaints.* **3. a.** To seize with the teeth and shake or tug at repeatedly: *a dog put down for worrying sheep.* **b.** To attack roughly and repeatedly; harass. **c.** To touch, move, or handle idly by: *worrying the sore tooth with his tongue.*
~n., pl. **worries. 1.** The act of worrying or the condition of being worried; mental uneasiness or anxiety. **2.** A source of nagging concern or uneasiness. —See Synonyms at **anxiety.** [Middle English *worien, wirien,* to seize by the throat, harass, Old English *wyrgan,* to strangle.] **—wor·ried·ly** adv. **—wor·ri·er** n.

worry beads pl.n. A bead bracelet kept in the hand and constantly toyed with to relieve boredom or tension, originally used by men in Greece and the Middle East.

worse (wurss). **1.** Comparative of **bad. 2.** Comparative of **ill.**
~adj. Also archaic **wors·er** (wúrssər). **1.** More inferior, as in quality, condition, or effect. **2.** More severe or unfavourable. **3.** Further from a standard; less desirable or satisfactory. **—worse luck.** Informal. Unfortunately. **—the worse for wear.** Shoddy or rundown.
~adv. In a worse way.
~n. Something that is worse. **—for the worse.** Into a worse state or condition. [Middle English *wors(e),* Old English *wyrsa.*]

wors·en (wúrss'n) v. **-ened, -ening, -ens.** —intr. To be or become worse. —tr. To make worse.

wor·ship (wúrship) n. **1.** The reverent love and allegiance accorded a deity, idol, or sacred object. **2.** A set of ceremonies, prayers, or other religious forms by which this love is expressed. **3.** Ardent devotion; adoration. **4.** Often capital **W.** Chiefly British. A title or form of address for magistrates, mayors, and certain other dignitaries. Used with *His, Her, Your,* or *Their.*
~v. **worshipped** or U.S. **worshiped, -shipping** or U.S. **-shiping, -ships.** —tr. **1.** To honour and love as a deity; venerate. **2.** To regard with great admiration or devotion; idolise. —intr. **1.** To participate in religious rites of worship. **2.** To perform any act of worship. —See Synonyms at **revere.** [Middle English *worschipe,* Old English *weorthscipe,* honour, dignity, reverence : *weorth,* WORTH + -SHIP.] **—wor·ship·per** n.

wor·ship·ful (wúrshipf'l) adj. **1.** Given to or expressive of worship; reverent or adoring. **2.** Chiefly British. Worthy of honour and respect; distinguished. Used especially as an honorific title for certain officers and for certain livery companies. **—wor·ship·ful·ly** adv. **—wor·ship·ful·ness** n.

worst (wurst). **1.** Superlative of **bad. 2.** Superlative of **ill.**
~adj. **1.** Most inferior, as in quality, condition, or effect. **2.** Most severe or unfavourable. **3.** Furthest from an ideal or standard; least desirable or satisfactory.
~n. Something that is worst: *at one's worst; do one's worst.* **—at worst. 1.** Under the worst foreseeable circumstances; if the worst should happen. **2.** From the least favourable point of view. **—get the worst of it.** To suffer a defeat or disadvantage. **—if the worst comes to the worst.** At the very worst.
~adv. In the worst manner or degree.
~tr.v. **worsted, worsting, worsts.** To gain the advantage over; defeat. [Middle English *worste, wurst,* Old English *wyrsta.*]

wor·sted (wŏŏss-tid, -təd ‖ wúrss-) n. **1.** Firm-textured, compactly twisted woollen yarn made from long-staple fibres. **2.** Fabric made from such yarn. [Middle English *worsted,* first made in *Worthstede* (now Worstead), a village in Norfolk.] **—wor·sted** adj.

wort (wurt ‖ wawrt) n. **1.** A plant, especially one formerly used as a medicinal herb. Now used only in combination: *liverwort; milkwort.* **2.** An infusion of malt fermented to make beer. [Middle English *wort, wurt,* Old English *wyrt,* plant, herb.]

worth¹ (wurth) n. **1.** The quality of something that renders it desirable, useful, or valuable: *the worth of higher education.* **2.** The material or market value of something: *have a worth of ten million pounds.* **3.** The number or quantity of something that may be purchased for a specified sum: *five pounds' worth of petrol.* **4.** The quality within a person that commands respect; merit.
~adj. **1.** Equal in value to something specified: *He's not worth her little finger.* **2.** Deserving of; meriting: *a proposal worth consideration.* **3.** Having wealth or riches amounting to: *He's worth a quarter of a million.* **—for all (one) is worth.** To the utmost of one's powers or ability. **—for what it's worth.** Even though it may not be important. [Middle English *worth,* Old English *weorth.*]

worth² intr.v. **worthed, worthing, worths.** Archaic. To befall; betide: *"Howl ye, Woe worth the day!"* (Ezekiel 30:2). [Middle English *worthen,* Old English *weorthan.*]

worth·less (wúrth-ləss, -liss) adj. **1.** Without worth, use, or value. **2.** Without moral worth; low and despicable. **—worth·less·ly** adv. **—worth·less·ness** n.

worth·while, worth-while (wúrth-wīl, -hwīl) adj. Sufficiently valuable or important to justify the expenditure of time or effort.
Usage: This is written as a whole, or with a hyphen, when used before a noun *(a worthwhile experience).* Used after a verb, it is usually written as two words *(the experience was worth while).*

wor·thy (wúrthi) adj. **-thier, -thiest. 1.** Having worth, merit, or value; useful or valuable. **2.** Honourable; admirable: *a worthy fel-*

THE WORLD (PHYSICAL)

low. **3.** Having sufficient worth; deserving: *worthy to be revered; worthy of acclaim.* **4.** Appropriate; suitable: *a large crowd, worthy of this great occasion.*
~*n., pl.* **worthies. 1.** A person esteemed for his worth, dignity, or importance. **2.** An eminent or distinguished person. Often used humorously: *local worthies.* —**wor·thi·ly** *adv.* —**wor·thi·ness** *n.*

–worthy *adj. comb. form.* Indicates: **1.** Of sufficient worth or importance for; for example, **newsworthy. 2.** Deserving of; for example, **blameworthy. 3.** Safe or suitable for travel by means of; for example, **roadworthy.**

wost. *Archaic.* Second person singular present tense of **wit** (to know).

wot. *Archaic.* First and third person singular present tense of **wit** (to know).

Wo·tan (vō′-taan) A Teutonic god identified with Woden.

wot·cher, wot·cha (wŏchər) *interj. Slang.* Used as a greeting or to attract attention.

would (wŏŏd; *weak forms* wəd, əd, d). Past tense of **will** (defective verb), often used as an auxiliary verb expressing various shades of attendant meaning indicating: **1.** A custom or habitual action in the past: *In her young days she would go skiing every winter.* **2.** *Chiefly British.* A stubborn action in the past: *Well, you would go and discuss politics with the barber.* **3.** A polite request or command: *Would you step this way, please.* **4.** Attempt or intention: *Those who*

would disregard the rules must bear the consequences. **5.** Desire or preference: *Treat others as you would have them treat you.* **6.** *Archaic.* A heartfelt wish: *Would that he were in my arms again.* **7.** *Chiefly British.* Approximation or estimate: *That house would cost about £80,000.* **8. a.** Probability: *He would be a millionaire by now if had taken my advice.* **b.** Condition; contingency of one condition upon another: *If you would only get home in time, we could have dinner together now and then.* **9.** Doubt, disdain, cynicism, or the like: *It would seem that I am under arrest again.* **10.** Moderation of the directness or bluntness of a request or statement: *My client would like to take issue with you there.*

Usage: **Would have** is sometimes used in conditional clauses introduced by *if*, but standard English prefers *had*, both in formal speech and in writing; *If John had gone, he would have seen her* (not *If John would have gone...*). Similarly, following the verb *wish*, *had* is the preferred form: *I wish that she had* (not *would have*) *gone.*

would-be (wŏŏd′-bee, -bi) *adj.* Desiring or pretending to be: *a would-be hero.*

would·n't (wŏŏd′nt). Contraction of *would not.*

wouldst (wŏŏdst), **would·est** (wŏŏd′dist). *Archaic.* Second person singular past tense of **will** (defective verb).

Woulfe bottle (wŏŏlf) *n.* A glass laboratory bottle with two necks or sometimes more, used for bubbling a gas through a liquid. [After Peter *Woulfe* (died 1803), British chemist.]

wound¹ (woond) *n.* **1.** An injury to a person or animal in which the skin or other external organic surface is torn, pierced, cut, or otherwise broken, as a result of violence, accident, or surgery. **2.** An injury to the tissue of a plant. **3.** An injury to the feelings. **—lick (one's) wounds.** To recuperate after a defeat.
~*v.* **wounded, wounding, wounds.** —*tr.* To inflict a wound or wounds upon. —*intr.* To inflict a wound or wounds. —See Synonyms at **injure.** [Middle English *wound(e)*, Old English *wund.*]

wound² (wownd). **1.** Past tense and past participle of **wind** (to wrap). **2.** Alternative past tense and past participle of **wind** (to sound).

wound·wort (woond-wurt ‖ -wawrt) *n.* **1.** Any of several plants of the genus *Stachys*, having downy leaves formerly used to treat wounds. **2.** Any of several similarly used plants.

wove. Past tense and *rare* past participle of **weave.**

woven. Past participle of **weave.**

wove paper (wōv) *n.* Paper made on a closely woven wire roller or mould and having a very faint mesh pattern or none at all. Compare **laid paper.**

wow¹ (wow) *interj. Informal.* Used in expressing wonder, amazement, or the like.
~*n. Chiefly U.S. Informal.* An outstanding success.
~*tr.v.* **wowed, wowing, wows.** *Chiefly U.S. Informal.* To have a strong and usually pleasurable impact on.

wow² *n.* A slow variation in the pitch of sound reproduced by a record player or tape recorder, usually the result of irregular movement of a mechanical part. [Imitative.]

wow·ser (wówzər) *n. Australian Slang.* An extremely puritanical person; a prude, killjoy, or teetotaller. [20th century : from English dialect *wow* (imitative), to wail, whine, complain.]

W.P.B., w.p.b. wastepaper basket.

W.P.C. woman police constable.

w.p.m. words per minute.

W.R. 1. *Medicine.* Wassermann reaction. **2.** Western Region.

W.R.A.C. Women's Royal Army Corps.

wrack¹ (rak) *n.* **1.** A remnant or vestige of something destroyed. **2.** Wreckage, especially of a ship cast ashore. **3.** A tangled mass of seaweed or other marine vegetation, cast ashore or floating. **4.** Variant of **rack** (ruin).
~*tr.v.* **wracked, wracking, wracks.** To cause the ruin of; wreck. [Middle English *wrack*, Old English *wrǣc*, punishment, vengeance, and Middle Dutch *wrak*, wreckage, wrecked ship.]

wrack² Variant of **rack** (clouds).

W.R.A.F. Women's Royal Air Force.

wraith (rayth) *n.* **1.** An apparition of a living person, supposed to appear just before he dies. **2.** The ghost of a dead person. **3.** Anything pale and insubstantial, such as a tree seen through mist. [16th century Scottish : origin obscure.]

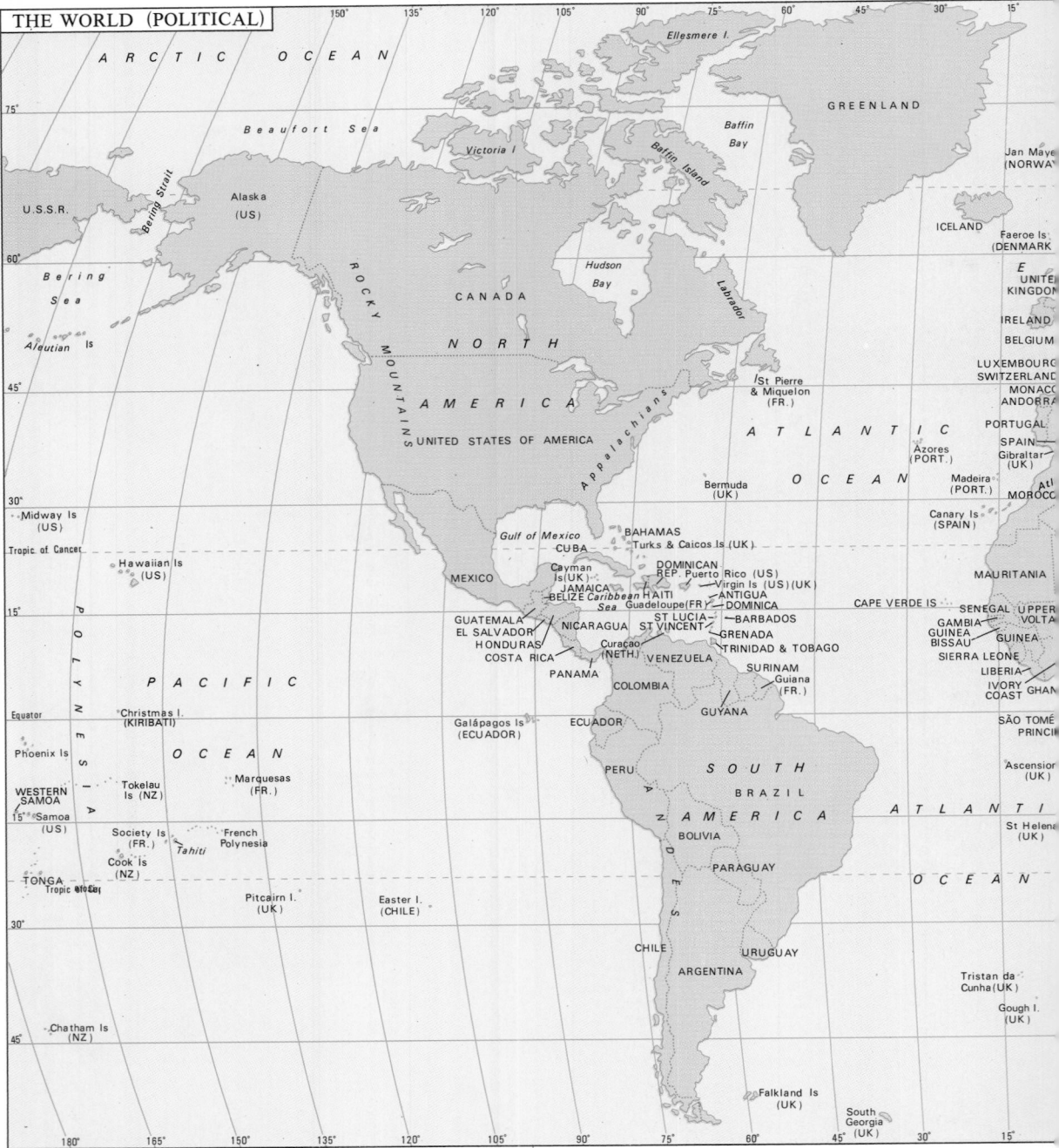

THE WORLD (POLITICAL)

wran·gle (ráng-g'l) v. **-gled, -gling, -gles.** —intr. **1.** To dispute nois-ily or angrily; quarrel; bicker. **2.** To engage in debate or contro-versy. —tr. **1. a.** To win or obtain by argument. **b.** To force or persuade (someone) by argument. **2.** *Western U.S.* To herd (horses or other livestock). —See Synonyms at **argue.**
~n. **1.** An angry, noisy, or vehement argument or dispute. **2.** The act of wrangling. [Middle English *wranglen,* probably of Low Ger-man origin; akin to Low German *wrangeln.*]
wran·gler (ráng-glər) n. **1.** One who wrangles. **2.** In Britain, a stu-dent who gains first-class honours in Part II of the tripos in mathe-matics at Cambridge University. **3.** *U.S.* A cowboy, especially one who tends saddle horses.
wrap (rap) v. **wrapped** or **wrapt, wrapping, wraps.** —tr. **1.** To ar-range or fold about in order to cover or protect something: *She wrapped her coat about her.* **2.** To cover, envelop, pack, or encase. **3.** To clasp, fold, or coil about something: *She wrapped her arms about his neck.* **4.** To envelop and obscure, often with the effect of concealing or disguising the nature of: *Fog wrapped the countryside.* **5.** To immerse in a specified condition. Usually used in the passive: *wrapped in grief; wrapped in thought.* —intr. To coil, wind, or twist about or around something: *The flag wrapped around the pole.*
~n. **1. a.** A garment to be wrapped or folded about a person, espe-cially about the shoulders, such as a cloak or shawl. **b.** *Plural.* Warm outer clothing: *First put on your wraps, and then you can go

out to play.* **2.** A blanket. **3.** A wrapping or wrapper. —**keep under wraps.** To keep secret or concealed. —**take the wraps off.** To disclose to the public; reveal. [Middle English *wrappen†.*]
wrap·a·round (ráp-ə-rownd) adj. Also **wrap·o·ver** (-ōvər), **wrap·round** (-rownd). **1.** Having ends that curve back or that overlap the sides. **2.** Designating a garment, such as a skirt, that is open to the hem and wrapped round the body before being fastened.
~n. Also **wrap·o·ver** (for sense 1), **wrap·round. 1.** A wraparound garment. **2.** *Printing.* A flexible relief plate wrapped round a cylin-der in letterpress printing.
wrap·per (ráppər) n. **1.** One that wraps. **2.** The paper or other ma-terial in which something is wrapped: *a sweet wrapper.* **3.** The pa-per encircling a magazine or newspaper sent by post. **4.** *Chiefly British.* A book jacket. **5.** The tobacco leaf covering a cigar. **6.** A loose dressing gown or negligee.
wrap·ping (rápping) n. *Sometimes plural.* The material in which something is wrapped.
wrapt. Alternative past tense of **wrap.**
wrap up tr.v. **1.** To settle finally or successfully; conclude: *wrap up a business deal.* **2.** *Chiefly U.S.* To encompass in a few words; sum-marise. —intr.v. **1.** To put on warm clothing. **2.** *Informal.* To stop talking; keep quiet. Usually used in the imperative. —**wrapped up.** Immersed or absorbed: *wrapped up in his research.*
wrap-up (ráp-up) n. *U.S.* A brief summary of the news.

wrasse (rass) *n.* Any of numerous chiefly tropical, often brightly coloured marine fishes of the family Labridae. [Cornish and Welsh *gwrach†,* "old woman".]

wrath (roth, rawth, raath ‖ rath) *n.* **1.** Violent, resentful anger; rage; fury. **2.** Divine retribution. **3.** *Archaic.* A fit of violent anger. —See Synonyms at **anger.**
~*adj. Archaic.* Wrathful. [Middle English *wrath(th)e,* Old English *wrǣththu,* from *wrāth,* angry.]

wrath·ful (róth-f'l, ráwth-, ráath- ‖ ráth-) *adj.* **1.** Full of wrath; fiercely angry. **2.** Proceeding from or expressing wrath: *wrathful vengeance.* —**wrath·ful·ly** *adv.* —**wrath·ful·ness** *n.*

wreak (reek) *tr.v.* **wreaked, wreaking, wreaks. 1.** To inflict (vengeance or punishment) upon a person. **2.** To express or gratify (anger, malevolence, or resentment); vent. **3.** To bring about; cause: *wreak havoc.* **4.** *Archaic.* To take vengeance for; avenge. [Middle English *wreken,* Old English *wrecan,* to drive, expel.] —**wreak·er** *n.*

wreath (reeth) *n., pl.* **wreaths** (reethz, reeths). **1. a.** A ring or circlet of flowers or leaves worn on the head, placed as a memorial, or used as a decoration. **b.** A representation of this, as in woodwork. **2.** A curling shape; a ring: *wreaths of smoke.* [Middle English *wrethe,* Old English *writha,* from weak grade of *writhan,* to WRITE.]

wreathe (reeth) *v.* **wreathed, wreathing, wreathes.** —*tr.* **1.** To twist, coil, or entwine into a wreath or a wreathlike shape or contour. **2.** To crown, decorate, or encircle with or as with a wreath. **3.** To coil or curl. **4.** To form a wreath around. —*intr.* **1.** To assume the form of a wreath. **2.** To curl, writhe, or spiral: *The smoke wreathed upwards.* [From WREATH.]

wreck (rek) *n.* **1. a.** The action of wrecking or the condition of being wrecked; destruction. **b.** The accidental destruction of a ship; shipwreck. **2.** The stranded hulk of a ship that has been gravely damaged, as by being driven onto rocks. **3.** The remains of something that has been wrecked or ruined. **4.** Fragments of a ship or its cargo cast ashore by the sea after a shipwreck; wreckage. **5.** A person, animal, or thing in a shattered, dilapidated, or debilitated state: *He's a nervous wreck.*
~*v.* **wrecked, wrecking, wrecks.** —*tr.* **1.** To cause to undergo shipwreck. **2.** To bring to a state of ruin; disable or destroy; undermine. —*intr.* To suffer destruction, ruin, or shipwreck. —See Synonyms at **ruin.** [Middle English *wrek,* from Anglo-French *wrec,* from Scandinavian; akin to Old Norse *(v)rek,* wreckage.]

wreck·age (réckij) *n.* **1.** The act of wrecking or the condition of being wrecked. **2.** The debris of anything wrecked.

wreck·er (réckər) *n.* **1.** One that wrecks or destroys: *a wrecker of dreams.* **2.** *Chiefly U.S.* A person who demolishes buildings or breaks up motor vehicles for a living. **3. a.** *Chiefly U.S.* A person, piece of equipment, or vehicle employed in recovering or removing a wreck; especially, a **breakdown van** *(see).* **b.** One who salvages wrecked cargo or parts. **4. a.** Formerly, one who lured a vessel to

Wren

ST. PAUL'S: MONUMENT TO A GENIUS
Wren planned his dome to rival St. Peter's, Rome

The dome of St. Paul's Cathedral dignifies the heart of London, a glorious memorial to England's greatest architect, Sir Christopher Wren (1632–1723). Wren was one of the geniuses of the age of learning that swept Europe after the Renaissance. He was a brilliant Oxford student, described by Isaac Newton as one of the greatest geometricians of his age. Wren was first a scientist, working in physics, and became professor of astronomy at Oxford when only 29.

His career as an architect began in 1663 when his uncle, the Bishop of Ely, asked him to design the chapel for Pembroke College, Cambridge. He went to France to study architecture in 1665.

The Fire of London (1666) gave Wren the opportunity to exercise his creative genius. He was one of the commissioners in charge of rebuilding, and although his ideas for sweeping avenues and spacious squares were not accepted, many of his 52 churches, built between 1670 and 1686 in distinctive classical styles, are still noted London landmarks.

St. Paul's, Wren's masterpiece, was begun in 1675, and his son Christopher laid the last stone in 1710. Wren himself was the first man to be buried there. Other Wren buildings include Trinity College library, Cambridge (1676–84), Chelsea Hospital (1682–92), and the south and east wings of Hampton Court Palace (1689–94). Wren was knighted in 1673.

SHELDONIAN THEATRE *This D-shaped theatre in Oxford, built between 1664 and 1669, was one of Wren's earliest buildings.*

THE FIRST DESIGN *The façade of Pembroke College chapel, Cambridge, Wren's first building (left). It led Wren to his life's work as an architect.*

PINNACLE OF GENIUS *Wren's great dome of St. Paul's has a bowl-shaped inner dome round which a brick cone supports an outer dome and the surmounting lantern. Only the windows at the base of the lantern are visible through the eye of the inner dome, casting light some 83 metres (274 feet) to the nave floor.*

destruction, as on a rocky coastline, in order to plunder. **b.** *Archaic.* A plunderer.

wreck·fish (rĕk-fish) *n., pl.* **-fishes** or collectively **wreckfish**. The **stone bass** *(see).* [From its often being found near wrecks.]

wren (ren) *n.* **1.** Any of various small, brownish birds of the family Troglodytidae. **2.** Any of various similar birds. [Middle English *wrenne,* Old English *wrenna,* from Germanic *wrend(il)a-* (unattested).]

Wren (ren) *n. British Informal.* A member of the Women's Royal Naval Service.

Wren, Sir Christopher (1632–1723). English architect and mathematician. Educated at Oxford, he became professor of astronomy at both London (1657) and Oxford (1661) and helped to form the Royal Society. He designed St. Paul's Cathedral, Greenwich Hospital, and Pembroke College chapel, Cambridge.

wrench (rench) *n.* **1.** A sudden sharp, forcible twist or turn. **2.** An injury produced by twisting or straining. **3.** A sudden tug at one's emotions; a surge of sorrow, anguish, or similar emotion. **4. a.** A break in relations or a parting that causes emotional distress. **b.** The pain this causes. **5.** A deliberate distortion in the original form or meaning of something written or spoken. **6.** *U.S.* A spanner. **b.** *British.* Any of various specialised adjustable spanners, especially a **monkey wrench** and a **torque wrench** *(both of which see).*

~*v.* **wrenched, wrenching, wrenches.** —*tr.* **1. a.** To twist or turn suddenly and forcibly. **b.** To twist and sprain: *wrenched her knee.* **2. a.** To force free by pulling at; yank; wrest. Usually used with *off* or *away.* **b.** To pull with a wrench. **3.** To pull at the feelings or emotions of; distress: *It wrenched her to say good-bye.* **4.** To distort or twist the original character or import of: *wrenched the text to prove her point.* —*intr.* To give a wrench, twist, or turn. [Middle English *wrenchen,* to twist, wrench, Old English *wrencan,* to twist.]

wrest (rest) *tr.v.* **wrested, wresting, wrests.** **1.** To obtain by or as by pulling with violent twisting movements: *wrest a book out of another's hands.* **2.** To usurp forcefully: *wrest power.* **3.** To obtain or extract by extortion, guile, or persistent effort: *wrest the meaning from an obscure poem.* **4. a.** To distort or twist the nature or meaning of: *wrested my words out of context.* **b.** To misapply.

~*n.* **1.** The action or an instance of wresting. **2.** *Archaic.* A small tuning key for the pins of a harp or piano. [Middle English *wresten,* Old English *wrǣstan,* to twist; akin to WRIST.] —**wrest·er** *n.*

wres·tle (rĕss'l) *v.* **-tled, -tling, -tles.** —*intr.* **1.** To take part in a fight or competition consisting of grappling and attempting to throw or immobilise one's opponent, especially under certain contest rules. **2.** To contend; struggle; grapple. Used with *with* or *against: town planners wrestling with budget cuts.* **3.** To strive in an effort to gain mastery: *wrestle with temptation.* —*tr.* **1. a.** To take part in (a wrestling match). **b.** To wrestle with. **2.** To make (one's way, for example) by or as if by wrestling: *wrestled her way through the crowd.* ~*n.* **1.** An act of wrestling; especially, a wrestling match. **2.** A struggle. [Middle English *wrest(e)len,* Old English *wrǣstlian.*] —**wres·tler** *n.*

wres·tling (rĕssling) *n.* Any of various sporting exercises or contests between two competitors and sometimes teams who attempt to throw or immobilise each other by grappling.

wrest pin *n.* Any of the pins to which the strings, especially of a keyboard stringed instrument, are attached and by which they are tuned.

wretch (rech) *n.* **1.** A miserable, unfortunate, or unhappy person. **2.** A base, mean, or despicable person: *"A stony adversary, an inhuman wretch"* (Shakespeare). [Middle English *wrecche,* Old English *wrecca,* wretch, exile.]

wretch·ed (rĕchid) *adj.* **1.** Living in degradation and misery; miserable: *wretched beggars huddling on the pavement.* **2.** Attended by misery and woes: *a wretched life.* **3.** Of a poor or mean character; dismal: *a wretched building.* **4.** Contemptible; despicable. **5.** Inferior in performance or quality: *a wretched translation.* **6.** Very unpleasant; deplorable. **7.** Used as an intensive: *a wretched nuisance.* —See Synonyms at **sad.** [Middle English *wrecched,* irregularly from *wrecche,* WRETCH.] —**wretch·ed·ly** *adv.* —**wretch·ed·ness** *n.*

wri·er. Alternative comparative of **wry.**

wri·est. Alternative superlative of **wry.**

wrig·gle (rĭgg'l) *v.* **-gled, -gling, -gles.** —*intr.* **1.** To turn or twist the body with sinuous writhing motions; squirm. **2.** To proceed with writhing motions. **3.** To worm one's way into or out of a situation; insinuate or extricate oneself by sly or subtle means: *He's always wriggling out of his responsibilities.* —*tr.* **1.** To move with a wriggling motion: *wriggle a toe.* **2.** To make (one's way, for example) by wriggling: *He wriggled his way into favour.*

~*n.* **1.** A wriggling movement. **2.** A sinuous path, line, marking, or the like. [Middle English *wrigglen,* from Middle Low German *wriggeln.*] —**wrig·gler** *n.* —**wrig·gly** *adj.*

wright (rīt) *n.* A person who constructs or repairs something. Now used only in combination: *playwright; shipwright.* [Middle English *wright,* Old English *wryhta, wyrhta.*]

Wright (rīt), **Frank Lloyd** (1869–1959). U.S. architect. He studied civil engineering and adapted its methods to architecture. Famous examples of his work include the Robie House (1909) in Chicago and the inside of the Guggenheim Museum (1946–56).

Wright, Judith (1915–). Australian poet. Examining Australian themes in a frequently introspective style, her works include *Woman to Man* (1950), *Alive* (1972), and *The Double Tree* (1978).

Wright, Orville (1871–1948), and **Wilbur** (1867–1912). U.S. pioneer aviators. The brothers ran a bicycle firm until they made the first successful powered flight in a heavier-than-air machine (1903). They later formed a production company.

wring (ring) v. **wrung** (rung) or rare **wringed, wringing, wrings.** —tr. **1.** To twist, squeeze, or compress, especially so as to extract liquid. Often used with out. **2.** To extract (liquid) by twisting or compressing. **3.** To wrench or twist forcibly or painfully: wring someone's neck. **4.** To clasp and twist or squeeze (one's hands), as in distress. **5.** To take hold of and shake energetically (someone's hand), as in congratulation. **6.** To cause distress to; affect with painful emotion: wring someone's heart. **7.** To obtain or extract by applying force or pressure: wring the truth out of a person. —intr. Archaic. To writhe or squirm, as in pain.
~n. The act or an instance of wringing; a squeeze or twist. [Middle English wringen, Old English wringan.]

wring·er (ring-ər) n. One that wrings; especially, a device in which laundry is pressed between rollers to extract water.

wring·ing (ring-ing) adv. Used as in intensive in the phrase wringing wet.

wrin·kle¹ (ringk'l) n. **1.** A small furrow, ridge, or crease on a normally smooth surface, caused by crumpling, folding, or shrinking. **2.** A line or crease in the skin, as from age.
~v. **wrinkled, -kling, -kles.** —tr. **1.** To make a wrinkle or wrinkles in. **2.** To draw up so as to form wrinkles; pucker: wrinkle one's nose in disdain. —intr. To acquire or be affected with wrinkles. [Middle English, back-formation from wrinkled, wrinkled, probably Old English gewrincled, serrated, winding, participle of gewrinclian, to wind.] —**wrin·kly** adj.

wrinkle² n. Informal. An ingenious trick or method; a useful or clever hint; a dodge. [Middle English wrinkel, crooked action, trick, specialised use of wrinkle, WRINKLE.]

wrist (rist) n. **1. a.** The junction between the hand and forearm. **b.** Anatomy. The system of bones forming this junction. Also called "carpus". **2.** The part of a sleeve or glove that encircles the wrist. [Middle English wrist, Old English wrist.]

wrist·band (rist-band) n. A band, as on a long sleeve or on a wristwatch, that encircles the wrist.

wrist-drop (rist-drop) n. Paralysis of the muscles that raise back the hand, caused by compression of the nerve or by damage to the nerve, as in lead poisoning.

wrist·let (rist-lət, -lit) n. **1.** A band of material worn round the wrist for warmth or support. **2.** A bracelet.

wrist-lock (rist-lok) n. A wrestling hold in which an opponent's wrist is gripped and twisted to immobilise him.

wrist pin n. **1.** A pin attached to a wheel parallel to its axle, to function as a bearing for a crank. **2.** Chiefly U.S. A **gudgeon pin** (see).

wrist-watch (rist-woch) n. A watch on a band worn about the wrist.

wris·ty (risti) adj. Using or characterised by flexible movements of the wrist: a wristy conducting style.

writ¹ (rit) n. **1.** Law. A written order issued by a court, in the name of the Crown or of the state commanding the person to whom it is addressed to perform or cease performing some stated act. **2.** Archaic. Writings: holy writ. [Middle English writ, Old English writ, from Germanic wrītan (unattested), to scratch. See write.]

writ². Archaic. Past tense and past participle of **write.** —**writ large.** On a magnified scale; in a large or emphasised form: He treated war just as a childhood game writ large.

write (rīt) v. **wrote** (rōt) or archaic **writ** (rit), **written** (ritt'n) or archaic **writ, writing, writes.** —tr. **1.** To form (letters, symbols, words, or sentences) on a surface such as paper, using a pen, pencil, or other tool. **2.** To spell: How do you write your name? **3.** To form (words) in cursive rather than printed script. **4.** To compose, especially as an author or musician: write a memo; write a symphony; write one's memoirs. **5.** To draw up in legal form; draft: write a will. **6.** To fill in with the required information: write a cheque. **7.** To cover with writing: wrote five pages in an hour. **8.** To set down; record: write one's thoughts. **9.** To relate or communicate by writing: wrote that he was planning to extend his holiday. **10.** To underwrite (an insurance policy). **11.** To have sufficient knowledge of (a language or writing system) to be able to compose in it in writing: able to read German but not write it. She can speak Chinese but can't write it. **12.** To depict clearly; mark: "Utter dejection was written on every face." (Winston Churchill). **13.** To ordain by fate or prophecy: It is written that the Empire will fall. **14.** To record (data) in a computer storage device. **15.** Chiefly U.S. To send a letter to. —intr. **1.** To trace or form letters, words, or symbols on paper or another surface. **2.** To produce articles, books, or other matter to be read. **3.** To compose a letter or letters; communicate by letter: wrote to say he'd be three days late; I wish you'd write more often. —**write out. 1.** To set down fully in writing. **2.** To remove (a character) from a long-running radio or television serial: was written out of "Crossroads" when her contract expired. [Middle English writen, Old English wrītan, from Germanic wrītan (unattested), to tear, scratch.]

write down tr.v. **1.** To put into writing. **2.** Accounting. To reduce the book value of (an asset). **3.** To disparage in writing. **4.** To write in an affectedly simple or condescending style. Often used with to.

write-down (rīt-down) n. Accounting. A reduction of the book value of an asset.

write in intr.v. To communicate or make a request by letter. —tr. U.S. **1.** To cast a vote for (one not listed on a ballot), as by inserting his name. **2.** To cast (a vote) in this way.

write-in (rīt-in) n. U.S. **1.** A vote for one not listed on a ballot,

usually cast by the insertion of his name in a space provided. **2.** A candidate voted for in this way. Also used adjectivally: a write-in campaign.

write off tr.v. **1.** To reduce to zero the book value of (an asset that has become worthless). **2.** To cancel from accounts as a loss. **3.** To consider with resignation as a loss or failure. **4.** Informal. To wreck beyond repair: wrote off his car on the M.1.

write-off (rīt-off, -awff) n. **1. a.** A cancellation in account books. **b.** The debt or asset thus cancelled. **c.** The amount cancelled or lost. **2.** Informal. Something regarded as being beyond repair or redemption; especially, a badly damaged car.

Wright

BUILDINGS FOR A "NEW TOMORROW"

Pioneer of open-plan interiors in homes and offices

Frank Lloyd Wright (1869–1959) first worked with L. H. Sullivan, the major architect of the "Chicago School". In 1901 he began building his revolutionary "prairie houses" – low, horizontal, ranch-type homes that were the first to have open-plan interiors. They demonstrated his theory of "organic architecture", in which buildings blend naturally into their surroundings, and were built in the Chicago outer suburbs of Riverside and Oak Park, where he lived. The most famous was the Robie House (1908–9).

The success of the middle-income houses led Wright to concentrate on homes and offices that, he said, would "reflect the personalities and characters of the people living and working in them". In these buildings, he either introduced or popularised many features now taken for granted – such as air-conditioning, indirect lighting, built-in furniture, fire-proofing, and central heating.

He began building his own canvas-roofed desert head-quarters at Taliesin West, near Phoenix, Arizona, from 1911, and produced a regular flow of unique and daring blueprints. They included those for the Johnson Wax Administration Building at Racine, Wisconsin (designed 1936, a windowless rectangle), and New York's Guggenheim Museum (completed in 1959) with its circular galleries that spiral wider at the top than the bottom.

Wright died as the museum was being completed. He once summed up his work by saying: "I am not interested in the architecture of yesterday, or today even. I am constructing a new tomorrow".

FALLING WATER A millionaire, Edgar Kaufmann, commissioned this house at Bear Run, Pennsylvania, as a holiday retreat. Built in 1939 of reinforced concrete, it has cantilevered terraces over a waterfall.

wren Only one species of wren, Troglodytes troglodytes (above), is found in Europe and Asia; it lives in hedges and undergrowth, feeding on insects and spiders. Most other species are native to South America.

PRONUNCIATION KEY

a, trap; aa, father; ai, fair; ar, star; aw, lawn; ay, play; b, bb, stab; rubber; ch, church; ck, ticket; d, dd, dead; ladder; e, dress; ee, bee; er, defer; ew, few; ewr, pure; ə, about; ər, letter; f, ff, fife; differ; g, gg, giggle; h, hat; i, kit; ī, price; īr, fire; j, judge; k, kick; l, ll, let; 'l, needle; m, mm, man; n, nn, no; 'n, sudden; ng, thing; o, lot; ō, no; ŏŏ, foot; ōō, shoe; oor, poor; ow, cow; owr, hour; oy, boy; p, pp, pepper; r, rr, red; s, ss, sauce; sh, ship; t, tt, totter; th, thick; th, this; smooth; u, cut; ur, turn; v, vv, valve; w, wet; y, yes; z, zz, zebra; zh, vision; pleasure

IN FOREIGN WORDS:

aN, oN, Saint-Saëns; hl, Llanelli; Hluhluwe; kh, loch; lough; Khaled

STRESS MARK:

in-sīt, insight; in-sīt, incite

Wyeth

THE PAINTER WHO REJECTED THE MODERN WORLD

Millions of Americans flock to Wyeth's exhibitions to view his vision of the past

The appeal of Andrew Wyeth – America's most popular living painter – is based on his rejection of the modern, commercialised world. His detailed and realistic canvases show artefacts and buildings that were made to last – such as rural houses in which generations of workers lived and died. His nostalgia for a lost America and his emphasis on the value of old-fashioned craftsmanship have drawn millions to his exhibitions. In the United States, only Picasso has a greater mass appeal.

Born in 1917, he learned his craft from his father, a book illustrator. He was 20 when he held his first one-man show, in Philadelphia. As a mature artist, he has confined his work to two rural areas of America, in the eastern states of Maine and Pennsylvania. Working mainly in tempera (a mixture of powder colour and egg yolk), he paints with a visionary quality that lifts his work above simple naturalism.

His major paintings include *Wind from the Sea* (1947), *Christina's World* (1948), *The Patriot* (1964), and *Witching Hour* (1977).

CHRISTINA'S WORLD *Christina Olson, a New England polio victim, reminded Wyeth of a "wounded seagull". He watched her hauling herself back home after gathering vegetables in a nearby field. The picture, he said, was more than just her portrait. "It really was her whole life."*

writ·er (rītər) *n.* **1.** One who writes, especially for a living. **2.** One who composes literary works. **3.** A composer of musical works.

writer's cramp *n.* A cramp chiefly affecting the muscles of the thumb and two adjacent fingers after prolonged writing.

Writer to the Signet *n. Abbr.* **W.S.** A member of the oldest and most influential society of solicitors in Scotland.

write up *tr.v.* **1.** To write a report or description of, as for publication. **2.** To bring (a journal, for example) up to date.

write-up (rīt-up) *n.* A published account, review, or notice, especially a favourable one.

writhe (rīth) *v.* **writhed**, **writhed** or *archaic* **writhen** (rĭth'n), **writhing**, **writhes.** —*intr.* **1.** To twist or squirm, as in pain, struggle, or embarrassment. **2.** To move with a twisting or contorted motion. —*tr.* To cause to twist or squirm; contort: *"He writhed himself quite off his stool in the excitement of his feelings"* (Charles Dickens). ~*n.* An act or instance of writhing; a contortion. [Middle English *writhen*, Old English *wrīthan*.] —**writh·er** *n.*

writ·ing (rīting) *n.* **1.** Written form: *Put it in writing.* **2. a.** Language symbols or characters written or imprinted on a surface. **b.** The art of using such symbols as a means of communication: *the invention of writing.* **3.** Any written work; especially, a literary composition. **4.** The activity, art, or occupation of a writer. **5.** Handwriting or handwritten matter: *couldn't read his writing.* —**the writing on the wall.** An indication of approaching defeat or catastrophe. ~*adj.* Of, pertaining to, or used in writing: *writing paper.*

Writ·ings (rītingz) *pl.n.* **Hagiographa** *(see).* Preceded by *the.*

writ of execution *n. Law.* A writ ordering the enforcement of a judgment.

writ of summons *n. Law.* A writ directing a person to appear in court to answer a complaint.

writ·ten. Past participle of **write.**

W.R.N.S. Women's Royal Naval Service.

wrnt. warrant.

Wroc·ław (vrōts-laaf, -lav; *Polish* -waaf). Capital and port of Wroclaw province, southwest Poland. Situated on the river Oder, it was a Hanseatic city (1368–1474) before passing to the Habsburgs (1526) and Prussia (1742).

wrong (rong ‖ rawng) *adj.* **1.** Not correct; erroneous. **2. a.** Contrary to conscience, morality, or law; wicked; immoral. **b.** Unfair or unjust. **3.** Not required, intended, or wanted: *We took a wrong turn.* **4.** Not fitting or suitable; inappropriate; improper: *the wrong moment.* **5.** Not in accordance with an established usage, method, or procedure. **6.** Not ·functioning properly; out of order; amiss. **7.** Unacceptable or undesirable according to social convention. ~*adv.* In a wrong manner or direction; mistakenly; erroneously. —**get wrong.** To misunderstand. —**go wrong. 1.** To take a wrong turn or make a wrong move: *Where did we go wrong?* **2.** To happen or turn out badly; go amiss. ~*n.* **1. a.** That which is morally wrong: *to know right from wrong.* **b.** An unjust, injurious, or immoral act or circumstance. **2. a.** An invasion or violation of another's legal rights. **b.** *Law.* An infringement, especially one leading to a civil action; a tort. **3.** The condition of being mistaken or to blame: *in the wrong.* —See Synonyms at **injustice.**

~*tr.v.* **wronged, wronging, wrongs. 1.** To treat unjustly or injuriously. **2.** To discredit unjustly; malign. **3.** To treat dishonourably; especially, to seduce (a woman). [Middle English *wrang, wrong,* probably from Scandinavian; akin to Danish *vrang,* Old Norse *rangr* and *vrangr* (unattested), awry; akin to WRING.] —**wrong·er** (róng-ər) *n.* —**wrong·ly** *adv.*

Usage: The adverbs *wrong* and *wrongly* are usually interchangeable, especially in the sense of "erroneously", when used after a verb. However *wrong* is somewhat informal, and should be avoided in careful writing or speech: *She spelt it wrongly/wrong.* Before the verb, or a verb form used adjectivally, *wrongly* is obligatory: *It was wrongly spelt; a wrongly conceived plan.*

wrong·do·er (róng-dōō-ər || ráwng-) *n.* One who does wrong morally or legally. —**wrong·do·ing** *n.*

wrong font *n. Abbr.* **wf** *Printing.* The incorrect font. Used, as in proofreading, to indicate a typeface of the wrong kind.

wrong-foot (róng-fóōt || ráwng-) *tr.v.* **-footed, -footing, -foots. 1.** In tennis and various other sports, to mislead (one's opponent) into balancing on the wrong foot, and thereby pass him on the other side. **2.** To mislead or surprise (a person) into an embarrassing or foolish action: *He wrong-footed me with a surprise question.*

wrong·ful (róng-f'l || ráwng-) *adj.* **1.** Wrong; injurious; marked by injustice or unfairness: *wrongful dismissal.* **2.** Contrary to law; unlawful; illegal. —**wrong·ful·ly** *adv.* —**wrong·ful·ness** *n.*

wrong-head·ed (róng-héddid || ráwng-) *adj.* **1.** Persistently erroneous in judgment. **2.** Wrong in stubborn defiance of the evidence. —**wrong-head·ed·ly** *adv.* —**wrong-head·ed·ness** *n.*

wrote. Past tense of **write.**

wroth (rōth, roth || rawth) *adj. Archaic.* Wrathful; angry. [Middle English *wrath, wroth,* Old English *wrāth.*]

wrought (rawt). *Archaic.* Past tense and past participle of **work.** ~*adj.* **1.** Created or put together with care and deliberation. **2.** Shaped by hammering with tools, rather than by casting. Said of metals or metalwork. **3.** Made or embellished delicately or elaborately: *wrought snuffboxes.* —**wrought up.** Agitated; excited.

wrought iron *n.* An easily welded or forged iron containing approximately 0.2 per cent carbon and total impurities less than approximately 0.5 per cent. —**wrought-i·ron** *adj.*

wrung. Past tense and past participle of **wring.**

W.R.V.S. Women's Royal Voluntary Service.

wry (rī) *adj.* **wrier** or **wryer, wriest** or **wryest. 1.** Temporarily twisted in an expression of distaste or displeasure: *On tasting the wine, she pulled a wry face.* **2.** Drily humorous, often with a touch of irony. **3.** Abnormally twisted or bent to one side; crooked. Said of the features or the neck. **4.** At variance with what is right, proper, or suitable; perverse. [Middle English *wrien,* to bend, twist, turn aside, Old English *wrīgian,* to proceed, turn.] —**wry·ly** *adv.* —**wry·ness** *n.*

wry·bill (rī-bil) *n.* A plover native to New Zealand, *Anarhynchus frontalis,* having a right-handed twist to its beak.

wry·neck (rī-nek) *n.* **1.** Either of two Old World birds, *Jynx torquilla* or *J. ruficollis,* that are capable of twisting the neck all the way round to look backwards. **2.** *Pathology.* **Torticollis** (see).

W.S. Writer to the Signet.

WSW west-southwest.

wt. weight.

Wu (wōō) *n.* Any of various Chinese dialects spoken in the valley and delta regions of the Chang Jiang (Yangtze river.) [Mandarin, *wú.*]

Wu·han (wōō-hán, -háan). Capital and port of Hubei province, People's Republic of China. Situated at the confluence of the Chang Jiang and Han Shui rivers, it is formed from the cities of Hanyang, Wuchang, and Hankou Yangtze.

Wuh·sien. See **Suzhou.**

wul·fen·ite (wōōlfə-nīt) *n.* A yellow to orange-red or brown mineral, PbMoO4, used as a molybdenum ore. [German *Wulfenit,* after Franz X. von *Wulfen* (1728–1805), Austrian mineralogist.]

Wun·der·kind (wúndər-kind; *German* vōōndər-kint) *n., pl.* **-kinds** or **-kinder** (kindər). *Sometimes small* **w. 1.** A person who attains great success or an advanced position in his profession, art, or the like at a relatively early age. **2.** A child prodigy. [German, "wonder child".]

Wup·per·tal (vōōpər-taal). Industrial city in North Rhine-Westphalia, West Germany. It lies on the river Wupper in the Ruhr valley, and was formed in 1929 from the twin towns of Elberfeld and Barmen, and Vohwinkel and several smaller towns.

wurst (wurst, vurst; *German* voorst || *U.S. also* wōōst, wōōsht) *n.* A large sausage of seasoned and usually cooked meat, of a type produced in German-speaking countries. [German *Wurst,* from Old High German *wurst.*]

Würt·tem·berg (vúrtəm-berg, wúrtəm-, -bairg; *German* vúrtəm-bairk). Former kingdom of southwest West Germany. A duchy from 1495, it was a kingdom (1806–1918) and joined the German Reich in 1870. It was incorporated (1952) into the newly formed state of Baden-Württemberg.

wuth·er·ing (wúthəring) *adj. Northern British.* **1.** Affected by swirling wind; blustery. **2.** Blowing strongly and noisily. Said of the wind. [Variant of dialect *whithering,* from *whither,* to bluster, from Scandinavian; akin to Old Norse *hvitha,* squall of wind, Old English *hwitha,* breeze.]

Wu·xian. See **Suzhou.**

W.W.I World War I.

W.W.II World War II.

WWF World Wildlife Fund.

Wy·att (wī-ət), **Sir Thomas,** (*c.* 1503–42). English poet and courtier. In Henry VIII's favour, he was sent on various missions abroad but was twice imprisoned on a charge of being the lover of Anne Boleyn (1536) and for suspected treason (1541). He is credited with the introduction of the Petrarchan sonnet into English poetry.

wych elm, wich elm (wich) *n.* **1.** An Old World elm, *Ulmus glabra,* often planted as a shade tree. **2.** The wood of this tree. [Middle English *wyche,* Old English *wice.*]

wych hazel. Variant of **witch hazel.**

Wyc·liffe (wicklif), **John** (*c.* 1329–84). English religious reformer. He spoke out against Church abuses and despite papal censure issued a condemnation of absolution, penances, and indulgences, denied transubstantiation, and issued the first translation of the Bible in English. He sent out itinerant preachers to spread his philosophy, but his followers, called Lollards, were imprisoned, although Wycliffe remained untouched. After his death, his works were again condemned by the Church. —**Wyc·lif·fite, Wyc·lif·ite** *n. & adj.*

Wye (wī). River of Wales and England. Rising in the Plynlimmons, it flows 210 kilometres (130 miles) mainly southeast to enter the estuary of the river Severn near Chepstow.

Wy·eth (wī-əth), **Andrew (Newell)** (1917–). U.S. painter. Working mainly in watercolour and egg tempera, he painted American landscapes and people in a restrained, naturalistic style. His many works include *Christina's World* (1948), *That Gentleman* (1960), *Garret Room* (1962), and *Day of the Fair* (1963).

Wyke·ham·ist (wickəmist) *n.* A pupil or former pupil of Winchester College, an English public school. [After William of *Wykeham* (1324–1404), Bishop of Winchester, Chancellor of England, and founder of the school.] —**Wyke·ham·ist** *adj.*

wynd (wīnd) *n. Scottish.* A narrow lane; an alley. [Middle English, probably from *wynden,* to go, Old English *windan,* to WIND.]

Wy·o·ming (wī-ōming). State of the western United States. With the Great Plains in the northeast, and crossed by the Rocky Mountains in the west, it is rich in mineral reserves. Its capital is Cheyenne.

wy·vern, wi·vern (wīvərn)*n.* A two-legged dragon with wings and a barbed and knotted tail. [17th century : Variant of earlier *wyver,* from Old French, from Latin *vīpera,* VIPER.]

wryneck *A European bird, the wryneck is a member of the woodpecker family and lives on insects which it picks from tree bark with its long tongue. It twists its head into odd angles when startled, and also during its courtship display.*

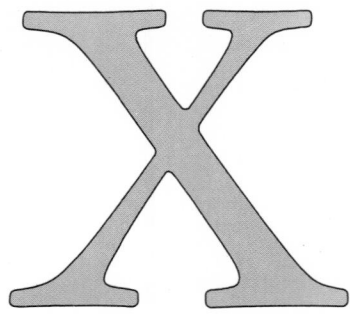

x, X (eks) *n., pl.* **x's** or *rare* **xs, Xs** or **X's. 1.** The 24th letter of the modern English alphabet. **2.** Any of the speech sounds represented by this letter. **3.** Anything shaped like the letter **X. 4.** The mark **X** inscribed to represent the signature of an illiterate person.

x, X, x., X. *Note:* As an abbreviation or symbol, *x* may be a small or a capital letter, with or without a full stop. Established forms or those generally preferred precede the definition. When no form is given, all four forms are in general use in that sense. **1. X** A symbol for Christ or Christian. **2. x.** *Finance.* ex. **3. x** *Printing.* A symbol used, as in proofreading, to indicate a mechanical defect in type. **4. X** The symbol for a kiss. **5. X** A symbol placed on a map or diagram to mark the location or position of a point. **6. X** A symbol placed on a ballot paper, questionnaire, or the like, to indicate one's preference among alternatives. **7. x, X** The Roman numeral for ten. **8. x** A symbol used in marking school exercises, examination papers, or the like, to indicate an error. **9.** *Mathematics.* **x** The symbol for: **a.** An unknown number. **b.** An algebraic variable. **10. X** The symbol for reactance. **11.** Any unknown or unnamed factor, thing, or person. **12.** The 24th in a series; 23rd when *J* is omitted. **13.** The first in a series consisting of *x, y,* and *z.*

x *tr.v.* **x'd** or **xed** (ekst), **x-ing** or **x'ing** (éksing), **x's** or **xes** (éksiz). **1.** To mark or sign with an *x.* **2.** To delete, cancel, or obliterate with a series of x's. Usually used with *out.*

X *n., pl.* **Xs** or **X's** (éksiz). Formerly, a film not permitted to be shown publicly to persons under a certain age, which in Britain is 18. Also used adjectively: *an X film.* Now indicated in Britain by the symbol 18.

xan·thate (zán-thayt) *n.* A salt or ester of a xanthic acid; especially, a simple xanthic acid salt, as of sodium or potassium, used as a flotation collector for copper, silver, and gold. [XANTH(O)- + -ATE.] —**xan·tha·tion** (zan-tháysh'n) *n.*

xan·thic acid (zánthik) *n.* Any of various unstable acids of the form ROC(S)SH, in which R is usually an alkyl radical. [Greek *xanthos†,* yellow (referring to the colour of its salts).]

xan·thine (zán-theen, -thīn, -thin) *n.* A yellowish-white purine base, $C_5H_4N_4O_2$, found in blood, urine, and some plants. [French *xanthine* : XANTH(O)- + -INE.]

Xan·thip·pe (zan-thíppi, gzan-, -típpi). The wife of Socrates; proverbial as a shrewish and scolding woman.

xantho-, xanth- *comb. form.* Indicates the colour yellow; for example, **xanthochroid, xanthoma.** [New Latin, from Greek *xanthos†,* yellow.]

xan·tho·chroid (zán-thō-kroyd, -thə-) *adj.* Having a light complexion and light hair.
~*n.* A xanthochroid individual. [New Latin *xanthochroi,* light-haired, fair-skinned people : XANTH(O)- + Greek *ōkhros,* pale, wan + -OID.]

xan·tho·ma (zan-thōmə) *n.* A skin disease characterised by nodular yellowish patches, especially on the eyelids. [New Latin : XAN-TH(O)- + -OMA.]

xan·tho·phyll (zán-thō-fil, -thə-) *n.* Any of a class of yellow carotenoid pigments, the commonest of which is lutein, found with chlorophyll in green plants and in egg yolk. [French *xanthophylle* : XANTHO- + -PHYLL.]

xan·thous (zánthəss) *adj.* **1.** Yellow. **2.** Having light-brown or yellowish skin. Compare **melanous.** [Greek *xanthos†,* yellow.]

Xan·thus (zánthəss). Ancient city of Lycia, west Asia Minor. Situated on the river Xanthus in modern Turkey, it was captured by the Persians (*c.* 546 B.C) and later the Romans (*c.* 42 B.C.).

x-ax·is (éks-ak-siss) *n., pl.* **x-axes** (-seez). **1.** The horizontal axis of a two-dimensional Cartesian coordinate system. **2.** One of three axes in a three-dimensional Cartesian coordinate system.

X-chro·mo·some (éks-krōmə-sōm) *n.* The larger of the two types of sex chromosome. It is associated with female characteristics in most animals, including humans, and occurs in pairs in such female animals, and paired with the **Y-chromosome** *(see)* in males.

Xe The symbol for the element xenon.

xe·bec, ze·bec, ze·beck (zée-bek) *n.* A small three-masted Mediterranean vessel with both square and triangular sails, once used commonly by Arab corsairs. [Earlier *chebec,* from French, from Italian *sciabecco,* from Arabic *shabbāk.*]

Xe·na·kis (ze-nǎakiss, *Greek* kse-), **Iannis** (1922–). Greek composer born in Romania. Applying mathematics to composition and sometimes employing a computer, he has written such works as *Poème électronique* (1958), *Duel* (1959), and *Pleiades* (1978).

xe·ni·a (zéeni-ə) *n. Botany.* An effect produced on a structure by the introduction of male genes; for example, a visible change in the endosperm of a seed caused by the pollen nucleus when it fuses with the endosperm nucleus. [New Latin, from Greek, the condition of a guest, from *xenos,* stranger, guest.]

xeno-, xen- *comb. form.* Indicates strange, foreign, or different; for example, **xenolith, xenophobe.** [New Latin, from Greek *xenos,* stranger.]

xen·o·cryst (zén-ə-krist, -ō-) *n.* A crystal foreign to the igneous rock in which it occurs. [XENO- + CRYST(AL).]

xe·nog·a·my (ze-nóggəmi, zee-, zi-) *n. Botany.* The transfer of pollen from one plant to another; cross-pollination. [XENO- + -GAMY.] —**xe·nog·a·mous** *adj.*

xen·o·gen·e·sis (zén-ə-jénni-siss, -ō-) *n. Biology.* **1.** The supposed production of offspring markedly different from and showing no relationship to either of its parents. **2. Alternation of generations** *(see).* [XENO- + -GENESIS.] —**xen·o·ge·net·ic** (-jə-néttik), **xen·o·gen·ic** (-jénnik) *adj.*

xen·o·graft (zén-ō-graaft, zéen-, -ō- ‖ -graft) *n.* A type of tissue graft, a **heterograft** *(see).* [XENO- + GRAFT.]

xen·o·lith (zén-ə-lith, zéen-, -ō-) *n.* A rock fragment foreign to the igneous mass in which it occurs. [XENO- + -LITH.]

xen·o·mor·phic (zén-ə-mórfik, zéen-, -ō-) *adj.* Designating a mineral constituent of an igneous rock that lacks its characteristic crystal form as a result of deformation. [XENO- + -MORPHIC.]

xen·on (zénnon, zée-non) *n. Symbol* **Xe** A colourless, odourless, highly unreactive gaseous element found in minute quantities in the atmosphere, extracted commercially from liquefied air, and used in stroboscopic, bactericidal, and flash lamps and lasers. Atomic number 54, atomic weight 131.30, melting point −111.9°C, boiling point −108.1°C, density (gas) 5.897 grams per cubic metre, relative density (liquid) 3.52 (−109°C). [Greek, neuter of *xenos,* stranger.]

xen·o·phobe (zén-ə-fōb, zéen-, -ō-) *n.* A person unduly fearful or contemptuous of strangers or foreigners, or of foreign ideas and cultures, especially as reflected in his political or cultural views. [XENO- + -PHOBE.] —**xen·o·pho·bi·a** (-fōbi-ə) *n.* —**xen·o·pho·bic** (-fōbik) *adj.*

Xen·o·phon (zénnəf'n) (*c.* 430–*c.* 354 B.C.). Greek soldier, essayist, and historian. A friend and pupil of Socrates, he gave an account of the philosopher's death in the *Apology.* He accompanied the expedition of Cyrus the Younger against King Artaxerxes Mnemon of Persia and on the death of Cyrus (401 B.C.) assumed command of 10,000 Greeks. He led his troops from the centre of the Persian empire to the Black Sea. He recorded their harrowing journey in the *Anabasis.*

xen·o·pus (zénnəpəss) *n.* Any clawed toad of the African genus *Xenopus;* especially *X. laevis,* which has been used in pregnancy testing since it produces eggs when injected with the urine of a pregnant woman. In its native South Africa the species *Xenopus laevis* is called the "platanna". [New Latin : XENO- + -*pus,* foot (see -**pod**).]

xe·ric (zéer-ik, zérrik) *adj.* Of, characterised by, or adapted to an extremely dry habitat. [Greek *xēros,* dry.]

xero-, xer- *comb. form.* Indicates dryness; for example, **xerophyte, xerosis.** [New Latin, from Greek *xēros,* dry.]

xe·ro·der·ma (zéer-ō-dérmə) *n.* Also **xe·ro·der·mi·a** (-dérmi-ə). **1.** Abnormal dryness of the skin. **2.** A skin disease, **ichthyosis** *(see).* [New Latin : XERO- + -DERMA.] —**xer·o·der·mat·ic** (-der-máttik), **xer·o·der·ma·tous** (-dérmətəss) *adj.*

xe·rog·ra·phy (zeer-róggrəfi, ze-) *n.* A dry photographic or photocopying process in which a negative image formed by a resinous powder on an electrically charged plate is electrically transferred to and thermally fixed as positive on a paper or other copying surface.

[XERO- + -GRAPHY.] —**xer·o·graph·ic** (zéer-ə-gráffik) adj. —**xe·rog·raph·er** (-róggrəfər) n.

xe·roph·i·lous (zeer-óffiləss) adj. Flourishing in or able to withstand a dry, hot environment. [XERO- + -PHILOUS.]

xe·roph·thal·mi·a (zeer-of-thálmi-ə, -op-) n. Extreme dryness of the conjunctiva, thought to result from vitamin A deficiency. [Late Latin xerophthalmia, from Greek xērophthalmia : XER(O)- + OPHTHALMIA.] —**xer·oph·thal·mic** (-thál-mik) adj.

xe·ro·phyte (zéer-ə-fīt, -ō-) n. A plant, such as a cactus, that grows in and is adapted to an environment deficient in moisture. Compare **hydrophyte, mesophyte**. [XERO- + -PHYTE.] —**xer·o·phyt·ic** (-fíttik) adj. —**xer·o·phyt·i·cal·ly** adv.

xe·ro·sere (zéer-ə-seer, -ō-) n. A sequence of ecological communities beginning in a dry area. [XERO- + SERE (series).]

xe·ro·sis (zeer-rō-siss, zi-) n. Abnormal dryness, especially of the skin, conjunctiva, or mucous membranes. [New Latin : XER(O)- + -OSIS.] —**xe·rot·ic** (-róttik) adj.

Xer·ox (zéer-oks) n. 1. A trademark for a photocopying process or machine using xerography. 2. A copy made on a Xerox machine. ~tr.v. **Xeroxed, -oxing, -oxes**. Sometimes small x. To reproduce or print by means of a Xerox machine. —**Xer·ox** adj.

Xer·xes I (zérkseez). (c. 519–465 B.C.). King of Persia (486–465 B.C.). Succeeding to the throne on the death of his father Darius I, he organised a vast army which defeated the Greeks at Thermopylae, and destroyed Athens (480 B.C.), but on the defeat of his navy at Salamis (480 B.C.) and of his army at Plataea (479 B.C.), he retreated to Persia where he was later assassinated.

x-height (éks-hīt) n. Printing. The height of a lower-case x. Compare **cap-height**.

Xho·sa (káw-sə, kó-, -zə. Note: the initial Xh properly denotes an aspirated voiceless alveolar lateral click). n., pl. **-sas** or collectively **Xhosa**. 1. A member of a southern African Bantu people living mainly in the Cape Province of the Republic of South Africa. 2. The Bantu language akin to Zulu spoken by the Xhosa, of the Niger-Congo family of languages.

xi (sī, ksī, zī; Greek ksee) n., pl. **xis**. 1. The 14th letter in the Greek alphabet, written Ξ, ξ. Transliterated in English as X, x, or ks. 2. Symbol Ξ Physics. Any of four elementary particles in the baryon family.

Xia·men or **Hsia·men** (syáa-mún). Also **A·moy** (ə-móy). Port of southeast China. Situated in Fujian province on Xiamen island, it stands opposite Taiwan. After its capture by the British during the Opium War (1841), it became a treaty port (1842). Formerly a chief port of the tea clipper trade, today it is an important industrial city and tourist centre.

Xi'an, Hsi-an, or **Sian** (shée-áan). Formerly **Changan**. Capital of Shaanxi province, northwest China. Situated in the valley of the river Wei, it was the capital of the Ch'in dynasty (255–206 B.C.), and at times of the Han and T'ang dynasties. Jiang Jieshi, leader of the Kuomintang, was held hostage here (1936) until he agreed to join with the communists against the Japanese.

Xiang Jiang (shée-áang jyáng). Also **Hsiang Chiang** or **Siang Kiang**. River of south central China. It rises in Guangxi Zhuang, and flows 1 150 kilometres (715 miles) through Hunan to the Dongting Hu (lake). Its valley is an ancient routeway and farming area.

Xi Jiang (sée jyáng). Also **Hsi Chiang** or **Si Kiang**; English **West River**. River of south China. Rising in Yunnan province, southwest China, it flows 1 900 kilometres (1,200 miles) eastwards to enter the South China Sea through a delta. Navigable by large ships, it passes Guangzhou (Canton).

Xin·jiang Uigur Zizhiqu. Also **Sin-kiang Uighur Autonomous Region** or **Chinese Turkestan**. Region of western China. It is a high plateau enclosed by the Pamirs, Kunlun Shan, Altun Shan, and Tian Shan, and includes the wastes of the Takla Makan desert, with the Tarim basin, and many salt lakes. Its many oases produce wheat, maize, and millet. There are considerable reserves of coal, tungsten, molybdenum, and oil. Most of the people are Turkic-speaking Muslims. The region came under Chinese control in the 16th century, but was later contested by Russia. Urumqi is the capital.

xiphi-, xiph- comb. form. Indicates sword; for example, **xiphisternum**. [New Latin, from Greek xiphos, sword, probably of Oriental origin.]

xiph·i·ster·num (ziffi-stér-nəm) n., pl. **-na** (-nə). The lowest or hindmost and smallest of the three divisions of the breastbone. Also called "**xiphoid**", "**xiphoid process**".

xiph·oid (zíffoyd, zī-foyd) adj. 1. Having the shape of a sword. 2. Of or pertaining to the xiphisternum. ~n. The xiphisternum. [Greek xiphoeidēs, "sword-shaped" : XIPHI- + -OID.]

xiph·o·su·ran (ziffə-séwr-ən, zīfə-, -sóor-) n. Any arthropod of the order Xiphosura, which includes the horseshoe crab and many extinct forms. ~adj. Of or belonging to the order Xiphosura. [New Latin Xiphosura, "sword-tailed ones" : XIPHI- + -ura, plural of -urus, -UROUS.]

Xizang. See Tibet.

XL extra large.

X·mas (kríss-məss, éks-) n. Informal. Christmas. [From the Greek letter X, transliterated as Kh (see **chi**) and representing Greek Khristos, CHRIST.]
Usage: This form occurs mainly in commercial writing, as on Christmas cards, and is not generally used in other contexts, unless there is a concern to save space (as in newspaper headlines).

XP See **chi-rho**.

X-ra·di·a·tion, x-ra·di·a·tion (éks-ráydi-áysh'n) n. 1. Treatment with or exposure to X-rays. 2. Radiation composed of X-rays.

X-ray, x-ray (éks-ray, -ráy) n. 1. a. A relatively high-energy photon with wavelength in the approximate range from 0.4 to 100 nanometres. b. Usually plural. A stream of such photons, used for their penetrating power in radiography, radiology, radiotherapy, and research. 2. A photograph taken with X-rays. In this sense, also called "X-ray photograph". ~tr.v. **X-rayed** or **x-rayed, -raying, -rays**. 1. To irradiate with X-rays. 2. To photograph by means of X-rays. [Translation of German X Strahlen (plural), so called because their exact nature was not known.] —**X-ray** adj.

X-ray astronomy n. The study of the X-rays emitted by celestial bodies as detected by satellites and rockets above the earth's atmosphere.

X-ray crystallography n. The study of crystal structure by means of X-ray diffraction.

X-ray diffraction n. The diffraction of X-rays by the atoms or ions of a crystal, according to a characteristic pattern that enables information to be obtained on the structure of the crystal.

X-ray microscope n. An instrument used to render a highly magnified image of the atomic structure of a crystalline system by means of the contrasts arising from the differences in such a structure's absorption or emission of X-rays.

X-ray star n. A star that emits most of its radiation in the X-ray part of the electromagnetic spectrum.

X-ray therapy n. Radiotherapy with X-rays.

X-ray tube n. A vacuum tube containing electrodes that accelerate electrons and direct them to a metal anode, where their impacts produce X-rays.

xy·lan (zī-lan) n. A yellow, gummy pentosan found in plant cell walls and yielding xylose upon hydrolysis. [XYL(O)- + -AN.]

xy·lem (zī-ləm, -lem) n. Botany. The supporting and water-conducting tissue of vascular plants, consisting primarily of tracheids and vessels; woody tissue. Compare **phloem**. [German Xylem, from Greek xulon, wood.]

xy·lene (zī-leen) n. 1. Any of three flammable isomeric hydrocarbons, $C_6H_4(CH_3)_2$, of the benzene series, obtained from wood and coal tar. Also called "xylol". 2. A mixture of these isomers used as a solvent in making lacquers and rubber cement and as an aviation fuel. [XYL(O)- + -ENE.]

xy·li·dine (zíli-deen, zílli-, -dīn, -din) n. 1. Any of six toxic isomers, $(CH_3)_2C_6H_3NH_2$, derived from xylene, used chiefly as dye intermediates. 2. Any of various mixtures of these isomers. [XYL(O)- + -IDINE.]

xylo-, xyl- comb. form. Indicates: 1. Wood; for example, **xylograph; xylophone**. 2. Xylene; for example, **xylidine**. [Greek xulon†, wood.]

xy·lo·graph (zílə-graaf, -graf) n. 1. An engraving on wood. 2. An impression from a wood block. ~tr.v. **xylographed, -graphing, -graphs**. To print from a wood engraving. —**xy·log·ra·pher** (zī-lóggrəfər) n.

xy·log·ra·phy (zī-lóggrəfi) n. 1. Wood engraving, especially of an early period. 2. The art of printing texts or illustrations, sometimes with colour, from wood blocks, as distinct from typography. [French xylographie : XYLO- + -GRAPHY.] —**xy·lo·graph·ic** (zīlə-gráffik) adj. —**xy·lo·graph·i·cal·ly** adv.

xy·loid (zī-loyd) adj. Of or similar to wood. [XYL(O)- + -OID.]

xy·loph·a·gous (zī-lóffəgəss) adj. Feeding on wood. Said especially of certain insects. [Greek xylophagos : XYLO- + -PHAGOUS.]

xy·lo·phone (zílə-fōn, zíllə-) n. A musical percussion instrument consisting of a mounted row of wooden bars graduated in length to sound a chromatic scale, played with two small mallets. [XYLO- + -PHONE.] —**xy·lo·phon·ic** (-fónnik) adj. —**xy·lo·phon·ist** (zī-lóf-fənist, zílə-fōnist) n.

xy·lose (zī-lōss, -lōz) n. A white crystalline aldose sugar, $C_5H_{10}O_5$, used in dyeing and tanning, and in diabetic diets. Also called "wood sugar". [XYL(O)- + -OSE.]

xy·lot·o·my (zī-lóttəmi) n. The preparation of sections of wood for microscopic study. [XYLO- + -TOMY.]

xyst (zist) n. Also **xys·tus** (zístəss). 1. In ancient Greece, a covered portico, used by athletes for exercise. 2. In ancient Rome, a long tree-lined garden walk or terrace. [Latin xystus, from Greek xustos, "scraped smooth", from xuein, to scrape.]

xys·ter (zístər) n. A surgical instrument for scraping bones. [New Latin, from Greek xuster, scraper, from xuein, to scrape.]

Y

yak *This domestic yak is much smaller than its wild cousin and is distributed widely through Central Asia. It is well suited to high altitudes because of its relatively small appetite and its ability to withstand extreme cold.*

y, Y (wī) *n., pl.* **y's** or *rare* **ys, Ys** or **Y's. 1.** The 25th letter of the modern English alphabet. **2.** Any of the speech sounds represented by this letter. **3.** Anything shaped like the letter **Y**.

y, Y, y., Y. *Note:* As an abbreviation or symbol, *y* may be a small or a capital letter, with or without a full stop. Established forms or those generally preferred precede the definition. When no form is given, all four forms are in general use in that sense. **1. Y** hypercharge. **2. y** ordinate. **3. y.** year. **4. Y** yen (currency). **5. Y, Y.** *U.S.* A shortened form of the abbreviations Y.M.C.A., Y.W.C.A. **6. Y** The symbol for the element yttrium. **7.** *Mathematics.* The symbol for an algebraic variable. **8.** The 25th in a series; 24th when *J* is omitted. **9.** The second in a series consisting of *x, y,* and *z*.

y-, i- *prefix. Archaic.* Indicates the past participle; for example, **yclept.** [Middle English *i-, y-,* Old English *ge-,* from Germanic *ga-* (unattested).]

-y¹, -ey *adj. suffix.* Indicates: **1.** The existence, possibility, or possession of something specified; for example, **curly, rainy. 2.** A relationship or resemblance to something specified; for example, **glassy, watery.** [Middle English *-ie, -y, -ey,* Old English *-ig, -ǣg,* from Common Germanic *-iga, -aga* (unattested).]

-y² *n. suffix.* Indicates: **1.** A condition, state of being, or quality; for example, **beggary, jealousy. 2.** An instance or result of engaging in a specified activity; for example, **entreaty, delivery.** [Middle English *-ie,* from Old French, from Latin *-ia, -*IA.]

-y³, -ey, -ie *n. suffix.* Indicates: **1.** Smallness or diminutiveness in a person or thing; for example, **kiddy, doggy. 2.** Familiarity or endearment; for example, **sweetie, daddy. 3.** A relationship or resemblance of a person or thing to a quality or thing specified; for example, **bookie, trendy.** [Middle English *-ie.*]

yab·ber (yábbər) *intr.v.* **-bered, -bering, -bers.** *Australian & N.Z. Informal.* To jabber.

yab·by (yábbi) *n., pl.* **-bies.** *Australian & N.Z. Informal.* A crab.

yacht (yot) *n.* Any of various sailing or powered vessels, generally with smart, graceful lines, used for pleasure cruises or racing.
~*intr.v.* **yachted, yachting, yachts.** To race, sail, or cruise in a yacht. [Earlier *yaught,* from obsolete Dutch *jaghte,* short for *jaght(schip),* "chasing (ship)", from *jagen,* to chase, hunt, from Germanic *jagojan* (unattested).] —**yacht·ing** *n. & adj.*

yachts·man (yóts-mən) *n., pl.* **-men** (-mən). A person who owns or sails a yacht. —**yachts·man·ship** *n.*

yachts·wom·an (yóts-woomən) *n., pl.* **-women** (-wimmin). A woman who owns or sails a yacht.

yaf·fle (yáff'l) *n.* The **green woodpecker** *(see).* [Imitative of its cry.]

ya·gi (yáagi, yággi) *n. Electronics.* A directional radio and television aerial consisting of a horizontal conductor with several insulated dipoles parallel to and in the plane of the conductor. Also called "yagi antenna". [After H. *Yagi* (1888–1976), Japanese engineer.]

yah¹ (yaa) *adv. Informal.* Yes. [Variant of YEA.]

yah² *interj.* Used to express derision, defiance, or disgust.

ya·hoo (yə-hoō, yaa- ‖ *U.S. also* yáa-hoō, yáy-) *n., pl.* **-hoos.** A crude or brutish person. [After the *Yahoos,* a race representing the brutish side of humanity in Jonathan Swift's *Gulliver's Travels.*]

Yahr·zeit (yáwrt-sīt, yáart-) *n. Judaism.* Any of the anniversary days of the death of a close relative, observed by saying Kaddish, lighting a memorial candle, and sometimes fasting. [Yiddish, from Middle High German *jārzīt,* anniversary : *jār,* YEAR + *zīt,* time, TIDE.]

Yah·weh, Jah·weh (yáa-way). Also **Jah** (yaa), **Yah·veh** (-vay), **Jah·veh.** A name for God assumed by modern scholars to be a rendering of the pronunciation of the **Tetragrammaton** *(see).* Compare **Elohim.**

Yah·wist, Jah·wist (yáa-wist) *n.* Also **Yah·vist** (-vist), **Jah·vist.** The author of the earliest sources of the Hexateuch, in which God is called Yahweh. Also called "Jehovist". Compare **Elohist.** —**Yah·wist, Yah·wis·tic** (yaa-wístik) *adj.*

yak¹ (yak) *n.* A long-haired bovine mammal, *Bos grunniens,* of the mountains of central Asia, where it is often domesticated. [Tibetan *gyag.*]

yak², yack (yak) *intr.v.* **yakked** or **yacked, yakking** or **yacking, yaks** or **yacks.** *Slang.* To talk or chatter persistently and meaninglessly. ~*n. Slang.* Continuous, meaningless chatter. [Imitative.]

Ya·kut (ya-koōt, yaa-) *n.* **1.** A member of a people living in the Yakut Autonomous Soviet Socialist Republic. **2.** The Turkic language of this people, of the Altaic family of languages.

Yale (yayl). See **New Haven** (Conn.).

Yale lock *n.* A trademark for a door lock having a revolving barrel operated by a flat, serrated key. Compare **deadlock, mortice lock.**

Yal·ta (yál-tə). City of the U.S.S.R. Situated on the Black Sea in the Crimea, south Ukrainian S.S.R., it is a health and holiday resort. It was the site of the Yalta Conference (1945), attended by Churchill, Stalin, and Roosevelt.

yam (yam) *n.* **1.** Any of various chiefly tropical vines of the genus *Dioscorea,* many of which have edible tuberous roots. **2.** The starchy root of such a vine, used in the tropics as food. **3.** *Chiefly U.S.* A sweet potato having reddish flesh. [Portuguese *inhame,* "edible", perhaps from Fulani *nyami,* to eat.]

ya·men (yáa-men, -mən) *n.* The office or residence of any public official in the Chinese Empire. [Mandarin Chinese *yá mén : yá,* office of a magistrate + *mén,* door.]

Yam Kinneret. See **Galilee, Sea of.**

yam·mer (yámmər) *v.* **-mered, -mering, -mers.** *Informal.* —*intr.* **1.** To complain peevishly or whimperingly. **2.** To talk volubly and loudly. —*tr.* To utter or say in a complaining or clamorous tone. ~*n. Informal.* An act or instance of yammering. [Alteration of earlier *yomer,* Middle English *yomeren,* Old English *geōmrian,* to lament, from *geōmor,* sorrowful, from Common Germanic.] —**yam·mer·er** *n.*

Yamuna. See **Jumna.**

Yan'an, Yen-an, Yen-an. Also **Fu-shih.** Industrial city of Shaanxi province, east central China. It was the refuge of the Chinese Communists following the Long March, and was their capital from World War II until they captured Beijing (Peking) in 1949.

yang (yang) *n. Sometimes capital* **Y.** In Chinese dualistic philosophy, the active, male cosmic element, force, or principle that is opposite but complementary to **yin** *(see).* [Mandarin Chinese *yáng,* the sun, masculine element.]

Yang (yang), **Chen Ning** (1922–). Chinese-born American physicist. He was awarded the Nobel prize (1957) with Tsung-Dao Lee for the theory discrediting the parity law.

Yangtze Kiang. See **Chang Jiang.**

yank (yangk) *v.* **yanked, yanking, yanks.** *Informal.* —*tr.* To pull or extract suddenly; jerk: *yanked her out of the chair.* —*intr.* To pull on something suddenly; jerk. ~*n.* A sudden vigorous pull; a jerk. [19th century : origin obscure.]

Yan·kee (yángki) *n.* Also **Yank** (yangk) (sense 1). *Informal.* **1.** A native or inhabitant of the United States; an American. **2.** A native or inhabitant of a Northern state of the United States; especially, a Union soldier during the American Civil War. **3.** A native or inhabitant of New England. Sometimes used derogatorily in all senses. [Perhaps from Dutch *Janke,* diminutive of *Jan,* John (used derisively of the Dutch in the 17th century, applied to inhabitants of New England in the 18th century).] —**Yan·kee** *adj.* —**Yan·kee·dom** *n.*

Yankee Doo·dle (dood'l) *n.* A Yankee. [From the title of a song popular during the War of American Independence.]

Yan·kee·ism (yángki-iz'm) *n.* **1.** The quality of being a Yankee, as in one's character or way of thinking. **2.** A Yankee custom or characteristic. **3.** A Yankee peculiarity, as of language or pronunciation.

Ya·oun·dé (yaa-oōn-dáy). Capital of the United Republic of Cameroon, West Central Africa. Founded by German traders (1888), it was capital of French Cameroon (1922–40, 1946–60).

yap (yap) *n.* **1.** A sharp, shrill bark, as of a small dog; a yelp. **2.** *Slang.* Noisy, stupid, or scolding talk; jabbering. **3.** *U.S. Slang.* A crude, loud, stupid person. **4.** *Chiefly U.S. Slang.* The mouth. ~*v.* **yapped, yapping, yaps.** —*intr.* **1.** To emit a yap or yaps; bark shrilly; yelp. **2.** *Slang.* To talk noisily, stupidly, annoyingly, or at excessive length; jabber. —*tr.* To utter or express by yapping: *The Queen of Hearts yapped her disapproval to Alice.* [Imitative.]

ya·pok, ya·pock (yə-pók) *n.* An aquatic marsupial mammal, *Chironectes minimus,* of tropical America, having dense fur, webbed hind feet, and a long tail. [After *Oyapock,* river in north Brazil.]

Yar·bor·ough (yár-bərə, -brə || *chiefly U.S.* -burrō) *n. Sometimes small* **y.** A full hand of 13 cards in bridge or whist containing no card higher than a nine. [After Charles Anderson Worsley (1809–97), Second Earl of *Yarborough,* who is said to have unsuccessfully bet 1,000 to 1 that such a hand would not occur.]

yard¹ (yard) *n.* **1.** *Abbr.* **yd** A unit of length in the British Imperial System, equal to 0.9144 metre (3 feet). **2.** *Nautical.* A long, tapering spar slung usually at right angles to a mast to support and spread the head of a square sail, lugsail, or lateen. [Middle English *yerde, yarde,* Old English *gerd,* staff, twig, measuring rod, from West Germanic *gazdjō* (unattested).]

yard² *n.* **1.** A tract of ground adjacent to, surrounding, or surrounded by a building or group of buildings. **2.** A tract of ground, often enclosed, used for a specific type of work, business, or other activity. Often used in combination: *shipyard; graveyard.* **3.** An area provided with a system of tracks where railway trains are made up and carriages are shunted, stored, or serviced. **4.** *U.S.* A winter pasture for deer or other grazing animals. **5.** An enclosed tract of ground in which animals, such as chickens or pigs, are kept. **6.** *U.S.* The garden of a house, especially if relatively small. **—the Yard.** *Informal.* In Britain, **Scotland Yard** *(see).*

~*v.* **yarded, yarding, yards.** —*tr.* To enclose, collect, or put in or as if in a yard. —*intr.* To gather in or as if in a yard. [Middle English *yarde, yard,* Old English *geard,* enclosure, residence, from Germanic *gardaz* (unattested).]

yard·age¹ (yárdij) *n.* **1.** The amount or length of something measured in yards. **2.** Cloth sold by the yard.

yardage² *n.* **1.** The use of a railway yard for loading and transporting cattle. **2.** The fee paid for such use.

yard·arm (yárd-aarm) *n.* Either end of the yard of a square sail.

yard grass *n.* Any of several weedy grasses of the genus *Eleusine.*

yard·man (yárd-mən, -man) *n., pl.* **-men** (-mən, -men). A man employed in a yard, especially a railway yard.

yard of ale *n.* **1.** An extremely long and narrow drinking glass, about a yard long, and having a volume usually of two or three pints. **2.** The beer or ale held by such a glass, sometimes drained in one draught in competitions in British pubs.

yard·stick (yárd-stik) *n.* **1.** A graduated measuring stick one yard in length. **2.** Any test or standard used in measurement, comparison, or judgment.

yare (yair) *adj. Archaic.* **1.** Responding easily; manageable; manoeuvrable. Said of a sea vessel. **2.** Bright; lively; quick. **3.** Ready; prepared.

~*adv. Obsolete.* Soon; quickly; promptly. [Middle English *yare,* Old English *gearo, gearu,* finished, ready.] **—yare·ly** *adv.*

Yarmouth. See **Great Yarmouth.**

yar·mul·ke (yárməlkə) *n., pl.* **-kes.** A small skullcap worn by male Jews on religious and celebratory occasions and by male Orthodox Jews at all times. [Yiddish, from Polish and Ukrainian *yarmulka,* perhaps from Turkish *yağmurluk,* raincoat, from *yağmur,* rain.]

yarn (yarn) *n.* **1.** A continuous strand of twisted threads of natural or synthetic material, such as wool, cotton, flax, or nylon, used in weaving or knitting. **2.** *Informal.* A long, involved story or a tale of real or fictitious adventures, often elaborated upon by the teller during the telling.

~*intr.v.* **yarned, yarning, yarns.** *Informal.* To tell a long, complicated story; spin a yarn. [Middle English *yarn,* Old English *gearn.*]

yarn-dyed (yárn-dīd) *adj.* Woven from yarn already dyed.

yar·row (yárrō) *n.* Any of several plants of the genus *Achillea;* especially, *A. millefolium,* native to Eurasia, having finely dissected foliage and flat clusters of usually white flowers. Also called "milfoil". [Middle English *yar(ro)we,* Old English *gearwe,* from West Germanic *garw-* (unattested).]

yash·mak, yash·mac (yásh-mak) *n.* A veil worn by Muslim women in public to cover their faces. [Arabic *yashmaq, yashmak.*]

Yass-Canberra. See **Australian Capital Territory.**

yat·a·ghan, yat·a·gan (yáttə-gən, -gan) *n.* Also **at·a·ghan** (áttə-). A Turkish single-edged sword or scimitar having a slightly S-shaped blade with a pommel or knob on the end, and lacking a handle guard. [Turkish *yatağan.*]

yau·ti·a (yáwti-ə) *n.* Any of various tropical American plants of the genus *Xanthosoma;* especially *X. sagittifolium,* which is cultivated for its starchy tubers. Also called "cocoyam". [American Spanish, from Taino.]

yaw (yaw) *v.* **yawed, yawing, yaws.** —*intr.* **1.** To deviate temporarily from the intended course. Used of a ship. **2.** To turn about the vertical axis. Used of an aircraft or projectile. —*tr.* To cause to yaw.

~*n.* **1.** The action of yawing. **2.** The extent of this movement, measured in degrees. [16th century : origin obscure.]

yawl (yawl) *n.* **1.** A two-masted fore-and-aft-rigged sailing vessel similar to the ketch but having a smaller jigger mast stepped abaft the rudder. Also called "dandy". **2.** A ship's small boat, manned by oarsmen. Compare **ketch.** [Middle Low German *jolle*†.]

yawn (yawn) *v.* **yawned, yawning, yawns.** —*intr.* **1.** To open the mouth wide with a deep intake of air, usually involuntarily, from drowsiness, fatigue, or boredom. **2.** To open wide; gape: *The chasm yawned at our feet.* —*tr.* To utter wearily, as if in yawning.

~*n.* **1.** An act or instance of yawning. **2.** *Informal.* A dull or boring event or person. [Middle English *yonen, yenen,* Old English *geonian, ginian.*] **—yawn·er** *n.* **—yawn·ing·ly** *adv.*

yawp (yawp) *intr.v.* **yawped, yawping, yawps.** *U.S.* **1.** To utter a sharp cry; bark; yelp. **2.** *Slang.* To talk loudly and stupidly.

~*n.* **1.** A bark; a yelp. **2.** *Slang.* Loud, stupid talk. [Middle English *yolpen,* perhaps variant of *yelpen,* YELP.]

yaws (yawz) *n. Used with a singular verb.* An infectious tropical skin disease, caused by a spirochaete, *Treponema pertenue,* and characterised by multiple red pimples. Also called "framboesia". [17th century : perhaps from a Cariban word.]

y-ax·is (wī-ak-siss) *n., pl.* **y-axes** (-seez). **1.** The vertical axis of a two-dimensional Cartesian coordinate system. **2.** One of three axes in a three-dimensional Cartesian coordinate system.

Yb The symbol for the element ytterbium.

Y-chro·mo·some (wī-krōmə-sōm) *n.* The smaller of the two types of sex chromosome, associated with male characteristics in most animals, including humans, and occurring paired with one **X-chromosome** *(see)* in the body cells of such male animals.

y·clept, y·cleped (i-klépt). *Archaic.* Past participle of **clepe.**

~*adj. Archaic.* Known as; named; called. [Middle English *ycleped,* Old English *gecleopod,* past participle of *clipian, cleopian,* to speak, call, CLEPE.]

yd yard (measurement).

ye¹ (thee, *also* yee) *adj. Archaic.* The. Still used in names to convey a sense of history: *ye olde taverne.* [Incorrect transcription resulting from the resemblance between the runic letter called thorn (properly transcribed as *th*) and the letter *y* in certain Middle English manuscripts. See **thorn.**]

ye² (yee) *pron.* **1.** *Poetic & Archaic.* You (plural). **2.** *Regional.* You (singular). [Middle English, Old English *gē.*]

yea (yay) *adv.* **1.** Yes; aye. Now archaic except in recording or expressing a vote. **2.** *Archaic.* Indeed; truly.

~*n.* **1.** A statement or vote in favour of a motion. **2.** One who votes in favour of a motion: *The ayes have it.* [Middle English *ye, ya,* Old English *gēa,* yes.]

yeah (yair) *adv. Informal.* Yes. [Informal pronunciation of *yes.*]

yean (yeen) *v.* **yeaned, yeaning, yeans.** —*intr.* To bear young. Used of sheep and goats. —*tr.* To bear; give birth to. [Middle English *yenen,* Old English *geēanian* (unattested) : *ge-,* Y- + *ēanian,* to bear young, to lamb.]

yean·ling (yéen-ling) *n.* The young of a sheep or goat; a lamb or kid. [YEAN + -LING (little).] **—yean·ling** *adj.*

year (yeer, yer) *n. Abbr.* **y., yr. 1.** The period of time as measured by the Gregorian calendar in which the earth completes a single revolution around the sun. It is divided into 12 months, 52 weeks, or 365 or 366 days, and begins on January 1 and ends on December 31. Also called "calendar year". **2.** See **sidereal year. 3.** See **tropical year. 4.** A period of about equal length in other calendars. **5.** Any period of approximately this duration: *We were married a year ago.* **6.** A period equal to the calendar year but beginning on a different date: *a fiscal year.* **7.** A set period of time, usually shorter than 12 months, devoted to some special activity: *the academic year.* **8.** A group of students that form any of a number of distinct levels of academic progress at a school, college, or other educational institution: *Sarah was in the same year as James at Cambridge; She's a third-year student.* **9.** *Plural.* Age; especially, old age: *feeling his years.* **10.** *Plural.* Time; especially, a long time: *It will take years to do it.* **—the year dot.** *Informal.* A very early stage or time. **—year and a day.** *Law.* In various legal matters, a period of time specified to ensure that a full year is completed. **—year in, year out.** Continuously or regularly over a long period of time. [Middle English *year, yere,* Old English *gēar.*]

year·book (yéer-bŏŏk, yér- || -bŏŏk) *n.* A documentary, memorial, or historical book published every year, containing information about the previous year and for the current year.

year·ling (yéer-ling, yér-) *n.* **1.** An animal that is one year old or has not completed its second year. **2.** A thoroughbred racehorse, regarded as a colt or filly one year old dating from January 1 of the year that it was foaled. **—year·ling** *adj.*

year·long (yéer-long, yér- || -lawng) *adj.* Lasting through one year.

year·ly (yéer-li, yér-) *adj.* **1.** Occurring once a year or every year; annual. **2.** Of or lasting for a year.

~*adv.* Once a year; annually.

yearn (yern) *intr.v.* **yearned, yearning, yearns. 1.** To have a strong or deep desire; be filled with longing. Usually used with *for* or *to: yearns for his native land.* **2.** *Literary.* To feel deep pity, sympathy, or tenderness. [Middle English *yernen,* Old English *gyrnan, giernan,* to strive, desire.] **—yearn·ing·ly** *adv.*

Synonyms: *yearn, long, pine, hanker, hunger, thirst.*

yearn·ing (yérning) *n.* A deep longing.

year-round (yéer-równd, yér-) *adj.* Existing, active, or continuous throughout the year; during all seasons.

yeast (yeest) *n.* **1.** Any of various unicellular fungi of the genus *Saccharomyces* and related genera, reproducing by budding and capable of fermenting carbohydrates. **2.** Froth consisting of yeast cells together with the carbon dioxide they produce in the process of fermentation, present in or added to fruit juices and other substances in the production of alcoholic beverages. **3.** A commercial preparation, either in powdered or compressed form, containing yeast cells and inert material such as meal, and used especially as a leavening agent or as a dietary supplement to treat vitamin B deficiency. **4.** Foam; froth. **5.** An agent of ferment or activity.

yashmak *These veils, which have been worn at least since the time of Christ, are thought to have developed originally as a way of protecting the face from sun and sand. Muslim custom later decreed that they should be worn by women in public – as here, by an Egyptian woman – as a gesture of modesty.*

yawl *Yawls are two-masted sailing boats with a fore-and-aft rig. The smaller mast is usually set behind the rudder post.*

~*intr.v.* **yeasted, yeasting, yeasts. 1.** To ferment. **2.** To froth or foam. [Middle English *yest*, Old English *gist*, *gyst*.]

yeast·y (yéesti) *adj.* **-ier, -iest. 1.** Of, similar to, or containing yeast. **2.** Causing or characterised by a ferment. **3.** Restless; turbulent. **4.** Frothy; frivolous. —**yeast·i·ly** *adv.* —**yeast·i·ness** *n.*

Yeats (yayts), **William Butler** (1865–1939). Irish poet and playwright. He helped to found the Irish National Theatre Company at the Abbey Theatre, Dublin; he wrote many short plays, mostly on mythological themes. His poetry is very varied, ranging from early love lyrics to the complex symbolist poems of such later collections as *The Winding Stair* (1929) and *Last Poems* (1939), and reflecting his deep interests in the occult, art, Celtic mythology, and Irish politics. He served in the Irish Senate (1922–28), and was awarded the Nobel prize for literature (1923).

yell (yel) *v.* **yelled, yelling, yells.** —*intr.* To cry out loudly, as in pain, fright, surprise, or enthusiasm. —*tr.* To utter loudly; shout. ~*n.* **1.** A loud cry; a shriek; a shout. **2.** *U.S.* A rhythmic cheer uttered or chanted in unison by a group: *a college yell.* [Middle English *yellen*, Old English *giellan*, to sound, shout, from Germanic *gel-, gal-* (unattested).] —**yell·er** *n.*

yel·low (yéllō) *n.* **1.** Any of a group of colours of a hue resembling that of ripe lemons and varying in lightness and saturation; the hue of that portion of the spectrum lying between green and orange; one of the psychological primary hues, evoked in the normal observer by radiant energy of wavelength approximately 580 nanometres; also one of the subtractive primaries. **2.** A pigment or dye having this hue. **3.** Something that has this hue, such as: **a.** Yellow clothing. **b.** The yellow ball in snooker. **c.** In the United States, an amber traffic light. **4.** The yolk of an egg. **5.** *Plural.* Any of various plant diseases usually caused by fungi of the genus *Fusarium* or viruses of the genus *Chlorogenus* and characterised by yellow or yellowish discoloration. ~*adj.* **1.** Of the colour yellow. **2.** Designating a person or a people, such as the mongoloid race, having yellowish skin. **3.** *Slang.* Cowardly. **4.** Treating news material in a sensational, exaggerated way. Said of newspapers and used especially in the phrase *the yellow press.* ~*v.* **yellowed, -lowing, -lows.** —*tr.* To make or render yellow. —*intr.* To become yellow. [Middle English *yelwa, yelow*, Old English *geolu*.] —**yel·low·ish, yel·low·y** *adj.* —**yel·low·ly** *adv.* —**yel·low·ness** *n.*

yellow archangel *n.* A creeping perennial woodland plant, *Lamiastrum galeobdolon*, resembling the white dead-nettle but having yellow flowers. Also called "yellow dead-nettle".

yel·low·bark (yéllō-baark) *n.* A kind of tree bark, **calisaya** (see).

yel·low·bel·lied (yéllō-béllid) *adj.* **1.** Having a belly yellow or yellowish in colour, as certain birds and fish do. **2.** *Slang.* Cowardly.

yel·low·bird (yéllō-burd) *n.* Any of various yellow or predominantly yellow birds.

yellow fever *n.* An acute infectious disease of subtropical and tropical New World areas, caused by a virus transmitted by a mosquito of the genus *Aëdes* and characterised by jaundice and dark-coloured vomit resulting from haemorrhages. Also called "yellow jack".

yellow flag *n.* A common yellow-flowered iris, *Iris pseudacorus*, found by streams and on marshy land.

yel·low·ham·mer (yéllō-hammər) *n.* A Eurasian bird, *Emberiza citrinella*, having brown and yellow plumage. Also called "yellow bunting". [Earlier *yelambre* : perhaps YELLOW + *-ambre*, ultimately from Old English *amore, omer*, an unidentified bird.]

yellow jack *n.* **1.** Yellow fever. **2.** *Nautical.* A yellow flag hoisted to request pratique or to warn of disease on board.

Yel·low·knife (yéllō-nīf). Capital of Northwest Territories, north Canada. Situated on the Great Slave Lake, it was founded (1935) after the discovery of gold and is a mining and commercial centre.

yel·low·legs (yéllō-legz) *n., pl.* **yellowlegs.** Either of two North American wading birds, *Tringa melanoleuca* or *T. flavipes*, having yellow legs and a long, narrow bill, occasionally found in Europe as vagrants. Formerly called "yellowshank", "yellowshanks".

yellow lines *pl.n.* In Britain, yellow stripes painted along the sides of a roadway to indicate parking restrictions. *Double yellow lines* forbid parking at all times; *single yellow lines* forbid parking at certain times.

yellow metal *n.* **1.** A form of brass containing about 60 per cent copper and 40 per cent zinc. **2.** **Gold** (see).

yellow pages *pl.n.* A telephone directory or section of a directory, printed on yellow pages, that lists names of people, companies, or other enterprises alphabetically according to the service they provide.

yellow peril *n.* The threat or the alleged threat that Oriental races, especially the Chinese, will invade or destroy Europe or Western civilised countries.

yellow pimpernel *n.* See **pimpernel.**

yellow poplar *n.* The **tulip tree** *(see).*

yellow rattle *n.* A semiparasitic annual plant, *Rhinanthus minor*, having two-lipped yellow flowers and an inflated fruit inside which the ripened seeds rattle.

Yellow River. See **Huang He.**

Yellow Sea. *Chinese* **Huang Hai** or **Hwang Hai** (hwáng hī). Inlet of the west Pacific Ocean. Situated between Korea and northeast China, it receives its name from the yellow silt carried into it by the Huang He (Yellow River), Yalü Jiang, and Liao He.

yellow spot *n.* A part of the human retina, the **macula lutea** *(see).*

Yel·low·stone National Park (yéllō-stōn). The oldest and largest

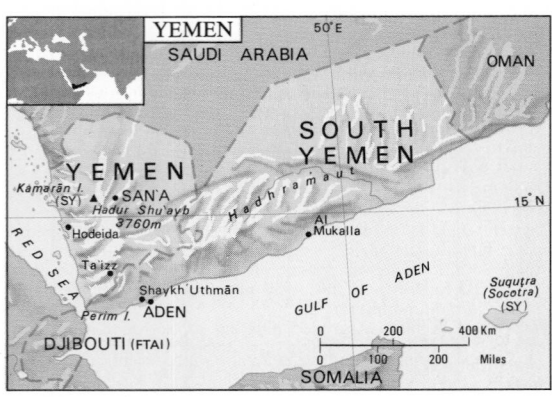

Yellowstone National Park *The first of the U.S. national parks (set up in 1872), Yellowstone is also the largest, covering almost 9000 square kilometres (3,475 square miles). The park contains thousands of geysers, boiling pools, and hot springs. At Mammoth Hot Springs, shown here, the springs bubble over terraces built of limestone deposited by the mineral-rich water.*

national park of the United States. Lying mainly in Wyoming, with small areas in Idaho and Montana, it is chiefly a volcanic plateau in the Rocky mountains. Established in 1872, it has over 3,000 geysers and hot springs, the best-known being Old Faithful, which erupts approximately once every hour.

yellow streak *n.* A proneness to cowardice and disloyalty.

yel·low-tail moth (yéllō-tayl) *n.* A white silky moth, *Euproctis similis*, with a tuft of yellow hairs at the end of the abdomen. See **palmer worm.**

yellow water lily *n.* A yellow-flowered aquatic plant, *Nuphar lutea*, having large floating leaves. Also called "brandy bottle".

yel·low-wood (yéllō-wōōd) *n.* **1.** A tree, *Cladrastis lutea*, of the southeast United States, having compound leaves, drooping clusters of white flowers, and yellow wood yielding a yellow dye. Also *U.S.* "gopherwood". **2.** Any of various other trees having yellow wood. **3.** The wood of any of these trees.

yelp (yelp) *v.* **yelped, yelping, yelps.** —*intr.* To utter a sharp, short bark or cry, as in pain or surprise. Used especially of a dog. —*tr.* To utter by yelping. ~*n.* A sharp, short cry or bark. [Middle English *yelpen*, to cry aloud, Old English *gielpan*, to boast, exult (imitative).] —**yelp·er** *n.*

Yem·en Arab Republic (yémmən). Also **North Yemen.** Mountainous country in the southwest Arabian Peninsula, southwest Asia. A poor country, it is largely agricultural, cotton and coffee (from the fertile, well watered coastal plain), and hides and skins being its chief exports. However, considerable foreign aid is being used for agricultural, fishing and industrial development. The country was part of the Ottoman Empire (1517–1919). Republican army officers overthrew the Iman (1962), but strife occurred until 1969. A military coup took place in 1974, but instability, and fluctuating relations with its neighbours, and East and West continue. Union with South Yemen has been proposed. Area, 195 000 square kilometres (75,270 square miles). Population, 5,500,000. Capital, San'a.

yen¹ (yen) *intr.v.* **yenned, yenning, yens.** *Informal.* To yearn; long. ~*n. Informal.* A yearning; a longing. [Cantonese *yan*, craving, corresponding to Mandarin Chinese *yīn*.]

yen² *n., pl.* **yen. 1.** *Symbol* **Y.** The basic monetary unit of Japan. **2.** A coin or note worth one yen. [Japanese *en*, from Mandarin Chinese *yuán*, "round (piece)", dollar.]

Yenan. See **Yan'an.**

yeo·man (yṓ-mən) *n., pl.* **-men** (-mən). **1.** An independent farmer; especially, formerly in England, a member of a class of small freeholding farmers below the gentry. **2.** A yeoman of the guard. **3.** Formerly, an attendant, servant, or lesser official in a royal or noble household. **4.** A petty officer chiefly concerned with signalling in the Royal Navy or with clerical duties in certain other navies. **5.** *Archaic.* An assistant or other subordinate, as of a sheriff or craftsman. **6.** A member of the British volunteer yeomanry. [Middle English *yoman, yuman*, perhaps contraction of *yongman* : YOUNG + MAN.]

yeo·man·ly (yṓmənli) *adj.* **1.** Pertaining to or ranking as a yeoman. **2.** Characteristic of or befitting a yeoman; sturdy, staunch, or workmanlike. —**yeo·man·ly** *adv.*

yeoman of the guard *n.* A member of a ceremonial guard attending the British sovereign and royal family, consisting of 100 yeomen with their officers.

yeo·man·ry (yṓmənri) *n.* **1.** The class or a body of yeomen. **2.** A British volunteer cavalry force organised in 1761 to serve as a home guard and later incorporated into the Territorial Army (1907).

yep (yep) *adv.* Also **yup** (yup). *Informal.* Yes. [From YES (after NOPE).]

yer·ba ma·té (yáir-bə máa-tay, yér-, maa-táy) *n.* A tree, the **maté** *(see).* [Spanish *yerba*, herb, from Latin *herba*, plant, HERB.]

Ye·re·van (yérri-ván, -váan). Also **Erevan** (érri-). Capital of the Armenian S.S.R., southwest U.S.S.R. Situated on the river Razdan, it passed several times between Persia and Turkey until ceded to Russia (1828). It is an industrial centre.

yes (yess) *adv.* **1.** It is so; as you say or ask; opposed to "no". Used in expressing affirmation, agreement, positive confirmation, or consent. **2.** Indeed; what is more. Used to introduce a more emphatic phrase: *I could do with a drink, yes, a very strong drink.* **3.** I hear you

and am ready to give my attention to you. Used in response to being addressed or summoned.
~n., pl. **yeses. 1.** An affirmative or consenting response. **2.** An affirmative vote or voter. [Middle English *yes,* Old English *gese* : probably *gēa,* YEA + *sīe,* "may it be", third-person singular present subjunctive of *bēon,* to BE.]

ye·shi·va, ye·shi·vah (yə-shée-və) *n., pl.* **-vas** or **-voth** (-vot, -vōt). **1.** An Orthodox Jewish school devoted to rabbinical and Talmudic studies. **2.** A Jewish day school providing religious and secular education.

yes-man (yéss-man) *n., pl.* **-men** (-men). *Informal.* A person who slavishly agrees with his superior or any other person with whom he wishes to ingratiate himself; a sycophant.

yester– *comb. form.* Indicates: **1.** The day before the present day; for example, **yestermorning. 2.** A previous and indeterminate period of time; for example, **yesteryear.** [Middle English *yister-,* Old English *geostra(n).*]

yes·ter·day (yéstər-di, -day) *n.* **1.** The day before the present day. **2.** *Sometimes plural.* Time in the immediate or recent past.
~adv. **1.** On the day before the present day. **2.** A short while ago. [Middle English *yesterdai,* Old English *geostran dæg* : YESTER- + DAY.]

yes·ter·year (yéstər-yeer, -yer) *n. Literary.* **1.** The year before the current one. **2.** Time past, especially as thought of nostalgically; yore. **—yes·ter·year** *adv.*

yes·treen (ye-stréen) *n. Scottish.* Yesterday evening. [Middle English : YESTER- + E'EN (evening).] **—yes·treen** *adj.*

yet (yet) *adv.* **1.** At this time; for the present; now: *Don't sing yet.* **2.** Up to a particular time; thus far: *The end had not yet come.* **3.** In the time remaining; still: *There is yet a solution to be found.* **4.** Besides; in addition: *Play the tape yet another time.* **5.** Even; still: *a yet sadder tale.* **6.** Nevertheless; but despite this: *young yet wise.* **7.** At some future time; eventually: *They may yet score a goal.* **—as yet.** Up to the present time; up to now.
~conj. Nevertheless; and despite this: *He said he would be late, yet he arrived on time.* —See Synonyms at **but.** [Middle English *yet, yit,* Old English *gīet(a)*†.]

Usage: *Yet,* as an adverb of time in the sense "up to the present", occurs with the perfect tenses: *Have they arrived yet?* However, it is often used, mainly in informal American English, with the simple past tense: *Did you eat yet?*

ye·ti (yétti) *n.* The **abominable snowman** *(see).*

Yev·tu·shen·ko (yév-tōō-shéngkō; *Russian* yiftōō-shéngkə), **Yevgeny (Alexandrovich)** (1933–). Russian poet. His works contain criticisms of the U.S.S.R. state, and include *A Precocious Autobiography* (1963) and *Stolen Apples* (1972).

yew (yōō || yew) *n.* **1.** Any of several evergreen trees or shrubs of the genus *Taxus,* of which the flat, dark-green needles and often the scarlet berries are poisonous. **2.** The wood of a yew; especially, the durable, fine-grained wood of an Old World species, *T. baccata,* used in cabinetmaking and for archery bows. [Middle English *ew,* Old English *ēow, īw.*]

Ygg·dra·sil, Yg·dra·sil (ígdrə-sil) *n. Norse Mythology.* The great ash tree that holds together earth, heaven, and hell by its roots and branches. [Old Norse, probably "the horse of Yggr" : *Yggr,* Odin, from *yggr,* variant of *uggr,* frightful (see **ugly**) + *drasill*†, horse.]

Y.H.A. Youth Hostels Association (in Britain).

YHWH, YHVH, JHWH, JHVH The Hebrew Tetragrammaton representing the name of God.

Yid·dish (yíddish) *n.* A language derived from High German dialects with additional vocabulary drawn from Hebrew and from Slavonic languages, written in Hebrew characters and spoken chiefly as a vernacular in eastern European Jewish communities and by emigrants from these communities throughout the world. Also called "Judaeo-German". [Yiddish *Yidish,* from Middle High German *jüdisch,* Jewish, from *Jüde,* Jew, from Old High German *judo,* from Latin *Jūdaeus,* JEW.] **—Yid·dish** *adj.*

Yid·dish·ism (yíddish-iz'm) *n.* **1.** The advocacy or promotion of Yiddish language and literature. **2.** A word, expression, or usage characteristic of Yiddish.

yield (yeeld) *v.* **yielded, yielding, yields.** *—tr.* **1.** To give forth by or as if by a natural process, especially by cultivation: *a field that yields much corn.* **2.** To provide or give in return; be productive of: *an investment that yields six per cent.* **3.** To surrender (something) in deference or defeat; relinquish: *yielded the field to a rival.* **4.** To grant or concede: *yield right of way; yield the point in the argument.* *—intr.* **1.** To provide or give a return; be productive. **2.** To give up; surrender; submit. **3.** To give way to pressure, force, or persuasion. **4.** To give way or precedence; be overcome. Used with *to*: *yielded to the logic of her case.* —See Synonyms at **relinquish.**
~n. **1.** The amount yielded or produced; a product. **2.** The profit obtained from investment; a return. **3.** The energy released by an explosion, especially by a nuclear explosion, expressed in units of weight of TNT required to produce an equivalent release: *a 100-megaton yield.* **4.** The amount of a specific product produced by a chemical reaction, often expressed as a percentage of the stoichiometric quantity obtainable. [Middle English *yieldan,* Old English *gieldan,* to yield, pay, from Germanic *geldhan* (unattested), to pay.] **—yield·er** *n.*

Synonyms: *yield, relent, bow, defer, submit, capitulate.*

yield·ing (yéelding) *adj.* Inclined to yield; submissive. **—yield·ing·ly** *adv.* **—yield·ing·ness** *n.*

yield point *n.* The point, beyond the elastic limit of a material, at which a sudden increase in strain occurs with only a small increase in stress.

yin (yin) *n. Often capital* **Y.** The passive, female cosmic element, force, or principle that is opposite but complementary to **yang** *(see)* in Chinese dualistic philosophy. [Mandarin Chinese *yīn,* the moon, shade, femininity.]

yip (yip) *n. U.S.* A sharp, high-pitched bark; a yelp.
~intr.v. **yipped, yipping, yips.** *U.S.* To make such sounds; yelp. [Imitative.]

yip·pee (yíppi, yi-pée) *interj.* Used to express joy, elation, or excitement.

–yl *n. comb. form. Chemistry.* Indicates a radical; for example, **carbonyl, ethyl.** [French *-yle,* from Greek *hulē,* wood, matter.]

y·lang-y·lang, i·lang-i·lang (éelang-éelang) *n.* **1.** A tropical Asian tree, *Cananga odorata* (or *Canangium odoratum*), having fragrant greenish-yellow flowers that yield an oil used in perfumery. **2.** An oil or perfume obtained from the flowers of this tree. [Tagalog *alang-ilang.*]

y·lem (ī-ləm, -lem) *n.* The hypothetical matter, thought to consist of neutrons, from which the chemical elements may have been derived, in the big-bang theory of the creation of the universe. [Middle English, from Old French, from Latin *hȳlē,* from Greek *hulē,* matter.]

Y.M.C.A. Young Men's Christian Association.

Y.M.H.A. Young Men's Hebrew Association.

–yne *n. comb. form. Chemistry.* Indicates a triple bond in a compound; for example, **alkyne, ethyne.**

yob (yob) *n.* Also **yob·bo** (yóbbō). *British Informal.* A loutish or ill-mannered youth or man. [Back-slang for BOY.]

yod[1], yodh (yod, yōd) *n.* The tenth letter of the Hebrew alphabet. [Hebrew *yōdh,* from *yādh,* hand.]

yod[2] *n.* The sound (y), especially when considered as a historical phonetic development. [Probably from YOD (Hebrew letter).]

yo·del (yṓd'l) *v.* **-delled** or *U.S.* **-deled, -delling** or *U.S.* **-deling, -dels.** *—intr.* To sing so that the voice fluctuates between the normal chest voice and a falsetto. *—tr.* To sing (a melody without words) in this fashion.
~n. A song or cry that is yodelled. [German *jodeln* (imitative).] **—yo·del·ler** *n.*

yo·ga (yṓgə) *n.* **1.** *Often capital* **Y.** A Hindu discipline aimed at training the consciousness for a state of perfect spiritual insight and union with the universal spirit. **2.** A system of exercises practised as part of this discipline to promote control of the body and mind. Also called "hatha yoga". [Sanskrit, union, yoking.] **—yo·gic** *adj.* **—yo·gism** *n.*

yogh (yog, yōg, yōk, yōkh) *n.* A Middle English letter representing a velar or palatal fricative, usually voiced. [Middle English *yogh, yok,* perhaps from *yok,* YOKE (from its shape).]

yog·hurt, yog·urt (yóggərt, yóggoort || *chiefly U.S.* yṓ-gərt, -goort) *n.* A food of a custard-like consistency, prepared from milk curdled by bacteria, especially *Lactobacillus bulgaricus* and *Streptococcus thermophilus,* and often sweetened or flavoured with fruit. [Turkish *yoğurt.*]

yo·gi (yṓgi) *n., pl.* **-gis.** Also **yo·gin** (yṓgin). **1.** One who practises yoga. **2.** One who teaches or is a master of yoga. [Hindi, from Sanskrit *yogin,* from *yoga,* YOGA.]

yo·him·bine (yō-hím-been) *n.* A poisonous alkaloid, $C_{21}H_{26}N_2O_3$, derived from the bark of a tree, *Corynanthe yohimbe,* and formerly used as an aphrodisiac. [New Latin *yohimbe* (the tree) from Bantu.]

yoicks (yoyks) *interj.* Used as a hunting cry to urge the hounds after the fox.

yoke (yōk) *n., pl.* **yokes** or **yoke** (for sense 2). **1.** A crossbar with two U-shaped pieces that encircle the necks of a pair of oxen, mules, or other draught animals working in a team. **2.** A pair of draught animals joined by such a device or trained to work together. **3.** A frame or crossbar designed to be carried across a person's shoulders with equally weighed loads, such as buckets of water, suspended from each end. **4.** A bar used with a double harness to connect the collar of each horse to the tongue of a wagon, coach, or other trailer. **5.** *Nautical.* A crossbar on a ship's rudder to which the steering cables are connected. **6.** A clamp or vice that holds a part in place or controls its movement or that holds two parts together. **7.** A piece of a garment that is closely fitted, either around the neck and shoulders or at the hips, and from which an unfitted or gathered part of the garment falls. **8.** Something that connects or joins together; a bond: *the yoke of marriage.* **9.** A structure made of two upright spears with a third laid across them, under which conquered enemies of ancient Rome were forced to march in subjection. **10.** Any form or symbol of subjugation or bondage: *the yoke of a dictator.* —See Synonyms at **couple.**
~v. **yoked, yoking, yokes.** *—tr.* **1.** To fit or join with a yoke. **2. a.** To harness a draft animal to. **b.** To harness (a draught animal) to something. **3.** To connect, join, or bind together. **4.** *Obsolete.* To force into bondage or servitude; oppress. *—intr.* To become connected, joined, or bound together. [Middle English *yok,* Old English *geoc.*]

yoke·fel·low (yṓk-fellō) *n.* A companion or partner, as in work or marriage. Also called "yokemate".

yo·kel (yṓk'l) *n.* A country bumpkin or rustic; especially, one who is gullible or naive. [Perhaps from dialectal *yokel,* green woodpecker (probably imitative of its note).]

Yo·ko·ha·ma (yōkō-haámə). Capital and port of Kanagawa prefecture, Honshu island, Japan. Situated on Tokyo Bay it was badly

yew Taxus baccata, *the common yew (above), is an evergreen conifer native to Eurasia and Mediterranean Africa. Sacred in European mythology, yews are often found in churchyards, and may have been planted on pagan sites before Christians built churches there. Because of its strong, closely grained wood, the yew was used in the Middle Ages for making longbows.*

PRONUNCIATION KEY

a, trap; aa, father; ai, **fair**; ar, star; aw, **lawn**; ay, **play**; b, bb, stab; **rubber**; ch, **church**; ck, ticket; d, dd, **dead**; **ladder**; e, dress; ee, bee; er, defer; ew, **few**; ewr, **pure**; ə, about; ər, letter; f, ff, **fife**; **differ**; g, gg, **giggle**; h, **hat**; i, **kit**; ī, price; īr, fire; j, **judge**; k, **kick**; l, ll, let; 'l, **needle**; m, mm, **man**; n, nn, **no**; 'n, **sudden**; ng, **thing**; o, **lot**; ō, no; ŏŏ, **foot**; ōō, **shoe**; oor, **poor**; ow, **cow**; owr, **hour**; oy, **boy**; p, pp, **pepper**; r, rr, **red**; s, ss, sauce; sh, **ship**; t, tt, totter; th, **thick**; th, **this**; smooth; u, cut; ur, **turn**; v, vv, valve; w, **wet**; y, **yes**; z, zz, zebra; zh, vision; pleasure

IN FOREIGN WORDS:

aN, oN, **Saint-Saëns**; hl, **Llanelli**; **Hluhluwe**; kh, loch; **lough**; **Khaled**

STRESS MARK:

ín-sīt, insight; in-sī́t, incite

damaged by an earthquake (1923) and bombing in World War II.

yolk (yōk) *n.* **1.** The nutritive material of an animal ovum, consisting primarily of protein and fat; especially, the yellow, usually spheroidal mass of the egg of a bird or reptile, surrounded by the albumen. **2.** A greasy substance found in unprocessed sheep's wool. [Middle English *yolke*, Old English *geoloca, geolca*, from *geolu*, YELLOW.] —**yolked** *adv.* —**yolk·y** *adj.*

yolk sac *n. Zoology.* A membranous sac attached to the embryo and providing early nourishment in the form of yolk in bony fishes, sharks, reptiles, birds, and primitive mammals, and functioning as the circulatory system of the human embryo prior to the initiation of internal circulation by the pumping of the heart.

Yom Kip·pur (yóm kíppər, ki-po͝or) *n.* The holiest Jewish holiday, celebrated on the tenth day of Tishri, on which fasting and prayer for the atonement of sins are prescribed. Also called "Day of Atonement". [Hebrew *yōm kippūr : yōm*, day + *kippūr*, atonement, from *kippēr*, they covered, they made atonement.]

yomp (yomp) *n. Slang.* The act of advancing on foot carrying one's equipment, especially military equipment, at a fast pace. [Perhaps imitative of the sound of rapid marching.] —**yomp** *intr.v.*

yon (yon) *adj.* **1.** *Chiefly Northern British.* That. **2.** *Poetic.* Yonder. ~*pron. Chiefly Northern British.* That. ~*adv. Poetic.* Yonder. [Middle English *yon*, Old English *geon.*]

yond (yond) *adj. Archaic & Poetic.* Yonder. ~*adv. Archaic & Poetic.* Yonder. [Middle English *yond*, Old English *geond.*]

yon·der (yóndər) *adj.* Being at an indicated distance, usually within sight. ~*adv.* In or at that indicated relatively distant place; over there. [Middle English *yonder*, from *yond*, YOND.]

yo·ni (yōni) *n.* In Hinduism, a representation of the vulva symbolising the feminine principle. [Sanskrit *yoni*†, abode, womb.]

yonks (yongks) *adv. Informal.* A long time; ages: *left yonks ago.*

yoo-hoo (yo͞o-ho͞o) *interj.* Used to attract someone's attention.

yore (yor ‖ yôr) *n.* Time long past. Now archaic except in the phrase *days of yore.* [Middle English *yore*, Old English *gēara*, formerly, once, perhaps from the genitive plural of *gēar*, YEAR.]

York¹ (york) *n.* The family name of the English royal family from 1461 to 1485.

York². *Latin.* **E·bo·ra·cum** (ēe-baw-ra'akəm, áy-). City of North Yorkshire, northeast England. Situated at the confluence of the rivers Ouse and Foss, it was a Roman military post and is where Constantine I was proclaimed emperor (A.D. 306). An important market for the wool trade during the Middle Ages, York is a walled city with many medieval remains and is overlooked by the cathedral York Minster (13th–15th century).

York, Richard Plantagenet, 3rd Duke of (1411–60). English nobleman. A descendant of the third son of Edward III, he was named by Henry VI as heir to the throne until Henry himself had a son. His claims led to the outbreak of the Wars of the Roses (1455) between the Yorkists and Lancastrians, and after Yorkist victories he was reinstated as heir. He was killed in battle at Wakefield.

york·er (yórkər) *n.* In cricket, a ball bowled with speed directly at the feet of the facing batsman. [Probably associated with Yorkshire County Cricket Club.]

York·ist (yórkist) *n.* A member of the Yorkist faction in the Wars of the Roses (1455–85). —**York·ist** *adj.*

York·shire (yórk-shər, -sheer). Former county of northeast England. Bordering the North Sea, in 1974 its area was redistributed between the counties of Humberside, North Yorkshire, West Yorkshire, and South Yorkshire. It was a centre of the woollen industry during the Middle Ages and developed around its western coalfield during the industrial revolution.

Yorkshire fog *n.* A common tufted grass, *Holcus lanatus*, having downy stems and leaves. [From the foggy impression made by its leaves and from its prevalence in Yorkshire.]

Yorkshire pudding *n.* A light, baked pudding made from a batter of eggs, flour, and milk, and traditionally served with roast beef.

Yorkshire terrier *n.* A toy terrier of a breed developed in Yorkshire, having a long, bluish-grey and tan coat.

Yorkshire tyke (tīk) *n. Informal.* A native or inhabitant of Yorkshire. Also called "tyke".

Yo·ru·ba (yórroōbə, yáw-roōbə) *n., pl.* **-bas** or collectively **Yoruba.** **1.** A member of a West African Negro people living chiefly in southwestern Nigeria. **2.** The Kwa language of this African people. —**Yo·ru·ban** *adj.*

Yo·sem·i·te National Park (yō-sémməti). Park in eastern California, United States. It is a mountainous region with many lakes, rivers, gorges, and falls, including the Yosemite falls, the highest in North America (739 metres; 2,425 feet).

you (yo͞o; *weak form* yoo ‖ yə) *pron.* The second person singular or plural pronoun in the nominative or objective case. **1.** Used to represent the one or ones addressed by the speaker: **a.** As subject: *You are always hounding me.* **b.** As the direct object of a verb: *I'll hit you.* **c.** As the indirect object of verb: *My friend will give you a thrashing.* **d.** As the object of a preposition: *He'll set his dog on you.* **2.** Used in apposition before a noun to indicate address: *You fool!* **3.** *Chiefly U.S. Informal.* Used in place of the reflexive pronouns *yourself* or *yourselves*, as the indirect object of a verb: *You went and bought you a new tractor.* **4.** Used in various elliptical, absolute, or interjectional phrases in which it is neither subject nor object: *You and your so-called friends!* **5.** Used to represent unspecified persons or people in general: *You have to be ruthless in a ruthless world.* In

more formal contexts, the pronoun *one* is often preferred. —**you know what** or **who.** One that is unspecified but felt by the speaker to be known to the person addressed. ~*n.* The individuality or image of the person being addressed: *the real you; That shirt is really you.* —See Usage note at **me.** [Middle English *you, eow*, Old English *ēow*, dative and accusative of *gē*, ye.]

you-all (yo͞o-áwl, yawl) *pl.pron. U.S. Regional.* You. Used in addressing two or more persons or referring to two or more persons.

you'd (yo͞od; *weak form* yŏod ‖ yəd). Contraction of *you had* or *you would.*

you'll (yo͞ol; *weak form* yŏol ‖ yəl). Contraction of *you will* or *you shall.*

young (yung) *adj.* **younger** (yúng-gər), **youngest** (yúng-gist). **1.** Being in the early or undeveloped period of life or growth; not old. **2. a.** Newly begun or formed; not advanced: *The evening is young.* **b.** Recently introduced; not long established: *a young firm.* **3. a.** Pertaining to or suggestive of youth or early life: *young for her age.* **b.** Vigorous or fresh; youthful. **c.** Lacking experience; immature; green: *Her sophistication made him feel very young.* **4.** Designating the junior of two people having the same name. Usually used in the comparative: *Pitt the younger.* **5.** *Often capital* **Y.** Designating a political group or movement, often adopting progressive ideas or policies, that aims its appeal at the younger members of a population or community. **6.** *Geology.* Being of an early stage in a geological cycle. Said of bodies of water and land formations. ~*n., pl.* **young. 1.** *Plural.* Young persons collectively; youth. Preceded by *the.* **2.** Offspring; brood: *a lioness with her young.* —**with young.** Pregnant. Said of an animal. [Middle English *yong*, Old English *geong.*] —**young·ish** *adj.*

Synonyms: *young, youth, juvenile, adolescent, teenager.*

Young (yung), **Thomas** (1773–1829). English physicist and physician. He revived the wave theory of light and postulated the three-colour theory of colour vision. Also an Egyptologist, he helped to decipher the hieroglyphics of the Rosetta Stone.

young blood *n.* Young people with energy, enthusiasm, fresh ideas, and similar qualities.

young·ling (yúng-ling) *n. Archaic.* **1.** A young person. **2.** A young animal. **3.** A young plant. [Middle English *yongling*, Old English *geongling* (YOUNG + -LING (noun suffix).] —**young·ling** *adv.*

Young Pretender. See Charles Edward **Stuart.**

young man *n.* A male lover or boyfriend.

Young's modulus *n.* The ratio of the stress per unit area of cross-section on a wire or rod under tension or compression to the longitudinal strain. Also called "Young's modulus of elasticity". [After Thomas YOUNG.]

young·ster (yúng-stər) *n.* **1.** A young person or child. **2.** A young animal.

Young Turk *n.* A progressive or rebellious member of a political party or other organised group. [Originally a member of a Turkish revolutionary party in the early 20th century.]

young woman *n.* A female lover or girlfriend.

youn·ker (yúngkər) *n. Archaic.* A young man; a youngster. [Dutch *jonker*, from Middle Dutch *jonckher, jonchere*, young nobleman : *jonc*, young + *here*, master, lord.]

your (yor, yoor ‖ yər, yôr). The possessive form of the pronoun *you.* *Abbr.* **yr. 1.** Used attributively to indicate possession, agency, or reception of an action by the one or ones addressed by the speaker: *your wallet; pursuing your tasks; suffered your first rebuff.* **2.** Used to designate something having special significance to you: *Today is your day.* **3.** *Informal.* Used to suggest a person or thing commonly experienced as being typical of a specified group or set: *not one of your scatterbrained philosophers.* **4.** Used to indicate possession, agency, or reception of an action by any unspecified person or persons: *The house is on your right.* In more formal contexts, the pronoun *one's* is often preferred in this sense. [Middle English *your*, Old English *ēower*, genitive of *gē*, ye. See **you.**]

you're (yoor, yor ‖ yər, yôr). Contraction of *you are.*

yours (yorz, yoorz ‖ yôrz). Possessive pronoun, absolute form of *your.* **1.** Belonging to you; your own. Used predicatively: *The brown boots are yours.* **2.** The one or ones belonging or pertaining to you. Used substantively: *If I can't find my hat, I'll take yours.* **3.** Used as convention in the closing of letters especially in the phrases *yours sincerely, yours faithfully,* and *yours truly.* —**of yours.** Belonging or pertaining to you: *a friend of yours.* —**you and yours.** You and your family. —**What's yours?** *Informal.* What do you want to drink? [Middle English *youres*, genitive of YOUR.]

your·self (yawr-sélf, yoor-, yər-) *pron., pl.* **-selves** (-sélvz). A specialised form of the second person pronoun. It is used: **1.** As a reflexive pronoun, forming the direct or indirect object of a verb or the object of a preposition: *hurt yourself; give yourself time; talk to yourself.* **2.** For emphasis: *Do it yourself; You yourself weren't certain.* **3.** As an emphasising substitute: *He invited only Tom and yourself; Yourself in debt, you couldn't help them.* **4.** As an indication of (your) real, normal, or healthy or condition identity: *You have not been yourself lately.*

Usage: Yourself is not acceptable as a substitute for *you* in formal style, though it is commonly so used informally: *She wants to see Joan and yourself; Yourself and the others will be expected later; How's yourself?* It is particularly common in Irish English. It is with *yourself* and *yourselves* that standard English now distinguishes singular from plural in the second person: *You yourself know your duty; You yourselves know your duty.*

yours truly *pron. Informal.* I; myself; me: *Yours truly had to pay.*

youse (yo͞oz) *pl. pron. Regional.* You (plural).

youth (yo͞oth) *n., pl.* **youths** (yo͞othz ‖ yo͞oths). **1.** The condition or quality of being young. **2.** Any quality such as vigour, enthusiasm, rashness, inexperience, or freshness, typically associated with youth. **3.** An early period of development or existence. **4. a.** The time of life between childhood and maturity. **b.** *Used with a plural verb.* Young people collectively. **c.** A young person; especially, a young man. —See Synonyms at **young.** [Middle English *youthe,* Old English *geoguth.*]

youth club *n.* A place where the young people of a particular area can go and join in leisure activities or social events.

youth·ful (yo͞othf'l) *adj.* **1.** Possessing youth; still young. **2.** Characteristic of youth; vigorous; fresh; active. **3.** Of or belonging to youth. **4.** In an early stage of development; new. **5.** *Geology.* Young. —**youth·ful·ly** *adv.* —**youth·ful·ness** *n.*

youth hostel *n.* A place offering simple accommodation and sometimes food to especially young people. Also called "hostel".

you've (yo͞ov; *weak form* yo͞ov ‖ yəv). Contraction of *you have.*

yowl (youl) *v.* **yowled, yowling, yowls.** —*intr.* To utter a loud, long, cry; howl; wail. —*tr.* To say or utter with such a cry. ~*n.* A loud, mournful cry; a wail. [Middle English *youlen* (imitative).]

Yo-yo (yō'-yō) *n., pl.* **-yos.** A trademark for a toy in the shape of a spool, around which a string is wound. The string is attached to the finger, and the yo-yo is spun up and down by moving the hand.

Ypres (eepr, éepr∂; *also facetiously* wīpərz). *Flemish* **Ieper** (éepər). Town of West Flanders, southwestern Belgium. Situated on the river Yperlee, it was a prosperous textile centre during the Middle Ages and was the site of three battles during World War I.

Y-quem (ee-kém) *n.* A variety of Sauterne wine. [After Château d'*Yquem,* an estate in southwest France, where it is produced.]

yr. **1.** year. **2.** younger. **3.** your.

yrs. **1.** years. **2.** yours.

-yse See Usage note at **-ise.**

Yseult. Variant of **Iseult.**

yt·ter·bi·a (i-térbi-ə) *n.* Ytterbium oxide. [New Latin, from YTTERBIUM.]

yt·ter·bite (i-tér-bīt) *n.* A mineral, **gadolinite** *(see).*

yt·ter·bi·um (i-térbi-əm) *n. Symbol* **Yb** A soft, bright, silvery rare-earth element occurring in two allotropic forms and used as an X-ray source for portable irradiation devices, in some laser materials, and in some special alloys. Atomic number 70, atomic weight 173.04, melting point 824°C, boiling point 1,427 °C, relative density 6.977 or 6.54 depending on allotropic form, valencies 2, 3. [New Latin; discovered at *Ytterby,* Sweden.] —**yt·ter·bic** *adj.*

ytterbium oxide *n.* A colourless hygroscopic compound, Yb_2O_3, used in certain alloys. Also called "ytterbia".

yt·tri·a (ittri-ə) *n.* Yttrium oxide.

yt·tri·um (íttri-əm) *n. Symbol* **Y.** A silvery, lustrous metallic element, not a rare earth but occurring in nearly all rare-earth minerals and resembling them chemically, used in various metallurgical applications, notably to increase the strength of magnesium and aluminium alloys. Atomic number 39, atomic weight 88.905, melting point 1,509°C, boiling point 3,338 °C, relative density 4.47, valency 3. [New Latin, from YTTR(IA).] —**yt·tric** *adj.*

yttrium oxide *n.* A yellowish powder, Y_2O_3, used in optical glasses, ceramics, and colour-television tubes. Also called "yttria".

yu·an (yo͞o-án) *n., pl.* **yuan. 1. a.** The basic monetary unit of the People's Republic of China, equal to 10 jiao or 100 fen. **b.** The basic monetary unit of Taiwan, equal to 100 cents. **2.** A coin or note worth one yuan. [Mandarin Chinese *yuán,* round (piece), dollar.]

Yu·ca·tán Peninsula (yo͞okə-taán, -tán). Peninsula of Central America. Separating the Gulf of Mexico from the Caribbean Sea, it is mainly a limestone plateau situated largely in southeast Mexico. It includes Belize and north Guatemala, and was once the centre of the Mayan civilisation of which there are many remains. Lumbering and fishing are its chief industries, and tourism is important.

Yuc·a·tec (yo͞okə-tek) *n., pl.* **-tecs** or collectively **Yucatec. 1.** A member of an American Indian people inhabiting the Yucatán Peninsula. **2.** The Mayan language of this people.

yuc·ca (yúckə) *n.* Any of various New World plants of the genus *Yucca,* often tall and stout-stemmed, and having a terminal cluster of white flowers. [Spanish *yuca,* from Cariban.]

yuck, yuk (yuk, yukh) *interj. Slang.* Used to express disgust or distaste. [Imitative.]

yuck·y, yuk·ky (yúcki) *adj.* **-ier, -iest.** *Slang.* Disgusting; revolting. [From YUCK.]

Yue, Yüeh (ywe) *n. Cantonese (see).*

Yu·ga (yo͞ogə) *n.* Also **Yug** (yo͞og). *Hinduism.* One of the four ages constituting the cycle of history. [Sanskrit, yoke, pair, age.]

Yu·go·sla·vi·a (yo͞o-gō-slaávi-ə, -gə-), **Socialist Federal Republic of.** Also **Ju·go·sla·vi·a.** Federal republic of southeast Europe. Situated in the Balkan peninsula and bordering the Adriatic sea, it is chiefly mountainous except in the northeast where fertile lowlands are drained by the river Danube. It was formed in 1918 as the Kingdom of the Serbs, Croats, and Slovenes, and gained its present

name in 1927. It was occupied by the Germans during World War II, after which Tito, a Communist, became president; he later broke with the U.S.S.R. (1948). Almost half the population is involved with agriculture: grains, potatoes, sugar beet, fruit, tobacco, and olives are grown. Mineral resources include copper, iron, gold, and coal, and industries include iron and steel, sugar refining, cement, textiles, and chemicals. Fishing and tourism are important on the Adriatic coast. Area 255 804 square kilometres (96,766 square miles). Population, 22,600,000. Capital, Belgrade. —**Yu·go·slav** (-slaav, -slaáv), **Yu·go·sla·vi·an** (-slaávi-ən) *n. & adj.*

Yu·ka·wa (yo͞o-kaá-wə), **Hideki** (1907–81). Japanese nuclear physicist. In 1935 he predicted the existence of the meson, later observed by scientists. He has also made important contributions to strong interaction and elementary-particle theory. He received the Nobel prize for physics (1949).

Yu·kon[1] (yo͞o-kon). Territory of northwest Canada, on the Beaufort Sea, it includes Mount Logan, Canada's highest peak (6 050 metres; 19,850 feet), and is sparsely populated. It was the site of the Klondike gold rush in the 1890s. Its capital is Whitehorse.

Yukon[2]. River of North America. Formed by the confluence of the rivers Lewes and Pelly in south central Yukon, Canada, it flows 3 220 kilometres (2,000 miles), first northwest to Alaska then southwest to enter the Bering Sea through a wide shallow delta.

yu·lan (yo͞o-lan) *n.* A tree, *Magnolia denudata,* native to China and often cultivated for its large, cup-shaped, fragrant white flowers. [Mandarin Chinese *yù lán,* "jade orchid" : *yù,* jade + *lán*[2], orchid.]

Yule (yo͞ol) *n.* Christmas or the season or feast celebrating Christmas. [Middle English *yole, yule,* Old English *gēol(a)†.*]

yule log *n.* A large log traditionally burned in the fireplace at Christmas.

Yule·tide (yo͞ol-tīd) *n.* The Christmas season.

Yu·ma (yo͞omə) *n., pl.* **-mas** or collectively **Yuma. 1.** A member of a Yuman-speaking North American Indian people of southwest Arizona and the adjacent parts of California and Mexico. **2.** The language of this people. [Spanish *Yuma†.*]

Yu·man (yo͞omən) *n.* A language family comprising the languages of the Yuma and Mohave Indians and other North American Indian languages. —**yu·man** *adj.*

yum·my (yúmmi) *adj.* **-mier, -miest.** *Informal.* Delightful; delicious. [From YUM YUM.]

yum yum (yúm-yúm) *interj. Informal.* Used to express appreciation of food. [Imitative of the sound made when food is tasted.]

Yun·nan or **Yün·nan** (yo͞o-nán, yo͞on-, *Chinese* yün-). Province of southwest China. It is chiefly mountainous and is crossed by the rivers Huang, Lancang (Mekong), and Nu (Salween). Its capital is Kunming.

yup. Variant of **yep.**

yurt (yoort) *n., pl.* **yurta** (yo͞órtə). A circular, domed, portable tent used by the nomadic Mongols of Siberia. [Russian *yurta,* from Turkic; akin to Turkish *yurt,* home.]

Y.W.C.A. Young Women's Christian Association.

Y.W.H.A. Young Women's Hebrew Association.

ywis. Variant of **iwis.**

yucca *There are about 40 species of yucca, ranging from small shrubs to trees which can reach 15 metres (50 feet). Native to southern North America and Central America, some species have leaves which are made into cloth, and the roots of others were once used as soap by American Indians.*

Z

z, Z (zed ‖ *U.S.* zee) *n., pl.* **z's** or *rare* **zs, Zs** or **Z's.** **1.** The 26th letter of the modern English alphabet. **2.** Any of the speech sounds represented by this letter. **3.** Anything shaped like the letter *z,* such as a **z-bend** *(see).*

z, Z, z., Z. Note: As an abbreviation or symbol, *z* may be a small or a capital letter, with or without a full stop. Established forms or those generally preferred precede the definition. When no form is given, all four forms are in general use in that sense. **1. Z** atomic number. **2. Z** impedance. **3. z.** zero. **4. z.** zone. **5.** The 26th in a series; 25th when *J* is omitted. **6.** The third in a series consisting of *x, y,* and *z.* **7.** The symbol of an algebraic variable, especially the third variable in a tertiary equation.

za·ba·glio·ne (zá-bəl-yŏni, zaá-, -bəl-, -yónay; *Italian* tsa-) *n.* A dessert consisting of egg yolks, sugar, and wine, usually Marsala wine, beaten until thick and frothy and served either hot or cold. [Italian *zaba(gl)ione.*]

Zach·a·ri·as (zácke-rī́-əss). Also **Zach·a·ri·ah** (-ə). The husband of Elizabeth and father of John the Baptist. Luke 1:5.

Zad·kine (zád-keen, *French* zat-kéen), **Ossip** (1890–1967). French sculptor. Born in Russia, he moved to Paris (1909) where he was heavily influenced by cubism in his representations of the human form. His most famous work is the memorial to the destruction of Rotterdam in World War II, *The Destroyed City* (1954).

zaf·fer, zaf·fre (záffər) *n.* An impure oxide of cobalt, used to produce a blue colour in enamel and in the making of smalt. [Italian *zaffera,* from Old French *safre,* from Arabic *ṣufr,* yellow copper.]

zag (zag) *n.* A sharp turn in a different direction.
~*intr.v.* **zagged, zagging, zags.** To make a sharp turn or change of course. [Shortened from ZIGZAG.]

Za·greb (zaá-greb). Capital of Croatia, north central Yugoslavia. Situated on the river Sava, it was a Roman city and became a centre for Yugoslav nationalism in the 19th century.

Zag·re·us (zággri-əss). *Greek Mythology.* A god worshipped in Orphic cults and identified with Dionysus.

zai·bat·su (zī́-bat-sŏo) *n., pl.* **zaibatsu.** Any powerful commercial combine of Japan controlled by a few leading families. [Japanese, from Chinese *cái fá,* plutocrat : *cái,* wealth + *fá,* powerful person or family.]

za·ire (zaa-éer, zī́-) *n.* The basic monetary unit of Zaire, equal to 100 makuta.

Za·ire (zaa-éer, zī-), also known as **Congo.** River of central Africa. Formed by the confluence of the rivers Lualaba and Luvua near the Zaire-Zambian border, it flows 4 667 kilometres (2,900 miles) west and southwest, forming the Zaire-Congo border, to enter the Atlantic Ocean through a wide delta at Boma. It was explored by Captain J. Tuckey (1816), David Livingstone (1871), and Henry Stanley (1874–77). It is navigable by shipping to Matadi, and is the second longest river of Africa.

Zaire, Republic of. *French* **Zaïre.** Formerly **Belgian Congo** (1908–60); **Democratic Republic of Congo** (1960–71). Republic of central Africa. Situated almost entirely in the basin of the Zaire river, with a small coastline on the Atlantic ocean, it is largely equatorial rain forest, with the Ruwenzori mountains in the southeast and savannah in the north and south. Discovered by the Portuguese (15th century), it was a source of slaves (17th to 19th century) and in 1908 was annexed by Belgium from whom independence was gained in 1960. The secession of Katanga region (1960) led to civil war and U.N. intervention. In 1965 Mobutu Sese Seko seized power and later defeated attempts by Katanganese forces, backed by Cuba and Angola, to assume power (1977–78). Crops include tea, coffee, rubber, cocoa, palm oil, and cotton, and there are reserves of copper, zinc, cobalt, diamonds, oil and natural gas. Area, 2 345 409 square kilometres (905,568 square miles). Population, 30,000,000. Capital, Kinshasa. —**Za·ir·e·an** (zaa-éer-i-ən), **Za·ir·ese** (-eer-éez ‖ -éess) *n. & adj.*

za·kat (zaá-kat) *n.* A proportion of the income of a devout Muslim set aside to be devoted to the poor. [Arabic.]

Zam·be·zi (zam-béezi). River of southern Africa. Rising in northwest Zambia, it flows 2 735 kilometres (1,700 miles) chiefly eastwards, forming the Zambia-Zimbabwe border, and enters the Indian Ocean through a wide delta near Chinde, Mozambique. Despite the many rapids along its length, it is navigable in stretches; it includes the Victoria Falls and the Kariba and Cabora Bassa dams.

Zam·bi·a (zámbi-ə), **Republic of.** Republic of southern central Africa. It consists chiefly of plateau, with mountains to the north and northeast, and the basins of the Zambezi and Kafue rivers to the west. It produces maize, groundnuts, cotton, tobacco, and sugar, while cattle-rearing is important in the east. Copper, zinc, cobalt, and emeralds are mined, and it has unexploited iron deposits. Explored by Livingstone (1850s to 1870s), it became the British protectorate of Northern Rhodesia (1911), was incorporated into the Federation of Rhodesia and Nyasaland (1953–63), and achieved independence (1964). Area, 752 614 square kilometres (290,586 square miles). Population, 6,000,000. Capital, Lusaka. —**Zam·bi·an** *n. & adj.*

za·mi·a (záymi-ə) *n.* Any of various chiefly tropical American cycads of the genus *Zamia,* having a thick, usually underground trunk and a crown of palmlike terminal leaves. [New Latin *Zamia,* from a misreading of *(nŭces) azániae,* pine (nuts), probably from Greek *azainein,* to dry, parch.]

za·min·dar, ze·min·dar (zə-mín-daar, -min-dár) *n.* **1.** An official in India during the Mogul empire assigned to collect the land taxes of his district. **2.** A native landholder in British colonial India, responsible for collecting and paying to the government the taxes on the land under his jurisdiction. [Persian *zamīndār* : *zamīn,* earth, land + *-dār,* holder, from Old Persian *dār-,* to hold.]

za·min·da·ri (zámmin-daári, zə-méen-) *n., pl.* **-is.** Also **ze·min·da·ry** (zémmin-, zə-méen-) *pl.* **-ies. 1.** The system of tax collection by zamindars. **2.** The area administered by a zamindar. [Hindi *zamīndāri,* from Persian, from *zamīndār,* ZAMINDAR.]

zanana. Variant of **zenana.**

Z.A.N.U., ZANU (zaá-nŏo). Zimbabwe African National Union.

za·ny (záyni) *n., pl.* **-nies. 1.** A ludicrous, buffoonish character in old comedies who attempts feebly to mimic the tricks of the clown.

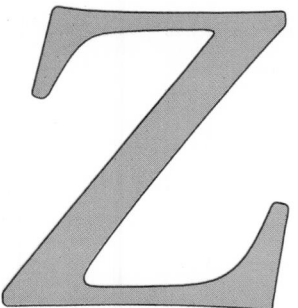

ZAIRE

2. A comical person given to extravagant or outlandish behaviour.
~adj. **zanier, -niest.** **1.** Inventively and eccentrically humorous; bizarrely funny. **2.** Ludicrously comical; clownish; droll. [Italian *zani, zanni,* buffoon, from *Zanni,* dialectal variant of *Gianni,* pet form for *Giovanni,* John.]

Zan·zi·bar (zánzi-bár, -baar). Coral island of Tanzania, east Africa, situated in the Indian Ocean. It was ruled by the Portuguese from 1503, before passing to the Arabs of Oman in 1698, and became a British protectorate in 1890. It achieved independence in 1963, and, with the exile of its Sultan (1964), was united with Tanganyika to form Tanzania. Cocoa, rice, cloves, and copra are exported. The capital is Zanzibar. **—Zan·zi·bar·i** (-baári) *n. & adj.*

zap (zap) *v.* **zapped, zapping, zaps.** *Slang. —tr.* **1.** To destroy or kill suddenly and violently, as with a burst of gunfire, flame, or electric current. **2.** To attack with heavy firepower; strafe or bombard. **3.** To hit suddenly and violently. *—intr.* To move very fast: *zapped along the road.*
~n. Slang. Vigour; vitality.
~interj. Used to express surprise or suddenness. [Imitative.]

Za·pa·ta (zə-paátə; *Spanish* sa-), **Emiliano** (*c.* 1877–1919). Mexican revolutionary. For the cause of agrarian reform he led an American Indian revolt (1910–15); he ruled the state of Morelos, and occupied Mexico City three times.

za·pa·te·a·do (záppə-tay-aádō; *Spanish* tháppa-, -aáthō) *n., pl.* **-dos.** *Spanish.* **1.** The rhythmic stamping of the heels characteristic of Spanish flamenco dances. **2.** A Spanish flamenco dance in which the performer stamps rhythmically with his heels. [Spanish, from *zapatear,* to tap with the shoe, from *zapáto,* shoe.]

Zap·o·tec (záppə-tek, zaápə-, saápə-) *n.* Any of a group of Central American languages spoken in southern Mexico. **—Zap·o·tec** *adj.*

Z.A.P.U., ZAPU (zaá-pōō). Zimbabwe African People's Union.

Za·ra·go·za (thárrə-gōthə). *English* **Sar·a·gos·sa** (sárrə-góssə). Capital of Zaragoza province, northeast Spain. Situated on the river Ebro, it lies in an agricultural region for which it is a market centre. Its industries include textiles, food processing, and leather goods. Held by the Moors (8th to early 12th century), it was capital of Aragon (12th to 15th century) and resisted sieges by the French (1808–09) during the Peninsula War.

Zarathustra. See **Zoroaster.**

zar·a·tite (zárrə-tīt) *n.* A green amorphous form of hydrated nickel carbonate, $NiCO_3 \cdot 2Ni(OH)_2 \cdot 4H_2O$. [Spanish *zaratita,* after G. *Zárate,* 19th-century Spanish mineralogist.]

za·re·ba, za·ri·ba, za·ree·ba (zə-réebə) *n.* **1.** An enclosure of bushes or stakes protecting a campsite or village in northeast Africa. **2.** A campsite or village so protected. [Arabic *zarībah,* pen for cattle, from *zarb,* sheepfold.]

zarf (zarf) *n.* A chalice-like holder for a hot coffee cup, typically made of ornamented metal, used in the Middle East. [Arabic *ẓarf,* "container".]

zastruga. Variant of **sastruga.**

Za·to·pek (záttə-pek), **Emil** (1922–). Czech athlete. The greatest long-distance runner of his day, he won the 10 000 metres at the London Olympic Games (1948), and at the Helsinki Olympic Games (1952) won the 5 000 metres, 10 000 metres, and marathon.

zax (zaks). Variant of **sax** (tool). [Variant of SAX (tool).]

z-ax·is (zéd-ak-siss || *U.S.* zée-) *n., pl.* **z-axes** (-akseez). **1.** One of the three axes in a three-dimensional Cartesian coordinate system. **2.** The vertical axis of an aircraft.

za·yin (zaá-yin, zīn) *n.* The seventh letter of the Hebrew alphabet. [Hebrew *zayin,* "weapon", from Aramaic.]

z-bend (zéd-bend || *U.S.* zée-) *n.* A pair of successive sharp bends on a road.

zeal (zeel) *n.* Enthusiastic and diligent devotion in pursuit of a cause, ideal, or goal; fervent adherence or service; extreme and ardent commitment: *religious zeal.* See Synonyms at **passion.** [Middle English *zele,* from Late Latin *zēlus,* from Greek *zēlos.*]

Zealand. See **Sjælland.**

zeal·ot (zéllət) *n.* **1.** One who is zealous; a fanatically committed person. See Synonyms at **fanatic.** **2.** *Capital* **Z.** A member of a Jewish sect that resisted Roman rule in Palestine during the first century A.D. [Late Latin *zēlōtes,* from Greek *zēlōtēs,* from *zēlos,* ZEAL.]

zeal·ot·ry (zéllətri) *n.* Excessive zeal; fanaticism.

zeal·ous (zélləss) *adj.* Filled with or motivated by zeal; ardent; enthusiastic; fervent. See Synonyms at **eager.** **—zeal·ous·ly** *adv.* **—zeal·ous·ness** *n.*

ze·a·tin (zée-ə-tin) *n. Botany.* A naturally occurring cytokinin (a plant growth substance) found in maize kernels. [New Latin *Zea,* genus name for maize (see **zein**) + *-tin,* as in *kinetin.*]

zebec, zebeck. Variants of **xebec.**

Zeb·e·dee (zébbi-dee). A fisherman whose sons James and John became disciples of Jesus. Matthew 4:21.

ze·bra (zéebrə, zébbrə) *n.* Any of several horselike African mammals of the genus *Equus,* having characteristic overall markings of conspicuous dark and whitish stripes. [Portuguese, from Old Spanish *zebra, zebro*†, wild ass.]

zebra crossing (*usually* zébbrə) *n.* A pedestrian crossing, in which the road is painted with broad white stripes, where pedestrians may cross at any time and have precedence over road-using vehicles. [From the zebra-like painted stripes.]

zebra finch *n.* A small Australian bird, *Poephila castanotis* (or *Taeniopygia castanotis* or *T. guttata),* having black and white striped markings, and popular as a cage bird.

zebra fish *n.* A small freshwater tropical fish, *Brachydanio rerio,* of India, having horizontal dark-blue and silvery stripes, and popular in home aquariums. Also called "zebra danio".

ze·bra·wood (zéebrə-wŏŏd, zébbrə-) *n.* **1.** Any of several African or tropical American trees having striped wood, especially *Connarus guianensis.* **2.** The wood of such a tree, used in cabinet-making.

ze·bu (zée-bōō, -bew) *n.* A domesticated bovine mammal, *Bos indicus,* of Asia and Africa, having a prominent hump on the back and a large dewlap. [French *zébu*†.]

Zeb·u·lon¹, Zeb·u·lun (zébbew-lən, ze-béw-). A son of Jacob and Leah. Genesis 30:20. [Hebrew *Zəbhūlōn,* from *zəbhūl,* dwelling, from *zābhal,* he dwelt.]

Zebulon², Zebulun *n.* A tribe of Israel descended from Zebulon.

zec·chi·no (ze-kée-nō, tse-) *n., pl.* **-ni** (-nee). Also **zec·chin** (zéckin, ze-kéen), **zech·in.** A coin, a **sequin** *(see).* [Italian, SEQUIN.]

Zech. Zechariah (Old Testament).

Zech·a·ri·ah¹ (zéckə-rī́-ə). A Hebrew prophet of the sixth century B.C.

Zechariah² *n. Abbr.* **Zech.** A book of the Old Testament.

zed (zed) *n. Chiefly British.* The letter *z.* [Middle English *zed,* from Old French *zede,* from Late Latin *zēta,* ZETA.]

Zed·e·ki·ah (zéddi-kī́-ə). The last king of Judah (597–586 B.C.), who died in captivity at Babylon. II Kings 24:17. [Hebrew, *Ṣidqīyāh(ū),* "the Lord is righteousness".]

zed·o·ar·y (zéddō-əri || *U.S.* -erri) *n.* The dried rhizome of a tropical Asian plant, *Curcuma zedoaria,* used as a stimulant and condiment and in the manufacture of cosmetics. [Middle English *zeodoarye,* from Medieval Latin *zeodoaria,* from Arabic *zadwār,* from Persian *zedwār*†.]

zee (zee) *n. U.S.* The letter *z.* [Variant (17th-century) of ZED.]

Zee·brug·ge (zée-brŏŏgə; *Dutch* záy-brükhə). Deep-water port of West Flanders, Belgium. It is situated on the North Sea and connected by canal with Bruges. It was a German submarine base during World War I.

Zee·land (záy-lənd, zée-; *Dutch* záy-lant). Province of southwest Netherlands. Situated on the Scheldt estuary, it is bordered by Belgium in the south and includes the islands of Walcheren and North and South Beveland. It produces sugar beet, grains, flax, and fruit, and has chemical and motor industries. Its capital is Middelburg.

Zee·man (zéemən; *Dutch* záy-man), **Pieter** (1865–1943). Dutch physicist. Famous for his work on magneto-optics, he discovered the **Zeeman effect.** In 1902 he shared the Nobel prize for physics with H.A. Lorentz.

Zeeman effect *n.* The splitting of single spectral lines of an emission spectrum into three or more polarised components when the radiation source is in a magnetic field. [After Pieter ZEEMAN.]

Zef·fi·rel·li (zéffi-rélli), **Franco** (1923–). Italian stage and film director. Beginning his career as an actor and stage designer, he achieved recognition for directing a series of operas, including *La Cenerentola* (1953) at La Scala and *I Pagliacci* (1959) at Covent Garden. His films include *The Taming of the Shrew* (1966), *Romeo and Juliet* (1967), and *Jesus of Nazareth* (1977).

ze·in (zée-in) *n.* A prolamine protein derived from maize and used in the manufacture of various plastics, coatings, and lacquers. [New Latin *Zea,* genus name for maize, from Greek *zea, zeia,* one-seeded wheat + -IN.]

Zeiss (zīss; *German* tsīss), **Carl** (1816–88). German industrialist and optician. After establishing his first workshop at Jena (1846), he joined Ernest Abbe (1866) to produce field glasses, microscopes, and later cameras, using new optical techniques and materials, including heat-resistant glass.

Zeit·geist (tsīt-gīst, zīt-) *n.* The spirit of the time; the taste and outlook characteristic of a period or generation. [German, "time-spirit".]

zemindar. Variant of **zamindar.**

zemindary. Variant of **zamindari.**

zemst·vo (zémst-vō) *n., pl.* **-vos.** An elective council responsible for the local administration of a provincial district in tsarist Russia. [Russian, from *zemlya,* land.]

ze·na·na (ze-naánə, zi-) *n.* Also **za·na·na** (zə-). The part of a house in Asian countries such as India and Pakistan reserved for the women of the household. [Hindi *zenāna,* from Persian, from *zan,* woman.]

Zen Buddhism (zen) *n.* A Chinese and Japanese school of Mahayana Buddhism that asserts that enlightenment can be attained through meditation, self-contemplation, and intuition rather than through the scriptures. Also called "Zen". [Japanese *zen,* meditation, from Chinese *chan*; akin to Sanskrit *dhyāna,* he meditates.] **—Zen Buddhist** *n. & adj.* See feature, next page.

Zend (zend) *n.* **1.** The Zend-Avesta. **2.** Formerly, a language, **Avestan** *(see).*

Zend-A·ves·ta (zénd-ə-véstə) *n.* The entire body of sacred writings of the Zoroastrian religion. Also called "Zend". [Persian *zandavastā, zendastā,* from *Avesta-va-zend,* Avesta with an interpretation : Middle Persian *apastāk,* AVESTA + *va,* with + *zend*†, interpretation.] **—Zend-A·ves·ta·ic** (-vess-táy-ik) *adj.*

Ze·ner current (zéenər) *n.* A current in certain p-n junctions produced, at the point of **Zener breakdown,** by electrons from the valency band that have been excited into the conduction band as a result of the application of a strong electric field. [After C.M. *Zener* (1905–), U.S. physicist.]

Zener diode *n.* A semiconductor diode used as a voltage regulator, in which at a specific reverse voltage there is a sharp increase in reverse current. [After C.M. *Zener;* see **Zener current.**]

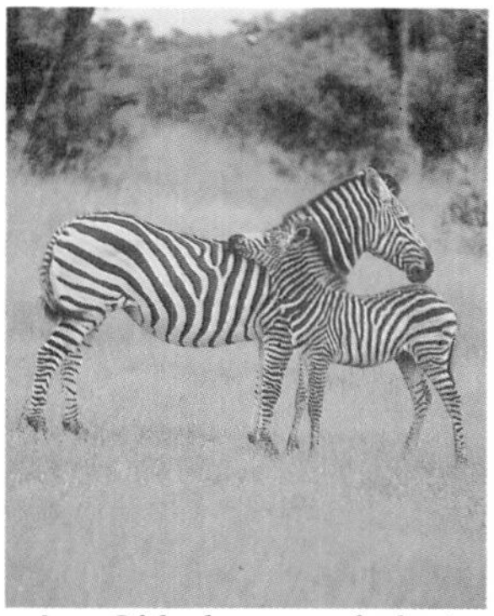

zebra *Of the three types of zebra in Africa, Burchell's zebra (above) – named after a 19th-century English naturalist – is the most common, ranging over most of the south and east of the continent.*

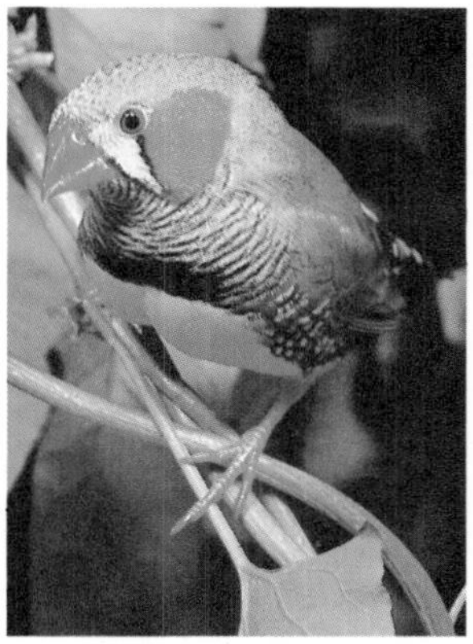

zebra finch *One of the Australian weaver finches, the zebra finch has been widely bred as a cage bird. In the wild it lives on open grassland.*

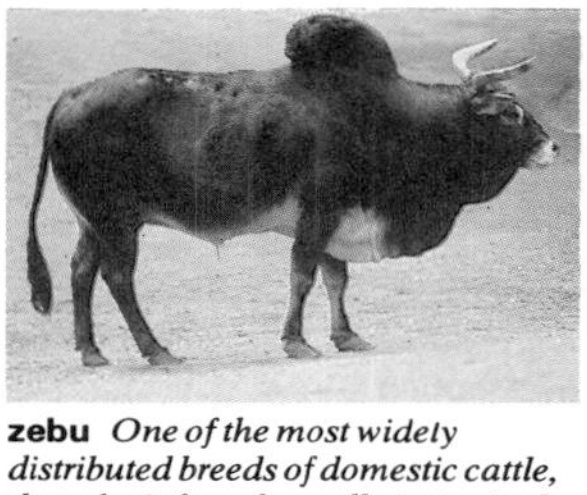

zebu *One of the most widely distributed breeds of domestic cattle, the zebu is found usually in tropical or semitropical climates because of its ability to cope with heat and its resistance to some tropical diseases. It is used as a beast of burden and reared for its milk and meat.*

Zen

JAPAN'S FORM OF BUDDHISM
Enlightenment through meditation and paradox

Zen is a branch of the Buddhist religion that has about nine million followers worldwide, most of whom live in Japan. In the 6th century B.C., Buddhism was brought from India to China where it was influenced by Taoism. In the 12th century, it was transferred in its new form to Japan.

The aim of Zen is the same as that of mainstream Buddhism – to achieve nirvana, or enlightenment, and release from the cycle of death and rebirth which binds man to the world. This release is said to be reached by looking beyond the reality of the world and becoming aware of one's own immortal nature. The two main branches of Zen believe different aspects of Buddhism to be the fundamental truth. In Soto Zen, meditation is the gradual path to self-awareness and liberation. In Rinzai Zen, mental concepts produced by language are seen as the chief barrier to spiritual development. Paradoxes, called koans, are used to destroy the hold of language on the mind and bring a person to liberation through a sudden awakening. An example is: "Imagine the sound of one hand clapping."

Zen, with its rejection of the intellect, developed partly as a reaction against the idolisation of scripture in mainstream Buddhism. It states that nirvana is possible for all people, not just reclusive monks, and aims to engender tranquillity, fearlessness, and spontaneity through a life of hard work and social concern.

Zen was the main religion of Japan in the 14th and 15th centuries and considerably influenced poetry, calligraphy, and painting. Disciplined spontaneity was developed by archery, flower arranging, and landscape gardening.

STONE GARDEN *A Zen stone garden is a place for meditation that goes beyond the normal concepts of conscious thought. The raked sand may represent the emptiness of mind which brings nirvana; the rocks may represent thoughts that obscure this enlightened state.*

STRICT REGIME *A monk sits in contemplation, part of the strict regime of the Koninji Temple, which is the cradle of Rinzai Zen in Japan.*

ze·nith (zénnith, zéenith) *n.* **1.** The point on the celestial sphere that is directly above the observer. **2.** The highest point above the observer's horizon attained by a celestial body. **3.** The highest point of any path or course; a point of culmination; a peak; a summit. —See Synonyms at **summit.** [Middle English, from Old French *cenith,* from Old Spanish *zenit,* from Arabic *samt,* road, in *samt ar-ra's,* road (over) the head.] —**zen·ith·al** *adj.*

zenithal projection *n.* A form of map projection in which a part of the earth's surface is projected onto a plane tangential to it such that all points have their true compass bearings from the central point.

Ze·no·bi·a (zi-nṓbi-ə, ze-) (third century A.D.). Queen of Palmyra (part of Syria) from 267 A.D. Acceding to the throne after the death of her husband Odenathus, she acted as regent for her son and extended her empire to include Syria, Egypt, and part of Asia Minor. In 272 she was defeated and captured by the Roman emperor Aurelian.

Ze·no (zéenō) **of Citium** (sítti-əm, kítti-) (c.334–c.262 B.C.). Greek philosopher. He founded the Stoic school of philosophy, which taught that virtue is necessarily good, and that most objects of desire, such as material possessions, family, and honours are morally indifferent or at best only relatively good.

ze·o·lite (zée-ə-līt) *n.* Any of a large group of hydrous calcium and aluminium silicate minerals or their corresponding synthetic compounds, used chiefly as molecular filters, water-softeners, and ion-exchange agents. [Swedish *zeolit,* "boiling stone" (because it swells and boils under the blowpipe) : Greek *zeein,* to boil + -LITE.]

Zeph. Zephaniah (Old Testament).

Zeph·a·ni·ah[1] (zéffə-nī-ə). A Hebrew prophet of the seventh century B.C.

Zephaniah[2] *n. Abbr.* **Zeph.** A book of the Old Testament containing the prophecies of Zephaniah.

zeph·yr (zéffər) *n.* **1. a.** A gentle breeze. **b.** The west wind. **2.** Any of various light, soft fabrics, yarns, or garments. **3.** Any airy, insubstantial, or passing thing. —See Synonyms at **wind.** [Middle English *Zephirus,* from Latin *zephyrus,* from Greek *zephuros,* akin to *zophos*†, darkness, west.]

Zeph·y·rus (zéffərəss). *Greek Mythology.* A god personifying the gentle west wind. [Latin, from Greek *Zephuros,* from *zephuros,* ZEPHYR.]

Zep·pe·lin (zéppə-lin; *German* tséppə-leen) *n.* Sometimes small **z.** A rigid airship having a long, cylindrical body. [After its inventor, Ferdinand von ZEPPELIN.]

Zeppelin, Ferdinand, Graf von (1838–1917). German inventor. After retiring from the army (1891), he designed and built the first motorised, rigid-frame dirigible balloon.

Zer·matt (zér-mat; *German* tsair-mát). Resort of Valas canton, south Switzerland. Situated at the foot of the Matterhorn, it is a mountaineering and winter sports centre.

ze·ro (zée-rō) *n., pl.* **-ros** or **-roes.** *Abbr.* **z. 1.** The numeral, or numerical symbol, "0"; a nought. **2.** *Mathematics.* **a.** An element of a set that when added to any other element in the set produces a sum identical with the element to which it is added. **b.** A cardinal number indicating the absence of any or all units under consideration. **c.** An ordinal number indicating an initial point or origin. **d.** An argument at which the value of a function vanishes. **3. a.** The starting point on a scale of measurement. **b.** The position on a scale marking the point between positive and negative values. **4.** The temperature indicated by the numeral 0 on a thermometer. **5.** A sight setting that enables a firearm to shoot on target. **6.** One having no influence or importance; a nonentity; a nobody. **7.** The lowest point: *His prospects were set at zero.* **8.** Nothing; nil.
~*adj.* **1.** Of, pertaining to, or being zero. **2. a.** Having no measurable or otherwise determinable value. **b.** Absent, inoperative, or irrelevant in specified circumstances: *zero energy.* **3. a.** Limited by cloud cover to little or no vertical visibility. **b.** Permitting little or no horizontal visibility. **4.** *Informal.* No; not any: *She showed zero interest in my problems.*
~*tr.v.* **zeroed, -roing, -roes.** To adjust (an instrument or device) to zero value. —**zero in. 1.** To aim or concentrate firepower on an exact target location. **2.** To adjust the aim or sight of by repeated firings. **3.** To converge intently; move near; close in: *The children zeroed in on the toy display.* [French *zéro,* from Italian *zero,* from Medieval Latin *zephirum,* from Arabic *şifr,* zero, CIPHER.]

zero gravity *n.* The state of weightlessness; the condition of not experiencing the effects of gravity.

zero hour *n.* The scheduled time for the start of an operation or action, especially a concerted military attack. Also called "H-hour".

ze·ro-point energy (zéer-ō-poynt) *n.* The irreducible minimum energy possessed by a substance at the temperature of absolute zero.

zero population growth *n. Abbr.* **ZPG** The limiting of population increase to the number of live births needed to maintain the existing population level.

ze·ro-rate (zéer-ō-rayt) *tr.v.* **-rated, -rating, -rates.** To exempt (goods or services) from value-added tax.

ze·roth (zéer-ōth) *n.* Anything, such as an element or term, that is considered to come before the first in a series. [ZERO + -TH (suffix of ordinals and fractions).] —**ze·roth** *adj. & adv.*

zest (zest) *n.* **1.** Added flavour or interest; piquancy; charm. **2.** Spirited enjoyment; wholehearted interest; gusto: *"At fifty-three he retains all the heady zest of adolescence"* (Kenneth Tynan). **3.** The outermost part of the rind of an orange or lemon, used as flavouring.

~*tr.v.* **zested, zesting, zests.** To give zest, charm, or spirit to. [French *zest†*, orange or lemon peel.] —**zest·ful** *adj.*

ze·ta (zéeta ‖ *U.S. also* záytə) *n.* The sixth letter in the Greek alphabet, written Z, ζ. Transliterated in English as Z, z. [Late Latin *zēta*, from Greek, probably from Semitic, akin to Hebrew *zayit*, Aramaic *zētā*.]

ZETA (zéetə) *n.* Zero-energy *t*hermonuclear *a*pparatus: a torus-shaped ring in which a plasma is contained by magnetic fields in order that thermonuclear reactions may be examined.

Zet·land (zetlənd). See **Shetland Islands.**

zeug·ma (zéwg-mə ‖ zōōg-) *n.* **1.** The use of a single word, especially a verb or adjective, to apply to two or more nouns, when its sense is appropriate to only one of them; for example, *He held his tongue and his oath*; *Pedal your bicycle rather than your car.* **2.** Loosely, a syllepsis. Compare **syllepsis.** [Latin, from Greek *zeugma*, a joining, uniting, yoking.]

Zeus (zewss ‖ zée-əss, zōōss). The presiding god of the Greek pantheon, ruler of the heavens and father of other gods and mortal heroes. [Greek.]

Zhan·jiang (ján-jyáng). Formerly **Guangzhon Bay.** Seaport in Guangdong Province, south China, having a large harbour. In 1898 it was made a French foreign concession and its architecture still retains some foreign influence.

Zhe·jiang or **Che-chiang** or **Che-kiang** (jə-jáng). China's smallest, most densely populated province, lying on the East China Sea coast. The north is part of the Chang Jiang valley, and the south, apart from the Fuchun Jiang valley, is mountainous. Zhejiang is a major rice, soya bean, wheat, cotton, and tea producing area. Its capital is the industrial port of Hangzhou.

Zheng·zhou or **Cheng-chou** or **Cheng-chow** (júng-jó). Also **Cheng·hsien.** Capital of Henan province, south central China. An important industrial city and rail centre, situated on the Huang He, it produces heavy machinery and textiles.

Zhi·to·mir (zhi-tómmeer). Capital of Zhitomir oblast, Ukraine, U.S.S.R. Situated on the river Teterev, it is a market centre for an agricultural region producing wheat and hops. Its industries include textiles and furniture.

Zhou *n.* See **Chou.**

Zhou En-lai or **Chou En-Lai** (jó en-lí) (1898–1976). Chinese statesman. After studying in Japan and Europe, he became an increasingly important leader in the Chinese Communist Party. He organised a general strike in Shanghai (1927) and later an insurrection in Nanching. He was the first prime minister (1949–76) and foreign minister (1949–58) of the People's Republic of China.

Zhu·jiang or **Chu-chiang** (jōō-jyáng). *English* **Pearl** or **Canton.** River of southeast China. On its large, fertile delta lie the cities of Guangzhou (Canton) and Macau, and the colony of Hong Kong.

Zhu·kov (zhōō-kov; *Russian* -kəf), **Georgi Konstantinovich** (1896–1974). Marshal of the U.S.S.R. Entering the Red Army in 1918, he rose to army chief of staff (1941). He directed the counteroffensive at Stalingrad (1943), relieved Leningrad (1943), and captured Berlin (1945). He served under Khrushchev as defence minister (1955–57) but was attacked for "political mistakes" (1957).

Zi·a ul-Haq (zée-ə ōōl-hák), **General Mohammed** (1924–). President of Pakistan. An army general, he led the military coup which overthrew President Bhutto (1977) and martial law administrator and then president (1978). Under his rule, general elections were postponed, Bhutto was executed, and strict Islamic laws were introduced.

zib·e·line, zib·el·line (zíbbə-līn, -lin, -leen) *n.* **1.** A thick, lustrous, soft fabric of wool and other animal hair, such as mohair, having a silky nap. **2.** *Rare.* The sable or its fur. [Old French, from Old Italian *zibellino*, from Slavic, akin to Russian *sobol†*.]

zib·et, zib·eth (zíbbit) *n.* A civet cat, *Viverra zibetha*, of southeast Asia. [Italian *zibetto*, from Medieval Latin *zibethum*, from Arabic *zabād*, CIVET.]

Zieg·feld (zéeg-feld, zíg-), **Flo(renz)** (1867–1932). U.S. theatre manager. Adapting the style of the Parisian Folies-Bergère, he became famous for his extravagant revues, known as the Ziegfeld Follies (1907–32). The discoverer of many entertainers, including Eddie Cantor and W.C. Fields, he produced musicals such as *Show Boat* (1927) and *Bitter Sweet* (1929).

Zieg·ler (zéeg-lər; *German* tséeg-), **Karl** (1898–1973). German organic chemist. For his work on long-chain polymers, and the use of catalysts to control polymerisation in plastics production, he shared the Nobel prize with Giulio Natta (1963).

Ziegler catalyst *n. Chemistry.* Any of a class of industrial catalysts that are mixed metal halides and organometallic compounds, used for promoting polymerisation reactions to make stereospecific plastics with improved strength and other properties. The original such catalyst was a mixture of titanium chloride ($TiCl_4$) and aluminium trimethyl ($Al(CH_3)_3$), used to make high-density polythene from ethylene. [After Karl ZIEGLER.]

zig·gu·rat (zíggōō-rat, zíggə-) *n.* Also **zik·ku·rat** (zíckōō-, zíckə-). A temple tower of the ancient Assyrians and Babylonians, having the form of a terraced pyramid of successively receding storeys. [Assyrian *ziqquratu*, summit, mountain top, from *zaqaru-*, to be high.]

zig·zag (zíg-zag) *n.* **1.** A line or course that proceeds by sharp turns in alternating directions. **2.** Any of a series of such sharp turns. **3.** Something exhibiting one or a series of sharp turns, such as a road or design.
~*adj.* Having or moving in a zigzag.
~*adv.* In a zigzag manner or pattern.

~*v.* **zigzagged, -zagging, -zags.** —*intr.* To move in or form a zigzag. —*tr.* To cause to move in or form a zigzag. [French, from German *Zickzack*, expressive formation.]

zig·zag·ger (zíg-zaggər) *n.* **1.** A person or thing that zigzags. **2.** A sewing-machine attachment for sewing zigzag stitches.

zilch (zilch) *n. U.S. Slang.* **1.** Zero; nothing. **2.** An insignificant person; a nonentity. [Variant of ZERO.]

zil·lion (zíl-yən, zilli-ən) *n. Chiefly U.S. Informal.* An extremely large indefinite number. Used humorously.
~*adj. Informal.* Very many. [z- (perhaps representing an indefinite large number) + (M)ILLION.]

Zil·pah (zílpə). The servant of Leah who bore Jacob two sons, Gad and Asher. Genesis 30:9-13.

Zim·ba·bwe (zim-baáb-wi, -báb-, -way). Landlocked country of south central Africa. It is made up of highveld and lowveld, including the Limpopo lowlands and forested Zambezi valley. Agriculture, mainly at subsistence level, accounts for only 16 per cent of its gross domestic product, and manufacturing 25 per cent. U.N. sanctions (imposed 1965) led to considerable diversification of manufacturing. The country has major reserves of timber and minerals, including coal. Its chief exports are gold, tobacco, iron and steel, chrome ore, asbestos, cotton, and nickel. Tourism is also important. Cecil Rhodes and his British South Africa Company obtained mineral rights in and claimed what are now Matabeleland and Mashonaland in the 1880s. From 1898 these formed the British colony of Southern Rhodesia, which became self-governing in 1923. The area was part of the Federation of Rhodesia and Nyasaland (1953–63), which broke up largely because of African opposition to the dominance of Southern Rhodesia's white minority. Led by Ian Smith, the minority government failed to arrive at an independence settlement with Britain, largely because it would not accept (black) majority rule, and made an illegal unilateral declaration of independence (1965). A republic was declared (1970), but Rhodesia was increasingly isolated in the world, and the government faced a protracted guerrilla war from the Zimbabwe African People's Union (ZAPU), led by Joshua Nkomo, and the Zimbabwe African National Union (ZANU), led by Robert Mugabe. Eventually, as an outcome of the Commonwealth Conference of 1979, a peace formula involving majority rule was agreed, and under British supervision, elections were held (March, 1980). Mugabe became independent Zimbabwe's first prime minister (April, 1980). Area, 390 580 square kilometres (150,764 square miles). Population, 8,000,000. Capital, Harare (formerly Salisbury).

Zim·mer (zímmər) *n.* A trademark for a lightweight, sturdy, metal frame that has four rubber-tipped feet and a wide, curved crossbar that is easy to hold, used as a support when walking by the elderly or disabled.

zinc (zingk) *n. Symbol* **Zn** A bluish-white, lustrous metallic element that is brittle at room temperatures but malleable when heated. It is used to form a wide variety of alloys including brass, bronze, German silver, various solders, and nickel silver, in galvanising iron and other metals, for electric fuses, anodes, and meter cases, and in roofing, gutters, and various household objects. Atomic number 30, atomic weight 65.37, melting point 419.5°C, boiling point 908°C, relative density 7.14 (25°C), valency 2.
~*tr.v.* **zinced** or **zincked, zincing** or **zincking, zincs.** To coat or treat with zinc; galvanise. [German *Zink*, perhaps from *Zinke*, prong (so named because it becomes jagged in the furnace), from Old High German *zinko*.]

zinc·ate (zíng-kayt) *n.* Any of several chemical compounds derived from the reaction of zinc or zinc oxide with certain alkali solutions.

zinc blende *n.* A mineral, **sphalerite** (*see*).

zinc chloride *n.* A white soluble solid, $ZnCl_2$, used as a wood

---

Map caption (top right):
ZIMBABWE · ZAMBIA · Rift Valley · 30° E · Zambezi · Dam · Lake Kariba · Shonaland · Victoria Falls · HARARE (SALISBURY) · Mt Inyangani ▲2595m · Wankie · ZIMBABWE · Gatooma · Kwekwe · Mutare · Ndebeleland · Gweru · 20° S · Bulawayo · Zimbabwe · MOZAMBIQUE · BOTSWANA · Matopo Hills · Kalahari · Limpopo · 0 200 Km · 0 100 Miles · S. AFRICA

Zeus *In Greek mythology, Zeus became king of the gods after he led them to victory over the Titans – the older gods who were the offspring of Heaven and Earth. This detail from an Athenian cup made in about 550 B.C., shows the birth of his daughter Athena who sprang fully clothed from Zeus's head when Hephaestus, the god of fire, split it open with an axe.*

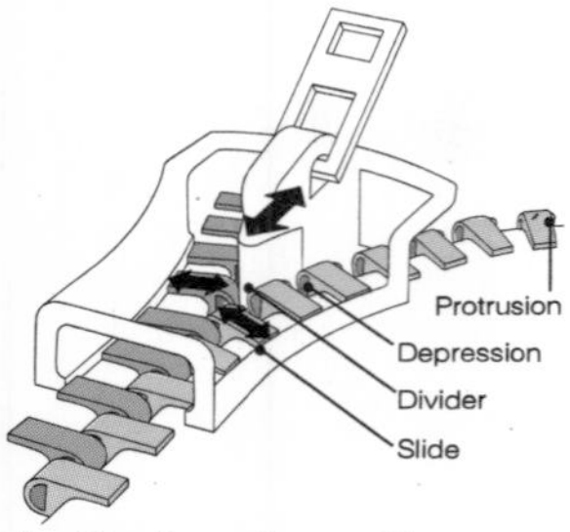

zip *The zip was invented by an American in 1893 as a quicker means of fastening boots, in place of buttons. It was unreliable until perfected by a Swede in 1912. The most common type of modern zip fastener consists of two tapes with rows of teeth joined by a slide. When the zip is closed, the slide draws together the rows of teeth, so that the protrusions and depressions of opposite teeth mesh. When the zip is opened, a divider on the slide pushes the teeth apart.*

PRONUNCIATION KEY

a, trap; aa, father; ai, fair; ar, star; aw, lawn; ay, play; b, bb, stab; rubber; ch, church; ck, ticket; d, dd, dead; ladder; e, dress; ee, bee; er, defer; ew, few; ewr, pure; ə, about; ər, letter; f, ff, fife; differ; g, gg, giggle; h, hat; i, kit; ī, price; īr, fire; j, judge; k, kick; l, ll, let; 'l, needle; m, mm, man; n, nn, no; 'n, sudden; ng, thing; o, lot; ō, no; ŏŏ, foot; ōō, shoe; oor, poor; ow, cow; owr, hour; oy, boy; p, pp, pepper; r, rr, red; s, ss, sauce; sh, ship; t, tt, totter; th, thick; th, this; smooth; u, cut; ur, turn; v, vv, valve; w, wet; y, yes; z, zz, zebra; zh, vision; pleasure

IN FOREIGN WORDS:

aN, oN, Saint-Saëns; hl, Llanelli; Hluhluwe; kh, loch; lough; Khaled

STRESS MARK:

ín-sīt, insight; in-sī́t, incite

preservative, soldering flux, and medical astringent. Also called "butter of zinc".

zinc·if·er·ous (zing-kíffərəss) *adj.* Designating a compound, ore, or mineral that contains zinc.

zinc·ite (zíng-kīt) *n.* A red to yellow-orange zinc ore, essentially ZnO.

zin·co·graph (zíngkə-graaf, -graf) *n.* **1.** A prepared zinc plate used in zincography. **2.** A print or picture obtained from such a plate. [ZINC + -GRAPH.]

zin·cog·ra·phy (zing-kóggrəfi) *n.* The process of engraving zinc printing plates. [ZINC + -GRAPHY.] **—zin·cog·ra·pher** *n.* **—zinc·o·graph·ic** (zíngkə-gráffik), **zinc·o·graph·i·cal** *adj.*

zinc ointment *n. Medicine.* A salve consisting of about 20 per cent zinc oxide with beeswax or paraffin and petrolatum, used in the treatment of skin diseases.

zinc oxide *n.* An amorphous white or yellowish powder, ZnO, used as a pigment, in compounding rubber, in the manufacture of plastics, and in pharmaceuticals and cosmetics. Also called "Chinese white", "zinc white".

zinc spinel *n.* A mineral, **gahnite** *(see).*

zinc sulphate *n.* A colourless crystalline compound, $ZnSO_4 \cdot 7H_2O$, used medicinally as an emetic and astringent, as a fungicide, and in wood and skin preservatives. Also called "white vitriol".

zinc white *n.* A paint pigment, zinc oxide.

zing (zing) *n.* **1.** A brief high-pitched humming or buzzing sound, such as that made by a swiftly passing object or a taut vibrating string. **2.** Zest; vigour.
~*intr.v.* **zinged, zinging, zings.** *Informal.* **1.** To make or move with such a sound. **2.** To move quickly or vigorously. [Imitative.]

zin·ga·ro (zíng-gə-rō, tséeng-, -gaa-) *n., pl.* **-ri** (-ree). *Feminine* **zin·ga·ra** (-rə, -raa) *pl.* **-re** (-ray). A Gypsy. [Italian *zingaro,* probably from Greek *Athinganoi*† (plural), name of an oriental people.]

zin·jan·thro·pus (zin-jánthrə-pəss, zín-jan-thrṓ-) *n.* Any extinct primate of the genus *Zinjanthropus.* See **australopithecine.** [New Latin : Arabic *Zinj,* East Africa + Greek *anthrōpos,* man.]

zink·en·ite, zinck·en·ite (zíngkə-nīt) *n.* A steel-grey mineral, essentially $Pb_6Sb_{14}S_{27}$. [German *Zinkenit,* after J.K.L. *Zinken* (1790–1862), German mineralogist.]

zin·ni·a (zínni-ə) *n.* Any of various plants of the genus *Zinnia,* native to tropical America; especially, *Z. elegans,* widely cultivated for its showy, variously coloured flowers. [New Latin *Zinnia,* after Johann Gottfried *Zinn* (1727–59), German botanist and physician.]

Zi·no·viev (zi-nṓv-i-ev; *Russian* -yif), **Gregory Evseyevich** (1883–1936). Soviet politician. Chairman of the Comintern from 1919, he was an influential government member until expelled from the party (1927). He was executed in a Stalinist purge. The publication in Britain of a forged letter allegedly from him contributed to the downfall of the Labour government (1924).

Zi·on (zī́-ən) *n.* Also **Si·on** (sī́-ən). **1. a.** The Jewish people; the Israelites. **b.** The Jewish homeland as a symbol of Judaism. **c.** *Literary.* Ancient Jerusalem. **2. a.** A place or religious community regarded as sacredly devoted to God; a city of God. **b.** Heaven. **3.** An idealised harmonious community; a utopia. **4.** In Rastafarian ideology, the promised land. [Middle English *Sion,* Old English, from Late Latin *Siōn,* from Greek *Seiōn,* from Hebrew *Ṣiyōn.*]

Zion, Mount. 1. The part of Jerusalem that constituted the City of David. **2.** The hill in Jerusalem on which Solomon's temple was built.

Zi·on·ism (zī́-ə-niz'm) *n.* **1.** A plan or movement of the Jewish people to return from the Diaspora to Palestine. **2.** A movement originally aimed at the re-establishment of a Jewish national homeland and state in Palestine and now concerned with the development of Israel. **—Zi·on·ist** *adj.* & *n.* **—Zi·on·is·tic** (-nístik) *adj.*

zip (zip) *n.* **1.** A fastening device consisting of parallel rows of metal or nylon teeth on adjacent edges of an opening which are interlocked by a sliding tab. Also called "zip fastener", *U.S.* "zipper". **2.** A brief, sharp, hissing sound, such as that made by a flying arrow. **3.** *Informal.* Energetic activity; zest; vim.
~*v.* **zipped, zipping, zips.** *—intr.* **1. a.** To move or act with a speed that makes or suggests a brief, sharp, hissing sound: *The cars zipped by endlessly.* **b.** To act or proceed swiftly and energetically. **2.** To become fastened by a zip. Often used with *up.* *—tr.* To fasten with a zip. Often used with *up.* [Imitative.]

zip code *n. Sometimes capital* **Z,** *capital* **C.** *U.S.* A **post code** *(see).* [Zone *I*mprovement *P*rogram.]

zip·py (zíppi) *adj.* **-pier, -piest.** *Informal.* Full of energy; brisk; lively; snappy.

zir·con (zúr-kən, -kon) *n.* A brown to colourless mineral, essentially $ZrSiO_4$, which is heated, cut, and polished to form a brilliant blue-white gem. [German *Zirkon,* from French *jargon,* from Italian *giargone,* from Arabic *zarqūn,* from Persian *zargūn,* gold-coloured : *zar,* gold + *gūn*-†.]

zir·con·ate (zúrkə-nayt) *n.* Any of several chemical compounds formed by heating zirconium oxide with a metal carbonate or oxide in the presence of an acid. [ZIRCON + -ATE.]

zir·co·ni·um (zur-kṓni-əm) *n. Symbol* **Zr** A lustrous, greyish-white, strong, ductile metallic element obtained primarily from zircon and used chiefly in ceramic and refractory compounds, as an alloying agent, in nuclear reactors, and in medical prosthesis. Atomic number 40, atomic weight 91.22, melting point 1,171°C, boiling point 4,377°C, relative density 6.53 (calculated), principal valency 4. [New Latin, from ZIRCON.]

zirconium oxide *n.* A hard, white, amorphous powder, ZrO_2, derived from zirconium and also found naturally, used chiefly in pigments, refractories, ceramics, and as an abrasive. Also called "zirconia".

zit (zit) *n. Slang.* A pimple. [20th century : imitative of bursting pimple.]

zith·er (zíth-ər, zíth-) *n.* Also **zith·ern** (-ərn). A musical instrument consisting of a flat sounding box with about 30 to 40 strings stretched over it and played horizontally with the fingertips or a plectrum. [German *Zither,* from Old High German *zithera, cithera,* from Latin *cithara,* from Greek *kithara,* CITHARA.] **—zith·er·ist** *n.*

zi·zith (tsítsiss, tsee-tséet) *pl.n.* The tassels or fringes of thread on the four corners of prayer shawls worn by orthodox Jewish males. [Hebrew *ṣīṣīth,* tassel.]

zizz (ziz) *n. British Informal.* A short sleep; a doze. [Probably from zzz.]

zlo·ty (zlótti) *n., pl.* **-tys** or **zloty. 1.** The basic monetary unit of Poland, equal to 100 groszy. **2.** A coin worth one zloty. [Polish *złoty,* "golden", from *złoto,* gold.]

Zn The symbol for the element zinc.

zo. Variant of **dzo.**

zo–. Variant of **zoo-.**

–zoa *n. comb. form.* Indicates certain animal organisms or taxonomic groups; for example, **entozoa, Protozoa.** [New Latin, from Greek *zōia,* plural of *zōion,* animal.]

–zoan *n. comb. form. Zoology.* Indicates animals within a taxonomic group; for example, **protozoan.** [From -ZOA.]

zo·di·ac (zṓdi-ak) *n.* **1. a.** *Astronomy.* A band of the celestial sphere, extending about eight degrees to either side of the ecliptic, that represents the path of the principal planets, the Moon, and the Sun. **b.** In astrology, this band divided into 12 equal parts called signs of the Zodiac, each 30 degrees wide, bearing the name of a constellation for which it was originally named but with which it no longer coincides owing to the precession of the equinoxes. **2.** A diagram or figure representing the signs of the zodiac. **3.** A complete circuit; a circle. [Middle English, from Old French *zodiaque,* from Latin *zōdiacus,* from Greek *zōidiakos (kuklos),* "(circle) of carved figures", from *zōidion,* carved figure, sign of the zodiac, diminutive of *zōion,* animal.] **—zo·di·a·cal** (zō-dī́-ək'l) *adj.*

zodiacal light *n.* A faint hazy cone of light, often visible in the west just after sunset or in the east just before sunrise, apparently caused by the reflection of sunlight from meteoric particles surrounding the sun.

zo·e·trope (zṓ-i-trōp) *n.* An optical toy consisting of a case containing a cylinder bearing pictures of figures which appear to move as they are viewed through a slit in the case while the cylinder revolves. [Originally a trademark; from Greek *zōē,* life + *tropos,* a turning, from *trepein,* to turn.]

Zof·fa·ny (zóffəni), **Johann** (*c.* 1733–1810). German painter. Living chiefly in London from 1761, he secured royal patronage and painted many royal portraits, as well as theatrical scenes.

Zog I (zog) (1895–1961). King of Albania (1928–43). Educated in Istanbul, he served as prime minister (1922–24) and president (1925–28) but fled the country after its invasion by Italy (1939). He first settled in England but later moved to Egypt and France. He abdicated in 1943.

–zoic *adj. comb. form.* Indicates: **1.** A specified kind of animal existence; for example, **holozoic. 2.** A specified geological division; for example, **Mesozoic.** [Greek *zōikos,* of animals, from *zōion,* animal.]

zois·ite (zóy-sīt) *n.* A grey or pink mineral, essentially $Ca_2Al_3(SiO_4)_3(OH)$. [German *Zoisit,* named after its discoverer, Baron S. *Zois* von Edelstein (1747–1819), Slovenian nobleman.]

Zo·la (zṓlə; *French* zō-laá), **Émile (Édouard Charles Antoine)** (1840–1902). French novelist. Leader of the naturalist movement, he worked as a clerk and journalist before establishing his reputation with *Thérèse Raquin* (1867). Through the portrayal of a single extended family in *Les Rougon-Macquart,* a series of 20 novels including *L'Assommoir* (1877), *Nana* (1880), and *Germinal* (1885), he provided a detailed account of contemporary social problems. He was obliged to flee France after publishing *J'accuse* (1898), a defence of Dreyfus.

zoll·ver·ein (zólvər-īn; *German* tsólfər-) *n.* **1.** *Often capital* **Z.** A union of German states during the 19th century that established a uniform tariff on imports from nonmembers and free trade among themselves. **2.** Any customs or tariff union. [German *Zollverein,* "custom union".]

zom·bie, zom·bi (zómbi) *n.* **1.** A snake god of voodoo cults in West Africa, Haiti, and the southern United States. **2. a.** A supernatural power or spell that according to voodoo belief can enter into and reanimate a dead body. **b.** A corpse revived in this way. **3.** *Informal.* One who appears lifeless, apathetic, or stupid. [Of West African origin.]

zo·nal (zṓn'l) *adj.* Also **zo·na·ry** (zṓnəri). **1.** Of or associated with a zone or zones. **2.** Divided into zones. **—zo·nal·ly** *adv.*

zonal soil *n.* A soil with a profile that depends largely on the type of vegetation it supports and the climate to which it is exposed.

zo·nate (zṓ-nayt) *adj.* Also **zo·nat·ed** (zō-náytid, zṓ-naytid). Having zones; belted, striped, or ringed.

zo·na·tion (zō-náysh'n) *n.* **1.** Arrangement or formation in zones; zonate structure. **2.** *Ecology.* The distribution of organisms in biogeographic zones.

zone (zōn) *n. Abbr.* **z. 1.** An area, region, or division distinguished from adjacent parts by some distinctive feature or character: *a danger zone; an erogenous zone.* **2. a.** *Geography.* Any of the five regions

zodiac

HOW ASTROLOGERS SEEK TO PREDICT HUMAN DESTINY

A 5,000-year-old Babylonian system based on the planets and constellations

The Zodiac with its 12 signs was devised about 3000 B.C. by Babylonian priests. The priests observed that the Sun, Moon, and planets seemed to move round the Earth in a yearly course which passed through 12 constellations. They divided the course into 12 parts, and called them after the constellations.

The Babylonians also saw that the Sun seemed to rise in a different part of the Zodiac each month, and, on that basis, they compiled a calendar. They also believed that the movements of the Sun, stars, and planets could be used to predict events on Earth and the destiny of individuals. Although the constellations have been moving apart since the system was devised, astrologers today still use the Babylonians' basic ideas.

Astrologers cast horoscopes to analyse a person's character and future, by linking the date, place, and time of birth with the exact position of the Moon and planets at the time. Then they calculate how the characteristics they associate with the Sun, Moon, and planets may affect the person's future. Below is a summary of the Zodiac signs' significance.

CAPRICORN (Dec 23–Jan 19)
Ruler: Saturn. Positive traits: careful, ambitious, determined. Negative traits: mean, pessimistic, rigid. Suggested partner: Taurus, Cancer, or Virgo.

AQUARIUS (Jan 20–Feb 19)
Rulers: Uranus and Saturn. Positive traits: independent, original. Negative traits: perverse, obstinate. Suggested partner: Gemini or Libra.

PISCES (Feb 20–Mar 21)
Rulers: Neptune and Jupiter. Positive traits: caring, intuitive, kind. Negative traits: vague, weak-willed. Suggested partner: Taurus or Cancer.

ARIES (Mar 22–Apr 20)
Ruler: Mars. Positive traits: energetic, brave, direct. Negative traits: impatient, selfish, unsubtle. Suggested partner: Gemini or Sagittarius.

TAURUS (Apr 21–May 21)
Ruler: Venus. Positive traits: warm, determined. Negative traits: stubborn, possessive. Suggested partner: Taurus, Capricorn, or Pisces.

GEMINI (May 22–June 22)
Ruler: Mercury. Positive traits: lively, versatile. Negative traits: superficial, inconsistent. Suggested partner: Gemini, Aries, or Libra.

CANCER (June 23–July 23)
Ruler: Moon. Positive traits: kind, imaginative, sensitive. Negative traits: overemotional, possessive. Suggested partner: Taurus or Capricorn.

LEO (July 24–Aug 23)
Ruler: Sun. Positive traits: strong, generous, creative. Negative traits: intolerant, pompous, conceited. Suggested partner: Aries or Libra.

VIRGO (Aug 24–Sept 23)
Ruler: Mercury. Positive traits: modest, practical. Negative traits: aloof, fussy, over-critical. Suggested partner: Virgo, Capricorn, or Taurus.

LIBRA (Sept 24–Oct 23)
Ruler: Venus. Positive traits: idealistic, charming, romantic. Negative traits: indecisive, frivolous. Suggested partner: Leo or Aquarius.

SCORPIO (Oct 24–Nov 22)
Rulers: Pluto and Mars. Positive traits: passionate, purposeful. Negative traits: jealous, secretive. Suggested partner: Capricorn or Cancer.

SAGITTARIUS (Nov 23–Dec 22)
Ruler: Jupiter. Positive traits: optimistic, active. Negative traits: lack of tact, restless. Suggested partner: Libra or Aquarius.

of the surface of the earth that are loosely divided according to prevailing climate and latitude, including the Torrid Zone, the North and South Temperate Zones, and the North and South Frigid Zones. **b.** A similar division on any planet. **3.** In geometry, a portion of a sphere bounded by the intersections of two parallel planes with the sphere. **4.** *Ecology.* An area characterised by distinct physical conditions and populated by communities of certain kinds of organism. **5.** *Geology.* A region or stratum distinguished by composition or content. **6. a.** A section or division of an area or territory established to distinguish it from other similar areas for a specific purpose: *a fare zone.* **b.** A municipal area in a city designated for a particular type of building, enterprise, or activity: *residential zone.* **7.** *Archaic.* A belt or girdle. —See Synonyms at **area.** ~*tr.v.* **zoned, zoning, zones. 1.** To divide into zones. **2.** To designate or mark off into zones. **3.** To surround or encircle with or as if with a belt or girdle. [Latin *zōna*, girdle, zone, from Greek *zōnē.*]

zone refining *n.* A method of redistributing the impurities in a semiconductor material by melting a small section or zone of a bar of the material and causing the molten zone to move along the length of the bar. Purification can be achieved by concentrating the impurities at the end of the bar, which is later removed.

zone·time (zōn-tīm) *n.* Standard time used at sea according to the time zone in which a ship is located.

zonked (zongkt) *adj. Chiefly U.S. Slang.* **1.** Intoxicated by alcohol or drugs. **2.** Extremely tired, confused, or disorientated. [20th century : origin obscure.]

zoo (zōō) *n., pl.* **zoos.** A public park or institution in which living animals are kept, bred, and exhibited to the public. Also called "zoological garden". [Short for ZOOLOGICAL GARDEN.]

zoo-, zo- *comb. form.* Indicates animals or animal forms; for example, **zoology, zoogeography, zooid.** [Greek *zōio-,* from *zōion, zōon,* living being, animal.]

zo·o·chem·is·try (zō-ə-kĕmmistri, -ō-) *n.* Animal biochemistry.

zo·o·chore (zō-ə-kawr, -ō- ‖ -kōr) *n.* A plant dispersed by animals. [ZOO- + -CHORE.]

zoogeog. zoogeography.

zoogeographic region *n.* An extensive region of the earth, such as central and southern Africa, characterised by the dominance of certain kinds of animal life.

zo·o·ge·og·ra·phy (zō-ə-jee-óggrəfi, zōō-, -ō-) *n. Abbr.* **zoogeog.** The biological study of the geographical distribution of animals. —**zo·o·ge·og·ra·pher** *n.* —**zo·o·ge·o·graph·ic** (-jée-ə-gráffik, -ō-), **zo·o·ge·o·graph·i·cal** *adj.* —**zo·o·ge·o·graph·i·cal·ly** *adv.*

zo·o·gloe·a, zo·o·gle·a (zō-ə-glée-ə) *n., pl.* **-ae** (-ee) or **-as.** Any of various bacteria of the genus *Zoogloea*, forming colonies in a jelly-like secretion. [New Latin : ZOO- + Medieval Greek *glia, gloia,* glue.]

zo·og·ra·phy (zō-óggrəfi) *n.* The biological description of animals. [ZOO- + -GRAPHY.] —**zo·og·ra·pher** *n.* —**zo·o·graph·ic** (zō-ə-gráffik), **zo·o·graph·i·cal** *adj.*

zo·oid (zō-oyd) *n.* **1.** *Biology.* An organic cell or organised body that has independent movement within a living organism; especially, a motile gamete such as a spermatozoon. **2.** *Zoology.* Any of the usually microscopic animals forming an aggregate or colony, as of polyzoans or hydrozoans. [ZO(O)- + -OID.] —**zo·oi·dal** (zō-óyd'l) *adj.*

zool. zoological; zoology.

zo·ol·a·try (zō-óllətri) *n., pl.* **-tries.** The worship of animals. [New Latin *zoolatria* : ZOO- + -LATRY.] —**zo·ol·a·ter** *n.* —**zo·ol·a·trous** *adj.*

zo·o·log·i·cal (zō-ə-lójik'l, zōō-; *sometimes* zōō-lójik'l) *adj.* Also *chiefly U.S.* **zo·o·log·ic** (-ə-lójik). *Abbr.* **zool. 1.** Of or pertaining to animals or animal life. **2.** Of or pertaining to the science of zoology. —**zo·o·log·i·cal·ly** *adv.*

zoological garden *n.* A zoo (*see*).

zo·ol·o·gist (zō-óllajist, zōō-) *n.* One who specialises in the study of animals.

zo·ol·o·gy (zō-óllaji, zōō-) *n., pl.* **-gies.** *Abbr.* **zool. 1.** The biological study of animals. **2.** The animal life of a particular area. **3.** The characteristics of an animal group or category: *the zoology of fish.* **4.** A book or scholarly work on animals. [New Latin *zoologia* : ZOO- + -LOGY.]

zoom (zōōm) *v.* **zoomed, zooming, zooms.** —*intr.* **1.** To make a continuous low-pitched buzzing or humming sound. **2.** To move while making such a sound. **3.** To climb suddenly and sharply in an aeroplane. **4.** To move or act very rapidly: *zoom up to town.* **5. a.** To move rapidly towards or away from a photographic subject. Used of a camera. Often used with *in* or *out.* **b.** To simulate such a movement, as by means of a zoom lens. Often used with *in* or *out.* —*tr.* To cause to zoom. —*n.* The act or sound of zooming. [Imitative.]

zo·om·e·try (zō-ómmətri) *n.* Measurement and comparison of the sizes of animals or animal parts, especially the measurement of bulk. [ZOO- + -METRY.] —**zo·o·met·ric** (zō-ə-méttrik), **zo·o·met·ri·cal** *adj.* —**zo·o·met·ri·cal·ly** *adv.*

zoom lens *n.* A camera lens whose focal length can be rapidly changed, allowing rapid change in the size of an image.

zo·o·mor·phism (zō-ə-mór-fiz'm) *n.* Also **zo·o·mor·phy** (-mórfi). **1.** The attribution of animal characteristics or qualities to a god or gods. **2.** The use of animal forms in symbolism, literature, or art. [ZOO- + -MORPH + -ISM.] —**zo·o·mor·phic** *adj.*

-zoon *n. comb. form.* Indicates an individual animal or independently moving organic unit; for example, spermatozoon. [New Latin, from Greek *zōion, zōon,* living being, animal.]

zo·o·no·sis (zō-ónnə-siss, zō-ə-nō-) *n., pl.* **-ses** (-seez). A disease such as rabies or malaria that can be transmitted from animals to man. [New Latin : ZOO- + Greek *nosos,* illness.]

zo·oph·a·gous (zō-óffagəss) *adj.* Feeding on animal matter. [ZOO- + -PHAGOUS.]

zo·o·phile (zō-ə-fīl ‖ -fil) *n.* A lover of animals; especially, one opposed to vivisection. [ZOO- + -PHILE.] —**zo·o·phil·ic** (-fíllik) *adj.* —**zo·oph·i·lism** (zō-óffiliz'm) *n.*

zo·oph·i·lous (zō-óffiləss) *adj.* **1.** *Botany.* Pollinated by animals. **2.** Of, pertaining to, or characterised by zoophilism.

zo·o·pho·bi·a (zō-ə-fṓbi-ə) *n.* An irrational fear of animals. [New Latin : ZOO- + -PHOBIA.] —**zo·oph·o·bous** (zō-óffəbəss) *adj.*

zo·o·phyte (zō-ə-fīt) *n.* An invertebrate animal such as a sea anemone or sponge that remains attached to a surface and superficially resembles a plant. [Greek *zōophuton* : ZOO- + -PHYTE.] —**zo·o·phyt·ic** (-fíttik), **zo·o·phyt·i·cal** *adj.*

zo·o·plank·ton (zō-ə-plángktən) *n.* Small crustaceans, fish larvae, and other, often microscopic, aquatic animals that make up the animal part of plankton.

zo·o·plas·ty (zō-ə-plasti) *n.* Surgical transfer of tissue from an animal to man. [ZOO- + -PLASTY.] —**zo·o·plas·tic** (-plástik) *adj.*

zo·o·sperm (zō-ə-sperm) *n. Biology.* A spermatozoon (*see*). [ZOO- + -SPERM.]

zo·o·spo·ran·gi·um (zō-ə-spaw-ránji-əm, -spə- ‖ -spō-) *n., pl.* **-gia** (-ji-ə). *Botany.* A sporangium in which zoospores develop.

zo·o·spore (zō-ə-spawr ‖ -spōr) *n.* A motile, flagellated asexual spore, as of certain algae and fungi. —**zo·o·spor·ic** (-spáwr-ik ‖ -spór-), **zo·o·spor·ous** (zō-óspərəss, zō-ə-spáwr-əss ‖ -spōr-) *adj.*

zo·os·ter·ol (zō-óstə-rol ‖ -rōl) *n. Biochemistry.* Any of several animal sterols, such as cholesterol.

zo·o·tech·nics (zō-ə-tékniks) *n. Used with a singular or plural verb.* Zootechny. [ZOO- + Greek *tekhnē,* art.]

zo·o·tech·ny (zō-ə-tekni) *n.* The domestication, breeding, and improvement of animals; the technology of animal husbandry. Also called "zootechnics". [ZOO- + Greek *tekhnē,* art.] —**zo·o·tech·ni·cal** (-téknik'l) *adj.* —**zo·o·tech·ni·cian** (-tek-nísh'n) *n.*

zo·ot·o·my (zō-óttəmi) *n.* **1.** Dissection of animals other than man. **2.** Comparative anatomy. [ZOO- + -TOMY.] —**zo·o·tom·ic**

(zō-ə-tómmik), **zo·o·tom·i·cal** *adj.* —**zo·o·tom·i·cal·ly** *adv.* —**zo·ot·o·mist** (zō-óttəmist) *n.*

zoot suit (zōōt) *n. Slang.* A man's suit, popular especially in the United States during the early 1940s, characterised by tapering trousers with turn-ups and a long jacket with wide lapels and wide, padded shoulders. [Zoot, rhyming formation based on SUIT.]

zor·ille, zor·il (zórril, zə-ríl) *n.* Also **zor·il·la** (zə-rílla). An African mammal, *Ictonyx striatus,* resembling the skunk in appearance and defensive action. [French, from Spanish *zorrillo, zorrilla,* "small fox", from *zorro,* fox, from Old Spanish *zorra†,* to drag.]

Zor·o·as·ter (zórrō-ástər) (c. 628–551 B.C.). Also **Zar·a·thus·tra** (zárrə-thṓostrə). Persian prophet. As a priest in northwest Persia, he founded the religion Zoroastrianism after he had a divine vision. He wrote the Gathas, a collection of hymns in honour of the god Ormazd.

Zor·o·as·tri·an·ism (zórrō-ástri-ə-niz'm ‖ zōrō-) *n.* The dualistic religious system founded in Persia by Zoroaster and set forth in the Zend-Avesta, teaching the worship of Ormazd, god of creation, light, and goodness, who is engaged in a continual struggle against Ahriman, spirit of evil and darkness. Also called "Mazdaism". —**Zor·o·as·tri·an** *adj. & n.*

zos·ter (zóstər) *n.* A belt or girdle worn by men in ancient Greece. [Latin, from Greek *zōstēr,* girdle.]

Zou·ave (zōō-áav, zwáav) *n.* **1.** A member of a French infantry unit, formerly composed of Algerian recruits, characterised by colourful oriental uniforms and precision drilling. **2.** A member of any group modelled on the French Zouaves; especially, a member of such a

---

Zoroaster

THE ONE GOD OF PERSIA

A religion that unified an empire

The ancient Persian mystic Zoroaster (*c.* 628–*c.* 551 B.C.), known by both this Greek form of his name and Zarathustra (the Persian form), originated a religion named after him. Virtually nothing is known of his life, except that his homeland was northwest Persia, from where he fled to achieve acceptance in eastern Persia. There Zoroastrianism was adopted by the Achaemenid rulers. Darius the Great (522–486 B.C.) saw it as a means of unifying his empire.

The original tenets of Zoroastrianism are obscure – its sacred text, the Zend-Avesta, is a body of oral tradition probably not written until about A.D. 400 – but it broke sharply with the Persians' previous belief in many gods. It taught that there is one God, Ormazd, assisted by a hierarchy of subordinate spirits. Ormazd created two opposing forces, Truth and Untruth, and rewarded or condemned men after death according to their actions on Earth. In certain respects, the religion seems to be a parallel to Judaism and a predecessor of Christianity. The priests were known as Magi, a term inherited from the previous Persian religion, from which comes the word "magic". Central to its rituals were the use of fire, the sacrifice of bulls, and the drinking of an intoxicant, "haoma".

Zoroastrianism was undermined when Alexander the Great conquered Persia in 330 B.C., but flourished again under Persia's Sassanid dynasty from A.D. 224 until 642, when the Muslims overran Persia. It is now practised by 10,000 in Iran and 85,000 Parsees ("Persians") in India, descendants of those who fled Muslim rule.

ZOROASTRIAN GOD *Ormazd, the source of truth, was symbolised by the pure light of the Sun. The earliest representations of the god were as a winged disc – from which various hovering, winged figures were developed.*

---

unit of the Union Army in the American Civil War. [French, from *zwāwa,* Algerian tribal name.]

zounds (zowndz, zŏŏndz) *interj.* Also **swounds** (zwowndz, zowndz, zŏŏndz), **swouns** (zwownz, zownz, zŏŏnz). *Archaic.* Used to express anger, surprise, or indignation. [Euphemism for *God's wounds.*]

zoy·si·a (zóyzi-ə) *n.* Any of several creeping grasses of the genus *Zoysia,* native to Asia and Australia, and widely cultivated as a lawn grass. [New Latin *Zoysia;* after Karl von *Zois* (died 1800), German botanist.]

ZPG zero population growth.

Z-pro·pyl·pi·per·i·dine (zéd-prō-pil-pi-pérri-deen, -pī-, -din) *n.* **Coniine** *(see).*

Zr The symbol for the element zirconium.

zuc·chet·to (zŏŏ-kéttō, tsŏō-) *n., pl.* **-tos.** *Roman Catholic Church.* A skullcap worn by clergymen, varying in colour according to the rank of the wearer. It is white, red, or purple for a pope, cardinal, or bishop respectively. [Italian, incorrect diminutive of *zucca,* gourd, head, from Late Latin *cucutia,* gourd, probably from Latin *cucurbita,* GOURD.]

zuc·chi·ni (zŏŏ-kéeni) *n., pl.* **zucchini.** *Chiefly U.S.* A courgette. [Italian, plural of *zuchino,* diminutive of *zucca,* gourd. See **zucchetto.**]

Zuck·er·man (zúckərmən), **Solly, Baron** (1904–). South African-born British scientist. Trained as an anatomist, he served as chief scientific adviser to the British government (1964–71). His books include *Scientists and War* (1966) and *From Apes to Warlords* (1978).

Zug·spitz·e (tsŏŏk-shpitsə). Mountain of southern West Germany. Situated in the Bavarian Alps near the Austrian border, it is the highest peak of West Germany, 2963 metres (9721 feet).

zug·zwang (tsŏŏk-tsvang) *n.* In chess, a situation in which a player must take his turn, even though it is to his disadvantage.

~*tr.v.* **zugzwanged, -zwanging, -zwangs.** To force (one's opponent) into such a situation. [German : *Zug,* (a) move + *Zwang,* force, compulsion.]

Zui·der Zee (zídər zée; *Dutch* zóydər záy). Former inlet of the North Sea, northeastern Netherlands. A drainage project (begun 1920) separated the inlet from the sea by a dyke (completed 1932), ·dividing it into the Ijsselmeer and the Waddenzee.

Zuid-Holland, Zuidholland. .See **South Holland.**

Zu·lu (zŏō-lōō) *n., pl.* **-lus** or collectively **Zulu. 1.** A member of a tall, Negroid people of southeastern Africa, formerly a powerful warrior nation, and now living chiefly in northeastern Natal. **2.** The Bantu language spoken by this people. —**Zu·lu** *adj.*

Zu·lu·land (zŏōlŏō-land). Southern African region, formerly in northeastern Natal province. The historic home of the Zulus, it rose to power during the early 19th century, resisting the Boer settlers until its final defeat by the British (1879). Part of Natal from 1897, it now corresponds approximately to the Bantu homeland of Kwa-Zulu.

zup·pa in·gle·se (tsŏŏppə ing-gláy-say) *n.* A pudding resembling a trifle, originally made with a macaroon base. [Italian, "English soup".]

Zü·rich (zéwr-ik, zóor-; *German* tsǘ-ri̱kh). Capital of Zürich canton, northeastern Switzerland. Situated on the river Limmat on the north shore of Lake Zurich, it is the cultural centre of German-speaking Switzerland, and is best known for its banking and financial facilities.

Zweig (tsvīk), **Stefan** (1881–1942). Austrian Jewish writer. Influenced by Freud, he was a prolific and popular writer of both fiction and non-fiction. His best-known work is the novel *Beware of Pity* (1939).

zwie·back (zwée-bak, -baak ‖ zwi̱-, swi̱-, swée-) *n.* A type of bread, usually sweetened, baked first as a loaf and later cut into slices and toasted. [German *Zwieback,* "twice-baked (bread)".]

Zwing·li (zwíng-li, swíng-; *German* tsvíng-). **Ulrich** (1484–1531). Swiss Protestant reformer. Ordained as a Roman Catholic priest (1506), he became a preacher in Zurich (1518) where he spoke out against the selling of indulgences. He became leader of the Reformation in Switzerland but was killed in an attack on Zurich by the Catholic forest cantons. He predated Luther in many of his ideas and greatly influenced Calvin.

Zwing·li·an (zwíng-li-ən, swíng-, tsvíng-, -gli-) *adj.* Of or pertaining to Zwingli or to his theological system, especially his doctrine that the physical body of Christ is not present in the Eucharist and that the ceremony is merely a symbolic commemoration of Christ's death.

~*n.* A follower of Zwingli. —**Zwing·li·an·ism** *n.* —**Zwing·li·an·ist** *n.*

zwit·ter·i·on (zwíttər-ī-ən, tsvíttər-) *n. Physics.* An ion carrying both a positive and a negative charge, thus forming an electrically neutral molecule. [German *Zwitterion,* "mongrel ion" : *Zwitter,* mongrel, hybrid, from Old High German *zwitar(a)n,* from *zwi-,* twice + ION.] —**zwit·ter·i·on·ic** (-ī-ónnik) *adj.*

Zwor·y·kin (zwáwrikin), **Vladimir Kosma** (1889–). U.S. physicist. Born in Russia, he took U.S. citizenship in 1924. He invented the iconoscope (1938), the first practical television camera, and helped to develop the electron microscope (1939).

zyg·a·poph·y·sis (zíggə-póffi-siss, zígə-) *n., pl.* **-ses** (-seez). *Anatomy.* Either of two usually paired processes of a vertebra that articulate with corresponding parts of·adjacent vertebrae. [ZYG(O)- + APOPHYSIS.] —**zyg·a·po·phys·e·al** (-sée-əl, -pə-fī-zi-əl) *adj.*

zygo-, zyg- *comb. form.* Indicates: **1.** Yoke or pair; for example, **zygodactyl, zygapophysis. 2.** Union or fusion; for example, **zygospore, zygomorphic.** [New Latin, from Greek *zugon,* yoke.]

zy·go·dac·tyl (zīgō-dáktil, zíggə-) *adj.* Also **zy·go·dac·tyl·ous** (-əss). Having two toes projecting forwards and two projecting backwards. Said of certain birds.

~*n.* A zygodactyl bird.

zy·go·ma (zī-gṓ-mə, zi-) *n., pl.* **-mata** (-mətə) or **-mas. 1.** The zygomatic bone. **2.** The zygomatic arch. [New Latin, from Greek *zugṓma,* bolt, bar, yoke, from *zugoun,* to yoke, connect.] —**zy·go·mat·ic** (zī-gō-máttik, -gə-, zi-) *adj.*

zygomatic arch *n.* The bony arch in vertebrates that extends along the side or front of the skull beneath the orbit. Also called "zygoma".

zygomatic bone *n.* A small quadrangular bone in vertebrates on the side of the face below the eye, forming, in mammals, part of the orbit and part of the zygomatic arch. Also called "cheekbone", "jugal", "malar", "zygoma".

zy·go·mor·phic (zīgō-mórfik, zíggō-) *adj.* Also **zy·go·mor·phous** (-fəss). Bilaterally symmetrical so as to be capable of being symmetrically divided only along a single longitudinal plane. Said of flowers. Compare **actinomorphic.** [ZYGO- + -MORPHIC.] —**zy·go·mor·phism** *n.*

zy·go·sis (zī-gṓ-siss, zi-) *n., pl.* **-ses** (-seez). The union of gametes to form a zygote; conjugation. [ZYG(O)- + -OSIS.]

zy·go·spore (zígō-spawr, zíggō- ‖ -spōr) *n.* A thick-walled spore formed from the zygote in certain algae or fungi.

zy·gote (zī-gōt, zíggōt) *n.* The cell formed by the union of two gametes. [Greek *zugōtos,* joined, yoked, from *zugoun,* to join, to yoke.] —**zy·got·ic** (zī-góttik, zi-) *adj.* —**zy·got·i·cal·ly** *adv.*

zy·go·tene (zígə-teen, zíggə-) *n.* The second stage of meiotic prophase during which the homologous chromosomes pair to form bivalents. [ZYGO(TE) + -TENE.]

zy·mase (zī-mayz, -mayss) *n.* The enzyme complex, first isolated from yeast, that converts hexose sugars to ethanol and carbon dioxide. [ZYM(O)- + -ASE.]

–zyme *n. comb. form.* Indicates an enzyme; for example, **lysozyme.** [Greek *zumē,* leaven.]

zymo-, zym– *comb. form.* Indicates fermentation; for example, **zymolysis, zymase.** [New Latin, from Greek *zumē,* leaven.]

zy·mo·gen (zī-mō-jen, -mə-, -jən) *n.* The inactive protein precursor of an enzyme. [ZYMO- + -GEN.]

zy·mo·gen·ic (zī-mō-jénnik, -mə-) *adj.* Also **zy·mog·e·nous** (zī-mójinəss, zi-). **1.** Of or pertaining to a zymogen. **2.** Capable of causing fermentation. **3.** Enzyme-producing.

zy·mol·o·gy (zī-móllǝji) *n.* The chemistry of fermentation. [New Latin *zymologia* : ZYMO- + -LOGY.] —**zy·mo·log·ic** (-mə-lójik), **zy·mo·log·ic·al** *adj.* —**zy·mol·o·gist** (zī-móllǝjist) *n.*

zy·mol·y·sis (zī-mólli-siss) *n.* Fermentation. Also called "zymosis". [ZYMO- + -LYSIS.] —**zy·mo·lyt·ic** (zímə-líttik) *adj.*

zy·mom·e·ter (zī-mómmitər) *n.* An instrument used for determining the degree of fermentation. [ZYMO- + -METER.]

zy·mo·scope (zímə-skōp) *n.* An instrument used to determine fermentation efficiency by measuring the amount of carbon dioxide produced. [ZYMO- + -SCOPE.]

zy·mo·sis (zī-mṓ-siss, zi-) *n.* **1.** Zymolysis. **2.** *Medicine.* The process of infection or an infectious disease. [New Latin, from Greek *zumōsis,* fermentation, from *zumoun,* to leaven, ferment, from *zumē,* leaven.] —**zy·mot·ic** (-móttik) *adj.* —**zy·mot·i·cal·ly** *adv.*

zy·mur·gy (zī-murji) *n.* The branch of chemistry concerned with fermentation processes in brewing. [ZYM(O)- + -URGY.]

zzz, zzzz. A convention used to indicate, as in a cartoon, that a person is asleep.

zygodactyl *Several types of climbing birds have zygodactyl feet – ones with four toes, two pointing forwards and two backwards – to help them balance against vertical surfaces such as tree trunks. This is the foot of a great spotted woodpecker.*

Acknowledgments

The artwork illustrating the entries listed below is reproduced by kind permission of the Publishers. Features are shown in capital letters.

MITCHELL BEAZLEY LTD:

BONE, COLOSSEUM, ECLIPSE, ESCALATOR, HYDROFOIL, MACHINE GUN, MOLLUSC, MOSQUE, MOUNTAIN, MUSCLES, NITROGEN CYCLE, PERIODIC TABLE, PERISCOPE, ROAD, SPEAR, SPINAL CORD, STAR, SWORDS, TIDAL POWER, TRAIN, TREE.

ARNOLDO MONDADORI LTD:

Aardvark, Abyssinian Cat, Agrimony, Anteater, Armadillo, Asparagus, Bedbug, Bryophyte, Drone, Emu, Ermine, Euphorbia, Fig, FISH, Fox, Hackney, HORSE, INSECT (Life Cycle of a Fly), Larva, Lemon, Manx Cat, Molerat, Okapi, Olive, Pomegranate, Porcupine, Prickly Pear, Remora, REPTILE, Shrew, Siamese Cat, SNAKE, Square, Sugar Cane, Tuatara, Vole, Walnut, Winter Aconite, Winter Cherry, Wolf.

Some of the illustrations in this dictionary are taken or adapted from the following books, first published by Reader's Digest.

Book of British Birds; Book of the British Countryside; Book of the Car; Complete Guide to Needlework; Do It Yourself; Family Health Guide; Food from your Garden; Heritage of Britain; Household Manual; Illustrated Guide to Britain; Inventions that Changed the World; The Last Two Million Years; Library of Modern Knowledge; Living World of Animals; Nature Lover's Library; North American Wildlife; The Past All Around Us; Success with House Plants; Things to Make and Do.

Artwork specially commissioned by Reader's Digest for the Great Illustrated Dictionary was produced by the artists listed below:

Hayward and Martin Ltd, Mike Jackson, Pavel Kostal, Malcolm McGregor, Eric Robson, Ted Williams.

Photographs appearing in Reader's Digest Great Illustrated Dictionary came from the sources listed below.
Entries are identified by the headword.
Features are shown in capital letters.
Work commissioned by Reader's Digest is shown in italics.
Where necessary, photographs in features are also identified by position within the feature: *T* = **Top**, *B* = **Bottom**, *L* = **Left**, *R* = **Right**, *C* = **Centre**.

Aardwolf: Simon Trevor/Bruce Coleman Ltd. **Abalone:** Jane Burton/Bruce Coleman Ltd. **Abu Simbel:** Gunter Heil/ZEFA. **Acanthus:** Michael Holford. **Accipiter:** Hans Reinhard/Bruce Coleman Ltd. **Acorn:** John Markham/Bruce Coleman Ltd. **Acorn Barnacle:** David & Katie Urry/Ardea London. **ADAM** Both from National Trust. **Adobe:** Gene Ahrens/Bruce Coleman Ltd. **Aeolipile:** Mary Evans Picture Library. **African Marigold:** Eric Crichton/Bruce Coleman Ltd. **African Violets:** Eric Crichton/Bruce Coleman Ltd. **Agama:** Mark N. Boulton/Bruce Coleman Ltd. **Agamemnon:** Konrad Helbig/ZEFA. **Agave:** B & C Calhoun/Bruce Coleman Ltd. **Ageratum:** Eric Crichton/Bruce Coleman Ltd. **Agouti:** Michael Freeman/Bruce Coleman Ltd. **Ajax:** Michael Holford. **Alabaster:** Michael Holford. **Alder Fly:** Jane Burton/Bruce Coleman Ltd. **Alexanders:** Eric Crichton/Bruce Coleman Ltd. **Alexander the Great:** P.H. Teuffen/ZEFA. **Ali Baba:** Mary Evans Picture Library. **ALLEGORY** Reproduced by courtesy of the Trustees, The National Gallery, London. **Aloe:** M.P. Kahl/Bruce Coleman Ltd. **Altamira:** Michael Holford. **Alyssum:** Eric Crichton/Bruce Coleman Ltd. **Amaranthus:** Eric Crichton/Bruce Coleman Ltd. **Amaryllis:** Francisco Futil/Bruce Coleman Ltd. **Amazons:** Michael Holford. **Ambulacrum:** Jane Burton/Bruce Coleman Ltd. **Amethyst:** Institute of Geological Sciences. **AMERICAN INDEPENDENCE** *TL* American Antiquarian Society, *TC* Charles Wilson Peale, Pennsylvania Academy of Fine Arts, *TR* Metropolitan Museum of Art, Gift of William H. Huntington, 1823, *CL* Rembrandt Peale, United States Information Service, London, *BL* National Gallery of Art, Washington, D.C., *BR* John Trumbull, Yale University Art Gallery. **Ammonite:** J. Fennell/Bruce Coleman Ltd. **Amoeba:** John Clegg/Ardea London. **Amphipod:** Inigo Everson/Bruce Coleman Ltd. **Amphitheatre:** Nick Holt/ZEFA. **Andes:** Michael Freeman/Bruce Coleman Ltd. **Andrea del Sarto:** Robert Harding Picture Library/Louvre. **Anemone:** B & C Calhoun/Bruce Coleman Ltd. **Angel Falls:** Adrian Warren/Ardea London. **Angel Fish:** Jane Burton/Bruce Coleman Ltd. **Angle Shades:** John Fennell/Bruce Coleman Ltd. **Annual Rings:** A.J. Deane/Bruce Coleman Ltd. **Anopheles:** Kim Taylor/Bruce Coleman Ltd. **Ansate Cross:** Michael Holford. **ANT** Graham Pizzey/Bruce Coleman Ltd. **Antarctica:** Edwin Mickleburgh/Ardea London. **Anthurium:** Eric Crichton/Bruce Coleman Ltd. **Antler:** Martin W. Grosnick/Ardea London. **Anubis:** Michael Holford. **Aphrodite:** Michael Holford. **Apis:** Michael Holford. **Apricot:** S. Roberts/Ardea London. **Aqueduct:** I.R. Beames/Ardea London. **Archaeopteryx:** Peter Green/Ardea London. **Archaic Smile:** Acropolis Museum, Athens/Robert Harding Picture Library. **Archer Fish:** P. Morris/Ardea London. **Arctic Fox:** Brian Hawkes/Robert Harding Picture Library. **Ard:** Foto Leidmann/ZEFA. **Aril:** Eric Lindgren/Ardea London. **Arjuna:** Michael Holford. **Armadillo:** Francois Gohier/Ardea London. **Armillary Sphere:** Michael Holford. **Armorial Bearing:** Mary Evans Picture Library. **Arrowhead:** Bob Gibbons/Ardea London. **ART DECO** *TL* Angelo Hornak/Vision International, *TR* Angelo Hornak/Vision International, *CL* Richard Bryant, *BL* Angelo Hornak/Vision International, *BR* H.E. Kiessling/Bridgeman Art Library. **ARTHURIAN LEGEND** *TL* Bibliotheque Nationale, Paris Ms FR95 fol 159 V, *TR* Bibliotheque Nationale, Paris Ms R577 fol 74V, *B* British Museum Add Ms 10294 fol 94. **ART NOUVEAU** *TL* Angelo Hornak/Vision International, *TC* Angelo Hornak/Vision International, *TR* Hunterian Art Gallery, University of Glasgow, Mackintosh Collection, *CL* ZEFA, *R* Bridgeman Art Library, *BL* Bridgeman Art Library, *BC* Bridgeman Art Library. **Ash:** Eric Crichton/Bruce Coleman Ltd. **Aspen:** Jeff Foott/Bruce Coleman Ltd. **Ass:** Ardea London. **Atahualpa:** Mary Evans Picture Library. **Athena:** National Museum Athens/Robert Harding Picture Library. **Aubergine:** Eric Crichton/Bruce Coleman Ltd. **Aubrietia:** Eric Crichton/Bruce Coleman Ltd. **Audubon:** Michael Holford. **Augustus:** British Museum/Robert Harding Picture Library. **Aurochs:** Mary Evans Picture Library. **Avatar:** Michael Holford. **Avocado:** Eric Crichton/Bruce Coleman Ltd. **Avocet:** M.P. Kahl/Bruce Coleman Ltd. **Axolotl:** Jane Burton/Bruce Coleman Ltd. **Ayers Rock:** Eric Crichton/Bruce Coleman Ltd. **AZTEC** *T* Biblioteca Nazionale, Florence, *B* Ianthe Ruthven/Michael Holford. **Azalea:** Eric Crichton/Bruce Coleman Ltd.

Ba: Michael Holford. **Baboon:** Norman Myers/Bruce Coleman Ltd. **Babylon:** L. Schranner/ZEFA. **Bacchae:** Michael Holford. **BACTERIUM** all Tony Brain/Science Photo Library. **Bactrian Camel:** J. Bitsch/ZEFA. **Badlands:** R. Everts/ZEFA. **BADGER** J.P. Ferrero/Ardea London. **Bagworm:** Peter Ward/Bruce Coleman Ltd. **Bald Eagle:** Jeff Foott/Bruce Coleman Ltd. **Balloon:** M.P. Kahl/Bruce Coleman Ltd. **Balm:** John Mason/Ardea London. **Baltimore Oriole:** John Dunning/Ardea London. **Bamboo:** Sybil Sassoon/Robert Harding Picture Library. **Banana:** Richard Nicholas/ZEFA. **Bandicoot:** Bruce Coleman Ltd. **Baneberry:** A.P. Paterson/Ardea London. **Banjo Clock:** Michael Holford. **Baobab:** Jane Burton/Bruce Coleman Ltd. **Barbary Ape:** Bruce Coleman Ltd. **Barge:** Starfoto/ZEFA. **Barge Board:** Andy Williams/Robert Harding Picture Library. **Barn Owl:** John Markham/Bruce Coleman Ltd. **Barometer:** Michael Holford. **Barque:** N. Bahnsen/ZEFA. **Barracuda:** P. Morris/Ardea London. **BAROQUE** *L* Bridgeman Art Library, *TR* Reproduced by courtesy of the Trustees, The National Gallery, London, *BR* James Austin/Robert Harding Picture Library. **Barrier Reef:** M.T. O'Keefe/Bruce Coleman Ltd. **Bartizan:** K. Praedel/ZEFA. **Basalt:** Trevor Wood/Robert Harding Picture Library. **Bascule:** Eric Crichton/Bruce Coleman Ltd. **Basilisk:** P. Morris/Ardea London. **Bas Relief:** Caroline Weaver/Ardea London. **Basset Hound:** Hans Reinhard/Bruce Coleman Ltd. **Bat:** R.J. Tulloch/Bruce Coleman Ltd. **Beagle:** Hans Reinhard/Bruce Coleman Ltd. **Bearberry:** J. Wightman/Ardea London. **Beardsley:** Mary Evans Picture Library. **Bearskin:** Jessica Anne Ehlers/Bruce Coleman Ltd. **BEAVER** Jack Swedberg/Ardea London. **Beefeaters:** Bruce Coleman Ltd. **Bellerophon:** Michael Holford. **Bellflower:** J.P. Ferrero/Ardea London. **Bell Jar:** Michael Holford. **Beluga:** Pat Morris/Ardea London. **Benin:** Michael Holford. **BERNINI** Dimitri Kessel, Life. © Time Inc/Colorific! **Bezant:** Michael Holford. **Bib:** Michael Holford. **Bilberry:** John Markham/Bruce Coleman Ltd. **Bird of Paradise:** Brian J. Coates/Bruce Coleman Ltd. **Bird of Paradise Flower:** M.P.L. Fogden/Bruce Coleman Ltd. **Bison:** Francisco Erize/Bruce Coleman Ltd. **Bittern:** Bruce Coleman Ltd. **Bittersweet:** Bob Gibbons/Ardea London. **Blackbird:** P.A. Hinchliffe/Bruce Coleman Ltd. **Blackcurrant:** Eric Crichton/Bruce Coleman Ltd. **BLACK HOLE** Dr. W.H. Fu/University of California/Science Photo Library. **Black Grouse:** Gunter Ziesler/Bruce Coleman Ltd. **Black Widow:** Jack Dermid/Bruce Coleman Ltd. **Bladder Campion:** Hans Reinhard/Bruce Coleman Ltd. **Bleeding Heart:** Bob & Clara Calhoun/Bruce Coleman Ltd. **Blesbok:** Ardea London. **Blister Beetle:** Jane Burton/Bruce Coleman Ltd. **BLOOD** *T* London Scientific Fotos, *C* Science Photo Library, *B* Dr. G.F. Leedale/Biophotos. **Bluebell:** Adrian Davies/Bruce Coleman Ltd. **Blueberry:** Pekka Helo/Bruce Coleman Ltd. **Blue Jay:** Bill Brooks/Bruce Coleman Ltd. **Bobcat:** Kenneth W. Fink/Ardea London. **Boll:** R. Bond/ZEFA. **Bonnet Monkey:** G.K. Brown/Ardea London. **Booby:** Brian Hawkes/Robert Harding Picture Library. **Bottle Nosed Dolphin:** Norman Tomalin/Bruce Coleman Ltd. **Bower Bird:** Cyril Laubscher/Bruce Coleman Ltd. **Bow Street Runner:** Mary Evans Picture Library. **Boxer:** Hans Reinhard/Bruce Coleman Ltd. **Bracken:** Sinclair Stammers/Bruce Coleman Ltd. **Brazil Nuts:** Denis Moore/Robert Harding Picture Library. **Breadfruit:** A.F. Soper/Bruce Coleman Ltd. **Breaker:** Dr. D. James/ZEFA. **Bream:** Allan Power/Bruce Coleman Ltd. **Bridle:** Blume/ZEFA. **Broadbean:** Eric Crichton/Bruce Coleman Ltd. **Broadbill:** Norman Tomalin/Bruce Coleman Ltd. **Broccoli:** Eric Crichton/Bruce Coleman Ltd. **Bromeliad:** John Mason/Ardea London. **BRONZE AGE** Hirmer Fotoarchiv. **Brooch:** Michael Holford. **Brown Bear:** Bruce Coleman Ltd. **BRUEGEL** Kunsthistoriches Museum, Vienna. **BRUNELLESCHI** both Scala. **Bryony:** J.A. Bailey/Ardea London. **Buck:** S.C. Porter/Bruce Coleman Ltd. **Buckeye:** Wardene Weisser/Ardea London. **BUDDHISM** *L* British Museum, *R* Bill O'Connor/Robert Harding Picture Library. **Budgerigar:** Bruce Coleman Ltd. **Buffalo:** Peter Davey/Bruce Coleman Ltd. **Bufflehead:** Joseph van Wormen/Bruce Coleman Ltd. **Bugloss:** Bob Gibbons/Ardea London. **Bulldog:** S. McKenna/ZEFA. **Bullfinch:** Bruce Coleman Ltd. **Bullfrog:** Hans & Judy Beste/Ardea London. **Burnous:** Konrad Helbig/ZEFA. **Bushbaby:** P. Davey/Bruce Coleman Ltd. **Bustard:** L.R. Dawson/Bruce Coleman Ltd. **Bustle:** Victoria & Albert Museum/Robert Harding Picture Library. **BUTTERFLY** All photographs by Eric Lingren/Ardea London except *B* Ian Beames/Ardea London. **Butterfly Fish:** Allan Power/Bruce Coleman Ltd. **BYZANTIUM** *TR* Scala, *B* Stylitzes Codex, Biblioteca Nacional, Madrid.

Cabbage: Bruce Coleman Ltd. **Cabriole:** Michael Holford. **Cacao:** M.P.L. Fogden/Bruce Coleman Ltd. **Cacomistle:** Kenneth W. Fink/Ardea London. **Cactus:** Eric Crichton/Bruce Coleman Ltd. **Caddis Worm:** Dr. R. Sauer/ZEFA. **Caesar:** Michael Holford. **Calculating Machine:** Michael Holford. **Californian Poppy:** Robert P. Carr/Bruce Coleman Ltd. **Camel:** G.K. Brown/Ardea London. **Camellia:** A.P. Paterson/Ardea London. **Camouflage:** G. Ziesler/ZEFA. **Campanile:** John Ross/Robert Harding Picture Library. **Canada Goose:** Jack Dermid/Bruce Coleman Ltd. **Canary:** John Markham/Bruce Coleman Ltd. **Cannabis Plant:** G. Mabbs/ZEFA. **Canoe:** Brian J. Coates/Bruce Coleman Ltd. **Capital:** Mary Evans Picture Library. **Capybara:** Francisco Erize/Bruce Coleman Ltd. **Caracal:** R.I.M. Campbell/Bruce Coleman Ltd. **Caracara:** Francisco Erize/Bruce Coleman Ltd. **Caribou:** Martin W. Grosnick/Ardea London. **Carnation:** Eric Crichton/Bruce Coleman Ltd. **Carnelian:** Institute of Geological Sciences. **Carrion Crow:** P.A. Hinchliffe/Bruce Coleman Ltd. **Cartouche:** ZEFA. **CARTIER-BRESSON** Henri Cartier-Bresson/John Hillelson Agency Ltd. **Caryatid:** Michael Holford. **Cashew:** T. Lancefield/ZEFA. **Cassowary:** Rod Williams/Bruce Coleman Ltd. **Catalpa:** Eric Crichton/Bruce Coleman Ltd. **Catfish:** Hans Reinhard/Bruce Coleman Ltd. **Cauliflower:** Bruce Coleman Ltd. **Cave Painting:** ZEFA. **Cedar of Lebanon:** Eric Crichton/Bruce Coleman Ltd. **CELL DIVISION** All: Eric V. Grave/Science Photo Library. **Centaur:** Mary Evans Picture Library. **Centipede:** C.S. Frith/Bruce Coleman Ltd. **Chalice:** Michael Holford. **Chambered Nautilus:** J.L. Mason/Ardea London. **Chameleon:** P. Davey/Bruce Coleman Ltd. **Chamois:** J.P. Ferrero/Ardea London. **Chariot:** Michael Holford. **Chateau:** Ronald Sheridan/ZEFA. **CHARTRES** All: Sonia Halliday. **Chaucer:** Mary Evans Picture Library. **Cheetah:** M.P. Kahl/Bruce Coleman Ltd. **Cherry:** Eric Crichton/Bruce Coleman Ltd. **Cheshire Cat:** Mary Evans Picture Library. **Chicory:** Hans Reinhard/Bruce Coleman Ltd. **Chillies:** Sybil Sassoon/Robert Harding Picture Library. **Chimpanzee:** Peter Jackson/Bruce Coleman Ltd. **Chinchilla:** Jane Burton/Bruce Coleman Ltd. **Chinoiserie:** Michael Holford. **Chiton:** Michael Holford. **CHRISTIANITY** *L* Bridgeman Art Library, *R* Scala. **Christmas Rose:** Hans Reinhard/Bruce Coleman Ltd. **Chrysalis:** W. Kratz/ZEFA. **Chrysanthemum:** Eric Crichton/Bruce Coleman Ltd. **Churn:** Mary Evans Picture Library. **Cicada:** John R. Brownlie/Bruce Coleman Ltd. **Cichlid:** P. Morris/Ardea London. **Cinquefoil:** Charlie Ott/Bruce Coleman Ltd. **Cithara:** Michael Holford. **Civet:** Francisco Erize/Bruce Coleman Ltd. **CIVIL WAR** Weidenfeld & Nicolson. **Clavichord:** Mary Evans Picture Library. **Clematis:** Eric Crichton/Bruce Coleman Ltd. **Cloisonne:** Michael Holford. **Cloisters:** Michael Holford. **CLOUD** Cirrus, Stratocumulus, Cirrostratus & Cumulus R.K. Pilsbury/Bruce Coleman Ltd. Nimbostratus, Cirrocumulus, Altocumulus, Altostratus & Cumulonimbus Alan Watts and Stratus Professor Scorer. **CLOWN** *L* BBC Hulton Picture Library, *R* Sylvie Mercier. **Cobra:** Dr. Frieder Sauer/Bruce Coleman Ltd. **Cobweb:** John Shaw/Bruce Coleman Ltd. **Cockatoo:** John R. Brownlie/Bruce Coleman Ltd. **Cockle:** Jane Burton/Bruce Coleman Ltd. **Cock of the Rock:** L.C. Marigo/Bruce Coleman Ltd. **Coconut Palm:** Adrian Warren/Ardea London. **Coffee Beans:** L.C. Marigo/Bruce Coleman Ltd. **Coley:** Jane Burton/Bruce Coleman Ltd. **Colobus Monkey:** R. Williams/Bruce Coleman Ltd. **Colorado Beetle:** Udo Hirsch/Bruce Coleman Ltd. **Colossus:** Michael Holford. **Columbine:** Wayne Lankinen/Bruce Coleman Ltd. **Compass:** B. Benjamin/ZEFA. **Composite Order:** Mary Evans Picture Library. **Compound Eye:** G. Doré/Bruce Coleman Ltd. **Conch Shell:** Nicholas Devore III/Bruce Coleman Ltd. **Condor:** J. van Wormer/Bruce Coleman Ltd. **Confucius:** Mary Evans Picture Library. **CONSTABLE** Reproduced by Courtesy of the Trustees, The National Gallery, London. **Containers:** Robert Harding Picture Library. **Contrail:** Walter Rawlings/Robert Harding Picture Library. **Coot:** Gordon Langsbury/Bruce Coleman Ltd. **Cope:** Michael Holford. **Coracle:** *Patrick Thurston.* **Coral:** Bill Wood/Robert Harding Picture

Library. **Coral Snake:** Jack Dermid/Bruce Coleman Ltd. **Corinthian:** Michael Holford. **Cormorant:** M. Dohrn/Bruce Coleman Ltd. **Corydalis:** Hans Reinhard/Bruce Coleman Ltd. **Cot:** G. Rettinghaus/ZEFA. **Cotton:** Stephen J. Krasemann/Bruce Coleman Ltd. **Cottontail:** Leonard Lee Rue III/Bruce Coleman Ltd. **Courgette:** Norman Owen Tomalin/Bruce Coleman Ltd. **Cowberry:** N.A. Callow/Robert Harding Picture Library. **Cowrie:** Adrian Davies/Bruce Coleman Ltd. **Cowslip:** E. Duscher/Bruce Coleman Ltd. **Coyote:** Tom Willock/Ardea London. **Crab:** Neville Fox-Davies/Bruce Coleman Ltd. **Cranberry:** Charlie Ott/Bruce Coleman Ltd. **Crane:** Bruce Coleman Ltd. **Crater:** ZEFA. **Creeping Jenny:** Hans Reinhard/Bruce Coleman Ltd. **Crocodile:** Simon Trevor/Bruce Coleman Ltd. **Crocus:** R. Carr/Bruce Coleman Ltd. **Crookes Radiometer:** Michael Holford. **Crossbill:** W. Lankinen/Bruce Coleman Ltd. **Crosswort:** Eric Crichton/Bruce Coleman Ltd. **Crucifix:** Michael Holford. **Crystal:** ZEFA. **Cubism:** Collection: State Museum Kroller-Muller, Otterlo, The Netherlands © A.D.A.G.P. 1984. **Cuckoo:** Hans Reinhard/Bruce Coleman Ltd. **Cuneiform:** Jennifer Fry/Bruce Coleman Ltd. **Cupid:** Michael Holford. **Curassow:** Hans Reinhard/Bruce Coleman Ltd. **Curlew:** Gordon Langsbury/Bruce Coleman Ltd. **Cuscus:** J.P. Ferrero/Ardea London. **Custard Apple:** J.L. Mason/Ardea London. **Cuttlefish:** P. Morris/Ardea London. **Cycad:** Jan Taylor/Bruce Coleman Ltd.

Dado: Duchcov Castle/Robert Harding Picture Library. **DADA** *T* Courtesy Sidney Janis Gallery, N.Y. © A.D.A.G.P. 1984. *B* Lord's Gallery, London © S.P.A.D.E.M. 1984. **Dagger:** Michael Holford. **Daisy:** Geoff Doré/Bruce Coleman Ltd. **Damascene:** Michael Holford. **Damson:** Eric Crichton/Bruce Coleman Ltd. **Dandelion:** Eric Crichton/Bruce Coleman Ltd. **Darwin:** Ardea London. **Davy Lamp:** Michael Holford. **DEAD SEA SCROLLS** Israel Museum, Jerusalem. **Death Watch Beetle:** J.L. Mason/Ardea London. **Decoy:** J.L. Mason/Ardea London. **Degas:** Courtauld Institute Galleries, London (Courtauld Collection). **Delphi:** Michael Holford. **Delphinium:** Eric Crichton/Bruce Coleman Ltd. **Demeter:** Michael Holford. **Denarius:** Michael Holford. **Dendrites:** Jane Burton/Bruce Coleman Ltd. **Derringer:** Rainbird/Robert Harding Picture Library. **DESERT** *T* Leidmann/ZEFA, *C* and *B* Tony Morrison. **Diamond:** Institute of Geological Sciences. **Diamondback:** Jack Dermid/Bruce Coleman Ltd. **DICKENS** Michael Holford. **Diffraction:** Michael Holford. **Dill:** Starfoto/ZEFA. **Dingo:** Jen & Des Bartlett/Bruce Coleman Ltd. **Diogenes:** Mary Evans Picture Library. **Dionysus:** Michael Holford. **Dip:** M. Pitner/ZEFA. **Dolphin:** Alain Compost/Bruce Coleman Ltd. **DOME** *T* Michael Holford, *B* Mike Yamashita/Aspect Picture Library. **Donjon:** Michael Holford. **Donkey:** ZEFA. **Doric Order:** Mary Evans Picture Library. **Dormer:** Margaret Collier/Robert Harding Picture Library. **Dormouse:** Hans Reinhard/Bruce Coleman Ltd. **Dourocouli:** R. Williams/Bruce Coleman Ltd. **Dove:** Bruce Coleman Ltd. **Downing Street:** Bruce Coleman Ltd. **DRAGON** *L* Narodni Galerie V Praze, *R* Gulbenkian Museum of Oriental Art, University of Durham. **Dragon Tree:** Brian Hawkes/Robert Harding Picture Library. **Dromedary:** K. Goebel/ZEFA. **Druids:** Bruce Coleman Ltd. **Drum:** Michael Holford. **Druse:** H. Schumacher/ZEFA. **Dry dock:** Robert Harding Picture Library. **Duiker:** Wardene Weisser/Ardea London. **Dunes:** Carol Hughes/Bruce Coleman Ltd. **DURER** Michael Holford. **Dutchman's Breeches:** Lynn M. Stone/Bruce Coleman Ltd. **Dyke-Sea:** E. Winter/ZEFA. **Dyke-Inland:** D.H. Teuffen/ZEFA.

EARTHQUAKE Stan Wayman/Life April, 1964/Time Inc. ©/Colorific! **Easter Egg:** Michael Holford. **Easter Island:** Colin Caket/ZEFA. **Echidna:** John Markham/Bruce Coleman Ltd. **Eclosion:** Dr. F. Sauer/ZEFA. **Edelweiss:** Eric Crichton/Bruce Coleman Ltd. **Egret:** Kenneth W. Fink/Ardea London. **EGYPT** all Michael Holford. **Eland:** Mark N. Boulton/Bruce Coleman Ltd. **Electrostatic Generator:** Michael Holford. **Elephant:** Lee Lyon/Bruce Coleman Ltd. **Elephant Seal:** Brian Hawkes/Robert Harding Picture Library. **Ely:** *Patrick Thurston.* **Embrasure:** Michael Holford. **Embroidery:** Michael Holford. **Enamel:** Michael Holford. **Endomorph:** Manfred Becker/ZEFA. **ENGRAVING** The Metropolitan Museum of Art, Fletcher Fund, 1919. **Epstein Sculpture:** Walter Rawlings/Robert Harding Picture Library. **Equestrian:** Konrad Helbig/ZEFA. **Escapement:** Michael Holford. **ETRUSCAN** *T* Michael Holford, *B* Scala. **Ewer:** George Rainbird/American Museum in Britain, Bath/Robert Harding Picture Library. **Excavator:** Schlodien/ZEFA.

Fabergé Egg: Collection of Wartski's/Michael Holford. **Faience:** Michael Holford. **Falconry:** M. Freeman/Bruce Coleman Ltd. **Fallow Deer:** Leonard Lee Rue III/Bruce Coleman Ltd. **Fan:** Victoria & Albert Museum/Robert Harding Picture Library. **Fanlight:** N.A. Callow/Robert Harding Picture Library. **Fantail Pigeon:** Jane Burton/Bruce Coleman Ltd. **Fan Vaulting:** Michael Holford. **FAUVISM** Museum of Modern Art, New York. Gift of Mr. and Mrs. Charles Zadok © S.P.A.D.E.M. 1984. **Feather:** Frieder Sauer/Bruce Coleman Ltd. **Feather Palm:** Knight & Hunt Photo/ZEFA. **Felucca:** Ardea London. **Fencing:** Ung. Werbestudio/ZEFA. **FERN** Paul Wakefield/Bruce Coleman Ltd. **Fiddler Crab:** G.B. Frittie/Bruce Coleman Ltd. **Fig Bird:** Brian Coates/Bruce Coleman Ltd. **Figurine:** Michael Holford. **Filefish:** Jane Burton/Bruce Coleman Ltd. **Filigree:** Michael Holford. **Finger Board:** Michael Holford. **Fjord:** Ziesmann/ZEFA. **Fireworks:** H. Armstrong/ZEFA. **Flight Deck:** Jack Novak/ZEFA. **Flint:** Adrian Davies/Bruce Coleman Ltd. **Flintlock:** Photo by Bill Monaghan © George Rainbird Ltd/Robert Harding Picture Library. **Floe:** Geoff Renner/Robert Harding Picture Library. **Fluting:** Michael Holford. **Font:** Mary Evans Picture Library. **Fore-and-Aft Rig:** Sybil Sassoon/Robert Harding Picture Library. **Forge:** *Neil Holmes.* **Fork:** Michael Holford. **Fosbury Flop:** UWS/ZEFA. **Four-Poster:** Christina Gascoigne/Robert Harding Picture Library. **Frame:** Ardea London. **Fresco:** Michael Holford. **Friar Bird:** Ellis McNamara/Ardea London. **Frost:** Jon Gardey/Robert Harding Picture Library. **Fruit Bat:** Bruce Coleman Ltd. **Fruit Fly:** Anthony Healy/Bruce Coleman Ltd. **Fuchsia:** Udo Hirsch/Bruce Coleman Ltd. **Fur Seal:** Clem Haagner/Ardea London. **FUTURISM** Mr. and Mrs. Estorick/Photo Herbert Michel.

Gable: F.A.H. Bloemendal/ZEFA. **GALAXY** *T* © 1961 California Institute of Technology & Carnegie Institution of Washington, *BL* Space Frontiers, *BR* Science Photo Library. **Galley:** Michael Holford. **Gannet:** Gordon Langsbury/Bruce Coleman Ltd. **Garnet:** Institute of Geological Sciences. **Gargoyle:** Michael Holford. **Gazelle:** Joe van Wormer/Bruce Coleman Ltd. **Gecko:** Eric Lindgren/Ardea London. **GEM** all photographs from the Institute of Geological Sciences. **Gemsbok:** Francisco Erize/Bruce Coleman Ltd. **Genet:** Clem Haagner/Ardea London. **Geode:** ZEFA. **Geothermal:** Paolo Koch/ZEFA. **Gerbil:** James Simon/Bruce Coleman Ltd. **Geyser:** James Simon/Bruce Coleman Ltd. **Gibbon:** Norman Tomalin/Bruce Coleman Ltd. **Gila Monster:** Norman Myers/Bruce Coleman Ltd. **Giraffe:** Leonard Lee Rue III/Bruce Coleman Ltd. **Girandole:** Michael Holford. **Glacier:** M.N. Boulton/Bruce Coleman Ltd. **Gladiolus:** Ardea London. **Glassfish:** Jane Burton/Bruce Coleman Ltd. **Glastonbury Abbey:** *Malcolm Aird.* **Globe Thistle:** Peter Ward/Bruce Coleman Ltd. **Gloxinia:** William McPherson/Bruce Coleman Ltd. **Glow Worm:** P.A. Hinchliffe/Bruce Coleman Ltd. **Glyph:** Ziesmann/ZEFA. **Gnu:** Kenneth W. Fink/Ardea London. **Goat:** Hans Reinhard/Bruce Coleman Ltd. **Go-Away Bird:** Bruce Coleman Ltd. **Goldfish:** Hans Reinhard/Bruce Coleman Ltd. **Gondola:** Charles Henneghien/Bruce Coleman Ltd. **Gorilla:** Norman Tomalin/Bruce Coleman Ltd. **GOTHIC** all Michael Holford. **Gourd:** Eric Crichton/Bruce Coleman Ltd. **Grand Canyon:** Stella Martin. **Grapefruit:** Norman Tomalin/Bruce Coleman Ltd. **Grape Hyacinth:** Eric Crichton/Bruce Coleman Ltd. **Great Dane:** Hans Reinhard/Bruce Coleman Ltd. **Great Auk:** Mary Evans Picture Library. **Great Wall of China:** Norman Myers/Bruce Coleman Ltd. **Green Algae:** Jane Burton/Bruce Coleman Ltd. **Grimaldi:** Mary Evans Picture Library. **Grizzly Bear:** Stouffer Productions/Bruce Coleman Ltd. **Ground Squirrel:** Clem Haagner/Ardea London. **Guinea Fowl:** M.P. Kahl/Bruce Coleman Ltd. **Guinea Pig:** J.P. Ferrero/Ardea London.

Hackle: R. Bond/ZEFA. **Haddock:** P. Morris/Ardea London. **Hadrian:** Michael Holford. **Hadrian's Wall:** Bergmann/ZEFA. **Halo:** Bruce Coleman Ltd. **Halter:** G. Mabbs/ZEFA. **Hammerhead Shark:** Ron & Valerie Taylor/Ardea London. **Hang Glider:** Eric Crichton/Bruce Coleman Ltd. **Harlequin:** Michael Holford. **Harebells:** Hans Reinhard/Bruce Coleman Ltd. **Harpy:** Kenneth W. Fink/Ardea London. **Harvester:** G. Heilman/ZEFA. **Hathor:** Mary Evans Picture Library. **Hauberk:** Stadtbibliothek Nuremberg/Robert Harding Picture Library. **Hawksbill:** J.L. Mason/Ardea London. **Hebe:** Eric Crichton/Bruce Coleman Ltd. **HEAVEN & HELL** *T* Michael Holford, *B* M. Thonig/ZEFA. **Hedgehog:** Hans Reinhard/ZEFA. **Helicopter:** Jane Burton/Bruce Coleman Ltd. **Helmet:** Michael Holford. **Henge:** *Penny Tweedie.* **Herbaceous:** Ardea London. **Hercules:** Michael Holford. **Hibiscus:** Eric Crichton/Bruce Coleman Ltd. **Hieratic:** Michael Holford. **Hieroglyphic:** Charles Henneghien/Bruce Coleman Ltd. **High Relief:** Michael Holford. **Hind:** Brian Hawkes/Robert Harding Picture Library. **Hilt:** Michael Holford. **HINDUISM** all Michael Holford. **Hippodrome:** Ardea London. **Hippopotamus:** M.D. England/Ardea London. **HOCKNEY** 'A Bigger Splash'. Acrylic on canvas, © David Hockney 1967, Courtesy Petersburg Press/Bridgeman Art Library. **Honesty Seeds:** John Flowerdew/ZEFA. **Honeycomb:** W. Kratz/ZEFA. **Honey Fungus:** Adrian Davies/Bruce Coleman Ltd. **Honeysuckle:** John Fennell/Bruce Coleman Ltd. **Honiton Lace:** *Patrick Thurston.* **Hooded Seal:** Nir Lightfoot/Bruce Coleman Ltd. **Horn:** Mary Evans Picture Library. **Hornbill:** Sybil Sassoon/Robert Harding Picture Library. **Horned Owl:** P. Morris/Ardea London. **Horse Brass:** G. Mabbs/ZEFA. **Horseshoe Crab:** C.B. Frith/Bruce Coleman Ltd. **Horus:** Michael Holford. **HOVERCRAFT** Paul Kamper/ZEFA. **Howdah:** Michael Holford. **Hull:** Dr. K. Heydermann/Mulle/ZEFA. **Hummingbird:** Wardene Weisser/Ardea London. **HYDROFOIL** Jonathan T. Wright/Bruce Coleman Ltd. **Hydroplane:** W. Ostgathe/ZEFA. **Hypocaust:** Michael Holford. **Hyrax:** Kenneth W. Fink/Ardea London.

Ibex: Leonard Lee Rue III/Bruce Coleman Ltd. **Iceberg:** Francisco Erize/Bruce Coleman Ltd. **I Ching:** Michael Holford. **Icicle:** Gordon Langsbury/Bruce Coleman Ltd. **Iguana:** Harold Schultz/Bruce Coleman Ltd. **Imbricate:** Michael Allen Bolton/ZEFA. **Impala:** M.F. Soper/Bruce Coleman Ltd. **IMPRESSIONISM** *TR* Musée Marmottan, *BL* Musée de Louvre/Cliché Musées Nationaux Paris, *BR* Musée de Louvre/Cliché Musées Nationaux Paris. **INCA** Tony Morrison. **Incuse:** Michael Holford. **INDUS VALLEY** *T & C* Robert Harding Picture Library, both *B* pictures Scala. **INDUSTRIAL REVOLUTION** *T* Science Museum, *B* Alan Hutchison Library. **Ingot:** Goebel/ZEFA. **Intarsia:** Michael Holford. **Intrusion:** Travel Photo International. **Ionic Order:** Mary Evans Picture Library. **Ironstone:** Neville Fox-Davies/Bruce Coleman Ltd. **ISLAM** *TL* A. Duncan/MEPhA, *TR* A. Duncan/MEPhA, *BL* British Museum, *BR* Metropolitan Museum of Art, Rogers Fund. **Ivory:** Michael Holford. **Ivy:** Ake Lindau/Ardea London.

Jackal: Ian Beames/Ardea London. **Jack-in-the-box:** *Eileen Tweedy*/Art Gallery & Museums, Brighton. **Jack Rabbit:** Stephen J. Kraseman/Bruce Coleman Ltd. **Jaguar:** Revers-Widaver/ZEFA. **Janus:** Michael Holford. **JELLYFISH** *L* Ron & Valerie Taylor/Ardea London, *R* Anthony & Elizabeth Bomford/Ardea London. **Jet:** *Michael Freeman.* **Joshua Tree:** P. Morris/Ardea London. **JUDAISM** *TR* Israel Museum, Jerusalem, *BL* Staats und Universitatsbibliothek, Hamburg (Ralph Kleinkempe from Aldus Books Ltd), *BR* Jewish Museum, London. **Juggernaut:** J. Pfaff/ZEFA. **Jagannath:** Michael Holford. **Jumping Jack:** *Graham Henderson*/Museum of London. **Junco:** Kenneth W. Fink/Ardea London. **Junk:** Sybil Sassoon/Robert Harding Picture Library. **JUPITER** Both pictures NASA.

Kabuki: R. Halin/ZEFA. **Kale:** Eric Crichton/Bruce Coleman Ltd. **Kangaroo:** P. Morris/Ardea London. **Kapok:** Norman Myers/Bruce Coleman Ltd. **Katydid:** Donald D. Burgess/Ardea London. **Kayak:** R. Theissen/ZEFA. **Kilauea:** Hawaii-Corn/ZEFA. **Kiln:** Joy Langsbury/Bruce Coleman Ltd. **Kimono:** Michael Holford. **Kiwi:** Jeff Foott/Bruce Coleman Ltd. **Kiwi Fruit:** R. Smith/ZEFA. **Klee:** Michael Holford © A.D.A.G.P., Cosmo Press 1984. **Koala:** Jen & Des Bartlett/Bruce Coleman Ltd. **Kohlrabi:** Eric Crichton/Bruce Coleman Ltd. **Kongoni:** Mark Boulton/Bruce Coleman Ltd. **Kookaburra:** Rainbird/Robert Harding Picture Library. **Krishna:** Michael Holford. **Kudu:** Clem Haagner/Ardea London.

Lace: *Patrick Thurston.* **Lacquer:** Michael Holford. **Ladybird:** W. Kratz/ZEFA. **LASER** © F. Goro/Life Magazine 1965/Colorific! **Lateen:** Sarah King/Robert Harding Picture Library. **Lattice:** Nedra Westwater/Robert Harding Picture Library. **Launcher:** Photri/ZEFA. **Lavender:** Eric Crichton/Bruce Coleman Ltd. **Leaf Insect:** Anton Thau/ZEFA. **LE CORBUSIER** ZEFA. **Leeboard:** B. Fleumer/ZEFA. **Leech:** Jane Burton/Bruce Coleman Ltd. **Leg of Mutton:** Mary Evans Picture Library. **Lei:** Erwin Christian/ZEFA. **Lemur:** Kenneth W. Fink/Ardea London. **LENS** Eaglemoss Publications Ltd. **Leopard:** Peter Jackson/Bruce Coleman Ltd. **LEONARDO DA VINCI** *L* Reproduced by courtesy of the Trustees, The National Gallery, London, *R* Reproduced by Gracious Permission of Her Majesty the Queen. **Lichen:** J.L. Mason/Ardea London. **Life Guards:** Clive Sawyer/ZEFA. **Lighthouse:** N.A. Callow/Robert Harding Picture Library. **LIGHTNING** C. Voit/ZEFA. **Lilac:** Eric Crichton/Bruce Coleman Ltd. **Lintel:** Michael Holford. **Lion:** Michael Putland/Ardea London. **Little Auk:** L.R. Dawson/Bruce Coleman Ltd. **Llama:** Bruce Coleman Ltd. **Lloyd, Christine Evert:** Tony Duffy/All Sport. **Lock:** Ingrid Rangnow/ZEFA. **Locust:** John Markham/Bruce Coleman Ltd. **Lodestone:** Michael Holford. **Longhorn:** V. Wentzel/ZEFA. **Longship:** Puck-Kornetzki/ZEFA. **Loris:** Rod Williams/Bruce Coleman Ltd. **Lotus:** Joanna Van Gruist/Ardea London. **Lungwort:** Hans Reinhard/Bruce Coleman Ltd. **Lupin:** M. Thonig/ZEFA. **Lychee:** Eric Crichton/Bruce Coleman Ltd. **Lynx:** W. Layer/ZEFA.

Macaque: Sybil Sassoon/Robert Harding Picture Library. **Macaw:** Hans Reinhard/Bruce Coleman Ltd. **Mace:** *Patrick Thurston.* **Mace-Seed:** Starfoto/ZEFA. **Magnolia:** Ardea London. **Majolica:** Michael Holford. **Malachite:** Adrian Davies/Bruce Coleman Ltd. **Mandala:** Michael Holford. **Mandrill:** Kenneth W. Fink/Ardea London. **Mangrove:** Bruce Coleman Ltd. **Mantis:** Martin Dohrn/Bruce Coleman Ltd. **Marabou:** Carol Hughes/Bruce Coleman Ltd. **Marduk:** Michael Holford. **Mare:** ZEFA. **Marionette:** R. Bond/ZEFA. **Marmot:** Wardene Weisser/Ardea London. **MARS** both NASA. **Marten:** ZEFA. **MASK** *TR* Michael Holford, *BL* Bob Croxford/ZEFA and *BC* and *BR* both Michael Holford. **MATISSE** Cliché Musées Nationaux Paris: Photo Bulloz © S.P.A.D.E.M. 1984. **Matterhorn:** Toni Hiebeler/ZEFA. **MAYA** *L* Michael Holford, *R* Ianthe Ruthven/Michael Holford. **Meadowlark:** Des Bartlett/Bruce Coleman Ltd. **Medicine Man:** Michael Holford. **Medusa:** Michael Holford. **Megalith:** Michael Holford. **Melon:** Ernst A. Weber/ZEFA. **MERCURY** both NASA. **Mesopotamia:** Michael Holford. **MICHELANGELO** Ted Spiegel/John Hillelson Agency. **Microfilm:** University Microfilms International/Business Week. **Milkweed:** Bob & Clara Calhoun/Bruce Coleman Ltd. **MILKY WAY** *T* Space Frontiers Ltd., *B* Science Photo Library. **Minaret:** Ch. Fetzer/ZEFA. **Miniature:** Michael Holford. **Minotaur:** Michael Holford. **Minstrel:** British Museum/Robert Harding Picture Library. **Mistletoe:** Bob Gibbons/Ardea London. **Mitre:** Michael Holford. **Moat:** G. Archbold/Robert Harding Picture Library. **Moccasin:** Rod Williams/Bruce Coleman Ltd. **Mockingbird:** Joe Van Wormer/Bruce Coleman Ltd. **MONEY** *TL* Michael Holford, *TR* Alan Hutchison Library. **Monkey Puzzle Tree:** Ardea London. **Monolith:** Michael Holford. **Monorail:** B. Anderson/ZEFA. **Monstera:** William McPherson/Bruce Coleman Ltd. **MOON** *T* Space Frontiers, *BL* Space Frontiers, *BC* Science Photo Library, *BR* Space Frontiers. **Montezuma:** Museo de America, Madrid/Robert Harding Picture Library. **Moonstone:** Institute of Geological Sciences. **MOORE** Walter Rawlings/Robert Harding Picture Library. **Moose:** Jeff Foott/Bruce Coleman Ltd. **Morel:** Hans Reinhard/Bruce Coleman Ltd. **Mosaic:** Michael Holford. **Mould:** Adrian Davies/Bruce Coleman Ltd. **Mountaineer:** Chris Bonnington/Bruce Coleman Ltd. **Mount Rushmore National Memorial:** M.P.L. Fogden/Bruce Coleman Ltd. **Mule:** J.L.G. Grande/Bruce Coleman Ltd. **Mullion:** Robert Harding Picture Library. **Mummy:** Michael Holford. **Murillo:** Michael Holford. **Muse:** Michael Holford. **Musk Ox:** Kenneth W. Fink/Ardea London.

Natterjack: J.P. Ferrero/Ardea London. **Neanderthal Man:** Rainbird/Robert Harding Picture Library. **NEBULA** © 1959 by California Institute of Technology and Carnegie Institution of Washington. **Nectarine:** Sybil Sassoon/Robert Harding Picture Library. **Nematode:** Dr. F. Sauer/ZEFA. **NEOCLASSICISM** *TL* © 1980 By the Metropolitan Museum of Art, *TR* Ole Woldbye/Thorvaldsens Museum, *BL Malcolm Aird, BR A. Howarth.* **Neptune:** Michael Holford. **Netsuke:** Michael Holford. **Newel:** *Malcolm Aird.* **Newt:** W. Kratz/ZEFA. **Niche:** Konrad Helbig/ZEFA. **Night Heron:** E. Hummel/ZEFA. **Nolan:** Marlborough Fine Art, London/Bridgeman Art Library. **NUCLEAR WEAPON** 1 to 4 US Dept. of Environment/Science Photo Library. 5 Aspect Picture Library. **Nutmeg:** Starfoto/ZEFA. **Oasis:** Foto Leidmann/ZEFA. **Ocelot:** Norman Tomalin/Bruce Coleman Ltd.

Octagon: Michael Holford. **Ogee:** Michael Holford. **Okra:** John Mason/Ardea London. **Olivine:** Institute of Geological Sciences. **Onion:** ZEFA. **OP ART** The Tate Gallery, London. **Opal:** Institute of Geological Sciences. **Opossum:** Leonard Lee Rue III/Bruce Coleman Ltd. **Opuntia:** Eric Crichton/Bruce Coleman Ltd. **Orang-utan:** ZEFA. **Organ:** G.M. Wilkins/Robert Harding Picture Library. **Oriel:** Michael Holford. **Oryx:** B. Croxford/ZEFA. **Osiris:** Michael Holford. **Ostrich:** W. Layer/ZEFA. **OTTOMAN EMPIRE** Sonia Halliday. **Outcrop:** Dr. Hans Kramarz/ZEFA. **Ovenbird:** Gunter Ziesler/Bruce Coleman Ltd.

Paddle Wheel: Klaus Benser/ZEFA. **Paddy:** Starfoto/ZEFA. **Pagoda:** Christina Gascoigne/Robert Harding Picture Library. **Painted Lady:** L.R. Dawson/Bruce Coleman Ltd. **PALLADIAN** John Bethell. **Palomino:** J.P. Ferrero/Ardea London. **Panda:** WWF/Kojo Tanaka/Bruce Coleman Ltd. **Pangolin:** R. Borland/Bruce Coleman Ltd. **PANTHEON** John Flowerdew/ZEFA. **Papyrus:** Michael Holford. **Parabola:** J. Pfaff/ZEFA. **Parachute:** A. Hubrick/ZEFA. **Parasite:** P. Morris/Ardea London. **Pargetting:** G.M. Wilkins/Robert Harding Picture Library. **Parrot:** Geoff Kalt/ZEFA. **Parsnip:** Eric Crichton/Bruce Coleman Ltd. **PARTHENON** Michael Holford. **Passion Flower:** Christian Zuber/Bruce Coleman Ltd. **Patchwork:** Michael Holford. **Peacock:** Wardene Weisser/Ardea London. **Pearl:** Orion Press/ZEFA. **Peat:** Hed Wiesner/ZEFA. **Peccary:** Hans D. Dessenbach/Ardea London. **Pegasus:** Michael Holford. **Pelican:** David Goulston/Bruce Coleman Ltd. **Penguin:** Jen & Des Bartlett/Bruce Coleman Ltd. **Pericles:** Michael Holford. **PERPENDICULAR** *T* John Bethell, *B* Angelo Hornak. **Persimmon:** J.L. Mason/Ardea London. **PERSIA** © Eric Lessing, Magnum. **PERSPECTIVE** Scala. **Petrified Forest:** ZEFA. **Pewter:** American Museum, Bath/Robert Harding Picture Library. **Pharaoh:** Robert Harding Picture Library. **Phonograph:** Michael Holford. **Photomicrograph:** Dr. David Corke/ZEFA. **Phrygian Cap:** Michael Holford. **PICASSO** MAS © S.P.A.D.E.M. 1984. **Pigmentation:** Dr. David Corke/ZEFA. **Pilaster:** G. Archbold/Robert Harding Picture Library. **Pineapple:** William E. Townsend Jnr./Bruce Coleman Ltd. **Pinnacle:** P. Bond/ZEFA. **Pistol:** Robert Harding Picture Library. **Pitcher Plant:** Jack Dermid/Bruce Coleman Ltd. **PLAYING CARDS** 1500 *Michael Holford*/Courtesy of Intercol. 1678 Yasha Beresiner, Intercol, London. Iran *Michael Holford*/Courtesy of Intercol. 1840 Tony Hutchins/Sunday Times. Modern *Michael Holford*/Waddingtons. India *Michael Holford*/ Courtesy of Intercol. **Plum:** Eric Crichton/Bruce Coleman Ltd. **PLUTO** both by courtesy of the Royal Astronomical Society, London. **Polar Bear:** Thor Larsen/Bruce Coleman Ltd. **Polo:** E.M. Bordis/ZEFA. **Polyphemus Moth:** George Laycock/Bruce Coleman Ltd. **Pompeii:** J. Schorken/ZEFA. **POP ART** *L* The Tate Gallery, London © S.P.A.D.E.M. 1984, *R* Collection, The Museum of Modern Art, New York. Elizabeth Bliss Parkinson Fund © S.P.A.D.E.M. 1984. **PORCELAIN** *TL* Robert Harding Picture Library, *TR* Bridgeman Art Library, *BL* Michael Holford/Victoria & Albert Museum, *BR* Michael Holford/Victoria & Albert Museum. **Portico:** Christina Gascoigne/Robert Harding Picture Library. **POSTIMPRESSIONISM** *TL* Kunsthalle Bremen, *TR* Museum Folkwang Essen, *BL* The Metropolitan Museum of Art, Bequest of Mrs. H.O. Havemeyer, 1929. The H.O. Havemeyer Collection. **POTTERY** *TR* Robert Harding Picture Library, *BL* John Bethell, *BR* Victoria & Albert Museum. **Potter's Wheel:** G.M. Wilkins/Robert Harding Picture Library. **Powder Horn:** *Patrick Thurston.* **Prairie Dog:** M.P.L. Fogden/Bruce Coleman Ltd. **Pre-Columbian Pottery:** Robert Harding Picture Library. **Pre-Raphaelite:** Photo John Webb/The Tate Gallery, London. **Primrose:** S.C. Porter/Bruce Coleman Ltd. **Proboscis:** E. Bleicher/ZEFA. **Prominence:** ZEFA. **Pronghorn:** Kenneth W. Fink/Ardea London. **Protective Colouring:** Kim Taylor/Bruce Coleman Ltd. **Pseudomorph:** ZEFA. **Pueblo:** Stefnmans/ZEFA. **Puffball:** Ake Lindau/Ardea London. **Puffer Fish:** ZEFA. **PUGIN** John Bethell. **Puma:** W. Weisser/Ardea London. **Pupa:** Dr. Sauer/ZEFA. **Puppet:** Dr. G. Haasch/ZEFA. **Pyramid:** Kim Taylor/Bruce Coleman Ltd. **Pyrite:** Hed Wiesner/ZEFA. **Pyrotechnics:** Starfoto/ZEFA.

Quarry: R. Jensen/ZEFA. **Quern:** Mary Evans Picture Library. **Quetzalcoatl:** Michael Holford.

Ra: Michael Holford. **Rabbit:** Ian Beames/Ardea London. **Raccoon:** Hans Reinhard/ZEFA. **Radial Symmetry:** J.E. Rhodes/Robert Harding Picture Library. **RADAR** Paul Brierley. **Radio Telescope:** V. Stapelberg/ZEFA. **Ragged Robin:** Bob Gibbons/Ardea London. **Rainbow:** ZEFA. **Ram-sheep:** Leonard Lee Rue III/Bruce Coleman Ltd. **Ram-god of Mendes:** Mary Evans Picture Library. **Ramses:** Michael Holford. **Rape:** Ian Sumner/Robert Harding Picture Library. **RAPHAEL** Scala. **Rattle:** Michael Holford. **Rattlesnake:** WWF/Urs Woy/Bruce Coleman Ltd. **Rayleigh Scattering:** K.D. Frohlich/ZEFA. **Redcurrant:** John Mason/Ardea London. **Red Deer:** W. Ostgate/ZEFA. **Red Fox:** H. Reinhard/ZEFA. **Red Squirrel:** Leonard Lee Rue III/Bruce Coleman Ltd. **Reed:** Norman Tomalin/Bruce Coleman Ltd. **Regency:** Michael Holford. **Reindeer:** Herta Grondal/ZEFA. **Reliquary:** Michael Holford. **REMBRANDT** The Greater London Council as Trustees of the Iveagh Bequest, Kenwood. **RENAISSANCE** *L* Scala, *R* National Gallery of Art, Washington; Ailsa Mellon Bruce Fund. **Resin:** Bert Leidmann/ZEFA. **Retort:** Michael Holford. **Rhea:** Bruce Coleman Ltd. **Rhesus Monkey:** Ardea London. **Rhinoceros:** ZEFA. **Rickshaw:** Sybil Sassoon/Robert Harding Picture Library. **Roadrunner:** Charlie Ott/Bruce Coleman Ltd. **Robin:** W. Layer/ZEFA. **Rocking Horse:** Mary Evans Picture Library. **Roe Deer:** ZEFA. **ROCOCO** *TL* Michael Holford, *TR* Wallace Collection, *BL* M. Thonig/ZEFA. **RODIN** Musée Rodin. **ROMANESQUE** S.H. & D.H. Cavanaugh/Robert Harding Picture Library. **Romulus & Remus:** ZEFA. **Rood Screen:** Michael Holford. **Rotifer:** Dr. F. Sauer/ZEFA. **Rotunda:** Michael Holford. **Royal Palm:** Bruce Coleman Ltd. **Rubber Tree:** J. Bitsch/ZEFA. **Ruff:** Michael Holford. **Russet:** Eric Crichton/Bruce Coleman Ltd. **RUSSIAN REVOLUTION** e.t. archive. **Rye:** Prato/Bruce Coleman Ltd.

Sable Antelope: Simon Trevor/Bruce Coleman Ltd. **Sage Grouse:** Leonard Lee Rue III/Bruce Coleman Ltd. **Saguaro:** Charlie Ott/Bruce Coleman Ltd. **Saiga:** Jane Burton/Bruce Coleman Ltd. **Sailing Ship:** N. Bahnsen/ZEFA. **Salamander:** W. Layer/ZEFA. **Salmon:** Hans Reinhard/Bruce Coleman Ltd. **Sampler:** Michael Holford. **Samurai:** Michael Holford. **SAN ANDREAS FAULT** John Shelton. **Sand Dollars:** Alan Weaving/Ardea London. **Sand Dunes:** R. Bond/ZEFA. **Sandstone:** Gunter Heil/ZEFA. **Sand Yacht:** ZEFA. **SATELLITE** NASA/Science Photo Library. **SATURN** both NASA. **Satyr:** Michael Holford. **Scale:** Eric Lindgren/Ardea London. **Scallop:** John Gregg/Ardea London. **Scarab:** *T* Jane Burton/Bruce Coleman Ltd., *B* Michael Holford. **Scat:** R. Beames/Ardea London. **Screamer:** Sullivan & Rogers/Bruce Coleman Ltd. **Scrimshaw:** Francois Gohier/Ardea London. **Sculpture:** ZEFA. **Sea Anemone:** Dr. Sauer/ZEFA. **Sea Cucumber:** Ron & Valerie Taylor/Ardea London. **Seal:** E. Mickleburgh/Ardea London. **Seaplane:** ZEFA. **Seashell:** John Ker/ZEFA. **Sea Snake:** Ron & Valerie Taylor/Ardea London. **Sea Urchin:** Adrian Davies/Bruce Coleman Ltd. **Secretary Bird:** ZEFA. **Seedhead:** N. Fox-Davies/Bruce Coleman Ltd. **Selfheal:** John Markham/Bruce Coleman Ltd. **Serow:** Kenneth W. Fink/Ardea London. **Seventeen-year Locust:** Leonard Lee Rue III/Bruce Coleman Ltd. **Sèvres Plate:** Michael Holford. **SEVEN DEADLY SINS** Prado, Madrid. **Shark:** Ron & Valerie Taylor/Ardea London. **Sheep:** ZEFA. **Sheepdog:** S. McKenna/ZEFA. **SHELLS** Mourning Cowrie: Heather Angel/Biofotos, Giant Clam: Heather Angel/Biofotos, Paper Nautilus: Ken Lucas/Seaphot, Queen Conch: Ken Lucas/Seaphot, others RD copyright. **Shield:** Michael Holford. **Ship Canal:** K. Kerth/ZEFA. **Shire Horse:** John S. Adams/ZEFA. **Shoe-billed Stork:** Ian Beames/Ardea London. **Shofar:** F. Paul/ZEFA. **Silkworm:** Dr. P. Thiele/ZEFA. **Silverfish:** J.L. Mason/Ardea London. **Skiing:** A. Hubrich/ZEFA. **Skimmer:** J.B. & S. Bottomley/Ardea London. **Skink:** Hans & Judy Beste/Ardea London. **Skunk Cabbage:** Gene Ahrens/Bruce Coleman Ltd. **Skylark:** Gunter Ziesler/Bruce Coleman Ltd. **Sloth:** Francisco Erize/Bruce Coleman Ltd. **Slow-worm:** J.L. Mason/Ardea London. **Slug:** Ardea London. **Smelting:** ZEFA. **Snail:** Eric Lingren/Ardea London. **Snake:** Donald Burgess/Ardea London. **Snake Charmer:** M. Freeman/Bruce Coleman Ltd. **Snipe:** Roger Wilmshurst/Bruce Coleman Ltd. **Snow Leopard:** Kenneth W. Fink/Ardea London. **Snowplough:** ZEFA. **Snuffbox:** Royal Naval Museum, Portsmouth/Robert Harding Picture Library. **SOLAR POWER** ZEFA. **SPACE SHUTTLE** © 1981 Douglas Kirkland/Colorific! **Sparrowhawk:** W. Layer/ZEFA. **Spawn:** Jane Burton/Bruce Coleman Ltd. **Speedboat:** ZEFA. **SPIDER** John H. Gerard. **Spider Crab:** Neville Coleman/Bruce Coleman Ltd. **Spinnaker:** A. Roberts/ZEFA. **Spinning Wheel:** Michael Holford. **Spire:** Michael Holford. **Spirogyra:** Bruce Coleman Ltd. **Spleenwort:** Prato/Bruce Coleman Ltd. **Spoonbill:** M.P. Kahl/Bruce Coleman Ltd. **Springbok:** Goetz D. Plage/Bruce Coleman Ltd. **Spurge:** Roger Wilmshurst/Bruce Coleman Ltd. **Squirrel:** Kenneth W. Fink/Ardea London. **Squirrel Monkey:** Michael Freeman/Bruce Coleman Ltd. **Stack:** P.J. Sharpe/ZEFA. **Stadium:** Michael Holford. **STAINED GLASS** *L* Gottfried Frenzel/Institut fur Glasgemalde forschung und Restaurierung, Nurnberg, *R* Dr. Wolff Kolnerdom/Sonia Halliday. **Stalagmites and Stalactites:** W. Ernest/ZEFA. **Stallion:** J.P. Ferrero/Ardea London. **Starfish:** Sybil Sassoon/Robert Harding Picture Library. **Star of Bethlehem:** Hans Reinhard/Bruce Coleman Ltd. **Steam:** Walter Rawlings/Robert Harding Picture Library. **Steam Engine:** J.M. Jarvis/ZEFA. **Steamroller:** Derek Cattani/ZEFA. **Steinbok:** Peter Steyn/Ardea London. **Stele:** Michael Holford. **Stereoscope:** Michael Holford. **Stilt:** Graeme Chapman/Ardea London. **Stoa:** Michael Holford. **Stoat:** Hans Reinhard/Bruce Coleman Ltd. **Stock Dove:** Hans Reinhard/Bruce Coleman Ltd. **STONE AGE** Flint handaxe: Trustees of the British Museum (Natural History), Flint dagger, stone battleaxe and flint arrowhead: Devizes Museum, *Eileen Tweedy*, Nambicuara Indian and stone axehead: Jesco Von Puttkamer/Alan Hutchison Library. **Stonechat:** R.K. Murton/Bruce Coleman Ltd. **Stone Marten:** ZEFA. **Stork:** ZEFA. **Stupa:** J.L. Peyromaure/Alan Hutchison Library. **Suffolk Punch:** J.P. Ferrero/Ardea London. **SUN** ZEFA. **Sun Bittern:** G. Ziesler/Bruce Coleman Ltd. **Sundial:** Nedra Westwater/Robert Harding Picture Library. **Supernova:** © 1959 by California Institute of Technology & Carnegie Institution of Washington. **Surgeon Fish:** Jane Burton/Bruce Coleman Ltd. **Suricate:** M.P. Kahl/Bruce Coleman Ltd. **SURREALISM** The Minneapolis Institute of Arts, Minneapolis, Minnesota © A.D.A.G.P. 1984. **Swan:** Hans D. Dossenbach/Ardea London. **Sweet Pea:** Eric Crichton/Bruce Coleman Ltd. **Sweet William:** Bruce Coleman Ltd. **Swordbill:** A.J. Mabbs/Bruce Coleman Ltd. **SYNAGOGUE** *Titanic Photography.*

Tahr: Bruce Coleman Ltd. **Talapoin Monkey:** Norman Tomalin/Bruce Coleman Ltd. **Tamandua:** Francisco Erize/Bruce Coleman Ltd. **Tanager:** Hans Reinhard/Bruce Coleman Ltd. **Tankard:** Robert Harding Picture Library. **Tanker:** Orion Press/ZEFA. **Tapestry:** The Metropolitan Museum of Art, The Cloisters Collection, Gift of John D. Rockefeller, Jnr., 1937/Robert Harding Picture Library. **TAOISM** Trustees of the British Museum. **Tapir:** ZEFA. **TAROT** Victoria & Albert Museum, London. **Tarsier:** J. Mackinnon/Bruce Coleman Ltd. **Telegraph:** Michael Holford. **TELESCOPE** *L* Firenze Museum della Scienza/Scala, *R* John Walsh/Aspect. **Temple:** Bob Croxford/ZEFA. **Tepee:** K.H. Kurz/ZEFA. **Termitarium:** Peter Ward/Bruce Coleman Ltd. **Termite:** Peter Ward/Bruce Coleman Ltd. **Tern:** Wayne Lankinen/Bruce Coleman Ltd. **Terpsichore:** Michael Holford. **Terracotta:** Michael Holford. **Terrapin:** Hans Reinhard/Bruce Coleman Ltd. **Thatch:** Colin Caket/ZEFA. **Thimble:** Michael Holford. **Thoth:** Michael Holford. **Tiger:** Pat Morris/Ardea London. **Tiki:** Michael Holford. **Tinamou:** Jen & Des Bartlett/Bruce Coleman Ltd. **TITIAN** Scala. **Toad:** ZEFA. **Toga:** Michael Holford. **Tomb:** ZEFA. **Topaz:** Institute of Geological Sciences. **Tope:** J.A. Bailey/Ardea London. **Topiary:** Eric Crichton/Bruce Coleman Ltd. **Toucan:** Francisco Erize/Bruce Coleman Ltd. **Tragopan:** P. Morris/Ardea London. **Trap-door Spider:** Jen & Des Bartlett/Bruce Coleman Ltd. **Tree Frog:** Pat Morris/Ardea London. **Triforium:** Michael Holford. **Triggerfish:** I.R. Beames/Ardea London. **Trillium:** Eric Crichton/Bruce Coleman Ltd. **Trilobite:** J. Fennell/Bruce Coleman Ltd. **Tripod:** Michael Holford. **Triptych:** ZEFA. **Trogan:** B & C Calhoun/Bruce Coleman Ltd. **Trompe l'oeil:** Michael Holford. **Trotter:** ZEFA. **Trumpeter Swan:** Joe Van Wormer/Bruce Coleman Ltd. **Tsetse Fly:** Kim Taylor/Bruce Coleman Ltd. **TSUNAMI** Michael Holford. **Turkey:** D.A.J. Mabbs/Bruce Coleman Ltd. **Turkey:** Kenneth W. Fink/Ardea London. **Turnip:** Eric Crichton/Bruce Coleman Ltd. **TURNER** National Gallery of Art, Washington: Widener Collection. **Turtle Dove:** J.L.G. Grande/Bruce Coleman Ltd. **Tuscan Order:** Mary Evans Picture Library. **Tutu:** ZEFA. **Tympanum:** Michael Holford.

Undercroft: Michael Holford. **UNICORN** Musée de Cluny/Cliché Musées Nationaux Paris. **UNITED NATIONS** *L* Frank Spooner, *R* Klaus Benser/ZEFA. **Untouchable:** Alan Hutchison Library. **Uraeus:** ZEFA.

Vampire Bat: Rod Williams/Bruce Coleman Ltd. **Vase:** Michael Holford. **VENUS** NASA. **Venus Flower Basket:** Jane Burton/Bruce Coleman Ltd. **Venus Flytrap:** ZEFA. **Verbena:** Eric Crichton/Bruce Coleman Ltd. **Vervet:** Peter Davey/Bruce Coleman Ltd. **Viaduct:** S. Sammer/ZEFA. **Viburnum:** Eric Crichton/Bruce Coleman Ltd. **VICTORIA CROSS** Michael Holford. **Victoriana:** Photograph by kind permission of the Victorian Society, of Linley Sambourne House, open to the public, details from the Victorian Society, 01-994-1019. **VIKING** Ray Sutcliffe. **Vineyard:** ZEFA. **Virginia Creeper:** Eric Crichton/Bruce Coleman Ltd. **Viscacha:** G. Ziesler/Bruce Coleman Ltd. **VOLCANO** Frank W. Lane. **Volute:** Neville Coleman/Bruce Coleman Ltd. **Vulture:** Peter Steyn/Ardea London.

Wailing Wall: H.J. Kreuger/ZEFA. **Wallaby:** F. Park/ZEFA. **Wall creeper:** Hans Reinhard/Bruce Coleman Ltd. **Walrus:** Leonard Lee Rue III/Bruce Coleman Ltd. **Wapiti:** Kenneth W. Fink/Ardea London. **War Bonnet:** A. Roberts/ZEFA. **Wart Hog:** Mark Boulton/Bruce Coleman Ltd. **Wasp Pupae:** Dr. David Corke/ZEFA. **Water Beetle:** Jane Burton/Bruce Coleman Ltd. **Water Boatman:** John Clegg/Ardea London. **Waterbuck:** Alan Weaving/Ardea London. **Water Bug:** Jack Dermid/Bruce Coleman Ltd. **Waterfall:** ZEFA. **Waxbill:** John Markham/Bruce Coleman Ltd. **Weather:** Dept. of Electrical Engineering & Electronics, Dundee University. **Weather Vane:** Robert Harding Picture Library. **Weaver Bird:** Pat Morris/Ardea London. **Wedgwood:** *John Cook (Whitecross Studios).* **Weevil:** Dr. Sauer/ZEFA. **White Clover:** Eric Crichton/Bruce Coleman Ltd. **White-eye:** Alan Paterson/Ardea London. **Whydah:** Bruce Coleman Ltd. **Wild Boar:** Leonard Lee Rue III/Bruce Coleman Ltd. **Winepress:** C. Maher/ZEFA. **Witch Doctor:** Robert Harding Picture Library. **Witch Hazel:** Eric Crichton/Bruce Coleman Ltd. **Wombat:** J.P. Ferrero/Ardea London. **Woodchuck:** P. Morris/Ardea London. **Woodcock:** Hans Reinhard/Bruce Coleman Ltd. **WONDERS OF THE ANCIENT WORLD** Adam Woolfitt/Susan Griggs Agency. **Woodlark:** Hans Reinhard/Bruce Coleman Ltd. **Woolly Bear Caterpillar:** Bob Gibbons/Ardea London. **WREN** *TL* John Bethell, *TR* John Bethell, *B* Rainbird/Robert Harding Picture Library. **FRANK LLOYD WRIGHT** Richard Bryant. **WYETH** Collection, The Museum of Modern Art, New York. **Wryneck:** R.M. Bloomfield/Ardea London.

Yak: Robert Harding Picture Library. **Yashmak:** ZEFA. **Yawl:** ZEFA. **Yellowstone National Park:** Hans Schmied/ZEFA. **Yucca:** Timothy O'Keefe/Bruce Coleman Ltd.

Zebra: Peter Steyne/Ardea London. **Zebra Finch:** John Markham/Bruce Coleman Ltd. **Zebu:** Bruce Coleman Ltd. **ZEN** *T* Carol Jopp/Robert Harding Picture Library, *B* © Elliott Erwitt–Magnum/John Hillelson Agency. **Zeus:** Michael Holford. **ZODIAC** Hunterian Collection, Library of University of Glasgow. **ZOROASTER** William McQuitty.

The publishers also wish to thank the following for assistance in verifying scientific entries:

Laurence Urdang Associates Ltd., Jeremy Bartlett, Mary Bickley, David Ellesmore, Anne Haysom, Bruce Ingram, Michael Malone, Veronique Mott, Christopher Townshend, Linda Young.